SUGGESTIONS FOR FAST, EFFECTIVE USE OF THE INDEX

1. PLEASE **READ THE FOREWORD** TO THE INDEX WHICH APPEARS IN THIS VOLUME.

2. STOP AND THINK ABOUT YOUR SUBJECT; TAKE A MOMENT TO **SELECT THE TERMS MOST DESCRIPTIVE OF YOUR RESEARCH SUBJECT.** IT HELPS TO SELECT THE PRINCIPAL SUBJECT RATHER THAN THE SECONDARY SUBJECT AND TO LOOK FOR NOUNS RATHER THAN ADJECTIVES.

3. IF YOU KNOW THE SHORT TITLE OR THE POPULAR NAME OF A STATUTE, YOU MAY CONSULT THE **SHORT TITLE/POPULAR NAME INDEX**, WHICH IMMEDIATELY PRECEDES THE GENERAL INDEX. ALSO PRECEDING THE GENERAL INDEX IS THE **EXECUTIVE AGENCY INDEX**, WHICH CONTAINS REFERENCES TO THE STATUTORY AND CONSTITUTIONAL PROVISIONS CREATING THE AGENCIES.

4. IF YOUR SEARCH DOES NOT LEAD YOU TO THE CODE SECTION SOUGHT, OR IF YOU HAVE QUESTIONS ABOUT OR SUGGESTIONS FOR THE INDEX, PLEASE FEEL WELCOME TO **CONTACT THE INDEXERS.** THE INDEXERS MAY BE REACHED DIRECTLY BY THE FOLLOWING METHODS: **TOLL-FREE INDEX HOTLINE, 1-800-897-7922,** BETWEEN 8:00 AM AND 4:30 PM, EASTERN TIME ZONE; **FAX NUMBER 1-434-972-7686; INTERNET E-MAIL** ADDRESSED TO **lng-cho-indexing@lexisnexis.com; POSTAGE-PAID CARDS** FOUND AT THE BACK OF THIS VOLUME.

GENERAL STATUTES OF NORTH CAROLINA

ANNOTATED

Volume 20

2004 INDEX

A to I

INDEX TO GENERAL LAWS OF NORTH CAROLINA
ENACTED BY THE GENERAL ASSEMBLY

Prepared under the Supervision of
THE DEPARTMENT OF JUSTICE
OF THE STATE OF NORTH CAROLINA
by
The Editorial Staff of the Publisher

LexisNexis®

4657721

ISBN 0-8205-9232-3

LexisNexis

Matthew Bender & Company, Inc.
P.O. Box 7587, Charlottesville, VA 22906-7587
www.lexisnexis.com

Customer Service: 1-800-833-9844

(Pub. 46405)

Foreword to the Indexes

Purpose–The purpose of this Foreword is to communicate to index users some of the characteristics of this particular index and also to provide insight into the way in which the Indexing staff tried to translate the years of contact with index users into a useful, efficient, and easy-to-use index. You know how to use an index; this Foreword and the suggestions for using the index are offered to aid in the effective use of this particular index.

Coverage–Each section of the General Statutes of North Carolina through legislation enacted during the 2004 Session, and each provision of the Constitutions of North Carolina and the United States has been thoroughly examined and covered in the index. Also included in the index is coverage of court rules of the state courts; the text of these rules appears in the soft-bound "Annotated Rules of North Carolina."

Special Indexes–Also contained in this index, at the beginning of the first index volume, are an updated index of executive agencies, containing references to the statutory and constitutional provisions creating them, and an updated combined index of short titles and popular names of legislation.

Citations–Statutory provisions are referred to in the index by section number (e.g., §48-10-101), including when indicated, subsections (e.g., §20-141, (h)). The constitutions are identified by abbreviations, a table of which follows this Foreword.

Philosophy–The index is a combination of two approaches to indexing, topical and descriptive word. LexisNexis® undertook this dual approach in order to provide index users with the advantages of each approach; the addition of thousands of descriptive main headings to a topical framework combines the access provided by the descriptive word approach and the organization and consistency of terminology provided by the topical approach. The result is a user-friendly and manageable index.

Cross References–Users sometimes question the necessity or desirability of cross references ("see" lines) in indexes. Cross references are used to keep indexes to a manageable size by reducing the amount of repetition of treatment under different headings. To make cross references even more useful and efficient, LexisNexis® has taken the following steps.

Double Jumps–"Double jump" cross references, which are cross references to other cross references, have been avoided.

Three Section Rule–Cross references have been used only to direct users to index entries covering three or more sections.

Group Section References–Group section references, which cite the user to the principal statutory treatment of a subject, have been attached to many of our cross references; this provides the user with the option to go immediately to the code for the cited material.

Main headings–Main headings were derived from the language of the General Statutes of North Carolina, from the phraseology commonly used in the courts of North Carolina and terminology commonly used in the legal profession. In addition, an effort was made to employ phrases commonly applied to General Statutes sections, such as frequently used nonlegal terms.

Communication with the Indexers–LexisNexis® solicits your help in keeping this index as useful as possible and asks that you inform us of any popular names that may have eluded us by returning the business reply cards found inside the back cover of each index volume. You may also use the cards to tell us of any errors we have made or improvements you think we should make. LexisNexis® also maintains a **toll-free index hotline (1-800-897-7922)** for use by those needing immediate help in locating a particular section or by those desiring to make comments or suggestions. Additionally, you may reach the Indexers by **fax (1-434-972-7686)**, or by **Internet E-mail(lng-cho-indexing@lexisnexis.com).** All suggestions, questions or comments receive serious consideration. For non-index questions and comments or to place orders, Customer Service may be reached by **toll-free telephone number (1-800-833-9844),** or by **toll-free fax (1-800-828-8341)**.

Scope of Index–The general index does not attempt to cover each topic in the vast field of law but refers only to those materials contained in the General Statutes. A thorough knowledge of the format and terminology of the General Statutes contributes to the efficient use of this index as a guide to subject matter.

Suggestions–LexisNexis® offers a few suggestions for efficient use of this index. Creating an index involves communicating with index users by anticipating where index users might look. It is hoped that these examples suggest to index users how the Indexers went about this process of anticipation and thus improve the communication between the Indexers and index users.

(1) *Gain familiarity with the contents of the General Statutes and the index.* Although it is not a predicate to using the index successfully, knowledge of the arrangement, terminology, topical treatment, analyses and reference system of both the General Statutes and the index is conducive to the efficient use of the index.

(2) *Consult the principal subject and not the secondary subject.* Thus, for motor vehicle registration, look under **MOTOR VEHICLE REGISTRATION** and not under **REGISTRATION;** for drivers' licenses, look under **DRIVERS' LICENSES** and not under **MOTOR VEHICLES;** for attorneys' fees, look under **ATTORNEYS' FEES** and not under **FEES.**

(3) *Search under commonly used phrases or terms of art.* Thus, for wrongful death, look under **WRONGFUL DEATH** and not under **DEATH;** for declaratory judgments, look under **DECLARATORY JUDGMENTS** and not under **JUDGMENTS**.

(4) *Look under specific areas of law and not under broad areas of law.* Thus, for life insurance, look under **LIFE INSURANCE** and not under **INSURANCE;** for nonprofit corporations, look under **NONPROFIT CORPORATIONS** and not under **CORPORATIONS.**

(5) *Consult the most pertinent subject.* Thus, for depositions, look under **DEPOSITIONS** and not under **EVIDENCE** or **TESTIMONY** or **WITNESSES;** for sales by executors and administrators, look under **EXECUTORS AND ADMINISTRATORS** and not under **WILLS** or **DESCENT AND DISTRIBUTION** or **INTESTATE SUCCESSION.**

(6) *Consult allied or related headings.* If your search under one heading is to no avail, try a related heading. Thus, if a search under the heading **PEACE OFFICERS** is fruitless, try **POLICE** or **HIGHWAY PATROL** or other related headings. Each section has itemized entries, but perhaps they appear under headings that may not have initially occurred to you.

(7) *Use descriptive words or phrases to aid in your search.* If you have

trouble expressing your search topically, use descriptive words or phrases. Thus, if it does not occur to you to search under concealment of merchandise in mercantile establishments for the crime of concealing unpurchased merchandise, look under **SHOPLIFTING;** if you want the provisions covering a motor vehicle manufacturer's duty as to new automobiles that cannot be repaired after a reasonable number of attempts, the index provides the option of looking under **LEMON LAW;** if public safety telephone service does not come to mind, try **911 SYSTEM.**

(8) *Begin your search with "starting point" headings.* "Starting point" headings are collections of entries or cross references that can provide assistance in getting a search started by exposing the index user to a diverse sampling of statutory terminology, which could suggest to the user other headings to consult. Although there is no formal list of "starting point" headings, the following have proven to be useful for that purpose: **DEFINED TERMS** (entries for all defined terms); **PRISON TERMS** (entries for each offense that carries a prison term); **CRIMINAL LAW AND PROCEDURE** (direction to all criminal offenses); **MISDEMEANORS** (all misdemeanor offenses); **FELONIES** (all felony offenses); **FINES** (all offenses carrying a fine); **BOARDS AND COMMISSIONS** (lists of all boards and commissions).

(9) *Use cross references.* Pay close attention to and make full use of the index cross references. An index cross reference is a direction, using the word "See", to the index user to go to another part of the index to find treatment. There are two types of cross references, external and internal. External cross references direct index users to another main heading. Thus, "**AERONAUTICS. Aircraft.** See AIRCRAFT" directs the index user from the main heading **AERONAUTICS** to the main heading **AIRCRAFT.** Internal cross references direct index users from one subheading within a main heading to another subheading within that same main heading. Thus, under the main heading **MOTOR VEHICLE EQUIPMENT, "Seat belts.** See within this heading 'Safety belts.'" directs the index user from the subheading **Seat belts** to the subheading **Safety belts.**

(10) *Keep in touch.* Let LexisNexis® know how you like the index. Contact the Indexers directly as indicated above under **Communication with the Indexers** if you have questions about or suggestions for the index.

LexisNexis®

Table of Abbreviations

Admission to Practice	Rules Governing Admission to the Practice of Law
Amd.	Amendment
App. Proc. Rule	North Carolina Rules of Appellate Procedure
Appx.	Appendix
Arbitration Rule	Rules for Court-Ordered Arbitration in North Carolina
Art.	Article
Bar Rules & Regs.	Rules and Regulations of the North Carolina State Bar
Childhood Vac. Rule	Rules of the Industrial Commission Relating to North Carolina Childhood Vaccine-Related Injury
CEA Rule	Canons of Ethics for Arbitrators
CJE Rule	Rules of Continuing Judicial Education
CLE Reg.	Regulations Governing Continuing Legal Education
CLE Rule	Rules for Continuing Legal Education Program
Code Jud. Cond.	Code of Judicial Conduct
Const. N. C.	Constitution of North Carolina
Const. U. S.	Constitution of the United States
Farm Med. Rule.	Prelitigation Farm Nuisance Mediation Program
Guideline	Medico-Legal Guidelines
I.C. Form	Workers' Compensation Rules of the North Carolina Industrial Commission Official Forms
I.C. Managed Care Orgs. R.	North Carolina Industrial Commission Rules for Managed Care Organizations
I.C. Mediated Settlmt. Conf. R.	Mediated Settlement and Neutral Evaluation Conferences Rules of the North Carolina Industrial Commission
I.C. Rule	Workers' Compensation Rules of the North Carolina Industrial Commission
I.C. Util. Rehab. Profs.	North Carolina Industrial Commission Rules for Utilization of Rehabilitation Professionals in Workers' Compensation Claims
IDS Rule	Rules for Indigent Defense Services
Indigent Rep.	Rules and Regulations Relating to the Appointment of Counsel for Indigent Defendants in Certain Criminal Cases

Jud. Stds. Comm. Rule	Rules of the Judicial Standards Commission
Prof. Cond. Rule	Rules of Professional Conduct of the North Carolina State Bar
Rehab. Services Guideline	Guidelines for Rehabilitation Services in North Carolina
SPCM Rule	Standards of Professional Conduct for Mediators
Sup. Ct. Library Rule	North Carolina Supreme Court Library Rules
Sup. Ct. Review (Jud. Stds. Comm.) Rule	Rules for Supreme Court Review of Recommendations of the Judicial Standards Commission
Sup. Ct. Y2K Mediation Rule	Rules of the North Carolina Supreme Court Implementing the Year 2000 Prelitigation Mediation Program
Super. Ct. Mediated Settlmt. Conf. R.	Rules Implementing Statewide Mediated Settlement Conferences in Superior Court Civil Actions
Super. Ct. Rule	General Rules of Practice for the Superior and District Courts
Tort Claim Rule	Rules of the Industrial Commission Relating to Tort Claims

The court rules appear in the softbound "Annotated Rules of North Carolina." The constitutions appear in Volume 19.

Executive Agency Index

A

ADMINISTRATIVE RULES REVIEW COMMISSION, §143B-30.1.

ADVISORY BUDGET COMMISSION, §143-4.

ADVISORY COMMITTEE ON ABANDONED CEMETERIES, §143B-128.

AERONAUTICS COUNCIL, §143B-356.

AGENCY FOR PUBLIC TELECOMMUNICATIONS, §143B-426.9.

AGRICULTURAL HALL OF FAME, §106-568.13.

AGRICULTURE, FORESTRY AND SEAFOOD AWARENESS STUDY COMMISSION, §120-150.

AIR CARGO AUTHORITY, §63A-3.

AIR QUALITY COUNCIL, §143B-317.

ALARM SYSTEMS LICENSING BOARD, §74D-4, (a).

ALCOHOLIC BEVERAGE CONTROL COMMISSION, §18B-200, (a).

AMERICA'S FOUR HUNDREDTH ANNIVERSARY COMMITTEE, §143B-85.

ANIMAL HEALTH DIVISION OF THE NORTH CAROLINA DEPARTMENT OF AGRICULTURE, §19A-22.

APPELLATE DEFENDER OFFICE, §7A-486.

APPRENTICESHIP COUNCIL, §94-2.

AQUACULTURE DEVELOPMENT ADVISORY BOARD, §106-760.

ARTS COUNCIL, §143B-87.

ARTS SOCIETY, INCORPORATED, §143B-89.

ATLANTIC STATES MARINE FISHERIES COMMISSION, §113-252.

B

BICYCLE COMMITTEE, §136-71.13, (a).

BOARD OF AGRICULTURE, §106-2.

BOARD OF ARCHITECTURE, §83A-2.

BOARD OF BOILER AND PRESSURE VESSEL RULES, §95-69.13, (a).

BOARD OF CERTIFIED PUBLIC ACCOUNTANT EXAMINERS, §93-12.

BOARD OF CORRECTION, §143B-265.

BOARD OF CROP SEED IMPROVEMENT, §143A-64.

BOARD OF DIETETICS/NUTRITION, §90-353.

BOARD OF ELECTROLYSIS EXAMINERS, §88A-5, (a).

BOARD OF EMPLOYEE ASSISTANCE PROFESSIONALS, §90-501.

BOARD OF EXAMINERS FOR SPEECH AND LANGUAGE PATHOLOGISTS AND AUDIOLOGISTS, §90-303, (a).

BOARD OF FUNERAL SERVICE, §90-210.18A.

BOARD OF LANDSCAPE ARCHITECTS, §89A-3, (a).

BOARD OF LAW EXAMINERS, §§84-24 to 84-26.

BOARD OF LICENSED PROFESSIONAL COUNSELORS, §90-333.

BOARD OF NURSING, §90-171.21.

BOARD OF PHARMACY, §90-85.6.

BOARD OF PHYSICAL THERAPY EXAMINERS, §90-270.25.

BOARD OF PODIATRY EXAMINERS FOR THE STATE OF NORTH CAROLINA, §90-202.4, (a).

BOARD OF TRANSPORTATION, §143B-350.

BOARD OF TRUSTEES OF THE NORTH CAROLINA FIREMEN'S AND RESCUE SQUAD WORKERS' PENSION FUND, §58-86-1.

BOARD OF TRUSTEES OF THE NORTH CAROLINA MUSEUM OF ART, §140-5.13.

BOARD OF TRUSTEES OF THE NORTH CAROLINA VOCATIONAL TEXTILE SCHOOL, §115D-68.

BRIDGE AUTHORITY, §§136-89.159 to 136-89.167.

BUILDING CODE COUNCIL, §143-136, (a).

BUREAU OF MINES, §113-26.1.

BUSINESS LICENSE INFORMATION OFFICE, §147-54.13.

BUTNER PLANNING COMMISSION, §122C-402.

C

CAPE FEAR NAVIGATION AND PILOTAGE COMMISSION, §76A-1.

CAPITAL PLANNING COMMISSION, §143B-373.

CEMETERY COMMISSION, §§65-49 to 65-54.

CERTIFICATION BOARD FOR SOCIAL WORK, §90B-5.

CHILD CARE COMMISSION, §143B-168.4.

CIVIL AIR PATROL DIVISION, §143B-490, (a).

COASTAL AREA MANAGEMENT COMMISSION, §113A-100.

COASTAL RESOURCES ADVISORY COUNCIL, §113A-105.

COASTAL RESOURCES COMMISSION, §113A-104.

CODE OFFICIALS QUALIFICATION BOARD, §143-151.9.

COMMISSION FOR HEALTH SERVICES, §130A-29.

COMMISSION FOR MENTAL HEALTH, DEVELOPMENTAL DISABILITIES AND SUBSTANCE ABUSE SERVICES, §143B-147.

COMMISSION FOR THE BLIND, §143B-157.

COMMISSION FOR THE STUDY OF PROBLEMS OF THE CARE OF THE AGED AND INTELLECTUALLY OR PHYSICALLY HANDICAPPED, §143-279.

COMMISSION OF ANATOMY, §130A-33.30.

COMMISSION ON AGRICULTURE, FORESTRY AND SEAFOOD AWARENESS, §120-150.

COMMISSION ON STATE PROPERTY, §§143-735 to 143-737.

COMMISSION TO STUDY THE CARE OF THE AGED AND HANDICAPPED, §143-279.

COMMITTEE ON INAUGURAL CEREMONIES, §143-533.

COMMUNITY APPEARANCE COMMISSION, §160A-451.

COMMUNITY DEVELOPMENT COUNCIL, §143B-437.1.

COMMUNITY OF BUTNER PLANNING COMMISSION, §122C-402.

COMMUNITY PENALTIES BOARD, §7A-775.

CONSUMER AND ADVOCACY ADVISORY COMMITTEE FOR THE BLIND, §143B-163.

COUNCIL OF STATE GOVERNMENTS, §143-186.

COUNCIL ON DEVELOPMENTAL DISABILITIES, §143B-177.

COUNCIL ON EDUCATIONAL SERVICES FOR EXCEPTIONAL CHILDREN, §115C-121, (a).

COUNCIL ON EMPLOYMENT OF THE HANDICAPPED, §143-283.2.

COUNCIL ON SICKLE CELL SYNDROME, §130A-131.2.

COUNCIL ON THE HOLOCAUST, §143A-48.1.

COUNCIL ON THE STATUS OF WOMEN, §143B-393.

COURTS COMMISSION, §7A-506.

CREDIT UNION COMMISSION, §143B-439.

CREDIT UNION DIVISION, §54-109.10.

CREMATORY AUTHORITY, §90-210.47.

CRIME CONTROL DIVISION, §143B-477.

CRIME VICTIMS COMPENSATION COMMISSION, §15B-3.

CRIMINAL JUSTICE EDUCATION AND TRAINING STANDARDS COMMISSION, §17C-3.

CROP IMPROVEMENT ASSOCIATION, §106-273.

D

DEPARTMENT OF ADMINISTRATION, §143B-366.

DEPARTMENT OF AGRICULTURE AND CONSUMER SERVICES, §143A-56.

DEPARTMENT OF AGRICULTURE, IMMIGRATION AND STATISTICS, §106-2.

DEPARTMENT OF COMMERCE, §143B-427.

DEPARTMENT OF CORRECTION, §143B-260.

DEPARTMENT OF CRIME CONTROL AND PUBLIC SAFETY, §143B-473.

DEPARTMENT OF CULTURAL RESOURCES, §143B-49.

DEPARTMENT OF ENVIRONMENT AND NATURAL RESOURCES, §143B-279.1.

DEPARTMENT OF HEALTH AND HUMAN SERVICES, §143B-136.1.

DEPARTMENT OF INSURANCE, §143A-73.

DEPARTMENT OF JUSTICE, §143A-49.

DEPARTMENT OF JUVENILE JUSTICE AND DELINQUENCY PREVENTION, §143B-511.

DEPARTMENT OF LABOR, §143A-67.

DEPARTMENT OF PUBLIC INSTRUCTION, §143A-44.1.

DEPARTMENT OF REVENUE, §143B-217.

DEPARTMENT OF STATE AUDITOR, §143A-24.

DEPARTMENT OF STATE TREASURER, §143A-30.

DEPARTMENT OF THE SECRETARY OF STATE, §143A-19.

DEPARTMENT OF TRANSPORTATION, §143B-345.

DIVISION OF AERONAUTICS, §143B-355.

DIVISION OF AGING, §143B-181.1.

DIVISION OF CRIMINAL STATISTICS, §114-10.

DIVISION OF LEGISLATIVE DRAFTING AND CODIFICATION OF STATUTES, §114-9.

DIVISION OF MOTOR VEHICLES OF THE DEPARTMENT OF TRANSPORTATION, §20-1.

DIVISION OF NORTH CAROLINA AQUARIUMS, §143B-289.40.

DIVISION OF PUBLICATIONS, §147-54.1.

E

ECONOMIC DEVELOPMENT BOARD, §143B-434.

ECONOMIC INVESTMENT COMMITTEE.
Job development investment grant program, §143B-437.48.

EDENTON HISTORICAL COMMISSION, §143B-95.

EDUCATION CABINET, §116C-1.

EMERGENCY MEDICAL SERVICES ADVISORY COUNCIL, §143-510, (a).

EMPLOYMENT SECURITY COMMISSION OF NORTH CAROLINA, §96-3, (a).

E-NC AUTHORITY, §143B-437.46.

ENERGY POLICY COUNCIL, §113B-2.

ENVIRONMENTAL MANAGEMENT COMMISSION, §143B-282.

EXECUTIVE MANSION FINE ARTS COMMITTEE, §143B-79.

F

FARMWORKER COUNCIL, §143B-426.25.

FEDERAL TAX REFORM ALLOCATION COMMITTEE, §143-433.7.

FORESTRY COUNCIL, §143B-308.

G

GASOLINE AND OIL INSPECTION BOARD, §119-26.

GENERAL STATUTES COMMISSION, §164-12.

GOVERNOR'S ADVISORY COUNCIL ON AGING, §143B-180.

GOVERNOR'S ADVOCACY COUNCIL FOR PERSONS WITH DISABILITIES, §143B-403.1.

GOVERNOR'S ADVOCACY COUNCIL ON CHILDREN AND YOUTH, §143B-414.

GOVERNOR'S COUNCIL ON PHYSICAL FITNESS AND HEALTH, §130A-33.40.

GOVERNOR'S CRIME COMMISSION, §143B-478.

GOVERNOR'S JOBS FOR VETERANS COMMITTEE, §143B-420.

GOVERNOR'S MANAGEMENT COUNCIL, §143B-426.22.

GRASSROOTS ARTS PROGRAM, §143B-121.

GRIEVANCE RESOLUTION BOARD, §148-118.6.

H

HAZARDOUS WASTE MANAGEMENT COMMISSION, §130B-6.

HEALTH AND WELLNESS TRUST FUND COMMISSION, §147-86.32.

HEALTH INSURANCE INNOVATIONS COMMISSION, §§58-90-1 to 58-90-30.

HISTORICAL COMMISSION, §143B-62.

HISTORIC BATH COMMISSION, §143B-99.

HISTORIC HILLSBOROUGH COMMISSION, §143B-103.

HISTORIC MURFREESBORO COMMISSION, §143B-107.

HOME INSPECTOR LICENSURE BOARD, §143-151.46.

HOUSING FINANCE AGENCY, §122A-4.

HUMAN RELATIONS COMMISSION, §143B-391.

I

INDUSTRIAL COMMISSION, §97-77.

INFORMATION RESOURCE MANAGEMENT COMMISSION, §147-33.78.

INSURANCE DEPARTMENT, §58-2-1.

INSURANCE GUARANTY ASSOCIATION, §58-48-25.

INSURANCE UNDERWRITING ASSOCIATION, §58-45-10.

INTERAGENCY COORDINATING COUNCIL FOR HANDICAPPED CHILDREN.

From birth to five years of age, §§143B-179.5, 143B-179.6.

INTERNSHIP COUNCIL, §143B-417.

INTERPRETER AND TRANSLITERATOR LICENSING BOARD, §90D-5.

J

JOB DEVELOPMENT INVESTMENT GRANT PROGRAM.

Economic investment committee, §143B-437.48.

JOHN MOTLEY MOREHEAD MEMORIAL COMMISSION, §143B-111.

JUDICIAL STANDARDS COMMISSION, §7A-375.

JUSTICE ACADEMY, §17D-2, (b).

JUSTUS-WARREN HEART DISEASE AND STROKE PREVENTION COUNCIL, §143B-216.60.

JUVENILE JUSTICE, OFFICE OF, §147-33.30.

L

LAKE WYLIE MARINE COMMISSION, §§77-30 to 77-38.

LAND CONSERVATION AND LAND DEVELOPMENT BUREAU, §54-49.

LAND POLICY COUNCIL, §113A-153.

LANDSCAPE CONTRACTORS' REGISTRATION BOARD, §89D-4, (a).

LEGISLATIVE COMMITTEE ON ENERGY CRISIS MANAGEMENT, §113B-21.

LIFE SCIENCES REVENUE BOND AUTHORITY, §159D-65 to 159D-69.

LOCAL GOVERNMENT COMMISSION, §159-3, (a).

M

MANUFACTURED HOUSING BOARD, §143-143.10.

MARINE FISHERIES COMMISSION, §143B-289.50.

MARRIAGE AND FAMILY THERAPY LICENSURE BOARD, §90-270.49, (a).

MEDICAL BOARD OF THE STATE OF NORTH CAROLINA, §90-2, (a).

MEDICAL CARE COMMISSION, §143B-165.

MILK COMMISSION, §106-266.7.

MINING COMMISSION, §143B-290.

MINORITY HEALTH ADVISORY COUNCIL, §130A-33.43.

MOTORBOAT COMMITTEE, §75A-3.

MOTOR VEHICLE DEALERS' ADVISORY BOARD, §20-305.4.

MOTOR VEHICLE REINSURANCE FACILITY, §58-37-5.

N

NATIONAL PARK, PARKWAY AND FORESTS DEVELOPMENT COMMISSION, §143-258.

NATIONAL PARK, PARKWAY AND FORESTS DEVELOPMENT COUNCIL, §143B-324.1.

NONGAME WILDLIFE ADVISORY COMMITTEE, §113-335.

NORTH CAROLINA COUNCIL ON THE HOLOCAUST, §143A-48.1.

NURSING SCHOLARS COMMISSION, §90-171.60.

O

OFFICE OF COORDINATOR OF SERVICES FOR VICTIMS OF SEXUAL ASSAULT, §143B-394.1.

OFFICE OF DIRECTOR OF THE BOILER AND PRESSURE VESSEL DIVISION, §95-69.12.

OFFICE OF ENVIRONMENTAL EDUCATION, §143B-285.22.

OFFICE OF INFORMATION TECHNOLOGY SERVICES, §147-33.75.

OFFICE OF LOCAL GOVERNMENT ADVOCACY, §143-506.14.

OFFICE OF OCCUPATIONAL SAFETY AND HEALTH, §95-133, (a).

P

PARKS AND RECREATION AUTHORITY, §143B-313.1.

PESTICIDE BOARD, §143-436.

PETROLEUM UNDERGROUND STORAGE TANK FUNDS COUNCIL, §143-215.94D.

PIEDMONT TRIAD RESEARCH INSTITUTE, §116-250.

PLANT CONSERVATION BOARD, §106-202.14, (a).

PORTS RAILWAY COMMISSION, §143B-469.

POSTAL HISTORY COMMISSION, §143-675.

POST-RELEASE SUPERVISION AND PAROLE COMMISSION, §143B-266.

PRIVATE PROTECTIVE SERVICES BOARD, §74C-4, (a).

PROFESSIONAL ADVISORY COMMITTEE, §143B-161.

PROGRESS BOARD, §143B-372.1.

PROPERTY TAX COMMISSION, §105-288, (b).

PUBLIC DEFENDER OFFICE, §7A-465.

PUBLIC EMPLOYEE DEFERRED COMPENSATION PLAN.

Board of trustees, §143B-426.24.

PUBLIC EMPLOYEE SPECIAL PAY PLAN.

Board of trustees, §143B-426.41.

PUBLIC HEALTH STUDY COMMISSION, §§120-195 to 120-203.

PUBLIC LIBRARIAN CERTIFICATION COMMISSION, §143B-67.

PUBLIC LIVESTOCK MARKET ADVISORY BOARD, §106-407.1.

PUBLIC RADIO ADVISORY COMMITTEE, §143B-426.12.

PUBLIC TELECOMMUNICATIONS AGENCY, §143B-426.9.

R

RADIATION PROTECTION COMMISSION, §104E-7.

RAIL COUNCIL, §143B-362.

RATE BUREAU, §58-36-1.

REAL ESTATE COMMISSION, §93A-3, (a).

ROANOKE ISLAND COMMISSION, §143B-131.1.

ROANOKE ISLAND HISTORICAL ASSOCIATION, §143B-92.

ROANOKE RIVER BASIN ADVISORY COMMITTEE, §§77-103 to 77-106.

ROANOKE RIVER BASIN BI-STATE COMMISSION, §§77-90 to 77-99.

RURAL ELECTRIFICATION AUTHORITY, §117-1.

RURAL REHABILITATION CORPORATION, §137-31.

S

SAFETY AND HEALTH REVIEW BOARD, §95-135, (a).

SALTWATER FISHING FUND.

Board of trustees, §§113-175 to 113-175.4.

SAVINGS INSTITUTIONS COMMISSION, §54B-53.

SCHOOL TECHNOLOGY COMMISSION, §115C-102.5.

SCIENCE AND TECHNOLOGY RESEARCH CENTER, §143B-442.

SEAFOOD INDUSTRIAL PARK AUTHORITY, §113-315.25, (a).

SEDIMENTATION CONTROL COMMISSION, §143B-299, (a).

Department of the environment and natural resources, §143B-298.

SENTENCING AND POLICY ADVISORY COMMISSION, §§164-35 to 164-45.

SHERIFFS' EDUCATION AND TRAINING STANDARDS COMMISSION, §17E-3.

SMALL BUSINESS CONTRACTOR AUTHORITY, §§143B-472.85 to 143B-472.97.

SOCIAL SERVICES COMMISSION, §143B-153.

SOIL AND WATER CONSERVATION COMMISSION, §143B-294.

SOUTH ATLANTIC FISHERY MANAGEMENT COUNCIL, §113-259.

SOUTHERN GROWTH POLICIES BOARD, §143-492.

SOUTHERN STATES ENERGY BOARD, §§104D-1, 104D-2.

SPECIAL PROSECUTION DIVISION, §114-11.6.

STATE ADVISORY COUNCIL ON OCCUPATIONAL SAFETY AND HEALTH, §95-134, (a).

STATE AGENCY FOR FEDERAL SURPLUS PROPERTY, §143-64.1.

STATE BOARD OF BARBER EXAMINERS, §86A-4, (a).

STATE BOARD OF CERTIFIED PUBLIC ACCOUNTANT EXAMINERS, §93-12.

STATE BOARD OF CHIROPRACTIC EXAMINERS, §90-139, (a).

STATE BOARD OF COMMUNITY COLLEGES, §115D-2.1, (a).

STATE BOARD OF COSMETIC ART EXAMINERS, §88B-3.

STATE BOARD OF DENTAL EXAMINERS, §90-22, (b).

STATE BOARD OF EDUCATION, §115C-10.

STATE BOARD OF ELECTIONS, §163-19.

STATE BOARD OF EXAMINERS FOR NURSING HOME ADMINISTRATORS, §90-277.

STATE BOARD OF EXAMINERS IN OPTOMETRY, §90-116.

STATE BOARD OF EXAMINERS OF ELECTRICAL CONTRACTORS, §87-39.

STATE BOARD OF EXAMINERS OF FEE-BASED PRACTICING PASTORAL COUNSELORS, §90-385.

STATE BOARD OF EXAMINERS OF PLUMBING AND HEATING CONTRACTORS, §87-16.

STATE BOARD OF EXAMINERS OF PRACTICING PSYCHOLOGISTS, §90-270.6.

STATE BOARD OF OPTICIANS, §90-238.

STATE BOARD OF OSTEOPATHIC EXAMINATION AND REGISTRATION, §90-130.

STATE BOARD OF REFRIGERATION EXAMINERS, §87-52.

STATE BOARD OF REGISTRATION FOR FORESTERS, §89B-3, (a).

STATE BOARD OF REGISTRATION FOR PROFESSIONAL ENGINEERS AND LAND SURVEYORS, §89C-4.

STATE BOARD OF SANITARIAN EXAMINERS, §90A-50.

STATE BOARD OF THERAPEUTIC RECREATION CERTIFICATION, §90C-5.

STATE BUILDING COMMISSION, §143-135.25.

STATE BUREAU OF INVESTIGATION, §114-12.

STATE COMMISSION FOR HEALTH SERVICES, §130A-29.

STATE COMMISSION OF INDIAN AFFAIRS, §143B-404.

STATE CRIMINAL JUSTICE PARTNERSHIP ADVISORY BOARD, §143B-273.6.

STATE EDUCATION ASSISTANCE AUTHORITY, §116-203.

STATE EDUCATION COMMISSION, §§116C-2, 143-261.

STATE FIRE AND RESCUE COMMISSION, §58-78-1.

STATE HEARING AID DEALERS AND FITTERS BOARD, §93D-3, (a).

STATE HIGHWAY PATROL, §20-184.

STATE INDIAN HOUSING AUTHORITY, §157-66.

STATE JUDICIAL COUNCIL, §§7A-409 to 7A-411.

STATE LIBRARY COMMISSION, §143B-90.

STATE LICENSING BOARD FOR GENERAL CONTRACTORS, §87-2.

STATE MARKETING AUTHORITY, §106-529.

STATE PERSONNEL COMMISSION, §126-2.

STATE PORTS AUTHORITY, §143B-452.

STATE SCHOOL HEALTH ADVISORY COMMITTEE, §115C-81.

STATE YOUTH ADVISORY COUNCIL, §143B-385.

STRUCTURAL PEST CONTROL COMMITTEE, §106-65.23.

STRUCTURAL PEST CONTROL DIVISION OF DEPARTMENT OF AGRICULTURE, §106-65.23.

STUDY COMMISSION ON AGING, §120-180.

SUBSTANCE ABUSE ADVISORY COUNCIL, §143B-270.

SUBSTANCE ABUSE PROFESSIONALS CERTIFICATION BOARD, §90-113.32.

SYMPHONY SOCIETY, INC., §143B-94.

T

TOBACCO TRUST FUND COMMISSION, §143-715.

TRAILS COMMITTEE, §143B-333.

TRAUMATIC BRAIN INJURY ADVISORY COUNCIL, §§143B-216.65, 143B-216.66.

TRAVEL AND TOURISM BOARD, §143B-434.1.

TRYON PALACE COMMISSION, §143B-71.

TURNPIKE AUTHORITY, §136-89.182.

U

U.S.S. NORTH CAROLINA BATTLESHIP COMMISSION, §143B-73.

UTILITIES COMMISSION, §62-10, (a).

V

VETERANS' AFFAIRS COMMISSION, §143B-399.

VETERANS' MEMORIAL COMMISSION, §143B-133.

VETERINARY MEDICAL BOARD, §90-182, (a).

W

WAGE AND HOUR DIVISION, §95-25.17.

WATER POLLUTION CONTROL SYSTEM OPERATORS.

Certification commission, §143B-300.

WATER TREATMENT FACILITY OPERATORS BOARD OF CERTIFICATION, §90A-21, (a).

WELL CONTRACTORS CERTIFICATION COMMISSION, §143B-301.10.

WILDLIFE RESOURCES COMMISSION, §143-240.

Z

ZOOLOGICAL AUTHORITY, §143-177.

Short Title/Popular Name Index

A

ABANDONMENT ACT, §§14-322 to 14-326.1.

ABC ACT, §§18B-100 to 18B-1119.

ABC STORE ACT, §§18B-800 to 18B-807.

ABORTION ACT, §§14-44 to 14-46.

ABSENTEE VOTING ACT, §§163-226 to 163-239.

ABUSED, NEGLECTED OR EXPLOITED DISABLED ADULT ACT, §§108A-99 to 108A-111.

ACCESS TO CIVIL JUSTICE ACT, §§7A-474.1 to 7A-474.5.

ACCOUNTANTS' ACT, §§93-1 to 93-13.

ACTUARIAL NOTE ACT, §§120-112 to 120-114.

ACUPUNCTURE PRACTICE ACT, §§90-450 to 90-459.

ADMINISTRATION DEPARTMENT ACT, §§143-334 to 143-345.9.

ADMINISTRATIVE PROCEDURE ACT, §§150B-1 to 150B-52.

ADULT CARE HOME RESIDENTS' BILL OF RIGHTS, §§131D-19 to 131D-34.

ADULT PROTECTION ACT, §§108A-99 to 108A-111.

ADVERTISING CONTROL ACT, §§136-126 to 136-140.

AERONAUTICS ACT, §§63-1 to 63-89.

AFDC, §§108A-27 to 108A-39.1.

AFTER-BORN CHILD ACT, §31-5.5.

AGRICULTURAL DEVELOPMENT ACT, §§106-580 to 106-587.

AGRICULTURAL FINANCE ACT, §§122D-1 to 122D-23.

AGRICULTURAL LIMING MATERIALS AND LANDPLASTER ACT, §§106-92.1 to 106-92.17.

AGRICULTURE EXTENSION SERVICE.
Agriculture development act, §§106-580 to 106-587.

AID TO FAMILIES WITH DEPENDENT CHILDREN ACT, §§108A-27 to 108A-39.1.

AIR AND WATER QUALITY REPORTING ACT, §§143-215.63 to 143-215.69.

AIR AND WATER RESOURCES ACT, §§143-211 to 143-215.74I.

AIR POLLUTION CONTROL, §§143-215.103 to 143-215.114C.

AIRPORT DEVELOPMENT ACT, §§63-65 to 63-73.

AIRPORT DISTRICTS ACT, §§63-78 to 63-89.

AIRPORT ZONING ACT, §§63-30 to 63-37.1.

ALARM SYSTEMS LICENSING ACT, §§74D-1 to 74D-13.

ALCOHOLIC BEVERAGE CONTROL ACT, §§18B-100 to 18B-1119.

ALIEN PROPERTY ACT, §§64-1 to 64-5.

ALIEN RECIPROCAL INHERITANCE ACT, §§64-3 to 64-5.

ALIMONY ACT, §§50-16.1A to 50-17.

AMBER ALERT SYSTEM, §143B-499.7.

AMBULATORY SURGICAL FACILITY LICENSURE ACT, §§131E-145 to 131E-152.

AMUSEMENT DEVICE SAFETY ACT, §§95-111.1 to 95-111.18.

AMY JACKSON LAW, §§14-208.5 to 14-208.13.

ANATOMICAL GIFT ACT, §§130A-402 to 130A-412.1.

ANIMAL WELFARE ACT, §§19A-20 to 19A-40.

ANNEXATION ACT, §§160A-29 to 160A-58.28.

ANTI-BLACKLISTING ACT, §14-355.

ANTI-CLOSED SHOP ACT, §§95-78 to 95-84.

ANTI-DEFICIENCY JUDGMENT ACT, §45-21.38.

ANTIFREEZE LAW OF 1975, §§106-579.1 to 106-579.14.

ANTILAPSE ACT, §31-42.

ANTI-MONOPOLY ACT, §§75-1 to 75-35.

ANTI-SLOT MACHINE ACT, §§14-304 to 14-309.1.

ANTITRUST ACT, §§75-1 to 75-35.

ANTI-VANDALISM ACT, §1-538.1.

APPALACHIAN TRAILS SYSTEM ACT, §§113A-72 to 113A-77.

APPORTIONMENT ACT, §§120-1 to 120-2.2.

APPRAISERS ACT, §§93E-1-1 to 93E-1-14.

AQUACULTURE DEVELOPMENT ACT, §§106-756 to 106-764.

ARBITRATION ACT.
International commercial arbitration act, §§1-567.30 to 1-567.67.

ARBITRATION OF LABOR DISPUTES, §§95-36.1 to 95-36.9.

ARCHAEOLOGICAL RECORD PROGRAM, §§70-46 to 70-52.

ARCHAEOLOGICAL RESOURCES PROTECTION ACT, §§70-10 to 70-20.

ARCHITECTS LICENSING ACT, §§83A-1 to 83A-17.

ARCHIVES AND HISTORY ACT, §§121-1 to 121-42.

ARMORY ACT, §§127A-161 to 127A-169.

ARREST WITHOUT WARRANT ACT, §§15A-401 to 15A-406.

ARTIFICIAL INSEMINATION, §§49A-1, 90-187.10.

ARTWORK ON CONSIGNMENT, §§25C-1 to 25C-5.

ASSET PROTECTION ACT, §§58-13-1 to 58-13-25.

ASSIGNED RISK ACT, §20-279.21.

ASSIGNMENT OF PUPILS ACT, §§115C-364 to 115C-372.

ASSISTED LIVING ADMINISTRATORS, §§90-288.10 to 90-288.20.

ASSOCIATE SAFETY PROFESSIONALS (ASP), §§90-671 to 90-674.

ASSUMED BUSINESS NAME ACT, §§66-68 to 66-71.

ATHLETE AGENTS.
Uniform athlete agent act, §§78C-85 to 78C-105.

ATHLETIC TRAINERS LICENSING ACT, §90-522.

ATLANTIC STATES MARINE FISHERIES COMPACT ACT, §§113-252 to 113-258.

ATTACHMENT ACT, §§1-440.1 to 1-440.46.

ATTENDANCE OF WITNESSES FROM WITHOUT STATE IN CRIMINAL PROCEEDINGS ACT, §§15A-811 to 15A-816.

AUTOPSIES, §§130A-398 to 130A-401.

B

BABY DROP OFF, §14-322.3.

BACKGROUND INVESTIGATIONS, §114-19.1 to 114-19.15.

BAD CHECK ACT, §§14-106 to 14-107.1.

BALANCED GROWTH POLICY ACT, §§143-506.6 to 143-506.14.

BALLOON PAYMENTS, §25A-34.

BANG'S DISEASE ACT, §§106-388 to 106-398.

BANK BRANCH ACT, §53-62.

BANK DEPOSITS AND COLLECTIONS-UNIFORM COMMERCIAL CODE, §§25-4-101 to 25-4-504.

BANK HOLDING COMPANY ACT OF 1984, §§53-225 to 53-232.

BANKING LAW, §§53-1 to 53-208.

BAR ACT, §§84-15 to 84-38.

BARBER ACT, §§86A-1 to 86A-26.

BARBITURATE AND STIMULANT DRUGS ACT, §§90-86 to 90-113.8.

BASEBALL PARK DISTRICT, §§160C-1, 160C-2.

BASTARDY ACT, §§49-1 to 49-17.

BATTLE ACT, §41-10.

BEE AND HONEY ACT OF 1977, §§106-634 to 106-644.

BEER AND WINE LOCAL OPTION ACT, §§18B-600 to 18B-605.

BETTERMENTS ACT, §§1-340 to 1-351.

BICYCLE AND BIKEWAY ACT OF 1974, §§136-71.6 to 136-71.13.

BILL OF RIGHTS FOR ADULT DAY CARE HOME RESIDENTS, §§131D-19 to 131D-34.

BIOLOGICAL ORGANISM ACT, §§106-65.42 to 106-65.49.

BIOLOGICS LAW OF 1981, §§106-707 to 106-715.

BLACKLISTING ACT, §14-355.

BLUE LAWS, §160A-191.

BLUE SKY LAW, §§78A-1 to 78A-65.

BOATING SAFETY ACT, §§75A-1 to 75A-19.

BOAT TITLING ACT, §§75A-32 to 75A-49.

BOILER AND PRESSURE VESSEL ACT, §§95-69.8 to 95-69.18.

BOLL WEEVIL ERADICATION ACT, §§106-65.67 to 106-65.78.

BORROWING ACT FOR LIMITATIONS, §1-21.

BRAIN DEATH ACT, §§90-320 to 90-323.

BRANCH BANK ACT, §53-62.

BREAKING AND ENTERING ACT, §14-54.

BREATH TESTS, §§20-16.2, 20-139.1.

BRIDGE LOAD LIMIT ACT, §136-72.

BROADCAST DEFAMATION ACT, §§99-1 to 99-5.

BROWN-BAGGING ACT, §18B-301.

BROWNFIELDS PROPERTY REUSE ACT OF 1997, §§130A-453.01 to 130A-453.11.

BRUCELLOSIS ACT, §§106-388 to 106-398.

BUCKET SHOP ACT, §§16-3 to 16-6.

BUDGET ACT, §§143-1 to 143-34.7.

BUDGET AND FISCAL CONTROL ACT FOR LOCAL GOVERNMENT, §§159-7 to 159-41.

BUGGING, §14-155.

BUILDING CODE, §§143-136 to 143-143.3.

BUILDING CONTRACT ACT, §§143-128 to 143-135.8.

BULK TRANSFERS-UNIFORM COMMERCIAL CODE, §§25-6-101 to 25-6-111.

BUREAU OF INVESTIGATION.
Background investigations, §§114-19.1 to 114-19.15.

BURGLARY ACT, §§14-51 to 14-57.

BURGLARY TOOLS ACT, §14-55.

BUSINESS CORPORATION ACT, §§55-1-01 to 55-17-05.

BUSINESS ENERGY INPROVEMENT PROGRAM, §§143-345.16 to 143-345.18.

BUSINESS TAX CREDIT, §§105-129.15 to 105-129.19.

BUSINESS UNDER ASSUMED NAME ACT, §§66-68 to 66-71.

C

CAMPAIGN CONTRIBUTIONS AND EXPENDITURES, §§163-278.6 to 163-278.40I.

CAPITAL FACILITIES FINANCING ACT, §§159D-1 to 159D-57.

CAPITAL IMPROVEMENT PLANNING ACT, §§143-34.40 to 143-34.45.

CAPITAL ISSUES LAW, §§78A-1 to 78A-65.

CARDIAC REHABILITATION CERTIFICATION PROGRAM, §§131E-165 to 131E-170.

CAROLYN SONZOGNI ACT, §90-600.

CARRIER ACT, §§62-259 to 62-279.

CARTWAY ACT, §§136-69, 136-70.

CAVE PROTECTION ACT, §§14-159.20 to 14-159.23.

CDL.
Commercial driver's license act, §§20-37.10 to 20-37.23.

CEMETERY ACT, §§65-46 to 65-73.

CENTENNIAL CAMPUS AND HORACE WILLIAMS CAMPUS FINANCING ACT, §§116-198.31 to 116-198.40.

CERTIFICATES OF TITLES ACT, §§20-50 to 20-71.1.

CERTIFIED PUBLIC ACCOUNTANTS ACT, §§93-1 to 93-13.

CERTIFIED SAFETY PROFESSIONALS (CSP), §§90-671 to 90-674.

CHANGE OF VENUE ACT, §1-83.

CHARITABLE REMAINDER TRUSTS ADMINISTRATION ACT, §§36A-59.1 to 36A-59.7.

CHARITABLE TRUSTS ADMINISTRATION ACT, §36A-53.

CHARTER SCHOOLS, §§115C-238.29A to 115C-238.29J.

CHATTEL MORTGAGE RECORDATION ACT, §47-20.

CHEMICAL TESTS FOR INTOXICATION OF DRIVERS ACT, §20-139.1.

CHILD BICYCLE SAFETY ACT, §§20-171.6 to 20-171.9.

CHILD CUSTODY AND SUPPORT ACT, §§50-13.1 to 50-13.12.

CHILD CUSTODY JURISDICTION AND ENFORCEMENT ACT, §§50A-101 to 50A-317.

CHILD PLACEMENT COMPACT, §§110-57.1 to 110-57.7.

CHILDREN'S SUPPORT ACT FOR ILLEGITIMATE CHILDREN, §§49-1 to 49-9.

CHILD SUPPORT ENFORCEMENT, §§110-128 to 110-142.2.

CHURCH SCHOOLS, §§115C-547 to 115C-554.

CIGARETTE TAX, §§105-113.5 to 105-113.33.

CITIZEN'S ARREST, §§15A-404, 15A-405.

CITY-COUNTY CONSOLIDATION ACT, §§160B-1 to 160B-21.

CIVIL PROCEDURE ACT, §§1-1 to 1-601.

CIVIL RIGHTS, INTERFERENCE WITH, §99D-1.

CLEAN WATER REVOLVING LOAN AND GRANT ACT OF 1987, §§159G-1 to 159G-18.

CLOSED SHOP ACT, §§95-78 to 95-84.

CLOSING-OUT SALES ACT, §§66-76 to 66-83.

COASTAL AREA MANAGEMENT ACT OF 1974, §§113A-100 to 113A-134.3.

COLOR OF TITLE, §§1-38, 98-8.

COMMERCIAL BANKING LAW, §§53-1 to 53-208.

COMMERCIAL CODE, §§25-1-101 to 25-11-108.

COMMERCIAL DRIVERS' LICENSE ACT, §§20-37.10 to 20-37.23.

COMMERCIAL FEED LAW OF 1973, §§106-284.30 to 106-284.46.

COMMERCIAL FERTILIZER LAW, §§106-655 to 106-677.

COMMERCIAL FISHERMEN'S HULL INSURANCE, PROTECTION AND INDEMNITY CLUB ACT, §§58-20-1 to 58-20-40.

COMMODITIES ACT, §§78D-1 to 78D-33.

COMMON TRUST FUND ACT, §§36A-90 to 36A-94.

COMMUNITY ACTION PARTNERSHIP ACT, §§108B-21 to 108B-26.

COMMUNITY COLLEGES, §§115D-1 to 115D-81.

COMMUNITY PROPERTY.
Uniform disposition of community property rights at death act, §§31C-1 to 31C-12.

COMMUNITY SCHOOLS ACT, §§115C-203 to 115C-209.

COMMUNITY TRUST FOR PERSONS WITH SEVERE CHRONIC DISABILITIES ACT, §§36A-59.10 to 36A-59.20.

COMPANY POLICE ACT, §§74E-1 to 74E-13.

COMPENSATING USE TAX ACT, §§105-164.1 to 105-164.44D.

COMPETENCY ACT FOR CRIMINAL DEFENDANTS, §8-54.

COMPULSORY ATTENDANCE ACT, §§115C-378 to 115C-383.

COMPULSORY INSURANCE ACT, §§20-309 to 20-319.

COMPULSORY MEAT INSPECTION ACT, §§106-549.15 to 106-549.28.

COMPULSORY POULTRY INSPECTION ACT, §§106-549.49 to 106-549.69.

CONCEALED WEAPONS ACT, §14-269.

CONDEMNATION ACT, §§40A-1 to 40A-70.

CONDOMINIUM ACT, §§47C-1-101 to 47C-4-120.

CONFIDENTIALITY OF LEGISLATIVE COMMUNICATIONS, §§120-129 to 120-134.

CONFORMITY ACT FOR JUDGMENTS, §1-237.

CONNOR ACT, §47-18.

CONSERVATION AND HISTORIC PRESERVATION AGREEMENTS ACT, §§121-34 to 121-42.

CONSOLIDATED CITY-COUNTY ACT OF 1973, §§160B-1 to 160B-21.

CONSOLIDATED JUDICIAL RETIREMENT ACT, §§135-50 to 135-74.

CONSPIRACY TO VIOLATE CIVIL RIGHTS, §99D-1.

CONSUMER FINANCE ACT, §§53-164 to 53-191.

CONTEMPT ACT, §§5A-11 to 5A-25.

CONTRIBUTING TO THE DELINQUENCY OF MINORS, §14-316.1.

CONTRIBUTION AMONG TORT-FEASORS ACT, §§1B-1 to 1B-6.

CONTRIBUTIONS TO POLITICAL CAMPAIGNS, §§163-278.6 to 163-278.40I.

CONTROLLED SUBSTANCES ACT, §§90-86 to 90-113.8.

CONTROL SHARE ACQUISITION ACT, §§55-9A-01 to 55-9A-09.

COOPERATIVE INNOVATION HIGH SCHOOL PROGRAMS, §§115C-238.50 to 115C-238.55.

COOPERATIVE MARKETING ASSOCIATIONS ACT, §§54-129 to 54-166.

CORNEAL TISSUE REMOVAL, §130A-391.

CORPORATE OFFICERS INDEMNIFICATION ACT, §§55-8-50 to 55-8-58.

CORPORATE TAKEOVERS, §§75E-1 to 75E-9.

CORPORATION INCOME TAX ACT, §§105-130 to 105-130.42.

S corporation income tax act, §§105-131 to 105-131.8.

CORRECTIONS COMPACT, §§148-119 to 148-121.

COSMETIC ART ACT, §§88B-1 to 88B-29.

COTTON WAREHOUSE ACT, §§106-451.6 to 106-451.28.

COUNTY-CITY CONSOLIDATION ACT, §§160B-1 to 160B-15.

COUNTY SERVICE DISTRICT ACT OF 1973, §§153A-300 to 153A-310.

COURTS-MARTIAL, §§127A-47 to 127A-61.

COVENTRY ACT, §§14-30, 14-30.1.

CREDIT CARD CRIME ACT, §§14-113.8 to 14-113.17.

CREDIT CARD INSURANCE ACT, §58-3-145.

CREDIT REPAIR SERVICES ACT, §§66-220 to 66-226.

CREDIT UNION ACT, §§54-109.1 to 54-110.10.

CREMATION, §130A-388.

CREMATORY ACT, §§90-210.40 to 90-210.54.

CRIME AGAINST NATURE, §14-177.

CRIME VICTIMS COMPENSATION ACT, §§15B-1 to 15B-38.

CRIME VICTIMS FINANCIAL RECOVERY ASSISTANCE ACT, §§15B-26 to 15B-38.

CRIMINAL EXTRADITION ACT, §§15A-721 to 15A-750.

CRIMINAL HISTORY RECORD CHECKS, §§114-19.1 to 114-19.15.

CRIMINAL JUSTICE PARTNERSHIP ACT, §§143B-273 to 143B-273.19.

CRIMINAL PROCEDURE ACT, §§15A-101 to 15A-2003.

CUSTODIAL TRUST ACT, §§33B-1 to 33B-22.

CUSTODY AND SUPPORT OF CHILDREN ACT, §§50-13.1 to 50-13.12.

CUSTOMER INFORMATION SAFEGUARDS ACT, §§58-39-130 to 58-39-165.

D

DAM SAFETY LAW, §§143-215.23 to 143-215.37.

DEATH BENEFITS ACT, §§143-166.1 to 143-166.7.

DEATH BY WRONGFUL ACT, §28A-18-2.

DECLARATORY JUDGMENTS ACT, §§1-253 to 1-267.

DEFAMATION ACT, §§99-1 to 99-5.

DEFAULTED STUDENT LOAN RECOVERY ACT, §§105B-1 to 105B-4.

DEFENSE OF PUBLIC SCHOOL EMPLOYEES, §§143-300.13 to 143-300.18.

DEFENSE OF STATE EMPLOYEES, §§143-300.2 to 143-300.10.

DEFERRED PROSECUTION, §15A-1341.

DEFICIENCY JUDGMENT ACT, §45-21.38.

DEMURRER TO THE EVIDENCE ACT, §15-173.

DENTAL HYGIENE ACT, §§90-221 to 90-233.1.

DENTAL PEER REVIEW PROTECTION ACT, §§90-48.7 to 90-48.11.

DEPARTMENT OF ADMINISTRATION ACT, §§143-334 to 143-345.9.

DEPOSITIONS ACT, §§8-74 to 8-83.

DESCENT AND DISTRIBUTION ACT, §§29-1 to 29-30.

DETAINER AGREEMENT ACT, §§15A-761 to 15A-767.

DIETETICS/NUTRITION PRACTICE ACT, §§90-350 to 90-369.

DISABILITY INCOME PLAN OF NORTH CAROLINA, §§135-100 to 135-114.

DISASTER SERVICE VOLUNTEER LEAVE, §§166A-30 to 166A-32.

DISSENT FROM WILL ACT, §§30-1 to 30-3.

DISTRIBUTION LAW, §§29-1 to 29-30.

DIVORCE ACT, §§50-2 to 50-22.

DNA DATABASE AND DATABANK ACT, §§15A-266 to 15A-270.

DOCUMENTS OF TITLE, §§25-7-101 to 25-7-603.

DO NOT CALL LAW, §§75-100 to 75-105.

DOOR CLOSING ACT, §45-21.38.

DRAM SHOP LIABILITY ACT, §18B-305, (a).

DRINKING WATER ACT, §§130A-311 to 130A-328.

DRIVER'S LICENSE ACT, §§20-5 to 20-37.
Commercial driver's license act, §§20-37.10 to 20-37.23.

DRIVER'S LICENSE COMPACT, §§20-4.21 to 20-4.30.

DRIVER TRAINING SCHOOL LICENSING LAW, §§20-320 to 20-328.

DRUG ACT, §§90-86 to 90-113.8.

DRUG AND COSMETIC ACT, §§106-120 to 106-145.12.

DRUG PARAPHERNALIA ACT, §§90-113.20 to 90-113.24.

DRUG TESTING REGULATION, §§95-230 to 95-235.

DRUG TREATMENT COURT, §§7A-790 to 7A-801.

DRUNKEN DRIVING ACT, §§20-138.1 to 20-139.1, 20-179.

DRY-CLEANING SOLVENT CLEANUP ACT OF 1997, §§143-215.104A to 143-215.104U.

DRY-CLEANING SOLVENT TAX, §§105-187.30 to 105-187.34.

DURABLE POWER OF ATTORNEY, §§32A-8 to 32A-14.

E

EDUCATIONAL PERSONNEL QUALIFICATIONS ACT, §§115C-349 to 115C-358.

EDUCATION COMPACT, §115C-104.

EGG LAW, §§106-245.13 to 106-245.28.

ELECTION LAWS, §§163-1 to 163-306.

ELECTRIC MEMBERSHIP CORPORATIONS ACT, §§117-6 to 117-26.

ELECTROLYSIS PRACTICE ACT, §§88A-1 to 88A-23.

ELEVATOR SAFETY ACT, §§95-110.1 to 95-110.15.

EMANCIPATION OF MARRIED PERSONS, §52-2.

EMANCIPATION OF MINORS, §§7B-3500 to 7B-3509.

EMERGENCY INTERIM LOCAL GOVERNMENT EXECUTIVE SUCCESSION ACT OF 1959, §§162B-5 to 162B-13.

EMERGENCY MANAGEMENT ACT OF 1977, §§166A-1 to 166A-16.

EMERGENCY MANAGEMENT ASSISTANCE COMPACT, §§166A-40 to 166A-53.

EMERGENCY MEDICAL SERVICES ACT OF 1973, §§143-507 to 143-517.

EMERGENCY WAR POWERS ACT, §§147-33.1 to 147-33.6.

EMINENT DOMAIN ACT, §§40A-1 to 40A-70.

EMPLOYEES' RETIREMENT SYSTEM ACT FOR LOCAL GOVERNMENTS, §§128-21 to 128-38.2.

EMPLOYMENT AND TRAINING ACT OF 1985, §§143B-438.1 to 143B-438.6.

EMPLOYMENT PREFERENCE FOR VETERANS, §§126-80 to 126-83, 128-15.

EMPLOYMENT SECURITY LAW, §§96-1 to 96-29.

E-NC INITIATIVE, §§143B-437.44 to 143B-437.47.

ENDANGERED WILDLIFE LAW, §§113-331 to 113-337.

ENERGY CONSERVATION FINANCE ACT, §§142-60 to 142-70.

ENERGY POLICY ACT, §§62-2, 113B-1 to 113B-24.

ENFORCEMENT OF FOREIGN JUDGMENTS ACT, §§1C-1701 to 1C-1708.

ENGINEERING AND LAND SURVEYING ACT, §§89C-1 to 89C-28.

ENTERPRISE CORPORATION ACT, §§53A-35 to 53A-47.

ENVIRONMENTAL COMPACT ACT, §§113A-21 to 113A-23.

ENVIRONMENTAL EDUCATION ACT OF 1993, §§143B-285.20 to 143B-285.25.

ENVIRONMENTAL POLICY ACT OF 1971, §§113A-1 to 113A-13.

EQUAL EMPLOYMENT OPPORTUNITY, §§126-16 to 126-39.

EQUAL EMPLOYMENT PRACTICES ACT, §§143-422.1 to 143-422.3.

EQUINE ACTIVITY LIABILITY, §§99E-1 to 99E-3.

EQUINE INFECTIOUS ANEMIA, §§106-405.15 to 106-405.20.

EROSION CONTROL.
Sedimentation pollution control act of 1973, §§113A-50 to 113A-66.

ESCHEAT LAW, §§116B-1 to 116B-4.

ETHICS, LEGISLATIVE ACT, §§120-85 to 120-106.

ETHNIC HATE CRIMES, §14-401.14.

EVIDENCE RULES, §8C-1, Rules 101 to 1102.

EXECUTIVE BUDGET ACT, §§143-1 to 143-34.7.

EXECUTIVE ORGANIZATION ACT OF 1971, §§143A-1 to 143A-245.

EXECUTIVE ORGANIZATION ACT OF 1973, §§143B-1 to 143B-499.6.

EXPUNGEMENT OF CRIMINAL RECORDS, §§15A-145 to 15A-148.

EXTRADITION ACT, §§15A-721 to 15A-750.

F

FACILITY AUTHORITY ACT, §§160A-480.1 to 160A-480.15.

FAIR HOUSING ACT, §§41A-1 to 41A-10.

FALSE ADVERTISEMENT ACT, §§66-76 to 66-83.

FAMILY PRESERVATION ACT, §§143B-150.5 to 143B-150.9.

FAMILY PURPOSE DOCTRINE, §75A-10.1.

FAMILY SUPPORT ACT, §§52C-1-100 to 52C-9-902.

FAMILY THERAPY LICENSURE ACT, §§90-270.45 to 90-270.62.

FARM AND HOME DEVELOPMENT PROGRAM.

Agriculture development act, §§106-580 to 106-587.

FARMLAND PRESERVATION ENABLING ACT, §§106-735 to 106-744.

FEDERAL LIEN REGISTRATION ACT, §§44-68.10 to 44-68.17.

FEDERAL WATER RESOURCES DEVELOPMENT PROJECTS ACT, §§143-215.38 to 143-215.43.

FEE-BASED PRACTICING PASTORAL COUNSELOR CERTIFICATION ACT, §§90-380 to 90-396.

FEED LAW OF 1973, §§106-284.30 to 106-284.46.

FELONY SENTENCING, §§15A-1340.13 to 15A-1340.17.

FERTILIZER LAW, §§106-655 to 106-677.

FICTITIOUS NAME ACT, §§66-68 to 66-71.

FIDUCIARIES ACT, §§32-1 to 32-13.

FIDUCIARY POWERS.

Renunciation of property and renunciation of fiduciary powers act, §§31B-1 to 31B-7.

FINANCIAL PRIVACY ACT, §§53B-1 to 53B-10.

FINANCIAL RESPONSIBILITY ACT OF 1953, §§20-279.1 to 20-279.39.

FINANCIAL RESPONSIBILITY ACT OF 1957, §§20-309 to 20-319.

FIREMEN'S AND RESCUE SQUAD WORKERS' PENSION FUND, §§58-86-1 to 58-86-91.

FIRE SALES ACT, §§66-76 to 66-83.

FIRST IN AMERICA INNOVATIVE EDUCATION ACT, §116C-4.

FIRST ONE-CENT LOCAL GOVERNMENT SALES AND USE TAX, §§105-463 to 105-474.

FIRST ONE-HALF CENT LOCAL GOVERNMENT SALES AND USE TAX, §§105-480 to 105-487.

FISCAL INFORMATION ACT FOR LOCAL GOVERNMENT, §§120-30.41 to 120-30.49.

FISHERIES LAW, §§113-127 to 113-316.

FISHERMAN'S ECONOMIC DEVELOPMENT ACT, §§113-315.15 to 113-315.19.

FISH FARMING.

Aquaculture development act, §§106-756 to 106-764.

FLANAGAN ACT, §§14-304 to 14-309.1.

FOOD, DRUG AND COSMETIC ACT, §§106-120 to 106-145.12.

FOOD STAMP PROGRAM, §§108A-1 to 108A-3.

FORECLOSURE ACT FOR TAX LIENS, §§105-374, 105-375.

FOREIGN INSURANCE COMPANIES ACT, §§58-16-1 to 58-16-55.

FOREIGN JUDGMENTS ENFORCEMENT.

Uniform enforcement of foreign judgments act, §§1C-1701 to 1C-1708.

FOREIGN LEGAL CONSULTANTS, §§84A-1 to 84A-8.

FOREIGN-MONEY CLAIMS ACT, §§1C-1820 to 1C-1834.

FOREIGN MONEY JUDGMENTS RECOGNITION ACT, §§1C-1800 to 1C-1808.

FOREST DEVELOPMENT ACT, §§113A-176 to 113A-183.

FOREST FIRE PROTECTION COMPACT, §§113-60.11 to 113-60.15.

FOREST PRODUCT ASSESSMENT ACT, §§113A-189 to 113A-196.

FRANCHISE TAX ACT, §§105-114 to 105-129.

FRAUDS, STATUTE OF, §§22-1 to 22-4.

FUEL USE TAX ACT FOR TRUCKERS, §§105-449.37 to 105-449.57.

FUNDS TRANSFERS-UNIFORM COMMERCIAL CODE, §§25-4A-101 to 25-4A-507.

G

GAMBLING LAW, §§14-292 to 14-309.1.

GAS CONSERVATION ACT, §§113-381 to 113-415.

GASOLINE AND OIL INSPECTION ACT, §§119-14 to 119-47.

GENERAL ASSEMBLY APPORTIONMENT ACT, §§120-1 to 120-2.2.

GENETIC IDENTIFICATION, §§15A-266 to 15A-270.

GEOLOGISTS LICENSING ACT, §§89E-1 to 89E-24.

GIFTED STUDENTS, §§115C-150.5 to 115C-150.8.

GIFTS TO MINORS.

Uniform transfers to minors act, §§33A-1 to 33A-24.

GIFT TAXES, §§105-188 to 105-197.1.

GLOBAL TRANSPARK AUTHORITY ACT, §§63A-1 to 63A-25.

GLOBAL TRANSPARK DEVELOPMENT ZONE ACT, §§158-30 to 158-42.

GLUE SNIFFING ACT, §§90-113.8A to 90-113.14.

GOING OUT OF BUSINESS SALES, §§66-76 to 66-83.

GOOD FUNDS SETTLEMENT ACT, §§45A-1 to 45A-7.

GOOD NEIGHBOR COUNCIL ACT, §§143B-391, 143B-392.

GOOD SAMARITAN ACT, §§20-166, 90-21.14.

GOVERNMENT COMPETITION ACT OF 1998, §§143-701 to 143-709.

GOVERNMENT EMPLOYEES INTERCHANGE ACT, §§126-51 to 126-58.

GOVERNMENT SALE OF MERCHANDISE ACT, §66-58.

GOVERNOR'S COUNCIL ON EMPLOYMENT OF THE HANDICAPPED ACT, §§143-283.1 to 143-283.8.

GROUP LIFE INSURANCE ACT, §§58-58-135 to 58-58-165.

GUARDIANSHIP FOR VETERANS, §§34-1 to 34-18.

H

HABEAS CORPUS ACT, §§17-1 to 17-46.

HABITUAL FELONS ACT, §§14-7.1 to 14-7.6.
Violent habitual felons, §§14-7.7 to 14-7.12.

HANDICAPPED EMPLOYMENT COUNCIL ACT, §§143-283.1 to 143-283.8.

HANDICAPPED PERSONS RIGHTS LAW, §§168-1 to 168-10.

HATE CRIMES, §14-401.14.

HAZARDOUS CHEMICALS RIGHT TO KNOW ACT, §§95-173 to 95-218.

HAZARDOUS MATERIALS EMERGENCY RESPONSE ACT, §§166A-20 to 166A-28.

HAZARDOUS RECREATION PARKS SAFETY AND LIABILITY, §§99E-21 to 99E-25.

HAZARDOUS SUBSTANCES CONTROL ACT, §§143-215.75 to 143-215.104.

HAZARDOUS WASTE MANAGEMENT COMMISSION ACT OF 1989, §§130B-1 to 130B-24.

HEALTH CARE FACILITIES FINANCE ACT, §§131A-1 to 131A-25.

HEALTH CARE POWERS OF ATTORNEY, §§32A-15 to 32A-26.

HEALTH CARE PURCHASING ALLIANCE ACT, §§143-621 to 143-636.

HEALTH INSURANCE PROGRAM FOR CHILDREN ACT OF 1998, §§108A-70.18 to 108A-70.28.

HEALTH MAINTENANCE ORGANIZATION ACT OF 1979, §§58-67-1 to 58-67-185.

HEATING CONTRACTORS' LICENSE ACT, §§87-16 to 87-27.1.

HIGHER EDUCATION BONDS.
Community colleges facilities finance, §§116D-41 to 116D-49.
Financing capital facilities, §§116D-6 to 116D-13.

HIGH-VOLTAGE LINE SAFETY ACT, §§95-229.5 to 95-229.13.

HIGHWAY PATROL ACT, §§20-184 to 20-196.3.

HIGHWAY RELOCATION ASSISTANCE ACT, §§133-5 to 133-18.

HIGHWAY USE TAX, §§105-187.1 to 105-187.11.

HISTORIC AND NATURE PRESERVE DEDICATION ACT, §§143-260.6 to 143-260.10G.

HIT AND RUN DRIVING, §20-166.

HITCHHIKING, §20-175.

HOG CHOLERA CONTROL ACT, §§106-316.1 to 106-316.4.

HOLDING OVER, §42-26.

HOME CARE AGENCY LICENSURE ACT, §§131E-135 to 131E-142.

HOME INSPECTOR LICENSURE ACT, §§143-151.43 to 143-151.63.

HOME SCHOOLS, §§115C-563 to 115C-565.

HONEY ACT, §§106-634 to 106-644.

HORSE INDUSTRY PROMOTION ACT, §§106-820 to 106-825.

HOSPICE LICENSURE ACT, §§131E-200 to 131E-207.

HOSPITAL AUTHORITIES ACT, §§131E-15 to 131E-34.

HOSPITAL DISTRICT ACT, §§131E-40 to 131E-47.

HOSPITAL LICENSURE ACT, §§131E-75 to 131E-99.

HOSPITAL, MEDICAL AND DENTAL SERVICE CORPORATION READABLE INSURANCE CERTIFICATES ACT, §§58-66-1 to 58-66-40.

HOTCHPOT, §§29-23 to 29-29.

HOUSEBREAKING, §§14-51 to 14-57.

HOUSEHOLD CLEANERS ACT, §§66-85 to 66-88.

HOUSING AUTHORITIES LAW, §§157-1 to 157-39.8.

HOUSING FINANCE AGENCY ACT, §§122A-1 to 122A-23.

HOUSING TRUST AND OIL OVERCHARGE ACT, §§122E-1 to 122E-9.

HULL INSURANCE ACT, §§58-20-1 to 58-20-40.

HUMAN BURIAL AND HUMAN SKELETAL REMAINS PROTECTION ACT, §§70-26 to 70-40.

HUMAN SERVICE AND VOLUNTEER TRANSPORTATION.
Remove barriers to coordinating act, §§62-289.1 to 62-289.7.

HUNTING OR FISHING ON POSTED PROPERTY, §§113-281 to 113-287.

I

IDENTIFICATION BADGES FOR HEALTH CARE PRACTITIONERS, §90-640.

IDENTITY FRAUD, §14-100.1.

ILLEGITIMATE CHILDREN'S LEGITIMATION LAW, §§49-10 to 49-13.1.

IMMUNIZATION, §§130A-152 to 130A-157.

IMPAIRED DRIVING, §§20-138.1 to 20-139.1.

IMPEACHMENT, §§123-1 to 123-13.

IMPLIED CONSENT ACT, §20-16.2.

INACTIVE HAZARDOUS SITES RESPONSE ACT OF 1987, §§130A-310 to 130A-310.13.

INCOME AND PRINCIPAL ACT, §§37-16 to 37-40.

INCOME TAX, §§105-130 to 105-163.44.

INCOME TAX ACT FOR ESTATES, TRUSTS AND BENEFICIARIES, §§105-160 to 105-160.8.

INCOME TAX WITHHOLDING ACT, §§105-163.1 to 105-163.24.

INDEMNIFICATION ACT FOR CORPORATE OFFICERS, §§55-8-50 to 55-8-58.

INDIGENT DEFENSE SERVICES, §§7A-450 to 7A-458.

INDIVIDUAL INCOME TAX ACT, §§105-133 to 105-159.1.

INDUSTRIAL AND POLLUTION CONTROL FACILITIES FINANCING ACT, §§159C-1 to 159C-27, 159D-1 to 159D-27.

INJUNCTION ACT, §§1-485 to 1-500.

INMATE LABOR ACT, §§148-26 to 148-49.

INSOLVENT DEBTORS ACT, §§23-23 to 23-38.

INSTITUTIONAL FUNDS.

Uniform management of institutional funds act, §§36B-1 to 36B-10.

INSURABLE INTEREST ACT, §§58-58-70 to 58-58-90.

INSURANCE GUARANTY ASSOCIATION ACT, §§58-48-1 to 58-48-130.

INSURANCE HOLDING COMPANY SYSTEM REGULATORY ACT, §§58-19-1 to 58-19-70.

INSURANCE INFORMATION AND PRIVACY PROTECTION ACT, §§58-39-1 to 58-39-76.

INSURANCE LAW, §§58-1-1 to 58-88-30.

INSURANCE REGULATORY REFORM ACT, §§58-41-1 to 58-41-55.

INSURERS FALSE ADVERTISING PROCESS ACT, §§58-29-1 to 58-29-25.

INTERCHANGE OF GOVERNMENTAL EMPLOYEES ACT OF 1977, §§126-51 to 126-58.

INTEREST ACT, §§24-1 to 24-17.

INTERFERENCE WITH CIVIL RIGHTS, §99D-1.

INTERNATIONAL BANKING ACT, §§53-232.1 to 53-232.17.

INTERNATIONAL COMMERCIAL ARBITRATION ACT, §§1-567.30 to 1-567.67.

INTERPRETERS AND TRANSLITERATORS LICENSURE ACT, §§90D-1 to 90D-13.

INTERSTATE AGREEMENT ON DETAINERS, §§15A-761 to 15A-767.

INTERSTATE BANKING ACT, §§53-209 to 53-218.

INTERSTATE BRANCH BANKING, §§53-224.9 to 53-224.31.

INTERSTATE COMPACT FOR THE SUPERVISION OF ADULT OFFENDERS, §§148-65.4 to 148-65.9.

INTERSTATE COMPACT ON JUVENILES, §§7B-2800 to 7B-2827.

INTERSTATE COMPACT ON THE PLACEMENT OF JUVENILES, §§7B-3800 to 7B-3806.

INTERSTATE FAMILY SUPPORT ACT, §§52C-1-100 to 52C-9-902.

INTESTATE SUCCESSION ACT, §§29-1 to 29-30.

INVESTMENT ADVISERS ACT, §§78C-1 to 78C-81.

INVESTMENT SECURITIES, §§25-8-101 to 25-8-511.

J

JACOB BATTLE ACT, §41-10.

JOB DEVELOPMENT INVESTMENT GRANT PROGRAM, §§143B-437.44 to 143B-437.56.

JOINT MUNICIPAL ELECTRIC POWER AND ENERGY ACT, §§159B-1 to 159B-52.

JOINT TORT-FEASORS CONTRIBUTION ACT, §§1B-1 to 1B-6.

JOY RIDING, §14-72.2.

JUDGMENT CONFORMITY ACT, §1-237.

JUDICIAL DEPARTMENT ACT OF 1965, §§7A-1 to 7A-801.

JUDICIAL RETIREMENT ACT, §§135-50 to 135-74.

JUNKYARD CONTROL ACT, §§136-141 to 136-155.

JUVENILE CODE, §§7B-100 to 7B-3806.

JUVENILE PLACEMENT, INTERSTATE COMPACT, §§7B-3800 to 7B-3806.

JUVENILES, INTERSTATE COMPACT ON, §§7B-2800 to 7B-2827.

K

KAITLYN'S LAW, §110-102.1A.

KICKBACKS, §§58-27-5, 95-47.6, 95-47.24.

KIDNAPPING ACT, §§14-39 to 14-43.3.

KU KLUX KLAN, §§14-12.2 to 14-12.15.

L

LABELING OF HOUSEHOLD CLEANERS ACT, §§66-85 to 66-88.

LABOR DISPUTES ARBITRATION ACT, §§95-36.1 to 95-36.9.

LABORERS' LIEN LAW, §§44A-1 to 44A-6.1.

LABOR OF PRISONERS ACT, §§148-26 to 148-49.

LAND CONTRACTS REGISTRATION ACT, §§47-17 to 47-36.

LANDLORD AND TENANT ACT, §§42-1 to 42-76.

LAND POLICY ACT OF 1974, §§113A-150 to 113A-159.

LAND TITLE REGISTRATION ACT, §§43-1 to 43-64.

LAPSED LEGACY ACT, §31-42.

LAW-ENFORCEMENT OFFICERS, FIREMEN'S, RESCUE SQUAD WORKERS AND CIVIL AIR PATROL MEMBERS.
Death benefit act, §§143-166.1 to 143-166.7.

LEAD POISONING IN CHILDREN, §§130A-131.5 to 130A-131.9G.

LEARNER'S PERMITS, §§20-7, 20-11, 20-30.

LEASES-UNIFORM COMMERCIAL CODE, §§25-2A-101 to 25-2A-532.

LEGISLATIVE APPORTIONMENT ACT, §§120-1 to 120-2.2.

LEGISLATIVE ETHICS ACT, §§120-85 to 120-106.

LEGITIMATION OF ILLEGITIMATE CHILDREN, §§49-10 to 49-13.1.

LEMON LAW, §§20-351 to 20-351.10.

LESSER INCLUDED OFFENSES, §§15-169, 15-170, 20-140.

LETTERS OF CREDIT, §§25-5-101 to 25-5-117.

LIBEL AND SLANDER ACT, §§99-1 to 99-5.

LIBRARY COMPACT, §§125-12 to 125-17.

LICENSE TAX ACT, §§105-33 to 105-102.6.

LICENSURE ACT FOR SPEECH AND LANGUAGE PATHOLOGISTS AND AUDIOLOGISTS, §§90-292 to 90-307.

LIEN LAW, §§44A-1 to 44A-35.

LIFE AND HEALTH INSURANCE GUARANTY ASSOCIATION ACT, §§58-62-2 to 58-62-95.

LIFE INSURANCE ACT FOR GROUP INSURANCE, §§58-58-135 to 58-58-165.

LIFE INSURANCE STANDARD NONFORFEITURE LAW, §58-58-55.

LIFE INSURANCE STANDARD VALUATION LAW, §58-58-50.

LIMING MATERIALS AND LANDPLASTER ACT, §§106-92.1 to 106-92.17.

LIMITATION OF ACTIONS FOR CIVIL CASES, §§1-15 to 1-56.

LIMITATION OF ACTIONS FOR MISDEMEANORS, §15-1.

LIMITED LIABILITY COMPANY ACT, §§57C-1-01 to 57C-10-07.

LIMITED PARTNERSHIP ACT, §§59-101 to 59-1106.

LIQUOR LAW, §§18B-100 to 18B-1119.

LIS PENDENS ACT, §§1-116 to 1-120.2.

LITTLE FTC ACT, §75-1.1.

LITTLE SMITH ACT FOR SUBVERSIVE ACTIVITIES, §§14-11 to 14-12.1.

LIVESTOCK DEALER LICENSING ACT, §§106-418.8 to 106-418.16.

LIVESTOCK LAW, §§68-15 to 68-46.

LIVESTOCK MARKETS, §§106-406 to 106-418.

LIVESTOCK PROMPT PAY LAW, §§106-418.1 to 106-418.7A.

LIVING WILLS ACT, §§90-320 to 90-323.

LOAD LIMIT FOR BRIDGES, §136-72.

LOBBYING, §§93B-6, 120-47.1 to 120-47.11.

LOCAL GOVERNMENT BOND ACT, §§159-43 to 159-79.

LOCAL GOVERNMENT BUDGET AND FISCAL CONTROL ACT, §§159-7 to 159-41.

LOCAL GOVERNMENT EXECUTIVE SUCCESSION ACT, §§162B-5 to 162B-13.

LOCAL GOVERNMENT FINANCE ACT, §§159-1 to 159-200.

LOCAL GOVERNMENT FISCAL INFORMATION ACT, §§120-30.41 to 120-30.49.

LOCAL GOVERNMENT RETIREMENT SYSTEM ACT, §§128-21 to 128-38.2.

LOCAL GOVERNMENT RISK POOL ACT, §§58-23-1 to 58-23-40.

LOCAL GOVERNMENTS ACT, §§160A-1 to 160A-588.

LOCAL GOVERNMENT SALES AND USE TAX.
First one-cent local government sales and use tax, §§105-463 to 105-474.
First one-half cent local government sales and use tax, §§105-480 to 105-487.
Second one-half cent local government sales and use tax, §§105-495 to 105-502.
Third one-half cent local government sales and use tax act, §§105-515 to 105-521.

LOCAL GOVERNMENT SALES AND USE TAX FOR BEACH NOURISHMENT, §§105-525 to 105-531.

LOCAL IMPROVEMENT ACT, §§160A-216 to 160A-238.

LOCAL OPTION ACT FOR ALCOHOLIC BEVERAGES, §§18B-600 to 18B-605.

LOCKSMITH LICENSING ACT, §§74F-1 to 74F-18.

LONDON LIBEL ACT, §§99-1 to 99-5.

LONG-TERM CARE INSURANCE ACT, §§58-55-1 to 58-55-35.

LOOTING, §§14-288.1 to 14-288.20.

LORD CAMPBELL'S ACT, §28A-18-2.

LOSE CONTROL, LOSE LICENSE, §20-11, (n1).

LOTTERY ACT, §§14-289 to 14-291.2.

LOW-INCOME HOUSING TAX CREDIT, §§105-129.40 to 105-129.45.

LOW-LEVEL RADIOACTIVE WASTE MANAGEMENT AUTHORITY ACT OF 1987, §§104G-1 to 104G-23.

LYNCHING, §§114-15, 162-23.

M

MACHINE GUN ACT, §14-409.

MACHINERY ACT, §§105-271 to 105-395.1.

MANUFACTURED HOMES STANDARDS CODE ACT, §§143-144 to 143-151.5.

MARINE FISHERIES COMPACT, §§113-252 to 113-258.

MARITAL DEDUCTION TRUSTS, §36A-130.

MARKETABLE TITLE ACT, §§47B-1 to 47B-9.

MARKETING ASSOCIATIONS ACT, §§54-129 to 54-166.

MARRIAGE AND FAMILY THERAPY LICENSURE ACT, §§90-270.45 to 90-270.62.

MARRIED PERSON'S ACT, §§52-1 to 52-12.

MARRIED PERSONS' EMANCIPATION ACT, §52-2.

MARTIN ACT, §52-2.

MASON ACT FOR NONSUIT, §15-173.

MASSAGE AND BODYWORK PRACTICE ACT, §§90-620 to 90-636.

MASSAGE PARLORS, §§14-202.10 to 14-202.12.

MASS GATHERINGS, §§130A-251 to 130A-258.

MATERNITY HOMES, §131D-1.

MAXIMUM HOUR LAW, §§95-25.1 to 95-25.25.

MEAT INSPECTION ACT, §§106-549.15 to 106-549.28.

MECHANICS' AND MATERIALMEN'S LIEN, §§44A-7 to 44A-24.

MEDICAID, §§108A-54 to 108A-70.5.

MEDICAL ASSISTANCE PROVIDER FALSE CLAIMS ACT, §§108A-70.10 to 108A-70.16.

MEDICAL CARE DATA ACT, §§131E-214 to 131E-214.4.

MEDICAL EXAMINERS ACT, §§130A-377 to 130A-395.

MEDICAL MALPRACTICE, §§90-21.11 to 90-21.14.

MEDICAL PRACTICE ACT, §§90-1 to 90-21.

MEMBERSHIP CAMPING ACT, §66-230.

MENTAL HEALTH, DEVELOPMENTAL DISABILITIES, AND SUBSTANCE ABUSE ACT OF 1985, §§122C-1 to 122C-411.

MERIT SYSTEM ACT, §§126-1 to 126-79.

METROPOLITAN SEWERAGE DISTRICTS ACT, §§162A-64 to 162A-81.

METROPOLITAN WATER DISTRICTS ACT, §§162A-31 to 162A-58.

M.I.A., §§28B-1 to 28B-10.

MIDWIFERY PRACTICE ACT, §§90-178.1 to 90-178.7.

MIGRANT HOUSING ACT OF NORTH CAROLINA, §§95-222 to 95-229.

MILEAGE ACT, §§20-340 to 20-350.

MILK CONTROL ACT, §§106-266.6 to 106-266.19.

MINE SAFETY AND HEALTH ACT OF NORTH CAROLINA, §§74-24.1 to 74-24.20.

MINING ACT OF 1971, §§74-46 to 74-68.

MINING COMPACT, §§74-37, 74-38.

MINOR VETERANS ENABLING ACT, §§165-12 to 165-16.

MISDEMEANOR SENTENCING, §§15A-1340.20 to 15A-1340.23.

MISSING IN ACTION.

Absentees in military service, §§28B-1 to 28B-10.

MISTRIAL, §§15A-1061 to 15A-1065.

MODEL AIRPORT ZONING ACT, §§63-30 to 63-37.1.

MODEL PAYMENT AND PERFORMANCE BOND, §§44A-25 to 44A-35.

MONEY TRANSMITTERS ACT, §§53-192 to 53-208.30.

MONOPOLIES ACT, §§75-1 to 75-35.

MORTGAGE ACT, §§45-4 to 45-80.

MORTGAGE LENDING ACT, §§53-243.01 to 53-243.15.

MORTUARY TABLES, §§8-46, 8-47.

MOTION PICTURE FAIR COMPETITION ACT, §§75C-1 to 75C-5.

MOTIONS TO SUPPRESS, §§15A-971 to 15A-980.

MOTORBUS ACT, §§62-259 to 62-279.

MOTOR CARRIER SAFETY REGULATION UNIT, §§20-376 to 20-397.

MOTOR FUEL MARKETING ACT, §§75-80 to 75-89.

MOTOR TRAFFIC LAW, §§20-138.1 to 20-171.

MOTOR VEHICLE ACT OF 1937, §§20-39 to 20-183.

MOTOR VEHICLE CERTIFICATES OF TITLE ACT, §§20-50 to 20-71.1.

MOTOR VEHICLE DEALERS AND MANUFACTURERS LICENSING LAW, §§20-285 to 20-308.2.

MOTOR VEHICLE RACING ACT, §20-141.3.

MOTOR VEHICLE REGISTRATION ACT, §§20-50 to 20-71.1.

MOTOR VEHICLE REPAIR ACT, §§20-354 to 20-354.9.

MOTOR VEHICLE SAFETY AND FINANCIAL RESPONSIBILITY ACT OF 1953, §§20-279.1 to 20-279.39.

MOTOR VEHICLE STOP ACT, §20-158.

MOTOR VOTERS, §163-82.19.

MOUNTAIN RIDGE PROTECTION ACT OF 1983, §§113A-205 to 113A-214.

MOUTH HYGIENE ACT, §§90-221 to 90-233.1.

MOVERS, §§20-356 to 20-372.

MULTISTATE TRUST INSTITUTIONS ACT, §§53-302 to 53-329.

MUNICIPAL CORPORATIONS ACT, §§160A-1 to 160A-588.

MUNICIPAL ELECTION LAW, §§163-279 to 163-306.

MUNICIPAL EMPLOYEES' RETIREMENT SYSTEM ACT, §§128-21 to 128-38.2.

MUNICIPAL FINANCE ACT, §§159-1 to 159-200.

MUNICIPAL HOSPITAL ACT, §§131E-5 to 131E-14.1.

MUNICIPAL SERVICE DISTRICTS ACT OF 1973, §§160A-535 to 160A-544.

MURDER, §§14-17, 14-18.

N

NARCOTICS ACT, §§90-86 to 90-113.8.

NATIONAL CRIME PREVENTION AND PRIVACY COMPACT, §114-19.50.

NATIONAL GUARD MUTUAL ASSISTANCE COMPACT, §§127A-175 to 127A-184.

NATIONAL GUARD TUITION ASSISTANCE ACT OF 1975, §127A-190.

NATURAL AND SCENIC RIVERS ACT OF 1971, §§113A-30 to 113A-44.

NATURE AND HISTORIC PRESERVE DEDICATION ACT, §§143-260.6 to 143-260.10G.

NATURE PRESERVES ACT, §§113A-164.1 to 113A-164.11.

NEGOTIABLE INSTRUMENTS-UNIFORM COMMERCIAL CODE, §§25-3-101 to 25-3-605.

NEW MOTOR VEHICLES WARRANTIES ACT, §§20-351 to 20-351.10.

NIMBLE DIVIDEND LAW, §55-6-40.

911 EMERGENCY TELEPHONE SYSTEM.
Public safety telephone act, §§62A-1 to 62A-12.

NO CALL LAW, §§75-100 to 75-105.

NONFORFEITURE ACT FOR LIFE INSURANCE, §58-58-55.

NONFORFEITURE FOR INDIVIDUAL DEFERRED ANNUITIES, §§58-58-60, 58-58-61.

NONPROFIT CORPORATIONS ACT, §§55A-1-01 to 55A-17-05.

NONPUBLIC SCHOOLS, §§115C-547 to 115C-565.

NONSUIT ACT FOR CRIMINAL CASES, §15-173.

NONSUPPORT ACT, §§14-322 to 14-326.1.

NORTH CAROLINA AMBER ALERT SYSTEM, §143B-499.7.

NORTH CAROLINA CAPITAL FACILITIES FINANCING ACT, §§159D-1 to 159D-57.

NORTH CAROLINA COSMETIC ART ACT, §§88B-1 to 88B-29.

NORTH CAROLINA FAMILY LAW ARBITRATION ACT, §§50-41 to 50-62.

NORTH CAROLINA GOVERNMENT COMPETITION ACT OF 1998, §§143-701 to 143-709.

NORTH CAROLINA INDUSTRIAL AND POLLUTION CONTROL FACILITIES FINANCING ACT, §§159D-1 to 159D-27.

NORTH CAROLINA MASSAGE AND BODYWORK THERAPY PRACTICE ACT, §§90-620 to 90-636.

NORTH CAROLINA MOTOR VEHICLE REPAIR ACT, §§20-354 to 20-354.9.

NORTH CAROLINA PERSONS WITH DISABILITIES PROTECTION ACT, §§168A-1 to 168A-12.

NORTH CAROLINA PLANNED COMMUNITY ACT, §§47F-1-101 to 47F-3-120.

NORTH CAROLINA PROJECT DEVELOPMENT FINANCING ACT, §§159-101 to 159-113.

NORTH CAROLINA RURAL INTERNET ACCESS AUTHORITY ACT, §§143B-437.40 to 143B-437.43.

NORTH CAROLINA RURAL REDEVELOPMENT AUTHORITY ACT, §§143B-437.20 to 143B-437.33.

NORTH CAROLINA STATE BUILDING CODE, §143-138.

NORTH CAROLINA STRUCTURED SETTLEMENT ACT, §§1-543.10 to 1-543.15.

NORTH CAROLINA UNCLAIMED PROPERTY ACT, §§116B-51 to 116B-80.

NORTH CAROLINA UNIFORM PARTNERSHIP ACT, §§59-31 to 59-73.

NORTH CAROLINA UNIFORM PRUDENT INVESTOR ACT, §§36A-161 to 36A-173.

NORTH CAROLINA VACATION RENTAL ACT, §§42A-1 to 42A-36.

NOTARY PUBLIC ACT, §§10A-1 to 10A-16.

NURSE LICENSURE COMPACT, §§90-171.80 to 90-171.94.

NURSES AIDES REGISTRY ACT, §90-171.55.

NURSING HOME ADMINISTRATOR ACT, §§90-275.1 to 90-288.

NURSING HOME LICENSURE ACT, §§131E-100 to 131E-131.

NURSING HOME PATIENTS' BILL OF RIGHTS, §§131E-115 to 131E-131.

NURSING POOL LICENSURE ACT, §§131E-154.1 to 131E-154.8.

NURSING PRACTICE ACT, §§90-171.19 to 90-171.53.

NUTRITION/DIETETICS PRACTICE ACT, §§90-350 to 90-369.

O

OCCUPATIONAL DISEASE ACT, §§97-52 to 97-76.

OCCUPATIONAL LICENSING ACT, §§105-33 to 105-113.

OCCUPATIONAL SAFETY AND HEALTH ACT OF NORTH CAROLINA, §§95-126 to 95-155.

ODOMETER ALTERATION.
Vehicle mileage act, §§20-340 to 20-350.

OIL AND GAS CONSERVATION ACT, §§113-381 to 113-415.

OIL AND GASOLINE INSPECTION ACT, §§119-14 to 119-47.

OIL POLLUTION AND HAZARDOUS SUBSTANCES CONTROL ACT OF 1978, §§143-215.75 to 143-215.104.

OPEN BURNING LAW, §§113-60.21 to 113-60.31.

OPEN MEETINGS ACT, §§143-318.9 to 143-318.18.

OPTOMETRY ACT, §§90-114 to 90-127.3.

OSTEOPATHY ACT, §§90-129 to 90-138.

OUTDOOR ADVERTISING CONTROL ACT, §§136-126 to 136-140.

OUT-OF-STATE PAROLEE SUPERVISION ACT, §§148-65.1 to 148-65.3.

OVERHEAD HIGH-VOLTAGE LINE SAFETY ACT, §§95-229.5 to 95-229.13.

P

PALMISTRY, §14-401.5.

PARAPHERNALIA ACT, §§90-113.20 to 90-113.24.

PARDONS, §§147-21 to 147-25; Const. N. C., art. III, §5; Const. U.S., Art. II, §2.

PARENTAL RESPONSIBILITY ACT, §1-538.1.

PARK COMMISSION ACT, §143-258.

PARKING AUTHORITIES LAW, §§160A-550 to 160A-565.

PAROCHIAL SCHOOLS, §§115C-547 to 115C-554.

PAROLE ACT, §§148-52.1 to 148-64.

PARTNERSHIP ACT, §§59-31 to 59-73.

PARTY LINES, §14-401.8.

PASSWORDS, §14-12.4.

PATERNITY ACT, §§49-1 to 49-17.

PATIENTS' BILL OF RIGHTS FOR NURSING HOME PATIENTS, §§131E-115 to 131E-131.

PAWNBROKERS MODERNIZATION ACT OF 1989, §§91A-1 to 91A-14.

PAYABLE ON DEATH ACCOUNTS, §§54-109.57, 54B-130.

PAYMENT BOND, §§44A-25 to 44A-35.

PAYMENT INTO COURT, §§1-508 to 1-510.

PEDERASTY, §14-202.1.

PEEPING TOM ACT, §14-202.

PEREMPTORY CHALLENGES, §§9-19 to 9-21.

PERFORMANCE BOND, §§44A-25 to 44A-35.

PERJURY ACT, §§14-209 to 14-211.

PERPETUITIES, RULE AGAINST.
Uniform statutory rule, §§41-15 to 41-22.

PERSONAL PROPERTY LIEN ACT, §§44A-1 to 44A-6.1.

PERSONNEL SYSTEM ACT, §§126-1 to 126-88.

PEST CONTROL ACT, §§106-65.22 to 106-65.41.

PEST CONTROL COMPACT, §§106-65.55 to 106-65.61.

PESTICIDE LAW OF 1971, §§143-434 to 143-470.1.

PET ADMITTANCE TO HOTEL ROOMS, §72-7.1.

PHARMACY PRACTICE ACT, §§90-85.2 to 90-85.40.

PHOTOGRAPHIC COPIES OF BUSINESS AND PUBLIC RECORDS AS EVIDENCE ACT, §§8-45.1 to 8-45.4.

PHRENOLOGY, §14-401.5.

PHYSICALLY HANDICAPPED ACT FOR SECOND INJURY, §97-35.

PHYSICAL THERAPY PRACTICE ACT, §§90-270.24 to 90-270.39.

PICKETING, §14-225.1.

PIPELINES, §62-50.

PLACEMENT OF JUVENILES, INTERSTATE COMPACT, §§7B-3800 to 7B-3806.

PLANNED COMMUNITY ACT, §§47F-1-101 to 47F-3-120.

PLANT PROTECTION AND CONSERVATION ACT, §§106-202.12 to 106-202.22.

PLUMBING AND HEATING CONTRACTORS ACT, §§87-16 to 87-27.1.

PODIATRY ACT, §§90-202.2 to 90-202.14.

POINTS SCHEDULE, §20-16, (c).

POLITICAL ACTIVITY OF STATE EMPLOYEES ACT, §§126-13 to 126-15.1.

POLITICAL CAMPAIGN CONTRIBUTIONS, §§163-278.6 to 163-278.40I.

POLLUTION CONTROL FACILITIES FINANCING ACT, §§159C-1 to 159C-27.

PORK PROMOTION ASSESSMENT ACT, §§106-790 to 106-796.

POST CONVICTION HEARING ACT, §§15A-1411 to 15A-1422.

POSTED PROPERTY.
Hunting and fishing, §§113-281 to 113-287.

POSTMORTEM MEDICAL EXAMINERS ACT, §§130A-377 to 130A-395.

POST-TOWING PROCEDURES, §§20-219.9 to 20-219.14.

POULTRY INDUSTRY ACT, §§106-539 to 106-549.

POULTRY PRODUCTS INSPECTION ACT, §§106-549.49 to 106-549.69.

POUR-OVER TRUST ACT, §31-47.

POWELL ACT, §§136-41.1 to 136-41.3.

PRACTICE OF MEDICINE ACT, §§90-1 to 90-21.

PREJUDGMENT ATTACHMENT ACT, §§1-440.1 to 1-440.46.

PREMARITAL AGREEMENT ACT, §§52B-1 to 52B-11.

PREMIUM TAX.
Taxes upon insurance companies, §§105-228.3 to 105-228.10.

PRESENTENCE REPORTS, §§15A-1332, 15A-1333.

PRESIDENTIAL PREFERENCE PRIMARY ACT, §§163-213.1 to 163-213.9.

PRESSURE VESSEL ACT, §§95-69.8 to 95-69.18.

PRETRIAL CRIMINAL PROCEDURE ACT, §§15A-901 to 15A-980.

PRICE GOUGING DURING STATE OF DISASTER, §§75-37, 75-37.1.

PRIMARY ELECTION LAWS, §§163-104 to 163-115, 163-119.

PRIMARY FOREST PRODUCT ASSESSMENT ACT, §§113A-189 to 113A-196.

PRISONERS OF WAR.
Absentees in military service, §§28B-1 to 28B-10.

PRISON LABOR ACT, §§148-26 to 148-49.

PRIVATE CAPITAL FACILITIES FINANCE ACT, §§159D-35 to 159D-57.

PRIVATE EDUCATIONAL FACILITIES FINANCE ACT, §§115E-1 to 115E-23.

PRIVATE PROTECTIVE SERVICES ACT, §§74C-1 to 74C-33.

PRIVATE SCHOOLS ACT, §§115C-547 to 115C-565.

PRIVILEGED COMMUNICATIONS ACT, §§8-53 to 8-53.5.

PROBATION ACT, §§15A-1341 to 15A-1347.

PRODUCTS LIABILITY ACT, §§99B-1 to 99B-11.

PROFESSIONAL CORPORATION ACT, §§55B-1 to 55B-16.

PROFESSIONAL EMPLOYER ORGANIZATION ACT, §§58-89-1 to 58-89-180.

PROJECT DEVELOPMENT FINANCING ACT, §§159-101 to 159-113.

PROMPT PAY LAW, §§106-418.1 to 106-418.7.

PROPERTY RECORDATION ACT, §§47-17 to 47-36.

PROPERTY TAXES.
Machinery act, §§105-271 to 105-395.1.

PROPRIETARY SCHOOLS ACT, §§115D-87 to 115D-97.

PROSECUTION BONDS, §§1-109 to 1-112.

PROSTITUTION ACT, §§14-203 to 14-208.

PROTECTION OF THE ABUSED, NEGLECTED OR EXPLOITED DISABLED ADULT ACT, §§108A-99 to 108A-111.

PRUDENT INVESTOR ACT, §§36A-161 to 36A-173.

PRUDENT PERSON RULE, §36A-2, (a).

PSYCHOLOGY PRACTICE ACT, §§90-270.1 to 90-270.21.

PSYCHOTHERAPY PATIENT/CLIENT SEXUAL EXPLOITATION ACT, §§90-21.41 to 90-21.48.

PUBLIC ACCOUNTANTS LAW, §§93-1 to 93-13.

PUBLIC ASSISTANCE ACT, §§108A-24 to 108A-70.5.

PUBLIC BUILDING CONTRACTS ACT, §§143-128 to 143-135.8.

PUBLIC HEALTH AUTHORITIES ACT, §§130A-45 to 130A-45.11.

PUBLIC HEALTH LAW, §§130A-1 to 130A-460.

PUBLIC HOSPITAL PERSONNEL ACT, §§131E-257 to 131E-257.2.

PUBLIC SAFETY TELEPHONE ACT, §§62A-1 to 62A-12.

PUBLIC SCHOOL ACT, §§115C-1 to 115C-546.2.

PUBLIC TRANSPORTATION AUTHORITIES ACT, §§160A-575 to 160A-588.
Regional public transportation authorities act, §§160A-600 to 160A-625.

PUBLIC UTILITIES ACT, §§62-1 to 62-333.

PUBLIC UTILITIES COMMISSION ACT, §§62-10 to 62-98.

PUBLIC UTILITIES COMMISSION PROCEDURE ACT, §§62-60 to 62-82.

PUBLIC WORKS ACT, §§133-1 to 133-33.

PUBLIC WORKS EMINENT DOMAIN LAW, §§40A-40 to 40A-56.

PURCHASE MONEY MORTGAGE ACT, §45-21.38.

PURE FOOD ACT, §§106-120 to 106-145.12.

Q

QUALIFIED BUSINESS INVESTMENT TAX CREDIT, §§105-163.010 to 105-163.015.

QUARRIES AND MINES ACT, §§74-24.1 to 74-68.

QUASHING INDICTMENTS, §§15-153, 15-155.

QUIETING TITLE ACT, §41-10.

R

RABIES, §§130A-184 to 130A-200.

RACING ACT FOR MOTOR VEHICLES, §20-141.3.

RACKETEER INFLUENCED AND CORRUPT ORGANIZATIONS ACT (RICO), §§75D-1 to 75D-14.

RADIATION PROTECTION ACT, §§104E-1 to 104E-29.

RADIO DEFAMATION ACT, §§99-1 to 99-5.

RAPE ACT, §§14-27.1 to 14-27.10.

READABLE INSURANCE POLICIES ACT, §§58-38-1 to 58-38-40.

REAL ESTATE APPRAISERS ACT, §§93E-1-1 to 93E-1-14.

REAL ESTATE LICENSE LAW, §§93A-1 to 93A-59.

REAL PROPERTY ACQUISITIONS POLICIES ACT, §§133-5 to 133-18.

REAL PROPERTY LIEN ACT, §§44A-7 to 44A-24.

REAL PROPERTY MARKETABLE TITLE ACT, §§47B-1 to 47B-9.

RECIPROCAL INHERITANCE ACT, §§64-3 to 64-5.

RECIPROCAL INTERSTATE BANKING ACT, §§53-209 to 53-218.

RECKLESS DRIVING ACT, §20-140.

RECORDATION ACT, §§47-17 to 47-36.

RECORDS AS EVIDENCE ACT, §§8-45.1 to 8-45.4.

RECREATIONAL TRESPASS, §§14-159.6, 113A-95.

RECREATION ENABLING LAW, §§160A-350 to 160A-356.

REDEVELOPMENT LAW, §§160A-500 to 160A-526.

REFUND ANTICIPATION LOAN ACT, §§53-245 to 53-254.

REFUNDING BOND ACT, §§142-29.1 to 142-29.7.

REGIONAL NATURAL GAS DISTRICT ACT, §§160A-660 to 160A-676.

REGIONAL PUBLIC TRANSPORTATION AUTHORITY ACT, §§160A-600 to 160A-625.

REGIONAL RECIPROCAL SAVINGS AND LOAN ACQUISITION ACT, §§54B-48.1 to 54B-48.9.

REGIONAL SEWAGE DISPOSAL PLANNING ACT OF 1971, §§162A-26 to 162A-30.

REGIONAL TRANSIT AUTHORITY VEHICLE RENTAL TAX, §§105-550 to 105-555.

REGIONAL TRANSPORTATION AUTHORITY ACT, §§160A-630 to 160A-651.

REGIONAL WATER SUPPLY PLANNING ACT OF 1971, §§162A-20 to 162A-25.

REGISTERED PUBLIC OBLIGATIONS ACT, §§159E-1 to 159E-15.

REGISTERS OF DEEDS SUPPLEMENTAL PENSION FUND ACT OF 1987, §§161-50 to 161-50.5.

REGISTRATION ACT, §§47-17 to 47-36.

REGISTRATION ACT FOR MAKERS OF MORTGAGES AND DEEDS OF TRUST, §§53-233 to 53-242.

REGISTRATION ACT FOR MOTOR VEHICLES, §§20-50 to 20-71.1.

REGISTRATION OF TRADEMARKS ACT, §§80-1 to 80-14.

REGISTRATION OF VOTERS ACT, §§163-82.1 to 163-82.26.

RELIGIOUS SCHOOLS, §§115C-547 to 115C-554.

RELOCATION ASSISTANCE ACT, §§133-5 to 133-18.

REMOVAL FROM OFFICE ACT, §§128-16 to 128-20.

REMOVE BARRIERS TO COORDINATING HUMAN SERVICE AND VOLUNTEER TRANSPORTATION ACT, §§62-289.1 to 62-289.7.

RENT-A-COPS, §§74E-1 to 74E-13.

RENUNCIATION OF PROPERTY AND RENUNCIATION OF FIDUCIARY POWERS ACT, §§31B-1 to 31B-7.

RESCUE WORKERS' PENSION FUND ACT, §§58-86-1 to 58-86-91.

RESIDENTIAL PROPERTY DISCLOSURE ACT, §§47E-1 to 47E-10.

RESPIRATORY CARE PRACTICE ACT, §§90-646 to 90-665.

RETAIL INSTALLMENT SALES ACT, §§25A-1 to 25A-45.

RETALIATORY EMPLOYMENT DISCRIMINATION, §§95-240 to 95-245.

RETIREMENT SYSTEM ACTUARIAL NOTE ACT, §§120-112 to 120-114.

RETIREMENT SYSTEM FOR COUNTIES, CITIES AND TOWNS ACT, §§128-21 to 128-38.2.

RETIREMENT SYSTEM FOR TEACHERS AND STATE EMPLOYEES, §§135-1 to 135-18.7.

REVENUE ACT, §§105-1 to 105-270.

REVENUE BOND ACT, §§159-80 to 159-97.

REVERSE MORTGAGE ACT, §§53-255 to 53-272.

REVISED UNIFORM ARBITRATION ACT, §§1-569.1 to 1-569.31.

REVISED UNIFORM LIMITED PARTNERSHIP ACT, §§59-101 to 59-1106.

RICO ACT, §§75D-1 to 75D-14.

RIDESHARING, §§136-44.21 to 136-44.26.

RIGHT-OF-WAY ACT, §§20-155 to 20-158.1.

RIGHT TO NATURAL DEATH, §§32A-15 to 32A-26, 90-320 to 90-323.

RIGHT TO WORK LAW, §§95-78 to 95-84.

ROAD ACT, §§136-4 to 136-155.

ROADWAY CORRIDOR OFFICIAL MAP ACT, §§136-44.50 to 136-44.53.

ROLLER SKATING RINK SAFETY AND LIABILITY, §§99E-10 to 99E-14.

RULE AGAINST PERPETUITIES.
Uniform statutory rule, §§41-15 to 41-22.

RULES OF EVIDENCE, §8C-1, Rules 101 to 1102.

RULES OF THE ROAD, §§20-138.1 to 20-171.

RURAL DEVELOPMENT PROGRAM.
Agriculture development act, §§106-580 to 106-587.

RURAL ELECTRIFICATION ACT, §§117-1 to 117-5.

RURAL INTERNET ACCESS AUTHORITY ACT, §§143B-437.40 to 143B-437.43.

RURAL REDEVELOPMENT ACT, §§143B-437.20 to 143B-437.33.

RURAL TELEPHONE ACT, §§117-29 to 117-35.

S

SAFECRACKING, §14-89.1.

SAFE HAVEN FOR INFANTS, §14-322.3.

SAFETY AND FINANCIAL RESPONSIBILITY ACT OF 1953, §§20-279.1 to 20-279.39.

SAFETY PROFESSIONALS, §§90-671 to 90-674.

SALES AND USE TAX.
Local government sales and use tax for beach nourishment, §§105-525 to 105-531.

SALES AND USE TAX —Cont'd
Uniform sales and use tax administration act, §§105-164.42A to 105-164.42J.

SALES AND USE TAX ACT, §§105-164.1 to 105-164.44D.

SALES-UNIFORM COMMERCIAL CODE, §§25-2-101 to 25-2-725.

SALVAGE TITLES, §§20-71.2 to 20-71.4.

SAVINGS AND LOAN ASSOCIATIONS, §§54B-1 to 54B-278.

SAVINGS AND LOAN INTERSTATE BRANCH ACT, §§54B-265 to 54B-278.

SAVINGS BANK INTERSTATE BRANCH ACT, §§54C-199 to 54C-212.

SAVINGS BANKS, §§54C-1 to 54C-212.

SCENIC RIVERS SYSTEM ACT, §§113A-30 to 113A-44.

SCHOOL-BASED MANAGEMENT AND ACCOUNTABILITY PROGRAM, §§115C-105.20 to 115C-105.39.

SCHOOL BUDGET AND FISCAL CONTROL ACT, §§115C-422 to 115C-452.

SCHOOL BUSES, §§115C-239 to 115C-262.

S CORPORATION INCOME TAX ACT, §§105-131 to 105-131.8.

SCRAP TIRE DISPOSAL ACT, §§130A-309.51 to 130A-309.63.

SCRAP TIRE DISPOSAL TAX, §§105-187.15 to 105-187.19.

SEARCH WARRANT ACT, §§15A-241 to 15A-259.

SECOND INJURY ACT, §97-35.

SECOND ONE-HALF CENT LOCAL GOVERNMENT SALES AND USE TAX, §§105-495 to 105-502.

SECRET SOCIETIES PROHIBITION ACT, §§14-12.2 to 14-12.15.

SECURED TRANSACTIONS, §§25-9-100 to 25-9-709.

SECURITIES ACT, §§78A-1 to 78A-65.

SEDIMENTATION POLLUTION CONTROL ACT OF 1973, §§113A-50 to 113A-66.

SEED LAW OF 1963, §§106-277 to 106-277.28.

SELF-SERVICE STORAGE FACILITIES LIENS, §§44A-40 to 44A-46.

SENTENCE SUSPENSION ACT, §§15A-1341 to 15A-1347.

SENTENCING SERVICES ACT, §§7A-770 to 7A-777.

SERVICE DISTRICT ACT FOR MUNICIPALITIES, §§160A-535 to 160A-544.

SETOFF DEBT COLLECTION ACT, §§105A-1 to 105A-16.

SEWAGE DISPOSAL PLANNING ACT, §§162A-26 to 162A-30.

SEWER AUTHORITIES ACT, §§162A-1 to 162A-19.

SEXUAL OFFENDER REGISTRATION PROGRAM, §§14-208.5 to 14-208.13.

SHAREHOLDER PROTECTION ACT, §§55-9-01 to 55-9-05.

SHAREHOLDER'S APPRAISAL ACT, §§55-13-30, 55-13-31.

SHELLEY'S CASE, §39-1.1, (a).

SHERIFFS' SUPPLEMENTAL PENSION FUND ACT OF 1985, §§143-166.80 to 143-166.85.

SHOP BOOK RULE, §§8-42 to 8-44.

SHOPLIFTING ACT, §14-72.1.

SIMULTANEOUS DEATH ACT, §§28A-24-1 to 28A-24-7.

SINGLE ACT LAW FOR FOREIGN CORPORATIONS, §§55-15-01 to 55-15-33.

SLANDER ACT, §§99-1 to 99-5.

SLAYER ACT, §§31A-3 to 31A-12.

SLOT MACHINE ACT, §§14-304 to 14-309.1.

SMALL BUSINESS CONTRACTOR ACT, §§143B-472.85 to 143B-472.97.

SMALL EMPLOYER GROUP HEALTH COVERAGE REFORM ACT, §§58-50-100 to 58-50-150.

SMALL LOANS ACT, §§53-164 to 53-191.

SMOKING IN PUBLIC PLACES, §§143-595 to 143-601.

SOCIAL SERVICES ACT, §§108A-1 to 108A-11.

SOCIAL WORKER CERTIFICATION ACT, §§90B-1 to 90B-14.

SOFT DRINK TAX ACT, §§105-113.41 to 105-113.64.

SOIL ADDITIVES ACT OF 1977, §§106-50.28 to 106-50.41.

SOIL AND WATER CONSERVATION DISTRICTS LAW, §§139-1 to 139-57.

SOIL SCIENTIST LICENSING ACT, §§89F-1 to 89F-25.

SOLID WASTE MANAGEMENT ACT OF 1989, §§130A-309.01 to 130A-309.29.

SOLID WASTE MANAGEMENT LOAN PROGRAM AND LOCAL GOVERNMENT SPECIAL OBLIGATIONS BOND ACT, §§159I-1 to 159I-30.

SOUTHEASTERN INTERSTATE FOREST FIRE PROTECTION COMPACT, §§113-60.11 to 113-60.15.

SOUTHEAST INTERSTATE LOW-LEVEL RADIOACTIVE WASTE MANAGEMENT COMPACT, §§104F-1 to 104F-5.

SOUTHERN GROWTH POLICIES AGREEMENT ACT, §§143-490 to 143-506.

SOUTHERN STATES ENERGY COMPACT, §§104D-1 to 104D-5.

SPECIAL AIRPORT DISTRICTS ACT, §§63-78 to 63-89.

SPECIAL ASSESSMENTS ACT, §§160A-216 to 160A-238.

SPECIAL EDUCATION, §§115C-106 to 115C-145.

SPEECH AND LANGUAGE PATHOLOGISTS AND AUDIOLOGISTS LICENSURE ACT, §§90-292 to 90-307.

SPEED ACT, §§20-141 to 20-141.3, 20-144, 20-145.

SPEED EXEMPTION ACT, §20-145.

SPEEDY TRIAL ACT, §15-10.

SPENDTHRIFT TRUST ACT, §36A-115.

STANDARD NONFORFEITURE LAW FOR INDIVIDUAL DEFERRED ANNUITIES, §§58-58-60, 58-58-61.

STANDARD NONFORFEITURE LAW FOR LIFE INSURANCE, §58-58-55.

STANDARD VALUATION LAW FOR LIFE INSURANCE, §58-58-50.

STATE AND LOCAL GOVERNMENT REVENUE BOND ACT, §§159-80 to 159-97.

STATE BAR ACT, §§84-15 to 84-38.

STATE CAPITAL FACILITIES FINANCE ACT, §§142-80 to 142-101.

STATE COLLEGES ACT, §§116-31 to 116-40.5.

STATE-COUNTY CRIMINAL JUSTICE PARTNERSHIP ACT, §§143B-273 to 143B-273.19.

STATE EMPLOYEE INCENTIVE BONUS PROGRAM, §§143-345.20 to 143-345.25.

STATE EMPLOYEES' POLITICAL ACTIVITY ACT, §§126-13 to 126-15.1.

STATE EMPLOYEES RETIREMENT ACT, §§135-1 to 135-18.7.

STATE ENERGY CONSERVATION FINANCE ACT, §§142-60 to 142-70.

STATE FAIR HOUSING ACT, §§41A-1 to 41A-10.

STATE NATURE AND HISTORIC PRESERVE DEDICATION ACT, §§143-260.6 to 143-260.10G.

STATE PARKS ACT, §§113-44.7 to 113-44.15.

STATE PERSONNEL SYSTEM ACT, §§126-1 to 126-88.

STATE PSYCHIATRIC HOSPITAL FINANCE ACT, §§142-100 to 142-113.

STATE REFUNDING BOND ACT, §§142-29.1 to 142-29.7.

STATE TRUST COMPANY CHARTER ACT, §§53-330 to 53-365.

STATE VETERANS HOME ACT, §§165-45 to 165-55.

STATEWIDE PRIMARY ACT, §§163-104 to 163-115, 163-119.

STATUTE OF FRAUDS, §§22-1 to 22-4.

STATUTE OF FRAUDS FOR SALES OF GOODS, §25-1-206.

STATUTE OF LIMITATIONS FOR CIVIL CASES, §§1-15 to 1-56.

STATUTE OF LIMITATIONS FOR MISDEMEANORS, §15-1.

STATUTE OF USES, §41-7.

STATUTORY SHORT FORM POWER OF ATTORNEY, §§32A-1 to 32A-3.

STERILIZATION ACT, §§35-36 to 35-50.

STERILIZATION OPERATION ACT, §§90-271 to 90-275.

STIMULANT DRUGS ACT, §§90-86 to 90-113.8.

STOCK LAW, §§68-15 to 68-46.

STOP ACT FOR MOTOR VEHICLES, §20-158.

STOP AND FRISK ACT, §15A-255.

STRAWBERRY ASSESSMENT ACT, §§106-781 to 106-786.

STREAMLINED SALES AND USE TAX AGREEMENT.

Uniform sales and use tax administration act, §§105-164.42A to 105-164.42J.

STREET AND HIGHWAY ACT, §§136-4 to 136-155.

STRUCTURAL PEST CONTROL ACT OF NORTH CAROLINA OF 1955, §§106-65.22 to 106-65.41.

STRUCTURED SENTENCING, §§15A-1340.10 to 15A-1340.23.

STUDENT LOANS.

Defaulted student loan recovery act, §§105B-1 to 105B-4.

STUDIES ACT OF 1995, §§14-415.10 to 14-415.23.

SUBDIVISIONS, CITIES, §§160A-371 to 160A-376.

SUBDIVISIONS, COUNTIES, §§153A-330 to 153A-335.

SUBSTANCE ABUSE PROFESSIONALS CERTIFICATION ACT, §§90-113.30 to 90-113.46.

SUBVERSIVE ACTIVITIES ACT, §§14-11 to 14-12.1.

SUMMER SCHOOLS, §§115C-232, 115C-233.

SUNDAY CLOSING ACT, §160A-191.

SUNDAY HUNTING ACT, §103-2.

SUNSHINE LAW, §§143-318.9 to 143-318.18.

SUPERFUND PROGRAM, §§130A-310.20 to 130A-310.23.

SUPPLEMENTAL PROCEEDINGS LAW, §§1-352 to 1-368.

SUPPLEMENTAL RETIREMENT INCOME ACT OF 1984, §§135-90 to 135-95.

SUPPORT ACT, §§52C-1-100 to 52C-9-902.

SUPPORT AND CUSTODY OF CHILDREN ACT, §§50-13.1 to 50-13.12.

SUPPORT OF CHILDREN OF PARENTS NOT MARRIED TO EACH OTHER, §49-1.

SUPPRESSION MOTIONS, §§15A-971 to 15A-980.

SURPLUS LINES ACT, §§58-21-1 to 58-21-105.

SURVIVAL LAW, §28A-18-1.

SUSPENSION OF SENTENCE ACT, §§15A-1341 to 15A-1347.

SWEEPSTAKES, §§14-289 to 14-291.2.

SWINE FAMILY SITING ACT, §§106-800 to 106-803.

T

TATTOOS, §130A-283.

TAX INCENTIVES FOR NEW AND EXPANDING BUSINESSES, §§105-129.2 to 105-129.11.

TAX LIEN FORECLOSURE ACT, §§105-374, 105-375.

TAX MACHINERY ACT, §§105-271 to 105-395.1.

TEACHERS' RETIREMENT ACT, §§135-1 to 135-18.7.

TEMPORARY LARCENY ACT, §14-72.2.

TENANT SECURITY DEPOSIT ACT, §§42-50 to 42-56.

TENDER OFFER DISCLOSURE ACT, §§78B-1 to 78B-11.

TENNESSEE VALLEY AUTHORITY, §§105-258, 105-458 to 105-462.

TENTATIVE TRUSTS, §28A-15-10.

TENURE, §§115C-304, 115C-325.

TEST-TUBE BABIES, §49A-1.

THE HEALTH INSURANCE PROGRAM FOR CHILDREN ACT OF 1998, §§108A-70.18 to 108A-70.28.

THERAPEUTIC RECREATION PERSONNEL CERTIFICATION ACT, §§90C-1 to 90C-19.

THIRD ONE-HALF CENT LOCAL GOVERNMENT SALES AND USE TAX ACT, §§105-515 to 105-521.

TIME SHARE ACT, §§93A-39 to 93A-59.

TOBACCO PRODUCTS TAX ACT, §§105-113.2 to 105-113.40.

TOBACCO RESERVE FUND AND ESCROW COMPLIANCE, §§66-290 to 66-294.1.

TOBACCO TRUST FUND, §§143-715 to 143-723.

TOLLING ACT, §1-21.

TORRENS TITLE REGISTRATION ACT, §§43-1 to 43-64.

TORT CLAIMS ACT, §§143-291 to 143-300.1A.

TORT-FEASORS CONTRIBUTIONS ACT, §§1B-1 to 1B-6.

TOXIC VAPORS ACT, §§90-113.8A to 90-113.14.

TRADEMARK REGISTRATION ACT, §§80-1 to 80-14.

TRADE SECRETS PROTECTION ACT, §§66-152 to 66-157.

TRAFFIC LAWS, §§20-138.1 to 20-171.

TRAILS SYSTEM ACT, §§113A-83 to 113A-95.
Appalachian trials system act, §§113A-72 to 113A-77.

TRAINING WAGE, §95-25.3A.

TRANSFERS TO MINORS.
Uniform transfers to minors act, §§33A-1 to 33A-24.

TRANSPORTATION AUTHORITIES ACT, §§160A-575 to 160A-588.
Regional public transportation authorities act, §§160A-600 to 160A-625.

TRAVEL AND TOURISM POLICY ACT, §143B-434.2.

TRESPASS ACT, §§14-127 to 14-165, 113A-95.

TRUANCY, §§115C-378 to 115C-383.

TRUCK ACT, §§62-259 to 62-279.

TRUCKERS' FUEL USE TAX ACT, §§105-449.37 to 105-449.57.

TRUSTEES' POWERS ACT, §§32-25 to 32-28.

TRUSTS ACT, §§36A-60 to 36A-84.

TUITION, §§116-143 to 116-144.

T.V.A., §§105-258, 105-458 to 105-462.

U

U.C.C., §§25-1-101 to 25-11-108.

UMSTEAD ACT FOR GOVERNMENT SALE OF MERCHANDISE, §66-58.

UNAUTHORIZED DOMESTIC INSURERS ACT, §§58-14-1 to 58-14-15.

UNAUTHORIZED INSURERS ACT, §§58-28-1 to 58-28-45.

UNAUTHORIZED INSURERS FALSE ADVERTISING PROCESS ACT, §§58-29-1 to 58-29-25.

UNAUTHORIZED INSURERS PROCESS ACT, §58-16-35.

UNCLAIMED PROPERTY ACT, §§116B-51 to 116B-80.

UNDERGROUND DAMAGE PREVENTION ACT, §§87-100 to 87-114.

UNEMPLOYMENT COMPENSATION LAW, §§96-1 to 96-29.

UNIFORM ACT FOR OUT-OF-STATE PAROLEE SUPERVISION, §148-65.2.

UNIFORM ACT TO SECURE THE ATTENDANCE OF WITNESSES FROM WITHOUT A STATE IN CRIMINAL PROCEEDINGS, §§15A-811 to 15A-816.

UNIFORM ANATOMICAL GIFT ACT, §§130A-402 to 130A-412.1.

UNIFORM ARBITRATION ACT, §§1-569.1 to 1-569.31.

UNIFORM ATHLETE AGENT ACT, §§78C-85 to 78C-105.

UNIFORM BOILER AND PRESSURE VESSEL ACT OF NORTH CAROLINA, §§95-69.8 to 95-69.18.

UNIFORM BOLL WEEVIL ERADICATION ACT, §§106-65.67 to 106-65.78.

UNIFORM CHILD CUSTODY JURISDICTION AND ENFORCEMENT ACT, §§50A-101 to 50A-317.

UNIFORM COMMERCIAL CODE, §§25-1-101 to 25-11-108.

UNIFORM COMMERCIAL CODE-BANK DEPOSITS AND COLLECTIONS, §§25-4-101 to 25-4-504.

UNIFORM COMMERCIAL CODE-BULK TRANSFERS, §§25-6-101 to 25-6-111.

UNIFORM COMMERCIAL CODE-DOCUMENTS OF TITLE, §§25-7-101 to 25-7-603.

UNIFORM COMMERCIAL CODE-FUNDS TRANSFERS, §§25-4A-101 to 25-4A-507.

UNIFORM COMMERCIAL CODE-INVESTMENT SECURITIES, §§25-8-101 to 25-8-511.

UNIFORM COMMERCIAL CODE-LEASES, §§25-2A-101 to 25-2A-532.

UNIFORM COMMERCIAL CODE-LETTERS OF CREDIT, §§25-5-101 to 25-5-117.

UNIFORM COMMERCIAL CODE-NEGOTIABLE INSTRUMENTS, §§25-3-101 to 25-3-605.

UNIFORM COMMERCIAL CODE-SALES, §§25-2-101 to 25-2-725.

UNIFORM COMMERCIAL CODE-SECURED TRANSACTIONS, §§25-9-101 to 25-9-709.

UNIFORM COMMON TRUST FUND ACT, §§36A-90 to 36A-94.

UNIFORM CRIMINAL EXTRADITION ACT, §§15A-721 to 15A-750.

UNIFORM CUSTODIAL TRUST ACT, §§33B-1 to 33B-22.

UNIFORM DECLARATORY JUDGMENT ACT, §§1-253 to 1-267.

UNIFORM DISPOSITION OF COMMUNITY PROPERTY RIGHTS AT DEATH ACT, §§31C-1 to 31C-12.

UNIFORM DRIVER'S LICENSE ACT, §§20-5 to 20-37.

UNIFORM ELECTRONIC TRANSACTIONS ACT, §§66-311 to 66-327.

UNIFORM ENFORCEMENT OF FOREIGN JUDGMENT ACT, §§1C-1701 to 1C-1708.

UNIFORM FEDERAL LIEN REGISTRATION ACT, §§44-68.10 to 44-68.17.

UNIFORM FIDUCIARIES ACT, §§32-1 to 32-13.

UNIFORM FRAUDULENT TRANSFERS ACT, §39-23.12.

UNIFORM INTERSTATE FAMILY SUPPORT ACT, §§52C-1-100 to 52C-9-902.

UNIFORM LIMITED PARTNERSHIP ACT.
Revised act, §§59-101 to 59-1106.

UNIFORM MANAGEMENT OF INSTITUTIONAL FUNDS ACT, §§36B-1 to 36B-10.

UNIFORM PARTNERSHIP ACT, §§59-31 to 59-73.

UNIFORM PHOTOGRAPHIC COPIES OF BUSINESS AND PUBLIC RECORDS AS EVIDENCE ACT, §§8-45.1 to 8-45.4.

UNIFORM PREMARITAL AGREEMENT ACT, §§52B-1 to 52B-11.

UNIFORM PRINCIPAL AND INCOME ACT, §§37A-1-101 to 37A-6-602.

UNIFORM RELOCATION ASSISTANCE AND REAL PROPERTY ACQUISITION POLICIES ACT, §§133-5 to 133-18.

UNIFORM SALES AND USE TAX ADMINISTRATION ACT, §§105-164.42A to 105-164.42J.

UNIFORM SIMULTANEOUS DEATH ACT, §28A-24-7.

UNIFORM STANDARDS FOR MANUFACTURED HOMES ACT, §§143-144 to 143-151.5.

UNIFORM STATUTORY RULE AGAINST PERPETUITIES, §§41-15 to 41-22.

UNIFORM TRANSFERS TO MINORS ACT, §§33A-1 to 33A-24.

UNIFORM TRUSTS ACT, §§36A-60 to 36A-84.

UNIFORM UNAUTHORIZED INSURERS ACT, §58-28-45.

UNIFORM VENDOR AND PURCHASER RISK ACT, §§39-36 to 39-39.

UNION SHOP ACT, §§95-78 to 95-84.

UNIT OWNERSHIP ACT, §§47A-1 to 47A-28.

UNIVERSITY OF NORTH CAROLINA, §§116-1 to 116-44.8.

UNMARKED HUMAN BURIAL AND HUMAN SKELETAL REMAINS PROTECTION ACT, §§70-26 to 70-40.

URBAN REDEVELOPMENT LAW, §§160A-500 to 160A-526.

USE TAX ACT, §§105-164.1 to 105-164.44D.

USURY ACT, §24-2.

UTILITIES ACT, §§62-1 to 62-333.

UTILITIES COMMISSION ACTS, §§62-10 to 62-98.

UTILITIES COMMISSION PROCEDURE ACT, §§62-60 to 62-82.

V

VACATION RENTAL ACT, §§42A-1 to 42A-36.

VAPORS ACT, §§90-113.8A to 90-113.14.

VARSER ACT, §1-500.

VEGETABLE PLANT LAW, §§106-284.14 to 106-284.22.

VEHICLE EQUIPMENT SAFETY COMPACT, §§20-183.13 to 20-183.21.

VEHICLE FINANCIAL RESPONSIBILITY ACT OF 1957, §§20-309 to 20-319.

VEHICLE MILEAGE ACT, §§20-340 to 20-350.

VENDOR AND PURCHASER RISK ACT, §§39-36 to 39-39.

VENUE FOR CIVIL CASES, §§1-76 to 1-87.

VENUE FOR CRIMINAL CASES, §§15A-131 to 15A-136.

VETERANS AFFAIRS ACT, §§165-1 to 165-44.

VETERANS ENABLING ACT FOR MINORS, §§165-12 to 165-16.

VETERANS' GUARDIANSHIP ACT, §§34-1 to 34-18.

VETERANS HOME ACT, §§165-45 to 165-55.

VETERANS' PREFERENCE, §§126-80 to 126-83, 128-15.

VETERANS' RECREATION AUTHORITIES LAW, §§165-23 to 165-38.

VETERINARY PRACTICE ACT, §§90-179 to 90-187.14.

VIATICAL SETTLEMENTS ACT, §§58-58-200 to 58-58-310.

VICTIMS COMPENSATION ACT, §§15B-1 to 15B-38.

VIRGINIA-NORTH CAROLINA INTERSTATE HIGH-SPEED RAIL COMPACT, §§136-220 to 136-222.

VITAL STATISTICS PROGRAM, §§130A-90 to 130A-120.

VOCATIONAL AND TECHNICAL EDUCATION, §§115C-151 to 115C-169.

VOLUNTARY STERILIZATION LAW, §§90-271 to 90-275.

VOTER REGISTRATION ACT, §§163-82.1 to 163-82.26.

VOTING TRUST ACT, §§55-7-30, 55-7-31.

W

WAGE AND HOUR ACT, §§95-25.1 to 95-25.25.

WAREHOUSE RECEIPTS, BILLS OF LADING AND OTHER DOCUMENTS OF TITLE, §§26-7-101 to 25-7-603.

WAR POWERS ACT, §§147-33.1 to 147-33.6.

WATER AND AIR QUALITY REPORTING ACT OF 1971, §§143-215.63 to 143-215.69.

WATER AND AIR RESOURCES ACT, §§143-211 to 143-215.74I.

WATER AND SEWAGE FACILITIES ACT, §§153A-283 to 153A-288.

WATER AND SEWER AUTHORITIES ACT, §§162A-1 to 162A-19.

WATERCRAFT SAFETY ACT, §§75A-1 to 75A-19.

WATERCRAFT TITLING ACT, §§75A-32 to 75A-49.

WATERED STOCK ACT, §§55-6-21, 55-6-22.

WATER RESOURCES DEVELOPMENT PROJECTS FOR FEDERAL WATER RESOURCES, §§143-215.38 to 143-215.43.

WATER SUPPLY PLANNING ACT, §§162A-20 to 162A-25.

WATER USE ACT OF 1967, §§143-215.11 to 143-215.22B.

WEAPONS OF MASS DEATH AND DESTRUCTION, §§14-288.21 to 14-288.24.

WEATHERIZATION ASSISTANCE PROGRAM, §108A-70.30.

WEIGHTS AND MEASURES ACT OF 1975, §§81A-1 to 81A-88.

WELL CONSTRUCTION ACT, §§87-83 to 87-96.

WELL CONTRACTORS CERTIFICATION ACT, §§87-98.1 to 87-98.13.

WELL DRILLER REGISTRATION ACT, §143-355, (e).

WETLANDS RECREATION PROGRAM, §§143-214.8 to 143-214.13.

WHISTLEBLOWER PROTECTION.
Protection for reporting improper government activities, §§126-84 to 126-88.
Retaliatory employment discrimination, §§95-240 to 95-245.

WHITE CANE LAW, §§20-175.1 to 20-175.3, 168-5.

WHITE GOODS, §§130A-309.80 to 130A-309.86.

WILDLIFE RESOURCES LAW, §§143-237 to 143-254.2.

WILLARD ACT FOR FOREIGN INSURANCE COMPANIES, §§58-16-1 to 58-16-55.

WILLS ACT, §§31-1 to 31-47.

WILLS REVOCATION ACT, §§31-5.1 to 31-5.8.

WIND POWER TAX CREDIT, §§105-130.31, 105-151.9.

WINE AND BEER LOCAL OPTION ACT, §§18B-600 to 18B-605.

WIRETAPPING ACT, §14-155.

WITHHOLDING, §§105-163.1 to 105-163.24.

WITNESS ACT, §§8-49 to 8-58.1.

WORKERS' COMPENSATION ACT, §§97-1 to 97-101.

WORKPLACE VIOLENCE PREVENTION.
Civil no-contact orders, §§95-265 to 95-276.

WORTHLESS CHECK ACT, §§14-106 to 14-107.1.

WRONGFUL DEATH ACT, §28A-18-2.

Z

ZONING ACT FOR AIRPORTS, §§63-30 to 63-37.1.

ZONING, COUNTIES, §§153A-340 to 153A-348.

ZONING, MUNICIPALITIES, §§160A-381 to 160A-392.

General Index

A

AARON'S ROD.
Taking, etc., of certain wild plants from land of another, §14-129.

ABANDONED AND DERELICT MOTOR VEHICLES, §§20-137.6 to 20-137.14.
Abandoned vehicles.
Defined, §20-137.7.
Accident involving parked or unattended vehicle.
Report to owner, §20-166.1, (c).
Accumulation of abandoned vehicles.
Prevention, §20-137.6.
Antique vehicles.
Exemption from provisions, §20-137.14.
Automobile graveyards defined, §136-143.
Contracts for disposal.
Authority of secretary, §20-137.12.
Public areas used for collection areas, §20-137.12.
Definitions, §20-137.7.
Demolishers.
Defined, §20-137.7.
Duties on purchasing or acquiring, §20-137.11.
Derelict vehicles.
Defined, §20-137.7.
Disabled vehicles.
Parking or leaving standing on highways, §20-161, (a).
Warning lights, display, trucks, §20-161, (c).
Enclosed vehicles.
Exemption from provisions, §20-137.14.
Exceptions from provisions.
Enclosed, antique, registered and certain other vehicles, §20-137.14.
Legislative declaration, §20-137.6.
Liens.
Identification of lienholders, §20-137.10, (d).
No liability for removal, §20-137.13.
Notice.
Sale, §20-137.10, (c) to (d1).
Tagging of vehicles, §20-137.10, (a), (c).
Ownership.
Identity of owner undetermined, §20-137.10, (d).
Parking or leaving standing on highways.
Clear to approaching drivers, §20-161, (b).
Disabled vehicles, §20-161, (a).
Warning lights, display, trucks, §20-161, (c).
Removal and storage.
Agent of owner or operator for removal.
Law enforcement officer deemed, §20-161, (d), (e).
Controlled access highway, §20-161, (f).
Costs, liability of owner, §20-161, (g).
Peace officers' duties, §20-114.
Private parking lots.
Removal of unauthorized vehicles, §20-219.2.
Private property.
Removal from, §§20-137.9, 20-219.2.
Provision for credit if new license purchased, §20-100.
Purpose of provisions, §20-137.6.

ABANDONED AND DERELICT MOTOR VEHICLES —Cont'd
Regulation, restraint and prohibition, §153A-132.2.
Removal, disposal or storage, §§20-137.9, 20-137.13, 153A-132, 160A-303.
Cities and towns, §160A-303.
Coastal area counties.
Service districts to provide, §153A-301, (b), (c).
No liability for, §20-137.13.
Parking or leaving standing on highways.
Agent of owner or operator for removal.
Law enforcement officer deemed, §20-161, (d), (e).
Controlled access highway, §20-161, (f).
Costs, liability of owner, §20-161, (g).
Private property, §20-137.9.
Unauthorized vehicle, §20-219.2.
Reports.
Duties of peace officers, §20-114, (c).
Rules and regulations.
Adoption, §20-137.8.
Sale.
Authority of secretary, §20-137.12.
Notice, §20-137.10, (c), (d).
When not required, §20-137.10, (d1).
Salvage yards.
Defined, §20-137.7.
Secretary of department of transportation to regulate, §20-137.8.
Tags.
Defined, §20-137.7.
Effect, §20-137.10, (c).
Generally, §20-137.10, (a).
Title.
Vesting in state, §20-137.11.
Towing.
Removal generally, §§20-137.9, 20-137.13, 153A-132, 160A-303.
Towing generally.
See TOWING OF VEHICLES.
Value.
Abandoned vehicles valued in excess of one hundred dollars, §20-137.10, (d).
Abandoned vehicles valued less than one hundred dollars, §20-137.10, (d1).
Appraisal or determination.
Authority of officers, §20-137.10, (e).
Warning lights, display, trucks.
Disabled vehicles.
Parking or leaving standing on highways, §20-161, (c).

ABANDONED, IDLE OR UNUSED PROPERTY.
Environmental contamination.
Brownfields property reuse act of 1997, §§130A-310.30 to 130A-310.40.
See BROWNFIELDS PROPERTY REUSE.
Unclaimed property generally, §§116B-51 to 116B-80.
See UNCLAIMED PROPERTY.

ABANDONMENT.
Acts barring rights of spouse, §31A-1, (a).

ABANDONMENT —Cont'd
Aid to families with dependent children.
Reports to district attorneys, §15-155.2.
Attorneys at law.
Entrusted property, Prof. Cond. Rule 1.15-2.
Birth of abandoned children.
Establishing facts relating to birth, §130A-107.
Cartways.
Manner of altering or abandoning, §136-70.
Cemeteries.
Advisory committee on abandoned cemeteries, §143B-128.
Historic preservation program, §121-8, (g).
Children and minors.
See ABANDONMENT OF CHILD.
Child support.
Child support enforcement program generally, §§110-128 to 110-142.2.
See CHILD SUPPORT.
Willful neglect or refusal to provide adequate support, §14-322.
Counties.
Junked motor vehicles, §§153A-132, 153A-132.2.
Cruelty to animals, §14-361.1.
Disposition of seized, confiscated or unclaimed property, §§15-11 to 15-17.
Disposition of unclaimed property generally, §§116B-51 to 116B-80.
See UNCLAIMED PROPERTY.
Divorce.
Grounds for divorce, §50-7.
Husband and wife.
Acts barring rights of spouse, §31A-1, (a).
Competency of spouse as witness against other, §8-57, (b).
Guardian's sale of abandoned incompetent spouse's estate, §35A-1306.
Willful abandonment, §14-322.
Junked motor vehicles.
Regulation in municipalities, §160A-303.2.
Landlord and tenant.
Ejectment of residential tenant.
Personal property of tenant abandoned.
Delivery of property to custody of nonprofit organization, §42-25.9.
Lost instruments and records.
See LOST INSTRUMENTS AND RECORDS.
Motor vehicles.
Generally, §§20-137.6 to 20-137.14.
See ABANDONED AND DERELICT MOTOR VEHICLES.
Navigable waters.
Removal of abandoned structures, §76-40, (c).
Oil and gas wells.
Abandoning wells, §113-395.
Parent and child.
Property rights.
Acts barring rights of parents, §31A-2.
Willful neglect or refusal to provide adequate support, §14-322.
Public utility franchises.
Abandonment or reduction of service, §62-118.
Railroads.
Easements.
Presumptive ownership of abandoned easements, §1-44.2, (a), (b).
Rights of way.
Presumption, §1-44.1.
Refrigerators, §14-318.1.
Repair business, disposal of unclaimed property.
Authorization, §66-67.1, (a).
Definitions, §66-67.1, (d).

ABANDONMENT —Cont'd
Repair business, disposal of unclaimed property —Cont'd
Liability, §66-67.1, (c).
Notice requirement, §66-67.1, (b).
Seized, confiscated or unclaimed property disposition, §§15-11 to 15-17.
Six month abandonment period.
Failure or refusal to provide adequate support, §14-322.1.
Willful abandonment, §14-322.1.
Streets and highways.
Cartways, tramways or railways.
Manner of altering or abandoning, §136-70.
Controlled-access facilities.
Authority to abandon, §136-89.50.
Dedication of road or street.
Deemed abandoned if not used within fifteen years, §136-96.
Secondary road system.
Municipality keeping open and assuming responsibility.
Roads within one mile of corporate limits, §136-63, (b).
Request to abandon or change.
Board of county commissioners, §136-63, (a).
State highway system.
Municipality keeping open and assuming responsibility.
Roads within one mile of corporate limits, §136-55.1, (b).
Notice, §136-55.1, (a).
Unclaimed property generally, §§116B-51 to 116B-80.
See UNCLAIMED PROPERTY.
Veterinarians.
Abandoned animals, §90-187.7.
Vital statistics.
Birth of abandoned children.
Establishing facts relating to birth, §130A-107.
Water or sewer utility service.
Abandonment of service without prior consent of utilities commission, §62-118, (b).
Inadequate service, §62-118, (c).
Welfare recipients, investigations, §15-155.2.

ABANDONMENT OF CHILD.
Acts barring rights of parents, §31A-2.
Baby drop off, §14-322.3.
Child abuse.
Exceptions, §§14-318.2, 14-318.4, (c).
Child abuse.
Exceptions, §§14-318.2, 14-318.4, 14-322.3, (c).
Reports of abandonment.
Investigation of reports, §7B-302.
Termination of parental rights proceedings.
Generally, §§7B-1100 to 7B-1113.
See TERMINATION OF PARENTAL RIGHTS.
Grounds for terminating, §7B-1111, (a).
Willful neglect or refusal to provide adequate support, §14-322.

ABANDONMENT OF RAILROAD EASEMENT.
Presumption of ownership, §1-44.2, (a), (b).

ABANDONMENT OF RAILROAD RIGHT-OF-WAY.
Presumption, §1-44.1.

ABATEMENT OF LEAD POISONING HAZARDS, §130A-131.9C.

ABATEMENT OF NUISANCES.
General provisions, §§19-1 to 19-8.3.
See NUISANCES.

ABATEMENT OF NUISANCES —Cont'd
Offenses against public morals, §§19-1 to 19-20.
See NUISANCES.

ABATEMENT, REVIVAL AND SURVIVAL OF ACTIONS.
Collaborative law procedures.
Equitable distribution, §50-79.
Death before limitation expires.
Action by or against personal representative or collector, §1-22.
Death, insanity or incompetency of party.
Abatement unless continued by proper party, §1A-1, Rule 25, (c).
No abatement after verdict, §1A-1, Rule 25, (g).
Death of receiver of corporation.
Continuance against successor or against corporation in case of new receiver, §1A-1, Rule 25, (e).
Equitable distribution, §50-20, (l).
Collaborative law procedures, §50-79.
Executors and administrators.
Death before limitation expires.
Action by or against personal representative or collector, §1-22.
Presentation of claims.
Substitution of personal representative to constitute, §28A-19-1, (c).
Rights of action surviving decedent, §28A-18-1.
Wrongful death, §28A-18-2.
Incompetency or insanity of party.
Action not to abate by reason of, §1A-1, Rule 25, (b).
Investment advisers.
Civil liabilities for violations, §78C-38, (c).
Public officers, death or separation from office.
Successor automatically substituted as party, §1A-1, Rule 25, (f).
Securities regulation.
Civil liabilities, §78A-56, (e).
Support of illegitimate children.
Death of mother not bar to proceeding, §49-5.

ABATTOIRS.
Biological residues in animals, §§106-549.81 to 106-549.89.
Meat inspection requirements, §§106-549.15 to 106-549.28.
Poultry products inspection, §§106-549.49 to 106-549.69.
Rendering plants and rendering operations, §§106-168.1 to 106-168.16.

ABC ACT.
See ALCOHOLIC BEVERAGES.

ABC BOARDS, LOCAL.
Accounts, §18B-205, (a).
System of accounting, §18B-205, (b).
Appointment.
City boards, §18B-700, (b).
County boards, §18B-700, (c).
Merged boards, §18B-703, (b).
Audits, §§18B-205, (c), 18B-702, (c).
Bonds, surety, §18B-700, (i).
Borrowing of money, §18B-702, (b).
Chairman, §18B-700, (a).
Compensation of members, §18B-700, (g).
Compliance with commission rules, §18B-702, (e).
Composition, §18B-700, (a).
Conflicts of interest, §18B-700, (h).
Corporate body, §18B-702, (a).

ABC BOARDS, LOCAL —Cont'd
Debts.
Governing body not responsible, §18B-702, (b).
Deposits, §18B-702, (d).
Distribution of revenue, §18B-805.
Embezzlement by members and employees, §18B-702, (f).
Financial operations, §18B-702.
Investments, §§18B-701, 18B-702, (d).
Joint store operation, §18B-703, (h).
Liability of members.
Limited liability, §18B-700, (j).
Malfeasance by members and employees, §18B-702, (f).
Merger of local operations.
Appointment of merged board, §18B-703, (b).
Conditions for merger, §18B-703, (a).
Dissolution, §18B-703, (e).
Distribution of profits, §18B-703, (c).
Jurisdiction of enforcement officials, §18B-703, (d).
Negotiation of details, §18B-703, (f).
Operation to follow general law, §18B-703, (g).
Officers, local, §18B-501.
Powers, §§18B-701, 18B-702.
Public authority.
Not to be considered public authority, §18B-702, (a).
Qualification of members, §18B-700, (d).
Removal of members, §18B-700, (f).
Reports, §18B-205, (a).
Revenue.
Distribution, §18B-805.
Rules and regulations.
Compliance with commission rules, §18B-702, (e).
Terms of office, §18B-700, (a).
Vacancies in office.
Filling, §18B-700, (e).

ABC LICENSES.
Local licenses, §§105-113.77 to 105-113.79.
Permits generally.
See ABC PERMITS.

ABC OFFICERS.
Alcohol law enforcement agencies, §18B-500.
Disposition of seized beverages, §18B-503.
Forfeitures, §18B-504.
Inspection of licensed premises, §18B-502.
Local ABC officers, §18B-501.
Appointment by local boards, §18B-501, (a).
Arrest authority, §18B-501, (b).
Assisting other local agencies, §18B-501, (b).
Assisting state and federal enforcement, §18B-501, (e).
Contractors who hire officers with other agencies, §18B-501, (f).
Designation as ABC officers, §18B-501, (a).
Discharge, §18B-501, (g).
Investigatory and enforcement authority, §18B-501, (b).
Local option elections.
Small resort town ABC elections, §18B-600, (e5).
Pursuit outside normal territorial jurisdiction, §18B-501, (c).
Subject matter jurisdiction, §18B-501, (b).
Territorial jurisdiction, §18B-501, (c).
Restitution to law enforcement agency, §18B-505.

ABC PERMITS.
ABC stores, §18B-603.

ABC PERMITS —Cont'd
Administrative procedure act.
Applicability, §18B-906, (a).
Exception on location of hearing, §18B-906, (b).
Adult establishments.
Local government regulation of adult establishments or other sexually oriented businesses.
Provisions not deemed to preempt, §18B-904, (g).
Applications.
False information, §18B-902, (c).
Form, §18B-902, (a).
Bottlers.
Authorization, §18B-1110, (a).
Commercial permit, §18B-1100.
Fee, §18B-902, (d).
Brewery permits.
Authorization, §18B-1104.
Commercial permit, §18B-1100.
Fee, §18B-902, (d).
Power to issue, §18B-1001.
Brew on premises.
Fee, §18B-902, (d).
Issuance, §18B-1001.
Brown-bagging permit, §18B-1001.
Fee, §18B-902, (d).
Business not operating.
Automatic expiration, §18B-904, (c).
Change in management, §18B-903, (d).
Change in ownership.
Automatic expiration, §18B-903, (c).
Child labor.
Restrictions on employment of minors, §95-25.5, (j).
Cider and vinegar manufacturers.
Commercial permit, §18B-1100.
Effect of permit, §18B-1114.2.
Fee, §18B-902, (d).
Commercial permits, §18B-1100.
Commercial transportation.
Permit required, §18B-1115.
Conduct on premises.
Certain conduct prohibited, §§18B-1005, (a), 18B-1005.1, (a), (c).
Supervision, §§18B-1005, (b), 18B-1005.1, (b).
Controlled substances.
Prohibited on licensed premises, §18B-1005, (a).
Cooking schools, §18B-1000.
Restrictions on sales at cooking schools, §18B-1006, (g).
Corporations.
Person to qualify, §18B-900, (c).
Culinary permit, §18B-1001.
Duration, §18B-903, (a).
Fee, §18B-902, (d).
Disorderly conduct.
Prohibited on licensed premises, §18B-1005, (a).
Distilleries.
Authorized acts, §18B-1105, (a).
Commercial permit, §18B-1100.
Fee, §18B-902, (d).
Fuel alcohol, §18B-1105, (b).
Drugs.
Prohibited on licensed premises, §18B-1005, (a).
Duration, §18B-903, (a).
Change in ownership.
Automatic expiration, §18B-903, (c).
Elections.
Permits not dependent on elections, §18B-603, (f).
Facsimile permits, §18B-1006, (e).

ABC PERMITS —Cont'd
Failure to surrender permit, §18B-1006, (f).
False permits, §18B-1006, (e).
Fees, §18B-902, (d).
Combined applications, §18B-902, (e).
Disposition, §18B-902, (g).
Duplicate, §18B-903, (f).
Name change.
Issuance of new permit, §18B-903, (g).
Nonrefundable, §18B-902, (f).
Registration of persons holding permits, §18B-903, (b1).
Renewal, §18B-903, (b).
Fighting.
Prohibited on licensed premises, §18B-1005, (a).
Firm, association or general partnership.
Person to qualify, §18B-900, (c).
Fortified wine permit.
Duration, §18B-903, (a).
Fortified winery permit.
Authorization, §18B-1102.
Commercial permit, §18B-1100.
Fee, §18B-902, (d).
Fuel alcohol permit.
Commercial permit, §18B-1100.
Fee, §18B-902, (d).
Gambling.
Prohibited on licensed premises, §18B-1005, (a).
Guest room cabinet permit.
Fee, §18B-902, (d).
Hearings.
Location, §18B-906, (b).
Recommendations.
Local government official designated to make.
Testimony at hearing, §18B-904, (f).
Investigations.
Prerequisite to issuance, §18B-902, (b).
Issuance.
Authority of commission, §18B-901, (d).
Commercial permits.
Types authorized, §18B-1100.
Commission, §18B-900, (a).
Factors to be considered, §18B-901, (c).
Investigations prior to issuance, §18B-902, (b).
Notice, §18B-904, (d).
Notice to local government, §18B-901, (b).
Places eligible, §18B-1001.
Temporary permits, §18B-905.
Who issues, §18B-901, (a).
Who permit issued to, §18B-904, (a).
Kinds of permits, §18B-1001.
Limited liability companies.
Person to qualify for permits, §18B-900, (c).
Limited partnerships.
Person to qualify, §18B-900, (c).
Limited winery permit.
Authorization, §18B-1103.
Commercial permit, §18B-1100.
Fee, §18B-902, (d).
Liquor importer/bottler permit.
Authorizations, §18B-1105.1.
Location no longer suitable.
Suspension or revocation of permit, §18B-904, (e).
Lost permits.
Issuance of duplicates, §18B-903, (f).
Malt beverages.
Importers, §18B-1108.
Commercial permit, §18B-1100.
Fee, §18B-902, (d).
Nonresident vendor, §18B-1113.

ABC PERMITS —Cont'd
Malt beverages —Cont'd
Wholesalers, §18B-1109.
Commercial permit, §18B-1100.
Fee, §18B-902, (d).
Mixed beverage permits, §18B-1001.
Additional requirements, §18B-1007.
Fee, §18B-902, (d).
Hotels and restaurants.
National historic landmark district, §18B-1006, (n).
Temporary permit, §18B-1007, (d).
Name change.
Issuance of new permit, §18B-903, (g).
National historic landmark district.
Mixed beverages permit.
Hotels and restaurants.
Issuance of permits in certain counties, §18B-1006, (n).
Nonresidents.
Nonresident malt beverage vendor permit.
Commercial permit, §18B-1100.
Fee, §18B-902, (d).
Nonresident wine vendor permit.
Commercial permit, §18B-1100.
Fee, §18B-902, (d).
Restrictions on sale by nonresident vendors, §18B-1118.
Nontransferable, §18B-903, (e).
Notice.
Issuance, §18B-904, (d).
Notice to local government, §18B-901, (b).
Off-premises fortified wine permit, §18B-1001.
Fee, §18B-902, (d).
Off-premises malt beverage permit, §18B-1001.
Duration, §18B-903, (a).
Fee, §18B-902, (d).
Off-premises unfortified wine permit, §18B-1001.
Fee, §18B-902, (d).
One-time permits, §18B-1002.
On-premises fortified wine permit, §18B-1001.
Fee, §18B-902, (d).
On-premises malt beverage permit, §18B-1001.
Duration, §18B-903, (a).
Fee, §18B-902, (d).
On-premises unfortified wine permit, §18B-1001.
Fee, §18B-902, (d).
Out of state purchases.
Suspension or revocation, §18B-104, (a), (d), (e).
Owner of business or management company.
Permit issued to, §18B-904, (a).
Partnerships.
Person to qualify, §18B-900, (c).
Permits based on existing permits, §18B-603, (h).
Places eligible, §18B-1001.
Posting, §18B-904, (b).
Private clubs.
Residential private clubs, §18B-1006, (k).
Prostitution.
Prohibited on licensed premises, §18B-1005, (a).
Purchase-transportation permits, §§18B-403 to 18B-405.
Purchasing in greater amounts than allowed, §18B-303, (c).
Qualifications for permits.
Convention centers, §18B-900, (e).
Conviction defined, §18B-900, (b).
Discretion of commission, §18B-901, (d).
ABC PERMITS —Cont'd
Qualifications for permits —Cont'd
Manager of off-premises establishment, §18B-900, (d).
Requirements, §18B-900, (a).
Who must qualify, §18B-900, (c).
Recreation districts, §18B-1006, (j).
Registration of persons holding, §18B-903, (b1).
Renewal, §18B-903, (b).
Responsibilities of permittees.
Employees, §18B-1003, (b).
Certain employees prohibited, §18B-1003, (c).
Financial responsibility, §18B-1003, (d).
Premises, §18B-1003, (a).
Retail business.
Restrictions on purchases by retail permittees, §18B-1006.
Rules and regulations.
Retail permits, §18B-1008.
Salesmen.
Authorized acts, §18B-1111.
Commercial permit, §18B-1100.
Duration, §18B-1111, (c).
Fee, §18B-902, (d).
Persons required to obtain, §18B-1111.
Term, §18B-1111, (c).
Schools.
Business located on property of public school, §18B-1006, (a).
Sexually explicit conduct.
Prohibited on licensed premises, §18B-1005.1, (a).
Exceptions, §18B-1005.1, (c).
Sole proprietorships.
Person associated with business to qualify, §18B-900, (c).
Special ABC areas.
Elections, §18B-603, (f2).
Special occasion permit, §18B-1001.
Fee, §18B-902, (d).
Limited special occasion permit, §18B-1001.
Duration, §18B-903, (a).
Fee, §18B-902, (d).
Special one-time permit.
Administrative procedure, §18B-1002, (d).
Conditions of permit, §18B-1002, (c).
Duration, §18B-903, (a).
Fee, §18B-902, (d).
Intent of section, §18B-1002, (b).
Kinds of permits, §18B-1002, (a).
Sports clubs, §18B-1006, (k).
Sale of malt beverages, unfortified wine or mixed beverages and operation of ABC system allowed in six cities and counties.
Issuance of permits to sports clubs throughout county, §18B-603, (h).
Stadiums.
In-stand sales, §18B-1009.
Supervision of business.
Permittee or manger, §§18B-1005, (b), 18B-1005.1, (b).
Surrender.
Failure to surrender, §18B-1006, (f).
Suspension or revocation.
Administrative penalties, §18B-104, (a).
Business or location no longer suitable, §18B-904, (e).
Effect on other permits, §18B-104, (e).
Summary suspension or revocation.
Violation by business in urban redevelopment area, §18B-904, (e).

ABC PERMITS —Cont'd
Suspension or revocation —Cont'd
Urban redevelopment areas.
Violation of sales restrictions, §18B-904, (e).
Wine distribution agreements.
Violations of article, §18B-1207, (c).
Temporary permits, §18B-905.
Term, §18B-903, (a).
Tour boats.
Restrictions on sales on tour boats, §18B-1006, (i).
Transferability, §18B-903, (e).
Unfortified wine permit.
Duration, §18B-903, (a).
Unfortified winery permit.
Authorization, §18B-1101.
Commercial permit, §18B-1100.
Fee, §18B-902, (d).
Universities and colleges.
Permit for business on campus, §18B-1006, (a).
Viticulture/oenology course authorization, §18B-1114.4.
Vendor representative.
Authorized acts, §18B-1112, (a).
Commercial permit, §18B-1100.
Fee, §18B-902, (d).
Number of permits, §18B-1112, (b).
Viticulture/oenology course authorization.
Generally, §18B-1114.4, (a).
Limitations on issuance, §18B-1114.4, (b).
Manufacture of wines, §18B-1114.4, (b), (c).
Winery.
Holder not deemed to be, §18B-1114.4, (d).
Wholesalers.
Malt beverages, §18B-1109.
Restrictions on sales by wholesalers to retail permittees, §18B-1006.
Supplier's financial interest in wholesaler, §18B-1119.
Wine, §18B-1107, (a).
Wine importer, §18B-1106, (a).
Commercial permit, §18B-1100.
Fee, §18B-902, (d).
Wine producer permit, §18B-902, (d).
Authorization, §18B-1114.3, (a).
Commercial permit, §18B-1100.
Limitation on total gallons sold annually, §18B-1114.3, (b).
Wine producer defined, §18B-1000.
Wineries.
Commercial permits, §18B-1100.
Fortified wineries, §18B-1102.
Limited wineries, §18B-1103.
Special event permit.
Authorization, §18B-1114.1, (a).
Fee, §18B-902, (d).
Jurisdictions permit valid, §18B-1114.1, (b).
Special show permit, §18B-1114.1, (a).
Commercial permit, §18B-1100.
Limitation, §18B-1114.1, (b).
Unfortified wineries, §18B-1101.
Viticulture/oenology course authorization.
Holder not deemed to be winery, §18B-1114.4, (d).
Wine distribution agreements.
Violations of article.
Suspension or revocation of winery permit, §18B-1207, (c).
Wine shipper permit.
Direct shipments into state.
Application, authorization, §18B-1001.1, (a).
Fee, §18B-902, (d).

ABC PERMITS —Cont'd
Wine shipper permit —Cont'd
Direct shipments into state —Cont'd
Manner of making, §18B-1001.1, (c).
Quarterly summary of shipped wine, §18B-1001.2, (a).
Registration of permittee, §18B-1001.2, (a).
Rules, adoption, §18B-1001.2, (b).
State jurisdiction, permittee subject to, §18B-1001.1, (d).
Wholesaler in state, appointment, §18B-1001.1, (b).
Wine tasting permit, §§18B-902, 18B-1001, (d).
Wine vendor.
Nonresident vendor, §18B-1114.
Wine wholesaler, §18B-1107, (a).
Commercial permit, §18B-1100.
Fee, §18B-902, (d).

ABC STORES.
Alcoholism funds, §18B-805, (h).
Expenditures, §18B-805, (h).
Bonds, surety.
Employees, §18B-803, (c).
Manager, §18B-803, (b).
Closing of stores.
Grounds, §18B-801, (c).
Insolvent ABC system, §18B-801, (d).
State of emergency, §18B-110.
Consumption at ABC store, §18B-301, (e), (f).
Credit cards.
Expansion of credit sales prohibited, §18B-800, (d).
Damaged alcoholic beverages, sale.
Not owned by local board, §18B-806, (b).
Owned by local board, §18B-806, (a).
Procedure, §18B-806, (c).
Records, §18B-806, (d).
Days of operation, §18B-802, (b).
Distribution of revenue.
Cities and counties, §18B-805, (e).
Gross receipts.
Defined, §18B-805, (a).
Mixed beverage profit shared, §18B-805, (f).
Primary distribution, §18B-805, (b).
Quarterly distributions, §18B-805, (g).
Statutory distributions, §18B-805, (c).
Sale at less than uniform price, §18B-805, (i).
Elections.
City elections, §18B-600, (d).
Form of ballot, §18B-602, (g).
Mixed beverage election held simultaneously, §18B-603, (d2).
Permits.
Effect of election on issuance, §18B-603, (c).
Not dependent on election, §18B-603, (f).
Required for mixed beverages, §18B-604, (e).
Ski resort.
ABC elections, §18B-600, (e2).
Expenditures of alcoholism funds, §18B-805, (h).
Hours of operation, §18B-802, (a).
Insolvent system.
Closing of stores, §18B-801, (d).
Joint store operation, §18B-703, (h).
Local ABC officers.
Appointment, §18B-501, (a).
Assisting other local agencies, §18B-501, (d).
Assisting state and federal enforcement, §18B-501, (e).
Contracts with other agencies.
Alternative to hiring local officers, §18B-501.
Discharge, §18B-501, (g).

ABC STORES —Cont'd
Local ABC officers —Cont'd
Jurisdiction, §18B-501, (b), (c).
Location of stores, §18B-801, (b).
Manager, §18B-803, (a), (b).
Merger of local operations.
Cities and counties, board for merged system, §18B-703.
Number of stores, §18B-801, (a).
Permits.
Effect of election on issuance, §18B-603, (c).
Permits not dependent on elections, §18B-603, (f).
Required for mixed beverages, §18B-604, (e).
Pregnancy, consumption during.
Signs warning of dangers.
Display, §18B-808, (a), (b).
Rules and regulations, §18B-807.
Sales.
Commission approval, §18B-800, (c).
Credit cards.
Expansion of credit sales prohibited, §18B-800, (d).
Damaged alcoholic beverages, §18B-806.
Spirituous liquor, §18B-800, (a).
Sundays and holidays, §18B-802, (b).
Wine, §18B-800, (b).
Sales price.
Fortified wine, §18B-804, (c).
Spirituous liquor, §18B-804, (b).
Spirituous liquor.
Approval of sale, §18B-800, (c).
Price, §18B-804, (b).
Sold only in ABC stores, §18B-800, (a).
Uniform price, §18B-804, (a).
State of emergency, governor closing, §18B-110.
Sundays and holidays sales, §18B-802, (b).
Time of operation, §18B-802, (a).
Uniform price of spirituous liquor, §18B-804, (a).
Working capital, §18B-805, (d).

ABDUCTION.
Kidnapping and abduction, §§14-39 to 14-41.
See KIDNAPPING AND ABDUCTION.

ABORTION, §§14-44 to 14-46.
Certification of fitness of institutions, §14-45.1, (a).
Concealing birth of child, §14-46.
Consent.
Legal counsel for indigent persons, §7A-451, (a).
Parental or judicial consent, §§90-21.6 to 90-21.10.
Department of health and human services reports.
Certification of fitness of health care institutions, §14-45.1, (a).
Statistical summary reports concerning medical and demographic characteristics of abortions, §14-45.1, (c).
Destroying unborn child by using drugs or instruments, §14-44.
First twenty weeks of woman's pregnancy, §14-45.1, (a).
Geographically based field program.
Limitations on eligible cases, §7A-474.3, (c).
Health care institutions.
Certification of fitness by health and human services department, §14-45.1, (a).
Requirement to perform abortion, §14-45.1, (f).
Health of woman gravely impaired, §14-45.1, (b).

ABORTION —Cont'd
Injunctions.
Obstruction of abortion clinic, §14-277.4, (d).
Injuring pregnant woman by using drugs, §14-45.
Life of woman threatened, §14-45.1, (b).
Minors.
Consent. See within this heading, "Consent."
Miscarriages.
Drugs or instruments to produce miscarriage.
Using drugs or instruments, §14-45.
Injury to pregnant woman resulting in miscarriage or stillbirth, §14-18.2.
Obstruction of abortion clinics, §14-277.4.
Access to or egress from clinic, §14-277.4, (a).
Exemptions, §14-277.4, (h).
Felony offense.
Habitual offenders, §14-277.4, (c).
Free speech not abridged, §14-277.4, (e).
"Health care facility" defined, §14-277.4, (f).
"Health care services" defined, §14-277.4, (g).
Injunctive relief, §14-277.4, (d).
Misdemeanor offense, §14-277.4, (c).
Personal injury, §14-277.4, (b).
Picketing right not abridged, §14-277.4, (e).
Parental or judicial consent for abortion, §§90-21.6 to 90-21.10.
Definitions, §90-21.6.
District court jurisdiction, §7B-200, (a).
Medical emergency exception to parental consent requirement, §90-21.9.
Misdemeanors for violations of provisions, §90-21.10.
Parental consent required, §90-21.7, (a).
Medical emergency exception, §90-21.9.
Waiver of requirement, §90-21.8.
Petition by pregnant minor, §90-21.7, (b).
Petition by pregnant minor on own behalf.
Waiver of parental consent requirement, §90-21.7, (b).
Waiver of parental consent requirement.
Appeal by minor, §90-21.8, (h).
Availability inapplicability to unemancipated minor seeking treatment in state, §90-21.8, (a).
Confidentiality of court proceedings, §90-21.8, (d).
Costs not required of minors, §90-21.8, (i).
Findings necessary, §90-21.8, (e).
Hearing, §90-21.8, (d).
Participation by minor in proceedings, §90-21.8, (c).
Petition by pregnant minor, §90-21.7, (b).
Assistance in preparing and filing by court, §90-21.8, (b).
Precedence of proceedings over pending matters, §90-21.8, (d).
Summons or notice not served upon parent, guardian, etc., upon request of petitioner, §90-21.8, (g).
Written findings of fact and conclusions of law, §90-21.8, (f).
Physicians and surgeons.
Producing or attempting to produce abortion contrary to law.
Grounds for denial, annulment, suspension or revocation of license, §90-14, (a).
Refusal of physician to perform or participate in medical procedures, §14-45.1, (e).
Remains of terminated pregnancies.
Manner of disposition, §130A-131.10.

ABORTION —Cont'd
Reports.
Statistical summary reports concerning medical and demographic characteristics of abortions, §14-45.1, (c).

ABORTION CLINICS.
Health and human services department.
Certification of facilities.
Department certification fee authorized, §131E-269.
Obstruction of health care facility, §14-277.4.
Access to or egress from, §14-277.4, (a).
Exemptions, §14-277.4, (h).
Felony offense.
Habitual offenders, §14-277.4, (c).
Free speech not abridged, §14-277.4, (e).
"Health care facility" defined, §14-277.4, (f).
"Health care services" defined, §14-277.4, (g).
Injunctive relief, §14-277.4, (d).
Misdemeanor offense, §14-277.4, (c).
Personal injury, §14-277.4, (b).
Picketing right not abridged, §14-277.4, (e).
Weapons at demonstrations at private health care facilities, §14-277.2.

ABSCONDING DEBTORS.
Arrest, §1-355.
Attachment.
Grounds for attachment, §1-440.3.

ABSCONDING JUVENILES.
Delinquent and undisciplined juveniles.
Taking juvenile into temporary custody without court order, §7B-1900.
Transporting to nearest secure custody facility, §7B-1901, (c).
Interstate compact on juveniles, §§7B-2800 to 7B-2827.
See INTERSTATE COMPACT ON JUVENILES.

ABSENCE FROM RESIDENCE.
Estates of missing persons, §§28C-1 to 28C-22.
See MISSING PERSONS.
Presumption of death.
Not presumed by mere absence, §28C-1, (a).

ABSENCE FROM SCHOOL.
Compulsory attendance law, §§115C-378 to 115C-383.
See COMPULSORY SCHOOL ATTENDANCE.

ABSENTEE BALLOTS, §§163-226 to 163-239.
Alternative procedures for requesting application and voting, §163-227.2, (a).
Application procedure, §163-227.2, (b).
Disapproval of application, §163-227.2, (d).
Furnishing voter with ballot, instruction sheets, entry of name in register, §163-227.2, (c).
Office hours for receipt of applications.
Counties running modified full-time office, §163-227.2, (f).
One or more sites in counties for applying for and casting ballots, §163-227.2, (g).
Plan of implementation, adoption, §163-227.2, (g).
Safe keeping of application, §163-227.2, (d).
Voting procedure, §163-227.2, (e).
Applications for.
Absence for sickness or physical disability, §163-230.1, (a1).
Alternate procedures, §163-227.2.
Completed applications and ballots.
Container-return envelope, §163-230.1, (b).
Invalid written requests, §163-230.2, (b).

ABSENTEE BALLOTS —Cont'd
Applications for —Cont'd
Method of requesting ballots, §163-230.2.
Military absentee voting.
Certified list of approved applications, §163-251, (a) to (c).
Consideration and approval, §163-249.
Methods of applying, §163-247.
Register of military absentee ballot applications and ballots issued, §163-248, (a).
Primary elections.
Second primary, §163-227.1.
Register of applications, §163-228.
Retention, §163-233.
Simultaneous issuance of ballots with application, §163-230.1, (a).
Valid written requests, §163-230.2, (a).
Candidate witnessing absentee ballots of nonrelative.
Misdemeanor, §163-237, (b1).
Certified list of executed absentee ballots, §163-232.
Challenge of voters.
Burden of proof, §163-89, (c).
Hearing, §163-89, (e).
Separate challenge to each ballot, §163-89, (c).
Signing of challenge, §163-89, (c).
Time for challenge, §163-89, (a).
To whom challenge addressed, §163-89, (d).
Who may challenge, §163-89, (b).
Container-return envelopes.
Application on, §163-229, (b).
Delivery to applicant, §163-230.1, (a2).
Military absentee voting, §163-248, (c).
County boards of elections.
Certified list of executed absentee ballots.
Preparation, §163-232.
Counting of absentee ballots by, §163-234.
Duties, §163-236.
Military absentee voting.
Absentee voting at office of board of elections, §163-255.
Consideration and approval of applications, §163-249.
Issuance of absentee ballots, §163-249.
Required meeting of county board, §163-230.1, (c1).
Retention of applications, §163-233.
Violations by.
Penalties, §163-236.
Curtained or private area for marking ballot.
One stop voting sites, §163-227.2, (i).
Date by which absentee ballots must be available for voting, §163-227.3, (a).
Definition of "near relative," §163-230.1, (f).
Delaying ballots pending appeal, §163-227.3, (a).
Election defined, §163-226, (c).
Facsimile, electronic mail or scanned transmission of election materials.
Military absentee voting, §163-257.
False statements.
Misdemeanors, §163-237, (a), (b).
Felonies, §163-226.3, (a).
Fire district elections.
Ballots not permitted, §163-226, (b).
Forgery, §163-237, (c).
Fraud, §163-237, (c).
In-person voting for person previously registered by mail, §163-166.12, (a).
Instruction sheets, §163-229, (c).

ABSENTEE BALLOTS —Cont'd
Issuance.
Delivery of absentee ballots and container-return envelope to applicant, §163-230.1, (a2).
Simultaneous issuance with application, §163-230.1, (a).
List.
Executed absentee ballots, §163-232.
Military absentee voting, §§163-245 to 163-257.
Applicability of provisions, §163-245, (b).
Effect on voting provisions generally, §163-239.
Inapplicable to persons after change of status, §163-253.
Applications for absentee ballots.
Certified list of approved applications, §163-251, (a) to (c).
Consideration and approval, §163-249.
Methods of applying, §163-247.
Register of military absentee ballot applications and ballots issued, §163-248, (a).
Authorized, §163-245, (a).
Challenges.
Hearing by county board of elections, §163-251, (d).
Change of status.
Provisions inapplicable after, §163-253.
Civilians.
Applicability of provisions to certain civilians, §163-245, (b).
Container-return envelopes, §163-248, (c).
Counting ballots, §163-251, (d).
County boards of elections.
Absentee voting at office of board of elections, §163-255.
Consideration and approval of applications, §163-249.
Issuance of absentee ballots, §163-249.
Day of primary or election.
Registration and voting on, §163-254.
Disqualified because of change in residence or conviction, §163-253.
Early turn-in of ballot, §163-245, (c).
Effect of provisions, §163-239.
Facsimile, electronic mail or scanned transmission of election materials, §163-257.
General absentee voting provisions.
Applicability, §163-246.
Instruction sheets, §163-248, (d).
Issuance of absentee ballots, §163-249.
List of applicants to whom ballots have been issued.
Distribution, §163-251, (b).
List constitutes registration, §163-251, (c).
Preparation, §163-251, (a).
Oaths or affirmations accompanying ballot, §163-245, (e).
Office of board of elections.
Absentee voting at, §163-255.
Peace Corps.
Applicability to members, §163-245, (b).
Primary or election day.
Registration and voting on, §163-254.
Proof of military status.
Presenting if requested, §163-253.
Register of military absentee ballot applications and ballots issued, §163-248, (a).
Regular official ballots, §163-248, (b).
Rejection of ballot.
Early turn-in, rejection prohibited, §163-245, (c).
Notice to voter, §163-245, (d).

ABSENTEE BALLOTS —Cont'd
Military absentee voting —Cont'd
State board of elections.
Duties generally, §163-256, (b).
Rules and regulations, §§163-246, 163-256.
Uniformed services defined, §163-246.
Veterans.
Applicability to certain disabled war veterans, §163-245, (b).
Voting procedure, §163-250, (a).
Transmitting executed absentee ballots to chairman of county board of elections, §163-250, (b).
Misdemeanors.
County boards of elections.
Violations by, §163-236.
Prohibited acts, §163-237.
Municipal elections, §§163-226.2, 163-302.
One stop voting.
Challenge entered against voter, §163-227.2, (h).
Procedure, §163-227.2.
Peace Corps.
Military absentee voting, applicability, §163-245, (b).
Penalties.
County boards of elections.
Violations by, §163-236.
General penalty, §163-237, (d).
Prohibited acts, §§163-226.3, (a), 163-237.
Persons previously registered by mail who have not voted for federal office.
Exemptions, §163-166.12, (d).
Identification proof submitted by voter.
County board to note, §163-166.12, (b1).
In-person voting, §163-166.12, (a).
Mail-in absentee voting, §163-166.12, (b).
Provisional voting, §163-166.12, (c).
Primary elections, §163-226.1.
Reduction of time by which absentee ballots required to be printed and distributed, §163-22, (k).
Second primary.
Applications for absentee ballots, §163-227.1.
Providing of ballots, §163-227.3, (b).
Prohibited acts, §§163-226.3, (a), 163-237.
Investigation and prosecution by boards of elections, §163-226.3, (b).
Qualifications of voters.
Primary elections, §163-226.1.
Register of absentee ballot applications and ballots issued, §163-228.
Regular official ballots, §163-229, (a).
Return of ballots, §163-230.1, (c).
Sickness or disability to last calendar year.
Application to constitute request for ballot in all primaries and elections during year, §163-226, (a2).
State board of elections.
Duties generally, §163-256, (b).
Method of requesting ballots.
Rules and regulations, §163-230.2, (c).
Military absentee voting.
Rules and regulations, §§163-246, 163-256.
Providing absentee ballots, §163-227.3.
Report of violations to district attorneys, §163-238.
Rules and regulations, §163-230.1, (e).
Single office responsible for procedures, §163-256, (b).
Violations of provisions.
Investigation and prosecution, §163-226.3, (b).

ABSENTEE BALLOTS —Cont'd
Violations of provisions.
Investigations by boards of elections, §163-226.3, (b).
Prohibited acts generally, §§163-226.3, (a), 163-237.
Reports of violations to district attorneys, §163-238.
Voting procedures, §§163-227.2, (e), 163-231, (a).
Transmitting executed ballots to chairman of county boards of elections, §163-231, (b).
Voting system with retrievable ballots.
One stop voting procedure, §163-227.2, (e1).
Who may vote absentee, §163-226, (a).
Withdrawal of absentee ballots not allowed, §163-233.1.

ABSENTEE INSURANCE FUND.
Missing persons, §28C-19.

ABSENTEES.
Estates of missing persons, §§28C-1 to 28C-22.
See MISSING PERSONS.
Habeas corpus.
Party ill or infirm.
Cause determined in his absence, §17-37.
Presumption of death, §28C-1.
Service of process.
Personal jurisdiction.
Alternative methods of service on party that cannot be served or found within state, §1A-1, Rule 4, (j).

ABSENTEES IN MILITARY SERVICE, §§28B-1 to 28B-10.
Bonds, surety.
Receivers, §28B-5, (a).
Complaint.
Hearing, §28B-3, (b).
Notice of hearing, §28B-3, (a).
Death of absentee.
Termination of receivership, §28B-8, (b).
Defined, §28B-1.
Evidence.
Transfer of property valued at less than $5,000.
Court order authorizing transfer, §28B-9, (c).
Transfer of property valued at more than $5,000.
Court order authorizing transfer, §28B-10.
Final accounting upon termination of receivership, §28B-8, (c).
Guardian ad litem.
Appointment by court, §28B-3, (c).
Hearings.
Transfer of property valued at more than $5,000, §28B-10, (c).
Husband and wife.
Transfer of property valued at less than $5,000.
Application to superior court, §28B-9, (a).
Transfer of property valued at more than $5,000, §28B-10.
Inventories.
Final inventory upon termination of receivership, §28B-8, (c).
Receiver to file, §28B-5, (b).
Jurisdiction.
Action for appointment of receiver, §28B-2.
Limitation of actions.
Suits against receivers after released from duties, §28B-8, (d).
Maintenance and support of dependents.
Powers of receiver, §28B-6.

ABSENTEES IN MILITARY SERVICE —Cont'd
Receivers.
Action for appointment, §28B-2, (a).
Actions against receiver.
Limitation of action, §28B-8, (d).
Appointment.
Action for appointment, §28B-2, (a).
Order of appointment, §28B-4, (a).
Spouses or next of kin, §28B-4, (b).
Bonds, surety, §28B-5, (a).
Complaints.
Contents, §28B-2, (b).
Inventory.
Filing required, §28B-5, (b).
Maintenance and support of dependents, §28B-6.
Misconduct.
Report of clerk, §28B-5, (b).
Modification.
Addition or subtraction from statutory powers of receiver, §28B-6, (b).
Order of appointment, §28B-4.
Powers and duties, §28B-6, (a).
Release from duties.
Termination of receivership, §28B-8, (d).
Removal, §28B-7, (b).
Resignation, §28B-7, (a).
Termination.
Filing of final inventory, §28B-8, (c).
Order of court, §28B-8, (a).
Transfer of property.
Order of court, §28B-9, (b).
Evidence of validity of proceedings, §28B-9, (c).
Property valued at less than $5,000.
Application.
Form, §28B-9, (a).
Property valued at more than $5,000, §28B-10.

ABSENT PARENTS.
Child support enforcement program generally, §§110-128 to 110-142.2.
See CHILD SUPPORT.

ABSENT WITNESSES.
Depositions, use in court proceedings, §1A-1, Rule 32, (a).

ABSOLUTE DIVORCE.
Acts barring rights of spouse, §31A-1, (a).
Cost of final action filed in district court, §7A-305, (a2).
Divorce generally.
See DIVORCE.
Effect of answer of summons by defendant, §50-9.
Effects of absolute divorce, §50-11.
Equitable distribution judgment not entered prior to decree, §50-21, (a).
Former section 52-6, effect of decree or certificate not complying with, §52-9.
Incurable insanity, §50-5.1.
Judgments entered prior to January 1, 1981 validated, §50-11.3.
Maiden or premarriage surname.
Resumption by woman or man, §50-12.
Separation for one year, §50-6.
Summary judgment.
Applicability of provisions, §50-10, (d).

ABSTRACTS.
Evidence.
Certified copies of abstracts of grants, §§8-6, 8-7.
Recording of certified copies, §8-8.
Validation, §8-9.

ABSTRACTS —Cont'd
Property taxes, §§105-309 to 105-311.

ABUSED, NEGLECTED OR DEPENDENT JUVENILES, §§7B-101 to 7B-1414.
See CHILD ABUSE, NEGLECT OR DEPENDENCY.

ABUSED, NEGLECTED OR EXPLOITED DISABLED ADULTS, §§108A-99 to 108A-111.
Abuse.
Criminal offense defined, §14-32.3, (a).
Defined, §108A-101, (a).
Reports.
Director to notify district attorney, §108A-109.
Appeals.
Motion in the cause.
Review of orders issued pursuant to provisions, §108A-107.
Caretaker.
Defined, §§14-32.3, (d), 108A-101, (b).
Protective services.
Interference with provision of protective services.
Injunction, §108A-104, (b).
Citation of act.
Short title, §108A-99.
Consent.
Lack of capacity to consent.
Defined, §108A-101, (l).
Protective services.
Provision to disabled adults who lack capacity to consent, §108A-105.
Provision of protective services to disabled adults who lack capacity to consent, §108A-105.
Protective services.
Provision with consent of person, §108A-104, (a).
Withdrawal of consent, §108A-104, (c).
County directors of social services.
Contracts for provision of medical evaluations, §108A-103, (c).
Cooperation by certain agencies with, §108A-103, (b).
Definition of "director," §108A-101, (c).
Director to notify district attorney of abuse, §108A-109.
Duties on receiving reports, §§108A-14, 108A-103, (a), (d).
Definitions, §108A-101.
Disabled adults.
Defined, §§14-32.3, (d), 108A-101, (d), (e).
Protective services.
Provision to disabled adults who lack capacity to consent, §108A-105.
District courts.
Defined, §108A-101, (f).
Domestic setting.
Defined, §14-32.3, (d).
Elder adult.
Defined, §14-32.3, (d).
Emergencies.
Defined, §108A-101, (g).
Emergency services.
Defined, §108A-101, (h).
Entry of premises without disabled adult's consent, §108A-106, (e).
Financial records of disabled adult.
Order for inspection, §108A-106, (f).
Order for, §108A-106, (a), (b).

ABUSED, NEGLECTED OR EXPLOITED DISABLED ADULTS —Cont'd
Emergency services —Cont'd
Petition for, §108A-106, (c).
Immunity of petitioner, §108A-106, (g).
Notice of filing, §108A-106, (d).
Essential services.
Defined, §108A-101, (i).
Payment for, §108A-108.
Exploitation.
Criminal offense defined, §14-32.3, (c).
Defined, §108A-101, (j).
Finance.
Funding of protective services, §108A-110.
Immunity from civil or criminal liability, §108A-102, (c).
Indigent persons.
Definition of "indigent," §108A-101, (k).
Legislative intent, §108A-100.
Motion in the cause.
Review of orders issued pursuant to provisions, §108A-107.
Neglect.
Criminal offense defined, §14-32.3, (b).
Defined, §108A-101, (m).
Payment for essential services, §108A-108.
Protective services.
Caretaker.
Interference with provision of protective services.
Injunction, §108A-104, (b).
Consent.
Lack of capacity to consent.
Provision of protective services to disabled adults to lack capacity to consent, §108A-105.
Provision with consent of person, §108A-104, (a).
Withdrawal of consent, §108A-104, (c).
Defined, §108A-101, (n).
Funding, §108A-110.
Lack of capacity to consent.
Effect of determination of lack of capacity to consent, §108A-105, (d).
Guardian ad litem, §108A-105, (b).
Notice of hearing, §108A-105, (b).
Order authorizing, §108A-105, (c).
Petition, §108A-105, (a).
Purpose of act, §108A-100.
Reports.
Content of report, §108A-102, (b).
Director to notify district attorney of abuse, §108A-109.
Duty to report, §108A-102, (a).
Immunity, §108A-102, (c).
Short title of act, §108A-99.
Standards.
Adoption, §108A-111.

ABUSE OF PATIENTS.
Unlawful to physically abuse patient, §14-32.2, (a).
Criminal process, issuance, request of attorney general, §14-32.2, (g).
Defenses, §14-32.2, (f).
Definitions, §14-32.2, (c) to (e1).
Provisions not to supersede other offenses, §14-32.2, (h).
Punishment, §14-32.2, (b).

ACADEMIC CREDIT OR DEGREE.
Obtaining by fraudulent means, §14-118.2.

ACCELERATION.
Commercial code.
Option to accelerate at will, §25-1-208.
High cost home loans, §24-1.1E, (b).
Leases, UCC.
Consumer leases.
Option to accelerate at will, §25-2A-109, (2).

ACCEPTANCE OF GOODS.
Leases, UCC, §25-2A-515.
Acceptance of part of unit acceptance of entire unit, §25-2A-515, (2).
Accessions.
Lessor's and lessee's rights when goods become accessions, §25-2A-310.
Burden of establishing default after acceptance, §25-2A-516.
Damages.
Lessors' damages for noncompliance, §25-2A-528.
Effect, §25-2A-516.
Firm offers, §25-2A-205.
Nonconforming goods or delivery of goods, §25-2A-509.
Notice of default, §25-2A-516.
Offer and acceptance generally, §25-2A-206.
Revocation of acceptance, §25-2A-517.
Damages, §25-2A-519.
Justifiable revocation, §25-2A-517.
Lessors' rights and remedies, §25-2A-508.
Wrongful revocation, §25-2A-523.
Sales, UCC.
Breach after acceptance.
Burden of establishing, §25-2-607, (4).
Buyer's damages, §25-2-714.
Documents deliverable on acceptance, §25-2-514.
Effect of acceptance, §25-2-607.
Generally, §25-2-606.
Improper delivery.
Buyer's rights, §25-2-601.
Installment contracts, §25-2-612.
Nonacceptance.
Seller's damages, §25-2-708.
Revocation in whole or in part, §25-2-608.

ACCEPTANCE OF PAYMENT ORDER.
Funds transfers, UCC, §25-4A-209.

ACCEPTANCE OF SERVICE.
Personal jurisdiction by, §1A-1, Rule 4, (j5).

ACCESSIONS.
Leases, UCC.
Defined, §§25-2A-103, (2), 25-2A-310.
Secured transactions.
Perfection and priority of security interests, §25-9-335.

ACCESSORIES.
Generally.
See ACCOMPLICES AND ACCESSORIES.

ACCESSORY AFTER THE FACT, §14-7.

ACCESSORY BEFORE THE FACT, §14-5.2.

ACCESS TO CIVIL JUSTICE ACT.
General provisions, §§7A-474.1 to 7A-474.5.
See GEOGRAPHICALLY BASED FIELD PROGRAMS.

ACCESS TO JUDICIAL PROCEEDINGS AND RECORDS, §1-72.1.

ACCIDENT AND HEALTH INSURANCE.
Actions for negligent decisions.
Health care liability, §§90-21.50 to 90-21.56.
See HEALTH CARE LIABILITY.

ACCIDENT AND HEALTH INSURANCE —Cont'd
Additional coverage mandates prohibited, §58-50-63, (a).
Employer not prohibited from expanding coverage, §58-50-63, (b).
Insurer and health benefit plan defined, §58-50-63, (c).
Adopted children.
Definitions, §58-51-125, (a).
Policies to cover, §§58-51-30, (a) to (f), 58-51-125, (a) to (c).
Preexisting conditions, §58-51-125, (c).
Advance practice registered nurse.
Payment or reimbursement, §58-50-30, (d).
Right to choose services, §58-50-30, (a1) to (a3), (g), (h).
Applicability of acts of general assembly to health benefit plans.
Health benefit plan defined, §58-3-167, (a).
Law enacted by general assembly, definition applicable, §58-3-167, (b).
Insurer defined, §58-3-167, (a).
Renewal of health benefit plan.
Date of renewal when law enacted by general assembly applies to health benefit plans, §58-3-167, (c).
Authorized, §58-7-15.
Blanket insurance.
Benefits.
To whom payable, §58-51-75, (b).
Defined, §58-51-75, (a).
Legal liability of policyholders not affected, §58-51-75, (c).
Policies, §58-51-75, (a).
Approval of forms, §58-51-85.
Breast cancer.
Mammograms.
Coverage, §58-51-57.
Cancer treatment.
Cervical cancer screening.
Coverage, §58-51-57.
Colorectal cancer examinations, laboratory tests and screening.
Coverage required of all health benefit plans, §58-3-179, (a).
Limitations applicable to services, §58-3-179, (b).
Small employer group health plans, §58-50-155, (a).
Coverage of certain prescribed drugs.
Applicability of provisions, §58-51-59, (c).
Generally, §58-51-59, (a), (b).
Mammograms.
Coverage, §58-51-57.
Ovarian cancer.
Surveillance tests for women at risk, coverage, §§58-3-270, 58-50-155, (a).
Cervical cancer.
Screening for early detection.
Coverage requirements, §58-51-57, (a), (e).
Defined, §58-51-57, (a1).
Chemical dependency treatment.
Coverage for, §58-51-50, (a) to (e).
Childbirth.
Maternity coverage, §58-3-170.
Child support, medical support orders and agreements, §50-13.11.
Chiropractors.
Right to choose services, §58-50-30, (a1) to (a3), (g), (h).

ACCIDENT AND HEALTH INSURANCE —Cont'd
Choice of service providers, §58-50-30, (a1) to (a3).
Pediatrician for minors, §58-3-240.
Provider directories, §58-3-245.
Specialist selected as primary care provider, §58-3-235.
Uniform provider credentialing, §58-3-230.
Claims.
Health care providers claims not timely processed due to year 2000 date change.
Interim payments by insurer to providers, §58-2-235.
Definitions, §58-2-235, (c).
Payment in full, when considered, §58-2-235, (c).
Recovery of excess payment, §58-2-235, (c).
Report by insurer, §58-2-235, (a).
Notice.
Claim denial, §58-3-172, (a).
Health benefit plans defined, §58-3-172, (b).
Required policy provisions, §58-51-15, (a).
Payment.
Prompt claim payments under health benefit plans, §58-3-225.
Required policy provisions, §58-51-15, (a).
Prompt payments under health benefit plans, §58-3-225.
Uniform claim forms, §58-3-171, (a).
Health benefit plans defined, §58-3-171, (c).
Workers' compensation insurance policies as health benefit plans, §58-3-171, (b).
Claims submission and reimbursement policies of insurers.
Disclosure to contracted providers, §58-3-227, (d).
Availability of information.
Notifying providers, §58-3-227, (e).
Changes to information.
Advance notification, §58-3-227, (f).
Definitions, §58-3-227, (a).
Inapplicability of provisions, §58-3-227, (i).
Purpose of provisions, §58-3-227, (b).
Reference information.
Instructions provided, §58-3-227, (g).
Clinical social workers.
Defined, §58-50-30, (c).
Right to choose services, §58-50-30, (a1) to (a3), (g), (h).
Clinical trials, coverage, §58-3-255, (b).
Costs not required to be covered, §58-3-255, (d).
Covered clinical trials defined, §58-3-255, (a).
Definitions, §58-3-255, (a).
Medical necessary costs covered, §58-3-255, (c).
Closed formularies or restricted access to prescription drugs, §58-3-221.
Colorectal cancer examinations, laboratory tests and screening.
Coverage required of every health benefit plan, §58-3-179, (a).
Limitations applicable to services, §58-3-179, (b).
Small employer group health plans, §58-50-155, (a).
Commissioner.
Forms.
Approval, §§58-51-1, 58-51-85, 58-51-95, (a) to (f).
Hearings.
Withdrawal of approval of forms, §58-51-95, (e).
Premiums.
Approval of rates, §58-51-95, (f).
Increased rates, §58-51-95, (f).

ACCIDENT AND HEALTH INSURANCE —Cont'd
Confidentiality of consumer and customer information.
Generally, §§58-39-1 to 58-39-165.
See INSURANCE CONSUMER AND CUSTOMER INFORMATION PRIVACY.
Continuing care retirement community residents, §58-3-200, (f).
Contraceptive drugs or devices and outpatient contraceptive services.
Coverage by insurer providing health benefit plan, §58-3-178, (a), (b).
Definitions, §58-3-178, (c).
Prohibited acts, §58-3-178, (d).
Religious employer requesting exclusion of coverage, §58-3-178, (e).
Conversion privileges.
Generally. See within this heading, "Group insurance."
Credentialing providers.
Health benefit plan and insurer defined, §58-3-230, (c).
Process requirements, §58-3-230, (a).
Time limit on processing applications, §58-3-230, (a).
Uniform provider credentialing application form.
Commissioner to adopt by rule, §58-3-230, (b).
Credit insurance.
Defined, §58-51-100.
Generally, §§58-57-1 to 58-57-115.
See CREDIT INSURANCE.
Definitions.
Blanket accident and health insurance, §58-51-75, (a).
Credit accident and health insurance, §58-51-100.
Franchise accident and health insurance, §58-51-90.
Group accident and health insurance, §58-51-80, (a).
Hospitalization insurance, §58-51-105.
Industrial sick benefit insurance, §58-51-65.
Joint action to insure elderly, §58-52-1.
Pharmacy of choice, §58-51-37, (b).
Prompt claim payments under health benefit plans, §58-3-225, (a).
Denial of claim, notice, §58-3-172.
Dental procedures performed in hospital or ambulatory surgical facility.
Children under age nine, persons with serious mental and physical condition and persons with significant behavior problems.
Definitions, §58-3-122, (b).
Health benefit plans to provide coverage for payment of anesthesia and facility charges, §58-3-122, (a).
Dentists.
Right to choose services, §58-50-30, (a1) to (a3), (g), (h).
Determinations as to coverage, §58-3-200, (c).
Diabetes.
Coverage for certain treatment, §58-51-61, (a).
Definition of "physician," §58-51-61, (b).
Directories of providers, §58-3-245.
Direct payment to government agencies, §58-3-175.
Disability income insurance, policy standards, §58-51-130.
Applicability of provisions, §58-51-130, (b).
Definitions, §58-51-130, (a).
Disclosure standards, §58-51-130, (c).

ACCIDENT AND HEALTH INSURANCE —Cont'd
Disability income insurance, policy standards —Cont'd
Exceptions, §58-51-130, (e).
Other income sources, §58-51-130, (h).
Other provisions applicable, §58-51-130, (g).
Preexisting conditions, when denial of claim prohibited, §58-51-130, (d).
Required provisions, §58-51-130, (f).
Disclosure requirements for health benefit plans, §58-3-191, (b).
Disclosures to contracted providers.
Fee schedules, claim and reimbursement policies of insurers, §58-3-227, (c).
Availability of information.
Notifying providers, §58-3-227, (e).
Changes to information.
Advance notification, §58-3-227, (f).
Definitions, §58-3-227, (a).
During contract negotiations, §58-3-227, (h).
Inapplicability of provisions, §58-3-227, (i).
Purpose of provisions, §58-3-227, (b).
Reference information.
Instructions provided, §58-3-227, (g).
Discrimination.
Children of insured, §58-51-120, (a).
Mentally ill and chemically dependent, §58-51-55.
Drive-thru deliveries, §58-3-169.
Electronic or on-line system for up-to-date network information.
Plan to provide, §58-3-245, (a).
Emergency care.
Coverage required, §58-3-190.
Employer distinguishing between employees based on use or nonuse of lawful products, §95-28.2, (d).
Evidence of coverage.
Notice, expenses may exceed covered amount, §58-3-250, (b).
Payment obligations, explanation by insurer, §58-3-250, (a).
Exemptions from provisions, §58-50-65.
External review, §§58-50-75 to 58-50-95.
Applicability of part, §58-50-75, (b).
Approval of independent review organization.
Accreditation program, §58-50-85, (c).
Application for approving, §58-50-85, (a), (b).
Commission to approve, §58-50-85, (a).
Duration of approval, §58-50-85, (d).
Termination, §58-50-85, (e).
Assigned organization.
Approval of independent review organization, §58-50-85.
Expedited review, request.
Decision of organization, time for, §58-50-82, (e).
Notice of decision or written conformation, §58-50-82, (f).
Review of documents, considerations in reaching decision, §58-50-82, (c), (d).
Hold harmless provision, §58-50-89.
Minimum qualifications for independent organization, §58-50-87.
Notice of decision, time period, included in, §58-50-90, (j), (k).
Records review organization, §58-50-90, (a), (d), (e).
Report by review organization, §58-50-90, (b), (c).

ACCIDENT AND HEALTH INSURANCE —Cont'd
External review —Cont'd
Assigned organization —Cont'd
Review of information and documents, considerations in reaching decision, §58-50-90, (i).
Selection of review organization, §58-50-94.
Binding nature of decision.
Covered person, binding on, §58-50-84, (b).
Insurer, binding on, §58-50-84, (a).
Clinical peer reviewers assigned by organization.
Hold harmless provision, §58-50-89.
Minimum qualifications, §58-50-87, (b).
Conflicts of interest.
Independent review organization, §58-50-87, (d), (e).
Definitions, §58-50-75, (c).
Description of procedures.
Insurer to provide, §58-50-93, (a).
Release of medical records.
Statement informing covered person, §58-50-93, (c).
Statement of right to file request, §58-50-93, (b).
Exhaustion of internal appeal and grievance procedure.
Noncertification involving retrospective review determination, §58-50-79, (c).
Request for external review may be made before exhaustion, §58-50-79, (d).
Required, §58-50-79, (a).
When person considered to exhaust internal procedure, §58-50-79, (b).
Expedited review, request, §58-50-77, (c).
Assigned organization.
Decision of organization, time for, §58-50-82, (e).
Notice of decision or written conformation, §58-50-82, (f).
Review of documents, considerations in reaching decision, §58-50-82, (c), (d).
Commission's duties after reviewing request, time period, §58-50-82, (b).
Decisions subject to, §58-50-82, (a).
Retrospective noncertification, inapplicability, §58-50-82, (g).
Reversal of noncertification appeal or grievance review, §58-50-82, (f).
Fees charged by review organization.
Reimbursement by insurer, §58-50-92.
Funding, §58-50-92.
Hold harmless provision.
Commissioner, medical professionals, and review organizations, §58-50-89.
Immunity of commissioner, medical professionals, and review organizations, §58-50-89.
Independent review organization.
Approval, §58-50-85.
Hold harmless provision, §58-50-89.
Minimum qualifications for independent organization, §58-50-87.
Records review organization, §58-50-90, (a), (d), (e).
Report by review organization, §58-50-90, (b), (c).
Selection, §58-50-94.
Medical professionals.
Hold harmless provision, §58-50-89.
Minimum qualifications for independent organization, §58-50-87, (a).
Clinical peer reviewers assigned by organization, §58-50-87, (b).

ACCIDENT AND HEALTH INSURANCE —Cont'd
External review —Cont'd
Minimum qualifications for independent organization —Cont'd
Conflicts of interest, §58-50-87, (d), (e).
Health benefit plan owning or controlling, prohibition, §58-50-87, (c).
Notice of right, §58-50-77, (a).
Appeal decision, §58-50-77, (c).
Copy of procedure included, §58-50-77, (e).
Final second level grievance review, §58-50-77, (d).
Noncertified decision, §58-50-77, (b).
Purposes of part, §58-50-75, (a).
Records of requests, §58-50-90, (a), (d), (e).
Reimbursement by insurer.
Fees charged by review organization, §58-50-92.
Release of medical records.
Disclosure by insurer, §58-50-93, (c).
Report by commissioner, §58-50-95.
Report by review organization, §58-50-90, (b), (c).
Request for review.
Assigned review committee.
Information to consider, §58-50-80, (i).
Commission's duties on receiving request, time period, §58-50-80, (b).
Making before exhaustion of internal procedures, §58-50-79, (d).
Not complete request, additional information to be furnished, §58-50-80, (c) to (f).
Notice that request not accepted, §58-50-80, (d).
Reconsideration.
Additional information supplied commission, §58-50-80, (g), (h).
Records of requests, §58-50-90, (a), (d), (e).
Statement of right to file request.
Included in insurer's disclosure of procedures, §58-50-93, (b).
Subsequent request prohibited, §58-50-84, (c).
Time for filing after receipt of notice, §58-50-80, (a).
Reversal of noncertification appeal or grievance review.
Assigned review committee.
Notice of decision, §58-50-80, (j), (k).
Expedited review, request, §58-50-82, (f).
Insurer's duty on receipt of notice of organization decision, §58-50-80, (l).
Notice, presumption when received, §58-50-80, (m).
Selection of independent review organization.
Modifying or withdrawing proposals, §58-50-94, (c).
Request for proposals by commissioner, §58-50-94, (a).
Review of proposals after public opening, selection, §58-50-94, (b).
Subsequent request for review.
Covered person may not file, §58-50-84, (c).
Fee based pastoral counselor.
Defined, §58-50-30, (c1).
Right to choose services, §58-50-30, (a1) to (a3), (g), (h).
Fee schedules of insurers.
Disclosure to contracted providers, §58-3-227, (c).
Availability of information.
Notifying providers, §58-3-227, (e).
Changes to information.
Advance notification, §58-3-227, (f).
Definitions, §58-3-227, (a).

ACCIDENT AND HEALTH INSURANCE —Cont'd
Fee schedules of insurers —Cont'd
Disclosure to contracted providers —Cont'd
During contract negotiations, §58-3-227, (h).
Inapplicability of provisions, §58-3-227, (i).
Purpose of provisions, §58-3-227, (b).
Reference information.
Instructions provided, §58-3-227, (g).
Financial incentives to delay, deny or reduce coverage.
Plan prohibited from offering provider, §58-3-265.
Forms.
Approval by commissioner, §58-51-95, (a) to (f).
Group or blanket accident and health insurance, §58-51-85.
Policies, §58-51-5, (a).
Approval of forms by commissioner, §58-51-1.
Other states, §58-51-5, (b).
Franchise accident and health insurance.
Defined, §58-51-90.
Fraternal benefit societies.
Exemptions from provisions, §58-50-65, (c).
Genetic information in health insurance.
Definitions, §58-3-215, (a).
Measurements and tests not considered genetic tests, §58-3-215, (b).
Prohibited acts by insurers, §58-3-215, (c).
Government agencies, direct payments to.
Generally, §58-3-175, (b).
Health benefit plan defined, §58-3-175, (a).
Inapplicability of provisions, §58-3-175, (c).
When direct payment not required, §58-3-175, (d).
Grace period, §58-51-15, (a).
Grievance procedures for insurers.
Availability of process, §58-50-62, (b).
Discrimination based on actions taken by provider.
Prohibited, §58-50-62, (j).
External review of decision, §§58-50-75 to 58-50-95.
First-level grievance review, §58-50-62, (e).
Generally, §58-50-62, (c).
Informal consideration of grievances, §58-50-62, (b1).
Propose of provisions, §58-50-62, (a).
Records maintenance, §58-50-62, (d).
Second-level grievance review, §58-50-62, (f) to (i).
Violations of provisions.
Effect on insurer, §58-50-62, (k).
Group insurance.
Alternative plans, insurer's option to offer, §58-53-105.
Basic coverage plans, §58-53-105.
Eligible persons, §58-53-110, (c).
Notice, §58-53-110, (e).
Provision of group coverage in lieu of issuance of individual policy, §58-53-110, (d).
Retirement plan offering continuation of coverage.
Applicability of conversion rights, §58-53-110, (a).
Benefits.
To whom payable, §58-51-80, (e), (f).
Children of insured, §58-51-120, (d).
Chemical dependency treatment.
Contracts to cover, §58-51-50, (b).
Coverage not required, §58-51-55, (c).
Definition of "chemical dependency," §58-51-55, (a).
Discrimination prohibited, §58-51-55, (b), (c).

ACCIDENT AND HEALTH INSURANCE —Cont'd
Group insurance —Cont'd
Continuation privileges.
Benefits not included, §58-53-20.
Dates for termination of continuation privileges, §58-53-35, (a).
Exceptions, §58-53-35, (b).
Conversion privileges.
Alternative plans, §58-53-100.
Applicability of provisions, §58-53-115.
Basic coverage plans, §58-53-90, (a).
Alternative plans, §58-53-100.
Maximum amounts, §58-53-90, (b).
Benefits.
Excess benefits, §58-53-80.
Coverage.
Alternative plans, §58-53-100.
Basic coverage plans, §58-53-90, (a).
Individual policy, §58-53-65.
Major medical plans, §58-53-95.
Preexisting conditions covered under group policy, §58-53-85.
Definitions, §58-53-1.
Delivery outside state, §58-53-110, (f).
Excess benefits, §58-53-80.
Exclusions from conversion privilege, §58-53-70.
Extent of coverage, §58-53-65.
Grounds for excluding persons from coverage, §58-53-70.
Grounds for not converting policy, §58-53-50.
Information requested from policyholders, §58-53-75.
Limitation on exercising privilege to convert, §58-53-55.
Major medical plans, §58-53-95.
Alternative plans, §58-53-100.
Maximum amounts of basic coverage plans, §58-53-90, (b).
Notice of by insurance fiduciary, §58-50-40, (g).
Option of insurer to offer alternative plans in addition to those required by part, §58-53-105.
Permissible provisions in individual policy.
Information provisions, §58-53-75.
Premium for individual policy.
Authorized increase in premiums, §58-53-60, (b).
Determination, §58-53-60, (a).
Rates and adjustments to be filed with commissioner of insurance, §58-53-60, (c).
Rate existing conditions covered by group policy to be covered by converted policy, §58-53-85.
Restrictions, §58-53-50.
Right to obtain individual policy.
Termination of group coverage, §58-53-45.
Self-insurance of employer.
Inapplicability of provisions, §58-53-115.
Termination of group coverage.
Right to obtain individual policy, §58-53-45.
Time limitation, §58-53-55.
Definitions, §58-53-1.
"Agents," §58-51-80, (d).
Continuation of conversion privileges, §58-53-1.
"Employees," §58-51-80, (c).
Generally, §58-51-80, (a).
Discrimination.
Mentally ill and chemically dependent.
Applicability, §58-51-55, (d).
Coverage, §58-51-55, (b1), (c).

ACCIDENT AND HEALTH INSURANCE —Cont'd
Group insurance —Cont'd
Discrimination —Cont'd
Mentally ill and chemically dependent —Cont'd
Definitions, §58-51-55, (a).
Prohibited acts, §58-51-55, (b), (c).
Eligibility, §58-53-10.
Children of insured, §58-51-120, (b).
Exceptions to eligibility, §58-53-15.
Exceptions to provisions, §58-51-80, (h).
Excluded benefits, §58-53-20.
Hospital, surgical and major medical coverage.
Notice.
Form of notice to employee, §58-53-25.
Inclusion in individual certifications of coverage, §58-53-40.
Premiums.
Payments, §58-53-30.
Requirements for eligibility, §58-53-25.
Self-insurance.
Inapplicability of provisions, §58-53-115.
Termination of continuation privileges.
Dates of termination, §58-53-35.
Termination of employment or membership.
Group hospital, surgical and major medical coverage continued, §58-53-5.
Insurance fiduciary.
Causing cancellation or nonrenewal by willfully failing to pay premiums, §58-50-40, (b).
Cessation of individual contributions, inapplicability, §58-50-40, (j).
Conversion policies.
Notice of, §58-50-40, (g).
Defined, §58-50-40, (a).
Exhibiting books and papers to commissioner, §58-50-40, (f).
Felony for conviction under provisions, §58-50-40, (c).
Restitution, §58-50-40, (e).
Insolvency of fiduciary, §58-50-40, (h).
Notice of obligations by insurer, §58-50-45, (a).
Form, §58-50-45, (b).
Portability and accountability.
Notice of, §58-50-40, (g).
Restitution.
Felony for conviction under provisions, §58-50-40, (e).
Willfully failing to deliver notice of intention to stop payment of premiums, §58-50-40, (b), (h).
Policies, §58-51-80, (a), (b).
Approval of forms, §58-51-85.
Renewal, §58-51-110, (a).
Replacement, §58-51-110, (b).
Portability and accountability.
Notice of by insurance fiduciary, §58-50-40, (g).
Premiums.
Adjustment of rate, §58-51-80.
Conversion privileges.
Authorized increase in premiums, §58-53-60, (b).
Determination of premium for individual policy, §58-53-60, (a).
Rates and adjustments to be filed with commissioner of insurance, §58-53-60, (c).
Payment of premiums.
Continuation privileges, §58-53-30.
Public schools.
Coverage of students, §58-51-81, (a), (b).
Renewal of insurance, §58-51-110, (a).

ACCIDENT AND HEALTH INSURANCE
—Cont'd
Group insurance —Cont'd
Replacement of contracts, §58-51-110, (b).
Retirement plans.
Choosing conversion rights in lieu of continuation upon retirement, §58-53-110, (a).
Eligibility of spouses and children for retirement benefits, §58-53-110, (c).
Provision of group coverage in lieu of issuance of individual policy, §58-53-110, (d).
Reduction or termination of coverage when Medicare eligible, §58-53-110, (b).
Termination.
Acts of insurance fiduciary causing, §58-50-40, (b) to (h).
Notice by insurer, §58-50-40, (i).
Of continuation, §58-53-35, (a).
Exceptions, §58-53-35, (b).
Gynecologist, direct access to, §58-51-38, (a).
Information on to be provided, §58-51-38, (b).
Handicapped children.
Insurers to afford coverage to, §58-51-35, (a).
Applicability of provisions, §58-51-35, (c).
Revocation of license for noncompliance, §58-51-35, (b).
Policy coverage to continue as to, §58-51-25.
Health benefit plan provisions generally, §§58-3-168 to 58-3-178, 58-3-190 to 58-3-265.
Health insurance innovations commission, §§58-90-1 to 58-90-25.
Health insurance portability and accountability, §§58-68-25 to 58-68-75.
See HEALTH INSURANCE PORTABILITY AND ACCOUNTABILITY.
Health maintenance organizations, §§58-67-1 to 58-67-185.
See HEALTH MAINTENANCE ORGANIZATIONS.
High-risk populations.
Nondiscrimination against, §58-3-200, (e).
Hospitalization insurance.
Defined, §58-51-105.
Hospital, medical and dental service corporations, §§58-65-1 to 58-66-40.
See HOSPITAL, MEDICAL AND DENTAL SERVICE CORPORATIONS.
Hospital, surgical and major medical coverage.
Continued coverage.
Date of termination, §58-53-35.
Eligibility, §58-53-10.
Termination of employment or membership, group coverage, §58-53-5.
Eligibility requirements, §58-53-25.
Form of notice to employee, §58-53-25.
Notice included in individual certificates, §58-53-40.
Premium payments, §58-53-30.
Self-insurance, inapplicability, §58-53-115.
Incentives to delay, deny or reduce coverage.
Plan prohibited from offering provider, §58-3-265.
Incontestability, §58-51-15, (a).
Industrial sick benefit insurance.
Defined, §58-51-65.
Policy provisions, §58-51-70.
Insurers to afford coverage to.
Applicability of provisions, §58-51-35, (c).
Interim payment of health care providers' claims.
Claims not timely processed due to year 2000 date change.
Definitions, §58-2-235, (c).

ACCIDENT AND HEALTH INSURANCE
—Cont'd
Interim payment of health care providers' claims —Cont'd
Claims not timely processed due to year 2000 date change —Cont'd
Payment in full, when considered, §58-2-235, (c).
Recovery of excess payment, §58-2-235, (c).
Report by insurer, §58-2-235, (a).
Intoxicants and narcotics, §58-51-16, (a) to (c).
Job development investment grant program.
Health insurance requirements, §143B-437.53, (c).
Joint action to insure elderly, §§58-52-1 to 58-52-25.
Associations.
Articles of association, §58-52-20.
Authorized, §58-52-5.
Defined, §58-52-1.
Mutual insurers may participate, §58-52-20.
Powers, §58-52-20.
Statements.
Annual statements, §58-52-20.
Authorized, §58-52-5.
Regional plans, §58-52-10.
Definitions, §58-52-1.
Licenses.
No additional licensing required, §58-52-25.
Policies, §58-52-5.
Approval of forms by commissioner, §58-52-15.
Premiums.
Approval of rates by commissioner, §58-52-15.
Regional plans.
Authorized, §58-52-10.
Jurisdiction over providers of health care benefits.
Determination of generally, §§58-49-1 to 58-49-25.
See HEALTH CARE BENEFITS PROVIDERS.
Law enforcement officers.
Separate insurance benefits plan for state and local officers, §143-166.60, (a) to (h).
Life and health insurance guaranty association, §§58-62-2 to 58-62-95.
See LIFE AND HEALTH INSURANCE GUARANTY ASSOCIATION.
Local government risk pools, §58-23-5, (c).
Long-term care insurance, §§58-55-1 to 58-55-50.
See LONG-TERM CARE INSURANCE.
Mammograms.
Low-dose screening mammography.
Coverage requirement, §58-51-57, (a), (c).
Deductibles, coinsurance and other limitations, applicability, §58-51-57, (a).
Defined, §58-51-57, (b).
Reimbursement, §58-51-57, (d).
Marriage and family therapists.
Defined, §58-50-30, (c4).
Right to choose services, §58-50-30, (a1) to (a3).
Mastectomy.
Coverage for reconstructive breast surgery resulting from, §58-51-62, (a).
Definitions, §58-51-62, (b).
Prohibited acts, §58-51-62, (c).
Written notice of available coverage, §58-51-62, (d).
Postmastectomy inpatient care coverage, §58-3-168.
Maternity coverage requirement, §58-3-170, (a).
Health benefit plans defined, §58-3-170, (b).
Minimum hospital stay following birth, §58-3-169.
Definitions, §58-3-169, (a).
Effect on mother, §58-3-169, (g).

ACCIDENT AND HEALTH INSURANCE —Cont'd
Maternity coverage requirement —Cont'd
Minimum hospital stay following birth —Cont'd
Exceptions, §58-3-169, (c).
Generally, §58-3-169, (b).
Postdelivery follow-up care, §58-3-169, (d).
Prohibited acts, §58-3-169, (e), (f).
Reimbursements, level and type, §58-3-169, (h).
Timely care, §58-3-169, (e).
Medicaid.
Coordination, §58-51-115, (b).
Definitions, §58-51-115, (a).
Employer-provided family health benefit plans.
Required coverage of children, §108A-69.
Medical necessity.
Requirements for health benefit plans that limit coverage to medically necessary services and supplies, §58-3-200, (b).
Medical support orders and agreements for children, §50-13.11.
Medicare supplement insurance, §§58-54-1 to 58-54-40.
See MEDICARE.
Mental health area authorities.
Life or health insurance for officers and employees, §122C-156, (b), (c).
Mentally retarded children.
Insurers to afford coverage to, §58-51-35, (a).
Revocation of license for noncompliance, §58-51-35, (b).
Policy coverage to continue as to, §58-51-25.
Multiple employer welfare arrangements.
Regulation generally, §§58-49-30 to 58-49-65.
See HEALTH CARE BENEFITS PROVIDERS.
Mutual insurance companies.
Surplus, §58-7-75.
Narcotics and intoxicants, §58-51-16, (a) to (c).
Negligent decisions by plan providers.
Health care liability, §§90-21.50 to 90-21.56.
See HEALTH CARE LIABILITY.
Newborns.
Newborn hearing screening.
Coverage required, §58-3-260, (b).
Health benefit plan and insurer defined, §58-3-260, (a).
Policies to cover, §58-51-30, (a) to (f).
Notice.
Acknowledgment by insurer of receipt of notice under policy.
No waiver of rights of insurer, §58-50-1.
Claims.
Denied, §58-3-172.
Required policy provisions as to notice of claims, §58-51-15, (a).
Nonpayment of premium.
Notice required before forfeiture, §58-50-35.
Renewability of individual and blanket hospitalization and accident and health insurance policies, §58-51-20, (a).
Right to return policy and have premium refunded, §58-51-10.
Utilization review.
Noncertification, §58-50-61, (h).
Nurses' services, §58-50-25, (a).
Direct payments to nurse, §58-50-25, (b).
Obstetricians, direct access to, §58-51-38, (a).
Information to be provided, §58-51-38, (b).
Offset or reversal of payment, §58-50-57, (a).
Contract with provider not to contain provision authorizing, §58-50-57, (b).

ACCIDENT AND HEALTH INSURANCE —Cont'd
Optometrists.
Right to choose services, §58-50-30, (a1) to (a3), (g), (h).
Osteoporosis or low bone mass.
Bone mass measurement for diagnosis and evaluation.
Health benefit plan to provide coverage, §58-3-174, (a).
Definitions, §58-3-174, (d).
Frequency of coverage, §58-3-174, (b).
Screening for nonqualified individuals not covered, §58-3-174, (c).
Ovarian cancer.
Surveillance tests for women at risk for ovarian cancer.
Coverage requirement, §§58-3-270, (a), 58-50-155, (a).
Deductibles, coinsurance and other limitations, §58-3-270, (b).
Definitions, §58-3-270, (a).
Parent and child.
Employer-provided family health benefit plan.
Parent required to provide coverage for child.
Employer obligations, §108A-69, (b).
Definitions, §108A-69, (a).
Recoupment of amount spent on medical care.
Health benefit plan coverage required to be provided for child, §108A-70, (a).
Payment obligations for covered services.
Explanation by insurer, §58-3-250, (a).
Notice that actual expenses may exceed covered amount, §58-3-250, (b).
Payment to government agencies.
Direct payment, §58-3-175.
Pediatrician.
Direct access for minors, §58-3-240.
Pharmacist.
Payment or reimbursement, §58-50-30, (e).
Right to choose services, §58-50-30, (a1) to (a3), (g), (h).
Pharmacy of choice.
Applicability of provisions, §58-51-37, (a).
Definitions, §58-51-37, (b).
Generally, §58-51-37, (c) to (e).
Rebates or marketing incentives.
Offering on equal basis, §58-51-37, (f).
Violations of provisions.
Sanctions and effect, §58-51-37, (g) to (k).
Physician assistant.
Denial of reimbursement to agency, institution or physician, §58-50-26.
Payment or reimbursement, §58-50-30, (f).
Right to choose services, §58-50-30, (a1) to (a3), (g), (h).
Plan summaries.
Notice, expenses may exceed covered amount, §58-3-250, (b).
Payment obligations, explanation by insurer, §58-3-250, (a).
Podiatrists.
Right to choose services, §58-50-30, (a1) to (a3), (g), (h).
Policies.
Adopted children.
Policies to cover, §§58-51-30, (a) to (f), 58-51-125, (a) to (c).
Preexisting conditions, §58-51-125, (c).
Age limits, §58-50-20.

ACCIDENT AND HEALTH INSURANCE —Cont'd

Policies —Cont'd
Applications for, §58-50-5, (a).
Alteration, §58-50-5, (b).
False statements.
Effect, §58-50-5, (c).
Blanket accident and health insurance, §58-51-75, (a).
Approval of forms, §58-51-85.
Disability income insurance.
Standards for policies, §58-51-130.
Exemption of certain policies from provisions, §58-50-65.
Filing.
Rules and regulations as to, §58-51-15, (g).
Forfeiture.
Notice of nonpayment of premium required before forfeiture, §58-50-35.
Forms, §58-51-5, (a).
Approval by commissioner, §58-51-1.
Other states, §58-51-5, (b).
Generally.
See INSURANCE POLICIES OR CONTRACTS.
Group accident and health insurance, §58-51-80, (a), (b).
Approval of forms, §58-51-85.
Renewal, §58-51-110, (a).
Replacement, §58-51-110, (b).
Industrial sick benefit insurance.
Provisions, §58-51-70.
Intoxicants and narcotics, §58-51-16, (a) to (c).
Mentally retarded or physically handicapped children.
Policy coverage to continue as to, §58-51-25.
Narcotics and intoxicants, §58-51-16, (a) to (c).
Newborn infants.
Policies to cover, §58-51-30, (a) to (f).
Nonconforming policies, §58-50-15, (b).
Preexisting condition exclusion.
Adopted children, §58-51-125, (c).
Clarification, §58-51-15, (h).
"Preexisting conditions."
Meaning of term, §58-51-60.
Provisions.
Generally, §58-51-15, (a), (b).
Inapplicable or inconsistent provisions, §58-51-15, (c).
Industrial benefit insurance, §58-51-70.
Order of certain policy provisions, §58-51-15, (d).
Other policy provisions.
Effect, §58-50-15, (a).
Requirements of other jurisdictions, §58-51-15, (f).
Renewability.
Applicability of provisions, §58-51-20, (d).
Notice, §58-51-20, (a).
Policies issued during grace period construed to be continuation of first policy, §58-51-20, (c).
Unilateral acts by insurers prohibited, §58-51-20, (b).
Requirements, §58-51-5, (a).
Other states, §58-51-5, (b).
Return of policy.
Notice of right to return policy, §58-51-10.
Third-party ownership not precluded, §58-51-15, (e).

Portability and accountability, §§58-68-25 to 58-68-75.
See HEALTH INSURANCE PORTABILITY AND ACCOUNTABILITY.

ACCIDENT AND HEALTH INSURANCE —Cont'd

Preexisting conditions.
Adopted children, §58-51-125, (c).
Disability income insurance, §58-51-130, (d).

Preferred providers.
Advertising restrictions, §58-50-56, (k).
Contract provisions, §58-50-56, (d) to (f).
Contracts or arrangements, §58-50-56, (b).
Coverage from nonparticipating provider, §58-50-56, (i).
Definitions, §58-50-56, (a).
Disclosures by insurers, §58-50-56, (h).
List of participating providers, §58-50-56, (j).
Proposals for participation, §58-50-56, (c).
Rules, §58-50-56, (g).

Premiums.
Approval of rates by commissioner, §§58-51-1, 58-51-95, (f).
Increased rates, §58-51-95, (f).
Filing of rates.
Group or blanket accident and health insurance, §58-51-85.
Group accident and health insurance.
Continuation privileges, §58-53-30.
Conversion privileges, §58-53-60.
Joint action to insure elderly.
Approval of rates by commissioner, §58-52-15.
Nonpayment.
Notice of nonpayment required before forfeiture, §58-50-35.
Refund.
Notice of right to return policy and have premium refunded, §58-51-10.

Prescription drug identification cards.
Plan issuing prescription drug cards to issue uniform identification cards, §58-3-177, (a).
Definitions, §58-3-177, (e).
Electronic verification of claim, §58-3-177, (d).
Exceptions, §58-3-177, (f).
Information contained in card, §58-3-177, (a), (b).
Issued annually if change in coverage, §58-3-177, (c).

Prescription drugs.
Closed formularies or restricted access to perspiration drugs or devices.
Definitions, §58-3-221, (c).
Medically necessary nonformulary or restricted access drug or device prescribed.
Voiding or refusing to renew contract prohibited, §58-3-221, (b).
Payment for drugs or devices specifically excluded from coverage not required, §58-3-221, (d).
Requirements of insurers maintaining, §58-3-221, (a).
Contraceptive drugs or devices.
Coverage by insurer providing health benefit plan, §58-3-178.

Primary care provider, specialist selected.
Insured diagnosed with serious or chronic degenerative, disabling or life threatening disease, §58-3-235, (a).
Care authorized by specialist, §58-3-235, (b).
Denial of access by insurer, §58-3-235, (a).
Treatment plan approved by insurer, selection under, §58-3-235, (b).

Professional counselor.
Defined, §58-50-30, (c3).

ACCIDENT AND HEALTH INSURANCE —Cont'd
Professional counselor —Cont'd
Right to choose services, §58-50-30, (a1) to (a3), (g), (h).
Professional employer organizations.
Health benefit plans.
Licensee offering plan not fully insured by authorized insurer, §58-89A-105, (c), (d).
Prompt claim payments under health benefit plans.
Claim status report, §58-3-225, (g).
Definitions, §58-3-225, (a).
Denial of claim.
Additional information required by insurer, §58-3-225, (c), (d).
Notice, §58-3-225, (b), (c).
Duties of insurer, §58-3-225, (b).
Interest, §58-3-225, (e).
Overpayments.
Recovery by insurer, §58-3-225, (h).
Patient's liability not limited or impaired, §58-3-225, (m).
Records of insurers, §58-3-225, (i).
Submission of claims.
Time for, §58-3-225, (f).
Violations by insurers, §58-3-225, (j).
Exceptions, §58-3-225, (k).
Proof of loss.
Required policy provisions, §58-51-15, (a).
Prostate-specific antigen (PSA) tests.
Coverage, §58-51-58, (a), (c).
Defined, §58-51-58, (b).
Provider credentialing.
Health benefit plan and insurer defined, §58-3-230, (c).
Process requirements, §58-3-230, (a).
Time limit on processing applications, §58-3-230, (a).
Uniform provider credentialing application form.
Commissioner to adopt by rule, §58-3-230, (b).
Provider directories.
Allied health professionals, listing, §58-3-245, (c).
Information included in directory listing, §58-3-245, (b).
Plan required to provide, §58-3-245, (a).
Provider networks.
Services outside, §58-3-200, (d).
Psychologists.
Defined, §58-50-30, (b).
Right to choose services, §58-50-30, (a1) to (a3), (g), (h).
Public school employees, §115C-340, (a), (b).
Railroad ticket policies.
Exemptions from certain provisions, §58-50-65, (d).
Rates.
Exceptions to applicability of rating provisions, §58-40-15.
Reinsurance.
Life and health insurance reinsurance agreements, §58-7-31.
Renewal of health benefit plan.
Date of renewal when law enacted by general assembly applies to health benefit plans, §58-3-167, (c).
Reports.
Health benefit plan reporting requirements, §58-3-191, (a).
Access to reports, §58-3-191, (b1).

ACCIDENT AND HEALTH INSURANCE —Cont'd
Risk based capital requirements.
Insurance companies, §§58-12-2 to 58-12-70.
See INSURANCE COMPANIES.
School employees, §115C-340, (a), (b).
Secured transactions.
Health-care-insurance receivables.
Third party assignments.
Claims and defenses against assignee, taking subject to.
Inapplicability of provisions, §25-9-404, (e).
Modification of assigned contract, §25-9-405, (d).
Restrictions on assignments, §§25-9-406, (i), 25-9-408.
Sickle cell trait or hemoglobin C trait.
Policies to be issued to person possessing, §58-51-45.
Simultaneous death of insured and beneficiary.
Disposition of proceeds, §28A-24-4.
Site development grants.
Health insurance for employees.
Required for project eligiblity, §143B-437.02, (e).
Small employer group health coverage, §§58-50-105 to 58-50-150.
See SMALL EMPLOYER GROUP HEALTH COVERAGE.
Specialist care referral.
In-plan specialists.
Definitions, §58-3-223, (b).
Duties of insurer providing health benefit plan, §58-3-223, (a).
Specialist selected as primary care provider.
Insured diagnosed with serious or chronic degenerative, disabling or life threatening disease, §58-3-235, (a).
Care authorized by specialist, §58-3-235, (b).
Denial of access by insurer, §58-3-235, (a).
Treatment plan approved by insurer, selection under, §58-3-235, (b).
Stock accident and health insurance companies.
Capital and/or surplus.
Amount required, §58-7-75.
Substance abuse professional.
Defined, §58-50-30, (c2).
Right to choose services, §58-50-30, (a1) to (a3), (g), (h).
Supplemental contract.
Exemptions from provisions, §58-50-65, (b).
Tax-supported institutions.
Coverage for active medical treatment in.
Insurers to afford, §58-51-40, (a), (b).
Applicability of provisions, §58-51-40, (c).
Teachers and state employees.
Comprehensive major medical plan, §§135-39 to 135-40.14.
See MEDICAL PLAN FOR TEACHERS AND STATE EMPLOYEES.
Telephone system for up-to-date network information.
Plan to provide, §58-3-245, (a).
Third party administrators, §§58-56-2 to 58-56-66.
See THIRD PARTY ADMINISTRATORS.
Transplants.
Request for determination of coverage.
Required response time, §58-3-102.

ACCIDENT AND HEALTH INSURANCE —Cont'd
Treatment discussions.
Limiting prohibited, §58-3-176, (a).
Construction of provisions, §58-3-176, (b).
Definitions, §58-3-176, (c).
Uniform prescription drug identification cards, §58-3-177.
Uniform provider credentialing, §58-3-230.
Utilization review.
Definitions, §58-50-61, (a).
Disclosures requirements, §58-50-61, (m).
External review, §§58-50-75 to 58-50-95.
Insurer oversight, §58-50-61, (b).
Insurer responsibility, §58-50-61, (e).
Noncertification.
Appeals, §58-50-61, (j) to (l).
Notice, §58-50-61, (h).
Program.
Operations, §58-50-61, (d).
Scope and content, §58-50-61, (c).
Prospective and concurrent reviews, §58-50-61, (f).
Reconsideration.
Requests for, §58-50-61, (i).
Records maintenance, §58-50-61, (n).
Retrospective reviews, §58-50-61, (g).
Violations.
Effect on insurer, §58-50-61, (o).
Waiver by insurer.
Acts which do not constitute, §58-50-1.
Workers' compensation insurance.
Exemption from provisions, §58-50-65, (a).
Workers' compensation proceedings.
Insurers not party in interest to proceedings, §97-90.1.
Reimbursement from employer, §97-90.1.
Year 2000 date change.
Health care providers insurance payment claims not timely processed due to year 2000 date change.
Definitions, §58-2-235, (c).
Interim payments by insurer to providers, §58-2-235.
Payment in full, when considered, §58-2-235, (c).
Recovery of excess payment, §58-2-235, (c).
Report by insurer, §58-2-235, (a).

ACCIDENT INVESTIGATORS.
Safety professionals, §§90-671 to 90-674.

ACCIDENTS.
Aircraft.
Liability determination, §63-15.
Use of aircraft to discover certain motor vehicle violations.
Primarily for accident prevention, §20-196.2.
Amusement devices, §95-111.10.
Boat operators duties, §75A-11.
Violations of provisions, §75A-18, (a).
Boilers.
Investigations, §95-69.11.
Elevators, §95-110.9.
Landlord and tenant.
Liability for accidental damage, §42-10.
Liquefied petroleum gases.
Limitations on liability, §119-60.
Mine accidents.
Bureau of mines, §113-26.1.
Defined, §74-24.2.
Mine safety and health, §§74-24.1 to 74-24.20.
See MINE SAFETY AND HEALTH.

ACCIDENTS —Cont'd
Mine accidents —Cont'd
Powers of commissioner of labor, §74-24.7, (c) to (e).
Reporting, §74-24.13.
Motor carriers.
Reports not to be used as evidence, §62-274.
Motor vehicles.
Generally.
See MOTOR VEHICLE ACCIDENTS.
Public utilities.
Investigation by commission, §62-41.
Safety professionals, §§90-671 to 90-674.
School buses.
Claims for death or injury to pupil, §§115C-257 to 115C-259.
See SCHOOL BUSES.
Skier safety and skiing accidents, §§99C-1 to 99C-5.
Workers' compensation.
Compensation, death resulting, §97-38.
Compensation from other states, §97-36.
Notice to employer, §§97-22, 97-23.
Reports, §97-92.

ACCIDENT-TRAUMA VICTIM IDENTIFICATION, §§90-600 to 90-604.
Body information tags.
Contents, §90-604, (b).
Use, §90-604, (a).
Citation of article, §90-600.
Next of kin.
Timely notification, §90-603.
Organ donors.
Routine search for information, §90-602.
Personal effects.
Search, §90-602, (a), (c).
Policy of state, §90-601.
Purpose of article, §90-601.
Search of driver record, §90-602, (b).
Short title, §90-600.

ACCOMMODATION ENDORSER.
Joinder of debtor by surety.
Surety defined to include, §26-12, (a).
Surety's recovery on obligation paid.
Surety defined to include, §26-3.1.

ACCOMMODATION MAKER.
Joinder of debtor by surety.
Surety defined to include, §26-12, (a).
Surety's recovery on obligation paid.
Surety defined to include, §26-3.1, (b).

ACCOMPLICES AND ACCESSORIES.
After the fact accessories.
Punishment of accessories, §14-7.
Alcoholic beverages.
Sale to or purchase by minors, §18B-302, (c).
Fines and other penalties, §18B-302.1, (b), (c).
Before the fact accessories.
Punishment of accessories, §14-5.2.
Collections out of state of employee earnings.
Resident as aider, §95-74.
Continuing criminal enterprise, §14-7.20.
Eggs.
Violation of egg act, §106-245.27, (a).
Escape.
Assisting escape from state prison, §148-45.
Conveying messages to convicts and other prisoners, §14-258.
Use of deadly weapon, §14-258.2.
Futures contracts, §16-4.

ACCOMPLICES AND ACCESSORIES —Cont'd
Habeas corpus.
Concealing party entitled to writ, §17-28.
Larceny, §14-70.
Prisoner injuries.
Inflicting or assisting in infliction of self injury to prisoner resulting in incapacity, §148-46.1.
Prostitution, §14-204.
Punishment of accessories.
After the fact accessories, §14-7.
Before the fact accessories, §14-5.2.
Taxation.
Violations by officers, agents or employees, §105-234.

ACCORD AND SATISFACTION.
Advance payments to person claiming bodily injury, §1-540.3.
Affirmative defense, §1A-1, Rule 8, (c).
Assignments.
Secured transactions.
Inapplicability of article 9.
Accounts, chattel paper, etc., assigned to satisfy preexisting obligation, §25-9-109, (d).
By agreement receipt of less sum is discharge, §1-540.
Motor vehicle accident settlements, §1-540.2.
Negotiable instruments.
Use of instrument, §25-3-311.
Secured transactions.
Assignment to satisfy preexisting obligation, inapplicability, §25-9-109, (d).
Collateral accepted in full or partial satisfaction of obligation, §§25-9-620 to 25-9-622.

ACCOUNTANTS, §§93-1 to 93-13.
See CERTIFIED PUBLIC ACCOUNTANTS.

ACCOUNTS AND ACCOUNTING.
Absentees in military service.
Final accounting upon termination of receivership, §28B-8, (c).
Accountants, §§93-1 to 93-13.
See CERTIFIED PUBLIC ACCOUNTANTS.
Agricultural finance authority, §122D-18, (a).
Alcoholic beverages.
Required accounts and systems, §18B-205, (a), (b).
Animals.
Spay/neuter account, §19A-62.
Distributions to counties and cities, §19A-64.
Eligibility for distributions, §19A-63.
Assignments for benefit of creditors.
Final account in twelve months, §23-11.
Quarterly accounts, §23-11.
Trustee of deed of trust to account for property coming into hands, §23-2.
Attorneys at law.
Deposit of funds, Prof. Cond. Rule 1.15-2.
Records and accountings, Prof. Cond. Rule 1.15-3.
Banks.
Deposits.
Statement of account from bank to depositor.
Deemed final adjustment if not objected to within five years, §53-75.
Depositor not relieved from exercising diligence to errors, §53-76.
Rendering annually or on request, §53-75.
False entries in banking accounts.
Felony, §53-130.
Savings banks. See within this heading, "Savings banks."

ACCOUNTS AND ACCOUNTING —Cont'd
Bedding law account, §130A-270.
Book accounts, evidence.
Accounts under $10, §8-42.
Copies, §8-44.
Executors or administrators to approve, §8-43.
Book debt oath.
Administrators, §11-11.
Form of oath, §11-11.
Boxing commission revenue account, §143-655, (c).
Budget.
Clean water management trust fund.
Established, §143-15.3B, (a).
Use of funds, §143-15.3B, (b).
Director of the budget.
Records, §143-20.
Repairs and renovations reserve account.
Allocations and expenditures, §143-15.3A, (c).
Established, §143-15.3A, (a).
Use of funds in account, §143-15.3A, (b).
Cemeteries.
Trust funds for care of cemeteries.
Separate record of accounts to be kept, §65-8.
Certified public accountants, §§93-1 to 93-13.
See CERTIFIED PUBLIC ACCOUNTANTS.
Clean water management trust fund, §143-15.3B.
Collection agencies.
Application of funds where there is debtor-creditor relationship, §58-70-85.
Furnishing acknowledgment of account, §58-70-60, (a).
Remittance trust account, §58-70-65, (a) to (c).
Return of accounts.
Request by creditor, §58-70-75.
Termination of permit, §58-70-80.
Collegiate and cultural attraction plate account, §20-79.7, (b).
Commerce department.
Industrial development fund.
Utility account, §143B-437.01, (b1).
Community colleges, §115D-58.5.
Community trust for persons with severe chronic disabilities.
Settlement of trust, §36A-59.20.
Statements, §36A-59.14.
Constitution of the United States.
Receipts and expenditures of public money.
Publication of statement and account, Const. U. S., art. I, §9.
Corporations.
Business corporations.
Accounting records, §55-16-01, (b).
Court process.
Collection of accounts.
Simulation of court process in connection with collection, §14-118.1.
CPAs, §§93-1 to 93-13.
See CERTIFIED PUBLIC ACCOUNTANTS.
Current accounts.
Accrual of action to recover balance due, §1-31.
Custodial trusts.
Accounting by custodial trustee, §33B-15.
Establishment of checking, savings or other accounts, §33B-9, (c).
Decedents' estates.
Collectors.
Duty to file inventories, accounts and other reports, §28A-11-3.
Settlement of accounts, §28A-11-4, (b).

ACCOUNTS AND ACCOUNTING —Cont'd
Decedents' estates —Cont'd
General provisions, §§28A-21-1 to 28A-21-5.
See EXECUTORS AND ADMINISTRATORS.
Inventories, §§28A-20-1 to 28A-20-4.
See DECEDENTS' ESTATES.
Default judgments.
Clerk to ascertain interest upon default judgment on account, §24-6.
Detectives.
Collection of claims, accounts, etc., by detective.
Misdemeanor offense for detective to collect, §14-401.2.
Drainage districts.
Filing account of expenses, §156-77.
Durable power of attorney.
Incapacity or incompetency of principal.
Filing annual and final accounts, §32A-11, (b).
Evidence.
Book accounts.
Copies of book accounts in documentary evidence, §8-44.
Documentary evidence of book accounts under $60, §8-42.
Executors and administrators to approve book accounts, §8-43.
Documentary evidence.
Itemized and verified accounts, §8-45.
Executors and administrators.
Book accounts.
Proved by personal representative, §8-43.
Generally, §§28A-21-1 to 28A-21-5.
See EXECUTORS AND ADMINISTRATORS.
Facility authorities.
Fiscal accountability, §160A-480.3, (f).
Fiduciaries.
Personal accounts.
Deposit in fiduciary's personal account, §32-10.
Film industry development account, §143B-434.4.
Firemen's relief fund.
Disbursement of funds by trustees.
Account of moneys received and disbursed to be kept, §58-84-40, (a) to (d).
Fiscal year, §147-85.
Fraud.
Court process in connection with collection of account.
Simulation of court process, §14-118.1.
Guardians.
Annual accounts.
Approval, §35A-1264.
Compelling accounting, §35A-1265, (a).
Contempt, §35A-1265, (a).
Corporation as guardian, §35A-1265, (b).
Costs of proceedings, §35A-1265, (a).
Required, §35A-1264.
Applicability of article, §35A-1260.
Commissions, §35A-1269.
Exhibition of investments and bank statements, §35A-1268.
Expenses and disbursements.
Chargeable in annual account, §35A-1267.
Final account and discharge of guardian, §35A-1266.
Responsibility of guardian for accounting until discharged, §35A-1295, (b).
Inventory or account required within three months, §35A-1261.
Compelling inventory or account, §35A-1262, (a).
Contempt, §35A-1262, (a).

ACCOUNTS AND ACCOUNTING —Cont'd
Guardians —Cont'd
Inventory or account required within three months —Cont'd
Compelling inventory or account —Cont'd
Costs of proceedings.
Personal liability of guardian, §35A-1262, (b).
Supplemental inventory, §35A-1263.1.
Removal or resignation of guardian or guardian stopped serving, §35A-1294, (a).
Standby guardians for minor children, §35A-1381.
Highway patrol.
Oversized and hazardous shipment escort fee.
Escort fee account, §20-196.4, (d), (e).
Housing authorities and projects.
Local government finance.
Special provisions pertaining to public housing authorities, §159-42, (f).
Systems as part of city or county accounting system, §157-4.2.
Housing trust fund.
Separate accounts, §122E-5, (c).
Incompetence, restoration.
Filing an approval of final accounts from guardian, §35A-1130, (e).
Judicial sales.
Private sale.
Filing of account of receipts and disbursements, §1-339.40, (a), (b).
Public sale.
Filing of account by commissioner or trustee, §1-339.31, (a).
Limitation of actions.
Mutual, open and current account.
Action upon, §1-31.
Local development.
Expenditures, §158-7.2.
Local government finance, §§159-1 to 159-188.
See LOCAL GOVERNMENT FINANCE.
Marine fisheries commission.
Examination of accounts and books by state auditor, §113-257.
Missing persons.
Limitations on accounting, §28C-14.
Mortgage bankers and brokers.
Prohibited acts, §53-243.11.
Mortgages and deeds of trust.
Sales under power of sale.
Clerk to audit account and record, §45-21.33, (b).
Trustees of deed of trust.
Assignment of benefit of creditors.
Accounting of property, §23-2.
Motor carriers, §62-269.
Mutual accounts.
Accrual of action to recover balance due, §1-31.
Naval militia.
Accounting officer, §127A-71.
Rendition of accounts, §127A-72.
Oil pollution and hazardous substances discharges.
Expenses of agencies for removal, §143-215.86, (e).
Open accounts.
Accrual of action to recover balance due, §1-31.
Partnerships.
Right of partner to formal account as to partnership affairs, §59-52.
Surviving partners.
Compelling accounting, §59-83.
Duty to account and settle, §59-82.

ACCOUNTS AND ACCOUNTING —Cont'd
Power of attorney.
Durable power of attorney.
Incapacity or incompetency of principal.
Filing annual and final accounts, §32A-11, (b).
Principal and income act.
Allocation of receipts during administration of trust.
Separate accounting for business and other activities, §37A-4-403.
Prisons and prisoners.
Trustee for estate of debtor, §23-20.
Public schools.
Accounting system, §115C-440.
Audit.
Annual independent audit, §115C-447.
Budgetary accounting for appropriations, §115C-441.
Public warehousemen.
Books of account, §66-39.
Referees meetings.
Statement of accounts, §1A-1, Rule 53, (f).
Repairs and renovations reserve account, §143-15.3A.
General fund credit balance.
Transfer of funds from unreserved credit balance to account, §143-15.2, (c).
Rescue squad workers' relief fund, §58-88-15.
Retail installment sales, statement of accounts.
Additional statements, §25A-35, (b).
Annual statement free of charge, §25A-35, (a).
Request of information for income tax purposes.
Seller to provide such information, §25A-35, (c).
Savings banks.
Deposit accounts, §54C-164.
Generally accepted accounting principles, §54C-161.
Joint accounts, §54C-165, (a).
Additional nature of provisions, §54C-165, (a1).
Deposits and withdrawals.
Effect, §54C-165, (c).
Estate taxes.
Provisions not to repeal or modify estate tax laws, §54C-165, (b).
Personal agency accounts, §54C-167, (a).
Checks on account, payment by bank, §54C-167, (d).
Contract establishing, §54C-167, (a), (c).
Payments by savings bank, §54C-167, (b).
Survivorship.
No right of survivorship on death of principal, §54C-167, (b).
Trust accounts, §54C-166, (a), (b).
Additional nature of provisions, §54C-166, (a1).
Deposits and withdrawals.
Effect, §54C-166, (c).
Estate tax laws.
Provisions not to repeal or modify, §54C-166, (d).
Septage management account, §130A-291.1, (e3).
Small claim actions.
Form of complaint on account, §7A-232.
Small estates.
Savings accounts.
Collection of property by affidavits.
Transfer of ownership rights on presentation of affidavit, §28A-25-1, (c).
Soil and water conservation districts.
Annual audit, §139-7.
Solid waste management.
Regional solid waste management authorities.
Fiscal accountability, §153A-428, (a).

ACCOUNTS AND ACCOUNTING —Cont'd
Southern growth policies agreement.
Board, §143-497, (d), (e), (f).
Spay/neuter account, §19A-62.
Eligibility for distributions, §19A-63.
Special proceedings.
Commissioner of sale to account, §1-406.
Special registration plate account, §20-79.7, (b), (c).
State-county criminal justice partnership account, §§143B-273 to 143B-273.19.
See STATE-COUNTY CRIMINAL JUSTICE PARTNERSHIP.
State departments and agencies.
Annual financial statements, §143-20.1.
Comprehensive annual financial report, §143-20.1.
Expenditures for departments and institutions, §143-154.
Fiscal year, §147-85.
Investigations and audits, §143-157.
Statewide accounts receivable program, §§147-86.20 to 147-86.27.
State treasurer.
Fiscal year, §147-85.
Office of treasurer declared office of deposit and disbursement, §147-74.
Pool accounts for local government unemployment compensation, §147-86.1.
Separate funds.
Accounts of funds kept separate, §147-82.
Statewide accounts receivable program.
State departments and agencies, §§147-86.20 to 147-86.27.
See STATEWIDE ACCOUNTS RECEIVABLE PROGRAM.
Superior courts.
Clerks of court.
Fees and other receipts, §7A-108.
Transfers to minors.
Accounting by and determination of liability of custodian, §33A-19.
Trust companies.
Seizure by commissioner.
Administration of accounts, §53-383, (c).
Trustees of deed of trust.
Assignment for benefit of creditors.
Accounting of property coming into hands, §23-2.
Trusts and trustees.
Charitable trusts.
Actions for account, §36A-48.
Trustees to file accounts, §36A-47.
Class in esse.
Sale of property held by, §41-11.1, (l).
Payable on death accounts in financial institutions.
Governing statutes, §36A-120.
Resignation of trustees.
Final accounting before resignation, §36A-29, (b).
When required, §36A-29, (a).
Uniform common trust fund act.
Court accounting, §36A-91.
Uniform trusts act.
Bank account to pay special debts, §36A-61.
Wills.
Filing inventories and accounts, §36A-107, (a).
Testamentary trust created under will, §36A-107, (b).
Unemployment compensation.
Training and employment account, §96-6.1, (b).

ACCOUNTS AND ACCOUNTING —Cont'd
Utilities commission.
Power to establish system of accounts, §62-35, (a).
Veterans' guardianship act.
Filing accounts, §34-10.
Failure to file, §34-11.
Cause for removal, §34-11.
Hearing on accounts, §34-10.
Warrants for payment of money.
Issuance of warrants upon state treasurer.
Disbursing accounts, §143-3.2, (a).
Wastewater treatment.
Certification of water pollution control system operator.
Establishment of water pollution control system account, §90A-42, (b).
Water and air resources.
Department of environment and natural resources.
Separate nonreverting accounts established within, §143-215.3A, (a) to (b1).
Funds.
Wastewater treatment works emergency maintenance, operation and repair fund.
Department to provide annual accounting to general assembly, §143-215.3B, (e).
Wetlands restoration fund, §143-214.12, (c).
Wetlands restoration program.
Receipts and disbursements of fund, §143-214.13.
Wildlife conservation account, §143-247.2.
Wills.
Trusts and trustees.
Filing inventories and accounts, §36A-107, (a).
Testamentary trust created under will, §36A-107, (b).
Year.
Fiscal year, §147-85.

ACCOUNTS RECEIVABLE.
Statewide accounts receivable program.
State departments and agencies, §§147-86.20 to 147-86.27.
See STATEWIDE ACCOUNTS RECEIVABLE PROGRAM.

ACCRUAL OF ACTIONS.
Action upon mutual, open and current account, §1-31.
Fraud or mistake, relief on ground of, §1-52.
Personal injury or physical damage to claimant's property, §1-52.
Wrongful death actions, §1-53.

ACCRUAL OF INTEREST.
Time from which interest runs, §24-3.

ACETYLENE HEADLAMPS.
Vehicles eligible for historic vehicle owner special registration, §20-132.

ACID-FREE (ALKALINE) PAPER.
State publications of historical and enduring value.
Compliance with requirement, monitoring, §125-11.13, (b).
Designation of publications on annual basis, §125-11.13, (a), (b).
Identification that publication printed on permanent paper, §125-11.13, (a).
Notice to agencies responsible for publishing designated titles, §125-11.13, (b).
Report as to titles designated for printing on alkaline paper, §125-11.13, (c).

ACID-FREE (ALKALINE) PAPER —Cont'd
State publications of historical and enduring value —Cont'd
Required to be printed on, §§125-11.13, (a), 143-170.5.
Responsibility of agency to print on alkaline paper, §125-11.13, (b).

ACIDS.
Malicious throwing, §14-30.1.
Municipal corporations.
Regulation of corrosive substances, §160A-183.

ACKNOWLEDGMENTS.
Attorney-in-fact.
Form of certificate of acknowledgment of instrument executed by, §47-43.
Attorneys at law.
Execution and acknowledgment of instruments, §47-43.1.
Banks.
Stockholders, officers or directors, §47-93.
Building and loan associations.
Officers or stockholders, §47-94.
Child support.
Acknowledgment of paternity in agreement to support, §110-132, (a).
Agreement to support.
Filing fees, §110-134.
Paternity acknowledged, §110-132.
Clerk of superior court.
Party, validation, §47-106.
Seal of clerk omitted, validation, §47-53.1.
Clerk's certificate upon probate by justice of peace or magistrate, §47-44.
Clerk's certificate upon probate by nonresident official without seal, §47-45.
Clerks, deputies.
Before deputy clerks of courts of other states, §47-79.
Validation of acts, §47-108.7.
Clerk's seal omitted, §47-86.
Clerks without seals, §47-99.
Commissioners of the United States.
Validation of instruments acknowledged before, §47-108.12.
Conditional sales or leases of railroad property, §47-24.
Consuls.
Probate of deeds before consular or agents of the United States, §47-91.
Consuls general, §47-83.
Vice-consuls and vice-consuls general, §47-84.
Conveyances.
Certification of correctness.
Failure of register of deeds to certify.
Validation of registration, §47-50.1.
Defective acknowledgment on old instruments validated, §47-52.
Corporations.
Admission to record of certain corporate deeds declared valid, §47-108.1.
By president and attested by treasurer under corporate seal, §47-70.
Interested corporations.
Probates before officer, §47-63.
Probates before officers, stockholders or directors of corporations prior to January 1, 1945, §47-64.
Proof of corporate articles before officer authorized to probate, §47-75.

ACKNOWLEDGMENTS —Cont'd
Corporations —Cont'd
Validation of corporate deeds containing error and acknowledgment, §47-97.1.
Curative statutes.
See CURATIVE ACTS AND STATUTES.
Deeds.
Certification of correctness.
Failure of register of deeds to certify.
Validation of registration, §47-50.1.
Defective acknowledgment on old deeds validated, §47-52.
Defective acknowledgment on old deeds, §47-52.
Defective certification or adjudication of clerk, etc., admitting to registration, §47-49.
Division of motor vehicles.
Officers and employees.
Power to acknowledge signatures, §20-42, (a).
Durable power of attorney.
Substitution of attorney-in-fact, §32A-12, (b).
Electronic signature or record, §66-321.
Fee of magistrate for proving, §7A-309.
Forms.
Acknowledgment by grantor, §47-38.
Certificate of acknowledgment of instrument executed by attorney-in-fact, §47-43.
Handwriting.
Proof of handwriting of maker refusing to acknowledge, §47-57.
Husband and wife.
Absence of wife does not affect deed as to husband, §39-9.
Before different officers, §39-8.
Different times and places, §39-8.
Fraud.
Certain conveyances not affected by fraud, §39-11.
Husband's and wife's acknowledgment before same officer, §47-40.
Order immaterial, §39-8.
Powers of attorney.
Acknowledgment of spouse of grantor unnecessary, §39-12.
Liens.
Discharge of lien.
Filing acknowledgments, §44-48.
Limitation of actions.
Party to obligation, co-obligor or guarantor.
Effect of acknowledgment by, §1-27, (a).
Notaries public.
Acknowledgment omitting seal of notary.
Validation, §47-53.1.
Powers, §10A-9.
Underage notaries, §47-108.
Partnerships.
Limitation of actions.
Effect of acknowledgment by partner, §59-39.1.
Paternity.
Child support.
Agreement to support, §110-132.
Filing fee, §110-134.
Power of attorney.
Durable power of attorney.
Substitution of attorney-in-fact, §32A-12, (b).
Form of certificate of acknowledgment of instrument executed by attorney-in-fact, §47-43.
Prior certificates, §47-48.
Registers of deeds.
Fee for taking acknowledgment, §161-10, (a).

ACKNOWLEDGMENTS —Cont'd
Savings and loan associations.
Officer or stockholder in association, §47-94.
Seal of clerk or notary omitted.
Validation, §47-53.1.
Secured transactions.
Filing office.
Filing of written record, §25-9-523, (a).
Timeliness of acknowledgment, §25-9-523, (e).
Perfection of security interests.
Possession by secured party to perfect, §25-9-313, (f), (g).
Self authentication of acknowledged documents, §8C-1, Rule 902.
Superior courts.
Clerks of court.
Authority of clerk to take acknowledgment, §7A-103.
Trademarks.
Assignment of registration.
Acknowledgment as prima facie evidence, §80-6, (d).
Who authorized to take, §47-2.

ACQUIRED IMMUNE DEFICIENCY SYNDROME.
Anatomical gifts.
Information for potential donors, §130A-148, (b).
Laboratory tests for AIDS virus infection.
Immunity of facility or institution, §130A-148, (e).
Required, §130A-148, (c), (d).
Arrest.
Initial appearance before magistrate.
Detention for communicable diseases, §15A-534.3.
Basic education program, §115C-81, (a2).
Blood donors.
Information for potential donors, §130A-148, (b).
Laboratory tests for AIDS virus infection.
Immunity of facility or institution, §130A-148, (e).
Required, §130A-148, (c).
Confidentiality.
Records identifying person who has AIDS virus infection, §130A-143.
Different treatment for individual with AIDS.
Not unlawful, §130A-148, (j).
Handling dead body of person infected with HIV.
Notification to person handling, §130A-395, (a), (c).
Laboratory tests for AIDS virus infection, §130A-148, (i).
Blood transfusion.
Immunity of facility or institution, §130A-148, (e).
Information for potential donors, §130A-148, (b).
Testing required, §130A-148, (c).
Consent.
Organ or tissue transplant, §130A-148, (d).
When not required, §130A-148, (f).
Notification of results, §130A-148, (g).
Organ or tissue transplant.
Immunity of facility or institution, §130A-148, (e).
Information for potential donors, §130A-148, (b).
Testing required, §130A-148, (d).
Protection of public health.
Commission may authorize or require tests when necessary to protect, §130A-148, (h).

ACQUIRED IMMUNE DEFICIENCY SYNDROME —Cont'd
Laboratory tests for AIDS virus infection —Cont'd
Rules establishing standards, §130A-148, (a).
Semen, §130A-148, (b), (c), (e).
Referral of individual with AIDS to another provider or facility.
Not unlawful, §130A-148, (j).
Sexually transmitted diseases, tests, §15A-615, (a).
Treating individual with AIDS differently than individual without AIDS.
Not unlawful, §130A-148, (j).

ACTIONS.
Absentees in military service.
Receivers.
Powers to bring and defend actions, §28B-6.
Release from duties, limitation of actions, §28B-8.
Access to civil justice act, §§7A-474.1 to 7A-474.5.
See GEOGRAPHICALLY BASED FIELD PROGRAMS.
Access to judicial proceeding or record.
Effect of provision on other laws, §1-72.1, (f).
Effect of provision on other types of relief, §1-72.1, (g).
Motion to determine, §1-72.1, (a).
Procedures upon filing of motion, §1-72.1, (b).
Ruling on motion, §1-72.1, (c).
Sealing of document or testimony, §1-72.1, (d).
Service of motion, §1-72.1, (b).
Status of movant, §1-72.1, (a).
Accrual of actions, §1-15.
Administration department.
Coal and petroleum suppliers.
Stocks of coals and petroleum fuel capacity, §143-345.14, (e).
Adoption.
Failure to disclose nonidentifying information.
Civil action for equitable or monetary relief, §48-10-104.
Unauthorized disclosure of identifying information.
Civil action for equitable or monetary relief, §48-10-105, (d).
Visitation of adopted grandchild.
Action by biological grandparent, §50-13.2A.
Adult care homes.
Residents' bill of rights, §131D-28.
Instituting civil actions, §131D-28.
Agricultural finance authority.
Power to sue and be sued, §122D-6.
Agriculture fees and taxes.
Suits to prevent collection prohibited, §106-9.6.
Air pollution control.
Failure to pay penalties, §143-215.114A, (f).
Alarm systems licensing.
Licensee's failure to pay penalties, §74D-11, (e).
Aliens.
Suits against state, Const. U. S., amd. XI.
Alimony.
Maintenance of certain actions as independent actions, §50-19, (a).
Separate action during pendency, §50-19, (b).
Without action, §50-16.10.
Ancient minerals claims.
Extinguished in certain counties, §§1-42.1 to 1-42.9.

ACTIONS —Cont'd
Appeals.
See APPEALS.
Apportionment or redistricting.
State legislative or congressional districts.
Challenge to plan, §§1-81.1, 1-267.1, 120-2.3 to 120-2.5.
Three-judge panel, §1-267.1.
Arbitration and award.
Statewide court-ordered nonbinding arbitration in certain civil actions.
Amount in controversy, §7A-37.1, (c).
Arbitrators.
Immunity as judges from civil liability for official conduct, §7A-37.1, (e).
Fees, §7A-37.1, (c1).
Findings of general assembly, §7A-37.1, (a).
Implementation of procedure, §7A-37.1, (d).
Supreme court.
Adoption of rules, §7A-37.1, (b).
Supervising implementation and operation, §7A-37.1, (b).
Architects.
Civil penalty for violations of provisions, §83A-16, (b), (c).
Associations.
Suits by or against unincorporated associations, §1-69.1.
Athlete agents.
Civil remedies against for violations, §78C-100.
Attorney general.
Duties of attorney general as to civil litigation, §114-6.
Bailments.
Trespass committed during existence of bailment, §99A-1.
Boats liens.
Action to regain possession of vessel, §44A-6.1, (a).
Bonds, surety.
Action on bond generally, §§58-76-1 to 58-76-30.
See BONDS, SURETY.
Limitation of actions, §§1-50, (a), 1-52.
Model payment and performance bond, §44A-27.
Prosecution bonds, §§1-109 to 1-112.
Satisfaction.
Defendant may plead satisfaction, §1-60.
Business trusts.
Authority to sue and be sued, §39-45.
Business under assumed name.
Recovery in civil action not prevented for violations, §66-71, (b).
Cable television systems.
Theft, §14-118.5.
Campaign contributions and expenditures.
Civil remedies other than penalties, §163-278.34, (c).
District attorney, notifying and consulting with, §163-278.34, (f).
Collection of penalty, §163-278.34, (e).
Late filing penalty, §163-278.34, (a1).
Carriers.
Joinder of causes of action, §62-205.
Lost or damaged goods.
Generally, §§62-203, 62-204.
Rights against prior carrier, §62-206.
Change of venue, §§1-83 to 1-87.
Charitable solicitation.
Enforcement actions, §§131F-23, (c), 131F-24.
Child care provider criminal history record check.
Disagreement with department's decision, §110-90.2, (d).

ACTIONS —Cont'd
Child custody or visitation, §§50-13.1, 50-13.5.
Attorneys' fees, §50-13.6.
Childhood vaccine-related injury compensation.
Right of state to bring action, §130A-430, (a).
Child labor violations.
Civil penalty, §95-25.23, (b).
Child support, §§50-13.4, 50-13.5.
Attorneys' fees, §50-13.6.
Independent actions for divorce.
Maintenance of certain actions as independent actions permissible, §50-19.
Civil no-contact orders.
Workplace violence prevention, §§95-265 to 95-276.
See WORKPLACE VIOLENCE PREVENTION.
Civil rights, interference with, §99D-1, (b) to (c).
Claim and delivery of personal property.
Recovery of personal property, §1-230.
Class actions, §1A-1, Rule 23, (a).
Class in esse.
Special proceeding to sell, lease or mortgage property held by.
Membership subject to increase by persons not in esse, §41-11.1.
Commissioner of banks.
Nonliability to suit, §53-94.
Power to sue and defend, §53-94.
Commodities, §78D-22, (a).
Community college board of trustees.
Tort actions against, §115D-58.12, (b), (c), (d).
Community college construction contract claim.
Contract completed, contractor dissatisfied with director's decision, §143-135.6, (c).
Condominiums.
Assessments.
Lien for, action to recover, §47C-3-116.
Breach of warranty.
Limitation of action, §47C-4-116.
Tort or contract liability.
Owners' association and declarant, §47C-3-111.
Consolidated city-county act.
Assumption of debt.
Action to set aside referendum, §160B-19, (i).
Constitution of North Carolina.
Civil cases.
Jury trial, Const. N. C., art. I, §25.
Form of action, Const. N. C., art. IV, §13.
Constitution of the United States.
Actions to which United States a party, Const. U. S., art. III, §2.
Contracts with forum selection provisions.
Void as against public policy, §22B-3.
Contracts to improve real property, §22B-2.
Contribution among joint tort-feasors, §§1B-1 to 1B-7.
Enforcement, §1B-3.
Release or covenant not to sue, §1B-4.
Controlled substance examination and screening of employees.
Recovery of civil penalty imposed, §95-234, (b).
Corporations.
Actions against directors of public corporations, §55-7-48.
Derivative actions by shareholders, §1A-1, Rule 23, (b).
Applicability to foreign corporations, §55-7-47.
Definitions, §55-7-40.1.
Demand requirement, §55-7-42.

ACTIONS —Cont'd
Corporations —Cont'd
Derivative actions by shareholders —Cont'd
Discontinuance or settlement, §55-7-45.
Dismissal, §55-7-44.
Jurisdiction, §55-7-40.
Nonprofit corporations, §55A-7-40.
Payment of costs and expenses, §55-7-46.
Privileged communications, §55-7-49.
Standing, §55-7-41.
Stays, §55-7-43.
Drainage.
Payment of bonds authorized, §156-53.
Foreign corporations.
Certificates of authority.
Consequences of failure to obtain, §55-15-02, (a).
Indemnification generally.
Business corporations, §§55-8-50 to 55-8-58.
Nonprofit corporations, §§55A-8-50 to 55A-8-58.
Nonprofit corporations.
Corporations already in existence, §55A-17-03, (b).
Creditors action against member, §55A-6-24.
Derivative actions, §55A-7-40.
Judicial dissolution, §§55A-14-30 to 55A-14-33.
Power to sue and be sued, §55A-3-02, (a).
Voluntary dissolution.
Claims against dissolved corporations, §55A-14-09, (a).
Savings provisions, §55-17-03, (b).
Costs.
General provisions, §§6-1 to 6-62.
See COSTS.
Counties.
Damages.
Suits against counties involving governmental functions, §153A-435, (a), (b).
Defense of employees and officers, §160A-167.
Inspection departments.
Failure to take corrective action, §153A-368.
Outdoor advertising.
Regulation of nonconforming off-premises outdoor advertising.
Payment of monetary compensation for removal.
Determination, §153A-143, (f).
Public officers.
Retention of county funds by delinquent official.
Citizen to recover funds, §128-10.
Riparian owners.
Venue for actions, §153A-288.
County alcoholic beverage control board.
Defense of employees and officers, §160A-167.
Credit device fraud.
Civil action for damages, §14-113.6, (c).
Credit unions.
Power to sue and be sued, §54-109.21.
Crime victims.
Recovery of profits or funds, §15B-35, (a).
Commission, responsibilities of, §15B-35, (c).
Criminal acts.
Civil actions seeking to recover damages.
Statutes of limitation and repose, §1-15.1.
Cruelty to animals.
Civil remedies, §§19A-1 to 19A-4.
Dam safety law.
Civil penalties, §143-215.36, (b).
Debtors.
Joint and several debtors, §§1-113, 1-114.

ACTIONS —Cont'd
Decedents' estates.
Collectors for estates.
Power to maintain and defend actions, §28A-11-3.
Powers of personal representatives or fiduciaries, §28A-13-3, (a).
Survival of actions, §28A-18-1.
Actions in favor of decedent which do not survive, §28A-18-1, (b).
Transfers or conveyances by decedent to defraud creditors.
Actions by personal representative to recover, §28A-15-10.
Declaratory judgments, §§1-253 to 1-267.
See DECLARATORY JUDGMENTS.
Definitions.
Civil action, §1-6.
Criminal action, §1-5.
Generally, §1-2.
Kinds of actions, §1-4.
Special proceedings, §1-3.
Department of health and human services.
Costs to be paid by persons admitted to institutions, §§143-117 to 143-127.1.
See HEALTH AND HUMAN SERVICES DEPARTMENT.
Derivative actions, §1A-1, Rule 23, (b).
Applicability to foreign corporations, §55-7-47.
Definitions, §55-7-40.1.
Demand requirement, §55-7-42.
Discontinuance or settlement, §55-7-45.
Dismissal, §55-7-44.
Jurisdiction, §55-7-40.
Limited liability companies, §57C-8-01.
Limited partnerships, §§59-1001 to 59-1006.
Nonprofit corporations, §55A-7-40.
Payment of costs and expenses, §55-7-46.
Privileged communications, §55-7-49.
Secondary action by shareholders, §1A-1, Rule 23, (b).
Standing, §55-7-41.
Stays, §55-7-43.
Disabled persons.
Civil actions for discriminatory practices, §§168A-11, 168A-12.
Discharge of employee for lawful use of lawful products during nonworking hours, §95-28.2, (e).
Discrimination in business.
Enforcement of provisions, §75B-4.
Dismissal, discontinuance and nonsuit.
See DISMISSAL, DISCONTINUANCE AND NONSUIT.
Divorce.
General provisions.
See DIVORCE.
Dogs.
Dangerous dogs.
Damages for injuries or property damage inflicted by dog.
Strict liability, §67-4.4.
Domestic violence.
Institution of civil action, §50B-2, (a).
Who may institute, §50B-2, (a).
Drainage corporations.
Payment of bonds authorized, §156-53.
Payment of bonds enforced, §156-53.
Drainage districts.
Bondholder's remedy, §156-99.
Dredging permits, §113-229.

ACTIONS —Cont'd
Drugs law violations.
Employing or intentionally using minor to commit drug law violations, §90-95.5.
Dry-cleaning solvent cleanup.
Collection of unpaid civil penalties, §143-215.104P, (f).
Reimbursement for cost of remediation of uncertified site, §143-215.104O, (b), (c).
Elections.
State board of elections.
Authority to assist in litigation, §163-25.
Electrical materials, devices, appliances and equipment sales, §66-27.01.
Electrologists.
Reports of violations of chapter.
Immunity from suit, §88A-23.
Venue for actions brought under chapter, §88A-22, (b).
Electronic surveillance.
Civil cause of action for violation of article.
Damages authorized, §15A-296.
Emancipation of juvenile.
Generally, §§7B-3500 to 7B-3509.
See EMANCIPATION.
Right to sue and be sued as adult, §7B-3507.
Embezzlement.
Civil liability, §1-538.2, (a) to (d).
Eminent domain.
Generally.
See EMINENT DOMAIN.
Right of entry prior to condemnation.
Action by owner for damages resulting, §40A-11.
Employee assistance professionals.
Civil action to enforce article, §90-506, (a).
Employee drug screening.
Recovery of civil penalty imposed, §95-234, (b).
Employee theft, §1-538.2, (a) to (d).
Employer discrimination for lawful use of lawful products during nonworking hours, §95-28.2, (e).
Employment security.
Claims for benefits, §96-15.
Equine activity liability.
Limiting and preventing liability generally, §§99E-1 to 99E-3.
Excise stamp tax.
Recoverable by action, §105-228.33.
Execution sales.
Defective title.
Remedy of purchaser against defendant, §1-323.
Executors and administrators.
Actions brought by or against in representative capacity, §28A-18-3.
Bonds, surety.
Action against obligors on bond, §28A-8-6.
Costs.
When costs against representative allowed, §28A-19-18.
Creditors.
When creditors may sue on claim, §28A-18-5.
False imprisonment.
Rights of action not surviving decedent, §28A-18-1.
Libel and slander.
Rights of actions which do not survive, §28A-18-1.
Liens.
Commencement of actions against personal representatives not lien, §28A-19-17.

ACTIONS —Cont'd
Executors and administrators —Cont'd
Representative capacity.
To sue or defend in representative capacity, §28A-18-3.
Revocation of letters.
Actions to continue, §28A-18-8.
Service on or appearance of one binds all, §28A-18-4.
Survival of actions, §28A-18-1.
Actions which do not survive, §28A-18-1, (b).
Venue of actions against executors and administrators, §1-78.
Wrongful death.
Power to maintain actions, §28A-13-3, (a).
Expedited evictions.
Nature of cause of action of landlord, §42-60.
Parties.
Defendants to action, §42-62, (b).
Who may bring action, §42-62, (a).
Standard of proof, §42-61.
Expenses of litigation.
See COSTS.
Facility authorities.
Powers of authority, §160A-480.4.
Fair housing, §41A-7, (h) to (k).
False pretenses and cheats.
Civil liability for obtaining property by, §1-538.2, (a) to (d).
Felony, forfeiture of gain, §14-2.3, (b).
Fiduciaries.
Claims against estate or trust.
Powers which may be incorporated by reference in trust instrument, §32-27.
Forfeiture of gain from felony, §14-2.3, (b).
Forms of action.
Civil actions, Const. N. C., art. IV, §13.
One form of action, §1A-1, Rule 2.
Forum selection.
Contracts with forum selection provisions.
Void and unenforceable, §22B-3.
Contracts to improve real property, §22B-2.
Frivolous actions.
Inmates presenting frivolous complaints.
Court determination, dismissal, §1-110, (b).
Gain from felony, forfeiture, §14-2.3, (b).
Geographically based field program.
Access to civil justice act, §§7A-474.1 to 7A-474.5.
Governor.
Employment of counsel in cases where state is interested, §147-17, (a).
Payment of counsel, §147-17, (c).
Grain dealers.
Action on bond, §106-605, (b).
Guardian's powers in administering incompetent's estate, §35A-1251.
Guardian's powers in administering minor ward's estate, §35A-1252.
Hazardous materials emergency response.
Action for recovery of costs, §166A-27.
Health.
Forfeiture of money or property unlawfully acquired, §130A-28.
Recovery of money or property, §130A-27.
Health benefit plans.
Negligent decisions of plan providers, §§90-21.50 to 90-21.56.
See HEALTH CARE LIABILITY.
Health care facilities.
Certificate of public advantage.
Decisions on issuing or allowing to remain in effect, §131E-192.10, (a) to (d).

ACTIONS —Cont'd
Highway construction contracts with department of transportation.
Civil action in lieu of claim by contractor, §136-29, (c).
Housing authorities and projects.
Remedies of obligee, §§157-18 to 157-22.
Husband and wife.
Quieting title, §41-10.
Torts between husband and wife, §52-5.
Acts arising outside state, §52-5.1.
Identity fraud.
Action for damages, §1-539.2C.
Illegitimacy.
Support of illegitimate children.
When prosecution may be commenced, §49-4.
Indigent persons.
Access to civil justice act, §§7A-474.1 to 7A-474.5.
See GEOGRAPHICALLY BASED FIELD PROGRAMS.
Affidavit that person unable to advance court costs, required to sue as indigent, §1-110, (a).
Courts may authorize person to sue as indigent, §1-110, (a).
Criteria for meeting status as indigent, §1-110, (a).
Dismissal of case and charge of court costs.
Allegations in affidavit untrue, §1-110, (a).
Inmates filing pro se motion to proceed as indigent, §1-110, (b).
Complaint frivolous, determination by court, dismissal, §1-110, (b).
Insurance.
Agents.
Soliciting agent represents the company, §58-58-30.
Unauthorized insurers.
Soliciting, negotiating or selling insurance for, §58-33-95, (b).
Brokers.
Unauthorized insurers.
Soliciting, negotiating or selling insurance for, §58-33-95, (b).
False statement to procure or deny benefit of policy or certificate, §58-2-161, (b).
Foreign or alien insurance company deposit liens, §58-5-70.
Fraud.
False statement to procure or deny benefit of policy or certificate, §58-2-161, (b).
Limited representatives.
Unauthorized insurers.
Soliciting, negotiating or selling insurance for, §58-33-95, (b).
Policies or contracts.
Conditions or stipulations.
Court or jurisdiction for bringing action or suit.
Prohibited, §58-3-35, (a).
Prohibited conditions or stipulations void, §58-3-35, (c).
Time for bringing action or suit.
Less than period prescribed by law, prohibited, §58-3-35, (b).
Soliciting agent represents the company, §58-58-30.
Supervision, rehabilitation and liquidation of insurers.
Rehabilitation.
Actions by and against rehabilitator, §58-30-90.

ACTIONS —Cont'd
Insurance —Cont'd
Surplus lines insurer.
Actions against, §58-21-100.
Unauthorized insurers, §§58-28-10, 58-28-15.
Insurance consumer and customer information privacy.
Action by individual for violations, §58-39-105.
Interlocal agreements concerning economic development.
Binding effect, action to specifically enforce, §158-7.4, (c).
International banking.
Actions against international banking corporations, §53-232.7.
Interstate family support.
Minor parent, §52C-3-302.
Inverse condemnation, §40A-51.
Investment advisers.
Civil liabilities for violations, §78C-38.
Jail keepers causing injuries to prisoners, §162-55.
Joint and several debtors, §§1-113, 1-114.
Journalist's qualified privilege against disclosure in any legal proceeding, §8-53.11, (b).
Definitions, §8-53.11, (a).
Eyewitness observation of criminal or tortuous conduct, no privilege, §8-53.11, (d).
Order to compel disclosure, notice to journalist and hearing, §8-53.11, (c).
Overcoming privilege, person seeking to compel disclosure, §8-53.11, (c).
Judgments.
Declaratory judgments, §§1-253 to 1-267.
See DECLARATORY JUDGMENTS.
Generally.
See JUDGMENTS.
Limitation of actions.
Periods prescribed generally, §1-46.
Ten-year limitation, §1-47.
Judicial sales.
Party to action by purchaser, §1-62.
Jurisdiction generally, §§1-75.1 to 1-75.12.
See JURISDICTION.
Jury duty, discharge of employee called to serve, §9-32, (b), (c).
Kinds of actions, §1-4.
Landlord and tenant.
Expedited evictions, §§42-60 to 42-62. See within this heading, "Expedited evictions."
Lien on crops.
Disputes between parties, §42-17.
Residential rental agreements.
Rights and remedies enforceable by civil action, §42-44, (a).
Tenant security deposit act.
Recovery of deposit, §42-55.
Law enforcement peer support group counselor's privilege, §8-53.10.
Leave for parent involved in school, discharge of employee, §95-28.3, (c).
Legal services of North Carolina, Inc.
Access to civil justice act.
See GEOGRAPHICALLY BASED FIELD PROGRAMS.
Libel and slander.
Notice.
Action against newspaper, §99-1, (a).
Action against radio or television station, §99-1, (b).

ACTIONS —Cont'd
Liens.
Failure to commence action for enforcement.
Discharge of liens, §44-48.
Mechanics, laborers and materialmen dealing with owner.
Enforcement of lien, §44A-13, (a).
Possessory liens on personal property.
Action to regain possession of motor vehicle or vessel, §44A-6.1, (a).
Immediate possession of property.
Action by owner or person dealing with lienor, §44A-4, (a).
Motor vehicles or vessels.
Action to regain possession, §44A-6.1.
Storage charges.
Action on debt, §44A-4, (a).
Limitation of actions.
See LIMITATION OF ACTIONS.
Limited liability companies.
Derivative actions by members, §57C-8-01.
Foreign limited liability companies.
Certificate of authority required to maintain action or proceeding in court, §57C-7-03, (a).
Members as parties to proceedings by or against company, §57C-3-30, (b).
Limited partnerships.
Suits by or against, §1-69.1.
Lis pendens, §§1-116 to 1-120.2.
Litigation expenses.
See COSTS.
Livestock prompt pay law.
Failure of payment, §106-418.6.
Local boards of education.
Against board.
Burden of proof on complaining party, §115C-44, (b).
Order or action of board presumed correct, §115C-44, (b).
Breach of bond by treasurer of county school fund.
County commissioners to institute action, §115C-44, (a).
Defense of members and employees, §115C-43, (a) to (c).
Recovery of money or property due board.
Board to institute action, §115C-44, (a).
Tort or negligence action against board, §115C-42.
Local government finance.
Bond issues.
Enforcement of contract of sale, §159-133.
Funding and refunding bonds.
Costs of actions validating bonds, §159-75.
Testing validity of funding or refunding bonds, §159-74.
Setting aside supplemental tax referendum, §159-97, (d).
Local government officers and employees.
Defense of civil actions or proceedings, §160A-167.
Local governments.
Notice of claims against local units of government, §1-539.16.
Mediation.
Superior court civil actions.
Court ordered mediated settlement conference.
Rules implementing, Super. Ct. Mediated Settlmt. Conf. R. 1 to 15.
Superior court civil cases.
Mediated settlement conferences, §7A-38.1.

ACTIONS —Cont'd
Medicaid.
False claims by providers, §§108A-70.12, 108A-70.13.
Objection to or failing to comply with civil investigative demand, §108A-70.14, (i).
Medical expenses at issue.
Testimony of injured party as to medical expenses, §8-58.1.
Medical payments programs administered under chapter 130A.
Assignment to state of rights to third party benefits, §130A-13, (a) to (d).
Mental health area authorities.
Defense of agents, employees and board members, §122C-153, (a) to (d).
Waiver of governmental tort immunity.
Purchase of liability insurance, §122C-152, (a) to (f).
Methamphetamine watch program.
Immunity from civil and criminal liability.
Good faith actions, §114-43.
Metropolitan sewerage districts.
Inclusion of additional political subdivision or unincorporated areas.
Limitation on action to set aside, §162A-68, (f).
Militia.
Recovery of organization owned property, §127A-118.
Milk distributors.
Liens on tangible and intangible assets of milk distributors, §44-69.3, (e).
Missing persons.
Receivers.
Power to bring or defend suits, §28C-8.
Monopolies and restraint of trade.
Attorney general.
Mandatory order.
Action to obtain, §75-14.
Prosecution of civil actions generally, §75-15.
Attorneys' fees, §75-16.1.
Limitation of actions, §75-16.2.
Right of action by person injured, §75-16.
Mortgages and deeds of trust.
Consumer home loans.
Enforcement of section, §24-10.2, (e).
Foreclosures.
Attacking certain foreclosures on ground trustee was agent, etc., of owner of debt.
Limitation of time for attacking, §45-21.39, (a).
Reverse mortgages.
Actions by borrowers for damages, §53-271, (d).
Motion picture fair competition.
Enforcement of provisions, §75C-5.
Motor fuel marketing violations, §75-86.
Motor vehicle dealers, §20-308.1.
Motor vehicle repairs.
Remedies for violation of article, §20-354.9.
Motor vehicles.
Odometer violations, §20-348, (b).
Limitation of actions, §20-348, (b).
Possessory liens on personal property.
Action to regain possession, §44A-6.1, (a).
Sublease and loan assumption arranging, §20-106.2, (f).
Uninsured motorists, §20-279.21, (b).
Mountain ridge protection.
Civil action against persons alleged in violation, §113A-211, (b).

ACTIONS —Cont'd
Municipal corporations.
Civil penalty.
Recovery, §160A-175, (c).
Defense of employees and officers, §160A-167.
Effect of chapter upon prior laws, §160A-2.
Joint municipal electric power and energy act.
Bond issues.
Venue for actions relating to bonds or security for bonds, §159B-37.
Remedies of bondholders, §159B-19.
Notice of claims against local units of government, §1-539.16.
Outdoor advertising.
Regulation of nonconforming off-premises outdoor advertising.
Payment of monetary compensation.
Determination of compensation, §160-199, (f).
Power to sue and be sued, §160A-11.
Public officers.
Retention of funds of town by delinquent official.
Citizen to recover funds, §128-10.
Natural and scenic rivers system violations, §113A-42, (a).
Negotiable instruments.
Accrual of actions, §25-3-118.
Limitation of actions, §25-3-118.
911 system.
Injuries, death or loss by act or omission of service suppliers.
Liability in civil actions for, §62A-10.
911 charges.
Action for collection, §62A-5, (b).
Nonprofit corporations.
Corporations already in existence, §55A-17-03, (b).
Creditors action against member, §55A-6-24.
Derivative actions, §55A-7-40.
Judicial dissolution, §§55A-14-30 to 55A-14-33.
Power to sue and be sued, §55A-3-02, (a).
Removal of director by judicial proceeding, §55A-8-10.
Unlawful loans or distributions by directors, §55A-8-33.
Voluntary dissolution.
Claims against dissolved corporations, §55A-14-09, (a).
Non-state entities receiving and using state funds.
Recovery of state funds, §143-6.2, (k).
Nonsuits.
See DISMISSAL, DISCONTINUANCE AND NONSUIT.
Nuisances.
Abatement.
Offenses against public morals, §§19-2.1, 19-2.2.
Subjects of actions, §1-539.
Nursing home patient's bill of rights, §131E-123.
Nursing homes.
Medical directors of licensed homes.
Limitation on liability, §90-21.18.
Odometer violations with intent to defraud, §20-348, (b).
Oil and gas conservation.
Department of environment and natural resources.
Suits by department, §113-399.
Oil pollution and hazardous substances control.
Offshore oil and gas activities, §§143-215.94DD, (b), (c), 143-215.94FF, (b), (c).

ACTIONS —Cont'd
Oil pollution and hazardous substances control —Cont'd
Removal of oil discharges.
Limitation on liability of persons engaged in, §143-215.93A.
One form of action, §1A-1, Rule 2.
Ordinances.
Recovery of civil penalty, §160A-175, (c).
Parental authority over juvenile.
Enforcement of parental authority, juvenile leaving home and refusing to return, §7B-3404.
Parent and child.
Malicious or willful destruction of property by minors.
Action for recovery of damages from parents, §1-538.1.
Negligent supervision of minor.
Right of educational entity to recover against parents, §1-538.3.
Parking authorities.
Allegations required in actions against authority, §160A-563.
Parties.
See PARTIES.
Partition, §§46-1 to 46-44.
See PARTITION.
Partnerships.
Dissolution and winding up.
Accrual of actions, §59-73.
Parties to suits by or against partnerships, §1-69.1.
Paternity, establishing, §49-14.
Pawnbrokers.
Bonds, surety.
Action on bond, §91A-14.
Perpetuation of testimony, §1A-1, Rule 27, (c).
Personal property.
Interference with property rights.
Recovery of damages, §99A-1.
Recovery of personal property, §1-230.
Pesticides.
Power of board to institute action in superior court, §143-461.
Planned community act.
Tort and contract liability.
Association and lot owners, §47F-3-111.
Pleadings.
See PLEADINGS.
Principals or teachers.
Allowance of counsel fees and costs in certain cases, §6-21.4.
Prisoners.
Limitation of actions.
Persons under disability on January 1, 1976 as result of being imprisoned.
When statute commences to run, §1-17, (a1).
Pro se motion to proceed as indigent, §1-110, (b).
Frivolous complaint, determination by court, dismissal, §1-110, (b).
Private personnel services.
Overstated earnings expectations from employers.
Fees reimbursement from employers due to, §95-47.3A, (e).
Products liability, §§99B-1 to 99B-11.
Profit from felony, forfeiture, §14-2.3, (b).
Prosecution bonds, §§1-109 to 1-112.
Indigent, suit as, §1-110, (a).

ACTIONS —Cont'd
Prosecution bonds —Cont'd
Land actions.
Defendant's bond for costs, §1-111.
Plaintiff not entitled to recover, certification by attorney.
Bond not required, §1-112, (a).
Summary ejectment.
Bond not required, §1-112, (b).
Unable to give bond, not worth amount, affidavit by defendant.
Bond not required, §1-112, (a).
Plaintiff's bond for costs, §1-109.
Prisoners.
Pro se motion to proceed as indigent, §1-110, (b).
Protest of tax collected and demand for refund, §105-267.
Psychotherapy patient/client sexual exploitation act, §90-21.42.
Public contracts.
Adjustment and resolution of state construction contract claim.
Civil action by contractor on portion of claim denied, §143-135.3, (d).
Contractors action on behalf of subcontractor, §143-134.2.
Public lands.
Attorney general, §§146-69, 146-70.
Grants.
Vacation of grants, §146-61.
State action, §146-63.
Institution of actions by state, §146-70.
Pending entries, §146-38.
Service of process on state in land actions, §146-69.
Public officers and employees.
Action to try title to office.
Quo warranto, §§1-514 to 1-532.
See QUO WARRANTO.
Counsel.
Employment of counsel in cases where state is interested, §147-17.
Describing party by official title rather than by name, §1A-1, Rule 25, (f).
Improper government activities.
Reporting.
Civil actions for injunctive relief or remedies, §126-86.
Retention of funds of county or town by delinquent official.
Citizen to recover funds, §128-10.
Public safety telephone service.
Service supplier.
Injuries, death or loss as result of act or omission.
Liability for damages in civil actions, §62A-10.
Public warehousemen.
Bonds, surety.
Injured person may sue on bond, §66-37.
Quieting title, §41-10.
Quo warranto.
General provisions, §§1-514 to 1-532.
See QUO WARRANTO.
Radiation protection.
Expenses of state and local agencies, §104E-17.
Real property.
Contracts to improve real property.
Provisions making contract subject to laws of another state.
Void as against public policy, §22B-2.

ACTIONS —Cont'd
Real property —Cont'd
Defendant's bond for costs and damages in land actions, §§1-111, 1-112, (a), (b).
Marketable title.
Prima facie evidence of title ownership, §47B-2, (d).
Quieting title, §41-10.
Receivers.
Powers of receivers of corporations, §1-507.2.
Recorded device.
Owner's action, §14-436.
Records.
Public records.
Compelling disclosure, §132-9, (b).
Relief from judgment or order, §1A-1, Rule 60, (b).
Religious societies.
Power of trustees to sue and be sued, §61-2.
Remainders, reversions and executory interests.
Grantees of reversion and assigns of lease have reciprocal rights under covenants, §42-8.
Rental referral agencies.
Damages from violations of provisions.
Action for damages, §66-146, (a).
Action on bond, §66-145, (c).
Repairs, remedies for violating article, §20-354.9.
Rescue squads.
Defense of employees or officers in civil or criminal actions, §160A-167.
Retaliatory employment discrimination, §95-243.
Right-to-sue letter, §95-242, (a) to (c).
Retirement system for counties and cities.
Deficiency in payment of benefits.
Commencement of action, §128-27, (i).
Retirement system for teachers and state employees.
Payment of benefits.
Commencement of actions, §135-5, (n).
Right of access to judicial proceeding or record.
Appeal of ruling, §1-72.1, (e).
Effect of provision on other laws, §1-72.1, (f).
Effect of provision on other types of relief, §1-72.1, (g).
Motion to determine, §1-72.1, (a).
Procedures upon filing of motion, §1-72.1, (b).
Ruling on motion, §1-72.1, (c).
Sealing of document or testimony, §1-72.1, (d).
Service of motion, §1-72.1, (b).
Status of movant, §1-72.1, (a).
Roller skating rink safety and liability, §§99E-10 to 99E-14.
Sales and use tax.
Overcollections by seller.
Cause of action against seller, notice required, §105-164.11, (c).
Sales commission, §66-192, (a).
Frivolous actions.
Liability, §66-192, (b).
Savings banks.
Involuntary liquidation.
Commencement by attorney general, §54C-83, (l).
School employees.
Defense of board of education members and employees, §115C-43, (a) to (c).

ACTIONS —Cont'd
Secondary action by shareholders, §1A-1, Rule 23, (b).
Securities regulation.
Civil liabilities generally, §78A-56.
Manipulation of market, §78A-56, (b1).
Shoplifting.
Civil liability, §1-538.2, (a) to (d).
Skateboarding, inline skating and freestyle bicycling.
Assumption of inherent risks, limitation on liability, §§99E-21 to 99E-25.
Skier safety and skiing accidents, §§99C-1 to 99C-5.
Small claim actions, §§7A-210 to 7A-232.
See SMALL CLAIM ACTIONS.
Soil and water conservation districts.
Invalidity of expenditures, §139-8.1, (d).
Land-use regulations.
Enforcement, §§139-10, 139-11.
Special education.
Administrative review.
Right to file civil action, §115C-116, (k).
State.
Employment of counsel in cases where state is interested, §147-17.
State departments and agencies.
Deposit in unlawful depository.
Recovery of deposit, §147-80.
Executive organization act of 1973.
Pending actions and proceedings, §143B-19.
State treasurer.
Deposits in unlawful depository.
Recovery, §147-80.
May demand and sue for money and property of state, §147-71.
Statutes.
Repeal of statute not to affect actions, §12-2.
Statutes of limitation.
See LIMITATION OF ACTIONS.
Strawberry plant sellers.
Collection of assessment owed association, §106-785, (d).
Streets and highways.
Condemnation, §§136-103 to 136-121.1.
See STREETS AND HIGHWAYS.
County public roads incorporated into state highway system.
No court action against board of transportation, §136-59.
Sublease of motor vehicles and loan assumption arranging.
Violations of provisions, §20-106.2, (f).
Surety's recovery on obligation paid.
No assignment necessary, §26-3.1, (a).
Construction of term "surety," §26-3.1, (b).
Taxation.
Extraterritorial authority to enforce payment, §105-269.
Overpayment of tax.
Action to recover, §105-266.1, (c).
Precedence over other civil actions, §105-246.
Property taxes.
Foreclosure of tax lien.
Action in nature of action to foreclose mortgage, §105-374.
Public utilities.
Action for recovery of tax, §105-344.
Recovery of taxes by taxpayers, §105-381, (c), (d).

ACTIONS —Cont'd
Taxation —Cont'd
Protest of tax collected and demand for refund, §105-267.
Recovery of taxes, §§105-239, 105-241.4, 105-243.
Suits in other state to enforce collection, §105-269, (a).
Teachers or principals.
Allowance of counsel fees and costs in certain cases, §6-21.4.
Telephone solicitations.
Action by subscriber for violation, §75-105, (b).
Attorneys' fees, awarding, §75-105, (d).
Enforcement of federal law, §75-105, (e).
Mistake by solicitor, no action for, §75-105, (c).
Venue, §75-105, (f).
Theft by employees, §1-538.2, (a) to (d).
Time share violations.
Right of action by person injured by, §93A-55.
Title.
Quieting title, §41-10.
Torrens system registration.
Adverse claims.
Limitation of action, §43-19.
Assurance fund.
Action for indemnity, §43-50.
Trade secret misappropriation.
Limitation of actions, §66-157.
Preservation of secrecy by court, §66-156.
Right of action, §66-153.
Transportation department.
Enforcement of causes of action, §136-18.
Trespass.
Marketable title.
Prima facie evidence of title ownership, §47B-2, (d).
Trust companies.
Liability of directors for violation of provisions.
Action by shareholder, §53-356, (b).
Power of commissioner to bring actions, §53-413.
Trusts and trustees.
Charitable trusts.
Action for account, §36A-48.
Powers of trustees under express trust, §36A-136.
Unclaimed property act.
By another state on behalf of state, §116B-76, (d).
Enforcement of chapter by treasurer, §116B-75, (a).
Establishment of claim to property, §116B-68.
Limitation of action, proceeding by treasurer to enforce provisions, §116B-71, (b).
On behalf of another state, §116B-76, (c).
Underground petroleum storage tank leak cleanup.
Injunctive relief, §143-215.94Y.
Recovery of unpaid civil penalties by attorney general, §143-215.94W, (f).
Underground storage tanks.
Leaking petroleum cleanup.
Actions for fund reimbursement, §143-215.94G, (d), (e).
Groundwater protection loan fund.
Default or violation of loan agreement, §143-215.94P, (e).
Uniform contribution among tort-feasors, §§1B-1 to 1B-6.
Unincorporated associations, organizations, etc.
Suits by or against, §1-69.1.
Uninsured motorists, §20-279.21, (b).

ACTIONS —Cont'd
Unit ownership.
Common interests, §47A-26.
Exhaustion of remedies against association, §47A-26.
Service of process on designated agent, §47A-26.
University of North Carolina.
Nuclear reactors.
Damage or personal property arising from construction or operation of, §116-40.2.
Self-insurance.
Defense of suits or actions against covered persons, §116-220, (d).
Urban redevelopment.
Obligee of commission, §160A-518.
Venue.
General provisions, §§1-76 to 1-87.
See VENUE.
Vessel liens.
Action to regain possession, §44A-6.1, (a).
Veterans' recreation authorities.
Power to sue and be sued, §165-31.
Viatical settlements, §58-58-290, (b).
Victims of crime.
Recovery of profits or funds, §15B-35, (a).
Commission, responsibilities of, §15B-35, (c).
Visitation.
Action or proceeding for custody or visitation, §50-13.1.
Adopted grandchild, §50-13.2A.
Wages.
Recovery of unpaid wages, §95-25.22.
Water and air resources.
Civil penalties, §143-215.6A, (g).
Water and sewer authorities.
Riparian owners.
Actions against authority by, §162A-18.
Witnesses.
Arrest in civil cases.
Exemptions, §8-64.
Fees of witnesses, §6-53.
Hearing impaired.
Appointment of interpreters authorized, §8B-2.
Women's credit rights.
Enforcement of article, §25B-3, (a).
Workers' compensation.
Fines and penalties.
Collection by industrial commission, §97-101.
Insurance or proof of financial ability to pay benefits.
Actions against employers failing to comply with provisions, §97-95.
Workplace violence prevention.
Civil no-contact orders, §§95-265 to 95-276.
See WORKPLACE VIOLENCE PREVENTION.
Wrongful death.
Cause of action permitted, §28A-18-2.

ACTION TO PERPETUATE TESTIMONY, §1A-1, Rule 27, (c).

ACTIVITY BUSES.
Defects, §115C-248, (d).
Defined, §20-4.01.
Inspection, §115C-248, (d).
Maximum speed, §20-218, (b), (c).
Operating after consuming alcohol, §20-138.2B.
Purchase by local boards of education, §§115C-47, 115C-247.
Stopping at railroad grade crossings, §20-142.3, (a).

ACTORS.
Children and minors.
Artistic and creative services and talent agency contracts, §§48A-11 to 48A-18.
Wage and hour act.
Exemptions, §95-25.14, (a).
Youth employment, exemption from provisions, §95-25.5, (g).

ACTS.
Coded bill drafting, §120-20.1.
Francis X. Martin.
Collection of private acts.
Evidence, §8-2.
General laws.
Defined, Const. N. C., art. XIV, §3.
Style of the acts, Const. N. C., art. II, §21.
When acts take effect, §120-20.

ACTS BARRING PROPERTY RIGHTS.
Adultery, §31A-1, (a).
Killing decedent generally, §§31A-3 to 31A-15.
See SLAYER ACT.

ACTS BARRING RIGHTS OF PARENTS, §31A-2.

ACTUARIES.
Insurance commissioner hiring qualifications, §58-2-171.
Legislative actuarial notes.
Amendments in law relative to retirement system, §120-114.
Citation of act, §120-112.
Generally, §120-114.
Research division of legislative services commission.
Duties, §120-113.
Functions, §120-113.
Title of article, §120-112.
Mortality tables, §§8-46, 8-47.
Retirement system for counties and cities.
Board of trustees.
Duties of actuary, §128-28, (m) to (p).
Retirement system for general assembly.
Actuarial notes, §§120-112 to 120-114.
Retirement system for teachers and state employees.
Board of trustees to keep actuarial data, §135-6, (h).
Definition of actuarial equivalent, §135-53.
Duties of actuary, §135-6, (l) to (o).
Small employer group health coverage.
Certification, §58-50-130, (f).

ACUPUNCTURE.
Activities prohibited, §90-456.
Child support enforcement.
Forfeiture of licensing privilege, §50-13.12.
Chiropractors.
Exemption from licensing, §90-452, (b).
Definitions, §90-451.
Display of license, §90-458.
Exemptions.
Practice of acupuncture, §90-452, (b).
Fees, §90-457.
Felony convictions.
Forfeiture of license, §15A-1331A.
Identification badges required, §90-640.
Legislative declaration.
Purpose of, §90-450.
Licenses.
Display, §90-458.
Fees, §90-457.

ACUPUNCTURE —Cont'd
Licenses —Cont'd
Forfeiture.
Felony convictions, §15A-1331A.
Initial license, §90-455, (a).
Renewal, §90-455, (b).
Fee, §90-457.
Licensing board.
Compensation of members, §90-453, (d).
Duties, §90-454.
Meetings, §90-453, (c).
Membership, §90-453, (a).
Powers, §90-454.
Terms of members, §90-453, (b).
Names.
Use of title, §90-458.
Physicians and surgeons.
Exemption from licensing, §90-452, (b).
Practice of acupuncture.
Defined, §90-451.
Exemptions, §90-452, (b).
Unlawful acts, §90-452, (a).
Prohibited activities, §90-456.
Purpose of article, §90-450.
Reimbursements by third-party, §90-459.
Students practicing acupuncture.
Exemption from licensure, §90-452, (b).
Third-party reimbursements, §90-459.
Titles.
Use, §90-458.

AD DAMNUM CLAUSE.
Pleadings, §1A-1, Rule 8.

ADDITIONAL TIME AFTER SERVICE BY MAIL, §§1-593, 1A-1, Rule 6, (e).

ADDRESS CONFIDENTIALITY PROGRAM, §§15C-1 to 15C-13.
Application to participate, §15C-4, (a) to (c).
Assistance for applicants, §15C-10.
Falsifying application information, §15C-6.
Assistance for applicants, §15C-10.
Authorization card, §15C-4, (d), (e).
Boards of elections.
Substitute address, use by, §15C-8, (e).
Cancellation of certification of participant, §15C-7, (a) to (c).
Change of address or telephone number of participant.
Notification of attorney general, §15C-5, (b).
Change of name of participant.
Notification of attorney general, §15C-5, (a).
Definitions, §15C-2.
Disclosure of address, §15C-9, (a), (c).
Notification, §15C-9, (b).
Prohibited acts, §15C-9, (d), (e).
Penalties, §15C-9, (f).
Established, §15C-3.
Falsifying application information, §15C-6.
Immunities, §15C-11.
Marriage licenses.
Form of license for program participant, §51-16.1.
Public schools.
Actual address and telephone number of participants confidential, §115C-402, (f).
Assignment or admission purposes.
Use of actual address, confidentiality, §115C-366, (g).
Use of substitute address by administrative units, §15C-8, (i).
Purpose of provisions, §15C-1.

ADDRESS CONFIDENTIALITY PROGRAM —Cont'd
Registers of deeds.
Substitute address, use by, §15C-8, (h).
Rulemaking, §15C-12.
Substitute address.
Agencies of North Carolina.
Use by, §15C-8, (a) to (d).
Attorney general to designate, §15C-3.
Boards of elections.
Use by, §15C-8, (e).
Cessation of participation in program.
Notification to persons who use substitute address, §15C-7, (e).
Elections.
Use by boards of elections, §15C-8, (e).
Public record.
Not deemed to be, §15C-8, (j).
Registers of deeds.
Use by, §15C-8, (h).
School administrative units.
Use by, §15C-8, (i).
Taxation.
Use for purposes of, §15C-8, (f), (g).
Taxation.
Substitute address.
Use for purposes of, §15C-8, (f), (g).
Time.
Additional time for participants, §§1A-1, Rule 6, (f), 15C-13.

ADDRESSING ENVELOPES.
Work-at-home solicitations, advertising restrictions, §75-31.

ADET SCHOOLS.
Limited driving privilege, §20-179.3, (g2).
Restoration of license after conviction.
Obtaining certificate of completion, §20-17.6, (c).

ADJOURNMENT.
Clerks of court, §7A-103.
Congress, Const. U. S., art. I, §§5, 7; art. II, §3.
Sheriffs.
Superior courts.
Court adjourned by sheriff when judge not present, §7A-96.
Superior courts.
Sheriff to adjourn court when judge not present, §7A-96.

ADJUDICATION OF INCOMPETENCY, §§35A-1101 to 35A-1116.
See INCOMPETENCE.

ADJUDICATORY HEARINGS.
Abused, neglected or dependent juveniles, §§7B-801 to 7B-807.
Delinquent and undisciplined juvenile actions, §§7B-2403 to 7B-2412.

ADJUSTABLE INTEREST RATES.
Equity lines of credit, §24-1.2A, (a).

ADJUSTERS.
Debt adjusters, §§14-423 to 14-426.
Insurance adjusters generally.
See INSURANCE ADJUSTERS.

ADJUTANT GENERAL, §§127A-19, 127A-20.
Administrative and operational matters.
Relationships of adjutant general, §127A-20.
Appointment, §127A-19.
Assistant adjutant general for air national guard.
Appointment, §127A-19.

ADJUTANT GENERAL —Cont'd
Assistant adjutant general for army national guard.
Appointment, §127A-19.
Military head of militia, §127A-19.
Qualifications, §127A-19.
Staff members and other personnel, §127A-19.

ADMINISTRATION DEPARTMENT.
Allocation of property and space.
Rules governing, §143-342.
Appropriations.
Emergency contingent fund, §143-19.
Transfer of funds, property, records, etc., §143-344, (d).
Budget.
Appropriations.
Emergency contingent fund, §143-19.
Itemized statements and forms, §143-7.
Capital facilities finance act.
Generally, §§142-80 to 142-101.
See CAPITAL FACILITIES FINANCE ACT.
Capital planning commission.
Appointment, §143B-374, (a).
Clerical and other services, §143B-374, (b).
Composition, §143B-374, (a).
Creation, §143B-373, (a).
Duties, §143B-373, (a), (d).
Ex officio members, §143B-374, (a).
Expenses, §143B-374, (b).
Information to be provided to, §143B-373, (b), (c).
Meetings, §143B-374, (b).
Powers and duties, §143B-373, (a), (d).
Public lands.
State governmental complex, §146-22.1.
Quorum, §143B-374, (b).
Records.
Turned over to department of administration, §143B-374, (b).
Citation of article, §143-334.
Coal and petroleum suppliers.
Authority to collect data, §143-345.14, (a).
Civil enforcement, §143-345.14, (e).
Confidentiality of information, §143-345.14, (f).
Definitions, §143-345.14, (b), (f).
Refusal to supply data, §143-345.14, (d).
Rulemaking authority, §143-345.14, (c).
Stocks of coals and petroleum fuel capacity.
Reporting requirements, §143-345.13.
Contingency and emergency fund.
Use for construction and repair of public buildings, §143-345.3.
Costs.
Publications.
Statement of cost, §143-170.1.
Courier.
Evidence.
Chain of custody, §8-103.
Court of appeals.
Providing adequate quarters for court, §7A-19, (b).
Creation, §§143-335, 143B-366.
Definitions, §143-336.
Publications, §143-169.2.
Stocks of coal and petroleum fuels, §143-345.14, (b), (f).
Disorderly conduct in buildings, §143-345.2.
Domestic violence commission, §§143B-394.15, 143B-394.16.
Duties, §§143-341, 143B-367, 143B-368.
Functions, §143B-368, (a).

ADMINISTRATION DEPARTMENT —Cont'd
Energy improvement loan program, §§143-345.16 to 143-345.18.
Established, §143B-366.
Evacuation of state buildings and grounds.
Fire, bombs, bomb threats or other emergencies, §143-341.1.
Executive mansion.
Authority of department of administration not affected, §143-415.
Farmworker council, §§143B-426.25, 143B-426.26.
Fees.
Use of state-owned office space by self-supporting agencies, §143-342.1.
Flags.
Official "prisoner of war/missing in action" flag.
State capitol.
Department authorized to fly on certain holidays, §143-345.9.
Functions of department, §143B-368, (a).
Funds.
Contingency and emergency fund.
Use for construction and repair of public buildings, §143-345.3.
Future public buildings.
Program for location and construction, §143-345.5.
General services division.
Addition to administrative department, §143-343.
Governor's management council, §§143B-426.22, 143B-426.23.
Clerical services report, §143B-426.23.
Creation, §143B-426.22, (a).
Within department of administration, §143B-426.22, (a).
Meetings, §143B-426.23.
Membership, §143B-426.22, (a).
Powers and duties, §143B-426.22, (b).
Reports.
Annual report, §143B-426.23.
Head of department, §143B-369.
Internship council.
Clerical services, §143B-418.
Compensation, §143B-418.
Creation, §143B-417.
Duties, §143B-417.
Members, §143B-418.
Powers and duties, §143B-417.
Quorum, §143B-418.
Selection of members, §143B-418.
Mailing lists.
Updating, §143-169.1.
Certification, §143-169.1, (a).
Name, §143B-366.
North Carolina art society.
Authorization to provide space for art society, §140-12.
Office space.
Fees for use of state-owned office space by self-supporting agencies, §143-342.1.
Pistols, revolvers, shotguns or rifles.
Sale to local government, law enforcement agency or state, §143-63.1, (b).
Destruction of unsold weapons, §143-63.1, (c).
Powers and duties, §§143-341, 143B-367, 143B-368.
Functions, §143B-368, (a).
Progress board, §§143B-372.1 to 143B-372.3.
Property.
Surplus property of state.
State agency.
Federal surplus property, §§143-64.1 to 143-64.5.

ADMINISTRATION DEPARTMENT —Cont'd
Property —Cont'd
Surplus property of state —Cont'd
State agency —Cont'd
General provisions, §§143-64.01 to 143-64.05.
Transfer of property, §143-344, (b).
Appropriations, §143-344, (d).
Saving clause, §143-345.
Supervision of governor, §143-344, (c).
Publications.
Administrative review procedures for public documents, §143-170.2, (c).
State departments and agencies.
Failure to comply with provisions, §143-170.3, (a), (b).
Cost of public documents.
Reduction in printing budget for failure to comply with section, §143-170.1, (a3).
Statement of cost, §143-170.1, (a), (a1), (b).
Definitions, §143-169.2.
Limitations upon, §143-169.
Mailing lists.
Updating, §143-169.1.
North Carolina purchase directory, §143-345.8.
Procedures manuals for public documents, §143-170.2.
Administrative office of the courts, §143-170.4.
Alkaline paper.
Designated public documents to be printed on, §143-170.5.
Consultation with certain state departments and agencies, §143-170.2, (a).
Guidelines.
Final guidelines, §143-170.2, (b), (d1).
Initial guidelines, §143-170.2, (a).
Production elements for public documents, §143-170.2, (a).
Reporting requirements.
Failure to comply with provisions, §143-170.3, (a), (b).
Published at expense of state, §143-169, (b).
Recycling and reuse requirements.
Applicability, §143-169, (c).
Statement that document printed on recycled paper, §143-170.1, (a2).
Statement of cost of public documents, §143-170.1, (a), (a1), (b).
Public buildings and grounds.
Construction and repair of public buildings.
Use of contingency and emergency fund, §143-345.3.
Defined, §143-336.
Disorderly conduct in and injury to public buildings and grounds, §143-345.2.
Future public buildings.
Program for location and construction, §143-345.5.
Program for location and construction of future public buildings, §143-345.5.
Raleigh.
Moore and Nash squares and other public lots, §143-345.4.
Secretary powers and duties, §143-340.
Western residence of the governor.
Repair and reconstruction, §143-345.7.
Public employee deferred compensation plan.
Board of trustees, §143B-426.24.
Public employee special pay plan.
Board of trustees, §143B-426.41.
Public lands, §§146-1 to 146-83.
See PUBLIC LANDS.

ADMINISTRATION DEPARTMENT —Cont'd
Records transfer, §143-344, (b).
Appropriations, §143-344, (d).
Saving clause, §143-345.
Supervision of governor, §143-344, (c).
Reports.
Conciseness, §143-168.
Farmworker council, §143B-426.26, (b).
Governor's management council.
Annual report, §143B-426.23.
Publications.
State departments and agencies.
Failure to comply with reporting requirements, §§143-170.3, 143-170.4.
Rules and regulations.
Allocation of property and space, §143-342.
Governor shall adopt, §143-345.1.
Sale of merchandise by governmental units.
Exception to prohibition, §66-58, (b).
Saving clause.
Transfer of functions, §143-345.
School buses.
Purchase through department, §115C-249, (g).
Science and technology.
Board of science and technology, §§143B-472.80, 143B-472.81.
Secretary.
Duties, §143-340.
Head of department, §143B-369.
Powers, §143-340.
Public lands.
Service of process on state in land actions, §146-69.
Streets and highways.
Test drilling or boring.
Filing record of results with secretary, §136-102.3.
Self-supporting agencies using state-owned office space.
Fees, §143-342.1.
Short title, §143-334.
State energy office.
Guaranteed energy savings contracts.
Evaluation of use by state agencies.
Adoption of rules for evaluation, §143-64.17F, (b).
Recommendations as to savings, §143-64.17F, (c).
State veterans home.
Administration and operation, §165-46.
Streets and highways.
Test drilling or boring.
Filing record of results with secretary of administration, §136-102.3.
Surplus property of state.
State agency.
Federal surplus property, §§143-64.1 to 143-64.5.
General provisions, §§143-64.01 to 143-64.05.
Transfer of functions, §143-344, (b).
Appropriations, §143-344, (d).
Saving clause, §143-345.
Supervision of governor, §143-344, (c).
Veterans affairs department.
Transfer to department of administration, §143A-96.1.
Veterans homes.
Operation and administration, §165-46.
Youth councils.
Compensation of members, §143B-386.
Creation, §143B-385.

ADMINISTRATION DEPARTMENT —Cont'd
Youth councils —Cont'd
Duties, §143B-385.
Local youth council.
Purposes, §143B-388.
Members, §143B-386.
Powers and duties, §143B-385.
Purposes, §143B-388.
Quorum, §143B-386.
Selection of members, §143B-386.
State youth council.
Established, §143B-387.
Powers and duties, §143B-387.

ADMINISTRATION OF ESTATES.
Decedents' estates.
See DECEDENTS' ESTATES.
Executors and administrators.
See EXECUTORS AND ADMINISTRATORS.
Mentally ill and developmentally disabled, §7A-307.
Principal and income act.
General provisions, §§37A-1-101 to 37A-6-602.
See PRINCIPAL AND INCOME ACT.

ADMINISTRATIVE CODE AND REGISTRY.
Publication generally, §§150B-21.17 to 150B-21.25.
See PUBLICATION OF ADMINISTRATIVE CODE AND REGISTER.
Rebuttable presumption rule adopted.
Entry in administrative code, §150B-21.9, (a1).

ADMINISTRATIVE HEARINGS, OFFICE OF, §§7A-750 to 7A-759.
Administrative law judges.
Additional judges, §7A-753.
Appointment, §7A-753.
Availability to exempt agencies, §7A-758.
Expenses.
Reimbursement, §7A-755.
Temporary judges, §7A-757.
Longevity pay, §7A-151, (b).
Oaths, §7A-754.
Power to administer oaths, §7A-756.
Private practice of law, §7A-754.
Qualifications, §7A-754.
Reimbursement for expenses, §7A-755.
Removal from office, §7A-754.
Salary, §7A-151, (b).
Senior judge.
Designation by chief judge, §7A-152.
Performance of duties of chief judge.
Chief judge absent or unable to serve, §7A-152.
Specialization, §7A-753.
Subpoenas, §7A-756.
Temporary judges, §7A-757.
Age discrimination in employment.
Deferral agency, §7A-759, (b1).
Chief administrative law judge.
Absence or unable to serve.
Senior judge to perform duties, §7A-152.
Appointment, §7A-152.
Head of office, §7A-151, (a).
Longevity pay, §7A-151, (a).
Salary, §7A-151, (a).
Term, §7A-152.
Creation, §7A-750.
Deferral agency, §7A-759, (a) to (i).
Confidentiality, §7A-759, (g).
Contested cases, §7A-759, (d), (e).

ADMINISTRATIVE HEARINGS, OFFICE OF —Cont'd
Deferral agency —Cont'd
Contracts to serve as deferral agency, §7A-759, (b).
Designation, §7A-759, (a).
Federal authority not limited, §7A-759, (h).
Investigations, §7A-759, (c).
Monetary compliance with settlement or compromise, §7A-759, (f).
Duties, §7A-750.
E.E.O.C. actions.
Deferral agency, §7A-759, (b1).
Enforcement of powers, §7A-756.
Exempt agencies, §7A-758.
Availability of administrative law judges to, §7A-758.
Expenses reimbursed, §7A-755.
Head of office.
Chief administrative law judge, §7A-151, (a).
Municipal corporations.
Availability of administrative law judges to, §7A-758.
Oaths, §§7A-754, 7A-756, 7A-759, (c).
Political subdivisions.
Availability of administrative law judges to, §7A-758.
Purpose, §7A-750.
Qualifications of administrative law judges, §7A-754.
Reimbursement of expenses, §7A-755.
Removal of administrative law judges, §7A-754.
Salary.
Administrative law judges, §7A-151, (b).
Chief administrative law judge, §7A-151, (a).
Senior judge.
Designation by chief judge, §7A-152.
Performance of duties of chief judge.
Chief judge absent or unable to serve, §7A-152.
Specialization of administrative law judges, §7A-753.
Standards of conduct, §7A-754.
Status, §7A-750.
Subpoena issuance, §7A-756.
Subpoenas, §7A-756.
Temporary judges, §7A-757.

ADMINISTRATIVE LAW JUDGES, §150B-40, (e).
Administrative procedure generally, §§150B-1 to 150B-52.
See ADMINISTRATIVE PROCEDURE.
Assignment, §150B-32, (a).
Decisions, §§150B-34, (a), 150B-36, (d).
Applicability of provisions, §150B-34, (d).
Finality, §150B-36, (c).
Judgment on pleadings, power to grant, §150B-36, (d).
Recommended decisions, §150B-34, (c).
Adoption by agency, §150B-36, (b3).
Disqualification, §150B-32, (b), (c).
Ex parte communications.
Prohibited, §150B-35.
Office of administrative hearings.
See ADMINISTRATIVE HEARINGS, OFFICE OF.
Powers, §150B-33, (b).
Stays, §150B-33, (a).

ADMINISTRATIVE OFFICE OF THE COURTS, §§7A-340 to 7A-346.
Abused, neglected or dependent juvenile actions.
Guardian ad litem program to provide services, §§7B-1200 to 7B-1204.

ADMINISTRATIVE OFFICE OF THE COURTS —Cont'd
Advance sheets.
Contracting for printing of advance sheets, §7A-6, (b).
Designation of commercial advance sheets as official reports, §7A-6, (b1).
Furnishing of advance sheets, §7A-6, (c).
Sale of advance sheets, §7A-6, (b).
Remittance of proceeds of sale, §7A-6, (b).
Appellate division reports.
Distribution of copies, §7A-343.1.
Assistant director.
Appointment, §7A-342.
Compensation, §7A-342.
Duties, §7A-345.
Bad checks.
Collection of fees and restitution, §14-107.2, (a1), (d).
Reporting worthless check collection, §7A-346.2.
Worthless checks collection program.
Collection of worthless checks fund, §7A-308, (c).
Fees, superior court clerks, §7A-308, (c).
Contracts.
Assistant clerks.
Local government funding, §7A-102, (g).
Deputy clerks.
Local government funding, §7A-102, (g).
Judicial secretaries.
Local government funding, §7A-44.1, (d).
Copies.
Appellate division reports.
Distribution of copies, §7A-343.1.
Courts commission.
Ex officio member, §7A-507.
Director.
Appointment, §7A-341.
Assistant clerks.
Local funding assistance, §7A-102, (f).
Compensation, §7A-341.
Deputy clerks.
Local funding assistance, §7A-102, (f).
Duties, §7A-343.
Judicial secretaries.
Local funding assistance, §7A-44.1, (c).
Service equivalent to service as superior court judge, §7A-341.
Supervision of office, §7A-340.
Voting rights act of 1965.
Duties as to, §§120-30.9C, 120-30.9H.
Disability.
Retirement on account of total and permanent disability, §7A-55.
Applicability of provisions, §7A-56.
District attorneys, temporary assistance to, §7A-64.
Drug treatment courts, §§7A-790 to 7A-801.
See DRUG TREATMENT COURTS.
Duties of director, §7A-343.
Elections.
Submission of acts to United States attorney general, §120-30.9C.
Electronic access to superior court records in clerks office.
Contracts to provide public, §7A-109, (d), (e).
Employees.
Appointment, §7A-342.
Compensation, §7A-342.
Health and safety programs.
Authority of administrative office to establish, §143-589.

ADMINISTRATIVE OFFICE OF THE COURTS —Cont'd
Establishment, §7A-340.
Expungement of criminal records.
Confidential file of persons granted, §15A-146, (c).
Family court fee, §7A-314.1, (a).
Reduction, procedure, §7A-314.1, (b).
Guardian ad litem program.
Providing services to abused, neglected or dependent juveniles, §§7B-1200 to 7B-1204.
Indigent defense services.
Budgeting process, §7A-498.2, (e).
Clerical support, §7A-498.2, (c).
Information to be furnished to administrative officer, §7A-346.
Law clerks.
Salaries of law clerks set by administrative officer, §7A-7, (a).
Motor vehicle license plates.
Special license plate issuable to director, §20-79.4, (b).
Office of guardian ad litem services.
Established within administrative office of the courts, §7B-1200.
Officers, §7A-340.
Registration and indexing of testamentary trusts, §36A-108.
Reports.
Appellate division reports.
Distribution of copies, §7A-343.1.
Contracting for printing of reports, §7A-6, (b).
Designation of commercial reports as official report, §7A-6, (b1).
Legislative reporting.
Local government services contracts, §7A-346.2, (a).
Worthless check collection, §7A-346.2, (b).
Sale of reports, §7A-6, (b).
Remittance of proceeds of sale, §7A-6, (b).
Research assistants.
Salaries of research assistants set by administrative officer, §7A-7, (a).
Retirement.
Age requirements, §7A-51, (a) to (e).
Applicability of provisions, §7A-56.
Compensation for retirement, §7A-51, (a) to (e).
Applicability of provisions, §7A-56.
On account of total and permanent disability, §7A-55.
Applicability of provisions, §7A-56.
Service requirements, §7A-51, (a) to (e).
Applicability of provisions, §7A-56.
Safety and health programs for employees.
Authority to establish, §143-589.
Secretaries.
Determination of number and salaries of secretary, §7A-7, (b).
Sentencing services act, §§7A-770 to 7A-777.
See SENTENCING SERVICES.
Setoff debt collection, §§105A-1 to 105A-16.
See SETOFF DEBT COLLECTION.
Stenographers.
Determination of number and salaries of stenographers, §7A-7, (b).
Supervision of office, §7A-340.
Temporary assistance to district attorneys, §7A-64.
Termination of parental rights proceedings.
Payment of fees of court appointed guardian ad litem and court appointed counsel, §7B-1101.

ADMINISTRATIVE OFFICE OF THE COURTS —Cont'd
Total and permanent disability.
Retirement on account of, §7A-55.
Applicability of provisions, §7A-56.

ADMINISTRATIVE PROCEDURE, §§150B-1 to 150B-52.
Administrative code.
Publication generally, §§150B-21.17 to 150B-21.25.
Rebuttable presumption rule adopted.
Entry in administrative code, §150B-21.9, (a1).
Administrative hearings, office of, §§7A-750 to 7A-759. See within this heading, "Office of administrative hearings."
Administrative law judge.
Defined, §150B-2.
Agencies.
Defined, §150B-2.
Alcoholic beverages.
Applicability, §18B-906.
Ambulatory surgical facilities.
Adverse action on licenses.
Applicability of provisions, §131E-148, (b).
Answers.
Hearings, §150B-38, (d).
Appeals, §§150B-43 to 150B-52.
Appellate division, §150B-52.
Evidence.
New evidence, §150B-49.
Intervention.
Motion to intervene, §150B-46.
Jury.
Review by court without jury, §150B-50.
Manner of seeking review, §150B-45.
New evidence, §150B-49.
Petitions.
Contents, §150B-46.
Copies served on all parties, §150B-46.
Time for filing petition, §150B-45.
Power of court in disposing of case, §150B-51, (d).
Records, §150B-47.
Contents, §150B-47.
Costs, §150B-47.
Filing with clerk of superior court, §150B-47.
Review by court without jury, §150B-50.
Right to judicial review, §150B-43.
Decision unreasonably delayed, §150B-44.
Scope of review, §150B-51, (a), (a1), (c).
Service of process.
Copies of petition served on all parties, §150B-46.
Standard of review, §150B-51, (b).
Stays, §150B-48.
Obtaining stay of court's decision, §150B-52.
Unreasonable delay of decision.
Right to judicial intervention, §150B-44.
Waiver, §150B-45.
Applicability of provisions.
Exemptions, §150B-1, (c) to (f).
Assisted living administrators, applicability, §90-288.18, (b).
Banks.
Hearings.
Special provisions, §§150B-38 to 150B-42.
Cardiac rehabilitation certification program.
Adverse action on certificates, §131E-168, (b).
Code.
Publication generally, §§150B-21.17 to 150B-21.21.

ADMINISTRATIVE PROCEDURE —Cont'd
Codifier of rules.
Defined, §150B-2.
Publication of code and register.
Copies of register and code.
Distribution of free copies, §150B-21.24.
North Carolina administrative code.
Authority to revise form of rules, §150B-21.20, (a).
Duties, §150B-21.18.
Effect of codifier's revision of rule, §150B-21.20, (b).
North Carolina register.
Duties, §150B-21.17.
Publication of manual, §150B-21.23.
Commission.
Defined, §150B-2.
Community colleges.
Construction contract claims.
Adjustment and resolution, §143-135.6, (a) to (c).
State board of community colleges.
Applicability of administrative procedure act, §115D-80.
Consolidation.
Hearings, §150B-26.
Contested cases.
Commencement, §150B-23, (a).
Time for filing petition, §150B-23, (f).
Defined, §150B-2.
Exemptions, §150B-1, (e).
Hearings.
Generally, §§150B-22 to 150B-42. See within this heading, "Hearings."
Prehearing statement, filing, §150B-23, (a2).
Settlement through informal procedures, §150B-22.
Declaratory rulings, §150B-4, (a).
Definitions, §150B-2.
Depositions, §150B-39, (a).
Hearings, §§150B-28, (a), 150B-39, (a).
Subpoenas.
Witness fees, §150B-39, (c).
Discovery, §150B-39, (b).
Hearings, §§150B-28, (b), 150B-39, (a).
Subpoenas.
Witness fees, §150B-39, (c).
Educational agencies.
Subject to administrative procedure act, §115C-2.
Elections.
Precinct boundaries.
Exemption of state board of elections, §163-132.5B.
Evidence.
Appeals.
New evidence, §150B-49.
Dying declarations, §8-51.1.
Hearings, §150B-41, (a), (b).
Opportunity to present evidence, §§150B-25, (c), 150B-40, (a).
Rules of evidence, §150B-29, (a), (b).
Subpoenas, §§150B-27, 150B-39, (c).
Exempt agencies' rules.
Publication of code and register, §150B-21.21, (b), (c).
Exemptions.
Contested case provisions, §150B-1, (e).
Full exemptions, §150B-1, (c).
Rule making, §150B-1, (d).
University of North Carolina, §150B-1, (f).

ADMINISTRATIVE PROCEDURE —Cont'd
Fees.
Copies of register and code, §150B-21.25.
Subpoenas.
Witness fees, §150B-39, (c).
Foreign corporations.
Nonprofit corporations.
Revocation of certificates of authority.
Inapplicability of administrative procedure act, §55A-15-33.
General assembly.
Joint legislative administrative procedure oversight committee, §§120-70.100 to 120-70.103.
Health maintenance organizations, §58-67-155.
Hearings, §§150B-22 to 150B-42.
Absence of party.
Proceeding with hearing in absence of party, §§150B-25, (a), 150B-40, (a).
Administrative law judges, §150B-40, (e).
Assignment, §150B-32, (a).
Decisions, §§150B-34, 150B-36.
Disqualification, §150B-32, (b), (c).
Ex parte communications.
Prohibited, §150B-35.
Office of administrative hearings.
See ADMINISTRATIVE HEARINGS, OFFICE OF.
Powers, §150B-33, (b).
Stays, §150B-33, (a).
Answers, §150B-38, (d).
Arguments.
Opportunity to present, §150B-25, (c).
Banks.
Special provisions, §§150B-38 to 150B-42.
Consolidation, §150B-26.
Decisions.
Final decision, §§150B-36, 150B-42, (a).
Unreasonable delay of decision.
Right to judicial intervention, §150B-44.
Depositions, §150B-28, (a).
Discovery, §150B-28, (b).
Evidence, §150B-41, (a), (b).
Opportunity to present evidence, §§150B-25, (c), 150B-40, (a).
Rules of evidence, §150B-29, (a), (b).
Subpoenas, §§150B-27, 150B-39, (c).
Ex parte communications, §150B-40, (d).
Prohibited, §150B-35.
Final decision, §§150B-36, 150B-42, (a).
Findings of fact, §150B-36, (b) to (b2).
Informal procedures.
Settlement of contested cases, §150B-22.
Insurance.
Department of insurance and commissioner of insurance.
Special provisions, §§150B-38 to 150B-42.
Interpreters.
General provisions.
See INTERPRETERS.
Intervention, §§150B-23, (d), 150B-38, (f).
Licenses.
Occupational licensing agencies.
Special provisions, §§150B-38 to 150B-42.
Notice, §§150B-23, (b), (c), 150B-38, (b), (c).
Official notice, §§150B-30, 150B-41, (d).
Office of administrative hearings, §§7A-750 to 7A-759. See within this heading, "Office of administrative hearings."
Official notice, §§150B-30, 150B-41, (d).
Open to public, §§150B-23, (e), 150B-38, (e).

ADMINISTRATIVE PROCEDURE —Cont'd
Hearings —Cont'd
Opportunity for hearing to be provided, §150B-23, (a).
Presiding officer, §150B-40, (b), (c).
Records.
Official record, §§150B-37, (a), 150B-42, (b).
Forwarding copy to agency, §150B-37, (c).
Transcript, §§150B-37, (b), 150B-42, (c).
Scope of provisions.
Special provisions, §150B-38, (a).
Stipulations, §§150B-31, (a), 150B-41, (c).
Disposition of contested case by stipulation, §150B-31, (b).
Subpoenas, §150B-27.
Venue, §150B-24, (a).
Waiver of objection to venue, §150B-24, (b).
Witnesses.
Cross-examination, §§150B-25, (d), 150B-40, (a).
Subpoenas, §§150B-27, 150B-39, (c).
Hospitals.
Licenses.
Adverse action on licenses, §131E-78, (a) to (c).
Denial or revocation of license, §131E-78, (a).
Insurance.
Hearings.
Department of insurance and commissioner of insurance.
Special provisions, §§150B-38 to 150B-42.
Interpleader and intervention.
Appeals.
Motion to intervene, §150B-46.
Right to judicial intervention when agency unreasonably delays decision, §150B-44.
Hearings.
Motion to intervene, §§150B-23, (d), 150B-38, (f).
Joint hearings, §150B-38, (g).
Judgment on the pleadings, §150B-36, (d).
Judicial or official notice.
Publication of code and register.
Effect of inclusion of rule in code, §150B-21.22.
Judicial review, §§150B-43 to 150B-52. See within this heading, "Appeals."
Jury.
Appeals.
Review by court without jury, §150B-50.
Licenses.
Application of provisions, §150B-3, (d).
Defined, §150B-2.
Expiration, §150B-3, (a).
Hearings.
Occupational licensing agencies.
Special provisions, §§150B-38 to 150B-42.
Hospitals, §131E-78, (a) to (c).
Licensing defined, §150B-2.
Notice.
Suspension, revocation or cancellation of license, §150B-3, (b).
Nursing homes, §131E-103, (b).
Occupational licenses.
Defined, §150B-2.
Special provisions, §150B-3.
Suspension.
Notice, §150B-3, (b).
Summary suspension, §150B-3, (c).
Mediated settlement conferences.
Attendance, §150B-23.1, (d).
Costs, §150B-23.1, (i).
Definitions, §150B-23.1, (b).
Immunity, §150B-23.1, (h).

ADMINISTRATIVE PROCEDURE —Cont'd
Mediated settlement conferences —Cont'd
Inadmissibility of negotiations, §150B-23.1, (j).
Mediators, §150B-23.1, (e).
Order by administrative law judge, §150B-23.1, (c).
Purpose of section, §150B-23.1, (a).
Right to hearing, §150B-23.1, (k).
Sanctions, §150B-23.1, (f).
Standards, §150B-23.1, (g).
Mine safety and health standards.
Procedure utilized for adoption and promulgation, §74-24.4, (b).
Nonprofit corporations.
Administrative dissolution by secretary of state.
Inapplicability of administrative procedure act, §55A-14-24.
Foreign corporations.
Revocation of certificates of authority.
Inapplicability of administrative procedure act, §55A-15-33.
Notice.
Hearings, §§150B-23, (b), (c), 150B-38, (b), (c).
Official notice, §§150B-30, 150B-41, (d).
Licenses.
Suspension, revocation or cancellation, §150B-3, (b).
Nursing homes.
Adverse action on licenses, §131E-103, (b).
Occupational licensing agency.
Defined, §150B-2.
Office of administrative hearings, §§7A-750 to 7A-759.
Administrative law judges.
Longevity pay, §7A-151, (b).
Salary, §7A-151, (b).
Senior judge.
Designation by chief judge, §7A-152.
Performance of duties of chief judge.
Chief judge absent or unable to serve, §7A-152.
Age discrimination in employment.
Deferral agency, §7A-759, (b1).
Appointment of administrative law judges, §7A-753.
Chief administrative law judge.
Absence or unable to serve.
Senior judge to perform duties, §7A-152.
Appointment, §7A-152.
Head of office, §7A-151, (a).
Longevity pay, §7A-151, (a).
Salary, §7A-151, (a).
Term, §7A-152.
Civil rights division.
Investigating charges, authority, §7A-759, (c1).
Creation, §7A-750.
Deferral agency.
Broad construction of provisions, §7A-759, (i).
Confidentiality, §7A-759, (g).
Contested cases, §7A-759, (d), (e).
Contracts to serve as deferral agency, §7A-759, (b).
Designation, §7A-759, (a).
Federal authority not limited, §7A-759, (h).
Investigations, §7A-759, (c).
Monetary compliance with settlement or compromise, §7A-759, (f).
Duties, §7A-750.
E.E.O.C. actions.
Deferral agency, §7A-759, (b1).
Enforcement of powers, §7A-756.

ADMINISTRATIVE PROCEDURE —Cont'd
Office of administrative hearings —Cont'd
Exempt agencies.
Availability of administrative law judges to, §7A-758.
Expenses reimbursed, §7A-755.
Head of office.
Chief administrative law judge, §7A-151, (a).
Municipal corporations.
Availability of administrative law judges to, §7A-758.
Oath administration, §7A-756.
Deferral agency, §7A-759, (c).
Oaths and affirmations, §7A-759, (c).
Oaths of administrative law judges, §7A-754.
Political subdivisions.
Availability of administrative law judges to, §7A-758.
Purpose, §7A-750.
Qualifications of administrative law judges, §7A-754.
Reimbursement of expenses, §7A-755.
Removal of administrative law judges, §7A-754.
Salary.
Administrative law judges, §7A-151, (b).
Chief administrative law judge, §7A-151, (a).
Senior judge.
Designation by chief judge, §7A-152.
Performance of duties of chief judge.
Chief judge absent or unable to serve, §7A-152.
Specialization of administrative law judges, §7A-753.
Standards of conduct, §7A-754.
Status, §7A-750.
Subpoena issuance, §7A-756.
Temporary administrative law judges, §7A-757.
Parties.
Defined, §150B-2.
Petitions.
Appeals.
Time for filing petition, §150B-45.
Contents, §150B-46.
Copies served on all parties, §150B-46.
Policy of state, §150B-1, (a).
Prehearing statement.
Contested case, §150B-23, (a2).
Publication of administrative code and register, §§150B-21.17 to 150B-21.25.
See PUBLICATION OF ADMINISTRATIVE CODE AND REGISTER.
Purpose of provisions, §150B-1, (b).
Records.
Appeals, §150B-47.
Hearings.
Official record, §§150B-37, 150B-42, (b), (c).
Residence.
Defined, §150B-2.
Rulemaking procedure.
Abolition of part or all of agency.
Transfer of agency's duties.
Effect on rule, §150B-21.7.
Administrative code.
Publication, §§150B-21.17 to 150B-21.25.
Rebuttable presumption rule adopted.
Entry in administrative code, §150B-21.9, (a1).
Changes.
Permanent rules.
Response to commission objection, §150B-21.12, (c).

ADMINISTRATIVE PROCEDURE —Cont'd
Rulemaking procedure —Cont'd
Conduct of hearings, §150B-38, (h).
Coordinators.
Agencies to designate rulemaking coordinators, §150B-21, (a).
Duties of rulemaking coordinators, §150B-21, (b) to (f).
Definitions.
Substantial economic impact, §150B-21.4, (b1).
Effective dates.
Day of adjournment defined, §150B-21.3, (d).
Delayed effective dates, §150B-21.3, (b1).
Executive order exception, §150B-21.3, (c).
Fee increase or new fee established, §150B-21.3, (c1).
Legislative day defined, §150B-21.3, (d).
Objections to adoption, §150B-21.3, (b2).
OSHA standard, §150B-21.3, (e).
Permanent rules, §150B-21.3, (b).
Technical change, §150B-21.3, (f).
Temporary and emergency rules, §150B-21.3, (a).
Emergency rules.
Declaratory judgment.
Standing to file for, §150B-21.1A, (c).
Department of health and humans services.
When agency may adopt, §150B-21.1A, (a).
Effective date, §§150B-21.1A, (d), 150B-21.3, (a).
Expiration, §150B-21.1A, (d).
Publication, §150B-21.1A, (e).
Review, §§150B-21.1A, (b), 150B-21.8, (a).
Standing to file for declaratory judgment, §150B-21.1A, (c).
When agency may adopt, §150B-21.1A, (a).
Executive order exception.
Effective dates, §150B-21.3, (c).
Exemptions, §150B-18.
Fee increase or new fee established.
Effective dates, §150B-21.3, (c1).
Fiscal notes on rules.
Content, §150B-21.4, (b2).
Erroneous note, §150B-21.4, (c).
Local funds, §150B-21.4, (b).
State funds, §150B-21.4, (a).
Substantial economic impact, §150B-21.4, (b1).
Judicial review.
Permanent rule returned by commission, §150B-21.8, (d).
Limitations on what can be adopted as a rule, §150B-19.
Local governments.
Rules affecting, §§150B-21.26 to 150B-21.28.
Objections to adoption, §150B-21.3, (b2).
Commission objection, §150B-21.12.
OSHA standard.
Effective dates, §150B-21.3, (e).
Notice and hearing not required, §150B-21.5, (c).
Permanent rules.
Actions prior to adopting, §150B-21.2, (a).
Adoption of proposed rule, §150B-21.2, (g).
Amendment of rule.
Notice and hearing not required, §150B-21.5, (a).
Review by commission, scope, §150B-21.8, (c).
Approval by commission, §§150B-21.10, 150B-21.11.
Changes.
Response to commission objection, §150B-21.12, (c).

ADMINISTRATIVE PROCEDURE —Cont'd
Rulemaking procedure —Cont'd
Permanent rules —Cont'd
Comments, §150B-21.2, (f).
Effective dates, §150B-21.3, (b).
Executive order exception, §150B-21.3, (c).
OSHA standard, §150B-21.3, (e).
Technical change, §150B-21.3, (f).
Explanation as to why rule adopted, §150B-21.2, (h).
Extending period for review.
Public hearing on rule, §150B-21.14.
Fiscal notes, §150B-21.4, (a) to (c).
Judicial review.
Rule returned by commission, §150B-21.8, (d).
Mailing list of persons requesting notice, §150B-21.2, (d).
Notice of rulemaking.
When not required, §150B-21.5.
Notice of text, §150B-21.2, (c).
Objection by commission.
Action, §150B-21.12, (a).
Changes, §150B-21.12, (c).
Return of rule, §150B-21.12, (d).
Time limit, §150B-21.12, (b).
OSHA standard.
Effective dates, §150B-21.3, (e).
Public hearing, §150B-21.2, (e).
Public hearing for rule where review period has been extended, §150B-21.14.
Public hearing on proposed rule.
When not required, §150B-21.5.
Record of proceeding, §150B-21.2, (i).
Repeal of rule.
Notice and hearing not required, §150B-21.5, (b).
Report to joint legislative administrative procedure oversight committee, §150B-21.16.
Review by commission, §150B-21.8, (b).
Action on rule, §150B-21.10.
Amendment, scope, §150B-21.8, (c).
Approval procedures, §150B-21.11.
Extending period for review, §150B-21.13.
Time limit, §150B-21.9, (b).
Timetable for review.
Extension of time, §150B-21.13.
Public hearing on rule where time for review has been extended, §150B-21.14.
Steps for adopting, §150B-21.2, (a).
Technical change.
Effective dates, §150B-21.3, (f).
Petitioning agencies to adopt rules.
Denial of petition.
Procedure, §150B-20, (c), (d).
Generally, §150B-20, (a).
Granting or denying petition.
Generally, §150B-20, (b).
Publication of code and register, §§150B-21.17 to 150B-21.25.
Rebuttable presumption.
Rule adopted, entry in administrative code, §150B-21.9, (a1).
Reference to material.
Incorporation of material and rule by reference, §150B-21.6.
Register.
Publication, §§150B-21.17 to 150B-21.25.
Repeal of law authorizing agency to adopt rule.
Effect, §150B-21.7.

ADMINISTRATIVE PROCEDURE —Cont'd
Rulemaking procedure —Cont'd
Restrictions on what can be adopted as a rule, §150B-19.
Review by commission.
Criteria, determining whether rule meets, §150B-21.9, (a).
Emergency rules, §150B-21.8, (a).
Scope, amendment to permanent rule, §150B-21.8, (c).
Standards for review, §150B-21.9, (a).
Temporary and permanent rules, §150B-21.8, (b).
Time limit, §150B-21.9, (b).
Rulemaking coordinators.
Agencies to designate, §150B-21, (a).
Duties, §150B-21, (b) to (f).
Rule publication manual, §150B-21.23.
Rules affecting local governments.
Minimizing effects of rules on local budgets, §150B-21.27.
Office of state budget and management.
Duties, §150B-21.28.
Preliminary review by governor, §150B-21.26, (a).
Scope, §150B-21.26, (b).
Rules review commission, §§143B-30.1 to 143B-30.4.
Appointment, §143B-30.1, (a).
Compensation, §143B-30.1, (d).
Composition, §143B-30.1, (a).
Computer access to North Carolina administrative code, §143B-30.1, (f).
Creation, §143B-30.1, (a).
Employees.
Appointments, §143B-30.1, (e).
Expenses, §143B-30.1, (d).
Independent agency, §143B-30.1, (c).
Meetings, §143B-30.1, (c).
Number of members, §143B-30.1, (a).
Procedures and forms in submitting rules.
Commission to prescribe, §143B-30.1, (f).
Quorum, §143B-30.1, (c).
State personnel act.
Employees not exempt from, §143B-30.1, (e).
Terms, §143B-30.1, (a).
Expiration, §143B-30.1, (b).
Vacancies, §143B-30.1, (a).
Resignation, dismissal, ineligibility, etc., §143B-30.1, (c).
Scope of article, §150B-18.
State building code.
Notice and hearing not required, §150B-21.5, (d).
Technical change.
Effective dates, §150B-21.3, (f).
Temporary rules.
Comments on proposed rule.
Acceptance of written comments, time period, §150B-21.1, (a3).
Declaratory judgment.
Rule returned to agency, §150B-21.1, (b2), (c1).
Effective date, §§150B-21.1, (d), 150B-21.3, (a).
Environmental impact statements.
Class of minimum criteria projects, §150B-21.1, (a9).
Expiration, §150B-21.1, (d).
Findings of need for rule, written statement, §150B-21.1, (a4).
Statement not meeting criteria, §150B-21.1, (b1) to (b3).

ADMINISTRATIVE PROCEDURE —Cont'd
Rulemaking procedure —Cont'd
Temporary rules —Cont'd
Findings of need for rule, written statement —Cont'd
Supplementation, §150B-21.1, (b1).
Notice of intent to adopt and of public hearing, §150B-21.1, (a3).
Publication, §150B-21.1, (a3), (e).
Public hearing, §150B-21.1, (a3).
Recent act, change, regulation or order.
Defined, waiver 210 day requirement, §150B-21.1, (a2).
Review, §§150B-21.1, (b), 150B-21.8, (b).
Rule not entered into code, §150B-21.1, (b3).
Standing to file action for declaratory judgment, §150B-21.1, (c).
When agency may adopt, §150B-21.1, (a).
Validity of rules, §150B-18.
Erroneous fiscal note.
Effect, §150B-21.4, (c).
Rule publication manual, §150B-21.23.
Rules and regulations defined, §150B-2.
Service of process.
Appeals.
Copies of petition served on all parties, §150B-46.
State bar rules.
Publication of code and register, §150B-21.21, (a), (c).
Stays.
Appeals.
Administrative decision, §§150B-48, 150B-52.
Hearings, §150B-33, (a).
Stipulations.
Hearings, §§150B-31, (a), (b), 150B-41, (c).
Subpoenas, §150B-39, (c).
Hearings, §§150B-27, 150B-39, (c).
Witnesses.
Fees, §150B-39, (c).
Substantial evidence.
Defined, §150B-2.
University of North Carolina.
Exemption, §150B-1, (f).
Venue.
Hearings, §150B-24.
Waiver.
Appeals, §150B-45.
Hearings.
Venue.
Waiver of objection to venue, §150B-24, (b).
Witnesses.
Hearings.
Cross-examination, §§150B-25, (d), 150B-40, (a).
Subpoenas, §§150B-27, 150B-39, (c).
Subpoenas.
Fees, §150B-39, (c).

ADMINISTRATIVE SEARCH AND INSPECTION WARRANTS, §15-27.2.
Wildlife protectors, securing, §113-302.1, (c).

ADMINISTRATOR OF SAVINGS INSTITUTION DIVISION.
Savings and loan associations.
Generally.
See SAVINGS AND LOAN ASSOCIATIONS.
Savings banks.
Generally.
See SAVINGS BANKS.

ADMINISTRATORS.
See EXECUTORS AND ADMINISTRATORS.

ADMINISTRATORS OF PUBLIC SCHOOLS.
Qualifications and standards generally, §§115C-290.1 to 115C-290.9.
See SCHOOL ADMINISTRATOR QUALIFICATIONS AND STANDARDS.

ADMIRALTY.
Constitution of the United States, Const. U. S., art. I, §8.
Jurisdiction of courts, Const. U. S., art. III, §2.

ADMISSION FEES.
Privilege tax on gross receipts.
Dance or athletic contest for which admission fee charged, §105-37.1.

ADMISSIONS.
Adultery.
Admissibility of admission or confession as evidence, §14-184.
Compromise and settlement.
Advance or partial payments.
Not to constitute admission of liability, §1-540.3, (a).
Motor vehicle collisions or accidents.
Settlement of property damage claims not to constitute admission of liability, §1-540.2.
Contents of writings, recordings and photographs, §8C-1, Rule 1007.
Delinquent and undisciplined juvenile actions.
In-custody admission, §7B-2101, (b).
When admissions by juvenile accepted by court.
Determination factual basis for admission, §7B-2407, (c).
Determination that admission product of informed choice, §7B-2407, (b).
Duties of court before accepting, §7B-2407, (a).
Fornication.
Admissibility of admission or confession as evidence, §14-184.
Gambling contracts, §16-2.
Garnishment.
Garnishee, §1-440.28, (a) to (e).
Limitation of actions.
Party to obligation, co-obligor or guarantor.
Effect of admission by, §1-27, (a).
Partnerships.
Bound by admission of partner, §59-41.
Limitation of actions.
Effect of admission by partner, §59-39.1.
Payment into court.
Defendant ordered to satisfy admitted sum, §1-510.
Pre-trial conference to consider possibility of obtaining, §1A-1, Rule 16, (a).
Proof of service.
Written admission of defendant, §1-75.10.
Request for admission, §1A-1, Rules 26, (a); 36, (a).
Answer, §1A-1, Rule 36, (a).
Effect of admission, §1A-1, Rule 36, (b).
Expenses on failure to admit, §1A-1, Rule 37, (c).
Filing, §1A-1, Rule 5, (d).
Statements against interest.
Hearsay exception, §8C-1, Rule 804, (b).

ADMONITION.
Attorney discipline.
Imposition of discipline, Bar Rules & Regs., B, §.0123.
Issuance by grievance committee, Bar Rules & Regs., B, §.0113.

ADOPT-A-BEACH PROGRAM.
Rules promulgation, §143-673.

ADOPT-A-HIGHWAY PROGRAM, §136-140.1.

ADOPTION, §§48-1-101 to 48-10-105.
Abused, neglected or dependent juveniles.
Periodic review hearings as to placement.
Custody removed from parent, permanency plan, §7B-906.
Surrender of juvenile for adoption, agency plan for placement, §7B-909.
Termination of parental rights, permanent placement plan, §7B-908.
Action, §50-13.2A.
Failure to disclose nonidentifying information.
Civil action for equitable or monetary relief, §48-10-104.
Unauthorized disclosure of identifying information.
Civil action for equitable or monetary relief, §48-10-105, (d).
Visitation of adopted grandchild, §50-13.2A.
Adoptee.
Defined, §48-1-101.
Adoption facilitator.
Defined, §48-1-101.
Adoptive homes.
Regulation of agencies receiving or placing children in, §§131D-10.1 to 131D-10.9.
See CHILD PLACING AGENCIES.
Adult adoptions.
Adult.
Defined, §48-1-101.
Adults.
Applicability of article, §48-5-100.
Consent.
Contents, §48-5-102, (b).
Persons from whom consent required, §48-5-102, (a).
Revocation, §48-5-102, (d).
Spouse of petitioner in stepparent adoption, §48-5-102, (c).
Defined, §48-1-101.
Incompetent adults.
Consent of guardian, §48-5-103, (a), (b).
Guardian ad litem to investigate and report to court, §48-5-103, (c).
Petition for adoption.
Married prospective adoptive parent.
Joinder of both spouses, §48-5-101, (b).
Who may file, §48-5-101, (a).
Advertisements.
Desire to adopt, §48-10-101, (b1).
Unauthorized persons, misdemeanor, §48-10-101, (b), (c).
Affidavit of parentage.
Agency placements, §48-3-206, (b).
Contents, §48-3-206, (a).
Execution, §48-3-206, (a).
Filing with petition for adoption, §48-2-305.
Agencies.
Defined, §48-1-101.
Agency placements.
Acquisition of legal and physical custody of minor, §48-3-203, (a).
Adoption of minors, §48-3-201.
Affidavit of parentage, §48-3-205, (b).
Consent withheld contrary to best interest of minor.
Court order dispensing with consent, §48-3-603, (b).

ADOPTION —Cont'd
Agency placements —Cont'd
Criminal history investigation, §48-3-203, (d1).
Custody of minor pending adoption decree.
Legal custody with agency, §48-3-502, (a).
Petition by agency for full legal and physical custody, §48-3-502, (b).
Execution of consent, §48-3-605, (d).
Identifying information.
Release by agency, §§48-3-203, 48-9-109, (f).
Investigation required, §48-3-203, (d1).
Notice to parent when adoption decree issued, §48-3-203, (c).
Parties by whom consent required, §48-3-601.
Preplacement assessments.
Selection of prospective adoptive parent, §48-3-203, (d).
Promulgation of rules by social services commission, §48-3-203, (e).
Recruitment of adoptive parents, §48-3-204.
Relinquishment of one parent sufficient for placement for adoption, §48-3-201, (d).
Schedule of fees or expenses charged.
Statements of services to prospective adoptive parents, §48-3-203, (b).
Statement of services provided to prospective adoptive parents, §48-3-203, (b).
Time for execution of consent, §48-3-604.
Alien adoptees.
Contents of decree of adoption, §48-2-606, (b).
Alleged father of minor adoptee, no notice given.
Court to give notice, §48-2-404.
Appeals.
Consent of parent or guardian obtained by fraud or duress, §48-2-607, (c).
Procedure, notice, §48-2-607, (b).
Prohibited grounds for appeals, §48-2-607, (a).
Relinquishment of parent or guardian obtained by fraud or duress, §48-2-607, (c).
Statute of limitations.
Action for damages against adoptee or adoptive parent for fraud or duress, §48-2-607, (c).
Unfavorable preplacement assessments, §48-3-308, (a).
Appearances.
Hearing on petition to adopt adult, §48-2-605, (b).
Assistance for adoptive parents.
Interstate compact on adoption and medical assistance, §§7B-3900 to 7B-3906.
Attorneys at law.
Attorneys specializing in family law.
Certification standards, Bar Rules & Regs., D, §§.2401 to .2407.
Representation of adoptee, §48-2-201, (b).
Representation of parents, §48-2-201, (a).
Attorneys' fees.
Revocation of consent.
Fees awarded to person who revoked upon non-return of minor, §48-3-608, (c).
Revocation of relinquishment.
Failure to return minor, §48-3-706, (b).
Background information provided to prospective adoptive parents, §48-3-205.
Best interest of adoptee.
Standard of proof for hearings on petition, §48-2-603.
Biological parents.
Consent of biological father, §48-2-206.
Bringing or sending juvenile into state for purposes of placement for adoption.
Applicability of article, §7B-3705.

ADOPTION —Cont'd
Bringing or sending juvenile into state for purposes of placement for adoption —Cont'd
Bond required for person, agency, etc., bringing juvenile into state, §7B-3701.
Consent of department of health and human services, §7B-3700, (a).
Definitions, §7B-3704.
Misdemeanor for violating provisions, §7B-3703.
Responsibility for care and training of juvenile, §7B-3700, (b).
Burden of proof.
Hearing on petition to adopt adult, §48-2-605, (b).
Hearings on petition for adoption, §48-2-603, (a).
Certificate of identification for individual of foreign birth, §130A-108, (a).
Readoption in state, §130A-108, (b).
Child custody.
Failure to consent, §50-13.2, (d).
Visitation of adopted grandchild.
Action by biological grandparent, §50-13.2A.
Child, defined, §48-1-101.
Children and minors.
Affidavit of parentage, §48-3-206.
Agency placements generally. See within this heading, "Agency placements."
Applicability of article to stepparents, §48-3-100.
Consent required for direct placement of minor, §48-3-201, (b).
Consent to adoption generally. See within this heading, "Consent."
Consequences of consent to adopt minor, §48-3-607.
Custody of minor in health care facility.
Authorization to transfer custody to agency, §48-3-402.
Definitions, §48-3-401.
Custody of minor pending adoption decree, §§48-3-501, 48-3-502.
Custody of minor upon denial of petition to adopt, §48-2-604, (c).
Custody of minor upon execution of consent, §48-3-607, (b).
Denial of petition to adopt minor, §48-2-604, (c).
Direct placements generally. See within this heading, "Direct placements."
Disclosure of background information.
Forms to collect information, §48-3-205, (d).
General information provided to prospective adoptive parents, §48-3-205, (a).
Preservation of health information by agency, §48-3-205, (c).
Use against provider in pending civil or criminal actions prohibited, §48-3-205, (b).
Dismissal of petition, §48-2-604, (a).
Notice and hearing, §48-2-604, (b).
Interstate placements, §48-3-207.
Married and emancipated minors, adoption of, §48-5-100.
Notice to alleged father of minor adoptee, §48-2-404.
Placement of minors for adoption, §48-3-201.
Recruitment of adoptive parents.
Cooperation between agencies, §48-3-204, (c).
Photo-listing service, §48-3-204, (b).
Rules for agencies to follow, §48-3-204, (a).
Relinquishment generally. See within this heading, "Relinquishment."
Revocation of consent to adoption of minor, §§48-3-607 to 48-3-609.

ADOPTION —Cont'd
Children and minors —Cont'd
Stepparent's adoption of minor.
General provisions. See within this heading, "Stepparents."
Transfer of custody from health care facility.
Attending practitioner, defined, §48-3-401.
Authorization for transfer of minor to agency.
Duration of authorization, §48-3-402, (b).
Health care facility, defined, §48-3-401.
Who may place minors for adoption, §48-3-201, (a).
Child support.
Consequences of consent by parent to adoption, §48-3-607, (c).
Duty of former parent to make past-due payments.
Effect of decree of adoption, §48-1-106, (c).
Collateral agreements to consent.
Enforceability, effect on consent, §48-3-610.
Confidentiality.
Criminal history record check.
Prospective parent.
Privileged information, §48-3-309, (f).
Proceedings generally, §48-2-203.
Records.
General provisions, §§48-9-101 to 48-9-109. See within this heading, "Records."
Conflicts resolved in favor of minors, §48-1-100, (c).
Consent.
Adult adoptions.
Contents, §48-5-102, (b).
Persons from whom consent required, §48-5-102, (a).
Revocation, §48-5-102, (d).
Spouse of petitioner in stepparent adoption, §48-5-102, (c).
Agency placements, §48-3-601.
Consent withheld contrary to best interest of minor.
Court order dispensing with consent, §48-3-603, (b).
Execution of consent by agency, §48-3-605, (d).
Time for execution of consent, §48-3-604, (d).
Biological father.
Applicability of court decision, §48-2-206, (i).
Computation of time, §48-2-206, (g).
Hearings, §48-2-206, (d).
Jurisdiction, §48-2-206, (f).
Notice of intent to place for adoption, §48-2-206, (a).
Contents, §48-2-206, (b).
Failure to respond, §48-2-206, (c).
Service of process, §48-2-206, (e).
Transfers and appeals, §48-2-206, (h).
Bringing juvenile into state or taking or sending juvenile out of state for purposes of placement, §§7B-3700 to 7B-3705.
Collateral agreements, effect on consent, §48-3-610.
Consequences, §48-3-607.
Contents, mandatory provisions, §48-3-606.
Court order dispensing with consent in certain situations, §48-3-603, (b).
Custody of minor upon revocation, §48-3-608, (c).
Custody of minor upon voiding of consent, §48-3-609, (b).
Direct placements, §§48-3-201, (b), 48-3-601.
Dismissal of adoption proceeding upon voiding of consent, §48-3-609, (c).

ADOPTION —Cont'd
Consent —Cont'd
Effect, §48-3-607.
Execution.
Agencies, §48-3-605, (d).
Timing, §48-3-604, (d).
Contents, mandatory provisions, §48-3-606.
Foreign execution, §48-3-605, (e).
General provisions, §48-3-605, (c).
Guardian, timing, §48-3-604, (c).
Indian children, §48-3-605, (f).
Man whose consent is require, timing, §48-3-604, (a).
Minor twelve years of age or older, timing, §48-3-604, (e).
Mother, timing, §48-3-604, (b).
Parent or guardian of minor, §48-3-605, (a).
Parent under age of eighteen, §48-3-605, (b).
Final and irrevocable, §48-3-607, (a).
Foreign consent, §48-3-605, (e).
Fraud or duress in obtaining consent of parent or guardian.
Statute of limitations for appeal, §48-2-607, (c).
General provisions, §§48-3-601, 48-3-603.
Guardian ad litem for incompetent parents, §48-3-602.
Incompetent parents, §48-3-602.
Inheritance, succession, insurance, child support and other benefits or claims.
Minors, §48-3-607, (c).
Irrevocable consent.
Second consent to adoption by same adoptive parents, §48-3-608, (e).
Legal and physical custody in prospective adoptive parent, §48-3-607, (b).
Mandatory contents, §48-3-606.
Minor age twelve or older.
Consent required, §48-3-601.
Court order dispensing with consent, §48-3-603, (b).
Time for execution, §48-3-604, (e).
Persons whose consent not required, §48-3-603.
Persons whose consent required, §48-3-601.
Readoption after stepparent adoption.
Adoptee, §48-6-102, (d).
Adoptee's parent who was spouse of adoptive parent, §48-6-102, (g).
Adoptive parent, §48-6-102, (f).
Guardian of minor adoptee, §48-6-102, (h).
Petitioner's spouse, §48-6-102, (e).
Who must execute consent, §48-6-102, (c).
Revocation of consent.
Adoption cannot proceed without another consent, §48-3-608, (d).
Attorneys' fees to person who revoked upon non-return of minor, §48-3-608, (c).
Custody of minor, §48-3-608, (c).
Direct placement, §48-3-608, (b).
Generally, §48-3-608, (a).
Second consent by same adoptive parents.
Irrevocable, §48-3-608, (e).
Stepparent's adoption of stepchild, §48-4-102.
Timing of execution, §48-3-604.
Void, §48-3-609, (a).
Custody of minor, §48-3-609, (b).
Dismissal of adoption proceeding, §48-3-609, (c).
Construction of chapter, §48-1-100, (c).
Liberally construed generally, §48-1-100, (d).
Criminal history record checks.
Criminal history defined, §48-1-101.

ADOPTION —Cont'd
Criminal history record checks —Cont'd
Mandatory preplacement criminal checks of prospective adoptive parents of minor in custody or placement responsibility of county department of social services.
Department of justice.
Duties, §48-3-309, (c).
Performance of check by, §48-3-309, (h).
Forms, §48-3-309, (d).
Negligence in carrying out provisions.
No liability for, §48-3-309, (g).
Notification of results, §48-3-309, (e).
Privileged information, §48-3-309, (f).
Responsibility of department, §48-3-309, (a).
Unfavorable preplacement assessment, §48-3-309, (b).
Parents seeking to adopt minor in custody of county department of social services, §114-19.7.
Preplacement assessments, §48-3-303, (d).
Minor in custody or placement responsibility of county department of social services.
Mandatory preplacement criminal checks of prospective adoptive parents, §48-3-309.
Prospective adoptive parents, §114-19.3, (d).
Criminal law and procedure.
Prohibited placement activities, §48-10-101.
Unauthorized disclosure of identifying information, §48-10-105.
Unlawful payments related to adoption, §48-10-102.
Damages.
Failure to disclose nonidentifying information.
Civil action for monetary relief, §48-10-104.
Unauthorized disclosure of information.
Civil action for monetary relief, §48-10-105.
Death of joint petitioner pending final decree, §48-2-204.
Decedents' estates.
Inheritance rights of child subject to adoption.
Consequences of consent by parent to adoption, §48-3-607, (c).
Intestate succession, §29-17.
Share of after-adopted children, §28A-22-2.
Decree of adoption.
Alien adoptees, §48-2-606, (b).
Biological grandparents' rights, effect, §48-1-106, (f).
Child support arrearage of former parent not terminated, §48-1-106, (c).
Contents, §48-2-606, (a).
Former parent of adoptee not to be named on decree, §48-2-606, (c).
Former parents' rights, effect, §48-1-106, (c).
Inheritance rights of adoptee, §48-1-106, (b).
Instruments transferring ownership, language of kinship included in instrument.
Effect of decree, §48-1-106, (e).
Legal effect, §48-1-106, (a).
Omission of information from petition, effect on decree, §48-2-306, (b).
Parent and child relationship established, §48-1-106, (b).
Recognition of foreign decrees, §48-2-205.
Restoration of original certificate if decree set aside, §48-9-108.
Rights of biological grandparents, §48-1-106, (f).
Rights of former parents, §48-1-106, (c).
Stepparent adoption or readoption.
Effect on relationship between child and stepparent's spouse, §48-1-106.

ADOPTION —Cont'd
Definitions, §48-1-101.
Direct placements.
Custody of minor pending adoption decree, §48-3-501.
Information regarding prospective adoptive parent provided to parent or guardian, §48-3-202, (b).
Minor placed with relative, preplacement assessment not required, §48-3-301, (b).
Persons whose consent required, §48-3-601.
Preplacement assessments.
Provided to parent or guardian, §48-3-202, (b).
Recruitment of adoptive parents, §48-3-204.
Revocation of consent, §48-3-608, (b).
Selection of prospective adoptive parent, §48-3-202, (a).
Violation of preplacement assessment requirements, §48-3-301, (c).
Disclosure of confidential information.
General provisions, §§48-9-101 to 48-9-109. See within this heading, "Records."
Dismissal of petition, §48-2-604, (a).
Consent becomes void, §48-3-609, (c).
Notice and hearing, §48-2-604, (b).
Dispositional hearing on petition.
Disclosure of fees and charges, §48-2-602.
Extension of time for hearing, §48-2-601, (c).
No contest to petition, §48-2-601, (a).
Procedure generally, §48-2-603.
Time for hearing, §48-2-601, (b).
Division.
Defined, §48-1-101.
Divorce.
Visitation of adopted grandchild.
Action by biological grandparent, §50-13.2A.
Duress in execution of notice waiver, §48-2-406, (c).
Failure to disclose nonidentifying information, §48-10-104.
Fees.
Agency placements.
Schedule of fees included in statement of services, §48-3-203, (b).
Dispositional hearing on petition.
Disclosure of fees and charges, §48-2-602.
Lawful payments related to adoption.
Agency fees and charges, §48-10-103, (e).
Preplacement assessments, §48-3-304.
Report to court, §48-2-504.
Unlawful payments related to adoption, §48-10-102, (a).
Felonies.
Unlawful payments related to adoption.
Subsequent violations, §48-10-102, (b).
Fines.
Unlawful payments related to adoption, §48-10-102, (b).
Foreign adoption decrees, recognition, §48-2-205.
Foreign birth.
Certificate of identification for individual of foreign birth, §130A-108.
Former parent adoption, §§48-6-100 to 48-6-102. See within this heading, "Readoption."
Former parents of adoptees.
Child support arrearage not terminated by adoption decree, §48-1-106, (c).
Name prohibited on decree of adoption, §48-2-606, (c).
Foster care and adoption assistance payments, §§108A-48 to 108A-50.

ADOPTION —Cont'd
Foster homes.
Control over child caring facilities, §§110-45 to 110-48.
Foster care and adoption assistance payments, §§108A-48 to 108A-50.
Fraud in execution of notice waiver, §48-2-406, (c).
Grandparent visitation, §48-1-106, (f).
Actions, §50-13.2A.
Guardian ad litem.
Adoption of incompetent adults.
Investigation and report to court, §48-5-103, (c).
Consent execution for incompetent parents, §48-3-602.
Representation of adoptee, §48-2-201, (b).
Guardians.
Adoption of incompetent adults.
Consent, §48-5-103, (a), (b).
Appointment for minor child.
Consent not required from parent, §48-3-603, (a).
Defined, §48-1-101.
Execution of consent, time, §48-3-604, (c).
Relinquishment of child generally. See within this heading, "Relinquishment."
Hearings.
Confidentiality of hearings, §48-2-203.
Dispositional hearing on uncontested petition, §48-2-601.
Petition for adoption of adult.
Appearance of parties, §48-2-605, (a).
Burden of proof, §48-2-605, (b).
Procedure generally, §48-2-605, (b).
Petition for adoption of minor.
Continuance of hearing on court's motion, §48-2-603, (c).
Procedure generally, §48-2-603.
Sanctions for violations of chapter, §48-2-603, (b).
Standard of proof, §48-2-603, (a).
Hearsay exception.
Statement of personal or family history, §8C-1, Rules 803, 804.
Husband and wife.
Death of joint petitioner pending final decree, §48-2-204.
Prohibition on adoption, §48-1-103.
Spouse of petitioner must join in petition, §48-2-301, (b).
Identification of adoptees.
Confidentiality of records generally, §§48-9-101 to 48-9-109. See within this heading, "Records."
Indians.
Adoptee subject to Indian child welfare act, §48-1-108.
Execution of consent, §48-3-605, (f).
Information provided to prospective adoptive parents, §48-3-205.
Inheritance rights.
Consequences of consent by parent to adoption, §48-3-607, (c).
Effect of decree of adoption, §48-1-106, (b), (e).
Injunctions.
Prohibited placement activities, §48-10-101, (d).
Unauthorized disclosure of information, §48-10-105, (c).
Unlawful payments related to adoption, §48-10-102, (c).
Interstate compact on adoption and medical assistance, §§7B-3900 to 7B-3906.
Administrator, appointment by secretary of health and human services, §7B-3906.

ADOPTION —Cont'd
Interstate compact on adoption and medical assistance —Cont'd
Authorization to secretary of health and human services, §7B-3902.
Definitions, §7B-3901.
Federal government payment provisions, inclusion in compact, §7B-3905.
General assembly advice to enter into compact, §7B-3900, (b).
Medical assistance certification of child with special needs, §7B-3904, (a).
Applicability of provisions, §7B-3904, (c).
Entitlement of holder of certificate, §7B-3904, (b).
Provisions required to be included in compact, §7B-3903, (a).
Provision that may be included in compact, §7B-3903, (b).
Purposes and legislative findings, §7B-3900, (a).
Interstate compact on the placement of children, §§7B-3800 to 7B-3806.
Interstate placements, §48-3-207.
Intestate succession, §29-17.
Consequences of consent by parent to adoption, §48-3-607, (c).
Jurisdiction.
Adoptee also subject of pending proceeding in district court.
Jurisdiction of district court, §48-2-102, (b).
Foreign court exercising jurisdiction, §48-2-100, (c).
Requirements, §48-2-100, (b).
Superior court, §48-2-100, (a).
Jury trial.
No right to jury, §48-2-202.
Lawful payments related to adoption, §48-10-103.
Legal custody.
Defined, §48-1-101.
Legislative intent, §48-1-100, (a).
Liberal construction of chapter, §48-1-100, (d).
Limitation of actions.
Action for damages against adoptee or adoptive parent for fraud or duress in obtaining consent, §48-2-607, (c).
Medical assistance for children of adoptive parents.
Interstate compact on adoption and medical assistance, §§7B-3900 to 7B-3906.
Minors.
Adoption of minors generally. See within this heading, "Children and minors."
Defined, §48-1-101.
Misdemeanors.
Prohibited placement activities, §48-10-101.
Unauthorized disclosure of identifying information, §48-10-105.
Unlawful payments related to adoption, §48-10-102, (b).
Motion for release of information.
Protection of adoptee or public, §48-9-105.
Name.
Former parents' names not to be listed on decree, §48-2-606, (c).
Name of adoptee after adoption, §48-1-105.
Notice.
Agency placements, §48-3-203, (c).
Clerk of court to give notice of proceedings, §48-2-403.

ADOPTION —Cont'd
Notice —Cont'd
Consent of person not required, rights in proceeding, §48-2-405.
Court to give notice to alleged father, §48-2-404.
Dismissal of petition to adopt minor, §48-2-604, (b).
Filing of petition.
Adoption of adult, §48-2-401, (d).
Adoption of minor, §48-2-401, (c).
Generally, §48-2-401, (b).
Time for filing response, §48-2-401, (f).
Identity of biological parent cannot be ascertained, §48-2-402, (b).
Motion for release of information.
Notice of hearings, §48-9-105, (b).
Relinquishment, §48-3-706, (a).
Service of process, §48-2-402, (a).
Time for serving notice of petition, §48-2-401, (a).
Unknown biological parent, §48-2-402, (b).
Waiver.
Effect on person who executes waiver, §48-2-406, (b).
Motion to set aside for fraud or duress, §48-2-406, (c).
Procedure, §48-2-406, (a).
Who is entitled to notice, §48-2-401, (e).
Other rights of adoptee not divested by decree, §48-1-107.
Parental consent.
Biological father, §48-2-206.
Parent and child.
Adoption by former parent, §§48-6-100 to 48-6-102.
Definition of "parent," §48-1-102.
Execution of consent, §48-3-605.
Relinquishment of minors generally. See within this heading, "Relinquishment."
Parties.
Defined, §48-1-101.
Payments related to adoption.
Agency fees, §48-10-103, (e).
Contingent on placement for adoption, prohibited, §48-10-103, (c).
Lawful payments generally, §48-10-103, (a).
Preplacement assessment, §48-10-103, (b).
Recovery of payment.
Receipt by person with fraudulent intent to prevent adoption from being completed, §48-10-103, (d).
Sliding scale fees by agency.
Authorized, §48-10-103.
Unlawful payments, §48-10-102, (a).
Persons entitled to notice, consent not required.
Rights in adoption proceedings, §48-2-405.
Persons who may adopt, §48-1-103.
Persons who may be adopted, §48-1-104.
Petition for adoption.
Additional documents to be filed, §48-2-305.
Adults.
Hearing on petition to adopt adult, §48-2-605.
Caption, §48-2-303.
Contents, §48-2-304, (a).
Adoption of adult, §48-2-304, (e).
Adoption of minor, §48-2-304, (b) to (d).
Death of joint petitioner pending final decree, §48-2-204.
Denial of petition to adopt minor, §48-2-604, (c).
Dispositional hearing, §48-2-603.
Uncontested petition, §48-2-601.
Documents to be filed with, §48-2-305.

ADOPTION —Cont'd
Petition for adoption —Cont'd
Filing concurrently with petition to terminate parental rights, §48-2-302, (c).
Filing of additional information, §48-2-306, (a).
Form of caption, §48-2-303.
Granting.
Sanctions for violations of chapter, §48-2-603, (b).
Hearing on petition, §48-2-603.
Joinder.
Readoption after stepparent adoption.
Joinder of petitioner's spouse, §48-6-102, (b).
Spouse of petitioner, §48-2-301, (b).
Unmarried petitioner, §48-2-301, (c).
Joint petition between spouses.
Death of joint petitioner pending final decree, §48-2-204.
Jurisdiction, §48-2-100.
Notice, §48-2-401.
Omission of information, effect on decree, §48-2-306, (b).
Placement requirement, §48-2-301, (a).
Preplacement assessment not complete.
Affidavit of explanation attached to petition, §48-3-307, (b).
Readoption after stepparent adoption.
Joinder of petitioner's spouse, §48-6-102, (b).
Spouse of petitioner must join in petition, §48-2-301, (b).
Standard petition promulgated by department, §48-2-304, (f).
Stepparent's adoption of stepchild, §48-4-101.
Termination of parental rights.
Petitions filed concurrently, §48-2-302, (c).
Time of filing, §48-2-302, (a).
Failure to file timely, §48-2-302, (b).
Filing concurrently with petition to terminate parental rights, §48-2-302, (c).
Unmarried prospective adoptive parent.
Joinder by others prohibited, §48-2-301, (c).
Venue, §48-2-101.
Who may file, §48-2-301, (a).
Physical custody.
Defined, §48-1-101.
Placement.
Defined, §48-1-101.
Placement assessments.
Fees for preparation.
Agreement, §48-3-304, (a).
Authority to charge fee, §48-3-304, (a).
Maximum fees, basis for, §48-3-304, (c).
Review by court, §48-3-304, (b).
Waiver, unable to pay, §48-3-304, (c).
Time for completing, §48-3-303, (a).
Placement for adoption by unauthorized persons.
Misdemeanor, §48-10-101, (a), (c).
Placement of children.
Control over child caring facilities, §§110-45 to 110-48.
Foster care and adoption assistance payments, §§108A-48 to 108A-50.
Preplacement assessments.
Adoption of minors, §48-3-301, (a).
Agency assessment of individual, §48-3-302, (d).
Agency placements.
Selection of prospective adoptive parent, §48-3-203, (d).
Agency refusal to conduct.
Assessment prepared by county department of social services, §48-3-302, (e).

ADOPTION —Cont'd
Preplacement assessments —Cont'd
Contents of report, §48-3-303, (c).
Copies of favorable assessments, §48-3-306.
Copy of assessments retained by agency, §48-3-305, (b).
Copy sent to subjects of assessment, §48-3-305, (a).
Criminal record check, §48-3-303, (d).
Minor in custody or placement responsibility of county department of social services.
Mandatory preplacement criminal checks of prospective adoptive parents, §48-3-309.
Defined, §48-1-101.
Delivery of copy to parent or guardian who placed minor for adoption.
Certificate to be filed by prospective adoptive parent, §48-3-307, (c).
Determination of suitability to be adoptive parent.
Assessment to include factors in support of determination, §48-3-303, (f).
Determination of unsuitability to be adoptive parent.
Assessment to state specific concerns, §48-3-303, (g).
Filing of original assessment with division, §48-3-305, (a).
Direct placement for adoption of minor.
Information provided about prospective adoptive parents, §48-3-202, (b).
Placement made in violation of section, §48-3-301, (c).
Placement with relative of minor.
Assessment not required, §48-3-301, (b).
Favorable assessment.
Copies to be provided, §48-3-306.
Filing of petition before assessment complete, §48-3-307, (b).
Filing with adoption petition, §48-2-305.
Lawful payments related to adoption, §48-10-103, (b).
Multiple assessments.
Request by prospective adoptive parents, §48-3-302, (c).
Personal interview requirement, §48-3-303, (b).
Petition for adoption filed before assessment complete, §48-3-307, (b).
Placement occurring before assessment complete, §48-3-307, (a).
Prepared in other states, §48-1-109, (b).
Requested by prospective adoptive parent.
Agency refusal to conduct.
Assessment prepared by county department of social services, §48-3-302, (e).
Direct placements in violation of section, §48-3-301, (c).
Multiple assessments, §48-3-302, (c).
Permissibility of request generally, §48-3-302, (a).
Selection of prospective adoptee not required, §48-3-302, (b).
Review of information obtained, §48-3-303, (e).
Rules established by social services commission, §48-3-303, (i).
Sources of information, assessment to contain list, §48-3-303, (h).
Time for completion, §48-3-302, (a).
Unfavorable assessment.
Not public records, §48-3-308, (e).
Response filed with division, §48-3-308, (b) to (e).
Action to be taken by county department of social services, §48-3-308, (d).

ADOPTION —Cont'd
Preplacement assessments —Cont'd
Unfavorable assessment —Cont'd
Response filed with division —Cont'd
Authority of division to take action, §48-3-308, (c).
Review procedure, §48-3-308, (a).
Who may prepare, §48-1-109, (a).
Prohibited activities in placement, §48-10-101.
Property interest contingent on family relationship with former family divested by decree, §48-1-107.
Purpose of chapter, §48-1-100, (b).
Readoption.
Adoptee adopted by stepparent.
Consent, §48-6-102, (c) to (h).
Joinder in petition by petitioner's spouse, §48-6-102, (b).
Permissibility, §48-6-102, (a).
Applicability of article, §48-6-100.
Applicability of other articles, §48-6-101.
Custody orders already existing.
No effect, §48-6-102, (j).
Effect on relationship between child and parent, §48-1-106, (d).
Relationship between adoptee and parent who was married to adoptive parent.
Not affected by adoption under this section, §48-6-102, (i).
Recognition of foreign adoption decrees, §48-2-205.
Records.
Adoption or name change of minor, §48-9-102, (f).
Authorized disclosures, §48-9-109.
Birth certificates.
Motion for release of information may be accompanied by request for birth certificate, §48-9-105, (d).
New birth certificate.
Adoption by stepparent, §48-9-107, (b).
Adoption of adult, §48-9-107, (a).
Adoption of minor, §48-9-107, (a).
Copies to adoptee's new family, §48-9-107, (c).
Issuance only by state registrar, §48-9-107, (d).
Reference to adoption on certificate prohibited, §48-9-107, (a).
Removal of original birth certificate from records, §48-9-107, (d).
Reports of adoptions from other states, §48-9-107, (e).
Original birth certificate of adoptee.
Release by state registrar, §48-9-106.
Release of original certificate by state registrar, §48-9-106.
Removal from records upon decree, §48-9-107, (d).
Removal of original certificate from register of deeds, §48-9-107, (d).
Restoration of original certificate if decree set aside, §48-9-108.
Restoration upon setting aside of adoption decree, §48-9-108.
Sealing of original birth certificate, §48-9-107, (c).
Clerk of superior court to file records with division.
Priority, §48-9-102, (d).
Confidential nature generally, §48-9-102, (a).
Copy of final order, §48-9-102, (g).
Defined, §48-9-101.

ADOPTION —Cont'd
Records —Cont'd
Disclosures authorized, §48-9-109.
Failure to disclose nonidentifying information, §48-10-104.
Filing by clerk of superior court with division, §48-9-102, (d).
Inspection after final decree of adoption.
Prohibited generally, §48-9-102, (c).
Inspection during adoption proceeding, §48-9-102, (b).
Motion for release of information.
Determining factors of cause for release, §48-9-105, (c).
Notice of hearings, §48-9-105, (b).
Original birth certificate of adoptee.
Request for release authorized with filing of motion, §48-9-105, (d).
Protection of adoptee or public, §48-9-105, (a).
Service of process, §48-9-105, (b).
Order of name change, §48-9-102, (g).
Permanently indexed and filed, §48-9-102, (e).
Release of identifying information.
Agency placement adoption, §§48-3-203, 48-9-109, (f).
Prohibited, §48-9-104.
Protection of adoptee or public, §48-9-105.
Unauthorized disclosure, §48-10-105.
Release of nonidentifying health-related information.
Agency release to former parent or sibling, §48-9-103, (f).
Court release to adoptee or adoptive parent, §48-9-103, (e).
Express provisions for confidentiality, §48-9-103, (c).
Failure to disclose, §48-10-104.
Omission of identifying information, §48-9-103, (c).
Procedure for verifying identity of requester, §48-9-103, (g).
Protection of adoptee or public.
Motion for release of information not otherwise obtainable, §48-9-105.
Request to agency, §48-9-103, (b).
Request to court, §48-9-103, (b).
Request to state registrar of vital statistics prohibited, §48-9-103, (h).
Review of denial, §48-9-103, (d).
Unauthorized disclosure, §48-10-105.
Who may request, §48-9-103, (a).
Report of adoption or name change of minor, §48-9-102, (f).
Sealed, permanently retained, §48-9-102, (c).
Statistical research.
Disclosure not resulting in identification of adoptee authorized, §48-9-109.
Unauthorized disclosure of information, §48-10-105.
Generally, §48-10-105, (a).
Misdemeanor, §48-10-105, (b).
Relinquishment.
Agency acceptance of relinquishment, §48-3-702, (b), (c).
Agency placement of minors for adoption, §48-3-201, (c).
Relinquishment from one parent sufficient, §48-3-201, (d).
Contents, mandatory provisions, §48-3-703, (a).
Contents, optional provisions, §48-3-704.
Custody of minor upon execution, §48-3-705, (b).

ADOPTION —Cont'd
Relinquishment —Cont'd
Custody of minor upon revocation, §48-3-706, (b).
Defined, §48-1-101.
Dismissal of proceeding upon voiding of relinquishment, §48-3-707, (c), (d).
Effect, §48-3-705, (a).
General procedures, §48-3-702.
Guardian relinquishment of guardianship powers, §48-3-701, (a).
Timing of execution, §48-3-701, (c).
Irrevocable second relinquishment, §48-3-706, (d).
Mandatory contents, §48-3-703, (a).
Optional contents, §48-3-704.
Parental relinquishment of rights, §48-3-701, (a).
Timing of execution, §48-3-701, (b).
Procedures generally, §48-3-702, (a).
Revocation.
Adoption cannot proceed until other relinquishment obtained, §48-3-706, (c).
Condition precedent, §48-3-707, (b).
Custody of minor, §48-3-706, (b).
Procedure, §48-3-706, (a).
Second relinquishment irrevocable, §48-3-706, (d).
Termination of rights, §48-3-705, (c).
Certain rights not terminated until relinquishment filed, §48-3-705, (d).
Timing of execution, §48-3-701, (b), (c).
Void, §48-3-707, (a).
Dismissal of adoption proceeding, §48-3-707, (c), (d).
Reports.
Adoption or name change of adult, §48-9-102, (a).
Adoption or name change of minor, §48-9-102, (f).
Copies of report to court, §48-2-503, (c).
Fee for preparing.
Agreement, §48-2-504, (a).
Application of fees collected, §48-2-504, (c).
Court may charge petitioner, §48-2-504, (a).
Maximum fees.
Basis for, §48-2-504, (c).
Review by court, §48-2-504, (b).
Waiver of fees.
Unable to pay, §48-2-504, (c).
Filing of report to court, §48-2-503.
Interim report.
Specific concerns identified by agency, §48-2-503, (b).
Order for report to court, §§48-1-109, (c), 48-2-501, (a).
Adoption petition and additional documents provided to preparer, §48-2-501, (c).
Preparation, agency responsibility, §48-2-501, (b).
Preparation of report to court.
Adoption of rules to implement provisions, §48-2-502, (c).
Contents, §48-2-502, (b).
Fees, §48-2-504.
Procedure, §48-2-502, (a).
Preplacement assessments generally. See within this heading, "Preplacement assessments."
"Report to the court" defined, §48-1-101.
Specific concern identified by agency.
Supplemental report as to satisfaction of concerns, §48-2-504, (b1).
Stepparent adoptions, §48-2-501, (d).
Time for filing report to court, §48-2-503, (a).
Revocation of consent, §§48-3-607 to 48-3-609.

ADOPTION —Cont'd
Rights of adoptee.
Vested property interest not divested by decree, §48-1-107.
Service of process.
Agency placements.
Petition to terminate parental rights filed instead of serving notice, §48-2-402, (c).
Filing of proof of service, §48-2-407.
Identity of biological parent cannot be ascertained, §48-2-402, (b).
Motion for release of information, §48-9-105, (b).
Notice of filing of petition, §48-2-402, (a).
Proof of service, §48-2-407.
Unknown biological parent, §48-2-402, (b).
Solicitation of adoptees for adoption.
Unauthorized persons, §48-10-101, (a).
Specific performance.
Failure to disclose nonidentifying information.
Civil action for equitable relief, §48-10-104.
Statute of limitations.
Action for damages against adoptee or adoptive parent.
Fraud or duress in obtaining consent, §48-2-607, (c).
Stepparents.
Applicability of articles on adoption of minors, §§48-3-100, 48-4-100.
Consent to adoption of stepchild, §48-4-102.
Execution by adoptee, §48-4-103, (e).
Execution by guardian of minor stepchild, §48-4-103, (c).
Execution by stepchild's parent who is not a spouse of stepparent, §48-4-103, (b).
Execution by stepparent's spouse, §48-4-103, (a).
Final and irrevocable, §48-4-103, (d).
Defined, §48-1-101.
Effect on relationship between child and parent who is spouse of stepparent, §48-1-106, (d).
Petition for adoption.
Who may file, §48-4-101.
Report to court.
Exception to requirement, §48-2-501, (d).
Visitation rights of biological grandparents.
Previously existing rights not terminated, §48-4-105, (a).
Right to petition not affected by article, §48-4-105, (b).
Who may file petition, §48-4-101.
Taking and sending child out of state for purposes of placement.
Applicability of article, §7B-3705.
Consent of department of health and human services required, §7B-3702.
Definitions, §7B-3704.
Misdemeanor for violating provisions, §7B-3703.
Termination of parental rights.
Agency placements.
Legal and physical custody of minor with agency, §48-3-203, (a).
Petition to terminate filed instead of serving notice, §48-2-402, (c).
Certified copy of order to be filed with adoption petition, §48-2-305.
Consent not required from persons whose rights terminated, §48-3-603, (a).
Finding that clerk of superior court has jurisdiction for adoptions.
Required before court exercises jurisdiction to terminate parental rights, §7B-1101.

ADOPTION —Cont'd
Termination of parental rights —Cont'd
Generally, §§7B-1100 to 7B-1113.
See TERMINATION OF PARENTAL RIGHTS.
Permanent placement review hearing.
Cancellation, placement for adoption prior to review, §7B-908, (e).
Person filing adoption petition, right to file petition or motion, intervention, right, §7B-1103, (a), (b).
Petition for adoption filed concurrently with petition to terminate parental rights, §48-2-302, (c).
Selection of adoptive parents, responsibility, §7B-908, (f).
Time.
Notice of proceedings by clerk of court, §48-2-403.
Petition for adoption, time for filing, §48-2-302.
Placement assessments, completing, §48-3-303, (a).
Transfer of custody from health care facility.
Authorization to transfer minor to agency, §48-3-402, (a).
Unauthorized disclosure of information.
Civil action for equitable or monetary relief, §48-10-105, (d).
Injunctions, §48-10-105, (c).
Unknown biological parent.
Notice and service of process, §48-2-402, (b).
Unlawful payments related to adoption, §48-10-102.
Venue.
Petition for adoption, §48-2-101.
Transfer, stay or dismissal for improper venue, §48-2-102, (a).
Waiver of notice, §48-2-406.
Who may adopt, §48-1-103.
Who may be adopted, §48-1-104.
Wills.
After-born or after-adopted children, §31-5.5.

ADOPTIVE HOMES.
Regulation of agencies receiving or placing children in, §§131D-10.1 to 131D-10.9.
See CHILD PLACING AGENCIES.

ADULT CARE HOMES.
Actions, §131D-2, (i).
Residents' bill of rights.
Instituting civil actions, §131D-28.
Administrators of facilities.
Residents' bill of rights.
Implementation of provisions, §131D-25.
Alzheimer's disease.
Special care units.
Disclosure of information, §131D-8, (a), (b).
Applicability, §131D-8, (d).
Definition of "special care unit," §131D-8, (e).
License renewal.
Examination of disclosures for accuracy, §131D-8, (c).
Amenities exempted from licensure requirements, §131D-2, (c4).
Antitrust, antikickback or safe harbor law.
Not superseded, §131D-2, (c3).
Assistance granted to persons in adult care homes.
State-county special assistance for adults, §§108A-40 to 108A-47.
See SOCIAL SERVICES.
Audits, §131D-4.2, (f).

ADULT CARE HOMES —Cont'd
Bill of rights.
Actions.
Instituting civil action, §131D-28.
Address and telephone number of section responsible for enforcement, §131D-24, (b).
Administrator of facility.
Implementation of provisions, §131D-25.
Civil actions.
Institution of action, §131D-28.
Community advisory committees.
Appointment, §131D-31, (b).
Minimum qualifications for appointment, §131D-31, (g).
Establishment, §131D-31, (b).
Functions of committees, §131D-32, (a) to (j).
Joint nursing and adult care home community advisory committees, §131D-31, (c).
Minimum qualifications for appointment, §131D-31, (g).
Officers, §131D-31, (f).
Privileged communications, §131D-31, (i).
Purpose, §131D-31, (a).
Terms of office, §131D-31, (d).
Training, §131D-31, (h).
Vacancies, §131D-31, (e).
Compliance with provisions.
Insuring compliance, §131D-26, (c).
Confidentiality of information, §131D-27.
Copy of declaration of residents' rights.
Posting requirements, §131D-24, (a).
Declaration of residents' rights, §131D-21.
Copy of declaration, §131D-24, (a).
Definitions, §131D-20.
Disclosure of medical records to private peer review committee, §131D-21.1.
Enforcement of provisions.
Address and telephone number of section responsible for enforcement, §131D-24, (b).
Responsibility for enforcement, §131D-26, (a).
Enumeration of rights, §131D-21.
Fiduciaries.
Transfer of management responsibilities, §131D-22.
Guardians.
Transfer of management responsibilities, §131D-22.
Implementation of provisions, §131D-25.
Investigations.
Violations of provisions, §131D-26, (a1), (b).
Legislative intent, §131D-19.
Licenses.
Revocation of facilities license for violations of provisions, §131D-29.
Notice to resident, §131D-24.
No waiver of rights, §131D-23.
Peer review, §131D-21.1.
Penalties.
Actions to collect penalties, §131D-34, (g).
Amount of initial penalty.
Factors to be considered, §131D-34, (c).
Facts found to support factors.
Basis for determining amount, §131D-34, (c1).
Civil penalty and forfeiture fund, remission of proceeds, §131D-34, (i).
Commencement of penalty, §131D-34, (f).
Contesting penalties, §131D-34, (e).
Failure to correct violations within time specified, §131D-34, (b).

ADULT CARE HOMES —Cont'd
Bill of rights —Cont'd
Penalties —Cont'd
Inspections.
Refusal to allow inspection.
Civil penalty, §131D-34, (d).
Review committee, §131D-34, (h).
Staff training in lieu of assessing, §131D-34, (g1).
Telephone number of section responsible for enforcement, §131D-24, (b).
Transfer of management responsibilities, §131D-22.
Violations of provisions.
Classification of violations, §131D-34, (a).
Investigations, §131D-26, (a1), (b).
Penalties, §131D-34.
Reporting number of substantiated violations, §131D-26, (d).
Waiver of rights.
No waiver, §131D-23.
Compliance history provider file, §§131D-41, 131E-266.
Confidentiality of information.
Death of resident.
Reporting, §131D-34.1, (d).
Quality assurance, medical, or peer review committees, proceedings and records, §131D-21.2, (b).
Residents' bill of rights, §131D-27.
Contract agency.
Criminal history records check.
Requirement, §131D-40, (a1).
County's share of costs, §143B-139.5.
Criminal history record checks for providers and employees, §§114-19.3, 114-19.10, 131D-40.
Day care programs, §131D-6.
Death of resident.
Confidentiality, §131D-34.1, (d).
Notification to department, §131D-34.1, (a).
Duties of department upon receipt of, §131D-34.1, (b), (c).
Standard reporting format, §131D-34.1, (e).
Defined, §§131D-2, (a), 131E-101, 131E-231.
Department of Health and Human Services.
Compliance history provider file, §131D-41.
Share of costs, §143B-139.5.
Emergencies.
Waiver of rules for certain homes providing shelter or service during disaster or emergency, §131D-7, (a).
Definition of "emergency management agency," §131D-7, (b).
Employees.
Criminal history record checks.
Action on positive check, §131D-40, (b).
Conditional employment, §131D-40, (f).
Immunity from liability, §131D-40, (g).
Limited immunity, §131D-40, (c).
Penalty for furnishing false information, §131D-40, (e).
Relevant offenses, §131D-40, (d).
Required for certain employees, §131D-40, (a).
Immunization, §131D-9.
Enforcement of provisions, §131D-4.2, (g).
Evaluation of residents, §131D-2, (e).
Persons in need of medical and nursing care, §131E-106.
Evidence.
Temporary management.
Hearing on petition for appointment of temporary manager, §131E-233, (b).

ADULT CARE HOMES —Cont'd
Exemptions, §131D-2, (c).
Fiduciaries.
Bill of rights.
Transfer of management responsibilities, §131D-22.
General assembly.
Residents' bill of rights.
Legislative intent, §131D-19.
Guardians.
Bill of rights.
Transfer of management responsibilities, §131D-22.
Health facilities personnel registry, §131E-256.
Hospice care, §131D-2, (a3).
Immunization of residents and employees.
Definition of "employee," §131D-9, (g).
Determination of individual's status, §131D-9, (d).
Documentation, §131D-9, (c).
Notification of requirement, §131D-9, (b), (b1).
Requirement, §131D-9, (a).
Exceptions, §131D-9, (e).
Rules, §131D-9, (f).
Inspections, §§131D-2, (b), 131E-105.
Patients' bill of rights.
Refusal to allow inspection.
Civil penalty, §131D-34, (d).
Intent of legislature, §131D-4.1.
Investigations.
Death of resident within seven days of use of physical restraint, §131D-34.1, (c).
Residents' bill of rights.
Violations of provisions to be investigated, §131D-26, (a1), (b).
Legislative intent, §131D-4.1.
Licenses, §131D-2, (b).
Amenities exempted from licensure requirements, §131D-2, (c4).
Definitions, §131E-101.
Enforcement of provisions, §131D-4.3, (c).
Interference with.
Community advisory committee, §131D-2, (g).
Residents' bill of rights.
Revocation of license, §131D-29.
Revocation of license.
Residents' bill of rights.
Violations, §131D-29.
Special care units, §131D-4.6, (b), (c).
Long-term care ombudsman program, §§143B-181.15 to 143B-181.24.
See LONG-TERM CARE OMBUDSMAN.
Management.
Temporary management, §131D-35.
Medical care commission.
Powers, §§131D-4.5, 143B-165.
Notice.
Residents' bill of rights.
Notice to resident, §131D-24.
Nursing care.
Evaluation of residents, §131E-106.
Nursing homes.
General provisions.
See NURSING HOMES.
Patients' bill of rights, §§131E-115 to 131E-131.
See NURSING HOMES.
Penalties.
Residents' bill of rights, §131D-34.
Persons not to be cared for in, §131D-2, (a1).
Multiunit assisted housing with services, §131D-2, (a2).

ADULT CARE HOMES —Cont'd
Physical restraint.
Investigations.
Death of resident within seven days of use, §131D-34.1, (c).
Report on use, §131D-42.
Quality assurance, medical, or peer review committees.
Confidentiality of proceedings and records, immunity from discovery, §131D-21.2, (b).
Immunity, §131D-21.2, (a).
Rate adjustments.
Report documentation used, §131D-4.2, (h).
Records.
Peer review, §§131D-21.1, 131D-21.2, (b).
Quality assurance, medical, or peer review committee.
Confidentiality of records, immunity from discovery, §131D-21.2, (b).
Remedies.
Residents' bill of rights, §131D-34.
Reporting number of substantiated violations, §131D-26, (d).
Reports, §131D-4.2, (a).
Costs, §131D-4.2, (b).
First report due date, §131D-4.2, (e).
Exemptions, §131D-4.2, (d).
Physical restraint.
Use, §131D-42.
Suspension of admissions to facilities.
Failure to submit annual report, §131D-4.2, (g).
Rules and regulations, §131E-104.
Adoption as emergency rules, §131D-4.3, (b).
Adoption by medical care commission, §131D-2, (c2).
Adoption by social services commission, §131D-4.3, (a).
Immunization of residents and employees, §131D-9, (f).
Medical care commission, §131D-4.5.
Safety.
Minimum requirements, §131D-4.4.
Services not at expense of housing management.
Right of resident to obtain, §131D-2, (c1).
Severability, §131D-2, (f).
Special care units.
Cost reports, §131D-4.2, (a), (b).
Defined, §131D-4.6, (a).
Licensing, §131D-4.6, (b), (c).
Specialist fund, §131D-4.7.
Staffing requirements, §131D-4.3, (a).
Suspension of admissions, §131D-2, (h).
Failure to submit annual report, §131D-4.2, (g).
Temporary management, §131D-35.
Accounting after termination, §131E-244, (a).
Appointment of manager.
Alternatives, §131E-235, (a), (b).
Grounds, §§131E-233, (c), 131E-234.
Procedures, §131E-233, (a), (b).
Candidates for temporary manager, §131E-237.
Compensation of temporary manager, §131E-236.
Conditions on return to owner, §131E-243, (d).
Conflict of laws, §131E-246.
Contingency fund.
Department may maintain, §131E-242, (a).
Funds provided for management, court order, §131E-242, (b).
Reallocation, §131E-242, (c).
Continuing need, review, §131E-243, (a).

ADULT CARE HOMES —Cont'd
Temporary management —Cont'd
Correction of deficiencies in excess of $1,000.
Correction without prior approval, §131E-239, (d).
Written plan submitted by manager, §131E-239, (a).
Hearing on plan, §131E-239, (c).
Service of copy upon department and respondent, §131E-239, (b).
Definitions, §131E-231.
Expenses of management.
Accounting after termination, §131E-244, (a).
Deficiencies, liability, §131E-244, (b).
Lien for reasonable costs, §131E-244, (c).
Notice, §131E-244, (f).
Priority, §131E-244, (d).
Recording, §131E-244, (e).
Reasonableness, petition to determine, §131E-244, (b).
Repayment over time, §131E-244, (b).
Findings of legislature, §131E-230.
Leases, mortgages and contracts by respondent.
Manager not required to honor, §131E-241, (a).
Real estate or goods necessary for continued operation.
Application to court to set compensation for, §131E-241, (b), (c).
Liability for payment for goods and services, §131E-240, (a).
Action to enforce liability, §131E-240, (b).
Deposit of amounts received, §131E-240, (a).
Omission to pay respondent for payment to manager, §131E-240, (c).
Receipt given for payment, §131E-240, (a).
Lien for reasonable costs, §131E-244, (c) to (f).
Obligations of licensee, §131E-245.
Payment for goods or services.
Liability for, §131E-240, (a) to (c).
Petition, §131E-232.
Powers and duties of temporary manager, §131E-238.
Preexisting leases, mortgages and contracts.
Avoidance, §131E-241, (a) to (c).
Removal or remedying conditions.
Alternative to appointment of temporary manager, §131E-235, (a), (b).
Replacement of manager, mismanagement, §131E-243, (b).
Termination, court order, §131E-243, (c).
Accounting by manager after, §131E-244, (a).

ADULT DAY CARE PROGRAMS.
Alzheimer's disease.
Disclosure requirements for programs offering special care services for persons with, §131D-6, (b1) to (b4).
Civil penalty for violations, §131D-6, (c).
Defined, §131D-6, (b).
Exempt programs, §131D-6, (d).
Harming or willfully neglecting person under care, §131D-6, (c1).
Inspection and certification, §131D-6, (b).
Policy of state, §131D-6, (a).
Rules to protect health, safety and welfare, §131D-6, (b).
Transportation for participants, §131D-6, (a).

ADULT EDUCATION.
Entitlement to attend, §115C-231, (c).
Free tuition.
Persons 18 years of age or older not having completed high school, §115C-231, (b).

ADULT EDUCATION —Cont'd
Organization and administration of program, §115C-231, (a).
Removal or prohibiting enrollment.
Persons having attained age of 21 years, §115C-231, (c).

ADULTERATION.
Antifreeze.
Deemed to be adulterated, §106-579.5.
Commercial feed.
Deemed to be adulterated, §106-284.38.
Flour, cornmeal and grain, §§106-621 to 106-628.
Food, drug and cosmetic act, §§106-120 to 106-145.
See FOOD, DRUG AND COSMETIC ACT.
Gasoline and oil inspection.
Products offered for sale, §119-35.
Grains, §§106-621 to 106-628.
See GRAIN ADULTERATION.
Health.
Embargo of adulterated or misbranded food, §130A-21, (a) to (e).
Meat inspection.
Defined, §106-549.15.
Examinations and inspection before slaughter, §106-549.17.
Exemptions, §106-549.27, (e).
Motor vehicles.
Antifreeze.
Deemed to be adulterated, §106-579.5.
Poultry inspection.
Ante mortem inspections, §106-549.53, (a).
Condemnation, §106-549.53, (c).
Defined, §106-549.51.
Enforcement, §106-549.58, (b).
Exemptions, §106-549.62, (f).
Soil additives act, §§106-50.28 to 106-50.41.

ADULTERY, §14-184.
Acts barring rights of spouse, §31A-1, (a).
Admissibility of admission or confession as evidence, §14-184.
Divorce.
Grounds for divorce, §50-7.
Domestic violence.
Effect upon prosecuting for violation of section 14-184 or other offense against public morals, §50B-8.
Parties as witnesses, §8-50, (a).

ADULT ESTABLISHMENTS.
ABC permits.
Local government regulation of adult establishments or other sexually oriented businesses.
Provisions not deemed to preempt, §18B-904, (g).
Adult bookstores.
Defined, §14-202.10.
Adult live entertainment.
Defined, §14-202.10.
Adult mini motion picture theaters.
Defined, §14-202.10.
Restrictions on occupancy of viewing booths, §14-202.11, (b).
Adult motion picture theaters.
Defined, §14-202.10.
Definitions, §14-202.10.
Person, §14-202.12.
Local regulation, §14-202.11, (c).
Massage business defined, §14-202.10.

ADULT ESTABLISHMENTS —Cont'd
Massage defined, §14-202.10.
Restrictions as to adult establishments, §14-202.11, (a).
Penalty for violation of provisions, §14-202.12.
Sexually oriented devices.
Defined, §14-202.10.
Specified anatomical area defined, §14-202.10.
Specified sexual activities, §14-202.10.

ADULT HIGH SCHOOL DIPLOMAS.
Post-release supervision.
Reintegrative conditions, §15A-1364.4, (d).
World War II veterans.
Powers of board of education, §115C-12.

ADULT PROTECTION ACT, §§108A-99 to 108A-111.
See ABUSED, NEGLECTED OR EXPLOITED DISABLED ADULTS.

ADULTS.
Abused, neglected or exploited disabled adults, §§108A-99 to 108A-111.
See ABUSED, NEGLECTED OR EXPLOITED DISABLED ADULTS.
Adoption, §§48-5-100 to 48-5-103.
See ADOPTION.
Adult care homes.
Generally.
See ADULT CARE HOMES.
Education.
General provisions, §115C-231.
Health.
Establishment of program, §130A-223, (a), (b).
Homes.
Adult care homes.
Generally.
See ADULT CARE HOMES.

AD VALOREM TAXES.
Oil, gas and mineral interest severed or separated from surface fee.
Listing to be effective against surface fee holder, creditors, purchasers, heirs or assigns, §§1-42.1 to 1-42.9.
Property taxes.
Generally.
See PROPERTY TAXES.
Sales and use tax.
See SALES AND USE TAX.

ADVANCE HEALTH CARE DIRECTIVE REGISTRY, §§130A-465 to 130A-471.
Access to registry, §130A-469.
Documents to be registered, §130A-466, (a).
Effect of registration, §130A-468, (d).
Establishment, §130A-465.
Fee for filing, §130A-466, (e).
Amount, §130A-470, (a).
Subject to audit, §130A-470, (c).
File number and password, §130A-468, (a).
Access to registry, §130A-469.
Immunities, §130A-471.
Limitation of liability, §130A-471.
Notarization of documents, §130A-466, (b).
Original document returned to person who filed, §130A-468, (b).
Reproduction entered into database, §130A-468, (a).
Return address required, §130A-466, (d).
Revocation of registered document, §130A-468, (c).

ADVANCE HEALTH CARE DIRECTIVE REGISTRY —Cont'd
Unregistered documents, validity, §130A-467.
Voluntary contributions of funds, §130A-470, (b).
Who may file, §130A-466, (c).

ADVANCEMENTS.
Agriculture.
Landlord's lien on crops for rents, §42-15.
Death of advancee before intestate donor, §29-27.
Defined, §29-2.
Effect, §29-25.
Future advancements, §§29-23 to 29-29.
Generally, §29-23.
Gift inter vivos.
Presumption of gift, §29-24.
Guardians.
Parties to proceedings, §35A-1324.
Housing authorities and projects.
Municipal cooperation and aid.
Advances and donations by city and municipality, §157-43.
Intestate succession.
General provisions, §§29-23 to 29-29.
See INTESTATE SUCCESSION.
Inventory.
Failure to give inventory, §29-28.
Landlord and tenant.
Agricultural tenancies.
Lien on crops, §42-15.
Mental health and developmental disabilities.
Surplus income and advancements, §§35A-1321 to 35A-1330.
Mortgages and deeds of trust.
Advances and future obligations, §§45-68 to 45-74.
Nonprofit corporations.
Directors.
Notice to members, §55A-16-21.
Obtaining advances under promise to work and pay for, §14-104.
Obtaining advances under written promise to pay from designated property, §14-105.
Release by advancee, §29-29.
Sharecroppers.
Landlord failing to make advance, §14-359.
Receiving advance with intent to defraud, §§14-358, 14-359.
Taking into account and computation at estate, §29-23.
Valuation.
Determination, §29-26.

ADVANCE PAYMENTS TO PERSONS CLAIMING BODILY INJURIES, §1-540.3.

ADVANCES.
Contract rates and fees, §24-1.1.
Powers of fiduciaries incorporated by reference, §32-27.
Savings and loan association interest rates, §24-1.4.
State opt-out for federal preemptions, §24-2.3, (a), (b).

ADVANCES AND FUTURE OBLIGATIONS, INSTRUMENTS TO SECURE, §§45-67 to 45-74.
Article not exclusive, §45-74.
Cancellation of record, §45-73.
Electric or telephone membership corporations.
Instruments securing obligations, §45-70, (d).

ADVANCES AND FUTURE OBLIGATIONS, INSTRUMENTS TO SECURE —Cont'd
Fire and extended coverage insurance.
Security for payment, §45-70, (c).
Fluctuation of obligations within maximum amount, §45-69.
Instruments to secure equity lines of credit.
Future advances statute not to apply, §45-83.
Priorities.
Security instruments, §45-70, (a).
Probate and registration.
Termination of future optional advances, §45-72.
Requirements, §45-68.
Applicability, §45-68.
Satisfaction of security instrument, §45-71.
Security instruments.
Defined, §45-67.
Presentation of notes described in instrument, §45-73.
Priority, §45-70, (a).
Requirement, §45-70, (a).
Satisfaction, §45-71.
Termination of future optional advances, §45-72, (a).

ADVANCE SHEETS.
Administrative officer of the courts.
Designation of commercial advance sheets as official reports, §7A-6, (b1).
Furnishing advance sheets without charge, §7A-6, (c).
Sale of advance sheets, §7A-6, (b).
Printing.
Contracting for printing of advance sheets by administrative officer of the courts, §7A-6, (b).
Sales.
Administrative officer of the courts to sell, §7A-6, (b).

ADVERSE POSSESSION.
Boundaries.
Color of title.
Known and visible lines and boundaries, §1-38.
Canals.
No title by possession of right of way, §1-44.
Color of title, §1-38.
Seven years' possession under color of title, §1-38.
Commissioner's deeds in judicial sales.
Constitute color of title, §1-38, (a).
Definitions.
Public trust rights, §1-45.1.
Entry on land.
Action must be commenced within one year after entry, §1-41.
Evidence of seven years possession under color of title, §1-38, (b).
Highways.
No title by possession of public ways, §1-45.
Turnpike companies.
No title by possession of right of way, §1-44.
Landlord and tenant.
Tenant's possession is landlord's, §1-43.
Maps recorded prior to October 1, 1973.
Qualified as if certified, §1-38, (c).
Marriage.
Disability of marriage, §1-18.
Mineral rights.
Severance of surface and subsurface rights, §1-42.
Persons under disability.
Seven years possession under color of title.
Possession perpetual bar against, §1-38, (a).
Possession follows legal title, §1-42.

ADVERSE POSSESSION —Cont'd
Presumptions.
Effect of record chain of title, §1-42.
Railroad right of way.
Abandonment, §1-44.1.
Title presumed out of state, §1-36.
Public trust rights.
Defined, §1-45.1.
No adverse possession of property subject to, §1-45.1.
Public ways.
No title by possession of public ways, §1-45.
Railroads.
Abandonment of right of way.
Presumption, §1-44.1.
No title by possession of right of way, §1-44.
Record chain of title.
Prima facie evidence of possession, §1-42.
Right of way.
No title by possession of right of way, §1-44.
Railroad right of way.
Presumption of abandonment, §1-44.1.
Seizing within twenty years necessary, §1-39.
Seven years possession under color of title.
Entry or action against possessor barred, §1-38, (a).
State of North Carolina.
Title against state, §1-35.
Validity of possession against claimants under state, §1-37.
Title against state, §1-35.
Title conclusively deemed out of state, §1-36.
Torrens system registration.
No right by adverse possession, §43-21.
Trustee's deeds in foreclosure.
Constitute color of title, §1-38, (a).
Twenty year limitation, §1-40.
Seizing within twenty years necessary, §1-39.

ADVERTISEMENTS.
Adoption.
Desire to adopt, §48-10-101, (b1).
Unauthorized persons, misdemeanor, §48-10-101, (b), (c).
Affidavit of publication.
Legal advertising, §§1-598, 1-600, (a).
Prima facie evidence, §1-600, (b).
Alcoholic beverages.
Authority of commission to make rules, §18B-105, (b).
Compliance with rules of commission, §18B-105, (a).
Architects.
Rules and regulations prohibiting.
Board not to adopt, §83A-6, (b).
Attorneys at law, Prof. Cond. Rule 7.2.
Communications of fields of practice, Prof. Cond. Rule 7.4.
Dramatization depicting fictional situation, Prof. Cond. Rule 7.1.
False or misleading communications concerning services, Prof. Cond. Rule 7.1.
Auctions and auctioneers.
Misleading or untruthful advertising.
Grounds for suspension or revocation of license, §85B-8, (a).
Bids and bidding.
Public building contracts, §143-131, (a).
Billboards.
Blue Ridge parkway.
Control of outdoor advertising, §§113A-165 to 113A-170.

ADVERTISEMENTS —Cont'd
Billboards —Cont'd
Churches or schools.
Obstructing view at entrance, §136-102.
Outdoor advertising generally, §§136-126 to 136-140.
See OUTDOOR ADVERTISING.
Transportation department reporting requirements, §136-12.1.
Blue Ridge parkway.
Control of outdoor advertising, §§113A-165 to 113A-170.
Cemeteries.
Perpetual care fund.
Requirements for advertising, §65-63.
Chiropractors.
False or misleading advertisement, grounds for disciplinary actions, §90-154, (b).
Free or reduced rate service.
Notice to patient, §90-154.1, (b).
Cities.
Outdoor advertising.
Regulation of nonconforming off-premises outdoor advertising, §160A-199.
Closing-out sales.
Advertising sale contrary to provisions, §66-81.
False advertisements, §66-82.
Consumer finance act.
False or misleading statements, §53-183.
Continuing care retirement communities.
Marketing by unlicensed providers, §58-64-5, (a).
Contracts.
Public building contracts.
Second advertisement, §143-132, (a).
Purchases and contracts through department of administration.
Competitive bidding procedure, §143-52.
Setting of benchmarks, §143-53.1.
Counties.
Outdoor advertising.
Regulation of nonconforming off-premises outdoor advertising, §153A-143.
Deceptive and fraudulent advertising, §14-117.
Defacing or destroying advertisements, §14-385.
Diamonds.
Unfair trade practices in diamond industry, §66-74.
Drug paraphernalia, §90-113.24, (a), (b).
Eggs.
Designation in block letters, §106-245.20.
Electioneering communications.
Disclosures, prohibited sources, §§163-278.80 to 163-278.83.
Mass mailings and telephone banks, §§163-278.90 to 163-278.93.
Elections.
Contributions and expenditures in political campaigns.
Charges, §163-278.18, (a), (b).
Disclosure requirements for media advertisements, §§163-278.39 to 163-278.39C.
Electrologists.
Board of electrologist examiners.
Powers to regulate, §88A-6.
Electronic surveillance devices.
Felony, §15A-288, (a2).
Employee assistance professionals.
Representation as licensed professional, §90-508.

ADVERTISEMENTS —Cont'd
Food, drug and cosmetic act.
Definitions and general consideration, §106-121.
False advertising, §§106-122, 106-138, (a), (b).
Violations made misdemeanor, §106-124, (c).
Funeral service.
Defined, §90-210.20, (a).
Gasoline prices.
Drawing or pumping fuel by purchaser himself, §14-117.2, (a), (b).
Hatcheries and chick dealers.
False advertising, §106-545.
Health maintenance organizations.
False or misleading advertising, §58-67-65, (a).
Solicitation of enrollees.
Not deemed validation of law relating to advertising by health professionals, §58-67-170, (b).
Injuring advertisements, §14-384.
Insurance.
Medicare supplement insurance.
Filing requirements for advertising, §58-54-35.
Third party administrators.
Approval, §58-56-21.
Unauthorized insurers.
Domestic companies, §58-14-10.
Cease and desist orders, §58-14-15.
Unauthorized insurers false advertising process act.
Generally, §§58-29-1 to 58-29-25.
See UNAUTHORIZED INSURERS.
Unfair trade practices.
False advertising, §58-63-15.
Job listing services.
Identification of self by service, §95-47.26, (a).
Prerequisites, §95-47.26, (b).
Term "no fee" not to be used, §95-47.26, (d).
Judicial sales, §1-595.
Public sale.
Posting and publishing notices of sale of real property, §1-339.17, (a) to (e).
Posting notice of sale of personal property, §1-339.18, (a), (b).
Time for beginning advertisement, §1-339.16.
Law enforcement officers' association publications.
Soliciting advertisements for publications, §14-401.10.
Legal advertising.
Affidavit of publication, §§1-598, 1-600, (a).
Prima facie evidence, §1-600, (b).
Charges, §1-596.
Evidence of publication in newspaper.
Proof of publication of notice in newspaper prima facie evidence, §1-600, (b).
Sworn statement prima facie evidence of qualification, §1-598.
Judicial sales, §1-595.
Newspapers.
Affidavit of publication, §§1-598, 1-600, (a).
Prima facie evidence, §1-600, (b).
Charges, §1-596.
No qualified newspaper in county, §§1-597, 1-599.
Proof of publication of notice in newspaper, §1-600, (a).
Method of proof not exclusive, §1-600, (c).
Prima facie evidence, §1-600, (b).
Requisites for newspaper publication, §1-597.
Applicability of provisions, §1-599.

ADVERTISEMENTS —Cont'd
Legal advertising —Cont'd
Newspapers —Cont'd
Requisites for newspaper publication —Cont'd
Sworn statement prima facie evidence of qualification, §1-598.
Public sales, §1-595.
Rates and charges.
Newspapers, §1-596.
Sales.
Public sales, §1-595.
Validation.
Certain legal advertisements validated, §1-601.
Liquid fuels.
Sale of fuels different from advertised name prohibited, §119-8.
Locksmiths, §74F-12, (b).
Lotteries.
Misdemeanor offense of advertising lotteries, §14-289.
Lubricating oils.
Sale of lubricants different from advertised name prohibited, §119-8.
Mattresses and bedding.
Tags.
Advertising prohibited, §130A-265, (d).
Membership camping, §66-242.
Mobile homes.
Uniform standards code.
Disclosure of manner used in determining length of manufactured homes, §143-143.20.
Mortgage bankers and brokers.
Prohibited acts, §53-243.11.
Motor courts, rates and charges, §§72-50 to 72-52.
Motor vehicle dealers.
Coercing or attempting to coerce dealer to participate voluntarily in advertising campaign, §20-305.
Type and serial number of license to appear, §20-290, (c).
Motor vehicle manufacturers.
False or misleading advertising, §20-305.
Type and serial number of license to appear, §20-290, (c).
Motor vehicle servicing or repairing.
Private passenger vehicles.
Truthful advertisements of costs, §66-285.
Newspapers.
Legal advertising.
Affidavit of publication, §§1-598, 1-600, (a).
Prima facie evidence, §1-600, (b).
Charges, §1-596.
No qualified newspaper in county, §§1-597, 1-599.
Proof of publication of notice in newspaper, §1-600, (a).
Method of proof not exclusive, §1-600, (c).
Prima facie evidence, §1-600, (b).
Requisites for newspaper publication, §1-597.
Applicability of provisions, §1-599.
Sworn statement prima facie evidence of qualification, §1-598.
Validation of certain advertisements, §1-601.
Unfair competitive practices.
Applicability of provisions to publications, §75-1.1.
Notaries public.
False or misleading advertising, §10A-4, (c).
Immigration, prohibitions on advertising as consultant, §10A-9, (h).

ADVERTISEMENTS —Cont'd
Notaries public —Cont'd
Notice that notary is not an attorney, §10A-9, (g), (j).
Nurses.
Loans.
Consolidation of information on existing scholarships and loan programs, §90-171.50.
Need-based nursing scholarships fund.
Universities and colleges, §90-171.65, (c).
Salary levels, job opportunities, refresher courses and license renewal requirements.
Developing publicity on, §90-171.53.
Nursing home administrators.
Fraudulent, misleading or deceptive advertising.
Grounds for revocation or suspension of license, §90-285.1.
Obscenity.
Literature and exhibitions.
Advertising or otherwise promoting sale of obscene material, §14-190.1, (f).
Opticians.
Certain advertising as grounds for revocation or suspension of license, §90-249, (b).
Osteopaths.
False advertising.
Grounds for refusal, revocation or suspension of license, §90-136.
Outdoor advertising.
Blue Ridge parkway.
Control of advertising on parkway, §§113A-165 to 113A-170.
Cities.
Regulation of nonconforming off-premises outdoor advertising, §160A-199.
Counties.
Regulation of nonconforming off-premises outdoor advertising, §153A-143.
General provisions, §§136-126 to 136-140.
See OUTDOOR ADVERTISING.
Scenic highways, state and national parks and historic areas.
Advertising adjacent to park.
Limitations, §136-129.2, (a) to (c).
Podiatrists.
False advertising as grounds for suspension or revocation of license, §90-202.8, (a).
Posting.
Unlawful posting of advertisements.
Criminal trespass, §14-145.
Preneed funeral contracts and funds.
False or misleading advertising.
Refusal to issue or renew, suspension or revocation of license, §90-210.69, (c).
Prepaid legal services plans.
State bar approval prohibited, Bar Rules & Regs., E, §.0304.
Private personnel services, §95-47.6.
Private protective services.
Unlicensed persons, §74C-16, (c).
Prizes.
Representation of eligibility to win a prize, §75-33.
Representation of winning a prize, §75-32.
Professional counselors.
Persons claiming exemption from licensure, §90-332.1, (b).
Professional employer organizations, §58-89A-80, (d).
Public building contracts.
Procedure for letting of public contracts, §§143-129, 143-131.

ADVERTISEMENTS —Cont'd
Radio and television.
Unfair competitive practices.
Applicability of provisions to broadcasts, §75-1.1.
Real estate brokers and salespersons.
License required, §93A-1.
Rental vehicles.
Advertising and sales practices, §§66-200 to 66-207.
Representation of being specially selected, §75-34.
Representation of eligibility to win a prize, §75-33.
Representation of winning a prize, §75-32.
Retail installment sales, §25A-2, (e).
Sale of prints by art dealers, §25C-11, (a).
Sales and use tax.
Advertisement to absorb tax unlawful, §105-164.9.
Savings banks.
False or misleading advertising, §54C-64.
Scenic highways, state and national parks and historic areas.
Outdoor advertising adjacent to park.
Limitations, §136-129.2, (a) to (c).
Speech and language pathologists and audiologists.
False or misleading advertising, §§90-301A, 90-304, (b).
Structural pest control.
Name of company shown on license and identification card, §106-65.31, (b3).
Therapeutic recreation personnel, §90C-3.
Time shares.
Exchange programs.
Statement to be included, §93A-48, (d).
Prizes, §93A-46.
Tourist camps and homes.
Rate advertisements, §§72-50 to 72-52.
Trespass.
Posting of advertisements.
Unlawful posting, §14-145.
Truth in advertisement.
Cost of service or repair of private passenger vehicles, §66-285.
Unauthorized insurers false advertising process act.
Generally, §§58-28-1 to 58-28-25.
See UNAUTHORIZED INSURERS.
Unfair competitive practices.
Applicability of provisions, §75-1.1.
Viatical life insurance settlements, §58-58-260.
Viatical settlement contract securities, §78A-14.
"Wholesale."
Use of term "wholesale," §75-29.
Work-at-home solicitations, §75-31.
Workers' compensation.
Self-insurance.
Third-party administrators and service companies.
Approval of advertising, §58-47-175.

ADVERTISING CONTROL ACT, §§136-126 to 136-140.
See OUTDOOR ADVERTISING.

ADVISORY JURY, §1A-1, Rule 39, (c).

AERONAUTICS.
Aircraft.
See AIRCRAFT.

AERONAUTICS —Cont'd
Airports.
See AIRPORTS.

AERONAUTICS ADMINISTRATION.
Rules and regulations.
Enforcement, §63-47.

AERONAUTICS COUNCIL.
Appointment of members, §143B-357, (a).
Chairman, designation, §143B-357, (b).
Clerical and other services, §143B-357, (d).
Compensation of members, §143B-357, (c).
Creation, §143B-356.
Duties, §143B-356.
Members, §143B-357, (a).
Powers and duties, §143B-356.
Quorum, §143B-357, (c).
Removal of members, §143B-357, (b).
Selection of members, §143B-357, (a).
Terms, §143B-357, (a).
Within department of transportation, §143B-357, (a).

AERONAUTICS DIVISION, §143B-355.

AFDC.
Work first program generally, §§108A-27 to 108A-39.
See WORK FIRST PROGRAM.

AFFIDAVITS.
Advertisements.
Legal advertising.
Affidavit of publication, §§1-598, 1-600, (a).
Prima facie evidence, §1-600, (b).
Appeal bonds.
Justification assurance, §1-286.
Arrest in civil cases.
Plaintiff, §1-411.
Copy to defendant, §1-414.
Counter affidavits, §1-418.
Assignments for benefit of creditors.
Petition for assignment, §23-13.
Attachment.
Amendment, §1-440.11, (c), (d).
Bonds, §1-440.8, (b).
Complaint.
Verified complaint use as affidavit, §1-440.11, (b).
Discharge upon giving bonds, §1-440.39, (b).
Dissolution of order, §1-440.36, (c).
Filing.
Judge to require, §1-440.5, (c).
Motion by plaintiff to sell remaining debts and evidences of indebtedness, §1-440.46, (b).
Requirements, §1-440.11, (a).
Sheriffs.
Sale of debts and other evidences of indebtedness, §1-440.46, (b).
Attorney disciplinary proceedings.
Consent to disbarment, Bar Rules & Regs., B, §.0117.
Disbarred or suspended attorney to show compliance with order, Bar Rules & Regs., B, §.0124.
Grievance reduced to affidavit form, Bar Rules & Regs., B, §.0111.
Resignation while under investigation, Bar Rules & Regs., B, §.0117.
Attorneys at law.
Continuing legal education.
General compliance procedures, CLE Reg. 8.

AFFIDAVITS —Cont'd
Bail bondsmen and runners.
Affidavits filed with clerk of court, §58-71-140, (d).
Bonds, surety.
Mortgage in lieu of bond.
Value of property required, §58-74-30.
Campaign contribution and expenditure statements and reports.
Certified as true and correct, §163-278.32.
Change of venue.
Application for removal, §1-85.
Child support.
Acknowledgment of paternity in agreement to support, §110-132, (a).
Claim and delivery, §1-473.
Third parties.
Property claimed by third person, §1-482.
CLE compliance, Bar Rules & Regs., D, §.1608.
Color of title under destroyed instrument, §98-8.
Contempt.
Civil contempt.
Order or notice, §5A-23, (a).
Proceeding initiated on motion of aggrieved party, §5A-23, (a1).
Continuing legal education compliance, Bar Rules & Regs., D, §.1608.
Credits upon judgments, §1-242.
Criminal law and procedure.
Depositions of nonattending witness, §8-74.
Motion for appropriate relief.
Supporting affidavits, §15A-1420, (b).
Motion to suppress evidence.
Pretrial motion in superior court.
Affidavit supporting motion, §15A-977, (a).
Nontestimonial identification orders, §15A-273.
Decedents' estates.
Debts and claims.
Right of personal representative to require affidavit of claimant, §28A-19-2, (b).
Default judgment, §1A-1, Rule 55, (a).
Devisavit vel non.
Witness to will as evidence, §31-35.
District attorneys, removal, §7A-66.
Drivers' licenses.
False affidavits.
Perjury, §20-31.
Durable power of attorney.
Statement by attorney-in-fact of no actual knowledge of termination of power by revocation.
Conclusive proof of nonrevocation or nontermination of power, §32A-13, (c).
Equitable distribution of marital and divisible property.
Inventory affidavit, §50-21, (a).
Executors and administrators.
Domiciliary administration.
Payment of debt and delivery of property without ancillary administration, §28A-26-2, (a).
False affidavit.
Perjury, §20-112.
Foreign judgments.
Affidavit stating judgment final and unsatisfied, §1C-1703, (a).
Foreign-money claims.
Enforcement of judgment, §1C-1826, (i).
Seizure or restraint of assets, §1C-1830, (d).
Foresters.
Consulting foresters.
Affidavit of compliance with provisions, §89B-14, (b).

AFFIDAVITS —Cont'd
Funeral service.
Good moral character of license applicant, §90-210.26.
Incompetence, determination of.
Notice and petition mailed to respondent's next of kin.
Proof of mailing or acceptance, §35A-1109.
Indigent persons.
Small claims actions.
Appeals, §7A-228, (b1).
Suing as indigent, §1-110, (a).
In forma pauperis appeals, §1-288.
Injunctions.
Preliminary injunction, §1-485.
Insurance companies.
Affidavit of company president or other chief officer.
Compliance with insurance law.
Required to do business, §58-2-150.
Landlord and tenant.
Execution of judgments for possession more than thirty days old, §42-36.1A.
Larceny.
Mutilation, larceny or destruction of public records and papers, §14-76.
Letters testamentary and of administration.
Application, §28A-6-1.
Lis pendens notice, §1-119, (a).
Lost instruments and records.
Mortgages and deeds of trust, §47-46.3.
Petitions and motions.
Facts stated to be verified by affidavit of petitioner, §98-14.
Lost note.
Form, §47-46.3.
Magistrates.
Verification of pleadings.
Power of magistrate to take affidavit for verification, §7A-292.
Manufactured home qualifying as real property, §47-20.6.
Surrender of title certificate.
Affidavit of qualification by owner, §20-109.2, (b).
Marriage certificates, delayed issuance, §51-21.
Marriage license.
Issuance to applicant unable to appear, §51-8.2.
Medical records, subpoena commanding custodian to produce.
Certified copies and affidavit in lieu of appearance, §1A-1, Rule 45, (c).
Mental health, developmental disabilities and substance abuse.
Involuntary commitment.
Petition and affidavit before clerk or magistrate, §122C-261.
Substance abuser, §122C-281.
Mortgages and deeds of trust.
Lost note.
Form, §47-46.3.
Motion for appropriate relief, §15A-1420, (b).
Motions supported by affidavits.
Affidavit served with motion, §1A-1, Rule 6, (d).
Motor vehicles.
False affidavit.
Perjury, §20-112.
Licenses.
False affidavits.
Perjury, §20-31.

AFFIDAVITS —Cont'd
Motor vehicles —Cont'd
Municipal parking violations.
Rented or leased vehicles.
Responsibility of owner, §160A-301, (e).
Traffic control photographic system.
Evidence exempting owner from liability, §160A-300.1, (c).
New trial.
Motion.
Time for serving affidavits, §1A-1, Rule 59, (c).
Optometrists.
Persons in practice before passage of statute, §90-119.
Partition sales.
Notice.
Certification and affidavit of notice, §46-28, (b).
Paternity.
Acknowledging paternity, §130A-101, (f).
Perjury.
Punishment for perjury, §14-209.
Probate and registration.
Land titles or family history, §47-1.
Unregistered deeds prior to January, 1920, §47-19.
Probate of wills.
Compelling production of will, §31-15.
Examination of witnesses by, §31-24.
What shown on application for probate, §31-16.
Proof of service of process, §1-75.10.
Prosecution bonds.
Land actions.
Defendant unable to give, not worth amount.
Bond not required, §1-112, (a).
Publication, service by.
Proof of service, §1-75.10.
Public contracts.
Minority business participation goals.
Good faith efforts required.
Affidavit submitted with bid, §143-128.2, (c).
Public records, subpoena commanding custodian to produce.
Certified copies and affidavit in lieu of appearance, §1A-1, Rule 45, (c).
Public works.
Regulation of contractors.
Noncollusion affidavits, §133-30.
Perjury in affidavit, §133-31.
Removal for fair trial, §1-85.
Search warrants, §15A-244.
Self-proved wills, §31-11.6, (b), (c).
Service of process.
Mail in foreign country, §1A-1, Rule 4, (j3).
Motions supported by affidavits.
Affidavits served with motions, §1A-1, Rule 6, (d).
Proof of service, §1-75.10.
Registered or certified mail, §1A-1, Rule 4, (j2).
Small claims actions.
Indigents desiring to appeal, §7A-228, (b1).
Small estates.
Collection of property by affidavit.
See SMALL ESTATES.
Summary judgment, §1A-1, Rule 56, (c), (e) to (g).
Claimant, §1A-1, Rule 56, (a).
Defending party, §1A-1, Rule 56, (b).
Service, §1A-1, Rule 56, (c).
Superior court clerks, removal, §7A-105.
Supplemental proceedings.
Debtors earnings necessary for family support, §1-362.

AFFIDAVITS —Cont'd
Supplemental proceedings —Cont'd
Ordering debtor or judgment debtor to appear at specified time and place to answer, §1-360.
Temporary restraining order without notice, §1A-1, Rule 65, (b).
Time for, §§1-593, 1A-1, Rule 6, (d).
Torrens system registration.
Adverse claims existing at initial registry, §43-19.
Tort claims against state departments and agencies.
Claimant to provide affidavit, §143-297.
Demurrer or other pleading to affidavit, §143-297.
Trust companies.
Directors.
Affidavit of acceptance, §53-352, (b).
Seizure by commissioner.
Action following full settlement, §53-393.
Claims against company.
Notice of rejection by commissioner, §53-387.
Notice regarding presentation of claims, §53-386.
Usurpation office.
Arrest and bail of defendants, §1-519.
Utilities commission.
Use of affidavits in proceedings, §62-68.
Verification of pleadings, §§1-148, 1A-1, Rule 11, (b), (c).
Wage and hour act.
Power of commissioner of labor to take affidavits, §95-25.16, (b).
Wills.
Self-proved wills, §31-11.6, (b), (c).

AFFIRMATIONS.
Oaths.
Affirmation in lieu of oath, §11-4.
General provisions.
See OATHS.
Perjury, §§14-209 to 14-211.

AFFIRMATIVE DEFENSES, §1A-1, Rule 8, (c).
Accord and satisfaction.
Pleading, §1A-1, Rule 8, (c).
Arbitration and award.
Pleading, §1A-1, Rule 8, (c).
Assaulting law enforcement or assistance animals, §14-163.1, (f).
Assumption of risk.
Pleading, §1A-1, Rule 8, (c).
Bad checks, §6-21.3, (c).
Bankruptcy and insolvency.
Discharge, pleading, §1A-1, Rule 8, (c).
Commodities.
Failure to make physical delivery, §78D-33.
Commodities trading, §78D-33.
Consideration, failure.
Pleading, §1A-1, Rule 8, (c).
Contributory negligence.
Pleading, §1A-1, Rule 8, (c).
Defamation.
Truth, pleading, §1A-1, Rule 8, (c).
Disabled persons.
Protection act.
Affirmative defenses of employers, §168A-9.
Duress.
Pleading, §1A-1, Rule 8, (c).
Estoppel.
Pleading, §1A-1, Rule 8, (c).
Eviction.
Retaliatory eviction, §42-37.1.

AFFIRMATIVE DEFENSES —Cont'd
Expedited evictions.
Evidence of isolated or nonrecurring incidents.
Admissible only to support affirmative defense, §42-67.
Fellow servant doctrine.
Pleading, §1A-1, Rule 8, (c).
Fraud.
Pleading, §1A-1, Rule 8, (c).
Laches.
Pleading, §1A-1, Rule 8, (c).
Limitation of actions.
Pleading, §1A-1, Rule 8, (c).
Motor vehicles.
Lemon law, §20-351.4.
New motor vehicles warranties act, §20-351.4.
Obscenity.
Disseminating or exhibiting harmful materials to minors, §14-190.15, (c).
Pleading, §1A-1, Rule 8, (c).
Release.
Pleading, §1A-1, Rule 8, (c).
Res judicata.
Pleading, §1A-1, Rule 8, (c).
Statute of frauds.
Pleading, §1A-1, Rule 8, (c).
Statute of limitations.
Pleading, §1A-1, Rule 8, (c).
Unclaimed property act.
Payment, satisfaction, discharge and want of consideration, §116B-58.
Usury.
Pleading, §1A-1, Rule 8, (c).
Waiver.
Pleading, §1A-1, Rule 8, (c).

AFFRAYS.
Aggravated affrays.
Punishment for misdemeanor affrays, §14-33, (b), (c).
Factors determining classification of offense, §14-33, (b), (c).
Habitual misdemeanor assault, §14-33.2.
Arrest without warrant, §15A-401.
Misdemeanor affrays, §14-33, (b), (c).
Habitual misdemeanor assault, §14-33.2.
Self-defense.
Evidence of former threats upon plea of self-defense, §14-33.1.
Simple affray, §14-33, (a).
Punishment for misdemeanor affrays, §14-33, (a).

AFTER-ACQUIRED CLAUSE.
Definitions, §47-20.5, (a), (b).
Effectiveness, §47-20.5, (c).
Indexing by register of deeds, §47-20.5, (f).
Instruments creating security interest made by public utilities, §47-20.5, (h).
Notice of extension.
Operation, §47-20.5, (e).
Registration in lieu of registering instrument, §47-20.5, (d).
Passing title against lien creditors or purchasers for consideration, §47-20.5, (g).

AFTER-ACQUIRED PROPERTY.
Secured transactions.
Security interest in after-acquired property, §25-9-204, (a), (b).

AFTER-ADOPTED CHILDREN.
Will not revoked by, §31-5.5.

AFTERBORN CHILDREN.
Children's allowance, when entitled, §30-17.
Estates.
Taking of property by deed or writings, §41-5.
Intestate succession generally, §29-9.
Wills, §31-5.5.

AGE.
Accountants.
Minimum age, §93-2.
Adult education, §115C-231.
Anatomical gifts.
Blood.
Giving of blood by persons 17 years of age or more, §130A-411.
Persons who may execute anatomical gift, §130A-404, (a), (b).
Bail bondsmen and runners.
Licenses.
Minimum age, §58-71-50, (b).
Bus drivers.
Age limits for public passenger-carrying vehicles, §20-10.
Capital punishment.
Mitigating circumstances.
Age of defendant, §15A-2000, (f).
Commercial drivers' licenses.
Minimum age, §20-9, (a).
Congress.
Representatives, Const. U. S., art. I, §2.
Senators, Const. U. S., art. I, §3.
Credit union members.
Minimum age to hold office, §54-109.31, (e).
Minimum age to vote at meetings, §54-109.31, (d).
Deeds.
Married persons under eighteen made competent as to certain transactions, §39-13.2.
District courts.
Twenty-fifth judicial district judges.
Validation of official acts performed after mandatory retirement age, §7A-4.21.
Drivers' licenses.
Minimum age for drivers' licenses, §20-9, (a).
Elections.
Qualifications of voters.
Minimum age, §163-55.
Right to vote.
Not to be abridged on account of age, Const. U. S., amd. XXVI.
Persons eighteen years of age, Const. U. S., amd. XXVI.
Executors and administrators.
Persons disqualified to serve, §28A-4-2.
Farm tractors.
Minimum age for operation, §20-10.
Funeral service.
Qualifications for licenses, §90-210.25, (a).
Hearing aid dealers and fitters.
Qualifications for license, §93D-5, (a).
Implements of husbandry.
Minimum age for operation, §20-10.
Jury.
Excuse from jury service on account of age, §9-6.1.
Justices or judges of general court of justice.
Age limit for service as, §7A-4.20.
Marriage.
Capacity, §51-2.
Minors, §48A-2.
Mopeds.
Minimum age for operation, §20-10.1.

AGE —Cont'd
Mortality tables.
Evidence, §§8-46, 8-47.
Motor vehicle insurance.
Discriminatory practices, §58-3-25, (a).
Motor vehicles.
Commercial drivers' licenses.
Minimum age, §20-9, (a).
Farm tractors.
Minimum age for operation, §20-10.
Implements of husbandry.
Minimum age for operation, §20-10.
Licenses.
Minimum age for drivers' licenses, §20-9, (a).
Mopeds.
Minimum age for operation, §20-10.1.
Public passenger-carrying vehicles.
Age limits for drivers, §20-10.
Nursing home administrators.
Qualifications, §90-278.
Occupational licensing board.
Requirements for licensure, §93B-9.
Opticians.
Minimum age, §90-237.
President of the United States, Const. U. S., art. II, §1.
Private protective services.
Licenses.
Minimum age, §74C-8, (d).
Probate and registration.
Acknowledgments before notaries under age, §47-108.
Public passenger-carrying vehicles.
Age limits for drivers, §20-10.
Public schools.
Admission requirements, §115C-364, (a), (b).
Adult education, §115C-231.
Compulsory attendance.
Children required to attend, §115C-378.
Free tuition, §115C-1.
Kindergartens.
Age of eligibility for enrollment, §115C-81, (f).
Teachers.
Minimum age, §115C-295, (a).
Rape indictments.
Victim female child under age of 13, §15-144.1, (b).
Real estate brokers and salespersons.
Minimum age, §93A-4, (a).
Retirement system for teachers and state employees.
Local board of education to provide age, §115C-47.
School bus drivers.
Minimum age, §20-218, (a).
Sexual offense indictments.
Victim 13 years of age or less, §15-144.2, (b).
Sheriffs.
Minimum age, §162-2.
Special education.
Local boards of education.
Special programs for children of certain ages, §115C-139, (b).
Sterilization.
Persons over eighteen.
Operation lawful upon request, §90-271.
Persons under eighteen.
Married persons.
Operation lawful upon request, §90-271.
Unmarried persons, §90-272.
Teachers.
Minimum age, §115C-295, (a).
Tobacco products, §14-313.

AGE —Cont'd
Vice-president, Const. U. S., amd. XII.

AGED PERSONS.
Accident and health insurance.
Joint action to insure elderly, §§58-52-1 to 58-52-25.
See ACCIDENT AND HEALTH INSURANCE.
Adult protection, §§108A-99 to 108A-111.
See ABUSED, NEGLECTED OR EXPLOITED DISABLED ADULTS.
Advisory council on aging.
Creation within department of health and human services, §143B-180.
Alzheimer's disease.
Study commission on aging.
Alzheimer's subcommittee, §120-186.1.
Assistant secretary for aging.
Appointment, §143B-181.2, (a).
Duties, §143B-181.2, (a), (b).
Commission to study the care of the aged and handicapped.
Appointment of members, §143-281.
Compensation of members, §143-283.
Designation, §143-279.
Duties of commission, §143-282.
Establishment, §143-279.
Members, §143-280.
Appointment, §143-281.
Compensation, §143-283.
Removal, §143-281.
Purpose, §143-279.
Recommendations of commission, §143-282.
Removal of members, §143-281.
Definitions.
Long-term care ombudsman program, §143B-181.16.
Division of aging.
Calendar of conferences, training events and educational program.
Producing and distributing, §143B-181.1B, (b).
Clearinghouse for information, §143B-181.1B, (a).
Creation, §143B-181.1, (a).
Duties, §143B-181.1, (a).
Functioning under authority of department of health and human services, §143B-181.1, (b).
Information provided by state agencies and entities, §143B-181.1B, (c).
Inventory of existing data, §143B-181.1A, (b).
Plan for serving older adults.
Update of plan, §143B-181.1A, (a).
Powers and duties, §143B-181.1, (a).
Rules and regulations.
Promulgation, §143B-181.1, (c).
Education.
Tuition waiver for senior citizens, §§115B-1 to 115B-6.
Elections.
Accessible polling places, §163-131.
Curbside voting, §163-166.9.
Satellite voting places, §163-130.
Fair housing.
Familial status provisions of chapter.
Inapplicability to housing for older persons, §41A-6, (e).
Governor's advisory council on aging.
Appointments, §143B-181.
Compensation of members, §143B-181.
Creation, §143B-180.
Duties, §143B-180.
Members, §143B-181.

AGED PERSONS —Cont'd
Governor's advisory council on aging —Cont'd
Powers and duties, §143B-180.
Quorum, §143B-181.
Selection of members, §143B-181.
Terms of members, §143B-181.
Hearings.
Study commission on aging, §120-185.
Homestead exclusion.
Property taxes, §105-277.1.
Notice on abstract, §105-309, (f).
Human service and volunteer transportation, §§62-289.1 to 62-289.7.
Insurance.
Accident and health insurance.
Joint action to insure elderly, §§58-52-1 to 58-52-25.
See ACCIDENT AND HEALTH INSURANCE.
Medicare supplement insurance, §§58-54-1 to 58-54-50.
See MEDICARE.
Long-term care.
Legislative policy, §143B-181.5.
Purpose and intent of act, §143B-181.6.
Long-term care ombudsman program, §§143B-181.15 to 143B-181.24.
See LONG-TERM CARE OMBUDSMAN.
Medicare supplement insurance, §§58-54-1 to 58-54-50.
See MEDICARE.
Minimum wage.
Persons earning or productive capacity impaired by age, §95-25.3, (c).
Municipal corporations.
Senior citizens programs, §160A-497.
Policy act of the aging.
Implementation.
Responsibility for policy, §143B-181.4.
Principles.
Statement, §143B-181.3.
Responsibility for policy, §143B-181.4.
Statement of principles, §143B-181.3.
Property taxes.
Abstracts.
Information on tax relief for, §105-309, (f).
Failure to give information required, §105-309, (g).
Homestead exclusion, §105-277.1.
Notice on abstract, §105-309, (f).
Reduced valuation of permanent residence of aged persons.
Abstract notice, §105-309, (f).
Public transportation.
Elderly and disabled transportation assistance program.
General provisions, §136-44.27.
Reports.
Adult protection, §§108A-102, 108A-109.
Study commission on aging, §120-187.
Respite care program.
Administration of program, §143B-181.10, (d).
Eligibility, §143B-181.10, (b).
Established, §143B-181.10, (a).
Funding, §143B-181.10, (e).
Payment for services, §143B-181.10, (f).
Services provided, §143B-181.10, (c).
Salaries.
Commission to study the care of the aged and handicapped, §143-283.

AGED PERSONS —Cont'd
School bus use by senior citizen groups.
Agreement with locality or agency.
Authority of local board to enter into, §115C-243, (a).
No duty on board to enter into, §115C-243, (d).
Required provision, §115C-243, (b).
Charges for use of buses.
State board to adopt uniform schedule, §115C-243, (f).
Policy for use of buses by elderly.
Board to establish prior to agreement, §115C-243, (c).
Travel outside state prohibited, §115C-243, (e).
Senior Tarheel legislature.
Created, §143B-181.55, (a).
Delegates, §143B-181.55, (b).
Duties, §143B-181.55, (a).
Meetings, §143B-181.55, (c).
Report, §143B-181.55, (d).
Social security.
See SOCIAL SECURITY.
Study commission on aging.
Alzheimer's subcommittee, §120-186.1, (a).
Duties, §120-186.1, (b).
Appointment of members, §120-182.
Co-chairman, §120-183.
Composition, §120-182.
Creation, §120-180.
Duties, §120-181.
Expenses of members, §120-184.
Functions, §120-181.
Hearings, §120-185.
Long-term care subcommittee, §120-186.1, (a).
Duties, §120-186.1, (b).
Meetings, §120-183.
Place for, §120-188.
Number of members, §120-182.
Powers, §120-186.
Purpose, §120-180.
Reports, §120-187.
Staff, §120-188.
Subcommittees, §120-186.1.
Subpoenas.
Power of commission, §120-186.
Terms of members, §120-182.
Travel expenses of members, §120-184.
Vacancies.
Filling, §120-182.
Witnesses.
Powers as to, §120-186.
Tuition waiver for senior citizens, §§115B-1 to 115B-6.
Voting.
Accessible polling places, §163-131.
Curbside voting, §163-166.9.
Satellite voting places, §163-130.

AGED RECORDS.
Inspection of public records, §132-6, (f).

AGE LIMIT FOR JUSTICES AND JUDGES, §7A-4.20.
Validation of certain actions of district court judges of twenty fifth judicial district performed after mandatory retirement, §7A-4.21.

AGENCY FOR PUBLIC TELECOMMUNICATIONS, §§143B-426.8 to 143B-426.20.
See PUBLIC TELECOMMUNICATIONS, AGENCY FOR.

AGENTS.
ABC law enforcement agents, §18B-500.
ABC officers, local, §18B-501.
Alarm systems licensing.
Requirements, §74D-2, (c).
Athlete agents, §§78C-85 to 78C-105.
See ATHLETE AGENTS.
Attorneys at law.
Agent of lawyers' or judges' association.
Duty of confidentiality when acting as, Prof. Cond. Rule 1.6.
Banks.
Personal agency accounts.
Generally, §53-146.3.
Bonds, surety.
Actions on bonds.
Evidence against principal admissible against sureties, §58-76-25.
Indemnity bonds to state maximum liability and period of liability, §66-65.
Collection of debts or accounts.
Simulation of court process in connection with collection, §14-118.1.
Commissions to sales representatives, §§66-190 to 66-193.
Community colleges.
Negligence of agents.
Waiver of governmental immunity by act of obtaining liability insurance, §115D-24.
Compensation.
Powers which may be incorporated by reference in trust instrument, §32-27.
Trustees and other fiduciaries, §§32-53 to 32-62.
See FIDUCIARIES.
Consent to health care for minors.
Parent authorizing agent to consent, §§32A-28 to 32A-34.
Corporations.
Embezzlement.
Receipt of property by virtue of office or employment, §14-90.
Indemnification generally.
Business corporations, §§55-8-50 to 55-8-58.
Nonprofit corporations, §§55A-8-50 to 55A-8-58.
Misconduct in private office.
Malfeasance of corporation agents, §14-254, (a).
Oaths, §11-5.
Registered agent.
Business corporations.
Foreign corporations, §55-15-07.
Nonprofit corporations, §55A-5-01.
Foreign corporations, §55A-15-07.
Credit unions.
Personal agency accounts.
Generally, §54-109.63.
Deeds.
Execution of deed dated before 1835.
Evidence of due execution, §8-13.
Torrens system registration.
Instruments describing party as agent not to operate as notice, §§43-63, 43-64.
Disclosure of real parties.
Person trading as "agent" to disclose, §66-72.
Eggs.
Act of agent as that of principal, §106-245.28.
Embezzlement.
Receipt of property by virtue of office or employment, §14-90.

AGENTS —Cont'd
Employers and employees.
Violating duties owed employers.
Influencing agents in violating duties, §14-353.
Witness required to give self-incriminating evidence, §14-354.
No suit or prosecution to be founded thereon, §14-354.
Fiduciaries generally.
See FIDUCIARIES.
Futures contracts, §16-4.
Health care for minors.
Parent authorizing agent to consent, §§32A-28 to 32A-34.
Health maintenance organizations.
Licensing, §58-67-90.
Hospital authorities.
Corporate agents, §131E-23, (b).
Exercise of powers through agents, §131E-23, (b).
Hospital, medical and dental service corporations.
Licenses, §58-65-115.
Associations to transact business through licensed agents only, §58-65-120.
Required, §58-65-120.
Insurance agents generally.
See INSURANCE AGENTS.
Legislative agents.
Lobbying generally, §§120-47.1 to 120-47.12.
See LOBBYING.
Limited liability companies.
Agency law to apply under chapter, §57C-10-03, (c).
Agency power of managers, §57C-3-23.
Delegation of authority by managers, §57C-3-24, (c).
Insurance purchased on behalf of agent, §57C-3-32, (c).
Registered office and registered agent, §57C-2-40.
Lotteries.
Acting as agent for lotteries, §14-291.
Managing general insurance agents, §§58-34-2 to 58-34-15.
Marketing and branding farm products.
Power to employ agents and assistants, §106-186.
Missing persons.
When agent's acts binding on estates, §28C-21.
Mortgages and deeds of trust.
Appointment of agency.
Agency to sell under power may be appointed by parol or writing, §45-7.
Foreclosures.
Attacking foreclosures on ground trustee was agent, etc., of owner of debt, §45-21.39, (a).
Sales under power of sale.
Trustee agent of owner of debt.
Validation of foreclosure sale, §45-21.47.
Negotiable instruments.
Signature by authorized representative, §25-3-402.
Partnerships.
Applicability of law of agency, §59-34, (c).
Partner as agent of partnership as to partnership business, §59-39, (a).
Partner by estoppel.
Agent of persons consenting to representation, §59-46, (b).
Plant pests.
Inspections authorized, §106-422.
Powers of attorney.
Powers conferred by statutory short form.
Employment of agents, §32A-2.

AGENTS —Cont'd
Powers of fiduciaries generally, §§32-25 to 32-28.
Prudent person rule.
Investment and deposit of funds, §36A-2, (a).
Rendering plants and rendering operations.
Authority of agents of licensee, §106-168.11.
Residential property disclosure act.
Duty of agent to inform owner of rights and obligations, §47E-8.
Liability of agent for owner's refusal to provide disclosure statement, §47E-8.
Sales representative commissions, §§66-190 to 66-193.
Savings and loan associations.
Personal agency accounts.
Generally, §54B-139.
Service of process.
Process agents.
Appointment by agency of state, §1A-1, Rule 4, (j).
Sports agents, §§78C-85 to 78C-105.
See ATHLETE AGENTS.
State departments and agencies.
Identification cards for field agents or deputies of state departments, §128-14.
Structural pest control.
Designation of resident agent, §106-65.30, (b).
Torrens system registration.
Instruments describing party as agent not to operate as notice, §§43-63, 43-64.
Trader or merchant transacting business with addition of words agent.
Disclosure of name of principal or partner by sign placed conspicuously in place of business, §66-72.
Transfer agents.
Security transfers.
See FIDUCIARIES.
Transportation department.
Highway inspection reports.
Falsifying reports, §136-13.2, (a).
Trust and trustees.
Distribution of estates to nonresident trustees.
Appointment of process agent required, §28A-22-4.
Uniform fiduciaries act, §§32-1 to 32-13.
See FIDUCIARIES.

AGE OF EMANCIPATION.
Age of minor, §48A-2.

AGGRAVATED SENTENCING.
Felony structured sentencing, §15A-1340.16.

AGGRAVATING CIRCUMSTANCES.
Attorney disciplinary proceedings.
Imposition of discipline, Bar Rules & Regs., B, §.0114.
Capital felonies, §15A-2000, (e).
Impaired driving sentencing hearing.
Aggravating factors to be weighed, §20-179, (d).
Determining existence of grossly aggravating factors, §20-179.
Weighing aggravating and mitigating circumstances, §20-179, (f).

AGGRESSIVE DRIVING.
Elements of offense, §20-141.6, (a).
Misdemeanor, §20-141.6, (c).
Proof of offense, §20-141.6, (b).
Reckless driving as lesser included offense, §20-141.6, (d).

AGREEMENTS OF CHILD SUPPORT, §110-133.
Acknowledgment of paternity in agreement to support, §110-132.
Filing of affirmations, acknowledgments, etc., §110-134.

AGRIBUSINESS.
Motor vehicle license plates.
Special NC agribusiness plates, §§20-79.4, (b), 20-81.12, (b23).

AGRICULTURAL DEVELOPMENT, §§106-580 to 106-587.
Agricultural extension service.
Cooperation of departments and agencies with service, §106-583.
Appropriations.
By counties, §106-585.
Local appropriations, §106-587.
Authority granted by article supplementary, §106-586.
Citation of act, §106-580.
Congress.
Funds made available by congress, §106-585.
Cooperation of departments and agencies with agricultural extension service, §106-583.
Counties.
Appropriations by counties, §106-585.
Local appropriations, §106-587.
Utilizing facilities for installing and promoting programs, §106-582.
Declaration of intent, §106-581.
Declaration of policy, §106-583.
Definitions, §106-581.1.
Funds made available by congress, §106-585.
Intent of article, §106-581.
Municipal corporations.
Local appropriations, §106-587.
Policy declaration, §106-583.
Programs.
Counties authorized to utilize facilities for installing and promoting, §106-582.
Purpose of article, §106-581.
Research facilities.
Maximum use of existing facilities, §106-584.
Short title, §106-580.
State departments and agencies.
Cooperation with agricultural extension service, §106-583.
Supplementary grant of authority by article, §106-586.
Title of article, §106-580.

AGRICULTURAL EXTENSION SERVICE.
Agricultural development generally, §§106-580 to 106-587.
See AGRICULTURAL DEVELOPMENT.
Workers' compensation.
Employee defined, §97-2.

AGRICULTURAL FAIRS.
See FAIRS.

AGRICULTURAL FARM WORKERS.
See MIGRANT FARM WORKERS.

AGRICULTURAL FEES AND TAXES.
Assessment procedure.
Authority of commissioner of agriculture, §106-9.3, (f), (g).
Finality of assessment, §106-9.3, (d).
Hearing requested by objecting taxpayer, §106-9.3, (c).
Interest rate, §106-9.3, (e).

AGRICULTURAL FEES AND TAXES —Cont'd
Assessment procedure —Cont'd
Limitation of actions, §106-9.3, (a).
Notice to taxpayer, §106-9.3, (b).
Delivery of notice, §106-9.3, (b).
Time period for assessment, §106-9.3, (e).
Delinquent taxes.
Attachment.
Collection of delinquent taxes, §106-9.4, (b).
Collection of delinquent taxes.
Certificate of particulars, §106-9.4, (c).
Choses in action, §106-9.4, (b).
Cumulative nature of remedies, §106-9.4, (d).
Intangible personal property, §106-9.4, (b).
Order issued by commissioner of agriculture, §106-9.4, (a).
Other remedies, §106-9.4, (d).
Suits to prevent collection prohibited, §106-9.6.
Cumulative nature of remedies, §106-9.4, (d).
Garnishment.
Collection of delinquent taxes, §106-9.4, (b).
Order issued by commissioner of agriculture, §106-9.4, (a).
Other remedies, §106-9.4, (d).
Eastern North Carolina agricultural center fund, §106-6.2, (a).
Noncompliance cases.
Determination of amount due by commissioner, §106-9.2, (c).
Overpayment.
Refund of overpayment, §106-9.5.
Payment under protest.
Recovery of fee or tax so paid, §106-9.6.
Preventing collection.
Suits prohibited, §106-9.6.
Property taxes.
Agricultural, horticultural and forestland, §§105-277.2 to 105-277.7.
Exemptions, §105-275.
Reduced valuation.
Certain farm products classified for taxation at, §105-277.01.
Protest payments.
Recovery of fee or tax so paid, §106-9.6.
Records.
Examination of records, §106-9.2, (b).
Noncompliance cases.
Determination of amount due by commissioner, §106-9.2, (c).
Required of persons paying fees or taxes to commissioner or department, §106-9.2, (a).
Recovery of tax.
Payment under protest, §106-9.6.
Refund of overpayment, §106-9.5.
Reports.
Noncompliance cases.
Determination of amount due by commissioner, §106-9.2, (c).
Required of persons paying fees or taxes to commissioner or department, §106-9.2, (a).
Southeastern North Carolina agricultural center fund, §106-6.2, (b).
Suits to prevent collection prohibited, §106-9.6.

AGRICULTURAL FESTIVALS.
Winery special event permit authorization, §18B-1114.1.

AGRICULTURAL FINANCE AUTHORITY, §§122D-1 to 122D-23.
Accounts and accounting, §122D-18, (a).

AGRICULTURAL FINANCE AUTHORITY —Cont'd
Actions.
Power to sue and be sued, §122D-6.
Appointment of members, §122D-4, (b) to (d).
Audits, §122D-18, (b).
Bond issues, §122D-10.
Authorized, §122D-10, (a), (i).
Coupon bonds, §122D-10, (g).
Covenant of state, §122D-15.
Definition of "bonds" or "notes," §122D-3.
Deposits.
Bonds as security for public deposits, §122D-17.
Interim receipts or temporary bonds, §122D-10, (h).
Investments.
Bonds as legal investment, §122D-17.
Pledge.
Statutory pledge, §122D-11.
Powers of authority, §122D-6.
Proceeds.
Trust funds, §122D-16, (a).
Purchase of bonds by authority, §122D-13.
Refunding bonds, §122D-12.
Sale of bonds, §122D-10, (c), (e), (f).
Signatures on bonds, §122D-10, (d).
Taxation.
Exemption from taxes, §122D-14.
Terms and conditions of bonds, §122D-10, (b), (c).
Chairman.
Election, §122D-5, (a).
Citation of act.
Short title, §122D-1.
Composition, §122D-4, (b).
Construction and interpretation.
Liberal construction of provisions, §122D-20.
Severability of provisions, §122D-22.
Contracts.
Experts and consultants.
Employment on contractual basis, §122D-5, (d).
Power to contract, §122D-6.
Creation, §122D-4, (a).
Definitions, §122D-3.
Domicile of authority, §122D-4, (e).
Duties.
Delegation, §122D-4, (i).
Executive director, §122D-5, (b), (c).
Expenses of members, §122D-4, (g).
Experts and consultants.
Employment on contractual basis, §122D-5, (d).
Findings of legislature, §122D-2, (a) to (c).
General fund.
Termination of authority.
Deposits of assets in, §122D-21.
Immunities, §122D-23.
Insurance.
Agricultural loans, §122D-9.
Investments.
Bond issues.
Legal investments, §122D-17.
Moneys of authority.
Authorized investments, §122D-16, (a).
Legislative findings and declarations, §122D-2, (a) to (c).
Lending institutions.
Defined, §122D-3.
Loans.
Agricultural loans.
Defined, §122D-3.
Insurance, §122D-9.
Powers of authority, §122D-6.

AGRICULTURAL FINANCE AUTHORITY —Cont'd
Loans —Cont'd
Agricultural loans —Cont'd
Purchases and sales of agricultural loans, §122D-7.
Insurance of agricultural loans.
Agreements, §122D-9, (d).
Amount, §122D-9, (b).
Authorized, §122D-9, (a).
Default.
What constitutes, §122D-9, (c).
Maximum aggregate value of agricultural loans insured, §122D-9, (e).
Lending institutions.
Loans to, §122D-8.
Powers of authority, §122D-6.
Meetings, §122D-4, (h).
Powers, §122D-6.
Delegation, §122D-4, (i).
Quorum, §122D-4, (f).
Reports.
Annual report to governor and general assembly, §122D-18, (c).
Severability of provisions, §122D-22.
Short title of act, §122D-1.
State departments and agencies.
Cooperation of state agencies, §122D-19.
Taxation.
Exemption from taxes, §122D-14.
Termination of authority, §122D-21.
Terms of members, §122D-4, (c).
Trust funds, §122D-16, (a).
Vacancies.
Filling, §122D-4, (d).
Vice-chairman.
Election, §122D-5, (a).

AGRICULTURAL HALL OF FAME, §§106-568.13 to 106-568.17.
Acceptance of awards, §106-568.17.
Admission of candidates, §106-568.16.
Board of directors, §106-568.14.
Terms, §106-568.15.
Candidates.
Admission, §106-568.16.
Control of hall of fame, §106-568.14.
Creation, §106-568.13.
Display of awards, §106-568.17.
Established, §106-568.13.
State agency designation, §106-568.13.
Supervision of hall of fame, §106-568.14.
Terms of directors, §106-568.15.
Transfer to department of agriculture and consumer services, §143A-61.

AGRICULTURAL LIMING MATERIALS AND LANDPLASTER.
Limestone, marl and landplaster, §§106-92.1 to 106-92.17.
See LIMESTONE, MARL AND LANDPLASTER.

AGRICULTURAL OPERATION NUISANCE LIABILITY.
Declaration of policy, §106-700.

AGRICULTURAL PRODUCTS PROMOTION, §§106-550 to 106-568.
Activities deemed not illegal or in restraint of trade, §106-552.
Applicability of provisions.
Tobacco excluded, §106-550.

AGRICULTURAL PRODUCTS PROMOTION —Cont'd
Assessments.
Alternative method for collection, §106-564.1.
Cattle-related assessments, §106-564.3.
Further alternative method, §106-564.2.
Sweet potatoes, §106-564.4.
Amount and basis of proposed assessment, §106-557.
Cattle-related assessments.
Alternative method for collection, §106-564.3.
Collection of assessments, §106-564.
Alternative method of collection, §§106-564.1 to 106-564.4.
Further alternative method for collection, §106-564.2.
Continuance of assessments approved at prior referendum, §106-566.
Custody and use of funds, §106-564.
Dissatisfaction with assessments, §106-567.
Effect of more than one-third vote against assessment, §106-560.
Effect of two-third vote for assessment, §106-561.
Financial statement.
Publication by treasurer of agency, §106-568.
Financing program of production, use and sale, §106-553.
Growers and producers on question of assessments, §106-556.
Maximum assessment, §106-557.
Publication of financial statement by treasurer of agency, §106-568.
Bond required, §106-568.
Purpose of assessment, §106-557.
Refund.
Milk product assessments, §106-567.1.
Time for demanding, §106-567.
Rights of farmers dissatisfied with assessment, §106-567.
Sweet potato-related assessments.
Alternative method for collection, §106-564.4.
Time for demanding refund, §106-567.
Treasurer of agency.
Publication of financial statement, §106-568.
Associations deemed not illegal or in restraint of trade, §106-552.
Ballot by mail.
Alternative method of conducting referendum, §106-557.1, (a).
Applicability of provisions, §106-557.1, (b).
Board of agriculture.
Application to board for authorization of referendum, §106-554.
Action by board, §106-555.
Citation of federal act, §106-551.
Cotton promotion association.
Special referendum provisions, §106-559.
County agents.
Notice of referendum, §106-562.
Declaration of policy, §106-550.
Designation of federal law, §106-551.
Farmers' rights.
Dissatisfaction with assessments, §106-567.
Farm organizations.
Notice of referendum, §106-562.
Federal agricultural marketing act, §106-551.
Federal assessment programs.
Official state board, §106-555.1.
Subsequent referenda not required, §106-555.1.
Growers.
Conduct of referendum among growers on question of assessments, §106-556.

AGRICULTURAL PRODUCTS PROMOTION —Cont'd
Meetings deemed not illegal or in restraint of trade, §106-552.
Milk products.
Referendum.
Basis of vote, §106-559.1.
Supervision, §106-563.1.
Refund of assessment, §106-567.1.
Policy declaration, §106-550.
Producers.
Conduct of referendum among producers on question of assessments, §106-556.
Publications.
Financial statement by treasurer of agency, §106-568.
Referendum.
Alternative method of conducting, §106-557.1, (a).
Mail ballot, §106-557.1, (a).
Applicability of provisions, §106-557.1, (b).
Amount and basis of proposed assessment, §106-557.
Application to board of agriculture for authorization, §106-554.
Action by board, §106-555.
Area or statewide basis, §106-559.
Arrangements for holding referendum, §106-563.
Continuance of assessments approved at prior referendum, §106-566.
Declaration of results, §106-563.
Effect of more than one-third vote against assessment, §106-560.
Effect of two-thirds vote for assessment, §106-561.
Eligibility for participation, §106-559.
Expenses in connection therewith, §106-558.
Financing program of production, use and sale, §106-553.
Growers and producers on question of assessments, §106-556.
Management of referendum, §106-558.
Milk product assessment.
Basis of vote, §106-559.1.
Supervision of referendum, §106-563.1.
Notice of referendum, §106-557.
Notice to farm organizations and county agents, §106-562.
Preparation and distribution of ballots, §106-563.
Question to be submitted, §106-559.
Regulations as to referendum, §106-562.
Special provisions for cotton promotion association, §106-559.
Subsequent referendum, §106-565.
Restraint of trade.
Associations, meetings or activities deemed not in restraint of trade, §106-552.
Strawberries or strawberry plants excluded from article, §106-550.
Subsequent referendum, §106-565.
Surety bond.
Assessments.
Publication of financial statement by treasurer of agency, §106-568.
Tobacco excluded from article, §106-550.

AGRICULTURAL RESEARCH, §§106-568.1 to 106-568.12.
Assessments.
Collection of assessment, §106-568.8, (a).
Continuation of assessment, §106-568.10.
Dissatisfaction with assessments.
Refunds to farmers, §106-568.9.

AGRICULTURAL RESEARCH —Cont'd
Assessments —Cont'd
Effect of more than one-third vote against assessment, §106-568.11.
Effect of two-thirds vote in favor of assessment, §106-568.12.
Levy of assessment.
When assessment shall and shall not be levied, §106-568.5.
Policy as to assessment, §106-568.2.
Promotion of agricultural research and dissemination of findings, §106-568.2.
Purposes for assessment, §106-568.6.
Refunds to farmers dissatisfied with assessment, §106-568.9.
Remittance, §106-568.8, (b).
Statement of amount of proposed assessment, §106-568.6.
When assessment shall and shall not be levied, §106-568.5.
Board of agriculture.
Petition for referendum.
Action of board, §106-568.3, (a).
Development act.
Maximum use of existing research facilities, §106-584.
Disposition of assessment, §106-568.8, (a).
Report of receipts and disbursements, §106-568.8, (a), (b).
Notice of referendum.
Promotion of agricultural research and dissemination of findings, §106-568.6.
Promotion of agricultural research and dissemination of findings.
Declaration of policy, §106-568.1.
Joint action of farmers, §106-568.1.
Policy declaration, §106-568.1.
Referendum.
Announcements prior to referendum, §106-568.4.
Arrangements for poll holders, §106-568.7.
By whom referendum to be managed, §106-568.4.
Canvass and announcement of results, §106-568.7.
Continuation of assessment, §106-568.10.
Declaration of results, §106-568.7.
Effect of more than one-third vote against assessment, §106-568.11.
Effect of two-thirds vote in favor of assessment, §106-568.12.
Management of referendum, §106-568.4.
Notice of referendum, §106-568.6.
Petition for referendum.
Action of board of agriculture, §106-568.3, (a).
Policy as to referendum, §106-568.2.
Preparation and distribution of ballots, §106-568.7.
Promotion of agricultural research and dissemination of findings, §106-568.2.
Regulations as to referendum, §106-568.6.
Subsequent referendum, §106-568.10.
Regulations as to referendum.
Promotion of agricultural research and dissemination of findings, §106-568.6.
Reports.
Receipts and disbursements of assessment, §106-568.8, (a), (b).
Tobacco research commission, §106-568.3, (b).

AGRICULTURAL SEEDS.
Defined, §106-277.2.
Inspection, §106-277.21.
Labels, §106-277.10.

AGRICULTURAL SEEDS —Cont'd
Sampling and testing, §106-277.21.
Unlawful acts, §106-277.9.

AGRICULTURAL TOURISM SIGNS, §106-22.5, (a).
Qualification of agricultural facility for, §106-22.5, (b).

AGRICULTURE.
Adams act.
Experiment stations.
Legislative assent to act, §106-23.
Adulteration of grains, §§106-621 to 106-628.
See GRAIN ADULTERATION.
Advances.
Landlord's lien on crops for rents, §42-15.
Animals.
Generally.
See ANIMALS.
Animal waste management, §§143-215.10A to 143-215.10H.
See ANIMAL WASTE MANAGEMENT.
Animal waste management system operators, §§90A-47 to 90A-47.6.
See ANIMAL WASTE MANAGEMENT SYSTEM OPERATORS.
Apiaries.
See BEES AND HONEY.
Aquaculture development, §§106-756 to 106-760.
Auction of livestock.
Livestock markets.
Generally, §§106-406 to 106-418.
See LIVESTOCK MARKETS.
Prompt pay law, §§106-418.1 to 106-418.7A.
See LIVESTOCK MARKETS.
Bees and honey.
See BEES AND HONEY.
Biological organism act, §§106-65.42 to 106-65.49.
See BIOLOGICAL ORGANISM ACT.
Biologics.
General provisions, §§106-707 to 106-715.
See BIOLOGICS.
Board of agriculture.
See AGRICULTURE BOARD.
Boll weevil eradication, §§106-65.67 to 106-65.78.
Chickens.
Eggs.
See EGGS.
Cigarettes.
See CIGARETTES AND TOBACCO PRODUCTS.
Commercial feed.
General provisions, §§106-284.30 to 106-284.46.
See FEED.
Commercial fertilizers, §§106-655 to 106-677.
See FERTILIZERS.
Commissioner of agriculture.
See AGRICULTURE COMMISSIONER.
Commission on agriculture and forestry awareness, §§120-150 to 120-154.
Advisory committee, §120-151.
Appointment, §120-150.
Creation, §120-150.
Duties.
Generally, §120-154.
Expenses.
Subsistence and travel expenses, §120-152.
Facilities, §120-153.
Qualifications of members, §120-150.
Reports, §120-154.
Staff, §120-153.

AGRICULTURE —Cont'd
Commission on agriculture and forestry awareness —Cont'd
Terms of office, §120-150.
Travel expenses, §120-152.
Commodities.
Generally, §§78D-1 to 78D-33.
See COMMODITIES.
Conservation easements.
Applicability of provisions, §106-744, (d).
Construction of provisions, §106-744, (d).
Countywide farmland protection plans, §106-744, (e), (f).
Creation of lots.
Number, §106-744, (b).
Defined, §106-744, (b).
Duration, §106-744, (b).
Farmland preservation trust fund, §106-744, (c) to (c2).
Purchase by county.
Authorized, §106-744, (a).
Constitution of North Carolina.
Capital projects for agriculture.
Authorization for creation of agency to issue revenue bonds, Const. N. C., art. V, §11.
Commissioner of agriculture.
Acting commissioner, Const. N. C., art. III, §7.
Compensation and allowances, Const. N. C., art. III, §9.
Council of state.
Membership, Const. N. C., art. III, §8.
Duties, Const. N. C., art. III, §7.
Elective officers, Const. N. C., art. III, §7.
Incapacity.
Determination, Const. N. C., art. III, §7.
Interim commissioner, Const. N. C., art. III, §7.
Vacancies.
Filling, Const. N. C., art. III, §7.
Consumer protection.
Records of sales of farm products.
Dated sales confirmation slips inapplicable to consumers, §106-202.6, (b).
Contracts.
Purchases and contracts through department of administration.
Preference given to home projects, §143-59.
Cooperative associations.
Authorized purposes, §§54-111, 54-124.
Cosmetics.
Food, drugs and cosmetics, §§106-120 to 106-145.
See FOOD, DRUG AND COSMETIC ACT.
Cotton.
Generally.
See COTTON.
Cotton warehouses, §§106-451.6 to 106-451.28, 106-451.40 to 106-451.44.
See COTTON WAREHOUSES.
Countywide farmland protection plans, §106-744, (e), (f).
Crops.
General provisions.
See CROPS.
Crop seed improvement board, §§106-269 to 106-276.
Department of agriculture and consumer services.
Transfer to department, §143A-64.
Dairies and dairy products.
Ice cream plants, creameries and cheese factories.
Inspections generally, §§106-246 to 106-255.
See ICE CREAM PLANTS, CREAMERIES AND CHEESE FACTORIES.

AGRICULTURE —Cont'd
Dairies and dairy products —Cont'd
Production, distribution, inspection, grading and testing generally, §§106-267 to 106-268.1.
See MILK AND MILK PRODUCTS.
Damage to commodities or production systems.
Definitions, §1-539.2B, (c).
Double damage liability, §1-539.2B, (a).
Valuation, §1-539.2B, (b).
Decedents' estates.
Continuation of farming operations, §§28A-13-3, 28A-13-4.
Crops of deceased persons, §28A-15-1.
Definitions.
Conservation easements, §106-744, (b).
Development act, §106-581.1.
Nuisance liability of agricultural and forestry operations, §106-701, (b), (b1).
Department of agriculture and consumer services.
See AGRICULTURE AND CONSUMER SERVICES DEPARTMENT.
Development act generally, §§106-580 to 106-587.
See AGRICULTURAL DEVELOPMENT.
Drainage, §§156-1 to 156-141.
See DRAINAGE.
Drainage districts, §§156-54 to 156-138.4.
See DRAINAGE DISTRICTS.
Drugs.
Food, drugs and cosmetics, §§106-120 to 106-145.
See FOOD, DRUG AND COSMETIC ACT.
Easements.
Conservation easements, §106-744.
Eggs, §§106-245.13 to 106-245.28.
See EGGS.
Emblements.
In lieu of emblements, farm lessee holds out year, with rents apportioned, §42-7.
Equine activity liability, §§99E-1 to 99E-3.
Executors and administrators.
Continuation of farming operations, §28A-13-4.
Powers of personal representative, §28A-13-3, (a).
Crops.
Ungathered at death of deceased person, §28A-15-1, (d).
Experiment stations.
Legislative assent to Adams act, §106-23.
Extension service.
Agricultural development generally, §§106-580 to 106-587.
See AGRICULTURAL DEVELOPMENT.
Fairs, §§106-502 to 106-520.7.
See FAIRS.
Farm credit administration.
Banks.
Obligations of agencies supervised by.
Investments in, §53-44.1.
Securities for deposit of public funds, §53-43.1.
Farm equipment.
Age for operation, §20-10.
Certificate of title exemptions, §20-51.
Defined, §20-4.01.
Driver's license exemptions, §20-8.
Identification marks, removing, defacing, etc., §14-401.4.
Registration exemptions, §20-51.
Farmland preservation, §§113A-240, 113A-241.

AGRICULTURE —Cont'd
Farm machinery franchises, §§66-180 to 66-188.
Farm machinery tax credit.
Property taxes paid on, §105-151.21.
Farm name registration, §§80-33 to 80-39.
Farm nuisance dispute mediation, §7A-38.3; Farm Med. Rules 1 to 10.
Farm operations commission.
Sale of merchandise by governmental units.
Exception to prohibition, §66-58, (b).
Farm tractors.
Age for operation, §20-10.
Certificate of title exemptions, §20-51.
Defined, §20-4.01.
Driver's license exemptions, §20-8.
Registration exemptions, §20-51.
Tires, §20-122, (c), (d).
Farmworker council, §§143B-426.25, 143B-426.26.
Feed.
Advisory service.
Establishment of pilot program, §106-21.1.
Fee for test samples, §106-21.1.
Commercial feed, §§106-284.30 to 106-284.46.
See FEED.
Fees.
Feed advisory service.
Test samples, §106-21.1.
Generally.
See AGRICULTURAL FEES AND TAXES.
Fertilizers.
Commercial fertilizers, §§106-655 to 106-677.
See FERTILIZERS.
Soil additives act, §§106-50.28 to 106-50.41.
See SOIL ADDITIVES ACT.
Finance authority.
Agricultural finance authority, §§122D-1 to 122D-23.
See AGRICULTURAL FINANCE AUTHORITY.
Food, §§106-120 to 106-145.
See FOOD, DRUG AND COSMETIC ACT.
Food bank information and referral service.
Maintenance by department of agriculture and consumer services, §106-21.2.
Fruit handlers unfair practices, §§106-496 to 106-501.
See FRUIT HANDLERS UNFAIR PRACTICES.
Funds.
Eastern North Carolina agricultural center fund, §106-6.2, (a).
Farmland preservation trust fund, §106-744, (c) to (c2).
Southeastern North Carolina agricultural center fund, §106-6.2, (b).
Gasoline and oil inspection board.
Department of agriculture and consumer services.
Transfer to department, §143A-62.
Gleaning.
Exemption from civil liability for farmers permitting, §106-706.
Goodness grows.
Special license plates, §§20-79.4, (b), 20-81.12, (b16).
Grain dealers, §§106-601 to 106-615.
See GRAIN DEALERS.
Grape growers council, §§106-750, 106-751.
Hall of fame, §§106-568.13 to 106-568.17.
Honey.
See BEES AND HONEY.
Housing authorities and projects.
Housing applications by farmers, §157-39.
Rural housing projects, §157-38.

AGRICULTURE —Cont'd
Housing standards for migrant farm workers, §§95-222 to 95-229.
Ice cream plants, creameries and cheese factories.
Inspections generally, §§106-246 to 106-255.
See ICE CREAM PLANTS, CREAMERIES AND CHEESE FACTORIES.
Income tax credit.
Farm machinery.
Property taxes paid on, §105-151.21.
Insurance.
Farmowners' policies.
Ice, snow or sleet damage, §58-44-55.
Judicial sales.
Private sale of farm commodities or produce authorized, §1-339.34, (a).
Landlord and tenant.
Emblements.
In lieu of emblements, farm lessee holds out year, with rents apportioned, §42-7.
Holding out year in lieu of emblements, farm lessee holds out year, with rents apportioned, §42-7.
Landlord's lien on crops, §§42-15 to 42-23.
Termination.
Rights of tenant on termination, §42-7.
Terms of agricultural tenancies in certain counties, §42-23.
Turpentine and lightwood leases, §42-24.
Landplaster.
Limestone, marl and landplaster, §§106-92.1 to 106-92.17.
See LIMESTONE, MARL AND LANDPLASTER.
License plates.
Goodness grows special plates, §§20-79.4, (b), 20-81.12, (b16).
Liens.
Effective period for liens on peanuts, cotton and grains, §44-69.1.
Landlord's lien on crops, §§42-15 to 42-23.
Leaf tobacco.
Effective period for tobacco sold in auction warehouses, §44-69.
Secured transactions.
Collateral, disposition.
Rights of secured party, §25-9-315, (a).
Crops.
Priority of security interests in, §25-9-334, (i).
Production money security interests, §25-9-324.1.
Production-money crops.
Defined, §25-9-102, (a).
Status of security interest in, §25-9-103.1, (a).
Production-money obligation.
Application of payments, §25-9-103.1, (b).
Defined, §25-9-102, (a).
Production-money security interests.
Burden of establishing status, §25-9-103.1, (c).
Continuation of status, §25-9-103.1, (c).
Status, §25-9-103.1, (a).
Production of crops.
Defined, §25-9-102, (a).
Default.
Time of default, §25-9-606.
Perfection and priority.
Buyers receiving delivery.
Interests that take priority over or take free of agricultural lien, §25-9-317, (a).

AGRICULTURE —Cont'd
Liens —Cont'd
Secured transactions —Cont'd
Perfection and priority —Cont'd
Choice of law governing agricultural liens, §25-9-302.
Filed financing statement providing certain incorrect information.
Priority of agricultural lien perfected by, §25-9-338.
Filing.
Assigned perfected interests need not be refiled, §25-9-310, (c).
When filing not required to perfect lien, §25-9-310, (b).
When required to perfect lien, §25-9-310, (a).
Interests that take priority over or take free of agricultural lien, §25-9-317, (a).
Law governing, §25-9-302.
Lessees receiving delivery.
Interests that take priority over or take free of agricultural lien, §25-9-317, (c).
Multiple conflicting interests in same collateral.
Other UCC provisions governing, §25-9-322, (f).
Proceeds and supporting obligations, time of perfection, §25-9-322, (b).
Rules governing priority, §25-9-322, (a), (g).
When perfected, §25-9-308, (b).
Light-traffic road weight and load limitations.
Exceptions, §20-118, (c).
Limestone, §§106-92.1 to 106-92.17.
See LIMESTONE, MARL AND LANDPLASTER.
Livestock brands, §§80-45 to 80-66.
See LIVESTOCK BRANDS.
Livestock dealer licensing, §§106-418.8 to 106-418.16.
See LIVESTOCK DEALER LICENSING.
Livestock diseases.
Brucellosis, §§106-388 to 106-398.
See BRUCELLOSIS.
Cattle tick, §§106-351 to 106-363.
See CATTLE TICK.
Compensation for killing diseased animals, §§106-323 to 106-335.
See LIVESTOCK DISEASES.
Control of livestock diseases generally, §§106-400 to 106-405.
See LIVESTOCK DISEASES.
Equine infectious anemia, §§106-405.15 to 106-405.20.
Generally, §§106-304 to 106-307.7.
See LIVESTOCK DISEASES.
Hog cholera, §§106-310 to 106-322.3.
See HOG CHOLERA.
Tuberculosis, §§106-336 to 106-350.
See TUBERCULOSIS IN LIVESTOCK.
Livestock markets.
Generally, §§106-406 to 106-418.
See LIVESTOCK MARKETS.
Prompt pay law, §§106-418.1 to 106-418.7A.
See LIVESTOCK MARKETS.
Marketing and branding farm products, §§106-185 to 106-196.
See FARM PRODUCTS MARKETING AND BRANDING.
Marketing associations, §§54-129 to 54-166.
See MARKETING ASSOCIATIONS.

AGRICULTURE —Cont'd
Marketing authority, §§106-528 to 106-534.
See MARKETING AUTHORITY.
Marl.
Limestone, marl and landplaster, §§106-92.1 to 106-92.17.
See LIMESTONE, MARL AND LANDPLASTER.
Meat inspections, §§106-549.15 to 106-549.39.
See MEAT INSPECTIONS.
Mediation of farm nuisance disputes, §7A-38.3; Farm Med. Rules 1 to 10.
Migrant farm workers.
See MIGRANT FARM WORKERS.
Milk and milk products.
Ice cream plants, creameries and cheese factories.
Inspections generally, §§106-246 to 106-255.
See ICE CREAM PLANTS, CREAMERIES AND CHEESE FACTORIES.
Production, distribution, inspection, grading and testing generally, §§106-267 to 106-268.1.
See MILK AND MILK PRODUCTS.
Milk distributors and processors generally.
See MILK DISTRIBUTORS AND PROCESSORS.
Motor carrier safety regulation unit.
Exemptions from certain requirements, §20-381, (b).
Nonpoint source pollution control program.
Agriculture cost share program, §§143-215.74 to 143-215.74B.
North Carolina grape growers council, §§106-750, 106-751.
Nuisance liability of agricultural and forestry operations.
Agricultural operation defined, §106-701, (b).
Changed conditions in locality, §106-701, (a).
Applicability of provisions, §106-701, (c).
Construction of provisions, §106-701, (e).
Declaration of policy, §106-700.
Farm nuisance dispute mediation, §7A-38.3; Farm Med. Rules 1 to 10.
Forest operation defined, §106-701, (b1).
Legislative determination, §106-700.
Local ordinances affected, §106-701, (d).
Policy declaration, §106-700.
Purpose of article, §106-700.
Occupational safety and health.
Citations.
Contesting citations, §95-137, (b).
Standards.
Promulgation, §95-131, (g).
Organic products.
Certification.
Standards, guidelines and policies, §106-22.3, (a).
Organic food production act.
Compliance with, §106-22.3, (b).
Pest control.
Biological organism act, §§106-65.42 to 106-65.49.
Boll weevil eradication, §§106-65.67 to 106-65.78.
Compact, §§106-65.55 to 106-65.61.
Structural pest control, §§106-65.22 to 106-65.41.
Plant pests, §§106-419 to 106-423.1.
Plant protection and conservation, §§106-202.12 to 106-202.22.
See PLANT PROTECTION AND CONSERVATION.
Poultry generally.
See POULTRY AND POULTRY PRODUCTS.
Poultry products inspections, §§106-549.49 to 106-549.69.
See POULTRY PRODUCTS INSPECTIONS.

AGRICULTURE —Cont'd
Preservation of farmland, §§106-735 to 106-743.
See FARMLAND PRESERVATION.
Prisons and prisoners.
Employment of prisoners, §148-26, (d).
Promotion of use and sale of agricultural products, §§106-550 to 106-568.
See AGRICULTURAL PRODUCTS PROMOTION.
Prompt pay law.
Livestock, §§106-418.1 to 106-418.7A.
See LIVESTOCK MARKETS.
Property taxes.
Agricultural, horticultural and forestland, §§105-277.2 to 105-277.7.
See PROPERTY TAXES.
Pulverized limestone and marl, §§106-92.1 to 106-92.17.
See LIMESTONE, MARL AND LANDPLASTER.
Records of dated farm products sales.
Dated sales confirmation slips, §106-202.6, (a).
Inapplicable to consumers, §106-202.6, (b).
Rendering plants and rendering operations, §§106-168.1 to 106-168.16.
See RENDERING PLANTS AND RENDERING OPERATIONS.
Rents.
In lieu of emblements, farm lessee holds out year, with rents apportioned, §42-7.
Terms of agricultural tenancies in certain counties, §42-23.
Research, §§106-568.1 to 106-568.12.
See AGRICULTURAL RESEARCH.
Runoff.
Nonpoint source pollution control program.
Agriculture cost share program, §§143-215.74 to 143-215.74B.
Water supply watershed protection.
Local and statewide standards.
Requirements as to agriculture and silviculture activities, §143-214.5, (d1).
Sales and use tax.
Exemptions, §105-164.13.
Searches and seizures.
Lien on crops.
Unlawful seizure by landlord, §42-22.
Seed board, §§106-277.31 to 106-277.33.
Seeds, §§106-269 to 106-284.22.
See SEEDS.
Slaughterhouses generally.
See SLAUGHTERHOUSES.
Soil additives act, §§106-50.28 to 106-50.41.
See SOIL ADDITIVES ACT.
Soil and water conservation districts, §§139-1 to 139-57.
See SOIL AND WATER CONSERVATION DISTRICTS.
Southern dairy compact, §§106-810, 106-811.
State farm operations commission.
Sale of merchandise by governmental units.
Exception to prohibition, §66-58, (b).
State farms, §106-22.1.
States.
Cooperation of federal and state governments.
Legislative assent to Adams act for experiment station, §106-23.
Structural pest control, §§106-65.22 to 106-65.41.
See STRUCTURAL PEST CONTROL.
Taxation.
Generally.
See AGRICULTURAL FEES AND TAXES.

AGRICULTURE —Cont'd
Tobacco.
Cigarettes and tobacco products.
See CIGARETTES AND TOBACCO PRODUCTS.
Tobacco research commission, §106-568.3, (b).
Tobacco trust fund commission, §§143-715 to 143-723.
See TOBACCO TRUST FUND COMMISSION.
Tourism.
Agricultural tourism signs, §106-22.5.
Transportation department.
Seed planted by department of transportation.
Approval by department of agriculture and consumer services, §136-18.2.
Unfair practices by fruit handlers, §§106-496 to 106-501.
See FRUIT HANDLERS UNFAIR PRACTICES.
United States.
Cooperation of federal and state governments.
Legislative assent to Adams act for experiment station, §106-23.
Promotion of use and sale of agricultural products.
Federal agricultural marketing act, §106-551.
University of North Carolina.
Agricultural research stations.
Control by board of governors, §116-39.
Vegetable handlers unfair practices, §§106-496 to 106-501.
See VEGETABLE HANDLERS' UNFAIR PRACTICES.
Vegetable plant law, §§106-284.14 to 106-284.22.
See VEGETABLE PLANT LAW.
Vocational and technical education.
Acquisition of land for instructional programs, §115C-163.
Wage and hour act.
Exemptions from wage and hour act, §95-25.14, (a).
Warehouses.
Cotton warehouses, §§106-451.6 to 106-451.28, 106-451.40 to 106-451.44.
See COTTON WAREHOUSES.
Waste management, §§143-215.10A to 143-215.10H.
See ANIMAL WASTE MANAGEMENT.
Water and air resources, §§143-211 to 143-215.9B.
See WATER AND AIR RESOURCES.
Water pollution control.
Nonpoint source pollution control program.
Agriculture cost share program, §§143-215.74 to 143-215.74B.
Water supply watershed protection.
Local and statewide standards.
Requirements as to agriculture and silviculture activities, §143-214.5, (d1).
Workers' compensation.
Farm laborers.
Exceptions to provisions, §97-13, (b).
Sellers of agricultural products.
Exceptions to provisions, §97-13, (d).

AGRICULTURE AND CONSUMER SERVICES DEPARTMENT.
Adulteration of grains.
Generally, §§106-621 to 106-628.
See GRAIN ADULTERATION.
Agricultural hall of fame.
Transfer to department, §143A-61.

AGRICULTURE AND CONSUMER SERVICES DEPARTMENT —Cont'd
Animal health division.
Animal welfare section, §§19A-22, 19A-25.
Antifreeze.
Registration generally, §§106-579.1 to 106-579.14.
See ANTIFREEZE.
Aquaculture development.
Generally, §§106-756 to 106-760.
See AQUACULTURE DEVELOPMENT.
Lead agency, powers and duties, §106-759.
Bees and honey.
Generally, §§106-634 to 106-644.
See BEES AND HONEY.
Biologics.
Generally, §§106-707 to 106-715.
See BIOLOGICS.
Board of agriculture.
Transfer to department, §143A-59.
Boll weevil eradication.
Generally, §§106-65.67 to 106-65.78.
See BOLL WEEVIL ERADICATION.
Brucellosis.
Generally, §§106-388 to 106-398.
See BRUCELLOSIS.
Cattle tick.
Eradication generally, §§106-351 to 106-363.
See CATTLE TICK.
Collection and publication of information relating to agriculture, §106-24.
Classification as to prevent identification of information received from individual farm operators, §106-24.1.
Commercial feed law.
Generally, §§106-284.30 to 106-284.46.
See FEED.
Commercial fertilizers.
Generally, §§106-655 to 106-677.
See FERTILIZERS.
Commissioner of agriculture.
Transfer of powers and duties to department, §143A-58.
Confidentiality of information collected and published, §106-24.1.
Cooperation with United States department of agriculture, §106-24.
Cotton grower's organization, §§106-65.84 to 106-65.91.
See COTTON GROWER'S ORGANIZATION.
Cotton warehouses.
Generally, §§106-451.6 to 106-451.28, 106-451.40 to 106-451.44.
See COTTON WAREHOUSES.
Creation, §143A-56.
Crop seed improvement board.
Transfer to department, §143A-64.
Distribution of food, surplus commodities and agricultural products.
Contracts and agreements with federal government, §143-64.5.
Egg law.
Generally, §§106-245.13 to 106-245.28.
See EGGS.
Egg promotion tax.
Generally, §§106-245.30 to 106-245.39.
See EGG PROMOTION TAX.
Endangered plant species.
Conservation and protection generally, §§106-202.12 to 106-202.22.
See PLANT PROTECTION AND CONSERVATION.

AGRICULTURE AND CONSUMER SERVICES DEPARTMENT —Cont'd
Equine infectious anemia.
Generally, §§106-405.15 to 106-405.20.
See EQUINE INFECTIOUS ANEMIA.
Established, §106-2.
Extension service.
Agricultural development generally, §§106-580 to 106-587.
See AGRICULTURAL DEVELOPMENT.
Farmed deer.
Production and sale, §§106-549.97, 106-549.98.
Feed advisory service, §106-21.1.
Feeding garbage to swine.
Generally, §§106-405.1 to 106-405.9.
See FEEDING GARBAGE TO SWINE.
Fees, §106-6.1.
Fees and taxes paid to department generally.
See AGRICULTURAL FEES AND TAXES.
Food bank information and referral service, §106-21.2.
Food, drug and cosmetic act.
Generally, §§106-120 to 106-145.
See FOOD, DRUG AND COSMETIC ACT.
Gasoline and oil inspection board.
Transfer to department, §143A-62.
Grain dealers.
Generally, §§106-601 to 106-615.
See GRAIN DEALERS.
Hog cholera.
Generally, §§106-310 to 106-322.3.
See HOG CHOLERA.
Ice cream plants, creameries and cheese factories.
Inspections generally, §§106-246 to 106-255.
See ICE CREAM PLANTS, CREAMERIES AND CHEESE FACTORIES.
Land conservation and land development bureau, §54-49.
Limestone, marl and landplaster.
Generally, §§106-92.1 to 106-92.17.
See LIMESTONE, MARL AND LANDPLASTER.
Livestock dealer licensing.
Generally, §§106-418.8 to 106-418.16.
See LIVESTOCK DEALER LICENSING.
Livestock diseases.
Brucellosis generally, §§106-388 to 106-398.
See BRUCELLOSIS.
Cattle tick, §§106-351 to 106-363.
See CATTLE TICK.
Compensation for killing diseased animals, §§106-323 to 106-335.
See LIVESTOCK DISEASES.
Equine infectious anemia, §§106-405.15 to 106-405.20.
See EQUINE INFECTIOUS ANEMIA.
Generally, §§106-304 to 106-307.7.
See LIVESTOCK DISEASES.
Hog cholera generally, §§106-310 to 106-322.3.
See HOG CHOLERA.
Tuberculosis generally, §§106-336 to 106-350.
See TUBERCULOSIS IN LIVESTOCK.
Marketing and branding farm products.
Generally, §§106-185 to 106-196.
See FARM PRODUCTS MARKETING AND BRANDING.
Meat inspections.
Generally, §§106-549.15 to 106-549.39.
See MEAT INSPECTIONS.

AGRICULTURE AND CONSUMER SERVICES DEPARTMENT —Cont'd
Milk and milk products.
Production, distribution, inspection, grading and testing generally, §§106-267 to 106-268.1.
See MILK AND MILK PRODUCTS.
Pest control compact.
Filing of bylaws and amendments with department, §106-65.57.
Plant conservation scientific committee.
Creation within department, §106-202.17.
Plant protection and conservation.
Generally, §§106-202.12 to 106-202.22.
See PLANT PROTECTION AND CONSERVATION.
Pork.
Promotion assessments, §§106-790 to 106-796.
See PORK PROMOTION ASSESSMENTS.
Poultry and poultry products.
Generally.
See POULTRY AND POULTRY PRODUCTS.
Poultry products inspection.
Generally, §§106-549.49 to 106-549.69.
See POULTRY PRODUCTS INSPECTIONS.
Prescription drug distributors.
Wholesale distributors generally, §§106-145.1 to 106-145.12.
See WHOLESALE PRESCRIPTION DRUG DISTRIBUTORS.
Public livestock market advisory board.
Transfer to department, §143A-65.
Public livestock markets generally, §§106-406 to 106-418.
See LIVESTOCK MARKETS.
Quail.
Production and sale of pen-raised quail.
Regulation by department, §106-549.94, (a).
Records and reports required of persons paying fees or taxes to, §106-9.2.
Rendering plants and rendering operations, §§106-168.1 to 106-168.16.
See RENDERING PLANTS AND RENDERING OPERATIONS.
Research.
Generally, §§106-568.1 to 106-568.12.
See AGRICULTURAL RESEARCH.
Rest areas.
Promotion of North Carolina farm products, §136-89.59A.
Rural rehabilitation corporation.
Transfer to department, §143A-63.
Sale of merchandise by governmental units.
Exceptions to prohibition, §66-58, (c).
Seed law, §§106-269 to 106-284.22.
See SEEDS.
Serums, viruses, vaccines, biologics and other products for control of animal diseases.
Purchase for resale, §106-307.1.
Soil additives act, §§106-50.28 to 106-50.41.
See SOIL ADDITIVES ACT.
State farm program.
Management for department, §106-22.1.
Strawberries.
Assessments generally, §§106-781 to 106-786.
See STRAWBERRIES.
Structural pest control division, §106-65.23, (a).
Transfer to department, §143A-60.
Structural pest control generally, §§106-65.22 to 106-65.39.
See STRUCTURAL PEST CONTROL.

AGRICULTURE AND CONSUMER SERVICES DEPARTMENT —Cont'd
Surplus food, commodities and agricultural products.
Distribution under contracts and agreements with federal government, §143-64.5.
Transportation department.
Seed planted by transportation department.
Approval by department of agriculture and consumer services, §136-18.2.
Tuberculosis in livestock.
Generally, §§106-336 to 106-350.
See TUBERCULOSIS IN LIVESTOCK.
Vegetable plant law.
Generally, §§106-284.14 to 106-284.22.
See VEGETABLE PLANT LAW.
Wholesale prescription drug distributors.
Generally, §§106-145.1 to 106-145.12.
See WHOLESALE PRESCRIPTION DRUG DISTRIBUTORS.

AGRICULTURE AND FORESTRY AWARENESS, COMMISSION ON, §§120-150 to 120-154.

AGRICULTURE BOARD.
Appointment of members, §106-2.
Biological organism act.
General provisions, §§106-65.42 to 106-65.49.
See BIOLOGICAL ORGANISM ACT.
Biologics.
Definition of "board," §106-708.
Rules and regulations, §106-709.
Chairman, §106-2.
Commercial fertilizers.
Authority to make rules and regulations, §106-673.
General provisions, §§106-655 to 106-677.
See FERTILIZERS.
Commissioner of agriculture.
Joint duties of commissioner and board, §106-22.
Composition, §106-2.
Cotton warehouses.
Generally, §§106-451.6 to 106-451.28, 106-451.40 to 106-451.44.
See COTTON WAREHOUSES.
Fees.
Generally, §106-6.1.
Food, drugs and cosmetics.
Generally, §§106-120 to 106-145.
See FOOD, DRUG AND COSMETIC ACT.
Regulations of board, §106-139.
Standards of quality.
Establishment of reasonable standards, §106-128.
Investigations.
Marketing and branding farm products, §106-187.
Limestone, marl and landplaster.
Authority of board to make rules and regulations, §106-92.16.
Liquefied petroleum gases.
Power to set minimum standards, §119-55.
Livestock.
Prompt pay law.
Authority of board, §106-418.7.
Public livestock markets.
Revocation of permit by board, §106-407.2.
Llamas as livestock.
Rules adopted by board to refer to llamas as livestock, §106-22.4.
Marketing and branding farm products.
Investigating marketing of products, §106-187.

AGRICULTURE BOARD —Cont'd
Meat inspection.
Sanitary conditions of establishments.
Rules and regulations prescribed by board, §106-549.22.
Meetings of board, §106-4.
Membership, §106-2.
Milk and milk products.
Ice cream plants, creameries and cheese factories.
Tests by board, §106-250.
Production, distribution, inspection, grading and testing generally, §§106-267 to 106-268.1.
See MILK AND MILK PRODUCTS.
Plant pests.
Agents of board.
Inspection, §106-422.
Regulations.
Authority of board to adopt, §106-420.
Powers and duties.
Commissioner of agriculture.
Joint duties of commissioner and board, §106-22.
Joint duties of commissioner and board, §106-22.
Promotion of use and sale of agricultural products.
Application to board for authorization of referendum, §106-554.
Action by board on application, §106-555.
Prompt pay law.
Authority of board, §106-418.7.
Research.
Promotion of agricultural research and dissemination of findings.
Action of board on petition for referendum, §106-568.3, (a).
State fair.
Constructing and financing facilities and improvements for fair, §106-503.1.
Operation of state fair, §106-503, (a).
Terms of office, §106-2.
Transfer of powers and duties to department, §143A-59.
Vacancies in board, §106-2.
Weights and measures.
Establishment of standards, §81A-4.

AGRICULTURE COMMISSIONER.
Acting officers, Const. N. C., art. III, §7.
Bees and honey, §§106-634 to 106-644.
See BEES AND HONEY.
Biological organism act.
Definition of commissioner, §106-65.44.
Enforcement of article, §106-65.46.
General provisions, §§106-65.42 to 106-65.49.
See BIOLOGICAL ORGANISM ACT.
Board of agriculture.
Joint duties of commissioner and board, §106-22.
Boll weevil eradication.
Generally, §§106-65.67 to 106-65.78.
See BOLL WEEVIL ERADICATION.
Cigarettes and tobacco products.
Leaf tobacco sales, §§106-461 to 106-465.
See LEAF TOBACCO SALES.
Commercial feed.
Enforcing official, §106-284.32.
General provisions, §§106-284.30 to 106-284.46.
See FEED.
Commercial fertilizers.
Administration of article, §106-658.
Analysis.
Duty of commissioner to make analysis, §106-662.

AGRICULTURE COMMISSIONER —Cont'd
Commercial fertilizers —Cont'd
General provisions, §§106-655 to 106-677.
See FERTILIZERS.
Inspections.
Duty of commissioner to inspect, §106-662, (a).
Samples.
Duty of commissioner to sample, §106-662, (a).
Testing.
Duty of commissioner to test, §106-662, (a).
Compensation and allowances, Const. N. C., art. III, §9.
Cotton warehouses.
Generally, §§106-451.6 to 106-451.28, 106-451.40 to 106-451.44.
See COTTON WAREHOUSES.
Council of state.
Membership, Const. N. C., art. III, §8.
Department of agriculture and consumer services.
Transfer of powers and duties to department, §143A-58.
Eggs.
Definitions in egg law, §106-245.14.
Power of commissioner, §106-245.23.
Sanitary conditions.
Approval of method by commissioner, §106-245.22, (a).
Election, §106-10.
Date of election, §163-1, (a).
Vacancy in office, §163-8.
Elective officers, Const. N. C., art. III, §7.
Fairs.
Supervision of fairs, §106-520.3.
Fees and taxes paid to commissioner generally.
See AGRICULTURAL FEES AND TAXES.
Food, drugs and cosmetics.
Enforcement of article.
Further powers of commissioner, §106-140.
Report of minor violations in discretion of commissioner, §106-127.
Violations of article.
Report of minor violations in discretion of commissioner, §106-127.
Fruits.
Unfair practices by handlers of fruits.
Additional powers of commissioner to enforce article, §106-500.
Approval of contracts between handlers and producers, §106-499.
Gasoline and oil inspection.
Administration by commissioner of agriculture, §119-23.
Grain.
Adulteration of grains.
Definition of commissioner, §106-621.
General provisions, §§106-621 to 106-628.
Sign furnished by commissioner, §106-624.
Grain dealers.
Authority to investigate, §106-612.
Definition of commissioner, §106-601, (b).
General provisions, §§106-601 to 106-615.
See GRAIN DEALERS.
Incapacity.
Determination, Const. N. C., art. III, §7.
Interim officers, Const. N. C., art. III, §7.
Limestone, marl and landplaster.
Sale of agricultural liming materials and landplaster.
Appeals from assessments and orders of commissioner, §106-92.13.

AGRICULTURE COMMISSIONER —Cont'd
Liquefied petroleum gases.
Administration of article, §119-57.
Livestock.
Prompt pay law.
Authority of commissioner, §106-418.7.
Duties of commissioner, §106-418.4.
Public livestock markets.
Permits from commissioner for operation of markets, §106-406.
Transportation of livestock.
Establishment of regulations for transportation, §106-14.
Longevity pay, §106-10.
Lubricating oils.
Inspection duties devolve upon commissioner, §119-6.
Meat inspection.
Powers of commissioner.
Additional powers, §106-549.36, (a), (b).
Refusal of commissioner to inspect and certify meat, §106-549.30.
Milk and milk products.
Records and reports of milk distributors and processors.
Powers of commissioner, §106-262.
Natural History Museum.
Advisory commission.
Member of commission, §143B-344.18.
Pests.
Declaring wild animal or bird, §113-300.2.
Plant law.
Interference with commissioner, etc., or other violation a misdemeanor, §106-284.20.
Poultry products inspections.
Definition of commissioner, §106-549.51.
Limiting entry of products to establishment, §106-549.63.
Powers of commissioner, §106-549.68, (a) to (c).
Registration of poultry products brokers, renderers or animal food manufacturers, §106-549.58, (c).
Powers and duties, §143A-57; Const. N. C., art. III, §7.
Egg law, §106-245.23.
Food, drugs and cosmetics.
Further powers of commissioner for enforcement of article, §106-140.
Joint duties of commissioner and board, §106-22.
Milk or milk products.
Records and reports of distributors and processors, §106-262.
Prompt pay law, §106-418.4.
Rendering plants and rendering operations.
Receipt of application for license, §106-168.5.
Transfer to department, §143A-58.
Prompt pay law.
Authority of commissioner, §106-418.7.
Duties of commissioner, §106-418.4.
Records and reports required of persons paying fees or taxes to commissioner, §106-9.2.
Rendering plants and rendering operations.
Application for license.
Duties of commissioner upon receipt of application, §106-168.5.
Rules and regulations.
Authority to adopt, §106-168.12.
Rules and regulations.
Transportation of livestock, §106-14.

AGRICULTURE COMMISSIONER —Cont'd
Salary, §106-11.
Longevity pay, §106-11.
Seeds.
Administration of article, §106-277.14.
Enforcement of article, §106-277.14.
General provisions, §§106-277 to 106-277.34.
See SEEDS.
Soil additives act, §§106-50.28 to 106-50.41.
See SOIL ADDITIVES ACT.
Succession to office of governor, §147-11.1, (b).
Term of office, §§106-10, 163-1, (a).
Transportation of livestock.
Establishment of regulations, §106-14.
Vacancy in office.
Filling, §§106-10, 163-8; Const. N. C., art. III, §7.
Vegetables.
Unfair practices by handlers of vegetables.
Additional powers of commissioner to enforce article, §106-500.
Approval of contracts between handlers and producers, §106-499.
Weights and measures.
See WEIGHTS AND MEASURES.

AGRICULTURE COST SHARE PROGRAM.
Nonpoint source pollution control program, §§143-215.74 to 143-215.74B.

AIDING AND ABETTING.
Accessories.
After the fact, §14-7.
Before the fact, §14-5.2.
Alcoholic beverages.
Sale to or purchase by underage persons, §18B-302, (c).
Fines and other penalties, §18B-302.1, (b), (c).
Bigamy, §14-183.
Concealing birth of child, §14-46.
Eggs.
Violations of egg act.
Persons punishable as principals, §106-245.27.
Escape.
Aiding escape from state prison, §148-45.
Futures contracts, §16-4.
Habeas corpus.
Concealing party entitled to writ, §17-28.
Hazing, §14-35.
Impaired driving.
Aider and abettor punishment, §20-179, (f1).
Interstate commerce.
Earnings of employees in interstate commerce.
Collections out of state to avoid exemptions.
Resident not to abet collection out of state, §95-74.
Larceny, §14-70.
Marriage licenses.
Obtaining license by false pretenses, §51-15.
Minors purchasing or possessing alcohol, §§18B-302, (c), 18B-302.1, (b), (c).
Prisons and prisoners.
Aiding escape from state prison, §148-45.
Aiding in prisoner self-injury resulting in incapacity, §148-46.1.
Conveying messages to convicts and other prisoners, §14-258.
Use of deadly weapon during escape, §14-258.2.
Prostitution.
Acts abetting prostitution unlawful, §14-204.
Public officers and employees.
Misuse of confidential information, §14-234.1.

AIDING AND ABETTING —Cont'd
Taxation.
Violations by officers, agents or employees.
Penalty for aiding and/or abetting, §105-234.
Underage drinking, §18B-302, (c).
Fines and other penalties, §18B-302.1, (b), (c).
Worthless checks, §14-107, (b).

AIDS.
Anatomical gifts.
Information for potential donors, §130A-148, (b).
Laboratory tests for AIDS virus infection.
Immunity of facility or institution, §130A-148, (e).
Required, §130A-148, (c), (d).
Arrest.
Initial appearance before magistrate.
Detention of defendant for communicable diseases, §15A-534.3.
Blood donors.
Information for potential donors, §130A-148, (b).
Laboratory tests for AIDS virus infection.
Immunity of facility or institution, §130A-148, (e).
Required, §130A-148, (c).
Confidentiality.
Records identifying person who has AIDS virus infection, §130A-143.
Different treatment for individual with AIDS.
Not unlawful, §130A-148, (j).
Handling of dead body of person infected with HIV.
Notice to persons handling body, §130A-395, (a), (c).
Laboratory tests for AIDS virus infection, §130A-148, (i).
Blood transfusion.
Immunity of facilities or institutions, §130A-148, (e).
Information for potential blood donors, §130A-148, (b).
Testing required, §130A-148, (c).
Consent.
Organ or tissue transplant, §130A-148, (d).
When not required, §130A-148, (f).
Notification of results, §130A-148, (g).
Organ or tissue transplant.
Immunity of facilities or institutions, §130A-148, (e).
Information for potential donors, §130A-148, (b).
Testing required, §130A-148, (d).
Protection of public health.
Commission may authorize or require tests when necessary for, §130A-148, (h).
Rules establishing standards for, §130A-148, (a).
Semen, §130A-148, (b), (c), (e).
Public schools.
Basic education program.
AIDS prevention instructions, §115C-81, (a2).
Referral of individual with AIDS to another provider or facility.
Not unlawful, §130A-148, (j).
Sexually transmitted infections, tests, §15A-615, (a), (4).
Treating individual with AIDS differently than individual without AIDS.
Not unlawful, §130A-148, (j).

AID TO FAMILIES WITH DEPENDENT CHILDREN.
District attorneys, reports to, §§15-155.1 to 15-155.3.

AID TO FAMILIES WITH DEPENDENT CHILDREN —Cont'd
Setoff debt collection, §§105A-1 to 105A-16.
See SETOFF DEBT COLLECTION.
Work first program generally, §§108A-27 to 108A-39.
See WORK FIRST PROGRAM.

AIR AND WATER QUALITY REPORTING ACT, §§143-215.63 to 143-215.69.

AIR BAGS.
Unlawful installation or reinstallation, §20-136.2.

AIR CARGO AIRPORT AUTHORITY ACT, §§63A-1 to 63A-25.
See GLOBAL TRANSPARK AUTHORITY.

AIR CARGO AIRPORT FACILITIES.
Global TransPark development zone, §§158-30 to 158-42.
See GLOBAL TRANSPARK DEVELOPMENT ZONE.

AIR CARRIERS.
Alcoholic beverages for use in air commerce, §18B-107.
Exemption from wage and hour act, §95-25.14, (c).
Property taxes.
Public service corporations.
Generally, §§105-333 to 105-344.
See PROPERTY TAXES.
Sales and use tax.
Interstate air carrier defined, §105-163.3.
Tax incentives for new and expanding businesses.
Creating jobs credit.
Constructing or planning to construct hub, §105-129.8, (d).
Interstate air carriers.
Sunset provisions, §105-129.2A, (a1).
Investment in machinery or equipment.
Constructing or planning to construct hub, §105-129.9, (e).

AIR-CLEANING DEVICES.
Corporate franchise tax.
Deducted reserves, §105-122, (d).
Deductible liabilities, §105-122, (b).

AIR CONDITIONERS.
Chlorofluorocarbon refrigerants, §§130A-309.80 to 130A-309.87.
Public assistance.
Weatherization assistance program, §108A-70.30.
Service agreements, §§58-1-25 to 58-1-42.

AIR CONDITIONING CONTRACTORS.
Plumbing, heating and fire sprinkler contractors.
Generally, §§87-16 to 87-27.1.
See PLUMBING, HEATING AND FIRE SPRINKLER CONTRACTORS.

AIR-CONDITIONING INSPECTORS.
County inspection departments.
Generally, §§153A-350 to 153A-375.
See COUNTY INSPECTION DEPARTMENTS.

AIRCRAFT.
Accidents.
Collision of aircraft.
Liability, §63-15.

AIRCRAFT —Cont'd
Accidents —Cont'd
Use of aircraft to discover certain motor vehicle violations.
Primarily for accident prevention, §20-196.2.
Acrobatic flying.
Penalty, §63-18.
Aeronautics instructors.
Defined, §63-1, (a).
Air instruction.
Defined, §63-1, (a).
Airmen.
Defined, §63-1, (a).
Alcoholic beverages.
Forfeiture generally, §18B-504.
Use in air commerce, §18B-107, (a), (b).
Antique airplanes.
Property tax assessment.
Antique airplane defined, §105-277.12, (a).
Designated special class of property for assessment, §105-277.12, (b).
Bailment, lease or rental of vehicle or draft animals.
Protection of bailor against bailee's acts, §§14-165 to 14-169.
See BAILMENTS.
Burglary.
Breaking or entering into or breaking out of aircraft, §14-56.
Collision of aircraft.
Liability.
Determination, §63-15.
Commercial fishing.
Spotter planes in commercial fishing operations.
Coastal and estuarine commercial fishing licenses, §113-171.1, (d).
Construction, design and airworthiness.
Conformity to federal standards, §63-22.
Construction of provisions, §63-1, (b).
Contracts entered into while in.
Jurisdiction, §63-17.
Damages.
Forced landing, §63-13.
Definitions, §63-1, (a).
Division of motor vehicles.
Additional airplanes.
Purchase, §20-3.1.
Dropping objects.
Penalty, §63-18.
Drugs.
Forfeiture of conveyances used in controlled substances violations.
Generally, §§90-112, 90-112.1.
Operation of aircraft while impaired, §§63-27, 63-28.
Drunkenness.
Operation of aircraft while impaired, §§63-27, 63-28.
Federal license, §63-20.
Possession and exhibition of license certificates, §63-21.
Violations of provisions, §63-23.
Handicapped persons.
Right to use of public conveyances, §168-3.
Highway patrol.
Use of aircraft to discover certain motor vehicle violations, §20-196.2.
Hunting from, §113-291.1, (b).
Impaired operation.
Chemical analysis, §63-27, (d).
Defense precluded, §63-27, (b).

AIRCRAFT —Cont'd
Impaired operation —Cont'd
Infliction of serious bodily injury.
Defense precluded, §63-28, (b).
Felony, §63-28, (d).
Offense, §63-28, (a).
Pleading, §63-28, (c).
Misdemeanor, §63-27, (e).
Offense, §63-27, (a).
Pleading, §63-27, (c).
Joyriding, §14-72.2.
Jurisdiction.
Contracts, §63-17.
Crimes and torts, §63-16.
State jurisdiction retained, §63-24.
Larceny.
Motor-propelled conveyances used in committing larceny and similar crimes.
Seizure and forfeiture of conveyances, §14-86.1.
Taking of aircraft, §63-25.
Unauthorized use of motor-propelled conveyance, §14-72.2.
Lawfulness of flight, §63-13.
Mental disability or infirmity of pilot.
Report and testimony by physician, immunity, §90-21.20A, (a), (b).
Navigable air space.
Defined, §63-1, (a).
Obstructing takeoff and landing operations, §63-37.1.
Operation of aircraft.
Defined, §63-1, (a).
Impaired persons, §§63-27, 63-28.
Qualifications of operators, §63-20.
Overflights.
Municipal regulation, §160A-180.
Ownership of space, §63-12.
Peace officers.
Enforcement of provisions, §63-45.
Regulations of civil aeronautics administration, §63-47.
Pesticide applicator licenses, §§143-452 to 143-459.
Physical disability or infirmity, pilots.
Report by physician, immunity, §90-21.20A, (a).
Testimony by physician, immunity, §90-21.20A, (b).
Physician's report or testimony.
Pilot's physical disability or infirmity.
Immunity of physician for making report, §90-21.20A, (a), (b).
Real property.
Landing on lands or waters of another, §63-13.
Ownership of space, §63-12.
Registration of aircraft.
Federal registration, §§63-22, 63-23.
Restricted areas.
Defined, §63-1, (a).
Sales and use tax.
Periodic rental payments.
Souring payments, §105-164.4B, (b).
Rate of tax, §105-164.4, (a).
Sovereignty in space, §63-11.
Special use airspaces.
Applications, §63-91.
Approval.
Notification to federal aviation administration, §63-92, (a).
Legislative declaration.
Public purpose, §63-90.
Public purpose declared, §63-90.

AIRCRAFT —Cont'd
Special use airspaces —Cont'd
Rejection.
Notification to federal aviation administration, §63-92, (b).
Review of applications, §63-91.
State airways.
Defined, §63-1, (a).
State of North Carolina.
Jurisdiction.
Contracts, §63-17.
Crimes and torts, §§63-16, 63-24.
Sovereignty in space, §63-11.
Takeoff and landing operations.
Illegal obstructing, §63-37.1.
Taking of aircraft, §63-25.
Tampering with aircraft, §63-26.
Torts.
Jurisdiction, §63-16.
State jurisdiction retained, §63-24.
Trick or acrobatic flying, §63-18.
Wage and hour act.
Exemption as to employees of air carriers, §95-25.14, (c).

AIRCRAFT FACILITY PROPERTY TAX CREDIT, §105-129.12.

AIR FORCE.
Generally.
See MILITARY AFFAIRS.

AIR FORCE CROSS.
Special registration plates issued to recipient, §20-79.4, (b).

AIR PISTOLS.
Firearms generally.
See FIREARMS.
Minors.
Permitting young children to use dangerous weapons.
Whether air pistol deemed dangerous firearm, §14-316, (b).
Possessing or carrying on campus or other educational property, §14-269.2.
Weapons generally.
See WEAPONS.

AIR POLLUTION CONTROL.
Action for failure to pay civil penalty, §143-215.114A, (f).
Administration of air quality program.
Department of natural resources and community development, §143-215.106.
Air quality compliance advisory panel, §§143B-317 to 143B-319.
Appointment, §143B-318, (a).
Chairman.
Calling of meetings, §143B-319.
Designation, §143B-318, (b).
Clerical and other services, §143B-318, (h).
Composition, §143B-318, (a).
Creation, §143B-317.
Duties, §143B-317.
Expenses, §143B-318, (e).
Meetings, §143B-319.
Membership generally, §143B-318, (a).
Number of members, §143B-318, (a).
Powers, §143B-317.
Quorum, §143B-318, (f).
Removal, §143B-318, (d).
Small business stationary source technical and environmental compliance assistance program.
Designation of ombudsman, §143B-318, (g).

AIR POLLUTION CONTROL —Cont'd
Air quality compliance advisory panel —Cont'd
Small business stationary source technical and environmental compliance assistance program —Cont'd
Secretariat for development and dissemination of reports by panel, §143B-318, (g).
Terms, §143B-318, (c).
Vacancies, §143B-318, (c).
Animal waste management, §§143-215.10A to 143-215.10H.
See ANIMAL WASTE MANAGEMENT.
Asbestos NESHAP for demolition and renovation.
Local air pollution control programs, §130A-452, (a), (b).
Assessments.
Title V program.
Assessment of program implementation fees, §143-215.106A.
Attorney general.
Civil action for failure to pay penalties, §143-215.114A, (f).
Bonds, surety.
Compliance bonds.
Special orders, §143-215.110, (e).
Cities regulating or restricting emissions, §160A-185.
Civil penalties.
Amount, §143-215.114A, (c).
Coal-fired generating units.
Emissions of oxides of nitrogen and sulfur dioxide by investor-owned utilities, §143-215.114A, (b1).
Contested case petitions.
Filing, §143-215.114A, (d).
Continuing violations, §143-215.114A, (b), (b1).
Disposition of proceeds, §143-215.114A, (h).
Enforcement procedures generally, §143-215.114A.
Failure to pay.
Civil action, §143-215.114A, (f).
Grounds for imposition, §143-215.114A, (a).
Notice of assessment, §143-215.114A, (d).
Remission request, §143-215.114A, (e).
Coal-fired generating units.
Emissions of oxides of nitrogen and sulfur dioxide by investor-owned utilities, §143-215.107D.
Civil penalties for violations, §143-215.114A, (b1).
Compliance with provisions, §143-215.107D, (f), (g).
Criminal penalties for violations, §143-215.114B, (f) to (h).
Definitions, §143-215.107D, (a).
Environmental compliance costs, accelerated recovery, §62-133.6, (b).
Adjustments or reductions in rate base, §62-133.6, (e), (f).
Amortization, §62-133.6, (b).
Compliance plans, filing, §62-133.6, (c).
Defined, §62-133.6, (a).
Emissions limitations, statement by utilities subject to, §62-133.6, (i), (j).
Enforcement of utility compliance, §62-133.6, (h).
Final agency action not subject to review, §62-133.6, (k).
Hearing to review compliance costs, §62-133.6, (d).
Market based rates and services, authority to implement, §62-133.6, (g).

AIR POLLUTION CONTROL —Cont'd
Coal-fired generating units —Cont'd
Emissions of oxides of nitrogen and sulfur dioxide by investor-owned utilities —Cont'd
Environmental compliance costs, accelerated recovery —Cont'd
Rate base to remain unchanged, §62-133.6, (e).
Permits to include certain conditions, §143-215.107D, (h).
Prohibited acts, §143-215.107D, (b) to (e).
Statements by utility, §143-215.107D, (j).
Voluntary agreement to transfer to state certain emissions allowances, §143-215.107D, (i).
Complex sources.
Construction or modification.
Approval or disapproval of environmental management commission, §143-215.109, (b).
Control by commission, §143-215.109.
Comprehensive plan or plans for prevention, abatement and control of air pollution, §143-215.107, (a).
Consent orders.
Public notice and review, §143-215.110, (a1).
Corporate franchise tax.
Deducted reserves, §105-122, (d).
Deductible liabilities, §105-122, (b).
Counties.
Local air pollution control programs authorized, §143-215.112.
Criminal penalties, enforcement procedures.
Actual knowledge, circumstantial evidence, §143-215.114B, (c).
Coal-fired generating units.
Emissions of nitrogen and sulfur dioxide by investor-owned utilities, §143-215.114B, (f) to (h).
Defenses, affirmative defense and bars to prosecutions, applicability, §143-215.114B, (e).
False statements, certifications or representation, §143-215.114B, (i).
Knowingly or willfully, state of mind not found, §143-215.114B, (d).
Person defined, §143-215.114B, (a).
Previous federal conviction, no proceeding based on, §143-215.114B, (b).
Declaration of policy, §143-215.105.
Definitions, §143-215.105.
Coal-fired generating units.
Emissions of oxides of nitrogen and sulfur dioxide by investor-owned utilities, §143-215.107D, (a).
Department of natural resources and community development.
Administration of program, §143-215.106.
Dry-cleaning equipment not using hazardous substances.
Business and energy tax credits, §105-129.16C, (a) to (c).
Dry-cleaning solvent cleanup fund.
Transfer of sales and use taxes to fund, §105-164.44E.
Dumping toxic substances, §14-284.2.
Enforcement procedures, §§143-215.114A to 143-215.114C.
Injunctive relief, §143-215.114C.
Engineers certifying application for permit.
Expedited review of applications, §143-215.108, (h).
Environmental management commission.
Auxiliary powers, §143-215.111.

AIR POLLUTION CONTROL —Cont'd
Environmental management commission —Cont'd
Complex sources.
Adoption and development of rules and regulations, §143-215.109, (a).
Approval or disapproval of construction or modification, §143-215.109, (b).
Enforcement procedures, §§143-215.114A to 143-215.114C.
General powers, §143-215.111.
Local air pollution control programs, §143-215.112.
Permits.
Generally, §143-215.108.
Powers.
General powers, §143-215.111.
Special orders, §143-215.110.
Supervision of programs, §143-215.106.
Environmental policy act, §§113A-1 to 113A-13.
See ENVIRONMENTAL POLICY ACT.
Expedited review of permit applications certified by professional engineer, §143-215.108, (h).
Fees.
Title V program.
Assessment of implementation fees, §143-215.106A.
Fires and fire protection.
Open burning regulated, §§113-60.25, 113-60.27.
Industrial and pollution control facilities financing.
Industrial and pollution control facilities financing act, §§159C-1 to 159C-27.
See INDUSTRIAL AND POLLUTION CONTROL FACILITIES FINANCING.
North Carolina capital facilities financing act.
North Carolina industrial and pollution control facilities financing act, §§159D-1 to 159D-27.
See INDUSTRIAL AND POLLUTION CONTROL FACILITIES FINANCING.
Injunctions.
Enforcement procedures, §143-215.114C.
Investigations.
Permits, §143-215.108, (d).
Limitation of actions.
Civil action for failure to pay penalties, §143-215.114A, (f).
Local air pollution control programs.
Asbestos NESHAP for demolition and renovation, §130A-452, (a), (b).
Certification by environmental management commission, §143-215.112, (b).
Environmental management commission.
Oversight and supervision, §143-215.112, (a).
Establishment.
Certification by commission required, §143-215.112, (b).
Counties and municipalities may establish with approval of commission, §143-215.112, (c).
Finance, §143-215.112, (d1).
Hearings.
Circumstances under which commission may hold, §143-215.112, (e).
Judicial review of final administrative decisions, §143-215.112, (d2).
Misdemeanors, §143-215.112, (d).
Oversight and supervision by commission, §143-215.112, (a).

AIR POLLUTION CONTROL —Cont'd
Local air pollution control programs —Cont'd
Rules and regulations.
Violations constitute misdemeanors, §143-215.112, (d).
Motor vehicles emission control.
Enforcement of provisions, §20-128.1, (c).
Inspections generally.
See MOTOR VEHICLE INSPECTIONS.
Requirements generally, §§20-128, (c), 20-128.1, (a).
Exception for pollution reduction modifications, §20-128, (d).
Safety inspections, scope, §20-183.3, (a).
Standards.
Rules and regulations, §20-128.2, (a).
Violations of provisions.
Penalty, §20-128.1, (d).
Time for bringing vehicle into conformity with provisions, §20-128.1, (b).
Municipal corporations.
Emission of pollutants.
Prohibited, §160A-185.
Local air pollution control programs authorized, §143-215.112.
New facilities.
Construction of containment source, equipment or cleaning device.
Activities allowed prior to obtaining permit, §143-215.108A, (a).
Permit required, §143-215.108A, (a).
Nitrogen oxides.
Investor-owned utilities.
Emissions by coal-fired generating units owned or operated by, §143-215.107D.
Statewide goals for reduction, report, §143-215.107B.
Notice.
Civil penalties.
Assessment, §143-215.114A, (d).
Title V program.
Assessment of implementation fees, §143-215.106A, (a).
Orders.
Special orders, §143-215.110.
Permits.
Activities requiring permits, §143-215.108, (a).
Alteration or expansion of existing facilities.
Modification of permit, §143-215.108A, (b) to (j).
Changes without requiring revision.
Adoption of rules, §143-215.108, (a1).
Contested cases.
Filing of petition, §143-215.108, (e).
Expedited review of applications certified by professional engineer, §143-215.108, (h).
Investigations, §143-215.108, (d).
Modification, §143-215.108, (a2).
Alteration or expansion of existing facilities, §143-215.108A, (b) to (j).
New facilities, §143-215.108A, (a).
Powers of commission, §143-215.108, (c).
Purposes of section.
Actions upon applications to effectuate, §143-215.108, (b).
Reduction of emission of air contaminants.
Submission of written description of current and projected plans, §143-215.108, (g).
Required.
Activities requiring permits, §143-215.108, (a).
Review of applications other than those certified by professional engineers, §143-215.108, (i).

AIR POLLUTION CONTROL —Cont'd
Permits —Cont'd
Term, §143-215.108, (d1).
Title V program.
Assessment of program implementation fees, §143-215.106A.
Zoning or subdivision ordinances.
Request to local government to determine applicability, §143-215.108, (f).
Petitions.
Civil penalties.
Contested cases, §143-215.114A, (d).
Permits.
Contested cases, §143-215.108, (e).
Policy declaration, §143-215.105.
Rules and regulations.
Complex sources.
Adoption and development of rules and regulations by commission, §143-215.109, (a).
Solid waste management.
General provisions, §§130A-290 to 130A-305.
See SOLID WASTE MANAGEMENT.
Sources of air pollution.
Complex sources, §143-215.109.
Construction or modification, §143-215.109, (b).
Control generally, §143-215.108.
Special orders.
Compliance bonds, §143-215.110, (e).
Effect of compliance, §143-215.110, (d).
Issuance, §143-215.110, (a).
Procedure, §143-215.110, (b).
Standards and classifications.
Criteria for standards, §143-215.107, (b).
Duty to prepare and develop comprehensive plan or plans for prevention, abatement and control of air pollution, §143-215.107, (a).
Provisions governing adoption and publication of rules, §143-215.107, (c).
State plans to reduce emissions from job-related travel.
Alternative-fueled or low emission vehicles, purchase by state, §143-215.107C, (a) to (c).
Plan for private sector employees, §143-215.107C, (e).
Plan for state employees, §143-215.107C, (d).
Sulfur dioxide (SO2).
Investor-owned utilities.
Emissions by coal-fired generating units owned or operated by, §143-215.107D.
Superior courts.
Civil penalties.
Civil action for failure to pay, §143-215.114A, (f).
Supervision of program.
Environmental management commission to review and supervise program, §143-215.106.
Title V program assessment of implementation fees, §143-215.106A, (a).
Notices of assessments, §143-215.106A, (a).
Reduction.
Fee becoming due and payable during fiscal year permit holder paid assessment, §143-215.106A, (c).
Schedule of assessments, §143-215.106A, (b).
Transportation projects.
Planning regionally significant transportation projects, §136-202.
Venue.
Civil action for failure to pay penalties, §143-215.114A, (f).

AIR POLLUTION CONTROL —Cont'd
Violations.
Enforcement procedures, §§143-215.114A to 143-215.114C.
Water and air quality reporting, §§143-215.63 to 143-215.69.
See WATER AND AIR QUALITY REPORTING.
Water and air resources, §§143-211 to 143-215.9B.
See WATER AND AIR RESOURCES.
Zoning permits.
Applicability of zoning or subdivision ordinance.
Request to local government to determine, §143-215.108, (f).

AIR POLLUTION EPISODES.
Open burning prohibited statewide, §113-60.25.

AIRPORT AUTHORITIES.
Security interest.
Entering into contracts creating, §160A-20.

AIRPORT BOARDS OR COMMISSIONS.
Security interest.
Entering into contracts creating, §160A-20.

AIRPORT DEVELOPMENT ACT.
State aid, §§63-65 to 63-73.
See AIRPORTS.

AIRPORTS.
Air cargo airports and related facilities.
Global TransPark development zone, §§158-30 to 158-42.
See GLOBAL TRANSPARK DEVELOPMENT ZONE.
Air navigation facilities.
Defined, §63-1, (a).
Airport authorities.
Sales and use tax refunds, §105-164.14, (c).
Air schools.
Defined, §63-1, (a).
Alcoholic beverages.
Mixed beverages.
Effect of election on permit issuance, §18B-603, (e).
Appropriations.
Municipal airports, §63-8.
State aid.
Sources of funds, §§63-68, 63-69.
Transportation department.
Continuing aviation appropriations, §§136-16.4, 136-16.5.
Construction and interpretation.
Singular and plural, §63-1, (b).
Contracts.
Transportation department.
Airport construction, repair, etc., §63-73.
Counties.
Establishment of airport, §63-3.
Public enterprises.
Operating, financing and fixing rates, §§153A-274 to 153A-277.
Definitions, §63-1, (a).
Special airport districts, §63-79.
Disorderly conduct, §14-275.1.
Federal aid.
Acceptance, §§63-70, 63-71, (a).
Department of transportation.
Powers as to, §63-71.
Global TransPark authority.
General provisions, §§63A-1 to 63A-25.
See GLOBAL TRANSPARK AUTHORITY.

AIRPORTS —Cont'd
Jurisdiction.
Municipal jurisdiction exclusive, §63-58.
Legislative declaration.
Airports a public purpose, §63-50.
Local development.
Global TransPark development zone, §§158-30 to 158-42.
See GLOBAL TRANSPARK DEVELOPMENT ZONE.
Misdemeanors.
Obstructing takeoff and landing operations, §63-37.1.
Zoning violations, §63-35.
Municipal airports, §§63-1 to 63-9.
Acquisition of property, §63-49, (a) to (c).
Sites, §§63-5, 63-6.
Validation of prior acquisitions, §63-51.
Appropriations, §63-8.
Cities.
Establishment by cities.
Authorized, §63-2.
Counties.
Establishment by counties, §63-3.
Powers of municipalities granted to counties, §63-57, (b).
Purpose of provisions declared county purposes, §63-57, (a).
Eminent domain, §§63-5, 63-6, 63-49, (b).
Joint operation of airports, §63-56, (h).
Establishment.
Cities and towns authorized to establish, §63-2.
Counties authorized to establish, §63-3.
Joint airports.
Establishment by cities, towns and counties, §63-4.
Existing airports.
Powers of governing bodies as to, §63-7.
Federal aid, §63-54.
Acceptance, §63-54, (a).
Compliance with federal regulations, §63-54, (b), (c).
Fees.
Establishment for existing airports, §63-7.
Gift or devise.
Acquisition of property by, §63-6.
Joint airports established by cities, towns and counties, §63-4.
Joint operation of airports, §63-56.
Agreements, §63-56, (b), (c).
Specific performance, §63-56, (k).
Authorized, §63-56, (a).
Board.
Composition, §63-56, (d), (l).
Generally, §63-56, (d) to (f), (l) to (n).
Officers, §63-56, (e).
Powers and duties, §63-56, (d), (f), (m).
Cessation of use of facilities for aeronautical purposes, §63-56, (o).
Eminent domain, §63-56, (h).
Expansion or enlargement of facilities, §63-56, (p).
Funds.
Joint fund, §63-56, (i), (j).
Ordinances, §63-56, (g).
Water and sewer systems.
Operation, §63-56, (q).
Jurisdiction.
Municipal jurisdiction exclusive, §63-58.
Legislative declaration.
Airports a public purpose, §63-50.

AIRPORTS —Cont'd
Municipal airports —Cont'd
Powers of municipalities operating airports, §63-53.
Airports on public waters and reclaimed land, §63-55, (a), (b).
Powers declared granted to counties, §63-57, (b).
Property taxes.
Authorized purposes, §160A-209, (c).
Public purpose.
Airports declared public purpose, §63-5.
Reclaimed land, §63-55, (a), (b).
Regulation of aircraft overflights, §160A-180.
Rules and regulations.
Powers of municipalities operating airports, §63-53.
Severability of provisions, §63-9.
Towns.
Establishment by towns, §63-2.
Trees and other vegetation.
Encroachment upon airport protection privileges prohibited, §63-49, (d).
Waters.
Airports on public waters, §63-55, (a), (b).
Municipal corporations.
Public enterprises generally, §§160A-311 to 160A-326.
See MUNICIPAL UTILITIES.
Peace officer enforcement of provisions, §§63-45, 63-47.
Powers of general assembly as to airport facilities, Const. N. C., art. V, §13.
Protection privileges.
Acquisition by municipalities, §63-49, (c).
Defined, §63-1, (a).
Encroachments upon.
Prohibited, §63-49, (d).
Rural airports.
State aid.
Sources of funds, §63-68.
Special airport districts, §§63-78 to 63-89.
Advances, §63-88.
Aeronautical facilities.
Defined, §63-79.
Bond issues.
Elections, §63-87.
Powers of districts, §§63-83, 63-84.
Taxes for supplementing airport revenue bond projects, §§63-85, 159-97, (i).
Citation of act.
Short title, §63-78.
Conflict of laws.
Inconsistent laws declared inapplicable, §63-89.
Contracts.
Powers of districts, §63-83.
Creation, §63-80.
Action to set aside.
Limitation of actions, §63-80, (e).
Advances for preliminary expenses, §63-88.
Election, §63-80, (c).
Hearing.
Notice, §63-80, (b).
Limitation of actions.
Actions to set aside creation, §63-80, (e).
Notices, §63-80, (d).
Hearing, §63-80, (b).
Resolution of governing body, §63-80, (a).
Definitions, §63-79.
District board.
Appointment of members, §63-81, (a).
Composition, §63-81, (a).

AIRPORTS —Cont'd
Special airport districts —Cont'd
District board —Cont'd
Defined, §63-79.
Inclusion of additional units of local government.
Appointment of new members, §63-82, (e).
Meetings, §63-81, (b).
Notice, §63-81, (b).
Oath of office of members, §63-81, (a).
Officers.
Election, §63-81, (c).
Quorum, §63-81, (b).
Vacancies, §63-81, (a).
Elections.
Bond elections, §63-87.
Creation of district, §63-80, (c).
Eminent domain.
Powers of districts, §63-83.
Fiscal impact of bills, resolutions or rules.
Local government fiscal information, §§120-30.41 to 120-30.49.
Inclusion of additional units of local government, §63-82.
Actions to set aside inclusion, §63-82, (d).
Annexation by participating unit of local government.
Effect, §63-82, (f).
Limitation of actions.
Actions to set aside inclusion, §63-82, (d).
New members of district board.
Appointment, §63-82, (e).
Procedure generally, §63-82, (a) to (c).
Limitation of actions.
Actions to set aside creation, §63-80, (e).
Actions to set aside inclusion of additional units of local government, §63-82, (d).
Notice.
Creation of district, §63-80, (d).
Hearing, §63-80, (b).
District board.
Meetings, §63-81, (b).
Powers of districts, §63-83.
Seals and sealed instruments.
Power to adopt official seal, §63-83.
Taxation.
Levy and collection of taxes generally, §63-86.
Levy for supplementing airport revenue bond project, §§63-85, 159-97, (i).
Powers of districts, §63-83.
Rate of tax.
Determination by district board, §63-86.
Title of act.
Short title, §63-78.
State aid.
Acceptance authorized, §63-70.
Activities eligible, §63-67.
Amount.
Limitations, §63-68.
Appropriations.
Source of funds, §§63-68, 63-69.
Conditions, §63-68.
Department of transportation.
Powers of department as to, §§63-65, 63-66.
Eligibility.
Activities eligible, §63-67.
Limitations, §63-68.
Rural airports, §63-68.
Source of funds, §§63-68, 63-69.
Streets and highways.
Connection of airports with state highway system.
Powers of department of transportation, §136-18.

AIRPORTS —Cont'd
Traffic signs and traffic control devices.
Uniform signs and devices.
Exemption as to informational and directional signs, §136-30, (d).
Transportation department.
Agent of public agency which applies for federal aid, §63-71, (b).
Appropriations.
Continuing aviation appropriations, §§136-16.4, 136-16.5.
Connection of state airports with public highway system, §136-18.
Contracts.
Airport construction, repair, etc., §63-73.
Federal aid.
Powers as to, §63-71.
Operation of airports by department, §63-72.
Powers, §§63-65, 63-66, 63-71, 63-72.
Public highway system.
Connection of state airports with system.
Powers of department, §136-18.
State aid.
Powers of department as to, §§63-65, 63-66.
Trespass upon airport property, §63-26.1, (b).
Unlawful, §63-26.1, (a).
Waters and watercourses.
Municipal airports.
Airports on public waters and reclaimed land, §63-55, (a), (b).
Zoning, §§63-30 to 63-37.
Air cargo airport authority.
Political subdivision not to adopt regulation in violation, §63-31, (f).
Air rights.
Acquisition, §63-36.
Board of appeals.
Appeals to board, §63-33, (c).
Composition, §63-33, (c).
Judicial review, §63-34.
Copies of papers may be returned, §63-34, (c).
Costs, §63-34, (e).
Jurisdiction of court, §63-34, (d).
Petition, §63-34, (a).
Writ of certiorari, §63-34, (b).
Meetings, §63-33, (c).
Powers, §63-33, (c).
Citation of act.
Short title, §63-37.
Eminent domain.
Acquisition of air rights, §63-36.
Enforcement of act, §63-35.
General zoning ordinances.
Effect, §63-31, (b).
Hearings.
Adoption of zoning regulations, §63-33, (a).
Injunctions.
Violations of provisions, §63-35.
Joint boards, §63-31, (c).
Legislative declaration, §63-30.
Misdemeanors.
Violations of provisions, §63-35.
Notice.
Hearing on adoption of zoning regulations, §63-33, (a).
Penalties.
Violations of provisions, §63-35.
Permits, §63-32, (a).
Obstruction marking and lighting may be required, §63-32, (c).

AIRPORTS —Cont'd
Zoning —Cont'd
Regulations.
Administrative agency, §63-33, (b).
Adoption.
Authorized, §63-31, (a).
Procedure, §63-33, (a).
Area affected by, §63-31, (d).
Restrictions on, §63-31, (e).
Title of act.
Short title, §63-37.
Variances, §63-32, (b).
Obstruction marking and lighting may be required, §63-32, (c).
Violations of provisions.
Injunctions, §63-35.
Penalties, §63-35.

AIR RESOURCES ACT, §§143-211 to 143-215.9B.
See WATER AND AIR RESOURCES.

AIR RIFLES.
Firearms generally.
See FIREARMS.
Minors.
Permitting young children to use dangerous firearms.
Whether air rifle deemed dangerous firearm, §14-316, (b).
Possessing or carrying on campus or other educational property, §14-269.2.
Weapons generally.
See WEAPONS.

AIRSPACE.
Special use airspaces, §§63-90 to 63-92.

ALAMANCE COUNTY.
Agricultural tendencies in certain counties.
Terms of, §42-23.
Ambulance services.
Attachment or garnishment and lien for, §§44-51.4 to 44-51.8.
Obtaining ambulance services without intending to pay, §14-111.2.
Requesting ambulance falsely, §14-111.3.
Board of county commissioners.
Filling vacancies on board, §153A-27.1.
Condemnation or acquisition of land by local government unit outside county.
Consent of board of commissioners necessary, §153A-15.
Coroner elected as nominee of political party.
Filling vacancy in office, §152-1.
County boards of education elected on partisan basis.
Vacancies in office, §115C-37.1.
Cropper or tenant neglecting or refusing to perform terms of contract without just cause.
Forfeiture of right of possession to premises, §42-27.
Dog collars.
Unlawful removal of electronic dog collars, §14-401.17.
Dogs used in hunting.
Regulation by wildlife resources commission, §113-291.5, (a).
On-premises unfortified wine licenses.
Discretion to decline to issue, §105-113.71, (b).
School property.
Acquisition and improvement, §153A-158.1.

ALAMANCE COUNTY —Cont'd
Sheriff.
Vacancy, performance of duties until vacancy filled, §162-5.1.
Small city mixed beverage elections.
Inapplicability of subsection to, §18B-600, (e1).

ALARMS.
Fire alarms.
Giving false alarm, §14-286.
Molesting alarms, §14-286.

ALARM SYSTEMS LICENSING, §§74D-1 to 74D-13.
Action for failure to pay civil penalty, §74D-11, (e).
Agents.
Requirements, §74D-2, (c).
Alarm systems recovery fund, §§74D-30 to 74D-33.
Appeals.
Suspension or revocation of license, §74D-10, (b).
Apprenticeship registration permit.
Duration, §74D-8.1, (b).
Issuance, §74D-8.1, (a).
Restrictions on holder, §74D-8.1, (c).
Assignment of license.
Prohibited, §74D-7, (b).
Attorney general.
Investigative powers, §74D-5.2.
Background investigations.
Persons applying for license, §74D-2, (d).
Criminal history record checks, §74D-2, (c).
Board.
Appointment of members, §74D-4, (c), (d).
Chairman, §74D-4, (f).
Compensation of members, §74D-4, (e).
Composition, §74D-4, (b).
Director, §74D-5.1.
Established, §74D-4, (a).
Exclusive jurisdiction, §74D-11, (c).
Expenses of members.
Reimbursement, §74D-4, (e).
Hearings, §74D-5, (b).
Meetings, §74D-4, (g).
Powers, §74D-5, (a).
Quorum, §74D-4, (g).
Removal of members, §74D-4, (d).
Terms of members, §74D-4, (c).
Vacancies.
Filling, §74D-4, (d).
Branch offices, §74D-7, (d).
Notification requirements to board, §74D-7, (d).
Citation of act.
Short title, §74D-1.
Confidentiality of information.
Certain information concerning applicants and licensees, §74D-2, (f).
Criminal history record checks.
Persons applying for license, §74D-2, (c).
Denial of license.
Grounds, §74D-6.
Employee registration, §74D-8, (a).
Registration card, §74D-8, (c), (d).
Termination of employment.
Notice, §74D-8, (b).
Examinations.
Oral or written examinations.
Board may require, §74D-2, (e).
Exemptions from provisions, §74D-3.
Fees, §74D-7, (e).
Transfer of certain fees, §74D-13.
Form of license, §74D-7, (a).

ALARM SYSTEMS LICENSING —Cont'd
Fraud.
Conviction of crime involving fraud.
Grounds for denial of license, §74D-6.
Funds.
Transfer of funds, §74D-13.
Hearings.
Board, §74D-5, (b).
Injunctions, §74D-11, (a).
Invalidity of provisions.
Severability, §74D-12.
Investigations.
Background investigation of license applicant, §74D-2, (d).
Powers of board, §74D-5, (a).
Liability insurance.
Cancellation of policy, §74D-9, (e).
Certificate of insurance to be maintained on file, §74D-9, (f).
Requirements, §74D-9, (d).
Local governments.
Permits.
Requirement by ordinance, §74D-11, (c).
Misdemeanors, §74D-11, (b).
Name of licensee.
Engaging in business under, §74D-7, (c).
License to state, §74D-7, (a).
Penalties.
Civil penalties in lieu of suspension or revocation of license, §74D-11, (d).
Violations of provisions, §74D-11, (b).
Qualifications for licensing, §74D-2, (d).
Registration.
Denial of registration, §74D-6.
Employees of licensees, §74D-8.
Required, §74D-2, (a).
Exceptions, §74D-3.
Rules and regulations.
Powers of board, §74D-5, (a).
Violations as grounds for suspension or revocation of license, §74D-10, (a).
Severability of provisions, §74D-12.
Subpoenas.
Powers of board, §74D-5, (a).
Suspension or revocation of license.
Appeal, §74D-10, (b).
Civil penalties in lieu of, §74D-11, (d).
Grounds, §74D-10, (a).
Powers of board generally, §74D-5, (a).
Term of license, §74D-7, (b).
Title of act.
Short title, §74D-1.

ALARM SYSTEMS RECOVERY FUND, §§74D-30 to 74D-33.
Application for payment out of fund, §74D-31.
Creation, §74D-30.
Hearings, §74D-31.
Management, §74D-30.
Payment out of fund, §§74D-31 to 74D-33.
Application for, §74D-31.
Maximum liability, §74D-33.
Order directing payment, §74D-32.
Pro rata distribution, §74D-33.
Payments to fund, §74D-30.
Use of funds, §74D-30.

ALBEMARLE.
Traffic control photographic systems, §160A-300.1, (d).

ALBEMARLE SOUND.
Obstructions.
Lumbermen to remove, §76-42.

ALCOHOL AND DRUG EDUCATION PROGRAM.
Basic education program, §115C-81, (a3).

ALCOHOL AND DRUG EDUCATION TRAFFIC SCHOOLS.
Limited driving privilege.
Driving for other than work-related purposes, §20-179.3, (g2).
Restoration of license.
Under 21 years, impaired driving or driving after consuming alcohol or drugs.
Requirement for obtaining certificate of completion, §20-17.6, (c).

ALCOHOLIC BEVERAGE CONTROL COMMISSION.
Advertisements.
Authority to promulgate rules, §18B-105, (b).
Appointment, §18B-200, (b).
Bond issues, §18B-208, (a).
Chairman.
Salary, §18B-200, (a).
Compensation, §18B-200, (a).
Composition, §18B-200, (a).
Conflicts of interest.
Dealing for family members, §18B-201, (c).
Financial interest restricted, §18B-201, (a).
Self-dealing, §18B-201, (b).
Creation, §18B-200, (a).
Department of crime control and public safety.
Transfer to department, §143A-243.
Employees.
Authority to employ, §18B-200, (d).
Orders.
Service of orders, §18B-500, (d).
Powers.
General provisions, §18B-203.
Implied powers, §18B-203, (b).
Pregnancy, consumption during.
Signs warning of dangers.
Distribution and posting, §§18B-203, (a), 18B-808.
Service of orders, §18B-500, (d).
Special fund, §18B-208, (b).
State warehouse, §18B-204.
Vacancies in office.
Filling, §18B-200, (c).

ALCOHOLIC BEVERAGE CONTROL LICENSES.
ABC permits generally.
See ABC PERMITS.
Local licenses, §§105-113.77 to 105-113.79.

ALCOHOLIC BEVERAGE CONTROL PERMITS.
Generally.
See ABC PERMITS.

ALCOHOLIC BEVERAGES.
ABC boards, local.
See ABC BOARDS, LOCAL.
ABC stores.
See ABC STORES.
Accounts and accounting.
Required, §18B-205, (a), (b).
Administrative procedure act.
Applicability, §18B-906, (a).
Exception on hearing location, §18B-906, (b).
Exception on new evidence, §18B-906, (c).
Advertisements.
Authority of commission, §18B-105, (b).

ALCOHOLIC BEVERAGES —Cont'd
Advertisements —Cont'd
Compliance with rules of commission, §18B-105, (a).
Aiding and abetting.
Sale to or purchase by underage persons, §§18B-302, (c), 18B-302.1, (b), (c).
Airports and airplanes.
Forfeiture generally, §18B-504.
Mixed beverages.
Effect of elections on issuance of permits, §18B-603, (e).
Use in air commerce.
Purchase and storage, §18B-107, (a).
Sale, §18B-107, (b).
Alcoholism research authority, §§122C-431 to 122C-433.
Alcohol law enforcement.
Agents for law enforcement, §18B-500.
Department of crime control and public safety.
Alcohol law enforcement agents.
Appointment by secretary, §18B-500.
Alcohol law enforcement division.
Defined, §18B-101.
Transfer to department, §§143A-243, 143B-475.
Forfeitures, §18B-504.
Inspection of licensed premises, §18B-502.
Local ABC officers, §18B-501.
Restitution to law enforcement agency, §18B-505.
Seized beverages.
Disposition, §18B-503.
Alcohol treatment center.
Joint security force, §122C-421, (a), (b).
Amounts that may be purchased.
Kegged malt beverages, §18B-303, (a).
Liquor and fortified wine, §18B-303, (a).
Malt beverages, §18B-303, (a).
Purchase-transportation permit.
Purchasing in grater amounts, §18B-303, (c).
Unfortified wine, §18B-303, (a).
Unlawful purchases in greater amounts, §18B-303, (b).
Without permit, §18B-303, (a).
Amusement device operators.
Operating device equipment under the influence.
Prohibition, §95-111.11, (b).
Applications for permits, §18B-902.
Athletic contests.
Publicly displaying fortified wine, spirituous liquor or mixed beverages at athletic contests, §18B-301, (f).
Audits.
Local ABC boards, §§18B-205, (c), 18B-702, (c).
Local ABC stores, §18B-205, (c).
State warehouse, §18B-204.
Ball parks.
In-stand sales, §18B-1009.
Beer.
Definition of "malt beverage," §18B-101.
Malt beverages generally. See within this heading, "Malt beverages."
Beer franchises, §§18B-1300 to 18B-1308.
See BEER FRANCHISES.
Bingo games.
Sale or consumption, §18B-308.
Boards.
Local ABC boards.
See ABC BOARDS, LOCAL.
Boating safety.
Operation of boat or manipulation of water skis while intoxicated, §75A-10, (b).

ALCOHOLIC BEVERAGES —Cont'd
Boating safety —Cont'd
Operation of motorboat or motor vessel while under the influence, §75A-10, (b1).
Bootlegging, §18B-304.
Unauthorized substances taxes, §§105-113.105 to 105-113.113.
See UNAUTHORIZED SUBSTANCES TAXES.
Bottlers.
Distribution agreements, §18B-1110, (b).
Permits.
Authorization, §18B-1110, (a).
Commercial permit, §18B-1100.
Brown-bagging permit, §§18B-301, 18B-1001.
Burden of proof.
Compensation for injury caused by sales to underage persons, §18B-122.
Charities.
Furnishing alcoholic beverages to inmates of charitable institutions, §14-258.1, (b).
Chemical analysis of impairing substances in blood generally.
See IMPAIRED DRIVING.
Child labor.
ABC permit holders.
Restrictions on employment of minors by, §95-25.5, (j).
Cider.
Commercial permit, manufacturers, §18B-1100.
Exemption from alcoholic beverage provisions, §18B-103.
Commercial transportation, §18B-1115.
Commercial vehicles.
Operating a commercial vehicle after consuming alcohol, §20-138.2A.
Odor of alcohol.
Evidentiary effect, §20-138.2A, (b1).
Screening test for alcohol, §20-138.2A, (b2).
Operating while possessing alcoholic beverages, §20-138.2C.
Commission for mental health, developmental disabilities and substance abuse services, §§143B-147 to 143B-150.
Community service.
Minors.
Aiding and abetting sale to or purchase by underage persons, §18B-302, (c).
Fines and other penalties, §18B-302.1, (b), (c).
Sales to, §18B-302, (a).
Fines and other penalties, §18B-302.1, (a), (c).
Community theatre.
Defined, §18B-1000.
Compensation for injury caused by sales to underage persons, §§18B-121 to 18B-129.
Burden of proof, §18B-122.
Claims for relief.
Creation, §18B-121.
Exception, §18B-125.
Limitation on damages, §18B-123.
Clerk of superior court.
Duties, §18B-127.
Common-law rights not abridged, §18B-128.
Definitions, §18B-120.
Evidence.
Admissibility, §18B-122.
Exemptions from article, §18B-125.
Holding of documents.
No liability for holding, §18B-129.
Joint and several liability, §18B-124.
Limitation of actions, §18B-126.
Limitation on damages, §18B-123.

ALCOHOLIC BEVERAGES —Cont'd
Compensation for injury caused by sales to underage persons —Cont'd
Refusal to sell.
No liability, §18B-129.
Statute of limitations, §18B-126.
Superior court.
Duty of clerk, §18B-127.
Complimentary alcoholic beverages.
Air carriers serving, §18B-107, (b).
Conduct not permitted on licensed premises, §§18B-1005, (a), 18B-1005.1, (a), (c).
Conduct on licensed premises, §18B-1005.
Conflicts of interest.
Alcoholic beverage control commission, §18B-201.
Local ABC boards, §18B-700, (h).
Wholesalers.
Supplier's financial interest in wholesaler, §18B-1119.
Congressionally chartered veterans organizations.
Defined, §18B-1000.
Constitution of the United States, Const. U. S., amds. XVIII, XXI.
Construction of chapter, §18B-100.
Consumption.
Bingo games, §18B-308.
Fortified wine and spirituous liquor.
Restrictions, §18B-301, (d).
Where lawful, §18B-301, (d).
Hours of consumption, §18B-1004, (a).
Malt beverages and unfortified wine.
General provisions, §18B-300, (a).
Off-premises establishments, §18B-300, (b).
Ordinances.
Property owned or occupied by city or county, §18B-300, (c).
Unlawful possession or consumption.
Consumption not authorized by permits, §18B-1006, (d).
Controlled substances.
Prohibited on licensed premises, §18B-1005, (a).
Convention center.
Defined, §18B-1000.
Cooking school.
Defined, §18B-1000.
Permits, §18B-1001.
Restrictions on sales at cooking schools, §18B-1006, (g).
Counties.
Confinement facilities.
Furnishing alcoholic beverages to inmates, §14-258.1.
Licenses.
Beer and wine retail licenses, §105-113.78.
Local option elections, §18B-600, (b).
Favorable county vote.
Effect on city, §18B-604, (b).
Negative county vote.
Effect on city, §18B-604, (c).
Ordinances.
Consumption.
Malt beverages and unfortified wine, §18B-300, (c).
Restriction on adoption, §18B-100.
Regulation of places of amusement, §153A-135.
County boards of alcoholic control.
Defense of employees and officers, §160A-167.
Damaged alcoholic beverage sales, §18B-806.
Definitions, §18B-101.
ABC stores.
Gross receipts, §18B-805, (a).
Beer franchises, §18B-1301.

ALCOHOLIC BEVERAGES —Cont'd
Definitions —Cont'd
Compensation for injury caused by sales to underage persons, §18B-120.
Malt beverage, §18B-101.
Oceangoing vessel, §18B-106, (b).
Permits.
Conviction, §18B-900, (b).
Retail activities, §18B-1000.
Transportation.
Passenger area of a motor vehicle, §18B-401, (c).
Wine distribution agreements, §18B-1201.
Denatured alcohol.
Exemption from alcoholic beverage provisions, §18B-103.
Dentists.
Exemption from chapter, §18B-103.
Department of crime control and public safety.
Alcohol law enforcement agents.
Appointment by secretary, §18B-500.
Alcohol law enforcement division.
Defined, §18B-101.
Transfer to department, §§143A-243, 143B-475.
Direct shipment into state.
Applicability of sections, §18B-102.1, (c).
Armed forces installations, §18B-109, (b).
Notice to bureau of alcohol, tobacco and firearms, §18B-102.1.
Prohibited, §18B-109, (a).
Wholesaler receiving from out-of-state retail or wholesale dealer, §18B-102.1, (a).
Wine purchased while visiting winery premises, §18B-109, (d).
Wine shipper permittees, §§18B-109, (c), 18B-1001.1, 18B-1001.2.
Disabled persons.
Refusal to sell not to be discriminatory, §18B-305, (c).
Disasters.
Prohibitions and restrictions during state of emergency.
County powers, §14-288.13.
Municipal powers, §14-288.12.
Discrimination.
Refusal to sell not to be discriminatory, §18B-305, (c).
Disorderly conduct.
Prohibited on licensed premises, §18B-1005, (a).
Disposition of seized beverages, §§18B-503, 18B-504.
Distilleries.
Permits.
Authorized acts, §18B-1105, (a).
Commercial permits, §18B-1100.
Fuel alcohol, §18B-1105, (b).
Searches and seizures.
Disposition of seized, confiscated or unclaimed property.
Provisions not applicable to whiskey distilleries, §15-17.
Divorce.
Excessive use.
Grounds for divorce, §50-7.
Drivers' licenses.
Issuance to habitual drunkards, §20-9, (c).
Revocation or suspension.
Mental incompetents, alcoholics and habitual users, §20-17.1.
Underage purchasers of alcohol, §20-17.3.
Driving by person less than 21 years old after consuming alcohol or drugs, §20-138.3.

ALCOHOLIC BEVERAGES —Cont'd
Driving by provisional licensee after consuming alcohol.
Restoration of license after conviction, §20-17.6.
Driving instruction.
Impaired instruction, §20-12.1.
Driving under the influence.
Generally.
See IMPAIRED DRIVING.
Drugs.
Prohibited on licensed premises, §18B-1005, (a).
Drunk driving.
Generally.
See IMPAIRED DRIVING.
Drunkenness, §§14-443 to 14-447.
Eating establishment.
Defined, §18B-1000.
Education.
Alcohol addicted children.
Appropriate education provided for.
Policy of state to insure, §115C-149.
Children with special needs.
Alcohol addicted children excluded from article, §115C-149.
Policy of state, §115C-149.
State board of education to adopt rules, §115C-150.
Elections, §§18B-600 to 18B-605.
See LOCAL OPTION ELECTIONS.
Emergencies.
Powers of governor, §18B-110.
Prohibitions and restrictions during state of emergency.
County powers, §14-288.13.
Municipal powers, §14-288.12.
Employer discrimination for lawful use of lawful products during nonworking hours, §95-28.2.
Ethyl alcohol.
Exemption from alcoholic beverage provisions, §18B-103.
Evidence.
Compensation for injury caused by sales to underage persons.
Admissibility, §18B-122.
Possession for purpose of sale.
Prima facie evidence.
Possession by person not permitted to possess, §18B-304, (b).
Exclusive outlets.
Prohibited, §18B-1116, (a).
Exemptions, §18B-1116, (b).
Exemptions from chapter, §18B-103.
Exclusive outlets.
Prohibited, §18B-1116, (b).
Fake ID used to purchase.
Sale to or purchase by underage persons, §18B-302, (e).
Fighting.
Prohibited on licensed premises, §18B-1005, (a).
Flavor extracts.
Exemption from alcoholic beverage provisions, §18B-103.
Food business.
Defined, §18B-1000.
Urban redevelopment area location.
Sales of beverages, §18B-309.
ABC permit suspension or revocation for violation, §18B-904, (e).
Food, drug and cosmetic act.
Foods deemed to be adulterated, §106-129.

ALCOHOLIC BEVERAGES —Cont'd
Forfeiture.
Custody until trial, §18B-504, (d).
Defendant unavailable, §18B-504, (i).
Disposition.
After trial, §18B-504, (e).
Manner of disposition, §18B-504, (f).
Exemptions from forfeiture, §18B-504, (b).
Innocent parties.
Protection of interest, §18B-504, (h).
Property subject to forfeiture, §18B-504, (a).
Return of property.
Innocent parties, §18B-504, (h).
When no charges made, §18B-504, (j).
Sales.
Disposition of forfeited property, §18B-504, (f).
Proceeds of sale, §18B-504, (g).
Seizure of property, §18B-504, (c).
Unavailability of defendant, §18B-504, (i).
Fortified wine.
Consumption, §18B-301, (d).
Defined, §18B-101.
Possession, §18B-301.
Transportation.
Holder of permit for retail sales, §18B-405.
Fraudulent use of identification to purchase, §18B-302, (e).
Allowing use of identification, §18B-302, (f).
Fuel alcohol.
Distilleries.
Permits, §18B-1105, (b).
Gambling.
Prohibited on licensed premises, §18B-1005, (a).
Gaming.
Allowing gambling in houses of public entertainment, §14-293.
Handicapped persons.
Refusal to sell not to be discriminatory, §18B-305, (c).
Hearing officers.
Appointment, §18B-200, (d).
Home brewing.
Making wines and malt beverages for private use, §18B-306.
Hospitals.
Exemption from provisions, §18B-103.
Hospitals for mentally disordered.
Furnishing to inmates, §14-258.1, (b).
Hotel.
Defined, §18B-1000.
Hours for sale and consumption, §18B-1004.
ABC stores, §18B-802.
Identification documents used to purchase.
Allowing use of identification, §18B-302, (f).
Fraudulent use of identification, §18B-302, (e).
Illicit mixed beverages or spirituous liquors.
Unauthorized substances taxes, §§105-113.105 to 105-113.113.
See UNAUTHORIZED SUBSTANCES TAXES.
Impaired driving.
Generally.
See IMPAIRED DRIVING.
Implied warranty of merchantability.
Sale of goods, UCC, §25-2-314.
Imports and exports.
Denatured alcohol.
Exemption from provisions, §18B-103.
Liquor importer/bottler permit, §18B-1105.1.
Malt beverages.
Authorization of permit, §18B-1108.

ALCOHOLIC BEVERAGES —Cont'd
Imports and exports —Cont'd
Unauthorized imports and exports prohibited, §18B-102, (a).
Violation a misdemeanor, §18B-102, (b).
Wine.
Distribution agreements, §18B-1106, (b).
Permits, §18B-1106, (a).
Inspections.
Authority to inspect licensed premises, §18B-502, (a).
Interference with inspections, §18B-502, (b).
State warehouse.
Private warehouses, §18B-204, (b).
In-stand sales at ball parks or stadiums, §18B-1009.
Instruction on driving vehicle.
Impaired instruction, §20-12.1.
Intent of chapter, §18B-100.
Interstate interchange economic development zones.
Permit for businesses, §18B-1006, (m).
Intoxicated persons.
Sales to, §18B-305, (a).
Intoxication in public, §§14-443 to 14-447.
Investigations.
Expenses.
Restitution, §18B-505.
Law enforcement agents, §18B-500.
Local ABC officers, §18B-501.
Permits.
Prior to issuance, §18B-902, (b).
Restitution.
Expenses, §18B-505.
Joint store operation, §18B-703, (h).
Jurisdiction.
Law enforcement agents, §18B-500.
Local ABC officers, §18B-501.
Law enforcement agents.
Appointment, §18B-500, (a).
Discharge, §18B-500, (e).
Jurisdiction.
Subject matter jurisdiction, §18B-500, (b).
Territorial jurisdiction, §18B-500, (c).
Service of process.
Orders of commission, §18B-500, (d).
Subject matter jurisdiction, §18B-500, (b).
Territorial jurisdiction, §18B-500, (c).
Licenses.
Local licenses.
City beer and wine retail licenses, §105-113.77, (a).
City wholesaler license, §105-113.79.
County beer and wine retail licenses, §105-113.78.
Suspension or revocation of permit.
Effect on licenses, §18B-104, (d).
Local ABC boards.
See ABC BOARDS, LOCAL.
Local ABC officers.
Appointment, §18B-501, (a).
Assisting other local agencies, §18B-501, (d).
Assisting state and federal enforcement, §18B-501, (e).
Contracts with other agencies.
Alternative to hiring local officers, §18B-501.
Discharge, §18B-501, (g).
Jurisdiction.
Subject matter jurisdiction, §18B-501, (b).
Territorial jurisdiction, §18B-501, (c).

ALCOHOLIC BEVERAGES —Cont'd
Local option elections, §§18B-600 to 18B-605.
See LOCAL OPTION ELECTIONS.
Lockers.
Private clubs, §18B-1006, (b).
Magistrates.
Powers in cases involving alcohol offenses, §7A-273.
Mailing alcoholic beverages from outside state, §18B-109, (a).
Malt beverages.
Beer franchises generally, §§18B-1300 to 18B-1308.
See BEER FRANCHISES.
Breweries.
Authorization permit, §18B-1104.
Power to issue, §18B-1001.
Commercial permits, §18B-1100.
Consumption, §18B-300.
Defined, §18B-101.
Elections.
Determination of results, §18B-602, (b).
Effect, §18B-604.
Issuance of permits, §18B-603, (a).
Form of ballot, §18B-602, (e).
Subsequent elections, §18B-602, (c).
Hours for sale, §18B-1004.
Importers.
Permits.
Authorization, §18B-1108.
Making for private use, §18B-306.
Permits.
Commercial permits, §18B-1100.
Elections.
Effect on issuance of permits, §18B-603, (a).
Transportation.
Holder of permit for retail sales, §18B-405.
Vendors.
Nonresident vendors.
Authorization of permit, §18B-1113.
Wholesalers.
Beer franchises generally, §§18B-1300 to 18B-1308.
See BEER FRANCHISES.
Permits.
Authorization, §18B-1109.
Manufacturers.
Cider.
Commercial permits, §18B-1100.
Exemption from provisions, §18B-103.
Private use.
Wines and malt beverages, §18B-306.
Second offense of manufacturing, §18B-307, (c).
Unauthorized manufacture prohibited, §18B-102, (a).
Violation a misdemeanor, §18B-102, (b).
Unlawful manufacturing, §18B-307, (a), (b).
Vinegar.
Commercial permits, §18B-1100.
Exemption from provisions, §18B-103.
Wines and malt beverages.
Private use, §18B-306.
Merchantability, implied warranty.
Sale of goods, UCC, §25-2-314.
Merger of local operations.
Cities and counties, board for merged system, §18B-703.
Military affairs.
Direct shipment of beverages into state.
Armed forces installations, §18B-109, (b).

ALCOHOLIC BEVERAGES —Cont'd
Minors.
Alcoholism.
Consent of minor to treatment, §90-21.5, (a).
Defenses.
Sales to, §18B-302, (d).
Driving after consuming alcohol.
Restoration of driver's license after conviction, §20-17.6.
Driving by person less than 21 years old after consuming alcohol or drugs, §20-138.3.
Employment of youth by person holding ABC permits, §95-25.5, (j).
Handling in course of employment, §18B-302, (h).
Purchase or possession.
Aiding and abetting, §18B-302, (c).
Conviction reports to division of motor vehicles, §18B-302, (g).
Driver's license.
Allowing use of license, §18B-302, (f).
Revocation for underage purchase of alcohol, §20-17.3.
Use of fraudulent license, §18B-302, (e).
Nineteen or twenty year olds, §18B-302, (i).
Prohibited, §18B-302, (b), (i).
Sales to.
Aiding and abetting, §18B-302, (c).
Defense to violation of subsection, §18B-302, (d).
Fines and other penalties, §18B-302.1, (a), (b).
Prohibited, §18B-302, (a).
Mixed beverages.
ABC stores.
Required for mixed beverages, §18B-604, (e).
Airports.
Elections.
Effect of election on issuance of permit, §18B-603, (e).
Defined, §18B-101.
Elections.
ABC store election held simultaneously, §18B-603, (d2).
Airports.
Effect of election on issuance of permits, §18B-603, (e).
City elections, §18B-600, (e).
Small city elections, §18B-600, (e1).
Form of ballot, §18B-602, (h).
Permits.
Effect of election on issuance, §18B-603, (d).
Three cities within county approving.
When county may approve mixed beverage sales throughout county, §18B-603, (d1).
Handling of bottles.
Restrictions, §18B-1007, (b).
Hours for sale, §18B-1004.
Permits, §18B-1001.
Additional requirements for permittees, §18B-1007.
Elections.
Effect of elections on issuance, §18B-603, (d).
Airports, §18B-603, (e).
Hotels and restaurants in national historic landmark district, §18B-1006, (n).
Temporary permit for new permittee to continue business at same location, §18B-1007, (d).
Price list.
Available to customers, §18B-1007, (c).
Purchases.
Designated ABC store, §18B-1007, (a).
Transportation.
Permits, §18B-404.

ALCOHOLIC BEVERAGES —Cont'd
Moonshining, §18B-307.
Unauthorized substances taxes, §§105-113.105 to 105-113.113.
See UNAUTHORIZED SUBSTANCES TAXES.
Motor vehicles.
Chemical analysis of impairing substances in blood generally.
See IMPAIRED DRIVING.
Commercial vehicle, operating after consuming alcohol, §20-138.2A.
Odor of alcohol.
Evidentiary effect, §20-138.2A, (b1).
Screening test for alcohol, §20-138.2A, (b2).
Confiscation.
Vehicles used in illegal transportation.
Reports by officers, §20-114, (c).
Habitual drunkards.
Issuance of drivers' licenses prohibited, §20-9, (c).
Impaired driving generally.
See IMPAIRED DRIVING.
Impaired instruction, §20-12.1.
Manner of transportation, §18B-401.
Minors.
Drivers' licenses.
Revocation for underage purchases, §20-17.3.
Use of fraudulent license to purchase, §18B-302.
Open bottle violations, §18B-401, (a).
Mandatory revocation of driver's license, §20-17, (a).
Period of suspension or revocation, §20-19, (g1).
Motor vehicles defined, §20-138.7, (a3).
Ordinances regulating, §18B-300, (c).
Possession or consumption of alcoholic beverage in passenger compartment, §20-138.7, (a1).
Exceptions, §20-138.7, (a2).
Transporting open container in passenger area and while driver consuming alcohol, §20-138.7.
Alcoholic beverage defined, §20-138.7, (f).
General offense, §20-138.7, (a).
Implied consent law, offense subject to, §20-138.7, (b).
Implied driving offense also charged, §20-138.7, (e).
Limited driving privilege, §20-138.7, (h).
Misdemeanor for violating, §20-138.7, (e).
Motor vehicle defined, §20-138.7, (a3).
Odor insufficient to prove alcohol remaining in driver body, §20-138.7, (c).
Open container defined, §20-138.7, (f).
Passenger area of motor vehicle defined, §20-138.7, (f).
Pleading in prosecution for violation, §20-138.7, (g).
Possession or consumption in passenger compartment, §20-138.7, (a1), (a2).
Screening test, §20-138.7, (d).
School bus, operating after consuming alcohol, §20-138.2B.
Municipal corporations.
Confinement facilities.
Furnishing alcoholic beverages to inmates, §14-258.1.
Licenses.
City beer and wine retail licenses, §105-113.77, (a).
City wholesaler license, §105-113.79.

ALCOHOLIC BEVERAGES —Cont'd
Municipal corporations —Cont'd
Local option elections generally, §§18B-600 to 18B-605.
See LOCAL OPTION ELECTIONS.
Ordinances.
Consumption.
Malt beverages and unfortified wine, §18B-300, (c).
Restriction on ordinances, §18B-100.
National origin.
Refusal to sell not to be discriminatory, §18B-305, (c).
Nonresidents.
Malt beverage vendor.
Permit.
Authorization, §18B-1113.
Permits.
Restrictions on sale by nonresident vendors, §18B-1118.
Wine vendors.
Authorization of permit, §18B-1114.
Nuisances.
Abatement of offenses against public morals.
General provisions.
See NUISANCES.
Oceangoing ships.
Use on, §18B-106.
Off-premises establishment.
Consumption.
Malt beverages and unfortified wine, §18B-300, (b).
Open container law, §18B-401, (a).
Mandatory revocation of driver's license, §20-17, (a).
Period of suspension or revocation, §20-19, (g1).
Manner of transportation, §18B-401, (a).
Ordinances regulating open containers, §18B-300, (c).
Transporting open container in passenger area and while driver consuming alcohol.
Alcohol beverage defined, §20-138.7, (f).
General offense, §20-138.7, (a).
Implied consent law, offense subject to, §20-138.7, (b).
Implied driving offense also charged, §20-138.7, (e).
Limited driving privilege, §20-138.7, (h).
Misdemeanor for violation, §20-138.7, (e).
Motor vehicle defined, §20-138.7, (a3).
Odor on breath of driver insufficient to prove alcohol remaining in body, §20-138.7, (c).
Open container defined, §20-138.7, (f).
Passenger area of vehicle defined, §20-138.7, (f).
Pleading in prosecution, §20-138.7, (g).
Possession or consumption in passenger compartment, §20-138.7, (a1), (a2).
Screening test, §20-138.7, (d).
Operating a commercial vehicle after consuming alcohol, §20-138.2A.
Odor of alcohol.
Evidentiary effect, §20-138.2A, (b1).
Screening test for alcohol, §20-138.2A, (b2).
Operating a school bus, school activity bus, or child care vehicle after consuming alcohol, §20-138.2B.
Odor of alcohol.
Evidentiary effect, §20-138.2B, (b1).
Screening for alcohol, §20-138.2B, (b2).
Ordinances.
Consumption.
Malt beverages and unfortified wine, §18B-300, (c).

ALCOHOLIC BEVERAGES —Cont'd
Ordinances —Cont'd
Restrictions on ordinances, §18B-100.
Out-of-state purchases.
Limitation, §18B-402.
Transportation, §18B-402.
Penalties.
Administrative penalties, §18B-104.
Compromise, §18B-104, (b).
Disposition, §18B-104, (c).
Permits.
See ABC PERMITS.
Pharmaceutical products.
Exemption from provisions, §18B-103.
Physicians and surgeons.
Exemption from chapter, §18B-103.
Poisons.
Manufacture of poisonous liquors, §14-329, (a).
Trafficking in, transporting or possessing poisonous liquors, §14-329, (b) to (d).
Possession.
Evidence.
Possession for purpose of sale.
Possession by person not permitted to possess, §18B-304, (b).
Fortified wine and spirituous liquor.
Amount, §18B-301, (b).
Incident to sale, §18B-301, (e).
Possession at home, §18B-301, (a).
Special occasions, §18B-301, (c).
Unlawful possession or use, §18B-301, (f).
Malt beverages and unfortified wine.
General provisions, §18B-300, (a).
Sales.
Possession for purpose of sale, §18B-304, (a).
Unauthorized possession prohibited, §18B-102, (a).
Violation a misdemeanor, §18B-102, (b).
Unlawful possession or consumption.
Possession not authorized by permits, §18B-1006, (d).
Pregnancy, consumption during.
Signs warning of dangers.
Design, size, contents, §18B-808, (c).
Development, §18B-808, (b).
Display, ABC stores, §18B-808, (a), (d).
Distribution and posting, §18B-203, (a).
Fee, §18B-808, (b).
Prisons and prisoners.
Employees.
Use of intoxicants, narcotic drugs or profanity, §148-23.
Furnishing alcoholic beverages to inmates, §14-258.1, (b).
Substance abuse program, §§143B-262, 143B-262.1.
Private club.
Defined, §18B-1000.
Lockers, §18B-1006, (b).
Permits.
Residential private clubs, §18B-1006, (k).
Private use, making wines and malt beverages for, §18B-306.
Property.
Allowing property to be used for manufacture of beverage, §18B-307, (a).
Prostitution.
Prohibited on licensed premises, §18B-1005, (a).
Public schools.
Alcohol addicted children.
Appropriate education provided for.
Policy of state to insure, §115C-149.

ALCOHOLIC BEVERAGES —Cont'd
Public schools —Cont'd
Alcohol addicted children —Cont'd
Children with special needs.
Excluded from provisions of article, §115C-149.
Policy of state, §115C-149.
State board of education to adopt rules, §115C-150.
Basic education program.
Alcohol and drug education program, §115C-81, (a3).
Instruction in dangers of harmful or illegal drugs, including alcohol, §115C-81, (c).
Discipline of students.
Driving eligibility certificate.
Effect of disciplinary action for enumerated student conduct, §20-11, (n1).
Property owned or leased by local board of education and used for school purposes.
Possession and consumption of fortified wine and spirituous liquor upon, §18B-301, (f).
Purchases.
Amount purchased, §18B-303, (a).
Greater amounts, §18B-303, (c).
Unlawful purchases, §18B-303, (b).
Exclusive outlets.
Prohibited, §18B-1116, (a).
Exemptions, §18B-1116, (b).
Malt beverages and unfortified wine.
General provisions, §18B-300, (a).
Minors, prohibition, §18B-302, (b), (i).
Mixed beverages.
Designated ABC store, §18B-1007, (a).
Out of state purchases.
Transportation, §18B-402.
Purchase-transportation permits, §§18B-403 to 18B-405.
Purchasing in greater amounts than allowed, §18B-303, (c).
Purpose of chapter, §18B-100.
Racial minorities.
Refusal to sell not to be discriminatory, §18B-305, (c).
Raffles.
Sale or consumption, §18B-308.
Railroads.
Operating trains and streetcars while intoxicated, §14-281.
Sale on trains, §18B-108.
Recreation districts.
Permits, §18B-1006, (j).
Refusal to sell, discretion for seller, §18B-305, (b).
Religion.
Sacramental wine.
Exemption from provisions, §18B-103.
Religious discrimination.
Refusal to sell not to be discriminatory, §18B-305, (c).
Reports.
Required reports, §18B-205, (a).
Residential private club.
Defined, §18B-1000.
Responsibilities of permittee, §18B-1003.
Restaurant.
Defined, §18B-1000.
Restitution.
Expenses of investigation, §18B-505.
Retail business.
Defined, §18B-1000.

ALCOHOLIC BEVERAGES —Cont'd
Retail business —Cont'd
Permits.
Restrictions on purchases by retail permittees, §18B-1006.
Riots and civil disorders.
Prohibitions and restrictions during state of emergency.
County powers, §14-288.13.
Roller skating rink operators.
Duty to prohibit sale or use, §99E-11.
Rules and regulations.
ABC stores.
Promulgation, §18B-807.
Advertisements.
Authority of commission, §18B-105, (b).
Commission.
Local ABC boards to comply, §18B-702, (e).
Effective date.
Promulgation by commission, §18B-207.
Permits.
Retail permits.
Promulgation by commission, §18B-1008.
Promulgation.
Authority of commission, §18B-207.
Ships and shipping.
Use on oceangoing ships, §18B-106, (c).
State warehouse.
Promulgation, §18B-204, (d).
Sacramental wine.
Exemption from provisions, §18B-103.
Salaries.
Commission.
Chairman, §18B-200, (a).
Sales.
ABC stores.
See ABC STORES.
Aviation.
Use in air commerce, §18B-107, (b).
Ball parks or stadiums.
In-stand sales, §18B-1009.
Bingo games, §18B-308.
Cider.
Exemption from provisions, §18B-103.
Damaged alcoholic beverages, §18B-806.
Defined, §18B-101.
Discretion for seller, §18B-305, (b).
Discriminatory refusals prohibited, §18B-305, (c).
Exclusive outlets.
Prohibited, §18B-1116, (a).
Exemptions, §18B-1116, (b).
Hours of sale, §18B-1004, (a).
Applicability of section, §18B-1004, (e).
Exemption from section, §18B-1004, (e).
Local option, §18B-1004, (d).
Sunday hours, §18B-1004, (c).
Implied warranty of merchantability, §25-2-314.
In-stand sales.
Ball parks or stadiums, §18B-1009.
Intoxicated persons, §18B-305, (a).
Minors.
Prohibited sales, §18B-302.
Nonresidents.
Restrictions on sales by nonresident vendors, §18B-1118.
Nontaxpaid alcoholic beverages, §18B-111.
Out-of-state purchases.
Limitation, §18B-402.
Possession for purpose of sale.
Prima facie evidence.
Possession by person not permitted to possess, §18B-304, (b).

ALCOHOLIC BEVERAGES —Cont'd
Sales —Cont'd
Possession for purpose of sale —Cont'd
Unlawful possession, §18B-304, (a).
Refusal to sell.
Discretion for seller, §18B-305, (b).
Discriminatory refusals prohibited, §18B-305, (c).
Salesmen.
Permits, §18B-1111.
Seized alcoholic beverages, §§18B-503, 18B-504.
Trains, §18B-108.
Unauthorized sales prohibited, §18B-102, (a).
Violation a misdemeanor, §18B-102, (b).
Urban redevelopment areas.
Sales within, §18B-309.
ABC permit suspension or revocation for violation, §18B-904, (e).
Vinegar.
Exemption from provisions, §18B-103.
When sales stop.
Effect of election, §18B-604, (f).
Wine.
List of approved wines, §18B-1006, (c).
Sales and use tax.
Rate of tax on sale of spirituous liquor other than mixed beverages, §105-164.4, (a).
Subject to tax, §105-164.13B, (a).
School buses.
Operating after consuming alcohol, §20-138.2B.
Odor of alcohol.
Evidentiary effect, §20-138.2B, (b1).
Screening for alcohol, §20-138.2B, (b2).
Schools.
Discipline of students.
Driving eligibility certificate.
Effect of disciplinary action for enumerated student conduct, §20-11, (n1).
Permits.
Business located on campus, §18B-1006, (a).
Property owned or leased by local board of education and used for school purposes.
Possession and consumption of fortified wine and spirituous liquor upon, §18B-301, (f).
Searches and seizures.
Disposition of seized alcoholic beverages, §§18B-503, 18B-504.
Whiskey distilleries.
Disposition of seized, confiscated or unclaimed property.
Provisions not to apply to whiskey distilleries, §15-17.
Secured transactions.
Wholesalers.
Security interest of supplier in inventory or property of wholesaler, §18B-1119, (c).
Sexual discrimination.
Refusal to sell not to be discriminatory, §18B-305, (c).
Sexually explicit conduct.
Prohibited on licensed premises, §18B-1005.1, (a).
Exceptions, §18B-1005.1, (c).
Ships and shipping.
Commercial transportation.
Malt beverages and wine, §18B-1115, (f).
Use on oceangoing ships.
Delivery permitted, §18B-106, (a).
"Oceangoing vessel" defined, §18B-106, (b).
Promulgation of rules and regulations, §18B-106, (c).

ALCOHOLIC BEVERAGES —Cont'd
Special education.
Alcohol addicted children excluded from provisions of article, §115C-149.
Spirituous liquor.
ABC stores.
See ABC STORES.
Consumption, §18B-301.
Defined, §18B-101.
Possession, §18B-301.
Transportation.
Commercial transportation, §18B-1115.
Sports clubs.
Defined, §18B-1000.
Permits, §18B-1006, (k).
Sale of malt beverages, unfortified wine, or mixed beverages and operation of ABC system allowed in six cities and counties.
Issuance of permits to sports clubs throughout county, §18B-603, (h).
Stadiums.
In-stand sales, §18B-1009.
Standards for alcoholic beverages.
Authority to establish, §18B-206, (a).
Effective date, §18B-206, (b).
Testing, §18B-206, (c).
State of emergency.
Powers of governor, §18B-110.
Prohibitions and restrictions during.
County powers, §14-288.13.
Municipal powers, §14-288.12.
State warehouse.
Audits, §18B-204, (b).
Commercial transportation, §18B-1115, (g).
Contracts.
Private warehouses, §18B-204, (a).
Inspections, §18B-204, (b).
Private warehouses.
Contracting for private warehouses, §18B-204, (a).
Emergency operation, §18B-204, (c).
Temporary operation, §18B-204, (c).
Rules and regulations.
Promulgation, §18B-204, (d).
Transportation by state warehouse carrier, §18B-1115, (g).
Storage.
Warehouse receipts.
Storage under government bond, §25-7-201, (2).
Sundays.
Hours of sale, §18B-1004, (c).
Supervision of licensed premises.
Permittee or manager, §§18B-1005, (b), 18B-1005.1, (b).
Taxation.
General provisions.
See ALCOHOLIC BEVERAGES TAX.
Local license taxes, §§105-113.77 to 105-113.78.
Nontaxpaid alcoholic beverages.
Defined, §18B-101.
Possession, transportation or sale, §18B-111.
Unauthorized substances taxes, §§105-113.105 to 105-113.113.
See UNAUTHORIZED SUBSTANCES TAXES.
Taxicabs.
Transportation of alcoholic beverages, §18B-401, (b).
Time.
Hours for sale and consumption, §18B-1004.
Tour boats.
Permits.
Restrictions on sales on tour boats, §18B-1006, (i).

ALCOHOLIC BEVERAGES —Cont'd
Tourism ABC establishment.
Defined, §18B-101.
Transportation.
Alcoholic beverages purchased out of state, §18B-402.
Amounts that may be transported, §18B-400.
Transportation in greater amounts, §18B-406.
Commercial transportation.
Boats.
Malt beverages and wine, §18B-1115, (f).
Common carriers, §18B-1115, (c).
Motor vehicle carriers, §18B-1115, (d).
Permit.
Required, §18B-1115.
Spirituous liquor, §18B-1115, (e).
State warehouse carrier, §18B-1115, (g).
When transportation legal, §18B-1115, (b).
Wine.
Boats, §18B-1115.
Definitions.
Passenger area of a motor vehicle, §18B-401, (c).
Direct shipment into state, §18B-109.
Excess amounts, §18B-406.
Limitation upon out-of-state purchases, §18B-402.
Malt beverages and unfortified or fortified wines.
Transportation by permittee, §18B-405.
Manner of transportation.
Open container, §18B-401, (a).
Mandatory revocation of license, §20-17, (a).
Ordinances regulating, §18B-300, (c).
Transporting open container in passenger area of vehicle and while driver consuming alcohol, §20-138.7.
Taxis, §18B-401, (b).
Nontaxpaid alcoholic beverages, §18B-111.
Open container, §18B-401, (a).
Mandatory revocation of driver's license, §20-17, (a).
Open container in passenger area of vehicle and while driver consuming alcohol, §20-138.7.
Ordinances regulating, §18B-300, (c).
Out of state purchases, §18B-402.
Purchase-transportation permits.
Amount authorized to purchase and transport, §18B-403, (a).
Commercial transportation, §18B-1115.
Display, §18B-403, (e).
Disqualifications of applicant, §18B-403, (c).
Form, §18B-403, (d).
Issuance, §18B-403, (b).
Disqualifications of applicant, §18B-403, (c).
Mixed beverage permits, §18B-404, (b).
Malt beverages and unfortified or fortified wine.
Transportation by permittee, §18B-405.
Mixed beverage permits.
Designated employee, §18B-404, (a).
Designated stores, §18B-404, (c).
Issuance, §18B-404, (b).
Size of bottles, §18B-404, (d).
Purchasing in greater amounts than allowed, §18B-303, (c).
Restrictions on permit, §18B-403, (e).
Special occasions, §18B-403, (g).
Time permit valid, §18B-403, (f).
Taxis.
Restrictions, §18B-401, (b).
Unauthorized transportation prohibited, §18B-102, (a), (b).
Unlawful transportation.
Excess amounts, §18B-406.

ALCOHOLIC BEVERAGES —Cont'd
Unfortified wine.
Consumption, §18B-300.
Permits.
Elections.
Effect of election on issuance, §18B-603, (b).
Transportation.
Holder of permit for retail sales, §18B-405.
Unincorporated areas.
Defined, §18B-101.
Universities and colleges.
Permits.
Business located on campus, §18B-1006, (a).
Viticulture/oenology course authorization, §18B-1114.4.
Urban redevelopment designated areas.
Percentage of total alcohol sales to total business sales, §18B-309, (a).
Investigation and report by commission, §18B-309, (b).
Records required of business, filing requirements, §18B-309, (c).
Suspension or revocation of permit.
Business in violation of provisions
Vendors.
Malt beverages.
Nonresident vendor.
Authorization, §18B-1113.
Restrictions on sales by nonresident vendor, §18B-1118.
Representatives.
Permits.
Authorization, §18B-1112.
Wine vendors.
Nonresident vendor.
Authorization of permit, §18B-1114.
Restrictions on sale by nonresident vendor, §18B-1118.
Vinegar.
Commercial permit, manufacturers, §18B-1100.
Exemption from alcoholic beverage provisions, §18B-103.
Violation of chapter.
Discharge of employees, §18B-202.
Viticulture/oenology courses.
Authorization, §18B-1114.4.
Warehouse receipts.
Storage under government bond, §25-7-201, (2).
Warehouses.
State warehouse, §18B-204.
Warranties.
Implied warranty of merchantability, §25-2-314.
Weapons.
Establishments where alcoholic beverages are sold and consumed.
Carrying weapons into establishments, §14-269.3, (a).
Applicability of provisions, §14-269.3, (b).
Wholesalers.
Beer franchises generally, §§18B-1300 to 18B-1308.
See BEER FRANCHISES.
Permits.
Malt beverages.
Authorization, §18B-1109.
Restrictions on sales by wholesalers to retail permittees, §18B-1006.
Supplier's financial interest in wholesaler.
Generally, §18B-1119.
Wine.
Authorization, §18B-1107, (a).

ALCOHOLIC BEVERAGES —Cont'd
Wholesalers —Cont'd
Suppliers.
Financial interest in wholesaler.
Financial assistance to proposed purchasers, §18B-1119, (a), (b).
Security interest in inventory or property of wholesaler, §18B-1119, (c).
Wine.
Distribution agreements, §18B-1107, (b).
Permits.
Authorization, §18B-1107, (a).
Wine generally.
See WINE.
Wine producer.
Defined, §18B-1000.
Permit, §18B-902, (d).
Authorization, §18B-1114.3, (a).
Commercial permit, §18B-1100.
Limitation on total gallons sold annually, §18B-1114.3, (b).
Wine shippers.
Direct shipments into state, §18B-109, (c).
Manner of making, §18B-1001.1, (c).
Permit.
Application authorization, §18B-1001.1, (a).
Fee, §18B-902, (d).
Quarterly summary of shipped wine, §18B-1001.2, (a).
Registration, §18B-1001.2, (a).
Rules, adoption, §18B-1001.2, (b).
Sales and use tax.
Collection responsibility, §105-164.8, (b).
Subject to state jurisdiction, §18B-1001.1, (d).
Wholesaler in state, appointment, §18B-1001.1, (b).
Wine tasting, §18B-1001.
Witnesses.
Illicit sale.
Testimony enforced in certain criminal investigations, §8-55.
Immunity of witness, §8-55.
Zero tolerance law.
Driving by person less than 21 years old after consuming alcohol or drugs, §20-138.3.

ALCOHOLIC BEVERAGES TAX.
Applicability of tax, §105-113.68, (b).
Bonds, surety.
Nonresident vendors, §105-113.86, (b).
Wholesalers and importers, §105-113.86, (a).
Definitions, §105-113.68, (a).
Excise tax on beer, wine and liquor, §§105-113.80 to 105-113.87.
Discount.
Expenses incurred in preparing reports and records, §105-113.85.
Distribution of part of beer and wine taxes.
City defined, §105-113.82, (f).
County in which ABC stores established by petition, §105-113.82, (c).
Department of agriculture and consumer affairs.
Credit of amount of wine sold bottled in state, §105-113.81A.
Local revenue.
Governor may not reduce distribution, §105-113.82, (d).
Municipality incorporated on or after January 1, 2000, §105-113.82, (h).

ALCOHOLIC BEVERAGES TAX —Cont'd
Excise tax on beer, wine and liquor —Cont'd
Distribution of part of beer and wine taxes —Cont'd
Percentages of net amount distributed, §105-113.82, (a).
Population estimates, §105-113.82, (e).
Time of distribution, §105-113.82, (d).
Use of funds for any public purpose, §105-113.82, (g).
Wine taxes attributable to North Carolina wine, §105-113.81A.
Exemptions.
Armed forces, sales to, §105-113.82, (c).
Free testing, §105-113.82, (e).
Major disasters.
Beverages rendered unsalable by, §105-113.82, (a).
Oceangoing vessels, sales to, §105-113.82, (b).
Out-of-sate sales, §105-113.82, (d).
Expenses incurred in preparing reports and records.
Discount, §105-113.85.
Monthly reports, §105-113.84.
North Carolina wine, distribution of taxes attributable, §105-113.81A.
Payment.
Beer and wine tax, §105-113.83, (b).
Liquor tax, §105-113.83, (a).
Railroad sales, §105-113.83, (b).
Railroad sales.
Monthly reports, §105-113.83, (b).
Rate of tax.
Beer, §105-113.80, (a).
Liquor, §105-113.80, (c).
Wine, §105-113.80, (b).
Refund for tax paid on sacramental wine, §105-113.87, (a), (b).
Sacramental wine.
Refunds, §105-113.87, (a), (b).
Licenses.
Counties.
Beer and wine retail licenses, §105-113.78.
Local exceptions, §105-113.71, (b).
Refusal to issue, §105-113.71, (a).
Defined, §105-113.68, (a).
Duration, §105-113.70, (b).
Effect of license, §105-113.69.
Exclusive license, §105-113.70, (d).
Issuance, §105-113.70, (a).
License tax, §105-113.69.
Municipal corporations.
City beer and wine retail licenses.
Additional license, tax on, §105-113.77, (b).
Amount, §105-113.77, (a).
City wholesaler license, §105-113.79.
Local exceptions, §105-113.71, (b).
Refusal to issue, §105-113.71, (a).
Other applicable administrative provisions, §105-113.89.
Qualifications of licensee, §105-113.70, (a).
Records.
Length of time records to be kept, §105-113.88, (b).
Requirements, §105-113.88, (a).
Transfers, §105-113.70, (c).
Malt beverages.
Defined, §105-113.68, (a).
Misdemeanors.
Violations, §105-113.73.

ALCOHOLIC BEVERAGES TAX —Cont'd
Sales and use tax.
Rate of tax on sale of spirituous liquor other than mixed beverages, §105-164.4, (a).
Subject to tax, §105-164.13B, (a).
Spirituous liquors.
Defined, §105-113.68, (a).
Wine.
Fortified wine.
Defined, §105-113.68, (a).
Unfortified wine.
Defined, §105-113.68, (a).

ALCOHOLISM.
Chiropractors.
Grounds for disciplinary action, §90-154, (b).
Drug treatment courts, §§7A-790 to 7A-801.
See DRUG TREATMENT COURTS.
Grants.
Research authority.
Application for grants, §122C-433.
Lawyers and judges impaired by substance abuse or addiction.
Lawyer assistance program, Bar Rules & Regs., D, §§.0601 to .0623.
See LAWYERS ASSISTANCE PROGRAM.
Mental health, developmental disabilities and substance abuse.
General provisions.
See MENTAL HEALTH, DEVELOPMENTAL DISABILITY, SUBSTANCE ABUSE.
Physicians and surgeons.
Grounds for denial, revocation or suspension of license, §90-14, (a).
Referral of physician to state medical society physician health and effectiveness committee, §90-14, (b).
Research authority, §§122C-431 to 122C-433.
Specialty hospitals.
Alcohol detoxification programs, §131E-65.
Work First program recipients of assistance.
Treatment required, drug testing, §108A-29.1.

ALCOHOLISM RESEARCH AUTHORITY, §§122C-431 to 122C-433.
Appointment of members, §122C-431, (a).
Authorized to receive and expend funds, §122C-432.
Chairman, §122C-431, (b).
Composition, §122C-431, (a).
Creation of alcoholism research authority, §122C-431, (a).
Executive secretary, §122C-431, (b).
Expenditures.
Authorized to receive and expend funds, §122C-432.
Expenses of members, §122C-431, (b).
Funds.
Authority to receive and expend funds, §122C-432.
Grants.
Application for grant, §122C-433.
Rules and regulations.
Promulgation, §122C-433.
Terms of office, §122C-431, (a).
Vacancies in office, §122C-431, (a).
Vice-chairman, §122C-431, (b).

ALCOHOL LAW ENFORCEMENT AGENTS, §18B-500.
Appointment by secretary of crime control and public safety, §18B-500, (a).
Arrest authority, §18B-500, (b).

ALCOHOL LAW ENFORCEMENT AGENTS —Cont'd
Controlled substances act, enforcement, §18B-500, (b).
Department of crime control and public safety.
Alcohol law enforcement division.
Defined, §18B-101.
Transfer to department, §§143A-243, 143B-475.
Discharge, §18B-500, (e).
Forfeitures, §18B-504.
Inspections of licensed premises, §18B-502.
Investigatory and enforcement actions, §18B-500, (b).
Local ABC officers, §18B-501.
Resignation as alcohol law-enforcement agents, §18B-500, (a).
Restitution to law enforcement agency, §18B-505.
Seized beverages.
Disposition, §18B-503.
Service of commission order, §18B-500, (b).
State officer with jurisdiction throughout state, §18B-500, (c).
Subject matter jurisdiction, §18B-500, (b).
Territorial jurisdiction, §18B-500, (c).

ALCOHOL REHABILITATION CENTER.
Joint security force, §122C-421, (a), (b).

ALCOHOL SCREENING TEST.
Commercial vehicles.
Operating a commercial vehicle after consuming alcohol, §20-138.2A, (b2).
Impaired driving checks, §20-16.3A.
Limited driving privileges.
Use of results or fact of refusal to take screening, §20-179.3, (j).
Open container law violations.
Evidence in determining whether alcohol present in driver's body, §20-138.7, (d).
Required of certain drivers, §20-16.3.
School buses.
Operating a school bus, school activity bus, or child care vehicle after consuming alcohol, §20-138.2B, (b2).

ALCOHOL, TOBACCO AND FIREARMS LAWS.
Agents authorized to enforce criminal laws, §15A-406.

ALDERMEN, BOARDS OF.
Generally.
See CITY COUNCILS.

ALEXANDER COUNTY.
Ambulance service, attachment or garnishment and lien for, §§44-51.4 to 44-51.8.
Board of county commissioners.
Filling vacancies on board, §153A-27.1.
Cropper or tenant neglecting or refusing to perform terms of contract without just cause.
Forfeiture of right of possession to premises, §42-27.
Maps in special proceedings, recording and photographing copies, §47-32.
On-premises unfortified wine licenses.
Discretion to decline to issue, §105-113.71, (b).
School property.
Acquisition and improvement, §153A-158.1.
Sheriff.
Vacancy, performance of duties until vacancy filled, §162-5.1.

ALEXANDER COUNTY —Cont'd
Special school tax, election to abolish.
Number of petitions required, §115C-505.
Tax elections for industrial development purposes, §§158-16 to 158-24.

ALFALFA.
Weights and measures.
Standard weights and measures, §81A-42.

ALIAS.
Orders of attachment, §1-440.13, (b).

ALIAS SUMMONS, §1A-1, Rule 4, (d).
Discontinuance for failure to issue within time specified, §1A-1, Rule 4, (e).
Docketing, §1A-1, Rule 4, (g).
Judgments based on summons erroneously designated validated, §1-217.1.

ALIEN INSURANCE COMPANIES.
Generally.
See FOREIGN OR ALIEN INSURANCE COMPANIES.

ALIEN PROPERTY ACT, §§64-1 to 64-5.

ALIENS.
Actions.
Suits against state, Const. U. S., amd. XI.
Adoption of persons born outside United States, §48-2-606, (b).
Congress.
Eligibility to be representative, Const. U. S., art. I, §2.
Contracts.
Real property.
Validation of contracts to purchase or sell real property, §64-2.
Conveyances.
Right to convey real property, §64-1.
Deeds.
Certified copies.
Registration allowed, §47-33.
Evidence.
Certified copies of deeds made by alien property custodians, §47-34.
Employment security.
Benefits.
Eligibility, §96-13, (f).
Escheat.
Personal property.
Reciprocal rights.
Escheat in absence of reciprocity, §64-4.
Evidence.
Real property.
Certified copies of deeds made by alien property custodians.
Admissible in evidence, §47-34.
Fair housing, §§41A-1 to 41A-10.
See FAIR HOUSING.
Intestate succession, §29-11.
Limitation of actions.
War.
Effect on limitation period, §1-34.
Mental health, developmental disabilities and substance abuse.
Proceedings, §122C-344.
Naturalization, Const. U. S., art. I, §§8, 9.
Personal property.
Escheat, §64-4.
Reciprocal rights, §64-3.
Burden of proof, §64-5.
Escheat in absence of reciprocity, §64-4.

ALIENS —Cont'd
President of the United States.
Ineligible for presidency, Const. U. S., art. II, §1.
Probate and registration.
Certified copies of deeds.
Registration authorized, §47-33.
Psychologists.
Licensure of foreign graduates, §90-270.11, (c).
Real property.
Contracts.
Validation, §64-2.
Custodians.
Certified copies of deeds.
Admissible in evidence, §47-34.
Registration, §47-33.
Right to hold and convey, §64-1.
Secretary of state.
Information as to foreign ownership of real property.
Secretary of state to collect, §64-1.1.
Reciprocity.
Personal property.
Escheat, §64-4.
Reciprocal rights, §64-3.
Burden of proof, §64-5.
Escheat in absence of reciprocity, §64-4.
Registration cards.
False or fraudulent, §14-100.1.
Secretary of state.
Information as to foreign ownership of real property.
Secretary of state to collect, §64-1.1.
Suits against state, Const. U. S., amd. XI.
Unemployment compensation.
Employment, exclusion of services performed by, §96-8.
Validation.
Contracts to purchase or sell real property, §64-2.
Workers' compensation, §97-38.

ALIMONY.
Absolute divorce.
Effects, §50-11, (c).
Divorce obtained outside state in which jurisdiction over dependent spouse not obtained.
Right to alimony not impaired or destroyed, §50-11, (d).
Actions.
Competency of witnesses.
Communication between marital counselor and parties, §8-53.6.
Independent actions.
Maintenance of certain actions as independent actions permissible, §50-19, (a).
Separate action prosecuted during pendency, §50-19, (b).
Without action, §50-16.10.
Amount, §50-16.3A, (b).
Arbitration.
Family law arbitration generally, §§50-41 to 50-62.
See FAMILY LAW ARBITRATION.
Arrest.
Remedy available, §50-16.7, (d).
Attachment, actions when attachment may be had, §§1-440.2, 50-16.7, (e).
Attorneys' fees, §50-16.4.
Barred by separation agreement or premarital agreement provisions, §50-16.6, (b).

ALIMONY —Cont'd
Attorneys specializing in family law.
Certification standards, Bar Rules & Regs., D, §§.2401 to .2407.
Bail and recognizance.
Remedy available, §50-16.7, (d).
Barred by separation agreement or premarital agreement provisions, §50-16.6, (b).
Bonds, surety.
Bond for costs unnecessary, §50-2.
Change in circumstances.
Modification.
Family law arbitration act, §50-56.
Cohabitation of dependent spouse.
Termination of alimony, §50-16.9, (b).
Compromise and settlement.
District court actions.
Mediated settlement conferences or other settlement procedures, §7A-38.4A.
Confession of judgment.
Alimony without action, §50-16.10.
Force and effect, §1A-1, Rule 68.1, (e).
Contempt.
Willful disobedience of order, §50-16.7, (j).
Costs.
Bond for costs unnecessary, §50-2.
Cruel or barbarous treatment.
Grounds for alimony, §50-16.3A.
Decrees.
Enforcement, §50-16.7.
Definitions, §50-16.1A.
Dependent spouse deemed creditor, §50-16.7, (h).
Dependent spouse defined, §50-16.1A.
Distribution by court of marital and divisible property.
Discovery.
Prejudicial delay.
Sanctions, §50-21, (e).
Equitable distribution without regard to alimony, §50-20, (f).
District court actions.
Mediated settlement conferences or other settlement procedures, §7A-38.4A.
Divorce generally.
See DIVORCE.
Duration, §50-16.3A, (b).
Effects of absolute divorce, §50-11, (c).
Divorce obtained outside state in which jurisdiction over dependent spouse not obtained.
Right to alimony not impaired or destroyed, §50-11, (d).
Entitlement, §50-16.3A, (a).
Execution, execution sales and supplemental proceedings.
Remedies available, §50-16.7, (k).
Time limitation as to execution not to apply, §1-306.
Exempt property from enforcement of claims of creditors.
Exception, §1C-1601, (e).
Family law arbitration generally, §§50-41 to 50-62.
See FAMILY LAW ARBITRATION.
Findings of fact, §50-16.3A, (c).
Garnishment.
Remedy available, §50-16.7, (e).
General assembly.
Local, private and special legislation prohibited, Const. N. C., art. II, §24.

ALIMONY —Cont'd
Grounds for alimony, §50-16.3A.
Illicit sexual behavior.
Defined, §50-16.1A.
Dependent or supporting spouse participating in, §50-16.3A, (a).
Income withholding.
Application to court by dependent spouse, §50-16.7, (l1).
Limitation on amount withheld, §110-136.6, (b1).
Incompetent spouses.
Actions on behalf of, §50-22.
Independent actions.
Maintenance of certain actions as independent actions permissible, §50-19, (a).
Separate action prosecuted during pendency, §50-19, (b).
Injunctions.
Remedy available, §50-16.7, (f).
Judgment for alimony not lien, §50-16.7, (i).
Jury trial, §50-16.3A, (d).
Local, private and special legislation prohibited, Const. N. C., art. II, §24.
Lump sum payments, §50-16.7, (a).
Marital misconduct.
Defined, §50-16.1A.
Mediated settlement conferences or other settlement procedures.
District court actions, §7A-38.4A.
Rules implementing, Settle. Proc. Equitable Distribution Rules 1 to 15.
See MEDIATED SETTLEMENT CONFERENCES.
Military affairs.
Residence of military personnel, §50-18.
Modification.
Change in circumstances.
Family law arbitration act, §50-56.
Resumption of marital relations, §50-16.9, (a).
Mortgages and deeds of trust.
Securing payment by mortgage, §50-16.7, (b).
Orders.
Modification, §50-16.9, (a).
Payment.
How paid, §50-16.7.
Willful disobedience of order, §50-16.7, (j).
Contempt to enforce payment, §50-16.7, (j).
Pendente lite, §50-11, (c).
Personal property.
Transfer as part of order, §50-16.7, (c).
Postseparation support.
Attorneys' fees, §50-16.4.
Court's duty, §50-16.8.
Defined, §50-16.1A.
Enforcement of decree, §50-16.7.
How paid, §50-16.7.
Income withholding.
Limitation on amount withheld, §110-136.6, (b1).
Maintenance of certain actions as independent actions permissible, §50-19.
Modification of order, §50-16.9.
Procedure, §50-16.8.
Real property.
Transfer of property as part of alimony order, §50-16.7, (c).
Writ of possession issued, §50-17.
Receivers.
Appointment, §50-16.7, (g).
Reference by consent, §1A-1, Rule 53, (a).

ALIMONY —Cont'd
Remarriage of dependent spouse.
Termination of alimony, §50-16.9, (b).
Remedies supplemental, §50-16.7, (l).
Separation agreements.
Authorization and requisites, §52-10.1.
Settlement.
District court actions.
Mediated settlement conferences or other settlement procedures, §7A-38.4A.
Supporting spouse.
Defined, §50-16.1A.
Termination, §50-16.9, (b).
Resumption of marital relations, §50-16.9, (a).
Travel expenses.
Payment, §50-18.
Venue, §50-3.
Without action, §50-16.10.

ALIMONY PENDENTE LITE.
Absolute divorce not to affect rights of spouse to, §50-11, (c).

ALKALI.
Malicious throwing, §14-30.1.
Municipal corporations.
Regulation of corrosive substances, §160A-183.

ALKALINE PAPER.
State publications of historical and enduring value.
Compliance with requirement, monitoring, §125-11.13, (b).
Designation of publications on annual basis, §125-11.13, (a), (b).
Identification that publication printed on permanent paper, §125-11.13, (a).
Notice to agencies responsible for publishing designated titles, §125-11.13, (b).
Report as to titles designated for printing on alkaline paper, §125-11.13, (c).
Required to be printed on, §§125-11.13, (a), 143-170.5.
Responsibility of agency to print on alkaline paper, §125-11.13, (b).

ALLEGHANY COUNTY.
Ambulance service, attachment or garnishment and lien for, §§44-51.4 to 44-51.8.
Blank or master forms of mortgages, deeds of trust, etc.
Indexing and recording, inapplicability of provisions, §47-21.
Board of county commissioners.
Filling vacancies on board, §153A-27.1.
Condemnation or acquisition of land by local government unit outside county.
Consent of board of commissioners necessary, §153A-15.
Coroner elected as nominee of political party.
Filling vacancy in office, §152-1.
Counties generally.
See COUNTIES.
County boards of education elected on partisan basis.
Vacancies in office, §115C-37.1.
Cropper or tenant refusing to perform terms of contract.
Forfeiture of right of possession to premises, §42-27.
Game laws, local acts not repealed, §113-133.1, (e).

ALLEGHANY COUNTY —Cont'd
Maps in special proceedings, recording of photographic copies, §47-32.
Violation as misdemeanor, inapplicability of provisions, §47-32.2.
Oil, gas or mineral interest separated from surface interest, extinguished, title in surface fee holder.
Failure to list interest for tax purposes for 10 years prior to January 1, 1981, §1-42.6, (a) to (c).
Failure to list interest for tax purposes for 10 years prior to January 1, 1974.
Protection of interest from surface estate, §1-42.3, (d).
Failure to list interest for tax purposes for 10 years prior to January 1, 1981,
Protection of interest from surface fee holder, §1-42.6, (b), (d).
Registration of deeds.
Tax certification, no delinquent taxes due, §161-31, (b).
Room occupancy taxes.
Uniform provisions, §153A-155.
School property.
Acquisition and improvement, §153A-158.1.
Sheriff.
Vacancy, performance of duties until vacancy filled, §162-5.1.
Tax sales, notices by publication validated.
Inapplicability of provisions, §47-108.24.

ALLEYS.
Judicial sales.
Dedication of real property subdivided for sale, §1-339.9, (b).
Littering, §14-399.
No title by possession of public ways, §1-45.
Poisons.
Putting poisonous foodstuffs, etc., in certain public places prohibited, §14-401.
Right of way.
Left turns into, §20-155, (b).
Pedestrians, §20-173, (c).
Vehicles emerging from or entering highway from, §20-156, (a).
Secret societies.
Wearing masks, hoods, etc., on public ways, §14-12.7.

ALLIGATORS.
Propagation and production of American alligators.
Facility requirements, §106-763.1, (b).
License required, §106-763.1, (a).
Untagged or undocumented alligators possessed by facility operator, §106-763.1, (c).

ALL-TERRAIN VEHICLES.
Amusement device safety.
Amusement device defined as not including, §95-111.3, (a).
Trespass to land on motorized all terrain vehicle, §14-159.3.
Utility easements.
Operating vehicle upon after being forbidden to do so, §14-134.2.

ALPACAS.
Llamas classified as livestock.
Definition of llama including, §106-22.4.

ALPHA AND BETA PARTICLES.
Radiation protection act generally, §§104E-1 to 104E-29.
See RADIATION PROTECTION.

ALTERATION OF JUDGMENT.
Motions, §1A-1, Rule 59, (e).

ALTERNATIVE CLAIMS OR DEFENSES, §1A-1, Rule 8, (e).
Joinder of claims, §1A-1, Rule 18, (a).

ALTERNATIVE DISPUTE RESOLUTION.
Arbitration.
Family law arbitration generally, §§50-41 to 50-62.
See FAMILY LAW ARBITRATION.
Generally.
See ARBITRATION.
Revised uniform arbitration act, §§1-569.1 to 1-569.31.
See ARBITRATION.
Collaborative law proceedings, §50-78.
Community mediation centers, §7A-38.5.
Negotiation not discoverable or admissible in evidence, §8-110.
Mediated settlement conferences.
Court ordered mediated settlement conferences, Super. Ct. Mediated Settlmt. Conf. R. 1 to 12.
See MEDIATED SETTLEMENT CONFERENCES.
Mediation.
Generally.
See MEDIATION.
Persons with disabilities.
Public service discrimination cases, §168A-10.1.

ALTERNATIVE FUEL, §§105-449.130 to 105-449.139.
Bond or letter of credit.
Required as condition of obtaining and keeping licenses.
Amount, §105-449.133, (b).
Persons required to have bond, §105-449.133, (a).
Bulk-end users.
Bond or letter of credit required as condition of license, §105-449.133.
Defined, §105-449.130.
Informational return, §105-449.138, (a).
Liability for tax, §105-449.137, (a).
Marking of storage facility, §105-449.138, (b).
Persons required to have license, §§105-449.131, 105-449.139.
Definitions, §105-449.130.
Due date of tax.
Change by licensee, §105-449.135, (b).
Imposition of tax, §105-449.136.
Informational return.
Bulk-end users and retailers, §105-449.138, (a).
Inspection, §§119-14 to 119-47.
See GASOLINE AND OIL INSPECTION.
Liability for tax imposed, §105-449.137, (a).
Licenses.
Application for, §105-449.132.
Bond or letter of credit as condition of obtaining and keeping.
Amount, §105-449.133, (b).
Persons required to have bond, §105-449.133, (a).
Denial or cancellation, §105-449.134.
Issuance, §105-449.135, (a).
Notification of changes, §105-449.135, (b).
Persons required to have license, §105-449.131.
Liquid alternative fuel, tax imposed, §105-449.136.
List of providers, §105-449.139, (c).

ALTERNATIVE FUEL —Cont'd
Notice.
Changes by licensee, §105-449.135, (b).
Offenses, §105-449.139, (b).
Payment of tax, §105-449.137, (b).
Providers.
Bond or letter of credit as condition of license, §105-449.133.
Liability for tax, §105-449.137, (a).
Persons required to have license, §105-449.139.
Providers of alternative fuel.
Defined, §105-449.130.
List, §105-449.139, (c).
Persons required to have license, §105-449.131.
Records kept by license holders, §105-449.139, (a).
Retailers.
Bond or letter of credit required as condition of license, §105-449.133.
Defined, §105-449.130.
Informational return, §105-449.138, (a).
Liability for tax, §105-449.137, (a).
Marking of storage facility, §105-449.138, (b).
Persons required to have license, §105-449.131.
Return.
Informational return.
Bulk-end users and retailers, §105-449.138, (a).
Storage facilities.
Marking by bulk-end users or retailers, §105-449.138, (b).
Tax at motor fuel rate imposed, §105-449.136.
Violation, §105-449.139, (b).

ALTERNATIVE FUELED OR LOW EMISSION VEHICLES.
State goal to purchase new or replacement vehicles, §143-215.107C, (b).
Alternative fueled vehicle defined, §143-215.107C, (a).
Report on progress, §143-215.107C, (c).

ALTERNATIVE FUEL VEHICLES.
Special license plates, §20-79.4, (b).

ALTERNATIVE LEARNING PROGRAMS AND ALTERNATIVE SCHOOLS.
Driving eligibility certificate.
Effect of disciplinary action for enumerated student conduct, §20-11, (n1).
Establishment, development of rules and policies, local boards of education, §115C-47.
Placement of at-risk or disruptive students.
Determination of support services and intervention strategies, §115C-105.48, (b).
Document procedures used to identify student prior to referring student, §115C-105.48, (a).
Reasons for referring student, school to provide, §115C-105.48, (a).
Student records, providing alternative schools, §115C-105.48, (a).

ALUMINUM CANS.
Incineration, disposal by prohibited, §130A-309.10, (f1).
Landfills, disposal in prohibited, §130A-309.10, (f).

ALZHEIMER'S DISEASE.
Adult care homes.
Special care units.
Disclosure of information, §131D-8, (a), (b).
Adult day care programs.
Disclosure requirements for programs offering special care services for persons with, §131D-6, (b1) to (b4).

ALZHEIMER'S DISEASE —Cont'd
Long-term care insurance.
Coverage for, §58-55-35, (b).
Study commission on aging.
Alzheimer's subcommittee, §120-186.1.

AMATEUR RADIO OPERATORS.
Specialized license plates, §20-79.4, (b).

AMATEUR SPORTS.
Limited food establishment.
Preparing and serving food in conjunction with events.
Defined, §130A-247.
Permits, issuance, §130A-248, (a4).
Sanitation, rules governing, adoption, §130A-248, (a4).
State games.
Insurance.
Liability insurance coverage required, §143-299.3, (b).
State departments and agencies.
Motor vehicles.
No liability for damages, §143-299.3, (b).

AMBASSADORS.
Constitution of the United States, Const. U. S., art. II, §§2, 3; art. III, §2.
Probate and registration.
Authorized to take probate, §47-2.

AMBER ALERT SYSTEM.
Center for missing persons.
Duty to develop and maintain system, §143B-499.2.
Criteria for dissemination of information, §143B-499.7, (b).
Education and training, providing, §143B-499.7, (c).
Emergency alert system, development, §143B-499.7, (e).
Established, §143B-499.7, (a).
Grants, contributions, devises, bequests and gifts.
Authority to accept, §143B-499.7, (f).
Purpose, §143B-499.7, (a).
Quick dissemination of information.
Duty of system, §143B-499.7, (b).
Statewide implementation.
Guidelines and procedures, development, §143B-499.7, (c).
Streets and highways.
Overhead permanent changeable message signs.
Development of procedure for use, §143B-499.7, (d).

AMBER LIGHTS.
Use on certain vehicles, §20-130.2.

AMBULANCES.
Approach of ambulance.
Duties of motorists, §20-157, (a).
Assault on emergency personnel, §14-288.9.
Attachment.
Liens.
County or city ambulance services, §§44-51.4 to 44-51.8.
Automated external defibrillator (AED), §90-21.15.
Counties.
County or city ambulance service lien, §§44-51.4 to 44-51.8.
EMS services in fire protection districts, §153A-309, (a), (b).

AMBULANCES —Cont'd
Counties —Cont'd
Health services, §153A-250.
Making false ambulance request, §14-111.3.
Obtaining ambulance services without intending to pay, §§14-111.1, 14-111.2, (a).
Named counties, §14-111.2, (b).
Service districts, §§153A-300 to 153A-310.
Crossing median of divided highway.
When permitted, §20-140.3.
Emergency medical services, §§143-507 to 143-519.
See EMERGENCY MEDICAL SERVICES.
Emergency medical technicians.
Offenses against.
Aggravating factor in sentencing, §15A-1340.16.
False pretenses and cheats.
Making false ambulance request, §§14-111.3, 14-286.1.
Obtaining ambulance services without intending to pay, §§14-111.1, 14-111.2, (a).
Named counties, §14-111.2, (b).
Franchises.
County ambulance services, §153A-250.
Garnishment.
Liens.
County or city ambulance service, §§44-51.4 to 44-51.8.
Horns and warning devices, §20-125, (b).
Liens.
County or city ambulance service.
Attachment or garnishment.
Collection authorization, §44-51.4.
Counties to which article applicable, §44-51.8.
Discharging lien, §44-51.7.
Filing, §44-51.6.
General lien for service, §44-51.5.
Recoveries for personal injuries, §44-49.
Attorneys' fees, §44-50.
Charges, §44-50.
Creation of lien, §44-49.
Disputed claims to be settled before payments, §44-51.
Evidence, §44-50.
Limit on recovery, §44-50.
Receiving person charged with duty of retaining fund, §44-50.
Services by county or municipality.
Discharge, §44-51.3.
Filing, §44-51.2.
Real property of recipient, §44-51.1.
Lights.
Electronically modulated headlamps, §20-130, (d).
Red lights.
Exception to prohibition, §20-130.1, (b).
Limitation of actions.
County or city ambulance services.
Enforcement of lien for, §44-51.1.
Municipal property taxes.
Authorized purposes, §160A-209, (c).
Obtaining ambulance services without intending to pay, §§14-111.1, 14-111.2, (a).
Named counties, §14-111.2, (b).
Parked or standing on roadway and giving warning signal.
Duties of driver approaching, §20-157, (f).
Parking within 100 feet of ambulance, §20-157, (e).
Personnel.
Offenses against.
Aggravating factor in sentencing, §15A-1340.16.
Red lights, §20-130.1, (b).

AMBULANCES —Cont'd
Regulation of emergency medical services, §§131E-155 to 131E-161.
See EMERGENCY MEDICAL SERVICES.
Requesting ambulance falsely, §§14-111.3, 14-286.1.
Right-of-way, §20-156, (b).
Sanitary districts.
Corporate powers of sanitary district board, §130A-55.
Sirens.
Vehicles on which authorized, §20-125, (b).
Speeding.
When speed limits not applicable, §20-145.
Traffic lights.
Preempting.
Local authority to permit, §20-169.
Window tinting exceptions, §20-127, (c).

AMBULATORY SURGICAL FACILITIES, §§131E-145 to 131E-152.
Abuse and neglect of patients, §14-32.2.
Administrative regulations.
Adverse action on licenses, §131E-148, (b).
Certificates of need, §§131E-175 to 131E-190.
See HEALTH CARE FACILITIES.
Definitions.
Licensing of facilities, §131E-146.
Hiring nurses.
Verification of licensure status, §90-171.43A, (a), (b).
Injunctions.
Hindering secretary's performance of duties, §131E-152, (b).
Operation without license, §131E-152, (a).
Procedure, §131E-152, (c).
Licenses.
Adverse action on licenses, §131E-148, (a), (b).
Applications for licenses, §131E-147, (b).
Renewal application, §131E-147, (c).
Assignability of license, §131E-147, (d).
Definitions, §131E-146.
Denial of license, §131E-148, (a).
Applicability of provisions, §131E-148, (b).
Development of standards, §131E-145, (b).
Enforcement of standards, §§131E-145, (b), 131E-149, (b).
Establishment of standards, §131E-145, (b).
Injunctive relief, §131E-152, (a) to (c).
Inspections, §131E-150, (a), (b).
Issuance, §131E-147, (d).
Penalties for violation of provisions, §131E-151.
Posting of license on premises, §131E-147, (e).
Purpose of part, §131E-145, (b).
Renewal of license, §131E-147, (c).
Required, §131E-147, (a).
Revocation of license, §131E-148, (a).
Applicability of provisions, §131E-148, (b).
Rules and regulations, §131E-149, (a).
Enforcement, §131E-149, (b).
Suspension of license, §131E-148, (a).
Applicability of provisions, §131E-148, (b).
Title of part.
Ambulatory surgical facility licensure act, §131E-145, (a).
Transferability of license, §131E-147, (d).
Violations of provisions.
Penalties, §131E-151.
Medical care commission.
Defined, §131E-146.

AMBULATORY SURGICAL FACILITIES —Cont'd
Nurses, hiring.
Verification of licensure status, §90-171.43A, (a), (b).
Obstruction of health care facility, §14-277.4.

AMBUSHING.
Secret assault, §14-31.

AMENDED STATUTES.
Construction and interpretation, §12-4.

AMENDING PLEADING, §1A-1, Rule 15, (a) to (d).

AMENDMENT OF JUDGMENT.
Motions, §1A-1, Rule 59, (e).

AMERICAN ALLIGATORS.
Propagation and production.
License required, §106-763.1, (a).
Operator of facility possessing untagged or undocumented alligators, §106-763.1, (c).
Requirements of facility raising, §106-763.1, (b).

AMERICAN EX-PRISONERS OF WAR HIGHWAY, §136-102.1.

AMERICAN FAMILY DAY.
Designation, §103-7.

AMERICAN HOLLY.
Taking, etc., of certain wild plants from land of another, §14-129.

AMERICAN INDIANS.
See INDIANS.

AMERICAN LEGION.
Emblem.
Commercialization of American Legion emblem, §14-395.
Wearing by nonmembers, §14-395.
Junior or youth baseball.
Certification of birth dates furnished to veterans' organizations, §130A-120.
Motor vehicle special license plates, §20-79.4, (b).
Property taxes.
Exclusion of real and personal property, §105-275.
Specialized registration plates, §20-79.4, (b).

AMERICAN REVOLUTION BICENTENNIAL COMMISSION.
Department of cultural resources.
Transfer of commission to department, §143B-51.

AMERICA'S FOUR HUNDREDTH ANNIVERSARY COMMITTEE, §§143B-85, 143B-86.

AMICUS CURIAE BRIEFS, App. Proc. Rule 28, (i).

AMMUNITION.
Dealers.
Door lock exemption permit, §§58-79-22, 143-143.4.
Furnishing bullets to inmates of charitable, mental or penal institutions, §14-258.1.
Persons subject to domestic violence orders.
Surrender and disposal of firearms.
Emergency or ex parte order, §50B-3.1.
Products liability lawsuits involving, §99B-11.
Teflon-coated bullets.
Manufacture sale, purchase or possession unlawful, §14-34.3, (a).
Inapplicability of provisions, §14-34.3, (b).
Misdemeanor, §14-34.3, (c).

AMNESTY.
Attorney disciplinary amnesty in illicit drug use cases, Bar Rules & Regs., B, §.0130.
Underground petroleum storage tank leak cleanup.
Reports of suspected discharge or release.
Limited amnesty, §143-215.94F.

AMOUNT IN CONTROVERSY.
District courts.
Proper division for trial of civil actions.
Determination by amount in controversy, §7A-243.
Small claims actions in district courts, §7A-210.
Statewide court-ordered-nonbinding arbitration in certain cases, §7A-37.1.
Superior courts.
Proper division for trial of civil actions.
Determination by amount in controversy, §7A-243.

AMPHETAMINES.
Methamphetamine watch program.
Immunity from civil and criminal liability.
Good faith actions, §114-43.
Precursor chemicals.
Possession or distribution with intent to manufacture, §90-95, (d1).
List of chemicals to which subsection applies, §90-95, (d2).
Schedule II controlled substances, §90-90, (c).
Trafficking, §90-95, (h).

AMPLIFIED SPEECH REGULATION BY CITIES, §160A-184.

AMPUTATION.
Podiatry.
Amputation of entire foot excluded from definition, §90-202.2, (a).
Podiatrist to perform at licensed hospital, §90-202.2, (b).
Workers' compensation.
Computation of compensation for amputation, I.C. Rule 405.

AMUSEMENT DEVICE SAFETY, §§95-111.1 to 95-111.18.
Accidents.
Investigations, §95-111.10, (b).
Removing of damaged parts, §95-111.10, (d).
Reports.
Required, §95-111.10, (a).
Use or moving of device, §95-111.10, (c).
Alcohol or other impairing substance.
Operating device equipment under the influence.
Prohibition, §95-111.11, (b).
Applicability of article, §95-111.2, (a).
Attorney general.
Representing department of labor, §95-111.15.
Certificate of operation.
Liability insurance required, §95-111.12, (b).
Required, §95-111.7, (a).
Suspension, revocation or refusal to issue or renew.
Appeals, §95-111.6, (c).
Operation of device after revocation or refusal to issue certificate, §95-111.7, (c).
Violations of article or rules and regulations, §95-111.6, (b).
Citation of article, §95-111.1, (a).
Civil penalties, §95-111.13, (a) to (e).
Administrative proceeding.
Final determination, §95-111.13, (g).
Copy of final order, filing, §95-111.13, (h).

AMUSEMENT DEVICE SAFETY —Cont'd
Civil penalties —Cont'd
Exception to determination.
Time for taking, §95-111.13, (g).
Factors considered, §95-111.13, (f).
Finality of determination, §95-111.13, (g).
Commissioner of labor.
Powers and duties, §95-111.4.
Compliance with article and rules and regulations, §95-111.7, (b).
Confidentiality.
Trade secrets, §95-111.17.
Construction of article and rules and regulations, §95-111.18.
Criminal penalties, §95-111.13, (i).
Death resulting from violation.
Criminal penalty, §95-111.13, (i).
Definitions, §95-111.3.
Department of labor.
Elevator and amusement device division, §95-110.4.
Entrance to amusement device.
Authority of owner or operator to deny, §95-111.14.
Exemptions from article, §95-111.2, (b).
Federal laws.
Agreements to enforce, §95-111.16.
Findings of general assembly, §95-111.1, (b).
Inspection.
Pre-opening inspection and test, §95-111.5.
Intent of article, §95-111.1, (c).
Liability insurance.
Amount, §95-111.12, (a).
Proof of insurance, §95-111.12, (c).
Required, §95-111.12, (a), (b).
Waterslides.
Notification to commission of personal injuries involving, §95-111.12, (d).
Location.
Notice, §95-111.8.
Noncomplying devices.
Stopping or limiting use, §95-111.6, (a).
Notice.
Location notice, §95-111.8.
Operators.
In attendance at all times, §95-111.11, (a).
Operating device equipment under the influence.
Prohibition, §95-111.11, (b).
Operating more than one device.
Restrictions, §95-111.11, (a).
Qualifications, §95-111.11, (a).
Reports.
Accidents, §95-111.10, (a).
Rules and regulations.
Adoption, §95-111.4.
Construction, §95-111.18.
Severability of article, §95-111.18.
Short title, §95-111.1, (a).
Tests.
Pre-opening inspection and test, §95-111.5.
Trade secrets.
Confidentiality, §95-111.17.
Unsafe device.
Operation of, §95-111.9.
Violations of article.
Civil penalties, criminal penalties, §95-111.13.
Waterslides.
Defined, §95-111.3, (h).
Insurance.
Liability insurance, §95-111.12, (a).

AMUSEMENT LICENSING AND LICENSE TAXES.
Amusement or entertainment not otherwise taxed.
Cities may levy but counties may not, §105-37.1, (d).
Application for license for privilege of engaging in business, §105-33, (a).
Charities.
Exemption, §105-40.
Circus, §105-37.1, (d).
Dance or athletic contest for which admission fee charge.
Cities may levy but counties may not, §105-37.1, (d).
Dog shows, §105-37.1, (d).
Educational purposes.
Exemption, §105-40.
Exemptions from tax, §105-40.
Exhibiting performance, show or exhibition, §105-37.1, (d).
Religious societies.
License taxes.
Exemption, §105-40.

AMUSEMENT OR ENTERTAINMENT NOT OTHERWISE TAXED.
License tax by city but not county, §105-37.1, (d).
Privilege tax on gross receipts, admission fee charged, §105-37.1.
Rate and payment, §105-37.1, (b).

AMUSEMENT PARKS.
Amusement device safety generally, §§95-111.1 to 95-111.18.
See AMUSEMENT DEVICE SAFETY.

AMUSEMENTS.
Counties.
Regulation of places of amusement, §153A-135.
Handicapped persons.
Right to use of places of public amusement, §168-3.
Municipal corporations.
Regulating and licensing businesses, etc., §§160A-181, 160A-194.

AMY JACKSON LAW.
Sex offender and public protection registration generally, §§14-208.5 to 14-208.32.
See SEX OFFENDER AND PUBLIC PROTECTION REGISTRATION.

ANABOLIC STEROIDS.
Controlled substances.
Schedule III, §90-91.
Unauthorized substances taxes, §§105-113.105 to 105-113.113.
See UNAUTHORIZED SUBSTANCES TAXES.

ANALINGUS.
Rape.
See RAPE.
Sexual offenses generally.
See SEXUAL OFFENSES.

ANATOMICAL GIFTS, §§130A-402 to 130A-412.1.
Advance health care directive registry, §§130A-465 to 130A-471.
Age.
Giving of blood by persons 17 years of age or more, §130A-411.

ANATOMICAL GIFTS —Cont'd
Age —Cont'd
Persons who may execute anatomical gift, §130A-404, (a), (b).
AIDS.
Information for potential donors, §130A-148, (b).
Laboratory tests for AIDS virus infection.
Immunity of facility or institution, §130A-148, (e).
Required, §130A-148, (c), (d).
Amendment of gift, §130A-408, (a) to (d).
Autopsies.
Applicability of provisions as to autopsies, §130A-409, (d).
Bank or storage facility.
Defined, §130A-403.
Citation of part.
Uniform anatomical gift act, §130A-402.
Consent for organ or tissue donation in order of priority established.
Duties of federally designated organ procurement organization, §130A-412.2, (c).
Construction and interpretation.
Uniformity of interpretation, §130A-412.
Damages.
Persons acting with due care not liable, §130A-409, (c).
Decedent.
Defined, §130A-403.
Definitions, §130A-403.
Discretion and sensitivity with respect to beliefs of families and potential donors.
Federally designated organ procurement organization to encourage, §130A-412.2, (d).
Document of gift.
Amendment, §130A-408, (a) to (d).
Delivery, §130A-407.
Deposit for safe keeping, §130A-407.
Documents other than wills, §130A-406, (b).
Donee.
Specified or unspecified donee, §130A-406, (c).
Medical records of donor.
Gift deemed to include authorization to donee to review records, §130A-406, (g).
Physicians and surgeons.
Designating physician or surgeon, §130A-406, (d).
Revocation, §130A-408, (a) to (d).
Will, §130A-406, (a).
Donee.
Acceptance of gift, §130A-409, (a).
Document of gift.
Specified or unspecified donee, §130A-406, (c).
Notice of contrary indications by decedent.
Donee not to accept gift, §130A-404, (d).
Persons who may become donees, §130A-405.
Rights and duties at death of donor, §130A-409, (a).
Priority, §130A-404, (f).
Donor.
Death of donor.
Rights and duties of donee on, §130A-409, (a).
Time of death.
Determination, §130A-409, (b).
Defined, §130A-403.
Persons who may execute anatomical gift, §130A-404, (a), (b).
Donor cards.
Availability at division of motor vehicles offices, §20-7.3.

ANATOMICAL GIFTS —Cont'd
Evaluation of donation potential.
Duty of federally designated organ procurement organization, §130A-412.2, (a).
Examinations.
Gift authorizes examinations, §130A-404, (e).
Eyes.
Manner of making gift of eye, §130A-406, (e).
Financial liability for cost related to evaluation of suitability of donor's organ or tissue.
Family of person whose organ or tissue to be donated not liable, §130A-412.1, (c).
Guardians.
Manner of making anatomical gifts, §130A-406, (f).
Persons who may execute anatomical gift, §130A-404, (c).
Hospitals.
Defined, §130A-403.
Federally designated organ procurement organizations and tissue banks.
Access to patient's medical records, §130A-412.1, (b).
Written agreement with addresses requirements of provisions, §130A-412.1, (e).
Hold harmless provision.
Hospital made party to action arising out of failure of federally designated organ procurement organization, §130A-412.2, (f).
Medical records.
Access by federally designated organ procurement organization and tissue bank.
Deceased patient's medical records, §130A-412.1, (d).
Protocols for organ procurement, §130A-412.1, (a).
Immunity of hospitals and hospital personnel in good faith compliance, §130A-412.1, (g).
Requirements not to exceed protocol provisions of Title XI of social security act, §130A-412.1, (f).
Signed statement with federally designated organ procurement organization, §130A-412.1, (a).
Human tissue donation programs, §§130A-413, 130A-415.
Husband and wife.
Persons who may execute anatomical gift, §130A-404, (b).
Irrevocable, when, §130A-404, (a).
Legislative declaration.
Use of tissue declared service, §130A-410.
Liability, §130A-410.
Damages.
Persons acting with due care not liable, §130A-409, (c).
License to give trust fund, §§20-7.4 to 20-7.6.
Manner of making anatomical gifts, §130A-406.
Medical records.
Access by federally designated organ procurement organizations and tissue banks.
Hospitals to provide, §130A-412.1, (b).
Negligence.
Liability, §130A-410.
Notice.
Contrary indications by decedent.
Donee not to accept gift, §130A-404, (d).
Options of organ or tissue donation and option to decline.
Families of potential organ donors made aware of by federally designated organ procurement organization, §130A-412.2, (b).

ANATOMICAL GIFTS —Cont'd
Parent and child.
Blood.
Giving of blood by persons 17 years or more.
Consent of parent or guardian not required, §130A-411.
Persons who may execute anatomical gift, §130A-404, (b).
Part.
Defined, §130A-403.
Physicians and surgeons.
Defined, §130A-403.
Document of gift.
Designating physician or surgeon, §130A-406, (d).
Time of death.
Determination, §130A-409, (b).
Privileged and confidential information.
Hospital and patient information, interviews, reports, etc., §130A-412.2, (e).
Purposes for which anatomical gifts may be made, §130A-405.
Qualified individual.
Defined, §130A-403.
Revocation of gift, §130A-408, (a) to (d).
Short title.
Uniform anatomical gift act, §130A-402.
Standard of care, §130A-410.
State.
Defined, §130A-403.
Surgeon.
Defined, §130A-403.
Time of death.
Determination, §130A-409, (b).
Tissue banks.
Defined, §130A-403.
Title of part.
Uniform anatomical gift act, §130A-402.
Unclaimed bodies.
Exemption of body for which deceased has made anatomical gift, §130A-415, (f).
Use of tissue declared a service, §130A-410.
Warranties.
No liability in warranty, §130A-410.
Wills.
Manner of making anatomical gifts, §130A-406, (a).

ANATOMY COMMISSION.
Appointments, §130A-33.31, (a), (b).
Autopsies.
Unclaimed bodies.
Consent of commission, §130A-415, (d).
Board of anatomy.
References to former board in testamentary dispositions, §130A-33.32.
Chairman, §130A-33.31, (d).
Clerical and other services, §130A-33.31, (g).
Creation, §130A-33.30.
Duties, §130A-33.30.
Meetings, §130A-33.31, (f).
Members, §130A-33.31, (a).
Powers and duties, §130A-33.30.
Quorum, §130A-33.31, (e).
Removal of members, §130A-33.31, (c).
Terms, §130A-33.31, (a).
Testamentary dispositions.
References to former board of anatomy, §130A-33.32.
Unclaimed bodies.
Adoption of rules, §130A-416.

ANATOMY COMMISSION —Cont'd
Unclaimed bodies —Cont'd
Autopsies.
Consent of commission, §130A-415, (d).
Consent of commission for autopsy, §130A-415, (d).
Notification to commission, §130A-415, (a), (g), (i).
Minors in custody of county at time of death, §130A-415, (g).
Vacancies, §130A-33.31, (b).

ANCESTRAL PROPERTY.
Intestate succession.
Distinction between ancestral and nonancestral property abolished, §29-3.

ANCESTRY.
Hearsay exception.
Records of religious organizations, §8C-1, Rule 803.
Statement of personal or family history, §8C-1, Rule 804, (b).

ANCIENT AND ARABIC ORDER NOBLES OF THE MYSTIC SHRINE.
Property tax exclusion, §105-275.

ANCIENT DOCUMENTS.
Authentication and identification of evidence, §8C-1, Rule 901, (b).
Hearsay exception, §8C-1, Rule 803.

ANCIENT EGYPTIAN ORDER NOBLES OF THE MYSTIC SHRINE.
Property tax exclusion, §105-275.

ANCILLARY ADMINISTRATION, §§28A-26-1 to 28A-26-9.
Assets.
Assets in jurisdiction outside state subject to ancillary administration, §28A-26-1.
Nonresident decedents.
Assets subject to claims, allowances, etc., §28A-26-8, (a).
Remission of surplus assets, §28A-26-9.
Bonds, surety.
Personal representatives granted ancillary letters, §28A-26-4, (a).
Claims.
Certain claims binding, §28A-26-8, (b).
Limitation on presentation, §28A-26-8, (c).
Payment, §28A-26-8, (d).
Duties of personal representatives in ancillary administration, §28A-26-8.
Foreign corporations.
Authority to act as ancillary personal representative, §28A-26-3, (a).
General provisions, §28A-26-1.
Granting ancillary letters, §28A-26-3, (a).
Bond for personal representatives, §28A-26-4.
Nonexistence of domiciliary personal representative, §28A-26-3, (b).
No ancillary administrator within ninety days.
Payment of debt and delivery of property to nonresident domiciliary, §28A-26-2, (c).
Nonresident decedents.
Assets subject to claims, etc., §28A-26-8, (a).
Payment of debt and delivery of property without ancillary administration in state, §28A-26-2.

ANDREW JACKSON HISTORIC MEMORIAL COMMITTEE.
Administrative and staff services, §143B-132, (e).

ANDREW JACKSON HISTORIC MEMORIAL COMMITTEE —Cont'd
Compensation of members.
No compensation, §143B-132, (d).
Composition, §143B-132, (b).
Creation, §143B-132, (b).
Duties, §143B-132, (c).
Funds, §143B-132, (f).
Legislative declaration, §143B-132, (a).
Terms of members, §143B-132, (b).

ANESTHESIA.
Dentists.
Anesthesia and parenteral sedation, §90-29, (b).
Standards for general anesthesia and parenteral sedation.
Board of dental examiners to establish by regulation, §90-30.1.
Medical plan for teachers and state employees.
Benefits, §135-40.6.
Podiatry.
Administration of anesthetic other than local excluded from definitions, §90-202.2, (a).

ANESTHESIOLOGISTS.
Professional corporations.
Formation authorized, §55B-14, (c).

ANIMAL AUCTIONS.
Licensing public auctions, §19A-28.
Changes in ownership, management, etc., §19A-31.
Fees, §19A-28.
Operation without license, §19A-33.
Refusal, suspension or revocation, §19A-32.
Transfer prohibited, §19A-31.
Public auction defined, §19A-23.

ANIMAL BAITING, §14-362.1.
Dog baiting, §14-362.2.

ANIMAL CONTROL OFFICERS.
County appointment authorized, §67-30.
Powers and duties of county dog warden, §67-31.

ANIMAL CRUELTY INVESTIGATORS.
Appointment, §19A-45, (a).
Badges, §19A-45, (b).
Care of seized animals, §19A-47.
Complaints.
Filing, §19A-46, (a), (c).
Costs of proceedings, §19A-46, (d).
Educational requirements, §19A-49.
Expenses.
Reimbursement, §19A-45, (d).
Forcible entry.
Order by district court judge, §19A-46, (e).
Interference with investigator.
Penalty, §19A-48.
Oath of office, §19A-45, (c).
Powers, §19A-46, (a), (b).
Removal from office, §§19A-45, (b), 19A-49.
Seizure of animal.
Care of seized animals, §19A-47.
Magistrate's order, §19A-46, (a).
Execution of order, §19A-46, (b), (c).
Terms of office, §19A-45, (b).

ANIMAL DEALERS.
Defined, §19A-23.
Licensing, §19A-29.
Change in ownership, management, etc., §19A-31.
Fees, §19A-28.

ANIMAL DEALERS —Cont'd
Licensing —Cont'd
Operation without license, §19A-33.
Refusal, suspension or revocation, §19A-30.
Appeals, §19A-32.
Transfer prohibited, §19A-31.

ANIMAL-DRAWN VEHICLE.
Traffic laws apply, §20-171.

ANIMAL FIGHTING, §14-362.1.
Cockfighting, §14-362.
Dog fighting, §14-362.2.

ANIMAL INSURANCE.
Mandatory or voluntary risk sharing plans.
See MANDATORY OR VOLUNTARY RISK SHARING PLANS.
Types of insurance authorized, §58-7-15.

ANIMAL LOVERS.
Motor vehicle license plates.
Special license plates, §§20-79.4, (b), 20-81.12, (b11).

ANIMAL RESEARCH FACILITIES.
Interference with, §14-159.2.

ANIMALS.
Animal cruelty investigators, §§19A-45 to 19A-49.
Auctions.
Licensing public auctions, §§19A-28 to 19A-33.
Livestock markets.
Generally, §§106-406 to 106-418.
See LIVESTOCK MARKETS.
Prompt pay law, §§106-418.1 to 106-418.7A.
See LIVESTOCK MARKETS.
Bailments.
Vehicles and draft animals, §§14-165 to 14-169.
Bang's disease, §§106-388 to 106-398.
See BRUCELLOSIS.
Bears.
Protection of black bears, §§19A-10 to 19A-14.
Biological residues in animals, §§106-549.81 to 106-549.89.
See BIOLOGICAL RESIDUES IN ANIMALS.
Biologics.
General provisions, §§106-707 to 106-715.
See BIOLOGICS.
Black bears.
Protection, §§19A-10 to 19A-14.
Brands.
Livestock generally, §§80-45 to 80-66.
See LIVESTOCK BRANDS.
Brucellosis, §§106-388 to 106-398.
See BRUCELLOSIS.
Cattle tick, §§106-351 to 106-363.
See CATTLE TICK.
Counties.
Abuse of animals.
Prohibition, §153A-127.
Dangerous animals.
Possession or harboring of dangerous animals.
Regulation, §153A-131.
Licenses.
Taxation, §153A-153.
Shelters.
Establishing, standards, §153A-442.
Taxation, §153A-153.
Criminal interference with animal research, §14-159.2.
Cruelty to animals.
General provisions.
See CRUELTY TO ANIMALS.
Investigators, §§19A-45 to 19A-49.

ANIMALS —Cont'd
Dangerous animals.
Possession or harboring.
Regulation by counties, §153A-131.
Dangerous dogs, §§67-4.1 to 67-4.5.
Dead animals.
Dead domesticated animals.
Disposition of, §106-403.
Transportation department.
Removal of dead animals.
Powers of department, §136-18.
Dealers.
Livestock dealer licensing generally, §§106-418.8 to 106-418.16.
See LIVESTOCK DEALER LICENSING.
Definitions, §19A-1.
Dangerous dogs, §67-4.1, (a).
Welfare Act, §19A-23.
Discharge of oil or hazardous substances.
Liability for damages to animal life, §143-215.90, (a) to (c).
Dogs.
See DOGS.
Equine infectious anemia, §§106-405.15 to 106-405.20.
Exempt property from enforcement of claims of creditors, §1C-1601, (a).
False pretenses and cheats.
Pedigree of animals.
Obtaining property by false representation of pedigree, §14-102.
Registration of animals.
Obtaining certificate of registration by false representation, §14-103.
Fish and fishing.
See FISH AND FISHING.
Hog cholera, §§106-310 to 106-322.3.
See HOG CHOLERA.
Horses.
General provisions.
See HORSES.
Hotels, inns and other transient lodging places.
Admitting to rooms, §72-7.1.
Hunting and wildlife.
See HUNTING AND WILDLIFE.
Impoundment.
Livestock running at large, §§68-17 to 68-24.
See LIVESTOCK RUNNING AT LARGE.
Interference with animal research, §14-159.2, (c).
Landlord and tenant.
Tenant security deposit act.
Pet deposits, §42-53.
Larceny.
Animals subject to larceny, §14-84.
Horses, mules, swine, cattle or dogs, §14-81.
Temporary purposes, §14-82.
Law enforcement animals.
Injuring, maiming or killing agency animal, §14-163.1.
Leases, UCC.
Unborn young.
Definition of "goods," §25-2A-103, (1).
Identification, §25-2A-217.
Liens.
Boarding animals.
Possessory liens on personal property.
Persons entitled to, §44A-2, (c).
Livestock.
Brucellosis, §§106-388 to 106-398.
See BRUCELLOSIS.

ANIMALS —Cont'd
Livestock —Cont'd
Cattle tick, §§106-351 to 106-363.
See CATTLE TICK.
Compensation for killing diseased animals, §§106-323 to 106-335.
See LIVESTOCK DISEASES.
Control of livestock diseases generally, §§106-400 to 106-405.
See LIVESTOCK DISEASES.
Diseases generally, §§106-304 to 106-307.7.
See LIVESTOCK DISEASES.
Equine infectious anemia, §§106-405.15 to 106-405.20.
Hog cholera, §§106-310 to 106-322.3.
See HOG CHOLERA.
Impoundment of animals running at large, §§68-17 to 68-24.
See LIVESTOCK RUNNING AT LARGE.
Quarantine.
See LIVESTOCK DISEASES.
Livestock brands, §§80-45 to 80-66.
See LIVESTOCK BRANDS.
Livestock dealer licensing generally, §§106-418.8 to 106-418.16.
See LIVESTOCK DEALER LICENSING.
Livestock diseases.
Tuberculosis, §§106-336 to 106-350.
See TUBERCULOSIS IN LIVESTOCK.
Livestock markets.
Generally, §§106-406 to 106-418.
See LIVESTOCK MARKETS.
Prompt pay law, §§106-418.1 to 106-418.7A.
See LIVESTOCK MARKETS.
Meat inspections, §§106-549.15 to 106-549.39.
See MEAT INSPECTIONS.
Milk and milk products.
Ice cream plants, creameries and cheese factories.
Animals prohibited, §106-246.
Motor vehicles.
Applicability of traffic laws to persons riding animals or driving animal-drawn vehicles, §20-171.
Passing horses or other draft animals.
Reasonable care, §20-216.
Municipal corporations.
Abuse of animals.
Define and prohibit abuse of animals, §160A-182.
Animal shelters.
Establishment, standards, §160A-493.
Dangerous animals.
Possession or harboring, §160A-187.
Domestic animals.
Regulation, §160A-186.
Taxation.
License tax, §160A-212.
Oaths.
Animal cruelty investigators, §19A-45, (c).
Pedigree of animals.
Obtaining property by false representation of pedigree, §14-102.
Poultry generally.
See POULTRY AND POULTRY PRODUCTS.
Poultry products inspections, §§106-549.49 to 106-549.69.
See POULTRY PRODUCTS INSPECTIONS.
Prompt pay law.
Livestock, §§106-418.1 to 106-418.7A.
See LIVESTOCK MARKETS.

ANIMALS —Cont'd
Quarantine of livestock with diseases generally.
See LIVESTOCK DISEASES.
Rabies.
General provisions, §§130A-184 to 130A-201.
See RABIES.
Registration of animals.
Obtaining certificate of registration by false representation, §14-103.
Rendering plants and rendering operations generally, §§106-168.1 to 106-168.16.
See RENDERING PLANTS AND RENDERING OPERATIONS.
Reports.
Spay/neuter program.
Animal shelters receiving state or local funding, §19A-65.
Research.
Criminal interference, §14-159.2.
Restitution.
Interference with animal research.
Conditions of probation, §14-159.2, (d).
Interpretation of provisions, §14-159.2, (e).
Sale of goods, UCC.
Identification of goods, §25-2-501, (1).
Sale of unborn animals, §25-2-501.
Definition of goods, §25-2-105, (1).
Identification of goods, §25-2-501, (1).
Sale of meat of diseased animals.
Regulation of sale, §14-342.
Shelters.
Counties.
Establishing, standards, §153A-442.
Municipalities.
Establishment, standards, §160A-493.
Slaughterhouses generally.
See SLAUGHTERHOUSES.
Spay/neuter program, §§19A-60 to 19A-65.
Account, §19A-62.
Application for reimbursement, §19A-64, (b).
Counties or cities.
Eligibility for distributions, §19A-63, (a).
Creation, §19A-62, (a).
Distributions to counties and cities, §19A-64.
Eligibility for distributions, §19A-63.
Low-income persons defined.
Eligibility for distributions, §19A-63, (b).
Priorities for distribution, §19A-64, (c).
Reimbursable costs, §19A-64, (a).
Sources of funding, §19A-62, (a).
Uses, §19A-62, (b).
Components, §19A-61.
Establishment, §19A-61.
Legislative findings, §19A-60.
Purpose, §19A-60.
Reports.
Animal shelters receiving state or local funding, §19A-65.
Taxation.
Counties may levy animal tax, §153A-153.
Traffic laws.
Applicability to persons riding animals or driving animal-drawn vehicles, §20-171.
Trusts for pets, §36A-147.
Veterinarians.
General provisions, §§90-179 to 90-187.13.
See VETERINARIANS.
Wildlife.
Hunting and wildlife.
See HUNTING AND WILDLIFE.

ANIMAL SHELTERS.
Certificate of registration, §19A-26.
Refusal, suspension or revocation, §19A-30.
Appeals, §19A-32.
Counties.
Establishing, standards, §153A-442.
Municipalities.
Establishment, standards, §160A-493.
Spay/neuter program, §§19A-60 to 19A-65.

ANIMALS RUNNING AT LARGE.
Dogs.
Dangerous dog going beyond owner's property without leash or muzzle, §67-4.2, (a).
Female dogs in heat, §67-2.
Nighttime, §67-12.
Sheep-killing dogs, §67-3.
Wildlife management areas.
Impoundment of unmuzzled dogs running at large, §67-14.1, (b) to (e).
Impoundment.
Livestock, §§68-17 to 68-24.
See LIVESTOCK RUNNING AT LARGE.
Livestock generally.
See LIVESTOCK RUNNING AT LARGE.

ANIMAL WASTE MANAGEMENT, §§143-215.10A to 143-215.74B.
Action on permit application, §143-215.10C, (c).
Application for permit, contents, §143-215.10C, (d).
Bird operations, §143-215.10C, (f).
Certification of animal waste management system operators, §§90A-47 to 90A-47.6.
Construction and design of system, §143-215.10C, (b).
Definitions, §§143-215.10B.
Discharge of waste, publication of notice or press release, §143-215.10C, (h).
Dry litter poultry facility.
Animal waste management plan, §143-215.10C, (f1).
Application for permit, §143-215.10C, (a1).
Fees, §143-215.10G, (a) to (c).
Permits, §143-215.3D, (a).
Inspections, §143-215.10F.
Notice of discharge, §143-215.10C, (h).
Permit requirement, §143-215.10C, (a).
Violation points system applicable to swine farms, §143-215.6E.
Plan requirements, §143-215.10C, (e).
Press release, discharge, §143-215.10C, (h).
Property taxes.
Special classes of property excluded from tax base, §105-275.
Publication of notice of discharge, §143-215.10C, (h).
Public livestock markets.
Permit holders, exemption from requirements, §143-215.10C, (i).
Purpose of act, §143-215.10A.
Reports.
Contents, §143-215.10M, (a).
Itemization of information, §143-215.10M, (b).
Review of operations.
Conflicts of interest, §143-215.10D, (c).
Reporting procedure, §143-215.10D, (a).
Requirement, §143-215.10D, (b).
Swine integrators.
Definitions, §143-215.10H, (a).
Disclosure of violations, §143-215.10H, (d).

ANIMAL WASTE MANAGEMENT —Cont'd
Swine integrators —Cont'd
Notice of termination or new relationship, §143-215.10H, (c).
Registration.
Required, §143-215.10H, (b).
Technology development, §143-215.10C, (g).
Violation points system applicable to swine farms.
Appeals process to be provided for, §143-215.6E, (c).
Determinations in developing, §143-215.6E, (b).
Development, §143-215.6E, (a).
Provisions of system, §143-215.6E, (a).
Violations requiring immediate notification.
Federal employees, §143-215.10E, (b).
State employees, §143-215.10E, (a).

ANIMAL WASTE MANAGEMENT SYSTEM OPERATORS, §§90A-47 to 90A-47.6.
Certification program.
Operators in charge, §90A-47.3, (a).
Certification required, §90A-47.2, (a).
Contracts.
Reports, §90A-47.2, (b).
Definitions, §90A-47.1.
Enforcement.
Rules, §90A-47.6.
Examinations, §90A-47.3, (b).
Fees.
Certification, §90A-47.4, (a).
Renewal fee, §90A-47.4, (b).
Fines.
Willful violations, §90A-47.5, (b).
Goals, §90A-47.
Operators in charge.
Certification program, §90A-47.3, (a).
Contracts with more than one owner, §90A-47.2, (b).
Qualifications for certification, §90A-47.2, (a).
Training program, §90A-47.3, (b).
Purpose of part, §90A-47.
Renewal of certificate, §90A-47.4, (b).
Reports.
Operators in charge contracting with more than one owner, §90A-47.2, (b).
Revocation of certificate, §90A-47.5, (a).
Rules, §90A-47.6.
Suspension of certification, §90A-47.5, (a).
Training program.
Operators in charge, §90A-47.3, (b).

ANIMAL WELFARE, §§19A-20 to 19A-40.
Animal shelters.
Certificates of registration.
Duration, §19A-26.
Refusal, suspension or revocation, §19A-30.
Appeals, §19A-32.
Required, §19A-26.
Defined, §19A-23.
Appeals.
Denial, suspension or revocation of license or certificate, §19A-32.
Applicability of provisions, §19A-37.
Exemptions, §§19A-37, 19A-39.
Assessment of civil penalty, §19A-40.
Auctions.
Defined, §19A-23.
Licenses.
Change in ownership, management or operation of business, §19A-31.
Fees, §19A-28.

ANIMAL WELFARE —Cont'd
Auctions —Cont'd
Licenses —Cont'd
Penalty for operation without license, §19A-33.
Refusal, suspension or revocation, §§19A-30, 19A-32.
Required, §19A-28.
Transfer prohibited, §19A-31.
Boarding kennel.
Defined, §19A-23.
License.
Change in ownership, management or operation of business, §19A-31.
Fee, §19A-28.
Penalty for operation without license, §19A-33.
Refusal, suspension or revocation, §§19A-30, 19A-32.
Required, §19A-28.
Transfer prohibited, §19A-31.
Board of agriculture.
Hearings, §19A-32.
Refusal, suspension or revocation of certificate or license, §19A-30.
Powers, §19A-24.
Rules and regulations, §19A-24.
Citation of act.
Short title, §19A-20.
Civil penalty, §19A-40.
Dealers.
Defined, §19A-23.
Licenses.
Change in ownership, management or operation of business, §19A-31.
Fees, §19A-29.
Penalty for acting as dealer without license, §19A-34.
Refusal, suspension or revocation, §19A-30.
Appeals, §19A-32.
Required, §19A-29.
Transfer prohibited, §19A-31.
Definitions, §19A-23.
Department of agriculture and consumer services.
Animal health division.
Animal welfare section, §19A-22.
Employees, §19A-25.
Investigations, §19A-25.
Dog wardens.
Violations of provisions by, §19A-36.
Euthanasia.
Defined, §19A-23.
Fees for licenses, §§19A-27 to 19A-29.
Use of fees, §19A-38.
Hearings, §19A-32.
Refusal, suspension or revocation of certificate or license, §19A-30.
Hunting dogs.
Training establishments.
Inapplicability of provisions, §19A-39.
Investigations.
Director of animal welfare section, §19A-22.
Legislative declaration.
Purposes of act, §19A-21.
Misdemeanors.
Acting as dealer without license, §19A-34.
Dog wardens.
Violations of provisions by, §19A-36.
Failure to adequately care for animals, §19A-35.
Operation of pet shop, kennel or auction without license, §19A-33.

ANIMAL WELFARE —Cont'd
Motor vehicle license plates.
Animal lovers special license plates, §§20-79.4, (b), 20-81.12, (b11).
Pet shops.
Defined, §19A-23.
Licenses, §19A-27.
Change in ownership, management or operation of business, §19A-31.
Fee, §19A-27.
Penalty for operation without license, §19A-33.
Refusal, suspension or revocation, §19A-30.
Appeals, §19A-32.
Required, §19A-27.
Transfer prohibited, §19A-31.
Purposes of act, §19A-21.
Research facilities.
Defined, §19A-23.
Exemptions from provisions, §19A-37.
Right of entry.
Director of animal welfare section, §19A-25.
Rules and regulations.
Board of agriculture, §19A-24.
Title of act.
Short title, §19A-20.
Use of fees for enforcing and administering article, §19A-38.

ANNE CARTER LEE GRAVE SITE.
Maintenance of grave, §136-44.

ANNEXATION.
Annexation agreements.
Approval, §160A-58.23.
Authority not granted by part, §160A-58.26.
Authorized, §160A-58.23.
Binding on parties, §160A-58.27, (a).
Contents, §160A-58.24, (a).
Definitions, §160A-58.22.
Duration, §160A-58.23.
Effect, §160A-58.25.
Effect of part on prior local acts, §160A-58.28.
Execution, §160A-58.23.
Hearings, §160A-58.24, (c).
Modification, §160A-58.24, (d).
Notice, §160A-58.24, (b).
Part grants no annexation authority, §160A-58.26.
Prohibiting city from annexing into area.
Petition to annex area, §160A-58.27, (i).
Purpose of part, §160A-58.21.
Scope of part, §160A-58.21.
Termination, §160A-58.24, (d), (f).
Territorial limits, §160A-58.24, (e).
Violation.
Relief from, §160A-58.27, (a) to (i).
Violations, §160A-58.25.
Annexation by petition.
Authority of governing board, §160A-31, (a).
Citizens and property subject to debts, laws, etc., §160A-31, (e).
Contiguous defined, §160A-31, (f).
Form of petition, §160A-31, (b).
Hearings, §160A-31, (c).
Ordinance annexing territory, §160A-31, (d).
Resolution in lieu of petition.
Property owned by municipality, §160A-31, (g).
Statement by petitioners as to vested rights, §160A-31, (h).
Annexation of noncontiguous areas.
Assumption of debt.
Rural fire departments, §160A-58.2A, (a).
Exemption from section, §160A-58.2A, (c).
Payments, calculation, §160A-58.2A, (b).

ANNEXATION —Cont'd
Annexation of noncontiguous areas —Cont'd
Assumption of debt —Cont'd
Rural fire departments —Cont'd
Schedule for payment, §160A-58.2A, (d).
Authority, §160A-58.1, (a).
Definitions, §160A-58.
Extraterritorial powers, §160A-58.4.
Hearing, §160A-58.2.
Ordinances.
Annexed area subject to city taxes and debts, §160A-58.3.
Petition for annexation, §160A-58.1, (a).
Contents, §160A-58.1, (c).
Form, §160A-58.1, (c).
Resolution in lieu of petition.
Property owned by municipality, §160A-58.7.
Signatures required, §160A-58.1, (a).
Statement by petitioners concerning vesting rights, §160A-58.1, (d).
Powers.
Extraterritorial powers, §160A-58.4.
Primary corporate limits.
Defined, §160A-58.
Transition from satellite to primary limits, §160A-58.6.
Property owned by municipality.
Resolution in lieu of petition, §160A-58.7.
Recordation, §160A-58.8.
Reports, §160A-58.8.
Satellite corporate limits.
Defined, §160A-58.
Transition from satellite to primary limits, §160A-58.6.
Standards.
Annexing area not meeting standards, §160A-58.1, (b2).
Inapplicability of certain standard to specified cities and towns, §160A-58.1, (b).
Noncontiguous areas proposed for annexation, §160A-58.1, (b).
Taxation.
Annexed area subject to city taxes and debts, §160A-58.3.
Water and sewer rates.
Special rates, §160A-58.5.
Assumption of debt.
Rural fire departments, §160A-31.1, (a).
Exemption from section, §160A-31.1, (c).
Payment.
Calculation, §160A-31.1, (b).
Schedule, §160A-31.1, (d).
Camp Butner hospital.
Annexation of territory extending into Camp Butner reservation, §122C-410, (a).
City prohibited from annexing area.
Petition seeking permission to annex, §160A-58.27, (i).
Contiguous area defined, §160A-31, (f).
Municipalities less than five thousand, §160A-41.
Municipalities of five thousand or more, §160A-53.
County service districts.
Authority, findings required, §153A-303, (a).
By petition of owners, §153A-303, (b).
County research and production service districts.
Removal of territory from.
Applicability of general annexation law to removed territory, §153A-314.1, (d).
Fire protection district.
Chapter 69 district annexing, §153A-304.2, (a), (b).

ANNEXATION —Cont'd
County service districts —Cont'd
Fire protection district —Cont'd
Municipality annexing all or part of district, §153A-304.1, (a) to (d).
Hearing on resolution, §153A-303, (e).
Notice of hearing, §153A-303, (e).
Report, §153A-303, (d).
Required provision or maintenance of services, §153A-305, (b).
Sanitary districts within city limits, §153A-303, (c).
Definitions, §§160A-41, 160A-53.
Development financing district.
District established by county, §159-107, (e).
Economic development and training districts.
County extending district, §153A-317.14.
Effective date of certain annexation ordinances.
Ordinances adopted from January 1, 1987 to August 3, 1987, §160A-58.9.
Ordinances adopted under Article 4A of Chapter 160A, §160A-58.9A, (a), (b).
Applicability of provisions, §160A-58.9A, (c).
Elections.
Registration of voters in areas proposed for incorporation or annexation, §163-288.2.
Firemen's and rescue squad workers' pension fund.
Firemen whose residence is annexed by a city.
Monthly pensions upon retirement, §58-86-55.
Fire protection district.
Municipality annexing all or part of district, §153A-304.1, (a) to (d).
Garbage and trash.
Annexation of area where private collection firm providing services, §160A-324.
Local acts.
Effect of part on prior local acts, §160A-58.28.
Map of annexed area.
Population less than five thousand, §§160A-35, 160A-35.1.
Population of five thousand or more, §§160A-47, 160A-47.1.
Recordation, §160A-29.
Metropolitan sewerage districts.
Inclusion of additional political subdivision or unincorporated areas.
Annexation of area lying outside district not construed as inclusion, §162A-68, (h).
Municipal service districts.
Petition, §160A-538, (b).
Personal property.
Tax liability of newly annexed territory, §160A-58.10.
Petition.
Agreement prohibiting city from annexing into area.
Permission to annex, §160A-58.27, (i).
Annexation by petition, §160A-31.
Violations of part or agreement.
Review of action by city, §160A-58.27, (a) to (i).
Population less than five thousand.
Appeals.
Actions of court, §160A-38, (g).
Appeals from judgment of court, §160A-38, (h).
Conduct of review by court, §160A-38, (f).
Consolidation of petitions, §160A-38, (d).
Contents of petition, §160A-38, (b).
Effective date of ordinance, §160A-38, (i), (j).

ANNEXATION —Cont'd
Population less than five thousand —Cont'd
Appeals —Cont'd
Lost property tax revenue pending appeal, §160A-38, (k).
Material solicited by municipality, §160A-38, (c).
Right of appeal, §160A-38, (a).
Settlements, presentation to superior court, §160A-38, (l).
Stay of annexation ordinance, §160A-38, (e).
Authority to annex, §160A-34.
Authorized expenditures, §160A-40.
Character of area to be annexed, §160A-36.
Boundaries, §160A-36, (d).
Extension of corporate limits, §160A-36, (a).
Purposes for development, §160A-36, (c).
Standards for total area to be annexed, §160A-36, (b).
Water and sewer districts, §160A-36, (e).
Contiguous area.
Defined, §160A-41.
Contracts with private solid waste collection firms.
Amount of payment, §160A-37.3.
Appeals, §160A-37.3, (g).
Authorized under certain circumstances, §160A-37.3, (a).
Contents of contract, §160A-37.3, (c).
Determination of payment, §160A-37.3, (d).
Economic loss.
Defined, §160A-37.3, (f).
Information to be disclosed by firm or firms, §160A-37.3, (h).
Offer to be made to firm prior to annexation ordinance becoming effective, §160A-37.3, (g).
Resolution of intent, §160A-37.3, (b).
Termination, §160A-37.3, (e).
Contracts with rural fire departments, §160A-37.1.
Declaration of policy, §160A-33.
Definitions, §160A-41.
Effective date for certain property, §160A-37, (f2).
Estimates.
Land estimates, §160A-42.
Expenditures.
Authorized expenditures, §160A-40.
Failure to delivery police protection, fire protection, solid waste or street maintenance services, §160A-37, (k).
Hearings, §160A-37, (d).
Notice of public hearing, §160A-37, (b).
Informational meetings, §160A-37.
Actions prior to meeting, §160A-37, (c).
Questions and answers, §160A-37, (c1).
Land estimates, §160A-42.
Notice.
Hearings, §160A-37, (b).
Intent to annex, §160A-37, (a).
Ordinance.
Effect of annexation ordinance, §160A-37, (f).
Passage of annexation ordinance, §160A-37, (e).
Plans, §§160A-35, 160A-35.1.
Policy declaration, §160A-33.
Power to annex, §160A-34.
Prerequisites to annexation, §§160A-35, 160A-35.1.
Procedure for annexation, §160A-37.
Property subject to present-use value appraisal, §160A-37, (f1).

ANNEXATION —Cont'd
Population less than five thousand —Cont'd
Recordation.
Annexation recorded, §160A-39.
Remedies for failure to provide services, §160A-37, (h).
Report, §§160A-35, 160A-35.1.
Resolution of intent, adoption, §§160A-37, (i), (j).
Rural fire departments.
Assumption of debt, §160A-37.2, (a), (b).
Contracts with, §160A-37.1.
Services.
Ability to service territory annexed, §§160A-35, 160A-35.1.
Remedies for failure to provide services, §160A-37, (h).
Settlements by parties to appeal.
Presentation to superior court, §160A-38, (l).
Simultaneous annexation proceedings, §160A-37, (g).
Solid waste collection.
Contract with private solid waste collection firms, §160A-37.3.
Used for residential purposes.
Defined, §160A-41.
Population of five thousand or more.
Appeals.
Amendment of annexation ordinance, §160A-50, (i), (k).
Approval of settlement by court, §160A-50, (m).
Consolidation of petitions, §160A-50, (d).
Court of appeals.
Appeal from supreme court to, §160A-50, (h).
Date for review, §160A-50, (f).
Disposition alternatives, §160A-50, (g).
Evidence, §160A-50, (f).
Information to be transmitted to reviewing court, §160A-50, (c).
Lost property tax revenue caused by appeal, §160A-50, (l).
Petition for appeal, §160A-50, (a), (b).
Petition for review.
Effect of filings, §160A-50, (j).
Stays, §160A-50, (e).
Time for appeal, §160A-50, (a).
Authority to annex, §160A-46.
Character of area to be annexed, §160A-48.
Adjacent areas, §160A-48, (d).
Boundaries, §160A-48, (e).
Extension of corporate limits, §160A-48, (a).
Purposes for development, §160A-48, (c).
Standards for area to be annexed, §160A-48, (b).
Water and sewer districts, §160A-48, (f).
Contiguous area.
Defined, §160A-53.
Contracts with rural fire departments, §160A-49.1.
Contract with private solid waste collection firms.
Appeals, §160A-49.3, (g).
Authorized, §160A-49.3, (a).
Contents of contract, §160A-49.3, (c).
Determination of amount paid by city, §160A-49.3, (d).
Economic loss.
Defined, §160A-49.3, (f).
Information to be disclosed to city by firm, §160A-49.3, (h).
Offer to be made to private firm prior to annexation ordinance becoming effective, §160A-49.3, (g).

ANNEXATION —Cont'd
Population of five thousand or more —Cont'd
Contract with private solid waste collection firms —Cont'd
Payment.
Determination of amount, §160A-49.3, (d).
Resolution of intent to contract, §160A-49.3, (b).
Termination of contract, §160A-49.3, (e).
Declaration of policy, §160A-45.
Definitions, §160A-53.
Effective date of annexation, §160A-49, (f2).
Estimates.
Population and land estimates, §160A-54.
Expenditures.
Authorized, §160A-52.
Hearings.
Conduct of hearings, §160A-49, (d).
Notice of public hearing, §160A-49, (b).
Informational meetings, §160A-49, (c1).
Actions prior to, §160A-49, (c).
Notice.
Intent to annex, §160A-49, (a), (i), (j).
Public hearings, §160A-49, (b).
Ordinance.
Effect of annexation ordinance, §160A-49, (f).
Passage of annexation ordinance, §160A-49, (e).
Plans, §§160A-47, 160A-47.1.
Police protection, fire protection, solid waste or street maintenance services.
Failure to deliver by city, §160A-49, (l).
Policy declaration, §160A-45.
Power to annex, §160A-46.
Prerequisites to annexation, §§160A-47, 160A-47.1.
Property subject to present-use value appraisal, §160A-49, (f1).
Recordation.
Annexation recorded, §160A-51.
Remedies for failure to provide services, §160A-49, (h).
Report, §§160A-47, 160A-47.1.
Rural fire departments.
Assumption of debt, §160A-49.2, (a), (b).
Contracts with, §160A-49.1.
Services.
Ability to service territory annexed, §§160A-47, 160A-47.1.
Remedies for failure to provide services, §160A-49, (h).
Simultaneous annexation proceedings, §160A-49, (g).
Solid waste collection.
Contract with private solid waste collection firms, §160A-49.3.
Used for residential purposes.
Defined, §160A-53.
Water or sewer lines extensions not completed.
Petition for abatement of taxes, §160A-49, (k).
Property tax liability of newly annexed territory, §160A-58.10.
Referendum on question of extension.
Election results recorded, §160A-29.
Regional sports authorities, §160A-479.17.
Register of deeds.
Annexation recorded, §§160A-39, 160A-51.
Recordation of maps and election results, §160A-29.
Right of entry.
Surveys of proposed new areas, §160A-30.
Rural fire protection districts.
Annexation by municipality furnishing fire protection, §69-25.15.

ANNEXATION —Cont'd
Sanitary district and municipality extending simultaneously, §130A-70, (a) to (h).
Sanitary districts.
Extension of district, §130A-69.
Satellite annexation in conjunction with municipal annexation, §130A-70.1.
Satellite annexation.
Annexation of noncontiguous areas, §§160A-58.1 to 160A-158.8.
Solid waste collection.
Annexation of area where private firm providing services, §160A-324.
Surveys of proposed new areas, §160A-30.
Taxation.
Applicability of section, §160A-58.10, (a).
Property tax liability for newly annexed territory, §160A-58.10.
Prorated taxes, §160A-58.10, (b).
Taxes in subsequent fiscal years, §160A-58.10, (c).
Transfer of tax records, §160A-58.10, (d).
Violation of part or agreement.
Petition seeking review of action by city, §160A-58.27, (a).
Appeal from final decision of superior court, §160A-58.27, (g).
Conducted by court without jury, §160A-58.27, (d).
Date for review, court to fix, §160A-58.27, (d).
Finding that city in violation.
Relief granted by court, §160A-58.27, (f).
Finding that city not in violation.
Affirmance of action, §160A-58.27, (f).
Oral argument, briefs, evidence, §160A-58.27, (d).
Ordinance deemed amended, §160A-58.27, (h).
Respondent, information supplied, duty, §160A-58.27, (c).
Service of copies, §160A-58.27, (b).
Stay of operation of ordinance, granting or denying, §160A-58.27, (e).
Wills.
Executors and administrators.
Powers and duties, §28A-13-8.

ANNUAL CHARGE FOR REVOLVING CREDIT PLANS, §24-11, (a).
Disclosure requirements for charge cards, §24-11.2, (b).
Disclosure requirements for credit cards, §24-11.1, (b).

ANNUITIES.
Authorized, §58-7-15.
Charitable gift annuities.
Authorized, §58-3-6, (a).
Business of insurance.
Issuance not to constitute engaging in, §58-3-6, (e).
Definition of "educational institution," §58-3-6, (f).
Enforcement of provisions by insurance department, §58-3-6, (d).
Information to be made available to insurance commissioner, §58-3-6, (c).
Notice to insurance department, §58-3-6, (b).
Decedents' estates.
Killing decedents.
Additional liability for annuity company, §31A-11, (c).
Proceeds payable to slayer, §31A-11, (a).
Funding agreements.
Insurers authorized to write life insurance and annuities, §58-7-16.

ANNUITIES —Cont'd
Gift tax.
Manner of determining value, §105-195.
Group annuity contracts, §58-58-145.
Assignment of interest in, §58-58-155.
Killing decedents.
Additional liability for annuity companies, §31A-11, (c).
Proceeds payable to slayer, §31A-11, (a).
Mortality tables.
Worth of annuities.
Establishing present worth, §8-47.
Principal and income act.
Insurance policies.
Allocation of receipts not normally apportioned during administration of trust, §37A-4-407, (a) to (c).
Public officers and employees, §§147-9.2 to 147-9.4.
Rates.
Exemption from applicability of rating provisions, §58-40-15.
Renunciation of succession, §31B-1.
Retirement system for counties and cities, §128-30.
Retirement system for teachers and state employees.
Annuity reserve fund, §135-8, (c).
Merger with pension reserve fund into pension accumulation fund, §135-8, (g).
Annuity savings fund, §135-8, (b).
Transfer of credits from local governmental employees' retirement system, §135-18.1, (b).
Definitions, §135-1.
Merger of annuity reserve fund and pension reserve fund into pension accumulation fund, §135-8, (g).
State institutions of higher education.
Optional retirement program.
Underwriting program by purchase of annuity contracts, §135-5.1, (a).
School employees.
Annuity contracts, §115C-341.
Custodial accounts in lieu of, §115C-341.
Standard nonforfeiture law for deferred annuities, §58-58-61.
Cash surrender value, §58-58-61, (h).
Effective date, §58-58-61, (o).
Inapplicability of section, §58-58-61, (b).
Interest rates used in determining minimum amounts, §58-58-61, (e).
Lapse of time considerations, §58-58-61, (l).
Limited death benefits, disclosure, §58-58-61, (k).
Maturity date, §58-58-61, (j).
Minimum values, §58-58-61, (d).
Paid-up annuity benefits, §58-58-61, (i).
Present value, §58-58-61, (f), (g).
Proration of values, §58-58-61, (m).
Required contract provision, §58-58-61, (c).
Rules, §58-58-61, (n).
Title of law, §58-58-61, (a).
Standard provisions, §58-58-23.
Teachers.
Annuities and deferred compensation, §§147-9.2 to 147-9.4.
Third party administrators.
Generally, §§58-56-2 to 58-56-66.
See THIRD PARTY ADMINISTRATORS.
Transfers to minors.
Creating custodial property and effecting transfer, §33A-9.

ANNUITIES —Cont'd
Transfers to minors —Cont'd
Custodian investing in, §33A-12.
University of North Carolina.
Purchase of annuity or retirement income contracts for faculty members, officers and employees, §116-17.
Custodial accounts in lieu of, §116-17.
Worth of annuities.
Mortality tables.
Establishing present worth of annuities, §8-47.

ANNULMENT OF MARRIAGE.
Action for child custody or support, procedure, §50-13.5.
Acts barring rights of spouse, §31A-1, (a).
Appearances.
Failure of defendant to appear in action.
Notice of trial not required, §50-10, (b).
Child born of voidable or bigamous marriage legitimate, §50-11.1.
Complaints.
Material facts deemed denied by defendant, §50-10, (a).
District courts.
Proper division for trial of civil actions, §7A-244.
Fraudulent misrepresentation as to age in obtaining license for marriage, §51-2, (c).
Grounds for annulment.
Void and voidable marriages, §51-3.
Guardians.
Incompetent spouses.
General guardian may commence, defend or maintain actions, §50-22.
Incompetent spouses.
Actions on behalf of, §50-22.
Judgments.
Material facts found by judge or jury.
Judgment not given in favor of plaintiff until, §50-10, (a).
Jurisdiction in rem or quasi in rem, §1-75.8.
Jury trial or trial before judge without jury.
Determination, §50-10, (c).
Material facts found by judge or jury.
Judgment not given in favor of plaintiff until, §50-10, (a).
Material facts found by judge or jury.
Genuine issue of material fact.
Determination, §50-10, (d).
Judgment not given in favor of plaintiff until, §50-10, (a).
Material facts in complaint deemed denied by defendant, §50-10, (a).
Notice.
Failure of defendant to appear in action.
Notice of trial not required, §50-10, (b).
Reference by consent, §1A-1, Rule 53, (a).
Registration, §130A-111.
Summary judgment.
When summary judgment provisions applicable, §50-10, (d).
Trial.
Jury trial or trial before judge without jury.
Determination, §50-10, (c).
Notice of trial.
Failure of defendant to appear in action.
Notice not required, §50-10, (b).
Vital statistics.
Registration of annulments, §130A-111.
Void and voidable marriages, §51-3.

ANNULMENT OF MARRIAGE —Cont'd
What marriages may be declared void, §§50-4, 51-3.
Wills.
Revocation by annulment, §31-5.4.
Revival, §31-5.4.

ANONYMOUS COMMUNICATIONS AND PUBLICATIONS.
Libelous articles by newspapers or broadcasts by radio and television, §99-3.
Threatening letters, §14-394.

ANSON COUNTY.
Agricultural tendencies in certain counties.
Terms of, §42-23.
Ambulance service.
Attachment or garnishment and lien for, §§44-51.4 to 44-51.8.
Obtaining ambulance services without intending to pay, §14-111.2.
Condemnation or acquisition of land by local government unit outside county.
Consent of board of commissioners necessary, §153A-15.
Counties generally.
See COUNTIES.
Cropper or tenant refusing to perform terms of contract.
Forfeiture of right of possession to premises, §42-27.
Dangerous firearm use by young children, permitting.
Air rifles, air pistols and bb guns not dangerous firearm, §14-316, (b).
Deeds in Anson.
Evidence of records of deeds, §8-26.
Dog collars.
Unlawful removal of electronic dog collars, §14-401.17.
Dogs used in hunting.
Regulation by wildlife resources commission, §113-291.5, (a).
Game laws, local acts not repealed, §113-133.1, (e).
Officers compensated from fees.
Statement to be rendered, §128-13.
Oil, gas and mineral interests separated from surface fee, extinguished, title in surface fee holder.
Failure to list interest for tax purposes 10 years prior to January 1, 1965.
Protection of subsurface interest from surface fee holder, §1-42.1, (d).
Failure to list interest for tax purposes for 10 years prior to January 1, 1971.
Protection of surface interest from surface estate holder, §1-42.2, (d).
Registration of deeds.
Tax certification, no delinquent taxes due, §161-31, (b).
Room occupancy tax levied by county, uniform provisions, §153A-155.
School property.
Acquisition and improvement, §153A-158.1.
Special school tax, election to abolish.
Petition required, §115C-505.
Wills in Anson.
Evidence of records of wills, §8-26.

ANSWERS, §1A-1, Rule 7, (a).
Administrative procedure.
Hearings, §150B-38, (b).

ANSWERS —Cont'd
Attorney disciplinary proceedings, Bar Rules & Regs., B, §.0114.
Cases removed to United States district court.
Time for filing upon remand to state court, §1A-1, Rule 12, (a).
Crossclaims, §1A-1, Rule 7, (a).
Defenses, §1A-1, Rule 8, (b).
Affirmative defenses, §1A-1, Rule 8, (c).
Denials.
Failure to deny.
Effect, §1A-1, Rule 8, (d).
Form, §1A-1, Rule 8, (b).
Discipline of attorneys, Bar Rules & Regs., B, §.0114.
Emancipation of juvenile.
Time for filing, §7B-3502.
Eminent domain.
Private condemnors.
Petitions.
Answer to petition, §40A-25.
Public condemnors, §40A-45, (a).
Determination of issues raised, §40A-42, (d).
Failure to answer, §40A-46.
Reply to answer, §40A-45, (b).
Service of answer, §40A-45, (b).
Time for filing answer, §40A-46.
Expedited evictions.
Time for filing, §42-68.
Forms, §1A-1, Rule 84.
Interrogatories, §1A-1, Rule 33, (a).
Interrogatories to discover assets of judgment debtors, §1-352.1.
Inverse condemnation, §40A-51, (a).
Judicial standards commission proceedings, Jud. Stds. Comm. Rule 10.
Amendments, Jud. Stds. Comm. Rule 16.
Libel and slander.
Proof of matter charged or mitigating circumstances, §1A-1, Rule 9, (i).
Payment into court.
Admissions.
Defendant ordered to satisfy admitted sum, §1-510.
Quo warranto.
Defendant undertaking before answer, §1-523.
Judgment by default and inquiry on failure of defendant to give bond, §1-525.
Request for admission, §1A-1, Rule 36, (a).
Small claims actions, §7A-218.
Assigned actions, §7A-220.
Special proceedings.
Contested proceedings, §1-394.
Streets and highways.
Condemnation, §§136-106, 136-107.
Termination of parental rights proceedings, §7B-1108.
Failure of respondent to answer, §7B-1107.
Time for filing.
Summons to notify respondent, §7B-1106, (a).
Third party answer, §1A-1, Rule 7, (a).
Time for serving, §1A-1, Rule 12, (a).
When presented, §1A-1, Rule 12, (a).

ANTE LITEM NOTICE.
Local acts not to require notice to local unit of government of claim, §1-539.16.

ANTENUPTIAL AGREEMENTS AND CONTRACTS, §§52B-1 to 52B-11.
Acts barring rights of spouse.
Property rights lost, §31A-1, (b).
Amendment, §52B-6.

ANTENUPTIAL AGREEMENTS AND CONTRACTS —Cont'd
Applicability of provisions, §52B-10.
Child support not affected, §52B-4, (b).
Citation of chapter, §52B-1.
Construction and interpretation, §52B-10.
Severability, §52B-11.
Content, §52B-4, (a).
Definitions, §52B-2.
Effect, §52B-5.
Formalities, §52B-3.
Liability of married persons for debts, contracts or damages incurred before marriage, §52-11.
Limitation of actions, §52B-9.
Revocation, §52B-6.
Severability of chapter provisions, §52B-11.
Short title, §52B-1.
Support ordered, §52B-7, (b).
Unconscionability, §52B-7, (a), (c).
Unenforceable, §52B-7, (a).
Void marriages, §52B-8.
Vote consideration, §52B-3.
Writing, §52B-3.

ANTHRAX.
Mass death and destruction weapons.
Nuclear, biological or chemical weapons, §§14-288.21 to 14-288.24.
See WEAPONS OF MASS DEATH AND DESTRUCTION.
Nuclear, biological or chemical agents.
Terrorist incident using, §§130A-475 to 130A-479.
See TERRORIST INCIDENT USING NUCLEAR, BIOLOGICAL OR CHEMICAL AGENTS.
Students communicating false threats of harm, §115C-391, (d4).

ANTIBIOTICS.
Biological residues in animals, §§106-549.81 to 106-549.89.
See BIOLOGICAL RESIDUES IN ANIMALS.
Food, drug and cosmetic act.
Drugs deemed misbranded, §106-134.

ANTIBLACKLISTING ACT, §14-355.

ANTICIPATION NOTES.
Bond issues.
Local government finance.
General provisions, §§159-160 to 159-165.
See LOCAL GOVERNMENT FINANCE.
Housing finance agency, §122A-8.

ANTICIPATORY REPUDIATION.
Leases, UCC, §25-2A-402.
Retraction, §25-2A-403.
Sales, UCC, §25-2-610.
Retraction, §25-2-611.

ANTICLOSED SHOP ACT, §§95-78 to 95-84.
See LABOR.

ANTIDEFICIENCY JUDGMENT ACT, §45-21.38.

ANTIFREEZE, §§106-579.1 to 106-579.14.
Administration of article.
Commissioner of agriculture to administer, §106-579.7, (b).
Adulteration.
Deemed adulterated, §106-579.5.
Analysis.
Reporting results of examination, §106-579.8.

ANTIFREEZE —Cont'd
Appeals.
Judicial review of acts, orders or rulings, §106-579.12, (e).
Board of agriculture.
Defined, §106-579.3.
Exclusive jurisdiction, §106-579.14.
Commissioner of agriculture.
Administration of article, §106-579.7, (b).
Defined, §106-579.3.
Exclusive jurisdiction, §106-579.14.
Condemnation.
Enforcement of article, §106-579.10, (b).
Court orders.
Reports summarizing court orders, §106-579.13, (b).
Decrees.
Reports summarizing decrees, §106-579.13, (b).
Definitions, §106-579.3.
District attorneys.
Instituting and prosecuting proceedings, §106-579.12, (c).
Enforcement of article.
Condemnation orders, §106-579.10, (b).
Seizure of antifreeze, §106-579.10, (b).
"Stop sale" orders, §106-579.10, (a).
"Withdrawal from distribution" orders, §106-579.10, (a).
Supplying distribution data, §106-579.10, (d).
Evidence.
Copy of analysis administered as evidence, §106-579.10, (c).
Fees.
Inspection fee, §106-579.4.
License fee, §106-579.4.
Incineration, disposal by prohibited, §130A-309.10, (f1).
Injunctions, §106-579.12, (d).
Inorganic salts.
Antifreeze solutions compounded with.
Manufacture or sale prohibited, §66-66.
Inspections.
Authorized, §106-579.8.
Fee, §106-579.4.
Sampling and analysis, §106-579.8.
Judgments.
Reports summarizing judgments, §106-579.13, (b).
Judicial review of acts, orders or rulings, §106-579.12, (e).
Jurisdiction.
Exclusive jurisdiction vested in board and commissioner, §106-579.14.
Landfills, disposal in prohibited, §130A-309.10, (f).
Licenses.
Application for license.
Confidential formula information, §106-579.11.
Furnishing statement of formula or contents of antifreeze, §106-579.11.
Confidential formula information, §106-579.11.
Cancellation of license, §106-579.4.
Fee, §106-579.4.
Issuance, §106-579.4.
List of brands and classes or types of antifreeze.
Publishing or furnishing list, §106-579.13, (a).
Misbranding.
Deemed misbranded, §106-579.6.
Misdemeanors.
Manufacture or sale of antifreeze solutions compounded with inorganic salts or petroleum distillates, §66-66.

ANTIFREEZE —Cont'd
Notice.
Repeal of existing regulation, §106-579.7, (a).
Warning notice for minor violations, §106-579.12, (b).
Open containers.
Placing in public places, §14-401.
Petroleum distillates.
Antifreeze solutions compounded with.
Manufacture or sale prohibited, §66-66.
Prohibited acts, §106-579.9.
Publications.
Dissemination of certain information, §106-579.13, (c).
List of brands and classes or types of antifreeze, §106-579.13, (a).
Report summarizing judgments, decrees and court orders, §106-579.13, (b).
Purpose of article, §106-579.2.
Registration.
Application for registration, §106-579.4.
Modifying application, §106-579.4.
Refusal to register, §106-579.4.
Reports.
Sampling and analysis, §106-579.8.
Summarization of judgments, decrees and court orders, §106-579.13, (b).
Rules and regulations.
Execution of rules or regulations, §106-579.7, (b).
Issuance, amendment or repeal of any rule or regulation, §106-579.7, (a).
Notice to repeal existing regulation, §106-579.7, (a).
Sampling and analysis.
Evidentiary value of copy of analysis, §106-579.10, (c).
Reporting results of examination, §106-579.8.
Seizure of article.
Enforcement of article, §106-579.10, (b).
Short title, §106-579.1.
"Stop sale" orders.
Enforcement of article, §106-579.10, (a).
Temporary restraining orders.
Violations of article, §106-579.12, (d).
Title of article, §106-579.1.
Uniformity of requirements, §106-579.2.
Unlawful acts, §106-579.9.
Violations of article.
Continuing violations constitutes separate violation, §106-579.12, (a).
Instituting proceedings, §106-579.12, (c).
Minor violations.
Notice of warning, §106-579.12, (b).
Preliminary or permanent injunctions, §106-579.12, (d).
Prosecution of violations, §106-579.12, (c).
Temporary restraining orders, §106-579.12, (d).
"Withdrawal from distribution" orders.
Enforcement of article, §106-579.10, (a).
Supplying distribution data, §106-579.10, (d).

ANTILAPSE STATUTE.
Generally, §31-42.

ANTI-PYRAMID STATUTE, §14-291.2.

ANTIQUE AIRPLANES.
Property tax assessment.
Antique airplane defined, §105-277.12, (a).
Designated special class of property for assessment, §105-277.12, (b).

ANTIQUE FIREARMS.
Defined, §§14-402, (c), 14-409.11.
Permit or license to sell pistols.
Inapplicability of provisions to, §14-402, (b).

ANTIQUE SLOT MACHINES.
Defense in prosecution for possession of slot machine, §14-309.1.

ANTIQUE VEHICLES.
Abandoned and derelict motor vehicles.
Exemption from provisions, §20-137.14.
Dealers.
Temporary supplemental license.
Off-premises sales, §20-292.1.
Historic vehicle owner special registration, §20-132.
Property taxes.
Defined, §105-330.9, (a).
Special class, assessment, §105-330.9, (b).
Special plates, §20-79.4, (a).

ANTIQUE WEAPONS.
Mass death and destruction weapons.
Applicability of section, §14-288.8.

ANTITRUST.
Cooperative agreements among physicians or between physician, hospital or other person.
Immunity from scrutiny of federal and state antitrust laws, §§90-21.26, (a), 90-21.36, (a).
Federal or state antitrust laws defined, §90-21.25.
Monopolies and restraint of trade, §§75-1 to 75-89.
See MONOPOLIES AND RESTRAINT OF TRADE.
Motor fuel marketing generally, §§75-80 to 75-89.
See MOTOR FUEL MARKETING.

APARTMENTS.
Landlord and tenant.
General provisions.
See LANDLORD AND TENANT.
Liens.
Possessory liens on personal property.
Persons entitled to lien, §44A-2, (e).
Unit ownership, §§47A-1 to 47A-28.
See UNIT OWNERSHIP.

APIARIES.
Bees and honey.
See BEES AND HONEY.

APPALACHIAN STATE UNIVERSITY.
University of North Carolina.
Constituent institution of university of North Carolina, §116-4.
Traffic and parking.
Specific provisions applicable to Appalachian state university, §116-44.5.

APPALACHIAN TRAILS SYSTEM, §§113A-72 to 113A-77.
Acquisition of rights of way and lands, §113A-76.
Manner of acquiring, §113A-76.
Administration of lands acquired by state outside of boundaries, §113A-75, (e).
Appropriations.
Expenditures authorized, §113A-77.
Citation of article, §113A-72.

APPALACHIAN TRAILS SYSTEM —Cont'd
Connecting or side trails, §113A-74.
Coordination with national trails system act, §113A-74.
Conveyance of land acquired within certain distance of right-of-way to forest service, §113A-75, (d).
Cooperation and assistance of board of transportation, §113A-75, (c).
Due consideration to conservation of environment, advice and assistance from local governments and organizations, §113A-75, (b).
Expenditures.
Authorization, §113A-77.
Legislative declaration, §113A-73.
Motor vehicles.
Use regulated, §113A-75, (g).
Policy, §113A-73, (a).
Purpose, §113A-73, (b).
Real property.
Acquisition, §113A-76.
Regulations, establishing, §113A-75, (f).
Rights of way.
Acquisition, §113A-76.
Cooperation with federal agencies to develop, §113A-75, (a).
Short title, §113A-72.
Title, §113A-72.

APPEAL BONDS, App. Proc. Rule 17.
Appeal to appellate division, §1-270.
Cap on amount.
Judgment directing payment of money.
Noncompensatory damages of $25,000,000 or more, §1-289, (b), (c).
Certiorari, §1-269.
In forma pauperis, §1-288; App. Proc. Rule 17, (d).
Injunctions.
Restraining orders and injunctions in effect pending appeals, §1-500.
Judgment directing payment of money, stay, §1-289, (a).
Cap on bond amount, noncompensatory damages of $25,000,000 or more, §1-289, (b), (c).
Deposit into court in lieu of, §1-289, (a).
Dismissal of appeal, failure to give bond, §1-289, (a).
Perishable property, sale, proceeds deposited or invested, §1-289, (a).
Justification of sureties, §1-286.
Physician or surgeon review of revocation or suspension of license, §90-14.9, (a).
Medical board not required to give, §90-14.11, (a).
Quo warranto, §1-529.
Recordari, §1-269.
Record on appeal.
Undertaking as part of record, §1-297.
Stays.
Fiduciaries.
Security limited for, §1-294.
Judgment directing conveyance, §1-291.
Judgment directing payment of money, §1-289, (a).
Cap on bond amount, noncompensatory damages of $25,000,000 or more, §1-289, (b), (c).
Deposit into court in lieu of, §1-289, (a).
Dismissal of appeal, failure to give bond, §1-289, (a).

APPEAL BONDS —Cont'd
Stays —Cont'd
Judgment directing payment of money —Cont'd
Perishable property, sale, proceeds deposited or invested, §1-289, (a).
Judgment for personal property, §1-290.
Judgment for real property, §1-292.
Service of undertaking on appellee, §1-295.
Undertaking in one or more instruments, §1-295.
Supersedeas, §1-269.
Supreme court.
Appeals of right from court of appeals, App. Proc. Rule 17, (a).
Discretionary review on certification, App. Proc. Rule 17, (b), (c).
Undertaking on appeal, §1-285, (a).
Exception as to state, city, county, local board of education or an officer or agency thereof, §1-285, (b).
Justification of sureties, §1-286.

APPEAL INFORMATION STATEMENT, App. Proc. Rule 41.

APPEALS.
Abortion.
Parental or judicial consent to abortion.
Waiver of parental consent requirement, §90-21.8, (h).
Abused, neglected or dependent juvenile actions.
Final order of court.
Contents of final order, requirements, §7B-1001.
Modification of original order after affirmation by appellate court, §7B-1004.
Notice of appeal, §7B-1001.
Parties, §7B-1002.
Return of juvenile to parent pending disposition of appeal, §7B-1003.
Right to appeal, §7B-1001.
Temporary order affecting custody pending disposition of appeal, compelling reasons, §7B-1003.
Time for giving notice, §7B-1001.
Access to judicial proceeding or record.
Ruling on motion, appeal of, §1-72.1, (e).
Accident and health insurance.
Utilization review.
Noncertification, §58-50-61, (j) to (l).
Administrative boards and agencies.
Appeal from superior court review.
Record on appeal, App. Proc. Rule 9, (b).
Further procedures for perfecting and prosecuting the appeal, App. Proc. Rule 18, (e).
General provisions, §§150B-43 to 150B-52.
See ADMINISTRATIVE PROCEDURE.
Miscellaneous provisions of law governing in agency appeals, App. Proc. Rule 20.
Record on appeal.
Composition, App. Proc. Rule 18, (c).
Settling the record, App. Proc. Rule 18, (d).
Superior courts.
Proper division for review or appeal of administrative agency decisions, §7A-250, (a).
Taking appeal.
Extensions of time, App. Proc. Rule 18, (f).
Generally, App. Proc. Rule 18, (a).
Time and method, App. Proc. Rule 18, (b).
Administrative rules.
Permanent rules.
Judicial review.
Rule returned by commission, §150B-21.8, (d).

APPEALS —Cont'd
Adoption.
Consent of parent or guardian obtained by fraud or duress, §48-2-607, (c).
Procedure, notice, §48-2-607, (b).
Prohibited grounds for appeals, §48-2-607, (a).
Relinquishment of parent or guardian obtained by fraud or duress, §48-2-607, (c).
Unfavorable preplacement assessments, §48-3-308, (a).
Affirmance of judgment.
Power of court, §1-297.
Agriculture.
Marketing and branding of farm products.
Classification of farm products, §106-191.
Air pollution control.
Local air pollution control programs.
Judicial review of final administrative decisions, §143-215.112, (d2).
Airports.
Zoning.
Board of appeals, §63-33, (c).
Judicial review of board, §63-34.
Alarm systems licensing.
Suspension or revocation of license, §74D-10, (b).
Amicus curiae briefs, App. Proc. Rule 28, (i).
Antifreeze.
Judicial review of acts, orders or rulings, §106-579.12, (e).
Appeal information statement.
Adoption by court of appeals, App. Proc. Rule 41, (a).
Appellant's to complete, file and serve, App. Proc. Rule 41, (b).
Purpose, App. Proc. Rule 41, (a).
Appearances.
Attorneys at law, App. Proc. Rule 33, (a).
Appellants.
Briefs.
Contents, App. Proc. Rule 28, (b).
Joinder of parties on appeal, App. Proc. Rule 5, (a).
Supreme court review.
Discretionary review on certification.
Definition of appellant, App. Proc. Rule 15, (i).
Scope of review of decisions.
Definition of appellant, App. Proc. Rule 16, (c).
Appellees.
Briefs.
Contents.
Preservation of additional questions, App. Proc. Rule 28, (c).
Joinder of parties on appeal, App. Proc. Rule 5, (b).
Supreme court review.
Discretionary review on certification.
Definition of appellee, App. Proc. Rule 15, (i).
Scope of review of decisions.
Definition of appellee, App. Proc. Rule 16, (c).
Apportionment and redistricting.
Action challenging state legislative or congressional plan.
Direct appeal to supreme court, §120-2.5.
Arbitration.
How taken, §1-569.28.
Preaward ruling by arbitrators.
Appealability of arbitrator's ruling, §1-569.18, (b), (c).
When may be taken, §1-569.28.

APPEALS —Cont'd
Arguments.
Oral argument, App. Proc. Rule 30.
Attorneys at law.
Admission to practice, Admission to Practice, §§.1401 to .1405.
Agreements, App. Proc. Rule 33, (c).
Appearances, App. Proc. Rule 33, (a).
Disciplinary proceedings, §84-28, (h).
From board of law examiners, §84-24.
Signatures on electronically filed documents.
More than one attorney representing party, App. Proc. Rule 33, (b).
Specialization.
Denial of certification or continued certification, Bar Rules & Regs., D, §§.1805, .1806.
Bail and recognizance.
Bond forfeiture.
Release from final judgment, §15A-544.8, (f).
Setting aside, §15A-544.5, (h).
Correction of errors by appellate division.
Authority of court to act pending appeal, §15A-1453, (a).
Bank commissioner.
Branch banking, interstate, §53-224.30.
Orders appealed to commission.
Appellate review panel, §53-92, (d).
Banking commission.
Final orders of, §53-92, (d).
Banks.
Bank holding companies.
Decisions of commissioner, §53-231.
International banking.
Commissioner's decisions, §53-232.17.
Regional reciprocal banking.
Decisions of commissioner, §53-215.
Trust terminated on insolvency of trustee bank.
Appointment of new trustee, §53-29.
Biological residues in animals.
Detention or quarantine of animal, animal product or feed, §106-549.83.
Blind persons.
Aid to the blind.
Denial of application for aid, §111-16.
Boat liens.
Action to regain possession of vessel.
Appeal to district court for trial de novo, §44A-6.1, (b).
Bonds, surety, App. Proc. Rule 17.
Appeal to appellate division, §1-270.
Cap on amount of bond.
Noncompensatory damages of $25,000,000 or more awarded, §1-289, (b), (c).
Certiorari, §1-269.
In forma pauperis, §1-288; App. Proc. Rule 17, (d).
Injunctions.
Restraining orders and injunctions in effect pending appeals, §1-500.
Judgment directing payment of money, §1-289, (a).
Cap on amount, noncompensatory damages of $25,000,000 or more, §1-289, (b), (c).
Justification of sureties, §1-286.
Physician or surgeon review of revocation or suspension of license, §90-14.9, (a).
Medical board not required to give, §90-14.11, (a).
Quo warranto, §1-529.
Recordari, §1-269.
Record on appeal.
Undertakings as part of record, §1-297.

APPEALS —Cont'd
Bonds, surety —Cont'd
Stays.
Fiduciaries.
Security limited for, §1-294.
Judgment directing conveyance, §1-291.
Judgment directing payment of money, §1-289, (a).
Cap on amount, noncompensatory damages of $25,000,000 or more, §1-289, (b), (c).
Judgment for personal property, §1-290.
Judgment for real property, §1-292.
Service of undertaking on appellee, §1-295.
Undertaking in one or more instruments, §1-295.
Supersedeas, §1-269.
Supreme court.
Appeals of right from court of appeals, App. Proc. Rule 17, (a).
Discretionary review on certification, App. Proc. Rule 17, (b), (c).
Undertaking on appeal, §1-285, (a).
Exception as to state, city, county, local board of education or an officer or agency thereof, §1-285, (b).
Justification of sureties, §1-286.
Boundaries.
Special proceeding to establish boundaries.
Appeal to session, §38-3, (b).
Briefs.
Additional authorities, App. Proc. Rule 28, (g).
Amicus curiae briefs, App. Proc. Rule 28, (i).
Appendices to briefs, App. Proc. Rule 28, (d).
Contents.
Appellant's brief, App. Proc. Rule 28, (b).
Appellee's brief, App. Proc. Rule 28, (c).
Presentation of additional questions, App. Proc. Rule 28, (c).
Form, App. Proc., Appx. E.
Copies reproduced by clerk, App. Proc. Rule 13, (b).
Filing and service.
Consequence of failure to file and serve, App. Proc. Rule 13, (c).
Copies reproduced by clerk, App. Proc. Rule 13, (b).
Failure to file.
Consequences, App. Proc. Rule 13, (c).
Time, App. Proc. Rule 13, (a).
Functions, App. Proc. Rule 28, (a).
Joinder of multiple parties in briefs, App. Proc. Rule 28, (f).
Page limitations, App. Proc. Rule 28, (j).
References to record, App. Proc. Rule 28, (e).
Reply briefs, App. Proc. Rule 28, (h).
Submission of case on written briefs in lieu of oral argument, App. Proc. Rule 30, (d).
Supreme court review.
Appeal of right from court of appeals, App. Proc. Rule 14, (d).
Discretionary review on certification by supreme court, App. Proc. Rule 15, (g).
Termination of parental rights and juvenile matters.
Name of juvenile and identifying matter not included, App. Proc. Rule 28, (k).
Type style and size, App. Proc. Rule 28, (j).
Word count limits, App. Proc. Rule 28, (j).
Brownfields property reuse.
Decision by department as to whether or not to enter into agreement, §130A-310.36.

APPEALS —Cont'd
Budget.
Judgment of joint committee, §143-14.
Building code council, §143-141.
Building codes.
Door lock exemptions.
Revocation of permit, §143-143.4, (f).
Calendar of cases for hearing, App. Proc. Rule 29, (b).
Capital punishment.
Automatic review of judgment and sentence, §15A-2000, (d).
Direct appeal to supreme court.
Death sentences included in superior court judgments, §7A-27, (a).
Indigent persons.
Representation of indigent persons, §7A-451, (c) to (e).
Appellate appointments, Indigent Rep., Model Plan, art. VIII, §8.2.
New trial.
Notice of new trial, §15-193.
Prisoner taken to place of trial when new trial granted, §15-195.
Notice of appeals, §15-189.
Notice of reprieve or new trial, §15-193.
Cap on amount of bond to stay execution.
Judgment directing payment of money.
Noncompensatory damages of $25,000,000 or more, §1-289, (b), (c).
Certificate of determination of appeal.
Procedure after determination, §1-298.
Certification by supreme court, §7A-31, (a) to (d).
Discretionary review, App. Proc. Rule 15.
Certiorari.
See CERTIORARI.
Child custody jurisdiction and enforcement, §50A-314.
Child custody order enforcement pending appeal.
Enforcement by civil contempt proceedings, §50-13.3, (a).
Childhood vaccine-related injury compensation.
Decisions of commission, §130A-428, (c).
Children's health insurance program.
Benefits eligibility, §108A-70.26, (c).
Child support.
Enforcement pending appeal.
Civil contempt, §50-13.4, (f).
Expedited process.
Orders of child support hearing officer, §50-38.
Civil cases.
How and when taken, App. Proc. Rule 3.
Judgments and orders rendered, App. Proc. Rule 3, (a).
Notice of appeal.
Content, App. Proc. Rule 3, (d).
Service, App. Proc. Rule 3, (e).
Record on appeal, App. Proc. Rule 9, (b).
Stay pending appeal, App. Proc. Rule 8.
Time when taken by written notice, App. Proc. Rule 3, (c).
Claim and delivery.
Issuance or refusal to issue order to sheriff, §1-474, (a).
Clerks of court.
Briefs.
Copies reproduced by clerk, App. Proc. Rule 13, (b).

APPEALS —Cont'd
Clerks of court —Cont'd
Docket book, App. Proc. Rule 39, (b).
Duties generally, App. Proc. Rule 39, (a).
In forma pauperis.
Fees of clerk, §1-288.
Judgment docket, App. Proc. Rule 39, (b).
Minute book, App. Proc. Rule 39, (b).
Records, App. Proc. Rule 39.
Superior court clerks.
Civil actions, §1-301.1.
Estate matters, §1-301.3.
Special proceedings, §1-301.2.
Coastal area management.
Denial of permits, §113A-123.
Collection agencies.
Denial of permit, §58-70-30.
Commercial feed.
Judicial review of act, orders or rulings, §106-284.44, (e).
Computation of time.
Generally, App. Proc. Rule 27.
Concealed handgun permit.
Denial, revocation or nonrenewal of permit, §§14-415.15, (c), 14-415.18, (a).
Consolidation of actions on appeal, App. Proc. Rule 40.
Constitution of North Carolina.
Court of appeals.
Jurisdiction, Const. N. C., art. IV, §12.
Right of appeals from certain decisions directly to supreme court, §7A-30.
Jurisdiction of the general court of justice, Const. N. C., art. IV, §12.
Supreme court.
Jurisdiction, Const. N. C., art. IV, §12.
Constitution of the United States.
Court of appeals decisions.
Right of direct appeal from certain decisions, §7A-30.
Review of facts tried by jury, Const. U. S., amd. VII.
Consumer finance act.
Commission may review rules, orders or acts of commissioner, §53-188.
Contempt.
Civil contempt, §5A-24.
Criminal contempt, §5A-17.
Content of notice of appeal, App. Proc. Rule 3, (d).
Continuing legal education board of trustee decisions, Bar Rules & Regs., D, §.1610.
Cooperative agreements among physicians or between physician, hospital or other person.
Judicial action as to certificates of public advantage, §90-21.33.
Copies.
Briefs.
Reproduction by clerk, App. Proc. Rule 13, (b).
Extraordinary writs, App. Proc. Rule 24.
Record on appeal, App. Proc. Rule 12, (c).
Filing of security for cost with record on appeal, App. Proc. Rule 6, (c).
Corporations.
Administrative dissolution of business corporation.
Denial of reinstatement, §55-14-23.
Foreign corporations.
Revocation of certificate of authority, §55-15-32.

APPEALS —Cont'd
Corporations —Cont'd
Refusal of secretary of state to file documents, §55D-16.
Costs, §6-33; App. Proc., Appx. F.
Criminal appeals.
No security for cost, App. Proc. Rule 6, (e).
Discretion of appellate court in recovery of cost, §6-33.
Execution to collect costs in appellate courts, App. Proc. Rule 35, (d).
Federal courts.
State costs on appeals to federal courts, §6-17.
Forma pauperis, App. Proc. Rule 6, (b).
Frivolous appeals, App. Proc. Rule 34.
Generally, §6-33; App. Proc. Rule 6.
Magistrates.
Recovery of cost, §6-33.
Mandates of the courts.
Direction as to cost, App. Proc. Rule 35, (b).
Prosecution bonds.
Sureties on bonds liable for costs, §6-3.
Record on appeal.
Inclusion of unnecessary matter.
Penalty for inclusion, App. Proc. Rule 9, (b).
Security for costs.
Criminal appeals.
No security for costs, App. Proc. Rule 6, (e).
Dismissal of appeal for failure to file or for defect in security, App. Proc. Rule 6, (d).
Filing with record on appeal, App. Proc. Rule 6, (c).
In forma pauperis appeals, App. Proc. Rule 6, (b).
Regular course, App. Proc. Rule 6, (a).
Taxable in tribunals, App. Proc. Rule 35, (c).
To whom allowed, App. Proc. Rule 35, (a).
Counties.
Bonds, surety.
Exception as to, §1-285, (b).
Inspection departments.
General appeal to commissioner of insurance, §153A-374.
Orders to take corrective action, §153A-370.
Stop orders, §153A-361.
Planning and zoning.
Board of adjustment, §153A-345, (b).
Superior court.
Review of decisions of board of commissioners, §153A-340, (f).
Special assessments.
General court of justice, §153A-197.
Court of appeals, §§7A-16 to 7A-21.
See COURT OF APPEALS.
Credit unions.
Suspension and conservation.
Decisions of administrator, §54-109.92, (k).
Criminal justice education and training standards commission.
Denial, suspension or revocation of certification, §17C-11, (b).
Criminal procedure.
Appellate division.
Certiorari, §15A-1444, (e), (g).
Burden of proof.
Prejudicial error, §15A-1443, (a).
Capital punishment.
Automatic review, §15A-2000, (d).
Direct review by supreme court, §7A-27, (a).
New trial.
Notice, §15-193.
Taking prisoner to place of new trial, §15-195.

APPEALS —Cont'd
Criminal procedure —Cont'd
Capital punishment —Cont'd
Notice of appeal, §15-189.
Reprieve.
Notice, §15-193.
Certiorari, §15A-1444, (e), (g).
Correction of errors by appellate division, §15A-1448, (c).
Content of notice of appeal, App. Proc. Rule 4, (b).
Correction of errors by appellate division, §§15A-1441 to 15A-1453.
Affirmance of sentence, §15A-1447, (e).
Duties of clerk of superior court upon, §15A-1452, (b).
Ancillary actions during appeal, §15A-1453.
Authorized, §15A-1441.
Bail and recognizance.
Authority of court to act pending appeal, §15A-1453, (a).
Capital cases, §15A-1441.
Certiorari, §15A-1448, (c).
Compliance with directive of appellate court.
Duties of clerk of superior court, §15A-1452.
Double jeopardy.
When charges must be dismissed with prejudice, §15A-1447, (g).
Grounds, §15A-1442.
Jurisdiction, §15A-1448, (a).
Lack of jurisdiction on part of trial court.
Errors which may be reviewed even though no objection, exception or motion made, §15A-1446, (d).
New trial.
Duties of clerk of superior court upon order of new trial, §15A-1452, (c).
Relief available upon appeal, §15A-1447, (a).
Notice of appeal, §15A-1448, (b).
Time for, §15A-1448, (a).
Prejudice to defendant.
Burden of showing prejudice, §15A-1443, (a).
Grounds for correction of errors generally, §15A-1442.
No prejudice by granting of relief which defendant has sought, §15A-1443, (c).
When prejudice exists, §15A-1443, (a), (b).
Preservation of right to appeal, §15A-1446, (a).
Errors subject to review even though no objection, exception or motion made, §15A-1446, (d).
Waiver of right to assert error upon appeal.
Failure to make appropriate and timely motion or objection, §15A-1446, (b).
Procedures, §15A-1444, (d).
Relief available upon appeal, §15A-1447.
Reversal.
Relief available upon appeal, §15A-1447, (b), (c).
Security for costs not required, §15A-1449.
Sentencing.
Relief available upon appeal, §15A-1447, (d), (f).
State may appeal, §15A-1445, (a).
Order granting motion to suppress, §15A-1445, (b).
Stays, §15A-1451, (a).
No stay when state appeals, §15A-1451, (b).
Time for entry of appeal, §15A-1448, (a).
Waiver of right to assert error upon appeal.
Failure to make appropriate and timely motion or objections, §15A-1446, (b).

APPEALS —Cont'd
Criminal procedure —Cont'd
Correction of errors by appellate division —Cont'd
Withdrawal of appeal, §15A-1450.
Order to be entered by clerk of superior court, §15A-1452, (a).
Right to appeal not waived, §15A-1448, (a).
Cost on appeal, §6-33.
No security for cost, App. Proc. Rule 6, (e).
Defined, §15A-101.
District courts, §7A-290.
Appeal by defendant from, §15A-1431, (b).
Compliance with judgment no bar, §15A-1431, (d).
Notice of appeal, §15A-1431, (c).
Appeal after compliance with judgment, §15A-1431, (d).
Pretrial release.
Order remains in effect pending appeal, §15A-1431, (e).
Procedure, §15A-1444, (c).
Stays, §15A-1431, (f).
Withdrawal of appeal, §15A-1431, (c), (g).
Appeal by state from, §15A-1432, (a).
Affirmance of judgment of district court, §15A-1432, (e).
Hearing on motion, §15A-1432, (c).
Motion, §15A-1432, (b).
Remand to district court for further proceedings, §15A-1432, (d).
Bail bond status, §7A-290.
Notice of appeal, §7A-290.
Appeal by defendant from district court, §15A-1431, (c), (d).
How and when taken, App. Proc. Rule 4.
Magistrates.
Appeal by defendant from, §15A-1431, (a).
Compliance with judgment no bar, §15A-1431, (d).
Notice of appeal, §15A-1431, (c).
Appeal after compliance with judgment, §15A-1431, (d).
Pretrial release.
Order remains in effect pending appeal, §15A-1431, (e).
Procedure, §15A-1444, (b).
Stays, §15A-1431, (f).
Withdrawal of appeal, §15A-1431, (c), (g).
Cost on appeal, §6-33.
Manner of taking, App. Proc. Rule 4, (a).
Motion for appropriate relief.
Correction of errors by appellate division.
Ancillary actions during appeal, §15A-1453, (b).
Denial of motion.
No effect on right to assert error upon appeal, §15A-1422, (e).
Finality of decision, §15A-1422, (f).
Making of motion not prerequisite to asserting error on appeal, §15A-1422, (a).
Motion in appellate division, §15A-1418.
Ruling of court subject to review, §15A-1444, (f).
Ruling on motion, §15A-1422, (b) to (d).
Motion to suppress evidence.
Order denying motion, §15A-979, (b).
Order granting motion, §15A-979, (c).
Notice of appeals, App. Proc. Rule 4.
Petition for rehearing.
Not entertained, App. Proc. Rule 31, (g).
Plea bargaining.
Noncompliance with provisions.
Limitation on collateral attack on conviction, §15A-1027.

APPEALS —Cont'd
Criminal procedure —Cont'd
Prejudicial error.
Burden of proof, §15A-1443, (a).
Constitutional error, §15A-1443, (b).
Defined, §15A-1443, (a).
Preservation of right to appeal.
Post-trial motions.
Not prerequisite to assertion of error on appeal, §15A-1446, (c).
Prosecutorial appeal, §15A-1445.
Appeal by state from district court, §15A-1432.
Record on appeal, App. Proc. Rule 9, (b).
Relief from errors, §15A-1401.
Restitution to victims of crime.
Effect of appeal of conviction upon which order based, §15A-1340.38, (d).
Right of appeal, §15A-1444, (a), (a1), (a2).
Service of notice of appeal, App. Proc. Rule 4, (c).
State of North Carolina.
Correction of errors by appellate division.
Appeal by state, §15A-1445, (a).
Order granting motion to suppress, §15A-1445, (b).
Stays.
No stay when state appeals, §15A-1451, (b).
District courts.
Appeal by state from, §15A-1432.
Stays.
Correction of errors by appellate division, §15A-1451, (a).
No stay when state appeals, §15A-1451, (b).
Sufficiency of evidence.
Reviewable on appeal regardless of whether motion made during trial, §15A-1227, (d).
Time for taking appeal, App. Proc. Rule 4, (a).
To which appellate court addressed, App. Proc. Rule 4, (d).
Trial de novo, Const. N. C., art. IV, §12.
Dam safety law.
Applications for construction, §143-215.33.
Death.
Substitution of parties, App. Proc. Rule 38, (a).
Decedents' estates.
Examination of persons or corporations believed to have possession of property, §28A-15-12, (b).
Declaratory judgments.
Review, §1-258.
Definitions.
Supreme court review.
Appellants and appellees defined, App. Proc. Rules 15, (i), 16, (c).
Trial tribunal, App. Proc. Rule 1, (c).
Delinquent and undisciplined juvenile actions.
County appeal, limitations, §7B-2604, (c).
Disposition after appeal, §7B-2606.
Disposition pending appeal, §7B-2605.
Parties, §7B-2604, (a).
Right to appeal, §7B-2602.
Transfer decision, §7B-2603.
State appeal, limitations, §7B-2604, (b).
Depositions pending appeal, §1A-1, Rule 27, (b).
Directed verdict.
Action on motion, §1A-1, Rule 50, (b).
Dismissal.
Appeal bond to stay execution on money judgment.
Failure to give bond, §1-289, (a).
District attorneys, removal from office, §7A-66.
District courts.
Appeal from judge, §1-277, (a).
Clerk to judge, §7A-251, (b).

APPEALS —Cont'd
District courts —Cont'd
Costs in civil action, §7A-305, (b), (c).
Costs in criminal actions, §7A-304, (b).
Determination, §7A-304, (d).
Criminal procedure, §7A-290.
Appeal by defendant, §15A-1431.
Appeal by state, §15A-1432.
Final judgment of court in civil action.
Direct appeal to court of appeals, §7A-27, (c).
Game commission rulings.
Heard in district court division, §7A-250, (a).
Interlocutory orders.
Direct appeal to court of appeals, §7A-27, (d).
Liens.
Possessory liens on personal property.
Action to regain possession of motor vehicle or vessel.
Appeal to district court for trial de novo, §44A-6.1, (b).
Procedure after determination of appeal, §1-298.
Settling record on appeal.
Power of trial judge, §1-283.
Small claim actions.
Indigent persons, §7A-228, (b1).
Jury trial on appeal, §7A-230.
Priority of judgment when appeal taken, §7A-226.
Stay of execution on appeal, §7A-227.
Trial de novo, §7A-228, (a).
Dismissal of appeal, §7A-228, (c).
How appeal perfected, §7A-228, (b).
Oral notice of appeal, §7A-228, (a).
Perfection of appeal, §7A-228, (b).
Procedure generally, §7A-229.
Trial tribunals.
Inclusion within term, App. Proc. Rule 1, (c).
Dockets, App. Proc. Rule 12, (b).
Clerks of court.
Docket book, App. Proc. Rule 39, (b).
Judgment docket, App. Proc. Rule 39, (b).
Stays.
Docket entry of stay, §1-293.
Dogs.
Dangerous dogs.
Determination that dog is potentially dangerous dog, §67-4.1, (c).
Double jeopardy.
Correction of errors by appellate division.
When charges must be dismissed with prejudice, §15A-1447, (g).
Drainage.
Canals.
Right to drain into canal, §156-10.
Petitions.
Agreement for construction, §156-29.
Drainage districts.
Acquiring title for purpose of easements or rights-of-way, §156-70.1.
Bonds, surety, §156-66.
Construction of drainage law, §156-135.
Easements, §156-70.1.
Hearings.
Final hearings, §156-75.
Improvement, renovation, enlargement and extension of canals, structures and boundaries, §§156-93.2, 156-93.3.
Notice, §156-70.1.
Publication in case of unknown owners, §156-58.
Public or private ways.
Maintenance of drainage across, §156-88.

APPEALS —Cont'd
Drainage districts —Cont'd
Railroads.
Drainage across railroads, §156-90.
Right of appeal, §156-66.
Rights of way, §156-70.1.
Drivers' licenses.
Denial, cancellation, etc., §20-25.
Drugs.
Controlled substances.
Judicial review of drug commission, §90-113.2.
Dry-cleaning solvent cleanup, §143-215.104S.
Education.
Budget dispute between board of education and board of county commissioners.
Procedure for resolution, §115C-431, (c) to (e).
Education programs at residential schools.
Decisions of school personnel.
Appeals to secretary, §143B-146.14.
Employees.
Repayment of money owed to state.
Delinquent employees, §143-554, (a).
Local boards of education.
Appeals to local boards, §115C-45, (c).
Appeals to superior court, §115C-45, (c).
Education programs at residential schools.
Decisions of school personnel.
Appeals to secretary, §143B-146.14.
Elections.
Contributions and expenditures in political campaigns.
State board of elections.
Appeals from board, §163-278.26.
Protest of election.
Appeal of decision to state board, §163-182.11.
Appeal of decision to superior court, §163-182.14.
Public campaign financing fund.
Adverse agency decisions, §163-278.68, (c).
Voter registration.
Denial of registration, §163-82.18.
Elective share of surviving spouse.
Appeal from decision of clerk to superior court, §30-3.4, (g).
Electronic filing, App. Proc. Rule 26, (a).
Signatures.
More than one attorney representing party, App. Proc. Rule 33, (b).
Electronic surveillance.
Order granting motion to suppress, §15A-294, (h).
Elevator safety act.
Convictions for violation of article, §95-110.10.
Emancipation of juvenile, §7B-3508.
Eminent domain, §40A-13.
Private condemnors, §40A-28, (c).
Jury trial, §40A-29.
Employer safety and health program.
Penalties, §95-256, (c).
Employment security.
Claims for benefits, §96-15, (c) to (i).
Decisions of commission, §96-4, (m), (n).
Engineers and land surveyors.
Disciplinary action.
Judicial review, §89C-22, (d).
Entries.
Form, App. Proc., Appx. D.
Error.
Cross-assignment of error, §1-271.
Writs of error abolished, §1-268.
Evidence.
Exceptions, §1-186, (b).

APPEALS —Cont'd
Exceptions.
Decisions on matters of law, §1-186, (a).
Evidence, §1-186, (b).
Executions.
Costs.
Collection of costs in appellate courts, App. Proc. Rule 35, (d).
Executors and administrators.
Resignation, §28A-10-6.
Revocation of letters, §28A-9-4.
Extensions of time.
Administrative boards and agencies.
Taking appeal, App. Proc. Rule 18, (f).
Granting, App. Proc. Rule 27, (c).
Extraordinary writs, App. Proc. Rule 24.
Failure to comply with appellate rules.
Dismissal for failure, App. Proc. Rule 25.
Fair housing commission, §41A-7, (m).
Felony guilty or no contest pleas in district court.
Appeals authorized, §15A-1029.1, (b).
Fertilizers.
Commercial fertilizers.
Assessments of penalties, orders or rulings, §106-670.
Filing, App. Proc. Rule 26, (a).
Format and style of documents, App. Proc., Appx. B.
Form of papers, App. Proc. Rule 26, (g).
Index required, App. Proc. Rule 26, (g).
Juvenile's name and identifying information.
Exclusion, App. Proc. Rule 26, (g).
Letter size, type size, paper type, double space, App. Proc. Rule 26, (g).
Findings by court.
Review on appeal, §1A-1, Rule 52, (c).
Fish and fisheries resources.
Dredging permits, §113-229.
Food stamps, §108A-79, (h).
Foreign money judgments recognition.
Stay pending appeal, §1C-1806.
Forests and forestry.
Protection and development corporations, §113-66.
Forma pauperis, §1-288.
Appeal bonds, App. Proc. Rule 17, (d).
Cost.
Security for cost, App. Proc. Rule 6, (b).
Extraordinary writs, App. Proc. Rule 24.
Record on appeal, App. Proc. Rule 9, (c).
Format of documents for filing, App. Proc., Appx. B.
Forms.
Briefs, App. Proc., Appx. E.
Entries, App. Proc., Appx. D.
Petition for discretionary review, App. Proc., Appx. D.
Petition for writ of supersedeas and motion for temporary stay, App. Proc., Appx. D.
Frivolous appeals.
Cost, App. Proc. Rule 34.
Sanctions, App. Proc. Rule 34.
Game commission rulings.
Heard in district court division, §7A-250, (a).
General assembly.
Investigating committees.
Appeal from denial of right to be heard, §120-18.
General court of justice.
Appellate division, Const. N. C., art. IV, §5.

APPEALS —Cont'd
Geologists.
Judicial review of final agency decision, §89E-20, (c).
Grade crossings.
Elimination or safeguarding of crossings.
Procedure for appeal, §136-20, (g).
Guardians.
Determination of incompetence.
Orders of clerk, §35A-1115.
Sterilization of mentally ill or retarded ward.
Mentally necessity, appeal of clerk's order, §35A-1245, (f).
Health, §130A-24.
Applicability of provisions to actions taken by department of environment and natural resources, §130A-24, (e).
Decisions of local boards of health, §130A-24, (d).
Interpretation and enforcement of rules.
Adopted by commission, §130A-24, (a).
Adopted by local board of health, §130A-24, (b).
Petition for contested case, §130A-24, (a1).
Local boards of health.
Hearings, §130A-24, (c).
Procedure, §130A-24.
Health care facilities.
Certificates of need.
Administrative and judicial review, §131E-188.
Health care liability.
Exhaustion of administrative remedies and appeals, §90-21.54.
Highway use tax, §105-187.10, (c).
Hospitals.
Certificate of need law.
Administrative and judicial review, §131E-188.
Licenses.
Adverse action on licenses, §131E-78, (c).
Denial or revocation of license.
Judicial review, §131E-78, (c).
Housing authorities and projects.
Eminent domain.
Certificate of convenience and necessity.
Issuance, §157-28.
How and when taken.
Civil actions, App. Proc. Rule 3.
Incompetence, determination of.
Order adjudicating incompetence, §35A-1115.
Industrial commission.
Awards, §97-86.
Interest on awards after hearing, §97-86.2.
Payment of award pending appeal in certain cases, §97-86.1.
Court of appeals.
Review of final orders, §7A-250, (b).
Inclusion in term "trial tribunal," App. Proc. Rule 1, (c).
Insurers.
Expenses of appeals brought by insurers, §97-88.
Right of appeal from industrial commission to court of appeals, §7A-29, (a).
Tort claim rules.
Appeal to court of appeals, Tort Claim Rule T401 to T404.
Appeal to full commission, Tort Claim Rule T301 to T310.
In forma pauperis, §1-288.
Appeal bonds, App. Proc. Rule 17, (d).
Cost.
Security for cost, App. Proc. Rule 6, (b).
Extraordinary writs, App. Proc. Rule 24.

APPEALS —Cont'd
In forma pauperis —Cont'd
Record on appeal, App. Proc. Rule 9, (c).
Information statement, App. Proc. Rule 41.
Infractions.
Review of disposition by superior court, §15A-1115.
Appeal of district court decision, §15A-1115, (a).
Review of infractions originally disposed of in superior court, §15A-1115, (b).
Injunctions.
Injunction pending appeal, §1A-1, Rule 62, (c).
Restraining orders and injunctions in effect pending appeals, §1-500.
Bonds, surety, §1-500.
Insurance.
Accident and health insurance.
Utilization review.
Noncertification, §58-50-61, (j) to (l).
Beach area property essential property insurance.
Commissioner to superior court, §58-45-50.
Commissioner's orders and decisions.
Appeal from supreme court, §58-2-75, (d).
Credit insurance, §58-57-75.
Direct right of appeal to court of appeals, §7A-29, (a).
Jurisdiction of trial judge, §58-2-75, (c).
Motor vehicle reinsurance facility, §58-37-65, (f).
Orders with respect to plan of operation, §58-37-40, (d).
Petition, §58-2-75, (a).
Place of hearing.
Change, §58-2-75, (b).
Post assessment insurance guaranty association, §58-48-45, (c).
Rates, §58-40-105, (b).
Stays.
Commencement of proceedings not to operate as stay, §58-2-75, (e).
Transcript of hearing.
Commissioner to provide, §58-2-75, (b).
Unauthorized insurers.
Domestic companies, §58-14-15.
Credit insurance.
Orders of commissioner, §58-57-75.
Revocation or suspension of license, §58-57-80.
Fair access to insurance requirements, §58-46-30.
Holding companies.
Orders of commissioner, §58-19-70, (a).
Post-assessment insurance guaranty association.
Appeals to commissioner, §58-48-42.
Commissioner.
Judicial review, §58-48-45, (c).
Rate bureau, §58-36-35.
Administration review, §58-36-85.
Commissioner of insurance.
Appeals from orders of commissioner, §58-36-25.
Motor vehicle insurance.
Termination review, §58-36-85, (d) to (g).
Rates.
Orders and decisions of commissioner, §58-40-105, (b).
Unauthorized insurers.
Domestic companies.
Judicial review of orders of commissioner, §58-14-15.
Unfair trade practices.
Cease and desist orders.
Judicial review, §58-63-35.

APPEALS —Cont'd
Insurance —Cont'd
Unfair trade practices —Cont'd
Undefined practices.
Judicial review by intervenor, §58-63-45.
Insurance consumer and customer information privacy.
Final order of commissioner, §58-39-100.
Interlocutory orders.
Discretionary review on certification, App. Proc. Rule 15, (h).
Review on appeal from judgment, §1-278.
International commercial arbitration and conciliation, §1-567.67, (a), (b).
Internet.
Electronic filing site, App. Proc. Rule 26, (a).
Investment advisers.
Judicial review of orders, §78C-29.
Joinder of actions and parties, App. Proc. Rule 5.
Briefs.
Joinder of multiple parties in brief, App. Proc. Rule 28, (f).
Consolidation of actions on appeal, App. Proc. Rule 40.
Procedure after joinder, App. Proc. Rule 5, (c).
Service of process, App. Proc. Rule 26, (e).
Judges.
Trial judges authorized to enter orders.
Death, incapacity or absence of particular judge authorized, App. Proc. Rule 36, (b).
When particular judge not specified by rule, App. Proc. Rule 36, (a).
Judgments and orders in session, App. Proc. Rule 3, (a).
Judgments and orders not in session, App. Proc. Rule 3, (b).
Orders for perfecting appeal.
Clerk authorized to make, §1-281.
Junkyard control.
Final decisions of secretary of transportation, §136-149.1.
Jurisdiction.
Adverse ruling as to jurisdiction.
Right of immediate appeal, §1-277, (b).
Rules of appellate procedure do not affect, App. Proc. Rule 1, (b).
Stay of proceedings to permit trial in foreign jurisdiction.
Review of rulings on motion, §1-75.12, (c).
Juvenile code.
Abused, neglected or dependent juvenile actions, §§7B-1001 to 7B-1004.
Delinquent and undisciplined juvenile actions, §§7B-2602 to 7B-2606.
Juvenile matters.
Appeal information statement.
Juvenile's name not used, App. Proc. Rule 41, (b).
Briefs in juvenile matters.
Name of juvenile or identifying information excluded, App. Proc. Rul e28, (k).
Identifying information of juvenile subject to action.
Exclusion from filings, documents, exhibits and argumanrs, App. Proc. Rules 3, (b), 26, (g).
Motion or response to motion.
Juvenile's name not used, App. Proc. Rule 37, (c).
Name of juvenile subject of action.
Referenced by initials, App. Proc. Rules 3, (b), 26, (g).

APPEALS —Cont'd
Juvenile matters —Cont'd
Oral argument in juvenile matters.
Name of juvenile not used, App. Proc. Rule 30, (g).
Verbatim transcripts.
Submitted to court in signed, sealed envelope, App. Proc. Rule 9, (c).
Landlord and tenant.
Lien on crops.
Tenant's undertaking on continuance or appeal, §42-18.
Summary ejectment.
Appeal to district court, §42-32.
Surety on crops.
Landlord, §42-19.
Tenant, §42-18.
Law-enforcement officers.
Salary continuation plan.
Determination of cause and extent of incapacity, §143-166.19.
Liens.
Action to regain possession of motor vehicle or vessel.
Involuntary relinquishment of possession by lienor, §44A-6.1, (a).
Limestone, marl and landplaster.
Assessments and orders of commissioner of agriculture, §106-92.13.
Limited liability companies.
Revocation of certificate of authority of foreign limited liability companies, §57C-7-14, (b).
Local government finance.
Executive committee to commission, §159-4, (b).
Magistrates.
Cost on appeal, §6-33.
Criminal procedure, §§15A-1431, 15A-1444.
Removal of magistrate, §7A-173, (d).
Trial de novo on appeal, Const. N. C., art. IV, §12.
Mail.
Additional time after service by mail, App. Proc. Rule 27, (b).
Filing papers by, App. Proc. Rule 26, (a).
Mandamus, App. Proc. Rule 22.
Determination by court, App. Proc. Rule 22, (c).
Petition for writ.
Contents, App. Proc. Rule 22, (b).
Filing and service, App. Proc. Rule 22, (b).
Response, App. Proc. Rule 22, (c).
To which appellate court addressed, App. Proc. Rule 22, (a).
Mandates of the courts.
Cost.
Direction as to cost in mandates, App. Proc. Rule 35, (b).
Generally, App. Proc. Rule 32, (a).
Time of issuance, App. Proc. Rule 32, (b).
Meat inspection.
Enforcement against condemned meat, §106-549.32, (a).
Mental health, developmental disability, substance abuse, etc.
Appeals panel, §122C-151.4.
Area authorities.
Appeals panel, §122C-151.4.
Procedure for appeal by, §122C-151.2, (c).
Right of appeal, §122C-151.2, (a), (b).
County programs.
Appeals panel, §122C-151.4.
Procedure for appeal by, §122C-151.2, (c).
Right of appeal, §122C-151.2, (a), (b).

APPEALS —Cont'd
Mental health, developmental disability, substance abuse, etc —Cont'd
Facilities.
Licenses.
Adverse action on license, §122C-24.
Involuntary commitment.
District court hearing, §122C-272.
Substance abusers, §122C-288.
Surplus income and advancements.
Mental health and retardation, §35A-1328.
Merger of actions on appeal, App. Proc. Rule 40.
Mines and minerals.
Decisions on mine safety, §74-24.10, (a).
Modification of safety and health standards, §74-24.5.
Permits, §§74-51, 74-61.
Miscellaneous provisions of law governing in agency appeals, App. Proc. Rule 20.
Modification of judgment.
Powers of court, §1-297.
Money transmitters.
Rules review by commission, §53-208.27, (b).
Mortgage bankers and brokers.
Review of rules or orders by commissioner, §53-243.03.
Mortgages and deeds of trust.
Reverse mortgages.
Commissioner's decisions, §53-272.
Sales under power of sale, §45-21.16, (e).
Motion for appropriate relief, §15A-1422.
Motions in appellate courts.
Contents, App. Proc. Rule 37, (a).
Determination, App. Proc. Rule 37, (b).
Juvenile's name or identifying information not used, App. Proc. Rule 37, (c).
Response, App. Proc. Rule 37, (a).
Time, App. Proc. Rule 37, (a).
Motor clubs and associations.
Judicial review of commissioner of insurance, §58-69-25.
Motor vehicle dealers' and manufacturers' licenses.
Actions of commissioner, §20-300.
Motor vehicle inspections.
Licenses to perform inspections.
Denial, revocation or suspension, or assessment of civil penalty, §20-183.8G, (g).
Municipal corporations.
Assessments.
Appeal to general court of justice, §160A-230.
Bonds, surety.
Undertaking on appeal.
Exception as to, §1-285, (b).
Building inspection, §160A-434.
Extension of corporate limits.
Municipalities less than five thousand, §160A-38.
Population less than five thousand.
Contract with private solid waste collection firms, §160A-37.3, (g).
Population of five thousand or more, §160A-50.
Contract with private solid waste collection firms, §160A-49.3.
Streets.
Building setback lines.
Appeals by property owners for variance or modification, §160A-306, (c).
Zoning.
Boards of adjustment, §160A-388.

APPEALS —Cont'd
Mutual burial associations.
Dispute over liability for benefits, §90-210.102.
Revocation of license or authority, §90-210.94.
Noncompliance with appellate rules, App. Proc. Rule 25.
Nonprofit corporations.
Denial of reinstatement following administrative dissolution by secretary of state, §55A-14-23, (b) to (d).
Foreign corporations.
Revocation of certificate of authority, §55A-15-32.
Notice, App. Proc. Rule 3.
Abused, neglected or dependent juvenile actions, §7B-1001.
Civil actions, App. Proc. Rule 3, (c), (d), (e).
Content of notice of appeal.
Criminal cases, App. Proc. Rule 4, (b).
Criminal procedure, App. Proc. Rule 4.
Correction of errors by appellate division, §15A-1448, (a), (b).
District courts, §7A-290.
Appeal by defendant from, §15A-1431, (c), (d).
Magistrates.
Appeal by defendant from, §15A-1431, (c), (d).
Delinquent and undisciplined juvenile actions, §7B-2602.
Appeal of order transferring jurisdiction of juvenile to superior court, §7B-2603, (a).
Forms, App. Proc., Appx. D.
Physician or surgeon review of revocation or suspension of license, §90-14.9, (a).
Service of notice of appeal.
Criminal cases, App. Proc. Rule 4, (c).
Small claims actions, §7A-228.
Termination of parental rights proceedings, §7B-1113.
Time and manner for giving notice.
Appeal to appellate division in civil actions and special proceedings, §1-279.1.
Tolling of time for filing and serving notice of appeal, App. Proc. Rule 3, (c).
Tolling of time for filing and serving notice, App. Proc. Rule 3, (c).
Utilities commission decisions, §62-90, (a), (b).
Occupational safety and health.
Judicial review of administrative decisions, §95-141.
Oil and gas conservation.
Hearings before department, §113-401.
Application for court review, §113-403.
Effect of pendency of judicial review, §113-406.
Oil pollution and hazardous substances control.
Civil penalties.
Time for filing petition, §143-215.88A, (a).
Damages.
Contesting liability for damage to public resources.
Time for filing petition, §143-215.90, (b).
Oral argument.
Briefs.
Submission on written brief, App. Proc. Rule 30, (d).
Contents, App. Proc. Rule 30, (a).
Decision of appeal without publication of opinion, App. Proc. Rule 30, (e).
Decision without oral argument, App. Proc. Rule 30, (f).
Juvenile's name not used, App. Proc. Rule 30, (a).

APPEALS —Cont'd
Oral argument —Cont'd
Nonappearance of parties, App. Proc. Rule 30, (c).
Order of argument, App. Proc. Rule 30, (a).
Pre-argument review, App. Proc. Rule 30, (f).
Time allowed for argument, App. Proc. Rule 30, (b).
Orders.
Trial judges authorized to enter orders.
Death, incapacity or absence of particular judge authorized, App. Proc. Rule 36, (b).
When particular judge not specified by rule, App. Proc. Rule 36, (a).
Outdoor advertising.
Final decisions of secretary of transportation, §136-134.1.
Parental authority over juvenile.
Civil action to enforce, juvenile leaving home and refusing to return, §7B-3404.
Parties.
Abused, neglected or dependent juvenile actions, §7B-1002.
Joinder on appeal, App. Proc. Rule 5.
Multiple parties.
Service of process upon numerous parties proceeding separately, App. Proc. Rule 26, (f).
Substitution of parties.
Death of party, App. Proc. Rule 38, (a).
Public officers.
Death or separation from office, App. Proc. Rule 38, (c).
Reasons other than death, App. Proc. Rule 38, (b).
Who may appeal, §1-271.
Partition.
Report of commissioners.
Order of confirmation, §46-19, (c).
Passenger tramways.
Commission of labor order, §95-123.
Perpetuation of testimony.
Depositions, §1A-1, Rule 27, (b).
Personnel system.
Grievances and disciplinary action, §§126-34 to 126-39.
Veteran believing preference not received.
Appeals directly to state personnel commission, §126-82, (d).
Pesticide dealers and manufacturers.
Denial, suspension or revocation of license, §143-451, (b).
Petitions.
Discretionary review.
Form, App. Proc., Appx. D.
Rehearing, App. Proc. Rule 31.
Supersedeas, App. Proc. Rule 23, (c).
Supreme court review.
Discretionary review on certification, App. Proc Rule 15.
Physicians and surgeons.
Revocation or suspension of license.
Appeal bond, §90-14.9, (a).
Medical board not required to give bond, §90-14.11, (a).
Notice of appeal, §90-14.9, (a).
Parties who may appeal from decision of superior court, §90-14.11, (a).
Scope of review, §90-14.10.
Stay of medical board decision, §90-14.9, (b).
Stay of superior court decisions, §90-14.11, (b).

APPEALS —Cont'd
Podiatrists.
Denial, revocation or suspension of license, §90-202.8, (c).
Pollution control.
Applicability of article.
Additional methods, §159C-24.
Environmental documents.
Administrative and judicial review, §113A-13.
Environmental policy act.
Review of agency actions involving major adverse changes or conflicts, §113A-5.
Powers of attorney.
Gifts.
Court order authorizing gift, §32A-14.11.
Pre-argument review, App. Proc. Rule 30, (f).
Preneed funeral contracts and funds.
Judicial review, §90-210.69, (e).
Prisons and prisoners.
Release pending appeal, §15A-1353, (e).
Repair or replacement of personal property of employees that is damaged or stolen by inmates.
Secretary to establish appeal process, §143B-261.2, (e).
Private protective services.
Licenses.
Suspension or revocation, §74C-12, (b).
Probation.
Post-trial relief from judgment of probation, §15A-1342, (f).
Revocation of probation or imposition of special probation upon violation, §15A-1347.
Prohibition, App. Proc. Rule 22.
Determination by court, App. Proc. Rule 22, (c).
Petition for writ.
Contents, App. Proc. Rule 22, (b).
Filing and service, App. Proc. Rule 22, (b).
Response, App. Proc. Rule 22, (c).
To which appellate court addressed, App. Proc. Rule 22, (a).
Property tax commission.
Right of appeal from commission to court of appeals, §7A-29, (a).
Property taxes.
Motor vehicles.
Special committee for motor vehicle appeals, §105-325.1.
Personal property.
Value, situs or taxability, §105-317.1, (c).
Power of board of equalization to hear, §105-322, (g).
Proprietary schools.
Suspension, revocation or refusal of license, §115D-93, (b).
Prosecution bonds.
Liability for costs.
Sureties on prosecution bonds liable, §6-3.
Public lands.
Allocated state lands.
Right of appeal to governor and council of state, §146-31.
Public officers and employees.
Death or separation from office.
Substitution of parties, App. Proc. Rule 38, (c).
Public schools.
Assignment of students to schools.
Decision denying reassignment, §115C-370.
Student disciplinary measures, §115C-392.
Teachers.
Dismissal or demotion, §115C-325, (n).

APPEALS —Cont'd
Public school student's suspension.
Appeal to local board of education, §115C-391, (e).
Judicial review of local board of education decision, §115C-391, (e).
Public utilities commission decisions, §§62-90 to 62-98.
Court of appeals.
Review of final orders, §7A-250, (b).
Purchases and contracts through department of administration.
Law applicable to printing supreme court reports not affected, §143-62.
Quo warranto, §1-529.
Bonds of parties, §1-529.
Radiation protection.
Denial, suspension or revocation of licenses, §104E-13, (c).
Radioactive wastes.
Privilege license tax on radioactive and hazardous waste facilities.
Appeals of tax rate to board, §160A-211.1, (c).
Recordari.
Authorized, §1-269.
Bonds, surety, §1-269.
Issuance as substitute for appeal, §1-269.
Rehearing.
Petition for rehearing, App. Proc. Rule 31.
Content, App. Proc. Rule 31, (a).
Determination, App. Proc. Rule 31, (c).
Filing, App. Proc. Rule 31, (b).
How addressed, App. Proc. Rule 31, (b).
No petition in criminal cases, App. Proc. Rule 31, (g).
Procedure upon granting, App. Proc. Rule 31, (d).
Stay of execution, App. Proc. Rule 31, (e).
Time for filing, App. Proc. Rule 31, (a).
Waiver by appeal from court of appeals, App. Proc. Rule 31, (f).
Restitution.
Effect of appeal of conviction upon which order based, §15A-1340.38, (d).
Reversal or modification of judgment.
Court may make restitution, §1-297.
Reversal of judgment.
Powers of court, §1-297.
Right to appeal.
Appeal from courts of trial divisions, §7A-27.
Appeal from superior or district court judge, §1-277, (a).
Immediate appeal, §1-277, (b).
Jurisdictional rulings.
Right of immediate appeal from adverse ruling, §1-277, (b).
Who may appeal, §1-271.
Rules of administrative agency.
Permanent rules.
Judicial review.
Rule returned by commission, §150B-21.8, (d).
Savings and loan associations.
Branch offices.
Final decision on application, §54B-22, (j).
Cease and desist orders.
Judicial review, §54B-71.
Fines.
Judicial review, §54B-71.
Incorporation.
Final decision of commission, §54B-16.
Interstate branches.
Agency decision, §54B-277.

APPEALS —Cont'd
Savings and loan associations —Cont'd
Supervisory control of associations, §54B-68, (b), (d).
Savings banks.
Branch offices.
Applications for permission to establish.
Final decision of commissioner of banks on, §54C-23, (g).
Cease and desist orders.
Judicial review, §54C-84.
Fines.
Judicial review, §54C-84.
Incorporation.
Application to organize savings bank.
Final decision of commission, §54C-16.
Interstate branch banks.
Commissioner of banks' decisions, §54C-211.
School employee injured during episode of violence.
Entitlement to salary and other benefits.
Appeal of board of education decision, §115C-338, (c).
Scope of review.
Record on appeal.
Function in limiting scope, App. Proc. Rule 10, (a).
Supreme court review.
Appeal based solely upon dissent, App. Proc. Rule 16, (b).
How determined, App. Proc. Rule 16, (a).
Scope of rules, App. Proc. Rule 1, (a).
Secured transactions.
Filing office.
Refusal to accept record or cancellation of record, §25-9-520, (e).
Securities regulation.
Cease and desist orders, §78A-47, (b).
Judicial review of administrator's orders, §78A-48, (a).
Cease and desist orders, §78A-47, (b).
Not to operate as stay, §78A-48, (b).
Saving provision, §78A-65, (e).
Seeds.
Licensing of dealers.
Revocation or refusal of license for cause, §106-277.19.
Stop-sale orders.
Right of appeal, §106-277.22.
Sentencing.
Release pending appeal, §15A-1353, (e).
Resentencing after appellate review, §15A-1335.
Service of process.
Copies of all papers required to be served, App. Proc. Rule 26, (b).
Form of papers, App. Proc. Rule 26, (g).
Joint appellants and appellees, App. Proc. Rule 26, (e).
Mail.
Additional time after service by mail, App. Proc. Rule 27, (b).
Manner of service, App. Proc. Rule 26, (c).
Notice of appeal, App. Proc. Rules 3, 4.
Numerous parties to appeal proceeding separately, App. Proc. Rule 26, (f).
Proof of service, App. Proc. Rule 26, (d).
Size of papers, App. Proc. Rule 26, (g).
Stays.
Bonds, surety.
Service of undertaking on appellee, §1-295.

APPEALS —Cont'd
Service of process —Cont'd
Supreme court review.
Appeal of right from court of appeals, App. Proc. Rule 14, (a).
Sessions of court, App. Proc. Rule 29, (a).
Setoff debt collection act.
Actions taken at hearings, §105A-9.
Sheriffs' education and training standards commission.
Denial, suspension or revocation of certificate, §17E-9, (b).
Social services.
Adult protection.
Motion in the cause.
Review of orders issued pursuant to provisions, §108A-107.
Applicability of certain provisions, §108A-73.
Conflict of laws, §108A-79, (l).
Food stamps, §108A-79, (h).
Judicial review, §108A-79, (k).
Right of appeal, §108A-79, (a).
Termination or modification of assistance.
Further appeal to department, §108A-79, (g).
Hearing, §108A-79, (i), (j).
Hearings, §108A-79, (d), (e).
Decision, §108A-79, (f).
Notice of action and right to appeal, §108A-79, (b), (c).
Right of appeal, §108A-79, (a).
Solid waste management.
Hazardous waste facilities.
Preempting local ordinance, §130A-293, (e).
Special education.
Administrative review.
Civil actions.
Right to file, §115C-116, (k).
Decision of administrative law judge, §115C-116, (h).
Generally, §115C-116, (d).
Hearing closed, §115C-116, (g).
Review by review officer, §115C-116, (i).
Appointment of review officer, §115C-116, (i).
Decisions of review officer, §115C-116, (i).
Qualifications, §115C-116, (i).
Scope of review, §115C-116, (e).
State board of education.
Final decision.
Power to enforce, §115C-116, (j).
Venue of hearing, §115C-116, (f).
Right of review of proposed decisions, §115C-116, (c).
Special proceedings.
Manner and time for giving notice of appeals, §1-279.1.
Surveys ordered by clerk, §1-408.1.
Undertaking on appeal, §1-285.
State bar.
Right of appeal from North Carolina state bar to court of appeals, §7A-29, (a).
State departments and agencies.
Attorneys' fees.
Parties appeals or defending against agency decision, §6-19.1.
Bonds, surety.
Exception as to state agencies, §1-285, (b).
Decisions of administrative agencies.
Final judgment of superior court upon review of decision.
Appeals of right from superior courts to court of appeals, §7A-27, (b).

APPEALS —Cont'd
State departments and agencies —Cont'd
Right of appeal from certain administrative agencies to court of appeals, §7A-29, (a).
State institutions.
Damage of personal property, §143-127.6.
State of North Carolina.
Criminal law and procedure.
Appeals by state.
Correction of errors, §15A-1445, (a), (b).
From district court, §15A-1432.
Stay, §15A-1451, (b).
Exception as to state, §1-285, (b).
Stays, §1A-1, Rule 62, (d).
Appeal to appellate division, §1-270.
Attachment.
Orders dissolving or modifying, §1-440.38.
Bonds, surety.
Judgment directing conveyance, §1-291.
Judgment directing payment of money, §1-289, (a).
Cap on amount, noncompensatory damages of $25,000,000 or more, §1-289, (b), (c).
Judgment for personal property, §1-290.
Judgment for real property, §1-292.
Security limited for fiduciaries, §1-294.
Service of undertaking on appellee, §1-295.
Undertaking in one or more instruments, §1-295.
Cap on amount of bond to stay execution.
Noncompensatory damages of $25,000,000 or more awarded, §1-289, (b), (c).
Docket entry of stay, §1-293.
Fiduciaries.
Security limited for fiduciaries, §1-294.
Incompetence, determination of.
Order adjudicating incompetence, §35A-1115.
Judgment directing conveyance, §1-291.
Judgment directing payment of money, §1-289, (a).
Cap on amount, noncompensatory damages of $25,000,000 or more, §1-289, (b), (c).
Judgment for personal property, §1-290.
Judgment for real property, §1-292.
Judgment not vacated by stay, §1-296.
Pending appeal, App. Proc. Rule 8.
Petition for rehearing, App. Proc. Rule 31, (e).
Petition for writ of supersedeas and motion for temporary stay.
Form, App. Proc., Appx. D.
Physician or surgeon review of revocation or suspension of license, §90-14.9, (b).
Superior court decisions, §90-14.11, (b).
Power of appellate court not limited, §1A-1, Rule 62, (f).
Scope of stay, §1-294.
Service of process.
Bonds, surety.
Service of undertaking on appellee, §1-295.
Small claims actions, §7A-227.
Supersedeas, App. Proc. Rule 23.
Streets and highways.
Cartways, church roads or mill roads.
Special proceeding for establishment, alteration or discontinuance.
Procedure for appeal, §136-68.
Condemnation proceedings.
Right of appeal, §136-119.
County public roads incorporated into state highway system.
Filing of complaints, §136-64.

APPEALS —Cont'd
Streets and highways —Cont'd
Drainage of highway.
Judgment of commissioners.
Right to appeal, §136-23.
Style of documents for filing, App. Proc., Appx. B.
Substitution of parties, App. Proc. Rule 38.
Superior courts.
Administrative agency decision.
Proper division for review or appeal of decisions, §7A-250, (a).
Appeal from judge, §1-277, (a).
Clerks entering appeals, §§1-301.1 to 1-301.3.
Clerk to judge, §7A-251, (a).
Costs in criminal actions.
Determination, §7A-304, (d).
Criminal actions.
Correction of errors in appellate division.
General provisions, §§15A-1441 to 15A-1453.
Procedure after determination of appeal, §1-298.
Settling record on appeal.
Power of trial judge, §1-283.
Trial tribunals, App. Proc. Rule 1, (c).
Supersedeas, App. Proc. Rule 23.
Authorized, §1-269.
Bonds, surety, §1-269.
Determination by court, App. Proc. Rule 23, (d).
Issuance to suspend execution, §1-269.
Petition.
Content, App. Proc. Rule 23, (c).
Filing and service, App. Proc. Rule 23, (c).
Form, App. Proc., Appx. D.
Response, App. Proc. Rule 23, (d).
Stays, App. Proc. Rule 23.
Supreme court review.
Pending review by supreme court, App. Proc. Rule 23, (b).
Temporary stay, App. Proc. Rule 23, (e).
Trial tribunal judgments and orders.
Pending review of trial tribunal judgments and orders, App. Proc. Rule 23, (a).
Supreme court of the United States.
Costs of state on appeals, §6-17.
Supreme court review.
Appeal bonds.
Forma pauperis, App. Proc. Rule 17, (d).
Appeal of right from court of appeals, App. Proc. Rule 14.
Appeal bond, App. Proc. Rule 17, (a).
Briefs, App. Proc. Rule 14, (d).
Content of notice, App. Proc. Rule 14, (d).
Definition of appellant and appellee, App. Proc. Rule 16, (c).
Notice of appeal.
Contents, App. Proc. Rule 14, (b).
Filing and service, App. Proc. Rule 14, (a).
Record on appeal, App. Proc. Rule 14, (c).
Scope of review, App. Proc. Rule 16, (a).
Appeal based solely upon dissent, App. Proc. Rule 16, (b).
Discretionary review on certification.
Appeal bonds, App. Proc. Rule 17, (b), (c).
Appellant.
Defined, App. Proc. Rules 15, (i), 16, (c).
Appellee.
Defined, App. Proc. Rules 15, (i), 16, (c).
Briefs.
Filing and service, App. Proc. Rule 15, (g).
Interlocutory orders, App. Proc. Rule 15, (h).

APPEALS —Cont'd
Supreme court review —Cont'd
Discretionary review on certification —Cont'd
Petition of party, App. Proc. Rule 15, (a).
Content, App. Proc. Rule 15, (c).
Filing and service, App. Proc. Rule 15, (b).
Procedure for certification, App. Proc. Rule 15, (e).
Response to petition, App. Proc. Rule 15, (d).
Record on appeal, App. Proc. Rule 15, (f).
Response to petition of party, App. Proc. Rule 15, (d).
Scope of review, App. Proc. Rule 16, (a).
Forma pauperis.
Appeal bonds, App. Proc. Rule 17, (d).
Scope of review of decisions of court of appeals.
Appeals based solely upon dissent, App. Proc. Rule 16, (b).
How scope determined, App. Proc. Rule 16, (a).
Terms and sittings, App. Proc. Rule 29, (a).
Surviving spouses.
Year's allowance.
Assignment, §§30-23, 30-24.
Suspension of appellate rules.
Grounds, App. Proc. Rule 2.
Suspension of public school student.
Appeal to local board of education, §115C-391, (e).
Judicial review of local board of education decision, §115C-391, (e).
Taxation.
Action to recover tax paid, §105-241.4.
Collection of taxes.
Attachment or garnishment, §105-242, (b).
Overpayment of taxes, recovery, §105-266.1, (b).
Tax review board.
Administrative review, §§105-241.2, 105-241.4.
Appeal without payment of tax, §105-241.3.
Termination of parental rights proceedings, §7B-1113.
Appeal information statement.
Juvenile's name not used, App. Proc. Rule 41, (b).
Briefs.
Name of juvenile and identifying information excluded, App. Proc. Rule 28, (k).
Identifying information of juvenile subject to action.
Exclusion from filings, documents, exhibits and argumanrs, App. Proc. Rules 3, (b), 26, (g).
Motion or response to motion.
Juvenile's name not used, App. Proc. Rule 37, (c).
Name of juvenile subject of action.
Referenced by initials, App. Proc. Rules 3, (b), 26, (g).
Oral argument.
Juvenile's name not used, App. Proc. Rule 30, (a).
Verbatim transcripts.
Submitted to court in signed, sealed envelope, App. Proc. Rule 9, (c).
Terms and sittings of courts, App. Proc. Rule 29, (a).
Time.
Administrative agencies.
Extensions of time, App. Proc. Rule 18, (f).
Method and time of taking appeal, App. Proc. Rule 18, (b).
Civil cases, App. Proc. Rule 3.
Computation of time, App. Proc. Rule 27.

APPEALS —Cont'd
Time —Cont'd
Criminal cases, App. Proc. Rule 4, (a).
Correction of errors by appellate division, §15A-1448, (a).
Extensions of time.
Granting, App. Proc. Rule 27, (c).
Mail.
Additional time after service by mail, App. Proc. Rule 27, (b).
Mandates of the courts.
Time of issuance, App. Proc. Rule 32, (b).
Motions in appellate courts, App. Proc. Rule 37, (a).
Oral argument.
Allowable time for argument, App. Proc. Rule 30, (b).
Petition for rehearing, App. Proc. Rule 31, (a).
Record on appeal.
Filing, App. Proc. Rule 12, (a).
Settling the record.
Extensions of time, App. Proc. Rule 11, (f).
Service by mail.
Additional time, App. Proc. Rule 27, (b).
Taking by written notice, App. Proc. Rule 3, (c).
Appeals to appellate division in civil actions and in special proceedings, §1-279.1.
Timetables for appeals, App. Proc., Appx. A.
Tolling of time for filing and serving notice of appeal, App. Proc. Rule 3, (c).
Title of appellate rules, App. Proc. Rule 42.
Tolling of time for filing and serving notice of appeal, App. Proc. Rule 3, (c).
Torrens system registration.
Report of examiners.
Exceptions to report, §43-11, (c).
Tort claims against state departments and agencies.
Appeal to court of appeals, Tort Claim Rule T401 to T404.
Appeal to full commission, Tort Claim Rule T301 to T310.
Cost, §143-291.1.
Court of appeals, §143-293.
Supersedeas, §143-294.
Full commission, §143-292.
Transcript copies, §143-291.1.
Rules of industrial commission.
Appeals to court of appeals, Tort Claim Rule T401 to T404.
Appeals to full commission, Tort Claim Rule T301 to T310.
Supersedeas.
Appeal to court of appeals to act as supersedeas, §143-294.
Toxic substance identification complaints.
Judicial review of commission orders, §95-195, (d).
Transcripts.
Delivery, App. Proc. Rule 7, (b).
Indigency of party.
Ordering of transcript in civil and special proceedings, App. Proc. Rule 7, (a).
Ordering of transcript, App. Proc. Rule 7, (a).
Preparation, App. Proc. Rule 7, (b).
Trial tribunal.
Defined, App. Proc. Rule 1, (c).
Trust companies.
Hearings.
Appeal of decisions generally, §53-412, (d).
Venue, §53-412, (e).

APPEALS —Cont'd
Trusts and trustees, §36A-27.
Resignation of trustee, §36A-27.
Underpasses or overpasses.
Elimination or safeguarding of inadequate underpasses or overpasses.
Procedure for appeal, §136-20, (g).
United States.
Costs of state on appeals to federal courts, §6-17.
Uranium exploration.
Administrative review of decisions of department, §74-85.
Judicial review of decisions of department, §74-85.
Utilities commission.
Court of appeals.
Review of final orders, §7A-250, (b).
Inclusion within term "trial tribunal," App. Proc. Rule 1, (c).
Vacation rentals.
Expedited evictions, §42A-25.
Variances of appellate rules.
Grounds for variance, App. Proc. Rule 2.
Vessel liens.
Action to regain possession, §44A-6.1, (b).
Waiver.
Failure to make motion or objection, §15A-1446, (b).
Water and air resources.
Abatement of existing pollution.
Special orders, §143-215.2, (a).
Hearings.
Judicial review, §143-215.5, (a).
Judicial review of actions under article, §143-215.5, (a).
Permit applications, §143-215.5, (b).
Use of water resources.
Capacity use areas, §143-215.13.
Workers' compensation.
Administrative decisions appealed, I.C. Rule 703.
Appeal to court of appeals, I.C. Rule 702.
Awards, §97-86.
Interest on awards after hearing, §97-86.2.
Judgment on award.
Decision as to certificate of accrued arrearages, §97-87, (c).
Payment of award pending appeal in certain cases, §97-86.1.
Commission appeals, I.C. Rule 701.
Insurers.
Expenses of appeals brought by insurers, §97-88.
Parties to appeal from agencies, App. Proc. Rule 18, (b).
Work First program.
Mismanagement of assistance, appointment of personal representative, §108A-37, (c).
Program of temporary public assistance for purposes of appeal, §108A-27.15, (b).
Writs.
Copies, App. Proc. Rule 24.
Extraordinary writs, App. Proc. Rule 24.
Form of papers, App. Proc. Rule 24.
Writs of error abolished, §1-268.
Www.ncappellatecourts.org.
Electronic filing site, App. Proc. Rule 26, (a).

APPEARANCES.
Abused, neglected or dependent juvenile actions.
Failure of parent, guardian, etc., personally served to appear, §7B-407.

APPEARANCES —Cont'd
Adoption.
Hearing on petition to adopt adult, §48-2-605, (b).
Annulment of marriage.
Failure of defendant to appear in action.
Notice of trial not required, §50-10, (b).
Appeals.
Attorneys at law, App. Proc. Rule 33, (a).
Bail and recognizance.
Failure to appear, §15A-543, (a).
Imposition of conditions of pretrial release.
Prior failure to appear and answer charges, §15A-534, (d1).
Penalties, §15A-543, (b), (c).
Corporations.
Organizations generally.
Appearance by counsel or agent, §15A-773, (b).
Delinquent and undisciplined juvenile actions.
Failure of parent, guardian or custodian to appear.
Contempt, §§7B-1805, (b), (c), 7B-1806.
First appearance of juvenile for felony cases, §7B-1808.
Parent, guardian or custodian to attend hearings, §7B-2700.
Excusing appearance, §7B-2700.
District courts.
Attorneys at law.
Withdrawal of appearance, Super. Ct. Rule 16.
First appearance before district court judge, §§15A-601 to 15A-606.
Divorce.
Failure of defendant to appear in action.
Notice of trial not required, §50-10, (b).
Executors and administrators.
Actions against personal representatives or collectors.
Service on or appearance of one binds all, §28A-18-4.
Failure to appear.
Abused, neglected or dependent juvenile actions, §7B-407.
Delinquent and undisciplined juvenile actions.
Contempt of parent, guardian or custodian for failure to appear, §§7B-1805, (b), (c), 7B-1806.
Dismissal with leave when defendant fails to appear and cannot readily be found, §15A-932.
Divorce or annulment, notice of trial not required, §50-10, (b).
Garnishees, §1-440.27.
Motor vehicle offenses.
Court to report failure to appear, §20-24.2.
Revocation of drivers' license, §20-24.1.
Penalties, §15A-543.
Referees meetings, §1A-1, Rule 53, (f).
Service of pleadings and other papers on party in default not required, §1A-1, Rule 5, (a).
Small claims actions.
Appeals, §7A-228, (c).
First appearance before district court judge.
Charges.
Defendant to be informed of charges against him, §15A-605.
Sufficiency.
Determination, §15A-604, (a).
Proceedings on finding of insufficiency, §15A-604, (b).
Clerk of court.
When clerk may conduct appearance, §15A-601, (e).

APPEARANCES —Cont'd
First appearance before district court judge —Cont'd
Continuance, §15A-601, (d).
Charges found to be insufficient, §15A-604, (b).
Determination whether defendant had retained or been assigned counsel, §15A-603, (a).
Generally, §15A-601, (a).
Indigent persons.
Determination whether defendant has been assigned counsel.
Duty of judge, §15A-603, (a).
Proceedings when defendant asserts indigence and desires counsel, §15A-603, (c).
Right to be furnished counsel.
Defendant to be informed by judge, §15A-603, (b).
Information to be given defendant, §§15A-602, 15A-603, 15A-605.
Initial appearance.
Consolidation of proceedings, §15A-601, (b).
Probable cause hearing.
Attorneys at law.
Defendant to be informed of right to counsel, §15A-606, (e).
Continuance, §15A-606, (f).
Scheduling by judge, §15A-606, (a), (d).
Waiver, §15A-606, (a).
After first appearance, §15A-606, (g).
Evidence not to be admitted in trial, §15A-606, (b).
Proceedings on, §15A-606, (c).
Required, §15A-601, (a).
Right to counsel.
Defendant to be informed by judge, §15A-603, (b), (d).
Self-incrimination.
Warning of right against self-incrimination, §15A-602.
Sufficiency of charge.
Determination, §15A-604, (a).
Procedure if insufficient, §15A-604, (b).
Time for, §15A-601, (c).
Waiver not allowed, §15A-601, (d).
Waiver of representation by counsel, §15A-603, (e).
First appearance before magistrate, §15A-511.
Audio and video transmission.
Conducting of proceeding by, §15A-511, (a1).
Bail and recognizance.
Release, §15A-511, (e).
Communicable disease.
Detention of defendant, §15A-534.3.
First appearance before district court judge.
Consolidation and proceedings, §15A-601, (b).
Generally, §15A-511, (a).
Impaired drivers.
Administration of test, §15A-534.2, (d).
Compliance with provisions, §15A-534.2.
Conditions for release, §15A-534.2, (c).
Detention in custody, §15A-534.2.
Officers other than magistrates.
Authority to conduct initial appearance, §15A-511, (f).
Probable cause.
Arrest without warrant.
Determination of probable cause, §15A-511, (c).
Statement by magistrate, §15A-511, (b).
Warrant.
Procedure when arrest is pursuant to warrant, §15A-511, (d).

APPEARANCES —Cont'd
First appearance before magistrate —Cont'd
Warrantless arrest.
Procedure on, §15A-511, (c).
Garnishees.
Failure to appear, §1-440.27.
Infractions.
Appearance bonds, §15A-1113, (c).
Failure to appear to answer charge.
No order for arrest, §15A-1116, (b).
Jurisdiction.
Grounds for personal jurisdiction without service of summons, §1-75.7.
Judgment against nonappearing defendant.
Proof of jurisdiction, §1-75.11.
Organizations.
Appearance by counsel or agent, §15A-773, (b).
Securing attendance of organizations as defendants, §15A-773.
Parental authority over juvenile.
Order directing juvenile to appear before court.
Juvenile leaving home and refusing to return, §7B-3404.
Partnerships.
Organizations generally.
Appearance by counsel or agent, §15A-773, (b).
Personal jurisdiction without service of summons.
General appearance in action, §1-75.7.
Real estate appraisal board.
Enforcement of chapter, §93E-1-13, (b).
Referees meetings.
Failure to appear, §1A-1, Rule 53, (f).
Service of pleadings and other papers, §1A-1, Rule 5, (a).
Superior courts.
Attorneys at law.
Withdrawal of appearance, Super. Ct. Rule 16.
Two-way audio and video transmissions, §15A-601, (a1), (a2).
Waiver.
Defendant may execute written waiver and plead not guilty, §15A-1011, (d), (e).

APPELLATE COURTS PRINTING AND COMPUTER OPERATIONS FUND, §7A-343.3.

APPELLATE DEFENDER.
Appointment by commission, §7A-498.8, (a).
Appointment of assistants and staff, §7A-498.8, (c).
Consultation on capital cases, §7A-498.8, (b4).
Continuing legal education, §7A-498.8, (b3).
Counsel of record in capital cases, §7A-498.8, (b7).
Federal capital cases, §7A-498.8, (b7).
Funding, §7A-498.8, (d).
Indigent defense services.
Capital cases.
Appointment, compensation eligibility, IDS Rules 2B.1 to 2B.4.
Standards for, IDS Appx. 2B.1 to 2B.3.
Non-capital criminal and non-criminal cases.
Appointment, compensation eligibility, IDS Rules 3.1 to 3.7.
Legal representation, §7A-498.8, (b1).
Maintenance of clearinghouse, §7A-498.8, (b2).
Recruitment of appointed counsel, §7A-498.8, (b5).
Vacancy in office, §7A-486.2, (b).

APPELLATE DIVISION OF GENERAL COURT OF JUSTICE.
Advance sheets.
Contracting for printing by administrative officer of the court, §7A-6, (b).
Designation of commercial advance sheets as official reports, §7A-6, (b1).
Furnishing without charge, §7A-6, (c).
Sale to general public, §7A-6, (b).
Remittance of proceeds, §7A-6, (b).
Appellate division reports.
Distribution of copies, §7A-343.1.
Court of appeals.
See COURT OF APPEALS.
Distribution of appellate division reports, §7A-343.1.
Division within general court of justice, §7A-4.
Judicial conduct.
Authority of supreme court to prescribe standards, §7A-10.1.
Law clerks.
Justices or judges entitled to services of one clerk, §7A-7, (a).
Salaries of clerks, §7A-7, (a).
Organization, §7A-5.
Reporters.
Appointment by supreme court, §7A-6, (a).
Duties, §7A-6, (a).
Salary, §7A-6, (a).
Reports.
Contracting for printing of reports by administrative officer of the courts, §7A-6, (b).
Designation of commercial reports as official reports, §7A-6, (b1).
Sale of reports to general public, §7A-6, (b).
Remittance of proceeds of sales, §7A-6, (b).
Research assistants.
Justice or judges entitled to services of one research assistant, §7A-7, (a).
Salaries of research assistants, §7A-7, (a).
Rules of practice and procedure.
Supreme court to prescribe rules, §7A-33.
Secretaries.
Determination of number and salaries of secretaries, §7A-7, (b).
Stenographers.
Determination of number and salaries of stenographers, §7A-7, (b).
Supreme court.
See SUPREME COURT.

APPELLATE DIVISION REPORTS.
Distribution of copies, §7A-343.1.

APPENDICITIS.
Food, drug and cosmetic act.
False advertising of drug or device, §106-138, (b).

APPLES.
Dried apples.
Standard weight and measure, §81A-42.
Immature apples.
Grade standards, requirements for maturity, adoption, §106-189.2, (a).
Criminal penalty for violating, §106-189.2, (b).
Marketing and branding farm products.
Generally, §§106-185 to 106-196.
See FARM PRODUCTS MARKETING AND BRANDING.
Promotion of use and sale of agricultural products.
Generally, §§106-550 to 106-568.
See AGRICULTURAL PRODUCTS PROMOTION.

APPLES —Cont'd
Unfair practices.
Practices by handlers, §§106-496 to 106-501.
See FRUIT HANDLERS UNFAIR PRACTICES.

APPLE SEEDS.
Standard weight and measure, §81A-42.

APPLIANCES.
Bailment, lease or rental of vehicle or draft animal.
Protection of bailor against bailee's acts, §§14-165 to 14-169.
See BAILMENTS.
Electric appliance sales.
Actions.
Enforcement of provisions, §66-27.01.
Compliance with provisions required, §66-23.
Evidence.
Acceptable listings as to safety of goods, §66-25.
Identification marks.
Removal, alteration, changing or defacement.
Prohibited, §66-24.
Required, §66-24.
Installation.
Legal responsibility for proper installation unaffected, §66-26.
Liability.
Effect of provisions, §66-26.
Merchantability.
Acceptable listings as to safety of goods, §66-25.
Safety.
Acceptable listings as to safety of goods, §66-25.
Testing.
Acceptable listings as to safety of goods, §66-25.
Violations of provisions, §66-27.
Exempt property from enforcement of claims of creditors, §1C-1601, (a).
Interfering with gas, electric and steam appliances.
Criminal trespass, §14-151.
Service agreements, §§58-1-25 to 58-1-42.

APPLICATORS OF PESTICIDES, §§143-452 to 143-459.
See PESTICIDE APPLICATORS.

APPOINTMENT OF COUNSEL FOR INDIGENT PERSONS.
Abused, neglected or dependent juvenile actions.
Appointment for parent, §7B-602, (a).
Notice in summons of right to counsel and appointment information, §7B-406, (b).
Payment of court-appointed counsel, §7B-603, (a) to (b).
Delinquent and undisciplined juvenile actions, §7B-2000, (a).
Payment, §7B-2002.
Presumption of indigence, §7B-2000, (b).
Secure or nonsecure custody hearings.
Appointment of counsel for juvenile, §7B-1906, (c).
Summons to notify parent of right, §7B-1805, (b).
Interstate compact on juvenile.
Return of escapees or absconders, §7B-2805, (c).
Mental health, developmental disability, substance abuse.
Involuntary commitment.
Substance abuser's commitment hearing, §122C-286, (d).
Representation of indigent persons.
General provisions, §§7A-450 to 7A-458.
See INDIGENT DEFENSE SERVICES.

APPOINTMENT OF COUNSEL FOR INDIGENT PERSONS —Cont'd
Representation of indigent persons —Cont'd
Indigent defense services act, §§7A-498 to 7A-498.8.
See INDIGENT DEFENSE SERVICES.
Indigent services rules, Rules 1.1 to 3.7.
See INDIGENT DEFENSE SERVICES.
Model plan, Indigent Rep., Model Plan, arts. I to X.
See INDIGENT DEFENSE SERVICES.
Termination of parental rights proceedings.
Adjudicatory hearing, parents, §7B-1109, (b).
Payment of fees, §7B-1101.

APPOINTMENT TO PUBLIC OFFICE.
Notice, §143-47.7.
Definitions, §143-47.6.
Per diem compensation and travel allowances, §143-47.9.

APPORTIONMENT.
Action challenging plans apportioning state legislature and congressional districts.
Appeal to supreme court.
Direct appeal, §120-2.5.
Contents of judgments invalidating plan, requirements, §120-2.3.
Filed in Wake county superior court, §1-81.1, (b).
Opportunity given general assembly to remedy defects, §120-2.4.
Three-judge panel, §1-267.1, (a).
Appointment of two additional judges to panel, §1-267.1, (b).
Copy of complaint.
Service on senior resident judge, §1-267.1, (b).
Decision, §1-267.1, (c).
Disqualification of judge.
Replacement, appointment, §1-267.1, (b).
Former member of general assembly.
Prohibited from setting, §1-267.1, (b).
Majority of court prevails, §1-267.1, (c).
Organization, §1-267.1, (b).
Presiding judge, §1-267.1, (b).
Required to enter order or judgment affecting act of assembly, §1-267.1, (c).
Venue in Wake county superior court, §1-81.1, (a).
Approval of act, amending, deleting, adding to, modifying or repealing plan.
Attorney general to seek, §120-30.9B, (b).
Congress, Const. U. S., art. I, §§2, 3; amds. XIV, XVII.
Drainage.
Expenses for repairs, §156-11.
General assembly.
Dividing precincts.
Compliance with federal law, §120-2.2, (c).
Prohibited, §120-2.2, (a).
Rejection based upon federal law, §120-2.2, (a), (b).
House of representatives, §120-2, (a) to (c); Const. N. C., art. II, §5.
Senate, §120-1, (a) to (c); Const. N. C., art. II, §3.
Severability of apportionment acts, §120-2.1.
Municipal corporations.
Council.
Electoral districts, §160A-23, (b).
Redistricting after 2000 census, §160A-23.1.

APPRAISALS AND APPRAISERS.
Chattel mortgages.
Insurance companies.
Investments, §58-7-180, (c).

APPRAISALS AND APPRAISERS —Cont'd
Commissioner of banks.
Appraisal of assets of doubtful value, §53-112.
Compensation for killing diseased livestock.
Cattle affected with Bang's disease and tuberculosis, §106-324.
Report of appraisal, §106-326.
Glanders affected animals, §106-325.
Report of appraisal of cattle affected with Bang's disease and tuberculosis, §106-326.
Decedents' estates.
Employment, §28A-20-4.
Eminent domain.
Right of entry prior to condemnation, §40A-11.
Fiduciaries.
Employment and compensation of appraisers.
Powers which may be incorporated by reference in trust instrument, §32-27.
Homestead exemption.
Costs.
Laying off homestead and exemption, §6-28.
Reassessment of homestead, §6-29.
Insurance companies.
Chattel mortgages.
Investments, §58-7-180, (c).
Valuation.
Assets of doubtful value, §58-7-197, (c).
Real property, §58-7-193, (d).
Mortgage bankers and brokers.
Prohibited acts, §53-243.11.
Mortgages and deeds of trust.
Appraisal by financial institution employee.
Fee charge authorized, §24-10, (h).
Motor vehicle damage appraisers generally.
See MOTOR VEHICLE DAMAGE APPRAISERS.
Property taxes.
See PROPERTY TAXES.
Public lands.
State allocated lands.
Acquisitions, §146-22.2, (a), (b).
Real estate appraisers, §§93E-1-1 to 93E-1-14.
See REAL ESTATE APPRAISERS.

APPRENTICESHIP.
Alarm systems licensing.
Apprenticeship registration permit, §74D-8.1.
Apprenticeship agreements.
Approval by director, §94-8.
Contents, §94-7.
Defined, §94-5, (a).
Director of apprenticeship.
Approval of agreements, §94-8.
Rotation of employment.
Agreements may provide for, §94-9.
Signatures, §94-8.
Terms, §94-7.
Apprenticeship committees.
Appointment, §94-5, (b).
Defined, §94-5, (a).
Functions, §94-5, (c).
Sponsors.
Functions, §94-5, (c).
Apprenticeship council.
Appointment of members, §94-2.
Chairman.
Appointment, §94-2.
Compensation of members, §94-2.
Composition, §94-2.
Director of apprenticeship.
Confirmation of appointment of director, §94-3.
Duties, §94-2.

APPRENTICESHIP —Cont'd
Apprenticeship council —Cont'd
Meetings, §94-2.
Number of members, §94-2.
Qualifications of members, §94-2.
Reports, §94-2.
Terms of members, §94-2.
Transfer to department of labor, §143A-71.
Apprenticeship programs.
Defined, §94-5, (a).
Sponsors.
Defined, §94-5, (a).
Barbers, §86A-24.
Collective agreements between employers and employees.
Apprenticeship provisions not invalidated, §94-11.
Definitions, §§94-5, (a), 94-6.
Director of apprenticeship.
Appointment, §94-3.
Apprenticeship agreements.
Approval of agreements, §94-8.
Apprenticeship council.
Confirmation of appointment of director, §94-3.
Duties, §94-4.
Powers, §94-4.
Hearing aid dealers and fitters.
Registration, §93D-9.
Legislative declaration.
Purposes of provisions, §94-1.
Locksmiths, §74F-7.1.
Exemptions from provisions, §74F-16.
Minimum wage, §95-25.3, (b).
Opticians.
Provisions not to apply to apprentices, §90-236.
Qualifications for admission on basis of apprenticeship, §90-240, (a), (f).
Registration of apprentices, §90-243.
Purposes of provisions, §94-1.
Reports.
Apprenticeship council, §94-2.
Rotation of employment, §94-9.
Signatures.
Apprenticeship agreements, §94-8.

APPROPRIATE RELIEF, MOTION FOR.
Generally, §§15A-1411 to 15A-1422.
See MOTION FOR APPROPRIATE RELIEF.

APPROPRIATIONS.
Administration department.
Transfer of funds, property, records, etc., §143-344, (d).
Agriculture.
Development act, §§106-585, 106-587.
Airports.
Municipal airports, §63-8.
State aid.
Sources of funds, §§63-68, 63-69.
Transportation department.
Continuing aviation appropriations, §§136-16.4, 136-16.5.
Archives and history.
Department of cultural resources.
Responsibility for administering appropriations for grants-in-aid, §121-12.1.
Expending appropriations for grants-in-aid, §121-12.2.
Armories.
Supplementing available funds authorized, §127A-167.
Unexpended portion of state appropriation, §127A-169.

APPROPRIATIONS —Cont'd
Art.
Promotion of arts, §143-407.
Beaufort and Morehead railroad company.
Continuing appropriation, §136-16.6, (c).
Black Mountain advancement center for women.
General assembly not obligated to appropriate funds, §143B-269, (h).
Blind persons.
Aid to the blind.
County appropriations, §111-17.
Budget.
Administration department.
Emergency contingent fund, §143-19.
Building code.
Code officials qualification board, §143-151.20.
Cemeteries.
Rural cemeteries.
Appropriations by county commissioners for care, §65-2.
Charities.
Additional to receipts, §143-27.
Community colleges.
Financial support.
Elections on questions of appropriations, §§115D-33 to 115D-37.
Congress, Const. U. S., art. I, §§7, 9.
Constitution of the United States, Const. U. S., art. I, §9.
Army, Const. U. S., art. I, §8.
Revenue bills, Const. U. S., art. I, §7.
Counties.
Agricultural development act, §§106-585, 106-587.
Beach erosion control, §153A-438.
Economic development commissions, §158-12.
Health services.
Counties may appropriate revenues, §153A-248, (a).
Ordinances, §153A-248, (b).
Hurricanes.
Flood and hurricane protection works, §153A-438.
Inspection departments.
Financial support, §153A-354.
Private entities.
Appropriation of money to private entity to carry out public purpose, §153A-449.
State highway fund.
Allocation of funds, §136-41.1, (a) to (c).
Annual appropriation out of fund, §136-41.1, (a).
Contracts for maintenance, etc., of streets, §136-41.3.
Eligible municipalities, §§136-41.1, (b), 136-41.2, (a) to (c).
Incorporated since January 1, 1945, §136-41.2, (d).
Excess accumulation of funds, §136-41.3.
Nature of funds distributed, §136-41.1, (d).
Records and annual statement, §136-41.3.
Use of funds, §136-41.3.
Western North Carolina Development Association, Inc., §153A-447, (a), (b).
County boards of elections.
Boards of county commissioners to make appropriations for, §163-37.
Crime victims compensation.
Compensation payable.
Available to extent general assembly appropriates funds, §15B-25.

APPROPRIATIONS —Cont'd
Cultural resources department.
Promotion of arts, §143-407.
Current operations appropriations act, §143-15.1, (a).
Education.
Additional to receipts, §143-27.
School districts.
Allocation by purpose, function or project.
Discretion of county commissioners, §115C-429, (b).
Basic education program.
Supplemental nature of funds appropriated for program, §115C-81.1.
Budget, §§115C-425 to 115C-434.
Capital outlay appropriations by county.
Inadequacy of county appropriation, petition by board of education, §115C-440.1, (c).
Report on by local government commission, §115C-440.1, (a), (b).
Capital outlay fund.
Included in fund, §115C-426, (f).
Commissioners to determine amount appropriated, §115C-429, (b).
County appropriations.
Allocation to local administrative units, §115C-437.
Apportionment among local school administrative units, §115C-430.
Dispute between board of education and county commissioners.
Procedure for resolution, §115C-431.
Driver education, §115C-216.
Local current expense fund.
Included in fund, §115C-426, (e).
Other funds.
Included in funds, §115C-426, (g).
State public school fund.
Included in fund, §115C-426, (d).
Transfer of funds appropriated, §115C-433, (c).
Emergencies, amendment of budget, §115C-433, (d).
Elections.
County boards of elections.
Boards of county commissioner to make appropriations for, §163-37.
Emergency contingent fund, §143-19.
Advisory budget commission.
Increase or decrease of projects, §143-18.1, (a), (b).
Recommendations, §143-12, (c).
Reduction of appropriations, §143-15.
Allocation for emergency allotment, §143-12, (b).
Use of allocated funds, §143-12, (b).
Allotments.
Records of allotments to be kept by director, §143-20.
Requisition for allotment, §143-17.
Article governs all departmental and agency appropriations, §143-16.
Balances.
Unencumbered balances to revert to treasury, §143-18.
Capital appropriations excepted, §143-18.
Definition of "unencumbered," §143-18.
Bills containing current operations appropriations, §143-12, (a).
Capital appropriations, §143-18.
Increase or decrease of projects, §143-18.1, (a), (b).

APPROPRIATIONS —Cont'd
Emergency contingent fund —Cont'd
Charitable institutions.
Appropriations are in addition to receipts, §143-27.
Correctional institutions.
Appropriations are in addition to receipts, §143-27.
Current operations appropriations act, §143-15.1, (a).
Director of the budget.
Copies of reports and bills, §143-13.
Reduction of appropriations, §143-25, (a).
Disbursements, §143-5.
Educational institutions.
Appropriations are in addition to receipts, §143-27.
Expenditure of appropriations.
Wrongful expenditures.
Recovery, §143-32, (a).
General fund financial model, §143-15.1, (b).
General fund operating budget.
Size limit.
Generally, §143-15.4.
Historic and archaeological property, §143-31.2.
Prerequisites to allotment and expenditures, §143-31.2.
Intent of article, §143-33.
Joint meetings of committees, §143-14.
Maintenance appropriations.
Adequacy of revenues, §143-25, (a).
Legislative declaration, §143-25, (b).
Itemized purposes, §143-23, (a).
Payment.
Director to have discretion as to manner of paying annual appropriations, §143-26, (a).
Printing of bills, §143-13.
Records, §143-20.
Reduction of appropriations, §143-15.
Power of director, §143-25, (a).
Reports.
Office of state budget and management to report, §143-27.
Printing copies of budget report and bills, §143-13.
Reports to or of appropriations committees, etc., of general assembly.
Effect, §143-15.
Rules and regulations, §143-5.
Savings reserve account, §143-15.3, (a).
State highway fund, §143-28.1.
Transfers between objects and items, §143-23.
Energy.
Southern states energy compact.
Supplementary agreements ineffective until funds appropriated, §104D-4.
Fire departments.
State volunteer fire department.
Local appropriations, §58-80-55.
Firemen's and rescue squad workers' pension fund.
Administrative expenses of fund, §58-86-20.
Firemen's relief fund.
State appropriation, §§58-85-10, 58-85-15, 58-85-25.
Fire protection grant fund, §58-85A-1, (c).
Forests and forestry.
Forest management appropriation, §113-33.
General assembly.
Current operations appropriations act.
Enactment, §143-15.1, (a).

APPROPRIATIONS —Cont'd
General assembly —Cont'd
General fund credit balance.
Appropriation of anticipated credit balance not expected to be reserved.
Capital improvements or other one-time expenditures only, §143-15.2, (e).
General fund financial model, §143-15.1, (b).
Legislative research commission.
Payment of expenses from appropriations, §120-30.18.
No expenditures for purposes for which general assembly has considered but not enacted appropriation, §143-16.3.
Savings reserve account, §143-15.3, (a).
Historic districts and landmarks, §160A-400.12.
Hospital authorities, §131E-30.
Housing finance agency.
Authorization to accept appropriated moneys, §122A-18.
Receipt, administration and compliance with conditions and requirements of appropriation.
General power of agency, §122A-5.
Inaugural ceremonies committee.
Payments from appropriations, §143-539.
Interlocal cooperation.
Joint agencies, §160A-462, (b).
Internal improvements.
State deemed shareholder in corporation accepting appropriation, §124-2.
Libraries.
Interstate library compact, §125-12, art. IX.
Public library service.
State policy as to public library service.
Annual appropriation therefore, §125-7.
Livestock.
Combating animal and fowl diseases, §106-308.
Disposition of surplus funds, §106-309.
Tuberculosis.
Counties to appropriate funds for eradication of tuberculosis, §106-343.
Amount of appropriation, §106-346.
Local development.
Authorized activities.
Approval of appropriations, §158-7.1, (c).
Economic development commissions.
Localities, §158-12.
Encouragement of developments, §158-7.1.
Limitation on appropriations and expenditures, §158-7.1, (f).
Local government budget and fiscal control acts.
Applicability, §158-7.1, (e).
Local governments.
Open space.
Acquisition, §160A-406.
Parks and recreation, §160A-353.
Matching funds.
Non-state match restrictions, §143-31.4.
Mental health, developmental disabilities and substance abuse.
Area authorities, §§122C-147, 122C-147.1.
Militia.
Support of militia.
Local appropriations, §127A-138, (a).
Municipal corporations.
Agricultural development act.
Local appropriations, §106-587.
Continuing contracts.
Appropriation of sufficient funds, §160A-17.
Contract with and appropriating money to private entities.
Authorization, §160A-20.1.

APPROPRIATIONS —Cont'd
Municipal corporations —Cont'd
Local development.
Economic development commissions, §158-12.
Public safety.
Resources to protect public.
Appropriations under contract with state, §160A-289.1.
State highway fund.
Allocation of funds, §136-41.1, (a) to (c).
Annual appropriation out of fund, §136-41.1, (a).
Contracts for maintenance, etc., of streets, §136-41.3.
Eligible municipalities, §§136-41.1, (b), 136-41.2, (a) to (c).
Incorporated since January 1, 1945, §136-41.2, (d).
Excess accumulation of funds, §136-41.3.
Nature of funds distributed, §136-41.1, (d).
Records and annual statement, §136-41.3.
Use of funds, §136-41.3.
North Carolina center for nursing.
State budget support, §90-171.72.
North Carolina railroad.
Continuing appropriations, §136-16.6, (a), (b).
Nurses.
North Carolina center for nursing.
State budget support, §90-171.72.
Occupational safety and health.
Commissioner of labor.
Request for sufficient appropriations, §95-150.
Parks and recreation.
Local governments, §160A-353.
Post-war reserve fund, §§143-191 to 143-194.
Public officers and employees.
Diversion of appropriations to state institutions, §143-114.
Public transportation.
Transportation department.
Continuing appropriations for public transportation, §§136-16.8, 136-16.9.
Railroads.
Transportation department.
Continuing rail appropriations, §§136-16.6, (a) to (c), 136-16.7.
Regional planning commissions, §153A-396.
Regional sports authorities, §160A-479.9, (a).
Reports.
Budget.
Reports to appropriation committees.
Effect, §143-15.
Salaries and wages.
Use of funds appropriated for, §143-23, (a2).
School districts.
Allocation by purpose, function or project.
Discretion of county commissioners, §115C-429, (b).
Basic education program.
Supplemental nature of funds appropriated for program, §115C-81.1.
Budget, §§115C-425 to 115C-434.
Capital outlay appropriations by county.
Inadequacy of county appropriation, petition by board of education, §115C-440.1, (c).
Report on by local government commission, §115C-440.1, (a), (b).
Capital outlay fund.
Included in fund, §115C-426, (f).
Commissioners to determine amount appropriated, §115C-429, (b).

APPROPRIATIONS —Cont'd
School districts —Cont'd
County appropriations.
Allocation to local administrative units, §115C-437.
Apportionment among local school administrative units, §115C-430.
Dispute between board of education and county commissioners.
Procedure for resolution, §115C-431.
Driver education, §115C-216.
Local current expense fund.
Included in fund, §115C-426, (e).
Other funds.
Included in funds, §115C-426, (g).
State public school fund.
Included in fund, §115C-426, (d).
Transfer of funds appropriated, §115C-433, (c).
Emergencies, amendment of budget, §115C-433, (d).
Solid waste management.
Regional solid waste management authorities.
State and local governments, §153A-428, (b).
Special education.
Nonreduction provision, §115C-142.
State debt, §§142-1 to 142-29.7.
State literary fund.
Special appropriation from fund, §115C-465.
State-owned railroad company.
Continuing appropriations, §136-16.6, (a), (b).
State treasurer.
Short-term notes in emergencies.
Authorization to make, §147-70.
Streets and highways.
Primary, secondary and urban road systems, §136-44.2.
Reports to appropriations committees of general assembly, §136-44.2B.
Special appropriations for highway construction, §136-44.2C.
Superior court judges.
Hiring of secretaries, §7A-44.1, (b).
Transportation department.
Allocations by department controller to eliminate overdraft, §136-16.10.
Aviation.
Continuing aviation appropriations, §136-16.4.
Purposes, §136-16.5.
Public transportation.
Continuing appropriations for, §136-16.8.
Purposes, §136-16.9.
Rail appropriations.
Continuing rail appropriations, §136-16.6, (a) to (c).
Purposes, §136-16.7.
Reports to appropriations committees of general assembly, §136-44.2B.
United States, Const. U. S., art. I, §9.
Universities and colleges.
Additional to receipts, §143-27.
University of North Carolina.
Carryforward of funds not used in fiscal year, §116-30.3, (e).
Constituent institutions.
Special responsibility constituent institutions, §116-30.2, (a).
Reversions, §116-30.3, (a).
School of science and mathematics, §116-30.2, (b).
Distinguished professors endowment trust fund, §116-41.18, (c).

APPROPRIATIONS —Cont'd
University of North Carolina —Cont'd
General fund for operation of university.
Receipt by president, administration, powers and responsibilities, §116-14, (b1), (b2).
Urban redevelopment.
Municipalities may appropriate funds to commission, §160A-520.
Veterans, §165-9.
Vocational and technical education.
State funds, §115C-156.
Weights and measures.
Funds for administration of act, §81A-6.

AQUACULTURE DEVELOPMENT, §§106-756 to 106-764.
Advisory board.
Advisory committees.
Appointment, §106-760, (b).
Chairman, §106-760, (b).
Clerical and other assistance, §106-760, (b).
Composition, §106-760, (a).
Created, §106-760, (a).
Powers and duties, §106-760, (c).
Quorum, §106-760, (b).
Alligators.
Propagation and production of American alligators, §106-763.1.
American alligators.
Propagation and production, §106-763.1.
Citation of article.
Short title, §106-757.
Damage to agricultural commodities or production systems.
Definitions, §1-539.2B, (c).
Double damage liability, §1-539.2B, (a).
Valuation, §1-539.2B, (b).
Definitions, §106-758.
Department of agriculture and consumer services.
Lead agency, §106-759, (a).
Powers and duties, §106-759, (b).
Findings of legislature, §106-756.
Fish disease management.
Development and implementation of plans, §106-762, (a).
Release of fish, §106-762, (b).
Fish hatcheries and production facilities.
Aquarium or ornamental trade in fish, §106-761, (h).
Commercial catchout facilities, §106-761, (e).
Holding pond/tank permit, §106-761, (f).
Hybrid striped bass, §106-761, (c).
Licenses, §106-761, (d).
Revocation, §106-761, (c).
Possession of species other than those listed, §106-761, (g).
Registration, §106-761, (a).
Species subject to section, §106-761, (b).
Fish passage, §106-763, (a).
Joint legislative commission on seafood and aquaculture, §§120-70.60 to 120-70.66.
Legislative findings and purpose, §106-756.
Natural watercourses.
Blocking, §106-763, (a).
Penalties.
Violation of act, §106-764.
Purpose of article, §106-756.
Residual stream flow, §106-763, (b).
Robbing or injuring hatchery or other aquaculture operation, §113-269, (g).

AQUACULTURE DEVELOPMENT —Cont'd
Shellfish leases.
Water column leases for aquaculture, §113-202.1.
Title of article.
Short title, §106-757.
Violation of provisions, §106-764.

AQUARIUMS.
North Carolina aquariums, §§143B-289.40 to 143B-289.44.
See NORTH CAROLINA AQUARIUMS.

AQUATIC WEED CONTROL, §§113A-220 to 113A-227.
Citation of article, §113A-220.
Definitions, §113A-221.
Injunctions.
Violation of article, §113A-226, (b).
Noxious aquatic weeds.
Areas of state, §113A-222, (b).
Commissioner of agriculture.
Powers, §113A-224, (a), (b).
Control, removal or destruction.
Compliance with applicable federal and state laws, §113A-223, (d).
Cost-efficiency and effectiveness, §113A-223, (c).
Secretary, §113A-223, (b).
Defined, §113A-221.
Designation, §113A-222, (a).
Modification or withdrawal, §113A-222, (d).
Rules, §113A-222, (c).
Importation, sale, etc.
Regulation by commissioner, §113A-224, (a), (b).
Secretary.
Powers and duties.
Generally, §113A-223, (a).
State departments and agencies.
Cooperation with secretary, §113A-225.
Penalties.
Violation of article, §113A-226, (a).
Rules and regulations.
Adoption, §113A-227.
Secretary.
Defined, §113A-221.
Powers and duties.
Generally, §113A-223, (a).
Short title of article, §113A-220.
State departments and agencies.
Cooperation with secretary, §113A-225.
Violation of article.
Injunctions, §113A-226, (b).
Penalties, §113A-226, (a).

ARBITRATION, §§1-569.1 to 1-569.31.
Actions subject to arbitration, Arbitration Rule 1.
Exceptions, Arbitration Rule 1.
Affirmative defense, pleading, §1A-1, Rule 8, (c).
Agreements to arbitrate.
Arbitration by agreement, Arbitration Rule 1.
Case or controversy, §1-569.6, (b).
Challenge to proceedings, §1-569.6, (d).
Conditions precedent, §1-569.6, (c).
Effect of, §1-569.4.
Nonwaivable provisions, §1-569.4, (c).
Prohibitions, §1-569.4, (b).
Validity of, §1-569.6, (a).
Amount in issue.
Maximum amount, Arbitration Rule 1.
Exceptions, Arbitration Rule 1.
Excessive claims, Arbitration Rule 1.

ARBITRATION —Cont'd
Appeals.
How taken, §1-569.28.
Preaward ruling by arbitrators.
Appealability of arbitrator's ruling, §1-569.18, (b), (c).
When may be taken, §1-569.28.
Applicability of article, §1-569.3, (a), (b).
Applicability of rules, Arbitration Rules 1, 9.
Arbitrators.
Appointment, §1-569.11.
Canons of ethics for arbitrators. See within this heading, "Ethics."
Conflicts of interest, §§1-569.11, (b), 1-569.12.
Continuing duty to disclosure, §1-569.12, (b).
Defined, §1-569.1.
Disclosure requirements, §1-569.12.
Disqualification, Arbitration Rule 2.
Eligibility of arbitrators, Arbitration Rule 2.
Ex parte communications with arbitrator.
Prohibited, Arbitration Rule 3.
Expenses.
Rules for court-ordered arbitration, Arbitration Rule 2.
Fees.
Rules for court-ordered arbitration, Arbitration Rule 2.
Immunity from civil liability, §1-569.14, (a).
Impartiality, disclosure of, §1-569.12, (a).
Loss of immunity, §1-569.14, (c).
Method of appointment, §1-569.11, (a).
Motor vehicle accidents.
Immunity prohibited, §1-569.14, (f).
Nature of immunity, §1-569.14, (b).
Oath of office.
Rules for court-ordered arbitration, Arbitration Rule 2.
Objections to appointment.
Conflicts of interest, §1-569.12, (c).
Panel of arbitrators.
Action by majority, §1-569.13.
Presumption of impartiality, §§1-569.12, (e), 1-569.23, (a).
Replacement arbitrator, §1-569.7, (e).
Replacement of arbitrator, Arbitration Rule 2.
Selection of arbitrators, Arbitration Rule 2.
Service as neutral arbitrator, §1-569.11.
Statewide court-ordered nonbinding arbitration in certain civil actions.
Immunity as judges from civil liability for official conduct, §7A-37.1, (e).
Testimony as witness, §1-569.14, (d).
Attorneys at law.
Attorneys representation at hearings, Arbitration Rule 3.
Former arbitrators.
Conflict of interest, Prof. Cond. Rule 1.12.
Lawyers serving as third-party neutrals, Prof. Cond. Rule 2.4.
Representation by lawyer, §1-569.16.
Attorneys' fees.
Civil action against arbitrator, §1-569.14, (e).
Client assistance committee, Bar Rules & Regs., D, §§.0701 to .0704.
Model plan for district bar, Bar Rules & Regs., D, §§.0801 to .0808.
Awards.
Contested judicial proceedings.
Court submission to arbitrator, §1-569.20, (d).
Copies.
Delivery to parties, Arbitration Rule 4.
Correction of award, §1-569.24.

ARBITRATION —Cont'd
Awards —Cont'd
Filing of award, Arbitration Rule 4.
Findings of fact and conclusions of law.
Not required, Arbitration Rule 4.
Judgment on award, §1-569.25.
Modification or correction of award, §1-569.24.
Change by arbitrator, §1-569.20, (a).
Grounds, §1-569.20, (a).
Notice to parties, §1-569.20, (b).
Notice to parties.
Modification or correction of award, §1-569.20, (b).
Objection to motion to modify award, §1-569.20, (d).
Opinions supporting award.
Not required, Arbitration Rule 4.
Preaward ruling by arbitrators.
Incorporation into award, §1-569.18, (a).
Record of award, §1-569.19, (a).
Scope of award, Arbitration Rule 4.
Signature of arbitrators.
Rules for court-ordered arbitration, Arbitration Rule 4.
Time limit for award, §1-569.19, (b).
Vacating award.
Conflicts of interest of arbitrator, §1-569.12, (d).
Contested judicial proceedings, §1-569.23.
Failure to follow established procedures, §1-569.12, (f).
Motion to vacate award, §1-569.23.
Writing.
Award to be in writing, Arbitration Rule 4.
Child support or custody.
Family law arbitration generally, §§50-41 to 50-62.
See FAMILY LAW ARBITRATION.
Citation of act, §1-569.31.
Civil actions.
Application for judicial relief, §1-569.5.
Venue, §1-569.27.
Collaborative law proceedings.
Alternative dispute resolution permitted, §50-78.
Commencement of proceedings, §1-569.9.
Waiver of objections, §1-569.9, (b).
Conduct of hearing, §1-569.7, (d).
Conferences.
Arbitrator's discretion, §1-569.15, (a).
Confidentiality of information.
Canons of ethics for arbitrators.
Faithfulness to relationship of trust and confidentiality inherent in office, CEA Rule 6.
Confirmation of award, §1-569.22.
Contested judicial proceedings, §1-569.22.
Modification or correction of award, §1-569.24, (b).
Motion to vacate award.
Denial of motion as confirmation, §1-569.23, (d).
Conflicts of interest.
Arbitrators, §§1-569.11, (b), 1-569.12.
Canons of ethics for arbitrators.
Disclosures required, CEA Rule 2.
Vacating award.
Conflicts of interest of arbitrator, §1-569.12, (d).
Consolidation of separate arbitration proceedings, §1-569.10.
Construction of act.
Applicability of article, §1-569.3, (a), (b).
Federal electronic signatures in global and national commerce act.
Relationship to federal act, §1-569.30.
Short title, §1-569.31.

ARBITRATION —Cont'd
Construction of act —Cont'd
Uniformity of application and construction, §1-569.29.
Contempt of arbitration proceedings, §1-569.17, (h).
Contested judicial proceedings, §§1-569.22 to 1-569.25.
Confirmation of award, §1-569.22.
Court submission of award to arbitrator, §1-569.20, (d).
Litigation expenses, §1-569.25, (c).
Modification or correction of award, §1-569.24.
Vacating award, §§1-569.12, (e), 1-569.23.
Contracts with forum selection provisions.
Void and against public policy, §22B-3.
Contracts to improve real property, §22B-2.
Costs, Arbitration Rule 7.
Judgment on award, §1-569.25, (b).
Counties.
Outdoor advertising.
Regulation of nonconforming off-premises outdoor advertising.
Relocating and reconstructing outdoor advertising, §153A-143, (i).
Courts.
Extent of intervention, §1-567.35.
International commercial arbitration.
Applications to superior court, §1-567.66.
Extent of court intervention, §1-567.35.
Damages.
Additional remedies, §1-569.21, (c).
Award by arbitrator, §1-569.21, (b).
Exemplary relief, §1-569.21, (a).
Grounds for awarding, §1-569.21, (b).
Payment of arbitrator's expenses, §1-569.21.
Punitive damages, §1-569.21, (a), (e).
Decedents' estates.
Disputed claims, §28A-19-15.
Definitions, §1-569.1.
Court.
Rules of court-ordered arbitration, Arbitration Rule 8.
International commercial arbitration, §1-567.32, (a).
Arbitration agreement, §1-567.37, (a).
Delegation of nonjudicial functions by court, Arbitration Rule 8.
Depositions.
Discovery permitted, §1-569.17, (b).
Designation of actions by court, Arbitration Rule 8.
Discovery.
Grounds for permitting, §1-569.17, (c).
Issuance of process, §1-569.17, (d).
Divorce.
Family law arbitration generally, §§50-41 to 50-62.
See FAMILY LAW ARBITRATION.
Effective date of rules.
Applicability to cases filed on or after, Arbitration Rule 9.
Employers and employees.
Conciliation service, §§95-32 to 95-36.
Voluntary arbitration of labor disputes, §§95-36.1 to 95-36.9.
Ethics.
Canons of ethics for arbitrators.
Appointment by one party.
Ethical considerations relating to arbitrators appointed by one party, CEA Rule 7.

ARBITRATION —Cont'd
Ethics —Cont'd
Canons of ethics for arbitrators —Cont'd
Choice of law, CEA Rule 8.
Communications with parties.
Avoidance of impropriety or appearance of the propriety, CEA Rule 3.
Conflicts of interest.
Disclosures, CEA Rule 2.
Decision-making in just, independent and deliberate manner, CEA Rule 5.
Diligence.
Conducting proceedings diligently, CEA Rule 4.
Fairness of arbitration process.
Conducting proceedings fairly, CEA Rule 4.
Upholding, CEA Rule 1.
Integrity of arbitration process.
Upholding, CEA Rule 1.
Professional responsibility principles.
Canons subject to, CEA Rule 8.
Relationship of trust and confidentiality inherent in office.
Faithfulness to, CEA Rule 6.
Evidence.
Compelling attendance of witnesses, §1-569.17, (a).
Depositions permitted, §1-569.17, (b).
Exhibits.
Copies admissible, Arbitration Rule 3.
Law of evidence used as guide, Arbitration Rule 3.
Presentation of case, §1-569.7, (c).
Rules of evidence.
Applicability to proceedings, §1-569.7, (f).
Trial de novo.
No evidence of arbitration admissible, Arbitration Rule 5.
Executors and administrators.
Referral of disputed claim, §28A-19-15.
Exemption and withdrawal from arbitration, Arbitration Rule 1.
Family law arbitration generally, §§50-41 to 50-62.
See FAMILY LAW ARBITRATION.
Fees.
Trial de novo.
Filing fee, Arbitration Rule 5.
Witnesses fees, §1-569.17, (f).
Forms, Arbitration Rule 8.
Forum selection.
Contracts with forum selection provisions.
Void and unenforceable, §22B-3.
Contracts to improve real property, §22B-2.
Guardian's powers in administering incompetent's estate, §35A-1251.
Guardian's powers in administering minor ward's estate, §35A-1252.
Hearings.
Attorneys at law.
Right to representation by attorney, Arbitration Rule 3.
Conclusion of hearing, Arbitration Rule 3.
Conduct of hearing, §1-569.7, (d).
Date.
Advancement by agreement, Arbitration Rule 8.
Setting, Arbitration Rule 8.
Evidence.
Exhibits.
Copies admissible, Arbitration Rule 3.
Law of evidence used as guide, Arbitration Rule 3.

ARBITRATION —Cont'd
Hearings —Cont'd
Exhibits.
Copies admissible, Arbitration Rule 3.
Ex parte communications with arbitrator.
Prohibited, Arbitration Rule 3.
Failure to appear, Arbitration Rule 3.
Indigent persons.
Proceedings in forma pauperis, Arbitration Rule 3.
Limits, Arbitration Rule 3.
Motions, Arbitration Rule 3.
Notice, Arbitration Rule 8.
Pre-hearing exchange of information, Arbitration Rule 3.
Presence at hearing, Arbitration Rule 3.
Record of testimony and evidence.
No record of hearing made, Arbitration Rule 3.
Scheduled by court, Arbitration Rule 3.
Subpoenas, Arbitration Rule 3.
Time for.
Advancement of date by agreement, Arbitration Rule 8.
Setting of date, Arbitration Rule 8.
Witnesses, Arbitration Rule 3.
Subpoenas, Arbitration Rule 3.
Immunities.
Arbitrators, §1-569.14, (a).
State court-ordered nonbinding arbitration in certain civil actions.
Arbitrators.
Immunity as judges from civil liability for official conduct, §7A-37.1, (e).
Indigent persons.
Hearings.
Proceedings in forma pauperis, Arbitration Rule 3.
Initiation of arbitration, §1-569.9.
Injunctions.
Motion to compel arbitration, §1-569.7, (a).
International commercial arbitration and conciliation, §§1-567.30 to 1-567.87.
See INTERNATIONAL COMMERCIAL ARBITRATION AND CONCILIATION.
Judgment on award.
Costs, §1-569.25, (b).
Recordation, docketing and enforcement, §1-569.25, (a).
Rules for court-ordered arbitration, Arbitration Rule 6.
Jurisdiction.
Exclusive jurisdiction, §1-569.26, (b).
Subject-matter jurisdiction, §1-569.26, (a).
Labor disputes.
Conciliation service and mediation, §§95-32 to 95-36.
See LABOR DISPUTES.
Voluntary arbitration, §§95-36.1 to 95-36.9.
See LABOR DISPUTES.
Law firm disputes.
State bar rules for arbitration of internal disputes, Bar Rules & Regs., E, §§.0401 to .0410.
Marriage.
Family law arbitration generally, §§50-41 to 50-62.
See FAMILY LAW ARBITRATION.
Mediation generally.
See MEDIATION.
Modification or correction of award, §1-569.24.
Change by arbitrator, §1-569.20, (a).
Criteria, §1-569.24, (a).

ARBITRATION —Cont'd
Modification or correction of award —Cont'd
Grant deemed confirmation, §1-569.24, (b).
Grounds, §1-569.20, (a).
Joinder of motions, §1-569.24, (c).
Notice to parties, §1-569.20, (b).
Motions.
Application for judicial relief, §1-569.5, (a).
Notice of initial motion, §1-569.5, (b).
Service of motion, §1-569.5, (c).
Enforceability of agreement, §1-569.7, (c).
Modification or correction of award.
Joinder of motions, §1-569.24, (c).
Motion to compel arbitration, §1-569.7, (a).
Order of court.
Court action pending, §1-569.7, (e).
Judicial discretion, §1-569.7, (d).
Provisional remedies, §1-569.8, (a).
Stay of proceedings, §1-569.7, (f), (g).
Summary disposition, §1-569.7, (b).
Vacating award, §1-569.23.
Municipal corporations.
Outdoor advertising.
Regulation of nonconforming off-premises outdoor advertising.
Relocation and reconstruction of sign.
Resolution of disputes, §160A-199, (i).
Nonbinding arbitration in certain civil actions.
Statewide court-ordered.
Amount in controversy.
Limitations on, §7A-37.1, (c).
Arbitrators.
Immunity as judges from civil liability for official conduct, §7A-37.1, (e).
Fees, §7A-37.1, (c1).
Findings of general assembly, §7A-37.1, (a).
Implementation of procedure, §7A-37.1, (d).
Supreme court.
Adoption of rules, §7A-37.1, (b).
Supervising implementation and operation, §7A-37.1, (b).
Notice, Arbitration Rule 8.
Awards.
Modification or correction of award, §1-569.20, (c).
Objection to motion to modify award, §1-569.20, (d).
Effective notice, §1-569.2, (a).
Hearings.
Rules for court-ordered arbitration, Arbitration Rule 8.
Motions.
Notice of initial motion, §1-569.5, (b).
Receipt of notice, §1-569.2, (c).
What constitutes, §1-569.2, (b).
Nurse licensure compact, §90-171.92.
Oaths.
Arbitrators, Arbitration Rule 2.
Objections to proceedings.
Waiver of, §1-569.9, (b).
Panel of arbitrators.
Action by majority, §1-569.13.
Partnerships.
Power of partner to submit partnership to arbitration, §59-39, (c).
Preaward ruling by arbitrators.
Appealability of arbitrator's ruling, §1-569.18, (b), (c).
Incorporation into award, §1-569.18, (a).
Judicial enforcement, §1-569.18.

ARBITRATION —Cont'd
Protective orders.
Issuance by arbitrator, §1-569.17, (e).
Provisional remedies, §1-569.8, (b).
Interim awards, §1-569.8, (b).
Issuance by arbitrator, §1-569.8, (b).
Order of court, §1-569.8, (a).
Service of process.
Service of subpoenas in civil action, §1-569.17, (a).
Signatures.
Award.
Arbitrators' signatures, Arbitration Rule 4.
State boundaries, §§141-3, 141-4.
Statewide court-ordered nonbinding arbitration in certain civil actions.
Amount in controversy.
Limitation on, §7A-37.1, (c).
Arbitrators.
Immunity.
Same immunity as judges from civil liability for official conduct, §7A-37.1, (e).
Fees, §7A-37.1, (c1).
Findings of general assembly, §7A-37.1, (a).
Implementation of procedure, §7A-37.1, (d).
Supreme court.
Adoption of rules governing procedure, §7A-37.1, (b).
Implementation and operation.
Supervising, §7A-37.1, (b).
Stay of proceedings, §1-569.7, (f), (g).
Subpoenas, Arbitration Rule 3.
Summary disposition.
Authority of arbitrator, §1-569.15, (b).
Motions, §1-569.7, (b).
Superior courts.
Other settlement procedures in civil actions.
Arbitration authorized as other settlement procedure, Super. Ct. Mediated Settlmt. Conf. R. 10(B).
Award, Super. Ct. Mediated Settlmt. Conf. R. 12(D).
Binding arbitration, agreement, Super. Ct. Mediated Settlmt. Conf. R. 12(G).
Canon of ethics for arbitrators, Super. Ct. Mediated Settlmt. Conf. R. 12(A).
Exchange of information, Super. Ct. Mediated Settlmt. Conf. R. 12(B).
General rules applicable to other settlement procedures, Super. Ct. Mediated Settlmt. Conf. R. 10(C).
Hearings, Super. Ct. Mediated Settlmt. Conf. R. 12(C).
Judgment on award, Super. Ct. Mediated Settlmt. Conf. R. 12(F).
Modification procedure, Super. Ct. Mediated Settlmt. Conf. R. 12(H).
Order authorizing other settlement procedures, Super. Ct. Mediated Settlmt. Conf. R. 10(A).
Rules for arbitration specifically, Super. Ct. Mediated Settlmt. Conf. R. 12.
Trial de novo, dissatisfaction with award, Super. Ct. Mediated Settlmt. Conf. R. 12(E).
Supreme court.
Statewide court-ordered nonbinding arbitration in certain civil actions.
Adoption of rules, §7A-37.1, (b).
Supervising implementation and operation, §7A-37.1, (b).
Termination of action by agreement before judgment.
Rules for court-ordered arbitration, Arbitration Rule 6.

ARBITRATION —Cont'd
Title of act, §1-569.31.
Trial de novo.
Costs following trial de novo, Arbitration Rule 7.
Demand for.
Filing, Arbitration Rule 5.
Fee, Arbitration Rule 5.
Service on parties, Arbitration Rule 5.
Evidence.
No evidence of arbitration admissible, Arbitration Rule 5.
Fees.
Filing fee, Arbitration Rule 5.
Judicial immunity, Arbitration Rule 5.
Jury.
No reference to arbitration in presence of jury, Arbitration Rule 5.
Reference to arbitration in presence of jury.
Prohibited, Arbitration Rule 5.
Right to, Arbitration Rule 5.
Witnesses.
Arbitrator not to be called as witness, Arbitration Rule 5.
Trusts and trustees.
Powers of trustees under express trust, §36A-136.
Vacating award.
Conflicts of interest of arbitrator, §1-569.12, (d).
Contested judicial proceedings, §§1-569.12, (e), 1-569.23.
Failure to follow established procedures, §1-569.12, (f).
Motion to vacate award.
Denial of motion as confirmation, §1-569.23, (d).
Filing requirements, §1-569.23, (b).
Grounds, §1-569.23, (a).
Rehearing, §1-569.23, (c).
Waiver of rights.
Effect of provisional remedies, §1-569.8, (c).
Witnesses.
Compelling testimony, §1-569.17, (a).
Deposition of witness, §1-569.17, (b).
Fees for attending arbitration proceedings, §1-569.17, (f).
Hearings, Arbitration Rule 3.
Subpoenas, Arbitration Rule 3.
Subpoenas, Arbitration Rule 3.

ARBORETUM.
Western North Carolina arboretum, §§116-240 to 116-244.
See WESTERN NORTH CAROLINA ARBORETUM.

ARBOR WEEK.
Designation, §103-6.

ARCHAEOLOGICAL RECORD, §§70-46 to 70-52.
Archaeological investigations.
Defined, §70-48.
Permits.
Application, §70-51, (a).
Issuance, §70-51, (b).
Notice, §70-51, (d).
Suspension, §70-51, (e).
Terms, conditions or limitations, §70-51, (c).
Archaeological resource.
Defined, §70-48.
Citation of article, §70-46.
Contents, §70-49, (b).
Definitions, §70-48.
Establishment, §70-49, (b).
Findings of general assembly, §70-47.

ARCHAEOLOGICAL RECORD —Cont'd
Program.
Defined, §70-48.
Establishment, §70-49, (a).
Purposes, §70-49, (a).
Voluntary participation, §70-49, (a).
Purpose of article, §70-47.
Removal of resource from record, §70-49, (c).
Rules and regulations.
Adoption, §70-52.
Short title of article, §70-46.
Site steward program.
Administration, §70-50.
Establishment, §70-50.
State archaeologist.
Defined, §70-48.

ARCHAEOLOGICAL RESOURCES PROTECTION, §§70-10 to 70-20.
Archaeological investigations.
Defined, §70-12.
Permits.
Applications, §70-13, (a).
Issuance.
Findings required, §70-13, (b).
Required, §70-15, (a), (b).
Terms, conditions or limitations, §70-13, (c).
Religious or cultural sites.
Procedure when permit may result in harm to, §70-13, (d).
Suspension or revocation, §70-13, (e).
Citation of act.
Short title, §70-10.
Confidentiality of information, §70-18.
Definitions, §70-12.
Department of cultural resources.
Cooperation with private individuals, §70-19.
Delegation of responsibilities, §70-20.
Forfeitures.
Violations of provisions, §70-17.
Historical commission.
Rules and regulations, §70-14.
Indians.
Permits for archaeological investigations.
Procedure when permit may harm cultural or religious site, §70-13, (d).
Legislative findings, §70-11, (a).
Penalties.
Violations of provisions, §70-15, (c).
Civil penalties, §70-16.
Permits.
Archaeological investigations, §70-13.
Private individuals.
Cooperation with, §70-19.
Purpose of provisions, §70-11, (b).
Rights of way.
Objects on highway right-of-way, §136-42.1.
Rules and regulations.
Historical commission, §70-14.
Short title of act, §70-10.
Streets and highways.
Objects on highway right-of-way, §136-42.1.
Title of act.
Short title, §70-10.
Underwater archaeological sites.
Salvage of abandoned shipwrecks and other underwater sites, §§121-22 to 121-28.
Unmarked human burial and human skeletal remains, §§70-26 to 70-40.
See UNMARKED HUMAN BURIAL AND SKELETAL REMAINS PROTECTION.

ARCHAEOLOGICAL RESOURCES PROTECTION —Cont'd
Violations of provisions.
Forfeitures, §70-17.
Penalties, §70-15, (c).
Civil penalties, §70-16.
Separate offense for each day on which violation occurs, §70-15, (d).

ARCHITECTS.
Actions.
Civil penalty for violations of provisions, §83A-16, (b), (c).
Advertising.
Rules and regulations prohibiting.
Board not to adopt, §83A-6, (b).
Board.
Administration of provisions, §83A-2, (a).
Appointment of members, §83A-2, (b).
Bonds, surety.
Treasurer, §83A-2, (c).
Composition, §83A-2, (b).
Defined, §83A-1.
Disciplinary actions, §83A-14.
Expenses of members, §83A-3, (a).
Fees, §83A-4.
Finances, §83A-3, (b).
Injunctions.
Power to seek, §83A-17.
Meetings, §83A-2, (c).
Number of members, §83A-2, (b).
Officers, §83A-2, (c).
Quorums, §83A-2, (c).
Records, §83A-5, (a).
Roster, §83A-5, (b).
Rules and regulations.
Administrative procedure act.
Applicability, §83A-6, (c).
Powers generally, §83A-6, (a), (b).
Seal, §83A-5, (c).
Vacancies, §83A-2, (b).
Child support enforcement.
Forfeiture of licensing privilege, §50-13.12.
Civil penalty, §83A-16, (a).
Actions to recover, §83A-16, (b), (c).
Condominium plats or plans.
Certification, §47C-2-109.
Conflicts of interest.
Public works.
Employment of architects when interested in use of materials prohibited, §133-1.
Construction.
Exemptions from provisions as to architects, §83A-13, (c).
Contractors.
Exemptions from provisions as to architects, §83A-13, (b).
Corporations.
Corporate certificate, §83A-3.
Corporate practice, §83A-8.
Professional corporations generally, §§55B-1 to 55B-16.
See PROFESSIONAL CORPORATIONS.
Definitions, §83A-1.
Disasters.
Qualified immunity for volunteers during a disaster, §83A-13.1.
Disciplinary actions, §83A-14.
Emergencies.
Qualified immunity during an emergency, §83A-13.1.

ARCHITECTS —Cont'd
Engineers.
Exemption of architectural work incidental to engineering project, §83A-13, (a).
Examinations.
Licensing by examination, §83A-7, (a).
Exemptions from provisions, §83A-13.
Fees.
Board, §83A-4.
Felony convictions.
Forfeiture of license, §15A-1331A.
Injunctions, §83A-17.
Landscape architects.
General provisions, §§89A-1 to 89A-8.
See LANDSCAPE ARCHITECTS.
Licenses.
Corporate certificate.
Application for, §83A-8, (a).
Defined, §83A-1.
Reciprocity, §83A-8, (b).
Subject to rules and regulations of board, §83A-8, (c).
Denial.
Grounds, §83A-15.
Examinations, §83A-7, (a).
Qualification requirements, §83A-7, (a).
Expiration, §83A-11.
Forfeiture.
Felony convictions, §15A-1331A.
Reciprocity, §83A-7, (b).
Corporate certificates, §83A-8, (b).
Renewal, §83A-11.
Fees, §83A-4.
Required, §83A-12.
Suspension or revocation.
Grounds, §83A-15.
Taxation.
Professional licenses generally, §105-41.
Limitation of actions.
Real property improvements.
Recovery of damages for defective or unsafe conditions, §1-50, (a).
Misdemeanors.
Violations of provisions, §83A-16, (a).
Motor vehicles.
Volunteer architects during an emergency or disaster.
Inapplicability of qualified immunity, §83A-13.1, (c).
Partnerships.
Practice of architecture, §83A-9.
Practice of architecture.
Corporate practice.
Defined, §83A-1.
Qualification for, §83A-8.
Partnership practice, §83A-9.
Prohibited practice, §83A-12.
Professional corporations, §55B-14, (a).
Generally, §§55B-1 to 55B-16.
See PROFESSIONAL CORPORATIONS.
Public buildings and grounds.
Bids and bidding.
Architectural, engineering and surveying services, §§143-64.31 to 143-64.34.
Certain buildings involving public funds to be designed, etc., by architect, §133-1.1.
Public works.
Bids and bidding.
Architectural, engineering and surveying services, §§143-64.31 to 143-64.34.

ARCHITECTS —Cont'd
Public works —Cont'd
Buildings involving expenditure of public funds.
Certain buildings involving public funds to be designed, etc., by architect, §133-1.1.
Employment of architects when interested in use of materials prohibited, §133-1.
Relocation assistance, §§133-5 to 133-18.
Reciprocity.
Licensing by reciprocity, §83A-7, (b).
Corporate certificates, §83A-8, (b).
Records.
Board, §83A-5, (a).
Roster, §83A-5, (b).
Rules and regulations.
Administrative procedure act.
Applicability, §83A-6, (c).
Powers of board generally, §83A-6, (a), (b).
Seals and sealed instruments.
Board, §83A-5, (c).
Professional seals, §83A-10.
Signatures.
Plans or specifications under exemptions, §83A-13, (e).
Subcontractors.
Payments to for improvements upon real property, §§22C-1 to 22C-6.
Unit ownership.
Plans of buildings.
Certificate of architects, §47A-15, (a).
Violations of provisions.
Injunction, §83A-17.
Penalties, §83A-16, (a).
Civil penalty, §83A-16, (a).
Actions to recover, §83A-16, (b), (c).

ARCHITECTURE.
Promotion of arts, §§143-403 to 143-407.1.

ARCHIVES AND HISTORY.
Advisory commission for state museum of natural history, §§143B-344.18 to 143B-344.21.
Alkaline (acid-free) paper.
Historical publications.
Printing state publications of historical value on, §§125-11.13, (a) to (c), 143-170.5.
Appropriations.
Department of cultural resources.
Responsibility for administering appropriations for grants-in-aid, §121-12.1.
Expending appropriations for grants-in-aid, §121-12.2.
Archaeological resources protection, §§70-10 to 70-20.
See ARCHAEOLOGICAL RESOURCES PROTECTION.
Artifacts owned by state and in custody or curated by office of archives and history.
Selling, trading or loaning by department, §121-7, (a).
Budget requests.
Preparation of budget requests.
Procedures for preparing, §121-12.2.
Cemeteries.
Historic preservation program.
Abandoned cemeteries, §121-8, (g).
Citation of act, §121-1.
Colonial North Carolina.
Historical publications, §121-6, (c).
Conservation and historic preservation agreements, §§121-34 to 121-42.

ARCHIVES AND HISTORY —Cont'd
Corporations.
Outdoor historical dramas, §143-204.8.
Counties.
Historic preservation program.
Cooperation with local governments, §121-8, (e).
Historic properties.
Acquisition, maintenance, etc., of property.
Procedures where assistance extended to counties, §121-11.
Definitions, §121-2.
Department of cultural resources.
Archival and historical agency of state, §121-3.
Artifacts owned by state and in custody of office of archives and history.
Selling, trading or placing on permanent loan, §121-7, (a).
Budget requests.
Procedures for preparing budget requests, §121-12.2.
Defined, §121-2.
Duties.
Enumerated, §121-4.
Grants-in-aid.
Expending appropriations, §121-12.2.
Responsibility for administering appropriations, §121-12.1.
Museum of history.
Maintenance and administration of museum by department, §121-7, (a).
Powers.
Enumerated, §121-4.
Transfer of commission to department, §143B-51.
Tryon's palace, §§121-14 to 121-21.
Division.
General assembly.
Retention of books, records, etc., §120-37, (f).
General assembly.
Retention of books, records, etc., by office of archives and history, §120-37, (f).
Governor.
Historical publications.
Editing and publishing of official messages and other papers of governor, §121-6, (b).
Portrait of governor.
Acquisition of portrait during term of office, §121-13.
Security of historic properties.
Designated employees commissioned special peace officers by governor, §121-10, (a).
Grants.
Department of cultural resources, §121-12.1.
Responsibility for administering appropriations for grants-in-aid, §121-12.1.
Expending appropriations for grants-in-aid, §121-12.2.
Historical publications, §121-6.
Alkaline (acid-free) paper.
Printing state publications of historical value on, §§125-11.13, (a) to (c), 143-170.5.
Historic preservation and conservation agreements, §§121-34 to 121-42.
Historic preservation program, §121-8.
Defined, §121-2.
Historic properties.
See HISTORIC PROPERTIES.
Murfreesboro historical commission, §§143B-107 to 143B-110.
Museums.
Administration, §121-7.
Branches established, §121-7.

ARCHIVES AND HISTORY —Cont'd
Museums —Cont'd
Defined, §121-2.
Maintenance, §121-7.
Maritime museum.
Disposition of artifacts, §121-7.1.
Natural History Museum.
Advisory commission, §§143B-344.18 to 143B-344.21.
Nonstate owners of history museums.
Procedures where assistance extended, §121-11.
North Carolina museum of forestry.
Satellite museum of state museum of natural sciences, §143B-344.23.
Records, §121-7, (b).
State aid.
Criteria for state aid to historical museums, §121-12, (c1).
Titles to artifacts, §121-7, (c), (d).
Name.
Archival and historical agency, §121-3.
Natural History Museum.
Advisory commission, §§143B-344.18 to 143B-344.21.
Nature and historic preserves, §§143-260.6 to 143-260.10C.
North Carolina register of historic places, §121-4.1.
Outdoor historical dramas.
Allotments to outdoor historical dramas.
Audits, §143-204.8, (d).
Authorization, §143-204.8, (a).
Definition, §143-204.8, (c).
Guidelines for approval, §143-204.8, (b).
Amusement tax exemptions, §105-40.
Wage and hour act.
Exemptions, §95-25.14, (a).
Youth employment, §95-25.5, (h).
Youth employment.
Exemptions from certain provisions, §95-25.5, (h).
Portrait of governor.
Acquisition of portrait during term of office, §121-13.
Public records.
Assistance to public officers, §121-5, (c).
Defined, §121-2.
Designation of state archival agency, §121-5, (a).
Destruction of records regulated, §121-5, (b).
Preservation of permanently valuable records, §121-5, (d).
Public officers.
Assistance to officers, §121-5, (c).
Regulation of destruction of records, §121-5, (b).
State archival agency designated, §121-5, (a).
Register of historic places, §121-4.1.
Salvage of abandoned shipwrecks and other underwater sites, §§121-22 to 121-28.
Short title, §121-1.
State aid.
Department of cultural resources.
Responsibility for administering appropriations for grants-in-aid, §121-12.1.
Expending appropriations for grants-in-aid, §121-12.2.
Historical commission.
Criteria for state aid to historical museums, §121-12, (c1).
Criteria for state aid to historic properties, §121-12.

ARCHIVES AND HISTORY —Cont'd
State archives.
Larceny of records, §14-72, (b).
Mutilation or defacement of records, §14-76.1.
Title.
Museums.
Archives, §121-7, (c), (d).
Tryon's palace and Tryon's palace commission, §§121-14 to 121-21.
See TRYON'S PALACE.

ARENAS.
Facility authorities.
Seating at regional facility arena, §160A-480.7.
Smoking in public places.
Applicability of article to local government, §143-601.
Nonsmoking areas in state-controlled buildings, §143-597.

ARGUMENT OF COUNSEL.
Court's control of argument, §7A-97.
Limitations on arguments to jury.
Criminal proceedings, §15A-1230.
Opening and concluding arguments, Super. Ct. Rule 10.
Oral argument on appeal, App. Proc. Rule 30.

ARMED FORCES.
Military affairs.
See MILITARY AFFAIRS.
Military property, care of, §§127A-125 to 127A-131.
See MILITARY PROPERTY, CARE OF.
Militia.
Generally.
See MILITIA.
Naval militia, §§127A-67 to 127A-74.
See NAVAL MILITIA.
State defense militia, §§127A-80, 127A-81.
Unorganized militia, §§127A-87 to 127A-91.
See UNORGANIZED MILITIA.
Missing in action.
Estates of absentees in military service, §§28B-1 to 28B-10.
See ABSENTEES IN MILITARY SERVICE.
National guard.
General provisions.
See NATIONAL GUARD.
Naval militia, §§127A-67 to 127A-74.
See NAVAL MILITIA.
Pay of militia, §§127A-105 to 127A-111.
See MILITIA.
Prisoners of war.
Estates of absentees in military service, §§28B-1 to 28B-10.
See ABSENTEES IN MILITARY SERVICE.
State defense militia, §§127A-80, 127A-81.
Unorganized militia, §§127A-87 to 127A-91.
See UNORGANIZED MILITIA.
Veterans.
General provisions.
See VETERANS.

ARMED PRIVATE SECURITY OFFICERS.
Defined, §74C-13, (a).
Firearm registration permits.
Application, §74C-13, (c).
Denial, §74C-13, (g).
Fees.
Expenditure, §74C-13, (k).
Form, §74C-13, (d).

ARMED PRIVATE SECURITY OFFICERS —Cont'd
Firearm registration permits —Cont'd
Issuance.
Prerequisites, §74C-13, (i).
Renewal, §74C-13, (d).
Required, §74C-13, (a), (b).
Rules and regulations, §74C-13, (j).
Suspension or revocation, §74C-13, (g).
Temporary employment, §74C-13, (f).
Termination of employment.
Expiration and return of permit, §74C-13, (e).
Training program, §74C-13, (h).

ARMED ROBBERY, §14-87, (a).
Seizure and forfeitures of conveyances used in committing robbery, §14-86.1.

ARMORED CARS.
Private protective services generally, §§74C-1 to 74C-33.
See PRIVATE PROTECTIVE SERVICES.

ARMORIES, §§127A-161 to 127A-169.
Alcoholic beverage permits.
Civic center defined to include, §18B-1000.
Mixed beverage permit.
Kind of permit that may be issued, §18B-1001.
On-premises fortified wine permit.
Kind of permit that may be issued, §18B-1001.
On-premises malt beverage permit.
Kind of permit that may be issued, §18B-1001.
On-premises unfortified wine permit.
Kind of permit that may be issued, §18B-1001.
Appropriations.
Supplementing available funds authorized, §127A-167.
Unexpended portion of state appropriation, §127A-169.
Contracts.
Department of crime control and public safety.
Making contracts, etc., §127A-164.
Conveyances.
Counties and municipalities may lease, convey or acquire property for use as armory, §127A-165.
Prior conveyances validated, §127A-166.
Validation of prior conveyances, §127A-166.
Counties.
Lease, conveyance or acquisition of property for use as armory, §127A-165.
Local financial support, §127A-168.
Definitions, §127A-161.
Department of crime control and public safety.
Defined, §127A-161.
Powers.
Acquisition of land, §127A-164.
Contracts.
Making contracts, etc., §127A-164.
Enumerated, §127A-163.
Specified, §127A-163.
Fostering development of armories and facilities, §127A-162.
Leases.
Counties and municipalities may lease, convey or acquire property for use as armory, §127A-165.
Local financial support, §127A-168.
Municipal corporations.
Lease, conveyance or acquisition of property for use as armory, §127A-165.
Local financial support, §127A-168.

ARMOR-PIERCING BULLETS.
Teflon-coated bullets.
Manufacture, sale, purchase or possession, §14-34.3.

ARMS.
Workers' compensation.
Loss of arms.
Rates of compensation, I.C. Rule 405.

ARMY.
Absentees in military service.
Estates of absentees, §§28B-1 to 28B-10.
See ABSENTEES IN MILITARY SERVICE.
Guardian and ward.
Veterans' guardianship act, §§34-1 to 34-18.
See VETERANS' GUARDIANSHIP ACT.
Military affairs.
General provisions.
See MILITARY AFFAIRS.
Veterans.
General provisions.
See VETERANS.

ARRAIGNMENT.
Closed circuit television, §15A-941.
Generally, §15A-941.
Order of proceedings in jury trial, §15A-1221, (a).
Right to counsel, §15A-942.
Superior court.
Not guilty plea.
Effect, §15A-943, (b).
Optional calendaring, §15A-944.
Required calendaring, §15A-943, (a), (c).
Waiver, §15A-945.
Written request for arraignment, §15A-941, (d).
Right to counsel, §15A-942.

ARREST.
Alimony.
Remedy available, §50-16.7, (d).
Arson.
Power of attorney general, §58-79-5.
Assistance by private persons.
Authority, §15A-405, (a).
Benefits to private persons, §15A-405, (b).
Liability.
Freedom of private person from, §15A-405, (a).
Request by officer, §15A-405, (a).
Avoiding arrest.
Aggravating factors in sentencing, §15A-1340.16.
Bail bondsmen and runners.
Surrender of defendant by surety.
Arrest of defendant for purpose of surrender, §58-71-30.
Bank examiners.
Power to make arrest, §53-121.
Campus police officers, §74E-6.
Territorial jurisdiction of officer to make arrest.
Immediate and continuous flight, §15A-402, (f).
Child support enforcement.
Remedy of arrest available, §50-13.4, (f).
Citizens' arrest, §§15A-404, 15A-405.
Civil cases, §§1-409 to 1-439.
See ARREST IN CIVIL CASES.
Clerks of court.
Warrant for arrest.
Clerk may issue, §15A-304, (f).
Commitment to detention facility pending trial, §15A-521.
Congress.
Privilege from, Const. U. S., art. I, §6.
Cost, nonpayment, §6-48.

ARREST —Cont'd
Costs in criminal actions in superior or district courts, §7A-304, (a).
County officers outside territory.
Felonies, §15A-402, (e).
Court of appeals.
Warrant for arrest.
Judges may issue, §15A-304, (f).
Criminal contempt.
Custody of person charged with criminal contempt, §5A-16, (b).
Deaf or hearing impaired person.
Interpreter, officer to procure, §8B-2, (d).
Debt collectors.
Representing that nonpayment may result in arrest, §75-51.
Debtor leaving state or concealing himself, §1-355.
Definitions.
Order for arrest, §15A-305, (a).
Warrant for arrest, §15A-304, (a).
Diabetes.
Police assistance to persons arrested while unconscious or semiconscious, §15A-503.
District courts.
Costs in criminal actions, §7A-304, (a).
Warrants for arrest.
Judges may issue, §15A-304, (f).
Dog wardens.
Power of arrest, §67-31.
Domestic violence.
Violation of order, §50B-4, (b).
Duties upon arrest, §§15A-401, (c), 15A-501.
Elections.
County boards of elections.
Power to maintain order, §163-34.
Offenses by voters.
Election officers to cause violators to be arrested, §163-273, (b).
Precinct election officials.
Power to maintain order, §163-48.
State board of elections.
Power to maintain order, §163-24.
Entry on private premises or vehicle, §15A-401, (e).
Environment and natural resources.
Special peace officers.
Arrest powers, §113-28.2.
Epilepsy.
Police assistance to persons arrested while unconscious or semiconscious, §15A-503.
Escape.
Persons escaped from penal institutions, §162-35.
Prevention of escape, use of force, §15A-401, (d).
Executions.
Debtor leaving state or concealing self, §1-355.
Extradition, §§15A-721 to 15A-750.
Fugitives from other states, §§15A-728, 15A-729.
Arrest prior to requisition, §15A-733.
Confinement in jail when necessary, §15A-732.
Rights of accused person, §§15A-730, 15A-731.
Warrantless arrest, §15A-734.
Warrant of arrest, §15A-741.
Execution, §§15A-728, 15A-729.
Issuance, §15A-727.
Federal law enforcement officers.
Assistance in enforcing criminal laws in state, §15A-406.
Fingerprints.
Person arrested, §15A-502, (a).
Exceptions, §15A-502, (b), (c).

ARREST —Cont'd
Fingerprints —Cont'd
Person arrested —Cont'd
Law-enforcement agencies.
Forwarding of fingerprints to, §15A-502, (e).
Fish and wildlife inspectors and protectors.
Arrest without warrant, §113-136, (d).
Search on arrest, §113-137, (a).
Service of arrest warrant, §113-136, (e).
Fleeing or attempting to elude arrest or apprehension.
Impaired driving.
Aggravating factor to be weighed, §20-179, (d).
Police chases, speed limit not applicable, §20-145.
Speeding, §20-141.5.
Force.
Use of deadly force to resist arrest, §15A-401, (f).
Use of force in arrest, §15A-401, (d), (e).
Forest law-enforcement officers.
Powers, §113-55.1.
General assembly.
Duty and privilege of members.
Protection from arrest, §120-9.
Highway patrol, §§20-49, 20-188.
Historic property.
Special police, powers, §121-10, (b).
Hot pursuit.
Campus police officers.
Immediate and continuous flight, §15A-402, (f).
Company police.
Power to make arrest, §74E-6.
County and city officers.
Immediate and continuous flight, §15A-402, (d).
Officers from other states, §15A-403.
How arrest made, §15A-401, (c).
Identification as peace officer.
Requirement upon making arrest, §15A-401, (c).
Impaired drivers.
Initial appearance before magistrate, §15A-534.2.
Information as to arrest public record, §132-1.4, (c).
Information to arrested person.
Requirements upon making arrest, §§15A-401, (c), 15A-501.
Infractions.
Detention of person charged, §15A-1113, (b).
Territorial jurisdiction, §15A-1113, (d).
Failure to appear to answer charge.
No order for arrest, §15A-1116, (b).
Initial appearance before magistrate.
Audio and video transmission.
Conducting of proceeding by, §15A-511, (a1).
Bail and recognizance.
Release, §15A-511, (e).
Communicable disease.
Detention of defendant, §15A-534.3.
First appearance before district court judge.
Consolidation of proceedings, §15A-601, (b).
Generally, §15A-511, (a).
Impaired drivers.
Administration of test, §15A-534.2, (d).
Compliance with provisions, §15A-534.2.
Conditions for release, §15A-534.2, (c).
Detention in custody, §15A-534.2.
Officers other than magistrates.
Authority to conduct initial appearance, §15A-511, (f).
Probable cause.
Arrest without warrant.
Determination of probable cause, §15A-511, (c).

ARREST —Cont'd
Initial appearance before magistrate —Cont'd
Statement by magistrate, §15A-511, (b).
Warrant.
Procedure when arrest is pursuant to warrant, §15A-511, (d).
Warrantless arrest.
Procedure on, §15A-511, (c).
Insurance commissioner powers, §58-2-50.
Interpreter for deaf or hearing impaired person.
Officer to procure, §8B-2, (d).
Judicial officer.
Taking person arrested before, §15A-501.
Magistrates.
Initial appearance before magistrate, §15A-511.
Impaired driver, §15A-534.2.
Warrants for arrest.
Issuance, §15A-304, (f).
Mental health facilities.
State facilities.
Special policemen, §122C-183.
Militia.
Power of arrest in certain emergencies, §127A-149.
Minors.
Notification of parent or guardian, §15A-505, (a), (b).
Notification of principal of school, §15A-505, (c).
Photographs and fingerprints.
Not authorized for juveniles, §15A-502, (c).
Motor vehicle offenses.
Authority of state highway patrol, §20-188.
Lights.
Violations of provisions.
Time to bring lamps into conformance with requirements, §20-133, (b).
Nonresidents, reciprocal provisions, §§20-4.18 to 20-4.20.
Photographs and fingerprints.
Not authorized for misdemeanors under motor vehicles provisions, §15A-502, (b).
Police authority of division, §20-49.
Offense in presence of officer.
Arrest without warrant, §15A-401, (b).
Offense out of presence of officer.
Arrest without warrant, §15A-401, (b).
Officers from other states, §15A-403, (a).
Applicability of provisions, §15A-403, (c).
Hearing before judicial officer, §15A-403, (b).
Unlawful arrest by officers, §14-43.1.
Order for arrest.
Criminal process generally, §15A-301.
Defined, §15A-305, (a).
Delivery, execution and service of criminal process, §15A-301.
Indictment.
Copy of indictment, §15A-305, (c).
Issuance, §15A-305, (b).
Who may issue, §15A-305, (d).
Service and execution of criminal process, §15A-301.
Statement of cause and order, §15A-305, (c).
Parole.
Violations of parole, §15A-1376, (a).
Photography.
Person arrested, §15A-502, (a).
Exceptions, §15A-502, (b), (c).
Intoxication.
Photographs for purpose of showing, §15A-502, (d).

ARREST —Cont'd
Photography —Cont'd
Person arrested —Cont'd
Law-enforcement agencies.
Forwarding of photographs to, §15A-502, (e).
Police.
Unlawful arrest by officers from other states, §14-43.1.
Preliminary examinations, §15A-521.
Preventing arrest.
Aggravating factors in sentencing, §15A-1340.16.
Prisons and prisoners.
Debtor and creditor.
Discharge of insolvent prisoners.
Persons taken in arrest proceedings, §23-29.
Private persons.
Assistance to law-enforcement officers.
Benefits to private person, §15A-405, (b).
Request by officer, §15A-405, (a).
Authority, §15A-405, (a).
Detention of offenders.
Authorized, §15A-404, (a), (b).
Manner of detention, §15A-404, (c).
Period of detention, §15A-404, (d).
Surrender of offender to officer, §15A-404, (e).
Liability.
Freedom from, §15A-405, (a).
Privilege from arrest.
Congress, Const. U. S., art. I, §6.
Probable cause.
Arrest by officer without warrant, §15A-401, (b).
Initial appearance before magistrate.
Arrest without warrant.
Determination of probable cause, §15A-511, (c).
Warrant for arrest.
Showing of probable cause, §15A-304, (d).
Probation.
Probation officers, §15-205.
Violation of probation, §15A-1345, (a).
Public record.
Information as to arrest public record, §132-1.4, (c).
Requirements upon making arrest, §§15A-401, (c), 15A-501.
Resisting arrest.
Aggravating factors in sentencing, §15A-1340.16.
Obstruction of justice for assisting officers in performance of duties, §14-223.
Use of deadly weapon or deadly force to resist arrest, §15A-401, (f).
Return of released person.
Immunity of officer, §15A-504, (b).
Lack of probable cause for arrest, §15A-504, (a).
Revenue law enforcement agents, §105-236.1, (b).
Rewards.
Information leading to arrest and conviction.
Governor may offer rewards, §15-53.1.
Right of entry.
Entry on private premises or vehicle, §15A-401, (e).
Right to counsel.
Peace officers to advise person arrested of right to counsel, §15A-501.
Sealing by court order to withhold public record, §132-1.4, (k).
Sex offender and public protection registration.
Failure to register, §14-208.11, (a1).

ARREST —Cont'd
Shoplifting.
Detention or arrest of suspect.
Liability for detention, malicious prosecution, false imprisonment or false arrest, §§14-72, (d), 14-72.1.
Snake handling.
Persons violating provisions to be arrested, §14-420.
Speeding to elude arrest, §20-141.5.
Superior courts.
Costs in criminal actions, §7A-304, (a).
Warrant for arrest.
Judges may issue, §15A-304, (f).
Supplemental proceedings.
Debtor leaving state or concealing self, §1-355.
Supreme court.
Warrant for arrest.
Justices may issue, §15A-304, (f).
Territorial jurisdiction of officers to make arrest.
Campus police officers.
Immediate and continuous flight, §15A-402, (f).
City officers, §15A-402, (b).
Immediate and continuous flight, §15A-402, (d).
Outside territory, §15A-402, (c).
County officers, §15A-402, (b).
Immediate and continuous flight, §15A-402, (d).
Outside territory.
Felonies, §15A-402, (e).
State officers, §15A-402, (a).
Transportation of persons in custody, §15A-402, (c).
Unconscious or semiconscious persons.
Assistance to persons arrested while unconscious or semiconscious, §15A-503, (a), (b).
Cost of medical care, §15A-503, (c).
Unlawful arrest by officers from other states, §14-43.1.
Warrantless arrest.
Extradition of fugitives from other states, §15A-734.
Warrants.
Amendment.
Criminal warrants may be amended to show ownership of property, §15-24.1.
Arrest by officer pursuant to warrant, §15A-401, (a).
Arrest by officer without warrant, §15A-401, (b).
Contents, §15A-304, (c) to (e).
Criminal process generally, §15A-301.
Criminal summons.
Enforcement, §15A-303, (e).
Defined, §15A-304, (a).
District court judges.
Power of judge to issue arrest warrants, §7A-291.
Execution, delivery and service of criminal process, §15A-301.
Extradition.
Fugitives from other states, §15A-741.
Execution, §§15A-728, 15A-729.
Issuance, §15A-727.
Initial appearance before magistrate.
Procedure when arrest is pursuant to warrant, §15A-511, (d).
Issuance, §15A-304, (b).
Who may issue, §15A-304, (f).
Law enforcement officers.
Power of officer to issue arrest warrant.
Termination of power upon establishment of district court, §7A-274.

ARREST —Cont'd
Warrants —Cont'd
Magistrates.
Power of magistrate to issue arrest warrant in criminal action, §7A-273.
Mayors.
Power of mayor to issue arrest warrant.
Termination of power upon establishment of district court, §7A-274.
Mental health facilities.
State facilities.
Special policemen, §122C-183.
Order for arrest, §15A-304, (e).
Peace officers.
Arrest pursuant to warrant, §15A-401, (a).
Arrest without warrant, §15A-401, (b).
Probable cause.
Showing of probable cause, §15A-304, (d).
Public records, §132-1.4, (k).
Service of criminal process generally, §15A-301.
Statement of the crime, §15A-304, (c).
Weights and measures.
Powers of commissioner of agriculture, §81A-16.
Wildlife protectors.
Arrest without warrant, §113-136, (d).
Search on arrest, §113-137, (a).
Service of arrest warrants, §113-136, (e).
Witnesses.
Civil cases.
Exemption from arrest, §8-64.
Criminal cases.
Material witnesses.
Order of arrest, §15A-803, (g).
Witnesses from without state.
Exemption from arrest, §15A-814.

ARREST IN CIVIL CASES.
Affidavit by plaintiff, §1-411.
Copy to defendant, §1-414.
Counter affidavits, §1-418.
Attorneys at law.
Indigent persons.
Right to counsel, §1-413.
Bail and recognizance.
Civil cases.
See BAIL AND RECOGNIZANCE.
Bonds, surety.
Order for arrest.
Undertaking before order, §1-412.
Cases in which arrest allowed, §1-410.
Concealment.
Cases in which arrest allowed, §1-410.
Congress.
Privilege from arrest, Const. U. S., art. I, §6.
Contempt.
Exclusive nature of provisions.
Exception as to contempt, §1-409.
Copies of affidavit and order to defendant, §1-414.
Debtor leaving state or concealing self, §1-355.
Debtor removing or disposing property with intent to defraud creditors.
Cases in which arrest allowed, §1-410.
Embezzlement.
Cases in which arrest allowed, §1-410.
Exclusive nature of provisions, §1-409.
Exception as to contempt, §1-409.
Execution against the person, §1-311.
Form of execution, §1-313.
Fraud.
Cases in which arrest allowed, §1-410.

ARREST IN CIVIL CASES —Cont'd
Habeas corpus.
Party held in execution not to be discharged, §17-36.
Indigent persons.
Order for arrest.
Information to be included in order, §1-413.
Jury.
Petit jury.
Exemption from civil arrest, §9-16.
Motion to vacate order, §1-417.
Order for arrest, §1-411.
Copy to defendant, §1-414.
Execution of order, §1-415.
Form, §1-413.
Issuance, §1-413.
Motion to vacate, §1-417.
Jury trial on, §1-417.
Return, §1-413.
Undertaking before order, §1-412.
Vacation of order.
Failure to serve, §1-416.
Privilege from arrest.
Congress, Const. U. S., art. I, §6.
Quo warranto.
Defendant usurping office, §1-519.
Scope of provisions.
Cases in which arrest allowed, §1-410.
Seduction.
Cases in which arrest allowed, §1-410.
Supplemental proceedings.
Debtor leaving state or concealing self, §1-355.
Torts.
Cases in which arrest allowed, §1-410.
Usurpation of office.
Defendant usurping office, §1-519.
Witnesses.
Attendance of witnesses.
Exemption from civil arrest, §8-64.

ARREST OF JUDGMENT.
Prosecuting witness, §6-49.
Relief now available by motion for appropriate relief, §15A-1411, (c).

ARSENIC.
Pesticides.
Coloration or discoloration required, §143-443, (a).

ARSON.
Arrest.
Power of attorney general, §58-79-5.
Attempts to commit crime.
Burning or attempting to burn buildings not covered by other provisions, §14-67.1.
Barges, §14-63.
Barns, §14-62.
Bridges, §14-61.
Buildings.
Defined, §14-58.1.
Not covered by other provisions.
Burning or attempting to burn, §14-67.1.
Public buildings.
Bureau of investigation.
Authority over, §114-15.
Burning certain public buildings, §14-59.
Bureau of investigation.
Investigations of misuse of state property, §114-15.1.
Public buildings.
Authority over, §114-15.

ARSON —Cont'd
Capital punishment.
Aggravating circumstances.
Capital punishment in commission of arson, §15A-2000, (e).
Crimes punishable by death, Const. N. C., art. XI, §2.
Chapels, §§14-49, (b1), 14-62.2.
Churches, §§14-49, (b1), 14-62.2.
Coach houses, §14-62.
Construction.
Burning of building or structure in process of construction, §14-62.1.
Cotton ginhouses, §14-64.
Definitions.
Building, §14-58.1.
House, §14-58.1.
Destructive devices.
Making false report concerning devices, §14-69.1.
Dwelling houses.
Fraudulently setting fire, §14-65.
Educational institution buildings, §14-60.
Emergency medical technicians.
Serious injury to, §14-69.3.
False bomb or other device.
False reports concerning destructive devices, §14-69.1, (a).
Definition of "report," §14-69.1, (e).
Public buildings, §14-69.1, (c).
Restitution, §14-69.1, (d).
Perpetrating hoax by use of bomb or device, §14-69.2, (a).
Public building, §14-69.2, (c).
Restitution, §14-69.1, (d).
Ferries, §14-63.
Fire-engine houses, §14-61.
Firefighters.
Serious injury to, §14-69.3.
Fire investigations and inspection of premises, §§58-79-1 to 58-79-45.
First degree, §14-58.
Fraudulently setting dwelling on fire, §14-65.
Ginhouses, §14-64.
Granaries, §14-62.
Hoaxes.
False bombs or other devices, §14-69.2.
House.
Defined, §14-58.1.
Fraudulently burning dwelling, §14-65.
Manufactured-type house, §14-58.2.
Insurance.
Burning of personal property, §14-66.
Dwelling house fraudulently set fire to, §14-65.
Investigations.
Failure of officers to investigate incendiary fires, §14-69.
Manufactured-type house, §14-58.2.
Masjids, §14-49, (b1).
Meeting houses, §14-62.2.
Mills, §14-62.
Mobile homes, §14-58.2.
Mosques, §14-49, (b1).
Murder committed during commission of felony.
First degree murder, §14-17.
Outhouses, §14-62.
Personal property, §14-66.
Property owners.
Compliance with orders of public authorities.
Failure of owner to comply with orders, §14-68.

ARSON —Cont'd
Public authorities.
Compliance with orders of public authorities.
Failure of owner of property to comply with orders, §14-68.
Public buildings and grounds, §14-59.
Punishment for arson, §14-58.
Recreational trailer home, §14-58.2.
Rescue-squad building, §14-61.
Schoolhouses, §14-60.
Second degree, §14-58.
Shops, §14-62.
Stables, §14-62.
State capitol, §14-59.
Synagogues, §14-49, (b1).
Tobacco houses, §14-64.
Toll bridges, §14-61.
Warehouses, §14-62.
Watercraft, §14-63.

ART.
Arts council, §§143B-87, 143B-88.
Artwork on consignment, §§25C-1 to 25C-5.
Composer-laureate for state.
Appointment, §143-407.1, (a), (b).
Consignments.
Artwork on consignment, §§25C-1 to 25C-5.
Cultural resources department, §§143-403 to 143-415.
See CULTURAL RESOURCES DEPARTMENT.
Definitions, §143-403.
Sale of prints, §25C-10.
Executive mansion fine arts committee, §§143B-79, 143B-80.
Grassroots arts program, §§143B-121 to 143B-125.
Local governments.
Powers as to museums and arts programs, §160A-488.
Municipal corporations.
Powers as to museums and arts programs, §160A-488.
Property taxes.
Authorized purposes, §160A-209, (c).
North Carolina art society, §§140-12 to 140-14.
North Carolina museum of art, §§140-5.12 to 140-5.17.
Promotion of arts, §§143-403 to 143-407.1.
Sale of fine prints, §§25C-10 to 25C-16.
Sales and use tax.
Sales to North Carolina museum of art.
Exemption, §105-164.13.
Society, Inc., §143B-89.
State art museum, §§140-5.12 to 140-5.17.
Theft or destruction of art.
Property of public museums or galleries, §14-398.
University of North Carolina.
School of the arts, §§116-63 to 116-69.
See UNIVERSITY OF NORTH CAROLINA.

ART DEALERS.
Artwork on consignment.
Creditors may not reach works, §25C-4.
Defined, §25C-1.
Interest of dealer who accepts work, §25C-2.
Status of works subsequently purchased by dealer from own account, §25C-3.
Sale of prints, §§25C-10 to 25C-16.
Disclosure requirement, §25C-14.
General prohibitions, §25C-11.
Rights and liabilities not inclusive, §25C-15.

ARTERIOSCLEROSIS.
Food, drug and cosmetic act.
Drug or device, false advertising, §106-138, (b).

ARTHRITIS PROGRAM, §130A-222, (a).

ARTHROPODS.
Mosquito and vector control program, §§130A-346 to 130A-349.

ARTICLES OF INCORPORATION.
Amendment, §§55-10-01 to 55-10-09.
Defined, §55-1-40.
Filing, §55-2-03.
Nonprofit corporations.
Amendment, §§55A-10-01 to 55A-10-07.
Conclusive proof of incorporation, §55A-2-03, (b).
Contents, §55A-2-02, (a), (b).
Existence begins when articles filed, §55A-2-03, (a).
Powers of corporation need not be set forth, §55A-2-02, (c).
Restated articles, §55A-10-06.
Statutory powers need not be set out, §§55-2-02, 55-3-02.
Trust companies, §53-332.

ARTIFICIAL COLORING.
Food, drug and cosmetic act.
Foods deemed misbranded, §106-130.

ARTIFICIAL FLAVORING.
Food, drug and cosmetic act.
Foods deemed misbranded, §106-130.

ARTIFICIAL INSEMINATION.
Status of child born, §49A-1.

ARTIFICIAL INSEMINATION OF ANIMALS.
Sales and use tax rate on semen, §105-164.4, (a).
Veterinarians.
Exemption from provisions regulating veterinarians, §90-187.10.

ARTIFICIAL LIMBS.
Sales and use tax.
Exemption, §105-164.13.

ARTISTIC AND CREATIVE SERVICES CONTRACTS.
Minors, §§48A-11 to 48A-16.

ARTISTIC ORGANIZATIONS.
Solicitation of contributions, §§131F-1 to 131F-24.
See CHARITABLE SOLICITATION.

ARTS COUNCIL, §§143B-87, 143B-88.
Compensation of members, §143B-88.
Creation, §143B-87.
Department of cultural resources.
Transfer of commission to department, §143B-51.
Duties, §143B-87.
Members, §143B-88.
Powers, §143B-87.
Quorum, §143B-88.
Selection of members, §143B-88.

ARTS FESTIVALS.
Amusement license taxes.
Exemption, §105-40.

ARTS, PROMOTION OF.
Appropriations, §143-407.
Cultural resources department.
Duties, §143-406.
Executive Mansion.
Authority of administration department not affected, §143-415.

ARTS, PROMOTION OF —Cont'd
Cultural resources department —Cont'd
Executive Mansion —Cont'd
Powers of department, §143-411.
Purpose of provisions, §143-410.
Definitions, §143-403.
Funds, §143-407.
Gifts.
Acceptance by cultural resources department, §143-407.
Reports.
Submission of biennial report to governor, §143-406.

ARTS SOCIETY, INC.
Department of cultural resources.
Transfer of society to department, §143B-51.
Generally, §143B-89.

ARTWORK ON CONSIGNMENT, §§25C-1 to 25C-5.
Art dealers.
Acceptance of works of fine art on consignment.
Interest of art dealer who accepts, §25C-2.
Creditors of art dealer may not reach works of fine art on consignment with art dealer, §25C-4.
Defined, §25C-1.
Subsequent purchase of work of fine art for own account.
Status of works of fine art subsequently purchased, §25C-3.
Debts.
Art dealers.
Creditors of art dealer may not reach works of fine art on consignment with art dealer, §25C-4.
Definitions, §25C-1.
Insurance.
Provisions as to insurable interest.
Not affected, §25C-5.
Risk of loss.
Provisions not affected, §25C-5.
Works of fine art.
Acceptance on consignment.
Interest of art dealer who accepts, §25C-2.
Defined, §25C-1.
Subsequent purchase by art dealer for own account.
Status of works of fine art subsequently purchased, §25C-3.

ASBESTOS HAZARD MANAGEMENT, §§130A-444 to 130A-451.
Accreditation of persons performing management.
Exemptions, §130A-447, (c).
Fee, §130A-448, (a).
Required, §130A-447, (a).
Temporary accreditation, §130A-447, (b).
Administrative penalties, §130A-22, (b1), (b2).
Asbestos NESHAP for demolition and renovation.
Local air pollution programs.
Adoption and enforcement, §130A-452, (a), (b).
Definitions, §130A-444.
Exposure standards.
Public areas, §130A-446.
Fees.
Removal permits, §130A-450.
Local air pollution programs.
Asbestos NESHAP for demolition and renovation.
Adoption and enforcement, §130A-452, (a), (b).

ASBESTOS HAZARD MANAGEMENT —Cont'd
Penalties.
Administrative penalties, §130A-22, (b1), (b2).
Permits.
Material removal permits, §130A-449.
Removal permits.
Fees, §130A-450.
Public areas.
Exposure standards, §130A-446.
Removal.
Permits, §130A-449.
Fees, §130A-450.
Rules and regulations.
Adoption, §130A-451.
Schools.
Inspection, §130A-445.
School management plans.
Rules and regulations, §130A-445.
Training courses.
Approval, fee, §130A-448, (b).

ASBESTOSIS.
Workers' compensation.
Defined, §97-62.
Disability or death from.
Compensation, §97-61.6.
Disablement defined, §97-54.
Discontinued benefits.
Claims for further benefits, §97-66.
Exposure deemed injurious, §97-57.
First examination of and report on employee, §§97-61.1, 97-61.2.
General provisions of act to control benefits, §97-64.
Hearings on reports, §§97-61.1, 97-61.5, 97-61.6.
Injurious exposure.
Period necessary, §97-63.
Occupational diseases enumerated, §97-53.
Occupational diseases generally.
See WORKERS' COMPENSATION.
Rates of compensation, §§97-61.5, (b), 97-61.6.
Reduction of rate where tuberculosis developed, §97-65.
Removal from hazardous condition.
Compensation upon.
Waiver of right to compensation as alternative to forced change of occupation, §97-61.7.
Removal from hazardous occupation.
Compensation upon, §97-61.5, (b).
Second examination and report, §97-61.3.
Third examination and report, §97-61.4.

ASHEBORO MUNICIPAL AIRPORT.
Location of North Carolina aviation hall of fame and North Carolina aviation museum, §145-21.

ASHE COUNTY.
Acquisition of property, power, §153A-158.1, (a).
Agricultural tendencies in certain counties.
Terms of, §42-23.
Ambulances.
Obtaining ambulance services without intending to pay, §14-111.2.
Requesting ambulance falsely, §14-111.3.
Ambulance service.
Attachment or garnishment and lien for, §§44-51.4 to 44-51.8.
Blank or master forms of mortgages, deeds of trust, etc.
Indexing and recording, inapplicability of provisions, §47-21.

ASHE COUNTY —Cont'd
Condemnation or acquisition of land by local government unit outside county.
Consent of board of commissioners necessary, §153A-15.
Counties generally.
See COUNTIES.
Cropper or tenant refusing to perform terms of contract.
Forfeiture of right of possession to premises, §42-27.
Game laws, local acts not repealed, §113-133.1, (e).
Maps in special proceedings, recording of photographic copies, §47-32.
Violation as misdemeanor, inapplicability of provisions, §47-32.2.
Oil, gas or mineral interest separated from surface fee, extinguished, title in surface fee holder.
Failure to list property for tax purposes for 10 years prior to January 1, 1977, §1-42.4, (a) to (c).
Protection of interest against surface fee, §1-42.4, (b), (d).
On-premises unfortified wine licenses.
Discretion to decline to issue, §105-113.71, (b).
Probates and registration orders before clerks of inferior courts.
Validation, §47-59.
Real estate mortgage loans.
Interest, commissions and repayment, §45-43.
School property.
Acquisition and improvement, §153A-158.1.

ASPHALT.
Disposal of demolition debris consisting of used asphalt, §130A-294, (m).

ASSAULT AND BATTERY.
Acid or alkali, malicious throwing, §14-30.1.
Aggravated assault and battery.
Habitual misdemeanor assault, §14-33.2.
Punishment for misdemeanor assaults, §14-33, (b), (c).
Factors determining classification of offense, §14-33, (b), (c).
Arrest without warrant, §15A-401.
Attempts to commit crime.
Discharging certain barreled weapons or a firearm into occupied property, §14-34.1.
Blind persons, §14-32.1.
Castration, §§14-28, 14-29.
Children as victims.
Bail and recognizance, §15A-534.4.
Costs.
Allowance of costs to defendant, §6-19.
Allowance of costs to plaintiff, §6-18.
Crossing county lines.
Assault in one county, death in another, §15-130.
Crossing state lines.
Assault in this state, death in another, §15-131.
Deadly weapons.
See ASSAULT WITH DEADLY WEAPON.
Defenses.
Plea of self-defense.
Evidence of former threats upon plea, §14-33.1.
Detention facilities.
Person employed at state or local detention facility.
Assault on, §14-34.7, (b).

ASSAULT AND BATTERY —Cont'd
Domestic violence, §§50B-1 to 50B-9.
See DOMESTIC VIOLENCE.
Emergency personnel.
Assault or affray upon while discharging duties, §14-34.6, (a).
Infliction of bodily injury, §14-34.6, (b).
Use of deadly weapons other than firearms, §14-34.6, (b).
Use of firearms, §14-34.6, (c).
Assault with firearm upon, §14-34.2.
Riots and civil disorders, §14-288.9.
Endangering executive, legislative or court officers.
Applicability of article, §14-16.9.
Assault on executive, legislative or court officers, §14-16.6.
Definitions, §14-16.10.
Inflicting serious bodily injury, §14-16.6, (c).
Officers-elect to be covered, §14-16.9.
Threats against officers, §14-16.7.
Mailing threatening letters or documents, §14-16.7, (b).
No requirement of receipt of threat, §14-16.8.
Serious bodily injury, §14-16.7, (a).
Use of deadly weapons, §14-16.6, (b).
Violent attacks against persons or dwellings, §14-16.6, (a).
Evidence.
Plea of self-defense.
Evidence of former threats upon plea, §14-33.1.
Felonious assault with deadly weapon, §14-32.
Firearms.
Detention facilities.
Person employed at state or local detention facility.
Assault with firearm upon in performance of duties, §14-34.5, (b).
Discharging into occupied property, §14-34.1.
Emergency medical services personnel.
Assault with firearm upon, §§14-34.2, 14-34.6, (c).
Firemen.
Assault with firearm upon fireman, §14-34.2.
Habitual misdemeanor assault, §14-33.2.
Law enforcement officers.
Assault with firearm upon law enforcement officer, §14-34.2.
Assault with firearm upon law enforcement officer in performance of duties, §14-34.5, (a).
Pointing gun at person, §14-34.
Probation or parole officers.
Assault with firearm upon while in performance of duties, §14-34.5, (a).
Habitual misdemeanor assault, §14-33.2.
Handicapped persons, §14-32.1.
Aggravated assault, §14-32.1, (e).
Definition of handicapped person, §14-32.1, (a).
DNA analysis.
Blood sample required upon conviction, §15A-266.4.
Simple assault, §14-32.1, (f).
Hearing impaired.
Assault upon handicapped persons, §14-32.1.
Lesser included offenses.
Conviction of assault, when included in charge, §15-169.
Limitation of actions, §1-52.
Maliciously assaulting in secret manner, §14-31.

ASSAULT AND BATTERY —Cont'd
Mentally ill.
Assault upon handicapped persons, §14-32.1.
Minors.
Bail and recognizance, §15A-534.4.
Inflicting serious injury or using deadly weapon in presence of minor, §14-33, (d).
Misdemeanor assaults, batteries and affrays, §14-33, (b), (c).
Habitual misdemeanor assault, §14-33.2.
Motor vehicle assault.
Mandatory revocation of license, §20-17, (a).
Patient abuse, §14-32.2.
Police.
Assault on a law enforcement officer, §14-34.7.
Probation or parole officers.
Assault on, §14-34.7, (a).
Public school property.
Principals to report offenses occurring on school property, §115C-288, (g).
Public schools student.
Assault on teacher or other employee or other student.
Removal to alternative educational setting, §115C-391, (d2).
Rape.
See RAPE.
Riots and civil disorders.
Assault on emergency personnel, §14-288.9.
Secret manner.
Maliciously assaulting in secret manner, §14-31.
Self-defense.
Evidence of former threats upon plea of self-defense, §14-33.1.
Serious bodily injury.
Assault inflicting, §14-32.4, (a).
Sexual battery.
Elements of offense, §14-27.5A, (a).
Punishment, §14-27.5A, (b).
Sexual offenses generally.
See SEXUAL OFFENSES.
Simple assault and battery, §14-33, (a).
Strangulation, §14-32.4, (b).
Student at public school.
Assault on teacher or other employee or other student.
Removal to alternative educational setting, §115C-391, (d2).
Threats.
See THREATS.
Venue.
Assault in one county, death in another, §15-130.
Assault in this state, death in another, §15-131.
Warrantless arrest, §15A-401.

ASSAULT WITH DEADLY WEAPON.
Detention facilities.
Person employed at state or local detention facility.
Assault with firearm upon in performance of duties, §14-34.5, (b).
Emergency medical services.
Personnel assaulted with deadly weapon, §§14-34.2, 14-34.6, (b).
Fire protection.
Firemen assaulted with deadly weapon, §14-34.2.
Handicapped persons.
Assaults upon, §14-32.1.
Highway patrol.
Law enforcement officer assaulted with deadly weapon, §14-34.2.

ASSAULT WITH DEADLY WEAPON —Cont'd
Inflicting serious injury.
Punishment for felonious assault, §14-32, (b).
Intent to kill.
Punishment for felonious assault, §14-32, (a), (b).
Law enforcement officers.
Assault with deadly weapon upon law enforcement officer, §14-34.2.
Assault with firearm upon law enforcement officer in performance of duties, §14-34.5, (a).
Probation or parole officers.
Assault with firearm upon in performance of duties, §14-34.5, (a).
Punishment for felonious assault.
Inflicting serious injury, §14-32, (b).
Intent to kill and inflict serious injury, §14-32, (a), (c).

ASSAULT WITH MOTOR VEHICLE.
Mandatory revocation of license, §20-17, (a).

ASSEMBLY.
Mass gatherings, §§130A-251 to 130A-258.
See MASS GATHERINGS.
Right to assembly, Const. N. C., art. I, §12; Const. U. S., amd. I.
Weapons.
Carrying into assemblies, §14-269.3, (a).

ASSES.
Brands generally, §§80-45 to 80-66.
See LIVESTOCK BRANDS.
Equine infectious anemia, §§106-405.15 to 106-405.20.

ASSESSMENT COMPANIES, §§58-11-1 to 58-11-35.
Advance assessments.
Requirements, §58-11-20.
Bylaws.
Contracts must accord with, §58-11-5.
Filing of copies, §58-11-1.
Charters.
Contracts must accord with, §58-11-5.
Filing of copies, §58-11-1.
Contracts.
Conformance with charter and bylaws required, §58-11-5.
Deposit requirements, §58-11-20.
Foreign assessment companies, §58-11-25.
Revocation for noncompliance, §58-11-30.
Foreign companies.
Deposits by, §58-11-25.
Mutual life insurance companies.
Assessments prohibited, §58-11-35.
Policies.
"Assessment plan" to be printed on, §58-11-10.
Revocation for noncompliance, §58-11-15.
Conformance with charter and bylaws required, §58-11-5.
Revocation of authority to do business, §§58-11-15, 58-11-30.

ASSESSMENTS.
Agricultural fees and taxes.
Procedure, §106-9.3.
Agricultural products promotion.
See AGRICULTURAL PRODUCTS PROMOTION.
Agricultural research.
See AGRICULTURAL RESEARCH.
Air pollution control.
Title V program.
Assessment of program implementation fees, §143-215.106A.

ASSESSMENTS —Cont'd
Banks.
Impairment of capital, §53-42.
Banks and consumer finance licensees.
Operating and maintaining office of commissioner of banks, §53-122, (a), (e), (f).
Cigarettes and tobacco products.
Promotion of sale and use of tobacco.
See TOBACCO SALES.
Coastal fishery and seafood industry promotion, §§113-315.4 to 113-315.8.
Condominium owners' associations.
Common expenses, §47C-3-115.
Lien for assessment, §47C-3-116.
Conservation and historic preservation agreements.
Assessment of land or improvements subject to agreement, §121-40.
Cotton grower's organization, §§106-65.88, 106-65.90.
County water and sewer districts.
Special assessments authorized, §162A-92.
Drainage.
Deficiencies.
Supplemental assessments to make up deficiencies, §156-22.
Jurors.
Vacancy appointments of assessment jurors, §156-22.
Liens.
Drainage assessments declared liens, §156-21.
Petitions.
Agreement for construction.
Viewers, §156-28.
Subsequent owners bound, §156-14.
Supplemental assessment to make up deficiencies, §156-22.
Vacancy appointments of assessment jurors, §156-22.
Drainage corporations, §156-42.
Canals already constructed, §156-43.
Payment of dues entitles to use of canal, §156-46.
Penalty for nonpayment of assessments, §156-51.
Shareholders to pay assessments, §156-45.
Drainage districts, §§156-54 to 156-138.4.
See DRAINAGE DISTRICTS.
Fiduciaries.
Establishing and maintaining reserves.
Powers which may be incorporated by reference in trust instrument, §32-27.
Fraternal orders.
Collection, §58-25-15.
Funds derived from, §58-25-10.
Horse industry promotion, §§106-823 to 106-825.
Jurisdiction.
Personal jurisdiction.
Grounds, §1-75.4.
Life and health insurance guaranty association, §58-62-41.
Limestone, marl and landplaster.
Sale of agricultural liming materials and landplaster.
Appeals from assessments and orders of commissioner of agriculture, §106-92.13.
Marketing authority.
Exemptions, §106-534.
Mortgages and deeds of trust.
Reverse mortgages.
Contractual provisions for payment, §53-261.
Mutual insurance companies, §§58-8-40 to 58-8-55.

ASSESSMENTS —Cont'd
Nature preserves.
Land subject to permanent dedication agreement, §113A-164.11.
Oil and gas conservation.
Taxation, §113-387.
Collection, §113-388.
Planned community act.
Common expenses, §§47F-3-115, 47F-3-116.
Pork promotion assessment, §§106-790 to 106-796.
Primary forest product assessment act, §§113A-189 to 113A-196.
See FOREST PRODUCTS ASSESSMENT.
Sanitary districts.
Levy of tax, §130A-62, (b) to (d).
Seafood industry and coastal fishery promotion, §§113-315.4 to 113-315.8.
Social security.
Coverage of governmental employees under title II of social security act.
Contribution fund, §135-24, (f).
Strawberries, §§106-781 to 106-786.
Street light assessments, §153A-206.
Trust companies, §53-368.

ASSESSORS.
Generally.
See COUNTY ASSESSORS.
Magistrates.
Appointment of assessors by magistrate.
Fees of assessors, §7A-310.

ASSET-BACKED SECURITIES FACILITATION.
Definitions, §53-425.
Exceptions to provisions, §53-426, (b).
Waiver of equity of redemption, §53-426, (a).

ASSETS OF JUDGMENT DEBTORS.
Discovery.
Additional method, §1-352.2.
Generally, §§1-352 to 1-368.
See SUPPLEMENTAL PROCEEDINGS.
Interrogatories to discover assets generally, §1-352.1.
Supplemental proceedings generally, §§1-352 to 1-368.
See EXECUTIONS.

ASSIGNED RISK INSURANCE.
Workers' compensation.
Rate bureau.
Duties, §58-36-1.

ASSIGNMENT OF CASES FOR TRIAL, §1A-1, Rule 40, (a).

ASSIGNMENT OF PUPILS ACT, §§115C-364 to 115C-372.
See PUBLIC SCHOOLS.

ASSIGNMENT OF THING IN ACTION.
Action by assignee without prejudice to setoff or defense existing, §1-57.

ASSIGNMENTS.
Action by assignee on assignment of thing in action.
Action without prejudice to setoff or other defense, §1-57.
Assignments for benefit of creditors.
See ASSIGNMENTS FOR BENEFIT OF CREDITORS.
Child support.
Public assistance.
Acceptance of assistance constitutes assignment of support rights to state or county, §110-137.

ASSIGNMENTS —Cont'd
Child support —Cont'd
Unemployment compensation benefits, §110-136.2.
Wages, §110-136.1.
Claims against the state.
Charitable organization.
Approved by local board of education or community college board.
Deductions from employee's salary or wages, §143-3.3, (i).
Approved by University of North Carolina.
Deductions from employee's salary or wages, §143-3.3, (j).
Credit unions.
Deductions from state employee's salary or wages.
Authorization by state employee, §143-3.3, (f).
Definitions, §143-3.3, (a).
Domiciled employees' association.
Deductions from employee's salary or wages.
Authorization, §143-3.3, (g).
Exceptions to section, §143-3.3, (c), (d), (e).
Pledge to state employees combined campaign.
Deductions from employee's salary or wages.
Authorization, §143-3.3, (h).
Void unless duly audited and allowed by state, §143-3.3, (b).
Community trust for persons with severe chronic disabilities.
Life insurance policy proceeds assignments.
Acceptance by trust, §36A-59.13, (g), (h).
Consumer finance act.
Earnings.
Prohibited, §53-180, (b).
Contracts.
Real property pledged as security, §47-17.2.
Conveyances.
Real property pledged as security, §47-17.2.
Cost.
Liability of assignee for cost, §6-32.
Deeds.
Real property pledged as security, §47-17.2.
Default, secured obligation assigned.
Secured transactions.
Rights and duties of secondary obligors, §25-9-618.
Definitions.
Claims against the state, §143-3.3, (a).
Financing statements.
Secured party of right.
Powers assigned, §25-9-514.
Firemen's and rescue squad workers' pension fund.
Rights nonassignable, §58-86-90.
Issues.
Probate and registration.
Assignment of leases, rents, issues or profits, §47-20, (b) to (e).
Judgments.
Docketing.
Entry on judgment docket, §1-246.
Recordation.
Photographic process, §1-239.1.
Signing.
Required, §1-246.
Witnessing, §1-246.
Leases, rents, issues or profits.
Probate and registration, §47-20, (b) to (e).
Leases, UCC, §25-2A-303.
Limited liability company membership interest, §57C-5-02.
Right of assignee to become member, §57C-5-04.

ASSIGNMENTS —Cont'd
Mechanics, laborers and materialmen dealing with owner.
Claim of lien.
Notice of assignment of claim, §44A-12, (e).
Medical payments programs administered under chapter 130A.
Assignment to state of rights to third party benefits, §130A-13, (a) to (d).
Mortgage bankers and brokers.
Licenses.
Assignment prohibited, §53-243.06, (c).
Mortgages and deeds of trust.
Real property pledged as security, §47-17.2.
Parties.
Assignees, §1-57.
Partner's interest in partnership, §59-57, (a).
Rights of assignee in case of dissolution, §59-57, (b).
Partner's right in specific partnership property, §59-55, (b).
Preneed funeral contracts and funds, §90-210.68, (b), (c), (e).
Probate and registration, §47-1.
Leases, rents, issues or profits, §47-20, (b) to (e).
Renunciation of property or interest.
Bar to right to renounce, §31B-4, (a).
Sale of goods, UCC.
Rights of buyer and seller, §25-2-210.
Secured transactions.
Assignment of perfected interest.
Refiling not needed to perfect, §25-9-310, (c).
Inapplicability of article, §25-9-109, (d).
Real property pledged as security, §47-17.2.
Third party rights, §§25-9-401 to 25-9-409.
State departments, agencies and institutions.
Claims against state.
Generally, §143-3.3.
Surety's recovery on obligation paid.
No assignment necessary, §26-3.1, (a).
Construction of term "surety," §26-3.1, (b).
Surviving spouses.
Year's allowance, §§30-19 to 30-33.
See SURVIVING SPOUSES.
Trademarks.
Registration, §80-6.
Wages.
Acceptance by employer of assignment.
Employer not responsible until, §95-31.
Child support, §110-136.1.
Consumer finance act.
Assignment of earnings prohibited, §53-180, (b).
Usurious loans, §14-391.
Year's allowance, §§30-19 to 30-33.
See SURVIVING SPOUSES.

ASSIGNMENTS FOR BENEFIT OF CREDITORS.
Accounts and accounting.
Final account in twelve months, §23-11.
Quarterly accounts, §23-11.
Affidavits.
Petition for assignment, §23-13.
Appointment of trustees.
Insolvent trustee.
Substitute appointed, §23-5.
Order of appointment, §23-15.
Removal of trustee upon petition of creditors.
Substitute appointed, §23-6.
Substitute for incompetent trustee appointed in special proceedings, §23-4.

ASSIGNMENTS FOR BENEFIT OF CREDITORS —Cont'd
Bankruptcy and insolvency.
Insolvent trustee, §23-5.
Bonds, surety.
Release of insolvent upon giving bond, §23-40.
Substituted trustee to give bond, §23-7.
Surrender of principal.
Surety may surrender, §23-41.
Trustees.
Insolvent trustee removed unless bond given, §23-5.
Claims.
Creditors to file verified claims with clerk, §23-9.
Clerks of court.
Notice of petition.
Clerk to give, §23-14.
Discharge, §23-16.
Opposition.
Suggestion of fraud by opposing creditor, §23-17.
Execution of assignment.
Debts mature on executions, §23-1.
Executors and administrators.
Summary revocation of letters testamentary and of administration, §28A-9-2.
False swearing as to verified claims filed with clerk, §23-9.
Fraud.
Judgment of fraud by opposing creditor, §23-17.
Superior or district court to try issue, §23-39.
Fraudulent conveyances.
Trustee to recover property conveyed fraudulently, §23-3.
Limited liability companies.
Cessation of membership, §57C-3-02.
Misdemeanors.
Filing of verified claims by creditors with clerk.
False swearing, §23-9.
Trustees.
Violations of duties generally, §23-12.
Notice.
Petition.
Clerk to give notice of petition, §23-14.
Orders.
Discharge of insolvent, §23-15.
Terms and effect of order, §23-16.
Trustees.
Appointment, §23-15.
Payments.
Trustees.
Priority of payments by trustee, §23-10.
Perishable property.
Sale within ten days of registration, §23-8.
Petitions, §23-13.
Notice.
Clerk to give notice of petition, §23-14.
Preferences.
No preferences, §23-1.
Trustee to recover property fraudulently conveyed, §23-3.
Priority of payments by trustee, §23-10.
Prudent person rule.
Trustees.
Investments and deposit of funds, §36A-2, (a).
Sales.
Perishable property.
Sale within ten days of registration, §23-8.
Schedule of property.
Filing by trustee, §23-2.

ASSIGNMENTS FOR BENEFIT OF CREDITORS —Cont'd
Trust companies.
Seizure by commissioner.
Directors' resolution to place control under commissioner, §53-378.
Trustees.
Accounts quarterly, §23-11.
Appointment.
Order of appointment, §23-15.
Fraudulent conveyances.
Recovery of property fraudulently conveyed, §23-3.
Incompetent trustees.
Substitute appointed in special proceedings, §23-4.
Insolvent trustee removed unless bond given, §23-5.
Substitute appointed, §23-5.
Misdemeanors.
Violations of duties generally, §23-12.
Payments.
Priority of payments by trustee, §23-10.
Powers.
Generally, §23-44.
Removal upon petition of creditors.
Substitute appointed, §23-6.
Schedule of property to be filed by trustee, §23-2.
Substitute trustees.
Bonds, surety, §23-7.
Incompetent trustees, §23-4.
Removal of trustee on petition of creditors, §23-6.
Uniform fiduciaries act generally, §§32-1 to 32-13.
See FIDUCIARIES.
Verified claims filed by creditor with clerk, §23-9.
Violation of trustee duty, §23-12.

ASSISTANCE DOGS.
Assaulting law enforcement or assistance animals, §14-163.1.
Blind persons pedestrian rights and privileges without guide dog, §20-175.3.
Common carrier fares for blind person accompanied by, §62-144, (b).
Donation of service animal for training, §168-4.6.
Misdemeanors.
Prohibited acts, §168-4.5.
Mobility impaired persons.
Defined, §168-4.2.
Penalties.
Prohibited acts, §168-4.5.
Registration of service animal, §168-4.3.
Responsibility for service animal, §168-4.4.
Right to be accompanied by service animal, §168-4.2.
Penalty for depriving of right, §168-4.5.
Tags, §168-4.2.
Trainers.
Right to be accompanied by service animal, §168-4.2.
Training of service animal, §168-4.3.
Donation, §168-4.6.

ASSISTANT PRINCIPALS.
Dismissal.
Low-performing schools, §115C-325, (q).

ASSISTED LIVING ADMINISTRATORS, §§90-288.10 to 90-288.20.
Administrative procedures, applicability, §90-288.18, (b).

ASSISTED LIVING ADMINISTRATORS —Cont'd
Adverse actions on certificates, §90-288.18.
Applicability, §90-288.12, (b).
Certification.
Administrative procedures, applicability, §90-288.18, (b).
Adverse actions, §90-288.18.
Amendments, authority, §90-288.18, (a).
Contents, §90-288.15, (a).
Expiration, §90-288.15, (b).
Issuance, §90-288.15, (a).
Lost, destroyed or mutilated certificates, §90-288.15, (c).
Posting of certificates, §90-288.17.
Practicing without certificate, §90-288.20.
Procedures, §90-288.14.
Qualifications, §90-288.14.
Recall, suspension or revocation, §90-288.18, (a).
Reciprocity, §90-288.16.
Renewal, §90-288.15, (b).
Replacement certificates, §90-288.15, (c).
Required, §90-288.12, (a).
Validity of certificate, §90-288.12, (a).
Citation of act, §90-288.10.
Criminal penalty.
Practicing without certificate, §90-288.20.
Defined terms, §90-288.13.
Exemptions, §90-288.12, (b).
Findings, §90-288.11.
Posting of certificates, §90-288.17.
Preceptors.
Defined, §90-288.13.
Purpose of act, §90-288.11.
Qualifications, §90-288.14.
Reciprocity, §90-288.16.
Reports, §90-288.19.
Title of act, §90-288.10.
Validity of certificate, §90-288.12, (a).

ASSISTED LIVING RESIDENCES.
Generally.
See ADULT CARE HOMES.

ASSOCIATE SAFETY PROFESSIONALS (ASP), §§90-671 to 90-674.

ASSOCIATIONS.
Actions.
Parties.
Suits by or against unincorporated associations, §1-69.1.
Agriculture products promotion.
Meetings, activities or associations deemed not in restraint of trade, §106-552.
Automobile dealers.
Declaratory and injunctive relief, §20-308.1, (d).
Averment of capacity, §1A-1, Rule 84.
Building and loan associations.
See SAVINGS AND LOAN ASSOCIATIONS.
Burning of unincorporated association's buildings, §14-61.
Cemetery associations or corporations, §§65-16 to 65-17.1.
Class actions.
Secondary action by members, §1A-1, Rule 23, (b).
Community colleges.
Trustee association regions.
Division of regions, §115D-62.
Cooperative associations, §§54-111 to 54-128.
See COOPERATIVE ASSOCIATIONS.
Declaratory judgments.
Word "person" construed as including unincorporated association or society, §1-265.

ASSOCIATIONS —Cont'd
Depositions, use in court proceedings, §1A-1, Rule 32, (a).
Deposition upon oral examination, §1A-1, Rule 30, (b).
Health maintenance organizations, §§58-67-1 to 58-67-185.
See HEALTH MAINTENANCE ORGANIZATIONS.
Interrogatories to parties, §1A-1, Rule 33, (a).
Judgments and decrees.
Binding effect of judgments against associations, §1-69.1.
Land and loan associations, §§54-45 to 54-73.
See LAND AND LOAN ASSOCIATIONS.
Life and health insurance guaranty association, §§58-62-2 to 58-62-95.
See LIFE AND HEALTH INSURANCE GUARANTY ASSOCIATION.
Lloyds insurance associations, §58-17-1.
Marketing associations, §§54-129 to 54-166.
See MARKETING ASSOCIATIONS.
Motor clubs and associations, §§58-69-2 to 58-69-55.
See MOTOR CLUBS AND ASSOCIATIONS.
Mutual burial associations, §§90-210.80 to 90-210.107.
See MUTUAL BURIAL ASSOCIATIONS.
Parties.
Suits by or against unincorporated associations, §1-69.1.
Political contributions.
Prohibited acts, §163-278.19.
Post assessment insurance guaranty association, §§58-48-1 to 58-48-130.
See POST ASSESSMENT INSURANCE GUARANTY ASSOCIATION.
Real estate appraisers.
License or certificate not issued to, §93E-1-3, (a).
Use of term "state-licensed real estate appraiser" or "state-certified real estate appraiser prohibited," §93E-1-3.1, (c).
Real property conveyances by voluntary organizations and associations, §§39-24 to 39-27.
Authority to acquire and hold real estate, §39-24.
Prior deeds validated, §39-27.
Probate, §39-25.
Trustees.
Effect as to conveyances by trustees, §39-26.
Vesting title, §39-25.
Religious societies, §§61-1 to 61-7.
Restraint of trade.
Promotion of use and sale of agricultural products.
Meetings, activities or associations deemed not in restraint of trade, §106-552.
Roanoke Island historical association, §§143-199 to 143-202.
Savings and loan associations.
See SAVINGS AND LOAN ASSOCIATIONS.
Secondary actions by members, §1A-1, Rule 23, (b).
Seeds.
North Carolina crop improvement association, §106-273.
Service of process.
Personal jurisdiction.
Manner of service to exercise, §1A-1, Rule 4, (j).

ASSOCIATIONS —Cont'd
Social security.
Coverage of governmental employees under title II of social security act.
Transfers from state to certain association service, §135-27.
Unincorporated associations.
Declaratory judgments.
Word "person" construed, §1-265.
Property tax abstracts.
Content requirements, §105-309, (b).
Secondary action by members, §1A-1, Rule 23, (b).
Service of process.
Personal jurisdiction, manner of service, §1A-1, Rule 4, (j).
Suit by or against, §1-69.1.

ASSUMED NAMES.
Boxing under fictitious or assumed name, §143-655, (b).
Business under assumed name, §§66-68 to 66-71.
Accountants.
Partnerships engaged in practice of certified public accountancy.
Exemption from provisions, §66-68, (e).
Actions.
Violations of provisions.
Recovery in civil action not prevented, §66-71, (b).
Certificates.
Copy.
Prima facie evidence, §66-69.1.
Filing required, §66-68, (a).
Exceptions, §66-68, (d), (e).
Index of certificates.
Register of deeds to keep, §66-69.
Transfer of assumed name, §66-69.
Withdrawal of assumed name, §66-69.
Signing, §66-68, (b).
Transfer of assumed name, §66-68, (f).
Index, §66-69.
Withdrawal of assumed name, §66-68, (f).
Index, §66-69.
Evidence.
Copy of certificate prima facie evidence, §66-69.1.
Misdemeanors.
Violations of provisions, §66-71, (a).
Partnerships.
Public accountancy.
Exemption of partnerships engaged in practice of certified public accountancy, §66-68, (e).
Withdrawal of partner or new partner.
New certificate, §66-68, (c).
Transfer of assumed name, §66-68, (f).
Violations of provisions.
Penalties, §66-71, (a).
Recovery in civil action not prevented, §66-71, (b).
Withdrawal of assumed name, §66-68, (f).
Defendant sued in fictitious name.
Amendment of pleading or proceeding upon discovery of true name, §1-166.
Hotels, inns and other transient lodging places.
Registration of guests to be in true name, §72-30.
Insurance producers.
Commissioner notified, §58-33-83.
Optometrists.
Practicing under other than own name, §90-125.

ASSUMED NAMES —Cont'd
Osteopaths.
Prohibited acts, §90-136.
Partnerships.
Applicability of "assumed name" statute, §59-84.1, (a).
Plumbing, heating and fire sprinkler contractors.
Licenses.
Issuance in trade name, §87-26, (c) to (e).
Professional employer organizations.
Fictitious or assumed name.
Conducting business under, §58-89A-80, (a).

ASSUMPTION OF LOANS.
Sublease and loan assumption arranging.
Motor vehicles, §20-106.2.

ASSUMPTION OF RISK.
Affirmative defense, pleading, §1A-1, Rule 8, (c).
Minor employed to commit drug violation.
Doctrine defense to civil liability, §90-95.5.
Roller skaters and spectators.
Obvious and necessary inherent risks, §99E-12.
Defense to suit against operator, §99E-14.
Skateboarding, inline skating and freestyle bicycling, §99E-24.
Skiing competitions, §99C-4.

ASSUMPTION REINSURANCE, §§58-10-20 to 58-10-65.
See REINSURANCE.

ASYLUM.
Extradition.
No immunity from other criminal prosecution while in this state, §15A-748.

ATHLETE AGENTS, §§78C-85 to 78C-105.
Action by education institution against agent or student-athlete, §78C-100, (a).
Damages, §78C-100, (b).
Discovery of violation, accrual of action, §78C-100, (c).
Rights, remedies or defenses not limited, §78C-100, (e).
Several and joint liability, §78C-100, (d).
Administrative penalty, §78C-101.
Agency contracts.
Cancellation by student-athlete.
Consequences, §78C-96, (c).
Notice of cancellation, §78C-96, (a).
Waiver of right, §78C-96, (b).
Defined, §78C-86.
Notice by student-athlete of existence of contract.
To athletic director, §78C-95, (b).
To educational institution, §78C-95, (a).
Prohibited conduct, §78C-98, (a).
Provisions required, §78C-94, (b).
Record of contract, providing student-athlete, §78C-94, (e).
Registration requirements.
Contract in violation void, §78C-88, (d).
Requirements, §78C-94, (a).
Voidable, nonconforming contracts, §78C-94, (d).
Waiver of attorney client privilege, §78C-94, (c), (f).
Warning to student-athlete as to consequences of signing, §78C-94, (c).
Attorney-client privilege.
Waiver of attorney client privilege.
Records maintained by agent, §78C-97, (c).
Signing agency contract, §78C-94, (c), (f).

ATHLETE AGENTS —Cont'd
Attorneys licensed and resident of state.
Acting without certificate of registration, §78C-88, (c).
Child support enforcement.
Forfeiture of licensing privilege, §50-13.12.
Suspension or revocation of license, §110-142.1.
Civil penalty, §78C-101.
Civil remedies, §78C-100.
Criminal penalties, §78C-99.
Damages.
Action by education institution against agent or student-athlete, §78C-100, (b).
Definitions, §78C-86.
Electronic records and signature.
Law governing, §78C-103.
Fees.
Registration, §78C-93.
Felony convictions.
Forfeiture of certificate, §15A-1331A.
Nonresidents agents acting as agent in state.
Secretary of state.
Agent for service of process, §78C-87, (a).
Notice by student-athlete of cancellation of agency contract, §78C-96, (a).
Notice by student-athlete of existence of agency contract.
To athletic director, §78C-95.
Prohibited conduct, §78C-98, (a), (b).
Civil remedies, §78C-100.
Criminal penalties, §78C-99.
Prudent person rule.
Investment and deposit of funds, §36A-2, (a).
Records required to be maintained, §78C-97, (a).
Attorney-client privilege waived, §78C-97, (c).
Open to public inspection, §78C-97, (b).
Prohibited conduct, §78C-98, (b).
Registration.
Acting without certificate.
Attorneys licensed and resident of state, §78C-88, (c).
When permitted, §78C-88, (b).
Agency contract resulting from conduct in violation of provisions.
Void, §78C-88, (d).
Application, §78C-89, (a).
Copy of application in lieu of.
Agent registered in another state, §78C-89, (b).
Public record, §§78C-89, (c), 78C-90, (g).
Renewal, §78C-90, (d), (e).
Duration, §78C-90, (f).
Fees, §78C-93.
Forfeiture of certificate.
Felony convictions, §15A-1331A.
Issuance of certificate, §78C-90, (a).
Prohibited conduct, §78C-98, (b).
Refusal to issue certificate, §78C-90, (b).
Consideration in making determination, §78C-90, (c).
Renewal, §78C-90, (d), (e).
Required to act as agent in state, §78C-88, (a).
Suspension, revocation or refusal to renew.
Authority of secretary, §78C-91, (a).
Notice and opportunity for hearing required, §78C-91, (b).
Temporary registration, §78C-92.
Rules, adoption, §78C-105.

ATHLETE AGENTS —Cont'd
Service of process.
Secretary of state.
Agent for service of process.
Appointed for nonresident athlete agents, §78C-87, (a).
Severability of provisions, §78C-104.
Subpoenas.
Secretary of state, authority to issue, §78C-87, (b).
Uniform athlete agents act.
Article cited as, §78C-85.
Uniformity of application and construction, §78C-102.

ATHLETIC CLUBS.
Prepaid entertainment contracts, §§66-118 to 66-125.

ATHLETIC CONTESTS.
Admission fee charged.
License tax.
Cities may levy but counties may not, §105-37.1, (d).
Privilege tax on gross receipts, §105-37.1, (a).
Rate and payment, §105-37.1, (b).
Alcoholic beverages.
Publicly displaying fortified wine, spirituous liquor or mixed beverages at athletic contests, §18B-301, (f).
Assault and battery.
Evidence of threats upon plea of self defense, §14-33.1.
Sports officials, §14-33.
Bonuses.
Not forbidden, §14-379.
Boxing, §§143-651 to 143-658.
See BOXING.
Bribery.
Acceptance of bribes by players, managers, etc., §14-374.
Completion of offenses, §14-375.
Definition of bribe, §14-376.
Elements of offense of bribery of players, managers, etc., §14-373.
Compensation.
Extra compensation not forbidden, §14-379.
First aid or emergency treatment, liability limitation.
Services provided by volunteer health care provider.
Services deemed not to be a normal and ordinary course of provider's business or profession, §90-21.14, (b).
Intentionally losing contests, §14-377.
Leave of state employees.
Paid leave for certain athletic competition, §126-8.1.
Limited food establishment.
Preparing and serving food in conjunction with amateur sporting events.
Defined, §130A-247.
Permits, issuance, §130A-248, (a4).
Sanitation, rules governing, adoption, §130A-248, (a4).
Limiting margin of victory or defeat, §14-377.
Throwing, dropping, etc., objects at sporting events.
Offenses against the public safety, §14-281.1.
Venue.
Protection of athletic contests.
Proper venue of prosecutions under article, §14-378.

ATHLETIC TEAMS.
First aid or emergency treatment, liability limitation.
Services provided by volunteer health care provider.
Deemed not to be a normal and ordinary course of provider's business or profession, §90-21.14, (b).

ATHLETIC TRAINERS.
Board of examiners.
Compensation, §90-524, (f).
Composition and terms, §90-524, (b).
Contributions.
Acceptance, §90-526, (b).
Creation, §90-524, (a).
Duties, §90-525.
Expenses, §90-534, (a).
Fees, §90-534, (b).
Funds.
Custody and use, §90-526, (a).
Meetings, §90-524, (h).
Officers, §90-524, (g).
Powers, §90-525.
Qualifications, §90-524, (c).
Removal of members, §90-524, (e).
Vacancies, §90-524, (d).
Citation of article, §90-522, (a).
Continuing education.
Renewal of license, §90-533.
Definitions, §90-523.
Actively engaged, §90-530, (b).
Disciplinary actions.
Complaints, §90-539.
Grounds, §90-536, (a).
Sanctions, §90-536, (b).
Expenses, §90-534, (a).
Funds.
Custody and use of, §90-526, (a).
Identification badges required, §90-640.
Immunities.
Good faith reports of misconduct or incapacity, §90-539.
Injunctions.
Illegal practices, §90-537.
Licenses.
Applications, §90-528, (a).
Continuing education, §90-533.
Examination.
Licensure without examination, §90-530.
Exemptions, §90-527, (b).
Issuance, §90-528, (c).
Trainers previously certified, §90-529.
Lapse, §90-532.
Qualifications of applicant, §90-528, (b).
Reciprocity, §90-531.
Renewal, §90-532.
Continuing education, §90-533.
Required, §90-527, (a).
Trainers previously certified, §90-529.
Misdemeanors, §90-538.
Purpose of article, §90-522, (b).
Reciprocity.
Licenses, §90-531.
Reimbursements.
Third-party reimbursements, §90-540.
Schools.
Hiring by school units, §90-535.
Third-party reimbursements, §90-540.
Violations, §90-538.
Penalties, §90-538.

ATLANTIC BEACH.
Eminent domain.
Exercise of power, purposes, modified provisions, §40A-3, (b1).
Vesting of title and right to possession, §40A-42, (a).
Ordinances to regulate and control swimming, personal watercraft operation, surfing and littering in Atlantic Ocean, §160A-176.2.

ATLANTIC OCEAN.
Jurisdiction over marine fisheries resources.
Marine fisheries commission, §113-134.1.
Municipal corporations.
Ordinances effective in beach towns, §160A-176.1.
Ordinances to regulate and control swimming, personal watercraft operation, surfing and littering in Atlantic Ocean, §§160A-176.1, 160A-176.2.

ATLANTIC STATES MARINE FISHERIES COMPACT AND COMMISSION, §§113-251 to 113-258.

ATM CARDS.
Financial transaction card crime act, §§14-113.8 to 14-113.17.
See FINANCIAL TRANSACTION CARDS.

A TOAST TO NORTH CAROLINA.
State toast, §149-2.

ATOMIC ENERGY, RADIOACTIVITY AND IONIZING RADIATION.
Confidentiality.
Disclosure authorization, §104E-29, (b).
Protection of information, §104E-29, (a).
Criminal penalties for violation, §104E-29, (c).
Counties.
Privileged license taxes.
Low-level radioactive and hazardous waste facilities, §153A-152.1, (a) to (c).
Regulation of radioactive substances, §153A-128.
Definitions.
Dumping of radioactive material, §14-284.2.
Radiation protection, §104E-5.
Dumping of radioactive material.
Definitions, §14-284.2, (b) to (d).
Elements of offense, §14-284.2, (a).
Penalty for willful violations, §14-284.2, (a).
Dumping of toxic substances.
Willful violations of provisions, §14-284.2, (a).
Fees for facilities producing electricity in state, §166A-6.1, (a), (b).
Fire insurance.
Nuclear reaction, nuclear radiation or radioactive contamination.
Optional policy provisions as to loss or damage from, §58-44-25.
Mass death and destruction weapons.
Manufacture, assembly, etc., §14-288.8.
Nuclear, biological or chemical weapons, §§14-288.21 to 14-288.24.
See WEAPONS OF MASS DEATH AND DESTRUCTION.
Municipal corporations.
Regulation of radioactive substances, §160A-183.
Radiation protection act.
Generally, §§104E-1 to 104E-29.
See RADIATION PROTECTION.
Radioactive waste.
See RADIOACTIVE WASTE.
Spent nuclear fuel.
Transportation of spent nuclear fuel, §20-167.1.

ATOMIC ENERGY, RADIOACTIVITY AND IONIZING RADIATION —Cont'd
Taxation.
Property taxes.
Exemptions.
Special nuclear materials, §105-275.
Transportation of spent nuclear fuel, §20-167.1.
University of North Carolina.
Damage or personal injury arising from construction or operation of nuclear reactors.
Actions, §116-40.2.
Insurance in connection with construction or operation of nuclear reactors.
Authorization to purchase, §116-40.2.
Water and air resources.
Prohibited discharges, §143-214.2, (a).

AT-RISK STUDENTS.
Extended services programs, §§115C-238.30 to 115C-238.33.
Based on needs assessments of children, §115C-238.31, (c).
Collaboratively based programs, §115C-238.31, (d).
Community-based locations, §115C-238.31, (d).
Goals and expected outcomes based on needs assessment, §115C-238.32, (b).
Implementation of services, §115C-238.31, (a).
Integrated with existing classroom and school activities, §115C-238.31, (c).
Intent of general assembly, §115C-238.30.
Model plans developed by state board, §115C-238.33, (a).
Needs assessment, §115C-238.32, (a).
Purposes, §115C-238.30.
School based programs, §115C-238.31, (d).
Target of programs, §115C-238.31, (b).

ATTACHMENT.
Affidavits.
Amendment, §1-440.11, (c), (d).
Complaint.
Verified complaint used as affidavit, §1-440.11, (b).
Filing.
Judge to require, §1-440.5, (c).
Requirements, §1-440.11, (a).
Sheriffs.
Sale of debts and other evidences of indebtedness, §1-440.46, (b).
Agriculture.
Delinquent fees and taxes.
Collection of delinquent fees and taxes, §106-9.4, (b).
Alimony.
Remedies available, §50-16.7, (e).
Ambulances.
County or city ambulance services, §§44-51.4 to 44-51.8.
Ancillary proceedings, §1-440.1, (a).
Authority to fix and determine procedural details.
Court of proper jurisdiction, §1-440.9.
Bank deposits and collections.
When item subject to legal process, §25-4-303, (a).
Bills of lading.
Attachment of goods covered by a negotiable document, §25-7-602.
Blind persons.
Aid to the blind.
Payment of awards.
Exemption from attachment, §111-18.

ATTACHMENT —Cont'd
Bonds, surety.
Actions on bond.
Defenses.
Certain defenses disallowed, §1-440.8, (d).
Affidavit of surety, §1-440.8, (b).
Amount of bond, §1-440.10.
Approval by court.
Bonds subject to, §1-440.8, (c).
Conditions of bond, §1-440.10.
Discharge of attachment upon giving bond.
Amount of bond, §1-440.39, (b).
Effect, §1-440.39, (c), (d).
Motion for, §1-440.39, (a).
Execution of bonds, §1-440.8, (a).
Filing.
Judge to require, §1-440.5, (c).
Increased or new bond.
Order to furnish, §§1-440.40, (a), 1-440.42, (a).
Failure to comply, §1-440.42, (c).
Objections to bond or surety.
Defendant, §1-440.40, (b).
Plaintiff, §1-440.42, (a), (b).
Recovery on bond.
When defendant prevails in principal action, §1-440.45, (c).
When plaintiff prevails in principal action, §1-440.46, (d).
Requirements, §1-440.10.
Stay of order dissolving or modifying.
Plaintiff's bond, §1-440.38.
Child support.
Enforcement of support.
Remedy available, §50-13.4, (f).
Corporations.
Grounds for attachment, §1-440.3.
Death of defendant after levy, §1-440.34.
Discharge of attachment upon giving bond.
Amount of bond, §1-440.39, (b).
Effect, §1-440.39, (c), (d).
Motion for, §1-440.39, (a).
Dissolution, dismissal or setting aside of attachment.
Proceedings after, §1-440.45, (a), (b).
Dissolution of attachment.
Failure to serve summons or give notice by publication within time, §1-440.7, (b).
Jury trial, §1-440.36, (c).
Motion for, §1-440.36, (a).
Hearing of motion, §1-440.36, (b), (c).
Remedies of third person claiming attached property or interest therein, §1-440.43.
Service of process.
Noncompliance with time limit, §1-440.7, (b).
Stay of order dissolving order of attachment, §1-440.38.
Documents of title.
Attachment of goods covered by a negotiable document, §25-7-602.
Family law arbitration, §50-44, (c).
Federal liens.
Certificate of nonattachment, §44-68.14, (b), (c).
Firemen's and rescue squad workers' pension fund.
Exemption of pensions from attachment, §58-86-90.
Fraternal benefit societies.
Benefits subject to attachment, §58-24-85.
Funds transfers, UCC.
Creditor process served on receiving bank, §25-4A-502.

ATTACHMENT —Cont'd
Garnishment.
See GARNISHMENT.
Grounds for attachment, §1-440.3.
Habeas corpus.
County may be called on to aid execution, §17-22.
Failure to obey writ, §17-16.
Refusal of attachment.
Liability of judge refusing attachment, §17-17.
Sheriffs.
Attachment against sheriff to be directed to coroner, §17-18.
Order of discharge.
Compelling obedience, §17-23.
Injunctions.
Transfer of certificate of stock, §1-440.19, (c).
Transfer of negotiable warehouse receipts, §1-440.20, (b).
Insurer supervision, rehabilitation and liquidation.
Attachment prohibited during pendency of liquidation proceeding, §58-30-295.
Intent to defraud creditors.
Grounds for attachment, §1-440.3.
Judgments.
Jurisdiction required for rendering personal judgment against defendant, §1-440.1, (b).
Procedure after judgment.
When defendant prevails in principal action, §1-440.45, (a), (b).
When plaintiff prevails in principal action, §1-440.46.
Sale of attached property before judgment, §1-440.44.
Satisfaction of judgment.
When plaintiff prevails in principal action, §1-440.46, (a).
Satisfaction of plaintiff's claim.
Rendering judgment providing for application of attached property to, §1-440.1, (c).
Jurisdiction.
In rem or quasi in rem jurisdiction.
Grounds, §1-75.8.
Required for rendering personal judgment against defendant, §1-440.1, (b).
Jury.
Dissolution of order of attachment.
Jury trial of motion, §1-440.36, (c).
Legislative retirement system.
Exemption from attachment, §120-4.29.
Levy.
Death of defendant after levy, §1-440.34.
Goods in warehouses, §1-440.20, (a).
Order of attachment.
Delivery of copy of order to defendant not required, §1-440.15, (c).
Methods of execution generally, §1-440.15, (a).
Personal property.
Levy upon personal property before real property, §1-440.15, (b).
Tangible personal property in defendant's possession, §1-440.18.
Real property.
Docketing levy, §1-440.17, (b).
How levy made, §1-440.17, (a).
Levy on personal property before real property, §1-440.15, (b).
Stock in corporation, §1-440.19.
Liens.
County or city ambulance service, §§44-51.4 to 44-51.8.

ATTACHMENT —Cont'd
Liens —Cont'd
Death of defendant after levy, §1-440.34, (b).
Mechanics, laborers and materialmen dealing with owner.
Remedy available to lien claimant, §44A-15.
Priority of liens, §1-440.33, (f), (g).
When lien of attachment begins, §1-440.33, (a) to (e).
Lis pendens.
Docketing notice of attachment upon lis pendens docket, §§1-116, (a), 1-440.33, (a).
When notice of suit required to be filed, §1-116, (a).
Motor vehicles.
Delinquent taxes.
Remedies for collection, §20-99.
Municipal corporations.
Remedies for collecting taxes, §160A-207.
Nature of attachment, §1-440.1, (a) to (c).
Nonresidents.
Grounds for attachment, §1-440.3.
Notice.
Order of attachment.
Filing in county where real property of defendant located, §1-440.33, (a).
Publication.
Issuance of notice of order when no personal service, §1-440.14, (a) to (c).
Order of attachment.
Additional orders of attachment at time of original order, §1-440.13, (a).
Alias and pluries orders, §1-440.13, (b).
Contents, §1-440.12, (a).
Dissolution of order, §1-440.36.
Execution.
Methods, §1-440.15, (a).
Return, §1-440.16, (a) to (c).
Form, §1-440.12, (a).
Issuance.
By whom issued, §1-440.5, (a).
Time for, §§1-440.5, (b), 1-440.6, (a), (b).
Levy.
Delivery of copy of order to defendant not required, §1-440.15, (c).
Methods of execution generally, §1-440.15, (a).
Modification of order, §1-440.37.
Remedies of third person claiming attached property or interest therein, §1-440.43.
Stay of order modifying order of attachment, §1-440.38.
More than one order issued.
Priority of liens, §1-440.33, (c) to (e).
Notice.
Filing in county where real property of defendant located, §1-440.33, (a).
Publication.
Notice of issuance when no personal service, §1-440.14, (a) to (c).
Publication.
Notice of issuance when no personal service, §1-440.14, (a) to (c).
Return after execution, §1-440.16, (a).
Garnishee process issued, §1-440.16, (b).
No levy made, §1-440.16, (c).
Return date.
Order not to contain, §1-440.12, (b).
Personal property.
Levy upon personal property before real property, §1-440.15, (b).
Levy upon tangible personal property in defendant's possession, §1-440.18.

ATTACHMENT —Cont'd
Powers of court.
Procedural details, §1-440.9.
Procedural details, statute fails to make definite provision.
Authority of court to fix procedural details, §1-440.9.
Property subject to attachment, §1-440.4.
Property taxes, §§105-366, 105-368.
Publication.
Issuance of notice of order when no personal service.
Original order issued after publication, §1-440.14, (b).
Service by publication subsequent to issuance of order, §1-440.14, (a).
No newspaper published in county where action pending, §1-440.14, (c).
Real property.
Docketing levy, §1-440.17, (b).
How levy made, §1-440.17, (a).
Levy upon personal property before real property.
Not required, §1-440.15, (b).
Lien.
Attachment when levy docketed and indexed, §1-440.33, (b).
Notice of issuance of order of attachment.
Filing in county where real property of defendant located, §1-440.33, (a).
Remedies.
Remedies of defendant not exclusive, §1-440.41.
Third person claiming attached property or interest therein, §1-440.43.
Residue of attached property or proceeds thereof.
Delivery to defendant after judgment and costs paid, §1-440.46, (e).
Retirement system for teachers and state employees.
Exemption from attachment, §135-9.
Return.
Sheriff's return, §1-440.16, (a) to (c).
Sales.
Sale of attached property before judgment, §1-440.44.
Proceeds.
Disposition, §1-440.44, (b).
When sheriff to apply for authority to sell property, §1-440.44, (a).
Satisfaction of judgment.
When plaintiff prevails in principal action, §1-440.46, (a).
Sales and use tax.
Delinquent taxes, §105-164.39.
Scope of provisions.
Actions in which attachment may be had, §1-440.2.
Grounds for attachment, §1-440.3.
Property subject to attachment, §1-440.4.
Secured transactions.
Security interest attachment, §25-9-203, (a).
Financial asset.
Security interest arising in purchase or delivery of, §25-9-206.
Payment against delivery transactions, §25-9-206, (c), (d).
Purchase through securities intermediary, §25-9-206, (a), (b).
Service of process.
Publication.
Notice of issuance of order of attachment where no personal service, §1-440.14, (a) to (c).

ATTACHMENT —Cont'd
Service of process —Cont'd
Publication —Cont'd
Time for service by publication, §1-440.7, (a).
Time for, §1-440.7, (a).
Dissolution of attachment for noncompliance, §1-440.7, (b).
Sheriffs.
Affidavits.
Sale of debts and other evidences of indebtedness, §1-440.46, (b).
Care of attached property.
Expenses, §1-440.35.
Liability for, §1-440.35.
Residue of attached property or proceeds thereof.
Delivery to defendant after judgment and costs paid, §1-440.46, (e).
Return, §1-440.16, (a) to (c).
Sale of attached property before judgment.
Proceeds.
Retention by sheriff, §1-440.44, (b).
When sheriff to apply for authority to sell property, §1-440.44, (a).
Satisfaction of judgment.
Duties as to, §1-440.46, (a) to (c).
Stay of order dissolving or modifying order or attachment, §1-440.38.
Stock and stockholders.
Levy on stock in corporation, §1-440.19, (a), (b).
Plaintiff prevailing in principal actions, §1-440.46, (c).
Sale of stock.
Certificate of sale, §1-440.46, (c).
Transfer of certificate of stock.
Restraining order or injunction, §1-440.19, (c).
Support and maintenance.
Actions in which attachment may be had, §1-440.2.
Taxation.
Collection of taxes, §105-242, (b).
Exempt property, §105-242, (e).
Property taxes, §§105-366, 105-368.
Third parties.
Remedies of third person claiming attached property or interest therein, §1-440.43.
Warehouse receipts.
Attachment of goods covered by a negotiable document, §25-7-602.
Transfer of negotiable warehouse receipt.
Restraining order or injunction, §1-440.20, (b).
Warehouses.
Levy on goods in warehouses, §1-440.20, (a).
Plaintiff prevailing in principal actions, §1-440.46, (c).

ATTAINDER.
Bill of attainder.
Constitutional provisions, Const. U. S., art. I, §§9, 10; art. III, §3.

ATTEMPTS TO COMMIT CRIME.
Arson.
Burning or attempting to burn buildings not covered by other provisions, §14-67.1.
Bribery of horse show judges or officials, §14-380.2.
Drugs.
Controlled substances, §90-98.
Felonies, punishment for, §14-2.5.
Firearms.
Discharging into occupied property, §14-34.1.

ATTEMPTS TO COMMIT CRIME —Cont'd
Lesser included offenses.
Conviction for attempt, §15-170.
Malicious use of explosive or incendiary.
Property occupied by persons, §14-49.1.
Misdemeanors, punishment for, §14-2.5.
Robbery.
Common law robbery, §14-87.1.
Use of firearms or weapons in robbery, §14-87, (a).
Weapons.
Discharging certain barreled weapons or a firearm into occupied property, §14-34.1.

ATTENDANCE AT PUBLIC SCHOOLS.
Compulsory attendance law, §§115C-378 to 115C-383.
See COMPULSORY SCHOOL ATTENDANCE.

ATTENDANCE OF DEFENDANT.
Securing attendance of criminal defendants confined in institutions within state, §15A-711.

ATTENDANCE OF WITNESSES.
Securing attendance in criminal proceedings.
Out-of-state witnesses, §§15A-811 to 15A-816.
Prisoners as witnesses, §§15A-821 to 15A-823.

ATTESTATION.
Bank conveyances by secretary or cashier, §47-42.
Coroner's inquest.
Stenography transcript of proceedings, §152-7.
Corporate conveyances.
Filing corporations.
Validation of certain conveyances of foreign dissolved corporations, §47-108.6.
Forms of probate for deeds and other conveyances, §47-41.02.
Elections.
Registration of voters.
Contents of application form, §§163-82.4, 163-82.20.
Federal liens.
Execution of certificate, §44-68.13.
Global TransPark development zone.
Incorporation of zone.
County clerk's attestation of resolution, §158-33.
Notaries public, §10A-9, (b).
Oaths.
How attested.
May be self-proved, §31-11.6.
Public lands.
Conveyance of state land, §146-75.
Self-authentication of public documents, §8C-1, Rule 901.
Wills, §31-3.3.

ATTESTED WRITTEN WILL, §31-3.3.
Manner of probate, §31-18.1.

ATTORNEY-CLIENT PRIVILEGE.
Client-lawyer confidentiality, Prof. Cond. Rule 1.6.
Waiver.
Athlete agency contracts.
Records maintained by agent, §78C-97, (c).
Student-athlete signing, §78C-94, (c), (f).
Motion for appropriate relief, §15A-1415, (e).

ATTORNEY GENERAL.
Acting officers, Const. N. C., art. III, §7.
Actions.
Duties of attorney general as to civil litigation, §114-6.

ATTORNEY GENERAL —Cont'd
Additional clerical help, §114-5.
Address confidentiality program.
General provisions, §§15C-1 to 15C-13.
See ADDRESS CONFIDENTIALITY PROGRAM.
Air pollution control.
Civil penalties.
Civil action for failure to pay, §143-215.114A, (f).
Alarm systems licensing.
Investigative powers, §74D-5.2.
Amusements.
Amusement device safety.
Representing department of labor, §95-111.15.
Arson.
Powers as to arrest and prosecution, §58-79-5.
Assistants.
Assignments, §114-4.
Authority to appoint staff, §114-4.
Compensation, §114-4.
State insurance department.
Assignment to department, §114-4.2A.
Attorney general interns, §114-8.1.
Attorneys at law.
Impracticability of representing state entity.
Advice to governor to employ outside counsel, §147-17.
Auctions and auctioneers.
Enforcement of provisions.
Commission entitled to services of attorney general, §85B-9, (c).
Biologics.
Prosecution of violations.
Concurrent jurisdiction with district attorneys, §106-714, (a).
Boards and commissions.
Charges for legal services to state boards and commissions, §114-8.2.
Boundaries of state.
Jurisdiction over territory within state, §141-6, (c).
Budget.
Witnesses.
Prosecution of offenses, §143-21.
Wrongful expenditures.
Prosecution, §143-32, (b).
Charges for legal services to state boards and commissions, §114-8.2.
Charitable solicitation.
Civil action to enforce chapter, §131F-24, (a).
Investigations by, §131F-24, (b).
Voluntary compliance.
Termination of investigation or enforcement action, §131F-24, (c).
Charitable trusts.
Action for accounting, §36A-48.
Civil investigative demand.
Medicaid.
False claims by providers, §108A-70.14.
Civil litigation.
Duties as to, §114-6.
Clerical help.
Additional assistants, §114-5.
Common law.
Powers at common law, §114-1.1.
Company police.
Fees, §74E-12.
Powers, §74E-4.
Records.
Legal custodian, §74E-5.

ATTORNEY GENERAL —Cont'd
Compensation and allowances, Const. N. C., art. III, §9.
Control share acquisitions.
Investigative and regulatory powers, §75E-3.
Cooperative agreements among physicians or between physician, hospital or other person.
Authority, §90-21.35.
Copy of report submitted to attorney general, §90-21.32, (a).
Defined, §90-21.25.
Objection to issuance of certificate of public advantage, §90-21.29.
Review after issuance of certificate of public advantage, §90-21.31.
Suit to authorize cancellation of certificate, §90-21.33, (c).
Council of state.
Membership, Const. N. C., art. III, §8.
Crime victims compensation.
Representation of state, §15B-5.
Criminal justice education and training standards commission.
Chairman, §17C-5, (a).
Custody of books, §17C-7, (b).
Staff assistant, §17C-7, (a).
Dam safety law.
Civil penalties.
Action to recover, §143-215.36, (b).
Injunctive relief, §143-215.36, (c).
Declaratory judgments.
Party to proceedings involving constitutionality, §1-260.
Department of commerce.
Energy division.
Employment of attorney for, §114-4.2D.
Department of health and human services actions to recover costs of care.
Prosecution of actions by attorney general, §143-124.
Department of transportation.
Assistant attorneys general.
Legal assistance for department of transportation, §114-4.2.
Deputies.
Authority to designate, §114-4.4.
Discrimination in business.
Enforcement of provisions.
Actions, §75B-4.
District attorneys.
Consulting and advising prosecutors.
Duties of attorney general, §114-2.
Dry-cleaning solvent cleanup.
Institution of civil action to collect civil penalty, §143-215.104P, (f).
Duties, Const. N. C., art. III, §7.
Civil litigation, §114-6.
Department of justice, §114-2.
Devotion of full time to duties, §114-3.
Economic and community development.
Energy division of department.
Employment of attorney for division, §114-4.2D.
Elections.
Date of election, §163-1, (a).
Elective officers, Const. N. C., art. III, §7.
Vacancy in office.
Election to fill, §163-8.
Voting rights act of 1965.
Duties under, §§120-30.9H, 120-30.9I.

ATTORNEY GENERAL —Cont'd
Electronic surveillance generally, §§15A-286 to 15A-298.
See ELECTRONIC SURVEILLANCE.
Elevators.
Representing department of labor, §95-110.12.
Energy efficiency program.
Assignment of attorney for, §114-4.2D.
Energy policy council.
Assignment of attorney for, §114-4.2D.
Engineers and land surveyors.
Legal advisor to board, §89C-23.
Execution sales.
Notification of attorney general, §1-339.55.
Financial identity fraud.
Investigation of complaints, §14-113.23.
Fire investigations.
Authorized investigations, §58-79-1.
Forest fires.
Deputy investigators, §58-79-25.
Powers of attorney general, §§58-79-5, 58-79-10.
Right of entry, §58-79-10.
Subpoenas, §58-79-10.
Contempt for failure to comply, §58-79-15.
Witnesses, powers as to, §58-79-10.
Fish and fisheries resources.
Attorney for agencies, §113-131, (d).
Foreign limited liability companies.
Action to restrain violations, §57C-7-13.
Foreign or alien insurance companies.
Actions to enforce compliance with provisions, §58-16-50.
General assembly.
Lobbying.
Enforcement of article by attorney general, §120-47.10.
Opinion on questions of law.
Duties of attorney general, §114-2.
Geologists.
Legal advisor to board, §89E-24.
Governor.
Succession to office of governor, §147-11.1, (b).
Handicapped persons.
Designation of attorney specializing in law of the handicapped, §114-4.2F.
Hospital, medical and dental service corporations.
Conversion.
Enforcement authority, §§58-65-132, (d), 58-65-133, (d).
Foundation to receive fair market value of corporation.
Approval of determination of fair market value, §58-65-133, (h).
Hospitals.
University of North Carolina hospital at Chapel Hill.
Employment of attorney for hospital, §114-4.2B.
Hunting and wildlife.
Attorney for agency, §113-131, (d).
Incapacity.
Determination, Const. N. C., art. III, §7.
Incompetence, determination of.
Representation of petitioner on appeal by respondent to appellate division, §35A-1115.
Interim officers, Const. N. C., art. III, §7.
Interns, §114-8.1.
Job development investment grant program.
Approval of agreements, §143B-437.57, (b).
Judgments.
Consent judgments.
State departments and agencies.
Approval, §114-2.2, (a) to (c).

ATTORNEY GENERAL —Cont'd
Judicial standards commission.
Specific cases authorizing attorney general to furnish counsel for commission, §7A-377, (b).
Justice department.
Actions.
Duties of attorney general as to civil litigation, §114-6.
Assistants.
Assignments, §114-4.
Assignment to state insurance department, §114-4.2A.
Authority to appoint, §114-4.
Compensation, §114-4.
Legal assistance for department of transportation, §114-4.2.
Boards and commissions.
Charges for legal services to state boards and commissions, §114-8.2.
Charges for legal services, §114-8.2.
Civil litigation.
Duties as to, §114-6.
Clerical assistants.
Additional clerical help, §114-5.
Creation of department under supervision of attorney general, §114-1.
Deputies.
Authority to designate, §114-4.4.
Duties, §114-2.
Devotion of full time to duties, §114-3.
General provisions, §§114-1 to 114-20.1.
See JUSTICE DEPARTMENT.
Handicapped persons.
Designation of attorney specializing in law of the handicapped, §114-4.2F.
Real estate commission.
Employment of attorney, §114-4.2C.
Revisor of statutes, §114-9.1.
Salary, §114-7.
Longevity pay, §114-7.
Special prosecution division.
Duties, §114-11.6.
Established, §114-11.6.
Supervision and direction of attorney general, §114-1.
University of North Carolina hospital at Chapel Hill.
Employment of attorney, §114-4.2B.
Labor.
Enforcement of rules and regulations, §95-13.
Landscape contractors.
Services to board, §89D-4, (e).
Limited liability companies.
Foreign limited liability companies.
Actions by, §57C-7-13.
Interrogatories by secretary of state disclosing violations.
Certification to attorney general for actions, §57C-1-31.
Limited liability partnerships.
Foreign limited liability partnerships.
Action to restrain from transacting business, §59-94.
Local government finance.
Legal advisor to commission, §159-3, (d).
Offending officers.
Quo warranto proceedings, §159-182.
Marine fisheries commission.
Legal services, §143B-289.54, (l).
Master settlement agreement.
Cigarette and tobacco products manufacturers.
Duties as to enforcing against nonparticipating members, §105-113.4C.

ATTORNEY GENERAL —Cont'd
Medicaid.
False claims by providers.
Authority to investigate, institute proceedings, etc., §108A-70.13, (a).
Civil investigative demand, §108A-70.14.
Mines and minerals.
Safety and health.
Legal representation of department of labor, §74-24.18.
Monopolies and restraint of trade, §§75-9 to 75-15.
New motor vehicles warranties act.
Civil action by, §20-351.6.
Nonprofit corporations.
Exercise of corporate franchises not granted.
Authority of attorney general, §55A-3-05.
Mergers.
Limitations of charitable or religious corporations.
Notice and approval, §55A-11-02, (a), (b), (c).
Notaries public.
Injunctions for violations of chapter, §10A-12, (f).
Nuisances against public morals, action to abate, §19-2.1.
Oaths.
Form of oaths of office, §11-11.
Occupational safety and health.
Legal representation of department of labor, §95-142.
Offshore oil and gas activities.
Removal of prohibited discharges.
Referral of unexplained discharges to state and federal law enforcement agencies, §143-215.94EE, (b).
Pesticides.
Board may call upon attorney general for advice, §143-461.
Physicians and surgeons.
Practicing without license.
Prosecution of violation, §90-21.
Post-secondary education.
Nonpublic post-secondary educational institutions.
Licensing.
Enforcement authority of attorney general, §116-15, (j).
Powers.
Address confidentiality program.
Rulemaking, §15C-12.
Common-law powers, §114-1.1.
Justice department.
Transfer of powers to department, §§143A-49.1, 143A-50.
Practice of law.
Authorization to practice in North Carolina.
Prerequisite to appointment or election, Const. N. C., art. III, §7.
Preclearance.
Voting rights act of 1965.
Duties under, §§120-30.9H, 120-30.9I.
Price gouging during state of disaster.
Seller not in violation.
Statement issued by attorney general, §75-37.1, (b).
Private protective services.
Appointment of director, §74C-6.
Investigative powers, §74C-7.
Prosecution of violations, §74C-17, (b).
Training.
Certified trainers.
Establishment of training program, §74C-13, (l).

ATTORNEY GENERAL —Cont'd
Private protective services —Cont'd
Training —Cont'd
Unarmed security guards.
Establishment of training program, §74C-13, (m).
Public lands.
Grants.
Vacation of grants.
State action, §146-63.
Institution of actions by state, §146-70.
Service of process on state in land actions, §146-69.
Public officers and employees.
Defense of state employees.
Compromise and settlement of claims, §143-300.6, (b).
Public utilities.
Actions against to recover penalties, institution and prosecutions, §62-312.
Utilities commission.
Participation in commission proceedings, §62-20.
Witnesses.
Expert witnesses.
Power to employ, §62-20.
Qualifications, Const. N. C., art. III, §7.
Quo warranto, §159-182.
Action by attorney general.
Complaint of private party, §1-515.
Grounds, §1-515.
Own information.
Action upon, §1-515.
Racketeer influenced and corrupt organizations.
Civil remedies instituted by, §75D-8, (b).
Real estate brokers and salespersons.
Commission.
Employment of attorney for commission, §114-4.2C.
Services to board, §93A-3, (e).
Retirement system for counties and cities.
Board of trustees.
Legal advisor of board, §128-28, (k).
Retirement system for teachers and state employees.
Legal advisor to board of trustees, §135-6, (j).
Revisor of statutes, §114-9.1.
Roanoke Island commission.
Assignment of legal counsel to commission, §143B-131.7.
Salaries, §114-7.
Longevity pay, §114-7.
Savings banks.
Involuntary liquidation.
Commencement of action by attorney general, §54C-83, (l).
School bus accidents.
Claims, authority to pay, §115C-257.
Defense of claim by attorney general, §143-300.1, (d).
Duties of attorney general, §143-300.1, (b).
Service of process.
Personal jurisdiction.
Service on local public bodies, §1A-1, Rule 4, (j).
Service on state or agency thereof, §1A-1, Rule 4, (j).
Setoff debt collection, §§105A-1 to 105A-16.
See SETOFF DEBT COLLECTION.

ATTORNEY GENERAL —Cont'd
Settlement or resolution of litigation or potential litigation.
Agreements entered into by state or state department, agency, etc.
Report as to payments received and terms or conditions of payment, §114-2.5, (a).
Attorney general's authority to negotiate settlement of cases not affected, §114-2.5, (b).
Report on agreements, §114-2.4, (b).
Review of agreements, §114-2.4, (a).
Report on pending lawsuits in which state is a party, §114-2.6.
Shareholder protection act.
Investigative and regulatory powers, §75E-3.
Sheriffs education and training standards commission.
Custody of records, §17E-5, (b).
Staff assistance, §17E-5, (a).
Soil scientists.
Legal advisor to board for licensing, §89F-24.
Special prosecution division.
Duties, §114-11.6.
Established, §114-11.6.
State auditor.
Comparing warrants drawn by auditor.
Duties of attorney general, §114-2.
State banking commission.
Staff attorney as full time legal assistant to commission, §53-96.
State boundaries.
Jurisdiction over territory within state, §141-6, (c).
State debt.
Payment of moneys received for debts due state.
Duties of attorney general, §114-2.
State departments and agencies.
Collection of money owed to agencies, §147-86.11, (e).
Consent judgments.
Approval, §114-2.2, (a) to (c).
Counsel for departments, agencies and institutions, §147-17, (b).
Private counsel.
Employment.
Permission from attorney general, §114-2.3.
Private investigators.
Consent of attorney for use of, §114-15.2.
Representation of departments, agencies and institutions, §114-2.
Settlement or resolution of litigation or potential litigation.
Report by attorney general as to payment received and terms or conditions of payment, §114-2.5, (a).
Report on agreements, §114-2.4, (b).
Review of terms of proposed agreements, §114-2.4, (a).
State forests.
Gifts of land to state or acquisition of land for state forests.
Duty to See that deeds properly executed, §113-34, (a).
State treasurer.
Deposits in unlawful depositories.
Recovery, §147-80.
Streets and highways.
Condemnation proceedings.
Employment of outside counsel, §136-103.1.

ATTORNEY GENERAL —Cont'd
Structured settlement agreements.
Standing to raise issues relating to transfer, §1-543.14, (d).
Telephone solicitations.
Do not call registry.
Bill insert informing subscriber of existence.
Drafting, §75-102, (m).
Providing and maintaining.
Federal registry not ready for use, §75-102, (n).
Investigation of violations, action for civil penalties, §75-105, (a).
Term of office, §163-1, (a).
Textbooks.
Contracts with publishers.
Advice from and suits by attorney general, §115C-93.
Tobacco escrow compliance.
Duties, §66-294.1.
Generally, §§66-292 to 66-294.1.
Torrens system registration.
Rules of practice prescribed by attorney general, §43-3.
Tort claims against state departments and agencies.
Duty of attorney general, §143-298.
Underground petroleum storage tank leak cleanup.
Injunctive relief, §143-215.94Y.
Institution of actions to recover civil penalties, §143-215.94W, (f).
Underground storage tanks.
Leaking petroleum cleanup.
Groundwater protection loan fund.
Default or violation of loan agreement, §143-215.94P, (e).
University of North Carolina.
Self-insurance.
Defense of actions or suits against covered persons, §116-220, (d).
Vacancy in office, Const. N. C., art. III, §7.
Filling, §163-8.
Voting rights act of 1965.
Duties under, §§120-30.9H, 120-30.9I.
Wage and hour act.
Representation of department of labor, §95-25.18.
Warrants for payment of money.
Comparing warrants drawn by state auditor.
Duties of attorney general, §114-2.
Water and air resources.
Civil penalties.
Failure to pay.
Institution of civil actions, §143-215.6A, (g).
Wells.
Construction.
Injunctive relief.
Institution of actions, §87-95.

ATTORNEY GENERAL OF UNITED STATES.
Voting rights act of 1965.
Submissions to attorney general of United States, §§120-30.9A to 120-30.9I.

ATTORNEYS AT LAW.
Abused, neglected or dependent juvenile actions.
Attorney advocate.
Appointment when guardian ad litem nonattorney, standing, §7B-601.
Local guardian ad litem program, conflict of interest.
Appointment of district bar member, §7B-1202.

ATTORNEYS AT LAW —Cont'd
Abused, neglected or dependent juvenile actions —Cont'd
Notice in summons of right to counsel and appointment information, §7B-406, (b).
Parent's right to counsel, appointment of counsel, §7B-602, (a).
Payment of court-appointed counsel, §7B-603, (a) to (c).
Accounts.
Deposit of funds, Prof. Cond. Rule 1.15-2.
Records and accountings, Prof. Cond. Rule 1.15-3.
Acknowledgments.
Execution and acknowledgment of instruments, §47-43.1.
Addiction.
Lawyer assistance program, Bar Rules & Regs., D, §§.0601 to .0623.
See LAWYERS ASSISTANCE PROGRAM.
Administrative committee.
Continuing legal education hearings before committee, rules governing, Bar Rules & Regs., D, §§.1001 to .1011.
Failure to pay membership fees or costs, Bar Rules & Regs., D, §.0903.
Reinstatement after suspension, Bar Rules & Regs., D, §.0904.
Reinstatement from inactive status, Bar Rules & Regs., D, §.0902.
Transfer to inactive status, Bar Rules & Regs., D, §.0901.
Admission to practice, Bar Rules & Regs., C, §.0103.
Appeals.
From board of law examiners, §84-24.
Jurisdiction.
Wake county superior court, Admission to Practice, §.1404.
Notice, Admission to Practice, §.1402.
Records, Admission to Practice, §.1403.
Right of appeal, Admission to Practice, §.1401.
Supreme court.
Appeal from superior court to, Admission to Practice, §.1405.
Wake county superior court, Admission to Practice, §.1404.
Appeal to supreme court from, Admission to Practice, §.1405.
Bar candidate committee, Admission to Practice, §.0604.
Bar examinations, Bar Rules & Regs., C, §.0102.
Board of law examiners.
Powers, §84-24.
Dates, Admission to Practice, §.0902.
Fees.
Review of written bar examination, Admission to Practice, §.1002.
Frequency, Admission to Practice, §.0901.
Passing score, Admission to Practice, §.0904.
Review of written bar examinations.
Board representative, Admission to Practice, §.1005.
Fees, Admission to Practice, §.1002.
Generally, Admission to Practice, §.1001.
Multistate bar examination.
No provision for review, Admission to Practice, §.1003.
Scores.
Release, Admission to Practice, §.1004.
Subject matter, Admission to Practice, §.0903.

ATTORNEYS AT LAW —Cont'd
Admission to practice —Cont'd
Bar examinations —Cont'd
Written examinations, Admission to Practice, §.0901.
Board of law examiners, §§84-24 to 84-26; Admission to Practice, §§.0101 to .0103.
Address, Admission to Practice, §.0101.
Approval of rules and regulations, Bar Rules & Regs., C, §.0104.
Chair, §84-24; Admission to Practice, §.0103.
Compensation of members, §84-26.
Composition, §84-24.
Creation, §84-24.
Executive secretary.
Board may employ, §84-24.
Expenses of members, §84-26.
Membership, Admission to Practice, §.0103.
Number of members, Admission to Practice, §.0103.
Office hours, Admission to Practice, §.0101.
Powers, §84-24.
Prescription of applicant fees, §84-25.
Purpose, Admission to Practice, §.0102.
Subpoena and summons, power, §84-24.
Teachers in law schools.
Ineligibility to be members, §84-24.
Terms, §84-24.
Burden of proof.
Good moral character, Admission to Practice, §.0601.
Comity applicants, Admission to Practice, §.0203.
Interim permits, Admission to Practice, §.1301.
Licenses, Admission to Practice, §.1301.
Qualifications, Admission to Practice, §.0502.
Compliance with rules.
Required, Admission to Practice, §.0201.
Continuances.
Hearings, Admission to Practice, §.1204.
Criminal record check, §84-24.
Definitions, Admission to Practice, §.0202.
Depositions.
Board of law examiners.
Election, Bar Rules & Regs., C, §.0101.
Executive secretary, Admission to Practice, §.0103.
Use in hearings, Admission to Practice, §.1206.
Education.
General education requirement, Admission to Practice, §.0701.
Legal education requirement, Admission to Practice, §.0702.
False statements, failure to disclose, Prof. Cond. Rule 8.1.
Fees.
Bar examinations.
Review of written bar examinations, Admission to Practice, §.1002.
Comity applicants, Admission to Practice, §.0502.
General applicants, Admission to Practice, §.0404.
Late filing fee, Admission to Practice, §.0403.
Refund of fees, Admission to Practice, §.0405.
Nonpayment, Admission to Practice, §.0206.
Fingerprinting applicants, §84-24.
General applicants, Admission to Practice, §.0203.
Deadline for filing application, Admission to Practice, §.0403.

ATTORNEYS AT LAW —Cont'd
Admission to practice —Cont'd
General applicants —Cont'd
Fees, Admission to Practice, §.0404.
Late filing fee, Admission to Practice, §.0403.
Refund of fees, Admission to Practice, §.0405.
Form of application, Admission to Practice, §.0402.
How to apply, Admission to Practice, §.0401.
Licenses.
Issuance, Admission to Practice, §.1302.
Lists, Admission to Practice, §.0204.
Qualifications, Admission to Practice, §.0501.
Good moral character.
Burden of proof, Admission to Practice, §.0601.
Requirements, Admission to Practice, §§.0501, .0502.
Hearings, Admission to Practice, §.1201.
Applicants, Admission to Practice, §.0205.
Conduct of hearings, Admission to Practice, §.1203.
Continuances, Admission to Practice, §.1204.
Discovery, Admission to Practice, §.1206.
Notice, Admission to Practice, §.1202.
Request by applicant for hearing de novo, Admission to Practice, §.1203.
Protest of applications, Admission to Practice, §.0804.
Reopening of case, Admission to Practice, §.1207.
Subpoenas, Admission to Practice, §.1205.
Information concerning applicant, Admission to Practice, §.0602.
Failure to disclose, Admission to Practice, §.0603.
Inherent powers of courts unaffected, §84-36.
Jurisdiction.
Appeals.
Wake county superior court, Admission to Practice, §.1404.
Law schools.
Requirement of degree from approved law schools, Bar Rules & Regs., C, §.0105.
Licenses, Bar Rules & Regs., C, §§.0102, .0103.
Comity applicants, Admission to Practice, §.1301.
General applicant, Admission to Practice, §.1302.
Notice.
Hearings, Admission to Practice, §.1202.
Request by applicant for hearing de novo, Admission to Practice, §.1203.
Oath, Bar Rules & Regs., C, §.0103.
Protest of application.
Format, Admission to Practice, §.0802.
Hearing, Admission to Practice, §.0804.
Nature of protest, Admission to Practice, §.0801.
Notice to applicant, Admission to Practice, §.0803.
Refusal by board on own motion to license, Admission to Practice, §.0805.
Withdrawal by applicant.
Right to withdraw, Admission to Practice, §.0803.
Qualifications, Admission to Practice, §§.0501, .0502.
Requirement of degree from approved law schools, Bar Rules & Regs., C, §.0105.
Re-application, Admission to Practice, §.0605.
Rules and regulations.
Power of board of law examiners, §84-24.

ATTORNEYS AT LAW —Cont'd
Admission to practice —Cont'd
Subpoenas.
Power of board, Admission to Practice, §.1205.
Supreme court.
Appeal from superior court to, Admission to Practice, §.1405.
Wake county superior court.
Appeals, Admission to Practice, §.1404.
Appeal to supreme court from, Admission to Practice, §.1405.
Admonition.
Attorney discipline.
Imposition of discipline, Bar Rules & Regs., B, §.0123.
Issuance by grievance committee, Bar Rules & Regs., B, §.0113.
Adoption.
Representation of adoptee, §48-2-201, (b).
Representation of parents, §48-2-201, (a).
Affidavits.
Continuing legal education.
General compliance procedures, CLE Reg. 8.
Disbarred or suspended attorney to show compliance with provisions of order, Bar Rules & Regs., B, §.0124.
"Ambulance chasing."
Prohibited acts, §84-38.
Amnesty in elicit drug use cases, Bar Rules & Regs., B, §.0130.
Annual state bar membership fees.
Suspension for nonpayment of dues, Bar Rules & Regs., D, §.0903.
Reinstatement after suspension, Bar Rules & Regs., D, §.0904.
Appeals.
Admission to practice of law, Admission to Practice, §§.1401 to .1405.
Agreements, App. Proc. Rule 33, (a).
Appearances, App. Proc. Rule 33, (a).
Disciplinary proceedings, §84-28, (h).
From board of law examiners, §84-24.
Signatures on electronically filed documents.
More than one attorney representing party, App. Proc. Rule 33, (b).
Specialization.
Denial of certification or continued certification, Bar Rules & Regs., D, §§.1805, .1806.
Appearances.
Authority.
Filing or producing if requested, §84-11.
Employment contract.
Filing or producing if requested, §84-11.
Evidence of attorney-client relationship.
Filing or producing if requested, §84-11.
First appearance before district court judge, §15A-603.
Retainer agreement.
Filing or producing if requested, §84-11.
Withdrawal, Super. Ct. Rule 16.
Appointment of counsel.
Abused, neglected or dependent juvenile actions, §§7B-602, 7B-603.
Attorney disappearance, death or transfer to disability inactive status.
Protection of clients' interests, Bar Rules & Regs., B, §.0122.
Delinquent and undisciplined juvenile actions, §§7B-1906, (c), 7B-2000, 7B-2002.
Indigent defense services act, §§7A-498 to 7A-498.8.
See INDIGENT DEFENSE SERVICES.

ATTORNEYS AT LAW —Cont'd
Appointment of counsel —Cont'd
Indigent services rules, Rules 1.1 to 3.7.
See INDIGENT DEFENSE SERVICES.
Interstate compact on juvenile.
Return of escapees or absconders, §7B-2805, (c).
Mental health, developmental disability, substance abuse.
Involuntary commitment.
Substance abuser's commitment hearing, §122C-286, (d).
Representation of indigent person generally, §§7A-450 to 7A-458.
See INDIGENT DEFENSE SERVICES.
Termination of parental rights proceeding, §§7B-1101, 7B-1109, (b).
Arbitration.
Representation by lawyer, §1-569.16.
Arbitration and award.
Fee disputes.
Client assistance committee, Bar Rules & Regs., D, §§.0701 to .0704.
Model plan for district bar, Bar Rules & Regs., D, §§.0801 to .0808.
Hearings.
Right to representation by attorney, Arbitration Rule 3.
Internal law firm disputes, Bar Rules & Regs., E, §§.0401 to .0410; Arbitration Rule 3.
Arguments in trials in superior court.
Court's control, §7A-97.
Arraignment.
Right to counsel, §15A-942.
Arrest.
Right to counsel.
Peace officers to advise person arrested of right to counsel, §15A-501.
Arrest in civil cases.
Indigent persons.
Right to counsel, §1-413.
Athlete agents.
Acting without certificate of registration.
Attorneys licensed and resident of state, §78C-88, (c).
Attorney-client privilege.
Client-lawyer confidentiality, Prof. Cond. Rule 1.6.
Waiver.
Athlete agency contracts.
Records maintained by agent, §78C-97, (c).
Student-athlete signing, §78C-94, (c), (f).
Motion for appropriate relief, §15A-1415, (e).
Audits.
Continuing legal education, CLE Rule 13.
Lawyers trust accounts, Bar Rules & Regs., B, §.0128.
Authorized practice committee.
Procedures to prevent and restrain unauthorized practice of law, Bar Rules & Regs., D, §§.0201 to .0207.
Chairpersons' powers and duties, Bar Rules & Regs., D, §.0205.
Counsel's powers and duties, Bar Rules & Regs., D, §.0207.
Definitions, Bar Rules & Regs., D, §.0203.
Generally, Bar Rules & Regs., D, §.0202.
Powers and duties of committee.
Generally, Bar Rules & Regs., D, §.0206.
Purposes for establishing, Bar Rules & Regs., D, §.0201.
State bar councils' powers and duties, Bar Rules & Regs., D, §.0204.

ATTORNEYS AT LAW —Cont'd
Bail bondsmen and runners.
Prohibited from becoming sureties or runners, §§15A-541, (a), 58-71-105.
Bank accounts.
Deposit of funds, Prof. Cond. Rule 1.15-2.
Records and accountings, Prof. Cond. Rule 1.15-3.
Bank directive.
Lawyer maintaining trust or fiduciary accounts, Prof. Cond. Rule 1.15-2.
Bank receipts.
Record requirements, Prof. Cond. Rule 1.15-3.
Bankruptcy and insolvency.
Appearance for creditor in insolvency proceedings.
Unlawful for anyone except attorney, §§84-9, 84-10.
Bankruptcy law specialty, Bar Rules & Regs., D, §§.2201 to .2207.
Applicability of other requirements, Bar Rules & Regs., D, §.2207.
Certification standards, Bar Rules & Regs., D, §.2205.
Continuing legal education, Bar Rules & Regs., D, §.2205.
Continued certification, Bar Rules & Regs., D, §.2206.
Definition of specialty, Bar Rules & Regs., D, §.2202.
Establishment of specialty field, Bar Rules & Regs., D, §.2201.
Examination for specialty, Bar Rules & Regs., D, §.2205.
Peer review, Bar Rules & Regs., D, §.2205.
Continued certification, Bar Rules & Regs., D, §.2206.
Plan of legal specialization, applicability of provisions, Bar Rules & Regs., D, §.2204.
Recognition of specialist, Bar Rules & Regs., D, §.2203.
Suspension or revocation of certification.
Continued certification, Bar Rules & Regs., D, §.2206.
Bank statements.
Record requirements, Prof. Cond. Rule 1.15-3.
Bar examinations, Admission to Practice, §§.0901 to .1005.
Blind persons.
Aid to the blind.
Lending North Carolina reports to blind lawyers, §111-29.
Board of law examiners, §§84-24 to 84-26; Admission to Practice, §§.0101 to .0103.
Address, Admission to Practice, §.0101.
Approval of rules and regulations, Bar Rules & Regs., C, §.0104.
Chair, §84-24; Admission to Practice, §.0103.
Compensation of members, §84-26.
Composition, §84-24.
Creation, §84-24.
Executive secretary.
Board may employ, §84-24.
Expenses of members, §84-26.
Membership, Admission to Practice, §.0103.
Number of members, Admission to Practice, §.0103.
Office hours, Admission to Practice, §.0101.
Powers, §84-24.
Prescription of applicant fees, §84-25.
Purpose, Admission to Practice, §.0102.
Subpoena and summons, power, §84-24.

ATTORNEYS AT LAW —Cont'd
Board of law examiners —Cont'd
Teachers in law schools.
Ineligibility to be members, §84-24.
Terms, §84-24.
Business transactions with clients.
Conflict of interest, Prof. Cond. Rule 1.8.
Campaign contributions and expenditures.
Public campaign financing fund.
Opportunity to contribute, §105-41, (a).
Candidates for judicial office.
Compliance with code of judicial conduct, Prof. Cond. Rule 8.2.
False statements regarding, Prof. Cond. Rule 8.2.
Censure.
Imposition of discipline, Bar Rules & Regs., B, §.0123.
Issuance by grievance committee, Bar Rules & Regs., B, §.0113.
Checks.
Canceled checks, copies.
Record requirements, Prof. Cond. Rule 1.15-3.
Child support.
Procedure to insure payment.
Appointment to represent party support payment owed, §50-13.9, (f).
List of attorneys willing to undertake representation, §50-13.9, (e).
Choice of law.
Disciplinary authority of North Carolina, Prof. Cond. Rule 8.5.
CLE. See within this heading, "Continuing legal education."
Client-lawyer confidentiality, Prof. Cond. Rule 1.6.
Client security fund, Bar Rules & Regs., D, §§.1401 to .1420.
Appropriate uses of fund, Bar Rules & Regs., D, §.1416.
Audit of accounts, Bar Rules & Regs., D, §.1413.
Authority to establish fund, Bar Rules & Regs., D, §.1402.
Board of trustees.
Annual report, Bar Rules & Regs., D, §.1415.
Appointment and removal of members, Bar Rules & Regs., D, §.1406.
Chairperson, appointment, Bar Rules & Regs., D, §.1410.
Lay participation, Bar Rules & Regs., D, §.1405.
Meetings, Bar Rules & Regs., D, §.1414.
Operational responsibility of fund, Bar Rules & Regs., D, §.1403.
Size of board, Bar Rules & Regs., D, §.1404.
Succession, Bar Rules & Regs., D, §.1409.
Term of office, Bar Rules & Regs., D, §.1407.
Staggered terms, Bar Rules & Regs., D, §.1408.
Vice-chairperson, appointment, Bar Rules & Regs., D, §.1411.
Definitions, Bar Rules & Regs., D, §.1401.
Disbursement of funds, Bar Rules & Regs., D, §.1413.
Investment criteria, Bar Rules & Regs., D, §.1413.
Jurisdiction of state bar, Bar Rules & Regs., D, §.1402.
Maintenance of accounts, Bar Rules & Regs., D, §.1413.
Purposes, Bar Rules & Regs., D, §.1401.
Reimbursement applications, Bar Rules & Regs., D, §.1417.
Processing, Bar Rules & Regs., D, §.1418.
Source of funds, Bar Rules & Regs., D, §.1412.

ATTORNEYS AT LAW —Cont'd
Client security fund —Cont'd
Subrogation for reimbursement, Bar Rules & Regs., D, §.1419.
Supreme court, authority reserved by, Bar Rules & Regs., D, §.1420.
Uses of fund, Bar Rules & Regs., D, §.1416.
Clients' interests protected.
Appointment of counsel when attorney disappears, dies or transferred to disability inactive status, Bar Rules & Regs., B, §.0122.
Clients to be notified by disbarred or suspended member, Bar Rules & Regs., B, §.0124.
Collection agencies.
Practice of law by collection agencies, §58-70-120.
Shared office space, §58-70-125.
Committees, CLE Reg. 1.
Communications.
Concerning lawyer's services, Prof. Cond. Rule 7.1.
Fields of practice, Prof. Cond. Rule 7.4.
With clients, Prof. Cond. Rule 1.4.
Fees and expenses, Prof. Cond. Rule 1.5.
With judge or jurors.
Ex parte communications, Prof. Cond. Rule 3.5.
With person represented by counsel, Prof. Cond. Rule 4.2.
Concurrent conflict of interest, Prof. Cond. Rule 1.7.
Specific rules, Prof. Cond. Rule 1.8.
Conference between attorney and prisoner.
Secret listening, §§14-227.1, 14-227.3.
Confidentiality of information, Prof. Cond. Rule 1.6.
Confidential government information.
Lawyer acquiring as public officer or employees.
Representing client with interest adverse to information, Prof. Cond. Rule 1.11.
Defined, Prof. Cond. Rule 1.0.
Discussions with prospective clients, Prof. Cond. Rule 1.18.
Conflicts of interest.
Current clients, Prof. Cond. Rule 1.7.
Specific rules, Prof. Cond. Rule 1.8.
Former clients.
Duties to, Prof. Cond. Rule 1.9.
Former judges, arbitrators, mediators or other third party neutrals, Prof. Cond. Rule 1.12.
Government officers and employees.
Special conflicts, former and current officers and employees, Prof. Cond. Rule 1.11.
Imputation, Prof. Cond. Rule 1.10.
Lawyer as witness, Prof. Cond. Rule 3.7.
Prospective clients, matters with, Prof. Cond. Rule 1.18.
Sale or purchase of practice, notice, Prof. Cond. Rule 1.17.
Consent.
Informed consent.
Aggregate settlement or agreement for two or more clients, Prof. Cond. Rule 1.8.
Communicating with client when client's consent required, Prof. Cond. Rule 1.4.
Defined, Prof. Cond. Rule 1.0.
Consent to disbarment, Bar Rules & Regs., B, §.0117.
Constitution of North Carolina.
Rights of accused to counsel, Const. N. C., art. I, §23.

ATTORNEYS AT LAW —Cont'd
Constitution of the United States.
Right to counsel, Const. U. S., amd. VI.
Consultants.
Foreign legal consultants, §§84A-1 to 84A-8; Bar Rules & Regs., F, §§.0101 to .0113.
Administrative committee recommendations, Bar Rules & Regs., F, §.0107.
Adoption of rules, §84A-8.
Appeals, Bar Rules & Regs., F, §.0108.
Applications, Bar Rules & Regs., F, §.0101.
Denial, Bar Rules & Regs., F, §.0113.
Fees, Bar Rules & Regs., F, §.0111.
Forms, Bar Rules & Regs., F, §.0102.
Audits, §84A-5.
Board of law examiners.
Delegation of duties by state bar, §84A-7.
Certificate of registration, §84A-2.
Application, §84A-2, (a).
Accompanying documents, §84A-2, (d).
Fee, §84A-2, (c).
Photograph of applicant, §84A-2, (b).
Evidence of applicant's application, qualifications, etc., §84A-2, (e).
Good moral character of applicant, §84A-3, (c).
Issuance of certificate, §84A-3, (b).
Failure to satisfy all provisions, §84A-3, (d).
Review by North Carolina state bar, §84A-3, (a).
Committee recommendations, Bar Rules & Regs., F, §.0107.
Delegation of duties by state bar, §84A-7.
Duties, §84A-5.
Failure to disclose, Bar Rules & Regs., F, §.0105.
Fees.
Certificate of registration, §84A-2, (c).
Duties of consultant, §84A-5.
Foreign country.
Defined, §84A-1.
Good moral character of applicant.
Certificate of registration, §84A-3, (c).
Hearings, Bar Rules & Regs., F, §.0109.
Investigations, Bar Rules & Regs., F, §.0106.
Licenses, §84A-1.
Examinations, §84A-1, (b).
Issuance, §84A-1, (a).
Moral character and general fitness.
Burden of proof, Bar Rules & Regs., F, §.0104.
Permanent record, Bar Rules & Regs., F, §.0112.
Prohibited activities, §84A-4, (b).
Public records, §84A-2, (f).
Reciprocity, §84A-2, (g).
Requirements for applicants, Bar Rules & Regs., F, §.0103.
Review and order of council, Bar Rules & Regs., F, §.0110.
Rules and regulations.
Adoption of rules, §84A-8.
Scope of practice, §84A-4.
Service of process, §84A-6.
Written legal advice.
Jurisdiction other than admitted to practice in, §84A-4, (c).
Contempt.
Clerks of court.
Certification of orders, §84-36.1.
Disciplinary hearing commission of state bar.
Power to hold in contempt, §84-28.1, (b1).

ATTORNEYS AT LAW —Cont'd
Contempt —Cont'd
Suspended or disbarred attorney failing to comply with obligations, Bar Rules & Regs., B, §.0124.
Contingent fees and contingent fee agreements, Prof. Cond. Rule 1.5.
Continuing legal education, Bar Rules & Regs., D, §§.1501 to .1610.
Accreditation of prerecorded and live programs, Bar Rules & Regs., D, §.1604.
Accreditation of sponsors and programs, Bar Rules & Regs., D, §.1520.
Accreditation standards, Bar Rules & Regs., D, §.1519; CLE Rule 19.
Program, CLE Rule 20.
Sponsors, CLE Rule 20.
Accredited sponsors, Bar Rules & Regs., D, §.1603.
Application requirements, CLE Reg. 3.
Defined, CLE Rule 1.
Active members.
Defined, CLE Rule 1.
Administrative committee.
Defined, CLE Rule 1.
Adoption of regulations for program, Bar Rules & Regs., D, §.1527.
Affidavit of compliance, Bar Rules & Regs., D, §.1608.
Agency appeals, CLE Reg. 10.
Announcement of approval of courses by accredited sponsors, Bar Rules & Regs., D, §.1602.
Annual report by members of state bar, Bar Rules & Regs., D, §.1522.
Appeals, Bar Rules & Regs., D, §.1610.
Applicability of rules, CLE Rule 17.
Approval of courses, Bar Rules & Regs., D, §.1602.
Approved activities.
Defined, CLE Rule 1.
Armed forces of the United States.
Applicability of rules, CLE Rule 17.
Attendee fee, Bar Rules & Regs., D, §.1606.
Computation, CLE Reg. 6.
Source of funding, CLE Rule 12.
Audit of accounts, Bar Rules & Regs., D, §.1513.
Authority for agency appeals, CLE Reg. 10.
Bankruptcy law specialty, Bar Rules & Regs., D, §.2205.
Continued certification, Bar Rules & Regs., D, §.2206.
Bar examiner of board of law examiners, credit earned through service, Bar Rules & Regs., D, §.1607.
Bar review/refresher courses, approval, Bar Rules & Regs., D, §.1602; CLE Reg. 2.
Board of continuing legal education.
Annual report, Bar Rules & Regs., D, §.1515.
Appointment and removal of members, Bar Rules & Regs., D, §.1506; CLE Rule 6.
Chairperson, appointment, Bar Rules & Regs., D, §.1510; CLE Rule 10.
Meetings, CLE Rule 14.
Referral of matters to board by grievance committee.
Failure of respondent in disciplinary proceeding to practice sound office management, Bar Rules & Regs., B, §.0112.
Reporting requirements, CLE Rule 15.
Size, CLE Rule 4.

ATTORNEYS AT LAW —Cont'd
Continuing legal education —Cont'd
Board of continuing legal education —Cont'd
Term of office, CLE Rule 7.
Staggered terms, CLE Rule 8.
Vice chairperson, CLE Rule 11.
Broadcast programs, Bar Rules & Regs., D, §.1604.
CLE.
Defined, CLE Rule 1.
Compliance procedures, CLE Reg. 8.
Computation of credit, Bar Rules & Regs., D, §.1605.
Hours, CLE Reg. 5.
Computer-based CLE, accreditation, Bar Rules & Regs., D, §.1611.
Confidentiality of records, CLE Rule 25.
Congress.
Applicability of rules, CLE Rule 17.
Council.
Defined, CLE Rule 1.
Course materials, approval, Bar Rules & Regs., D, §.1602.
Course requirements, CLE Rule 18.
Accreditation of video or other audiovisual programs, CLE Reg. 4.
General course approval, CLE Reg. 2.
Practical skills courses.
Defined, CLE Rule 1.
Credit hours, Bar Rules & Regs., D, §.1521; CLE Rule 21.
Computation, CLE Reg. 5.
Defined, CLE Rule 1.
Criminal law specialty, Bar Rules & Regs., D, §.2505.
Continued certification, Bar Rules & Regs., D, §.2506.
Defined, Bar Rules & Regs., D, §.1601; CLE Rule 1.
Definitions, Bar Rules & Regs., D, §§.1501, .1601; CLE Rule 1.
Disabilities, substitute programs for attorneys with, Bar Rules & Regs., D, §.1607.
Disbursement of funds, Bar Rules & Regs., D, §.1513.
Duties, CLE Rule 16.
Effective date of CLE rules, CLE Rule 26.
Effective date of rules governing administration of program, Bar Rules & Regs., D, §.1526.
Estate planning and probate law specialty, Bar Rules & Regs., D, §.2305.
Continued certification, Bar Rules & Regs., D, §.2306.
Executive committee, Bar Rules & Regs., D, §.1601.
Exemptions from continuing education requirement, Bar Rules & Regs., D, §.1517.
Facilities to be provided by sponsors, Bar Rules & Regs., D, §.1602.
Family law specialty, Bar Rules & Regs., D, §.2405.
Continued certification, Bar Rules & Regs., D, §.2406.
Fees, Bar Rules & Regs., D, §.1606.
Attendee's fees.
Computation, CLE Reg. 6.
Source of funding, CLE Rule 12.
Fiscal responsibility, CLE Rule 13.
Funding, CLE Rule 12.
Reinstatement fee, CLE Reg. 9.
Review of fees, CLE Reg. 6.

ATTORNEYS AT LAW —Cont'd
Continuing legal education —Cont'd
Fees —Cont'd
Sponsors.
Computation, CLE Reg. 6.
Source of funding, CLE Rule 12.
Uniform application, CLE Reg. 6.
Funding for program, Bar Rules & Regs., D, §.1512.
General assembly.
Applicability of rules, CLE Rule 17.
General compliance procedures, Bar Rules & Regs., D, §.1608.
General course approval, Bar Rules & Regs., D, §.1602.
Governor.
Applicability of rules, CLE Rule 17.
Hearings before administrative committee of state bar, Bar Rules & Regs., D, §§.1001 to .1011.
Hearing generally, Bar Rules & Regs., D, §.1006.
Hearing panel, Bar Rules & Regs., D, §.1007.
Notice of hearing, Bar Rules & Regs., D, §.1005.
Purposes of regulations, Bar Rules & Regs., D, §.1001.
Referral from board of continuing legal education, Bar Rules & Regs., D, §.1003.
Reinstatement hearing, Bar Rules & Regs., D, §.1009.
Report by committee to council, Bar Rules & Regs., D, §.1011.
Report by panel to committee, Bar Rules & Regs., D, §.1010.
Review of recommendation of hearing panel, Bar Rules & Regs., D, §.1002.
Suspension hearing, Bar Rules & Regs., D, §.1008.
Time of hearing, Bar Rules & Regs., D, §.1004.
Hours required, Bar Rules & Regs., D, §.1518.
Immigration law specialty, Bar Rules & Regs., D, §§.2601 to .2607.
Inactive members.
Defined, CLE Rule 1.
In-house CLE and self-study, approval, Bar Rules & Regs., D, §.1602.
Defined, CLE Rule 1.
General course approval, CLE Reg. 2.
Institute of government.
Applicability of rules, CLE Rule 17.
Investment criteria for funds, Bar Rules & Regs., D, §.1513.
Judges.
Applicability of rules, CLE Rule 17.
Jurisdiction, CLE Rule 2.
Jurisdiction and authority, Bar Rules & Regs., D, §.1502.
Law school courses, approval, Bar Rules & Regs., D, §.1602; CLE Reg. 2.
Lay participation, Bar Rules & Regs., D, §.1505; CLE Rule 5.
Lay participation prohibition, CLE Rule 5.
Lieutenant governor.
Applicability of rules, CLE Rule 17.
Maintenance of accounts, Bar Rules & Regs., D, §.1513.
Meetings, Bar Rules & Regs., D, §.1414; CLE Rule 14.
Members' annual report.
Noncompliance, CLE Rule 23.
Reinstatement of members, CLE Rule 24.

ATTORNEYS AT LAW —Cont'd
Continuing legal education —Cont'd
Newly admitted active members.
Defined, CLE Rule 1.
Noncompliance by members, CLE Rule 23.
Noncompliance procedures, Bar Rules & Regs., D, §.1609; CLE Reg. 9.
Noncompliance with requirement, Bar Rules & Regs., D, §.1523.
Nonlegal educational activities, approval, Bar Rules & Regs., D, §.1602.
Nonresidents.
Active member nonresidents.
Applicability of rules, CLE Rule 17.
Operational responsibility, Bar Rules & Regs., D, §.1503; CLE Rule 3.
Operational responsibility, CLE Rule 3.
Organization, CLE Rule 3.
Other committees, Bar Rules & Regs., D, §.1601.
Penalty for late filing of affidavit of compliance, Bar Rules & Regs., D, §.1608.
Powers and duties, Bar Rules & Regs., D, §.1516; CLE Rule 16.
Practical skills courses.
Defined, CLE Rule 1.
Prerecorded and live programs, accreditation of, Bar Rules & Regs., D, §.1604.
Procedures.
Compliance, CLE Reg. 8.
Noncompliance, CLE Reg. 9.
Review of board decision, CLE Reg. 10.
Professional responsibility.
Defined, CLE Rule 1.
Program, Bar Rules & Regs., D, §.1518; CLE Rule 18.
Accreditation standards, CLE Rule 20.
Purposes of rules, Bar Rules & Regs., D, §.1501; CLE Rule 1.
Quorum, Bar Rules & Regs., D, §.1601.
Real property law specialty, Bar Rules & Regs., D, §.2105.
Continued certification, Bar Rules & Regs., D, §.2106.
Records of sponsors, Bar Rules & Regs., D, §.1602.
Regulations, CLE Rule 17.
Regulations.
Adoption, CLE Rule 27.
Reinstatement after suspension for noncompliance, Bar Rules & Regs., D, §.1524; CLE Rule 24.
Reinstatement fee, Bar Rules & Regs., D, §.1609.
Reports.
Annual report of board, CLE Rule 15.
Members' annual report, CLE Rule 22.
Revenues applied to expense of administration, Bar Rules & Regs., D, §.1513.
Rules concerning administration, Bar Rules & Regs., D, §§.1601 to .1610.
Rules governing administration of program, Bar Rules & Regs., D, §§.1501 to .1527.
Scope and exemptions of CLE rules, CLE Rule 17.
Scope of rules governing administration of program, Bar Rules & Regs., D, §.1517.
Size of board, Bar Rules & Regs., D, §.1504.
Source of funds for program, Bar Rules & Regs., D, §.1512.
Special cases and exemptions, Bar Rules & Regs., D, §.1607; CLE Reg. 7.

ATTORNEYS AT LAW —Cont'd
Continuing legal education —Cont'd
Specialization certification, rules governing accreditation, Bar Rules & Regs., D, §§.1901 to .1908.
Accreditation of courses, Bar Rules & Regs., D, §.1906.
Accreditation of sponsor, Bar Rules & Regs., D, §.1907.
Computation of hours of instruction, Bar Rules & Regs., D, §.1904.
Definitions, Bar Rules & Regs., D, §.1902.
General provisions, Bar Rules & Regs., D, §.1901.
Lecture-type CLE activities, Bar Rules & Regs., D, §.1903.
Alternatives to course instruction, Bar Rules & Regs., D, §.1905.
Showing by applicants, Bar Rules & Regs., D, §.1908.
Sponsor fee, Bar Rules & Regs., D, §.1606.
Sponsors.
Accreditation standards, CLE Rule 20.
Accredited sponsors.
Application requirements, CLE Reg. 3.
Defined, CLE Rule 1.
Fees.
Source of funding, CLE Rule 12.
Substitute compliance, Bar Rules & Regs., D, §.1607.
Succession in office, Bar Rules & Regs., D, §.1509; CLE Rule 9.
Suspension for noncompliance, Bar Rules & Regs., D, §.1523.
Noncompliance with reporting requirements, CLE Rule 3.
Reinstatement, CLE Rule 24.
Term of office, Bar Rules & Regs., D, §.1507; CLE Rule 7.
Staggered terms, Bar Rules & Regs., D, §.1508; CLE Rule 9.
Vice-chairman, appointment, Bar Rules & Regs., D, §.1511; CLE Rule 11.
Videotape programs, accreditation, CLE Reg. 4.
Year.
Defined, CLE Rule 1.
Contracts.
Contingent fee agreements, Prof. Cond. Rule 1.5.
Restriction on practice, Prof. Cond. Rule 5.6.
Conviction of criminal offense.
Clerks of court.
Certification of orders, §84-36.1.
Corporations.
Practice of law.
Nonprofit corporations.
Indigent legal services by, §84-5.1.
Professional corporations, regulations for practicing law, Bar Rules & Regs., D, §§.0101 to .0106.
Prohibition as to practice of law by corporation, §84-5.
Violations of provisions.
Misdemeanor, §84-8.
Professional corporations generally, §§55B-1 to 55B-16.
See PROFESSIONAL CORPORATIONS.
Receivers.
Counsel fees, §1-507.9.
Costs.
Failure to file complaint on time.
Attorney liable for cost, §84-12.
County attorneys, §153A-114.

ATTORNEYS AT LAW —Cont'd
Court appointed counsel.
Abused, neglected or dependent juvenile actions, §§7B-602, 7B-603.
Delinquent and undisciplined juvenile actions, §§7B-1906, (c), 7B-2000, 7B-2002.
Indigent defense services act, §§7A-498 to 7A-498.8.
See INDIGENT DEFENSE SERVICES.
Indigent services rules, Rules 1.1 to 3.7.
See INDIGENT DEFENSE SERVICES.
Interstate compact on juvenile.
Return of escapees or absconders, §7B-2805, (c).
Mental health, developmental disability, substance abuse.
Involuntary commitment.
Substance abuser's commitment hearing, §122C-286, (d).
Representation of indigent persons generally, §§7A-450 to 7A-458.
See INDIGENT DEFENSE SERVICES.
Termination of parental rights proceeding, §§7B-1101, 7B-1109, (b).
Credit unions.
Selection of attorneys to handle loan-closing proceedings, §54-109.18.
Criminal case records to identify attorney representing defendant, §7A-109.2.
Criminal conduct.
Client engaging in, remedial measures, Prof. Cond. Rule 3.3.
Lawyer not to counsel client to engage in, Prof. Cond. Rule 1.2.
Criminal history record checks.
Applicants for admission to practice, §84-24.
Criminal law and procedure.
Abiding by client's decision, Prof. Cond. Rule 1.2.
Appearance.
Recordation.
Requirement that clerk record entry, §15A-142.
When entry of attorney in criminal proceeding occurs, §15A-141.
Appointment of counsel.
Indigent defense services act, §§7A-498 to 7A-498.8.
See INDIGENT DEFENSE SERVICES.
Representation of indigent persons generally.
See INDIGENT DEFENSE SERVICES.
Arraignment.
Right to counsel, §15A-942.
Arrest.
Right to counsel, §15A-501.
Contingent fees, charging prohibited, Prof. Cond. Rule 1.5.
Defendant representing himself.
Standby counsel, §15A-1243.
Entry of attorney in criminal proceeding.
General entry.
Attorney making general entry obligated to represent defendant at all subsequent stages, §15A-143.
Recordation.
Requirement that clerk record entry, §15A-142.
When entry of attorney occurs, §15A-141.
Meritorious claims and contentions, Prof. Cond. Rule 3.1.
Motion for appropriate relief.
Appointment of counsel for indigent defendant, §15A-1421.

ATTORNEYS AT LAW —Cont'd
Criminal law and procedure —Cont'd
Nontestimonial identification.
Right to counsel, §15A-279.
Pleas.
Aid of counsel, §15A-1012, (a).
Probable cause hearings.
Defendant to be advised of right to counsel, §15A-606, (e).
Determination whether right to counsel waived, §15A-611, (c).
Representation of state and defendant, §15A-611, (a).
Probation revocation hearings.
Right to counsel, §15A-1345, (e).
Prosecutors, special responsibilities, Prof. Cond. Rule 3.8.
Right to counsel generally, §15-4; Const. N. C., art. I, §23; Const. U. S., amd. VI.
Waiver of counsel.
Indigent persons, §7A-457.
Withdrawal of attorney with permission of court, §15A-144.
Criminal law specialty, Bar Rules & Regs., D, §§.2501 to .2507.
Applicability of other requirements, Bar Rules & Regs., D, §.2507.
Certification standards, Bar Rules & Regs., D, §.2505.
Continuing legal education, Bar Rules & Regs., D, §.2505.
Continued certification, Bar Rules & Regs., D, §.2506.
Definition of specialty, Bar Rules & Regs., D, §.2502.
Establishment of specialty field, Bar Rules & Regs., D, §.2501.
Examination for specialty, Bar Rules & Regs., D, §.2505.
Lapse of certification, Bar Rules & Regs., D, §.2506.
Peer review, Bar Rules & Regs., D, §.2505.
Plan of legal specialization.
Applicability of provisions, Bar Rules & Regs., D, §.2504.
Recognition of specialist, Bar Rules & Regs., D, §.2503.
Suspension or revocation of certificate.
Continued certification, Bar Rules & Regs., D, §.2506.
Damages.
Fraudulent practice.
Liability of attorney in double damages, §84-13.
Death.
Appointment of counsel to protect clients' interests, Bar Rules & Regs., B, §.0122.
Debtor and creditor.
Appearance for creditor in insolvency and certain other proceedings.
Unlawful for anyone except attorney, §§84-9, 84-10.
Declining representation, Prof. Cond. Rule 1.16.
Dedicated trust account.
Defined, Prof. Cond. Rule 1.15-1.
Deposit of trust funds in, Prof. Cond. Rule 1.15-2.
Defense of public school employees.
Employee's obligation for attorney fees, §143-300.17.
Defense of state employees.
See PUBLIC OFFICERS AND EMPLOYEES.

ATTORNEYS AT LAW —Cont'd
Definitions.
Admission to practice, Admission to Practice, §.0202.
Continuing legal education, CLE Rule 1.
Discipline and disability rules of state bar, Bar Rules & Regs., B, §.0103.
Practice of law, §84-2.1.
State bar.
Judicial districts, §84-19.
Delinquent and undisciplined juvenile actions.
Appointment of counsel for juvenile generally, §7B-2000, (a).
Payment, §7B-2002.
Presumption of indigence, §7B-2000, (b).
Right to counsel, §7B-2000, (a).
Secure or nonsecure custody hearings.
Appointment of counsel for juvenile, determining if juvenile retained counsel, §7B-1906, (c).
Summons to notify parent of right to counsel and appointment of counsel, §7B-1805, (b).
Deposit of fiduciary funds, Prof. Cond. Rule 1.15-2.
Deposit of trust funds, Prof. Cond. Rule 1.15-2.
Deposits.
State bar.
Securing of deposits, §84-34.1.
Diligence in representation, Prof. Cond. Rule 1.3.
Diminished capacity.
Client with, Prof. Cond. Rule 1.14.
Direct contact with prospective clients, Prof. Cond. Rule 7.3.
Disability, CLE substitute program, Bar Rules & Regs., D, §.1607.
Disability proceedings.
Address of record, Bar Rules & Regs., B, §.0126.
Appointment of counsel to protect clients' interests when attorney transferred to disability inactive status, Bar Rules & Regs., B, §.0122.
Chairperson of hearing commission, powers and duties, Bar Rules & Regs., B, §.0108.
Clerks of court.
Certification of orders, §84-36.1.
Confidentiality, Bar Rules & Regs., B, §.0129.
Counsel's powers and duties, Bar Rules & Regs., B, §.0107.
Defendant alleges disability in disciplinary proceeding, Bar Rules & Regs., B, §.0118.
Definitions, Bar Rules & Regs., B, §.0103.
Evidence, preservation, Bar Rules & Regs., B, §.0118.
Fees and costs, Bar Rules & Regs., B, §.0118.
Final determination of incapacity or disability.
Entry upon judgment docket of superior court, Bar Rules & Regs., B, §.0123.
Hearing committee's powers and duties, Bar Rules & Regs., B, §.0109.
Hearings, Bar Rules & Regs., B, §.0118.
Initiation of hearing by hearing committee, Bar Rules & Regs., B, §.0118.
Involuntary commitment of member, proceedings, Bar Rules & Regs., B, §.0118.
Judicial declaration of incompetence of a member, proceedings, Bar Rules & Regs., B, §.0118.
Petition for reinstatement after transfer to disability inactive status, Bar Rules & Regs., B, §.0125.
Proceedings initiated by state bar, Bar Rules & Regs., B, §.0118.

ATTORNEYS AT LAW —Cont'd
Disability proceedings —Cont'd
Protection of clients' interests when attorney transferred to disability inactive status, Bar Rules & Regs., B, §.0122.
Appointment of counsel, Bar Rules & Regs., B, §.0122.
Reinstatement after transfer to disability inactive status, Bar Rules & Regs., B, §.0125.
Secretary's powers and duties, Bar Rules & Regs., B, §.0110.
State bar council's powers and duties, Bar Rules & Regs., B, §.0104.
Disappearance of attorney.
Appointment of counsel to protect clients' interests, Bar Rules & Regs., B, §.0122.
Disaster response plan of the state bar, Bar Rules & Regs., D, §§.0301 to .0303.
Disaster response team, Bar Rules & Regs., D, §.0301.
General policy and objectives, Bar Rules & Regs., D, §.0302.
Report on results, Bar Rules & Regs., D, §.0303.
Disbarment, §84-28, (c).
Consent to disbarment, Bar Rules & Regs., B, §.0117.
Employing as legal clerk or assistant, Prof. Cond. Rule 5.5.
Forfeiture of license.
Felony convictions, §15A-1331A.
Imposition of discipline, Bar Rules & Regs., B, §.0123.
Obligations of disbarred attorney, Bar Rules & Regs., B, §.0124.
Reinstatement, Bar Rules & Regs., B, §.0125.
Resignation while under investigation, order disbarring member, Bar Rules & Regs., B, §.0117.
Restoration of license, §84-28, (c).
Disciplinary proceedings.
Action on grievance.
Notice to complainant, Bar Rules & Regs., B, §.0121.
Notice to member, Bar Rules & Regs., B, §.0120.
Address of record, Bar Rules & Regs., B, §.0126.
Administration of reciprocal discipline, Bar Rules & Regs., B, §.0116.
Admissions.
Prehearing conference for purposes of obtaining, Bar Rules & Regs., B, §.0114.
Admonition.
Imposition of discipline, Bar Rules & Regs., B, §.0123.
Issuance by grievance committee, Bar Rules & Regs., B, §.0113.
Affidavit consenting to disbarment, Bar Rules & Regs., B, §.0117.
Affidavit form, grievances, Bar Rules & Regs., B, §.0111.
Affidavit stating member's desire to resign, Bar Rules & Regs., B, §.0117.
Aggravating factors in imposing discipline, Bar Rules & Regs., B, §.0114.
Amendment of judgments, Bar Rules & Regs., B, §.0114.
Amnesty in elicit drug use cases, Bar Rules & Regs., B, §.0130.
Answer.
Filing by defendant, Bar Rules & Regs., B, §.0114.

ATTORNEYS AT LAW —Cont'd
Disciplinary proceedings —Cont'd
Appeals, §84-28, (h).
Appearance by defendant in his or her own behalf.
Filing of proof of delivery of copy, Bar Rules & Regs., B, §.0114.
Appearance by defendant represented by counsel.
Filing by counsel of proof of delivery of copy, Bar Rules & Regs., B, §.0114.
Audit of trust accounts, investigative subpoenas, Bar Rules & Regs., B, §.0128.
Censure.
Imposition of discipline, Bar Rules & Regs., B, §.0123.
Issuance by grievance committee, Bar Rules & Regs., B, §.0113.
Public censure, §84-28, (c).
Chairperson of grievance committee, powers and duties, Bar Rules & Regs., B, §.0105.
Proceedings before committee, Bar Rules & Regs., B, §.0113.
Chairperson of hearing commission, powers and duties, Bar Rules & Regs., B, §.0108.
Clerks of court.
Certification of orders, §84-36.1.
Complaint.
Amendments, Bar Rules & Regs., B, §.0113.
Content requirements, Bar Rules & Regs., B, §.0114.
Filing, Bar Rules & Regs., B, §.0114.
Issuance, Bar Rules & Regs., B, §.0113.
Service, Bar Rules & Regs., B, §.0114.
Concurrent jurisdiction of state bar and courts, Bar Rules & Regs., B, §.0102.
Conference prior to hearing for obtaining admissions or narrowing issues, Bar Rules & Regs., B, §.0114.
Confidentiality, Bar Rules & Regs., B, §.0129.
Consent orders after trial, Bar Rules & Regs., B, §.0114.
Consent to disbarment, Bar Rules & Regs., B, §.0117.
Continuance of hearing, Bar Rules & Regs., B, §.0114.
Convening grievance to consider grievance, Bar Rules & Regs., B, §.0112.
Conviction in criminal case, effect of finding of guilt, Bar Rules & Regs., B, §.0115.
Counsel's powers and duties, Bar Rules & Regs., B, §.0107.
Courts.
Enforcement of powers of council, §84-28, (i), (j).
Default.
Failure to file answer, Bar Rules & Regs., B, §.0114.
Order imposing discipline, Bar Rules & Regs., B, §.0114.
Definitions, Bar Rules & Regs., B, §.0103.
Depositions.
Investigations of professional misconduct, §84-29.
Disability alleged by defendant in disciplinary proceeding, Bar Rules & Regs., B, §.0118.
Disbarment, §84-28, (c).
Consent to, Bar Rules & Regs., B, §.0117.
Imposition of discipline, Bar Rules & Regs., B, §.0123.
Obligations of disbarred attorney, Bar Rules & Regs., B, §.0124.
Reinstatement, §84-32, (d); Bar Rules & Regs., B, §.0125.

ATTORNEYS AT LAW —Cont'd
Disciplinary proceedings —Cont'd
Disbarment —Cont'd
Resignation while under investigation, order debarring member, Bar Rules & Regs., B, §.0117.
Restoration of license, §84-32, (c).
Disciplinary authority of North Carolina.
Choice of law, Prof. Cond. Rule 8.5.
Lawyer admitted to practice in state subject to, Prof. Cond. Rule 8.5.
Discovery, Bar Rules & Regs., B, §.0114.
Dismissal.
Notice of action, Bar Rules & Regs., B, §.0120.
Dispositional alternatives, §84-28, (c).
Disqualification of member of council or hearing commission due to interest, Bar Rules & Regs., B, §.0127.
District bars not to conduct separate proceedings, Bar Rules & Regs., B, §.0102.
District grievance committees, Bar Rules & Regs., B, §§.0201 to .0207.
Acknowledgment of receipt of grievance from state bar, Bar Rules & Regs., B, §.0204.
Appearances by complainants and respondents at meetings, Bar Rules & Regs., B, §.0203.
Appointment of members, Bar Rules & Regs., B, §.0201.
Assignment of grievance to investigating member, Bar Rules & Regs., B, §.0204.
Assistance in questions, Bar Rules & Regs., B, §.0206.
Authority, Bar Rules & Regs., B, §.0202.
Confidentiality of meetings, Bar Rules & Regs., B, §.0203.
Conflicts of interest, Bar Rules & Regs., B, §.0207.
Creation, Bar Rules & Regs., B, §.0201.
Decision reports, Bar Rules & Regs., B, §.0204.
Deliberations by committee, Bar Rules & Regs., B, §.0204.
Fee disputes, grievances involving, Bar Rules & Regs., B, §.0202.
Filing grievances with committees, Bar Rules & Regs., B, §§.0202, .0204.
Form letters, Bar Rules & Regs., B, §§.0208 to .0217.
Investigation of grievance, Bar Rules & Regs., B, §.0204.
Judicial districts eligible to form, Bar Rules & Regs., B, §.0201.
Jurisdiction and authority, Bar Rules & Regs., B, §.0202.
Letter of notice to respondent attorney and responses, Bar Rules & Regs., B, §.0204.
Meetings, Bar Rules & Regs., B, §.0203.
Missing attorneys, Bar Rules & Regs., B, §.0206.
Notice of meetings, Bar Rules & Regs., B, §.0203.
Notice to state bar of locally filed grievances, Bar Rules & Regs., B, §.0204.
Organization, Bar Rules & Regs., B, §.0201.
Procedure upon institution of grievance, Bar Rules & Regs., B, §.0204.
Quorum for meetings, Bar Rules & Regs., B, §.0203.
Recordkeeping, Bar Rules & Regs., B, §.0204.
Referral of grievances to committees, Bar Rules & Regs., B, §.0202.

ATTORNEYS AT LAW —Cont'd
Disciplinary proceedings —Cont'd
District grievance committees —Cont'd
Report of committee's decision, Bar Rules & Regs., B, §.0204.
Rules of the state bar, committees subject to, Bar Rules & Regs., B, §.0202.
Drug use cases, amnesty, Bar Rules & Regs., B, §.0130.
Enforcement of powers, Bar Rules & Regs., B, §.0119.
Evidence, §84-29.
Formal hearings, Bar Rules & Regs., B, §.0114.
Imposition of discipline, Bar Rules & Regs., B, §.0114.
Record of evidence, §84-32, (a).
Failure to employ sound office management techniques.
Referral of case to board of continuing legal education, Bar Rules & Regs., B, §.0112.
False statements, failure to disclose, Prof. Cond. Rule 8.1.
Federal courts, administration of reciprocal discipline, Bar Rules & Regs., B, §.0116.
Felony convictions.
Forfeiture of license, §15A-1331A.
Filing of grievance, Bar Rules & Regs., B, §.0111.
Formal hearing, Bar Rules & Regs., B, §.0114.
Form grievance to be in, Bar Rules & Regs., B, §.0111.
Form letters, district grievance committees, Bar Rules & Regs., B, §§.0208 to .0217.
Letter of notice to respondent attorney, Bar Rules & Regs., B, §.0216.
Letter to complainant acknowledging grievance, Bar Rules & Regs., B, §.0213.
Letter to complainant from investigating attorney, Bar Rules & Regs., B, §.0215.
Letter to complainant/respondent where district grievance committee recommends finding of no probable cause, Bar Rules & Regs., B, §.0210.
Letter to complainant where district committee recommends finding of probable cause, Bar Rules & Regs., B, §.0212.
Letter to complainant where local grievance alleges fee dispute only, Bar Rules & Regs., B, §.0208.
Letter to complainant where local grievance alleges fee dispute with other violations, Bar Rules & Regs., B, §.0209.
Letter to investigating attorney assigning grievance, Bar Rules & Regs., B, §.0214.
Letter to respondent where district grievance committee recommends finding of probable cause, Bar Rules & Regs., B, §.0211.
Letter transmitting completed file to North Carolina state bar, Bar Rules & Regs., B, §.0217.
Grievance committee.
Powers and duties, Bar Rules & Regs., B, §.0106.
Grounds for discipline, §84-28, (b).
Guilt in criminal case, effect of finding, Bar Rules & Regs., B, §.0115.
Hearing commission, §84-28.1.
Appointment of members, §84-28.1, (a).
Compensation of members, §84-28.1, (c).
Composition, §84-28.1, (a).
Contempt.
Power to hold in contempt, §84-28.1, (b1).
Number of members, §84-28.1, (a).

ATTORNEYS AT LAW —Cont'd
Disciplinary proceedings —Cont'd
Hearing commission —Cont'd
Powers, §84-28.1, (b), (b1).
Hearing committee, designation, Bar Rules & Regs., B, §.0114.
Hearing committee's powers and duties, Bar Rules & Regs., B, §.0109.
Immunity from suit.
Persons immune, §84-28.2.
Imposition of discipline, Bar Rules & Regs., B, §.0123.
Inactive status.
Transfer to inactive status for mental incompetence or physical disability, §84-28, (g).
Inherent powers of courts unaffected, §84-36.
Initial determination, Bar Rules & Regs., B, §.0112.
Injunctions.
Practice of law by attorney, §84-28, (f).
Interim report of council concerning grievance, Bar Rules & Regs., B, §.0112.
Investigations.
Initial determination, Bar Rules & Regs., B, §.0112.
Investigators, §84-31.
Judgment or order, relief from, Bar Rules & Regs., B, §.0114.
Judgments, §84-32, (a).
Amendment, Bar Rules & Regs., B, §.0114.
Judicial district grievance committees, rules governing, Bar Rules & Regs., B, §§.0201 to .0207.
Form letters, Bar Rules & Regs., B, §§.0208 to .0217.
Jurisdiction of council, §84-28, (a).
Letter of caution.
Issuance by grievance committee, Bar Rules & Regs., B, §.0113.
Letter of notice sent to respondent, Bar Rules & Regs., B, §.0112.
Letter of warning.
Issuance by grievance committee, Bar Rules & Regs., B, §.0113.
Lifting stay of suspension with conditions, Bar Rules & Regs., B, §.0114.
Mitigating factors in imposing discipline, Bar Rules & Regs., B, §.0114.
Motion to lift stay of suspension, Bar Rules & Regs., B, §.0114.
New trial, Bar Rules & Regs., B, §.0114.
Notice of findings of incapacity or disability, Bar Rules & Regs., B, §.0123.
Notice of imposition of discipline, Bar Rules & Regs., B, §.0123.
Notice to complainant of action, Bar Rules & Regs., B, §.0121.
Notice to member of action or dismissal, Bar Rules & Regs., B, §.0120.
Obligations of disbarred or suspended attorneys, Bar Rules & Regs., B, §.0124.
Open hearings, Bar Rules & Regs., B, §.0114.
Other jurisdictions.
Effect of disciplinary proceedings in, §84-28, (e).
Petition for reinstatement after disbarment or suspension, Bar Rules & Regs., B, §.0125.
Post-trial motions, Bar Rules & Regs., B, §.0114.
Prehearing conferences, Bar Rules & Regs., B, §.0114.

ATTORNEYS AT LAW —Cont'd
Disciplinary proceedings —Cont'd
Preliminary hearings held by grievance committee.
Quorum and vote required for finding probable cause, Bar Rules & Regs., B, §.0113.
Pretrial motions.
Hearing and disposing of, Bar Rules & Regs., B, §.0114.
Probable cause determination by grievance committee, Bar Rules & Regs., B, §.0113.
Procedure at formal hearings, Bar Rules & Regs., B, §.0114.
Procedure for discipline, Bar Rules & Regs., B, §.0102.
Procedure on reciprocal discipline, Bar Rules & Regs., B, §.0116.
Proceedings before grievance committee, Bar Rules & Regs., B, §.0113.
Production of books, papers and other documents.
Subpoena issued at formal hearings, Bar Rules & Regs., B, §.0114.
Subpoena issued in proceedings before grievance committee, Bar Rules & Regs., B, §.0113.
Subpoena to compel during initial determination, Bar Rules & Regs., B, §.0112.
Prosecutor.
Appointment, §84-31.
Purposes of discipline for misconduct, Bar Rules & Regs., B, §.0101.
Reciprocal discipline, Bar Rules & Regs., B, §.0116.
Record at formal hearings, Bar Rules & Regs., B, §.0114.
Record of proceedings, §84-32, (a).
Referral of case to board of continuing legal education.
Respondent failing to employ sound office management, Bar Rules & Regs., B, §.0112.
Refusal to obey lawful orders.
Enforcement of powers, Bar Rules & Regs., B, §.0119.
Reinstatement after disbarment or suspension, §84-32, (d); Bar Rules & Regs., B, §.0125.
Relief from judgment or order, Bar Rules & Regs., B, §.0114.
Reprimand.
Imposition of discipline, Bar Rules & Regs., B, §.0123.
Issuance by grievance committee, Bar Rules & Regs., B, §.0113.
Private reprimand, §84-28, (c).
Resignation while under investigation, Bar Rules & Regs., B, §.0117.
Rights of accused person, §84-30.
Rules of civil procedure.
Pleadings and proceedings to conform to, Bar Rules & Regs., B, §.0114.
Secretary's powers and duties, Bar Rules & Regs., B, §.0110.
Service of complaints and other documents or papers, Bar Rules & Regs., B, §.0114.
Settlement of case.
Meeting of parties prior to hearing, Bar Rules & Regs., B, §.0114.
Size of papers presented to commission for filing, Bar Rules & Regs., B, §.0114.
State bar council's powers and duties, Bar Rules & Regs., B, §.0104.

ATTORNEYS AT LAW —Cont'd
Disciplinary proceedings —Cont'd
Stay of period of suspension, Bar Rules & Regs., B, §.0114.
Stipulation of issues, facts or matters of law.
Meeting of parties prior to hearing, Bar Rules & Regs., B, §.0114.
Subpoenas.
Issuance at formal hearings, Bar Rules & Regs., B, §.0114.
Issuance by chairperson of grievance committee during initial determination, Bar Rules & Regs., B, §.0112.
Issuance in proceedings before grievance committee, Bar Rules & Regs., B, §.0113.
Surrender of license.
Voluntary surrender, §84-32, (b).
While under investigation, Bar Rules & Regs., B, §.0117.
Suspension, §84-28, (c), (d).
Imposition of discipline, Bar Rules & Regs., B, §.0123.
Obligation of suspended attorney, Bar Rules & Regs., B, §.0124.
Reinstatement, §84-32, (d); Bar Rules & Regs., B, §.0125.
Restoration of license, §84-32, (c).
Stay of period of suspension with conditions, Bar Rules & Regs., B, §.0114.
Time for filing answer, Bar Rules & Regs., B, §.0114.
Time for scheduling hearing, Bar Rules & Regs., B, §.0114.
Trust account, audit.
Investigative subpoena, Bar Rules & Regs., B, §.0128.
Witnesses, §84-29.
Rights of accused person as to, §84-30.
Subpoena compelling attendance in proceedings before grievance committee, Bar Rules & Regs., B, §.0113.
Subpoenas to compel attendance during initial determination, Bar Rules & Regs., B, §.0112.
Subpoena to compel attendance at formal hearing, Bar Rules & Regs., B, §.0114.
Disclosure of confidential information, Prof. Cond. Rule 1.6.
Discovery.
Frivolous discovery, Prof. Cond. Rule 3.4.
Dispute as to fees.
Lawyer responsibilities, Prof. Cond Rule 1.5.
Disqualification.
Former judge, clerk, arbitrator, mediator or third party neutral, Prof. Cond. Rule 1.12.
Imputed disqualification.
Principles of, Prof. Cond. Rule 1.10.
Public officers and employees.
Special conflicts, former and current officers and employees, Prof. Cond. Rule 1.11.
District courts.
Courtroom decorum, Super. Ct. Rule 12.
Scheduling conflicts.
Guidelines for resolving, Super. Ct. Rule 3.1.
Withdrawal of appearance, Super. Ct. Rule 16.
District grievance committees, rules governing, Bar Rules & Regs., B, §§.0201 to .0207.
Form letters, Bar Rules & Regs., B, §§.0208 to .0217.

ATTORNEYS AT LAW —Cont'd
Division of fees, Prof. Cond Rule 1.5.
Lawyer or firm sharing fees with nonlawyer, Prof. Cond. Rule 5.4.
Drug use.
Disciplinary amnesty in elicit drug use cases, Bar Rules & Regs., B, §.0130.
Electronic contact with prospective clients, Prof. Cond. Rule 7.3.
Employment agreements.
Restriction on practice, Prof. Cond. Rule 5.6.
Employment security.
Representation of parties to proceedings before commission, §96-17, (b).
Representation of state and commission in civil actions, §96-7, (a).
Entrusted property, Prof. Cond. Rule 1.15-2.
Defined, Prof. Cond. Rule 1.15-1.
Estate planning and probate law specialty, Bar Rules & Regs., D, §§.2301 to .2307.
Applicability of other requirements, Bar Rules & Regs., D, §.2307.
Certification standards, Bar Rules & Regs., D, §.2305.
Continued certification standards, Bar Rules & Regs., D, §.2306.
Continuing legal education, Bar Rules & Regs., D, §.2305.
Definition of specialty, Bar Rules & Regs., D, §.2302.
Establishment of specialty field, Bar Rules & Regs., D, §.2301.
Examination for specialty, Bar Rules & Regs., D, §.2305.
Peer review, Bar Rules & Regs., D, §.2305.
Plan of legal specialization, applicability of provisions, Bar Rules & Regs., D, §.2304.
Recognition of specialist, Bar Rules & Regs., D, §.2303.
Ethics opinions and ethics advisories, Bar Rules & Regs., D, §§.0101 to .0104.
Definitions, Bar Rules & Regs., D, §.0101.
Ethics, Bar Rules & Regs., D, §.0103.
Ethics opinions and decisions, Bar Rules & Regs., D, §.0104.
Requests, Bar Rules & Regs., D, §.0102.
Evidence.
Altering, destroying or concealing, Prof. Cond. Rule 3.4.
False evidence offered, Prof. Cond. Rule 3.3.
Obstructing party's access to, Prof. Cond. Rule 3.4.
Prohibited acts as to opposing party and counsel, Prof. Cond. Rule 3.4.
Excessive fees and expenses.
Charging client prohibited, factors in determining, Prof. Cond. Rule 1.5.
Executions, §47-43.1.
Execution against the person.
Indigent defendants.
Appointment of counsel, §1-311.
Executors and administrators.
Counsel fees allowable to attorneys serving as representatives, §28A-23-4.
Employing attorneys.
Powers of personal representatives and fiduciaries, §28A-13-3, (a).
Ex parte communications with judge or jurors, Prof. Cond. Rule 3.5.
Ex parte proceedings.
Information to tribunal, Prof. Cond. Rule 3.3.
Expediting litigation, Prof. Cond. Rule 3.2.

ATTORNEYS AT LAW —Cont'd
Extrajudicial statements, Prof. Cond. Rule 3.6.
Fairness to opposing party and counsel, Prof. Cond. Rule 3.4.
False communications concerning services, Prof. Cond. Rule 7.1.
False evidence offered, Prof. Cond. Rule 3.3.
False or misleading statements.
Bar admission, disciplinary matters, Prof. Cond. Rule 8.1.
Communications concerning services, Prof. Cond. Rule 7.1.
Regarding judges or candidates for judicial office, Prof. Cond. Rule 8.2.
To third persons, Prof. Cond. Rule 4.1.
To tribunal, Prof. Cond. Rule 3.3.
Family law arbitration, §50-48.
Family law specialty, Bar Rules & Regs., D, §§.2401 to .2407.
Applicability of other requirements, Bar Rules & Regs., D, §.2407.
Certification standards, Bar Rules & Regs., D, §.2405.
Continued certification standards, Bar Rules & Regs., D, §.2406.
Continuing legal education, Bar Rules & Regs., D, §.2405.
Definition of specialty, Bar Rules & Regs., D, §.2402.
Establishment of specialty field, Bar Rules & Regs., D, §.2401.
Peer review, Bar Rules & Regs., D, §.2405.
Plan of legal specialization, applicability of provisions, Bar Rules & Regs., D, §.2404.
Recognition of specialist, Bar Rules & Regs., D, §.2403.
Fee arbitration, model plan for district bar, Bar Rules & Regs., D, §§.0801 to .0808.
Appointment of committee on fee arbitration members, Bar Rules & Regs., D, §.0801.
Chairperson of committee, Bar Rules & Regs., D, §.0802.
Decision of arbitrators, Bar Rules & Regs., D, §.0806.
Enforcement of decisions of arbitrators, Bar Rules & Regs., D, §.0807.
Jurisdiction of committee, Bar Rules & Regs., D, §.0803.
Proceedings.
Generally, Bar Rules & Regs., D, §.0805.
Recordkeeping by coordinator of fee arbitration, Bar Rules & Regs., D, §.0808.
Request for arbitration, processing, Bar Rules & Regs., D, §.0804.
Fees generally.
See ATTORNEYS' FEES.
Fiduciaries.
Counsel fees allowed attorneys serving as fiduciaries, §32-61.
Employment and compensation.
Powers which may be incorporated by reference in trust instrument, §32-27.
Fiduciary funds.
Defined, Prof. Cond. Rule 1.15-1.
Deposit, Prof. Cond. Rule 1.15-2.
Financial assistance to client, Prof. Cond. Rule 1.8.
Fingerprinting.
Applicants for admission to practice, §84-24.
Firm names and letterheads, Prof. Cond. Rule 7.5.

ATTORNEYS AT LAW —Cont'd
Foreign legal consultants. See within this heading, "Consultants."
Forfeiture.
Contingent fee.
Charging in criminal or civil forfeiture proceeding, Prof. Cond. Rule 1.5.
Former clients.
Duties to, Prof. Cond. Rule 1.9.
Form letters involving disciplinary matters.
District grievance committees, Bar Rules & Regs., B, §§.0208 to .0217.
Fraud.
Client engaging in fraudulent conduct, remedial measures, Prof. Cond. Rule 3.3.
Defined, Prof. Cond. Rule 1.0.
Lawyer not to counsel client to engage in fraudulent conduct, Prof. Cond. Rule 1.2.
Liability for fraudulent practice.
Double damages, §84-13.
Frivolous claims and contentions, Prof. Cond. Rule 3.1.
Frivolous discovery, Prof. Cond. Rule 3.4.
General trust account.
Defined, Prof. Cond. Rule 1.15-1.
Deposit of trust funds in, Prof. Cond. Rule 1.15-2.
Gift from client.
Soliciting, Prof. Cond. Rule 1.8.
Government officers and employees.
Action as public official, Prof. Cond. Rule 6.6.
Conflict of interest.
Special conflicts, former and current officers and employees, Prof. Cond. Rule 1.11.
Guardian ad litem.
Discharge and appointment.
Attorney as guardian ad litem, §35A-1107, (a), (b).
Immigration law specialty, Bar Rules & Regs., D, §§.2601 to .2607.
Impairment.
Lawyer assistance program, Bar Rules & Regs., D, §§.0601 to .0623.
See LAWYERS ASSISTANCE PROGRAM.
Impeachment.
Accused entitled to counsel, §123-9.
Implied authorization to take action, Prof. Cond. Rule 1.2.
Disclosure of confidential informations, Prof. Cond. Rule 1.6.
Imputation of conflict of interest, Prof. Cond. Rule 1.10.
Imputed disqualification.
Principles of, Prof. Cond. Rule 1.10.
Inactive status.
Reinstatement from, Bar Rules & Regs., D, §.0902.
Transfer to, Bar Rules & Regs., D, §.0901.
Incompetence, determination of.
Attorney as guardian ad litem, §35A-1107, (a), (b).
Right to counsel, §35A-1107, (a).
Incompetence, restoration.
Right to counsel, §35A-1130, (c).
Indigent persons.
Access to civil justice act, §§7A-474.1 to 7A-474.5.
See GEOGRAPHICALLY BASED FIELD PROGRAMS.
Indigent defense services act, §§7A-498 to 7A-498.8.
See INDIGENT DEFENSE SERVICES.
Representation of indigent persons generally.
See INDIGENT DEFENSE SERVICES.

ATTORNEYS AT LAW —Cont'd
Industrial commission.
Utilization of rehabilitation professionals and workers' compensation claims, I.C. Util. Rehab. Profs. VII.
Industrial commission mediated settlement conferences.
Attendance, I.C. Mediated Settlmt. Conf. R. 4(a).
Influencing judge or juror, Prof. Cond. Rule 3.5.
Interest on lawyer's trust accounts, Prof. Cond. Rule 1.15-4.
Rules governing administration of plan, Bar Rules & Regs., D, §§.1301 to .1316.
Interest on trust or fiduciary accounts, Prof. Cond. Rule 1.15-2.
International commercial arbitration and conciliation.
Representation by attorney, §1-567.48, (b).
Conciliation proceedings, §1-567.79.
Interstate and international law firm registration, Bar Rules & Regs., E, §§.0201 to .0206.
Certificate, Bar Rules & Regs., E, §.0204.
Conditions, Bar Rules & Regs., E, §.0202.
Effect, Bar Rules & Regs., E, §.0205.
Fee, Bar Rules & Regs., E, §.0203.
Nonrenewal of registration, Bar Rules & Regs., E, §.0206.
Required, Bar Rules & Regs., E, §.0201.
Iolta, Prof. Cond. Rule 1.15-4.
Rules governing administration of plan, Bar Rules & Regs., D, §§.1301 to .1316.
Judges.
Ex parte communications with, Prof. Cond. Rule 3.5.
False statements regarding, Prof. Cond. Rule 8.2.
Former judges.
Conflict of interest, Prof. Cond. Rule 1.12.
Influencing, Prof. Cond. Rule 3.5.
Judgments.
Attorney in action not to probate papers therein.
Final judgments in which documents verified in violation of section.
Validation of certain documents verified by attorneys, §47-8.1.
Judicial district grievance committees, rules governing, Bar Rules & Regs., B, §§.0201 to .0207.
Form letters, Bar Rules & Regs., B, §§.0208 to .0217.
Jury.
Argument of counsel, §7A-97.
Court's control of argument, §7A-97.
Communicating with after discharge, Prof. Cond. Rule 3.5.
Ex parte communications with, Prof. Cond. Rule 3.5.
Influencing, Prof. Cond. Rule 3.5.
Juvenile code.
Custody hearings.
Determining need for continued secure or nonsecure custody.
Right to counsel at hearing, §7B-506.
Knowledge and skill.
Competent representation, Prof. Cond. Rule 1.1.
Land examiners.
Torrens system registration, §§43-4, 43-5.
Law firms.
Arbitration of internal disputes, Bar Rules & Regs., E, §§.0401 to .0410.
Administration of program, Bar Rules & Regs., E, §.0404.

ATTORNEYS AT LAW —Cont'd
Law firms —Cont'd
Arbitration of internal disputes —Cont'd
Authority to adopt amendments and regulations, Bar Rules & Regs., E, §.0410.
Confidentiality, Bar Rules & Regs., E, §.0409.
Expenses and fees of arbitrators, Bar Rules & Regs., E, §.0408.
Jurisdiction, Bar Rules & Regs., E, §.0403.
List of arbitrators, Bar Rules & Regs., E, §.0406.
Purposes of state bar rules, Bar Rules & Regs., E, §.0401.
Selection of arbitrators, Bar Rules & Regs., E, §.0407.
Submission to arbitration, Bar Rules & Regs., E, §.0402.
Uniform arbitration act to govern procedures, Bar Rules & Regs., E, §.0405.
Voluntary program, Bar Rules & Regs., E, §.0402.
Defined, Prof. Cond. Rule 1.0.
Fee sharing with non-lawyer, Prof. Cond. Rule 5.4.
Forming partnership with non-lawyer, Prof. Cond. Rule 5.4.
Imputation of conflict of interest, Prof. Cond. Rule 1.10.
Names and letterheads, Prof. Cond. Rule 7.5.
Non-lawyer assistants, responsibilities, Prof. Cond. Rule 5.3.
Professional corporation or association.
Practice in, Prof. Cond. Rule 5.4.
Professional corporations and professional limited liability companies practicing law, regulations, Bar Rules & Regs., E, §§.0101 to .0106.
Professional independence of lawyer, Prof. Cond. Rule 5.4.
Registration of interstate law firms, Bar Rules & Regs., E, §§.0201 to .0206.
Responsibilities of partners, managers and supervisory lawyers, Prof. Cond. Rule 5.1.
Restriction on practice, Prof. Cond. Rule 5.6.
State bar.
Interstate and international law firm registration, Bar Rules & Regs., E, §§.0201 to .0206.
Subordinate lawyer, responsibilities, Prof. Cond. Rule 5.2.
Unauthorized practice of law, Prof. Cond. Rule 5.5.
Law students, rules governing practical training, Bar Rules & Regs., C, §§.0201 to .0207.
Activities permitted by students, Bar Rules & Regs., C, §.0206.
Certification as legal intern, Bar Rules & Regs., C, §.0204.
Definitions, Bar Rules & Regs., C, §.0202.
Eligibility to engage in activities permitted, Bar Rules & Regs., C, §.0203.
Form of withdrawal of dean's certificate, Bar Rules & Regs., C, §.0210.
Purposes, Bar Rules & Regs., C, §.0201.
Supervising attorneys, Bar Rules & Regs., C, §.0205.
Use of student's name, Bar Rules & Regs., C, §.0207.
Lawyer referral service.
Participation, Prof. Cond. Rule 7.2.

ATTORNEYS AT LAW —Cont'd
Lawyer's trust accounts.
Audit.
By investigative subpoena, Bar Rules & Regs., B, §.0128.
Interest on lawyer's trust accounts (IOLTA).
Audit of accounts, Bar Rules & Regs., D, §.1313.
Disbursement of funds, Bar Rules & Regs., D, §.1313.
Funding for program, Bar Rules & Regs., D, §.1312.
Investment criteria, Bar Rules & Regs., D, §.1313.
IOLTA board of trustees, Bar Rules & Regs., D, §§.1301 to .1316.
Annual report of board, Bar Rules & Regs., D, §.1315.
Appointment and removal of members, Bar Rules & Regs., D, §.1306.
Chairperson, appointment, Bar Rules & Regs., D, §.1310.
Funding for program carried out by board, Bar Rules & Regs., D, §.1312.
Jurisdiction and authority of board, Bar Rules & Regs., D, §.1302.
Lay participation, Bar Rules & Regs., D, §.1305.
Meetings of board, Bar Rules & Regs., D, §.1314.
Purposes of board, Bar Rules & Regs., D, §.1301.
Responsibility for operating program of board, Bar Rules & Regs., D, §.1303.
Severability of provisions, Bar Rules & Regs., D, §.1316.
Size of board, Bar Rules & Regs., D, §.1304.
Staggered terms, Bar Rules & Regs., D, §.1308.
Succession in office, Bar Rules & Regs., D, §.1309.
Terms of office, Bar Rules & Regs., D, §.1307.
Vice-chairperson, appointment, Bar Rules & Regs., D, §.1311.
Maintenance of accounts, Bar Rules & Regs., D, §.1313.
Legal ethics, procedures for ruling on questions, Bar Rules & Regs., D, §§.0101 to .0104.
Legal knowledge and skill.
Competent representation, Prof. Cond. Rule 1.1.
Legal services organizations.
Limited legal services programs, Prof. Cond. Rule 6.5.
Membership in, Prof. Cond. Rule 6.3.
Legal services provided by law students.
Rules governing, Bar Rules & Regs., C, §§.0201 to .0207.
Letterheads.
Law firm names and letterheads, Prof. Cond. Rule 7.5.
Letter of warning.
Issuance by grievance committee, Bar Rules & Regs., B, §.0113.
Letters of caution.
Issuance by grievance committee, Bar Rules & Regs., B, §.0113.
Licenses.
Forfeiture of license.
Felony convictions, §15A-1331A.
Inherent powers of courts unaffected, §84-36.

ATTORNEYS AT LAW —Cont'd
Licenses —Cont'd
Issuance, Bar Rules & Regs., C, §§.0102, .0103.
Comity applicants, Admission to Practice, §.1301.
General applicants, Admission to Practice, §.1302.
Restoration of license ordered.
Duty of board of law examiners to issue, §84-24.
Surrender while under investigation, Bar Rules & Regs., B, §.0117.
Taxation.
Professional licenses generally, §105-41.
Limited legal services programs, Prof. Cond. Rule 6.5.
Limited liability companies.
Professional limited liability companies, regulations for practicing law, Bar Rules & Regs., E, §§.0101 to .0106.
Limiting liability.
Prospective agreement limiting lawyer's liability.
Prohibition, Prof. Cond. Rule 1.8.
Limiting scope of representation, Prof. Cond. Rule 1.2.
List of attorneys.
Secretary of revenue.
Clerk of superior court to furnish list to secretary, §7A-110.
Literary or media rights.
Negotiating agreement with client, Prof. Cond. Rule 1.8.
Lobbying.
Lawyer holding public office, Prof. Cond. Rule 6.6.
Local government finance.
Bond issues.
Contract involving legal services, §159-131.
Employment of bond attorneys, §159-123, (e), (f).
Malpractice.
Agreement limiting lawyer's liability or settling claim, Prof. Cond. Rule 1.8.
Failure to file complaint on time.
Attorney liable for cost, §84-12.
Fraudulent practice.
Liability of attorney in double damages, §84-13.
Professional liability insurance.
Certificate of coverage provided by bar members, Bar Rules & Regs., A, §.0204.
Mediation.
Former mediators.
Conflict of interest, Prof. Cond. Rule 1.12.
Lawyers serving as third-party neutrals, Prof. Cond. Rule 2.4.
Medicolegal guidelines for attorney-physician relationship, MLG Rules 1 to 6.
Mental health, developmental disabilities and substance abuse.
Involuntary commitment.
District court hearing.
Discharge of counsel.
Substance abusers, §122C-289.
Duty of assigned counsel.
Substance abusers, §122C-289.
Representation of state's interest, §122C-268, (b).
Respondent's right to counsel, §122C-268, (d).
Lawyer assistance program, Bar Rules & Regs., D, §§.0601 to .0623.
See LAWYERS ASSISTANCE PROGRAM.
Rights of clients.
Release of information to attorney, §122C-53, (i).

ATTORNEYS AT LAW —Cont'd
Mental health, developmental disabilities and substance abuse —Cont'd
Rights of clients —Cont'd
24-hour facilities.
Contact and consultation with legal counsel, §122C-62, (a).
Special counsel to represent the respondent and the state.
Employment, §122C-270.
Misappropriation of entrusted property.
Duty to report, Prof. Cond. Rule 1.15-2.
Misconduct, Prof. Cond. Rule 8.4.
Disciplinary rules of state bar generally, Bar Rules & Regs., B, §§.0101 to .0217. See within this heading, "Disciplinary proceedings."
Reporting, Prof. Cond. Rule 8.3.
Misdemeanors.
Appearance for creditor in insolvency and certain other proceedings by anyone except attorney, §84-10.
Practice of law by disqualified persons, §84-2.
Solicitation of retainer or contract for legal services, §84-38.
Unauthorized practice of law, §84-8.
Motions.
Out-of-state attorneys.
Motion for admission to practice law in state, §84-4.1.
Municipal corporations.
Defense of employees and officers, §160A-167.
Voting rights act of 1965.
Publications in North Carolina register, §120-30.9H.
Submission of charges to United States attorney general by municipal attorney, §120-30.9F.
Nonresidents.
Out-of-state attorneys.
Admission to practice law, §84-4.1.
Nontestimonial identification.
Right to counsel, §15A-279, (d).
Oaths.
Admission to practice of law, §84-1.
Attorney in action not to probate papers therein.
Validation of certain documents verified by attorneys, §47-8.1.
Form of oaths of office, §11-11.
Obstructing party's access to evidence, Prof. Cond. Rule 3.4.
Opposing party and counsel.
Fairness to, Prof. Cond. Rule 3.4.
Organization as client.
Representing, Prof. Cond. Rule 1.13.
Out-of-state attorneys.
Practice of law.
Admission to practice, §84-4.1.
Summary revocation of permission, §84-4.2.
Parole.
Indigent parolees.
Entitlement to counsel, §148-62.1.
Partnerships.
Fee sharing with non-lawyer, Prof. Cond. Rule 5.4.
Firm names and letterheads, Prof. Cond. Rule 7.5.
Forming partnership with non-lawyer, Prof. Cond. Rule 5.4.
Imputation of conflict of interest, Prof. Cond. Rule 1.10.
Non-lawyer assistants, responsibilities, Prof. Cond. Rule 5.3.

ATTORNEYS AT LAW —Cont'd
Partnerships —Cont'd
Professional independence of lawyer, Prof. Cond. Rule 5.4.
Responsibilities of partners, managers and supervisory lawyers, Prof. Cond. Rule 5.1.
Restriction on practice, Prof. Cond. Rule 5.6.
Subordinate lawyer, responsibilities, Prof. Cond. Rule 5.2.
Unauthorized practice of law, Prof. Cond. Rule 5.5.
Pleading, signing and verifying, §1A-1, Rule 11.
Electronic filing.
Signatures, App. Proc. Rule 33, (b).
Practice of law.
Accountants.
Engaging in practice of law prohibited, §93-1, (b).
Collection agencies.
Unauthorized practice of law, §58-70-120.
Corporations.
Nonprofit corporations.
Indigent legal services by, §84-5.1.
Prohibition as to practice of law by corporation, §84-5.
Violations of provisions.
Misdemeanor, §84-8.
Defined, §84-2.1.
Disqualification of certain persons, §84-2.
Foreclosures.
Fee for conducting foreclosures.
Prohibited to all except licensed attorneys, §84-6.
Inherent powers of courts unaffected, §84-36.
Oath on admission to practice, §84-1.
Out-of-state attorneys.
Admission to practice, §84-4.1.
Summary revocation of permission, §84-4.2.
Professional corporations and professional limited liability companies.
Regulations for practicing law, Bar Rules & Regs., E, §§.0101 to .0106.
Pro hac vice, §84-4.1.
State bar.
Persons other than members of state prohibited from practicing law, §84-4.
Suspension from practice.
Noncompliance with reporting requirements, CLE Rule 23.
Reinstatement, CLE Rule 24.
Unauthorized practice.
Actions by state bar, §84-37, (a).
Additional nature of provisions, §84-37, (e).
Advisory opinions, §84-37, (f).
Injunction, §84-37, (b).
Plaintiff may examine adverse party, §84-37, (d).
Venue, §84-37, (c).
Appearance for creditor in insolvency and certain other proceedings by anyone except attorney, §§84-9, 84-10.
Authorized practice committee procedures, Bar Rules & Regs., D, §§.0201 to .0207.
Collection agencies, §58-70-120.
Disqualified persons, §84-2.
Foreclosures.
Fee for conducting foreclosures.
Prohibited to all except licensed attorneys, §84-6.
Indictments.
Duty of district attorneys to indict persons upon receipt of information of violation, §84-7.

ATTORNEYS AT LAW —Cont'd
Practice of law —Cont'd
Unauthorized practice —Cont'd
Injunctions, §84-37, (b).
District attorneys to bring injunction proceedings upon application, §84-7.
Investigation by state bar, §84-37, (a).
Legal clinics of law schools.
Exception, §84-8.
Misdemeanor, §84-8.
Persons other than members of state bar, §84-4.
Prepaid legal services plans, Bar Rules & Regs., E, §§.0301 to .0309.
Advertising of state bar approval prohibited, Bar Rules & Regs., E, §.0304.
Amendments, filing requirement, Bar Rules & Regs., E, §.0303.
Annual registration, Bar Rules & Regs., E, §.0305.
Index of registered plans, Bar Rules & Regs., E, §.0307.
Jurisdiction of state bar, Bar Rules & Regs., E, §.0309.
Registration fee, Bar Rules & Regs., E, §.0306.
Registration required, Bar Rules & Regs., E, §.0301.
Registration site, Bar Rules & Regs., E, §.0302.
State bar may not approve or disapprove plans, Bar Rules & Regs., E, §.0308.
Prepaid or group legal services plans.
Participation, Prof. Cond. Rule 7.3.
Prisoner and attorney conference.
Secret listening, §§14-227.1, 14-227.3.
Probate and registration.
Attorney in action not to probate papers therein.
Validation of certain documents verified by attorneys, §47-8.1.
Execution and acknowledgment of instruments by attorneys or attorneys-in-fact, §47-43.1.
Probate law specialty.
Certification standards for estate planning and probate law specialty, Bar Rules & Regs., D, §§.2301 to .2307.
Probation.
Revocation hearing.
Right to counsel, §15A-1345, (e).
Pro bono work.
Legal services provided by law students, Bar Rules & Regs., C, §§.0201 to .0207.
Professional conduct.
Abandoned property.
Entrusted property, Prof. Cond. Rule 1.15-2.
Accounts.
Deposit of funds, Prof. Cond. Rule 1.15-2.
Records and accountings, Prof. Cond. Rule 1.15-3.
Actions impliedly authorized.
Disclosure of confidential information, Prof. Cond. Rule 1.6.
Lawyer may take, Prof. Cond. Rule 1.2.
Admission to bar.
False statements, failure to disclose, Prof. Cond. Rule 8.1.
Adverse interest to client.
Acquiring, conflict of interest, Prof. Cond. Rule 1.8.
Advertising, Prof. Cond. Rule 7.2.
Communications of fields of practice, Prof. Cond. Rule 7.4.
Dramatization depicting fictional situation, Prof. Cond. Rule 7.1.

ATTORNEYS AT LAW —Cont'd
Professional conduct —Cont'd
Advertising —Cont'd
False or misleading communications concerning services, Prof. Cond. Rule 7.1.
Advisor, Prof. Cond. Rule 2.1.
Agent of lawyers' or judges' association.
Duty of confidentiality when acting as, Prof. Cond. Rule 1.6.
Aggregate settlement or agreement.
Two or more clients, Prof. Cond. Rule 1.8.
Agreements restricting practice, Prof. Cond. Rule 5.6.
Allocation of authority between client and lawyer, Prof. Cond. Rule 1.2.
Arbitrators.
Former arbitrators.
Conflict of interest, Prof. Cond. Rule 1.12.
Lawyers serving as third-party neutrals, Prof. Cond. Rule 2.4.
Attorney-client privilege.
Client-lawyer confidentiality, Prof. Cond. Rule 1.6.
Audit by state bar, Prof. Cond. Rule 1.15-3.
Bank accounts.
Deposit of funds, Prof. Cond. Rule 1.15-2.
Records and accountings, Prof. Cond. Rule 1.15-3.
Bank directive.
Lawyer maintaining trust or fiduciary accounts, Prof. Cond. Rule 1.15-2.
Bank receipts.
Record requirements, Prof. Cond. Rule 1.15-3.
Bank statements.
Record requirements, Prof. Cond. Rule 1.15-3.
Bar admission.
False statements, failure to disclose, Prof. Cond. Rule 8.1.
Business transactions with clients.
Conflict of interest, Prof. Cond. Rule 1.8.
Canceled checks.
Record requirements, Prof. Cond. Rule 1.15-3.
Candidates for judicial office.
Compliance with code of judicial conduct, Prof. Cond. Rule 8.2.
False statements regarding, Prof. Cond. Rule 8.2.
Candor toward tribunal, Prof. Cond. Rule 3.3.
Capacity of client diminished, Prof. Cond. Rule 1.14.
Checks.
Canceled checks, copies.
Record requirements, Prof. Cond. Rule 1.15-3.
Choice of law.
Disciplinary authority of North Carolina, Prof. Cond. Rule 8.5.
Client-lawyer confidentiality, Prof. Cond. Rule 1.6.
Client's decisions.
Lawyer to abide by, Prof. Cond. Rule 1.2.
Client with diminished capacity, Prof. Cond. Rule 1.14.
Communications concerning lawyer's services, Prof. Cond. Rule 7.1.
Communications of fields of practice, Prof. Cond. Rule 7.4.
Communications with clients, Prof. Cond. Rule 1.4.
Fees and expenses, Prof. Cond. Rule 1.5.
Communications with judge or jurors.
Ex parte communications, Prof. Cond. Rule 3.5.

ATTORNEYS AT LAW —Cont'd
Professional conduct —Cont'd
Communications with person represented by counsel, Prof. Cond. Rule 4.2.
Compensation.
Acceptance of compensation from other than client, Prof. Cond. Rule 1.8.
Fees and expenses, Prof. Cond. Rule 1.5.
Law firm.
Fee sharing with non-lawyer, Prof. Cond. Rule 5.4.
Sale or purchase of practice.
Increase in fees, Prof. Cond. Rule 1.17.
Competence to handle legal matter, Prof. Cond. Rule 1.1.
Concurrent conflict of interest, Prof. Cond. Rule 1.7.
Specific rules, Prof. Cond. Rule 1.8.
Confidential information, Prof. Cond. Rule 1.6.
Confidential government information.
Lawyer acquiring as public officer or employees.
Representing client with interest adverse to information, Prof. Cond. Rule 1.11.
Defined, Prof. Cond. Rule 1.0.
Discussions with prospective clients, Prof. Cond. Rule 1.18.
Confirmed in writing.
Defined, Prof. Cond. Rule 1.0.
Conflict of interest.
Current clients, Prof. Cond. Rule 1.7.
Specific rules, Prof. Cond. Rule 1.8.
Former clients.
Duties to, Prof. Cond. Rule 1.9.
Former judges, arbitrators, mediators or other third party neutrals, Prof. Cond. Rule 1.12.
Government officers and employees.
Special conflicts, former and current officers and employees, Prof. Cond. Rule 1.11.
Imputation, Prof. Cond. Rule 1.10.
Lawyer as witness, Prof. Cond. Rule 3.7.
Prospective clients, matters with, Prof. Cond. Rule 1.18.
Sale or purchase of practice, notice, Prof. Cond. Rule 1.17.
Consent.
Informed consent.
Aggregate settlement or agreement for two or more clients, Prof. Cond. Rule 1.8.
Communicating with client when client's consent required, Prof. Cond. Rule 1.4.
Defined, Prof. Cond. Rule 1.0.
Consultations with client, Prof. Cond. Rule 1.4.
Contingent fees and contingent fee agreements, Prof. Cond. Rule 1.5.
Contracts.
Contingent fee agreements, Prof. Cond. Rule 1.5.
Restriction on practice, Prof. Cond. Rule 5.6.
Criminal cases.
Abiding by client's decision, Prof. Cond. Rule 1.2.
Contingent fees, charging prohibited, Prof. Cond. Rule 1.5.
Meritorious claims and contentions, Prof. Cond. Rule 3.1.
Prosecutors, special responsibilities, Prof. Cond. Rule 3.8.
Criminal conduct.
Client engaging in, remedial measures, Prof. Cond. Rule 3.3.

ATTORNEYS AT LAW —Cont'd
Professional conduct —Cont'd
Criminal conduct —Cont'd
Lawyer not to counsel client to engage in, Prof. Cond. Rule 1.2.
Dealing with unrepresented person, Prof. Cond. Rule 4.3.
Decisions of client.
Lawyer to abide by, Prof. Cond. Rule 1.2.
Declining representation, Prof. Cond. Rule 1.16.
Dedicated trust account.
Defined, Prof. Cond. Rule 1.15-1.
Deposit of trust funds in, Prof. Cond. Rule 1.15-2.
Definitions, Prof. Cond. Rule 1.0.
Law-related services, Prof. Cond. Rule 5.7.
Prepaid legal services plan or group services plan, Prof. Cond. Rule 7.3.
Prospective client, Prof. Cond. Rule 1.18.
Safekeeping property, Prof. Cond. Rule 1.15-1.
Sexual relations with clients, Prof. Cond. Rule 1.19.
Deposit of fiduciary funds, Prof. Cond. Rule 1.15-2.
Deposit of trust funds, Prof. Cond. Rule 1.15-2.
Deposit slips.
Record requirements, Prof. Cond. Rule 1.15-3.
Diligence in representation, Prof. Cond. Rule 1.3.
Diminished capacity.
Client with, Prof. Cond. Rule 1.14.
Direct contact with prospective clients, Prof. Cond. Rule 7.3.
Disbarred attorney.
Employing as legal clerk or assistant, Prof. Cond. Rule 5.5.
Disciplinary authority of North Carolina.
Choice of law, Prof. Cond. Rule 8.5.
Lawyer admitted to practice in state subject to, Prof. Cond. Rule 8.5.
Disciplinary matters.
False statements, failure to disclose, Prof. Cond. Rule 8.1.
Disclosure of confidential information, Prof. Cond. Rule 1.6.
Discovery.
Frivolous discovery, Prof. Cond. Rule 3.4.
Dispute as to fees.
Lawyer responsibilities, Prof. Cond Rule 1.5.
Disqualification.
Former judge, clerk, arbitrator, mediator or third party neutral, Prof. Cond. Rule 1.12.
Imputed disqualification.
Principles of, Prof. Cond. Rule 1.10.
Public officers and employees.
Special conflicts, former and current officers and employees, Prof. Cond. Rule 1.11.
Disrupting tribunal, Prof. Cond. Rule 3.5.
Division of fees, Prof. Cond Rule 1.5.
Lawyer or firm sharing fees with nonlawyer, Prof. Cond. Rule 5.4.
Dramatization depicting fictional situation, Prof. Cond. Rule 7.1.
Elections.
Lawyer candidate for judicial office.
Compliance with Code of Judicial Conduct, Prof. Cond. Rule 8.2.
Electronic contact with prospective clients, Prof. Cond. Rule 7.3.
Employment agreements.
Restriction on practice, Prof. Cond. Rule 5.6.

ATTORNEYS AT LAW —Cont'd
Professional conduct —Cont'd
Entity as client.
Representing organization, Prof. Cond. Rule 1.13.
Entrusted property, Prof. Cond. Rule 1.15-2.
Defined, Prof. Cond. Rule 1.15-1.
Evaluation for use by third parties, Prof. Cond. Rule 2.3.
Evidence.
Altering, destroying or concealing, Prof. Cond. Rule 3.4.
False evidence offered, Prof. Cond. Rule 3.3.
Obstructing party's access to, Prof. Cond. Rule 3.4.
Prohibited acts as to opposing party and counsel, Prof. Cond. Rule 3.4.
Excessive fees and expenses.
Charging client prohibited, factors in determining, Prof. Cond. Rule 1.5.
Ex parte communications with judge or jurors, Prof. Cond. Rule 3.5.
Ex parte proceedings.
Information to tribunal, Prof. Cond. Rule 3.3.
Expediting litigation, Prof. Cond. Rule 3.2.
Explaining matter to client, Prof. Cond. Rule 1.4.
Extrajudicial statements, Prof. Cond. Rule 3.6.
Fairness to opposing party and counsel, Prof. Cond. Rule 3.4.
False communications concerning services, Prof. Cond. Rule 7.1.
False evidence offered, Prof. Cond. Rule 3.3.
False or misleading statements.
Bar admission, disciplinary matters, Prof. Cond. Rule 8.1.
Communications concerning services, Prof. Cond. Rule 7.1.
Regarding judges or candidates for judicial office, Prof. Cond. Rule 8.2.
To third persons, Prof. Cond. Rule 4.1.
To tribunal, Prof. Cond. Rule 3.3.
Fees and expenses, Prof. Cond. Rule 1.5.
Acceptance of compensation from other than client, Prof. Cond. Rule 1.8.
Law firm.
Fee sharing with non-lawyer, Prof. Cond. Rule 5.4.
Sale or purchase of practice, increase, Prof. Cond. Rule 1.17.
Fiduciary funds.
Defined, Prof. Cond. Rule 1.15-1.
Deposit, Prof. Cond. Rule 1.15-2.
Financial assistance to client, Prof. Cond. Rule 1.8.
Firm.
Defined, Prof. Cond. Rule 1.0.
Fee sharing with non-lawyer, Prof. Cond. Rule 5.4.
Forming partnership with non-lawyer, Prof. Cond. Rule 5.4.
Imputation of conflict of interest, Prof. Cond. Rule 1.10.
Names and letterheads, Prof. Cond. Rule 7.5.
Non-lawyer assistants, responsibilities, Prof. Cond. Rule 5.3.
Professional corporation or association.
Practice in, Prof. Cond. Rule 5.4.
Professional independence of lawyer, Prof. Cond. Rule 5.4.
Responsibilities of partners, managers and supervisory lawyers, Prof. Cond. Rule 5.1.

ATTORNEYS AT LAW —Cont'd
Professional conduct —Cont'd
Firm —Cont'd
Restriction on practice, Prof. Cond. Rule 5.6.
Subordinate lawyer, responsibilities, Prof. Cond. Rule 5.2.
Unauthorized practice of law, Prof. Cond. Rule 5.5.
Firm names and letterheads, Prof. Cond. Rule 7.5.
Forfeiture.
Contingent fee.
Charging in criminal or civil forfeiture proceeding, Prof. Cond. Rule 1.5.
Former clients.
Duties to, Prof. Cond. Rule 1.9.
Former judges, arbitrators, mediators or other third party neutrals.
Conflict of interest, Prof. Cond. Rule 1.12.
Fraud.
Client engaging in fraudulent conduct, remedial measures, Prof. Cond. Rule 3.3.
Defined, Prof. Cond. Rule 1.0.
Lawyer not to counsel client to engage in fraudulent conduct, Prof. Cond. Rule 1.2.
Frivolous claims and contentions, Prof. Cond. Rule 3.1.
Frivolous discovery, Prof. Cond. Rule 3.4.
General trust account.
Defined, Prof. Cond. Rule 1.15-1.
Deposit of trust funds in, Prof. Cond. Rule 1.15-2.
Gift from client.
Soliciting, Prof. Cond. Rule 1.8.
Government officers and employees.
Action as public official, Prof. Cond. Rule 6.6.
Conflict of interest.
Special conflicts, former and current officers and employees, Prof. Cond. Rule 1.11.
Impartiality and decorum of tribunal.
Respecting, Prof. Cond. Rule 3.5.
Implied authorization to take action, Prof. Cond. Rule 1.2.
Disclosure of confidential informations, Prof. Cond. Rule 1.6.
Imputation of conflict of interest, Prof. Cond. Rule 1.10.
Imputed disqualification.
Principles of, Prof. Cond. Rule 1.10.
Inadvertent receipt of writing, Prof. Cond. Rule 4.4.
Independent professional judgment.
Lawyer to exercise, Prof. Cond. Rule 2.1.
Influencing judge or juror, Prof. Cond. Rule 3.5.
Informed consent.
Aggregate settlement or agreement for two or more clients, Prof. Cond. Rule 1.8.
Communicating with client when client's consent required, Prof. Cond. Rule 1.4.
Defined, Prof. Cond. Rule 1.0.
Informing client as to status of matter, Prof. Cond. Rule 1.4.
In-person contact with prospective clients, Prof. Cond. Rule 7.3.
Interest on lawyers' trust accounts, Prof. Cond. Rule 1.15-4.
Interest on trust or fiduciary accounts, Prof. Cond. Rule 1.15-2.
Iolta, Prof. Cond. Rule 1.15-4.
Judges.
Ex parte communications with, Prof. Cond. Rule 3.5.

ATTORNEYS AT LAW —Cont'd
Professional conduct —Cont'd
Judges —Cont'd
False statements regarding, Prof. Cond. Rule 8.2.
Former judges.
Conflict of interest, Prof. Cond. Rule 1.12.
Influencing, Prof. Cond. Rule 3.5.
Jurors.
Communicating with after discharge, Prof. Cond. Rule 3.5.
Ex parte communications with, Prof. Cond. Rule 3.5.
Influencing, Prof. Cond. Rule 3.5.
Jury trial.
Waiver in criminal case.
Abiding by client's decision, Prof. Cond. Rule 1.2.
Knowingly.
Defined, Prof. Cond. Rule 1.0.
Knowledge and skill.
Competent representation, Prof. Cond. Rule 1.1.
Law firm.
Defined, Prof. Cond. Rule 1.0.
Fee sharing with non-lawyer, Prof. Cond. Rule 5.4.
Forming partnership with non-lawyer, Prof. Cond. Rule 5.4.
Imputation of conflict of interest, Prof. Cond. Rule 1.10.
Names and letterheads, Prof. Cond. Rule 7.5.
Non-lawyer assistants, responsibilities, Prof. Cond. Rule 5.3.
Professional corporation or association.
Practice in, Prof. Cond. Rule 5.4.
Professional independence of lawyer, Prof. Cond. Rule 5.4.
Responsibilities of partners, managers and supervisory lawyers, Prof. Cond. Rule 5.1.
Restriction on practice, Prof. Cond. Rule 5.6.
Subordinate lawyer, responsibilities, Prof. Cond. Rule 5.2.
Unauthorized practice of law, Prof. Cond. Rule 5.5.
Law reform activities affecting client's interest, Prof. Cond. Rule 6.4.
Law-related services.
Responsibilities regarding, Prof. Cond. Rule 5.7.
Lawyer referral service.
Participation, Prof. Cond. Rule 7.2.
Lawyer's or judge's assistance programs.
Confidentiality when lawyer acting as agent for, Prof. Cond. Rule 1.6.
Legal entity as client.
Representing, Prof. Cond. Rule 1.13.
Legal knowledge and skill.
Competent representation, Prof. Cond. Rule 1.1.
Legal services organizations.
Limited legal services programs, Prof. Cond. Rule 6.5.
Membership in, Prof. Cond. Rule 6.3.
Letterheads.
Firm names and letterheads, Prof. Cond. Rule 7.5.
Limited legal services programs, Prof. Cond. Rule 6.5.
Limiting liability.
Prospective agreement limiting lawyer's liability.
Prohibition, Prof. Cond. Rule 1.8.

ATTORNEYS AT LAW —Cont'd
Professional conduct —Cont'd
Limiting scope of representation, Prof. Cond. Rule 1.2.
Literary or media rights.
Negotiating agreement with client, Prof. Cond. Rule 1.8.
Lobbying.
Lawyer holding public office, Prof. Cond. Rule 6.6.
Malpractice.
Agreement limiting lawyer's liability or settling claim, Prof. Cond. Rule 1.8.
Mediators.
Former mediators.
Conflict of interest, Prof. Cond. Rule 1.12.
Lawyers serving as third-party neutrals, Prof. Cond. Rule 2.4.
Mental impairment.
Client with diminished capacity, Prof. Cond. Rule 1.14.
Meritorious claims and contentions, Prof Cond. Rule 3.1.
Minority.
Client with diminished capacity, Prof. Cond. Rule 1.14.
Misappropriation of entrusted property.
Duty to report, Prof. Cond. Rule 1.15-2.
Misconduct, Prof. Cond. Rule 8.4.
Reporting, Prof. Cond. Rule 8.3.
Names.
Firm names and letterheads, Prof. Cond. Rule 7.5.
Nonlawyers in law firms.
Responsibility for, Prof. Cond. Rule 5.3.
Notice of sale or purchase of practice, Prof. Cond. Rule 1.17.
Obstructing party's access to evidence, Prof. Cond. Rule 3.4.
Opposing party and counsel.
Fairness to, Prof. Cond. Rule 3.4.
Organization as client.
Representing, Prof. Cond. Rule 1.13.
Partnerships.
Fee sharing with non-lawyer, Prof. Cond. Rule 5.4.
Firm names and letterheads, Prof. Cond. Rule 7.5.
Forming partnership with non-lawyer, Prof. Cond. Rule 5.4.
Imputation of conflict of interest, Prof. Cond. Rule 1.10.
Non-lawyer assistants, responsibilities, Prof. Cond. Rule 5.3.
Partner defined, Prof. Cond. Rule 1.0.
Professional independence of lawyer, Prof. Cond. Rule 5.4.
Responsibilities of partners, managers and supervisory lawyers, Prof. Cond. Rule 5.1.
Restriction on practice, Prof. Cond. Rule 5.6.
Subordinate lawyer, responsibilities, Prof. Cond. Rule 5.2.
Unauthorized practice of law, Prof. Cond. Rule 5.5.
Person represented by counsel.
Communications with, Prof. Cond. Rule 4.2.
Plea in criminal case.
Abiding by client's decision, Prof. Cond. Rule 1.2.
Political, economic, social or moral views of client.
Representation not endorsement, Prof. Cond. Rule 1.2.

ATTORNEYS AT LAW —Cont'd
Professional conduct —Cont'd
Preamble, Prof. Cond. Rule 0.1.
Prepaid or group legal services plans.
Participation, Prof. Cond. Rule 7.3.
Professional corporation or association.
Practice in, Prof. Cond. Rule 5.4.
Professional judgment.
Independent professional judgment, Prof. Cond. Rule 2.1.
Lawyer may exercise, Prof. Cond. Rule 1.2.
Professional misconduct, Prof. Cond. Rule 8.4.
Reporting, Prof. Cond. Rule 8.3.
Prompt representation, Prof. Cond. Rule 1.3.
Proprietary interest in cause action.
Acquiring, Prof. Cond. Rule 1.8.
Prosecutors.
Special responsibilities, Prof. Cond. Rule 3.8.
Prospective clients.
Direct contact with, Prof. Cond. Rule 7.3.
Duties to, Prof. Cond. Rule 1.18.
Protective action.
Client with diminished capacity, Prof. Cond. Rule 1.14.
Publicity during trial, Prof. Cond. Rule 3.6.
Public officers and employees.
Action as public official, Prof. Cond. Rule 6.6.
Conflict of interest.
Special conflicts, former and current officers and employees, Prof. Cond. Rule 1.11.
Purchase of practice, Prof. Cond. Rule 1.17.
Reasonable.
Defined, Prof. Cond. Rule 1.0.
Reasonable belief.
Defined, Prof. Cond. Rule 1.0.
Reasonable diligence and promptness in representation, Prof. Cond. Rule 1.3.
Reasonably should know.
Defined, Prof. Cond. Rule 1.0.
Records and accountings, Prof. Cond. Rule 1.15-3.
Referral service.
Participation, Prof. Cond. Rule 7.2.
Reform activities affecting client's interest, Prof. Cond. Rule 6.4.
Reporting professional misconduct, Prof. Cond. Rule 8.3.
Requests for information.
Compliance with client's reasonable request, Prof. Cond. Rule 1.4.
Respect for third persons rights, Prof. Cond. Rule 4.4.
Restriction on practice, Prof. Cond. Rule 5.6.
Safekeeping property, Prof. Cond. Rule 1.15.
Definitions, Prof. Cond. Rule 1.15-1.
General rules, Prof. Cond. Rule 1.15-2.
Interest on lawyers' trust accounts, Prof. Cond. Rule 1.15-4.
Records and accounting, Prof. Cond. Rule 1.15-3.
Sale of practice, Prof. Cond. Rule 1.17.
Scope of representation, Prof. Cond. Rule 1.2.
Organization as client, Prof. Cond. Rule 1.13.
Scope of rules, Prof. Cond. Rule 0.2.
Screened.
Defined, Prof. Cond. Rule 1.0.
Securities.
Holding in fiduciary account, Prof. Cond. Rule 1.15-2.
Segregation of lawyer's funds, Prof. Cond. Rule 1.15-2.

ATTORNEYS AT LAW —Cont'd
Professional conduct —Cont'd
Settlements.
Abiding by client's decision, Prof. Cond. Rule 1.2.
Aggregate settlement for two or more clients, Prof. Cond. Rule 1.8.
Sexual relations with clients, Prof. Cond. Rule 1.19.
Sharing fees with nonlawyer, Prof. Cond. Rule 5.4.
Soliciting professional employment, Prof. Cond. Rule 7.3.
Advertising, Prof. Cond. Rule 7.2.
Communications of fields of practice, Prof. Cond. Rule 7.4.
Specialists.
Communications of fields of practice, Prof. Cond. Rule 7.4.
Stock.
Holding, identification, Prof. Cond. Rule 1.15-2.
Substantial.
Defined, Prof. Cond. Rule 1.0.
Suspended attorney.
Employing as legal clerk or assistant, Prof. Cond. Rule 5.5.
Tampering with evidence, Prof. Cond. Rule 3.4.
Telephone contact with prospective clients, Prof. Cond. Rule 7.3.
Terminating representation, Prof. Cond. Rule 1.16.
Terminology, Prof. Cond. Rule 1.0.
Third parties.
Communications with persons represented by counsel, Prof. Cond. Rule 4.2.
Dealing with unrepresented person, Prof. Cond. Rule 4.3.
Evaluation for use by, Prof. Cond. Rule 2.3.
Respect for third persons rights, Prof. Cond. Rule 4.4.
Truthfulness to third persons, Prof. Cond. Rule 4.1.
Third-party neutrals.
Former neutrals.
Conflict of interest, Prof. Cond. Rule 1.12.
Lawyers serving as, Prof. Cond. Rule 2.4.
Thoroughness and preparation.
Competent representation, Prof. Cond. Rule 1.1.
Trial publicity, Prof. Cond. Rule 3.6.
Tribunal.
Defined, Prof. Cond. Rule 1.0.
Trust funds.
Accounting, Prof. Cond. Rule 1.15-3.
Defined, Prof. Cond. Rule 1.15-1.
Deposit, Prof. Cond. Rule 1.15-2.
Interest on lawyers' trust accounts, Prof. Cond. Rule 1.15-4.
Quarterly reconciliation of accounts, Prof. Cond. Rule 1.15-3.
Truthfulness in statements to others, Prof. Cond. Rule 4.1.
Unauthorized practice of law, Prof. Cond. Rule 5.5.
Unclaimed entrusted property, Prof. Cond. Rule 1.15-2.
Unrepresented persons.
Dealing with, Prof Cond. Rule 4.3.
Violation of rules of professional conduct.
Acts constituting professional misconduct, Prof. Cond. Rule 8.4.

ATTORNEYS AT LAW —Cont'd
Professional conduct —Cont'd
Violation of rules of professional conduct —Cont'd
Lawyer in firm.
Nonlawyer's violations, Prof. Cond. Rule 5.3.
Responsibility for other lawyer's violations, Prof. Cond. Rule 5.1.
Reporting professional misconduct, Prof. Cond. Rule 8.3.
Waiver of jury trial in criminal case.
Abiding by client's decision, Prof. Cond. Rule 1.2.
Withdrawal from representation, Prof. Cond. Rule 1.16.
Witness.
Lawyer as, Prof. Cond. Rule 3.7.
Writing.
Contingent fee agreements, required, Prof. Cond. Rule 1.5.
Defined, Prof. Cond. Rule 1.0.
Inadvertent receipt of writing, Prof. Cond. Rule 4.4.
Professional corporations.
Practice in, Prof. Cond. Rule 5.4.
Professional counselors.
Exemption from licensure, §90-332.1.
Professional judgment.
Independent professional judgment, Prof. Cond. Rule 2.1.
Lawyer may exercise, Prof. Cond. Rule 1.2.
Professional liaility insurance.
Certificate of coverage.
State bar members to provide, Bar Rules & Regs., A, §.0204.
Professional limited liability companies.
Regulations for practicing law, Bar Rules & Regs., E, §§.0101 to .0106.
Additional information furnished state bar, Bar Rules & Regs., E, §.0105.
Administration of regulations, Bar Rules & Regs., E, §.0105.
Appeal to state bar council, Bar Rules & Regs., E, §.0105.
Application for certificate of registration.
Form, Bar Rules & Regs., E, §.0106.
Application for renewal of certificate of registration.
Form, Bar Rules & Regs., E, §.0106.
Articles of amendment, merger and dissolution.
Filing with secretary of state bar, Bar Rules & Regs., E, §.0105.
Authority of state bar to adopt regulations, Bar Rules & Regs., E, §.0101.
Authority over professional matters, Bar Rules & Regs., E, §.0104.
Certificate of registration.
Form, Bar Rules & Regs., E, §.0106.
Certification by council of North Carolina state bar.
Form, Bar Rules & Regs., E, §.0106.
Deceased or retired member's name may be retained in name of company, Bar Rules & Regs., E, §.0102.
Definitions, Bar Rules & Regs., E, §.0101.
Disqualified member's name not to appear in company's name, Bar Rules & Regs., E, §.0102.
Disqualified person not to receive income, Bar Rules & Regs., E, §.0104.
Expiration of certificate of registration, Bar Rules & Regs., E, §.0103.

ATTORNEYS AT LAW —Cont'd
Professional limited liability companies —Cont'd
Regulations for practicing law —Cont'd
Filing fees, Bar Rules & Regs., E, §.0105.
Forms, Bar Rules & Regs., E, §.0106.
Management, Bar Rules & Regs., E, §.0104.
Member becoming judge or official, name appearing in company name.
Change of company name, Bar Rules & Regs., E, §.0102.
Name of company, Bar Rules & Regs., E, §.0102.
Records of state bar, Bar Rules & Regs., E, §.0105.
Registration, Bar Rules & Regs., E, §.0103.
Registration fees, Bar Rules & Regs., E, §.0103.
Renewal of certificate of registration, Bar Rules & Regs., E, §.0103.
Supplementation of statutory law, Bar Rules & Regs., E, §.0101.
Trade name allowed, Bar Rules & Regs., E, §.0102.
Words professional limited liability company to appear in name, Bar Rules & Regs., E, §.0102.
Professional misconduct, Prof. Cond. Rule 8.4.
Reporting, Prof. Cond. Rule 8.3.
Pro hac vice.
Practice of law, §84-4.1.
Prompt representation, Prof. Cond. Rule 1.3.
Proprietary interest in cause action.
Acquiring, Prof. Cond. Rule 1.8.
Prosecuting attorneys.
See DISTRICT ATTORNEYS.
Prospective clients.
Direct contact with, Prof. Cond. Rule 7.3.
Duties to, Prof. Cond. Rule 1.18.
Public campaign financing fund.
Opportunity to contribute, §105-41, (a).
Publicity during trial, Prof. Cond. Rule 3.6.
Purchase of practice, Prof. Cond. Rule 1.17.
Real property law specialty, Bar Rules & Regs., D, §§.2101 to .2107.
Applicability of other requirements, Bar Rules & Regs., D, §.2107.
Certification standards, Bar Rules & Regs., D, §.2105.
Continued certification, Bar Rules & Regs., D, §.2106.
Continuing legal education, Bar Rules & Regs., D, §.2105.
Continued certification, Bar Rules & Regs., D, §.2106.
Definition of specialty, Bar Rules & Regs., D, §.2102.
Establishment of specialty field, Bar Rules & Regs., D, §.2101.
Examination, Bar Rules & Regs., D, §.2105.
Peer review, Bar Rules & Regs., D, §.2105.
Continued certification, Bar Rules & Regs., D, §.2106.
Plan of legal specialization, applicability of provisions, Bar Rules & Regs., D, §.2104.
Recognition as specialist, Bar Rules & Regs., D, §.2103.
Standards for certification, Bar Rules & Regs., D, §.2105.
Standards for continued certification, Bar Rules & Regs., D, §.2106.

ATTORNEYS AT LAW —Cont'd
Real property law specialty —Cont'd
Suspension or revocation of certification.
Continued certification, Bar Rules & Regs., D, §.2106.
Reasonable diligence and promptness in representation, Prof. Cond. Rule 1.3.
Records, Prof. Cond. Rule 1.15-3.
Public records.
Confidential communications by legal counsel to public board or agency, §132-1.1.
Referral service.
Participation, Prof. Cond. Rule 7.2.
Reinstatement after disbarment, suspension or transfer to disability in active status, Bar Rules & Regs., B, §.0125.
Reinstatement after suspension for failure to comply with continuing legal education rules.
Reinstatement hearing before administrative committee of state bar, Bar Rules & Regs., D, §.1009.
Reinstatement after suspension for failure to pay fees, Bar Rules & Regs., D, §.0904.
Reinstatement from inactive status, Bar Rules & Regs., D, §.0902.
Reporting professional misconduct, Prof. Cond. Rule 8.3.
Representation of indigent persons generally.
See INDIGENT DEFENSE SERVICES.
Reprimand.
Imposition of discipline, Bar Rules & Regs., B, §.0123.
Issuance by grievance committee, Bar Rules & Regs., B, §.0113.
Resignation while under investigation, Bar Rules & Regs., B, §.0117.
Restoration of license ordered.
Duty of board of law examiners to issue, §84-24.
Restriction on practice, Prof. Cond. Rule 5.6.
Retail installment sales.
Fees.
Provisions included in provisions, §25A-21.
Rules for continuing legal education, CLE Rules 1 to 27. See within this heading, "Continuing legal education."
Rules governing admission to practice of law.
See within this heading, "Admission to practice."
Rules of professional conduct, Prof. Cond. Rules 1.0 to 8.5. See within this heading, "Professional conduct."
Safekeeping property, Prof. Cond. Rule 1.15.
Definitions, Prof. Cond. Rule 1.15-1.
General rules, Prof. Cond. Rule 1.15-2.
Interest on lawyers' trust accounts, Prof. Cond. Rule 1.15-4.
Records and accounting, Prof. Cond. Rule 1.15-3.
Sale of practice, Prof. Cond. Rule 1.17.
Savings and loan associations.
Legal services in connection with loans, §54B-165.
Scheduling conflicts.
Guidelines for resolving.
District and superior courts, Super. Ct. Rule 3.1.
Scope of representation, Prof. Cond. Rule 1.2.
Organization as client, Prof. Cond. Rule 1.13.
Seals and sealed instruments.
Execution and acknowledgment of instruments by attorneys, §47-43.1.

ATTORNEYS AT LAW —Cont'd
Secret listening.
Conference between prisoner and his attorney, §14-227.1, (a).
Admissibility as evidence, §14-227.1, (b).
Violations made misdemeanors, §14-227.3.
Securities.
Holding in fiduciary account, Prof. Cond. Rule 1.15-2.
Segregation of lawyer's funds, Prof. Cond. Rule 1.15-2.
Settlements.
Abiding by client's decision, Prof. Cond. Rule 1.2.
Aggregate settlement for two or more clients, Prof. Cond. Rule 1.8.
Sexual relations with clients, Prof. Cond. Rule 1.19.
Sharing fees with nonlawyer, Prof. Cond. Rule 5.4.
Sheriffs.
Practicing attorneys disqualified for office, §162-2.
Signing discovery requests, responses, etc., §1A-1, Rule 26, (g).
Signing pleadings, §1A-1, Rule 11.
Social services.
Special county attorneys for social service matters, §§108A-16 to 108A-18.
Solicitation of clients, §84-38.
Soliciting professional employment, Prof. Cond. Rule 7.3.
Advertising, Prof. Cond. Rule 7.2.
Communications of fields of practice, Prof. Cond. Rule 7.4.
Solicitors.
See DISTRICT ATTORNEYS.
Specialists.
Communications of fields of practice, Prof. Cond. Rule 7.4.
Specialization, Bar Rules & Regs., D, §§.1701 to .2707.
Appeal to state bar council, Bar Rules & Regs., D, §.1804.
Appeal to Wake county superior court, Bar Rules & Regs., D, §.1805.
Applicant not in compliance with certification standards, Bar Rules & Regs., D, §.1801.
Applications incomplete, Bar Rules & Regs., D, §.1801.
Areas of specialty, Bar Rules & Regs., D, §.1725.
Audit of accounts maintained, Bar Rules & Regs., D, §.1713.
Bankruptcy law specialty, Bar Rules & Regs., D, §§.2201 to .2207.
Board of legal specialization.
Annual report, Bar Rules & Regs., D, §.1715.
Appointment and removal of members, Bar Rules & Regs., D, §.1706.
Chairperson, appointment, Bar Rules & Regs., D, §.1710.
Hearing and appeal rules, Bar Rules & Regs., D, §§.1801 to .1805.
Jurisdiction and authority, Bar Rules & Regs., D, §.1702.
Lay participation, Bar Rules & Regs., D, §.1705.
Meetings, Bar Rules & Regs., D, §.1714.
Operational responsibility, Bar Rules & Regs., D, §.1703.
Powers and duties, Bar Rules & Regs., D, §.1716.
Size of board, Bar Rules & Regs., D, §.1704.

ATTORNEYS AT LAW —Cont'd
Specialization —Cont'd
Board of legal specialization —Cont'd
Succession in office, Bar Rules & Regs., D, §.1709.
Term of office, Bar Rules & Regs., D, §.1707.
Staggered terms, Bar Rules & Regs., D, §.1708.
Vice-chairperson, appointment, Bar Rules & Regs., D, §.1711.
Certification of specialists.
Denial of continued certification, Bar Rules & Regs., D, §.1802.
Establishment of additional standards, Bar Rules & Regs., D, §.1722.
Hearing and appeal on denial of certification or continued certification, Bar Rules & Regs., D, §.1724.
Minimum standards for continued certification, Bar Rules & Regs., D, §§.1720, 1721.
Suspension or revocation of certification, Bar Rules & Regs., D, §.1723.
Procedure, Bar Rules & Regs., D, §.1803.
Continuing legal education, accreditation standards, Bar Rules & Regs., D, §§.1901 to .1908.
Accreditation of courses, Bar Rules & Regs., D, §.1906.
Accreditation of sponsors, Bar Rules & Regs., D, §.1907.
Alternatives to lecture-type CLE course instruction, Bar Rules & Regs., D, §.1905.
Applicants to make satisfactory showing of requisite number of hours, Bar Rules & Regs., D, §.1901.
Computation of hours of instruction, Bar Rules & Regs., D, §.1904.
Definitions, Bar Rules & Regs., D, §.1902.
Lecture-type CLE activities, Bar Rules & Regs., D, §.1903.
Lecture-type CLE course instruction.
Alternatives, Bar Rules & Regs., D, §.1905.
Showing by applicants, Bar Rules & Regs., D, §.1908.
Criminal law specialty, certification standards, Bar Rules & Regs., D, §§.2501 to .2507.
Dependent certifying organizations, rules for approval, Bar Rules & Regs., D, §§.2001 to .2006.
Application procedure, Bar Rules & Regs., D, §.2005.
Effect of approval, Bar Rules & Regs., D, §.2006.
Factors considered, Bar Rules & Regs., D, §.2003.
Policy statement as to guidelines, Bar Rules & Regs., D, §.2001.
Procedure generally, Bar Rules & Regs., D, §.2002.
Standards for approval, Bar Rules & Regs., D, §.2004.
Disbursement of funds, Bar Rules & Regs., D, §.1713.
Establishment of additional standards for certification, Bar Rules & Regs., D, §.1722.
Estate planning and probate law specialty, Bar Rules & Regs., D, §§.2301 to .2307.
Examination for specialty.
Failure of written examination, Bar Rules & Regs., D, §.1801.

ATTORNEYS AT LAW —Cont'd
Specialization —Cont'd
Family law specialty, certification standards, Bar Rules & Regs., D, §§.2401 to .2407.
Funding for program, Bar Rules & Regs., D, §.1712.
Hearing and appeal on denial of certification or continued certification, Bar Rules & Regs., D, §.1724.
Appeal to state bar council, Bar Rules & Regs., D, §.1804.
Applications incomplete or applicant not in compliance with certification standards, Bar Rules & Regs., D, §.1801.
Denial of continued certification, Bar Rules & Regs., D, §.1802.
Expenses related to, Bar Rules & Regs., D, §.1806.
Failure of written examination, Bar Rules & Regs., D, §.1801.
Judicial review of state bar council decisions, Bar Rules & Regs., D, §.1805.
Notices, Bar Rules & Regs., D, §.1806.
Suspension or revocation of certification, Bar Rules & Regs., D, §.1803.
Investment criteria of funds, Bar Rules & Regs., D, §.1713.
Judicial review of state bar council decisions, Bar Rules & Regs., D, §.1805.
Limitations imposed on specialists, Bar Rules & Regs., D, §.1718.
Maintenance of accounts, Bar Rules & Regs., D, §.1713.
Minimum standards for certification, Bar Rules & Regs., D, §.1720.
Continued certification, Bar Rules & Regs., D, §.1721.
Petition for review by board.
Application rejected by specialty committee, Bar Rules & Regs., D, §.1801.
Previous decisions approving standards reaffirmed, Bar Rules & Regs., D, §.1726.
Privileges conferred on specialists, Bar Rules & Regs., D, §.1718.
Purposes of plan of certified legal specialization, Bar Rules & Regs., D, §.1701.
Reaffirmance of previous decisions approving standards, Bar Rules & Regs., D, §.1726.
Real property law specialty, certification standards, Bar Rules & Regs., D, §§.2101 to .2107.
Source of funds for program, Bar Rules & Regs., D, §.1712.
Specialty committees, Bar Rules & Regs., D, §.1719.
Review of incomplete applications and applications not in compliance, Bar Rules & Regs., D, §.1801.
Suspension or revocation of certification, Bar Rules & Regs., D, §.1723.
Procedure, Bar Rules & Regs., D, §.1803.
Workers' compensation law, Bar Rules & Regs., D, §§.2700 to .2707.
State bar.
Active members, §84-16; Bar Rules & Regs., A, §.0201.
Administrative suspensions, Bar Rules & Regs., A, §.0201.
Admission to practice.
Rules governing admission to practice of law. See within this heading, "Admission to practice."

ATTORNEYS AT LAW —Cont'd
State bar —Cont'd
Agency of state, §84-15.
Annual meeting, §84-33; Bar Rules & Regs., A, §.0501.
Council to provide suitable program for, Bar Rules & Regs., A, §.0105.
Reports made to, Bar Rules & Regs., A, §.0106.
Annual membership fees, Bar Rules & Regs., A, §.0203.
Failure to pay membership fees, Bar Rules & Regs., D, §.0903.
Reinstatement after suspension for failure to pay fees, Bar Rules & Regs., D, §.0904.
Appeals.
Right of appeal from state bar to court of appeals, §7A-29, (a).
Appointment of counsel for indigent defendants in certain criminal cases.
Model plan for appointment, Bar Rules & Regs., D, §§.0501 to .0510.
Rules and regulations relating to, Bar Rules & Regs., D, §§.0401 to .0406.
Approval of bylaws, Bar Rules & Regs., A, §.0901.
Arbitration of internal law firm disputes, Bar Rules & Regs., E, §§.0401 to .0410.
Bankruptcy law specialty, Bar Rules & Regs., D, §§.2201 to .2207.
Bar examination.
Fees of applicants, §84-25.
Board of continuing legal education.
Referral of matters to board by grievance committee, Bar Rules & Regs., B, §.0112.
Rules concerning administration of program, Bar Rules & Regs., D, §§.1601 to .1610.
Rules governing administration of program, Bar Rules & Regs., D, §§.1501 to .1527.
Board of law examiners.
Compensation of members, §84-26.
Expenses of members, §84-26.
Prescription of applicant fees, §84-25.
Board of legal specialization.
Bankruptcy law specialty, certification standards, Bar Rules & Regs., D, §§.2201 to .2207.
Continuing legal education, rules concerning accreditation, Bar Rules & Regs., D, §§.1901 to .1908.
Criminal law specialty, certification standards, Bar Rules & Regs., D, §§.2501 to .2507.
Estate planning and probate law specialty, certification standards, Bar Rules & Regs., D, §§.2301 to .2307.
Family law specialty, certification standards, Bar Rules & Regs., D, §§.2401 to .2407.
Hearing and appeal rules, Bar Rules & Regs., D, §§.1801 to .1806.
Independent certified organization, rules for approval, Bar Rules & Regs., D, §§.2001 to .2006.
Plan of legal specialization, Bar Rules & Regs., D, §§.1701 to .1726.
Real property law specialty, certification standards, Bar Rules & Regs., D, §§.2101 to .2107.
Workers' compensation law specialty, certification standards, Bar Rules & Regs., D, §§.2700 to .2707.
Bylaws, Bar Rules & Regs., A, §.0901.
Model bylaws, Bar Rules & Regs., A, §§.1001 to .1012.
Amendment, Bar Rules & Regs., A, §.1012.

ATTORNEYS AT LAW —Cont'd
State bar —Cont'd
Bylaws —Cont'd
Model bylaws —Cont'd
Annual membership fee, Bar Rules & Regs., A, §.1006.
Authority and purpose, Bar Rules & Regs., A, §.1002.
Board of directors, Bar Rules & Regs., A, §.1011.
Committees, Bar Rules & Regs., A, §.1010.
Counselor, Bar Rules & Regs., A, §.1005.
District bar finances, Bar Rules & Regs., A, §.1008.
Meetings, Bar Rules & Regs., A, §.1007.
Membership, Bar Rules & Regs., A, §.1003.
Name, Bar Rules & Regs., A, §.1001.
Officers, Bar Rules & Regs., A, §.1004.
Prohibited activities, Bar Rules & Regs., A, §.1009.
Classes of membership, Bar Rules & Regs., A, §.0201.
Classification or division of work under appropriate sections and committees, Bar Rules & Regs., A, §.0102.
CLE, Bar Rules & Regs., D, §§.1501 to .1610.
Specialization certification, rules governing accreditation, Bar Rules & Regs., D, §§.1900 to .1908.
Client assistance committee, Bar Rules & Regs., D, §§.0701 to .0704.
Client security fund board of trustees.
Rules governing administration of fund, Bar Rules & Regs., D, §§.1401 to .1420.
Code of professional conduct. See within this heading, "Professional conduct."
Committee on consumer protection.
Procedures for committee, Bar Rules & Regs., D, §§.0201 to .0207.
Committee on grievances.
Judicial district grievance committees, rules governing, Bar Rules & Regs., B, §§.0201 to .0207.
Form letters, Bar Rules & Regs., B, §§.0208 to .0217.
Powers and duties in disciplinary matters, Bar Rules & Regs., B, §.0106.
Powers and duties of chairperson of committee in disciplinary matters, Bar Rules & Regs., B, §.0105.
Committee on indigent appointments, Bar Rules & Regs., D, §.0504.
Committee on membership and fees.
Continuing legal education hearings before committee, rules governing, Bar Rules & Regs., D, §§.1001 to .1011.
Procedures for, Bar Rules & Regs., D, §§.0901 to .0904.
Committees generally, §84-22.
Compensation of officers, Bar Rules & Regs., A, §.0401.
Continuing legal education, Bar Rules & Regs., D, §§.1501 to .1610.
Specialization certification, rules governing accreditation, Bar Rules & Regs., D, §§.1901 to .1908.
Cooperation with local bar association committees, Bar Rules & Regs., A, §.0103.
Corporations.
Regulations for professional corporations practicing law, Bar Rules & Regs., E, §§.0101 to .0106.

ATTORNEYS AT LAW —Cont'd
State bar —Cont'd
Council.
Appointment of councilors, §84-18, (b).
Compensation of councilors, §84-20.
Composition, §84-17.
Courts commission.
Representative of council to be ex officio member, §7A-507.
Discipline and disability matters, powers and duties, Bar Rules & Regs., B, §.0104.
Election and appointment of councilors, §84-18, (b); Bar Rules & Regs., A, §§.0801 to .0805.
Geographical rotation or division of representation by district bar, Bar Rules & Regs., A, §.0806.
Indigent persons.
Representation of indigent persons.
Implementing regulations by council, §§7A-451, (d), 7A-459.
Number of members, §84-17.
Organization, §84-21.
Per diem and mileage, §84-20.
Powers, §84-23.
Property, powers as to, §84-23, (d).
Publication of official journal, §84-23, (c).
Public members, §84-17.
Term of office, §84-18, (c).
Quorum at meeting, Bar Rules & Regs., A, §.0604.
Regular meetings, Bar Rules & Regs., A, §.0601.
Rules and regulations.
Indigent persons.
Representation of indigent persons, §§7A-451, (d), 7A-459.
Publication, §84-21.
Rulemaking authority, §84-23, (a).
Special meetings, Bar Rules & Regs., A, §.0602.
Notice of call, Bar Rules & Regs., A, §.0603.
Subpoena power, §84-23, (b).
Terms of councilors, §84-18, (a).
Public members, §84-18, (c).
Travel and subsistence expenses, §84-20.
Vacancies, Bar Rules & Regs., A, §.0805.
Court of appeals.
Appeals of right for state bar, §7A-29, (a).
Courts inherent powers unaffected, §84-36.
Creation, §84-15.
Criminal law specialty, certification standards, Bar Rules & Regs., D, §§.2501 to .2507.
Definitions.
Judicial districts, §84-19.
Deposits.
Securing, §84-34.1.
Disability inactive members, Bar Rules & Regs., A, §.0201.
Disability rules generally, Bar Rules & Regs., B, §§.0101 to 0217. See within this heading, "Disability proceedings."
Disaster response plan, Bar Rules & Regs., D, §§.0301 to .0303.
Disaster response team, Bar Rules & Regs., D, §.0301.
General policies and objectives, Bar Rules & Regs., D, §.0302.
Reports on results, Bar Rules & Regs., D, §.0303.
Disciplinary rules generally, Bar Rules & Regs., B, §§.0101 to .0217. See within this heading, "Disciplinary proceedings."

ATTORNEYS AT LAW —Cont'd
State bar —Cont'd
Disciplinary suspension/disbarments.
Category of inactive members, Bar Rules & Regs., A, §.0201.
District bars.
Membership fees, §84-18.1, (b).
District court judges.
Selection of nominees, Bar Rules & Regs., A, §.1013.
District grievance committees, rules governing, Bar Rules & Regs., B, §§.0201 to .0207.
Form letters, Bar Rules & Regs., B, §§.0208 to .0217.
Domestic violence victim assistance act.
Funding, §7A-474.19.
Duties of officers, Bar Rules & Regs., A, §§.0401 to .0404.
Election of councilors.
Mail elections, Bar Rules & Regs., A, §.0804.
Nominations, Bar Rules & Regs., A, §.0802.
Notice, Bar Rules & Regs., A, §.0802.
Purposes of rules, Bar Rules & Regs., A, §.0801.
Vacancies, Bar Rules & Regs., A, §.0805.
Voting procedure, Bar Rules & Regs., A, §.0803.
When election held, Bar Rules & Regs., A, §.0802.
Election of officers, Bar Rules & Regs., A, §.0304.
Nominating committee, Bar Rules & Regs., A, §.0305.
Eligibility for office, Bar Rules & Regs., A, §.0302.
Enumeration of officers, Bar Rules & Regs., A, §.0301.
Estate planning and probate law specialty, certification standards, Bar Rules & Regs., D, §§.2301 to .2307.
Ethics opinions and ethics advisories, Bar Rules & Regs., D, §§.0101 to .0104.
Family law specialty, certification standards, Bar Rules & Regs., D, §§.2401 to .2407.
Fee arbitration committee.
Model plan for district bar fee obligation, Bar Rules & Regs., D, §§.0801 to .0808.
Fees.
Annual membership fees, Bar Rules & Regs., A, §.0203.
Filing papers under rules and regulations, Bar Rules & Regs., A, §.1201.
Form letters involving disciplinary matters, district grievance committees, Bar Rules & Regs., B, §§.0208 to .0217.
Geographical rotation or division of representation of district bar, Bar Rules & Regs., A, §.0806.
Immediate past president.
Duties, Bar Rules & Regs., A, §.0403.
Inactive members, §84-16; Bar Rules & Regs., A, §.0201.
Inactive status.
Reinstatement from, Bar Rules & Regs., D, §.0902.
Transfer to, Bar Rules & Regs., D, §.0901.
Indigent defendants.
Appointment of counsel in certain criminal cases.
Model plan for appointment, Bar Rules & Regs., D, §§.0501 to .0510.
Rules and regulations relating to, Bar Rules & Regs., D, §§.0401 to .0406.
Interstate and international law firm registration, Bar Rules & Regs., E, §§.0201 to .0205.

ATTORNEYS AT LAW —Cont'd
State bar —Cont'd
IOLTA board of trustees.
Rules governing administration of plan, Bar Rules & Regs., D, §§.1301 to .1316.
Judicial district grievance committees, rules governing, Bar Rules & Regs., B, §§.0201 to .0207.
Form letters, Bar Rules & Regs., B, §§.0208 to .0217.
Judicial districts.
Defined, §84-19.
Organization of judicial district bars, Bar Rules & Regs., A, §§.0902, .0903.
Law students, rules governing practical training, Bar Rules & Regs., C, §§.0201 to .0207.
Legal ethics, procedures for ruling on questions of, Bar Rules & Regs., D, §§.0101 to .0104.
Limited liability companies.
Regulations for professional limited liability companies practicing law, Bar Rules & Regs., E, §§.0101 to .0106.
Local bar associations.
Savings clause as to, §84-35.
Meetings of council.
Quorum, Bar Rules & Regs., A, §.0604.
Regular meetings, Bar Rules & Regs., A, §.0601.
Special meetings, Bar Rules & Regs., A, §.0602.
Notice of call, Bar Rules & Regs., A, §.0603.
Meetings of state bar.
Annual meeting, Bar Rules & Regs., A, §.0501.
Annual program provided by council, Bar Rules & Regs., A, §.0105.
Reports made, Bar Rules & Regs., A, §.0106.
Notice of meetings, Bar Rules & Regs., A, §§.0501, .0502.
How given, Bar Rules & Regs., A, §.0503.
Parliamentary rules, Bar Rules & Regs., A, §.0505.
Quorum, Bar Rules & Regs., A, §.0504.
Special meetings, Bar Rules & Regs., A, §.0502.
Membership, §84-18.1, (a); Bar Rules & Regs., A, §.0201.
Annual membership fees, Bar Rules & Regs., A, §.0203.
Failure to pay, Bar Rules & Regs., D, §§.0903, .0904.
Fees, §84-34.
Active members, §84-16.
District bars, §84-18.1, (b).
Failure to pay, Bar Rules & Regs., D, §.0903.
Reinstatement after suspension, Bar Rules & Regs., D, §.0904.
List of members, §84-34.
Privileges, §84-16.
Records of state bar, Bar Rules & Regs., A, §.0202.
Register of members, Bar Rules & Regs., A, §.0202.
Waiving or rebating annual membership fee, Bar Rules & Regs., A, §.0203.
Model bylaws, Bar Rules & Regs., A, §§.1001 to .1012.
Amendments, Bar Rules & Regs., A, §.1012.
Annual membership fee, Bar Rules & Regs., A, §.1006.
Authority and purpose, Bar Rules & Regs., A, §.1002.
Board of directors, Bar Rules & Regs., A, §.1011.
Committees, Bar Rules & Regs., A, §.1010.
Counselor, Bar Rules & Regs., A, §.1005.

ATTORNEYS AT LAW —Cont'd
State bar —Cont'd
Model bylaws —Cont'd
District bar finances, Bar Rules & Regs., A, §.1008.
Meetings, Bar Rules & Regs., A, §.1007.
Membership, Bar Rules & Regs., A, §.1003.
Name, Bar Rules & Regs., A, §.1001.
Officers, Bar Rules & Regs., A, §.1004.
Prohibited activities, Bar Rules & Regs., A, §.1009.
Nominating committee appointed to nominate candidates, Bar Rules & Regs., A, §.0305.
North Carolina bar association.
Savings clause as to, §84-35.
Notice of call of special meeting of council, Bar Rules & Regs., A, §.0603.
Notice of election of councilors, Bar Rules & Regs., A, §.0802.
Notice of meetings of state bar, Bar Rules & Regs., A, §§.0501 to .0503.
Office of state bar, Bar Rules & Regs., A, §.1101.
Officers, §84-22.
Compensation, Bar Rules & Regs., A, §.0401.
Election, Bar Rules & Regs., A, §.0304.
Nominating committee, Bar Rules & Regs., A, §.0305.
Enumerated, Bar Rules & Regs., A, §.0301.
Immediate past president's duties, Bar Rules & Regs., A, §.0403.
Need not be members of council at time of election, Bar Rules & Regs., A, §.0302.
President elect duties, Bar Rules & Regs., A, §.0403.
President's duties, Bar Rules & Regs., A, §.0402.
Removal, Bar Rules & Regs., A, §.0307.
Secretary's duties, Bar Rules & Regs., A, §.0404.
Succession upon vacancy, Bar Rules & Regs., A, §.0306.
Term of office, Bar Rules & Regs., A, §.0303.
Vacancies, Bar Rules & Regs., A, §.0306.
Vice-president duties, Bar Rules & Regs., A, §.0403.
Organization of local bar associations encouraged and fostered, Bar Rules & Regs., A, §.0104.
Parliamentary rules at meetings of state bar, Bar Rules & Regs., A, §.0505.
Positive action for lawyers (PALS) committee.
Disciplinary amnesty in elicit drug use cases, Bar Rules & Regs., B, §.0130.
Practice of law.
Persons other than members of state bar prohibited from practicing law, §84-4.
Prepaid legal services, §84-23.1.
Additional nature of provisions, §84-23.1, (a).
Insurance.
When subject to regulation under insurance provisions, §84-23.1, (d).
Registration of plans, §84-23.1, (b1).
Rules governing, Bar Rules & Regs., E, §§.0301 to .0309.
President.
Duties, Bar Rules & Regs., A, §.0402.
President-elect duties, Bar Rules & Regs., A, §.0403.
Professional corporations.
Regulations for practicing law, Bar Rules & Regs., E, §§.0101 to .0106.
Professional liability insurance.
Certificate of coverage, member to provide, Bar Rules & Regs., A, §.0204.

ATTORNEYS AT LAW —Cont'd
State bar —Cont'd
Professional limited liability companies.
Regulations for practicing law, Bar Rules & Regs., E, §§.0101 to .0106.
Publication of notice of meetings of state bar, Bar Rules & Regs., A, §.0503.
Purpose of state bar, Bar Rules & Regs., A, §.0101.
Quorum at meeting of council, Bar Rules & Regs., A, §.0604.
Quorum for meetings of state bar, Bar Rules & Regs., A, §.0504.
Real property law specialty, certification standards, Bar Rules & Regs., D, §§.2101 to .2107.
Records of state bar membership, Bar Rules & Regs., A, §.0202.
Register of members, Bar Rules & Regs., A, §.0202.
Regular meetings of council, Bar Rules & Regs., A, §.0601.
Removal from office, Bar Rules & Regs., A, §.0307.
Reports made to annual meeting, Bar Rules & Regs., A, §.0106.
Retired/nonpracticing members.
Category of inactive member, Bar Rules & Regs., A, §.0201.
Rules of professional conduct, Prof. Cond. Rules 1.0 to 8.5. See within this heading, "Professional conduct."
Seal, form and custody, Bar Rules & Regs., A, §.1301.
Secretary.
Discipline and disability matters, powers and duties, Bar Rules & Regs., B, §.0110.
Duties, Bar Rules & Regs., A, §.0404.
Serving papers under rules and regulations, Bar Rules & Regs., A, §.1201.
Specialization of lawyers.
Bankruptcy law specialty, certification standards, Bar Rules & Regs., D, §§.2201 to .2207.
Continuing legal education, rules governing accreditation, Bar Rules & Regs., D, §§.1901 to .1908.
Criminal law specialty, certification standards, Bar Rules & Regs., D, §§.2501 to .2507.
Estate planning and probate law specialty, certification standards, Bar Rules & Regs., D, §§.2301 to .2307.
Family law specialty, certification standards, Bar Rules & Regs., D, §§.2401 to .2407.
Hearing and appeal rules of legal specialization, Bar Rules & Regs., D, §§.1801 to .1806.
Independent certified organizations, rules for approval, Bar Rules & Regs., D, §§.2001 to .2006.
Plan of legal specialization, Bar Rules & Regs., D, §§.1701 to .1726.
Real property law specialty, certification standards, Bar Rules & Regs., D, §§.2101 to .2107.
Special meetings of council, §84-33; Bar Rules & Regs., A, §.0602.
Notice of call, Bar Rules & Regs., A, §.0603.
Special meetings of state bar, Bar Rules & Regs., A, §.0502.
Standing committees and boards, Bar Rules & Regs., A, §.0701.

ATTORNEYS AT LAW —Cont'd
State bar —Cont'd
Succession to office upon vacancy, Bar Rules & Regs., A, §.0306.
Term of office, Bar Rules & Regs., A, §.0303.
Training of law students, rules governing, Bar Rules & Regs., C, §§.0201 to .0207.
Unauthorized practice.
Actions, §84-37, (a).
Additional nature of provisions, §84-37, (e).
Advisory opinions, §84-37, (f).
Injunction, §84-37, (b).
Plaintiff may examine adverse party, §84-37, (d).
Venue, §84-37, (c).
Investigation, §84-37, (a).
Vacancies in office, Bar Rules & Regs., A, §.0306.
Vacancies on council, Bar Rules & Regs., A, §.0805.
Vice-president duties, Bar Rules & Regs., A, §.0403.
Waiver for rebating annual membership fee, Bar Rules & Regs., A, §.0203.
Workers' compensation law specialty, certification standards, Bar Rules & Regs., D, §§.2700 to .2707.
State departments and agencies.
Private counsel.
Employment, §147-17.
Use limited, §114-2.3.
Stock.
Holding, identification, Prof. Cond. Rule 1.15-2.
Substance abuse.
Lawyer assistance program, Bar Rules & Regs., D, §§.0601 to .0623.
See LAWYERS ASSISTANCE PROGRAM.
Superior courts.
Courtroom decorum, Super. Ct. Rule 12.
List of attorneys furnished to secretary of revenue.
Clerk to furnish list, §7A-110.
Scheduling conflicts.
Guidelines for resolving, Super. Ct. Rule 3.1.
Secure leave periods for attorneys, Super. Ct. Rule 26.
Withdrawal of appearance, Super. Ct. Rule 16.
Surrender of license while under investigation, Bar Rules & Regs., B, §.0117.
Suspension.
Continuing legal education hearings before administrative committee, Bar Rules & Regs., D, §.1008.
Employing as legal clerk or assistant, Prof. Cond. Rule 5.5.
Failure to pay membership fees, Bar Rules & Regs., D, §.0902.
Imposition of discipline, Bar Rules & Regs., B, §.0123.
Obligations of suspended attorney, Bar Rules & Regs., B, §.0124.
Reinstatement after suspension, Bar Rules & Regs., B, §.0125.
Tampering with evidence, Prof Cond. Rule 3.4.
Terminating representation, Prof Cond. Rule 1.16.
Termination of parental rights.
Adjudicatory hearing, appointment for indigent parents, §7B-1109, (b).
Appointment to assist nonattorney guardian ad litem, §7B-1108, (b).

ATTORNEYS AT LAW —Cont'd
Termination of parental rights —Cont'd
Indigent defense services act, §§7A-498 to 7A-498.8.
See INDIGENT DEFENSE SERVICES.
Right to counsel, appointment of counsel, payment of appointed counsel's fees, §7B-1101.
Third parties.
Communications with persons represented by counsel, Prof Cond. Rule 4.2.
Dealing with unrepresented person, Prof Cond. Rule 4.3.
Evaluation for use by, Prof Cond. Rule 2.3.
Respect for third persons rights, Prof. Cond. Rule 4.4.
Truthfulness to third persons, Prof Cond. Rule 4.1.
Third-party neutrals.
Former neutrals.
Conflict of interest, Prof. Cond. Rule 1.12.
Lawyers serving as, Prof Cond. Rule 2.4.
Training of law students, rules governing, Bar Rules & Regs., C, §§.0201 to .0207.
Trial publicity, Prof Cond. Rule 3.6.
Trust accounts of lawyers.
Audit by investigative subpoena, Bar Rules & Regs., B, §.0128.
Interest on lawyer's trust accounts (IOLTA).
Rules governing administration of plan, Bar Rules & Regs., D, §§.1301 to .1316.
Trust funds.
Accounting, Prof Cond. Rule 1.15-3.
Defined, Prof. Cond. Rule 1.15-1.
Deposit, Prof. Cond. Rule 1.15-2.
Interest on lawyers' trust accounts, Prof Cond. Rule 1.15-4.
Quarterly reconciliation of accounts, Prof Cond. Rule 1.15-3.
Truthfulness in statements to others, Prof Cond. Rule 4.1.
Unauthorized practice of law, Prof. Cond. Rule 5.5.
Actions by state bar, §84-37, (a).
Additional nature of provisions, §84-37, (e).
Advisory opinions, §84-37, (f).
Injunction, §84-37, (b).
Plaintiff may examine adverse party, §84-37, (d).
Venue, §84-37, (c).
Appearance for creditor in insolvency and certain other proceedings by anyone except attorney, §§84-9, 84-10.
Authorized practice committee procedures, Bar Rules & Regs., D, §§.0201 to .0207.
Collection agencies, §58-70-120.
Disqualified persons, §84-2.
Foreclosures.
Fee for conducting foreclosures.
Prohibited to all except licensed attorneys, §84-6.
Indictments.
Duty of district attorneys to indict persons upon receipt of information of violation, §84-7.
Injunctions, §84-37, (b).
District attorneys to bring injunction proceedings upon application, §84-7.
Investigation by state bar, §84-37, (a).
Legal clinics of law schools.
Exception, §84-8.
Misdemeanor, §84-8.
Persons other than members of state bar, §84-4.

ATTORNEYS AT LAW —Cont'd
Unclaimed entrusted property, Prof. Cond. Rule 1.15-2.
Unrepresented persons.
Dealing with, Prof Cond. Rule 4.3.
Verifying pleadings, §1A-1, Rule 11.
Waiver of counsel.
Indigent persons, §7A-457.
Withdrawal from representation, Prof Cond. Rule 1.16.
Collaborative law proceedings, §50-76, (c).
Obligations of disbarred or suspended attorney, Bar Rules & Regs., B, §.0124.
Withdrawal of appearance, Super. Ct. Rule 16.
Witness.
Lawyer as, Prof Cond. Rule 3.7.
Workers' compensation law specialty, Bar Rules & Regs., D, §§.2700 to .2707.
Work product.
Collaborative law proceedings.
Privilege, inadmissible, §50-77, (a), (b).
Scope of discovery, §1A-1, Rule 26, (b).

ATTORNEYS' FEES, Prof. Cond. Rule 1.5.
Abused, neglected or dependent juvenile actions.
Payment of court-appointed counsel, §7B-603, (a) to (c).
Acceptance of compensation from other than client, Prof. Cond. Rule 1.8.
Administration of estates, §7A-307, (c).
Admissions.
Failure of party to admit, §1A-1, Rule 37, (c).
Adoption.
Revocation of consent.
Fees awarded to person who revoked upon non-return of minor, §48-3-608, (c).
Revocation of relinquishment.
Failure to return minor to person who revoked, §48-3-706, (b).
Agency decisions, parties appealing or defending, §6-19.1.
Alimony.
Actions, §50-16.4.
Allowance of counsel fees as part of costs in certain cases, §6-21.1.
Appellate defender.
Judgment for legal fees, §7A-486.7.
Arbitration of disputes.
Client assistance committee, Bar Rules & Regs., D, §§.0701 to .0704.
Model plan for district bar, Bar Rules & Regs., D, §§.0801 to .0808.
Arbitrators.
Civil action against arbitrator, §1-569.14, (e).
Automobile dealers.
Actions by, §20-308.1, (b).
Bonds, surety.
Model payment and performance bonds.
Suits under provisions, §44A-35.
Business combinations or control share acquisitions unlawful, §75E-4.
Business corporations.
Dissenting shareholders.
Judicial appraisal of shares, §55-13-31, (b), (c).
Inspection of records by shareholders.
Court-ordered inspection, §55-16-04, (c).
Stock and stockholders.
Derivative actions by shareholders, §55-7-46.
Business opportunity sales violations.
Action for recovery of damages, §66-100, (b).
Cases involving principals or teachers, §6-21.4.

ATTORNEYS' FEES —Cont'd
Chattel mortgages.
Attorneys' fees in addition to interest, §6-21.2.
Child custody.
Action or proceeding for custody or visitation, §50-13.6.
Childhood vaccine-related injury compensation, Childhood Vac. Rule 203.
Child support.
Action for support of minor child, §50-13.6.
Income withholding.
Computation of amount to be withheld, §110-136.6, (a).
Limitations on amount withheld, §110-136.6, (b).
Civil rights, interference with, §99D-1, (b), (b1).
Condominium assessment lien.
Judgment, decree or order to include, §47C-3-116, (c).
Condominium law violations, §47C-4-117.
Condominium owners' associations and declarant.
Declarant liable to association, §47C-3-111, (d).
Consumer finance act.
Loan agreement not to provide for payment by borrower, §53-180, (e).
Contingent fees and contingent fee agreements, Prof. Cond. Rule 1.5.
Credit device fraud.
Telecommunication services, §14-113.6, (c).
Credit repair service violations, actions to recover damages, §66-225, (a).
Credit rights of married women.
Actions to enforce articles, §25B-3, (a).
Defense of public school employees.
Employee's obligation for attorney fees, §143-300.17.
Delinquent and undisciplined juvenile actions.
Court appointed attorney, §7B-2002.
Depositions.
Failure of party to attend, §1A-1, Rule 37, (d).
Oral examination.
Failure to attend or serve subpoena, §1A-1, Rule 30, (g).
Derivative actions.
Payment, §55-7-46.
Discount buying club violations, action to recover damages, §66-136, (a).
Discovery conference.
Failure to participate, §1A-1, Rule 37, (g).
Discovery, failure to comply with order, §1A-1, Rule 37, (b).
Discovery, motion compelling.
Granting or denying, §1A-1, Rule 37, (a).
Discrimination against employees for lawful use of lawful products during nonworking hours.
Civil actions for violations, §95-28.2, (e).
Division of fees, Prof. Cond. Rule 1.5.
Lawyer or firm sharing fees with nonlawyer, Prof. Cond. Rule 5.4.
Divorce.
Barred by separation agreement or premarital agreement provisions, §50-16.6, (b).
Custody and support of minor children, §50-13.6.
Domestic violence, §50B-3, (a).
Drainage district petitions, §§156-60, 156-61.
Dry-cleaning solvent cleanup.
Remediation of uncertified sites.
Civil action for reimbursement cost, §143-215.104O, (c).

ATTORNEYS' FEES —Cont'd
Electronic surveillance.
Civil action for violation of article, §15A-296, (a).
Eminent domain.
Appointment of attorney for unknown parties, §40A-32.
Petitioner abandoning condemnation proceeding taxed with fee for respondent's attorney, §1-209.1.
Right of entry prior to condemnation.
Recovery for damages resulting, §40A-11.
Employee's use of lawful products during nonworking hours.
Actions brought pursuant to section, §95-28.2, (e), (f).
Enhanced 911 wireless system for wireless communications.
Collection action for service charge, §62A-24, (c).
Evidence of indebtedness.
Attorneys' fees and notes, etc., in addition to interest, §6-21.2.
Excessive fees and expenses.
Charging client prohibited, factors in determining, Prof. Cond. Rule 1.5.
Execution sales.
Special proceeding to determine ownership of surplus, §1-339.71, (d).
Executors and administrators.
Counsel fees allowable to attorneys serving as representatives, §28A-23-4.
Fee arbitration, model plan for district bar, Bar Rules & Regs., D, §§.0801 to .0808.
Fiduciaries.
Counsel fees allowed attorneys serving as fiduciaries, §32-61.
Frivolous actions.
Cases involving principals or teachers, §6-21.4.
Punitive damages, §1D-45.
Funds transfers.
Improper execution or failure to execute payment order, §25-4A-305, (e).
Grievances involving fee disputes.
Jurisdiction and authority of district grievance committees, Bar Rules & Regs., B, §.0202.
Guardians.
Procedure to compel accounting, §35A-1265, (a).
Incompetence, determination of, §35A-1116, (a).
Court-appointed counsel, §35A-1116, (b).
Indigent person representation, §7A-452, (b).
Fixing of counsel fees, §7A-458.
Inspection of land or documents.
Failure to respond to request, §1A-1, Rule 37, (d).
Insurance.
Allowance of counsel fees as part of costs in certain cases, §6-21.1.
Insurance consumer and customer information privacy.
Action by individual for violations, §58-39-105, (c).
International commercial arbitration and conciliation.
Awarding, order of costs, §1-567.61, (h).
Interrogatories.
Failure of party to serve answers, §1A-1, Rule 37, (d).
Interstate family support, §52C-3-312, (b).
Law firm.
Fee sharing with non-lawyer, Prof. Cond. Rule 5.4.
Leases, UCC.
Unconscionable lease contracts or clauses, §25-2A-108, (4).

ATTORNEYS' FEES —Cont'd
Letters of credit.
Damages for wrongful dishonor or breach, §25-5-111, (e).
Liens.
Past-due child support, §44-50.
Possessory liens on personal property.
Enforcement of lien by sale.
Noncompliance, §44A-4, (g).
Recoveries for personal injuries.
Enforcement of lien rights, §44-50.1, (a) to (c).
Limited liability company derivative actions by members, §57C-8-01, (e).
Actions brought by reasonable cause, §57C-8-01, (f).
Limited partnerships.
Derivative actions, §59-1004.
Mediated settlement conferences or other settlement procedures in district court.
Actions involving equitable distribution, alimony or support.
Monetary sanction for failure of party to attend mediated settlement conference, §7A-38.4A, (e).
Membership camping contract violations, purchaser's remedies, §66-247, (a).
Model plan for district bar fee arbitration, Bar Rules & Regs., D, §§.0801 to .0808.
Monopolies and restraints of trade, §75-16.1.
Mortgages and deeds of trust.
Consumer home loans.
Actions under provisions, §24-10.2, (f).
Foreclosure, §84-6.
Reverse mortgages.
Actions by borrowers for damages, §53-271, (d).
Motion picture fair competition violations, §75C-5.
Motor fuel marketing violations, private actions, §75-86.
Motor vehicle repairs.
Remedies for violation of article, §20-354.9.
Motor vehicles.
New motor vehicle warranties act, §20-351.8.
Sublease and loan assumption arranging.
Violations of provisions, §20-106.2, (f).
Mountain ridge protection.
Civil action against persons alleged in violation, §113A-211, (b).
New motor vehicles warranties act, §20-351.8.
Nonjusticiable cases, §6-21.5.
Nuisances against public morals.
Actions abating, §19-8.
Defendant's expenses incurred in defending actions, §19-2.1.
Lien on real and personal property, §19-6.
Oil pollution and hazardous substances control.
Offshore oil and gas activities, §143-215.94CC, (c).
Outpatient involuntary commitment proceedings, §7A-451.1.
Personal injury suits, §6-21.1.
Planned community act.
Assessments for common expenses.
Foreclosure of lien for assessments, §47F-3-116, (e).
Declaration limits on attorneys' fees, §47F-3-120.
Pork promotion assessments.
Recovery of unpaid assessments, §106-790.
Post assessment insurance guaranty association.
Right to recover, §58-48-50, (a1).

ATTORNEYS' FEES —Cont'd
Prepaid entertainment contracts, actions for damages, §66-125, (a).
Principals of schools, allowance in cases involving, §6-21.4.
Property damage suits, §6-21.1.
Psychotherapy patient/client sexual exploitation act, §90-21.43.
Public meetings.
Declaratory relief for violations of provisions.
Assessment and award, §143-318.16B.
Public officers and employees.
Improper government activities.
Reporting, §126-87.
Public records.
Action to compel disclosure, §132-9, (c), (d).
Punitive damages.
Frivolous or malicious actions, §1D-45.
Quo warranto.
Appropriation of public funds to pay, §1-521.
Receivers of corporations.
Counsel fees, §1-507.9.
Rental referral agency violations, action to recover damages, §66-146, (a).
Requests for admission, failure to admit, §1A-1, Rule 37, (c).
Retail installment sales.
Fee provisions included, §25A-21.
Retaliatory employment discrimination, §95-243, (c).
Returned checks, §6-21.3, (b).
Sale of prints by art dealers.
Wrongful refusal to repay purchaser, §25C-15, (b).
Sale or purchase of practice.
Increase in fees, Prof Cond. Rule 1.17.
Sales commissions.
Civil actions, §66-192, (a).
Frivolous actions, §66-192, (b).
Sharing fees with nonlawyer, Prof. Cond. Rule 5.4.
Shoplifting and theft by employees.
Civil liability, §1-538.2, (a).
State departments and agencies.
Defending actions arising from activities of state employees, §147-17.
Structured settlement agreements.
Violation of provisions, §1-543.15, (b).
Summary judgment.
Affidavits made in bad faith, §1A-1, Rule 56, (g).
Teachers, allowance in cases involving, §6-21.4.
Telephone solicitations.
Action for violation, awarding, §75-105, (d).
Termination of parental rights proceedings.
Appointed counsel, payment, §7B-1101.
Trade secrets, claim of misappropriation, §66-154, (d).
Underground storage tanks.
Leaking petroleum cleanup.
Actions for fund reimbursement, §143-215.94G, (e).
Groundwater protection loan fund.
Civil action for default or violation of loan agreement, §143-215.94P, (e).
Vehicle mileage act violations, private civil actions, §20-348, (a).
Visitation.
Action or proceeding for custody or visitation, §50-13.6.
Vocational rehabilitation.
Subrogation.
Payment of fees based upon established fee schedule, §143-547, (a).

ATTORNEYS' FEES —Cont'd
Workers' compensation.
Approval by industrial commission, §97-90, (a).
Determination of reasonableness of fee, §97-90, (c).
Filing agreement for fee or compensation, §97-90, (c).
Receipt of fees not approved by commission, §97-90, (b).
Industrial commission hearings, §97-88.1.

ATTORNEYS IN FACT.
Powers of attorney.
Advance instruction for mental health treatment, §§122C-71 to 122C-77.
See MENTAL HEALTH, DEVELOPMENTAL DISABILITY, SUBSTANCE ABUSE.
General provisions, §§32A-1 to 32A-14.
See POWER OF ATTORNEY.
Health care powers of attorney, §§32A-15 to 32A-26.
See HEALTH CARE POWERS OF ATTORNEY.
Renunciation of succession, §31B-1.
Service of process on partnerships.
Personal jurisdiction, manner of service, §1A-1, Rule 4, (j).
Trusts and trustees.
Parties to trust proceedings.
Representation by others, §36A-26.3.

ATTORNMENT.
Unnecessary on conveyance or reversions, etc., §42-2.

AUCTIONS AND AUCTIONEERS, §§85B-1 to 85B-9.
Advertisements.
Misleading or untruthful advertising.
Grounds for suspension or revocation of license, §85B-8, (a).
Agreement with owner of property.
Required for auction, §85B-7, (a).
Animals, public auctions.
Defined, §19A-23.
Licenses.
Change in ownership, management or operation of business, §19A-31.
Fees, §19A-28.
Penalty for operation without license, §19A-33.
Refusal, suspension or revocation, §§19A-30, 19A-32.
Required, §19A-28.
Transfer prohibited, §19A-31.
Applicability of provisions, §85B-2.
Exceptions, §85B-2.
Apprentice auctioneers.
Licenses.
Applications, §85B-4, (c).
Fees, §85B-6.
Forfeiture.
Felony convictions, §15A-1331A.
Qualifications for license, §85B-4, (b).
Required, §85B-4, (a).
Supervisor of apprentice, §85B-4, (c1).
Attorney general.
Enforcement of provisions.
Commission entitled to services of attorney general, §85B-9, (c).
Auctioneer recovery fund.
Failure to make required contribution.
Grounds for suspension or revocation of license, §85B-8, (a).

AUCTIONS AND AUCTIONEERS —Cont'd
Auctioneer recovery fund —Cont'd
Fee to be included in fund, §85B-4.1, (a).
Investments, §85B-4.1.
Licenses.
Contribution to fund as prerequisite to license, §85B-4, (f).
Payments from fund.
Application to commission, §85B-4.2.
Hearings, §85B-4.3.
Attorneys' fees, §85B-4.7.
Automatic suspension of license, §85B-4.8.
Board directing payment, §85B-4.6.
Compromise of claim, §85B-4.6.
Determination of small claims without prior judicial determination, §85B-4.5.
Disciplinary action against licensee, §85B-4.12.
Grounds, §85B-4.2.
Limitations, §85B-4.7.
Notice, §85B-4.2.
Persons ineligible to recovery from, §85B-4.11.
Proof of conversion and other fraudulent act, §85B-4.4.
Pro rata distribution, §85B-4.7.
Repayment to fund, §85B-4.8.
Disciplinary action against licensee, §85B-4.12.
Required showings, §85B-4.3.
Response and defense by commission, §85B-4.4.
Small claims.
Determination without prior judicial determination, §85B-4.5.
Subrogation of rights, §85B-4.9.
Persons ineligible to recovery from, §85B-4.11.
Sources of funding, §85B-4.1, (a).
License fees, §85B-4, (g).
Nonresidents.
License fees, §85B-5.
Use of funds, §85B-4.1, (c).
Waiver of rights, §85B-4.10.
Charities.
Exemptions from auction provisions, §85B-2.
Child support enforcement.
Forfeiture of licensing privilege, §50-13.12.
Clients' funds.
Handling, §85B-7.1.
Commercial code.
Sale by auction, §25-2-328.
Commission.
Appointment of members, §85B-3, (a).
Attorneys at law.
Employment of attorney to assist in enforcement, §85B-9, (c).
Chairman, §85B-3, (e).
Compensation, §85B-3, (g).
Duties, §85B-3.1, (a).
Employees, §85B-3, (c).
Hearings, §85B-8, (e).
Investigations, §85B-8, (e).
Number of members, §85B-3, (a).
Public member, §85B-3, (b).
Purchase of equipment and supplies, §85B-3.1, (d).
Qualifications of members, §85B-3, (b).
Real property, powers, §85B-3.1, (c).
Terms of members, §85B-3, (a).
Vacancies, §85B-3, (a).
Vote required for actions, §85B-3, (d).
Conduct of auction, §85B-7.
Continuing education.
License renewal, §85B-4, (e1).

AUCTIONS AND AUCTIONEERS —Cont'd
Corporations.
Licenses, §85B-4, (g).
Criminal history record checks.
Applicants for auctioneer license, §§85B-3.2, 114-19.8.
Decedents' estates.
Sales in settlement of decedents' estates.
Exemptions from auction provisions, §85B-2.
Definitions, §85B-1.
Electronic auction service.
State surplus property.
Sale or disposal by, §143-64.03, (d).
Escrow accounts, §85B-7.1.
Exemptions from provisions, §85B-2.
Fees.
Auctioneer recovery fund.
Fee to be included in fund, §85B-4.1, (a).
Licenses, §85B-6.
Felony convictions.
Forfeiture of license, §15A-1331A.
Fines.
Civil penalties.
Imposition by commission, §85B-3.1, (b).
Hearings.
Commission, §85B-8, (e).
Injunctions.
Violations of provisions, §85B-9, (b).
Investigations.
Commission, §85B-8, (e).
Judicial sales.
Exemptions from auction provisions, §85B-2.
Licenses.
Applications, §85B-4, (c), (d).
Apprentice auctioneers.
Applications, §85B-4, (c).
Fees, §85B-6.
Qualifications for license, §85B-4, (b).
Required, §85B-4, (a).
Supervisor of apprentice, §85B-4, (c1).
Auctioneer recovery fund.
Contribution to fund as prerequisite to license, §85B-4, (f).
Availability at auction, §85B-7, (c).
Corporations, §85B-4, (g).
Criminal history record checks of applicants, §114-19.8.
Definitions, §85B-3.2, (a).
Denial of license, §85B-3.2, (d), (e).
Disposition of fees collected, §85B-3.2, (g).
Duties of commission, §85B-3.2, (b).
Release of information, §85B-3.2, (c).
Review of information by applicant, §85B-3.2, (f).
Denial.
Grounds, §85B-8, (a).
Fees, §85B-6.
List of licensees.
Publication, §85B-4, (h).
Local governments.
Charging fees or requiring licenses prohibited, §85B-6.
Nonresidents, §85B-5.
Partnerships, §85B-4, (g).
Qualifications for licensure, §85B-4, (b), (d).
Reciprocity, §85B-5.
Renewal, §85B-4, (e), (e1).
Required, §85B-4, (a).
Suspension or revocation, §85B-8, (e).
Applying for license, §85B-8, (f).
Felony convictions, §15A-1331A.

AUCTIONS AND AUCTIONEERS —Cont'd
Licenses —Cont'd
Suspension or revocation —Cont'd
Grounds, §85B-8, (a).
Payments from auctioneer recovery fund, §85B-4.8.
Livestock markets.
Exemptions from auction provisions, §85B-2.
Generally, §§106-406 to 106-418.
See LIVESTOCK MARKETS.
Prompt pay law, §§106-418.1 to 106-418.7A.
See LIVESTOCK MARKETS.
Local governments.
Licenses.
Charging fees or requiring licenses prohibited, §85B-6.
Misdemeanors.
Violations of provisions, §85B-9, (a).
Motor vehicle repairs.
Applicability of repair provisions to work done for motor vehicle auctions, §20-354.1.
Motor vehicles.
Exemptions from auction provisions, §85B-2.
Municipalities.
Public auction of real or personal property, §160A-270.
Nonresidents.
Licenses, §85B-5.
Partnerships.
Licenses, §85B-4, (g).
Prompt pay law.
Livestock, §§106-418.1 to 106-418.7A.
See LIVESTOCK MARKETS.
Public schools.
Sale of school property, §115C-518.
Reciprocity.
Licenses, §85B-5.
Records.
Auctioneer to maintain records, §85B-7, (b), (d).
Religious societies.
Exemptions from auction provisions, §85B-2.
State surplus property.
Electronic auction service.
Sale or disposal by, §143-64.03, (d).
Subrogation.
Auctioneer recovery fund.
Payments from fund, §85B-4.9.
Tobacco.
Exemptions from auction provisions, §85B-2.
Liens.
Effective period for lien on leaf tobacco sold in auction warehouse, §44-69.
Trust accounts, §85B-7.1.
Violations of provisions.
Grounds for suspension or revocation of license, §85B-8, (a).
Injunctions, §85B-9, (b).
Misdemeanors, §85B-9, (a).
Waiver.
Auctioneer recovery fund.
Failure to comply with chapter.
Waiver of right, §85B-4.10.

AUDIO-CASSETTE TAPE TEXTBOOKS.
Textbook contracts to include clause granting state board of education license to produce, §115C-90.

AUDIO EQUIPMENT.
Service agreements, §§58-1-25 to 58-1-42.

AUDIOLOGISTS.
General provisions, §§90-292 to 90-307.
See SPEECH AND LANGUAGE PATHOLOGISTS AND AUDIOLOGISTS.
Professional corporations.
Formation authoized, §55B-14, (c).
Self-referrals, §§90-405 to 90-408.

AUDIO RECORDINGS.
Secret listening.
Electronic surveillance, §§15A-286 to 15A-298.
See ELECTRONIC SURVEILLANCE.

AUDIO VIDEO EQUIPMENT.
Service agreements, §§58-1-25 to 58-1-42.

AUDITORIUMS.
Alcoholic beverage permits.
Mixed beverage permit.
Kind of permit that may be issued, §18B-1001.
On-premises fortified wine permit.
Kind of permit that may be issued, §18B-1001.
On-premises malt beverage permit.
Kind of permit that may be issued, §18B-1001.
On-premises unfortified wine permit.
Kind of permit that may be issued, §18B-1001.
Municipal corporations.
Power to establish and support, §160A-489.
Smoking in public places.
Applicability of article to local government, §143-601.
Nonsmoking areas in state-controlled buildings, §143-597.

AUDITS.
Advance health care directive registry.
Fee for filing, §130A-470, (c).
Agricultural finance authority, §122D-18, (b).
Alcoholic beverages.
Local ABC boards, §§18B-205, (c), 18B-702, (c).
State warehouse.
Private warehouses, §18B-204, (b).
Attorneys at law.
Audit by state bar, Prof Cond. Rule 1.15-3.
Continuing legal education, CLE Rule 13.
Lawyers trust accounts, Bar Rules & Regs., B, §.0128.
Boards and commissions.
Occupational licensing board.
Annual audit of books and records, §93B-4.
Settlement of affairs of certain inoperative boards and agencies, §143-272.
Bridge authority, §136-89.166.
Commissioner of banks.
Confidentiality of official records, §53-99.
Community colleges, §147-64.6, (a).
Correction department.
Security staffing, §143B-262.5.
Court of appeals.
Clerk of court.
Financial accounts of clerk audited, §7A-20, (b).
Credit unions.
Supervisory committee, §54-109.49.
Department of health and human services.
Office of internal auditor, §§143B-216.50, 143B-216.51.
Enhanced 911 wireless system for wireless communications.
Wireless fund, §62A-28.
Executors and administrators.
Employment of auditors.
Powers of personal representatives, §28A-13-3, (a).

AUDITS —Cont'd
Fish and fisheries resources.
Promotion of coastal fisheries and seafood industry, §113-315.9.
Seafood industrial park authority.
Oversight of state auditor, §113-315.35.
Foreign legal consultants, §84A-5.
Gasoline tax, §105-449.121, (b).
Health care facilities.
Finance act.
Books and accounts to be audited, §131A-19.
Hospital authorities.
Reports to be filed, §131E-29.
Housing authorities and projects.
Local government finance.
Special provisions pertaining to public housing authorities, §159-42, (g).
Insurance.
Financial statements.
CPA audits, §58-2-205.
Supervision, rehabilitation and liquidation of insurers.
External audit of receiver's books, §58-30-255.
Job development investment grant program.
Records of recipient, §143B-437.58, (c).
Judicial sales.
Public sale.
Accounts and reports of commissioner or trustee, §1-339.31, (b).
Local development.
Industrial development commission.
Bureau.
Annual audit, §158-23.
Local government finance, §159-34.
Nonprofit corporation receiving public funds, §159-40, (a) to (d).
Mental health, developmental disability, substance abuse.
Area authorities, §122C-144.1, (c).
Mortgage bankers and brokers.
Disciplinary action.
Audit of books and records, §53-243.12, (i).
Motor carrier safety regulation unit.
Department of crime control and public safety.
Audit of motor carriers for compliance, §20-379.
Motor vehicle registration.
International registration plan.
Audit of vehicle registrations under, §20-91.
Mutual burial associations.
Assessment by board of funeral service, §90-210.81.
Nonprofit corporation receiving public funds, §159-40, (a) to (d).
Non-state entities receiving and using state funds.
Audit oversight, §143-6.2, (h).
North Carolina art society.
Operations of society.
Subject to oversight of state auditor, §140-13.
North Carolina symphony society.
Operations of society.
Subject to oversight of state auditor, §140-8.
Nurses.
Board of nursing.
Funds, §90-171.25.
Oaths.
Form of oath, §11-11.
Occupational licensing board.
Annual audit of books and records, §93B-4.
Outdoor historical dramas.
State auditor to audit, §143-204.8, (d).
Piped natural gas tax, §105-187.46, (b).

AUDITS —Cont'd
Public schools.
Annual independent audit, §115C-447.
Public utilities.
Utilities commission, §62-37, (b).
Rescue squad workers' relief fund, §58-88-15.
River basins advisory commissions, §77-115, (b).
Roanoke river basin bi-state commission.
Accounts and records, §77-96, (c).
Savings banks.
Dissolution.
Involuntary liquidation.
Final distribution, §54C-83, (p).
Examinations by commissioner of banks.
Extended audit, §54C-56, (a).
Payment of expenses, §54C-56.
Service corporations, §54C-144, (c).
Southern growth policies agreement.
Board.
Compliance with audit or inspection laws, §143-497, (f).
State auditor.
General provisions, §§147-64.1 to 147-64.14.
See STATE AUDITOR.
State departments and agencies.
Settlement of affairs of certain inoperative boards and agencies.
Affairs of board or agency, §143-272.
Strawberry plant sellers, §106-785, (c).
Superior courts.
Clerks of court.
Accounting for fees and other receipts.
Annual audits, §7A-108.
Supreme court.
Financial accounts of the clerk of supreme court, §7A-11.
Teachers' and state employees' comprehensive major medical plan, §135-39.1.
Tobacco trust fund commission.
State auditor to conduct, §143-723.
Transportation department.
Operations of department.
Subject to oversight of state auditor, §136-10.
Turnpike authority, §136-89.186.
Unit ownership.
Annual audit of records, §47A-20.
University of North Carolina.
Functions and programs.
Internal auditors.
Access to records, data or other information, §116-40.7, (b).
Confidentiality of audit work papers, exceptions, §116-40.7, (c).
Independent reviews and analysis, §116-40.7, (a).
Retention of reports and records, §116-40.7, (c).

AUDUBON NORTH CAROLINA.
Motor vehicle license plates, §20-79.4, (b).

AULANDER, CITY OF.
On-premises unfortified wine licenses.
Discretion to decline to issue, §105-113.71, (b).

AUNTS.
Intestate succession.
Distribution.
Among uncles and aunts and their lineal descendents, §29-16, (c).

AUTHENTICATION AND IDENTIFICATION OF EVIDENCE.
Copies of official records, §1A-1, Rule 44, (a).
General provisions, §8C-1, Rule 901, (a).

AUTHENTICATION AND IDENTIFICATION OF EVIDENCE —Cont'd
Illustration of examples, §8C-1, Rule 901, (b).
Medical records, subpoena commanding custodian to produce.
Certified copies in lieu of appearance, §1A-1, Rule 45, (c).
Public records, subpoena commanding custodian to produce.
Certified copies in lieu of appearance, §1A-1, Rule 45, (c).
Self-authentication, §8C-1, Rule 902.
Subscribing witness.
Testimony not necessary to authenticate, §8C-1, Rule 903.

AUTHENTICATION OF COPY OF OFFICIAL RECORD, §1A-1, Rule 44, (a).

AUTHENTICATION OF DOCUMENTS.
Certificates of authentication.
Authority of secretary of state, §66-270.
Definitions, §66-271.
Issuance of certificate, §66-272.
Limitation on authority of secretary, §66-274, (c).
Non-certifiable documents, §66-274, (b).
Other methods of authentication, §66-275.
Prerequisites to authentication, §66-273.
Purpose of certificate precluding issuance, §66-274, (a).

AUTHORITIES.
Agricultural finance authority, §§122D-1 to 122D-23.
See AGRICULTURAL FINANCE AUTHORITY.
Alcoholism research authority, §§122C-431 to 122C-433.
Bridge authority, §§136-89.159 to 136-89.167.
Capital projects for industry.
Authorities may issue bonds, Const. N. C., art. V, §9.
Community colleges.
Tax-levying authorities, §§115D-32, (a), 115D-33, (a).
Constitution of North Carolina.
Bond issues to finance capital projects for industry, Const. N. C., art. V, §9.
Education assistance authority, §§116-201 to 116-209.35.
See EDUCATION ASSISTANCE AUTHORITY.
Electrification.
Rural electrification authority, §§117-1 to 117-5.
Eminent domain.
Power of eminent domain, §40A-3, (c).
E-NC authority, §§143B-437.44 to 143B-437.47.
Energy conservation loan authority.
Housing finance agency, §§122A-5.3, 122A-6.1.
Facility authorities, §§160A-480.1 to 160A-480.15.
See FACILITY AUTHORITIES.
Global TransPark authority, §§63A-1 to 63A-25.
See GLOBAL TRANSPARK AUTHORITY.
Hospital authorities, §§131E-15 to 131E-34.
See HOSPITAL AUTHORITIES.
Housing authorities and projects, §§157-1 to 157-70.
See HOUSING AUTHORITIES AND PROJECTS.
Housing finance agency.
Energy conservation loan authority, §§122A-5.3, 122A-6.1.
Mortgage insurance authority, §122A-5.2.
Life sciences revenue bond authority, §§159D-65 to 159D-69.

AUTHORITIES —Cont'd
Mortgage insurance authority, §122A-5.2.
North Carolina rural redevelopment authority, §§143B-437.20 to 143B-437.33.
See RURAL REDEVELOPMENT AUTHORITY.
Parking authorities, §§160A-550 to 160A-565.
Parks and recreation authority, §§143B-313.1, 143B-313.2.
Public health authorities, §§130A-45 to 130A-45.12.
See PUBLIC HEALTH AUTHORITIES.
Public transportation authorities.
General provisions, §§160A-575 to 160A-588.
See PUBLIC TRANSPORTATION AUTHORITIES.
Regional public transportation authority, §§160A-600 to 160A-626.
See REGIONAL PUBLIC TRANSPORTATION AUTHORITY.
Regional sports authorities, §§160A-479 to 160A-479.17.
See REGIONAL SPORTS AUTHORITIES.
Regional transportation authorities, §§160A-630 to 160A-651.
See REGIONAL TRANSPORTATION AUTHORITIES.
Rural electrification authority, §§117-1 to 117-5.
Rural redevelopment authority, §§143B-437.20 to 143B-437.33.
See RURAL REDEVELOPMENT AUTHORITY.
Sale, lease or exchange of property between governmental units.
Action taken by governmental unit, §160A-274, (c).
Authority, §160A-274, (b).
Governmental unit defined, §160A-274, (a).
Seafood industrial park authority, §§113-315.25 to 113-315.39.
See SEAFOOD INDUSTRIAL PARK AUTHORITY.
Small business contractor authority, §§143B-472.85 to 143B-472.97.
See SMALL BUSINESS CONTRACTOR ACT.
Solid waste management.
Regional solid waste management authorities, §§153A-421 to 153A-432.
See REGIONAL SOLID WASTE MANAGEMENT AUTHORITIES.
Tennessee Valley Authority.
Taxation, §§105-458 to 105-462.
Turnpike authority, §§136-89.180 to 136-89.197.
See TURNPIKE AUTHORITY.
Veterans' recreation authorities, §§165-23 to 165-38.
See VETERANS' RECREATION AUTHORITIES.
Water and sewer authorities, §§162A-1 to 162A-19.
See WATER AND SEWER AUTHORITIES.

AUTISM.
Defined, §35A-1101.
Determination of incompetence, §§35A-1101 to 35A-1116.
See INCOMPETENCE.
Special education.
See SPECIAL EDUCATION.

AUTOMATED EXTERNAL DEFIBRILLATORS (AED), §90-21.15.
Definitions, §90-21.15, (b).
Immunity from liability, §90-21.15, (d) to (f).
Products liability claims, §90-21.15, (f).

AUTOMATED EXTERNAL DEFIBRILLATORS (AED) —Cont'd
Public policy, §90-21.15, (a).
Seller's notification requirements, §90-21.15, (g).
Use of device construed, §90-21.15, (c).

AUTOMATED TELEPHONE SYSTEMS.
State government agency systems.
Minimization of number of menus, §143-162.1.

AUTOMATED TELLER MACHINES, §53-62, (d1).
Cards, §§14-113.8 to 14-113.17.
See FINANCIAL TRANSACTION CARDS.

AUTOMATIC DIALING AND RECORDED MESSAGE PLAYERS.
Circumstances allowing, §75-104, (b).
Restriction, §75-104, (a).

AUTOMATIC STAY TO ENFORCE JUDGMENT, §1A-1, Rule 62, (a).

AUTOMATIC WEAPONS.
Mass death and destruction weapons.
Manufacture, assembly, etc., §14-288.8.

AUTOMOBILE ACCIDENTS.
See MOTOR VEHICLE ACCIDENTS.

AUTOMOBILE DEALERS' LICENSE ACT, §§20-285 to 20-308.2.
See MOTOR VEHICLE DEALERS.

AUTOMOBILE MANUFACTURERS' LICENSE ACT, §§20-285 to 20-308.2.
See MOTOR VEHICLE MANUFACTURERS.

AUTOMOBILE MECHANICS.
Motor vehicle mechanic and storage liens.
Assignment of actions to enforce to magistrates, §7A-211.1.

AUTOMOBILE REPAIR FACILITIES.
Motor vehicle repairs generally, §§20-354 to 20-354.9.
See MOTOR VEHICLE REPAIRS.

AUTOMOBILES.
Abandoned and derelict motor vehicles, §§20-137.6 to 20-137.14.
See ABANDONED AND DERELICT MOTOR VEHICLES.
Accidents.
See MOTOR VEHICLE ACCIDENTS.
Clubs and associations, §§58-69-2 to 58-69-55.
See MOTOR CLUBS AND ASSOCIATIONS.
Commissioner.
See MOTOR VEHICLES COMMISSIONER.
Damage appraisers.
See MOTOR VEHICLE DAMAGE APPRAISERS.
Dealers.
See MOTOR VEHICLE DEALERS.
Division.
See MOTOR VEHICLES DIVISION.
Drivers' licenses.
Commercial drivers' licenses, §§20-37.10 to 20-37.23.
See COMMERCIAL DRIVERS' LICENSES.
Generally.
See DRIVERS' LICENSES.
Drunk driving.
See IMPAIRED DRIVING.
Equipment.
See MOTOR VEHICLE EQUIPMENT.
Financial responsibility, §§20-279.1 to 20-284.
See MOTOR VEHICLE FINANCIAL RESPONSIBILITY.

AUTOMOBILES —Cont'd
Generally.
See MOTOR VEHICLES.
Impaired driving.
See IMPAIRED DRIVING.
Inspections, §§20-183.2 to 20-183.8G.
See MOTOR VEHICLE INSPECTIONS.
Insurance.
See MOTOR VEHICLE INSURANCE.
Lemon law, §§20-351 to 20-351.10.
See LEMON LAW.
License plates.
See MOTOR VEHICLE LICENSE PLATES.
Manufacturers.
See MOTOR VEHICLE MANUFACTURERS.
New motor vehicles warranty act, §§20-351 to 20-351.10.
See LEMON LAW.
Odometers, §§20-340 to 20-350.
See ODOMETERS.
Railroad grade crossings, §§20-142.1 to 20-142.5.
See RAILROAD GRADE CROSSINGS.
Reckless driving.
See RECKLESS DRIVING.
Registration.
See MOTOR VEHICLE REGISTRATION.
Rentals.
See RENTAL VEHICLES.
Service agreement companies, §§58-1-30 to 58-1-42.
See MOTOR VEHICLE SERVICE AGREEMENT COMPANIES.
Size, weight and loads.
See MOTOR VEHICLE SIZE, WEIGHT AND LOADS.
Speed.
See SPEED RESTRICTIONS AND VIOLATIONS.
Stolen vehicles.
See STOLEN VEHICLES.
Taxicabs.
See TAXICABS.
Tires.
See TIRES.
Titling.
See MOTOR VEHICLE TITLING.
Towing.
See TOWING OF VEHICLES.
Traffic laws.
See TRAFFIC LAWS.
Traffic lights.
See TRAFFIC LIGHTS.
Traffic tickets.
See TRAFFIC TICKETS.
Trailers.
See TRAILERS.

AUTOMOBILE THEFT REWARD SERVICE.
Motor clubs and associations, §58-69-2.

AUTOPSIES.
Anatomical gifts.
Applicability of provisions as to autopsies, §130A-409, (d).
Authorization.
Who may authorize, §130A-398.
Fees.
Medical examiners, §130A-389, (a).
Homicide investigations, §15-7.
Inmates of certain public institutions, §130A-399.
Written consent required, §130A-400.

AUTOPSIES —Cont'd
Medical examiners, §130A-389.
Performance of autopsies or other pathological examinations, §130A-389, (a), (b).
Postmortem medicolegal examinations and services generally, §§130A-377 to 130A-394.
See MEDICAL EXAMINERS.
Reports.
Autopsies performed pursuant to next of kin request, §130A-389, (d).
Requests by next of kin for autopsy, §130A-389, (b), (c).
When autopsies or other pathological examinations to be performed, §130A-389, (a), (b).
Medical schools.
Postmortem examinations in medical schools, §130A-401.
Written consent required, §130A-400.
Postmortem medicolegal examinations and services generally, §§130A-377 to 130A-394.
See MEDICAL EXAMINERS.
Reports.
Medical examiners, §130A-389, (a), (d).
Right to perform autopsy.
Limitation on right, §130A-398.
Unclaimed bodies.
Consent of commission of anatomy, §130A-415, (d).
Who may authorize, §130A-398.
Workers' compensation.
Employer or industrial commission may require, §97-27, (a).

AUTO RACING EVENTS.
Alcoholic beverage permit to recreation district, §18B-1006, (j).

AUTREFOIS, ACQUIT OR CONVICT.
Double jeopardy.
See DOUBLE JEOPARDY.

AUXILIARY POLICE, §160A-283.
City authorized to organize, §160A-282, (a).
Workers' compensation benefits, §160A-282, (b), (c).

AVERAGE WEEKLY WAGES.
Workers' compensation.
Defined, §97-2.
Rates for total incapacity, §97-29.

AVERASBORO, TOWNSHIP OF.
Room occupancy tax levied by county, uniform provisions, §153A-155.

AVERY COUNTY.
Acquisition of property, power, §153A-158.1, (a).
Blank or master forms of mortgages, deeds of trust, etc.
Indexing and recording, inapplicability of provisions, §47-21.
Board of county commissioners.
Filling vacancies on board, §153A-27.1.
Coroner elected as nominee of political party.
Filling vacancy in office, §152-1.
Counties generally.
See COUNTIES.
County boards of education elected on partisan basis.
Vacancies in office, §115C-37.1.
Dog collars.
Unlawful removal of electronic dog collars, §14-401.17.

AVERY COUNTY —Cont'd
Forestland sales, distribution of funds, §113-38.
Game laws, local acts not repealed, §113-133.1, (e).
Housing authority commissioners.
Tenant serving as commissioner, exemption from provision of law allowing, §157-5.
Oil, gas or mineral interest, extinguished, title in surface fee holder, §1-42.5, (a) to (c).
Protection of interest from surface fee holder, §1-42.5, (b), (d).
On-premises unfortified wine licenses.
Discretion to decline to issue, §105-113.71, (b).
School property.
Acquisition and improvement, §153A-158.1.
Sheriff.
Vacancy, performance of duties until vacancy filled, §162-5.1.
Small city mixed beverage elections.
Inapplicability of subsection to, §18B-600, (e1).
Western North Carolina Development Association, Inc.
Appropriation of funds to, §153A-447, (a), (b).

AVIATION.
Aircraft.
See AIRCRAFT.
Airports.
See AIRPORTS.
Aviation hall of fame.
Official location, §145-21.
North Carolina aviation museum.
Official location, §145-21.

AVIATION HALL OF FAME.
Official location, §145-21.

AVIATION MAINTENANCE TECHNICIANS.
Motor vehicle license plates, §20-79.4, (b).

AWARDS.
Agriculture.
Hall of fame.
Acceptance of awards, §106-568.17.
Annual award to native living outside state, §140A-3.
Design, §140A-1.
Established, §140A-1.
Expenses, §140A-6.
Fields of recognition, §140A-2.
Form, §140A-1.
Funds.
Expenses of administration, §140A-6.
Nonresidents.
Annual award to native living outside state, §140A-3.
Periods covered, §140A-2.
Recipients.
Selection for awards, §140A-5.
Arbitration and awards.
Generally.
See ARBITRATION.
International commercial arbitration and conciliation generally, §§1-567.30 to 1-567.87.
See INTERNATIONAL COMMERCIAL ARBITRATION AND CONCILIATION.
National guard.
Authority to wear medals, ribbons and other awards, §127A-46.
Creation of additional awards, §127A-45.5A.
Design of additional awards, §127A-45.5A.
Meritorious civilian service award, §127A-45.5.

AWARDS —Cont'd
National guard —Cont'd
Outstanding unit award, §127A-45.2A.
State active duty award, §127A-45.
State awards system, §§140A-1 to 140A-6.

AWARDS COMMITTEE.
Appointment, §143B-84.
Compensation, §143B-84.
Creation, §143B-83.
Department of cultural resources.
Transfer of committee to department, §143B-51.
Duties.
Generally, §143B-83.
Members, §143B-84.
Powers and duties.
Generally, §143B-83.
Quorum, §143B-84.
Selection of members, §143B-84.

AZALEAS.
Trespass.
Taking, etc., of certain wild plants from land of another, §14-129.

B

BABCOCK TESTS.
Milk and milk products.
Scales and weights, §106-267.5.

BABY CHICKS.
Disposing of as pets or novelties forbidden, §14-363.1.
Sales and use tax.
Exemption, §105-164.13.

BABY DROP OFF.
Abandonment of child, §14-322.3.
Child abuse or neglect.
Exceptions, §§14-318.2, 14-318.4, 14-322.3, (c).
Temporary custody without court order.
Immunity from civil and criminal liability, §7B-500, (e).
Individual's responsibilities toward infant, §7B-500, (c), (d).
Inquiries of parents, §7B-500, (c), (d).
Notification of law enforcement or social services, §7B-500, (c), (d).
Persons authorized to do so, §7B-500, (b).
Voluntarily delivered to individual, §7B-500, (d).
Termination of parental rights.
Grounds for termination, §7B-1111, (a).

BABYSITTERS.
Wage and hour act.
Exemptions from wage and hour act, §95-25.14, (a).

BACKGROUND INVESTIGATIONS, §§114-19.1 to 114-19.15.
Abuse, neglect or dependency of juvenile reports.
When juvenile removed from home.
Check of alleged abuser or abusers, §§7B-302, 7B-503, (b).
Adoption.
Agency placements.
Investigation required, §48-3-203, (d1).
Definition of criminal history, §48-1-101.
Preplacement assessments, §48-3-303, (d).
Minor in custody or placement responsibility of county department of social services, §§48-3-309, 114-19.7.

BACKGROUND INVESTIGATIONS —Cont'd
Adult care home providers and employees, §§114-19.3, 114-19.10, 131D-40.
Alarm systems licensing.
Persons applying for license, §74D-2, (d).
Criminal history record checks, §74D-2, (c).
Area mental health, developmental disabilities, and substance abuse services authorities.
Criminal record checks, §114-19.10.
Auctioneer, apprentice auctioneer or auction firm licenses.
Criminal record checks of applicants, §§85B-3.2, 114-19.8.
Charter schools, §115C-238.29K.
Child care providers, §114-19.5.
Mandatory checks, §110-90.2.
Concealed handgun permit, §14-415.15, (a).
Fees, §14-415.19, (a).
Dental hygienists.
Criminal records checks for license applicants, §90-224, (c).
Dentists.
Criminal records checks for license applicants, §90-30, (b).
Department of health and human services employees and applicants for employment, §114-19.6.
Department of juvenile justice and delinquency prevention employees and applicants for employment, §114-19.6.
Division of criminal statistics, §§114-10, 114-10.01.
Drug detection dog handlers, §90-102.1, (d).
Fees for performance.
Conducted for purpose of other than administration of criminal justice, §114-19.1, (a).
Foster parents, §114-19.4.
Funeral service.
Criminal records checks for license applicants, §90-210.25, (a).
General assembly appointees, §§114-15, (a), 120-19.4, (a).
Home care agencies.
Applicant for employment, §131E-265.
Criminal record checks, §114-19.10.
Insurance company incorporators and key persons, §58-7-37.
Interpreters and transliterators.
Criminal records checks for license applicants, §90D-7, (c).
Locksmith licensing.
Criminal history record checks on applicants, §74F-18.
Requesting department of justice to conduct on applicants.
Power of board, §74F-6.
Manufactured home manufacturer, dealer, salesperson or set-up contractor.
Applicants for licensure as, §143-143.10A.
McGruff house program volunteers.
Criminal record checks, §114-19.9.
Mental health, developmental disability, substance abuse.
Area authorities, §§114-19.3, 114-19.10, 122C-80.
Mortgage bankers and brokers, §53-243.16.
Authority of commissioner to require, §53-243.12, (l).
License application to contain consent to, §53-243.05, (a).
Licensee to furnish consent to, §53-243.06, (b1).

BACKGROUND INVESTIGATIONS —Cont'd
Nursing home employees and applicants for employment, §§114-19.10, 131E-265.
Pharmacists and pharmacies.
Criminal records checks for license applicants, §90-85.15, (c).
Physicians and surgeons.
Criminal records checks for license applicants, §90-11, (b).
Police information network, §114-10.1.
Positions that must be confirmed by general assembly, §§114-15, 120-19.4A.
Precious metals dealers.
Criminal record check of applicants for permits.
Department of justice may provide law enforcement agency, §66-165, (c).
Priority in processing, §114-19.1, (c).
Private personnel services.
Criminal records checks for license applicants, §95-47.2, (d).
Private protective services.
Criminal history record checks.
Persons applying for license, §74C-8, (c), (d).
Professional employer organizations.
Criminal history of license applicant furnished department upon request, §58-89A-60, (d).
Providers of treatment for or services to children, the elderly, mental health patients, the sick and the disabled, §114-19.3.
Public utility employees, screening employment applications, §62-333.
Real estate appraisers and registered trainees, §93E-1-6, (c), (d).
Real estate brokers and salespersons.
Criminal records checks for license applicants, §93A-4, (b1).
Respiratory care practitioners.
Applicants for license.
Discretion of board to investigate, §90-652.
Right to receive records of bureau.
Not enlarged, §114-19.1, (d).
School employees, §§114-19.2, 115C-332.
Charter schools, §115C-238.29K.
Concealed handgun permit, §§14-415.15, (a), 14-415.19, (a).
Residential schools, §143B-146.16.

BACKING OF VEHICLE.
Movement to be safe and without interfering with traffic, §20-154.

BACK PAY.
Retaliatory employment discrimination civil actions.
Award to employee, §95-243, (c).

BAD CHECKS.
Applicability of provisions.
Prima facie evidence in worthless check cases, §14-107.1, (b).
Collection program.
Administrative office of the courts, §14-107.2, (a1), (d).
Check passer and check taker defined, §14-107.2, (a).
District attorney may establish, §14-107.2, (b).
Eligibility criteria, district attorney may establish, §14-107.2, (b).
Participation, check passer not prosecuted, §14-107.2, (c).

BAD CHECKS —Cont'd
Collection program —Cont'd
Remitting fee and providing restitution.
Procedures established by administrative office of the courts, §14-107.2, (d).
Costs.
Remedies for returned check, §6-21.3, (b).
Credit defined, §14-107, (c).
Damages.
Remedies for returned check, §6-21.3, (a), (d).
Defenses.
Affirmative defense, §6-21.3, (c).
Definitions.
Credit, §14-107, (c).
Prima facie evidence in worthless check cases, §14-107.1, (a).
Delivery of check or draft to acceptor by mail or delivery other than in person.
Prima facie evidence in worthless check cases.
Applicability of provisions, §14-107.1, (c).
Demand letter.
Form, §6-21.3, (a2).
Dishonor.
Introduction of check or draft as evidence of fact of dishonor, §14-107.1, (e).
Drawing, making, uttering or issuing and delivering, unlawful, §14-107, (a).
Soliciting or aiding and abetting, §14-107, (b).
Identified check passer, §14-107.1, (d).
Magistrates.
Powers in worthless check cases, §7A-273.
Mail.
Delivery of check or draft to acceptor by mail.
Prima facie evidence in worthless check cases, §14-107.1, (c).
Motor vehicle dealers or manufacturers.
Highway use taxes.
Submitting bad check in payment of taxes collected by licensee.
Suspension or revocation of license, §20-294.
Motor vehicle fees or taxes, §20-178.
Notification letter.
Form, §6-21.3, (a1).
Obtaining property in return for worthless check, draft or order, §14-106.
Prima facie evidence in worthless check cases, §14-107.1.
Affidavit of employee of bank or depository, §14-107.1, (f).
Applicability of provisions, §14-107.1, (b), (c).
Conditions making provisions applicable, §14-107.1, (b), (c).
Definitions, §14-107.1, (a).
Dishonor of check or draft, §14-107.1, (e).
Identifying check passer, §14-107.1, (d).
Processing fees, payment, judge may order, §14-107, (e).
Punishment for worthless checks, §14-107, (d).
Remedies, §6-21.3.
Restitution, judge may order, §14-107, (e).
Returned checks.
Remedies, §6-21.3.
Services charges, payment, judge may order, §14-107, (e).
Taxation.
Penalty for bad checks in payment, §105-236.
Property taxes.
Payment of taxes.
Penalty, §105-357, (b).
Waiver of penalty, §105-358, (a).

BAD CHECKS —Cont'd
Worthless checks collection program.
Collection of worthless checks fund, §7A-308, (c).
Fees, superior court clerks, §7A-308, (c).

BAD FAITH.
Abused, neglected or exploited disabled adults.
Immunity from civil or criminal liability for reporting.
Effect of bad faith or malicious purpose report, §108A-102.
Airports.
Zoning board of appeals.
Judicial review of agency decision, §63-34.
Arson.
Fire incident reports, §58-79-45, (a).
Attorneys' fees.
Oil pollution and hazardous substance control.
Award of attorneys' fees to prevailing defendant, §143-215.94CC.
Trade secrets.
Awarding attorneys' fees in misappropriation actions, §66-154, (d).
Auctions and auctioneers.
Disciplinary actions against licensee.
Dishonest or bad faith conduct as grounds, §85B-8.
Bank deposits and collections.
Damages.
Measure of damages, §25-4-103, (e).
Best evidence rule.
Lost or destroyed originals.
When original document not required, §8C-1, Rule 1004.
Business corporations.
Stock and stockholders.
Financial statements for stockholders.
Time for mailing, §55-16-20.
Cost where executor, administrator, trustee or person authorized by statute a party, §6-31.
Damages.
Bank deposits and collections.
Measure of damages, §25-4-103, (e).
Decedents' estates.
Claims against the estate.
Pleading statute of limitations, §28A-19-11.
Depositions upon oral examination.
Motion to terminate or limit, §1A-1, Rule 30, (b).
Emergency management personnel.
Governmental immunity, §166A-14.
Fiduciaries.
Negotiable instruments.
Checks drawn payable to third persons, §32-6.
Checks payable to fiduciary, §32-7.
Deposit in fiduciary's personal account.
Check drawn by fiduciary upon account, §32-10.
Deposit in name of fiduciary, §32-8.
Deposit in name of principal.
Check drawn upon account of principal and bank by fiduciary, §32-9.
Deposit in names of two or more trustees.
Checks drawn upon trust account, §32-11.
Transfer of negotiable instruments, §32-5.
Trust and trustees.
Powers which may be incorporated by reference in trust agreement in absence of bad faith, §32-27.
Fire incident reports, §58-79-45, (a).
Fraud.
Insurance fraud.
Immunity from liability for reporting, §58-2-160, (a), (b).

BAD FAITH —Cont'd
Governmental immunity.
Emergency management personnel, §166A-14.
Health care benefits providers.
Multiple employer welfare arrangements.
Qualifications for licensure, §58-49-40.
Insurance companies.
Cessations of business.
Liability for statements or communications made in bad faith, §58-41-40, (a).
Insurance fraud.
Immunity from liability for reporting fraud, §58-2-160, (a), (b).
Insurance market assistance program.
Good faith immunity from operation of programs, §58-40-135.
Mechanics' and materialmen' liens.
Dealings with one other than owner.
Priority of lien, §44A-22.
Motor vehicle insurance.
Reinsurance facility.
Information to policyholder upon cession, §58-37-25, (c).
Safe driver incentive plan.
Furnishing statement or information in bad faith, §58-36-65, (f).
Municipal corporations.
Warranted deeds.
Effect of fraud, malice or bad faith on immunity, §160A-275.
Negotiable instruments.
Fiduciaries.
Checks drawn payable to third persons, §32-6.
Checks payable to fiduciary, §32-7.
Deposit in fiduciary's personal account.
Check drawn by fiduciary upon account, §32-10.
Deposit in name of fiduciary, §32-8.
Deposit in name of principal.
Check drawn upon account of principal and bank by fiduciary, §32-9.
Deposit in names of two or more trustees.
Checks drawn upon trust account, §32-11.
Transfer by fiduciary, §32-5.
Oil pollution and hazardous substance control.
Attorneys' fees.
Award of attorneys' fees to prevailing defendant, §143-215.94CC.
Open meetings of public bodies.
Additional remedies for violations of article, §143-318.16A, (c).
Partnerships, knowledge of fact within meaning of article.
Knowledge of other facts as in circumstances to show bad faith, §59-33, (a).
Statute of limitations.
Decedents' estates.
Pleading statute of limitations, §28A-19-11.
Stock and stockholders.
Business corporations.
Financial statements for stockholders.
Time for mailing, §55-16-20.
Summary judgment affidavits made in bad faith, §1A-1, Rule 56, (g).
Trade secrets.
Attorneys' fees.
Awarding attorneys' fees in misappropriation actions, §66-154, (d).
Trust and trustees.
Powers which may be incorporated by reference in trust agreement in absence of bad faith, §32-27.

BAD FAITH —Cont'd
Warranted deeds.
Municipal corporations.
Effect of fraud, malice or bad faith on immunity, §160A-275.

BADGES.
Company police, §74E-7.
Fraternal orders.
Unauthorized wearing, §58-25-70.

BAGGAGE.
Carriers.
Careful handling, §62-202.
Checks, §62-203.
Sale of unclaimed baggage, §62-209.
Emergency operating authority granted to duly licensed owner of vehicle or vehicles, §62-265.
Hotels.
Liability for loss, §72-2.
Fire loss, §72-4.

BAGGAGE CHECKS, §62-203, (d), (e).

BAGS.
Plastic bags.
Retail outlet providing.
Recyclable material, requirements, §130A-309.10, (c).

BA'HAI.
Marriage, §51-1.

BAIL AND RECOGNIZANCE.
Alimony.
Remedy available, §50-16.7, (d).
Appeals.
Correction of errors by appellate division.
Authority of court to act pending appeal, §15A-1453, (a).
Appearance.
Failure to appear, §15A-543, (a).
Imposing conditions on pretrial release, §15A-534, (d1).
Penalties, §15A-543, (b), (c).
Appearance bond.
Failure to appear and answer on prior occasions.
Secured appearance bond required, no conditions set, §15A-534, (d1).
Arrest in civil cases.
Action on sheriff's bond.
Where judgment recovered against sheriff, §1-432.
Allowance of bail, §1-425.
Amendment of process or pleading.
Bail not discharged, §1-439.
Authorized, §1-419.
Bail may arrest defendant, §1-435.
Bail not discharged by amendment of process or pleading, §1-439.
Death of defendant.
Bail exonerated, §1-433.
Defendant in jail.
Sheriff may take bail, §1-430.
Defendants undertaking, §1-420.
Delivery of defendants undertaking to clerks, §1-421.
Deposit in lieu of bail, §1-426.
Application of deposit to plaintiff's judgment, §1-429.
Authorized, §§1-419, 1-426.
Bail substituted for deposit, §1-428.
Certificate of deposit, §1-426.

BAIL AND RECOGNIZANCE —Cont'd
Arrest in civil cases —Cont'd
Deposit in lieu of bail —Cont'd
Judgment.
Deposit applied to plaintiff's judgment, §1-429.
Payment of deposit into court, §1-427.
Sheriff.
Liability on sheriff's bond, §1-427.
Payment of deposit into court, §1-427.
Substitution of bail for deposit, §1-428.
Discharge of defendant, §1-419.
Examination of bail, §1-424.
Exception to bail.
New bail, §1-422.
Notice, §1-421.
Notice of justification, §1-422.
Exoneration of bail, §1-433.
Imprisonment of defendant.
Bail exonerated, §1-433.
Justification of bail, §1-424.
Liability of bail to sheriff, §1-437.
Motion, proceedings against bail, §1-436.
Motion to reduce bail, §1-417.
New bail, §1-422.
Notice by plaintiff of not accepting bail, §1-421.
Notice to plaintiff of justification, §1-422.
Proceedings against bail by motion, §1-436.
Qualification of bail, §1-423.
Quo warranto.
Defendant usurping office, §1-519.
Sheriff.
Bonds, surety.
Liability on bond, §§1-427, 1-432.
Defendant in jail.
Sheriff may take bail, §1-430.
Substitute for deposit, §1-428.
Surrender of defendant, §1-434.
When bail to pay costs, §1-438.
When sheriff liable as bail, §1-431.
Attorney prohibited from becoming surety, §15A-541, (a).
Bail bond.
Defined, §15A-531.
Bail bondsmen and runners, §§58-71-1 to 58-71-195.
See BAIL BONDSMEN AND RUNNERS.
Breach of condition.
Forfeiture, §§15A-544.1 to 15A-544.8.
Surrender of principal, §15A-540.
Capias.
Bond of prisoner committed on capias in civil action, §162-32.
Capital punishment.
Discretion of judge as to pretrial release, §15A-533, (c).
Child support.
Enforcement of support.
Remedy of arrest and bail available, §50-13.4, (f).
Illegitimate children.
Continuance, surety of person accused of being father, §49-5.
Child victims.
Violent crimes against, §15A-534.4.
Community penalties program.
Remission of bail bond if defendant sentenced to community or intermediate punishment, §15A-547.1.
Concealed handgun permit.
Proceedings pending for disqualifying crime.
Grounds for denial of permit, §14-415.12, (b).

BAIL AND RECOGNIZANCE —Cont'd
Conditions, §15A-534.
Controlled substance offenses.
Presumptions concerning conditions, §15A-533, (d).
Determination.
Judicial officers may determine, §15A-532.
Excessive bail, Const. N. C., art. I, §27; Const. U. S., amd. VIII.
Release after conviction in superior court.
Determination, §15A-536, (b), (c).
Evidence to be considered, §15A-536, (f).
Right to have conditions determined, §15A-533, (b).
Surrender of principal by surety.
After breach of condition, §15A-540, (b).
Going off the bond before breach, §15A-540, (a).
New conditions of pretrial release, §15A-540, (c).
Contempt.
Power of court to punish for contempt not affected, §15A-546.
Controlled substance offenses.
Conditions of pretrial release.
Presumptions concerning conditions in controlled substance cases, §15A-533, (d).
Costs.
Civil cases.
When bail to pay costs, §1-438.
Pretrial release services in district or superior courts, §7A-304, (a).
Several actions on one recognizance.
Allowance of costs to defendant, §6-19.
Allowance of costs to plaintiff, §6-18.
Criminal contempt.
Custody of person charged with criminal contempt, §5A-16, (b).
Defendant sentenced to community or intermediate punishment.
Remission of bail bond, §15A-547.1.
Definitions, §15A-531.
Delinquent and undisciplined juvenile actions.
Pretrial release of delinquent juvenile.
Transferring jurisdiction of juvenile to superior court, §§7B-2204, 7B-2603, (b).
Deposit in lieu of bail.
Civil cases, §§1-419, 1-426 to 1-429.
District courts.
Criminal actions.
Status of bail bond, §7A-290.
Judges of district court.
Power to set bail, §7A-291.
Domestic violence, §15A-534.1, (a).
Retention of defendant in custody without action.
Time limitation, §15A-534.1, (b).
Effecting release.
Persons authorized, §15A-537, (a).
Duties of person effecting release, §15A-537, (b).
Powers of law-enforcement or custodial officers, §15A-537, (c).
Evidence, rules of.
Inapplicability, §8C-1, Rule 1101, (b).
Excessive bail.
Liability as bail, §1-437.
Action on sheriff's bond, §1-432.
Liability on sheriff's bond, §1-427.
Payment of deposit into court, §1-427.
When liable, §1-431.
Surrender of defendant.
Bail exonerated, §1-433.
Bail may arrest defendant, §1-435.

BAIL AND RECOGNIZANCE —Cont'd
Excessive bail —Cont'd
Surrender of defendant —Cont'd
Surrender of defendant.
Detention of defendant, §1-434.
Usurpation of office.
Defendant usurping office, §1-519.
Written undertaking, §1-420.
Delivery to clerk, §1-421.
Exoneration.
Civil cases, §§1-433, 1-434.
Extradition, §§15A-736, 15A-738.
Fugitives from other states, §15A-735.
Failure to appear.
Imposition of conditions on pretrial release.
Prior failure to appear and answer charges, §15A-534, (d1).
Penalty, §15A-543.
Felonies.
Failure to appear, §15A-543, (b).
Forfeiture, §§15A-544.1 to 15A-544.8.
Contents of forfeiture, §15A-544.3, (b).
Entry of forfeiture, §15A-544.3, (a).
Final judgment, §15A-544.6.
Docketing as civil judgment, §15A-544.7, (a).
Execution, §15A-544.7, (c), (d).
Lien of judgment, §15A-544.7, (b).
No final judgment after forfeiture set aside, §15A-544.5, (g).
Relief from final judgment of forfeiture, §15A-544.8.
Identifying information on bond, §15A-544.2, (a).
Effect of release on bond that does not contain, §15A-544.2, (b).
Jurisdiction, §15A-544.1.
Notice of forfeiture, §15A-544.4, (a), (c).
Mailing, §15A-544.4, (b), (d), (e).
Relief from final judgment of forfeiture.
Appeals, §15A-544.8, (f).
Exclusive nature of relief, §15A-544.8, (a).
Finality of judgment as to other parties not affected, §15A-544.8, (e).
Procedure, §15A-544.8, (c), (d).
Reasons, §15A-544.8, (b).
Setting aside forfeiture.
Appeals, §15A-544.5, (h).
Exclusive nature of relief, §15A-544.5, (a).
Procedure, §15A-544.5, (c) to (e).
Reasons, §15A-544.5, (b).
Restrictions, §15A-544.5, (e) to (g).
Fugitives from other states awaiting extradition, §15A-735.
Guaranteed arrest bond certificates issued by motor clubs.
Acceptance in lieu of cash bail or other bond, §58-69-55, (a).
Forfeiture and enforcement, applicable provisions, §58-69-55, (b).
Surety company becoming surety with respect to.
Filing undertaking, amount, §58-69-50, (a).
Form of undertaking, §58-69-50, (b).
Habeas corpus.
Right of habeas corpus not abridged, §15A-547.
When party bailed or remanded, §17-35.
Initial appearance before magistrate.
Release on bail, §15A-511, (e).
Law enforcement officers.
Power of officer to set bail.
Termination of power upon establishment of district court, §7A-274.

BAIL AND RECOGNIZANCE —Cont'd
Limitation of actions.
Action against bail, §1-52.
Mayors.
Power of mayor to set bail.
Termination of power upon establishment of district court, §7A-274.
Mental health, developmental disability, substance abuse.
Involuntary commitment.
Escape and commission of crime after escape or while resident of facility.
Pretrial release denied, §122C-254, (a).
Misdemeanors.
Failure to appear, §15A-543, (c).
False qualification by surety, §15A-542, (b).
Surety.
Persons prohibited from becoming surety.
Violation of provisions, §15A-541, (b).
Mortgage in lieu of bond.
Recognizance for appearance in criminal proceeding, §58-74-5.
Required for recognizance in criminal proceeding.
Cancellation of mortgage in such proceedings, §58-74-10.
Motor clubs and associations.
Bail or cash appearance bond service, §58-69-2.
Guaranteed arrest bond certificates issued by motor clubs, §58-69-50.
Obligor.
Effect of bail bond upon, §15A-534, (h).
Orders.
Modification.
Motion of person detained, §15A-538, (a).
Motion of prosecutor, §15A-539.
Substitution of surety, §15A-538, (b).
Pretrial release, §15A-534, (d).
Modification of orders, §15A-534, (e).
Evidence to be considered, §15A-534, (g).
Revocation of order, §15A-534, (f).
Evidence to be considered, §15A-534, (g).
Release after conviction in superior court, §15A-536, (d).
Modification or revocation of order, §15A-536, (e).
Evidence to be considered, §15A-536, (f).
Peace officers.
Power of peace officer to set bail.
Termination of power upon establishment of district court, §7A-274.
Prohibited from becoming surety, §15A-541, (a).
Pretrial release.
Audio and video transmissions.
Conduct of proceedings, §15A-532, (b).
Capital cases.
Discretion of judge, §15A-533, (c).
Closed-circuit television.
Conduct of proceedings, §15A-532.
Conditions.
Controlled substance offenses.
Presumptions concerning conditions, §15A-533, (d).
Determination.
Conditions which must be imposed, §15A-534, (a), (b).
Evidence to be considered, §15A-534, (g).
Factors, §15A-534, (c).
Judicial officers may determine, §15A-532.
Right to have conditions determined in noncapital cases, §15A-533, (b).

BAIL AND RECOGNIZANCE —Cont'd
Pretrial release —Cont'd
Conditions —Cont'd
Prior failure of defendant to appear and answer charges, §15A-534, (d1).
Delinquent and undisciplined juvenile actions.
Transferring jurisdiction to superior court, §§7B-2204, 7B-2603, (b).
Domestic violence, §15A-534.1, (a).
Retention of defendant in custody without action, time limitation, §15A-534.1, (b).
Failure to appear and answer on prior occasions, §15A-534, (d1).
Mental health, developmental disability, substance abuse.
Involuntary commitment.
Escape and commission of crime after escape or while resident of facility.
Pretrial release denied, §122C-254, (a).
Noncapital cases, §15A-532, (b).
Orders, §15A-534, (d).
Modification, §15A-534, (e).
Evidence to be considered, §15A-534, (g).
Revocation, §15A-534, (f).
Evidence to be considered, §15A-534, (g).
Persons committed to mental health facility, §15A-533, (a).
Policies.
Issuance, §15A-535.
Public health.
Denial to protect, §15A-534.5.
Restrictions on travel, associations, conduct or place of abode.
Prior failure of defendant to appear and answer charges, §15A-534, (d1).
Secured appearance bond.
Prior failure of defendant to appear and answer charges, §15A-534, (d1).
Sex offenses and crimes of violence against child victims, §15A-534.4.
Two or more failures to appear and answer on prior occasions, §15A-534, (d1).
Two-way audio and video transmissions.
Conduct of proceedings, §15A-532, (b).
Prisons and prisoners.
Discharge of insolvent prisoners.
Persons taken in bail proceedings, §23-29.
Probation.
Violation of probation.
Bail following arrest, §15A-1345, (b).
Probation officers.
Prohibited from becoming surety, §15A-541, (a).
Public health.
Detention to protect, §15A-534.5.
Quo warranto.
Defendant usurping office, §1-519.
Right to bail.
Noncapital offenses.
Right to have conditions of pretrial release determined, §15A-533, (b).
Rules of evidence.
Inapplicability, §8C-1, Rule 1101, (b).
Runners.
Bail bondsmen and runners, §§58-71-1 to 58-71-195.
See BAIL BONDSMEN AND RUNNERS.
Sexual offenses, §15A-534.4.
Sheriffs.
Bond of prisoner committed on capias in civil action, §162-32.

BAIL AND RECOGNIZANCE —Cont'd
Sheriffs —Cont'd
Civil cases.
Defendant in jail.
Sheriff may take bail, §1-430.
Liability on bond, §§1-427, 1-432.
Prohibited from becoming surety, §15A-541, (a).
Superior courts.
Pretrial release.
Policies.
Issuance, §15A-535.
Release after conviction.
Authorized, §15A-536.
Conditions.
Determination, §15A-536, (b), (c).
Evidence to be considered, §15A-536, (f).
Order, §15A-536, (d).
Modification or revocation, §15A-536, (e).
Evidence to be considered, §15A-536, (f).
Surety.
Defined, §15A-531.
False qualification by surety, §15A-542, (a).
Penalty, §15A-542, (b).
Persons prohibited from becoming sureties, §15A-541, (a).
Penalty for violation, §15A-541, (b).
Surrender of principal.
After breach of condition, §15A-540, (b).
Going off the bond before breach, §15A-540, (a).
New conditions of pretrial release, §15A-540, (c).
Surrender of principal.
Breach of condition, §15A-540.

BAIL BONDSMEN AND RUNNERS, §§58-71-1 to 58-71-195.
Accommodation bondsmen.
Defined, §58-71-1.
Affidavit filed with commissioner.
Appointment of bondsman, §58-71-141, (a).
Affidavits filed with clerk of court, §58-71-140, (d).
Age.
Licenses.
Minimum age, §58-71-50, (b).
Amount of bail bond.
Limit on amount of bond to be written by professional bondsman, §58-71-175.
Appointment of bondsman.
Affidavit filed with commissioner, §58-71-141, (a).
Former insurer defined, §58-71-141, (c).
Rules, §58-71-141, (b).
Arrest.
Surrender of defendant by surety.
Arrest of defendant for purpose of surrender, §58-71-30.
Attorneys at law.
Prohibited from becoming sureties or runners, §58-71-105.
Bankruptcy and insolvency.
Notice of receivership, §58-71-81.
Breach of undertaking.
Surrender of defendant, §§58-71-20, 58-71-25.
Arrest of defendant, §58-71-30.
Child support enforcement.
Forfeiture of licensing privilege, §50-13.12.
Collateral.
Receipts for, §58-71-100.
Commissioner of insurance.
Administration of provisions, §58-71-5, (a).
Evidence of commissioners' actions, §58-71-5, (b).
Examinations, §58-71-170.

BAIL BONDSMEN AND RUNNERS —Cont'd
Commissioner of insurance —Cont'd
Rules and regulations, §58-71-5, (a).
Confidentiality of information.
Runners.
Notice of termination of appointment, §58-71-125.
Surety bondsmen.
Notice of termination of appointment, §58-71-115.
Conflict of laws, §58-71-195.
Continuing education, §58-71-71, (b), (c).
Failure to comply with requirements, §58-71-71, (e).
Death of bail bondsman, §58-71-121.
Defects not to invalidate undertakings, §58-71-10, (a).
Definitions, §58-71-1.
Deposit of securities.
Local requirements prohibited, §58-71-190.
Professional bondsmen.
Deficiencies.
Deposit of additional securities, §58-71-160, (a).
Failure to give notice, §58-71-160, (b).
Disposition of securities.
Authority of commissioner, §58-71-150.
Power of attorney.
Bondsman to furnish with securities, §58-71-155.
Required, §58-71-145.
Securities held in trust by commissioner, §58-71-150.
Release and cancellation of undertaking.
Deposit for defendant admitted to bail authorizes, §58-71-135.
Substituting bail by sureties for deposit, §58-71-130.
Discontinuance of business.
Cancellation of license, §58-71-120.
Notice, §58-71-120.
Education.
Approval of courses, §58-71-71, (d).
Continuing education, §58-71-71, (b), (c).
Failure to comply with requirements, §58-71-71, (e).
False representation that requirements met, §58-71-71, (e).
Exemptions, §58-71-71, (c).
Qualifications of instructors, §58-71-72, (a), (b).
Requirements, §58-71-71, (a), (b).
Rules and regulations, §58-71-71, (f).
Employment of staff for office duties, §58-71-40, (e).
Evidence.
Commissioners' actions, §58-71-5, (b).
Examinations.
Commissioner of insurance, §58-71-170.
Educational requirements for taking, §58-71-71, (a).
Licenses, §58-71-70.
Fees, §58-71-70.
Fees.
Disposition, §58-71-180.
Licenses, §58-71-55.
Examinations, §58-71-70.
Renewal, §58-71-75.
Dual license holding, §58-71-82.
Felonies.
Conviction of felony.
Grounds for denial, suspension, revocation or refusal to renew license, §§15A-1331, (a), 58-71-80, (b).

BAIL BONDSMEN AND RUNNERS —Cont'd
Felonies —Cont'd
Monthly report.
Knowingly and willfully falsifying, §58-71-165.
Fingerprints.
Licenses.
Applications, §58-71-50, (a).
First-year licensees, §58-71-41, (a) to (e).
Defined, §58-71-1.
Exceptions to provisions, §58-71-41, (e).
Inability to become employed.
Affidavit, §58-71-41, (d).
Notice of completing supervision, §58-71-41, (b).
Supervision, §58-71-41, (a), (b).
Termination of contract or employment.
Notification to commissioner, §58-71-41, (c).
Suspension, revocation or refusal to renew license, §58-71-80, (c).
Forfeiture of bail.
Procedure, §58-71-35, (a).
Remission of judgment, §58-71-35, (b).
Fraud.
Grounds for denial, suspension, revocation or refusal to renew license, §58-71-80, (a).
Hearings.
Licenses.
Denial, suspension, revocation or refusal to renew, §58-71-85.
Identification cards, §58-71-40, (d).
Incapacitated or incompetence of bail bondsman, §58-71-121.
Jailers.
Prohibited from becoming sureties or runners, §58-71-105.
Licenses.
Applications, §58-71-40, (b).
Fingerprints and photographs of applicants, §58-71-50, (a).
Reapplication, §58-71-40, (c).
Runners.
Contents of application for runner's license, §58-71-65.
Disclosure of prior licensure as professional bondsman or runner, §58-71-65.
Endorsement by bail bondsman, §58-71-65.
Denial, suspension, revocation or refusal to renew.
Conviction of felony, §58-71-80, (b).
Dual license holding, §58-71-82.
Felony convictions, §15A-1331A.
First-year licensee whose employment or contract terminated, §58-71-80, (c).
Grounds, §58-71-80, (a).
Hearing, §58-71-85.
Notice, §58-71-85.
Discontinuance of business.
Cancellation of license, §58-71-120.
Dual license holding, §58-71-82.
Examinations, §58-71-70.
Fees, §58-71-70.
Fees, §58-71-55.
Examinations, §58-71-70.
Renewal, §58-71-75.
Dual license holding, §58-71-82.
First-year licensees, §58-71-41, (a) to (e).
Identification cards, §58-71-40, (d).
Individual natural persons only, §58-71-40, (a).
Investigation of applicant, §58-71-40, (b).
Local licenses prohibited, §58-71-190.
Monetary penalty for violations, §58-2-70, (c), (d), (g).
Qualifications, §58-71-50, (b).

BAIL BONDSMEN AND RUNNERS —Cont'd
Licenses —Cont'd
Registration, §58-71-140, (a) to (c).
Renewal, §§58-71-45, 58-71-75.
Dual license holding, §58-71-82.
Fees, §58-71-75.
Refusal to renew, §§58-71-80 to 58-71-85.
Required, §58-71-40, (a).
Restitution for violations, §58-2-70, (e), (f), (g).
Runners.
Applications.
Contents of application for runner's license, §58-71-65.
Disclosure of prior licensure as professional bondsman or runner, §58-71-65.
Endorsement by bail bondsman, §58-71-65.
Cancellation, §58-71-45.
Qualifications, §58-71-50, (b).
Registration, §58-71-140, (c).
Required, §58-71-40, (a).
Surrender, §58-2-65.
Suspension or revocation, §§58-71-80 to 58-71-85.
Applicable provisions, §58-2-70, (h).
Criminal convictions, §§15A-1331A, 58-2-60, (b).
Notice and hearing, §58-2-70, (b).
Term of license, §58-71-45.
Limit on amount of bond to be written by professional bondsman, §58-71-175.
Local governments.
Duplication of regulations prohibited, §58-71-190.
Misdemeanors.
Violations of provisions, §58-71-185.
Notice.
Bankruptcy.
Notice of receivership, §58-71-81.
Discontinuance of business, §58-71-120.
First-year licensees.
Completion of supervision, §58-71-41, (b).
Licenses.
Denial, suspension, revocation or refusal to renew, §58-71-85.
Runners.
Appointments and terminations, §58-71-125.
Surety bondsmen.
Appointments and terminations, §58-71-115.
Obligors.
Defined, §58-71-1.
Office staff, license exemption, §58-71-40, (e).
Parole or probation officers.
Prohibited from becoming sureties or runners, §58-71-105.
Payment of bond.
Deferral, §58-71-167, (a), (b).
Peace officers.
Prohibited from becoming sureties or runners, §58-71-105.
Penalties.
Violations of provisions, §58-71-185.
Personation of law-enforcement officer, §58-71-95.
Photography.
Licenses.
Applications.
Fingerprints and photographs of applicants, §58-71-50, (a).
Powers of attorney.
Deposit of securities by professional bondsmen.
Bondsmen to furnish power of attorney with securities, §58-71-155.
Premiums.
Payments.
Deferral, §58-71-167, (a), (b).

BAIL BONDSMEN AND RUNNERS —Cont'd
Professional bondsmen.
Defined, §58-71-1.
Deposit of securities.
Deficiencies.
Deposit of additional securities, §58-71-160, (a).
Failure to give notice, §58-71-160, (b).
Disposition of securities.
Authority of commissioner, §58-71-150.
Power of attorney.
Bondsman to furnish with securities, §58-71-155.
Required, §58-71-145.
Securities held in trust by commissioner, §58-71-150.
Examination, §58-71-170, (a).
Licenses.
Generally. See within this heading, "Licenses."
Reports.
Monthly report, §58-71-165.
Rebates.
Prohibited practices, §58-71-95.
Receipts for collateral, §58-71-100, (a).
Records.
Separate from records of other businesses, §58-71-168.
Registration.
Licenses and power of appointment, §58-71-140, (a) to (c).
Reports.
Professional bondsmen.
Monthly report, §58-71-165.
Runners.
Bail bondsman to annually report runners, §58-71-125.
Surety bondsmen.
Insurers to annually report surety bondsmen, §58-71-115.
Rules and regulations.
Commissioner of insurance, §58-71-5, (a).
Educational requirements, §58-71-71, (f).
Runners.
Defined, §58-71-1.
Eligibility to be runner, §58-71-125.
Licenses.
Applications.
Contents of application for runner's license, §58-71-65.
Disclosure of prior licensure as professional bondsman or runner, §58-71-65.
Endorsement by bail bondsman, §58-71-65.
Cancellation, §58-71-45.
General provisions. See within this heading, "Licenses."
Qualifications, §58-71-50, (b).
Registration, §58-71-140, (c).
Required, §58-71-40, (a).
Notice.
Appointments and terminations, §58-71-125.
Persons prohibited from becoming runners, §58-71-105.
Reports.
Bail bondsman to annually report runner, §58-71-125.
Security deposits. See within this heading, "Deposit of securities."
Shared trust accounts, §58-71-100, (b).
Sheriffs.
Prohibited from becoming sureties or runners, §58-71-105.

BAIL BONDSMEN AND RUNNERS —Cont'd
Signatures.
Bonds not to be signed in blank, §58-71-110.
Countersigning.
Authority given only to licensed employees, §58-71-110.
Solicitation.
Prohibited practices, §58-71-95.
Sureties.
Appointment.
Notice, §58-71-115.
Defined, §58-71-1.
Examination, §58-71-170, (b).
Insurers to annually report surety bondsmen, §58-71-115.
Liability not affected by agreement or lack of qualifications, §58-71-10, (b).
Notice.
Appointments and terminations, §58-71-115.
Persons prohibited from becoming sureties, §58-71-105.
Prerequisites, §58-71-15.
Qualifications, §58-71-15.
Registration of power of appointment, §58-71-140, (b).
Surrender of defendant by surety, §§58-71-20 to 58-71-30.
Termination of appointment.
Notice, §58-71-115.
Surrender of defendant by surety.
Arrest of defendant for purpose of surrender, §58-71-30.
Authorized, §58-71-20.
Procedure, §58-71-25.
Return of premium.
When not required, §58-71-20.
Term of licenses, §58-71-45.
Trust accounts, §58-71-100, (b).
Violations of provisions.
Grounds for denial, suspension, revocation or refusal to renew license, §58-71-80, (a).
Penalties, §58-71-185.
Prohibited practices, §58-71-95.

BAIL EXONERATED.
Arrest in civil cases, §1-433.
Surrender of defendant, §1-434.

BAILMENTS.
Artwork on consignment, §§25C-1 to 25C-5.
Civil action for interference with property.
Trespass committed during existence of bailment, §99A-1.
Embezzlement.
Master and servant.
Larceny by servant or employee, §14-74.
Receipt of property by bailee by virtue of office or employment, §14-90.
Leases, UCC.
Risk of loss passing to lessee.
Goods held by bailee and delivered without being moved, §25-2A-219, (2).
Motor vehicle repairs.
Exceeding estimate.
Shop not to retain vehicle for refusal to pay excessive charges, §20-354.5, (d).
Sales, UCC.
Seller's remedy of stoppage of delivery in transit, §25-2-705.
Trespass committed during existence of bailment.
Civil action for interference with property, §99A-1.

BAILMENTS —Cont'd
Vehicles and draft animals, protection of bailor against bailee's act, §§14-165 to 14-169.
Attorney in fact.
Conversion by attorney in fact, §14-168.1.
Bailee.
Conversion by bailee, §14-168.1.
Conversion.
Bailees, lessees, tenants or attorneys in fact, §14-168.1.
Evidence of intent to convert property.
Prima facie evidence of intent, §14-168.3.
Definitions, §14-168.2.
Failure to return hired property, §14-167.
Fraud.
Hiring with intent to defraud, §14-168.
Lessee.
Conversion by lessee, §14-168.1.
Malicious or willful injury to hired personal property, §14-165.
Options to purchase.
Failing to return rented property on which there is purchase option.
Intent to commit crime, presumption, §14-168.4, (b).
Misdemeanor, §14-168.4, (a).
Prosecution of violations, §14-168.4, (c).
Subletting of hired property, §14-166.
Tenant.
Conversion by tenant, §14-168.1.
Violations made misdemeanors, §14-169.
Willful injury to hired personal property, §14-165.

BAIL OR CASH APPEARANCE BOND SERVICE.
Motor clubs and associations, §58-69-2.

BAITING ANIMALS, §14-362.1.
Dog baiting, §14-362.2.

BALANCED GROWTH POLICY ACT, §§143-506.6 to 143-506.14.
Citation of article, §143-506.6.
Citizen participation.
Governor to establish process of citizen participation, §143-506.11.
Cooperation of agencies.
Endorsement by general assembly, §143-506.9.
Declaration of policy, §143-506.8.
Governor.
Citizen participation.
Governor to establish process, §143-506.11.
Designation of growth centers, §143-506.10.
Growth centers.
Designation, §143-506.10.
Legislative declaration, §§143-506.7, 143-506.8.
Local government advocacy council.
Composition, §143-506.14, (a).
Cooperation of other departments, §143-506.14, (f).
Duties.
General duties and responsibilities, §143-506.14, (d).
Expenses, §143-506.14, (b).
Meetings, §143-506.14, (b).
Members not considered public officers, §143-506.14, (c).
Number of members, §143-506.14, (a).
Terms, §143-506.14, (a).
Transferred to office of local government advocacy, §143-506.14, (a).

BALANCED GROWTH POLICY ACT —Cont'd
Local government advocacy office.
Established, §143-506.14, (a).
Local government advocacy council.
Transferred to office, §143-506.14, (a).
Staff, §143-506.14, (e).
Partnerships.
Implementation of a state-local partnership, §143-506.13.
Policy areas.
Delineation of program area guidelines, §143-506.12.
Program area guidelines.
Delineation, §143-506.12.
Purposes, §143-506.7.
Policy areas, §143-506.12.
State departments and agencies.
Cooperation of agencies encouraged by general assembly, §143-506.9.
State-local partnership.
Implementation, §143-506.13.
Title, §143-506.6.

BALD EAGLES.
Unlawfully taking, possessing, etc., §113-294, (l).

BALD HEAD ISLAND.
Eminent domain.
Vesting of title and right to possession, §40A-42, (a).

BALLISTIC KNIVES.
Possession and sale, §14-269.6, (a), (b).

BALLOON PAYMENTS.
High cost home loans, §24-1.1E, (b).
Home loans for term in excess of six months, §24-1.1A, (a).
Retail installment sales, §25A-34.

BALLOON RACES.
Winery special event permit authorization, §18B-1114.1.

BALLOT COUNTERS, §163-43.

BALLOTS.
Absentee ballots.
Generally, §§163-226 to 163-239.
See ABSENTEE BALLOTS.
Military voting absentee, §§163-245 to 163-257.
See ABSENTEE BALLOTS.
Generally.
See ELECTIONS.

BALL PARKS.
Instand sales of alcoholic beverages, §18B-1009.

BANG'S DISEASE, §§106-388 to 106-398.
See BRUCELLOSIS.

BANK BILLS.
Limitation of actions not affecting actions to enforce payment, §1-32.

BANK BRANCH ACT, §53-62.

BANK DEPOSITS AND COLLECTIONS, §§25-4-101 to 25-4-504.
Account.
Defined, §25-4-104, (a).
Afternoon.
Defined, §25-4-104, (a).
Agents.
Agency status of collecting banks, §25-4-201, (a).
Alteration of instruments.
Customer's duty to discover and report, §25-4-406.
Applicability of article, §25-4-102, (a).

BANK DEPOSITS AND COLLECTIONS —Cont'd
Attachment and garnishment.
When item subject to legal process, §25-4-303, (a).
Banking day.
Defined, §25-4-104, (a).
Branch or separate offices deemed separate bank, §25-4-106.
Burden of proof.
Stop payment order.
Burden of proof of loss, §25-4-403, (c).
Care.
Certain action constituting ordinary care, §25-4-103, (c).
Citation of article, §25-4-101.
Clearinghouse.
Defined, §25-4-104, (a).
Effect, §25-4-103, (b).
Collection by depositary and collecting banks.
Action.
When action seasonable, §25-4-202, (b).
Agency status.
Item indorsed "pay any bank," §25-4-201, (b).
Presumption and duration of agency status of collecting banks, §25-4-201, (a).
Provisional status of credits, §25-4-201, (a).
Bills of lading.
Warranties of collecting bank as to documents, §25-7-508.
Charge-back.
Right of charge-back, §25-4-212, (a) to (f).
Delayed, §25-4-108, (a), (b).
Direct return, §25-4-212, (a) to (f).
Documents of title.
Warranties of collecting bank as to documents, §25-7-508.
Duration of agency status of collecting banks, §25-4-201, (a).
Holder in due course.
When bank gives value for purposes of holder in due course, §25-4-209.
Indorsements.
Missing indorsement, §25-4-205.
Insolvency, §25-4-214, (a) to (d).
Instructions.
Effect of instructions, §25-4-203.
Liability for insolvency, neglect, etc., §25-4-202, (c).
Methods of sending and presenting, §25-4-204, (a), (b).
Payment.
Deposit of money.
Availability, §25-4-213, (f).
When deposit becomes final, §25-4-213, (e).
Final payment of item by payor bank, §25-4-213, (a).
Liability of bank, §25-4-213, (d).
Provisional debits and credits.
When provisional debits and credits become final, §25-4-213, (b), (c).
Suspends payment.
Defined, §25-4-104, (a).
When provisional debits and credits become final, §25-4-213, (b), (c).
Preference, §25-4-214, (a) to (d).
Presentment.
By notice of item not payable by, through or at bank, §25-4-210, (a).
Liability of secondary parties, §25-4-210, (b).
Method of sending and presenting, §25-4-204, (a), (b).

BANK DEPOSITS AND COLLECTIONS —Cont'd
Collection by depositary and collecting banks —Cont'd
Refund.
Right of refund, §25-4-212, (a) to (f).
Responsibility for collection or return, §25-4-202, (a).
Security interests.
Accompanying documents and proceeds, §25-4-208, (a).
Credit given, §25-4-208, (b).
Final settlement, §25-4-208, (c).
Sending and presenting.
By notice of item not payable by, through or at bank, §25-4-210, (a).
Liability of secondary parties, §25-4-210, (b).
Direct to payor bank, §25-4-204, (c).
Methods for sending and presenting, §25-4-204, (a), (b).
Settlement by bank.
Final settlement, §25-4-211, (d).
Medium of settlement, §25-4-211, (a).
Midnight deadline, §25-4-211, (c).
Time of settlement, §25-4-211, (a).
Status.
Agency status.
Presumption and duration of agency status of collecting banks, §25-4-201, (a).
Provisional status of credits, §25-4-201, (a).
Transfer between banks, §25-4-206.
Value.
When bank gives value for purposes of holder in due course, §25-4-209.
Warehouse receipts.
Warranties of collecting bank as to receipts, §25-7-508.
Warranties.
Documents of title.
Warranties of collecting bank as to receipts and bills, §25-7-508.
When action seasonable, §25-4-202, (b).
When provisional debits and credits become final, §25-4-213, (b), (c).
Liability of banks, §25-4-213, (d).
Withdrawal.
When certain credits become available for withdrawal, §25-4-213, (e).
Collection of documentary drafts.
Definition of documentary draft, §25-4-104, (a).
Dishonor.
Duty to notify customer of dishonor, §25-4-501.
Referee in case of need, §25-4-503.
Report of reasons for dishonor, §25-4-503.
Handling of documentary drafts, §25-4-501.
"On arrival" drafts.
Presentment, §25-4-502.
Presentment.
Duty to send for presentment, §25-4-501.
"On arrival" drafts, §25-4-502.
Responsibility of presenting bank for documents and goods, §25-4-503.
Privilege of presenting bank to deal with goods, §25-4-504, (a).
Security interest for expenses, §25-4-504, (b).
Referee, §25-4-503.
Responsibility of presenting bank for documents and goods, §25-4-503.
Security interest for expenses, §25-4-504, (b).
Conflict of laws.
Liability of bank, §25-4-102, (b).

BANK DEPOSITS AND COLLECTIONS —Cont'd
Contributory negligence.
Unauthorized signature or alteration, §25-4-406, (c), (d).
Customer.
Defined, §25-4-104, (a).
Damages.
Certain action constituting ordinary care, §25-4-103, (e).
Limitation by agreements, §25-4-103, (a).
Measure of damages, §25-4-103, (e).
Definitions.
Agreement for electronic presentment, §25-4-110, (a).
Banks generally, §25-4-105.
Collecting bank, §§25-4-105, 25-4-105.1.
Depositary bank, §25-4-105.
Generally, §25-4-104.
Index of definitions, §25-4-104.
Intermediary bank, §25-4-105.
Payable at bank, §25-4-105.1.
Payable through bank, §25-4-105.1.
Payor banks, §25-4-105.
Presenting bank, §25-4-105.
Remitting bank, §25-4-105.
Delays, §25-4-108, (a), (b).
Depositary and collecting banks.
Collection by. See within this heading, "Collection by depositary and collecting banks."
Defined, §25-4-105.
Documentary drafts.
Collection. See within this heading, "Collection of documentary drafts."
Defined, §25-4-104, (a).
Draft.
Defined, §25-4-104, (a).
Executions.
When item subject to legal process, §25-4-303, (a).
Federal reserve regulations.
Effect, §25-4-103, (b).
Forgery.
Customer's duty to discover and report, §25-4-406.
Intermediary bank.
Defined, §25-4-105.
Item.
Defined, §25-4-104, (a).
Limitation of actions, §25-4-111.
Negligence.
Unauthorized signature or alteration, §25-4-406, (c), (d).
Payment.
Properly payable.
Defined, §25-4-104, (a).
Suspends payment.
Defined, §25-4-104, (a).
Payor banks.
Alteration of instruments.
Customer's duty to discover and report unauthorized alteration, §25-4-406.
Attachment and garnishment.
When item subject to legal process, §25-4-303, (a).
Certifying items.
Order in which items may be certified, §25-4-303, (b).
Charging items.
Order in which items may be charged, §25-4-303, (b).
Clearinghouse.
Defined, §25-4-104, (a).

BANK DEPOSITS AND COLLECTIONS —Cont'd
Payor banks —Cont'd
Collection by depositary and collecting banks.
Final payment of item by payor bank, §25-4-213, (a).
Sending direct to payor bank, §25-4-204, (c).
Suspension of payments, §25-4-214, (a) to (d).
Customer relationship.
Customer's duty to discover and report unauthorized signature or alteration, §25-4-406.
Customer's right to stop payment, §25-4-403, (a).
Burden of proof of loss, §25-4-403, (c).
Oral stop payment order, §25-4-403, (b).
Death of customer, §25-4-405, (a), (b).
Controlling provisions, §25-4-405, (c).
Definition of customer, §25-4-104, (a).
Dishonor.
Liability to customer for wrongful dishonor, §25-4-402, (a).
Damages, §25-4-402, (b).
Time for determining account insufficiency, §25-4-402, (c).
Improper payment.
Bank's right to subrogation on improper payment, §25-4-407.
Incompetence of customer, §25-4-405, (a), (b).
Controlling provisions, §25-4-405, (c).
No obligation to pay check more than six months old, §25-4-404.
Stop payment order.
Bank's right to subrogation on improper payment, §25-4-407.
Customer's right to stop payment, §25-4-403, (a).
Oral order, §25-4-403, (b).
Subrogation.
Bank's right to subrogation on improper payment, §25-4-407.
When bank may charge customer's account, §25-4-401, (a) to (d).
Customer not liable, §25-4-401, (b).
Wrongful dishonor.
Bank's liability to customer, §25-4-402, (a).
Damages, §25-4-402, (b).
Death of customer, §25-4-405, (a), (b).
Controlling provisions, §25-4-405, (c).
Defined, §25-4-105.
Delays, §25-4-108, (a), (b).
Responsibility for late return of item, §25-4-302, (a).
Defenses, §25-4-302, (d).
Dishonor.
Liability to customer for wrongful dishonor, §25-4-402, (a).
Damages, §25-4-402, (b).
Time of dishonor, §25-4-301, (c).
Executions.
When items subject to legal process, §25-4-303, (a).
Forgery.
Customer's duty to discover and report, §25-4-406.
Incompetence of customer, §25-4-405, (a), (b).
Controlling provisions, §25-4-405, (c).
Late return of item.
Responsibility, §25-4-302, (a).
Defenses, §25-4-302, (b).
Legal process.
When items subject to legal process, §25-4-303, (a).

BANK DEPOSITS AND COLLECTIONS —Cont'd
Payor banks —Cont'd
Notice.
When items subject to notice, §25-4-303, (a).
Order in which items may be charged or certified, §25-4-303, (b).
Payment.
Definition of suspending payment, §25-4-104, (a).
Final payment, §25-4-213, (a).
Improper payment.
Bank's right to subrogation on improper payment, §25-4-407.
No obligation to pay check more than six months old, §25-4-404.
Recovery of payment by return of items, §25-4-301, (b).
Posting.
Deferred posting, §25-4-301, (a).
Recovery of payment by return of items, §25-4-301, (b).
Responsibility for late return of item, §25-4-302, (a).
Defenses, §25-4-302, (b).
Return of items.
Recovery of payment by return of items, §25-4-301, (b).
When item deemed return, §25-4-301, (d).
Setoff.
When items subject to setoff, §25-4-303, (a).
Signature.
Unauthorized signature.
Customer's duty to discover and report, §25-4-406.
Stopping payment.
Bank's right to subrogation on improper payment, §25-4-407.
Burden of proof of loss, §25-4-403, (c).
Customer's right, §25-4-403, (a).
Duration of order, §25-4-403, (b).
When items subject to stop-order, §25-4-303, (a).
Subrogation.
Right to subrogation on improper payment, §25-4-407.
Suspension of payments, §25-4-214, (a) to (d).
Defined, §25-4-104, (a).
Time of dishonor, §25-4-301, (c).
Unauthorized signature or alteration.
Customer's duty to discover and report, §25-4-406.
When bank may charge customer's account, §25-4-401, (a) to (d).
Customer not liable, §25-4-401, (b).
When items subject to notice, stop-order, legal process or setoff, §25-4-303, (a).
Wrongful dishonor.
Liability to customer, §25-4-402, (a).
Damages, §25-4-402, (b).
Posting.
Deferred posting, §25-4-301, (a).
Presenting banks.
Defined, §25-4-105.
Electronic presentment, §25-4-110, (a).
Presentment notice, §25-4-110, (b), (c).
Presumptions.
Agency status of collecting banks, §25-4-201, (a).
Provisional status of credits, §25-4-201, (a).
Procedure.
Specification or approval of, §25-4-103, (d).
Receipt of items.
Time of receipt, §25-4-107, (a), (b).

BANK DEPOSITS AND COLLECTIONS —Cont'd
Remitting bank.
Defined, §25-4-105.
Secured transactions.
Collecting bank.
Security interest of collecting bank in items, accompanying documents and proceeds, §25-4-208, (a).
Credit given, §25-4-208, (b).
Final settlement, §25-4-208, (c).
Collection of documentary drafts.
Privilege of presenting bank to deal with goods.
Security interest for expenses, §25-4-504, (b).
Setoffs.
When items subject to setoff, §25-4-303, (a).
Settle.
Defined, §25-4-104, (a).
Short title of article, §25-4-101.
Statute of limitations, §25-4-111.
Stopping payment.
Bank's right to subrogation on improper payment, §25-4-407.
Burden of proof of loss, §25-4-403, (c).
Customer's right, §25-4-403, (a).
Duration of order, §25-4-403, (b).
When items subject to stop-order, §25-4-303, (a).
Time.
Afternoon.
Defined, §25-4-104, (a).
Collection by depositary and collecting banks.
Finality of deposit of money, §25-4-213, (e).
Availability, §25-4-213, (f).
Finality of provisional debits and credits, §25-4-213, (b), (c).
Delays, §25-4-108, (a), (b).
Midnight deadline.
Defined, §25-4-104, (a).
Receipt of items, §25-4-107, (a), (b).
Time of dishonor, §25-4-301, (c).
When action seasonable, §25-4-202, (b).
Unauthorized signature or alteration.
Customer's duty to discover and report, §25-4-406.
Variation of article by agreement, §25-4-103, (a).
Warranties.
Encoding warranties, §25-4-207.2, (a).
Damages, §25-4-207.2, (c).
Presentment warranties, §25-4-207.1, (a).
Accrual of cause of action, §25-4-207.1, (f).
Breach of warranty claim, §25-4-207.1, (d).
Damages, §25-4-207.1, (b).
Defenses, §25-4-207.1, (c).
Disclaimers, §25-4-207.1, (e).
Retention warranties, §25-4-207.2, (b).
Damages, §25-4-207.2, (c).
Transfer warranties, §25-4-207, (a).
Accrual of cause of action, §25-4-207, (e).
Damages, §25-4-207, (c).
Disclaimers, §25-4-207, (d).
Dishonored items, §25-4-207, (b).
When action seasonable, §25-4-202, (b).
Withdrawal.
When certain credits become available for withdrawal, §25-4-213, (e).

BANK EXAMINERS, §§53-117 to 53-123.
Appointment, §53-117, (a).
Arrest.
Power to make arrest, §53-121.
Bribery.
Accepting bribes, §§14-233, 53-124.

BANK EXAMINERS —Cont'd
Commissioner of banks.
Appointment of bank examiners, §53-117, (a).
Confidentiality of information.
Disclosure, §53-125.
Examination of banks.
Duties generally, §53-118.
Refusal to be examined.
Taking possession of and liquidating banks, §53-118.
Reports which commissioner of banks is authorized to accept as part of examination, §53-117, (c), (d).
Rules and regulations as to, §53-117, (b).
Felonies.
Bribery.
Keeping or accepting bribe or gratuity, §53-124.
False reports, §53-124.
Loans.
Prohibited loans or gratuities, §53-126.
Misconduct in public office.
Bribes.
Accepting bribes, §14-233.
Reports.
Making of false report by bank examiners, §14-233.
Misdemeanors.
Disclosing confidential information, §53-125.
Oaths.
Power to administer, §53-120.
Reports, §53-123.
False reports, §§14-233, 53-124.
Rules and regulations.
Examination of banks, §53-117, (b).
State banking commission.
Rules and regulations.
Examination of banks, §53-117, (b).
Witnesses.
Power to summon, §53-120.

BANK HOLDING COMPANIES, §§53-225 to 53-232.
Acquisitions.
Commercial banks, §53-17.1, (e), (f).
Criteria, §55-227.1, (a).
No criteria in state where company has principal place of business, §55-227.1, (b).
Appeals.
Decisions of commissioner, §53-231.
Citation of article, §53-225, (a).
Commissioner.
Appeal of commissioner's decision, §53-231.
Rules and regulations, §53-230.
Criteria for certain bank holding company acquisitions, §53-227.1.
Definitions, §53-226.
Dividends.
Income tax.
Adjustment to expenses related to, §105-130.6A, (c), (e), (f), (h).
Fees.
Registration, §53-232.
Income tax.
Dividends.
Adjustment to expenses related to, §105-130.6A, (c), (e), (f), (h).
Reciprocal interstate banking, §§53-209 to 53-218.
See RECIPROCAL INTERSTATE BANKING.
Registration.
Fees, §53-232.
Forms, §53-227.

BANK HOLDING COMPANIES —Cont'd
Registration —Cont'd
Required, §53-227.
Rules and regulations.
Promulgation by commissioner, §53-230.
Scope of act, §53-225, (d).
Short title of article, §53-225, (a).
Violation of banking laws.
Cease and desist orders.
Issuance, §53-228.
Penalties, §53-228.

BANKING CARDS.
Credit cards.
See CREDIT CARDS.
Financial transaction card crimes, §§14-113.8 to 14-113.17.
See FINANCIAL TRANSACTION CARDS.

BANKING COMMISSION.
Administrative orders of commissioner.
Penalties for violations.
Imposition of civil money penalties, §53-107.2, (b).
Review by banking commission, §53-107.2, (a).
Appeals from final orders, §53-92, (d).
Appointment, §53-92, (b).
Bank examiners.
Rules and regulations.
Examination of banks, §53-117, (b).
Borrowing public.
Appointment as members, §53-92, (b).
Branch banks.
Review of actions of commissioner, §53-62, (f).
Chairman.
State treasurer, §53-92, (c).
Commissioner of banks.
Commission bound by requirements imposed on commissioner as to certain matters, §53-92.1.
Executive director, §53-92, (c).
Generally, §§53-92 to 53-116.
See BANKS COMMISSIONER.
Orders appealed to commission.
Appellate review panel, §53-92, (d).
Powers of commissioner.
Exercise of powers under supervision of banking commission, §53-95.
Review of exercise of powers, duties and functions, §53-92, (d).
Compensation, §53-92, (b).
Conflicts of interest.
Interest in financial institution, restriction, §53-92, (b), (c).
Executive director.
Commissioner of banks, §53-92, (c).
Incorporation.
Review of actions of commissioner, §53-4.
Interest in financial institution, restriction, §53-92, (b), (c).
International banking.
Rules and regulations, §53-232.15.
Legal assistance.
Attorney on staff of attorney general, §53-96.
Limited service facilities.
Review of actions of commissioner, §53-62, (f).
Meetings, §53-92, (c).
Number of members, §53-92, (b).
Powers.
Generally, §§53-92, 53-114.
Practical bankers.
Appointment as members, §53-92, (b).
Quorum, §53-92, (c).

BANKING COMMISSION —Cont'd
Rules and regulations, §53-115, (a).
Additional nature of rule-making authority, §53-115, (b).
Books, accounts and records of banks, §53-110, (a).
Classification and retention of records, §53-110, (b).
Industrial banks, §53-144.
International banking, §53-232.15.
State treasurer.
Chairman, §53-92, (c).
Ex officio member, §53-92, (b).
Supervision of common trust funds, §36A-92.

BANKING COMMISSIONER.
Commissioner of banks.
Generally, §§53-92 to 53-116.
See BANKS COMMISSIONER.

BANKRUPTCY AND INSOLVENCY.
Alcoholic beverage ownership acquired through.
Special one-time permit issued, §18B-1002, (a).
Assets.
Liens.
Wages for two months' lien on assets, §44-5.1.
Assignments for benefit of creditors.
Insolvent trustee, §23-5.
Attorney appearance for creditor in insolvency proceedings.
Unlawful for anyone except attorney, §§84-9, 84-10.
Attorneys specializing in bankruptcy law.
Certification standards, Bar Rules & Regs., D, §§.2201 to .2207.
Bail bondsmen and runners.
Notice of receivership, §58-71-81.
Banks.
Defined, §53-1.
Deposits.
Receiving deposits in insolvent banks, §53-132.
Dissolution and liquidation.
Receivers.
Statute relating to receivers applicable to insolvent banks, §53-22.
Records.
Destruction of records of liquidation insolvent banks, §53-24.
Trusts terminated on insolvency of trustee bank, §§53-25 to 53-32.
Fiduciaries.
Revocation of license to do business, §53-163.
Investigations.
General or special investigations of insolvent banks, §53-100.
Receivers.
Statute relating to receivers applicable to insolvent banks, §53-22.
Trust terminated on insolvency of trustee bank, §§53-25 to 53-32.
When commissioner of banks may take charge, §§53-19, 53-20, (a).
Congress.
Powers of congress, Const. U. S., art. I, §8.
Consolidated city-county act.
Authority of counties, cities, towns and villages to avail themselves of bankruptcy law, §23-48.
Constitution of the United States.
Powers of congress, Const. U. S., art. I, §8.
Corporations.
Receivers generally, §§1-507.1 to 1-507.11.
See CORPORATIONS.

BANKRUPTCY AND INSOLVENCY —Cont'd
Counties.
Authority to avail themselves of bankruptcy law, §23-48.
Credit unions.
Suspension and conservation, §54-109.92.
Discharge as affirmative defense, pleading, §1A-1, Rule 8, (c).
Discharge of insolvent prisoners.
Generally.
See DISCHARGE OF INSOLVENT PRISONERS.
Employment security.
Lack of work caused by employer.
Eligibility for benefits, §96-14.
Exempt property generally.
See EXEMPTION OF PROPERTY FROM CREDITOR CLAIMS.
Homestead exemptions.
See HOMESTEAD EXEMPTIONS.
Jeopardy.
Unlawful to solicit claims of creditors in proceedings, §23-46.
Misdemeanor, §23-47.
Judgments.
Cancellation of judgments discharged through bankruptcy proceedings, §1-245.
Leases, UCC.
Lessee's rights to goods on lessor's insolvency, §25-2A-522.
Liens.
Wages for two months.
Lien on employer's assets, §44-5.1.
Limited liability companies.
Cessation of membership, §57C-3-02.
Local improvement districts.
Authority to avail themselves of bankruptcy law, §23-48.
Manufactured homes.
Notice to board of bankruptcy of licensee, §143-143.11A, (d).
Misdemeanors.
Solicitation of claims of creditors in proceedings, §§23-46, 23-47.
Money transmitters.
Extraordinary reports required, §53-208.13, (a).
Permissible investments.
Held in trust during bankruptcy of licensee, §53-208.6, (b).
Surety bond.
Proceeds held in trust, §53-208.8, (e).
Mortgages and deeds of trust.
Sales under power of sale.
Procedure upon lifting of automatic bankruptcy stay, §45-21.22, (c).
Motor vehicle reinsurance facility members, §58-37-15.
Municipal corporations.
Authority to avail themselves of bankruptcy law, §23-48.
Partnerships.
Defined, §59-32.
Dissolution and winding up, §§59-61, 59-70.
Prisoners.
Generally.
See DISCHARGE OF INSOLVENT PRISONERS.
Probate and registration.
Recording bankruptcy records, §47-29.
Provider sponsored organizations.
Continuation of benefits, §131E-300.

BANKRUPTCY AND INSOLVENCY —Cont'd
Provider sponsored organizations —Cont'd
Covered services offered to beneficiaries, §131E-301, (a).
Allocations by division, §131E-301, (b), (c).
Hold harmless agreements, §131E-299, (a), (c).
Protection against insolvency.
Deposits, §131E-298, (a).
Failure to comply with net worth requirements.
Appropriate action by division, §131E-298, (b).
Plan, §131E-298, (c).
Special deposit, §131E-299, (b), (c).
Receivers generally, §§1-501 to 1-507.11.
See RECEIVERS.
Recording of bankruptcy records, §47-29.
Reinsurance.
Ceding insurer, §58-7-30.
Sale of goods, UCC.
Buyer's right to goods on seller's insolvency, §25-2-502.
Promise to revive debt of bankruptcy.
Statute of frauds, §22-4.
Sales and use tax.
Taxpayer going into bankruptcy.
Tax constitutes prior lien, §105-164.37.
School districts.
Authority to avail themselves of provisions of bankruptcy law, §23-48.
Solicitation.
Unlawful to solicit claims of creditors in proceedings, §23-46.
Misdemeanor, §23-47.
Statute of frauds.
Revival of debt of bankruptcy, §22-4.
Taxing districts.
Authority to avail themselves of bankruptcy law, §23-48.
Towns.
Authority to avail themselves of bankruptcy law, §23-48.
Trespass on land.
Insolvency of defendant.
When allegation of insolvency unnecessary, §1-486.
Villages.
Authority to avail themselves of bankruptcy law, §23-48.

BANKRUPTCY LAW SPECIALTY.
Certification standards, Bar Rules & Regs., D, §§.2201 to .2207.

BANKS, §§53-1 to 53-163.
Abandoned property.
Disposition of unclaimed property generally, §§116B-51 to 116B-80.
See UNCLAIMED PROPERTY.
Acceptances.
Definition of "trade acceptance," §53-55.
Generally, §53-56.
Loans.
When acceptance considered direct loan to drawer, §53-56.
Restrictions, §53-56.
Accounts and accounting.
False entries in banking accounts, §53-130.
Statement of account from bank to depositor.
Deemed final adjustment if not objected to within five years, §53-75.
Depositor not relieved from exercising diligence to errors, §53-76.
Rendering annually or on request, §53-75.

BANKS —Cont'd
Accounts and accounting —Cont'd
Worthless checks, §14-107.
Acknowledgments.
Stockholders, officers or directors, §47-93.
Acquisitions.
State associations.
Supervisory acquisitions, §53-17.1.
Administrative procedure.
Hearings.
Special provisions, §§150B-38 to 150B-42.
Agents.
Personal agency accounts.
Generally, §53-146.3.
Appraisal fees.
Loans secured by real property, §24-10, (h).
Assessments.
Expenses of operating office of commissioner of banks, §53-122.
Impairment of capital, §53-42.
Assets.
Appraisal of assets of doubtful value, §53-112.
Conservatorship, §§53-148 to 53-158.
Misrepresenting assets and liability of banks, §53-130.
Uncollectible assets.
Writing off, §53-91.1.
Automated teller machines or banking facilities, §53-62, (d1).
Bank bills.
Limitation of action not affecting actions to enforce payment, §1-32.
Bank examiners, §§53-117 to 53-123.
See BANK EXAMINERS.
Bank holding companies.
Generally, §§53-225 to 53-232.
See BANK HOLDING COMPANIES.
Reciprocal interstate banking act generally, §§53-209 to 53-218.
See RECIPROCAL INTERSTATE BANKING.
Banking commission.
See BANKING COMMISSION.
Bond issues.
Fiduciaries.
Deposit of securities in clearing corporation, §53-159.1.
Bonds, surety.
Dissolution and liquidation.
Commissioner of banks.
Taking possession, §53-20, (h).
Employees, §53-90.
Officers, §53-90.
Branch banks.
Authorized, §53-62, (b).
Capital requirements for establishment, §53-62, (c).
Commissioner of banks.
Approval of establishment, §53-62, (b).
Capital requirements, §53-62, (c).
Review of commissioner's actions by state banking commission, §53-62, (f).
Definition of "branch," §53-1.
Discontinuance, §53-62, (e).
Industrial banks.
Power to establish, §53-141.
Interstate banking, §§53-224.9 to 53-224.31.
See BRANCH BANKS.
Limited service facilities.
Conversion of limited service facility to branch, §53-62, (d).
Loan committee, §53-78.

BANKS —Cont'd
Branch banks —Cont'd
Officers, §53-62, (c).
Operation, §53-62, (c).
School thrift or savings plan.
Acceptance of deposits not construed as establishment or operation of branch, §53-43.6, (b).
State banking commission.
Review of actions of commissioner, §53-62, (f).
Bribery.
Directors or officers accepting fees or gifts.
Prohibited, §53-86.
Loans or gratuities to commissioner of banks or bank examiners.
Prohibited, §53-126.
Building and loan associations.
See SAVINGS AND LOAN ASSOCIATIONS.
Business paper.
Acceptance generally, §53-56.
Defined, §53-55.
Certificates of deposit.
Unlawful issuance, §53-63.
Certificates of incorporation, §§53-2 to 53-5.
Charters.
Approval, §53-17.1, (c).
Authorization, §53-17.1, (a).
Bank holding companies, §53-17.1, (e), (f).
Date of applicability of provisions, §53-17.1, (i).
Effect of charter on commercial bank, §53-17.1, (g).
Eligible state associations, §53-17.1, (b).
Governing provisions, §53-17.1, (d).
Prerequisites to commencement of business, §53-17.1, (h).
Checks.
Bad checks generally.
See BAD CHECKS.
False certification of check.
Penalty, §53-131.
Fees on remittances covering checks.
Prohibited, §53-70.
Payable in exchange, §53-71.
Exemptions.
Checks in payment of obligations due state and federal government, §53-73.
Remittances covering checks.
Fees not to be charged, §53-70.
Child support enforcement.
Location of absent parents.
Information to be provided, §110-139, (d).
Clearinghouse certificates.
State banking commissioner may require or permit, §53-114.
Clerks of court.
Superior court.
Deposit of money held by clerk, §7A-112.1.
Closed accounts.
Worthless checks, §14-107.
Closed banks.
Reopening effect upon certain contracts, §53-38.
Collection agencies.
Not included in definition of "collection agency," §58-70-15, (c).
Collections.
Bank deposits and collections generally, §§25-4-101 to 25-4-504.
See BANK DEPOSITS AND COLLECTIONS.
Commencement of business.
Payment of capital stock as prerequisite, §53-6.
Surplus fund, §53-39.
Statement as prerequisite, §53-7.

BANKS —Cont'd
Commencement of business —Cont'd
Time for, §53-5.
Transactions preliminary to, §53-9.
When authorized, §53-8.
Commercial loan commitments to be in writing, §22-5.
Commercial paper.
Acceptances.
Generally, §53-56.
Branch or separate offices deemed separate bank, §25-4-106.
Defined, §53-55.
Instructions.
Effect of instructions, §25-4-203.
Commissioner of banks, §§53-92 to 53-116.
See BANKS COMMISSIONER.
Confidential records.
Compliance review documents, §53-99.1, (b).
Regulatory rating prepared by bank commissioner, §53-99, (d).
Conservatorship, §§53-148 to 53-158.
Appointment of conservator, §53-148.
Creditors.
Special funds for paying creditors ratably, §53-151.
Deposits.
New deposits, §53-151.
Segregation of recent deposits not effective after bank turned back to officers, §53-153.
Rate of organization on agreement of depositors and stockholders, §53-152.
Segregation of new deposits, §53-151.
Not effective after bank turned back to officers, §53-153.
Special funds for paying depositors ratably, §53-151.
Dissolution and liquidation.
Naming of conservator not liquidation, §53-158.
Duties of conservator, §53-148.
Embezzlement and misapplication of funds.
Applicability of general provisions to conservator, §53-157.
Examination of bank, §53-149.
Expenses of conservator, §53-148.
Liquidation.
Naming of conservator not liquidation, §53-158.
Notice.
Turning bank back to officers, §53-153.
Powers of conservator, §53-148.
Reorganization on agreement of depositors and stockholders, §53-152.
Rights and liabilities of conservator.
Applicability of certain general provisions, §53-157.
Salary of conservator, §53-148.
Stock and stockholders.
Reorganization on agreement of depositors and stockholders, §53-152.
Termination of conservatorship, §53-150.
Turning bank back to officers.
Notice, §53-153.
Segregation of recent deposits not effective after, §53-153.
Consolidated banks.
Authority to consolidate, §53-12, (a).
Deemed one bank, §53-13.
Investigation by commission, §53-12, (a).
Notice, publication, §53-12, (a).
Procedure, §53-12, (a).

BANKS —Cont'd
Consolidated banks —Cont'd
Proceedings of directors and stockholders.
Certified copies, filing, §53-12, (a).
State banks or trust companies with national banks, §53-16.
Subsidiaries, §53-12, (b).
Substitution as executor or trustee under will, §31-19.
Consumer finance act, §§53-164 to 53-191.
See CONSUMER FINANCE ACT.
Conversions.
Bank to stock association, §54B-46.
Actions subject to review, §54B-46, (d).
Applicability of provisions, §54B-46, (a).
Approval by stockholders, §54B-46, (g).
Authority of resulting stock association, §54B-46, (h).
Board approval as prerequisite, §54B-46, (b).
Conditions, §54B-46, (e).
Effect of conversion, §54B-46, (i).
Plan of conversion, §54B-46, (c).
Submission of plan to stockholders, §54B-46, (f).
Savings association to state bank.
Application to convert, §53-17.2, (b).
Authority, §53-17.2, (a).
Conditions to be met for approval, §53-17.2, (e).
Effect, §53-17.2, (i).
Plan of conversion, §53-17.2, (c).
Approval by stockholders or members, §53-17.2, (g).
Submission to stockholders or members, §53-17.2, (f).
Resulting bank.
Authorization by commissioner, §53-17.2, (h).
Continuation of former institution, §53-17.2, (i).
Review of action taken by commissioner, §53-17.2, (d).
Rules, promulgation, §53-17.2, (d).
Supervising and monitoring process, §53-17.2, (f).
Transactions included in term conversion, §53-17.2, (a).
Cooperative associations generally, §§54-111 to 54-129.
See COOPERATIVE ASSOCIATIONS.
Copies.
Records, §§53-110, (b), 53-113.
Corporations.
International banking.
Applicability of business corporation act, §53-232.5.
Corporations law.
General corporation law to apply, §53-135.
Creation.
Incorporation, §§53-2 to 53-17.1.
Credit cards.
General provisions.
See CREDIT CARDS.
Credit unions, §§54-109.1 to 54-110.10.
See CREDIT UNIONS.
Customer-bank communications terminals.
Establishment off premises, §53-62, (d1).
Damages.
Directors.
Liability, §53-82.
Days of operation, §53-77.1A.
Deeds.
Attestation of conveyances by secretary or cashier, §47-42, (a).

BANKS —Cont'd
Deeds —Cont'd
Validation of deeds executed by nonresident bank, §47-108.16.
Validation of deeds executed prior to February 14, 1939, §47-42, (b).
Defamation.
Willfully and maliciously making derogatory reports, §53-128.
Definitions, §53-1.
Acceptances.
Trade acceptance, §53-55.
Bank holding companies, §53-226.
Capital, §53-62, (a).
Cash, §53-51, (b).
Commercial or business paper, §53-55.
Emergency suspension of business, §53-77.3, (a).
Federal reserve system, §53-61, (a).
Financial privacy, §53B-2.
Industrial banks, §53-136.
International banking, §53-232.2, (a).
Regional reciprocal banking, §53-210.
Reserve, §53-51, (a).
Stock and stockholders, §53-108.
Shareholder, §53-108.
Term "stock" to include preferred stock, §53-156.
Deposit insurance.
Securing through FDIC or successor corporation.
Powers in securing, §53-9.1, (b).
Required to engage in business, §53-9.1, (a).
Depositories.
Directors.
Designation by directors, §53-84.
Industrial banks.
Designation, §53-142.
Deposits.
Bank deposits and collections generally, §§25-4-101 to 25-4-504.
See BANK DEPOSITS AND COLLECTIONS.
Certificate of deposit.
Unlawful issuance, §53-63.
Clerks of superior courts.
Deposit of money held by clerk, §7A-112.1.
Collateral required as security for deposits.
Debentures issued by secretary of housing and urban development or federal housing administration, §53-45, (d).
Collection of taxes.
Bank deposits subject to attachment or garnishment, §105-242, (b).
Exempt property, §105-242, (e).
Conservatorship.
New deposits, §53-151.
Segregation of recent deposits not effective after bank turned back to officers, §53-153.
Rate of organization on agreement of depositors and stockholders, §53-152.
Segregation of new deposits, §53-151.
Not effective after bank turned back to officers, §53-153.
Special funds for paying depositors ratably, §53-151.
Demand deposits.
Defined, §53-1.
Deposits payable on demand, §53-65.
Dissolution and liquidation.
Commissioner taking possession.
Unlocated depositor, §53-20, (x).
Voluntary liquidation.
Unclaimed deposits, §53-18.

BANKS —Cont'd
Deposits —Cont'd
Failure to meet deposit demands.
Commissioner not to take over banks failing to meet, §53-116.
Insolvency.
Receiving deposits in insolvent banks, §53-132.
Insurance, §53-9.1.
Joint deposits, §§41-2.1, 53-146 to 53-146.3.
Minors.
Operating deposit account in name of minor, §53-43.5, (a).
Payable on death accounts, §§54-109.57, 54B-130.
Payable on demand, §53-65.
School thrift or savings plan, §53-43.6, (a).
Branch acceptance of deposits in furtherance of plan not construed as establishment, §53-43.6, (b).
Secured transactions.
Security interests in deposit accounts.
Perfection and priority, §§25-9-304, 25-9-327.
Rights of banks, §25-9-341.
Rights of banks, control agreements, §25-9-342.
Set-off or recoupment, §25-9-340.
Transfer of funds, §25-9-332, (b).
Securities for deposit of public funds.
Obligations of agencies supervised by farm credit administration, §53-43.1.
Obligations of agencies supervised by federal home loan bank board, §53-43.2.
Solicitation of deposits.
Prohibited.
Consumer finance act, §53-180, (j).
State and state officials.
Statements showing deposits of, §53-68.
Statement of account from bank to depositor.
Deemed final adjustment if not objected to within five years, §53-75.
Depositor not relieved from exercising diligence as to errors, §53-76.
Rendering annually or on request, §53-75.
Superior court clerks.
Deposit of money held by clerk, §7A-112.1.
Survivorship in bank deposit created by written agreement, §41-2.1.
Time deposits.
Defined, §53-1.
Unclaimed property generally, §§116B-51 to 116B-80.
See UNCLAIMED PROPERTY.
Directors.
Acceptance of fees and gifts prohibited, §53-86.
Acknowledgments taken by director, §47-93.
Appointment of advisory directors, §53-91.3, (b).
Depositories.
Designation by directors, §53-84.
Dissolution and liquidation.
Placing assets and business under control of commissioner.
Resolution of majority of directors, §53-20, (b).
Dividends.
Power to declare dividends, §53-87.
Election, §53-67.
Embezzlement or misapplication of funds, §53-129.
Examining committee, §53-83.
Executive committee, §53-78.
Minutes of meetings, §53-79.
Liability, §53-82.

BANKS —Cont'd
Directors —Cont'd
Limitation of action to recover penalty or forfeiture imposed, §1-33.
Meetings, §53-67.
Minutes, §53-79.
Number of directors, §53-67.
Additional directorships.
Stockholders may authorize, §53-67.
Oath of office, §53-81.
Penalty or forfeiture imposed by statute.
Limitation of actions, §1-33.
Powers, §53-67.
Probates before directors, §47-92.
Qualifications, §53-80.
References to, §53-91.3, (a).
Removal of directors.
Commissioner may require, §53-119.
Reports.
Changes in directors, §53-42.1, (d).
Stockholders.
Book of shareholders.
Directors to provide, §53-85.
Election of directors, §53-67.
Terms of office, §53-67.
Disposition of unclaimed property generally, §§116B-51 to 116B-80.
See UNCLAIMED PROPERTY.
Dissolution and liquidation, §§53-18 to 53-36.
Commissioner taking possession.
Accountants and other experts.
Employment, §53-20, (o).
Applicability of provisions, §53-20, (v).
Attorneys at law.
Employment of local attorneys, §53-20, (o).
Bond, surety, §53-20, (h).
Claims against bank.
Action on claims, §53-20, (k).
Lists of claims presented, §53-20, (l).
Notice and time for filing claims, §53-20, (j).
Powers and duties as to, §53-20, (g).
Rejection of claims, §53-20, (k).
Compensation of commissioner, §53-20, (t).
Deposits.
Funds collected, §53-20, (n).
Unlocated depositor, §53-20, (x).
Directors may act by resolution, §53-20, (b).
Dividends.
Declaration, §53-20, (m).
Unclaimed dividends held in trust, §53-20, (p).
Exclusive method of liquidation, §53-20, (u).
Failure to meet deposit demands.
Commissioner not to take over banks failing to meet, §53-116.
Injunction, §53-20, (f).
Inventory, §53-20, (i).
Liquidation by commissioner of all banks in receivership required, §53-20, (w).
Notices, §53-20, (c), (d).
Answer to notice, §53-20, (f).
Claims, §53-20, (j), (k).
Remedy by bank for seizure, §53-20, (f).
Reopening of closed banks, §§53-37, 53-38.
Report, §53-20, (q).
Annual report, §53-20, (s).
Report to secretary of state concerning certain matters relative to liquidation of closed banks, §53-36.
Resumption of business.
Permission, §53-20, (e).

BANKS —Cont'd
Dissolution and liquidation —Cont'd
Commissioner taking possession —Cont'd
Settlement.
Action by commissioner after full settlement, §53-20, (r).
When authorized, §§53-19, 53-20, (d).
Conservatorship.
Naming of conservator not liquidation, §53-158.
Deeds of trusts.
Validation.
Acts of officers of insolvent banks as trustees in deeds of trust, §53-33.
Foreclosures and executions of deeds by commissioner of banks, §53-35.
Sales by commissioner of banks under deeds of trust giving banks power of sale, §53-34.
Deposits.
Commissioner of banks.
Taking possession.
Unlocated depositor, §53-20, (x).
Voluntary liquidation.
Unclaimed deposits, §53-18.
Directors.
Placing assets and business under control of commissioner.
Resolution of majority of directors, §53-20, (b).
Dividends.
Commissioner taking possession.
Declaration of dividends, §53-20, (m).
Unclaimed dividends held in trust, §53-20, (p).
Voluntary liquidation.
Unclaimed dividends, §53-18.
Injunctions.
Taking possession by commissioner, §53-20, (f).
Insolvency.
Receivers.
Statute relating to receivers applicable to insolvent banks, §53-22.
Records.
Destruction of records of liquidated insolvent banks, §53-24.
Trust terminated on insolvency of trustee bank, §§53-25 to 53-32.
When commissioner of banks may take charge, §§53-19, 53-20, (a).
Notice.
Commissioner taking possession, §53-20, (c), (d).
Answer to notice, §53-20, (f).
Claims, §53-20, (j), (k).
Publication.
Report by commissioner to secretary of state concerning certain matters relative to liquidation of closed banks, §53-36.
Receivers.
Commissioner of banks.
Liquidation by commissioner of all banks in receivership required, §53-20, (w).
Statutes relating to receivers.
Applicability to insolvent banks, §53-22.
Records.
Destruction of records of liquidated insolvent banks, §53-24.
Disposition of books and records, §53-23.
Reopening of closed banks.
Conditions under which banks may reopen, §53-37.
Contracts.
Certain contracts not affected, §53-38.
When authorized, §53-37.

BANKS —Cont'd
Dissolution and liquidation —Cont'd
Stock and stockholders.
Sale of stock of defunct banks validated, §53-21.
Voluntary liquidation.
Vote of owners of two thirds of stock, §53-18.
Taking possession by commissioner of banks, §§53-19, 53-20.
Trust terminated on insolvency of trustee bank.
Additional remedy, §53-32.
Appeals.
Appointment of new trustee, §53-29.
Appointment of new trustee.
Additional remedy, §53-32.
Appeal from order, §53-29.
Applicability of petition and all instruments involved, §53-31.
Final order.
Registration, §53-30.
Hearing where objection made, §53-29.
No objection made, §53-28.
Petition, §§53-26, 53-27.
Registration of final order, §53-30.
Generally, §53-25.
Objection to new trustee.
Appointment where no objection made, §53-28.
Hearing where objection made, §53-29.
Petition for new trustee, §53-26.
Applicability to all instruments involved, §53-31.
Contents, §53-27.
Notice.
Publication, §§53-26, 53-27.
Voluntary liquidation, §53-18.
Dividends.
Declaration of dividends, §53-87.
Directors.
Power to declare dividends, §53-87.
Dissolution and liquidation.
Commissioner taking possession.
Declaration of dividends, §53-20, (m).
Voluntary liquidation.
Unclaimed dividends, §53-18.
Generally, §53-87.
Preferred stock, §53-155.
Requirements for declaration of dividends, §53-87.
Surplus.
Use of surplus, §53-88.
Drafts.
Negotiable instruments.
Generally, §§25-3-101 to 25-3-605.
See NEGOTIABLE INSTRUMENTS.
Embezzlement.
Conservators, §53-157.
Prohibited acts, §53-129.
Emergency suspension of business.
Authorization, §53-77.3, (b).
Construction and interpretation, §53-77.3, (d).
Definitions, §53-77.3, (a).
Legal holiday for certain purposes, §53-77.3, (c).
Employees.
Acceptance fees and gifts prohibited, §53-86.
Bonds, surety, §53-90.
Embezzlement or misapplication of funds, §53-129.
Overdraft liability, §53-89.
Removal of employees.
Commissioner may require, §53-119.
Share purchase and option plans, §53-43.3.

BANKS —Cont'd
Evidence.
Records.
Certified copies, §53-113.
Examiners.
Generally, §§53-117 to 53-123.
See BANK EXAMINERS.
Executors and administrators.
Acting as executor or administrator authorized, §53-159.
Stock and stockholders.
Executors and administrators not personally liable, §53-40.
Farm credit administration.
Investments in obligations of agencies supervised by, §53-44.1.
Obligations of agencies supervised by.
Securities for deposit of public funds, §53-43.1.
Federal deposit insurance corporation.
Deposit insurance, §53-9.1.
Federal home loan bank board.
Investment in obligations of agencies supervised by, §53-44.2.
Obligations of agencies supervised by.
Securities for deposit of public funds, §53-43.2.
Federal reserve system.
Definitions, §53-61, (a).
Membership in federal reserve bank, §53-61, (b).
Compliance with reserve requirements required, §53-61, (d).
Powers vested by federal act, §53-61, (c).
Supervision and examination of bank, §53-61, (e).
Reserve requirements.
Compliance, §53-61, (d).
Members of system, §53-50, (b).
Savings banks.
Authority to join federal reserve bank, §54C-177.
Fees.
Checks.
Remittances covering checks.
No fees to be charged, §53-70.
Directors.
Acceptance prohibited, §53-86.
Fiduciaries.
Licensed to do business, §53-160.
Officers.
Acceptance prohibited, §53-86.
Operating and maintaining office of commissioner of banks, assessment, §53-122, (a), (e), (f).
Out-of-state, state banks.
Branch banking in North Carolina.
Supervisory and examination fees, §53-224.24, (d).
Felonies.
Deposits.
Insolvent banks.
Receiving deposits, §53-132.
Embezzlement or misapplication of funds, §53-129.
False certification of check, §53-131.
False entries in banking accounts, §53-130.
Misrepresenting assets and liabilities of banks, §53-130.
Fiduciary capacity, acting in, §§53-159 to 53-163.
Bank holding companies.
Retaining stock.
Fiduciary authorized to retain, §36A-3, (b).
Clearing corporations.
Deposit of securities in, §53-159.1.

BANKS —Cont'd
Fiduciary capacity, acting in —Cont'd
Deposit in name of fiduciary.
Bank authorized to pay amount of deposit, §32-8.
Examination as to solvency, §53-161.
Licensed to do business.
Fee, §53-160.
Generally, §53-160.
Notification of clerk of superior court, §53-163.
Required, §53-160.
Revocation, §53-163.
Notification of clerk of superior court, §53-163.
Merger or consolidation.
Fiduciary powers and liabilities of banks or trust, §53-17.
Securities.
Deposit in clearing corporation, §53-159.1.
Solvency.
Certificate of solvency, §53-162.
Examination as to solvency, §53-161.
Stock and stockholders.
Fiduciaries not personally liable, §53-40.
Finance companies.
Consumer finance act, §§53-164 to 53-191.
See CONSUMER FINANCE ACT.
Financial records privacy, §§53B-1 to 53B-10.
See FINANCIAL RECORDS PRIVACY.
Financial transaction cards.
General provisions, §§14-113.8 to 14-113.17.
See FINANCIAL TRANSACTION CARDS.
Forgery.
Notes, checks and other securities, §14-119.
Connecting genuine parts, §14-125.
Governor.
Holidays.
Power to proclaim banking holidays, §53-77.
Guardians.
Acting as guardian authorized, §53-159.
Deposit of ward's money held by applicant for letters, §35A-1232, (b) to (d).
Stock and stockholders.
Personal liability of guardians, §53-40.
Holding companies.
Generally, §§53-225 to 53-232.
See BANK HOLDING COMPANIES.
Reciprocal interstate banking act generally, §§53-209 to 53-218.
See RECIPROCAL INTERSTATE BANKING.
Holidays.
Emergency suspension of business.
Legal holiday for certain purposes, §53-77.3, (c).
Governor empowered to proclaim banking holidays, §53-77.
Opening for transactions on holidays not required, §53-54.
Savings banks, §54C-175.
Hours of business, §53-77.1A.
Transactions not performed during banking hours, §53-54.
Income tax.
Refund anticipation loans, §§53-245 to 53-254.
See INCOME TAX.
Incompetency of customer.
Authority as payor or as collecting bank.
Controlling provisions, §25-4-405, (c).
Incorporation.
Certificate of incorporation.
Acknowledgment, §53-3.
Certification, §53-5.

BANKS —Cont'd
Incorporation —Cont'd
Certificate of incorporation —Cont'd
Contents, §53-2.
Evidentiary effect, §53-5.
Filing, §53-3.
Industrial banks, §53-137.
Issuance, §53-4.
Recordation, §53-5.
Refusal.
Grounds, §53-4.
Signing, §53-3.
Commencement of business.
Payment of capital stock as prerequisite, §53-6.
Surplus fund, §53-39.
Statement as prerequisite, §53-7.
Time for, §53-5.
Transactions preliminary to, §53-9.
When authorized, §53-8.
Examination of proposed bank, §53-4.
General corporation law to apply, §53-135.
How incorporated, §53-2.
Industrial banks, §53-137.
Certificate of incorporation.
Contents, §53-137.
Number of incorporators, §53-137.
Number of incorporators, §53-2.
Review of actions by commission, §53-4.
State banking commission.
Review of actions of commissioner, §53-4.
Industrial banks, §§53-136 to 53-145.
See INDUSTRIAL BANKS.
Injunctions.
Dissolution and liquidation.
Taking possession by commissioner, §53-20, (f).
Insolvency.
Defined, §53-1.
Deposits.
Receiving deposits in insolvent banks, §53-132.
Dissolution and liquidation.
Receivers.
Statute relating to receivers applicable to insolvent banks, §53-22.
Records.
Destruction of records of liquidated insolvent banks, §53-24.
Trust terminated on insolvency of trustee bank, §§53-25 to 53-32.
When commissioner of banks may take charge, §§53-19, 53-20, (a).
Fiduciaries.
Revocation of license to do business, §53-163.
Investigations.
General or special investigations of insolvent banks, §53-100.
Receivers.
Statute relating to receivers applicable to insolvent banks, §53-22.
Trust terminated on insolvency of trustee bank, §§53-25 to 53-32.
Insurance.
Deposit insurance, §53-9.1.
Insurance companies.
Disclosure of regulatory rating prepared by bank commissioner, §53-99, (d).
Insurance premium financing.
Exemption from license requirement, §58-35-10, (a).
International banking, §§53-232.1 to 53-232.17.
See INTERNATIONAL BANKING.

BANKS —Cont'd
Interstate banking.
Branch banks, §§53-224.9 to 53-224.31.
See BRANCH BANKS.
Investigations.
Insolvent banks.
General or special investigations, §53-100.
Official communications relating to, §53-109.
Investments.
Bonds guaranteed by United States, §53-44, (a).
Fiduciaries.
Bonds deemed cash in settlements by fiduciaries, §53-44, (c).
Security for loans and deposits, §53-44, (b).
Capital stock or other securities of financial institution, §53-47, (a).
Farm credit administration.
Obligations of agencies supervised by, §53-44.1.
Farm loan bonds, §53-60.
Federal home loan bank board.
Obligations of agencies supervised by, §53-44.2.
Federal housing administration, secretary of housing and urban development or veterans administrations, securities approved by.
Insured mortgages and obligations of national mortgage associations and federal home loan banks, §53-45, (a).
Financial institution's capital stock or other securities, §53-47, (a).
Industrial banks.
Limitations.
Applicability of general provisions, §53-143.
International banking.
Restrictions on international banking corporations, §53-232.11, (b).
Limitations on investments.
Securities, §53-46.
Suspension of limitation, §53-49.
Mutual funds, §53-46.1.
Powers generally, §53-43.
Protection of bank from loss.
Investment in corporation, partnership, firm or company, §53-47, (b).
Prudent person rule.
Directors and officers, §36A-2, (a).
Stock or assets of other business.
Completion of investment, time for, §53-47, (e).
Discrimination against nonbanks, prohibition, §53-47, (d).
Disposal of stock exceeding limitations, §53-47, (f).
Monitoring impact on bank, §53-47, (f).
Other financial institutions, §53-47, (a).
Without limitation, certain circumstance, §53-47, (b).
Subsidiaries.
Investing in without limitation, §53-47, (b).
Unimpaired capital fund in stock or assets of other businesses, §53-47, (c).
Investment securities.
Dealing in investment securities.
Engaging in business not authorized, §53-43.
Joint accounts.
Additions.
Effect, §53-146.1, (c).
Common law provisions, applicability, §53-146.1, (a1).
Establishment, §53-146.1, (a).
Estate tax provisions not repealed, §53-146.1, (b).
Section not deemed exclusive, §53-146.1, (a1).

BANKS —Cont'd
Joint accounts —Cont'd
Withdrawals.
Effect, §53-146.1, (c).
Joint deposits, §§41-2.1, 53-146 to 53-146.3.
Deposits in two names, §53-146.
Joint accounts.
Generally, §53-146.1.
Payable on death accounts, §§53-146.2, 54-109.57, 54B-130.
Personal agency accounts.
Generally, §53-146.3.
Right of survivorship, §41-2.1.
Larceny.
Choses in action, §14-75.
Lead-based paint presence on property or other health-related issues.
Providing financial assistance, §130A-131.9F.
Licenses.
Fiduciary business, §§53-160, 53-163.
International banking corporations, §§53-232.8, 53-232.9.
Taxation, §105-102.3.
Limitation of actions.
Actions against bank directors or stockholders, §1-33.
Actions to enforce payment of bank bills.
Limitations not applicable to, §1-32.
Limited service facilities.
Approval of establishment, §53-62, (b).
Authorized, §53-62, (b).
Branch banks.
Conversion of limited service facility to branch, §53-62, (d).
Commissioner of banks.
Approval of establishment, §53-62, (b).
Review of commissioner's actions by state banking commissioner, §53-62, (f).
Defined, §53-1.
Discontinuance of operation, §53-62, (d).
Notice.
Discontinuance of operation, §53-62, (d).
Operation, §53-62, (c).
Discontinuance, §53-62, (d).
State banking commission.
Review of actions of commissioner, §53-62, (f).
Liquidation. See within this heading, "Dissolution and liquidation."
Loan committee, §53-78.
Minutes of meetings, §53-79.
Loans.
Acceptances.
When acceptance considered direct loan to drawer, §53-56.
Bank examiners.
Prohibited loans or gratuities, §53-126.
Commercial loan commitments to be in writing, §22-5.
Commissioner of banks.
Prohibited loans or gratuities, §53-126.
Consumer finance act.
General provisions, §§53-164 to 53-191.
See CONSUMER FINANCE ACT.
Federal housing administration, secretary of housing and urban development or veterans administrations, securities approved by.
Credit insurance, eligibility for, §53-45, (c).
General laws not applicable, §53-45, (d).
Insured or guaranteed loans, §53-45, (b).
General powers, §53-43.

BANKS —Cont'd
Loans —Cont'd
Income tax.
Refund anticipation loans, §§53-245 to 53-254.
See INCOME TAX.
Industrial banks.
Limitations.
Applicability of general provisions, §53-143.
Powers generally, §53-141.
Limitations.
Suspension of limitations, §53-49.
Total loans and extension of credit to one person, §53-48, (a), (b).
Person defined, §53-48, (d).
Things not considered money borrow, §53-48, (c).
Officers.
Loans to executive officers, §53-91.2.
Refund anticipation loans, §§53-245 to 53-254.
See INCOME TAX.
Reports.
Loan secured by ten percent or more of voting stock, §53-42.1, (b).
Contents of report, §53-42.1, (b).
Stock of bank or parent holding company, secured by.
Purchase of or to carry stock, prohibition, §53-64, (b).
Unlawful, §53-64, (a).
Total loans and extension of credit to one person.
Limitations, §53-48.
Mentally ill.
Incompetency of customer.
Authority of payor or collecting bank, §25-4-405, (a), (b).
Merger and consolidation.
Authority to consolidate, §53-12, (a).
Conditions for interstate merger prior to June 1, 1997, §53-224.21.
Deemed one bank, §53-13.
Fiduciary powers and liabilities of banks and trust companies merging or transferring assets and liabilities, §53-17.
Interstate bank mergers.
North Carolina state banks.
Establishment of out-of-state branches by merger, §53-224.18.
Out-of-state banks.
Establishing of North Carolina state branches by merger, §53-224.19.
Purpose of law, §53-224.17.
Investigation by commission, §53-12, (a).
National banks.
Merger or consolidation of state banks or trust companies with, §53-16.
North Carolina state banks.
Powers of branches resulting from merger, §53-224.22, (b).
Notice and filing requirements, §53-224.20.
Notice, publication, §53-12, (a).
Out-of-state banks.
Powers of branches resulting from merger, §53-224.22, (a).
Procedure, §53-12, (a).
Proceedings of directors and stockholders.
Certified copies, filing, §53-12, (a).
Savings banks, §§54C-35 to 54C-40.
Subsidiaries, §53-12, (b).
Surviving bank.
Vesting of property and rights of several companies into surviving company, §53-13.

BANKS —Cont'd
Microfilm.
Records, §53-110, (b).
Minors.
Deposits.
Operating deposit account in name of minor, §53-43.5, (a).
Safe-deposit boxes.
Leasing or renting to minors, §53-43.5, (b), (c).
Misdemeanors.
Acceptance of fees or gifts by directors, officers or employees, §53-86.
Bank examiners.
Disclosing confidential information, §53-125.
Deposits.
Certificate of deposit.
Unlawful issuance, §53-63.
Derogatory reports.
Willfully and maliciously making, §53-128.
Loans or gratuities to commissioner of banks or bank examiners, §53-126.
Names.
Unlawful use of "bank," "banking" or "trust" incorporate name, §53-127, (d).
Offenses generally, §53-134.
Money transmitters, §§53-208.1 to 53-208.30.
See MONEY TRANSMITTERS.
Mortgage bankers and brokers, §§53-243.01 to 53-243.16.
See MORTGAGE BANKERS AND BROKERS.
Mortgages and deeds of trust.
Dissolution and liquidation.
Validation.
Acts of officers of insolvent banks as trustees in deeds of trust, §53-33.
Foreclosures and executions of deeds by commissioner of banks, §53-35.
Sales by commissioner of banks under mortgages and deeds of trust giving banks power of sale, §53-34.
Mortgages held by banks, §45-44.
Powers generally, §53-43.
Reverse mortgages, §§53-255 to 53-272.
See REVERSE MORTGAGES.
Mutual funds.
Investments, §53-46.1.
Names.
Certificate of incorporation to set forth, §53-2.
Industrial banks.
Certificate of incorporation to set forth, §53-137.
Corporate title, §53-138.
Misleading names.
Grounds for refusal for certificate of incorporation, §53-4.
Unlawful use of "banks," "banking," "banker" or "trust company" in nonbanking entity name, §53-127.
National banks.
Conversion, consolidation or merger of state banks with.
Authorized, §53-16, (a).
Effect, §53-16, (b), (e).
Stock and stockholders.
Approval of holders of two thirds of each class of voting stock, §53-16, (a).
Dissenting shareholders.
Rights, §53-16, (c).
Value as debt of resulting national bank, §53-16, (d).
Negotiable instruments.
Generally, §§25-3-101 to 25-3-605.
See NEGOTIABLE INSTRUMENTS.

BANKS —Cont'd
Newspapers.
Reports of banks to commissioner.
Publication of summary of report, §53-105.
Special report, §53-106.
Nonbanking affiliates.
Commissioner of banks.
Examination, §53-104.1.
Nonbanking entity using terms indicating bank or trust company business.
Unlawful use, §53-127.
Nonresidents.
Validation of deeds executed by nonresident banks, §47-108.16.
Notice.
Administrative orders of commissioner.
Hearings on, §53-107.1, (b).
Branch banks, interstate banking.
Branch banks resulting from interstate merger, §53-224.20.
Notice of subsequent merger or other change in control, §53-224.28.
Conservatorship.
Turning bank back to officers, §53-153.
Dissolution and liquidation.
Commissioner taking possession, §53-20, (c), (d).
Answer to notice, §53-20, (f).
Claims, §53-20, (j), (k).
Impairment of capital, §53-42.
Limited service facilities.
Discontinuance of operation, §53-62, (d).
Regional bank holding companies.
Acquisition by.
Publication by commissioner of notice of intent to acquire, §53-211, (d).
Reserves.
Deficiency in reserve fund, §53-50, (c).
Stock and stockholders.
Impairment of capital, §53-42.
Sale of stock if subscription unpaid, §53-41.
Oaths.
Directors.
Oath of office, §53-81.
Officers, §§53-78 to 53-91.3.
Acceptance of gifts or fees prohibited, §53-86.
Acknowledgments taken by officer, §47-93.
Bonds, surety, §53-90.
Directors. See within this heading, "Directors."
Embezzlement or misapplication of funds, §53-129.
Executive officers.
Loans to, §53-91.2.
Overdraft liability, §53-89.
Removal of officers.
Commissioner may require, §53-119.
Reports.
Changes in executive officers, §53-42.1, (d).
Stock and stockholders.
Share purchase and option plans, §53-43.3.
Off-premises customer-bank communications terminals, §53-62, (d1).
Out-of-state branch banks.
Generally, §§53-224.9 to 53-224.31.
See BRANCH BANKS.
Overdrafts.
Payment by officer or employee, §53-89.
Payable on death (POD) accounts, §§54-109.57, 54B-130.
Change to account, not affecting status, §53-146.2, (c).
Establishment, §53-146.2, (a).

BANKS —Cont'd
Payable on death (POD) accounts —Cont'd
Estate tax laws, effect, §53-146.2, (d).
Interest and incidents, §53-146.2, (a).
Section not deemed exclusive, §53-146.2, (a1).
Penalties, §§53-124 to 53-146.3.
Administrative orders of commissioner.
Civil money penalties, §§53-107.1, (d), 53-107.2, (b).
Advertising larger amount of capital stock than actually paid in, §53-133.
Deposits.
Insolvent bank receiving, §53-132.
Embezzlement or misapplication of funds, §53-129.
Failure of bank to make report to commissioner, §53-107.
False certification of check, §53-131.
False entries in banking accounts, §53-130.
Loans or gratuities to bank examiners or commissioner of banks, §53-126.
Misrepresenting assets and liabilities of banks, §53-130.
Names.
Unlawful use of "bank," "banking" or "trust" incorporate name, §53-127, (d).
Personal agency accounts.
Establishment, §53-146.3, (a), (c).
Effect, §53-146.3, (d).
Survivorship, §53-146.3, (b).
Point-of-sale terminals, §53-62, (d1).
Powers.
Generally, §53-43.
Practical banker.
Defined, §53-1.
Preferred stock, §§53-154 to 53-156.
Privacy of financial records.
Generally, §§53B-1 to 53B-10.
See FINANCIAL RECORDS PRIVACY.
Private banker.
Acting as private banker, §14-401.7.
Probate and registration.
Attestation of bank conveyances by secretary or cashier, §47-42, (a).
Nonresident banks.
Validation of certain deeds, §47-108.16.
Probate before stockholders or directors in banking corporations, §§47-10, 47-92.
Promissory notes.
Discount and negotiation.
Powers of banks generally, §53-43.
Prudent person rule.
Investments.
Directors and officers, §36A-2, (a).
Publication.
Conservatorship.
Notice of turning bank back to officers, §53-153.
Reports of banks to commissioner.
Summary of report, §53-105.
Special report, §53-106.
Public officers and employees.
Deposits.
Statements showing deposits of state officials, §53-68.
Real property.
Powers as to, §53-43.
Receivers.
Acting as receiver authorized, §53-159.
Dissolution and liquidation.
Commissioner of banks.
Liquidation by commissioner of all banks in receivership required, §53-20, (w).

BANKS —Cont'd
Receivers —Cont'd
Dissolution and liquidation —Cont'd
Statutes relating to receivers.
Applicability to insolvent banks, §53-22.
Insolvency.
Statute relating to receivers applicable to insolvent banks, §53-22.
Reciprocal interstate banking, §§53-209 to 53-218.
See RECIPROCAL INTERSTATE BANKING.
Records.
Copies, §53-110, (b).
Evidence.
Certified copies, §53-113.
Disposition, §53-110, (b).
Dissolution and liquidation.
Destruction of records of liquidated insolvent banks, §53-24.
Disposition of books and records, §53-23.
Evidence.
Certified copies, §53-113.
Reproduction, §53-110, (b).
Retention, §53-110, (b).
Refund anticipation loans, §§53-245 to 53-254.
See INCOME TAX.
Reopening of closed banks, §§53-37, 53-38.
Reorganization, §53-14.
Reports.
Banks to report to commissioner, §53-105.
Failure to make report, §53-107.
Publication of summary of report, §53-105.
Special reports, §53-106.
Directors.
Changes in directors, §53-42.1, (d).
Dissolution and liquidation.
Commissioner taking possession, §53-20, (q), (s).
Loans.
Loan secured by ten percent or more of voting stock, §53-42.1, (b).
Contents of report, §53-42.1, (b).
Officers.
Changes in executive officers, §53-42.1, (d).
Out-of-state banks.
Branch banking in North Carolina, §53-224.24.
Stock and stockholders.
Changes in control, §53-42.1, (a).
Reserves.
Deficiency in reserve fund.
Notice to commissioner of banks, §53-50, (c).
Defined, §53-51, (a).
Falling below legal requirement.
Powers and duties of commissioner of banks, §53-111.
Notice.
Deficiency in reserve fund, §53-50, (c).
Requirement of reserve fund, §53-50, (a), (b).
Reverse mortgages, §§53-255 to 53-272.
See REVERSE MORTGAGES.
Safe-deposit boxes.
Abandoned property.
Unpaid rentals.
Delivery of contents to state treasurer, §53-43.7, (c), (d).
Minors.
Leasing or renting to minors, §53-43.5, (b), (c).
Unpaid rentals.
Abandoned property.
Delivery of contents to state treasurer, §53-43.7, (c), (d).
Notice, §53-43.7, (c).

BANKS —Cont'd
Safe-deposit boxes —Cont'd
Unpaid rentals —Cont'd
Opening of box, §53-43.7, (a).
Destruction of items of little apparent value, §53-43.7, (b).
Notice, §53-43.7, (a).
Printing of provisions on contracts for rental of safe-deposit boxes, §53-43.7, (f).
Salaries.
Commissioner of banks, §53-96.
Savings and loan associations.
Conversion.
Bank to stock association, §54B-46.
General provisions, §§54B-1 to 54B-278.
See SAVINGS AND LOAN ASSOCIATIONS.
Investments.
Deposits in banks, §54B-185.
Merger of banks and associations, §54B-47.
Sale of loans to banks, §54B-161.
Savings banks, §§54C-1 to 54C-141.
See SAVINGS BANKS.
School thrift or savings plan.
Authorized, §53-43.6, (a).
Branches.
Acceptance of deposits in furtherance of plan not construed as establishment, §53-43.6, (b).
Secured transactions.
Rights of banks.
Control agreement.
Refusal to enter into or disclose existence of, §25-9-342.
Security interests in deposit accounts.
Control agreements.
Rights of banks with respect to agreements, §25-9-342.
Perfection and priority.
Law governing, §25-9-304.
Rules of priority, §25-9-327.
Rights and duties of banks, §25-9-341.
Set-off or recoupment, §25-9-340.
Transfer of funds from deposit account, §25-9-332, (b).
Transfer of accounts excluded from article, §25-9-104, (l).
Securities.
Asset-backed securities facilitation, §§53-425, 53-426.
Dealing in securities on commission.
Taxed as private banker, §14-401.7.
Security broker.
When deemed security broker, §14-401.7.
Small loan companies, §§53-164 to 53-191.
See CONSUMER FINANCE ACT.
State banking commission, §53-92, (b) to (d).
See BANKING COMMISSION.
State of North Carolina.
Checks payable in exchange.
Exemption of checks for obligations due state, §53-73.
Deposits.
Statements showing deposits of state and state officials, §53-68.
Stock and stockholders, §§53-39 to 53-42.1.
Acknowledgments by stockholders, §47-93.
Advertising larger amount of capital stock than actually paid in.
Penalty, §53-133.
Authorized but unissued stock, §53-10, (b).
Book of stockholders, §53-85.

BANKS —Cont'd
Stock and stockholders —Cont'd
Capital notes.
Issuance, §53-43.4.
Changes in control.
Report to commissioner, §53-42.1, (a).
Consolidation.
Approval of owners of two thirds of stock, §53-12, (a).
Debentures.
Issuance, §53-43.4.
Decrease of capital stock, §53-11.
Definitions.
Shareholder, §53-108.
Term "stock" to include preferred stock, §53-156.
Directors.
Book of shareholders.
Directors to provide, §53-85.
Election of directors, §53-67.
Qualifications of directors.
Stock ownership, §53-80.
Dissolution and liquidation.
Preferred stock, §53-155.
Sale of stock of defunct banks validated, §53-21.
Use of surplus, §53-88.
Voluntary liquidation.
Vote of owners of two thirds of stock, §§53-18, 53-87.
Employees.
Share purchase and option plans, §53-43.3.
Fiduciaries not personally liable, §53-40.
Forfeiture or penalty imposed.
Limitation of actions, §1-33.
Impairment of capital, §53-42.
Assessments, §53-42.
Increase of capital stock.
Authorized, §53-10, (a).
Unissued stock, §53-10, (b).
Industrial banks.
Amount of authorized capital stock, §53-139.
Certificate of incorporation to set forth, §53-137.
Sale of capital stock, §53-140.
Investments.
Limitations on investment in stock, §53-47.
Suspension of limitation, §53-49.
Limitation of action to recover penalty or forfeiture imposed, §1-33.
List of shareholders, §53-108.
Loans.
Secured by banks own stock or stock of holding company, §53-64.
Merger and consolidation.
Approval of owners of two thirds of stock, §53-12, (a).
National banks.
Conversion, consolidation or merger of state banks or trust companies with, §53-16.
Notice.
Impairment of capital, §53-42.
Sale of stock if subscription unpaid, §53-41.
Officers.
Share purchase and option plans, §53-43.3.
Payment of capital stock, §53-6.
Surplus fund, §53-39.
Penalties.
Advertising larger amount of capital stock than actually paid in, §53-133.
Preferred stock.
Approval by commissioner, §53-154.
Authorized, §53-154.

BANKS —Cont'd
Stock and stockholders —Cont'd
Preferred stock —Cont'd
Dividends, §53-155.
Issuance, §53-154.
Rights and liabilities of preferred stockholders, §53-155.
Term "stock" to include preferred stock, §53-156.
Probates before stockholders, §47-92.
Purchase of own shares or shares of parent holding company.
Prohibition, §53-64, (c).
Reorganization.
Approval of owners of two thirds of capital stock, §53-14.
Reports.
Changes in control, §53-42.1, (a).
Subscriptions.
Stock sold if subscription unpaid, §53-41.
Surplus.
Conversion of portion of surplus into capital stock, §53-88.
Stock broker.
Acting as stock broker, §14-401.7.
Supervisory acquisitions.
State associations, §53-17.1.
Surplus.
Defined, §53-1.
Dividends.
Use of surplus, §53-88.
Stock and stockholders.
Conversion of portion of surplus into capital stock, §53-88.
Use of surplus, §53-88.
Surplus fund.
Commencement of business.
Payment of capital stock as prerequisite, §53-39.
Survivorship.
Bank deposits created by written agreement, §41-2.1.
Joint deposits, §53-146.
Personal agency accounts, §53-146.3, (b).
Suspension of business.
Emergencies, §53-77.3.
Taxation.
Collection of taxes.
Bank deposits subject to attachment or garnishment, §105-242, (b).
Exempt property, §105-242, (e).
License taxes, §105-102.3.
Terms indicating business bank or trust company.
Unlawful use by nonbanking entity.
Definitions, §53-127, (a).
Restrictions on use, §53-127, (b).
Exceptions, §53-127, (c).
Penalty for violations, §53-127, (d).
Totten trust.
Payable on death accounts, §§54-109.57, 54B-130.
Trust companies and interstate trust business, §§53-301 to 53-415.
See TRUST COMPANIES.
Trusts and trustees.
Acting as trustee authorized, §53-159.
Bank account to pay special debts, §36A-61, (a).
Deposits.
In name of two or more trustees, §32-11.
Dissolution and liquidation.
Trust terminated on insolvency of trustee bank, §§53-25 to 53-32.

BANKS —Cont'd
Trusts and trustees —Cont'd
Funds held by corporation exercising fiduciary powers awaiting investment of distribution, §36A-63.
Investments in securities by banks or trust companies, §36A-66.1.
Payable on death accounts in financial institutions.
Governing statutes, §36A-120.
Separate records of securities required, §36A-71.
Stock and stockholders.
Trustees not personally liable, §53-40.
Uniform common trust fund act.
Establishment of common trust funds, §36A-90, (a).
State banking commission.
Supervision by commission, §36A-92.
When bank considered owned, controlled or affiliated, §36A-90.
Unclaimed property generally, §§116B-51 to 116B-80.
See UNCLAIMED PROPERTY.
Uncollectible assets.
Writing off, §53-91.1.
Uniform commercial code.
Bank deposits and collections, §§25-4-101 to 25-4-504.
See BANK DEPOSITS AND COLLECTIONS.
United States.
Checks payable in exchange.
Exemptions of checks in payment of obligations due federal government, §53-73.
Federal reserve system, §53-61.
Validation.
Dissolution and liquidation, §§53-33 to 53-35.
Transactions not performed during banking hours, §53-54.
Wills.
Probate of wills.
Substitution of consolidated bank as executor or trustee under will, §31-19.

BANKS COMMISSIONER, §§53-92 to 53-116.
Actions.
Nonliability to suit, §53-94.
Power to sue and defend, §53-94.
Administrative orders.
Civil money penalties for violations, §§53-107.1, (d), 53-107.2, (b).
Hearings.
Notice and opportunity for hearing, §53-107.1, (b).
Powers of commissioner, §53-107.1, (a), (c).
Review by banking commission, §53-107.2, (a).
Appeals.
Branch banking, interstate, §53-224.30.
Appointment, §53-92, (a).
Assessments for operating office, §53-122.
Assets.
Appraisal of assets of doubtful value, §53-112.
Attorneys at law.
Employment of counsel to prosecute offenses, §53-134.
Bank examiners.
Appointment of bank examiners, §53-117, (a).
Branch banks.
Approval of establishment, §53-62, (b).
Capital requirements, §53-62, (c).
Interstate banks.
Appeal of commissioner's decisions, §53-224.30.

BANKS COMMISSIONER —Cont'd
Branch banks —Cont'd
Interstate banks —Cont'd
Approval by commissioner, §53-224.15.
Interstate branching by merger, §53-224.18.
Cooperative agreements, §53-224.24, (c).
Enforcement of law, §53-224.25.
Examination of branches, §53-224.24, (a).
Rulemaking authority, §53-224.26.
Review of commissioner's actions by state banking commission, §53-62, (f).
Cease and desist orders.
Administrative orders generally, §§53-107.1, 53-107.2.
Clerical help, §53-101.
Confidentiality of records, §53-99, (b).
Conservatorship.
Appointment of conservator, §53-148.
Examination of bank, §53-149.
Termination of conservatorship, §53-150.
Consumer finance act generally, §§53-164 to 53-191.
See CONSUMER FINANCE ACT.
Deputy commissioner, §53-93.1, (b).
Appointment, §53-93.1, (b).
Chief, §53-93.1, (a).
Powers, §53-93.1, (b).
Directors of banks.
Removal of directors.
Commissioner may require, §53-119.
Dissolution and liquidation.
Deeds of trust.
Validation of certain acts of commissioner as to, §§53-34, 53-35.
Taking possession.
Accountants and other experts.
Employment, §53-20, (o).
Applicability of provisions, §53-20, (v).
Attorneys at law.
Employment of local attorneys, §53-20, (o).
Bond, surety, §53-20, (h).
Claims against bank.
Lists of claims presented, §53-20, (l).
Notice and time for filing claims, §53-20, (j).
Powers and duties as to, §53-20, (g).
Rejection of claims, §53-20, (k).
Compensation of commissioner, §53-20, (t).
Debts and claims.
Action on claims, §53-20, (k).
Lists of claims presented, §53-20, (l).
Notice and time for filing claims, §53-20, (j).
Powers and duties as to, §53-20, (g).
Rejection of claims, §53-20, (k).
Deposits.
Deposit of funds collected, §53-20, (n).
Unlocated depositor, §53-20, (x).
Directors may act by resolution, §53-20, (b).
Dividends.
Declaration, §53-20, (m).
Unclaimed dividends held in trust, §53-20, (p).
Exclusive method of liquidation, §53-20, (u).
Failure to meet deposit demands.
Commissioner not to take over banks failing to meet, §53-116.
Injunction, §53-20, (f).
Inventory, §53-20, (i).
Notices, §53-20, (c), (d).
Answer to notice, §53-20, (f).
Claims, §53-20, (j), (k).

BANKS COMMISSIONER —Cont'd
Dissolution and liquidation —Cont'd
Taking possession —Cont'd
Receivership.
Liquidation by commissioner of all banks in receivership required, §53-20, (w).
Remedy by bank for seizure, §53-20, (f).
Reopening of closed banks, §§53-37, 53-38.
Report, §53-20, (q).
Annual report, §53-20, (s).
Report to secretary of state concerning certain matters relative to liquidation of closed banks, §53-36.
Resumption of business.
Permission, §53-20, (e).
Settlement.
Action by commissioner after full settlement, §53-20, (r).
When authorized, §§53-19, 53-20, (a).
Voluntary liquidation.
Approval, §53-18.
Duties.
Generally, §§53-93, 53-104.
Employees of banks.
Removal of employees.
Commissioner may require, §53-119.
Executive director.
State banking commission, §53-92, (c).
Fees and assessments for operating office.
Banks, §53-122, (a).
Collection annually or in installments, §53-122, (f).
Consumer finance licensees, §53-122, (a).
Expenses not to exceed fees collected, §53-122, (d).
Processing applications or proceedings, §53-122, (b).
Reduction.
Estimated fees and assessments exceed operating costs, §53-122, (e).
Special assessments, §53-122, (a).
Incorporation.
Examination of proposed bank, §53-4.
Review of actions by commission, §53-4.
Industrial banks.
Supervision by, §53-144.
International banking.
Appeal of commissioner's decisions, §53-232.17.
Cease and desist orders, §53-232.16.
Definition of "commissioner," §53-232.2, (a).
International representative offices.
Review of operations, §53-232.14, (c).
Investigations.
Insolvent banks, §53-100.
Official communications relating to, §53-109.
Legal assistance, §53-96.
Limited service facilities.
Approval of establishment, §53-62, (b).
Review of commissioner's actions by state banking commissioner, §53-62, (f).
Loans.
Prohibited loans or gratuities, §53-126.
Money transmitters.
Generally, §§53-208.1 to 53-208.30.
See MONEY TRANSMITTERS.
Mortgage bankers and brokers.
Generally, §§53-243.01 to 53-243.16.
See MORTGAGE BANKERS AND BROKERS.
Nonbanking affiliates.
Examination, §53-104.1.
Officers of banks.
Removal of officers.
Commissioner may require, §53-119.
Offices, §53-102.

BANKS COMMISSIONER —Cont'd
Official communications, §53-109.
Orders.
Administrative orders, §§53-107.1, 53-107.2.
Powers.
Actions, §53-94.
Examination of nonbanking affiliate, §53-104.1.
Exercise under supervision of banking commission, §53-95.
Generally, §53-93.
Investigations of insolvent banks, §53-100.
Supervision of banks, §53-104.
Prosecution of offenses against banking laws, §53-134.
Raleigh.
Offices for commissioner, §53-102.
Records.
Confidentiality of certain records, §53-99, (b).
Generally, §53-99, (a).
Reports.
Banks to report to commissioner, §53-105.
Failure to make report.
Notice of violation, §53-107.
Penalty, §53-107.
Publication of summary of report, §53-105.
Special reports, §53-106.
Special reports, §53-106.
Reserves below legal requirement.
Powers and duties of commissioner, §53-111.
Reverse mortgages generally, §§53-255 to 53-272.
See REVERSE MORTGAGES.
Review of exercise of powers, duties and functions.
State banking commission, §53-92, (d).
Salary, §53-96.
Savings and loan associations.
Annual statements of associations, §54B-76.
Cease and desist orders, §54B-59.
Confidentiality of information, §54B-63.
Conflicts of interest, §54B-62.
Deputy commissioner.
Powers and duties, §54B-54, (a), (b).
Dividends.
Approval required, §54B-43.
Duties, §54B-52.
Examination and investigation, §§54B-56 to 54B-58.
Fees.
Supervision and examination fees, §54B-57, (a).
Holding companies.
Supervision by, §54B-262.
Incorporation applications.
Consideration, §54B-11.
Criteria for recommendation of approval, §54B-12.
Jurisdiction, §54B-67.
Liquidation of associations.
Involuntary liquidation, §54B-70.
Lists of stockholders.
Filing in office of commissioner, §54B-21.
Loans.
Collateral.
Test appraisal of collateral, §54B-61.
Granting to commissioner prohibited, §54B-62, (a).
Rule-making power of commissioner, §54B-155.
Mergers, §54B-246.
Mutual and stock associations.
Simultaneous conversion/mergers, §54B-37.1.

BANKS COMMISSIONER —Cont'd
Savings and loan associations —Cont'd
Oaths.
Power to administer, §54B-60, (a).
Powers generally, §54B-52.
Records.
Access to books and records of associations, §54B-60, (a).
Regional reciprocal savings and loan acquisition.
Appeals of decisions, §54B-48.7.
Removal of directors, officers and employees, §54B-69.
Service corporations, §54B-194.
Subpoena power, §54B-60, (a), (b).
Failure to comply with subpoena, §54B-60, (c).
Supervisory consolidations, §54B-44.
Supervisory control, §54B-68.
Supervisory conversions, §54B-44.
Supervisory mergers, §54B-44.
Withdrawable accounts.
Holding withdrawable accounts permitted, §54B-62, (c).
Witnesses.
Powers as to, §54B-60, (a).
Seal of office, §53-98.
Secretarial help, §53-101.
State banking commission.
Commission bound by requirements imposed on commissioner as to certain matters, §53-92.1.
Executive director, §53-92, (c).
Powers of commissioner.
Exercise of powers under supervision of banking commission, §53-95.
Review of exercise of powers, duties and functions, §53-92, (d).
Stock and stockholders.
Authorized but unissued stock.
Approval of commissioner, §53-10, (b).
Decrease of capital stock.
Approval by commissioner, §53-11.
Preferred stock.
Approval of issuance, §53-154.
Subpoenas.
Administrative orders.
Powers in connection with, §53-107.1, (c).
Investigations of insolvent banks, §53-100.
Supervision of banks, §53-104.
Taking possession, §§53-19, 53-20.
Tellers' windows.
Approval of establishment, §53-62, (b).
Term of office, §53-92, (a).
Trust companies and interstate trust business.
Generally, §§53-301 to 53-415.
See TRUST COMPANIES.
Vacancy, §53-92, (a).
Witness fees.
Employees of office used as witness, §53-122, (c).

BANK SERVICES CARDS.
Credit cards.
See CREDIT CARDS.
Financial transaction card crimes, §§14-113.8 to 14-113.17.
See FINANCIAL TRANSACTION CARDS.

BANNER ELK.
Room occupancy tax, uniform provision, §160A-215.

BANQUETS.
Utility commission members attending banquets sponsored by public utilities, §62-327.

BAPTISMAL CERTIFICATES.
Hearsay exceptions, §8C-1, Rule 803.

BAR ASSOCIATION.
Court commission.
Ex officio member, §7A-507.
State bar, §§84-15 to 84-38.
See ATTORNEYS AT LAW.

BARBERS, §§86A-1 to 86A-27.
Apprenticeship, §86A-24.
Examinations, §86A-24, (a).
Retaking.
Requirement, §86A-24, (c).
Supervision of apprentices.
Required, §86A-24, (b).
Board of barber examiners.
Appointment of members, §86A-4, (a), (b).
Bonds, surety.
Executive secretary, §86A-6.
Civil penalties.
Generally, §86A-27, (a) to (c).
Compensation of members, §86A-7, (a).
Composition, §86A-4, (a).
Costs.
Disciplinary costs, §86A-27, (d).
Duties, §86A-5, (a).
Employees, §86A-7, (b).
Executive secretary, §86A-6.
Duties, §86A-6.
Expenses of members, §86A-7, (a).
Inspections, §86A-15, (b).
Number of members, §86A-4, (a).
Office, §86A-6.
Officers, §86A-6.
Powers, §86A-5, (a).
Public-at-large member, §86A-4, (d).
Qualifications of members, §86A-4, (a).
Record of proceedings, §86A-21.
Removal of members, §86A-4, (c).
Reports.
Annual report to governor, §86A-7, (e).
Right of entry.
Inspections, §86A-15, (b).
Rules and regulations, §86A-5, (b).
Seal, §86A-6.
Terms of members, §86A-4, (a).
Bonds, surety.
Schools.
Guaranty bond required for approval, §86A-22.
Certificates of registration.
Criteria for issuance, §86A-10.
Data on registrants.
Board to keep, §86A-21.
Denial, §§86A-18, 86A-19.
Display, §86A-16.
Expiration, §86A-17, (a).
Restoration, §86A-17, (b).
Issuance, §86A-10.
Qualifications, §86A-3.
Reciprocity, §86A-12.
Effect, §86A-12, (c).
Qualifications of applicants, §86A-12, (a).
Waiver of certain qualifications, §86A-12, (b).
Renewal, §86A-17, (a), (c).
Required, §86A-1.
Suspension or revocation, §§86A-18, 86A-19.
Felony convictions, §15A-1331A.
Practicing during period of suspension or revocation.
Penalty, §86A-20.

BARBERS —Cont'd
Certificates of registration —Cont'd
Temporary permits.
Graduates of barber schools, §86A-11, (a).
Persons licensed in other state, §86A-11, (c), (d).
Persons whose licenses expired, §86A-11, (b).
Child support enforcement.
Forfeiture of licensing privilege, §50-13.12.
City privilege license tax.
Barbershops or beauty salons, §160A-211, (b).
Civil penalties, §86A-27, (a) to (c).
Cosmetic art.
Exemptions from barbering provisions, §86A-14.
Costs.
Disciplinary costs, §86A-27, (d).
Definitions.
Practice of barbering.
What constitutes, §86A-2.
Drunkenness.
Disqualifications for certificates or permits, §86A-18.
Equipment and instruments.
Requirements, §86A-15, (a).
Examinations.
Applications, §86A-8.
Apprenticeship, §86A-24, (a).
Retaking.
Requirement, §86A-24, (c).
Fees, §86A-25.
Payment required, §86A-8.
Frequency, §86A-9.
Instructors, §86A-23, (a).
Applications for, §86A-23, (b).
Qualifications for certificate of registration, §86A-3.
Times and places, §86A-9.
Exemptions from provisions, §86A-14.
Members of same family, §86A-26.
Family members.
Exemption from provisions, §86A-26.
Fees.
Examinations, §86A-25.
Payment required, §86A-8.
Generally, §86A-25.
Felony convictions.
Disqualification for certificate or permit, §86A-18.
Forfeiture of license, §15A-1331A.
Fraud.
Prohibited acts, §86A-20.
Injunctions.
Illegal practice, §86A-20.1.
Inspections, §86A-15, (b).
Instructors, §86A-23.
Certificates, §86A-23.
Examinations, §86A-23, (a).
Applications for, §86A-23, (b).
Military.
Exemptions from barbering provisions, §86A-14.
Misdemeanors.
Prohibited acts, §86A-20.
Municipal corporations.
Privilege license tax.
Barbershops or beauty salons, §160A-211, (b).
Nurses.
Exemptions from barbering provisions, §86A-14.
Practice of barbering.
What constitutes, §86A-2.
Prohibited acts, §86A-20.
Reciprocal licensing, §86A-12.
Effect of reciprocity, §86A-12, (c).

BARBERS —Cont'd
Reciprocal licensing —Cont'd
Qualifications of applicants, §86A-12, (a).
Waiver of certain qualifications, §86A-12, (b).
Reports.
Board of barber examiners.
Annual report to governor, §86A-7, (e).
Right of entry.
Board of barber examiners.
Inspections, §86A-15, (b).
Rules and regulations.
Sanitary rules and regulations, §86A-15, (a).
Schools, §86A-22.
Sanitary rules and regulations, §86A-15, (a).
Violations.
Disqualifications for certificates or permits, §86A-18.
Schools.
Approval by board, §86A-22.
Attendance at approved school.
Qualifications for certificate of registration, §86A-3.
Bonds, surety.
Guaranty bond required for approval, §86A-22.
Permits, §86A-13.
Applications, §86A-13.
Denial, §§86A-18, 86A-19.
Display, §86A-16.
Fees, §86A-25.
Renewal, §86A-13, (b).
Required, §86A-1.
Suspension or revocation, §§86A-18, 86A-19.
Requirements, §86A-22.
Rules and regulations, §86A-22.
Shops.
Permits, §86A-13.
Applications, §86A-13, (a).
Display, §86A-16.
Fees, §86A-25.
Renewal, §86A-13, (b).
Required, §86A-1.
Suspension or revocation, §§86A-18, 86A-19.
Violations of provisions.
Prohibited acts, §86A-20.

BARBITAL.
Schedule II controlled substance, §90-92, (a).

BARBITURATES.
Controlled substances generally, §§90-86 to 90-113.8.
See CONTROLLED SUBSTANCES.
Driver's license not to be issued to habitual user, §20-9, (c).

BARBITURIC ACID.
Food, drug and cosmetic act.
Drugs deemed misbranded, §106-134.

BAR EXAMINATION, Admission to Practice, §§.0901 to .1005.

BARGES.
Burning of barges, §14-63.

BARLEY.
Adulteration of grains.
Generally, §§106-621 to 106-628.
See GRAIN ADULTERATION.
Grain dealers.
Generally, §§106-601 to 106-615.
See GRAIN DEALERS.
Standard weight and measure, §81A-42.

BARNS.
Burning of barn, §14-62.

BARRELS.
Trucks of leaf tobacco in barrels.
Load to be securely fastened, §20-120.

BARROOMS.
ABC permits generally.
See ABC PERMITS.
Gaming.
Allowing gambling in houses of public entertainment, §14-293.
Minors.
Permitting minors to enter barrooms, §14-317.

BAR TO PROPERTY RIGHTS.
Killing decedent generally, §§31A-3 to 31A-15.
See SLAYER ACT.

BAR TO RIGHT TO RENOUNCE PROPERTY OR INTEREST, §31B-4, (a).

BASEBALL.
Athletic contests generally.
See ATHLETIC CONTESTS.
Junior or youth baseball.
Certification of birth dates furnished to veterans' organizations, §130A-120.

BASIC EDUCATION PROGRAM, §115C-81.

BASINWIDE WATER QUALITY MANAGEMENT PLANS, §143-215.8B.

BASKETBALL.
Athletic contests generally.
See ATHLETIC CONTESTS.

BASTARDY.
General provisions, §§49-1 to 49-17.
See ILLEGITIMACY.
Legitimation by subsequent marriage, §49-12.
Legitimation when mother marries, §49-12.1.

BATH HISTORICAL COMMISSION, §§143B-99 to 143B-102.
Appointments, §143B-102.
Compensation of members, §143B-102.
Creation, §143B-99.
Department of cultural resources.
Transfer of commission to department, §143B-51.
Duties, §143B-99.
Exemption from provisions, §143B-100.
Members, §143B-102.
Powers and duties, §143B-99.
Quorum, §143B-102.
Reports, §143B-101.
Selection of members, §143B-102.
Status, §143B-100.

BATHROOMS.
See RESTROOMS.

BATTERIES.
Lead-acid batteries, §§130A-309.70 to 130A-309.73.
Incineration, disposal by prohibited, §§130A-309.10, (f1), 130A-309.70, (a), (b).
Civil penalty for violation, §130-309.70, (c).
Inspection of retailers, §130A-309.73, (a).
Landfills, disposal in prohibited, §§130A-309.10, (f), 130A-309.70, (a), (b).
Civil penalty for violation, §130A-309.70, (c).
Persons not selling.
Not prohibited from collecting and recycling, §130A-309.73, (b).

BATTERIES —Cont'd
Lead-acid batteries —Cont'd
Retailers.
Acceptance for recycling required, §130A-309.71, (a).
Posting of notice, §130A-309.71, (b).
Civil penalty for failure to post, §130A-309.71, (c).
Inspection.
Authorized, §130A-309.73, (a).
Warning to person for noncompliance.
Issuance by department, §130A-309.73, (a).
Wholesalers.
Acceptance for recycling required, §130A-309.72, (a).
Civil penalties for violations, §130A-309.72, (b).

BATTERY.
See ASSAULT AND BATTERY.

BATTLE ACT.
Quieting title, §41-10.

BATTLE OF THE FORMS.
Sale of goods, UCC.
Additional terms in acceptance or confirmation, §25-2-207.

BATTLESHIP COMMISSION, §§143B-73 to 143B-74.3.

BAWDY HOUSES.
Abatement of nuisances against public morals, §§19-1 to 19-8.3.
See NUISANCES.
Bad character of inmates and frequenters.
Prima facie evidence, §14-188, (a).
Definitions.
Keeper, §14-188.
Keeper.
Defined, §14-188.
Misdemeanor offense, §14-188, (b).

BB GUNS.
County regulation, §153A-130.
Firearms generally.
See FIREARMS.
Municipal regulation, §160A-190.
Permitting young children to use dangerous firearms.
Whether BB gun deemed dangerous firearm, §14-316, (b).
Possessing or carrying on campus or other educational property, §14-269.2.
Weapons generally.
See WEAPONS.

BEACH ACCESS PROGRAM, §§113A-134.1 to 113A-134.3.
Acquisition, improvement and maintenance of system, §113A-134.3, (a).
Administration of program, §113A-134.2, (a).
Coordination of state and local programs, §113A-134.3, (b).
Creation of program, §113A-134.2, (a).
Definitions, §113A-134.2, (b).
Funding of program, §113A-134.3, (c).
Legislative findings, §113A-134.1, (a), (b).
Priorities, §113A-134.3.
Purposes, §§113A-134.1, (a), (b), 113A-134.2, (a).
Standards, §113A-134.3.

BEACH AREA ESSENTIAL PROPERTY INSURANCE, §§58-45-1 to 58-45-90.
Appeals, §58-45-50, (a).
Commissioner to superior court, §58-45-50.
Costs of recording and transcribing, §58-45-50, (b).

BEACH AREA ESSENTIAL PROPERTY INSURANCE —Cont'd
Appeals —Cont'd
Denial of policy, §58-45-35, (c).
Proposed order, submitting, §58-45-50, (b).
Statement of case and evidence.
Appellant and appellee to file, §58-45-50, (b).
Assessments.
Inability to pay, §58-45-85.
Commissioner.
Appeal from commissioner to superior court, §58-45-50.
Appeals from acts of association, §58-45-50.
Examination of affairs of association, §58-45-70.
Immunity of commissioner from liability, §58-45-60.
Plan of operation of association, §58-45-30, (a) to (f).
Action on, §58-45-30.
Rules and regulations, §58-45-75.
Definitions, §§58-45-5, 58-45-6.
Plan of operation defined, §§58-45-30, (f).
Homeowners' insurance policy.
Insurance underwriting association.
Issuance, §58-45-35, (b1).
Special surcharges, schedule, adoption, §58-45-45, (c).
Insolvent insurer.
Reassessments, §58-45-85.
Insurance underwriting association.
Agent.
Authority to temporarily bind coverage, §58-45-35, (d).
Insurance agent not deemed agent of association, §58-45-35, (d).
Appeals from acts of association, §58-45-50.
Applications to association for coverage, §58-45-35, (a).
Board of directors.
Temporary board of directors, §58-45-20.
Ceding of insurance to association by members, §58-45-40.
Composition, §58-45-10.
Creation, §58-45-10.
Examination by commissioner, §58-45-70.
Homeowners' insurance policy.
Issuance, §58-45-35, (b1).
Special surcharges, schedule, adoption, §58-45-45, (c).
Immunity from liability, §58-45-60.
Inspections.
Reports made available, §58-45-55.
Meetings.
Open meetings act, §58-45-90.
Membership, §58-45-10.
Ceding of insurance to association by members, §58-45-40.
Credit for voluntarily written policies.
Members to receive, §58-45-25, (b).
Participation by members, §58-45-25, (a).
Open meetings act, §58-45-90.
Participation by members, §58-45-25, (a).
Plan of operation.
Amendments, §58-45-30, (c).
Approval, §58-45-30, (b).
Defined, §58-45-30, (f).
Homeowners' insurance policy defined, §58-45-30, (d).
Manufacturing risks coverage, §58-45-30, (e).
Principal residence policies, §58-45-30, (d).

BEACH AREA ESSENTIAL PROPERTY INSURANCE —Cont'd
Insurance underwriting association —Cont'd
Plan of operation —Cont'd
Submission to commissioner, §§58-45-20, 58-45-30, (a).
Policies.
Issuance, §58-45-35, (b).
Temporary binders of insurance, §58-45-36.
Authority of agents, §58-45-35, (d).
Powers, §58-45-15.
Rates, rating plans, rate rules and forms.
Applicability to association, §58-45-45, (a).
Windstorm and hail insurance.
Filing of rates, rating plans and rating rules for approval, §58-45-45, (b).
Reports.
Annual report to commissioner, §58-45-65.
Inspections by or on behalf of association.
Reports to be made available, §58-45-55.
Reserves.
Unearned premiums, losses, and loss expenses.
Association shall make provisions for, §58-45-46.
"Take out" program.
Use, §58-45-25, (c).
Temporary binders of insurance, §58-45-36.
Authority of agents, §58-45-35, (d).
Unearned premium, loss, and loss expense reserves.
Association shall make provisions for, §58-45-46.
Wind, storm or hail insurance, §58-45-35, (e).
Legislative declarations, §58-45-1.
Market of last resort.
Legislative declaration, §58-45-1, (b).
Plan of operation of association, §58-45-30, (a) to (f).
Premium taxes.
Payment through association, §58-45-80.
Purpose of provisions, §58-45-1, (a).
Reinsurance.
Powers of association, §58-45-15.
Reports.
Association to file annual report with commissioner, §58-45-65.
Inspections by or on behalf of association.
Availability of reports, §58-45-55.
Rules and regulations.
Commissioner may promulgate, §58-45-75.

BEACH BINGO.
Applicability of bingo article to, §14-309.14.

BEACH EROSION CONTROL.
Counties.
Service districts, §§153A-300 to 153A-310.
Special assessments.
Authority to make, §153A-185.
Municipal corporations.
Assessments.
Authority to make assessments for beach erosion control, §160A-238.
Powers in connection with, §160A-491.
Property taxes.
Authorized purposes, §160A-209, (c).

BEACH EROSION PROTECTION WORKS.
Special assessments by counties, §§153A-185 to 153A-206.
See SPECIAL ASSESSMENTS BY COUNTIES.

BEACHES.
Access program, §§113A-134.1 to 113A-134.3.
Adverse possession of property subject to public trust rights.
No adverse possession, §1-45.1.
Coastal area management.
General provisions.
See COASTAL AREA MANAGEMENT.
Hurricane flood protection and beach erosion control project revolving fund, §143-215.62.
Income tax credit.
Donations of real property for public beach access or use, §105-151.12.
Littering, §14-399.
Management plan, §§113A-134.11, 113A-134.12.
Ocean beaches.
Public trust rights in, §77-20, (d), (e).
Offshore oil and gas activities, §§143-215.94AA to 143-215.94JJ.
See OFFSHORE OIL AND GAS ACTIVITIES.
Oil or hazardous substances discharges, §§143-215.83 to 143-215.94.
See OIL OR HAZARDOUS SUBSTANCES DISCHARGES.
Ordinances of beach towns on Atlantic Ocean, §§160A-176.1, 160A-176.2.
Property insurance.
Essential property insurance, §§58-45-1 to 58-45-90.
See BEACH AREA ESSENTIAL PROPERTY INSURANCE.
Public trust rights, no adverse possession, §1-45.1.
Sales and use tax for beach nourishment.
Local government tax, §§105-525 to 105-531.
Water quality of coastal fishing waters.
Monitoring, §§130A-233, 130A-233.1, (a), (b).

BEACH MANAGEMENT PLAN, §§113A-134.11, 113A-134.12.

BEACH MOUNTAIN.
Room occupancy tax.
Uniform provisions for municipalities authorized to levy, §160A-215.

BEACONS.
Displaying false lights on seashore, §14-282.
Interfering with, §76-58.
Rafts to exercise care in passing, §76-57.

BEAGLES.
Field trials for beagles.
Hunting license exemption, §113-276, (k).

BEAM INDICATORS.
Motor vehicle headlamp requirements, §20-131, (a).

BEANS.
Standard weight and measures, §81A-42.

BEARS.
Black bears.
Captivity licenses.
Applicability to, §113-272.5, (f).
Protection, §§19A-10 to 19A-14.
Dogs.
Injuring or killing bear on wildlife management areas, killing dogs, §67-14.1, (a).
Hunting and wildlife generally.
See HUNTING AND WILDLIFE.
Open seasons, §113-291.7.
Protection of black bears.
Enclosure.
Prohibited except as provided, §19A-10.
Enforcement of provisions, §19A-14.

BEARS —Cont'd
Protection of black bears —Cont'd
Exemptions from provisions, §19A-11.
Forfeiture of bear held on July 1, 1975, §19A-12.
Misdemeanors, §19A-13.
Peace officers.
Enforcement of provisions, §19A-14.
Penalties, §19A-13.
Purchase.
Prohibited except as provided, §19A-10.
Sale.
Prohibited except as provided, §19A-10.
Surrender of bear held on July 1, 1975, §19A-12.
Violations of provisions.
Penalty, §19A-13.
Zoos.
Exemption from provisions, §19A-11.
Regulation of taking, §113-291.7.
Sale of parts prohibited, §113-291.3, (b).
Unlawfully taking, possessing, transporting, etc., §113-294, (c1).

BEAUFORT AND MOREHEAD RAILROAD COMPANY.
Appropriations.
Continuing appropriation, §136-16.6, (c).

BEAUFORT COUNTY.
Ambulances.
Attachment or garnishment and lien for, §§44-51.4 to 44-51.8.
Obtaining ambulance services without intending to pay, §14-111.2.
Blank or master forms of mortgages, deeds of trust, etc.
Indexing and recording, inapplicability of provisions, §47-21.
Board of county commissioners.
Filling vacancies on board, §153A-27.1.
Coroner elected as nominee of political party.
Filling vacancy in office, §152-1.
Counties generally.
See COUNTIES.
County boards of education elected on partisan basis.
Vacancies in office, §115C-37.1.
Cropper or tenant refusing to perform terms of contract.
Forfeiture of right of possession to premises, §42-27.
Dog collars.
Unlawful removal of electronic dog collars, §14-401.17.
Game laws, local acts not repealed, §113-133.1, (e).
Grants in navigable waters, registration, §113-205, (a).
Housing authority commissioners.
Tenant as commissioner, exemption from provision of law allowing, §157-5.
Low-income housing tax credits.
Qualified building eligible for credit, §105-129.41, (c).
Maps in special proceedings, recording of photographic copies, §47-32.
Violation as misdemeanor, inapplicability of provisions, §47-32.2.
Northeastern North Carolina regional economic development commission, §158-8.2.
Open fires in high hazard counties.
Applicability of provisions, §113-60.23, (a).

BEAUFORT COUNTY —Cont'd
Open fires in high hazard counties —Cont'd
Ground clearing fires, special permit required, §113-60.23, (c).
Woodland fires, permits required, §113-60.23, (b).
Probate and registration orders before clerks of inferior courts validated, §47-59.
Registration of deeds.
Tax certification, no delinquent taxes due, §161-31, (b).
Sheriff.
Vacancy, performance of duties until vacancy filled, §162-5.1.
Special school tax, election to abolish.
Petition required, §115C-505.
Tax sales, notices by publication validated.
Inapplicability of provisions, §47-108.24.

BEAUTIFICATION DISTRICTS.
Alcoholic beverage elections, places eligible to hold, §18B-600, (g).

BEAUTY SALONS.
City privilege license taxes, §160A-211, (b).
Cosmetic art generally, §§88B-1 to 88B-29.
See COSMETIC ART.

BEAVER.
Beaver damage control advisory boards, §113-291.10.
Control of beaver damage on private and public lands.
Beaver damage control advisory board.
Development of statewide program to control beaver damage, §113-291.10, (b).
Established, §113-291.10, (a).
Implementation of program, advisory capacity to wildlife resources commission, §113-291.10, (b).
Membership, §113-291.10, (a).
Conflict with other provisions, section prevails, §113-291.10, (e).
Implementation of program developed by advisory board.
Wildlife resources commission to implement, §113-291.10, (c).
Notification to county of wish to participate.
Counties volunteering to participate, §113-291.10, (f).
Snares, use when trapping beaver pursuant to damage control program, §113-291.10, (d).
Depredation permits.
Landowner's property damaged or destroyed, §113-291.9, (f).
Use or sale of beaver parts taken under, §113-291.9, (b).
Hunting and wildlife.
General provisions.
See HUNTING AND WILDLIFE.
Landowner's property damaged or destroyed.
Taking without depredation permit, §113-291.9, (f).
Open season for taking with firearms, §113-291.9, (a).
Sales.
Beaver parts taken under depredation permits, §113-291.9, (b).
Snares, §113-291.9, (d).
Use when trapping pursuant to beaver damage control program, §113-291.10, (d).
Trapping.
Use of snares when trapping, §113-291.9, (d).
Trapping pursuant to beaver damage control program, §113-291.10, (d).

BEAVER —Cont'd
Trapping —Cont'd
Use of trap number 330 of connibear type, §§113-291.6, (d), 113-291.9, (c).
Unlawfully selling, possessing for sale or buying, §113-294, (f).

BED AND BREAKFAST ESTABLISHMENTS.
Defined, §130A-247.
Defrauding innkeeper, §14-110.
Sanitation of food and lodging establishments.
Exemption from provisions, §130A-250.
Sanitation of private homes offering accommodations as.
Adoption, §130A-248, (a2), (a3).

BEDDING.
Mattresses and bedding.
General provisions, §§130A-261 to 130A-273.
See MATTRESSES AND BEDDING.

BEEF.
Standard weight and measure, §81A-42.

BEER.
Alcoholic beverages.
Malt beverages.
See ALCOHOLIC BEVERAGES.
Definition of "malt beverage," §18B-101.
Excise tax, §§105-113.80 to 105-113.87.
Oceangoing ships, alcoholic beverages for use on, §18B-106.

BEER FRANCHISES, §§18B-1300 to 18B-1308.
Agreement.
Alteration of provisions of article by parties.
Prohibited, §18B-1308.
Existence of franchise agreement.
When deemed to exist, §18B-1302, (b).
Filing of distribution agreement, §18B-1303, (a).
Nature of franchise agreement, §18B-1302, (a).
Price maintenance.
Prohibited, §18B-1303, (c).
Provisions of article as part of all agreements, §18B-1308.
Termination.
Good cause.
Absence of good cause, §18B-1305, (d).
Notice of cause, §18B-1305, (b).
Termination for cause without advance notice, §18B-1305, (c).
What constitutes, §18B-1305, (a).
Notice of cause, §18B-1305, (b).
Termination for cause without advance notice, §18B-1305, (c).
Wrongful termination.
Damages, §18B-1306, (b).
Injunctive relief, §18B-1306, (a).
Coercion.
Prohibited acts by suppliers, §18B-1304.
Damages.
Transfer of wholesaler's business.
Disapproval or prevention of transfer, §18B-1307, (c).
Wrongful termination of agreement, §18B-1306, (b).
Definitions, §18B-1301.
Discrimination.
Prohibited, §18B-1303, (b).
Injunctions.
Wrongful termination of agreement, §18B-1306, (a).
Legislative declaration.
Purpose of provisions, §18B-1300.
Purpose of provisions, §18B-1300.

BEER FRANCHISES —Cont'd
Suppliers.
Defined, §18B-1301.
Prohibited acts, §18B-1304.
Transfer of wholesaler's business.
Approval of certain transfers, §18B-1307, (b), (c).
Damages for disapproval or prevention of transfer, §18B-1307, (c).
Death.
Right of transfer to designated family member upon, §18B-1307, (a).
Wholesalers.
Defined, §18B-1301.
Discrimination.
Prohibited, §18B-1303, (b).
Remedies for wrongful termination of agreement, §18B-1306.
Transfer of wholesaler's business.
Approval of certain transfers, §18B-1307, (b), (c).
Damages for disapproval or prevention of transfer, §18B-1307, (c).
Death.
Right of transfer to designated family member upon, §18B-1307, (a).

BEES AND HONEY, §§106-634 to 106-644.
Administration of article.
Designation of persons to administer, §106-643.
Apiary defined, §106-635.
Bees defined, §106-635.
Beeyard defined, §106-635.
Board.
Authority to accept donations, gifts or grants, §106-637.
Contracts.
Authority to enter into contracts, §106-637.
Defined, §106-635.
Regulations.
Authority of board to adopt, §106-638.
Boll weevil eradication.
Authority to regulate honeybee colonies in elimination zones and other areas, §106-65.76.
Brazilian or African bee, §106-635.
Colonies.
Defined, §106-635.
Minimum standards for colony strength, §106-638.
Comb defined, §106-635.
Commercial beekeeper, §106-635.
Commissioner.
Defined, §106-635.
Diseases.
Authority of commissioner to protect industry from diseases and disorders, §106-640.
Giving false information to commissioner, §106-641.
Duties, §106-636.
Emergency action by commissioner, §106-642.
Powers, §106-635.
Contracts.
Authority of board to enter into contracts, §106-637.
Declaration of policy, §106-634.
Definitions, §106-625.
Diseases.
Authority of commissioner to protect industry from diseases, §106-640.
Giving false information to commissioner, §106-641.
Defined, §106-635.

BEES AND HONEY —Cont'd
Diseases —Cont'd
Minimum standards for disease tolerance levels, §106-638.
Moveable frame hives, §106-641.
Regulations for control and prevention, §106-639.
Disorders.
Authority of commissioner to protect industry from diseases and disorders, §106-640.
Defined, §106-635.
Moveable frame hives, §106-641.
Regulations for control and prevention, §106-639.
Donations.
Authority of board to accept, §106-637.
Duties of commissioner, §106-636.
Emergencies.
Action by commissioner, §106-642.
Exposed defined, §106-635.
General assembly.
Legislative declaration, §106-634.
Gifts.
Authority of board to accept, §106-637.
Grants.
Authority of board to accept, §106-637.
Health certificates.
Defined, §106-635.
Issuance, §106-641.
Hives.
Defined, §106-635.
Moveable frame hives.
Inspection for disease or disorder, §106-641.
Honeybees defined, §106-635.
Honey defined, §106-635.
Honeyflow defined, §106-635.
Honey plants defined, §106-635.
Infested or infected defined, §106-635.
Inspections.
Conduct of inspections and other activities, §106-643.
Moveable frame hives.
Inspection for disease or disorder, §106-641.
Penalties for preventing inspection, §106-644, (a), (b).
Legislative declarations, §106-634.
Marketing associations, §§54-129 to 54-166.
See MARKETING ASSOCIATIONS.
Moveable frame hives.
Defined, §106-635.
Diseases, §106-641.
Disorders, §106-641.
Inspection for disease or disorder, §106-641.
Penalties.
Violations of provisions, §106-644, (a), (b).
Permits.
Defined, §106-635.
Moving permits.
Issuance, §106-641.
Selling bees, §106-639.1.
Policy declaration, §106-634.
Registration.
Adoption of regulations for registration of honeybees, §106-641.
Rules and regulations.
Authority of board to adopt regulations, §106-638.
Control and prevention of diseases and disorders, §106-639.
Sales.
Permit to sell bees, §106-639.1.
Symptomless carrier defined, §106-635.
Violations of article.
Penalties, §106-644, (a), (b).

BEETS.
Standard weight and measure, §81A-42.

BEGGING.
Counties.
Regulation of begging, §153A-126.
Municipal corporations.
Regulation of begging, §160A-179.
Obtaining money by false representation of physical defect, §14-113.

BELOW-COST SALES.
Motor fuels, §75-82.

BENCH TRIAL.
Trial of issues by court, §1A-1, Rule 39, (b).

BENEVOLENT AND PROTECTIVE ORDER OF ELKS.
Property taxes.
Exclusion, §105-275.

BENEVOLENT ASSOCIATIONS.
Property taxes.
Exemption of real and personal property, §105-278.7.

BENNETT PLACE MEMORIAL COMMISSION.
Department of cultural resources.
Transfer of commission to department, §143B-51.

BENZINE.
Household cleaners labeling, §§66-85 to 66-88.

BEQUESTS.
Agriculture.
Hall of fame.
Acceptance of bequests, §106-568.17.
Libraries.
Acceptance of gifts, bequests and endowments.
Powers and duties of department of cultural resources, §125-2.
Wills generally.
See WILLS.

BERRIES.
Promotion of use and sale of agricultural products.
Generally, §§106-550 to 106-568.
See AGRICULTURAL PRODUCTS PROMOTION.
State berries, §145-18, (b), (c).

BERTIE COUNTY.
Condemnation or acquisition of land by local government unit outside county.
Consent of board of commissioners necessary, §153A-15.
Cropper or tenant refusing to perform terms of contract.
Forfeiture of right of possession to premises, §42-27.
Game laws, local acts not repealed, §113-133.1, (e).
Grants in navigable waters, registration, §113-205, (a).
Housing authority commissioners.
Tenant as commissioner, exemption from provision of law allowing, §157-5.
Low-income housing tax credits.
Qualified building eligible for credit, §105-129.41, (c).
Multi-county water conservation and infrastructure district.
Generally, §158-15.1.

BERTIE COUNTY —Cont'd
Northeastern North Carolina regional economic development commission, §158-8.2.
Officers compensated from fees.
Statement to be rendered, §128-13.
Probate and registration orders before clerks or inferior courts validated, §47-59.
Wastewater systems.
Innovative septic tank systems.
Ordinance billing fee as property tax, §130A-343.1, (c).

BEST EVIDENCE.
Contents of writings, recordings and photographs, §8C-1, Rules 1001 to 1008.
Admission of party, §8C-1, Rule 1007.
Collateral matters, §8C-1, Rule 1004.
Definitions, §8C-1, Rule 1001.
Duplicates, admissibility, §8C-1, Rule 1003.
Functions of court and jury, §8C-1, Rule 1008.
Lost or destroyed originals, §8C-1, Rule 1004.
Not obtainable original, §8C-1, Rule 1004.
Opponent possesses original, §8C-1, Rule 1004.
Original, requirement, §8C-1, Rule 1002.
Public records, §8C-1, Rule 1005.
Summaries, §8C-1, Rule 1006.
Copies of official records, authentication, §1A-1, Rule 44, (a).
Copy of destroyed record as evidence, §98-1.
Medical records, subpoena commanding custodian to produce.
Certified copies in lieu of appearance, §1A-1, Rule 45, (c).
Proof of official record.
Authentication of copy, §1A-1, Rule 44, (a).
Lack of record, proof of, §1A-1, Rule 44, (b).
Public records, subpoena commanding custodian to produce.
Certified copies in lieu of appearance, §1A-1, Rule 45, (c).

BEST INTEREST OF CHILD.
Child custody, §50-13.2, (a).
Parent presumed to know, §35A-1225, (a).

BETTERMENTS, §§1-340 to 1-351.
Assessment of damages.
Annual value of land and waste charged against defendant, §1-341.
Execution suspended for, §1-340.
Value of improvements estimated, §1-342.
Value of premises without improvements.
Estimate, §1-346.
Disabilities.
Procedure where plaintiff is under disability, §1-349.
Election by plaintiff that defendant take premises, §1-347.
Eviction of defendant.
Recovery from plaintiff, §1-350.
Executions.
Suspension of execution for assessment, §1-340.
Judgments, §1-344.
Jury.
Verdict, §1-344.
Liens, §1-344.
Life estates.
Life tenant recovers from remainderman, §1-345.
Mentally ill.
Procedure where plaintiff is under disability, §1-349.

BETTERMENTS —Cont'd
Minors.
Procedure where plaintiff is under disability, §1-349.
Mortgages and deeds of trust.
Provisions not applicable to suit by mortgagee, §1-351.
Payments to court, §1-348.
Petitions.
Claimant, §1-340.
Property taxes.
Increase or decrease of real property appraised value in years a reappraisal not made.
Reasons for making increase or decrease, §105-287, (b).
Rents.
Improvements to balance rents, §1-343.
Sales.
Default.
Land sold on default, §1-348.

BETTING.
Elections.
Bet or wager on election, §163-274.
Futures contracts, §§16-3 to 16-6.
Gaming.
See GAMING.
Lotteries, §§14-291 to 14-291.2.
Racing vehicles on streets and highways, §20-141.3, (c).

BEVERAGE CONTAINER DEPOSITS.
Sales and use tax.
Exemption, §105-164.13.

BEVERAGES.
Alcoholic beverages.
See ALCOHOLIC BEVERAGES.
High-calcium foods and beverages.
Local boards of education.
Preference in purchasing contracts, §115C-264.1, (a), (b).
Implied warranty of merchantability.
Sale of goods, UCC, §25-2-314.
Juice and bottled water.
Contracts for sale of.
Educational institutions to competitively bid, §143-64.
Milk and milk products.
Production, distribution, inspection, grading and testing generally, §§106-267 to 106-268.1.
See MILK AND MILK PRODUCTS.
Milk distributors and processors.
Generally.
See MILK DISTRIBUTORS AND PROCESSORS.
Warranties.
Implied warranty of merchantability, §25-2-314.

BEYOND REASONABLE DOUBT.
Delinquent and undisciplined juvenile actions.
Quantum of proof where petition alleges delinquency, §7B-2409.

BFP.
See BONA FIDE PURCHASERS.

BIBLES.
Administration of oath upon Holy Scriptures, §11-2.
Hearsay exception, family records, §8C-1, Rule 803.
Sales and use tax.
Exemption, §105-164.13.

BIBLE SCHOOLS.
Child care facilities.
Schools conducted during vacation periods not included in term, §110-86.

BICYCLE AND BIKEWAY ACT, §§136-71.6 to 136-71.13.
Citation of article, §136-71.6.
Committee.
Appointment of bicycle committee members, §136-71.13, (a).
Composition of bicycle committee, §136-71.13, (a).
Coordination of bicycle activities, §136-71.13, (d).
Creation of North Carolina bicycle committee, §136-71.13, (a).
Duties of bicycle committee, §136-71.13, (c).
Expenses of bicycle committee, §136-71.13, (a).
Meetings of bicycle committee, §136-71.13, (b).
Quorum, §136-71.13, (b).
Terms of bicycle committee members, §136-71.13, (a).
Coordination of program, §136-71.9.
Bicycle committee, §136-71.13, (d).
Definitions, §136-71.7.
Designation of bikeways, §136-71.11.
Development of program, §136-71.
Duties, §136-71.10.
Bicycle committee, §136-71.13, (c).
Functions of department.
Duties generally, §136-71.10.
Funds, §136-71.12.
General assembly.
Authorization of funds, §136-71.12.
How article cited, §136-71.6.
Legislative findings, §136-71.8.
Program development, §136-71.9.
Public roads.
Designation of bikeways, §136-71.11.

BICYCLE RACING, §20-171.2.

BICYCLES.
Alleys, building entrances, private roads or driveways.
Driver emerging from or entering to yield to person on bicycle, §20-173, (c).
Amusement device safety.
Amusement device defined as not including, §95-111.3, (a).
Bicycle and bikeway act, §§136-71.6 to 136-71.13.
See BICYCLE AND BIKEWAY ACT.
Child bicycle safety act, §§20-171.6 to 20-171.9.
Article known and cited as, §20-171.6.
Civil fine assessed parent or guardian found responsible, §20-171.9, (d).
Definitions, §20-171.8.
Infraction for violation, §20-171.9, (d).
Legislative findings and declaration, §20-171.7, (a).
Negligence or liability not assessed for violation, §20-171.9, (c).
Passenger on bicycle, requirements, §20-171.9, (b).
Protective bicycle helmet.
Wearing while riding roadway, bicycle path, required, §20-171.9, (a).
Purposes of article, §20-171.7, (b).
Restraining seat for small children.
Requirement to be passenger, §20-171.9, (b).
Short title of act, §20-171.6.
Subsequent purchase of helmet or restraining seat.
Waiver of fine for violation, §20-171.9, (e).
Definitions, §20-171.1.

BICYCLES —Cont'd
Freestyle bicycling.
Assumption of risks, limitation on liability, §§99E-21 to 99E-25.
General penalty provisions, penalty not specified.
Infractions, §20-176, (a).
Maximum penalty authorized, §20-176, (b).
Misdemeanors, §20-176, (a).
Class 2 misdemeanors, §20-176, (c).
Imprisonment for certain violations, limitation, §20-176, (c1).
Negligence per se, determining.
Crimes and infractions treated identically, §20-176, (d).
Lamps.
Requirements, §20-129, (e).
Racing.
Approved racing events, §20-171.2, (b).
Exemptions from compliance with traffic laws, §20-171.2, (c).
Highways.
Prohibited generally, §20-171.2, (a).
Exception as to approved racing events, §20-171.2, (b).
Searches and seizures.
Unclaimed bicycles.
Advertisement and sale or donation, §15-12, (b).

BIDS AND BIDDING.
Advisory budget commission.
Certain purchases exempted from provisions of articles, §§143-56, 143-57.
Rules.
Covering certain purposes, §143-60.
Architectural, engineering and surveying services.
Public building contracts, §§143-64.31 to 143-64.34.
Drainage districts.
Construction of improvements, §156-84.
Facility authorities.
Construction contracts, §160A-480.6.
Judicial sales.
Upset bids.
See JUDICIAL SALES.
Motion pictures.
Fair competition, §§75C-2 to 75C-5.
North Carolina purchase directory, §143-345.8.
Public contracts.
Architectural, engineering and surveying services, §§143-64.31 to 143-64.34.
Generally, §§143-128 to 143-135.9.
See PUBLIC CONTRACTS.
Public works.
Regulation of contractors.
List of bidders, §133-33.
Suspension from bidding, §133-27.
Purchase directory.
North Carolina purchase directory, §143-345.8.
Purchases and contracts through department of administration, §§143-48 to 143-64.
See PURCHASES THROUGH DEPARTMENT OF ADMINISTRATION.
Sanitary districts.
Plan for accomplishing objective of district, §130A-63, (b).
State departments and agencies.
Consultant services.
Architectural, engineering and surveying services, §§143-64.31 to 143-64.34.

BIDS AND BIDDING —Cont'd
State departments and agencies —Cont'd
Consultant services —Cont'd
General provisions, §§143-64.20 to 143-64.24.
Streets and highways.
Letting of contracts to bidders after advertisement, §136-28.1, (a) to (k).
Unclaimed property.
Public sale of abandoned property by treasurer, §116B-65.
Upset bids.
See JUDICIAL SALES.

BIENNIAL STATE OF ENVIRONMENT REPORT, §143B-279.5.

BIFURCATED TRIAL.
Punitive damages, §1D-30.

BIGAMY, §14-183.
Acts barring rights of spouse, §31A-1, (a).
Children born of voidable marriage legitimate, §50-11.1.
Competency of witnesses.
Husband and wife, §8-57, (b).
Marriage void, §51-3.

BILLBOARDS.
Alcoholic beverage advertising, §18B-105, (b).
Blue Ridge parkway.
Control of outdoor advertising, §§113A-165 to 113A-170.
Cities.
Outdoor advertising.
Regulation of nonconforming off-premises outdoor advertising, §160A-199.
Counties.
Outdoor advertising.
Regulation of nonconforming off-premises outdoor advertising, §153A-143.
Obstructing view at entrance to school, church or public institution, §136-102, (a), (b).
Outdoor advertising control act, §§136-126 to 136-140.
See OUTDOOR ADVERTISING.
Scenic highways, state and national parks and historic areas.
Outdoor advertising adjacent to park.
Limitations, §136-129.2, (a) to (c).
Transportation department.
Legislative reporting requirements, §136-12.1.

BILLIARDS.
Counties.
Regulation of places of amusement, §153A-135.
Minors.
Permitting minors to enter billiard rooms, §14-317.
Municipal corporations.
Regulation of pool and billiard halls, §160A-181.

BILL OF PARTICULARS, §1A-1, Rule 84.
Criminal procedure, §15A-925.
Motion for more definite statement, §1A-1, Rule 12, (e).

BILL OF RIGHTS.
Adult care homes, §§131D-19 to 131D-34.
See ADULT CARE HOMES.
Constitution of North Carolina.
Declaration of rights, Const. N. C., art. I, §§1 to 37.
Constitution of the United States, Const. U. S., amds. I to X.

BILL OF RIGHTS —Cont'd
Nursing homes.
Patients' bill of rights, §§131E-115 to 131E-131.
See NURSING HOMES.

BILLS AND NOTES.
Negotiable instruments.
General provisions, §§25-3-101 to 25-3-605.
See NEGOTIABLE INSTRUMENTS.

BILLS BY GAS AND ELECTRIC LIGHT COMPANIES.
Reading of meter to be shown on bill, §66-9.

BILLS OF ATTAINDER.
Constitutional provisions, Const. U. S., art. I, §§9, 10; art. III, §3.

BILLS OF COSTS.
Attachment execution for unpaid costs, §6-4.

BILLS OF EXCHANGE.
Commercial paper generally.
See NEGOTIABLE INSTRUMENTS.
Costs.
Several suits or actions on one instrument.
Allowance of costs to defendant, §6-19.
Allowance of costs to plaintiff, §6-18.
Default judgments.
Clerk to ascertain interest upon default judgment on bill of exchange, §24-6.
Fiduciaries drawing, §32-7.
Payable to third persons, §32-6.
Forgery, §14-122.
Selling of certain forged securities, §14-121.
Larceny of choses in action, §14-75.
Negotiable instruments generally.
See NEGOTIABLE INSTRUMENTS.
Powers of attorney.
Powers conferred by statutory short form, §32A-2.

BILLS OF GENERAL ASSEMBLY.
Action on bills, Const. N. C., art. II, §22.
Approval of bills, §120-29.1.
Coded bill drafting.
Act in law defined, §120-20.1, (c).
Applicability of section, §120-20.1, (d).
Deleted material and added material only changes, §120-20.1, (b1).
New section, subsection or subdivision added, §120-20.1, (b2).
Struck through or underlined material, §120-20.1, (a), (b).
Enrolling clerk.
Deposit of original bills and resolutions enrolled for application, §120-33, (f).
Duties, §120-33.
Presenting true ratified copies, §120-33, (d) to (d2).
Proofreading bills, §120-33, (c).
Ratification of enrolled bills, §120-33, (a).
Substituting corresponding Arabic numerals for written words, §120-33, (b).
Typewritten bills, §120-33, (c).
Governor's approval of bill, §120-29.1, (a).
Calculation of time for approval, §120-29.1, (d).
Failure to take action on bill, §120-29.1, (b).
Objections, §120-29.1, (c).
Veto, Const. N. C., art. II, §22; art. III, §5.
Local government fiscal information act, §§120-30.41 to 120-30.49.
Local, private and special legislation, Const. N. C., art. II, §24.

BILLS OF GENERAL ASSEMBLY —Cont'd
Reconvening of legislature, Const. N. C., art. II, §22; art. III, §5.
Request that session not be held, §120-6.1, (a).
Form of request, §120-6.1, (b).
Revenue bills, Const. N. C., art. II, §23.
Signing by presiding officers of both houses required, Const. N. C., art. II, §22.
Style of acts, Const. N. C., art. II, §21.
Three readings required, Const. N. C., art. II, §22.
Veto by governor, Const. N. C., art. II, §22; art. III, §5.
Voting rights act of 1965.
Submission of changes to United States attorney general, §§120-30.9A to 120-30.9H.
When acts take effect, §120-20.

BILLS OF INDICTMENT.
General provisions, §§15-144 to 15-155.
See INDICTMENTS.

BILLS OF LADING.
Alcoholic beverages transported by motor carriers, §18B-1115, (d).
Carriers.
Issuance on receiving property for transportation in interstate commerce, §62-203, (a).
Counterfeiting, §21-42.
Discovery.
Actions by or against common or connecting carriers.
Bills of lading as evidence, §8-41.
Documents of title generally, §§25-7-101 to 25-7-603.
See COMMERCIAL CODE.
Evidence.
Actions by or against common or connecting carriers, §8-41.
False bills.
Issuing false bills made felony, §21-42.
Forgery, §21-42.
Gasoline and oil transporters.
Required to have in possession an invoice, bill of sale or bill of lading, §119-42.
Suretyship.
Indorser not guarantor for other parties, §25-7-505.
Uttering, §21-42.

BILLS OF SALE.
Execution sales, §1-339.62.
Judicial sales.
Person holding public sale may execute and deliver, §1-339.23, (c).
Private sale of personal property, §1-339.39.
Sale under execution, §1-315, (b).

BINDERS.
Fire insurance policies, §58-44-20.
Lenders engaged in mortgage or deed of trust loans.
Acceptance or denial of temporary insurance contracts, §58-3-140.
Motor vehicle insurance, §20-279.21, (k).

BINGO.
Alcoholic beverage sale or consumption, §18B-308.
Beach bingo.
Applicability of article, §14-309.14.
Conduct of bingo game, §14-309.5.
Certain property, §14-309.7, (d).

BINGO —Cont'd
Conduct of bingo game —Cont'd
Charitable or nonprofit causes.
Purposes of conduct of bingo, §14-309.5, (a).
Limit on number of sessions, §14-309.8.
Payment of member of organization to conduct game, §14-309.7, (c).
Penalties for violations, §14-309.5, (b).
Public sessions, §14-309.13.
Responsibility of special committee, §14-309.10.
Definitions, §14-309.6.
Exempt organization.
Defined, §14-309.6.
False information in audit, §14-309.11, (c).
Licenses.
Applications, §14-309.7, (a).
Contents, §14-309.7, (b).
Fee, §14-309.7, (a).
Limit on number of sessions, §14-309.8.
Permits.
Single occasion permit, §14-309.7, (e).
Prizes.
Maximum, §14-309.9, (a).
Applicability of section, §14-309.9, (c).
Proceeds.
Audit, §14-309.11, (b).
False information, §14-309.11, (c).
Deposit, §14-309.11, (a).
False information in audit, §14-309.11, (c).
Use, §14-309.11, (a).
Public sessions, §14-309.13.
Raffles.
Not to be conducted in conjunction with bingo, §14-309.15, (e).
Records.
Open for inspection, §14-309.11, (d).
Single occasion permit, §14-309.7, (e).
Video bingo.
Ban on new machines, regulation of existing machines, §14-306.1.
Violations, §14-309.12.

BIODIESEL FUEL.
Renewable fuel facility construction tax credit, §105-129.16D.

BIOLOGICAL AGENTS.
Mass death and destruction weapons.
Nuclear, biological or chemical weapons, §§14-288.21 to 14-288.24.
See WEAPONS OF MASS DEATH AND DESTRUCTION.
Murder as a result of the use of, §14-17.
Prohibited discharges into air or water, §143-214.2, (a).
Terrorist incident using nuclear, biological or chemical agents, §§130A-475 to 130A-479.
See TERRORIST INCIDENT USING NUCLEAR, BIOLOGICAL OR CHEMICAL AGENTS.

BIOLOGICAL AGENTS REGISTRY, §130A-479.
Confidentiality of information, §130A-479, (e).
Definitions, §130A-479, (b).
Generally, §130A-479, (a).
Penalty for violations, §130A-479, (f).
Reports, §130A-479, (d).
Rules, §130A-479, (c).

BIOLOGICAL ORGANISM ACT, §§106-65.42 to 106-65.49.
Article not applicable in certain cases, §106-65.49.

BIOLOGICAL ORGANISM ACT —Cont'd
Authority under other statutes not abrogated, §106-65.47.
Board of agriculture.
Adoption of regulations, §106-65.45.
Defined, §106-65.44.
Further authority of board, §106-65.46.
Commissioner of agriculture.
Defined, §106-65.44.
Enforcement of article, §106-65.46.
Criminal penalties, §106-65.48.
Definitions, §106-65.44.
Division of entomology.
Defined, §106-65.44.
Enforcement of article, §106-65.46.
Environmental protection.
Purpose of article, §106-65.43.
Intergovernmental cooperation.
Memoranda of understanding, §106-65.47.
Memoranda of understanding.
Intergovernmental cooperation, §106-65.47.
Purpose of article, §106-65.43.
Short title, §106-65.42.
States.
Memoranda of understanding, §106-65.47.
Title of article, §106-65.42.
United States.
Memoranda of understanding, §106-65.47.
Violation of law or regulations, §106-65.48.

BIOLOGICAL RESIDUES IN ANIMALS, §§106-549.81 to 106-549.89.
Animal defined, §106-549.81.
Animal feed defined, §106-549.81.
Animal produce defined, §106-549.81.
Appellate review.
Detention or quarantine, §106-549.83.
Bond.
Preservation or disposition of animal, animal product or feed, §106-549.83.
Burden of proof.
Content of biological residue, §106-549.82.
Civil penalties, §106-549.89.
Definitions, §106-549.81.
Detention of animal, animal product or feed, §106-549.82.
Movement of contaminated animals forbidden, §106-549.84, (a).
Fines, §106-549.89.
Inspections.
Examining facilities, inventory, etc., §106-549.85.
Investigations.
Discovering violations of article, §106-549.86.
Movement of contaminated animals forbidden, §106-549.84, (a), (b).
Penalties for violations of provisions.
Civil penalties, §106-549.89.
Fines, §106-549.89.
Quarantine of animal, animal product or feed, §106-549.82.
Movement of contaminated animals forbidden, §106-549.84, (a).
Records.
Examining and/or copying records, §106-549.85.
Right of entry.
Inspection of facilities, inventory, etc., §106-549.85.
Rules and regulations.
Promulgation of, §106-549.87.
Violations of article.
Investigations to discover violation, §106-549.86.

BIOLOGICAL RESIDUES IN ANIMALS —Cont'd
Violations of article —Cont'd
Misdemeanors, §106-549.88.
Civil penalties, §106-549.89.
Fines, §106-549.89.

BIOLOGICS, §§106-707 to 106-715.
Attorney general.
Prosecution of violations, §106-714, (a).
Board of agriculture.
Definition of "board," §106-708.
Rules and regulations, §106-709.
Definitions, §106-708.
District attorneys.
Prosecution of violations, §106-714, (a).
Fines, §106-715.
Injunctions, §106-714, (b).
License to produce.
Applications, §106-710, (c).
Inspection of establishment applying, §106-710, (b).
Fees, §106-710, (d).
Issuance, §106-710, (d).
Renewal, §106-710, (d).
Required, §106-710, (a).
Revocation or suspension, §106-711.
Penalties.
Civil penalties, §106-715.
Purpose of law, §106-707.
Registration.
Application for registration.
Information to accompany, §106-712, (b).
Generally, §106-712, (a).
Revocation or suspension, §106-713.
Short title of law, §106-707.
Violations of provisions.
Injunctions, §106-714, (b).
Penalties, §106-714, (a).
Civil penalties, §106-715.
Fines, §106-715.

BIOMASS EQUIPMENT.
Corporations.
Income tax.
Definitions, §105-130.28, (b).

BIOMASS RESOURCES.
Business and energy tax credits, §§105-129.15 to 105-129.19.

BIOPROCESSING INDUSTRIES.
Bioprocessing defined, §105-164.14, (j).
Life sciences revenue bond authority, §§159D-65 to 159D-69.
Sales and use tax refund, §105-164.14, (j).

BIOTERRORISM.
Nuclear, biological or chemical agents.
Terrorist incident using, §§130A-475 to 130A-479.
See TERRORIST INCIDENT USING NUCLEAR, BIOLOGICAL OR CHEMICAL AGENTS.

BIRD-FOOT VIOLET.
Taking, etc., of certain wild plants from land of another, §14-129.

BIRDS.
Animal waste management, §§143-215.10A to 143-215.10H.
See ANIMAL WASTE MANAGEMENT.
Cardinal.
State bird, §145-2.
Certificate of registration obtained by false representation, §14-103.

BIRDS —Cont'd
Hunting and wildlife generally.
See HUNTING AND WILDLIFE.
Municipal corporations.
Sanctuaries, §160A-188.
Poultry generally.
See POULTRY AND POULTRY PRODUCTS.
Poultry products inspections, §§106-549.49 to 106-549.69.
See POULTRY PRODUCTS INSPECTIONS.

BIRTH CERTIFICATES.
Adoption.
Confidentiality of records generally, §§48-9-101 to 48-9-109.
See ADOPTION.
Affidavit of paternity.
Listing declaring father on certificate and presumption as natural father, §130A-101, (f).
Amendment of birth certificate, §130A-118, (a).
Fee, §130A-118, (d).
Certificate of identification.
Birth of unknown parentage, §130A-107.
Foreign births, §130A-108.
Children born out of wedlock, §130A-101, (f).
Affidavit acknowledging paternity.
Listing declaring father on certificate and presumption as natural father, §130A-101, (f).
Contents, §130A-102.
Copies, §130A-93.
Duties of local registrars, §130A-97.
Establishing fact of birth by person without certificate, §130A-106, (a) to (c).
Evidentiary value, §130A-104, (d), 130A-109.
Fee for registering or amending, copies, §161-10, (a).
Felonies and misdemeanors.
Generally, §130A-26A, (a), (b).
Filing of birth certificate, §130A-101.
Illegitimate children judicially determined.
Furnishing facts as to paternity, §130A-119.
Irregular registration of birth certificates.
Validation of registration, §130A-105.
Legitimation.
Names entered upon birth certificates, §130A-101, (f).
New certificate upon legitimation, §§49-12.1, 49-13.
Local registrar's duties, §130A-97.
Name of husband entered on certificate, §130A-101, (e).
New certificates, §130A-118, (b), (c), (e).
Copies, §130A-93, (f).
Fee, §130A-118, (d).
Filing, §130A-118, (e).
Paternity of illegitimate children judicially determined.
Furnishing facts as to paternity, §130A-119.
Registers of deeds.
Copies to be forwarded by local registrars, §130A-97.
Registration of birth certificate, §130A-101.
More than five days and less than one year after birth, §130A-103.
One year or more after birth, §130A-104.
Social security numbers.
Parents to provide, §130A-101, (g).
Validation of irregular registration of birth certificates, §130A-105.

BIRTH CERTIFICATES —Cont'd
Where parentage cannot be established.
Certificate as identification in lieu of birth certificate, §130A-107.
Without certificate.
Establishing fact of birth by person without certificate, §130A-106, (a), (c).
Cumulative nature of provisions, §130A-106, (a), (c).
Fees, §130A-106, (b).

BIRTH CONTROL.
Health benefit plan coverage.
Prescription contraceptive drugs and devices and outpatient contraceptive services, §58-3-178.
Small employer group health coverage.
Contraceptive drugs and devices, §58-50-155, (a).
Surgical interruption of vas deferens or fallopian tubes.
Operation lawful upon request of married person or person over 18, §90-271.
No liability for nonnegligent performance of operation, §90-274.

BIRTH DEFECTS MONITORING PROGRAM.
Birth defect defined, §130A-131.16, (b).
Confidentiality of information, §130A-131.17, (a).
Persons other than authorized program staff, §130A-131.17, (b).
Record of all persons given access to information, §130A-131.17, (d).
Contacting case subjects, §130A-131.17, (c).
Established, §130A-131.16, (a).
Program defined, §130A-131.16, (b).
Review of medical records, §130A-131.16, (c).
Civil or, §130A-131.16, (d).
Statistical compilations, §130A-131.17, (e).

BIRTHS.
Abandoned children.
Establishing facts relating to birth, §130A-107.
Abortion generally.
See ABORTION.
Birth certificates.
See BIRTH CERTIFICATES.
Concealing birth of child, §14-46.
Defects.
Monitoring program, §§130A-131.16, 130A-131.17.
Hearsay exception.
Records of religious organizations, §8C-1, Rule 803.
Statement of personal or family history, §8C-1, Rule 804, (b).
Vital statistics.
General provisions, §§130A-90 to 130A-120.
See VITAL STATISTICS.

BISHOPS.
See CLERGYMEN.

BISON.
Inspections, §106-549.39.
Meat inspections, §§106-549.15 to 106-549.39.
See MEAT INSPECTIONS.

BITCH DOGS.
Permitting at large, §67-2.

BLACK BEARS.
Captivity licenses.
Applicability to, §113-272.5, (f).
Protection, §§19A-10 to 19A-14.

BLACKBERRIES.
Standard weights and measures, §81A-42.

BLACKJACKS.
Weapons generally.
See WEAPONS.

BLACKLISTING.
Antiblacklisting act, §14-355.

BLACKMAIL, §14-118.

BLACK MOUNTAIN ADVANCEMENT CENTER FOR WOMEN.
Description of grounds, §143B-269, (b).
Educational and vocational training for inmates, §143B-269, (f).
Established, §143B-269, (a).
General assembly not obligated to appropriate funds, §143B-269, (h).
Inmates, §143B-269, (c).
Training.
Educational and vocational training, §143B-269, (f).
Transfer, §143B-269, (d).
Work release, §143B-269, (g).
Joint security force, §122C-421, (a), (b).
Medical services and food services contracts, §143B-269, (e).
Work release, §143B-269, (g).

BLACK PEOPLE.
Discrimination.
See DISCRIMINATION.
Racial minorities generally.
See RACIAL MINORITIES.

BLADEN COUNTY.
Acquisition of property, power, §153A-158.1, (a).
Agricultural tendencies in certain counties.
Terms of, §42-23.
Ambulance service.
Attachment or garnishment and lien for, §§44-51.4 to 44-51.8.
Blank or master forms of mortgages, deeds of trust, etc.
Indexing and recording, inapplicability of provisions, §47-21.
Condemnation or acquisition of land by local government unit outside county.
Consent of board of commissioners necessary, §153A-15.
Counties generally.
See COUNTIES.
Cropper or tenant refusing to perform terms of contract.
Forfeiture of right of possession to premises, §42-27.
Game laws, local acts not repealed, §113-133.1, (e).
Grants in navigable waters, registration, §113-205, (a).
Low-income housing tax credits.
Qualified building eligible for credit, §105-129.41, (c).
Officers compensated from fees.
Statement to be rendered, §128-13.
Open fires in high hazard counties.
Applicability of section, §113-60.23, (a).
Ground clearing activities, special permit required, §113-60.23, (c).
Woodland fires, permit required, §113-60.23, (b).
Records in Bladen.
Copies of lost records, §8-33.
School property.
Acquisition and improvement, §153A-158.1.

BLADEN COUNTY —Cont'd
Southeastern North Carolina regional economic development commission, §158-8.3.

BLANK CARTRIDGE PISTOLS.
Sale, §14-407.1.

BLANKET ACCIDENT AND HEALTH INSURANCE, §58-51-75.
Approval of policy form, §58-51-85.

BLANKET BONDS.
Clerks of superior courts, §7A-107.

BLAZE ORANGE.
Hunters wearing hunter orange material, §113-291.8, (a) to (c).

BLENDED FUEL TAX.
Gasoline tax generally, §§105-449.60 to 105-449.127.
See GASOLINE TAX.

BLIND BIDDING FOR FIRST RUN MOTION PICTURES, §75C-3.

BLIND PERSONS.
Aid to the blind.
Administration of assistance, §111-13.
Alternate sources of income, §111-21.
Appeals.
Denial of application for aid, §111-16.
Application for aid, §111-14.
Denial of application, §111-16.
Notice requirements, §111-16.
Appropriations by counties, §111-17.
Attachment.
Payment of awards exempt from attachment, §111-18.
Attorneys at law.
Lending North Carolina reports to blind lawyers, §111-29.
Awards.
Change in condition.
Reopening awards upon change, §111-20.
Death of recipient, §111-18.1, (a).
Exemption from execution, attachment or garnishment, §111-18.
Notice of award, §111-16.
Payment of award, §111-18.
Death of recipient, §111-18.1, (a).
Reopening upon change in condition, §111-20.
Beneficiaries not deemed paupers, §111-22.
Business operations.
Authority to conduct certain operations, §111-27.1.
Cash payment service.
Death of recipient, §111-18.1, (b).
Commission for the blind.
Denial of application for aid.
Appeal to commission, §111-16.
Rules and regulations, §111-13.
Counties.
Appropriations by counties, §111-17.
Intercounty transfer of recipients, §111-19.
Court reports.
Lending North Carolina reports to blind lawyers, §111-29.
Department of health and human services.
Conducting certain business operations, §111-27.1.
Cooperation with federal government in rehabilitation of blind and visually impaired, §111-28.1.

BLIND PERSONS —Cont'd
Aid to the blind —Cont'd
Department of health and human services —Cont'd
Federal grants.
Authority to receive, §111-28.
Promoting employment of needy blind persons, §111-27.
State grants.
Authority to receive, §111-28.
Director of social services.
Authority of director, §111-35.
Direct relief, §111-6.
Matching of federal funds, §111-6.
Disqualifications for relief, §111-21.
Eligibility for relief, §111-15.
Employment of needy blind persons.
Promoting employment, §111-27.
Vending stands on public property, §111-27.
Estimating of number of needy blind persons, §111-17.
Evidence.
Personal representatives for certain recipients of aid.
Findings not competent as evidence in other proceedings, §111-32.
Executions.
Payment of awards exempt from execution, §111-18.
Federal aid.
Acceptance of aid, §111-25.
Authority of department of health and human services to receive, §111-28.
Grants affording maximum aid, §111-29.
Grants from federal government, §111-24.
Matching federal funds, §111-6.
Termination of aid, §111-26.
Use of aid, §111-25.
Fraud in obtaining assistance, §111-23.
Funds.
Expenditure of equalizing funds, §111-29.
Source of funds, §111-17.
Garnishment.
Payment of awards exempt from garnishment, §111-18.
Grants.
Federal aid, §111-24.
Affording maximum aid, §111-29.
Information concerning blind persons.
Use of information, §111-28.
Intercounty transfer of recipients, §111-19.
Investigations.
Application for aid, §111-14.
Minors.
Personal representatives for certain recipients of aid.
Affecting provisions for payments for minors, §111-33.
Misrepresentation or fraud in obtaining assistance, §111-23.
Notice, §111-16.
Objective standards for qualifications of personnel, §111-13.
Paupers.
Beneficiaries not deemed paupers, §111-22.
Payment of monthly relief, §111-17.
Personal representatives for certain recipients of aid, §111-30.
Courts for purposes of article, §111-31.
Findings not competent as evidence in other proceedings, §111-32.

BLIND PERSONS —Cont'd
Aid to the blind —Cont'd
Personal representatives for certain recipients of aid —Cont'd
Minors.
Affecting provisions for payments for minors, §111-33.
Personnel.
Objective standards for qualifications of personnel, §111-13.
Public assistance.
Death of recipient of cash payment service, §111-18.1, (b).
Qualifications for eligibility for relief, §111-15.
Records.
Personal representatives for certain recipients of aid.
Adoption as courts, §111-31.
Retirement benefits.
Vending-stand operators, §111-27.2.
Rules and regulations.
Commission for the blind to make, §111-13.
Social services.
Authority of director, §111-35.
Source of funds, §111-17.
State aid.
Authority of department of health and human services to receive, §111-28.
Transfer of recipients.
Intercounty transfer, §111-19.
United States.
Cooperation with federal departments or agencies, §111-24.
Department of health and human services authorized to cooperate with federal government, §111-28.1.
Vending stands on public property.
Operation of vending facilities on state property, §§111-41 to 111-47.
Promoting employment of needy blind persons, §111-27.
Retirement benefits for operators, §111-27.2.
Assault on handicapped persons, §14-32.1.
DNA analysis.
Blood sample required upon conviction, §15A-266.4.
Coin-operated vending machines.
Installation of machines, §111-43.
Commission for the blind.
Aid to the blind.
Appeal to the commission for denial of application for aid, §111-16.
Rules and regulations made by commission, §111-13.
Appointments, §143B-158, (b).
Officers, §143B-160.
Blind persons, majority of commission members, §143B-158, (c).
Chairperson, §§143B-158, (d), 143B-160.
Clerical and other services, §143B-158, (j).
Consumer and advocacy advisory committee for the blind, §§143B-163, 143B-164.
Creation, §143B-157.
Duties, §143B-157.
Establishment, §143B-157.
Financial interest of member, §143B-158, (g).
Meetings.
Regular and special meetings, §143B-159.
Number of members, representatives of state programs, §143B-158, (a).
Officers, §143B-160.

BLIND PERSONS —Cont'd
Commission for the blind —Cont'd
Per diem, travel and subsistence expenses, §143B-158, (h).
Powers and duties, §143B-157.
Professional advisory committee.
Compensation, §143B-162.
Creation, §143B-161.
Members, §143B-162.
Powers and duties, §143B-161.
Quorum, §143B-162.
Selection, §143B-162.
Quorum, §143B-158, (i).
Removal by governor, §143B-158, (g).
Special meetings, §143B-159.
Terms, consecutive terms, §143B-158, (e), (f).
Vice-chairman, §143B-160.
Commission to study the care of the aged and handicapped, §§143-279 to 143-283.
Common carrier fares.
Blind person accompanied by guide dog, §62-144, (b).
Community-based support groups.
In-home services, §111-7.
Consumer and advocacy advisory committee for the blind.
Applicability of provisions, §143B-163, (d).
Chairman, §143B-164, (b).
Clerical services, §143B-164, (e).
Compensation, §143B-164, (f).
Creation, §143B-163, (a).
Meetings.
Regular and special meetings, §143B-164, (d).
Members, §143B-164, (a).
Powers and duties, §143B-163, (b), (c).
Quorum, §143B-164, (c).
Shifts in budget items, §143B-163, (e).
Special meetings, §143B-164, (d).
Contributions for particular facilities.
Acceptance of contributions authorized, §111-12.1.
Rules and regulations as to receiving and expending contributions, §111-12.3.
Treating contributions as state funds to match federal funds, §111-12.2.
Definitions, §111-11.
Operation of highway vending facilities, §111-49, (a) to (c).
Operation of vending facilities on state property, §111-42, (a) to (d).
Department of health and human services.
Aid to the blind, §§111-27 to 111-28.1. See within this heading, "Aid to the blind."
Operation of highway vending facilities.
Preference to blind persons.
Responsibility of department, §111-48.
Operation of vending facilities on state property.
Locations for vending facilities.
Duty to inform department, §111-45.
Preference to blind persons.
Responsibility of department, §111-41.
Deposit with or transferred to state treasurer.
Disposition of funds, §111-12.6.
Education of blind children.
Governor Morehead school.
State school for sight impaired children, §§143B-164.10 to 143B-164.17.
See GOVERNOR MOREHEAD SCHOOL.
Elections.
Assistance to voters, §163-166.8.
Eye examinations.
Aid to the blind.
Application for aid, §111-14.

BLIND PERSONS —Cont'd
Eye examinations —Cont'd
Arranging for examination of eyes, §111-8.
Medical and surgical treatment, §111-8.
Facsimile signatures.
Use of signature facsimile by visually handicapped person, §22A-1.
False representation as to physical defect to obtain money, §14-113.
Rehabilitation center for the blind and visually impaired.
Authority to receive federal grants-in-aid, §111-6.1.
Governor Morehead school.
State school for sight impaired children, §§143B-164.10 to 143B-164.17.
See GOVERNOR MOREHEAD SCHOOL.
Governor's council on the employment of the handicapped, §§143-283.1 to 143-283.8.
Guide dogs.
Common carrier fares for blind persons accompanied by, §62-144, (b).
Duties of drivers approaching person using guide dog, §168-5.
Pedestrians rights and privileges without guide dog, §20-175.3.
Service animals generally, §§168-4.2 to 168-4.6.
Signal for blind persons crossing streets, §20-175.2.
In-home services, §111-7.
Insurance on motor vehicles.
Discriminatory practices prohibited, §58-3-25, (b).
Mattresses and bedding.
Exemptions for blind persons.
Bedding manufactured, sanitized or renovated by nonprofit agency for the blind, §130A-272, (a).
Medical and surgical treatment.
Arranging for examination of eyes.
Securing and paying for treatment, §111-8.
Motor vehicle insurance.
Discriminatory practices prohibited, §58-3-25, (b).
Nonprofit work centers for the blind and severely disabled.
Public contracts.
Purchases from, §143-129.5.
Purchases through department of administration.
Agency procurement of goods directly from center, §143-48.2, (a).
Agency procurement of services directly from center, §143-48.2, (b).
Bids or making offers by center, §143-48.2, (c).
Procurement program, §143-48.2, (b).
Operation of highway vending facilities.
Contracts, §111-50, (a).
Definitions, §111-48.
Preference to visually handicapped persons, §111-48.
Current operators, §111-51.
Priority for specific line vendors, §111-51.
Profits.
Deposits, §111-52.
Use, §111-52.
Rules and regulations, §111-50, (c).
Operation of vending facilities on state property.
Applicability of article.
Exclusions, §111-47, (a), (b).
Coin-operated vending machines.
Installation of machines, §111-43.
Definitions, §111-42, (a) to (d).

BLIND PERSONS —Cont'd
Operation of vending facilities on state property —Cont'd
Exclusions from article, §111-47, (a), (b).
Installation of coin-operated vending machines, §111-43.
Location provided by state agency, §111-44.
Duties to inform department of health and human services, §111-45.
North Carolina aquariums contracting for food or vending services.
Authority to contract not withstanding provisions of article, §111-47.1, (a).
Existing contracts not altered, §111-47.1, (b).
Preference to visually handicapped persons, §111-41.
Responsibility of department of health and human services, §111-41.
Services provided by state agency, §111-44.
Those other than blind persons, §111-46.
Visually handicapped.
Facilities operated by those other than blind persons, §111-46.
Pedestrians.
Guide dogs.
Duties of drivers approaching person using guide dog, §168-5.
Signal for blind persons crossing streets, §20-175.2.
Rights and privileges of blind persons without white cane or guide dog, §20-175.3.
Rights of way, §20-175.2.
White canes.
Public use by other than blind persons, §20-175.1.
Signal for blind persons crossing streets, §20-175.2.
Private contributions.
Acceptance of contributions for particular facilities authorized, §111-12.1.
Rules and regulations as to receiving and expending contributions, §111-12.3.
Treating contributions as state funds to match federal funds, §111-12.2.
Professional advisory committee, §§143B-161, 143B-162.
Public contracts.
Nonprofit work centers for the blind and severely disabled.
Purchases from, §143-129.5.
Register of blind in state.
Facts to be described, §111-4, (a).
Maintenance of complete register, §111-4, (a).
Reports of examinations by physicians and optometrists, §111-4, (b).
Rehabilitation center for the blind and visually impaired.
Established, §111-6.1.
Federal aid.
Authority to receive grants-in-aid, §111-6.1.
Grants.
Authority to receive federal grants-in-aid, §111-6.1.
Intent of center, §111-6.1.
Operation of center, §111-6.1.
Purposes of center, §111-6.1.
Rules and regulations, §111-6.1.
Rehabilitative services to visually impaired persons.
Jurisdiction of certain divisions within department of health and human services, §111-11.1.

BLIND PERSONS —Cont'd
Reserve and operating capital fund.
Expending funds, §111-12.5.
Retaining funds, §111-12.5.
Retirement system for teachers and state employees.
Enrollment of blind or visually handicapped employees, §135-16.1, (a) to (c).
Sale of merchandise by governmental units.
Exceptions, §66-58, (b), (c).
Sales and use tax.
Exemption of sales by blind persons, §105-164.13.
Sales by training schools and workshops.
Distribution and sale of products, §111-6.
School for sight impaired children.
Governor Morehead school, §§143B-164.10 to 143B-164.17.
See GOVERNOR MOREHEAD SCHOOL.
Seeing-eye dogs.
Common carrier fares for blind persons accompanied by, §62-144, (b).
Duties of drivers approaching persons using guide dog, §168-5.
Pedestrians rights and privileges without guide dog, §20-175.3.
Service animals generally, §§168-4.2 to 168-4.6.
Signal for blind persons crossing street, §20-175.2.
Signatures.
Facsimile signatures.
Use by visually handicapped person, §22A-1.
Special education.
See SPECIAL EDUCATION.
State treasurer.
Funds deposited with or transferred to state treasurer.
Disposition of funds, §111-12.6.
Teachers.
Blind teachers not to be discriminated against, §115C-299, (b).
Training schools and workshops, §111-6.
Special educational opportunities outside state, §111-6.
Vending facilities.
Operation of highway vending facilities, §§111-48 to 111-52.
Operation of vending facilities on state property, §§111-41 to 111-47.
Visually impaired persons defined, §111-11.
Voting.
Assistance to voters, §163-166.8.
White canes.
Duties of drivers approaching person using such cane, §168-5.
Public use by other than blind persons prohibited, §20-175.1.
Signal for blind persons crossing streets, §20-175.2.
Workers' compensation.
Loss of vision.
Rates of compensation, §97-31.
Workshops.
Training schools and workshops, §111-6.

BLOCK GRANTS.
Block grant plans.
Submission by agency receiving federal grants, §143-16.1, (b).
Department of administration duties and powers, §143-341.

BLOOD BANKS.
AIDS.
Information for potential donors, §130A-148, (b).

BLOOD BANKS —Cont'd
AIDS —Cont'd
Laboratory tests for AIDS virus infection, §130A-148, (c), (e).
Anatomical gifts generally, §§130A-402 to 130A-412.1.
See ANATOMICAL GIFTS.
Applicability of provisions.
Limitations, §90-220.14.
Hepatitis.
Selection of donors.
Risk of transmission of agents that may cause hepatitis to be minimized, §90-220.13.
Supervision by licensed physician required, §90-220.12.

BLOOD DONORS.
Anatomical gifts.
General provisions, §§130A-402 to 130A-412.1.
See ANATOMICAL GIFTS.
Selection of donors.
Risk of disease transmission to be minimized, §90-220.13.

BLOOD GROUPS.
Physical examination of persons, §1A-1, Rule 35, (a).

BLOOD POISON.
Food, drug and cosmetic act.
Drug or device, false advertising, §106-138, (b).

BLOODROOT.
Taking, etc., of certain wild plants from land of another, §14-129.

BLOOD TESTS AND SAMPLES.
Child support.
Expedited procedures to establish paternity in IV-D cases.
Subpoena to appear for blood tests to establish paternity, §110-132.2.
Competency of blood tests, §8-50.1.
Discovery in criminal cases.
Disclosure of results by defendant, §15A-905.
DNA analysis, §§15A-266 to 15A-270.
See DNA DATABASE AND DATABANKS.
Impaired driving.
Chemical analysis of impairing substances in blood.
Generally.
See IMPAIRED DRIVING.
Livestock.
Brucellosis, §106-390.
Nontestimonial identification.
Delinquent and undisciplined juvenile actions, §§7B-2103 to 7B-2109.
Generally, §§15A-271 to 15A-282.
See IDENTIFICATION.
Paternity, actions to establish, §49-14, (d).
Competency of blood tests, §8-50.1.
Expedited procedures to establish paternity in IV-D cases, §110-132.2.

BLUEBERRY.
Official berry of state, §145-18, (c).

BLUE DOGBANE.
Taking, etc., of certain wild plants from land of another, §14-129.

BLUE LIGHTS.
Use on vehicles prohibited, §20-130.1, (c).

BLUE RIDGE PARKWAY.
Control of outdoor advertising, §§113A-165 to 113A-170.
Advertisements prohibited within one thousand feet of center line, §113A-165.
Billboards.
Existing billboards, §113A-167.
Center line.
Advertisements prohibited within one thousand feet, §113A-165.
Condemnation procedure, §113A-169.
Existing billboards, §113A-167.
Injunctions, §113A-170.
Misdemeanor, §113A-170.
Rules and regulations.
Adoption, §113A-166.
Secretary of environment and natural resources.
Rules at option, §113A-166.
Unlawful advertising.
Removal, etc., §113A-168.
National park, parkway and forest development council, §§143B-324.1 to 143B-324.3.

BLUE SKY LAW.
Securities regulation.
General provisions, §§78A-1 to 78A-66.
See SECURITIES REGULATION.

BLUE STAR MEMORIAL HIGHWAY, §136-102.1.

BOARDING HOUSES.
Hotels, inns and other transient lodging places.
See HOTELS, INNS AND OTHER TRANSIENT LODGING PLACES.

BOARD OF ALDERMEN.
Generally.
See CITY COUNCILS.

BOARD OF AWARDS, §143-52.1.

BOARD OF DIRECTORS.
Corporations generally.
See CORPORATIONS.
Nonprofit corporations.
See NONPROFIT CORPORATIONS.

BOARD OF EDUCATION.
Local boards of education generally.
See LOCAL BOARDS OF EDUCATION.
State board of education.
See STATE BOARD OF EDUCATION.

BOARD OF LAW EXAMINERS.
Address, Admission to Practice, §.0101.
Appeals from board, §84-24.
Approval of rules and regulations, Bar Rules & Regs., C, §.0104.
Chair, §84-24; Admission to Practice, §.0103.
Compensation of members, §84-26.
Composition, §84-24.
Creation, §84-24.
Executive secretary.
Board may employ, §84-24.
Expenses of members, §84-26.
Membership, Admission to Practice, §.0103.
Number of members, Admission to Practice, §.0103.
Office hours, Admission to Practice, §.0101.
Powers, §84-24.
Prescription of applicant fees, §84-25.
Purpose, Admission to Practice, §.0102.
Subpoena and summons, power, §84-24.

BOARD OF LAW EXAMINERS —Cont'd
Teachers in law schools.
Ineligibility to be members, §84-24.
Terms, §84-24.

BOARDS AND COMMISSIONS.
Accountants.
Board of examiners, §93-12.
Administrative rules review commission, §§143B-30.1 to 143B-30.4.
Advisory budget commission.
See BUDGETS.
Advisory commission for state museum of natural history, §§143B-344.18 to 143B-344.21.
Aged persons.
Commission to study the care of the aged and handicapped, §§143-279 to 143-283.
Study commission on aging, §§120-180 to 120-188.
Agricultural, horticultural and forestland.
Special classification for property taxes purposes.
Use-value advisory board, §105-277.7.
Agriculture and forestry awareness, commission on, §§120-150 to 120-154.
Agriculture, board of.
See AGRICULTURE BOARD.
Alarm systems licensing board, §§74D-4 to 74D-5.1.
Alcoholic beverages.
Commission.
See ALCOHOLIC BEVERAGE CONTROL COMMISSION.
Local ABC boards.
See ABC BOARDS, LOCAL.
Allowances officials conditioned on filing of notice, §143-47.9.
Anatomy commission, §§130A-33.30 to 130A-33.32.
Aquaculture development advisory board, §106-760.
Architects.
Board, §§83A-2 to 83A-6.
Assets.
Settlement of affairs of certain inoperative boards and agencies.
Conversion and allocation of assets, §143-268.
Delivery to secretary of administration, §143-267.
Attorney general.
Charges for legal services to state boards and commissions, §114-8.2.
Attorneys at law.
Board of continuing legal education.
See ATTORNEYS AT LAW.
Board of law examiners, §§84-24 to 84-26; Admission to Practice, .0101 to .0103.
Auctioneer's commission, §85B-3.
Audits and auditing.
Occupational licensing board.
Annual audit of books and records, §93B-4.
Settlement of affairs of certain inoperative boards and agencies, §143-272.
Banking commission.
See BANKING COMMISSION.
Barbers.
Board of barber examiners, §§86A-4 to 86A-7.
Bath historical commission, §§143B-99 to 143B-102.
Battleship commission, §§143B-73 to 143B-74.3.
Beaver damage control advisory board, §113-291.10.

BOARDS AND COMMISSIONS —Cont'd
Bees and honey, §§106-635, 106-637, 106-638.
Blind persons.
Commission for the blind, §§143B-157 to 143B-160.
Boilers.
Board of boiler and pressure vessel rules, §95-69.13.
Building codes.
Code officials' qualification board.
See BUILDING CODES.
Building commission, §§143-135.25 to 143-135.28.
Cape Fear river navigation and pilotage commission, §§76A-1 to 76A-25.
Capital planning commission, §§143B-373, 143B-374.
Cemeteries.
Commission, §§65-48 to 65-54.
Child care commission, §§110-86, 110-88, 143B-168.4, 143B-168.5.
Children with special health care needs commission, §§143-682 to 143-684.
Chiropractors.
Board of examiners, §§90-139 to 90-142.
Cigarettes and tobacco products.
Tobacco boards of trade, §106-465.
Coastal resources commission, §113A-104.
Commission to study the care of the aged and handicapped, §§143-279 to 143-283.
Community appearance commissions, §§160A-451 to 160A-455.
Community colleges.
State board.
See COMMUNITY COLLEGES.
Compensation for services.
Per diem, subsistence and travel allowances, §138-5, (a) to (f).
Compensation to officers conditioned on filing of notice, §143-47.9.
Congressional districts.
Appointment of members from each district, statute requiring.
Extra position due to congressional redistricting, §143B-13, (f2).
Residency lost due to congressional redistricting, §143B-13, (f1).
Two or members from same district due to congressional redistricting, §143B-13, (f).
Consolidated human services boards.
See CONSOLIDATED HUMAN SERVICES AGENCY.
Constitutional amendments publication commission, §§147-54.8 to 147-54.10.
Correction, board of, §143B-265.
Cosmetic art.
Board of cosmetic art.
See COSMETIC ART.
Counties.
Boards of commissioners.
See COUNTY BOARDS OF COMMISSIONERS.
Courts commission, §§7A-506 to 7A-510.
Creation.
Writing required, §147-16.2, (d).
Credit unions.
Commission, §143B-439.
Crime victims compensation commission, §15B-3.
Criminal justice information network governing board, §§143-660 to 143-664.
Crop seed improvement board, §143A-64.

BOARDS AND COMMISSIONS —Cont'd
Definitions.
Fees and charges by agencies, §12-3.1, (b).
Notice of appointments to public office, §143-47.6.
Occupational licensing boards, §93B-1.
Dental hygienists.
Board of dental examiners, §§90-222, 90-223.
Dentists.
Board of dental examiners.
See DENTISTS.
Dietitians and nutritionists.
North Carolina board of dietetics/nutrition, §§90-352 to 90-356.
Discrimination against lawful use of lawful products during nonworking hours, §95-28.2.
Domestic violence commission, §§143B-394.15, 143B-394.16.
Drainage district commission, §§156-79 to 156-93.1.
Drug commission, §§143B-147 to 143B-150.
Economic development board, §§143B-434 to 143B-437.
Economic development commissions, §§158-8 to 158-15.
Economic development plan, §143B-434.01, (a).
Edenton historical commission, §§143B-95 to 143B-98.
Education.
Education commission, §§143-261 to 143-266.
Local boards of education, §§115C-35 to 115C-50.
See LOCAL BOARDS OF EDUCATION.
School technology commission, §§115C-102.5 to 115C-102.7.
State board of education.
Generally.
See STATE BOARD OF EDUCATION.
State board of higher education.
Powers and duties, §116-158.
State education commission, §§143-261 to 143-266.
See EDUCATION COMMISSION.
Teaching fellows commission, §§115C-363.22, 115C-363.23.
Elections.
County boards of elections, §§163-30 to 163-37.
See COUNTY BOARDS OF ELECTIONS.
State board of elections generally, §§163-19 to 163-28.
See STATE BOARD OF ELECTIONS.
Electrical contractors.
Board of examiners, §§87-39 to 87-42.
Electrologists.
Board of electrolysis examiners, §§88A-5 to 88A-8.
Employment security commission.
Unemployment compensation generally, §§96-1 to 96-29.
See UNEMPLOYMENT COMPENSATION.
Engineers.
Board of examiners, §§89C-4 to 89C-12.
Environmental management commission, §§143B-282 to 143B-285.
Environmental review commission, §§120-70.41 to 120-70.47.
Expiration of board or commission created by governor or other state officials.
Constitutional elective officers creating, §147-16.2, (b).
Executive branch officials creating, §147-16.2, (c).
Executive order of governor creating, §147-16.2, (a).

BOARDS AND COMMISSIONS —Cont'd
Fees and charges.
Agencies establishing fees and charges by rule, §12-3.1, (a), (c).
Definitions, §12-3.1, (b).
Fire and rescue commission, §§58-78-1 to 58-78-20.
First flight centennial commission, §§143-640 to 143-643.
Foresters.
Board of registration, §§89B-3 to 89B-8.
Funeral service.
Board of funeral service, §§90-210.18A to 90-210.24.
Future of the North Carolina railroad study commission, §§120-245 to 120-255.
Gasoline and oil inspection board, §119-26.
Gender based appointments.
Appointing members to statutorily created decision making or regulatory entities.
Appointments to reflect proportion that gender represents in population of state, §143-157.1, (a).
Report by appointing authority of number appointments of each gender, §143-157.1, (b).
General assembly.
Appointments, §120-121.
Employees and consultants.
Legislative commissions and committees.
Contracting for employment and consultant services, §120-32.02, (a) to (c).
Environmental review commission, §§120-70.41 to 120-70.47.
Grants, contributions and loans.
Legislative commissions and committees.
Applying for, receiving and accepting, §120-32.03, (a), (b).
Joint legislative commission on future strategies for North Carolina, §§120-84.6 to 120-84.11.
Joint legislative commission on governmental operation, §§120-71 to 120-79.
Joint legislative commission on municipal incorporation, §§120-158 to 120-174.
Joint legislative commission on seafood and aquaculture, §§120-70.60 to 120-70.66.
Legislative research commission, §§120-30.10 to 120-30.18.
Legislative services commission, §§120-31 to 120-36.
Reports for state institutions and departments, §120-12.
Service by general assembly members, §120-123.
General contractors.
Board, §§87-2 to 87-8, 87-9.1.
General statutes commission, §§164-12 to 164-19.
See GENERAL STATUTES COMMISSION.
Geologists.
Board for licensing geologists, §§89E-4, 89E-5.
Global TransPark development commission, §§158-35, 158-36.
Governor's crime commission, §§143B-478 to 143B-480.
Grievance resolution board.
Prisoners' grievance procedure, §§148-118.6 to 148-118.9.
Handicapped persons.
Commission to study the care of the aged and handicapped, §§143-279 to 143-283.

BOARDS AND COMMISSIONS —Cont'd
Hazardous waste management commission.
See HAZARDOUS WASTE MANAGEMENT.
Health and wellness trust fund commission, §§147-86.32 to 147-86.36.
Health insurance innovations commission, §§58-90-1 to 58-90-25.
Health services, commission for.
Generally.
See HEALTH SERVICES COMMISSION.
Hearing aid dealers and fitters.
Board, §93D-3.
High Rock lake marine commission, §§77-50 to 77-58.
Hillsborough historical commission, §§143B-103 to 143B-106.
Historical commission, §§143B-62 to 143B-65.
Historic Bath commission, §§143B-99 to 143B-102.
Home inspectors.
Licensure board, §§143-151.43 to 143-151.63.
Human relations commission, §§143B-391, 143B-392.
Indians.
Commission of Indian affairs, §§143B-404 to 143B-411.
Indigent defense services.
Commission on, §§7A-498.4, 7A-498.5.
Industrial commission.
Generally.
See INDUSTRIAL COMMISSION.
Industrial development commission, §§158-21 to 158-24.
John Motley Morehead memorial commission, §§143B-111 to 143B-115.
Joint legislative commission on future strategies for North Carolina, §§120-84.6 to 120-84.11.
Joint legislative commission on governmental operation, §§120-71 to 120-79.
Joint legislative commission on municipal incorporation, §§120-158 to 120-174.
See MUNICIPAL CORPORATIONS.
Joint legislative commission on seafood and aquaculture, §§120-70.60 to 120-70.66.
Judicial standards commission, §§7A-375 to 7A-377.
Jury commissions, §9-1.
Justice department.
Rules review commission, §§143B-30.1 to 143B-30.4.
Lake Lure marine commission, §§77-80 to 77-88.
See LAKE LURE MARINE COMMISSION.
Lake Wylie marine commission, §§77-30 to 77-38.
Landscape architects.
Board, §89A-3.
Landscape contractors.
Board, §89D-4.
Land surveyors.
Board of examiners, §§89C-4 to 89C-12.
See ENGINEERS.
Legislative appointments to boards and commissions, §120-121, (d).
Bill enactment required, §120-121, (a).
Conflicts of interest.
Service by members of general assembly on certain boards and commissions, §120-123.
Contents of bills, §120-121, (c).
Multiple appointments, §120-121, (b).

BOARDS AND COMMISSIONS —Cont'd
Legislative appointments to boards and commissions —Cont'd
Service by members of general assembly on certain boards and commissions, §120-123.
Vacancies in appointments, §120-122.
Legislative research commission, §§120-30.10 to 120-30.18.
See LEGISLATIVE RESEARCH COMMISSION.
Legislative services commission, §§120-31 to 120-36.
Legislative study commission on children and youth, §§120-215 to 120-220.
Legislative study commission on mental health, developmental disabilities and substance abuse services, §§120-204 to 120-207.
Liability insurance commission, §§58-32-1 to 58-32-30.
See LIABILITY INSURANCE COMMISSION.
Libraries and librarians.
Public librarian certification commission, §§143B-67 to 143B-70.
State library commission, §§143B-90, 143B-91.
License to give trust fund commission, §§20-7.5, 20-7.6.
Limitation of actions.
Settlement of affairs of certain inoperative boards and agencies.
Claims settlement, §143-270.
Livestock market advisory board, §106-407.1.
Local government finance commission.
See LOCAL GOVERNMENT FINANCE.
Local governments commission, §128-12.
Locksmith licensing board, §74F-5.
Lodging expenses, §138-5, (a) to (f).
Manufactured housing board, §143-143.8.
Marine fisheries commission, §§143B-289.50 to 143B-289.61.
See MARINE FISHERIES COMMISSION.
Marine fisheries compact commission, §§113-254 to 113-257.
Marriage and family therapists.
Board, §§90-270.49 to 90-270.51.
Martin Luther King, Jr., commission, §§143B-426.34A, 143B-426.34B.
Massage and bodywork therapy.
Board of massage and bodywork therapy, §§90-625 to 90-628.
See MASSAGE AND BODYWORK THERAPY.
Medical board, §§90-2 to 90-8.
See MEDICAL BOARD.
Medical care commission, §§143B-165 to 143B-168.
Meetings.
Legislative commissions, committees and standing subcommittees, §143-318.14A.
Meetings of public bodies generally, §§143-318.9 to 143-318.18.
See MEETINGS.
Mental health, developmental disabilities and substance abuse services commission, §§143B-147 to 143B-150.
See MENTAL HEALTH, DEVELOPMENTAL DISABILITY, SUBSTANCE ABUSE.
Metropolitan sewerage districts.
District boards, §§162A-65 to 162A-67.
Metropolitan water districts.
District board, §§162A-32 to 162A-34.
Midwives.
Joint subcommittee of medical board and board of nursing, §§90-178.4, 90-178.7.

BOARDS AND COMMISSIONS —Cont'd
Military affairs.
Advisory commission on military affairs, §§127C-1 to 127C-4.
Mining commission, §§143B-290 to 143B-293.
Morehead City navigation and pilotage commission, §§76A-31 to 76A-54.
See MOREHEAD CITY NAVIGATION AND PILOTAGE COMMISSION.
Mountain Island lake marine commission, §§77-70 to 77-78.
See MOUNTAIN ISLAND LAKE.
Municipal boards of elections, §163-280.
Abolished, exception, §163-280.1.
Municipal zoning adjustment boards, §160A-388.
Murfreesboro historical commission, §§143B-107 to 143B-110.
Natural History Museum Advisory Commission, §§143B-344.18 to 143B-344.21.
Northeastern North Carolina regional economic development commission, §158-8.2.
Notice and record of appointment.
Filing, contents, §143-47.7.
Nurses.
Board of nursing, §§90-171.20 to 90-171.27.
Nursing home administrators.
Board of examiners, §§90-277 to 90-285.1.
Nursing scholars commission, §90-171.60.
Nutritionists and dietitians.
North Carolina board of dietetics/nutrition, §§90-352 to 90-356.
Occupational licensing boards.
General provisions, §§93B-1 to 93B-13.
See OCCUPATIONAL LICENSING BOARDS.
New boards, §§120-149.1 to 120-149.6.
See OCCUPATIONAL LICENSING BOARDS.
Occupational safety and health board, §95-135.
Occupational therapists board, §§90-270.68, 90-270.69.
Official appearance commission, §§160A-451 to 160A-455.
Officials qualification board, §143-151.8.
Opticians.
Board, §§90-238, 90-239.
Optometrists.
Board of examiners, §§90-116 to 90-122.
Osteopaths.
Board of osteopathic examination and registration, §90-130.
Pastoral counselors.
Fee-based practicing pastoral counselors.
State board of examiners, §90-385.
Per diem, subsistence and travel allowances.
Applicability of schedules, §138-5, (b).
Convention registration fees, §138-5, (a).
Per diem, amount, §138-5, (a).
Members whose salaries paid from state funds, §138-5, (f).
Subsistence expenses, amount, §138-5, (a).
Documentation of actual lodging expenses, required, §138-5, (d).
General assembly members, §138-5, (f).
Travel expenses, amount, §138-5, (a).
General assembly members, §138-5, (f).
Out-of-state travel, §138-5, (e).
Personnel system.
Commission, §§126-2, 126-4.
Final agency decisions, §126-4.1.

BOARDS AND COMMISSIONS —Cont'd
Pesticide board generally, §§143-434 to 143-470.1.
See PESTICIDE BOARD.
Pharmacists and pharmacies.
Board of pharmacy, §§90-85.6 to 90-85.12.
Physical therapists.
Board of examiners, §§90-270.24 to 90-270.26.
Plant protection and conservation board, §§106-202.12 to 106-202.15.
Plumbing, heating and fire sprinkler contractors.
Board, §§87-16 to 87-20.
Podiatrists.
Board of podiatry examiners, §90-202.4.
Post-release supervision and parole commission, §§143B-266, 143B-267.
Prisons and prisoners.
Grievance resolution board.
Administrative remedy procedure generally, §§148-118.1 to 148-118.9.
Private protective services board, §§74C-4 to 74C-6.
Progress board, §§143B-372.1 to 143B-372.3.
Property tax commission.
See PROPERTY TAX COMMISSION.
Property taxes.
Agricultural, horticultural and forestland.
Special classification for property taxes purposes.
Use-value advisory board, §105-277.7.
Public employee special pay plan.
Board of trustees, §143B-426.41.
Public health study commission, §§120-195 to 120-203.
Public librarian certification commission, §§143B-67 to 143B-70.
Public records, §§132-1 to 132-10.
See RECORDS.
Purchases through department of administration.
Board of awards, §143-52.1.
Radiation protection.
Commission, §§104E-7, 104E-8.
Real estate brokers and salespersons.
Commission, §93A-3.
Records.
Public records, §§132-1 to 132-10.
See RECORDS.
Settlement of affairs of certain inoperative boards and agencies.
Official records turned over to department of cultural resources, §143-268.
Redevelopment commission, §§160A-504 to 160A-512.
Refrigeration contractors.
Board of examiners, §§87-52 to 87-56.
Regional planning commissions, §§153A-391 to 153A-398.
Regional response team advisory committee.
Hazardous materials emergency response, §166A-26.
Reports.
From state institutions and departments to general assembly, §120-12.
Respiratory care board, §§90-649 to 90-652.
River basins advisory commissions, §§77-110 to 77-118.
See RIVER BASINS ADVISORY COMMISSIONS.
Roanoke Island commission, §§143B-131.1 to 143B-131.10.

BOARDS AND COMMISSIONS —Cont'd
Roanoke river basin bi-state commission, §§77-90 to 77-99.
Rules review commission, §§143B-30.1 to 143B-30.4.
Salaries.
Exceptions to provisions, §138-7.
Moving expenses of state employees, §138-8.
Sale, lease or exchange of property between governmental units.
Action taken by governmental unit, §160A-274, (c).
Authority, §160A-274, (b).
Governmental unit defined, §160A-274, (a).
Sanitarians.
Board of examiners, §§90A-50 to 90A-60.
Sanitary districts.
Boards, §§130A-50 to 130A-56.
Science and technology.
Board of science and technology, §§143B-472.80, 143B-472.81.
Secretary of state.
Appointments, §147-36.
Sedimentation control commission, §§113A-54 to 113A-56, 143B-298, 143B-299.
Seed board, §§106-277.31 to 106-277.33.
Seeds.
Board of crop seed improvement, §§106-269 to 106-276.
Sentencing and policy advisory commission, §§164-35 to 164-45.
See NORTH CAROLINA SENTENCING AND POLICY ADVISORY COMMISSION.
Service of process.
Personal jurisdiction.
Manner of service, §1A-1, Rule 4, (j).
Process agent, appointment, §1A-1, Rule 4, (j).
Settlement of affairs of certain inoperative boards and agencies.
Allocation of certain assets to state agency or department, §143-268.
Audits.
Affairs of board or agency, §143-272.
Payment for audit and other expenses, §143-272.
Claims.
Certification to state treasurer, §143-271.
Escheat of balance to University of North Carolina, §143-271.
Payment, §143-271.
Statement of claims against board of agency, §143-270.
Conversion of certain assets into cash, §143-268.
Delivery of certain assets to secretary of administration, §143-267.
Deposit of funds by state treasurer, §143-269.
Escheat of balance to University of North Carolina, §143-271.
Limitation of actions.
Claims against board of agency, §143-270.
Official records turned over to department of cultural resources, §143-268.
Release and payment of funds to state treasurer, §143-267.
Sheriffs' education and training standards commission.
General provisions, §§17E-1 to 17E-12.
Social services commission, §§143B-153 to 143B-156.
Social workers.
Certification and licensure board, §§90B-3 to 90B-6.

BOARDS AND COMMISSIONS —Cont'd
Soil and water conservation commission.
General provisions, §§143B-294 to 143B-297.
Soil scientists.
Board for licensing, §§89F-4, 89F-5.
Southern dairy compact commission, §106-811.
Southern growth policies agreement board, §§143-492 to 143-497.
Southern states energy compact board, §§104D-1 to 104D-5.
Southwestern North Carolina regional economic development commission, §158-8.3.
Speech and language pathologists and audiologists.
Board of examiners, §90-303.
State banking commission.
See BANKING COMMISSION.
State board of pensions, §143A-29.
State education commission, §§143-261 to 143-266.
State farms operation commission, §66-58.
State fire and rescue commission, §§58-78-1 to 58-78-20.
See FIRE AND RESCUE COMMISSION.
State library commission, §§143B-90, 143B-91.
State property.
Commission on state property, §§143-735 to 143-737.
Subsistence expenses, §138-5, (a) to (f).
Survey of operation and management.
Director of the budget, §143-11, (a).
Tax review board, §143A-38.
Teaching fellows commission, §§115C-363.22 to 115C-363.23A.
Textbook commission, §§115C-87, 115C-88.
Therapeutic recreation personnel.
Board, §§90C-4 to 90C-8.
Tobacco boards of trade.
Membership, §106-465.
Organization, §106-465.
Tobacco research commission, §106-568.3.
Tobacco trust fund.
General provisions, §§143-715 to 143-723.
See TOBACCO TRUST FUND COMMISSION.
Transportation board.
See TRANSPORTATION BOARD.
Travel and tourism board, §143B-434.1.
Travel expenses, §138-5, (a) to (f).
Tryon Palace commission, §§143B-71, 143B-72.
Universities and colleges.
State board of higher education.
Powers and duties, §116-158.
University of North Carolina.
Board of governors.
See UNIVERSITY OF NORTH CAROLINA.
Constituent institutions.
Boards of trustees, §§116-31 to 116-33.
See UNIVERSITY OF NORTH CAROLINA.
Urban redevelopment commission.
See URBAN REDEVELOPMENT.
Use-value advisory board.
Agricultural, horticultural and forestland.
Special classification for property taxes purposes, §105-277.7.
U.S.S. North Carolina battleship commission, §§143B-73 to 143B-74.3.
Utilities commission.
Generally, §§62-10 to 62-98.
See UTILITIES COMMISSION.
Veterans commission, §§143B-399 to 143B-401.

BOARDS AND COMMISSIONS —Cont'd
Veterans employment priority.
Priority in employment assistance for United States armed forces veterans, §§165-44.1 to 165-44.6.
Veterans' memorial commission, §§143B-133, 143B-133.1.
Veterinarians.
Board, §§90-181 to 90-186.
Virginia-North Carolina interstate high-speed rail compact commission, §136-222.
War manpower commission, §135-16.
Water pollution control.
System operators certification commission, §§143B-300 to 143B-301.1.
Water treatment facility operators.
Board of certification, §§90A-21 to 90A-28.
Welfare.
Board of public welfare, Const. N. C., art. XI, §4.
Well contractor certification commission, §§143B-301.10 to 143B-301.12.
Western North Carolina regional economic development commission, §158-8.1.
Wildlife resources commissions, §§143-237 to 143-254.2.
See WILDLIFE RESOURCES COMMISSION.
Wireless 911 board, §62A-22.
Workforce development boards, local, §143B-438.11.
Workforce development commission, §143B-438.10.
Writing required to create, §147-16.2, (d).
Zoning.
Municipal corporations.
Adjustment boards, §160A-388.

BOARDS OF CITY COMMISSIONERS.
Generally.
See CITY COUNCILS.

BOARDS OF COUNTY COMMISSIONERS.
Generally.
See COUNTY BOARDS OF COMMISSIONERS.

BOARDS OF EDUCATION.
Local boards of education generally.
See LOCAL BOARDS OF EDUCATION.
State board of education.
See STATE BOARD OF EDUCATION.

BOARDS OF ELECTIONS.
County boards of elections generally, §§163-30 to 163-37.
See COUNTY BOARDS OF ELECTIONS.
Municipal boards of elections, §163-280.
Abolished, exception, §163-280.1.
Political activities by board members, §§163-38 to 163-40.1.
State board of elections generally, §§163-19 to 163-28.
See STATE BOARD OF ELECTIONS.

BOATING SAFETY, §§75A-1 to 75A-26.
Accidents.
Duties of operator involved in, §75A-11.
Violations of provisions, §75A-18, (a).
Alcoholic beverages.
Operation of boat or manipulation of water skis while intoxicated, §75A-10, (b), (b1).
Boat liveries.
Compliance with provisions.
Prerequisite to rental of vessels, §75A-8.
Equipment.
Duty to equip rented vessels as required, §75A-8.

BOATING SAFETY —Cont'd
Collisions.
Duties of operators involved in, §75A-11.
Violations of provisions, §75A-18, (a).
Commercial fishing boats.
Defined, §75A-5.1, (b).
Identification numbers.
False information, §75A-5.1, (d).
Renewal of number, §75A-5.1, (a), (c).
Muffling devices.
Exemption from provisions, §75A-9.1.
Dealers.
Operation of watercraft by.
Rules and regulations, §75A-19.
Death.
Collision or accident resulting in.
Duty of operator involved, §75A-11, (b).
Definitions, §75A-2.
Commercial fishing boats, §75A-5.1, (b).
Diver's flag, §75A-13.1.
Violations of provisions, §75A-18, (c).
Drugs.
Operation of boat or manipulation of water skis while under influence of drugs, §75A-10, (b), (b1).
Penalty, §75A-18, (b).
Drunkenness.
Operation of boat or manipulation of water skis while intoxicated, §75A-10, (b), (b1).
Penalty, §75A-18, (b).
Enforcement of provisions.
Department of environment and natural resources.
Agreement with wildlife resources commission to enforce, §75A-17, (b).
Law enforcement officers, §75A-17, (a).
Wildlife resources commission, §75A-3, (a).
Funds for enforcement, §75A-3, (c).
Evidence.
Proof of ownership of motorboat, §75A-10.2.
Family purpose doctrine.
Applicability of doctrine, §75A-10.1.
Fire extinguishers.
Requirements, §75A-6, (g).
Exceptions, §75A-6, (h).
Flags.
Diver's flag, §75A-13.1.
Violations of provisions, §75A-18, (c).
Garbage and trash.
Depositing or discharging litter, §75A-10, (c).
Medical waste, §75A-10, (d).
Penalties, §75A-18, (d).
Heads.
Marine toilets, §75A-6, (o).
Identification numbers, §§75A-5, 75A-7.
Agents for awarding of certificates, §75A-5, (e), (l).
Applications, §75A-5, (a).
Change of address of owner of vessel.
Notification to wildlife resources commission, §75A-5, (j).
Change of ownership, §75A-5, (c).
Display, §75A-5, (a).
Other numbers, §75A-5, (k).
Exemptions from requirement, §75A-7, (a).
Federal overall systems of identification numbering.
Conformity with, §75A-5, (d).
Fees.
Application fee, §75A-5, (a).
Change of ownership of vessel, §75A-5, (c).
Renewal fee, §75A-5, (h).

BOATING SAFETY —Cont'd
Identification numbers —Cont'd
Government-owned vessels.
Permanent certificate of number, §75A-7, (c).
Voluntary numbering, §75A-7, (b).
Lifeboats.
Exemption from requirement, §75A-7, (a).
Period of numbering, §75A-5, (a), (g).
Reciprocity, §75A-5, (b).
Records.
Public records, §75A-5, (f).
Renewal, §75A-5, (h).
Required, §75A-4.
Exemptions, §75A-7, (a).
Transfer of interest in vessels.
Notification to wildlife resources commission, §75A-5, (i).
Unauthorized numbers, §75A-5, (k).
Lake Norman no-wake zone, §75A-14.1.
Legislative declaration, §75A-1.
Lifeboats.
Identification numbers for vessels.
Exemption from requirement, §75A-7, (a).
Life preservers, etc.
Requirements, §75A-6, (f), (n).
Lights.
Motorboats, §75A-6, (n).
Local water safety committees.
Administrative and staff services, §75A-26, (d).
Authorized, §75A-26, (a).
Duties of members, §75A-26, (g).
Existing organizations or committees, §75A-26, (c).
Expenses of members, §75A-26, (d).
Meetings, §75A-26, (b), (f).
Notification of sponsorship or withdrawal of sponsorship, §75A-26, (e).
Selection of members, §75A-26, (b).
Magistrate's powers in cases involving boating offenses, §7A-273.
Manufacturers.
Operation of watercraft by.
Rules and regulations, §75A-19.
Misdemeanors.
Depositing or discharging litter, §75A-10, (c).
Medical waste, §75A-18, (d).
Identification numbers for vessels.
Agents for awarding of certificates of number.
Violations of provisions, §75A-5, (e), (l).
Commercial fishing boats.
Renewal of number.
False information, §75A-5.1, (d).
Violations of provisions generally, §75A-18, (a).
Liability insurance.
Violation of certain requirements, §75A-18, (c1).
Operation of boat or manipulation of water skis in reckless or negligent manner, §75A-18, (b).
Operation of boat or manipulation of water skis while intoxicated or under influence of drugs, §75A-18, (b).
Regatta or race.
Violations of provisions, §75A-18, (a).
Violations generally, §75A-18.
Motorboats.
Bells, §75A-6, (h).
Carburetors, §75A-6, (i).
Classification, §75A-6, (a).
Defined, §75A-2.
Equipment.
Federal boat safety act of 1971.
Conformance with, §75A-6, (m).
Generally, §75A-6.

BOATING SAFETY —Cont'd
Motorboats —Cont'd
Equipment —Cont'd
Muffling devices, §§75A-9, 75A-9.1.
Permission for operation of vessel.
Compliance as prerequisite, §75A-6, (l).
Fire extinguishers, §75A-6, (g).
Exceptions, §75A-6, (h).
Identification numbers.
Violations of provisions generally, §75A-18, (a).
Length.
Classification, §75A-6, (a).
Life preservers, etc., §75A-6, (f), (n).
Lights, §75A-6, (n).
Muffling devices, §§75A-9, 75A-9.1.
Proof of ownership, §75A-10.2, (a), (b).
Regatta or race.
Equipment requirements, §75A-6, (h).
Ventilation, §75A-6, (j).
Whistles, §75A-6, (h).
Muffling devices, §§75A-9, 75A-9.1.
Navigation rules.
Compliance with, §75A-6.1, (a).
Enforcement, §75A-6.1, (b).
Violations, §75A-6.1, (c).
Negligence.
Operation of boat or manipulation of water skis in reckless or negligent manner, §75A-10, (a).
Penalty, §75A-18, (b).
Personal watercraft.
Defined, §75A-13.3, (a).
Following too closely, §75A-13.3, (e).
Lanyard-type engine cut-off device.
Requirement, §75A-13.3, (d).
Local governments, marine commission or lake authorities.
Regulation, authorization, §75A-13.3, (h).
Narrow channel.
Defined, §75A-13.3, (f1).
No-wake speed, operating at greater speed, §75A-13.3, (a1).
No-wake speed.
Operating at speed greater than in certain areas, prohibition, §75A-13.3, (a1).
Performers engaged in professional exhibition.
Inapplicable of provisions, §75A-13.3, (f).
Personal floatation device.
Requirement, §75A-13.3, (d).
Persons at least 12 years of age but under 16 years of age operating, §75A-13.3, (b).
Persons under 16 years of age operating, §75A-13.3, (b).
Infraction, §75A-18, (e).
Leasing, hiring or renting to, §75A-13.3, (c).
Reasonable and prudent operation.
Requirement, §75A-13.3, (e).
Reckless operation, §75A-13.3, (e).
Renting to public.
Liability insurance requirements, §75A-13.3, (c1).
Misdeameanor, fine, failure to carry, §75A-18, (c1).
Persons under 16 years of age, §75A-13.3, (c).
Safety equipment requirements, §75A-13.3, (d).
Sunset and sunrise.
Operating at any time between prohibited, §75A-13.3, (a).
Swerving at last moment to avoid collision, §75A-13.3, (e).
Towing another, §75A-13.3, (d1).
Wake jumping, §75A-13.3, (e).

BOATING SAFETY —Cont'd
Personal watercraft —Cont'd
Weaving through congested traffic, §75A-13.3, (e).
Policy of state.
Legislative declaration, §75A-1.
Regatta or race.
Equipment requirements.
Exceptions, §75A-6, (h).
Muffling devices.
Exceptions to requirements, §§75A-9, 75A-9.1.
Violations of provisions, §75A-18, (a).
Rules and regulations.
Agencies which may apply for rules, §75A-15, (b).
Effect of rules, §75A-15, (d).
Electric generating facilities, §75A-15, (e).
Navigation rules, §75A-6.1, (a) to (c).
Operation of watercraft by manufacturers, dealers, etc., §75A-19.
Scope of rules, §75A-15, (a).
Special regulations, §75A-15.
Uniform state waterway marking system.
Rules implementing, §75A-15, (c).
Violations, §75A-18, (a).
Skin and scuba divers.
Diver's flag, §75A-13.1.
Description, §75A-13.1, (b).
Duties of operators of vessels as to, §75A-13.1, (c).
Required, §75A-13.1, (a).
Violations of provisions.
Penalty, §75A-18, (c).
Violations of provisions, §75A-18, (a), (b).
Surfboards.
Hours for surfboarding, §75A-13, (c).
Manipulation in reckless or negligent manner, §75A-10, (a).
Manipulation while intoxicated or under influence of drugs, §75A-10, (b).
Requirements for vessels towing, §75A-13, (a), (b), (d).
Exceptions, §75A-13, (c).
Toilets.
Marine toilets, §75A-6, (o).
Torts.
Family purpose doctrine.
Applicability, §75A-10.1.
Uniform state waterway marking system.
Adoption, §75A-15, (c).
United States.
Furnishing information to agencies of United States.
Duty of wildlife resources commission, §75A-12.
Vessels.
Defined, §75A-2.
Water skis.
Hours for water skiing, §75A-13, (b).
Manipulation in reckless or negligent manner, §75A-10, (a).
Manipulation while intoxicated or under influence of drugs, §75A-10, (b).
Personal watercraft.
Towing person on water skis, §75A-13.3, (d1).
Requirements for vessels towing, §75A-13, (a), (b), (d).
Exceptions, §75A-13, (c).
Violations of provisions as to, §75A-18, (a), (b).
Wildlife protectors jurisdiction, §113-136, (c).
Wildlife resources commission.
Administration and enforcement of provisions, §75A-3, (a).
Funding, §75A-3, (c).

BOATING SAFETY —Cont'd
Wildlife resources commission —Cont'd
Information.
Furnishing to agencies of United States, §75A-12.
Motorboat committee, §75A-3, (b).

BOATING UNDER THE INFLUENCE, §75A-10, (b), (b1).

BOAT LIVERIES.
Compliance with boating safety requirements, §75A-8.

BOATS.
Alcoholic beverages.
Forfeiture generally, §18B-504.
Use on oceangoing ships, §18B-106.
Boating safety, §§75A-1 to 75A-26.
See BOATING SAFETY.
Breaking or entering into or breaking out of boats or other watercraft, §14-56.
Bridges.
Fastening vessels to bridges a misdemeanor, §136-80.
Burning of boats and barges, §14-63.
Certificate of title, §§75A-32 to 75A-48.
See BOAT TITLING.
Discharges of oil or hazardous substances, §§143-215.83 to 143-215.94.
See OIL OR HAZARDOUS SUBSTANCES DISCHARGES.
Discharging firearm into occupied property, §14-34.1.
Duties and import taxes.
Vessels traveling between states, Const. U. S., art. I, §9.
Forfeiture, §18B-504.
Controlled substances, §§90-112, 90-112.1.
Handicapped persons.
Right to use of public conveyances, §168-3.
Hazardous waste.
Storage of certain waste on vessels, §143-214.2B.
Hunting from vessels, §113-291.1, (b).
Taking wild animals or birds from vessels equipped with motors, §113-294, (g).
Insurance.
Department of transportation.
Authority to insure operated by department, §136-82.1.
Lights.
Displaying false lights on seashore, §14-282.
Malt beverages and wine transported by boats, §18B-1115, (f).
Obstructing passage in rivers or creeks, §77-12.
Parks and recreation.
State parks and state lakes.
Operation and use rules, §113-35, (c).
Personal watercraft.
Regulation of operation, §75A-13.3.
Ports authority, §§143B-452 to 143B-467.
See PORTS AUTHORITY.
Possessory liens on personal property.
Action to regain possession of vessel.
Involuntary relinquishment of possession by lienor, §44A-6.1, (a).
Appeal to district court for trial de novo, §44A-6.1, (b).
General provisions, §§44A-1 to 44A-6.1.
Vessel defined, §44A-1.
Records.
Title, §75A-38, (a).

BOATS —Cont'd
Registration.
Prima facie evidence of ownership, §75A-49.
Rules affecting general public.
Notification, §113-301.1.
Sales and use tax.
Rate of tax, §105-164.4, (a).
Seizure and forfeiture of conveyances used in committing larceny and similar crimes, §14-86.1.
Shad boat.
State historical boat, §145-11.
Ships and shipping.
See SHIPS AND SHIPPING.
Title, §§75A-32 to 75A-49.
See BOAT TITLING.
Tour boats.
Alcoholic beverage permits, §18B-1006, (i).
Transportation department.
Insuring vessels operated by department, §136-82.1.
Trespass.
Removing boats, §14-162.
Unmooring or turning adrift, §14-162.
Waste.
Storage of waste on vessels, §143-214.2B.

BOAT TITLING, §§75A-32 to 75A-49.
Certificate of title, §§75A-32 to 75A-48.
Application.
Contents, §75A-35, (a), (b).
Form, §75A-35, (b).
Who may apply for, §75A-34, (a).
Change of address.
Notice by owner, §75A-36.
Duplicate certificates, §75A-39.
Duration, §75A-37, (a).
Evidence, §75A-37, (a).
Fees, §75A-38, (b).
Leases, UCC.
Leases applicable to certificate of title statute, §25-2A-104, (1).
Levy of execution, §75A-48.
Lost, stolen, etc.
Certificate, §75A-39.
Security interest, §75A-40.
Filing, §75A-43.
Legal holder subject to security interest, §75A-45.
Notice of interest, §75A-42.
Priority shown on certificate, §75A-44.
Release, §75A-46.
Subsequently created interest, §75A-41.
Surrender of certificate when interest paid, §75A-47.
Transfer, §75A-37, (b).
Change of address.
Notice by owner, §75A-36.
Citation of article, §75A-32.
Commission.
Authority of employee, §75A-34, (b).
Definitions, §75A-33.
Evidence.
Certificate of title.
Prima facie evidence of ownership, §75A-37, (a).
Execution.
Levy, §75A-48.
Records, §75A-38, (a).
Registration.
Prima facie evidence of ownership, §75A-49.

BOAT TITLING —Cont'd
Security interest, §§75A-40 to 75A-47.
Certificate of title to show, §75A-40.
Filing, §75A-43.
Interest subsequently created, §75A-41.
Legal holder subject to interest, §75A-45.
Notice of interest, §75A-42.
Priority of interest shown on certificate, §75A-44.
Release, §75A-46.
Surrender when security interest paid, §75A-47.
Short title of article, §75A-32.
Transfer of title, §75A-37, (b).
Fees, §75A-38, (b).

BOBCATS.
Rabies emergencies.
Plan to reduce threat of rabies exposure to humans and domestic animals, §130A-201.
Rabies emergency for particular county.
Plan to reduce exposure to humans and domestic animals, §113-291.2, (a1).
Sale of parts, §113-291.3, (b).

BODYGUARDS.
Generally, §§74C-1 to 74C-33.
See PRIVATE PROTECTIVE SERVICES.

BODY MEASUREMENTS.
Nontestimonial identification, §§15A-271 to 15A-282.
See IDENTIFICATION.

BODY PIERCING.
Children and minors.
Without consent of parents, §14-400, (b).

BODY SHOPS.
Repair of motor vehicles, §§20-354 to 20-354.9.
See MOTOR VEHICLE REPAIRS.

BODYWORK THERAPY, §§90-620 to 90-636.
See MASSAGE AND BODYWORK THERAPY.

BOILER AND MACHINERY INSURANCE, §58-7-15.
Mandatory or voluntary risk sharing plans.
See MANDATORY OR VOLUNTARY RISK SHARING PLANS.

BOILER ROOM OPERATIONS.
Telephone rooms, securities regulation, §78A-11.
Criminal penalties, §78A-57, (a) to (a4).

BOILERS, §§95-69.8 to 95-69.18.
Accident investigations, §95-69.11.
Appeals.
Administrative and judicial review of decisions, §95-69.17.
Applicability of provisions, §95-69.10, (a).
Exceptions, §95-69.10, (b) to (e).
Board of boiler and pressure vessel rules.
Chairman, §95-69.13.
Composition, §95-69.13, (a).
Creation, §95-69.13, (a).
Definition of "board," §95-69.9, (a).
Duties, §95-69.13, (b).
Expenses of members, §95-69.13, (c).
Meetings, §95-69.13, (b).
Number of members, §95-69.13, (a).
Qualifications of members, §95-69.13, (a).
Review of final decisions of board, §95-69.17.
Terms of members, §95-69.13, (a).
Building code.
Enforcement of code, §143-139, (c).

BOILERS —Cont'd
Citation of act.
Short title, §95-69.8.
Commissioner of labor.
Accident investigations, §95-69.11.
Definition of "commissioner," §95-69.9, (c).
Duties, §95-69.11.
Injunctions, §95-69.11.
Powers, §95-69.11.
Rules and regulations, §95-69.14.
Powers and duties of commissioner, §95-69.11.
Subpoenas, §95-69.11.
Definitions, §95-69.9.
Director of boiler and pressure vessel division.
Creation of office, §95-69.12.
Defined, §95-69.9, (d).
Duties, §95-69.12.
Review of final decisions of director, §95-69.17.
Exemptions from provisions, §95-69.10, (b) to (e).
Fines, §95-69.18.
Hot water heaters, §§66-27.1 to 66-27.4.
Injunctions, §95-69.11.
Inspections.
Certificates, §95-69.16.
Definition of "inspection certificate," §95-69.9, (e).
Refusal to issue or renew certificate.
Final decision, §95-69.17, (b).
Judicial review of final decision, §95-69.17, (c).
Required, §95-69.18.
Suspension or revocation of certificate.
Final decision, §95-69.17, (a).
Judicial review of final decision, §95-69.17, (c).
Powers and duties of commissioner, §95-69.11.
Required, §95-69.16.
Inspectors.
Classification of inspectors, §95-69.15, (a).
Commissions, §95-69.15, (b).
Definition of "inspector's commission," §95-69.9, (f).
Suspension or revocation.
Final decisions, §95-69.17, (a).
Judicial review of final decisions, §95-69.17, (c).
Misrepresentation of self as inspector.
Penalty, §95-69.18.
Qualifications, §95-69.15, (c).
Misdemeanors.
Misrepresentation of self as inspector, §95-69.18.
Operation or use of boiler or pressure vessel without certificate of inspection, §95-69.18.
Pressure vessels.
Defined, §95-69.9, (g).
Subpoenas, §95-69.11.
Tampering with boilers, §14-153.
Title of act.
Short title, §95-69.8.

BOLL WEEVIL ERADICATION, §§106-65.67 to 106-65.78.
Bees and honey.
Authority to regulate honeybee colonies in elimination zones and other areas, §106-65.76.
Certificates.
Defined, §106-65.69.
Citation of act, §106-65.67.
Commissioner of agriculture.
Defined, §106-65.69.

BOLL WEEVIL ERADICATION —Cont'd
Cooperative programs.
Authorized, §106-65.70.
Cotton.
Authority to prohibit planting of cotton, §106-65.74.
Defined, §106-65.69.
Elimination zones.
Destruction and treatment of cotton in zones, §106-65.75.
When compensation payable, §106-65.75.
Participation in eradication program.
Authority to require participation, §106-65.74.
Criminal penalties.
Violations of provisions, §106-65.78, (a), (b).
Declaration of policy, §106-65.68.
Definitions, §106-65.69.
Elimination zones.
Cotton.
Destruction and treatment of cotton in zones, §106-65.75.
When compensation payable, §106-65.75.
Designation, §106-65.74.
Honeybee colonies.
Authority to regulate, §106-65.76.
Pasturage.
Authority to regulate, §106-65.76.
Right of entry, §106-65.76.
Entry of premises.
Eradication activities, §106-65.71.
Inspections, §106-65.71.
Forged or counterfeited documents.
Criminal penalties, §106-65.78, (a).
Host.
Defined, §106-65.69.
Infested.
Defined, §106-65.69.
Inspections.
Entry of premises, §106-65.71.
Moving regulated article into state.
Criminal penalties, §106-65.78, (b).
Participation in eradication program.
Authority to require participation, §106-65.74.
Pasturage.
Elimination zones.
Authority to regulate pasturage, §106-65.76.
Permits.
Defined, §106-65.69.
Policy declaration, §106-65.68.
Purpose of article, §106-65.68.
Quarantine.
Regulations governing quarantining, §106-65.73.
Regulated article.
Defined, §106-65.69.
Reports.
Information contained in report, §106-65.72.
Right of entry.
Authority to regulate entry in elimination zones and other areas, §106-65.76.
Eradication activities, §106-65.71.
Inspections, §106-65.71.
Rules and regulations.
Authority to adopt, §106-65.77.
Quarantining, §106-65.73.
Short title, §106-65.67.
States.
Cooperative programs authorized, §106-65.70.
United States.
Cooperative programs authorized, §106-65.70.
Violations of provisions.
Criminal penalties, §106-65.78, (a), (b).

BOMBS.
Burglary with explosives, §14-57.
Civil disorders.
Certain weapons at civil disorders, §14-288.20.
Exploding, §14-283.
Explosives generally.
See EXPLOSIVES.
Keeping for sale or selling without license, §14-284.
Mass death and destruction weapons.
Manufacture, assembly, etc., §14-288.8.
Nuclear, biological or chemical weapons, §§14-288.21 to 14-288.24.
See WEAPONS OF MASS DEATH AND DESTRUCTION.
Minors detonating in schools.
Parental liability for damages, §1-538.3.
Possessing or carrying on campus or other educational property, §14-269.2.
Regulation of sale of explosives, §14-284.1.
Weapons generally.
See WEAPONS.

BOMB SCARES.
Drivers' licenses.
Revocation or suspension of license.
Minors, §20-13.2, (c2).
False reports concerning destructive device.
Destructive device located in any building or vehicle, §14-69.1, (a).
Destructive device located in public building, §14-69.1, (c).
Report defined, §14-69.1, (d).
Restitution, costs and consequential damages, ordering, §14-69.1, (d).
General assembly.
Evacuation of state legislative buildings and grounds, §120-32.1A.
Hoax by use of false bomb or other device, §14-69.2, (a).
Public buildings, §14-69.2, (c).
Restitution, costs and consequential damages, ordering, §14-69.2, (d).
Minors causing in schools.
Parental liability for disruption, §1-538.3.
Suspension of students.
False threats to destroy or damage property by explosion, blasting or burning, §115C-391, (d3).

BONA FIDE PURCHASERS.
Conveyances.
Husband and wife.
Certain conveyances not affected by fraud, §39-11.
Registration necessary to pass title as against creditors and bona fide purchasers, §47-18.
Execution against property of judgment debtor not lien on personal property as against, §1-313.
Investment securities.
Enforcement of completed or altered instrument, §25-8-206.
Judgments and decrees.
Title not affected when judgment set aside, §1-108.
Marriage settlements.
Registration necessary for validity as against creditors and bona fide purchasers, §47-25.
Notice of pending litigation.
Filing to be effective against, §1-116, (d).

BONA FIDE PURCHASERS —Cont'd
Partition.
Impeachment of commissioner's report.
Purchases not affected, §46-19, (a).
Title not affected when judgment set aside, §1-108.
Sale of goods, UCC.
Title acquired by bona fide purchasers, §25-2-403, (1).

BOND ISSUES.
Agricultural finance authority, §§122D-10 to 122D-17.
Definition of "bonds" or "notes," §122D-3.
Powers of authority, §122D-6.
Airports.
Special airport districts, §§63-83, 63-84, 63-87.
Alcoholic beverages commission, §18B-208, (a).
Banks.
Investments, §§53-44 to 53-46.
Capital facilities finance act.
Special indebtedness generally, §§142-80 to 142-101.
See CAPITAL FACILITIES FINANCE ACT.
Community colleges.
Financial support.
Elections on question of issuance, §115D-36.
Previously established institutions, §115D-34, (b).
Local financial support of institutions.
Authority to issue bonds and notes, §115D-38.
Consolidated city-county act, §§160B-13 to 160B-15.
Constitution of North Carolina.
Capital projects for industry.
Authorities may be created, Const. N. C., art. V, §9.
General assembly.
Actions on revenue bills, Const. N. C., art. II, §23.
Health care facilities.
Authorized, Const. N. C., art. V, §8.
Higher education facilities.
Authorized, Const. N. C., art. V, §12.
Hospitals, Const. N. C., art. V, §8.
Seaport and airport facilities.
Authorized powers as to, Const. N. C., art. V, §13.
Corporations.
Drainage, §§156-52, 156-53.
Interest.
Sale below par permitted, §24-2.
Payment of bonds enforced, §156-53.
Costs.
Several suits on one instrument.
Allowance of costs to defendant, §6-19.
Allowance of costs to plaintiff, §6-18.
Counties.
Local government bond act.
General provisions, §§159-43 to 159-78.
See LOCAL GOVERNMENT FINANCE.
Local government revenue bond act.
General provisions, §§159-80 to 159-97.
See LOCAL GOVERNMENT FINANCE.
Relocation of county seat.
Procedures if county votes to relocate, §159-67.
Savings banks.
Investment in county obligations, §54C-137.
School bonds.
Election required, §115C-501, (f).

BOND ISSUES —Cont'd
Counties —Cont'd
Service districts.
Authorization, §153A-308.
Streets and highways.
Prohibition of local road bonds, §136-98, (a), (b).
County service districts, §153A-308.
County water and sewer districts.
Authorized, §162A-90.
Drainage.
Corporations, §§156-52, 156-53.
Payment of bonds authorized, §156-53.
Educational institutions.
Private capital facilities finance act.
Institutions for higher education and elementary and secondary education, §§159D-35 to 159D-57.
See CAPITAL FACILITIES FINANCE AGENCY.
Electric membership corporations, §117-21.
Covenants or agreements for security of bonds, §117-22.
Purchase and cancellation of bonds, §117-23.
Specific grant of power, §117-18.
Embezzlement, §14-90.
Facility authorities, §§160A-480.8 to 160A-480.14.
Powers of authority, §160A-480.4.
Fairs.
State fair.
Constructing and financing facilities and improvements for fair, §106-503.1, (a).
Fiduciaries.
Investments.
Powers which may be incorporated by reference in trust instrument, §32-27.
Fish and fisheries resources.
Seafood industrial park authority, §113-315.31.
Forests and forestry.
Protection and development corporations.
Issuance of securities restricted, §113-68.
Forgery, §14-122.
Selling of certain forged securities, §14-121.
General assembly.
Requirements for passage of revenue bills, Const. N. C., art. II, §23.
Governor.
Council of state.
Duties performed by other officers, §142-9.
Health care facilities.
Authority to finance by bond, Const. N. C., art. V, §8.
Health care facility financing generally, §§131A-1 to 131A-25.
See HEALTH CARE FACILITY FINANCING.
Hospital authorities.
Definition of bonds, §131E-16.
Exemption from taxation, §131E-28, (c).
Revenue bonds and notes, §131E-26, (a), (b).
Hospitals.
Authority to finance by bond issue, Const. N. C., art. V, §8.
Housing authorities and projects.
See HOUSING AUTHORITIES AND PROJECTS.
Housing finance agency.
See HOUSING FINANCE AGENCY.
Income tax.
Exemption from federal income taxation.
Registered public obligations act.
Generally, §§159E-1 to 159E-15.
See REGISTERED PUBLIC OBLIGATIONS.

BOND ISSUES —Cont'd
Income tax —Cont'd
Exemption from federal income taxation —Cont'd
Registered public obligations act —Cont'd
Purpose of act, §159E-3, (a), (b).
Federal tax reform allocation committee, §§143-433.6 to 143-433.9.
Industrial and pollution control facilities financing.
Industrial and pollution control facilities financing act, §§159C-1 to 159C-27.
See INDUSTRIAL AND POLLUTION CONTROL FACILITIES FINANCING.
North Carolina capital facilities financing act.
North Carolina industrial and pollution control facilities financing act, §§159D-1 to 159D-27.
See INDUSTRIAL AND POLLUTION CONTROL FACILITIES FINANCING.
Industry.
Capital projects for industry.
County may create authorities to issue bonds, Const. N. C., art. V, §9.
Interest.
Corporate bonds may be sold below par, §24-2.
Refunding bonds.
State debt, §§142-29.6, (a), 142-29.7.
Interest rate swap agreements for governmental units, §§159-193 to 159-200.
See SWAP AGREEMENTS.
Investment securities, §§25-8-101 to 25-8-511.
See COMMERCIAL CODE.
Joint municipal electric power and energy.
See JOINT MUNICIPAL ELECTRIC POWER AND ENERGY ACT.
Land and loan associations.
Powers, §54-53.
Larceny of choses in action, §14-75.
Local government bond act.
General provisions, §§159-43 to 159-78.
See LOCAL GOVERNMENT FINANCE.
Local government revenue bond act.
General provisions, §§159-80 to 159-97.
See LOCAL GOVERNMENT FINANCE.
Metropolitan sewerage districts, §§162A-69, 162A-70.
Metropolitan water districts, §§162A-36, (a), 162A-37.
Mosquito control districts.
Power to issue bonds, §130A-357.
Municipal corporations.
Joint municipal electric power and energy.
See JOINT MUNICIPAL ELECTRIC POWER AND ENERGY ACT.
Local government bond act.
General provisions, §§159-43 to 159-78.
See LOCAL GOVERNMENT FINANCE.
Local government revenue bond act.
General provisions, §§159-80 to 159-97.
See LOCAL GOVERNMENT FINANCE.
Sinking funds.
Local government finance, §§159-1 to 159-188.
See LOCAL GOVERNMENT FINANCE.
Municipal hospitals.
Power of municipality to issue, §131E-7, (a).
Sale to nonprofit corporation.
General obligation or revenue bonds outstanding.
Escrow fund, placement of money in by corporation, §131E-8, (b).
Municipal service districts, §160A-543.

BOND ISSUES —Cont'd
Parking authorities, §§160A-556, 160A-560 to 160A-562.
Ports and harbors.
Constitution of North Carolina.
Seaport and airport facilities, Const. N. C., art. V, §13.
Ports authority, §143B-456.
Special user projects.
Generally, §143B-456.1.
Powers of attorney.
Powers conferred by statutory short form, §32A-2.
Private activity bonds.
Federal tax reform allocation committee.
Composition, §143-433.7.
Duties, §143-433.8.
Established, §143-433.7.
Formulas for allocation, §143-433.9.
Legislative findings, §143-433.6.
Private educational facilities finance.
Authorized, Const. N. C., art. V, §12.
Private nonprofit educational institutions.
Private capital facilities finance act.
Institutions for higher education and elementary and secondary education, §§159D-35 to 159D-57.
See CAPITAL FACILITIES FINANCE AGENCY.
Project development financing debt instruments.
Local governmental units, §§159-101 to 159-113.
See LOCAL GOVERNMENT FINANCE.
Public schools.
Merged school administrative units consisting of one entire county and part of second county.
Issuance, §115C-513, (a), (b).
Qualified zone academy bonds, §§115C-489.5, 115C-489.6.
School districts, §§115C-481 to 115C-484.
See SCHOOL DISTRICTS AND ADMINISTRATIVE UNITS.
Public utilities.
Securities regulation.
Generally, §§62-160 to 62-171.
See PUBLIC UTILITY SECURITIES.
Railroads.
Powers of railroad corporations, §136-190.
Refunding bonds.
Local government finance.
See LOCAL GOVERNMENT FINANCE.
State debt, §§142-29.1 to 142-29.7.
See STATE DEBT.
Regional natural gas districts, §160A-673.
Regional sports authorities, §160A-479.12.
Taxation.
Exemption on interest of bonds, §160A-479.14, (c).
Regional transportation authorities, §160A-647.
Registered public obligations, §§159E-1 to 159E-15.
See REGISTERED PUBLIC OBLIGATIONS.
Sanitary districts, §130A-61.
Validation of bonds, §130A-77.
Tax levy for validated bonds, §130A-78.
Savings and loan associations.
Investments.
County obligations, §54B-188.
Fannie Mae obligations, §54B-187.
Federal home loan bank obligations, §54C-134.
Municipal obligations, §54B-188.
North Carolina obligations, §54B-183.

BOND ISSUES —Cont'd
Savings and loan associations —Cont'd
Investments —Cont'd
United States obligations, §54B-182.
Loans.
Security, §54B-151, (d).
State associations, powers, §54B-77, (b).
Savings banks.
Investments.
County obligations, §54C-137.
Federal government-sponsored enterprise obligations, §54C-136.
Municipal obligations, §54C-137.
North Carolina obligations, §54C-133.
United States obligations, §54C-132.
Stock savings banks.
Power to issue bonds, §54C-146, (b).
School districts.
General provisions, §§115C-481 to 115C-484.
See SCHOOL DISTRICTS AND ADMINISTRATIVE UNITS.
Securities regulation.
General provisions, §§78A-1 to 78A-66.
See SECURITIES REGULATION.
Sinking funds.
Local government finance, §§159-1 to 159-188.
See LOCAL GOVERNMENT FINANCE.
Soil and water conservation districts.
Watershed improvement works or projects, §139-49, (a) to (g).
Solid waste management.
Local governments.
Solid waste management loans and special obligation bonds, §§159I-1 to 159I-30.
See SOLID WASTE MANAGEMENT LOANS AND SPECIAL OBLIGATION BONDS.
Regional solid waste management authorities.
Revenue bonds and notes.
Advances, §153A-432.
Issuance, §153A-431.
State capital facilities finance act.
Special indebtedness generally, §§142-80 to 142-101.
See CAPITAL FACILITIES FINANCE ACT.
State debt, §§142-1 to 142-29.7.
See STATE DEBT.
State departments and agencies.
Amount of bonds, §143-163.
Covenants in resolutions authorizing bonds, §143-165.
Federal aid.
Acceptance of federal loans and grants.
Permitted, §143-164.
Financing of certain public undertakings, §143-163.
Governor.
Approval by governor and council of state, §143-165.
Security, §§143-163, 143-165.
Terms, §143-163.
State education assistance authority.
General provisions.
See EDUCATION ASSISTANCE AUTHORITY.
Local road bonds.
Prohibition, §136-98, (a), (b).
Taxation.
Exemption of state bonds, §§142-12, 142-17.
Continuation of state tax exemptions, §142-12.1.
Federal taxation of interest income on state or local bonds on issuance thereof.
Effect, §142-12.1.

BOND ISSUES —Cont'd
Trust companies.
Investment in bonds, §53-342.
Turnpike authority.
Revenue bonds.
See TURNPIKE AUTHORITY.
Unclaimed property generally, §§116B-51 to 116B-80.
See UNCLAIMED PROPERTY.
Universities and colleges.
Private capital facilities finance act.
Institutions for higher education and elementary and secondary education, §§159D-35 to 159D-57.
See CAPITAL FACILITIES FINANCE AGENCY.
University of North Carolina.
See UNIVERSITY OF NORTH CAROLINA.
Urban redevelopment.
Definition of "bonds," §160A-503.
Liability on bonds.
Limitations on, §160A-516, (b).
Powers of redevelopment commission, §§160A-512, 160A-516, (a), 160A-517.
Presumptions as to issuance, §160A-516, (f).
Rights of obligees of commission, §§160A-517, (b), 160A-518.
Sale of bonds, §160A-516, (d).
Security.
Powers of redevelopment commission as to securing bonds, §160A-517, (a).
Signatures on bonds, §160A-516, (e).
Usury.
Corporate bonds may be sold below par, §24-2.
Water and sewer authorities.
Bondholder's remedies, §162A-12.
Power of authority, §162A-6, (a).
Refunding bonds.
Generally, §162A-13.
Power to issue, §162A-13.
Revenue bonds.
Power to issue, §162A-8.
Remedies of bondholders, §162A-12.
Trust funds.
Moneys received deemed trust funds, §162A-11.

BONDS, SURETY.
Absentees in military service.
Receivers.
Required, §28B-5, (a).
Actions, §§58-76-1 to 58-76-30.
Complaint shows party interest, §58-76-10.
Election to sue officer individually, §58-76-10.
Damages.
Officer unlawfully detaining money liable, §58-76-20.
Debts.
Officer liable for negligence in collecting, §58-76-30.
Destroyed bonds, §98-9.
Election of rights of remedies.
Suing officer individually, §58-76-10.
Evidence against principal admissible against sureties, §58-76-25.
Liability and right of action on official bonds, §58-76-5.
Summary remedy on bond, §58-76-15.
Limitation of actions, §§1-50, (a), 1-52.
Model payment and performance bond, §44A-27.
Negligence in collecting debt, §58-76-30.

BONDS, SURETY —Cont'd
Actions —Cont'd
Payable to court officer.
Suit in name of state, §58-76-1.
Principals.
Evidence against principal admissible against sureties, §58-76-25.
Satisfaction.
Defendant may plead satisfaction, §1-60.
State of North Carolina.
Bonds in actions payable to court officer.
Suit in name of state, §58-76-1.
Summary remedy on official bonds, §58-76-15.
Surety's recovery on obligation paid.
No assignment necessary, §26-3.1, (a).
Construction of term "surety," §26-3.1, (b).
Unlawfully detaining money, §58-76-20.
Administrators, §§28A-8-1 to 28A-8-6.
Agents.
Indemnity bonds to state maximum liability and period of liability, §66-65.
Agriculture.
Promotion of use and sale of agricultural products.
Publication of financial statement by treasurer of agency, §106-568.
Air pollution control.
Compliance bonds.
Special orders, §143-215.110, (e).
Alcoholic beverages.
ABC stores.
Employees, §18B-803, (c).
Managers, §18B-803, (b).
Local ABC boards, §18B-700, (i).
Alcoholic beverages tax.
Nonresident vendors, §105-113.86, (b).
Wholesalers and importers, §105-113.86, (a).
Alimony.
Bond for costs unnecessary, §50-2.
Securing payment, §50-16.7, (b).
Alternative fuel.
Bond required as condition of obtaining and keeping licenses, §105-449.133.
Appeals.
See APPEAL BONDS.
Architects.
Board.
Treasurer, §83A-2, (c).
Arrest in civil cases.
Bail and recognizance.
See BAIL AND RECOGNIZANCE.
Order for arrest.
Undertaking before order, §1-412.
Assignments.
Surety's recovery on obligation paid.
No assignment necessary, §26-3.1, (a).
Construction of term "surety," §26-3.1, (b).
Assignments for benefit of creditors.
Release of insolvent upon giving bond, §23-40.
Substituted trustee to give bond, §23-7.
Surrender of principal.
Surety may surrender, §23-41.
Trustees.
Insolvent trustee removed unless bond given, §23-5.
Attachment.
See ATTACHMENT.
Attorneys' fees.
Model payment and performance bonds.
Suits under provisions, §44A-35.

BONDS, SURETY —Cont'd
Bail and recognizance.
See BAIL AND RECOGNIZANCE.
Bail bondsmen and runners, §§58-71-1 to 58-71-195.
See BAIL BONDSMEN AND RUNNERS.
Banks.
Dissolution and liquidation.
Commissioner of banks.
Taking possession, §53-20, (h).
Employees, §53-90.
Officers, §53-90.
Barber schools.
Guaranty bond required for approval, §86A-22.
Bills of lading.
Indorser not guarantor for other parties, §25-7-505.
Biological residues in animals.
Preservation or disposition of animal, animal product or feed.
Posting of bond required, §106-549.83.
Blanket bonds.
Clerks of superior courts, §7A-107.
Boxing promoter's license, §143-654, (c).
Building codes.
Manufactured buildings, structures or components.
Securing permits to erect modular buildings, §143-139.1, (a).
Business opportunity sales.
Filing of copies with secretary of state, §66-97, (c).
Requirements, §66-96.
Caveat to will, §31-33.
Cemeteries.
Trust funds for care of cemeteries.
Clerk of superior court.
Official bond liable for funds, §65-11.
Certiorari, §1-269.
Charitable solicitations.
Solicitors, §131F-16, (d).
Child placement.
Bringing or sending child into state for purposes of placement or adoption.
Person, agency, association, etc., bringing child into state, §7B-3701.
Child support.
Payments secured by bond, §50-13.4, (f).
Claim and delivery.
Defendant's undertaking for replevy, §1-478.
Qualification and justification of defendant's surety, §1-479.
Plaintiff's undertaking, §1-475.
Exceptions to undertaking, §1-477.
Sheriffs.
Liability for sufficiency of sureties, §§1-477, 1-479.
Third parties.
Property claimed by third person, §1-482.
Clerk of board of county commissioners.
Approval of official bonds.
Recording votes approving bond, §58-72-55.
Closing-out sales.
Required for license, §66-77, (b).
Collection agencies.
Amount, §58-70-20.
Permit applications, §58-70-5, (e).
Prerequisite to issuance of permit, §58-70-20.
Commercial code.
Definition of surety, §25-1-201, (40).
Documents of title.
Indorser not guarantor for other parties, §25-7-505.

BONDS, SURETY —Cont'd
Commodities.
Power of court to grant injunctive relief.
When surety bond not required, §78D-23, (b).
Community colleges.
Investment of idle cash, §115D-58.10.
Compliance bonds.
Execution sales.
Upset bids on real property, §1-339.64, (b).
Judicial sales.
Upset bid on real property at public sales, §1-339.25, (b).
Mortgages and deeds of trust.
Compliance bond in case of upset bids on real property, §45-21.27.
Condition of official bonds, §58-72-10.
Continuing care facilities.
Rehabilitation of facilities.
Refusal or vacation of orders, §58-64-45, (g).
Contracts.
Principal and surety distinguished in judgment and execution, §26-1.
Contribution among sureties, §26-5.
Coroners.
Certified copies as evidence, §152-4.
Execution, §152-3.
Official bonds of county officers generally, §§58-72-1 to 58-72-70.
See OFFICIAL BONDS OF COUNTY OFFICERS.
Registration, §152-4.
Cosmetic art.
Private cosmetic art schools, §88B-17.
Costs.
Defendant's liability in criminal actions.
Confession of judgment, §6-47.
Bond given to secure fine and cost, §6-47.
Several suits on one instrument.
Allowance of costs to defendant, §6-19.
Allowance of costs to plaintiff, §6-18.
Cotton warehouses, §106-451.11, (a).
Action on bond by person injured, §106-451.12.
Inspectors, §106-451.25.
Registration, §106-451.42, (b).
Counties.
When county may pay premiums on official bonds, §58-72-15.
County commissioners.
Clerk of board.
Approval of official bonds.
Recording votes approving bond, §58-72-55.
Official bonds.
Liability of commissioner as surety, §58-72-60.
Record of board conclusive as to facts stated, §58-72-65.
Vacancy declared.
Judge to file statement of proceedings with commissioners, §58-72-45.
Surety companies.
Clerk to notify county commissioners of condition of company, §58-73-10.
County officers.
Official bonds generally, §§58-72-1 to 58-72-70.
See OFFICIAL BONDS OF COUNTY OFFICERS.
Court of appeals.
Clerk of court, §7A-20, (a).
Credit repair services, §66-222.
Credit unions.
Blanket fidelity bond.
Purchase by board of directors, §54-109.44.
Generally, §54-109.11.

BONDS, SURETY —Cont'd
Custodial trustees, §33B-14.
Damages.
Actions on bonds.
Officer unlawfully detaining money liable for damages, §58-76-20.
Debtor and creditor.
Joinder of debtor by surety, §26-12.
Notice to creditor to take action, §§26-7 to 26-9.
Decedents' estates.
Collectors, §28A-11-2.
Debts and claims.
Distribution of estate despite contingent or unliquidated claim.
Bond of heirs and devisees, §28A-19-5.
Examination of persons or corporations believed to have possession of property, §28A-15-12, (b).
Default judgments.
Plaintiff, §1A-1, Rule 55, (c).
Definitions.
Model payment and performance bond, §44A-25.
"Surety," §26-3.1, (b).
Deposit in lieu of bond.
Cash or securities deposited in lieu of bond, §58-75-1.
Deposits.
State funds, §147-79.
Discount buying clubs, §66-135.
Divorce.
Bonds for costs unnecessary, §50-2.
Documents of title.
Indorser not guarantor for other parties, §25-7-505.
Drainage.
Petitions.
Agreement for construction, §156-26, (d).
Drainage districts.
Amount of penalty, §156-57.
Appeals, §156-66.
Construction of improvements.
Contractors, §156-84.
Penalties.
Amount of penalty, §156-57.
Petitions.
Filing with petition, §156-57.
Treasurer, §156-81.1.
Election of rights and remedies.
Actions on bonds.
Suing officer individually, §58-76-10.
Elective share of surviving spouse.
Recovery of assets by personal representative, §30-3.5, (e).
Electrical contractors.
Board of examiners.
Secretary-treasurer, §87-40.
Energy conservation.
Guaranteed energy savings contracts, §143-64.17B, (c), (d).
Engineers and land surveyors.
Board of examiners.
Executive director, §89C-9.
Examinations.
Annual examination of official bonds, §58-72-20.
Executions.
Debtor leaving state or concealing self, §1-355.
Execution sales.
Special proceedings to determine ownership of surplus.
Transfer of proceedings to civil issue docket of superior court, §1-339.71, (c).

BONDS, SURETY —Cont'd
Executions —Cont'd
Execution sales —Cont'd
Upset bid on real property.
Compliance bond, §1-339.64, (b).
Forthcoming bond for personal property, §§1-318 to 1-320.
Principal and surety distinguished in judgment and execution, §26-1.
Principal liable on execution before surety, §26-2.
Stay of execution.
Dissenting surety not liable to surety on stay of execution, §26-6.
Executors and administrators.
See EXECUTORS AND ADMINISTRATORS.
Exempt property from enforcement of claims of creditors.
Exceptions, §1C-1601, (e).
Federal estate tax apportionment.
Distribution before final apportionment.
Distributee to provide security for tax liability, §28A-27-7.
Fiduciaries.
Removal of fiduciary funds.
Local fiduciaries appointed to receive property administered in another state, §36A-15.
Surety companies.
Expense of fiduciary bond charged to fund, §58-73-35.
Firemen's relief fund.
Treasurer of state firemen's association.
State appropriation.
Bond to be given by treasurer, §58-85-10.
Trustees.
Treasurer of board of trustees, §58-84-30.
Fish and fisheries resources.
Promotion of coastal fisheries and seafood industry.
Financial officers, §113-315.9, (a), (b).
Foresters.
Board of registration.
Secretary, §89B-7.
Forfeitures.
Failure of surety companies to pay judgment is forfeiture, §58-73-25.
Forthcoming bond for personal property, §1-318.
Procedure on giving bond, §1-319.
Subsequent levies, §1-319.
Summary remedy, §1-320.
Fraternal benefit societies.
Organization.
Filing with articles of incorporation, §58-24-45, (b).
Fruits.
Unfair trade practices by handlers of fruits.
Required bond, §106-498.
Garnishment.
Garnishee retaining possession, §1-440.32, (b).
Gasoline and oil inspection.
Cancellation of license, §119-19.
Inspectors to be bonded, §119-25.
Gasoline tax.
Failure to file replacement bond or additional bond, §105-449.120, (a).
Required as condition of obtaining and keeping certain licenses, §105-449.72.
Grain dealers.
Application for license, §§106-604, 106-605.
Guardians.
Action on bond.
Persons injured by breach of condition, §35A-1234.

BONDS, SURETY —Cont'd
Guardians —Cont'd
Action on bond —Cont'd
Relief of endangered guardians, §35A-1237.
Several wards with estate in common, §35A-1235.
Adjusting guardian's bond.
Authority of clerks of superior court, §35A-1203, (c).
Approval, §35A-1230.
Breach of condition.
Action on bond by person issued by, §35A-1234.
Clerk.
Approval, §35A-1230.
Liability of official bond, §35A-1238.
Recording, §35A-1231, (a).
Reduced penalty, §35A-1233.
Renewal of bond.
Duties of clerk upon failure to renew, §35A-1236.
Common wards for one guardian, §35A-1235.
Conditions of bond, §35A-1231, (a).
Deposited or invested money, ward's estate including.
Exclusion when computing amount of bond, §35A-1232, (a).
Disinterested public agents.
Health and human services bond, §35A-1239.
Health and human services bond, §35A-1239.
Increase on sale of realty or personal property, §35A-1231, (b).
Judicial sale, holding, §1-339.10, (b), (c).
Limitation of action against surety, §1-52.
Nonresident guardian, §35A-1230.
Penalty.
Reduction by clerk, §35A-1233.
Public guardian, §35A-1271.
Real property.
Increase on sale of realty, §35A-1231, (b).
Recording, §35A-1231, (a).
Renewal, §35A-1236.
Failure to renew, §35A-1236.
Required, §35A-1230.
Standby guardians for minor children, §35A-1380.
Sureties.
Relief of endangered sureties, §35A-1237.
Terms of bond, §35A-1231, (a).
Hearing aid dealers and fitters.
Board.
Secretary-treasurer, §93D-3, (d).
Historic properties.
Special peace officers to be bonded, §121-10, (c).
Home inspectors, §143-151.58, (b).
Illegitimacy.
Support of illegitimate children.
Bond for future appearance of defendant, §49-9.
Industrial development commission, §158-21.
Infractions.
Appearance bonds, §15A-1113, (c).
Injunctions, §1A-1, Rule 65, (c).
Appeals.
Restraining orders and injunctions in effect pending appeals, §1-500.
Insurance.
Reciprocal insurance.
Domestic reciprocals.
Attorney's bond, §§58-15-105, 58-15-110.
Supervision, rehabilitation and liquidation of insurers.
Claims of surety, §58-30-210.

BONDS, SURETY —Cont'd
Insurance —Cont'd
Supervision, rehabilitation and liquidation of insurers —Cont'd
Commissioner and deputies.
Responsibility on official bonds, §58-30-30.
Insurance brokers, §58-33-30, (f).
Insurance premium financing.
Licensees, §58-35-15, (a).
Interest.
Default judgments.
Clerk to ascertain interest, §24-6.
Penal bonds.
Exceptions to contract rate, §24-5, (a).
Legal rate from date of entry of judgment, §24-5, (a1).
Investment advisers, §78C-17, (e).
Job listing services.
Licensure requirement, §95-47.22, (b).
Required, §95-47.24.
Judges.
Official bonds.
Vacancy declared.
Statement of proceedings filed with commissioners, §58-72-45.
Judgments.
Cancellation as to surety, §26-11.
Failure of surety companies to pay judgment, §58-73-25.
Principal and surety distinguished in judgment and execution, §26-1.
Judicial sales.
Bond of person holding sale, §1-339.10.
Upset bid on real property at public sales, §1-339.25, (b).
Justification of sureties.
Official bonds, §58-72-30.
Compelling justification before judge.
Effect of failure.
Successor bonded, §58-72-40.
Considered debts and liabilities, §58-72-40.
Oath required, §58-72-30.
Successor bonded, §58-72-40.
Kerosene distributors, suppliers and terminal operators.
License requirement, §119-15.3.
Landlord and tenant.
Summary ejectment.
Payment to stay execution of judgment, §§42-34, (b) to (c1), 42-34.1, (b).
Undertaking to stay order of execution.
Form of undertaking, §42-34, (d).
Tenant security deposit act.
Landlord may furnish bond from insurance company, §42-50.
Limitation of actions.
Bail and recognizance.
Action against bail, §1-52.
Fiduciaries, §1-50, (a).
Action against surety, §1-52.
Model payment and performance bond.
Actions on payment bonds, §44A-28, (b).
Personal representatives, §1-50, (a).
Action against surety, §1-52.
Public officers and employees, §1-52.
Liquefied petroleum gases.
Dealers.
Bond as substitute for liability insurance, §119-56.
Livestock markets.
Required bonds of operators of public livestock markets, §106-407.

BONDS, SURETY —Cont'd
Loan brokers.
Requirements as to bond or trust account, §66-108, (a).
Noncompliance misdemeanor, §66-108, (b).
Local governments.
Finance.
Blanket performance bond, §159-29, (c).
Finance officer's bond, §159-29, (a).
Individuals handling money, §159-29, (b).
Lost instruments and records.
Action on destroyed bond, §98-9.
Magistrates, §7A-174.
Mass gatherings.
Provisional permit.
Forfeiture of bond, §130A-256, (d).
Performance bond or other surety to be filed, §130A-255, (a).
Mechanics, laborers and materialmen dealing with owner.
Deposit of bond and satisfaction of lien.
Discharge of record lien, §44A-16.
Medical board secretary, §90-7.
Membership camping.
Nondisturbance agreement.
Surety bond in lieu of agreement, §66-246.
Military property sales facilities, §127B-4, (c).
Militia.
Property and fiscal officer of North Carolina, §127A-22, (c).
Mines and minerals.
Forfeiture, §§74-56, (d), 74-59.
Generally, §74-54.
Permits, §§74-51, 74-54.
Bond required, §74-50, (c).
Modifications, §74-52, (d).
Release, §74-56, (c).
Missing persons.
Temporary, §28C-3.
Mobile homes and trailers.
Approval by board, §143-143.12.
Model payment and performance bonds, §§44A-26 to 44A-35.
Money transmitters.
Licenses, §53-208.8.
Mortgage bankers and brokers.
Licenses, §53-243.05, (f).
Mortgage in lieu of bond, §§58-74-1 to 58-74-35.
Affidavit of value of property required, §58-74-30.
Civil cases.
Prosecuting or defending civil case, §58-74-25.
Clerk of superior court.
Depositing mortgage with register of deeds, §58-74-20.
Executing mortgage on real estate of value of required bond, §58-74-1.
Official bonds, §58-74-1.
Recognizance for appearance in criminal proceeding, §58-74-5.
Cancellation of mortgage in such proceedings, §58-74-10.
Register of deeds.
Clerk of court may give surety by mortgage deposited with register, §58-74-20.
Security of costs or fine in criminal action, §58-74-5.
Cancellation of mortgage in such proceedings, §58-74-10.
Special proceedings.
Prosecuting or defending special proceeding, §58-74-25.

BONDS, SURETY —Cont'd
Mortgage in lieu of bond —Cont'd
Statute.
Validating statute, §58-74-15.
Validating statute, §58-74-15.
Value of property required.
Affidavit of value, §58-74-30.
When additional security required, §58-74-35.
When additional security required, §58-74-35.
Motor carriers.
Joinder of surety prohibited, §62-274.
Road tax on carriers using fuel purchased outside state.
Refunds to motor carriers who give bond, §105-449.40.
Security for protection of public, §62-268.
Motor clubs and associations.
Prerequisite to issuance of license, §58-69-10.
Motor vehicle dealers' or manufacturers' licenses, §20-288, (e).
Motor vehicles.
Actions against company executing, §20-279.24, (b).
Authorized surety companies, §20-279.24, (a).
Brokers, §62-263, (e).
Cancellation of surety, §20-279.29.
Financial responsibility.
Proof of financial responsibility, §§20-279.18, 20-279.24.
Methods, §20-279.18.
Real estate, §20-279.24, (a).
Municipal corporations.
Cemetery trustees.
Secretary and treasurers, §160A-349.2.
Order of abatement, §160A-175, (e).
Solicitation campaigns.
Adequate bond posted to protect public from fraud, §160A-178.
Mutual burial associations.
Secretary or secretary-treasurer, §90-210.95.
Navigation and pilotage.
Pilots, §76-45.
Cape Fear river, §76A-5, (e).
Nonpublic post-secondary educational institutions.
Licensing.
Guaranty bond required of applicant, §116-15, (f1).
Notice.
Surety companies.
Clerk to notify county commissioners of condition of company, §58-73-10.
Surety, indorser or guarantor may notify creditor to take action, §26-7, (a).
Applicability of provisions, §26-7, (d).
Effect of failure of creditor to take action.
Discharge of parties, §26-9, (a).
Separate notice of co-sureties, co-indorsers or co-guarantors, §26-9, (c).
Waiver of defense provisions, §26-9, (b).
Evidence of notice, §26-8, (c).
Extent of notice, §26-7, (b).
Holder or owner of obligation to disclose other sureties, indorsers and guarantors, etc., §26-7, (c).
Method of notice, §26-8, (a).
Return of service, §26-8, (b).
Nuisances.
Abatement.
Offenses against public morals.
Preliminary injunction, §19-2.1.

BONDS, SURETY —Cont'd
Nurses.
Board of nursing.
Executive director, §90-171.24.
Nurses aides registry, §90-171.55, (b).
Nurses aides registry, §90-171.55, (b).
Oaths.
Justification of sureties on official bonds, §58-72-30.
Official bonds of county officers generally, §§58-72-1 to 58-72-70.
See OFFICIAL BONDS OF COUNTY OFFICERS.
Oil and gas conservation.
Hearings before department.
Stay bond, §113-407.
Persons drilling for oil or gas to register and furnish bond, §113-378.
Violations, §113-380.
Ordinances.
Enforcement of ordinances.
Unlawful use of real property, §160A-175, (e).
Parties.
Satisfaction.
Defendant may plead satisfaction, §1-60.
Partnerships.
Surviving partners, §§59-74, 59-75.
Purchase by surviving partner, §59-81, (c).
Pawnbrokers, §91A-14.
Payment bonds.
Model payment and performance bonds generally, §§44A-25 to 44A-35.
See PAYMENT AND PERFORMANCE BONDS.
Penal bonds, interest, §24-5, (a), (a1).
Performance bonds.
Model payment and performance bonds generally, §§44A-25 to 44A-35.
See PAYMENT AND PERFORMANCE BONDS.
Pesticides.
Licenses.
Financial responsibility of licensees, §143-467, (a), (b).
Rules and regulations, §143-467, (c).
Physicians and surgeons.
Revocation or suspension of license.
Appeal bond, §90-14.9, (a).
Medical board not required to give, §90-14.11, (a).
Pilots.
Navigation and pilotage.
Cape Fear river, §76A-5, (e).
Pleadings.
Surety companies.
Not to plead ultra vires, §58-73-20.
Post-secondary educational institutions.
Nonpublic institutions.
Licensing.
Guaranty bond required of applicant, §116-15, (f1).
Precious metal dealers.
Permits.
Bond or trust account required, §66-168.
Preliminary injunctions, §1A-1, Rule 65, (c).
Premiums on bonds.
Official bonds.
When county may pay premiums, §58-72-15.
Prepaid entertainment contracts, §66-124.
Records, §66-124.1.
Principal and agent.
Actions on bonds.
Evidence against principal admissible against sureties, §58-76-25.

BONDS, SURETY —Cont'd
Principal and agent —Cont'd
Death of principal.
Subrogation of surety paying debt, §26-4.
Distinguish between surety and principal in judgment and execution, §26-1.
Liability on execution before surety, §26-2.
Remedies of surety against principal.
Summary remedy of surety, §26-3.
Prisons and prisoners.
Persons authorized to collect or receive moneys, §148-2, (a).
Private personnel services.
Licensees, §95-47.2, (j).
Private protective services, §74C-10.
Professional counselors.
Injunctive relief.
Board not required to post bond, §90-342.
Professional employer organizations.
Surety bond filed by applicant for license, §58-89A-50.
Proprietary schools.
Guaranty bond.
Operating school without bond, §115D-96.
Required for school's license to operate, §115D-95.
Prosecution bonds, §§1-109 to 1-112.
Indigent, suit as, §§1-110, (a).
Land actions.
Defendant's bond for costs, §§1-111.
Plaintiff not entitled to recover, certification by attorney.
Bond not required, §§1-112, (a).
Summary ejectment.
Bond not required, §§1-112, (b).
Unable to give bond, not worth amount, affidavit by defendant.
Bond not required, §§1-112, (a).
Plaintiff's bond for costs, §§1-109.
Prisoners.
Pro se motion to proceed as indigent, §§1-110, (a), (b).
Public building contracts.
Bid bond in lieu of cash deposits, §143-129, (b).
Performance bonds, §143-129, (c).
Procurement from particular surety, agent, producer or broker.
Officer or employee requiring prohibited, §58-31-66.
Public officers and employees.
Acting as officer before qualifying as such, §14-229.
Actions on bonds.
Venue, §1-78.
Official bonds.
County officers generally, §§58-72-1 to 58-72-70.
See OFFICIAL BONDS OF COUNTY OFFICERS.
On presentation of proper bond officer to be inducted, §58-73-30.
Penalty for officer acting without bond, §58-72-5.
Retention of funds of county or town by delinquent official.
Citizen to recover funds, §128-10.
Surety companies.
State officers may be bonded in surety company, §58-73-1.
Public schools.
School finance officer and other officers, employees and agents, §115C-442, (a) to (c).

BONDS, SURETY —Cont'd
Public utilities.
Generally, §62-64.
Rates.
Temporary rates, §62-135, (c).
Quo warranto.
Action by private person with leave, §1-516.
Leave withdrawn and action dismissed for insufficient bond, §1-518.
Solvent sureties required, §1-517.
Appeals, §1-529.
Defendant's undertaking before answer, §1-523.
Judgment by default and inquiry on failure of defendant to give bond, §1-525.
Radiation protection.
Security for emergency response and perpetual maintenance costs, §104E-18, (a).
Powers of commission as to, §104E-18, (b).
Real estate brokers and salespersons.
Private real estate schools, §93A-36.
Real property.
Defendant's bond for costs and damages in land actions, §§1-111, 1-112, (a), (b).
Warranties.
Required for certain warranties, §58-1-20, (b).
Receivers, §1-504.
Applicant for receiver.
Furnishing bond to adverse party, §1-502.1.
Receivers of corporations, §1-507.2.
Refusal of appointment on bond being given, §1-503.
Recordari, §1-269.
Records.
Approval of official bonds.
Clerk records vote approving bond, §58-72-55.
Register of deeds, §161-4, (a).
Mortgage in lieu of bond.
Clerk of court may give surety by mortgage deposited with register, §58-74-20.
Official bonds of county officers generally, §§58-72-1 to 58-72-70.
See OFFICIAL BONDS OF COUNTY OFFICERS.
Vacancies in office.
Assistant or deputy register of deeds holding over, §161-4, (b).
Rental referral agencies, §66-145, (b).
Actions on bond, §66-145, (c).
Restraining orders, §1A-1, Rule 65, (c).
Retirement system for teachers and state employees.
Management of funds.
Personal profit or acting as surety prohibited, §135-7, (e).
Savings and loan associations.
Blanket indemnity bond, §54B-109, (a).
Collection agents, §54B-109, (b).
Examination by commissioner, §54B-109, (e).
Unauthorized investments.
Indemnity bond, §54B-109, (c), (d).
Savings banks.
Blanket indemnity bond, §54C-109, (a).
Collection agents, §54C-109, (b).
Securities regulation.
Dealers and salesmen, §78A-37, (d).
Service of process.
Habeas corpus ad testificandum.
Applicant to give bond, §17-44.
Model payment and performance bond.
Service of notice, §44A-27, (c).

BONDS, SURETY —Cont'd
Service of process —Cont'd
Surety, indorser or guarantor may notify creditor to take action.
Method of notice, §26-8, (a).
Sheriffs.
Boards of county commissioners.
Duties as to bond of sheriff, §§162-9, 162-10.
Generally, §162-8.
Liability of surety, §162-12.
Official bonds of county officers generally, §§58-72-1 to 58-72-70.
See OFFICIAL BONDS OF COUNTY OFFICERS.
Small business contractor act.
Bonding assistance authorized, §§143B-472.92, 143B-472.93.
Small business surety bond fund, §143B-472.91.
Surety bonding line.
Establishment, §143B-472.94.
Soil and water conservation districts.
Board of supervisors, §139-7.
Solicitors of contributions, §131F-16, (d).
Special proceedings.
Commissioners.
Sale of property, §§1-407 to 1-407.2.
Mortgage in lieu of bond.
Prosecuting or defending special proceeding, §58-74-25.
State treasurer.
Depositories, §147-78.
State funds, §147-79.
Stay of execution.
Dissenting surety not liable to surety on stay of execution, §26-6.
Subrogation.
Surety paying debt of deceased principal subrogated, §26-4.
Summary remedy of surety, §26-3.
Summary remedy on official bond, §58-76-15.
Superior courts.
Clerks of court, §7A-107.
Employees of office of clerk, §7A-107.
Mortgage in lieu of bond.
Depositing mortgage with register of deeds, §58-74-20.
Supersedeas.
Issuance to suspend execution, §1-269.
Supreme court.
Appeal of right from court of appeals, App. Proc. Rule 17, (a).
Clerk of the supreme court to be bonded, §7A-11.
Forma pauperis, App. Proc. Rule 17, (d).
Surety companies, §§58-73-1 to 58-73-35.
See SURETY COMPANIES.
Surveyors of counties.
Official bonds of county officers generally, §§58-72-1 to 58-72-70.
See OFFICIAL BONDS OF COUNTY OFFICERS.
Telephonic sellers.
Gift or prize, §66-263.
Terms of official bonds, §58-72-10.
Tobacco products tax.
Dealers.
Wholesale dealer or retail dealer, §105-113.38.
Transfers to minors.
Custodians, §33A-15, (c).
Treasurers of counties.
Official bonds of county officers generally, §§58-72-1 to 58-72-70.
See OFFICIAL BONDS OF COUNTY OFFICERS.

BONDS, SURETY —Cont'd
Trust companies.
Directors.
Surety and indemnity bond, §53-358, (a), (b).
Seizure by commissioner, §53-384.
Injunction of action by commissioner, §53-382, (a).
Trusts and trustees.
Calculation of amount, §36A-31, (b).
Class in esse.
Sale of property held by, §41-11.1, (d).
Governing instrument excuses bond requirement, §36A-31, (b).
Special trustees, §36A-36.
Testamentary trust created under will, §36A-31, (a).
When bond required, §36A-31.
Tryon's Palace.
Financial officer and treasurer designated by commission to disburse funds and property, §121-20, (a).
Ultra vires.
Surety companies not to plead ultra vires, §58-73-20.
Universities and colleges.
Nonpublic post-secondary educational institutions.
Licensing.
Guaranty bond required of applicant, §116-15, (f1).
Uranium exploration permits, §§74-78 to 74-81, 74-83.
Vegetables.
Unfair practices by handlers of vegetables.
Required bond, §106-498.
Veterans' guardianship act.
Guardians.
Separate bond for each appointment, §34-4.
Warehouses.
Public warehousemen, §66-36.
Injured person may sue on bond, §66-37.
Warehouse receipts.
Indorser not guarantor for other parties, §25-7-505.
Warranties.
Real property.
Required for certain warranty, §58-1-20, (b).
Water and sewer companies.
Required, §62-110.3.
Water supply and waterworks.
Water and sewer companies.
Required, §62-110.3.
Wills.
Caveat to wills.
See WILLS.
Contests.
Prosecution bond required, §31-34.
Executors and administrators.
Executing will without giving bond, §28A-26-4.
Workers' compensation.
Self-insurance.
Employer groups, §58-47-90, (e), (f).
Self-insurers.
Security deposits and surety bonds, §97-185.

BONE DISEASE.
Food, drug and cosmetic act.
Drug or device, false advertising, §106-138, (b).

BONE MASS MEASUREMENT.
Diagnosis and evaluation of osteoporosis and low bone mass.
Health benefit plan coverage, §58-3-174.

BONUSES FOR COST SAVINGS SUGGESTIONS OR INNOVATIONS.
State employee incentive bonus program, §§143-345.20 to 143-345.25.

BOOK ACCOUNTS.
Shop-book rule, §§8-42 to 8-44.

BOOK CLUBS.
Discount buying clubs generally, §§66-131 to 66-136.
See DISCOUNT BUYING CLUBS.

BOOKMAKING.
Gambling and betting contracts.
Prohibited, §§16-1, 16-2.

BOOK OF ORDERS APPOINTING RECEIVERS OF JUDGMENT DEBTORS.
Clerk of court to file and record appointment, §1-364.

BOOTLEGGING, §18B-304.
Unauthorized substances taxes, §§105-113.105 to 105-113.113.
See UNAUTHORIZED SUBSTANCES TAXES.

BORROWING MONEY.
Bond issues.
See BOND ISSUES.
Consolidated city-county act.
Authorized, §160B-13.
Debt limitations, §160B-15.
Credit unions.
Powers of credit unions generally, §54-109.21.
Electric membership corporations.
Specific grant of power, §117-18.
Fairs.
State fair.
Constructing and financing facilities and improvements, §106-503.1, (a).
Hospital authorities.
Contracts with federal government, §131E-27.
Housing finance agency.
General power of agency, §122A-5.
Loans.
See LOANS.
Local government finance.
Regulation, Const. N. C., art. V, §4.
Mosquito control districts.
Corporate powers of board of commissioners, §130A-355.
Railroads.
Powers of railroad corporations, §136-190.
Savings and loan associations.
Mutual deposit guaranty associations.
Powers of associations, §54B-244, (b).
Power to borrow money, §54B-162.
Savings banks.
Power to borrow money, §54C-176.
State debt.
See STATE DEBT.

BOTTLED WATER.
Contracts for sale of.
Educational institutions to competitively bid, §143-64.

BOTTLER PERMIT.
Authorization, §18B-1110.
Distribution agreements, §18B-1110, (b).

BOTTLES AND BOTTLING.
Alcoholic beverages.
Bottler's permits.
Authorization, §18B-1110, (a).
Distribution agreements, §18B-1110, (b).

BOTTLES AND BOTTLING —Cont'd
Polluting bottles.
Unlawful to pollute bottles used for beverages, §14-288.

BOUNCED CHECKS.
Bad checks generally.
See BAD CHECKS.

BOUNDARIES.
Adverse possession.
Color of title.
Known and visible lines and boundaries, §1-38.
Annexation.
Extension of corporate limits generally, §§160A-29 to 160A-58.28.
See ANNEXATION.
Coastal lands.
Seaward boundary.
High water mark, §77-20, (a) to (c).
Condominiums.
Relocation of boundaries between adjoining units, §47C-2-112.
Units, §47C-2-102.
Declaration amendment changing, §47C-2-117, (d).
Constitution of North Carolina.
State boundaries, Const. N. C., art. XIV, §2.
Conveyances.
Use of word adjoining instead of words bounded by, §39-2.
Coordinate system.
Use in descriptions, §102-6.
Counties, §§153A-17 to 153A-22.
Criminal trespass.
Landmarks.
Removing, altering or defacing landmarks, §14-147.
Drainage districts.
Establishment, §156-65.
Extension, §156-93.3.
Existing districts may act together, §156-93.7.
Election precincts, §§163-132.3 to 163-132.5F.
Establishing boundaries and interest where conveyance and copy lost, §98-3.
Fires and fire protection.
Rural fire protection districts.
Changes in area of district, §69-25.11.
Hearsay exception, reputation concerning, §8C-1, Rule 803.
Hospital authorities.
Creation of authority, §131E-17, (a) to (c).
Housing authorities and projects.
Area of operation, §157-39.1, (a) to (c).
Land boundary corners.
Use of coordinate system in description, §102-6.
Landmarks.
Removing, altering or defacing landmarks.
Criminal trespass, §14-147.
Lost instruments and records.
Establishing boundaries where conveyance and copy lost, §98-3.
Metropolitan sewerage districts.
Description, §162A-65, (b).
Metropolitan water districts.
Description, §162A-32, (b).
Municipal corporations.
Corporate limits.
General provisions, §§160A-21 to 160A-58.28.
See MUNICIPAL CORPORATIONS.
Sanitary district and municipality extending boundaries simultaneously, §130A-70, (a) to (h).

BOUNDARIES —Cont'd
Parking authorities.
Coterminous with boundaries of city, §160A-552.
Petitions.
Special proceeding to establish, §38-3, (a).
Public health authorities.
Operating facilities outside territorial limits, §130A-45.6.
Public lands.
Allocated state lands, §§146-33, 146-34.
Grants.
Correction of grants.
Change of county line before grant issued or registered, §146-47.
Public schools.
Special taxing districts.
Superintendents to furnish boundaries, §115C-500.
Referees, compulsory reference, §1A-1, Rule 53, (a).
Sanitary districts, §130A-49, (a).
Extension of boundaries.
Municipality and district extending boundaries simultaneously, §130A-70, (a) to (h).
Validation of extension, §130A-75, (a), (b).
Industrial villages.
Status within boundaries of district, §130A-49, (b).
Seaward boundary of coastal lands.
High water mark, §77-20, (a) to (c).
Special proceeding to establish, §§38-1 to 38-4.
Appeals, §38-3, (b).
Authorized, §38-1.
Disputed boundaries.
Surveys, §38-4, (a).
Hearing, §38-3, (a).
Judgments.
Survey after judgment, §38-3, (c).
Notice.
Appeals, §38-3, (b).
Occupation sufficient ownership, §38-2.
Petition, §38-3, (a).
Procedure, §38-3, (d).
Summons.
Failure to answer, §38-3, (a).
Issuance by clerk, §38-3, (a).
Surveys.
After final judgment, §38-3, (c).
Appointment of surveyor, §38-4, (b).
Calling surveyors as witnesses, §38-4, (c).
Disputed boundaries, §38-4, (a).
Fees for surveyors, §38-4, (d).
Order by clerk, §38-3, (a).
Venue, §38-1.
Witnesses.
Surveyors, §38-4, (c).
State boundaries, §§141-1 to 141-8; Const. N. C., art. XIV, §2.
Subdivisions.
Control corners.
Use to fix boundaries prima facie evidence of correct method, §39-32.4.
Summons and process.
Special proceeding to establish boundaries, §38-3, (a).
Townships, §143A-19, (a) to (c).
Transportation engineering divisions.
Designation of boundaries by department, §136-14.1.
Trees and timber.
Unlawful cutting or removal of timber as result of misrepresentation of property lines, §1-539.1, (c).

BOUNDARIES —Cont'd
Trespass.
Criminal trespass.
Removing, altering or defacing landmarks, §14-147.
Veterans' recreation authorities, §165-26.

BOUNTY HUNTERS.
Governor authorized to employ, §15-53.

BOW HUNTING.
Method of taking wild animals or wild birds, §113-291.1, (a).
Nongame fish.
Taking in inland and joint fishing waters, §113-275, (k).

BOWIE KNIVES.
Carrying concealed, §14-269, (a), (b) to (d).
Confiscation and disposition, §14-269.1.
Possessing and carrying on educational property, §14-269.2.
Sale to minor, §14-315.
Weapons generally.
See WEAPONS.

BOWLING ALLEYS.
Child care facilities.
Drop-in or short-term child care not included in term child care, §110-86.

BOXES.
Flat trucks loaded with.
Load to be securely fastened, §20-120.

BOXING, §§143-651 to 143-658.
Athletic contests generally.
See ATHLETIC CONTESTS.
Bond for promoter's license, §143-654, (c).
Civil penalties, §143-658, (a).
Contract requirements, §143-656.
Corporations.
Licenses for manager or promoter issued to, §143-654, (b).
Criminal penalties, §143-658, (b).
Definitions, §143-651.
Department of crime control and public safety.
Alcohol law enforcement division.
Regulation of boxing, rules, authority to issue, §143-652.1.
Fees for licenses, §143-655, (a).
Fees for permits, §143-655, (b).
Fictitious or assumed names.
Persons may not participate under, §143-654, (b).
Financial arrangements, §143-656.
Injunctions, §143-658, (c).
Licenses.
Bond for promoter's license, §143-654, (c).
Fees, §143-655, (a).
Generally, §143-654, (b).
Required, §143-654, (a).
Partnerships.
Licenses for manager or promoter issued to, §143-654, (b).
Permits.
Fees, §143-655, (b).
Promoters.
Required, §143-654, (a).
Valid for single match, §143-654, (d).
Promoters.
Bond for license, §143-654, (c).
Permits.
Fees, §143-655, (b).
Valid for single match, §143-654, (d).

BOXING —Cont'd
Rules regulating boxing, §143-652.1.
Sanctioned amateur matches, §143-657.1.
State boxing commission revenue account, §143-655, (c).
Ultimate warrior matches prohibited, §143-653.

BOXING COMMISSION REVENUE ACCOUNT, §143-655, (c).

BOYCOTTS.
Insurance.
Unfair trade practices.
Prohibited acts, §58-63-15.

BPOL TAXES.
License taxes generally, §§105-33 to 105-109.
See LICENSE TAXES.

BRAILLE.
Textbook contracts to include clause granting state board of education license to produce, §115C-90.

BRAIN DEATH.
Defined, §90-323.
Right to natural death generally, §§90-320 to 90-323.
See RIGHT TO NATURAL DEATH.
Use as sole basis for determination of death, §90-323.

BRAIN INJURIES.
Traumatic brain injury advisory council, §§143B-216.65, 143B-216.66.
Chair, §143B-216.66, (c).
Clerical and other assistance, §143B-216.66, (f).
Duties, §143B-216.65.
Established, §143B-216.65.
Meetings, quorum, §143B-216.66, (d).
Members, terms, vacancies, expenses, §143B-216.66, (a), (b), (e).

BRAKE LININGS.
Type and brand to be approved by commissioner of motor vehicles, §20-124, (h).

BRAKES.
Hydraulic brake fluid.
Restrictions on sale, §20-124, (h).
Linings.
Approved brake lining, §20-124, (h).
Motorcycles and motor-driven cycles, §20-124, (d).
Repair of motor vehicles, §§20-354 to 20-354.9.
See MOTOR VEHICLE REPAIRS.
Requirements generally, §20-124, (a), (c).
Safety inspections.
Scope of inspections, §20-183.3, (a).
Sales.
Restrictions, §20-124, (h).
Trailers.
Requirements, §20-124, (f), (g).
Tractor-truck with semitrailer attached.
Requirements, §20-124, (e), (e1).
Trucks.
Requirements for motor trucks, §20-124, (e), (e1).
Truck tractors.
Requirements, §20-124, (e), (e1).
Violations of restriction on sales, §20-124, (h).

BRAN.
Standard weights and measures, §81A-42.

BRANCH BANKS.
Authorized, §53-62, (b).

BRANCH BANKS —Cont'd
Capital requirements for establishment, §53-62, (c).
Commissioner of banks.
Approval of establishment, §53-62, (b).
Capital requirements, §53-62, (c).
Review of commissioner's actions by state banking commission, §53-62, (f).
Definition of "branch," §53-1.
Discontinuance, §53-62, (e).
Industrial banks.
Power to establish, §53-141.
Interstate banking, §§53-224.9 to 53-224.31.
Acquisition of a branch, §53-224.13.
Conditions for acquiring and maintaining, §53-224.14, (b), (c).
Conditions for approval, §53-224.15.
Notice of desire to acquire and maintain, §53-224.14, (a).
Additional branches, §53-224.27.
Appeal of commissioner's decisions, §53-224.30.
Bank mergers, §§53-224.17 to 53-224.22.
Closing of branches, §53-224.29.
Cooperative agreements, §53-224.24, (c).
Definitions, §53-224.9.
De novo banks, §53-224.12.
Conditions for approval, §53-224.15.
Conditions for establishing and maintaining, §53-224.14, (b), (c).
Notice of desire to establish and maintain, §53-224.14.
Enforcement of laws, §53-224.25.
Examination of out-of-state, state bank branches, §53-224.24, (a).
Fees to be paid by out-of-state, state banks, §53-224.24, (d).
North Carolina state banks in other states.
Application process, §53-224.11, (b).
Authorized, §53-224.11, (a).
Notice of subsequent merger or other change in control, §53-224.28.
Periodic reports of out-of-state, state banks, §53-224.24, (b).
Powers of North Carolina state banks doing business in other states, §53-224.16, (b).
Powers of out-of-state banks, §53-224.16, (a).
Purpose of law, §53-224.10.
Rulemaking authority, §53-224.26.
Severability of supervisory provisions, §53-224.31.
Supervisory authority.
Applicability, §53-224.23.
Generally, §§53-224.24 to 53-224.31.
Interstate bank mergers.
Conditions for interstate merger prior to June 1, 1997, §53-224.21.
North Carolina state banks.
Establishing of out-of-state branches by merger, §53-224.18.
Powers of branches resulting from merger, §53-224.22, (b).
Notice and filing requirements, §53-224.20.
Out-of-state banks.
Establishing of North Carolina state branches by merger, §53-224.19.
Powers of branches resulting from merger, §53-224.22, (a).
Purpose of law, §53-224.17.
Limited service facilities.
Conversion of limited service facility to branch, §53-62, (d).
Loan committee, §53-78.

BRANCH BANKS —Cont'd
Officers, §53-62, (c).
Operation, §53-62, (c).
Out-of-state branch banks, §§53-224.9 to 53-224.31. See within this heading, "Interstate banking."
School thrift or savings plan.
Acceptance of deposits not construed as establishment or operation of branch, §53-43.6, (b).
State banking commission.
Review of actions of commissioner, §53-62, (f).

BRANDISHING.
Habitual misdemeanor assault, §14-33.2.
Pointing firearm at person, §14-34.

BRANDS AND MARKS.
Farm products.
Marketing and branding farm products, §§106-185 to 106-196.
See FARM PRODUCTS MARKETING AND BRANDING.
Fertilizers.
Registration of brands, §106-660.
Gold, §80-40.
Articles of gold plate, §80-42.
Violations of provisions.
Misdemeanors, §80-44.
Greases.
Juggling mark prohibited, §119-10.
Mixing different brands for sale under standard trade name prohibited, §119-11.
Health.
Embargo of adulterated or misbranded food, §130A-21, (a) to (e).
Labels generally.
See LABELS.
Limestone, marl and landplaster.
Sale of agricultural liming materials and landplaster.
Registration of brands by distributors, §106-92.7.
Liquid fuels.
Juggling trademark prohibited, §119-10.
Mixing different brands for sale under standard trade name prohibited, §119-11.
Livestock generally, §§80-45 to 80-66.
See LIVESTOCK BRANDS.
Lubricating oils.
Display of brand or trade name of lubricating oil, §119-2.
Imitation of standard equipment prohibited, §119-9.
Juggling mark prohibited, §119-10.
Misrepresentation of brands for sale, §119-3.
Mixing different brands for sale under standard trade name prohibited, §119-11.
Secretary of state.
Duties as to, §147-36.
Silver, §80-41.
Articles of silver plate, §80-43.
Violations of provisions.
Misdemeanors, §80-44.
Timber marks, §§80-15 to 80-23.
See TIMBER MARKS.
Trademarks.
See TRADEMARKS.

BRASS.
Dealing in regulated, §66-11.

BRASS KNUCKLES.
Carrying concealed, §14-269, (a), (b) to (d).
Confiscation, §14-269.1.
Possessing or carrying on educational property, §14-269.2.
Sale to minor, §14-315.
Weapons generally.
See WEAPONS.

BREACH OF THE PEACE.
Assault and battery.
See ASSAULT AND BATTERY.
Disorderly conduct, §§14-132, 14-275.1, 143-345.2.
Nuisances.
Offenses against public morals.
Definition of breach of the peace, §19-1.1.
Riots and civil disorders, §§14-288.1 to 14-288.20.
See RIOTS AND CIVIL DISORDERS.
Secured transactions.
Default.
Agreements as to rights and duties inapplicable to breach of the peace, §25-9-603, (b).
Repossession.
No sanctioning of breach of the peace, §25-9-609, (b).

BREAKFASTS.
Utility commission members attending public breakfasts sponsored by public utilities, §62-327.

BREAKING AND ENTERING.
Alarm systems licensing, §§74D-1 to 74D-13.
See ALARM SYSTEMS LICENSING.
Buildings, §14-54.
Burglary generally, §§14-51 to 14-57.
See BURGLARY.
Coin or currency operated machine, §14-56.1.
Deadly force.
Use against intruder.
Justification, §14-51.1, (a).
No duty to retreat, §14-51.1, (b).
Other defenses not repealed, expanded or limited, §14-51.1, (c).
Defense of home or residence.
Use of deadly force against intruder.
Justification, §14-51.1, (a).
No duty to retreat, §14-51.1, (b).
Other defenses not repealed, expanded or limited, §14-51.1, (c).
Executing officer may break and enter premises, §15A-251.
Jails.
Intent to injure prisoners, §14-221.
Prevention of felonies.
Authorized, §15-43.
Railroad cars, motor vehicles, aircraft, etc., §14-56.

BREAKING OUT OF DWELLING HOUSE, §14-53.

BREAST CANCER.
Accident and health insurance.
Mammograms.
Coverage, §58-51-57.
Health maintenance organizations, coverage.
Mammograms, §58-67-76.
Hospital, medical and dental services corporations.
Mammograms.
Coverage, §58-65-92.

BREAST CANCER —Cont'd
Mammograms.
Accident and health insurance.
Coverage, §58-51-57.
Accreditation of facilities performing, §143B-165.
Health maintenance organizations, coverage, §58-67-76.
Hospital, medical and dental services corporations.
Coverage, §58-65-92.
Small employer group health coverage, §58-50-155, (a).
Mastectomy.
Post-mastectomy inpatient care coverage.
Health benefit plans, §58-3-168.
Motor vehicle license plates.
Breast cancer awareness, §20-79.4, (b).
Reconstructive breast surgery.
Small employer group health coverage, §58-50-155, (a).
Reconstructive breast surgery resulting from mastectomy.
Accident and health insurance coverage, §58-51-62.
Health maintenance organizations, coverage, §58-67-79.
Hospital, medical and dental services corporations, coverage, §58-65-96.

BREAST FEEDING.
Not indecent exposure, §14-190.9, (b).

BREATHALYZERS.
Arrest.
Used as condition of release, §15A-534.2.
Impaired driving generally.
See IMPAIRED DRIVING.
Required for certain drivers, §20-16.3.

BREWERIES.
Commercial permits, §18B-1100.
Consumption on premises.
Authorization of brewery permit, §18B-1104.
Exclusive outlets, §18B-1116, (a).
On-premises malt beverage permit.
Kind of permit that may be issued, §18B-1001.
Permit authorization, §18B-1104.
Sale of breweries malt beverages.
Authorization of brewery permits, §18B-1104.
Vendor representative permit.
Authorization, §18B-1112.

BRIBERY.
Advisory budget commission.
Purchases and contracts through department of administration.
Acceptance of bribes by officers, §143-63.
Athletic contests.
Acceptance of bribes by players, managers, etc., §14-374.
Completion of offenses, §14-375.
Completion of offenses, §14-375.
Definition of bribe, §14-376.
Elements of offense of bribery of players, managers, etc., §14-373.
Bank directors or officers accepting fees or gifts, §53-86.
Bank examiners.
Accepting bribes, §14-233.
Keeping or accepting bribe or gratuity.
Penalties, §53-124.
Bank loans or gratuities to commissioner of banks or bank examiners, §53-126.

BRIBERY —Cont'd
Commercial bribery, §14-353.
Constitution of the United States, Const. U. S., art. II, §4.
Definitions.
Athletic contests, §14-376.
Horse show judges or officials, §14-380.3.
Election officers, §163-275.
Electrologists.
Grounds for disciplinary actions, §88A-21, (a).
Electronic surveillance orders, §15A-290, (b).
Employees violating duties owed employers, §14-353.
General assembly.
Legislative ethics act, §120-86, (a).
Horse show judges or officials.
Attempts at bribery to be reported, §14-380.2.
Definition of "bribe," §14-380.3.
Printing provisions of article in horse show schedules, §14-380.4.
Protection of horse shows, §14-380.1.
Jurors, §14-220.
Meat inspectors, §106-549.26.
Mortgage bankers and brokers.
Prohibited acts, §53-243.11.
Offering bribes, §14-218.
Acceptance of bribe not required, §14-218.
Public officers and employees.
Bribery of officials, §14-217.
Purchases and contracts through department of administration.
Acceptance of bribes, §143-63.
Utilities commission.
Gifts to members, employees or staff, §62-327.
Vice-president of the United States, Const. U. S., art. II, §4.

BRIDGE AUTHORITY, §§136-89.159 to 136-89.167.
Audits, §136-89.166.
Bridge from Currituck county to Outer Banks.
Duty to construct, §136-89.159, (b).
Bylaws, §136-89.161, (g).
Chair and vice-chair, §136-89.161, (d).
Composition, §136-89.161, (b).
Dissolution, §136-89.167.
Election of officers, §136-89.161, (d).
Executive director, §136-89.161, (h).
Expenses of projects, §136-89.160.
Fees, §136-89.160.
Members, §136-89.161, (b).
Need for creating, §136-89.159, (a).
Oath of office, §136-89.161, (c).
Powers.
Enumerated, §136-89.162, (a).
Execution, §136-89.162, (b).
Public agency status, §136-89.161, (a).
Quorum, §136-89.161, (d).
Required for execution of powers, §136-89.162, (b).
Real property.
Acquisition, disposition or exchange, §136-89.164.
Removal of members, §136-89.161, (c).
Reports, §136-89.166.
Salaries, §136-89.161, (e).
Secretary, §136-89.161, (d).
State departments and agencies.
Authority as public agency, §136-89.161, (a).
Cooperation by other agencies, §136-89.165.
Successor members, §136-89.161, (c).
Taxation.
Exemption, §136-89.163.

BRIDGE AUTHORITY —Cont'd
Transportation, department of.
Location of authority, §136-89.161, (f).

BRIDGES.
Burning public bridge, §14-61.
Counties.
Authorizing bridges over navigable waters, §153A-243.
Fishing from bridges.
Regulation or prohibition, §153A-242.
Criminal trespass.
Injuring bridges, §14-146.
Destroying, breaking, tearing down, etc., §14-146.
Drainage districts.
Control and repairs, §156-92.
Maintenance of drainage, §156-88.
Draws in bridges.
Commissioners for opening and clearing streams, §77-10.
Railroad companies to provide draws, §136-78.
Eminent domain.
By whom right may be exercised, §40A-3, (a).
Environmental policy act.
Replacement program for bridges, §136-76.1, (b).
Fastening vessels to bridges misdemeanor, §136-80.
Fishing from bridges.
Counties regulating, §153A-242.
Municipal corporations.
Power to prohibit or regulate, §160A-302.1.
Signs on bridges, §136-102.5.
Footways.
Maintenance of footways by department of transportation, §136-81.
Load limits for bridges.
Determination of safe load-carrying capacity, §136-72.
Penalty for violations of provisions, §136-72.
Local, private and special legislation prohibited, Const. N. C., art. II, §24.
Monuments and memorials.
Historical commission.
Approval before acceptance by state, §100-3.
Motor vehicle speed limitations, §20-144.
Municipal corporations.
Fishing from bridges.
Power to prohibit or regulate, §160A-302.1.
North Carolina bridge authority, §§136-89.159 to 136-89.167.
Parks and recreation.
Toll bridges.
Private operation in public parks, §100-16.
Privately owned bridges, construction and maintenance.
State highway or road right of way.
Use and encroachment, §136-18.
Railroads.
Companies to provide draws, §136-78.
Replacement program.
Completion of program, §136-76.1, (a).
Environmental policies.
Applicability of act to bridge replacement program, §136-76.1, (b).
Initiation, §136-76.1, (a).
Removal of bridges not replaced, §136-76.1, (a).
Ships and shipping.
Fastening vessels to bridges misdemeanor, §136-80.

BRIDGES —Cont'd
Signs.
Fishing bridges, §136-102.5.
Speed limitations, §20-144.
Toll bridges.
Authority of county commissioners with regard to toll bridges, §136-88.
Authority to charge, length requirement, amount, §136-82.2, (a).
Burning of certain bridges, §14-61.
Owners of toll bridges not under supervision of department of transportation.
Rights and liabilities of owners, §136-88.
Private operation in parks, §100-16.
Public toll roads and bridges.
Turnpike authority, §§136-89.180 to 136-89.197.
See TURNPIKE AUTHORITY.
Report on amount collected, §136-82.2, (b).
Transportation department.
Disposal of debris, §136-97, (b).
Maintenance of footways, §136-81.
Vessels.
Fastening vessels to bridges misdemeanor, §136-80.

BRIEFS.
Additional authorities, App. Proc. Rule 28, (g).
Amicus curiae briefs, App. Proc. Rule 28, (i).
Appendices to briefs, App. Proc. Rule 28, (d).
Contents.
Appellant's brief, App. Proc. Rule 28, (b).
Appellee's brief, App. Proc. Rule 28, (c).
Presentation of additional questions, App. Proc. Rule 28, (c).
Form, App. Proc., Appx. E.
Copies reproduced by clerk, App. Proc. Rule 13, (b).
Filing and service.
Consequence of failure to file and serve, App. Proc. Rule 13, (c).
Copies reproduced by clerk, App. Proc. Rule 13, (b).
Dispositive motions.
Briefs in support or opposition, §1A-1, Rule 5, (a1).
Failure to file.
Consequences, App. Proc. Rule 13, (c).
Time, App. Proc. Rule 13, (a).
Functions, App. Proc. Rule 28, (a).
Joinder of multiple parties in briefs, App. Proc. Rule 28, (f).
Motions seeking final determination.
Service of briefs in support or opposition, §1A-1, Rule 5, (a1).
Page limitations, App. Proc. Rule 28, (j).
References to record, App. Proc. Rule 28, (e).
Reply briefs, App. Proc. Rule 28, (h).
Submission of case on written briefs in lieu of oral argument, App. Proc. Rule 30, (d).
Supreme court review.
Appeal of right from court of appeals, App. Proc. Rule 14, (d).
Discretionary review on certification by supreme court, App. Proc. Rule 15, (g).
Termination of parental rights and juvenile matters.
Name of juvenile and identifying matter not included, App. Proc. Rule 28, (k).
Type style and size, App. Proc. Rule 28, (j).
Utilities commission proceedings.
Exceptions to recommended decision or order, §62-78, (b).

BRIEFS —Cont'd
Utilities commission proceedings —Cont'd
Proposed findings of fact and conclusions of law prior to decision or order, §62-78, (a).
Word count limits, App. Proc. Rule 28, (j).

BRIGHT'S DISEASE.
Food, drug and cosmetic act.
Drug or device, false advertising, §106-138, (b).

BROADCAST DEFAMATION ACT, §§99-1 to 99-5.
See DEFAMATION.

BROADCASTERS AND BROADCASTING.
Alcoholic beverage advertising, §18B-105, (b).
Contempt.
Criminal contempt.
Basis for holding in contempt, §5A-11, (b).
Court orders prohibiting publication or broadcast of reports of open court proceedings or public records, §7A-276.1.
Electioneering communications.
Disclosures, prohibited sources, §§163-278.80 to 163-278.83.
Journalist's qualified privilege, §8-53.11.
Libel and slander.
See DEFAMATION.
Radio.
See RADIO.
Television.
See TELEVISION.

BROADCASTING MACHINERY SALES.
Sales and use tax rate, §105-164.4A.

BROADCAST JOURNALISTS.
Journalist's qualified privilege against disclosure in any legal proceeding, §8-53.11, (b).
Definitions, §8-53.11, (a).
Eyewitness observation of criminal or tortuous conduct, no privilege, §8-53.11, (d).
Order to compel disclosure, notice to journalist and hearing, §8-53.11, (c).
Overcoming privilege, person seeking to compel disclosure, §8-53.11, (c).

BROKERS.
Cemetery brokers.
Defined, §65-48.
Licenses, §65-57.
Commodities.
General provisions, §§78D-1 to 78D-33.
See COMMODITIES.
Insurance brokers generally.
See INSURANCE BROKERS.
Loan brokers, §§66-106 to 66-112.
Mortgage bankers and brokers, §§53-243.01 to 53-243.16.
See MORTGAGE BANKERS AND BROKERS.
Motor carriers.
Bonds, surety, §62-263, (e).
Licenses, §62-263.
Utilities commission.
Regulation of brokers, §62-261.
Pawnbrokers, §§91A-1 to 91A-14.
See PAWNBROKERS.
Real estate brokers and salespersons, §§93A-1 to 93A-10.
See REAL ESTATE BROKERS AND SALESPERSONS.
Stockbrokers.
Acting as stockbroker, §14-401.7.

BROKERS' LIENS.
Secured transactions, §25-9-206, (a), (b).

BRONZE.
Dealing in regulated, §66-11.

BRONZE STAR.
Motor vehicle license plates.
Special plates for recipients, §20-79.4, (b).

BROOMCORN.
Standard weight and measure, §81A-42.

BROTHELS.
Abatement of nuisances against public morals, §§19-1 to 19-8.3.
See NUISANCES.
Keeping a disorderly or bawdy house, §14-188.
Prostitution.
Generally, §§14-203 to 14-208.
See PROSTITUTION.

BROUGHTON HOSPITAL.
Joint security force, §122C-430.

BROWN BAGGING ACT, §18B-301.

BROWN-BAGGING PERMIT, §18B-1001.
Fee, §18B-902, (d).

BROWNFIELDS PROPERTY REUSE, §§130A-310.30 to 130A-310.40.
Additional remediation of property.
Prospective buyer or other person completing remediation or redevelopment required, §130A-310.33, (c).
Appeals.
Decision by department as to whether or not to enter into agreement, §130A-310.36.
Brownfields agreement defined, §130A-310.31, (b).
Brownfields property or Brownfields site defined, §130A-310.31, (b).
Brownfields property reuse act implementation account, §130A-310.38.
Fees imposed credited to, §130A-310.39, (b).
Brownfields property reuse act of 1997.
Short title, §130A-310.30.
Cancellation of notice of Brownfields property, §130A-310.35, (e).
Comment period during public meeting.
Department to take into account, §130A-310.34, (d).
Construction of provisions, §130A-310.37, (a).
Deed when Brownfields property sold, lease, conveyed or transferred, §130A-310.35, (d).
Definitions, §130A-310.31, (a), (b).
Description of Brownfields property.
Brownfields agreement to contain, §130A-310.32, (c).
Enforcement of land-use restriction, §130A-310.35, (f).
Entry into Brownfields agreement, §130A-310.32.
Environmental assessment conducted on Brownfields property.
Person conducting not potentially responsible person, §130A-310.33, (b).
Environmental contamination defined, §130A-310.31, (b).
Failure to comply with Brownfields agreement.
Violation of provisions, §130A-310.32, (d).
Federal superfund sites.
Department not to enter into Brownfields agreement where Brownfields sites identified as, §130A-310.37, (c).

BROWNFIELDS PROPERTY REUSE —Cont'd
Fees.
Credit to Brownfields property reuse act implementation account, §130A-310.39, (b).
Failure to pay fees, §130A-310.39, (c).
Schedule of fees to be collected, §130A-310.39, (a).
Immunity of state, agencies, officers, employees or agents, §130A-310.37, (b).
Information provided by prospective developer, §130A-310.32, (a).
Interest.
Unpaid fees, §130A-310.39, (c).
Land-use restrictions.
Enforcement, §130A-310.32, (a).
Liability for remediation to current standards, §130A-310.33, (c).
Reliance on negotiating Brownfields agreement, §130A-310.32, (b).
Liability for remediation of areas of contaminants identified in Brownfields agreement.
Limitation on liability, §130A-310.33, (a).
Liens.
Unpaid fees, §130A-310.39, (c).
Noncompliance with Brownfields agreement.
Violation of provisions, §130A-310.32, (d).
Notice of Brownfields property, §130A-310.35, (a).
Applicability of provisions, §130A-310.35, (g).
Cancellation, §130A-310.35, (e).
Filing copy in register of deeds office, §130A-310.35, (b).
Notice of intent to redevelop Brownfields property, §130A-310.34, (a).
Publication, §130A-310.34, (b).
Notice to public and community by prospective developer desiring to enter into Brownfields agreement, §130A-310.34, (a).
Persons to whom liability protection applies, §130A-310.33, (a).
Property taxes.
Definitions, §105-277.13, (b).
Qualifying improvements, §105-277.13, (a).
Table of percentage of appraised value, §105-277.13, (c).
Publication of notice of intent to redevelop Brownfields property, §130A-310.34, (b).
Public meeting on Brownfields agreement, §130A-310.34, (c).
Comment received during.
Taken into consideration by department, §130A-310.34, (d).
Recording notice of Brownfields property, §§47-29.1, (c), 130A-310.35, (b), (c).
Register of deeds.
Filing copy of notice of Brownfields property in office of register of deeds, §130A-310.35, (b).
Recording notice of Brownfields property, §130A-310.35, (c).
Remedial standards based on land-use restrictions.
Brownfields agreement may provide for, §130A-310.32, (b).
Reports by department to environmental review commission, §130A-310.40.
Statement of remediation activities to be included in Brownfields agreement, §130A-310.32, (c).
Violation of provisions.
Failure to comply with Brownfields agreement, §130A-310.32, (d).

BRUCELLOSIS, §§106-388 to 106-398.
Blood sample testing, §106-390.
Compulsory testing of animals, §106-393.
Brands.
Diseased animals to be branded and quarantined, §106-390.
Compensation for killing diseased animals.
Appraisal of cattle affected with Bang's disease, §106-324.
Report of appraisal, §106-326.
Generally, §§106-323 to 106-335.
See LIVESTOCK DISEASES.
Marketing of cattle affected with Bang's disease, §106-327.
Compulsory testing, §§106-393, 106-395.
Blood sample testing, §106-390.
Control and eradication of brucellosis.
Cooperation with United States department of agriculture, §106-389.
Control of livestock diseases generally, §§106-400 to 106-405.
See LIVESTOCK DISEASES.
County boards of commissioners.
Cooperation of county boards, §106-394.
Defined, §106-389.
Duties of state veterinarian, §106-393.
Liability of vendors.
Civil liability, §106-391.
Livestock diseases generally, §§106-304 to 106-307.7.
See LIVESTOCK DISEASES.
Misdemeanors.
Sale of animals known to be infected or under quarantine, §106-398.
Violations made misdemeanor, §106-397.
Program for vaccination, §106-389.
Sale, etc., of vaccine, §106-389.
Quarantine, §§106-388, 106-390.
Duties of state veterinarian, §106-393.
Rules and regulations.
Authority to promulgate and enforce, §106-396.
Sale of diseased animals, §106-390.
Civil liability of vendors, §106-391.
Nonresident sales, §106-392.
Punishment for sale, §106-398.
Removal of identification marks, §106-390.
State veterinarian.
Duties, §106-393.
Quarantine of animals, §106-393.
United States department of agriculture.
Cooperation with department in control and eradication of brucellosis, §106-389.
Vaccination.
Program for vaccination, §106-389.
Sale, etc., of vaccine, §106-389.
Violations made misdemeanor, §106-397.

BRUNSWICK COUNTY.
Acquisition of property, power, §153A-158.1, (a).
Agricultural tenancies in certain counties.
Terms of, §42-23.
Ambulance service.
Attachment or garnishment and lien for, §§44-51.4 to 44-51.8.
Board of county commissioners.
Filling vacancies on board, §153A-27.1.
Condemnation or acquisition of land by local government unit outside county.
Consent of board of commissioners necessary, §153A-15.

BRUNSWICK COUNTY —Cont'd
Coroner elected as nominee of political party.
Filling vacancy in office, §152-1.
Counties generally.
See COUNTIES.
County boards of education elected on partisan basis.
Vacancies in office, §115C-37.1.
Cropper or tenant refusing to perform terms of contract.
Forfeiture of right of possession to premises, §42-27.
Dog collars.
Unlawful removal of electronic dog collars, §14-401.17.
Game laws, local acts not repealed, §113-133.1, (e).
Grants in navigable waters, registration, §113-205, (a).
Low-income housing tax credits.
Qualified building eligible for credit, §105-129.41, (c).
Maps in special proceedings, recording of photographic copies, §47-32.
Room occupancy tax levied by county, uniform provision, §153A-155.
Room occupancy tax levied by municipalities in county.
Uniform provisions for municipalities authorized to levy, §160A-215.
School property.
Acquisition and improvement, §153A-158.1.
Sheriff.
Vacancy, performance of duties until vacancy filled, §162-5.1.
Southeastern North Carolina regional economic development commission, §158-8.3.
Swimming, surfing and littering in Atlantic Ocean.
City ordinances effective in Atlantic Ocean, §160A-176.1.
Wills.
Evidence.
Records of wills in Brunswick, §8-27.

BRUSH FIRES.
Criminal trespass.
Setting fire to grass, brushlands and woodlands, §14-136.

BUCKET SHOP ACT.
Futures contracts, §§16-3 to 16-6.
Securities regulation, §§78A-1 to 78A-66.
See SECURITIES REGULATION.

BUCK SPRINGS.
Transportation department.
Maintenance of grounds at home of Nathaniel Macon, §136-44.

BUCKWHEAT.
Standard weight and measure, §81A-42.

BUDGETS, §§143-1 to 143-34.7.
Accounts and accounting.
Clean water management trust fund.
Established, §143-15.3B, (a).
Use of funds, §143-15.3B, (b).
Director of the budget.
Records, §143-20.
Repairs and renovations reserve account.
Allocations and expenditures, §143-15.3A, (c).
Established, §143-15.3A, (a).

BUDGETS —Cont'd
Accounts and accounting —Cont'd
Repairs and renovations reserve account —Cont'd
Use of funds in account, §143-15.3A, (b).
Savings reserve account.
Appropriations, §143-15.3, (a).
Established, §143-15.3, (a).
Reserving to account unreserved credit balance remaining in general fund, §143-15.3, (a1).
Use of funds in account, §143-15.3, (b).
Administration department.
Appropriations.
Emergency contingent fund, §143-19.
Itemized statements and forms, §143-7.
Advisory budget commission.
Allotments.
Requisitions, §143-17.
Appointment of members, §143-4, (a).
Appropriations.
Increase or decrease of projects, §143-18.1, (a), (b).
Recommendations, §143-12, (c).
Reduction of appropriations, §143-15.
Chairman.
Expenses, §143-4, (b).
Compensation, §143-4, (b).
Conflicts of interest, §143-63.
Director of the budget.
Appropriations.
Increase or decrease of projects, §143-18.1, (a), (b).
Expenses, §143-4, (b).
General assembly.
Appointment of members, §143-4, (a).
Governor.
Appointment of members, §143-4, (a).
Calling meetings, §143-4, (c).
Inspections.
Biennial inspection of physical facilities, §143-4.1.
Legislative officers.
Participation by, §143-34.7.
Meetings, §143-4, (c).
Agenda for meetings, §143-4, (d).
Attendance by legislative officers, §143-34.7.
Persons not members addressing commission, §143-4, (d).
Oath of office, §143-4, (c).
Purchases and contracts through department of administration.
Acceptance of bribes, §143-63.
Conflicts of interest, §143-63.
Rules.
Covering certain purposes, §143-60.
Quorum, §143-4, (f).
Recommendations.
Intent of article, §143-33.
Secretary.
Designation, §143-4, (c).
Staff, §143-4, (c).
State auditor's office.
Audit of receipts and expenditures, §143-4, (e).
Vacancies.
Filling, §143-4, (d).
Witnesses.
Generally, §143-21.
Agencies.
Examinations, §143-3.
Allotments.
Advisory budget commission.
Requisitions, §143-17.

BUDGETS —Cont'd
Allotments —Cont'd
Director of the budget.
Approval, §143-17.
Records of allotments to be kept by director, §143-20.
Requisitions, §143-17.
State auditor.
Check for compliance with allotments, §143-17.
State treasurer.
Quarterly allotments to office, §143-17.
Appeals.
Judgment of joint committee, §143-14.
Applicability of provisions, §143-28.
Appropriations.
Administration department.
Emergency contingent fund, §143-19.
Advisory budget commission.
Increase or decrease of projects, §143-18.1, (a), (b).
Reduction of appropriations, §143-15.
Allocation for emergency allotment, §143-12, (b).
Use of allotted funds, §143-12, (b).
Allotments, §143-17.
Article governs all departmental and agency appropriations, §143-16.
Balances to revert to treasury, §143-18.
Capital appropriations, §143-18.
Increase or decrease of projects, §143-18.1, (a), (b).
Charitable institutions.
Appropriations are in addition to receipts, §143-27.
Correctional institutions.
Appropriations are in addition to receipts, §143-27.
Current operations appropriations, §143-12, (a).
Current operations appropriations act, §143-15.1, (a).
Director of the budget.
Copies of reports and bills, §143-13.
Reduction of appropriations, §143-25, (a).
Requests for payment appropriations, §143-33.
Disbursements, §143-5.
Educational institutions.
Appropriations are in addition to receipts, §143-27.
Expenditure of appropriations.
Wrongful expenditures.
Recovery, §143-32, (a).
Expenditures beyond appropriated amounts.
Deviations from total, §143-23, (f).
General assembly, §143-23, (c) to (e2).
Reports.
Expenditures beyond appropriated amounts, §143-23, (a1).
General fund financial model, §143-15.1, (b).
General fund operating budget.
Size limit, §143-15.4.
Historic and archaeological property, §143-31.2.
Prerequisites to allotment and expenditures, §143-31.2.
Intent of article, §143-33.
Introduction of bills, §143-13.
Joint meetings of committees, §143-14.
Maintenance appropriations.
Adequacy of revenues, §143-25, (a).
Legislative declaration, §143-25, (b).
Maintenance funds.
Itemized purposes, §143-23, (a).

BUDGETS —Cont'd
Appropriations —Cont'd
Payment.
Director to have discretion as to manner of paying annual appropriations, §143-26, (a).
Printing of bills, §143-13.
Records, §143-20.
Reduction of appropriations, §143-15.
Power of director, §143-25, (a).
Reports.
Appropriations committees, etc., of general assembly.
Effect, §143-15.
Office of state budget and management to report, §143-27.
Printing copies of budget report and bills, §143-13.
Rules and regulations, §143-5.
Savings reserve account, §143-15.3, (a).
State highway fund, §143-28.1.
Transfers or changes between objects and line items, §143-23, (c) to (e2).
Attorney general.
Witnesses.
Prosecution of offenses, §143-21.
Wrongful expenditures.
Prosecution, §143-32, (b).
Budget message by director of budget, §143-11, (b).
Building and permanent improvement funds.
Director of the budget.
Study and review of plans and specifications, §143-31.1.
Spending in accordance with budget, §143-31.
Capital improvement planning and budgeting process, §§143-34.40 to 143-34.45.
Automated inventory of facilities owned by state agencies, §143-34.42.
Capital improvement defined, §143-34.40.
Elements of process, §143-34.41, (b).
Needs estimate submitted by state agencies, §143-34.44, (a).
First part of estimate, §143-34.44, (b).
Second part of estimate, §143-34.44, (c).
Recognition by general assembly for need to establish, §143-34.41, (a).
Responsibility for management of planning process, §143-34.41, (c).
Six-year capital improvement plan, §143-34.45, (a).
First part of plan, §143-34.45, (b).
Second part of plan, §143-34.45, (c).
State agency defined, §143-34.40.
Weighted list of factors to evaluate need for capital improvement projects, §143-34.43.
Capital improvements.
Construction of improvements not specifically authorized or provided for, §143-18.1, (c).
Special reserve account, §143-18.1, (c).
Increase or decrease of projects, §143-18.1, (a), (b).
Acceptance of gifts or grants for construction, §143-18.1, (c).
Cemeteries.
Commission.
Annual budget, §65-54.
Clean water management trust fund.
Established, §143-15.3B, (a).
Use of funds, §143-15.3B, (b).
Community colleges.
See COMMUNITY COLLEGES.

BUDGETS —Cont'd
Condominium owners' associations.
Summary provided, meeting to ratify, §47C-3-103, (c).
Contempt.
Punishment for violation of rules before joint meetings, §143-14.
Continuation and expansion costs.
Preparation of the budget, §143-10.1A.
Contracts.
State departments and agencies, §143-34.2.
Criminal procedure.
Wrongful expenditures.
Prosecution, §143-32, (b).
Current operations appropriations act, §143-15.1, (a).
Definitions, §143-1.
Dependent care assistance.
Providing to eligible officers and employees, §143-34.1, (c).
Deposits.
Payroll deductions.
State employees, §143-34.6.
Director of the budget.
Advisory budget commission.
Appropriations.
Increase or decrease of projects, §143-18.1, (a), (b).
Allotments.
Approval, §143-17.
Appropriations.
Copies of reports and bills, §143-13.
Reduction of appropriations, §143-25, (a).
Requests for payment appropriations, §143-33.
Borrowing money, §143-24.
Budget message supporting recommendations and outlining financial policy and program for ensuing biennium, §143-11, (b).
Building and permanent improvement funds.
Study and review of plans and specifications, §143-31.1.
Capital improvement planning and budgeting, §§143-34.40 to 143-34.45.
Coordination of statistics, §143-3.5, (a), (c).
Dependent care assistance.
Providing to eligible officers and employees, §143-34.1, (c).
Fiscal analysis, §143-3.5, (a).
Forms and reports in use by state departments and institutions.
Review by director through office of state budget and management, §143-10.7.
Furnishing information upon request to director, §143-9.
Health and welfare agencies.
Submission of appropriation requests, §143-31.3.
Help for director, §143-19.
Historical and archaeological properties.
Allotment and expenditure of funds, §143-31.2.
Legislative expenditures.
Recommendations, §143-8.
Payment.
Discretion as to manner of paying annual appropriations, §143-26, (a).
Nonprofit corporations, §143-26, (b).
Payroll.
Submission to, §143-34.1, (a).
Powers.
Delegation, §143-29.

BUDGETS —Cont'd
Director of the budget —Cont'd
Public lands fund.
Administration, §146-73.
Approval of expenditures, §146-73.
Creation, §146-71.
Purposes, §146-72.
Records, §143-20.
Reports.
Employees, §143-19.
State aid.
Departments and agencies asking state aid, §143-6, (d).
Savings reserve account.
Use, §143-15.3, (b).
State aid.
Departments and agencies asking state aid.
Reports, §143-6, (d).
State treasurer, §147-84.
Statistics.
Coordination, §143-3.5, (a), (c).
Summons and process.
Issuance of subpoenas, §143-21.
Survey of operation and management of departments, bureaus, divisions, etc., §143-11, (a).
Budget message supporting recommendations and outlining financial policy and program for ensuing biennium, §143-11, (b).
Witnesses.
Generally, §143-21.
Work first program.
Duty to approve and recommend adoption, §108A-27.10, (a).
Report as to permanent state employees who have been recipients, §108A-27.10, (b).
Disbursements, §143-3.
Rules and regulations, §143-5.
Disbursing officer.
Building and permanent improvement funds.
Spending in accordance with budget, §143-31.
Warrants for payment of money.
Compensation of help for director, §143-19.
District health departments.
Dissolution of department.
Distribution of budgetary surplus, §130A-38, (d).
Education.
Public school budgets, §§115C-425 to 115C-434.
See SCHOOL DISTRICTS AND ADMINISTRATIVE UNITS.
Energy.
Southern states energy compact.
Submission of budgets of board, §104D-3.
Examinations.
Agencies, §143-3.
Officers, §143-3.
Surveys, studies and examinations of departments and institutions, §143-22.
Expenditures.
Reporting as to legislative and judicial expenditures and finances, §143-8.
Wrongful expenditures.
Recovery, §143-32, (a), (b).
Federal block grants.
Submission of block grant plans by agency receiving, §143-16.1, (b).
Federal funds.
Expending and reporting, §143-16.1, (a).
Fiscal analysis, §143-3.5, (a).
Bill proposed by state agency that affects budget.
Requirement of fiscal analysis, §143-3.5, (b).

BUDGETS —Cont'd
Forms.
Itemized statements and forms, §143-7, (a).
Account codes, §143-7, (b).
Limit on number of state employees, §143-10.2.
Functions.
Transfer, §143-3.1.
Funds.
Building and permanent improvement funds.
Spending in accordance with budget, §143-31.
Maintenance funds.
All funds for itemized purposes, §143-23, (a).
Definitions, §143-23, (f).
Savings reserve account.
Established as special fund in state treasury, §143-15.3, (a).
General assembly.
Advisory budget commission.
Appointment of members, §143-4, (a).
Participation by legislative officers, §143-34.7.
Appropriations.
Bills containing proposed appropriations, §143-12, (a).
Reduction, §143-15.
Reports.
Appropriations committees or subcommittees of general assembly.
Effect of report, §143-15.
Expenditures beyond appropriated amounts, §143-23, (a1).
Current operations appropriations act.
Enactment, §143-15.1, (a).
Expenditures.
Reporting as to legislative and judicial expenditures and finances, §143-8.
General fund financial model, §143-15.1, (b).
General fund operating budget size limit.
Research division.
Tentative estimate, §143-15.4, (c).
House of representatives.
Transfer between objects and line items in budget of, §143-23, (d).
Joint meetings of committees, §143-14.
No expenditures for purposes for which general assembly has considered but not enacted appropriation, §143-16.3.
Other than senate or house.
Transfer between objects and line items in budget of, §143-23, (e).
Savings reserve account.
Appropriations, §143-15.3, (a).
Senate.
Transfer between objects and line items in budget of, §143-23, (c).
General fund operating budget.
Size limit, §143-15.4, (a).
Estimates, §143-15.4, (c).
Increase, §143-15.4, (b).
Governor.
Advisory budget commission.
Appointment of members, §143-4, (a).
Calling of meetings, §143-4, (c).
Borrowing money, §143-24.
Dismissals from office, §143-34.
Duties of governor, Const. N. C., art. III, §5.
Transfer between objects and line items in budget of, §143-23, (e1).
Health trust account.
Settlement reserve fund, §143-16.4, (a1).
Hearings.
Joint meetings.
Appeals, §143-14.
Procedure, §143-14.

BUDGETS —Cont'd
Historical and archaeological properties.
Allotment and expenditure of funds, §143-31.2.
Prerequisites, §143-31.2.
Historical commission.
Allotment and expenditure of funds, §143-31.2.
Housing authorities and projects.
Local government finance.
Special provisions pertaining to public housing authorities, §159-42, (c).
System as part of city or county system, §157-4.2.
Indigent defense services, office of, §7A-498.2, (d), (e).
Industrial development commission.
Bureau.
Furnishing county commissioners with proposed budget, §158-22.
Information.
State departments and agencies.
Requests for nonstate funds for projects imposing obligation on state, §143-34.2.
Inspections.
Advisory budget commission.
Biennial inspection of physical facilities, §143-4.1.
Surveys, studies and examinations of departments and institutions, §143-22.
Itemized statements and forms, §143-7, (a).
Account codes, §143-7, (b).
JDIG reserve fund, §143-15.3E.
Joint municipal electric power and energy act.
Balanced budget, §159-41, (a) to (f).
Judges.
Expenditures.
Reporting as to legislative and judicial expenditures and finances, §143-8.
Legislative findings, §143-2.
Lieutenant governor.
Transfer between objects and line items in budget of, §143-23, (e2).
Local government budget and fiscal control act, §§159-7 to 159-42.
See LOCAL GOVERNMENT FINANCE.
Matching funds.
Non-state match restrictions, §143-31.4.
Mental health, developmental disability, substance abuse.
Area authorities, §122C-144.1, (a).
Bridge funding, §143-15.3D.
Transfer of funds for, §143-23.3.
Occupational safety and health.
Commissioner of labor to submit to general assembly, §95-150.
Office of information technology services, §147-33.88, (a).
Office of state budget and management.
Advisory budget commission.
Staff to commission.
Serving as staff, §143-4, (c).
Forms and reports in use by state departments and institutions.
Director to review through office, §143-10.7.
General fund operating budget size limit.
Tentative estimate, §143-15.4, (c).
Job training, education and placement information management, §§96-30 to 96-35.
See JOB TRAINING, EDUCATION AND PLACEMENT INFORMATION MANAGEMENT.
Non-state entities receiving and using state funds (eff 7/1/2005).
Power to suspend disbursement, §143-6.2, (g).
Report, §143-6.2, (i).

BUDGETS —Cont'd
Office of state budget and management —Cont'd
Non-state entities receiving and using state funds (eff 7/1/2005) —Cont'd
Rules, adoption, §143-6.2, (d) to (f).
Personal services contracts utilized by state departments, agencies and institutions.
Submission of report to office, §143-64.70, (a).
Compiling and analyzing information, §143-64.70, (b).
State aid.
Departments and agencies asking state aid.
Reports, §143-6, (d).
Officers.
Examinations, §143-3.
Payrolls.
Establishment of new receipt-supported positions, §143-34.1, (a).
Submission to director of budgets, §143-34.1, (a).
Performance budgeting.
Community colleges, §115D-31.3.
Preparation of the budget.
Continuation and expansion costs, §143-10.1A.
Public officers and employees.
Limit on number of state employees, §143-10.2.
Public schools.
Generally, §§115C-425 to 115C-434.
See SCHOOL DISTRICTS AND ADMINISTRATIVE UNITS.
Purposes, §143-2.
Records.
Appropriations.
Accounting records, §143-20.
Recovery of wrongful expenditures, §143-32, (a).
Repairs and renovations reserve account.
Allocations and expenditures, §143-15.3A, (c).
Established, §143-15.3A, (a).
General fund credit balance.
Transfer of funds from unreserved credit balance to repairs and renovation reserve account, §143-15.2, (c).
Use of funds in account, §143-15.3A, (b).
Repayment of certain unexpended and unencumbered sums, §143-31.5, (a).
Reports, §143-31.5, (b).
Reports, §143-16.2.
Appropriations.
Office of state budget and management to report, §143-27.
Printing copies of budget report and bills, §143-13.
Reports to appropriation committees.
Effect, §143-15.
Copies of budget report, §143-13.
Director of the budget.
Employees, §143-19.
State aid, §143-6, (d).
Joint meetings of committees.
Consideration of report and appropriation bill, §143-14.
Repayment of certain unexpended and unencumbered sums, §143-31.5, (b).
State aid.
Departments and agencies asking state aid, §143-6, (d).
Requirements, §143-30.
Requisitions.
Allotments, §143-17.

BUDGETS —Cont'd
Retirement.
Payment of benefits and other salary-related items.
Paid from same source as salary, §143-34.1, (b).
River basins advisory commissions, §77-115, (a).
Rules and regulations.
Appropriations, §143-5.
Disbursements, §143-5.
Salaries.
Benefits and other salary-related items.
Paid from same source as salary, §143-34.1, (b).
Flexible compensation to eligible employees, §143-34.1, (d).
Submission of payrolls to director of budgets, §143-34.1, (a).
Use of funds appropriated for, §143-23, (a2).
Sanitary districts.
Annual budget, §130A-62, (a).
Operation under annual budget, §130A-62, (a).
Savings reserve account.
Appropriations, §143-15.3, (a).
Established, §143-15.3, (a).
Reserving to account unreserved credit balance remaining in general fund, §143-15.3, (a1).
Transfer of funds from unreserved credit balance to savings reserve account, §143-15.2, (b).
Use, §143-15.3, (a).
School districts.
Generally, §§115C-425 to 115C-434.
See SCHOOL DISTRICTS AND ADMINISTRATIVE UNITS.
Scope of provisions, §143-1.
Settlement reserve fund, §143-16.4.
Health trust account, §143-16.4, (a1).
Social security.
Payment of benefits and other salary-related items.
Paid from same source as salary, §143-34.1, (b).
Southern growth policies agreement.
Board, §143-497.
State aid.
Departments and agencies asking state aid.
Information from, §143-6, (a).
Certification of construction, §143-6, (b1).
Constructing or renovating state building, utility or other property, §143-6, (b).
Information required, §143-6, (c).
Reports, §143-6, (d).
Information technology projects, §143-6, (b2).
Use by non-state entities.
Audit oversight, §143-6.1.
State auditor.
Advisory budget commission.
Audit of state auditor's office, §143-4, (e).
Allotments.
Check for compliance with allotments, §143-17.
Information.
Furnishing upon request to director, §143-9.
State controller.
Budget request, §143B-426.38, (f).
State debt, §§142-1 to 142-29.7.
See STATE DEBT.
State departments and agencies.
All state agencies under provisions of article, §143-28.
Fiscal analysis.
Required for bill proposed by state agency that affects budget, §143-3.5.
Forms and reports in use by state departments and institutions.
Review, §143-10.7.

BUDGETS —Cont'd
State departments and agencies —Cont'd
Information.
Departments and agencies asking state aid, §143-6, (a).
Certification of construction, §143-6, (b1).
Constructing or renovating state buildings, utilities or other property development, §143-6, (b).
Information required, §143-6, (c).
Information technology projects, §143-6, (b2).
Reports, §143-6, (d).
Requests for nonstate funds for projects imposing obligation on state, §143-34.2.
Purpose of article, §143-33.
Requirements.
Generally, §143-30.
State aid, §143-6.
Survey of operation and management of departments, bureaus, divisions, officers, etc., §143-11, (a).
State institutions, §143-30.
Statements.
Itemized statements and forms, §143-7, (a).
Account codes, §143-7, (b).
State treasurer.
Allotments.
Quarterly allotments to office, §143-17.
Borrowing money, §143-24.
Director of the budget, §147-84.
State veterans home.
Annual budget, §165-55, (b).
Statistics.
Director of the budget.
Coordination by director, §143-3.5, (a), (c).
Streets and highways.
State highway fund.
Appropriations, §143-28.1.
State primary, secondary and urban road systems, §136-44.2.
Subpoenas.
Issuance, §143-21.
Taxation.
Borrowing money.
Consent of governor and council, §143-24.
Transfer of functions, §143-3.1.
Transfer of funds for certain services, §143-23.3.
University of North Carolina.
Duties of board of governors, §116-11.
Urban redevelopment.
Commission budgeting and accounting systems as part of municipality budgeting accounting systems, §160A-505.1.
Vending facilities.
State agencies and institutions.
Application of provisions, §143-12.1, (h).
Appropriation of net proceeds, §143-12.1, (c).
Contents of budget, §143-12.1, (e).
Definition of vending facilities, §143-12.1, (g).
Deposit of receipts or payments, §143-12.1, (b).
Inclusion of departmental budgets, §143-12.1, (d).
Revenue deemed state funds, §143-12.1, (a).
Use of net proceeds, §143-12.1, (f), (f1).
Venue.
Witnesses.
Prosecution of offending witnesses, §143-21.
Punishment for contempt at joint meetings of committees, §143-14.

BUDGETS —Cont'd
Venue —Cont'd
Wrongful expenditures.
Prosecution, §143-32, (b).
Violations of provisions, §§143-32, 143-34.
Wages.
Deposit of payroll deductions, §143-34.6.
Flexible compensation to eligible employees, §143-34.1, (d).
Payment of benefits and other salary-related items.
Paid from same source as salary, §143-34.1, (b).
Submission of payrolls to director of budget, §143-34.1, (a).
Warrants for payment of money.
Issuance, §143-3.2.
Fee, §143-3.2, (b).
Witnesses.
Advisory budget commission.
Generally, §143-21.
Director of the budget.
Generally, §143-21.

BUGGERY.
Rape.
See RAPE.
Sexual offenses generally.
See SEXUAL OFFENSES.

BUGGIES.
Bailment, lease or rental of vehicle or draft animals.
Protection of bailor against bailee's acts, §§14-165 to 14-169.
See BAILMENTS.
Traffic laws apply to animal-drawn vehicles, §20-171.

BUGGING.
Electronic eavesdropping, §§14-227.1 to 14-227.3.

BUILDING AND LOAN ASSOCIATIONS.
Acknowledgments.
Officers or stockholders, §47-94.
Claims against the state.
Assignments in favor of association.
Section inapplicable to, §143-3.3, (c).
Collection agencies.
Not included in definition of "collection agency," §58-70-15, (c).
Mortgages and deeds of trust.
Mortgages held by associations, §45-44.
Probate before stockholders in association, §47-9.
Officers.
Acknowledgment and registration by officer, §47-94.
Probate before stockholders in association, §47-9.
Savings and loan associations, §§54B-1 to 54B-278.
See SAVINGS AND LOAN ASSOCIATIONS.
Small estates.
Transfer of ownership rights by presentation of affidavit, §28A-25-1, (c).
State of North Carolina.
Assignment of claims against state.
Section inapplicable to assignments in favor of associations, §143-3.3, (c).
Stock and stockholders.
Acknowledgment and registration by stockholder, §47-94.

BUILDING CODES, §§143-136 to 143-143.4.
Adoption of North Carolina state building code, §143-138, (a).
Standards to be followed, §143-138, (c).
Amendments to code, §143-138, (d).
Applicability of article, §143-143.
Appropriations.
Code officials qualification board, §143-151.20.
Boilers.
Enforcement of building code, §143-139, (c).
Bonds, surety.
Manufactured buildings, structures or components.
Securing permits to erect modular buildings, §143-139.1, (a).
Building code council.
Adoption and preparation of state code, §143-138, (a).
Amendment of state code, §143-138, (d).
Appeals.
Further appeals to courts, §143-141, (d).
Interpretations of code, §143-141, (b).
Method of appeal, §143-141, (a).
Variations of code, §143-141, (c).
Committees, §143-137, (a).
Compensation, §143-136, (b).
Creation, §143-136, (a).
Duties.
Further duties of council, §143-142, (a), (b).
Enforcement agencies.
Recommending changes in enforcement procedures, §143-142, (b).
Expenses, §143-136, (b).
First meeting, §143-137, (a).
Fiscal affairs, §143-137, (d).
Manufactured buildings, structures or components.
Certification, §143-139.1, (a).
Meetings.
First meeting, §143-137, (a).
Regular meetings, §143-137, (b).
Membership, §143-136, (a).
Organization, §143-137, (a).
Per diem, §143-136, (b).
Recommending statutory changes, §143-142, (a).
Revision committees, §143-137, (a).
Rules and regulations, §143-137, (a).
Staff, §143-137, (c).
Terms, §143-136, (a).
Business occupancy buildings.
Special safety to life requirements applicable to existing high-rise buildings.
Inapplicability of provisions to, §143-138, (j).
Certificates for code enforcement officials.
Actions under section, §143-151.17, (c).
Administration, §143-151.19.
Clerical and staff services, §143-151.19, (a).
Contents, §143-151.19, (d).
County electrical inspectors, §143-151.13, (e).
Denial, §143-151.17, (d).
Duplicate certificates, §143-151.19, (e).
Examinations, §143-151.13, (a).
Fees, §143-151.16, (a).
Indian tribe employing officials to enforce codes.
Applicability of provisions to federally recognized tribe, §143-151.17, (e).
Injunctions, §143-151.18.
Investigations, §143-151.17, (b).
Issuance, §143-151.13, (f).
Reissuance by board, §143-151.15.
Penalties, §143-151.18.

BUILDING CODES —Cont'd
Certificates for code enforcement officials —Cont'd
Performance levels, §143-151.13, (b).
Probationary or temporary certificates, §143-151.13, (d).
Records of names and addresses of officials, §143-151.19, (c).
Reissuance by board, §143-151.15.
Renewal, §143-151.16, (b).
When examination required, §143-151.16, (c).
Required, §143-151.13, (a).
Return of certificate to board, §143-151.15.
Rules and regulations.
Certified copies, §143-151.19, (b).
Suspension, revocation or refusal to grant.
Grounds, §143-151.17, (a).
Tenure, §143-151.13, (c).
Violations, §143-151.18.
Certificates for occupancy.
Electric service, §143-139.2, (b).
Applicability of provisions, §143-139.2, (c).
Certification of manufactured buildings, structures or components, §143-139.1, (a).
Child care facilities.
Mandatory standards for licensing, §110-91.
Classes for various trades affected by state building code, §143-138.1.
Code officials qualification board.
Appointments, §143-151.9, (b).
Appropriations, §143-151.20, (b).
Chairman, §143-151.11, (a).
Code enforcement.
Defined, §143-151.8, (a).
Comity, §143-151.14.
Compensation, §143-151.10.
Definitions, §143-151.8.
Donations.
Acceptance by board, §143-151.20, (a).
Duties, §143-151.12.
Established, §143-151.9, (a).
Expenses, §143-151.10.
Fees.
Certificates for code enforcement officials.
Schedule of fees, §143-151.16, (a).
Disposition, §143-151.21.
Gifts.
Acceptance by board, §143-151.20, (a).
Grants.
Board may provide, §143-151.20, (b).
Local inspection departments.
Defined, §143-151.8, (a).
Meetings, §143-151.11, (c).
Members, §143-151.9, (a).
Population.
Determination, §143-151.8, (b).
Powers, §143-151.12.
Reciprocity, §143-151.14.
Reports.
Submission, §143-151.11, (d).
Rules and regulations.
Promulgation, §143-151.12.
Salaries, §143-151.10.
Standards.
Generally, §143-151.13.
Terms, §143-151.9, (b).
Vacancies, §143-151.9, (c).
Vice-chairman, §143-151.11, (b).
Construction and interpretation.
Existing laws.
Effect of article upon existing laws, §143-143.
Contents of state building code, §143-138, (b).

BUILDING CODES —Cont'd
Definitions.
Code officials qualification board, §143-151.8.
Electric wiring of houses, buildings and structures.
Definition of building, §143-143.2.
Distribution of state code, §143-138, (g).
Door lock exemption permits.
Businesses applicable, §143-143.4, (a).
Conditions for permit, §143-143.4, (b).
Definitions, §143-143.4, (g).
Filing of permit, §143-143.4, (c).
Implementation rules, §143-143.4, (i).
Inspections by insurance department, §143-143.4, (d).
Penalty for violation of provisions, §143-143.4, (h).
Revocation of permit, §143-143.4, (e).
Appeal of decision, §143-143.4, (f).
Effect of state code upon local codes, §143-138, (e).
Electric service.
Certificates for occupancy, §143-139.2, (b).
Applicability of provisions, §143-139.2, (c).
Insulation requirements, §143-139.2, (a), (b).
Applicability of provisions, §143-139.2, (c).
Wiring of houses, buildings and structures.
Requirements, §143-143.2.
Elevators.
Enforcement of building code, §143-139, (d).
Special safety to life requirements applicable to existing high-rise buildings.
Requirements for buildings, §143-138, (i).
Emergency electrical power supply.
Special safety to life requirements applicable to existing high-rise buildings.
Requirements for buildings, §143-138, (i).
Enforcement.
Boilers, §143-139, (c).
Elevators, §143-139, (d).
General building regulations, §143-139, (b).
Procedural requirements, §143-139, (a).
Remedies, §143-139, (b1).
Enforcement agencies.
Building code council.
Recommending changes in enforcement procedures, §143-142, (b).
Hearings.
Questions under building code, §143-140.
Existing laws.
Effect of article upon existing laws, §143-143.
Exit requirements.
Special safety to life requirements applicable to existing high-rise buildings.
Requirements for buildings, §143-138, (i).
Fair housing.
Unlawful discriminatory housing practices provisions.
Inapplicability to code provisions applicable to handicapped, §41A-6, (d).
Family care home.
Defined, §143-138, (k).
Fees.
Code officials qualification board.
Certificates for code enforcement officials, §143-151.16.
Disposition, §143-151.21.
Fire alarm systems.
Special safety to life requirements applicable to existing high-rise buildings.
Requirements for buildings, §143-138, (i).

BUILDING CODES —Cont'd
Fire protection of electrical conductors.
Special safety to life requirements applicable to existing high-rise buildings.
Requirements for class III buildings, §143-138, (i).
Fire stopping for vertical shafts.
Special safety to life requirements applicable to existing high-rise buildings.
Requirements for buildings, §143-138, (i).
General building regulations.
Enforcement, §143-139, (b).
Hearings.
Enforcement agencies.
Questions under building code, §143-140.
High-rise buildings to be provided with safety to life facilities, §143-138, (i).
Injunctions.
Code officials qualification board.
Certificates for code enforcement officials, §143-151.18.
Inspections.
Local inspection departments.
Code officials qualification board.
Defined, §143-151.8, (a).
Instructional classes for various trades affected by state building code, §143-138.1.
Insulation and energy utilization standards.
Applicability of provisions, §143-139.2, (c).
Electric service, §143-139.2, (a), (b).
Applicability of provisions, §143-139.2, (c).
Electric wiring of houses, buildings and structures, §143-143.2.
Enforcement, §143-139.2, (a).
Judicial notice, §143-138, (l).
Life requirements for existing high-rise buildings, §143-138, (i).
Liquefied petroleum gas.
Residential structures.
Inspection of liquefied petroleum gas piping systems for, §143-139.3.
Local codes, effect of state code upon, §143-138, (e).
Local inspection departments.
Code officials qualification board.
Defined, §143-151.8, (a).
Manufactured buildings, structures and components.
Agencies offering testing, evaluation, inspection and certification.
Rules for approving, adoption, §143-139.1, (a).
Bonds, surety.
Securing permits to erect modular buildings, §143-139.1, (a).
Building code council.
Certification, §143-139.1, (a).
Certification, §143-139.1, (a).
Eave projection, standards, §143-139.1, (b).
Exterior wall, standards, §143-139.1, (b).
Foundations, standards, §143-139.1, (b).
Labels and seals.
Evidence of approval, §143-139.1, (a).
Minimum standards, §143-139.1, (b).
Roof pitch, standards, §143-139.1, (b).
Siding and roofing materials, standards, §143-139.1, (b).
Testing, evaluation, inspection and certification, §143-139.1, (a).
Unlicensed persons erecting.
Rules, adoption, §143-139.1, (a).

BUILDING CODES —Cont'd
Manufactured homes generally, §§143-144 to 143-151.5.
See MANUFACTURED HOMES.
Misdemeanors.
Violation of state code, §143-138, (b).
Nonbusiness occupancy building built prior to adoption of 1953 code.
Compliance with certain provisions by December 31, 2006 required, §143-138, (j1).
North Carolina state building code, §143-138.
Preparation of North Carolina state building code, §143-138, (a).
Pressurized fans.
Special safety to life requirements applicable to existing high-rise buildings.
Requirements for class II buildings, §143-138, (i).
Publication of code, §143-138, (g).
Refuge areas required in class III high-rise buildings.
Special safety to life requirements applicable to existing high-rise buildings, §143-138, (i).
Reports.
Code officials qualification board, §143-151.11.
Rulemaking procedure.
Notice and rule-making hearing not required.
State building code, §150B-21.5, (d).
Smoke compartmentation for institutional buildings.
Special safety to life requirements applicable to existing high-rise buildings.
Requirements for buildings, §143-138, (i).
Smoke detectors.
Business occupancy buildings, §143-138, (j).
Special safety to life requirements applicable to existing high-rise buildings.
Requirements for buildings, §143-138, (i).
Smoke venting in class III high-rise buildings.
Special safety to life requirements applicable to existing high-rise buildings, §143-138, (i).
Special safety to life requirements applicable to existing high-rise buildings, §143-138, (i).
Specific activities and functions of state code.
Enumeration, §143-138, (b).
Sprinkler systems.
Special safety to life requirements applicable to existing high-rise buildings.
Requirements for class III buildings, §143-138, (i).
Standards to be followed in adopting state code, §143-138, (c).
State building code, §143-138.
State buildings.
Applicability of county or municipal building code, §143-135.1, (a), (c).
Toilets.
Shopping malls.
Horizontal travel distance for access, §143-143.5.
Temporary toilet facilities at construction sites.
Requirements, §143-143.3, (a).
Standards to be established, §143-143.3, (b).
Violations of state code, §143-138, (h).
Voice communication system.
Special safety to life requirements applicable to existing high-rise buildings.
Requirements for buildings, §143-138, (i).

BUILDING COMMISSION, §§143-135.25 to 143-135.27.
Appointment of members, §143-135.25, (c).

BUILDING COMMISSION —Cont'd
Capital improvement project.
Defined, §143-135.27.
Chairman.
Election, §143-135.25, (c).
Compensation, §143-135.25, (e).
Composition, §143-135.25, (c).
Conflicts of interest.
Interested members not to participate in authorization of contract, §143-135.28.
Creation, §143-135.25, (a).
Department of administration.
Created within, §143-135.25, (a).
Designer.
Final selection.
Duty as to, §143-135.26.
Exception, §143-135.26.
Duties, §143-135.26.
Expenses.
Reimbursement for travel and subsistence, §143-135.25, (e).
Meetings, §143-135.25, (d).
Number of members, §143-135.25, (c).
Powers, §143-135.26.
Staff.
Provided by state construction office, §143-135.25, (b).
State construction office.
Director.
Qualifications, §143-135.25, (b).
Staff provided by, §143-135.25, (b).
Terms, §143-135.25, (c).
Vacancies, §143-135.25, (c).

BUILDING CONTRACTORS.
Electrical contractors.
Generally, §§87-39 to 87-51.
See ELECTRICAL CONTRACTORS.
General contractors.
Generally, §§87-1 to 87-15.3.
See GENERAL CONTRACTORS.
Plumbing, heating and fire sprinkler contractors.
Generally, §§87-16 to 87-27.1.
See PLUMBING, HEATING AND FIRE SPRINKLER CONTRACTORS.
Refrigeration contractors, §§87-52 to 87-64.1.
See REFRIGERATION CONTRACTORS.

BUILDING ENTRANCES.
Right of way.
Vehicle about to enter or cross, §20-156, (a).

BUILDING INSPECTIONS AND INSPECTORS.
County inspection departments, §§153A-350 to 153A-375.
See COUNTY INSPECTION DEPARTMENTS.
Filing of lis pendens by cities and counties in certain cases, §1-120.2.
Municipal building inspection, §§160A-411 to 160A-438.
See MUNICIPAL BUILDING INSPECTION.

BUILDINGS.
Allocated state lands.
Acquisition.
Buildings having historic, architectural or cultural significance, §146-23.1.
Arson.
Defined, §14-58.1.
General provisions, §§14-58 to 14-69.2.
Not covered by other provisions.
Burning or attempting to burn, §14-67.1.

BUILDINGS —Cont'd
Arson —Cont'd
Public buildings.
Bureau of investigation.
Authority, §114-15.
Burning certain public buildings, §14-59.
Building and permanent improvement funds, §§143-31, 143-31.1.
Burglary, §§14-51 to 14-57.
Child care facilities.
Mandatory standards, §110-91.
Claim and delivery.
Property concealed in buildings, §1-480.
Code, §§143-136 to 143-143.4.
See BUILDING CODES.
Community colleges.
Fire and casualty insurance on institutional buildings and contents, §115D-58.11, (a) to (c).
Public building contracts.
Construction contract claims.
Adjustment and resolution, §143-135.6.
Concealed property in buildings.
Claim for delivery of personal property, §1-480.
Condemnation of unsafe buildings.
Municipalities generally, §§160A-411 to 160A-438.
See MUNICIPAL BUILDING INSPECTION.
Condominium act, §§47C-1-101 to 47C-4-120.
See CONDOMINIUMS.
Construction indemnity agreements invalid, §22B-1.
Counties.
Care and use of county property, §153A-169.
Damages.
Rewards for information, §153A-446.
Defined, §153A-350.
Failure of owner to comply with orders of public authorities, §14-68.
Inspection departments, §§153A-350 to 153A-375.
See COUNTY INSPECTION DEPARTMENTS.
Joint buildings, §153A-164.
Planning and zoning.
Applicability of provisions, §153A-347.
Sites of county buildings, §153A-169.
Disorderly conduct.
Public buildings and facilities.
Trespasses to land and fixtures, §14-132.
Eminent domain.
Removal of structures on condemned land, §40A-9.
Evacuation of public buildings.
Governor may order in emergency, §14-288.19, (a).
Penalty for willful refusal to leave, §14-288.19, (b).
Firearms.
Discharging firearm into occupied property, §14-34.1.
Attempt, §14-34.1.
General assembly.
State legislative building.
Official name, §129-12.1.
Hospital authorities.
Subject to building laws, ordinances and regulations, §131E-25.
Housing authorities and projects.
Applicability of building laws, §157-13.
General provisions, §§157-1 to 157-70.
See HOUSING AUTHORITIES AND PROJECTS.
Indemnity agreements.
Construction indemnity agreements invalid, §22B-1.

BUILDINGS —Cont'd
Joint tenants and tenants in common.
Dismantling portion of building.
Damages, §1-539.2.
Mountain ridge construction.
Certain building prohibited, §113A-209, (a) to (c).
Mountain ridge protection.
Existing buildings, §113A-210.
Municipal corporations.
Building inspection, §§160A-411 to 160A-438.
See MUNICIPAL BUILDING INSPECTION.
Generally.
See MUNICIPAL CORPORATIONS.
Nuisances.
Abatement.
Offenses against public morals, §§19-1 to 19-8.3.
See NUISANCES.
Party walls, §1-539.2.
Ports authority.
Removal of buildings, §143B-458.
Public building contracts.
Architectural, engineering and surveying services, §§143-64.31 to 143-64.34.
See PUBLIC CONTRACTS.
Generally, §§143-128 to 143-135.9.
See PUBLIC CONTRACTS.
Public buildings.
Burning of certain public buildings, §14-59.
General provisions.
See PUBLIC BUILDINGS AND GROUNDS.
Public lands.
Allocated state lands.
Severance approval delegation, §146-35.
Public officers and employees.
Failure of owner to comply with orders of public authorities, §14-68.
Public works.
General provisions, §§133-1 to 133-4.1.
See PUBLIC WORKS.
School buildings and property.
Generally, §§115C-517 to 115C-528.
See SCHOOL BUILDINGS AND PROPERTY.
State legislative building.
Designation, §129-12.1.
Official name, §129-12.1.
State prison system.
Additional facilities.
Authorized, §148-37, (a).
Structural pest control, §§106-65.22 to 106-65.41.
See STRUCTURAL PEST CONTROL.
Subversion.
Use of public buildings, §14-11.
Transportation department.
Acquisition of buildings, §136-19.3.
Trespass.
Injuring buildings, §14-159.
Public buildings and facilities.
Disorderly conduct in and injuries to buildings and facilities, §14-132.
Unit ownership, §§47A-1 to 47A-28.
See UNIT OWNERSHIP.
Unsafe building, condemnation, correction of defects, §§160A-411 to 160A-438.
See MUNICIPAL BUILDING INSPECTION.
Veterans' recreation authorities.
Projects subject to building laws, §165-32.
Wildlife resources commission.
Transfer, §143-248.

BUILDING TRADES TRAINING.
Vocational and technical education generally, §§115C-151 to 115C-169.
See VOCATIONAL AND TECHNICAL EDUCATION.

BULBS.
Promotion of use and sale of agricultural products.
Generally, §§106-550 to 106-568.
See AGRICULTURAL PRODUCTS PROMOTION.

BULLDOZERS.
Mechanical breakdown service agreement, §58-1-42.

BULLET-PROOF VESTS.
Defendant wearing or having in possession during commission of felony.
Enhanced sentence, §15A-1340.16C, (a).
Burden of proof, §15A-1340.16C, (d).
Exceptions, §15A-1340.16C, (b), (e).
Indictments or informations, §15A-1340.16C, (c).

BULLETS.
Furnishing bullets to inmates of charitable, mental or penal institutions, §14-258.1.
Products liability lawsuits involving ammunition, §99B-11.
Teflon-coated bullets.
Manufacture, sale, purchase or possession, §14-34.3.

BUNCOMBE COUNTY.
Alcohol detoxification program.
Facility not to be removed from county without prior approval of general assembly, §131E-65.
Ambulances.
Attachment or garnishment and lien for, §§44-51.4 to 44-51.8.
Obtaining services without intending to pay, §14-111.1.
Requesting ambulance falsely, §14-111.3.
Board of county commissioners.
Filling vacancies on board, §153A-27.1.
Condemnation or acquisition of land by local government unit outside county.
Consent of board of commissioners necessary, §153A-15.
Coroner elected as nominee of political party.
Filling vacancy in office, §152-1.
Counties generally.
See COUNTIES.
County boards of education elected on partisan basis.
Vacancies in office, §115C-37.1.
Dog collars.
Unlawful removal of electronic dog collars, §14-401.17.
Forestland sales, distribution of funds, §113-38.
Game laws, local acts not repealed, §113-133.1, (e).
Oil, gas and mineral interests separated from surface fee, extinguished, title in surface fee holder.
Failure to list interest for tax purposes for 10 years prior to January 1, 1965.
Protection of subsurface interest from surface fee holder, §1-42.1, (d).
Failure to list interest for tax purposes for 10 years prior to January 1, 1971.
Protection of surface interest from surface estate holder, §1-42.2, (d).

BUNCOMBE COUNTY —Cont'd
Probates and registration orders before clerks of inferior courts validated, §47-59.
Real estate mortgage loans.
Interest, commissions and repayment, §45-43.
Room occupancy tax levied by county, uniform provisions, §153A-155.
Sheriff.
Vacancy, performance of duties until vacancy filled, §162-5.1.
Special police officers, joint security force, §122C-421, (a).
Special school tax, election to abolish.
Petition required, §115C-505.
Western North Carolina Development Association, Inc.
Appropriation of funds to, §153A-447, (a), (b).
Western North Carolina regional economic development commission, §158-8.1.

BUNDLED SERVICES.
Sales and use tax.
Telecommunications services, §105-164.4C, (d).

BUNDLED TRANSACTIONS.
Sales and use tax, §105-164.12B.

BUOYS.
Interfering with, §76-58.
Rafts to exercise care in passing, §76-57.

BUPRENORPHINE.
Prescribing or dispensing for treatment of opiate dependence.
Registration of physicians, §90-101, (a1).

BURDEN OF PROOF.
Abused, neglected or dependent juvenile actions.
Adjudicatory hearing, §7B-805.
Nonsecure custody hearings, §7B-506, (b).
Adoption.
Hearing on petition to adopt adult, §48-2-605, (b).
Hearings on petition for adoption, §48-2-603, (a).
Alcoholic beverages.
Compensation for injury caused by sales to underage persons, §18B-122.
Attorney discipline.
Reinstatement after disbarment, Bar Rules & Regs., B, §.0125.
Bank deposits and collections.
Stop payment order.
Burden of proof of loss, §25-4-403, (c).
Biological residues in animals.
Content of biological residue, §106-549.82.
Bullet-proof vests.
Defendant wearing or having in possession during commission of felony.
Enhanced sentence, §15A-1340.16C, (d).
Business and energy tax credit.
Eligibility and amount of credit, §105-129.18.
Capital punishment.
Death penalty for mentally retarded defendants prohibited.
Defendant's burden, §15A-2005, (a), (c), (f).
Civil actions and proceedings.
Presumptions, §8C-1, Rule 301.
Commercial paper.
Order to stop payment.
Burden of proof of loss, §25-4-403, (c).
Common carriers duty to transport freight within reasonable time.
Delay in shipping, §62-200, (c).

BURDEN OF PROOF —Cont'd
Contempt.
Civil contempt.
Proceeding initiated on motion of aggrieved party, §5A-23, (a1).
Contributory negligence, §1-139.
Controlled substances.
Exemptions or exceptions, §90-113.1, (a).
Registration or order form, §90-113.1, (b).
Credit repair service violations, actions for damages.
Proving exemption or exception, §66-225, (d).
Criminal investigation information records.
Preventing disclosure of information considered public record, §132-1.4, (e).
Criminal law and procedure.
Appeals.
Prejudice to defendant, §15A-1443, (a).
Death penalty for mentally retarded defendants prohibited.
Defendant's burden, §15A-2005, (a), (c), (f).
Delinquent and undisciplined juvenile actions.
Adjudicatory hearing, §7B-2409.
Prior adjudication of delinquent.
Delinquency history level determination, §7B-2507, (f).
Secure or nonsecure custody hearing, §7B-1906, (d).
Discharge of employee called to jury duty.
Action for damages, §9-32, (b).
Employment security.
Benefits, §96-14.
Eligibility conditions, §96-14.
Claims for benefits.
Witnesses.
Discharge, demotion or intimidation, §96-15.1, (b).
Enhanced sentence.
Bullet-proof vests.
Defendant wearing or having in possession during commission of felony, §15A-1340.16C, (d).
Firearms.
Use or display during commission of felony, §15A-1340.16A, (e).
Methamphetamine manufacture.
Serious injury inflicted upon law enforcement or emergency personnel, §15A-1340.16D, (c).
Expedited evictions.
Affirmative defense to subsequent action for complete eviction, §42-64, (b).
Civil causes of action, §42-61.
Exemption from complete eviction where grounds established, §42-64, (c).
Firearms.
Use or display during commission of felony.
Enhanced sentence, §15A-1340.16A, (e).
Foreign judgments.
Motion for enforcement of foreign judgment, §1C-1705, (b).
Infractions, §15A-1114, (f).
International commercial arbitration and conciliation.
Tribunal conducting proceeding, §1-567.49, (b).
Investment advisers.
Civil or administrative proceedings, §78C-40.
Leases, UCC.
Default of lessor.
Burden of establishing default after acceptance of goods, §25-2A-516.

BURDEN OF PROOF —Cont'd
Legitimation of illegitimate children.
Legitimation where mother married, §49-12.1, (b).
Life imprisonment without parole.
Second or subsequent conviction of class B1 felony, §15A-1340.16B, (e).
Livestock markets.
Transportation, sale, etc., of diseased livestock.
Burden of proving health, §106-414.
Local boards of education.
Actions against board, §115C-44, (b).
Medicaid.
False claims by providers.
Civil actions, §108A-70.13, (c).
Medical malpractice.
Standard of health care, §90-21.12.
Mental health, developmental disability, substance abuse.
Involuntary commitment.
Hearing following automatic commitment, §122C-268.1, (i).
Substance abuser's commitment hearing, §122C-286, (h).
Methamphetamine manufacture.
Serious injury inflicted upon law enforcement or emergency personnel.
Enhanced sentence, §15A-1340.16D, (c).
Monopolies and restraint of trade.
Unfair methods of competition, acts and practices.
Party claiming exemption from prohibition, §75-1.1, (d).
Motion for appropriate relief.
Denial.
Defendant's burden of proof, §15A-1419, (b), (c).
Ordinances, §160A-79, (c).
Partition sales.
Sale in lieu of partition.
Order for sale, §46-22, (d).
Paternity, civil action to establish, §49-14, (b).
Presumptions.
See PRESUMPTIONS.
Products liability.
Claims based on inadequate design or formulation, §99B-6, (a).
Claims based on inadequate warning or instruction, §99B-5, (a).
Products liability lawsuits involving firearms, §99B-11, (b).
Public records.
Actions to compel disclosure of certain public records, §132-9.
Punitive damages.
Aggravating factors, §1D-15, (b).
Sale of goods, UCC.
Burden of establishing breach after acceptance, §25-2-607, (4).
Sales and use tax.
Seller who accepts certificate of resale.
Burden of proving sale not retail sale, §105-164.28.
Secured transactions.
Purchase-money security interest.
Non-consumer goods, §25-9-103, (g).
Securities regulation.
Exemptions.
Burden of proving exemption on person claiming it, §78A-18, (b).
Tax incentives for new and expanding businesses.
Eligibility for credit and amount of credit, §105-129.7, (a).

BURDEN OF PROOF —Cont'd
Telephonic sellers.
Exemptions or exceptions, §66-266, (e).
Termination of parental rights proceedings.
Adjudicatory hearing, §7B-1109, (f).
Establishing grounds for terminating, §7B-1111, (b).
Tort claims against state departments and agencies.
Contributory negligence, §143-299.1.
Trade secrets.
Misappropriation, §66-155.
Trusts and trustees.
Uniform trusts act.
Plaintiff's burden of proof, §36A-76.
Unclaimed property act.
Existence and amount of property and abandonment, §116B-58.
Utilities commission.
Proceedings instituted by commission, §62-75.
Water resources.
Capacity use areas, §143-215.15, (f).
Workers' compensation.
Person claiming exemption or forfeiture, §97-12.

BUREAU OF ALCOHOL, TOBACCO AND FIREARMS.
Agents authorized to enforce criminal laws, §15A-406.

BUREAU OF INVESTIGATION, §§114-12 to 114-20.1.
Abuse, neglect or dependency of juvenile.
Report by director upon finding evidence of sexual abuse in child care facility, §7B-307, (c).
Background investigations, §§114-19.1 to 114-19.15.
Child care providers.
Criminal record checks, §114-19.5.
Education.
Criminal record checks of school personnel, §114-19.2.
Fees for performance.
Conducted for purposes other than administration of criminal justice, §114-19.1, (a).
Foster parents.
Criminal record check, §114-19.4.
Positions must be confirmed by general assembly, §114-15, (a).
Priority in processing, §114-19.1, (c).
Providers of treatment for or services to children, the elderly, mental health patients, the sick and the disabled.
Criminal record checks, §114-19.3.
Rights to receive records of bureau.
Not enlarged, §114-19.1, (d).
Central prison identification bureau.
Transfer of activities to new bureau, §114-18.
Child sexual abuse in child care.
Investigation, §114-15.3.
Clinical facilities, §114-16.
Concealed handgun permit.
Permittee list, maintenance, §14-415.17.
Submission of fingerprints to FBI for records check, §14-415.13, (b).
Created, §114-12.
Crimes authorized to investigate, §114-15, (a), (b).
Criminal justice information network governing board, §§143-660 to 143-664.

BUREAU OF INVESTIGATION —Cont'd
Criminal statistics.
Duties, §114-19, (a).
Reception and collection, §114-18.
Criminologists.
Employment, §114-16.
Delinquent or undisciplined juvenile actions.
Fingerprinting or photographing juveniles.
Proper format for transfer to bureau, §7B-2102, (c).
Director.
Appointment by attorney general, §114-13.
Assistants, §114-13.
Duties, §114-14.
Mileage payments, §114-15, (d).
Powers, §114-14.
Salary, §114-13.
DNA database and databank.
Expungement of records.
Charges dismissed on appeal or pardon of innocence granted, §15A-148, (b).
Generally, §§15-266 to 15-266.12.
Duties, §114-12.
Election fraud.
Investigation, §114-15, (a).
Electronic surveillance generally, §§15A-286 to 15A-298.
See ELECTRONIC SURVEILLANCE.
Evidence.
Availability to district attorneys, §114-15, (c).
Expungement of criminal records.
Charges dismissed or person found not guilty or not responsible.
Law enforcement agencies ordered to expunge records, §15A-146, (b).
As result of identity fraud, §15A-147, (c).
DNA records, §15A-148, (b).
Fees.
Performance of certain background investigations, §114-19.1, (a).
Fingerprinting.
Records, §114-18.
Firearms.
Surplus weapons.
Sale, trade or disposal, §143-63.1, (d).
Fires and fire prevention.
Investigations.
Attorney general acting through bureau, §58-79-1.
Gaming.
Investigation of gaming law violations, §114-15, (a).
General assembly.
Background investigation of person who must be confirmed by legislative action.
Requests to bureau of investigation, §120-19.4A.
Governor.
Services subject to call of governor, §114-15, (a).
Laboratory and clinical facilities, §114-16.
List of crimes authorized to investigate, §114-15, (a), (b).
Local law enforcement officers.
Cooperation, §114-17.
Lotteries.
Investigation of lottery law violations, §114-15, (a).
Lynchings.
Investigation, §114-15, (a).
Mileage.
Director and assistants, §114-15, (d).

BUREAU OF INVESTIGATION —Cont'd
Misuse of state property.
Reports of department heads, §114-15.1.
Mob violence.
Investigations of, §114-15, (a).
Personnel.
Transfer, §114-14.1.
Photography.
Records, §114-18.
Police.
Cooperation of local enforcement officers, §114-17.
Powers, §114-12.
Protection of public officials.
Authority to provide protection, §114-20.
Designation of areas for protection of public officials, §114-20.1, (a).
Promulgation of rules and regulations governing ingress to or egress from buildings, §114-20.1, (b).
Public buildings and grounds.
Arson, damage or theft, §114-15.
Public lands.
Investigation of cases involving misuse of state property, §114-15.1.
Public utilities.
Employment applications.
Criminal history record from state bureau of investigation, §62-333.
Radio system.
State system available to bureau, §114-16.
Records.
Availability to district attorneys, §114-15, (c).
Photographing and fingerprinting records, §114-18.
Reports.
Violations of criminal statutes involving misuse of state property, §114-15.1.
Social security fraud.
Investigations, authority, §114-15, (a).
State radio system.
Availability to bureau, §114-16.
Transfer of personnel, §114-14.1.
Transfer to department, §143A-51.
Waste discharges.
Referral by secretary for review, §143-215.6B, (k).
Weapons.
Surplus weapons.
Sale, trade or disposal, §143-63.1, (d).
Witnesses.
Fees, §114-15, (d).

BURGLAR ALARMS.
Alarm systems licensing, §§74D-1 to 74D-13.
See ALARM SYSTEMS LICENSING.
Private protective services generally, §§74C-1 to 74C-33.
See PRIVATE PROTECTIVE SERVICES.

BURGLARY, §§14-51 to 14-57.
Airplanes.
Breaking or entering into or breaking out of aircraft, §14-56.
Boats.
Breaking or entering into or breaking out of boats or other watercraft, §14-56.
Breaking or entering buildings.
Definition of "building," §14-54, (c).
Felony offenses, §14-54, (a).
Generally, §14-54.
Misdemeanor offenses, §14-54, (b).
Breaking out of dwelling, §14-53.

BURGLARY —Cont'd
Capital punishment.
Aggravating circumstances.
Capital felony in commission of burglary, §15A-2000, (e).
Crimes punishable by death, Const. N. C., art. XI, §2.
Coin-operated machines.
Breaking into or forcibly opening, §14-56.1.
Damaging or destroying machine, §14-56.2.
Deadly force.
Use against intruder.
Justification, §14-51.1, (a).
No duty to retreat, §14-51.1, (b).
Other defenses not repealed, expanded or limited, §14-51.1, (c).
Defense of home or residence.
Use of deadly force against intruder.
Justification, §14-51.1, (a).
No duty to retreat, §14-51.1, (b).
Other defenses not repealed, expanded or limited, §14-51.1, (c).
Definitions.
Buildings.
Breaking or entering buildings, §14-54, (c).
First degree burglary, §14-51.
Second degree burglary, §14-51.
Dwelling houses.
Breaking out of dwelling house, §14-53.
Explosives.
Use of explosives in burglary, §14-57.
First degree burglary, §§14-51, 14-52.
Implements of housebreaking.
Preparation to commit burglary or other housebreakings, §14-55.
Mobile homes.
Breaking or entering into or breaking out of trailers, §14-56.
Motor vehicles.
Breaking or entering into or breaking out of vehicles, §14-56.
Murder during commission, §14-17.
Paper currency machines.
Breaking into machine, §14-56.3.
Preparation to commit burglary or other housebreakings, §14-55.
Punishment for burglary, §14-52.
Mandatory period of incarceration, §14-52.
Railroad cars.
Breaking or entering into or breaking out of cars, §14-56.
Second degree burglary, §§14-51, 14-52.
Explosives used in burglary, §14-57.
Slot machines.
Breaking into or forcibly opening, §14-56.1.
Trailers.
Breaking or entering into or breaking out of trailers, §14-56.
Watercraft.
Breaking or entering into or breaking out of boats or other watercraft, §14-56.
Weapons.
Preparation to commit burglary or other housebreakings, §14-55.

BURGLARY AND THEFT INSURANCE, §58-7-15.
Mandatory or voluntary risk sharing plans.
See MANDATORY OR VOLUNTARY RISK SHARING PLANS.

BURGLARY TOOLS.
Preparation to commit burglary, §14-55.

BURIAL.
Animals.
Disposition of dead domesticated animals, §106-403.
Burial at sea, §§130A-113, (b), 130A-388, (b).
Certification and duties of medical examiners, §130A-388, (b).
Cemeteries.
General provisions.
See CEMETERIES.
Community trust for persons with severe chronic disabilities.
Expenditure of funds for burial of beneficiaries, §36A-59.13, (d).
Cremation.
General provisions, §§90-210.40 to 90-210.54.
See CREMATION.
Decedents' estates.
Funeral and burial expenses deemed obligation of estate, §28A-19-8.
Discrimination.
Burial without regard to race or color, §65-72, (a).
Violations of provisions misdemeanors, §65-72, (b).
Disposition of remains of terminated pregnancies, §130A-131.10.
Executors and administrators.
Carrying out burial arrangements prior to appointment, §28A-13-1.
Franchise tax.
Mutual burial associations, §105-121.1.
Funeral service.
General provisions, §§90-210.18A to 90-210.29.
See FUNERAL SERVICE.
Hog cholera.
Burial of hogs and other livestock dying in transit, §106-319.
Burial of hogs dying natural death, §106-310.
Identification of bodies before burial or cremation, §90-210.29A.
Medical examiners.
Postmortem medicolegal examinations and services.
Burial at sea.
Certification and duties of medical examiners, §130A-388, (b).
When examiner's permission necessary before burial, §130A-388, (a), (b).
Minimum burial depth, §§65-77, 90-210.25A.
Property taxes.
Real property set aside for burial.
Exemption, §105-278.2, (a).
Real property defined, §105-278.2, (c).
Special class, designation, assessment, §105-278.2, (b).
Racial minorities.
Burial without regard to race or color, §65-72, (a).
Violations of provisions misdemeanors, §65-72, (b).
Sales and use tax.
Exemption of funeral expenses, §105-164.13.
Maintenance and repair of ingress and egress to burial grounds.
Powers of department, §136-18.
Unmarked human burial and human skeletal remains protection, §§70-26 to 70-40.
See UNMARKED HUMAN BURIAL AND SKELETAL REMAINS PROTECTION.

BURIAL —Cont'd
Veterans' cemeteries.
Days for burial, §65-44.
Workers' compensation.
Expenses of burial, §97-38.

BURIAL ASSOCIATIONS.
Mutual burial associations, §§90-210.80 to 90-210.107.
See MUTUAL BURIAL ASSOCIATIONS.

BURIAL AT SEA, §§130A-113, (b), 130A-388, (b).

BURKE COUNTY.
Ambulance service.
Attachment or garnishment and lien for, §§44-51.4 to 44-51.8.
Board of county commissioners.
Filling vacancies on board, §153A-27.1.
Condemnation or acquisition of land by local government unit outside county.
Consent of board of commissioners necessary, §153A-15.
Copies of grants in Burke.
Admission into evidence, §8-10.
Coroner elected as nominee of political party.
Filling vacancy in office, §152-1.
Counties generally.
See COUNTIES.
County boards of education elected on partisan basis.
Vacancies in office, §115C-37.1.
Cropper or tenant refusing to perform terms of contract.
Forfeiture of right of possession to premises, §42-27.
Dog collars.
Unlawful removal of electronic dog collars, §14-401.17.
Forestland sales, distribution of funds, §113-38.
Game laws, local acts not repealed, §113-133.1, (e).
Highway system.
County participation in improvements to, §136-66.3, (k).
Housing authority commissioners.
Tenant as commissioner, exemption from provision of law allowing, §157-5.
Oil, gas or mineral interest separated from surface interest, extinguished, title in surface fee holder.
Failure to list interest for tax purposes for 10 years prior to January 1, 1974.
Protection of interest from surface estate, §1-42.3, (d).
School property.
Acquisition and improvement, §153A-158.1.
Sheriff.
Vacancy, performance of duties until vacancy filled, §162-5.1.
Small city mixed beverage elections.
Inapplicability of provisions to, §18B-600, (e1).
Tax elections for industrial development purposes, §§158-16 to 158-24.
Western North Carolina Development Association, Inc.
Appropriation of funds to, §153A-447, (a), (b).

BURLAP.
Dealers of scrap, salvage or surplus, failure to keep records of purchases, §66-10, (b).

BURNING BOATS AND BARGES, §14-63.

BURNING BUILDING UNDER CONSTRUCTION, §14-62.1.

BURNING GINHOUSES AND TOBACCO HOUSES, §14-64.

BURNING OF CERTAIN BRIDGES AND BUILDINGS, §14-61.

BURNING OF CERTAIN PUBLIC BUILDINGS, §14-59.

BURNING OF CHURCHES AND OTHER BUILDINGS OF WORSHIP, §§14-49, (b1), 14-62.2.

BURNING OF DWELLING.
Fraudulently setting fire, §14-65.

BURNING OF MOBILE HOME, MANUFACTURED HOME OR TRAILER HOME, §14-58.2.

BURNING OF PERSONAL PROPERTY, §14-66.

BURNING OF SCHOOLS OR EDUCATIONAL INSTITUTION BUILDINGS, §14-60.

BURNING OF TIMBER.
Damages for unlawful burning, §1-539.1, (a).

BURNING WILL.
Revocation of written will, §31-5.1.

BUS COMPANIES.
Certificates of authority, §62-262.1.
Fees, §62-300.
Charter service rates, fares and charges.
Exempt from regulations, §62-146.1, (j).
Complaints about rates, fares, charges, etc., §62-146.1, (h).
Defined, §62-3.
Discontinuance or reduction in service.
Certificate or permit.
Inapplicability of provisions to bus companies, §62-262.2, (e).
Granting permission, §62-262.2, (c).
Hearings.
Determination with or without public hearing, §62-262.2, (d).
Notice to be given, §62-262.2, (a).
Objections to granting permission, §62-262.2, (b).
Petitions for permission, §62-262.2, (a).
Fare, just and reasonable rates, fares and charges.
Establishment pursuant to this section, §62-146.1 (i).
Fixed service, petition for new or revised rates, fares or charges, §62-146.1, (d).
Franchises.
Fixed routes, franchise to specify, §62-113, (b).
Hearings on proposed new or revised rates, fares or charges, §62-146.1, (e).
Interlining of passengers, §62-146.1, (b).
Investigation, suspension, etc., of proposed new revised rates, fares or charges, §62-146.1, (g).
Joint rates between companies, §62-146.1, (c).
Policy of state, §62-259.1.
Proof of financial responsibility, §62-268.
Rates, §62-146.1.
Revenue levels authorized by utilities commission, §62-146.1, (f).
Safe and adequate service, equipment and facilities.
Duty to provide, §62-146.1, (a).

BUS COMPANIES —Cont'd
Service, §62-146.1.
Discontinuance or reduction, §62-262.2.

BUSES.
Disorderly conduct at bus station, §14-275.1.
Drivers.
Age limits for public passenger-carrying vehicles, §20-10.
Handicapped persons.
Right to use of public conveyances, §168-3.
Lights.
Additional lighting equipment required on certain vehicles, §20-129.1.
Motor carriers generally, §§62-259 to 62-279.
See MOTOR CARRIERS.
Motor vehicle license plates.
Permanent license plates for city-owned buses or trolleys, §20-84, (b).
Nonprofit activity buses.
Railroad grade crossings.
Stopping at, §20-142.3, (a).
Violation of speed limit, §20-218.2.
Property taxes.
Public service corporations.
Generally, §§105-333 to 105-344.
See PROPERTY TAXES.
Railroad grade crossings.
Activity buses.
Stopping at crossings, §20-142.3, (a).
Rearview mirrors.
Requirements, §20-117.1, (a).
Registration.
Common carriers of passengers.
Fees, §20-87.
Interchange of buses with nonresident common carriers, §20-87.1.
Repair of motor vehicles, §§20-354 to 20-354.9.
See MOTOR VEHICLE REPAIRS.
School buses.
Generally.
See SCHOOL BUSES.
Speed limits.
Nonprofit activity buses, §20-218.2.
School buses, §20-218, (b).
Penalty for violation, §20-218, (c).
Stations.
Disorderly conduct at bus station, §14-275.1.
Transitway lanes, §20-146.2, (a1).
Width, §20-116, (k).
Window tinting exception for hire passenger vehicles, §20-127, (c).

BUSHELS.
Standard weights and measures, §81A-42.

BUSINESS AND ENERGY TAX CREDITS, §§105-129.15 to 105-129.19.
Burden of proving eligibility and amount, §105-129.19.
Cap on credit, §105-129.17, (b).
Carryforwards.
Claimed against franchise or income tax, §105-129.17, (a).
Credit.
Business property placed in service before January 1, 2002, §105-129.16, (a).
Definitions, §105-129.15.
Dry-cleaning equipment not using hazardous substances, §105-129.16C, (a) to (c).
Election of tax against which credit claimed, §105-129.17, (a).

BUSINESS AND ENERGY TAX CREDITS —Cont'd
Expiration of credit.
Business property placed in service before January 1, 2002, §105-129.16, (b).
Franchise tax.
Election of tax against which credit claimed, §105-129.17, (a).
Income tax.
Election of tax against which credit claimed, §105-129.17, (a).
Information required to supplied secretary of revenue, §105-129.18.
Investing in business property.
Sunset provision, §105-129.15A.
No double credit.
Business property placed in service before January 1, 2002, §105-129.16, (c).
Renewable energy property investment, §105-129.16A, (a).
Ceiling on credit, §105-129.16A, (c).
Double credit not allowed, §105-129.16A, (d).
Expiration, property sold, taken out of service, etc., §105-129.16A, (b).
Nonresidential property ceiling, §105-129.16A, (c).
Residential property ceiling, §105-129.16A, (c).
Renewable fuel facilities construction credit.
Dispensing credit, §105-129.16D, (a).
No double credit, §105-129.16D, (c).
Production credit, §105-129.16D, (b).
Sunset, §105-129.16D, (d).
Reports, §105-129.19.
Sunset provisions, §105-129.15A.

BUSINESS AND INDUSTRIAL EXPANSION.
Site development grants, §143B-437.02.

BUSINESS COMBINATIONS.
Chapter not to supersede, restrict or limit other applicable laws, §75E-7.
Civil penalties for unlawful activities, §75E-5.
Cumulative effect of remedies for unlawful activities, §75E-6.
Investigative and regulatory powers of attorney general, §75E-3.
Nonresidents deemed to appoint secretary of state as agent for service, §75E-8.
Preventing or restraining violations, attorney general, §75E-4.
Private action by person injured, §75E-4.
Saving clause as to provisions of chapter, §75E-9.
Unlawful activities, §75E-2.

BUSINESS CORPORATIONS.
Generally, §§55-1-01 to 55-17-05.
See CORPORATIONS.

BUSINESS DISCRIMINATION, §§75B-1 to 75B-7.
Actions not prohibited, §75B-3.
Chapter not exclusive, §75B-7.
Contracts void, §75B-6.
Definitions, §75B-1.
Enforcement of chapter, §75B-4.
Prohibited, §75B-2.
Remedies cumulative, §75B-5.

BUSINESS INVESTMENT TAX CREDIT.
Qualified business investments, §§105-163.010 to 105-163.015.

BUSINESS LICENSES.
Clearinghouse for license information.
Department of commerce.
Authorized to establish, §143B-431, (e).

BUSINESS LICENSES —Cont'd
License information service.
Department of commerce.
Authorized to establish, §143B-431, (e).
Municipal regulations, §160A-194.
Occupational licensing boards generally, §§93B-1 to 93B-13.
See OCCUPATIONAL LICENSING BOARDS.

BUSINESS LICENSE TAXES.
Generally, §§105-33 to 105-109.
See LICENSE TAXES.

BUSINESS NECESSITY.
Fair housing violation, §41A-5, (a).

BUSINESS OPPORTUNITY SALES, §§66-94 to 66-100.
Bonds, surety.
Filing of copies with secretary of state, §66-97, (c).
Requirements, §66-96.
Contracts.
Provisions, §66-99, (b).
Voiding of contract.
Remedy of purchaser, §66-100, (a).
Written contracts required, §66-99, (a).
Damages.
Remedy of purchaser, §66-100, (b).
Definition of "business opportunity," §66-94.
Disclosure statement.
Contents, §66-95.
Filing with secretary of state, §66-97, (a).
Failure to file.
Misdemeanor, §66-97, (e).
Fee, §66-97, (a).
Uniform statements, §66-97, (d).
Required, §66-95.
Injunctions.
Violations of provisions, §66-100, (c).
Misrepresentations.
Prohibited acts, §66-98.
Prohibited acts, §66-98.
Remedies of purchasers.
Additional nature of remedies, §66-100, (d).
Generally, §66-100, (a) to (c).
Responsible sellers exemption.
Information to be filed with secretary of state, §66-94.1, (c).
Qualifications, §66-94.1, (a), (b).
Secretary of state.
Bonds, surety.
Filing with secretary, §66-97, (c).
Disclosure statement.
Filing with secretary of state, §66-97, (a).
Uniform statements, §66-97, (d).
Responsible sellers exemption.
Filing information with secretary, §66-94.1, (b).
Service of process.
Appointment of secretary as attorney to receive process, §66-97, (b).
Service of process.
Appointment of secretary of state as attorney to receive process.
Seller to file consent, §66-97, (b).
Trademarks.
Prohibited acts, §66-98.
Trust accounts.
When required, §66-96.
Violations of provisions.
Remedies of purchaser, §66-100, (a) to (c).
Additional nature of remedies, §66-100, (d).
Unfair practices, §66-100, (e).

BUSINESS PROPERTY INVESTMENT TAX CREDIT.
Business and energy tax credits generally, §§105-129.15 to 105-129.19.

BUSINESS RECORDS.
Hearsay exceptions.
Records of regularly conducted activity, §8C-1, Rule 803.
Absence of entry in records, §8C-1, Rule 803.
Interrogatories, option to produce, §1A-1, Rule 33, (c).

BUSINESS RETENTION AND EXPANSION.
One North Carolina fund, §§143B-437.70 to 143B-437.74.
See ONE NORTH CAROLINA FUND.

BUSINESS TAX INCENTIVES.
Business and energy tax credits, §§105-129.15 to 105-129.19.
Tax incentives for new and expanding businesses, §§105-129.2 to 105-129.13.
See TAX INCENTIVES FOR NEW AND EXPANDING BUSINESSES.

BUSINESS, TRADE AND CORRESPONDENCE SCHOOLS.
Defined, §115D-87.
National guard.
Tuition assistance, §§127A-190 to 127A-195.
Private schools.
General provisions.
See PRIVATE SCHOOLS.
Proprietary schools, §§115D-87 to 115D-97.
See PROPRIETARY SCHOOLS.
Vocational and technical education, §§115C-151 to 115C-169.
See VOCATIONAL AND TECHNICAL EDUCATION.

BUSINESS TRUSTS.
Actions.
Authority to sue and be sued, §39-45.
Conveyances, §39-46.
Deeds.
Prior deeds validated, §39-47.
Definition, §39-44.
Probate of conveyances.
Applicability of law for conveyances by corporations, §§39-46, 47-41.01, 47-41.02.
Real property.
Authority to acquire and hold, §39-45.
Conveyances, §39-46.
Title vested, §39-46.

BUSINESS UNDER ASSUMED NAME.
Accountants.
Partnerships engaged in practice of certified public accountancy.
Exemption from provisions, §66-68, (e).
Actions.
Violations of provisions.
Recovery in civil action not prevented, §66-71, (b).
Certificates.
Copy.
Prima facie evidence, §66-69.1.
Filing required, §66-68, (a).
Exceptions, §66-68, (d).
Index of certificates.
Register of deeds to keep, §66-69.
Transfer of assumed name, §66-69.
Withdrawal of assumed name, §66-69.

BUSINESS UNDER ASSUMED NAME —Cont'd
Certificates —Cont'd
Signing, §66-68, (b).
Transfer of assumed name, §66-68, (f).
Index, §66-69.
Withdrawal of assumed name, §66-68, (f).
Index, §66-69.
Evidence.
Copy of certificate prima facie evidence, §66-69.1.
Partnerships.
Public accountancy.
Exemption of partnerships engaged in practice of certified public accountancy, §66-68, (e).
Withdrawal of partner or new partner.
New certificate, §66-68, (c).
Transfer of assumed name, §66-68, (f).
Violations of provisions.
Penalties, §66-71, (a).
Recovery in civil action not prevented, §66-71, (b).
Withdrawal of assumed name, §66-68, (f).

BUS STATIONS.
Disorderly conduct at bus station, §14-275.1.
Eminent domain.
By whom right may be exercised, §40A-3, (a).

BUTNER ADVISORY COUNCIL, §§122C-413, 122C-413.1.

BUTNER PLANNING COUNCIL, §§122C-412 to 122C-412.2.

BUTTER AND EGG LOTTERY.
Selling numbers tickets, §14-291.1.

BUTTERFLY BALLOTS.
Use prohibited, §163-165.4B.

BUY BACKS.
Business opportunity sales, §§66-94 to 66-100.
See BUSINESS OPPORTUNITY SALES.

BUYING AND SELLING PUBLIC OFFICES, §14-228.

BYLAWS.
Corporations, §55-2-06.
Amendment, §§55-10-20, 55-10-22.
Emergency bylaws, §55-2-07.
Nonprofit corporations, §55A-2-06.
Amendment, §§55A-10-20, 55A-10-21.
Emergency bylaws, §55A-2-07.
Mutual burial associations.
Operation in noncompliance with, §90-210.88.
Requirements, §90-210.81.

BYSTANDERS.
Trials.
Exclusion in rape cases, §15-166.

C

CABARRUS COUNTY.
Acquisition of property, power, §153A-158.1, (a).
Ambulance service.
Attachment or garnishment and lien for, §§44-51.4 to 44-51.8.
Obtaining ambulance services without intending to pay, §14-111.2.
Requesting ambulance falsely, §14-111.3.
Board of county commissioners.
Filling vacancies on board, §153A-27.1.
Condemnation or acquisition of land by local government unit outside county.
Consent of board of commissioners necessary, §153A-15.

CABARRUS COUNTY —Cont'd
Coroner elected as nominee of political party.
Filling vacancy in office, §152-1.
County boards of education elected on partisan basis.
Vacancies in office, §115C-37.1.
Cropper or tenant refusing to perform terms of contract.
Forfeiture of right of possession to premises, §42-27.
Highway system.
County participation in improvements to, §136-66.3, (k).
Motor vehicle emission inspections.
Counties inspections required to be performed in, §143-215.107A, (c).
Officers compensated from fees.
Statement to be rendered, §128-13.
Registration of deeds.
Tax certification, no delinquent taxes due, §161-31, (b).
Room occupancy tax levied by county, uniform provisions, §153A-155.
School property.
Acquisition and improvement, §153A-158.1.
Sheriff.
Vacancy, performance of duties until vacancy filled, §162-5.1.
Tax sales, notices by publication validated.
Inapplicability of provisions, §47-108.24.
Wild plants, taking of certain plants from land of another.
Inapplicability of provisions, §14-129.

CABBAGE.
Standard weights and measures, §81A-42.

CABLE CAR.
Passenger tramways, §§95-116 to 95-125.
See TRAMWAYS.

CABLE TELEVISION.
Counties.
Regulation, §153A-137.
Taxes, §153A-154.
Electioneering communications.
Disclosures, prohibited sources, §§163-278.80 to 163-278.83.
Mass mailings and telephone banks, §§163-278.90 to 163-278.93.
Environmental document for constructing, maintaining or removal of lines.
Not required for lines across right of way of street or highway, §113A-12.
Municipal corporations, §160A-319.
Franchise tax, §160A-212.
Public enterprises generally, §§160A-311 to 160A-326.
See MUNICIPAL UTILITIES.
Overhead high-voltage line safety.
Exemption from act, §95-229.11, (a).
Theft of service, §14-118.5.
Actual damages not prerequisite to civil actions, §14-118.5, (d).
Applicability of provisions, §14-118.5, (e).
Charges for cable television service.
Avoiding lawful charge by use of instruments, apparatus, etc., §14-118.5, (a).
Civil penalties, §14-118.5, (c).
Facilities or equipment of cable television company.
Rearranging, tampering, etc., of facilities or equipment of company, §14-118.5, (a).

CABLE TELEVISION —Cont'd
Theft of service —Cont'd
Prima facie evidence, §14-118.5, (e).
Refusal to provide service to alleged violators, §14-118.5, (g).
Sale, distribution, etc., of converters, decoders, etc., §14-118.5, (b).
Satellite dish or antenna, §14-118.5, (f).
Winning prizes.
Representation of eligibility broadcast by, §75-33, (c).

CADAVERS.
Anatomical gifts, §§130A-402 to 130A-412.1.
See ANATOMICAL GIFTS.
General provisions.
See DEAD BODIES.

CAFES.
Alcoholic beverage permits.
Eating establishment defined to include, §18B-1000.
Off-premises malt beverage permit.
Kind of permit that may be issued, §18B-1001.
On-premises malt beverage permit.
Kind of permit that may be issued to, §18B-1001.
On-premises unfortified wine permit.
Kind of permit that may issued, §18B-1001.
Special occasion permit.
Kind of permit that may be issued, §18B-1001.

CAFETERIA PLANS.
Community colleges.
Flexible compensation plan, §115D-25.2.
University of North Carolina.
Flexible compensation plans, §116-17.2.

CAFETERIAS.
Alcoholic beverage permits.
Eating establishment defined to include, §18B-1000.
Off-premises malt beverage permits.
Kind of permit that may be issued, §18B-1001.
On-premises malt beverage permit.
Kind of permit that may be issued to, §18B-1001.
On-premises unfortified wine permit.
Kind of permit that may be issued, §18B-1001.
Special occasion permit.
Kind of permit that may be issued, §18B-1001.
Governmental units operating, §66-58, (a).
Public schools operating, §66-58, (c).
State legislative building, operation in, §66-58, (c).

CALABASH.
Ordinances to regulate and control swimming, personal watercraft operation, surfing and littering in Atlantic Ocean, §160A-176.2.
Satellite annexation.
Limitation on area of satellite corporate limits, inapplicability, §160A-58.1, (b).

CALCIUM.
High-calcium foods and beverages.
Local boards of education.
Preference in purchasing contracts, §115C-264.1, (a), (b).

CALCIUM CHLORIDE.
Antifreeze solutions compounded with, prohibited, §66-66.

CALDWELL COUNTY.
Ambulances.
Attachment or garnishment and lien for, §§44-51.4 to 44-51.8.

CALDWELL COUNTY —Cont'd
Ambulances —Cont'd
Obtaining ambulance services without intending to pay, §14-111.2.
Board of county commissioners.
Filling vacancies on board, §153A-27.1.
Condemnation or acquisition of land by local government unit outside county.
Consent of board of commissioners necessary, §153A-15.
Coroner elected as nominee of political party.
Filling vacancy in office, §152-1.
Counties generally.
See COUNTIES.
County boards of education elected on partisan basis.
Vacancies in office, §115C-37.1.
Dangerous firearm use by young children, permitting.
Air rifles, air pistols and BB guns not dangerous firearm, §14-316, (b).
Dog collars.
Unlawful removal of electronic dog collars, §14-401.17.
Foxes, open season for taking with firearms, §113-291.4A, (a), (b).
Game laws, local acts not repealed, §113-133.1, (e).
Housing authority commissioners.
Tenant as commissioner, exemption from provision of law allowing, §157-5.
Oil, gas or mineral interest separated from surface interest, extinguished, title in surface fee holder.
Failure to list interest for tax purposes for 10 years prior to January 1, 1974.
Protection of interest from surface estate, §1-42.3, (d).
Real estate mortgage loans.
Interest, commissions and repayment, §45-43.
School property.
Acquisition and improvement, §153A-158.1.
Sheriff.
Vacancy, performance of duties until vacancy filled, §162-5.1.
Small city mixed beverage elections.
Inapplicability of provisions to, §18B-600, (e1).

CALENDARING OF ACTIONS FOR TRIAL, §1A-1, Rule 40, (a).
Caveats to wills.
Priority trial settings, §31-33.
Criminal law and procedure.
Calendaring by district attorney for administrative purposes, §15A-941, (e).
Superior courts, criminal case docketing, §7A-49.4.
Evidence.
Proof of dates.
Clerk's calendar may be used, §8-48, (a).

CALIBRATION OF SPEED-MEASURING INSTRUMENTS.
Testing standards.
Admissibility of results as evidence, §8-50.2, (c).
Photographic speed-measuring instruments, §8-50.3, (c).

CALL BEFORE YOU DIG.
Underground damage prevention.
Generally, §§87-100 to 87-114.
See UNDERGROUND DAMAGE PREVENTION.

CALLER ID.
Exception from trace device regulations, §15A-261.
Sales and use tax on telecommunications services.
Gross receipts, §105-164.4C, (b).
Telephone solicitations.
Solicitor blocking or circumventing, prohibition, §75-102, (h).

CALL FORWARDING.
Sales and use tax on telecommunications services.
Gross receipts, §105-164.4C, (b).

CALLIGRAPHY.
Artwork on consignment, §§25C-1 to 25C-5.
Sale of prints, §§25C-10 to 25C-16.

CALL WAITING.
Sales and use tax on telecommunications services.
Gross receipts, §105-164.4C, (b).

CAMDEN COUNTY.
Ambulance service.
Attachment or garnishment and lien for, §§44-51.4 to 44-51.8.
Obtained without intending to pay, §14-111.2.
Requesting ambulance falsely, §14-111.3.
Blank or master forms of mortgages, deeds of trust, etc.
Indexing and recording, inapplicability of provisions, §47-21.
Condemnation or acquisition of land by local government unit outside county.
Consent of board of commissioners necessary, §153A-15.
Cropper or tenant refusing to perform terms of contract.
Forfeiture of right of possession to premises, §42-27.
Dog collars.
Unlawful removal of electronic dog collars, §14-401.17.
Game laws, local acts not repealed, §113-133.1, (e).
Grants in navigable waters, registration, §113-205, (a).
Housing.
Tenant as commissioner, exemption from provision of law allowing, §157-5.
Maps in special proceedings, recording of photographic copies, §47-32.
Violation as misdemeanor, inapplicability of provisions, §47-32.2.
Northeastern North Carolina regional economic development commission, §158-8.2.
Open fires, §113-60.23.
Applicability of provisions, §113-60.23, (a).
Ground clearing activities, special permit required, §113-60.23, (c).
Woodland fires, permit required, §113-60.23, (b).
Registration of deeds.
Tax certification, no delinquent taxes due, §161-31, (b).
School property.
Acquisition and improvement, §153A-158.1.
Tax sales, notices by publication validated.
Inapplicability of provisions, §47-108.24.
Wastewater systems.
Innovative septic tank systems.
Ordinance billing fee as property tax, §130A-343.1, (c).

CAMERAS.
Photography and photographs generally.
See PHOTOGRAPHY AND PHOTOGRAPHS.

CAMPAIGN CONTRIBUTIONS AND EXPENDITURES, §§163-278.5 to 163-278.38.
Actions.
Civil remedies other than penalties, §163-278.34, (c).
District attorney, notifying and consulting with, §163-278.34, (f).
Collect of penalty, §163-278.34, (e).
Advertisement charges, §163-278.18, (a).
Discrimination prohibited, §163-278.18, (b).
Advertisements broadcast or distributed naming candidate or prospective candidate.
Indication of name of political party or political committee, §163-278.16, (g).
Amounts of contributions, limitations.
Exemption from provisions, §163-278.13, (e).
Generally, §163-278.13, (a) to (c).
Penalties for violations, §163-278.13, (f).
Annual report.
Referendum committee, §163-278.9A, (a).
Anonymous contributions.
Acceptance prohibited, §163-278.14, (a).
Applicability of provisions.
General provisions as to corruption, §163-278.33.
Candidates.
Defined, §163-278.6.
Inactive candidates.
Procedure for, §163-278.10.
Cease and desist orders.
Civil remedy other than penalty, §163-278.34, (c).
Certificate of election.
Filing of statements as prerequisite, §163-278.25.
Certified as true and correct.
Statements and reports required to be filed, §163-278.32.
Checks.
Contributions in excess of one hundred dollars, §163-278.14, (b).
Expenditures by check, §163-278.8, (e), (f).
Civil penalties.
Calculation and assessment, §163-278.34, (e).
Civil action to collect, §163-278.34, (e).
Contesting, time period, §163-278.34, (e).
District attorney, notifying and consulting with, §163-278.34, (f).
Illegal contributions, §163-278.34, (b).
Late filing, §163-278.34, (a).
Mitigation, facts, §163-278.34, (d).
Civil remedies other than penalties, §163-278.34, (c).
District attorney, notifying and consulting with, §163-278.34, (f).
Collection of penalty, civil action, §163-278.34, (e).
Corporations.
Acceptance of contributions by corporations, §163-278.15.
Defined, §163-278.6.
Prohibited acts, §163-278.19, (a).
Exceptions, §163-278.19, (b), (d), (f).
Penalties, §163-278.19, (c).
Council of state candidates.
Restrictions on using state funds for advertising or public service announcements, §163-278.16A.

CAMPAIGN CONTRIBUTIONS AND EXPENDITURES —Cont'd
Criminal penalty and prosecution of violations.
Costs incurred by board to investigate.
Payment by violator as condition of probation, §163-278.27, (d).
Criminal penalty, §163-278.27, (a).
Duty of district attorney to prosecute.
Receipt of report of violation, §163-278.27, (c).
Reports by board of violations to prosecutorial authorities, §163-278.27, (b).
Statute of limitation on prosecutions, §163-278.27, (a).
Definitions, §163-278.6.
Disclosure requirements for media advertisements, §163-278.38Z.
Election, §§163-278.6, 163-278.13, (d).
Political party, §§163-278.6, 163-278.13, (e).
Electronically filed reports, §163-278.9, (j).
Evidence.
Communications are "to support or oppose the nomination or election of one or more clearly identified candidates," §163-278.14A, (a).
Exceptions, §163-278.14A, (b).
Exemptions to reporting requirement.
Threshold amount for financial reports, §163-278.10A.
Federal election campaign act of 1971.
Reports by political parties.
Required to file reports under, §163-278.9, (e), (f).
Federal offices.
Candidates to file information reports, §163-278.30.
Federal political committees, gifts from, §163-278.7A.
Filing of reports, statements or other documents required.
Late filing.
Civil late penalty, §163-278.34, (a).
Manual delivery or by mail, §163-278.34, (a).
Timely filing, §163-278.34, (a).
Final report.
Referendum committee, §163-278.9A, (a).
Forty-eight hour report, §163-278.9, (a).
Referendum committee, §163-278.9A, (a).
Fundraising during legislative session, limitation.
Definitions, §163-278.13B, (a).
Exceptions, §163-278.13B, (d).
Misdemeanor for violating provisions, §163-278.13B, (e).
Prohibited contributions by limited contributor, §163-278.13B, (c).
Prohibited solicitations by limited contributor, §163-278.13B, (b).
General provisions as to corruption.
Applicability, §163-278.33.
Gifts from federal political committees, §163-278.7A.
Illegal contributions.
Civil penalties, §163-278.34, (b).
Independent expenditures.
Defined, §163-278.6.
Special reporting, §163-278.12, (a), (c), (d).
Individuals.
Defined, §163-278.6.
Injunctions, §163-278.28, (a).
Insurance companies.
Defined, §163-278.6.

CAMPAIGN CONTRIBUTIONS AND EXPENDITURES —Cont'd
Insurance companies —Cont'd
Prohibited acts, §163-278.19, (a).
Exceptions, §163-278.19, (b), (d), (f).
Penalties, §163-278.19, (c).
Intentional violations of reporting provisions.
Costs incurred by board to investigate.
Payment by violator as condition of probation, §163-278.27, (d).
Criminal penalty, §163-278.27, (a).
Duty of district attorney to prosecute.
Receipt of report of violation, §163-278.27, (c).
Reports by board of violations to prosecutorial authorities, §163-278.27, (b).
Statute of limitation on prosecutions, §163-278.27, (a).
Labor unions.
Prohibited acts, §163-278.19, (a).
Exceptions, §163-278.19, (b), (d), (f).
Penalties, §163-278.19, (c).
Late filing penalty, §163-278.34, (a).
Late penalty.
Untimely filing, §163-278.34, (a).
Limitation of actions.
Civil action to collect penalty, §163-278.34, (e).
Limitations on contributions.
Exemptions from provisions, §163-278.13, (e).
Generally, §163-278.13, (a) to (c).
Penalties for violations, §163-278.13, (f).
Loans.
Recording separately, detailed analysis, §163-278.8, (g).
Lobbyists.
Limitation on fund-raising during legislative session, §163-278.13B.
Media.
Authorizations of expenditures.
Media to require, §163-278.17, (b).
Defined, §163-278.6.
Disclosure requirements for media advertisements, §§163-278.39 to 163-278.39C.
Definitions, §163-278.38Z.
Misrepresentation of authorization.
Misdemeanor, §163-278.39, (c).
Requirements, §163-278.39, (a), (b).
Scope, §163-278.39C.
Television and radio advertisements supporting or opposing the nomination or election of one or more clearly identified candidates, §163-278.39A.
Scope of requirements, §163-278.39C.
Television and radio advertisements supporting or opposing the nomination or election of one or more clearly identified candidates.
Choice of supporting or opposing a candidate, §163-278.39A, (e).
Communications act of 1934.
Relation to, §163-278.39A, (g).
Criminal liability not created, §163-278.39A, (i).
Expanded disclosure requirements, §163-278.39A, (a).
Radio, §163-278.39A, (c).
Television, §163-278.39A, (b).
Immunity of television or radio outlets, §163-278.39A, (h).
Join sponsors, §163-278.39A, (e1).
Legal remedy, §163-278.39A, (f).
Placement of disclosure statement in advertisements, §163-278.39A, (d).

CAMPAIGN CONTRIBUTIONS AND EXPENDITURES —Cont'd
Media —Cont'd
Expenditures for media expenses, §163-278.8, (e).
Expenditures for nonmedia expenses, §163-278.8, (f).
Misdemeanors.
Disclosure requirements for media advertisements.
Misrepresentation of authorization, §163-278.39, (c).
Limitations on contributions.
Violations, §163-278.13, (f).
Violations generally, §163-278.27, (a).
Municipal campaign reporting, §§163-278.9, (d), 163-278.40 to 163-278.40I.
Accounts.
Organizational report, §163-278.40A, (b).
Board.
Defined, §163-278.40.
Contents, §163-278.40G.
Contributions.
Report to list, §163-278.40G.
Definitions, §163-278.40.
Filing, §163-278.40D.
Form, §163-278.40F.
Nonpartisan elections, §163-278.40C.
Nonpartisan plurality, §163-278.40E.
Primary elections, §163-278.40D.
Nonpartisan plurality method, §163-278.40E.
Notice of reports due, §163-278.40H.
Organizational report.
Contents, §163-278.40A, (b).
Partisan elections, §163-278.40B.
Part 1 to apply, §163-278.40I.
Primary elections, §§163-278.40B, 163-278.40D.
Runoffs, §163-278.40C.
Treasurers.
Appointment by candidate, §163-278.40A, (a).
Names.
Contributions in name of others.
Acceptance prohibited, §163-278.14, (a).
Reports to recipient, §163-278.14, (c).
Oath.
Certified as true and correct.
Statements and reports required to be filed, §163-278.32.
Organizational report, §163-278.9, (a).
Referendum committee, §163-278.9A, (a).
Person or entity not otherwise required to report.
Contributions in excess of $100, reporting, §163-278.12, (b), (c), (d).
Political committees.
Defined, §163-278.6.
Federal political committees, gifts from, §163-278.7A.
Inactive committee.
Procedure for, §163-278.10.
Political parties financing fund, §§163-278.41 to 163-278.45.
Political party headquarters building funds.
Donations to, §163-278.19B.
Postprimary report, §163-278.9, (a).
Pre-referendum report.
Referendum committee, §163-278.9A, (a).
Prerequisites to receipts of contributions, §163-278.16, (a).
Preservation of reports, records and accounts, §163-278.35.
County boards of election to preserve reports, §163-278.37.

CAMPAIGN CONTRIBUTIONS AND EXPENDITURES —Cont'd
Presidential election year candidates fund, §§163-278.41 to 163-278.45.
Presumptions.
Generally, §163-278.34A.
Printed material identifying candidate or potential candidate.
Name of political party or political committee, §163-278.16, (g).
Professional associations.
Defined, §163-278.6.
Prohibited acts, §163-278.19, (a).
Exceptions, §163-278.19, (b), (d), (f).
Penalties, §163-278.19, (c).
Public campaign financing fund.
Attorneys at law.
Opportunity to contribute, §105-41, (a).
Generally, §§163-278.61 to 163-278.70.
See ELECTIONS.
Individual income taxpayer.
Allocation to fund by individual, §105-159.2, (a).
Instructions for individual to designate allocation, §105-159.2, (c).
Returns to give individual opportunity to designate allocation, §105-159.2, (b).
Quarterly reports, §163-278.9, (a).
Radio.
Disclosure requirements for media advertisements, §§163-278.39 to 163-278.39C.
Records, §163-278.19, (e).
Referenda, §163-278.19A.
Defined, §163-278.6.
Failure to comply with provisions not to invalidate results, §163-278.38.
Referendum committees.
Defined, §163-278.6.
Inactive committees.
Procedure for, §163-278.10.
Restrictions, §163-278.13, (e1).
Remedial action.
Civil remedy other than penalty, §163-278.34, (c).
Reports.
Cumulative totals reflected, §163-278.9, (h).
Declaration of nomination or certificate of election.
Filing of statements as prerequisite, §163-278.25.
Elected officials to report funds, §163-278.36.
Electronically filed reports, §163-278.9, (j).
Examination of statements within four months, §163-278.24.
Exemptions.
Threshold amount for financial reports, §163-278.10A, (a).
Inapplicability of exemption, §163-278.10A, (b).
Federal election campaign act of 1971, §163-278.9, (e), (f).
Federal officers.
Candidates to file information reports, §163-278.30.
Filing, late filing penalty, §163-278.34, (a).
Inactive candidate or committee, §163-278.10.
Independent expenditures, §163-278.12, (a), (c), (d).
Information required, §163-278.9, (g).
Municipal candidates and committees, §163-278.9, (b).
Oath required, §163-278.9, (i).
Person or entity not otherwise required to report.
Contributions in excess of $100, §163-278.12, (b), (c), (d).

CAMPAIGN CONTRIBUTIONS AND EXPENDITURES —Cont'd
Reports —Cont'd
Preservation, §163-278.35.
County boards of elections to preserve reports, §163-278.37.
Treasurer, §163-278.9, (a), (b).
Anything of value paid to be reflected, §163-278.11, (b).
Best efforts used to obtain, maintain and submit information, §163-278.11, (c).
Contents generally, §163-278.11, (a).
Referendum committee, §163-278.9A, (a), (b).
Violations of provisions.
Board to report to prosecuting authorities, §163-278.27, (b).
Reprimand of violators.
Civil remedy other than penalty, §163-278.34, (c).
Rules and regulations.
State board of elections, §163-278.21.
Scope of provisions, §163-278.5.
Semiannual reports, §163-278.9, (a).
Severability of provisions, §163-278.5.
Soliciting contributions.
Disclosure required, §163-278.20, (a).
Penalty for violation, §163-278.20, (b).
State board of elections.
Administration of provisions, §163-278.21.
Appeals from board, §163-278.26.
Duties, §163-278.22.
Executive director.
Duties, §163-278.23.
Powers, §163-278.22.
Rules and regulations, §163-278.21.
Statute of limitations.
Civil action to collect penalty, §163-278.34, (e).
Television.
Disclosure requirements for media advertisements, §§163-278.39 to 163-278.39C.
Transfer of funds to committee or political party account.
When deemed contribution, §163-278.19, (a1).
Treasurers.
Accounts and accounting, §163-278.8, (a), (b).
Appointment, §163-278.7, (a).
Prerequisite to receipt of contributions, §163-278.16, (a).
Defined, §163-278.6.
Prosecution of violations, §163-278.27, (c).
Special prosecutors, §163-278.28, (b).
Removal, §163-278.7, (d).
Changes in information, §163-278.7, (c).
Contents, §163-278.7, (b).
Filing, §163-278.7, (b).
Reports, §163-278.9, (a), (b).
Anything of value paid to be reflected, §163-278.11, (b).
Best efforts used to obtain, maintain and submit information, §163-278.11, (c).
Contents generally, §163-278.11, (a).
Referendum committee, §163-278.9A, (a), (b).
Training as duties of office, §163-278.7, (e).
True and correct.
Certification.
Statements and reports required to be filed, §163-278.32.
Witnesses.
Self-incrimination.
Immunity from prosecution, §163-278.29.

CAMP BUTNER RESERVATION.
Administrative procedure act.
Full exemption given department of health and humans services, §150B-1, (c).
Butner advisory council, §§122C-413, 122C-413.1.
Butner town manager vacancy, selection, §122C-413.1, (b).
Chair, §122C-413, (e).
Created, §122C-413, (a).
Election, §122C-413, (a) to (d1).
Resolutions, advising secretary of health and human services, §122C-413.1, (a).
Vacancies, §122C-413, (f).
Butner planning council, §§122C-412 to 122C-412.2.
Advisory capacity to secretary of health and human services, §122C-412.1, (a).
Chairman, vice-chairman, clerk, §122C-412, (l).
Created, §122C-412, (a).
Expenses, travel, per diem, subsistence, reimbursement, §122C-412, (k).
Meetings, §122C-412, (i), (m).
Membership, appointments, terms, §122C-412, (a), (g), (h).
Removal, §122C-412, (j).
Resolution, adoption, approval or disapproval, §122C-412.1, (b).
Responsibilities, §122C-412.2.
Rule of procedure, adoption, §122C-412, (n).
Butner public safety division.
Authorized, §122C-408, (a).
Butner town manager vacancy, selection, §122C-413.1, (b).
Community of Butner comprehensive emergency management plan, §122C-409.
County ordinances.
Application to Camp Butner reservation, §122C-410, (b).
Department of crime control and public safety.
Butner public safety division, §122C-408, (a).
Enforcement of part.
Ordinances and rules for enforcement, §122C-403.
Fire prevention contracts, §122C-411.
Hospitals generally.
See HOSPITALS.
Lyons station sanitary district.
No jurisdiction over, §122C-413, (g).
Municipal corporations.
Annexation.
Territory extending into Camp Butner reservation, §122C-410, (a).
Extraterritorial jurisdiction.
Extension into Camp Butner reservation, §122C-410, (a).
Ordinances.
Enforcement of part, §122C-403.
Rules and regulations.
Procedures applicable to rules, §122C-405.
Violations of rules, §122C-405.
Special police officers.
Authorized, §122C-408, (a).
Powers and duties, §122C-408, (b).
Traffic laws.
Application of state highway and motor vehicle laws to roads, etc., at reservation, §122C-402.
Use authorized, §122C-401.
Violations made misdemeanor, §122C-406.
Water and sewer system, §122C-407, (a) to (c).

CAMPERS.
Trailers generally.
See TRAILERS.

CAMPGROUNDS.
Cabin camps.
General provisions.
See CABIN CAMPS.
Defrauding campground owner, §14-110.
Littering, §14-399.
Membership camping, §§66-230 to 66-247.
See MEMBERSHIP CAMPING.

CAMPING TRAILERS.
Recreational vehicle, defined as, §20-4.01.

CANAL COMPANIES.
No title by possession company's right-of-way, §1-44.

CANALS.
Adverse possession.
No title by possession of right of way, §1-44.
Draining districts.
Improvement, renovation, enlargement and extension, §§156-93.2, 156-93.3.
Public or private ways.
Maintenance of drainage across, §156-88.
Earth from canal removed or leveled, §156-8.
Eminent domain.
By whom right may be exercised, §40A-3, (a).
Magistrates.
Assessment of contribution for damages or for work done on canal, §7A-292.
Maintenance for seven years presumed a necessity, §156-21.
Protection of canals, ditches and natural drains, §156-25.
Right to drain into canal, §156-10.

CANARY SEEDS.
Standard weight and measure, §81A-42.

CANCELLATION OF DISCOUNT BUYING CLUB CONTRACTS.
Customer's right, §66-133.

CANCELLATION OF INSURANCE.
Applicability of article, §58-41-10, (a).
Citation of article, §58-41-1.
Commercial general liability insurance.
Extended reporting periods, §58-40-140.
Grounds, §58-41-15, (a).
Intent of legislature, §58-41-5, (a), (b).
In-term cancellation of entire book of business, §58-41-45, (b).
Legislative findings, §58-41-5, (a), (b).
Loss of reinsurance, §58-41-30.
Nonpayment of premium, §58-41-15, (d).
Notice.
Copies sent to agent or broker, §58-41-15, (e).
Required, §58-41-15, (b).
Timing of notice to insured, §58-41-40, (b).
Penalties, §58-41-55.
Policy in effect for less than sixty days, §58-41-15, (c).
Provisions not exclusive, §58-41-10, (b).
Short title, §58-41-1.
Statements or communications made in good faith.
No liability for, §58-41-40, (a).

CANCELLATION OF JUDGMENT AS TO SURETY, §26-11.

CANCELLATION OF LIS PENDENS NOTICE, §§1-119, (b), 1-120.

CANCELLATION OF MEMBERSHIP CAMPING CONTRACTS.
Purchaser's right, §66-240.

CANCELLATION OF PREPAID ENTERTAINMENT CONTRACTS.
Buyer's right, §66-121.

CANCELLATION OF WILL.
Revocation of written will, §31-5.1.

CANCELLATION OF WINE DISTRIBUTION AGREEMENTS, §18B-1204.
Judicial remedies, §18B-1207.
Notice of intent, §18B-1205.

CANCELLATION, UCC.
Funds transfers.
Payment orders, §25-4A-211.
Leases.
Defined, §25-2A-103, (1).
Effect on rights and remedies, §25-2A-505, (1), (3).
Lessee's remedies, §25-2A-508, (1).
Negotiable instruments indorsement, §25-3-604.
Sale of goods, §25-2-209.
Antecedent breach.
Effect of cancellation on claims for, §25-2-720.
Defined, §25-2-106, (4).

CANCER, §§130A-205 to 130A-215.
Accident and health insurance.
Breast cancer.
Mammograms.
Coverage, §58-51-57.
Cervical cancer screening.
Coverage, §58-51-57.
Colorectal cancer examinations, laboratory tests and screening.
Coverage, §58-3-179.
Small employer group health plans, §58-50-155, (a).
Drugs for cancer treatment.
Coverage of certain prescribed drugs, §58-51-59, (a), (b).
Mammograms.
Coverage, §58-51-57.
Ovarian cancer.
Surveillance tests for women at risk, coverage, §§58-3-270, 58-50-155, (a).
Administration of program.
Care and treatment of persons with cancer, §130A-205, (a).
Prevention and detection of cancer, §130A-205, (a).
Advisory committee on cancer coordination and control.
Administrative staff, §130A-33.50, (f).
Appointment, §130A-33.50, (b).
Compensation, §130A-33.50, (d).
Composition, §130A-33.50, (b).
Established, §130A-33.50, (a).
Meetings, §130A-33.50, (b).
Quorum, §130A-33.50, (e).
Reports.
Annual reports, §130A-33.51, (b).
Responsibilities, §130A-33.51, (a).
Vacancies, §130A-33.50, (c).
Breast cancer.
Mammograms.
Accident and health insurance.
Coverage, §58-51-57.
Health maintenance organizations.
Coverage, §58-67-76.
Hospital, medical and dental services corporations.
Coverage, §58-65-92.

CANCER —Cont'd
Breast cancer —Cont'd
Motor vehicle license plates.
Breast cancer awareness, §20-79.4, (b).
Cancer committee of North Carolina medical society, §130A-213.
Consultation with committee, §130A-213.
Care and treatment of persons with cancer.
Establishment and administration of program, §130A-205, (a).
Facilities made available, §130A-206.
Financial aid for diagnosis and treatment, §130A-206.
Central cancer registry, §130A-208.
Functions, §130A-208.
Incidence reporting of cancer, §130A-209.
Information to be received, §130A-208.
Reports.
Incidence reporting of cancer, §130A-209.
Cervical cancer screening.
Accident and health insurance.
Coverage, §58-51-57.
Hospital, medical and dental services corporations.
Coverage, §58-65-92.
Clinics, §130A-207.
Authority to establish, §130A-207.
Confidentiality of records, §130A-212.
Minimum standards, §130A-207.
Colorectal cancer examinations, laboratory tests and screening.
Health benefit plan coverage, §58-3-179.
Small employer group health plans, §58-50-155, (a).
Confidentiality.
Records of cancer, §130A-212.
Control program.
Administration of program, §130A-205, (a).
Authority to establish clinic, §130A-207.
Committee of North Carolina medical society, §130A-213.
Financial aid for diagnosis and treatment, §130A-206.
Health and human services department.
Duties of department, §130A-214.
Incidence reporting of cancer.
Central cancer registry, §130A-208.
Medical society.
Cancer committee of the North Carolina medical society, §130A-213.
Records.
Confidentiality of records, §130A-212.
Reports.
Immunity of persons who report cancer, §130A-211.
Incidence reporting of cancer, §130A-209.
Secretary of health and human services to make report, §130A-215.
Rules and regulations, §130A-205, (b).
Department of environment and natural resources.
Duties of department, §130A-214.
Secretary.
Reports by secretary, §130A-215.
Diagnosis of cancer.
Facilities made available, §130A-206.
Financial aid, §130A-206.
Establishment of program.
Care and treatment of persons with cancer, §130A-205, (a).

CANCER —Cont'd
Establishment of program —Cont'd
Prevention and detection of cancer, §130A-205, (a).
Financial aid.
For diagnosis and treatment, §130A-206.
To sponsored cancer clinics, §130A-207.
Food, drug and cosmetic act.
Drug or device, false advertising, §106-138, (b).
Health maintenance organizations.
Colorectal cancer examinations, laboratory tests and screening.
Coverage, §58-3-179.
Drugs for cancer treatment.
Coverage of certain prescribed drugs.
Exceptions, §58-67-78, (b), (c).
Generally, §58-67-78, (a).
Prostate-specific antigen (PSA) tests.
Coverage, §58-67-77, (a), (c).
Defined, §58-67-77, (b).
Hospital, medical and dental service corporations.
Cervical cancer screening.
Coverage, §58-65-92.
Colorectal cancer examinations, laboratory tests and screening.
Coverage, §58-3-179.
Drugs for cancer treatment.
Coverage of certain prescribed drugs.
Exceptions, §58-65-94, (b), (c).
Generally, §58-65-94, (a).
Mammograms.
Coverage, §58-65-92.
Prostate-specific antigen (PSA) tests.
Coverage, §58-65-93, (a), (c).
Defined, §58-65-93, (b).
Hospitals.
Cancer clinics, §130A-207.
Confidentiality of records, §130A-212.
Immunities.
Persons who report cancer, §130A-211.
Reporting of cancer, §130A-211.
Indigent persons.
Financial aid for diagnosis and treatment, §130A-206.
Mammograms.
Accident and health insurance.
Coverage, §58-51-57.
Accreditation of facilities performing.
Medical care commission, §143B-165.
Health maintenance organizations.
Coverage, §58-67-76.
Hospital, medical and dental services corporations.
Coverage, §58-65-92.
Small employer group health coverage, §58-50-155, (a).
Medical facilities.
Cancer clinics, §130A-207.
Confidentiality of records, §130A-212.
North Carolina medical society.
Cancer committee, §130A-213.
Ovarian cancer.
Accident and health insurance.
Surveillance tests for women at risk, coverage, §§58-3-270, 58-50-155, (a).
Pap smears.
Accreditation of facilities performing.
Medical care commission, §143B-165.
Small employer group health coverage, §58-50-155, (a).

CANCER —Cont'd
Prevention and detection of cancer.
Establishment and administration of program, §130A-205, (a).
Prostate-specific antigen (PSA) tests.
Small employer group health coverage, §58-50-155, (a).
Records.
Central cancer registry, §130A-208.
Incidence reporting of cancer, §130A-209.
Confidentiality of records, §130A-212.
Registry.
Central cancer registry, §130A-208.
Incidence reporting of cancer, §130A-209.
Reports, §130A-215.
Central cancer registry, §130A-208.
Incidence reporting of cancer, §130A-209, (a).
Control program.
Secretary of health and human services to make report, §130A-215.
Immunity of persons who report cancer, §130A-211.
Incidence reporting of cancer, §130A-209.
Central cancer registry, §130A-208.
Definitions, §130A-209, (c).
Failure to report.
Charge for collection, §130A-209, (b).
To governor and general assembly, §130A-215.
Rules and regulations.
Control program, §130A-205, (b).
Establishment and administration of program, §130A-205, (b).
Small employer group health insurance.
Coverage of certain prescribed drugs for cancer treatment, §58-50-156.
Treatment of cancer.
Financial aid for treatment, §130A-206.

C. & F.
Sale of goods, UCC, §25-2-320.
Form of bill of lading required in overseas shipment, §25-2-323.
Net landed weight, §25-2-321.
Payment on arrival, §25-2-321.
Warranty of condition on arrival, §25-2-321.

CANNABIS.
Controlled substances generally, §§90-86 to 90-113.8.
See CONTROLLED SUBSTANCES.
Food, drug and cosmetic act.
Drugs deemed misbranded, §106-134.
Marijuana.
See MARIJUANA.

CANS.
Containers generally.
See CONTAINERS.

CANTALOUPES.
Standard weight and measure, §81A-42.

CAPACITY OF MARRIED PERSONS TO CONTRACT, §52-2.

CAPACITY TO MARRY, §51-2.
Want of capacity, §51-3.

CAPACITY TO SUE.
Pleading special matter, §1A-1, Rule 9, (a).

CAPE CARTERET.
Ordinances to regulate and control swimming, personal watercraft operation, surfing and littering in Atlantic Ocean, §160A-176.2.

CAPE FEAR RIVER NAVIGATION AND PILOTAGE.
Commission.
Appointment of members, §76A-2.
Chairman.
Designation, §76A-2.
Composition, §76A-2.
Established, §76A-1.
Expenses, §76A-24.
Jurisdiction.
Disputes as to pilotage, §76A-5, (f).
Majority to constitute quorum, §76A-4.
Powers, §76A-1.
Quorum, §76A-4.
Rules and regulations, §76A-5, (a).
Terms of members, §76A-3.
Vacancies.
Filling, §76A-3.
Widows and orphans fund.
Dissolution, §76A-25.
Mutual association for pilots.
Recognition of pilotage association by commission, §76A-13.
Pilots.
Age.
Apprentices, §76A-12.
Apprentices, §76A-12.
Association.
Payments to commission for expenses, §76A-24.
Recognition by commission, §76A-13.
Bonds, surety, §76A-5, (e).
Compulsory use of pilots, §76A-16.
Exceptions, §76A-18.
Disciplinary measures, §76A-5, (d).
Docking masters.
Not deemed pilots, §76A-14.
Examination, §76A-5, (b).
Licenses.
Apprentices, §76A-6.
Classes, §76A-6.
Full license, §76A-6.
Limited license, §76A-6.
Renewal, §76A-5, (c).
Suspension or revocation, §76A-5, (d).
Term, §76A-5, (b).
Number of pilots, §76A-14.
Rates of pilotage, §76A-17.
Retirement, §76A-15.
Vessels not liable for pilotage, §76A-18.

CAPIAS.
Arrest in civil cases.
See ARREST IN CIVIL CASES.
Bail and recognizance.
Bond of prisoner committed on capias in civil action, §162-32.
General provisions.
See BAIL AND RECOGNIZANCE.
Costs.
Arrest for nonpayment, §6-48.
Executions.
See EXECUTIONS.
Sundays.
Execution on Sundays, §103-3.

CAPITAL FACILITIES FINANCE ACT, §§142-80 to 142-101.
Acquisition and construction, §142-94.
Alternative financing methods.
Purposes of act, §142-81.
Certificates of participation indebtedness.
Defined, §142-82.
Documentation required, §142-87, (a).

CAPITAL FACILITIES FINANCE ACT —Cont'd
Certificates of participation indebtedness —Cont'd
Interest, §142-87, (c).
Other conditions, §142-87, (e).
Procedure for delivery and sale, §142-87, (b).
Sale, §142-87, (c).
Trust agreement, delivered pursuant to, §142-87, (d).
Debt affordability.
Annual study to establish guidelines for maintaining prudent debt levels, §142-100.
Debt affordability advisory committee.
Duties, §142-101, (d).
Established, §142-101, (a).
Members, §142-101, (a).
Officers and staff, §142-101, (b).
Per diem and allowances, §142-101, (c).
Reports, §142-101, (e).
Definitions, §142-82.
Financing contract indebtedness.
Bidding, §142-86, (c).
Certificates of participation indebtedness, §142-87.
Credit facility, delivery to secure payment, §142-86, (e).
Defined, §142-82.
Documentation required, §142-86, (a).
Execution, §142-86, (d).
Interest component, §142-86, (b).
Terms and conditions, §142-86, (f).
Findings of general assembly, §142-81.
Investments.
Special indebtedness, §142-93.
Limited obligation bonds and notes.
Authorization to issue and sell, §142-88.
Defined, §142-82.
Denominations, §142-89, (b).
Expenses in preparation, sale and issuance, §142-89, (c).
Form of issuance, §142-89, (b).
Notes, §142-89, (e).
Refunding bonds and notes, §142-89, (f).
Registration, §142-89, (b).
Repayment of notes, §142-89, (e).
Sale, §142-89, (c).
Security for payment, §142-89, (g).
Signatures required, §142-89, (b).
Terms and conditions, §142-89, (a).
Trust agreement securing, §142-89, (h).
Use of proceeds, §142-89, (d).
Managing debt capacity.
Annual debt affordability study, §142-100.
Debt affordability advisory committee, §142-101.
North Carolina industrial and pollution control facilities financing act, §§159D-1 to 159D-27.
See INDUSTRIAL AND POLLUTION CONTROL FACILITIES FINANCING.
Private capital facilities finance act.
Institutions for higher education and elementary and secondary education, §§159D-35 to 159D-57.
See CAPITAL FACILITIES FINANCE AGENCY.
Procurement of capital facilities, §142-94.
Purposes of act, §142-81.
Real estate certificates of participation indebtedness.
Addition state property exception, §142-95, (f).
Authorization, §142-95, (a).
Interest, payment, §142-95, (e).

CAPITAL FACILITIES FINANCE ACT —Cont'd
Real estate certificates of participation indebtedness —Cont'd
Principal, maturity, reduction, §142-95, (d).
Purposes for incurring, §142-95, (b).
Secured by property or interest in property, §142-95, (c).
RECOP indebtedness, §142-95.
Special indebtedness.
Appropriations necessary to make payments.
Including in governor's budget, §142-85, (c).
Authorization to finance costs, §142-83.
Certificates of participation indebtedness, §142-87.
Certification that special indebtedness desirable.
State treasurer, §142-84, (a).
Consultants, fiduciaries and other agents, employment, §142-84, (g).
Deficiency judgment not rendered against state, §142-85, (e).
Defined, §142-82.
Designation of facilities, §142-84, (e).
Determination that indebtedness appropriate.
Notice to state treasurer, §142-84, (a).
Documents for use, development, §142-84, (g).
Final approval, §142-84, (c).
Financing contract indebtedness, §142-86.
Financing terms, §142-84, (d).
Investments, §142-93.
Lien or security interest.
Multiple liens, §142-85, (b).
Required as security, §142-85, (a).
Value, §142-85, (b).
Limited obligation bonds and notes, §§142-88, 142-89.
Nonsubstitution clause prohibited, §142-85, (f).
Notice to department of administration.
Appropriate to finance facilities, §142-84, (a).
Notice to state treasurer.
Determination that indebtedness appropriate, §142-84, (a).
Other agreements, §142-91.
Oversight by joint legislative commission, §142-84, (h).
Preliminary approval, §142-84, (b).
Protection of lender, §142-85, (g).
Repayment, source, §142-85, (d).
Satisfaction of payment obligations.
Net proceeds from sale or disposition of property, §142-85, (e).
State property law exemption, §142-85, (h).
Tax exemption, §142-92.
Taxing power of state not pledged, §142-85, (e).
Type of debt and security, determination, §142-84, (f).
Variable rate demand bonds and notes, §142-90, (a), (b).
State capital facilities finance act.
Short title, §142-80.
Tax exemption.
Special indebtedness, §142-92.
Tobacco trust fund.
Priority use.
Debt service for special indebtedness authorized by capital facilities act of 2004, §143-719, (c).
Variable rate demand bonds and notes, §142-90, (a), (b).

CAPITAL FACILITIES FINANCE AGENCY.
Board of directors, §159D-38, (a).
Quorum, §159D-38, (d).

CAPITAL FACILITIES FINANCE AGENCY —Cont'd
Contained within department of state treasurer, §159D-38, (e).
Created, §159D-38, (a).
General powers, §159D-39.
North Carolina industrial and pollution control facilities financing act, §§159D-1 to 159D-27.
See INDUSTRIAL AND POLLUTION CONTROL FACILITIES FINANCING.
Private capital facilities finance act, §§159D-35 to 159D-57.
Annual report on activities, §159D-53.
Bonds or notes.
Approval by local government commission, §159D-45, (b).
Authority to issue, §159D-45, (a).
Consent of other agencies not required, §159D-45, (e).
Credit of state not pledged, §159D-44.
Holders rights not limited or altered, §159D-47, (d).
Interim receipts or temporary bonds, §159D-45. (d).
Investing in, §159D-51.
Investment securities, §159D-50.
Members or officers not personally liable, §159D-54.
Payment of principal and interest, source, §159D-45, (a).
Proceeds, use, §159D-45. (c).
Public hearing, §159D-45, (f).
Refunding bonds or notes.
Authority to issue, §159D-52, (a).
Purposes, §159D-52, (a).
Sale or exchange, §159D-52, (b).
Terms and conditions, provision governing, §159D-52, (b).
Remedies of holders, §159D-49.
Secured by trust agreement or resolution, §159D-46.
Tax exemption, interest paid, §159D-55.
Terms and conditions, §159D-45, (a).
Conflict of interest, disclosure, §159D-56.
Construction contracts, awarding by agency, §159D-43.
Conveyance of possessory or ownership interest acquired, §159D-42, (b).
Cost of project, institution bearing, §159D-47, (a).
Criteria and requirements in undertaking project, §159D-40, (a).
Factors in making determination, §159D-40, (b).
Definitions, §159D-37.
Exemption from taxation, §159D-55.
Expenses incurred by agency, §159D-44.
Fees, loan repayments, purchase price payments, rents and charges.
Fixing and collecting, §159D-47, (a) to (c).
Trust funds, §159D-48.
General powers, §159D-39.
Interest directly or indirectly in contract, disclosure, §159D-56.
Investing in bonds or notes, §159D-51.
Investment securities, bonds, notes and interest coupons, §159D-50.
Legislative finding, §159D-36.
Lending money to institution, §159D-42, (a).
Loan agreement or agreement for sale or lease, provisions, §159D-42, (a).
Procedural requirements, §159D-41.

CAPITAL FACILITIES FINANCE AGENCY —Cont'd
Private capital facilities finance act —Cont'd
Proposal for financing project, submittal by institution, procedure, §159D-41.
Public hearing on proposed project and bonds, §159D-45, (f).
Refunding bonds or notes, §159D-52.
Remedies of holders of bonds and notes, §159D-49.
Report on activities, §159D-53.
Sale or lease of project to institution, §159D-42, (a).
Short title, §159D-35.
Supplemental and additional method for doing things authorized, §159D-57.
Tax exemption, §159D-55.
Trust agreement or resolution securing bonds, §159D-46.
Trust funds, money received, §159D-48.
Revenues or assets not to inure to benefit of private persons, §159D-38, (b).
Secretary-treasurer, §159D-38, (c).

CAPITAL IMPROVEMENT PLANNING AND BUDGETING PROCESS, §§143-34.40 to 143-34.45.
Automated inventory of facilities owned by state agencies, §143-34.42.
Capital improvement defined, §143-34.40.
Elements of process, §143-34.41, (b).
Joint legislative oversight committee on capital improvements, §§120-258 to 120-260.
Needs estimates, §143-34.44, (a).
First part, §143-34.44, (b).
Second part, §143-34.44, (c).
Recognition by general assembly of need to establish process, §143-34.41, (a).
Responsibility for management, §143-34.41, (c).
Six-year capital improvement plan, §143-34.45, (a).
First part, §143-34.45, (b).
Second part, §143-34.45, (c).
State agency defined, §143-34.40.
Weighted list to evaluate needs, §143-34.43.

CAPITAL ISSUES LAW, §§78A-1 to 78A-66.
See SECURITIES REGULATION.

CAPITAL PLANNING COMMISSION, §143B-374.

CAPITAL PROJECT FINANCING.
Development financing.
Local units of government, §158-7.3.
Project development financing debt instruments.
Project development financing act, §§159-101 to 159-113.
See LOCAL GOVERNMENT FINANCE.

CAPITAL PUNISHMENT.
Age of defendant.
Mitigating circumstances, §15A-2000, (f).
Aggravating circumstances.
Consideration by jury, §15A-2000, (b), (c).
Enumerated, §15A-2000, (e).
Agreement to accept life imprisonment.
Plea of guilty to first degree murder, §15A-2001, (b).
State may agree at any point in prosecution, §15A-2004, (a).
Upon remand from Supreme Court.
State may agree, §15A-2001, (d).

CAPITAL PUNISHMENT —Cont'd
Appeals.
Automatic review of judgment and sentence, §15A-2000, (d).
Direct appeal to supreme court.
Death sentences included in superior court judgments, §7A-27, (a).
Indigent persons, representation of, §7A-451, (c) to (e); Indigent Rep., Model Plan, art. VIII, §8.2.
New trial.
Notice of new trial, §15-193.
Prisoner taken to place of trial when new trial granted, §15-195.
Notice of appeals, §15-189.
Notice of reprieve or new trial, §15-193.
Arson.
Aggravating circumstances.
Capital punishment in commission of arson, §15A-2000, (e).
Bail and recognizance.
Discretion of judge as to pretrial release, §15A-533, (c).
Burglary.
Aggravating circumstances.
Capital felony in commission of burglary, §15A-2000, (e).
Certiorari in death penalty cases, App. Proc. Rule 21, (f).
Clerks of court.
Certificate of execution.
Filing, §15-192.
Duties on sentence of death, §15-189.
Confidentiality.
Witnesses to and persons carrying out execution, §15-190.
Contact with victims' family members.
Death row inmates, §148-10.2, (a).
Crimes punishable by death, Const. N. C., art. XI, §2.
Discretion of prosecutor to seek death penalty, §15A-2004, (a).
District attorneys.
Argument for death penalty, §15-176.1.
Duties on sentence of death, §15-189.
Drugs.
Manner of execution, §15-187.
Duress.
Mitigating circumstances, §15A-2000, (f).
Electrocution.
Abolished, §15-187.
Electrocution, death by.
Abolished, §15-187.
Enumeration of permissible punishments, Const. N. C., art. XI, §1.
Escape.
Aggravating circumstances.
Capital felony committed for purpose of effecting escape, §15A-2000, (e).
Execution, §§15-187 to 15-195.
Certificate of execution, §15-192.
Confidentiality of witnesses and executioner, §15-190.
Designation of person or persons to execute sentence, §15-190.
Electrocution.
Abolished, §15-187.
Fee, §15-190.
Manner of execution, §§15-187, 15-188.
Pending sentences unaffected, §15-191.
Pending sentences unaffected, §15-191.
Place of execution, §15-188.

CAPITAL PUNISHMENT —Cont'd
Execution —Cont'd
Supervision of execution, §15-190.
Time for execution, §15-194.
Who shall be present, §15-190.
Findings in support of sentence of death, §15A-2000.
Guilty plea entered to capital offense.
Entry of plea at any time after indictment, §15A-201, (a).
Jury impanel for limited purpose of sentence recommendation.
Notice given of intent to seek death penalty, §15A-201, (c).
Life imprisonment.
Agreement by state or defendant to accept life imprisonment, §15A-201, (b).
Notice of intent to seek death penalty not given, §15A-201, (b).
Notice of intent to seek death penalty given by state, §15A-201, (c).
Habeas corpus.
Procedure when considering application, Super. Ct. Rule 25.
Indictment may not be waived in capital case, §15A-642, (b).
Indigent persons, representation of.
Appointment of counsel in capital cases, Indigent Rep., Model Plan, art. VII.
Appellate appointments, §7A-451, (c) to (e); Indigent Rep., Model Plan, art. VIII, §8.2.
Indigent defense services.
Generally, §§7A-450 to 7A-458.
See INDIGENT DEFENSE SERVICES.
Indigent defense services act, §§7A-498 to 7A-498.8.
See INDIGENT DEFENSE SERVICES.
Indigent services rules, Rules 1.1 to 3.7.
See INDIGENT DEFENSE SERVICES.
Judges.
Duties on sentence of death, §15-189.
Judgments, §15-189.
Jury.
Alternate jurors in capital cases, §15A-1215, (b).
Arguments of counsel to jury.
Consequences of guilty verdict, §15-176.5.
District attorney may argue for death penalty, §15-176.1.
No limit as to number, §7A-97.
Informing potential jurors on consequences of guilty verdict, §15-176.3.
Instructions to jury on consequences of guilty verdict, §15-176.4.
Peremptory challenges.
Number in capital cases, §15A-1217, (a).
Questioning potential jurors on consequences of guilty verdict, §15-176.3.
Selection of jurors in capital cases, §15A-1214, (j).
Sentencing proceedings.
Generally, §15A-2000, (a).
Recommendation by jury as to sentence, §15A-2000, (b).
Findings in support of sentence of death, §15A-2000, (c).
Sentencing upon, §15A-2002.
Kidnapping.
Aggravating circumstances.
Capital felony in commission of kidnapping, §15A-2000, (e).
Lethal injection.
Manner of carrying out, obtaining drugs, §15-187.
Manner of execution, §15-187.

CAPITAL PUNISHMENT —Cont'd
Mentally ill.
Mitigating circumstances, §15A-2000, (f).
Mentally retarded defendants.
Death sentence prohibited, §15A-2005, (b).
Burden of proof on defendant, §15A-2005, (a), (c), (f).
Definitions, §15A-2005, (a).
Jury determination of aggravating or mitigating circumstance.
Consideration of evidence of retardation, §15A-2005, (g).
Legal defenses not precluded by pretrial determination, §15A-2005, (d).
Motion seeking appropriate relief.
Post conviction determination of mental retardation, §15A-2006.
Noncapital case, court declaration, §15A-2005, (c).
Other sentence not precluded, §15A-2005, (h).
Post conviction determination of mental retardation, §15A-2006.
Pretrial hearing to determine retardation, §15A-2005, (c).
Special issue submitted to jury.
Pretrial determination of retardation not found, §15A-2005, (e).
Minors who commit murder, §14-17.
Mitigating circumstances.
Consideration by jury, §15A-2000, (b), (c).
Enumerated, §15A-2000, (f).
Motions.
Superior courts.
Motions for appropriate relief in capital cases, Super. Ct. Rule 25.
New trial.
Notice of reprieve or new trial, §15-193.
Prisoner taken to place of trial when new trial granted, §15-195.
Noncapital proceeding.
Notice of intent to seek death penalty not given, §15A-2001, (c).
Notice of intent to seek death penalty.
Required to impose sentence, §15A-2001, (b).
Offenses punishable by death, Const. N. C., art. XI, §2.
Peace officers.
Aggravating circumstances.
Capital felony committed against peace officer, §15A-2000, (e).
Place of execution, §15-188.
Plea of guilty to first degree murder.
Entry of plea at any time after indictment, §15A-201, (a).
Jury impanel for limited purpose for sentence recommendation.
Notice given of intent to seek death penalty, §15A-201, (c).
Life imprisonment.
Agreement by state or defendant to accept life imprisonment, §15A-201, (b).
Notice of intent to seek death penalty not given, §15A-201, (b).
Notice of intent to seek death penalty given by state, §15A-201, (c).
Pretrial conference in capital cases, Super. Ct. Rule 24.
Prisoner taken to penitentiary, §15-189.
Prosecutorial discretion to seek death penalty, §15A-2004, (a).

CAPITAL PUNISHMENT —Cont'd
Rape.
Aggravating circumstances.
Capital punishment in commission of rape, §15A-2000, (e).
Remand of case from Supreme court.
Agreement to accept life imprisonment, §15A-2001, (d).
Reprieve.
Notice, §15-193.
Review of judgment and sentence, §15A-2000, (d).
Sentencing, §15A-2002.
Aggravating circumstances.
Consideration by jury, §15A-2000, (b), (c).
Enumerated, §15A-2000, (e).
Enumeration of permissible punishments, Const. N. C., art. XI, §1.
Mitigating circumstances.
Consideration by jury, §15A-2000, (b), (c).
Enumerated, §15A-2000, (f).
Offenses punishable by death, Const. N. C., art. XI, §2.
Review of sentence.
Automatic review, §15A-2000, (d).
Separate sentencing proceeding.
Disability of trial judge.
Chief justice to designate judge to conduct proceedings, §15A-2003.
Generally, §15A-2000, (a).
Recommendation by jury as to sentence, §15A-2000, (b).
Findings in support of sentence of death, §15A-2000, (c).
Sentencing upon, §15A-2002.
Superior courts.
Motions for appropriate relief in capital cases, Super. Ct. Rule 25.
Time.
Execution, §15-194.
Time for filing notice of intent to seek death penalty, §15A-2001, (b).
Verdict.
Consequences of guilty verdict.
Argument to jury, §15-176.5.
Informing and questioning potential jurors, §15-176.3.
Instruction to jury, §15-176.4.
Warden.
Presence at execution, §15-190.
Supervision of execution, §15-190.
Witnesses.
Aggravating circumstances.
Capital felony committed against witness, §15A-2000, (e).

CAPITAL RESERVE ACTS.
Local government finance.
General provisions, §§159-1 to 159-188.
See LOCAL GOVERNMENT FINANCE.

CAPITATION TAX.
Constitution of North Carolina.
Prohibited, Const. N. C., art. V, §1.
Constitution of the United States, Const. U. S., art. I, §9.
Elections.
Denial or abridgement of right to vote for failure to pay tax prohibited, Const. U. S., amd. XXIV.

CAPITOL OF THE STATE.
Arson, §14-59.
Historic properties, §121-9, (h).

CAPITOL OF THE STATE —Cont'd
"Prisoner of war/missing in action" flag display, §143-345.9.

CAP ON AMOUNT OF APPEAL BOND.
Staying execution of money judgment.
Noncompensatory damages of $25,000,000 or more, §1-289, (b), (c).

CAP ON COMPENSATORY OR CONSEQUENTIAL DAMAGES.
Employee theft, larceny, shoplifting, embezzlement or obtaining by false pretenses.
Civil liability, §1-538.2, (a), (b).

CAP ON PUNITIVE DAMAGES, §1D-25, (b).
Exemption, DWI, injury or harm arising, §1D-26.
Not made known to trier of fact, §1D-25, (c).

CAP ON TAX CREDITS.
Business and energy tax credit, §105-129.17, (b).
Tax incentives for new and expanding businesses, §105-129.5, (b).

CARAT.
Standard unit for designation of weight of diamonds, §66-74.

CARBON MONOXIDE.
Motor vehicle emission standards, §20-128.2.

CARBUNCLES.
Food, drug or cosmetic act.
Drug or device, false advertising, §106-138, (b).

CARCASSES.
Meat inspection.
Examination and inspection of carcasses, §106-549.18.
Application of article, §106-549.19.
Equine carcasses.
Slaughter, sale and transportation of carcasses, §106-549.25.
Exemptions from article, §106-549.27.
Misbranding information required, §106-549.21, (b).
Place of inspection, §106-549.19.
Marking, stamping, etc., carcass, §106-549.18.
Poultry inspections.
Condemnation of adulterated poultry, §106-549.53, (c).
Postmortem inspection of carcass, §106-549.53, (b).
Rendering plants and rendering operations, §§106-168.1 to 106-168.16.
See RENDERING PLANTS AND RENDERING OPERATIONS.
Transportation department.
Removal of dead animals, §136-18.

CARDIAC ARREST.
Automated external defibrillator (AED), §90-21.15.

CARDIAC REHABILITATION CERTIFICATION PROGRAM, §§131E-165 to 131E-170.
Administrative procedure.
Applicability of provisions, §131E-168, (b).
Adverse action on certificates, §131E-168, (a), (b).
Applications for certification, §131E-167, (a).
Definitions, §131E-166.
Denial or suspension of certificates.
Adverse action on certificates, §131E-168, (a), (b).
Enforcement of provisions, §131E-169, (b).

CARDIAC REHABILITATION CERTIFICATION PROGRAM —Cont'd
Granting of certificates, §131E-167, (a).
Inspection, evaluation and certification of programs, §131E-167, (c).
Inspections, §131E-170, (a), (b).
Issuance of certification, §131E-167, (a).
Nontransferable or nonassignable, §131E-167, (e).
Posting, §131E-167, (f).
Provisional certificates, §131E-167, (b).
Purpose of article, §131E-165, (b).
Renewal of certificates, §131E-167, (d).
Requirements for certification, §131E-167, (a) to (f).
Rules and regulations, §131E-169, (a).
Title of article.
Cardiac rehabilitation certification program, §131E-165, (a).

CARDINAL.
State bird, §145-2.

CARDINAL-FLOWER.
Taking, etc., of certain wild plants from land of another, §14-129.

CARDIOPULMONARY RESUSCITATION.
Basic education program, §115C-81, (c).

CARGO AIRPORT FACILITIES.
Global TransPark development zone, §§158-30 to 158-42.
See GLOBAL TRANSPARK DEVELOPMENT ZONE.

CARNAL KNOWLEDGE.
Sexual offenses.
See SEXUAL OFFENSES.

CARNIVALS.
Amusement device safety generally, §§95-111.1 to 95-111.18.
See AMUSEMENT DEVICE SAFETY.
Counties.
Regulation of places of amusement, §153A-135.
Municipal corporations.
Regulation of carnivals and circuses, §160A-181.

CAROLINA BEACH.
Eminent domain.
Exercise of power, purposes, modified provisions, §40A-3, (b1).
Vesting of title and right to possession, §40A-42, (a).
Ordinances to regulate and control swimming, personal watercraft operation, surfing and littering in Atlantic Ocean, §160A-176.2.

CAROLINA LILY.
State wildflower, §145-20.

CAROLYN SONZOGNI ACT.
Accident-trauma victim identification, §§90-600 to 90-604.
See ACCIDENT-TRAUMA VICTIM IDENTIFICATION.

CAR REPAIRS.
Motor vehicle repairs, §§20-354 to 20-354.9.
See MOTOR VEHICLE REPAIRS.

CARRIAGES.
Bailment, lease or rental of vehicle or draft animal.
Protection of bailor against bailee's acts, §§14-165 to 14-169.
See BAILMENTS.

CARRIAGES —Cont'd
Traffic laws apply to animal drawing vehicles, §20-171.

CARRIERS.
Actions.
Carrier's right against prior carrier, §62-206.
Joinder of causes of action, §62-205.
Lost or damaged goods.
Generally, §§62-203, 62-204.
Alcoholic beverage transportation.
Commercial transportation permits, §18B-1115, (c).
Baggage.
Careful handling required, §62-202.
Checks, §62-203, (d), (e).
Sale of unclaimed baggage, §62-209.
Motor carriers of passengers.
Exemption from provisions, §62-209, (d).
Notice, §62-209, (a).
Record, §62-209, (c).
Bills of lading.
Issuance on receiving property for transportation in interstate commerce, §62-203, (a).
Bus companies.
See BUS COMPANIES.
Cash-on-delivery shipments.
Common carriers.
Prompt settlement, §62-208.
Commercial code.
Documents of title, §§25-7-101 to 25-7-603.
See COMMERCIAL CODE.
Common carriers.
See COMMON CARRIERS.
Confidentiality of information.
Disclosure of information as to shipments unlawful, §62-324, (a).
Exceptions, §62-324, (b).
Contract carriers.
Motor carriers.
Defined, §62-3.
Rates.
Conflict of laws.
Provisions controlling, §62-146, (e).
Damages.
Limitation of liability.
Carrier issuing bill of lading, §25-7-309, (2).
Discrimination between connecting lines prohibited, §62-210.
Documents of title, §§25-7-101 to 25-7-603.
See COMMERCIAL CODE.
Drunkenness.
Ejection of intoxicated person, §62-151.
Ticket may be refused intoxicated person, §62-150.
Prohibited entry, §62-150.
Duty of carrier.
Carrier issuing bill of lading, §25-7-309, (1).
Escheat.
Unclaimed baggage or freight, §62-209, (c).
Evidence.
Actions by or against common or connecting carriers.
Bills of lading in evidence, §8-41.
Franchise carriers generally.
See FRANCHISE CARRIERS.
Freight.
Bills of lading, §62-203, (a).
Careful handling required, §62-202.
Lost or damaged goods and property.
Additional nature of provisions, §62-203, (g).
Causes of action may be united, §62-203, (f).

CARRIERS —Cont'd
Freight —Cont'd
Lost or damaged goods and property —Cont'd
Claims.
Notice, §62-204.
Time for adjustment and payment, §62-203, (b).
Penalty for failure to adjust and pay claim during time, §62-203, (c).
Liability for, §62-203, (a), (c).
Limitation of actions, §62-204.
Motor carriers.
Exemptions from provisions, §62-203, (h).
Rates.
Charges to be at legal rates, §62-201.
Damages for failure or refusal to comply with provisions, §62-201.
Reasonable time for transportation, §62-200, (a), (b).
Motor carriers of passengers.
Provisions not applicable, §62-200, (d).
Violations of provisions.
Forfeiture, §62-200, (b).
Sale of unclaimed freight, §62-209, (a).
Motor carriers of passengers.
Exemption from provisions, §62-209, (d).
Notice, §62-209, (a).
Record, §62-209, (c).
Gasoline and oil transporters.
Invoice, bill of sale or bill of lading.
Required to be in possession of transporters, §119-42.
Handicapped persons.
Right to use of public conveyances, §168-3.
Human service and volunteer transportation.
Inapplicability of laws and regulations, §62-289.5.
Joinder.
Claims between shippers and common carriers, §62-205.
Liens, §25-7-307.
Enforcement, §25-7-308.
Limitation of actions.
Lost or damaged goods claims, §62-204.
Lost or damaged goods.
Failure to adjust and pay claims within required period, §62-203, (c).
Motor carriers.
General provisions, §§62-259 to 62-279.
See MOTOR CARRIERS.
Notice.
Lost or damaged goods claims, §62-204.
Sale of unclaimed baggage or freight, §62-209, (a).
Passengers.
Ejection.
Passengers refusing to pay fare or violating rules, §62-151.
Poultry inspections.
Violations of article, §106-549.59, (b).
Prescriptions.
Rules pertaining to common-carrier delivery of prescription orders, §90-85.32, (b).
Property taxes.
Public service corporations.
Generally, §§105-333 to 105-344.
See PROPERTY TAXES.
Radioactive waste.
Safety regulations, §20-167.1, (c).
Railroads.
See RAILROADS.
Rates.
Bus companies, §62-146.1.

CARRIERS —Cont'd
Rates —Cont'd
Common carriers, §62-152.1.
Motor common carriers, §62-146.
Freight, §62-201.
Joint rates.
Common carriers, §62-152.1.
Motor common carriers, §62-146.
Mileage between points connected by more than one route, §62-145.
Motor carriers.
Allowance to shippers for transportation services, §62-272.
Collection rates and charges of carriers of property, §62-271.
Common carriers, §62-146.
Points connected by more than one route, §62-145.
Standard transportation practices, §62-152.2.
Sales of unclaimed baggage or freight, §62-209.
School buses.
See SCHOOL BUSES.
Tickets.
Intoxicated persons.
Ticket may be refused, §62-150.
Redemption, §62-149.
Utilities commission.
Free transportation for members.
Common carriers to furnish, §62-144, (a).

CARROTS.
Weights and measures.
Standard weights and measures, §81A-42.

CARRYFORWARDS OF TAX CREDITS.
Business and energy tax credits.
Claimed against franchise or income tax, §105-129.17, (a).
Income tax credits for manufacturing cigarettes for exportation.
Increasing employment and utilizing state ports, §105-130.46, (h).
Low-income housing tax credits.
Claimed against tax for which credit taken, §105-129.41, (a1).
Unused portion, §105-129.41, (a2).
Tax incentives for new and expanding businesses, §105-129.5, (c).

CARRYING CONCEALED WEAPONS.
Burden of proving defense, §14-269, (c).
Concealed handgun permits, §§14-415.10 to 14-415.24.
See CONCEALED HANDGUN PERMIT.
Deadly weapons.
Unlawful to carry, §14-269, (a).
Class 1 felony, second or subsequent offense, §14-269, (c).
Class 2 misdemeanor, §14-269, (c).
Ordinary pocket knife, inapplicability, §14-269, (d).
Defenses to prosecution, §14-269, (c).
Ordinary pocket knife.
Inapplicability, §14-269, (d).
Permits.
Concealed handgun permit, §§14-415.10 to 14-415.24.
See CONCEALED HANDGUN PERMIT.
Persons to which prohibition inapplicable, §14-269, (b).
Pistol or gun.
Unlawful to carry, exceptions, §14-269, (a1).
Class 1 felony, second or subsequent offense, §14-269, (c).

CARRYING CONCEALED WEAPONS —Cont'd
Pistol or gun —Cont'd
Unlawful to carry, exceptions —Cont'd
Class 2 misdemeanor, §14-269, (c).

CARS.
Abandoned and derelict motor vehicles, §§20-137.6 to 20-137.14.
See ABANDONED AND DERELICT MOTOR VEHICLES.
Accidents.
See MOTOR VEHICLE ACCIDENTS.
Clubs and associations, §§58-69-2 to 58-69-55.
See MOTOR CLUBS AND ASSOCIATIONS.
Commissioner.
See MOTOR VEHICLES COMMISSIONER.
Damage appraisers.
See MOTOR VEHICLE DAMAGE APPRAISERS.
Dealers.
See MOTOR VEHICLE DEALERS.
Division.
See MOTOR VEHICLES DIVISION.
Driver's license.
Commercial drivers' licenses, §§20-37.10 to 20-37.23.
See COMMERCIAL DRIVERS' LICENSES.
Generally.
See DRIVERS' LICENSES.
Drunk driving.
See IMPAIRED DRIVING.
Equipment.
See MOTOR VEHICLE EQUIPMENT.
Financial responsibility, §§20-279.1 to 20-284.
See MOTOR VEHICLE FINANCIAL RESPONSIBILITY.
Generally.
See MOTOR VEHICLES.
Impaired driving.
See IMPAIRED DRIVING.
Inspections, §§20-183.2 to 20-183.8G.
See MOTOR VEHICLE INSPECTIONS.
Insurance.
See MOTOR VEHICLE INSURANCE.
Lemon law, §§20-351 to 20-351.10.
See LEMON LAW.
License plates.
See MOTOR VEHICLE LICENSE PLATES.
Manufacturers.
See MOTOR VEHICLE MANUFACTURERS.
New motor vehicles warranty act, §§20-351 to 20-351.10.
See LEMON LAW.
Odometers, §§20-340 to 20-350.
See ODOMETERS.
Railroad grade crossing, §§20-142.1 to 20-142.5.
See RAILROAD GRADE CROSSINGS.
Reckless driving.
See RECKLESS DRIVING.
Registration.
See MOTOR VEHICLE REGISTRATION.
Rentals.
See RENTAL VEHICLES.
Service agreement companies, §§58-1-30 to 58-1-42.
See MOTOR VEHICLE SERVICE AGREEMENT COMPANIES.
Size, weight and loads.
See MOTOR VEHICLE SIZE, WEIGHT AND LOADS.
Speed.
See SPEED RESTRICTIONS AND VIOLATIONS.

CARS —Cont'd
Stolen vehicles.
See STOLEN VEHICLES.
Taxicabs.
See TAXICABS.
Tires.
See TIRES.
Titling.
See MOTOR VEHICLE TITLING.
Towing.
See TOWING OF VEHICLES.
Traffic laws.
See TRAFFIC LAWS.
Traffic lights.
See TRAFFIC LIGHTS.
Traffic tickets.
See TRAFFIC TICKETS.
Trailers.
See TRAILERS.

CARTERET COUNTY.
Acquisition of property, power, §153A-158.1, (a).
Ambulances.
Obtaining ambulance services without intending to pay, §14-111.2.
Requesting ambulance falsely, §14-111.3.
Blank or master forms of mortgages, deeds of trust, etc.
Indexing and recording, inapplicability of provisions, §47-21.
Board of county commissioners.
Filling vacancies on board, §153A-27.1.
Condemnation or acquisition of land by local government unit outside county.
Consent of board of commissioners necessary, §153A-15.
County boards of education elected on partisan basis.
Vacancies in office, §115C-37.1.
Cropper or tenant refusing to perform terms of contract.
Forfeiture of right of possession to premises, §42-27.
Eminent domain.
Exercise of power, purposes, modified provisions, §40A-3, (b1).
Game laws, local acts not repealed, §113-133.1, (e).
Global TransPark development zone, §§158-30 to 158-42.
Grants in navigable waters, registration, §113-205, (a).
Low-income housing tax credits.
Qualified building eligible for credit, §105-129.41, (c).
Officers compensated from fees.
Statement to be rendered, §128-13.
Open fires, §113-60.23.
Applicability of provisions, §113-60.23, (a).
Ground clearing activities, special permit required, §113-60.23, (c).
Woodland fires, permit required, §113-60.23, (b).
Registration of deeds.
Tax certification, no delinquent taxes due, §161-31, (b).
Room occupancy tax levied by county, uniform provisions, §153A-155.
School property.
Acquisition and improvement, §153A-158.1.
Sheriff.
Vacancy, performance of duties until vacancy filled, §162-5.1.

CARTERET COUNTY —Cont'd
Small city mixed beverage elections.
Inapplicability of provisions to, §18B-600, (e1).
Special school tax, election to abolish.
Petition required, §115C-505.
Swimming, surfing and littering in Atlantic Ocean.
City ordinances effective, §160A-176.1.
Tax sales, notices by publication validated.
Inapplicability of provisions, §47-108.24.
Wild plants, taking of certain plants from land of another.
Inapplicability of provisions, §14-129.

CARTRIDGES.
Firearms generally.
See FIREARMS.
Inmates of charitable institutions.
Furnishing cartridges or ammunition for firearms, §14-258.1, (a).
Teflon coated bullets.
Manufacture, sale, etc., §14-34.3.
Weapons generally.
See WEAPONS.

CARTWAYS.
Abandonment or discontinuance, §§136-68, 136-70.
Application, §6-21.
Alteration, §§136-68, 136-70.
Application, §6-21.
Establishment, §§136-68, 136-69, (a) to (c).
Application, §6-21.
Laying out, §136-69, (a) to (c).

CAR WRECKS.
See MOTOR VEHICLE ACCIDENTS.

CASH FLOW CARDS.
Financial transaction card crime.
General provisions, §§14-113.8 to 14-113.17.
See FINANCIAL TRANSACTION CARDS.

CASHIER'S CHECKS.
Presumption of abandonment, time, §116B-53, (c).

CASH MANAGEMENT ACT, §§147-86.10 to 147-86.15.

CASH ON DELIVERY.
Common carriers to settle shipments promptly, §62-208.
Motor carriers, embezzlement of shipments, §62-273.
Sales, UCC.
Buyers not entitled to inspect goods, §25-2-513.

CASH SHORTAGES.
Deductions from employees' wages, §95-25.9.
Combined amounts of deductions and recoupments, §95-25.10.
Employers' remedies preserved, §95-25.11.

CASINOS.
Houses of public entertainment, §14-293.

CASTRATION, §14-29.
Malicious castration, §14-28.

CASUALTY INSURANCE.
Community college buildings and contents, §115D-58.11, (a) to (c).
Confidentiality of consumer and customer information.
Generally, §§58-39-1 to 58-39-165.
See INSURANCE CONSUMER AND CUSTOMER INFORMATION PRIVACY.

CASUALTY INSURANCE —Cont'd
Foreign or alien insurance companies.
Deposits required, §58-5-10.
Motor vehicle insurance.
Generally.
See MOTOR VEHICLE INSURANCE.

CASWELL BEACH.
Eminent domain.
Vesting of title and right to possession, §40A-42, (a).
Ordinances to regulate and control swimming, personal watercraft operation, surfing and littering in Atlantic Ocean, §160A-176.2.

CASWELL COUNTY.
Ambulance services.
Attachment or garnishment and lien for, §§44-51.4 to 44-51.8.
Obtaining ambulance services without intending to pay, §14-111.2.
Condemnation or acquisition of land by local government unit outside county.
Consent of board of commissioners necessary, §153A-15.
Counties generally.
See COUNTIES.
Cropper or tenant refusing to perform terms of contract.
Forfeiture of right of possession to premises, §42-27.
Dangerous firearm use by young children, permitting.
Air rifles, air pistols and BB guns not dangerous firearms, §14-316, (b).
Dog collars.
Unlawful removal of electronic dog collars, §14-401.17.
Foxes, open seasons for taking.
Wildlife resources commission authorized to continue seasons from year to year, §113-291.4, (f1).
Game laws, local acts not repealed, §113-133.1, (e).
Tax elections for industrial development purposes, §§158-16 to 158-24.
Tax sales, notices by publication validated.
Inapplicability of provisions, §47-108.24.

CATALOGS.
Sale of prints.
General prohibitions applicable to art dealers, §25C-11, (a).

CATASTROPHES.
State of emergency.
Government powers and proclamations generally, §§14-288.12 to 14-288.18.
See STATE OF EMERGENCY.

CATAWBA COUNTY.
Ambulance services.
Attachment or garnishment and lien for, §§44-51.4 to 44-51.8.
Obtaining ambulance services without intending to pay, §14-111.2.
Condemnation or acquisition of land by local government unit outside county.
Consent of board of commissioners necessary, §153A-15.
Counties generally.
See COUNTIES.
Game laws, local acts not repealed, §113-133.1, (e).

CATAWBA COUNTY —Cont'd
Oil, gas and mineral interests separated from surface fee, extinguished, title in surface fee holder.
Interest not listed for tax purposes for 10 years prior to January 1, 1971.
Protection of surface interest from surface estate holder, §1-42.2, (d).
School property.
Acquisition and improvement, §153A-158.1.
Special school tax, election to abolish.
Petition required, §115C-505.
Wild plants, taking of certain plants from land of another.
Inapplicability of provisions, §14-129.

CATAWBA RIVER.
Mountain Island lake marine commission, §§77-70 to 77-78.
See MOUNTAIN ISLAND LAKE.

CATAWBA, TOWN OF.
Satellite annexation.
Limitation on area of satellite corporate limits, inapplicability, §160A-58.1, (b).

CATAWBA/WATEREE RIVER BASIN ADVISORY COMMISSION.
River basins advisory commissions generally, §§77-110 to 77-118.
See RIVER BASINS ADVISORY COMMISSIONS.

CATERING BUSINESS.
Alcoholic beverage permits.
Culinary permit.
Kind of permit that may be issued, §18B-1001.
Mixed beverages catering permit.
Kind of permit that may be issued, §18B-1001.

CATS.
Hotel rooms, admittance of pets, §72-7.1.
Persons bitten by cats.
Confinement of all biting dogs and cats, §130A-196.
Notice to local health director, §130A-196.
Reports by physicians, §130A-196.
Rabies.
Defined, §130A-184.
Generally, §§130A-184 to 130A-201.
Infected cats to be destroyed, §130A-197.
Quarantine, §130A-198.
Cats brought into state, §130A-193.
Confinement of all biting dogs and cats, §130A-196.
Districts infected with rabies.
Destroying stray dogs and cats in quarantine districts, §130A-195.
Tags.
Dogs and cats not wearing, §130A-192.
Vaccinations.
Administration of vaccine, §130A-185, (a).
Cats brought into state.
Confinement and vaccination, §130A-193.
Protection of vaccinated cats, §130A-197.
Required, §130A-185.
Tags, §130A-190.
Dogs and cats not wearing, §130A-192.
Time of vaccination, §130A-185, (a).
Spay/neuter program, §§19A-60 to 19A-65.

CATTLE.
Allowance to officers for keeping and maintaining cattle taken into custody under legal process, §1-322.

CATTLE —Cont'd
Brands generally, §§80-45 to 80-66.
See LIVESTOCK BRANDS.
Brucellosis, §§106-388 to 106-398.
See BRUCELLOSIS.
Cattle tick, §§106-351 to 106-363.
See CATTLE TICK.
Certificate of registration obtained by false representation, §14-103.
Compensation for killing diseased animals generally, §§106-323 to 106-335.
See LIVESTOCK DISEASES.
Control of livestock diseases generally, §§106-400 to 106-405.
See LIVESTOCK DISEASES.
Dealer licensing generally, §§106-418.8 to 106-418.16.
See LIVESTOCK DEALER LICENSING.
Diseases generally, §§106-304 to 106-307.7.
See LIVESTOCK DISEASES.
Dogs killing cattle.
Any person may kill, §67-14.
Larceny.
Felony, §14-81, (a).
Probation, conditions required, §14-81, (b).
Sentencing to active sentence.
Judge's authority not limited, §14-81, (b).
Livestock generally.
See LIVESTOCK.
Livestock markets, §§106-406 to 106-418.
See LIVESTOCK MARKETS.
Meat inspections generally, §§106-549.15 to 106-549.39.
See MEAT INSPECTIONS.
Promotion of use and sale of agricultural products.
Generally, §§106-550 to 106-568.
See AGRICULTURAL PRODUCTS PROMOTION.
Pursuing or injuring with intent to steal, §14-85.
Quarantine of diseased animals generally.
See LIVESTOCK DISEASES.
Rendering plants and rendering operations, §§106-168.1 to 106-168.16.
Signs for protection of cattle, §136-33.1.

CATTLE GUARDS.
Railroads, §136-194.

CATTLE RUSTLING.
Larceny of livestock, §14-81.

CATTLE TICK, §§106-351 to 106-363.
Compelling county commissioners to comply, §106-355.
Control of livestock diseases generally, §§106-400 to 106-405.
See LIVESTOCK DISEASES.
Counties.
Quarantine zones, §106-352.
Dipping of cattle or horses, §106-351.
Counties to provide dipping vats, §106-353.
Damaging dipping vats a felony, §106-363.
Expense of owner, §106-358.
Lien on animal, §106-359.
Owners of stock to have same dipped, §106-356.
Period of dipping, §106-356.
Service of dipping notice, §106-357.
Supervision of dipping, §106-356.
Dipping vats.
Damaging dipping vats a felony, §106-363.

CATTLE TICK —Cont'd
Enforcement of article.
Duty of sheriff, §106-360.
State veterinarian, county commissioners failing to comply, §106-355.
Liens.
Expense of dipping as lien on animals, §106-359.
Livestock diseases generally, §§106-304 to 106-307.7.
See LIVESTOCK DISEASES.
Mandamus.
Enforcement of compliance by state veterinarian, §106-355.
Misdemeanor, §106-362.
Notice.
Service of quarantine and dipping notice, §106-357.
Quarantine.
Cattle placed in quarantine, §106-358.
Counties not embraced in quarantine zones, §106-352.
Service of notice, §106-357.
Rules and regulations, §106-361.
Sheriffs.
Duty of sheriff in enforcing article, §106-360.
State veterinarian.
Enforcement of compliance with law, §106-355.
Violation of provisions, §106-362.

CAUSAL EMPLOYEES.
Workers' compensation.
Not included in definition of employee, §97-2.

CAUSEWAYS.
Special speed limitations, §20-144.

CAVEAT TO WILL.
Bonds, surety, §31-33.
By whom filed, §31-32.
Costs.
Allowance of costs to either or apportioned in discretion of court, §6-21.
Docketing.
Transferring of cause to trial docket, §31-33.
Judgments.
Final judgment entered, §31-37.
Settlement agreements, §31-37.1.
Notice.
Caveator to notify all heirs, §31-33.
Superior court clerks to enter notice on will book, §31-37.
Priority trial setting, §31-33.
Settlement agreements.
Parties may enter into, §31-37.1.
Superior court clerks.
Notice of caveat, §31-37.
Suspension of proceedings, §31-36.
Transfer of cause to superior court for trial, §31-33.
When filed, §31-32.
Wills probated prior to May 1, 1951, §31-32.

CAVE PROTECTION.
Definitions, §14-159.20.
Owners and agents liability, §14-159.23.
Speleothems.
Defined, §14-159.20.
Sale, §14-159.22.
Vandalism, §14-159.21.

CB RADIOS.
Special license plates, §20-79.4, (a).

CEASE AND DESIST ORDERS.
Alcoholic beverages.
Notice regarding direct shipment into state, §18B-102.1, (b).

CEASE AND DESIST ORDERS —Cont'd
Banks.
Commissioner of banks.
Administrative orders generally, §§53-107.1, 53-107.2.
International banking, §53-232.16.
Campaign contributions and expenditures.
Civil remedy other than penalty, §163-278.34, (c).
Consumer finance act, §53-187.
Continuing care retirement communities, §58-64-10, (c).
Health maintenance organizations, §58-67-165, (c), (d).
Injunctions.
See INJUNCTIONS.
Insurance consumer and customer information privacy, §58-39-90.
Penalty for violating, §58-39-95, (b).
Insurance unfair trade practices, §58-63-35.
Issuance, modification or setting aside, §58-63-32.
Penalty for violating, §58-63-50.
Mortgage bankers and brokers.
Disciplinary action, §53-243.12, (d).
Mortgages and deeds of trust.
Reverse mortgages, §53-271, (a), (b).
Producer-controlled property or casualty insurers.
Lack of material compliance with section, §58-3-165, (l).
Professional employer organizations, §58-89A-165, (b).
Emergency orders, §58-89A-165, (c).
Provider sponsored organizations.
Division of medical assistance, §131E-307, (d), (e).
Savings and loan associations, §54B-59, (a).
Judicial review, §54B-71.
Temporary cease and desist orders, §54B-59, (b).
Savings banks.
Generally, §54C-76, (a).
Judicial review, §54C-84.
Temporary cease and desist orders, §54C-76, (b).
Violations of orders, §54C-79, (b).
Securities regulation, §78A-47, (b).
Trust companies.
Administrative enforcement, §53-369, (a).
Unauthorized insurers, §§58-28-20 to 58-28-35.
Additional nature provisions, §58-28-35.
Adducing additional evidence, §58-28-25, (b).
Domestic companies.
Unauthorized acts by, §58-14-15.
Finality, §58-28-25, (c).
Judicial review, §58-28-25, (a).
Modification or setting aside, §58-28-20, (b), (c).
Penalties for violations, §58-28-30.
Power of commissioner, §58-28-20, (a), (d).
Viatical settlements, §58-58-290, (c).
Emergency cease and desist orders, §58-58-290, (d).

CELLULAR COMMUNICATIONS.
Enhanced 911 system for wireless communications, §§62A-21 to 62A-32.
See 911 SYSTEM.
Secret listening.
Electronic surveillance, §§15A-286 to 15A-298.
See ELECTRONIC SURVEILLANCE.

CEMENT.
Standard weights and measures, §81A-42.
Street and highway construction contracts.
Production in United States.
Contract requirements relating to construction materials, §136-28.7, (a) to (d).

CEMETERIES, §§65-46 to 65-73.
Abandonment.
Advisory committee.
Compensation of members, §143B-128, (c).
Composition, §143B-128, (a).
Creation, §143B-128, (a).
Expenses, §143B-128, (c).
Officers, §143B-128, (e).
Terms of members, §143B-128, (b).
Vacancies, §143B-128, (d).
Historic preservation program, §121-8, (g).
Public cemeteries.
Access and maintenance.
Persons who may enter to maintain or visit grave, §65-74.
Without consent, §65-75, (a).
Rural cemeteries, §§65-1, 65-3.
Cemetery associations or corporations.
Change of control, §65-59.
Change of name, §65-17.
Land holdings, §65-16.
Stockholder's meetings, §65-17.1.
Cemetery brokers.
Defined, §65-48.
Licenses, §65-57.
Cemetery commission, §§65-49 to 65-54.
Cemetery management organizations.
Defined, §65-48.
Licenses, §65-57.
Cemetery sales organizations.
Defined, §65-48.
Licenses, §65-57.
Charitable trusts.
Not invalidated by rule against perpetuities, §36A-49.
Cities or towns.
Cemetery trustees generally, §§160A-349.1 to 160A-349.15.
See MUNICIPAL CEMETERIES.
Generally, §§160A-341 to 160A-348.
See MUNICIPAL CEMETERIES.
Columbarium.
Defined, §65-48.
Commission, §§65-49 to 65-54.
Confederate cemetery.
Labor for care of cemetery.
Department of correction to furnish, §65-4.
Contracts.
Individual contracts for care and maintenance, §65-62.
Conveyances, §65-69, (b), (c).
Corporate trustees.
Application for approval, §65-60.1, (b).
Defined, §65-60.1, (a).
Investments, §65-60.1, (e).
Records, §65-60.1, (c).
Removal of trustee, §65-60.1, (d).
Counties.
Cemeteries for inmates of county homes.
County commissioners may establish, §65-5.
Removal and reinterment of bodies, §65-6.
Rural cemeteries, §§65-1 to 65-3.
Service districts, §§153A-300 to 153A-310.
Cremation.
General provisions, §§90-210.40 to 90-210.54.
See CREMATION.
Deeds.
Validation of certain deeds for cemetery lots executed by suspended corporations, §65-73.
Defacing or desecrating grave sites.
Applicability of provisions, §14-148, (b).

CEMETERIES —Cont'd
Defacing or desecrating grave sites —Cont'd
Archaeologists.
Applicability of provisions, §§14-148, 14-149, (b).
Plowing over or covering up graves, §14-149, (a).
Prohibited, §14-148, (a).
Violation constitutes misdemeanor, §14-148, (c).
Definitions, §65-48.
Discrimination.
Burial without regard to race or color, §65-72, (a), (b).
Disinterment and reinterment, §65-13.
Eminent domain.
Powers of local public condemnors, §40A-3, (b).
Fees.
Change of control of cemetery company.
Application.
Filing fee, §65-59.
Commission, §65-54.
Licenses, §65-54.
Cemetery companies, §65-55, (c).
Sales organizations, management organizations and brokers, §65-57, (c).
Fraternal orders and societies.
Exemptions from North Carolina cemetery act, §65-47, (b).
Funeral service.
General provisions, §§90-210.18A to 90-210.29.
See FUNERAL SERVICE.
Grave space.
Defined, §65-48.
Historic preservation program.
Abandoned cemeteries, §121-8, (g).
Identification of bodies before burial or cremation, §90-210.29A.
Inscriptions on gravestone or monument.
Unlawful inscriptions.
Charging person with commission of crime, §14-401.3.
Investments.
Corporate trustees, §65-60.1, (e).
Trust funds for care of cemeteries, §65-10.
Licenses.
Cemetery companies, §§65-55, 65-56.
Application, §65-55, (b).
Action by commission on, §65-55, (d), (e).
Filing fee, §65-55, (c).
Defined, §65-48.
Denial of license, §65-55, (e).
Existing companies.
Grant of license to, §65-56.
Investigation of applicant, §65-55, (c).
Notice.
Granting of license, §65-55, (f).
Required, §65-55, (a).
Preneed funeral establishment license and preneed sales license, §90-210.67.
Renewal license.
Application, §65-67.
Assignment or transfer prohibited, §65-68.
Sale of preneed grave space, etc., §65-58.
Application, §65-58, (b).
Filing fee, §65-58, (c).
Fees, §65-58, (c).
Judicial review of orders or decisions of commission.
Applicability of certain provisions, §65-58, (f).
Notice.
Grant of license, §65-58, (e).
Refusal of license, §65-58, (d).
Required, §65-58, (a).

CEMETERIES —Cont'd
Licenses —Cont'd
Sales organizations, management organizations and brokers.
Application, §65-57, (b).
Action by commission on, §65-57, (e) to (g).
Filing fee, §65-57, (c).
Investigation of applicant, §65-57, (d).
Notice.
Denial of application, §65-57, (f).
Granting of application, §65-57, (g).
Required, §65-57, (a).
Violations of provisions.
Misdemeanor, §65-57, (h).
Local, private and special legislation prohibited, Const. N. C., art. II, §24.
Mausoleums.
Defined, §65-48.
Sale of space before construction.
Time for construction, §65-70, (a).
Failure to complete in time, §65-70, (e).
Trust account, §65-70, (b), (c).
Bond in lieu of payment to, §65-70, (f).
Withdrawal of funds from, §65-70, (d).
Minimum acreage, §65-69, (a).
Exceptions, §65-69, (d).
Minimum burial depth, §§65-77, 90-210.25A.
Minor's malicious or willful destruction of property.
Recovery of damages from parents, §1-538.1.
Municipal cemeteries.
Generally, §§160A-341 to 160A-348.
See MUNICIPAL CEMETERIES.
Parent responsibility for damages.
Malicious or willful destruction of property by minors, §1-538.1.
Perpetual care funds, §§65-61 to 65-65.
Plowing over or covering up graves, §14-149.
Preneed funeral contracts and funds, §§90-210.60 to 90-210.73.
See PRENEED FUNERAL CONTRACTS AND FUNDS.
Private graves, access and maintenance.
Consent of landowner.
Persons who may enter private property to maintain or visit grave with consent, §65-74.
Special proceedings where consent cannot be obtained, §65-75, (a).
Order allowing access to and maintenance of private grave, §65-75, (a), (b).
Petition and petitioners, §65-75, (a).
Private way to public road.
Cartway, tramway or railway.
Laying off, procedure, §136-69, (a) to (c).
Property taxes.
Burial property.
Assessment, special class, §105-278.2, (b).
Exemption, §105-278.2, (a).
Real property defined, §105-278.2, (c).
Racial minorities.
Burial without regard to race or color, §65-72, (a).
Violations of provisions misdemeanors, §65-72, (b).
Records, §65-60.
Corporate trustees, §65-60.1, (c).
Removal of graves.
Certificate.
Filing after removal, §65-13, (c).
Fee, §65-13, (c).
Rules and regulations concerning, §65-13, (e).

CEMETERIES —Cont'd
Removal of graves —Cont'd
Eminent domain.
Power not granted, §65-13, (h).
Expenses, §65-13, (d).
Notice, §65-13, (b).
Reinterment site.
Duties as to, §65-13, (f).
Supervision of county commissioners, §65-13, (g).
Who may disinter, move and reinter, §65-13, (a).
Rural cemeteries.
Abandoned cemeteries.
Boards of trustees, §65-3.
County commissioners to have control, §65-3.
List, §65-1.
Appropriations for care, §65-2.
County commissioners.
Appropriations for care, §65-2.
Control of abandoned cemeteries, §65-3.
List of public and abandoned cemeteries, §65-1.
Sale of personal property or services.
Applicability of provisions, §65-66, (a).
Cancellation of contract by purchaser, §65-66, (m).
Examination of business by commission, §65-66, (h).
Exemptions from provisions, §65-66, (k).
Interest.
Prepayments, §65-66, (f).
Policy of state, §65-66, (a).
Reports, §65-66, (b).
Failure to make, §65-66, (l).
Requirements of contracts, §65-66, (b) to (e).
Trust account.
Deposit of proceeds, §65-66, (b).
Bond in lieu of, §65-66, (g).
Waiver of provisions.
Prohibited, §65-66, (i).
Sanitary districts.
Acceptance of gifts for nonprofit cemetery.
Corporate powers of sanitary district board, §130A-55.
Scope of act, §65-47, (a).
Exceptions, §65-47, (b), (c).
Taxation.
Exemption from tax, Const. N. C., art. V, §2.
Property taxes.
Exemption of burial property, §105-278.2.
Title of act.
Short title, §65-46.
Tombstones.
Defacing or desecrating grave sites, §§14-148, 14-149.
Transportation department.
Maintenance and repair of ingress and egress to public or church cemeteries, §136-18.
Trespass.
Defacing or desecrating grave sites, §§14-148, 14-149.
Trust funds for care of cemeteries.
Generally.
See CEMETERY CARE TRUST FUNDS.
Perpetual care fund, §§65-61 to 65-65.
Trusts for cemetery lots, §36A-146.
Veterans.
Burial.
Days for, §65-44.
Costs, §65-43.6.
Definitions, §65-43.
Disinterment, §65-43.4.
Interment, §65-43.1.
Bars to eligibility, §65-43.3.

CEMETERIES —Cont'd
Veterans —Cont'd
Interment —Cont'd
Death of family member prior to qualified veteran, §65-43.1, (c).
Eligibility, §65-43.1, (a).
Number of gravesites authorized, §65-43.1, (b).
Proof, §65-43.2.
Land acquisition, §65-41.
Location of cemeteries, §65-42.
Reinterment, §65-43.5.
Violations of North Carolina cemetery act, §65-71, (a).

CEMETERIES TRUSTEES.
Generally, §§160A-349.1 to 160A-349.15.
See MUNICIPAL CEMETERIES.

CEMETERY ASSOCIATIONS OR CORPORATIONS.
Change of control of cemetery company.
Application, §65-59.
Filing fee, §65-59.
Change of name, §65-17.
Land holdings authorized, §65-16.
Licensing of cemetery company, §§65-55, 65-56.
Meetings of certain nonprofit cemetery corporations.
Amendment of charter.
Required vote, §65-17.1.
Calling of meeting, §65-17.1.
Notice, §65-17.1.
Quorum, §65-17.1.
Names.
Change of name, §65-17.

CEMETERY BROKERS.
Defined, §65-48.
Licenses, §65-57.

CEMETERY CARE TRUST FUNDS.
Accounts.
Separate record of accounts to be kept, §§65-8, 65-9.
Perpetuity, §65-9.
Amount, §65-7.
Clerk of superior court.
Bonds, surety.
Official bond liable for funds, §65-11.
Commission, §65-11.
Money deposited with, §65-7.
Substitution of bank or trust company as trustee, §65-11.
Investment of funds, §65-10.
Perpetual care fund, §§65-61 to 65-65.
Advertising.
Requirements for advertising of perpetual care fund, §65-63.
Corporate trustee.
Designation, §65-61.
Financial reports, §65-65.
Deposits, §§65-61, 65-64.
Conversion to private cemetery, §65-64, (b).
Individual cemetery.
Requirements as to grave memorial markers, §65-63.
Investment of amounts deposited, §65-64, (e).
Items subject to, §65-64, (d).
Special endowments, §65-64, (f).
Time for, §65-64, (a).
Individual contracts for care and maintenance, §65-62.

CEMETERY CARE TRUST FUNDS —Cont'd
Perpetual care fund —Cont'd
Misdemeanors.
Failure to make required contributions, §65-71, (b).
Reports.
Financial reports, §65-65.
Required trust fund, §65-61.
Withdrawal or transfer of portion of fund.
Consent of commission required, §65-61.
Preneed funeral contracts and funds, §§90-210.60 to 90-210.73.
Taxation.
Exemption, §65-12.

CEMETERY COMMISSION.
Attorneys at law.
Employment of, §65-53.
Budget.
Annual budget, §65-54.
Chairperson, §65-50, (e).
Composition, §65-50.
Defined, §65-48.
Employment of staff, §65-53.
Established, §65-49.
Fees, §65-54.
Injunctions.
Power to bring action for, §65-53.
Investigations, §65-53.
Meetings.
Notice, §65-51.
Regular meetings, §65-52.
Special meetings, §65-52.
Notice.
Meetings, §65-51.
Number of members, §65-50, (a).
Office.
Principal office, §65-51.
Officers.
Election, §65-50.
Powers, §65-53.
Qualifications of members, §65-50.
Quorum, §65-50, (d).
Removal of members, §65-50, (c).
Rules and regulations, §65-49.
Powers of commission generally, §65-53.
Selection of members, §65-50.
Term of members, §65-50, (b).

CEMETERY MANAGEMENT ORGANIZATIONS.
Defined, §65-48.
Licenses, §65-57.

CEMETERY SALES ORGANIZATIONS.
Defined, §65-48.
Licenses, §65-57.

CENSURE.
Attorney discipline.
Imposition of discipline, Bar Rules & Regs., B, §.0123.
Issuance by grievance committee, Bar Rules & Regs., B, §.0113.

CENSUS.
Constitution of the United States, Const. U. S., art. I, §§2, 9.
Municipal corporations.
Electoral districts.
Reapportionment, §160A-23.
Estimates of population, §160A-486.
Special education.
Annual census of children with special needs, §115C-110, (j).

CENSUS —Cont'd
Traffic census.
Established, §136-18.

CENTENNIALS.
America's four hundredth anniversary committee.
Compensation of members, §143B-86.
Creation, §143B-85.
Members, §143B-86.
Powers and duties, §143B-85.
Quorum, §143B-86.
Selection of members, §143B-86.

CENTER FOR APPLIED TEXTILE TECHNOLOGY, §§115D-68 to 115D-71.

CENTER FOR GEOGRAPHIC INFORMATION AND ANALYSIS.
Role, §143-725, (b).

CENTER FOR HEALTH STATISTICS, §§130A-371 to 130A-374.

CENTER FOR MISSING PERSONS, §§143B-495 to 143B-499.7.

CENTER FOR NURSING, §§90-171.70 to 90-171.72.

CENTER LINES.
Marking street or highway with, §136-30.1, (a), (b).

CENTRAL NORTH CAROLINA SCHOOL FOR THE DEAF AT GREENSBORO.
Education programs in residential schools generally, §§143B-146.1 to 143B-146.21.
See EDUCATION.
Schools for the deaf generally, §§143B-216.40 to 143B-216.44.
See HEARING IMPAIRED.

CENTRAL OFFICE OR AIRCRAFT FACILITY PROPERTY TAX CREDIT, §105-129.12.

CENTRAL PIEDMONT COMMUNITY COLLEGE.
Community colleges generally, §§115D-1 to 115D-81.
See COMMUNITY COLLEGES.
Financial support.
Authority to provide local financial support, §115D-60, (a).
Sale, exchange or lease of property, §115D-60, (b).

CENTRAL PRISON.
Delivery of prisoners to prison, §148-28.
Employees, §148-31.
Identification bureau.
Transfer to state bureau of investigation, §114-18.
Maintenance, §148-31.
Sentencing of prisoners, §148-28.
Warden.
Powers and duties.
Generally, §148-31.
Youthful offenders, §148-28.

CENTRAL REGISTRY.
Abuse, neglect or dependency of juvenile cases or child fatalities, §7B-311.
Report by director of social services where maltreatment involved, §7B-307, (c).

CEREBRAL PALSY.
Defined, §35A-1101.

CEREBRAL PALSY —Cont'd
Determination of incompetence, §§35A-1101 to 35A-1116.
See INCOMPETENCE.

CERTIFICATE OF DETERMINATION OF APPEAL.
Procedure after determination of appeal, §1-298.

CERTIFICATE OF ENVIRONMENTAL COMPATIBILITY.
Construction of transmission line by utility.
Application for certificate, §62-102.

CERTIFICATE OF PUBLIC ADVANTAGE.
Cooperative agreements among hospitals generally, §§131E-192.1 to 131E-192.13.
See HEALTH CARE FACILITIES.

CERTIFICATES OF BIRTH.
See BIRTH CERTIFICATES.

CERTIFICATES OF DEATH.
Amendment by medical examiner, §130A-385, (c).
Amendment of death certificate, §130A-118, (a).
Contents of death certificate, §130A-116.
Cremation.
Authorization for cremation, §130A-113, (b).
Duties of local registrars, §130A-97.
Duties of medical examiners, §130A-385.
Filing of death certificate, §130A-115, (a).
Information to be obtained, §130A-115, (b).
Local registrar's duties, §130A-97.
Register of deeds.
Copies to be forwarded by local registrars, §130A-97.
Standard certificate of death.
Contents of death certificate, §130A-116.
Vital statistics generally.
See VITAL STATISTICS.

CERTIFICATES OF DEPOSIT.
Banks.
Unlawful issuance, §53-63.

CERTIFICATES OF MARRIAGE.
Delayed marriage certificate.
Issuance, §51-21.
Registration of marriage certificates.
Duty of registers of deeds, §130A-110, (a) to (d).
Evidentiary value of copies, §130A-110, (b).
Forms, §130A-110, (a).
Furnishing copies, §130A-110, (b), (c).

CERTIFICATES OF NEED.
Health care facilities, §§131E-175 to 131E-190.
See HEALTH CARE FACILITIES.

CERTIFICATES OF PUBLIC CONVENIENCE AND NECESSITY.
Coin, coinless or key-operated pay telephone service.
Special certificate issued to utility offering, §62-110, (c).
Construction, acquisition or operation of utility plant or system.
Required, §62-110, (a).
Construction of transmission line by utility.
Application for certificate, §62-102.
Generating facilities, certificates for construction.
Analysis for needs for expansion, §62-110.1, (c).
Appeal from award order, §62-82, (b).

CERTIFICATES OF PUBLIC CONVENIENCE AND NECESSITY —Cont'd
Generating facilities, certificates for construction —Cont'd
Application.
Factors in action, §62-110.1, (d).
Notice in hearing, §62-82, (a).
Electric membership corporations.
Inclusion in definition of public utility, §62-110.1, (b).
Estimate of construction costs.
Conditions for receiving, §62-110.1, (e).
Exceptions to requirements, §62-110.1, (g).
Required, §62-110.1, (a).
Review of construction by commission, §62-110.1, (f).
Local telephone exchange or exchange access services, §62-110, (f1).
Long distance service.
Issuance to utility offering, §62-110, (b).
Motor carriers, certificate or permit, §62-262.
Bus companies.
Certificates of authority, §62-262.1.
Fees, §62-300.
Discontinuance or reduction in service.
Inapplicability of provision to bus companies, §62-262.2, (e).
Fees, §62-300, (a).
Nonprofit colleges or universities.
Telephone service to, §62-110, (e).
Public transportation authorities.
Power to issue, §160A-579.
Public utilities, §62-110.
Alternative operator services, §62-110.4.
Applications.
Fees, §62-300, (a).
Definition of "certificate," §62-3.
Long distance telephone and telegraph services, §62-110.
Pay telephone service, §62-110.
Taxicabs, §20-87.
Telephone network.
Shared use or resale of services, §62-110, (b).

CERTIFICATES OF TITLE.
Boats generally, §§75A-32 to 75A-48.
See BOAT TITLING.
Motor vehicles generally.
See MOTOR VEHICLE TITLING.
Real property.
Torrens system registration, §§43-13 to 43-25.
See TORRENS SYSTEM REGISTRATION.

CERTIFICATION FOR REVIEW BY SUPREME COURT.
Discretionary review, §7A-31, (a) to (d).

CERTIFICATION OF DEPOSITIONS, §1A-1, Rule 30, (f).

CERTIFICATION OF LEGAL SPECIALISTS.
Bankruptcy law specialty, Bar Rules & Regs., D, §§.2201 to .2207.
Continuing legal education, accreditation rules, Bar Rules & Regs., D, §§.1901 to .1908.
Criminal law specialty, Bar Rules & Regs., D, §§.2501 to .2507.
Estate planning and probate law specialty, Bar Rules & Regs., D, §§.2301 to .2307.
Family law specialty, Bar Rules & Regs., D, §§.2401 to .2407.
Hearing and appeal rules, Bar Rules & Regs., D, §§.1801 to .1806.

CERTIFICATION OF LEGAL SPECIALISTS —Cont'd
Independent certifying organizations, rules of approval, Bar Rules & Regs., D, §§.2001 to .2006.
Plan of legal specialization, Bar Rules & Regs., D, §§.1701 to .1726.
Real property law specialty, Bar Rules & Regs., D, §§.2101 to .2107.

CERTIFIED CHECKS.
Checks generally.
See CHECKS.
Presumption of abandonment, time, §116B-53, (c).

CERTIFIED MAIL.
Personal jurisdiction.
Manner of service to exercise, §1A-1, Rule 4, (j).
Proof of service, §1A-1, Rule 4, (j2).
Physician or surgeon licensure to practice medicine.
Service of notices required by chapter, §90-14.3.
Proof of service by, §1-75.10.
Subpoenas.
Service, §1A-1, Rule 45, (e).
Workers' compensation.
Notice of accident to employer, §97-23.

CERTIFIED PUBLIC ACCOUNTANTS, §§93-1 to 93-13.
Age.
Minimum age, §93-2.
Assistants.
Certification not required, §93-9.
Board of examiners, §93-12.
Records.
Confidentiality, §93-12.2.
Business under assumed name.
Partnerships engaged in practice of certified public accountancy.
Exemption from provisions, §66-68, (e).
Certificates of qualification.
Assistants need not be certified, §93-9.
Issuance.
Powers and duties of board, §93-12.
Reciprocity, §93-10.
Required, §§93-3 to 93-6.
Revocation or suspension.
Disciplinary action by board, §93-12.
Child support enforcement.
Forfeiture of licensing privilege, §50-13.12.
Civil penalties.
Power of board to assess, §93-12.
Confidentiality of information.
Records of board, §93-12.2.
Corporations.
Professional corporations generally, §§55B-1 to 55B-16.
See PROFESSIONAL CORPORATIONS.
Public practice of accountancy.
Prohibited, §93-8.
Use of title "certified public accountant," §93-5.
Definitions, §93-1, (a).
Disciplinary action.
Board of examiners, §93-12.
Education.
Continuing education.
Powers of board of examiners as to, §93-12.
Qualifications of applicants for examination, §93-12.

CERTIFIED PUBLIC ACCOUNTANTS —Cont'd
Examinations.
Powers and duties of board as to, §93-12.
Qualifications of applicants, §93-12.
New requirements.
Effect, §93-12.1.
Fees, §93-12.
Fiduciaries.
Employment and compensation.
Powers which may be incorporated by reference in trust instrument, §32-27.
License taxes.
Professional licenses generally, §105-41.
Nonresidents.
Certificates of qualification.
Persons certified in other states, §93-10.
Partnerships.
Use of title "certified public accountant," §93-4.
Peer review.
Board of examiners, §93-12.
Practice of law.
Prohibited, §93-1, (b).
Professional corporations.
Generally, §§55B-1 to 55B-16.
See PROFESSIONAL CORPORATIONS.
Public accountants.
Defined, §93-1, (a).
Public officers and employees.
Accountancy provisions not applicable to, §93-11.
Public practice of accountancy.
Cooperation, §93-8.
Defined, §93-1, (a).
Prohibited practice, §93-6.
Qualifications, §§93-2, 93-12.
Reciprocity.
Certification, §93-10.
Records.
Board of examiners, §93-12.
Referees meetings.
Statement of account by, §1A-1, Rule 53, (f).
Registration.
Required, §93-6.
Rules for registration, §93-12.
Reports.
Board of examiners.
Annual report to governor, §93-12.
Peer review, §93-12.
Rules and regulations.
Board of examiners, §93-12.
Peer review.
Authority of board to adopt, §93-12.
Rules of professional conduct.
Power of board to adopt, §93-12.
Title.
Misleading titles.
Prohibited, §93-6.
Use of titles, §93-4.
Corporations, §93-5.
Individuals, §93-3.
Violations of provisions, §93-13.

CERTIFIED SAFETY PROFESSIONALS (CSP), §§90-671 to 90-674.

CERTIORARI.
Authorized, §1-269.
Bonds, surety, §1-269.
Undertakings to be made part of record sent up to appellate division, §1-297.
Court of appeals.
Issuance of remedial writs, §7A-32, (b).
Criminal procedure, §15A-1444.

CERTIORARI —Cont'd
Death penalty cases, App. Proc. Rule 21, (f).
Deposition of witnesses to perpetuate testimony, §1A-1, Rule 27, (b).
Forms.
Petition for writ, App. Proc., Appx. D.
Generally, App. Proc. Rule 21, (a).
Issuance as substitute for appeal, §1-269.
Jurisdiction.
Stay of proceedings to permit trial in foreign jurisdiction.
Review of rulings on motion, §1-75.12, (c).
Petition for writ.
Contents, App. Proc. Rule 21, (c).
Filing and service, App. Proc. Rule 21, (c).
Post-conviction matters, App. Proc. Rule 21, (e).
To which appellate court addressed, App. Proc. Rule 21, (b).
Response.
Determination by court, App. Proc. Rule 21, (d).
Scope of the writ, App. Proc. Rule 21, (a).
Supreme court.
Issuance of remedial writs, §7A-32, (b).

CERVICAL CANCER.
Accident and health insurance.
Screening for early detection.
Coverage requirements, §58-51-57, (a), (e).
Defined, §58-51-57, (a1).
Hospital, medical and dental services corporations.
Screening for early detection.
Coverage, §58-65-92.

CFC.
Containers manufactured with, restrictions, §130A-309.10, (b).

CHAIN GANGS, §§148-26, (b), 162-58.

CHAIN LETTERS.
Pyramid and chain schemes, §14-291.2.

CHAIN OF CUSTODY.
Evidence.
Courier service or common carrier, §8-103.

CHAINS.
Tire chains.
Permissible use, §20-122, (b).

CHAIN SAWS.
Mechanical breakdown service agreement, §58-1-42.

CHAIRLIFTS.
Passenger tramway safety, §§95-116 to 95-125.
See TRAMWAYS.

CHALLENGE OF JUROR.
Challenges for cause.
Civil cases, §§1A-1, Rule 47, 9-15, (c).
Criminal cases, §9-15, (c).
Appeal on grounds that challenge for cause not allowed.
Prerequisites, §15A-1214, (h).
Challenge to the panel, §15A-1211, (c).
Grounds, §15A-1212.
Renewal of challenge for cause previously denied, §15A-1214, (i).
Questioning jurors without challenge, §9-15, (a).
Valid cause for challenge, §9-15, (b).
Criminal cases.
After juror accepted but before jury impaneled, §15A-1214, (g).

CHALLENGE OF JUROR —Cont'd
Criminal cases —Cont'd
Challenge for cause, §9-15, (c).
Appeal on grounds that challenge for cause not allowed.
Prerequisites, §15A-1214, (h).
Challenge to the panel, §15A-1211, (c).
Grounds, §15A-1212.
Renewal of challenge for cause previously denied, §15A-1214, (i).
Judge to decide all challenges, §15A-1211, (b).
Peremptory challenges, §§9-21, 15A-1214, (d), (e).
Governing statutory provisions, §9-21.
Number of peremptory challenges, §15A-1217.
Peremptory challenges.
Civil cases, §9-19.
Number of peremptory challenges, §9-19.
Several defendants, §9-20.
Apportionment of challenges, §9-20.
Discretion of judge, §9-20.
Criminal cases, §§9-21, 15A-1214, (d), (e).
Governing statutory provisions, §9-21.
Number of peremptory challenges, §15A-1217.
Defendants.
Civil cases having several defendants, §9-20.
Apportionment of challenges, §9-20.
Discretion of judge, §9-20.

CHALLENGE OF VOTERS.
Absentee ballots, §163-89.
Answer to challenge as felon not to be used on prosecution, §163-90.
Burden of proof, §163-90.1, (b).
Challenge to absentee ballots, §163-89, (c).
Day of primary or election, §163-87.
Hearing, §163-88.
Request for challenged ballot, §163-88.1.
Hearings.
Challenge on day of primary or election, §163-88.
Challenge other than on day of primary or election, §163-86.
Challenge to absentee ballots, §163-89, (e).
Municipal elections, §163-289.
Notice.
Challenge on other than day of primary or election, §163-86, (d).
Oaths.
Challenge on day of primary or election, §163-88.
Challenge other than on day of primary or election, §§163-85, 163-86, (c).
False swearing, §163-90.3.
Overruled or dismissed challenge.
Action by board on, §163-90.2, (c).
Appeals, §163-90.2, (d).
Reasonable belief by challenger required, §163-90.1, (a).
Sustained challenge.
Action by board on, §163-90.2, (a), (b).
Appeals, §163-90.2, (d).
Other than day of primary or election, §163-85, (a) to (e).

CHAMBERS OF COMMERCE.
Franchise tax.
Exemption, §105-125, (a).
Securities regulation.
Exempt securities, §78A-16.

CHANGE MACHINES.
Breaking into, §14-56.3.

CHANGE OF NAME.
Abandoned child, consent of abandoning parent not required, §101-2.

CHANGE OF NAME —Cont'd
Address confidentiality program participant.
Notification of attorney general, §15C-5, (a).
Application.
Contents, §101-3.
Filing, §101-2.
Certificate, §101-5.
Clerk to order change, §101-5.
Consent of parent to change minor's name, §101-2.
Effect, §101-6.
Elections.
Registration of voters, §163-82.16.
General but not private law, §101-1.
Good character, proof filed with petition, §101-4.
Hospital authorities, §131E-19, (c).
Joinder of application to change minor's name with parent's application, §101-2.
Marriage licenses.
Amendment of license, §51-18.1, (b).
Minors.
Procedure, §101-2.
Two change limitation, §101-6, (b).
One change only, §101-6, (a).
Exception from minors, §101-6, (b).
Petition.
Contents of application, §101-3.
Filing application, §101-2.
Procedure, §101-2.
Professional employer organizations, §58-89A-80, (b).
Proof of good character, filed with petition, §101-4.
Recordation, §§101-5, 101-7.
Secured transactions.
Financing statement.
Effect of change of name, §25-9-507, (c).
Special proceedings, §§101-1 to 101-8.
Substance abuse professionals.
Certification or registration, §90-113.41B.
Venue.
Filing application, §101-2.
Widow or widower.
Resumption of name, §101-8.

CHANGE OF VENUE.
Affidavits.
Application for removal, §1-85.
Conflicts of interest.
Judge interested as party or counsel, §1-83.
Costs.
Liability of counties where trial removed from one county to another, §6-40.
Criminal procedure.
Motion for change of venue, §15A-957.
Divorce, §1-83.
General provisions, §§1-76 to 1-87.
See VENUE.
Grounds, §1-83.
Incompetence, determination of.
Hardship or prejudice to respondent, §35A-1104.
Judges.
Interest as party or counsel, §1-83.
Removal for fair trial, §1-84.
Affidavits on hearing, §1-85.
Order for removal, §1-85.
Subsequent proceedings, §1-87, (b).
Transcript of record, §1-87, (a).
Witnesses.
Convenience of witnesses, §1-83.

CHANGES AFFECTING VOTING.
Voting rights act of 1965.
Submissions to attorney general of United States, §§120-30.9A to 120-30.9I.

CHANNEL BASS.
State saltwater fish, §145-6.

CHAPEL HILL.
Traffic control photographic systems, §160A-300.1, (d).

CHAPEL HILL TELEPHONE COMPANY.
Retirement system for teachers and state employees.
Eligibility for benefits, §135-5.2.

CHAPELS.
Burning of churches and certain other religious buildings, §14-62.2.
Churches generally.
See CHURCHES.
Malicious use of explosive or incendiary, §14-49, (b1).

CHAPLAINS.
Clergymen.
See CLERGYMEN.
Prisons and prisoners.
Employment of clinical chaplains, §148-10.1.

CHARACTER EDUCATION.
Public schools, §115C-81, (h).

CHARACTER EVIDENCE.
Accused's character, §8C-1, Rule 404, (a).
Credibility of witness attacked or supported, §8C-1, Rule 608.
Hearsay exception, reputation, §8C-1, Rule 803.
Juvenile's character.
Other crimes, wrongs or acts, §8C-1, Rule 404, (b).
Methods of proving character, §8C-1, Rule 405.
Not admissible to prove conduct.
Exceptions, §8C-1, Rule 404, (a).
Opinion, §8C-1, Rule 405, (a).
Other crimes, wrongs or acts, §8C-1, Rule 404, (b).
Reputation, §8C-1, Rule 405, (a).
Specific instances of conduct, §8C-1, Rule 405, (b).
Victim's character, §8C-1, Rule 404, (a).
Witness's character, §8C-1, Rule 404, (a).

CHARCOAL.
Standard weights and measures, §81A-42.

CHARGE ACCOUNTS.
Powers of attorney.
Powers conferred by statutory short form, §32A-2.
Revolving charge account contracts.
Collateral.
Inapplicability of provisions, §25A-23, (d).
Defined, §25A-11.
Finance charge.
Default or deferral charges, §25A-14, (c).
Insurance.
Additional charges for insurance, §25A-17, (b).
Rates, §25A-14, (a).
Security interest.
Rates, §25A-14, (b).
Security interests.
Finance charges, §25A-14, (b).

CHARGE CARDS.
Credit cards generally.
See CREDIT CARDS.

CHARGE CARDS —Cont'd
Credit device fraud.
See CREDIT DEVICE FRAUD.
Disclosure requirements, §24-11.2.
Applicability, §24-11.2, (a).
Construction and interpretation, §24-11.2, (f).
Federal requirements, §24-11.2, (c).
Generally, §24-11.2, (b).
Penalty for violation, §24-11.2, (d).
Severability of provisions, §24-11.2, (e).

CHARGE OF COURT.
Instructions.
See INSTRUCTIONS TO JURY.

CHARGE REDUCTIONS.
Criminal law and procedure.
Witnesses, §15A-1054.

CHARITABLE CONTRIBUTIONS INCOME TAX CREDIT.
Individual income tax.
Nonitemizers, §105-151.26.

CHARITABLE GIFT ANNUITIES.
Authorized, §58-3-6, (a).
Definition of education institution, §58-3-6, (f).
Enforcement by insurance department, §58-3-6, (d).
Information to insurance commissioner, §58-3-6, (c).
Issuance not business of insurance, §58-3-6, (e).
Notice to insurance department, §58-3-6, (b).

CHARITABLE IMMUNITY, §1-539.11.
Abolition of common law defense, §1-539.9.

CHARITABLE SOLICITATION, §§131F-1 to 131F-24.
Actions to enforce chapter.
Attorney general bringing, §131F-24, (a).
Department bringing, §131F-23, (c).
Voluntary compliance.
Termination of enforcement action, §131F-24, (c).
Adoption of rules.
Rule-making authority, §131F-33.
Annual report, §131F-30, (c).
Attorney general.
Civil action to enforce chapter, §131F-24, (a).
Investigations by, §131F-24, (b).
Voluntary compliance.
Termination of investigation or enforcement action, §131F-24, (c).
Charitable contributions to governmental agencies.
Exemption from chapter, §131F-3.
Collection of contributions in name of charitable organization or sponsor, §131F-16, (i).
Community trust.
Exemption from chapter, §131F-3.
Continuing care retirement communities.
Exemption of nonprofit facility from provisions, §131F-3.
Conventurers conducting sales promotion.
Accounting prepared by, §131F-18, (c).
Consent from organization or sponsor.
Required prior to conducting, §131F-18, (a).
Conventurers defined, §131F-2.
Disclosures in advertising.
Adoption of rules by department, §131F-18, (b).
Prohibited acts, §131F-20.

CHARITABLE SOLICITATION —Cont'd
Deceptive or unfair trade practices.
Violation of act so designated, §131F-21.
Definitions, §131F-2.
Deposits of contributions.
Duty of solicitor, §131F-16, (i).
Disclosures by organization or sponsor, §131F-9, (b), (c).
Disclosures by solicitors, §131F-17, (a).
Distribution of contributions.
Power of attorney general to seek, §131F-24, (a).
Educational institution contributions.
Exemption from chapter, §131F-3.
Exemptions from chapter.
Enumerated, §131F-3.
Expressed purpose set forth in license application.
Solicitation only for, §131F-9, (a).
Fees.
Licensing, §131F-8, (a) to (d).
Fund-raising consultants, §131F-15, (c), (f).
Fund-raising consultants.
Change in information, reporting, §131F-15, (g).
Contracts or agreements, requirements, §131F-15, (d).
Licensing.
Application, §131F-15, (b).
Partnership or corporation acting as, §131F-15, (c).
Examination of application by department, §131F-15, (e).
Failure to satisfy requirements, notice, hearing, §131F-15, (e).
Fees, §131F-15, (c).
Deposited in solicitation of contributions find, §131F-15, (f).
Partnership or corporation acting as, §131F-15, (c).
Required to act as, §131F-15, (a).
Prohibited acts, §131F-20.
Hospital contributions.
Exemption from chapter, §131F-3.
Injunctions.
Power of attorney general to seek, §131F-24, (a).
Power of department to seek, §131F-23, (c).
Investigations by attorney general, §131F-24, (b).
Voluntary compliance.
Termination, §131F-24, (c).
Investigations by department, §131F-23, (a).
Legislative intent, §131F-1.
Licensing.
Fund-raising consultants, §131F-15, (a) to (g).
Organizations, sponsors or individuals, §§131F-5 to 131F-8.
Solicitor's license, §131F-16, (a) to (n).
Masters.
Power of attorney general to seek appointment, §131F-24, (a).
Named individual trust accounts.
Required, §131F-31, (a).
Use of trust funds, §131F-31, (b).
Noncommercial radio or television contributions.
Exemption from chapter, §131F-3.
Notice of solicitation.
Solicitor to give, §131F-16, (f).
Organizations, sponsors or individuals.
Disclosures, §131F-9, (b).
Printed on solicitation or contribution, §131F-9, (c).

CHARITABLE SOLICITATION —Cont'd
Organizations, sponsors or individuals —Cont'd
Licensing.
Consolidated application.
Election to file, §131F-7, (a).
Examination of license application, §131F-5, (b).
Extension of time.
Renewal or updating information, §131F-5, (d).
Fees.
Exemption from payment, §131F-8, (b).
Late filing fee.
Failure to file renewal information on time, §131F-8, (d).
Schedule of required fees, §131F-8, (a).
Parent organization or association filing, §131F-8, (c).
Financial report required, §131F-6, (a).
Consolidated report, §131F-7, (b).
Information required, §131F-6, (a), (b).
License requirements not satisfied, notice, hearing, decision, §131F-5, (b).
Renewal, §131F-5, (c).
Extensions of time, §131F-5, (d).
Information required, §131F-6, (b).
Consolidated form, §131F-7, (c).
Late filing fee, failure to file on time, §131F-8, (d).
Required of organization, sponsor or person, §131F-5, (a).
Public information.
Generally, §131F-30, (a).
Included information, §131F-30, (b).
Purpose expressed in license application.
Solicitation only for, §131F-9, (a).
Purpose of act, §131F-1.
Receivers.
Power of attorney general to seek appointment, §131F-24, (a).
Power of department to seek appointment of, §131F-23, (c).
Records, §131F-32.
Religious institution charitable solicitation.
Exemption from chapter, §131F-3.
Rules and regulations, §131F-33.
Sales promotions conducted by coventurers.
Accounting prepared by, §131F-18, (c).
Consent from organization or sponsor.
Required prior to conducting, §131F-18, (a).
Disclosures in advertising.
Adoption of rules by department, §131F-18, (b).
Sequestration of assets.
Power of attorney general to seek, §131F-24, (a).
Solicitors.
Bond, §131F-16, (d).
Certificate of deposit in lieu of bond, §131F-16, (d1).
Change of information filed with department, §131F-16, (m).
Collection of contribution in name of charitable organization or sponsor, §131F-16, (i).
Contract or agreement with charitable organization, §131F-16, (g).
Deposit of contribution, §131F-16, (i).
Disclosures, §131F-17, (a).
Financial report of campaigns, §131F-16, (h).
Licensing.
Applications, §131F-16, (b).
Bonds, §131F-16, (d).
Examination of applications by department, §131F-16, (e).

CHARITABLE SOLICITATION —Cont'd
Solicitors —Cont'd
Licensing —Cont'd
Fees, §131F-16, (c).
Permanent loss of license, grounds, §131F-16, (n).
Required, §131F-16, (a).
Notice of solicitation, §131F-16, (f).
Prohibited acts, §131F-20.
Recordkeeping requirements, §131F-16, (j).
Review of records, §131F-16, (l).
Tickets, §131F-16, (k).
Tickets.
Donation for use by another person, representing, §131F-17, (b).
Recordkeeping, §131F-16, (k).
Subpoenas and subpoenas duces tecum.
Noncompliance with, §131F-23, (c).
Power of department to issue, §131F-23, (b).
Tickets.
Donation for use by another person.
Solicitor representing, §131F-17, (b).
Records, §131F-16, (k).
Violations of act, §131F-23, (d).
Criminal penalties, §131F-22.
Deceptive or unfair trade practice designation, §131F-21.
Penalties, §§131F-23, (e) to (g), 131F-24, (a).
Voluntary compliance.
Termination of investigation or enforcement action, §131F-24, (c).
Volunteer fire and rescue squad contributions.
Exemption from chapter, §131F-3.

CHARITABLE TRUSTS, §§36A-47 to 36A-54.
Accounts.
Action for account, §36A-48.
Trustees to file accounts, §36A-47.
Administration act, §36A-53.
Amendments, §36A-54, (b).
Estate tax deductions, §36A-53, (b).
Applicability of provisions.
Other states, §36A-51.
Attorney general.
Investigations, §36A-48.
Cemetery trusts.
Rule against perpetuities not invalidating, §36A-49.
Charitable.
Defined, §36A-53, (c).
Charitable trusts administration act.
General provisions, §36A-53.
Charity.
Defined, §36A-53, (c).
Construction with other acts, §36A-52, (d).
Contents of governing instrument, §36A-54, (a1).
Conveyances.
Effect as to conveyance by trustee, §39-26.
Declaration of policy, §36A-52, (a).
Enforcement, §36A-52, (c).
Court to enforce trust, §36A-48.
Federal estate tax deductions, §36A-53, (b).
Illegal trusts.
Administration, §36A-53, (a).
Impracticable of fulfillment.
Defined, §36A-53, (d).
Indefiniteness.
Gifts, etc., not to be void, §36A-52, (b).
Not void, §36A-49.

CHARITABLE TRUSTS —Cont'd
Mandamus.
Method of enforcement, §36A-52, (c).
Other states.
Application of law, §36A-51.
Validity of trusts created, §36A-50.
Personal property.
Section inapplicable to property granted by deed, will, etc., §36A-47.
Prudent investor act.
Effect on charitable remainder trusts, §36A-170.
Real property.
Section inapplicable to property granted by deed, will, etc., §36A-47.
Remainder trusts administration, §§36A-59.1 to 36A-59.7.
Annuity trusts and unitrusts.
Creation of remainder interests in charity, §36A-59.4, (a).
Distribution from trust used to administer an estate to charitable remainder trust, §36A-59.4, (f).
Distribution to charity during term of noncharitable interest and distributions in kind, §36A-59.4, (d).
Investment restrictions on trustee, §36A-59.4, (e).
Noncharitable beneficiaries.
Payment of taxes by noncharitable beneficiary, §36A-59.4, (g).
Payment of taxes by noncharitable beneficiaries, §36A-59.4, (g).
Prohibitions governing trustees, §36A-59.4, (c).
Selection of alternate charitable beneficiary if remaindermen do not qualify, §36A-59.4, (b).
Failure of remaindermen to qualify under section 170(b) (1) (A) of code at time of distribution, §36A-59.4, (b1).
Taxation.
Payment of taxes by noncharitable beneficiary, §36A-59.4, (g).
Annuity trusts only.
Additional contributions prohibited, §36A-59.5, (c).
Annuity amount may be allocated among class of noncharitable beneficiaries, §36A-59.5, (f).
Computation of annuity amount in short and final taxable years, §36A-59.5, (b).
Creation of annuity amount for period of years or life, §36A-59.5, (a).
Deferral of annuity amount during period of administration or settlement, §36A-59.5, (d).
Dollar amount annuity may be stated at fraction or percentage, §36A-59.5, (e).
Reduction of annuity amount if part of corpus is paid to charity, §36A-59.5, (g).
Retention of testamentary power to revoke noncharitable interest, §36A-59.5, (i).
Termination of annuity amount on payment date preceding termination of interest, §36A-59.5, (h).
Citation of article, §36A-59.1.
Construction of article, §36A-59.7.
Definitions, §36A-59.3.
General rule, §36A-59.2.
Interpretation of article, §36A-59.7.
Rules and regulations.
General rule, §36A-59.2.
Short title, §36A-59.1.

CHARITABLE TRUSTS —Cont'd
Remainder trusts administration —Cont'd
Unitrusts only.
Additional contributions, §36A-59.6, (e).
Adjustment of incorrect valuation, §36A-59.6, (c).
Allocation of amount among class of noncharitable beneficiaries in discretion of trustee, §36A-59.6, (g).
Computation of unitrust amount in short and final taxable years, §36A-59.6, (d).
Creation of unitrust amount for a period of years or life, §36A-59.6, (a).
Deferral of unitrust amount during period of administration or settlement, §36A-59.6, (f).
Reduction of amount if part of corpus is paid to charity at expiration of term, §36A-59.6, (h).
Retention of testamentary power to revoke interest, §36A-59.6, (j).
Termination of amount on payment date preceding termination of interests, §36A-59.6, (i).
Unitrust amount expressed as the lesser of income or fixed percentage, §36A-59.6, (b).
Rule against perpetuities.
Cemetery trust not invalidated by, §36A-49.
Taxation.
Exempt status, §36A-54, (a).
References to code, §36A-54, (c).
Title.
Legal title and trustee, §36A-49.
Trusts or wills executed before December 31, 1977.
Administration, §36A-53, (b).
Vacancies, §36A-49.
Validity.
Trusts created in other states, §36A-50.

CHARITIES.
Alcoholic beverage permits.
Special one-time permits, §18B-1002, (a).
Alcoholic beverages furnished to inmates of charitable institutions, §14-258.1, (b).
Amusements.
License taxes.
Exemption, §105-40.
Annuities.
Charitable gift annuities, §58-3-6.
Appropriations.
Additional to receipts, §143-27.
Auctions and auctioneers.
Exemptions from auction provisions, §85B-2.
Bingo.
General provisions, §§14-309.5 to 14-309.14.
See BINGO.
Purposes of conduct of bingo games, §14-309.5.
Cartridges or ammunition for firearms.
Furnishing to inmates of charitable institutions, §14-258.1, (a).
Charitable immunity, §1-539.11.
Common law defense abolished, §1-539.9.
Community colleges.
Contributions to organizations approved by community college board.
Deduction from employee's salary or wage, §143-3.3, (i).
Controlled substances.
Furnishing substances to inmates of charitable institutions, §14-258.1, (a).

CHARITIES —Cont'd
Conventurers conducting sales promotion.
Accounting prepared by, §131F-18, (c).
Consent from organization or sponsor.
Required prior to conducting, §131F-18, (a).
Disclosures in advertising.
Adoption of rules by department, §131F-18, (b).
Conveyances.
Authorized, §39-25.
Effect as to conveyances by trustees, §39-26.
Prior deeds validated, §39-27.
Corporations.
Exemptions from business corporation act, §§55-3-01, (b), 55-17-01, (b).
Management of institutional funds, §§36B-1 to 36B-10.
See MANAGEMENT OF INSTITUTIONAL FUNDS.
Deeds.
Prior deeds validated, §39-27.
Definitions.
Charitable organizations, §1-539.11.
Soliciting charitable contributions by telephone, §14-401.12, (b).
Volunteers, §1-539.11.
Donated food.
Immunity for, §99B-10.
Inspections by department of agriculture and consumer services, §106-141.1.
Drugs.
Controlled substances.
Furnishing to inmates of charitable institutions, §14-258.1, (a).
Embezzlement.
Funds embezzled by public officers and trustees, §14-92.
Treasurers of charitable organizations, §14-93.
Establishment and operation by state, Const. N. C., art. XI, §3.
Franchise tax.
Exemptions, §105-125, (a).
Fund-raising.
Solicitation of contributions generally, §§131F-1 to 131F-24.
See CHARITABLE SOLICITATION.
Gift tax.
Exemptions, §105-188, (h).
Handicapped persons.
Governor's council on employment of the handicapped.
Council to be nonpartisan and nonprofit, §143-283.8.
Hospitals.
Property tax exemptions.
Property used for charitable hospital purposes, §105-278.8.
Immunities.
Defense of charitable immunity abolished, §1-539.9.
Volunteers for charitable organizations, §1-539.10, (a) to (c).
Definitions, §1-539.11.
Income tax on corporations.
Contributions.
Deductions, §105-130.9.
Exemption of charitable corporations, §105-130.11, (a), (b).
Income tax on individuals.
Credit for charitable contributions by nonitemizers, §105-151.26.

CHARITIES —Cont'd
Institutional funds.
Management of institutional funds, §§36B-1 to 36B-10.
See MANAGEMENT OF INSTITUTIONAL FUNDS.
Licensing, §§131F-5 to 131F-8.
Life insurance.
Insurable interest of charitable organizations, §58-58-86, (a), (b).
Management of institutional funds, §§36B-1 to 36B-10.
See MANAGEMENT OF INSTITUTIONAL FUNDS.
Municipal corporations.
Regulation of solicitation campaigns, §160A-178.
Nonprofit corporations.
Certain associations deemed incorporated, §55A-17-02.
General provisions, §§55A-1-01 to 55A-17-05.
Poisons.
Furnishing poison to inmates of charitable institution, §14-258.1, (a).
Possibility of reverter, right of entry or executory interest.
Time limit.
Inapplicability to charity, §41-32, (b).
Property taxes.
Exemptions, §105-275.
Agencies which may obtain exemption, §§105-278.6, (a), 105-278.7, (c).
Property used for charitable hospital purposes, §105-278.8.
Property used for charitable purposes, §§105-278.6, 105-278.7.
Public officers and employees.
Deductions from salary or wages.
Local boards of education or community colleges.
Charitable organizations approved by, §143-3.3, (i).
University of North Carolina constituent institutions.
Charitable organization approved by, §143-3.3, (j).
Public schools.
Charitable organization approved by local board of education.
Contributions.
Deduction from local board employee's salary or wage, §143-3.3, (i).
Real property.
Authority to acquire and hold, §39-24.
Conveyances.
Authorized, §39-25.
Effect as to conveyance by trustees, §39-26.
Prior deeds validated, §39-27.
Probate, §39-25.
Trustees.
Effect as to conveyance by trustee, §39-26.
Vesting title, §39-25.
Sales and use tax.
Contributions deductible as charitable contributions.
Exemption, §105-164.13.
Refunds.
Nonprofit organizations, §105-164.14, (b).
Sales promotion conducted by coventurers.
Accounting prepared by, §131F-18, (c).
Consent from organization or sponsor.
Required prior to conducting, §131F-18, (a).

CHARITIES —Cont'd
Sales promotion conducted by coventurers —Cont'd
Disclosures in advertising.
Adoption of rules by department, §131F-18, (b).
Securities regulation.
Exempt securities, §78A-16.
Solicitation of funds, §§131F-1 to 131F-24.
See CHARITABLE SOLICITATION.
State debt.
Educational and charitable institutions.
Interest.
Reimbursement of treasurer for interest, §142-15.
State of North Carolina.
Establishment and operation of charitable and correctional institutions and agencies by state, Const. N. C., art. XI, §3.
Tax exemption, Const. N. C., art. V, §2.
Telephones.
Soliciting charitable contributions by telephone.
Definitions, §14-401.12, (b).
Misdemeanor, §14-401.12, (a).
Section construed, §14-401.12, (c).
Treasurers.
Embezzlement by treasurers of charitable organizations, §14-93.
Trusts and trustees.
Charitable trust, §§36A-47 to 36A-54.
See CHARITABLE TRUSTS.
Conveyances.
Effect as to conveyance by trustee, §39-26.
University of North Carolina.
Charitable organization approved by constituent institution.
Contributions.
Deduction from employee's salary or wage, §143-3.3, (j).
Volunteers for charitable organizations.
Immunity, §1-539.10, (a).
Definitions, §1-539.11.
Liability insurance, waiver, §1-539.10, (b).
Professional services, standard of care or liability not altered, §1-539.10, (c).
Weapons.
Furnishing deadly weapons to inmates of charitable institutions, §14-258.1, (a).

CHARLES B. AYCOCK MEMORIAL COMMISSION.
Department of cultural resources.
Transfer of commission to department, §143B-51.

CHARLOTTE, CITY OF.
Private parking lots.
Removal of unauthorized vehicles, §20-219.2.
Traffic control photographic systems, §160A-300.1, (d).

CHARON COUNTY.
Acquisition of property, power, §153A-158.1, (a).

CHARTER SCHOOLS, §§115C-238.29A to 115C-238.29K.
Admission requirements, §115C-238.29F, (g).
Advisory committee, §115C-238.29I, (d).
Alternative timeline for submissions, §115C-238.29I, (e).
Application, §115C-238.29B, (b) to (d).
Assistance to applicants and potential applicants, §115C-238.29J, (c).
Final approval, §115C-238.29D.
Conditional approval, §115C-238.29D, (c).

CHARTER SCHOOLS —Cont'd
Application —Cont'd
Final approval —Cont'd
Limitations on number of approved schools, §115C-238.29D, (b).
Standards, §115C-238.29D, (a).
Material revision, approval required, §115C-238.29D, (d).
Preliminary approval, §115C-238.29C.
Appeal process, §115C-238.29C, (c).
Standards, §115C-238.29C, (b).
Time period, §115C-238.29C, (a).
Submission for preliminary approval, §115C-238.29B, (c).
Assets, §115C-238.29F, (i).
Audits, §115C-238.29F, (f).
Board of directors, §115C-238.29E, (d).
Contract, §115C-238.29E, (c).
Conversion of existing public schools, §115C-238.29B, (a).
Course of instruction, §115C-238.29F, (d).
Criminal history checks.
Definitions, §115C-238.29K, (a).
Determination based on results.
Duty of state board, §115C-238.29K, (d).
Notification to board of directors of schools, §115C-238.29K, (e).
Findings made by state board, §115C-238.29K, (d).
Supplying board of directors of school, §115C-238.29K, (e).
Immunity for carrying out provisions, §115C-238.29K, (g).
Notification to board of directors of schools.
Determination based on results made by state board, §115C-238.29K, (e).
Privileged nature of information, §115C-238.29K, (f).
Release or disclosure of personnel's criminal history.
Prohibition, §115C-238.29K, (e).
Review of results by state board, §115C-238.29K, (d).
State board of education.
Duties, §115C-238.29K, (b) to (e).
Definitions.
Criminal history checks, §115C-238.29K, (a).
Department of revenue.
Change in school status.
Notice to department, §115C-238.29J, (d).
Driving eligibility certificates.
Designee of board of directors, duties, §115C-238.29F, (j).
Employees, §115C-238.29F, (e).
Criminal history checks, §115C-238.29K.
Exemption from various statutes and rules, §115C-238.29E, (f).
Flu and meningitis and vaccine information.
Information provided parents and guardians, §115C-238.29F, (a).
Funding, §115C-238.29H, (a), (a1).
Grievance procedures.
State board of education to develop, §115C-238.29G, (b).
Health and safety standards, §115C-238.29F, (a).
Increase in enrollment.
Material revision of charter application requiring approval, §115C-238.29D, (d).
Insurance, §115C-238.29F, (c).
Liability to civil suit, §115C-238.29F, (c).
Local board of education.
Accountability of charter schools to, §115C-238.29E, (a).

CHARTER SCHOOLS —Cont'd
Location, §115C-238.29E, (e).
Mediation.
Differences between charter school and state board, §115C-238.29G, (c).
Medical plan for teachers and state employees.
Participation by charter school operated by nonprofit corporation.
Election by board of directors, §135-40.3A, (a), (b).
Effect of election or failure to elect, §135-40.3A, (c), (d).
Notification to employees, §135-40.3A, (e).
Premium rates.
Total of amount of premiums, §135-39.6A, (e).
Motor fuel excise tax exemption, §105-449.88.
Nonrenewal of charter, §115C-238.29G, (a).
Nonsectarian requirement, §115C-238.29F, (b).
Number authorized per year, §115C-238.29D, (b).
Operation.
Private nonprofit corporations, §115C-238.29E, (b).
Per pupil local current expense appropriations.
Transfer to charter school for students attending, §115C-238.29H, (b).
Private contributions, §115C-238.29J, (b).
Private nonprofit corporations establishing, §115C-238.29B, (a).
Public assistance from local school administrative units, §115C-238.29J, (a).
Publicity to local community, §115C-238.29I.
Purpose, §115C-238.29A.
Renewal of charter, §115C-238.29D, (d).
Nonrenewal or termination, §115C-238.29G, (a).
Reporting requirements, §115C-238.29F.
Report to joint legislative education oversight committee.
State board recommendations to modify, expand or terminate approach, §115C-238.29I, (c).
Retirement system for teachers and state employees.
Creditable service.
Credit for employment in charter school operated by private nonprofit corporation, §135-4, (cc).
Participation by charter school operated by nonprofit corporation.
Election by board of directors, §135-5.3, (a), (b).
Effect of election or failure to elect, §135-5.3, (c), (d).
Notification to employees, §135-5.3, (e).
Review and evaluation of charter school approach.
Duty of state board, §115C-238.29I, (c).
Teachers, §115C-238.29F, (e).
Termination of charter, §115C-238.29G, (a).
Term of initial charter, §115C-238.29D, (c).
Transportation, §115C-238.29F, (h).

CHARTERS OF CORPORATIONS, Const. N. C., art. VIII, §8.
Counterfeiting.
Forfeiture, §14-15.
Kidnapping.
Forfeiture, §14-39.

CHARTERS OF MUNICIPAL CORPORATIONS.
Amendments.
By ordinance, §160A-102.
Charter to remain in force, §160A-110.
Referendum, §160A-103.

CHARTERS OF MUNICIPAL CORPORATIONS —Cont'd
Amendments —Cont'd
Copies.
Filing, §160A-111.
Effective date, §160A-109.
Filing copies, §160A-111.
Initiative petition, §160A-104.
Plan to continue for two years, §160A-107.
Officers to carry out plan, §160A-108.
Provisions dependent on form of government, §160A-106.
Applicability of provisions, §160A-82.
Code sections and conflict repealed, §160A-77, (c).
Construction, §160A-4.
Defined, §160A-1.
Effect of provisions upon prior laws, §160A-2.
General laws.
Alternative procedure, §160A-3, (a).
Superseding charter, §160A-3, (c).
Supplementary charters, §160A-3, (b).
Incorporation into charter.
Definition of "charter," §160A-496, (c).
Local acts.
Incorporation into charter, §160A-496, (a), (b).
Name, §160A-11.
New form of government.
Charter to remain in force, §160A-110.

CHARTERS OF TRUST COMPANIES, §§53-330 to 53-365.
See TRUST COMPANIES.

CHASES BY POLICE OF VIOLATORS OF LAW.
Speed limits not applicable, §20-145.

CHATHAM COUNTY.
Ambulance services.
Attachment or garnishment and lien for, §§44-51.4 to 44-51.8.
False pretenses and cheats.
Obtaining ambulance services without intending to pay, §14-111.2.
Condemnation or acquisition of land by local government unit outside county.
Consent of board of commissioners necessary, §153A-15.
Counties generally.
See COUNTIES.
Cropper or tenant refusing to perform terms of contract.
Forfeiture of right of possession to premises, §42-27.
Dogs used in hunting.
Regulation by wildlife resources commission, §113-291.5, (a).
False pretenses and cheats.
Ambulance services.
Obtaining services without intending to pay, §14-111.2.
Game laws, local acts not repealed, §113-133.1, (e).
Oil, gas or mineral interest, extinguished, title in surface fee holder.
Failure to list interest for tax purposes for 10 years prior to January 1, 1979, §1-42.7, (a) to (c).
Protection of interest from surface fee holder, §1-42.7, (b), (d).
On-premises unfortified wine licenses.
Discretion to decline to issue, §105-113.71, (b).

CHATHAM COUNTY —Cont'd
Special school tax, election to abolish.
Petition required, §115C-505.

CHATTEL MORTGAGES.
Corporations.
Forms of probate for deeds and other conveyances, §47-41.02, (f).
Costs.
Attorneys' fees in addition to interest, §6-21.2.
Insurance companies.
Investments in chattel mortgages, §58-7-180, (a) to (d).
Valuation of personal property acquired, §58-7-193, (c).
Registration, §47-20.
Secured transactions, §§25-9-101 to 25-9-710.
See COMMERCIAL CODE.
Tobacco.
Leaf tobacco sold in auction.
Effective period for lien, §44-69.

CHATTEL PAPER.
Secured transactions.
Perfection of security interests in, §25-9-312.
Purchaser of chattel paper.
Priority, §25-9-330.

CHEATING.
Education.
Academic credit obtained by fraudulent means, §14-118.2.
False pretenses and cheats.
See FALSE PRETENSES AND CHEATS.

CHECK-CASHING BUSINESSES, §§53-275 to 53-289.
Advancing money on security of check.
Requirements, §53-280, (b).
Banks and other financial institutions.
Exemptions to provisions, §53-277, (a).
Books, accounts and records, §53-282, (a).
Examination by commissioner, §53-282, (c).
Definitions, §53-275.
Delayed deposit checks, §53-281.
Deposit of check cashed for fee.
Time, §53-280, (b).
Endorsement of instrument presented by licensee for payment, §53-280, (d).
Examination by commissioner.
Books, accounts and records, §53-282, (c).
Exemptions.
Banks and other financial institutions, §53-277, (a).
Money transmitters, §53-277, (b).
Retailer incidentally cashing checks, §53-277, (a).
Fees.
License applications, §53-278, (c).
Service fees, §53-280, (a).
Notice of fees charged, posting, §53-280, (c).
Government checks.
Fee for cashing, §53-280, (a).
Hearings.
Denial of license, §53-279, (b).
Incidental to retailers business.
Exemptions to provisions, §53-277, (a).
Investigation for licenses, §53-278, (b).
Licenses.
Application, §53-278, (a).
Fee, §53-278, (c).
Denial of license, §53-279, (b).
Hearing, §53-279, (b).
Issuance, findings required, §53-279, (b).

CHECK-CASHING BUSINESSES —Cont'd
Licenses —Cont'd
Liquid assets requirement, §53-279, (a).
Posting at place of business, §53-280, (c).
Requirement, §53-276.
Suspension or revocation.
Grounds, §53-284, (a).
Notice and opportunity for hearing required, §53-284, (b).
Money orders.
Fee for cashing, §53-280, (a).
Money transmitters.
Exemptions to provisions, §53-277, (b).
Personal checks.
Fee for cashing, §53-280, (a).
Postdated checks, §53-281.
Privilege tax, §105-88.
Prohibited acts, §53-283.
Cease and desist orders, §53-285.
Civil penalty, §53-286.
Criminal penalty, §53-287.
Receipts, customer provided, §53-282, (b).
Restitution.
Prohibited acts, §53-286.
Rules.
Adoption, §53-288.
Review of, §53-289.
Service fees, §53-280, (a).
Notice of fees charged, posting, §53-280, (c).
Taxation.
Privilege tax, §105-88.
Time.
Deposit of checked cashed for fee, §53-280, (b).

CHECK GUARANTEE CARDS.
Credit cards.
See CREDIT CARDS.
Financial transaction card crimes, §§14-113.8 to 14-113.17.
See FINANCIAL TRANSACTION CARDS.

CHECK LOAN.
Interest and service charges, §24-11, (b).

CHECKOFFS.
Income tax refund contributions.
Candidates financing fund, §105-269.6.
Wildlife conservation account, §105-269.5.

CHECKS.
Accord and satisfaction.
Use of negotiable instrument, §25-3-311.
Bad checks.
See BAD CHECKS.
Banks.
Exchange.
Payable in exchange, §53-71.
Exemptions.
Checks in payment of obligations due state or federal government, §53-73.
False certification of check.
Penalty, §53-131.
Fees on remittances covering checks.
Prohibited, §53-70.
Payable in exchange, §53-71.
Exemptions.
Checks in payment of obligations due state and federal government, §53-73.
Remittances covering checks.
Fees not to be charged, §53-70.
Check-cashing businesses, §§53-275 to 53-289.
See CHECK-CASHING BUSINESSES.

CHECKS —Cont'd
Costs for returned checks.
Remedies for returned check, §6-21.3, (b).
Damages.
Remedies for returned check, §6-21.3, (a), (d).
Defenses.
Returned checks.
Affirmative defense, §6-21.3, (c).
Electronic transactions.
Retention of electronic records, §66-322, (e).
Embezzlement, §14-90.
Employment security.
Uncertified check in payment of contribution.
Penalty, §96-10, (h).
Reduction or waiver of penalty, §96-10, (j).
Fees.
Remittances covering checks.
Banks and trust companies not to charge fees, §53-70.
Fiduciaries.
Checks drawn payable to third persons, §32-6.
Deposit in fiduciary's personal account.
Check drawn by fiduciary upon account, §32-10.
Deposit in name of fiduciary.
Payment by bank upon check of fiduciary, §32-8.
Deposit in name of principal.
Check drawn upon account of principal and bank by fiduciary, §32-9.
Payable to fiduciary, §32-7.
Forgery, §14-119.
Larceny of choses in action, §14-75.
Leaf tobacco warehouses.
Purchases to be paid for by cash or check to order, §106-455.
Letters of notification and demand.
Returned checks, §6-21.3, (a1), (a2).
Loans.
Unsolicited checks to secure loans, §75-20.
Money transmitters.
Check-cashing businesses, §§53-275 to 53-289.
See CHECK-CASHING BUSINESSES.
Generally, §§53-208.1 to 53-208.30.
See MONEY TRANSMITTERS.
Motor vehicles.
Bad check in payment of fee or tax, §20-178.
Negotiable instruments generally, §§25-3-101 to 25-3-605.
See NEGOTIABLE INSTRUMENTS.
Payment in full.
Accord and satisfaction.
Use of negotiable instrument, §25-3-311.
Powers of attorney.
Powers conferred by statutory short form, §32A-2.
Releases.
Accord and satisfaction.
Use of negotiable instrument, §25-3-311.
Remedies.
Returned checks, §6-21.3.
Returned checks.
Collection of processing fee, §25-3-506.
Remedies for returned check, §6-21.3.
Saving and loan associations.
Fees, §54B-147.
Savings banks.
Processing fee, §54C-168.
Sale of goods, UCC.
Payment by check, §25-2-511, (3).
Savings banks.
Returned checks.
Processing fee, §54C-168.

CHECKS —Cont'd
Simulation.
Prohibited, §75-35.
Taxation.
Bad checks in payment, §§105-236, 105-357, (b).
Property taxes.
Payment of taxes.
Acceptance of checks, §105-357, (b).
Bad checks.
Penalty, §105-357, (b).
Tobacco warehouses.
Purchases of leaf tobacco to be paid for by cash or check to order, §106-455.
Trusts and trustees.
Deposit in names of two or more trustees.
Checks drawn upon trust account.
Duty to inquire as to breach of trust, §32-11.
Unclaimed property generally, §§116B-51 to 116B-80.
See UNCLAIMED PROPERTY.
Worthless checks.
See BAD CHECKS.

CHEESE FACTORIES.
Inspections generally, §§106-246 to 106-255.
See ICE CREAM PLANTS, CREAMERIES AND CHEESE FACTORIES.

CHEMICAL ANALYSIS OF IMPAIRING SUBSTANCES IN BLOOD.
Generally.
See IMPAIRED DRIVING.

CHEMICAL DEPENDENCY.
Accident and health insurance.
Coverage for treatment, §58-51-50, (a) to (e).
Group accident and health insurance.
Contracts to cover, §58-51-50, (b).
Coverage not required, §58-51-55, (c).
Definition of "chemical dependency," §58-51-55, (a).
Discrimination prohibited, §58-51-55, (b), (c).
Chiropractors.
Grounds for disciplinary action, §90-154, (b).
Health maintenance organizations.
Contracts to cover treatment, §58-67-70, (a) to (f).
Coverage not required, §58-67-75, (c).
Defined, §58-67-75, (a).
Discrimination.
Applicability of section, §58-67-75, (d).
Prohibited acts, §58-67-75, (b).
Hospital, medical and dental service corporations.
Contracts to cover treatment, §58-65-75, (a) to (e).
Incompetence, determination of, §§35A-1101 to 35A-1116.
See INCOMPETENCE.
Lawyers and judges impaired by substance abuse or addiction.
Lawyer assistance program, Bar Rules & Regs., D, §§.0601 to .06023.
See LAWYERS ASSISTANCE PROGRAM.
Physicians and surgeons.
Grounds for denial, revocation or suspension of license, §90-14, (a).
Probation.
Drug alcohol recovery treatment program as condition.
Screening and assessing for chemical dependency, §15A-1343, (b3).
Substance abuse.
General provisions.
See MENTAL HEALTH, DEVELOPMENTAL DISABILITY, SUBSTANCE ABUSE.

CHEMICAL DEPENDENCY —Cont'd
Work first program recipients of assistance.
Treatment required, drug testing, §108A-29.1.

CHEMICAL DEPENDENCY TREATMENT FACILITIES.
Certificates of need, §§131E-175 to 131E-190.
See HEALTH CARE FACILITIES.

CHEMICAL PRESERVATIVES.
Food, drug and cosmetic act.
Foods deemed misbranded, §106-130.

CHEMICALS.
Discharges of oil or hazardous substances generally, §§143-215.83 to 143-215.94.
See OIL OR HAZARDOUS SUBSTANCES DISCHARGES.
Mass death and destruction weapons.
Nuclear, biological or chemical weapons, §§14-288.21 to 14-288.24.
See WEAPONS OF MASS DEATH AND DESTRUCTION.
Offshore oil and gas activities, §§143-215.94AA to 143-215.94JJ.
See OFFSHORE OIL AND GAS ACTIVITIES.
Oil pollution and hazardous substances control generally, §§143-215.75 to 143-215.82.
See OIL POLLUTION AND HAZARDOUS SUBSTANCES CONTROL.
Terrorist incident using nuclear, biological or chemical agents, §§130A-475 to 130A-479.
See TERRORIST INCIDENT USING NUCLEAR, BIOLOGICAL OR CHEMICAL AGENTS.
Water and air resources.
Prohibited discharges, §143-214.2, (a).

CHEROKEE COUNTY.
Ambulance services.
Attachment or garnishment and lien for, §§44-51.4 to 44-51.8.
Obtaining service without intending to pay, §14-111.2.
Requesting ambulance falsely, §14-111.3.
Board of county commissioners.
Filling vacancies on board, §153A-27.1.
Condemnation or acquisition of land by local government unit outside county.
Consent of board of commissioners necessary, §153A-15.
Coroner elected as nominee of political party.
Filling vacancy in office, §152-1.
Counties generally.
See COUNTIES.
County boards of education elected on partisan basis.
Vacancies in office, §115C-37.1.
Dog collars.
Unlawful removal of electronic dog collars, §14-401.17.
Housing authority commissioners.
Tenant as commissioner, exemption from provision of law allowing, §157-5.
Oil, gas or mineral interest separated from surface interest, extinguished, title in surface fee holder.
Failure to list interest for tax purposes for 10 years prior to January 1, 1974.
Protection of interest from surface estate, §1-42.3, (d).
Registration of deeds.
Tax certification, no delinquent taxes due, §161-31, (b).

CHEROKEE COUNTY —Cont'd
School property.
Acquisition and improvement, §153A-158.1.
Sheriff.
Vacancy, performance of duties until vacancy filled, §162-5.1.
Western North Carolina Development Association, Inc.
Appropriation of funds to, §153A-447, (a), (b).
Western North Carolina regional economic development commission, §158-8.1.
Wild plants, taking of certain plants from land of another.
Inapplicability of provisions, §14-129.

CHEROKEE INDIANS.
Amusement tax exemptions, §105-40.
Fishing license provisions.
Inapplicability to Eastern Band of the Cherokee Indians, §113-276, (l).
Full faith and credit to judgments, decrees, and orders.
Eastern band of the Cherokee Indians.
Considered a foreign judgment, §1E-1, (b).
Subject to certain provisions, §1E-1, (b).
Tribal court.
Subject to full faith and credit of tribal court, §1E-1, (a).
Maps of Cherokee lands.
Evidence.
Certified copies of maps, §8-14.
Motor fuel or special fuel taxes.
Refund.
Eastern band of the Cherokee Indians, §105-449.114.
National park system.
Jurisdiction over lands.
Inapplicable to lands held in trust, §104-33.
Robeson county.
Provision inapplicable to certain bands of Indians, §71A-2.
Rights and privileges, §71A-1.
Sales and use tax.
Exemption of sales on Cherokee Indian reservation, §105-164.13.

CHERRIES.
Standard weights and measures, §81A-42.
Unfair practices by handlers, §§106-496 to 106-501.
See FRUIT HANDLERS UNFAIR PRACTICES.

CHERRY BOMBS.
Fireworks generally, §§14-410 to 14-415.

CHERRY HOSPITAL.
Hospitals generally.
See HOSPITALS.
Joint security force, §122C-430.10.
Mental health, developmental disabilities and substance abuse.
General provisions.
See MENTAL HEALTH, DEVELOPMENTAL DISABILITY, SUBSTANCE ABUSE.

CHESTNUTS.
Standard weight and measure, §81A-42.

CHEWING TOBACCO.
Sale or distribution of tobacco products to minors, §14-313.

CHICK DEALERS.
Civil penalties, §106-549.01.
Defined, §106-541.

CHICK DEALERS —Cont'd
Diseases.
Compulsory testing for disease, §106-548.
False advertising, §106-545.
Fines, §106-549.01.
Grade of chicks.
Notice describing grade to be posted, §106-546.
License needed to operate, §106-542.
Misdemeanor offenses, §106-549.
Quarantine on premises, §106-548.
Records to be kept, §106-547.
Shipments from out of state, §106-544.
Violations of provisions a misdemeanor, §106-549.

CHICKENS.
Egg law, §§106-245.13 to 106-245.28.
See EGGS.
Poultry generally.
See POULTRY AND POULTRY PRODUCTS.
Poultry products inspections, §§106-549.49 to 106-549.69.
See POULTRY PRODUCTS INSPECTIONS.
Promotion of use and sale of agricultural products.
Generally, §§106-550 to 106-568.
See AGRICULTURAL PRODUCTS PROMOTION.

CHIEF INFORMATION OFFICER.
See INFORMATION TECHNOLOGY SERVICES.

CHIEF JUSTICE.
Assignment of judges, Const. N. C., art. IV, §11.
Death penalty sentencing proceedings.
Designation of judge on disability of trial judge, §15A-2003.
Election of, §7A-10, (a).
Emergency justices.
Recall of justices by chief justice.
Finality of decisions regarding, §7A-39.9, (a).
Termination of recall by chief justice, §7A-39.9, (b).
Impeachment of governor.
Presiding judge, §123-2.
Incapacity of chief justice.
Procedure when chief justice incapacitated, §7A-39.9, (c).
Salary, §7A-10, (b).
Longevity pay, §7A-10, (c).
Terms of office, §7A-10, (a).

CHILD ABDUCTION, §14-41, (a).
Bail and recognizance, §15A-534.4.
Child custody.
Transporting child outside state.
Intent to violate custody order, §14-320.1.
Electronic surveillance orders, §15A-290, (c1).
Enticing minors out of state for purposes of employment, §14-40.
Kidnapping and abduction generally, §§14-39 to 14-41.
See KIDNAPPING AND ABDUCTION.

CHILD ABUSE, NEGLECT OR DEPENDENCY, §§7B-100 to 7B-1414.
Abandonment, reports of.
Investigation of reports, §7B-302.
Abortion.
Consent for abortion on unemancipated minor.
Records not public record and maintained separately from juvenile records, §7B-2901, (d).

CHILD ABUSE, NEGLECT OR DEPENDENCY —Cont'd
Abused juvenile defined, §7B-101.
Adjudication of juvenile, §7B-807.
Court's findings on allegations in petition, §7B-807, (a).
Order of adjudication.
Requirements for, §7B-807, (b).
Adjudicatory hearing, §§7B-801 to 7B-807.
Clear and convincing evidence required to prove allegations, §7B-805.
Closed hearing.
Court determination, §7B-801, (a).
Juvenile requesting opening hearing, §7B-801, (b).
Conduct, §7B-802.
Continuance, §7B-803.
Dismissal with prejudice, court finds allegation not proven, §7B-807, (a).
Due process of law, protection of juvenile's and parent's rights, §7B-802.
Finding that allegations proved, statement by court, §7B-807, (a).
Held at time and place as designated by court, §7B-801, (c).
Record of hearing, §7B-806.
Rules of evidence to apply, §7B-804.
Transcript.
Reducing record to transcript upon notice of appeal, §7B-806.
Adoption.
Bringing dependents into state for placement or adoption, §§7B-3700 to 7B-3705.
See CHILD PLACEMENT.
Periodic review hearing as to placement.
Surrender of juvenile for adoption, agency plan for placement, §7B-909.
Termination of parental rights, permanent placement plan, §7B-908.
Sending dependents out of state for placement, §§7B-3702 to 7B-3705.
Alcohol and other drug abuse and dependence.
Drug treatment courts, §§7A-790 to 7A-801.
See DRUG TREATMENT COURTS.
Alternative dispositions, §7B-903, (a).
Amendment of petition alleging abuse, neglect or dependency, §7B-800.
Appeal of final order of court.
Contents of final order, requirements, §7B-1001.
Modification of original order after affirmation by appellate court, §7B-1004.
Notice of appeal, §7B-1001.
Parties, §7B-1002.
Return of juvenile to parent pending disposition of appeal, §7B-1003.
Right to appeal, §7B-1001.
Temporary order affecting custody pending disposition of appeal, compelling reasons, §7B-1003.
Time for giving notice, §7B-1001.
Appearance of parent, guardian, etc., personally served.
Failure to appear, contempt, §7B-407.
Appointment of counsel for parent, §7B-602, (a).
Payment of court-appointed counsel, §7B-603, (a) to (c).
Summons to contain information about how to seek appointment, §7B-406, (b).
Appointment of guardian, §7B-600, (a).
Court's inquiry into person's qualifications to act as guardian, §7B-600, (c).

CHILD ABUSE, NEGLECT OR DEPENDENCY —Cont'd
Appointment of guardian ad litem, §7B-601, (a).
Armed forces enlistment, authority of guardian to consent, §7B-600, (a).
Attorney advocate.
Appointment when guardian ad litem nonattorney, §7B-601, (a).
Standing to represent juvenile, §7B-601, (a).
Attorney-client privilege, grounds for excluding evidence, §7B-310.
Baby drop off, §14-322.3.
Exceptions to child abuse, §§14-318.2, 14-318.4, (c).
Best interest of juvenile.
Appointment of guardian, §7B-600, (a).
Bringing dependents into state for placement or adoption, §§7B-3700 to 7B-3705.
See CHILD PLACEMENT.
Burden at adjudicatory hearing, §7B-805.
Burden at hearing on nonsecure custody, §7B-506, (b).
Burden of proof in cessation of interference with investigation proceedings, §7B-303, (c).
Caretaker defined, §7B-101.
Casework.
Protective services to include, §7B-300.
Central registry.
Maintained by department of health and human services, §7B-311.
Report submitted by director to, §7B-307, (c).
Cessation of obstruction or interference with investigation, order of court, §7B-303, (c).
Child care facilities.
See CHILD CARE FACILITIES.
Child fatality prevention system, §§7B-1400 to 7B-1414.
See CHILD FATALITY PREVENTION SYSTEM.
Children's trust fund, §7B-1302.
Clear and convincing evidence.
Adjudicatory hearing, proving allegations, §7B-805.
Clerk's office closed, magistrate issuing petition, §7B-404, (a).
Authority limited to emergency situations, §7B-404, (b).
Clerk to maintain complete records of juvenile cases, §7B-2901, (a).
Closed hearings.
Adjudicatory hearing, §7B-801, (a), (b).
Commencement of action by filing petition, §7B-405.
Community-based educational and service programs.
Program on prevention of abuse and neglect, §7B-1301.
Community-level services provided juvenile and family, §7B-900.
Conferences during prosecutor's review of director's decision, §7B-306.
Confidential information, records or reports.
Examination of records without court order.
Persons who may examine, §7B-2901, (a).
Guardian ad litem demanding, respect for confidentiality, §7B-601, (c).
Information received during investigation, §7B-302, (a).
Records and social reports generally, §7B-2901.
Refusal to allow director access.
Interference with investigation, §7B-303, (b).
Consent judgment or order, §7B-902.

CHILD ABUSE, NEGLECT OR DEPENDENCY —Cont'd
Consent of department of health and human services for placement of juvenile.
Sending into state or sending out of state for placement or adoption, §§7B-3700 to 7B-3705.
Consent to actions on part of juvenile.
Power of guardian, §7B-600, (a).
Construction and interpretation of subchapter to implement purposes, §7B-100.
Consultation with private or public agencies.
Performing duties related to investigation, §7B-302, (e).
Contempt.
Failure of parent, guardian, etc., personally served to appear, §7B-407.
Failure of parent to comply with dispositional order, §7B-904, (e).
Show cause orders, §7B-904, (e).
Failure to comply with order generally, §7B-406, (c).
Order to cease interference with investigation, enforcement, §7B-303, (f).
Payment of fees for court-appointed attorney or guardian ad litem.
Failure to comply with order of payment, §7B-603, (c).
Show cause orders.
Failure of parent to comply with dispositional order, §7B-904, (e).
Continuance of adjudicatory hearing, §7B-803.
Continuance of hearing on nonsecure custody, §7B-506, (a).
Continuance of placement review hearing.
Termination of parental rights, §7B-908, (b).
Continued jurisdiction of court to modify or vacate dispositional order, §7B-1000, (b).
Contracts to operate community-based educational and service programs, §7B-1301, (b).
Copies of petition, sufficient number, §7B-402.
Counseling services.
Protective services to include, §7B-300.
Criminal history check of alleged abuser.
Criminal history defined, §7B-101.
When juvenile removed from home, §§7B-302, (d1), 7B-503, (b).
Criminal investigation when evidence of abuse found, §7B-307, (a).
Criminal prosecution of alleged abuse determined by district attorney, §7B-307, (a).
Custodian defined, §7B-101.
Custody of juvenile.
Alternative dispositions, §7B-903, (a).
Medical professionals obtaining custody in abuse cases, §7B-308.
Nonsecure custody.
Authority of court to order placement of juvenile, §7B-502.
Continued custody hearing, §7B-506.
Criteria, §7B-503.
Delegation of authority to other than district court judges, §7B-502.
Factual basis for ordering, §7B-503, (a).
Hearing to determine need for continued custody, §7B-506.
Order, §7B-504.
Place of nonsecure custody, §7B-505.
Release of juvenile to parent, relative, etc.
Court's first consideration on request for nonsecure custody, §7B-503, (a).

CHILD ABUSE, NEGLECT OR DEPENDENCY —Cont'd
Custody of juvenile —Cont'd
Notices, orders, authorizations and request made by telephone, §7B-508.
Placement of juvenile, periodic review hearings.
Custody removed from parent, §7B-906.
Dispositional order to direct holding of hearing, §7B-905, (b).
Surrender of juvenile for adoption, agency plan, §7B-909.
Termination of parental rights, §7B-908.
Secure custody prohibited, §7B-503.
Temporary custody without court order, §7B-500, (a).
Duties of person taking into temporary custody, §7B-501, (a).
Time limit on holding in temporary custody, §7B-501, (b).
Voluntary foster care placement, §7B-910.
Death due to maltreatment.
Duty to report, §7B-301.
Investigation of report, protective services for and removal of other juveniles, §7B-302, (b).
Death of juvenile generally.
Child fatality prevention system, §§7B-1400 to 7B-1414.
See CHILD FATALITY PREVENTION SYSTEM.
Definitions, §7B-101.
Obstruction of or interference with investigation, §7B-303, (b).
Temporary custody, §7B-500, (a).
Department of health and human services to receive results of investigation and report, §7B-307, (b), (c).
Dependent juvenile defined, §7B-101.
Director of department of social services in each county to establish protective services, §7B-300.
Director of social services to maintain record of cases, §7B-2901, (b).
Disclosure of investigation records.
Law governing, §132-1.4, (l).
Predisposition reports, §7B-808, (c).
Discovery.
Court ordering discovery be denied, restricted or deferred, §7B-700, (a).
In camera inspection of affidavits or statements.
Party seeking relief from court order, §7B-700, (b).
Dismissal of petition with prejudice.
Finding by court that allegations not proved, §7B-807, (a).
Dispositional hearing, §7B-901.
Notice in summons that court will conduct, §7B-406, (b).
Dispositional order, §7B-905.
Notice in summons as types of disposition, §7B-406, (b).
Disposition of juvenile, §§7B-900 to 7B-910.
Allowing parent or others to take appropriate action, §7B-903, (a).
Alternatives for disposition, §7B-903, (a).
Appeal.
Before court of appeals, §7B-1001.
Disposition after appeal, §7B-1004.
Disposition pending appeal, §7B-1003.
Final order, §7B-1001.
Modification or alteration of original order upon affirmation by appellate court, §7B-1004.

CHILD ABUSE, NEGLECT OR DEPENDENCY —Cont'd
Disposition of juvenile —Cont'd
Appeal —Cont'd
Notice of appeal, §7B-1001.
Parties, §7B-1002.
Return of custody to parent or guardian pending appeal, §7B-1003.
Time for giving notice, §7B-1001.
Authority of court to direct parents' actions, §7B-904, (d1).
Closed hearing unless juvenile moves to open hearing, §7B-901.
Community-level services, providing juvenile and family, §7B-900.
Consent order or judgment, §7B-902.
Contempt.
Failure of parent to comply with dispositional order, §7B-904, (e).
Show cause orders, §7B-904, (e).
Court's inquiry into person's qualifications as to custody, §7B-903, (c).
Custody of juvenile removed from parent.
Review of order, §7B-906.
Calendaring case, timely request by director, §7B-906, (a).
Court relieved of duty to conduct review, restoration of custody to parent, §7B-906, (d).
Court's inquiry into person's qualifications as to custody or guardianship, §7B-906, (g).
Criteria considered by court, written findings by court, §7B-906, (c).
Disposition by court after findings, §7B-906, (d).
Disposition order to set time and date of hearing, §7B-905, (b).
Foster care placement, applicability of provisions, §7B-906, (f).
Guardian, appointment by court after making findings, §7B-906, (d).
Information considered at review hearing, §7B-906, (c).
Notice of review, §7B-906, (a).
Permanency-planning hearing, §7B-906, (e).
Reports to court in lieu of review, §7B-906, (b).
Return of juvenile to parent, hearing and findings required, §7B-906, (d).
Second or subsequent reviews, time for conducting, §7B-906, (a).
Time for review, §7B-906, (a).
Visitation plan, placement of juvenile with department of social services, §7B-906, (d).
Waiver of review, court authority, §7B-906, (b).
Examination by physician, psychiatrist, psychologist or other expert, §7B-903, (a).
Findings or fact and conclusions of law, order to contain, §7B-905, (a).
Foster care, order directing placement of juvenile, §7B-905, (c).
Foster care placement, voluntary agreements, review.
Addition review hearings, time for holding, §7B-909, (c).
Authority of court on making findings, §7B-909, (b).
Findings to be made by court, §7B-909, (a).
Notice, §7B-909, (c).

CHILD ABUSE, NEGLECT OR DEPENDENCY —Cont'd
Disposition of juvenile —Cont'd
Foster care placement, voluntary agreements, review —Cont'd
Time for conducting review, §7B-909, (c).
Time limit on placement, §7B-909, (c).
Hearing, §7B-901.
History of violent behavior, individual responsible for physical abuse.
Mental health professional's opinion considered, §7B-803, (a).
Medical, psychiatric, psychological, surgical, educational evaluations, examinations or treatment, §7B-903, (a).
Participation of parent in juvenile's treatment, §7B-904, (b).
Payment of costs, §7B-904, (a), (c).
Mental health professional.
Opinion considered by court, physical abuse suffered by juvenile, §7A-903, (b).
Mentally ill or developmentally disabled juveniles, §7B-903, (a).
Modification or vacation of dispositional order.
Continuance of jurisdiction until terminated by court order or emancipation, §7B-1000, (b).
Original order modified after affirmation by appellate court, §7B-1004.
Review hearing, §7B-1000, (a).
Order, §7B-905.
Parents' actions.
Authority of court to direct, §7B-904, (d1).
Permanent placement plan.
Placement review.
Adoption placement prior to review, notice, cancellation of review, §7B-908, (e).
Considerations by court during review, §7B-908, (c).
Continuance of case, §7B-908, (b).
Court authority after making findings of fact, §7B-907, (d).
Court's inquiry into person's qualifications as to custody or guardianship, §7B-907, (f).
Guardian ad litem, appointment, §7B-908, (b).
Notice of review, §7B-908, (b).
Purpose, §7B-908, (a).
Selection of specific adoptive parents, responsibility, §7B-908, (f).
Time for conducting, §7B-908, (b).
Placement review, custody of juvenile removed from parent, §7B-906.
Calendaring case, timely request by director, §7B-906, (a).
Court relieved of duty to conduct review, restoration of custody to parent, §7B-906, (d).
Court's inquiry into person's qualifications as to custody or guardianship, §7B-906, (g).
Criteria considered by court, written findings by court, §7B-906, (c).
Disposition by court after findings, §7B-906, (d).
Disposition order to set time and date of hearing, §7B-905, (b).
Foster care placement, applicability of provisions, §7B-906, (f).
Guardian, appointment by court after making findings, §7B-906, (d).
Information considered at review hearing, §7B-906, (c).
Notice of review, §7B-906, (a).
Permanency-planning hearing, §7B-906, (e).

CHILD ABUSE, NEGLECT OR DEPENDENCY —Cont'd
Disposition of juvenile —Cont'd
Placement review, custody of juvenile removed from parent —Cont'd
Reports to court in lieu of review, §7B-906, (b).
Return of juvenile to parent, hearing and findings required, §7B-906, (d).
Second or subsequent reviews, time for conducting, §7B-906, (a).
Time for review, §7B-906, (a).
Visitation plan, placement of juvenile with department of social services, §7B-906, (d).
Waiver of review, court authority, §7B-906, (b).
Placement review, parental rights terminated.
Adoption placement prior to review, notice, cancellation of review, §7B-908, (e).
Considerations by court during review, §7B-908, (c).
Continuance of case, §7B-908, (b).
Court authority after making findings of fact, §7B-907, (d).
Court's inquiry into person's qualifications as to custody or guardianship, §7B-907, (f).
Guardian ad litem, appointment, §7B-908, (b).
Notice of review, §7B-908, (b).
Purpose, §7B-908, (a).
Selection of specific adoptive parents, responsibility, §7B-908, (f).
Time for conducting, §7B-907, (b).
Placement review, surrender of juvenile for adoption by parent or parents.
Dismissal or withdrawal of adoption.
Notice of return of juvenile to department or agency, §7B-909, (b).
Notice to clerk to calendar case, §7B-909, (a).
Petition for review, notice required by, §7B-909, (c).
Time for conducting review, §7B-909, (c).
Placement review, voluntary foster care placements.
Addition review hearings, time for holding, §7B-909, (c).
Authority of court on making findings, §7B-909, (b).
Findings to be made by court, §7B-909, (a).
Notice, §7B-909, (d).
Time for conducting review, §7B-909, (c).
Time limit on placement, §7B-909, (c).
Placing juvenile with department of social services, §7B-903, (a).
Requirements of dispositional order, §7B-905, (c).
Placing juvenile with suitable person or agency, §7B-903, (a).
Predisposition investigation and report, §7B-808, (a).
Administrative orders, §7B-808, (c).
Preparation of report, §7B-808, (b).
Rulemaking, §7B-808, (c).
Purpose, §7B-900.
Show cause orders.
Contempt.
Failure of parent to comply with dispositional order, §7B-904, (e).
Support of juvenile, parent ordered to pay.
Legal custody of juvenile vested in someone other than parent, §7B-904, (d).
Terms of disposition to be stated in order, §7B-905, (a).

CHILD ABUSE, NEGLECT OR DEPENDENCY —Cont'd
Disposition of juvenile —Cont'd
Working with juvenile and family in home, initial approach, §7B-900.
Dispute between social services departments.
Legal residence of child.
Referral to division of social services for resolution, §153A-257, (d).
District attorney notified when evidence of abuse found, §7B-307, (a).
District court jurisdiction.
Cases involving juvenile alleged to be abused, neglected or dependent, §7B-200, (a).
Parent or guardian of child adjudicated abused, neglected or dependent, §7B-200, (b).
Retention or jurisdiction until terminated by court or emancipation of juvenile, §7B-201.
Drug treatment courts, §§7A-790 to 7A-801.
See DRUG TREATMENT COURTS.
Due process of law.
Adjudicatory hearing, §7B-802.
Duty to report abuse, neglect or dependency, §7B-301.
Entry into private residences.
Investigations by director or director's representative, §7B-302, (h).
Evaluation of juvenile, refusal to allow director to arrange.
Interference with investigation, §7B-303, (b).
Evidence.
Dispositional hearings, §7B-901.
Permanency planning hearings, §7B-907, (b).
Placement review, parental rights terminated, §7B-908, (a).
Review hearings, §7B-906, (c).
Evidence, excluding based on privilege, §7B-310.
Evidence of abuse or neglect found by director, report, §7B-307, (a), (b).
Excluding evidence based on privilege, §7B-310.
Execution of order for nonsecure custody, §7B-504.
Ex parte order for protection and assistance to juvenile, §7B-303, (d).
Failure of parent, guardian, etc., personally served to appear.
Contempt, §7B-407.
Fatality or near fatality cases, disclosure of records.
Application for order compelling disclosure, request denied, §7B-2902, (e).
Child fatality prevention team records, provisions governing access, §7B-2902, (f).
Confidential records, access prohibited, §7B-2902, (c).
Criminal investigative reports and criminal intelligence information, provisions governing access, §7B-2902, (f).
Definition of public record not limited or narrowed, §7B-2902, (h).
Definitions, §7B-2902, (a).
Immunity of public agency or employee acting in good faith, §7B-2902, (g).
Providing findings and information upon request, §7B-2902, (d).
Request to public agency for disclosure, §7B-2902, (b).
Time for providing findings and information upon request, §7B-2902, (d).

CHILD ABUSE, NEGLECT OR DEPENDENCY —Cont'd
Fees for court appointed attorney or guardian ad litem.
Payment, §7B-603, (a) to (c).
Felony child abuse, §14-318.4, (a) to (a3).
Additional offense to other civil and criminal provisions, §14-318.4, (b).
Exceptions, §14-318.4, (c).
Filing petition, commencement of action, §7B-405.
Final order.
Appeal, §§7B-1001 to 7B-1004.
Required to be included in order, §7B-1001.
Foster care.
Dispositional order directing placement of juvenile, §7B-905, (c).
Voluntary foster care placement agreement, review hearing, §7B-910.
Clerk to give notice of hearings, §7B-910, (d).
Courts' authority over placements, §7B-910, (b).
Evidence considered at hearing, §7B-910, (a).
Filing of petitions of abuse, neglect or dependency.
Time limitation in placement without filing petition, §7B-910, (c).
Timing of hearings, §7B-910, (c).
Generally, 1999 provisions, §§7B-100 to 7B-1414.
Geographically based field programs.
Eligible cases, §7A-474.3, (b).
Guardian.
Appointment, powers, §7B-600, (a).
Court's inquiry into person's qualifications to act as guardian, §7B-600, (c).
Review of placement, custody removed from parent.
Appointment after making findings, §7B-906, (d).
Court's inquiry into person's qualifications to act as guardian, §7B-906, (g).
Termination of relationship, reintegration of juvenile into parent's home, §7A-600, (b).
Guardian ad litem.
Accompanying juvenile to court in criminal matters, §7B-601, (b).
Appointment by court, §7B-601, (a).
Attorney appointed when nonattorney appointed as guardian ad litem, §7B-601, (a).
Confidentiality of information or reports demanded.
Guardian to respect, §7B-601, (c).
Demanding information or reports, authority, §7B-601, (c).
Duties, §7B-601, (a).
Fellow-up investigations to ensure orders executed, §7B-601, (b).
Husband-wife privilege inapplicable.
Demand for information by guardian, §7B-601, (c).
Parents.
Appointed for parents when incapable or underage, §7B-602, (b).
Payment, §7B-603, (a) to (c).
Petition alleging abuse, neglect or dependency.
Copy of petition to be provided to guardian ad litem office, §7B-408.
Physician-patient privilege inapplicable.
Demand for information by guardian, §7B-601, (c).
Reappointment on showing good cause, §7B-601, (a).

CHILD ABUSE, NEGLECT OR DEPENDENCY —Cont'd
Guardian ad litem —Cont'd
Report to court when orders not being met, §7B-601, (b).
Standing to represent juvenile in all actions under subchapter, §7B-601, (a).
Termination of appointment, §7B-601, (a).
Termination of parental rights, placement review, §7B-908, (b).
Two years, termination of appointment, §7B-601, (a).
Guardian ad litem program to provide services to juveniles, §§7B-1200 to 7B-1204.
Alternative plans, §7B-1203.
Appointment of district bar member to represent juvenile.
Conflict of interest of local program, §7B-1202.
Attorney for local program, §7B-1200.
Conflict of interest prohibiting local program from providing representation.
Appointment of member of district bar to represent juvenile, §7B-1202.
Coordinator of local program, paid state employee, §7B-1200.
District court operation of program.
No local program established, §7B-1201, (a).
Guardian ad litem advisory committee, §7B-1201, (b).
Immunity of volunteer from civil liability, §7B-1204.
Impractical to establish local program.
Waiver of establishment, §7B-1202.
Local program, §7B-1200.
Conflict of interest, appointment of district bar member, §7B-1202.
Implementation and administration, §7B-1201, (a).
Impractical to establish or alternative established, waiver of establishment, §7B-1202.
Office of guardian ad litem services.
Established within administrative of office of the courts, §7B-1200.
Rules and regulation adopted by administrative office of the courts, §7B-1200.
Volunteer guardians.
Immunity from civil liability, §7B-1204.
Part of local program, §7B-1200.
Waiver of establishment of local program, §7B-1202.
Alternative plans, §7B-1203.
Hearing on disposition, §7B-901.
Hearing on petition to cease interference with investigation, §7B-303, (c).
Hearings to review placement of juvenile.
Custody removed from parent, §7B-906.
Dispositional order to direct holding of hearing, §7B-905, (b).
Surrender of juvenile for adoption, agency plan, §7B-909.
Termination of parental rights, §7B-908.
Voluntary foster care placement, §7B-910.
Hearing to determine need for continued nonsecure custody, §7B-506.
Hearing to develop safe permanent home for juvenile.
Permanency planning hearing, custody removed from parent, §7B-906, (e).
History of violent behavior, person responsible for abuse.
Mental health professional's opinion considered, §7B-803, (a).

CHILD ABUSE, NEGLECT OR DEPENDENCY —Cont'd
Hospital, clinic or other medical facility administrators.
Authority in abuse cases.
Retention of physical custody of juvenile in medical facility, §7B-308, (a), (f).
Husband and wife.
Privilege.
Waiver of husband-wife privilege in child abuse cases, §8-57.1.
Husband-wife privilege, inapplicability.
Demand for information by guardian ad litem, §7B-601, (c).
Identity of reporter, confidentiality.
Order to reveal in interference with investigation proceeding, §7B-303, (e).
Immediate protection and assistance to juvenile.
Interference with investigation, §7B-303, (d).
Immunity of persons reporting and cooperating in investigation, §7B-309.
In camera inspection of affidavits or statements.
Relief from order denying, restricting or deferring discovery, §7B-700, (b).
Interference with investigation, §7B-303.
Investigation of report, §7B-302, (a).
Confidentiality of information received, §7B-302, (a).
Consultation with private or public agency, §7B-302, (e).
Disclosure of record, law governing, §132-1.4, (l).
Entry into private residences, §7B-302, (h).
Immunity of persons cooperating in investigation, §7B-309.
Interference with investigation, §7B-303.
Notice that custody of juvenile retained by medical facility.
Director to treat as report of abuse and conduct immediate investigation, §7B-308, (b).
Notice to person making report of action taken, §7B-302, (f).
Notice to person making report of findings, §7B-302, (g).
Protective services determination, §7B-302, (b), (c).
Protective services to include investigation and screening of complaint, §7B-300.
Removal of from home or facility determination, §7B-302, (b), (c).
Report on finding evidence of abuse or neglect, §7B-307, (a), (b).
Result of investigation, notice by director, §7B-307, (c).
Time for initiating investigation, §7B-302, (a).
Issuance of summons, §7B-406.
Jurisdiction of district court.
Cases involving juvenile alleged to be abused, neglected or dependent, §7B-200, (a).
Parent or guardian of child adjudicated abuse, neglected or dependent, §7B-200, (b).
Retention of jurisdiction until terminated by court or emancipation of juvenile, §7B-201.
Juvenile defined, §7B-101.
Law enforcement officers.
Return and execution of order for nonsecure custody, §7B-504.
Taking juvenile into temporary custody.
Authority, §7B-500, (a).

CHILD ABUSE, NEGLECT OR DEPENDENCY —Cont'd
Law enforcement officers —Cont'd
Taking juvenile into temporary custody —Cont'd
Duties upon taking juvenile into temporary custody, §7B-501, (a).
Legal residence of child.
Dispute between social services departments.
Referral to division of social services for resolution, §153A-257, (d).
Magistrate authorized to issue petition.
Clerk's office closed, §7B-404, (a).
Authority limited to emergency situations, §7B-404, (b).
Maltreatment of juvenile, death due to.
Duty of person or institution to report, §7B-301.
Marriage by underage parties.
District court jurisdiction, §7B-200, (a).
Marriage of juvenile, authority of guardian to consent, §7B-600, (a).
Medical professionals, authority in abuse cases.
Retention of physical custody in medical facility, §7B-308, (a), (f).
Medical, psychiatric or psychological examination, treatment or care, §7B-903.
Certification by physician, nonsecure custody order, cost of treatment, §7B-308, (b), (d).
Consent by guardian, §7B-600, (a).
Parent ordered to undergo psychiatric or psychological examination or treatment, §7B-904, (c).
Participation of parent in juvenile treatment, §7B-904, (b).
Payment of cost of treatment, §7B-904, (a), (c).
Mental health professional.
Opinion as to disposition considered by court.
Physical abuse suffered by juvenile, §7A-903, (b).
Mental health records of alleged abuser, review.
When juvenile removed from home, §§7B-302, (d1), 7B-503, (b).
Mentally ill or developmentally disabled.
Disposition on finding by court, §7B-903, (a).
Misdemeanor child abuse, §14-318.2, (a).
Additional offense to other civil and criminal provisions, §14-318.2, (b).
Exceptions, §14-318.2, (c).
Modification or vacation of dispositional order.
After affirmation by appellate court, §7B-1004.
Authority of court, §7B-1000, (a).
Continued jurisdiction of court after finding abuse, neglect or dependency, §7B-1000, (b).
More than one juvenile.
Petition containing information on, §7B-402.
Nature of proceeding.
Summons to contain notice, §7B-406, (b).
Neglected juvenile defined, §7B-101.
Nonsecure custody hearing, §7B-506.
Nonsecure custody of juvenile.
Administrative order delegating authority, §7B-502.
Authority of court to place juvenile, §7B-502.
Burden at custody hearing on state, §7B-506, (b).
Continuance of hearing, §7B-506, (a).
Copy of order to parent, guardian, custodian or caretaker, §7B-504.
Criteria for ordering, §7B-503.

CHILD ABUSE, NEGLECT OR DEPENDENCY —Cont'd

Nonsecure custody of juvenile —Cont'd
Criteria in determining whether to continue custody, §7B-506, (c).
Delegation of authority to other than district court judges, §7B-502.
Evidence and testimony at custody hearing, §7B-506, (b).
Execution of order in accordance with terms, §7B-504.
Factual basis for ordering, §7B-503, (a).
Findings of fact, order to contain, §7B-506, (d).
Hearing to determine need for continued custody, §7B-506.
Mental health professional performing evaluation of alleged abuser.
Considered in determining need for continued custody, §7B-506, (c1).
Missing parent inquiries, §7B-506, (h).
Order, §7B-504.
Order continuing custody, §7B-506, (d).
Findings as reasonable efforts to prevent need for placement, §7B-506, (g).
Paternity inquiries, §7B-506, (h).
Placing juvenile, §7B-505.
Reasonable efforts to eliminate need for placement, §7B-507.
Reasonable factual basis required to place in nonsecure custody, §7B-503.
Relatives, inquiries of.
Providing proper care and supervision in safe home, §7B-506, (h).
Relative willing and able to provide care, placement with, §7B-505.
Temporary placement, §7B-506, (h).
Release of juvenile first consideration when request made, §7B-503.
Release of juvenile to parent, relative, etc.
Court's first consideration on request for nonsecure custody, §7B-503, (a).
Remaining juveniles in home from which juvenile removed.
Inquiry, §7B-506, (h).
Return on order, §7B-504.
Rules of evidence, inapplicability at hearing, §7B-506, (b).
Secure custody, placement in prohibited, §7B-503.
Subsequent hearing, continued custody ordered, §7B-506, (e).
Waiver, §7B-506, (f).
Time for hearing, §7B-506, (a).
Subsequent hearing where continued custody ordered, §7B-506, (e).
Waiver of subsequent hearing, §7B-506, (f).

North Carolina child fatality prevention system, §§7B-1400 to 7B-1414.
See CHILD FATALITY PREVENTION SYSTEM.

Notice of appeal of final order, §7B-1001.

Notice of permanency planning hearing, §7B-906, (e).

Notice of review of placement hearing.
Custody removed from parent, §7B-906, (a).
Surrender of juvenile for adoption, agency placement plan, §7B-909, (a), (b).
Termination of parental rights, §7B-908, (b).
Cancellation, placement for adoption prior to review, §7B-908, (e).
Voluntary foster care placement, §7B-909, (c).

Notices contained in summons, §7B-406, (b).

CHILD ABUSE, NEGLECT OR DEPENDENCY —Cont'd

Notice that juvenile taken into temporary custody, §7B-501, (a).

Notice to director of retention of juvenile in medical facility, §7B-308, (b).

Notice to person making report.
Action taken on report by director, §7B-302, (f).
Findings of abuse, neglect or dependency, §7B-302, (g).
Prosecutor's review, §7B-305.

Notification to department or state bureau of investigation.
Results of investigation, §7B-307, (c).

Obstructing or interfering with investigation, §7B-303.

Order for nonsecure custody.
Reasonable efforts to eliminate need for placement.
Findings required, §7B-507.

Parent and child.
Protection of minors.
Contributing to delinquency and neglect by parents and others, §14-316.1.

Parents' actions.
Disposition of juvenile.
Authority of court to direct, §7B-904, (b1).

Parent's right to counsel and appointment of counsel, §7B-602, (a).

Parties to appeal of final order, proper parties, §7B-1002.

Payment of court-appointed attorney or guardian ad litem, §7B-603, (a) to (c).

Periodic review of placement of child.
Custody removed from parent, §7B-906.
Dispositional order to direct holding of hearing, §7B-905, (b).
Surrender of juvenile for adoption, agency plan, §7B-909.
Termination of parental rights, §7B-909.
Voluntary foster care placement, §7B-910.

Permanency planning hearing.
Reasonable efforts not required, time for hearing, §7B-507, (c).
Removal of custody from parent, §7B-906, (e).

Personal access to juvenile, refusal to allow director.
Interference with investigation, §7B-303, (b).

Petition alleging abuse, neglect or dependency, §7B-402.
Amendment, §7B-800.
Commencement of action by filing, §7B-405.
Copies, sufficient number, §7B-402.
Guardian ad litem office, provision of copy to, §7B-408.
Medical treatment needed, nonsecure custody, §7B-308, (b), (e).
More than one juvenile, petition containing information on, §7B-402.
Pleading in action by petition, §7B-401.
Report filed as petition, §7B-403, (a).

Petition for review.
Surrender of juvenile for adoption, agency placement plan review, §7B-909, (c).

Petition to cease obstruction or interference with investigation, §7B-303, (a).

Physician-patient privilege.
Waiver in child abuse cases, §8-53.1.

Physician-patient privilege, inapplicability.
Demand for information by guardian ad litem, §7B-601, (c).

CHILD ABUSE, NEGLECT OR DEPENDENCY —Cont'd
Physicians, authority in abuse cases.
Retention of physical custody of juvenile in medical facility, §7B-308, (a), (f).
Placement of juvenile.
Alternative dispositions, §7B-903, (a).
Bringing dependents into state for placement or adoption, §§7B-3700 to 7B-3705.
See CHILD PLACEMENT.
Nonsecure custody, §7B-505.
Reasonable efforts to eliminate need for placement.
Findings required in order, §7B-507, (a).
Health and safety of juvenile as primary concern in determination of need for reasonable efforts, §7B-507, (d).
Permanency planning hearing, time for when reasonable efforts not required, §7B-507, (c).
When reasonable efforts not required, §7B-507, (b).
Review hearings.
Custody removed from parent, §7B-906.
Surrender of juvenile for adoption, agency plan for placement, §7B-909.
Termination of parental rights, §7B-908.
Voluntary foster care placement, §7B-910.
Sending juvenile out of state for placement, §§7B-3702 to 7B-3705.
Pleading is by petition, §7B-401.
Post-release condition.
Required conditions.
Offenses involving abuse of minors, §15A-1368.4, (b1).
Predisposition investigation and report, §7B-808, (a).
Administrative orders, §7B-808, (c).
Preparation of report, §7B-808, (b).
Rulemaking, §7B-808, (c).
Prehearing diversion.
Director to consider when notified that juvenile in temporary custody, §7B-501, (a).
Private observation or interview with juvenile, refusal to allow director.
Interference with investigation, §7B-303, (b).
Privilege not grounds for failure to report or exclude evidence, §7B-310.
Process is summons, §7B-401.
Program on prevention of abuse and neglect, §§7B-1300 to 7B-1302.
Children's trust fund.
Deposit of contributions, grants or gifts received, §7B-1301, (c).
Establishment, §7B-1302.
Contracts to operate community-based educational and service programs, §7B-1301, (b).
Contributions, grants or gifts, assistance in implementing article, §7B-1301, (c).
Definition of abuse and neglect prevention program, §7B-1301, (d).
Implementation of program.
State board of education through department of public instruction, §7B-1301, (a).
Intent of programs contracted for under provisions, §7B-1301, (d).
Prevention as priority of state, purposes, §7B-1300.
Purposes of provisions, §7B-1300.
Staff and support services provided by department of public instruction, §7B-1301, (a).

CHILD ABUSE, NEGLECT OR DEPENDENCY —Cont'd
Program on prevention of abuse and neglect —Cont'd
State-level programs to coordinate community-based programs, limit on funding, §7B-1301, (e).
Prosecutor's review of director's decision, §7B-305.
Prosecutor's review of director's decision not to file report, §7B-403, (b).
Protective orders.
Discovery, court order denying, restricting or deferring, §7B-700.
Protective services for juveniles, §7B-300.
Investigation of report reveling abuse or neglect, §7B-302, (b), (c).
Psychologist-client or patient privilege.
Exception to privilege, §8-53.3.
Publication service of summons.
Parent, guardian, custodian or caretaker not found, §7B-407.
Public schools.
Duty to report, §115C-400.
Purposes, §7B-100.
Reasonable efforts.
Defined, §7B-101.
Elimination of need for placement, §7B-507.
Prevention of need for placement, §7B-506, (g).
Reasonable factual basis.
Placing juvenile in nonsecure custody, §7B-503.
Record of adjudicatory proceedings, §7B-806.
Records and social reports in cases generally, §§7B-2900 to 7B-2902.
Abortion of unemancipated minor, proceeding involving complaint.
Record or proceeding not public record, maintained separately from juvenile record, §7B-2901, (d).
Child fatality or near fatality cases, disclosure.
Application for order compelling disclosure, request denied, §7B-2902, (e).
Child fatality prevention team records, provisions governing disclosure, §7B-2902, (f).
Confidential records not authorized to be disclosed, §7B-2902, (c).
Criminal investigative reports and criminal intelligence information, provisions governing disclosure, §7B-2902, (f).
Definition of public record not narrowed or limited, §7B-2902, (h).
Definitions, §7B-2902, (a).
District attorney not required to disclose information, §7B-2902, (f).
Immunity of public agency or employees for disclosing in good faith, §7B-2902, (g).
Order compelling disclosure, request denied, §7B-2902, (e).
Providing findings and information upon request, §7B-2902, (d).
Request of public agency for disclosure, §7B-2902, (b).
Time for providing findings and information upon request, §7B-2902, (d).
Clerk to maintain complete set of records of juvenile cases, §7B-2901, (a).
Definitions, §7B-2900.
Director of social services to maintain records of cases, §7B-2901, (b).

CHILD ABUSE, NEGLECT OR DEPENDENCY —Cont'd
Records and social reports in cases generally —Cont'd
Examination of records without court order.
Persons who may examine, §7B-2901, (a).
Investigative records.
Law governing disclosure, §132-1.4, (l).
Sharing of information among public agencies in case of child victim, §7B-2901, (c).
Transcript, record reduced to only when notice of appeal timely given, §7B-2901, (a).
Referral of report to director for screening, §7B-403, (a).
Rehabilitative treatment.
Defendant may pay cost as condition of probation, §15A-1343, (b1).
Reintegration of juvenile into parent's home.
Termination of guardian relationship, §7A-600, (b).
Relative willing and able to provide care.
Placing juvenile with, §7B-505.
Release of juvenile taken into temporary custody, §7B-501, (a).
Removal of custody from parents.
Periodic review hearing as to placement, §7B-906.
Removal of juvenile from home or facility.
Complaint by director, immediate removal necessary, §7B-302, (d).
Determination after receipt of report, §7B-302, (b), (c).
Review of background of alleged abuser or abusers, §§7B-302, (d1), 7B-503, (b).
Nonsecure custody request, §7B-503, (b).
Report by director on finding evidence of abuse or neglect, §7B-307, (a), (b).
Reporting abuse, neglect, dependency or death due to maltreatment.
Confidentiality of reporter's identity.
Order to reveal in interference with investigation proceeding, §7B-303, (e).
Duty of person or institution with cause to suspect, §7B-301.
Immunity of persons reporting, §7B-309.
Information to be included in report, §7B-301.
Investigation.
Interference with investigation, §7B-303.
Investigation of report, §7B-302.
Privilege not grounds for failure to report, §7B-310.
School personnel to report child abuse, §115C-400.
Results of investigation, notice by director, §7B-307, (c).
Retention of jurisdiction by district court.
Jurisdiction to continue until terminated by court or emancipation of juvenile, §7B-201.
Retention of physical custody of juvenile in medical facility.
Authority of medical professionals in abuse cases, §7B-308, (a), (f).
Return of juvenile to parent pending disposition of appeal, §7B-1003.
Return on order for nonsecure custody, §7B-504.
Request for review, §7B-305.
Review hearings, placement of juvenile.
Custody removed from parent, §7B-906.
Dispositional order to direct holding of hearing, §7B-905, (b).
Surrender of juvenile for adoption, agency plan, §7B-909.

CHILD ABUSE, NEGLECT OR DEPENDENCY —Cont'd
Review hearings, placement of juvenile —Cont'd
Termination of parental rights, §7B-908.
Voluntary foster care placement, §7B-910.
Review of director's decision by prosecutor, §§7B-305, 7B-403, (b).
Request by reporter, §7B-305.
Review of final order of court, §§7B-1001 to 7B-1004.
Right to counsel.
Parents right, §7B-602, (a).
Summons to contain notice, §7B-406, (b).
Rules of evidence.
Applicable during adjudicatory hearing, §7B-804.
Dispositional hearings, §7B-901.
Permanency planning hearings, §7B-907, (b).
Placement review, parental rights terminated, §7B-908, (a).
Review hearings, §7B-906, (c).
Safe haven for infants, §§14-318.2, 14-318.4, 14-322.3, (c).
School enrollment, authority of guardian to consent, §7B-600, (a).
Screening of report by director of social services, §7B-403, (a).
Secure custody of juvenile prohibited, §7B-503.
Sending dependent out of state for placement, §§7B-3702 to 7B-3705.
Service of summons, §7B-407.
Proceeding to cease interference with investigation, §7B-303, (c).
Process in action by summons, §7B-401.
Summons delivered to person authorized to serve process, §7B-406, (d).
Summons directed to person summoned to appear, §7B-406, (d).
Sexual abuse in child care facility.
Notice of results of investigation and report to state bureau of investigation, §7B-307, (b), (c).
Notification to state bureau of investigation upon receipt of report, §7B-301.
Shelter care.
Defined, §7B-101.
Show cause orders.
Contempt.
Failure of parent to comply with dispositional order, §7B-904, (e).
Social services workers.
Taking juvenile into temporary custody.
Authority, §7B-500, (a).
Duties upon taking juvenile into temporary custody, §7B-501, (a).
State bureau investigation of report of sexual abuse in child care facility.
Formation of task force to investigate report, §7B-301.
Sexual abuse in child care facility found, §7B-307, (b), (c).
Summons.
Contempt on failure to comply with order, summons to advise parent, §7B-406, (c).
Delivered to person authorized to serve process, §7B-406, (d).
Directed to person summoned to appear, §7B-406, (d).
Form and contents, §7B-404, (b).
Issuance, §7B-406, (a).
Jurisdiction over parent obtained upon service, summons to advise, §7B-406, (c).

CHILD ABUSE, NEGLECT OR DEPENDENCY —Cont'd
Summons —Cont'd
Process in action by summons, §7B-401.
Service, §7B-407.
Supervision of juvenile in own home, §7B-903, (a).
Support of juvenile, payment by parent.
Legal custody vested in someone other than parent, §7B-904, (d).
Suspicion that juvenile abused, neglected or dependent.
Duty of person or institution to report, §7B-301.
Telephone communication authorized.
Temporary or nonsecure custody matters, §7B-508.
Temporary custody of juvenile without court order.
Authority of law enforcement officer or social services worker, §7B-500, (a).
Communication with director of social services, §7B-501, (a).
Duties of person taking into temporary custody, §7B-501, (a).
Notice to parent, guardian, custodian or caretaker, §7B-501, (a).
Release to parent, guardian, custodian or caretaker.
Decision that continued custody unnecessary, §7B-501, (a).
Right to be present with juvenile, parent, guardian, etc., to be advised, §7B-501, (a).
Temporary custody defined, §7B-500, (a).
Time limit on holding in temporary custody, §7B-501, (b).
Termination of guardian relationship, reintegration of juvenile into parent's home, §7A-600, (b).
Termination of parental rights.
Generally, §§7B-1100 to 7B-1113.
See TERMINATION OF PARENTAL RIGHTS.
Grounds for terminating, §7B-1111, (a).
Pending abuse, neglect or dependency proceeding.
Consolidation, petition filed during pending proceeding, §7B-1102, (c).
Motion filed during, service, §7B-1102, (a), (b).
Periodic review hearing as to placement, §7B-908.
Time for giving notice of appeal, §7B-1101.
Time for hearing on nonsecure custody, §7B-506, (a).
Time for holding review hearing as to placement.
Custody removed from parent, §7B-906, (a).
Surrender of juvenile for adoption, agency plan, §7B-909, (a).
Termination of parental rights, §7B-908, (b).
Voluntary foster care placement, §7B-909, (c).
Time for initiating investigation, §7B-302, (a).
Time for service of summons, §7B-407.
Time limit on holding juvenile in temporary custody, §7B-501, (b).
Transcript.
Reducing record to transcript upon notice of appeal, §§7B-806, 7B-2901, (a).
Transfer of juvenile to department of social services in county of residence, §7B-308, (c).
Transfer of proceeding to court in district where juvenile resides.
Proceeding commenced in district other than that of juvenile's residence, §7B-400.
Venue for proceeding, §7B-400.

CHILD ABUSE, NEGLECT OR DEPENDENCY —Cont'd
Violent behavior of person responsible for abuse, history of.
Mental health professional's opinion considered, §7B-803, (a).
Visitation.
Removal of custody from parent, supervision by department of social services, §7B-906, (d).
Waiver of time for service, §7B-407.
Whereabouts of juvenile, refusal to disclose.
Interference with investigation, §7B-303, (b).

CHILD BICYCLE SAFETY ACT, §§20-171.6 to 20-171.9.

CHILD BORN OUT OF WEDLOCK.
Illegitimacy generally, §§49-1 to 49-17.
See ILLEGITIMACY.

CHILD CARE ADMINISTRATORS.
Qualifications, §110-91.

CHILD CARE CENTERS.
Child care facilities generally, §§110-85 to 110-107.
See CHILD CARE FACILITIES.
Defined, §110-86.
Mandatory standards for licensing, §110-91.
Staff-child ratio, §110-91.

CHILD CARE COMMISSION, §143B-168.3, (a).
Appointment of members, §143B-168.4, (b).
Child abuse or neglect.
Investigation of reports and administrative action.
Commission to make rules for, §143B-168.5.
Clerical and other services, §143B-168.4, (c).
Expenses, §143B-168.4, (c).
Meetings, §143B-168.4, (c).
Membership, §143B-168.4, (a).
Officers, §143B-168.4, (c).
Powers and duties, §110-88.
Religious training offered in religious-sponsored child care facilities.
Commission not to interfere with, §110-88.1.
Rules, adoption, §143B-168.3, (b).
Vacancies, §143B-168.4, (c).

CHILD CARE FACILITIES.
Administrative penalty, §110-102.2.
Administrative procedure.
Applicability of act, §110-94.
Administrators.
Qualifications, §110-91.
Alcohol abusers.
Persons not to be employed, §110-91.
Announced and unannounced visits, §110-105, (a).
Building standards, §110-91.
Child abuse and neglect.
Administrative action, sanctions.
Rules, adoption by commission, §110-88.
Child abuse and neglect defined, §110-105.2, (a).
Child care commission.
Investigation of reports and administrative actions, §143B-168.5.
Corrective action, §110-105.2, (d).
Investigation of child sexual abuse in child care facilities, §114-15.3.
Notice by director to department of health and human services and state bureau of investigation.
Finding evidence of abuse or neglect or sexual abuse in facility, §7B-307, (b).

CHILD CARE FACILITIES —Cont'd
Child abuse and neglect —Cont'd
Protective services provided juveniles alleged to be abused, neglected or dependent.
Applicability of provisions to child care facilities, §7B-300.
Special provisional status, §110-105.2, (c).
Special unit within department of health and human services.
Established to deal primarily with violations involving, §143B-168.5.
Unannounced visit after issuance of written warning, §110-105.2, (b).
Use of other statutory or administrative remedies, §110-105.2, (e).
Violations, §110-105.2.
Written warning issued, §110-105.2, (b).
Child abuse or neglect convictions.
Persons not to be employed, §110-91.
Child care defined, §110-86.
Child care licensing commission.
Transfer, recodification and renaming as child care commission, §143B-168.3.
Child care provider criminal history checks, §114-19.5.
Civil action by child care provider on disagreement with department decision, §110-90.2, (d).
Cost of fingerprinting and local check, §110-90.2, (g).
Definitions, §110-90.2, (a).
Department of justice to provide criminal history, §110-90.2, (c).
Duties of department of health and human services, §110-90.2, (b).
Duties of division of child placement, department of health and human services, §110-90.2, (c).
Immunity from liability, §110-90.2, (f).
Notice to child care provider and employer as to qualifications to provide child care, §110-90.2, (d).
Privileged information, §110-90.2, (e).
Providers of treatment for or services to children, §114-19.3.
Statement as to criminal history check, §110-90.2, (c).
Civil penalty, §110-103.1, (a).
Determining amount, §110-103.1, (b).
Notice of penalty, §110-103.1, (c).
Remittance of proceeds, §110-103.1, (d).
Communicable diseases.
Report by child care operators, §130A-136.
Compliance with provisions.
Mandatory compliance, §110-98.
Contracts with state agencies and local boards of education.
Authorization to contract, §143-64.50.
Financial and legal responsibility assumed by operators, §143-64.52.
Licensing and regulating, §143-64.51.
Procedure for approving location, §143-64.50.
Control over facilities.
Abrogation of regulations of institution, §110-46.
Authority of institution as same as parent or guardian, §110-45.
Enticing a child from institution, §110-47.
Exception, §110-47.
Guardian.
Institution has authority of guardian, §110-45.
Institution has authority of parent or guardian, §110-45.

CHILD CARE FACILITIES —Cont'd
Control over facilities —Cont'd
Misdemeanors.
Violations a misdemeanor, §110-48.
Parent.
Institution has authority of parent, §110-45.
Rules and regulations.
Abrogation of regulations, §110-46.
Violations a misdemeanor, §110-48.
Conviction of crime involving child neglect, child abuse or moral turpitude.
Persons not to be employed, §110-91.
Corporal punishment.
Banned in certain nonlicensed homes, §110-101.1.
Prohibited, §110-91.
Criminal history checks.
Child care providers, §110-90.2.
Criminal penalties, §110-103.
Exemptions, §110-103, (a).
Felonies.
Subsequent offenses, §110-103, (d).
Violation causing serious injury to a child, §110-103, (c).
Willful violations, §110-103, (b).
Misdemeanors, §110-103, (a).
Unauthorized administration of medicine, §110-102.1A, (c), (d).
Willful violations, §110-103, (b).
Criminal record checks, §§110-90.2, 114-19.3, 114-19.5. See within this heading, "Child care provider criminal history checks."
Death of child while in child care.
Reporting, §110-102.1, (b).
Definitions, §110-86.
Department of health and human services.
Special unit.
Child abuse and neglect in child care arrangements.
Established to deal primarily with violations involving, §143B-168.5.
Developmentally appropriate activities and play materials, §110-91.
Development of staff requirements, §110-91.
Disciplinary policy, §110-91.
Diseases.
Communicable diseases.
Report by operators of child care facility, §130A-136.
Drop-in or short-term child care.
Notice to department, §110-99, (b).
Drug abusers.
Persons not to be employed, §110-91.
Drugs.
Unauthorized administration of medicine, §110-102.1A.
Duties of local and district health departments, §110-92.
Early childhood administration credential.
Requirement for center administrators, §110-91.
Equipment requirements, §110-91.
Existence of child care.
Prima facie evidence, §110-98.1.
Family child care home capacity, §110-91.
Fire prevention and safe evacuation standards, §110-91.
Fire prevention inspection, §110-92.
Food and beverage standards, §110-91.
Fraud.
Fraudulent misrepresentation, §110-107, (a), (b).
Definitions, §110-107, (c).
Furnishings requirements, §110-91.

CHILD CARE FACILITIES —Cont'd
General assembly.
Legislative intent, §110-85.
Group sizes for infants and toddlers, §110-91.
Health assessments, §110-91.
Immunization certificate.
Maintenance of record, §130A-155, (b).
Report to be filed, §130A-155, (c).
Submission of certificate to child care facility, §130A-155, (a).
Information for parents, guardians or full-time custodians, §110-102.
Injunctive relief, §110-104.
Inspections.
Fire departments, §110-91.
Refusal to allow.
Administrative warrant, §110-105, (b).
Standards and rules for, §110-105, (a).
Kaitlyn's law.
Unauthorized administration of medicine, §110-102.1A.
Lead poisoning in children.
Generally, §§130A-131.5 to 130A-131.9H.
See LEAD POISONING IN CHILDREN.
Legislative intent, §110-85.
Licenses.
Applications, §110-93, (a).
Display, §110-99, (a1).
Initial licensing inspection, §110-105, (a).
Issuance, §110-93, (b).
Mandatory standards, §110-91.
Provisional licenses.
Rules for issuance, adoption by commission, §110-88.
Required, §110-99, (a).
Temporary licenses.
Issuance, rules, adoption by commission, §110-88.
Location of facility.
Standards, §110-91.
Mandatory child care provider criminal history checks, §110-90.2.
Mandatory compliance with provisions, §110-98.
Mandatory standards for license, §110-91.
Medical care procedures, §110-91.
Unauthorized administration of medicine, §110-102.1A.
Medicine, administration, §110-102.1A.
Applicability, §110-102.1A, (a).
Emergency medical condition, §110-102.1A, (b).
Exceptions.
Bona fide medical care provider, §110-102.1A, (b).
Penalty, §110-102.1A, (c).
Written authorization required, §110-102.1A, (a).
Missing children.
Reporting, §110-102.1, (a).
Nutrition standards, §110-91.
Out-of-doors activities, §110-91.
Powers of child care commission, §110-88.
Prima facie evidence of existence of child care facility, §110-98.1.
Public schools.
Students.
Assignments to schools.
Children living in, cared for and supported by, §115C-366, (a1).
Purpose of article, §110-85.
Qualifications for staff, §110-91.
Recordkeeping requirements, §110-91.

CHILD CARE FACILITIES —Cont'd
Records.
Immunization.
Certificate of immunization.
Maintenance of record, §130A-155, (b).
Religious sponsored child care facilities.
Conviction of crime involving child neglect, child abuse or moral turpitude, §110-106, (d).
Corporal punishment banned in certain nonlicensed homes.
Exemptions from provisions, §110-101.1.
Defined, §110-106, (a).
Exemption from certain provisions, §110-106, (c).
Procedure, §110-106, (b).
Staff requirements, §110-106, (e).
Reporting of missing or deceased children, §110-102.1.
Reports.
Communicable diseases, §130A-136.
Immunization.
Certificate of immunization.
Report to be filed, §130A-155, (c).
Rest periods for children, §110-91.
Restraint employed by residential facility.
Collection of data on use, §131D-10.5A.
Rules.
Adoption by commission, §110-88.
Safe sleep policy, §110-91.
Sale of merchandise by governmental units.
Exception to child care facilities receiving state aid, §66-58, (b).
Sanitation standards, §110-91.
Secretary of health and human services.
Powers and duties, §110-90.
Sexual abuse in facilities.
Investigation by bureau of investigation, §114-15.3.
SIDS prevention.
Safe sleep policy, §110-91.
Smoking in public places.
No smoking except in teacher's lounge, §143-599.
Space requirements, §110-91.
Staff-child ratio, §110-91.
Staff development standards, §110-91.
Staff qualifications, §110-91.
Standards for license, §110-91.
Summary of provisions for parents, guardian, etc., §110-102.
Supervision of children, §110-91.
Transportation, §110-91.
Visitation and inspection of child care centers, §110-92.
Visual supervision of children, §110-91.

CHILD CARE SERVICES IN STATE BUILDINGS AND PUBLIC SCHOOLS, §§143-64.50 to 143-64.52.
Authorization to contract with city, county or other political subdivision, etc., §143-64.50.
Financial and legal responsibility assumed by operators, §143-64.52.
Licensing and regulating, §143-64.51.
Location of program, procedure for approving, §143-64.50.

CHILD CUSTODY.
Abused, neglected or dependent juvenile.
Alternative dispositions, §7B-903, (a).
Nonsecure custody, §§7B-502 to 7B-508.
Periodic review hearings, placement of juvenile.
Custody removed from parent, §7B-906.
Surrender of child for adoption, §7B-909.

CHILD CUSTODY —Cont'd
Abused, neglected or dependent juvenile —Cont'd
Periodic review hearings, placement of juvenile —Cont'd
Termination of parental rights, §7B-908.
Voluntary foster care agreement, §7B-910.
Support of juvenile paid by parent.
Custody in someone other than parent, §7B-904, (d).
Suspected abused juvenile brought to medical facility.
Physician or administrator obtaining judicial authority to retain custody, §7B-308.
Temporary custody without court order, §§7B-500, (a), 7B-501.
Accident and health insurance.
Coverage of children, §58-51-120, (b).
Action or proceeding for custody or visitation generally, §50-13.1.
Adoption.
Failure to consent, §50-13.2, (d).
Visitation of adopted grandchild.
Action by biological grandparent, §50-13.2A.
Arbitration.
Family law arbitration generally, §§50-41 to 50-62.
See FAMILY LAW ARBITRATION.
Attorneys' fees, §50-13.6.
Attorneys specializing in family law.
Certification standards, Bar Rules & Regs., D, §§.2401 to .2407.
Best interest and welfare of child.
Persons entitled to custody, §50-13.2, (a).
Change in circumstances.
Modification of order, §50-13.7.
Family law arbitration act, §50-56.
Confidentiality.
Mediation, §50-13.1, (e).
Contempt.
Enforcement of orders, §50-13.3, (a).
Contracts.
Mediation program.
Exemption from competitive bidding contracts, §7A-494, (b).
Costs.
Allowance of costs to either party or apportioned in discretion of court, §6-21.
Delinquent and undisciplined juvenile actions.
Authority to issue orders, delegation of authority, §7B-1902.
Secure or nonsecure custody, §§7B-1903 to 7B-1906.
Telephone communications, notices, etc., §7B-1907.
Temporary custody without court order, §§7B-1900, 7B-1901.
Dismissal on prejudicial grounds, §50-13.1, (d).
District courts.
Proper division for trial of civil actions, §7A-244.
Divorce.
Action or proceeding for custody or visitation, §50-13.1.
Enforcement of order, §50-13.3.
Grandparents' visitation, §50-13.2, (b1).
Adopted grandchild.
Action by biological grandparent, §50-13.2A.
Independent actions permissible, §50-19.
Judgment provisions pertaining to custody, §50-11.2.
Change in conditions.
Jurisdiction requirements, §50-11.2.

CHILD CUSTODY —Cont'd
Divorce —Cont'd
Judgment provisions pertaining to custody —Cont'd
Change in conditions —Cont'd
Modification upon substantial change, §50-11.2.
Mediation program, §§7A-494, 7A-495.
Modification of orders, §50-13.7.
Persons entitled, §50-13.2, (a), (b).
Persons incapable of self-support upon reaching majority, §50-13.8.
Taking child outside state, §50-13.2, (c).
Domestic violence.
Award of temporary custody, §§50B-2, (c1), (c2), 50B-3, (a), (a1).
Emergency relief ex parte orders, §50B-2, (c), (c1), (c2).
Emancipation.
Persons incapable of self-support upon reaching majority.
Rights same as minor child for custody purposes, §50-13.8.
Enforcement.
Uniform child custody jurisdiction and enforcement, §§50A-101 to 50A-317.
See CHILD CUSTODY JURISDICTION AND ENFORCEMENT.
Enforcement of custody orders, §50-13.3.
Contempt, §50-13.3, (a).
Injunctions, §50-13.3, (b).
Pending appeals.
Enforcement by civil contempt proceedings, §50-13.3, (a).
Exclusive custody, §50-13.2, (b).
Family law arbitration generally, §§50-41 to 50-62.
See FAMILY LAW ARBITRATION.
General requirements for orders, §50-13.2.
Modification of order.
Change of circumstances, §50-13.7, (a).
Orders entered by court of another state, §50-13.7, (b).
Grandparents.
Custody and visitation rights, §50-13.5, (j).
Grandparent defined, §50-13.5, (j).
Visitation, §50-13.2, (b1).
Adopted grandchild.
Action by biological grandparent, §50-13.2A.
Handicapped persons.
Persons incapable of self-support upon reaching majority.
Rights same as minor child for custody purposes, §50-13.8.
Health insurance.
Coverage of children, §58-51-120, (b).
Hearings by judge, §50-13.5, (h).
Independent actions for divorce.
Maintenance of certain actions as independent actions permissible, §50-19.
Injunctions.
Enforcement of custody orders, §50-13.3, (b).
Institution of action or proceeding.
Persons who may institute, §50-13.1, (a).
Interlocutory orders, §50-13.5, (d).
Joint custody, §50-13.2, (a), (b).
Jurisdiction.
Action or proceeding for custody or visitation, §50-13.5, (c).
Costs.
Allowance of costs to either party or apportioned in discretion of court, §6-21.

CHILD CUSTODY —Cont'd
Jurisdiction —Cont'd
Uniform child custody jurisdiction and enforcement, §§50A-101 to 50A-317.
See CHILD CUSTODY JURISDICTION AND ENFORCEMENT.
Kidnapping.
Abduction of child, §14-41, (a).
Bail and recognizance, §15A-534.4.
Transporting child outside state.
Intent to violate custody order, §14-320.1.
Mediation, §50-13.1, (b).
Advisory committee.
Established, §7A-495, (b).
Agreements.
Effect of reference as parenting agreement, §50-13.1, (h).
Requirements, §50-13.1, (g).
Competency to testify to communications, §50-13.1, (f).
Confidentiality, §50-13.1, (e).
Contracts.
Exemption from competitive bidding requirements, §7A-494, (b).
Dismissal, §50-13.1, (d).
Establishment of program.
Administrative office of courts to establish, §7A-494, (a).
Local district programs.
Establishment, §7A-494, (b).
Implementation and administration, §7A-495, (a).
Orders.
Incorporation of agreements, §50-13.1, (g).
Parenting agreement deemed order, §50-13.1, (h).
Prejudice.
Dismissal, §50-13.1, (e).
Privileged communications.
Communications with mediator, §50-13.1, (e).
Purposes, §§7A-494, (a), 50-13.1, (b).
Qualifications to provide mediation services, §7A-494, (c).
Rules for custody and visitation mediation.
Administration of program, Rule 4.
Attendance at mediation session, Rule 10.
Best interest of child.
Mediator to be aware of, Rule 11.
Caucus with parties, Rule 12.09.
Complaints about mediators or program, Rule 12.11.
Confidentiality of mediation, Rule 12.03.
Continuing education.
Mediators, Rule 6.02.
Custody mediation advisory committee, Rule 4.05.
Definitions.
Mediation, Rule 3.01.
Mediator, Rule 3.02.
Parenting agreement, Rule 3.03.
Delinquents, placement issues.
Referral to mediation, Rule 7.02.
Dismissal of mediation, Rule 12.06.
Evaluation of program, Rule 12.10.
Funds appropriated by general assembly.
Administration, Rule 4.03.
Goals of mediation, Rule 1.
Juvenile placement issues.
Referral, Rule 7.02.
Length of mediation session, Rule 10.
Local district programs, Rule 5.

CHILD CUSTODY —Cont'd
Mediation —Cont'd
Rules for custody and visitation mediation —Cont'd
Location of mediation, Rule 12.02.
Mandatory referral procedure, Rule 7.01.
Mediators.
Authority, Rule 12.01.
Best interest of child.
Mediator to be aware of, Rule 11.
Caucus with parties, Rule 12.09.
Complaints about, Rule 12.11.
Continuing education, Rule 6.02.
Defined, Rule 3.02.
Duties in mediation process, Rule 12.
Employment, Rule 4.01.
Ethics, Rule 6.04.
In-house contracts for delivery of services, Rule 4.02.
Initial training period, Rule 6.01.
Neutral stance, Rule 11.
Performance evaluation, Rule 6.03.
Qualification, Rule 6.
Speaking with child, Rule 12.08.
Multi-district programs, Rule 4.04.
Number of mediation sessions, Rule 10.
Order to mediation, Rule 7.01.
Orientation session.
Prior to mediation, Rule 9.
Parenting plan, Rule 12.04.
Defined, Rule 3.03.
Incorporation into court order, Rule 12.05.
Performance evaluation.
Mediators, Rule 6.03.
Placement of juveniles.
Referral of placement issues, Rule 7.02.
Process of mediation, Rule 12.
Purpose of program, Rule 2.
Referral of placement issues, Rule 7.02.
Referral to mediation, Rule 7.01.
Return to mediation.
Unable to resolve problems, change in circumstances, Rule 12.07.
Termination of mediation, Rule 12.06.
Undisciplined juveniles, placement issues.
Referral to mediation, Rule 7.02.
Waiver of mediation, Rule 8.
Staff support, §7A-494, (a).
Waiver of mandatory setting.
Good cause, §50-13.1, (c).
Mental health, developmental disabilities and substance abuse.
Persons incapable of self-support upon reaching majority.
Rights same as minor child for custody purposes, §50-13.8.
Modification of order, §50-13.7.
Family law arbitration act, §50-56.
Motions.
Modification of orders, §50-13.7.
Notice, §50-13.5, (d).
Notice.
Motions, §50-13.5, (d).
Paternity established, §49-15.
Persons entitled to custody, §50-13.2, (a).
Preliminary injunction enjoining spouse from interfering with, threatening or molesting plaintiff during pendency of suit.
Bonds not required, §1A-1, Rule 65, (c).

CHILD CUSTODY —Cont'd
Privileged communications.
Mediation.
Communications with mediator, §50-13.1, (e).
Procedure, §50-13.5, (a).
Rape.
Child born as result of commission of rape.
Effect of conviction.
First degree rape, §14-27.2, (c).
Second degree rape, §14-27.3, (c).
Records.
Health, education and welfare records of child.
Equal access, §50-13.2, (b).
Service of process.
Action or proceeding for custody or visitation, §50-13.5, (d).
Taking child outside of state.
Orders providing for, §50-13.2, (c).
Temporary orders pending service and notice, §50-13.5, (d).
Temporary restraining order enjoining spouse from interfering with, threatening or molesting plaintiff during pendency of suit.
Bond not required, §1A-1, Rule 65, (c).
Termination of parental rights proceedings.
Finding that court has jurisdiction to make custody determination.
Required before court exercises jurisdiction to terminate parental rights, §7B-1101.
Transporting child outside state.
Intent to violate custody order, §14-320.1.
Type of actions, §50-13.5, (b).
Uniform child custody jurisdiction and enforcement, §§50A-101 to 50A-317.
See CHILD CUSTODY JURISDICTION AND ENFORCEMENT.
Venue.
Action or proceeding for custody or visitation, §50-13.5, (f).
Visitation.
Abused, neglected or dependent juvenile.
Custody removed from parent, §7B-906, (d).
Action or proceeding for custody or visitation generally, §50-13.1.
Attorneys' fees, §50-13.6.
Denial of parental visitation rights.
Written findings of fact, §50-13.5, (i).
Grandparents, §50-13.2, (b1).
Adopted grandchild.
Action by biological grandparent, §50-13.2A.
Custody and visitation rights, §50-13.5, (j).
Mediation.
Custody and visitation mediation program, §§7A-494, 7A-495.
Waiver.
Action or proceeding for custody or visitation.
Mediation, §50-13.1, (c).
Who may institute action or proceeding, §50-13.1, (a).

CHILD CUSTODY JURISDICTION AND ENFORCEMENT, §§50A-101 to 50A-317.
Adoption.
Application of provisions, §50A-103.
Appeals, §50A-314.
Appearances, §50A-210.
Expenses, §50A-210, (d).
Limited immunity, §50A-109, (a).
Exceptions, §50A-109, (b), (c).
Notice, §50A-210, (b).

CHILD CUSTODY JURISDICTION AND ENFORCEMENT —Cont'd
Appearances —Cont'd
Orders, §50A-210, (a), (c).
Application of provisions, §50A-103.
Indian tribes, §50A-104.
International application, §50A-105.
Notice, §50A-205, (b).
Communication between courts, §50A-110.
Notice, §50A-110, (c).
Participation of parties, §50A-110, (b).
Permitted, §50A-110, (a).
Records, §50A-110, (d).
Defined, §50A-110, (e).
Temporary emergency jurisdiction, §50A-204, (d).
Confidentiality.
Sealed information, §50A-209, (e).
Cooperation between courts, §50A-112.
Expenses, §50A-112, (c).
Permissible requests, §50A-112, (a).
Hearings, §50A-112, (b).
Preservation of records, §50A-112, (d).
Costs and fees, §50A-310, (b).
Assessed against a state, §50A-312, (b).
Awarded to prevailing party, §50A-312, (a).
Hague convention, §50A-317.
Declining jurisdiction by reason of conduct, §50A-208, (a).
Remedies, §50A-208, (b), (c).
Definitions, §50A-102.
Duty to enforce, §50A-303.
Available remedies, §50A-303, (b).
Out of state custody determinations, §50A-303, (a).
Effect of child custody determination, §50A-106.
Emergency jurisdiction, §50A-204.
Emergency medical care.
Application of provisions, §50A-103.
Enforcement, §§50A-301 to 50A-317.
Definitions, §50A-301.
Exclusive continuing jurisdiction, §50A-202, (a).
Modification of determination, §50A-202, (b).
Expedited enforcement, §50A-308.
Petition, §50A-308, (a).
Filing, §50A-308, (c).
Orders, §50A-308, (d).
Requirements, §50A-308, (b).
Expenses, §50A-310, (b).
Assessed against a state, §50A-312, (b).
Awarded to prevailing party, §50A-312, (a).
Hague convention, §50A-317.
Forum non conveniens, §§50A-206, (a), 50A-207.
Full faith and credit, §50A-313.
Hague convention, §50A-302.
Costs and expenses, §50A-317.
Prosecutor or public official, role of, §50A-315.
Actions by law enforcement officer, §50A-316.
Hearings.
Enforcement, §50A-310.
Inconvenient forum, §§50A-206, (a), 50A-207.
Considerations, §50A-207, (b).
Declined to exercise jurisdiction, §50A-207, (d).
Motion, §50A-207, (a).
Stays, §50A-207, (c).
Indian tribes, §50A-104.
Applicable proceedings, §50A-104, (a).
Previous determinations, §50A-104, (c).
Tribe treated as state, §50A-104, (b).
Information to be submitted to court, §50A-209.
Additional information, §50A-209, (c).
Duty to inform, §50A-209, (d).

CHILD CUSTODY JURISDICTION AND ENFORCEMENT —Cont'd
Information to be submitted to court —Cont'd
Not furnished, §50A-209, (b).
Required information, §50A-209, (a).
Sealed information, §50A-209, (e).
Initial child custody jurisdiction, §50A-201.
Exclusive basis, §50A-201, (a), (b).
Physical presence or personal jurisdiction, §50A-201, (c).
Injunctions.
Simultaneous proceedings, §50A-206, (c).
International application, §50A-105.
Applicable proceedings, §50A-105, (c).
Foreign country treated as state, §50A-105, (a).
Previous determinations, §50A-105, (b).
Interpretation of provisions.
Third party proceedings, §50A-205, (c).
Intervention, §50A-205, (c).
Jurisdiction, §§50A-201 to 50A-210.
Appearances, §50A-210.
Limited immunity, §50A-109.
Basis for determination, §50A-201.
Declined by reason of conduct, §50A-208.
Exclusive continuing jurisdiction, §50A-202.
Inconvenient forum, §50A-207.
Simultaneous proceedings, §50A-206, (a).
Information to be submitted to court, §50A-209.
Modification of determination, §50A-203.
Notice, §50A-205.
Persons outside state, §50A-108.
Priority of determination, §50A-107.
Simultaneous proceedings, §50A-206.
Temporary emergency jurisdiction, §50A-204.
Law-enforcement officers.
Action by, §50A-316.
Modification of determination, §§50A-202, (b), 50A-203.
Notice.
Jurisdiction, §50A-205, (a).
Persons outside state, §50A-108, (a), (c).
Proof of service, §50A-108, (b).
Orders.
Expedited enforcement, §50A-308, (d).
Full faith and credit, §50A-313.
Hearing and order, §50A-310.
Immediate physical custody, §50A-310, (a).
Service of petitioner in order, §50A-309.
Petitions.
Expedited enforcement, §50A-308.
Service of petition and order, §50A-309.
Physical custody of child, warrant for, §50A-311.
Conditions, §50A-311, (f).
Enforcement, §50A-311, (e).
Petition, §50A-311, (a).
Reasons for issuance, §50A-311, (b).
Requirements, §50A-311, (c).
Service, §50A-311, (d).
Privilege, §50A-310, (d).
Proceedings governed by other law, §50A-103.
Prosecutor or public official, role of.
Hague convention, §50A-315, (a), (b).
Registration of child custody determination, §50A-305.
Confirmation, §50A-305, (e), (f).
Contesting validity, §50A-305, (d).
Enforcement, §50A-306, (a), (b).
Notice, §50A-305, (b), (c).
Procedure, §50A-305, (a).
Service of process, §50A-109, (b).

CHILD CUSTODY JURISDICTION AND ENFORCEMENT —Cont'd
Short title, §50A-101.
Simultaneous proceedings, §50A-206.
Enforcement, §50A-307.
Exercise of jurisdiction, §50A-206, (a).
Permissible actions, §50A-206, (b), (c).
Spousal privilege, §50A-310, (d).
Temporary emergency jurisdiction, §50A-204.
Communication between courts, §50A-204, (d).
No previous determination, §50A-204, (b).
Previous determination exists, §50A-204, (c).
Requirements, §50A-204, (a).
Temporary visitation, §50A-304.
Orders, §50A-304, (b).
Visitation schedule, §50A-304, (a).
Testimony.
Failure to testify, inferences drawn, §50A-310, (c).
Taking in another state, §50A-111.
Electronic means, §50A-111, (b).
Evidence, §50A-111, (c).
Permitted, §50A-111, (a).
Title, §50A-101.
Warrants.
Physical custody of child, §50A-311.
Witnesses.
Failure to testify, inferences drawn, §50A-310, (c).

CHILD FATALITY PREVENTION SYSTEM, §§7B-1400 to 7B-1414.
Access to records by state team, local teams and task force, §7B-1413, (a).
Assessment of prevention system, duty of state team, §7B-1405.
Child fatality prevention team.
Chair, §7B-1407, (b).
Duties, §7B-1406, (b).
Establishment in county to conduct reviews, §7B-1406, (b).
Local team defined, §7B-1401.
Meetings, §7B-1407, (f), (g).
Membership, §7B-1407, (a) to (c).
Reports to team coordinator, §7B-1406, (c).
Statement of confidentiality requirement, §7B-1413, (d).
Child fatality prevention team coordinator.
Duties, §7B-1408.
Ex officio member of local team, §7B-1407, (d).
Closed meetings of state team and local teams, §7B-1413, (b).
Community child protection team.
Chair, §7B-1407, (e).
Director of county department of social services as member of team, duties, §7B-1409.
Duties, §7B-1406, (a).
Establishment in counties of state, §7B-1406, (a).
Geographic or governmental area larger than one county, no team to encompass, §7B-1407, (a).
Local team defined, §7B-1401.
Meetings, §7B-1407, (f), (g).
Membership, §7B-1407, (b).
Public and nonpublic agencies in community, representation by, §7B-1407, (a).
Rules in connection with reviews, adoption by social services commission, §7B-1413, (f).
Statement of confidentiality requirement, §7B-1413, (d).
Technical assistance provided by state team, §7B-1405.
Training of members, responsibility, §7B-1411.

CHILD FATALITY PREVENTION SYSTEM —Cont'd
Community responsibility, prevention of abuse, neglect and death, §7B-1400.
Confidentiality of information and records acquired by team, §7B-1413.
Definitions, §7B-1401.
Director of county department of social services.
Calling first meeting of community child protection team, §7B-1407, (g).
Duties as member of community child protection team, §7B-1409.
Director of local department of health.
Calling first meeting of child fatality prevention team, §7B-1407, (g).
Duties as member of local team, §7B-1410.
Disclosure of records in child fatality or near child fatality cases, §7B-2902.
Provisions governing access to child fatality prevention team and fatality task force records, §7B-2902, (f).
Discovery of information and records acquired by local teams, prohibition, §7B-1413, (c).
Division of social services, department of health and human services.
Duty to train local team members, §7B-1411.
Entry in child's protective services records that case reviewed by local team, §7B-1413, (e).
Guidelines for selecting child deaths to received detailed reviews.
Duty of state team to develop, §7B-1405.
Intent of provisions, §7B-1400.
Local team.
Composition, §7B-1407.
Creation and duties, §7B-1406.
Defined, §7B-1401.
Rules in connection with reviews, adoption by social services commission, §7B-1413, (f).
Statement as to understanding of confidentiality requirements, §7B-1413, (d).
Technical assistance to provided by state team, §7B-1405.
Minutes of public meetings, §7B-1413, (b).
Multidisciplinary review of child deaths.
Duty of task force to develop system, §7B-1403.
Periodic public meetings held by local teams, §7B-1413, (b).
Prevention of abuse, neglect and death of juveniles.
Public policy of state, §7B-1400.
Report by task force to governor and general assembly, §7B-1412.
Report to task force during existence of task force.
Duty of state team, §7B-1405.
Review of deaths attributable to abuse or neglect.
Duty of state team, §7B-1405.
Rules as to reviews conducted by community child protection team.
Social services commission to adopt, §7B-1413, (f).
Statement of understanding as to confidentiality requirements.
Member of local team to sign, §7B-1413, (d).
State team.
Created, §7B-1404, (a).
Defined, §7B-1401.
Duties, §7B-1405.
Membership, §7B-1404, (b).

CHILD FATALITY PREVENTION SYSTEM —Cont'd
State team —Cont'd
Staff or consultants, hiring, §7B-1414, (a).
Travel and subsistence expenses for members, staff and consultants, §7B-1414, (b).
Vacancies, §7B-1404, (c).
Study of incidences and causes of child deaths and establishment of profile.
Duty of task force, §7B-1403.
Task force.
Chair, §7B-1402, (c).
Created, §7B-1402, (a).
Defined, §7B-1401.
Duties, §7B-1403.
Membership, §7B-1402, (b).
Office space in legislative building and legislative office building, §7B-1414, (c).
Report to governor and general assembly, §7B-1412.
Staff or consultants, hiring, §7B-1414, (a).
Travel and subsistence expenses for members, staff and consultants, §7B-1414, (b).
Vacancies, §7B-1402, (c).
Testimony as to what transpired at meeting of team, prohibition, §7B-1413, (c).
Training of local teams, §7B-1411.

CHILD FATALITY REVIEW TEAM.
Confidentiality requirement, members to sign statement of understanding, §143B-150.20, (g).
Disclosure of information, order for.
Failure to receive information requested, §143B-150.20, (d).
Established, §143B-150.20, (a).
Findings and recommendations developed for each fatality review.
Division of social service to make public, not admissible, §143B-150.20, (b).
Medical, hospital and other records, access to, §143B-150.20, (d).
Meetings not subject to open meetings law, holding public meetings, §143B-150.20, (e).
Records, confidentiality, not discoverable, not admissible, §143B-150.20, (f).
Report on activities, §143B-150.20, (h).
Representatives included on team, §143B-150.20, (c).
Reviews of child fatalities.
Purpose, §143B-150.20, (b).
Steps, §143B-150.20, (a).

CHILD FATALITY TASK FORCE.
Generally, §§7B-1400 to 7B-1414.

CHILDHOOD VACCINE-RELATED INJURY COMPENSATION, §§130A-422 to 130A-434.
Actions.
Health care providers.
Right of state to bring action against, §130A-430, (a).
Manufacturers.
Right of state to bring action against, §130A-430, (b).
Appeals.
Decisions of commission, §130A-428, (c).
Applicability of provisions, §130A-432.
Attorneys' fees, Childhood Vac. Rule 203.
Awards, §§130A-426, (b), 130A-427, (a).
Amount, §130A-427, (b).

CHILDHOOD VACCINE-RELATED INJURY COMPENSATION —Cont'd
Claims.
Determination by commission, §130A-426, (a).
Notice, §130A-428, (b).
Entry of case upon hearing docket.
Duty of commission on receipt, §130A-425, (c).
Filing, §130A-425, (b).
Contents of petition, §130A-425, (b).
Required, §130A-425, (a).
Time limit, §130A-429, (a) to (c).
Notice of date and place of hearing.
Duty of commission on receipt, §130A-425, (c).
Requirements for filing petition, §130A-423, (b1).
Rules of court.
Applicability, §130A-425, (d).
Secretary party to all proceedings, §130A-425, (c).
Service of copy of petition.
Duty of commission on receipt, §130A-425, (c).
Contempt.
Industrial commission.
Power to punish for contempt, §130A-424.
Superior court of Wake county.
Power to punish for contempt, §130A-425, (d).
Contracts.
Purchase of vaccines, §130A-433.
Covered vaccines.
Contracts for purchase, §130A-433.
Defined, §130A-422.
Distribution, §130A-433.
Fees for providing, §130A-433.
Damages.
Action by state against health care provider, §130A-430, (a).
Action by state against manufacturer, §130A-430, (b).
Damages awarded against vaccine manufacturers.
Duplicate damages, prevention, §130A-423, (c).
Limitation on amount, §130A-423, (d).
Definitions, §130A-422.
Diversion of vaccines, §130A-431.
Establishment of program, §130A-423, (a).
Exclusive nature of remedy, §130A-423, (b).
Fees.
Covered vaccines.
Providing, §130A-433.
Forms.
Official forms of the industrial commission, Childhood Vac. Rule 103.
Fund.
Established, §130A-434, (a).
Payments from fund, §130A-434, (a).
Transfer of appropriations and receipts, §130A-434, (b).
Guardian ad litem.
Filing of claims on behalf of minors or incompetent persons, §130A-429, (a).
Guardian and ward.
Filing of claims on behalf of minors or incompetent persons, §130A-429, (a).
Hearings.
Industrial commission.
Power to hear and determine claims, §130A-424.
Industrial commission.
Appeals from decisions, §130A-428, (c).
Attorneys' fees, Childhood Vac. Rule 203.
Decisions, §130A-426, (b).
Appeals from, §130A-428, (c).
Finality, §130A-428, (a).

CHILDHOOD VACCINE-RELATED INJURY COMPENSATION —Cont'd
Industrial commission —Cont'd
Definition of "commission," §130A-422.
Forms.
Official forms, Childhood Vac. Rule 103.
Hearings.
Power to hear and determine claims, §130A-424.
Hours of business, Childhood Vac. Rule 101.
Location of offices, Childhood Vac. Rule 101.
Powers, §130A-424.
Procedural rules of commission, Childhood Vac. Rule 202.
Rules of civil procedure.
Applicability, Childhood Vac. Rule 201.
Transaction of business by commission, Childhood Vac. Rule 102.
Limitation of actions.
Claims, §130A-429, (a) to (c).
Notice.
Decisions of commission, §130A-428, (b).
Oaths.
Industrial commission.
Power to administer oaths, §§130A-424, 130A-425, (d).
Parent and child.
Filing of claims on behalf of minors or incompetent persons, §130A-429, (a).
Petitions.
Information required, §130A-425, (b).
Requirements for filing, §130A-423, (b1).
Service, §130A-425, (c).
Record of proceedings, §130A-425, (d).
Rules and regulations.
Governing proceedings, commission to adopt, §130A-425, (d).
Secretary of health and human services, §130A-433.
Rules of civil procedure.
Industrial commission.
Applicability of rules of civil procedure, Childhood Vac. Rule 201.
Scope of provisions, §130A-432.
Service of process.
Notice of date and place of hearing, petition, §130A-425, (c).
Subpoenas.
Industrial commission.
Powers, §§130A-424, 130A-425, (d).
Subrogation.
Claims under national childhood vaccine injury act.
Filing with appropriate court, §130A-423, (f).
Witnesses.
Industrial commission.
Power to require witnesses to testify, §130A-425, (d).

CHILD LABOR.
ABC permit holders.
Restrictions on employment of minors by, §95-25.5, (j).
Actors or performers.
Exemption from certain provisions, §95-25.5, (g).
Civil penalty, §95-25.23.
Employment certificates, §95-25.5, (a).
Exemptions, §§95-25.5, (g) to (k), 95-25.14, (a).
Fair labor standards act.
Employment by parents.
Exemption from certain provisions, §95-25.5, (i).
Newspaper distribution, §95-25.5, (d).

CHILD LABOR —Cont'd
Fair labor standards act —Cont'd
Persons and establishments subject to.
Exemption from certain provisions, §95-25.5, (k).
Hazardous occupations, §95-25.5, (b).
Hours worked.
Restrictions, §95-25.5, (c), (e).
Limitation of actions.
Violations of provisions.
Assessment of penalties, §95-25.23, (d).
Models.
Exemption from certain provisions, §95-25.5, (g).
Motor vehicles.
Eligibility to drive as part of employment, §95-25.5, (l).
Outdoor dramas.
Exemptions from certain provisions, §95-25.5, (h).
School term employment.
Hours of employment, §95-25.5, (a1).
Violations of provisions.
Civil penalty, §95-25.23, (a).
Action to recover, §95-25.23, (b).
Collection, §95-25.23, (b).
Limitation of actions, §95-25.23, (d).
Payments of sums collected into general fund, §95-25.23, (c).
Waiver of provisions for minors over twelve years of age.
Power of commissioner, §95-25.5, (f).

CHILD MOLESTATION.
Bail and recognizance, §15A-534.4.
DNA analysis.
Blood sample required upon conviction, §15A-266.4.
Rehabilitative treatment.
Defendant may pay cost as condition of probation, §15A-1343, (b1).
Statutory rape, §14-27.7, (a).
Defendant at least six years older than victim, §14-27.7A, (a).
Defendant between four and six years older than victim, §14-27.7A, (b).
Taking indecent liberties with children, §14-202.1.
Indecent liberties between children, §14-202.2.
Testing of defendant for sexually transmitted diseases, §15A-615.
Venue, §15A-136.

CHILDNAPPING.
See CHILD ABDUCTION.

CHILD PASSENGER RESTRAINTS, §20-137.1.
Child care facilities.
Compliance with law required, §110-91.
Placement of small children within vehicle, §20-137.1, (a1).

CHILD PLACEMENT.
Abused, neglected or dependent juvenile actions.
Alternative dispositions, §7B-903, (a).
Disposition generally, §§7B-900 to 7B-1004.
See CHILD ABUSE, NEGLECT OR DEPENDENCY.
Periodic review hearings, §§7B-906 to 7B-910.
Adoption and medical assistance for adoptive parents.
Interstate compact on adoption and medical assistance, §§7B-3900 to 7B-3906.
See ADOPTION.

CHILD PLACEMENT —Cont'd
Adoption generally, §§48-1-101 to 48-10-105.
See ADOPTION.
Agencies.
General provisions, §§131D-10.1 to 131D-10.9.
See CHILD PLACING AGENCIES.
Bringing or sending into state child for purposes of placement or adoption, §§7B-3700 to 7B-3705.
Bond required of person, agency, association, etc., bringing or sending child into state, §7B-3701.
Definitions, §7B-3704.
Inapplicability of provisions, §7B-3705.
Misdemeanor for violating provisions, §7B-3703.
Responsibility for child's proper care and training, person within whom child placed, §7B-3700, (a).
Visitation and supervision, right of department of health and human services, §7B-3700, (b).
Written consent of department of health and human services required, §7B-3700, (a).
Consent of department of health and human services for adoption or placement of juvenile.
Bringing child into state or sending out of state, §§7B-3700 to 7B-3705.
Delinquent and undisciplined juvenile actions.
Secure or nonsecure custody, §§7B-1902 to 7B-1906.
Interstate compact, §§7B-3800 to 7B-3806.
Administrator, §7B-3806.
Agreements under compact, §7B-3802.
Applicability of compact.
Adoptions, §48-3-207.
Conditions for placement, §7B-3800.
Construction and severability of provisions, §7B-3800.
Default of performance for financial responsibility, §7B-3801.
Definitions, §7B-3800.
Delinquent children, institutional care, §7B-3800.
Delinquent children, placement generally, §7B-3805.
District court jurisdiction, §§7B-200, (a), 7B-1603.
Enactment into law, §7B-3800.
Financial responsibility for child placed pursuant to contract, §7B-3801.
Governor authorized to appoint compact administrator, §7B-3806.
Limitations on compact, §7B-3800.
Officers and agencies of state, agreement, §7B-3802.
Penalty for illegal placement, §7B-3800.
Placement of delinquents generally, §7B-3805.
Placements made pursuant to compact, applicability of provisions, §7B-3804.
Provisions governed between party states, §7B-3804.
Requirements for visitation, inspection or supervision, §7B-3803.
Retention of jurisdiction by sending state, §7B-3800.
Text of compact, §7B-3800.
Visitation, inspection or supervision of children, §7B-3803.
Reasonable efforts to eliminate need for placement.
Findings required in order, §7B-507, (a).
Health and safety of juvenile as primary concern in determination of need for reasonable efforts, §7B-507, (d).

CHILD PLACEMENT —Cont'd
Reasonable efforts to eliminate need for placement —Cont'd
Permanency planning hearing, time for when reasonable efforts not required, §7B-507, (c).
When reasonable efforts not required, §7B-507, (b).
Sending child out of state for purposes of placement.
Applicability of article, §7B-3705.
Consent of department of health and human services required, §7B-3702.
Definitions, §7B-3704.
Misdemeanor, §7B-3703.
Special education.
Change in placement pending administrative review or subsequent judicial review, §115C-116, (l).
Termination of parental rights.
Generally, §§7B-1100 to 7B-1113.
See TERMINATION OF PARENTAL RIGHTS.

CHILD PLACING AGENCIES, §§131D-10.1 to 131D-10.9.
Access to premises.
Licensee or license applicant to permit department, §131D-10.3, (b).
Administrative procedures act.
Applicability to notifications, hearings and appeals, §131D-10.9.
Applicability of article, §131D-10.3, (d).
Criminal history records checks of foster parents.
Annual check, §131D-10.3A, (b).
Confidential and privileged information, §131D-10.3A, (f), (g).
Department of justice to provide information, §131D-10.3A, (d).
Destruction of information, §131D-10.3A, (g).
Fee for check, §131D-10.3A, (i).
Hearing, request by foster parent, §131D-10.3A, (f).
Immunity for action taken in carrying out provision, §131D-10.3A, (h).
Mandatory checks, §131D-10.3A, (a).
Notice of mandatory checks.
Placement on application, §131D-10.3A, (e).
Prohibiting person from providing foster care, §131D-10.3A, (c).
Review of information, right of individual, §131D-10.3A, (f).
Death of resident of facility.
Civil penalty, failure to notify department, §131D-10.6B, (a).
Disclosure of information, restriction, §131D-10.6B, (d).
Governor's advocacy council for persons with disabilities.
Department to notify, §131D-10.6B, (b).
Notice to department, §131D-10.6B, (a).
Physical restraint, death occurring within 7 days of use.
Immediate investigation, §131D-10.6B, (c).
Standard reporting format, secretary to establish, §131D-10.6B, (e).
Declaratory rulings, commission issuing, §131D-10.5.
Definitions, §§131D-10.2, 48-1-101.
Exemptions from article, §131D-10.4.
Injunctions.
Interference with department carrying out duties, §131D-10.8, (b).

CHILD PLACING AGENCIES —Cont'd
Injunctions —Cont'd
Operating without license, §131D-10.8, (a).
Interference with department carrying out duties.
Injunctions, §131D-10.8, (b).
License to operate or provide foster care or place children.
Access to premises.
Applicant to permit department, §131D-10.3, (b).
Document of compliance, §131D-10.3, (g).
Duration and expiration, §131D-10.3, (e).
Exemptions from article, §131D-10.4.
Injunction, operating without license, §131D-10.8, (a).
Periodic review of persons licensed, §131D-10.3, (c).
Powers and duties of department, §131D-10.6.
Provisional license, granting, §131D-10.3, (f).
Required, §131D-10.3, (a).
Unlicensed practice.
Fine, §131D-10.7.
Injunction, §131D-10.8, (a).
Periodic review of persons licensed, §131D-10.3, (c).
Policy of state, §131D-10.1.
Powers and duties of department, §131D-10.6.
Powers of commission, §131D-10.5.
Purpose of article, §131D-10.1.
Restraint employed by child care facility.
Collection of data on use, §131D-10.5A.
Rules, adoption by commission, §131D-10.5.
Training.
Child welfare services staff, §131D-10.6A, (b).
Foster parents, §131D-10.6A, (a).
Unlicensed practice.
Fine, §131D-10.7.
Injunction, §131D-10.8, (a).

CHILD PORNOGRAPHY.
Electronic surveillance orders, §15A-290, (c1).
Sexual exploitation of a minor, §§14-190.16, 14-190.17.

CHILD PROTECTION TEAMS.
Generally, §§7B-1400 to 7B-1414.
See CHILD FATALITY PREVENTION SYSTEM.

CHILDREN AND MINORS.
Abandonment.
Baby drop off, §§14-318.2, 14-318.4, 14-322.3, (c).
Willful neglect or refusal to provide support, §14-322.
Abduction of children, §14-41, (a).
Abortion.
Parental or judicial consent, §§90-21.6 to 90-21.10.
Administration of estates.
Additional costs assessed before clerk, §7A-307, (d).
Assessment of costs, §7A-307, (a).
Completeness and exclusivity of costs, §7A-307, (c).
Courtroom and related judicial facilities.
Amount of facilities fee, §7A-307, (b).
Use of facilities, §7A-307, (a).
General court of justice.
Support of court, §7A-307, (a).
Liability of parties for costs, §7A-307, (e).
Adoption generally.
See ADOPTION.

CHILDREN AND MINORS —Cont'd
Adoptive homes.
Regulation of agencies receiving or placing children, §§131D-10.1 to 131D-10.9.
See CHILD PLACING AGENCIES.
Air pistols or rifles.
Permitting young children to use dangerous weapons, §14-316, (b).
Alcoholic beverages.
Compensation for injury caused by sales to underage persons, §§18B-120 to 18B-129.
See ALCOHOLIC BEVERAGES.
Driving after consuming alcohol.
Restoration of license after conviction, §20-17.6.
Driving by person less than 21 years old after consuming alcohol or drugs, §20-138.3.
Employment of youth by person holding ABC permits, §95-25.5, (j).
Handling in course of employment.
Authorized, §18B-302, (h).
Purchase or possession, §18B-302, (b), (i).
Aiding and abetting, §18B-302, (c).
Fines and other penalties, §18B-302.1, (b), (c).
Allowing use of license, §18B-302, (f).
Conviction reports to division of motor vehicles, §18B-302, (g).
Drivers' licenses.
Revocation for underage purchases, §20-17.3.
Use of fraudulent license, §18B-302, (e).
Nineteen or twenty year olds, §18B-302, (i).
Sales to.
Aiding and abetting, §18B-302, (c).
Fines and other penalties, §18B-302.1, (b), (c).
Defense to violation of subsection, §18B-302, (d).
Fines and other penalties, §18B-302.1, (a), (c).
Prohibited, §18B-302, (a).
Alcoholism.
Consent of minor to treatment sufficient, §90-21.5, (a).
AMBER alert system, §143B-499.7.
Appeals involving juvenile matters.
Appeal information statement.
Juvenile's name not used, App. Proc. Rule 41, (b).
Briefs in juvenile matters.
Name of juvenile or identifying information excluded, App. Proc. Rul e28, (k).
Identifying information of juvenile subject to action.
Exclusion from filings, documents, exhibits and argumanrs, App. Proc. Rules 3, (b), 26, (g).
Motion or response to motion.
Juvenile's name not used, App. Proc. Rule 37, (c).
Name of juvenile subject of action.
Referenced by initials, App. Proc. Rules 3, (b), 26, (g).
Oral argument in juvenile matters.
Name of juvenile not used, App. Proc. Rule 30, (g).
Verbatim transcripts.
Submitted to court in signed, sealed envelope, App. Proc. Rule 9, (c).
Arrest.
Notification of parent or guardian, §15A-505, (a), (b).
Notification of principal of school, §15A-505, (c).
Photographs and fingerprints.
Not authorized for juveniles, §15A-502, (c).
Artificial insemination.
Status of child, §49A-1.

CHILDREN AND MINORS —Cont'd
Artistic and creative services contracts, §§48A-11 to 48A-16.
Assault and battery.
Assault of child under certain age, §14-33.
Inflicting serious injury or using deadly weapon in presence of minor, §14-33, (d).
At-risk students.
Extended service programs, §§115C-238.30 to 115C-238.33.
Authority of parent over juvenile, §§7B-3400 to 7B-3404.
Baby drop off, §§14-318.2, 14-318.4, 14-322.3, (c).
Banks.
Deposits.
Operating deposit account in name of minor, §53-43.5, (a).
Safe-deposit boxes.
Leasing or renting to minors, §53-43.5, (b), (c).
Bars.
Permitting minors to enter barrooms, §14-317.
Bastardy.
General provisions, §§49-1 to 49-17.
See ILLEGITIMACY.
BB guns.
Permitting young children to use dangerous firearms, §14-316, (b).
Betterments.
Procedure where plaintiff is under disability, §1-349.
Bicycles.
Child bicycle safety act, §§20-171.6 to 20-171.9.
Article known and cited as, §20-171.6.
Civil fine assessed parent or guardian found responsible, §20-171.9, (d).
Definitions, §20-171.8.
Infraction for violation, §20-171.9, (d).
Legislative findings and declaration, §20-171.7, (a).
Negligence or liability not assessed for violation, §20-171.9, (c).
Passenger on bicycle, requirements, §20-171.9, (b).
Protective bicycle helmet.
Wearing while riding roadway, bicycle path, required, §20-171.9, (a).
Purposes of article, §20-171.7, (b).
Restraining seat for small children.
Requirement to be passenger, §20-171.9, (b).
Short title of act, §20-171.6.
Subsequent purchase of helmet or restraining seat.
Waiver of fine for violation, §20-171.9, (e).
Billiard rooms.
Permitting minors to enter billiard rooms, §14-317.
Birth of child, concealing, §14-46.
Blind persons.
Personal representatives for certain recipients of aid.
Affecting provisions for payments of minors, §111-33.
Boating safety.
Personal watercraft.
Persons under 16 years of age operating, §75A-13.3, (b).
Renting, hiring or leasing to persons under 16 years, §75A-13.3, (c).
Body piercing.
Without consent of parents, §14-400, (b).

CHILDREN AND MINORS —Cont'd
Capital punishment.
Persons under 17 years of age, §14-17.
Caveat to will.
Time for filing after removal of disability, §31-32.
Center for missing persons.
General provisions, §§143B-495 to 143B-499.7.
See MISSING PERSONS.
Change of name.
Procedure, §101-2.
Two change limitation, §101-6, (b).
Child abuse, neglect or dependency.
Generally, §§7B-100 to 7B-1414.
See CHILD ABUSE, NEGLECT OR DEPENDENCY.
Child care facilities.
Adoption generally.
See ADOPTION.
Control over child care facilities, §§110-45 to 110-48.
See CHILD CARE FACILITIES.
General provisions, §§110-85 to 110-107.
See CHILD CARE FACILITIES.
Child custody generally.
See CHILD CUSTODY.
Child custody jurisdiction and enforcement, §§50A-101 to 50A-317.
See CHILD CUSTODY JURISDICTION AND ENFORCEMENT.
Child fatality prevention system.
Generally, §§7B-1400 to 7B-1414.
See CHILD FATALITY PREVENTION SYSTEM.
Child placement compact, §§7B-3800 to 7B-3806.
Child placing agencies.
Regulation of agencies receiving or placing children, §§131D-10.1 to 131D-10.9.
See CHILD PLACING AGENCIES.
Child pornography.
Sexual exploitation of minors, §§14-190.16, 14-190.17.
Children's trust fund, §7B-1302.
Child restraint systems, §20-137.1.
Child bicycle safety act.
Restraining seat.
Small children as passengers, §§20-171.6 to 20-171.9.
Placement of small children within vehicle, §20-137.1, (a1).
Points for violations, §§20-16, (c), 20-137.1, (d).
Transporting children under 12 years of age in open bed or open cargo area of vehicle.
Exception to prohibition when child secured or restrained by seat belt, §20-135.2B, (b).
Child support generally.
See CHILD SUPPORT.
Cigarettes and tobacco products.
Sale or distribution of tobacco products to minors, §14-313.
Use of minors by department of health and human services to test compliance with provisions, §14-313, (d).
Use of minors by law enforcement agencies to test compliance with provisions, §14-313, (d).
Common-law definition abrogated, §48A-1.
Community colleges.
Students under the age of 16, §115D-1.1.
Complaints.
Harmful materials, §19-14.
Consent to health care for minors.
Authorization.
Duration, §32A-32.
Revocation, §32A-32.

CHILDREN AND MINORS —Cont'd
Consent to health care for minors —Cont'd
Authorization —Cont'd
Who may make an authorization, §32A-30.
Custodial parents.
Authority, §32A-30.
Person who may make authorization, §32A-30.
Disagreement regarding health care.
Revocation of authorization, §32A-32, (c).
Form for authorization, §32A-34.
Full power and authority.
Parent authorized to grant agent, §32A-31, (a).
Incapacity or mental incompetence of authorizing parent.
Authorization not effected by, §32A-32, (d).
Limitations and restrictions on authority.
Authorization may contain, §32A-31, (b).
Protection of health care provider.
Good faith reliance on authorization, §32A-33, (b).
Public policy, statement of, §32A-28, (a).
Purpose of article, §32A-28, (b).
Reliance on authorization.
Physician, dentist or other health care provider, §32A-33, (a), (b).
Revocation of authorization.
Automatic revocation, §32A-32, (a).
Disagreement regarding health care, §32A-32, (c).
Procedure for exercising right to revoke, §32A-32, (b).
Right to revoke, §32A-32, (b).
Treatment by physician.
Consent of minor sufficient, §90-21.5, (a).
Consent of parent or guardian.
When not required, §90-21.1.
Who may make an authorization to consent, §32A-30.
Withholding or discontinuing life sustaining procedures.
Authorization may not contain, §32A-31, (c).
Consent to intercourse and sexual offenses.
No defense as to certain victims, §14-27.7, (a).
Contempt.
Harmful materials.
Disobedience of injunctions, §19-20.
Contracts.
Artistic and creative services and talent agency contracts, §§48A-11 to 48A-18.
Applicability of article, §48A-11.
Artistic and creative services defined, §48A-11.
Disaffirmance during minority prohibited.
Contract approved by superior court, §48A-12, (a).
Documents to be provided to other party, §48A-13.
Earnings set aside in trust.
Contracts approved by court.
Change in facts, notice, §48A-14, (h).
Continuing jurisdiction over trust established, §48A-14, (g).
Deposit or disbursement of funds by employer, §48A-14, (d) to (f).
Percentage required to be set aside, §48A-14, (a).
Trustee, appointment, §48A-14, (b).
Trustee's statement, providing employer, §48A-14, (c).
Contracts not approved by court.
Amendment or termination, §48A-15, (e).
Change in facts, notice, §48A-15, (f).

CHILDREN AND MINORS —Cont'd
Contracts —Cont'd
Artistic and creative services and talent agency contracts —Cont'd
Earnings set aside in trust —Cont'd
Contracts not approved by court —Cont'd
Deposit or disbursement by employer, §48A-15, (c), (d).
Fiduciary relationship, parent or guardian, §48A-15, (g).
Gross earnings defined, §48A-15, (h).
Percentage of earning set aside, §48A-15, (a).
Trustee, appointment, §48A-15, (b).
Establishment of trust, §48A-16, (a).
Financial institutions, establishing with, §48A-16, (d).
Methods of handling by trustee, §48A-16, (e).
Withdrawals, restrictions, §48A-16, (b).
Written statement by trustee, §48A-16, (c).
Guardian ad litem during proceeding, §48A-12, (d).
Superior court approval of contracts, §48A-12, (a) to (d).
Talent agency contracts, §§48A-17, 48A-18.
Talent agency contracts.
Definitions, §48A-17, (a), (b).
Disaffirmance prohibited.
Court approval, §48A-18.
Deposit accounts.
Banks operating in name of minor, §53-43.5, (a).
Disaffirmance of minors contracts.
Determining applicable period of time, §48A-3.
Safe deposit boxes.
Banks leasing or renting to minors, §53-43.5, (b), (c).
Contributing to delinquency.
Elements of offense, §14-316.1.
Controlled substances.
Driving after consuming drugs, §20-138.3.
Restoration of license after conviction, §20-17.6.
Promoting drug sales by a minor, §90-95.6, (a), (c).
Mistake of age not a defense, §90-95.6, (b).
Treatment for abuse of controlled substances or alcohol.
Consent of minor to treatment sufficient, §90-21.5, (a).
Violations of provisions.
Employing or intentionally using minor to commit drug law violations, §90-95.4, (a), (b).
Civil liability, §90-95.5.
Definition of "minor," §90-95.4, (d).
Mistake of age, §90-95.4, (c).
Expunction of records, §90-96, (b), (d).
Immunity from prosecution, §90-96.1.
Participating in a drug violation by a minor, §90-95.7, (a), (c).
Mistake of age not a defense, §90-95.7, (b).
Control over child caring facilities, §§110-45 to 110-48.
See CHILD CARE FACILITIES.
Conveyances.
Infant trustees, §39-4.
Costs.
Administration of estates, §7A-307.
Responsibility of guardian for costs against infant plaintiff, §6-30.
Credit union members.
Minimum age for holding office, §54-109.31, (e).

CHILDREN AND MINORS —Cont'd
Credit union members —Cont'd
Minimum age for voting at meetings, §54-109.31, (d).
Criminal law and procedure.
Expungement of criminal records.
First offenders under age eighteen, §15A-145.
Parent or guardian may be present during testimony, §15A-1225.
Prosecution of juvenile as adult.
Commission of criminal offense by juvenile after superior court conviction, §7B-1604, (b).
Commission of criminal offense on or after juveniles sixteenth birthday, §7B-1604, (a).
Emancipated juveniles prosecuted as adult for commission of offense, §7B-1604, (a).
Transfer of jurisdiction of juvenile to superior court, §§7B-2200 to 7B-2204.
Curfews.
Cities imposing by appropriate ordinance.
Persons of age less than 18, §160A-198.
Custody generally.
See CHILD CUSTODY.
Damages.
Malicious or willful destruction of property by minors.
Recovery of damages from parents, §1-538.1.
Negligent supervision of minor.
Right of educational entity to recover against parents, §1-538.3.
Death.
Child fatality prevention system, §§7B-1400 to 7B-1414.
See CHILD FATALITY PREVENTION SYSTEM.
Maltreatment of juvenile, report, §7B-301.
Death sentence, §14-17.
Decedents' estates.
Distribution to parent or guardian of minor, §28A-22-7.
Default judgments.
Harmful materials, §19-16, (b).
Defenses.
Employing or intentionally using minor to commit drug law violations.
Assumption of risk or contributory negligence, §90-95.5.
Mistake of age.
Criminal prosecution, §90-95.4, (c).
Intercourse and sexual offenses with certain victims.
Consent no defense, §14-27.7, (a).
Participating in a drug violation by a minor.
Mistake of age.
Criminal prosecution, §90-95.7, (b).
Promoting drug sales by a minor.
Mistake of age.
Criminal prosecution, §90-95.6, (b).
Prostitution.
Participating in prostitution of a minor.
Mistake of age not a defense, §14-190.19, (b).
Promoting prostitution of a minor.
Mistake of age not a defense, §14-190.18, (b).
Sexual exploitation of a minor.
Mistake of age not a defense, §§14-190.16, (c), 14-190.17, (c), 14-190.17A, (c).
Definitions.
Age of minors, §48A-2.
Common-law definition of minor abrogated, §48A-1.
Harmful material, §19-12.

CHILDREN AND MINORS —Cont'd
Definitions —Cont'd
Stand by guardians for minor children, §35A-1370.
Deformed children.
Exhibition of certain children prohibited, §110-20.1.
Delinquency.
Contributing to delinquency, §14-316.1.
Generally, §§7B-1500 to 7B-2827.
See DELINQUENT AND UNDISCIPLINED JUVENILES.
Juvenile code.
See JUVENILE CODE.
Youth services.
See YOUTH SERVICES.
Divorce.
Custody generally.
See CHILD CUSTODY.
Support generally.
See CHILD SUPPORT.
Domestic violence generally, §§50B-1 to 50B-9.
See DOMESTIC VIOLENCE.
Drainage.
Corporations.
Rights of infant owners protected, §156-47.
Drivers' licenses.
Alcohol purchases by underage persons.
Revocation of license, §20-17.3.
Application, §20-11, (i).
Driving eligibility certificate, §20-11, (n).
Charter school's designee of board of directors, duties, §115C-238.29F, (j).
Principals of schools, duties, §115C-288, (k).
Private and home schools, duties, §115C-566.
Provisional license revocation, §20-13.2, (c1).
School disciplinary actions.
Effect on eligibility for certificate, §20-11, (n1).
State board of community colleges, adoption of rules, §115D-5, (a3).
State board of education, rules, duty to develop, §115C-12.
Fees, §20-11, (j).
Full provisional license, §20-11, (f).
Restrictions, §20-11, (g).
Insurance, §20-11, (m).
Limited learner's permit, §20-11, (b).
Restrictions, §20-11, (c).
Limited provisional license, §20-11, (d).
Restrictions, §20-11, (e).
Lose control, lose license, §20-11, (n1).
Nonresidents, §20-11, (h) to (h2).
Federally issued licenses, §20-11, (h3).
Permitting unlicensed minor to drive vehicle, §20-32.
Process for expanding privilege, §20-11, (a).
Provisional licensee defined, §20-4.01, (31a).
Revocation of license or provisional license.
Driving by provisional licensee after consuming alcohol or drugs, §20-13.2, (a).
Driving eligibility certificate not maintained, §20-13.2, (c1).
Explosives offenses, §20-13.2, (c2).
Issuance of license during revocation or suspension, §20-9, (b1).
Impaired driving conviction, §20-13.2, (b).
Length of revocation, §20-13.2, (d).
Restoration of license, proof of financial responsibility, §20-13.2, (e).

CHILDREN AND MINORS —Cont'd
Drivers' licenses —Cont'd
Revocation of license or provisional license —Cont'd
Willful refusal to submit to chemical analysis, §20-13.2, (c).
Rules for issuance of driving eligibility certificates.
Duty of state board of education to develop, §115C-12.
Supervising driver, §20-11, (k).
Suspension of license of provisional licensee for moving violation, §20-13, (a).
Length of suspension, §20-13, (b).
Motor vehicle moving violation defined, §20-13, (a).
Probation, placing licensee on, §20-13, (b).
Restoration of license on probationary status, hearing request, §20-13, (b).
Retention of license until hearing, §20-13, (a).
Suspension in addition to other remedies, §20-13, (d).
Two or more offenses committed on single occasion, §20-13, (c).
Term of license, §20-11, (j).
Underage purchase of alcohol.
Revocation, §20-17.3.
Violations, §20-11, (l).
Driving by person less than 21 years old after consuming alcohol or drugs, §20-138.3.
Driving by provisional licensee after consuming alcohol or drugs.
Restoration of license after conviction, §20-17.6.
Driving motor vehicle unlicensed.
Permitting prohibited, §20-32.
Drug paraphernalia.
Delivery of drug paraphernalia to certain younger persons, §90-113.23, (c).
Drugs.
Delivery of drug paraphernalia to certain youths, §90-113.23, (c).
Driving after consuming drugs.
Restoration of license after conviction, §20-17.6.
Driving by person less than 21 years old after consuming alcohol or drugs, §20-138.3.
Employing or intentionally using minors to commit drug law violations, §90-95.4, (a), (b).
Civil liability, §90-95.5.
"Minor" defined, §90-95.4, (d).
Mistake of age, §90-96, (b), (d).
Expunction of records, §90-96, (b), (d).
Immunity from prosecution, §90-96.1.
Participating in a drug violation by a minor, §90-95.7, (a), (c).
Mistake of age not a defense, §90-95.7, (b).
Promoting drug sales by a minor, §90-95.6, (a), (c).
Mistake of age not a defense, §90-95.6, (b).
Treatment for drug or alcohol abuse.
Consent of minor to treatment, §90-21.5, (a).
Drug treatment courts, §§7A-790 to 7A-801.
See DRUG TREATMENT COURTS.
Education.
Public schools generally.
See PUBLIC SCHOOLS.
Violations of provisions.
Expunction of records, §90-96, (b), (d).
Immunity from prosecution, §90-96.1.
Emancipation, §§7B-3500 to 7B-3509.
Actions by and against juvenile after final decree, §7B-3507.
Appeals, §7B-3508.

CHILDREN AND MINORS —Cont'd
Emancipation —Cont'd
Burden of showing that emancipation in best interest of petitioner, §7B-3503.
Common law provisions suspended, §7B-3509.
Considerations in determining best interest of petitioner and need for emancipation, §7B-3504.
Continuance of hearing and order of investigation, §7B-3503.
Contract rights of juvenile upon emancipation, §7B-3507.
Conveyances, right of juvenile upon final decree, §7B-3507.
Costs of proceedings, §7B-3506.
Criminal prosecution of emancipated juveniles as adult, §7B-1604, (a).
District court jurisdiction, §§7B-200, (a), 7B-1603.
Entry of final decree, §7B-3505.
Examination by psychiatrist, psychologist or physician.
Court ordering juvenile, §7B-3503.
Hearing by court sitting without jury, §7B-3503.
Husband-wife or physician-patient privilege not grounds for excluding evidence, §7B-3503.
Irrevocability of final decree, §7B-3507.
Juveniles sixteen years of age or older filing, §7B-3500.
Legal effect of final decree of emancipation, §7B-3507.
Married juvenile emancipated by provisions, §7B-3509.
Notice of appeal, §7B-3508.
Parent relieved of legal duties and obligations upon final decree, §7B-3507.
Petition.
Signing and verification, content requirements, §7B-3501.
Service of summons, §7B-3502.
Summons, §7B-3502.
Taxing costs of proceedings, §7B-3506.
Temporary order pending disposition of appeal, §7B-3508.
Transacting business as adult, effect of final decree, §7B-3507.
Emergency medical or surgical treatment, judicial consent, §7B-3600.
District court jurisdiction, §7B-1603.
Eminent domain.
Private condemnors.
Acquisition of title of infant, §40A-30.
Employment, enticing out of state, §14-40.
Employment security.
Employment of and assistance to minors, §96-22.
Evidence of other crimes, wrongs or acts.
Admissibility against juvenile, §8C-1, Rule 404, (b).
Execution for murder, §14-17.
Executors and administrators.
Persons disqualified to serve as personal representative, §28A-4-2.
Settlement.
Payment into court of fund due minor, §28A-23-2.
Exemptions.
Homestead exemption.
Exemption for benefit of children, Const. N. C., art. X, §2.
Exhibition of children.
Deformed children.
Prohibited exhibition, §110-20.1, (a).
Applicability of provisions, §110-20.1, (d).

CHILDREN AND MINORS —Cont'd
Exhibition of children —Cont'd
Deformed children —Cont'd
Prohibited exhibition —Cont'd
Penalty for violations of provisions, §110-20.1, (e).
Mentally ill or retarded children.
Prohibited exhibition, §110-20.1, (a).
Applicability of provisions, §110-20.1, (d).
Penalty for violations of provisions, §110-20.1, (e).
Participating in prohibited exhibition, §110-20.1, (b), (c).
Applicability of provisions, §110-20.1, (d).
Penalty for violations of provisions, §110-20.1, (e).
Procuring or arranging for prohibited exhibition, §110-20.1, (c).
Applicability of provisions, §110-20.1, (d).
Penalty for violations of provisions, §110-20.1, (e).
Expungement of criminal records.
First offenders under age eighteen, §15A-145.
Extradition.
Harmful materials.
Persons guilty of contempt, §19-20, (c).
Family preservation act, §§143B-150.5, 143B-150.6.
Family purpose doctrine.
Strict liability for damage to person or property by minors, §1-538.1.
Felonies.
Prostitution.
Participating in prostitution of a minor, §14-190.19, (c).
Promoting prostitution of a minor, §14-190.18, (c).
Sexual exploitation of a minor.
First degree, §14-190.16, (d).
Second degree, §14-190.17, (d).
Third degree, §14-190.17A, (d).
Taking indecent liberties with minors, §14-202.1.
Felonious restraint, §14-43.3.
Fiduciaries.
Payments to or for minors, §32-27.
Firearms.
Permitting young children to use dangerous firearms, §14-316, (a).
Air rifles, air pistols and BB guns not deemed dangerous firearms, §14-316, (b).
Fires.
Exposing children to fire, §14-318.
Fireworks.
Sale of pyrotechnics to minors, §14-410, (b).
Fishing licenses.
Salt water fishing license.
Exemption, persons 18 or younger, §113-174.2, (d).
Foster care and adoption assistance.
Payments generally, §§108A-48 to 108A-50.
Foster homes.
Regulation of agencies receiving or placing children, §§131D-10.1 to 131D-10.9.
See CHILD PLACING AGENCIES.
Fraternal benefit societies.
Life insurance, §58-24-75, (b).
Lodge systems.
Organization and operation of lodges for children, §58-24-5, (b).

CHILDREN AND MINORS —Cont'd
Fraternal orders.
Insurance, §58-25-35.
Certificates and contributions, §58-25-40.
Continuation of certificate, §58-25-60.
Exchange of certificates, §58-25-45.
Medical examination, §58-25-40.
Reserve fund, §58-25-45.
Gifts to minors generally, §§33A-1 to 33A-24.
See TRANSFERS TO MINORS.
Governor's advocacy council on children and youth.
Access to information, §143B-416.
Appointment, §143B-415, (a).
Chairman, §143B-415, (c).
Clerical and other services, §143B-415, (d).
Composition, §143B-415, (a).
Duties, §143B-414.
Expenses, §143B-415, (c).
Initial members, §143B-415, (b).
Meetings, §143B-415, (c).
Powers and duties, §143B-414.
Removal, §143B-415, (c).
Terms, §143B-415, (b).
Vice-chairman, §143B-415, (c).
Guardian ad litem, §1A-1, Rule 17.
Appointment of guardian, Super. Ct. Rule 7.1.
Generally.
See GUARDIAN AD LITEM.
Services to abused, neglected or dependent juveniles, §§7B-1200 to 7B-1204.
Guardians generally.
See GUARDIANS.
Handgun possession, §14-269.7.
Handicapped children.
Interagency coordinating council for children from birth to five with disabilities and their families.
Agency cooperation, §143B-179.6.
Compensation, §143B-179.5, (e).
Composition, §143B-179.5, (b).
Duties, §143B-179.5, (d).
Agency cooperation, §143B-179.6.
Establishment, §143B-179.5, (a).
Organization, §143B-179.5, (c).
Clerical and staff services, §143B-179.5, (f).
Regional councils.
Annual report, §143B-179.5A, (f).
Cochairs, §143B-179.5A, (d).
Composition, §143B-179.5A, (c).
Early intervention plan, development, §143B-179.5A, (e).
Established, number, §143B-179.5A, (a).
Meetings, quorum, §143B-179.5A, (d).
Members, appointment, number, term, removal, vacancy, §143B-179.5A, (b).
Reporting, §143B-179.5, (f).
Harmful materials.
Citation of act, §19-9.
Commencement of actions, §§19-13, (a), 19-14.
Rules of civil procedure, §19-13, (b).
Complaint.
Commencement of action, §19-14.
Examination and reading by court, §19-15, (a).
Filing, §19-14.
Generally, §19-14.
Contempt.
Defenses, §19-20, (a).
Disobedience of injunction, §19-20, (a).
Extradition, §19-20, (c).
Persons not to be guilty of contempt, §19-20, (b).

CHILDREN AND MINORS —Cont'd
Harmful materials —Cont'd
Default judgment, §19-16, (b).
Definitions, §19-12.
Dismissal of action.
No probable cause, §19-15, (b).
Extradition.
Persons guilty of contempt, §19-20, (c).
Injunctions.
Disobedience.
Contempt, §19-20, (a).
Permanent injunction, §19-18, (b).
Preliminary injunction, §19-19, (c), (d).
Temporary restraining order, §19-19, (a), (b).
Judgments, §19-18, (a), (b).
Territorial restrictions on, §19-18, (c).
Jury.
Right to trial by jury, §19-17, (c).
Legislative declaration, §§19-10, 19-11.
Notice.
Preliminary injunction, §19-19, (d).
Obscenity generally. See within this heading, "Obscenity or pornography."
Policy of state, §19-11.
Purposes of provisions, §19-10.
Respondent.
Appearance, §19-16, (a).
Right to trial by jury, §19-17, (c).
Right to trial of issues, §19-17, (b).
Rules of civil procedure.
Applicability to proceedings, §19-13, (b).
Summons.
Issuance, §19-15, (c).
Title of law, §19-9.
Trial.
Right of respondent to trial by jury, §19-17, (c).
Right of respondent to trial of issues, §19-17, (b).
Setting of date, §19-17, (a).
Health.
Childhood vaccine-related injury compensation, §§130A-422 to 130A-434.
See CHILDHOOD VACCINE-RELATED INJURY COMPENSATION.
Maternal and child health services.
County appropriations.
Local health departments not to reduce, §130A-4.1, (a).
Income earned by local health departments.
Departments required to budget and expend, §130A-4.1, (b).
Metabolic and other hereditary and congenital defect screening of newborns.
Establishment and administering of program, §130A-125, (a).
Fees, §130A-125, (c).
Rules, §130A-125, (b), (b1).
Teen pregnancy prevention, §130A-131.15A.
Health benefit plan coverage.
Newborn hearing screening, §58-3-260.
Health insurance program for children, §§108A-70.18 to 108A-70.28.
Hearing impaired.
Schools for the deaf.
See HEARING IMPAIRED.
Helmet law.
Bicycle safety act, §§20-171.6 to 20-171.9.
Homestead exemption.
Exemption for benefit of children, Const. N. C., art. X, §2.

CHILDREN AND MINORS —Cont'd
Homicide.
Punishment for persons under 17 years of age, §14-17.
Hunting and trapping licenses.
Persons under 16 years of age, license exemption, §113-276, (d).
Husband and wife.
Conveyances.
Married persons under 18 competent as to certain transactions, §39-13.2, (a).
Iceboxes.
Discarding or abandoning iceboxes, §14-318.1.
Illegitimacy.
General provisions, §§49-1 to 49-17.
See ILLEGITIMACY.
Immunities.
Motor vehicles.
Parent-child immunity, §1-539.21.
Immunization, §130A-153, (d).
Childhood vaccine-related injury compensation, §§130A-422 to 130A-434.
See CHILDHOOD VACCINE-RELATED INJURY COMPENSATION.
Generally, §§130A-152 to 130A-158.
See IMMUNIZATION.
Impaired driving.
Grossly aggravating factor.
Child under age of 16 in vehicle at time of offense, §20-179, (c).
Income tax credits, §105-151.24, (a).
Nonresident or part-time resident claiming, limitation, §105-151.34, (b).
Incompetence.
Determination generally, §§35A-1101 to 35A-1116.
See INCOMPETENCE.
Indian child welfare.
Health and human services department.
Collaboration between division of social services and commission of Indian affairs, §143B-139.5A.
Insurance proceeds belonging to minor as beneficiary after death of insured.
Payment to and receipt by clerk of superior court or public guardian, §7A-111, (a), (c).
Interstate compact on juveniles, §§7B-2800 to 7B-2827.
See INTERSTATE COMPACT ON JUVENILES.
Interstate compact on the placement of children, §§7B-3800 to 7B-3806.
Judicial consent for emergency surgical or medical treatment, §7B-3600.
District court jurisdiction, §7B-1603.
Judicial sales.
Confirmation of public sale of real property, §1-339.28, (b).
Juvenile delinquents.
Generally, §§7B-1500 to 7B-2827.
See DELINQUENT AND UNDISCIPLINED JUVENILES.
Juvenile records and social reports, §§7B-2900 to 7B-3202.
See JUVENILE RECORDS AND SOCIAL REPORTS.
Juvenile services generally.
See YOUTH SERVICES.
Kidnapping and abduction.
Abduction of children, §14-41, (a).
Electronic surveillance orders, §15A-290, (c1).
Employment purposes.
Enticing minors out of state for purposes of employment, §14-40.

CHILDREN AND MINORS —Cont'd
Kidnapping and abduction —Cont'd
Public officers and employees, §14-41, (b).
Labor.
See CHILD LABOR.
Larceny, shoplifting, employee theft, embezzlement or false pretenses.
Civil liability for minors acts, §1-538.2, (b).
Shoplifting.
Minors detained by merchants, agents or employees, §§14-72, (d), 14-72.1, (c).
Lead-based paint hazard management program, §§130A-453.01 to 130A-453.11.
See LEAD-BASED PAINT.
Lead poisoning in children.
Generally, §§130A-131.5 to 130A-131.9H.
See LEAD POISONING IN CHILDREN.
Lead-based paint hazard management program, §§130A-453.01 to 130A-453.11.
See LEAD-BASED PAINT.
Legislative study commission on children and youth, §§120-215 to 120-220.
Limitation of actions.
Disabilities.
Time for bringing action, §1-17, (a).
Time for bringing action.
Malpractice, §1-17, (b).
Tolled because of minority.
Persons not yet twenty-one, §48A-3.
Lose control, lose license, §20-11, (n1).
Maltreatment of juvenile, report of death due to, §7B-301.
Marriage.
Age to lawfully marry, §51-2, (a).
Consent to marry.
Persons over 16 years of age and under 18 years of age.
Required for issuance of licensee, §51-2, (a1).
District court jurisdiction.
Marriage by underage parties, §7B-200, (a).
Emancipated minor.
Consent to marry not required, §51-2, (a1).
Fraud or misrepresentation in procuring license, §51-2, (c).
Persons over 14 years of age and under 16 years of age, §§51-2, (b), 51-2.1.
Persons under 14 years of age.
Unlawful to marry, §51-2, (b1).
Want of capacity, §51-3.
Maternal and child health program, §130A-124, (a) to (c).
County appropriations for services.
Local health departments not to reduce, §130A-4.1, (a).
Income earned by local health departments.
Departments required to budget and expend, §130A-4.1, (b).
Medical treatment of minor by physician.
Abuse of controlled substances or alcohol.
Consent of minor sufficient, §90-21.5, (a).
Consent of minor.
Sufficient for certain medical health services, §90-21.5.
Consent of parent, guardian or person in loco parentis.
When not required, §90-21.1.
Consent to health care.
Authorization.
Duration, §32A-32.
Revocation, §32A-32.
Who may take on authorization, §32A-30.

CHILDREN AND MINORS —Cont'd
Medical treatment of minor by physician —Cont'd
Consent to health care —Cont'd
Custodial parents.
Authority, §32A-30.
Person who may make authorization, §32A-30.
Definitions, §32A-29.
Disagreement regarding health care.
Revocation of authorization, §32A-32, (c).
Form for authorization, §32A-34.
Full power and authority.
Parent authorized to grant agent, §32A-31, (a).
Incapacity or mental incompetence of authorizing parent.
Authorization not effected by, §32A-32, (d).
Limitations and restrictions on authority.
Authorization may contain, §32A-31, (b).
Protection of health care provider.
Good faith reliance on authorization, §32A-33, (b).
Public policy, statement of, §32A-28, (b).
Purpose of article, §32A-28, (b).
Reliance on authorization.
Physician, dentist or other health care provider, §32A-33, (a), (b).
Revocation of authorization.
Automatic revocation, §32A-32, (a).
Disagreement regarding health care, §32A-32, (c).
Procedure for exercising right to revoke, §32A-32, (b).
Right to revoke, §32A-32, (b).
Treatment by physician.
Consent of minor sufficient, §90-21.5, (a).
Consent of parent or guardian.
When not required, §90-21.1.
Who may make an authorization to consent, §32A-30.
Withholding or discontinuing life sustaining procedures.
Authorization may not contain, §32A-31, (c).
Definition of "treatment," §90-21.2.
Surgery included, §90-21.3.
Emancipated minor.
Consent by, §90-21.5, (b).
Emotional disturbance.
Consent of minor sufficient, §90-21.5, (a).
Liability of physician, §90-21.4, (a).
Notification of parent, guardian or person in loco parentis.
Physician not to notify without consent of minor, §90-21.4, (b).
Pregnancy.
Consent of minor sufficient, §90-21.5, (a).
Surgery.
Second opinion as to necessity, §90-21.3.
Venereal diseases.
Consent of minor sufficient, §90-21.5, (a).
Mental health, developmental disability, substance abuse.
Alcoholism or drug abuse.
Consent of minor to treatment sufficient, §90-21.5, (a).
Declaring trust irrevocable and making gift of life interest.
Notice to minors, §35A-1353.
Discharge of voluntarily admitted minors.
Developmentally disabled, §122C-242.

CHILDREN AND MINORS —Cont'd
Mental health, developmental disability, substance abuse —Cont'd
Discharge of voluntarily admitted minors —Cont'd
Notice and consultation with responsible person, §122C-57, (d1).
Exhibition of certain children prohibited, §110-20.1.
Rights of clients, §122C-62, (c), (d).
Sexual offense.
Engaging in act with minor client constituting, §122C-65, (a), (b).
Voluntary admissions.
Facilities for the mentally ill and substance abusers, §§122C-221 to 122C-224.7.
See MENTAL HEALTH, DEVELOPMENTAL DISABILITY, SUBSTANCE ABUSE.
Metabolic and other hereditary and congenital disorders.
Screening of newborns, §130A-125.
Missing children.
Center for missing persons.
General provisions, §§143B-495 to 143B-499.7.
See MISSING PERSONS.
Mistake of age.
Controlled substances.
Employing or intentionally using minor to commit drug law violations, §90-95.4, (c).
Participating in a drug violation by a minor, §90-95.7, (b).
Promoting drug sales by a minor, §90-95.6, (b).
Molestation.
See CHILD MOLESTATION.
Money belonging to minor as beneficiary after death of insured.
Payment to and receipt by clerk of superior court or public guardian, §7A-111, (a), (c).
Mortgages and deeds of trust.
Conveyances by infant trustees, §39-4.
Motor vehicle financial responsibility, §20-279.6A.
Motor vehicles.
Child restraint systems, §20-137.1.
Placement of small children within vehicle, §20-137.1, (a1).
Points for violations, §§20-16, (c), 20-137.1, (d).
Driving by person less than 21 years old after consuming alcohol or drugs, §20-138.3.
Driving by provisional licensee after consuming alcohol or drugs.
Restoration of license after conviction, §20-17.6.
Driving eligibility certificate, §20-11, (n).
Charter school's designee, duties, §115C-238.29F, (j).
Principals of schools, duties, §115C-288, (k).
Private or home schools, duties, §115C-366.
School disciplinary actions.
Effect on eligibility, §20-11, (n1).
Revocation of provisional license, §20-13.2, (c1).
State board of community colleges, rules, duty to adopt, §115D-5, (a3).
State board of education, rules, duty to develop, §115C-12.
Grounds for revoking provisional license, §20-13.2.
Driving by provisional licensee after consuming alcohol or drugs, §20-13.2, (a).
Driving eligibility certificate not maintained, §20-13.2, (c1).
Explosives offenses, §20-13.2, (c2).
Impaired driving conviction, §20-13.2, (b).

CHILDREN AND MINORS —Cont'd
Motor vehicles —Cont'd
Grounds for revoking provisional license —Cont'd
Issuance of license during revocation or suspension, §20-9, (b1).
Length of revocation, §20-13.2, (d).
Restoration of license, proof of financial responsibility, §20-13.2, (e).
Willful refusal to submit to chemical analysis, §20-13.2, (c).
Mandatory usage of restraint for child passengers, §20-137.1, (a).
Suspension of license of provisional licensee for moving violation, §20-13, (a).
Length of suspension, §20-13, (b).
Motor vehicle moving violation defined, §20-13, (a).
Probation, placing licensee on, §20-13, (b).
Restoration of license on probationary status, hearing request, §20-13, (b).
Retention of license until hearing, §20-13, (a).
Suspension in addition to other remedies, §20-13, (d).
Two or more offenses committed on single occasion, §20-13, (c).
Transporting children under 12 years of age in open bed or open cargo area of vehicle, §20-135.2B, (a).
Driver's license points or insurance surcharge not assessed for violation, §20-135.2B, (d).
Exceptions, §20-135.2B, (b).
Infraction for violating, §20-135.2B, (c).
Unlicensed driving, §20-32.
Murder in the first degree, §14-17.
Name change.
Procedure, §101-2.
Two change limitation, §101-6, (b).
Negligent supervision of child by parent.
Right of educational entity to recover against parent, §1-538.3.
Newborn hearing screening.
Health benefit plan coverage, §58-3-260.
Nonsupport.
Child support generally.
See CHILD SUPPORT.
Compelling disclosure of information respecting nonsupporting parent, §110-131.
Support of illegitimate children, §§49-1 to 49-9.
See ILLEGITIMACY.
Willful nonsupport by supporting spouse, §14-322.
North Carolina center for missing persons.
General provisions, §§143B-495 to 143B-499.7.
See MISSING PERSONS.
North Carolina child fatality prevention system, §§7B-1400 to 7B-1414.
See CHILD FATALITY PREVENTION SYSTEM.
Obscenity or pornography.
Definitions.
Certain offenses concerning minors, §14-190.13.
Displaying material harmful to minors, §14-190.14, (a).
Penalty, §14-190.14, (b).
Disseminating harmful material to minors, §14-190.15, (a).
Defenses, §14-190.15, (c).
Penalties, §14-190.15, (d).
Dissemination to minors under the age of 13 years, §14-190.8.
Dissemination to minors under the age of 16 years, §14-190.7.

CHILDREN AND MINORS —Cont'd
Obscenity or pornography —Cont'd
Employing or permitting minor to assist in offense under article, §14-190.6.
Exhibiting harmful performance, §14-190.15, (b).
Defenses, §14-190.15, (c).
Penalties, §14-190.15, (d).
Harmful materials, §§19-9 to 19-20. See within this heading, "Harmful materials."
Harmful to minors.
Defined, §14-190.13.
Prostitution, §§14-190.18, 14-190.19.
Defined, §14-190.13.
Sexual activity.
Defined, §14-190.13.
Sexual exploitation of a minor, §§14-190.16, 14-190.17.
Sexually explicit nudity.
Defined, §14-190.13.
Other crimes, wrongs or acts.
Admissibility against juvenile, §8C-1, Rule 404, (b).
Parental authority over juvenile, §§7B-3400 to 7B-3404.
Parental liability for minors acts.
Larceny, shoplifting, employee theft, embezzlement or false pretenses.
Civil liability for minors acts, §1-538.2, (b).
Parent and child generally.
See PARENT AND CHILD.
Parties.
Administration of estates.
Liability for costs in administration, §7A-307, (e).
Infants to sue or defend by guardian or guardian ad litem, §1A-1, Rule 17, (b).
Partition.
Owelty.
Infant's share due at majority, §46-12.
Partition sales.
Shares to persons not sui juris secured, §46-34.
Payment for work.
Failing to pay minors for doing certain work, §14-321.
Pederasty.
Bail and recognizance, §15A-534.4.
Taking indecent liberties with children, §14-202.1.
Penalties.
Control over child-caring facilities.
Violation a misdemeanor, §110-48.
Exhibition of children.
Prohibited exhibitions, §110-20.1, (e).
Prostitution.
Participating in prostitution of a minor, §14-190.19, (c).
Sexual exploitation of a minor.
First degree, §14-190.16, (d).
Second degree, §14-190.17, (d).
Third degree, §14-190.17A, (d).
Perinatal health care, §130A-127.
Personal watercraft.
Persons under 16 years of age operating, §75A-13.3, (b).
Renting, hiring or leasing to persons under 16 years, §75A-13.3, (c).
Pimping.
Electronic surveillance orders, §15A-290, (c1).
Participating in prostitution of a minor.
Generally, §14-190.19.
Promoting prostitution of a minor.
Definitions for certain offenses concerning minors, §14-190.13.

CHILDREN AND MINORS —Cont'd
Pimping —Cont'd
Promoting prostitution of a minor —Cont'd
Generally, §14-190.18.
Placement of children.
Bringing child into state or taking child out of state for purposes of adoption.
Consent of department of health and human services, §§7B-3700 to 7B-3705.
Child placing agencies generally.
See CHILD PLACING AGENCIES.
Control over child placing and child care, §§131D-10.1 to 131D-10.9.
See CHILD PLACING AGENCIES.
Foster care and adoption assistance payments, §§108A-48 to 108A-50.
See SOCIAL SERVICES.
Interstate compact on the placement of children, §§7B-3800 to 7B-3806.
Social services generally.
See SOCIAL SERVICES.
Precious metal dealers.
Purchasing from juvenile, §66-171.
Pregnancy.
Consent of minor to treatment sufficient, §90-21.5, (a).
Teen pregnancy prevention, §130A-131.15A.
Prior crimes, wrongs or acts.
Admissibility against juvenile, §8C-1, Rule 404, (b).
Prisons and prisoners.
Disposition of child born of female prisoner, §148-47.
Program on prevention of abuse and neglect of juveniles, §§7B-1300 to 7B-1302.
Property.
Malicious or willful destruction.
Recovery of damages from parents, §1-538.1.
Prostitution.
Defined, §14-190.13.
Electronic surveillance orders, §15A-290.
Participating in prostitution of a minor.
Definitions of certain offenses concerning minors, §14-190.13.
Elements of offense, §14-190.19, (a).
Mistake of age.
Not a defense, §14-190.19, (b).
Penalties, §14-190.19, (c).
Sentencing, §14-190.19, (c).
Promoting prostitution of a minor.
Definitions of certain offenses concerning minors, §14-190.13.
Elements of offense, §14-190.18, (a).
Mistake of age.
Not a defense, §14-190.18, (b).
Penalties, §14-190.18, (c).
Sentencing, §14-190.18, (c).
Protection of minors, §§14-313 to 14-321.
Public officers and employees.
Abduction of children, §14-41, (b).
Public schools generally.
See PUBLIC SCHOOLS.
Rape indictments.
Essentials of bill.
Victim female child under 13 years, §15-144.1, (b).
Real property.
Conveyances by infant trustees, §39-4.
Refrigerators.
Discarding or abandoning refrigerators, §14-318.1.
Precautions required, §14-318.1.

CHILDREN AND MINORS —Cont'd
Remainders, reversions and executory interests.
Sale, lease or mortgage in case of remainders, §41-11.
Report of abuse, neglect, dependency or death due to maltreatment, §7B-301.
Restraint.
Felonious restraint, §14-43.3.
Safe deposit boxes.
Banks.
Leasing or renting to minors, §53-43.5, (b), (c).
Savings and loan associations, §54B-132, (b).
Savings banks, §54C-170, (b).
Safe haven for infants, §§14-318.2, 14-318.4, 14-322.3, (c).
Safety belts.
Child restraint systems, §20-137.1.
Placement of small children within vehicle, §20-137.1, (a1).
Points for violations, §§20-16, (c), 20-137.1, (d).
Mandatory usage of restraint for child passengers, §20-137.1, (a).
Transporting children under 12 years of age in open bed or open cargo area of vehicle.
Exception to prohibition when child secured or restrained by seat belt, §20-135.2B, (b).
Salt water fishing license.
Exemption, persons 18 or younger, §113-174.2, (d).
Savings and loan associations.
Safe deposit boxes.
Leasing to minors, §54B-132, (b).
Withdrawable accounts.
Minors as account holders, §54B-132, (a).
Savings banks.
Deposit accounts.
Minors as deposit account holders, §54C-170, (a).
Safe-deposit boxes.
Leased to minors, §54C-170, (b).
Schools for the deaf.
See HEARING IMPAIRED.
Seat belts.
Child restraint systems, §20-137.1.
Effect of violations, §20-137.1, (d).
Placement of small children within vehicle, §20-137.1, (a1).
Points for violations, §§20-16, (c), 20-137.1, (d).
Mandatory usage of restraint for child passengers, §20-137.1, (a).
Transporting children under 12 years of age in open bed or open cargo area of vehicle.
Exception to prohibition when child secured or restrained by seat belt, §20-135.2B, (b).
Service of process.
Personal jurisdiction.
Manner of service on natural person under disability, §1A-1, Rule 4, (j).
Sexual exploitation of a minor.
Definitions for certain offenses concerning minor, §14-190.13.
Electronic surveillance orders, §15A-290.
First degree.
Elements of offense, §14-190.16, (a).
Inference, §14-190.16, (b).
Mistake of age not a defense, §14-190.16, (c).
Sentencing, §14-190.16, (d).
Second degree.
Elements of offense, §14-190.17, (a).
Inference, §14-190.17, (b).

CHILDREN AND MINORS —Cont'd
Sexual exploitation of a minor —Cont'd
Second degree —Cont'd
Mistake of age.
Not a defense, §14-190.17, (c).
Penalties, §14-190.17, (d).
Sentencing, §14-190.17, (d).
Third degree.
Elements of offense, §14-190.17A, (a).
Inferences, §14-190.17A, (b).
Mistake of age.
Not defense, §14-190.17A, (c).
Punishment and sentencing, §14-190.17A, (d).
Sexual offenses.
Bail and recognizance, §15A-534.4.
Electronic surveillance orders, §15A-290, (c1).
Incapacity to commit sex offense.
No presumption, §14-27.9.
Indecent liberties between children, §14-202.2.
Indictments.
Victim age 13 or less, §15-144.2, (b).
Intercourse and sexual offenses with certain victims, §14-27.7, (a).
Defendant at least six years older than victim, §14-27.7A, (a).
Defendant between four and six years older than victim, §14-27.7A, (b).
School personnel.
Acts with victim who is student, §14-27.7, (b).
Taking indecent liberties with children.
Elements of offense, §14-202.1.
Felony offense, §14-202.1, (b).
Venue, §15A-136.
Shoplifting.
Detention of minors by merchants or agents or employees.
Notification to parent or guardian during period of detention, §§14-72, (d), 14-72.1.
Notice to parent or guardian, §§14-72, (d), 14-72.1, (c).
Special education.
See SPECIAL EDUCATION.
Special proceedings.
Ex parte.
Infant petitioner.
Approval by judge, §1-402.
Standby guardians for minor children, §§35A-1370 to 35A-1382.
See GUARDIANS.
Sterilization.
Married minors.
Operation lawful upon request, §90-271.
Unmarried minors, §90-272.
Streets and highways.
Condemnation proceedings.
Appointment of guardian ad litem, §136-110.
Strict liability for damage to person or property by minors, §1-538.1.
Supervision and control of juvenile by parents.
Armed forces members, exception to parental authority, §7B-3402.
Criminal liability not created by provisions, §7B-3403.
Definitions, §7B-3401.
Enforcement of parental authority, §7B-3404.
Juvenile leaving home and refusing to return.
Civil action to enforce parental authority, §7B-3404.
Juveniles under eighteen subject to parental control, §7B-3400.
Married juveniles, exception, §7B-3402.

CHILDREN AND MINORS —Cont'd
Support and maintenance.
Child support.
See CHILD SUPPORT.
Illegitimate children, §§49-1 to 49-9.
See ILLEGITIMACY.
Surgery.
Second opinion as to necessity, §90-21.3.
Talent agency contracts, §§48A-17, 48A-18.
Tanning equipment.
Use by persons 13 or younger.
Prescription required, §104E-9.1, (a).
Tattooing.
Prohibited tattooing of persons under eighteen years of age, §14-400, (a).
Tax credits, §105-151.24.
Teen court programs, §143B-520, (a), (b).
Termination of parental rights.
Generally, §§7B-1100 to 7B-1113.
See TERMINATION OF PARENTAL RIGHTS.
Testamentary recommendation by parent for appointment of guardian for minor, §35A-1224, (d).
Incompetent minor, §35A-1225.
Tobacco products.
Sale or distribution of tobacco products to minors, §14-313.
Torrens system registration.
Infants may sue by guardian or trustee, §43-8.
Torts.
Malicious or willful destruction of property by minors.
Recovery of damages from parents, §1-538.1.
Transfers to minors, §§33A-1 to 33A-24.
See TRANSFERS TO MINORS.
Trial.
Harmful materials, §19-17.
Trusts and trustees.
Conveyances by infant trustees, §39-4.
Payments to or for minors, §32-27.
Talent contracts.
Earnings to be set aside in trust, §§48A-14 to 48A-16.
Unborn infants.
Taking by deed or writing, §41-5.
Undisciplined juveniles.
Generally, §§7B-1500 to 7B-2827.
See DELINQUENT AND UNDISCIPLINED JUVENILES.
Uniform child custody jurisdiction and enforcement, §§50A-101 to 50A-317.
See CHILD CUSTODY JURISDICTION AND ENFORCEMENT.
Uniform reciprocal enforcement of support act.
See SUPPORT AND MAINTENANCE.
Uniform transfers to minors act, §§33A-1 to 33A-24.
See TRANSFERS TO MINORS.
Vandalism.
Malicious or willful destruction of property by minors.
Recovery of damages from parents, §1-538.1.
Venereal diseases.
Consent of minor to treatment sufficient, §90-21.5, (a).
Veterans.
Minor spouses of veterans, §§165-17, 165-18.
Minor veterans, §§165-12 to 165-16.
Visitation rights.
See VISITATION.

CHILDREN AND MINORS —Cont'd
Weapons.
Exceptions, §14-269.7, (b).
Handgun sales, §14-315, (a1).
Possession of handgun.
Misdemeanor, §14-269.7, (a).
Sale of handguns, §14-315, (a1).
Sale of weapons other than handguns, §14-315, (a).
Selling or giving weapons to minors, §14-315.
Defense, §14-315, (b1).
Storage of firearms to protect minors, §14-315.1.
Close proximity of weapon, §14-315.1, (b).
Exemptions, §14-315.1, (c).
"Minor" defined, §14-315.1, (d).
Posting of warning sign, §14-315.2, (b), (c).
Prohibited conduct, §14-315.1, (a).
Written notice requirements, §14-315.2, (a), (c).
Will of parent recommending appointment of guardian, §35A-1224, (d).
Incompetent minors, §35A-1225.
Wills.
Caveat to will.
Time for filing after removal of disability, §31-32.
Witnesses.
Criminal proceedings.
Parent or guardian may be present, §15A-1225.
Work.
Failing to pay minors for certain work, §14-321.
Workers' compensation.
Agreements or receipts for payments to.
Effect, §97-48, (d).
Illegally employed minors.
Compensable under provisions, §97-10.3.
Limitation of actions.
Not to run against minor, §97-50.
Trusts and trustees.
Benefits of minor employees may be paid to trustee, §97-49.
Year's allowance, when children entitled, §30-17.
Youth councils, §§143B-385 to 143B-388.
Youthful offenders.
Sentencing committed offender to central prison, §148-28.
Zero tolerance law.
Driving by person less than 21 years old after consuming alcohol or drugs, §20-138.3.
Driving by provisional licensee after consuming alcohol or drugs.
Restoration of license after conviction, §20-17.6.

CHILDREN FROM BIRTH TO FIVE WITH DISABILITIES AND THEIR FAMILIES.
Interagency coordinating council, §§143B-179.5, 143B-179.6.
Regional councils, §143B-179.5A.

CHILDREN'S HEALTH INSURANCE PROGRAM, §§108A-70.18 to 108A-70.28.
Administration, §108A-70.20.
Application for benefits, §108A-70.26, (a).
Benefits available under program, §108A-70.21, (b).
Claims for benefits.
Administration and processing, §108A-70.24, (a).
Funds provisions, §108A-70.24, (b).
Special needs claims, §108A-70.24, (c).
Cost sharing and copayments, §108A-70.21, (d).
Maximum out of pocket amounts, §108A-70.21, (e).

CHILDREN'S HEALTH INSURANCE PROGRAM —Cont'd
Data collection requirements, §108A-70.27, (a).
Definitions, §108A-70.18.
Dental coverage, §108A-70.21, (b).
Eligibility requirements, §108A-70.21, (a).
Appeal of determination, §108A-70.26, (c).
Establishment, §108A-70.20.
Extended coverage, §108A-70.21, (g).
Use of state funds prohibited, §108A-70.21, (h).
Fee for enrollment, §108A-70.21, (c).
Fraud.
Aiding and abetting in fraudulent activity, §108A-70.28, (c).
Criminal penalty, §108A-70.28, (d).
Misrepresentation on application, §108A-70.28, (a).
Misrepresentation on behalf of another, §108A-70.28, (b).
Misuse of program card, §108A-70.28, (c).
Person defined, §108A-70.28, (e).
Hearing coverage, §108A-70.21, (b).
Implementation plan, §108A-70.25.
Information dissemination and publication, §108A-70.26, (b).
Outreach efforts, §108A-70.26, (b).
Private plan coverage, §108A-70.21, (f).
Purpose of provisions, §108A-70.19.
Reporting requirements, §108A-70.27, (b), (c).
Special needs children.
Case management services, §108A-70.23, (e).
Claims for benefits, processing, §108A-70.24, (c).
Eligibility for services, §108A-70.23, (b).
Enrollment requirement, §108A-70.23, (d).
Entitlement not conferred, §108A-70.23, (g).
Funds to be allocated for payment and program implementation, §108A-70.22.
Recommendations of commission on children with special health care needs, §108A-70.23, (f).
Services authorized, §108A-70.23, (a).
Services provided, §108A-70.23, (c).
State plan to implement program, §108A-70.25.
Title of part, §108A-70.19.
Vision coverage, §108A-70.21, (b).

CHILDREN'S TRUST FUND, §7B-1302, (a), (b).

CHILDREN'S YEAR'S ALLOWANCE.
When child entitled, §30-17.

CHILDREN WITH SPECIAL HEALTH CARE NEEDS COMMISSION.
Chairperson, §143-682, (c).
Children's health insurance program.
Recommendations for health care needs, §108A-70.23, (f).
Compensation, §143-684.
Composition, §143-682, (b).
Duties, §143-683.
Establishment, §143-682, (a).
Expenses, §143-684.
Powers, §143-683.
Terms of office, §143-682, (c).

CHILD RESTRAINT SYSTEMS, §20-137.1.
Child bicycle safety act.
Restraining seat.
Small children as passengers, §§20-171.6 to 20-171.9.
Child care facilities.
Compliance with law required, §110-91.
Placement of small children within vehicle, §20-137.1, (a1).

CHILD RESTRAINT SYSTEMS —Cont'd
Points for violations, §§20-16, (c), 20-137.1, (d).

CHILD SUPPORT.
Abandonment.
Willful neglect or refusal to provide adequate support, §14-322.
Magistrate's finding, §110-138.1.
Absent parents.
Location of parents, §110-139.
Abused, neglected or dependent juvenile action.
Parent to pay, custody of juvenile in someone other than parent, §7B-904, (d).
Acknowledgment of paternity.
Agreements of support.
Filing fees, §110-134.
Force and effect of agreements, §110-132, (a).
Show cause orders, §110-132, (b).
Action for support of minor child generally, §50-13.4.
Administration of program, §110-128.
Adoption.
Consequences of consent by parent to adoption, §48-3-607, (c).
Duty of former parent to make past-due payments.
Effect of decree of adoption, §48-1-106, (c).
AEI.
High-volume, automated administrative enforcement in interstate cases, §110-139.3.
Agreements of support, §§110-132 to 110-134.
Acknowledgment of paternity.
Filing fees, §110-134.
Force and effect of agreements, §110-132, (a).
Show cause orders, §110-132, (b).
Medical support, §50-13.11.
Responsible parents.
Enforceability of agreement, §110-133.
Filing fees, §110-134.
Modification of agreements, §110-133.
Voluntary support agreements, §110-133.
Acknowledgment of paternity and agreement to support, §110-132.
Filing fees, §110-134.
Filing fees, §110-134.
Amount of support, §50-13.4, (c), (c1).
Employee verification form.
Amount of obligor's gross income, establishing by, §110-139, (c1).
Factors considered, §50-13.4, (c).
Guidelines for computation.
Uniform statewide presumptive guidelines.
Application in determining amount, §50-13.4, (c).
Prescribed by conference of chief district judges, §50-13.4, (c1).
Hearings on request of party, §50-13.4, (c).
Modification of amount, §50-13.4, (c).
Past due child support, §50-13.10.
Procedure to insure payment, §50-13.9.
Reasonable needs of child, §50-13.4, (c).
Appeals.
Enforcement pending appeal.
Civil contempt, §50-13.4, (f).
Expedited process.
Orders of child support hearing officer, §50-38.
Arbitration.
Family law arbitration generally, §§50-41 to 50-62.
See FAMILY LAW ARBITRATION.

CHILD SUPPORT —Cont'd
Arrearages.
At termination of support, §50-13.4, (c).
Enforcement orders, §50-13.9, (d).
Vesting of past due support, §50-13.10.
Arrest.
Enforcement of support.
Remedy of arrest available, §50-13.4, (f).
Assignments.
Public assistance.
Acceptance of assistance constitutes assignment of support rights to state or county, §110-137.
Unemployment compensation benefits, §110-136.2.
Wages, §110-136.1.
Attachment.
Actions in which attachment may be had, §1-440.2.
Enforcement of support.
Remedy available, §50-13.4, (f).
Attorneys at law.
Procedure to insure payment.
Appointment to represent party support payment owed, §50-13.9, (f).
List of attorneys willing to undertake representation, §50-13.9, (e).
Attorneys' fees.
Action for support of minor child, §50-13.6.
Attorneys specializing in family law.
Certification standards, Bar Rules & Regs., D, §§.2401 to .2407.
Bail and recognizance.
Enforcement of support.
Remedy of arrest and bail available, §50-13.4, (f).
Illegitimate children.
Continuance, surety of person accused of being father, §49-5.
Blood tests.
Expedited procedures to establish paternity in IV-D cases.
Subpoena to appear for blood tests to establish paternity, §110-132.2.
Bonds, surety.
Enforcement of support.
Payments secured by bond, §50-13.4, (f).
Change in circumstances.
Modification of order, §50-13.7.
Family law arbitration act, §50-56.
Child support collection and disbursement unit.
Establishment, §110-139, (f).
Claims against the state.
Assignments made to meet child support obligations.
Section not applicable to, §143-3.3, (d).
Clerks of court.
Duty of judicial officials to assist in obtaining support, §110-138.1.
Hearing officer, §7A-183.
Past due child support.
Payments made to clerk.
When payments not past due, §50-13.10, (e).
Procedure to insure payment.
Notice of delinquency.
Non-IV-D cases, §50-13.9, (d).
Payments made to, §50-13.9.
Responsibilities in non-IV-D cases, §50-13.9, (b2).
Collection of spousal support, §110-130.2.

CHILD SUPPORT —Cont'd
Commission of offense of failure to support child.
When offense deemed committed in state, §14-325.1.
Compromise and settlement.
District court actions.
Mediated settlement conferences or other settlement procedures, §7A-38.4A.
Computation of support, §50-13.4, (c).
Guidelines.
Uniform statewide presumptive guidelines, §50-13.4, (c), (c1).
Confidentiality of information.
District attorneys.
Reports to district attorneys of aid to dependent children and illegitimate births, §15-155.3.
Location of absent parents, §110-139.
Conflicting provisions.
Conformity with federal requirements, §110-140, (a).
Contempt.
Compelling disclosure of information respecting nonsupporting parent.
Parent of dependent child receiving public assistance failing or refusing to cooperate, §110-131, (b).
Enforcement of support, §50-13.4, (f).
Garnishment.
Wage garnishment order.
Garnishee violating terms of order, §110-136, (e).
Procedure to insure payment.
Civil contempt.
Independent initiation of proceeding not precluded, §50-13.9, (g).
Wage garnishment to enforce, garnishee violating terms, §110-136, (e).
Counties.
Assignment of support rights to state or county.
Acceptance of public assistance constitutes assignment, §110-137.
Duty of county to obtain support, §110-138.
County commissioners.
Action by designated representatives, §110-130.
Responsibility for administration of program, §110-141.
Court orders.
Defined, §110-129.
Data match systems.
Agreements with financial institutions, §110-139.2.
Definitions, §§110-129, 110-142.
Abandonment and failure to support spouse and children, §14-322, (a).
Expedited process, §50-31.
Garnishment for enforcement of child-support obligation.
Disposable earnings, §110-136, (a).
Past due child support.
Child support payments, §50-13.10, (c).
Delinquencies.
Drivers' licenses, forfeiture, §§20-17, (b), 50-13.12.
Drivers' licenses, refusal to renew or issue, §20-17, (b).
Enforcement order, §50-13.9, (d).
Motor vehicle registration.
Refusal to register, §20-50.4, (b).

CHILD SUPPORT —Cont'd
Delinquencies —Cont'd
Occupational licenses revocation when privilege forfeited for nonsupport, §93B-13, (a).
Applicability of revocation period imposed by occupational licensing board, §93B-13, (c).
Notice of intent, §93B-13, (b).
Reinstatement upon payment of support, §93B-13, (d).
Past due child support, §50-13.10.
Procedure to insure payment, §50-13.9.
Delinquent and undisciplined juvenile actions.
Parent ordered to pay, §7B-2704.
Dependent children.
Defined, §110-129.
Designated representatives.
Action by representatives of county commissioners, §110-130.
Defined, §110-129.
Responsible parents.
Duty of county to obtain support, §110-138.
Directory of new hires.
Access to information by employment security commission, §110-129.2, (g).
Confidentiality of information, §110-129.2, (i).
Contracts with other state or private entities to perform services, §110-129.2, (h).
Definitions, §110-129.2, (j).
Employer reporting, §110-129.2, (b).
Civil penalty for failure to report, §110-129.2, (d).
Contents, §110-129.2, (c).
Entry of data into directory, §110-129.2, (e).
Established, §110-129.2, (a).
Withholding of income notice, §110-129.2, (f).
Distribution by court of marital and divisible property.
Equitable distribution without regard to child support, §50-20, (f).
District attorneys.
Duty to assist in enforcing support, §110-138.1.
Reports to district attorneys of aid to dependent children and illegitimate births, §15-155.1.
Confidentiality of information, §15-155.3.
Criminal offenses.
Indictments, §15-155.2, (b).
Disclosure of information by district attorney or agent, §15-155.3.
Investigations, §15-155.2, (a).
District courts.
Mediated settlement conferences or other settlement procedures, §7A-38.4A.
Proper division for trial of civil actions, §7A-244.
Divorce.
Action for support of minor child, §50-13.4.
Procedure, §50-13.5.
Distribution by court of marital and divisible property.
Equitable distribution without regard to child support, §50-20, (f).
Independent actions permissible, §50-19.
Judgment provisions pertaining to care, tuition and maintenance, §50-11.2.
Change of conditions.
Modification upon substantial change, §50-11.2.
Modification of orders, §50-13.7.
Past due child support, §50-13.10.
Procedure to insure payment, §50-13.9.

CHILD SUPPORT —Cont'd
Domestic violence, §50B-3, (a).
Drivers' licenses.
Access to information or data storage and retrieval system maintained by department of transportation.
Powers of department of health and human services, §110-129.1, (a).
Forfeiture of licensing privilege for nonpayment, §50-13.12.
Refusal to renew or issue, §20-17, (b).
Driver's license suspension or revocation.
Obligors delinquent in court-ordered support or not in compliance with orders, §§110-142, 110-142.2.
Actions authorized, §110-142.2, (a).
Certification that individual no longer delinquent or that individual in compliance with subpoena, §110-142.2, (d).
Definitions, §110-142.
Entry of order instituting sanctions, §110-142.2, (b).
Forms and procedures, development, §110-142.2, (i).
Limited driving privilege issued.
License to operate necessary to individual's livelihood, §110-142.2, (c).
Reinstatement, §110-142.2, (e) to (g).
Violation of terms and conditions of stay, §110-142.2, (h).
Due process requirements met, §110-131.1.
Duties of department of health and human services, §110-129.1, (a).
Secretary defined, §110-129.1, (b).
Effectuation of intent of article, §110-141.
Emancipation.
Termination of support, §50-13.4, (c).
Exceptions, §50-13.4, (c).
Employee verification form.
Amount of obligor's gross income, establishing by, §110-139, (c1).
Employer reporting of new hires to directory, §110-129.2, (b) to (e).
Enforcement of support.
Past due child support, §50-13.10.
Procedure to insure payment, §50-13.9.
Remedies, §50-13.4, (f).
Establishment of program, §110-128.
Establishment of spousal support obligation.
Child support enforcement program not authorized to assist, §110-130.2.
Evidence.
Employee verification form, §110-139, (c1).
Executions.
Enforcement of support, §50-13.4, (f).
Exempt property from enforcement of claims of creditors.
Exception, §1C-1601, (e).
Expedited process, §§50-30 to 50-39.
Appeal of order of hearing officer, §50-38, (a).
Order not stayed pending appeal, §50-38, (b).
Definitions, §50-31.
Disposition of cases within 60 days, §50-32.
Extension of time, §50-32.
Establishment.
Districts required to have process, §50-34, (a).
Procedure, §50-34, (b).
Findings of general assembly, §50-30, (a).
Hearing de novo.
Appeal of order of hearing officer, §50-38, (a).

CHILD SUPPORT —Cont'd
Expedited process —Cont'd
Hearing officers.
Authority, §50-35.
Contempt, §50-37.
Duties, §50-35.
Enforcement authority, §50-37.
Qualifications, §50-39, (a).
Training, §50-39, (b).
Hearings.
Place, §50-36, (b).
Procedure, §50-36, (c).
Record of proceedings, §50-36, (d).
Transfer to district court judge, §50-36, (e).
Public to be informed, §50-34, (c).
Purpose and policy, §50-30, (b).
Scheduling of cases, §50-36, (a).
Waiver of requirement.
Department to seek, §50-33, (a).
Districts not qualifying, §50-33, (b).
Failure to support child, §14-322.
Clerks of court.
Duty to assist in obtaining support, §110-138.1.
Competency of witnesses in prosecution.
Husband and wife, §8-57, (b).
Enforcement order, §50-13.9, (d).
Forfeiture of driver's license, §§20-17, (b), 50-13.12.
Judicial officials.
Duty to assist in obtaining support, §110-138.1.
When offense deemed committed in state, §14-325.1.
Family law arbitration generally, §§50-41 to 50-62.
See FAMILY LAW ARBITRATION.
Federal aid.
Conformity with federal requirements, §110-140, (a).
Federal parent locator service.
Access to, §110-139.1, (a).
Fees.
Filing of affirmations, acknowledgments, agreements and orders, §110-134.
Files.
Support files not to be released, §110-139.
Financial institutions data match system.
Financial institution defined, §110-139.2, (c).
Immunity of financial institution for disclosure of information, §110-139.2, (b).
Lien and levy on obligor's account, §110-139.2, (b1).
Mutual agreement department and financial institutions, §110-139.2, (a).
Notice to financial institution.
Lien and levy on obligor's account, §110-139.2, (b1).
Forfeiture of licensing privilege for nonpayment.
Certification obligor no longer delinquent, §50-13.12, (c).
Definitions, §50-13.12, (a).
Duties of licensing boards, §50-13.12, (f).
Findings by court, §50-13.12, (b).
Petition for reinstatement of privileges, §50-13.12, (d), (e).
Fraudulent conveyances.
Enforcement of support.
Minor child creditor within meaning of chapter, §50-13.4, (f).
Full faith and credit.
Past due child support judgment, §50-13.10, (b).

CHILD SUPPORT —Cont'd
Full faith and credit —Cont'd
Paternity determination by another state, §110-132.1.
Garnishment.
Continuing wage garnishment proceedings.
Method for instituting, §110-136, (b), (b1).
Time period for responding to pleadings, §110-136, (b1).
Verification of petition and statement, §110-136, (b1).
Enforcement of support.
Remedy available, §50-13.4, (f).
Wage garnishment order.
Contempt.
Garnishee violating terms of order, §110-136, (e).
Definition of disposable earnings, §110-136, (a).
Disposable earnings defined, §110-136, (a).
Dissolution of order, §110-136, (c).
Employer third-party garnishee, §110-136, (b).
Modifying order, §110-136, (c).
Payment of amount order to be garnished, §110-136, (d).
Percentage of disposable earnings, §110-136, (c).
Review for modification and dissolution, §110-136, (c).
Time period for responding to pleadings, §110-136, (b).
Verification of motion and statement, §110-136, (b).
Genetic testing.
Expedited procedures to establish paternity in IV-D cases.
Subpoena to appear for genetic testing, §110-132.2.
Guidelines.
Child support guidelines (court rules).
See Court Rules Volume.
Computation of support.
Uniform statewide presumptive guidelines.
Applied in determining amount, §50-13.4, (c).
Criteria for applying, §50-13.4, (c1).
Modification by conference of chief district judges, §50-13.4, (c1).
Prescribed by conference of chief district judges, §50-13.4, (c1).
Purposes, §50-13.4, (c1).
Review by conference of chief district judges, §50-13.4, (c1).
Health insurance.
Medical support, orders and agreements, §50-13.11.
Hearings.
Action for support of minor child.
Heard by judge without jury, §50-13.5, (h).
Amount of support payments.
Request of party, §50-13.4, (c).
Expedited process.
Appeal from orders of child support hearing officer.
De novo hearing, §50-38, (a).
Procedure to insure payment.
Cases heard for enforcement.
Informing district court judge, §50-13.9, (f).
Delinquency in non-IV-D cases.
Enforcement order, §50-13.9, (d).
High-volume, automated administrative enforcement in interstate cases, §110-139.3.

CHILD SUPPORT —Cont'd
Hunting, fishing or trapping licenses.
Forfeiture of licensing privilege for nonpayment, §50-13.12.
Suspension or revocation of license of delinquent obligors, §§110-142, 110-142.2.
Actions authorized, §110-142.2, (a).
Certification that individual no longer delinquent or in compliance, §110-142.2, (d).
Definitions, §110-142.
Forms and procedures, development, §110-142.2, (i).
Order instituting sanctions, §110-142.2, (b).
Reinstatement, §110-142.2, (e) to (g).
Stay of order, §110-142.2, (b).
Violations of terms of stay, §110-142.2, (h).
Husband-wife privilege.
Actions by designated representatives of county commissioners.
Privilege not grounds for excusing mother or father from testifying, §110-130.
Illegitimate child, §§49-1 to 49-9.
Amount.
Determination by court, §49-7.
Bond for future appearance of defendant, §49-9.
Child defined, §49-2.
Commencement of action, §49-4.
Continuances, surety of person accused of being father, §49-5.
Death of mother not bar to proceeding, §49-5.
Immunity of mother testifying, §49-6.
Issues determined by court, §49-7.
Nonsupport of illegitimate child by parents, §49-2.
Orders, §49-7.
Power of court to modify, §49-8.
Paternity.
Custody and support when paternity established, §49-15.
Temporary order of support.
Entry when paternity determination pending, §49-14, (f).
Place of child.
No consideration, §49-3.
Preliminary proceeding to determine, §49-5.
Reports to district attorneys of aid to dependent children and illegitimate births, §15-155.1.
Confidentiality of information, §15-155.3.
Criminal offenses.
Indictments, §15-155.2, (b).
Disclosure of information by district attorney or agent, §15-155.3.
Investigations, §15-155.2, (a).
Self-incrimination.
Mother not excused on grounds of self-incrimination, §49-6.
Sentencing.
Power of court to extend sentence, §49-8.
Time for commencing prosecutions, §49-4.
Title of article, §49-1.
Venue, §49-5.
Income information for both parents.
Revealing to establish child support obligation, §110-139, (b).
Income withholding, §§110-136.3 to 110-136.14.
See within this heading, "Withholding of income."
Independent actions for divorce.
Maintenance of certain actions as independent actions permissible, §50-19.

CHILD SUPPORT —Cont'd
Information respecting nonsupporting responsible parent.
Compelling disclosure of information, §110-131, (a).
Failure to cooperate.
Penalty for violation of provisions, §110-131, (b).
Penalty for failure to cooperate, §110-131, (b).
Refusal to cooperate, §110-131, (a).
Declaration of ineligibility for public assistance, §110-131, (a).
Needs of remaining family members, §110-131, (c).
Injunctions.
Enforcement of support, §50-13.4, (f).
Institution of action.
Persons who may institute, §50-13.4, (a).
Insurance.
Medical insurance, §50-13.11.
Insurance settlements.
Lien on insurance settlement of child support obligor, §§58-3-135, 58-3-185, (a), (b).
Receiving person charged with duty of retaining funds, §44-50.
Intent of article.
Effectuation of intent, §110-141.
Interlocutory orders, §50-13.5, (d).
Interstate family support, §§52C-1-100 to 52C-9-902.
See INTERSTATE FAMILY SUPPORT.
Intervention.
Action for support of minor child, §50-13.5, (e).
Job search, order of parents to perform, §50-13.4, (b).
Judgments.
Lien, §50-13.4, (f).
Past due child support.
Full faith and credit, §50-13.10, (b).
Judicial officials.
Duty to assist in obtaining support, §110-138.1.
Jurisdiction.
Action for support of minor child, §50-13.5, (c).
Transfer of IV-D cases to another jurisdiction, §50-13.4, (e1).
Liability.
Primary liability, §50-13.4, (b).
Secondary liability, §50-13.4, (b).
License suspension or revocation.
Drivers' licenses, hunting, fishing or trapping licenses, §§110-142, 110-142.2.
Occupational, professional or business licenses, §§110-142, 110-142.1.
Licensing privileges, forfeiture for nonpayment, §50-13.12.
Liens.
Creation, §44-86, (b).
Definitions, §44-86, (a).
Discharge, §44-87, (a).
Penalty for failure to discharge, §44-87, (b).
Execution, §44-86, (f).
Filing and perfection, §44-86, (d).
Insurance settlements owed to obligor, §§58-3-135, 58-3-185, (a), (b).
Judgment for child support, §50-13.4, (f).
Liens arising out-of-state, §44-86, (g).
Statement of child support delinquency, §44-86, (c).
Superior to subsequent liens, §44-86, (e).
Location of absent parents, §110-139.
Access to federal parent locator service, §110-139.1, (a).

CHILD SUPPORT —Cont'd
Location of absent parents —Cont'd
Banks.
Information to be provided, §110-139, (d).
Confidentiality of information, §110-139.
Nonjudicial records, §110-139.1, (c).
Cooperation of state, county and city agencies, officers and employees, §110-139, (b).
Custody determination.
Defined, §110-139.1, (b).
Employers.
Information to be provided, §110-139, (c).
Financial institutions.
Information to be provided, §110-139, (d).
Registry for receipt of information, §110-139, (a).
Savings and loan associations.
Information to be provided, §110-139, (d).
Utility companies.
Exemptions, §110-139, (e).
Provision of information, §110-139, (d).
Magistrates.
Child support hearing officer, §7A-178.
Duty to assist in enforcing support, §110-138.1.
Mediated settlement conferences or other settlement procedures.
District court actions, §7A-38.4A.
Rules implementing, Settle. Proc. Equitable Distribution Rules 1-15.
See MEDIATED SETTLEMENT CONFERENCES.
Medical support and health insurance coverage.
Agreement to provide medical support.
Authority of parties to enter into, §50-13.11, (a).
Change in applicable health insurance policy.
Notice provided by party ordered to provide, §50-13.11, (b).
Change in employment by obligor and health available through new employer.
Custodial obligee to notify new employer, §50-13.11, (f).
Failure to maintain health insurance for benefit of child.
Liability of person ordered to maintain, §50-13.11, (e).
Order to maintain health insurance for benefit of child.
Authority of court to order, §50-13.11, (a1).
Order to provide medical support.
Authority of court to order, §50-13.11, (a).
Payment of health related expenses.
Order or agreement may require, §50-13.11, (a).
Reasonable in cost.
When health insurance considered, §50-13.11, (a1).
Release of information on child's health insurance.
Ordering employer or insurer, §50-13.11, (c).
Signature of each party.
Authorization for insurer to process claim, §50-13.11, (d).
Modification of order, §50-13.7.
Family law arbitration act, §50-56.
Mortgages and deeds of trust.
Enforcement of support.
Securing payment, §50-13.4, (f).
Motions.
Action for support of minor child.
Notice, §50-13.5, (d).
Modification of orders, §50-13.7.

CHILD SUPPORT —Cont'd
Motor vehicle registration.
Access to information or data storage and retrieval system maintained by department of transportation.
Powers of department of health and human services, §110-129.1, (a).
Delinquent child support, refusal to register vehicles, §20-50.4, (b).
Refusal to issue to delinquent obligor or individual not in compliance with order, §110-142.2.
National medical support notice, §§110-136.11 to 110-136.14.
New hires, state directory, §110-129.2.
Nonrecipients of work first services.
Eligibility for collection and paternity determination services, §110-130.1, (a).
Actions brought in name of county or state agency, §110-130.1, (c).
Fees.
Deduction from amount collected, §110-130.1, (d).
Location of absent and deserting parent.
Use of electronic and print media authorized, §110-130.1, (c1).
Recovery of costs, §110-130.1, (b1).
Nonsupporting responsible parent.
Compelling disclosure of information respecting parent, §110-131, (a).
Declaration of ineligibility for public assistance, §110-131, (a).
Needs of remaining family members, §110-131, (c).
Failure to cooperate, §110-131, (a).
Penalty for violation of provisions, §110-131, (b).
Penalty for failure to cooperate, §110-131, (b).
Willful nonsupport by supporting spouse, §14-322.
Notice.
Action for support of minor child.
Additional persons, §50-13.5, (e).
Motions, §50-13.5, (d).
Procedure to insure payment.
Delinquency in non-IV-D cases, §50-13.9, (d).
Withholding of income.
Amount to be withheld.
Contents of order and notice, §110-136.6, (c).
IV-D cases.
Advance notice of withholding, §110-136.4, (a).
Non-IV-D cases.
Order for withholding, §110-136.5, (d).
Payor, §110-136.8, (a).
Occupational, professional or business licenses, §93B-13, (a).
Forfeiture of licensing privileges for nonpayment, §50-13.12.
Suspension and revocation of licenses of delinquent obligors, §§93B-13, (a), 110-142, 110-142.1.
Administrative procedure act, inapplicability, §110-142.1, (n).
Applicability of revocation period imposed by occupational licensing board, §93B-13, (c).
Definitions, §110-142.
Forms and procedures to implement provisions, development, §110-142.1, (c).
Forms for use by designated representative, §110-142.1, (l).

CHILD SUPPORT —Cont'd
Occupational, professional or business licenses —Cont'd
Suspension and revocation of licenses of delinquent obligors —Cont'd
Furnishing licensing agency with certified list, §110-142.1, (b).
Inquiry into license status of applicant, §110-142.1, (o).
Interagency agreements, §110-142.1, (m).
Motion for judicial review, §110-142.1, (j).
Notice of intent to revoke or suspend license, §§93B-13, (b), 110-142.1, (d), (f).
Notice of request for review, §110-142.1, (h).
Notice of right to request judicial review, judicial determination of compliance or modification of order, §110-142.1, (i).
Notice that person licensed not in compliance with order, §110-142.1, (a).
Reinstatement of license, individual no longer in arrears, §§93B-13, (d), 110-142.1, (k).
Review procedures to be developed, §110-142.1, (g).
Review request, §110-142.1, (h).
Severability of provisions, §110-142.1, (p).
Stay of action pending review, §110-142.1, (h).
Submission of certified list by designated representative, §110-142.1, (b).
Time license revoked or suspended after notice, §110-142.1, (e).
Orders.
Acknowledgment of paternity in agreement to support.
Same force and effect as order of support, §110-132, (a).
Agreements of support to have force and effect as order of court, §110-133.
Attorneys' fees, §50-13.6.
Collection of spousal support, §110-130.2.
Contents, §50-13.4, (h).
Definition of court order, §110-129.
Generally, §50-13.4.
Interlocutory orders, §50-13.5, (d).
Medical support, §50-13.11.
Modification.
Change of circumstances, §50-13.7, (a).
Orders entered by court of another state, §50-13.7, (b).
Procedure generally, §50-13.5.
Procedure to insure payment, §50-13.9.
Temporary orders, §50-13.5, (d).
Wage garnishment order, §110-136.
Withholding of income.
Amount to be withheld, §110-136.6, (c).
Expiration of order, §110-136.10.
Non-IV-D cases, §110-136.5, (c).
Notice to payor and obligor, §110-136.5, (d).
Required contents of support orders, §110-136.3, (a).
Paternity.
Acknowledgment of paternity, agreement to support.
Filing fees, §110-134.
Force and effect of agreement, §110-132, (a).
Show cause orders, §110-132, (b).
Determination by another state.
Full faith and credit, §110-132.1.
Established, §49-15.
Establishing paternity.
Powers of department of health and human services, §110-129.1, (a).

CHILD SUPPORT —Cont'd
Paternity —Cont'd
Expedited procedures to establish paternity in IV-D cases.
Subpoena to appear for blood or genetic testing to establish paternity, §110-132.2, (a).
Contesting subpoena, §110-132.2, (b).
Preliminary proceeding, §49-5.
Temporary order of support.
Entry when paternity determination pending, §49-14, (f).
Payment history of obligor parent, §110-139, (b).
Payment of support.
Arrearages at termination of support, §50-13.4, (c).
Methods of payment, §50-13.4, (e).
Past due child support.
Child support payments defined, §50-13.10, (c).
Clerks of court.
Payments made to clerk.
When payments not past due, §50-13.10, (e).
Divestment, §50-13.10, (a).
Full faith and credit, §50-13.10, (b).
Judgments, §50-13.10, (b).
Modification, §50-13.10, (a).
Vested when it accrues, §50-13.10, (a).
When support not past due, §50-13.10, (d), (e).
Procedure to insure payment, §50-13.9.
Arrearage.
Delinquency in non-IV-D cases, §50-13.9, (d).
Attorneys at law.
Appointment to represent party support payment owed, §50-13.9, (f).
List of attorneys willing to undertake representation, §50-13.9, (e).
Change of address or other conditions.
Information to clerk, §50-13.9, (c).
Contempt.
Independent initiation of proceeding not precluded, §50-13.9, (g).
Delinquency.
Enforcement order, §50-13.9, (d).
IV-D cases.
Transmission of payments to health and human services department, §50-13.9, (b).
Hearings.
Delinquency in non-IV-D cases, §50-13.9, (d).
Non-IV-D cases.
Clerks' responsibilities, §50-13.9, (b2).
Delinquency, §50-13.9, (d).
Notice.
Delinquency in non-IV-D cases, §50-13.9, (d).
Payments made to clerk, §50-13.9, (a).
Informing clerk of change of address, §50-13.9, (c).
Records listing amount of payment, §50-13.9, (a).
Transmission payments to health and human services department in IV-D cases, §50-13.9, (b).
Withholding of income.
Independent initiation of proceeding not precluded, §50-13.9, (g).
To whom payments made, §50-13.4, (d).
Powers of department of health and human services, §110-129.1, (a).
Secretary defined, §110-129.1, (b).
Premarital agreements.
Not affected, §52B-4, (b).

CHILD SUPPORT —Cont'd
Presumptions.
Computation of support.
Uniform statewide presumptive guidelines, §50-13.4, (c), (c1).
Probation.
Condition of probation.
Procedure to insure payment of child support, §15A-1344.1.
Procedure generally, §50-13.5, (a).
Production of documents and things.
Subpoena issued by department of health and human services, §110-129.1, (a).
Professional licenses. See within this heading, "Occupational, professional or business licenses."
Public assistance.
Assignment of support rights to state or county.
Acceptance of public assistance constitutes assignment, §110-137.
Debt to state created, §110-135.
Nonsupporting responsible parent.
Compelling disclosure of information respecting parent, §110-131.
Purposes of article, §110-128.
Transfer of property.
Order transferring title, §50-13.4, (f).
Receivers.
Enforcement of support, §50-13.4, (f).
Registry for receipt of information relating to identity or location of absent parents.
Department of health and human services to serve as, §110-139, (a).
Remedies.
Enforcement of support, §50-13.4, (e), (f).
Reports.
Directory of new hires.
Employer reporting, §110-129.2, (b) to (e).
Responsible parents.
Agreements of support.
Enforceability of agreement, §110-133.
Filing fees, §110-134.
Modification of agreements, §110-133.
Compelling disclosure of information respecting nonsupporting parent, §110-131, (a).
Declaration of ineligibility for public assistance, §110-131, (a).
Needs of remaining family, §110-131, (c).
Failure to cooperate, §110-131, (a).
Penalty for violation of provisions, §110-131, (b).
Penalty for failure to cooperate, §110-131, (b).
Defined, §110-129.
Designated representatives.
Duty of county to obtain support, §110-138.
Location of absent parents, §110-139.
Salaries.
Assignment of wages, §110-136.1.
Garnishment, §110-136.
Withholding of income, §§110-136.3 to 110-136.14. See within this heading, "Withholding of income."
Schedule of basic child support obligations.
Child support guidelines (court rules). See Court Rules Volume.
Service of process.
Action for support of minor child, §50-13.5, (d).
Services provided to nonrecipients of work first services, §110-130.1.
Setoff debt collection, §§105A-1 to 105A-16. See SETOFF DEBT COLLECTION.

CHILD SUPPORT —Cont'd
Settlement.
Mediated settlement conferences or other settlement procedures.
District court actions, §7A-38.4A.
Show cause orders.
Acknowledgment of paternity.
Agreements to support, §110-132, (b).
Filing fees, §110-134.
Social security number, §50-13.4, (g).
State child support collection and disbursement unit.
Establishment, §110-139, (f).
State debt.
Creating debt to state, §110-135.
State directory of new hires, §110-129.2.
Subpoenas.
Actions by designated representatives of county commissioners, §110-130.
Expedited procedures to establish paternity in IV-D cases.
Appearance for blood tests or genetic tests, §110-132.2.
Powers of department of health and human services, §110-129.1, (a).
Support and maintenance.
General provisions.
See SUPPORT AND MAINTENANCE.
Uniform reciprocal enforcement of support act.
See SUPPORT AND MAINTENANCE.
Temporary assistance for needy families (TANF) block grant program.
Distribution options for families receiving cash assistance under, §110-140, (b).
Temporary orders pending service and notice, §50-13.5, (d).
Termination of parental rights.
Failure of noncustodial parent to pay, grounds for terminating, §7B-1111, (a).
Termination of support, §50-13.4, (c).
Transfers to minors.
Delivery, payment or expenditure of custodial property.
Support obligation not affected by, §33A-14, (c).
Types of actions, §50-13.5, (b).
Unemployment compensation.
Deductions for support obligations, §96-17, (c).
Income withholding of unemployment compensation benefits.
Absence of voluntary assignment, §110-136.2, (f).
Voluntary assignment of unemployment compensation benefits to child support agency, §110-136.2, (a).
Assignment effective until employment security commission receives notification of revocation, §110-136.2, (d).
Notification to department of health and human services, §110-136.2, (b).
Payment of amount deducted and withheld by employment security commission, §110-136.2, (c).
Proper credit ensured by department of health and human services, §110-136.2, (e).
Uniform reciprocal enforcement of support act.
See SUPPORT AND MAINTENANCE.
Uniform statewide presumptive guidelines, §50-13.4, (c), (c1).
Venue.
Action for support of minor child, §50-13.5, (f).

CHILD SUPPORT —Cont'd
Venue —Cont'd
Actions by designated representatives of county commissioners, §110-130.
Voluntary assignment of unemployment compensation benefits, §110-136.2.
Voluntary support agreements, §110-133.
Acknowledgment of paternity and agreement to support, §110-132.
Filing fees, §110-134.
Filing fees, §110-134.
Wages.
Assignment of wages for child support, §110-136.1.
Attachment.
Enforcement of support, §50-13.4, (f).
Garnishment, §110-136.
Withholding of income, §§110-136.3 to 110-136.14.
Welfare.
Assignment of support rights to state or county.
Acceptance of public assistance constitutes assignment, §110-137.
Debt to state created, §110-135.
Nonsupporting responsible parent.
Compelling disclosure of information respecting parent, §110-131.
Who may institute action, §50-13.4, (a).
Withholding of income, §§110-136.3 to 110-136.14.
Amount to be withheld.
Computation, §110-136.6, (a).
Contents of order and notice, §110-136.6, (c).
Limits, §110-136.6, (b), (b1).
Applicability of provisions.
IV-D cases, §110-136.4, (f).
Based on arrearage, §110-136.5, (a).
Based on obligor's request, §110-136.5, (b).
Disposable income.
Defined, §110-129.
Distribution of payments received, §110-136.9.
Employer reporting to directory of new hires.
Notice to employer to withhold income, §110-129.2, (f).
IV-D cases.
Applicability of provisions, §110-136.4, (f).
Contested withholding, §110-136.4, (a).
Defenses.
Payment not a defense to withholding, §110-136.4, (a).
Defined, §110-129.
Immediate income withholding, §110-136.4, (b).
Modification of withholding, §110-136.4, (e).
Multiple withholdings, §110-136.4, (d).
Notice.
Advance notice of withholding, §110-136.4, (a).
Subsequent payors, §110-136.4, (c).
Uncontested withholding, §110-136.4, (a).
Immediate income withholding, §110-136.5, (c1).
Effective date, application of provision, §50-13.4, (d1).
IV-D cases, §110-136.4, (b).
Interstate cases, §110-136.3, (d).
Interstate family support act, §§52C-5-501 to 52C-5-507.
See INTERSTATE FAMILY SUPPORT.
Modification of withholding.
IV-D cases, §110-136.4, (e).
Non-IV-D cases, §110-136.5, (e).
Multiple withholdings, §110-136.7.
IV-D cases, §110-136.4, (d).

CHILD SUPPORT —Cont'd
Withholding of income —Cont'd
National medical support notice.
Contest of order, §110-136.13, (h).
Definition of employer, §110-136.13, (a).
Determination if qualified medical child support order, §110-136.14, (a).
Employer not to retaliate for withholding order, §110-136.13, (i).
Employer transfer of notice, §110-136.13, (b).
When notice not transferred, §110-136.13, (c).
Enrollment in plan, §110-136.14, (b).
Health insurer violations, §110-136.14, (e).
IV-D agency notice to employer, §110-136.12, (a).
IV-D notice of order expiration, §110-136.12, (c).
Liabilities of employer, §110-136.13, (j).
Newly hired employees, §110-136.12, (b).
Notice not a qualified medical child support order, §110-136.13, (e).
Not used, §110-136.11, (b).
Options for health care, §110-136.12, (d).
Selection of plan from options, §110-136.14, (c).
Termination of employment, notice, §110-136.13, (g).
Waiting period for enrollment, §§110-136.13, (f), 110-136.14, (d).
When used, §110-136.11, (a).
Withholding amount, §110-136.13, (d).
Non-IV-D cases.
Defined, §110-129.
Modification of withholding, §110-136.5, (e).
Order for withholding.
Notice to payor and obligor, §110-136.5, (d).
Notice.
Amount to be withheld.
Contents of order and notice, §110-136.6, (c).
IV-D cases.
Advance notice of withholding, §110-136.4, (a).
Non-IV-D cases.
Order for withholding, §110-136.5, (d).
Payor, §110-136.8, (a).
Obligee.
Defined, §110-129.
Obligor.
Change in obligor's employment, §110-136.8, (c).
Defined, §110-129.
When obligor subject to withholding, §110-136.3, (b).
Orders.
Amount to be withheld.
Contents of order and notice, §110-136.6, (c).
Expiration of order.
Termination of withholding, §110-136.10.
Non-IV-D cases, §110-136.5, (c).
Notice to payor and obligor, §110-136.5, (d).
Required contents of support orders, §110-136.3, (a).
Payment of withheld funds, §110-136.9.
Payment plan, §110-136.3, (a).
Payor.
Civil penalties, §110-136.8, (e), (f).
Combining amounts withheld from obligor's disposable income, §110-136.8, (d).
Defined, §110-129.
Notice to payor, §110-136.8, (a).
Prohibited conduct, §110-136.8, (e).
Responsibilities, §110-136.8, (b).
Priority.
Multiple withholdings, §110-136.7.

CHILD SUPPORT —Cont'd
Withholding of income —Cont'd
Procedure to insure payment.
Independent initiation of proceeding not precluded, §50-13.9, (g).
Rules and regulations, §110-136.3, (e).
Subsequent payors.
IV-D cases, §110-136.4, (c).
Termination of withholding, §110-136.10.
Unemployment compensation benefits, §110-136.2, (f).
Work requirement for past-due support, §110-136.3, (a1).

CHILD SUPPORT AGREEMENTS, §110-133.
Acknowledgment of paternity in agreement to support, §110-132.
Filing of affirmations, acknowledgments, etc., §110-134.

CHILD SUPPORT COLLECTION AND DISBURSEMENT UNIT.
Establishment, §110-139, (f).

CHILD SUPPORT ENFORCEMENT PROGRAM.
Generally, §§110-128 to 110-142.2.
See CHILD SUPPORT.

CHILD SUPPORT GUIDELINES.
Child support guidelines (court rules).
See Court Rules Volume.
Computation of support.
Uniform statewide presumptive guidelines.
Applied in determining amount, §50-13.4, (c).
Criteria for applying, §50-13.4, (c1).
Modification by conference of chief district judges, §50-13.4, (d).
Prescribed by conference of chief district judges, §50-13.4, (c1).
Purposes, §50-13.4, (c1).
Review by conference of chief district judges, §50-13.4, (c1).
Uniform statewide presumptive guidelines, §50-13.4, (c), (c1).

CHILD TAX CREDIT, §105-151.24.

CHIROPRACTORS, §§90-139 to 90-157.3.
Acceptable care in practice of chiropractic.
Adoption of rules to establish and define standards, §90-154.3, (b).
Lawful scope of practice not altered, §90-154.3, (d).
Unlawful to render service not conforming to standards, §90-154.3, (a).
Usual and customary method taught in majority of recognized chiropractic colleges.
Standard of care if rule not promulgated defining, §90-154.3, (c).
Acupuncture.
Exemption from licensing, §90-452, (b).
Advertisements.
False or misleading advertisement, grounds for disciplinary actions, §90-154, (b).
Free or reduced rate service.
Notice to patient, §90-154.1, (b).
Board of examiners.
Appointment of members, §§90-139, (a), 90-140.
Certification of diagnostic imaging technicians, §90-143.2, (a), (b).
Composition, §90-139, (a).
Creation, §90-139, (a).
Expenditures, §90-156.

CHIROPRACTORS —Cont'd
Board of examiners —Cont'd
Expenses of members, §90-156.
Meetings, §90-144.
Number of members, §90-139, (a).
Officers.
Election, §90-141.
Qualifications of members, §90-139, (a).
Quorum, §90-141.
Records, §90-148.
Removal of members, §90-139, (c).
Rules and regulations, §90-142.
Selection of members, §90-140.
Terms of members, §§90-139, (b), 90-140.
Business corporations.
Limitations on ownership of practice, §90-157.3, (c).
Censure of practitioner.
Powers of board of chiropractic examiners, §90-154, (a).
Certification.
Diagnostic imaging technicians, §90-143.2, (a), (b).
Charge or fee violations.
Grounds for disciplinary action, §90-154, (b).
Child support enforcement.
Forfeiture of licensing privilege, §50-13.12.
Control of contagious and infectious diseases.
Chiropractors subject to state and municipal regulations as to, §90-157.
Conviction of felony or crime involving moral turpitude.
Grounds for disciplinary action, §90-154, (b).
Corporations.
Professional corporations generally, §§55B-1 to 55B-16.
See PROFESSIONAL CORPORATIONS.
Costs.
Contested disciplinary hearings.
Assessment of costs upon guilty verdict, §90-154, (c).
Definitions.
Chiropractic, §90-143, (a).
Unethical conduct, §90-154.2.
Diagnostic imaging technicians.
Certification by board, §90-143.2, (a), (b).
Discipline.
Costs of hearing upon guilty verdict, §90-154, (c).
Grounds, §90-154, (b).
Powers of board of examiners, §90-154, (a).
Drugs.
Addiction or severe dependency.
Grounds for disciplinary action, §90-154, (b).
Prescriptions.
Prohibited, §90-151.
Drunkenness.
Addiction or severe dependency upon alcohol.
Grounds for disciplinary action, §90-154, (b).
Education requirements, §90-143, (b).
Diploma, §90-143, (c).
Examination scores, §90-143, (d).
Fees.
Collection of certain fees prohibited, §90-154.1.
Diagnostic imaging technicians, §90-143.2, (b).
Licenses.
Application fee, §90-149.
Renewal, §90-155.
Felony convictions.
Forfeiture of licenses, §15A-1331A.
Fines.
Unlicensed practice, §90-147.

CHIROPRACTORS —Cont'd
Fraud, deception or misrepresentation.
Grounds for disciplinary action, §90-154, (b).
Free choice by patient guaranteed, §90-157.1.
Free or reduced rate services.
Bills sent to patients, §90-154.1, (d).
Notice to prospective patients, §90-154.1, (b).
Refusal to pay certain fees.
Right of patient, §90-154.1, (a).
Health benefit plans.
Right of subscriber to choose service, payment, §58-50-30.
Identification badges required, §90-640.
Injunctions.
Unlicensed practice, §90-147.
Insurers or third-party payors.
Charging fee greater than advertised for same service, §90-154, (b).
Lewd or immoral conduct toward patient.
Ground for disciplinary action, §90-154, (b).
Licenses.
Denial.
Disciplinary powers of board of examiners, §90-154, (a).
Grounds, §90-154, (b).
Educational requirements, §90-143, (b).
Fees.
Application fee, §90-149.
Renewal, §90-155.
Issuance, §90-145.
Privileges of licensees, §90-151.
Qualifications, §90-143, (b).
Reciprocity, §§90-143.1, 90-146.
Renewal, §90-155.
Revocation or suspension.
Disciplinary powers of board of examiners, §90-154, (a).
Felony convictions, §15A-1331A.
Grounds, §90-154, (b).
Unlicensed practices, §90-147.
License taxes, §105-41.
Limited partnerships.
Limitations on ownership of practice, §90-157.3, (b).
Malpractice actions generally, §§90-21.11 to 90-21.14.
See MEDICAL MALPRACTICE.
Malpractice, negligence or incompetence in practice.
Grounds for disciplinary actions, §90-154, (b).
Medical records, §§90-410, 90-411.
Electronic medical records, §90-412.
Misdemeanors.
Unlicensed practice, §90-147.
North Carolina chiropractic association.
Meetings, §90-144.
Nutritional supplements.
Selling to patients, §90-151.1.
Sales and use tax exemption, §105-164.13.
Ownership of practice limited, §90-157.3.
Partnerships.
Limitations on ownership of practice, §90-157.3, (a).
Physical therapy modalities, use not restricted, §90-270.39.
Probationary status.
Placement on, powers of board, §90-154, (a).
Professional corporations generally, §§55B-1 to 55B-16.
See PROFESSIONAL CORPORATIONS.

CHIROPRACTORS —Cont'd
Rebates to patients.
Grounds for disciplinary action, §90-154, (b).
Reciprocity.
Licenses, §§90-143, (b), 90-143.1, 90-146.
Records.
Board of examiners, §90-148.
Referral fees and solicitation payments, §§90-400 to 90-402.
Health care provider defined, §90-400.
Prohibited, §90-401.
Sanctions, §90-402.
Reprimand.
Issuance of letter, powers of board, §90-154, (a).
Rules and regulations, §90-154.3, (b).
Board of examiners, §90-142.
Rules establishing and defining standards of acceptable care, §90-154.3, (b).
Sales.
Nutritional supplements, §90-151.1.
Self-referral, §§90-405 to 90-408.
Solicitation.
Direct solicitation prohibited, §90-401.1.
Payment prohibitions, §90-401.
Sanctions for violating prohibitions, §90-402.
Standard of acceptable care and practice of chiropractic.
Rules establishing and defining standards of acceptable care, §90-154.3, (b).
Scope or practice not altered, §90-154.3, (d).
Unlawful to render service not conforming to standards of acceptable care, §90-154.3, (a).
Usual and customary method as taught in majority of recognized chiropractic colleges.
Standard of acceptable care if rule not defining, §90-154.3, (c).
Unethical conduct.
Defined, §90-154.2.
Unlicensed practice, §90-147.
Witnesses.
Expert witnesses, §90-157.2.

CHLAMYDIA.
Testing of persons for sexually transmitted infections, §15A-615, (a), (1).

CHLOROFLUOROCARBONS REFRIGERANTS.
Management of discarded white goods, §§130A-309.80 to 130A-390.87.
See WHITE GOODS.

CHOICE OF LAW.
Conflict of laws generally.
See CONFLICT OF LAWS.
Electronic transactions.
Computer information agreement, §66-329.
Insurance policies or contracts.
Court or jurisdiction in which action or suit may be brought.
Condition or stipulation in policy prohibited, §58-3-35, (a).

CHOLERA.
Hog cholera, §§106-310 to 106-322.3.
See HOG CHOLERA.

CHOSES IN ACTION.
Agriculture.
Delinquent fees and taxes.
Collection of delinquent fees and taxes, §106-9.4, (b).
Execution sales.
Property liable to sale under execution, §1-315, (a).

CHOSES IN ACTION —Cont'd
Larceny, §14-75.
Obtaining property by false pretenses, §14-100.

CHOWAN COLLEGE.
Community colleges.
General provisions, §§115D-1 to 115D-81.
See COMMUNITY COLLEGES.

CHOWAN COUNTY.
Ambulance service.
Attachment or garnishment and lien for, §§44-51.4 to 44-51.8.
Blank or master forms of mortgages, deeds of trust, etc.
Indexing and recording, inapplicability of provisions, §47-21.
Dangerous firearm use by young children, permitting.
Air rifles, air pistols and BB guns not dangerous firearm, §14-316, (b).
Dog collars.
Unlawful removal of electronic dog collars, §14-401.17.
Game laws, local acts not repealed, §113-133.1, (e).
Grants in navigable waters, registration, §113-205, (a).
Housing authority commissioners.
Tenant as commissioner, exemption from provision of law allowing, §157-5.
Northeastern North Carolina regional economic development commission, §158-8.2.
Officers compensated from fees.
Statement to be rendered, §128-13.
Open fires, §113-60.23.
Applicability of provisions, §113-60.23, (a).
Ground clearing activities, special permit required, §113-60.23, (c).
Woodland fires, permit required, §113-60.23, (b).
Registration of deeds.
Tax certification, no delinquent taxes due, §161-31, (b).
School property.
Acquisition and improvement, §153A-158.1.
Special school tax, election to abolish.
Petition required, §115C-505.
Tax elections for industrial development purposes, §§158-16 to 158-24.
Wastewater systems.
Innovative septic tank systems.
Ordinance billing fee as property tax, §130A-343.1, (c).
Wild plants, taking of certain plants from land of another.
Inapplicability of provisions, §14-129.

CHRISTIAN SCIENCE.
Communications between practitioner and communicant.
Competency of Christian Science practitioner as witness, §8-53.2.

CHRISTMAS DAY.
Public holiday, §103-4, (a).

CHRISTMAS GREENS.
Taking, etc., of certain wild plants from land of another, §14-129.

CHURCH BUSES.
Motor vehicle license plates.
Permanent license plates for Sunday transportation vehicles, §20-84, (b).

CHURCH BUSES —Cont'd
Speed limit for nonprofit activity buses, §20-218.2.

CHURCHES.
Alcoholic beverage permits.
Factors considered, establishment located within 50 feet, §18B-901, (c).
Billboards.
Obstructing view at entrance to church on public highway, §136-102.
Burning of churches and certain other religious buildings, §14-62.2.
Buses.
License plates.
Permanent plates for Sunday transportation vehicles, §20-84, (b).
Speed limit for nonprofit activity buses, §20-218.2.
Child care facilities.
Drop-in or short-term child care not included in term child care, §110-86.
Injuring churches, §14-144.
Malicious use of explosive or incendiary, §14-49, (b1).
Obstructing place of worship, §14-199.
Pastoral counselors.
Certification of fee-based practicing pastoral counselors, §§90-380 to 90-395.
See PASTORAL COUNSELORS.
Professional counselors generally, §§90-329 to 90-344.
See PROFESSIONAL COUNSELORS.
Powers of attorney.
Powers conferred by statutory short form.
Continued payments incidental to membership or affiliation, §32A-2.
Religious organizations and societies.
See RELIGIOUS ORGANIZATIONS AND SOCIETIES.
Roads.
Special proceedings.
Establishment, alteration or discontinuance of church road, §136-68.
Sacramental wine.
Exemptions from alcoholic beverage control regulations, §18B-103.
Sales and use tax.
Refunds, §105-164.14, (b).
Schools.
Church schools and schools of religious charter, §§115C-547 to 115C-554.
See CHURCH SCHOOLS AND SCHOOLS OF RELIGIOUS CHARTER.
Streets and highways.
Billboard obstructing view at entrance to church on public highway, §136-102.
Swine houses, lagoons and land areas.
Siting requirements near, §106-803, (a), (b).
Volunteer immunity, §§1-539.10, 1-539.11.

CHURCH ROADS.
Establishment, alteration or discontinuance, §136-68.

CHURCH SCHOOLS AND SCHOOLS OF RELIGIOUS CHARTER, §§115C-547 to 115C-554.
Alcoholic beverage permits.
Factors considered, establishment located within 50 feet, §18B-901, (c).
Attendance.
Records, §115C-548.

CHURCH SCHOOLS AND SCHOOLS OF RELIGIOUS CHARTER —Cont'd
Competency testing.
High school competency testing, §115C-550.
Voluntary participation in state programs, §115C-551.
Compulsory attendance.
Records to be kept, §115C-548.
Disease immunization records, §115C-548.
Exclusivity of requirements, §115C-554.
Flu and meningitis and vaccines.
Information provided parents and guardians, §115C-548.
High school competency testing, §115C-550.
Voluntary participation in state programs, §115C-551.
Inspections, §115C-548.
Testing records, §115C-549.
Leave for parent involved in school, §95-28.3.
New schools.
Duly authorized representative of state, §115C-553.
Notice requirements, §115C-552, (a).
Policy of state, §115C-547.
Records.
Attendance and disease immunization records, §115C-548.
Requirements exclusive, §115C-554.
Sanitation.
Corrective action, §130A-237.
Inspections by department, §130A-236.
Regulation of sanitation by commission for health services, §§130A-235, 130A-236.
Reports, §130A-236.
Standardized testing requirements, §115C-549.
Voluntary participation in state programs, §115C-551.
State programs.
Voluntary participation in, §115C-551.
Termination of schools.
Duly authorized representative of state, §115C-553.
Notice requirements, §115C-552, (b).
Testing requirements.
High school competency testing, §115C-550.
Standardized testing requirements, §115C-549.
Voluntary participation in state programs, §115C-551.
Transportation of students.
Exemption of motor carriers from regulations, §62-260, (a).

CHURCH-SPONSORED CHILD CARE FACILITIES, §110-106.
Drop-in or short-term child care not included in term child care, §110-86.
Religious training offered in.
Commission not to interfere with, §110-88.1.

CIDER.
Exemption from alcoholic beverage provisions, §18B-103.

CIDER AND VINEGAR MANUFACTURERS.
ABC permits, §18B-1114.2.
Commercial permits for manufacturers, §18B-1100.

C.I.F.
Sale of goods, UCC, §25-2-320.
Form of bill of lading required in overseas shipment, §25-2-323.
Net landed weight, §25-2-321.

C.I.F —Cont'd
Sale of goods, UCC —Cont'd
Payment on arrival, §25-2-321.
Warranty of condition on arrival, §25-2-321.

CIGARETTES AND TOBACCO PRODUCTS.
Administration, §105-113.3, (b).
Agricultural products promotion.
Exclusion of tobacco from article, §106-550.
Auctions and auctioneers.
Exemptions from auction provisions, §85B-2.
Liens.
Effective period for lien on leaf tobacco sold in auction warehouse, §44-69.
Cigarette tax, §§105-113.5 to 105-113.33.
See CIGARETTE TAX.
Citation of title.
Short title, §105-113.2.
Contraband.
Cigarette packages violating certain label requirements, §14-401.18, (c).
Discrimination by employers for lawful use of lawful products during nonworking hours, §95-28.2.
Distribution to minors, §14-313.
Failure of tenant to account for sales under tobacco marketing cards, §42-22.1.
Federal cigarette labeling and advertising act.
Selling cigarettes in packages differing from requirements, §14-401.18, (b).
"For export only" selling cigarettes with label in state, §14-401.18, (b).
"For use outside U. S." selling cigarettes with label in state, §14-401.18, (b).
Funds.
Settlement reserve fund, §143-16.4.
Income tax credits for manufacturing cigarettes for exportation, §105-130.45.
Amount of credit allowed, §105-130.45, (b).
Cap, §105-130.45, (c).
Definitions, §105-130.45, (a).
Increasing employment and utilizing state ports.
Allocation, §105-130.46, (f).
Allowance of credit, amount, §105-130.46, (d).
Ceiling, §105-130.46, (g).
Definitions, §105-130.46, (b).
Documentation, §105-130.46, (i).
Employment level, eligibility for full credit, §105-130.46, (c).
No double credit, §105-130.46, (j).
Partial credit, §105-130.46, (e).
Purpose, §105-130.46, (a).
Reports, §105-130.46, (k).
Information required by corporation attaining credit, §105-130.45, (d).
No double credit, §105-130.45, (e).
Labels.
Sale of packages of cigarettes, labeling violations, §14-401.18, (b).
Tobacco seed.
Limitation on requirements, §106-277.10, (c).
Landlord's lien on crops.
Failure of tenant to account for sales under tobacco marketing cards, §42-22.1.
Larceny.
Ungathered crops, §14-78.
Leaf tobacco sales, §§106-461 to 106-465.
See LEAF TOBACCO SALES.
Leaf tobacco warehouses, §§106-452 to 106-455.
License plates.
Tobacco heritage special plates, §20-79.4, (b).

CIGARETTES AND TOBACCO PRODUCTS —Cont'd
Licenses.
Cancellation.
Reasons, §105-113.4B, (a).
Request of license holder, §105-113.4B, (a).
Summary cancellation by secretary, §105-113.4B, (a), (b).
Duplicate or amended license, §105-113.4A, (c).
Generally, §105-113.4A, (a).
Refund of license taxes, §105-113.4A, (b).
Liens.
Effective period for lien on leaf tobacco sold in auction warehouse, §44-69.
Lien on crops.
Failure of tenant to account for sales under tobacco marketing cards, §42-22.1.
Master settlement agreement.
Enforcement of provisions as to nonparticipating manufacturers.
Duties of attorney general and secretary of revenue, §105-113.4C.
Minors.
Sale or distribution to minors, §14-313.
Use of minors to test compliance with provisions, §14-313, (d).
Motor vehicles, size and loads.
Hogsheads of tobacco.
Maximum width, §20-116, (a).
Trucks hauling leaf tobacco in barrels or hogsheads.
Restrictions, §20-120.
Museums.
Establishment, §143-431.
Location of museums, §143-432.
Purposes, §143-431.
Tobacco museum board.
Transfer of board to department of cultural resources, §143B-51.
National tobacco grower settlement trust.
Board of directors of certification entity.
Appointment, §143-300.30, (b).
Creation, proposal by tobacco companies, §143-300.30, (a).
Decedents' estates.
Phase II payments.
List of distributees.
Definitions, §28A-21-3.1, (a).
Filing, conditions required, §28A-21-3.1, (b).
Information required, §28A-21-3.1, (c).
Payment to distributees, §28A-21-3.1, (e).
Reopening estate to file, §28A-21-3.1, (f).
Review by clerk, §28A-21-3.1, (d).
Payments while decedent alive.
Considered cash, §28A-21-3.1, (g).
Property of distributees, §28A-15-9.1.
Desire of tobacco companies, §143-300.30, (a).
Immunity of certification entity member, §143-300.30, (c).
Oaths.
Tobacco weighers, §106-453.
Packages of cigarettes.
Sale of certain packages prohibited.
Contraband, §14-401.18, (c).
Definitions, §14-401.18, (a).
Offenses, §14-401.18, (b).
Price fixing.
Leaf tobacco sales.
Tobacco boards of trade, §106-465.
Promotion of sale and use of tobacco, §§106-568.18 to 106-568.37.
See TOBACCO SALES.

CIGARETTES AND TOBACCO PRODUCTS —Cont'd
Public weighmasters.
Weighing tobacco, §81A-59.
Research commission, §106-568.3, (b).
Sales.
Leaf tobacco sales, §§106-461 to 106-465.
See LEAF TOBACCO SALES.
Minors, §14-313.
Packages of cigarettes.
Sale of certain packages prohibited, §14-401.18.
Promotion of sale and use of tobacco, §§106-568.18 to 106-568.37.
See TOBACCO SALES.
Tobacco escrow compliance.
Sale of cigarettes on compliant nonparticipating manufacturer's list, §66-293.
Tobacco reserve fund.
Escrow compliance, §§66-292 to 66-294.1.
Scope of tax, §105-113.3, (a).
Seeds.
Label requirement for tobacco seeds, §106-277.10, (c).
Settlement reserve fund, §143-16.4.
Established, §143-16.4, (a).
Federal funds, allocation, §143-16.4, (b).
Health trust account, §143-16.4, (a1).
Tobacco trust account, §143-16.4, (a2).
Short title, §105-113.2.
Taxation.
Cigarette tax, §§105-113.5 to 105-113.33.
See CIGARETTE TAX.
Tobacco products tax, §§105-113.2 to 105-113.4, 105-113.35 to 105-113.40.
See TOBACCO PRODUCTS TAX.
Tobacco boards of trade.
Membership, §106-465.
Organization, §106-465.
Tobacco heritage license plates, §20-79.4, (b).
Tobacco products tax, §§105-113.2 to 105-113.4, 105-113.35 to 105-113.40.
See TOBACCO PRODUCTS TAX.
Tobacco reserve fund.
Tobacco product manufacturers selling cigarettes, §§66-290, 66-291.
Escrow compliance, §§66-292 to 66-294.1.
Tobacco trust fund commission, §§143-715 to 143-723.
See TOBACCO TRUST FUND COMMISSION.
Tobacco warehouses.
See TOBACCO WAREHOUSES.
"U. S. tax exempt" selling cigarettes with label in state, §14-401.18, (b).

CIGARETTE TAX, §§105-113.5 to 105-113.33.
Confiscation.
Non-tax-paid cigarettes, §105-113.32.
Vehicles or vessels transporting, §105-113.31, (b).
Conflict of laws.
Federal constitution and statutes, §105-113.8.
Criminal penalties, §105-113.33.
Definitions, §105-113.4.
Interstate business, §105-113.9.
Place of business.
Distributors, §105-113.12, (b).
Discount.
Expenses incurred in preparing records and reports, §105-113.21, (a1).
Distributors.
Licenses.
Bond, §105-113.13, (b).
Investigation of applicants, §105-113.13, (a).

CIGARETTE TAX —Cont'd
Distributors —Cont'd
Licenses —Cont'd
Out-of-state distributors, §§105-113.12, (c), 105-113.24, (d).
Place of business.
Defined, §105-113.12, (b).
Required, §105-113.12, (a).
Tax, §105-113.12, (a).
Out-of-state distributors, §105-113.12, (c).
Out-of-state distributors.
Examination of books, accounts and records, §105-113.24, (b).
Licenses, §§105-113.12, (c), 105-113.24, (d).
Service of process.
Secretary of state as attorney for, §105-113.24, (c).
Stamps.
Sale to out-of-state distributors, §105-113.24, (a).
Reports, §105-113.18.
Exemptions.
Activities tax in violation of federal constitution and statutes, §105-113.8.
Manufacturers shipping to distributors, §105-113.10.
Identification of dispensers on vending machines, §105-113.17.
Imposition of taxes, §§105-113.5, 105-113.6.
Inventories.
Tax with respect to inventory on effective date of tax increase, §105-113.7.
Levy of taxes, §§105-113.5, 105-113.6.
Licenses, §105-113.11.
Distributors.
Bond, §105-113.13, (b).
Investigation of applicants, §105-113.13, (a).
Out-of-state distributors, §§105-113.12, (c), 105-113.24, (d).
Place of business.
Defined, §105-113.12, (b).
Required, §105-113.12, (a).
Tax, §105-113.12, (a).
Out-of-state distributors, §105-113.12, (c).
Required, §105-113.11.
Distributors, §105-113.12, (a).
Unlicensed place of business.
Prohibited, §105-113.29.
Manufacturers shipping to distributors.
Exempt, §105-113.10.
Non-tax-paid cigarettes.
Confiscation, §105-113.32.
Vehicle or vessel transporting, §105-113.31, (b).
Possession.
Prima facie evidence, §105-113.27, (c).
Prohibited acts, §§105-113.27, 105-113.31, (a).
Sale.
Prohibited acts, §105-113.27, (a), (b).
Transportation, §105-113.31, (a).
Requirements, §105-113.31, (b).
Seizure and confiscation of vehicle or vessel, §105-113.31, (b).
Out-of-state shipments, §105-113.9.
Prohibited acts.
Criminal penalties, §105-113.33.
Non-tax-paid cigarettes, §§105-113.27, 105-113.31, (a).
Records and reports, §105-113.30.
Unlicensed place of business, §105-113.29.
Rate, §105-113.5.

CIGARETTE TAX —Cont'd
Records.
Required records, §105-113.26.
Prohibited acts, §105-113.30.
Refunds, §105-113.21, (b).
Reports.
Required reports, §105-113.18.
Prohibited acts, §105-113.30.
Stale or unsaleable cigarettes.
Refund, §105-113.21, (b).
Stamps.
Out-of-state distributors.
Sale to, §105-113.24, (a).
Use tax.
Levy, §105-113.6.
Vending machines.
Identification of dispensers, §105-113.17.

CIGARETTE WRAPPING PAPERS.
Sale or distribution to minors, §14-313.

CIO.
State chief information officer.
See INFORMATION TECHNOLOGY SERVICES.

CIRCUSES.
Counties.
Regulation of places of amusement, §153A-135.
License tax, §105-37.1, (d).
Municipal corporations.
Regulation of carnivals and circuses, §160A-181.
Privilege tax on gross receipts, §105-37.1, (a).
Advance report when bringing show from outside to state, §105-37.1, (c).
Rate and payment, §105-37.1, (b).

CITATIONS.
Costs of criminal process in superior or district courts, §7A-304, (a).
Delivery, execution and service of criminal process, §15A-301.
Forest rangers.
Authority to issue, §113-55, (b).
Infractions.
Summons and process, §15A-1113, (a).
Mental health, development disability, substance abuse.
Facility licensing.
Classification of violations, §122C-24.1, (a).
National guard.
Governor's unit citation, §127A-45.1.
Meritorious unit citation, §127A-45.2.
Occupational safety and health.
Contest by employee of period of time fixed for correction violation, §95-130.
Enforcement procedure, §95-137, (b).

CITIES.
Annexation.
Extension of corporate limits generally, §§160A-29 to 160A-58.28.
See ANNEXATION.
Boards of education.
Local boards of education generally, §§115C-35 to 115C-50.
See LOCAL BOARDS OF EDUCATION.
Cemeteries.
Generally, §§160A-341 to 160A-348.
See MUNICIPAL CEMETERIES.
Condemnation of unsafe buildings.
Generally, §§160A-411 to 160A-438.
See MUNICIPAL BUILDING INSPECTION.
Council generally.
See CITY COUNCILS.

CITIES —Cont'd
Council-manager cities, §§160A-147 to 160A-152.
See COUNCIL-MANAGER CITIES.
Demolition of unsafe building.
Dwellings, §160A-443.
Nonresidential building, §160A-432, (b), (b1).
Ordinance, §160A-443.
Education.
Local boards of education, §§115C-35 to 115C-50.
Public schools generally.
See PUBLIC SCHOOLS.
Elections, §§163-279 to 163-306.
See MUNICIPAL ELECTIONS.
Electric service in urban areas, §§160A-331 to 160A-338.
See ELECTRIC SERVICE IN URBAN AREAS.
Extension of corporate limits generally, §§160A-29 to 160A-58.28.
See ANNEXATION.
Generally.
See MUNICIPAL CORPORATIONS.
Gross receipts tax on vehicle short-term leases and rentals, §160A-215.1.
Hospitals.
Municipal corporations, §§131E-5 to 131E-14.2.
See MUNICIPAL HOSPITALS.
Inspection of building, §§160A-411 to 160A-438.
See MUNICIPAL BUILDING INSPECTION.
Joint municipal electric power and energy, §§159B-1 to 159B-52.
See JOINT MUNICIPAL ELECTRIC POWER AND ENERGY ACT.
License taxes generally, §§105-33 to 105-109.
See MUNICIPAL LICENSE TAXES.
Local government finance, §§159-1 to 159-188.
See LOCAL GOVERNMENT FINANCE.
Local governments.
See LOCAL GOVERNMENTS.
Military property sales facilities.
Licensing, §127B-4, (a) to (c).
Motor vehicle short-term leases or rentals, gross receipts tax.
Authority to levy, §160A-215.1, (a).
Collection and administration, §160A-215.1, (d).
Definitions, §160A-215.1, (e).
Location of transaction giving rise to tax, §160A-215.1, (b).
Notation of tax in agreement, §160A-215.1, (b).
Penalties and remedies, §160A-215.1, (f).
Proceeds belong to city, not subject to creditor liens, §160A-215.1, (c).
Rate, §160A-215.1, (a).
Officers and employees generally.
See MUNICIPAL OFFICERS AND EMPLOYEES.
Outdoor advertising.
Regulation of nonconforming off-premises outdoor advertising, §160A-199.
Planning generally, §§160A-360 to 160A-366.
See MUNICIPAL PLANNING AND REGULATION OF DEVELOPMENT.
Property taxes.
Municipal corporations.
See PROPERTY TAXES.
Removal of unsafe building.
Dwellings, §160A-443.
Nonresidential building, §160A-432, (b), (b1).
Ordinance, §160A-443.
Retirement, §§128-21 to 128-38.3.
See RETIREMENT SYSTEM FOR COUNTIES AND CITIES.

CITIES —Cont'd
Room occupancy tax, uniform provisions.
Administration by taxing city, §160A-215, (d).
Applicability of section, §160A-215, (a).
Charge for furnishing taxable accommodation.
Tax collected as part of, §160A-215, (c).
Civil or criminal penalties.
Failure to file return or pay tax, §160A-215, (e).
Collection by operator of business subject to tax, §160A-215, (c).
Discount allowed operator for collecting tax, §160A-215, (c).
Effective date of tax, §160A-215, (f).
Levied by resolution, §160A-215, (b).
Liability attaching before repeal not affected, §160A-215, (f).
Public notice and hearing on levy, §160A-215, (b).
Repeal or reduced by resolution, §160A-215, (f).
Return, §160A-215, (d).
Sales price, tax added to, borne by purchaser, §160A-215, (c).
Waiver of civil or criminal penalties, §160A-215, (e).
When due and payable, §160A-215, (d).
Satellite annexation.
Annexation of noncontiguous areas, §§160A-58 to 160A-58.8.
See ANNEXATION.
Schools.
Generally.
See PUBLIC SCHOOLS.
Local boards of education, §§115C-35 to 115C-50.
See LOCAL BOARDS OF EDUCATION.
Special assessments, §§160A-216 to 160A-236.
See SPECIAL ASSESSMENTS BY CITIES.
Subdivision regulation generally, §§160A-371 to 160A-376.
See MUNICIPAL PLANNING AND REGULATION OF DEVELOPMENT.
Traffic control photographic systems, §160A-300.1.
Unsafe building, condemnation, correction of defects, §§160A-411 to 160A-438.
See MUNICIPAL BUILDING INSPECTION.
Zoning generally, §§160A-381 to 160A-392.
See MUNICIPAL PLANNING AND REGULATION OF DEVELOPMENT.

CITIZENS' ARREST, §§15A-404, 15A-405.

CITIZENS' AWARENESS MONTH.
Voter registration drive, §163-82.25.

CITIZENS BAND RADIO.
Interception of communications not unlawful, §15A-287, (b).
Special motor vehicle license plates.
Class D citizens radio station operators, §20-79.4, (a).
Unauthorized use, §62-328.

CITIZENSHIP.
Concealed handgun permit qualifications, §14-415.12, (a).
Constitutional provisions, Const. U. S., art. IV, §2; amd. XIV.
Convicted persons.
Restoration of citizenship, §13-1.
Filing of certificate or order of restoration, §13-2, (a).
Issuance of certificate or order of restoration, §13-2, (a).

CITIZENSHIP —Cont'd
Convicted persons —Cont'd
Restoration of citizenship —Cont'd
Pardon.
Conditional pardon, §13-4.
Unconditional pardon, §13-3.
Person convicted of crime against another state or United States.
Rights restored, provision applicable, §13-2, (b).
Elections.
Presidential elections.
Residence period for presidential elections, Const. N. C., art. VI, §2.
State elections.
Residence period for state elections, Const. N. C., art. VI, §2.
Indians, §§71A-3 to 71A-7.2.
Pardon.
Conditional pardon.
Endorsement of warrant, service and filing of conditional pardon, §13-4.
Unconditional pardon.
Restoration of citizenship.
Issuance, service and filing of warrant, §13-3.
Restoration of citizenship.
Certificate or order of restoration.
Filing of certificate, §13-2, (a).
Issuance, §13-2, (a).
Conditions for restoration, §13-1.
Pardon.
Conditional pardon.
Endorsement of warrant, service and filing, §13-4.
Unconditional pardon.
Warrant, issuance, service, §13-3.
Person convicted of crime against another state or United States.
Rights restored, provision applicable, §13-2, (b).
Rights and immunities of citizens, Const. U. S., amd. XIV.

CITY CLERKS.
Deputy clerk, §160A-172.
Duties, §160A-171.
Office created, §160A-171.

CITY COUNCILS.
Abolish office, position, etc.
Power limited, §160A-146.
Applicability of part 3, §160A-82.
Charter.
Amendment, §160A-102.
City attorney.
Appointment by council, §160A-173.
Compelling production of evidence, §160A-80, (a).
Compensation, §160A-64, (a), (b).
Composition, §160A-66.
Deeds.
Validation of certain deeds, §160A-18.
Defined, §160A-1.
Elections, §160A-66.
Districts.
Map, §160A-23, (a).
Optional form, §160A-101.
Reapportionment, §160A-23, (b).
Redistricting after 2000 census, §160A-23.1.
Optional form, §160A-101.
Hearings, §160A-81.
Investigation, §160A-80, (a).

CITY COUNCILS —Cont'd
Journal.
Kept by city clerk, §160A-171.
Mayor.
Preside over council, §160A-69.
Pro tempore.
Elected by council, §160A-70.
Voting.
Right to vote, §160A-69.
Meetings.
Notice.
Given by city clerk, §160A-171.
Organizational meeting.
Date and time, §160A-68, (a).
Repeal of charter and local act provisions, §160A-68, (c).
Qualifying of mayor and councilmen, §160A-68, (b).
Regular meetings.
Recess and adjourn meetings, §160A-71, (b1).
Time and place, §160A-71, (a).
Special meetings.
Calling, §160A-71, (b).
Recess and adjourn meetings, §160A-71, (b1).
Minutes.
Contents, §160A-72.
Keeping, §160A-72.
Number of members, §160A-66.
Amendment of charter.
Provisions affecting charter definition of quorum, §160A-106.
Optional form, §160A-101.
Oaths.
Administration, §160A-80, (a).
Organization.
City government, §160A-146.
Meetings, §160A-68.
Powers.
Exercise of corporate powers, §160A-12.
Generally, §160A-67.
Investigation, §160A-80, (a).
Subpoena powers, §160A-80, (a).
Procedure.
Rules of procedure, §160A-71, (c).
Quorum, §160A-74.
Filling vacancies to make quorum, §160A-63.
Subpoena, §160A-80, (a).
Terms of office, §160A-66.
Optional form, §160A-101.
Vacancies.
Filling, §160A-63.
Voting by members.
Ayes and noes.
Taken upon request of member, §160A-72.
Excused from voting, §160A-75.
Failure to vote.
Counted as affirmative vote, §160A-75.
Majority vote required, §160A-75.
Results of votes recorded in minutes, §160A-72.
Two thirds of membership.
Affirmative vote to adopt ordinance on date introduced, §160A-75.
Withdrawal of member from meeting without being excused.
Counted for purposes of quorum, §160A-74.
Witnesses.
Enforcement of subpoena, §160A-80, (b).
Perjury, §160A-80, (b).
Power to subpoena, §160A-80, (a).
Use of evidence against witness prohibited, §160A-80, (b).

CITY-COUNTY CONSOLIDATION ACT, §§160B-1 to 160B-21.
See CONSOLIDATED CITY-COUNTY ACT.

CITY MANAGERS.
Council-managers cities, §§160A-147 to 160A-152.
See COUNCIL-MANAGER CITIES.
Service of process.
Personal jurisdiction on city, town or village, §1A-1, Rule 4, (j).

CITY SCHOOL ADMINISTRATIVE UNITS.
Administrative units generally.
See SCHOOL DISTRICTS AND ADMINISTRATIVE UNITS.

CIVIC CENTERS.
Alcoholic beverage permits.
Convention center defined to include, §18B-1000.
Mixed beverage permit.
Kind of permit that may be issued, §18B-1001.
On-premises fortified wine permit.
Kind of permit that may be issued, §18B-1001.
On-premises malt beverage permit.
Kind of permit that may be issued, §18B-1001.
On-premises unfortified wine permit.
Kind of permit that may be issued, §18B-1001.

CIVIC CLUB LICENSE PLATES, §20-79.4, (b).

CIVIC LITERACY.
Basic education program, §115C-81, (g).

CIVIC ORGANIZATIONS.
Alcoholic beverage permits.
Special one-time permits, §18B-1002, (a).
Amusement tax exemptions, §105-40.
Solicitation of contributions, §§131F-1 to 131F-24.
See CHARITABLE SOLICITATION.

CIVIL ACTIONS.
Actions.
See ACTIONS.

CIVIL AERONAUTICS ADMINISTRATION.
Rules and regulations.
Enforcement, §63-47.

CIVIL AIR PATROL.
Death benefits, §§143-166.1 to 143-166.7.
See DEATH BENEFITS.
Division of department of crime control and public safety.
Benefits, §143B-491, (b).
Established, §143B-490, (a).
Liability of state, §143B-492.
Personnel, §143B-491, (a).
Powers and duties, §143B-490, (b).
Transfer to department, §143A-241.
Motor vehicle license plates.
Permanent license plates for patrol vehicles, §20-84, (b).
Special license plates, §20-79.4, (a).
Transfer to department of crime control and public safety, §143A-241.
Workers' compensation.
Employee defined, §97-2.

CIVIL ARREST.
See ARREST IN CIVIL CASES.

CIVIL CONTEMPT, §§5A-21 to 5A-25.
See CONTEMPT.

CIVIL DEFENSE.
Agency.
Transfer to department of crime control and public safety, §143A-240.

CIVIL DEFENSE —Cont'd
Emergency management.
General provisions, §§166A-1 to 166A-16.
See EMERGENCY MANAGEMENT.
Interception of radio communications not unlawful, §15A-287, (b).
Municipal corporations.
Property taxes.
Authorized purposes, §160A-209, (c).

CIVIL DISORDERS.
Riots and civil disorders, §§14-288.1 to 14-288.20.
See RIOTS AND CIVIL DISORDERS.

CIVIL DRIVER'S LICENSE REVOCATIONS, §20-16.5.

CIVIL INVESTIGATIVE DEMAND.
Medicaid.
False claims by providers, §108A-70.14.

CIVIL NO-CONTACT ORDERS, §§50C-1 to 50C-11.
Additional nature of remedy, §50C-11.
Address of victim.
Omission from documents, §50C-2, (d).
Commencement of action for, §50C-2, (a).
Contempt.
Violations, §50C-10.
Notice that violation punishable as contempt, §50C-5, (c).
Costs not to be assessed, §50C-2, (b).
Definitions, §50C-1.
Expiration of orders, §50C-8, (d).
Extension of orders, §50C-8, (c).
Delivery of order to sheriff, §50C-9, (d).
Issuance, §50C-5, (a).
Default, §50C-3, (c).
Permanent order, §50C-7.
Non-exclusive nature of remedy, §50C-11.
Notice of orders, §50C-9, (a).
Police department or sheriff.
Issuance to and retention by, §50C-9, (c).
Service, §50C-9, (b).
Notice that violation punishable as contempt, §50C-5, (c).
Permanent order, §50C-7.
Duration, §50C-8, (b).
Prior sexual activity of victim inadmissible, §50C-4.
Relief which may be granted, §50C-5, (b).
Summons.
Action for order, §50C-3, (a).
Service of summons and attachments, §50C-3, (b).
Temporary orders, §50C-6, (a), (b).
Appearance in court for, §50C-6, (c).
Court not in session, §50C-6, (d).
Duration, §50C-8, (a).
Venue of action for, §50C-2, (c).
Workplace violence prevention, §§95-265 to 95-276.
See WORKPLACE VIOLENCE PREVENTION.

CIVIL PENALTY AND FORFEITURE FUND, §§115C-457.1 to 115C-457.3.
Administration, §115C-457.1, (b).
Creation, §115C-457.1, (a).
Deposits in, §115C-457.2.
Remittance of moneys to, §115C-457.2.
State school technology fund.
Transfer of funds to, §115C-457.3.

CIVIL PREPAREDNESS.
Agency.
Transfer to department of crime control and public safety, §143A-240.
Emergency management.
General provisions, §§166A-1 to 166A-16.
See EMERGENCY MANAGEMENT.
Hazardous materials emergency response, §§166A-20 to 166A-28.
See HAZARDOUS MATERIALS EMERGENCY RESPONSE.
Municipal corporations.
Property taxes.
Authorized purposes, §160A-209, (c).

CIVIL PROCEDURE.
Actions.
Commencement of actions, §§1-105 to 1-120.2.
See COMMENCEMENT OF ACTIONS.
Definitions.
Generally, §1-2.
General provisions.
See ACTIONS.
Joinder.
See JOINDER.
Adverse possession.
See ADVERSE POSSESSION.
Advertisements.
Legal advertising, §§1-595 to 1-600.
Alimony.
See ALIMONY.
Appeals.
Appellate rules of procedure.
See APPEALS.
Arbitration.
Generally.
See ARBITRATION.
International commercial arbitration and conciliation, §§1-567.30 to 1-567.87.
See INTERNATIONAL COMMERCIAL ARBITRATION AND CONCILIATION.
Revised uniform arbitration act, §§1-569.1 to 1-569.31.
See ARBITRATION.
Arrest.
Civil cases, §§1-409 to 1-439.
See ARREST IN CIVIL CASES.
Attachment.
See ATTACHMENT.
Bail and recognizance.
Civil cases.
See BAIL AND RECOGNIZANCE.
Bankruptcy and insolvency.
General provisions.
See BANKRUPTCY AND INSOLVENCY.
Receivers, §§1-501 to 1-507.11.
See RECEIVERS.
Betterments, §§1-340 to 1-351.
See BETTERMENTS.
Bonds, surety.
Prosecution bonds, §§1-109 to 1-112.
Change of venue, §§1-83 to 1-87.
Claim and delivery, §§1-472 to 1-484.1.
See CLAIM AND DELIVERY.
Class actions, §1A-1, Rule 23.
Clerks of court.
General provisions.
See CLERKS OF COURT.
Commencement of actions, §§1-105 to 1-120.2.
See COMMENCEMENT OF ACTIONS.

CIVIL PROCEDURE —Cont'd
Complaints.
See COMPLAINTS.
Compromise and settlement, §§1-540 to 1-540.3.
See COMPROMISE AND SETTLEMENT.
Constitution of North Carolina.
Jury trial.
Right to jury trial in civil cases, Const. N. C., art. I, §25.
Rules of procedure, Const. N. C., art. IV, §13.
Contempt.
Civil contempt, §§5A-21 to 5A-25.
See CONTEMPT.
Costs, §§6-1 to 6-62.
See COSTS.
Counterclaims and cross-claims.
See COUNTERCLAIMS AND CROSS-CLAIMS.
Debtors.
Joint and several debtors, §§1-113, 1-114.
Declaratory judgments, §§1-253 to 1-267.
See DECLARATORY JUDGMENTS.
Defendants, §1-10.
Defenses.
See DEFENSES.
Definitions.
Actions.
Civil action, §1-6.
Criminal action, §1-5.
Generally, §1-2.
Kinds of actions, §1-4.
Court.
When court means clerk, §1-7.
Remedies, §1-1.
Special proceedings, §1-3.
Delivery.
Claim and delivery, §§1-472 to 1-484.1.
See CLAIM AND DELIVERY.
Depositions.
See DEPOSITIONS.
Deposit or delivery of money or other property, §§1-508 to 1-510.
Discovery.
See DISCOVERY.
Dismissal, discontinuance and nonsuit.
See DISMISSAL, DISCONTINUANCE AND NONSUIT.
District courts.
Applicability of civil procedure generally, §7A-193.
Jury trials, §7A-196, (a).
Divorce.
See DIVORCE.
Evidence.
See EVIDENCE.
Executions, §§1-302 to 1-368.
See EXECUTIONS.
Execution sales, §§1-339.41 to 1-339.71.
See EXECUTION SALES.
Frauds, statute of.
See STATUTE OF FRAUDS.
Garnishment.
See GARNISHMENT.
Habeas corpus, §§17-1 to 17-46.
See HABEAS CORPUS.
Improvements.
Betterments, §§1-340 to 1-351.
See BETTERMENTS.
Injunctions.
See INJUNCTIONS.
Interpleader and intervention.
See INTERPLEADER AND INTERVENTION.

CIVIL PROCEDURE —Cont'd
Interrogatories.
See INTERROGATORIES.
Joinder.
General provisions.
See JOINDER.
Joint and several debtors.
Defenses.
Parties summoned after judgment, §1-114.
Judgments, §1-113.
Summoning after judgment, §1-114.
Partners, §1-113.
Proceedings generally, §1-113.
Summons and process, §1-113.
Summoning after judgment, §1-114.
Judgments.
Declaratory judgments, §§1-253 to 1-267.
See DECLARATORY JUDGMENTS.
Executions, §§1-302 to 1-368.
See EXECUTIONS.
General provisions.
See JUDGMENTS.
Jurisdiction.
See JURISDICTION.
Jury.
See JURY.
Jury trial.
See JURY TRIAL.
Legal advertising, §§1-595 to 1-600.
Limitation of actions, §§1-15 to 1-56.
See LIMITATION OF ACTIONS.
Lis pendens, §§1-116 to 1-120.2.
See LIS PENDENS.
Nonsuits.
See DISMISSAL, DISCONTINUANCE AND NONSUIT.
Nuisances.
See NUISANCES.
Offer of judgment, §1A-1, Rule 68, (a).
Conditional offer of judgment for damages, §1A-1, Rule 68, (b).
Parties.
See PARTIES.
Payment into court, §§1-508 to 1-510.
Plaintiff, §1-10.
Pleadings.
See PLEADINGS.
Prosecution bonds, §§1-109 to 1-112.
Quo warranto.
See QUO WARRANTO.
Receivers, §§1-501 to 1-507.11.
See RECEIVERS.
Referees.
See REFEREES.
Remedies.
Civil and criminal remedies not merged, §1-8.
Enumeration, §1-1.
Merger.
Civil and criminal remedies not merged, §1-8.
Service of process.
See SERVICE OF PROCESS.
Settlement, §§1-540 to 1-540.3.
See SETTLEMENT.
Special proceedings.
See SPECIAL PROCEEDINGS.
Statute of frauds.
See STATUTE OF FRAUDS.
Statutes of limitation.
See LIMITATION OF ACTIONS.
Stays.
See STAYS.

CIVIL PROCEDURE —Cont'd
Summary judgment.
See SUMMARY JUDGMENT.
Supersedeas.
See SUPERSEDEAS.
Supreme court.
Rules of procedure.
Promulgation, Const. N. C., art. IV, §13.
Time.
See TIME.
Trial.
See TRIAL.
Venue.
Change of venue, §§1-83 to 1-87.
See CHANGE OF VENUE.
General provisions, §§1-76 to 1-87.
See VENUE.
Verdict.
See VERDICTS.
Waste, §§1-533 to 1-538.
Witnesses.
See WITNESSES.

CIVIL RIGHTS.
Discrimination.
See DISCRIMINATION.
Interference with.
Civil action.
Compensatory and punitive damages, §99D-1, (b), (b1).
Costs and attorney's fees, §99D-1, (b), (b1).
Government unit or government official.
Restriction on bringing against, §99D-1, (c).
Human relations commission bringing, §99D-1, (b1).
Personal action, §99D-1, (b).
Conduct constituting, §99D-1, (a).
Future acts.
Restraining and enjoining, §99D-1, (b), (b1).
Mental health, developmental disabilities and substance abuse.
Rights of clients.
Retention of right to exercise all civil rights, §122C-58.
Nursing homes.
Patients' bill of rights, §§131E-115 to 131E-131.
See NURSING HOMES.
Restoration of citizenship, §§13-1 to 13-4.
Automatic restoration, §13-1.
Certificate or order of restoration.
Issuance and filing, §13-2, (a), (b).
Conditional pardon.
Endorsement of warrant, service and filing, §13-4.
Unconditional pardon.
Issuance, service and filing of warrant, §13-3.
Voting rights act of 1965.
Submissions to attorney general of the United States, §§120-30.9A to 120-30.9I.

CIVIL SERVICE.
County personnel system.
Generally, §§153A-92 to 153A-99.
See COUNTY PERSONNEL SYSTEM.
Municipal personnel system, §§160A-162 to 160A-169.
See MUNICIPAL OFFICERS AND EMPLOYEES.
Public officers and employees generally.
See PUBLIC OFFICERS AND EMPLOYEES.
State personnel system, §§126-1 to 126-90.
See PERSONNEL SYSTEM.

CLAIM AND DELIVERY, §§1-472 to 1-484.1.
Affidavits, §1-473.
Third parties.
Property claimed by third person, §1-482.
Appeals.
Issuance or refusal to issue order to sheriff, §1-474, (a).
Bonds, surety.
Defendant's undertaking for replevy, §1-478.
Qualification and justification of defendant's surety, §1-479.
Plaintiff's undertaking, §1-475.
Exceptions to undertaking, §1-477.
Sheriffs.
Liability for sufficiency of sureties, §§1-477, 1-479.
Third parties.
Property claimed by third person, §1-482.
Buildings.
Property concealed in buildings, §1-480.
Construction and interpretation.
Remedy not exclusive, §1-484.1.
Forms.
Notice of hearing, §1-474.1, (c).
Waiver of hearing, §1-474.1, (c).
Hearings.
Notice, §1-474.1, (a).
Form, §1-474.1, (c).
Waiver of rights to notice and hearing, §1-474.1, (b).
Form, §1-474.1, (c).
Injunctions.
Notice containing order enjoining defendant from disposing of property, §1-474.1, (a).
Notice.
Bonds, surety.
Notice to sureties to justify, §§1-477, 1-479.
Hearing, §1-474.1, (a).
Form of notice, §1-474.1, (c).
Orders of court, §1-474, (a).
Expiration of certain orders, §1-474, (b).
Recovery of personal property, §1-230.
Remedy not exclusive, §1-484.1.
Requisites, §1-473.
Rights of plaintiff, §1-472.
Service of process.
Notice of hearing, §1-474.1, (a).
Property claimed by third person, §1-482.
Sheriffs.
Bonds, surety.
Liability for sufficiency of sureties, §§1-477, 1-479.
Care and delivery of seized property, §1-481.
Duties, §1-476.
Care and delivery of seized property, §1-481.
Property concealed in buildings, §1-480.
Order to take and deliver property, §1-474, (a).
Expiration of certain orders, §1-474, (b).
Return of papers, §1-484.
Third parties.
Property claimed by third person.
Delivery of property to intervener, §1-483.
Small claims actions.
Provisional and incidental remedies, §7A-231.
Taxation.
Property taxes.
Order not to be issued, §105-379, (b).
Third parties.
Property claimed by third person.
Delivery of property to intervener, §1-483.
Proceedings, §1-482.

CLAIM AND DELIVERY —Cont'd
Time, §1-472.
Waiver.
Rights to notice and hearing, §1-474.1, (b).
Form of waiver, §1-474.1, (c).

CLAIMS AGAINST BOARD OF EDUCATION MEMBER OR EMPLOYEE.
Local boards paying, §115C-43, (b), (c).

CLAIMS AGAINST LOCAL UNITS OF GOVERNMENT.
Notice of claim.
Local acts not to require notice, §1-539.16.

CLAIMS AGAINST THE STATE.
Amateur sports.
State vehicles.
No liability for damages, §143-299.3, (b).
Assignments, §143-3.3.
Deductions from employee's salary or wages.
Enumeration of authorized deductions, §143-3.3, (e) to (j).
Definitions, §143-3.3, (a).
Exceptions to section, §143-3.3, (c), (d), (e).
Void unless duly audited and allowed, §143-3.3, (b).
Atomic energy.
Radiation.
Tort claims against persons rendering emergency assistance, §104E-22.
Counsel.
Employment where state is interested, §147-17.
Defending actions arising from activities of state employees in course of employment, §147-17.
Department of transportation contracts.
Claims by contractors on completed contracts, §136-29, (a) to (d).
Jurisdiction.
Original jurisdiction of the supreme court, §7A-25.
Tort claims against state departments and agencies, §§143-291 to 143-300.1A.
See TORT CLAIMS AGAINST STATE DEPARTMENTS AND AGENCIES.

CLAIMS FOR RELIEF.
General rules of pleading, §1A-1, Rule 8, (a).

CLAIMS TO PUBLIC OFFICE.
Quo warranto.
Generally, §§1-514 to 1-532.
See QUO WARRANTO.

CLAMS.
Clamming on posted oyster rocks, §113-207.
Cultivation of shellfish, §§113-201 to 113-210.
See SHELLFISH.
Sanitation of shellfish, §§130A-230, 130A-231.

CLARK'S CALENDAR.
Proof of dates.
Use, §8-48, (a).
Secretary of state.
Perpetual calendar similar to Clark's calendar.
Preparation and publication, §8-48, (b).

CLASS ACTIONS.
Authorized, §1A-1, Rule 23, (a).
Compromise and settlement.
Approval of judge required, §1A-1, Rule 23, (c).
Notice, §1A-1, Rule 23, (c).
Dismissal, §1A-1, Rule 23, (c).
Limited liability companies.
Derivative actions by members, §57C-8-01.

CLASS ACTIONS —Cont'd
Motion picture fair competition act.
Class actions not available under provisions, §75C-5.
Secondary action by shareholders, §1A-1, Rule 23, (b).

CLASSIC CARS.
Abandoned and derelict motor vehicles.
Exemption from provisions, §20-137.14.
Property taxes.
Motor vehicle taxes on antique automobiles, §105-330.9.
Special plates, §20-79.4, (a).

CLASSIFIED MOTOR VEHICLES.
Property taxes, §§105-330 to 105-330.9.
See PROPERTY TAXES.

CLASS IN ESSE.
Sale, lease or mortgage of property held by.
Membership subject to increase by persons not in esse, §41-11.1.

CLASS SIZE REDUCTION FUND, §115C-472.10.

CLAY COUNTY.
Ambulances.
Obtaining ambulance services without intending to pay, §14-111.2.
Requesting ambulance falsely, §14-111.3.
Board of county commissioners.
Filling vacancies on board, §153A-27.1.
Condemnation or acquisition of land by local government unit outside county.
Consent of board of commissioners necessary, §153A-15.
Coroner elected as nominee of political party.
Filling vacancy in office, §152-1.
Counties generally.
See COUNTIES.
County boards of education elected on partisan basis.
Vacancies in office, §115C-37.1.
Dog collars.
Unlawful removal of electronic dog collars, §14-401.17.
Foxes, open seasons for taking.
Wildlife resources commission authorized to continue seasons from year to year, §113-291.4, (f1).
Housing authority commissioners.
Tenant as commissioner, exemption from provision of law allowing, §157-5.
Maps in special proceedings, recording of photographic copies, §47-32.
Violation as misdemeanor, inapplicability of provisions, §47-32.2.
Oil, gas or mineral interest separated from surface interest, extinguished, title in surface fee holder.
Failure to list interest for tax purposes for 10 years prior to January 1, 1974.
Protection of interest from surface estate, §1-42.3, (d).
On-premises unfortified wine licenses.
Discretion to decline to issue, §105-113.71, (b).
Sheriff.
Vacancy, performance of duties until vacancy filled, §162-5.1.
Western North Carolina Development Association, Inc.
Appropriation of funds to, §153A-447, (a), (b).

CLAY COUNTY —Cont'd
Western North Carolina regional economic development commission, §158-8.1.

CLE.
Bankruptcy law specialty, Bar Rules & Regs., D, §§.2205, .2206.
Criminal law specialty, Bar Rules & Regs., D, §§.2505, .2506.
Estate planning and probate law specialty, Bar Rules & Regs., D, §§.2305, .2306.
Family law specialty, Bar Rules & Regs., D, §§.2405, .2406.
Immigration law specialty, Bar Rules & Regs., D, §§.2601 to .2607.
Real property law specialty, Bar Rules & Regs., D, §§.2105, .2106.
Regulations generally, CLE Regs. 1 to 10.
Rules concerning administration of program, Bar Rules & Regs., D, §§.1601 to .1610.
Rules for continuing legal education.
See ATTORNEYS AT LAW.
Rules governing administration of program, Bar Rules & Regs., D, §§.1501 to .1527.
Rules of state bar generally, CLE Rules 1 to 27.
Specialization certification, rules governing accreditation, Bar Rules & Regs., D, §§.1901 to .1908.

CLEANING AGENTS CONTAINING PHOSPHORUS.
Manufacture, storage, sale prohibited, §143-214.4, (a).
Cleaning agent defined, §143-214.4, (b).
Exceptions, §143-214.4, (c), (d).
No adequate substitute, §143-214.4, (e).
Infractions, §143-214.4, (g).
Misdemeanor, fine, §143-214.4, (f).

CLEANING ESTABLISHMENTS.
Cleaning agents.
Certain cleaning agents containing phosphorus prohibited, §143-214.4, (a) to (g).
Notice.
Unclaimed articles, §66-67, (a) to (c).
Sales and use tax.
Exemption of sales to, §105-164.13.
Unclaimed articles.
Disposition, §66-67, (a) to (c).

CLEANUP OF LEAKING PETROLEUM UNDERGROUND STORAGE TANKS, §§143-215.94A to 143-215.94Y.
See UNDERGROUND PETROLEUM STORAGE TANK LEAK CLEANUP.

CLEAN WATER MANAGEMENT TRUST FUND, §§113A-251 to 113A-259, 143-15.3B.
See WATERS AND WATERCOURSES.

CLEAN WATER REVOLVING LOANS AND GRANTS, §§159G-1 to 159G-18.
Applications.
Eligibility, §159G-9.
Environmental assessments, §159G-8, (b).
Failure to qualify, §159G-10, (d).
Filing, §159G-8, (a).
Forms, §159G-8, (a).
Hearings, §159G-8, (c).
Appropriations.
Allocations, §159G-4, (b).
Matching of federal funds.
Allocation to water pollution control revolving fund, §159G-4, (a).

CLEAN WATER REVOLVING LOANS AND GRANTS —Cont'd
Citation of chapter, §159G-1.
Debt instruments.
Execution payable to state, §159G-18, (a).
Definitions, §159G-3.
Disbursements.
Certificate of eligibility required, §159G-12, (a).
Determination of lump sum or installment payments, §159G-12, (c).
Installments, §159G-12, (b).
Distribution of funds.
Revolving loans and grants, §159G-6, (a).
Wastewater accounts, §159G-6, (b).
Water pollution control revolving fund, §159G-6, (e).
Water supply accounts, §159G-6, (c).
Eligibility, §159G-9.
Arrangement to borrow amounts necessary, §159G-13, (a).
Environmental assessments.
Contents, §159G-8, (b).
Filing, §159G-8, (b).
Failure to arrange necessary financing or award contract.
Withdrawal of commitment, §159G-11.
Federal grants and loans, §159G-16.
Funds.
Administration, §159G-5, (a).
Drinking water treatment revolving loan fund, §159G-5, (d).
Establishment, §159G-5, (a).
Investment of funds, §159G-5, (b).
Water pollution control revolving fund.
Special account, §159G-5, (c).
Hearings, §159G-8, (c).
Inspections of projects, §159G-14.
Intent of legislature, §159G-2.
Interest.
Credited to proper accounts, §159G-4, (c).
Rates, §159G-4, (c).
Land-use plans, §159G-10, (e).
Local government commission.
Review and approved proposed loans, §159G-18, (b).
Priorities.
Assignment, §159G-10, (c).
Determination, §159G-10, (a).
Factors, §159G-10, (b).
Purpose of chapter, §159G-2.
Reports.
Environmental management commission and division of environmental health, §159G-17, (c).
Office of state budget and management, §159G-17, (b).
Preparation, §159G-17, (a).
Signing, §159G-17, (d).
Rules and regulations.
Adoption, modification and repeal, §159G-15, (a).
Copies, §159G-15, (b).
Federal grants and loans, §159G-16.
Sales and use taxes.
Use of revenues for payment on loans, §159G-13, (b).
Short title of chapter, §159G-1.
Withdrawal of commitment, §159G-11.

CLEAR AND CONVINCING EVIDENCE.
Abused, neglected or dependent juvenile actions.
Adjudicatory hearing, §7B-805.

CLEAR AND CONVINCING EVIDENCE —Cont'd
Delinquent and undisciplined juvenile actions.
Petition alleging undisciplined behavior, §7B-2409.
Secure or nonsecure custody hearing, §7B-1906, (d).
Legitimacy presumption, when mother married.
Overcome by clear and convincing evidence, §49-12.1, (b).
Termination of parental rights proceedings.
Establishing grounds for terminating, §7B-1111, (b).
Evidence standard at adjudicatory hearing, §7B-1109, (f).

CLEAR LIGHTS.
Use on rear of vehicles, §20-130.3.

CLEATS.
Tires not to have, §20-122, (b).

CLERGYMEN.
Communications between clergymen and communicants, §8-53.2.
Employee assistance professional practice by members of other professional groups, §90-511.
Income tax.
Withholding of income taxes from wages.
Ordained or licensed clergyman may elect to be self-employed, §105-163.1A.
Marriage.
Confirmation of vows before ordained ministers, §51-6.
Solemnization, §51-1.
Without license, §51-6.
Marriage and family therapists.
Exemptions from article, §90-270.48A.
Pastoral counselors.
Certification of fee-based practicing pastoral counselors, §§90-380 to 90-395.
See PASTORAL COUNSELORS.
Professional counselors generally, §§90-329 to 90-344.
See PROFESSIONAL COUNSELORS.
Property of church or religious sect, society or denomination.
Authority to acquire, hold and transfer, §61-5.
Religious organizations and societies.
See RELIGIOUS ORGANIZATIONS AND SOCIETIES.
State prison.
Employment of clinical chaplain for inmates, §148-10.1.

CLERICAL MISTAKES.
Relief from judgment or order, §1A-1, Rule 60, (a).

CLERKS.
County clerks.
Boards of commissioners, §153A-11.
Misconduct in public office.
Swearing falsely to official reports, §14-232.
General assembly.
Approval of bills, §120-29.1.
Journals.
Indexing of journals by clerks, §120-28.
Preparation and filing by clerks, §120-27.
Legislative services commission.
Duties of enrolling clerk, §120-33.

CLERKS —Cont'd
General assembly —Cont'd
Principal clerk.
Bills and resolutions.
Retention in office for certain periods, §120-37, (f).
Duties.
Assignment of additional duties, §120-37, (d).
Election, §120-37, (a).
Employing temporary assistance, §120-37, (e).
Retention of books, records, etc., §120-37, (f).
Salary, §120-37, (c).
Staff employees of office.
Additional full-time employees, §120-37, (d).
Term, §120-37, (a).
Reading clerk.
Election, §120-37, (a).
Salary, §120-37, (b).
Term, §120-37, (a).
Municipal corporations.
Deputy clerk.
Powers and duties.
Generally, §160A-172.
Provided by council, §160A-172.
Duties.
Generally, §160A-171.
Office created, §160A-171.

CLERKS OF COURT.
Appeals.
Briefs.
Copies reproduced by clerk, App. Proc. Rule 13, (b).
District courts.
Clerk to judge, §7A-251, (b).
Docket book, App. Proc. Rule 39, (b).
Duties generally, App. Proc. Rule 39, (a).
In forma pauperis.
Fees of clerk, §1-288.
Judgment docket, App. Proc. Rule 39, (b).
Minute book, App. Proc. Rule 39, (b).
Superior courts.
Civil actions.
Applicability of provisions, §1-301.1, (a).
Concurrent authority of judge, §1-301.1, (d).
Duty of judge hearing appeal, §1-301.1, (c).
Filing of appeal, §1-301.1, (b).
Clerk to judge, §7A-251, (a).
Estates of decedents, minors and incompetents.
Applicability of provisions, §1-301.3, (a).
Duty of judge, §1-301.3, (d).
Entry of judgment by clerk, §1-301.3, (b).
Filing of appeal, §1-301.3, (c).
Recording of hearings, §1-301.3, (f).
Remand to clerk, §1-301.3, (e).
Special proceedings.
Appeal of clerk's decision, §1-301.2, (e).
Applicability of provisions, §1-301.2, (a).
Clerk's decision-authority, §1-301.2, (d).
Duty of judge, §1-301.2, (c).
Exceptions, §1-301.2, (g), (h).
Grounds for transfer, §1-301.2, (b).
Service of process, §1-301.2, (f).
Arrest.
Warrant for arrest.
Clerk may issue, §15A-304, (f).
Assignments for benefit of creditors.
Notice of petition.
Clerk to give, §23-14.
Banks.
Superior court.
Deposit of money held by clerk, §7A-112.1.

CLERKS OF COURT —Cont'd
Book of orders appointing receivers of judgment debtors.
Filing and recording appointment in book, §1-364.
Capital punishment.
Certificate of execution.
Filing, §15-192.
Duties on sentence of death, §15-189.
Child support.
Past due child support.
Payments made to clerk.
When payments not past due, §50-13.10, (e).
Procedure to insure payment.
Notice of delinquency.
Non-IV-D cases, §50-13.9, (d).
Payments made to, §50-13.9, (a).
Informing clerk of change of address, §50-13.9, (c).
Records listing amount of payment, §50-13.9, (b).
Transmission to health and human services department in IV-D cases, §50-13.9, (b).
Constitution of North Carolina.
Removal, Const. N. C., art. IV, §17.
Vacancies in office, Const. N. C., art. IV, §19.
Court of appeals.
Appointment of clerk, §7A-20, (a).
Assistants to clerk, §7A-20, (a).
Audit of financial accounts of clerk, §7A-20, (b).
Bond required of clerk, §7A-20, (a).
Fee bill for services of clerk, §7A-20, (b).
Oath of office by clerk, §7A-20, (a).
Salary of clerk, §7A-20, (a).
Seal of office.
Adoption by clerk, §7A-20, (a).
Crime victims compensation.
Notice.
Award made from crime victims compensation fund, §15B-15.
Deeds.
Probate and registration.
Where clerk appointed himself to sell, §47-65.
District courts.
Equipment and supplies in clerk's office, §7A-303.
Estate taxes.
Liability of clerk.
Personal representative allowed to make final settlement without presenting affirmation or certificate, §105-32.3, (c).
Executions.
Directing execution to clerk in counties which office of coroner abolished, §1-313.
Execution sales.
Procedural details.
Authority to fix, §1-339.42.
Issuance, failure to issue, requirements, §1-305, (a), (b).
Returns.
Entry on judgment docket, §1-321.
Subscribed by clerk, §1-303.
Failure to discharge duties, §14-230.
Fees.
Court of appeals.
Fee bill for services, §7A-20, (b).
Limitation of actions for, §1-52.
Superior courts.
Accounting for fees and other receipts, §7A-108.
Deposit of money held by clerk, §7A-308.1.
Investment of funds in clerk's hands, §7A-308.1.
Statement rendered by county officer compensated from fees, §128-13.

CLERKS OF COURT —Cont'd
Foreign-money claims.
Powers and liabilities, §1C-1826, (j).
Illegitimacy.
Paternity of illegitimate children judicially determined.
Furnishing state registrar with facts as to paternity, §130A-119.
In forma pauperis.
Fees upon, §1-288.
Judgments.
Entry of judgment, §1A-1, Rule 58.
Foreign judgments.
Filing in office of clerk of superior court, §1C-1703, (a).
Judicial sales.
Applicability of provisions to sales ordered by clerk, §1-339.3, (a).
Compensation of person holding sale.
Fixing, §1-339.11.
Judge's approval of clerk's order of public sale, §1-339.14.
Power to order public or private sale, §1-339.3A.
Procedural details.
Authority to fix, §1-339.3, (c).
Report or accounting.
Authority to compel, §1-339.12.
Landlord and tenant.
Summary ejectment.
Issuance of summons by clerk, §42-28.
Limitation of actions.
Fee actions, §1-52.
Mortgages and deeds of trust.
Sales under power of sale.
Auditing and recording final account, §45-21.33, (d).
Motor vehicle license plates.
Special license plates for superior court clerks, §20-79.4, (a).
Oaths.
Who may administer oaths of office, §11-7.1, (a).
Offenses against.
Aggravating factor in sentencing, §15A-1340.16.
Pardons.
Duty of sheriff and clerk when pardon granted, §147-25.
Partition.
Docketing of owelty charges, §46-21.
Partition sales.
Clerk not to appoint self, etc., to sell, §46-31.
Paternity.
Illegitimate children judicially determined.
Furnishing state registrar with facts as to paternity, §130A-119.
Practice of law.
Private practice prohibited, §84-2.
Probate and registration.
Authorized to take probate, §47-2.
Before clerks in other states, §47-77.
Before judges of supreme or superior court or clerks before 1889, §47-58.
Certificates of clerks without seal, §47-99.
Nonresident officials without seal, §47-45.
Deeds.
Where clerk appointed himself to sell, §47-65.
Defective acknowledgment on old deeds validated, §47-52.
Deputy clerks of superior court.
Validation of acknowledgments, etc., §47-108.7.
Inferior courts.
Before clerks of inferior courts, §47-59.

CLERKS OF COURT —Cont'd
Probate and registration —Cont'd
Interested clerk.
Order of registration by interested clerk, §47-61.
Justices of the peace.
Clerk's certificate upon probate by justice of the peace.
Validation, §47-56.
Nonresident officials without seals.
Clerk's certificate, §47-45.
Omission of official seal by clerks of court of other states, §47-86.
Other states.
Before deputy clerks of courts of other states, §47-79.
Parties.
Order of registration by judge where clerk party, §47-60.
Probate by justice of peace or magistrate.
Clerk's certificate, §47-44.
Validation of instruments in which clerk was party, §47-106.
Receivers appointed in supplemental proceeding.
Recording in book of orders appointing receivers of judgment debtors, §1-364.
Renunciation of property and renunciation of fiduciary powers.
Filing renunciation with clerk, §31B-2, (c).
Search warrants.
Issuance, §15A-243, (b).
Service of process.
Sheriff a party.
Clerk to act in absence of office of coroner, §162-16.
Special proceedings.
Commissioners.
Fees.
Powers of clerk as to, §1-408.
Ex parte.
Summary action by clerks, §1-401.
Surveys.
Power to order in proceedings involving sale of land, §1-408.1.
Superior court clerks of court generally.
See SUPERIOR COURTS.
Supreme court.
Appellate division reports.
Lending prohibited, §147-51.
Responsibility of clerk, §147-51.
Appointment, §7A-11.
Assistant clerk, §7A-11.
Audit of financial accounts, §7A-11.
Bond required, §7A-11.
Duties, §7A-11.
Fees, §7A-11.
Oath of office, §7A-11.
Salaries, §7A-11.
Seal of office, §7A-11.
Torrens system registration.
Examiners.
Appointment and removal by clerk, §43-4.
Liens on registered lands.
Docketed judgments.
Duty of clerk to certify, §43-45.
Transfer of civil causes.
Retention and docketing of causes in originally designated trial division, §7A-256.
Vital statistics.
Paternity of illegitimate children judicially determined.
Furnishing state registrar with facts as to paternity, §130A-119.

CLERKS OF COURT —Cont'd
When court means clerk, §1-7.
Year's allowance, §§30-19 to 30-33.
See SURVIVING SPOUSES.

CLEVELAND COUNTY.
Ambulance service.
Attachment or garnishment and lien for, §§44-51.4 to 44-51.8.
Obtaining without intending to pay, §14-111.2.
Blank or master forms of mortgages, deeds of trust, etc.
Indexing and recording, inapplicability of provisions, §47-21.
Board of county commissioners.
Filling vacancies on board, §153A-27.1.
Condemnation or acquisition of land by local government unit outside county.
Consent of board of commissioners necessary, §153A-15.
Coroner elected as nominee of political party.
Filling vacancy in office, §152-1.
Counties generally.
See COUNTIES.
County boards of education elected on partisan basis.
Vacancies in office, §115C-37.1.
Cropper or tenant refusing to perform terms of contract.
Forfeiture of right of possession to premises, §42-27.
Dangerous firearm use by young children, permitting.
Air rifles, air pistols and bb guns not dangerous firearm, §14-316, (b).
Game laws, local acts not repealed, §113-133.1, (e).
Housing authority commissioners.
Tenant as commissioner, exemption from provision of law allowing, §157-5.
Oil, gas or mineral interest separated from surface interest, extinguished, title in surface fee holder.
Failure to list interest for tax purposes for 10 years prior to January 1, 1974.
Protection of interest from surface estate, §1-42.3, (d).
Registration of deeds.
Tax certification, no delinquent taxes due, §161-31, (b).
Sheriff.
Vacancy, performance of duties until vacancy filled, §162-5.1.
Small city mixed beverage elections.
Inapplicability of provisions to, §18B-600, (e1).
Special school tax, election to abolish.
Petition required, §115C-505.
Western North Carolina regional economic development commission, §158-8.1.

CLIENT SECURITY FUND.
Rules governing administration, Bar Rules & Regs., D, §§.1401 to .1420.

CLINICAL LABORATORIES.
Financing health care facilities generally, §§131A-1 to 131A-25.
See HEALTH CARE FACILITY FINANCING.

CLINICAL TRIALS.
Health benefit plan coverage, §58-3-255.

CLINTON.
Condemnation of unsafe buildings, §§160A-425.1, 160A-426, (d), 160A-432, (a1).

CLIPPING NEWSPAPER AND MAGAZINE ARTICLES.
Work-at-home solicitations, advertising restrictions, §75-31.

CLOSED-CIRCUIT TELEVISION.
Arraignment, §15A-941.
First appearance before district court judge, §15A-601.
Pretrial release.
Two-way audio and video transmissions authorized, §15A-532.

CLOSED FORMULARIES.
Health insurers maintaining, §58-3-221.

CLOSED HEARINGS.
Delinquent and undisciplined juvenile actions, §7B-2402.
Mental health, developmental disability, substance abuse.
Involuntary commitment.
Substance abuser's commitment hearing, §122C-286, (d).

CLOSED SHOPS.
Right to work law, §§95-78 to 95-84.

CLOSING ARGUMENTS, Super. Ct. Rule 10.
Court's control of argument, §7A-97.
Criminal proceedings.
Limitations on arguments to jury, §15A-1230.

CLOSING FORESTS AND WOODLANDS TO FISHING, HUNTING AND TRAPPING.
Annulment of proclamation, §113-60.2.
Authority of governor, §113-60.1.
Publication of proclamation, §113-60.2.
Violation of proclamation, misdemeanor, §113-60.3.

CLOSING-OUT SALES, §§66-76 to 66-83.
Additions to stock in contemplation of sale, §66-78.
Advertisements.
Advertising sale contrary to provisions, §66-81.
False advertisements, §66-82.
Applicability of provisions.
Exception of certain sales, §66-82.
Bonds, surety.
Required for license, §66-77, (b).
Continuation of sale or business beyond termination date.
Prohibited, §66-80.
Definitions, §66-76.
Distress sales.
Defined, §66-76.
Inventory not required, §66-77, (a).
Fees.
License fee, §66-77, (b).
Injunctions, §66-83.
Inventories.
Required of applicants for licenses, §66-77, (a).
Licenses.
Applications, §66-77, (a).
Date of filing to be endorsed on application, §66-77, (c).
False statements.
Perjury, §66-77, (d).
Bonds, surety.
Required, §66-77, (b).
Fees, §66-77, (b).
Issuance, §66-77, (b).
Required, §66-77, (a).

CLOSING-OUT SALES —Cont'd
Misdemeanor.
Advertising or conducting sale contrary to provisions, §66-81.
Perjury.
False statements in application, §66-77, (d).
Prohibited acts.
Additions to stock in contemplation of sale, §66-78.
Continuation of sale or business beyond termination date, §66-80.
Replenishment of stock, §66-79.
Replenishment of stock, §66-79.
Violations of provisions.
Advertising or conducting sale contrary to provisions, §66-81.
Prohibited acts, §§66-78 to 66-80.
Restraining or enjoining, §66-83.

CLOSING THE ACHIEVEMENT GAP.
Annual performance standards, §115C-105.35, (b).
Board of education model, §115C-12.

CLOTH.
Dealers of scrap, salvage or surplus, failure to keep records of purchases, §66-10, (b).

CLOTHES.
Exempt property from enforcement of claims of creditors, §1C-1601, (a).
Peeping Toms.
Secretly or surreptitiously peeping underneath or through clothing worn by another, §14-202, (a1).
Property taxes.
Exclusion of non-business property, §105-275.
Sales and use tax.
Defined, §105-164.3.
Tax holiday, §105-164.13C, (a).
Unclaimed clothing and other articles.
Disposition by laundries and dry-cleaning establishments, §66-67, (a) to (c).

CLOTHING ACCESSORIES OR EQUIPMENT.
Sales and use tax.
Defined, §105-164.3.
Tax holiday, inapplicability, §105-164.13C, (b).

CLOUD ON TITLE.
Judgments by default removed.
Validated, §1-217.2.

CLOVER.
Standard weights and measures, §81A-42.

CLOVER SEEDS.
Standard weights and measures, §81A-42.

CLUB FEET.
Podiatrist to surgically correct, §90-202.2, (b).
Infant two years of age or less excluded from definition of podiatry, §90-202.2, (a).

CLUBS.
Civic club license plates, §20-79.4, (b).
Franchise tax.
Exemption, §105-125, (a).
Hull insurance, protection and indemnity clubs, §§58-20-1 to 58-20-40.
See HULL INSURANCE, PROTECTION AND INDEMNITY CLUBS.
Motor vehicle special license plates.
Civic clubs, §20-79.4, (b).
Powers of attorney.
Powers conferred by statutory short form.
Continued payments incidental to membership, §32A-2.

CLUBS —Cont'd
Private clubs.
Alcoholic beverage permits.
Alcoholic beverages defined, §18B-1000.
Brown-bagging permit.
Kind of permit that may be issued, §18B-1001.
Lockers to be provided for storing alcoholic beverages, §18B-1006, (b).
Mixed beverage permit.
Kind of permit that may be issued, §18B-1001.
On-premises fortified wine permit.
Kind of permit that may be issued, §18B-1001.
On-premises malt beverage permit.
Kind of permit that may be issued, §18B-1001.
On-premises unfortified wine permit.
Kind of permit that may be issued, §18B-1001.
Permits.
Residential private clubs, §18B-1006, (k).
Rules concerning retail permits, §18B-1008.
Special occasion permit.
Kind of permit that may be issued, §18B-1001.
Fair housing.
Unlawful discriminatory practices provisions.
Exemption, §41A-6, (a).
Sanitation of food and lodging establishments.
Definition of private club, §130A-247.
Exemption from provisions, §130A-250.
Telephone service, shared service, §62-110, (d).

COACH HOUSES.
Burning of coach houses, §14-62.

COAL.
Coke.
Weights and measures, §81A-42.
Generally.
See MINES AND MINERALS.
Mine safety and health act generally, §§74-24.1 to 74-24.20.
See MINE SAFETY AND HEALTH.
Mining act of 1971, §§74-46 to 74-68.
See MINING ACT OF 1971.
Mining permits generally.
See MINING PERMITS.
Reports.
Standard weights and measures, §81A-42.
Suppliers.
Stocks of coal, §§143-345.13, 143-345.14.

COAL-FIRED GENERATING UNITS.
Emissions of oxides of nitrogen and sulfur dioxide by investor-owned utilities, §143-215.107D.
Civil penalties for violations, §143-215.114A, (b1).
Compliance with provisions, §143-215.107D, (f), (g).
Criminal penalties for violations, §143-215.114B, (f) to (h).
Definitions, §143-215.107D, (a).
Environmental compliance costs, accelerated recovery, §62-133.6, (b).
Adjustments or reductions in rate base, §62-133.6, (e), (f).
Amortization, §62-133.6, (b).
Compliance plans, filing, §62-133.6, (c).
Defined, §62-133.6, (a).

COAL-FIRED GENERATING UNITS —Cont'd
Emissions of oxides of nitrogen and sulfur dioxide by investor-owned utilities —Cont'd
Environmental compliance costs, accelerated recovery —Cont'd
Emissions limitations, statement by utilities subject to, §62-133.6, (i), (j).
Enforcement of utility compliance, §62-133.6, (h).
Final agency action not subject to review, §62-133.6, (k).
Hearing to review compliance costs, §62-133.6, (d).
Market based rates and services, authority to implement, §62-133.6, (g).
Rate base to remain unchanged, §62-133.6, (e).
Permits to include certain conditions, §143-215.107D, (h).
Prohibited acts, §143-215.107D, (b) to (e).
Statements by utility, §143-215.107D, (j).
Voluntary agreement to transfer to state certain emissions allowances, §143-215.107D, (i).

COASTAL AREA MANAGEMENT, §§113A-100 to 113A-134.3.
Advisory council.
Chairman, §113A-105, (e).
Compensation, §113A-105, (f).
Creation, §113A-105, (a).
Defined, §113A-103.
Duties, §113A-105, (c).
Functions, §113A-105, (c).
Members, §113A-105, (b).
Multiple offices, §113A-105, (d).
Vice-chairman, §113A-105, (e).
Appeals.
Denial of permits, §113A-123.
Areas of environmental concern.
Additional grounds for designation prohibited unless enacted by general assembly, §113A-113, (d).
Designation.
Adding new areas, §113A-115, (c).
Additional grounds for designation prohibited unless enacted into law by general assembly, §113A-113, (d).
Deleting areas, §113A-115, (c).
Generally, §113A-113.
Geographic areas, §113A-113, (a).
Hearings, §113A-115, (a).
Notice, §113A-115, (b).
Procedural requirements, §113A-115.
Review of designated areas, §113A-115, (c).
Rules and regulations.
Adoption, §§113A-113, 113A-115.
Erosion control structures, §113A-115.1.
Generally, §113A-113.
Hearings.
Designation of areas, §113A-115, (a).
Notice, §113A-115, (b).
Identification, §113A-113, (b), (c).
Notice.
Hearings, §113A-115, (b).
Outstanding resource areas of environmental concern.
Development in, §113A-118.2.
Permits.
Outstanding resource water areas of environmental concern.
Development in, §113A-118.2.

COASTAL AREA MANAGEMENT —Cont'd
Attorney general.
Representation of commission, §113A-124, (d).
Beach access program.
Administration of program, §113A-134.2, (a).
Creation of program, §113A-134.2, (a).
Definitions, §113A-134.2, (b).
Legislative findings, §113A-134.1.
Priorities, §113A-134.3.
Purposes, §§113A-134.1, 113A-134.2, (a).
Standards, §113A-134.3.
Beach management plan.
Duties of department, §113A-134.11.
Multiyear beach management and restoration plan.
Purposes, §113A-134.12, (a).
Revision, §113A-134.12, (b).
Boats.
Defined, §113A-103.
Citation of article, §113A-100.
Civil penalties.
Permits, §113A-126, (d).
Coastal habitat protection plans.
Adoption by commission, §113A-106.1.
Coastal reserves, §§113A-129.1 to 113A-129.3.
Acquisitions or dispositions of property, §113A-129.2, (d).
Administration of system, §113A-129.2, (b).
Area system established within, §113A-129.2, (c).
Creation of system, §113A-129.2, (a).
Hunting, fishing, navigation and recreation, §113A-129.2, (e).
Legislative findings, §113A-129.1, (a).
National estuarine reserve research system.
Coordination with, §113A-129.3, (a).
Nature and historic preserve.
Dedicated as components of, §113A-129.3, (b).
Purposes, §113A-129.1, (b).
Research and education.
Lands and water within system primarily used for, §113A-129.2, (e).
Coastal sound.
Defined, §113A-103.
Commission.
Appointments, §113A-104, (c).
Women and minorities, §113A-104, (k).
Attorney general.
Representation of commission, §113A-124, (d).
Chairman, §113A-104, (i).
Compensation, §113A-104, (j).
Composition, §113A-104, (b).
Defined, §113A-103.
Establishment, §113A-104, (a).
Meetings.
Attendance, §113A-104, (l).
Multiple offices, §113A-104, (f).
Nominating categories, §113A-104, (d).
Office may be held concurrently with elective or appointive offices, §113A-104, (f).
Powers and duties, §113A-124, (c).
Residence requirements, §113A-104, (e).
Terms, §113A-104, (g).
Vacancies, §113A-104, (h).
Failure to attend meetings, §113A-104, (l).
Women and minorities, §113A-104, (k).
Cooperative state-local program.
Establishment, §113A-101.
Coordination with federal government, §113A-127.
Definitions, §113A-103.
Permits, §113A-118.
Designated local officials, §113A-119, (c).

COASTAL AREA MANAGEMENT —Cont'd
Development.
Defined, §113A-103.
Discharge of oil or hazardous substances, §§143-215.83 to 143-215.94.
See OIL OR HAZARDOUS SUBSTANCES DISCHARGES.
Dredging permits, §113-229.
Eminent domain.
Commission order not applicable to certain land.
Acquisition of fee or lesser interest in land, §113A-123, (c).
Energy development, generation or transmission.
Permit for utility facility obtained from commission.
Facility subject to regulation under article, §113A-118, (e).
Erosion control structures, §113A-115.1.
Construction limitations, §113A-115.1, (b).
Defined terms, §113A-115.1, (a).
Permanent structures, limitations, §113A-115.1, (b).
Temporary structures, limitations, §113A-115.1, (b).
Variance permits, §113A-115.1, (c).
Fees.
Permits, §113A-119.1, (a), (b).
Findings, §113A-102.
Floating structures.
Defined, §113A-103.
Grants.
Planning grants, §113A-112.
Hearings.
Areas of environmental concern.
Designation of areas, §113A-115, (a).
Notice, §113A-115, (b).
Planning processes.
Land-use plans.
Adoption, §113A-110, (e).
Injunctions.
Permits, §113A-126, (a).
Judicial review.
Denial of permits, §113A-123, (a), (b).
Key facilities.
Defined, §113A-103.
Landowners' rights.
Protection, §113A-128.
Land-use plans and programs.
Approval by commission, §113A-110, (f).
Contents, §113A-110, (a).
Copies of approval plans, §113A-110, (g).
Delegation of responsibilities, §113A-110, (b).
Effect, §113A-111.
Hearings, §113A-110, (e).
Responsibilities of bodies charged with adoption, §113A-110, (c), (d).
Timetable for preparation, §113A-109.
Lead regional organizations.
Defined, §113A-103.
Legislative findings, §113A-102, (a).
Legislative goals, §113A-102, (b).
Letters of intent.
Planning processes, §113A-109.
Local government.
Defined, §113A-103.
Notice.
Areas of environmental concern.
Hearings, §113A-115, (b).
Permits.
Issuance of public notice of proposed development, §113A-119, (b).

COASTAL AREA MANAGEMENT —Cont'd
Notice —Cont'd
Permits —Cont'd
Quasi-judicial procedures.
Giving notice by registered or certified mail, §113A-122, (d).
Nursery areas.
Primary nursery areas.
Development in, §113A-118.2.
Offshore oil and gas activities, §§143-215.94AA to 143-215.94JJ.
See OFFSHORE OIL AND GAS ACTIVITIES.
Outstanding resource water areas of environmental concern.
Development in, §113A-118.2.
Permits.
Appeals.
Denial of permits, §113A-123, (a), (b).
Permit deemed suspended, §113A-121.1, (c).
Applications, §113A-119, (a).
Areas of environmental concern.
Outstanding resource water areas of environmental concern.
Development in, §113A-118.2.
Civil penalties, §113A-126, (d).
Definitions, §113A-118, (d).
Denial of permit, §§113A-120, (b1), 113A-123, (a), (b).
Appeals.
Permit deemed suspended, §113A-121.1, (c).
Hearing upon denial.
Procedures, §113A-122.
Request, §113A-121.1, (a), (b).
Judicial review, §113A-123, (a), (b).
Review of grant or denial of permits, §113A-121.1.
Procedure, §113A-122.
Designated local officials.
Defined, §113A-119, (c).
Expedited procedures, §113A-121, (b).
Fees.
Submitted with application, §113A-119, (a).
Issuance of public notice of proposed developments, §113A-119, (b).
Minor developments, §113A-121, (b), (c).
Notice.
Issuance of public notice of proposed developments, §113A-119, (b).
Dredging permits, §113-229.
Energy development, generation or transmission.
Permit for utility facility obtained from commission.
Facility subject to regulation under article, §113A-118, (e).
Enforcement programs, §113A-117, (c), (d).
Erosion control structures.
Variance permits, §113A-115.1, (c).
Fees.
Applications.
Submitted with application, §113A-119, (a).
Credited to general fund, §113A-119.1, (b).
Graduated fee schedule.
Establishment, §113A-119.1, (a).
Limitations, §113A-119.1, (a).
Uses, §113A-119.1, (b).
General permits.
Designation of certain classes of development, §113A-118.1, (a).
Issuance, §113A-118.1, (b).
Notice, §113A-118.1, (c).

COASTAL AREA MANAGEMENT —Cont'd
Permits —Cont'd
General permits —Cont'd
Outstanding resource water areas of environmental concern.
Development in, §113A-118.2.
Primary nursery areas.
Development in, §113A-118.2.
Riprap, use of, §113A-118.1, (e).
Variances, appeals and enforcements, §113A-118.1, (d).
Granting of permits, §113A-120, (a), (b).
Review of grant or denial of permits, §113A-121.1.
Procedure, §113A-122.
Implementation programs, §113A-117, (a), (b).
Injunctive relief, §113A-126, (a).
Intent.
Local government letter of intent, §113A-116.
Judicial review.
Denial of permits, §113A-123, (a), (b).
Local government letter of intent, §113A-116.
Minor developments.
Applications, §113A-121, (b), (c).
Expedited procedures, §113A-121, (a).
Notice.
Issuance of public notice of proposed development, §113A-119, (b).
Quasi-judicial procedures.
Giving notice by registered or certified mail, §113A-122, (d).
Obtaining permits.
Expedited procedure, §113A-118, (b), (c).
Outstanding resource water areas of environmental concern.
Development in.
Issuance of general permit, §113A-118.2.
Primary nursery areas.
Development in, §113A-118.2.
Publication.
Notice of proposed development, §113A-119, (b).
Quasi-judicial procedures.
Applicability of provisions, §113A-122, (b).
Failure of commission to approve or deny applications, §113A-122, (c).
Notices.
Giving by registered or certified mail, §113A-122, (d).
Requirements, §113A-118, (a).
Secretary of environment and natural resources.
Powers and duties, §113A-124, (a), (b).
Special emergency permits, §113A-118, (f).
Time limit on considering record of applicant, §113A-120, (b2).
Transitional provisions.
Existing regulatory permits, §113A-125, (a), (c).
Permit changeover date, §113A-125, (b).
Unified systems studies, §113A-125, (d).
Variances, §113A-120.1.
Violations, §113A-126, (a), (b), (c).
Petitions.
Variances, §113A-120.1, (a).
Planning processes.
County letter of intent, §113A-109.
Effect of land-use plans, §113A-111.
Effect of state guidelines, §113A-108.
Grants.
Authorization to make annual grants, §113A-112.
Hearings.
Land-use plans.
Adoption, §113A-110, (e).

COASTAL AREA MANAGEMENT —Cont'd
Planning processes —Cont'd
Land-use plans and programs.
Approval by commission, §113A-110, (f).
Contents, §113A-110, (a).
Copies of approval plans, §113A-110, (g).
Delegation of responsibilities, §113A-110, (b).
Effect, §113A-111.
Hearings, §113A-110, (e).
Responsibilities of bodies charged with adoption, §113A-110, (c), (d).
Timetable for preparation, §113A-109.
Letters of intent, §113A-109.
Scope, §113A-106.
State guidelines.
Amendment, §113A-107, (f).
Contents, §113A-107, (a).
Effect, §113A-108.
Preparation, adoption and amendment, §113A-107, (b).
Submission of proposed guidelines, §113A-107, (c).
Timetable for preparation of land-use plans, §113A-109.
Policy, §113A-102.
Primary nursery areas.
Development in primary nursery areas, §113A-118.2.
Protection of landowners' rights, §113A-128.
Publication.
Permits.
Public notice of proposed development, §113A-119, (b).
Public beach and coastal waterfront access program, §§113A-134.1 to 113A-134.3.
Purposes, §113A-102.
Rules and regulations.
Areas of environmental concern, §§113A-113, 113A-115.
Protection of landowners' rights, §113A-128.
Secretary of environment and natural resources.
Permits.
Powers and duties, §113A-124, (a), (b).
Short title, §113A-100.
Title, §113A-100.
Transitional provisions.
Permits.
Existing regulatory permits, §113A-125, (a), (c).
Permit changeover date, §113A-125, (b).
Unified systems studies, §113A-125, (d).
United States.
Coordination with federal government, §113A-127.
Variances, §113A-120.1, (a).
Conditions and safeguards may be imposed, §113A-120.1, (b).

COASTAL CAROLINA COMMUNITY COLLEGE.
Community colleges, §§115D-1 to 115D-81.
See COMMUNITY COLLEGES.
Financial support.
Authority to provide local financial support, §115D-61.

COASTAL FISHERIES.
Commercial fishing.
See COMMERCIAL FISHING.
Fish and fishing generally.
See FISH AND FISHING.

COASTAL FISHERIES —Cont'd
Promotion of coastal fisheries and seafood industry.
Generally, §§113-308 to 113-315.9.
See SEAFOOD INDUSTRY AND COASTAL FISHERIES PROMOTION.

COASTAL FISHING WATERS.
Monitoring program.
Protection of public health of swimmers and others using waters, §§130A-233, 130A-233.1, (a), (b).

COASTAL HABITAT PROTECTION PLANS.
Actions to be consistent with plan adopted, §143B-279.8, (c).
Adoption, §113A-106.1.
Explanation of inconsistent action by commissions, §143B-279.8, (d).
Goals, §143B-279.8, (a).
Preparation by department of environment and natural resources, §143B-279.8, (a).
Reports, §143B-279.8, (e), (f).
Review commission, §143B-279.8, (b).
Revision of plan by review commission and department, §143B-279.8, (b).

COASTAL RESERVES, §§113A-129.1 to 113A-129.3.
Acquisitions or dispositions of property, §113A-129.2, (d).
Administration of system, §113A-129.2, (b).
Area system established within, §113A-129.2, (c).
Creation.
North Carolina coastal reserve system, §113A-129.2, (a).
Hunting, fishing, navigation and recreation.
Other public uses, §113A-129.2, (e).
Legislative findings, §113A-129.1, (a).
National estuarine reserve research system.
Coordination with, §113A-129.3, (a).
Nature and historic preserve.
Dedicated as components of, §113A-129.3, (b).
Purposes, §113A-129.1, (b).
Research and education.
Lands and water within system primarily used for, §113A-129.2, (e).

COASTAL RESOURCES COMMISSION.
Coastal habitat protection plans, §143B-279.8.

COASTAL WATERS.
Seaward boundary of private property adjoining ocean high water mark, §77-20, (a) to (c).

COAST GUARD AUXILIARY.
Motor vehicle special license plates, §20-79.4, (a).

COASTS AND SHORES.
Coastal area management, §§113A-100 to 113A-134.3.
See COASTAL AREA MANAGEMENT.
Discharges of oil or hazardous substances, §§143-215.83 to 143-215.94.
See OIL OR HAZARDOUS SUBSTANCES DISCHARGES.
Habitat protection, §143B-279.8.
Lights.
Displaying false lights on seashore, §14-282.
Offshore oil and gas activities, §§143-215.94AA to 143-215.94JJ.
See OFFSHORE OIL AND GAS ACTIVITIES.
Reserves, §§113A-129.1 to 113A-129.3.

COCAINE.
Controlled substances generally, §§90-86 to 90-113.8.
See CONTROLLED SUBSTANCES.
Food, drug and cosmetic act.
Drugs deemed misbranded, §106-134.
Schedule II controlled substances, §90-90.

COCKFIGHTING.
Cruelty to animals, §14-362.

COCOA.
Food, drug and cosmetic act.
Drugs deemed misbranded, §106-134.

C.O.D.
Common carriers to settle shipments promptly, §62-208.
Motor carriers.
Embezzlement of C.O.D. shipments, §62-273.
Sale of goods, UCC.
Buyer not entitled to inspect goods, §25-2-513, (3).

CODED BILL DRAFTING, §120-20.1.

CODEINE.
Controlled substances generally, §§90-86 to 90-113.8.
See CONTROLLED SUBSTANCES.
Food, drug and cosmetic act.
Drugs deemed misbranded, §106-134.
Murder in second degree.
Ingestion of substance causing death of user, §14-17.
Schedule II controlled substances, §90-90.

CODE OF JUDICIAL CONDUCT.
See JUDGES.

CODE OF NORTH CAROLINA.
General statutes.
See GENERAL STATUTES.
Revisor of statutes.
Creation of office, §114-9.1.
Statutes.
See STATUTES.

CODES.
Administrative code and registry.
Publication generally, §§150B-21.17 to 150B-21.25.
See PUBLICATION OF ADMINISTRATIVE CODE AND REGISTER.
Building codes.
General provisions, §§143-136 to 143-143.4.
See BUILDING CODES.
Juvenile code, §§7B-100 to 7B-1414.
Ordinances.
City having population of five thousand or more, §160A-77, (a) to (c).
Counties, §153A-49.

CODICILS.
Concealment, larceny or destruction of codicils, §14-77.
Included within term will, §12-3.
Revocation of nuncupative will, §31-5.2.
Revocation of written wills, §31-5.1.
Wills generally.
See WILLS.

COERCION.
Collection agencies.
Prohibited practices, §58-70-95.
Debt collectors.
Prohibited acts, §75-51.

COERCION —Cont'd
Farm machinery franchises.
Suppliers, §66-187.1.
Insurance.
Unfair trade practices.
Prohibited acts, §58-63-15.
Involuntary servitude, §14-43.2.
Mortgage bankers and brokers.
Prohibited acts, §53-243.11.
Notaries public.
Coercing notary to commit official misconduct, §10A-12, (d).
Obscene materials.
Coercing acceptance of obscene materials by franchises, §14-190.4.
Political activities of public employees.
Coercing employee to support or contribute to political candidate, committee or party, §§126-14, 126-14.1.
Private personnel services contracts, §95-47.4, (d).
Wine distribution agreements, §18B-1202.

COGENERATING POWER PLANTS.
Income tax credit.
Corporation or partnership constructing in state, §105-130.25.

COHABITATION.
Misdemeanor, §14-184.

COHARIE INDIAN TRIBE.
Indians generally.
See INDIANS.
Rights, privileges, immunities, obligations and duties, §71A-6.

COIN-OPERATED MACHINES.
Blind persons.
Operation of highway vending facilities, §§111-48 to 111-52.
See BLIND PERSONS.
Operation of vending facilities on state property, §§111-41 to 111-47.
See BLIND PERSONS.
Breaking into or forcibly opening, §14-56.1.
Damaging or destroying machine, §14-56.2.
Manufacture, sale or gift of devices for cheating slot machines, §14-109.
Obtaining property or services from machine by false coins or tokens, §14-108.
Slot machines.
Gaming.
See GAMING.

COIN-OPERATED TELEPHONE SERVICE.
Certificate of convenience and necessity, §62-110, (c).

COINS.
Counterfeiting, §14-13.
Generally.
See COUNTERFEITING.
False coins or tokens.
Manufacture, sale or gift, §14-109.
Obtaining property or services by use of, §14-108.

CO-INSURANCE.
Contract or policy clauses, §58-3-15.

COKE.
Standard weights and measures, §81A-42.

COLISEUMS.
Alcoholic beverage permits.
Convention center defined to include, §18B-1000.

COLISEUMS —Cont'd
Alcoholic beverage permits —Cont'd
Mixed beverage permit.
Kind of permit that may be issued, §18B-1001.
On-premises fortified wine permit.
Kind of permit that may be issued, §18B-1001.
On-premises malt beverage permit.
Kind of permit that may be issued, §18B-1001.
On-premises unfortified wine permit.
Kind of permit that may be issued, §18B-1001.
Municipal corporations.
Power to establish and support, §160A-489.
Smoking in public places.
Applicability of article to local government, §143-601.
Nonsmoking areas in state-controlled buildings, §143-597.

COLLABORATIVE LAW PROCEEDINGS, §§50-70 to 50-79.
Agreements.
Defined, §50-71.
Judgment or order effectuating agreement, §50-75.
Notice, §50-74, (a), (b).
Requirements, §50-72.
Tolling of time periods, §50-73.
Alternative dispute resolution permitted, §50-78.
Death of a party.
Survival of proceeding, §50-79.
Definitions, §50-71.
Dismissal of civil action.
Notice of agreement filed with court, restrictions, §50-74, (b).
Failure to reach settlement, §50-76, (a) to (c).
Filing with court.
Notice of agreement.
Civil action pending, §50-74, (b).
Judgment or order effectuating agreement, §50-75.
Notice, §50-74, (a), (b).
Privileged evidence, §50-77, (a), (b).
Purpose, §50-70.
Tolling of time periods, §50-73.

COLLAGE.
Artwork on consignment, §§25C-1 to 25C-5.
Sale of prints, §§25C-10 to 25C-16.

COLLATERAL.
Retail installment sales.
Liens.
Inapplicability of section to rights or liens granted by chapter 44A, §25A-23, (c).
Permissible collateral, §25A-23, (a).
Revolving charge account contracts.
Inapplicability of provisions, §25A-23, (d).
Substitution of collateral, §25A-26.
Fee, §25A-26.
Transfer of equity.
Imposition of transfer fee, §25A-16.
Voidness of impermissible collateral, §25A-23, (d).
Secured transactions.
See SECURED TRANSACTIONS.
Trust companies.
Multistate trust institutions.
Deposits, §53-309, (d).

COLLATERAL CONTRACTS.
Sale of goods, UCC.
Remedies for breach not impaired, §25-2-701.

COLLATERAL KINSHIP.
Computation of degrees of kinship, §104A-1.

COLLATERAL SOURCE RULE.
Crime victims compensation.
Award reduction, §15B-11, (d).
Claim denial, §15B-11, (d).
Definitions, §15B-2.
Subrogation, §15B-19.
Workers' compensation.
Proceedings against third parties, §97-10.2, (a).

COLLATERAL WARRANTIES.
Abolished, §41-8.

COLLECTION AGENCIES, §§58-70-1 to 58-70-130.
Accounts.
Acknowledgment of accounts received.
Furnishing, §58-70-60, (a).
Application of funds where there is a debtor-creditor relationship, §58-70-85.
Remittance trust account, §58-70-65, (a) to (c).
Return of accounts.
Creditor may request, §58-70-75.
Termination of permit, §58-70-80.
Acknowledgment of accounts received.
Furnishing, §58-70-60, (a).
Appeals.
Denial of permit, §58-70-30.
Attorneys at law.
Practice of law by collection agencies, §58-70-120.
Shared office space, §58-70-125.
Banks.
Not included in definition of "collection agency," §58-70-15, (c).
Bonds, surety.
Amount, §58-70-20.
Prerequisite to issuance of permit, §58-70-20.
Building and loan associations.
Not included in definition of "collection agency," §58-70-15, (c).
Civil penalties, §58-70-130, (b), (c), (e).
Cumulative nature of provisions, §58-70-130, (d).
Coercion.
Prohibited practices, §58-70-95.
Correspondence.
Identification of collection agency in correspondence, §58-70-50.
Court process.
Simulation of court process in connection with collection of accounts, §14-118.1.
Damages.
Violations of provisions, §58-70-130, (a).
Cumulative nature of provisions, §58-70-130, (d).
Debt collectors.
Prohibited acts by debt collectors.
Collection agencies exempted from provisions, §75-50.
Deceptive representation.
Prohibited acts, §58-70-110.
Definitions, §§58-70-15, 58-70-90.
Deposits.
Remittance trust account, §58-70-65, (a) to (c).
Detectives.
Prohibited from acting as collection agency, §14-401.2.
Doing business without permit, §58-70-1.
False accusations.
Prohibited practices, §58-70-95.

COLLECTION AGENCIES —Cont'd
Fees.
Permit fees, §§58-70-35, (a), 58-70-45.
Fraud.
Deceptive representation.
Prohibited acts, §58-70-110.
Simulation of court process in connection with collection, §14-118.1.
Harassment.
Prohibited practices, §58-70-100.
Hearings.
Denial of permit, §58-70-30.
Hours of business, §58-70-55.
Injunctions.
Restraining orders, §§58-2-60, (a), 58-70-40, (a).
Office hours, §58-70-55.
Payment records, §58-70-70.
Permits.
Applications, §58-70-5.
Balance sheet, §58-70-5, (k).
Certification of no unsatisfied judgments, §58-70-5, (h).
Collection method statement, §58-70-5, (g).
Contents, §58-70-5, (a).
Corporations, §58-70-5, (b).
Fees, §§58-70-5, (j), 58-70-35, (a).
Foreign corporations, §58-70-5, (o).
Information to accompany, §58-70-5.
Intended business address, §58-70-5, (l).
Moral turpitude statement, §58-70-5, (m).
Nonresident applicants, §58-70-5, (n).
Surety bond, §58-70-20, (c).
Partnerships, §58-70-5, (c).
Renewal of permit, §58-70-10.
Stockholder statements, §58-70-5, (f).
Surety bond, §58-70-5, (e).
Telephone number list, §58-70-5, (i).
Trade name used, §58-70-5, (d).
Assignable or transferable, §58-70-35, (c).
Bond, surety, §58-70-20, (a).
Application for permit, §58-70-5, (e).
Cash deposit in lieu of bond, §58-70-20, (b).
Nonresidents, §58-70-20, (c).
Denial, §58-70-30.
Display, §58-70-50.
Doing business without permit, §58-70-1.
Duration, §58-70-35, (b).
Fees.
Application fee, §58-70-35, (a).
Disposition, §58-70-45.
Monetary penalty for violations, §58-2-70, (c), (d), (g).
Renewal.
Application, §58-70-10.
Required, §58-70-1.
Restitution for violations, §58-2-70, (e), (f), (g).
Return of accounts and all valuable papers upon termination of permit, §58-70-80.
Revocation.
Notice and hearing, §58-2-70, (b).
Violations of provisions, §58-70-40, (b), (c).
Surrender, §58-2-65.
Suspension.
Applicable provisions, §58-2-70, (h).
Criminal conviction, §58-2-60, (b).
Notice and hearing, §58-2-70, (b).
Violations of provisions, §58-70-40, (b), (c).
Practice of law.
Unauthorized practice of law, §58-70-120.
Prohibited practices, §§58-70-95, 58-70-125.
Civil liability, §58-70-130.

COLLECTION AGENCIES —Cont'd
Publication.
Unreasonable publication as to consumer's debt.
Prohibited practices, §58-70-105.
Receipts.
Requirements, §58-70-70.
Records.
Contents, §58-70-25, (b).
Required, §58-70-25, (a).
Remittances, §58-70-60, (b).
Statements to accompany, §58-70-60, (b).
Trust account, §58-70-65, (a) to (c).
Restraining orders, §§58-2-60, (a), 58-70-40, (a).
Savings and loan associations.
Not included in definition of "collection agency," §58-70-15, (c).
Shared office space.
Prohibited, §58-70-125.
Telephones.
Harassment.
Prohibited practices, §58-70-100.
Threats.
Prohibited practices, §58-70-95.
Unconscionability.
Prohibited practices, §58-70-115.
Unlawful practices, §§58-70-95, 58-70-125.
Civil liability, §58-70-130.

COLLECTION OF WORTHLESS CHECKS FUND, §7A-308, (c).

COLLECTORS FOR ESTATES.
Actions against collectors.
Service on or appearance of one binds all, §28A-18-4.
Appointment, §28A-11-1.
Termination.
Duties upon termination, §28A-11-4, (b).
Bond, §28A-11-2.
Commissions, §28A-23-3.
Collectors guilty of misconduct not entitled to commission, §28A-23-3, (e).
Computation, §28A-23-3, (f).
Construction of section, §28A-23-3, (d).
Determination of amount, §28A-23-3, (b).
Limitation on amount, §28A-23-3, (c).
Compensation, §28A-11-5.
Counsel fees.
Attorneys serving as collectors, §28A-23-4.
Death of person entitled to bring action before limitation expires.
Action by or against personal representative or collector, §1-22.
Defined, §28A-1-1, (1).
Duties, §28A-11-3.
Examination of accounts, §28A-11-4, (c).
Letters of collection.
Issuance, §28A-11-1.
Oaths, §28A-11-2.
Personal property.
Court ordered sale or lease, §28A-16-2.
Powers, §28A-11-3.
When collectors' powers ceased, §28A-11-4, (a).
Qualifications, §28A-11-1.
Small estates.
Subsequently appointed collectors, §28A-25-5.

COLLECTORS OF WINE OR DECORATIVE DECANTERS.
Alcoholic beverage permits.
Special one-time permits, §18B-1002, (a).

COLLECT TELEPHONE CALLS.
Debt collectors, harassment, §75-52.

COLLEGES.
Community colleges.
See COMMUNITY COLLEGES.
Generally.
See UNIVERSITIES AND COLLEGES.

COLLEGIATE INSIGNIA LICENSE PLATES, §§20-79.4, (b), 20-81.12, (a).
Application, §20-81.12, (c).

COLLISION INSURANCE.
Authorized, §58-7-15.
Mandatory or voluntary risk sharing plans.
See MANDATORY OR VOLUNTARY RISK SHARING PLANS.

COLLISIONS.
Boat operators.
Duties when involved in collision, §75A-11.
Violations, §75A-18, (a).
Motor vehicles.
Generally.
See MOTOR VEHICLE ACCIDENTS.

COLLUSION.
Suit for penalty.
Reply by plaintiff that former judgment obtained by covin, §1-59.

COLOR ADDITIVES.
Food, drug and cosmetic act.
Additives deemed unsafe, §106-132.
Cosmetics deemed adulterated, §106-136.
Cosmetics deemed misbranded, §106-137.
Drugs deemed misbranded, §106-134.
Drugs deemed to be adulterated, §106-133.
Foods deemed misbranded, §106-130.
Foods deemed to be adulterated, §106-129.

COLORECTAL CANCER.
Health benefit plan coverage.
Examinations, tests and screening, §58-3-179.
Small employer group health plans, §58-50-155, (a).

COLOR OF OFFICE.
Limitation of action against public officer for trespass, §1-52.
Venue, §1-77.

COLOR OF SKIN.
Discrimination generally.
See DISCRIMINATION.
Racial minorities generally.
See RACIAL MINORITIES.

COLOR OF TITLE.
Adverse possession, §1-38.
Seven years' possession under color of title, §1-38.
Lost instruments and records.
Destroyed instrument, §98-8.

COLORS, STATE, §144-6.

COLUMBINE.
Taking, etc., of certain wild plants from land of another, §14-129.

COLUMBUS COUNTY.
Acquisition of property, power, §153A-158.1, (a).
Agricultural tendencies in certain counties.
Terms of, §42-23.
Ambulance service.
Attachment or garnishment and lien for, §§44-51.4 to 44-51.8.

COLUMBUS COUNTY —Cont'd
Blank or master forms of mortgages, deeds of trust, etc.
Indexing and recording, inapplicability of provisions, §47-21.
Condemnation or acquisition of land by local government unit outside county.
Consent of board of commissioners necessary, §153A-15.
Cropper or tenant refusing to perform terms of contract.
Forfeiture of right of possession to premises, §42-27.
Dog collars.
Unlawful removal of electronic dog collars, §14-401.17.
Fair Bluff watermelon festival.
Official Southeastern North Carolina festival, §145-16, (b).
Game laws, local acts not repealed, §113-133.1, (e).
Grants in navigable waters, registration, §113-205, (a).
Low-income housing tax credits.
Qualified building eligible for credit, §105-129.41, (c).
School property.
Acquisition and improvement, §153A-158.1.
Southeastern North Carolina regional economic development commission, §158-8.3.

COLUMBUS DAY.
Public holiday, §103-4, (a).

COMBAT INFANTRY BADGE RECIPIENTS.
Motor vehicle license plates, §20-79.4, (b).

COMBAT VETERANS LICENSE PLATES.
Special registration plates, §20-79.4, (b).

COMBINATIONS IN RESTRAINT OF TRADE.
Illegality, §75-1.

COMEDIANS.
Artistic and creative services and talent agency contracts.
Minors, §§48A-11 to 48A-18.

COMITY.
Conflict of laws generally.
See CONFLICT OF LAWS.
Geologists.
Licenses, §89E-11.
Soil scientist licenses, §89F-12.
Taxation.
Reciprocal comity, §105-268.

COMMENCEMENT OF ACTIONS, §1A-1, Rule 3, (a).
Abused, neglected or dependent juvenile actions, §7B-405.
Bond for costs and damages.
Prosecution bonds, §§1-109 to 1-112.
Civil no-contact orders.
Workplace violence prevention.
Filing complaint or motion, §95-267, (a).
Complaints.
Filing, §1A-1, Rule 3, (a).
Death before limitation expires.
Action by or against personal representative or collector, §1-22.
Defendant out of state, §1-21.
Delinquent and undisciplined juvenile actions.
Filing of petition, §7B-1804, (a).

COMMENCEMENT OF ACTIONS —Cont'd
Joint and several debtors.
Defenses.
Parties summoned after judgment, §1-114.
Judgments, §1-113.
Summoning after judgment, §1-114.
Partners, §1-113.
Proceedings generally, §1-113.
Summons and process, §1-113.
Summoning after judgment, §1-114.
Limitation of actions generally.
See LIMITATION OF ACTIONS.
Lis pendens, §§1-116 to 1-120.2.
See LIS PENDENS.
Medical malpractice.
Index of actions provided senior district judge, §1A-1, Rule 3, (a).
Prosecution bonds, §§1-109 to 1-112.
Small claims actions, §7A-213.
Special proceedings.
Contested proceedings, §1-394.
Summons.
Issuance, §1A-1, Rule 3, (a).
Workplace violence prevention.
Civil no-contact orders.
Filing complaint or motion, §95-267, (a).

COMMENT BY JUDGE ON VERDICT, §1-180.1.

COMMERCE.
Commercial code, §§25-1-101 to 25-11-108.
See COMMERCIAL CODE.
Commodities, §§78D-1 to 78D-33.
See COMMODITIES.
Constitution of North Carolina.
Local, private and special legislation.
Limitation, Const. N. C., art. II, §24.
Constitution of the United States, Const. U. S., art. I, §§8, 9.
Counties.
Inspectors of articles of commerce, §§66-1 to 66-7.
Electronic commerce in government, §§66-58.1 to 66-58.12.
See ELECTRONIC COMMERCE IN GOVERNMENT.
Limited liability companies.
Generally, §§57C-1-01 to 57C-10-07.
See LIMITED LIABILITY COMPANIES.
Monopolies and restraints of trade, §§75-1 to 75-35.
See MONOPOLIES AND RESTRAINT OF TRADE.
Tax incentives for new and expanding businesses, §§105-129.2 to 105-129.13.
See TAX INCENTIVES FOR NEW AND EXPANDING BUSINESSES.
Unfair competitive practices.
Regulation of method, §75-1.1.

COMMERCE DEPARTMENT.
Accounts and accounting.
Industrial development fund.
Utility account, §143B-437.01, (b1).
Alcoholic beverages.
Commission.
See ALCOHOLIC BEVERAGE CONTROL COMMISSION.
Allocation of economic development responsibilities.
Economic development board, §143B-437.03.
Attorney general.
Energy division of department.
Employment of attorney for division, §114-4.2D.

COMMERCE DEPARTMENT —Cont'd
Business license information service.
Authorized to establish, §143B-431, (e).
Clearinghouse for business license information.
Authorized to establish, §143B-431, (e).
Comprehensive strategic economic development plan, §143B-434.01.
Annual report, §143B-434.01, (k).
Data, plans and reports.
Availability to general assembly, §143B-434.01, (l).
Economic distress defined, §143B-434.01, (a).
Environmental scan, §143B-434.01, (e).
Formulation of strategy, §143B-434.01, (i).
Goals and objectives, §143B-434.01, (h).
Implementation plan, §143B-434.01, (j).
Needs assessment, §143B-434.01, (f).
Plan defined, §143B-434.01, (a).
Preparation of plan by board, §143B-434.01, (b).
Public and private input, §143B-434.01, (d).
Purpose, §143B-434.01, (c).
Region defined, §143B-434.01, (a).
Vision and mission statements, §143B-434.01, (g).
Creation, §143B-427.
Credit unions.
Commission, §143B-439.
Declaration of policy, §143B-428.
Department of natural resources and economic development.
Divisions, councils and units transferred to department of commerce, §143B-432, (a) to (c).
Division of employment and training, §143B-438.13.
Division of tourism, film and sports development.
Duties and responsibilities, §143B-434.2.
Film industry development account, §143B-434.4.
Duties, §§143B-429, 143B-430, (a), (b).
Federal programs, §143B-431, (d).
Local planning assistance, §143B-431, (c).
Economic development board.
Advertising of resources and advantages, §143B-436.
Advice and staff, §143B-434, (c).
Allocation of responsibilities, §143B-437.03.
Block grants, §143B-437.04, (a).
Qualifications, §143B-437.04, (b).
Chairman, §143B-434, (c).
Clerical services, §143B-434, (b).
Creation, §143B-434, (a).
Duties, §143B-434, (a).
Impact studies.
Investigation of impact of proposed new and expanding industries, §143B-437.
Investigation of impact of proposed new and expanding industries, §143B-437.
Membership, §143B-434, (a), (b).
Powers and duties, §143B-434, (a).
Publication, §143B-435.
Reports.
Publication, §143B-435.
Review of annual report, §143B-437.05.
Employment and training grant program, §143B-438.13.
E-NC authority, §§143B-437.44 to 143B-437.47.
Energy division.
Attorney general.
Employment of attorney for division, §114-4.2D.

COMMERCE DEPARTMENT —Cont'd
Energy improvement loan program, §§143-345.16 to 143-345.18.
Established, §143B-427.
Federal funds.
Power of secretary to accept, §143B-430, (b).
Federal programs.
Powers and duties with respect to, §143B-431, (d).
Film industry development account, §143B-434.4.
Functions, §143B-431, (a).
Funds.
Industrial development fund, §143B-437.01.
Main street financial incentive fund, §143B-472.35.
Application for grants and loans, §143B-472.35, (c) to (e).
Disbursements, §143B-472.35, (f), (g).
Establishment, §143B-472.35, (a).
Inspections, §143B-472.35, (j).
Repayment, §143B-472.35, (h).
Reports, §143B-472.35, (i), (l).
Rules, §143B-472.35, (k).
Use of moneys, §143B-472.35, (b).
Grants.
Main street financial incentive fund.
Application for grants and loans, §143B-472.35, (c), (d), (e).
Power to apply for and accept, §143B-431, (d).
Housing assistance information.
Toll-free telephone number to provide information.
Established in department, §143B-431.1.
Industrial development fund.
Creation, §143B-437.01, (a).
Definitions, §143B-437.01, (a1).
Reports.
Annual report to general assembly, §143B-437.01, (c).
Utility account, use of funds, §143B-437.01, (c1).
Rules, §143B-437.01, (a).
Utility account, §143B-437.01, (b1).
Information resource management commission.
Administrative procedure.
Special provisions, §§150B-38 to 150B-42.
Inspections.
Main street financial incentive fund, §143B-472.35, (j).
Job development investment grant program, §§143B-437.50 to 143B-437.63.
Legislative declaration, §143B-428.
Limitation on grant or loan.
Entity currently in default on loan to department, §143B-431.2.
Loans.
Main street financial incentive fund.
Application for grants and loans, §143B-472.35, (c), (d), (e).
Major industrial projects.
Preparation of proposals.
Authority to contract for, §143B-431, (b1).
Navigation and pilotage commissions transferred to department, §143B-451.
One North Carolina fund, §§143B-437.70 to 143B-437.74.
See ONE NORTH CAROLINA FUND.
Organization, §143B-433.
Planning.
Local planning assistance, §143B-431, (c).
Policy, §143B-428.

COMMERCE DEPARTMENT —Cont'd
Powers, §§143B-430, (a), (b), 143B-431.
Federal programs, §143B-431, (d).
Local planning assistance, §143B-431, (c).
Reports.
Economic development board.
Publication, §143B-435.
Industrial development fund.
Annual report, §143B-437.01, (c).
Utility account, use of funds, §143B-437.01, (c1).
Main street financial incentive fund.
Reporting requirements, §143B-472.35, (h), (i).
One North Carolina fund, §143B-437.74.
Trade jobs for success initiative, §143B-438.17.
Rules and regulations.
Main street financial incentive fund.
Promulgation by department, §143B-472.35, (k).
Rural redevelopment authority, §§143B-437.20 to 143B-437.33.
See RURAL REDEVELOPMENT AUTHORITY.
Science and technology.
See SCIENCE AND TECHNOLOGY.
Seafood industrial park authority, §§113-315.25 to 113-315.39.
See SEAFOOD INDUSTRIAL PARK AUTHORITY.
Secretary.
Head of department, §143B-430, (a).
Powers and duties, §143B-430, (a), (b).
Rules, power to adopt, §143B-430, (c).
Site development funding, §143B-437.02.
Small businesses.
Nonprofit corporations for aiding development of.
Establishment authorized, §143B-431, (b).
Small business ombudsman.
Created in department, purposes, §143B-432.1.
Tax incentives for new and expanding businesses generally, §§105-129.2 to 105-129.13.
See TAX INCENTIVES FOR NEW AND EXPANDING BUSINESSES.
Trade jobs for success initiative.
Components, §143B-438.16, (c).
Established within department, §143B-438.16, (a).
Legislative findings, §143B-438.15, (a).
Policy of state, §143B-438.15, (b).
Purpose, §143B-438.15, (c).
Report, §143B-438.17.
Trade jobs for success fund, §143B-438.16, (b).
Transfers to department.
Divisions and councils of department of natural resources and economic development, §143B-432, (a), (c).
Navigation and pilotage commission, §143B-451.
Subunits of department of natural resources and economic development, §143B-432, (b).
Travel and tourism.
Board, §143B-434.1.
Policy act, §143B-434.2.
Workforce development, §§143B-438.10 to 143B-438.13.
Workforce development commission, §143B-438.10.

COMMERCIAL ABC PERMITS, §18B-1100.

COMMERCIAL BANKING LAW, §§53-1 to 53-208.30.
See BANKS.

COMMERCIAL BRIBERY, §14-353.

COMMERCIAL CODE, §§25-1-101 to 25-11-108.
Acceleration.
Option to accelerate at will, §25-1-208.
Acceptance under reservation of rights, §25-1-207.
Accessions.
Defined, §§25-2A-103, (2), 25-2A-310.
Action.
Defined, §25-1-201, (1).
Enforceability of rights or obligations, §25-1-106.
Aggrieved party.
Defined, §25-1-201, (2).
Agreements.
Defined, §§25-1-201, (3), 25-2-106, (1).
Applicability of act.
Territorial application, §25-1-105.
Bank deposits and collections, §§25-4-101 to 25-4-504.
Account.
Defined, §25-4-104, (a).
Afternoon.
Defined, §25-4-104, (a).
Agents.
Agency status of collection banks, §25-4-201, (a).
Agreement for electronic presentment.
Defined, §25-4-110, (a).
Alteration of instruments.
Customer's duty to discover and report, §25-4-406.
Applicability of article, §25-4-102, (a).
Attachment and garnishment.
When item subject to legal process, §25-4-303, (a).
Banking day.
Defined, §25-4-104, (a).
Branch or separate offices deemed separate bank, §25-4-106.
Burden of proof of loss.
Stop payment order, §25-4-403, (c).
Care.
Certain action constituting ordinary care, §25-4-103, (c).
Caution by depositary and collecting banks.
Security interests.
Accompanying documents and proceeds.
Credit given, §25-4-208, (b).
Certificates of deposit.
Defined, §25-3-104.
Citation of article, §25-4-101.
Clearinghouse.
Defined, §25-4-104, (a).
Effect, §25-4-103, (b).
Collection by depositary and collecting banks, §25-4-105.1.
Action.
When action seasonable, §25-4-202, (b).
Agency status.
Item indorsed "pay any bank," §25-4-201, (b).
Presumption and duration of agency status of collecting banks, §25-4-201, (a).
Provisional status of credits, §25-4-201, (a).
Bills of lading.
Warranties of collecting bank as to documents, §25-7-508.
Charge-back.
Right of charge-back, §25-4-212, (a) to (f).
Delayed, §25-4-108, (a), (b).
Direct return, §25-4-212, (a) to (f).
Documents of title.
Warranties of collecting bank as to documents, §25-7-508.

COMMERCIAL CODE —Cont'd
Bank deposits and collections —Cont'd
Collection by depositary and collecting banks —Cont'd
Duration of agency status of collecting banks, §25-4-201, (a).
Holder in due course.
When bank gives value for purposes of holder in due course, §25-4-209.
Indorsements, missing, §25-4-205.
Insolvency, §25-4-214, (a) to (d).
Instructions.
Effect of instructions, §25-4-203.
Liability for insolvency, neglect, etc., §25-4-202, (c).
Methods of sending and presenting, §25-4-204, (a), (b).
Payment.
Deposit of money.
Availability, §25-4-213, (f).
When deposit becomes final, §25-4-213, (e).
Final payment of item by payor bank, §25-4-213, (a).
Liability of banks, §25-4-213, (d).
Provisional debits and credits.
When provisional debits and credits become final, §25-4-213, (b), (c).
Suspends payment.
Defined, §25-4-104, (a).
When provisional debits and credits become final, §25-4-213, (b), (c).
Preference, §25-4-214, (a) to (d).
Presentment.
By notice of item not payable by, through or at bank, §25-4-210, (1).
Liability of secondary parties, §25-4-210, (b).
Method of sending and presenting, §25-4-204, (a), (b).
Refund.
Right of refund, §25-4-212, (a) to (f).
Responsibility for collection or return, §25-4-202, (a).
Security interests.
Accompanying documents and proceeds, §25-4-208, (a).
Final settlement, §25-4-208, (c).
Sending and presenting.
By notice of item not payable by, through or at bank, §25-4-210, (a).
Liability of secondary parties, §25-4-210, (b).
Direct to payor bank, §25-4-204, (c).
Methods for sending and presenting, §25-4-204, (a), (b).
Settlement, §25-4-211, (a).
Final settlement, §25-4-211, (d).
Midnight deadline, §25-4-211, (c).
Tender, §25-4-211, (b).
Status.
Agency status.
Presumption and duration of agency status of collecting banks, §25-4-201, (a).
Provisional status of credits, §25-4-201, (1).
Time, §25-4-207.
Finality of deposit, provisional debits and credits, §25-4-213.
Transfer between banks, §25-4-206.
Value.
When bank gives value for purposes of holder in due course, §25-4-209.

COMMERCIAL CODE —Cont'd
Bank deposits and collections —Cont'd
Collection by depositary and collecting banks —Cont'd
Warehouse receipts.
Warranties of collecting bank as to receipts, §25-7-508.
Warranties.
Documents of title.
Warranties of collecting bank as to receipts and bills, §25-7-508.
Of customer in collecting bank, §§25-4-207 to 25-4-207.2.
When action seasonable, §25-4-202, (b).
When provisional debits and credits become final, §25-4-213, (b), (c).
Withdrawal.
When certain credits become available for withdrawal, §25-4-213, (e).
Collection of documentary drafts.
Definition of documentary draft, §25-4-104, (a).
Dishonor.
Duty to notify customer of dishonor, §25-4-501.
Referee in case of need, §25-4-503.
Report of reasons for dishonor, §25-4-503.
Handling of documentary drafts, §25-4-501.
"On arrival" drafts.
Presentment, §25-4-502.
Presentment.
Duty to send for presentment, §25-4-501.
"On arrival" drafts, §25-4-502.
Responsibility of presenting bank for documents and goods, §25-4-503.
Privilege of presenting bank to deal with goods, §25-4-504, (a).
Security interest for expenses, §25-4-504, (b).
Referee, §25-4-503.
Responsibility of presenting bank for documents and goods, §25-4-503.
Security interest for expenses, §25-4-504, (b).
Conflict of laws.
Liability of bank, §25-4-102, (b).
Contributory negligence.
Unauthorized signature or alteration, §25-4-406, (c), (d).
Customer.
Defined, §25-4-104, (a).
Damages.
Certain action constituting ordinary care, §25-4-103, (e).
Limitation by agreements, §25-4-103, (a).
Measure of damages, §25-4-103, (e).
Definitions, §§25-4-104, 25-4-105, 25-4-105.1.
Index of definitions, §25-4-104.
Delays, §25-4-108, (a), (b).
Depositary and collecting banks.
Collection by. See within this subheading, "Collection by depositary and collecting banks."
Defined, §25-4-105.
Documentary drafts.
Defined, §25-4-104, (a).
Draft.
Defined, §25-4-104, (a).
Executions.
When item subject to legal process, §25-4-303, (a).
Federal reserve regulations.
Effect, §25-4-103, (b).

COMMERCIAL CODE —Cont'd
Bank deposits and collections —Cont'd
Forgery.
Customer's duty to discover and report, §25-4-406.
Intermediary bank.
Defined, §25-4-105.
Item.
Defined, §25-4-104, (a).
Limitations of actions, §25-4-111.
Negligence.
Unauthorized signature or alteration, §25-4-406, (c), (d).
Payable at bank, §25-4-105.1.
Payable through bank, §25-4-105.1.
Payment.
Properly payable.
Defined, §25-4-104, (a).
Suspends payment.
Defined, §25-4-104, (a).
Payor banks.
Alteration of instruments.
Customer's duty to discover and report unauthorized alteration, §25-4-406.
Attachment and garnishment.
When item subject to legal process, §25-4-303, (a).
Certifying items.
Order in which items may be certified, §25-4-303, (b).
Charging items.
Order in which items may be charged, §25-4-303, (b).
Clearinghouse.
Defined, §25-4-104, (a).
Collection by depositary and collecting banks.
Final payment of item by payor bank, §25-4-213, (a).
Sending direct to payor bank, §25-4-204, (c).
Suspension of payments, §25-4-214, (a) to (d).
Customer relationship.
Customer's duty to discover and report unauthorized signature or alteration, §25-4-406.
Customer's right to stop payment, §25-4-403, (a).
Burden of proof of loss, §25-4-403, (c).
Oral stop payment order, §25-4-403, (b).
Death of customer, §25-4-405, (a), (b).
Controlling provisions, §25-4-405, (c).
Definition of customer, §25-4-104, (a).
Dishonor.
Damages, §25-4-402, (b).
Liability to customer for wrongful dishonor, §25-4-402, (a).
Time for determining account balance, §25-4-402, (c).
Improper payment.
Bank's right to subrogation on improper payment, §25-4-407.
Incompetence of customer, §25-4-405, (a), (b).
Controlling provisions, §25-4-405, (c).
No obligation to pay check more than six months old, §25-4-404.
Stop payment order.
Bank's right to subrogation on improper payment, §25-4-407.
Customer's right to stop payment, §25-4-403, (a).
Oral order, §25-4-403, (b).

COMMERCIAL CODE —Cont'd
Bank deposits and collections —Cont'd
Payor banks —Cont'd
Customer relationship —Cont'd
Subrogation.
Bank's right to subrogation on improper payment, §25-4-407.
When bank may charge customer's account, §25-4-401, (a) to (d).
Customer not liable, §25-4-401, (b).
Wrongful dishonor.
Bank's liability to customer, §25-4-402, (a).
Damages, §25-4-402, (b).
Death of customer, §25-4-405, (a), (b).
Controlling provisions, §25-4-405, (c).
Defined, §25-4-105.
Delays, §25-4-108, (a), (b).
Responsibility for late return of item, §25-4-302, (a).
Defenses, §25-4-302, (b).
Dishonor.
Liability to customer for wrongful dishonor, §25-4-402, (a).
Damages, §25-4-402, (b).
Time of dishonor, §25-4-301, (c).
Executions.
When items subject to legal process, §25-4-303, (a).
Forgery.
Customer's duty to discover and report, §25-4-406.
Incompetence of customer, §25-4-405, (a), (b).
Controlling provisions, §25-4-405, (c).
Late return of item.
Responsibility, §25-4-302, (a).
Defenses, §25-4-302, (b).
Legal process.
When items subject to legal process, §25-4-303, (a).
Notice.
When items subject to notice, §25-4-303, (a).
Order in which items may be charged or certified, §25-4-303, (b).
Payment.
Definition of suspending payment, §25-4-104, (a).
Final payment, §25-4-213, (a).
Improper payment.
Bank's right to subrogation on improper payment, §25-4-407.
No obligation to pay check more than six months old, §25-4-404.
Recovery of payment by return of items, §25-4-301, (b).
Posting.
Deferred posting, §25-4-301, (a).
Recovery of payment by return of items, §25-4-301, (b).
Responsibility for late return of item, §25-4-302, (a).
Defenses, §25-4-302, (b).
Return of items.
Recovery of payment by return of items, §25-4-301, (b).
When item deemed return, §25-4-301, (d).
Setoff.
When items subject to setoff, §25-4-303, (a).
Signature.
Unauthorized signature.
Customer's duty to discover and report, §25-4-406.

COMMERCIAL CODE —Cont'd
Bank deposits and collections —Cont'd
Payor banks —Cont'd
Stopping payment.
Bank's right to subrogation on improper payment, §25-4-407.
Burden of proof of loss, §25-4-403, (c).
Customer's right, §25-4-403, (a).
Duration of order, §25-4-403, (b).
When items subject to stop-order, §25-4-303, (a).
Subrogation.
Right to subrogation on improper payment, §25-4-407.
Suspension of payments, §25-4-214, (a) to (d).
Defined, §25-4-104, (a).
Time of dishonor, §25-4-301, (c).
Unauthorized signature or alteration.
Customer's duty to discover and report, §25-4-406.
When bank may charge customer's account, §25-4-401, (a) to (d).
Customer not liable, §25-4-401, (b).
When items subject to notice, stop-order, legal process or setoff, §25-4-303, (a).
Wrongful dishonor.
Liability to customer, §25-4-402.
Damages, §25-4-402, (b).
Posting.
Deferred posting, §25-4-301, (a).
Presenting banks.
Defined, §25-4-105.
Electronic presentment, §25-4-110, (a).
Presentment notice, §25-4-110, (b), (c).
Presumptions.
Agency status of collecting banks, §25-4-201, (a).
Provisional status of credits, §25-4-201, (a).
Procedure.
Specification or approval of, §25-4-103, (d).
Receipt of items.
Time of receipt, §25-4-107, (a), (b).
Remitting bank.
Defined, §25-4-105.
Secured transactions.
Collecting banks.
Security interest of collecting bank in items, accompanying documents and proceeds, §25-4-208, (a).
Credit given, §25-4-208, (b).
Final settlement, §25-4-208, (c).
Collection of documentary drafts.
Privilege of presenting bank to deal with goods.
Security interest for expenses, §25-4-504, (b).
Setoffs.
When items subject to setoff, §25-4-303, (a).
Settle.
Defined, §25-4-104, (a).
Short title of article, §25-4-101.
Statute of limitations, §25-4-111.
Stopping payment.
Bank's right to subrogation on improper payment, §25-4-407.
Burden of proof of loss, §25-4-403, (c).
Customer's right, §25-4-403, (a).
Duration of order, §25-4-403, (b).
When items subject to stop-order, §25-4-303, (a).
Time.
Afternoon.
Defined, §25-4-104, (a).

COMMERCIAL CODE —Cont'd
Bank deposits and collections —Cont'd
Time —Cont'd
Collection by depositary and collecting banks.
Finality of deposit of money, §25-4-213, (e).
Finality of provisional debits and credits, §25-4-213, (b), (c).
Delays, §25-4-108, (a), (b).
Midnight deadline.
Defined, §25-4-104, (a).
Receipt of items, §25-4-107, (a), (b).
Time of dishonor, §25-4-301, (c).
When action seasonable, §25-4-202, (b).
Unauthorized signature or alteration.
Customer's duty to discover and report, §25-4-406.
Variation of article by agreement, §25-4-103, (a).
When action seasonable, §25-4-202, (b).
Withdrawal.
When certain credits become available for withdrawal, §25-4-213, (e).
Bankruptcy and insolvency.
Definitions, §25-1-201, (22), (23).
Banks and financial institutions.
Branches.
Defined, §25-1-201, (7).
Defined, §25-1-201, (4).
Bearer.
Defined, §25-1-201, (5).
Breach of contract.
Claim or right arising out of breach.
Waiver or renunciation, §25-1-107.
Burden of proof.
Definition of burden of establishing a fact, §25-1-201, (8).
Option to accelerate at will.
Burden of establishing lack of good faith, §25-1-208.
Buyer in ordinary course of business.
Defined, §25-1-201, (9).
Captions.
Section captions are part of chapter, §25-1-109.
Citation.
Short title, §25-1-101.
Commercial paper.
Banks.
Branch or separate offices deemed separate bank, §25-4-106.
Instructions.
Effect of instructions, §25-4-203.
Bearer.
Defined, §25-1-201, (5).
Burden of proof.
Order to stop payment.
Burden of proof of loss, §25-4-403, (c).
Checks.
Bad checks.
Power to transfer title when check dishonored, §25-2-403, (1).
Bank's right to subrogation on improper payment, §25-4-407.
Incompetence of maker except for payment, §25-4-405, (a), (b).
Payment by check, §25-2-511, (3).
Sales.
Power to transfer title when check dishonored, §25-2-403, (1).
Stale check.
No obligation to pay check more than six months old, §25-4-404.

COMMERCIAL CODE —Cont'd
Commercial paper —Cont'd
Checks —Cont'd
Stop payment order.
Relationship between payor bank and customer, §25-4-403.
Definitions.
Delivery, §25-1-201, (14).
Dishonor.
Power to transfer title when check dishonored, §25-2-403, (1).
Holder.
Defined, §25-1-201, (20).
Holder in due course.
Value.
When bank gives value for purposes of holder in due course, §25-4-209.
Honor.
Defined, §25-1-201, (21).
Value.
Defined, §25-1-201, (44).
When bank gives value for purposes of holder in due course, §25-4-209.
Conflicting provisions.
Severability of chapter, §25-1-108.
Conflict of laws.
Parties' powers to choose applicable law, §25-1-105.
Conspicuous.
Defined, §25-1-201, (10).
Construction and interpretation.
Course of dealing, §25-1-205.
Implicit repeal.
Construction against implicit repeal, §25-1-104.
Option to accelerate at will, §25-1-208.
Overseas, §25-2-323, (3).
Reasonable time, §25-1-204.
Seasonably, §25-1-204, (3).
Time, §25-1-204.
Usage of trade, §25-1-205.
Contracts.
Defined, §§25-1-201, (11), 25-2-106, (1).
Obligation of good faith, §25-1-203.
Reservation of rights.
Performance or acceptance under reservation of rights, §25-1-207.
Time.
Fixing reasonable time, §25-1-204.
Course of dealing, §25-1-205.
Creditors.
Defined, §25-1-201, (12).
Subordinated obligations, §25-1-209.
Custom.
Course of dealing and usage of trade, §25-1-205.
Date act effective, §25-10-101.
Definitions, general provisions.
Action, §25-1-201, (1).
Aggrieved party, §25-1-201, (2).
Agreements, §§25-1-201, (3), 25-2-106, (1).
Bank, §25-1-201, (4).
Bearer, §25-1-201, (5).
Bills of lading, §25-1-201, (6).
Branch, §25-1-201, (7).
Burden of establishing a fact, §25-1-201, (8).
Buyer in ordinary course of business, §25-1-201, (9).
Conspicuous, §25-1-201, (10).
Contracts, §§25-1-201, (11), 25-2-106, (1).
Creditors, §25-1-201, (12).
Defendant, §25-1-201, (13).
Delivery, §25-1-201, (14).

COMMERCIAL CODE —Cont'd
Definitions, general provisions —Cont'd
Fault, §25-1-201, (16).
Funds transfers, §25-4A-104.
Creditor process, §25-4A-502.
Executed, §25-4A-301.
Execution dates, §25-4A-301.
Funds-transfer system rule, §25-4A-501.
Other definitions, §25-4A-105.
Payment date, §25-4A-401.
Payment order, §25-4A-103.
Security procedure, §25-4A-201.
Sender.
Authorized and verified payment orders, §25-4A-202.
Fungible, §25-1-201, (17).
Genuine, §25-1-201, (18).
Good faith, §25-1-201, (19).
Holder, §25-1-201, (20).
Honor, §25-1-201, (21).
Insolvency proceedings, §25-1-201, (22).
Insolvent, §25-1-201, (23).
Installment contracts, §25-2-612, (1).
Money, §25-1-201, (24).
Notice, §25-1-201, (25).
Organization, §25-1-201, (28).
Party, §25-1-201, (29).
Person, §25-1-201, (30).
Presumption, §25-1-201, (31).
Purchase, §25-1-201, (32).
Purchaser, §25-1-201, (33).
Remedy, §25-1-201, (34).
Representative, §25-1-201, (35).
Rights, §25-1-201, (36).
Sales, §§25-2-103 to 25-2-106.
Security interest, §25-1-201, (37).
Send, §25-1-201, (38).
Signed, §25-1-201, (39).
Surety, §25-1-201, (40).
Telegram, §25-1-201, (41).
Term, §25-1-201, (42).
Unauthorized, §25-1-201, (43).
Value, §25-1-201, (44).
Warehouse receipt, §25-1-201, (45).
Writing, §25-1-201, (46).
Delivery.
Defined, §25-1-201, (14).
Documents.
Prima facie evidence by third party documents, §25-1-202.
Documents of title, §§25-7-101 to 25-7-603.
Alteration of instruments.
Bills of lading, §25-7-306.
Warehouse receipts, §25-7-208.
Applicability of chapter, §25-7-103.
Attachment of goods covered by a negotiable document, §25-7-602.
Bailee.
Defined, §25-7-102.
Bills of lading.
Altered bills, §25-7-306.
Attachment of goods covered by a negotiable document, §25-7-602.
Care.
Contractual limitation of carrier's liability, §25-7-309, (2).
Duty of care, §25-7-309, (1).
Change of instructions, §25-7-303, (1).
Claims.
Time and manner of presentation, §25-7-309, (3).

COMMERCIAL CODE —Cont'd
Documents of title —Cont'd
Bills of lading —Cont'd
Damages.
Limitation of liability, §25-7-309, (2).
Defined, §25-1-201, (6).
Destination bills, §25-7-305, (1).
Substitute bills, §25-7-305, (2).
Diversion, §25-7-303, (1).
Duty of carrier, §25-7-309, (1).
Handling.
Proper handling, §25-7-301, (1).
In a set, §25-7-304.
Instructions.
Change of instructions, §25-7-303, (1).
Liability for non-receipt or misdescription.
"Said to contain," §25-7-301, (1).
"Shipper's weight, load and count," §25-7-301, (1), (2).
Liability of carrier.
Contractual limitation of liability of carrier, §25-7-309, (2).
Duty of carrier, §25-7-309, (1).
Lien of carrier, §25-7-307, (1), (2).
Enforcement, §25-7-308.
Limitation of actions.
Limitations in bill of lading or tariff, §25-7-309, (1).
Misdescription.
Liability for misdescription, §25-7-301, (5).
Negotiability, §25-7-104, (1).
Negotiation. See within this subheading, "Negotiation."
Non-negotiable bills of lading, §25-7-104, (2).
Non-receipt.
Liability for non-receipt, §25-7-301, (1), (5).
Original terms.
Holding to original terms, §25-7-303, (2).
Overseas shipment.
Form of bill, §25-2-323.
Reconsignment, §25-7-303, (1).
"Said to contain," §25-7-301, (1).
Sets.
Bills of lading in a set, §25-7-304.
"Shipper's weight, load and count," §25-7-301, (1), (3).
Substitute bills, §25-7-305, (2).
Third party documents.
Prima facie evidence, §25-1-202.
Through bills of lading and similar documents, §25-7-302, (1), (2).
Issuers, §25-7-302, (3).
Citation of chapter.
Short title, §25-7-101.
Claims.
Conflicting claims, §25-7-603.
Consignee.
Defined, §25-7-102.
Consignor.
Defined, §25-7-102.
Construction against negative implication, §25-7-105.
Damages.
Limitation of liability in bill of lading, §25-7-309, (2).
Limitation of warehouseman's liability, §25-7-204, (1), (2).
Defeated.
Document of title to goods defeated in certain cases, §25-7-503.

COMMERCIAL CODE —Cont'd
Documents of title —Cont'd
Definitions, §§25-1-201, 25-7-102.
Bills of lading, §25-1-201, (6).
Warehouse receipts, §25-1-201, (45).
Delivery.
Excuse, §25-7-403, (1).
Good faith delivery.
No liability for good faith delivery pursuant to receipt or bill, §25-7-404.
Liens.
Satisfaction before delivery, §25-7-403, (2).
No liability for good faith delivery pursuant to receipt or bill, §25-7-404.
Obligation of warehouseman or carrier to deliver, §25-7-403, (1).
Seller's stoppage of delivery, §25-7-504, (4).
Without indorsement, §25-7-506.
Delivery order.
Defined, §25-7-102.
Destroyed documents, §25-7-601, (1).
Delivery by bailee, §25-7-601, (2).
Due negotiation.
Absence of due negotiation.
Rights acquired in absence, §25-7-504, (1), (2).
Duplicates, §25-7-402.
Evidence.
Prima facie evidence by third party documents, §25-1-202.
Executions.
Lien on goods covered by a negotiable document, §25-7-602.
Fungible goods.
Buyer in the ordinary course of business.
Delivery by warehouseman, §25-7-205.
Goods.
Defined, §25-7-102.
Guaranty.
Indorser not guarantor for other parties, §25-7-505.
Indorsement, §25-7-501, (1).
Compelling indorsement.
Right to compel, §25-7-506.
Delivery to compel indorsement, §25-7-506.
Indorser not guarantor for other parties, §25-7-505.
Negotiation. See within this subheading, "Negotiation."
Power to compel indorsement, §25-7-506.
Requirements of due negotiation, §25-7-501.
Injunctions.
Enjoining negotiations of document, §25-7-602.
Interpleader, §25-7-603.
Determination of conflicting claims, §25-7-603.
Irregularities in issue or conduct of issuer, §25-7-401.
Issuance.
Irregularities in issue, §25-7-401.
Overissue, §25-7-402.
Issuer.
Conduct.
Irregularities in conduct of issuer, §25-7-401.
Defined, §25-7-102.
Irregularities in conduct of issuer, §25-7-401.
Liability.
No liability for good faith delivery pursuant to receipt or bill, §25-7-404.
Liens.
Satisfaction before delivery, §25-7-403, (2).
Warehouseman, §25-7-209, (1).
Enforcement of lien, §25-7-210.

COMMERCIAL CODE —Cont'd
Documents of title —Cont'd
Limitation of actions.
Bill of lading or tariff, §25-7-309, (3).
Warehouse receipt or tariff, §25-7-204, (3).
Lost documents, §25-7-601, (1).
Delivery by bailee, §25-7-601, (2).
Missing documents, §25-7-601, (1).
Delivery by bailee, §25-7-601, (2).
Negative implication.
Construction against, §25-7-105.
Negotiation.
Absence of due negotiation.
Rights acquired in the absence of due negotiation, §25-7-504, (1), (2).
Attachment of goods covered by a negotiable document, §25-7-602.
Contract.
When adequate compliance with commercial contract, §25-7-509.
Defeated.
Document of title to goods defeated in certain cases, §25-7-503.
Delivery.
Seller's stoppage of delivery, §25-7-504, (1).
Without indorsement, §25-7-506.
Diversion.
Change of shipping instructions, §25-7-504, (3).
Effect of diversion, §25-7-504, (3).
Due negotiation.
Rights acquired by due negotiation, §25-7-502, (1), (2).
Rights acquired in the absence of due negotiation, §25-7-504, (1), (2).
Enjoining negotiation of document, §25-7-602.
Form of negotiation, §25-7-501.
Indorsement.
Compelling indorsement, §25-7-506.
Delivery without indorsement, §25-7-506.
Due negotiation, §25-7-501, (1).
Form of negotiation, §25-7-501.
Indorser not guarantor for other parties, §25-7-505.
Non-negotiable document, §25-7-501, (5).
Power to compel, §25-7-506.
Right to compel, §25-7-506.
Negotiability, §25-7-104.
Non-negotiable documents.
Indorsement, §25-7-501, (1), (5).
Warranties, §25-7-507.
Collecting bank.
Warranties of collecting bank as to documents, §25-7-508.
Non-negotiable documents, §25-7-104, (2).
Indorsement, §25-7-501, (1), (5).
Rights acquired by due negotiation, §25-7-502, (1), (2).
Warranties.
Collecting bank, §25-7-508.
Negotiation or transfer of receipt or bill, §25-7-507.
When adequate compliance with commercial contract, §25-7-509.
Obligation of warehouseman or carrier to deliver, §25-7-403, (1).
Overissue, §25-7-402.
Relation of chapter to treaties, statutes, tariffs, etc., §25-7-103.
Sales.
When documents deliverable on acceptance and on payment, §25-2-514.

COMMERCIAL CODE —Cont'd
Documents of title —Cont'd
Secured transactions.
Priority of security interests, §25-9-331.
Short title of chapter, §25-7-101.
Stolen documents, §25-7-601, (1).
Delivery by bailee, §25-7-601, (2).
Storage.
Termination of storage at warehouseman's option, §25-7-206.
Suretyship.
Indorser not guarantor for other parties, §25-7-505.
Tariffs.
Relation of chapter to tariffs, §25-7-103.
Transfer.
Warranties, §25-7-507.
Treaties.
Relation of chapter to treaty, §25-7-103.
United States statutes.
Relation of chapter to statute, §25-7-103.
Warehouseman.
Defined, §25-7-102.
Warehouse receipts.
Agricultural commodities stored under government bond, §25-7-201, (2).
Alcoholic beverages.
Distilled spirits stored under government bond, §25-7-201, (2).
Altered warehouse receipts, §25-7-208.
Contractual limitation of warehouseman's liability, §25-7-204, (4).
Crops.
Storage under government bond, §25-7-201, (2).
Defined, §§25-1-201, (45), 25-7-201, (2).
Distilled spirits.
Storage under government bond, §25-7-201, (2).
Duty of care, §25-7-204, (1).
Forms, §25-7-202, (1).
Fungible goods, §25-7-207, (2).
Title of buyer in ordinary course of business, §25-7-205.
Goods must be kept separate, §§25-7-204, 25-7-207, (1).
Issuance.
Who may issue, §25-7-201, (1).
Liability for non-receipt or misdescription, §25-7-203.
Contractual limitation of warehouseman's liability, §25-7-204, (4).
Lien of warehouseman, §25-7-209, (1), (2).
Enforcement, §25-7-210.
Limitation of actions.
Contractual limitation of warehouseman's liability, §25-7-204, (3), (4).
Misdescription.
Liability for, §25-7-203.
Non-negotiable warehouse receipts, §25-7-104, (2).
Non-receipts.
Liability for, §25-7-203.
Storage.
Under government bond, §25-7-201, (2).
Termination of storage at warehouseman's option, §25-7-206.
Terms.
Essential terms, §25-7-202, (1), (2).
Optional terms, §25-7-202, (3).

COMMERCIAL CODE —Cont'd
Documents of title —Cont'd
Warehouse receipts —Cont'd
Title under warehouse receipt defeated in certain cases, §25-7-205.
Who may issue, §25-7-201, (1).
Warranties.
Collecting banks.
Warranties of collecting bank as to documents, §25-7-508.
Negotiation, §25-7-507.
Duties.
Obligation of good faith, §25-1-203.
Effective date of act, §25-10-101.
Evidence.
Prima facie evidence by third party documents, §25-1-202.
Usage of trade, §25-1-205.
Executors and administrators.
Representative.
Defined, §25-1-201, (35).
Fault.
Defined, §25-1-201, (16).
Funds transfers, §§25-4A-101 to 25-4A-507.
Applicability of article, §25-4A-102.
Exclusion of consumer transactions governed by federal law, §25-4A-108.
Attachment and garnishment.
Creditor process served on receiving bank, §25-4A-502.
Attorneys' fees.
Improper execution or failure to execute payment order, §25-4A-305, (e).
Beneficiary.
Defined, §25-4A-103.
Payment order misdescription, §25-4A-207.
Beneficiary's bank.
Defined, §25-4A-103.
Payment orders.
Misdescription, §25-4A-208.
Obligation to pay and give notice to beneficiary, §25-4A-404.
Payment to beneficiary, §25-4A-405.
Setoff by, §25-4A-502.
Choice of law, §25-4A-507.
Citation of title, §25-4A-101.
Conflict of laws.
Choice of law, §25-4A-507.
Exclusion of consumer transactions governed by federal law, §25-4A-108.
Federal reserve regulations and operating circulars, §25-4A-107.
Consumer transactions governed by federal law.
Exclusion, §25-4A-108.
Creditor process served on receiving bank, §25-4A-502.
Damages.
Improper execution or failure to execute payment order, §25-4A-305, (c).
Obligation of beneficiary's bank to pay and give notice to beneficiary.
Refusal to pay after demand and receipt of notice, §25-4A-404, (a).
Definitions.
Authorized account, §25-4A-105.
Bank, §25-4A-105.
Beneficiary, §25-4A-103.
Beneficiary's bank, §25-4A-103.
Creditor process, §25-4A-502.
Customer, §25-4A-105.
Executed, §25-4A-301.

COMMERCIAL CODE —Cont'd
Funds transfers —Cont'd
Definitions —Cont'd
Execution date, §25-4A-301.
Funds-transfer business day, §25-4A-105.
Funds-transfer system, §25-4A-105.
Funds-transfer system rule, §25-4A-501.
Good faith, §25-4A-105.
Index of definitions, §25-4A-105.
Intermediary bank, §25-4A-104.
Originator, §25-4A-104.
Originator's bank, §25-4A-104.
Payment date, §25-4A-401.
Payment order, §25-4A-103.
Prove, §25-4A-105.
Receiving bank, §25-4A-103.
Security procedure, §25-4A-201.
Sender, §25-4A-103.
Authorized and verified payment orders, §25-4A-202.
Federal reserve regulations and operating circulars, §25-4A-107.
Funds-transfer system rule.
Defined, §25-4A-501.
Effect of, §25-4A-501.
Variation by agreement, §25-4A-501.
Injunctive relief, §25-4A-503.
Interest.
Rate of interest, §25-4A-506.
Intermediary bank.
Defined, §25-4A-104.
Payment order misdescription, §25-4A-208.
Limitation of actions.
Objection to debt of customer's account, §25-4A-505.
Notice.
Cancellation and amendment of payment orders, §25-4A-211.
Payment orders.
Obligation of beneficiary's bank to give notice to beneficiary, §25-4A-404.
Rejection of payment order, §25-4A-210.
Payment orders.
Acceptance, §25-4A-209.
Amendment, §25-4A-211.
Authorized payment orders, §25-4A-202.
Cancellation, §25-4A-211.
Cut-off time, §25-4A-106.
Defined, §25-4A-103.
Discharge of underlying obligation, §25-4A-406.
Erroneous payment orders, §25-4A-205.
Execution by receiving bank.
Erroneous execution, §25-4A-303.
Duty of sender to report, §25-4A-304.
"Executed" defined, §25-4A-301.
"Execution date" defined, §25-4A-301.
Failure to execute.
Liability for, §25-4A-305.
Improper execution.
Liability for, §25-4A-305.
Late execution.
Liability for, §25-4A-305.
Obligations of receiving bank, §25-4A-302.
Instruction to make more than one payment to beneficiary.
Instruction separate payment order, §25-4A-103, (b).
Issuance, §25-4A-103, (c).
Misdescription.
Beneficiary, §25-4A-207.
Beneficiary's bank, §25-4A-208.

COMMERCIAL CODE —Cont'd
Funds transfers —Cont'd
Payment orders —Cont'd
Misdescription —Cont'd
Intermediary bank, §25-4A-208.
Objection to debit of customer's account.
Preclusion of objection, §25-4A-505.
Obligation of beneficiary's bank, §25-4A-404.
Obligation of sender to pay receiving bank, §25-4A-402.
Order in which payment orders may be charged to account, §25-4A-504.
Order of withdrawals from account, §25-4A-504.
Payment by beneficiary's bank to beneficiary, §25-4A-405.
Payment by originator to beneficiary, §25-4A-406.
Payment by sender to receiving bank, §25-4A-403.
Payment date.
Defined, §25-4A-401.
Preclusion of objection to debit of customer's account, §25-4A-505.
Rejection, §25-4A-210.
Liability and duty of receiving bank regarding unaccepted payment order, §25-4A-212.
Security procedure.
Commercial reasonableness, §25-4A-202, (c).
Defined, §25-4A-201.
Time of acceptance, §25-4A-209.
Time received, §25-4A-106.
Transmission through communications system, §25-4A-206.
Transmission through funds-transfer system, §25-4A-206.
Unauthorized payment orders.
Duty of customer to report, §25-4A-204.
Refund of payment, §25-4A-204.
Verified payment orders, §25-4A-202.
Unenforceability of, §25-4A-203.
Refund of unauthorized payment order, §25-4A-204.
Scope of article, §25-4A-102.
Exclusion of consumer transactions governed by federal law, §25-4A-108.
Service of process.
Creditor process on receiving bank, §25-4A-502.
Setoff by beneficiary's bank, §25-4A-502.
Short title, §25-4A-101.
Title of article, §25-4A-101.
Fungible.
Defined, §25-1-201, (17).
Gender.
Masculine includes feminine and neuter, §25-1-102.
General repealing provision, §25-10-103.
Genuine.
Defined, §25-1-201, (18).
Global TransPark authority.
Bond issues.
Status of bonds and notes under code, §63A-17.
Good faith.
Defined, §25-2-103, (1).
Exercising option to accelerate, §25-1-208.
Holder.
Defined, §25-1-201, (20).
Honor.
Defined, §25-1-201, (21).
Indorsements.
Unauthorized indorsements.
Defined, §25-1-201, (43).

COMMERCIAL CODE —Cont'd
Insurance.
Policy or certificate as prima facie evidence, §25-1-202.
Investment securities, §§25-8-101 to 25-8-511.
Acquisition of security, asset or interest therein, §25-8-104.
Generally, §25-8-104, (a).
Satisfying condition of transfer or delivery, §25-8-104, (d).
Security entitlement, §§25-8-104, (b), (c).
Applicability of provisions, §25-8-110.
Assurance that indorsement or instruction is effective, §25-8-402.
Additional assurance, §25-8-402, (b).
Appropriate evidence of appointment or incumbency.
Defined, §25-8-402, (d).
Generally, §25-8-402, (a).
Guarantee of the signature, defined, §25-8-402, (c).
Bona fide purchasers.
Enforcement of completed or altered instrument, §25-8-206.
Choice of law, §25-8-110.
Citation of chapter, §25-8-101.
Clearing corporation rules, §25-8-111.
Completion of instrument.
Enforceable only according to its original terms, §25-8-206, (b).
Instrument contains all needed signatures, §25-8-206, (a).
Control, §25-8-106.
Bearer form certificated securities, §25-8-106, (a).
Registered form certificated securities, §25-8-106, (b).
Required, §25-8-106, (g).
Satisfaction of purchaser, §25-8-106, (f).
Security entitlements, §25-8-106, (d), (e).
Uncertificated securities, §25-8-106, (c).
Creditor's legal process, §25-8-112.
Certificated securities, §25-8-112, (a).
Debtor is the owner of, §25-8-112, (e).
In possession of secured party, §25-8-112, (d).
Generally, §25-8-112, (a).
Security entitlements, §25-8-112, (c).
Uncertificated securities, §25-8-112, (b).
Defenses, §§25-8-202, 25-8-203.
Additional issuer's defenses, §25-8-202, (d).
Applicability of provisions, §25-8-202, (e).
Entitlement holder, §25-8-202.
Issuer asserts security is not valid, §25-8-202, (b).
Lack of genuineness, §25-8-202, (c).
Terms of certificated securities, §25-8-202, (a).
Definitions, §25-8-102.
Index of definitions, §25-8-102.
Investment company security, §25-8-103.
Issuer's jurisdiction, §25-8-110.
Determination of security or financial asset, §25-8-103.
Application of provisions, §25-8-103, (d).
Clearing corporation, §25-8-103, (e).
Commodity contract, §25-8-103, (f).
Investment company security, defined, §25-8-103, (b).
Partnership or limited liability company, §25-8-103, (c).
Share of corporation or company, §25-8-103, (a).

COMMERCIAL CODE —Cont'd
Investment securities —Cont'd
Effectiveness of indorsement, instruction or entitlement.
Appropriate person, defined, §25-8-107, (a).
Change of capacity, §25-8-107, (d).
Change of circumstances, §25-8-107, (e).
Conditions for being appropriate, §25-8-107, (b).
Additional considerations, §25-8-107, (c).
Entitlements.
Effectiveness, §25-8-107.
Evidentiary rules concerning certificated securities, §25-8-114.
Indorsement.
Effectiveness, §25-8-107.
Instructions.
Effectiveness, §25-8-107.
Intermediary as purchaser for value, §25-8-116.
Issue and issuer.
Assurance that indorsement or instruction is effective, §25-8-402.
Demand that issuer not register transfer, §25-8-403.
Duty of issuer to register transfer, §25-8-401.
Effect of unauthorized signature, §§25-8-103, 25-8-205.
Lien of issuer, §25-8-103.
Notice.
Notice of defect or defense, §25-8-202, (4).
Staleness as notice of defects or defenses, §25-8-203, (1).
Calls which have been revoked, §25-8-203, (2).
Overissue, §25-8-104, (1).
Effect, §25-8-104, (1).
Owners.
Registered owners.
Effect of article on liability, §25-8-207, (7).
Rights of issuer with respect to registered owners, §25-8-207, (1).
Uncertificated security, §25-8-207, (2), (3).
Registered owners.
Effect of article on liability
Rights of issuer with respect to registered owners, §25-8-207, (a).
Interpretation of provisions, §25-8-207, (b).
Replacement of lost, destroyed or wrongfully taken security certificate, §25-8-405.
Signature.
Effect of signature authenticating trustee, registrar or transfer agent, §25-8-208.
Transfer.
Effect of issuer's restrictions on transfer, §25-8-204.
Effect of signature authenticating trustee, registrar or transfer agent, §25-8-208.
Warranties.
Effect of signature authenticating trustee, registrar or transfer agent, §25-8-208.
Wrongful registration, §25-8-404.
Issuer, §25-8-201.
Generally, §25-8-201, (a).
Guarantors, §25-8-201, (b).
Jurisdiction, §25-8-110, (a), (d).
Transfers, §25-8-201, (c).
Issuer's liens, §25-8-209.
Liability to adverse claimant, §25-8-115.
Lost, destroyed or wrongfully taken security certificates, §25-8-405.
Authenticating trustee, transfer agent and registrar, §25-8-407.

COMMERCIAL CODE —Cont'd
Investment securities —Cont'd
Lost, destroyed or wrongfully taken security certificates —Cont'd
Obligation to notify issuer, §25-8-406.
Notice of adverse claim, §25-8-105.
Events which do constitute notice, §25-8-105, (d).
Events which do not constitute notice, §25-8-105, (c).
Filing of a financial statement, §25-8-105, (e).
Generally, §25-8-105, (a).
Transfer of financial asset or interest therein, §25-8-105, (b).
Overissue, §25-8-210.
Application of provisions, §25-8-210, (b).
Compelling purchase, §25-8-210, (c).
Generally, §25-8-210, (a).
Recovery of price, §25-8-210, (d).
Registration.
Demand that issuer not register transfer, §25-8-403.
Generally, §25-8-403, (a).
Liability, §25-8-403, (d), (e).
Notice, §25-8-403, (b).
Withholding of registration, §§25-8-403, (b), (c).
Duty of issuer to register transfer, §25-8-401.
Generally, §25-8-401, (a).
Liability, §25-8-401, (b).
Effect of signature authenticating trustee, registrar or transfer agent, §25-8-208.
Wrongful registration, §25-8-404.
Liability, §25-8-404.
Effective indorsement or instruction, §25-8-404, (c).
Restitution, §25-8-404, (b).
Replacement of lost, destroyed or wrongfully taken security certificate, §25-8-405.
Issuance of new certificate, §25-8-405, (a).
Liability, §25-8-405, (b).
Secured transactions.
Priority of security interests, §25-9-331.
Securities intermediary.
Duty to change entitlement holder's position, §25-8-508.
Duty to comply with entitlement order, §25-8-507.
Duty to exercise rights as directed by entitlement holder, §25-8-506.
Duty to maintain financial asset, §25-8-504.
Duty with respect to payments and distributions, §25-8-505.
Financial asset held by.
Property interest of entitlement holder in, §25-8-503.
Jurisdiction, §25-8-110, (b), (e), (f).
Securities account, defined, §25-8-501.
Specification of duties by other statute or regulation, §25-8-509.
Security entitlements.
Account, §25-8-501.
Assertion of adverse claim against entitlement holder, §25-8-502.
Securities intermediary, §§25-8-503 to 25-8-509.
Short title of chapter, §25-8-101.
Signatures.
Effect of signature authenticating trustee, registrar or transfer agent, §25-8-208.
Effect of unauthorized signature, §25-8-205.
Statute of frauds, §25-8-113.

COMMERCIAL CODE —Cont'd
Investment securities —Cont'd
Transfer.
Effect of signature authenticating trustee, registrar or transfer agent, §25-8-208.
Transfer of securities.
Delivery, §25-8-301.
Certificated securities, §25-8-301, (a).
Uncertificated securities, §25-8-301, (b).
Effect of guaranteeing signature, indorsement or instruction, §25-8-306.
Breach of warranties, §25-8-306, (h).
Indorser of security certificate, §25-8-306, (a).
Originator of an instruction, §25-8-306, (b), (c).
Rightfulness of transfer, §25-8-306, (d) to (f).
Special guarantee, §25-8-306, (g).
Indorsement, §25-8-304.
Bearer form, §25-8-304, (e).
Blank or special, §25-8-304, (a).
Delivery, §25-8-304.
Effect of guaranteeing, §25-8-306.
Obligations assumed, §25-8-304, (f).
Protected purchasers, §25-8-304, (d).
Separately transferable units, §25-8-304, (b).
Instruction, §25-8-305.
Effect of guaranteeing, §25-8-306.
Incomplete, §25-8-305, (a).
Obligations assumed, §25-8-305, (b).
Protected purchaser, §25-8-303.
Defined, §25-8-303, (a).
Interest free of adverse claim, §25-8-303, (b).
Purchaser's right to requisites for registration of transfer, §25-8-307.
Rights of purchaser, §25-8-302.
Generally, §25-8-302, (a).
Limited interests, §25-8-302, (b).
Previous holder, §25-8-302, (c).
Signature.
Effect of guaranteeing, §25-8-306.
Warranties in authentication.
Additional assumptions of responsibility, §25-8-208, (b).
Effect of signature authenticating trustee, registrar or transfer agent, §25-8-208.
Person signing as authenticator, §25-8-208, (a).
Warranties in direct holding, §25-8-108.
Agents, §25-8-108, (g).
Brokers, §25-8-108, (i).
Generally, §25-8-108, (a).
Indorsements.
Effectiveness, §25-8-108, (e).
Security certificate, §25-8-108, (d).
Person who originates transfer, §25-8-108, (b).
Presenting certificated security for registration, transfer, payment or exchange, §25-8-108, (f).
Redelivery, §25-8-108, (h).
Uncertificated securities, §25-8-108, (c).
Warranties in indirect holding, §25-8-109.
Delivering security certificate, §25-8-109, (b).
Entitlement holders, §25-8-109, (c).
Generally, §25-8-109, (a).
Uncertificated security credited to securities account, §25-8-109, (b).
Where security certificate located, §25-8-110, (c).
Leases, §§25-2A-101 to 25-2A-532.
Acceleration.
Option to accelerate at will, §25-2A-109.
Acceptance of goods, §25-2A-515.
Accessions.
Lessor's and lessee's rights when goods become accessions, §25-2A-310.

COMMERCIAL CODE —Cont'd
Leases —Cont'd
Acceptance of goods —Cont'd
Burden of establishing default after acceptance, §25-2A-516.
Damages.
Lessor's damages for nonacceptance, §25-2A-528.
Effect, §25-2A-516.
Nonconforming goods or delivery of goods, §25-2A-509.
Notice of default, §25-2A-516.
Revocation of acceptance, §25-2A-517.
Damages, §25-2A-519.
Justifiable revocation, §25-2A-517.
Lessee's rights and remedies, §25-2A-508, (5).
Wrongful revocation, §25-2A-523.
Accessions.
Defined, §§25-2A-103, (2), 25-2A-310.
Lessor's and lessee's rights.
When goods become accessions, §25-2A-310.
Adequate assurance of performance, §25-2A-401.
Alienability of interest.
Lessor's residual interest in goods, §25-2A-303.
Party's interest under lease contract, §25-2A-303.
Animals.
Unborn young.
Definition of "goods," §25-2A-103, (1).
Identification, §25-2A-217.
Anticipatory repudiation, §25-2A-402.
Retraction, §25-2A-403.
Applicability of article.
Certificates of title.
Territorial application of article to goods covered by certificates, §25-2A-105.
Leases subject to other statutes, §25-2A-104.
Scope, §25-2A-102.
Assignments, §25-2A-303.
Attorneys' fees.
Unconscionable lease contracts or clauses, §25-2A-108.
Bankruptcy and insolvency.
Lessee's rights to goods on lessor's insolvency, §25-2A-522.
Burden of proof.
Acceptance of goods.
Establishing default after acceptance, §25-2A-516.
Cancellation.
Defined, §25-2A-103.
Effect on rights and remedies, §25-2A-505, (1), (3).
Lessee's remedies, §25-2A-508, (1).
Lessor's remedies, §25-2A-523.
Casualty to identified goods, §25-2A-221.
Choice of applicable law and judicial forum.
Limitation on power of parties to consumer lease, §25-2A-106.
Citation of article, §25-2A-101.
Claims.
Limitation of actions, §25-2A-506.
Notice of claim to person answerable over, §25-2A-516.
Rent.
Action by lessor, §25-2A-529.
Third parties.
Standing to sue for injury to goods, §25-2A-531.
Waiver or renunciation, §25-2A-107.

COMMERCIAL CODE —Cont'd
Leases —Cont'd
Conflict of laws.
Leases subject to other statutes, §25-2A-104.
Limitation on power of parties to choose applicable law and judicial forum, §25-2A-106.
Construction of lease agreements.
Course of performance, §25-2A-207.
Practical construction, §25-2A-207.
Consumer leases.
Choice of judicial forum, §25-2A-106.
Defined, §25-2A-103.
Option to accelerate at will, §25-2A-109, (2).
Unconscionability, §25-2A-108, (2).
Course of dealing.
Course of performance control, §25-2A-207, (2).
Explaining or supplementing terms, §25-2A-202, (a).
Implied warranties may arise from, §25-2A-212, (3).
Course of performance.
Explaining or supplementing terms, §25-2A-202, (a).
Cover by lessor, §25-2A-518.
Creditors' special rights, §25-2A-308.
Damages.
Acceptance of goods.
Nonacceptance.
Lessor's damages, §25-2A-528.
Consequential damages, §25-2A-520.
Limiting, altering or excluding, §25-2A-503, (3).
Cover by lessor.
Effect, §25-2A-518.
Incidental damages, §25-2A-520.
Lessor's damages, §25-2A-530.
Lessee's incidental and consequential damages.
Generally, §25-2A-520.
Lessee's remedies for default by lessor, §25-2A-508, (1), (4).
Lessor's damages.
Generally, §25-2A-523.
Incidental damages, §25-2A-530.
Nonacceptance or repudiation by lessee, §25-2A-528.
Liquidation, §25-2A-504.
Market rent.
Proof, §25-2A-507.
Nondelivery of goods, §25-2A-519.
Rejection of goods, §25-2A-519.
Repudiation by lessee.
Lessor's damages, §25-2A-528.
Repudiation by lessor, §25-2A-519.
Revocation of acceptance of goods, §25-2A-519.
Default.
Anticipatory repudiation, §25-2A-402.
Retraction, §25-2A-403.
Cover.
Right of lessor, §25-2A-518.
Installment lease contracts.
Lessee's rights and remedies, §25-2A-508.
Rejection and default, §25-2A-510.
Limitation of actions, §25-2A-506.
Modification or impairment, §25-2A-503.
Notice, §§25-2A-502, 25-2A-516.
Procedure generally, §25-2A-501.
Replevin of goods, §§25-2A-508, (2), 25-2A-521.
Rights and remedies.
Default by lessee.
Identification of goods to lease contract, §25-2A-524.

COMMERCIAL CODE —Cont'd
Leases —Cont'd
Default —Cont'd
Rights and remedies —Cont'd
Default by lessee —Cont'd
Rent action by lessor, §25-2A-529.
Default by lessor.
Cover, §25-2A-518.
Lessee's rights and remedies generally, §25-2A-508.
Nonconforming goods or delivery of goods, §§25-2A-509, 25-2A-510.
Replevin of goods, §§25-2A-508, (2), 25-2A-521.
Specific performance, §§25-2A-508, (2), 25-2A-521.
Substitute goods, §25-2A-518.
Replevy of goods, §§25-2A-508, (2), 25-2A-521.
Specific performance, §§25-2A-508, (2), 25-2A-521.
Waiver or renunciation of rights after default, §25-2A-107.
Risk of loss.
Effect of default on risk, §25-2A-220.
Transfers made event of default, §25-2A-303.
Defenses.
Unconscionability, §25-2A-108, (3).
Definitions, §25-2A-103.
Accessions, §25-2A-310.
At will.
Option to accelerate at will, §25-2A-109, (1).
Creation of a security interest, §25-2A-303, (1).
Fixtures, §§25-2A-103, (2), 25-2A-309.
Index of definitions, §25-2A-103, (2), (3).
When he deems himself insecure.
Option to accelerate at will, §25-2A-109, (1).
Delay or nondelivery.
Excused performance, §25-2A-405.
Procedure on excused performance, §25-2A-406.
Delegation of performance, §25-2A-303.
Enforcement of lease contract, §25-2A-301.
Evidence.
Extrinsic evidence, §25-2A-202.
Proof of market rent, §25-2A-507.
Unconscionability.
Parties afforded opportunity to present, §25-2A-108, (3).
Excused performance, §25-2A-405.
Procedure on excused performance, §25-2A-406.
Express warranties.
Displacement of inconsistent implied warranties, §25-2A-215, (c).
Generally, §25-2A-210.
Third-party beneficiaries, §25-2A-216.
Extrinsic evidence, §25-2A-202.
Final written expression, §25-2A-202.
Finance leases.
Defined, §25-2A-103, (1).
Effect of acceptance, §25-2A-516, (2).
Irrevocable promises, §25-2A-407.
Lessee under finance lease as beneficiary of supply contract, §25-2A-209.
Losses.
Casualty to identified goods, §25-2A-221.
Risk of loss, §25-2A-219.
Notice of delay or nondelivery, §25-2A-405, (c).
Supply contracts.
Lessee under finance lease as beneficiary, §25-2A-209.

COMMERCIAL CODE —Cont'd
Leases —Cont'd
Finance leases —Cont'd
Warranties.
Implied warranty of fitness for particular purpose, §25-2A-213.
Implied warranty of merchantability, §25-2A-212.
Warranty against infringement, §25-2A-211.
Firm offers, §25-2A-205.
Fitness for particular purpose.
Implied warranties, §25-2A-213.
Exclusion or modification, §25-2A-214, (2).
Express warranty not to displace inconsistent warranty for fitness, §25-2A-215, (c).
Fixtures.
Defined, §§25-2A-103, (2), 25-2A-309.
Lessor's and lessee's rights.
When goods become fixtures, §25-2A-309.
Formation.
Firm offers, §25-2A-205.
Generally, §25-2A-204.
Offer and acceptance.
Firm offers, §25-2A-205.
Generally, §25-2A-206.
Fraud.
Effect on rights and remedies, §25-2A-505, (4).
Fraudulent transfers.
Special rights of creditors, §25-2A-308.
Identification of goods, §25-2A-217.
Casualty to identified goods, §25-2A-221.
Insurable interest in existing goods.
Vesting in lessee, §25-2A-218.
Lessor's right to identify goods upon lessee's default, §25-2A-524.
Implied warranties.
Exclusion or modification, §25-2A-214, (2), (3).
Express warranties to displace inconsistent implied warranty, §25-2A-215, (c).
Fitness for particular purpose, §25-2A-213.
Merchantability, §25-2A-212.
Third-party beneficiaries, §25-2A-216.
Infringement.
Warranty against, §25-2A-211.
Warranty against exclusion or modification, §25-2A-214, (4).
Insecurity.
Adequate assurance of performance, §25-2A-401.
Insolvency of lessor.
Lessee's rights to goods, §25-2A-522.
Installment lease contracts.
Default.
Lessee's rights and remedies, §25-2A-508.
Rejection and default, §25-2A-510.
Defined, §25-2A-103, (1).
Insurance, §25-2A-218.
Interference with goods.
Warranty against interference, §25-2A-211.
Exclusion or modification, §25-2A-214, (4).
Irrevocable promises, §25-2A-407.
Liens.
Defined, §25-2A-103, (1).
Priority of certain liens arising by operation of law, §25-2A-306.
Priority of liens arising by attachment or levy on, security interests in and other claims to goods, §25-2A-307.
Limitation of actions.
Action for default, §25-2A-506.

COMMERCIAL CODE —Cont'd
Leases —Cont'd
Losses.
Casualty to identified goods, §25-2A-221.
Risk of loss, §25-2A-219.
Effect of default, §25-2A-220.
Market rent.
Proof, §25-2A-507.
Merchantability.
Implied warranties, §25-2A-212.
Exclusion or modification, §25-2A-214, (2).
Merchant lessees.
Defined, §25-2A-103, (1).
Rightfully rejected goods.
Duties, §25-2A-511.
Modification, §25-2A-208.
Notice.
Claim or litigation to person answerable over, §25-2A-516.
Cure by lessor of improper tender or delivery, §25-2A-513.
Default, §§25-2A-502, 25-2A-516.
Delay or nondelivery.
Termination or modification of lease, §25-2A-406, (1).
Excused performance, §25-2A-405.
Revocation of accepted goods, §25-2A-517.
Objections to goods.
Part acceptance of entire unit, §25-2A-515, (2).
Waiver of lessee's objections, §25-2A-514.
Offer and acceptance.
Firm offers, §25-2A-205.
Generally, §25-2A-206.
Parol evidence, §25-2A-202.
Payment or performance.
Adequate assurance of performance, §25-2A-401.
Course of performance.
Construction of lease agreements, §25-2A-207.
Delegation of performance, §25-2A-303.
Excused performance, §25-2A-405.
Procedure on excused performance, §25-2A-406.
Insecurity.
Adequate assurance of performance, §25-2A-401.
Option to accelerate at will, §25-2A-109, (1).
Substituted performance, §25-2A-404.
Possession of goods, §25-2A-302.
Priorities.
Liens.
Certain liens arising by operation of law, §25-2A-306.
Liens arising by attachment or levy on, security interests in and other claims to goods, §25-2A-307.
Promises.
Irrevocable promises, §25-2A-407.
Rent.
Action by lessor for rent, §25-2A-529.
Proof of market rent, §25-2A-507.
Replevin, §§25-2A-508, (2), 25-2A-521.
Repudiation.
Anticipatory repudiation, §25-2A-402.
Retraction, §25-2A-403.
Damages.
Lessee's damages, §25-2A-519.
Lessor's damages, §25-2A-528.
Insecurity.
Failure to provide adequate assurance of performance, §25-2A-401, (3).

COMMERCIAL CODE —Cont'd
Leases —Cont'd
Repudiation —Cont'd
Lessee's rights and remedies.
Damages for repudiation, §25-2A-519.
Lessor's remedies, §25-2A-523.
Rescission, §25-2A-208.
Effect on rights and remedies, §25-2A-505, (3), (5).
Residual interest of lessor.
Lessor's rights to, §25-2A-532.
Restitution to lessee.
Lessor justifiably withholding or stopping delivery, §25-2A-504, (3), (4).
Retraction of anticipatory repudiation, §25-2A-403.
Rights and remedies.
Default by lessee.
Identification of goods to lease contract, §25-2A-524.
Lessor's remedies generally, §25-2A-523.
Rent.
Action by lessor, §25-2A-529.
Residual interest of lessor.
Lessor's rights to, §25-2A-532.
Default by lessor.
Lessee's rights and remedies generally, §25-2A-508.
Nonconforming goods or delivery of goods, §§25-2A-509, 25-2A-510.
Replevin of goods, §25-2A-508, (2).
Specific performance, §25-2A-508, (2).
Goods.
Lessor's right to dispose of goods, §25-2A-527.
Lessor's right to possession of goods, §25-2A-525.
Installment lease contracts.
Lessee's rights and remedies, §25-2A-508.
Lessor's right to dispose of goods, §25-2A-527.
Lessor's right to possession of goods, §25-2A-525.
Liquidation of damages, §25-2A-504.
Modification or impairment, §25-2A-503.
Risk of loss, §25-2A-219.
Effect of default, §25-2A-220.
Sale of goods by lessee, §25-2A-305.
Scope of article, §25-2A-102.
Seals.
Inoperative to render lease a sealed instrument, §25-2A-203.
Secured transactions.
Rejected goods, buyer's security interest.
Applicability of article, §25-9-110.
Security interests arising under provisions, §25-9-110.
Shipment and delivery.
Acceptance of goods, §25-2A-515.
Accessions.
Lessor's and lessee's rights when goods become accessions, §25-2A-310.
Burden of establishing default after acceptance, §25-2A-516.
Damages.
Lessor's damages for nonacceptance, §25-2A-528.
Effect, §25-2A-516.
Nonconforming goods or delivery, §25-2A-509.
Notice of default, §25-2A-516.
Revocation of acceptance, §25-2A-517.
Damages, §25-2A-519.

COMMERCIAL CODE —Cont'd
Leases —Cont'd
Shipment and delivery —Cont'd
Acceptance of goods —Cont'd
Revocation of acceptance —Cont'd
Justifiable revocation, §§25-2A-508, (5), 25-2A-517.
Wrongful revocation, §25-2A-523.
Casualty to identified goods, §25-2A-221.
Failure to deliver goods.
Lessee's rights and remedies, §25-2A-508.
Identification of goods, §25-2A-217.
Improper tender or delivery.
Burden of establishing default after acceptance of goods, §25-2A-516.
Cure by lessor, §25-2A-513.
Lessee's rights.
Installment lease contracts, §25-2A-510.
Notice of default after acceptance of goods, §25-2A-516.
Objection by lessee.
Waiver, §25-2A-514.
Notice of default.
Accepted goods, §25-2A-516.
Rejection of goods.
Accepted goods.
Rejection precluded, §25-2A-516.
Cure by lessor, §25-2A-513.
Damages, §25-2A-519.
Installment lease contracts, §25-2A-510.
Replacement of rejected goods.
Cure by lessor, §25-2A-513.
Rightfully rejected goods, §25-2A-509.
Lessee's duties generally, §25-2A-512.
Lessee's rights and remedies, §25-2A-508, (5).
Merchant lessee's duties, §25-2A-511.
Wrongfully rejected goods.
Lessor's remedies, §25-2A-523.
Revocation of acceptance of goods, §25-2A-517.
Damages, §25-2A-519.
Justifiable revocation, §25-2A-517.
Lessee's rights and remedies, §25-2A-508, (5).
Wrongful revocation, §25-2A-523.
Stoppage of delivery.
Failure of agreed means or manner of payment, §25-2A-404.
Subsequent lease of goods by lessor, §25-2A-304.
Withholding delivery.
Failure of agreed means or manner of payment, §25-2A-404.
Special rights of creditors, §25-2A-308.
Specific performance, §§25-2A-508, (2), 25-2A-521.
Statute of frauds, §25-2A-201.
Statute of limitations.
Action for default, §25-2A-506.
Stoppage of delivery.
Failure of agreed means or manner of payment, §25-2A-404, (2).
Fraud by lessee.
Stoppage of delivery of goods, §§25-2A-523, 25-2A-526.
Sublease by lessee, §25-2A-305.
Subsequent lease of goods by lessor, §25-2A-304.
Substituted performance, §25-2A-404.
Substitute goods, §25-2A-518.
Cover by lessor, §25-2A-518.
Supply contracts.
Beneficiaries.
Lessee under finance lease, §25-2A-209.
Defined, §25-2A-103, (1).

COMMERCIAL CODE —Cont'd
Leases —Cont'd
Termination.
Effect on rights and remedies, §25-2A-505, (2).
Territorial application of article.
Goods covered by certificate of title, §25-2A-105.
Third parties.
Standing to sue for injury to goods, §25-2A-531.
Warranties.
Third-party beneficiaries, §25-2A-216.
Title of article.
Short title, §25-2A-101.
Title to goods, §25-2A-302.
Infringement.
Warranty against, §25-2A-211.
Subsequent lease of goods by lessor, §25-2A-304.
Unconscionability, §25-2A-108.
Usage of trade.
Course of dealing control, §25-2A-207, (2).
Explaining or supplementing terms, §25-2A-202, (a).
Implied warranties may arise from, §25-2A-212, (3).
Waiver.
Claims, rights after default or breach of warranty, §25-2A-107.
Course of performance relevant to show waiver or modification of term, §25-2A-207, (3).
Generally, §25-2A-208.
Objections by lessee to goods, §25-2A-514.
Warranties.
Breach of warranty.
Damages, §§25-2A-508, (4), 25-2A-519.
Notice of claim or litigation answerable over, §25-2A-516.
Waiver or renunciation of rights after breach, §25-2A-107.
Cumulation and conflict, §25-2A-215.
Damages.
Breach of warranty, §§25-2A-508, (4), 25-2A-519.
Exclusion, §25-2A-214.
Express warranties.
Displacement of inconsistent implied warranties, §25-2A-215, (c).
Generally, §25-2A-210.
Third-party beneficiaries, §25-2A-216.
Extension of benefit of suppliers' warranties to lessee, §25-2A-209, (2).
Fitness for particular purpose.
Implied warranties, §25-2A-213.
Exclusion or modification, §25-2A-214, (2).
Express warranty not to displace inconsistent warranty for fitness, §25-2A-215, (c).
Implied warranties.
Exclusion or modification, §25-2A-214, (2), (3).
Express warranties to displace inconsistent implied warranty, §25-2A-215, (c).
Fitness for particular purpose, §25-2A-213.
Merchantability, §25-2A-212.
Third-party beneficiaries, §25-2A-216.
Infringement.
Warranty against, §25-2A-211.
Exclusion or modification, §25-2A-214, (4).
Interference with goods.
Warranty against, §25-2A-211.
Exclusion or modification, §25-2A-214, (4).
Merchantability.
Implied warranties, §25-2A-212.
Exclusion or modification, §25-2A-214, (2).
Modification, §25-2A-214.

COMMERCIAL CODE —Cont'd
Leases —Cont'd
Warranties —Cont'd
Statute of limitation for breach, §25-2A-506.
Third-party beneficiaries, §25-2A-216.
Letters of credit, §§25-5-101 to 25-5-117.
Advisers.
Breach of obligation, remedies, §25-5-111, (c).
Defined, §25-5-102, (a).
Rights and obligations, §25-5-107, (c).
Agreements to vary terms of article, §25-5-103, (c).
Amendment, §25-5-106, (b).
Anticipatory repudiation.
Remedy, §25-5-111, (a).
Applicability of article, §25-5-103, (a).
Applicants.
Reimbursement of issuer.
Subrogation of rights, §25-5-117, (b).
Assignment of proceeds, §25-5-114.
Beneficiaries right to assign, §25-5-114, (b).
Issuer's consent to assignment, §25-5-114, (c).
Unreasonably withholding, §25-5-114, (d).
Nominated person's consent to assignment, §25-5-114, (c).
Unreasonably withholding, §25-5-114, (d).
Nominated person's rights, §25-5-114, (e).
Proceeds of a letter of credit defined, §25-5-114, (a).
Security interests, rights, §25-5-114, (f).
Transferee beneficiaries.
Rights, §25-5-114, (e).
Attorneys' fees.
Remedies, §25-5-111, (e).
Beneficiaries.
Name change, effect, §25-5-113, (f).
Right to assign proceeds, §25-5-114, (b).
Secured transactions.
Superior rights of beneficiary or nominated person under letter, §25-9-109, (c).
Warranties on presentment, §25-5-110, (a).
Additional to other warranties in commercial code, §25-5-110, (b).
Choice of law and forum, §25-5-116.
Citation of chapter.
Short title, §25-5-101.
Confirmers.
Defined, §25-5-102, (a).
Rights and obligations, §25-5-107, (a).
Conflict of laws.
Choice of law in document, §25-5-116, (a).
Governing law not specified, §25-5-116, (b).
Other articles of commercial code, §25-5-116, (d).
Rules and custom of practice, §25-5-116, (c).
Consideration, §25-5-105.
Contracts.
Issuer not responsible for underlying contracts, §25-5-108, (f).
Rights and obligations independent of underlying contract, §25-5-103, (d).
Creditors.
Sales.
Rights of creditors, §25-2-326.
Definitions, §25-5-102.
Discrepancies.
Limits on dishonor, §25-5-108, (c).
Dishonor.
Discrepancies, limits on dishonor, §25-5-108, (c).
Documents, disposition, §25-5-108, (h).
Fraud, forgery or expiration, §25-5-108, (d).

COMMERCIAL CODE —Cont'd
Letters of credit —Cont'd
Dishonor —Cont'd
Noncomplying presentation, obligation of issuer, §25-5-108, (a).
Remedy for improper dishonor, §25-5-111, (a), (b).
Time limit, §25-5-108, (b).
Expiration, §25-5-106, (c).
Basis for dishonor, §25-5-108, (d).
Perpetual letters of credit, §25-5-106, (d).
Forgery.
Basis for dishonor, §25-5-108, (d).
Bogus identification as successor, §25-5-113, (d).
Injunction on honoring, §25-5-109, (b).
Issuer allowed to honor despite, §25-5-109, (a).
Formal requirements, §25-5-104.
Fraud.
Basis for dishonor, §25-5-108, (d).
Injunction on honoring, §25-5-109, (b).
Issuer allowed to honor despite, §25-5-109, (a).
Honor.
Complying presentation, obligation of issuer, §25-5-108, (a).
Issuer's responsibilities, §25-5-108, (i).
Time limit, §25-5-108, (b).
Injunctions.
Fraud or forgery.
Injunction on honoring, §25-5-109, (b).
Interest.
Damages, §25-5-111, (d).
Issuance, §25-5-106, (a).
Issuers.
Anticipatory repudiation, remedies, §25-5-111, (a).
Assignment of proceeds.
Consent to assignment, §25-5-114, (c).
Unreasonably withholding, §25-5-114, (d).
Breach of obligation, remedies, §25-5-111, (c).
Fraud, forgery or expiration.
Injunction on honoring, §25-5-109, (b).
Issuer allowed to honor despite fraud or forgery, §25-5-109, (a).
Limitations on responsibility, §25-5-108, (f).
Nondocumentary conditions, disregard, §25-5-108, (g).
Rights and obligations, §25-5-108.
Security interest of issuer, §25-5-118.
Subrogation of rights.
Honoring beneficiary, §25-5-117, (a).
Reimbursement by applicant, §25-5-117, (b).
Successors to beneficiary.
Disclosure of status not required, §25-5-113, (a).
Honor despite status, consequences, §25-5-113, (d).
Not obligated to determine status, §25-5-113, (c).
Obligations upon disclosure, §25-5-113, (b).
Right to decline to recognize, §25-5-113, (e).
Transfers.
Refusal to recognize or carry out, §25-5-112, (b).
Wrongful dishonor, remedies, §25-5-111, (a), (b).
Liquidated damages, §25-5-111, (f).
Nominated persons.
Assignment of proceeds.
Consent to assignment, §25-5-114, (c).
Unreasonably withholding, §25-5-114, (d).
Rights, §25-5-114, (e).
Breach of obligation, remedies, §25-5-111, (c).

COMMERCIAL CODE —Cont'd
Letters of credit —Cont'd
Nominated persons —Cont'd
Defined, §25-5-102, (a).
Payment of drafts.
Subrogation of rights, §25-5-117, (c).
Rights and obligations, §25-5-107, (b).
Secured transactions.
Superior rights of beneficiary or nominated person under letter, §25-9-109, (c).
Security interest of nominated person, §25-5-118.
Nondocumentary conditions.
Issuer to disregard, §25-5-108, (g).
Notice to transferee beneficiary, §25-5-107, (d).
Perpetual letters of credit.
Expiration, §25-5-106, (d).
Remedies, §25-5-111.
Repudiation.
Remedy for anticipatory repudiation, §25-5-111, (a).
Requirements.
Formal requirements, §25-5-104.
Revocability, §25-5-106, (a).
Sales.
Letters of credit term, §25-2-325.
Scope of chapter, §25-5-103.
Secured transactions.
Applicability of article 9.
Superior rights of beneficiary or nominated person under letter, §25-9-109, (c).
Transfers, exclusions from article, §25-9-104, (m).
Security interests.
Assignment of proceeds.
Effect on rights, §25-5-114, (f).
Issuer or nominated person, §25-5-118.
Short title of chapter, §25-5-101.
Signing, §25-5-104.
Statement of rule, applicability, §25-5-103, (b).
Statute of limitations, §25-5-115.
Subrogation of rights, §25-5-117.
Applicant who reimburses issuer, §25-5-117, (b).
Issuer honoring beneficiary, §25-5-117, (a).
Nominated person who pays a draft, §25-5-117, (c).
When arising, §25-5-117, (d).
Successors of beneficiary.
Beneficiary who's name has changed, §25-5-113, (f).
Disclosure of status not required, §25-5-113, (a).
Honor despite status, consequences, §25-5-113, (d).
Issuer not obligated to determine status, §25-5-113, (c).
Issuer's obligations upon disclosure, §25-5-113, (b).
Issuer's right to decline to recognize, §25-5-113, (e).
Transfers by operation of law, §25-5-113.
Transferee beneficiaries.
Assignment of proceeds.
Rights, §25-5-114, (e).
Person who notifies or advises acts as adviser, §25-5-107, (d).
Transfers.
By operation of law, §25-5-113.
Generally not transferable, §25-5-112, (a).
Issuer's refusal to recognize or carry out, §25-5-112, (b).

COMMERCIAL CODE —Cont'd
Letters of credit —Cont'd
Transfers —Cont'd
Secured transactions, exclusion from article, §25-9-104, (m).
Warranties on transfer, §25-5-110.
Venue, §25-5-116, (e).
Specified in document, §25-5-116, (a).
Warranties.
Transfer and presentment, §25-5-110.
Local government finance.
Status of revenue bonds under code, §159-92.
Money.
Defined, §25-1-201, (24).
Negotiable instruments.
Acceptance.
Defined, §25-3-409.
Drafts, §25-3-409.
Acceptance varying drafts, §25-3-410.
Obligation of acceptor, §25-3-413.
Incomplete drafts, §25-3-409.
Mistake, §25-3-418.
Obligation of acceptor, §25-3-413.
Preparation of, §25-3-409.
Presentment.
Time allowed for acceptance, §25-3-501.
Unaccepted draft.
Drawee not liable, §25-3-408.
Varying of draft, §25-3-410.
Writing required, §25-3-409.
Accommodation party.
Discharge, §25-3-605.
Accord and satisfaction.
Use of instrument, §25-3-311.
Actions.
Accrual of actions, §25-3-118.
Limitation of actions, §25-3-118.
Alteration of instruments, §25-3-604.
Ambiguous terms, §25-3-114.
Applicability of article, §25-3-102.
Bearer.
Payable to bearer, §25-3-109.
Cancellation.
Discharge, §25-3-604.
Cashier's checks.
Defined, §25-3-104.
Payment.
Obligation of issuer, §25-3-412.
Refusal to pay, §25-3-411.
Certificates of deposit.
Defined, §25-3-104.
Certified checks.
Refusal to pay, §25-3-411.
Check-cashing businesses, §§53-275 to 53-289.
See CHECK-CASHING BUSINESSES.
Checks.
Defined, §25-3-104.
Incompetence of maker except for payment.
Controlling provisions, §25-4-405, (c).
Returned checks, collection of processing fee, §25-3-506.
Citation of article.
Short title, §25-3-101.
Claims.
Claim to the instrument, §25-3-306.
Claims in recoupment, §25-3-305.
Consideration.
Absence of, §25-3-303.
Conversion.
When instrument converted, §25-3-420.

COMMERCIAL CODE —Cont'd
Negotiable instruments —Cont'd
Date.
Antedating, §25-3-113.
Failure to date, §25-3-113.
Postdating, §25-3-113.
Defenses.
Burden of establishing signature and status as holder in due course, §25-3-308.
Generally, §25-3-305.
Defined terms, §§25-3-103, 25-3-104.
Acceptance, §25-3-409.
Alteration, §25-3-407.
Fiduciary, §25-3-307.
Holder in due course, §25-3-302.
Index of definitions, §25-3-103.
Indorsement, §25-3-204.
Issue, §25-3-105.
Negotiation, §25-3-201.
Person entitled to enforce, §25-3-301.
Presentment, §25-3-501.
Represented person, §25-3-307.
Demand.
Date of payment, §25-3-113.
Overdue instruments, §25-3-304.
Demand paper.
Generally, §25-3-108.
Destroyed instruments.
Cashier's check, teller's check or certified check, §25-3-312.
Enforcement, §25-3-309.
Discharge.
Accommodation of party, §25-3-605.
Accord and satisfaction.
Use of instrument, §25-3-311.
Certification of check, §25-3-310.
Effect of discharge, §25-3-601.
Generally, §25-3-601.
Holder in due course.
Effect of discharge against, §25-3-601.
Indorser, §25-3-605.
Joint and several liability of parties.
Effective discharge, §25-3-116.
Payment.
Discharge upon payment, §25-3-602.
Tender of payment, §25-3-603.
Renunciation, §25-3-604.
Dishonor.
Bank deposits and collections.
Time for determining account balance, §25-4-402, (c).
Wrongful dishonor.
Damages, §25-4-402, (b).
Liability of bank to customer, §25-4-402, (a).
Evidence of dishonor, §25-3-505.
Generally, §25-3-502.
Notice of dishonor, §§25-3-503 to 25-3-506.
Obligation of drawer, §25-3-414.
Obligation of indorser, §25-3-415.
Processing fee for returned checks, collection, §25-3-506.
When instrument is dishonored, §25-3-502.
Wrongful dishonor.
Liability of bank to customer, §25-4-402, (a).
Damages, §25-4-402, (b).
Drafts.
Dishonor, §25-3-502.
Unaccepted drafts.
Drawee not liable on, §25-3-408.

COMMERCIAL CODE —Cont'd
Negotiable instruments —Cont'd
Effect of instrument on obligation for which taken, §25-3-310.
Evidence.
Dishonor.
Evidence of dishonor, §25-3-505.
Notice of dishonor, §25-3-505.
Fiduciaries.
Breach of fiduciary duty, §25-3-307.
Foreign money.
Instrument payable in, §25-3-107.
Fraud.
Indorsements.
Responsibility of employer for fraudulent indorsement by employee, §25-3-405.
Holder in due course.
Defined, §25-3-302.
Discharge.
Effect of discharge against, §§25-3-302, 25-3-601.
Free of claim to the instrument, §25-3-306.
Proof of status as, §25-3-308.
Identification.
Person to whom instrument payable, §25-3-110.
Incomplete instruments, §25-3-115.
Indorsement.
Anomalous indorsement, §25-3-205.
Blank indorsement, §25-3-205.
Collection by depository and collecting banks.
Missing indorsement, §25-4-205.
Discharge of indorser, §25-3-605.
Fraud.
Responsibility of employer for fraudulent indorsement of employee, §25-3-405.
Generally, §25-3-204.
Impostors, §25-3-404.
Missing indorsement.
Collection by depositary and collecting banks, §25-4-205.
Obligation of indorser, §25-3-415.
Reacquisition, §25-3-207.
Restrictive indorsements, §25-3-206.
Signatures.
Proof of signature, §25-3-308.
Special indorsement, §25-3-205.
Transfer of security interest, §25-3-204.
Interest.
Payment, §25-3-112.
Rate, §25-3-112.
Issue.
Defined, §25-3-105.
Liability of parties.
Employers.
Responsibility for fraudulent indorsement by an employee, §25-3-405.
Fictitious payees, §25-3-404.
Impostors, §25-3-404.
Joint and several liability, §25-3-116.
Signatures.
Authorized representative, §25-3-402.
Person not liable unless signature appears, §25-3-401.
Signing of instrument, §25-3-401.
Unaccepted draft.
Drawee not liable, §25-3-408.
Limitation of actions, §25-3-118.
Lost instruments.
Cashier's check, teller's check or certified check, §25-3-312.
Enforcement, §25-3-309.

COMMERCIAL CODE —Cont'd
Negotiable instruments —Cont'd
Negligence.
Contributing to forged signature or alteration of instrument, §25-3-406.
Negotiability.
Incomplete instruments, §25-3-115.
Other writings affecting instrument, §25-3-117.
Negotiation.
Defined, §25-3-201.
Rescission, §25-3-202.
Notes.
Dishonor, §25-3-502.
Notice of breach of fiduciary duty, §25-3-307.
Notice of dishonor.
Delay.
Excused delay, §25-3-504.
Evidence of, §25-3-505.
Excused notice of dishonor, §25-3-504.
Generally, §25-3-503.
Protests, §25-3-505.
When necessary, §25-3-503.
Notice to third parties.
Right to defend action, §25-3-119.
Order.
Payable to order, §25-3-109.
Unconditional.
When order unconditional, §25-3-106.
Other agreements affecting instrument, §25-3-117.
Payment.
Bearer.
Payable to bearer, §25-3-109.
Demand.
Date of payment, §25-3-113.
Payment on demand or at a definite time, §25-3-108.
Discharge, §§25-3-602, 25-3-603.
Foreign money, §25-3-107.
Identification of person to whom instrument payable, §25-3-110.
Interest, §25-3-112.
Mistakes, §25-3-418.
Money.
Foreign currency, §25-3-107.
Obligation of issuer.
Note or cashier's check, §25-3-412.
Order.
Payable to order, §25-3-109.
Overdue instruments, §25-3-304.
Place of payment, §25-3-111.
Refusal to pay.
Cashier's checks, teller's checks and certified checks, §25-3-411.
Time.
When payable at definite time, §25-3-108.
Two or more persons.
Instruments payable to two or more persons, §25-3-116.
Place of payment, §25-3-111.
Presentment.
Acceptance.
Time allowed for acceptance, §25-3-501.
Defined, §25-3-501.
Dishonor.
When instrument is dishonored, §25-3-502.
Excused presentment, §25-3-504.
How made, §25-3-501.
Place of presentment, §25-3-501.
Rights of party to whom presentment made, §25-3-501.
Time of presentment, §25-3-501.

COMMERCIAL CODE —Cont'd
Negotiable instruments —Cont'd
Presentment —Cont'd
Unconditional.
When promise unconditional, §25-3-106.
Recoupment.
Claims in recoupment, §25-3-305.
Renunciation.
Discharge, §25-3-604.
Rescission.
Negotiation subject to rescission, §25-3-202.
Restrictive indorsements, §25-3-206.
Returned checks.
Collection of processing fee, §25-3-506.
Secured transactions.
Priority of security interests, §25-9-331.
Signatures.
Accommodation party, §25-3-419.
How made, §25-3-401.
Impostors, §25-3-404.
Liability.
Person not liable unless signature appears, §25-3-401.
Signature by authorized representative, §25-3-402.
Negligence.
Contributing to forged signature, §25-3-406.
Proof of signature, §25-3-308.
Representative, §25-3-402.
Trade or assumed name, §25-3-401.
Unauthorized signature, §25-3-403.
Stolen instruments.
Cashier's check, teller's check or certified check, §25-3-312.
Enforcement, §25-3-309.
Teller's checks.
Defined, §25-3-104.
Refusal to pay, §25-3-411.
Third parties.
Notice of right to defend action, §25-3-119.
Title of article.
Short title, §25-3-101.
Transfer.
Generally, §25-3-203.
Reacquisition, §25-3-207.
Rights vested in transferee, §25-3-203.
Traveler's checks.
Defined, §25-3-104.
Unconditional promises or orders, §25-3-106.
Value.
Defined, §25-1-201.
Issued or transferred for value, §25-3-303.
When bank gives value for purposes of holder in due course, §25-4-209.
Warranties.
Negligence contributing to forged signature or alteration of instrument, §25-3-406.
Presentment warranties, §25-3-417.
Transfer warranties, §25-3-416.
What constitutes, §25-3-407.
Notice.
Defined, §25-1-201, (25), (26), (27).
Options.
Acceleration at will, §25-1-208.
Organization.
Defined, §25-1-201, (28).
Parties.
Aggrieved party.
Defined, §25-1-201, (2).
Defendants.
Defined, §25-1-201, (13).
Defined, §25-1-201, (29).

COMMERCIAL CODE —Cont'd
Performance under reservation of rights, §25-1-207.
Person.
Defined, §25-1-201, (30).
Presumptions.
Defined, §25-1-201, (31).
Principles of law.
Supplementary general principles applicable, §25-1-103.
Prior registration statutes.
Covered transactions not subject to, §25-10-106.
Protests.
Performance or acceptance under reservation of rights, §25-1-207.
Purchasers.
Defined, §25-1-201, (33).
Purchases.
Defined, §25-1-201, (32).
Purpose of chapter, §25-1-102.
Registration.
Covered transactions not subject to prior registration statutes, §25-10-106.
Remedies.
Defined, §25-1-201, (34).
Liberal administration of remedies, §25-1-106.
Repeals.
Construction against implicit repeal of code, §25-1-104.
Documents of title.
Certain provisions not repealed, §25-10-104, (1).
Fiduciary security transfers.
Act for simplification of fiduciary security transfers not repealed, §25-10-104, (2).
General repealer, §25-10-103.
Specific repealer, §25-10-102, (1).
Transition provision, §25-10-102, (2).
Representatives.
Defined, §25-1-201, (35).
Reservation of rights.
Performance or acceptance under reservation of rights, §25-1-207.
Rules of construction, §25-1-102.
Sales, §§25-2-101 to 25-2-725.
Acceptance of goods.
Breach, repudiation and excuse.
Buyer's rights on improper delivery, §25-2-601.
Burden of establishing breach after acceptance, §25-2-607, (4).
Buyer's damages for breach in regard to accepted goods, §25-2-714.
Buyer's rights on improper delivery, §25-2-601.
Effect of acceptance, §25-2-607.
Installment contracts, §25-2-612.
Revocation of acceptance in whole or in part, §25-2-608.
Seller's damages for nonacceptance, §25-2-708.
What constitutes acceptance, §25-2-606.
When documents deliverable on acceptance, §25-2-514.
Actions. See within this subheading, "Remedies."
Agreement.
Defined, §25-2-106, (1).
Alcoholic beverages.
Implied warranty of merchantability, §25-2-314.
Animals.
Identification of goods, §25-2-501, (1).
Sale of unborn young, §25-2-501.
Anticipatory repudiation.
Generally, §25-2-610.

COMMERCIAL CODE —Cont'd
Sales —Cont'd
Anticipatory repudiation —Cont'd
Retraction of anticipatory repudiation, §25-2-611.
Approval.
Sales on approval, §25-2-326.
Risk of loss, §25-2-327, (1).
Special incidents, §25-2-327.
Assignment.
Rights of buyer or seller, §25-2-210.
Auctions.
Sale by auction, §25-2-328.
Bailment.
Seller's remedy of stoppage of delivery in transit, §25-2-705.
Bankruptcy and insolvency.
Buyer's right to goods on seller's insolvency, §25-2-502.
"Battle of the forms."
Additional terms in acceptance or confirmation, §25-2-207.
Bills of lading.
Form of bill of lading required in overseas shipment, §25-2-323.
Bona fide purchasers.
Title acquired, §25-2-403, (1).
Breach, repudiation and excuse.
Absence of breach.
Risk of loss in absence, §25-2-509.
Acceptance of goods.
Burden of establishing breach after acceptance, §25-2-607, (4).
Buyer's damages for breach in regard to accepted goods, §25-2-714.
Buyer's rights on improper delivery, §25-2-601.
Effect of acceptance, §25-2-607.
Installment contracts, §25-2-612.
Revocation of acceptance in whole or in part, §25-2-608.
Seller's damages for nonacceptance, §25-2-708.
What constitutes acceptance of goods, §25-2-606.
Antecedent breach.
Effect of cancellation or rescission on claims for antecedent breach, §25-2-720.
Anticipatory repudiation.
Generally, §25-2-610.
Retraction of anticipatory repudiation, §25-2-611.
Assurance of performance.
Right to adequate assurance of performance, §25-2-609.
Burden of establishing breach after acceptance, §25-2-607, (4).
Casualty to identified goods, §25-2-613.
Collateral contracts.
Remedies for breach not impaired, §25-2-701.
Cover.
Merchant buyer's duties as to rightfully rejected goods, §25-2-603.
Cure by seller of improper tender or delivery, §25-2-508.
Damages.
Buyer's remedies for repudiation, §25-2-713.
Seller's damages for repudiation, §25-2-708.
Delivery.
Buyer's rights on improper delivery, §25-2-601.

COMMERCIAL CODE —Cont'd
Sales —Cont'd
Breach, repudiation and excuse —Cont'd
Effect of breach on risk of loss, §25-2-510.
Failure of presupposed conditions, §25-2-615.
Procedure on notice claiming excuse, §25-2-616.
Identification of goods.
Casualty to identified goods, §25-2-613.
Improper tender or delivery.
Cure by seller, §25-2-508.
Installment contract breach, §25-2-612.
Notice of breach, §25-2-607, (3).
Notice of claim or litigation to person answerable over, §25-2-607, (5).
Notice of failure of presupposed conditions, §25-2-615.
Procedure on notice claiming excuse, §25-2-616.
Perishable goods.
Buyer's options as to salvage of rightfully rejected goods, §25-2-604.
Merchant buyer's duties as to rightfully rejected goods, §25-2-603.
Presupposed conditions.
Excuse by failure of presupposed conditions, §25-2-615.
Procedure on notice claiming excuse, §25-2-616.
Rejection of goods.
Buyer's rights as to salvage of rightfully rejected goods, §25-2-604.
Buyer's rights on improper delivery, §25-2-601.
Cover.
Merchant buyer's duties as to rightfully rejected goods, §25-2-603.
Installment contracts, §25-2-612.
Manner and effect of rightful rejection, §25-2-602.
Merchant buyer's duties as to rightfully rejected goods, §25-2-603.
Perishable goods, §§25-2-603, 25-2-604.
Waiver of buyer's objections by failure to particularize, §25-2-605.
Replacement, §25-2-608.
Revocation of acceptance, §25-2-608.
Risk of loss in absence of breach, §25-2-509.
Substituted performance, §25-2-614.
Waiver or renunciation of claim or right after breach, §25-1-107.
Buildings.
Contract for sale of building, §25-2-107, (1).
Burden of proof.
Burden of establishing breach after acceptance, §25-2-607, (4).
Buyer.
Defined, §25-2-103, (1).
Failure by seller to deliver.
Buyer's right to goods, §25-2-502.
In ordinary course of business.
Defined, §25-1-201, (9).
Insolvency of seller.
Buyer's right to goods, §25-2-502.
Repudiation by seller.
Buyer's right to goods, §25-2-502.
Checks.
Payment by check, §25-2-511, (3).
C.I.F. and C. & F. terms, §25-2-320.
Form of bill of lading required in overseas shipment, §25-2-323.

COMMERCIAL CODE —Cont'd
Sales —Cont'd
C.I.F. and C. & F. terms —Cont'd
Net landed weight, §25-2-321.
Payment on arrival, §25-2-321.
Warranty of condition on arrival, §25-2-321.
Citation of article.
Short title, §25-2-101.
C.O.D. terms.
Buyer not entitled to inspect goods before payment, §25-2-513, (3).
Commercial unit.
Defined, §25-2-105, (6).
Confirmed credit term, §25-2-325, (3).
Consequential damages.
Buyer's remedies, §25-2-715, (2).
Consignment sales, §25-2-326.
Sale or return, §25-2-326.
Risk of loss, §25-2-327, (2).
Special incidents, §25-2-327, (2).
Construction and interpretation.
Course of performance or practical construction of contracts, §25-2-208.
Exclusion or modification of warranties, §25-2-316.
Offer and acceptance in formation of contract, §25-2-206.
Contracts.
Absence of specified place for delivery, §25-2-308.
Absence of specified time provisions, §25-2-309.
Assignment of rights, §25-2-210.
"Battle of the forms," §25-2-207.
Cancellation, §25-2-209.
Defined, §25-2-106, (4).
Effect of cancellation on claims for antecedent breach, §25-2-720.
Collateral contracts.
Remedies for breach not impaired, §25-2-701.
Conforming to contract, §25-2-106, (2).
Construction.
Course of performance or practical construction, §25-2-208.
Cooperation respecting performance, §25-2-311.
Course of dealing.
Used to explain terms of contracts, §25-2-202.
Course of performance, §25-2-208.
Used to explain terms of contracts, §25-2-202.
Defined, §25-2-106, (1).
Delegation of performance, §25-2-210.
Delivery in single lot or several lots, §25-2-307.
Exclusive dealings, §25-2-306, (2).
Final written expression, §25-2-202.
Firm offers, §25-2-205.
Formal requirements, §25-2-201.
Formation.
Generally, §25-2-204.
Offer and acceptance, §25-2-206.
General obligations of parties, §25-2-301.
Identification of goods, §25-2-501, (1).
Installment contracts, §25-2-612.
Limitation of actions, §25-2-725.
Liquidation or limitation of damages, §§25-2-718, 25-2-719.
Modification.
Liquidation or limitation of damages, §25-2-719.
Procedure on notice claiming excuse by failure of presupposed conditions, §25-2-616.
Modification by agreement of parties, §25-2-209.
Notice of termination, §25-2-309, (3).

COMMERCIAL CODE —Cont'd
Sales —Cont'd
Contracts —Cont'd
Obligations.
General obligations of parties, §25-2-301.
Offer and acceptance.
Additional terms in acceptance or confirmation, §25-2-207.
"Battle of the forms."
Additional terms in acceptance or confirmation, §25-2-207.
Firm offers, §25-2-205.
Generally, §25-2-206.
Irrevocable offers, §25-2-205.
Methods of acceptance, §25-2-206.
Open price term, §25-2-305.
Option, §25-2-311.
Output of seller, §25-2-306, (1).
Parol or extrinsic evidence, §25-2-202.
Performance.
Cooperation respecting performance, §25-2-311.
Course of performance, §25-2-208.
Delegation of performance, §25-2-210.
General obligations of parties, §25-2-301.
Right to adequate assurance of performance, §25-2-609.
Presupposed conditions.
Excuse by failure of presupposed conditions, §25-2-615.
Price payable in money, goods, realty, etc., §25-2-304.
Recordation.
Goods to be severed from realty, §25-2-107.
Remedies for breach of collateral contracts not impaired, §25-2-701.
Requirements of buyer, §25-2-306, (1).
Formal requirements, §25-2-201.
Resale.
Seller's resale including contract for resale, §25-2-706.
Rescission, §25-2-209.
Effect of rescission on claims for antecedent breach, §25-2-720.
Risk of loss.
Allocation or division of risks, §25-2-303.
Seals inoperative, §25-2-203.
Statute of frauds, §§25-2-201, 25-2-209, (3).
Kinds of personal property not otherwise covered, §25-1-206.
When writing not required, §25-2-201.
Statute of limitations in contracts for sale, §25-2-725.
Termination.
Defined, §25-2-106, (3).
Notice of termination, §25-2-309, (3).
Terms.
Liquidation or limitation of damages, §§25-2-718, 25-2-719.
Unconscionable contract or clause, §25-2-302.
Void contracts.
Casualty to identified goods, §25-2-613.
Waiver of executory portion, §25-2-209, (5).
Written expression.
Final written expression, §25-2-202.
Course of dealing.
Implied warranties, §25-2-314, (3).
Exclusion or modification by course of dealing, §25-2-316, (3).
Course of performance, §25-2-208.
Used to explain terms of contracts, §25-2-202.

COMMERCIAL CODE —Cont'd
Sales —Cont'd
Cover.
Buyer's inability to effect cover.
Right to specific performance, §25-2-716.
Buyer's remedies, §§25-2-711, 25-2-712.
Merchant buyer's duties as to rightfully rejected goods, §25-2-603.
Credit.
Running of credit.
Open time for running of credit, §25-2-310, (d).
Creditor's rights.
Approval.
Sale on approval, §25-2-326.
Consignment sales, §25-2-326.
Rights of seller's creditors against sold goods, §25-2-402.
Sale on approval, §25-2-326.
Sale or return, §25-2-326.
Crops.
Contract for sale, §25-2-107, (2).
Definition of goods, §25-2-105, (1).
Identification of goods, §25-2-501, (1).
Cure by seller.
Improper tender or delivery, §25-2-508.
Damages.
Buyer's damages, §§25-2-713 to 25-2-718.
Effect of cancellation or rescission on claims for antecedent breach, §25-2-720.
Liquidation or limitation of damages, §§25-2-718, 25-2-719.
Proof of market price, §25-2-723.
Market price.
Admissibility of market quotations, §25-2-724.
Proof, §25-2-723.
Time and place, §25-2-723.
Proof of market price, §25-2-723.
Seller's damages for repudiation, §25-2-708.
Seller's incidental damages, §25-2-710.
Third parties.
Who can sue third parties for injury to goods, §25-2-722.
Definitions, §§25-2-103 to 25-2-106.
Fungible goods, §25-1-201.
Installment contracts, §25-2-612, (1).
Delivery.
Absence of specified place for delivery, §25-2-308.
Authority to ship under reservation, §25-2-310, (b).
Buyer's rights on improper delivery, §25-2-601.
Cure by seller of improper tender or delivery, §25-2-508.
Damages.
Buyer's damages for nondelivery, §25-2-713.
Defined, §25-1-201, (14).
Delivery ex-ship, §25-2-322.
Delivery on condition, §25-2-507.
Documents of title.
When documents deliverable on acceptance and on payment, §25-2-514.
Effect of seller's tender, §25-2-507.
Excuse by failure of presupposed conditions, §25-2-615.
Ex-ship, §25-2-322.
General obligation of seller, §25-2-301.
Improper tender or delivery.
Buyer's rights on improper delivery, §25-2-601.
Cure by seller, §25-2-508.

COMMERCIAL CODE —Cont'd
Sales —Cont'd
Delivery —Cont'd
Manner of seller's tender of delivery, §25-2-503.
No arrival, no sale term, §25-2-324.
Nonconforming tender or delivery.
Cure or replacement by seller, §25-2-508.
Nondelivery.
Buyer's damages for nondelivery, §25-2-713.
Place of delivery, §25-2-308.
Replacement, §25-2-508.
Restitution.
Seller justifiably withholding delivery, §25-2-718.
Seller's remedy of stoppage of delivery in transit, §25-2-705.
Shipment by seller, §25-2-504.
Shipment under reservation.
Authority to ship under reservation, §25-2-310, (b).
Single lot or several lots, §25-2-307.
Stoppage in transit, §25-2-705.
Substituted performance, §25-2-614.
Withheld delivery.
Restitution where seller justifiably withholds delivery, §25-2-718.
Deposits.
Liquidation or limitation of damages, §25-2-718.
Disclaimer of warranties, §25-2-316.
Disputed goods.
Preserving evidence of goods in dispute, §25-2-515.
Documents of title.
When deliverable on acceptance and when on payment, §25-2-514.
Doubtfulness of performance.
Right to adequate assurance of performance, §25-2-609.
Entrusting, §25-2-403.
Evidence.
Contracts.
Parol or extrinsic evidence, §25-2-202.
Preserving evidence of goods in dispute, §25-2-515.
Remedies.
Admissibility of market quotations, §25-2-724.
Proof of market price, §25-2-723.
Exclusions from article.
Certain security and other transactions excluded, §25-2-102.
Exclusive dealings, §25-2-306, (2).
Excuse. See within this subheading, "Breach, repudiation and excuse."
Express warranties, §25-2-313.
Cumulation and conflict, §25-2-317.
Third party beneficiaries, §25-2-318.
Factors.
Consignment sales, §25-2-326.
Entrusting, §25-2-403.
Rights of creditors, §25-2-326.
Sale on approval, §25-2-326.
Sale or return, §25-2-326.
Title.
Power to transfer title, §25-2-403.
F.A.S. terms, §25-2-319.
Financing agency.
Defined, §25-2-104, (2).
Rights of financing agency, §25-2-506.
Fitness for a particular purpose.
Implied warranties, §25-2-315.

COMMERCIAL CODE —Cont'd
Sales —Cont'd
F.O.B. terms, §25-2-319.
Form of bill of lading required in overseas shipment, §25-2-323.
Fraud.
Remedies for fraud, §25-2-721.
Transfer of title obtained by fraud, §25-2-403, (1).
Good faith.
Defined, §25-2-103, (1).
Purchase of goods, §25-2-403.
Identification of goods.
Breach of contract.
Seller's right to identify goods to the contract notwithstanding breach, §25-2-704.
Casualty to identified goods, §25-2-613.
Manner of identification, §25-2-501, (1).
Seller's right to identify goods to the contract notwithstanding breach, §25-2-704.
Implied warranties.
Course of dealing, §25-2-314, (3).
Exclusion or modification by course of dealing, §25-2-316, (3).
Cumulation and conflict, §25-2-317.
Fitness for a particular purpose, §25-2-315.
Merchantability, §25-2-314.
Third party beneficiaries, §25-2-318.
Usage of trade, §25-2-314, (3).
Exclusion or modification by usage of trade, §25-2-316, (3).
Impossibility of performance.
Excuse by failure of presupposed conditions, §25-2-615.
Procedure on notice claiming excuse, §25-2-616.
Substituted performance, §25-2-614.
Incidental damages.
Buyer's remedies, §25-2-715, (1).
Seller's incidental damages, §25-2-710.
Infringement.
Buyer's obligation against infringement, §25-2-312, (3).
Notice of claim or litigation to person answerable over, §25-2-607.
Warranty against infringement, §25-2-312, (3).
Insolvency.
Buyer's right to goods on seller's insolvency, §25-2-502.
Seller's remedies on discovery of buyer's insolvency, §25-2-702.
Inspection of goods.
Buyer's right to inspect goods, §25-2-513.
Disputed goods.
Preserving evidence of goods in dispute, §25-2-515.
Preserving evidence of goods in dispute, §25-2-515.
Installment contracts, §25-2-612.
Breach, §25-2-612.
Defined, §25-2-612, (1).
Insurance.
C.I.F. and C. & F. terms, §25-2-320.
Form of bill of lading required in overseas shipment, §25-2-323.
Net landed weight, §25-2-321.
Payment on arrival, §25-2-321.
Warranty of condition on arrival, §25-2-321.
Insurable interest in goods, §25-2-501.
Larceny.
Power to transfer voidable title, §25-2-403, (1).

COMMERCIAL CODE —Cont'd
Sales —Cont'd
Layaway contracts.
Defined, §25-2-106.
Restitution where seller justifiably withholds delivery, §25-2-718.
Limitation of actions, §25-2-725.
Liquidation of damages, §25-2-718.
Livestock.
Manner of identification, §25-2-501, (1).
Lot.
Defined, §25-2-105, (5).
Market price.
Admissibility of market quotations, §25-2-724.
Proof of market price, §25-2-723.
Time and place, §25-2-723.
Merchantability.
Implied warranty of merchantability, §25-2-314.
Merchants.
Between merchants.
Defined, §25-2-104, (3).
Defined, §25-2-104, (1).
Mines and minerals.
Contract for sale of minerals, §25-2-107, (1).
Misrepresentation.
Remedies, §25-2-721.
Models.
Express warranties upon model, §25-2-313.
No arrival, no sale term, §25-2-324.
Notice.
Breach, §25-2-607, (3).
Claim or litigation to person answerable over, §25-2-607, (5).
Contracts.
Notice of breach, §25-2-607, (3).
Excuse by failure of presupposed conditions, §25-2-615.
Procedure on notice claiming excuse, §25-2-616.
Resale by seller.
Notice to buyer, §25-2-706.
Termination, §25-2-309, (3).
Offer and acceptance, §§25-2-205 to 25-2-207.
Options, §25-2-311.
Output or requirements, §25-2-306, (1).
Overseas shipments.
Construction of "overseas," §25-2-323, (3).
Form of bill of lading required in overseas shipment, §25-2-323.
Letter of credit or banker's credit terms, §25-2-325.
Patents.
Buyer's obligations against infringement, §25-2-312, (3).
Notice of claim or litigation to person answerable over, §25-2-607.
Warranty against infringement, §25-2-312, (3).
Payment.
Before inspection, §25-2-512.
Check payment, §25-2-511, (3).
General obligation of buyer, §25-2-301.
Inspection of goods.
Buyer's right to inspect goods prior to payment, §25-2-513.
Payment before inspection, §25-2-512.
Open price term, §25-2-305.
Open time for payment, §25-2-310.
Price payable in money, goods, realty, etc., §25-2-304.
Seller's action for price, §25-2-709.
Substituted performance, §25-2-614.

COMMERCIAL CODE —Cont'd
Sales —Cont'd
Payment —Cont'd
Tender of payment by buyer, §25-2-511.
When documents deliverable on payment, §25-2-514.
Performance.
Assurance of performance.
Right to adequate assurance, §25-2-609.
Breach, repudiation and excuse. See within this subheading, "Breach, repudiation and excuse."
Cooperation respecting performance, §25-2-311.
Course of performance, §25-2-208.
Delegation of performance, §25-2-210.
Delivery on condition, §25-2-507.
Doubtfulness of performance.
Right to adequate assurance of performance, §25-2-609.
General obligations of parties, §25-2-301.
Impossibility of performance.
Excuse by failure of presupposed conditions, §25-2-615.
Procedure on notice claiming excuse, §25-2-616.
Substituted performance, §25-2-614.
Manner of tender of delivery, §25-2-503.
Right to adequate assurance of performance, §25-2-609.
Shipment by seller, §25-2-504.
Seller's shipment under reservation, §25-2-505.
Substituted performance, §25-2-614.
Tender of delivery.
Cure by seller of improper tender, §25-2-508.
Effect of seller's tender, §25-2-507.
Manner of tender, §25-2-503.
Tender of payment by buyer, §25-2-511.
Perishable goods.
Buyer's options as to salvage of rightfully rejected goods, §25-2-604.
Merchant buyer's duties as to rightfully rejected goods, §25-2-603.
Present sale.
Defined, §25-2-106, (1).
Preserving evidence of goods in dispute, §25-2-515.
Presumptions.
Burden of establishing breach after acceptance, §25-2-607, (4).
Prices.
Action for price, §25-2-709.
Admissibility of market quotations, §25-2-724.
Deduction of damages from price, §25-2-717.
Open price term, §25-2-305.
Prices payable in money, goods, realty, etc., §25-2-304.
Proof of market price, §25-2-723.
Time and place of market price, §25-2-723.
Quantity.
Output or requirements contracts, §25-2-306, (1).
Real property.
Goods to be severed from realty, §25-2-107.
Price payable in realty, §25-2-304, (2).
Receipt.
Defined, §25-2-103, (1).
Rejection of goods.
Buyer's options as to salvage of rightfully rejected goods, §25-2-604.
Buyer's rights on improper delivery, §25-2-601.

COMMERCIAL CODE —Cont'd
Sales —Cont'd
Rejection of goods —Cont'd
Cover.
Merchant buyer's duties as to rightfully rejected goods, §25-2-603.
Effect of rightful rejection, §25-2-602.
Installment contracts, §25-2-612.
Manner of rightful rejection, §25-2-602.
Merchant buyer's duties as to rightfully rejected goods, §25-2-603.
Perishable goods.
Buyer's options as to salvage of rightfully rejected goods, §25-2-604.
Merchant buyer's duties as to rightfully rejected goods, §25-2-603.
Secured transactions.
Applicability of article, §25-9-110.
Waiver of buyer's objections by failure to particularize, §25-2-605.
Remedies.
Anticipatory repudiation, §25-2-610.
Assurance of performance.
Right to adequate assurance of performance, §25-2-609.
Breach of collateral contracts.
Remedies for breach of collateral contracts not impaired, §25-2-701.
Breach of warranty.
Limitation of remedy, §25-2-316, (4).
Buyer's remedies.
Breach of warranty.
Limitation of remedies, §25-2-316, (4).
Consequential damages, §25-2-715, (2).
Cover, §§25-2-711, 25-2-712.
Buyer's right to replevin if unable to effect cover, §25-2-716.
Damages for breach in regard to accepted goods, §25-2-714.
Damages for nondelivery or repudiation, §25-2-713.
Deduction of damages from price, §25-2-717.
Generally, §25-2-711.
Incidental damages, §25-2-715, (1).
Price.
Deduction of damages from price, §25-2-717.
Procurement of substitute goods, §25-2-712.
Replevin, §25-2-716.
Security interest.
Rejected goods, §25-2-711, (3).
Specific performance, §25-2-716.
Claims for antecedent breach.
Effect of cancellation or rescission on, §25-2-720.
Contractual modification or limitation of remedies, §25-2-719.
Fraud.
Remedies for fraud, §25-2-721.
Injury to goods.
Who can sue third parties for injury to goods, §25-2-722.
Limitation of actions, §25-2-725.
Limitation of remedies, §25-2-719.
Liquidation or limitation of damages, §25-2-718.
Deposits, §25-2-718.
Market price.
Proof of market price, §25-2-723.
Market price.
Admissibility of market quotations, §25-2-724.
Time and place, §25-2-723.

COMMERCIAL CODE —Cont'd
Sales —Cont'd
Remedies —Cont'd
Seller's remedies.
Action for the price, §25-2-709.
Damages for nonacceptance or repudiation, §25-2-708.
Discovery of buyer's insolvency, §25-2-702.
Generally, §§25-2-703, 25-2-704.
Incidental damages, §25-2-710.
Person in the position of a seller, §25-2-707.
Resale including contract for resale, §25-2-706.
Right to identify goods to the contract notwithstanding breach, §25-2-704.
Right to salvage unfinished goods, §25-2-704.
Stoppage of delivery in transit or otherwise, §25-2-705.
Statute of limitations in contracts for sale, §25-2-725.
Third parties.
Who can sue third parties for injury to goods, §25-2-722.
Replacement, §25-2-508.
Replevin.
Buyer's right to replevin, §25-2-716, (3).
Repudiation. See within this subheading, "Breach, repudiation and excuse."
Requirement contracts, §25-2-306, (1).
Resales.
Merchant buyer's duties as to rightfully rejected goods, §25-2-603.
Sale or return, §25-2-326.
Risk of loss, §25-2-327, (2).
Special incidents, §25-2-327, (2).
Seller's resale including contract for resale, §25-2-706.
Res judicata.
Effect of notice to person answerable over, §25-2-607, (5).
Restitution.
Seller justifiably withholding delivery, §25-2-718.
Risk of loss.
Allocation or division of risks, §25-2-303.
Breach.
Effect of breach on risk of loss, §25-2-510.
Risk in absence of breach, §25-2-509.
C.I.F. and C. & F. terms, §25-2-320.
Form of bill of lading required in overseas shipment, §25-2-323.
Net landed weight, §25-2-321.
Payment on arrival, §25-2-321.
Warranty of condition on arrival, §25-2-321.
Delivery ex-ship, §25-2-322.
Effect of breach on risk of loss, §25-2-510.
F.O.B. and F.A.S. terms, §25-2-319.
Form of bill of lading required in overseas shipment, §25-2-323.
Generally, §25-2-509.
In absence of breach, §25-2-509.
Sale on approval, §25-2-327, (1).
Sale or return, §25-2-327, (2).
Sale on approval, §25-2-326.
Risk of loss, §25-2-327, (1).
Special incidents, §25-2-327, (1).
Sale or return, §25-2-326.
Risk of loss, §25-2-327, (2).
Special incidents, §25-2-327, (2).
Salvage.
Buyer's options as to salvage of rightfully rejected goods, §25-2-604.

COMMERCIAL CODE —Cont'd
Sales —Cont'd
Salvage —Cont'd
Seller's remedies.
Right to salvage unfinished goods, §25-2-704.
Samples.
Express warranties by sample, §25-2-313.
Scope of article, §25-2-102.
Seals inoperative, §25-2-203.
Secured transactions.
Buyer's security interest in rejected goods, §25-2-711, (3).
Applicability of article 9, §25-9-110.
Exclusions from article, §25-2-102.
Reservation for security, §25-2-501, (2).
Reservation of title, §§25-2-310, (b), 25-2-401.
Applicability of article 9, §25-9-110.
Security interests arising under provisions, §25-9-110.
Shipment under reservation, §25-2-505.
Warranty against liens or encumbrances, §25-2-312.
Seller.
Defined, §25-2-103, (1).
Severance from realty.
Goods to be severed, §25-2-107.
Shipment by seller, §25-2-504.
Shipment under reservation, §25-2-505.
Authority to ship under reservation, §25-2-310, (b).
Short title of article, §25-2-101.
Specially manufactured goods.
When writing not required for contract, §25-2-201, (3).
Specific performance.
Buyer's right to specific performance, §25-2-716.
Statute of frauds, §25-2-201.
Kinds of personal property not otherwise covered, §25-1-206.
Modification of contract, §25-2-209, (3).
Sales contracts, §25-2-201.
When writing not required, §25-2-201, (3).
Statute of limitations in contracts for sale, §25-2-725.
Stoppage of delivery.
Failure of agreed means or manner of payment, §25-2-614.
Stoppage of delivery in transit or otherwise.
Seller's remedies, §25-2-705.
Tender of delivery by seller.
Cure by seller of improper tender or delivery, §25-2-508.
Effect of seller's tender, §25-2-507.
Manner of tender of delivery, §25-2-503.
Tender of payment by buyer, §25-2-511.
Terms.
Absence of specified place for delivery, §25-2-308.
Absence of specified time provisions, §25-2-309.
Banker's credit, §25-2-325, (3).
C.I.F. and C. & F. terms, §25-2-320.
Form of bill of lading required in overseas shipment, §25-2-323.
Net landed weights, §25-2-321.
Payment on arrival, §25-2-321.
Warranty of condition on arrival, §25-2-321.
C.O.D. terms.
Buyer not entitled to inspect goods before payment, §25-2-513, (3).
Confirmed credit, §25-2-325, (3).
Delivery ex-ship, §25-2-322.

COMMERCIAL CODE —Cont'd
Sales —Cont'd
Terms —Cont'd
Exclusive dealing, §25-2-306, (2).
F.O.B. and F.A.S. terms, §25-2-319.
Bill of lading required in overseas shipment, §25-2-323.
Letter of credit, §25-2-325.
No arrival, no sale, §25-2-324.
Open price term, §25-2-305.
Output or requirement contracts, §25-2-306, (1).
Quantity.
Output or requirement contracts, §25-2-306, (1).
Third parties.
Injury to goods.
Who can sue third parties for injury to goods, §25-2-722.
Time.
Absence of specified time provisions, §25-2-309.
Notice of termination, §25-2-309, (3).
Open time for payment or running of credit, §25-2-310.
Title.
Creditor's rights, §25-2-402.
Entrusting, §25-2-403.
Fraud.
Transfer of title obtained by fraud, §25-2-403, (1).
Good faith purchase of goods, §25-2-403.
Larceny.
Power to transfer voidable title, §25-2-403, (1).
Passing of title, §25-2-401.
Limited applicability of section, §25-2-401.
Reservation for security, §25-2-401.
Power to transfer, §25-2-403.
Reservation for security, §25-2-401.
Applicability of article 9, §25-9-110.
Retention of title, §25-2-505.
Shipment under reservation, §25-2-505.
Transfer, §25-2-403.
Warranty of title and against infringement, §25-2-312.
Transferability, §25-2-105.
Trees and timber.
Contract for sale of timber, §25-2-107, (2).
Unconscionable contract or clause, §25-2-302.
Usage of trade.
Implied warranties, §25-2-314, (3).
Exclusion or modification by usage of trade, §25-2-316, (3).
Used to explain terms of contract, §25-2-202.
Waiver.
Buyer's objections by failure to particularize, §25-2-605.
Warranties.
Breach of warranty.
Limitation of remedies for breach, §25-2-316, (4).
C.I.F. and C. & F. terms.
Warranty of condition on arrival, §25-2-321.
Conflict of warranty, §25-2-317.
Course of dealing, §25-2-314, (3).
Exclusion or modification by course of dealing, §25-2-316.
Cumulation of warranties, §25-2-317.
Disclaimer of warranties, §25-2-316.
Exclusion, §25-2-316.
Persons to whom warranties extend, §25-2-318.

COMMERCIAL CODE —Cont'd
Sales —Cont'd
Warranties —Cont'd
Express warranties, §25-2-313.
Cumulation and conflict, §25-2-317.
Samples, §25-2-313.
Third party beneficiaries, §25-2-318.
Fitness for a particular purpose, §25-2-315.
Implied warranties.
Course of dealing, §25-2-314, (3).
Exclusion or modification by course of dealing, §25-2-316, (3).
Cumulation and conflict, §25-2-317.
Fitness for a particular purpose, §25-2-315.
Merchantability, §25-2-314.
Third party beneficiaries, §25-2-318.
Usage of trade, §25-2-314, (3).
Exclusion or modification by usage of trade, §25-2-316, (3).
Merchantability, §25-2-314.
Modification, §25-2-316.
Persons to whom warranties extend, §25-2-318.
Notice of claim or litigation to person answerable over, §25-2-607, (5).
Third party beneficiaries, §25-2-318.
Usage of trade, §25-2-314, (3).
Exclusion or modification by usage of trade, §25-2-316, (3).
Warranty of title and against infringement, §25-2-312.
Seasonably.
Construed, §25-1-204, (3).
Section captions.
Part of chapter, §25-1-109.
Secured transactions, §§25-9-101 to 25-9-710.
Accessions.
Perfection and priority of security interest in, §25-9-335.
Accounting.
Request for.
Charge for response, §25-9-210, (f).
Damages for noncompliance, §25-9-625, (f).
Defined, §25-9-210, (a).
Duty to respond to, §25-9-210, (b).
Limitation of security interest for noncompliance, §25-9-625, (g).
List of collateral, §25-9-210, (c), (d).
No interest claimed, §25-9-210, (e).
After-acquired collateral.
Security agreement may provide for security by, §25-9-204, (1).
After-acquired property.
Security interest in, §25-9-204, (a).
When after-acquired property clause not effective, §25-9-204, (b).
Agricultural liens.
Default.
Time of default, §25-9-606.
Perfection and priority.
Filed financing statement providing certain incorrect information.
Priority of agricultural lien perfected by, §25-9-338.
Filing.
Assigned perfected interest need not be refiled, §25-9-310, (c).
When filing not required to perfect lien, §25-9-310, (b).
When required to perfect lien, §25-9-310, (a).

COMMERCIAL CODE —Cont'd
Secured transactions —Cont'd
Agricultural liens —Cont'd
Perfection and priority —Cont'd
Interests that take priority over or take free of agricultural lien, §25-9-317, (a).
Law governing, §25-9-302.
Multiple conflicting interests in same collateral.
Other UCC provisions governing, §25-9-322, (f).
Proceeds and supporting obligations, time of perfection, §25-9-322, (b).
Rules governing priority, §25-9-322, (a), (g).
When perfected, §25-9-308, (b).
Amendatory act.
Definitions, §25-11-101.1.
Effective date, §25-11-101.
Filing.
Change of place of filing, §25-11-105, (1), (2).
Change of requirement for filing, §25-11-104.
Continuation statement, §25-11-105, (3).
Mortgages or deeds of trust, §25-11-105, (4).
Refilings.
Required refilings, §25-11-106.
Perfected security interest.
Transition to new article 9, §25-11-103, (2).
Presumption that rule of law continues unchanged, §25-11-108.
Priorities.
Transition provisions, §25-11-107.
Refilings.
Financing statement may be filed within six months before perfection of security interest which would otherwise lapse, §25-11-106, (4).
Security interest perfected by filing, refiling or recording under law repealed under act, §25-11-106, (3).
Security interest perfected or has priority when act takes effect, §25-11-106, (1).
Security interest perfected when new article 9 takes effect, §25-11-106, (2).
Transition provisions.
Filing.
Change of place of filing, §25-11-105.
Change of requirement for filing, §25-11-104.
General rule as to transition to new article 9, §25-11-103, (1).
Preservation of old transition provisions, §25-11-102.
Priorities, §25-11-107.
Applicability of provisions.
Articles 2 and 2A security interests, §25-9-110.
Conflict of laws, §25-9-109, (c).
Exclusions from article, §25-9-109, (d).
General scope, §25-9-109, (a).
Letters of credit.
Beneficiaries and nominated persons rights superior, §25-9-109, (c).
Secured interest in obligation secured outside of article 9, §25-9-109, (b).
Assignments.
Applicability of article 9.
Certain assignments not covered by provisions, §25-9-109, (d).

COMMERCIAL CODE —Cont'd
Secured transactions —Cont'd
Attachment of security interest, §25-9-203, (a).
Financial asset.
Security interest arising in purchase or delivery of, §25-9-206.
Payment against delivery transactions, §25-9-206, (c), (d).
Purchase through securities intermediary, §25-9-206, (a), (b).
Bank deposits and collections.
Documentary drafts.
Privilege of presenting bank to deal with goods.
Security interest for expenses, §25-4-504, (b).
Security interest of collecting bank in items, accompanying documents and proceeds, §25-4-208, (a).
Credit given, §25-4-208, (b).
Final settlement, §25-4-208, (c).
Banks and financial institutions.
Control agreement.
Refusal to enter into or disclose existence of, §25-9-342.
Rights of banks.
Deposit accounts, §§25-9-340, 25-9-341.
Transfer of accounts excluded from article, §25-9-104, (l).
Chattel paper.
Perfection of security interests in, §25-9-312, (a).
Purchaser of chattel paper or instrument.
Priority, §25-9-330.
Choice of law.
Debtor's location.
Applicability of section limited, §25-9-307, (k).
Continuation of location, §25-9-307, (d), (f).
Foreign air carriers, §25-9-307, (j).
General rules, §25-9-307, (b).
Limitation, §25-9-307, (c).
Place of business.
Defined, §25-9-307, (a).
Registered organizations, §25-9-307, (e).
Continuation of location, §25-9-307, (g).
Federally registered organizations, §25-9-307, (f).
Investment property, §25-9-305, (a).
Commodity intermediary jurisdiction determinations, §25-9-305, (b).
Exceptions to general rule, §25-9-305, (c).
Perfection and priority.
Agricultural liens, §25-9-302.
Certificates of title covering goods.
Applicability of section, §25-9-303, (a).
Determination of coverage of certificate, §25-9-303, (b).
Law of jurisdiction of certificate governs, §25-9-303, (c).
Deposit accounts.
Bank's jurisdiction's law governs, §25-9-304, (a).
Determining jurisdiction of bank, §25-9-304, (b).
Letter-of-credit rights, §25-9-306.
Security interests, §25-9-301.
Citation of chapter.
Short title, §25-9-101.
Citation of provisions, §25-9-101.
Classification of goods, §25-9-109.

COMMERCIAL CODE —Cont'd
Secured transactions —Cont'd
Collateral.
Default.
Acceptance in full or partial satisfaction of obligation, §§25-9-620 to 25-9-622.
Disposition after default, §§25-9-610 to 25-9-617.
Redemption.
Persons who may redeem, §25-9-623, (a).
Right to redeem collateral, §25-9-623.
Time for redemption, §25-9-623, (b).
Waiver of right, §25-9-624, (c).
Title transfers, legal or record.
Effect of transfer statement, §25-9-619, (b), (c).
Transfer statement defined, §25-9-619, (a).
Description.
Investment property, §25-9-108, (d).
Reasonable identification.
Examples, §25-9-108, (b).
Sufficiency, §25-9-108, (a).
Supergeneric descriptions, §25-9-108, (c).
Type, description by, §25-9-108, (e).
Disposition.
Permissible, §25-9-205, (a).
Possession requirement not relaxed, §25-9-205, (b).
Disposition after default.
Power of sale barred when foreclosure barred, §25-9-509, (1).
List of collateral.
Request regarding, §25-9-210, (c), (d).
Limitation of security interest for noncompliance, §25-9-625, (g).
Possession of collateral.
Rights and duties of secured party having, §25-9-207.
Repossession, §25-9-503.
Secured party in possession or control.
Buyers of accounts, paper, notes, etc, §25-9-207, (d).
Care, duty of, §25-9-207, (a).
Deposit account, electronic chattel paper, investment property or letter-of-credit right as collateral, §25-9-208, (a).
Demand from debtor, §25-9-208, (b).
Discharge of account debtor.
Applicability of section, §25-9-209, (a).
Demand from debtor, §25-9-209, (b).
Expenses to preserve collateral, §25-9-207, (b).
Preservation of collateral, §25-9-207, (b).
Proceeds from collateral, §25-9-207, (c).
Risk of loss, §25-9-207, (b).
Security interest in collateral, §25-9-207, (c).
Title immaterial, §25-9-202.
Transferred collateral.
Priority of security interests in, §25-9-325.
Use.
Permissible, §25-9-205, (a).
Possession requirement not relaxed, §25-9-205, (b).
Commingled goods.
Priority of security interests, §25-9-336.
Compliance with article. See within this subheading, "Remedies for noncompliance with article."
Conflict of laws.
Multiple state transactions.
Perfection of security interest, §25-9-103.

COMMERCIAL CODE —Cont'd
Secured transactions —Cont'd
Conflict of laws —Cont'd
Perfection of security interest in multiple state transactions, §25-9-103.
Consumer finance act.
Transactions also subject to, §25-9-203, (4).
Crops.
Priority of security interests in, §25-9-334, (i).
Production money security interests, §25-9-324.1.
Production-money crops.
Defined, §25-9-102, (a).
Status of security interest in, §25-9-103.1, (a).
Production-money obligation.
Application of payments, §25-9-103.1, (b).
Defined, §25-9-102, (a).
Production-money security interests.
Status, §25-9-103.1, (a).
Burden of establishing, §25-9-103.1, (c).
Continuation of status, §25-9-103.1, (c).
Production of crops.
Defined, §25-9-102, (a).
Debtor.
Defined, §25-9-102.
Location, §25-9-307.
Default.
Acceptance of collateral in full or partial satisfaction of obligation.
Conditions to acceptance, §25-9-620, (a).
Consent of debtor, §25-9-620, (c).
Consumer goods, mandatory disposition, §25-9-620, (e), (f).
Waiver of mandatory disposition, §25-9-624, (b).
Noncompliance with provisions.
Effect, §25-9-622, (b).
Notification of objection, §25-9-620, (d).
Notification of proposal.
Partial satisfaction, secondary obligors to be notified, §25-9-621, (b).
Partial satisfaction, §25-9-620, (g).
Purported acceptance, §25-9-620, (b).
Agricultural lien.
Time of default, §25-9-606.
Assembly of collateral for convenience of secured party, §25-9-609, (c).
Assignments, transfers or subrogations.
Effect, §25-9-618, (b).
Rights and duties of secondary obligors, §25-9-618, (a).
Collateral.
Acceptance in full or partial satisfaction of obligation, §§25-9-620 to 25-9-622.
Disposition after default, §§25-9-610 to 25-9-617.
Redemption.
Persons who may redeem, §25-9-623, (a).
Right to redeem collateral, §25-9-623.
Time for redemption, §25-9-623, (b).
Waiver of right, §25-9-624, (c).
Title transfers, legal or record.
Effect of transfer statement, §25-9-619, (b), (c).
Transfer statement defined, §25-9-619, (a).
Collection and enforcement by secured party, §25-9-607, (a).
Application of proceeds, §25-9-608, (a).
Commercial reasonableness, §25-9-607, (c).
Determination of commercial reasonableness, §25-9-627.

COMMERCIAL CODE —Cont'd
Secured transactions —Cont'd
Default —Cont'd
Collection and enforcement by secured party —Cont'd
Deficiency, responsibility for, §25-9-608, (a).
Certain sales, §25-9-608, (b).
Damage actions when surplus or deficiency an issue, §25-9-626.
Duty to secured party not affected by section, §25-9-607, (e).
Expenses, §25-9-607, (d).
Nonjudicial enforcement of mortgage, §25-9-607, (b).
Surplus, application, §25-9-608, (a).
Certain sales, §25-9-608, (b).
Damage actions when surplus or deficiency an issue, §25-9-626.
Disposition of collateral after, §25-9-610, (a).
Commercially reasonable disposition, §25-9-610, (b).
Determination of commercial reasonableness, §25-9-627.
Compulsory disposition, §25-9-620, (e).
Waiver of mandatory disposition, §25-9-624, (b).
Notification before, §25-9-611, (b).
Collateral other than consumer goods, other secured parties, §25-9-611, (e).
Consumer goods transactions, contents and form, §25-9-614.
Definition of notification date, §25-9-611, (a).
Nonconsumer transactions, timeliness, §25-9-612, (b).
Perishable collateral exception to notice requirement, §25-9-611, (d).
Persons to be notified, §25-9-611, (c).
Recognized market exception to notification requirement, §25-9-611, (d).
Timeliness, §25-9-612, (a).
Waiver, §25-9-624, (a).
Perishable collateral exception to notification requirement, §25-9-611, (d).
Proceeds.
Application, §25-9-615, (a).
Noncash proceeds, §25-9-615, (c).
Subordinate interest, §25-9-615, (b), (g).
Purchase by secured party, §25-9-610, (c).
Recognized market exception to notification requirement, §25-9-611, (d).
Surplus or deficiency, §25-9-615, (d).
Calculation, §25-9-615, (f).
Damage actions when surplus or deficiency an issue, §25-9-626, (a), (b).
Explanation of calculation, §25-9-616, (b).
Explanation of calculation, charges for additional explanations, §25-9-616, (e).
Explanation of calculation, definition, §25-9-616, (a).
Explanation of calculation, limitation of liability, §25-9-628, (d).
Explanation of calculation, required information, §25-9-616, (c).
Explanation of calculation, substantial compliance, §25-9-616, (d).
Sales of rights to payment, §25-9-615, (e).
Transferee's rights.
Effect of disposition, §25-9-617, (a).
Good faith transferees, §25-9-617, (b).
Taking subject to limitations, §25-9-617, (c).

COMMERCIAL CODE —Cont'd
Secured transactions —Cont'd
Default —Cont'd
Disposition of collateral after —Cont'd
Warranties on disposition, §25-9-610, (d).
Disclaimer, §25-9-610, (e), (f).
Fixtures.
Procedure if security agreement covers, §25-9-604, (b).
Removal, §25-9-604, (c).
Injury caused by, §25-9-604, (d).
Judicial enforcement, §25-9-601.
Nonjudicial enforcement of mortgage, §25-9-607, (b).
Real property.
Procedure if security agreement covers, §25-9-604, (a).
Rendering equipment unusable, §25-9-609, (a).
Breach of the peace not sanctioned, §25-9-609, (b).
Process, §25-9-609, (b).
Repossession, §25-9-609, (a).
Breach of the peace not sanctioned, §25-9-609, (b).
Process, §25-9-609, (b).
Right of secured party to take possession after default, §25-9-503.
Rights after default, §25-9-601, (a), (c).
Agreement on standards concerning, §25-9-603, (a).
Breach of the peace not covered by agreements, §25-9-603, (b).
Consignors or buyers of accounts, etc., §25-9-601, (g).
Debtors' rights and obligations, §25-9-601, (d).
Execution sales, §25-9-601, (f).
Lien of levy after judgment, §25-9-601, (e).
Waiver and variance, §25-9-602.
Secondary obligor.
Rights and duties, §25-9-618.
Secured party.
Right to take possession after default, §25-9-503.
Secured party in possession of collateral, §25-9-601, (b), (c).
Unknown debtor or secondary obligor, §25-9-605.
Waiver of certain rights, §25-9-624.
Defenses.
Agreement not to assert defenses against assignee, §25-9-206, (1).
Definitions.
Amendatory act, §25-11-101.1.
Article 9 definitions, §25-9-102, (a).
Commingled goods, priority of security interests, §25-9-336, (a).
Explanation of calculation.
Disposition of collateral after default, surplus or deficiency, §25-9-616, (a).
Former-article-9 records, transitional provisions regarding filing office, §25-9-710, (a).
General provisions article definitions.
Applicability, §25-9-102, (c).
Licensee of general intangible, priority of security interests, §25-9-321, (a).
Local-filing office, transitional provisions regarding filing office, §25-9-710, (a).
Non-article 9 definitions, §25-9-102, (b).
Notification date.
Disposition of collateral after default, notification before, §25-9-611, (a).

COMMERCIAL CODE —Cont'd
Secured transactions —Cont'd
Definitions —Cont'd
Place of business, debtor's location for choice of law issues, §25-9-307, (a).
Possessory liens, priority of security interests, §25-9-333, (a).
Pre-effective-date financing statement, transitional provisions, §25-9-707, (a).
Purchase money security interests, §25-9-103, (a).
Request for accounting, §25-9-210, (a).
Transfer statement defined, title transfers upon default, §25-9-619, (a).
Value, third parties, §25-9-403, (a).
Delivery.
Defined, §25-1-201, (14).
Deposit account.
Bank's rights and duties with respect to, §25-9-341.
Setoff or recoupment against deposit account.
Effectiveness, §25-9-340, (b), (c).
Exercise, §25-9-340, (a).
Control, §25-9-104.
Extent of control, §25-9-104, (b).
Requirements, §25-9-104, (a).
Inapplicability of article 9.
Consumer transaction assignments, §25-9-109, (d).
Perfection and priority of security interest in, §25-9-312, (b).
Perfection by control, §25-9-314, (a).
Priority of security interests, §25-9-327.
Transfer of funds from deposit account.
Transferee takes funds free of security interest, §25-9-332, (b).
Description of property.
Investment property, §25-9-108, (d).
Reasonable identification.
Examples, §25-9-108, (b).
Sufficiency, §25-9-108, (a).
Supergeneric description, §25-9-108, (c).
Type, description by, §25-9-108, (e).
Documents.
Multiple state transactions.
Perfection of security interest, §25-9-103, (1).
Effective date of provisions, §25-9-701.
Action taken before.
Effectiveness, §25-9-705.
Financing statement.
Pre-effective-date financing statement, §25-9-707.
Governmental transactions.
Special rule, §25-9-702, (d).
Pre-effective date proceedings, §25-9-702, (c).
Pre-effective date transactions, §25-9-702, (a).
Security interest not perfected before effective date, §25-9-704.
Priority, §25-9-703, (b).
Security interest perfected before effective date, §25-9-703, (a).
Electronic chattel paper.
Control, §25-9-105.
Perfection by control, §25-9-314, (a).
Perfection and priority of security interests in.
Perfection by control, §25-9-314, (a).
Enforceability of security interest.
Conditions for enforceability, §25-9-203, (b).
Lien securing right to payment.
Attachment of security interest in the security interest, §25-9-203, (g).

COMMERCIAL CODE —Cont'd
Secured transactions —Cont'd
Enforceability of security interest —Cont'd
Proceeds, right to, §25-9-203, (f).
Securities accounts, §25-9-203, (h).
Security agreement of another binding person, §25-9-203, (d), (e).
Supporting obligations for collateral.
Attachment of interest in supporting obligations, §25-9-203, (f).
UCC provisions from other articles overriding enforceability, §25-9-203, (c).
Exclusion from article, §25-9-104.
Filing.
Refilings.
Required refilings under amendatory act, §25-11-106.
Transition provisions, §§25-11-104 to 25-11-106.
Filing office, §25-9-501, (a).
Acknowledgments.
Filing of other records, §25-9-523, (b).
Filing of written record, §25-9-523, (a).
Timeliness, §25-9-523, (e).
Cancellation of record.
Appeals, §25-9-520, (e).
Communication concerning, §25-9-520, (b).
Communication of requested information, §25-9-523, (c), (g).
Fee, §25-9-525, (d).
Medium, §25-9-523, (d).
Timeliness, §25-9-523, (e).
Delay by.
Excuse for delay, §25-9-524.
Destruction of records, §25-9-522, (b).
Duties, §§25-9-519, 25-9-520, 25-9-522, 25-9-523.
Generally, §25-9-519, (a).
Fees, §25-9-525.
Initial statements or records, §25-9-525, (a).
Number of names immaterial, §25-9-525, (c).
Record of mortgage as financing statement, §25-9-525, (e).
Response to information request, §25-9-525, (d).
File numbers, §25-9-519, (b), (i).
Indexing.
Assignments.
Real property-related assignments, §25-9-519, (e).
Financing statements, §25-9-519, (c).
Real property-related financing statements, §25-9-519, (d).
Information from, §25-9-523.
Fee, §25-9-525, (d).
Maintenance of records, §25-9-522, (a).
Name of debtor.
Removal, §25-9-519, (g).
Refusal to accept record, §25-9-520, (a).
Amend form.
Prohibition on refusal when in proper form, §25-9-521, (b).
Appeals, §25-9-520, (e).
Communication regarding, §25-9-520, (b).
Effectiveness of certain refused records, §25-9-520, (c).
Initial financing statement form.
Prohibition on refusal when in proper form, §25-9-521, (a).
Multiple debtors, separate applications, §25-9-520, (d).
Reports on operation, §25-9-526.

COMMERCIAL CODE —Cont'd
Secured transactions —Cont'd
Filing office —Cont'd
Retrieval and association of records, §25-9-519, (f).
Timeliness of performance, §25-9-519, (h).
Transitional provisions.
Deadline for acceptance of records, §25-9-710, (b).
Former-article-9 records.
Defined, §25-9-710, (a).
Destruction, §25-9-710, (e).
Maintenance, duration, §25-9-710, (c).
Response to information requests, §25-9-710, (d).
Transmitting utilities, §25-9-501, (b).
Filing-office rules, §25-9-526, (a).
Harmonization of rules, §25-9-526, (b).
Financial asset.
Priority of certain interests in, §25-9-331.
Purchase or delivery of.
Security interest arising in, §25-9-206.
Financing statement.
Amendment, §25-9-512, (a).
Collateral added, §25-9-512, (c).
Debtor added, §25-9-512, (d).
Deleting secured party of record, §25-9-511, (c).
Extension of period of effectiveness not accomplished by, §25-9-512, (b).
Form, §25-9-521, (b).
Multiple secured parties of record, §25-9-509, (e).
Naming secured party of record, §25-9-511, (b).
Persons entitled to file, §25-9-509, (d).
Pre-effective-date financing statement.
Additional fee not to be charged, §25-9-707, (f).
Continuation by amendment, methods, §25-9-707, (d).
Definition, §25-9-707, (a).
Governing provisions, §25-9-707, (b).
Method of amendment, §25-9-707, (c).
Termination by amendment, methods, §25-9-707, (e).
Prohibited amendments, §25-9-512, (e).
Collateral.
Indication of collateral, §25-9-504.
Consignors, lessors, and other bailors.
Filing financing statement permitted, §25-9-505, (a).
Effect, §25-9-505, (b).
Contents, §25-9-502, (a).
Continuation statement.
Effect of filing, §25-9-515, (e).
Time for filing, §25-9-515, (d).
Transitional provisions, §§25-9-705, (d), 25-9-708.
Correction statements, §25-9-518.
Debtor information.
Multiple debtor names, §25-9-503, (e).
Name of debtor, §25-9-503, (a), (b).
Change of name, §25-9-507, (c).
Trade names, §25-9-503, (c).
Representative capacity not required, §25-9-503, (d).
Disposition of collateral, §25-9-507, (a).
Duration of effectiveness.
Five year period, §25-9-515, (a).

COMMERCIAL CODE —Cont'd
Secured transactions —Cont'd
Financing statement —Cont'd
Duration of effectiveness —Cont'd
Manufactured home transactions, §25-9-515, (b).
Public finance transactions, §25-9-515, (b).
Record of mortgage as financing statement, §25-9-515, (g).
Transmitting utilities, §25-9-515, (f).
Effective date of provisions.
Pre-effective-date financing statement, §25-9-707.
Errors and omissions.
Correction statement, §25-9-518, (a).
Effect, §25-9-518, (c).
Sufficiency, §25-9-518, (b), (b1).
Effect.
Indexing errors, §25-9-517.
Minor errors and omissions, §25-9-506, (a).
Name of debtor, §25-9-506, (d).
Not seriously misleading statement, §25-9-506, (c).
Seriously misleading statement, §25-9-506, (b).
Events with impact on effectiveness, §25-9-507.
Filing.
Amendments, §25-9-512, (a).
Collateral added, §25-9-512, (c).
Debtor added, §25-9-512, (d).
Extension of period of effectiveness not accomplished by, §25-9-512, (b).
Form, §25-9-521, (b).
Multiple secured parties of record, §25-9-509, (e).
Persons entitled to file, §25-9-509, (d).
Pre-effective date financing statements, §25-9-707.
Prohibited amendments, §25-9-512, (e).
Authorization by debtor.
Collateral acquisition, §25-9-509, (c).
Security agreement, §25-9-509, (b).
Continuation statements, §25-9-510, (c).
Amendment to continue financing statement, §25-9-512, (a).
Transitional provisions, §25-9-708.
Effectiveness of filed record.
Authorization, §25-9-510, (a).
Continuation statements, §25-9-510, (c).
One of multiple secured parties authorizing, §25-9-510, (b).
Initial financing statement.
Transitional provisions, §25-9-708.
When filing suffices to continue effectiveness of financing statement, §25-9-706.
Permissive filing.
Consignors, lessors and other bailors, §25-9-505.
Persons entitled to file record, §25-9-509, (a).
Amendments, §25-9-509, (d), (e).
Effectiveness of filed record, §25-9-510.
Pre-effective date filing, §25-9-705, (b), (c).
Prior to attachment or security agreement, §25-9-502, (d).
Refusal to accept record for filing, §25-9-516, (b), (c).
When effective as filed record, §25-9-516, (d).
Termination statements, §25-9-513.
What constitutes, §25-9-516, (a).

COMMERCIAL CODE —Cont'd
Secured transactions —Cont'd
Financing statement —Cont'd
Form, §25-9-521, (a).
Indexing errors, §25-9-517.
Correction statements, §25-9-518.
Information becoming seriously misleading, §25-9-507, (b).
Lapse, §25-9-515, (c).
Mortgage record as statement, §25-9-502, (c).
Name of debtor and secured party.
Errors and omissions, §25-9-506, (d).
Pre-effective date statement with post-effective date continuation statement, §25-9-705, (f).
Real property-related statements, §25-9-502, (b).
Secured party of record, §25-9-511, (a).
Assignment of powers of.
Filed statement assigned, §25-9-514, (b).
Record of mortgage assigned, §25-9-514, (c).
Reflection on initial statement, §25-9-514, (a).
Deletion by amendment, §25-9-511, (c).
Naming by amendment, §25-9-511, (b).
Subsequent or new debtor.
Effectiveness of statement naming original debtor, §25-9-508, (a).
Effect of 25-9-507, (a), §25-9-508, (c).
Seriously misleading statement as result, §25-9-508, (b).
Termination statement.
Amendment to terminate statement, §25-9-512, (a).
Collateral other than consumer goods, §25-9-513, (c).
Consumer goods, §25-9-513, (a).
Time for filing, §25-9-513, (b).
Effect of filing, §25-9-513, (d).
Transitional provisions.
Initial statement in lieu of continuation statement, §25-9-706, (a).
Period of continuing effectiveness, §25-9-706, (b).
Requirements, §25-9-706, (c).
Transmitting utility.
Transitional provisions, §25-9-705, (e).
Fixtures.
Priority of security interests in, §25-9-334.
Fraudulent transfers.
Enforcement of security interest in compliance with UCC secured transactions article.
Transfers not voidable, §39-23.8, (e).
Fungible.
Defined, §25-1-201, (17).
Future advances.
Priority of security interests, §25-9-323.
Security interest in, §25-9-204, (c).
Government transfers.
Excluded transactions, §25-9-104, (e).
Grandfather clause, §25-9-702, (b).
Identification and proof of assignment, §25-9-406.
Instruments.
Perfected security interest in instruments, §25-9-304.
Insurance.
Transfer of interest or claim in policy excluded, §25-9-104, (g).
Investment property.
Description of property, §25-9-108, (d).
Perfection and priority of security interests in, §25-9-312, (a).
Law governing, §25-9-305.
Perfection by control, §25-9-314, (a).

COMMERCIAL CODE —Cont'd
Secured transactions —Cont'd
Investment property —Cont'd
Perfection and priority of security interests in —Cont'd
Priority of security interests, §25-9-328.
Temporary perfection, §25-9-312, (e) to (h).
Judgments and decrees.
Transactions excluded from article, §25-9-104, (h).
Landlord and tenant.
Landlord's lien.
Applicability of secured transactions article, §25-9-104, (b).
Leases.
Restrictions on security interest in leasehold interest or in lessor's residual interest, §25-9-407.
Leases, UCC.
Rejected goods, buyer's security interest.
Applicability of article 9, §25-9-110.
Letter-of-credit right.
Assignment.
Restrictions on assignment ineffective, §25-9-409, (a).
Exceptions, §25-9-409, (b).
Control, §25-9-107.
Perfection and priority of security interests in, §25-9-312, (b).
Law governing, §25-9-306.
Perfection by control, §25-9-314, (a).
Priority of security interests, §25-9-329.
Letters of credit.
Security interest of issuer or nominated person, §25-5-118.
Transfer of interest.
Excluded transactions, §25-9-104, (m).
Liens.
Transactions excluded from article, §25-9-104, (c).
Noncompliance with article. See within this subheading, "Remedies for noncompliance with article."
Perfection of security interests.
Attachment.
Security interests perfected upon attachment, §25-9-309.
Chattel paper, §25-9-312, (a).
Commodity accounts, §25-9-308, (g).
Continuity of perfection, §25-9-308, (c).
Change in governing law, §25-9-316, (a).
Bank's, issuer's, nominated person's, intermediary's jurisdiction changes, §25-9-316, (f), (g).
Certificates of title, §25-9-316, (d), (e).
Perfection or unperfection under law of new jurisdiction, §25-9-316, (b).
Possessory security interest in collateral moved to new jurisdiction, §25-9-316, (c).
Control, perfection by.
Duration of perfection by control, §25-9-314, (b).
Investment property, §25-9-314, (c).
Security interests perfectible by control, §25-9-314, (a).
Delivery to secured party to perfect, §25-9-313, (a).
Duration of perfection by delivery, §25-9-313, (e).

COMMERCIAL CODE —Cont'd
Secured transactions —Cont'd
Perfection of security interests —Cont'd
Deposit accounts, §25-9-312, (b).
Perfection by control, §25-9-314, (a).
Effective date of provisions.
Security interest not perfected before, §25-9-704.
Priority, §25-9-703, (b).
Security interest perfected before, §25-9-703, (a).
Filing.
Assigned perfected interests need not be refiled, §25-9-310, (c).
Instruments.
Permissive filing, §25-9-312, (a).
Laws, treaties, etc., making filing unnecessary or ineffective, §25-9-311, (a).
Duration and renewal of perfection, §25-9-311, (c).
Effect of compliance with, §25-9-311, (b).
Inventories held for sale, §25-9-311, (d).
Permissive filing, §25-9-312.
When filing not required, §25-9-310, (b).
When required, §25-9-310, (a).
Instruments, §25-9-312, (a).
Investment property, §25-9-312, (a).
Perfection by control, §25-9-314, (a), (c).
Temporary perfection, §25-9-312, (e) to (h).
Law governing, §25-9-301.
Deposit accounts, §25-9-304.
Goods covered by certificate of title, §25-9-303.
Investment property, §25-9-305.
Letter-of-credit rights, §25-9-306.
Letter-of-credit rights, §25-9-312, (b).
Law governing, §25-9-306.
Perfection by control, §25-9-314, (a).
Lien securing right to payment, §25-9-308, (e).
Money, §25-9-312, (b).
Negotiable documents governing goods, §25-9-312, (c).
Nonnegotiable documents governing goods, §25-9-312, (d).
Possession by secured party to perfect, §25-9-313, (a).
Certificate of title covering goods, §25-9-313, (b).
Collateral in possession of person other than debtor, §25-9-313, (c).
Acknowledgments, §25-9-313, (f), (g).
Delivery by secured party to third party, §25-9-313, (h), (i).
Pre-effective date actions to perfect, §25-9-705, (a).
Proceeds, §25-9-315, (c).
Duration of perfection, §25-9-315, (d), (e).
Securities account, §25-9-308, (f).
Supporting obligations, §25-9-308, (d).
Temporary perfection.
Availability of goods or documents to debtor, §25-9-312, (f).
Delivery to debtor, §25-9-312, (g).
Expiration, §25-9-312, (h).
New value, §25-9-312, (e).
Treaties.
Security interest in property subject to certain treaties, §25-9-311.
When perfected, §25-9-308, (a).
Priorities.
Persons who take priority over unperfected security interests, §25-9-301.

COMMERCIAL CODE —Cont'd
Secured transactions —Cont'd
Priorities —Cont'd
Transition provisions, §25-11-107.
Priority of security interests.
Accessions, §25-9-335, (c).
Certificates of title, §25-9-335, (d).
Creation and continuation of interest in accession, §25-9-335, (a).
Perfection of interest in accession, §25-9-335, (b).
Removal of accession, §25-9-335, (e).
Reimbursement following, §25-9-335, (f).
Agricultural liens.
Buyers receiving delivery.
Interests that take priority over or take free of, §25-9-317, (b).
Filed financing statement providing certain incorrect information.
Agricultural lien perfected by, §25-9-338.
Interests that take priority over or take free of, §25-9-317, (a).
Law governing, §25-9-302.
Lessees receiving delivery.
Interests that take priority over or take free of, §25-9-317, (c).
Multiple conflicting interests in same collateral.
Other UCC provisions governing, §25-9-322, (f).
Proceeds and supporting obligations, time of perfection, §25-9-322, (b).
Rules governing priority, §25-9-322, (a), (g).
Buyer of goods, §25-9-320.
Consumer goods buyers, §25-9-320, (b).
Filing, effectiveness, §25-9-320, (c).
Ordinary course of business, §25-9-320, (a).
Wellhead or minehead, buyers at, §25-9-320, (d).
Possessory security interests, §25-9-320, (e).
Buyers receiving delivery.
Interests that take priority over or take free of, §25-9-317, (b).
Certificate of title.
Security interest in goods covered by, §25-9-337.
Chattel paper or instrument purchasers' priorities.
Assignment indication constituting knowledge, §25-9-330, (f).
Nonpossessory perfection, §25-9-330, (d).
Other interests, §25-9-330, (b).
Proceeds, §25-9-330, (a), (c).
Purchase money security interest holder giving new value, §25-9-330, (e).
Commingled goods.
Definition of commingled goods, §25-9-336, (a).
Transformation of interest in goods to interest in product or mass, §25-9-336, (b).
Attachment to product or mass, §25-9-336, (c).
Conflicting interests in product or mass, §25-9-336, (f).
Continuation of perfected interest, §25-9-336, (d).
Determining priority, §25-9-336, (e).
Consignees.
Rights and title with respect to creditors and purchasers, §25-9-319, (a).
Conflict of laws, §25-9-319, (b).

COMMERCIAL CODE —Cont'd
Secured transactions —Cont'd
Priority of security interests —Cont'd
Crops.
Security interest in, §25-9-334, (i).
Deposit account, §25-9-327.
Transfer of funds from, §25-9-332, (b).
Filed financing statement providing certain incorrect information.
Security interest perfected by, §25-9-338.
Financial asset.
Priority of certain interests in, §25-9-331.
Fixtures, §25-9-334, (a).
Consent, disclaimer, or right to remove fixture.
Effect on priority, §25-9-334, (f).
Construction mortgage, §25-9-334, (h).
Continuation of interest, §25-9-334, (g).
Purchase money priority, §25-9-334, (d).
Real property, interests in, §25-9-334, (e).
Real property law security interests, §25-9-334, (b).
Subordination, §25-9-334, (c).
Future advances.
Buyers of goods, ordinary course of business, §25-9-323, (d).
Commitment, advances pursuant to, §25-9-323, (e).
Buyers of receivables holding interest, §25-9-323, (c).
Lessees of goods, §25-9-323, (f).
Commitment, advances pursuant to, §25-9-323, (g).
Lien creditors, §25-9-323, (b).
Time of advance basis, §25-9-323, (a).
General intangibles, accounts, electronic chattel paper, or investment property.
Buyers or licensees of certain collateral.
Interests that take priority over or take free of, §25-9-317, (d).
Investment property, §25-9-328.
Law governing, §25-9-301.
Agricultural liens, §25-9-302.
Deposit accounts, §25-9-304.
Goods covered by certificate of title, §25-9-303.
Investment property, §25-9-305.
Letter-of-credit rights, §25-9-306.
Lessee of goods in ordinary course of business, §25-9-321, (c).
Lessees receiving delivery.
Interests that take priority over or take free of, §25-9-317, (c).
Letter-of-credit right, §25-9-329.
Law governing, §25-9-306.
Licensee of general intangible, §25-9-321, (b).
Defined, §25-9-321, (a).
Liens arising by operation of law.
Possessory liens, §25-9-333, (b).
Defined, §25-9-333, (a).
Money transfers.
Transferee takes money free of security interest, §25-9-332, (a).
Multiple conflicting interests in same collateral.
Chattel paper, deposit accounts, negotiable documents, instruments, etc., §25-9-322, (d), (e).
Other UCC provisions governing, §25-9-322, (f).
Proceeds and supporting obligations, special priority rules, §25-9-322, (c).

COMMERCIAL CODE —Cont'd
Secured transactions —Cont'd
Priority of security interests —Cont'd
Multiple conflicting interests in same collateral —Cont'd
Proceeds and supporting obligations, time of perfection, §25-9-322, (b).
Rules governing priority, §25-9-322, (a).
Negotiable instrument holders, negotiable documents of title holders or security purchasers.
Filing under article 9 not considered notice, §25-9-331, (c).
Operation of other articles of UCC, §25-9-331, (a), (b).
Subordination.
Priority subject to, §25-9-339.
Transition provisions.
Attachment, §25-9-709, (b).
Governing provisions, §25-9-709, (a).
Proceeds.
Rights of secured party in, §25-9-315, (b).
Purchase money security interests.
Application of payments.
Non-consumer goods, §25-9-103, (e).
Consignments.
Security interests in consignor's inventory, §25-9-103, (d).
Definitions, §25-9-103, (a).
Goods.
Security interests in goods, §25-9-103, (b).
Non-consumer goods.
Application of payments, §25-9-103, (e).
Burden of proof, §25-9-103, (g).
Inferences as to consumer goods from rules governing non-consumer goods not to be drawn, §25-9-103, (h).
Maintenance of status as purchase money security interest, §25-9-103, (f).
Priority, §25-9-324.
Software.
Security interests in software, §25-9-103, (c).
Real property.
Excluded transactions, §25-9-104, (j).
Remedies for noncompliance with article.
Commercial reasonableness.
Approval by court or on behalf of creditors, §25-9-627, (c).
Not required, §25-9-627, (d).
Dispositions considered commercially reasonable, §25-9-627, (b).
Low price not necessarily unreasonable, §25-9-627, (a).
Damages, §25-9-625, (b).
Consumer goods transactions.
Statutory damages, §25-9-625, (c).
Limitation of liability, §25-9-628.
Statutory damages.
Consumer goods transactions, §25-9-625, (c).
Generally, §25-9-625, (e).
Requests for accounting, collateral, etc., §25-9-625, (f).
Surplus or deficiency an issue.
Deficiency eliminated or reduced, §25-9-625, (d).
General rules, §25-9-626, (a).
Nonconsumer transactions, §25-9-626, (b).
Injunctions, §25-9-625, (a).
Limitation of liability, §25-9-628.

COMMERCIAL CODE —Cont'd
Secured transactions —Cont'd
Remedies for noncompliance with article —Cont'd
Limitation of liability of secured party.
Debtors not known, §25-9-628, (a).
Explanation of surplus or deficiency, §25-9-628, (d).
Multiple liability for statutory damages, §25-9-628, (e).
Reasonable belief that transaction nonconsumer, §25-9-628, (c).
Status as secured party, §25-9-628, (b).
Limitation of security interest.
Requests for accounting, collateral, etc., §25-9-625, (g).
Repossession, §25-9-503.
Salaries.
Transactions excluded from article, §25-9-104, (d).
Sale of business, sale of accounts and chattel papers.
Excluded transactions, §25-9-104, (f).
Sale of goods, UCC.
Buyer's security interest in rejected goods.
Applicability of article 9, §25-9-110.
Reservation of title.
Applicability of article 9, §25-9-110.
Savings and loan associations.
Transfer of accounts excluded from article, §25-9-104, (l).
Savings clause, §25-9-702.
Security agreement.
Collateral.
Title to collateral immaterial, §25-9-202.
Effectiveness.
Conflict of laws, §25-9-201, (c).
Consumer laws, §25-9-201, (b), (d).
General effectiveness, §25-9-201, (a).
Enforceability of security interest.
Security agreement of another binding person, §25-9-203, (d).
Title to collateral immaterial, §25-9-202.
Security interest.
Bank deposits and collections.
Collection of documentary drafts, §25-4-504, (2).
Security interest of collecting bank in items, accompanying documents or proceeds, §25-4-208.
Costs.
Attorneys' fees in addition to interest, §6-21.2.
Defined, §25-1-201, (37).
Perfected security interest. See within this subheading, "Perfection of security interests."
Sales.
Buyer's security interest in rejected goods, §25-2-711, (3).
Reservation for security, §§25-2-501, (2), 25-2-505.
Reservation of title for security, §25-2-310, (b).
Unperfected security interest.
Priority over, §25-9-301.
Setoff.
Transactions excluded from article, §25-9-104, (i).
Short title of chapter, §25-9-101.
Statement of account.
Request regarding, §25-9-210, (e).
Damages for noncompliance, §25-9-625, (f).
Subordinated obligations, §25-1-209.

COMMERCIAL CODE —Cont'd
Secured transactions —Cont'd
Third parties.
Alienability of debtor's rights.
Agreements against transfer do not prevent transfer, §25-9-401, (b).
Governing law, §25-9-401, (a).
Assignments.
Agreement not to assert defenses against assignee, §25-9-403, (b), (c).
Conflict of laws generally, §25-9-403, (f).
Consumer transaction missing required statement, §25-9-403, (d).
Governing law for individual account debtor, §25-9-403, (e).
Value defined, §25-9-403, (a).
Claims and defenses against assignee, taking subject to, §25-9-404, (a).
Asserting debtor's claim against assignor to reduce amount owed to assignee, §25-9-404, (b).
Consumer transaction lacking required statement, §25-9-404, (d).
Governing law for individuals assigning under other provisions, §25-9-404, (c).
Health care insurance receivables, inapplicability, §25-9-404, (e).
Discharge of account debtor, §25-9-406.
Leases.
Material impairment, security interest not considered, §25-9-407, (c).
Restrictions on assignments, §25-9-407, (a), (b).
Modification of assigned contract.
Effect, §25-9-405, (a), (b).
Governing law for individuals indebted for certain purposes, §25-9-405, (c).
Health care insurance receivable, inapplicability, §25-9-405, (d).
Notes and general intangibles.
Conflicting laws, §25-9-408, (d), (e).
Legal restrictions on assignments, §25-9-408, (c), (f).
Restrictions on assignments, §25-9-408, (a), (b).
Notice to debtor of assignment.
Conflicting provisions, §25-9-406, (j).
Effect, §25-9-406, (a).
Governing law for debtors indebted for certain purposes, §25-9-406, (h).
Health care insurance receivables, §25-9-406, (i).
Ineffective notice, §25-9-406, (b), (g).
Proof to debtor of assignment, §25-9-406, (c).
Restrictions on assignment, §25-9-406, (d), (e).
Legal restrictions, §25-9-406, (f), (i).
Rights acquired by assignee, §25-9-404.
Contract of debtor.
Secured party not obligated on, §25-9-402.
Torts of debtor.
Secured party not obligated on, §25-9-402.
Title to collateral.
Immaterial, §25-9-202.
Torts.
Transfer of claims excluded from article, §25-9-104, (k).
Transition provisions, §§25-11-102 to 25-11-107.
United States statutes or treaties.
Property subject to.
Excluded transactions, §25-9-104, (a).

COMMERCIAL CODE —Cont'd
Secured transactions —Cont'd
Unperfected security interest.
Persons who take priority over, §25-9-301.
Wages.
Transactions excluded from article, §25-9-104, (d).
Send.
Defined, §25-1-201, (38).
Severability of chapter, §25-1-108.
Short title, §25-1-101.
Signed.
Defined, §25-1-201, (39).
Singular includes plural and vice versa, §25-1-102.
Statute of frauds.
Kinds of personal property not otherwise covered, §25-1-206.
Subordinated obligations, §25-1-209.
Supplementary general principles applicable, §25-1-103.
Suretyship.
Defined, §25-1-201, (40).
Telegram.
Defined, §25-1-201, (41).
Territorial application, §25-1-105.
Time.
Collection by depositary and collecting banks.
Finality of deposit of money.
Availability, §25-4-213, (f).
Reasonable time, §25-1-204.
"Seasonably" construed, §25-1-204, (3).
Unless otherwise agreed.
Construction of phrase, §25-1-102.
Usage of trade, §25-1-205.
Value.
Defined, §25-1-201, (44).
Variation by agreement, §25-1-102.
Waiver or renunciation of claim or right after breach, §25-1-107.
Warranties.
Encoding warranties, §25-4-207.2, (a).
Damages, §25-4-207.2, (c).
Presentment warranties, §25-4-207.1, (a).
Accrual cause of actions, §25-4-207.1, (f).
Breach of warranty claims, §25-4-207.1, (d).
Damages, §25-4-207.1, (b).
Defenses, §25-4-207.1, (c).
Disclaimers, §25-4-207.1, (e).
Retention warranties, §25-4-207.2, (b).
Damages, §25-4-207.2, (c).
Transfer warranties, §25-4-207, (a).
Accrual of action, §25-4-207, (e).
Damages, §25-4-207, (c).
Disclaimers, §25-4-207, (d).
Dishonored items, §25-4-207, (b).
Weights and measures.
Official certificate as prima facie evidence, §25-1-202.
Written.
Defined, §25-1-201, (46).

COMMERCIAL DETECTION SERVICES.
Drug detection dogs utilized, §90-102.1, (h).

COMMERCIAL DRIVERS' LICENSES, §§20-37.10 to 20-37.23.
Address.
Change of address.
Applications for duplicates, §20-37.15, (b).
Age.
Minimum age for, §20-9, (a).

COMMERCIAL DRIVERS' LICENSES —Cont'd
Applications.
Contents, §20-37.15, (a).
Duplicates.
Change of name or address, §20-37.15, (b).
Fees, §20-37.15, (a1).
Cancellation of driving privileges.
Driving commercial motor vehicle prohibited, §20-37.12, (b).
Notification required by drivers, §20-37.18, (c).
Change of address.
Duplicates.
Applications for, §20-37.15, (b).
Change of names.
Duplicates.
Applications for, §20-37.15, (b).
Chemical analysis of impairing substances in blood.
Refusal to submit to chemical test.
Disqualification, §20-17.4, (a).
Effect, §20-17.5, (c).
Child support enforcement.
Forfeiture of licensing privilege for failure to pay, §50-13.12.
Suspension, revocation or restriction of license, §110-142.2.
Citation of article, §20-37.10.
Classes, §20-37.16, (b).
Commissioner of motor vehicles.
Authority to enter agreements, §20-37.23.
Content of licenses, §20-37.16, (a).
Controlled substances.
Use of commercial motor vehicle in commission of a felony involving.
Lifetime disqualification, §20-17.4, (c).
Convictions of violations of state law or local ordinances relating to motor vehicle traffic control.
Nonresidents.
Notification of traffic convictions, §20-37.20, (a).
Notification required by drivers, §20-37.18, (a), (b).
Defined, §20-4.01, (3c).
Disqualification.
Additional disqualification period.
Driving while disqualified, §20-28, (d).
Article governing revocation of drivers' licenses and disqualification of commercial drivers' licenses, §20-24, (d).
Defined, §20-4.01, (5a).
Driving while disqualified, §20-28, (d).
Duration, §20-17.4.
Effect.
Conviction that requires both disqualification and revocation, §20-17.5, (b).
Conviction that requires disqualification but not revocation, §20-17.5, (a).
Disqualification for refusing to take chemical tests, §20-17.5, (c).
Restoration fee.
When disqualified person must pay, §20-17.5, (e).
Right to obtain regular class C driver's license, §20-17.5, (d).
Employers prohibited from allowing, permitting or authorizing driver to drive commercial motor vehicle during period of, §20-37.19, (b).
Grounds, §20-17.4.
Issuance of driver's license or learner's permit while person disqualified.
Prohibited, §20-37.13, (d).

COMMERCIAL DRIVERS' LICENSES —Cont'd
Disqualification —Cont'd
Lifetime disqualification, §20-17.4, (c).
Life without reduction, §20-17.4, (b1).
Modified life, §20-17.4, (b).
Multiple serious traffic violations, §20-17.4, (d).
Notification required by drivers, §20-37.18, (c).
Out-of-state violations, §20-17.4, (i).
Persons without commercial drivers' licenses, §20-17.4, (j).
Railroad grade crossing offenses, §20-17.4, (k).
Revocation or suspension of drivers' licenses generally.
See DRIVERS' LICENSES.
Revocation period, §20-17.4, (f).
Violation of out-of-service order, §20-17.4, (g).
Hazardous materials and passenger offenses, §20-17.4, (h).
Division of motor vehicles.
Rulemaking authority, §20-37.22.
Driving commercial motor vehicle without license, §20-37.21, (a).
Driving while disqualified, §20-28, (d).
Drugs.
Controlled substances.
Lifetime disqualification for use of commercial motor vehicle in felony involving, §20-17.4, (c).
Duplicates.
Change of name or address, §20-37.15, (b).
Employers.
Defined, §20-4.01, (7a).
Disqualification.
Prohibited from allowing, permitting or authorizing driver to drive commercial motor vehicle during period of, §20-37.19, (b).
Drivers possessing more than one driver license.
Employer prohibited from allowing, permitting or authorizing driver to drive commercial motor vehicle, §20-37.19, (b).
Information required to be supplied by drivers, §20-37.18, (d).
Employers to require, §20-37.19, (a).
Endorsements.
Categories, §20-37.16, (c).
Examinations.
Administering, §20-37.13, (b).
Qualification standards, §20-37.13, (a).
Waiver, §20-37.13, (c).
Exemptions from provisions.
Persons taking up residence in state on permanent basis exempt for thirty days, §20-37.12, (e).
Failure to carry license.
Production of license on date of court appearance.
No conviction, §20-37.12, (f).
Federal commercial motor vehicle safety act of 1986.
Purpose of article to implement, §20-37.11.
Fees.
Applications for commercial driver licenses, §20-37.15, (a1).
Issuance, §20-37.16, (d).
Felonies.
Forfeiture of driving privilege after conviction, §15A-1331A.
Using commercial motor vehicle in commission of felony.
Disqualification, §20-17.4, (a).

COMMERCIAL DRIVERS' LICENSES —Cont'd
Forfeiture of driving privilege after conviction of felony, §15A-1331A.
Forfeiture of licensing privilege for failure to pay child support, §50-13.12.
Hazardous materials.
Disqualification, offenses while transporting hazardous materials, §20-17.4, (e).
Hit and run driving.
Disqualification, §20-17.4, (a).
Impaired driving.
Disqualification, §20-17.4, (a).
Infractions.
Violation of employer responsibilities, §20-37.21, (c).
Violations of notice requirements by drivers, §20-37.21, (b).
Issuance.
Fees, §20-37.16, (d).
Record check and notification of license issuance, §20-37.17.
Learners' permits, §20-37.13, (e).
Misdemeanors, §20-37.21, (a).
Names.
Change of names.
Applications for duplicates, §20-37.15, (b).
Nonresidents.
Issuance of nonresident commercial driver's license, §20-37.14.
Notification of traffic violations, §20-37.20, (a).
Requirements, §20-37.12, (d).
Notice.
Drivers.
Notification required by drivers, §20-37.18.
Issuance of commercial drivers' licenses.
Notification to commercial driver license information system, §20-37.17.
Nonresidents.
Traffic violations, §20-37.20, (a).
Out of service order.
Defined, §20-4.01.
Penalties, §20-37.21.
Points.
Schedule of point values, §20-16, (c).
Possessing more than one license.
Employers prohibited from allowing, permitting or authorizing driver to drive commercial motor vehicle, §20-37.19, (b).
Prohibited, §20-30.
Purposes of article, §20-37.11.
Qualifications, §20-37.13, (a).
Railroad grade crossing offenses.
Disqualification, §20-17.4, (k).
Record check prior to issuance, §20-37.17.
Required, §20-37.12, (a).
Waiver of requirement.
Classes of vehicles, §20-37.16, (e).
Revocation or suspension.
Disqualification. See within this heading, "Disqualification."
Driving privileges.
Driving commercial motor vehicle prohibited, §20-37.12, (b).
Employers prohibited from allowing, permitting or authorizing driver to drive commercial motor vehicle during period of, §20-37.19, (b).
Issuance of commercial driver's license or learner's permit while driver's license suspended or revoked, §20-37.13, (d).
Notification required by drivers, §20-37.18, (c).

COMMERCIAL DRIVERS' LICENSES —Cont'd
Rules and regulations.
Rulemaking authority of division, §20-37.22.
School bus drivers required to hold, §20-218, (a).
School buses.
S endorsement, required to drive, §20-37.16, (c).
School bus defined, §20-37.16, (f).
Waiver of test for S endorsement, §20-37.16, (c1).
Serious traffic violations.
Defined, §20-4.01.
Multiple serious traffic violations, §20-17.4, (d).
Standards.
Qualification standards, §20-37.13, (a).
Suspension for child support delinquency, §110-142.2.
Title of article, §20-37.10.
Waiver of licenses.
Classes of vehicles, §20-37.16, (e).

COMMERCIAL FEED, §§106-284.30 to 106-284.46.
See FEED.

COMMERCIAL FERTILIZERS, §§106-655 to 106-677.
See FERTILIZERS.

COMMERCIAL FISHING.
Aircraft.
Spotter planes in commercial fishing operations.
Coastal and estuarine commercial fishing licenses, §113-171.1, (d).
Boats.
Identification numbers, renewal of number, §75A-5.1.
Coastal and estuarine commercial fishing licenses, §§113-168 to 113-173.
Licenses.
Coastal and estuarine commercial fishing licenses, §§113-168 to 113-173.
Penalties, §113-187.
Promotion of coastal fisheries and seafood industry, §§113-308 to 113-315.9.
Sales and use tax.
Exemption of commercial fisheries, §105-164.13.

COMMERCIAL GENERAL LIABILITY INSURANCE.
Extended reporting periods, §58-40-140, (a).
Health care provider professional liability insurance, §58-40-140, (b), (c).

COMMERCIAL LOAN COMMITMENTS TO BE IN WRITING, §22-5.

COMMERCIAL PUBLICATIONS.
Hearsay exception, §8C-1, Rule 803.

COMMERCIAL VEHICLES.
Alcoholic beverages.
Operating a commercial vehicle after consuming alcohol, §20-138.2A.
Odor of alcohol.
Evidentiary effect, §20-138.2A, (b1).
Screening test for alcohol, §20-138.2A, (b2).
Operating while possessing alcoholic beverages, §20-138.2C.
Alcohol screening test.
Operating a commercial vehicle after consuming alcohol, §20-138.2A, (b2).
Double penalties for driving offenses, §20-16.01.
Drivers' licenses generally, §§20-37.10 to 20-37.23.
See COMMERCIAL DRIVERS' LICENSES.
Driving while disqualified, §20-28, (d).

COMMERCIAL VEHICLES —Cont'd
Evidence.
Operation after consuming alcohol.
Odor of alcohol, §20-138.2A, (b1).
Felony using commercial motor vehicles.
Special information in judgment for conviction, §20-24, (e).
Financial responsibility, §20-309, (a1).
Fines.
Out of service fines, §20-17.7.
Hit and run.
Special information in judgment for conviction, §20-24, (e).
Impaired driving.
Chemical analysis of impairing substances in blood.
Applicability, §20-138.2, (g).
Defenses.
Legally entitled to use alcohol or drug.
Defense precluded, §20-138.2, (b).
Effect when impaired driving offense also charged, §20-138.2, (e).
Implied consent offense, §20-138.2, (d).
Misdemeanor, §20-138.2, (e).
Offense defined, §20-138.2, (a).
Operating a commercial vehicle after consuming alcohol.
Generally, §20-138.2A, (a).
Implied-consent offense, §20-138.2A, (b).
Penalty, §20-138.2A, (c).
Second or subsequent conviction.
Punishment, §20-138.2A, (c).
What constitutes, §20-138.2A, (d).
Pleading.
Sufficiency, §20-138.2, (c).
Restoration of driver's license after conviction, §20-17.6.
Special information required in judgment for conviction, §20-24, (e).
Motor vehicle financial responsibility, §20-309, (a1).
Operating while possessing alcoholic beverages, §20-138.2C.
Out of service fines, §20-17.7.
Points.
Double penalties, §20-16.01.
Schedule of point values, §20-16, (c).
Reckless driving.
Schedule of point values, §20-16, (c).
Repair of motor vehicles, §§20-354 to 20-354.9.
See MOTOR VEHICLE REPAIRS.
Special mobile equipment.
Towing certain vehicles, §20-140.5.
Speeding.
Schedule of point values, §20-16, (c).

COMMINGLED GOODS IN SECURED TRANSACTIONS.
Priority of security interests.
Provisions effective July 1, 2001, §25-9-336.

COMMISSIONER OF AGRICULTURE.
See AGRICULTURE COMMISSIONER.

COMMISSIONER OF BANKS, §§53-92 to 53-116.
See BANKS COMMISSIONER.

COMMISSIONER OF INSURANCE.
Generally, §§58-2-1 to 58-2-230.
See INSURANCE COMMISSIONER.

COMMISSIONER OF LABOR.
Generally.
See LABOR COMMISSIONER.

COMMISSIONER OF MOTOR VEHICLES.
Generally.
See MOTOR VEHICLES COMMISSIONER.

COMMISSIONERS.
Agriculture.
See AGRICULTURE COMMISSIONER.
Appointment.
Fees of commissioners appointed by magistrate, §7A-310.
Compensation.
Deposition taking.
Allowance of costs to either party or apportioned in discretion of court, §6-21.
Costs.
Deposition taking.
Allowance of costs to either party or apportioned in discretion of court, §6-21.
County boards of commissioners.
See COUNTY BOARDS OF COMMISSIONERS.
Fees.
Appointment by magistrate, §7A-310.
Insurance commissioner.
Generally, §§58-2-1 to 58-2-230.
See INSURANCE COMMISSIONER.
Labor.
See LABOR COMMISSIONER.
Magistrates.
Appointment of commissioner by magistrate.
Fees of commissioners, §7A-310.
Issuing notices to commissioners.
Fee of magistrate, §7A-309.
Motor vehicles.
See MOTOR VEHICLES COMMISSIONER.
Oaths.
Form of oath, §11-11.
Opening and clearing streams, §§77-1 to 77-11.
See STREAMS.
Special proceedings.
See SPECIAL PROCEEDINGS.

COMMISSIONERS OF SALE.
Special proceedings.
See SPECIAL PROCEEDINGS.

COMMISSIONS.
Boards and commissions.
See BOARDS AND COMMISSIONS.

COMMITMENT FEES.
Home loan secured by first mortgage or first deed of trust, §24-1.1A, (c).

COMMITMENT FOR LOANS.
Contract rates and fees, §24-1.1.
Savings and loan association interest rates, §24-1.4.

COMMITMENT ORDERS.
Prisoners, §15A-1301.
Sentencing, §15A-1353.

COMMITMENTS AND PRELIMINARY EXAMINATIONS.
Generally, §15A-521, (a).
Involuntary commitments.
Mental health, developmental disabilities and substance abuse.
See MENTAL HEALTH, DEVELOPMENTAL DISABILITY, SUBSTANCE ABUSE.
National guard.
Courts-martial, §127A-59.
Orders, §15A-521, (b).
Delivery, §15A-521, (c).
Modification, §15A-521, (b).

COMMITMENTS AND PRELIMINARY EXAMINATIONS —Cont'd
Receipt of prisoner, §15A-521, (c).
Witnesses, §15A-521, (d).

COMMITTEES.
Powers generally, §§32-25 to 32-28.
See FIDUCIARIES.
Uniform fiduciaries act, §§32-1 to 32-13.
See FIDUCIARIES.

COMMITTEES (PUBLIC BODIES).
Advisory committee on abandoned cemeteries, §143B-128.
America's four hundredth anniversary committee, §§143B-85, 143B-86.
Andrew Jackson historic memorial committee, §143B-132.
Aquaculture development advisory committee, §106-760.
Committee on inaugural ceremonies, §§143-532 to 143-539.
Compensation for services.
Per diem, subsistence and travel expenses, §138-5, (a) to (f).
Consumer and advocacy advisory committee for the blind, §§143B-163, 143B-164.
Economic investment committee.
Job development investment grant program, §143B-437.54.
Executive Mansion fine arts committee, §§143-410 to 143-415, 143B-79 to 143B-80.1.
Expiration of council created by governor or other state officials.
Constitutional elective officers creating, §147-16.2, (b).
Executive branch officials creating, §147-16.2, (c).
Executive order of governor creating, §147-16.2, (a).
Gender based appointments.
Appointing members to statutorily created decision making or regulatory entities.
Appointments to reflect proportion that gender represents in population of state, §143-157.1, (a).
Report by appointing authority of number appointments of each gender, §143-157.1, (b).
Job development investment grant program.
Economic investment committee, §143B-437.54.
Jobs for veterans committee, §§143B-420, 143B-421.
Joint legislative administrative procedure oversight committee, §§120-70.100 to 120-70.103.
Joint legislative corrections, crime control, and juvenile justice oversight committee, §§120-70.93 to 120-70.95.
Joint legislative growth strategies oversight committee, §§120-70.120 to 120-70.122.
Joint legislative health care oversight committee, §§120-70.110 to 120-70.112.
Joint legislative transportation oversight committee, §§120-70.50 to 120-70.52.
Joint legislative utility review committee, §§120-70.1 to 120-70.6.
Joint select committee on low-level radioactive waste, §§120-70.31 to 120-70.37.
Legislative ethics committee, §§120-99 to 120-106.
Nonpoint source pollution control program committee, §143-215.74B.

COMMITTEES (PUBLIC BODIES) —Cont'd
North Carolina awards committee, §§143B-83, 143B-84.
North Carolina trails committee, §§143B-333, 143B-334.
Per diem, subsistence and travel expenses, §138-5, (a) to (f).
Pesticide advisory committee, §143-439.
Professional advisory committee, §§143B-161, 143B-162.
Revenue laws study committee, §§120-70.105 to 120-70.108.
School committees.
Discipline of students.
Use of force may not be prohibited, §115C-390.
Third party administrators, §58-56-65.
Writing required to create, §147-16.2, (d).

COMMODITIES, §§78D-1 to 78D-33.
Actions.
Civil penalties.
Enforcement of act, §78D-22, (a).
Declaratory judgments.
Enforcement of act, §78D-22, (b).
Enforcement of chapter, §78D-22.
Power of court to grant injunctive relief, §78D-23.
Injunctive relief, §78D-23.
Enforcement of act, §78D-22, (b).
Judicial review.
Orders, §78D-31.
Restitution of reparation.
Enforcement of act, §78D-22, (a).
Activities.
Fraudulent conduct, §78D-6.
Unlawful commodity activities, §78D-5.
Board of trade.
Failure to obtain authority of federal government, §78D-5, (b).
Licenses.
Temporary license.
Failure to obtain, §78D-5, (a).
Registration.
Failure to obtain, §78D-5, (a).
Administration of act, §78D-25.
Confidentiality of information, §78D-25, (c).
Exceptions, §78D-25, (c).
Insider trading prohibited, §78D-25, (b).
Prohibited disclosures, §78D-25, (b).
Cooperation with other agencies, §78D-26.
Powers and duties of administrator, §78D-25, (a).
Secretary of state defined as administrator, §78D-1.
Bonds, surety.
Power of court to grant injunctive relief.
When surety bond not required, §78D-23, (b).
Buys or offers to buy in state, §78D-29, (b).
Cease and desist orders.
Enforcement of act, §78D-22, (a).
Civil penalties, §78D-22, (a).
Confidentiality of information, §78D-25.
Conflict of laws.
Securities and other laws unaffected, §78D-8.
Construction and interpretation.
Comity with other agencies.
Uniform application and interpretation of act, §78D-26, (a).
Criminal penalties.
Violations of act, §78D-24, (e).
Liability.
Good faith compliance with agency rules, orders or forms, §78D-27, (d).

COMMODITIES —Cont'd
Construction and interpretation —Cont'd
Purpose of act, §78D-9.
Scope of act, §78D-29.
Cooperation with other agencies, §78D-26.
Activities for which cooperation authorized, §78D-26, (b).
Uniform application and interpretation of act, §78D-26, (a).
Criminal penalties, §78D-24.
Criminal procedure.
Referral for prosecution to attorney general or district attorney, §78D-24, (d).
Defenses.
Affirmative defenses, §78D-33.
Definitions, §78D-1.
Qualified seller, §78D-4, (b).
Enforcement of act, §78D-22.
Power of court to grant injunctive relief, §78D-23.
Evidence.
Power of court to grant injunctive relief, §78D-23.
Exempt person transactions.
Defined, §78D-3.
Exempt transactions.
Defined, §78D-4.
Enumeration, §78D-4, (a).
Limitations on authority to engage in business as a qualified seller, §78D-4, (d).
When limitations proper, §78D-4, (d).
Revocation of exemption.
Business dissolution, §78D-4, (f).
Disability warranting revocation, §78D-4, (f).
Rules and regulations.
Authority of administrator to issue rules or orders, §78D-4, (g).
Suspension of exemption.
Public interest or the protection of investors, §78D-4, (e).
Waiver of exemption requirements.
Conditional or unconditional, §78D-4, (c).
Felonies.
Violations of act, §78D-24, (a).
Fines.
Power of court to grant injunctive relief.
Imposition of civil penalty, §78D-23.
Violations of chapter.
When allowed, §78D-24, (b), (c).
Forms.
Adoption or modification.
Approval of administrator required, §78D-27, (b).
Authority of administrator to create, §78D-27, (a).
Publication authority of administrator, §78D-27, (c).
Fraudulent conduct, §78D-6.
Futures contracts.
Void, §16-3.
Good faith compliance with agency rules, orders or forms, §78D-27, (d).
Hearings.
Commencement of administrative proceedings, §78D-30.
Investigations, §78D-21.
Injunctions, §78D-22, (b).
Power of court to grant injunctive relief, §78D-23.
Investigations.
Application of administrator to court to compel production of documents and attendance of witnesses, §78D-21, (d).
Authority of administrator to conduct, §78D-21, (a).

COMMODITIES —Cont'd
Investigations —Cont'd
Discretion of administrator in appointment of law enforcement officers, §78D-21, (e).
Powers and duties of administrator in investigatory proceedings, §78D-21, (c).
Publication by administrator of information on violations authorized, §78D-21, (b).
Mandatory injunctions.
Power of court to grant relief, §78D-23.
Negligence, §78D-7, (a).
Offer of sales or to buy in state.
Defined, §78D-29, (d).
Parties' presence in state immaterial, §78D-29, (c).
When not made in state, §78D-29, (e).
Orders.
Adoption or modification.
Approval of administrator required, §78D-27, (b).
Authority of administrator to issue, §78D-27, (a).
Enforcement of act, §78D-22, (a).
Final orders, §78D-30.
Judicial review, §78D-31.
How obtained, §78D-31, (a).
Commencement of proceedings, §78D-31, (b).
Procedure for entry of an order, §78D-30.
Summary orders, §78D-30.
Finality of summary orders, §78D-30.
Packages.
Information required, §81A-27.
Unit price, declaration, §81A-28.
Pleadings.
Exemptions, §78D-32.
Powers of attorney.
Powers conferred by statutory short form, §32A-2.
Principals, consulting persons and others, §78D-7.
Procedure for entry of an order.
Finality of summary orders.
When final, §78D-30, (d).
Final orders.
When final, §78D-30, (f).
How administrative proceedings commenced, §78D-30, (a).
Notice to interested parties of hearing, §78D-30, (e).
Notification to interested parties, §78D-30, (b).
When matter may be set for hearing, §78D-30, (c).
Prohibited commodity transactions.
Defined, §78D-2.
Purpose, §78D-9.
Qualified sellers.
Defined, §78D-4, (b).
Receivers.
Power of court to grant injunctive relief, §78D-23.
Respondeat superior, §78D-7, (b).
Restitution or reparation, §78D-22, (a).
Rules and regulations.
Adoption or modification.
Approval of administrator required, §78D-27, (b).
Authority of administrator to adopt, §78D-27, (a).
Exempt transactions.
Authority of administrator to issue rules or orders, §78D-4, (g).
Sales or offer of sales in state, §78D-29, (a).
Scope of act, §§78D-9, 78D-29.
Securities.
Conflict of laws, §78D-8.
Service of process.
Consent to service of process, §78D-28.

COMMODITIES —Cont'd
Unlawful commodity activities, §78D-5.
Board of trade.
Failure to obtain authority of federal government, §78D-5, (b).
Fraudulent conduct, §78D-6.
Registration.
Failure to obtain, §78D-5, (a).
Temporary license.
Failure to obtain, §78D-5, (a).
Unlawful commodity transactions.
Defined, §78D-2.
Exempt person transactions, §78D-3.
Exempt transactions, §78D-4.
Fraudulent conduct, §78D-6.
Weights and measures.
Generally, §§81A-1 to 81A-88.
See WEIGHTS AND MEASURES.

COMMON CARRIERS.
Alcoholic beverages.
Commercial transportation, §18B-1115.
Commercial transportation permits, §18B-1115, (a).
Wine shippers.
Direct shipments into state, §18B-1001.1, (c).
Baggage.
Careful handling required, §62-202.
Checks affixed to parcels of baggage, §62-203, (d), (e).
Unclaimed baggage, sale, §62-209.
Bills of lading.
Actions by or against common carriers.
Evidence, §8-41.
Carriers generally.
See CARRIERS.
Cash-on-delivery shipments.
Prompt settlement, §62-208.
Checks affixed to parcels of baggage, §62-203, (d), (e).
Connecting lines, discrimination between, §62-210.
Ejection of passengers.
Passengers refusing to pay fare or violating rules, §62-151.
Free transportation.
Prohibited acts, §62-144, (b).
Exceptions, §62-144, (d).
Misdemeanors, §62-144, (c).
Utilities commission members, §62-144, (a).
Freight.
Careful handling required, §62-202.
Duty to transport within reasonable time, §62-200, (a).
Forfeiture to party aggrieved for violating provisions, §62-200, (b).
Inapplicability of section to motor carriers of passengers, §62-200, (d).
Reasonable time, determining, §62-200, (c).
Freight charges settled according to rate stipulated in bill of lading, §62-201.
Loss, damage or injury to property received for transportation, §62-203.
Rights and remedies against prior carriers, §62-206.
Unclaimed freight, sale, §62-209.
Human service and volunteer transportation.
Inapplicability of laws and regulations, §62-289.5.
Intoxicated persons.
Ticket may be refused, §62-150.

COMMON CARRIERS —Cont'd
Joinder of causes of action.
Overcharges by carriers or undercharges by shippers, §62-205.
Long and short hauls.
Prohibited charges, §62-141, (a).
Authorization from commission, §62-141, (b).
Provisions inapplicable to bus companies, §62-141, (c).
Motor carriers.
Definition of "common carrier by motor vehicle," §62-3.
Duties, §62-146, (a).
Generally, §§62-259 to 62-279.
See MOTOR CARRIERS.
Rates, §62-146.
Additional nature of provisions, §62-146, (i).
Complaints as to, §62-146, (e).
Joint rates, §62-146, (b), (d).
Powers of commission as to, §62-146, (f).
Utilities commission.
Powers, §62-146, (e) to (h).
Routes.
Deviation from regular route operations, §62-267, (a).
Overcharges.
Joinder causes of actions by shipper, §62-205.
Policy and authority of utilities commission.
Carriers of passengers, §62-2, (c).
Presumption of negligence.
Injury to baggage or freight in possession or control of carrier, §62-202.
Property taxes.
Public service corporations.
Generally, §§105-333 to 105-344.
See PROPERTY TAXES.
Railroads.
See RAILROADS.
Rates.
Definitions, §62-152.1, (a).
Standard transportation practices, §62-152.2, (a).
Joint rate agreements, §62-152.1, (b), (c).
Antitrust law.
Exemption of parties to agreements, §62-152.1, (h).
Approval by commission, §62-152.1, (d), (e), (i).
Order terminating or modifying approval, §62-152.1, (f), (g).
Investigations by commission, §62-152.1, (f).
Motor common carriers, §62-146.
Standard transportation practices, §62-152.2.
Uniform rates, §62-152.1, (b).
Undercharges by shippers.
Joinder of causes of actions by carrier, §62-205.
Utilities commission members.
Free transportation to, §62-144, (a).
Window tinting exception for common carrier of passengers, §20-127, (c).

COMMON LAW.
Alcoholic beverages.
Compensation for injury caused by sales to underage persons.
Common-law rights not abridged, §18B-128.
Attorney general.
Powers at common law, §114-1.1.
Charities.
Common law defense of charitable immunity abolished, §1-539.9.

COMMON LAW —Cont'd
Constitution of the United States.
Suits at common law, Const. U. S., amd. VII.
Contempt.
Criminal contempt.
Specified grounds for criminal contempt exclusive, §5A-11, (a).
Declared to be in force, §4-1.
Emancipation of minor.
Common law provisions superseded by article on emancipation, §7B-3509.
Felony.
Defined, §14-1.
Jurisdiction.
Rule as to statutes in derogation of common law not applicable, §1-75.1.
Laws of foreign countries or states.
Proof by oral evidence, §8-3, (a).
Partnerships.
Rule that statutes in derogation of common law strictly construed.
Not applicable, §59-34, (a).
Phonograph records.
Restriction of or collection of royalties on commercial use.
Common law rights abrogated, §66-28.
Proof of official record.
Methods authorized by rules of evidence at common law, §1A-1, Rule 44, (c).
Public lands.
Unallocated state lands.
Common law riparian or littoral rights not limited or expanded, §146-1, (d).
Restraint of trade in violation of common law, §75-2.
Retaliatory employment discrimination.
Effect of article on other rights of employees under, §95-244.
Riots and civil disorders.
Provisions of article intended to supplement common law, §14-288.3.
Robbery.
Punishment for common law robbery, §14-87.1.
Rule against perpetuities.
Superseded by statutory rule, §41-22.
Securities regulation.
Crimes at common law.
Power of state to punish not restricted, §78A-57, (c).
Trademarks.
Registration.
Common-law rights not adversely affected, §80-13.

COMMON TRUST FUNDS, §§36A-90 to 36A-94.
Approval of accounting, §36A-91.
Banks.
Establishing of common trust funds, §36A-90, (a).
Investment of funds held by bank, §36A-90, (d).
When deemed owned, controlled or affiliated, §36A-90, (b).
Court accounting, §36A-91.
Establishment of funds, §36A-90, (a).
Funds held under agency agreement, §36A-90, (c).
Short title of act, §36A-94.
State banking commission.
Supervision by commission, §36A-92.
Uniformity of interpretation, §36A-93.

COMMUNICABLE DISEASES, §§130A-134 to 130A-148.
AIDS.
See AIDS.
Child care operators to report, §130A-136.
Commission for health services.
Establishing lists of communicable diseases and conditions to be reported, §130A-134.
Rules of commission, §130A-147.
Confidentiality.
Records, §130A-143.
Control measures, §130A-144, (d), (e).
Compliance required, §130A-144, (f).
Immunity.
From, §130A-144, (h).
Rules to prescribe, §130A-144, (g).
Death by reportable diseases.
Transportation of bodies, §130A-146.
First responders.
Vaccination program, §130A-485, (a).
Hospitals.
Emergency departments, reports to state health director, detection of public health threats, §130A-480, (a), (b).
Reports by medical facilities, §130A-137.
Immunization generally, §§130A-152 to 130A-158.
See IMMUNIZATION.
Initial appearance before magistrate.
Detention of defendant for communicable diseases, §15A-534.3.
Investigations by local health directors, §130A-144, (a).
Access to medical records, §130A-144, (b).
Immunity of persons permitting, §130A-144, (c).
Isolation authority, §130A-145, (a).
Entry into isolation premises, §130A-145, (b).
Restrictions on applying authority, §130A-145, (c), (d).
Lists of communicable diseases and conditions to be reported, §130A-134.
Local health directors.
Investigations, §130A-144, (a) to (c).
Quarantine and isolation authority, §130A-145.
Reports, §130A-140.
Mass death and destruction weapons.
Nuclear, biological or chemical weapons, §§14-288.21 to 14-288.24.
See WEAPONS OF MASS DEATH AND DESTRUCTION.
Medical facilities may report, §130A-137.
Physicians.
Report of diseases, §130A-135.
Quarantine authority, §130A-145, (a).
Entry onto quarantine premises, §130A-145, (b).
Restrictions on applying authority, §130A-145, (c), (d).
Rabies, §§130A-184 to 130A-201.
See RABIES.
Records.
Confidentiality, §130A-143.
Reports.
Child care operators, §130A-136.
Emergency departments, reports to state health director, detection of public health threats, §130A-480, (a), (b).
Form and content of reports, §130A-141.
Immunity of persons who report, §130A-142.
Laboratories, §130A-139.
List of communicable diseases and conditions to be reported, §130A-134.

COMMUNICABLE DISEASES —Cont'd
Reports —Cont'd
Local health directors to report, §130A-140.
Medical facilities may report, §130A-137.
Physicians to report diseases, §130A-135.
Restaurants and other food or drink establishments, §130A-138.
School principals to report, §130A-136.
Temporary order to report health related information, §130A-141.1.
Time limits for reporting, §130A-141.
Rules and regulations.
Control measures, §130A-144, (g).
Detection, control and prevention of communicable diseases, §130A-147.
School principals to report, §130A-136.
Sexually transmitted diseases.
Testing persons, §15A-615.
Transportation of bodies of persons who have died of reportable diseases, §130A-146.
Venereal diseases.
Consent of minor for treatment sufficient, §90-21.5, (a).
Failure to obtain treatment.
Imprisonment, §130A-25, (b).
Discharge, §130A-25, (c).
Form and content of reports, §130A-141.
Laboratory reports.
Positive laboratory tests.
Persons in charge of laboratories to report, §130A-139.
Prostitution.
Probation or parole of infected persons, §14-208.
Temporary order to report health related information, §130A-141.1.

COMMUNICATIONS.
Secret listening.
Electronic surveillance, §§15A-286 to 15A-298.
See ELECTRONIC SURVEILLANCE.
Telegraph companies.
See TELEGRAPH COMPANIES.
Telephone companies.
See TELEPHONE COMPANIES.

COMMUNICATIONS WITH JURORS, §14-225.2.

COMMUNICATION TOWERS.
Lease of public lands, §146-29.2.

COMMUNIST PARTY.
Emergency management.
Members of Communist party ineligible as emergency management personnel, §166A-13, (a).

COMMUNITY ACTION PROGRAMS.
Agencies.
Activities, §108B-25.
Board of directors.
Organization, §108B-26, (a).
Responsibilities, §108B-26, (b).
Development zone project tax credit, §105-129.13.
Eligible agencies.
Designation, §108B-24.
Department of health and human services.
Authority, §108B-23, (b).
Definition of "department," §108B-23, (a).
Municipal corporations.
Powers as to, §160A-492.
Purpose of article, §108B-22.
Title of article.
Short title, §108B-21.

COMMUNITY APPEARANCE COMMISSIONS, §§160A-451 to 160A-455.
Advisory councils.
Authorized, §160A-453.
Appointment of members, §160A-451.
Authorized, §160A-451.
Composition, §160A-451.
Duties, §160A-452.
Expenses of members.
Reimbursement, §160A-451.
Funds.
Receipt and expenditure, §160A-455.
Joint commissions, §160A-451.
Number of members, §160A-451.
Powers, §160A-452.
Qualifications of members, §160A-451.
Reports.
Annual report to municipal or county governing body, §160A-454.
Staff and technical services, §160A-453.
Terms of members, §160A-451.

COMMUNITY BASED CORRECTIONS.
State-county criminal justice partnership, §§143B-273.12 to 143B-273.16.

COMMUNITY BASED DEVELOPMENT ORGANIZATION.
Development zone project tax credit, §105-129.13.

COMMUNITY CHILD PROTECTION TEAMS.
Generally, §§7B-1400 to 7B-1414.
See CHILD FATALITY PREVENTION SYSTEM.

COMMUNITY COLLEGES, §§115D-1 to 115D-81.
Academic credit.
Fraudulent means in obtaining credit, §14-118.2.
Accounts and accounting.
Annual audits, §115D-58.5, (c).
Contracts.
Approval requirements, §115D-58.5, (b).
State auditor.
Responsibilities, §115D-58.5, (c).
System to be maintained, §115D-58.5, (a).
Actions.
Tort actions against board of trustees, §115D-58.12, (b), (c), (d).
Additional support for regional institutions, §115D-31, (a).
Additions, improvements, renovations and repairs to property.
Acquisition of property from county, §115D-15.1, (c).
Sale, lease or disposition to county in which property located, §115D-15.1, (a).
Approval of state board, §115D-15.1, (d).
Financing contract, county responsibility, §115D-15.1, (e).
Transfer back to college after completion of project, §115D-15.1, (b).
Administration of institutions.
State board of community colleges, §115D-5, (a).
Administrative areas.
Board of trustees.
To be residents of administrative area, §115D-12, (b).
Defined, §115D-2.
Multiple-county administrative areas, §115D-59.
Admission of students under the age of 16.
Conditions, §115D-1.1, (a).
Rules promulgation, §115D-1.1, (b).

COMMUNITY COLLEGES —Cont'd
Agents.
Negligence of agents.
Waiver of governmental immunity by act of obtaining liability insurance, §115D-24.
Annuity contracts.
Employees of institutions.
Purchase of annuity contracts for employees, §115D-25.
Appropriations.
Elections on questions of appropriations. See within this heading, "Financial support."
Armed forces personnel on active duty.
Tuition assistance.
Active duty members, in-state rate, §116-143.3.
Associations.
Trustee association regions.
Division into regions, §115D-62.
Audits, §147-64.6A.
Statistical sample for program audits, §115D-5, (m).
Benefits of public institutions of higher education to be extended to people of state free of charge, Const. N. C., art. IX, §9.
Board of trustees.
Body corporate, §115D-14.
Compensation, §115D-17.
Composition, §115D-12, (a).
Conflicts of interest, §115D-26.
Cooperative innovative high school programs.
Established by local boards and community college board of trustees, §§115C-238.50 to 115C-238.55.
See COOPERATIVE INNOVATIVE HIGH SCHOOL PROGRAMS.
Duties, §115D-20.
Elective officials serving as trustees, §115D-16.
Eminent domain, §40A-3, (c).
Exchange of property, §115D-15.
Former employees.
Service on board prohibited, §115D-12, (b1).
Governmental immunity.
Waiver of immunity by act of obtaining liability insurance, §115D-24.
Information.
Access to information, §115D-78.
Lease of property, §115D-15.
Liability insurance, §115D-58.12, (a) to (e).
Waiver of governmental immunity by act of obtaining insurance, §115D-24.
Meetings, §115D-18.
Failure to attend three consecutive meetings without a justifiable cause.
Office declared vacant, §115D-19, (b).
Official meetings open to public, §115D-79.
Motor vehicle citations, fines and registration, §115D-21, (c).
Negligence of agents and employees of institutions.
Waiver of governmental immunity by act of obtaining liability insurance, §115D-24.
Official title, §115D-14.
Organization of boards, §115D-18.
Powers, §§115D-14, 115D-20.
Public building contracts.
Construction contract claims.
Adjustment and resolution, §143-135.6, (a) to (f).
Public/private partnerships.
Power to enter into, requirements, §115D-20.

COMMUNITY COLLEGES —Cont'd
Board of trustees —Cont'd
Records.
Public records.
Availability for examination and reproduction, §115D-78.
Removal of trustees, §115D-19, (a).
Resident of administrative area, §115D-12, (b).
Sale of property, §115D-15.
Selection of trustees.
Group one, §115D-12, (a).
Group two, §115D-12, (a).
Group three, §115D-12, (a).
Group four, §115D-12, (a).
Spouses and children of employees.
Prohibited service on board, §115D-12, (b1).
Terms of office, §115D-13, (a).
Commencement, §115D-13, (b).
Title to property, §115D-14.
Tort actions against, §115D-58.12, (b) to (d).
Traffic regulations, §115D-21, (b), (c).
Vacancy.
Failure to attend meetings, §115D-19, (b).
Filling, §115D-12, (c).
Board reserve fund.
Use, §115D-5, (j).
Bond issues.
Community colleges facilities finance, §§116D-41 to 116D-49.
See HIGHER EDUCATION BONDS.
Elections on question of issuance, §115D-36.
Local financial support of institutions.
Authority to issue bonds and notes, §115D-38.
Previously established institutions, §115D-34, (b).
Bonds, surety.
Investment of idle cash, §115D-58.10.
Budgets.
Adoption, §115D-56.
Interim budget, §115D-57.
Allocation of revenue to the institution by local tax-levying authority.
Provision of funds, §115D-58.2, (a).
Purpose of funds, §115D-58.2, (b).
Amendments.
Appropriations, §115D-58, (b).
Rules and regulations, §115D-58, (a).
Appropriations, §115D-58, (b), (c).
Contracts.
Federal contracts and grants, §115D-58.1.
Disbursements.
Provision for disbursement of local money, §115D-58.4.
Provision for disbursement of state money, §115D-58.3.
Federal contracts and grants, §115D-58.1.
Final adoption, §115D-56.
Grants.
Federal contracts and grants, §115D-58.1.
Interim budget, §115D-57.
Management.
Approval of budget by local tax-levying authority, §115D-55, (a).
Approval of budget by state board of community colleges, §115D-55, (b).
Performance budgeting.
Publication of performance, §115D-31.3.
State board to create new accountability measures and performance standards, §115D-31.3, (a).
Preparation and submission.
Annual submission required, §115D-54, (a).

COMMUNITY COLLEGES —Cont'd
Budgets —Cont'd
Preparation and submission —Cont'd
Procedures for preparation and submission, §115D-54, (b).
Provision of public funds, §115D-54, (c).
Responsibility of county finance officer, §115D-54, (d).
Trust and agency fund, §115D-54, (e).
Rules and regulations.
Amendments, §115D-58, (a).
Vending facilities.
Disposition of revenue, §115D-58.13.
Buildings.
Construction contract claims.
Adjustment and resolution, §143-135.6, (a) to (f).
Fire and casualty insurance on institutional buildings and contents, §115D-58.11, (a) to (c).
Cafeteria plans.
Flexible compensation plans, §115D-25.2.
Campus law enforcement agencies.
Board of trustees may establish and employee police officers, §115D-21.1, (a).
Joint agreement with county to extend enforcement authority, §115D-21.1, (c).
Joint agreement with municipality to extend enforcement authority, §115D-21.1, (b).
Qualifications and requirements for police officers, powers, §115D-21.1, (a).
Territorial jurisdiction of police officers, §115D-21.1, (a).
Capital improvements, §115D-4.
Captive or co-opted group students.
Course of instruction, §115D-5, (c).
Cash management for community colleges, §147-86.13.
Central Piedmont community college.
Local financial support, §115D-60, (a).
Sale, exchange or lease of property, §115D-60, (b).
Charitable organization approved by community college board.
Deduction of contributions from employee's salary or wage, §143-3.3, (i).
Coastal Carolina community college.
Authority to provide local financial support, §115D-61.
College transfer program.
Addition of program to community colleges.
Approval of addition to community college, §115D-4.1, (b).
Criteria and standards to regulate addition of program, §115D-4.1, (d), (e).
Election on question of addition, §115D-36.
Reports on academic performance of transfer students, §115D-4.1, (f).
Restrictions, §115D-4.1, (c).
Community colleges instructional trust fund, §115D-42.
Community college system office.
Chief administrative officer, §115D-3.
Information.
Access to information, §115D-78.
Motorcycle safety instruction program.
Delivered and implemented through department, §115D-72.
Operation of department, §115D-3.
President, §115D-3.
Compensation, §115D-3.
Professional staff members, §115D-3.
Compensation, §115D-3.
Establishing staff complement, §115D-3.

COMMUNITY COLLEGES —Cont'd
Community college system office —Cont'd
Public records.
Availability for examination and reproduction, §115D-78.
Conflicts of interest.
Employees of institutions, §115D-26.
Construction contract claims.
Adjustment and resolution.
Contract completed and amount claimed not received, §143-135.6, (b).
Civil action, limitation period, venue, §143-135.6, (c).
Contract not completed and amount claimed not received, §143-135.6, (a).
Definitions, §143-135.6, (e).
Provisions applicable to community colleges only, §143-135.6, (f).
Provisions part of every contract, §143-135.6, (d).
Continuation of existing law, §115D-81, (a).
Rights and liabilities, §115D-81, (b).
Contracts.
Annuity or retirement income contract.
Conflicts of interest, §115D-26.
Purchase of contracts for employees, §115D-25.
Local school administrative units.
Restrictions, §115D-41.
Public building contracts.
Construction contract claims.
Adjustment and resolution, §143-135.6, (a) to (f).
Cooperative innovative high school programs.
Established by local boards and community college board of trustees, §§115C-238.50 to 115C-238.55.
See COOPERATIVE INNOVATIVE HIGH SCHOOL PROGRAMS.
Correction education programs.
Reports of full-time student hours, §115D-5, (c1).
Counties.
Multiple-county administrative areas, §115D-59.
Satellite campuses.
Contracts for construction, §153A-450, (a) to (c).
Deadly weapons.
Possessing or carrying on campus or educational property, §14-269.2.
Defenses.
Tort actions against board of trustees, §115C-58.12, (c).
Definitions, §115D-2.
Construction contract claims.
Adjustment and resolution, §143-135.6, (c).
Department of revenue, list of colleges provided to, §115D-5, (n).
Dependent care assistance program.
Providing eligible employees, §115D-25.1.
Disbursements.
Provision for disbursement of local money, §115D-58.4.
Provision for disbursement of state money, §115D-58.3.
Discrimination.
Nondiscrimination policy, §115D-77.
Donated property to support specific educational purpose.
Use of proceeds from sale or lease according to terms of donation, §115D-15, (b).
Driving eligibility certificates.
Rules established by state board, §115D-5, (a3).
Education cabinet, §116C-1.

COMMUNITY COLLEGES —Cont'd
Elections on questions of appropriations.
Financial support. See within this heading, "Financial support."
Employees of institutions.
Annuity contracts.
Purchase of annuity contracts for employees, §115D-25.
Custodial accounts in lieu of, §115D-25.
Conflicts of interest, §115D-26.
Dependent care assistance program.
Providing eligible employees, §115D-25.1.
Flexible compensation plans, §115D-25.2.
Health insurance, §115C-340.
Negligence.
Waiver of governmental immunity by act of obtaining liability insurance, §115D-24.
Payroll deductions.
Charitable organization approved by community college board.
Contributions deducted from employee's salary or wage, §143-3.3, (i).
Records.
Confidential information, §115D-29.
Contents, §115D-28.
Employee objecting to material in file.
Remedy of employee, §115D-30.
Maintenance, §115D-28.
Objections to material in file.
Remedy of employee, §115D-30.
Personnel file.
Inspections, §115D-27.
Public inspection, §115D-28.
Retirement income contracts.
Purchase of contracts for employees, §115D-25.
Custodial accounts in lieu of, §115D-25.
Shared leave with family member.
Family member employed by community college, school or public agency, §115D-25.3.
Voluntary shared leave.
Family member employed by community college, school or public agency, §115D-25.3.
Workers' compensation act applicable to employees, §115D-23.
Equipment.
Allocation of funds to institutions in accordance with equipment allocation formula, §115D-31, (d).
Lease purchase and installment purchase contracts.
Authority of board of trustees, §115D-58.15, (a).
Deficiency judgment not to be rendered for breach of contractual obligation, §115D-58.15, (f).
Nonsubstitution clauses prohibited, §115D-58.15, (e).
Review and approval of contracts, §115D-58.15, (b).
Determining whether contract subject to approval, §115D-58.15, (d).
Local government commission approval, §115D-58.15, (c).
Taxing power of tax-levying authority and state not to be pledged, §115D-58.15, (f).
Purchases from noncertified sources, §115D-58.14, (a).
Cost of purchase not to exceed bid value benchmark, §115D-58.14, (a).
Policies and procedures for monitoring implementation, adoption, §115D-58.14, (b).
Purchasing price, §115D-58.14, (a).

COMMUNITY COLLEGES —Cont'd
Establishment of institutions, §115D-4.
Elections on questions of appropriations, §115D-33, (c).
Granting final approval for establishment of institution, §115D-33, (e).
State board of community colleges, §115D-5, (a).
Exchange of real or personal property no longer desirable for purposes of institution, §115D-15, (a).
Explosives.
Possessing or carrying on campus or educational property, §14-269.2.
Extension courses.
Curricular courses and noncurricular courses authorized, §115D-5, (b).
Fees, §115D-5, (b).
Recreation extension courses.
Financing on self-supporting basis, §115D-5, (g).
Tuition charge, §115D-5, (b).
Federal aid.
Budgets, §115D-58.1.
State board of community colleges.
Authority to accept, receive, use or reallocate federal funds or aid, §115D-31, (b).
Fees.
Extension courses, §115D-5, (b).
Fixing and regulating fees charged to students, §115D-39, (a).
Receipts state funds, deposit, §115D-39, (a).
Financial assistance for students.
Administration, §115D-40.1, (c).
Counselors, §115D-40.1, (c).
Low-enrollment programs targeted for high-demand occupations, §115D-40.1, (b).
Needs-based eligibility, §115D-40.1, (a).
Targeted assistance, §115D-40.1, (b).
Financial support, §§115D-31 to 115D-39.
Application for funds by board, §115D-32, (c).
Capital outlay.
Responsibility for budget item, §§115D-31, (a), 115D-32, (a).
Central Piedmont community college.
Authority to provide local financial support, §115D-60, (a).
Coastal Carolina community college.
Authority to provide local financial support, §115D-61.
Contracts.
Local school administrative units.
Restrictions, §115D-41.
Current expenses.
Responsibility for budget items, §§115D-31, (a), 115D-32, (a).
Supplemental current expense budget, §115D-32, (b).
Elections on questions of appropriations.
Ballot to be furnished, §115D-33, (b).
Bond issues, §115D-36.
Construction of provisions, §115D-33, (f).
Establishment of institution, §115D-33, (c).
Granting final approval for establishment of institution, §115D-33, (e).
Holding elections, §115D-33, (d).
Power to hold elections, §115D-35, (d).
Origination of formal requests for elections, §115D-35, (a).
Payment of expenses of special elections, §115D-37.
Requests for elections to provide funds for institutions, §115D-35.

COMMUNITY COLLEGES —Cont'd
Financial support —Cont'd
Elections on questions of appropriations —Cont'd
Special elections.
Payment of expenses, §115D-37.
Special tax levies.
Maximum annual rate sort stated on formal requests, §115D-35, (c).
Submitting formal requests for elections, §115D-35, (a), (b).
Wording of ballots, §115D-33, (b).
Federal aid.
Authority to accept, receive, use or reallocate funds, §115D-31, (b).
Fees.
Fixing and regulating fees charged to students, §115D-39, (a).
Local financial support of institutions, §115D-32, (a), (b).
Appropriating nontax revenues, §115D-38.
Authority to issue bonds and notes, §115D-38.
Central Piedmont community college, §115D-60, (a).
Coastal Carolina community college, §115D-61.
Levying special taxes, §115D-38.
Previously established institutions, §115D-34, (a), (c).
Bond issues, §115D-34, (b).
Satellite campuses.
Maintenance and utility costs.
Acceptance by counties, §115D-32, (d).
Tax-levying authority, §§115D-32, (a), 115D-33, (a).
Local school administrative units.
Contracts.
Restrictions, §115D-41.
Regional institutions.
Responsibility for additional support, §115D-31, (a).
Satellite campuses.
Maintenance and utility costs.
Acceptance by counties, §115D-32, (d).
State board of community colleges.
Budget items, §115D-31, (a).
Federal aid.
Authority to accept, receive, use or reallocate, §115D-31, (b).
Reversion of funds to general fund, §115D-31, (c).
State financial support of institutions, §115D-31.
Tax-levying authority.
Defined, §115D-2.
Local financial support of institutions, §§115D-32, (a), 115D-33, (a).
Responsibility for budget items, §115D-32, (a).
Tuition.
Fixing and regulating tuition, §115D-39, (a) to (c).
Withdrawal or withholding state support of institutions, §115D-6.
Fines.
Traffic regulations, §115D-21, (b), (c).
Fire and casualty insurance on institutional buildings and contents.
Funding, §115D-58.11, (b).
Purchase authorized, §115D-58.11, (c).
Purchase required, §115D-58.11, (a).
Firearms.
Possessing or carrying on campus or educational property, §14-269.2.

COMMUNITY COLLEGES —Cont'd
Governmental immunity.
Negligence of agents and employees of institutions.
Waiver of governmental immunity by act obtaining liability insurance, §115D-24.
Grants.
Federal contracts and grants, §115D-58.1.
Health insurance for employees, §115C-340, (a), (b).
Income withholding.
Charitable organization approved by community college board.
Contributions.
Deduction from employee's salary or wage, §143-3.3, (i).
Information.
Access to information, §115D-78.
In-plant training program.
Assisting in pre-employment and in-service training of certain employees, §115D-5, (d).
Instructional trust fund.
Allocation, §115D-42, (b).
Audit, §115D-42, (e).
Established, §115D-42, (a).
Matching funds, §115D-42, (c), (d).
Purpose, §115D-42, (a).
Rules, §115D-42, (b).
State funds and matching funds raised by foundation.
Use, §115D-42, (c).
Interest.
Deposits.
Investment of idle cash, §115D-58.6.
Investment of idle cash, §§115D-58.6 to 115D-58.10.
Bonds, surety, §115D-58.10.
Daily deposits, §115D-58.9.
Deposits.
Daily deposits, §115D-58.9.
Form, §115D-58.6, (b), (c).
Generally, §115D-58.6, (a).
Securing deposits, §115D-58.7, (b).
Selection of depository, §115D-58.7, (a).
Facsimile signatures, §115D-58.8.
Interest earned on deposits, §115D-58.6, (e).
Investment securities, §115D-58.6, (d), (f).
Signatures.
Facsimile signatures, §115D-58.8.
Surety bonds, §115D-58.10.
Juice and bottled water.
Contracts for sale of.
Competitive bid required, §143-64.
Law enforcement agencies, §115D-21.1.
Lease of property no longer desirable for purposes of institution, §115D-15, (a).
Lease purchase and installment purchase contracts.
Equipment, §115D-58.15.
State board to review, §115D-5, (l).
Liability insurance.
Negligence of agents and employees of institutions.
Waiver of governmental immunity by act of obtaining insurance, §115D-24.
Professional liability insurance.
Acquisition of insurance by commission, §58-32-15, (a), (b).
Declaration of public purpose, §58-32-15, (d).
Sovereign immunity.
Not deemed waiver of, §58-32-15, (c).
Purchase by board of trustees, §115C-58.12, (a).

COMMUNITY COLLEGES —Cont'd
Liability insurance —Cont'd
State funds to pay premiums, §115D-31.1.
List of colleges to department of revenue, §115D-5, (n).
Maintenance of system of higher education, Const. N. C., art. IX, §8.
Meetings.
Official meetings open to public, §115D-79.
Military affairs.
Tuition assistance.
Armed forces personnel on active duty.
In-state rate, §116-143.3.
Motorcycle safety instruction program.
Delivered and implemented through department of community colleges, §115D-72.
Motor fuel excise tax exemption, §105-449.88.
Motor vehicles.
Citations, fines and registration.
Establishing system, §115D-21, (c).
Operation of motor vehicles on campus of institutions, §115D-21, (a).
National guard.
Tuition assistance, §§127A-190 to 127A-195.
Negligence.
Liability of negligence of agents and employees of institutions.
Waiver of governmental immunity by act of obtaining liability insurance, §115D-24.
New and expanding industry program.
Guidelines for appropriations, §115D-5, (k).
Report on expenditures, §115D-5, (i).
New program.
Approval, §115D-5, (f).
North Carolina community colleges instructional trust fund, §115D-42.
Operation of institutions.
State board of community colleges, §115D-5, (a).
Operation of plant.
Out-of-county head count over fifty percent of total.
Funds provided to college, §115D-31.2.
Payroll deductions.
Charitable organization approved by community college board.
Contributions.
Deduction from employee's salary or wage, §143-3.3, (i).
Performance budgeting.
Mandatory performance measures, §115D-31.3, (e).
Publication of performance, §115D-31.3.
Publication of performance ratings, §115D-31.3, (f).
State board to create new accountability measures and performance standards, §115D-31.3, (a).
Successful performance.
Carryforward of funds for indicators achieved, §115D-31.3, (g).
Superior performance recognition, §115D-31.3, (h).
Uses of funds, §115D-31.3, (i).
Personal property.
Title to property, §115D-14.
Personnel system.
Exempt employees, §126-5, (c2).
Exempt from provisions of state personnel act, §115D-5, (a).
Exemption for employees, §126-5, (c6).
Police, §115D-21.1.

COMMUNITY COLLEGES —Cont'd
President of system of community colleges, §115D-3.
Private, nonprofit corporations.
Establishment to support community college system.
State employees may assist, §115D-7.
Program audits.
Statistical sample for program audits, §115D-5, (m).
Publications.
Administrative review procedures for public documents, §143-170.2.
Procedures manuals for public documents, §143-170.2.
Public buildings and grounds.
Fire and casualty insurance on institutional buildings and contents, §115D-58.11, (a) to (c).
Public/private partnerships.
Power of trustees to enter into, requirements, §115D-20.
Public records.
Availability for examination and reproduction, §115D-78.
Purchasing flexibility.
Supplies, equipment and materials, §115D-58.14.
Purposes of chapter, §115D-1.
Real estate continuing education courses.
Offer on self-supporting basis, §115D-5, (h).
Real property.
Acquisition, §153A-158.2, (a).
Additions, improvements, renovations and repairs.
Acquisition from county, §115D-15.1, (c).
Sale, lease or other disposition to county in which property located, §115D-15.1, (a), (b), (d), (e).
Central Piedmont community college.
Sale, exchange or lease of property, §115D-60, (b).
Construction or improvement, §153A-158.2, (b).
Disposition, §153A-158.2, (b).
Public hearing, §153A-158.2, (c).
Right-of-way easements for highway construction, §115D-15, (a).
Title to property, §115D-14.
Records.
Public records.
Available for examination and reproduction, §115D-78.
Recreation extension courses.
Financing on self-supporting basis, §115D-5, (g).
Regional institutions.
Defined, §115D-2.
Reports, §115D-5, (o).
Retirement income contracts for employees.
Purchase of contracts for employees, §115D-25.
Retirement system for teachers and state employees.
Applicability of provisions, §115D-22.
Optional retirement program.
Administration, §135-5.4, (e).
Beneficiaries, §135-5.4, (g).
Contracts with investment companies, §135-5.4, (d).
Contributions, §135-5.4, (c).
Election to participate, §135-5.4, (b).
Establishment, §135-5.4, (a).
Governance, §135-5.4, (b).
Participation, ineligibility for other programs, §135-5.4, (f).
Underwriting, §135-5.4, (a).

COMMUNITY COLLEGES —Cont'd
Retirement system for teachers and state employees —Cont'd
Purchase of retirement income contracts of employees, §115D-25.
Right-of-way easements for highway construction, §115D-15, (a).
Rules and regulations.
Available for examination and reproduction, §115D-78.
Salaries.
Community college system office.
Professional staff members, §115D-3.
Compensation of trustees, §115D-17.
Payroll deductions.
Charitable organization approved by community college board.
Deduction of contributions from employee's salary or wage, §143-3.3, (i).
Sale of real or personal property undesirable for purposes of institution, §115D-15, (a).
Satellite campuses.
Counties.
Contracts for construction, §153A-450, (a) to (c).
Saving clauses.
Continuation of existing law, §115D-81, (a).
Existing rights and liabilities, §115D-81, (b).
Shared leave with family member.
Family member employed by community college, public school or public agency, §115D-25.3.
State aid.
Financial support generally. See within this heading, "Financial support."
Withdrawal or withholding state support of institutions, §115D-6.
State board of community colleges.
Administration of institutions, §115D-5, (a).
Administrative procedure.
Applicability of administrative procedure act, §115D-80.
Bookstore sales.
Adoption of rules governing expenditures of funds derived from, §115D-5, (a1).
Chairman, §115D-2.1, (e), (f).
Composition, §115D-2.1, (b).
Defined, §115D-2.
Dependent care assistance program.
Providing to eligible employees of constituent institutions, §115D-25.1.
Eligibility to serve on board, §115D-2.1, (d).
Established, §115D-2.1, (a).
Establishment of institutions, §115D-5, (a).
Exchange of information between public schools and institutions of higher education.
Planning and implementation, §115D-5, (a2).
Financial support of institutions.
Authority to accept, receive, use or reallocate federal funds or aid, §115D-31, (b).
Responsibility for budget items, §115D-31, (a).
Reversion of funds to general fund, §115D-31, (c).
Flexible compensation plans.
Authorization to provide, §115D-25.2.
Information.
Access to information, §115D-78.
Meetings, §115D-2.1, (e) to (g).
Official meetings open to public, §115D-79.
Regular meetings, §115D-2.1, (g).
Special meetings, §115D-2.1, (g).
State board of education.
Annual meeting with, §115C-11, (b1).
Officers, §115D-2.1, (e), (f).

COMMUNITY COLLEGES —Cont'd
State board of community colleges —Cont'd
Operation of institutions, §115D-5, (a).
Organization, §115D-2.1, (b).
Records.
Public records.
Available for examination and reproduction, §115D-78.
Removal of trustees, §115D-19, (a).
Rules to assist colleges in administration of procedures, adoption, §115D-5, (a3).
Setoff debt collection.
Generally, §§105A-1 to 105A-16.
See SETOFF DEBT COLLECTION.
State board of education.
Annual meeting with, §115C-11, (b1).
Terms of members, §115D-2.1, (b), (c).
Vacancies, §115D-2.1, (h), (i).
Withdrawal or withholding state support of institutes, §115D-6.
Statement of purpose, §115D-1.
State of emergency.
Injunctions.
Public or private educational institutions, §14-288.18, (a), (b).
Statistical sample for program audits, §115D-5, (m).
Streets and highways.
Applicable provisions, §115D-21, (a).
Student activity fees.
Receipts state funds, deposit, §115D-39, (a).
Student head count from outside county of more than half of student body.
Funds provided for "operation of plant," §115D-31.2.
Students under the age of 16.
Enrollment, §115D-1.1.
Supplies.
Purchasing from noncertified sources, §115D-58.14, (a).
Cost of purchase not to exceed bid value benchmark, §115D-58.14, (a).
Policies and procedures for monitoring implementation, adoption, §115D-58.14, (b).
Purchase price, §115D-58.14, (a).
Tax-levying authority.
Defined, §115D-2.
Local financial support of institutions, §§115D-32, (a), 115D-33, (a).
Responsibility for budget items, §115D-32, (a).
Textiles.
Center for applied textile technology, §§115D-68 to 115D-71.
See TEXTILE TECHNOLOGY, CENTER FOR.
Title to property, §115D-14.
Tort actions against board of trustees, §115C-58.12, (b).
Defenses, §115C-58.12, (c).
Liability insurance.
Payment of premiums, §115C-58.12, (e).
Reading or mentioning in presence of jury, §115C-58.12, (d).
Traffic regulations.
Applicable provisions, §115D-21, (a).
Fines and penalties, §115D-21, (b), (c).
Trustee association regions.
Division into regions, §115D-62.
Tuition.
Armed forces personnel on active duty.
In-state rate, §116-143.3.

COMMUNITY COLLEGES —Cont'd
Tuition —Cont'd
Eligibility for resident tuition rate.
Persons lawfully admitted to United States, §115D-39, (b), (c).
Fixing and regulating.
State board, §115D-39, (a).
Legal resident limitation, §115D-39, (a).
Persons lawfully admitted to United States.
Eligibility for resident tuition rate, §115D-39, (b), (c).
Receipts state funds, deposit, §115D-39, (a).
Tuition and fees exceeding amount certified in general fund codes.
Transfer of excess to equipment reserve fund, §115D-31, (e).
Tuition assistance, §115D-40.1.
Extension courses, §115D-5, (b).
National guard, §§127A-190 to 127A-195.
Vending facilities.
Defined, §115D-2.
Disposition of revenue, §115D-58.13.
Viticulture or oenology program.
Authorization, §18B-1114.4.
Inapplicability of prohibition on governmental units selling merchandise, §66-58, (c).
Voluntary shared leave, §115D-25.3.
Weapons.
Possessing or carrying on campus or educational property, §14-269.2.
Withdrawal of state support.
State board of community colleges may withdraw, §115D-6.
Workers' compensation.
Applicability of workers' compensation act to institutional employees, §115D-23.

COMMUNITY COLLEGES INSTRUCTIONAL FUND, §115D-42.

COMMUNITY COLLEGE SYSTEM OFFICE, §115D-3.

COMMUNITY CORRECTIONS.
Basis of sentencing and policy advisory commissions recommendations, §164-42.2.
Probation.
Structured sentencing provisions.
Persons sentenced to community punishment, special rules, §15A-1343.2.
Sentencing services act, §§7A-770 to 7A-777.
See SENTENCING SERVICES.
Structured sentencing, §§15A-1340.10 to 15A-1340.23.
See SENTENCING.
Victims of crime.
Notification, responsibilities, §15A-837, (a).
Time period for notifying, §15A-837, (b).

COMMUNITY DEVELOPMENT CORPORATION.
Development zone project tax credit, §105-129.13.

COMMUNITY DEVELOPMENT COUNCIL.
Appointments, §143B-437.2, (a).
Chairman, §143B-437.2, (b).
Clerical services, §143B-437.2, (g).
Compensation of members, §143B-437.2, (e).
Creation, §143B-437.1.
Duties, §143B-437.1.
Meetings, §143B-437.3.
Powers and duties, §143B-437.1.

COMMUNITY DEVELOPMENT COUNCIL —Cont'd
Quorum, §143B-437.2, (f).
Removal of members, §143B-437.2, (d).
Special meetings, §143B-437.3.
Terms of members, §143B-437.2, (c).

COMMUNITY FESTIVALS.
Amusements.
License taxes.
Exemption, §105-40.

COMMUNITY HOUSING DEVELOPMENT ORGANIZATION.
Development zone project tax credit, §105-129.13.

COMMUNITY MEDIATION CENTERS.
Determination of percentages of funding, §7A-38.6, (g).
Dispute resolution fee for cases resolved in mediation, §7A-38.7, (a).
Proof of payment required, §7A-38.7, (b).
Evidence of statements made during negotiations not discoverable or admissible, §8-110, (a).
Mediator not compelled to testify in civil or criminal proceeding, §8-110, (b), (c).
Good faith effort to maintain level of non-state funding, §7A-38.6, (f).
Local government entity, function as, §7A-38.6, (j).
Management-related services.
State funds not to be used for such indirect costs, §7A-38.6, (j).
Nonprofit organization, function as, §7A-38.6, (j).
Non-state match restrictions not to apply, §7A-38.6, (i).
Public interest to encourage establishment, §7A-38.5, (a).
Referrals from courts, law enforcement agencies and other public agencies, §7A-38.5, (b).
Reports on centers, §7A-38.6.
Annual funding and activities report, §7A-38.6, (a).
Non-state funding, percentage of.
After second year, §7A-38.6, (c).
Six years or more, §7A-38.6, (e).
Third, fourth, and fifth years, §7A-38.6, (d).
Requesting state funding for first time, §7A-38.6, (b).
Waiver or special consideration for funding ratio difficulty, §7A-38.6, (h).

COMMUNITY ORGANIZATIONS.
Property taxes.
Exemption of real and personal property, §105-278.7.

COMMUNITY PROPERTY, DIVORCE.
Equitable distribution of marital property generally, §§50-11, 50-20 to 50-22.
Cross-actions, jurisdiction, §7A-244.
Decedents' estates.
Claim for distribution of marital or divisible property, §28A-19-19.
Mediated settlement conferences, district courts, §7A-38.4A.

COMMUNITY PROPERTY RIGHTS, DISPOSITION AT DEATH, §§31C-1 to 31C-12.
Altering interest of married persons, §31C-9.

COMMUNITY PROPERTY RIGHTS, DISPOSITION AT DEATH —Cont'd
Applicability of provisions, §31C-1.
Uniformity, §31C-11.
Citation of act, §31C-12.
Construction and interpretation, §31C-11.
Creditors' rights, §31C-8.
Elective share of spouse.
Property not subject to surviving spouses right, §31C-3.
General rule, §31C-3.
Perfection of personal representative, heir or devisee, §31C-5.
Perfection of title of surviving spouse, §31C-4.
Presumptions, §31C-2.
Purchaser for value or lender.
Inquiry as to whether lender or borrower acted properly, §31C-7, (c).
Rights generally, §31C-7, (a), (b).
Sale proceeds or creation of security interest, §31C-7, (d).
Scope of provisions, §31C-1.
Severing interest of married persons, §31C-9.
Short title of act, §31C-12.
Testamentary disposition, §31C-10.
Title.
Perfection of title of personal representative, heir or devisee, §31C-5.
Perfection of title of surviving spouse, §31C-4.
Wills.
Elective share.
Property not subject to surviving spouses right, §31C-3.
Limitations on testamentary disposition, §31C-10.
Written demand, §31C-6, (a).
Delivery, §31C-6, (b).

COMMUNITY SCHOOLS ACT, §§115C-203 to 115C-209.
Citation of article, §115C-203.
Community schools advisory councils, §115C-208.
Defined, §115C-205.
Community schools coordinators.
Defined, §115C-205.
Funds for employment, §115C-206.
Responsibilities, §115C-209.
Terms and conditions of employment, §115C-207.
Definitions, §115C-205.
Interagency council.
Defined, §115C-205.
Local boards of education.
Authority and responsibility, §115C-207.
Parents of students.
Membership on community schools advisory councils, §115C-208.
Public school facility.
Defined, §115C-205.
Purpose of article, §115C-204.
State board of education.
Duties and responsibilities, §115C-206.
Title of article, §115C-203.

COMMUNITY SERVICE.
Alcoholic beverages.
Minors.
Aiding and abetting sale to or purchase by underage persons, §§18B-302, (c), 18B-302.1, (a), (c).
Fines and other penalties, §18B-302.1, (b), (c).
Sales to, §18B-302, (a).
Fines and other penalties, §18B-302.1, (a), (c).

COMMUNITY SERVICE —Cont'd
Bail bond remission if defendant sentenced to, §15A-547.1.
Bomb scares, §§14-69.1, 14-69.2.
Deferred prosecution, community service restitution and volunteer program.
Boundaries of community service program district, §143B-262.4, (e).
Coordinator of program.
Secretary of department, §143B-262.4, (c).
Department of crime control and public safety may conduct, §143B-262.4, (a).
Fee paid by persons participating in program, §143B-262.4, (b).
Gross negligence of intentional wrongdoing.
Liability for damages sustained by individual performing service under program, §143B-262.4, (d).
Significant violations of probation or deferred compensation.
Community service staff to report, §143B-262.4, (f).
Delinquent juveniles, ordering to perform, §7B-2506.
Domestic violence.
Special probation conditions in addition to, §15A-1382.1, (b).
Drivers' licenses.
Noncompliance with community service obligation.
Revocation of license, §20-17, (b).
Impaired driving.
Coordinators assigned to district court districts, §20-179.4, (b).
Coordinator to report violations, §20-179.4, (e).
Department of correction to conduct alternative punishment program, §20-179.4, (a).
Fee for serving community service sentence, §20-179.4, (c).
Deposited in general fund, §20-179.4, (d).
Hearings on violation, §20-179.4, (e).
Level three punishment, §20-179, (i).
Level four punishment, §20-179, (j).
Level five punishment, §20-179, (k).
Method of serving sentence, §20-179, (s).
Time limit for performance, §20-179, (n).
Limited driving privilege.
Driving for other than work-related purposes, §20-179.3, (g2).
Littering, §14-399, (c), (d), (e).
Probation, §15A-1343, (b1).
Person sentenced under structured sentencing provisions.
Special rules, §15A-1343.2.
Sentencing services act, §§7A-770 to 7A-777.
See SENTENCING SERVICES.
Shoplifting, §14-72.1, (e), (f).
Structured sentencing.
Community punishments generally, §§15A-1340.10 to 15A-1340.23.
See SENTENCING.

COMMUNITY THEATERS.
Alcoholic beverage permits.
Brown-bagging permit.
Kind of permit that may be issued, §18B-1001.
Defined, §18B-1000.
Mixed beverage permit.
Kind of permit that may be issued, §18B-1001.
On-premises fortified wine permit.
Kind of permit that may be issued, §18B-1001.

COMMUNITY THEATERS —Cont'd
Alcoholic beverage permits —Cont'd
On-premises malt beverage permit.
Kind of permit that may be issued, §18B-1001.
On-premises unfortified wine permit.
Kind of permit that may be issued, §18B-1001.

COMMUNITY TRUST FOR PERSONS WITH SEVERE CHRONIC DISABILITIES, §§36A-59.10 to 36A-59.20.
Accounts and accounting.
Settlement of trust, §36A-59.20.
Statements, §36A-59.14.
Applicability of provisions, §36A-59.12.
Beneficiary.
Defined, §36A-59.11.
Interest in trust not asset for income eligibility determination, §36A-59.18.
Special requests on behalf of beneficiary, §36A-59.16.
Bequests.
Acceptance, §36A-59.13, (g), (h).
Board, §36A-59.13, (a).
Bylaws, §36A-59.13, (c).
Compensation of trustees, §36A-59.13, (b).
Incorporation as nonprofit corporation, §36A-59.12.
Staff, §36A-59.13, (d).
Status of trustees, §36A-59.13, (b1).
Burial.
Expenditure of funds for burial of beneficiaries, §36A-59.13, (d).
Citation of act.
Short title, §36A-59.10, (a).
Community trust.
Defined, §36A-59.11.
Contributions.
Acceptance, §36A-59.13, (g), (h).
Definitions, §36A-59.11.
Follow along services.
Defined, §36A-59.11.
Paid staff, §36A-59.13, (d).
Funds.
Trustee of funds as corporation, §36A-59.13.
Gifts.
Acceptance, §36A-59.15.
Guardians.
Acceptance of appointment as guardian by community trust, §36A-59.13, (f).
Impossibility of fulfillment, §36A-59.17.
Interest of beneficiary in trust not asset for income eligibility determination, §36A-59.18.
Irrevocability of trust, §36A-59.17.
Legislative findings, §36A-59.10, (b).
Liberal construction of act, §36A-59.10, (c).
Life insurance.
Assignment of insurance proceeds.
Acceptance by trust, §36A-59.13, (g), (h).
Merger, §36A-59.20.
Nonprofit corporations.
Administration of trust.
Board to incorporate as nonprofit corporation, §36A-59.12.
Dissolution of corporation.
Termination or merger of trust, §36A-59.20.
Perpetuities.
Not subject to law against perpetuities, §36A-59.19.
Public assistance.
Income eligibility determinations.
Trust interest not asset, §36A-59.18.
Purposes of act, §36A-59.10, (c).

COMMUNITY TRUST FOR PERSONS WITH SEVERE CHRONIC DISABILITIES —Cont'd
Reports.
Annual report, §36A-59.14.
Restraints on alienation.
Trusts not subject to laws against, §36A-59.19.
Scope of provisions, §36A-59.12.
Services.
Certain services not to be provided, §36A-59.13, (e).
Severe chronic disability.
Defined, §36A-59.11.
Social services.
Income eligibility determinations.
Interest in trust not asset, §36A-59.18.
Special requests on behalf of beneficiary, §36A-59.16.
Support and maintenance.
Interest of beneficiary in trust not reachable, §36A-59.18.
Surplus trust funds, §36A-59.15.
Defined, §36A-59.11.
Termination of trust, §36A-59.20.
Title of act.
Short title, §36A-59.10, (a).
Trustee.
Defined, §36A-59.11.
Trustee for individual trusts.
Authorized, §36A-59.16.
Welfare.
Income eligibility determinations.
Interest in trust not asset, §36A-59.18.

COMMUNITY WATER SYSTEMS.
Local water supply plans, §143-355.
Operating permit.
Fee, §130A-328, (b).
Required, §130A-328, (a).

COMMUTATION OF SENTENCE, Const. N. C., art. II, §5.
Notice of, §147-16, (b).

COMPACT DISKS.
Record and tape piracy.
See RECORD AND TAPE PIRACY.

COMPACTS.
Adoption.
Interstate compact on adoption and medical assistance, §§7B-3900 to 7B-3906.
See ADOPTION.
Atlantic States Marine Fisheries Compact and Commission, §§113-251 to 113-257.
Child placement.
Interstate compact on the placement of children, §§7B-3800 to 7B-3806.
Constitution of the United States.
Between state and foreign power, Const. U. S., art. I, §10.
Between the states, Const. U. S., art. I, §10.
Corrections compact, §§148-119 to 148-121.
Criminal history record checks.
National crime prevention and privacy compact, §114-19.50.
Criminal law and procedure.
National crime prevention and privacy compact, §114-19.50.
Detainers.
Interstate agreement on detainers, §§15A-761 to 15A-767.
Driver's license compact, §§20-4.21 to 20-4.30.

COMPACTS —Cont'd
Education.
Interstate compact on education, §115C-104.
Educational personnel.
Interstate agreement on qualifications, §§115C-349 to 115C-358.
See SCHOOL EMPLOYEES.
Emergency management assistance compact, §§166A-40 to 166A-53.
Environmental compact, §§113A-21 to 113A-23.
Forest fire protection.
Southeastern interstate forest fire protection compact, §§113-60.11 to 113-60.15.
High-speed rail transportation.
Virginia-North Carolina interstate high-speed rail compact, §§136-220 to 136-222.
Juveniles, interstate compact, §§7B-2800 to 7B-2827.
See INTERSTATE COMPACT ON JUVENILES.
Libraries.
Interstate library compact, §§125-12 to 125-16.
Marine fisheries compact, §§113-251 to 113-257.
Mental health.
Interstate compact on mental health, §§122C-361 to 122C-366.
Mines and minerals.
Interstate mining compact, §§74-37, 74-38.
Motor vehicles.
Driver's license compact, §§20-4.21 to 20-4.30.
Vehicle equipment safety compact, §§20-183.13 to 20-183.21.
National crime prevention and privacy compact, §114-19.50.
National guard.
Mutual assistance compact, §§127A-175 to 127A-184.
See NATIONAL GUARD.
Nurse licensure compact, §§90-171.80 to 90-171.94.
See NURSE LICENSURE COMPACT.
Parole.
Interstate compact for the supervision of adult offenders, §§148-65.4 to 148-65.9.
See INTERSTATE COMPACT FOR THE SUPERVISION OF ADULT OFFENDERS.
Pest control compact, §§106-65.55 to 106-65.61.
Placement of children.
Interstate compact, §§7B-3800 to 7B-3806.
Probation.
Interstate compact for the supervision of adult offenders, §§148-65.4 to 148-65.9.
See INTERSTATE COMPACT FOR THE SUPERVISION OF ADULT OFFENDERS.
Southeastern interstate forest fire protection compact, §§113-60.11 to 113-60.15.
Southern dairy compact, §§106-810, 106-811.
Southern growth policies agreement, §§143-490 to 143-506.
See SOUTHERN GROWTH POLICIES AGREEMENT.
Southern states energy compact, §§104D-1 to 104D-5.
Vehicle equipment safety compact, §§20-183.13 to 20-183.21.

COMPANIONS.
Wage and hour act.
Exemptions for persons employed as, §95-25.14, (a).

COMPANIONSHIP.
Death by wrongful act of another.
Damages for loss of companionship, §28A-18-2, (b).

COMPANY POLICE, §§74E-1 to 74E-13.
Assault and battery upon, §14-33.
Evidence of former threats upon plea of self-defense, §14-33.1.
Assault with deadly weapon.
Law enforcement officer assaulted with deadly weapon, §14-34.2.
Attorney general.
Fees, §74E-12.
Immunity, §74E-11.
Powers, §74E-4.
Records.
Legal custodian, §74E-5.
Authority of officers, §74E-6.
Badges, §74E-7.
Certification of agency.
Expiration, renewal and termination, §74E-10.
Citation of chapter, §74E-1.
Classification, §74E-6.
Compensation, §74E-9.
Insurance.
Certificate of self-insurance, §74E-3.
Liability insurance policy required, §74E-3.
Justice department.
Transfer of powers and duties to department, §143A-54.
Minimum standards for officers, §74E-8.
Motor vehicles, §74E-7.
Oaths, §74E-6.
Officer commission.
Expiration, renewal and termination, §74E-10.
Payment of compensation, §74E-9.
Powers, §74E-6.
Private protective services.
Exemption from private protective services act, §74C-3, (b).
Purpose of chapter, §74E-2.
Records.
Attorney general legal custodian, §74E-5.
Scope of chapter, §74E-2.
Short title of chapter, §74E-1.
Standards for officers.
Minimum standards, §74E-8.
Uniforms, §74E-7.
Violation of chapter.
Penalties, §74E-13.
Weapons, §74E-7.

COMPELLING PRODUCTION OF WILLS, §31-15.

COMPENSATING USE TAX, §§105-164.1 to 105-164.44F.
See SALES AND USE TAX.

COMPENSATION FOR KILLING DISEASED ANIMALS, §§106-323 to 106-335.
See LIVESTOCK DISEASES.

COMPENSATION OF TRUSTEES AND OTHER FIDUCIARIES, §§32-53 to 32-62.
See FIDUCIARIES.

COMPENSATION TO PERSONS ERRONEOUSLY CONVICTED OF FELONIES.
Action by parole commission, §148-84.
Amount of compensation, §148-84.
Evidence, §148-84.
Forms, §148-83.
Hearings.
Nature of hearing, §148-83.
Payment of compensation, §148-84.

COMPENSATION TO PERSONS ERRONEOUSLY CONVICTED OF FELONIES —Cont'd
Petitions, §148-83.
Provision for compensation, §148-82.

COMPENSATORY DAMAGES.
Civil rights, interference with, §99D-1, (b), (b1).

COMPETENCY OF WITNESSES.
Alcoholic beverage illicit sales.
Testimony enforced and immunity of witness, §8-55.
Child abuse cases.
Husband and wife privilege waived, §8-57.1.
Clergymen and communicants, §8-53.2.
Counselors, privileged communications, §8-53.8.
Dead man's statute, §8C-1, Rule 601, (c).
Defendant competent but not compelled to testify, §8-54.
Disqualifications.
Generally, §8C-1, Rule 601, (b).
Dying declarations, §8-51.1.
Wrongful death, §28A-18-2.
Exclusion by interest or crime, §8-49.
Gaming investigations.
Testimony enforced and immunity of witness, §8-55.
General rule, §8C-1, Rule 601, (a).
Husband and wife privilege.
Child abuse cases, waiver, §8-57.1.
Civil actions, §8-56.
Criminal actions, §8-57, (a) to (c).
Interested persons disqualified, §8C-1, Rule 601, (c).
Judges, §8C-1, Rule 605.
Jurors, §8C-1, Rule 606, (a), (b).
Lack of personal knowledge, §8C-1, Rule 602.
Marriage and family therapists.
Communications with clients, §§8-53.5, 8-53.6.
Optometrists, privileged communications, §8-53.9.
Parties competent as witness, §8-50, (a).
Personal knowledge, §8C-1, Rule 602.
Psychologist communications with client, §§8-53.3, 8-53.6.
School counselor privilege, §§8-53.4, 115C-401.
Social worker privilege, §8-53.7.

COMPETENCY TO STAND TRIAL, §§15A-1001 to 15A-1008.
Capacity regained by defendant, §15A-1006.
Commitment.
Civil commitment, §15A-1003, (a), (b).
Evidence admissible at proceedings, §15A-1003, (c).
Institution of proceedings, §15A-1002, (b).
Observation and treatment, §15A-1002, (b).
Confidentiality of information.
Reports to court, §15A-1002, (d).
Determination of incapacity, §15A-1002, (b).
Dismissal of charges, §15A-1008.
Supplemental hearing, §15A-1007, (c).
Dismissal with leave, §15A-1009.
Motion, §15A-1002, (a).
No proceedings when defendant mentally incapacitated, §15A-1001, (a).
Exceptions as to motions which can be handled by counsel without assistance of defendant, §15A-1001, (b).

COMPETENCY TO STAND TRIAL —Cont'd
Orders for safeguarding defendant, §15A-1004, (a) to (c).
Amendment or supplementation, §15A-1004, (f).
Reports to court, §15A-1004, (d).
Return of defendant to stand trial, §15A-1004, (e).
Reports to court, §§15A-1002, (b), (b1), (d), 15A-1005.
Hospital or institution with custody of defendant, §15A-1002, (d).
Return of defendant for trial upon gaining capacity, §§15A-1004, (e), 15A-1006.
Supplemental hearings, §15A-1007, (a).
Court's own determination, §15A-1007, (b).
Dismissal of charges, §15A-1007, (c).
Temporary confinement of defendant, §15A-1002, (c).

COMPLAINING WITNESSES.
Name, sex, age and address public record, §132-1.4, (c).
Temporarily withholding, law enforcement agencies, §132-1.4, (d).

COMPLAINTS.
Account.
Form, §1A-1, Rule 84.
Allowed pleadings, §1A-1, Rule 7, (a).
Amendment changing nature of action or relief.
Acquiring of interest in property prior to amendment not barred, §1-164.
Annulment of marriage.
Material facts deemed denied by defendant, §50-10, (a).
Attachment.
Verified complaint used as affidavit required, §1-440.11, (b).
Attorney discipline.
Amendment, Bar Rules & Regs., B, §.0113.
Content requirements, Bar Rules & Regs., B, §.0114.
Filing, Bar Rules & Regs., B, §.0114.
Issuance, Bar Rules & Regs., B, §.0113.
Service, Bar Rules & Regs., B, §.0114.
Child support, income withholding in non-IV-D cases, §110-136.5, (a).
Civil no-contact orders.
Workplace violence prevention.
Filing, commencement of action, §95-267, (a).
Commencement of actions.
Filing of complaint, §1A-1, Rule 3, (a).
Contractors.
Complaints against general contractors, §87-11, (a1).
Cruelty to animals, civil remedy.
Verified complaint, §19A-3.
Delinquent and undisciplined juvenile actions.
Filing complaint as petition, §7B-1803, (a).
Screening of delinquency and undisciplined complaints generally, §§7B-1700 to 7B-1706.
Delivery of complaint and summons to proper person for service, §1A-1, Rule 4, (a).
Divorce.
Contents and verification, §50-8.
Expedited evictions.
Service of complaint on defendant, §42-62, (c).
Fair housing, §41A-7.
Forms, §1A-1, Rule 84.
Fraud.
Form, §1A-1, Rule 84.
General contractors, §87-11, (a1).

COMPLAINTS —Cont'd
Geologists, §89E-17, (a).
Harmful material sales to minors, §19-14.
Insanity or incompetency of party.
Supplemental complaint, §1A-1, Rule 25, (b).
In the alternative.
Form, §1A-1, Rule 84.
Inverse condemnation, §40A-51, (a).
Limited liability companies.
Derivative actions by members, §57C-8-01, (b).
Lis pendens.
Failure to file within time limit.
Notice inoperative, §1-119, (b).
Medical malpractice.
Requirement where complaint alleges failure to comply with applicable standard of care, §1A-1, Rule 9, (j).
Money paid by mistake.
Form, §1A-1, Rule 84.
Negligence.
Forms, §1A-1, Rule 84.
Nuisances against public morals, action to abate, §19-2.2.
Pleadings generally.
See PLEADINGS.
Private personnel services, §95-47.9.
Promissory notes.
Form, §1A-1, Rule 84.
Retaliatory employment discrimination, §95-242, (a).
Secondary action by shareholders.
Verification by oath, §1A-1, Rule 23, (b).
Sheriffs.
Delivery to for service, §1A-1, Rule 4, (a).
Small claims actions, §7A-213.
Form of complaints, §7A-216.
Pleading required in assigned actions, §7A-220.
Specific performance.
Form, §1A-1, Rule 84.
Summary ejectment, §7A-223.
Supplemental complaints.
Insanity or incompetency of party, §1A-1, Rule 25, (b).
Temporary restraining order without notice.
Verified complaint, §1A-1, Rule 65, (b).
Third party complaint, §1A-1, Rule 7, (a).
Title of action, §1A-1, Rule 10, (a).
Utilities commission proceedings.
Complaints against public utilities, §62-73.
Complaints by public utilities, §62-74.
Workplace violence prevention.
Civil no-contact orders.
Filing, commencement of action, §95-267, (a).

COMPLETENESS RULE, §8C-1, Rule 106.

COMPLIANCE BONDS.
Execution sales.
Upset bids on real property, §1-339.64, (b).
Judicial sales.
Upset bid on real property at public sales, §1-339.25, (b).

COMPLIMENTARY ALCOHOLIC BEVERAGES.
Air carriers serving, §18B-107, (b).

COMPOSER-LAUREATE FOR STATE.
Appointment, §143-407.1, (a), (b).
Governor.
Appointment, §143-407.1, (a).

COMPOST.
Classification, §130A-309.11, (c).

COMPOST —Cont'd
Criteria.
Establishment, §130A-309.11, (a).
Investigation of potential markets, §130A-309.14, (d).
Nonstandard compost.
Disposal, §130A-309.11, (e).
Rules and regulations, §130A-309.11, (b).
State procurement, §130A-309.14, (f).
Use and application rates, §130A-309.11, (d).

COMPOUND INTEREST.
Obligations due guardians, §24-4.

COMPREHENSIVE MAJOR MEDICAL PLAN.
Teachers and state employees, §§135-39 to 135-40.14.
See MEDICAL PLAN FOR TEACHERS AND STATE EMPLOYEES.

COMPROMISE AND SETTLEMENT.
Admission to liability.
Advance or partial payment not admission, §1-540.3.
Motor vehicle accident settlement of property damage claim.
Not admission of liability, §1-540.2.
Advance payments not to constitute admission, §1-540.3.
Alcoholic beverage control penalties, §18B-104, (b).
Alimony.
District court actions.
Mediated settlement conferences or other settlement procedures, §7A-38.4A.
Annexation.
Population less than five thousand.
Settlements by parties to appeal.
Presentation to superior court, §160A-38, (l).
Attorney disciplinary proceedings, Bar Rules & Regs., B, §.0114.
Attorneys at law.
Abiding by client's decision, Prof. Cond. Rule 1.2.
Aggregate settlement for two or more clients, Prof. Cond. Rule 1.8.
By agreement receipt of less sum is discharged, §1-540.
Caveat to will.
Settlement agreements by party, §31-37.1.
Class actions, §1A-1, Rule 23, (c).
Community mediation centers, §7A-38.5.
Negotiation not discoverable or admissible in evidence, §8-110.
Derivative actions.
Business corporations, §55-7-45.
Limited liability company members, §57C-8-01, (d).
Shareholders, §55-7-45.
District courts.
Mediated settlement conferences or other settlement procedures.
Actions involving equitable distribution, alimony and support, §7A-38.4A.
Divorce.
Collaborative law proceedings, §§50-70 to 50-79.
See COLLABORATIVE LAW PROCEEDINGS.
Equitable distribution of marital property.
District court actions.
Mediated settlement conferences or other settlement procedures, §7A-38.4A.
Evidence of offering or accepting settlement, §8C-1, Rule 408.

COMPROMISE AND SETTLEMENT —Cont'd
Guardian's powers in administering incompetent's estate, §35A-1251.
Guardian's powers in administering minor ward's estate, §35A-1252.
Insurance companies.
Unfair claims settlement practices, §58-63-15.
International commercial arbitration and conciliation, §1-567.60.
Labor disputes.
Voluntary arbitration of labor disputes, §§95-36.1 to 95-36.9.
Lemon law.
Uniform settlement procedures, §20-351.7.
Liens for recovery for personal injuries.
Disputed claims settled before payment, §44-51.
Life insurance.
Viatical settlements, §§58-58-200 to 58-58-310.
See VIATICAL LIFE INSURANCE SETTLEMENTS.
Limited liability company contributions.
Obligation to pay, §57C-4-02, (c).
Limited liability company derivative action, §57C-8-01, (d).
Mediated settlement conferences in superior court civil actions, §7A-38.1.
Regulation of mediators, §7A-38.2.
Medical malpractice.
Effect of release of original wrongdoer on liability of physicians and surgeons, §1-540.1.
Money transmitters.
Civil penalties, §53-208.24, (b).
Motor vehicle collisions or accidents.
Settlement of property damage claims arising from, §1-540.2.
Negotiable instruments.
Use of instrument, §25-3-311.
New motor vehicles warranties act.
Utilization of informal settlement procedure.
Manufacturer requiring, §20-351.7.
Property taxes.
Restrictions, §105-380.
Receipt of less sum.
Release of whole debt, §1-540.
Record on appeal.
Power of trial judge to settle record, §1-283.
Settlement reserve fund, §143-16.4.
State or state department, agency, etc., entering into agreements.
Review by attorney general, §114-2.4.
Report as to payments received, §114-2.5.
Structured settlement protection.
Secured transactions.
Third parties.
Assignments.
Restrictions on assignments, §§25-9-406, (i), 25-9-408, (f).
Structured settlements.
Authority to transfer payment rights, §1-394.1.
Protection of structured settlement agreements, §§1-543.10 to 1-543.15.
Tax liability.
Power of secretary of revenue, §105-237.1, (a), (b).
Trusts and trustees.
Powers of trustees under express trust, §36A-136.
Underground petroleum storage tank leak cleanup.
Rights and obligations of owners or operators.
Payment or reimbursement for approved settlement agreement, §143-215.94E, (e1).
Unfair claims settlement practices, §58-63-15.

COMPROMISE AND SETTLEMENT —Cont'd
Viatical settlements, §§58-58-200 to 58-58-310.
See VIATICAL LIFE INSURANCE SETTLEMENTS.
Wills.
Caveat to wills, §31-37.1.
Workers' compensation, §97-17.

COMPULSORY COUNTERCLAIMS, §1A-1, Rule 13, (a).

COMPULSORY REFERENCE, §1A-1, Rule 53, (a).

COMPULSORY SCHOOL ATTENDANCE, §§115C-378 to 115C-383; Const. N. C., art. IX, §3.
Age children required to attend, §115C-378.
Blind children, §115C-383.
Church schools and schools of religious charter, §115C-548.
Deaf children, §115C-383.
Delinquent and undisciplined juvenile.
Alternative dispositions for delinquent juveniles.
Excusing juvenile from compliance with law, §7B-2506.
Alternative dispositions for undisciplined juveniles.
Excusing from compliance with law, §7B-2503.
Enforcement.
Method of enforcement, §115C-379.
Excessive absences.
Notice to parent, §115C-378.
Parent's responsibility of absence, §115C-378.
Indigency.
Investigation of indigency, §115C-382.
Investigations.
Indigency, §115C-382.
School social workers, §115C-381.
Indigency, §115C-382.
Nonpublic schools.
Required attendance, §115C-378.
Notice to parent.
Excessive absences, §115C-378.
Parent's responsibility for absence.
Prima facie case, §115C-378.
Penalty for violation, §115C-380.
Private schools, §115C-556.
Records.
Nonpublic schools, §115C-378.
Reports, §115C-381.
Nonpublic schools, §115C-378.
Required ages of attendance, §115C-378.
School social workers.
Allocation, §115C-381.
Employment, §115C-381.
General provisions, §115C-381.
Investigations, §115C-381.
Indigency, §115C-382.
Salary schedule.
State board of education to develop, §115C-381.
State board of education.
Enforcement, §115C-379.
Teachers.
Discouragement of nonattendance.
Duty of teachers, §115C-307, (f).
Violations.
Penalty for violation, §115C-380.
Prima facie evidence of violations, §115C-381.

COMPUTATION OF TIME, §§1-593, 1A-1, Rule 6, (a).
Act to be done falls on Saturday, Sunday or holiday, §103-5, (a), (b).

COMPUTER BASED CLE.
Accreditation, Bar Rules & Regs., D, §.1611.

COMPUTER GAMES.
Criminal offense to make unlawful payout, §14-306, (d).
Devices not considered slot machines, §14-306, (b).
Paying more than allowed by law.
Warning sticker or message as to criminal penalty affixed to machine, §14-306, (c).
Pay off in cash.
Exception to slot machine definition inapplicable, §14-306, (d).
Repurchase of prize for cash or reward in cash.
Inapplicability of exception to slot machine definition, §14-306, (d).

COMPUTER INFORMATION TRANSACTIONS.
Electronic transactions.
Choice of law, §66-329.

COMPUTER LOAN REVOLVING FUND, §115C-472.5.

COMPUTER RELATED CRIME.
Accessing or causing to be accessed.
Defined, §§14-453, 14-454, (c).
Felony offense of accessing computers, §14-454, (a).
Misdemeanor offense of accessing computers, §14-454, (b).
Applicability of provisions.
Exceptions, §14-453.1.
Authorization.
Defined, §14-453.
Computer.
Defined, §14-453.
Computer network.
Defined, §14-453.
Computer program.
Defined, §14-453.
Computer software.
Defined, §14-453.
Computer system.
Defined, §14-453.
Computer trespass, §14-458.
Damages for.
Jurisdiction, §1-539.2A, (b).
Limitations period, §1-539.2A, (b).
Right to damages, §1-539.2A, (a).
Damaging computers and computer resources.
Application of provisions, §14-455, (b).
Unlawful acts, §14-455, (a), (a1).
Viruses.
Computer viruses, §14-454, (b).
Data.
Defined, §14-453.
Denial of computer services to authorized user, §14-456, (a), (b).
Electronic mail.
Defined, §14-453.
Exceptions, §14-453.1.
Extortion, §14-457.
Financial instrument.
Defined, §14-453.
Government computers.
Accessing.
Definition, §14-454.1, (d).
Prohibited acts, §14-454.1, (a) to (c).
Altering, damaging or destroying, §14-455, (a1).
Defined, §14-453.

COMPUTER RELATED CRIME —Cont'd
Government computers —Cont'd
Denial of government computer services to an authorized user, §14-456.1, (a).
Applicability of provisions, §14-456.1, (b).
Internet.
Solicitation of child by computer, §14-202.3.
Jurisdiction, §14-453.2.
Property.
Defined, §14-453.
Resource.
Defined, §14-453.
Services.
Defined, §14-453.
Sexual offenses.
Solicitation of child by computer, §14-202.3, (a).
Solicitation of child by computer, §14-202.3, (a).
Viruses.
Introducing computer virus, §14-455, (b).
Denial of government computer services to an authorized user, §14-456.1, (b).

COMPUTERS.
Child custody jurisdiction and enforcement.
Testimony of witnesses, §50A-111.
Computer related crime, §§14-453 to 14-458.
Electronic transactions, §§66-311 to 66-330.
See ELECTRONIC TRANSACTIONS.
E-mail spam.
Damage recovery, §1-539.2A.
Personal jurisdiction for actions regarding, §1-75.4.
Employment security commission.
Reproduction of records.
Records stored on permanent computer-readable media, §8-45.3, (b).
Geographical information systems databases, §132-10.
Jury list.
Preparation of list.
Alternate procedure in certain counties, §9-2.1, (a).
Randomized list, §9-2.1, (b).
Medical care data, §§131E-214 to 131E-214.4.
See MEDICAL CARE DATA.
Office of information technology services.
Generally, §§147-33.75 to 147-33.103.
See INFORMATION TECHNOLOGY SERVICES.
Public schools.
Computer loan revolving fund, §115C-472.5.
Lease purchase or installment purchase contracts by local boards.
Purchase of computers, hardware, software and related services, §115C-528.
Records, §132-6.1.
Copies of databases, §132-6.2, (c).
Registration of voters, §§163-82.11, 163-82.12.
Revenue department.
Reproduction of records.
Records stored on permanent computer-readable media, §8-45.3, (b).
Sales and use tax.
Customer computer program.
Defined, §105-164.3.
Defined, §105-164.3.
Tax holiday, §105-164.13C, (a).
Service agreements, §§58-1-25 to 58-1-42.

COMPUTER SOFTWARE.
Property tax exemptions, §105-275.

COMPUTER SOFTWARE —Cont'd
Sales and use tax.
Defined, §105-164.3.
Exemption, §105-164.13.

COMPUTER TRESPASS.
Action by injured party, §14-458, (c).
Jurisdiction, §1-539.2A, (b).
Limitation period, §1-539.2A, (b).
Right to damages, §1-539.2A, (a).
Penalties, §14-458, (b).
Prohibited acts, §14-458, (a).

COMPUTER VIRUSES.
Computer related crime, §14-455, (b).
Denial of government computer services to an authorized user, §14-456.1, (b).

CONCEALED DEBTORS.
Arrest, §1-355.
Attachment.
Grounds for attachment, §1-440.3.

CONCEALED HANDGUN PERMIT, §§14-415.10 to 14-415.24.
Age limitation.
Qualifications of applicant, §14-415.12, (a).
Alcohol consumption.
Concealed handgun prohibited, §14-415.11, (c).
Appeals.
Denial, revocation or nonrenewal of permit, §14-415.15, (c).
Revocation or nonrenewal of permit, §14-415.18, (a).
Application, §14-415.13, (a).
Contents of form, §14-415.14, (a).
Warning on form, §14-415.14, (b).
Areas where concealed handgun unauthorized in spite of permit, §14-415.11, (c).
Bail and recognizance.
Proceedings pending for disqualifying crime.
Grounds for denial of permit, §14-415.12, (b).
Banks and financial institutions.
Concealed handgun prohibited, §14-415.11, (c).
Bureau of investigation.
Permittee list, maintenance, §14-415.17.
Submission of fingerprints to FBI for records check, §14-415.13, (b).
Carrying a concealed handgun without permit.
Applicability of provisions, §14-415.22.
Infraction, §14-415.21, (a).
Carrying of permit, §14-415.11, (a).
Change of address.
Permittee to notify sheriff, §14-415.11, (d).
Citizenship.
Qualifications of applicant, §14-415.12, (a).
Conflict of laws.
Warning required on application, §14-415.14, (b).
Construction of article, §14-415.22.
Controlled substance consumption.
Concealed handgun prohibited, §14-415.11, (c).
Convicted felon disqualifications, §14-415.12, (b).
Correctional facilities.
Concealed handgun prohibited, §14-415.11, (c).
Criminal history record checks.
Fees, §14-415.19, (a).
Procedure for issuance of permit, §14-415.15, (a).
Criminal justice education and training standards commission.
Approved courses for firearms safety, §14-415.12, (a).

CONCEALED HANDGUN PERMIT —Cont'd
Criminal justice education and training standards commission —Cont'd
Certificate of completion of firearms safety course, §14-415.13, (a).
Filing of course description by instructor, §14-415.12, (a).
Definitions, §14-415.10.
Denial of permit, §14-415.15, (a).
Appeal, §14-415.15, (c).
Grounds, §14-415.12, (b).
No liability of sheriff, §14-415.20.
Notice, stating grounds for denial, §14-415.15, (c).
Destruction of permit.
Notification to sheriff, §14-415.11, (d).
Discharge from armed forces, other than honorable.
Grounds for denial of permit, §14-415.12, (b).
Display to law enforcement officer upon request, §14-415.11, (a).
Failure to disclose, §14-415.21, (a).
Domestic violence, orders issued by court.
Suspension of permit, §14-415.18, (b).
Duplicate permit.
Replacement of lost or destroyed permits, §14-415.11, (d).
Unauthorized, grounds for revocation or suspension, §14-415.18, (a).
Duration of permit, §14-415.11, (b).
Emergencies.
Temporary permit issuance, §14-415.15, (b).
Exception.
Prohibition against carrying concealed pistol or gun, §14-269, (a).
Failure to disclose permit to law enforcement officer.
Infraction, §14-415.21, (a).
Federal office buildings.
Concealed handgun prohibited, §14-415.11, (c).
Federal prosecution for possession of handgun.
Warning required on application, §14-415.14, (b).
Fees, §14-415.13, (a).
Criminal records checks, §14-415.19, (a).
Fingerprint processing, §14-415.19, (b).
Retired sworn law enforcement officer, §14-415.19, (a1).
Schedule of fees, §14-415.19, (a).
Fingerprints.
Fees for processing, §14-415.19, (b).
Renewal of permit, new set of fingerprints, §14-415.16.
Submitted to state bureau of investigation for record check, §14-415.13, (b).
Submitted with application, §14-415.13, (a).
Firearms safety and training course.
Certificate of completion submitted with application, §14-415.13, (a).
Qualifications of applicant, §14-415.12, (a).
Qualified sworn law enforcement officers.
Exemption for, §14-415.12A.
Form of application, §14-415.13, (a).
Contents of form, §14-415.14.
Form of permit, §14-415.17.
Fraud.
Revocation or suspension for fraud in obtaining, §14-415.18, (a).
Fugitives from justice.
Grounds for denial of permit, §14-415.12, (b).
Handgun, defined, §14-415.10.
Identification required, §14-415.11, (a).

CONCEALED HANDGUN PERMIT —Cont'd
Impaired driving.
Conviction is grounds for denial of permit, §14-415.12, (b).
Indictment for felony.
Grounds for denial of permit, §14-415.12, (b).
Infractions.
Surrender of permit in lieu of paying fine, §14-415.21, (a).
Violations of article, §14-415.21, (a).
Issuance, §14-415.15, (a).
Sheriffs, §14-415.11, (b).
Liability, §14-415.20.
Law enforcement facilities.
Concealed handgun prohibited, §14-415.11, (c).
Liability of sheriff for issuance or denial, §14-415.20.
Local laws regarding concealed handgun permits prohibited, §14-415.23.
Local laws regarding posting of prohibitions.
Permissible, §14-415.23.
Lost permits.
Notification to sheriff, §14-415.11, (d).
Mental health, developmental disability, substance abuse.
Disclosure of records regarding mental health and capacity, §14-415.14, (c).
Drug addict or user.
Grounds for denial of permit, §14-415.12, (b).
Mentally ill or incompetent.
Grounds for denial of permit, §14-415.12, (b).
Release of records concerning mental health submitted with application, §14-415.13, (a).
Military affairs.
Discharge under conditions other than honorable.
Grounds for denial of permit, §14-415.12, (b).
Misdemeanors.
Grounds for denial of permit, §14-415.12, (b).
Violations of article, §14-415.21, (b).
Misrepresentation.
Revocation or suspension for misrepresentation in obtaining, §14-415.18, (a).
Misuse of permit.
Grounds for revocation or suspension, §14-415.18, (a).
National rifle association.
Approved course for firearms safety, §14-415.12, (a).
Notice.
Denial of permit, §14-415.15, (c).
Permit, defined, §14-415.10.
Permittee list kept by state bureau of investigation, §14-415.17.
Physical or mental infirmity preventing safe handling of handgun.
Qualifications of applicant, §14-415.12, (a).
Probable cause of commission of felony.
Grounds for denial of permit, §14-415.12, (b).
Property posting prohibition of concealed handguns, §14-415.11, (c).
Qualifications of applicant, §14-415.12, (a).
Reciprocity, §14-415.25, (a).
Annual written inquiry to permitting authorities in other states, §14-415.25, (c).
Registry of states that meet requirements, §14-415.25, (b).
Records.
Release of mental health records submitted with application, §14-415.13, (a).
Renewal of permit, §14-415.16.

CONCEALED HANDGUN PERMIT —Cont'd
Revocation of permit, §14-415.18, (a).
Sheriff, authority, §14-415.18, (a).
State bureau of investigation.
Permittee list, §14-415.17.
Submission of fingerprints for records check, §14-415.13, (b).
State office buildings.
Concealed handgun prohibited, §14-415.11, (c).
Statewide uniformity, §14-415.23.
Surrender of permit in lieu of paying fine.
First offense infractions, §14-415.21, (a).
Suspension of permit, §14-415.18, (a).
Part of orders issued in domestic violence case, §14-415.18, (b).
Temporary permit for emergencies, §14-415.15, (b).
Transferring permit to another person.
Grounds for revocation or suspension, §14-415.18, (a).
Validity period, §14-415.11, (b).
Violations of article.
Punishment, §14-415.21.
Revocation or suspension of permit, §14-415.18, (a).

CONCEALED PROPERTY IN BUILDINGS.
Claim for delivery of personal property, §1-480.

CONCEALED WEAPONS, §§14-269, 14-269.1.
Concealed handgun permit generally, §§14-415.10 to 14-415.24.
See CONCEALED HANDGUN PERMIT.

CONCEALING BIRTH OF CHILD, §14-46.

CONCEALMENT OF MERCHANDISE.
Shoplifting, §14-72.1.

CONCERTS.
Records and tapes.
Live concert recordings, §14-433, (a) to (c).
Scalping tickets, §14-344.

CONCESSIONS.
State forests and state parks.
Operation of public service facilities.
Authority of department of environment and natural resources, §113-35, (d).

CONCILIATION.
Custody and visitation mediation program, §§7A-494, 7A-495.
Fair housing complaints.
Commission to seek to informally resolve complaints, §41A-7, (g).
Labor disputes, §§95-32 to 95-36.
New motor vehicles warranties act.
Utilization of informal settlement procedure.
Manufacturer requiring, §20-351.7.
Retaliatory employment discrimination.
Commissioner's attempt to eliminate violation by informal method, §95-242, (a).

CONCURRENT SENTENCES, §15A-1354.

CONDEMNATION.
Fertilizers.
Noncompliance with commercial fertilizer article, §106-667.
Generally.
See EMINENT DOMAIN.
Meat, adulterated or misbranded, §106-549.52, (a), (b).
Poultry, adulterated or misbranded, §106-549.53, (a) to (c).

CONDEMNATION —Cont'd
Streets and highways.
Generally, §§136-103 to 136-121.1.
See STREETS AND HIGHWAYS.
Unsafe buildings.
Municipalities generally, §§160A-411 to 160A-438.
See MUNICIPAL BUILDING INSPECTION.

CONDITIONAL JUDGMENTS.
Garnishees.
Failure to appear, §1-440.27.

CONDITIONAL OFFER OF JUDGMENT FOR DAMAGES, §1A-1, Rule 68, (b).

CONDITIONAL SALES.
Attorneys' fees in conditional sale contract in addition to interest, §6-21.2.
Corporations.
Forms of probate for deeds and other conveyances, §47-41.02, (f).
Effect of registration, §47-20, (a).
Railroad property.
Conditional sales or leases of railroad property, §47-24.

CONDITIONAL SALES CONTRACTS.
Attorneys' fees, §6-21.2.
Claim for delivery of personal property.
Expiration of certain orders, §1-474, (b).
Sale under execution.
Interests of vendee, §1-315, (a).

CONDITION OF MIND.
Special matters, pleading, §1A-1, Rule 9, (b).
Then existing state or condition, hearsay exception, §8C-1, Rule 803.

CONDITIONS BROKEN, RIGHTS OF ENTRY.
Property passed by will, §31-40.

CONDITIONS PRECEDENT.
Pleading special matters, §1A-1, Rule 9, (c).

CONDOMINIUMS, §§47C-1-101 to 47C-4-120.
Actions.
Assessments.
Lien for, action recover, §47C-3-116.
Breach of warranty.
Limitation of action, §47C-4-116.
Tort or contract liability.
Owners' association and declarant, §47C-3-111.
Allocation of common element, interests, votes and common expenses liabilities, §47C-2-107.
Amendment to declaration changing, §47C-2-117, (d).
Limited common elements, §47C-2-108.
Merger or consolidation of condominiums.
Reallocation of allocated interests, §47C-2-121, (c).
Alterations.
Units, §47C-2-111.
Applicability of chapter.
Generally, §47C-1-102, (a).
Unit ownership act, §47C-1-102, (b).
Units located outside state, §47C-1-102, (c).
Applicability of supplemental general principles of law, §47C-1-108.
Assessments.
Lien for assessment, §47C-3-116.
Owners' associations.
Common expenses, §47C-3-115.
Attorneys' fees.
Declarant liable to association, §47C-3-111, (d).

CONDOMINIUMS —Cont'd
Attorneys' fees —Cont'd
Lien for assessment.
Included in judgment, decree or order, §47C-3-116, (d).
Protection of purchasers, §47C-4-117.
Boundaries.
Relocation of boundaries between adjoining units, §47C-2-112, (a), (b).
Units, §47C-2-102.
Declaration amendment changing, §47C-2-117, (d).
Building codes.
Applicability of local building codes, §47C-1-106.
Bylaws.
Conflict with declaration, §47C-2-103, (c).
Fines, §47C-3-107.1.
Owners' association, §47C-3-106, (a), (b).
Rule against perpetuities.
Not applied to defeat provisions, §47C-2-103, (b).
Severability of provisions, §47C-2-103, (a).
Cancellation of purchase contract.
Purchasers right, manner of canceling, §47C-4-108, (a), (b).
Citation of chapter, §47C-1-101.
Common elements.
Allocation, §47C-2-107, (a), (b), (d).
Limited common elements, §47C-2-108.
Conveyance, encumbrance, subjecting to security interest.
Access and support, unit owners not deprived of, §47C-3-112, (e).
Agreement and ratification, evidencing agreement, §47C-3-112, (b).
Contract by association, §47C-3-112, (c).
Proceeds of sale or financing, §47C-3-112, (a).
Void transactions, noncompliance with provisions, §47C-3-112, (d).
Votes required, §47C-3-112, (a).
Damages to.
Assessment of liability for damages by adjudicatory panel, §47C-3-107, (d).
Hearing by adjudicatory panel to assess responsibility, §47C-3-107, (d).
Repair by association when agent responsible for, §47C-3-107, (c).
Repair by unit owner responsible for, §47C-3-107, (b).
Easement rights of declarants, §47C-2-116.
Insurance.
Property insurance, §47C-3-113.
Limited common elements.
Allocation, §47C-2-108, (a).
Element not previously allocated as limited element, §47C-2-108, (c).
Maintenance, repair or replacement.
Assessment of unit owners to recover costs, §47C-3-115, (c).
Reallocation, §47C-2-108, (b).
Maintenance, repair or replacement.
Assessment of unit owners to recover costs, §47C-3-107, (a).
Limited common elements, §47C-3-115, (c).
Association responsibility, §47C-3-107, (a).
Partition, not subject to, §47C-2-107, (d).
Property insurance, §47C-3-113.
Security interest in common elements.
Exercise against common elements before enforced against unit, §47C-3-117, (b).

CONDOMINIUMS —Cont'd
Common elements —Cont'd
Transfer of undivided interest without unit to which interest allocated.
Void, §47C-2-107, (d).
Common expenses.
Allocation, §47C-2-107, (a), (b), (d).
Assessment.
Allocations.
Assessment against units in accordance with, §47C-3-115, (b).
Annual assessment required, §47C-3-115, (a).
Benefiting fewer than all units, §47C-3-115, (c).
Insurance costs, §47C-3-115, (c).
Judgments against association, §47C-3-115, (d).
Lien for assessment, §47C-3-116.
Limited common elements.
Maintenance, repair or replacement, §47C-3-115, (c).
Misconduct of unit owner, §47C-3-115, (e).
Past due, interest, §47C-3-115, (b).
Payment by declarant until assessment made, §47C-3-115, (a).
Recalculation.
Reallocation of expenses, §47C-3-115, (f).
Consolidation, §47C-2-121.
Contracts.
Conveyance or encumbrance of common elements, §47C-3-112, (c).
Owners' associations.
Tort and contract liability, §47C-3-111.
Termination of contracts and leases of declarant, §47C-3-105.
Conversion buildings.
Public offering statement, §47C-4-106.
Conveyance of common elements, §47C-3-112.
Corporations.
Master associations.
Powers exercised or delegated to corporation, §47C-2-120.
Cost of litigation.
Declarant liable to association, §47C-3-111, (d).
Lien for assessment.
Included in judgment, decree or order, §47C-3-116, (d).
Declarations.
Allocation of common element, interests, votes and common expenses liabilities, §47C-2-107.
Amendment.
Action to challenge validity, time limitation, §47C-2-117, (b).
Affirmative vote or written agreement by unit owners, percentage, §47C-2-117, (a).
Exercising development rights, §47C-2-110.
Recording and indexing, §47C-2-117, (c), (e).
Unanimous consent of unit owners.
Required for certain matters, §47C-2-117, (d).
Conflict with bylaws, §47C-2-103, (c).
Development rights.
Exercise, §47C-2-110.
Execution, §47C-2-101, (a).
Fines.
Violations of declaration, §47C-3-107.1.
Leasehold condominiums.
Every lessor must sign, §47C-2-106, (a).
Provisions required, §47C-2-106, (a).
Recording, §47C-2-106, (a).
Limited common elements, §47C-2-108.
Nonmaterial errors or omissions, §47C-1-104, (c).
Other provisions permitted, §47C-2-105, (b).
Plats and plans, §47C-2-109.

CONDOMINIUMS —Cont'd
Declarations —Cont'd
Recordation, §47C-2-101.
Required provisions, §47C-2-105, (a).
Leasehold condominiums, §47C-2-106, (a).
Rule against perpetuities.
Not applied to defeat provisions, §47C-2-103, (b).
Sales uses, §47C-2-115.
Severability of provisions, §47C-2-103, (a).
Special declarant rights.
Amendment creating or increasing, unanimous consent required, §47C-2-117, (d).
Transfer, §47C-3-104.
Subdividing units.
Amending declaration, §47C-2-113, (a), (b).
Substantial failure to comply.
Marketability of title impaired, determining, §47C-2-103, (d).
Surplus funds, §47C-3-114.
Transfer of special declarant rights, §47C-3-104.
Violation of declarations.
Fines, §47C-3-107.1.
Definitions, §47C-1-103.
Description of units, §47C-2-104.
Development rights.
Condominium subject to development right, §47C-4-104.
Exercise of rights.
Amendment to declaration, §47C-2-110, (a).
Recording amendment to declaration, §47C-2-110, (a).
Maintenance, repair and expenses.
Responsibility of declarant, §47C-3-107, (e).
Reserving rights in real estate added to condominium, §47C-2-110, (b).
Subdividing or converting units, §47C-2-110, (c).
Withdrawal, rights subject to, §47C-2-110, (d).
Easements.
Declarant's right to easements through common elements, §47C-2-116.
Encroachments, §47C-2-114, (a), (b).
Eminent domain.
Awards, §47C-1-107, (a).
Common elements, §47C-1-107, (c).
Partial taking, §47C-1-107, (b).
Recordation of court decree, §47C-1-107, (d).
Encroachments.
Easement for encroachment, §47C-2-114, (a), (b).
Escrow of deposits.
Deposit made in connection with purchase or reservation of unit, §47C-4-110, (a), (b).
Fines.
Violations of declaration, bylaws or rules and regulations, §47C-3-107.1.
Foreclosure or enforcement of lien or encumbrance, §47C-2-118, (i), (j).
Lien for assessment, §47C-116, (a).
Foreclosure or sale of special declarant rights, §47C-3-104, (c), (d).
Impairment of marketability of title.
Substantial failure of declaration to comply.
Determining, §47C-2-103, (d).
Implied warranty of quality.
Accrual of cause of action for breach.
Warranty of quality extending to future performance or duration, §47C-4-116, (b).
Exclusion or modification.
Agreement or expression, §47C-4-115, (a).
Purchaser of unit used for residential purposes, restrictions, §47C-4-115, (b).

CONDOMINIUMS —Cont'd
Improvements.
Completion of improvements labeled "must be built," §47C-4-119.
Declarant's obligation to complete and restore, §47C-4-119.
Inconsistent time share provisions, §47C-1-109.
Insurance.
Assessment to pay costs, §47C-3-115, (c).
Property and liability insurance, §47C-3-113.
Judgments against association.
Assessment to pay, §47C-3-115, (d).
Indexing, §47C-3-117, (d).
Lien in favor of judgment lienholder, §47C-3-117, (a).
Labels.
Completion of improvements labeled "must be built," §47C-4-119.
Promotional material, §47C-4-118.
Late payment charges, §47C-3-107.1.
Leasehold condominiums.
Declarations.
Every lessor must sign, §47C-2-106, (a).
Recording, §47C-2-106, (a).
Required provisions, §47C-2-106, (a).
Merger of leasehold and fee simple.
Acquisition of leasehold by owner of reversion or remainder, §47C-2-106, (c).
Reallocation of allocated interests as though units taken by eminent domain.
Expiration or termination of leasehold reducing units, §47C-2-106, (d).
Termination after recording declaration, restrictions, §47C-2-106, (b).
Leases of declarant.
Termination, §47C-3-105.
Liens or encumbrances.
Assessments, §47C-116, (a).
Action to recover not prohibited, §47C-116, (d).
Costs and attorneys' fees.
Judgment, decree or order must include, §47C-116, (e).
Deed in lieu of foreclosure, taking, §47C-116, (d).
Extinguished, statute of limitation, §47C-116, (c).
Fees, charges, late charges fines and interest.
Enforced as assessment, §47C-116, (a).
Foreclosure, §47C-116, (a).
Holder of first mortgage or deed of trust or purchaser.
Liability for, §47C-116, (f).
Priority, §47C-116, (b).
Common elements.
Subjecting common elements to encumbrance, §47C-3-112.
Foreclosure or enforcement of lien or encumbrance, §47C-2-118, (i), (j).
Judgment for money against association, §47C-3-117, (a).
Release of liens or encumbrances.
Conveying real estate to association, §47C-4-111, (b).
Covering unit of owner paying lienholder, §47C-3-117, (c).
Sale of unit requiring public offering statement.
Purchaser not agreeing to take subject to or assume, §47C-4-111, (a).
Security interest in common elements.
Exercise against common elements before enforced against unit, §47C-3-117, (b).

CONDOMINIUMS —Cont'd
Liens or encumbrances —Cont'd
Two or more units effected by lien.
Release lien attributable to owner paying, §47C-3-117, (c).
Limitation of actions.
Challenging validity of declaration amendment, §47C-2-117, (b).
Lien for assessment, §47C-116, (c).
Warranties, §47C-4-116.
Limited common elements, §47C-2-108.
Marketability of title impaired.
Substantial failure of declaration to comply.
Determining, §47C-2-103, (d).
Master associations, §47C-2-120.
Merger or consolidation.
Agreement, §47C-2-121, (b).
Authority, consequences, §47C-2-121, (a).
Reallocation of allocated interests, §47C-2-121, (c).
Nonprofit corporations.
Master associations.
Powers exercised or delegated to corporation, §47C-2-120.
Ordinances.
Applicability of local ordinances, §47C-1-106.
Owners' associations.
Assessment.
Common expenses, §47C-3-115.
Lien for, §47C-3-116.
Budget.
Summary provided, meeting to ratify, §47C-3-103, (c).
Bylaws, §47C-3-106, (a), (b).
Contract liability, §47C-3-111.
Corporate nature, §47C-3-101.
Declarant control of association.
Appointment and removal of executive board members, termination of control, §47C-3-103, (d).
Tort or contract liability to association, §47C-3-111, (c), (d).
Executive board.
Budget.
Summary provided, meeting to ratify, §47C-3-103, (c).
Declarant control of association.
Appointment and removal of executive board members, §47C-3-103, (d).
Election by unit owners, §47C-3-103, (e), (f).
Fiduciary relationship to association and unit owners, §47C-3-103, (a).
Power to act on behalf of association, §47C-3-103, (a).
Restrictions, §47C-3-103, (b).
Quorum, §47C-3-109, (b).
Removal, §47C-3-103, (b).
Franchise tax.
Exemption, §105-125, (a).
Judgments against.
Assessment to pay, §47C-3-115, (d).
Indexing, §47C-3-117, (d).
Lien in favor of judgment lienholder, §47C-3-117, (a).
Liabilities in tort in contract, §47C-3-111.
Liens.
Assessment, §47C-3-116.
Maintenance, repair or replacement of common elements.
Property covered by insurance, §47C-3-113, (h).
Responsibility, damages to, assessment, §47C-3-107.

CONDOMINIUMS —Cont'd
Owners' associations —Cont'd
Master associations.
Corporation, nonprofit corporation or unincorporated association.
Powers exercised by or delegated to, §47C-2-120, (a).
Delegation of powers.
Liability of members of executive board, §47C-2-120, (c).
Executive board, election, §47C-2-120, (e).
Exercise of powers, restrictions, §47C-2-120, (b).
Rights and responsibilities of unit owners, applicability, §47C-2-120, (d).
Meetings, §47C-3-108.
Quorum, §47C-3-109, (a).
Membership, §47C-3-101.
Organization, §47C-3-101.
Powers, §47C-3-102, (a).
Restrictions on powers to deal with unit owners, §47C-3-102, (b).
Property and liability insurance.
Association to maintain, §47C-3-113, (a).
Proxies, §47C-3-110, (b).
Records, §47C-3-118.
Release of liens or encumbrances.
Conveying real estate to association, §47C-4-111, (b).
Surplus funds, §47C-3-114.
Tort and contract liability.
Action against association, §47C-3-111, (b).
Wrongs occurring during declarant control, §47C-3-111, (c).
Declarant liable to association.
Litigation expenses, §47C-3-111, (d).
Wrong occurring during declarant control, §47C-3-111, (c).
Declarant's torts, §47C-3-111, (a).
Trustees, §47C-3-119.
Voting.
Allocation of votes, §47C-2-107, (c).
Common elements.
Conveyance, encumbrance, subjecting to security interest, §47C-3-112, (a).
Lessees casting votes, §47C-3-110, (c).
Multiple owners of unit, §47C-3-110, (a).
Proxy, §47C-3-110, (b).
Subgroup voting on specified matters, §47C-3-110, (e), (f).
Unit allocated to association, votes not cast, §47C-3-110, (d).
Partition.
Common elements, not subject to, §47C-2-107, (d).
Plats or plans.
Altered boundaries between adjoining units.
Preparation and recording plat or plan showing, §47C-2-112, (b).
Certification by architect required, §47C-2-109, (a).
Considered part of declaration, §47C-2-109, (a).
Improvement contemplated.
Intended location and dimensions shown, labeling, §47C-2-109, (c).
Indexing by register of deeds, §47C-2-109, (a).
New plats or plans, acquisition of development rights.
Recording, §47C-2-109, (d).
Recording, §47C-2-109, (a).
Fee, §47C-2-109, (f).
New plats or plans, acquisition of development rights, §47C-2-109, (d).

CONDOMINIUMS —Cont'd
Plats or plans —Cont'd
Recording —Cont'd
Requirements, §47C-2-109, (e).
Required to show, §47C-2-109, (b).
Subdividing units, §47C-2-113, (a).
Powers of attorney.
Use to evade chapter, §47C-1-104, (d).
Promotional material.
Labeling, §47C-4-118.
Property and liability insurance.
Assessment to pay costs, §47C-3-115, (c).
Association to maintain, §47C-3-113, (a).
Certificates or memoranda of insurance.
Issuance by insurer, §47C-3-113, (g).
Insurance not readily available.
Notice to unit owners, §47C-3-113, (c).
Losses covered by property insurance, §47C-3-113, (e).
Policies, required provisions, §47C-3-113, (d).
Repair or replacement of property covered by insurance.
Association's duty, §47C-3-113, (h).
Unit owner not prevented from obtaining, §47C-3-113, (f).
Units having horizontal boundaries, §47C-3-113, (b).
Varying or waiving provisions of section, §47C-3-113, (i).
Protection of purchasers.
Applicability of article, §47C-4-101, (a).
Attorneys' fees for violations, §47C-4-117.
Cancellation of contract by purchaser, §47C-4-108, (a), (b).
Deposits made in connection with purchase or reservation.
Escrow, §47C-4-110, (a), (b).
Escrow of deposit.
Deposit made in connection with purchase or reservation, §47C-4-110, (a), (b).
Improvements.
Declarant's obligation to complete and restore, §47C-4-119.
Labeling of promotional material, §47C-4-118.
Public offering statement.
Amendment.
Material change in information, §47C-4-103, (b).
Condominium registered with securities and exchange commission, §47C-4-107, (a).
Condominium subject to development right, §47C-4-104.
Conversion buildings, §47C-4-106.
Disclosures required, §47C-4-103, (a).
False or misleading statements, liability for, §47C-4-102, (c).
Investment contracts or other securities, condominiums deemed, §47C-4-107, (b).
Material change in information.
Amendment, §47C-4-103, (b).
Offer of unit for own account.
Required to prepare prior to offering, §47C-4-102, (c).
Required provisions, §47C-4-103, (a).
Required to prepare prior to offering, §47C-4-102, (a).
Exceptions, §47C-4-101, (b).
Offer of unit for own account, §47C-4-102, (c).
Single statement.
Unit part of condominium and other real estate regime, §47C-4-102, (d).

CONDOMINIUMS —Cont'd
Protection of purchasers —Cont'd
Public offering statement —Cont'd
Time shares, §47C-4-105, (a), (b).
Transfer of responsibility for preparing, §47C-4-102, (b).
False or misleading statements, responsibility for, §47C-4-102, (c).
When not required to prepare or deliver, §47C-4-101, (b).
Release of liens or encumbrances.
Conveying real estate to association, §47C-4-11, (a).
Sale of unit where public offering statement required.
Furnishing purchaser, §47C-4-11, (a).
Surety bond, substitute collateral or insurance against, providing, §47C-4-11, (a).
Resale certificate.
When not required to prepare or deliver, §47C-4-101, (b).
Resale of unit, §47C-4-109.
Rights of action.
Effect of violations upon, §47C-4-117.
Statutes of limitations.
Warranties, §47C-4-116.
Substantial completion of unit, §47C-4-120.
Warranties.
Breach.
Limitation of action, §47C-4-116.
Express warranty of quality, §47C-4-113.
Implied warranty of quality, §47C-4-114.
Accrual of cause of action for breach.
Warranty of quality extending to future performance or duration, §47C-4-116, (b).
Exclusion or modification.
Agreement or expression, §47C-4-115, (a).
Purchaser of unit used for residential purposes, restrictions, §47C-4-115, (b).
Limitation of action, §47C-4-116, (a).
Warranty of quality extending to future performance or duration.
Accrual of cause of action, §47C-4-116, (b).
Proxies.
Owners' associations, §47C-3-110, (b).
Public offering statement, §§47C-4-102 to 47C-4-107.
Purchase of unit.
Protection of purchaser, §§47C-4-101 to 47C-4-120.
Recordation.
Amendment to declaration, §47C-2-118, (c), (e).
Declarations.
Adding units to condominium, §47C-2-101, (b).
Creation of condominium, §47C-2-101, (a).
Plats or plans, §47C-2-109.
Records.
Owners' association, §47C-3-118.
Release of liens or encumbrances.
Conveying real estate to association, §47C-4-111, (b).
Sale of unit requiring public offering statement.
Purchaser not agreeing to take subject to or assume, §47C-4-111, (a).
Resales of units.
Protection of purchasers, §47C-4-109.
Rights of action.
Effect of violations upon, §47C-4-117.

CONDOMINIUMS —Cont'd
Rule against perpetuities.
Not applied to defeat provisions of declarations, bylaws or rules and regulations, §47C-2-103, (b).
Rules and regulations.
Applicability of local ordinances, regulations and building codes, §47C-1-106.
Violations.
Fines, §47C-3-107.1.
Sales.
Resales of units, §47C-4-109.
Sales offices, §47C-2-115.
Sales uses.
Declaration, §47C-2-115.
Securities or investment contracts.
Public offering statement, §47C-4-107, (a), (b).
Security interest.
Exercise against common elements before enforced against unit, §47C-3-117, (b).
Subjecting common elements to, §47C-3-112.
Short title, §47C-1-101.
Special declarant rights.
Amendment creating or increasing, unanimous consent required, §47C-2-117, (d).
Foreclosure or sale, §47C-3-104, (c), (d).
Transfer.
Foreclosure or sale, §47C-3-104, (c), (d).
Instrument evidencing, required, recording, §47C-3-104, (a).
Liability of persons who succeed to rights, §47C-3-104, (e).
Liability of transferor declarant, §47C-3-104, (b).
Statute of limitations.
Breach of warranty, §47C-4-116.
Challenging validity of declaration amendment, §47C-2-117, (b).
Lien for assessment, §47C-116, (c).
Subdivision of unit, §47C-2-113.
Substantial completion of unit, §47C-4-120.
Supplemental general principles of law applicable, §47C-1-108.
Surplus funds.
Owners' associations, §47C-3-114.
Taxation.
Common elements, §47C-1-105, (c).
No unit owner other than declarant, §47C-1-105, (d).
Unit owners other than declarant, §47C-1-105, (a), (b).
Termination.
Agreement of unit owners, §47C-2-118, (a).
Condominium containing units having only horizontal boundaries, §47C-2-118, (c).
Condominium containing units not having only horizontal boundaries, §47C-2-118, (d).
Evidenced by execution of termination agreement, §47C-2-118, (b).
Assets and proceeds from real estate sale.
Held by association as trustees, §47C-2-118, (g).
Creditors liens, enforcement, §47C-2-118, (g).
Interest of unit owners, §47C-2-118, (h).
Sale of real estate, §47C-2-118, (e).
Title to real estate.
No sale following termination, §47C-2-118, (f).
Sale following termination, §47C-2-118, (e).
Time share provisions.
Inconsistent provisions, §47C-1-109.
Public offering statement, §47C-4-105, (a), (b).

CONDOMINIUMS —Cont'd
Tort and contract liability of associations, §47C-3-111.
Transfer of special declarant rights, §47C-3-104.
Trust or escrow account.
Deposits made in connection with purchase of unit, §47C-4-110, (a), (b).
Trusts and trustees.
Owners' associations, §47C-3-119.
Unit boundaries, §47C-2-102.
Unit ownership, §§47A-1 to 47A-28.
See UNIT OWNERSHIP.
Units.
Access through unit.
Owner to afford association or other owners, §47C-3-107, (a).
Alteration, §47C-2-111.
Boundaries, §47C-2-102.
Declaration amendment changing, §47C-2-117, (d).
Relocation of boundaries between adjoining units, §47C-2-112, (a), (b).
Description of unit, §47C-2-104.
Encroachments.
Easement for encroachment, §47C-2-114.
Increasing number.
Amendment to declaration, §47C-2-117, (d).
Maintenance, repair or replacement.
Responsibility of owner of unit, §47C-3-107, (a).
Purchase of unit.
Protection of purchaser, §§47C-4-101 to 47C-4-120.
Restrictions on uses.
Amendment to declaration, §47C-2-117, (d).
Subdividing, §47C-2-113, (a), (b).
Variations.
Agreement, §47C-1-104, (b).
Declaration or bylaws, §47C-1-104, (a).
Voting.
Owners' associations, §47C-3-110.
Allocation of votes, §47C-2-107, (c).
Common elements.
Conveyance, encumbrance, subjecting to security interest, §47C-3-112, (a).
Warranties.
Breach.
Limitation of action, §47C-4-116.
Express warranty of quality, §47C-4-113.
Implied warranty of quality, §47C-4-114.
Exclusion or modification.
Agreement or expression, §47C-4-115, (a).
Purchaser of unit used for residential purposes, restrictions, §47C-4-115, (b).
Limitation of action, §47C-4-116, (a).
Warranty of quality extending to future performance or duration.
Accrual of cause of action, §47C-4-116, (b).

CONDUCT OF WITNESS.
Credibility attacked or supported, §8C-1, Rule 608.

CONDUCT RULES GOVERNING ATTORNEYS.
See ATTORNEYS AT LAW.

CONDUITS, §136-27.

CONFEDERATE CEMETERY.
Labor for care of cemetery.
Correction department to furnish, §65-4.

CONFEDERATE MEMORIAL DAY.
Public holiday, §103-4, (a).

CONFESSION OF JUDGMENT.
Alimony.
Alimony without action, §50-16.10.
Force and effect, §1A-1, Rule 68.1, (e).
Authorized, §1A-1, Rule 68.1, (a).
Consumer finance act.
Licensees not to take, §53-181, (c).
Costs.
Defendant's liability in criminal action, §6-47.
Entry.
Form of entry, §1A-1, Rule 68.1, (d).
Where entered, §1A-1, Rule 68.1, (c).
Executions.
Issuance and enforcement of executions, §1A-1, Rule 68.1, (e).
Force and effect, §1A-1, Rule 68.1, (e).
Insurance premium financing.
Provisions in agreements giving power of attorney to confess judgment in state.
Prohibited, §58-35-60.
Partnerships.
Power of partner to confess judgment, §59-39, (c).
Procedure, §1A-1, Rule 68.1, (b).
Retail installment sales.
Consumer credit sale.
Prohibited claims, §25A-18.
Prohibited clauses, §25A-18.
Summary ejectment, §42-30.

CONFESSIONS.
Admissions.
See ADMISSIONS.
Adultery and fornication.
Admissibility of admission or confession as evidence, §14-184.
Delinquent and undisciplined juvenile actions.
Court acceptance of admission by juvenile.
Determination that admission product of informed choice, §7B-2407, (b).
Determination that there is factual basis for admission, §7B-2407, (c).
Duties of court before accepting, §7B-2407, (a).
In-custody confession.
Admission into evidence, §7B-2101, (b).

CONFIDENTIALITY.
Abortion.
Parental or judicial consent to abortion.
Waiver of parental consent requirement proceedings, §90-21.8, (b).
Abused, neglected or dependent juveniles.
Authority of guardian ad litem to demand confidential information or reports, §7B-601.
Investigation, §7B-302.
Records and social reports generally, §§7B-2900 to 7B-2902.
Acquired immune deficiency syndrome.
Records identifying person who has AIDS virus infection, §130A-143.
Address confidentiality program, §§15C-1 to 15C-13.
See ADDRESS CONFIDENTIALITY PROGRAM.
Adoption.
Criminal history record check.
Prospective parent seeking adoption of child.
Privileged information, §48-3-309, (f).
Records, §§48-9-101 to 48-9-109.
See ADOPTION.
Adult care homes.
Death of resident.
Reporting, §131D-34.1, (d).

CONFIDENTIALITY —Cont'd
Adult care homes —Cont'd
Quality assurance, medical, or peer review committees, proceedings and records, §131D-21.2, (b).
Residents' bill of rights, §131D-27.
Aged persons.
Long-term care ombudsman program, §143B-181.22.
AIDS.
Records identifying person who has AIDS virus infection, §130A-143.
Alarm systems licensing.
Certain information concerning applicants and licensees, §74D-2, (f).
Amusement device safety.
Trade secrets, §95-111.17.
Anatomical gifts.
Hospital and patient information, interview, etc., §130A-412.2, (a).
Antifreeze.
Application for license.
Confidential formula information, §106-579.11.
Arbitration.
Canons of ethics for arbitrators.
Faithfulness to relationship of trust and confidentiality inherent in office, CEA Rule 6.
Archaeological resources protection, §70-18.
Atomic energy, radioactivity and ionizing radiation.
Disclosure limitations, §104E-29.
Attorney disability proceedings, Bar Rules & Regs., B, §.0129.
Attorney disciplinary proceedings, Bar Rules & Regs., B, §.0129.
Meetings of district grievance committees, Bar Rules & Regs., B, §.0203.
Attorneys at law, Prof. Cond. Rule 1.6.
Confidential government information.
Lawyer acquiring as public officer or employees.
Representing client with interest adverse to information, Prof. Cond. Rule 1.11.
Defined, Prof. Cond. Rule 1.0.
Discussions with prospective clients, Prof Cond. Rule 1.18.
Bail bondsmen and runners.
Runners.
Notice of termination of appointment, §58-71-125.
Surety bondsmen.
Notice of termination of appointment, §58-71-115.
Bank compliance review documents, §53-99.1, (b).
Bank examiners.
Disclosing confidentiality information, §53-125.
Bank's regulatory rating.
Disclosure to insurance carriers, §53-99, (d).
Biological agents registry, §130A-479, (e).
Birth data not public record, §130A-93, (b).
Birth defects monitoring program, §130A-131.17.
Cancer.
Records of cancer, §130A-212.
Capital punishment.
Witnesses to and persons carrying out execution, §15-190.
Carriers.
Disclosure of information as to shipments unlawful, §62-324, (a), (b).

CONFIDENTIALITY —Cont'd
Center for missing persons.
Improper release of information, §143B-499.6.
Child abuse, neglect or dependency action.
Records and social reports generally, §§7B-2900 to 7B-2902.
Child care provider criminal history record check, §110-90.2, (e).
Child custody.
Mediation, §50-13.1, (e).
Child custody jurisdiction and enforcement, §50A-209, (e).
Child fatality or near fatality case records.
Access to confidential records prohibited, §7B-2902, (c).
Disclosure by public agency on request generally, §7B-2902.
Child fatality prevention system.
Proceedings of state team and local teams, §7B-1413, (c).
Child placing agencies.
Death of resident of facility.
Reporting, §131D-10.6B, (d).
Child support enforcement.
Directory of new hires, §110-129.2, (i).
Reports to district attorneys of aid to dependent children and illegitimate births, §15-155.3.
Clergymen.
Communications between clergymen and communicants, §8-53.2.
Coal and petroleum suppliers stocks and fuel capacity, §143-345.14, (f).
Collaborative law proceedings.
Privileged and inadmissible evidence, §50-77, (a), (b).
Commercial detection services.
Utilization of drug detection dogs.
Client records, §90-102.1, (h).
Commercial feed.
Information obtained to be confidential, §106-284.44, (f).
Commissioner of banks.
Records.
Certain records not to be disclosed or be subject to public inspection, §53-99, (b).
Sharing of information with state and federal agencies, §53-99, (c).
Communicable diseases.
Records, §130A-143.
Controlled substances.
Practitioners.
Treatment and rehabilitation services, §90-109.1, (a).
Research, §90-113.3, (e).
Corporations.
Interrogatories by secretary of state, §55-1-33.
Counselors.
Privileged communications, §8-53.8.
Credit unions.
Agencies of state, other states or United States.
Exchange of information permitted, §54-109.105, (d).
Application for new credit union.
Public information, §54-109.105, (c).
Disclosure.
Court of competent jurisdiction may order, §54-109.105, (b).
Liability for damages, §54-109.105.
Misdemeanors for violations, §54-109.105, (f).
Penalties for violation, §54-109.105, (e).

CONFIDENTIALITY —Cont'd
Credit unions —Cont'd
Records of information of credit union division, administrator or agents, §54-109.105, (a).
Criminal law and procedure.
Address confidentiality program, §§15C-1 to 15C-13.
See ADDRESS CONFIDENTIALITY PROGRAM.
Mental incapacity of defendant to proceed.
Reports to court, §15A-1002, (d).
Public officers and employees.
Misuse of confidential information, §14-234.1.
Delinquent and undisciplined juvenile actions.
Records and social reports generally, §§7B-3000, 7B-3001.
Dental hygienists.
Criminal records checks for license applicants, §90-224, (c).
Dentists.
Criminal records checks for license applicants, §90-30, (b).
Peer review organizations, §§90-48.2, (e), 90-48.10.
Department of agriculture and consumer services.
Information collected and published, §106-24.1.
Department of health and human services.
Privileged patient medical records, §143B-139.6.
DNA database and databanks records, §15A-266.12, (a).
Domestic violence.
Programs for victims.
Privileged communications, §8-53.12.
Driver's license photographic image or signature recorded, §20-43, (a).
Education.
Contractors prohibited from selling personally identifiable student information, §115C-401.1.
Penalty for disclosure of certain information, §115C-13.
State board of education.
Duty to maintain confidentiality of certain information, §115C-13.
Statewide testing program.
Public records exemption, §115C-174.13.
Student records, §115C-402.
Elevators.
Trade secrets, §95-110.14.
Emergency medical services.
Confidentiality of patient information, §143-518.
Emergency response plans.
Universities and hospitals, §132-1.6.
Employment security.
Records, reports and information from claimants, employers or government, §96-4, (t).
Enhanced 911 wireless system for wireless communications.
Customer records, §62A-29.
Proprietary information and trade secrets, §62A-30.
Expunged criminal records.
File of person granted expungement, §15A-146, (c).
Fire insurance.
Information furnished by insurance companies, §58-79-40, (d).
Fish and fishing.
Coastal and estuarine commercial fishing licenses.
Records, §113-170.3, (c).
Funeral service.
Criminal records checks for license applicants, §90-210.25, (a).

CONFIDENTIALITY —Cont'd
General assembly.
Code of legislative ethics.
Disclosure of confidential information, §120-87, (a), (b).
Confidentiality of legislative communications, §§120-129 to 120-134.
Definitions, §120-129.
Documents prepared by legislative employees, §120-131.
Drafting requests, §120-130.
Fiscal note preparation requests, §120-131.1.
Information requests, §120-130.
Penalty, §§120-131.1, (c), 120-134.
Redistricting communications, §120-133.
Testimony by legislative employees, §120-132.
General contractors.
Identity of complaining party, §87-15.3.
Geologists.
Examination test scores, applications, etc., §89E-14, (c).
Investigations of complaints, §89E-17, (c).
Grand jury proceedings, §15A-623.
Guardians.
Status report for incompetent wards.
Restrictions on person with access to information, §35A-1242, (c).
Health care facilities.
Competitive health care information, §131E-97.3.
Credentialing information, §131E-97.2.
Employee information, §131E-97.1.
Health care contracts, §131E-99.
Hospices, §131E-207, (a) to (c).
Patient information, §131E-97, (a), (b).
Health maintenance organizations, §58-67-180.
Hearing impaired.
Interpreters for hearing impaired.
Criminal records checks for license applicants, §90D-7, (c).
Privileged communications, §8B-5.
Home care agency employee criminal records checks, §131E-265, (a).
Hospices, §131E-207, (a) to (c).
Hospital employee personnel files, §131E-257.2.
Hospitals.
Emergency departments, reports to state health director, §130A-480, (b).
Health care contracts, §131E-99.
Husband and wife.
Competency as witnesses.
Child abuse cases, §8-57.1.
Civil actions, §8-56.
Criminal actions, §8-57, (c).
Paternity proceedings, §8-57.2.
Illegitimacy.
District attorneys.
Reports to district attorneys of aid to dependent children and illegitimate births, §15-155.3.
Insurance.
Consumer and customer information.
Generally, §§58-39-1 to 58-39-165.
See INSURANCE CONSUMER AND CUSTOMER INFORMATION PRIVACY.
Holding companies.
Information obtained by commissioner, §58-19-40.
Medical records, §58-2-105, (a).
Credentialing of medical professionals, §58-2-105, (c).
Independent review organization, disclosure to, §58-2-105, (b).

CONFIDENTIALITY —Cont'd
Insurance —Cont'd
Misuse of borrowers' confidential information.
Prohibited, §58-63-15.
Reinsurance reports, §58-10-55, (b).
Asset acquisitions and dispositions, §58-10-60, (a) to (d).
Risk based capital requirements.
Hearings on commissioner's determinations, §58-12-30.
Information filed with commissioner, §58-12-35, (a).
Small employer group health coverage, §58-50-130, (g).
Supervision, rehabilitation and liquidation of insurers.
Hearings, §58-30-70.
Interpreters for hearing impaired.
Criminal records checks for license applicants, §90D-7, (c).
Privileged communications, §8B-5.
Interstate family support, §52C-3-311.
Journalist's qualified privilege against disclosure in any legal proceeding, §8-53.11, (b).
Definitions, §8-53.11, (a).
Eyewitness observation of criminal or tortuous conduct, no privilege, §8-53.11, (d).
Order to compel disclosure, notice to journalist and hearing, §8-53.11, (c).
Overcoming privilege, person seeking to compel disclosure, §8-53.11, (c).
Judicial standards commission proceedings, Jud. Stds. Comm. Rule 4.
Juvenile records and social reports.
Cases of abuse, neglect and dependency generally, §§7B-2900 to 7B-2902.
Cases of delinquency and undiscipline, §§7B-3000, 7B-3001.
Disclosure of information to local agencies, §7B-3100.
Labor dispute conciliation service, §95-36.
Law enforcement peer support group counselor's privilege, §8-53.10, (b).
Child abuse or neglect.
Privilege not grounds for failure to report or excluding evidence, §8-53.10, (d).
Definitions, §8-53.10, (a).
Disabled adult in need of protective services.
Privilege not grounds for failure to report or excluding evidence, §8-53.10, (d).
Inapplicability of privilege, §8-53.10, (c).
Law firm dispute arbitration, Bar Rules & Regs., E, §.0409.
Libraries and librarians.
User records, §125-19.
Limited liability companies.
Answers to interrogatories by secretary of state, §57C-1-33.
Trade secrets, §57C-3-04, (e).
Marine fisheries commission.
Personal information provided by license applicant.
Disclosure by commission prohibited, §143B-289.52, (h).
Marriage and family therapists.
Communications between therapists and clients, §8-53.5.
Alimony and divorce actions, §8-53.6.
Mediation.
Standards of professional conduct for mediators, SPCM Rule 3.

CONFIDENTIALITY —Cont'd
Medical records.
Electronic medical records, §90-412, (c).
Health care facilities.
Patient information, §131E-97, (a).
Insurance companies, §58-2-105, (a).
Credentialing of medical professionals, §58-2-105, (c).
Independent review organization, disclosure to, §58-2-105, (b).
Medical care data concerning patients, §131E-214.3, (a) to (d).
Privileged patient medical records in possession of department of health and human services, §143B-139.6.
Public health authorities, §130A-45.8, (a).
Viatical life insurance settlements, §58-58-250, (g).
Medical review and quality assurance committees.
Confidentiality of records and materials produced by committee, §90-21.22A, (c).
Medical review committee.
Introduction of records into evidence.
Testimony of members of committees, §131E-95, (b), (c).
Meningococcal disease vaccination information.
Information provided students in institution of higher education, §116-260, (b).
Mental health, developmental disability, substance abuse.
Area authorities.
Personnel records, privacy, §122C-158, (a) to (h).
Consumer advocacy program, §122C-17.
Death of client.
Adherence to laws concerning prohibited disclosures, §122C-31, (e).
Facility licenses.
Peer review and quality assurance committees' records and materials, §122C-30.
Restrictions on disclosure, §122C-25, (b).
Quality assurance activities by secretary.
Review and protection of information, §122C-192, (a) to (d).
Records.
Court records to be confidential, §122C-207.
Rights of clients.
See MENTAL HEALTH, DEVELOPMENTAL DISABILITY, SUBSTANCE ABUSE.
Militia.
Records of national guard, §127A-17.1.
Money transmitters, §53-208.17.
Motor vehicle records, personal information, §20-43.1.
Municipal tax records, §160A-208.1.
National guard.
Records of national guard, §127A-17.1.
911 database, §132-1.5.
Nurse licensure compact.
Coordinated licensure information system, §90-171.88, (d), (e).
Nurses.
Privileged communications, §8-53.13.
Nursing home employee criminal records checks, §131E-265, (a).
Nursing home patients' bill of rights.
Registration of complaints, §131E-124, (c).
Nursing homes.
Nursing home medication management advisory committee.
Meetings and proceedings, confidentiality of, §131E-128.1, (e).

CONFIDENTIALITY —Cont'd
Occupational licensing boards.
Social security numbers of applicants, §93B-14.
Occupational safety and health.
Trade secrets, §95-152.
Office of information technology services, §147-33.83, (b).
Optometrists.
Privileged communications, §8-53.9.
Patient health records, §130A-12.
Personnel files, §126-24.
Access to such information, §126-24.
Penalty for permitting access to unauthorized person, §126-27.
Examining, copying, etc., without authority, §126-28.
School employees, §115C-319.
Pharmacists and pharmacies.
Criminal records checks for license applicants, §90-85.15, (c).
Impaired pharmacist peer review organizations, §90-85.41, (e).
Records.
Availability of patient records, §90-85.35.
Availability of pharmacy records, §90-85.36, (a).
Physicians and surgeons.
Communications between physician and patient, §8-53.
Alimony and divorce actions, §8-53.6.
Waiver of privilege in child abuse cases, §8-53.1.
Criminal records checks for license applicants, §90-11, (b).
Disciplinary matters, inquiries or interviews conducted in connection with, §90-16.
Information about issuance, denial, suspension or revocation, voluntary surrender, etc., of license.
Release to health care licensure board in state, §90-14, (d).
Peer review agreements, §90-21.22, (e).
Precious metal dealers.
Files of local law-enforcement agencies, §66-169.
Preneed funeral contracts and funds, §90-210.73.
Presentence reports, §15A-1333.
Primary forest product assessment act.
Disclosure of information prohibited, §113A-195, (f).
Prisons and prisoners.
Administrative remedy procedure.
Records to be confidential, §148-118.5.
Capital punishment.
Witnesses to and persons carrying out execution, §15-190.
Private personnel services.
Criminal records checks for license applicants, §95-47.2, (d).
Privileged communications.
See PRIVILEGED COMMUNICATIONS.
Probation.
Records treated as privileged information, §15-207.
Provider sponsored organizations.
Medical information, §131E-310.
Psychologists.
Communications between psychologists and client or patient, §8-53.3.
Public health authorities.
Competitive health care information, §130A-45.11.
Credentialing information, §130A-45.10.

CONFIDENTIALITY —Cont'd
Public health authorities —Cont'd
Medical review committee.
Records and materials of proceedings, §130A-45.7, (b).
Patient information, §130A-45.8.
Personnel information, §130A-45.9.
Public officers and employees.
Misuse of confidential information, §14-234.1, (a), (b).
Repayment of money owed to state.
Exemption, §143-560.
Public records.
Communications by legal counsel to public board or agency to be confidential, §132-1.1.
911 database, §132-1.5.
Tax records, §132-1.1.
Public schools.
Address confidentiality program participants.
Actual address and telephone number confidential, §115C-402, (f).
Actual address used for admission or assignment, §115C-366, (g).
Contractors prohibited from selling personally identifiable student information, §115C-401.1.
Penalty for disclosure of certain information, §115C-13.
State board of education.
Duty to maintain confidentiality of certain information, §115C-13.
Statewide testing program.
Public records exemption, §115C-174.13.
Student records, §115C-402.
Public security information, §132-1.7, (a) to (c).
Public utilities.
Disclosure of information by commission employees unlawful, §62-316.
Rape crisis centers.
Privileged communications, §8-53.12.
Real estate brokers and salespersons.
Criminal records checks for license applicants, §93A-4, (b1).
Registration of voters.
Date of birth, §163-82.10B.
Retaliatory employment discrimination.
Commissioner's files and records relating to investigation and enforcement pleadings, §95-242, (e).
Informal procedures, §95-242, (d).
Retirement system for counties and cities.
List of members, §128-28, (q).
Retirement system for teachers and state employees.
Information concerning members, §135-6, (p).
Savings and loan associations, §54B-63.
Compliance review documents, §54B-63.1, (b).
Savings banks.
Compliance review documents, §54C-60.1, (b).
Records or information of commission or commissioner of banks, §54C-60.
School counselors.
Communications between counselors and students, §§8-53.4, 115C-401.
School employees' personnel files, §115C-319.
Schools.
Criminal record checks of school personnel, §115C-332, (f).
Setoff debt collection act, §105A-15.
Sexual assault.
Programs for victims.
Privileged communications, §8-53.12.

CONFIDENTIALITY —Cont'd
Social security numbers.
Occupational licensing boards, numbers for applicants, §93B-14.
Social services.
Aid to families with dependent children.
Reports to district attorneys, §15-155.3.
Records, §108A-80.
Applicability of certain provisions, §108A-73.
Reports to district attorney of aid to dependent children and illegitimate births.
Disclosure of information by district attorney or agent, §15-155.3.
Social workers.
Disciplinary hearings, §90B-11, (f).
Privileged communications, §8-53.7.
Soil scientists.
Board records, §89F-15, (b).
Special identification cards.
Photographic image or signature recorded, §20-43, (a).
State center for health statistics.
Security of health data, §130A-374, (a), (b).
State child fatality review team records, §143B-150.20, (f).
Members to sign statement of understanding, §143B-150.20, (g).
Student records, §115C-402.
Contractors prohibited from selling personally identifiable student information, §115C-401.1.
Taxation.
Disclosure of information.
Local tax records, §160A-208.1.
Preparers of tax forms and returns.
Unauthorized disclosure of tax information prohibited, §75-28.
Records, §132-1.1.
Tax information.
Definitions, §105-259, (a).
Disclosure prohibited, exceptions, §105-259, (b).
Misdemeanor for violations, §105-259, (c).
Municipal tax records, §160A-208.1.
Terrorist incident using nuclear, biological or chemical agents, §130A-476, (e).
Biological agents registry, §130A-479, (e).
Emergency departments, reports to state health director, §130A-480, (b).
Toxic substances.
Identification.
Emergency information, §95-194, (g).
Transportation board.
Misuse of confidential information by members, §136-14, (g).
Trust companies.
Acquisition of control.
Confidential information, §53-348, (c).
Private trust companies.
Application information, §53-364, (b).
Unemployment compensation.
Records, reports and information from claimants, employers or government, §96-4, (t).
University of North Carolina.
Audit of functions and programs.
Internal auditors work papers, exceptions, §116-40.7, (c).
Insurance.
Confidentiality of records, §116-222.
Mediation of personnel matters, §116-3.3, (a).
Uranium exploration.
Logs, surveys and reports, §74-88.

CONFIDENTIALITY —Cont'd
Veterans.
Records of department of administration, §165-11.1.
Viatical life insurance settlements.
Antifraud initiatives, §§58-58-268, (c), 58-58-280, (a).
Medical records, §58-58-250, (g).
Reports to commissioner of violation of provisions, §58-58-270.
Wage and hour act.
Files and other records relating to investigations and enforcement proceedings, §95-25.20.
Water and air resources, §143-215.3C.
Witnesses to execution, §15-190.

CONFIRMATION OF SALE.
Execution sales.
Real property, §1-339.67.
Judicial sales.
Private sale, §1-339.37.
Public sales, §1-339.28, (a) to (e).

CONFISCATION.
Controlled substances offenses.
Forfeitures of personal property used, §90-112.
Applicability of provisions, §90-113.7.
Mitigation and remission of forfeitures, §90-112.1.
Electronic surveillance devices, §15A-289.
Hunting and fishing.
Fruits and instrumentalities of offenses in question, §113-137, (i).
Motor vehicles.
Reports by peace officers, §20-114, (c).
Racing vehicles on streets and highways, §20-141.3, (g).
Searches and seizures.
Disposition of seized, confiscated or unclaimed property, §§15-11 to 15-17.
See SEARCHES AND SEIZURES.

CONFLICT OF LAWS.
Airports.
Special airport districts.
Inconsistent laws declared inapplicable, §63-89.
Bail bondsmen and runners, §58-71-195.
Bank deposits and collections.
Liability of bank, §25-4-102, (b).
Cigarette tax.
Federal constitution and statutes, §105-113.8.
Commercial code general provisions.
Parties' powers to choose applicable law, §25-1-105.
Commodities.
Securities and other laws unaffected, §78D-8.
Community colleges.
Construction contract claims.
Adjustment and resolution, §143-135.6.
Inconsistent contract provisions invalid, §143-135.6, (d).
Concealed handgun permit.
Warning required on application, §14-415.14, (b).
Contracts to improve real property.
Subject to laws of another state.
Void and against public policy, §22B-2.
Contracts with forum selection provisions.
Invalid and against public policy, §22B-3.
Counties.
Planning and zoning.
Rules and regulations, §153A-346.
Custodial trusts, §33B-19, (b).

CONFLICT OF LAWS —Cont'd
Determining foreign law, §1A-1, Rule 44.1.
Electronic commerce in government, §66-58.6, (d).
Eminent domain.
Exclusive nature of provisions, §40A-1.
Federal estate tax apportionment, §28A-27-8.
Foreign-money claims.
Interest rates, §1C-1828, (a).
Scope of article, §1C-1821, (b).
Forum selection.
Contracts to improve real property.
Provisions making contract subject to laws of other states.
Void and against public policy, §22B-2.
Contracts with forum selection provisions.
Invalid and against public policy, §22B-3.
Funds transfers, UCC.
Choice of law, §25-4A-507.
Exclusion of consumer transactions governed by federal law, §25-4A-108.
Federal reserve regulations and operating circulars supersede inconsistent provisions, §25-4A-107.
Good Samaritan act.
Medical malpractice, §90-21.14, (c).
Historic districts and landmarks, §160A-400.10.
Insurance.
Contract of insurance on property, lives or interest in this state.
State law governs, §58-3-1.
Health care benefits providers.
Jurisdiction over, §58-49-20.
Life insurance.
Interest rates on life insurance policy loans, §58-61-10, (i).
International commercial arbitration and conciliation.
Application of law as determined by conflict rules.
Failure of parties to designate applicable law, §1-567.58, (b).
Dispute decided on rules of law as chosen by parties, §1-567.58, (a).
Substantive law, designation construed to refer to, §1-567.58, (a).
Interstate family support.
Act or similar law not enacted by responding state.
State tribunal may make findings required by law of responding state, §52C-3-304, (b).
Leases, UCC.
Leases subject to other statutes, §25-2A-104.
Limitation on power of parties to choose applicable law and judicial forum, §25-2A-106.
Letters of credit.
Choice of law in document, §25-5-116, (a).
Governing law not specified, §25-5-116, (b).
Other articles of commercial code, §25-5-116, (d).
Rules and custom of practice, §25-5-116, (c).
Limited liability companies.
Applicability of provisions to foreign and interstate commerce, §57C-10-02.
Foreign limited liability companies.
Law governing, §57C-7-01.
Liability of members, managers, directors and executives, §57C-3-30, (c), (d).
Recognition of companies organized under chapter outside boundary of state, §57C-10-07.
Limited liability partnerships.
Foreign limited liability partnerships, §59-90.
Management of institutional funds, §36B-8.

CONFLICT OF LAWS —Cont'd
Marketing associations.
Conflicting laws not to apply, §54-138.
Metropolitan sewerage districts.
Inconsistent laws declared inapplicable, §162A-80.
Metropolitan water districts.
Inconsistent laws declared inapplicable, §162A-58.
Municipal corporations.
General laws and charters, §160A-3.
Railroad crossings.
Local act in conflict with provisions repealed, §160A-298.
Rail transportation liability, §160A-326, (e).
Zoning, §§160A-390, 160A-391.
Negotiable instruments, §25-3-102.
Offshore oil and gas activities.
Duties and obligations inconsistent with federal law, §143-215.94JJ.
Preemption of state law, §143-215.94JJ.
Oil and gas conservation, §113-415.
Open fires.
Effect on other laws, §113-60.30.
Overhead high-voltage line safety, §95-229.12.
Parking authorities.
Inconsistent provisions superseded, §160A-565.
Partnerships.
Liability of partners, §59-45, (f).
Pollution control.
Industrial and pollution control facilities financing act.
Inconsistent laws inapplicable, §159C-26.
Provider sponsored organizations, §131E-308, (a), (d).
Administrative procedures, §131E-305, (c).
Applicability of other laws, §131E-278.
Public transportation authorities.
Provisions controlling, §160A-586.
Racketeer influenced and corrupt organization.
Civil remedies as supplemental and cumulative, §75D-10.
Radiation protection, §104E-21, (a).
Real property improvement contracts.
Provisions making contract subject to laws of another state.
Void and against public policy, §22B-2.
Regional public transportation authority.
Rail transportation liability, §160A-626, (e).
Regional solid waste management authorities.
Compliance with other laws, §153A-430, (b).
Units of local government, §153A-430, (c), (d).
Retail installment sales.
Consumer credit protection act to control, §25A-45.
School budget and fiscal control act.
Conflicting laws superseded, §115C-424.
Secured transactions.
Applicability of article, §25-9-109, (c).
Investment property, §25-9-305, (a).
Commodity intermediary jurisdiction determinations, §25-9-305, (b).
Exceptions to general rule, §25-9-305, (c).
Perfection and priority.
Agricultural liens, §25-9-302.
Certificates of title covering goods, §25-9-303.
Consignees.
When other law governs priority, §25-9-319, (b).
Debtor's location, §25-9-307.
Letter-of-credit rights, §25-9-306.
Operation of other articles of UCC, §25-9-331.

CONFLICT OF LAWS —Cont'd
Secured transactions —Cont'd
Perfection and priority —Cont'd
Security interests, §25-9-301.
Security agreement, §25-9-201, (c).
Third party assignments.
Agreements not to assert defenses against assignees, §25-9-403, (e), (f).
Alienability of debtor's rights.
Governing law, §25-9-401, (a).
Notes, general intangibles and health care insurance receivables.
Restrictions on assignments, §25-9-408.
Notice to debtor of assignment, §25-9-406.
Social services.
Appeals, §108A-79, (l).
State education assistance authority, §§116-209.1, 116-209.23.
Transfers to minors.
Law of another state governing transfer, §33A-2, (b).
Trust companies.
Applicability of other laws, §53-366.
University of North Carolina.
Bond issues.
Compliance with other laws not required, §116-41.12.
Revenue bonds for student housing, student activities, physical education and recreation.
Inconsistent laws declared inapplicable, §§116-185, 116-198.
Urban redevelopment.
Controlling effect of provisions, §160A-524.
Venue.
Person in this state injuring one in another, §15-132.
Veterans' recreation authorities.
Provisions controlling, §165-38.
Viatical life insurance settlements.
Licenses, §58-58-210, (a).
Water and sewer authorities.
Inconsistent laws declared inapplicable, §162A-19.
Weights and measures.
Repeal of conflicting laws, §81A-88.
Wells.
Construction, §87-96.

CONFLICT RESOLUTION AND MEDIATION MODELS.
Basic education program, §115C-81, (a4).
Public schools.
School-based management and accountability program, §115C-105.32.

CONFLICTS OF INTEREST.
Advisory budget commission.
Purchases and contracts through department of administration, §143-63.
Alcoholic beverages.
Control commission, §18B-201.
Local ABC boards, §18B-700, (h).
Wholesalers.
Supplier's financial interest in wholesaler, §18B-1119.
Animal waste management.
Review of operations, §143-215.10D, (c).
Arbitration.
Arbitrators, §§1-569.11, (b), 1-569.12.
Canons of ethics for arbitrators, CEA Rule 2.
Arbitrators, §§1-569.11, (b), 1-569.12.

CONFLICTS OF INTEREST —Cont'd
Architects.
Public works.
Employment of architects when interest in use of materials prohibited, §133-1.
Attorney disciplinary proceedings.
Disqualification of council member or hearing commission member due to interest, Bar Rules & Regs., B, §.0127.
District grievance committee members, Bar Rules & Regs., B, §.0207.
Attorneys at law.
Current clients, Prof. Cond. Rule 1.7.
Specific rules, Prof. Cond. Rule 1.8.
Former clients.
Duties to, Prof. Cond. Rule 1.9.
Former judges, arbitrators, mediators or other third party neutrals, Prof. Cond. Rule 1.12.
Government officers and employees.
Special conflicts, former and current officers and employees, Prof. Cond. Rule 1.11.
Imputation, Prof. Cond. Rule 1.10.
Lawyer as witness, Prof Cond. Rule 3.7.
Prospective clients, matters with, Prof Cond. Rule 1.18.
Sale or purchase of practice, notice, Prof Cond. Rule 1.17.
Banking commission.
Interest in financial institution, restriction, §53-92, (b), (c).
Change of venue.
Judge interested as party or counsel, §1-83.
Commissioner of motor vehicles, §20-183.13.
Community colleges.
Board of trustees, §115D-26.
Employees of institutions, §115D-26.
Corporations.
Board of directors.
Business corporations, §55-8-31.
Cosmetic art.
Board of cosmetic art.
Employment of member by board for at least one year after member's term prohibited, §88B-3, (h).
Counties.
Inspection departments.
Members of departments, §153A-355.
Credit unions, §54-109.39.
Criminal justice information network governing board, §143-661, (c).
Decedents' estates.
Clerk of superior court.
Jurisdiction where clerk subscribing witness, §28A-2-3.
Depositions.
Persons before whom depositions may be taken.
Disqualification for interest, §1A-1, Rule 28, (c).
E-NC authority commission, §143B-437.46, (j).
Engineers.
Public works.
Employment of engineers when interest in use of materials prohibited, §133-1.
Fish and fisheries resources.
Inspectors, §113-225.
Gasoline and oil inspectors, §119-25.
General assembly.
Service by members of general assembly on certain boards and commissions, §120-123.
Global TransPark authority.
Members, officers or employees, §63A-21.

CONFLICTS OF INTEREST —Cont'd
Guardian ad litem program.
Services provided to abused, neglected or dependent juveniles.
Appointment of district bar member, conflict prohibiting local program representation, §7B-1202.
Health and wellness trust fund commission, §147-86.32, (i).
Health care facilities.
Finance act, §131A-22.
Hospital authorities, §131E-21.
Commissioners or employees, §157-7.
Housing finance agency, §122A-20.
Housing trust fund.
North Carolina housing partnership, §122E-4, (i).
Insurance commissioner examinations, §58-2-133, (a).
Job development investment grant program.
Economic investment committee, §143B-437.54, (c).
Judge interested as party or counsel, §1-83.
Judicial standards commission.
Interested party disqualified from acting in case, Jud. Stds. Comm. Rule 3.
Labor disputes.
Voluntary arbitration of labor disputes.
Disqualification of arbitrators, §95-36.4, (b).
License to give trust fund commission, §20-7.5, (d).
Marketing associations.
Directors, §54-146, (c).
Mediation.
Standards of professional conduct for mediators, SPCM Rule 7.
Mines and minerals.
Safety and health.
Commissioner of labor, director, etc., §74-24.19, (c).
Municipal hospitals, §131E-14.2.
Nonprofit corporations.
Board of directors, §55A-8-31.
Office of information technology services.
Procurement of information technology.
Certification that information technology bids submitted without collusion, §147-33.100.
Financial interest of officers in sources of supply, §147-33.99.
Unauthorized use of public purchase or contract procedures for private benefit, §147-33.98.
Parking authorities.
Commissioners or employees, §160A-555.
Pollution control.
Industrial and pollution control facilities financing act.
Conflict of public officers, §159C-16.
Prisoner grievance resolution board, §148-118.7.
Public contracts.
Public officers or employees benefiting from public contracts, §14-234.
Public officers or employees benefiting from public contracts, §14-234.
Public works.
Employment of architects, engineers, etc., when interest in use of materials prohibited, §133-1.
Purchases and contracts through department of administration.
Financial interest of officers in sources of supply, §143-63.

CONFLICTS OF INTEREST —Cont'd
Regional sports authorities.
Members, officers and employees, §160A-479.11.
Retirement system for teachers and state employees.
Management of funds.
Personal profit or acting as surety prohibited, §135-7, (e).
Rural redevelopment authority member, officer or employees, §143B-437.30.
Savings and loan associations, §54B-104.
Savings banks.
Directors, officers and employees, §54C-104.
Savings institutions division employees, §54C-59, (b) to (d).
Social services.
Medical assistance program, §108A-65.
State-county special assistance for adults.
No payments to facilities owned or operated by certain persons, §108A-47.
State auditor, §147-64.12, (a), (b).
State building commission.
Interested members not to participate in contract, §143-135.28.
State-county criminal justice partnership.
County board members, §143B-273.10, (g).
State board members, §143B-273.6, (g).
Tobacco trust fund commission.
Prohibited conduct, §143-717, (h).
Transportation board, §136-14, (b), (c), (e).
Criminal penalty, §136-14, (i).
Turnpike authority.
Board members, §136-89.182, (h).
Urban redevelopment.
Redevelopment commissions, §160A-511.
U.S.S. North Carolina battleship commission.
Employees not to have interest, §143B-74.3.
Veterans' recreation authorities.
Commissioners or employees, §165-29.
Vocational rehabilitation council, §143-548, (d5).
Wills.
Probate of wills.
Clerk of superior court, §28A-2-3.
Workers' compensation self-insurance.
Third-party administrators and service companies, §58-47-205.

CONFORMITY ACT.
Judgments, §1-237.

CONFUSION.
Exclusion of relevant evidence, §8C-1, Rule 403.

CONGRESS.
Absent members, Const. U. S., art. I, §5.
Adjournment, Const. U. S., art. I, §§5, 7; art. II, §3.
Admiralty, Const. U. S., art. I, §8.
Age.
Representative in congress, Const. U. S., art. I, §2.
Senator, Const. U. S., art. I, §3.
Agriculture development act.
Funds made available by congress, §106-585.
Aliens.
Eligibility to be representative, Const. U. S., art. I, §2.
Amendments to the constitution, Const. U. S., art. V.
Senate.
Equal suffrage in senate, Const. U. S., art. V.

CONGRESS —Cont'd
Apportionment, Const. U. S., art. I, §§2, 3; amds. XIV, XVII.
Action challenging state legislative or congressional plan, §§1-81.1, 1-267.1, 120-2.3 to 120-2.5.
Three-judge panel, §1-267.1.
Approval of act amending, deleting, adding to, modifying or repealing plan.
Attorney general to seek, §120-30.9B, (b).
Severability of congressional apportionment acts, §163-201.1.
Appropriations, Const. U. S., art. I, §§7, 9.
Approval by president of order, resolution or vote, Const. U. S., art. I, §7.
Army and navy.
Powers of congress, Const. U. S., art. I, §8.
Arrest of members, Const. U. S., art. I, §6.
Bankruptcy and insolvency.
Powers of congress, Const. U. S., art. I, §8.
Borrowing money, Const. U. S., art. I, §8.
Changing meeting of congress, Const. U. S., amd. XX.
CLE exemption to North Carolina members, Bar Rules & Regs., D, §.1517.
Commerce, Const. U. S., art. I, §§8, 9.
Compensation of members, Const. U. S., art. I, §6.
Laws varying compensation.
When to take effect, Const. U. S., amd. XXVII.
Consists of senate and house of representatives, Const. U. S., art. I, §1.
Continuing legal education exemption to North Carolina members of congress, Bar Rules & Regs., D, §.1517.
Copyright, Const. U. S., art. I, §8.
Counterfeiting.
Powers of congress, Const. U. S., art. I, §8.
Courts.
Power to constitute tribunals inferior to supreme court, Const. U. S., art. I, §8.
Debate, Const. U. S., art. I, §6.
Debts.
Powers of congress, Const. U. S., art. I, §8.
Declaration of war, Const. U. S., art. I, §8.
Defense.
Powers of congress, Const. U. S., art. I, §8.
Depositions.
Reading deposition on trial.
When depositions may be read, §8-83.
District of Columbia, Const. U. S., art. I, §8.
Districts.
Congressional districts specified, §163-201, (a).
Duties and imposts.
Powers of congress, Const. U. S., art. I, §8.
Elections.
Contributions and expenditures in political campaigns.
Candidates for federal office to file information report, §163-278.30.
Date of elections, §163-1, (a).
Districts.
Congressional district specified, §163-201, (a).
General assembly apportionment act.
Compliance with federal law, §163-201.2, (c).
Limitation on number of divisions, §163-201.2, (b).
Restriction, §163-201.2, (a).
Names and boundaries, §163-201, (b).
Additions or modifications, §163-201, (c).

CONGRESS —Cont'd
Elections —Cont'd
Districts —Cont'd
Names and boundaries —Cont'd
Change of precinct boundary, no effect on district, §163-201, (d).
Unassigned districts, §163-163, (e).
House of representatives, Const. U. S., art. I, §§2, 4.
District.
Congressional district specified, §163-201, (a).
Governor to issue commission upon certification of election, §163-182.16.
Judge of elections, returns and qualifications of members, Const. U. S., art. I, §5.
Qualifications of electors, Const. U. S., art. I, §2.
Reapportionment.
Election after reapportionment, §163-202.
Returns.
Judge of returns, Const. U. S., art. I, §5.
Taxation.
Denial or abridgement of right to vote for failure to pay tax prohibited, Const. U. S., amd. XXIV.
Times, places and manner of holding, Const. U. S., art. I, §4.
Payment of poll tax not required, Const. U. S., amd. XXIV.
Proclamation by governor of names of members of congress elected.
Judge of elections, returns and qualifications of members, Const. U. S., art. I, §5.
Senate.
Electors, Const. U. S., amds. XIV, XVII.
Judge of elections, returns and qualifications of members, Const. U. S., art. I, §5.
Qualifications of electors, Const. U. S., amd. XVII.
Times, places and manner of holding, Const. U. S., art. I, §4.
Vacancy in office, §§163-12, 163-115, (e).
Vacancies in office.
Filling.
House of representatives, §§163-13, 163-115, (b).
Senate, §§163-12, 163-115, (e).
Excises.
Powers of congress, Const. U. S., art. I, §8.
Foreign commerce, Const. U. S., art. I, §8.
Freedom of speech.
Members of congress, Const. U. S., art. I, §6.
Holding other office, Const. U. S., art. I, §6.
House of representatives, Const. U. S., art. I, §§1, 2, 4, 5.
Absent members, Const. U. S., art. I, §5.
Arrest of members, Const. U. S., art. I, §6.
Compensation of members, Const. U. S., art. I, §6.
Laws varying compensation.
When to take effect, Const. U. S., amd. XXVII.
Debate, Const. U. S., art. I, §6.
District.
Congressional district specified, §163-201, (a).
Elections, Const. U. S., art. I, §§2, 4.
District.
Congressional district specified, §163-201, (a).
Governor to issue commission upon certification of election, §163-182.16.
Judge of elections, returns and qualifications of members, Const. U. S., art. I, §5.
Qualifications of electors, Const. U. S., art. I, §2.

CONGRESS —Cont'd
House of representatives —Cont'd
Elections —Cont'd
Reapportionment.
Election after reapportionment, §163-202.
Returns.
Judge of returns, Const. U. S., art. I, §5.
Taxation.
Denial or abridgement of right to vote for failure to pay tax prohibited, Const. U. S., amd. XXIV.
Times, places and manner of holding, Const. U. S., art. I, §4.
Expulsion of member, Const. U. S., art. I, §5.
Freedom of speech, Const. U. S., art. I, §6.
Holding other office, Const. U. S., art. I, §6.
Impeachment, Const. U. S., art. I, §2.
Journals, Const. U. S., art. I, §§5, 7.
Libel and slander.
Privilege of members, Const. U. S., art. I, §6.
Officers, Const. U. S., art. I, §2.
Presidential elector.
Representative ineligible, Const. U. S., art. II, §1.
Punishment of members, Const. U. S., art. I, §5.
Qualifications.
Electors, Const. U. S., art. I, §2.
Members, Const. U. S., art. I, §2.
Judge of qualifications, Const. U. S., art. I, §5.
Reapportionment.
Election after reapportionment, §163-202.
Severability of congressional apportionment acts, §163-201.1.
Revenue bills, Const. U. S., art. I, §7.
Rules of procedure, Const. U. S., art. I, §5.
Speaker, Const. U. S., art. I, §2.
Term, Const. U. S., art. I, §2.
Vacancies in office, Const. U. S., art. I, §2.
Vice-president of the United States.
Vacancy in office.
Confirmation on nomination of president, Const. U. S., amd. XXV, §2.
Insurrections, Const. U. S., art. I, §8.
International law.
Power to punish offenses against, Const. U. S., art. I, §8.
Interstate commerce, Const. U. S., art. I, §§8, 9.
Invasions, Const. U. S., art. I, §8.
Legislative powers vested in, Const. U. S., art. I, §1.
Letters of marque and reprisal, Const. U. S., art. I, §8.
Libel and slander.
Privilege of members of congress, Const. U. S., art. I, §6.
Messages to congress, Const. U. S., art. II, §3.
Militia.
Powers of congress, Const. U. S., art. I, §8.
Money.
Powers of congress, Const. U. S., art. I, §8.
Motor vehicle license plates.
U.S. house.
Special plates, §20-79.4, (b).
Motor vehicle special license plates, §20-79.4, (a).
Naturalization, Const. U. S., art. I, §8.
Navy.
Powers of congress, Const. U. S., art. I, §8.
Oath of office, Const. U. S., art. VI.
Patents, Const. U. S., art. I, §8.
CONGRESS —Cont'd
Piracy.
Powers of congress, Const. U. S., art. I, §8.
Post offices and post roads, Const. U. S., art. I, §8.
Powers of congress, Const. U. S., art. I, §8.
Limitations on powers, Const. U. S., art. I, §9.
President of the United States.
Adjourning congress, Const. U. S., art. II, §3.
Convening congress, Const. U. S., art. II, §3.
Declaration of president's disability.
Determination of issue, Const. U. S., amd. XXV, §4.
Messages to congress, Const. U. S., art. II, §3.
Special sessions of congress, Const. U. S., art. II, §3.
Qualifications of members of congress, Const. U. S., art. I, §§2, 3, 5.
Rules of procedure, Const. U. S., art. I, §5.
Secretary of state.
Distribution of acts of congress, §147-36.
Senate, Const. U. S., amd. XVII.
Absent members, Const. U. S., art. I, §5.
Adjournment, Const. U. S., art. I, §§5, 7; art. II, §3.
Arrest of members, Const. U. S., art. I, §6.
Compensation of members, Const. U. S., art. I, §6.
Laws varying compensation.
When to take effect, Const. U. S., amd. XXVII.
Debate, Const. U. S., art. I, §§4, 6.
Elections.
Electors, Const. U. S., amds. XIV, XVII.
Judge of elections, returns and qualifications of members, Const. U. S., art. I, §5.
Qualifications of electors, Const. U. S., amd. XVII.
Times, places and manner of holding, Const. U. S., art. I, §4.
Equal suffrage in senate, Const. U. S., art. V.
Expulsion of member, Const. U. S., art. I, §5.
Freedom of speech, Const. U. S., art. I, §6.
Holding other office, Const. U. S., art. I, §6.
Impeachment, Const. U. S., art. I, §3.
Journals, Const. U. S., art. I, §§5, 7.
Libel and slander.
Privilege of members, Const. U. S., art. I, §6.
Officers, Const. U. S., art. I, §3.
President.
Pro tempore, Const. U. S., art. I, §3.
Presidential elector.
Senator ineligible, Const. U. S., art. II, §1.
Punishment of members, Const. U. S., art. I, §5.
Qualifications.
Electors, Const. U. S., amd. XVII.
Members, Const. U. S., art. I, §3.
Judge of qualifications, Const. U. S., art. I, §5.
Revenue bills, Const. U. S., art. I, §7.
Rules of procedure, Const. U. S., art. I, §5.
Vice-president of the United States.
Vacancy in office.
Confirmation of president, Const. U. S., amd. XXV, §2.
Sessions, Const. U. S., art. I, §4; amd. XX, §2.
Special sessions, Const. U. S., art. II, §3.
Suffrage, Const. U. S., amds. XV, XIX, XXVI.
Taxation.
Powers of congress, Const. U. S., art. I, §8.
Territories, Const. U. S., art. IV, §3.
Vacancies in office.
House of representatives.
Nominating procedures, §163-13, (a).
Special elections, §§163-13, (a), 163-115, (b).

CONGRESS —Cont'd
Vacancies in office —Cont'd
Senate.
Elections to fill, §§163-12, 163-115, (e).
War.
Articles of war, Const. U. S., art. I, §8.
Declaration of war, Const. U. S., art. I, §8.
Weights and measures, Const. U. S., art. I, §8.
Welfare.
Power of congress to provide for general welfare, Const. U. S., art. I, §8.

CONGRESSIONAL MEDAL OF HONOR LICENSE PLATES, §20-79.4, (b).

CONIFEROUS TREES.
Taking, etc., of certain wild plants from land of another, §14-129.

CONNOR ACT.
Registration of conveyances, contracts to convey, options and leases of land, §47-18.

CONSCIENTIOUS OBJECTORS.
Exemptions from duty with the militia, §127A-8.

CONSECUTIVE SENTENCES, §15A-1354.
Commencement date of consecutive sentence, §15A-1355, (a).

CONSENT.
Abortion.
Parental or judicial consent, §§90-21.6 to 90-21.10.
Adoption.
Adoption of minors.
Persons whose consent is required, §48-3-601.
Agency placements, §48-3-601.
Execution of consent by agency, §48-3-605, (d).
Time for execution of consent, §48-3-604, (d).
Child consent, §48-3-601.
Collateral agreements, effect on consent, §48-3-610.
Consequences, §48-3-607.
Contents, mandatory provisions, §48-3-606.
Court order dispensing with consent in certain situations, §48-3-603, (b).
Custody of minor upon revocation, §48-3-608, (c).
Custody of minor upon voiding of consent, §48-3-609, (b).
Direct placement of minors for adoption, §48-3-201, (b).
Direct placements, §48-3-601.
Dismissal of adoption proceeding upon voiding of consent, §48-3-609, (c).
Effect, §48-3-607.
Execution procedures.
Agencies, §48-3-605, (d).
Contents, mandatory provisions, §48-3-606.
Foreign execution, §48-3-605, (e).
General provisions, §48-3-605, (c).
Indian children, §48-3-605, (f).
Parent or guardian of minor, §48-3-605, (a).
Parent under age of eighteen, §48-3-605, (b).
Foreign consent, §48-3-605, (e).
Fraud or duress in obtaining consent of parent or guardian.
Statute of limitations for appeal, §48-2-607, (c).
Guardian ad litem for incompetent parents, §48-3-602.
Incompetent parents, §48-3-602.
Irrevocable consent.
Second consent to adoption by same adoptive parents, §48-3-608, (e).

CONSENT —Cont'd
Adoption —Cont'd
Mandatory contents, §48-3-606.
Minor age twelve or older.
Consent required, §48-3-601.
Court order dispensing with consent, §48-3-603, (b).
Persons whose consent not required, §48-3-603.
Revocation of consent.
Adoption cannot proceed without another consent, §48-3-608, (d).
Attorneys' fees to person who revoked upon failure to return minor, §48-3-608, (c).
Custody of minor, §48-3-608, (c).
Direct placement, §48-3-608, (b).
Generally, §48-3-608, (a).
Second consent by same adoptive parents.
Irrevocable, §48-3-608, (e).
Stepparent's adoption of stepchild, §48-4-102.
Timing of execution, §48-3-604.
Void, §48-3-609, (a).
Custody of minor, §48-3-609, (b).
Dismissal of adoption proceeding, §48-3-609, (c).
Alcoholic beverages.
Implied consent law, §20-16.2.
Attorney disbarment, Bar Rules & Regs., B, §.0117.
Attorneys at law.
Informed consent.
Aggregate settlement or agreement for two or more clients, Prof. Cond. Rule 1.8.
Communicating with client when client's consent required, Prof. Cond. Rule 1.4.
Defined, Prof. Cond. Rule 1.0.
Early childhood initiatives.
Home-centered services, §143B-168.16.
Guardian of the person.
Powers, §35A-1241, (a).
Health care for minors, §§32A-28 to 32A-34.
Custodial parents.
Extent and limitations of authority, §32A-31.
Impaired driving.
Implied consent, §20-16.2.
Implied consent law, §20-16.2.
Insurance policies or contracts.
Excessive rates, §58-40-30, (c).
Minors.
Cigarettes and tobacco products.
Use of minors to test compliance with provisions.
Written parental consent required, §14-313, (d).
Placement of children.
When consent of department of health and human services required, §7B-3702.
Treatment of minors.
Consent of minors required, §90-21.5.
Consent of parent or guardian.
When not required, §90-21.1.
Health care consent generally, §§32A-28 to 32A-34.
Money transmitters.
Inspection, §53-208.20, (d).
Motor vehicles.
Implied consent law, §20-16.2.
Nonprofit corporations.
Action by directors on written consent, §55A-8-21.
Action by members by written consent, §55A-7-04.
Prisons and prisoners.
Self-inflicted injuries.
Treatment of injuries upon prisoners.
Procedure when consent is refused by prisoner, §148-46.2.

CONSENT —Cont'd
Psychotherapy patient/client sexual exploitation act.
Prohibited defense, §90-21.46.
Reference by consent, §1A-1, Rule 53, (a).
Jury trial, §1A-1, Rule 53, (b).
Reinsurance.
Assumption reinsurance, §58-10-40.
Searches and seizures.
By whom given, §15A-222.
Defined, §15A-221, (b).
Items seizable as result of consent search, §15A-223, (b).
Person from whom effective consent may be obtained, §15A-222.
Scope of consent search.
Items seizable as result of consent search, §15A-223, (b).
Limited by scope of consent, §15A-223, (a).
Sexual offenses.
No defense to offense with certain victims, §14-27.7, (a).
No defense to taking indecent liberties with students, §14-202.4, (c).
Rape shield law, §8C-1, Rule 412.
Trial by consent.
Jury verdict having same effect as trial by jury, §1A-1, Rule 39, (c).
Viatical life insurance settlements.
Viators consent to contract, §58-58-250, (e).

CONSENT JUDGMENTS.
Abused, neglected or dependent juvenile actions, §7B-902.
Clerks of superior courts authorized to enter, §1-209.
Money transmitters, §53-208.25, (b).
State departments and agencies.
Approval by attorney general, §114-2.2, (a) to (c).
Entering into, §114-2.1.

CONSENT TO HEALTH CARE FOR MINORS, §§32A-28 to 32A-34.
Authorization.
Duration, §32A-32.
Form, §32A-34.
Good faith reliance on, §32A-33.
Reliance on authorization, §32A-33.
Revocation, §32A-32.
Statutory form, §32A-34.
Who may make an authorization, §32A-30.
Custodial parents.
Authority, §32A-30.
Definitions, §32A-29.
Extent and limitations of authority, §32A-31.
Public policy, §32A-28, (a).
Purpose of article, §32A-28, (b).
Treatment by physician.
Consent of minor sufficient, §90-21.5, (a).
Consent of parent or guardian.
When not required, §90-21.1.
Who may make an authorization to consent, §32A-30.

CONSERVATION.
Animal waste management, §§143-215.10A to 143-215.10H.
See ANIMAL WASTE MANAGEMENT.
Department of environment and natural resources.
Generally.
See ENVIRONMENT AND NATURAL RESOURCES DEPARTMENT.

CONSERVATION —Cont'd
Energy conservation loan authority, §122A-5.3.
Energy improvement loan program, §§143-345.16 to 143-345.18.
Farmland preservation, §§113A-240, 113A-241.
Floodplain regulation, §§143-215.51 to 143-215.61.
See FLOODPLAIN REGULATION.
Income tax credit.
Donations of real property for land conservation purposes, §105-151.12.
Oil and gas conservation.
See OIL AND GAS CONSERVATION.
Open space preservation, §§113A-240, 113A-241.
Parks and recreation.
Acquisition of conservation lands not included in state parks system, §113-34.1.
Plant protection and conservation, §§106-202.12 to 106-202.22.
See PLANT PROTECTION AND CONSERVATION.
Policy of state, Const. N. C., art. XIV, §5.
Soil and water conservation commission, §§143B-294 to 143B-297.
Southern growth policies agreement, §§143-490 to 143-506.
See SOUTHERN GROWTH POLICIES AGREEMENT.
Stream watch program, §§143-215.74F to 143-215.74I.
Tillage equipment.
Income tax, §§105-130.36, 105-151.13.
Water and air quality reporting, §§143-215.63 to 143-215.69.
See WATER AND AIR QUALITY REPORTING.
Water and air resources, §§143-211 to 143-215.9B.
See WATER AND AIR RESOURCES.
Water resources development projects.
Federal projects, §§143-215.38 to 143-215.43.
See WATER RESOURCES DEVELOPMENT PROJECTS.
Generally, §§143-215.70 to 143-215.73A.
See WATER RESOURCES DEVELOPMENT PROJECTS.
Water supply watershed protection, §§143-214.5 to 143-214.7.
Wetlands restoration program, §§143-214.8 to 143-214.13.
See WETLANDS RESTORATION PROGRAM.

CONSERVATION AND HISTORIC PRESERVATION AGREEMENTS, §§121-34 to 121-42.
Acquisition of agreements, §§121-37, 121-38, (b).
Applicability of article, §121-36, (a).
Approval of agreements, §121-37.
Assessment of land or improvements subject to agreement, §121-40.
Citation of act, §§121-34, 121-42.
Construction and interpretation, §121-36, (b), (c).
Definitions, §121-35.
Duration of agreements, §121-38, (c).
Effectiveness of agreements, §121-38, (c).
Enforceability of agreements, §121-38, (a).
Right of entry, §121-39, (b).
Who may enforce, §121-39, (a).
Holders.
Defined, §121-35.
Enforceability of agreements, §121-39, (a).

CONSERVATION AND HISTORIC PRESERVATION AGREEMENTS —Cont'd
Public recording of agreements, §121-41.
Register of deeds.
Public recording of agreements, §121-41, (a).
Releases or terminations of agreements, §121-41, (b).
Right of entry.
Enforceability of agreements, §121-39, (b).
Short title, §121-34.
Taxation.
Assessment of land or improvements subject to agreement, §121-40.
Validity of agreements, §121-38.
Imposition of continuing obligations, §121-38, (d).

CONSERVATION EASEMENTS, §§113A-230 to 113A-235.
Applicability and construction of provisions, §106-744, (d).
Conservation grant fund.
Administration of grants from fund, §113A-234, (b).
Allowable uses of grants, §113A-233, (a).
Created, §113A-232, (a).
Eligibility for grant, §113A-232, (c), (c1).
Procedures and criteria for grants, §113A-234, (a).
Prohibited uses of grants, §113A-233, (b).
Sources, §113A-232, (b).
Use of revenue, §113A-232, (d).
Countywide farmland protection plans, §106-744, (e).
Creation of lots.
Number, §106-744, (b).
Defined, §106-744, (b).
Development of program to accomplish, §113A-231.
Duration, §106-744, (b).
Farmland preservation, §§113A-240, 113A-241.
Farmland preservation trust fund, §106-744, (c) to (c2).
Findings of general assembly, §113A-230.
Intent of general assembly, §113A-230.
Inventory, §113A-235, (c).
Open space preservation, §§113A-240, 113A-241.
Protection of ecological systems and appropriate public use through conservation easements, §113A-235, (a), (b).
Purchase by county, §106-744, (a).
Reports.
Implementation of provisions, §113A-235, (c).
Wetlands restoration program.
Recipient or grantee to grant in property acquired under program, §143-214.12, (a1).

CONSERVATION, FARMLAND, AND OPEN SPACE LAND PRESERVATION.
Generally, §113A-241, (a).
Legislative intent, §113A-240, (a), (b).
Secretary of environment and natural resources.
Duties, §113A-241, (b), (c).

CONSERVATION OF ENERGY.
Electric power rates to promote conservation, §62-155.

CONSERVATION OFFICERS.
Special conservation officers, §113-138.

CONSERVATION TILLAGE EQUIPMENT.
Income tax.
Corporations, §105-130.36.

CONSERVATION TILLAGE EQUIPMENT —Cont'd
Income tax —Cont'd
Individual income tax.
Credit for installation of conservation tillage equipment, §105-151.13.

CONSERVATORS.
Banks.
Conservatorship generally, §§53-148 to 53-158.
See BANKS.
Compensation of trustees and other fiduciaries, §§32-53 to 32-62.
See FIDUCIARIES.
Credit unions.
Conservation generally, §54-109.92.
Durable power of attorney.
Attorney-in-fact accountable to court appointed conservator, §32A-10, (a).
Nomination by durable power of attorney for consideration by court, §32A-10, (b).
Judicial sales.
Bond of person holding sale, §1-339.10, (b), (c).
Limited liability companies.
Incompetence of member, powers upon, §57C-5-05.
Powers of fiduciaries generally, §§32-25 to 32-28.
See FIDUCIARIES.
Prudent person rule.
Investment and deposit of funds, §36A-2, (a).
Securities regulation.
Appointment of conservator for defendant's assets, §78A-47, (a).
Exempt transactions, §78A-17.
Trust companies, §§53-401 to 53-405.
Uniform fiduciaries act, §§32-1 to 32-13.
See FIDUCIARIES.

CONSIDERATION.
Failure as affirmative defense, pleading, §1A-1, Rule 8, (c).
Gift tax.
Transfer for less than adequate and full consideration, §105-189.
Leases, UCC.
Modification needs no consideration, §25-2A-208, (1).
Letters of credit, §25-5-105.
Want of consideration.
Unclaimed property act, affirmative defense, §116B-58.

CONSIGNMENTS.
Artwork on consignment, §§25C-1 to 25C-5.
Embezzlement by consignees.
Receipt of property by virtue of office or employment, §14-90.
Sale of goods, UCC, §25-2-326.
Sale or return, §25-2-326.
Risk of loss, §25-2-327, (2).
Special incidents, §25-2-327, (2).
Sale of used goods on consignment.
Records, §66-67.2, (a) to (e).

CONSOLIDATED CITY-COUNTY ACT, §§160B-1 to 160B-21.
Assumption of debt, §§160B-16 to 160B-21.
Actions to set aside referendum, §160B-19, (i).
Acts by localities, effect, §160B-18, (c).
Applicability of article, §160B-16, (a).
Approval by referendum required, §160B-18, (a).
Budget preparation by governing board, §160B-17.
Canvassing of referendum, §160B-19, (h).

CONSOLIDATED CITY-COUNTY ACT —Cont'd
Assumption of debt —Cont'd
Consolidation effective date, §160B-18, (b).
Consolidation enactment publication.
Notice of assumption of debt, §160B-21, (a).
Consolidations study commission.
Referendum by commission may include referendum on assumptions of debt, §160B-19, (b).
Effective date of consolidation, §160B-18, (b).
Enactment of consolidation.
Limitation on action contesting validity, §160B-21, (b).
Form of referendum on assumption of debt, §160B-19, (d).
General assembly.
Referendum of consolidation may include referendum on assumption of debt, §160B-19, (c).
Governing board.
Budget preparation, §160B-17.
Organizational meeting, §160B-17.
Governing bodies of consolidating units.
Referendum on assumption of debt, §160B-19, (d).
Interim governing boards.
Referendum on assumption of debt, §160B-19, (d).
Limitation of local acts, §160B-18, (c).
Limitation on action contesting validity of consolidation enactment, §160B-21, (b).
Local government commission review, §160B-20, (a).
Notice of referendum, §160B-19, (g).
Organizational meeting of governing board, §160B-17.
Outstanding debt secured by pledge of faith and credit of consolidating city.
Approval by majority of voters, §160B-19, (e).
Procedure for assumption of debt, §160B-20, (b).
Referendum on assumption of debt, §160B-19, (a).
Publication of consolidation enactment.
Inclusion of assumption of debt, §160B-21, (a).
Referendum approval required, §160B-18, (a).
Referendum on assumption of debt.
Action to set aside, §160B-19, (i).
Form, §160B-19, (d).
Notice, §160B-19, (g).
Time for holding, §160B-19, (f).
Review by local government commission, §160B-20, (a).
Right to issue authorized debt.
Majority of approval of voters for assumption of right, §160B-19, (e).
Procedure for assumption of right, §160B-20, (c).
Referendum on assumption of right, §160B-19, (a).
Scope of article, §160B-16, (a).
Severability of article, §160B-16, (b).
Validity of article, §160B-16, (b).
Bankruptcy and insolvency.
Authority of counties, cities, towns and villages, etc., to avail themselves of bankruptcy law, §23-48.
Bond issues.
Authorized, §160B-13.
Debt limitations, §160B-15.
Elections on, §160B-14.
Procedure for issuance, §160B-14.

CONSOLIDATED CITY-COUNTY ACT —Cont'd
Borrowing money.
Authorized, §160B-13.
Debt limitations, §160B-15.
Citation of act.
Short title, §160B-1.
Constitution of North Carolina.
General assembly to provide for local government, Const. N. C., art. VII, §1.
Merged or consolidated counties, Const. N. C., art. VII, §3.
Debts.
Assumption of obligations and debts, §§160B-16 to 160B-21.
Limitation on indebtedness, §160B-15.
Definitions, §160B-2.
Dissolution.
Establishment of study commission, §160B-2.2, (a).
Study commission.
Established, §160B-2.2, (a).
Powers and duties generally, §160B-2.2, (b).
Effective date of act, §160B-1.
Elections.
Bond issues, §160B-14.
General assembly.
Local government to be provided for by general assembly, Const. N. C., art. VII, §1.
Governing board.
Defined, §160B-2.
Urban service districts.
Defining districts, §§160B-3 to 160B-6.
Limitation of actions.
Contesting validity of enactment of consolidation, §160B-21, (b).
Obligations.
Assumption of debts and obligations, §§160B-16 to 160B-21.
Powers of consolidated city-county.
Generally, §160B-2.1, (a).
Outside boundaries of urban service district, §160B-2.1, (b).
Statute of limitations.
Contesting validity of enactment of consolidation, §160B-21, (b).
Streets and highways.
Arrangements in consolidated city-county, §136-66.6.
Study commission for dissolution of city-county.
Establishment, §160B-2.2, (a).
Powers, §160B-2.2, (b).
Taxation.
Urban service districts.
Authorized, §160B-11.
Rates, §160B-11.
Title of act.
Short title, §160B-1.
Urban service districts, §§160B-3 to 160B-12.
Abolition of districts, §160B-10.
Administration, §160B-3, (b).
Consolidation of district.
Effective date, §160B-8, (d).
Findings required, §160B-8, (a).
Hearing, §160B-8, (c).
Notice of hearing, §160B-8, (c).
Report.
Prerequisite to hearing, §160B-8, (b).
Services, facilities and functions.
Required provision or maintenance by consolidated district, §160B-9, (c).

CONSOLIDATED CITY-COUNTY ACT —Cont'd
Urban service districts —Cont'd
Effective date.
Resolution defining district, §160B-6, (d).
Establishment, §160B-3, (a).
Defining of district prior to consolidation, §160B-4, (b).
Effective date of resolution, §160B-6, (c).
Findings required, §160B-6, (a).
Hearing, §160B-6, (c).
Notice of hearing, §160B-6, (c).
Replacing municipalities abolished subsequent to consolidation, §160B-5.
Replacing municipality abolished at time of consolidation, §160B-4, (a).
Report.
Prerequisite to hearing, §160B-6, (b).
Services, facilities and functions.
Required provision or maintenance by new district, §160B-9, (a).
Exercise of powers, §160B-3, (b).
Extension of district.
Annexation by petition, §160B-7, (b).
Effective date of resolution, §160B-7, (e).
Findings required, §160B-7, (a).
Hearing, §160B-7, (d).
Notice of hearing, §160B-7, (d), (d1).
Report.
Prerequisite to hearing, §160B-7, (c).
Restriction on use of provisions, §160B-7, (f).
Services, facilities and functions.
Required provision or maintenance by extended district, §160B-9, (b).
Governing board.
Defining districts, §§160B-3 to 160B-6.
Hearings.
Abolition of districts, §160B-10.
Consolidation of district, §160B-8, (c).
Establishment of district, §160B-6, (c).
Extension of district, §160B-7, (d).
Notice.
Abolition of districts.
Hearings, §160B-10.
Consolidation of district.
Hearing, §160B-8, (c).
Establishment of district.
Hearing, §160B-6, (c).
Extension of district.
Hearing, §160B-7, (d), (d1).
Purpose, §160B-3, (a).
Revenues.
Allocation to urban service district by consolidated city-county, §160B-12.
Taxes.
Authorized, §160B-11.
Rates, §160B-11.

CONSOLIDATED COUNTY HUMAN SERVICES, §143B-139.7.

CONSOLIDATED HUMAN SERVICES AGENCY.
Board.
Appointing authority.
County board of commissioners, §108A-3, (d).
Authority and powers generally, §§108A-15.1, (a), 153A-77, (d).
Chairperson, §153A-77, (c).
Composition, §153A-77, (c).
Creation, authority of county, §153A-77, (b).
Meetings, §153A-77, (c).
Number of members, §153A-77, (c).

CONSOLIDATED HUMAN SERVICES AGENCY —Cont'd
Board —Cont'd
Per diem, subsistence and travel expenses, §153A-77, (c).
Policy-making, rule-making and administrative board to agency, §153A-77, (c).
Powers and duties of area authority, §122C-127, (b).
Powers and duties of board of social services, §108A-15.1, (b).
Powers and duties of local health board, §130A-43, (b).
Quorum, §153A-77, (c).
Removal, §153A-77, (c).
Social services, power and authority, §108A-15.1, (a).
Creation.
Authority of county, §153A-77, (b).
County required to provide for health services, §130A-34, (b).
Department of county, §122C-116, (b).
Director.
Appointment, dismissal, §153A-77, (e).
Duties, powers, §153A-77, (e).
Director of area authority, powers and duties of, §122C-127, (c).
Director of social services, powers and duties of, §108A-15.1, (c).
Local health director, powers and duties of, §130A-43, (c).
Report to county manager, §153A-77, (e).
Duties of local health department.
Responsibility to carry out, §130A-43, (a).
Human services functions.
Assignment to agency, §153A-77, (b).
Local public health programs.
Authority to administer, §130A-43, (a).
Mental health programs.
Authority to carry, §122C-127, (a).

CONSOLIDATED JUDICIAL RETIREMENT ACT, §§135-50 to 135-75.
See RETIREMENT SYSTEM FOR TEACHERS AND STATE EMPLOYEES.

CONSOLIDATION.
Administrative procedure.
Hearings, §150B-26.
Arbitration.
Consolidation of separate arbitration proceedings.
Court order, §1-569.10, (a), (b).
Prohibited contract provisions, §1-569.10, (c).
Banks, §53-12.
Deemed one bank, §53-13.
National banks.
Consolidation, conversion or merger of state banks or trust companies with national banks, §53-16.
Wills.
Substitution as executor or trustee under will, §31-19.
Condominiums, §47C-2-121.
Counties, Const. N. C., art. VII, §3.
Commissions.
Powers, §153A-404.
Purposes, §153A-402.
Content of concurrent resolutions, §153A-403.
Establishment, §153A-401, (a).
General assembly action, §153A-405, (d).
Powers and duties.
Commissions, §153A-404.
Purposes of commission, §153A-402.

CONSOLIDATION —Cont'd
Counties —Cont'd
Referendum, §153A-405, (a) to (c), (e).
Ballot propositions, §153A-405, (b) to (e).
Resolutions.
Content of concurrent resolutions, §153A-403.
Support, §153A-401, (b).
Electric membership corporations.
Articles of consolidation, §117-41, (c).
Filing and recording of articles, §117-43.
Recording of articles, §117-43.
Compliance with provisions, §117-41, (a).
Effect of consolidation, §117-44.
Procedure, §117-41, (c).
Proposition for consolidation, §117-41, (b).
Validation, §117-45.
Fraternal benefit societies.
Insurance.
Reinsurance upon consolidation, §58-24-60, (b).
Procedure, §58-24-65.
Hospital, medical and dental service corporations, §58-65-155.
Insurance companies, §58-7-150.
Marketing associations.
Abandonment of consolidation, §54-161, (b).
Articles of consolidation, §54-162, (a), (b).
Authorized, §54-160, (a).
Domestic and foreign associations, §54-164.
Effect, §54-164, (d), (e).
Effect, §54-163.
Objecting members, §54-166.
Plan of consolidation, §54-160, (b).
Adoption, §54-161, (a).
Time consolidation effected, §54-162, (c).
Merger.
See MERGER.
Motor carriers, §62-111, (b), (c), (e).
Municipal service districts.
Effective date, §160A-539.
Required provision or maintenance of services by consolidated district, §160A-540, (c).
Mutual burial associations, §§90-210.80, 90-210.106, (a) to (d), 90-210.107, (a) to (f).
Public utilities, §62-111.
Retail installment sales.
Consolidation and refinancing, §§25A-27, (a), 25A-31.
School districts, §115C-72, (a), (b).
Administrative units in adjoining counties.
Merger of units, §115C-68.
Administrative units in same county.
Merger, §115C-67.
Administrative units merged by board of commissioners, §115C-68.1.
Administrative units merged by local boards of education, §115C-68.2.
Validation of plans, §115C-68.3.
Schools, §115C-72, (a), (b).
State agencies.
Powers of governor, §147-13.1, (a) to (c).
Telephone membership corporations, §117-41.
Effect of consolidation, §117-44.
Filing and recording of articles, §117-43.
Validation, §117-45.

CONSOLIDATION OF ACTIONS, §1A-1, Rule 42, (a).
Nuisances against public morals.
Action to abate and application for preliminary injunction, §19-2.4.

CONSOLIDATION OF COUNTIES, §§153A-401 to 153A-405.

CONSPIRACY.
Civil rights, interference with, §99D-1, (a).
Continuing criminal enterprise, §14-7.20.
Controlled substances.
Trafficking in certain drugs, §90-95, (i).
Violations of provisions, §90-98.
Criminal offense, §14-7.20, (c).
Monopolies and restraint of trade.
Illegal acts, §75-1.
Nuclear, biological or chemical weapons.
Use of weapons, §14-288.22, (b).
Odometer violations, §20-345.
Punishment for conspiracy to commit felony, §14-2.4, (a).
Sentencing.
Aggravating factors, §15A-1340.16.

CONSTITUTIONAL RIGHTS.
Enforcement or declaration of claim.
Superior court jurisdiction, §7A-245, (a).

CONSTITUTION OF NORTH CAROLINA.
Actions.
Civil cases.
Jury trial, Const. N. C., art. I, §25.
Form of action, Const. N. C., art. IV, §13.
Jury trial, Const. N. C., art. I, §25.
Acts.
General laws.
Defined, Const. N. C., art. XIV, §3.
Agriculture.
Capital projects for agriculture.
Authorization to create agency to issue bonds, Const. N. C., art. V, §11.
Commissioner of agriculture.
Acting commissioner, Const. N. C., art. III, §7.
Compensation and allowances, Const. N. C., art. III, §9.
Council of state.
Membership, Const. N. C., art. III, §8.
Duties, Const. N. C., art. III, §7.
Elective officers, Const. N. C., art. III, §7.
Incapacity.
Determination, Const. N. C., art. III, §7.
Interim commissioner, Const. N. C., art. III, §7.
Vacancies.
Filling, Const. N. C., art. III, §7.
Airports.
Powers of general assembly as to seaport and airport facilities, Const. N. C., art. V, §13.
Alimony.
Local, private and special legislation prohibited, Const. N. C., art. II, §24.
Allegiance to the United States, Const. N. C., art. I, §5.
Amendments.
Constitutional amendments publication commission, §§147-54.8 to 147-54.10.
Convention of the people.
Revision or amendment of constitution by convention of the people, Const. N. C., art. XIII, §3.
Legislative initiation.
Revision or amendment by legislative initiation, Const. N. C., art. XIII, §4.
Power to revise or amend constitution reserved to people, Const. N. C., art. XIII, §2.
Revision or amendment by legislative initiation, Const. N. C., art. XIII, §4.

CONSTITUTION OF NORTH CAROLINA —Cont'd
Amendments —Cont'd
Submission of acts to United States attorney general.
Secretary of state, §120-30.9D.
Appeals.
Court of appeals.
Decisions of the court of appeals.
Right of appeals from certain decisions directly to supreme court, §7A-30.
Jurisdiction, Const. N. C., art. IV, §12.
Jurisdiction of the general court of justice, Const. N. C., art. IV, §12.
Supreme court.
Jurisdiction, Const. N. C., art. IV, §12.
Arson.
Capital punishment.
Crimes punishable by death, Const. N. C., art. XI, §2.
Assemblies.
Right to assembly, Const. N. C., art. I, §12.
Attorney general.
Acting attorney general, Const. N. C., art. III, §7.
Compensation and allowances, Const. N. C., art. III, §9.
Council of state.
Membership, Const. N. C., art. III, §8.
Duties, Const. N. C., art. III, §7.
Elective officers, Const. N. C., art. III, §7.
Incapacity.
Determination, Const. N. C., art. III, §7.
Interim attorney general, Const. N. C., art. III, §7.
Qualifications, Const. N. C., art. III, §7.
Attorneys at law.
Rights of accused to counsel, Const. N. C., art. I, §23.
Authority.
Bond issues to finance capital projects for industry, Const. N. C., art. V, §9.
Bail and recognizance.
Excessive bail prohibited, Const. N. C., art. I, §27.
Bond issues.
Capital projects for industry.
Authorities may be created, Const. N. C., art. V, §9.
General assembly.
Actions on revenue bills, Const. N. C., art. II, §23.
Health care facilities.
Authorized, Const. N. C., art. V, §8.
Higher education facilities.
Authorized, Const. N. C., art. V, §12.
Hospitals, Const. N. C., art. V, §8.
Seaport and airport facilities.
Authorized powers as to, Const. N. C., art. V, §13.
Boundaries.
State boundaries, Const. N. C., art. XIV, §2.
Branches of government.
Separation of powers, Const. N. C., art. I, §6.
Bridges.
Local, private and special legislation prohibited, Const. N. C., art. II, §24.
Budget.
Governor.
Duties of governor, Const. N. C., art. III, §5.
Burglary.
Capital punishment.
Crimes punishable by death, Const. N. C., art. XI, §2.

CONSTITUTION OF NORTH CAROLINA —Cont'd
Capital projects.
Bond issues to finance.
Counties may establish authorities to finance capital projects for industry, Const. N. C., art. V, §9.
Capital punishment.
Enumeration of permissible punishments, Const. N. C., art. XI, §1.
Offenses punishable by death, Const. N. C., art. XI, §2.
Capitation tax.
Prohibited, Const. N. C., art. V, §1.
Cemeteries.
Local, private and special legislation prohibited, Const. N. C., art. II, §24.
Charities.
Establishment and operation by state, Const. N. C., art. XI, §3.
Charters.
Corporate charters, Const. N. C., art. VIII, §1.
Civil procedure.
Jury trial.
Right to jury trial in civil cases, Const. N. C., art. I, §25.
Rules of procedure, Const. N. C., art. IV, §13.
Clerks of court.
Removal, Const. N. C., art. IV, §17.
Vacancies in office, Const. N. C., art. IV, §19.
Community colleges and technical institutes.
Benefits of public institutions of higher education to be extended to people of state free of charge, Const. N. C., art. IX, §9.
Maintenance of system of higher education, Const. N. C., art. IX, §8.
Conservation.
Policy of state, Const. N. C., art. XIV, §5.
Consolidated city-county act.
General assembly to provide for local government, Const. N. C., art. VII, §1.
Merged or consolidated counties, Const. N. C., art. VII, §3.
Consolidation.
Counties.
Merged or consolidated counties, Const. N. C., art. VII, §3.
Constitutional amendments publication commission.
Composition, §147-54.8, (b).
Duties, §147-54.10.
Established, §147-54.8, (a).
Within department of secretary of state, §147-54.8, (a).
Explanation of amendment, revision or new constitution, §147-54.10.
Meetings, §147-54.9, (c).
Members, §147-54.8, (b).
Officers, §147-54.9, (a).
Powers, §147-54.10.
Quorum, §147-54.9, (b).
Summary amendment, revision or new constitution, §147-54.10.
Contracts.
State, political subdivisions or public corporations may make contracts, Const. N. C., art. V, §2.
Conventions.
Amendment to the constitution.
Revision or amendment by the convention of the people, Const. N. C., art. XIII, §3.
Composition, Const. N. C., art. XIII, §1.

CONSTITUTION OF NORTH CAROLINA —Cont'd
Conventions —Cont'd
Procedure for calling, Const. N. C., art. XIII, §1.
Corporations.
Charters, Const. N. C., art. VIII, §1.
Defined, Const. N. C., art. VIII, §2.
Corrections.
Establishment and operation of charitable and correctional institutions and agencies by state, Const. N. C., art. XI, §3.
Costs.
Revenues and expenses of the judicial department, Const. N. C., art. IV, §20.
Council of state.
Composition, Const. N. C., art. III, §8.
Counties.
Contracts.
Authority to contract, Const. N. C., art. V, §2.
Education.
County school fund.
Composition of fund, Const. N. C., art. IX, §7.
Elections.
Sheriffs, Const. N. C., art. VII, §2.
General assembly to provide for local government, Const. N. C., art. VII, §1.
Local treasury.
Drawing public money, Const. N. C., art. V, §7.
Merged or consolidated counties, Const. N. C., art. VII, §3.
Sheriffs.
Election, Const. N. C., art. VII, §2.
Taxation.
Exemption from taxation, Const. N. C., art. V, §2.
Special tax areas, Const. N. C., art. V, §2.
Court of appeals.
Composition, Const. N. C., art. IV, §7.
Decisions of court of appeals.
Appeals of right from certain decisions, §7A-30.
Judges.
Election, Const. N. C., art. IV, §16.
Removal, Const. N. C., art. IV, §17.
Salaries, fees and emoluments, Const. N. C., art. IV, §21.
Terms of office, Const. N. C., art. IV, §16.
Vacancies in office, Const. N. C., art. IV, §19.
Jurisdiction, Const. N. C., art. IV, §12.
Courts.
Administration by general assembly, Const. N. C., art. IV, §14.
Court of appeals.
Composition, Const. N. C., art. IV, §7.
Judges.
Election, Const. N. C., art. IV, §16.
Removal, Const. N. C., art. IV, §17.
Salaries, fees and emoluments, Const. N. C., art. IV, §21.
Terms of office, Const. N. C., art. IV, §16.
Vacancies, Const. N. C., art. IV, §19.
Jurisdiction, Const. N. C., art. IV, §12.
District courts, Const. N. C., art. IV, §10.
Judges.
Salaries, fees and emoluments, Const. N. C., art. IV, §21.
Vacancies in office, Const. N. C., art. IV, §19.
Jurisdiction, Const. N. C., art. IV, §12.
Magistrates, Const. N. C., art. IV, §12.
General court of justice.
Appeals.
Jurisdiction, Const. N. C., art. IV, §12.
Appellate division, Const. N. C., art. IV, §5.

CONSTITUTION OF NORTH CAROLINA —Cont'd
Courts —Cont'd
General court of justice —Cont'd
Court of appeals, Const. N. C., art. IV, §5.
Divisions, Const. N. C., art. IV, §2.
Judges and justices.
Retirement, Const. N. C., art. IV, §8.
Judicial power vested in general court of justice, Const. N. C., art. IV, §1.
Jurisdiction.
Waiver, Const. N. C., art. IV, §12.
Retirement of justices and judges, Const. N. C., art. IV, §8.
Supreme court, Const. N. C., art. IV, §5.
Unified judicial system, Const. N. C., art. IV, §2.
Judges.
Removal by general assembly, Const. N. C., art. IV, §17.
Salaries, fees and emoluments, Const. N. C., art. IV, §21.
Open courts, Const. N. C., art. I, §18.
Superior courts.
Clerks, Const. N. C., art. IV, §9.
Removal, Const. N. C., art. IV, §17.
Districts, Const. N. C., art. IV, §9.
Judges.
Assignment, Const. N. C., art. IV, §11.
Election, Const. N. C., art. IV, §16.
Salaries, fees and emoluments, Const. N. C., art. IV, §21.
Terms of office, Const. N. C., art. IV, §16.
Vacancies in office, Const. N. C., art. IV, §19.
Jurisdiction, Const. N. C., art. IV, §12.
Open at all times, Const. N. C., art. IV, §9.
Sessions.
Trial of cases, Const. N. C., art. IV, §9.
Supreme court.
Chief justice.
Assignment of judges, Const. N. C., art. IV, §11.
Jurisdiction, Const. N. C., art. IV, §12.
Justices.
Election, Const. N. C., art. IV, §16.
Removal, Const. N. C., art. IV, §17.
Salaries, emoluments and fees, Const. N. C., art. IV, §21.
Terms of office, Const. N. C., art. IV, §16.
Vacancies in office, Const. N. C., art. IV, §19.
Membership, Const. N. C., art. IV, §6.
Procedural rules.
Authority to make, Const. N. C., art. IV, §13.
Sessions, Const. N. C., art. IV, §6.
Crime victim rights, Const. N. C., art. I, §37.
Criminal law and procedure.
Capital punishment.
Crimes punishable by death, Const. N. C., art. XI, §2.
District courts.
Prosecution in district court division, Const. N. C., art. IV, §18.
Ex post facto laws.
Prohibited, Const. N. C., art. I, §16.
Forms of actions, Const. N. C., art. IV, §13.
Jury trial.
Right to trial by jury, Const. N. C., art. I, §24.
Modes of prosecution, Const. N. C., art. I, §23.
Rights of accused, Const. N. C., art. I, §23.
Rules of procedure, Const. N. C., art. IV, §13.

CONSTITUTION OF NORTH CAROLINA —Cont'd
Debts.
General assembly.
Actions on revenue bills, Const. N. C., art. II, §23.
Imprisonment for debt, Const. N. C., art. I, §28.
Personal property.
Exemptions from process, Const. N. C., art. X, §1.
Declaration of rights, Const. N. C., art. I, §§1 to 37.
Arms.
Right to bear arms, Const. N. C., art. I, §30.
Assembly.
Right of assembly, Const. N. C., art. I, §12.
Attorneys at law.
Right of accused to counsel, Const. N. C., art. I, §23.
Bail and recognizance.
Excessive bail prohibited, Const. N. C., art. I, §27.
Branches of government.
Separation of powers, Const. N. C., art. I, §6.
Civil cases.
Jury trial, Const. N. C., art. I, §25.
Confrontation.
Right of accused to confrontation of witnesses against him, Const. N. C., art. I, §23.
Counsel.
Right of accused to counsel, Const. N. C., art. I, §23.
Courts.
Open courts, Const. N. C., art. I, §18.
Crime victims, Const. N. C., art. I, §37.
Criminal law and procedure.
Ex post facto laws.
Prohibited, Const. N. C., art. I, §16.
Jury trial, Const. N. C., art. I, §24.
Prosecution.
Modes of prosecution, Const. N. C., art. I, §23.
Rights of accused, Const. N. C., art. I, §23.
Cruel and unusual punishment.
Prohibited, Const. N. C., art. I, §27.
Debt.
Imprisonment for debt, Const. N. C., art. I, §28.
Discrimination.
Jury service, Const. N. C., art. I, §26.
Due process.
Law of the land, Const. N. C., art. I, §19.
Education.
State's duty to guard and maintain, Const. N. C., art. I, §15.
Elections.
Free elections, Const. N. C., art. I, §10.
Frequent elections required, Const. N. C., art. I, §9.
Property qualifications prohibited, Const. N. C., art. I, §11.
Emoluments.
Exclusive emoluments, Const. N. C., art. I, §32.
Hereditary emoluments, Const. N. C., art. I, §33.
Equality of persons, Const. N. C., art. I, §1.
Equal protection of the law, Const. N. C., art. I, §19.
Exclusive emoluments.
Prohibited, Const. N. C., art. I, §32.
Ex post facto laws.
Prohibited, Const. N. C., art. I, §16.

CONSTITUTION OF NORTH CAROLINA —Cont'd
Declaration of rights —Cont'd
Fines.
Excessive fines prohibited, Const. N. C., art. I, §27.
Fraud.
Imprisonment for debt, Const. N. C., art. I, §28.
Fundamental principles.
Recurrence to fundamental principles, Const. N. C., art. I, §35.
General assembly.
Representation required, Const. N. C., art. I, §8.
Habeas corpus.
Inquiry into restraints on liberty, Const. N. C., art. I, §21.
Hereditary emoluments, Const. N. C., art. I, §33.
Honors.
Hereditary emoluments and honors prohibited, Const. N. C., art. I, §33.
Impeachment.
Modes of prosecution, Const. N. C., art. I, §22.
Incrimination.
Self-incrimination, Const. N. C., art. I, §23.
Indictments.
Modes of prosecution, Const. N. C., art. I, §22.
Right of accused to be informed of accusation, Const. N. C., art. I, §23.
Information of accusation.
Right of accused to be informed, Const. N. C., art. I, §23.
Inquiry into restraints on liberty, Const. N. C., art. I, §21.
Internal government of the state, Const. N. C., art. I, §3.
Involuntary servitude, Const. N. C., art. I, §17.
Jury.
Civil cases.
Right to jury trial in civil cases, Const. N. C., art. I, §25.
Criminal cases.
Right to jury trial in criminal cases, Const. N. C., art. I, §24.
Discrimination in jury service prohibited, Const. N. C., art. I, §26.
Law of the land, Const. N. C., art. I, §19.
Military affairs.
Militia, Const. N. C., art. I, §30.
Quartering of soldiers, Const. N. C., art. I, §31.
Militia.
Maintenance of militia, Const. N. C., art. I, §30.
Monopolies.
Prohibited, Const. N. C., art. I, §34.
Other rights of the people.
Enumeration does not impair or deny other rights retained by people, Const. N. C., art. I, §36.
Penalties.
Excessive fines prohibited, Const. N. C., art. I, §27.
Perpetuities.
Prohibited, Const. N. C., art. I, §34.
Petition.
Right of petition, Const. N. C., art. I, §12.
Presentments.
Modes of prosecution, Const. N. C., art. I, §22.
Press.
Freedom of press, Const. N. C., art. I, §14.
Property qualifications.
Political rights, privileges and offices not to be affected by property, Const. N. C., art. I, §11.

CONSTITUTION OF NORTH CAROLINA —Cont'd
Declaration of rights —Cont'd
Prosecution.
Modes of prosecution, Const. N. C., art. I, §22.
Public officers and employees.
Property qualifications not to affect right to hold office, Const. N. C., art. I, §11.
Recurrence to fundamental principles, Const. N. C., art. I, §35.
Religious liberty, Const. N. C., art. I, §13.
Remedies.
Inquiry into restraints on liberty, Const. N. C., art. I, §21.
Restraints of trade.
Prohibited, Const. N. C., art. I, §34.
Retention of other rights by the people, Const. N. C., art. I, §36.
Retrospective laws.
Prohibited, Const. N. C., art. I, §16.
Rights of accused, Const. N. C., art. I, §23.
Rights of persons, Const. N. C., art. I, §1.
Secession prohibited, Const. N. C., art. I, §4.
Self-incrimination, Const. N. C., art. I, §23.
Sentence and punishment.
Cruel and unusual punishment prohibited, Const. N. C., art. I, §27.
Separation of powers, Const. N. C., art. I, §6.
Servitude.
Involuntary servitude.
Prohibited, Const. N. C., art. I, §17.
Slavery, Const. N. C., art. I, §17.
Soldiers.
Quartering of soldiers, Const. N. C., art. I, §31.
Sovereignty of the people, Const. N. C., art. I, §2.
Speech.
Freedom of speech and press, Const. N. C., art. I, §14.
State of North Carolina.
Secession prohibited, Const. N. C., art. I, §4.
Separation of powers, Const. N. C., art. I, §6.
Suspending laws.
Prohibited, Const. N. C., art. I, §7.
Taxation.
Ex post facto laws.
Prohibited, Const. N. C., art. I, §16.
Representation required, Const. N. C., art. I, §8.
Treason.
Conduct constituting, Const. N. C., art. I, §29.
Trial.
Jury trial.
Criminal cases, Const. N. C., art. I, §24.
United States.
Allegiance to the United States, Const. N. C., art. I, §5.
Secession prohibited, Const. N. C., art. I, §4.
Warrants.
General warrants.
Prohibited, Const. N. C., art. I, §20.
Witnesses.
Confrontation.
Rights of accused, Const. N. C., art. I, §23.
Fees, costs, etc.
Rights of accused, Const. N. C., art. I, §23.
Deeds.
Giving effect to informal deeds.
Local, private and special legislation prohibited, Const. N. C., art. II, §24.
Definitions.
Corporations, Const. N. C., art. VIII, §2.
General laws, Const. N. C., art. XIV, §3.

CONSTITUTION OF NORTH CAROLINA —Cont'd
Definitions —Cont'd
Local government finance, Const. N. C., art. V, §4.
State debt, Const. N. C., art. V, §3.
Discrimination.
Jury service, Const. N. C., art. I, §26.
District attorneys.
Prosecutorial districts, Const. N. C., art. IV, §18.
District courts, Const. N. C., art. IV, §10.
Criminal cases.
Prosecutions, Const. N. C., art. IV, §18.
Judges.
Qualifications, Const. N. C., art. IV, §22.
Salaries, fees and emoluments, Const. N. C., art. IV, §21.
Vacancies in office, Const. N. C., art. IV, §19.
Jurisdiction, Const. N. C., art. IV, §12.
Districts.
General assembly.
House of representatives, Const. N. C., art. II, §5.
Senate districts, Const. N. C., art. II, §3.
Superior court districts, Const. N. C., art. IV, §9.
Divorce.
Local, private and special legislation prohibited, Const. N. C., art. II, §24.
Due process.
Law of the land, Const. N. C., art. I, §19.
Education.
Attendance.
School attendance, Const. N. C., art. IX, §3.
Encouragement of education, Const. N. C., art. IX, §1.
Escheats.
Disposition of escheats, Const. N. C., art. IX, §10.
Funds.
County school fund.
Composition, Const. N. C., art. IX, §7.
State fund.
Penalties, fines and forfeitures collected by state agencies (effective upon approval), Const. N. C., art. IX, §7.
State school fund.
Composition, Const. N. C., art. IX, §6.
Higher education.
Benefits of public institutions of higher education to be extended to people of state free of expense, Const. N. C., art. IX, §9.
Maintenance of public system of higher education, Const. N. C., art. IX, §8.
Public schools.
Local responsibility for public schools, Const. N. C., art. IX, §2.
Uniform system of schools to be established, Const. N. C., art. IX, §2.
State board of education.
Composition, Const. N. C., art. IX, §4.
Powers and duties, Const. N. C., art. IX, §5.
State school fund.
Composition of fund, Const. N. C., art. IX, §6.
State's duty to guard and maintain, Const. N. C., art. I, §15.
State superintendent of public instruction.
Acting superintendent, Const. N. C., art. III, §7.
Chief officer of state board of education, Const. N. C., art. IX, §4.
Compensation and allowances, Const. N. C., art. III, §9.

CONSTITUTION OF NORTH CAROLINA —Cont'd
Education —Cont'd
State superintendent of public instruction —Cont'd
Council of state.
Membership, Const. N. C., art. III, §8.
Duties, Const. N. C., art. III, §7.
Elective officers, Const. N. C., art. III, §7.
Incapacity.
Determination, Const. N. C., art. III, §7.
Interim superintendent, Const. N. C., art. III, §7.
Vacancies.
Filling, Const. N. C., art. III, §7.
Students.
Escheats.
Disposition of escheats, Const. N. C., art. IX, §10.
Elections.
Ballots.
Elections by people to be by ballots, Const. N. C., art. VI, §5.
Capitation tax prohibited, Const. N. C., art. V, §1.
Continuation in office, Const. N. C., art. VI, §10.
Convention of the people.
Procedure for calling, Const. N. C., art. XIII, §1.
Counties.
Sheriffs, Const. N. C., art. VII, §2.
Court of appeals.
Judges, Const. N. C., art. IV, §16.
Disqualifications for office, Const. N. C., art. VI, §8.
Dual office holding, Const. N. C., art. VI, §9.
Elected officers, Const. N. C., art. III, §7.
Eligibility to elective office, Const. N. C., art. VI, §6.
Eligibility to vote, Const. N. C., art. VI, §1.
Executive branch.
Joint ballot in both houses of general assembly to decide, Const. N. C., art. VI, §5.
Felonies.
Disqualification of felon, Const. N. C., art. VI, §2.
Free elections, Const. N. C., art. I, §10.
Frequent elections required, Const. N. C., art. I, §9.
General assembly, Const. N. C., art. II, §8.
Elections by general assembly to be by viva voce, Const. N. C., art. VI, §5.
Governor, Const. N. C., art. III, §2.
Lieutenant governor, Const. N. C., art. III, §2.
Literacy requirements, Const. N. C., art. VI, §4.
Poll tax prohibited, Const. N. C., art. V, §1.
Property qualifications prohibited, Const. N. C., art. I, §11.
Qualifications of voter, Const. N. C., art. VI, §2.
Registration, Const. N. C., art. VI, §3.
Literacy requirements, Const. N. C., art. VI, §4.
Qualifications for registration, Const. N. C., art. VI, §4.
Residence.
Presidential elections, Const. N. C., art. VI, §2.
State elections, Const. N. C., art. VI, §2.
Sheriffs.
County sheriffs, Const. N. C., art. VII, §2.
Superior court.
Judges, Const. N. C., art. IV, §16.
Supreme court.
Justices, Const. N. C., art. IV, §16.

CONSTITUTION OF NORTH CAROLINA —Cont'd
Elections —Cont'd
Voters.
Qualifications, Const. N. C., art. VI, §2.
Electricity.
Municipal corporations.
Joint ownership of generation and transmission facilities, Const. N. C., art. V, §10.
Emoluments.
Declaration of rights.
Hereditary emoluments, Const. N. C., art. I, §33.
Prohibited, Const. N. C., art. I, §33.
Equality of persons, Const. N. C., art. I, §1.
Equal protection, Const. N. C., art. I, §19.
Escheats.
Disposition of escheats, Const. N. C., art. IX, §10.
Executions.
Homestead exemption, Const. N. C., art. X, §2.
Personal property.
Exemption from process, Const. N. C., art. X, §1.
Exemptions from execution, Const. N. C., art. X, §1.
Executive branch, Const. N. C., art. III, §§1 to 11.
Elections.
Joint ballot in both houses of general assembly to decide, Const. N. C., art. VI, §5.
Exemptions.
Homestead exemption, Const. N. C., art. X, §2.
Married women.
Property of married women secured to them, Const. N. C., art. X, §4.
Personal property.
Exemption of property from execution or other process, Const. N. C., art. X, §1.
Ex post facto laws.
Prohibited, Const. N. C., art. I, §16.
Fees.
Judicial officers, Const. N. C., art. IV, §21.
Revenues and expenses of the judicial department, Const. N. C., art. IV, §20.
Felonies.
Disqualifications from holding office, Const. N. C., art. VI, §8.
Elections.
Disqualification of felon, Const. N. C., art. VI, §2.
Local, private and special legislation prohibited, Const. N. C., art. II, §24.
Ferries.
Local, private and special legislation prohibited, Const. N. C., art. II, §24.
Finances, Const. N. C., art. V, §§1 to 14.
Fines.
Enumeration of permissible punishments, Const. N. C., art. XI, §1.
Forfeitures.
Local, private and special legislation prohibited, Const. N. C., art. II, §24.
Forms.
Actions, Const. N. C., art. IV, §13.
Fraud.
Imprisonment for debt, Const. N. C., art. I, §28.
Funds.
Retirement fund.
Inviolability, Const. N. C., art. V, §6.
Sinking funds.
Inviolability, Const. N. C., art. V, §6.

CONSTITUTION OF NORTH CAROLINA —Cont'd
General assembly.
Acts.
Style of the acts, Const. N. C., art. II, §21.
Bills.
Action on bills, Const. N. C., art. II, §22.
Revenue bills.
Requirements for passage, Const. N. C., art. II, §23.
Veto by governor, Const. N. C., art. II, §22.
Bond issues.
Requirements for passage, Const. N. C., art. II, §23.
Bridges.
Local, private and special legislation prohibited, Const. N. C., art. II, §24.
Cemeteries.
Local, private and special legislation prohibited, Const. N. C., art. II, §24.
Cities, towns and townships.
Changing names not subject to local, private and special legislation, Const. N. C., art. II, §24.
Compensation and allowances, Const. N. C., art. II, §16.
Contested elections for executive office.
Joint ballot of both houses to determine, Const. N. C., art. VI, §5.
Convention of the people.
Procedure for calling, Const. N. C., art. XIII, §1.
Courts.
Administration, Const. N. C., art. IV, §15.
Divorce or alimony.
Local, private and special legislation prohibited, Const. N. C., art. II, §24.
Elections, Const. N. C., art. II, §8.
Viva voce.
Elections by general assembly to be by viva voce, Const. N. C., art. VI, §5.
Felonies.
Restoring citizenship rights of convicts.
Local, private and special legislation prohibited, Const. N. C., art. II, §24.
Ferries.
Local, private and special legislation prohibited, Const. N. C., art. II, §24.
Giving effect to informal deeds.
Local, private and special legislation prohibited, Const. N. C., art. II, §24.
Governor.
Information to general assembly, Const. N. C., art. III, §5.
Reconvening of legislature, Const. N. C., art. II, §22; art. III, §5.
Request that session not be held, §120-6.1, (a), (b).
Sessions.
Extra sessions, Const. N. C., art. III, §5.
Veto by governor, Const. N. C., art. II, §22.
Health, sanitation and abatement of nuisances.
Local, private and special limitation prohibited, Const. N. C., art. II, §24.
Highways, streets or alleys.
Local, private and special legislation prohibited, Const. N. C., art. II, §24.
House of representatives.
Apportionment of representatives, Const. N. C., art. II, §5.
Districts, Const. N. C., art. II, §5.

CONSTITUTION OF NORTH CAROLINA —Cont'd
General assembly —Cont'd
House of representatives —Cont'd
Impeachments.
Power to impeach, Const. N. C., art. IV, §4.
Number of representatives, Const. N. C., art. II, §4.
Officers of the house, Const. N. C., art. II, §15.
Qualifications for representatives, Const. N. C., art. II, §7.
Speaker, Const. N. C., art. II, §15.
Term of office, Const. N. C., art. II, §9.
Indebtedness of state.
Requirements for passage of bills, Const. N. C., art. II, §23.
Journals.
Printing of journals, Const. N. C., art. II, §17.
Record of votes, Const. N. C., art. II, §19.
Judges.
Removal, Const. N. C., art. IV, §17.
Jury.
Pay of jurors.
Local, private and special legislation prohibited, Const. N. C., art. II, §24.
Labor.
Local, private and special legislation prohibited, Const. N. C., art. II, §24.
Legislative power vested in general assembly, Const. N. C., art. II, §1.
Legitimating persons born out of wedlock.
Local, private and special legislation prohibited, Const. N. C., art. II, §24.
Lieutenant governor.
President of the senate, Const. N. C., art. II, §13.
Local government.
Provision for local government, Const. N. C., art. VII, §1.
Local, private and special legislation.
Limitations, Const. N. C., art. II, §24.
Prohibited subjects, Const. N. C., art. II, §24.
Repeals.
Partial repeal of general law prohibited, Const. N. C., art. II, §24.
Voidness of prohibited acts, Const. N. C., art. II, §24.
Magistrates.
Removal, Const. N. C., art. IV, §17.
Manufacturing.
Local, private and special legislation prohibited, Const. N. C., art. II, §24.
Mines and minerals.
Local, private and special legislation prohibited, Const. N. C., art. II, §24.
Municipal corporations.
Local, private and special legislation prohibited, Const. N. C., art. II, §24.
Names.
Altering name of person.
Local, private and special legislation prohibited, Const. N. C., art. II, §24.
Oaths of members, Const. N. C., art. II, §12.
Penalties.
Local, private and special legislation prohibited, Const. N. C., art. II, §24.
Powers of general assembly, Const. N. C., art. II, §20.
President pro tempore.
Temporary succession, Const. N. C., art. II, §14.
Protests of members, Const. N. C., art. II, §18.

CONSTITUTION OF NORTH CAROLINA —Cont'd
General assembly —Cont'd
Quorum, Const. N. C., art. II, §11.
Reconvening of legislature, Const. N. C., art. II, §22; art. III, §5.
Request that session not be held, §120-6.1, (a), (b).
Resolutions.
Actions on resolutions, Const. N. C., art. II, §22.
School districts.
Local, private and special legislation prohibited, Const. N. C., art. II, §24.
Senate.
Apportionment of senators, Const. N. C., art. II, §3.
Districts, Const. N. C., art. II, §3.
Impeachments.
Court for the trial of impeachments, Const. N. C., art. IV, §4.
Number of senators, Const. N. C., art. II, §2.
Officers of the senate, Const. N. C., art. II, §14.
President of the senate.
Lieutenant governor to preside over senate, Const. N. C., art. II, §13.
President pro tempore.
Succession to presidency, Const. N. C., art. II, §14.
Qualifications for senator, Const. N. C., art. II, §6.
Term of office, Const. N. C., art. II, §9.
Sessions.
Extra sessions on legislative call, Const. N. C., art. II, §11.
Regular sessions, Const. N. C., art. II, §11.
Taxation.
Classification of property, Const. N. C., art. V, §2.
Local, private and special legislation prohibited, Const. N. C., art. II, §24.
Representation required, Const. N. C., art. I, §8.
Requirements for passage, Const. N. C., art. II, §23.
Term of office, Const. N. C., art. II, §9.
Townships.
Local, private and special legislation prohibited, Const. N. C., art. II, §24.
Trade.
Local, private and special legislation prohibited, Const. N. C., art. II, §24.
Vacancies, Const. N. C., art. II, §10.
Veto by governor, Const. N. C., art. II, §22.
Votes.
Record votes.
Keeping in journals, Const. N. C., art. II, §19.
Waters and watercourses.
Nonnavigable streams.
Local, private and special legislation prohibited, Const. N. C., art. II, §24.
Wills.
Giving effect to informal wills.
Local, private and special legislation prohibited, Const. N. C., art. II, §24.
General laws.
Definition, Const. N. C., art. XIV, §3.
Governor.
Appointments, Const. N. C., art. III, §5.
Budget.
Duties of governor, Const. N. C., art. III, §5.
Clemency.
Granting reprieves, commutation and pardons, Const. N. C., art. III, §5.

CONSTITUTION OF NORTH CAROLINA —Cont'd
Governor —Cont'd
Commander-in-chief of military forces, Const. N. C., art. III, §5; art. XII, §1.
Commutation, Const. N. C., art. III, §5.
Duties, Const. N. C., art. III, §5.
Election, Const. N. C., art. III, §2.
Execution of laws, Const. N. C., art. III, §5.
Executive power of state vested in governor, Const. N. C., art. III, §1.
General assembly.
Information to general assembly, Const. N. C., art. III, §5.
Sessions.
Extra sessions, Const. N. C., art. III, §5.
Impeachment, Const. N. C., art. III, §3.
Mental incapacity.
Succession to office of governor, Const. N. C., art. III, §3.
Military affairs.
Commander-in-chief, Const. N. C., art. III, §5; art. XII, §1.
Oaths, Const. N. C., art. III, §4.
Pardons, Const. N. C., art. III, §5.
Physical incapacity.
Succession to office of governor, Const. N. C., art. III, §3.
Qualifications, Const. N. C., art. III, §2.
Reprieves, Const. N. C., art. III, §5.
Residence, Const. N. C., art. III, §5.
State departments and agencies.
Information from department heads.
Governor may require, Const. N. C., art. III, §5.
Reorganization of administration, Const. N. C., art. III, §5.
Succession as acting governor, Const. N. C., art. III, §3.
Succession as governor, Const. N. C., art. III, §3.
Term, Const. N. C., art. III, §2.
Habeas corpus.
Inquiry into restraints on liberty, Const. N. C., art. I, §21.
Remedy without delay for restraint of liberty, §17-1.
Suspension of habeas corpus, §17-2.
Health.
Local, private and special legislation prohibited, Const. N. C., art. II, §24.
Health care facilities.
Bond issues to finance, Const. N. C., art. V, §8.
Highways.
Local, private and special legislation prohibited, Const. N. C., art. II, §24.
Homestead exemption, Const. N. C., art. X, §2.
Hospitals.
Bond issues to finance, Const. N. C., art. V, §8.
House of representatives.
Apportionment of representatives, Const. N. C., art. II, §5.
Districts, Const. N. C., art. II, §5.
Elections, Const. N. C., art. II, §8.
Impeachment.
Power to impeach, Const. N. C., art. IV, §4.
Number of representatives, Const. N. C., art. II, §4.
Officers of the house, Const. N. C., art. II, §15.
Qualifications for representative, Const. N. C., art. II, §7.
Speaker, Const. N. C., art. II, §15.

CONSTITUTION OF NORTH CAROLINA —Cont'd

House of representatives —Cont'd
Term of office, Const. N. C., art. II, §9.

Husband and wife.
Women.
Property of married women secured to them, Const. N. C., art. X, §4.

Impeachment.
Court for the trial of impeachment.
Senate to be court, Const. N. C., art. IV, §4.
Vesting of judicial power, Const. N. C., art. IV, §1.
Governor, Const. N. C., art. III, §3.
House of representatives.
Power to impeach, Const. N. C., art. IV, §4.
Modes of prosecution, Const. N. C., art. I, §22.

Imprisonment.
Enumeration of permissible punishments, Const. N. C., art. XI, §1.

Income tax.
Limitations and restrictions, Const. N. C., art. V, §2.

Incrimination.
Self-incrimination.
Rights of accused, Const. N. C., art. I, §23.

Indictments.
Modes of prosecution, Const. N. C., art. I, §22.
Right of accused to be informed of accusation, Const. N. C., art. I, §23.

Indigent persons.
Welfare policy of state, Const. N. C., art. XI, §4.

Industry.
Capital projects for industry.
Bond issues to finance.
County may create authorities to issue bonds, Const. N. C., art. V, §9.

Insurance.
Commissioner of insurance.
Acting commissioner, Const. N. C., art. III, §7.
Compensation and allowances, Const. N. C., art. III, §9.
Council of state.
Membership, Const. N. C., art. III, §8.
Duties, Const. N. C., art. III, §7.
Elective officers, Const. N. C., art. III, §7.
Incapacity.
Determination, Const. N. C., art. III, §7.
Interim commissioner, Const. N. C., art. III, §7.
Vacancies.
Filling, Const. N. C., art. III, §7.

Involuntary servitude.
Prohibited, Const. N. C., art. I, §17.

Judges.
Assignment, Const. N. C., art. IV, §11.
Qualifications of judges and justices, Const. N. C., art. IV, §22.
Removal, Const. N. C., art. IV, §17.
Additional method, Const. N. C., art. IV, §17.
Retirement, Const. N. C., art. IV, §8.
Salaries.
Diminished during continuance in office prohibited, Const. N. C., art. IV, §21.
Terms of office, Const. N. C., art. IV, §16.
Vacancies in office, Const. N. C., art. IV, §19.

Judicial department, Const. N. C., art. IV, §§1 to 21.
Fees.
Revenues and expenses of the judicial department, Const. N. C., art. IV, §20.

CONSTITUTION OF NORTH CAROLINA —Cont'd

Jurisdiction.
Courts, Const. N. C., art. IV, §12.
Waiver, Const. N. C., art. IV, §12.

Jury.
Civil cases.
Right to trial in civil cases, Const. N. C., art. I, §25; art. IV, §13.
Waiver of jury trial, Const. N. C., art. IV, §14.
Criminal cases.
Right to jury trial in criminal cases, Const. N. C., art. I, §24.
Discrimination in jury service prohibited, Const. N. C., art. I, §26.
Pay of jurors.
Local, private and special legislation prohibited, Const. N. C., art. II, §24.

Labor.
Commissioner of labor.
Acting commissioner, Const. N. C., art. III, §7.
Compensation and allowances, Const. N. C., art. III, §9.
Council of state.
Membership, Const. N. C., art. III, §8.
Duties, Const. N. C., art. III, §7.
Elective officers, Const. N. C., art. III, §7.
Incapacity.
Determination, Const. N. C., art. III, §7.
Interim commissioner, Const. N. C., art. III, §7.
Vacancies.
Filling, Const. N. C., art. III, §7.
Local, private and special legislation prohibited, Const. N. C., art. II, §24.

Laborers' liens.
Exemptions from process.
Inapplicability of provisions, Const. N. C., art. X, §3.

Laws.
Continuity of laws, Const. N. C., art. XIV, §4.
General laws.
Defined, Const. N. C., art. XIV, §3.

Legitimation.
Local, private and special legislation prohibited, Const. N. C., art. II, §24.

Liens.
Mechanics' and materialmen's liens.
Inapplicability of exemption provisions, Const. N. C., art. X, §3.

Lieutenant governor.
Duties, Const. N. C., art. III, §6.
Election, Const. N. C., art. III, §2.
General assembly.
Senate.
President of the senate, Const. N. C., art. II, §13.
Qualifications, Const. N. C., art. III, §2.
Succession as acting governor, Const. N. C., art. III, §3.
Succession as governor, Const. N. C., art. III, §3.
Term, Const. N. C., art. III, §2.

Life insurance.
Exemption from process, Const. N. C., art. X, §5.

Local government finance.
Authorized purposes, Const. N. C., art. V, §4.
Certain debts barred, Const. N. C., art. V, §4.
Definitions, Const. N. C., art. V, §4.
Gifts or loans of credit regulated, Const. N. C., art. V, §4.
Limitations upon increase of local government debt, Const. N. C., art. V, §4.

CONSTITUTION OF NORTH CAROLINA —Cont'd
Local government finance —Cont'd
Outstanding debt, Const. N. C., art. V, §4.
Regulation of borrowing in debt, Const. N. C., art. V, §4.
Two-thirds limitation, Const. N. C., art. V, §4.
Local legislation.
Limitation, Const. N. C., art. II, §24.
Magistrates.
Appointment, Const. N. C., art. IV, §10.
Jurisdiction, Const. N. C., art. IV, §12.
Removal, Const. N. C., art. IV, §17.
General assembly to remove, Const. N. C., art. IV, §17.
Salaries, fees and emoluments, Const. N. C., art. IV, §21.
Vacancies in office, Const. N. C., art. IV, §19.
Manufacturing.
Local, private and special legislation prohibited, Const. N. C., art. II, §24.
Marriage.
Property of married women secured to them, Const. N. C., art. X, §4.
Merger.
Counties.
Consolidated or merged counties, Const. N. C., art. VII, §3.
Military affairs.
Governor.
Commander-in-chief, Const. N. C., art. III, §5; art. XII, §1.
Militia, Const. N. C., art. I, §30.
Quartering of soldiers, Const. N. C., art. I, §31.
Mines and minerals.
Local, private and special legislation prohibited, Const. N. C., art. II, §24.
Money.
Drawing public money, Const. N. C., art. V, §7.
Monopolies.
Prohibited, Const. N. C., art. I, §34.
Municipal corporations.
Contracts.
Authority to contract, Const. N. C., art. V, §2.
General assembly to provide for local government, Const. N. C., art. VII, §1.
Local, private and special legislation prohibited, Const. N. C., art. II, §24.
Local treasury.
Drawing public money, Const. N. C., art. V, §7.
Public utilities.
Joint ownership of generation and transmission facilities, Const. N. C., art. V, §10.
Taxation.
Exemption from taxation, Const. N. C., art. V, §2.
Special tax areas, Const. N. C., art. V, §2.
Murder.
Capital punishment.
Crimes punishable by death, Const. N. C., art. XI, §2.
Names.
Altering name of person.
Local, private and special legislation prohibited, Const. N. C., art. II, §24.
Natural resources and community development.
Policy of state, Const. N. C., art. XIV, §5.
Newspapers.
Freedom of speech and press, Const. N. C., art. I, §14.

CONSTITUTION OF NORTH CAROLINA —Cont'd
North Carolina school of the arts.
Benefits of public institutions of higher education to be extended to people of state free of charge, Const. N. C., art. IX, §9.
Maintenance of system of higher education, Const. N. C., art. IX, §8.
Nuisances.
Abatement of nuisances.
Local, private and special legislation prohibited, Const. N. C., art. II, §24.
Oaths.
General assembly, §11-7; Const. N. C., art. II, §12.
Governor, Const. N. C., art. III, §4.
Officers of state to take oath or affirmation supporting constitutions, §11-7.
Public officers and employees, Const. N. C., art. VI, §7.
Oil and gas conservation.
Policy of state, Const. N. C., art. XIV, §5.
Ordinances.
Consistent with constitution of North Carolina, §160A-174, (b).
Orphans.
Welfare policy of state, Const. N. C., art. XI, §4.
Pardons.
Governor.
Duties of governor, Const. N. C., art. III, §5.
Penalties.
Excessive fines prohibited, Const. N. C., art. I, §27.
Local, private and special legislation prohibited, Const. N. C., art. II, §24.
Perpetuities.
Prohibited, Const. N. C., art. I, §34.
Personal property.
Exemptions from process, Const. N. C., art. X, §1.
Petitions.
Right to petition, Const. N. C., art. I, §12.
Plant protection and conservation.
Policy of state, Const. N. C., art. XIV, §5.
Poll tax.
Prohibited, Const. N. C., art. V, §1.
Pollution control.
Policy of state, Const. N. C., art. XIV, §5.
Ports and harbors.
Powers of general assembly as to seaport and airport facilities, Const. N. C., art. V, §13.
Power of people to amend, Const. N. C., art. XIII, §2.
Presentments.
Modes of prosecution, Const. N. C., art. I, §22.
Press.
Freedom of press, Const. N. C., art. I, §14.
Private legislation.
Limitations, Const. N. C., art. II, §24.
Project development financing (effective upon certification of approval), Const. N. C., art. V, §14.
Property qualifications.
Political rights, privileges and offices not to be affected by property, Const. N. C., art. I, §11.
Public officers and employees.
Continuation in office, Const. N. C., art. VI, §10.
Disqualifications for office, Const. N. C., art. VI, §8.
Dual office holding, Const. N. C., art. VI, §9.
Eligibility to hold elective office, Const. N. C., art. VI, §6.
Holding office contrary to the constitution, §128-2.

CONSTITUTION OF NORTH CAROLINA —Cont'd
Public officers and employees —Cont'd
Oaths, Const. N. C., art. VI, §7.
Property qualifications not to affect right to hold office, Const. N. C., art. I, §11.
Protection of persons holding office at time of adoption of constitution, Const. N. C., art. XIV, §4.
Removal from office.
Enumeration of permissible punishments, Const. N. C., art. XI, §1.
Public schools.
Basic education program.
Knowledge and understanding required, §115C-81, (g).
Public utilities.
Municipal corporations.
Joint ownership of generation and transmission facilities, Const. N. C., art. V, §10.
Punishment.
Cruel and unusual punishment prohibited, Const. N. C., art. I, §27.
Enumeration of permissible punishments, Const. N. C., art. XI, §1.
Quartering of soldiers, Const. N. C., art. I, §31.
Raleigh.
Seat of government to be at city of Raleigh, Const. N. C., art. XIV, §1.
Rape.
Capital punishment.
Crimes punishable by death, Const. N. C., art. XI, §2.
Reconvening of legislature, Const. N. C., art. II, §22; art. III, §5.
Religion.
Liberty of religion, Const. N. C., art. I, §13.
Remedies.
Inquiry into restraints on liberty, Const. N. C., art. I, §21.
Restraints of trade.
Monopolies, Const. N. C., art. I, §34.
Retirement.
Funds.
Inviolability, Const. N. C., art. V, §6.
Judges and justices, Const. N. C., art. IV, §8.
Retrospective laws.
Prohibited, Const. N. C., art. I, §16.
Rights of crime victims, Const. N. C., art. I, §37.
Rights of persons, Const. N. C., art. I, §1.
Salaries.
General assembly, Const. N. C., art. II, §16.
Judicial officers, Const. N. C., art. IV, §21.
Sanitation.
Local, private and special legislation prohibited, Const. N. C., art. II, §24.
School districts.
Local, private and special legislation prohibited, Const. N. C., art. II, §24.
Seals.
State seal, Const. N. C., art. III, §10.
Seat of government, Const. N. C., art. XIV, §1.
Secretary of state.
Acting secretary, Const. N. C., art. III, §7.
Compensation and allowances, Const. N. C., art. III, §9.
Council of state.
Membership, Const. N. C., art. III, §8.
Duties, Const. N. C., art. III, §7.
Elective officers, Const. N. C., art. III, §7.

CONSTITUTION OF NORTH CAROLINA —Cont'd
Secretary of state —Cont'd
Incapacity.
Determination, Const. N. C., art. III, §7.
Interim secretary, Const. N. C., art. III, §7.
Vacancies.
Filling, Const. N. C., art. III, §7.
Self-incrimination.
Rights of accused, Const. N. C., art. I, §23.
Senate.
Apportionment of senators, Const. N. C., art. II, §3.
Districts, Const. N. C., art. II, §3.
Elections, Const. N. C., art. II, §8.
Impeachment.
Court for the trial of impeachments, Const. N. C., art. IV, §4.
Lieutenant governor.
President of the senate, Const. N. C., art. II, §13.
Number of senators, Const. N. C., art. II, §2.
President of the senate.
Lieutenant governor to preside, Const. N. C., art. II, §13.
President pro tempore.
Succession to presidency, Const. N. C., art. II, §14.
Temporary succession, Const. N. C., art. II, §14.
Qualifications for senator, Const. N. C., art. II, §6.
Term of office, Const. N. C., art. II, §9.
Sentencing.
Cruel and unusual punishment prohibited, Const. N. C., art. I, §27.
Enumeration of permissible punishments, Const. N. C., art. XI, §1.
Sessions.
Extra sessions.
Governor may call, Const. N. C., art. III, §5.
Reconvening of legislature, Const. N. C., art. II, §22; art. III, §5.
Sheriffs.
Election, Const. N. C., art. VII, §2.
Sinking funds.
Inviolability, Const. N. C., art. V, §6.
Slavery.
Prohibited, Const. N. C., art. I, §17.
Soldiers.
Declaration of rights.
Quartering of soldiers, Const. N. C., art. I, §31.
Sovereignty of the people, Const. N. C., art. I, §2.
Special legislation.
Limitations, Const. N. C., art. II, §24.
Speech.
Freedom of speech, Const. N. C., art. I, §14.
State auditor.
Acting auditor, Const. N. C., art. III, §7.
Compensation and allowances, Const. N. C., art. III, §9.
Council of state.
Membership, Const. N. C., art. III, §8.
Duties, Const. N. C., art. III, §7.
Elective officers, Const. N. C., art. III, §7.
Incapacity.
Determination, Const. N. C., art. III, §7.
Interim auditor, Const. N. C., art. III, §7.
Vacancies.
Filling, Const. N. C., art. III, §7.
State debt.
Authorized purposes, Const. N. C., art. V, §3.
Certain debts barred, Const. N. C., art. V, §3.

CONSTITUTION OF NORTH CAROLINA
—Cont'd
State debt —Cont'd
Definitions, Const. N. C., art. V, §3.
Gifts regulated, Const. N. C., art. V, §3.
Increase.
Limitations, Const. N. C., art. V, §3.
Limitations upon increase, Const. N. C., art. V, §3.
Loans regulated, Const. N. C., art. V, §3.
Standing debt, Const. N. C., art. V, §3.
Two-thirds limitation, Const. N. C., art. V, §3.
State departments and agencies.
Administrative departments.
Allocation, Const. N. C., art. III, §11.
Executive organization act of 1973.
References to constitution of North Carolina, §143B-26.
Judicial powers of administrative agencies, Const. N. C., art. IV, §3.
State of North Carolina.
Boundaries of state, Const. N. C., art. XIV, §2.
Contracts.
Authority to contract, Const. N. C., art. V, §2.
Declaration of rights.
Internal government of the state, Const. N. C., art. I, §3.
Secession prohibited, Const. N. C., art. I, §4.
Drawing public money, Const. N. C., art. V, §7.
Seal of state, Const. N. C., art. III, §10.
Seat of government, Const. N. C., art. XIV, §1.
Separation of powers, Const. N. C., art. I, §6.
Taxation.
Exemption from taxation, Const. N. C., art. V, §2.
State treasurer.
Acting treasurer, Const. N. C., art. III, §7.
Compensation and allowances, Const. N. C., art. III, §9.
Council of state.
Membership, Const. N. C., art. III, §8.
Drawing public money, Const. N. C., art. V, §7.
Duties, Const. N. C., art. III, §7.
Elective officers, Const. N. C., art. III, §7.
Incapacity.
Determination, Const. N. C., art. III, §7.
Interim treasurer, Const. N. C., art. III, §7.
Vacancies.
Filling, Const. N. C., art. III, §7.
Streets.
Local, private and special legislation prohibited, Const. N. C., art. II, §24.
Suffrage.
Eligibility to vote, Const. N. C., art. VI, §1.
Felonies.
Disqualification of felon, Const. N. C., art. VI, §2.
Qualifications of voter, Const. N. C., art. VI, §2.
Residence.
Presidential elections, Const. N. C., art. VI, §2.
State elections, Const. N. C., art. VI, §2.
Superior courts.
Clerks of court, Const. N. C., art. IV, §9.
Removal of clerks, Const. N. C., art. IV, §17.
Salaries, fees and emoluments, Const. N. C., art. IV, §21.
Vacancies in office, Const. N. C., art. IV, §19.
Districts, Const. N. C., art. IV, §9.
Judges.
Assignment, Const. N. C., art. IV, §11.
Election, Const. N. C., art. IV, §16.
Qualifications, Const. N. C., art. IV, §22.

CONSTITUTION OF NORTH CAROLINA
—Cont'd
Superior courts —Cont'd
Judges —Cont'd
Salaries, fees and emoluments, Const. N. C., art. IV, §21.
Terms of office, Const. N. C., art. IV, §16.
Vacancies in office, Const. N. C., art. IV, §19.
Jurisdiction, Const. N. C., art. IV, §12.
Open at all times, Const. N. C., art. IV, §9.
Sessions.
Trial of cases, Const. N. C., art. IV, §9.
Supreme court.
Chief justice.
Assignment of judges, Const. N. C., art. IV, §11.
Court of appeals decisions.
Appeals of right from certain decisions, §7A-30.
Jurisdiction, Const. N. C., art. IV, §12.
Justices.
Election, Const. N. C., art. IV, §16.
Qualifications, Const. N. C., art. IV, §22.
Removal, Const. N. C., art. IV, §17.
Salaries, fees and emoluments, Const. N. C., art. IV, §21.
Terms of office, Const. N. C., art. IV, §16.
Vacancies in office, Const. N. C., art. IV, §19.
Membership, Const. N. C., art. IV, §6.
Procedural rules.
Authority to make, Const. N. C., art. IV, §13.
Sessions, Const. N. C., art. IV, §6.
Suspending laws.
Prohibited, Const. N. C., art. I, §7.
Taxation.
Capitation tax prohibited, Const. N. C., art. V, §1.
Cemeteries.
Exemption from tax, Const. N. C., art. V, §2.
Charities.
Exemption from tax, Const. N. C., art. V, §2.
Classification of property, Const. N. C., art. V, §2.
Counties.
Exemption from taxation, Const. N. C., art. V, §2.
Special tax areas, Const. N. C., art. V, §2.
Education.
Exemption from taxation, Const. N. C., art. V, §2.
Exemptions, Const. N. C., art. V, §3.
Ex post facto laws.
Prohibited, Const. N. C., art. I, §16.
Local, private and special legislation prohibited, Const. N. C., art. II, §24.
Municipal corporations.
Exemption from taxation, Const. N. C., art. V, §2.
Special tax areas, Const. N. C., art. V, §2.
Poll tax prohibited, Const. N. C., art. V, §1.
Power of taxation, Const. N. C., art. V, §2.
Property taxes.
Purposes, Const. N. C., art. V, §2.
Religion.
Exemption from tax, Const. N. C., art. V, §2.
Representation required, Const. N. C., art. I, §8.
Special tax areas, Const. N. C., art. V, §2.
Statement.
Objects, Const. N. C., art. V, §5.
Purposes to be stated, Const. N. C., art. V, §5.
State of North Carolina.
Exemption from taxation, Const. N. C., art. V, §2.
Supremacy, §105-1.1.

CONSTITUTION OF NORTH CAROLINA —Cont'd
Towns.
General assembly to provide for local government, Const. N. C., art. VII, §1.
Townships.
Local, private and special legislation prohibited, Const. N. C., art. II, §24.
Trade.
Local, private and special legislation prohibited, Const. N. C., art. II, §24.
Treason.
Conduct constituting, Const. N. C., art. I, §29.
Disqualifications from holding office, Const. N. C., art. VI, §8.
Trial.
Jury trial.
Civil cases, Const. N. C., art. I, §25.
Criminal cases, Const. N. C., art. I, §24.
United States.
Allegiance to the United States, Const. N. C., art. I, §5.
Declaration of rights.
Secession from Union prohibited, Const. N. C., art. I, §4.
Universities and colleges.
Benefits of public institutions of higher education to be extended to people of state free of expense, Const. N. C., art. IX, §9.
Bond issues.
Higher education facilities.
Authorized, Const. N. C., art. V, §12.
Maintenance of public system of higher education, Const. N. C., art. IX, §8.
University of North Carolina.
Benefits of public institutions of higher education to be extended to people of state free of charge, Const. N. C., art. IX, §9.
Escheats.
Disposition of escheats prior to July 1, 1971, Const. N. C., art. IX, §10.
Maintenance of system of higher education, Const. N. C., art. IX, §8.
Warrants.
General warrants.
Prohibited, Const. N. C., art. I, §20.
Waters and watercourses.
Nonnavigable streams.
Local, private and special legislation prohibited, Const. N. C., art. II, §24.
Weapons.
Right to bear arms, Const. N. C., art. I, §30.
Welfare.
Board of public welfare.
Establishment required, Const. N. C., art. XI, §4.
Policy of state, Const. N. C., art. XI, §4.
Wills.
Giving effect to informal wills.
Local, private and special legislation prohibited, Const. N. C., art. II, §24.
Witnesses.
Confrontation.
Right of accused, Const. N. C., art. I, §23.
Fees, costs, etc.
Rights of accused, Const. N. C., art. I, §23.
Women.
Married women.
Property secured to them, Const. N. C., art. X, §4.

CONSTITUTION OF THE UNITED STATES.
Absence.
Congress.
Members of congress, Const. U. S., art. I, §5.
Vice-president.
Senate to choose president pro tem, Const. U. S., art. I, §3.
Accounts and accounting.
Receipts and expenditures of public money.
Publication of statement and account, Const. U. S., art. I, §9.
Actions to which United States a party, Const. U. S., art. III, §2.
Admiralty, Const. U. S., art. I, §8.
Jurisdiction of courts, Const. U. S., art. III, §2.
Age.
Congress.
Representatives, Const. U. S., art. I, §2.
Senators, Const. U. S., art. I, §3.
Elections.
Right to vote not to be abridged on account of age, Const. U. S., amd. XXVI.
Voting by persons eighteen years of age, Const. U. S., amd. XXVI.
President of the United States, Const. U. S., art. II, §1.
Vice-president, Const. U. S., amd. XII.
Alcoholic liquors, Const. U. S., amds. XVIII, XXI.
Aliens.
Eligibility to be representative, Const. U. S., art. I, §2.
Naturalization, Const. U. S., art. I, §8.
Presidency.
Ineligibility for presidency, Const. U. S., art. II, §1.
Suits against state, Const. U. S., amd. XI.
Ambassadors and consuls, Const. U. S., art. II, §§2, 3; art. III, §2.
Amendments, Const. U. S., art. V.
Bail, Const. U. S., amd. VIII.
Congress.
Compensation of members.
Laws varying compensation.
When to take effect, Const. U. S., amd. XXVII.
Sessions, Const. U. S., amd. XX, §2.
Terms of office, Const. U. S., amd. XX, §1.
Time of convening, Const. U. S., amd. XX, §2.
Criminal law, Const. U. S., amds. V, VI.
Due process of law, Const. U. S., amds. V, XIV.
Effect of enumeration of rights, Const. U. S., amd. IX.
Eminent domain, Const. U. S., amd. V.
Freedom of religion, speech and press, Const. U. S., amd. I.
Guarantees in criminal cases, Const. U. S., amds. V, VI.
House of representatives.
Terms of representatives, Const. U. S., amd. XX, §1.
Income tax, Const. U. S., amd. XVI.
Intoxicating liquors, Const. U. S., amds. XVIII, XXI.
Lame duck amendment, Const. U. S., amd. XX.
Manner of making amendments, Const. U. S., art. V.
Poll tax.
Denial or abridgement of right to vote upon failure to pay.
Prohibited, Const. U. S., amd. XXIV.

CONSTITUTION OF THE UNITED STATES —Cont'd
Amendments —Cont'd
President.
Death, Const. U. S., amd. XX.
Election, Const. U. S., amds. XII, XX.
Failure to qualify, Const. U. S., amd. XX.
Succession upon death, resignation or removal of president, Const. U. S., amd. XXV.
Terms of office, Const. U. S., amds. XX, XXII.
Limitation on terms, Const. U. S., amd. XXII.
Proposal and ratification of amendments, Const. U. S., art. V.
Punishments, Const. U. S., amd. VIII.
Quartering soldiers in houses, Const. U. S., amd. III.
Ratification of amendment, Const. U. S., art. V.
Repeal of the eighteenth amendment, Const. U. S., amd. XXI.
Restriction of judicial power, Const. U. S., amd. XI.
Rights and immunities of citizens, Const. U. S., amd. XIV.
Right to bear arms, Const. U. S., amd. II.
Right to vote, Const. U. S., amds. XV, XXVI.
Searches and seizures, Const. U. S., amd. IV.
Self-incrimination, Const. U. S., amd. V.
Senate.
Election of senators, Const. U. S., amd. XVII.
Terms of senators, Const. U. S., amd. XX, §1.
Slavery, Const. U. S., amd. XIII.
Suits against state, Const. U. S., amd. XI.
Terms of office, Const. U. S., amd. XX, §1.
Limitation on terms of president, Const. U. S., amd. XXII.
Trial by jury, Const. U. S., amds. VI, VII.
Vice-president.
Death, Const. U. S., amd. XX.
Election, Const. U. S., amds. XII, XX.
Failure to qualify, Const. U. S., amd. XX.
Terms of office, Const. U. S., amd. XX, §1.
Weapons.
Right to bear arms, Const. U. S., amd. II.
Women's suffrage, Const. U. S., amd. XIX.
Appeals.
Decisions of the court of appeals.
Right of appeals from certain decisions directly to supreme court, §7A-30.
Review of facts tried by jury, Const. U. S., amd. VII.
Apportionment.
Congress, Const. U. S., amds. XIV, XVII.
Appropriations, Const. U. S., art. I, §9.
Army, Const. U. S., art. I, §8.
Revenue bills, Const. U. S., art. I, §7.
Approval of laws by president, Const. U. S., art. I, §7.
Arms.
Right to bear, Const. U. S., amd. II.
Army and navy, Const. U. S., art. I, §8.
Commander-in-chief, Const. U. S., art. II, §2.
Arrest.
Privilege from arrest, Const. U. S., art. I, §6.
Assembly.
Right of, Const. U. S., amd. I.
Attainder, Const. U. S., art. III, §3.
Attorneys at law.
Right to counsel, Const. U. S., amd. VI.
Authors.
Protection of rights, Const. U. S., art. I, §8.
Autrefois, acquit or convict, Const. U. S., amd. V.

CONSTITUTION OF THE UNITED STATES —Cont'd
Bail.
Excessive bail, Const. U. S., amd. VIII.
Bankruptcy.
Powers of congress, Const. U. S., art. I, §8.
Bill of attainder, Const. U. S., art. I, §§9, 10.
Bill of rights, Const. U. S., amds. I to X.
Bills of credit, Const. U. S., art. I, §10.
Black people, Const. U. S., amds. XIV, XV.
Bribery, Const. U. S., art. II, §4.
Capitation tax, Const. U. S., art. I, §9.
Elections.
Denial or abridgement of right to vote prohibited, Const. U. S., amd. XXIV.
Census, Const. U. S., art. I, §§2, 9.
Commerce, Const. U. S., art. I, §§8, 9.
Common law.
Suits at, Const. U. S., amd. VII.
Compacts.
Between state and foreign power, Const. U. S., art. I, §10.
Between the states, Const. U. S., art. I, §10.
Congress.
Absent members, Const. U. S., art. I, §5.
Adjournment, Const. U. S., art. I, §§5, 7; art. II, §3.
Admiralty, Const. U. S., art. I, §8.
Amendments to the constitution, Const. U. S., art. V.
Appropriations, Const. U. S., art. I, §9.
Approval by president of order, resolution or vote, Const. U. S., art. I, §7.
Army and navy.
Powers of congress, Const. U. S., art. I, §8.
Arrest, Const. U. S., art. I, §6.
Bankruptcy.
Powers of congress, Const. U. S., art. I, §8.
Borrowing money, Const. U. S., art. I, §8.
Commerce, Const. U. S., art. I, §§8, 9.
Compensation of members, Const. U. S., art. I, §6.
Laws varying compensation.
When to take effect, Const. U. S., amd. XXVII.
Consists of senate and house of representatives, Const. U. S., art. I, §1.
Copyright, Const. U. S., art. I, §8.
Counterfeiting.
Powers of congress, Const. U. S., art. I, §8.
Courts.
Power to constitute tribunals inferior to supreme court, Const. U. S., art. I, §8.
Debate, Const. U. S., art. I, §6.
Debt.
Powers of congress, Const. U. S., art. I, §8.
Declaration of war, Const. U. S., art. I, §8.
Defense.
Powers of congress, Const. U. S., art. I, §8.
District of Columbia, Const. U. S., art. I, §8.
Duties and imposts.
Powers of congress, Const. U. S., art. I, §8.
Elections.
House of representatives, Const. U. S., art. I, §§2, 4.
Senate, Const. U. S., art. I, §4; amd. XVII.
Excises.
Powers of congress, Const. U. S., art. I, §8.
Foreign commerce, Const. U. S., art. I, §8.
Freedom of speech.
Members of congress, Const. U. S., art. I, §6.
Holding other office, Const. U. S., art. I, §6.

CONSTITUTION OF THE UNITED STATES —Cont'd

Congress —Cont'd

House of representatives, Const. U. S., art. I, §§1, 2.
Absent members, Const. U. S., art. I, §5.
Arrest of members, Const. U. S., art. I, §6.
Compensation of members, Const. U. S., art. I, §6.
Laws varying compensation.
When to take effect, Const. U. S., amd. XXVII.
Debate, Const. U. S., art. I, §6.
Elections.
Election of representatives, Const. U. S., art. I, §2.
Times, places and manner of holding, Const. U. S., art. I, §4.
Expulsion of member, Const. U. S., art. I, §5.
Freedom of speech, Const. U. S., art. I, §6.
Holding other office, Const. U. S., art. I, §6.
Impeachment, Const. U. S., art. I, §2.
Journal, Const. U. S., art. I, §§5, 7.
Libel and slander.
Privilege of members, Const. U. S., art. I, §6.
Officers, Const. U. S., art. I, §2.
Presidential elector.
Representative ineligible, Const. U. S., art. II, §1.
Punishment of members, Const. U. S., art. I, §5.
Qualifications.
Electors, Const. U. S., art. I, §2.
Members, Const. U. S., art. I, §2.
Judge of qualifications, Const. U. S., art. I, §5.
Revenue bills, Const. U. S., art. I, §7.
Rules of procedure, Const. U. S., art. I, §5.
Speaker, Const. U. S., art. I, §2.
Term, Const. U. S., art. I, §2.
Vacancies, Const. U. S., art. I, §2.
Vice-president.
Vacancy in office.
Confirmation of nomination of president, Const. U. S., amd. XXV, §2.
Insurrections, Const. U. S., art. I, §8.
International law.
Power to punish offenses against, Const. U. S., art. I, §8.
Interstate commerce, Const. U. S., art. I, §§8, 9.
Journals, Const. U. S., art. I, §§5, 7.
Legislative powers vested in, Const. U. S., art. I, §1.
Letters of marque and reprisal, Const. U. S., art. I, §8.
Messages to congress, Const. U. S., art. II, §3.
Militia.
Powers of congress, Const. U. S., art. I, §8.
Money.
Powers of congress, Const. U. S., art. I, §8.
Naturalization, Const. U. S., art. I, §8.
Navy.
Powers of congress, Const. U. S., art. I, §8.
Patents, Const. U. S., art. I, §8.
Piracy.
Powers of congress, Const. U. S., art. I, §8.
Post office and post roads, Const. U. S., art. I, §8.
Powers of congress, Const. U. S., art. I, §8.
Limitations on powers, Const. U. S., art. I, §9.
President of the United States.
Declaration of president's disability.
Determination of issue, Const. U. S., amd. XXV, §4.

CONSTITUTION OF THE UNITED STATES —Cont'd

Congress —Cont'd

Qualifications of members of congress, Const. U. S., art. I, §§2, 3, 5.
Rules of procedure, Const. U. S., art. I, §5.
Senate.
Absent members, Const. U. S., art. I, §5.
Arrest of members, Const. U. S., art. I, §6.
Compensation of members, Const. U. S., art. I, §6.
Laws varying compensation.
When to take effect, Const. U. S., amd. XXVII.
Debate, Const. U. S., art. I, §6.
Elections.
Election of senators, Const. U. S., amd. XVII.
Times, places and manner of holding, Const. U. S., art. I, §4.
Equal suffrage in senate, Const. U. S., art. V.
Expulsion of member, Const. U. S., art. I, §5.
Freedom of speech, Const. U. S., art. I, §6.
Holding other office, Const. U. S., art. I, §6.
Impeachment, Const. U. S., art. I, §3.
Journal, Const. U. S., art. I, §§5, 7.
Libel and slander.
Privilege of members, Const. U. S., art. I, §6.
Officers, Const. U. S., art. I, §3.
President, Const. U. S., art. I, §3.
Pro tempore, Const. U. S., art. I, §3.
Presidential elector.
Senator ineligible, Const. U. S., art. II, §1.
Punishment of members, Const. U. S., art. I, §5.
Qualifications.
Electors, Const. U. S., amd. XVII.
Members, Const. U. S., art. I, §3.
Judge of qualifications, Const. U. S., art. I, §5.
Quorum, Const. U. S., art. I, §5.
Revenue bills, Const. U. S., art. I, §7.
Rules of procedure, Const. U. S., art. I, §5.
Vacancies, Const. U. S., amd. XVII.
Vice-president of the United States.
Vacancy in office.
Confirmation of nomination of president, Const. U. S., amd. XXV, §2.
Sessions, Const. U. S., art. I, §4; amd. XX, §2.
Special sessions, Const. U. S., art. II, §3.
Taxation.
Powers of congress, Const. U. S., art. I, §8.
Territories, Const. U. S., art. IV, §3.
Vice-president.
Vacancy in office.
Nomination by president, Const. U. S., amd. XXV, §2.
Confirmation by majority of both houses of congress, Const. U. S., amd. XXV, §2.
War.
Articles of war, Const. U. S., art. I, §8.
Declaration of war, Const. U. S., art. I, §8.
Weights and measures, Const. U. S., art. I, §8.

Construction and interpretation.
Effect of enumeration of rights, Const. U. S., amd. IX.

Consuls, Const. U. S., art. II, §§2, 3; art. III, §2.

Contracts.
Impairment of obligations of contracts, Const. U. S., art. I, §10.

Copyright, Const. U. S., art. I, §8.

Corruption of blood.
Attainder of treason not to work, Const. U. S., art. III, §3.

CONSTITUTION OF THE UNITED STATES —Cont'd
Counsel for defense, Const. U. S., amd. VI.
Counterfeiting, Const. U. S., art. I, §8.
Court of appeals.
Decisions of court of appeals.
Appeals of right from certain decisions, §7A-30.
Courts.
Congress.
Power to constitute tribunals inferior to supreme court, Const. U. S., art. I, §8.
Inferior courts, Const. U. S., art. III, §1.
Judges.
Compensation, Const. U. S., art. III, §1.
Tenure, Const. U. S., art. III, §1.
Restriction of judicial power, Const. U. S., amd. XI.
Criminal procedure.
Cruel and unusual punishment, Const. U. S., amd. VIII.
Excessive bail, Const. U. S., amd. VIII.
Extradition, Const. U. S., art. IV, §2.
Fugitives from justice, Const. U. S., art. IV, §2.
Guarantees in criminal cases, Const. U. S., amds. V, VI.
Public trial, Const. U. S., amd. VI.
Self-incrimination, Const. U. S., amd. V.
Speedy trial, Const. U. S., amd. VI.
Cruel and unusual punishment, Const. U. S., amd. VIII.
Customs.
Congress.
Power to lay and collect, Const. U. S., art. I, §8.
Exportations from any state.
Duties not to be laid on, Const. U. S., art. I, §9.
Importation of persons, Const. U. S., art. I, §9.
Death.
President and vice-president of the United States.
Duty of congress, Const. U. S., art. II, §1; amd. XXV.
President elect.
Provisions in case of, Const. U. S., amd. XX.
Debts.
Aid of rebellion, Const. U. S., amd. XIV.
Debts and engagements contracted before adoption, Const. U. S., art. VI.
Not to be questioned, Const. U. S., amd. XIV.
Powers of congress, Const. U. S., art. I, §8.
Declaration of rights, Const. U. S., amds. I to X.
Defense.
Power of congress, Const. U. S., art. I, §8.
Discrimination, Const. U. S., amds. XIV, XV.
Double jeopardy, Const. U. S., amd. V.
Due process of law, Const. U. S., amds. V, XIV.
Duties and imposts.
Powers of congress, Const. U. S., art. I, §8.
States, Const. U. S., art. I, §§9, 10.
Elections.
Age.
Right to vote not to be abridged on account of age, Const. U. S., amd. XXVI.
Voting by persons eighteen years of age, Const. U. S., amd. XXVI.
House of representatives, Const. U. S., art. I, §§2, 4.
President and vice-president, Const. U. S., art. II, §1; amds. XII, XIV, XXIII.
Racial minorities, Const. U. S., amd. XV.
Senate, Const. U. S., art. I, §4; amd. XVII.
Suffrage, Const. U. S., amds. XV, XIX.
Eminent domain, Const. U. S., amd. V.

CONSTITUTION OF THE UNITED STATES —Cont'd
Emoluments, Const. U. S., art. I, §9.
Equal protection of the laws, Const. U. S., amd. XIV.
Equity.
Judicial power to extend to cases in, Const. U. S., art. III, §2.
Excessive bail, Const. U. S., amd. VIII.
Excessive fines, Const. U. S., amd. VIII.
Excises.
Powers of congress, Const. U. S., art. I, §8.
Execution of laws, Const. U. S., art. II, §3.
Expenditures.
Necessity for appropriations, Const. U. S., art. I, §9.
Publication of statement, Const. U. S., art. I, §9.
Exports and imports, Const. U. S., art. I, §§9, 10.
Ex post facto laws, Const. U. S., art. I, §§9, 10.
Extradition, Const. U. S., art. IV, §2.
Fines.
Excessive fines, Const. U. S., amd. VIII.
Foreign presents, Const. U. S., art. I, §9.
Former jeopardy, Const. U. S., amd. V.
Freedom of conscience, Const. U. S., amd. I.
Freedom of speech, Const. U. S., amd. I.
Members of congress, Const. U. S., art. I, §6.
Freedom of the press, Const. U. S., amd. I.
Fugitives, Const. U. S., art. IV, §2.
Full faith and credit clause, Const. U. S., art. IV, §1.
Gifts.
Foreign presents to United States officials, Const. U. S., art. I, §9.
Grand jury.
Presentments by, Const. U. S., amd. V.
Habeas corpus, Const. U. S., art. I, §9.
Immigration, Const. U. S., art. I, §9.
Immunities, Const. U. S., art. IV, §2.
Impairment of obligations of contracts, Const. U. S., art. I, §10.
Impeachment, Const. U. S., art. I, §§2, 3; art. II, §4; art. III, §2.
Imports and exports, Const. U. S., art. I, §§9, 10.
Income tax, Const. U. S., amd. XVI.
Indictments, informations and presentments, Const. U. S., amd. V.
Insurrection or rebellion, Const. U. S., art. I, §8.
International law.
Power of congress to punish offenses against, Const. U. S., art. I, §8.
Interstate commerce, Const. U. S., art. I, §§8, 9.
Intoxicating liquors.
Prohibition, Const. U. S., amds. XVIII, XXI.
Repeal of the eighteenth amendment, Const. U. S., amd. XXI.
Invasions, Const. U. S., art. I, §8.
Involuntary servitude, Const. U. S., amd. XIII.
Jeopardy.
Double jeopardy, Const. U. S., amd. V.
Journals.
Congress, Const. U. S., art. I, §§5, 7.
Judges.
Compensation, Const. U. S., art. III, §1.
Tenure, Const. U. S., art. III, §1.
Judgments.
Full faith and credit clause, Const. U. S., art. IV, §1.
Proof, Const. U. S., art. IV, §1.
Jury.
Jury of vicinage, Const. U. S., amd. VI.
Lame duck amendment, Const. U. S., amd. XX.

CONSTITUTION OF THE UNITED STATES —Cont'd
Legal tender, Const. U. S., art. I, §10.
Letters of marque and reprisal, Const. U. S., art. I, §§8, 10.
Libel and slander.
Congress.
Privilege of members of congress, Const. U. S., art. I, §6.
Limitations on powers of states, Const. U. S., art. I, §10.
Liquors, Const. U. S., amds. XVIII, XXI.
Messages to congress, Const. U. S., art. II, §3.
Militia.
Powers of congress, Const. U. S., art. I, §8.
Quartering soldiers, Const. U. S., amd. III.
Ministers.
Jurisdiction of cases affecting, Const. U. S., art. III, §2.
Receiving, Const. U. S., art. II, §3.
Money, Const. U. S., art. I, §§8, 10.
Coinage, Const. U. S., art. I, §§8, 10.
Counterfeiting, Const. U. S., art. I, §8.
Powers of congress, Const. U. S., art. I, §8.
Naturalization, Const. U. S., art. I, §8.
Navy.
Powers of congress, Const. U. S., art. I, §8.
New states, Const. U. S., art. IV, §3.
Nonresidents.
Jurisdiction of suits against state, Const. U. S., amd. XI.
Oaths.
General assembly.
Members to take oath supporting constitutions, §11-7.
Officers to take oath or affirmation supporting constitutions, §11-7.
Ordinances.
Consistent with constitution of the United States, §160A-174, (b).
Pardons, Const. U. S., art. II, §2.
Patents, Const. U. S., art. I, §8.
Payments.
Legal tender, Const. U. S., art. I, §10.
Petitions.
Right of, Const. U. S., amd. I.
Piracy.
Powers of congress, Const. U. S., art. I, §8.
Poll tax.
Failure to pay poll or other tax.
Denial or abridgement of right to vote.
Prohibited, Const. U. S., amd. XXIV.
Post offices, Const. U. S., art. I, §8.
Post roads, Const. U. S., art. I, §8.
Powers of congress, Const. U. S., art. I, §8.
Powers reserved to states and people, Const. U. S., amd. X.
President.
Age, Const. U. S., art. II, §1.
Ambassadors and consuls, Const. U. S., art. II, §§2, 3.
Appointment of officers, etc., Const. U. S., art. II, §2.
Approval of laws by president, Const. U. S., art. I, §7.
Approval of order, resolution or vote of congress, Const. U. S., art. I, §7.
Bribery, Const. U. S., art. II, §4.
Commander in chief, Const. U. S., art. II, §2.
Compensation, Const. U. S., art. II, §1.

CONSTITUTION OF THE UNITED STATES —Cont'd
President —Cont'd
Congress.
Adjourning congress, Const. U. S., art. II, §3.
Convening congress, Const. U. S., art. II, §3.
Messages to congress, Const. U. S., art. II, §3.
Special sessions of congress, Const. U. S., art. II, §3.
Death, Const. U. S., art. II, §1; amd. XX, §3.
Succession upon death, Const. U. S., amd. XXV, §1.
Disability, Const. U. S., art. II, §1.
Declaration by president.
Inability to perform duties, Const. U. S., amd. XXV, §3.
Declaration by vice-president and other officers, Const. U. S., amd. XXV, §4.
Determination of issue by congress, Const. U. S., amd. XXV, §4.
Duties, Const. U. S., art. II, §3.
Declaration by president of inability to perform duties, Const. U. S., amd. XXV, §3.
Transmittal to senate and house of representatives, Const. U. S., amd. XXV, §3.
Elections, Const. U. S., art. II, §1; amds. XII, XIV, XXIII.
Eligibility, Const. U. S., art. II, §1.
Execution of laws, Const. U. S., art. II, §3.
Executive power, Const. U. S., art. II, §1.
Failure to qualify, Const. U. S., amd. XX.
Impeachment, Const. U. S., art. I, §3; art. II, §4.
Inability, Const. U. S., art. II, §1.
Limitation on terms, Const. U. S., amd. XXII.
Message to congress, Const. U. S., art. II, §3.
Ministers.
Receiving, Const. U. S., art. II, §3.
Opinions from principal officers in executive departments, Const. U. S., art. II, §2.
Pardons, Const. U. S., art. II, §2.
Powers of president, Const. U. S., art. II, §§2, 3.
Public officers.
Commissions, Const. U. S., art. II, §3.
Qualifications, Const. U. S., art. II, §1.
Removal, Const. U. S., art. II, §§1, 4.
Succession upon removal, Const. U. S., amd. XXV, §1.
Resignation, Const. U. S., art. II, §1.
Succession upon resignation, Const. U. S., amd. XXV, §1.
Signing of bills, Const. U. S., art. I, §7.
Statutes.
Veto, Const. U. S., art. I, §7.
Succession to office, Const. U. S., art. II, §1; amd. XX.
Upon death, resignation or removal of president, Const. U. S., amd. XXV, §2.
Supreme court.
Appointment of justices, Const. U. S., art. II, §2.
Terms of office, Const. U. S., art. II, §1; amds. XX, XXII.
Limitation on terms, Const. U. S., amd. XXII.
Time of taking office, Const. U. S., amd. XX.
Treason, Const. U. S., art. II, §4.
Treaties, Const. U. S., art. II, §2.
Vacancy in office, Const. U. S., art. II, §1; amd. XX.
During senate recess, Const. U. S., art. II, §2.
Veto, Const. U. S., art. I, §7.

CONSTITUTION OF THE UNITED STATES
—Cont'd
Press.
Freedom of the press, Const. U. S., amd. I.
Privileges.
Privileged from arrest, Const. U. S., art. I, §6.
Prohibition, Const. U. S., amds. XVIII, XXI.
Protection and aid of states, Const. U. S., art. IV, §4.
Public debt, Const. U. S., art. I, §8.
Public officers and employees.
Appointment, Const. U. S., art. II, §2.
Senate recess, Const. U. S., art. II, §2.
Bribery, Const. U. S., art. II, §4.
Commissions, Const. U. S., art. II, §3.
Emoluments, Const. U. S., art. I, §9.
Foreign office or title, Const. U. S., art. I, §9.
Holding more than one office, Const. U. S., art. I, §6.
Impeachment, Const. U. S., art. II, §4.
Ineligibility of members of congress, Const. U. S., art. I, §6.
Presents from foreign states, Const. U. S., art. I, §9.
Presidential electors.
Eligibility, Const. U. S., art. II, §1.
Religious tests, Const. U. S., art. VI.
Removal, Const. U. S., art. II, §4.
Treason, Const. U. S., art. II, §4.
Vacancies during senate recess, Const. U. S., art. II, §2.
Public schools.
Basic education program.
Knowledge and understanding of constitution required, §115C-81, (g).
First amendment displayed on school property, §115C-81, (g3).
Public trial, Const. U. S., amd. VI.
Punishment.
Cruel and unusual punishment, Const. U. S., amd. VIII.
Quartering soldiers in houses, Const. U. S., amd. III.
Racial minorities, Const. U. S., amds. XIV, XV.
Ratification, Const. U. S., art. VII.
Records.
Full faith and credit clause, Const. U. S., art. IV, §1.
Proof, Const. U. S., art. IV, §1.
Redress of grievances.
Right to petition for, Const. U. S., amd. I.
Religious test, Const. U. S., art. VI.
Republican form of government, Const. U. S., art. IV, §4.
Reservation of rights of the people, Const. U. S., amd. IX.
Revenue bills, Const. U. S., art. I, §7.
Right of assembly, Const. U. S., amd. I.
Right of trial by jury, Const. U. S., art. III, §2.
Right to bear arms, Const. U. S., amd. II.
Right to counsel, Const. U. S., amd. VI.
Right to petition for a redress of grievances, Const. U. S., amd. I.
Searches and seizures, Const. U. S., amd. IV.
Self-incrimination, Const. U. S., amd. V.
Sentence and punishment, Const. U. S., amd. VIII.
Capital punishment, Const. U. S., amd. V.
Sessions of congress, Const. U. S., art. I, §4.
Special sessions, Const. U. S., art. II, §3.
Slavery, Const. U. S., amds. XIII, XIV, XV.

CONSTITUTION OF THE UNITED STATES
—Cont'd
Soldiers.
Quartering prohibited, Const. U. S., amd. III.
Speech.
Freedom of speech, Const. U. S., amd. I.
Speedy trial, Const. U. S., amd. VI.
States.
Admission of new states, Const. U. S., art. IV, §3.
Bill of attainder, Const. U. S., art. I, §10.
Bills of credit, Const. U. S., art. I, §10.
Commerce, Const. U. S., art. I, §§8, 9.
Compacts between the states or with foreign powers, Const. U. S., art. I, §10.
Contracts.
Impairing obligations of contracts, Const. U. S., art. I, §10.
Controversies between citizens of different states, Const. U. S., art. III, §2.
Controversies between states, Const. U. S., art. III, §2.
Duties and imposts, Const. U. S., art. I, §10.
Equal suffrage in senate, Const. U. S., art. V.
Exports, Const. U. S., art. I, §§9, 10.
Ex post facto laws, Const. U. S., art. I, §10.
Full faith and credit clause, Const. U. S., art. IV, §1.
Gold and silver coin tender in payment of debts, Const. U. S., art. I, §10.
Impairing obligations of contracts, Const. U. S., art. I, §10.
Imports and exports, Const. U. S., art. I, §10.
Invasion.
Protection against, Const. U. S., art. IV, §4.
Legal tender, Const. U. S., art. I, §10.
Letters of marque and reprisal, Const. U. S., art. I, §10.
Limitations on powers of states, Const. U. S., art. I, §10.
Money.
Coining money, Const. U. S., art. I, §10.
New states, Const. U. S., art. IV, §3.
Powers, Const. U. S., art. I, §10.
Reserved to states, Const. U. S., amd. X.
Protection and aid of states, Const. U. S., art. IV, §4.
Republican form of government guaranteed, Const. U. S., art. IV, §4.
Reservation of powers to states, Const. U. S., amd. X.
Right to coin money, Const. U. S., art. I, §10.
Suits against state, Const. U. S., amd. XI.
Tender in payment of debts, Const. U. S., art. I, §10.
Tonnage, Const. U. S., art. I, §10.
Treaties, Const. U. S., art. I, §10.
Troops or ships of war in time of peace, Const. U. S., art. I, §10.
War, Const. U. S., art. I, §10.
Statutes.
Approval of laws by president, Const. U. S., art. I, §7.
Ex post facto laws, Const. U. S., art. I, §§9, 10.
Full faith and credit clause, Const. U. S., art. IV, §1.
Limitations on legislation, Const. U. S., art. I, §9.
Proof, Const. U. S., art. IV, §1.
Revenue bills, Const. U. S., art. I, §7.
Supreme law of the land, Const. U. S., art. VI.
Veto, Const. U. S., art. I, §7.
Suits against state, Const. U. S., amd. XI.

CONSTITUTION OF THE UNITED STATES —Cont'd
Suits against the United States, Const. U. S., art. III, §2.
Supreme court.
Chief justice presides in impeachment of president, Const. U. S., art. I, §3.
Court of appeals decisions.
Appeals of right from certain decisions of court of appeals, §7A-30.
Jurisdiction, Const. U. S., art. III, §2.
Justices.
Appointment, Const. U. S., art. II, §2.
Compensation, Const. U. S., art. III, §1.
Tenure, Const. U. S., art. III, §1.
Supreme law of the land, Const. U. S., art. VI.
Taxation.
Capitation tax, Const. U. S., art. I, §9.
Elections.
Denial or abridgement of right to vote for failure to pay tax prohibited, Const. U. S., amd. XXIV.
Excises.
Powers of congress, Const. U. S., art. I, §8.
Exports, Const. U. S., art. I, §§9, 10.
Income tax, Const. U. S., amd. XVI.
Limitations on powers of states, Const. U. S., art. I, §10.
Powers of congress, Const. U. S., art. I, §8.
Revenue bills, Const. U. S., art. I, §7.
Tender, Const. U. S., art. I, §10.
Territories, Const. U. S., art. IV, §3.
Time when constitution effective, Const. U. S., art. VII.
Titles of nobility, Const. U. S., art. I, §§9, 10.
Tonnage, Const. U. S., art. I, §10.
Treason, Const. U. S., art. I, §6; art. II, §4; art. III, §3.
Trial.
Public trial, Const. U. S., amd. VI.
Speedy trial, Const. U. S., amd. VI.
Venue, Const. U. S., art. III, §2.
Vessels and boats.
Bound to and from one state not to be obliged to clear, etc., in another, Const. U. S., art. I, §9.
Veto, Const. U. S., art. I, §7.
Vice-president of the United States.
Age, Const. U. S., amd. XII.
Bribery, Const. U. S., art. II, §4.
Election, Const. U. S., art. II, §1; amd. XII.
Failure to qualify, Const. U. S., amd. XX.
Impeachment, Const. U. S., art. II, §4.
Oaths, Const. U. S., art. VI; amd. XIV.
President of senate, Const. U. S., art. I, §3.
Qualifications, Const. U. S., amd. XII.
Removal, Const. U. S., art. II, §4.
Succession to office of president, Const. U. S., art. II, §1; amds. XX, XXV.
Treason, Const. U. S., art. II, §4.
Vacancy in office, Const. U. S., art. II, §1; amd. XX.
Nomination by president, Const. U. S., amd. XXV, §2.
Confirmation by congress, Const. U. S., amd. XXV, §2.
War.
Articles of war, Const. U. S., art. I, §8.
Declaration by congress, Const. U. S., art. I, §8.
Grand jury.
Presentment as dispensable in certain cases, Const. U. S., amd. V.

CONSTITUTION OF THE UNITED STATES —Cont'd
War —Cont'd
Quartering of soldiers in times of war, Const. U. S., amd. III.
State engaging in, Const. U. S., art. I, §10.
Treason.
Levying against the United States, Const. U. S., art. III, §3.
Warrants.
Searches and seizures.
Conditions for issuance, Const. U. S., amd. IV.
Weapons.
Right to bear arms, Const. U. S., amd. II.
Weights and measures, Const. U. S., art. I, §8.
Welfare.
General welfare.
Powers of congress, Const. U. S., art. I, §8.
Witnesses.
Confrontation with witnesses, Const. U. S., amd. VI.
Process to obtain, Const. U. S., amd. VI.
Self-incrimination, Const. U. S., amd. V.
Treason.
Number in treason cases, Const. U. S., art. III, §3.
Women's suffrage, Const. U. S., amd. XIX.

CONSTRUCTION.
Building trades training.
Vocational and technical education generally.
See VOCATIONAL AND TECHNICAL EDUCATION.
Burning of building or structure in process of construction, §14-62.1.
Construction management at risk contracts.
Public contracts, §143-128.1.
Fairs.
State fair.
Board authorized to construct and finance facilities and improvements, §106-503.1.
Health care facilities.
Construction contracts, §131A-9.
Hospitals.
Construction and enlargement of local hospitals, §131E-70.
Indemnity.
Contracts for construction indemnity agreements against public policy, §22B-1.
Interest on construction loans.
Definition, §24-10, (c).
Maximum fees on loans secured by real property.
Less than three hundred thousand dollars, §24-10, (d).
Payment and performance bonds generally, §§44A-25 to 44A-35.
See PAYMENT AND PERFORMANCE BONDS.
Sanitary districts.
Water supply or sewerage systems construction by corporations or individuals, §130A-58.
State fair.
Authority to construct and finance facilities and improvements, §106-503.1.
Streets and highways.
See STREETS AND HIGHWAYS.
Transportation department.
State highway construction.
Powers of department, §136-18.
Water well construction, §§87-83 to 87-96.
See WATER WELL CONSTRUCTION.

CONSTRUCTION EQUIPMENT.
Inside rearview mirror requirement exemption from provision, §20-126, (a).

CONSTRUCTION INDEMNITY AGREEMENT.
Invalidity, §22B-1.

CONSTRUCTION LOANS.
Defined, §24-10, (c).
Fees chargeable at closing, §24-1.1A, (c).
Maximum fees for loans secured by real property, §24-10, (a).
Prepayment fees, §24-10, (b).

CONSTRUCTION OF STATUTES, §§12-2 to 12-4.
Amended statutes, §12-4.
Fees and charges by agencies, §12-3.1, (a).
Definitions, §12-3.1, (b).
Inapplicability to fees or charges to state, federal or local governmental units, §12-3.1, (c).
Governor, senate, solicitor, etc., §12-3.
Imprisonment for one month, §12-3.
Joint authority to three or more officers, §12-3.
Leap year, how counted, §12-3.
Masculine gender to extend and apply to females, §12-3.
Month, §12-3.
Oath to include affirmation, §12-3.
Personal property to include money, goods, etc., §12-3.
Person extended and applied to body politic and corporate, §12-3.
Preceding and following, §12-3.
Property to include all property, §12-3.
Real property.
Coextensive with land, tenements and hereditaments, §12-3.
Repeal of statute not to affect actions, §12-2.
Rules for construction generally, §12-3.
Seal, §12-3.
Single and plural number, §12-3.
State, §12-3.
Sworn to include affirmed, §12-3.
United States, §12-3.
Will to construed to include codicils, §12-3.
Written and in writing construed to include printing, engraving, etc., §12-3.
Year, §12-3.

CONSTRUCTIVE NOTICE.
Eminent domain.
Filing of notice of proceedings, §40A-21.
Lis pendens, §§1-116 to 1-120.2.
See LIS PENDENS.
Mortgages and deeds of trust.
Substitution of trustees, §45-15.

CONSTRUCTIVE SERVICE.
Service of process generally.
See SERVICE OF PROCESS.

CONSULS.
Constitution of the United States, Const. U. S., art. II, §§2, 3; art. III, §2.
Deeds probated before consular agents of the United States, §47-91.
Probate before, §47-83.
Vice-consuls and vice-consuls general, §47-84.

CONSULTANT SERVICES.
Private protective services.
Exemption of certain consultants from private protective services act, §74C-3, (b).
State departments and agencies, §§143-64.20 to 143-64.24.
See STATE DEPARTMENTS AND AGENCIES.

CONSUMER CREDIT SALES.
Acceleration clause.
Conditions for including clause, §25A-19.
Applicability of chapter, §25A-2, (b).
Attorneys' fees, §25A-21.
Confession of judgment.
Prohibited clause, §25A-18.
Credit cards.
Exceptions to provisions, §25A-2, (c).
Defined, §25A-2, (a).
Installment sale contracts.
Default charges, §25A-29.
Deferral charges, §25A-30.
Defined, §25A-12.
Finance charge, §25A-15.
Form, §25A-28.
Insurance.
Additional charges for insurance, §25A-17, (c).
Payment.
Prepayment.
Unearned finance charge credits.
Real property and mobile home loans, §25A-32.1.
Terms of payments, §25A-33.
Security interests.
Rate of finance charge, §25A-15, (d).
Remedies and penalties, §25A-44.
Retail installment sales generally, §§25A-1 to 25A-45.
See RETAIL INSTALLMENT SALES.
Unconscionability, §25A-43, (a).

CONSUMER FINANCE ACT, §§53-164 to 53-191.
Advertising.
False or misleading statements, §53-183.
Appeals.
Commission may review rules, orders or acts of commissioner, §53-188.
Assets.
Requirements for licensees, §53-168, (a), (d).
Assignments.
Earnings, §53-180, (b).
Attorneys' fees.
Loan agreement not to provide for payment by borrower, §53-180, (e).
Borrowers.
Defined, §53-165.
Cease and desist orders.
Commissioner of banks, §53-187.
Citation of act.
Short title, §53-164.
Commissioner of banks.
Cease and desist orders, §53-187.
Confidentiality of official records, §53-99.
Definition of "commissioner," §53-165, (e).
Fees.
Payment for expenses of supervision, §53-167.
Hearings, §53-186.
Injunctions, §53-187.
Oaths.
Power to administer, §53-186.
Powers, §§53-186, 53-187.
Publicity to investigations and findings, §53-186.
Review of rules, acts or orders by commission, §53-188.
Rules and regulations, §53-185.
State banking commission.
Commission may review rules, orders or acts of commissioner, §53-188.
Subpoenas, §53-186.
Witnesses, §53-186.

CONSUMER FINANCE ACT —Cont'd
Conduct of other business in same office.
Best interest of borrowing public.
Authorizing other business found not contrary to, §53-172, (b).
Revocation of authority where business contrary to, §53-172, (f).
Books, records and accounts of other loans, §53-172, (h).
Collections in violation of G.S. 53-190.
Section not to authorize, §53-172, (g).
Purchase of goods and services sold under authorization, §53-172, (d), (e).
Restriction on, §53-172, (a).
Truth-in-lending act regulations.
Requirements of other business under, §53-172, (c).
Confession of judgment.
Licensees not to take, §53-181, (c).
Contracts.
Out-of-state loans.
When contracts unenforceable, §53-190, (a).
Splitting contracts prohibited, §53-178.
Time and payment limitations, §53-180, (a).
Credit life and credit accident and health insurance, §53-189, (a).
Premiums, §53-189, (a).
Not deemed interest or charges, §53-189, (b).
Terms of agreements, §53-189, (a).
Credit unions.
Exemption of cooperative credit unions, §53-191.
Deceptive trade practices.
Prohibited, §53-180, (g).
Default charge.
Limitation of default provisions, §53-180, (c).
Definitions, §53-165.
Discrimination.
Prohibited acts, §53-180, (d).
Evasion of provisions, §53-166, (b).
Exemptions.
Businesses exempted, §53-191.
False or misleading statements, §53-183.
Fees.
Commissioner of banks.
Payment for expenses of supervision, §53-167.
Operating and maintaining office of commissioner of banks, §53-122, (a), (e), (f).
Processing loan.
Maximum fee, §§53-173, (a1), 53-176, (b).
Recording fees, §53-177.
Goods and services.
Purchase under authorization to conduct other business in same office, §53-172, (d), (e).
Hearings.
Commissioner of banks, §53-186.
License applications, §53-168, (b).
Home loans.
Limitation on condition to making loans, §53-180, (i).
Limitation on other loans, §53-180, (h).
Injunctions, §53-187.
Installment loans.
Corporations, §53-176, (f).
Due date of first payment, §53-176, (e).
Election to make loan under, §53-176, (d).
Loan processing fee, §53-176, (b).
Interest.
Computation of charges, §53-173, (b).
Credit life and credit accident and health insurance.
Premiums not deemed interest or charges, §53-189, (b).

CONSUMER FINANCE ACT —Cont'd
Interest —Cont'd
Judgments.
Limitation on interest after judgment, §53-173, (c).
Maturity of loan.
Limitation of interest after, §53-173, (d).
Optional maturities, §53-176.
Maximum rate, §53-173, (a).
Further charges prohibited, §53-178.
Optional rates, §53-176, (a), (c).
Schedule of charges, §53-181, (b).
Licenses.
Affiliation with other licensees.
Allocation of expense, §53-184, (c).
Applications, §53-169.
Assets.
Requirements, §53-168, (a), (d).
Change of location, ownership or management, §53-170, (c).
Contents, §53-168, (e).
Findings required for issuance, §53-168, (a).
Hearing on application, §53-168, (b).
Investigation of applicants, §53-168, (b).
Location of business, §53-170, (a).
Additional places of business, §53-170, (b).
Change of location, §53-170, (c).
Multiple-office loan limitations, §53-179.
Posting, §53-168, (e).
Prerequisite to issuance, §53-168, (a).
Records of licensees, §53-184, (a).
Reports by licensees, §53-184, (b).
Required, §53-168, (a).
Revocation or suspension, §53-171, (a).
Preexisting contracts.
Effect, §53-171, (c).
Reinstatement or issuance of new license, §53-171, (d).
Surrender of license, §53-171, (a), (b).
Limitations on loans.
Conditions to making loans, §53-180, (i).
Home loans and noncommercial loan over $25,000 prohibited, §53-180, (h).
Negotiable check or facsimile, §53-180, (k).
Misdemeanors.
Violation of provisions, §53-166, (c).
Multiple-office loan limitations, §53-179.
Noncommercial loans.
Limitation on other loans, §53-180, (h).
Oaths.
Power of commissioner to administer oaths, §53-186.
Out-of-state loans.
Licensees not to collect loan made by lender in another state, §53-190, (c).
Solicitation or other activities in state.
Subject to requirement of provisions, §53-190, (b).
When contracts unenforceable, §53-190, (a).
Pawnbrokers.
Exemption, §53-191.
Payment of loans.
Payment in full.
Duties of licensees upon, §53-182, (b).
Receipts, §53-182, (a).
Powers of attorney.
Licensee not to permit borrower to execute, §53-181, (c).
Processing fee.
Maximum fee, §§53-173, (a1), 53-176, (b).

CONSUMER FINANCE ACT —Cont'd
Purchase of goods and services.
Sold under authorization to conduct other business in same office, §53-172, (d), (e).
Racial minorities.
Discrimination prohibited, §53-180, (d).
Real property not security for loan, §53-180, (f).
Receipts.
Payment of loans, §53-182, (a).
Receivers.
Violators of provisions, §53-187.
Recording fees, §53-177.
Records.
Licensees, §53-184, (a).
Religion.
Discrimination prohibited, §53-180, (d).
Reports.
Licensees, §53-184, (b).
Rules and regulations.
Commissioner of banks, §53-185.
State banking commission, §53-185.
Savings and loan associations.
Exemption, §53-191.
Scope of act, §53-166, (a), (b).
Secured transactions.
Security agreements.
Effect of consumer protection and other laws, §25-9-201, (b), (d).
Third parties.
Assignments.
Restrictions on assignments, §§25-9-406, (i), 25-9-408, (f).
Solicitation of deposits.
Prohibited, §53-180, (j).
State banking commission.
Commission defined, §53-165, (d).
Statement to borrower, §53-181, (a).
Subpoenas.
Power of commissioner, §53-186.
Title of act.
Short title, §53-164.
Unfair competition, §53-180, (g).
Violation of provisions.
Penalties, §53-166, (c), (d).
Void contracts, §53-166, (d).
Wages.
Assignment of earnings prohibited, §53-180, (b).
Women.
Discrimination prohibited, §53-180, (d).

CONSUMER GOODS.
Food, drug and cosmetic act.
Declaration of net quantity of contents, §106-139.1.
General provisions.
See FOOD, DRUG AND COSMETIC ACT.
Regulations by board of agriculture, §106-139, (c).
Exemption from certain labeling requirements, §106-139, (b).

CONSUMER HOME LOANS, §24-10.2.

CONSUMER LEASES.
Choice of judicial forum, §25-2A-106.
Defined, §25-2A-103.
Leases, UCC generally, §§25-2A-101 to 25-2A-532.
See LEASES, UCC.
Option to accelerate at will, §25-2A-109.
Unconscionability, §25-2A-108.

CONSUMER PRICE INDEX.
Retirement system for teachers and state employees.
Post-retirement increases in allowances, §135-5, (o).
Years 1975 and 1976 increase in allowance, §135-5, (v).

CONSUMER PROTECTION.
Advertisements.
Use of term "wholesale" in advertising, §75-29.
Agriculture.
Records of sales of farm products.
Dated sales confirmation slips inapplicable to consumers, §106-202.6, (b).
Artwork on consignment, §§25C-1 to 25C-5.
Authorized practice committee of the state bar.
Procedures to prevent and restrain unauthorized practice of law, Bar Rules & Regs., D, §§.0201 to .0207.
Blind persons.
Consumer and advocacy advisory committee for the blind, §§143B-163, 143B-164.
Check-cashing businesses, §§53-275 to 53-289.
See CHECK-CASHING BUSINESSES.
Common carriers.
Unsolicited merchandise through common carriers, §75-27.
Consumer finance act, §§53-164 to 53-191.
See CONSUMER FINANCE ACT.
Credit cards.
See CREDIT CARDS.
Credit rights of women, §§25B-1 to 25B-4.
Damages.
Unfair competition and deceptive practices.
Treble damages, §75-16.
Debt collectors.
Prohibited acts, §§75-50 to 75-56.
See DEBT COLLECTORS.
Fines.
Violator subject to fine, §75-19.
Gifts.
Unsolicited merchandise.
Receipt through mail, §75-27.
Income tax.
Unauthorized disclosure of tax information, §75-28.
Injunctions, §75-19.
Insurance.
Injunctions, §75-19.
Lender may not require borrower to deal with particular insurer, §75-17.
Lender may require nondiscriminatory approval of insurer, §75-18.
Insurance information privacy, §§58-39-1 to 58-39-165.
See INSURANCE CONSUMER AND CUSTOMER INFORMATION PRIVACY.
Invoices.
Simulation of invoices, §75-35.
Leases, UCC.
Leases subject to consumer protection statute of state, §25-2A-104, (1).
Limestone, marl and landplaster.
Sale of agricultural liming materials and landplaster, §106-92.11.
Little FTC act, §75-1.1.
Loans.
General provisions.
See LOANS.

CONSUMER PROTECTION —Cont'd
Mail.
Unsolicited merchandise through mail, §75-27.
Manufactured homes generally.
See MANUFACTURED HOMES.
Monopolies and restraint of trade, §§75-1 to 75-35.
See MONOPOLIES AND RESTRAINT OF TRADE.
Mortgages and deeds of trust.
Home loan protection of consumers, §24-10.2.
Motion pictures.
Fair competition act, §§75C-1 to 75C-5.
Names.
Unfair and deceptive trade name, §75-29.
Negotiable instruments.
Check-cashing businesses, §§53-275 to 53-289.
See CHECK-CASHING BUSINESSES.
Simulation of checks and invoices, §75-35.
New motor vehicles warranties act, §§20-351 to 20-351.10.
See LEMON LAW.
Prizes.
Representation of eligibility to win a prize, §75-33.
Representation of winning a prize, §75-32.
Products liability, §§99B-1 to 99B-11.
Pyramid distribution plans, §14-291.2.
Rental referral agencies, §§66-142 to 66-146.
Representation of being specially selected, §75-34.
Retail installment sales, §§25A-1 to 25A-45.
See RETAIL INSTALLMENT SALES.
Secured transactions.
Security agreements.
Effect of consumer protection and other laws, §25-9-201, (b), (d).
Taxation.
Unauthorized disclosure of tax information, §75-28.
Timber marks, §§80-15 to 80-23.
See TIMBER MARKS.
Trademarks.
Generally, §§80-1 to 80-14.
See TRADEMARKS.
Unfair and deceptive trade names, §75-29.
Unauthorized practice of law.
Authorized practice committee of the state bar, Bar Rules & Regs., D, §§.0201 to .0207.
Unsolicited checks to secure loans, §75-20.
Unsolicited merchandise.
Receipt through mail, §75-27.
Women.
Credit rights of women, §§25B-1 to 25B-4.
Work-at-home solicitations, §75-31.
CONSUMER PROTECTION FUND OF INSURANCE DEPARTMENT, §58-2-215.
CONSUMER REPORTS.
Insurance institutions, agents or insurance-support organization.
Investigative consumer reports, §58-39-40.
CONSUMPTION AT OFF-PREMISES ESTABLISHMENTS.
Malt beverages or unfortified wine, §18B-300, (b).
CONTACT LENSES.
Prescriptions, §90-236.1.
CONTAGIOUS DISEASES.
Body of person dying infected with contagious disease.
Notice to persons handling body by physician.
Proper precautions to prevent infection, §130A-395, (a).
CONTAGIOUS DISEASES —Cont'd
Communicable diseases.
See COMMUNICABLE DISEASES.
Food, drug and cosmetic act.
Dissemination of certain information, §106-142, (b).
Meningococcal disease vaccination information.
Universities and colleges.
Providing students information, §116-260.
Nuclear, biological or chemical agents.
Terrorist incident using, §§130A-475 to 130A-479.
See TERRORIST INCIDENT USING NUCLEAR, BIOLOGICAL OR CHEMICAL AGENTS.
Rabies.
See RABIES.
Vaccinations.
See VACCINATIONS.
CONTAINERS.
Aluminum cans.
Incineration, disposal by prohibited, §130A-309.10, (f1).
Landfills, disposal in prohibited, §130A-309.10, (f).
Commodities.
Information required, §81A-27.
Unit price, declaration, §81A-28.
Eggs.
Defined, §106-245.14.
Designation of grade and class on containers required, §106-245.15.
Labeling on containers, §106-245.18, (a).
Descriptive terms, §106-245.18, (b).
Fully halogenated chlorofluorocarbons (CFC).
Containers manufactured with, restrictions, §130A-309.10, (b).
Gasoline and oil inspection.
Display required on containers used in making deliveries, §119-43.
Matches.
Shipping containers.
Requirements, §66-15.
Metal ring or tab.
Prohibition on selling beverages in containers opened by, §130A-309.10, (a).
Open container law, §18B-401, (a).
Mandatory revocation of driver's license, §20-17, (a).
Period of suspension or revocation, §20-19, (g1).
Transporting open container of alcoholic beverage after consuming alcohol or in passenger area of vehicle, §20-138.7.
Pesticides.
Prohibited acts, §143-443, (a).
Plastic containers.
Rigid containers, requirements, §130A-309.10, (e).
Plastic yokes or ring type holding devices.
"Degradable" defined, §14-399.2, (a).
Nondegradable devices.
Penalties for violation, §14-399.2, (c).
Prohibited, §14-399.2, (b).
Prosecution of violators.
Exemption, §14-399.2, (d).
Ports authority.
Shipping in containers, §143B-454.1.
Violations of provisions.
Penalties, §66-16.
Soil additives act.
Labeling of containers, §106-50.32.

CONTAMINATION OF SITE.
Deed or other instrument of conveyance, contaminated property statement, §143B-279.10, (e).
Land use restrictions imposed by secretary of environment and natural resources.
Reduction of danger to public health, §143B-279.9, (a) to (d).
Definitions, §§143B-279.9, (d), 143B-279.10, (d), (h).
Notice of contamination.
Cancellation after contamination eliminated, owner's request, §143B-279.10, (f).
Exceptions, §143B-279.10, (g).
Filing copy in register of deeds office, §143B-279.10, (b).
Recording copy, §143B-279.10, (c).
Secretary may prepare and file, owner's failure, §143B-279.10, (d).
Survey plat submitted by owner, §143B-279.10, (a).

CONTEMPT.
Abused, neglected or dependent juvenile actions.
Dispositional order, parent's failure to comply, §7B-904, (e).
Enforcement of order to cease interference with investigation, §7B-303, (f).
Failure to appear, §7B-407.
Failure to comply with order, §7B-406, (c).
Alimony.
Enforcement of payment by contempt, §50-16.7, (j).
Arbitration.
Grounds, §1-569.17, (h).
Arrest in civil cases.
Exclusive nature of provisions.
Exception as to contempt, §1-409.
Attorneys at law.
Clerks of court.
Certification of orders, §84-36.1.
Disciplinary hearing commission of state bar.
Power to hold in contempt, §84-28.1, (b1).
Suspended or disbarred attorney failing to comply with obligations, Bar Rules & Regs., B, §.0124.
Bail and recognizance.
Power of court to punish for contempt not affected, §15A-546.
Broadcasters and broadcasting.
Criminal contempt.
Basis for holding in contempt, §5A-11, (b).
Budget.
Punishment for violation of rules before joint meetings, §143-14.
Child custody orders.
Enforcement, §50-13.3, (a).
Childhood vaccine-related injury compensation.
Industrial commission.
Power to punish for contempt, §130A-424.
Superior court of Wake county.
Power to punish for contempt, §130A-425, (d).
Child support enforcement, §50-13.4, (f).
Compelling disclosure of information respecting nonsupporting parent.
Parent of dependent child receiving public assistance failing or refusing to cooperate, §110-131, (b).
Procedure to insure payment, §50-13.9, (g).

CONTEMPT —Cont'd
Child support enforcement —Cont'd
Wage garnishment to enforce, garnishee violating terms of order, §110-136, (e).
Civil contempt.
Affidavit or sworn statement.
Proceeding initiated on motion of aggrieved party, §5A-23, (a1).
Appeal procedures, §5A-24.
Burden of roof.
Proceeding initiated on motion of aggrieved party, §5A-21, (a1).
Child support.
Imprisonment for failure to pay, §5A-21, (b).
Commencement of proceedings, §5A-23, (a).
Criminal contempt finding, §5A-23, (g).
Dismissal of order, §5A-23, (c).
Failure or refusal to purge contempt within period of imprisonment.
Recommitted to imprisonment, §5A-21, (b1).
Failure to comply with order, §5A-21, (a).
Findings at conclusion of hearing, §5A-23, (e).
Imprisonment, §5A-21, (b).
Failure to obey nontestimonial identification order, §5A-21, (b1).
Maximum period, §5A-21, (b2).
Recommitted for one or more successive periods, §5A-21, (b2).
Imprisonment to compel compliance.
Release when civil contempt no longer continues, §5A-22, (a).
Procedure for motion of contemnor, §5A-22, (b).
Jurisdiction, §5A-23, (b).
Motion of aggrieved party.
Initiation of proceeding by, §5A-23, (a1).
Noncompliance with order, §5A-21, (a).
Nontestimonial identification order.
Imprisonment for failure to obey, §5A-21, (b1).
Presenting case for finding of contempt by interested persons, §5A-23, (f).
Proceedings for civil contempt, §§5A-23, 5A-25.
Release when civil contempt no longer continues, §5A-22, (a).
Procedure for motion of contemnor, §5A-22, (b).
Same conduct.
Person held in civil contempt not found in criminal contempt, §5A-21, (c).
Superior courts.
Authority of clerk to hold persons in civil contempt, §7A-103.
Authority of clerk to punish in civil contempt, §7A-103.
Trier of fact at show cause hearings, §5A-23, (d).
Venue for proceedings, §5A-23, (b).
Civil no-contact orders.
Violations, §50C-10.
Notice that violation punishable as contempt, §50C-5, (c).
Workplace violence prevention.
Violation, §95-274.
Commissioner of labor.
Information from employers.
Power to compel giving of information, §95-7.
Statistical report from employers to commissioner.
Refusal as contempt, §95-8.
Criminal contempt, §§5A-11 to 5A-17.
Appeal procedure, §5A-17.
Authority of court.
Impairing respect due its authority, §5A-11, (a).

CONTEMPT —Cont'd
Criminal contempt —Cont'd
Common law.
Specified grounds for criminal contempt exclusive, §5A-11, (a).
Court proceedings.
Failure to comply with schedules and practices of court, §5A-11, (a).
Interrupting proceedings, §5A-11, (a).
Report of proceedings.
Court orders prohibiting publication or broadcast of reports, §5A-11, (c).
Publication of inaccurate reports of court proceedings, §5A-11, (a).
Direct criminal contempt.
Custody of person charged with criminal contempt, §5A-16, (a).
Proceedings required, §5A-13, (a).
Summary proceedings for contempt, §5A-14, (a).
Direct criminal contempt.
Notice of charges, §5A-14, (b).
Notice of charges, §5A-14, (b).
What constitutes, §5A-13, (a).
Execution of court.
Interference with courts execution, §5A-11, (a).
Fines.
Circumstances for fines, §5A-12, (a).
Imposition of fine, §5A-12, (b).
Reduction or remittance of fine, §5A-12, (c).
Immunity of witnesses.
Refusal to testify or produce information, §5A-11, (a).
Imprisonment.
Circumstances for imprisonment, §5A-12, (a).
Credit for imprisonment resulting from contempt, §5A-12, (e).
Imposition of imprisonment for criminal contempt, §5A-12, (b).
Reduction of sentence, §5A-12, (c).
Indirect criminal contempt.
Proceedings required, §5A-13, (b).
Instances enumerated, §5A-11, (a).
Jury.
Improper attempt to influence deliberations, §5A-11, (a).
Officers of court.
Failure to perform official duties, §5A-11, (a).
Order in courtroom.
Power of judge to maintain, §15A-1035.
Plenary proceedings for contempt.
Commencement of proceedings, §5A-15, (a).
Custody of person charged with criminal contempt, §5A-16, (b).
Dismissal of order, §5A-15, (c).
Hearings.
Representation of court in hearings for criminal contempt, §5A-15, (g).
Jurisdiction of proceedings, §5A-15, (b).
Representation of court in hearings for contempt, §5A-15, (g).
Self-incrimination of witnesses, §5A-15, (e).
Show cause hearing.
Trier of facts at hearing, §5A-15, (b).
Trier of fact at show cause hearing.
Judge, §5A-15, (d).
Venue of proceedings, §5A-15, (b).
Verdicts.
Establishing facts beyond reasonable doubt, §5A-15, (f).
Witnesses.
Self-incrimination, §5A-15, (e).

CONTEMPT —Cont'd
Criminal contempt —Cont'd
Proceedings for civil contempt.
Finding of criminal contempt, §5A-23, (g).
Punishment, §5A-12.
Circumstances for fine or imprisonment, §5A-12, (a).
Imposition of fine or imprisonment, §5A-12, (b).
Other measures, §5A-12.
Reduction of punishment, §5A-12, (c).
Reports of public records banned.
Court orders prohibiting reports, §5A-11, (c).
Same conduct.
Person held in criminal contempt not found in civil contempt, §5A-12, (d).
Summary proceedings for contempt.
Direct criminal contempt, §5A-14, (a).
Witnesses.
Immunity of witness.
Refusal to testify or produce information, §5A-11, (a).
Refusal to be sworn or to testify, §5A-11, (a).
Delinquent and undisciplined juvenile actions.
Parent's noncompliance with orders, §7B-2706.
Undisciplined juveniles, failure to comply with disposition order, §7B-2505.
Depositions.
Commissioner may punish for contempt, §8-78.
Use outside state.
Disobeyance of subpoena, §1A-1, Rule 28, (d).
Direct criminal contempt, §§5A-13, 5A-14.
Discovery.
Criminal procedure.
Failure to comply with orders, §15A-910, (a).
Considerations of court before granting sanctions, §15A-910, (b).
Order compelling discovery.
Failure to comply, §1A-1, Rule 37, (b).
District court judges.
Power to punish for contempt, §7A-291.
Divorce.
Alimony.
Enforcement of payment by contempt, §50-16.7, (j).
Order for custody of minor child.
Enforcement, §50-13.3, (a).
Domestic violence.
Enforcement of orders, §50B-4.
Employment security.
Subpoenas of commission.
Failure to obey, §96-4, (i).
Evidence, rules of.
Inapplicability, §8C-1, Rule 1101, (b).
Executions.
Debtor leaving state or concealing self, §1-355.
Discovery of assets of judgment debtor.
Disobedience of orders of court, §§1-352.1, 1-352.2.
Disobedience of orders, §1-368.
Expedited evictions.
Violation of injunction or preliminary relief, §42-74.
Fire investigations.
Failure to comply with summons or subpoena, §58-79-15.
General assembly.
Committee activity.
Failure to respond to subpoena punishable as contempt, §120-19.4.
Refusal to testify punishable as contempt, §120-19.4.

CONTEMPT —Cont'd
General assembly —Cont'd
Legislative services commission.
Subpoena and contempt powers, §120-32.4.
Grand jury.
Confidentiality of information.
Unauthorized disclosures, §15A-623, (g).
Guardians.
Annual accounts.
Compelling accounting, §35A-1265, (a).
Inventory or account required within three months.
Compelling inventory or account, §35A-1262, (a).
Habeas corpus.
Remand of party in custody for contempt, §17-34.
Industrial commission.
Holding persons, firms or corporations in contempt, §§97-79, 97-80.
Infractions.
Enforcement of sanctions, §15A-1116, (a).
Interrogatories to discover assets of judgment debtors.
Disobeyance of order of court, §1-352.1.
Judgments for specific acts, §1A-1, Rule 70.
Judicial sales.
Report or accounting ordered.
Failure to comply, §1-339.12.
Judicial standards commission, Jud. Stds. Comm. Rule 18.
Local boards of education.
Power to punish for contempt, §115C-45, (a).
Magistrates.
Power of magistrate, §7A-292.
Medical assistance provider false claims.
Failure to comply with civil investigative demand order, §108A-70.14, (j).
Minors.
Harmful materials.
Disobedience of injunctions, §19-20.
Monopolies and restraint of trade.
Lender requiring borrower to deal with particular insurer.
Disregard of injunction or other court order, §75-19.
Mortgages and deeds of trust.
Sales under power of sale.
Failure to make report, §45-21.14.
Nontestimonial identification.
Failure to obey order to appear, §15A-276.
Resistance to compliance, §15A-279, (e).
Nuisances against public morals.
Temporary order restraining removal of personal property.
Violations generally, §19-2.3.
Occupational safety and health.
Subpoenas of commissioner of labor, §95-136, (b).
Witnesses, §95-135, (g).
Ordinances.
Enforcement of ordinance.
Unlawful use of real property, §160A-175, (e).
Partition.
Commissioners, §46-9.
Payment into court.
Refusal to obey order, §1-509.
Plenary proceedings for contempt, §§5A-15, 5A-16.
Probation.
Willful refusal by defendant to comply with conditions, §5A-11, (a).
Willful violation of condition, §15A-1344, (e1).

CONTEMPT —Cont'd
Receivers.
Corporations.
Refusal to answer, §1-507.5.
Referees.
Power to punish for contempt, §1A-1, Rule 53, (e).
Rules of evidence.
Inapplicability, §8C-1, Rule 1101, (b).
Sales and use tax.
Examination of records by secretary or agent.
Refusal to permit examination, §105-164.30.
Savings and loan associations.
Subpoenas, §54B-60, (c).
Witnesses, §54B-60, (c).
Savings banks.
Subpoenas issued by administrator, §54C-57, (c).
Securities regulation.
Subpoenas.
Refusal to obey, §78A-46, (c).
Special proceedings.
Failure of commissioner of sale to account, §1-406.
Subpoenas.
Failure to obey, §1A-1, Rule 45, (f).
Superior court clerks' authority, §7A-103.
Supplemental proceedings.
Disobedience of orders, §1-368.
Utilities commission.
Power to punish for contempt, §62-61.
Wills.
Probate of wills.
Failure to answer summons of clerk, §31-15.
Workplace violence prevention.
Civil no-contact orders.
Violation, §95-274.

CONTESTS.
Alcoholic beverage advertising, §18B-105, (b).
Athletic contests.
See ATHLETIC CONTESTS.
Contested special proceedings.
Commencement, §1-394.
Complaint or petition.
Commencement of proceedings generally, §1-394.
Filing.
Time for, §1-396.
Enlargement of time, §1-398.
Summons, §1-394.
Return, §1-395.
Elections.
Executive branch.
Joint ballot of both houses of general assembly.
General assembly to determine, Const. N. C., art. VI, §5.
Executors and administrators.
Right to contest appointment, §28A-6-4.
Wills.
Bonds, surety.
Prosecution bond required in content of will, §31-34.
Caveat to will, §§31-32 to 31-37.

CONTINGENT FEES AND CONTINGENT FEE AGREEMENTS.
Attorneys, Prof. Cond. Rule 1.5.

CONTINGENT INTEREST IN REAL OR PERSONAL ESTATE.
Property passed by will, §31-40.

CONTINGENT REMAINDERS.
Validation of transfer, §41-12.

CONTINUANCES, §1A-1, Rule 40, (b).
Abused, neglected or dependent juvenile actions.
Adjudicatory hearing, §7B-803.
Nonsecure custody hearings, §7B-506, (a).
Periodic review hearings, placement of juvenile.
Termination of parental rights, §7B-908, (b).
Amendments not conforming to evidence, §1A-1, Rule 15, (b).
Attorney disciplinary proceedings.
Formal hearings, Bar Rules & Regs., B, §.0114.
Criminal law and procedure.
Entry of PJC not considered entry of judgment, §15A-101.
Factors in superior or district court, §15A-952, (g).
Delinquent and undisciplined juvenile actions.
Adjudicatory hearing, §7B-2406.
Detainers, §15-10.2, (a).
District courts.
Rules of practice and procedure, Super. Ct. Rule 3.
Eminent domain.
Public condemnors.
Power of judge, §40A-50.
Expedited evictions.
Procedure and standards for continuances, §42-68.
Insurance.
Supervision, rehabilitation and liquidation of insurers.
Delinquency proceedings, §58-30-50.
Judge comment on verdict, §1A-1, Rule 51, (c).
Motor vehicles.
Convictions.
Third PJC filed in five-year period as conviction, §20-4.01.
Record of PJC's, §20-26, (a).
Prisons and prisoners.
Discharge of insolvent prisoner, §23-35.
Superior courts.
Criminal law and procedure, §15A-952, (g).
Rules of practice and procedure, Super. Ct. Rule 3.
Support of illegitimate children.
Surety of person accused of being father, §49-5.
Termination of parental rights.
Adjudicatory hearing, §7B-1109, (d).
Placement review hearing, §7B-908, (b).

CONTINUING CARE RETIREMENT COMMUNITIES, §§58-64-1 to 58-64-85.
Additional beds for facility.
Commissioner appointed as receiver, §58-64-46.
Books and papers.
Failure to exhibit or making false statements, §58-2-200.
Cease and desist orders, §58-64-10, (c).
Commissioner.
Cease and desist orders, §58-64-10, (c).
Examination of books and records, §58-64-55.
Investigations.
Generally, §58-64-50.
Rehabilitation or liquidation.
Generally, §58-64-45.
Rules and regulations, §58-64-65.
Committee, §58-64-80.
Contracts.
Disclosure statements.
Copy of standard form of contract for continuing care.
Attachment to disclosure statement, §58-64-20, (c).
Provisions of contract for continuing care, §58-64-25, (a), (b).

CONTINUING CARE RETIREMENT COMMUNITIES —Cont'd
Contracts as preferred claims on liquidation, §58-64-60.
Definitions, §58-64-1.
Applicability of certain definitions, §58-64-45, (b).
Department of health and human services.
Authority, §58-64-85.
Disclosure statements.
Amendment for disclosure to proposed residents, §58-64-20, (f).
Annual revised disclosure statement, §58-64-30, (a).
Filing fee, §58-64-30, (b).
Civil liability for violations, §58-64-70, (a), (b).
Limitation of actions, §58-64-70, (d).
Offer of refund.
Effect, §58-64-70, (c).
Contents, §58-64-20, (a).
Cover page, §58-64-20, (b).
Contracts for continuing care.
Copy of standard form to be attached, §58-64-20, (c).
Language requirements, §58-64-20, (e).
Standardized format.
Commissioner may prescribe, §58-64-20, (d).
Escrow account, §58-64-35, (a).
Release of funds, §58-64-35, (b) to (d).
Fees.
Disclosure statements.
Annual revised disclosure statement.
Filing fee, §58-64-30, (b).
Entrance fee.
Defined, §58-64-1.
Return of entrance fee held in escrow, §58-64-35, (d).
Licenses.
Application fee, §58-64-5, (b).
Nursing beds and adult care home beds.
Licensure fees, §131E-138.1.
Financial statements, §58-64-55.
Financing health care facilities generally, §§131A-1 to 131A-25.
See HEALTH CARE FACILITY FINANCING.
Investigations, §58-64-50, (a).
Powers of commissioner, §58-64-50, (b), (c).
Licenses.
Actuarial report, §58-64-5, (g).
Applications, §58-64-5, (b).
Correction of application, §58-64-5, (d).
Notice of filing, §58-64-5, (c).
Criminal convictions.
Suspension of license, §58-2-60, (b).
Fees.
Application fee, §58-64-5, (b).
Information to be provided by licensees, §58-64-5, (f).
Monetary penalty for violations, §58-2-70, (c), (d).
Required, §58-64-5, (a).
Restitution for violations, §58-2-70, (e) to (g).
Revocation.
Findings of fact, §58-64-10, (a).
Statement of underlying facts supporting, §58-64-10, (b).
Notice and hearings, §58-2-70, (b).
Surrender, §58-2-65.
Suspension.
Applicable provisions, §58-2-70, (h).
Criminal conviction, §58-2-60, (b).
Notice and hearing, §58-2-70, (b).

CONTINUING CARE RETIREMENT COMMUNITIES —Cont'd
Licenses —Cont'd
Transfer.
Prohibited, §58-64-15.
Limitation of actions.
Disclosure statements.
Civil liability for violations, §58-64-70, (d).
Liquidation of facilities.
Application for order authorizing, §58-64-45, (a), (f).
Preferred claims on.
Contracts as to, §58-64-60.
Refusal or vacation of orders, §58-64-45, (g).
Marketing by unlicensed providers, §58-64-5, (a).
Operating reserves, §58-64-33, (a) to (c).
Orders.
Rehabilitation or liquidation, §58-64-45.
Penalties.
Criminal penalties for violations, §58-64-75.
Marketing, unlicensed providers, §58-64-5, (a).
Receivership.
Additional beds for facility, §58-64-46.
Records.
Examination of books and records.
Powers of commissioner, §58-64-55.
Rehabilitation of facilities.
Application for order authorizing, §58-64-45, (a), (f).
Refusal or vacation of orders, §58-64-45, (g).
Termination of order, §58-64-45, (c).
Reserves.
Operating reserves, §58-64-33, (a) to (c).
Residents.
Defined, §58-64-1.
Meetings with residents.
Governing body to hold, §58-64-40, (b).
Organization.
Right to organization, §58-64-40, (a).
Rules and regulations.
Definition and description of "insolvency" and "hazardous financial condition," §58-64-45, (b).
Promulgation by commissioner, §58-64-65, (a).
Time to comply with rules, §58-64-65, (b).
Sale or transfer of ownership.
Approval by commissioner, §58-64-15.
Subpoenas.
Powers of commissioner, §58-64-50, (c).
Supervision proceedings.
Commencement, §58-64-45, (a).

CONTINUING CRIMINAL ENTERPRISE.
Defined, §14-7.20, (c).
Forfeiture of profits, §14-7.20, (b).
Punishment, §14-7.20, (a).

CONTINUING EDUCATION.
Attorneys.
See CONTINUING LEGAL EDUCATION.
Auctions and auction years.
License renewal, §85B-4, (e1).
Certified public accountants, §93-12.
Cosmetic art.
Inactive status.
Removal from list, §88B-21, (h).
Teachers, §88B-21, (e).
Dental hygienists, §90-225.1.
Dentists, §90-31.1.
Diagnostic imaging technicians, §90-143.2, (a).
Election officials, §163-82.24, (a).
Certification, §163-82.24, (b).
Electrical contractors, §87-44.1.

CONTINUING EDUCATION —Cont'd
Electrologists, §88A-13.
Engineers.
Sponsors of continuing professional competency activities, §89C-10, (h).
Foresters.
Registration renewal, §89B-11, (b).
Funeral directors, §90-210.25.
Home inspectors, §143-151.64.
Insurance adjusters, agents and brokers, §§58-33-130, 58-33-135.
Insurance instructors, §58-33-132.
Judges.
Accreditations.
Sponsors, CJE Rule III.
Applicability of rules, CJE Rule I.
Attendance, CJE Rule II.
Credit hours, CJE Rule II.
Delinquency.
Notice, CJE Rule IV.
Exemptions, CJE Rule V.
Expenses, CJE Rule VI.
Hours required, CJE Rule II.
Reports.
Active members.
Annual report, CJE Rule IV.
Scope of rules, CJE Rule I.
Sponsors.
Accreditation, CJE Rule III.
Manufactured housing dealers and salespersons, §143-143.11B.
Massage and bodywork therapy, §90-632.
Mortgage bankers and brokers, §53-243.07.
Nurses, §90-171.42, (a), (b).
Local health directors.
Nurse pilot program, §130A-40.1, (c).
Nursing home administrators, §90-286.
Occupational therapists, §90-270.75.
Optometrists, §90-123.1.
Pastoral counselors, §90-389.
Pharmacists, §90-85.18.
Physicians and surgeons.
Retired physician with inactive license status, §90-12, (d).
Podiatrists, §90-202.11.
Real estate appraisers, §93E-1-7, (b).
Minimum standards, §93E-1-8, (c).
Real estate brokers and salespersons, §93A-4A.
Sanitarians, §90A-63.
Social workers, §90B-9.
Veterinarians, §90-186.
Well contractors, §87-98.12, (a), (b).

CONTINUING LEGAL EDUCATION.
Accreditation standards, CLE Rules 19, 20.
Accredited sponsors.
Application requirements, CLE Reg. 3.
Defined, CLE Rule 1.
Active members.
Defined, CLE Rule 1.
Administrative committee.
Defined, CLE Rule 1.
Agency appeals, CLE Reg. 10.
Applicability of continuing education rules, CLE Rule 17.
Approved certificates.
Defined, CLE Rule 1.
Armed forces of the United States.
Applicability of rules, CLE Rule 17.
Attendee's fees.
Computation, CLE Reg. 6.
Source of funding, CLE Rule 12.

CONTINUING LEGAL EDUCATION —Cont'd
Authority for agency appeals, CLE Reg. 10.
Bankruptcy law specialty, Bar Rules & Regs., D, §§.2205, .2206.
Bar review/refresher course, CLE Reg. 2.
Board.
Appointment of members, Bar Rules & Regs., D, §.1506; CLE Rule 6.
Appointments, CLE Rule 6.
Chair, Bar Rules & Regs., D, §.1510; CLE Rule 10.
Chairperson, CLE Rule 10.
Committees, Bar Rules & Regs., D, §.1601; CLE Rule 1.
Confidentiality of material, CLE Rule 25.
Defined, Bar Rules & Regs., D, §.1601; CLE Rule 1.
Duties, Bar Rules & Regs., D, §.1516; CLE Rule 16.
Executive committee, Bar Rules & Regs., D, §.1601.
Funding, CLE Rule 12.
Jurisdiction, Bar Rules & Regs., D, §.1502.
Lay participation, Bar Rules & Regs., D, §.1505; CLE Rule 5.
Meetings, Bar Rules & Regs., D, §.1514; CLE Rules 14, 15.
Noncompliance of members with provisions, CLE Rule 23.
Operation or responsibility, Bar Rules & Regs., D, §.1503; CLE Rule 3.
Organization, CLE Reg. 9.
Powers, Bar Rules & Regs., D, §.1516; CLE Rule 16.
Quorum, Bar Rules & Regs., D, §.1601.
Referral of matters to board by grievance committee, Bar Rules & Regs., B, §.0112.
Regulations, CLE Rule 17.
Removal of members, Bar Rules & Regs., D, §.1506; CLE Rule 6.
Reports, Bar Rules & Regs., D, §.1515; CLE Rule 15.
Size, Bar Rules & Regs., D, §.1504; CLE Rule 4.
Succession in office, Bar Rules & Regs., D, §.1509; CLE Rule 9.
Term of members, Bar Rules & Regs., D, §.1507; CLE Rule 7.
Staggered terms, Bar Rules & Regs., D, §.1508; CLE Rule 6.
Succession, CLE Rule 9.
Term of office, CLE Rule 7.
Staggered terms, CLE Rule 8.
Vice-chairperson, Bar Rules & Regs., D, §.1511; CLE Rules 6, 11.
Compliance procedures, CLE Reg. 8.
Congress.
Applicability of rules, CLE Rule 17.
Council.
Defined, CLE Rule 1.
Course requirements, CLE Rule 18.
Accreditation of audiovisual programs, CLE Reg. 4.
Generally, CLE Reg. 2.
Practical skills courses.
Defined, CLE Rule 1.
Credit hours, CLE Rule 21.
Computation, CLE Reg. 5.
Defined, CLE Rule 1.
Criminal law specialty, Bar Rules & Regs., D, §§.2505, .2506.
Defined terms, CLE Rule 1.

CONTINUING LEGAL EDUCATION —Cont'd
Effective date of CLE rules, CLE Rule 26.
Estate planning and probate law specialty, Bar Rules & Regs., D, §§.2305, .2306.
Family law specialty, Bar Rules & Regs., D, §§.2405, .2406.
Fees.
Attendee's fees.
Computation, CLE Reg. 6.
Source of funding, CLE Rule 12.
Fiscal responsibility, CLE Rule 13.
Reinstatement fee, CLE Reg. 9.
Review of fees, CLE Reg. 6.
Sponsors.
Computation, CLE Reg. 6.
Source of funding, CLE Rule 12.
Uniform application, CLE Reg. 6.
General assembly.
Applicability of rules, CLE Rule 17.
Governor.
Applicability of rules, CLE Rule 17.
Immigration law specialty.
Applicability of other requirements, Bar Rules & Regs., D, §.2607.
Applicability of provisions.
North Carolina plan of legal specialization, Bar Rules & Regs., D, §.2604.
Definition, Bar Rules & Regs., D, §.2602.
Establishment, Bar Rules & Regs., D, §.2601.
Recognition as specialist, Bar Rules & Regs., D, §.2603.
Standards for certification, Bar Rules & Regs., D, §.2605.
Standards for continued certification, Bar Rules & Regs., D, §.2606.
Inactive members.
Defined, CLE Rule 1.
In-house continuing education.
Defined, CLE Rule 1.
General course approval, CLE Reg. 2.
Institute of government.
Applicability of rules, CLE Rule 17.
Judges.
Applicability of rules, CLE Rule 17.
Jurisdiction, CLE Rule 2.
Law school courses, CLE Reg. 2.
Lieutenant governor.
Applicability of rules, CLE Rule 17.
Members' annual report.
Noncompliance, CLE Rule 23.
Reinstatement of members, CLE Rule 24.
Newly admitted active members.
Defined, CLE Rule 1.
Noncompliance procedures, CLE Reg. 9.
Nonresidents.
Active member nonresidents.
Applicability of rules, CLE Rule 17.
Operational responsibility, CLE Rule 3.
Practical skills courses.
Defined, CLE Rule 1.
Procedures.
Compliance, CLE Reg. 8.
Noncompliance, CLE Reg. 9.
Review of board decision, CLE Reg. 10.
Professional responsibility.
Defined, CLE Rule 1.
Program, CLE Rule 18.
Accreditation standards, CLE Rule 20.
Purpose of continuing legal education rules, CLE Rule 1.

CONTINUING LEGAL EDUCATION —Cont'd
Real property law specialty, Bar Rules & Regs., D, §§.2105, .2106.
Regulations.
Adoption, CLE Rule 27.
Regulations governing administration of program, Bar Rules & Regs., D, §§.1601 to .1610.
Reinstatement, CLE Rule 24.
Reports.
Annual report of board, CLE Rule 15.
Members' annual report, CLE Rule 22.
Rules concerning administration of program, Bar Rules & Regs., D, §§.1501 to .1527.
Scope and exemptions, CLE Rule 17.
Special exemptions, CLE Reg. 7.
Special cases, CLE Reg. 7.
Specialization certification, rules governing accreditation, Bar Rules & Regs., D, §§.1901 to .1908.
Sponsors.
Accreditation.
Application requirements, CLE Reg. 3.
Standards, CLE Rule 20.
Defined, CLE Rule 1.
Fees.
Source of funding, CLE Rule 12.
Suspension from practice of law.
Noncompliance with reporting requirements, CLE Rule 3.
Reinstatement, CLE Rule 24.
Video and audiovisual program accreditation, CLE Reg. 4.
Year.
Defined, CLE Rule 1.

CONTRABAND.
Cigarettes.
Non-tax-paid cigarettes, §105-113.32.
Packages violate certain label requirements, §14-401.18, (c).
Credit cards and devices.
Devices for theft, §14-113.5.
Making, possessing or transferring device for theft, §14-113.5.
Unlawful telecommunications devices, §14-113.5, (b).
Litter disposal vehicles or machines, §14-399, (g).
Motion to suppress evidence.
Contraband not subject to motion, §15A-979.
Obscenity.
Dissemination of obscene materials, §14-190.1, (h).
Searches and seizures, §15A-242.
Telecommunications devices, §14-113.5, (b).
Trademarks.
Counterfeit trademarks, §80-11.1, (d).

CONTRACEPTIVES.
Health benefit plan coverage.
Prescription contraceptive drugs and devices and outpatient contraceptive services, §58-3-178.
Small employer group health coverage.
Contraceptive drugs and devices, §58-50-155, (a).

CONTRACT KILLER SENTENCING, §15A-1340.16.

CONTRACT MOTOR CARRIERS.
Defined, §62-3.

CONTRACTORS.
Architect exemption, §83A-13, (b).

CONTRACTORS —Cont'd
Child support enforcement.
Forfeiture of licensing privilege, §50-13.12.
Definitions.
Electrical contracting, §87-43.
Electrical contractors, §87-41.1.
General contractors, §87-1.
Homeowners recovery fund, §87-15.5.
Plumbing, heating and fire sprinkler contractors, §87-21, (a).
Refrigeration contractors, §87-58, (a), (b).
Subcontractors.
Payments to subcontractors, §22C-1.
Electrical contractors, §§87-39 to 87-51.
See ELECTRICAL CONTRACTORS.
Fraud.
Improvements to real property.
Furnishing false statements, §44A-24.
Furnishing false statements in connection with improvements, §44A-24.
General contractors, §§87-1 to 87-15.3.
See GENERAL CONTRACTORS.
Handicapped persons.
Public building contracts.
Cooperation in promoting use of physically handicapped contractors, §143-135.5.
Homeowners recovery fund, §§87-15.5 to 87-15.9.
Improvements to real property.
Provisions making contract subject to laws of another state, §22B-2.
Indemnity agreements against public policy, §22B-1.
Interest.
Subcontractors.
Payments to subcontractors.
Late payments, §22C-5.
Landscape contractors, §§89D-1 to 89D-10.
See LANDSCAPE CONTRACTORS.
License forfeiture for felony convictions, §15A-1331A.
Liens.
See MECHANICS' AND MATERIALMEN'S LIENS.
Limitation of actions.
Real property improvements.
Recovery of damages for defective or unsafe conditions.
Six-year limitation, §1-50, (a).
Subcontractors.
Real property improvements.
Recovery of damages for defective or unsafe conditions.
Six-year limitation, §1-50, (a).
Manufactured homes.
Set-up contractors.
Bonds, surety, §143-143.12, (a).
Licenses, §§143-143.10A to 143-143.14.
Mechanics' and materialmen's liens.
See MECHANICS' AND MATERIALMEN'S LIENS.
Minorities.
Public building contracts.
Cooperation in promoting use of minority contractors, §143-135.5.
Streets and highways.
Disadvantaged businesses.
Participation in highway contracts, §136-28.4.
Payment and performance bonds generally, §§44A-25 to 44A-35.
See PAYMENT AND PERFORMANCE BONDS.

CONTRACTORS —Cont'd
Plumbing, heating and fire sprinkler contractors, §§87-16 to 87-27.1.
See PLUMBING, HEATING AND FIRE SPRINKLER CONTRACTORS.
Property taxes.
Defined, §105-273.
Inventories owned by contractors.
Exemptions, §105-275.
Public policy.
Construction indemnity agreements invalid, §22B-1.
Improvements to real property contracts.
Provisions making contract subject to laws of another state, §22B-2.
Public works, §§133-23 to 133-33.
See PUBLIC WORKS CONTRACTORS.
Refrigeration contractors, §§87-52 to 87-64.1.
See REFRIGERATION CONTRACTORS.
Small business contractor act, §§143B-472.85 to 143B-472.97.
See SMALL BUSINESS CONTRACTOR ACT.
Small contractors.
Public building contracts.
Cooperation in promoting use, §143-135.5.
Steam or gas fitters.
Licenses.
Revocation or suspension.
Felony convictions, §15A-1331A.
Subcontractors.
Limitation of actions.
Real property improvements.
Recovery of damages for defective or unsafe conditions.
Six-year limitation, §1-50, (a).
Payments to subcontractors.
Applicability of provisions, §22C-6.
Conditions of payment, §22C-4.
Definitions, §22C-1.
Entitlement to payment.
Performance by subcontractor, §22C-2.
Interest.
Late payments, §22C-5.
Late payments.
Interest, §22C-5.
Performance by subcontractor.
Effect, §§22C-2, 22C-3.
Scope of provisions, §22C-6.
Time for, §22C-3.
Withholding by contractor, §22C-4.
Prompt payment.
Public building contracts, §143-134.1, (a), (b).
Workers' compensation.
Certificate that subcontractor has complied with law, §97-19.
Women.
Public building contracts.
Cooperation in promoting use of women contractors, §143-135.5.
Workers' compensation, §97-19.

CONTRACTS.
Abandoned property.
Agreement by owner to locate, deliver or recover, §116B-78.
Accident and health insurance.
Group insurance.
Contracts to cover treatment, §58-51-50, (b).
Accounts and accounting.
Itemized and verified accounts.
Evidence, §8-45.

CONTRACTS —Cont'd
Administrative office of the courts.
Assistant clerks.
Local government funding, §7A-102, (g).
Deputy clerks.
Local government funding, §7A-102, (g).
Judicial secretaries.
Local government funding, §7A-44.1, (d).
Reports.
Local government services contracts, §7A-346.2, (a).
Adopt-a-highway participants.
Use of contract services to clean roadside, §136-140.1, (b).
Advertisements.
Purchases and contracts.
Contracts through department of administration.
Bids and bidding.
Competitive bidding procedure, §143-52.
Setting of benchmarks, §143-53.1.
Advisory budget commission.
Financial interest of officers, §143-63.
Purchases exempted, §§143-56, 143-57.
Rules covering certain purposes, §143-60.
Aeronautics.
Jurisdiction, §63-17.
Against public policy.
Construction indemnity agreements, §22B-1.
Forum selection provisions, §22B-3.
Improving real property.
Provisions making contract subject to laws of another state, §22B-2.
Waiving jury trial, §22B-10.
Agricultural finance authority.
Experts and consultants.
Employment on contractual basis, §122D-5, (d).
Power to contract, §122D-6.
Agriculture.
Purchases and contracts through department of administration.
Preference given to home projects, §143-59.
Airport construction, repair, etc., §63-73.
Alcoholic beverages.
Local ABC officers.
Contracts with other agencies.
Alternative to hiring local officers, §18B-501, (f).
State warehouse.
Contracting for private warehouses, §18B-204, (a).
Aliens.
Real property.
Validation of contracts to purchase or sell real property, §64-2.
Animal waste management system operators.
Reports, §90A-47.2, (b).
Annuities generally.
See ANNUITIES.
Antenuptial agreements, §§52B-1 to 52B-11.
See ANTENUPTIAL AGREEMENTS AND CONTRACTS.
Artistic and creative services contracts.
Minors, §§48A-11 to 48A-16.
Assignments.
Secured transactions.
Inapplicability of article 9.
Payment right assigned to one obligated to perform under contract, §25-9-109, (d).
Athlete agents.
Agency contracts generally, §§78C-85 to 78C-105.
See ATHLETE AGENTS.

CONTRACTS —Cont'd
Attorneys at law.
Appearances.
Employment contract.
Filing or producing if requested, §84-11.
Contingent fee agreements, Prof. Cond. Rule 1.5.
Restriction on practice, Prof. Cond. Rule 5.6.
Bank reopening and closing.
Effect upon certain contracts, §53-38.
Book accounts.
Documentary evidence of book accounts under $60.00, §8-42.
Boxing, requirements, §143-656.
Charitable solicitation.
Contracts between solicitor and charitable organization or sponsor, §131F-16, (g).
Fund-raising consultants, §131F-15, (d).
Children and minors.
Artistic and creative services and talent agency contracts, §§48A-11 to 48A-18.
Applicability of article, §48A-11.
Artistic or creative services defined, §48A-11.
Disaffirmance during minority prohibited.
Contract approved by superior court, §48A-12, (a).
Documents to be provided to other party, §48A-13.
Earnings set aside in trust.
Contracts approved by court.
Change in facts, notice, §48A-14, (h).
Continuing jurisdiction over trust established, §48A-14, (g).
Deposit or disbursement of funds by employer, §48A-14, (d) to (f).
Percentage required to be set aside, §48A-14, (a).
Trustee, appointment, §48A-14, (b).
Trustee's statement, providing employer, §48A-14, (c).
Contracts not approved by court.
Amendment or termination, §48A-15, (e).
Change in facts, notice, §48A-15, (f).
Deposit or disbursement by employer, §48A-15, (c), (d).
Fiduciary relationship, parent or guardian, §48A-15, (g).
Gross earnings defined, §48A-15, (h).
Percentage of earning set aside, §48A-15, (a).
Trustee, appointment, §48A-15, (b).
Establishment of trust, §48A-16, (a).
Financial institutions, establishing with, §48A-16, (d).
Methods of handling by trustee, §48A-16, (e).
Withdrawals, restrictions, §48A-16, (b).
Written statement by trustee, §48A-16, (c).
Guardian ad litem during proceeding, §48A-12, (d).
Superior court approval of contracts, §48A-12, (a) to (d).
Talent agency contracts, §48A-18.
Deposit accounts.
Banks operating in name of minor, §53-43.5, (a).
Emancipation of juvenile.
Right to contract as adult, §7B-3507.
Safe deposit boxes.
Banks leasing or renting to minors, §53-43.5, (b), (c).
Commercial code.
Leases, §§25-2A-101 to 25-2A-532.
See LEASES, UCC.

CONTRACTS —Cont'd
Commercial code —Cont'd
Secured transactions.
General provisions, §§25-9-101 to 25-9-710.
See SECURED TRANSACTIONS.
Condominiums.
Conveyance or encumbrance of common elements, §47C-3-112, (c).
Constitution of North Carolina.
State, political subdivisions or public corporations may make contracts, Const. N. C., art. V, §2.
Constitution of the United States.
Impairment of obligations of contracts, Const. U. S., art. I, §10.
Construction and interpretation.
Power of court to construe when declaratory judgment preceding, §1-254.
Continuity of contracts.
European monetary union, §§53-295 to 53-300.
See EUROPEAN MONETARY UNION.
Cooperative agreements among physicians or between physician, hospital or others.
Contract law to govern disputes among parties, §90-21.36, (c).
County water and sewer districts.
Validation of certain contracts, §162A-94.
Criminal justice education and training standards.
Power of commission to enter into contracts, §17C-6.
Custodial trusts.
Liability to third persons, §33B-12.
Diversion contract with delinquent or undisciplined juvenile and parent, guardian or custodian, §7B-1706.
Electronic transactions.
General provisions, §§66-311 to 66-330.
See ELECTRONIC TRANSACTIONS.
Emancipation of juvenile.
Right to contract as adult, §7B-3507.
Energy conservation finance act.
Financing contract.
See ENERGY CONSERVATION FINANCE ACT.
Executors and administrators.
Sale of real property.
Death of vendor under contract.
Delivery of deed by executor, §28A-17-9.
Facility authorities.
Conflicts of interest.
Disclosure to authority, §160A-480.3, (g).
Construction contracts, §160A-480.6.
Investment of bonds, §160A-480.8, (k).
Powers of authority, §160A-480.4.
False pretenses and cheats.
Advance payments under promise to work and pay for same, §14-104.
Nonfulfillment of contract obligation, §14-100.
Financing contract indebtedness.
State capital facilities finance act.
Special indebtedness generally, §§142-80 to 142-101.
See CAPITAL FACILITIES FINANCE ACT.
Funeral contracts.
Preneed funeral contracts and funds generally, §§90-210.60 to 90-210.73.
See PRENEED FUNERAL CONTRACTS AND FUNDS.
Futures contracts, §§16-3 to 16-6.
Gaming and betting contracts, §§16-1, 16-2.

CONTRACTS —Cont'd
Guardian ad litem appointed for unborn persons.
In rem and quasi in rem actions involving construction of contracts, §1A-1, Rule 17, (b).
Guardian's powers in administering incompetent's estate, §35A-1251.
Health and human services department.
Nursing home medication error quality initiative.
Public or private contracting entities, §131E-128.5, (a), (b).
Husband and wife.
Antenuptial agreements, §§52B-1 to 52B-11.
See ANTENUPTIAL AGREEMENTS AND CONTRACTS.
Validation of contract executed by married women without private examination.
Contracts executed prior to Feb. 7, 1945, §39-13.1, (b).
Contracts executed since Nov. 7, 1944, §39-13.1, (a).
Improvement to real property defective or unsafe.
Limitation of action for breach of contract, §1-50, (a).
Industrial commission managed care organizations, I.C. Managed Care Orgs. R. VI.
Insurance policies or contracts.
Accident and health insurance.
See ACCIDENT AND HEALTH INSURANCE.
Credit insurance.
See CREDIT INSURANCE.
Fire insurance.
See FIRE INSURANCE.
Generally.
See INSURANCE POLICIES OR CONTRACTS.
Life insurance.
See LIFE INSURANCE.
Medicare, §58-54-10.
Motor vehicle insurance.
See MOTOR VEHICLE INSURANCE.
Interests.
Rates and fees, §24-1.1.
International commercial arbitration.
Severability of arbitration laws, §1-567.46, (a).
Joint contracts of partners in trade or others.
Persons jointly liable, §1-72.
Leases.
Residential rental agreements, §§42-38 to 42-46.
See LANDLORD AND TENANT.
Leases, UCC, §§25-2A-101 to 25-2A-532.
See LEASES, UCC.
Letters of credit.
Issuer not responsible for underlying contracts, §25-5-108, (f).
Rights and obligations independent of underlying contract, §25-5-103, (d).
Location and recovery of abandoned property.
Agreement by owner, §116B-78.
Mechanical breakdown service agreements, §58-1-42.
Missing persons.
Receivers.
Operation and management of business, §28C-8.
Money transmitters.
Delegates, §53-208.19.
Motor vehicle registration, registration plates and certificates of title.
Division contracts, §20-63, (h), (h1).
Municipal corporations.
See MUNICIPAL CORPORATIONS.

CONTRACTS —Cont'd
Municipal service districts.
Provision of services, etc., §160A-536, (d).
New or continuing contract.
Running of statute of limitations.
Writing required, §1-26.
Planned community act.
Tort and contract liability.
Association and lot owners, §47F-3-111.
Premarital agreements generally, §§52B-1 to 52B-11.
See ANTENUPTIAL AGREEMENTS AND CONTRACTS.
Preneed funeral contracts and funds, §§90-210.60 to 90-210.73.
See PRENEED FUNERAL CONTRACTS AND FUNDS.
Principals of schools.
Method of employment generally, §115C-287.1.
Prisons and prisoners.
See PRISONS AND PRISONERS.
Private personnel services.
Commission-based compensation.
Anticipated earnings included in written job order, §95-47.4, (h).
Defined, §95-47.1.
Filing of copy with commissioner.
License applicant to file, §95-47.3, (b).
Forms.
Filing with commissioner, §95-47.4, (c).
Opportunity for applicant to read contract, §95-47.4, (d).
Records of executed contracts, §95-47.5.
Refund policy.
Statements as to, §95-47.4, (f), (g).
Requirements, §95-47.4, (a), (b), (e) to (g).
Written contracts required, §95-47.4.
Professional employer organizations.
PEO agreement, §§58-89A-95, 58-89A-100.
Interpretation for insurance, bonding and employer's liability purposes, §58-89A-112.
Public contracts.
Generally, §§143-128 to 143-135.9.
See PUBLIC CONTRACTS.
Punitive damages.
Breach of contract, §1D-15, (d).
Railroads.
Municipal corporations.
Contracts allocating financial responsibility, §160A-326.
Rates and fees, §24-1.1.
Real property.
Subordination agreements, §39-6.6.
Regional public transportation authority.
Contracts allocating financial responsibility, §160A-626, (b).
Reverse mortgages.
Contracts for shared appreciation or shared value, §53-270.1.
Sales, §§25-2-101 to 25-2-725.
See SALE OF GOODS, UCC.
Seafood industrial park authority.
Building contracts, §113-315.36, (a).
Department of administration.
Services available to authority, §113-315.36, (b).
Self-service storage rental contracts, §§66-305 to 66-307.
Service agreement companies, §§58-1-25 to 58-1-42.

CONTRACTS —Cont'd
Sports agents.
Agency contracts generally, §§78C-85 to 78C-105.
See ATHLETE AGENTS.
State capital facilities finance act.
Special indebtedness generally, §§142-80 to 142-101.
See CAPITAL FACILITIES FINANCE ACT.
State veterans home.
Operation and management of homes may be contracted, §165-50.
Supervisors of schools.
Method of employing administrators generally, §115C-287.1.
Talent agency contracts.
Minors, §§48A-17, 48A-18.
Toner or inkjets.
Agreement prohibiting reusing, remanufacturing or refilling.
Void and unenforceable, §75-36.
Transfers to minors.
Liability for claims based on contracts entered into by custodian, §33A-17.
Turnpike authority.
See TURNPIKE AUTHORITY.
Unborn persons.
Guardian ad litem appointed in in rem and quasi in rem actions involving construction, §1A-1, Rule 17, (b).
Unclaimed property act.
Agreement by owner to locate, deliver or recover, §116B-78.
Viatical life insurance settlements.
Commissioner's approval, §58-58-220.
Rescission, §58-58-250, (h).

CONTRACTS AGAINST PUBLIC POLICY.
Construction indemnity agreements, §22B-1.
Forum selection provisions, §22B-3.
Improving real property.
Provisions making contract subject to laws of another state, §22B-2.
Waiving jury trial, §22B-10.

CONTRIBUTING TO DELINQUENCY OF MINORS, §14-316.1.

CONTRIBUTION AMONG JOINT TORT-FEASORS, §§1B-1 to 1B-7.
Actions.
Enforcement, §1B-3, (a) to (c).
Alcoholic beverage sales to underage persons, compensation for injury.
Joint and several liability, §18B-124.
Citation of provisions, §1B-6.
Title of act, §1B-6.
Compromise and settlement.
Right to contribution, §1B-1, (d).
Construction and interpretation, §1B-5.
Covenant not to sue.
Effect, §1B-4.
Enforcement, §1B-3, (a) to (c).
Fiduciaries.
Provisions not to apply to breaches of trust or other fiduciary obligations, §1B-1, (g).
Improvement to real property defective or unsafe.
Limitation of action for contributions, §1-50, (a).
Indemnification.
Right of indemnity not impaired, §1B-1, (f).
Insurance.
Rights of liability insurer, §1B-1, (e).

CONTRIBUTION AMONG JOINT TORT-FEASORS —Cont'd
Intentional tort-feasors.
No right of contribution in favor of, §1B-1, (c).
Judgment against joint obligors or joint tort-feasors, §1B-7.
Preserved, §1B-7, (b).
Judgment against other judgment defendants.
Motion for, enforcement by, §1B-3, (b).
Liability to claimant.
Judgment of court binding, §1B-3, (f).
Recovery against one tort-feasor does not discharge others, §1B-3, (e).
Liens.
Joint obligors or joint tort-feasors.
Lien of judgment preserved, §1B-7, (b).
Limitation of actions.
Enforcement of right, §1B-3, (c), (d).
Nonprofit corporations.
Unlawful loans or distributions by directors, §55A-8-33, (d).
Pro rata shares, §§1B-2, 1B-7, (a).
Disagreement as to, §1B-7, (c).
Railroads.
Applicability of provisions to employees, §1B-1, (i).
Release, §1B-4.
Right to contribution, §1B-1, (a).
Limitation on amount of recovery, §1B-1, (b).
Separate action.
Enforcement by, §1B-3, (a), (c).
Settlement with claimant.
Rights of tort-feasors who enter into, §1B-1, (d).
Shares, pro rata, §§1B-2, 1B-7, (a).
Disagreements as to, §1B-7, (c).
State of North Carolina.
Applicability of provisions to tort claims against state, §1B-1, (h).
Suretyship.
Contribution among sureties, §26-5.
Uniformity of interpretation, §1B-5.

CONTRIBUTIONS AMONG SURETIES, §26-5.

CONTRIBUTIONS AND EXPENDITURES IN POLITICAL CAMPAIGNS, §§163-278.5 to 163-278.40.
See CAMPAIGN CONTRIBUTIONS AND EXPENDITURES.

CONTRIBUTION SOLICITATION BY CHARITIES, §§131F-1 to 131F-24.
See CHARITABLE SOLICITATION.

CONTRIBUTORY NEGLIGENCE.
Bank deposits and collections.
Unauthorized signature or alteration, §25-4-406, (c), (d).
Burden of proof, §1-139.
Claims against state departments and agencies.
Doctrine a matter of defense, §143-299.1.
Controlled substances.
Employing or intentionally using minor to commit drug law violations, §90-95.5.
Failure of motorist to stop vehicle within radius of headlights or range of vision, §20-141, (n).
Failure to yield right of way at yield right of way signs, §20-158.1.
Motorcycle or moped overcrowded or operator and passengers without helmets, §20-140.4, (b).

CONTRIBUTORY NEGLIGENCE —Cont'd
Motorcycles.
Rearview mirror requirement, §20-126, (c).
Products liability.
Injured parties knowledge or lack of reasonable care, §99B-4.
Reply to answer alleging last clear chance, §1A-1, Rule 7, (a).

CONTROL CORNERS IN REAL ESTATE DEVELOPMENTS, §§39-32.1 to 39-32.4.
See SUBDIVISIONS.

CONTROLLED ACCESS HIGHWAYS/FACILITIES.
See STREETS AND HIGHWAYS.

CONTROLLED FOREST FIRE.
Prescribed burning of forestland, §§113-60.40 to 113-60.45.

CONTROLLED SUBSTANCE ANALOGUE.
Defined, §90-87.
Treated as schedule I substance, §90-89.1.

CONTROLLED SUBSTANCES, §§90-86 to 90-113.8.
Additional nature of penalties, §90-97.
Administrative proceedings.
Pending proceedings, §90-113.7, (c).
Alcoholic beverage permittees.
Certain conduct unlawful on premises, §18B-1005, (a).
Amphetamines trafficking, §90-95, (h).
Amusement device operators.
Operating device equipment under the influence.
Prohibition, §95-111.11, (b).
Anabolic steroids, §90-91.
Appeals.
Judicial review of drug commission, §90-113.2.
Applicability of provisions, §90-113.7, (d).
Attempts to commit crime, §90-98.
Bail and recognizance.
Conditions of pretrial release.
Presumptions concerning conditions in controlled substance cases, §15A-533, (d).
Board of pharmacy.
Enforcement of provisions, §90-113.5.
Buprenorphine for treatment of opiate dependence.
Physicians prescribing or dispensing, §90-101, (a1).
Burden of proof.
Exemptions or exceptions, §90-113.1, (a).
Registration or order form, §90-113.1, (b).
Charities.
Furnishing substances to inmates of charitable institutions, §14-258.1, (a).
Citation of act.
Short title, §90-86.
Commercial detection services.
Drug detection dogs utilized by service.
Certification of dogs, §90-102.1, (h).
Confidentiality of client records, exception, §90-102.1, (h).
Disclosure of dog alert or discovery of controlled substances, §90-102.1, (h).
Commission.
Defined, §90-87.
Judicial review, §90-113.2.
Power to add, delete or reschedule substances, §90-88, (a) to (d).
Rules and regulations, §90-100.

CONTROLLED SUBSTANCES —Cont'd
Conditions of prescribed punishments and degree of offenses, §90-95, (e).
Confidentiality of information.
Research, §90-113.3, (e).
Conspiracy.
Trafficking in certain drugs, §90-95, (i).
Violations of provisions, §90-98.
Continuing criminal enterprise.
Electronic surveillance orders, §15A-290, (a1).
Felony, §90-95.1, (a).
Forfeitures, §90-95.1, (b).
Grand juries.
Examination of witnesses by prosecutor, §15A-623, (h).
Petition for convening, §15A-622, (h).
What constitutes, §90-95.1, (c).
Controlled substance analogue.
Defined, §90-87.
Treated as schedule I substance, §90-89.1.
Counterfeit substances.
Defined, §90-87.
Prohibited acts, §90-95, (a).
Penalties, §90-95, (c).
Counties.
Confinement facilities.
Furnishing controlled substances to inmates, §14-258.1, (a).
Death from use.
Distributor liability, §14-17.
Decontamination of property used for manufacture of methamphetamine, §130A-284.
Defenses.
Employing or intentionally using minor to commit drug law violations, §§90-95.4, (c), 90-95.5.
Participating in a drug violation by a minor.
Mistake of age not a defense, §90-95.7, (b).
Promoting drug sales by a minor.
Mistake of age not a defense, §90-95.6, (b).
Definitions, §90-87.
Law enforcement agencies, §90-95.2, (b).
Depressants.
Schedule I, §90-89.
Schedule II, §90-90.
Exemption of compounds, mixtures or preparations, §90-92, (b).
Schedule IV, §90-92, (a).
Dispensing.
Date of dispensing.
Entry on face of prescription, §90-106, (h).
Defined, §90-87.
Prescriptions.
Generally. See within this heading, "Prescriptions."
Prohibited acts, §90-108, (a).
Registration of manufacturers, distributors and dispensers, §§90-101 to 90-104.
Schedule V, §90-106, (d).
Schedule VI, §90-106, (e).
Distribution.
Definition of "distribute," §90-87.
Order forms, §90-105.
Inspection, §90-107.
Prohibited acts, §90-108, (a).
Registration of manufacturers, distributors and dispensers, §§90-101 to 90-104.
Samples, §90-106, (i).
Drug detection dog handlers.
Acquisition of controlled substances for training purposes, §90-102.1, (e).
Record keeping and inventory maintenance, §90-102.1, (f).

CONTROLLED SUBSTANCES —Cont'd
Drug detection dog handlers —Cont'd
Criminal record check, §90-102.1, (d).
Definitions, §90-102.1, (a).
Disclosure of dog alert or discovery of controlled substances.
Notifying and informing law enforcement, §90-102.1, (g).
Disclosure of requirement in contracts, §90-102.1, (i).
Dog alert or finding controlled substances.
Notifying and informing law enforcement, §90-102.1, (g).
Disclosure of requirement in contracts, §90-102.1, (i).
Inapplicability to law enforcement agencies, §90-102.1, (k).
Investigation of complaints, §90-102.1, (j).
Registration, §90-102.1, (b).
Criminal record check, §90-102.1, (d).
Denial, suspension or revocation, §90-102.1, (j).
Prerequisites, §90-102.1, (c).
Drug detection dogs.
Certification of dogs utilized by commercial detection services, §90-102.1, (h).
Drug education schools, §90-96.01, (a).
Fees, §90-96.01, (a).
Failure to pay, §90-96.01, (b).
Drug treatment courts, §§7A-790 to 7A-801.
See DRUG TREATMENT COURTS.
Educational activities contracts, §90-113.3, (b).
Educational programs to prevent and deter misuse and abuse, §90-113.3, (a).
Embezzlement, §90-108, (a).
Employee examination and screening for controlled substances, §§95-230 to 95-235.
Employing or intentionally using minor to commit drug law violations, §90-95.4, (a), (b).
Enforcement of provisions, §90-113.5.
Advance of funds by state treasurer for, §90-113.6, (c).
Cooperative arrangements, §90-111.
No liability on authorized officers, §90-113.1, (c).
Evidence.
Chain of custody, §90-95, (g1).
Reports of analysis, §90-95, (g).
Exemptions and exclusions from provisions, §90-88, (e) to (g).
List, §90-88, (i).
Schedule III, §90-91.
Schedule IV, §90-92.
First offenders.
Conditional discharge, §90-96, (a), (a1), (e).
Superior courts to file names of persons granted conditional discharge, §90-96, (c).
Expunction of records, §90-96, (b), (d), (f).
Food stamp program.
Eligibility of individual convicted of felony offense to participate in, §108A-25.2.
Forfeiture of property.
Contraband, §90-112, (e).
Conveyances subject to forfeiture, §90-112, (f).
Custody, §90-112, (c).
Disposition of property, §90-112, (c), (d).
Manner of forfeitures, §90-112, (f).
Money, §90-112, (a), (d1).
Pending proceedings not affected, §90-113.7, (b).
Process, §90-112, (b).
When seizure without process authorized, §90-112, (b).

CONTROLLED SUBSTANCES —Cont'd
Forfeiture of property —Cont'd
Property subject to forfeiture, §90-112, (a).
Release, §90-112, (c).
Remission or mitigation of forfeitures, §90-112.1.
Joint claims, §90-112.1, (c).
Jurisdiction of courts, §90-112.1, (a).
Proof required, §90-112.1, (b).
Vehicles held for purpose of evidence, §90-112.1, (d).
Forgery.
Acquiring or obtaining possession by, §90-108, (a).
Fraud.
Prohibited acts, §90-108, (a).
Grand juries.
Examination of witnesses by prosecutor, §15A-623, (h).
Petition for convening, §15A-622, (h).
Hallucinogenic substances.
Schedule I, §90-89.
Schedule II, §90-90.
Heroin trafficking, §90-95, (h).
Conspiracy, §90-95, (i).
Penalties, §90-95, (h).
Immediate precursor.
Defined, §90-87.
Impaired driving generally.
See IMPAIRED DRIVING.
Injunctions.
Jurisdiction of superior court, §90-110, (a).
Violations of injunctions.
Trial, §90-110, (b).
Inspections, §90-107.
Intentionally committed prohibited acts, §90-108, (b).
Isomer.
Defined, §90-87.
Justice department.
Enforcement of provisions, §90-113.5.
Purchase of controlled substances.
Reimbursement, §90-113.6, (b).
Ketamine.
Schedule III controlled substances, §90-91, (m).
Lab cleanup costs.
Restitution to law enforcement agencies, §90-95.3, (c).
Labels.
Requirements, §90-106, (f).
Law enforcement agencies.
Cooperation between, §90-95.2, (a).
Jurisdiction or authority not reduced, §90-95.2, (c).
Definitions, §90-95.2, (b).
Restitution for illegal lab cleanup costs, §90-95.3, (c).
Undercover purchases.
Restitution to law enforcement agencies, §90-95.3, (a).
Licenses.
Nonprofessional treatment.
Required, §90-109.
Lists.
Schedule I, §90-89.
Schedule II, §90-90.
Schedule III, §90-91.
Schedule IV, §90-92.
Schedule V, §90-93.
Schedule VI, §90-94.
Manufacture.
Defined, §90-87.

CONTROLLED SUBSTANCES —Cont'd
Manufacture —Cont'd
Enhanced sentencing in certain cases, §15A-1340.16D.
Penalties, §90-95, (b).
Prohibited acts, §§90-95, (a), 90-108, (a).
Registration of manufacturers, distributors and dispensers, §§90-101 to 90-104.
Marijuana.
Conspiracy, §90-95, (i).
Defined, §90-87.
Schedule VI, §90-94.
Trafficking in, §90-95, (h).
MDA/MDMA trafficking, §90-95, (h).
Mentally ill.
Furnishing substances to inmates of mental institutions, §14-258.1, (a).
Methamphetamine.
Manufacture.
Committed in area where minors live, are present or are otherwise endangered.
Aggravating factors in sentencing, §15A-1340.16, (d).
Decontamination of property used for manufacture of drug, §130A-284.
Serious injury inflicted upon law enforcement or emergency personnel.
Enhanced sentencing, §15A-1340.16D.
Precursor chemicals.
Possession or distribution with intent to manufacture, §90-95, (d1).
List of chemicals to which subsection applies, §90-95, (d2).
Trafficking, §90-95, (h).
Methamphetamine watch program.
Immunity from civil and criminal liability.
Good faith actions, §114-43.
Minors.
Employing or intentionally using minor to commit drug law violations, §90-95.4, (a), (b).
Civil liability, §90-95.5.
Definition of "minor," §90-95.4, (d).
Mistake of age, §90-95.4, (c).
Expunction of records, §90-96, (b), (d).
Immunity from prosecutions, §90-96.1.
Participating in a drug violation by a minor, §90-95.7, (a), (c).
Mistake of age not a defense, §90-95.7, (b).
Promoting drug sales by a minor, §90-95.6, (a), (c).
Mistake of age not a defense, §90-95.6, (b).
Treatment for abuse of controlled substances or alcohol.
Abuse of controlled substances.
Consent of minor to treatment sufficient, §90-21.5, (a).
Misrepresentation.
Acquiring or obtaining possession by, §90-108, (a).
Motor vehicles.
Forfeiture of conveyances used in violations of provisions.
Generally, §§90-112, 90-112.1.
Municipal corporations.
Confinement facilities.
Furnishing controlled substances to inmates, §14-258.1.
Murder in the second degree, §14-17.
Narcotic drugs.
Defined, §90-87.
Schedule III, §90-91.
Schedule IV, §90-92, (a).
Schedule V, §90-93.

CONTROLLED SUBSTANCES —Cont'd
Nonprofessional treatment.
Licenses.
Required, §90-109.
Non-use as probation condition, §15A-1343, (b1).
Nuisances.
Abatement of offenses against public morals, §§19-1 to 19-8.3.
See NUISANCES.
Opiates.
Defined, §90-87.
Schedule I, §90-89.
Schedule II, §90-90.
Opium.
Schedule II, §90-90.
Opium derivatives.
Schedule I, §90-89.
Opium trafficking, §90-95, (h).
Conspiracy, §90-95, (i).
Penalties, §90-95, (h).
Order forms, §90-105.
Inspection, §90-107.
Participating in a drug violation by a minor, §90-95.7, (a), (c).
Mistake of age not a defense, §90-95.7, (b).
Peace officers.
Enforcement of provisions, §90-113.5.
Possession.
Penalties, §90-95, (d).
Prohibited, §90-95, (a).
Post-release supervision.
Controlling conditions, nonuse, §15A-1364.4, (e).
Practitioners.
Defined, §90-87.
Treatment and rehabilitation services.
Confidentiality of information, §90-109.1, (a).
Examination and evaluation by practitioner, §90-109.1, (b).
Reports, §90-109.1, (c).
Precursor chemicals.
Designation, §90-95, (d2).
Possession or distribution with intent to manufacture controlled substance or methamphetamine.
Penalties, §90-95, (d1), (d1a).
Prescriptions.
Copies.
Marking, §90-106, (g).
Defined, §90-87.
Inspection, §90-107.
Prohibited acts, §90-108, (a).
Schedule II, §90-106, (a).
Oral prescriptions, §90-106, (b).
Schedules III and IV, §90-106, (c).
Prisons and prisoners.
Furnishing substances to inmates, §14-258.1, (a).
Probation.
Conditional discharge on first offense, §90-96, (a), (a1), (e).
Drug alcohol recovery treatment program as condition.
Screening and assessing for chemical dependency, §15A-1343, (b3).
Non-use as condition, §15A-1343, (b1).
Prohibited acts generally, §90-108.
Public schools.
Discipline of students.
Driving eligibility certificate.
Effect of disciplinary action for enumerated student conduct, §20-11, (n1).

CONTROLLED SUBSTANCES —Cont'd
Records.
Registration of manufacturers, distributors and dispensers.
Records of registrants, §90-104.
Registration of manufacturers, distributors and dispensers.
Buprenorphine for treatment of opiate dependence.
Physicians prescribing or dispensing, §90-101, (a1).
Drug detection dog handlers, §90-102.1, (b) to (d).
Persons initially permitted to register, §90-102, (e).
Places of business.
Inspection, §90-101, (f).
Separate registration required at each principal place of business, §90-101, (e).
Privileges of registrants, §90-101, (b), (g).
Restrictions, §90-102, (b).
Public interest.
Determination.
Factors considered, §90-102, (a).
Records of registrants, §90-104.
Required, §90-101, (a).
Exceptions, §90-101, (c), (i).
Waiver of requirement by commission, §90-101, (d).
Research, §90-102, (c), (d).
Revocation or suspension.
Disposition of controlled substances possessed by registrant, §90-103, (e).
Grounds, §90-103, (a).
Imminent danger to public health or safety, §90-103, (d).
Notice of orders to bureau, §90-103, (f).
Order to show cause why registration should not be revoked or suspended, §90-103, (c).
Powers of commission, §90-103, (a), (b).
Research.
Authorization for possession and distribution of controlled substances, §90-113.3, (f).
Confidentiality of information, §90-113.3, (e).
Contracts for research activities, §90-113.3, (d).
Powers of department of health and human services, §90-113.3, (c).
Registration, §90-102, (c), (d).
Rules and regulations, §90-100.
Continuation of regulations, §90-113.8.
Sales.
Paregoric, U.S.P., §90-91.
Penalties, §90-95, (b).
Prohibited, §90-95, (a).
Samples.
Distribution, §90-106, (i).
Schedule I, §90-89.
Controlled substance analogue treated as, §90-89.1.
Schedule II, §90-90.
Prescriptions, §90-106, (a), (b).
Schedule III, §90-91.
Dispensing or distributing, §90-106, (c).
Schedule IV, §90-92.
Dispensing or distributing, §90-106, (c).
Schedule V, §90-93.
Dispensing or distributing, §90-106, (d).
Schedules, §90-94.
Dispensing or distributing, §90-106, (e).
Republishing, §90-99.

CONTROLLED SUBSTANCES —Cont'd
Schools.
Discipline of students.
Driving eligibility certificate.
Effect of disciplinary action for enumerated student conduct, §20-11, (n1).
Sentencing.
Conditions governing prescribed punishments and degree of offenses, §90-95, (e).
Trafficking in certain drugs, §90-95, (h).
Speedy disposition of offenders.
County appropriations for programs to protect the public, §153A-212.1.
State departments and agencies.
Cooperative arrangements, §90-111.
Steroids.
Anabolic steroids.
Schedule III, §90-91.
Stimulants.
Schedule I, §90-89.
Schedule II, §90-90.
Schedule IV, §90-92, (b).
Exempt compounds, mixtures or preparations, §90-92, (b).
Structures or vehicles.
Knowingly keeping or maintaining places resorted to by persons using, §90-108, (a).
Substance abuse professionals, §§90-113.30 to 90-113.46.
See SUBSTANCE ABUSE PROFESSIONALS.
Tax, §§105-113.105 to 105-113.113.
See UNAUTHORIZED SUBSTANCES TAXES.
Title of act.
Short title, §90-86.
Trademarks, trade names or identification marks.
Making, distributing, etc., thing designed to print, imprint or reproduce, §90-108, (a).
Trafficking in certain drugs, §90-95, (h).
Conspiracy, §90-95, (i).
Electronic surveillance orders, §15A-290, (a1).
Unauthorized substances taxes, §§105-113.105 to 105-113.113.
See UNAUTHORIZED SUBSTANCES TAXES.
Undercover purchases.
Restitution to law enforcement agencies, §90-95.3, (a).
Work first program.
Eligibility of individual convicted of felony offense to participate in, §108A-25.2.

CONTROL OF JUVENILE BY PARENTS, §§7B-3400 to 7B-3404.

CONTROL SHARE ACQUISITIONS.
Business combinations, §§75E-1 to 75E-9.
See BUSINESS COMBINATIONS.
Generally, §§55-9A-01 to 55-9A-09.
See CORPORATIONS.

CONVENIENCE STORE ALCOHOLIC BEVERAGE PERMITS.
Food business defined to include, §18B-1000.
Off-premises fortified wine permit.
Kind of permit that may be issued, §18B-1001.
Off-premises malt beverage permit.
Kind of permit that may be issued, §18B-1001.
On-premises malt beverage permit.
Kind of permit that may be issued, §18B-1001.

CONVENTION CENTERS.
Alcoholic beverage permits.
Defined, §18B-1000.

CONVENTION CENTERS —Cont'd
Alcoholic beverage permits —Cont'd
Mixed beverage permit.
Kind of permit that may be issued, §18B-1001.
On-premises fortified wine permit.
Kind of permit that may be issued, §18B-1001.
On-premises malt beverage permit.
Kind of permit that may be issued, §18B-1001.
On-premises unfortified wine permit.
Kind of permit that may be issued, §18B-1001.
Qualifications for permit, §18B-900, (e).
Municipal corporations.
Power to establish and support, §160A-489.

CONVENTIONS.
Centers.
See CONVENTION CENTERS.
Winery special event authorization, §18B-1114.1.

CONVENTS.
Property tax exemption, §105-278.6.

CONVERSION.
Arrest in civil cases, §1-410.
Bailments, §14-168.1.
District courts.
Small claim actions.
Form of complaint for conversion, §7A-232.
Leaf tobacco sales in auction tobacco warehouses.
Limitation of actions, §1-55.
Limitation of actions, §1-52.
Tobacco, §1-55.
Militia.
Care of military property.
Unlawful conversion or willful destruction of military property, §127A-131.
Preneed funeral contracts and funds, §90-210.70, (a), (c).
Streets and highways.
State highway fund.
Funds and property converted to state highway fund, §136-16.

CONVEYANCES.
Acknowledgments.
Certification of correctness.
Failure of register of deeds to certify.
Validation of registration, §47-50.1.
Defective acknowledgment on old instruments validated, §47-52.
Aliens.
Right to convey real property, §64-1.
Armories.
Counties and municipalities may lease, convey or acquire property for use as armory, §127A-165.
Prior conveyances validated, §127A-166.
Validation of prior conveyances, §127A-166.
Assignments.
Real property pledged as security, §47-17.2.
Attornment.
Unnecessary on conveyance of reversions, etc., §42-2.
Boundaries.
Use of word "adjoining" instead of words "bounded by," §39-2.
Burden of proof.
Fee presumed though word "heirs" omitted, §39-1.
Business trusts, §39-46.
Cemeteries, §65-69, (b), (c).

CONVEYANCES —Cont'd
Charities.
Authorized, §39-25.
Effect as to conveyances by trustees, §39-26.
Prior deeds validated, §39-27.
Children and minors.
Emancipation of juvenile.
Right to make conveyance as adult, §7B-3507.
Condominiums.
Common elements, §47C-3-112.
Construction and interpretation.
Court to give effect to intent of parties, §39-1.1, (a).
Fee presumed though word "heirs" omitted, §39-1.
Rule in Shelley's case.
Abolished, §41-6.3.
Section not to prevent application, §39-1.1, (b).
Use of word adjoining instead of words bounded by, §39-2.
Vagueness of description not to invalidate, §39-2.
Contaminated site.
Deed or other instrument of conveyance, contaminated property statement, §143B-279.10, (e).
Contingent limitations.
Failure of issue.
Limitations on failure, §41-4.
Contingent remainders.
Validation of transfer, §41-12.
Cooperative associations.
Authorized, §39-25.
Effect as to conveyances by trustees, §39-26.
Prior deeds validated, §39-27.
Coroners.
Official selling or empowered to sell property not in office, §39-5.
Corporations.
Corporate seal.
Required, §47-41.1.
Forms of probate for deeds and other conveyances, §47-41.01, (b), (c).
Contracts in writing for purchase of personal property, §47-41.02, (f).
Instrument executed by president or presiding member or trustee, §47-41.02, (b) to (d).
Other forms not excluded, §47-41.01, (a).
Validation of conveyances probated and recorded prior to February 14, 1939, §47-41.02, (e).
Validation of deeds and other conveyances executed on or before April 12, 1974, §47-41.02, (g).
Court to give effect to intent of parties in construing, §39-1.1, (a).
Covenants.
Grantees of reversion and assigns of lease have reciprocal rights under covenants, §42-8.
Standing seized to use.
Possession transferred to use in certain conveyances, §41-7.
Death.
Contingent limitations depending on death of person without heirs.
Limitations on failure of issue, §41-4.
Disclosure of death or illness of previous occupant, §39-50.
Defective acknowledgment validated, §47-52.
Descriptions.
Vagueness not to invalidate, §39-2.
Disclosures.
Death or illness of previous occupant, §39-50.
Registered sex offender living in area, §39-50.

CONVEYANCES —Cont'd
Diseases.
Disclosure of death or illness of previous occupant, §39-50.
Draftsman.
Designation of draftsman required on instrument in certain counties, §47-17.1.
Drainage districts, §156-114.
Emancipation of juvenile.
Right to make conveyance as adult, §7B-3507.
Eminent domain.
Private condemnors.
Change of ownership pending proceedings, §40A-33.
Excise stamp tax, §§105-228.28 to 105-228.37.
See EXCISE STAMP TAX ON CONVEYANCES.
Executors and administrators.
Contract for sale of real property by decedent.
Delivery of deed by personal representative, §28A-17-9.
Real property conveyed to personal representative, §28A-17-10.
Exempt property, §1C-1604, (a).
Failure of issue.
Limitations on failure, §41-4.
Fee simple.
Presumption of fee though word "heirs" omitted, §39-1.
Forgery.
Excise stamp tax.
Reproduction of tax stamps, §105-228.36.
Fraternal orders and societies.
Authorized, §39-25.
Effect as to conveyances by trustees, §39-26.
Prior deeds validated, §39-27.
Fraudulent transfers, §§39-23.1 to 39-23.12.
See FRAUDULENT TRANSFERS.
Future interests.
Inter vivos and testamentary conveyances of future interests permitted, §39-6.3, (a) to (c).
Revocation of conveyances to persons not in esse, §39-6.
Validation of deed, §39-6.1.
General services administration.
Conveyances by United States acting by and through general services administration, §47-108.14.
Good funds settlement act, §§45A-1 to 45A-7.
See GOOD FUNDS SETTLEMENT ACT.
Health care facility interests, §131A-8.
Hearsay exception.
Records or documents or statements in documents affecting interest in property, §8C-1, Rule 803.
Heirs.
Construed to be "children" in certain limitations, §41-6.
Fee presumed though word "heirs" omitted, §39-1.
Sale, lease or mortgage of real property, §28A-17-12.
Hospital authorities.
Lease, conveyance or transfers of property to authority, §131E-31, (a), (b).
Husband and wife.
Acknowledgments.
Absence of wife's acknowledgment does not affect deed as to husband, §39-9.
Different times and places, §39-8.
Acts barring property rights.
Conveyance of property by spouse not at fault, §31A-1, (d).

CONVEYANCES —Cont'd
Husband and wife —Cont'd
Conveyance by spouse to both spouses.
Tenants by the entirety, interest vested as, §39-13.3, (b).
Conveyance by spouse to other spouse.
Interest vested in grantee spouse, §39-13.3, (a).
Tenants by the entirety, dissolution of interest held as, §39-13.3, (c).
Deed of separation.
Conveyance by husband or wife under deed, §39-13.4.
G.S. 52-10 or 52-10.1.
Applicability of provisions to conveyances by spouses to spouses, §39-13.3, (e).
Instruments affecting married woman's title.
Validation of instruments not executed by husband, §39-7.1.
Joinder of spouse, §§39-7, (b), (c), 39-13.3, (d).
Joint execution.
Married persons under 18 made competent as to certain transactions, §39-13.2, (a), (b).
Minors.
Married persons under 18 made competent as to certain transactions, §39-13.2, (a).
Notaries.
Validation of certificates as to conveyances between husband and wife, §52-7.
Party to convey without joinder, §39-7, (b).
Purchase-money mortgages.
Spouse need not join, §39-13.
Title.
Validation of instruments not executed by husband, §39-7.1.
Validation of conveyance executed by married women without private examination.
Conveyances executed prior to Feb. 7, 1945, §39-13.1, (b).
Conveyances executed since Nov. 7, 1944, §39-13.1, (a).
Waiver of elective life estate.
Execution of conveyance, §39-7, (a), (c).
Infants.
Conveyances by infant trustees, §39-4.
Intent.
Court to give effect to intent of parties, §39-1.1.
Fee presumed though word "heirs" omitted, §39-1.
Judgments.
Directing party to execute conveyance, §1A-1, Rule 70.
Stay, §1-291.
Transfer of title.
Judgment regarded as deed of conveyance, §1-228.
Landlord and tenant.
Transfer of rental property.
Attornment by tenant unnecessary, §42-2.
Local development.
Authority of city or county to convey interest in real property.
Determinations arriving at consideration amount, §158-7.1, (d2).
Lost instruments and records.
Applicability of provisions, §98-18.
Court records.
Conveyances reciting court records.
Prima facie evidence of destroyed court records, §§98-16, 98-17.
Replacing lost official conveyances, §98-11.
Married women.
Registration of instruments not executed by wife, §39-9.

CONVEYANCES —Cont'd
Married women —Cont'd
Repeal of laws requiring private examination, §47-14.1.
Validation of conveyance executed by married women without private examination.
Conveyances executed prior to Feb. 7, 1945, §39-13.1, (b).
Conveyances executed since Nov. 7, 1944, §39-13.1, (a).
Validation of instruments not executed by husband, §39-7.1.
Minors.
Infant trustees, §39-4.
Mortgages and deeds of trust.
Validation of appointment of and conveyances to corporations as trustees, §45-21.
Next of kin, §41-6.1.
Notaries.
Husband and wife.
Validation of certificates of notaries as to conveyances between husband and wife, §52-7.
Partnerships.
Real property, §§59-38, (c), (d), 59-40.
Personal property.
Creation of interest or estate in, §39-6.2.
Planned community act.
Common elements, §47F-3-112.
Possession.
Transferred to use in certain conveyances, §41-7.
Power of sale, sales under, §§45-21.1 to 45-21.33.
See POWER OF SALE, SALES UNDER.
Presumptions and burden of proof.
Fee presumed though word "heirs" omitted, §39-1.
Probate generally.
See PROBATE.
Public lands, §§146-74 to 146-78.
Registration of instruments generally.
See REGISTRATION OF INSTRUMENTS.
Religious organizations.
Authorized, §39-25.
Effect as to conveyances as to trustees, §39-26.
Prior deeds validated, §39-27.
Remainders, reversions and executory interests.
Attornment unnecessary, §42-2.
Conveyances of future interests, §39-6.3, (a) to (c).
Grantees of reversion and assigns of lease have reciprocal rights under covenants, §42-8.
Validation of sales or mortgages, §41-12.
Renunciation of property or interest.
Bar to right to renounce property or interest, §31B-4, (a).
Revenue stamps.
Excise stamp tax, §§105-228.28 to 105-228.37.
Revocation of will by subsequent conveyance.
No revocation, §31-5.6.
Right of entry.
Inter vivos and testamentary conveyances of future interests, §39-6.3, (a) to (c).
Rule in Shelley's case.
Abolished, §41-6.3.
Section not to prevent application, §39-1.1, (b).
School districts.
Administrative units.
Enlargement of city administrative unit.
Conveyance of school property upon, §115C-509.
Seals and sealed instruments.
Probates omitting official seals, §47-53.

CONVEYANCES —Cont'd
Seals and sealed instruments —Cont'd
Real property interests.
Seal of signatory not necessary for valid conveyance, §39-6.5.
Sex offender registration.
Disclosure of registered sex offender in area not required, §39-50.
Shelley's case.
Abolished, §41-6.3.
Section not to prevent application of rule, §39-1.1, (b).
Sheriffs.
Death of sheriff.
Execution by successor in office, §39-5.
Official selling or empowered to sell not in office, §39-5.
Solid waste management.
Hazardous waste landfill facility.
Land used for facility conveyed to state, §130A-292.
Stamp tax, §§105-228.28 to 105-228.37.
See EXCISE STAMP TAX ON CONVEYANCES.
Statute of uses, §41-7.
Stays.
Appeals.
How judgment directing conveyance stayed, §1-291.
Subordination agreements.
Interest in real property, §39-6.6, (c).
Tax collectors.
Official selling or empowered to sell not in office, §39-5.
Tenants by the entirety.
Spouse conveying interest to other spouse.
Dissolution of interest held as, §39-13.3, (c).
Interest created by, §39-13.3, (b).
Title insurance.
Generally, §§58-26-1 to 58-27-15.
See TITLE INSURANCE.
Torrens system registration.
Method of transfer.
Conveyance of part of registered land, §43-32.
Register of deeds.
Duty of register upon part conveyance, §43-33.
Trusts and trustees.
Infant trustees, §39-4.
Survivorship among trustees, §41-3.
Unborn infants.
Taking by deed or writing, §41-5.
United States.
General services administration.
Conveyances by United States acting by and through general services administration, §47-108.14.
Real property.
Recordation of conveyances of land acquired, §104-4.
Use of word "adjoining" instead of words "bounded by," §39-2.
Vagueness of description.
Not to invalidate, §39-2.
Water and sewer authorities.
Political subdivisions and authority, §162A-14.
Wills.
General provisions, §§31-1 to 31-47.
See WILLS.
Inter vivos and testamentary conveyances of future interests, §39-6.3, (a) to (c).
No revocation by subsequent conveyance, §31-5.6.

CONVICTED FELON DISQUALIFICATIONS.
Alcoholic beverage permittees.
Certain employees prohibited, §18B-1003, (b).
Concealed handgun permit, §14-415.12, (b).
Executors and administrators.
Persons disqualified to serve, §28A-4-2.
Firearms possession, §14-415.1.
Physicians and surgeons.
Automatic revocation of license, §90-14, (c).
Voting, §163-55; Const. N. C., art. VI, §2.
Concealed handgun permit, §14-415.12, (b).

CONVICTION AND PJC.
Drivers' licenses.
Forwarding record to division, §20-24, (b).
Entry of PJC not considered entry of judgment, §15A-101.
Motor vehicles.
Convictions.
Third PJC filed in five-year period as conviction, §20-4.01.
Records of PJC's, §20-26, (a).

CONVICTION OF CRIME, IMPEACHMENT, §8C-1, Rule 609, (a).
Appeal, pendency, §8C-1, Rule 609, (e).
Juvenile adjudication, §8C-1, Rule 609, (d).
Pardon, effect, §8C-1, Rule 609, (c).
Time limit, §8C-1, Rule 609, (b).

CONVICT-MADE GOODS.
Sale prohibited, §14-346, (a), (b).

CONVICTS.
Discharge of insolvent prisoners.
Generally.
See DISCHARGE OF INSOLVENT PRISONERS.
Farming out convicts, §§148-66 to 148-70.
See PRISONER LABOR.
Generally.
See PRISONS AND PRISONERS.
Grievance procedure generally, §§148-118.1 to 148-118.9.
See PRISONER'S GRIEVANCE PROCEDURE.
Labor of prisoners generally, §§148-26 to 148-49.
See PRISONER LABOR.

COOKING SCHOOL ALCOHOLIC BEVERAGE PERMITS.
Culinary permit.
Kind of permit that may be issued, §18B-1001.
Defined, §18B-1000.
On-premises unfortified wine permit.
Kind of permit that may be issued, §18B-1001.
Restrictions on sales, §18B-1006, (g).

COOPERATIVE AGREEMENTS AMONG HOSPITALS.
Certificate of public advantage, §§131E-192.1 to 131E-192.13.
See HEALTH CARE FACILITIES.

COOPERATIVE AGREEMENTS AMONG PHYSICIANS OR BETWEEN PHYSICIANS, HOSPITAL OR OTHER PERSON, §§90-21.24 to 90-21.26.
Appeals.
Judicial action as to certificates of public advantage, §90-21.33.
Attorney general.
Authority, §90-21.35.
Copy of report submitted to attorney general, §90-21.32, (a).

COOPERATIVE AGREEMENTS AMONG PHYSICIANS OR BETWEEN PHYSICIANS, HOSPITAL OR OTHER PERSON —Cont'd
Attorney general —Cont'd
Defined, §90-21.25.
Objection to issuance of certificate of public advantage, §90-21.29.
Review after issuance of certificate of public advantage, §90-21.31.
Suit to authorize cancellation of certificate, §90-21.33, (c).
Authority of department of health and human services, §90-21.35.
Certificate of need, licensure or other regulatory requirements.
Physician or other persons not exempted from compliance, §90-21.36, (b).
Certificate of public advantage.
Application, §90-21.26, (b).
Fee, §90-21.34, (a).
Additional fee when consultants needed to complete review, §90-21.34, (b).
Review of department of health and human services, §90-21.27, (a).
Cancellation, suit by attorney general, §90-21.33, (c).
Conditions, §90-21.28.
Consultants needed to complete review of application.
Additional fee, §90-21.34, (b).
Determination of department of health and human services to issue certificate, §90-21.27, (b).
Evaluating potential benefits, considerations by department of health and human services, §90-21.27, (b).
Immunity from challenge or scrutiny under state antitrust laws, §90-21.36, (a).
Immunity from federal or state antitrust laws, §90-21.26, (a).
Issuance by department of health and human services, §90-21.28.
Judicial review of decisions.
Applicants or other person aggrieved by decision to issue or not issue, §90-21.33, (a).
Attorney general suit, §90-21.33, (c).
Party or other person aggrieved by decision to allow certificate to remain in effect or make changes, §90-21.33, (b).
Work product of attorney general not public record, §90-21.33, (b).
Objection by attorney general, §90-21.29.
Periodic reports during time certificate in effect, §90-21.32.
Public hearing by department of health and human services, §90-21.27, (a).
Recordkeeping by department of health and human services, §90-21.30.
Review after issuance of certificate, §90-21.31.
Revocation for failure to file periodic report or provide information, §90-21.32, (b).
Contract law to govern disputes among parties to agreement, §90-21.36, (c).
Definitions, §90-21.25.
Disputes among parties to cooperative agreement.
Governed by contract law, §90-21.36, (c).
Federal or state antitrust laws.
Certificate of public advantage, immunity, §90-21.26, (a).
Defined, §90-21.25.

COOPERATIVE AGREEMENTS AMONG PHYSICIANS OR BETWEEN PHYSICIANS, HOSPITAL OR OTHER PERSON —Cont'd
Fees for application for certificate and periodic reports, §90-21.34.
Findings of general assembly, §90-21.24.
Judicial review of decisions as to certificate of public advantage, §90-21.33.
Notice.
Objection by attorney general to issuance of certificate of public advantage, §90-21.29.
Notice of termination, §90-21.30.
Periodic reports during time certificate of public advantage in effect, §90-21.32.
Purposes of provisions, §90-21.24.
Recordkeeping by department of health and human services, §90-21.30.
Report during time certificate of public advantage in effect.
Contents, §90-21.32, (a).
Copy submitted to attorney general, §90-21.32, (a).
Failure to file report or provide information, §90-21.32, (b).
Fee for filings, §90-21.34, (a).
Review of department of health and human services, §90-21.32, (c).
Time for filing, §90-21.32, (a).
Termination.
Notice, §90-21.30.
Time for filing judicial action as to certificate of public advantage.
Applicant or other person aggrieved by decision to issue or not issue, §90-21.33, (a).
Party or other person aggrieved by decision to allow certificate to remain in effect or make changes, §90-21.33, (b).
Venue of suit by attorney general to cancel certificate of public advantage, §90-21.33, (c).

COOPERATIVE ASSOCIATIONS, §§54-111 to 54-129.
Agriculture.
Authorized purposes, §§54-111, 54-124.
Apportionment of earnings, §54-126.
Time of allocation, §54-127.
Articles of incorporation, §54-113.
Amendments, §54-125.
Fee for filing, §54-115.
Filing with secretary of state, §54-114.
Fee, §54-115.
Boards of directors, §54-123.
Businesses authorized, §§54-111, 54-124.
Bylaws, §54-116.
Conveyances.
Authorized, §39-25.
Effect as to conveyances by trustees, §39-26.
Prior deeds validated, §39-27.
Dairy products.
Authorized purposes, §§54-111, 54-124.
Deeds.
Prior deeds validated, §39-27.
Dividends, §54-126.
Time for, §54-127.
Duties, §§54-124 to 54-128.
Electricity.
Authorized purposes, §§54-111, 54-124.
Fees.
Incorporation, §54-115.

COOPERATIVE ASSOCIATIONS —Cont'd
Forests and forestry.
Authorized purposes, §§54-111, 54-124.
Franchise tax, §54-118.2.
Exemptions from provisions, §105-125, (a).
General corporation law.
Applicability, §54-117.
General nonprofit corporation law.
Applicability, §54-117.
Housing.
Authorized purposes, §§54-111, 54-124.
Incorporation.
Admission of other corporations, §54-118.
Articles of incorporation, §54-113.
Amendments, §54-125.
Fee for filing, §54-115.
Filing with secretary of state, §54-114.
Fee, §54-115.
Authorized, §54-111.
Certificate of incorporation, §54-114.
Fees, §54-115.
Number of incorporators, §54-111.
Injunctions.
Unauthorized use of term "mutual" in name.
Violators may be enjoined from doing business, §54-112.
Irrigation.
Authorized purposes, §§54-111, 54-124.
Land and loan associations, §§54-45 to 54-73.
See LAND AND LOAN ASSOCIATIONS.
Licenses.
Taxation, §54-118.1.
Marketing associations, §§54-129 to 54-166.
See MARKETING ASSOCIATIONS.
Mines and minerals.
Authorized purposes, §§54-111, 54-124.
Names.
Bylaws to provide for, §54-116.
Use of term "mutual" restricted, §54-112.
Nonmembers, §54-117.
Officers, §54-123.
Other corporations.
Admission to provisions, §54-118.
Purchase of business.
Shares issued on, §54-121.
Powers, §§54-124 to 54-128.
Purposes, §§54-111, 54-124.
Real property.
Authority to acquire and hold, §39-24.
Conveyances.
Authorized, §39-25.
Effect as to conveyances by trustees, §39-26.
Prior deeds validated, §39-27.
Probate, §39-25.
Trustees.
Effect as to conveyance by trustee, §39-26.
Vesting title, §39-25.
Reports.
Annual report to secretary of state, §54-128.
Restriction on ownership of shares, §54-120.
Sewers.
Authorized purposes, §§54-111, 54-124.
Stock and stockholders.
Amendment of articles of incorporation.
Majority vote of shareholders, §54-125.
Bylaws.
Matters to be provided for, §54-116.
Dividends, §§54-126, 54-127.
Election of directors, §54-123.
Increase or decrease of amount of capital, §54-125.

COOPERATIVE ASSOCIATIONS —Cont'd
Stock and stockholders —Cont'd
Information to be stated in articles of incorporation, §54-113.
Proxy voting, §54-122.
Purchase of business.
Shares issued on, §54-121.
Subscriptions.
Certificates not issued until fully paid, §54-119.
Voting of shares by subscriber, §54-119.
Voting.
Absent members, §54-122.
Storage.
Authorized purposes, §§54-111, 54-124.
Taxation.
Franchise taxes, §54-118.2.
Income tax.
Corporation income tax.
Exemptions, §105-130.11, (a), (b).
License taxes, §54-118.1.
Property taxes.
Certain farm products classified for taxation at reduced valuation, §105-277.01.
Telephones.
Authorized purposes, §§54-111, 54-124.
Trusts and trustees.
Conveyances.
Effect as to conveyance by trustee, §39-26.
Voting.
Restriction, §54-120.
Water supply and waterworks.
Authorized purposes, §§54-111, 54-124.

COOPERATIVE INNOVATIVE HIGH SCHOOL PROGRAMS, §§115C-238.50 to 115C-238.55.
Accelerated learning programs offered.
Requirements of programs, §115C-238.50, (d).
Accountable to local board of education, §115C-238.53, (a).
Agreement.
Operated under term of written agreement, §115C-238.53, (b).
Application.
Information required, §115C-238.51, (b).
Joint application, §115C-238.51, (a).
Review, joint advisory committee, §115C-238.51, (c).
Submission to state boards, §115C-238.51, (c).
Appropriation of funds.
County boards of commissioners, §115C-238.54, (d).
Approval, §115C-238.51, (d).
Assignment of funds, §115C-238.54, (a).
Dropouts.
Programs targeting at-risk students.
Requirements, §115C-238.50, (c).
Eligibility to attend, §115C-238.50, (f).
Evaluation of student success, §115C-238.55.
Exemption from rules, §115C-238.53, (f).
Facilities programs operated in, §115C-238.53, (c).
High school or technical center located on campus.
Program may include creation, §115C-238.50, (e).
Joint establishment.
Local boards and community college boards of trustee.
Purpose of part to authorize, §115C-238.50, (a).
Ninth graders, eligibility to attend, §115C-238.50, (f).
Number of days of instruction, §115C-238.53, (d).

COOPERATIVE INNOVATIVE HIGH SCHOOL PROGRAMS —Cont'd
Other educational partner who may participate, §115C-238.52, (a).
Requirements, §115C-238.52, (b).
Purpose of part, §115C-238.50, (a).
Requirements of programs, §115C-238.50, (b).
Accelerated learning programs offered, §115C-238.50, (d).
Students at risk of dropping out targeted, §115C-238.50, (c).
School within school.
Program may include creation, §115C-238.50, (e).
State, federal and local funds, use, §115C-238.53, (e).
Allocation, §115C-238.54, (b), (c).
Encouragement to seek other funds, §115C-238.54, (e).
Students with disabilities.
Compliance with law and policies relating to, §115C-238.53, (d).
Technical high school.
Program may include creation, §115C-238.50, (e).

COORDINATE SYSTEM, §§102-1 to 102-17.
See SURVEYS AND SURVEYORS.

COPIERS.
Toner or inkjets.
Agreement prohibiting reusing, remanufacturing or refilling.
Void and unenforceable, §75-36.

COPIES.
Authenticated copies of public records.
Evidence, §8-35.
Certified copies.
Laws of foreign countries or states.
Admission into evidence, §8-3, (b).
Ordinances.
Prima facie evidence of existence of ordinance, §8-5.
Public records.
Evidence, §8-34.
Wills.
Evidence, §8-28.
Photographic reproductions.
Department of revenue, §8-45.3, (a).
Employment security commission, §8-45.3, (a1).
Evidence, §8-45.1.
Uniformity of interpretation, §8-45.2.
Public records.
Authenticated copies.
Evidence, §8-35.
Official writings.
Evidence, §8-34.

COPPER.
Records.
Purchase of certain metals, §66-11.
Regulation of purchase of certain metals.
Violations of provisions, §66-11.
Transportation, §66-11.1.

COPYRIGHTS.
Authors.
Protection of rights, Const. U. S., art. I, §8.
Corporate income tax.
Allocation and apportionment of income, §105-130.4.
International commercial arbitrations.
Arbitration deemed commercial, §1-567.31, (e).
Invention development by employees, §§66-57.1, 66-57.2.

COPYRIGHTS —Cont'd
Phonograph records and tapes.
Prohibition of rights to further restrict or to collect royalties on commercial use, §66-28.
Real estate commission.
Publications, §93A-3, (f).
Tryon's palace.
Emblems.
Authority of commission to adopt and copyright certain emblems, §121-21.

CORAM NOBIS.
Relief now available by motion for appropriate relief, §15A-1411, (c).

CORDAGE.
Dealers of scrap, salvage or surplus, failure to keep records of purchases, §66-10, (b).

CORN.
Adulteration of grains generally, §§106-621 to 106-628.
See GRAIN ADULTERATION.
Grain dealers generally, §§106-601 to 106-615.
See GRAIN DEALERS.
Grain mills generally, §§73-1 to 73-28.
Granary arson, §14-62.
Larceny.
Ungathered crops, §14-78.
Liens.
Effective period, §44-69.1.
Unfair practices by handlers, §§106-498 to 106-501.
Weights and measures.
Standard weights and measures, §81A-42.

CORNEAL TISSUE REMOVAL.
Authorization, §130A-391, (a).
Conditions for removal, §130A-391, (a).
Liability.
Immunity from liability, §130A-391, (b).

CORNELIUS.
Traffic control photographic systems, §160A-300.1, (d).

CORNERS.
Control corners in real estate developments, §§39-32.1 to 39-32.4.
See SUBDIVISIONS.

CORONERS.
Appointments.
Clerk may appoint in special cases, §152-1.
Autopsies generally.
See AUTOPSIES.
Bonds, surety.
Certified copies as evidence, §152-4.
Execution, §152-3.
Official bonds of county officers generally, §§58-72-1 to 58-72-70.
See OFFICIAL BONDS OF COUNTY OFFICERS.
Registration, §152-4.
Conveyances.
Official selling or empowered to sell property not in office, §39-5.
Death.
Conveyances of real property when not in office, §39-5.
Deeds.
Official selling or empowered to sell not in office, §39-5.
Elections, §152-1.
Date of election, §163-1, (a).

CORONERS —Cont'd
Escape.
Allowing prisoners to escape, §14-239.
Burden of proof, §14-239.
District attorney to prosecute officer for escape, §14-240.
Evidence.
Bonds, surety.
Certified copies as evidence, §152-4.
Executions.
Directed to coroner where sheriff is party or interested in action, §1-313.
Failure to discharge duties, §14-230.
Fees.
Generally, §152-5.
Statement rendered by county officers compensated from fees, §128-13.
Penalty for failure to file statement, §128-13.
Habeas corpus.
Hearings by coroner, §152-10.
Hearings.
Preliminary hearings.
Duties of coroners, §152-7.
Hearings by coroner in lieu of other preliminary hearing, §152-10.
Inquests.
Compensation of jurors at inquest, §152-9.
Duties of coroners, §152-7.
Medical examiners to be notified of certain deaths.
Holding of inquests by coroner, §130A-394.
Jury.
Compensation of jurors at inquest, §152-9.
Liabilities of special coroner, §152-6.
Medical examiners generally, §§130A-377 to 130A-395.
See MEDICAL EXAMINERS.
Oaths.
Taking of oath, §152-2.
Penalties.
Special coroner, §152-6.
Statement rendered by county officers compensated from fees.
Failure to file statement, §128-13.
Powers and duties, §152-7.
Special coroners, §152-6.
Preliminary hearings.
Duties, §152-7.
Salaries.
Statement rendered by county officers compensated from fees, §128-13.
Penalty for failure to file statement, §128-13.
Service of process.
Process issued by coroner, §152-11.
Subpoenas, §1A-1, Rule 45, (e).
Sheriffs.
Acting as sheriff in certain cases, §152-8.
Service of process.
Sheriff a party.
When coroner acts, §162-16.
Vacancies in office of sheriff.
Duties performed by coroner or chief deputy, §162-5.1.
Performance of duties by coroner, §162-5.
Special coroners.
Liabilities, §152-6.
Penalties, §152-6.
Powers and duties, §152-6.
Sheriffs.
Acting as sheriff in certain cases, §152-8.
Subpoenas.
Service, §1A-1, Rule 45, (e).
Terms of office, §163-1, (a).

CORONERS —Cont'd
Vacancies in office, §152-1.

CORPORAL PUNISHMENT.
Attorneys' fees and costs in cases involving principals or teachers.
Frivolous actions, §6-21.4.
Child care facilities.
Banned in certain nonlicensed homes, §110-101.1.
Prohibited as form of discipline, §110-91.
Mental health, developmental disabilities and substance abuse.
Rights of clients.
Use of corporal punishment prohibited, §122C-59.
Public schools.
Attorneys' fees in frivolous actions, §6-21.4.
Employees who may administer, §115C-391, (a).
Immunity from civil liability when use consistent with state and local laws, §115C-391, (h).
Mandated policies, publication, §115C-391, (a).
Misconduct resulting in punishment, informing student body, §115C-391, (a).
Not administered in classroom with other students present, §115C-391, (a).
Notice to parent or guardian that punishment administered, §115C-391, (a).
Reasonable force, §115C-390.
Use to control certain behavior and self defense, §115C-391, (a).
State prison.
Rules and regulations, §148-20.

CORPORATE LIMITS.
Municipal corporations.
Annexation generally, §§160A-29 to 160A-58.28.
See ANNEXATION.

CORPORATIONS, §§55-1-01 to 55-17-05.
ABC permits.
Person to qualify for issuance, §18B-900, (c).
Accountants.
Public practice of accountancy.
Prohibited, §93-8.
Use of title "certified public accountant," §93-5.
Actions.
Against directors, §55-7-48.
Amendment of articles of incorporation.
Effect on actions, §55-10-09.
Derivative actions by shareholders, §§55-7-40 to 55-7-49.
Applicability of foreign corporations, §55-7-47.
Definitions, §55-7-40.1.
Demand requirement, §55-7-42.
Discontinuance or settlement, §55-7-45.
Dismissal, §55-7-44.
Jurisdiction, §55-7-40.
Payment of costs and expenses, §55-7-46.
Privileged communications, §55-7-49.
Standing, §55-7-41.
Stays, §55-7-43.
Foreign corporations.
Certificates of authority.
Consequences of failure to obtain, §55-15-02, (a).
Nonprofit corporations.
Corporations already in existence, §55A-17-03, (b).
Creditors action against member, §55A-6-24.
Derivative actions, §55A-7-40.
Judicial dissolution, §§55A-14-30 to 55A-14-33.
Power to sue and be sued, §55A-3-02, (a).

CORPORATIONS —Cont'd
Actions —Cont'd
Nonprofit corporations —Cont'd
Voluntary dissolution.
Claims against dissolved corporations, §55A-14-09, (a).
Saving provisions, §55-17-03, (b).
Agents.
Embezzlement.
Receipt of property by virtue of office or employment, §14-90.
Misconduct in private office.
Malfeasance of corporation agents, §14-254, (a).
Amendment of articles of incorporation, §§55-10-01 to 55-10-09.
Articles of amendment.
Contents, §55-10-06.
Delivery to secretary of state, §55-10-06.
Issuance of classes or series of stock, filing, §55-6-02, (b).
Authorized, §55-10-01, (a).
Board of directors.
Amendment by board, §55-10-02.
Proposal of amendments to shareholders, §55-10-03, (a) to (d).
Approval of proposed amendments by shareholders, §§55-10-03, (b), (e), 55-10-04.
Restated articles of incorporation.
Power of board, §55-10-07, (a).
Effect of amendment, §55-10-09.
Restated articles of incorporation.
Amendments may be included in, §55-10-07, (b).
Articles of restatement, §55-10-07, (d).
Certification by secretary of state, §55-10-07, (f).
Effect, §55-10-07, (e).
Power of board of directors, §55-10-07, (a).
Submission to shareholders, §55-10-07, (c).
Stock and stockholders.
Acquisition by corporation of own shares, §55-6-31, (b), (c).
Amendment before issuance of shares, §55-10-05.
Classes or series of stock, §55-6-02, (b).
Issuance of shares.
Amendment before issuance, §55-10-05.
Restated articles of incorporation.
Submission to shareholders, §55-10-07, (c).
Vested property right resulting from provisions in articles.
Stockholders not deemed to have, §55-10-01, (b).
Voting groups.
Classes of shares entitled to vote as separate voting groups, §55-10-04, (a).
Nonvoting shares entitled to vote as voting groups, §55-10-04, (d).
Series of classes of shares entitled to vote as voting groups, §55-10-04, (b), (c).
Voting on proposed amendments.
Required votes for adoption, §55-10-03, (b), (e).
Voting groups, §55-10-04.
Amendment of bylaws.
Board of directors.
Amendment by, §55-10-20, (a).
Quorum or voting requirements.
Bylaws increasing, §55-10-22.
Stock and stockholders.
Amendment by shareholders, §55-10-20, (b).
Bylaw increasing quorum or voting requirements for directors, §55-10-22.

CORPORATIONS —Cont'd
Appeals.
Dissolution.
Administrative dissolution.
Denial of reinstatement, §55-14-23.
Filing of documents.
Appeal from secretary of state's refusal to file, §55D-16.
Foreign corporations.
Revocation of certificate of authority, §55-15-32.
Appearance.
Organizations generally.
Appearance by counsel or agent, §15A-773, (b).
Applicability of act, §55-17-01, (a).
Exceptions, §55-17-01, (b).
Foreign corporations.
Qualified foreign corporations, §55-17-02.
Architects.
Licenses.
Corporate certificate, §§83A-1, 83A-8.
Practice of architecture.
Corporate practice, §§83A-1, 83A-8.
Archives and history.
Outdoor historical dramas, §143-204.8.
Articles of incorporation.
Amendments, §§55-10-01 to 55-10-09. See within this heading, "Amendment of articles of incorporation."
Contents, §55-2-02, (a), (b).
Conversion of business entity to domestic corporation, §§55-2-02, 55-11A-03, (a) to (c), (d).
Defined, §55-1-40.
Filing.
Commencement of corporate existence, §55-2-03, (a).
Effect, §55-2-03, (b).
Nonprofit corporations.
See NONPROFIT CORPORATIONS.
Powers of corporation.
Statutory powers need not be set forth, §§55-2-02, (c), 55-3-02, (b).
Suspension.
Failure to file tax report or return or pay tax or fee.
Suspension of articles of incorporation, §105-230, (a).
Invalidity of acts performed during suspension, §105-230, (b).
Receivership, liquidation, cessation of business, §105-232, (b).
Reinstatement of articles, §105-232, (a).
Attachment.
Grounds for attachment, §1-440.3.
Attorneys at law.
Practice of law.
Nonprofit corporations.
Indigent legal services by, §84-5.1.
Prohibition as to practice of law by corporation, §84-5.
Regulations for professional corporations practicing law, Bar Rules & Regs., E, §§.0101 to .0106.
Violations of provisions.
Misdemeanor, §84-8.
Receivers.
Counsel fees, §1-507.9.
Attorneys' fees.
Dissenting shareholders.
Judicial appraisal of shares, §55-13-31, (b), (c).

CORPORATIONS —Cont'd
Attorneys' fees —Cont'd
Records.
Inspection of records by shareholders.
Court-ordered inspection, §55-16-04, (c).
Stock and stockholders.
Derivative actions by shareholders.
Award, §55-7-46.
Auctions and auctioneers.
Licenses, §85B-4, (g).
Averment of capacity, §1A-1, Rule 84.
Banks, §§53-1 to 53-272.
See BANKS.
Board of directors.
Actions against, §55-7-48.
Amendment of articles of incorporation.
Amendment by board, §55-10-02.
Classes or series of stock.
Filing articles of amendment prior to issuance required, §55-6-02, (b).
Proposal of amendments to shareholders, §55-10-03, (a) to (d).
Approval of proposed amendments by shareholders, §§55-10-03, (b), (e), 55-10-04.
Restated articles of incorporation.
Power of board, §55-10-07, (a).
Amendment of bylaws.
Amendment by board of directors, §55-10-20, (a).
Quorum or voting requirements.
Bylaws increasing, §55-10-22.
Classes or series of stock.
Amendment of articles of incorporation.
Filing articles of amendment prior to issuance required, §55-6-02, (b).
Preferences, limitations or rights.
Determination by board, §55-6-02, (a).
Committees.
Approval of creation and appointment of members, §55-8-25, (b).
Authority, §55-8-25, (d).
Restrictions, §55-8-25, (e).
Creation, §55-8-25, (a).
Effect, §55-8-25, (f).
Meetings.
Applicability of provisions to committees, §55-8-25, (c).
Number of members, §55-8-25, (a).
Compensation of directors, §55-8-11.
Conflicts of interest.
Authorization, approval, or ratification of transaction, §55-8-31, (a), (c), (d).
What constitutes, §55-8-31, (a), (b).
Cumulative voting for, §55-7-28, (b) to (d).
Dissolution.
Voluntary dissolution, §§55-14-01 to 55-14-08.
Adoption of proposal by shareholders, §55-14-02, (b), (e).
Articles of dissolution, §55-14-03, (a).
Effective date of dissolution by, §55-14-03, (b).
Notice of shareholders meeting to consider proposal, §55-14-02, (d).
Proposal by directors, §55-14-02, (a), (c).
Revocation of dissolution by, §55-14-04.
Election of directors, §55-8-03, (d).
Classes of shareholders, §55-8-04.
Voting of shares, §55-7-28, (a).
Cumulative voting, §55-7-28, (b) to (e).
Indemnification, §§55-8-50 to 55-8-58.

CORPORATIONS —Cont'd
Board of directors —Cont'd
Liability of directors.
Standards of conduct.
Effect of provisions, §55-8-30, (d), (e).
Unlawful distributions.
Contribution and reimbursement, §55-8-33, (b).
Generally, §55-8-33, (a).
Limitation of proceedings, §55-8-33, (c).
Loans to directors.
Indirect loan or guarantee, §55-8-32, (d).
Restrictions, §55-8-32, (a), (b).
Exceptions, §55-8-32, (c).
Meetings.
Action without meeting.
Authorized, §55-8-21, (a).
Effect of signed consent, §55-8-21, (c).
Electronic consent, §55-8-21, (a).
When effective, §55-8-21, (b).
Assent to action taken at meeting.
When director deemed to have assented, §55-8-24, (d).
Committees.
Applicability of provisions to committees, §55-8-25, (c).
Communication methods, §55-8-20, (b).
Location, §55-8-20, (a).
Notice.
Regular meetings, §55-8-22, (a).
Special meetings, §55-8-22, (b).
Waiver of notice, §55-8-23.
Quorum, §55-8-24, (a) to (c).
Special meetings.
Calling, §55-8-20, (c).
Telephone conference calls.
Means of communication generally, §55-8-20, (b).
Waiver of notice, §55-8-23, (a).
Attendance at or participation in meeting, §55-8-23, (b).
Number of directors, §55-8-03, (a) to (c).
Change in number, §55-8-03, (b).
Effect of decrease on terms of office, §55-8-05, (c).
Powers.
Dispensing with or limiting authority, §55-8-01, (c).
Exercise by individual or group other than board, §55-8-01, (d).
Exercise of corporate powers, §55-8-01, (b).
Qualifications of directors, §55-8-02.
Quorum, §55-8-24, (a) to (c).
Bylaws increasing quorum or voting requirements.
Amendment, who may amend, §55-10-22, (a) to (c).
Repeal, §55-10-22, (a), (b).
Removal of directors.
Entire board, §55-8-08, (e).
Judicial proceeding.
Barring director from reelection, §55-8-09, (b).
Corporation as party defendant, §55-8-09, (c).
Generally, §55-8-09, (a).
Power of superior court, §55-8-09, (a).
Shareholders.
Cumulative voting, §55-8-08, (c).
Notice of meeting, §55-8-08, (d).
Power to remove directors, §55-8-08, (a).
Removal of entire board, §55-8-08, (e).
Voting groups, §55-8-08, (b).

CORPORATIONS —Cont'd
Board of directors —Cont'd
Required, §55-8-01, (a).
Residence of directors.
Not required to be resident of state, §55-8-02.
Resignation of directors, §55-8-07, (a).
When effective, §55-8-07, (b).
Staggered terms for directors, §55-8-06.
Standards of conduct for directors.
Conflicts of interest, §55-8-31.
Generally, §55-8-30, (a).
Liability.
Effect of provisions on, §55-8-30, (d), (e).
Reliance on information, opinions, reports or statements, §55-8-30, (b), (c).
Terms of directors, §§55-8-05, 55-8-06.
Decrease in number of directors.
Effect, §55-8-05, (c).
Expiration, §55-8-05, (a), (b), (d), (e).
Staggered terms, §55-8-06.
Vacancies.
Filling, §55-8-10, (a), (c).
Voting groups, §55-8-10, (b).
Bond issues.
Drainage, §§156-52, 156-53.
Interest.
Sale below par permitted, §24-2.
Payment of bonds enforced, §156-53.
Boxing.
Licenses for manager or promoter issued to, §143-654, (b).
Brokers.
Acting as stockbroker, §14-401.7.
Burning of corporate buildings, §14-61.
Bylaws.
Adoption, §55-2-06, (a).
Amendments, §§55-10-20, 55-10-22.
Contents, §55-2-06, (b).
Emergency bylaws.
Authorized, §55-2-07, (a).
Duration of effectiveness, §55-2-07, (b).
Effect, §55-2-07, (c).
Nonprofit corporations, §55A-2-07.
Regular bylaws remain effective, §55-2-07, (b).
When emergency exists, §55-2-07, (d).
Nonprofit corporations, §§55A-2-06, 55A-2-07.
Campaign contributions and expenditures.
Acceptance of contributions by corporations.
Prohibited, §163-278.15.
Defined, §163-278.6.
Prohibited acts, §163-278.19, (a).
Exceptions, §163-278.19, (b), (d), (f).
Penalties, §163-278.19, (c).
Cemetery corporations.
Change of name, §65-17.
Land holdings, §65-16.
Stockholder's meetings for certain nonprofit corporations, §65-17.1.
Charities.
Exemptions from business corporation act, §55-17-01, (b).
Management of institutional funds, §§36B-1 to 36B-10.
See MANAGEMENT OF INSTITUTIONAL FUNDS.
Nonprofit corporations, §§55A-1-01 to 55A-17-05.
See NONPROFIT CORPORATIONS.
Charter, Const. N. C., art. VIII, §1.
Forfeiture.
Counterfeiting, §14-15.

CORPORATIONS —Cont'd
Charter —Cont'd
Kidnapping and abduction.
Forfeiture of charter, §14-39.
Chattel mortgages.
Forms of probate for deeds and other conveyances, §47-41.02, (f).
Citation of act.
Short title, §55-1-01.
Class actions.
Stock and stockholders.
Secondary action by shareholders, §1A-1, Rule 23, (b).
Collection of debts.
Simulation, §14-118.1.
Conditional sales.
Forms of probate for deeds and other conveyances, §47-41.02, (f).
Condominium owners' associations.
Master associations.
Powers exercised or delegated to corporation, §47C-2-120.
Confidentiality of information.
Interrogatories by secretary of state.
Information disclosed by, §55-1-33.
Construction and interpretation.
Control share acquisitions, §§55-9A-07, 55-9A-08.
Severability of provisions, §55-17-04.
Contractors.
Electrical contractors.
Licenses, §87-43.2.
Plumbing, heating and fire sprinkler contractors.
Licenses, §87-26, (a), (d), (e).
Refrigeration contractors.
Licenses, §§87-57, 87-62.
Contracts.
Contracts in writing for purchase of personal property.
Lien on property or retention of title as security for purchase.
Forms of probate for deeds and other conveyances, §47-41.02, (f).
Joint assumption or underwriting of risks, §58-65-5.
Control share acquisitions, §§55-9A-01 to 55-9A-09, 75E-1 to 75E-9.
Acquiring person's statement, §55-9A-02.
Applicability of provisions.
Exemptions, §55-9A-09.
Citation of act.
Short title, §55-9A-01, (a).
Conflict of laws.
Provisions controlling, §55-9A-08.
Construction and interpretation.
Provisions controlling, §55-9A-08.
Severability of provisions, §55-9A-07.
Definitions, §55-9A-01, (b).
Violation of article, §75E-1.
Exemptions from provisions, §55-9A-09.
Meeting of shareholders.
Calling special meeting, §55-9A-03, (a).
Next special or annual meeting.
Consideration of voting rights at, §55-9A-03, (c).
Notice, §55-9A-04.
Time for, §55-9A-03, (b), (d).
Nonresidents.
Service of process.
Designation of secretary of state, §75E-8.
Notice.
Meeting of shareholders, §55-9A-04.

CORPORATIONS —Cont'd
Control share acquisitions —Cont'd
Notice —Cont'd
Right of redemption by shareholders, §55-9A-06, (b), (c).
Redemption.
Definition of "fair value," §55-9A-06, (e).
Notice, §55-9A-06, (b), (c).
Right of redemption by shareholders.
Generally, §55-9A-06, (a).
Written demand by shareholder, §55-9A-06, (d).
Severability of provisions, §§55-9A-07, 75E-9.
Statement by acquiring person, §55-9A-02.
Title of act.
Short title, §55-9A-01, (a).
Violation of article.
Attorney general.
Investigative and regulatory powers, §75E-3.
Chapter not exclusive, §75E-7.
Civil actions, §75E-4.
Damages, §75E-4.
Definitions, §75E-1.
Penalties.
Civil penalties, §75E-5.
Remedies cumulative, §75E-6.
Unlawful activities, §75E-2.
Voting rights of control shares.
Meeting of shareholders to consider, §§55-9A-03, 55-9A-04.
Resolution granting, §55-9A-05, (a).
Adoption, §55-9A-05, (b).
Conversion of business entity to domestic corporation, §§55-11A-01 to 55-11A-04.
Articles of incorporation.
Effect, §55-11A-03, (c).
Filing by converting entity, §55-11A-03, (a).
Requirements of articles filed to effect conversion, §55-2-02, (d).
Withdrawal if plan of conversion abandoned, §55-11A-03, (b).
Authorized, §55-11A-01.
Certificate of conversion.
Registration, §55-11A-03, (d).
Effect, §55-11A-04.
Plan of conversion.
Amendment or abandonment, §55-11A-02, (c).
Approval, §55-11A-02, (b).
Contents, §55-11A-02, (a).
Requirements, §55-11A-01.
Conversion of domestic corporation to different business entity, §§55-11A-10 to 55-11A-13.
Articles of conversion, §55-11A-12, (a), (b).
Effect, §55-11A-12, (d).
Withdrawal if plan of conversion abandoned, §55-11A-12, (c).
Authorized, §55-11A-10.
Certificate of conversion.
Registration, §55-11A-12, (e).
Dissenting shareholders.
General provisions, §§55-13-01 to 55-13-31. See within this heading, "Dissenting shareholders."
Effect, §55-11A-13, (a).
Resulting entity not limited liability company or limited partnership, §55-11A-13, (b).
Plan of conversion.
Amendment or abandonment, §55-11A-11, (g).
Approval, §55-11A-11, (b) to (f).
Contents, §55-11A-11, (a).
Requirements, §55-11A-10.

CORPORATIONS —Cont'd
Conveyances.
Corporate seal.
Required, §47-41.1.
Forms of probate for deeds and other conveyances, §47-41.01, (b), (c).
Instrument executed by president or presiding member or trustee, §47-41.02, (b) to (d).
Other forms not excluded, §47-41.01, (a).
Other forms of probate for corporate conveyances.
Contracts in writing for purchase of personal property, §47-41.02, (f).
Other forms not excluded, §47-41.02, (a).
Validation of conveyances probated and recorded prior to February 14, 1939, §47-41.02, (e).
Validation of deeds and other conveyances executed on or before April 12, 1974, §47-41.02, (g).
Cooperative associations, §§54-111 to 54-129.
See COOPERATIVE ASSOCIATIONS.
Costs.
Actions by state for corporation.
Liability for costs, §6-15.
Dissenting shareholders.
Judicial appraisal of shares, §55-13-31.
Records.
Inspection of records by shareholders.
Court-ordered inspection, §55-16-04, (c).
Stock and stockholders.
Derivative actions by shareholders.
Award, §55-7-46.
Counterfeiting.
Issuing substitutes for money without authority, §14-15.
Receiving or passing unauthorized substitutes for money, §14-16.
Counties.
Corporate powers of counties, §153A-11.
Exercise of corporate powers, §153A-12.
Credit unions, §§54-109.1 to 54-110.10.
See CREDIT UNIONS.
Criminal law and procedure.
Defendants.
Appearance by counsel or agent, §15A-773, (b).
Securing attendance of organizations, §15A-773, (a).
Definition of "organization," §15A-773.
Indictments.
Manner of alleging joint ownership of property, §15-148.
Securing attendance of organizations as defendants, §15A-773.
Cumulative voting for directors, §55-7-28, (b) to (d).
Curative statute, §55-17-05.
Declaratory judgments.
Word "person" construed, §1-265.
Deeds.
Corporate seal.
Imprinting required, §47-41.1.
Forms of probate for deeds and other conveyances, §47-41.01.
Other forms of probate for corporate conveyances.
Generally, §47-41.02.
Probate and registration.
Error in acknowledgment of probate, §47-97.1.
Mistake as to officer's name, §47-97.
Where corporation has ceased to exist, §47-16.

CORPORATIONS —Cont'd
Definitions, §55-1-40.
Boards of directors, §58-65-20, (a).
Indemnification, §55-8-50, (b).
Shareholder protection act, §55-9-01, (b).
Violation of article, §75E-1.
Constitutional definition, Const. N. C., art. VIII, §2.
Control share acquisitions, §55-9A-01, (b).
Dissenting shareholders, §55-13-01.
Foreign trade zones.
"Public corporation," §55C-2.
Shareholder protection act, §55-9-01, (b).
Violation of article, §75E-1.
Dental service corporations generally, §§58-65-1 to 58-65-40.
See HOSPITAL, MEDICAL AND DENTAL SERVICE CORPORATIONS.
Depositions, use in court proceedings, §1A-1, Rule 32, (a).
Deposition upon oral examination, §1A-1, Rule 30, (b).
Derivative actions by shareholders, §§55-7-40 to 55-7-49.
Applicability of foreign corporations, §55-7-47.
Definitions, §55-7-40.1.
Demand requirement, §55-7-42.
Discontinuance or settlement, §55-7-45.
Dismissal, §55-7-44.
Jurisdiction, §55-7-40.
Nonprofit corporations.
Members and directors, §55A-7-40.
Payment of costs and expenses, §55-7-46.
Privileged communications, §55-7-49.
Standing, §55-7-41.
Stays, §55-7-43.
Dissenting shareholders, §§55-13-01 to 55-13-31.
Beneficial shareholders.
Defined, §55-13-01.
Dissent by, §55-13-03, (b).
Definitions, §55-13-01.
Demand for payment.
Duty to demand payment, §55-13-23, (a).
Effect, §55-13-23, (b).
Failure to demand payment.
Effect, §55-13-23, (c).
Notice of intent to demand payment, §55-13-21.
Offer of payment, §55-13-25.
Shareholder dissatisfied with corporation's offer or failure to perform, §55-13-28, (a).
Waiver of right to demand payment under provisions, §55-13-28, (b).
Failure of corporation to take proposed action.
Duties of corporation upon, §55-13-26, (a).
Subsequently taking proposed action, §55-13-26, (b).
Judicial appraisal of shares.
Appraisers.
Appointment, §55-13-30, (d).
Compensation and expenses, §55-13-31, (a).
Attorneys' fees, §55-13-31, (b), (c).
Costs, §55-13-31, (a).
Fees and expenses of counsel and experts, §55-13-31, (b), (c).
Judgment.
Amount, §55-13-30, (e).
Jurisdiction of court, §55-13-30, (d).
Petition.
Service of copies on parties, §55-13-30, (c).
Time for, §55-13-30, (a).
Time limitations, §55-13-30, (a).

CORPORATIONS —Cont'd
Dissenting shareholders —Cont'd
Notice.
Dissenter's notice.
Contents, §55-13-22, (b).
Required, §55-13-22, (a).
Time for, §55-13-22, (b).
Notice of dissenter's rights.
Effect of failure to comply with provisions, §55-13-20, (c).
Required, §55-13-20, (a).
Time for, §55-13-20, (b).
Notice of intent to demand payment.
Effect of failure to satisfy requirements, §55-13-21, (b).
Generally, §55-13-21, (a).
Required, §55-13-21, (a).
Offer of payment.
Generally, §55-13-25, (a).
Information to accompany, §55-13-25, (b).
Restriction of transfer of uncertificated shares.
Authorized, §55-13-24, (a).
Effect, §55-13-24, (b).
Rights.
Beneficial shareholders.
Dissent by, §55-13-03, (b).
Judicial appraisal of shares, §§55-13-30, 55-13-31.
Nominees.
Dissent by, §55-13-03, (a).
Notice of dissenter's rights, §55-13-20.
Procedure for exercise of rights, §§55-13-20 to 55-13-28.
Right to dissent, §55-13-02, (a).
Restriction, §55-13-02, (b), (c).
Dissolution, §§55-14-01 to 55-14-40.
Administrative dissolution, §§55-14-20 to 55-14-24.
Administrative procedure act.
Inapplicability, §55-14-24.
Appeal from denial of reinstatement, §55-14-23.
Appeal of court's final decision, §55-14-23, (d).
Burden on corporation, §55-14-23, (b).
Notice of denial, §55-14-23, (a).
Orders of court, §55-14-23, (c).
Petition, §55-14-23, (b).
Time for, §55-14-23, (b).
Certificate of dissolution, §55-14-21, (b).
Claims against dissolved corporation.
Applicability of certain provisions, §55-14-21, (c).
Effect of dissolution.
Applicability of certain provisions, §55-14-21, (c).
Registered agent's authority not terminated, §55-14-21, (d).
Grounds, §55-14-20.
Nonprofit corporations, §§55A-14-20 to 55A-14-24.
Notice.
Denial of reinstatement, §55-14-23, (a).
Determination that grounds exist, §55-14-21, (a).
Reinstatement, §55-14-22.
Appeal from denial, §55-14-23.
Application, §55-14-22, (a).
Certificate of reinstatement, §55-14-22, (b).
Effect, §55-14-22, (c).
Name, §55-14-22, (a1).
Creditors.
Unavailable shareholders and creditors.
Disposition of amounts due to, §55-14-40.

CORPORATIONS —Cont'd
Dissolution —Cont'd
Forest protection and development corporations, §113-71.
Judicial dissolution, §§55-14-30 to 55-14-33.
Claims against dissolved corporation.
Notification of claimants, §55-14-33, (b).
Decree of dissolution, §55-14-33, (a).
Grounds, §55-14-30.
Injunctions.
Power of court to issue, §55-14-31, (c).
Nonprofit corporations, §§55A-14-30 to 55A-14-33.
Parties.
Shareholders need not be made parties, §55-14-31, (b).
Purchase of shares of complaining shareholder.
Dissolution not ordered, §55-14-31, (d).
Receiver.
Appointment, §§55-14-31, (c), 55-14-32, (a), (b).
Compensation, §55-14-32, (e).
Powers and duties, §55-14-32, (c).
Venue of proceedings, §55-14-31, (a).
Winding up of affairs, §55-14-33, (b).
Nonprofit corporations, §§55A-14-01 to 55A-14-33.
See NONPROFIT CORPORATIONS.
Saving provisions, §55-17-03, (c).
Superior court.
Judicial dissolution generally, §§55-14-30 to 55-14-33.
Unavailable shareholders and creditors.
Disposition of amounts due to, §55-14-40.
Voluntary dissolution, §§55-14-01 to 55-14-08.
Articles of dissolution.
Dissolution by board of directors and shareholders, §55-14-03, (a).
Dissolution by incorporators or initial directors, §55-14-01, (a).
Board of directors or shareholders.
Adoption of proposal by shareholders, §55-14-02, (b), (e).
Articles of dissolution, §55-14-03, (a).
Effective date of dissolution by, §55-14-03, (b).
Notice of shareholders meeting to consider proposal, §55-14-02, (d).
Proposal by directors, §55-14-02, (a), (c).
Revocation of dissolution by, §55-14-04.
Claims against dissolved corporation, §§55-14-06 to 55-14-08.
Barred claims, §§55-14-06, (c), 55-14-07, (c).
Disposal of known claims, §55-14-06, (a).
Enforcement, §55-14-08, (a).
Exceptions to term "claim," §55-14-06, (d).
Limitation of actions not extended by provisions, §55-14-08, (b).
Notices, §§55-14-06, (b), (c), 55-14-07.
Effective date.
Dissolution by board of directors or shareholders, §55-14-03, (b).
Dissolution by incorporators or initial directors, §55-14-01, (b).
Revocation of dissolution, §55-14-04, (d).
Effect of dissolution, §55-14-05, (a), (c).
Exceptions, §55-14-05, (b).
Incorporators or initial directors.
Articles of dissolution, §55-14-01, (a).
Effective date of dissolution by, §55-14-01, (b).
Nonprofit corporations, §§55A-14-01 to 55A-14-09.

CORPORATIONS —Cont'd
Dissolution —Cont'd
Voluntary dissolution —Cont'd
Notice of dissolution, §55-14-07, (a).
Contents, §55-14-07, (b).
Effect of publication, §55-14-07, (c).
Known claimants, §55-14-06, (b), (c).
Publication, §55-14-07, (b).
Revocation of dissolution.
Articles of revocation of dissolution, §55-14-04, (c).
Authorization, §55-14-04, (b).
Effective date, §55-14-04, (d).
Effect of revocation, §55-14-04, (e).
Time for, §55-14-04, (a).
Distributions to shareholders.
Authorization, §55-6-40, (a).
Restrictions, §55-6-40, (c) to (g).
Compelling payment of dividends.
Shareholders rights not impair, §55-6-40, (k).
Demand by shareholders, §55-6-40, (h) to (j).
Payment of additional dividends, §55-6-40, (i).
Parity with indebtedness to general unsecured creditors, §55-6-40, (f).
Record date for determining shareholders entitled to distribution, §55-6-40, (b).
Restrictions, §55-6-40, (c), (d).
Determination of effect, §55-6-40, (e) to (g).
Dividends.
Distributions to shareholders generally, §55-6-40.
Income tax.
Adjustment to expenses related to, §105-130.6A.
Information filed with secretary of revenue.
Resident taxpayers receiving dividends, §105-130.21, (b).
S corporations.
Income tax.
Distributions to shareholders, §105-131.6.
Share dividends.
Generally, §55-6-23, (a), (b).
Record date for shareholders entitled to share dividend, §55-6-23, (c).
Document execution.
Authority and proof generally, §47-18.3.
Officers.
Liability, §47-18.3, (d).
Power of representatives to bind corporation.
Section not deemed to exclude, §47-18.3, (c).
Seals and sealed instruments.
Instrument executed bearing seal.
Prima facie evidence seal duly adopted, §47-18.3, (b).
Third parties.
Validity as to innocent third parties, §47-18.3, (a).
Drainage by corporations, §§156-37 to 156-53.
See DRAINAGE BY CORPORATION.
Electioneering communications.
Prohibited disbursement for, §163-278.82, (a), (b).
Mass mailings and telephone banks, §163-278.92, (a), (b).
Penalties, §163-278.93.
Penalties for violations, §163-278.83.
Electric membership corporations, §§117-6 to 117-26.
See ELECTRIC MEMBERSHIP CORPORATIONS.
Electronic transactions.
Agreement to conduct, §55-1-50.
Embezzlement.
Officers or agents of corporation.
Receipt of property by virtue of office or employment, §14-90.

CORPORATIONS —Cont'd
Emergency bylaws, §55-2-07.
Emergency powers, §55-3-03.
Nonprofit corporations, §55A-3-03.
Eminent domain.
By whom right may be exercised, §40A-3, (a).
Engineers and land surveyors.
Practice of engineering or land surveying, §89C-24.
Enterprise corporations, §§53A-35 to 53A-47.
See NORTH CAROLINA ENTERPRISE CORPORATIONS.
Evidence.
Filing of documents.
Certificate of existence.
Evidentiary effect, §55-1-28, (c).
Evidentiary effect of copy of filed document, §55D-17.
Probate and registration.
Execution of corporate instruments.
Instruments executed bearing seal.
Prima facie evidence seal duly adopted, §47-18.3, (b).
Executions.
Agents of corporations.
Duties, §§1-324.2 to 1-324.4.
Penalty for violations, §1-324.5.
Books and records.
Nonresident custodian, §§1-324.6, 1-324.7.
Debts due corporations.
Subject to execution, §1-324.4.
Information as to corporate officers and property.
Duty of agents to furnish, §1-324.2.
Information as to corporate shares.
Duty of agents to furnish, §1-324.3.
Information as to debts due corporation.
Duty of agents to furnish, §1-324.4.
Judgment against corporation.
Property subject to execution, §1-324.1.
Nonresident custodian of corporate books.
Duties, §1-324.7.
Liability, §1-324.7.
Notice to, §1-324.6.
Proceedings, §1-324.6.
Stock and stockholders.
Shares subject to execution, §1-324.3.
Executors and administrators.
Disqualifications for service.
Not authorized as personal representative, §28A-4-2.
Incorporation of businesses or ventures.
Power of personal representative or fiduciary, §28A-13-3, (a).
Fiduciaries.
Participation in reorganizations.
Powers which may be incorporated by reference in trust instrument, §32-27.
Security transfers.
See FIDUCIARIES.
Filing of documents, §§55D-10 to 55D-18.
Advisory review of documents, §55D-12.
Appeal from secretary of state's refusal to file.
Appeal of court's final decision, §55D-16, (c).
Generally, §55D-16, (a).
Powers of court, §55D-16, (b).
Certificate of existence.
Application for, §55-1-28, (a).
Contents, §55-1-28, (b).
Evidentiary effect, §55-1-28, (c).
Copying, comparing or certifying documents.
Fees, §55-1-22, (c).

CORPORATIONS —Cont'd
Filing of documents —Cont'd
Correcting filed document, §55D-14, (a).
Articles of correction, §55D-14, (b).
When effective, §55D-14, (c).
Definitions, §55D-1.
Effective time and date of document, §55D-13, (a).
Delayed effective time and date, §55D-13, (b).
Validity or invalidity of document not affected, §55D-13, (c).
Evidence.
Certificate of existence.
Evidentiary effect, §55-1-28, (c).
Copy of filed document.
Evidentiary effect, §55D-17.
Expedited filings, §55D-11.
False documents.
Signing, §55D-18, (a).
Misdemeanor, §55D-18, (b).
Fees.
Copying, comparing or certifying documents, §55-1-22, (c).
Expedited filings, §55D-11.
Nonrefundable fee for annual reports, §55-1-22, (d).
Schedule of fees, §55-1-22, (a).
Service of process on secretary of state, §55-1-22, (b).
Forms.
Promulgation, §55-1-21, (a).
Additional forms, §55-1-21, (b).
Nonprofit corporations, §§55A-1-20 to 55A-1-22.
See NONPROFIT CORPORATIONS.
Professional corporations.
Applicability of provisions to, §55B-3, (b).
Reorganization proceedings, §55-14A-01, (b).
Requirements, §§55-1-20, (a), 55D-10, (b).
Execution of document, §55-1-20, (b).
Satisfaction of requirements, §55D-10, (a).
Rulemaking, §55D-5.
Secretary of state.
Duties, §55D-15, (a), (b).
Effect of filing or refusal to file by, §55D-15, (d).
Forms.
Promulgation, §55-1-21.
Refusal to file.
Appeal from, §55D-16.
Duties upon, §55D-15, (c).
Effect, §55D-15, (d).
Foreign corporations, §§55-15-01 to 55-15-33.
Actions.
Certificates of authority.
Consequences of failure to obtain, §55-15-02, (a).
Administrative procedure act.
Revocation of certificate of authority.
Inapplicability of administrative procedure act, §55-15-33.
Appeals.
Revocation of certificate of authority, §55-15-32.
Applicability of act.
Qualified foreign corporations, §55-17-02.
Certificates of authority.
Amendment.
Procedure, §55-15-04, (b).
When required, §55-15-04, (a).
Applications.
Certificate of existence to accompany, §55-15-03, (b).
Contents, §55-15-03, (a).
Effect, §55-15-05.

CORPORATIONS —Cont'd
Foreign corporations —Cont'd
Certificates of authority —Cont'd
Failure to obtain.
Actions may not be maintained, §55-15-02, (a).
Liability to state for fees and taxes, §55-15-02, (d).
Validity of corporate acts not impaired, §55-15-02, (e).
Insurance companies.
Exception to requirement, §55-15-01, (d).
Issuance, §55-15-03, (c).
Effect, §55-15-05.
Required, §55-15-01, (a).
Consequences of transacting business without authority, §55-15-02.
Exceptions, §§55-15-01, (b), (d), 55-17-02.
Revocation, §§55-15-30 to 55-15-33.
Secretary of state.
Action on application for certificate, §55-15-03, (c).
Dissolution.
Probate and registration.
Validation of conveyances of foreign dissolved corporations, §47-108.6.
Domestic corporations.
Certificate of authority to confer same rights and privileges, §55-15-05, (b).
Executors and administrators.
Granting of ancillary letters, §28A-26-3, (a).
Fiduciaries.
Restrictions on foreign corporations, §55-15-05, (a).
Franchise tax generally, §§105-114 to 105-129.
See FRANCHISE TAX.
Insurance companies.
See FOREIGN OR ALIEN INSURANCE COMPANIES.
Merger or share exchange with foreign corporation, §55-11-07.
Acquisition of shares of domestic corporation.
Power of foreign corporation not affected, §55-11-07, (c).
Authorized, §55-11-07, (a).
Effect, §55-11-07, (b).
Names, §55D-22.
Change of name to satisfy requirements, §55D-22, (a).
May not conduct business unless requirements satisfied, §55D-22, (b).
Registration of name.
Generally, §§55D-24, 55D-25.
Nonprofit corporations.
See NONPROFIT CORPORATIONS.
Probate and registration.
Validation of certain conveyances of foreign dissolved corporations, §47-108.6.
Professional corporations, §55B-16.
Qualified foreign corporations.
Exemption of previously qualified foreign corporation, §55-17-02.
Receivers.
Property within state of foreign corporations, §1-502.
Registered agent.
Required, §55-15-07.
Revocation of certificate of authority.
Authority of registered agent not terminated by, §55-15-31, (e).

CORPORATIONS —Cont'd
Foreign corporations —Cont'd
Registered office.
Required, §55-15-07.
Revocation of certificate of authority.
Administrative procedure act.
Not applicable, §55-15-33.
Appeal.
Appeal from court's final decision, §55-15-32, (c).
Petition, §55-15-32, (a).
Powers of court, §55-15-32, (b).
Time for, §55-15-32, (a).
Certificate of revocation, §55-15-31, (b).
Effect, §55-15-31, (c) to (e).
Grounds, §55-15-30, (a).
New certificate of authority.
Not granted until grounds for revocation corrected, §55-15-31, (f).
Notice of determination that grounds exist, §55-15-31, (a).
Revenue act.
Certain provisions not repealed or modified, §55-15-30, (b).
Service of process.
Effect on, §55-15-31, (d).
Saving provisions, §55-17-02.
Secretary of state.
Certificates of authority.
Action on application for, §55-15-03, (c).
Revocation generally, §§55-15-30 to 55-15-33.
Power to require compliance with provisions, §55-15-02, (f).
Revocation of certificate of authority.
Generally, §§55-15-30 to 55-15-33.
Service of process.
Merger or share exchange with foreign corporation, §55-11-07, (b).
Withdrawal of foreign corporation, §55-15-21, (c).
Service of process.
Manner of service on to exercise personal jurisdiction, §1A-1, Rule 4, (j).
Revocation of certificate of authority.
Effect, §55-15-31, (d).
Secretary of state.
Merger or share exchange with foreign corporation, §55-11-07, (b).
Withdrawal of foreign corporation, §55-15-21, (c).
Withdrawal of foreign corporation.
Effect, §55-15-20, (c).
Taxation.
Applicability of laws, §105-250.
Property taxes.
Property of foreign corporations not exempted, §105-274, (b).
Transacting business in state.
Activities not deemed to constitute, §55-15-01, (b).
Previously qualified foreign corporations, §55-17-02.
Requirement of certificate of authority, §55-15-01, (a).
Consequences of transacting business without authority, §55-15-02.
Venue of actions against, §1-80.
Withdrawal.
Application for certificate, §55-15-20, (b).
Action by secretary of state on, §55-15-20, (b1).

CORPORATIONS —Cont'd
Foreign corporations —Cont'd
Withdrawal —Cont'd
Certificate of withdrawal.
Application for, §55-15-20, (b), (b1).
Issuance, §55-15-20, (b1).
Required, §55-15-20, (a).
Withdrawal by reason of merger, consolidation, or conversion, §55-15-21.
Effect, §55-15-20, (c).
Merger.
Withdrawal by reason of merger, consolidation, or conversion, §55-15-21.
Service of process.
Effect on, §55-15-20, (c).
Withdrawal by reason of merger, consolidation, or conversion.
Actions by secretary of state and application, §55-15-21, (b).
Application for certificate, §55-15-21, (a).
Foreign trade zones.
Definitions.
"Public corporation," §55C-2.
Federal law.
Corporations establishing foreign trade zone to be governed by, §55C-4.
Private corporations.
Application for privilege for establishing foreign trade zone.
Authorized, §55C-3.
Federal law.
Private corporation establishing foreign trade zone to be governed by, §55C-4.
Public corporations.
Application for privilege of establishing foreign trade zone.
Authorized, §55C-1.
Defined, §55C-2.
Federal law.
Public corporation establishing foreign trade zone to be governed by, §55C-4.
Foresters.
Registration.
Prohibited, §89B-9, (b).
Forest protection and development corporation, §§113-61 to 113-77.
See FOREST PROTECTION AND DEVELOPMENT CORPORATIONS.
Forfeiture of charter.
Counterfeiting, §14-15.
Kidnapping and abduction, §14-39.
Forgery.
Certificates of corporate stock forged, §14-124.
Formation, §58-65-15.
Articles of incorporation.
Amendments, §§55-10-01 to 55-10-09. See within this heading, "Amendment of articles of incorporation."
Contents, §55-2-02, (a), (b).
Defined, §55-1-40.
Filing.
Commencement of corporate existence, §55-2-03, (a).
Effect, §55-2-03, (b).
Powers of corporation.
Statutory powers need not be set forth, §§55-2-02, (c), 55-3-02, (b).
Bylaws, §§55-2-06, 55-2-07.
Commencement of corporate existence, §55-2-03, (a).
Incorporators, §55-2-01.

CORPORATIONS —Cont'd
Formation —Cont'd
Nonprofit corporations.
Incorporators, §55A-2-01.
Organizational meeting, §55A-2-05.
When corporate existence begins, §55A-2-03.
Number of incorporators, §§55-2-01, 58-65-15.
Organizational meeting, §55-2-05, (a).
Location, §55-2-05, (c).
Taking action without meeting, §55-2-05, (b).
Purposes, §55-3-01, (a).
Business subject to regulation under other statute, §55-3-01, (b).
Saving provisions, §55-17-03, (a).
Subscription for shares before incorporation, §55-6-20.
Forms.
Conveyances.
Probate for deeds and other conveyances, §47-41.01, (b), (c).
Instrument executed by president or presiding member or trustee, §47-41.02, (b) to (d).
Other forms not excluded, §47-41.01, (a).
Other forms of probate for corporate conveyances.
Contracts in writing for purchase of personal property, §47-41.02, (f).
Other forms not excluded, §47-41.02, (a).
Validation of conveyances probated and recorded prior to February 14, 1939, §47-41.02, (e).
Validation of deeds and other conveyances executed on or before April 12, 1974, §47-41.02, (g).
Filing of documents, §55-1-21.
Franchise tax.
General provisions, §§105-114 to 105-129.
See FRANCHISE TAX.
Garnishment.
Summons and process.
Delivery of garnishment process to corporate garnishee, §1-440.26.
General assembly.
Reservation of power to amend or repeal provisions, §55-1-02.
Geologists, §89E-7, (a).
Guardian ad litem.
Rules of civil procedure, §1A-1, Rule 17, (b), (d).
Guardians.
Accounting, procedure to compel.
Persons proceeded against, §35A-1265, (a).
Administering incompetent's estate, §35A-1251.
Administering minor ward's estate, §35A-1252.
Appointment as guardian for incompetent, §35A-1213, (c).
Priorities for appointment, §35A-1214.
Status reports for incompetent wards.
Procedure to compel, §35A-1244.
Health maintenance organizations, §§58-67-1 to 58-67-185.
See HEALTH MAINTENANCE ORGANIZATIONS.
History.
Outdoor historical dramas, §143-204.8.
Holding companies.
Insurance holding companies generally, §§58-19-1 to 58-19-70.
See INSURANCE HOLDING COMPANIES.
Hospital, medical and dental service corporations, §§58-65-1 to 58-65-40.
See HOSPITAL, MEDICAL AND DENTAL SERVICE CORPORATIONS.

CORPORATIONS —Cont'd
Husband and wife.
Joint ownership of corporate stock and investment securities, §41-2.2, (a).
Death of joint tenant, §41-2.2, (c).
Inheritance laws unaffected, §41-2.2, (d).
When joint tenancy and shares of corporate stock or investment securities exist, §41-2.2, (b).
Immunity.
Nonprofit corporations.
Acceptance or rejection of member's vote.
Corporate action in good faith, §55A-7-27, (d).
Improvements.
Internal improvements, §§124-1 to 124-7.
See INTERNAL IMPROVEMENTS.
Income tax.
General provisions, §§105-130 to 105-130.41.
See INCOME TAX.
S corporations, §§105-131 to 105-131.8.
See INCOME TAX.
Indemnification, §§55-8-50 to 55-8-58.
Additional indemnification, §55-8-57, (a), (b).
Agents, §55-8-56.
Articles of incorporation.
Restrictions on indemnification, §55-8-58, (a).
Court-ordered indemnification.
Directors, §55-8-54.
Officers, employees and agents, §55-8-56.
Definitions, §55-8-50, (b).
Directors.
Advance for expenses, §55-8-53.
Authority to indemnify, §55-8-51, (a) to (c).
Determinations required, §55-8-55, (a), (b).
Manner of authorization, §55-8-55, (c).
Conflicts of interest.
Indemnification not void or voidable on grounds of, §55-8-51, (f).
Court-ordered indemnification, §55-8-54.
Expenses in defending proceedings.
Advance for expenses, §55-8-53.
Certain powers of corporation not limited, §55-8-58, (b).
Evaluation as to reasonableness, §55-8-55, (c).
Mandatory indemnification, §55-8-52.
Restrictions on indemnification, §55-8-51, (d), (e).
Effective date of article.
Restriction on applicability of provisions, §55-8-58, (c).
Employees, §55-8-56.
Insurance.
Purchase and maintenance, §55-8-57, (c).
Mandatory indemnification.
Directors, §55-8-52.
Officers, employees and agents, §55-8-56.
Nonprofit corporations, §§55A-8-50 to 55A-8-58.
See NONPROFIT CORPORATIONS.
Officers, §55-8-56.
Public policy of state, §55-8-50, (a).
Report to shareholders, §55-16-21, (a).
Inheritance taxes.
Joint ownership of corporate stock and investment securities.
Inheritance tax laws unaffected, §41-2.2, (d).
Injunctions.
Dissolution.
Judicial dissolution.
Powers of court, §55-14-31, (c).
Franchises.
Exercise of corporate franchises not granted, §55-3-05.

CORPORATIONS —Cont'd
Injunctions —Cont'd
Nonprofit corporations.
Corporate power to act.
Ultra vires, §55A-3-04.
Insurance companies.
Foreign or alien insurance companies, §§58-16-1 to 58-16-55.
See FOREIGN OR ALIEN INSURANCE COMPANIES.
Generally.
See INSURANCE COMPANIES.
Holding companies generally, §§58-19-1 to 58-19-70.
See INSURANCE HOLDING COMPANIES.
Mutual insurance companies generally, §§58-8-1 to 58-8-60.
See MUTUAL INSURANCE COMPANIES.
Interest.
Sale below par permitted, §24-2.
Internal improvements, §§124-1 to 124-7.
See INTERNAL IMPROVEMENTS.
Interrogatories.
Secretary of state.
Answer, §55-1-31.
Sanctions for failure or refusal to answer, §55-1-32.
Confidentiality of information disclosed by, §55-1-33.
Failure or refusal to answer.
Misdemeanor, §55-1-32, (b).
Suspension of articles or authority to do business, §55-1-32, (a).
Generally, §55-1-31.
Nonprofit corporations, §§55A-1-31 to 55A-1-33.
Interrogatories to parties, §1A-1, Rule 33, (a).
Investment securities, §§25-8-101 to 25-8-511.
See INVESTMENT SECURITIES.
Joint assumption or underwriting of risks.
Contracts for, §58-65-5.
Jurisdiction.
Dissenting shareholders.
Judicial appraisal of shares, §55-13-30, (d).
Personal jurisdiction.
Grounds, §1-75.4.
Stock and stockholders.
Derivative actions by shareholders, §55-7-40.
Kidnapping and abduction.
Punishment for kidnapping.
Firm or corporation, §14-39, (c).
Land and loan associations, §§54-45 to 54-73.
See LAND AND LOAN ASSOCIATIONS.
Landscape contractors.
Applicability of provisions, §89D-3.
Liens.
Contracts in writing for purchase of personal property.
Lien on property.
Forms on probate for deeds and other conveyances, §47-41.02, (f).
Wages for two months' lien on assets, §44-5.1.
Limitation of actions.
Cash or stock dividends.
Six-year limitation, §1-50, (a).
Limited liability companies, §§57C-1-01 to 57C-10-07.
See LIMITED LIABILITY COMPANIES.
Liquidation.
Voluntary dissolution proceedings.
Actions for liquidation by court after dissolution, §§55-14-30 to 55-14-33.

CORPORATIONS —Cont'd
Loans.
Board of directors.
Loans to directors, §55-8-32.
Malfeasance.
Officers and agents.
Misconduct in private office, §14-254.
Marketing associations, §§54-129 to 54-166.
See MARKETING ASSOCIATIONS.
Medical service corporations.
Hospital, medical and dental service corporations, §§58-65-1 to 58-65-40.
See HOSPITAL, MEDICAL AND DENTAL SERVICE CORPORATIONS.
Mergers, §§55-11-01 to 55-11-09.
Articles of merger.
Contents, §55-11-05, (a).
Delivery to secretary of state, §55-11-05, (a).
Subsidiary corporation, §55-11-04, (d), (e).
Authorized, §55-11-01, (a).
Certificates of merger, §55-11-05, (c).
Dissenting shareholders.
General provisions, §§55-13-01 to 55-13-31. See within this heading, "Dissenting shareholders."
Effective date, §55-11-05, (b).
Effect of merger, §55-11-06, (a).
Foreign corporations.
Merger with, §55-11-07.
Withdrawn by reason of merger, consolidation, or conversion, §55-15-21.
Nonprofit corporations, §55A-11-08.
Compliance with requirements, §55A-11-08, (a).
Generally, §§55A-11-01 to 55A-11-07.
See NONPROFIT CORPORATIONS.
Plan of merger, §55-11-01, (a).
Abandonment of plan, §55-11-03, (i).
Approval, §55-11-03, (b).
Notice of meeting, §55-11-03, (d).
Voting groups, §55-11-03, (e), (f).
Contents, §55-11-01, (b), (c).
Submission to shareholders, §55-11-03, (a), (c).
Subsidiary corporation, §55-11-04, (b) to (d).
When action by shareholders of surviving corporation not required, §55-11-03, (g), (h).
Probate and registration.
Adoption of uniform certificates of merger or consolidation, §47-18.1, (b).
Certain formalities not required, §47-18.1, (c).
Name of corporation formerly owning property to appear in grantor index, §47-18.1, (c).
Name of corporation owning property by virtue of merger shall appear in grantee index, §47-18.1, (c).
Registration of certificate, §47-18.1, (a).
Shareholder protection act, §§55-9-01 to 55-9-05.
Provisions of act to control, §55-11-08.
Subsidiary corporation, §55-11-04, (d), (e).
Articles of merger, §55-11-04, (d), (e).
Plan of merger, §55-11-04, (b).
Mailing of summary to shareholders of subsidiary, §55-11-04, (c), (d).
Power of parent corporation to merge subsidiary into itself, §55-11-04, (a).
Right of shareholders to dissent, §55-11-04, (f).
Trusts and trustees.
Consolidation, merger, etc., by corporate trustee, §36A-37.
Misdemeanors.
Filing of documents.
False document.
Signing, §55D-18, (b).

CORPORATIONS —Cont'd
Misdemeanors —Cont'd
Interrogatories by secretary of state.
Failure or refusal to answer, §55-1-32, (b).
Money transmitters licenses.
Applications, §53-208.7, (b).
Good standing required, §53-208.5, (b).
Mortgage bankers and brokers.
Licenses, §53-243.05, (g).
Mortgages and deeds of trust.
Chattel mortgages or chattel deeds of trust.
Forms of probate for deeds and other conveyances, §47-41.02, (f).
Conveyances.
Validation of appointment of and conveyances to corporations as trustees, §45-21.
Corporate seal.
Required, §47-41.1.
Discharge and release.
Cancellation of lost mortgages by register of deeds, §45-42.1.
Foreclosure.
Powers of receivers of corporations, §§1-507.2, 1-507.4.
Receivers.
Powers of receivers of corporations, §§1-507.2, 1-507.4.
Sales, §1-507.4.
Receivers of corporations.
Foreclosure.
Powers, §§1-507.2, 1-507.4.
Sales, §1-507.4.
Reorganization, §1-507.11.
Satisfaction of corporate mortgages by corporate officers, §45-42.
Motor vehicle certificates of title.
Change of name of corporation, §20-64, (b).
Mutual insurance companies, §§58-8-1 to 58-8-60.
See MUTUAL INSURANCE COMPANIES.
Names, §§55D-20 to 55D-26.
Assumed or fictitious names, §55D-20, (d).
Authorization to use.
Restrictions, §55D-20, (e).
Change of name.
Certificate.
Recordation, §55D-26, (a), (c).
Uniform certificates, §55D-26, (b).
Definitions, §55D-1.
Dissolved entity.
Restrictions on use of name of, §55D-21, (d).
Distinguishable names, §55D-21, (b).
Exceptions, §55D-21, (a), (c).
Foreign corporations, §55D-22.
Change of name to satisfy requirements, §55D-22, (a).
May not conduct business unless requirements satisfied, §55D-22, (b).
Registration of name.
Generally, §§55D-24, 55D-25.
Prohibitions, §55D-20, (b), (c).
Registration of name.
Authorized, §55D-24, (a).
Effect, §55D-24, (e).
Filing of application, §55D-24, (b).
Renewal, §55D-24, (d).
Revocation, §55D-25.
When effective, §55D-24, (c).
Reinstatement following administrative dissolution, §55-14-22, (a1).
Requirements, §55D-20, (a).

CORPORATIONS —Cont'd
Names —Cont'd
Reservation of name, §55D-23, (a), (c).
Revocation, §55D-25.
Transfer of reservation.
Requirements, §55D-23, (b).
Rulemaking, §55D-5.
Nonprofit corporations.
Exemptions from business corporation act, §55-17-01, (b).
Generally, §§55A-1-01 to 55A-17-05.
See NONPROFIT CORPORATIONS.
Mergers with, §55A-11-08.
North Carolina enterprise corporations, §§53A-35 to 53A-47.
See NORTH CAROLINA ENTERPRISE CORPORATIONS.
Notice, §55-1-41.
Board of directors.
Meetings, §§55-8-22, 55-8-23.
Conflict of laws.
Requirements which govern, §55-1-41, (g).
Control share acquisitions.
Meeting of shareholders, §55-9A-04.
Right of redemption by shareholders, §55-9A-06, (b), (c).
Discontinuance or settlement of derivative proceeding, §55-7-45, (a), (b).
Dissenting shareholders, §§55-13-20 to 55-13-22.
Dissolution.
Administrative dissolution.
Denial of reinstatement, §55-14-23, (a).
Determination that grounds exist, §55-14-21, (a).
Voluntary dissolution, §§55-14-06, (b), (c), 55-14-07.
Foreign corporations.
Revocation of certificate of authority.
Notice of determination that grounds exist, §55-15-31, (a).
How notice given, §55-1-41, (a), (b).
Meetings of shareholders.
Action without meeting, §55-7-04, (d), (e).
Adjournment of meeting, §55-7-05, (e).
Amendments to articles of incorporation, §55-10-03, (d).
Annual meeting.
Failure to hold, §55-7-01, (c).
Location, §55-7-01, (b).
Required, §55-7-01, (a).
Subject matter, §55-7-01, (d).
Control share acquisitions, §§55-9A-03, 55-9A-04.
Court-ordered meetings.
Powers of court as to, §55-7-03, (b).
Summary order for meeting to be held, §55-7-03, (a).
Dissolution of corporation by directors and shareholders, §55-14-02, (d).
Election of directors.
Generally. See within this heading, "Board of directors."
Merger or share exchange, §55-11-03, (d).
Record date, §55-7-05, (d).
Removal of directors by shareholders, §55-8-08, (d).
Requirements, §55-7-05, (a) to (c).
Restated articles of incorporation, §55-10-07, (c).
Transfer of assets other than in regular course of business, §55-12-02, (d).
Waiver of notice, §55-7-06.

CORPORATIONS —Cont'd
Notice —Cont'd
Nonprofit corporations.
Directors' meetings, §55A-8-22.
Generally, §55A-1-41.
Waiver by directors, §55A-8-23.
Publication.
Notice by publication, §55-1-42, (b).
Shareholder action without meeting, §55-7-04, (d), (e).
To whom addressed, §55-1-41, (d).
When effective, §55-1-41, (c), (e), (f).
Oaths, §11-5.
Officers, §§55-8-40 to 55-8-44.
Assistants.
Appointment, §55-8-40, (b).
Construction of references to specific office, §55-8-40, (e).
Contract rights.
Appointment not to create, §55-8-44, (a).
Removal of officer not to affect, §55-8-44, (b).
Duties, §55-8-41.
Embezzlement.
Receipt of property by virtue of office or employment, §14-90.
Generally, §55-8-40, (a).
Indemnification, §§55-8-50 to 55-8-58.
Individual liability for taxes, §105-253, (a), (b).
Misconduct in private office.
Malfeasance of corporation officers, §14-254, (a).
Mortgages and deeds of trust.
Satisfaction of corporate mortgages by corporate officers, §45-42.
Multiple office-holding by individual, §55-8-40, (d).
Nonprofit corporations.
See NONPROFIT CORPORATIONS.
Probate and registration.
Execution of corporate instruments.
Liability, §47-18.3, (d).
Removal by board of directors, §55-8-43, (b).
Effect on contract rights, §55-8-44, (b).
Resignation, §55-8-43, (a).
Secretary.
Responsibilities, §55-8-40, (c).
Standards of conduct.
Generally, §55-8-42, (a).
Liability of officers.
Effect of provisions on, §55-8-42, (d), (e).
Reliance on information, opinions, reports, or statements, §55-8-42, (b), (c).
Tax liability, §105-253, (a), (b).
Uniform fiduciaries act generally, §§32-1 to 32-13.
See FIDUCIARIES.
Workers' compensation.
Employee defined, §97-2.
Exclusion of executive officers by corporation, §97-2.
Personal property.
Contracts in writing for purchase of personal property.
Lien on property or retention of title as security for purchase.
Forms of probate for deeds and other conveyances, §47-41.02, (f).
Powers, §55-3-02, (a).
Articles of incorporation.
Statutory powers need not be set forth, §§55-2-02, (c), 55-3-02, (b).
Emergency powers, §55-3-03, (a), (b).
Effect of actions taken under, §55-3-03, (c).
Nonprofit corporations, §55A-3-03.

CORPORATIONS —Cont'd
Powers —Cont'd
Emergency powers —Cont'd
When emergency exists, §55-3-03, (d).
Nonprofit corporations, §§55A-3-01 to 55A-3-07.
Ultra vires, §55-3-04, (a).
Exceptions, §55-3-04, (b), (c).
Nonprofit corporations, §55A-3-04.
Practice of law by.
Regulations for professional corporations practicing law, Bar Rules & Regs., E, §§.0101 to .0106.
Premiums or dues.
Payment, §58-65-10.
Preneed funeral contracts and funds.
Embezzling, fraudulently misapplying or converting funds.
Liability of officers, directors, agents or employees, §90-210.70, (c).
Presumptions.
Annual report delinquent, §55-16-22, (h).
Principal office.
Residence for purpose of venue, §1-79, (a).
Private banker.
Acting as private banker, §14-401.7.
Probate and registration.
Admission to record of certain corporate deeds declared valid, §47-108.1.
By president and attested by treasurer under corporate seal, §47-70.
Conveyance forms, §47-41.01, (b), (c).
Definitions, §47-41.01, (d).
Other forms not excluded, §47-41.01, (a).
Other forms of probate for corporate conveyances.
Contracts in writing for purchase of personal property, §47-41.02, (f).
Instrument executed by president or presiding member or trustee, §47-41.02, (b) to (d).
Other forms not excluded, §47-41.02, (a).
Validation of conveyances probated and recorded prior to February 14, 1939, §47-41.02, (e).
Validation of deeds and conveyances executed on or before April 12, 1974, §47-41.02, (g).
Deeds.
Mistake as to officer's name.
Validation, §47-97.
Error in acknowledgment or probate.
Validation of corporate deeds, §47-97.1.
Execution of corporate instruments.
Authority and proof generally, §47-18.3.
Homeowners loan corporation.
Conveyance of lands or other properties, §47-18.3, (e).
Liability of corporate officers, §47-18.3, (d).
Power of corporate representative to bind corporation.
Section not deemed to exclude, §47-18.3, (c).
Seals and sealed instruments.
Instruments executed bearing seal.
Prima facie evidence seal duly adopted corporate seal, §47-18.3, (b).
Third parties.
Validity with respect to innocent third parties, §47-18.3, (a).
Foreign corporations.
Validation of certain conveyances of foreign dissolved corporations, §47-108.6.

CORPORATIONS —Cont'd
Probate and registration —Cont'd
Interested corporations.
Probates before officer, §47-63.
Merger, consolidation or conversion.
Adoption of uniform certificates, §47-18.1, (b).
Certain formalities not required for registration, §47-18.1, (c).
Name of corporation to appear in grantor index, §47-18.1, (c).
Registration of certificate, §47-18.1, (a).
Name.
Corporate name not affixed, but signed otherwise prior to January, 1973, §47-72.
Oath of subscribing witness, §47-73.
Officers, stockholders or directors prior of January 1, 1945, §47-64.
Probate of corporate deeds, where corporation has ceased to exist, §47-16.
Proof of articles before officer authorized, §47-75.
Seal omitted prior to January 1, 1991, §47-71.1.
Stamps of corporate seal, §47-41.1.
Professional corporations, §§55B-1 to 55B-16.
See PROFESSIONAL CORPORATIONS.
Professional counselors.
Licensed professional counselors.
Use of title by corporate entity, §90-332.
Provider sponsored organizations, §§131E-275 to 131E-314.
See PROVIDER SPONSORED ORGANIZATIONS.
Proxies, §55-7-22.
Appointment, §55-7-22, (b) to (h).
Authorized, §55-7-22, (a).
Death or incapacity of shareholder appointing proxy, §55-7-22, (e).
Revocation of appointment, §55-7-22, (d), (f), (g).
Quo warranto.
General provisions, §§1-514 to 1-532.
See QUO WARRANTO.
Railroads.
Joint construction of railroads having same location, §136-193.
Powers of railroad corporations, §136-190.
Real estate appraisers.
License or certificate not issued to, §93E-1-3, (a).
Use of term state-licensed real estate appraiser or state-certified real estate appraiser prohibited, §93E-1-3.1, (c).
Real property.
Change of name or transfer of title upon merger.
Recordation of certificate, §55D-26.
Real property donations.
Credits, §105-130.34.
Receivers, §§1-507.1 to 1-507.11.
Actions.
Powers of receivers, §1-507.2.
Agents.
Appointment by receiver, §1-507.2.
Appointment of receivers, §1-507.1.
Attorneys at law.
Counsel fees, §1-507.9.
Bonds, surety, §1-507.2.
Claims.
Presentation to receiver, §1-507.6.
Proof, §1-507.6.
Report on claims to court, §1-507.7.
Exceptions, §1-507.7.
Time limit, §1-507.6.
Notice, §1-507.6.
Compensation of receivers, §1-507.9.

CORPORATIONS —Cont'd
Receivers —Cont'd
Contempt.
Power of receiver to examine persons and papers.
Refusal to answer, §1-507.5.
Death.
Substitution of parties, §1A-1, Rule 25, (e).
Debts of corporation paid or provided for.
Discharge of receiver, §1-507.10.
Discharge of receiver, §1-507.10.
Expenses, §1-507.9.
Foreign corporations.
Property within state of foreign corporations.
Appointment of receiver, §1-502.
Inventory, §1-507.3.
Jury.
Claims.
Exceptions to report on claims, §1-507.7.
Mortgages and deeds of trust.
Foreclosure.
Powers of receivers of corporations, §§1-507.2, 1-507.4.
Notice.
Sale of property pending litigation, §1-507.8.
Oaths.
Claims.
Power of receiver to examine witnesses touching on claim, §1-507.6.
Power of receivers to examine persons under oath, §1-507.5.
Powers of receivers, §§1-507.2 to 1-507.6.
Property.
Inventory, §1-507.3.
Powers of receivers generally, §1-507.2.
Title, §1-507.3.
Removal of receivers, §1-507.1.
Reorganization, §1-507.11.
Sales.
Mortgages and deeds of trust.
Foreclosure.
Powers of receivers of corporations, §1-507.4.
Powers of receivers of corporations, §1-507.2.
Foreclosure sales, §1-507.4.
Property sold pending litigation, §1-507.8.
Superior courts.
Proper division for actions for corporate receiverships, §7A-249.
Records, §§55-16-01 to 55-16-22.
Accounting records, §55-16-01, (b).
Copies to be kept at principal office, §55-16-01, (e).
Inspection of records by shareholders.
Agent of shareholder.
Same rights as shareholder, §55-16-03, (a).
Attorney of shareholder.
Same rights as shareholder, §55-16-03, (a).
Charges.
Right of corporation to impose, §55-16-03, (c).
Court-ordered inspection.
Application for, §55-16-04, (b).
Attorneys' fees, §55-16-04, (c).
Costs, §55-16-04, (c).
Generally, §55-16-04, (a).
Restrictions may be imposed, §55-16-04, (d).
Definitions, §55-16-02, (f), (g).
List of shareholders.
Compliance by corporation with shareholder's demand for, §55-16-03, (d).
Photographic copies.
Scope of copying right, §55-16-03, (b).

CORPORATIONS —Cont'd
Records —Cont'd
Inspection of records by shareholders —Cont'd
Rights of shareholders, §55-16-02, (a), (b), (e).
Abolition or limitation by articles of incorporation or bylaws prohibited, §55-16-02, (d).
No common law rights, shareholders of public corporations, §55-16-02, (i).
Restrictions, §55-16-02, (c).
Scope of right, §55-16-03.
Shareholder having right to elect majority of directors of another corporation, §55-16-02, (h).
Minutes of meetings, §55-16-01, (a).
Nonprofit corporations, §§55A-16-01 to 55A-16-05.
See NONPROFIT CORPORATIONS.
Shareholders.
Inspection by shareholders, §§55-16-02 to 55-16-04.
Record of shareholders, §55-16-01, (c).
Written records required, §55-16-01, (d).
Registered agent, §§55D-30 to 55D-33.
Change, §55D-31, (a).
Effective date.
Statement included in annual report, §55-16-22, (g).
Inclusion of information in annual report, §55D-31, (c).
Definitions, §55D-1.
Dissolution.
Administrative dissolution.
Authority of registered agent not terminated, §55-14-21, (d).
Duty, §55D-30, (b).
Foreign corporations, §55-15-07.
Nonprofit corporations, §55A-5-01.
Foreign corporations, §55A-15-07.
Required, §55D-30, (a).
Resignation.
Effect, §55D-32, (c).
Statement, §55D-32, (a), (b).
Rulemaking, §55D-5.
Service of process on, §55D-33, (a).
Failure to maintain registered agent, §55D-33, (b).
Registered office, §§55D-30, 55D-31.
Change, §55D-31, (a), (b).
Effective date.
Statement included in annual report, §55-16-22, (g).
Inclusion of information in annual report, §55D-31, (c).
Definitions, §55D-1.
Foreign corporations, §55-15-07.
Nonprofit corporations, §55A-5-01.
Foreign corporations, §55A-15-07.
Required, §55D-30, (a).
Residence for purposes of venue, §1-79, (a).
Rulemaking, §55D-5.
Register of deeds.
Mortgages and deeds of trust.
Cancellation of lost mortgages by register of deeds, §45-42.1.
Religious organizations and societies.
Exemption from business corporation act, §55-17-01, (b).
Management of institutional funds, §§36B-1 to 36B-10.
See MANAGEMENT OF INSTITUTIONAL FUNDS.

CORPORATIONS —Cont'd
Reorganization, §1-507.11.
Dissenting shareholders.
Actions under provisions not to give rise to rights, §55-14A-01, (c).
Filings, §55-14A-01, (b).
Fundamental changes in reorganization proceedings, §55-14A-01.
Dissenting shareholders.
Actions not to give rise to dissenter's rights, §55-14A-01, (c).
Execution and filing of documents, §55-14A-01, (b).
Final decree.
Provisions not to apply after entry of, §55-14A-01, (d).
Powers of corporation, §55-14A-01, (a).
Generally, §55-14A-01, (a).
No action to be taken after final decree, §55-14A-01, (d).
Nonprofit corporations, §55A-14-01.
Scope, §55-14A-01, (a).
Trusts and trustees.
Reorganization by corporate trustee, §36A-37.
Reports.
Annual report, §55-16-22.
Administrative dissolution or revocation of certificate of authority for failure to file
Amendment, §55-16-22, (e).
Change of registered office or agent.
Statement filed in report, effective date of change, §55-16-22, (g).
Content requirements, §55-16-22, (a3).
Correction of report to include required information, §55-16-22, (d).
Delinquent, presumption, §55-16-22, (h).
Filing fee nonrefundable, §55-1-22, (d).
Form provided, §55-16-22, (a3).
Information to be included, §55-16-22, (a), (b).
Correction of report which does not include required information, §55-16-22, (d).
Insurance companies, §55-16-22, (a1).
Professional corporations, exemption, §55-16-22, (a2).
Required, §55-16-22, (a).
Time for delivery, §55-16-22, (c).
Corrected report, §55-16-22, (d).
Financial statements for shareholders, §55-16-20.
Mailing.
Time for, §55-16-20, (c).
Public accountant's report to accompany, §55-16-20, (b).
Required, §55-16-20, (a).
Indemnification of directors.
Report to shareholders, §55-16-21, (a).
Promissory notes or promises to render services in future.
Issuance of shares for.
Report to shareholders, §55-16-21, (b).
Royalties.
Corporate income tax.
Payments received on use of trademarks.
Option methods of reporting, §105-130.7A.
Sanitary districts.
Construction of systems by corporations or individuals, §130A-58.
Saving provisions, §55-17-03.
Foreign corporations, §55-17-02.
Savings and loan associations, §§54B-1 to 54B-278.
See SAVINGS AND LOAN ASSOCIATIONS.

CORPORATIONS —Cont'd
Savings banks, §§54C-1 to 54C-141.
See SAVINGS BANKS.
Seals and sealed instruments.
Probate and registration.
By president and attested by treasurer under corporate seal, §47-70.
Execution of corporate instruments.
Instruments executed bearing seal.
Prima facie evidence seal duly adopted, §47-18.3, (b).
Seal omitted prior to January 1, 1991, §47-71.1.
Required on certain instruments, §47-41.1.
Secretary of revenue.
Annual report, §55-16-22.
Secretary of state.
Advisory review of documents prior to submission for filing, §55D-12.
Copying and certifying documents.
Fees, §147-37.
Dissolution.
Administrative dissolution, §§55-14-20 to 55-14-24.
Duties as to, §147-36.
Filing of documents, §§55D-10 to 55D-18.
Foreign corporations.
Certificates of authority.
Action on application for, §55-15-03, (c).
Revocation generally, §§55-15-30 to 55-15-33.
Power to require compliance with provisions, §55-15-02, (f).
Revocation of certificate of authority.
Generally, §§55-15-30 to 55-15-33.
Service of process.
Merger or share exchange with foreign corporation, §55-11-07, (b).
Withdrawal of foreign corporation, §55-15-21, (c).
Service of process on secretary, §55D-33, (b), (c).
Fees, §55-1-22, (b).
Foreign corporations.
Merger or share exchange with foreign corporation, §55-11-07, (b).
Withdrawal of foreign corporation, §55-15-21, (c).
Securities.
Broker.
When deemed security broker, §14-401.7.
Dealing in securities on commission.
Taxed as private banker, §14-401.7.
Investment securities, §§25-8-101 to 25-8-511.
See INVESTMENT SECURITIES.
Security transfers.
See FIDUCIARIES.
Service of process.
Additional nature of provisions, §55D-33, (d).
After merger with nonprofit corporations, §55A-11-08, (b).
Dissenting shareholders.
Judicial appraisal of shares.
Petition, §55-13-30, (c).
Dissolution.
Administrative dissolution.
Notice of denial of reinstatement, §55-14-23, (a).
Foreign corporations.
Revocation of certificate of authority.
Effect, §55-15-31, (d).
Secretary of state.
Merger or share exchange with foreign corporation, §55-11-07, (b).

CORPORATIONS —Cont'd
Service of process —Cont'd
Foreign corporations —Cont'd
Secretary of state —Cont'd
Withdrawal of foreign corporation, §55-15-21, (c).
Withdrawal of foreign corporation.
Effect, §55-15-20, (c).
Manner of service on to exercise personal jurisdiction, §1A-1, Rule 4, (j).
Nonprofit corporations.
See NONPROFIT CORPORATIONS.
Personal service manner of service to exercise, §1A-1, Rule 4, (j).
Registered agent, §55D-33, (a).
Failure to maintain registered agent, §55D-33, (b).
Secretary of state, §55D-33, (b), (c).
Fees, §55-1-22, (b).
Foreign corporations.
Merger or share exchange with foreign corporation, §55-11-07, (b).
Withdrawal of foreign corporation, §55-15-21, (c).
Severability of provisions, §55-17-04.
Share exchange, §§55-11-01 to 55-11-09.
Articles of share exchange.
Contents, §55-11-05, (a).
Delivery to secretary of state, §55-11-05, (a).
Authorized, §55-11-02, (a).
Dissenting shareholders, §§55-13-01 to 55-13-31.
Effective date, §55-11-05, (b).
Effect of share exchange, §55-11-06, (b).
Foreign corporations.
Share exchange with, §55-11-07.
Merger with nonprofit corporations.
No limitation on corporate powers, §55A-11-08, (c).
Plan of exchange, §55-11-01, (a).
Abandonment of plan, §55-11-03, (i).
Approval, §55-11-03, (b).
Notice of meeting to consider, §55-11-03, (d).
Voting groups, §55-11-03, (e), (f).
Contents, §55-11-02, (b), (c).
Submission to shareholders, §55-11-03, (a), (c).
Shareholder protection act.
Provisions of act to control, §55-11-08.
Voluntary exchanges.
Power of corporation not limited by provisions, §55-11-02, (d).
Shareholder protection act, §§55-9-01 to 55-9-05.
Applicability, §55-9-04, (a), (b).
Determinations by directors, §55-9-04, (c).
Business combinations.
Defined, §55-9-01, (b).
Voting requirement, §55-9-02.
Exceptions, §55-9-03.
Exemptions, §55-9-05.
Citation of act.
Short title, §55-9-01, (a).
Definitions, §55-9-01, (b).
Fiduciary obligations.
Provisions not construed to relieve other entities from, §55-9-04, (d).
Merger or share exchange.
Applicability of act to, §55-11-08.
Nonresidents.
Service of process.
Designation of secretary of state for service, §75E-8.

CORPORATIONS —Cont'd
Shareholder protection act —Cont'd
Title of act.
Short title, §55-9-01, (a).
Transfer of assets.
Provisions not to modify act, §55-12-03.
Violation of article.
Attorney general.
Investigative and regulatory powers, §75E-3.
Chapter not exclusive, §75E-7.
Civil actions, §75E-4.
Damages, §75E-4.
Definitions, §75E-1.
Penalties.
Civil penalties, §75E-5.
Remedies cumulative, §75E-6.
Severability of provisions, §75E-9.
Unlawful activities, §75E-2.
Voting requirement, §55-9-02.
Exceptions, §55-9-03.
Exemptions, §55-9-05.
Soil scientists.
Practice of soil science, §89F-6.
Stock and stockholders, §§55-6-01 to 55-7-40.
Acceptance of votes by corporation.
Good-faith acceptance.
Generally, §55-7-24, (a), (b).
Rejection of vote, §55-7-24, (c), (d).
Validity of corporate action based upon, §55-7-24, (e).
Validity of corporate action based upon, §55-7-24, (e).
Action by shareholders without meeting.
All shareholders entitled to vote on certain actions, §55-7-04, (a), (a1).
Notice of proposed action, §55-7-04, (d), (e).
Record date, §55-7-04, (b).
Written consent, §55-7-04, (a) to (c).
Agreements among shareholders.
Validity, §55-7-31, (a).
Agreement among all shareholders, §55-7-31, (b), (c).
Amendment of articles of incorporation.
Acquisition by corporation of own shares, §55-6-31, (b), (c).
Amendment before issuance of shares, §55-10-05.
Classes or series of stock, §55-6-02, (b).
Issuance of shares.
Amendment before issuance, §55-10-05.
Restated articles of incorporation.
Submission to shareholders, §55-10-07, (c).
Vested property right resulting from provisions in articles.
Stockholders not deemed to have, §55-10-01, (b).
Voting groups.
Classes of shares entitled to vote as separate voting groups, §55-10-04, (a).
Nonvoting shares entitled to vote as voting groups, §55-10-04, (d).
Series of classes of shares entitled to vote as voting groups, §55-10-04, (b), (c).
Voting on proposed amendments.
Required votes for adoption, §55-10-03, (b), (e).
Voting groups, §55-10-04.
Amendment of bylaws, §§55-10-20, 55-10-22.
Beneficial owner of shares registered in name of nominee.
Recognition as shareholder by corporation.
Corporation may establish procedure, §55-7-23, (a).

CORPORATIONS —Cont'd
Stock and stockholders —Cont'd
Beneficial owner of shares registered in name of nominee —Cont'd
Recognition as shareholder by corporation —Cont'd
What procedure may set forth, §55-7-23, (b).
Certificates, §55-6-25, (a).
Contents, §55-6-25, (b), (c).
Shares without certificate, §55-6-26, (a).
Written statement of information to be supplied, §55-6-26, (b).
Signing, §55-6-25, (d), (e).
Classes of shares.
Articles of amendment.
Delivery to secretary of state before issuance, §55-6-02, (b).
Authorized classes, §55-6-01, (d), (e).
Directors.
Election by certain classes of shareholders, §55-8-04.
Generally, §55-6-01, (a).
Preferences, limitations and rights.
Directors may determine, §55-6-02, (a).
Required classes, §55-6-01, (c).
Series, §55-6-01, (a).
Designation, §55-6-01, (b).
Consideration for shares.
Determination before issuance, §55-6-21, (c).
Effect of payment, §55-6-21, (d).
Liability of purchaser to pay, §55-6-22, (a).
Control share acquisitions, §§55-9A-01 to 55-9A-09.
Conversion of domestic corporation to different business entity.
Approval of plan of conversion, §55-11A-11, (b) to (f).
Cumulative voting for directors, §55-7-28, (b) to (d).
Debt securities.
Rights of holders, §55-7-21.1.
Derivative actions by shareholders.
Applicability of foreign corporations, §55-7-47.
Attorney-client privilege of corporation.
Restrictions on access of shareholder to communication within, §55-7-49.
Attorneys' fees.
Award, §55-7-46.
Authorized, §55-7-40.
Compromise and settlement.
Approval of court, §55-7-45.
Costs.
Award, §55-7-46.
Definitions, §55-7-40.1.
Demand requirement, §55-7-42.
Discontinuance or settlement, §55-7-45.
Dismissal.
Approval of court, §55-7-44.
Burden of proving proceeding not in best interest of corporation, §55-7-44, (e).
Committee appointed by independent directors, inquiry and determination by, §55-7-44, (b), (c).
Determination that proceeding not in best interest of corporation, §55-7-44, (a).
Independent directors, inquiry and determination by, §55-7-44, (b), (c).
Panel of independent persons, inquiry and determination by, §55-7-44, (f).
Proceeding commenced after determination rejecting shareholder's demand, §55-7-44, (d).

CORPORATIONS —Cont'd
Stock and stockholders —Cont'd
Derivative actions by shareholders —Cont'd
Jurisdiction, §55-7-40.
Payment of costs and expenses, §55-7-46.
Privileged communications, §55-7-49.
Standing, §55-7-41.
Stays, §55-7-43.
Dissenting shareholders, §§55-13-01 to 55-13-31.
See within this heading, "Dissenting shareholders."
Dissolution.
Unavailable shareholders and creditors.
Disposition of amounts due to, §55-14-40.
Voluntary dissolution, §§55-14-01 to 55-14-08.
Adoption of proposal by shareholders, §55-14-02, (b), (e).
Articles of dissolution, §55-14-03, (a).
Effective date of dissolution by, §55-14-03, (b).
Notice of shareholders meeting to consider proposal, §55-14-02, (d).
Proposal by directors, §55-14-02, (a), (c).
Revocation of dissolution by, §55-14-04.
Distributions to shareholders.
Authorization, §55-6-40, (a).
Restrictions, §55-6-40, (c) to (g).
Compelling payment of dividends.
Shareholders rights not impair, §55-6-40, (k).
Demand by shareholders, §55-6-40, (h) to (j).
Demand for payment of additional dividends, §55-6-40, (i), (k).
Parity with indebtedness to general unsecured creditors, §55-6-40, (f).
Record date for determining shareholders entitled to distribution, §55-6-40, (b).
Restrictions, §55-6-40, (c), (d).
Determination of effect, §55-6-40, (e) to (g).
Unlawful distributions.
Liability of directors, §55-8-33.
Dividends.
Distributions to shareholders generally, §55-6-40.
Share dividends, §55-6-23, (a) to (c).
Expense of issue, §55-6-28.
Financial statements for shareholders, §55-16-20.
Fractional shares.
Authorized, §55-6-04, (a).
Rights of holders, §55-6-04, (c).
Script, §55-6-04, (a), (b).
Conditions of issuance, §55-6-04, (d).
Issuance of shares.
Consideration.
Determination before issuance, §55-6-21, (c).
Effect of payment, §55-6-21, (d).
Escrow.
Placing certain shares in escrow, §55-6-21, (e).
Expenses, §55-6-28.
Power to issue, §55-6-21, (a), (b).
Liability of shareholders, §55-6-22, (b).
Meetings of shareholders.
Action without meeting, §55-7-04.
Annual meeting.
Failure to hold, §55-7-01, (c).
Location, §55-7-01, (b).
Required, §55-7-01, (a).
Subject matter, §55-7-01, (d).
Control share acquisitions, §§55-9A-03, 55-9A-04.
Court-ordered meetings.
Powers of court as to, §55-7-03, (b).

CORPORATIONS —Cont'd
Stock and stockholders —Cont'd
Meetings of shareholders —Cont'd
Court-ordered meetings —Cont'd
Summary order for meeting to be held, §55-7-03, (a).
Election of directors, §55-8-03, (d).
Classes of shareholders, §55-8-04.
Voting shares, §55-7-28.
Electronic attendance, §55-7-08.
Notice.
Adjournment of meeting, §55-7-05, (e).
Amendments to articles of incorporation, §55-10-03, (d).
Control share acquisitions, §55-9A-04.
Dissolution of corporation by directors and shareholders, §55-14-02, (d).
Merger or share exchange, §55-11-03, (d).
Record date, §55-7-05, (d).
Removal of directors by shareholders, §55-8-08, (d).
Requirements, §55-7-05, (a) to (c).
Restated articles of incorporation, §55-10-07, (c).
Transfer of assets other than in regular course of business, §55-12-02, (d).
Waiver of notice, §55-7-06.
Record date.
Bylaws may fix, §55-7-07, (a).
Court-ordered adjournment of meeting, §55-7-07, (d).
Notice of meeting, §55-7-05, (d).
Restrictions, §55-7-07, (b), (c).
Special meetings, §55-7-02, (b).
Special meetings.
Location, §55-7-02, (c).
Record date, §55-7-02, (b).
Subject matter, §55-7-02, (d).
When held, §55-7-02, (a).
Voting groups.
Generally, §§55-7-25 to 55-7-27.
Voting of shares generally, §§55-7-20 to 55-7-31.
Voting trusts, §55-7-30.
Waiver of notice of meetings.
Attendance at meeting, §55-7-06, (b).
Generally, §55-7-06, (a).
Merger or share exchange.
Action on plan.
Generally, §55-11-03.
Nonprofit corporations.
Acquisition of shares of corporation, §55-11-09, (c).
Number of shareholders, §55-1-42, (a).
More than one shareholder not required, §55-2-03, (c).
Options, §55-6-24, (a).
Public corporations, §55-6-24, (b).
Outstanding shares, §55-6-03, (a), (c).
Reacquisition, redemption or conversion, §55-6-03, (b).
Preemptive rights of shareholders.
Definition of "shares," §55-6-30, (c).
Generally, §55-6-30, (a), (d).
Statement in articles of incorporation.
Effect, §55-6-30, (b).
Professional corporations.
Death of stockholder, §55B-7, (b).
Disqualification of licensee stockholder, severance of financial interest, §55B-7, (a).
Distributing corporation, issuance of capital stock to, §55B-6, (b).

CORPORATIONS —Cont'd
Stock and stockholders —Cont'd
Professional corporations —Cont'd
Issuance of capital stock, §55B-6, (a).
To another professional corporation, §55B-6, (b).
Nonlicensed employee owning stock, §55B-6, (a).
Percentage of stock allowed to be own by person, §55B-6, (a1).
Transfer of capital stock, §55B-6, (a).
Voting trust agreements prohibited, §55B-6, (a).
Proxies, §55-7-22.
Appointment, §55-7-22, (b) to (h).
Authorized, §55-7-22, (a).
Death or incapacity of shareholder appointing proxy, §55-7-22, (e).
Revocation of appointment, §55-7-22, (d), (f), (g).
Records.
Inspection of records by shareholders, §§55-16-02 to 55-16-04.
Record of shareholders, §55-16-01, (c).
Removal of director by shareholders, §55-8-08.
Reports to shareholders, §§55-16-20, 55-16-21.
Restrictions on transfer of shares.
Authorized, §55-6-27, (a).
Definition of "shares," §55-6-27, (e).
Provisions authorized, §55-6-27, (c), (d).
Validity, §55-6-27, (b).
Series of stock.
Articles of amendment.
Delivery to secretary of state before issuance, §55-6-02, (b).
Preferences, limitations and rights.
Directors may determine, §55-6-02, (a).
Share exchange, §§55-11-01 to 55-11-09.
Shareholder protection act, §§55-9-01 to 55-9-05.
Subscription for shares.
Contract.
Subscription agreement as contract, §55-6-20, (e).
Default by subscriber, §55-6-20, (d).
Irrevocable, §55-6-20, (a).
Payment terms, §55-6-20, (b).
Effect of payment, §55-6-20, (c).
Substantially similar names.
Shareholders registered in to constitute one shareholder, §55-1-42, (b).
Treasury shares.
Acquisition by corporation of own shares.
Amendment of articles of incorporation, §55-6-31, (b), (c).
Authorized, §55-6-31, (a).
Voting groups. See within this heading, "Voting groups."
Voting of shares.
Acceptance of votes by corporation, §55-7-24.
Agreements between shareholders, §55-7-31.
Conversion of domestic corporation to different business entity.
Approval of plan of conversion, §55-11A-11, (e), (f).
Election of directors, §55-7-28, (a).
Cumulative voting, §55-7-28, (b) to (e).
Electronic attendance at meetings, §55-7-08.
Entitlement to vote, §55-7-21, (a).
Debt securities, §55-7-21.1.
Exceptions, §55-7-21, (b) to (d).
Redeemable shares, §55-7-21, (d).
List of shareholders, §55-7-20.
Availability for inspection, §55-7-20, (b) to (e).
Preparation, §55-7-20, (a).

CORPORATIONS —Cont'd
Stock and stockholders —Cont'd
Voting of shares —Cont'd
Redeemable shares, §55-7-21, (d).
Shareholders' agreements, §55-7-31.
Voting trusts, §55-7-30.
Voting trusts.
Authorized, §55-7-30, (a).
Duration, §55-7-30, (b).
Extension, §55-7-30, (c).
When effective, §55-7-30, (b).
Warrants for purchase of shares, §55-6-24, (a).
Public corporations, §55-6-24, (b).
Streets and highways.
Defunct corporations.
Dedication of road or street.
Deemed abandoned if not used within fifteen years, §136-96.
Superior courts.
Dissolution.
Administrative dissolution.
Appeal from denial of reinstatement, §55-14-23.
Judicial dissolution generally, §§55-14-30 to 55-14-33.
Proper division for actions for corporate receiverships, §7A-249.
Surplus lines insurance.
Agents or brokers license, §58-21-65, (c).
Suspended corporations, §§55-14-20 to 55-14-24.
Administrative procedure act.
Inapplicability, §55-14-24.
Authority of registered agent, §55-14-21, (d).
Certificate of dissolution, §55-14-21, (b).
Claims against dissolved corporations.
Applicability of certain provisions, §55-14-21, (c).
Denial of reinstatement.
Appeal.
Appeal of court's final decision, §55-14-23, (d).
Orders of court, §55-14-23, (c).
Appeal from, §55-14-23.
Notice of denial, §55-14-23, (a).
Petition, §55-14-23, (b).
Grounds, §55-14-20.
Notice, §§55-14-21, (a), 55-14-23, (a).
Reinstatement, §55-14-22.
Application, §55-14-22, (a).
Certificate, §55-14-22, (b).
Denial of reinstatement.
Appeal from, §55-14-23.
Effect, §55-14-22, (c).
Name, §55-14-22, (a1).
Taxation.
Annual report, §105-256.1.
Foreign corporations.
Applicability of laws, §105-250.
Property taxes.
Property of foreign corporations not exempted, §105-274, (b).
Franchise tax.
General provisions, §§105-114 to 105-129.
See FRANCHISE TAX.
Income tax.
Generally, §§105-130 to 105-130.41.
See INCOME TAX.
S corporations, §§105-131 to 105-131.8.
See INCOME TAX.
Individual liability of officers, trustees or receivers for taxes, §105-253, (a), (b).

CORPORATIONS —Cont'd
Taxation —Cont'd
Officers, trustees or receivers liability for taxes, §105-253, (a), (b).
Suspension of articles of incorporation.
Failure to file report or return or pay tax or fee, §105-230, (a).
Invalidity of acts performed during suspension, §105-230, (b).
Receivership, liquidation, cessation of business, §105-232, (b).
Reinstatement of articles, §105-232, (a).
Telephone membership corporations, §§62-157, 117-28 to 117-46.
See TELEPHONE MEMBERSHIP CORPORATIONS.
Third parties.
Probate and registration.
Execution of corporate instruments.
Validity as to innocent third parties, §47-18.3, (a).
Title of act.
Short title, §55-1-01.
Torrens system registration.
Authority to sue, §43-8.
Certificates of title.
Dissolution of corporation.
Issuance of certificate upon dissolution, §43-17.1.
Transfer of assets.
Mortgage of assets, §55-12-01, (a).
Other than in regular course of business.
Abandonment of transaction, §55-12-02, (f).
Approval by shareholders, §55-12-02, (a), (b), (e).
Notice of meeting, §55-12-02, (d).
Voting groups, §55-12-02, (e).
Distribution to shareholders.
Not governed by provisions, §55-12-02, (g).
Submission of proposed transaction to shareholders, §55-12-02, (a) to (c).
Regular course of business, §55-12-01, (b).
Other than in regular course of business, §55-12-02.
Shareholder protection act.
Provisions not to modify act, §55-12-03.
Trust companies and interstate trust business, §§53-301 to 53-415.
See TRUST COMPANIES.
Trusts and trustees.
Consolidation, merger, reorganization, etc., by corporate trustee, §36A-37.
Criminal law and procedure.
Indictments.
Manner of alleging joint ownership of property, §15-148.
Powers of trustees under express trust generally, §36A-136.
Uniform trusts act.
Corporate trustee buying own stock, §36A-67.
Ultra vires, §55-3-04, (a).
Exceptions, §55-3-04, (b), (c).
Nonprofit corporations, §55A-3-04.
Unclaimed property generally, §§116B-51 to 116B-80.
See UNCLAIMED PROPERTY.
Usury.
Bonds may be sold below par, §24-2.
Uttering.
Forged stock certificates uttered, §14-124.

CORPORATIONS —Cont'd
Validation of instrument.
Curative statute, §55-17-05.
Venue.
Domestic corporations.
Residence, §1-79, (a).
Foreign corporations, §1-80.
Verification of pleadings by corporation, §1A-1, Rule 11, (d).
Veterinarians.
Practice of veterinary medicine, §90-187.11.
Voluntary dissolution, §§55-14-01 to 55-14-08. See within this heading, "Dissolution."
Voting groups.
Amendment of articles of incorporation.
Voting on amendments by voting groups, §55-10-04.
Directors.
Election of directors, §55-7-25, (e).
Greater quorum or voting requirements.
Authorization, §55-7-27, (a).
Amendment of provision for, §55-7-27, (b).
Merger or share exchange.
Approval of plan, §55-11-03, (e), (f).
Multiple voting groups.
Action by, §55-7-26, (b).
Quorum requirements, §55-7-25, (a) to (c).
Changes, §55-7-25, (d).
Greater quorum or voting requirements, §55-7-27.
Removal of directors by shareholders, §55-8-08, (b).
Single voting group.
Action by, §55-7-26, (a).
Vacancies in board of directors.
Filling, §55-8-10, (b).
When tax must be paid, §105-130.19, (a).
Worthless checks, §14-107.

CORRECTION BOARD, §143B-265, (a) to (d).

CORRECTION DEPARTMENT, §§143B-260 to 143B-264.
Chaplains.
Employment for inmates by department, §148-10.1.
Community service for impaired driving.
Conduct of alternative punishment program, §20-179.4, (a).
Confederate cemetery.
Labor for care of cemetery.
Department of correction to furnish, §65-4.
Creation, §143B-260.
Custodian of prisoners, §§148-4, 148-6.
Domestic violence treatment program.
Establishment, completion by inmates, §143B-262, (e).
Duties.
Generally, §§143B-261, 143B-262.
Established, §143B-260.
Functions.
Generally, §143B-262, (a).
Transfer to department, §143B-262, (b).
Head of department, §143B-263.
Hiring out of prisoners, §148-6.
Impaired driving.
Community service alternative punishment program, §20-179.4, (a).
Intensive supervision program.
Established within division of adult probation and parole, §143B-262, (c).

CORRECTION DEPARTMENT —Cont'd
Labor of prisoners, §§148-26 to 148-49.
See PRISONER LABOR.
Mental health, developmental disabilities and substance abuse.
Involuntary commitment.
Inmate becoming mentally ill and dangerous to himself or others, §122C-313, (a) to (e).
State facilities.
Voluntary admission of inmates, §122C-312.
Organization, §143B-264.
Powers, §143B-261.
Prisons and prisoners generally.
See PRISONS AND PRISONERS.
Reports.
Vacancies in office, §120-12.1.
Rules and regulations.
Adoption, §143B-261.1.
Controlling classification, §148-36.
Secretary of correction.
Community service for impaired driving.
Assignment of coordinator to each district court district, §20-179.4, (b).
Conduct of affairs of prison system, §148-5.
Control and custody of prisoners, §148-4.
Department of correction.
Head of department, §143B-263.
Head of department, §143B-263.
Management of prison property, §148-5.
Personal property.
Repair or replacement of personal property belonging to employees that is damaged or stolen by inmates.
Adoption of rules governing, §143B-261.2, (a).
Appeals.
Secretary to establish appeals process, §143B-261.2, (e).
Reimbursement, §143B-261.2, (b).
Limitation, §143B-261.2, (d).
Rules and regulations.
Authority to make, §148-11, (a).
Controlling classification and operation of facilities, §148-36.
Uniforms for prisoners, authority to designate, §148-11, (b).
Security staffing, §143B-262.5.
Sexual assault pilot program.
Established for inmates of units of state prison system, §143B-262.2.
Operation of program, §143B-262.2, (b).
Substance abuse program.
Administration of substance abuse programs by department, §143B-264.
Admission priorities, §143B-262.1, (h).
Assistant secretary for substance abuse.
Duties, §143B-262.1, (b).
Employment, §143B-262.1, (b).
Description of program, §143B-262, (d).
Establishment, §§143B-262.1, (a), 143B-262, (d).
Extensive follow-up component, §143B-262.1, (f).
Follow-up, §143B-262.1, (h).
Follow-up after period of treatment, §143B-262.1, (i).
Inmate involvement as ancillary staff, peer counselors, etc., §143B-262.1, (f).
Report to general assembly, §143B-262.3, (a), (b).
Self-contained facilities, §143B-262.1, (a).
Unit superintendent.
Responsibilities, §143B-262.1, (e).

CORRECTION DEPARTMENT —Cont'd
Superintendent of facility.
Repair or replacement of personal property belonging to employees damaged or stolen by inmates.
Reimbursement.
Determination of whether employee has made good faith effort to recover the loss, §143B-261.2, (c).
Vacancies in office.
Report on long-term vacancies, §120-12.1.

CORRECTIONS.
Board, §143B-265, (a) to (d).
Department, §§143B-260 to 143B-264.
See CORRECTION DEPARTMENT.
Generally.
See PRISONS AND PRISONERS.
Jails.
See JAILS.

CORRECTIONS ADMINISTRATIVE REMEDY PROCEDURE, §§148-118.1 to 148-118.9.
See PRISONER'S GRIEVANCE PROCEDURE.

CORRECTIONS COMPACT, §§148-119 to 148-121.
All documents public records, §148-121, (b), (c).
Citation of article, §148-119.
Form of compact, §148-120.
Governor to execute, §148-120.
Proceedings to be open, §148-121, (a).
Exceptions where safety of persons or property jeopardized, §148-121, (c).
Short title, §148-119.
Written documents deemed public records, §148-121, (b).

CORRESPONDENCE SCHOOLS.
General provisions, §§115D-87 to 115D-97.
See PROPRIETARY SCHOOLS.

CORROSIVE ACID OR ALKALI.
Malicious throwing, §14-30.1.

CORRUPT ELECTIONS.
Convicted officials.
Disqualification from voting, §163-276.
Removal from office, §163-276.
District attorneys.
Investigation and prosecution of violations, §163-278.
Felonies.
Certain acts declared felonies, §163-275.
Fraud.
Felonies, §163-275.
Interference with voters.
Duties of election officers upon, §163-273, (b).
Prohibited acts, §163-273, (a).
Intimidation of voters by officers, §163-271.
Misdemeanors.
Generally, §§163-271 to 163-274.
Offenses of voters, §163-273, (a).
Duties of election officers upon, §163-273, (b).
Penalties.
Felonies, §163-275.
State board of elections.
Investigation of violations, §163-278.
Witnesses.
Self-incrimination.
Immunity from prosecution, §163-277.
Subpoenas, §§163-277, 163-278.
Powers of district attorneys, §163-278.

CORRUPTION OF BLOOD.
Attainder of treason not to work, Const. U. S., art. III, §3.

CORRUPT LAW ENFORCEMENT.
Removal of unfit officers, §128-16.

CORRUPT ORGANIZATIONS AND RACKETEER INFLUENCE, §§75D-1 to 75D-14.
See RACKETEER INFLUENCED AND CORRUPT ORGANIZATIONS.

CORRUPT PRACTICES ACT, §§163-271 to 163-278.
See CORRUPT ELECTIONS.

COSMETIC ART, §§88B-1 to 88B-29.
Apprentices.
Licenses.
Display of license, §88B-23, (a).
Qualifications, §88B-8.
Renewal, §88B-21, (c).
Failure to renew, §88B-21, (f).
Practice under direct supervision of cosmetologist, §88B-22, (e).
Barbers.
Exemptions from barbering provisions, §86A-14.
Board of cosmetic art.
Compensation of members, §88B-5, (a).
Composition, §88B-3, (a).
Disciplinary measures, §88B-24.
Costs in disciplinary proceedings, §88B-29, (d).
Duties, §88B-4, (a).
Employment of member by board prohibited for at least one year after member's term expires, §88B-3, (h).
Established, §88B-3, (a).
Executive budget act.
Applicability, §88B-6, (f).
Executive director, §88B-6, (b).
Collection of fees, §88B-6, (e).
Inspection of shops and schools, §88B-4, (b).
Meetings, §88B-5, (b).
Office.
Location, §88B-6, (a).
Officers, §88B-3, (f).
Personnel, §88B-6, (c), (d).
Powers, §88B-4, (a).
Qualifications of members, §88B-3, (b).
Record of proceedings, §88B-4, (c).
Removal of members, §88B-3, (d).
Restraining orders, §88B-28.
Rules.
Posting, §88B-26.
State personnel act.
Applicability, §88B-6, (f).
Teacher's licenses not to be issued to board members, §88B-3, (g).
Terms of members, §88B-3, (c).
Vacancies, §88B-3, (e).
Bonds, surety.
Private cosmetic art schools, §88B-17.
Citation of act, §88B-1.
Civil penalties.
Authority to assess, §88B-29, (a).
Factors to be considered in assessing, §88B-29, (b).
Schedule, §88B-29, (c).
Conflicts of interest.
Board of cosmetic art.
Employment of member by board for at least one year after member's term prohibited, §88B-3, (h).

COSMETIC ART —Cont'd
Continuing education, §88B-21, (e).
Inactive status.
Removal from list, §88B-21, (h).
Cosmetic art schools.
Bond, surety.
Amount, §88B-17, (b).
Required, §88B-17, (a).
Waiver of requirement, §88B-17, (c).
Credits.
Expired school credits, §88B-19.
Expired school credits, §88B-19.
Licenses, §88B-16, (a).
Bond, §88B-17.
Posting of license, §88B-23, (b).
Renewal, §88B-21, (g).
Required, §88B-16, (b), (c).
Rules of board.
Posting, §88B-26, (a), (b).
Teachers. See within this heading, "Teachers."
Cosmetic art shops.
Licenses, §88B-14, (a).
Inspection for compliance.
Operation during inspection, §88B-14, (c).
List of licensed cosmetologists who practice in, §88B-14, (b).
Posting of license, §88B-23, (b).
Renewal, §88B-21, (a).
Transfer of license prohibited, §88B-14, (d).
Unlicensed operation prohibited, §88B-22, (c).
Practice outside shops, §§88B-15, (a), 88B-22, (b).
Licensed barber shop, §88B-15, (b).
Rules of board.
Posting, §88B-26, (a).
Cosmetologists.
Licenses.
Display of license, §88B-23, (a).
Qualifications, §88B-7.
Renewal, §88B-21, (b).
Failure to renew, §88B-21, (f).
Costs.
Disciplinary proceedings, §88B-29, (d).
Criminal law and procedure, §88B-22, (f).
Definitions, §88B-2.
Disciplinary measures, §88B-24.
Costs in disciplinary proceedings, §88B-29, (d).
Electrologists, §§88A-1 to 88A-23.
See ELECTROLOGISTS.
Estheticians.
Licenses.
Display of license, §88B-23, (a).
Qualifications, §88B-9.
Renewal, §88B-21, (c).
Failure to renew, §88B-21, (f).
Restrictions on practice, §88B-22, (d).
Examinations.
Licensure, §88B-18.
Fees, §88B-20, (a).
Exemptions from provisions, §88B-25.
Fees.
Board of cosmetic art.
Collection by executive director, §88B-6, (e).
Licensure, §88B-20.
Injunctions, §88B-28.
Inspections, §88B-27.
Board of cosmetic art.
Shops and schools, §88B-4, (b).
Cosmetic art shops, §88B-4, (b).
Operation while board inspects for compliance, §88B-14, (c).

COSMETIC ART —Cont'd
Licenses.
Applicants licensed in other states.
Qualifications, §88B-13, (a), (b).
Teachers.
Standards for issuing license to applicant who is licensed as teacher in another state, §88B-13, (c).
Apprentices. See within this heading, "Apprentices."
Cosmetic art schools. See within this heading, "Cosmetic art schools."
Cosmetic art shops. See within this heading, "Cosmetic art shops."
Disciplinary measures, §88B-24.
Costs in disciplinary proceedings, §88B-29, (d).
Display, §88B-23.
Estheticians. See within this heading, "Estheticians."
Examinations.
Applications for, §88B-18, (a).
Contents, §88B-18, (b).
Fees, §88B-20, (a).
Locations, §88B-18, (c).
Reexamination, §88B-18, (d).
Fees.
Application fees, §88B-20, (b).
Examination fees, §88B-20, (a).
Late fees and reinstatement fees, §88B-20, (d).
License fees, §88B-20, (c).
Proration of fees, §88B-20, (e).
Inactive status.
Request, effect, removal, continuing education, §88B-21, (h).
Manicurists. See within this heading, "Manicurists."
Qualifications.
Apprentices, §88B-8.
Cosmetologists, §88B-7.
Estheticians, §88B-9.
Manicurists, §88B-10.
Teachers, §88B-11.
Temporary employment permit, §88B-12, (a).
Renewal, §88B-21.
Refusal to renew.
Disciplinary measures generally, §88B-24.
Required, §88B-22, (a).
Revocation or suspension.
Disciplinary measures generally, §88B-24.
Teachers. See within this heading, "Teachers."
Temporary employment permit, §88B-12.
Unlicensed acts prohibited, §88B-22, (a) to (e).
Manicurists.
Licenses.
Display of license, §88B-23, (a).
Qualifications, §88B-10.
Renewal, §88B-21, (c).
Failure to renew, §88B-21, (f).
Restrictions on practice, §88B-22, (d).
Misdemeanors, §88B-22, (f).
Nurses.
Exemptions from cosmetic art provisions, §88B-25.
Penalties.
Civil penalties, §88B-29.
Physicians and surgeons.
Exemptions from cosmetic art provisions, §88B-25.
Reciprocity.
Licensing of applicants licensed in other states, §88B-13.
Records.
Board proceedings, §88B-4, (c).

COSMETIC ART —Cont'd
Teachers.
Continuing education.
License renewal, §88B-21, (e).
Licenses.
Applicants licensed as teachers in another state.
Standards for issuing licenses to, §88B-13, (c).
Display of license, §88B-23, (a).
Qualifications, §88B-11, (a).
Cosmetology teachers, §88B-11, (b).
Esthetician teachers, §88B-11, (c).
Manicurist teachers, §88B-11, (d).
Renewal, §88B-21, (d).
Continuing education, §88B-21, (e).
Failure to renew, §88B-21, (f).
Temporary employment permits.
Applicants for examination.
Applications, §88B-12, (a).
Extension, §88B-12, (c).
Expiration, §88B-12, (b).
Limits on practice, §88B-12, (c).
Qualifications, §88B-12, (a).
Title of act, §88B-1.

COSMETICS.
Food, drugs and cosmetics, §§106-120 to 106-145.
See FOOD, DRUG AND COSMETIC ACT.
Sales and use tax.
Clothing accessories or equipment.
Defined as including, §105-164.3.

COSTS.
Abortion.
Parental or judicial consent to abortion.
Waiver of parental consent proceedings.
Cost not required of minors, §90-21.8, (i).
Absolute divorce.
Final action filed in district court, §7A-305, (a2).
Administration department.
Publications.
Statement of cost, §143-170.1, (a), (a1), (b).
Admissions.
Failure of party to admit, §1A-1, Rule 37, (c).
Alimony.
Bond for costs unnecessary, §50-2.
Appeals, §6-33; App. Proc., Appx. F.
Criminal appeals.
No security for cost, App. Proc. Rule 6, (e).
Discretion of appellate court in recovery of cost, §6-33.
Execution to collect costs in appellate courts, App. Proc. Rule 35, (d).
Federal courts.
State costs on appeals to federal courts, §6-17.
Frivolous appeals, App. Proc. Rule 34.
Generally, §6-33; App. Proc. Rule 6.
In forma pauperis, App. Proc. Rule 6, (b).
Magistrates.
Recovery of cost, §6-33.
Mandates of the courts.
Direction as to cost, App. Proc. Rule 35, (b).
Prosecution bonds.
Sureties on bonds liable for costs, §6-3.
Record on appeal.
Inclusion of unnecessary matter.
Penalty for inclusion, App. Proc. Rule 9, (b).
Security for costs.
Criminal appeals.
No security for costs, App. Proc. Rule 6, (e).
Dismissal of appeal for failure to file or for defect in security, App. Proc. Rule 6, (d).

COSTS —Cont'd
Appeals —Cont'd
Security for costs —Cont'd
Filing with record on appeal, App. Proc. Rule 6, (c).
In forma pauperis appeals, App. Proc. Rule 6, (b).
Regular course, App. Proc. Rule 6, (a).
Taxable in tribunals, App. Proc. Rule 35, (c).
To whom allowed, App. Proc. Rule 35, (a).
Appraisals and appraisers.
Homestead exemption.
Laying off homestead and exemption, §6-28.
Reassessment of homestead, §6-29.
Arbitration and award, §§50-51, (f), (g), 50-55, (d).
Judgment on award, §1-569.25, (b).
Modification or correction of awards, §50-55, (d).
Rules for conducting arbitration, §50-45, (h).
Rules for court-ordered arbitration, Arbitration Rule 7.
Arrest.
Criminal cases in superior or district courts, §7A-304, (a).
Nonpayment of fine and cost, §6-48.
Assault.
Allowance of costs to defendant, §6-19.
Allowance of costs to plaintiff, §6-18.
Assignments.
Liability of assignee for cost, §6-32.
Attorney disability proceedings, Bar Rules & Regs., B, §.0118.
Attorneys at law.
Failure to file complaint on time.
Attorney liable for cost, §84-12.
Attorneys' fees, §§6-21.1, 6-21.2, 6-21.4, 6-21.5.
Allowance as part of costs in certain cases, §6-21.1.
Cases involving principals or teachers.
Allowance of counsel fees and costs, §6-21.4.
Chattel mortgages.
Attorneys' fees in addition to interest, §6-21.2.
Evidence of indebtedness.
Attorneys' fees in notes, etc., in addition to interest, §6-21.2.
Nonjusticiable cases, §6-21.5.
Automobile dealers.
Actions by, §20-308.1, (b).
Autopsies.
Homicide investigations.
Compensation of physician, §15-7.
Bad checks.
Remedies for returned check, §6-21.3, (b).
Bail and recognizance.
Civil cases.
When bail to pay costs, §1-438.
Pretrial release services in district or superior courts, §7A-304, (a).
Several actions on one recognizance.
Allowance of costs to defendant, §6-19.
Allowance of costs to plaintiff, §6-18.
Battery.
Allowance of costs to defendant, §6-19.
Allowance of costs to plaintiff, §6-18.
Bill of costs.
Execution for unpaid costs.
Attachment of bill of costs to execution, §6-4.
Bills of exchange.
Several actions on one instrument.
Allowance of costs to defendant, §6-19.
Allowance of costs to plaintiff, §6-18.

COSTS —Cont'd
Blood tests and samples.
Competency of blood tests.
Taxing of expenses as cost, §8-50.1.
Bond issues.
Several suits on one instrument.
Allowance of costs to defendant, §6-19.
Allowance of costs to plaintiff, §6-18.
Bonds, surety.
Defendant's liability in criminal actions.
Confession of judgment, §6-47.
Bond given to secure fine and cost, §6-47.
Mortgage in lieu of bond.
Security of costs or fine in criminal action, §58-74-5.
Cancellation of mortgage in such proceedings, §58-74-10.
Prosecution bonds, §§1-109 to 1-112.
Several suits on one instrument.
Allowance of costs to defendant, §6-19.
Allowance of costs to plaintiff, §6-18.
Cartways.
Application for establishment, alteration or discontinuance.
Allowance of costs to either party or apportioned in discretion of court, §6-21.
Case files.
Entering costs in case file, §6-7.
Chattel mortgages.
Attorneys' fees in addition to interest, §6-21.2.
Checks.
Returned check.
Remedies for returned check, §6-21.3, (b).
Child care provider criminal history record check, §110-90.2, (g).
Child custody.
Uniform child custody jurisdiction act.
Allowance of costs to either party or apportioned in discretion of court, §6-21.
Child support, income withholding.
Computation of amount to be withheld, §110-136.6, (a).
Limitations on amount withheld, §110-136.6, (b).
Chiropractors.
Contested disciplinary hearings.
Assessment of costs upon guilty verdict, §90-154, (c).
Citations.
Criminal process in superior or district courts, §7A-304, (a).
Civil rights, interference with, §99D-1, (b), (b1).
Commissioner deposition taking.
Allowance of costs to either party or apportioned in discretion of court, §6-21.
Commissioner's fees taxed as cost, §1-408.
Compromise and settlement.
Mediated settlement conferences in superior court civil actions, §7A-38.1, (k).
Conditional sale contracts.
Attorneys' fees and conditional sale contract in addition to interest, §6-21.2.
Condominium assessment lien.
Judgment, decree or order to include, §47C-3-116, (c).
Condominium owners' associations and declarant.
Declarant liable to association, §47C-3-111, (d).
Construction and interpretation.
Allowance to either party or apportioned in discretion of court, §6-21.

COSTS —Cont'd
Contracts.
Conditional sales contracts.
Attorneys' fees and contract in addition to interest, §6-21.2.
Usurious contracts.
No costs to be recovered by party seeking recovery on usurious contracts, §6-25.
Corporations.
Actions by state for corporation.
Liability for costs, §6-15.
Business corporations.
Dissenting shareholders.
Judicial appraisal of shares, §55-13-31.
Records.
Inspection of records by shareholders.
Court-ordered inspection, §55-16-04, (c).
Stock and stockholders.
Derivative actions by shareholders.
Award, §55-7-46.
Nonprofit corporations.
Court-ordered inspections of records, §55A-16-04, (c).
Cosmetic art.
Disciplinary proceedings, §88B-29, (d).
Counties.
Actions by state for county.
Liability for costs, §6-15.
Prisoners.
Removal of trial from one county to another.
Liability of county, §6-40.
Public health or mental health grants from federal government.
Recovery of indirect costs on certain grants by counties, §130A-8, (a).
Exception, §130A-8, (b).
Special assessments.
Determination of costs, §153A-193.
Discounts authorized, §153A-193.1.
Uniform costs and fees in trial divisions.
Requirement to advance certain fees, §7A-317.
Court of appeals.
New trials.
Discretion of court in awarding cost, §6-33.
Courtroom costs in criminal actions in superior or district courts, §7A-304, (a).
Credit device fraud.
Telecommunication services, §14-113.6, (c).
Criminal cases.
Actions in superior or district courts, §7A-304.
Confession of judgment.
Bond given to secure fine and cost, §6-47.
Defendant's liability in criminal actions.
Confession of judgment.
Bond given to secure fine and cost, §6-47.
Nonpayment of costs.
Persons imprisoned for nonpayment released upon compliance with article, §23-24.
Removal of trial from one county to another.
Liability of counties for cost, §6-40.
Criminal conversation.
Allowance of costs to defendant, §6-19.
Allowance of costs to plaintiff, §6-18.
Dams.
Lowlands draining or damming.
Petitioner to pay costs, §6-22.
Debt.
Evidence of indebtedness.
Attorneys' fees in notes, etc., in addition to interest, §6-21.2.

COSTS —Cont'd
Decedents' estates.
Administration of estates, §7A-307.
Debts and claims.
When cost allowed against representative, §28A-19-18.
Reference of claim against deceased person.
Recovery of fees and other necessary disbursements, §6-31.
Declaratory judgments, §1-263.
Defamation.
Allowance of costs to defendant, §6-19.
Allowance of costs to plaintiff, §6-18.
Defendants.
Allowance of costs, §6-19.
Discretion of court, §§6-20, 6-21.
Attorneys' fees.
Parties appealing or defending against agency decision, §6-19.1.
Bonds, surety.
Confession of judgment.
Bond given to secure fine and cost, §6-47.
Confession of judgment.
Bond given to secure fine and cost, §6-47.
Notice of no personal claim.
Payment of costs by defendant unreasonably defending after notice, §6-23.
Depositions.
Compensation of referees and commissioners.
Allowance of costs to either party or apportioned in discretion of court, §6-21.
Failure of party to attend, §1A-1, Rule 37, (d).
Oral examination.
Failure to attend or serve subpoena, §1A-1, Rule 30, (g).
Derivative actions.
Payment, §55-7-46.
Determination of incompetence.
Fees.
Payment, §35A-1116, (c).
Multidisciplinary evaluations.
Assessment of costs, §35A-1116, (b).
Disability of attorney proceedings, Bar Rules & Regs., B, §.0118.
Discovery conference.
Failure to participate, §1A-1, Rule 37, (g).
Discovery, failure to comply with order, §1A-1, Rule 37, (b).
Discovery, motion compelling.
Granting or denying motion, §1A-1, Rule 37, (a).
Discretion of court.
Allowance of costs, §§6-20, 6-21.
Appellate court's discretion in recovery of cost, §6-33.
Discrimination against employees for lawful use of lawful products during nonworking hours.
Court costs in civil actions for violations, §95-28.2, (e).
Dismissal of actions, §1A-1, Rule 41, (d).
District courts.
Civil actions, §7A-305.
Criminal actions, §7A-304.
Divorce.
Absolute divorce.
Final action filed in district court, §7A-305, (a2).
Allowance of costs to either party or apportioned in discretion of court, §6-21.
Bond for costs unnecessary, §50-2.
Drainage.
Allowance of costs to either party or apportioned in discretion of court, §6-21.

COSTS —Cont'd
Drainage —Cont'd
Amount of contribution for repair ascertained, §156-15.
Lowlands draining or damming.
Petitioner to pay costs, §6-22.
Repairs enforced by judgment, §156-18.
Drug treatment courts.
Payment of costs of treatment program, §7A-800.
Dry-cleaning solvent cleanup.
Reimbursement for assessment and remediation activities generally, §143-215.104N, (a) to (e).
Electric, telegraph and telephone companies.
Petition for condemnation of land.
Payment of costs by petitioner, §6-22.
Electronic surveillance.
Civil action for violation of article, §15A-296, (a).
Emancipation of juvenile proceedings, §7B-3506.
Eminent domain, §40A-13.
Award of costs, §40A-8, (a), (b).
Action against condemnor, §40A-8, (c).
Condemnation action denied or abandoned, §40A-8, (b).
Petitioner to pay costs in certain cases, §6-22.
Streets and highways, §136-119.
Streets and highways.
Condemnation proceedings, §136-119.
Employee use of lawful products during nonworking hours.
Actions brought pursuant to section, §95-28.2, (f).
Employer discrimination against employee for lawful use of lawful products during nonworking hours.
Court costs in civil actions for violation, §95-28.2, (e).
Estates.
Administration of estates, §7A-307.
Evidence.
Blood tests.
Competency of blood tests.
Taxing of expenses as cost, §8-50.1.
Executions.
Issuance of execution for unpaid costs, §6-4.
Livestock.
Cost of keeping.
Officer's account, §1-322.
Executors and administrators.
Actions for debts and claims.
When costs allowed against representative, §28A-19-18.
Recovery of costs when executor or administrator a party, §6-31.
When chargeable to estate, §6-31.
Extradition.
Fugitives from this state, §15A-744.
False imprisonment.
Allowance of costs to defendant, §6-19.
Allowance of costs to plaintiff, §6-18.
False report of nuclear, biological or chemical weapons, §14-288.23, (b).
Hoaxes, §14-288.24, (b).
Federal courts.
Appeals.
State costs on appeals to federal courts, §6-17.
State cases.
Expenses and costs of state in connection with state cases, §6-17.1.
Fees.
Attorneys' fees.
See ATTORNEYS' FEES.

COSTS —Cont'd
Fees —Cont'd
General provisions.
See FEES.
Witnesses, §§6-51 to 6-62.
See WITNESSES.
Ferries.
Application for establishment, alteration or discontinuance.
Allowance of costs to either party or apportioned in discretion of court, §6-21.
Filing.
Entering costs in case file, §6-7.
Fish and fisheries resources.
Replacement costs of resources, §113-267.
Foreign-money claims.
Assessment of cost in U. S. dollars, §1C-1826, (c).
Forests and forestry.
Owners and operators of forestland.
Services and advice, §113-81.2, (b).
Deposit of receipts with state treasury, §113-81.3.
Frivolous prosecutions.
Nonpayment of cost.
Imprisonment of prosecuting witness for willful nonpayment, §6-50.
Guardian ad litem.
Responsibility of guardian for costs against infant plaintiff, §6-30.
Guardians.
Accounts and accounting.
Annual accounts.
Compelling accounting, §35A-1265, (a).
Inventory or account required within three months.
Compelling inventory or account.
Personal liability of guardian for costs of proceedings, §35A-1262, (b).
Determination of incompetence.
Taxing of costs, §35A-1116, (a).
Responsibility of guardian for costs against infant plaintiff, §6-30.
Habeas corpus.
Allowance of costs to either party or apportioned in discretion of court, §6-21.
Health.
Public health or mental health grants from federal government.
Counties to recover indirect costs on certain grants, §130A-8, (a).
Exception, §130A-8, (b).
Highways.
Application for establishment, alteration or discontinuance.
Allowance of costs to either party or apportioned in discretion of court, §6-21.
Homestead exemption.
Appraising costs and expenses, §6-28.
Laying off homestead and exemption, §6-28.
Reallotment of homestead for increase in value.
Allowance of costs to either party or apportioned in discretion of court, §6-21.
Reassessment of homestead, §6-29.
Husband and wife.
Judgments against married persons for costs.
Levy and collection out of separate estate, §1-223.
Illegitimacy.
Allowance of costs to either party or apportioned in discretion of court, §6-21.

COSTS —Cont'd
Imprisonment for willful nonpayment.
Prosecuting witnesses.
Frivolous prosecution, §6-50.
Incompetence determinations.
Assessment in taxing, §35A-1116.
Multidisciplinary evaluation, §35A-1116.
Witness fees and fees of court-appointed counsel or guardian ad litem, §35A-1116.
Indigent persons.
Payment of costs, §6-24.
Suits in forma pauperis.
Dismissal of actions, §1A-1, Rule 41, (d).
Infant plaintiffs.
Responsibility of guardian for costs against infant plaintiff, §6-30.
In forma pauperis.
Dismissal of actions, §1A-1, Rule 41, (d).
Infractions, §15A-1118.
Inspection of land or documents.
Failure to respond to request, §1A-1, Rule 37, (d).
Insurance.
Attorneys' fees.
Allowance of counsel fees as part of costs, §6-21.1.
Examinations by insurance commissioner.
Reimbursement by insurer, §58-2-134.
Insurance consumer and customer information privacy.
Action by individual for violations, §58-39-105, (c).
Interest.
Attorneys' fees in notes, conditional sale contracts, etc., in addition to interest, §6-21.2.
Conditional sale contracts.
Attorneys' fees and conditional sale contracts in addition to interest, §6-21.2.
Evidence of indebtedness.
Attorneys' fees in notes, conditional sale contracts, etc., in addition to interest, §6-21.2.
Interest from verdict to judgment added as costs, §24-7.
Notes.
Attorneys' fees in notes in addition to interest, §6-21.2.
International commercial arbitration and conciliation.
Awarding, §1-567.61, (h).
Conciliation, §1-567.85.
Interrogatories.
Failure of party to serve answers, §1A-1, Rule 37, (d).
Interstate family support, §52C-3-312.
Items allowed as costs, §6-1.
Jails.
Removal of trial from one county to another.
Liability of counties for cost, §6-40.
Joinder of actions.
Plaintiff's costs.
Several suits for same cause of action, §6-18.
Judgments.
Confession of judgment.
Defendant's liability in criminal action, §6-47.
Foreign judgments.
Enforcement, §1C-1706.
Interest from verdict to judgment added as costs, §24-7.
Judicial department.
Purposes of chapter.
Uniform costs and fees in trial divisions, §7A-2.
Revenues and expenses, Const. N. C., art. IV, §20.

COSTS —Cont'd
Judicial department —Cont'd
Uniform costs and fees in trial divisions, §§7A-304 to 7A-318.
Juror fees, §7A-312.
Labor.
Discrimination against lawful use of lawful products during nonworking hours.
Court costs in civil actions for violations, §95-28.2, (e).
Retaliatory employment discrimination.
Award of costs in civil action, §95-243, (c).
Landlord and tenant.
Summary ejectment.
Costs tendered by tenant, §42-33.
Light companies.
Petitions for condemnation of land.
Payment of costs by petitioners, §6-22.
Limited liability company derivative actions by members, §57C-8-01, (a).
Actions brought without reasonable cause, §57C-8-01, (f).
Loans.
Evidence of indebtedness.
Attorneys' fees in addition to interest, §6-21.2.
Local government finance.
Bond issues.
Actions validating bonds, §159-75.
Lost instruments and records.
Proceedings under provisions, §98-14.
Magistrates.
Appeals from magistrate, §6-33.
Malicious prosecution.
Allowance of costs in civil cases, §§6-18, 6-19.
Mediated settlement conferences in superior court civil actions, §7A-38.1, (k).
Mediated settlement conferences or other settlement procedures in district court.
Actions involving equitable distribution, alimony or support, §7A-38.4A, (i).
Mediation.
Insurance claims, §7A-38.3A.
Medicaid.
False claims presented by providers, §108A-70.12, (b).
Mental health, developmental disabilities and substance abuse.
Administration of estates, §7A-307.
Mills.
Petitions for condemnation of water millsites.
Payment of costs, §6-22.
Mines and minerals.
Trespass.
Damages.
Survey, §74-36.
Minors.
Administration of estates, §7A-307.
Responsibility of guardian for costs against infant plaintiff, §6-30.
Missing persons' estate administration.
Additional costs assessed before clerk, §7A-307, (d).
Assessment of costs, §7A-307, (a).
Completeness and exclusivity of costs, §7A-307, (c).
Courtroom and related judicial facilities.
Amount of facilities fee, §7A-307, (b).
Use of facilities, §7A-307, (a).
General court of justice.
Support of court, §7A-307, (a).
Liability of parties for costs, §7A-307, (e).

COSTS —Cont'd
Mountain ridge protection.
Civil action against persons alleged in violation, §113A-211, (b).
Municipal corporations.
Actions by state for city, town or village.
Liability for costs, §6-15.
Condemnation of land.
Petitioner to pay costs in certain cases, §6-22.
Uniform costs and fees in trial divisions.
Requirement to advance certain fees, §7A-317.
Negotiable instruments.
Attorneys' fees in notes in addition to interest, §6-21.2.
Several actions on one instrument.
Allowance of costs to defendant, §6-19.
Allowance of costs to plaintiff, §6-18.
Nolle prosequi.
Prosecuting witness' liability for cost, §6-49.
Determination of prosecuting witness by court, §6-49.
Nonjusticiable cases.
Attorneys at law.
Fees, §6-21.5.
Nonpayment.
Arrest for nonpayment, §6-48.
Frivolous prosecution.
Imprisonment for willful nonpayment, §6-50.
Nonprofit corporations.
Court-ordered inspections of records, §55A-16-04, (c).
Notes.
Attorneys' fees in notes in addition to interest, §6-21.2.
Notice.
Defendants with no personal claim against.
Payment of costs by defendant unreasonably defending after notice of no personal claim, §6-23.
Nuisances.
Abatement.
Offenses against public morals, §19-8.
Lien, §19-6.
Nurses.
Disciplinary action.
Assessment of costs against nurse, §90-171.27, (d).
Office of information technology services.
Procurement of information technology.
Liability for violations, §147-33.102.
Oil and gas conservation.
Hearings, §113-400.
Oil pollution and hazardous substances control.
Discharges.
Removal costs and damages.
Liability of responsible party, §143-215.93A, (c).
Overhead high-voltage line safety.
Precautionary safety arrangements, §95-229.10, (f).
Parties.
Administration of estates, §7A-307.
Allowance of costs to either party or apportioned in discretion of court, §6-21.
Decedents' estates.
Liability for costs in administration of estates, §7A-307, (e).
District courts.
Civil actions in district court.
Liability for costs, §7A-305, (e).
Items allowed as costs, §6-1.

COSTS —Cont'd
Parties —Cont'd
Joinder of defendants.
Several suits for same cause of action.
Allowance of costs to defendant, §6-19.
Allowance of costs to plaintiff, §6-18.
Joinder of private party.
Civil actions by the state, §6-13.
Minors.
Administration of estates.
Liability for costs in administration, §7A-307, (e).
Superior courts.
Civil actions in superior court.
Liability for costs, §7A-305, (e).
Special proceedings.
Added to costs for appeal or transfer, §7A-306, (d).
Liability of parties for costs, §7A-306, (e).
Partition.
Allowance of costs to either party or apportioned in discretion of court, §6-21.
Paupers.
Suits in forma pauperis.
Dismissal of actions, §1A-1, Rule 41, (d).
Payment.
Nonpayment of fine and cost.
Arrest for nonpayment, §6-48.
Prosecuting witnesses.
Imprisonment for willful nonpayment if prosecution frivolous, §6-50.
Personal injury.
Attorneys' fees as part of costs.
Allowance in certain cases, §6-21.1.
Personal property.
Recovery or possession.
Allowance of costs to defendant, §6-19.
Allowance of costs to plaintiff, §6-18.
Pesticides.
Condemnation, §143-447, (d), (e).
Petitioners.
When petitioner to pay costs, §6-22.
Plaintiffs.
Allowance of costs, §6-18.
Infant plaintiff.
Responsibility of guardian for costs against infant plaintiff, §6-30.
Pleadings.
Real property.
Claim of title arising on pleadings.
Allowance of costs to defendant, §6-19.
Allowance of costs to plaintiff, §6-18.
Police.
Removal of unfit officers.
Taxing of costs against unreasonable filing of complaint, §128-20.
Pork promotion assessments.
Recovery of unpaid assessment, §106-790.
Post assessment insurance guaranty association.
Right to recover, §58-48-50, (a1).
Postmortem examinations.
Homicide.
Compensation of physician, §15-7.
Powers of attorney.
Assessment of costs under powers of attorney, §7A-307.
Gifts.
Court order authorizing, §32A-14.12.
Principals.
Actions against principals or teachers.
Allowance of counsel fees and costs, §6-21.4.

COSTS —Cont'd
Prisons and prisoners.
Removal of trial from one county to another.
Liability of counties for cost, §6-40.
Probation.
Costs of court and appointed counsel.
Payment by defendant, §15A-1343, (e).
Promissory notes.
Several actions on one instrument.
Allowance of costs to defendant, §6-19.
Allowance of costs to plaintiff, §6-18.
Property.
Damages.
Allowance of attorneys' fees as part of costs, §6-21.1.
Personal property recovery or possession, §§6-18, 6-19.
Real property recovery.
Claim of title arising on pleadings, §§6-18, 6-19.
Prosecuting witnesses.
Liability for cost in certain cases, §6-49.
Determination of prosecuting witness by court, §6-49.
Nonpayment of cost if prosecution frivolous, §6-50.
Imprisonment of prosecuting witness for willful nonpayment, §6-50.
Prosecution bonds.
Bond for costs and damages, §§1-109 to 1-112.
Liability for costs.
Sureties on prosecution bonds liable, §6-3.
Public institutions.
Condemnation of land for water supplies.
Petitioner to pay costs in certain cases, §6-22.
Public officers and employees.
Civil actions by and against state officers, §6-14.
Improper government activities.
Reporting.
Remedies, §126-87.
Public roads.
Application for establishment, alteration or discontinuance.
Allowance of costs to either party or apportioned in discretion of court, §6-21.
Public utilities.
Condemnation of land.
Petitioner to pay costs in certain cases, §6-22.
Public works.
Regulation of contractors.
Estimates of cost, §133-33.
Quo warranto.
Judgments.
Recovery of costs, §1-527.
Railroads.
Petitions for condemnation of land for railroads.
Petitioner to pay costs, §6-22.
Real property.
Claim of title arising on pleadings.
Allowance of costs to defendant, §6-19.
Allowance of costs to plaintiff, §6-18.
Recovery of real property.
Allowance of costs to defendant, §6-19.
Allowance of costs to plaintiff, §6-18.
Recognizance.
Several actions on one instrument.
Allowance of costs to defendant, §6-19.
Allowance of costs to plaintiff, §6-18.
Record inspections.
Nonprofit corporations.
Court-ordered, §55A-16-04, (c).
Referees.
Deposition taking.
Allowance of costs to either party or apportioned in discretion of court, §6-21.

COSTS —Cont'd
Referees —Cont'd
Reference of claim against deceased person.
Recovery of fees of referees, §6-31.
Remission or revocation of fine or costs, §§15A-1363, 15A-1364, (c).
Requests for admissions, failure to admit, §1A-1, Rule 37, (c).
Rescue squad workers' relief fund.
Administration costs.
Withholding, §58-88-30.
Retaliatory employment discrimination.
Award of reasonable costs in civil action, §95-243, (c).
Sale of prints by art dealers.
Wrongful refusal to repay purchaser, §25C-15, (b).
Sales representatives' commissions.
Frivolous actions by sales representatives, §66-192, (b).
Principal failing to comply with provisions, §66-192, (a).
Seduction.
Allowance of costs to defendant, §6-19.
Allowance of costs to plaintiff, §6-18.
Service of process.
Uniform civil process fees, §7A-311.
Service of process in criminal cases in superior or district courts, §7A-304, (a).
Sheriffs.
Execution for unpaid costs.
Levy of execution by sheriffs, §6-4.
Removal of unfit officers.
Taxing of costs against unreasonable filing of complaint, §128-20.
Special proceedings, §7A-306.
Allowance in civil actions, §6-26.
Commissioner's fees taxed as cost, §1-408.
Surveyors' fees.
Taxed as costs, §1-408.1.
State departments and agencies.
Industrial commission may tax cost, §143-291.1.
Publications.
Statement of cost, §143-170.1, (a), (a1), (b).
State of North Carolina, §§6-13 to 6-17.1.
Civil actions by the state.
Joinder of private party, §6-13.
Liability of state for cost, §6-13.
Officers of state in civil actions, §6-14.
Federal litigation.
Appeals, §6-17.
Expenses and costs in connection with state cases, §6-17.1.
Liability of state for costs.
Civil actions by the state, §6-13.
Corporations.
Actions by state for corporation, §6-15.
Counties.
Actions by state for county, §6-15.
Federal court appeals, §6-17.
Joinder of private party, §6-13.
Municipal corporations.
Actions by state for city, town or village, §6-15.
Officers of state.
Civil action by and against state officers, §6-14.
Private persons.
Actions by state for private persons, §6-15.
Private persons.
Actions by state for private persons, §6-15.

COSTS —Cont'd
State treasurer.
Banking operations of department.
Apportionment of costs, §147-68.1.
Statutes.
Persons expressly authorized by statute to prosecute or defend actions.
Recovery of cost, §6-31.
Street railways.
Petitions for condemnation of land for street railways.
Payment of costs, §6-22.
Streets and highways.
Condemnation proceedings, §136-119.
Connection of highways with improved streets.
Pipelines and conduits, §136-27.
Public roads.
Application for establishment, etc.
Allowance of costs, §6-21.
Subpoenas.
Criminal process in superior or district courts, §7A-304, (a).
Subrogation.
Vocational rehabilitation, §143-547, (c).
Suits by indigent.
Payment of costs, §6-24.
Summary judgment.
Affidavits made in bad faith, §1A-1, Rule 56, (g).
Superior courts.
Case file.
Entering costs in case file, §6-7.
Civil actions, §7A-305.
Clerks of court.
Authority of clerk to award costs and disbursements, §7A-103.
Criminal actions, §7A-304.
Execution for unpaid costs, §6-4.
Special proceedings, §7A-306.
Support and maintenance.
Years' support for surviving spouse or children.
Allowance to either party or apportioned in discretion of court, §6-21.
Supreme court of the United States.
Appeals to federal courts.
State costs on appeals, §6-17.
Surveyors' fees.
In actions involving sale of land.
Taxed as costs, §1-408.1.
Surviving spouses.
Allowance to either party or apportioned in discretion of court, §6-21.
Teachers.
Actions against teachers.
Allowance of counsel fees and costs in certain cases, §6-21.4.
Termination of parental rights proceedings.
Taxing, §7B-1110, (e).
Trusts and trustees.
Action or proceeding requiring construction of trust agreement.
Allowance of costs to either party or apportioned in discretion of court, §6-21.
Express trusts.
Recovery of costs, §6-31.
When chargeable to fund, §6-31.
Underground leaking petroleum storage tank cleanup.
Actions for fund reimbursement.
Recovery of costs, §143-215.94G, (e).
Applicability of part, §143-215.94N.

COSTS —Cont'd
Underground leaking petroleum storage tank cleanup —Cont'd
Groundwater protection loan fund.
Civil action for default or violation of loan agreement, §143-215.94P, (e).
Uniform civil process fees, §7A-311.
Uniform fees for jurors, §7A-312.
Uniform fees for witnesses, §7A-314.
United States courts.
Appeals to federal courts.
State costs on appeals, §6-17.
Federal litigation arising out of state cases.
Expenses and costs of state, §6-17.1.
Usury.
Party seeking recovery on usurious contracts.
No recovery of costs, §6-25.
Vehicle mileage act violations, private civil actions, §20-348, (a).
Venue changes.
Liability of counties where trial removed from one county to another, §6-40.
Vocational rehabilitation.
Subrogation, §143-547, (c).
Will caveats.
Allowance of costs to either party or apportioned in discretion of court, §6-21.
Witnesses.
Fees, §§6-51 to 6-62.
See WITNESSES.
Out of state witnesses, §15A-813.
Prosecuting witness.
Liability for cost in certain cases, §6-49.
Nonpayment of cost if prosecution frivolous, §6-50.
Reference of claim against deceased person.
Recovery of fees of witness, §6-31.
Uniform fees for witnesses, §7A-314.

COST SAVINGS SUGGESTIONS OR INNOVATIONS.
State employee incentive bonus program, §§143-345.20 to 143-345.25.

COTENANTS.
See JOINT TENANTS AND TENANTS IN COMMON.

COTTON.
Boll weevil eradication, §§106-65.67 to 106-65.78.
See BOLL WEEVIL ERADICATION.
Commodities generally, §§78D-1 to 78D-33.
See COMMODITIES.
Definitions.
Grower's organization, §106-65.85.
Warehouses, §106-451.7.
Gins.
See COTTON GINS.
Grower's organization, §§106-65.84 to 106-65.91.
See COTTON GROWER'S ORGANIZATION.
Labels.
Requirements for cottonseed labeling, §106-277.10, (c).
Larceny.
Ungathered crops, §14-78.
Liens.
Effective period, §44-69.1.
Official cotton grower's organization, §§106-65.84 to 106-65.91.
Promotion of use and sale of agricultural products.
Generally, §§106-550 to 106-568.
See AGRICULTURAL PRODUCTS PROMOTION.

COTTON —Cont'd
Referendum.
Promotion of use and sale of agricultural products.
Special provisions for cotton promotion association, §106-559.
Sales.
Promotion of use and sale of agricultural products.
Special referendum provisions for cotton promotion association, §106-559.
Seeds.
Label requirements for cottonseed, §106-277.10, (c).
Weights and measures.
Standard weights and measures, §81A-42.
Warehouses, §§106-451.6 to 106-451.28, 106-451.40 to 106-451.44.
See COTTON WAREHOUSES.
Weights and measures.
Seed.
Standard weights and measures, §81A-42.

COTTON BALES.
Flat trucks loaded with.
Load to be securely fastened, §20-120.

COTTON DUST PREVENTION OR REDUCTION.
Ventilation and air conditioning systems used for.
Property tax exemption, §105-275.

COTTON GINS.
Burning of ginhouses, §14-64.
Defined, §106-451.40.
Duties, §106-451.43, (a) to (d).
Injunctions.
Operation without registration, §106-451.44.
Misdemeanors.
Operation without registration, §106-451.44.
Registration.
Applications, §106-451.42, (a).
Certificate.
Display, §106-451.42, (c).
Denial, suspension or revocation, §106-451.43, (e).
Operation without registration, §106-451.44.
Required, §106-451.41.

COTTON GROWER'S ORGANIZATION, §§106-65.74 to 106-65.91.
Agreements.
Authority to enter into, §106-65.89.
Assessments.
Basis, §106-65.88, (b).
Disposition, §106-65.88, (e).
Failure to pay.
Destruction of plants, §106-65.90, (b).
Lien upon cotton, §106-65.90, (c).
Penalties, §106-65.90, (a).
Not state funds, §106-65.88, (g).
Referendum, §106-65.88, (a).
Audits.
Annual audit of accounts, §106-65.88, (f).
Authority to enter into agreements, §106-65.89.
Certification.
Authority of board, §106-65.86, (a).
Eligibility, §106-65.86, (b).
Purposes, §106-65.87, (a).
Revocation, §106-65.87, (b).
Definitions, §106-65.85.
Findings of fact, §106-65.84.
Purpose of article, §106-65.84.

COTTON GROWER'S ORGANIZATION —Cont'd
Referendum.
Assessments, §106-65.88, (a).
Votes necessary, §106-65.88, (d).
Eligibility to vote, §106-65.88, (c).
Votes necessary, §106-65.88, (d).
Rules and regulations.
Adoption by board, §106-65.91.

COTTON MERCHANTS.
Defined, §106-451.40.
Duties, §106-451.43, (a) to (d).
Injunctions.
Operation without registration, §106-451.44.
Misdemeanors.
Operation without registration, §106-451.44.
Registration.
Applications, §106-451.42, (a).
Certificate.
Display, §106-451.42, (c).
Denial, suspension or revocation, §106-451.43, (e).
Operation without registration, §106-451.44.
Required, §106-451.41.

COTTON WAREHOUSES, §§106-451.6 to 106-451.28, 106-451.40 to 106-451.44.
Administration of article, §106-451.9.
Use of income from warehouse fund, §106-451.27.
Bonds, surety, §106-451.11, (a).
Action on bond by person injured, §106-451.12.
Inspectors, §106-451.25.
Registration, §106-451.42, (b).
Citation of article, §106-451.6.
Classification, grading and weighing of cotton stored.
Delivery to warehouse presumed for storage, §106-451.16.
Licenses, §106-451.14.
Suspension or revocation, §106-451.15.
Commissioner of agriculture.
Powers and duties.
Generally, §106-451.9.
Compliance with provisions of article, rules and regulations, §106-451.23.
Definitions, §§106-451.7, 106-451.40.
Delivery of products stored on demand, §106-451.21.
Conditions to delivery, §106-451.21.
Deposit of cotton deemed subject to article, §106-451.17.
Duties, §106-451.43, (a) to (d).
Enforcement of article, §106-451.9.
Examination of books, records, etc., §106-451.24.
Fraudulent or deceptive acts, §106-451.28.
Fund for support of system, §106-435.
Injunctions.
Operation without registration, §106-451.44.
Inspectors.
Bonds, surety, §106-451.25.
Insurance, §106-451.11, (b).
Liability.
Officials and employees, §106-451.26.
Licenses.
Applications.
Contents, §106-451.10, (b).
Classification, grading and weighing of cotton stored, §106-451.14.
Suspension or revocation, §106-451.15.
Issuance, §106-451.10, (a).
Renewal, §106-451.10, (a).
Revocation, §106-451.13.

COTTON WAREHOUSES —Cont'd
Licenses —Cont'd
Suspension, §106-451.13.
Term, §106-451.10, (a).
Misdemeanors.
Operation without registration, §106-451.44.
Penalties.
Violation of article, §106-451.28.
Presumptions.
Delivery to warehouse, §106-451.16.
Subject to article, §106-451.17.
Receipts for cotton stored, §106-451.18.
Cancellation on delivery of cotton stored, §106-451.22.
Contents, §106-451.19.
Delivery.
Cancellation, §106-451.22.
Issuance.
Issuance of further receipt with original outstanding prohibited, §106-451.20.
Prohibited acts, §106-451.20.
Requirements, §106-451.19.
Records, §106-451.23.
Examination, §106-451.24.
Registration.
Applications, §106-451.42, (a).
Bonds, surety, §106-451.42, (b).
Certificate.
Display, §106-451.42, (c).
Denial, suspension or revocation, §106-451.43, (e).
Operation without registration, §106-451.44.
Required, §106-451.41.
Reports, §106-451.23.
Rules and regulations.
Board of agriculture, §106-451.8.
Short title of article, §106-451.6.
Tort actions.
Liability of officials and employees, §106-451.26.
Violation of article.
Penalties, §106-451.28.
Warehouse fund.
Use of income to administer article, §106-451.27.

COUGARS.
Captivity licenses, §113-272.5, (e).

COUNCIL-MANAGER CITIES, §§160A-147 to 160A-152.
Applicability of part, §160A-152.
Council.
Ineligible to serve or act as manager, §160A-151.
Employees.
Compensation.
Manager responsible, §160A-162, (a).
Manager.
Acting city manager, §160A-149.
Appointment, §160A-147, (a).
Chief administrator of city, §160A-148.
Duties.
Applicability of part, §160A-152.
Generally, §160A-148.
Eligibility.
Mayor and councilmen ineligible to serve or act as manager, §160A-151.
Employees.
Compensation, §160A-162, (a).
Holding elective office, §160A-147, (c).
Interim city manager.
Designated by council, §160A-150.
Population figures, determining, §160A-147, (d).
Powers.
Applicability of part, §160A-152.
Generally, §160A-148.

COUNCIL-MANAGER CITIES —Cont'd
Manager —Cont'd
Residence in city not required, §160A-147, (a).
Serving on county board of education.
Elected on non-partisan basis, §160A-147, (b).
Vacancy.
Interim city manager, §160A-150.
Mayor.
Ineligible to serve or act as manager, §160A-151.
Optional form, §160A-101.
Plan of government.
Officers to carry out plan, §160A-108.
Service upon manager is service upon city, §1A-1, Rule 4, (j).

COUNCIL OF STATE.
Advertisements or public service announcements by candidates for council.
State funds not to be used, §163-278.16A.
Capital facilities finance act.
Generally, §§142-80 to 142-101.
See CAPITAL FACILITIES FINANCE ACT.
Continuing legal education exemption, Bar Rules & Regs., D, §.1517.
Convening, §147-13, (a).
Internal improvements.
Control of internal improvements, §124-1.
Investigation of corporations.
Power of investigation, §124-7.
Journal, §147-13, (b).
Limitation on fund-raising during legislative session, §163-278.13B.
Members-elect.
Office space and expenses, §147-31.1.
Personnel system.
Competitive service.
Determination of competitive service by council of state, §126-12.
Quorum, §147-13, (a).
Service of process, §1A-1, Rule 4, (j).

COUNCIL OF STATE GOVERNMENTS.
Declared joint governmental agency, §143-186.

COUNCILS.
Aeronautics council, §143B-357.
Air quality control council, §§143B-317 to 143B-319.
Apprenticeship council, §143A-71.
Building code council, §§143-136, 143-137.
Community development council, §§143B-437.1 to 143B-437.3.
Compensation for services.
Per diem, subsistence and travel expenses, §138-5, (a) to (f).
Deaf and the hard of hearing, §§143B-216.30 to 143B-216.34.
Developmental disabilities.
Council on developmental disabilities, §§143B-177 to 143B-179.
Drought management advisory council, §143-355.1.
Emergency medical services.
Advisory council, §§143-507 to 143-519.
Energy policy council, §§113B-1 to 113B-12.
Expiration of council created by governor or other state officials.
Constitutional elective officers creating, §147-16.2, (b).
Executive branch officials creating, §147-16.2, (c).
Executive order of governor creating, §147-16.2, (a).

COUNCILS —Cont'd
Fees, §12-3.1, (a), (c).
Definitions, §12-3.1, (b).
Fish and fisheries resources.
Mid-Atlantic fishery management council.
North Carolina members, §113-260.
South Atlantic fishery management council.
North Carolina members, §113-259.
Forestry council, §§143B-308 to 143B-310.
Gender based appointments.
Appointing members to statutorily created decision making or regulatory entities.
Appointments to reflect proportion that gender represents in population of state, §143-157.1, (a).
Report by appointing authority of number appointments of each gender, §143-157.1, (b).
Governor's advisory council on aging, §§143B-180, 143B-181.
Governor's advocacy council for persons with disabilities, §§143B-403.1, 143B-403.2.
Governor's advocacy council on children and youth, §§143B-414 to 143B-416.
Governor's council on employment of the handicapped, §§143B-403.1, 143B-403.2.
Governor's management council, §§143B-426.22, 143B-426.23.
Housing coordination and policy council, §§122A-5.10 to 122A-5.12.
Interagency coordinating council for children from birth to five with disabilities and their families, §§143B-179.5, 143B-179.6.
Regional councils, §143B-179.5A.
Internship council, §§143B-417 to 143B-419.
Juvenile crime prevention councils, §§143B-543 to 143B-550.
Juvenile justice and delinquency prevention advisory council, §§143B-556, 143B-557.
Local government advocacy council, §143-506.14.
Minority health advisory council, §§130A-33.43, 130A-33.44.
National park, parkway and forest development council, §§143B-324.1 to 143B-324.3.
Nature and historic preserves.
Dedication of properties owned by local government, §143B-260.8.
North Carolina advisory council on the eastern band of the Cherokee, §§143B-411.1 to 143B-411.4.
North Carolina arts council, §§143B-87, 143B-88.
North Carolina council on the Holocaust, §143A-48.1.
North Carolina farmworker council, §§143B-426.25, 143B-426.26.
North Carolina zoological park council, §143B-336.1.
Per diem, subsistence and travel expenses, §138-5, (a) to (f).
Petroleum underground storage tank funds council, §143-215.94O.
Physical fitness and health council, §§130A-33.40, 130A-33.41.
Secretary of state.
Membership, Const. N. C., art. III, §8.
Sickle cell trait, §§130A-131 to 130A-131.2.
State of North Carolina.
Council of state.
See COUNCIL OF STATE.

COUNCILS —Cont'd
State youth advisory council, §§143B-385 to 143B-388.
Status of women, §§143B-393, 143B-394.
Substance abuse advisory council, §§143B-270, 143B-271.
Traumatic brain injury advisory council, §§143B-216.65, 143B-216.66.
Women.
Council for women, §§143B-393, 143B-394.
Writing required to create, §147-16.2, (d).
Zoological park council, §§143B-335, 143B-336.

COUNSELORS.
Employee assistance professionals, §§90-500 to 90-511.
See EMPLOYEE ASSISTANCE PROFESSIONALS.
Licensed professional counselors, §§90-329 to 90-344.
See PROFESSIONAL COUNSELORS.
Marriage and family therapists.
General provisions.
See MARRIAGE AND FAMILY THERAPISTS.
Pastoral counselors.
Certification of fee-based practicing pastoral counselors, §§90-380 to 90-395.
See PASTORAL COUNSELORS.
Privileged communications, §8-53.8.
Professional counselors, §§90-329 to 90-344.
See PROFESSIONAL COUNSELORS.
School counselors.
Privileged communications, §§8-53.4, 115C-401.

COUNTERCLAIMS AND CROSS-CLAIMS, §1A-1, Rule 7, (a).
Answer to crossclaim, §1A-1, Rule 7, (a).
Claims for relief.
Contents, §1A-1, Rule 8, (a).
Compulsory counterclaims, §1A-1, Rule 13, (a).
Counterclaim against state, §1A-1, Rule 13, (d).
Counterclaim exceeding opposing claim, §1A-1, Rule 13, (c).
Counterclaim maturing or acquired after pleading, §1A-1, Rule 13, (e).
Crosslaim against party, §1A-1, Rule 13, (g).
Default judgments.
Provisions of rule apply to parties pleading, §1A-1, Rule 55, (e).
Dismissal, discontinuance and nonsuit, §1A-1, Rule 41, (c).
Dismissal as to plaintiff's claim.
Effect on counterclaim, §1-183.1.
District courts.
Small claim actions.
Assigned actions, §7A-220.
Impermissible counterclaims and cross claims, §7A-219.
Divorce.
Resumption of maiden name or adoption of name of prior deceased or prior living husband.
Incorporation of petition for resumption or use of name in complaint or counterclaim for divorce, §50-12, (d).
Expedited evictions.
Time for filing reply to counterclaim, §42-68.
Foreign-money claims, §1C-1825, (c).
International commercial arbitration and conciliation.
Stating counterclaims, requirements, §1-567.53, (a).
Amending or supplementing, §1-567.53, (b).

COUNTERCLAIMS AND CROSS-CLAIMS —Cont'd
International commercial arbitration and conciliation —Cont'd
Stating counterclaims, requirements —Cont'd
More than two parties to arbitration, §1-567.53, (c).
Interpleader by way of crossclaim or counterclaim, §1A-1, Rule 22, (a).
Joinder of claims, §1A-1, Rule 18, (a).
Judgments, §1A-1, Rule 54, (b).
Jurisdiction.
Personal jurisdiction.
Grounds for without service of summons, §1-75.7.
Mistakenly designating defense as counterclaim or crossclaim, §1A-1, Rule 8, (c).
Omitted counterclaim, §1A-1, Rule 13, (f).
Parties.
Additional parties brought in, §1A-1, Rule 13, (h).
Permissive counterclaims, §1A-1, Rule 13, (b).
Reply to counterclaim, §1A-1, Rule 7, (a).
Seals and sealed instruments.
Limitation of actions, §1-47.
Separate trial, §1A-1, Rules 13, (i), 42, (b).
Service of process.
Numerous defendants, §1A-1, Rule 5, (c).
Pleading setting forth counterclaim or crossclaim, §1A-1, Rule 5, (b).
Small claims actions.
Assigned actions, §7A-220.
Impermissible counterclaims and crossclaims, §7A-219.
Stay of judgment as to multiple parties or multiple claims, §1A-1, Rule 62, (g).
Summary judgment, §1A-1, Rule 56.
Time for serving reply to counterclaim, §1A-1, Rule 12, (a).
Tort claims against state departments and agencies.
Counterclaims by state, §143-291.3.
Usurious notes or other evidences of debt, actions to recover upon.
Pleading penalty for usury as crossclaim, §24-2.

COUNTERFEIT DRUGS, §106-122.
Defined, §106-121.

COUNTERFEITING.
Bills of lading.
Felony, §21-42.
Coins, §14-109.
Counterfeiting coin and uttering coin that is counterfeit, §14-13.
Credit devices, fraudulent use, §§14-113.1 to 14-113.7A.
Forgery.
See FORGERY.
Issuing substitutes for money without authority, §14-15.
Notes, checks and other securities, §14-119.
Possessing tools for counterfeiting, §14-14.
Property obtained by, §14-108.
Receiving or passing unauthorized substitutes for money, §14-16.
Services obtained by, §14-108.
Substitutes for money.
Issuing substitutes without authority, §14-15.
Receiving or passing unauthorized substitutes for money, §14-16.

COUNTERFEITING —Cont'd
Tools.
Possessing tools for counterfeiting, §14-14.
Trademarks.
Infringement generally.
Criminal use of counterfeit trademark, §80-11.1.
Deceptive or unfair trade practices, §80-12.
Uttering.
Coin that is counterfeit, §14-13.

COUNTERINTELLIGENCE SERVICE.
Private protective services generally, §§74C-1 to 74C-33.
See PRIVATE PROTECTIVE SERVICES.

COUNTIES.
Abandoned motor vehicles, §§153A-132, 153A-132.2.
Abrogation.
Mass gatherings.
Local ordinances not abrogated, §130A-258.
Actions.
Damages.
Suits against counties involving governmental functions, §153A-435, (a), (b).
Defense of employees and officers, §160A-167.
Inspection departments.
Failure to take corrective action, §153A-368.
Outdoor advertising.
Regulation of nonconforming off-premises outdoor advertising.
Payment of monetary compensation for removal.
Determination, §153A-143, (f).
Public officers.
Retention of funds of county by delinquent official.
Citizen to recover funds, §128-10.
Riparian owners.
Venue for actions, §153A-288.
Adult care homes.
Share of costs, §143B-139.5.
Advertising.
Outdoor advertising.
Regulation of nonconforming off-premises outdoor advertising, §153A-143.
Agricultural extension services.
Support of activities, §153A-439.
Agriculture.
Agricultural extension services.
Support of activities, §153A-439.
Development act.
Appropriations by counties, §§106-585, 106-587.
Utilizing facilities for installing and promoting programs, §106-582.
Nuisance liability of agricultural and forestry operations.
Local ordinances affected, §106-701, (d).
Societies.
See COUNTY AGRICULTURAL SOCIETIES.
Air pollution control programs, §143-215.112.
Airports.
Authority to operate public enterprise, §153A-275.
Establishment by counties.
Authorized, §63-3.
Financing public enterprise, §153A-276.
Powers of municipalities granted to counties, §63-57, (b).
Purpose of provisions declared county purposes, §63-57, (a).
Rates for public enterprise services, §153A-277.

COUNTIES —Cont'd
Alcoholic beverages.
Confinement facilities.
Furnishing alcoholic beverages to inmates, §14-258.1.
County boards of alcoholic control.
Defense of employees and officers, §160A-167.
Elections, §§18B-600 to 18B-605.
See LOCAL OPTION ELECTIONS.
Excise tax on beer, wine and liquor.
Distribution of part of taxes, §105-113.82.
Ordinances.
Consumption.
Malt beverages and unfortified wine, §18B-300, (c).
Restrictions on adoption, §18B-100.
Regulation of places of amusement, §153A-135.
Alcoholic beverages tax generally.
See ALCOHOLIC BEVERAGES TAX.
Ambulances.
EMS services in fire protection districts, §153A-309, (a), (b).
False pretenses and cheats.
Making false ambulance request, §14-111.3.
Obtaining ambulance services without intending to pay, §§14-111.1, 14-111.2.
Health services, §153A-250.
Liens.
Attachment or garnishment.
Collection authorization, §44-51.4.
Counties to which article applicable, §44-51.8.
Discharging lien, §44-51.7.
Filing, §44-51.6.
General lien for service, §44-51.5.
Services provided by county or municipality.
Discharge of lien, §44-51.3.
Filing, §44-51.2.
Real property of recipient, §44-51.1.
Service districts, §§153A-300 to 153A-310.
Amusements.
Regulation of places of amusement, §153A-135.
Animal control officers.
Appointment authorized, §67-30.
Powers and duties of dog warden, §67-31.
Animals.
Abuse of animals, §153A-127.
Dangerous animals.
Possession or harboring of dangerous animals, §153A-131.
License taxes, §153A-153.
Shelters.
Establishing, standards, §153A-442.
Taxation, §153A-153.
Ante litem notice.
Local acts not to require notice to local unit of government claim, §1-539.16.
Applicability of chapter.
Local acts, §153A-3.
Prior laws and actions taken pursuant to prior laws, §153A-2.
Statutory references deemed amended to conform to chapter, §153A-5.
Appropriations.
Agricultural development act, §§106-585, 106-587.
Beach erosion control, §153A-438.
Economic development commissions, §158-12.
Health services.
Counties may appropriate revenues, §153A-248, (a).
Ordinances, §153A-248, (b).

COUNTIES —Cont'd
Appropriations —Cont'd
Hurricanes.
Flood and hurricane protection works, §153A-438.
Inspection departments.
Financial support, §153A-354.
Private entities.
Appropriation of money to private entity to carry out public purpose, §153A-449.
Public schools.
Apportionment among local school administrative units, §115C-430.
State highway fund.
Allocation of funds, §136-41.1, (a) to (c).
Annual appropriation out of fund, §136-41.1, (a).
Contracts for maintenance, etc., of streets, §136-41.3.
Eligible municipalities, §§136-41.1, (b), 136-41.2, (a) to (c).
Incorporated since January 1, 1945, §136-41.2, (d).
Excess accumulation of funds, §136-41.3.
Nature of funds distributed, §136-41.1, (d).
Records and annual statement, §136-41.3.
Use of funds, §136-41.3.
Western North Carolina Development Association, Inc., §153A-447, (a), (b).
Arbitration.
Outdoor advertising.
Regulation of nonconforming off-premises outdoor advertising.
Relocating and reconstructing outdoor advertising, §153A-143, (i).
Architectural, engineering and surveying services.
Procurement, §§143-64.31 to 143-64.34.
Armories.
Lease, conveyance or acquisition of property for use as armory, §127A-165.
Local financial support, §127A-168.
Arson.
Burning of certain public buildings, §14-59.
Assessments.
Special assessments, §§153A-185 to 153A-206.
See SPECIAL ASSESSMENTS BY COUNTIES.
Assessors, §§105-294 to 105-297.
See COUNTY ASSESSORS.
Atomic energy, radioactivity and ionizing radiation.
Privileged license taxes.
Low-level radioactive and hazardous waste facilities, §153A-152.1, (a) to (c).
Regulation of radioactive substances, §153A-128.
Attorneys.
See COUNTY ATTORNEYS.
Balanced growth policy act, §§143-506.6 to 143-506.14.
See BALANCED GROWTH POLICY ACT.
Bankruptcy and insolvency.
Authority to avail themselves of bankruptcy law, §23-48.
Beach erosion control.
Appropriations, §153A-438.
Service districts, §§153A-300 to 153A-310.
Special assessments.
Authority to make, §153A-185.
Beach nourishment.
Local government sales and use tax, §§105-525 to 105-531.

COUNTIES —Cont'd
Beaver damage control program.
Notification to county volunteering to participate, §113-291.10, (f).
Begging regulations, §153A-126.
Bids and bidding.
Public buildings and grounds.
Architectural, engineering and surveying services, §§143-64.31 to 143-64.34.
See PUBLIC CONTRACTS.
Billboards.
Outdoor advertising.
Regulation of nonconforming off-premises outdoor advertising, §153A-143.
Billiard hall regulation, §153A-135.
Blind persons.
Aid to the blind.
Appropriations by counties, §111-17.
Boards of commissioners.
See COUNTY BOARDS OF COMMISSIONERS.
Boards of education, §§115C-35 to 115C-50.
See LOCAL BOARDS OF EDUCATION.
Boards of elections, §§163-30 to 163-37.
See COUNTY BOARDS OF ELECTIONS.
Boards of health.
See COUNTY BOARDS OF HEALTH.
Boards of social services, §§108A-1 to 108A-11.
See COUNTY BOARDS OF SOCIAL SERVICES.
Bond issues.
Interest rate swap agreements, §§159-193 to 159-200.
See SWAP AGREEMENTS.
Local government bond act generally, §§159-43 to 159-78.
See LOCAL GOVERNMENT FINANCE.
Local government revenue bond act generally, §§159-80 to 159-97.
See LOCAL GOVERNMENT FINANCE.
Relocation of county seat.
Procedures if county votes to relocate, §159-67.
Savings banks.
Investment in county obligations, §54C-137.
School bonds.
Election required, §115C-501, (f).
Service districts.
Authorization, §153A-308.
Solid waste management loans and bonds, §§159I-1 to 159I-30.
See SOLID WASTE MANAGEMENT LOANS AND SPECIAL OBLIGATION BONDS.
Streets and highways.
Prohibition of local road bonds, §136-98, (a), (b).
Watershed improvement, §139-49, (a) to (g).
Bonds of county officers generally, §§58-72-1 to 58-72-70.
See OFFICIAL BONDS OF COUNTY OFFICERS.
Boundaries.
Disputed boundaries, §153A-18, (b).
Existing boundaries, §153A-17.
Townships, §143A-19.
Uncertain boundaries, §153A-18, (a), (c).
Bridges.
Authorizing bridges over navigable waters, §153A-243.
Fishing from bridges.
Regulation or prohibition, §153A-242.
Budget.
Local government budget, §§159-7 to 159-17.
See LOCAL GOVERNMENT FINANCE.
Building codes.
See BUILDING CODES.

COUNTIES —Cont'd
Building inspections generally, §§153A-350 to 153A-375.
See COUNTY INSPECTION DEPARTMENTS.
Buildings.
Arson.
Burning of certain public buildings, §14-59.
Bids and bidding.
Architectural, engineering and surveying services, §§143-64.31 to 143-64.34.
See PUBLIC CONTRACTS.
Care and use of county property, §153A-169.
Contracts, §§143-128 to 143-135.9.
See PUBLIC CONTRACTS.
Damages.
Rewards for information, §153A-446.
Defined, §153A-350.
Failure of owner to comply with orders of public authorities, §14-68.
Joint buildings, §153A-164.
Planning and zoning.
Applicability of provisions, §153A-347.
Limitation of actions, §153A-348.
Statute of limitations, §153A-348.
Rewards.
Persons damaging county property, §153A-446.
Setback lines.
Authority to regulate, §153A-326.
Sites of county buildings, §153A-169.
Cable television franchises, §153A-137.
Tax levy, §153A-154.
Camp Butner hospital.
Ordinances.
Application to Camp Butner reservation, §122C-410, (b).
Capital project financing.
Development financing, §158-7.3.
Project development financing debt instruments.
Project development financing act, §§159-101 to 159-113.
See LOCAL GOVERNMENT FINANCE.
Capital reserve act.
Local government finance, §§159-1 to 159-188.
See LOCAL GOVERNMENT FINANCE.
Carnivals and circuses.
Regulation of places of amusement, §153A-135.
Cattle tick.
Dipping vats provided by counties, §106-353.
Embraced in quarantine zones, §106-352.
Cemeteries.
Inmates of county homes.
County commissioners may establish, §65-5.
Removal and reinterment of bodies, §65-6.
Rural cemeteries, §§65-1 to 65-3.
Abandoned cemeteries.
Boards of trustees, §65-3.
County commissioners to have control, §65-3.
List, §65-1.
Appropriations for care, §65-2.
County commissioners.
Appropriations for care, §65-2.
Control of abandoned cemeteries, §65-3.
List of public and abandoned cemeteries, §65-1.
Service districts, §§153A-300 to 153A-310.
Central Piedmont community college.
Financial support of institution.
Authority to provide local financial support, §115D-60, (a).
Child support.
Assignment of support rights to state or county.
Acceptance of public assistance constitutes assignment, §110-137.

COUNTIES —Cont'd
Child support —Cont'd
Duty of county to obtain support, §110-138.
Institution of civil or criminal proceedings against responsible parent, §110-130.
Child welfare services not provided by county departments or boards of social services.
Action by secretary of health and human services, §108A-74.
Chlorofluorocarbons refrigerants.
Management of discarded white goods, §§130A-309.80 to 130A-390.87.
See WHITE GOODS.
Civil disorders.
State of emergency.
Generally, §§14-288.12 to 14-288.18.
See STATE OF EMERGENCY.
Powers of counties, §14-288.13.
Claims against local units of government.
Local acts not to require notice, §1-539.16.
Clerks.
Boards of commissioners, §153A-11.
Misconduct in public office.
Swearing falsely to official reports, §14-232.
Coastal area counties.
Service districts.
Removal of junked vehicles and street maintenance, §153A-301, (b), (c).
Coastal Carolina community college.
Financial support of institution.
Authority to provide local financial support, §115D-61.
Commissioners.
See COUNTY BOARDS OF COMMISSIONERS.
Community appearance commissions, §§160A-451 to 160A-455.
Community colleges.
Multiple-county administrative areas, §115D-59.
Satellite campuses.
Contracts for construction, §153A-450, (a) to (c).
Community development.
Acquisition and disposition of property for redevelopment, §153A-377.
Authority of boards to engage in programs and activities, §153A-76.
Boards of commissioners.
Advisory committees, §153A-376, (c).
Exercise of powers, §153A-376, (a), (b).
Loans, §153A-376, (d).
Low- and moderate-income housing programs.
Authority to establish and develop, §153A-378.
Program income from economic development grants.
Retention by economically distressed counties, §153A-376, (f).
Programs, §153A-376, (a).
Property.
Acquisition and disposition of property for redevelopment, §153A-377.
Small cities community development block grant program.
Retention of program income by economically distressed counties, §153A-376, (f).
Taxation, §153A-376, (e).
Confinement facilities.
See JAILS.
Conflict of laws.
Planning and zoning.
Rules and regulations, §153A-346.
Conflicts of interest.
Inspection departments.
Members of departments, §153A-355.

COUNTIES —Cont'd
Consolidated case management system.
Development, §153A-77.1.
Consolidated city-county act, §§160B-1 to 160B-21.
See CONSOLIDATED CITY-COUNTY ACT.
Consolidated human services agencies, boards and directors.
Generally.
See CONSOLIDATED HUMAN SERVICES AGENCY.
Human services director.
Powers and duties, §108A-15.1, (c).
Powers and duties, §108A-15.1, (a), (b).
Consolidation.
Commissions.
Powers, §153A-404.
Purposes, §153A-402.
Content of concurrent resolutions, §153A-403.
Establishment, §153A-401, (a).
General assembly action, §153A-405, (d).
Merged or consolidated counties, Const. N. C., art. VII, §3.
Powers and duties of commissions, §153A-404.
Purposes of commission, §153A-402.
Referendum, §153A-405, (a).
Ballot propositions, §153A-405, (b) to (e).
Resolutions.
Content of concurrent resolutions, §153A-403.
Support, §153A-401, (b).
Construction and interpretation.
Broad construction of chapter, §153A-4.
Contracts.
Authority to contract, Const. N. C., art. V, §2.
Continuing contracts.
Requirements, §153A-13.
Grants from other governments, §153A-14.
Health and social services, §§153A-250, 153A-259.
Library services, §153A-270.
Private entities.
Contracts with private entities to carry out public purposes, §153A-449.
Public building contracts.
Architectural, engineering and surveying services, §§143-64.31 to 143-64.34.
See PUBLIC CONTRACTS.
Rail transportation liability.
Contracts allocating financial responsibility, §153-279.
Streets and highways.
Appropriation to municipalities.
Contracts for maintenance, etc., of streets, §136-41.3.
Construction of roads by local authorities.
Existing contracts, §136-98, (a), (b).
Controlled substances.
Confinement facilities.
Furnishing controlled substances to inmates, §14-258.1, (a).
Speedy disposition of offenses.
County appropriations for programs to protect the public, §153A-212.1.
Corporate franchise tax.
Counties prohibited from levying, §105-122, (g).
Corporate powers of counties, §153A-11.
Exercise, §153A-12.
Costs.
Actions by state for county.
Liability for costs, §6-15.
Prisoners.
Removal of trial from one county to another.
Liability of county, §6-40.

COUNTIES —Cont'd
Costs —Cont'd
Public health or mental health grants from federal government.
Recovery of indirect costs on certain grants by counties, §130A-8, (a).
Exception, §130A-8, (b).
Special assessments.
Determination of costs, §153A-193.
Discounts authorized, §153A-193.1.
Uniform costs in fees in trial divisions.
Requirement to advance certain fees, §7A-317.
Countywide farmland protection plans, §106-744, (e), (f).
Cruelty to animals, §153A-127.
Curfews.
Imposition of curfew on persons under 18, §153A-142.
Dance hall regulation, §153A-135.
Dangerous animals.
Possession or harboring.
Regulation, §153A-131.
Dangerous substances.
Regulation of explosives, corrosives, inflammables or radioactive substances, §153A-128.
Data processing.
Common data base.
Providing, §153A-77.1.
Debts, Const. N. C., art. V, §4.
Limitation on indebtedness, §159-55, (c).
Local government finance, §§159-1 to 159-188.
See LOCAL GOVERNMENT FINANCE.
Definitions.
Buildings, §153A-350.
Inspection departments, §153A-351.
Ex officio service by county and city representatives and officials.
Official, §128-1.2.
Generally, §153A-1.
Inspection departments, §153A-351.
Library materials, §153A-262.
Local confinement facilities, §153A-217.
Managers, §153A-81.
Motor vehicles.
Junked or abandoned vehicles, §153A-132, (b).
Public enterprises, §153A-274.
Roads, §153A-238, (a).
Solid waste, §§153A-136, (d), 153A-294.
Subdivisions, §153A-335.
Demonstration forests.
Use of lands acquired by counties through tax foreclosures.
County commissioners turning over title to tax-delinquent lands, §113-30.
Department of environment and natural resources.
Cooperation with counties and municipal corporations, §113-20.
Demonstration forests.
Use of lands acquired by counties through tax foreclosures.
County commissioners turning over to department title to tax-delinquent lands, §113-30.
Forests and forestry.
Cooperation between counties and state in forest protection and development, §113-59.
Water resource surveys.
Cooperation of counties in making, §113-21.
Department of inspections, §§153A-350 to 153A-375.
See COUNTY INSPECTION DEPARTMENTS.

COUNTIES —Cont'd
Departments.
Acting department heads, §153A-88.
Inspection departments, §§153A-350 to 153A-375.
See COUNTY INSPECTION DEPARTMENTS.
Interim department heads, §153A-89.
Development.
Economic development commissions, §§158-8 to 158-15.
See ECONOMIC DEVELOPMENT COMMISSIONS.
Industrial development, §§158-16 to 158-24.
See INDUSTRIAL DEVELOPMENT.
Local development generally.
See LOCAL DEVELOPMENT.
Multi-county water conservation and infrastructure district, §158-15.1.
Development financing district, §158-7.3, (c).
Project development financing debt instruments, §§159-101 to 159-113.
See LOCAL GOVERNMENT FINANCE.
Development financing plan, §158-7.3, (d) to (j).
Directors of social services, §§108A-12 to 108A-15.
See COUNTY DIRECTORS OF SOCIAL SERVICES.
Disasters.
State of emergency.
Generally, §§14-288.12 to 14-288.18.
See STATE OF EMERGENCY.
Powers of counties, §14-288.13.
Discrimination or retaliatory action against employees generally, §§95-240 to 95-245.
See RETALIATORY EMPLOYMENT DISCRIMINATION.
District courts.
Additional seats of court, §7A-133, (c).
Appointment of judges, §7A-133, (a).
Composition of split districts, §7A-133, (b), (b1).
Facilities and courtrooms.
Responsibility of county for physical facilities, §7A-302.
Number of judges by districts, §7A-133, (a).
Unincorporated seats of court.
Disposition of fees in counties, §7A-317.1.
Dogs.
Annual license tax.
Power to levy, §153A-153.
Dangerous dogs.
Local ordinances for control of dangerous dogs.
Article not to prevent, §67-4.5.
Potentially dangerous dogs.
Persons or board responsible for determining.
Designation, §67-4.1, (c).
Provisions as to dogs applicable to all counties, §67-18.
Supplemental nature of provisions, §67-36.
Dog wardens.
Appointment of animal control officers, §67-30.
Powers and duties, §67-31.
Rabies control officers.
Dog warden as assistant, §67-31.
Domestic violence.
County appropriations for programs to protect the public, §153A-212.1.
Drainage districts.
See DRAINAGE DISTRICTS.
Drainage generally, §§156-139 to 156-141.
See DRAINAGE.
Drugs.
Confinement facilities.
Furnishing controlled substances to inmates, §14-258.1, (a).

COUNTIES —Cont'd
Drunk in public.
Employment of officers to assist individuals intoxicated in public, §122C-302.
Economic development.
Interlocal agreements, §158-7.4.
Economic development and training districts, §§153A-317.11 to 153A-317.17.
See ECONOMIC DEVELOPMENT AND TRAINING DISTRICTS.
Economic development commissions, §158-14.
Education.
County school fund.
Composition, Const. N. C., art. IX, §7.
Generally.
See PUBLIC SCHOOLS.
Local boards of education, §§115C-35 to 115C-50.
See LOCAL BOARDS OF EDUCATION.
Public schools.
Responsibility, Const. N. C., art. IX, §2.
Elections.
County boards of elections generally, §§163-30 to 163-37.
See COUNTY BOARDS OF ELECTIONS.
Generally.
See COUNTY ELECTIONS.
Electrical inspections generally, §§153A-350 to 153A-375.
See COUNTY INSPECTION DEPARTMENTS.
Embezzlement.
Funds embezzled by public officers and trustees, §14-92.
Emergency management, §166A-7, (a).
Appropriations, §166A-7, (c), (d).
Gifts and grants.
Acceptance, §166A-9.
Local state of emergency.
Declaration, §166A-8.
Mutual aid agreements, §166A-10, (b), (c).
Powers, §166A-7, (d).
State financial assistance, §166A-7, (e).
State of emergency.
Generally, §§14-288.12 to 14-288.18.
See STATE OF EMERGENCY.
Powers of counties, §14-288.13.
Emergency medical services.
Fire protection districts.
EMS services in fire protection districts, §153A-309, (a), (b).
Eminent domain.
Boards of commissioners.
Local government unit outside county.
Consent of board required, §153A-15.
Federal water resources projects.
Acquisition of lands, §143-215.42, (a) to (h).
Local government unit outside county.
City property within corporate limits, inapplicability of section, §153A-15, (d).
Consent of board required, §153A-15, (a), (b).
Applicability of requirement, §153A-15, (c).
Power to exercise, purposes, §§40A-3, (b), (b1), 153A-158.
Solid waste facility.
Purchasing site by condemnation, §153A-292, (c).
State psychiatric hospital.
Selection of county as site for.
Acquisition by county, conveyance to state, §153A-178.
Water and sewer districts.
Power of district, §162A-89.1.

COUNTIES —Cont'd
Eminent domain —Cont'd
Watershed improvement works on projects.
Powers conferred on counties in certain cases, §139-44, (a) to (f).
Employees generally.
See COUNTY OFFICERS AND EMPLOYEES.
Employment discrimination.
Retaliatory employment discrimination, §§95-240 to 95-245.
See RETALIATORY EMPLOYMENT DISCRIMINATION.
Enterprise tier.
Tax incentives for new and expanding businesses, §105-129.3.
Enumeration, §153A-10.
Environmental impact statements, major development projects.
Ordinance requiring statement of impact, §113A-8, (a) to (c).
Equal employment opportunity.
Assistance in obtaining state employment, §§126-16 to 126-18.
See PERSONNEL SYSTEM.
Escape.
Confinement facilities or officers.
Prison breach and escape from facilities or officers, §14-256.
Excise tax on beer, wine and liquor.
Distribution of part of tax, §105-113.82.
Execution sales, §153A-163.
Explosives, regulation, §153A-128.
Extortion.
Inspectors of articles of commerce.
Penalty, §66-7.
Fairs.
Application for license to commissioners, §106-517.
Penalty for violation of provisions, §106-518.
Refusal to license shows within five miles, §106-519.
County societies, §§106-505 to 106-511.
See FAIRS.
Local aid to agricultural, animal and poultry exhibits, §106-520.
Supervision of fairs, §106-520.4.
Farmland preservation trust fund.
Matching funds by counties receiving money, §106-744, (c1).
Farmland protection plans.
Countywide plans, §106-744, (e), (f).
Federal aid.
Public health or mental health grants.
Recovery of indirect cost on certain grants by counties, §130A-8, (a).
Exception, §130A-8, (b).
Federal prisoners.
Contracts for confinement, §148-37, (b).
Fees.
Boards of commissioners.
Commissioners to fix fees, §153A-102.
Inspectors of articles of commerce, §§66-3, 66-7.
Payment, §138-2.
Uniform fees in trial divisions.
Requirement to advance certain fees, §7A-317.
Finance.
Fiscal policy.
Commissioners to direct, §153A-101.
Fiscal year, §147-85.
Local government finance, §§159-1 to 159-188.
See LOCAL GOVERNMENT FINANCE.
Financing public improvements, §158-7.3.

COUNTIES —Cont'd
Firearms.
Confinement facilities.
Furnishing cartridges or ammunition for firearms to inmates, §14-258.1.
Regulation, §153A-129.
Statewide uniformity of local regulation, §14-409.40.
Fire department.
Deceased or retiring firefighters.
Honoring, awarding helmet, §153A-236.
State volunteer fire department.
Acceptance of provisions by counties, §58-80-35.
Appropriations.
Local appropriations generally, §58-80-55.
Contracts with municipalities which have accepted provisions, §58-80-35.
No authority to render assistance to nonaccepting counties, §58-80-30.
Fires and fire protection.
Fire-fighting and prevention services, §153A-233.
Fire marshal.
Appointment, §153A-234.
Firemen's association.
Membership, §58-58-20.
Investigations.
County officers, §58-79-1.
Prevention inspections generally, §§153A-350 to 153A-375.
See COUNTY INSPECTION DEPARTMENTS.
Regulation of explosive, corrosive, inflammable or radioactive substances, §153A-128.
Rural fire protection districts, §§69-25.1 to 69-25.17.
Service districts generally, §§153A-300 to 153A-310.
Fiscal control.
Finance officer, §§159-24 to 159-38.
See LOCAL GOVERNMENT FINANCE.
Fiscal impact of bills, resolutions or rules.
Local government fiscal information act, §§120-30.41 to 120-30.49.
Fiscal policy.
Commissioners to direct, §153A-101.
Fiscal year, §147-85.
Fish and fisheries resources.
Bridges.
Prohibition or regulation of fishing from bridges, §153A-242.
Flea markets.
Regulation, §153A-125.
Forests and forestry.
Cooperation between counties and state in forest protection and development, §113-59.
Demonstration forests.
Use of lands acquired by counties through tax foreclosures, §113-30.
Procedure for acquisition of delinquent tax lands from counties, §113-31.
Taxation.
Procedure for acquisition of delinquent tax lands from counties, §113-31.
Franchises.
Ambulance services, §153A-250.
Cable television franchises, §153A-137.
Taxation.
Power to levy annual tax, §153A-154.
Ordinances, §153A-46.
Franchise taxes on electric companies.
Additional tax imposed by county or city.
Companies not subject to, §105-116, (e1).

COUNTIES —Cont'd
Funded reserve.
Use against liability for damage persons or property.
Same as purchase of liability insurance, §153A-435, (a).
Funds.
Intragovernmental service funds.
Generally, §159-13.1.
Included in budget, §159-11, (d).
Local government finance, §§159-1 to 159-188.
See LOCAL GOVERNMENT FINANCE.
Garbage and trash.
Areas outside corporate limits.
Establishing and operating facilities, §153A-292, (a).
Authority to operate public enterprise, §153A-275.
Costs of providing and operating facility.
Determining for imposition of fees, §153A-292, (b).
Definitions, §§153A-136, (c), (d), 153A-294.
Disposal and removal of trash and garbage.
Boards of commissioners to provide for, §153A-132.1.
Equipment.
Agreement with department of transportation to make available, §153A-291.
Fees.
Collection, use of facility and availability of facility.
Authority to impose, determining amount, §153A-292, (b).
Property taxes, billing and collecting in same manner, §153A-293.
Financing public enterprise, §153A-276.
Gate across highway leading to facility.
Erecting, §153A-292, (c).
Hazardous waste facilities.
Local ordinances prohibiting facilities invalid, §130A-293.
Privilege license taxes, §153A-152.1, (a) to (c).
Highway rights-of-way, collection containers on.
Misdemeanor for placing garbage on right-of-way, inapplicability, §136-18.3, (b).
Permits, issuance by department of transportation, §136-18.3, (a).
Removal or change of location, order of department, §136-18.3, (d).
Written permission of owner of underlying fee, required, §136-18.3, (c).
Landfills.
Selection and approval of site, §153A-136, (c).
Loans and bonds, §§159I-1 to 159I-30.
See SOLID WASTE MANAGEMENT LOANS AND SPECIAL OBLIGATION BONDS.
Low-income persons, providing aid to, §153A-292, (f).
Ordinances, §153A-136, (b).
Department may authorize, §130A-294, (a).
Plan.
Development, §130A-309.04.
Prison and other labor.
Agreement with department of transportation to make available, §153A-291.
Rates for public enterprise services, §153A-277.
Regional solid waste management authorities, §§153A-421 to 153A-432.
See REGIONAL SOLID WASTE MANAGEMENT AUTHORITIES.
Regulation of disposal facilities, nature of disposal and method of disposal, §153A-292, (a).

COUNTIES —Cont'd
Garbage and trash —Cont'd
Regulation of solid wastes, §153A-136.
Regulation of storage, collection, transportation and use, §153A-136, (a).
Removal and disposal of trash and garbage.
Boards of commissioners to provide for, §153A-132.1.
Service districts, §§153A-300 to 153A-310.
Site for facility.
Acquiring by purchase or condemnation, §153A-292, (c).
Use of suitable vacant land, §153A-292, (c).
General assembly.
Dividing precincts in apportionment acts, §120-2.2.
House of representatives.
Apportionment, §120-2.
Local government fiscal information, §§120-30.41 to 120-30.49.
See GENERAL ASSEMBLY.
Local government to be provided for by general assembly, Const. N. C., art. VII, §1.
Senatorial districts, §120-1.
Severability of apportionment acts, §120-2.1.
Global TransPark authority.
Payments by county to authority, §63A-15.
Governmental immunity waiver, §153A-435, (b).
Governmental property.
Sale, exchange, lease to or lease from other governmental unit, §160A-274, (b).
Action taken by governing body, §160A-274, (c).
Governmental unit defined, §160A-274, (a).
Grants.
Contracts.
Acceptance of grants and loans from other governments, §153A-14.
Public health or mental health grants from federal government.
Recovery of indirect costs on certain grants by counties, §130A-8, (a).
Exception, §130A-8, (b).
Gross receipts tax on short-term vehicle leases or rentals, §153A-156, (a).
Collection of tax, §153A-156, (c), (d).
Definitions, §153A-156, (e).
Penalties and remedies, §153A-156, (f).
Provision noting in agreement, §153A-156, (b).
Harbor master for unincorporated community situated in county.
Appointment by board of county commissioner, §76-56.
Hazardous substances.
Radioactive substances.
Low-level radioactive and hazardous waste facilities.
Privilege license taxes, §153A-152.1, (a) to (c).
Regulation, §153A-128.
Health authorities.
Public health authorities generally, §§130A-45 to 130A-45.12.
See PUBLIC HEALTH AUTHORITIES.
Health boards.
See COUNTY BOARDS OF HEALTH.
Health care facilities.
Finance act.
Additional powers of public agencies, §131A-6.
Health departments generally, §§130A-34 to 130A-42.
See LOCAL HEALTH DEPARTMENTS.

COUNTIES —Cont'd
Health grants by federal government.
Recovery of indirect costs on certain grants by county, §130A-8, (a).
Exception, §130A-8, (b).
Health nuisances.
Abatement of public health nuisances, §153A-140.
Health services.
Ambulances.
Applicability of regulations, §153A-250, (e).
Contracts for services, §153A-250, (b), (d).
Franchises, §153A-250, (a).
Ordinances.
Adoption, §153A-250, (c).
Appropriations.
Counties may appropriate revenues, §153A-248, (a).
Ordinances, §153A-248, (b).
Consolidated county human services funding, §143B-139.7.
Consolidated human services agencies, boards and directors.
See CONSOLIDATED HUMAN SERVICES AGENCY.
Contracts for ambulance services, §153A-250.
Hospitals, §153A-249.
Ordinances.
Ambulances, §153A-250.
Appropriations, §153A-248, (b).
Provision for public health and mental health, §153A-247.
Hearings.
Boards of commissioners.
Conduct of public hearings, §153A-52.
Inspection departments, §153A-361.
Planning and zoning.
Board of adjustment, §153A-345, (b).
Research and production service districts.
Abolition of districts, §153A-316.
Establishment, §153A-312, (d).
Extension, §153A-314, (c).
Special assessments.
Preliminary assessment roll, §153A-195.
Preliminary resolutions, §153A-192.
Heating and air-conditioning inspectors generally, §§153A-350 to 153A-375.
See COUNTY INSPECTION DEPARTMENTS.
Heating systems.
Dwelling units leased as rental property, §160A-443.1.
Highway-rights-of way.
Garbage collection containers.
Location on rights-of-way, §136-18.3, (a) to (d).
Highways.
Generally.
See COUNTY STREETS AND HIGHWAYS.
Secondary road construction programs by department of transportation.
Adoption of annual construction program for each county, §136-44.8, (a) to (f).
Historical associations, assistance to.
Authorization to appropriate revenues, §153A-437, (a).
Office space, §153A-437, (b).
Section is supplemental, §153A-437, (c).
Historic districts and landmarks.
Exercise of same powers as cities, §160A-400.2.
Historic preservation program.
Cooperation with local governments, §121-8, (e).
Historic properties.
Acquisition, maintenance, etc., of property.
Procedures where assistance extended to counties, §121-11.

COUNTIES —Cont'd
Hog cholera.
Purchasing and supplying serum, §106-315.
Holidays.
Public officers and employees, §153A-94, (b).
Hospital authorities, §131E-30.
Hospitals.
Branch facilities, §131E-14.1.
Health services, §§153A-247 to 153A-250.
House of representatives.
Apportionment, §120-2.
Dividing precincts restricted, §120-2.2.
Severability of acts, §120-2.1.
Housing authorities and projects.
Area of operation, §157-39.1, (a) to (c).
Commissioners, §157-34.
Creation of authority.
Hearings, §157-33.
Notice, §157-33.
Powers of authority, §157-34.
Regional housing authority, §§157-39.1 to 157-39.5.
Housing by local governments generally, §§160A-441 to 160A-450.
See LOCAL GOVERNMENTS.
Housing inspectors generally, §§153A-350 to 153A-375.
See COUNTY INSPECTION DEPARTMENTS.
Human service and volunteer transportation.
Local licenses and taxes prohibited, §62-289.7.
Human services.
Consolidated human services agencies, boards and directors.
Generally.
See CONSOLIDATED HUMAN SERVICES AGENCY.
Human services director.
Powers and duties, §108A-15.1, (c).
Powers and duties, §108A-15.1, (a), (b).
Human services funding.
Consolidated county human services.
Allocation of funds, §143B-139.7, (a).
Definitions, §143B-139.7, (c).
Promulgation of rules, §143B-139.7, (a), (b).
Hunting and wildlife.
Dangerous animals.
Possession or harboring, §153A-131.
Hurricanes.
Flood and hurricane protection works.
Appropriations, §153A-438.
Special assessments.
Authority to make, §153A-185.
Immunity.
Waiver of governmental immunity.
Liability insurance, §153A-435, (b).
Improvements.
Development financing, §158-7.3.
Ordinances.
Submission of statement concerning improvements, §153A-325.
Project development financing debt instruments.
Project development financing act, §§159-101 to 159-113.
See LOCAL GOVERNMENT FINANCE.
Special assessments.
Authority to make, §153A-185.
Subdivision and residential streets, §153A-205.
Income tax.
Levy prohibited, §105-247.

COUNTIES —Cont'd
Industrial and pollution control facilities financing.
Industrial and pollution control facilities financing act, §§159C-1 to 159C-27.
See INDUSTRIAL AND POLLUTION CONTROL FACILITIES FINANCING.
North Carolina capital facilities financing act.
North Carolina industrial and pollution control facilities financing act, §§159D-1 to 159D-27.
See INDUSTRIAL AND POLLUTION CONTROL FACILITIES FINANCING.
Industrial development, §158-24.
Industrial or commercial parks or sites.
Interlocal agreement for development, §158-7.4.
Information technology procurement contracts.
Best value information technology procurement, §143-135.9.
Inheritance tax.
Levy prohibited, §105-247.
Injunctions.
Inspection departments.
Equitable enforcement of article, §153A-372.
Ordinances.
Enforcement, §153A-123, (d).
Subdivisions.
Transferring lots in unapproved subdivisions, §153A-334.
Inspection of departments, §§153A-350 to 153A-375.
See COUNTY INSPECTION DEPARTMENTS.
Inspectors of articles of commerce, §§66-1 to 66-6.
See COUNTY INSPECTORS OF ARTICLES OF COMMERCE.
Insurance.
Defense of employees and officers.
Civil and criminal actions.
Insurer provides defense, §160A-167.
Liability insurance, §153A-435, (a), (b).
Local government risk pools, §§58-23-1 to 58-23-40.
See LOCAL GOVERNMENT RISK POOLS.
Public officers and employees.
Health insurance, §153A-92.
Life insurance, §153A-92.
Rail transportation liability.
Contracts allocating financial responsibility.
Insurance required, §153-279, (c).
Interchange of governmental employees, §§126-51 to 126-58.
See PERSONNEL SYSTEM.
Interest rate swap agreements, §§159-193 to 159-200.
See SWAP AGREEMENTS.
Interlocal cooperation generally, §§160A-460 to 160A-478.
See INTERLOCAL COOPERATION.
Intoxicated in public.
Employment of officers to assist individuals intoxicated in public, §122C-302.
Intragovernmental service funds.
Generally, §159-13.1.
Included in budget, §159-11, (d).
Jails.
Generally, §§153A-216 to 153A-229.
See JAILS.
Juvenile facilities.
Regional detention services, §143B-529.
Implementation of statewide regional system, §143B-531.

COUNTIES —Cont'd
Jails —Cont'd
Juvenile facilities —Cont'd
Regional detention services —Cont'd
State subsidy to counties providing, §143B-530.
Transfer of detainees, §143B-531.
John Motley Morehead memorial commission.
Authorization for counties to assist, §143B-113.
Judicial department.
District court districts.
Additional seats of court, §7A-133, (c).
Appointment of judges, §7A-133, (a).
Composition of split districts, §7A-133, (b), (b1).
Number of judges by districts, §7A-133, (a).
Superior court division.
Organization into divisions and districts, §7A-41.
Judicial sales, §153A-163.
Junked or abandoned vehicles.
Coastal area counties.
Service districts to provide removal, §153A-301, (b), (c).
Regulation, restraint or prohibition.
Authority of county, §153A-132.2, (a).
Junked motor vehicle defined, §153A-132.2, (a).
Removal of vehicles in violation of ordinance.
Authority, request, hearing, no liability, §153A-132.2, (a1) to (a4).
Vehicle used on regular basis, removal prohibited, §153A-132.2, (d).
Removal or disposal, §53A-132, (c).
Definitions, §153A-132, (b).
Exceptions, §§153A-132, (h), 153A-132.2, (b).
Grant of power to remove and dispose of, §153A-132, (a), (a1).
Hearing procedure, §§153A-132, (d), 153A-132.2, (a3).
Immunity from liability, §§153A-132, (g), 153A-132.2, (a4).
Indemnification of county against loss, §153A-132.2, (a2).
Jurisdiction.
Boards of commissioners.
Authority of boards in certain counties over commissions, boards, agencies, etc., §153A-77.
Ordinances.
Territorial jurisdiction of county ordinances, §153A-122.
Planning and zoning.
Territorial jurisdiction, §153A-320.
Jury commissions, §9-1.
Juvenile detention facilities operated by county.
Standards and rules, §7B-1905, (b).
Juvenile facilities.
Regional detention services, §143B-529.
Implementation of statewide regional system, §143B-531.
State subsidy to counties providing, §143B-530.
Transfer of detainees, §143B-531.
Landfills.
Solid waste management loans and bonds, §§159I-1 to 159I-30.
See SOLID WASTE MANAGEMENT LOANS AND SPECIAL OBLIGATION BONDS.
Land records improvement program, financial assistance, §102-15.
Law enforcement.
Appropriations for programs to protect the public, §153A-212.1.

COUNTIES —Cont'd
Law enforcement —Cont'd
Assistance by state law-enforcement officers, §160A-288.1.
Assistance to state law-enforcement agencies, §160A-288.2.
Cooperation between law-enforcement agencies, §160A-288.
Cooperation in law enforcement matters, §153A-212.
Development programs for law enforcement, §153A-211.
Joint county and city auxiliary police, §160A-283.
Service districts, §§153A-300 to 153A-310.
Leases.
Personal property, §153A-165.
Real property, §153A-165.
Libraries.
See COUNTY LIBRARIES.
Licenses.
Animals.
Taxation, §153A-153.
Regulating and licensing businesses and trades, §153A-134.
License taxes.
General provisions, §§105-33 to 105-109.
See LICENSE TAXES.
Privilege license taxes, §153A-152.
Low-level radioactive and hazardous waste facilities, §153A-152.1, (a) to (c).
Liens.
Ambulances.
Attachment or garnishment.
Collection authorization, §44-51.4.
Counties to which article applicable, §44-51.8.
Discharging lien, §44-51.7.
Filing, §44-51.6.
General lien for service, §44-51.5.
Services provided by county or municipality.
Discharge of lien, §44-51.3.
Filing, §44-51.2.
Real property of recipient, §44-51.1.
Recovery for services to injured persons.
Lien created in favor of, §44-49, (a).
Special assessments.
Cotenants or joint owners paying special assessments, §153A-203.
Preliminary assessment roll, §153A-195.
Limitation of actions.
Planning and zoning, §153A-348.
Special assessments.
Enforcement, §153A-200, (d).
Lis pendens.
Filing by counties in building inspection and housing standards cases, §1-120.2.
Livestock.
Cattle tick.
Dipping vats provided by counties, §106-353.
Embraced in quarantine zones, §106-352.
Hog cholera.
Purchasing and supplying serum, §106-315.
Loan agencies, check cashing businesses and pawnbrokers.
Privilege tax.
Levy by counties authorized, §105-88, (e).
Loans.
Contracts.
Grants and loans from other governments, §153A-14.
Local government finance, §§159-1 to 159-188.
See LOCAL GOVERNMENT FINANCE.

COUNTIES —Cont'd
Loans —Cont'd
Solid waste management loans and bonds, §§159I-1 to 159I-30.
See SOLID WASTE MANAGEMENT LOANS AND SPECIAL OBLIGATION BONDS.
Local acts.
Alternative use of procedures contained in acts or chapter, §153A-3, (b), (c).
Broad construction, §153A-4.
Not repealed or amended by chapter, §153A-3, (a).
Superseded by chapter.
Act omitting or denying power, right, privilege or immunity granted by chapter, §153A-3, (d).
Local confinement facilities.
See JAILS.
Local development.
Economic development commissions, §§158-8 to 158-15.
See ECONOMIC DEVELOPMENT COMMISSIONS.
Generally.
See LOCAL DEVELOPMENT.
Industrial development, §§158-16 to 158-24.
See INDUSTRIAL DEVELOPMENT.
Multi-county water conservation and infrastructure district, §158-15.1.
Local government advocacy office, §143-506.14.
Local government finance generally, §§159-1 to 159-188.
See LOCAL GOVERNMENT FINANCE.
Local government fiscal information, §§120-30.41 to 120-30.49.
See GENERAL ASSEMBLY.
Local government risk pools, §§58-23-1 to 58-23-40.
See LOCAL GOVERNMENT RISK POOLS.
Local government sales and use tax.
First one-cent local government sales and use tax, §§105-463 to 105-474.
See SALES AND USE TAX.
Second one-half cent local government sales and use tax, §§105-495 to 105-502.
See SALES AND USE TAX.
Third one-half cent local government sales and use tax act, §§105-515 to 105-521.
See SALES AND USE TAX.
Local governments generally.
See LOCAL GOVERNMENTS.
Local option elections, §§18B-600 to 18B-605.
See LOCAL OPTION ELECTIONS.
Low-level radioactive waste facilities.
Notice to county in which facility proposed to be located, §104E-10.1, (c).
Ordinance preventing establishment, operation or construction of.
Invalidity, determining preemption, §104E-6.2.
Magistrates.
Number of magistrates for each county, §§7A-133, (c), 7A-171, (a).
Managers, §§153A-81 to 153A-84.
Acting county manager, §153A-83.
Adoption of county-manager plan, §153A-81.
Appointment, §153A-81.
Counties not having managers, §153A-87.
Acting department heads, §153A-88.
Interim department heads, §153A-89.
Defined, §153A-81.
Designation, §153A-81.
Duties, §153A-82.

COUNTIES —Cont'd
Managers —Cont'd
Interim county manager, §153A-84.
Officers of counties generally.
See COUNTY OFFICERS AND EMPLOYEES.
Powers, §153A-82.
Service of process.
Personal jurisdiction, manner of serving on county, §1A-1, Rule 4, (j).
Manufactured homes.
Zoning regulations, §153A-341.1.
Maps and plats.
Electoral districts, §153A-20.
Local government property mappers, §147-54.4.
Massage and bodywork therapy.
Regulation by counties, §90-636.
Mass gatherings.
Local ordinances not abrogated, §130A-258.
Medical examiners.
Appointment, §130A-382.
Cremation.
Medical examiner's permission necessary before cremation, §130A-388, (a), (b).
Duties.
Notification of medical examiners of certain deaths, §130A-385, (a).
Embalming.
When medical examiner's permission necessary before embalming, §130A-388, (a), (b).
Postmortem medicolegal examinations and services, §§130A-377 to 130A-394.
See MEDICAL EXAMINERS.
Subpoena authority, §130A-386.
Term of office, §130A-382.
Vacancies in office, §130A-382.
Meetings of public bodies generally, §§143-318.9 to 143-318.18.
See MEETINGS.
Mental health, developmental disabilities and substance abuse.
Business plan, §122C-115.2.
Consolidated county human services funding, §143B-139.7.
Consolidated human services agency.
Generally.
See CONSOLIDATED HUMAN SERVICES AGENCY.
Status as department of county, §122C-116, (b).
County programs, §122C-115.1.
Business plan, §122C-115.2.
Mental health authorities.
Local personnel systems, §126-11, (a1), (b1).
Powers and duties, §122C-115.
Provision for public health and mental health, §153A-247.
State psychiatric hospital.
Selection of county as site for.
Acquisition and conveyance of property, §153A-178.
Merger, Const. N. C., art. VII, §3.
Military property sales facilities.
Licensing, §127B-4, (a) to (c).
Militia.
Support of families of soldiers, airmen and sailors by county.
Privilege of organized militia, §127A-119.
Mobile homes and trailer parks.
Registration, §153A-138.
Zoning regulations, §153A-341.1.
Money.
Drawing public money.
Local treasury, Const. N. C., art. V, §7.

COUNTIES —Cont'd
Monuments, memorials and parks.
Confederate monuments.
Contributions toward erection, §100-10.
Fences to protect.
Power of county commissioners to expend fund for, §100-9.
Establishment, §153A-444.
Fences to protect confederate monuments.
Power of county commissioners to expend money for, §100-9.
Local governments, §§160A-350 to 160A-356.
World wars.
Contributions toward erection of memorials, §100-10.
Mosquito control districts, §§130A-352 to 130A-358.
See MOSQUITO CONTROL DISTRICTS.
Motor fuel excise tax exemption, §105-449.88.
Motor vehicle license plates.
Marking county vehicle, private plates, confidential plates, §20-39.1.
Permanent license plates for county vehicles, §20-84, (b).
Transporter plates.
County receiving donated vehicles for low income individuals, §20-79.2, (d).
Motor vehicle repairs.
Inapplicability of provisions to governmental functions, §20-354.1.
Motor vehicles.
Applicability of provisions to drivers of county vehicles, §20-168, (a).
Exception as to highway maintenance or construction work, §20-168, (b).
Driveways.
Regulation of traffic at parking areas and driveways, §153A-139.
Financial responsibility.
Exemptions, §§20-279.32, 20-318.
Gross receipts tax on short-term vehicle leases or rentals, §153A-156.
Junked and abandoned vehicles.
Regulation, removal and disposal, §§153A-132, 153A-132.2.
Ordinance making power, §153A-121, (b).
Ordinances.
Parking regulations, §153A-170.
Parking.
Parking on county property.
Regulation by ordinance, §153A-170.
Regulation of traffic at parking areas and driveways, §153A-139.
Powers of local authorities generally, §20-169.
Motor vehicle transporter plates.
County receiving donated vehicles for low income individuals, §20-79.2, (d).
Mountain ridges, counties containing.
Mountain ridge protection, §153A-448.
Ordinances, §153A-448.
Authority to adopt, §113A-208.
Service districts.
Maintenance of public roads, §153A-301, (d).
Municipal corporations.
Buildings.
Joint buildings, §153A-164.
Extension of corporate limits.
Counties excepted from part.
Part 1 continued for such counties, §160A-54.
Municipal securities.
Local government finance, §§159-1 to 159-188.
See LOCAL GOVERNMENT FINANCE.
Names, §153A-10.

COUNTIES —Cont'd
Natural gas.
Regional natural gas districts, §§160A-660 to 160A-676.
See REGIONAL NATURAL GAS DISTRICTS.
Natural gas lines located on department of transportation right-of-way.
Relocation, payment of nonbetterment cost, §136-27.2.
Nature and historic preserves.
Dedication of properties owned by local government, §143B-260.8.
911 system.
Persons residing outside counties but receiving local exchange telephone service.
Responsibility of county for, §62A-11.
Noise.
Regulation of noise by ordinance, §153A-133.
North Carolina symphony society.
Contributions, §140-10.
Notice.
Inspection departments.
Condemned buildings.
Removing prohibited, §153A-367.
Outdoor advertising.
Regulation of nonconforming off-premises outdoor advertising.
Notice to require removal, §153A-143, (c).
Posting notices, §153A-443.
Research and production service districts.
Abolition of districts.
Hearing, §153A-316.
Establishment.
Hearing, §153A-312, (d).
Extension.
Hearing, §153A-314, (c).
Special assessments.
Preliminary assessment roll.
Notice of confirmation, §153A-196.
Preliminary resolutions, §153A-191.
Nuisances.
Noise regulations, §153A-133.
Offenses against public morals.
Institution of action for abatement, injunction, §19-2.1.
Public health nuisances.
Abatement, §153A-140.
Number, §153A-10.
Nutbush conservation area.
Contributions from certain counties authorized, §143-289.
Oaths.
Entry-takers.
Form of oath, §11-11.
Public officers and employees, §153A-26.
Officers generally.
See COUNTY OFFICERS AND EMPLOYEES.
Oil pollution and hazardous substances control.
Ordinances.
Effect of article, §143-215.82.
Open fires in high hazard counties.
Enumeration of counties to which provisions applicable, §113-60.23, (a).
Ground clearing activities, special permit, §113-60.23, (c).
Woodland fires, permit required, §113-60.23, (b).
Open fires in non-high hazard counties.
Applicability of provisions, §113-60.24, (a).
Woodland fires, permit required, §113-60.24, (b).

COUNTIES —Cont'd
Ordinances.
See COUNTY ORDINANCES.
Organization of county government.
Boards of commissioners to organize, §153A-76.
Outdoor advertising.
Regulation of nonconforming off-premises outdoor advertising.
Agreement in lieu of paying compensation, §153A-143, (g).
Voluntary agreement for removal after set time, §153A-143, (k).
Amortization.
Use to phase out nonconforming uses, §153A-143, (o).
Arbitration to resolve disputes.
Relocating and reconstructing outdoor advertising, §153A-143, (i).
Authority to require removal and regulate, §153A-143, (b).
Eminent domain power not affected, §153A-143, (n).
Notice to require removal, §153A-143, (c).
Off-premises outdoor advertising defined, §153A-143, (a).
Ordinances in effect on effective date of section, §153A-143, (m).
Payment of monetary compensation for removal.
Action to for determination, §153A-143, (f).
Determining compensation, §153A-143, (e).
Monetary compensation defined, §153A-143, (e).
Not required, conditions, §153A-143, (d).
Relocation site not reasonably comparable to existing site, §153A-143, (j).
Time period for payment, §153A-143, (l).
Permit or other approval.
Relocating and reconstructing outdoor advertising, §153A-143, (h).
Relocating and reconstructing outdoor advertising.
Agreement in lieu of compensation, §153A-143, (g).
Arbitration to resolve disputes, §153A-143, (i).
Payment of compensation by county, §153A-143, (j).
Permit or other approval, §153A-143, (h).
Voluntary agreement for removal after set time, §153A-143, (k).
Parking facilities.
Authority to operate public enterprise, §153A-275.
Financing public enterprise, §153A-276.
Rates for public enterprise services, §153A-277.
Parks and recreation.
Establishment, §153A-444.
Local governments generally, §§160A-350 to 160A-356.
Service districts, §§153A-300 to 153A-310.
Partition.
Land lying in more than one county.
Appointment of commissioners, §46-7.
Venue, §46-2.
Paternity of dependent child.
Institution of civil or criminal proceedings against responsible parent, §110-130.
Pawnbrokers.
Ordinances.
Authority to adopt provisions of act by ordinance, §91A-12.
Rules and regulations.
Authority to adopt, §91A-12.

COUNTIES —Cont'd
Peddlers, itinerant merchants and specialty markets.
Local regulation not affected, §66-258.
Regulation of itinerant merchants, §153A-125.
Pellet gun regulation, §153A-130.
Personal watercraft.
Local governments regulating, §75A-13.3, (h).
Personnel system, §§153A-92 to 153A-99.
See COUNTY PERSONNEL SYSTEM.
Pesticide regulation.
Preemption by state, §143-465, (d).
Planning and zoning.
Generally, §§153A-320 to 153A-326, 153A-340 to 153A-348.
See COUNTY PLANNING AND ZONING.
Regional planning commissions.
Generally, §§153A-391 to 153A-398.
See REGIONAL PLANNING COMMISSIONS.
Plumbing inspectors generally, §§153A-350 to 153A-375.
See COUNTY INSPECTION DEPARTMENTS.
Poisons.
Confinement facilities.
Furnishing poison to inmates, §14-258.1.
Police.
Assistance by state law-enforcement officers, §160A-288.1.
Assistance to state law-enforcement agencies, §160A-288.2.
Cooperation between law-enforcement agencies, §160A-288.
Joint county and city auxiliary police, §160A-283.
Unmarked vehicles, confidential plates, private plates, §20-39.1.
Pool hall regulation, §153A-135.
Postmortem medicolegal examinations and services, §§130A-377 to 130A-394.
See MEDICAL EXAMINERS.
Powers and duties.
Acquisition of property, §153A-158.
Consolidation.
Commissions, §153A-404.
Corporate powers of counties, §153A-11.
Exercise of corporate powers, §153A-12.
Eminent domain.
Power conferred, §153A-158.
Enumeration not exclusive, §153A-124.
Inspection departments, §§153A-351, (a1), 153A-352.
Failure to perform duties, §153A-356.
Miscellaneous powers found in chapter 160A, §153A-445, (a).
Applicability of section, §153A-445, (b).
Outdoor advertising.
Regulation of nonconforming off-premises advertising, §153A-143.
Planning and zoning.
Grant of power, §153A-340, (a) to (e).
Supplemental powers, §153A-322.
Regional planning commissions, §153A-395.
Taxation.
General power to impose taxes, §153A-146.
Remedies for collecting taxes other than property taxes, §153A-147.
Prior laws.
Effect of chapter on prior laws and actions taken pursuant to prior laws, §153A-2.
Prisons and prisoners.
Local confinement facilities.
See JAILS.

COUNTIES —Cont'd
Prisons and prisoners —Cont'd
Removal of trial from one county to another.
Liability of counties for cost, §6-40.
State-county criminal justice partnership, §§143B-273 to 143B-273.19.
See STATE-COUNTY CRIMINAL JUSTICE PARTNERSHIP.
Private personnel services.
Exemption from provisions, §95-47.11.
Privileged communications.
Privacy of employee personnel records, §153A-98.
Privilege taxes on electric companies.
Additional tax imposed by county or city.
Companies not subject to, §105-116, (e1).
Procurement.
Public contracts.
Architectural, engineering and surveying services, §§143-64.31 to 143-64.34.
See PUBLIC CONTRACTS.
Generally, §§143-128 to 143-135.9.
See PUBLIC CONTRACTS.
Project development financing debt instruments.
Project development financing act, §§159-101 to 159-113.
See LOCAL GOVERNMENT FINANCE.
Property.
Acquisition of property.
Applicability of provisions, §153A-158.1, (a).
Community college property, §153A-158.2, (a).
Methods of acquisition, §153A-158.1, (a).
Power to acquire, §153A-158.
School property, §153A-158.1, (a).
Selection of county for state psychiatric hospital.
Conveyance to state, §153A-178.
Buildings, joint, §153A-164.
Care and use of county property, §153A-169.
Community college property.
Acquisition, §153A-158.2, (a).
Construction or improvement, §153A-158.2, (b).
Disposition, §153A-158.2, (b).
Public hearing, §153A-158.2, (c).
Community development.
Acquisition and disposition of property for redevelopment, §153A-377.
Disposition of property, §153A-176.
Reconveyance of property donated to local government, §153A-177.
Execution sales, §153A-163.
Judicial sales, §153A-163.
Leases, §153A-165.
Motor vehicle parking ordinances, §153A-170.
Open space acquisitions, §§160A-401 to 160A-407.
See LOCAL GOVERNMENTS.
Power to acquire, §153A-158.
Rewards.
Persons damaging county property, §153A-446.
School property.
Acquisition by county, §153A-158.1, (a).
Construction or improvement by county, §153A-158.1, (b).
Contract for construction by board of education, §153A-158.1, (d).
Lease or sale by board of education, §153A-158.1, (c).
Scope of provisions, §153A-158.1, (e).
Special assessments.
Lands exempt from, §153A-188.

COUNTIES —Cont'd
Property —Cont'd
Warranty deeds, power to execute and deliver, §160A-275.
Property taxes.
See PROPERTY TAXES.
Public enterprises.
Authority to operate, §153A-275, (a), (b).
Borrowing money.
Financing public enterprises, §153A-276.
Cooperation in providing enterprisory services, §153A-278.
Defined, §153A-274.
Delinquent accounts, §153A-277, (b).
Financing public enterprises, §153A-276.
Joint provision of enterprisory services, §153A-278.
Liens.
Rates, fees and charges do not constitute lien, §153A-277, (c).
Operation authorized, §153A-275, (a), (b).
Penalties, §153A-277, (d).
Rates.
Counties may establish, §153A-277, (a), (a1).
Enforcement, §153A-277, (b).
Public health authorities.
Generally, §§130A-45 to 130A-45.12.
See PUBLIC HEALTH AUTHORITIES.
Retirement system for counties and cities.
Membership of employees, §128-37.
Public lands.
Acquisition.
Local government unit outside county.
Consent of board required, §153A-15.
Condemnation.
Local government unit outside county.
Consent of board required, §153A-15.
Conveyances.
Admission to registration in counties, §146-77.
Grants.
Correction of grants.
Change of county line before grant issued or registered, §146-47.
Entries in wrong county, §146-48.
Public transportation systems.
Authority to operate public enterprise, §§136-44.20, (c), 153A-275.
Financing public enterprise, §153A-276.
Rates for public enterprise services, §153A-277.
Quarantine inspectors, §106-354.
Tuberculosis.
Appropriations by counties for eradication of tuberculosis, §106-343.
Amount of appropriation, §106-346.
Rabies.
County rabies vaccination clinics, §130A-187.
Fee for vaccination at clinics, §130A-188.
Radioactive and hazardous waste facilities.
Privilege license taxes, §153A-152.1, (a) to (c).
Radioactive substances.
Regulation, §153A-128.
Railroads.
Contracts allocating financial responsibility.
Applicability of provisions, §153-279, (f).
Authorized, §153-279, (b).
Definitions, §153-279, (a).
Effect on other laws, §153-279, (e).
Insurance required, §153-279, (c).
Limit on liability, §153-279, (d).
Corridors.
Acquisition of property for corridor preservation, §160A-498.

COUNTIES —Cont'd
Railroads —Cont'd
Revitalization programs.
Authorization to participate in, §153A-244.
Distribution of state financial assistance, §136-44.38, (a).
Records.
Boards of commissioners.
Meetings.
Minutes to be kept, §153A-42.
Evidence.
Admissibility, §153A-436, (e).
Inspection departments, §153A-373.
Legitimacy of reproductions, §153A-436, (d).
Media authorized for storage, §153A-436, (f).
Original copies, §153A-436, (c).
Photographic reproduction of county records, §153A-436, (a).
Privacy of employee personnel records, §153A-98.
Removal from depositories, §153A-436, (b).
State highway fund.
Appropriation to municipalities.
Records and annual statement, §136-41.3.
Recreation.
Service districts, §§153A-300 to 153A-310.
Referenda.
Consolidation, §153A-405, (a) to (c), (e).
Regional councils of governments generally, §§160A-470 to 160A-478.
See INTERLOCAL COOPERATION.
Regional planning commissions, §§153A-391 to 153A-398.
See REGIONAL PLANNING COMMISSIONS.
Registers of deeds, §§161-1 to 161-30.
See REGISTERS OF DEEDS.
Remedies.
Taxation.
Collection of taxes other than property taxes, §153A-147.
Rents.
Control of rent prohibited, §42-14.1.
Death, serious illness, or certain criminal convictions of previous occupant.
Deemed not a material fact in real property transactions, §42-14.2.
Reports.
Boards of commissioners may require reports, §153A-104.
Inspection departments, §153A-373.
Misconduct in public office.
Swearing falsely to official reports, §14-232.
Regional planning commissions, §153A-397.
Required by boards of commissioners, §153A-104.
Research and production service districts.
Establishment.
Required before hearing, §153A-312, (c).
Extension.
Required before hearing, §153A-314, (b).
Rescue.
Service districts, §§153A-300 to 153A-310.
Rescue squads.
County financial support for rescue squads, §160A-487.
EMS services in fire protection districts, §153A-309, (a), (b).
Research and production service districts, §§153A-311 to 153A-317.
See COUNTY RESEARCH AND PRODUCTION SERVICE DISTRICTS.
Retirement system for counties and cities.
General provisions, §§128-21 to 128-38.
See RETIREMENT SYSTEM FOR COUNTIES AND CITIES.

COUNTIES —Cont'd
Retirement system for teachers and state employees.
See RETIREMENT SYSTEM FOR TEACHERS AND STATE EMPLOYEES.
Rewards.
Persons damaging county property, §153A-446.
Rights of way.
Streets and highways.
Dedication of rights of way under local ordinances, §§136-66.10, 136-66.11.
Riots and civil disorders.
State of emergency.
Generally, §§14-288.12 to 14-288.18.
See STATE OF EMERGENCY.
Powers of counties, §14-288.13.
Riparian buffer protection program.
Delegation of responsibilities to local government, §143-214.23.
Roads generally.
See COUNTY STREETS AND HIGHWAYS.
Room occupancy tax, uniform provisions for counties authorized to levy.
Administered by taxing county, §153A-155, (d).
Charge for furnishing taxable accommodation, part of charge, §153A-155, (c).
Civil and criminal penalties.
Failure to file return or pay, §153A-155, (e).
Collection of tax by operator of business, §153A-155, (c).
Counties authorized to levy, applicability, §153A-155, (a), (g).
Disclosure of records, §153A-155, (d).
Discount allowed operator for collecting, §153A-155, (c).
Effective date, §153A-155, (b).
Levied only by resolution, §153A-155, (b).
Liability for tax attaching before repeal not affected, §153A-155, (f).
Passed on to purchaser, §153A-155, (c).
Public notice and public hearing on levy, §153A-155, (b).
Repeal or reduction by resolution, §153A-155, (f).
Return, §153A-155, (d).
Stated and charged separately, §153A-155, (c).
Waiver of penalties, §153A-155, (e).
When due and payable, §153A-155, (d).
Rules and regulations.
Boards of commissioners, §153A-41.
Licenses.
Regulating and licensing businesses and trades, §153A-134.
Local personnel systems, §126-11, (d).
Planning and zoning.
Conflict of laws, §153A-346.
Enforcement.
Boards of commissioners to determine method of procedure, §153A-343.
Purposes in view, §153A-341.
Public officers and employees.
Personnel rules, §153A-94, (a).
Streets and highways in and around municipalities, §136-66.4.
Sales.
Disposition of property.
Governmental property generally, §153A-163.
Merchandise by governmental units.
Exception to prohibition, §66-58, (b).
Real property.
Execution sales, §153A-163.
Judicial sale, §153A-163.

COUNTIES —Cont'd
Sales —Cont'd
Sale, lease or exchange of property between governmental units.
Action taken by governmental unit, §160A-274, (c).
Authority, §160A-274, (b).
Governmental unit defined, §160A-274, (a).
Sales and use tax.
Beach nourishment, §§105-525 to 105-531.
First one-cent local government sales and use tax, §§105-463 to 105-474.
See SALES AND USE TAX.
First one-half cent local government sales and use tax, §§105-480 to 105-487.
See SALES AND USE TAX.
Levy, §153A-151.
Limitations, §153A-151.
Modular homes, tax on.
Distribution of part of tax to counties, §105-164.44G.
Refunds, §105-164.14, (c).
Information to counties, §105-164.14, (f).
Second one-half cent local government sales and use tax, §§105-495 to 105-502.
See SALES AND USE TAX.
Third one-half cent local government sales and use tax act, §§105-515 to 105-521.
See SALES AND USE TAX.
Sanitary districts generally, §§130A-47 to 130A-85.
See SANITARY DISTRICTS.
Satellite jail/work release units, §§153A-230 to 153A-230.5.
See JAILS.
Savings and loan associations.
Investments.
County obligations, §54B-188.
Savings banks.
Investments.
County obligations, §54C-137.
School district indebtedness.
Assumption by counties, §§115C-473 to 115C-475.
Schools.
Generally.
See PUBLIC SCHOOLS.
Local boards of education.
Generally, §§115C-35 to 115C-50.
See LOCAL BOARDS OF EDUCATION.
Seats.
Relocation.
Bond issues.
Procedures if county votes to relocate county seat, §159-67.
Secondary road construction programs by department of transportation.
Adoption of annual construction program for each county.
Board of transportation, §136-44.8, (e).
Department of transportation to follow, §136-44.8, (f).
Map showing tentative road paving projects.
Posting in county courthouse, §136-44.8, (a).
Notice of public meeting of board of county commissioners.
Deviations or priority of paving projects, §136-44.8, (d).
Presentation by department of annual program for county, §136-44.8, (b).
Public meeting on annual construction program for county, §136-44.8, (c).
Notice, §136-44.8, (b).

COUNTIES —Cont'd
Secondary road construction programs by department of transportation —Cont'd
Public meeting on deviations or priority of paving projects, §136-44.8, (d).
Review of changes to which commissioners do not consent.
Petition by board, §136-44.8, (f).
Security interest.
Entering into contracts creating, §160A-20.
Senatorial districts.
Dividing precincts into apportionment acts, §120-2.2.
Established, §120-1.
Number of senators, §120-1.
Severability of apportionment acts, §120-2.1.
Service districts.
Economic development and training districts, §§153A-317.11 to 153A-317.17.
See ECONOMIC DEVELOPMENT AND TRAINING DISTRICTS.
Generally, §§153A-300 to 153A-310.
See COUNTY SERVICE DISTRICTS.
Research and production service districts, §§153A-311 to 153A-317.
See COUNTY RESEARCH AND PRODUCTION SERVICE DISTRICTS.
Service of process.
Personal jurisdiction.
Manner of service to exercise, §1A-1, Rule 4, (j).
Sewage collection and disposal systems.
Service districts, §§153A-300 to 153A-310.
Sewers.
Connections.
Power to require, §153A-284.
Districts.
County water and sewer districts, §§162A-86 to 162A-94.
See COUNTY WATER AND SEWER DISTRICTS.
Liability for failure to furnish water or sewer services, §153A-283.
Nonliability for failure to furnish water or sewer services, §153A-283.
Powers and duties.
Requiring connection, §153A-284.
Riparian rights.
Law not changed, §153A-286.
Venue for actions by riparian owners, §153A-288.
Special assessments.
Authority to make, §153A-185.
Venue for actions by riparian owners, §153A-288.
Sheriffs.
Generally.
See SHERIFFS.
Training programs for law enforcement, §153A-211.
Short-term vehicle leases or rentals.
Gross receipts tax on, §153A-156.
Signs.
Outdoor advertising.
Regulation of nonconforming off-premises outdoor advertising, §153A-143.
Single portal of entry.
Development, §153A-77.1.
Sinking funds.
Local government finance, §§159-1 to 159-188.
See LOCAL GOVERNMENT FINANCE.

COUNTIES —Cont'd
Skateboarding, inline skating and freestyle bicycling.
Limitation of liability, §99E-25, (b).
Duty of care not created, §99E-25, (d).
Exceptions, §99E-25, (c).
Independent concessionaires or other persons or organizations.
Liability not limited by section, §99E-25, (e).
Insurance carried by entity.
Not waiver of liability limits, §99E-25, (f).
Sovereign immunity not waived, §99E-25, (d).
Operating skateboard park not supervised on regular basis.
Helmet, elbow pads and kneepads requirement.
Satisfaction of requirement, §99E-21, (b).
Specifically designated areas for activities.
Required to participate on property owner or controlled by entity, §99E-25, (a).
Smallpox vaccination incident to homeland security act.
Adverse reaction, policy regarding sick leave, §153A-94.1.
Social services.
Appropriations.
Not to revert, §108A-91.
Authority to provide social service programs, §153A-255.
Boards of social services, §§108A-1 to 108A-11.
See COUNTY BOARDS OF SOCIAL SERVICES.
Child abuse, neglect or dependency cases.
Disagreement between departments as to legal residence of child.
Resolution, referral to division of social services, §153A-257, (d).
Child welfare services not provided by county.
Action by secretary of health and human services, §108A-74.
Consolidated county human services funding, §143B-139.7.
Consolidated human services agencies, boards, directors.
See CONSOLIDATED HUMAN SERVICES AGENCY.
Contracts with other agencies, §153A-259.
County home, §153A-256.
Director of social services, §§108A-12 to 108A-15.
See COUNTY DIRECTORS OF SOCIAL SERVICES.
Disagreement between departments as to legal residence of child.
Child abuse, neglect or dependency cases.
Resolution, referral to division of social services, §153A-257, (d).
Failure to pay public assistance costs.
Withholding of state moneys from counties failing to pay, §108A-93.
Programs.
Authority to provide, §153A-255.
Residence requirements.
Eligibility for financial support, §153A-257, (a).
Purpose of section, §153A-257, (c).
Termination, §153A-257, (b).
Special county attorneys for social service matters, §§108A-16 to 108A-18.
Taxation, §108A-90, (a).
Consolidated tax, §108A-90, (b).
Work first program generally, §§108A-27 to 108A-39.
See WORK FIRST PROGRAM.

COUNTIES —Cont'd
Soil and water conservation districts.
Drainage projects.
Establishment and maintenance by counties, §153A-440.1, (b).
Water resources development projects.
Establishment and maintenance by counties, §153A-440.1, (b).
Watershed improvement works or projects.
Bond issues.
Borrowing by local units for anticipated water supplies, §139-49, (a) to (g).
Establishment and maintenance of programs by counties, §153A-440.1, (a).
Extraterritorial powers of counties, §139-45.
Participation by, §139-48, (a).
Powers, §139-41, (a) to (i).
Counties not authorized to levy watershed improvement taxes, §139-41.1.
Extraterritorial powers of counties, §139-45.
Taxation.
Alternative method of financing watershed improvement programs by special county tax, §139-39.
Soil and water conservation promotion, §153A-440.
Solicitation.
Regulation of solicitation, §153A-125.
Solid waste management.
Areas outside corporate limits.
Establishing and operating facilities, §153A-292, (a).
Authority to operate public enterprise, §153A-275.
Costs of providing and operating facility.
Determining for imposition of fees, §153A-292, (b).
Definitions, §§153A-136, (c), (d), 153A-294.
Equipment.
Agreement with department of transportation to make available, §153A-291.
Fees.
Collection, use of facility and availability of facility.
Authority to impose, determining amount, §153A-292, (b).
Property taxes, billing and collecting in same manner, §153A-293.
Financing public enterprise, §153A-276.
Gate across highway leading to facility.
Erecting, §153A-292, (c).
Hazardous waste facilities.
Local ordinances prohibiting facilities invalid, §130A-293.
Privilege license taxes, §153A-152.1, (a) to (c).
Loans and bonds, §§159I-1 to 159I-30.
See SOLID WASTE MANAGEMENT LOANS AND SPECIAL OBLIGATION BONDS.
Low-income persons, providing aid to, §153A-292, (f).
Ordinances.
Department may authorize, §130A-294, (a).
Plan.
Development, §130A-309.04.
Prison and other labor.
Agreement with department of transportation to make available, §153A-291.
Rates for public enterprise services, §153A-277.
Regional solid waste management authorities, §§153A-421 to 153A-432.
See REGIONAL SOLID WASTE MANAGEMENT AUTHORITIES.

COUNTIES —Cont'd
Solid waste management —Cont'd
Regulation of disposal facilities, nature of disposal and method of disposal, §153A-292, (a).
Service districts, §§153A-300 to 153A-310.
Site for facility.
Acquiring by purchase or condemnation, §153A-292, (c).
Use of suitable vacant land, §153A-292, (c).
Southern growth policies agreement.
Rights of state and local governments not restricted, §143-506.
Special assessments, §§153A-185 to 153A-206.
See SPECIAL ASSESSMENTS BY COUNTIES.
State of emergency.
Generally, §§14-288.12 to 14-288.18.
See STATE OF EMERGENCY.
Powers of counties, §14-288.13.
State psychiatric hospital.
Selection of county as site for.
Acquisition and conveyance of property, §153A-178.
Stormwater management programs.
Authority to operate public enterprise, §153A-275.
Financing public enterprise, §153A-276.
Rates for public enterprise services, §153A-277.
Telecommunications systems for state agencies.
Access to, switched broadband, chief information officer to provide, §147-33.92, (a), (b).
Townships.
Boundaries and boundary changes, §153A-19, (a) to (c).
Establishing or abolishing, §153A-19, (a).
Transportation department.
Local consultation on transportation projects, §136-11.1.
Transporter plates.
County receiving donated vehicles for low income individuals, §20-79.2, (d).
Unemployment compensation benefits chargeable to.
Pool account for local government unemployment compensation, §147-86.1, (a) to (d).
Used oil collection, reuse or disposal.
Grants to local governments to encourage, §130A-309.22, (a) to (d).
Vagrancy.
Regulation of begging, §153A-126.
Vesting rights.
Planning and zoning.
Land-use planning process, §153A-344.1.
Veterans.
Priority in employment assistance for United States armed forces veterans, §§165-44.1 to 165-44.6.
Wage and hour act.
Exemption from provisions, §95-25.14, (d), (e).
Waiver of governmental immunity, §153A-435, (a).
Wastewater collection, treatment and disposal systems.
Authority to operate public enterprise, §153A-275.
Financing public enterprise, §153A-276.
Rates for public enterprise services, §153A-277.
Wastewater treatment, assessments.
Special assessments.
Authority to make, §153A-185.
Water and sewerage facility assessments, §153A-185.

COUNTIES —Cont'd
Water and sewer districts, §§162A-86 to 162A-94.
See COUNTY WATER AND SEWER DISTRICTS.
Water pollution and hazardous substances control.
Privilege license taxes.
Low-level radioactive and hazardous waste facilities, §153A-152.1, (a) to (c).
Waters and watercourses.
Commissioners for opening and clearing streams, §§77-1 to 77-11.
See STREAMS.
Landings.
Public landings, §77-11.
Watershed improvement projects.
Service districts, §§153A-300 to 153A-310.
Water supply and distribution systems.
Authority to operate public enterprise, §153A-275.
Financing public enterprise, §153A-276.
Rates for public enterprise services, §153A-277.
Service districts, §§153A-300 to 153A-310.
Weapons.
Confinement facilities.
Furnishing deadly weapons to inmates, §14-258.1.
Firearms.
Regulation, §153A-129.
Pellet guns.
Regulation by counties, §153A-130.
Regulation of firearms, §153A-129.
Western North Carolina Development Association, Inc.
Appropriations, §153A-447, (a), (b).
Wetlands.
Eminent domain.
Condemnor acquiring land for purposes of wetlands mitigation.
Payment to county where land located, §153A-15.1.
State agency acquiring land by purchase.
Payment to county sum equal to or in lieu of ad valorem taxes, §§146-22.3 to 146-22.5.
White goods.
Management of discarded white goods, §§130A-309.80 to 130A-390.87.
See WHITE GOODS.
Wills.
Recording of wills.
Copies of wills recorded in wrong county, §8-30.
Work first program.
Generally, §§108A-27 to 108A-39.
See WORK FIRST PROGRAM.
Zoning and planning.
Generally, §§153A-320 to 153A-326, 153A-340 to 153A-348.
See COUNTY PLANNING AND ZONING.
Regional planning commissions, §§153A-391 to 153A-398.
See REGIONAL PLANNING COMMISSIONS.
Zoning inspectors generally, §§153A-350 to 153A-375.
See COUNTY INSPECTION DEPARTMENTS.
Zoological authority.
Gifts, §143-177.2.

COUNTRY CLUBS.
Alcoholic beverage permits.
Residential sports club permit, §18B-1006, (k).
Sports club defined to include, §18B-1000.

COUNTY AGRICULTURAL SOCIETIES.
Evidence.
Records may be read in evidence, §106-511.

COUNTY AGRICULTURAL SOCIETIES —Cont'd
Exhibits exempt from state and county taxes, §106-507.
Funds to be used in paying premiums, §106-508.
Incorporation, §106-505.
New members, §106-506.
Officers, §106-506.
Organization, §106-506.
Powers, §106-505.
Premiums awarded by societies.
Funds to be awarded in paying premiums, §106-508.
Publication of statements required, §106-510.
Records to be kept, §106-511.
May be read in evidence, §106-511.
Statements.
Annual statements to state treasurer, §106-509.
Publications required, §106-510.
State treasurer.
Annual statement to treasurer, §106-509.
Taxation.
Exhibits exempt from state and county taxes, §106-507.
Term of existence, §106-505.

COUNTY ASSESSORS.
Alternative to separate office of county assessor, §105-294, (f).
Annual review, §105-296, (j) to (m).
Exempted or excluded property, §105-296, (l).
Transportation corridor official maps and amendments, §105-296, (m).
Appointment, §105-294, (a).
Assistant assessor, §105-297.
Bonds generally, §§58-72-1 to 58-72-70.
See OFFICIAL BONDS OF COUNTY OFFICERS.
Certification, §105-294, (c).
Change in appraisal, §105-296, (i).
Compensation, §105-294, (e).
Duties, §105-296, (a) to (c).
Instruction in appraisal or assessment of property, §105-294, (d).
Inventories.
Requiring, §105-296, (h).
Oath of office, §105-295.
Powers.
Generally, §105-296, (g), (h).
Qualifications, §105-294, (b).
Removal from office, §105-294, (a).
Studies conducted by department.
Furnishing information to department, §105-296, (k).
Subpoenas.
Powers, §105-296, (g).
Term of office, §105-294, (a).
Unknown owner.
Listing in name of, §105-302, (c).
Reports on properties listed in name of, §105-302.1.
Vacancy in office, §105-294, (a).

COUNTY ATTORNEYS.
Appointments, §153A-114.
Employees of counties generally.
See COUNTY OFFICERS AND EMPLOYEES.
Oaths.
Form of oaths of office, §11-11.
Police.
Removal of unfit officers.
Prosecution by county attorney, §128-17.
Powers and duties, §153A-114.

COUNTY ATTORNEYS —Cont'd
Sheriffs.
Removal of unfit officers.
Prosecution by county attorney, §128-17.
Voting rights act of 1965.
Duties as to, §§120-30.9E, 120-30.9H.

COUNTY BOARDS OF COMMISSIONERS.
Allowances, §153A-28.
Attorney.
Appointment, §153A-114.
Ayes and noes, §153A-42.
Boards, commissions and agencies.
Counties with population in excess of 450,000, authority of commissioners, §153A-77, (h).
Direct control of activities.
Assumption, §153A-77, (a).
Consolidation of human services, §153A-77, (b) to (e).
Public health rules, enforcement by civil penalty, §153A-77, (a).
Bonds, surety.
Official bonds, §58-72-60.
Liability of commissioners as surety.
Record of board conclusive as to facts stated, §58-72-65.
Vacancy declared.
Judge to file statement of proceedings with commissioners, §58-72-45.
Surety companies.
Clerk to notify county commissioners of condition of company, §58-73-10.
Brucellosis.
Cooperation of county boards, §106-394.
Buildings.
Designation of sites, §153A-169.
Chairman.
Duties, §153A-39.
Powers and duties, §153A-39.
Selection, §153A-39.
Optional methods of selection, §153A-58.
Temporary chairman, §153A-39.
Tie votes, §153A-39.
Vice-chairman, §153A-39.
Child support.
Action by designated representatives, §110-130.
Clerk.
Appointment, §153A-111.
Powers and duties, §153A-111.
Code of ordinances, §153A-49.
Community development.
Advisory committees, §153A-376, (c).
Exercise of powers, §153A-376, (b).
Loans, §153A-376, (d).
Compensation, §§153A-28, 153A-92.
Duties, failure to discharge, §14-230.
Effective dates of alterations, §153A-62.
Elections, §§153A-60, 153A-64.
Alteration of structure of board, §153A-60.
Filing results of election, §153A-64.
Altering mode of elections, §153A-58.
Manner of election, §153A-34.
Vacancy in office, §163-115, (d).
Voting systems.
Powers and duties as to, §163-165.8.
Eminent domain.
Local government unit outside county.
Consent of board required, §153A-15.
Employees in offices of register of deeds and sheriff.
Fixing number, §153A-103.

COUNTY BOARDS OF COMMISSIONERS —Cont'd
Employees in offices of register of deeds and sheriff —Cont'd
Relatives.
Approval of board not required for employment, §153A-103.
Fairs.
Application for license to commissioners, §106-517.
Penalty for violation of provisions, §106-518.
Refusal to license shows within five miles, §106-519.
Fees.
Commissioners to fix fees, §153A-102.
Ferries.
Authority of county commissioners with regard to ferries, §136-88.
Fiscal policy of counties.
Commissioners to direct, §153A-101.
Joint meetings with local boards of education, §115C-426.2.
Franchises.
Adoption, §153A-46.
Hearings.
Conduct of public hearing, §153A-52.
Hospital districts.
Alternative procedures for creation of district, §131E-41, (b).
Creation of district.
Alternative procedures, §131E-41, (b).
Governing body of district, §131E-47.
Human services.
Consolidation of human services.
Counties with population in excess of 450,000, §153A-77, (b) to (g).
Industrial development commission.
Functions and duties of commission, §158-23.
Larceny, §14-76.
Livestock.
Brucellosis.
Cooperation of county boards of commissioners, §106-394.
Meetings, §153A-42.
Adjournment, §153A-40, (a).
Joint meetings with local boards of education, §115C-426.2.
Location, §153A-40, (c).
Minutes to be kept, §153A-42.
Quorum, §153A-43.
Regular meetings, §153A-40, (a).
Special meetings, §153A-40, (b).
Time and place, §153A-40, (a).
Voting.
Ayes and noes, §153A-42.
Members excused from voting, §153A-44.
Modification in structures of boards.
Ballots.
Forms, §153A-61.
Effective date of alterations, §153A-62.
Elections.
Altering mode of elections, §153A-58.
Filing copies of resolutions, §153A-63.
Implementation when board has members serving a combination of four and two year terms, §153A-59.
Initiation of alterations by resolution, §153A-60.
Number of commissioners.
Options, §153A-58.
Optional structures, §153A-58.

COUNTY BOARDS OF COMMISSIONERS —Cont'd
Modification in structures of boards —Cont'd
Resolutions.
Filing copies, §153A-63.
Initiation of alterations by resolution, §153A-60.
Submission of proposition to voters, §153A-61.
Filing results of election, §153A-64.
Terms of commissioners, §153A-59.
Motor vehicle license plates.
Special plates, §20-79.4, (b).
Number of commissioners.
Options, §153A-58.
Oaths.
Chairman of the board of county commissioners.
Administration of oaths by chairman, §11-9.
Who may administer oaths of office, §11-7.1, (a).
Optional structures, §153A-58.
Ordinances.
Adoption, §153A-45.
Book, §153A-48.
Code, §153A-49.
Pleading and proving county ordinances, §153A-50.
Technical ordinances, §153A-47.
Organization of county government.
Boards to organize, §153A-76.
Fiscal policy of county, §153A-101.
Personnel boards.
Establishment, §153A-95.
Planning and zoning.
Method of procedure, §153A-343.
Review of decisions by superior court, §153A-340, (f).
Pleading and proving county ordinances, §153A-50.
Procedures, §153A-41.
Property.
Use of county property, §153A-169.
Public hearings.
Conduct, §153A-52.
Public schools.
Appropriations.
Allocation by purpose, function or project, discretion, §115C-429, (b).
Determining amount, §115C-429, (b).
Budget.
Action on, completion, time, duties, §115C-429, (b).
Approval of amendment, §115C-433, (b).
Transfer of funds, emergencies, §115C-433, (d).
Books, records and other financial information, available to, §115C-429, (c).
Deficit, not required to fund, §115C-429, (d).
Dispute between board and state board of education.
Procedure for resolution, §115C-431.
Submission to commissioners, §115C-429, (a).
Uniform budget format, §115C-426.
Elections.
Action of board on petition for election, §115C-506.
Loans from state literary fund.
Loans by county board to school districts, §115C-461.
Money dispute between board and state board of education.
Procedure for resolution, §115C-431.
Purchase of building site.
Expenditures, approval required, §115C-426, (f).
Disagreement between commissioners and board of education, §115C-426, (f).

COUNTY BOARDS OF COMMISSIONERS —Cont'd
Public schools —Cont'd
Supplementary taxes for school purposes.
Action of board on petition for election, §115C-506.
Tax levying authority, §115C-5, (j).
Quorum, §153A-43.
Records, §153A-42.
Registers of deeds.
Clerk to board, §161-23.
Reports.
Commissioners may require reports, §153A-104.
Misconduct in public office.
Swearing falsely to official reports, §14-232.
Resolutions.
Filing copy of alteration resolution, §153A-63.
Initiation of alterations, §153A-60.
Rules and regulations.
Adoption, §153A-41.
Secondary roads construction programs.
Filing of annual statement, §136-44.9.
Submission of programs to county commissioners, §136-44.8, (a) to (f).
Sheriffs.
Bond of sheriff.
Duties as to, §§162-9, 162-10.
Soil and water conservation districts.
Watershed improvement works or projects.
Powers, §139-41, (a) to (i).
Streets and highways.
Responsibility of counties for upkeep, etc., terminated, §136-97, (a).
Secondary roads construction programs.
Filing of annual statement, §136-44.9.
Submission of programs to county commissioners, §136-44.8, (a) to (f).
Structure, §153A-34.
Optional structures, §153A-58.
Technical ordinances, §153A-47.
Term of commissioners, §153A-59.
Implementation of optional structures.
Members serving combination of four and two year terms, §153A-59.
Toll bridges.
Authority of county commissioners with regard to toll bridges, §136-88.
Vacancies, §153A-27.
Certain enumerated counties.
Appointment to fill, §153A-27.1, (a).
County executive committee of political party.
Consulting, recommendation, §153A-27.1, (d), (e).
Filing, provisions repealed, §153A-27.1, (f).
Eligibility for appointment, §153A-27.1, (c).
Inapplicability of G.S. 53A-27, §153A-27.1, (g).
List of counties which section applies, §153A-27.1, (h).
Remainder of unexpired terms, §153A-27.1, (b).
Term of appointee, §153A-27.1, (b).
Nominations to fill.
Special provisions for obtaining nominations, §163-115, (d).
Voting.
Members excused from voting, §153A-44.
Tie votes, §153A-39.

COUNTY BOARDS OF ELECTIONS.
Absentee ballots.
Certified list of executed absentee ballots.
Preparation, §163-232.
Counting of absentee ballots by, §163-234.

COUNTY BOARDS OF ELECTIONS —Cont'd
Absentee ballots —Cont'd
Required meeting of county board, §163-230.1, (c1).
Absentee voting by military.
Absentee voting at office of board of elections, §163-255.
Consideration and approval of applications, §163-249.
Issuance of absentee ballots, §163-249.
Appointment of members, §§163-22, (c), 163-30.
Appropriations.
Boards of county commissioners to make appropriations for, §163-37.
Ballots.
Duties as to, §163-33.
Preparation and production of official ballots and instructions, §163-165.3, (b).
Canvassing votes, §163-182.5, (b).
Certificate of nomination, election or referendum results, §163-182.15.
Chairman.
Examination of voting machines, §163-33.2.
Power to administer oaths, §163-33.1.
Compensation of members, §§163-32, 163-35, (c).
Attendance at instructional meetings, §163-30.
Composition, §163-30.
Counting ballots.
Jurisdiction, §163-182.4, (a).
Director of elections.
Duties, §163-35, (d).
Training and certification, §163-35, (e).
Vacancy in office, §163-35, (a).
Disqualifications for office, §163-35, (a).
Duties, §§163-33, 163-35, (d).
Expenses of members, §163-32.
Full-time offices, §163-36.
Instructional meetings.
Compensation of members for attendance, §163-30.
Investigations, §163-33.
Littering notification, §163-33.3.
Meetings, §163-31.
Modified full-time offices, §163-36.
Municipal elections.
Administration of elections.
Mandatory administration, §163-284.
Optional by municipality.
Provisions applicable to municipality which elects to conduct own elections, §163-286, (b).
Special district elections, §163-284.1.
Conducted by county boards, §163-285, (a).
Maps of definitive outline of boundaries of municipality, requiring, §163-285, (b).
Optional in certain specified municipalities, §163-285, (a).
Ongoing county administration, §163-304, (d).
Registration, §163-288.
Special district elections.
Conducted by county board of elections, §163-284.1.
Notice.
Duties of boards, §163-33.
Number of members, §163-30.
Oaths.
Oath of office of members, §163-30.
Power of chairman to administer, §163-33.1.
Political activities by board members, §§163-38 to 163-40.1.
Applicability of provisions, §163-38.

COUNTY BOARDS OF ELECTIONS —Cont'd
Political activities by board members —Cont'd
Definitions and proof of terms used, provision applicable, §163-40.1.
Limitation on activities, §163-39.
Removal, violation grounds for, §163-40.
Powers, §163-33.
Maintenance of order, §163-34.
Precincts.
Map of precinct boundaries.
Duty to prepare, §163-128, (b).
Powers as to precincts, §163-128, (a).
Protest of election.
Appeal of decision to superior court, §163-182.14.
Appeal to state board after decision, §163-182.11.
Filing, §163-182.9.
Rules for conduct of hearing, §163-182.10.
Quorum, §163-31.
Recounts, §163-182.7.
Relative of candidate not eligible to serve, §163-30.
Removal of members, §163-22, (c).
Reports.
State board of elections may require reports from county boards, §163-22, (c).
Rules and regulations, §163-33.
Special district elections.
Conducted by county boards.
Maps of definitive outline of boundaries of municipality, requiring, §163-285, (b).
Special district defined, §163-285, (c).
Statement of economic interests.
Notifying candidates of requirements, §120-93.
Student election assistants.
Appointment, §163-42.1.
Summary of duties.
Counting votes, canvassing, abstracts and protests, §163-182.17, (c).
Termination of employment, §163-35, (b).
Terms of office, §163-30.
Vacancies in office, §§163-22, (c), 163-30.
Voting machines.
Examination, §163-33.2.
Voting places.
Duties as to, §§163-129, 163-166.1.
Voting systems.
Powers and duties as to, §§163-165.9, 163-165.10.

COUNTY BOARDS OF HEALTH.
Adjudicatory body, §130A-35, (a).
Appointment of members, §130A-35, (b).
Chairperson, §130A-35, (e).
Composition, §130A-35, (b).
Consolidated human services agencies, boards and directors.
See CONSOLIDATED HUMAN SERVICES AGENCY.
Expenses, §130A-35, (h).
Fees.
Power to impose for services rendered by local department, §130A-39, (g).
Meetings, §130A-35, (i).
Per diem, §130A-35, (h).
Policy-making body, §130A-35, (a).
Quorum, §130A-35, (f).
Removal of board members, §130A-35, (g).
Rules, §130A-35, (a).
Authority to adopt, §130A-39, (a).
Code, standard, rule or regulation.
Adoption by reference to, §130A-39, (f).
Copies, filing, §130A-39, (e).

COUNTY BOARDS OF HEALTH —Cont'd
Rules —Cont'd
More stringent rules, power to adopt, §130A-39, (b).
Municipalities, applicability to, §130A-39, (c).
Notice prior to adoption, repeal or amendment, §130A-39, (d).
Terms of office, §130A-35, (c).
Vacancies in office, §130A-35, (d).

COUNTY BOARDS OF SOCIAL SERVICES, §§108A-1 to 108A-11.
Appointment of members, §108A-3, (a), (b).
Filling of vacancies, §108A-6.
Chairman.
Election, §108A-7.
Term of office, §108A-7.
Child welfare services not provided by boards.
Action by secretary of health and human services, §108A-74.
Compensation of members, §§108A-3, (c), 108A-8.
Composition, §108A-2.
Consolidated human services boards.
Generally.
See CONSOLIDATED HUMAN SERVICES AGENCY.
Human services director.
Powers and duties, §108A-15.1, (c).
Powers and duties, §108A-15.1, (a), (b).
Contracts with governmental or private agencies, §108A-10.
Creation, §108A-1.
Duties, §§108A-1, 108A-9.
Fees, §108A-10.
Fraudulent public assistance program payments.
Garnishment of wages to recoup, §108A-25.3.
Meetings, §108A-7.
Number of members.
Change of number, §§108A-2, 108A-5, (c).
Per diem of members, §108A-8.
Records.
Inspection of records by members, §108A-11.
Reports.
Fees received, §108A-10.
Residence requirements for membership, §108A-3, (c).
Terms of members, §108A-4.
Expiration, §108A-5, (a), (b).
Vacancies.
Filling, §108A-6.

COUNTY CLERKS.
Boards of commissioners, §153A-11.
Reports.
Misconduct in public office.
Swearing falsely to official reports, §14-232.

COUNTY COMMISSIONERS.
See COUNTY BOARDS OF COMMISSIONERS.

COUNTY CONSOLIDATION, §§153A-401 to 153A-405.
Cities-counties, §§160B-1 to 160B-21.
See CONSOLIDATED CITY-COUNTY ACT.

COUNTY DIRECTORS OF SOCIAL SERVICES, §§108A-12 to 108A-15.
Abuse, neglect or dependency of juveniles.
Powers and duties generally, §§7B-100 to 7B-1414.
See CHILD ABUSE, NEGLECT OR DEPENDENCY.

COUNTY DIRECTORS OF SOCIAL SERVICES —Cont'd
Adult protection.
Abuse.
Director to notify district attorney, §108A-109.
Contracts for provision of medical evaluations, §108A-103, (c).
Cooperation by certain agencies with, §108A-103, (b).
Definition of "director," §108A-101, (c).
Duties of receiving reports, §§108A-14, 108A-103, (a), (d).
Appointment, §108A-12, (a).
Delegation of authority, §108A-14, (b).
Duties, §108A-14.
Guardians.
Director and assistant directors as public guardians, §108A-15.
Investigations.
Duties generally, §108A-14.
Joint employment by two or more boards, §108A-12, (b).
Merit system.
Selection or appointment of directors according to, §§108A-9, 108A-12, (a).
Salaries, §108A-13.
Youth employment certificates.
Designation of personnel to issue, §108A-14, (b).

COUNTY ECONOMIC DEVELOPMENT AND TRAINING DISTRICTS.
Economic development and training districts, §§153A-317.11 to 153A-317.17.
See ECONOMIC DEVELOPMENT AND TRAINING DISTRICTS.

COUNTY ELECTIONS.
Boards of commissioners, §153A-34.
Altering mode of elections, §153A-58.
Modification of structures of boards, §153A-61.
Filing results of election, §153A-64.
Boards of elections, §§163-30 to 163-37.
See COUNTY BOARDS OF ELECTIONS.
Consolidation.
Plans proposed by governmental study commissions, §153A-405, (a) to (e).
Districts.
Applicability of provisions, §153A-22, (g).
Certified copies of resolution, §153A-22, (f).
Change in boundaries.
Effect upon unexpired term of office of commissioner, §153A-22, (d).
Map of electoral districts, §153A-20.
Redefining electoral district boundaries, §153A-22, (b), (c).
Resolutions adopted pursuant to provisions, §153A-22, (e).
Substantial inequality of population among districts, §153A-22, (a).
Industrial development.
Tax elections, §§158-16 to 158-24.
Sales and use tax.
Local government sales and use tax.
Election on adoption.
First one-cent tax, §105-465.
Sheriffs, Const. N. C., art. VII, §2.
Structure of boards.
Alteration.
Effective date, §153A-62.
Initiation of alterations by resolution.
Filing copy, §153A-63.

COUNTY ELECTIONS —Cont'd
Structure of boards —Cont'd
Alteration —Cont'd
Submission of proposition to voters, §153A-61.
Filing results of election, §153A-64.
Submission of acts to United States attorney general.
Alternative submission authority, §120-30.9I.
County attorney, §120-30.9E.
Taxation.
Property taxes, §153A-149.
Time.
Generally, §163-1, (a).
Watershed improvement programs, §§139-39, 139-40.

COUNTY INSPECTION DEPARTMENTS, §§153A-350 to 153A-375.
Actions.
Corrective action.
Failure to take, §153A-368.
Appeals.
General appeal to commissioner of insurance, §153A-374.
Orders to take corrective action, §153A-370.
Stop orders, §153A-361.
Appropriations.
Financial support, §153A-354.
Buildings.
Defined, §153A-350.
Certificates of compliance.
Generally, §153A-363.
Composition, §153A-351, (a).
Condemnation.
Notice.
Removing notice from condemned building, §153A-367.
Unsafe buildings, §153A-366.
Conflicts of interest.
Members of department, §153A-355.
Correction of defects in buildings, §§153A-365 to 153A-371. See within this heading, "Defects in buildings."
Creation, §153A-351, (a).
Defects in buildings.
Correction, §153A-365.
Action in event of failure to take corrective action, §153A-368.
Orders to take corrective action, §153A-369.
Appeals, §153A-370.
Failure to comply with orders, §153A-371.
Finality of order not appealed, §153A-370.
Orders to take corrective action, §§153A-369 to 153A-371.
Removing notice from condemned building, §153A-367.
Unsafe buildings condemned, §153A-366.
Enforcement of article.
Equitable enforcement, §153A-372.
Equitable enforcement, §153A-372.
Establishment of fire limits, §153A-375.
Financial support, §153A-354.
Fire limits.
Establishment, §153A-375.
Funds.
Financial support, §153A-354.
Hazardous conditions.
Periodic inspections, §153A-364.
Hearings.
Stop orders, §153A-361.

COUNTY INSPECTION DEPARTMENTS —Cont'd
Injunctions.
Equitable enforcement of article, §153A-372.
Inspectors.
Certification, §153A-351, (b).
Conflicts of interest, §153A-355.
Duties, §§153A-351, 153A-352.
Failure to perform, §153A-356.
Generally, §153A-351, (a).
Periodic inspections, §153A-364.
Powers, §§153A-351, 153A-352.
Qualifications, §§153A-351, (b), 153A-351.1.
Responsibilities, §§153A-351, 153A-352.
Joint inspection departments.
Authorized, §153A-353.
Generally, §153A-353.
Other arrangements, §153A-353.
Notice.
Condemnation.
Removing prohibited, §153A-367.
Orders, failure to comply with, §14-68.
Permits.
Certificates of compliance.
Generally, §153A-363.
Changes in work, §153A-359.
Forms, §153A-357, (a).
Grounds for revocation, §153A-362.
Issuance.
Requirements, §153A-357, (a), (b).
Requirements.
Generally, §153A-357, (a), (b).
Revocation, §153A-362.
Time limitations on validity of permits, §153A-358.
Validity.
Time limitations, §153A-358.
Work in progress.
Changes in work, §153A-359.
Generally, §153A-360.
Powers and duties, §§153A-351, (a1), 153A-352.
Failure to perform duties, §153A-356.
Qualifications of inspectors, §§153A-351, (b), 153A-351.1.
Records, §153A-373.
Reports, §153A-373.
Responsibilities, §§153A-351, 153A-352.
Right of entry.
Periodic inspections, §153A-364.
State buildings.
Inspection by counties or municipal authorities, §143-135.1, (a), (b).
Stop orders.
Appeals, §153A-361.
Hearing, §153A-361.
Tribal lands, §153A-350.1.
Unlawful conditions.
Periodic inspections, §153A-364.
Unsafe buildings.
Condemnation, §153A-366.
Notice.
Removing from building, §153A-367.
Work in progress, §§153A-359, 153A-360.

COUNTY INSPECTORS OF ARTICLES OF COMMERCE, §§66-1 to 66-6.
Appointment.
County commissioners may appoint, §66-1.
Bonds, surety, §66-3.
Employees of counties generally.
See COUNTY OFFICERS AND EMPLOYEES.

COUNTY INSPECTORS OF ARTICLES OF COMMERCE —Cont'd
Extortion.
Penalty, §66-7.
Falsely acting as inspector.
Penalty, §66-4.
Fees, §66-3.
Payment, §66-7.
Penalties.
Extortion, §66-7.
Falsely acting as inspector, §66-4.
Sale without inspection, §66-5.
Vessels.
Master or commander receiving articles without inspection, §66-6.
Sale without inspection.
Penalty, §66-5.
Vessels.
Master or commander receiving articles without inspection.
Penalty, §66-6.

COUNTY LAND RECORDS IMPROVEMENT PROGRAM, §102-15.

COUNTY LIBRARIES.
Boards of trustees, §153A-265.
Powers and duties, §153A-266.
Capital outlay.
Local subdivisions to comply with laws governing capital outlay, §125-13.
Chief librarian.
Qualifications, §153A-267, (a).
Contracts for library services, §153A-270.
Declaration of state policy, §153A-261.
Definitions, §153A-262.
Employees, §153A-267, (b).
Financing library systems, §153A-268.
Free library services, §153A-264.
Joint libraries, §153A-270.
Legislative declaration, §153A-261.
Local acts.
Systems operated under local acts brought under this article, §153A-271.
Pledging of credit.
Interstate library compact, §125-13.
Powers and duties of trustees, §153A-266.
Public library systems.
Authorized, §153A-263.
Title to library property, §153A-269.

COUNTY MANAGERS, §§153A-81 to 153A-84.
Acting county manager, §153A-83.
Adoption of county-manager plan, §153A-81.
Appointment, §153A-81.
Counties not having, §153A-87.
Acting department heads, §153A-88.
Interim department heads, §153A-89.
Defined, §153A-81.
Designation, §153A-81.
Duties, §153A-82.
Interim county manager, §153A-84.
Officers of counties generally.
See COUNTY OFFICERS AND EMPLOYEES.
Powers, §153A-82.
Service of process.
Personal jurisdiction, manner of serving on county, §1A-1, Rule 4, (j).

COUNTY MEDICAL EXAMINERS.
Appointment, §130A-382.
Cremation.
Medical examiner's permission necessary before cremation, §130A-388, (a), (b).

COUNTY MEDICAL EXAMINERS —Cont'd
Duties.
Notification of medical examiners of certain deaths, §130A-385, (a).
Embalming.
When medical examiner's permission necessary before embalming, §130A-388, (a), (b).
Employees of counties generally.
See COUNTY OFFICERS AND EMPLOYEES.
Postmortem medicolegal examinations and services, §§130A-377 to 130A-394.
See MEDICAL EXAMINERS.
Subpoena authority, §130A-386.
Term of office, §130A-382.
Vacancies in office, §130A-382.

COUNTY OFFICERS AND EMPLOYEES.
Appointive offices.
Qualifications, §153A-25.
Vacancies, §153A-27.
Assessors, §§105-294 to 105-297.
See COUNTY ASSESSORS.
Attorneys.
See COUNTY ATTORNEYS.
Boards of commissioners.
See COUNTY BOARDS OF COMMISSIONERS.
Bonds, surety, §§58-72-1 to 58-72-70.
See OFFICIAL BONDS OF COUNTY OFFICERS.
Chief librarian.
Qualifications, §153A-267, (a).
Clerks.
Boards of commissioners, §153A-11.
Reports, §14-232.
Compensation, §§153A-28, 153A-92.
Fixing pay schedules, §153A-92, (a).
Defenses.
Civil or criminal actions, §160A-167.
Providing defenses for employees, §153A-97.
Dual office holding.
Ex officio service by county and city representatives and officials, §128-1.2.
Ex officio service by county and city representatives and officials, §128-1.2.
Fees.
Statement rendered by county officers compensated from fees, §128-13.
Penalty for failure to file statement, §128-13.
Fringe benefits, §153A-92, (d).
Health insurance, §153A-92, (d).
Holidays, §153A-94, (b).
Hours and days of work, §153A-94, (b).
Inspectors of articles of commerce, §§66-1 to 66-6.
See COUNTY INSPECTORS OF ARTICLES OF COMMERCE.
Insurance.
Defense of officers and employees, §160A-167.
Health insurance, §153A-92.
Life insurance, §153A-92.
Jury commissions, §9-1.
Leaves of absence, §153A-94, (a).
Sick leave.
Smallpox vaccination incident to homeland security act.
Adverse reaction, policy regarding sick leave, §153A-94.1.
Library employees, §153A-267, (b).
Life insurance, §153A-92, (d).
Managers, §§153A-81 to 153A-84.
See COUNTY MANAGERS.

COUNTY OFFICERS AND EMPLOYEES —Cont'd
Medical examiners.
See COUNTY MEDICAL EXAMINERS.
Mileage allowances.
Exempt of counties, §147-9.1.
Oath of office, §153A-26.
Official bonds of county officers generally, §§58-72-1 to 58-72-70.
See OFFICIAL BONDS OF COUNTY OFFICERS.
Personnel rules, §153A-94, (a).
Employees may be made subject to rules adopted by local governing body, §126-9, (a) to (c).
Personnel system generally, §§153A-92 to 153A-99.
See PERSONNEL SYSTEM.
Political activities, §153A-99.
Coercion of employee to support or contribute to political candidate, committee or party, §126-14.
Qualifications for appointive offices, §153A-25.
Records.
Privacy of employee personnel records, §153A-98.
Registers of deeds, §§161-1 to 161-30.
See REGISTERS OF DEEDS.
Reports.
Swearing falsely to official reports, §14-232.
Retaliatory employment discrimination, §§95-240 to 95-245.
See RETALIATORY EMPLOYMENT DISCRIMINATION.
Retention of funds of county by delinquent official.
Citizen to recover funds, §128-10.
Retirement, §§128-21 to 128-38.
See RETIREMENT SYSTEM FOR COUNTIES AND CITIES.
Rules and regulations.
Personnel rules, §153A-94, (a).
Salaries.
Limitations of authority of boards, §153A-92, (b).
Responsibilities of manager, §153A-92, (c).
Schedule, §153A-92, (a).
Statement rendered by county officers compensated from fees, §128-13.
Penalty for failure to file statement, §128-13.
Sheriffs.
See SHERIFFS.
Sick leave.
Smallpox vaccination incident to homeland security act.
Adverse reaction, policy regarding sick leave, §153A-94.1.
Smallpox vaccination incident to homeland security act.
Adverse reaction, policy regarding sick leave, §153A-94.1.
Social security.
Coverage of governmental employees under Title II of social security act, §§135-19 to 135-31.
See SOCIAL SECURITY.
Participation in social security act, §153A-96.
Social service directors, §§108A-12 to 108A-15.
See COUNTY DIRECTORS OF SOCIAL SERVICES.
Surveyors.
See COUNTY SURVEYORS.
Trade unions or labor unions.
Employees prohibited from becoming members of, §§95-98 to 95-100.

COUNTY OFFICERS AND EMPLOYEES —Cont'd
Treasurers.
See COUNTY TREASURERS.
Trust funds to be kept separate, §128-11.
Vacancies in appointive offices, §153A-27.
Veterans.
Priority in employment assistance for United States armed forces veterans, §§165-44.1 to 165-44.6.
Whistleblower protection.
Retaliatory employment discrimination, §§95-240 to 95-245.
See RETALIATORY EMPLOYMENT DISCRIMINATION.
Work days, §153A-94, (b).

COUNTY ORDINANCES.
Adoption, §153A-45.
Alcoholic beverages.
Restriction on adoption, §18B-100.
Amusements.
Regulation of places of amusement, §153A-135.
Book, §153A-48.
Camp Butner hospital.
Application of county ordinance to Camp Butner reservation, §122C-410, (b).
Civil penalty, §153A-123, (c).
Violation of fire prevention code, §153A-123, (c1).
Code of ordinances, §153A-49.
Construction.
Board construction, §153A-4.
Dogs.
Control of dangerous dogs.
Article not to prevent, §67-4.5.
Effect of prior laws and actions taken pursuant to prior laws, §153A-2.
Enforcement, §153A-123.
Abatement, §153A-123, (e).
Generally, §153A-123, (a).
Injunctions, §153A-123, (d).
Enumeration of powers not a limit on general authority to adopt, §153A-124.
Franchises, §153A-46.
Garbage and trash.
Regulation, §§153A-132.1, 153A-136.
General ordinance-making power, §153A-121, (a).
Limitations, §153A-121, (b), (c).
Health services.
Ambulances, §153A-250.
Appropriations, §153A-248, (b).
Improvements.
Submission of statement concerning improvements, §153A-325.
Jurisdiction.
Territorial jurisdiction of county ordinances, §153A-122.
Misdemeanors.
Violations of local ordinances, §153A-123, (b).
Mobile home and trailer parks.
Registration, §153A-138.
Motor vehicles.
Parking regulations, §153A-170.
Regulation of traffic at parking areas and driveways, §153A-139.
Mountain ridge protection, §153A-448.
Noise regulation, §153A-133.
Parking, §153A-170.
Planning and zoning.
Adoption.
Procedure, §153A-323.
Agency establishment, §153A-321.

COUNTY ORDINANCES —Cont'd
Planning and zoning —Cont'd
Amendment.
Procedure, §153A-323.
Enforcement, §153A-324.
Zoning ordinance.
Amendments, §153A-344, (a).
Consent of landowner in certain cases, §153A-344, (b).
Board of adjustment, §153A-345, (c).
Certificate to boards of commissioners, §153A-344, (a).
Preparation, §153A-344, (a).
Pleading and proving county ordinances, §153A-50.
See COUNTY ORDINANCES.
Subdivisions.
Contents, §153A-331.
Procedure for plat approval, §153A-332.
Plat approval, §153A-332.
Requirements, §153A-331.
Technical ordinances.
Adoption, §153A-47.
Violations.
Injunctions, §153A-123, (d).
Misdemeanors, §153A-123.
Separate and distinct offenses, §153A-123.

COUNTY PERSONNEL SYSTEM, §§153A-92 to 153A-99.
Application to local employees, §126-1.
Boards, §153A-95.
Compensation.
Governing body to set, §153A-92, (a).
County manager system, §153A-92, (c).
Insurance coverage as part of compensation, §153A-92, (d).
Limitations, §153A-92, (b).
Defense of employees, §§153A-97, 160A-167.
Deferred compensation plan, §153A-93, (e).
Hours and days of work, §153A-94, (b).
Interchange of governmental employees, §§126-51 to 126-58.
Local personnel system.
Approval, §126-11, (a).
Establishment, §126-11, (a).
Maintenance, §126-11, (a).
Mental health authorities.
Determination of whether system meets requirements, §126-11, (b1).
Establishment and maintenance, §126-11, (a1).
Monitoring, §126-11, (c).
Petitions regarding meeting of requirements, §126-11, (b).
Rules and regulations, §126-11, (d).
Office of state personnel.
Services and facilities available to local subdivisions of state, §126-10.
Political activity.
Conflicts with local regulations or ordinances, §153A-99, (f).
Definitions, §153A-99, (b).
Prohibitions, §153A-99, (c) to (e).
Purpose, §153A-99, (a).
Records.
Allowing unauthorized access, §153A-98, (e).
Confidential records, §153A-98, (c), (c1).
Use for research, etc., §153A-98, (c2).
Inspection and disclosure, §153A-98, (a).
Objection of employee to items in file, §153A-98, (d).

COUNTY PERSONNEL SYSTEM —Cont'd
Records —Cont'd
Open records, §153A-98, (b).
Unauthorized access, §153A-98, (f).
Retirement benefits.
Certification by actuary, §153A-93, (b).
Definition of certified actuary, §153A-93, (c).
Deferred compensation plan, §153A-93, (e).
Governing body may provide for, §153A-93, (a).
Health insurance, §153A-93, (d).
Rules.
Governing body may provide for, §153A-94, (a).
Hours and days of work, §153A-94, (b).
Rules adopted by local governing body.
Employees of county may be made subject to rules, §126-9, (a) to (c).
Social security act.
Participation, §153A-96.

COUNTY PLANNING AND ZONING, §§153A-320 to 153A-326, 153A-340 to 153A-348.
Agency, §153A-344, (a).
Established, §153A-321.
Appeals.
Board of adjustment, §153A-345, (b).
Superior court.
Review of decisions of board of commissioners, §153A-340, (f).
Applicability of provisions, §153A-347.
Board of adjustment.
Appeals, §153A-345, (b).
Appointment, §153A-345, (a).
Chairman, §153A-345, (f).
Compensation, §153A-345, (a).
Hearings, §153A-345, (b).
Modification of regulations, §153A-345, (d).
Planning agency.
Designation to perform duties of board of adjustment, §153A-345, (a).
Votes, §153A-345, (e).
Zoning ordinance, §153A-345, (c).
Boards of commissioners.
Method of procedure, §153A-343.
Review of decisions by superior court, §153A-340, (f).
Buildings.
Applicability of provisions, §153A-347.
Setback lines, §153A-326.
Changes caused by adoption or amendment of ordinance.
Notice, §153A-323, (b).
Conflict of laws, §153A-346.
Districts.
Designation, §153A-342.
Enforcement.
Ordinances, §153A-324.
Hearings.
Board of adjustment, §153A-345, (b).
Jurisdiction.
Territorial jurisdiction, §153A-320.
Zoning less than entire jurisdiction, §153A-342.
Limitation of actions, §153A-348.
Validity of ordinance or amendment contested, §1-54.1.
Manufactured homes.
Zoning regulations for, §153A-341.1.
Method of procedure, §153A-343, (a).
Exceptions, §153A-343, (b), (c).
Military bases.
Change of permitted uses near.
Adoption or modification of ordinance resulting in.
Notice, §153A-323, (b).

COUNTY PLANNING AND ZONING —Cont'd
Notice.
Changes.
Adoption or amendment of ordinance resulting in, §153A-323, (b).
Mail notice of public hearing, §153A-343, (a).
Exceptions to requirement, §153A-343, (b).
Public hearing.
Adoption or amendment of ordinance, §153A-323, (a).
Ordinances.
Adoption.
Procedure, §153A-323, (a), (b).
Agency establishment, §153A-321.
Amendment.
Procedure, §153A-323, (a), (b).
Enforcement, §153A-324.
Zoning ordinance.
Amendments, §153A-344, (a).
Consent of landowner in certain cases, §153A-344, (b).
Board of adjustment, §153A-345, (c).
Certification to boards of commissioners, §153A-344, (a).
Preparation, §153A-344, (a).
Powers and duties.
Grant of power, §153A-340, (a) to (e).
Supplemental powers, §153A-322.
Publication.
Notice of public hearing.
Adoption or amendment of ordinance, §153A-323, (a).
Public hearing.
Adoption or amendment of ordinance, §153A-323, (a).
Purposes in view, §153A-341.
Regional planning commissions, §§153A-391 to 153A-398.
See REGIONAL PLANNING COMMISSIONS.
Rules and regulations.
Conflict of laws, §153A-346.
Enforcement.
Boards of commissioners to determine method of procedure, §153A-343, (a).
Purposes in view, §153A-341.
Statute of limitations, §153A-348.
Subdivisions, §§153A-330 to 153A-335.
Supplemental powers, §153A-322.
Vesting rights, §153A-344.1.
Declaration of legislature, §153A-344.1, (a).
Definitions, §153A-344.1, (b).
Duration of vested right, §153A-344.1, (d).
Establishment of vested right, §153A-344.1, (c).
County's failure to adopt ordinance.
How established, §153A-344.1, (f).
Judicial determination, §153A-344.1, (f).
Subsequent changes.
When permitted, §153A-344.1, (e).
Vested right not a personal right, §153A-344.1, (f).
Subsequent changes.
When permitted, §153A-344.1, (e).
Termination of vested right, §153A-344.1, (d).
Zoning map changes.
Adoption or modification of ordinance resulting in.
Notice, §153A-323, (b).

COUNTY RESEARCH AND PRODUCTION SERVICE DISTRICTS, §§153A-311 to 153A-317.
Abolition, §153A-316.
Advisory committee, §153A-313.

COUNTY RESEARCH AND PRODUCTION SERVICE DISTRICTS —Cont'd
Establishment.
Effective date of resolution, §153A-312, (e).
Hearing, §153A-312, (d).
Multi-county districts, §153A-312, (b).
Purposes, §153A-311.
Report, §153A-312, (c).
Standards, §153A-312, (a).
Multi-county districts, §153A-312, (b).
Extension.
Effective date of resolution, §153A-314, (d).
Hearing, §153A-314, (c).
Notice.
Hearing, §153A-314, (c).
Provision or maintenance of services.
Requirements for extended district, §153A-315, (b).
Report.
Required prior to hearing, §153A-314, (b).
Standards, §153A-314, (a).
Hearings.
Abolition of districts, §153A-316.
Establishment, §153A-312, (d).
Extension, §153A-314, (c).
Removal of territory.
Public hearing, §153A-314.1, (c).
Multi-county districts.
Abolition, §153A-316.
Establishment, §153A-312, (b).
Notice.
Abolition of districts.
Hearing, §153A-316.
Establishment.
Hearing, §153A-312, (d).
Extension.
Hearing, §153A-314, (c).
Removal of territory.
Public hearing, §153A-314.1, (c).
Provision or maintenance of services.
Extended district, §153A-315, (b).
New district, §153A-315, (a).
Purposes, §153A-311.
Removal of territory.
Annexation, general law.
Applicability to removed territory, §153A-314.1, (d).
Effective date of resolution removing territory, §153A-314.1, (f).
Findings required, §153A-314.1, (a).
Notice of public hearing, §153A-314.1, (c).
Public hearing before adopting resolution, §153A-314.1, (c).
Report prior to public hearing, §153A-314.1, (b).
Resolution of board of commissioners, §153A-314.1, (a).
Reports.
Establishment.
Required before public hearing, §153A-312, (c).
Extension.
Required before hearing, §153A-314, (b).
Standards, §153A-312, (a).
Extension, §153A-314, (a).
Multi-county districts, §153A-312, (b).
Taxation.
Authorized taxes, §153A-317.
Rate limitation, §153A-317.

COUNTY SCHOOL ADMINISTRATIVE UNITS.
Administrative units generally.
See SCHOOL DISTRICTS AND ADMINISTRATIVE UNITS.

COUNTY SERVICE DISTRICTS, §§143A-300 to 153A-310.
Abolition, §153A-306.
Research and production service districts, §153A-316.
Ambulance and rescue.
Establishing district to provide, §143A-301, (a).
Property tax reduction in district, §153A-310, (a), (b).
Annexation.
Authority, findings required, §153A-303, (a).
By petition of owners, §153A-303, (b).
Fire protection district.
Chapter 69 district annexing, §153A-304.2, (a), (b).
Municipality annexing all or part of district, §153A-304.1, (a) to (d).
Hearing on resolution, §153A-303, (e).
Notice of hearing, §153A-303, (e).
Report, §153A-303, (d).
Required provision or maintenance of services, §153A-305, (b).
Sanitary districts within city limits, §153A-303, (c).
Beach erosion control.
Establishing district to provide, §143A-301, (a).
Bonds authorized, §153A-308.
Cemeteries.
Establishing district to provide, §143A-301, (a).
Coastal area counties.
Junk automobile removal and street maintenance.
Establishing districts for removal, §143A-301, (b), (c).
Considerations in establishing, §153A-302, (a).
Consolidation.
Authority, findings required, §153A-304, (a).
Effective date, §153A-304, (d).
Hearing on resolution, §153A-304, (c).
Notice of hearing on resolution, §153A-304, (c).
Report, §153A-304, (b).
Required provision or maintenance of services, §153A-305, (c).
County containing protected mountain ridge.
Maintenance of public roads, §153A-301, (d).
County service district act of 1973.
Article cited as, §143A-300.
Economic development and training districts, §§153A-317.11 to 153A-317.17.
See ECONOMIC DEVELOPMENT AND TRAINING DISTRICTS.
Effective date of resolution establishing, §153A-302, (d).
EMS in fire protection districts, §153A-309, (a), (b).
Establishment.
Research and production service districts, §§153A-311, 153A-312.
Extension.
Research and production service districts, §153A-314.
Findings for establishing, §153A-302, (a1).
Fire protection.
Annexation by chapter 69 district, §153A-304.2, (a), (b).
Annexation of all or part of district by municipality, §153A-304.1, (a).
Fire protection tax, levy by commissioners, §153A-304.1, (b) to (c).
EMS in fire protection districts, §153A-309, (a), (b).
Establishing district to provide, §143A-301, (a).

COUNTY SERVICE DISTRICTS —Cont'd
Fire protection —Cont'd
Property tax rate reduction, §153A-309.2, (a), (b).
Hearings.
Abolition, §153A-306.
Annexation of territory, §153A-303, (e).
Before adopting resolution, §153A-302, (c).
Consolidation, §153A-304, (c).
Junked automobile removal.
Coastal area counties.
Establishing districts for, §143A-301, (b), (c).
Law enforcement.
Establishing district to provide, requirement, §143A-301, (a).
Requirements not applicable to countywide district, §153A-302, (e).
Notice.
Abolition.
Public hearing, §153A-306.
Annexation of territory.
Public hearing, §153A-303, (e).
Consolidation.
Hearing on resolution, §153A-304, (c).
Public hearing before adopting resolution, §153A-302, (c).
Property taxes.
Authorized, rate, §153A-307.
Ambulance and rescue district, rate reduction, §153A-310, (a), (b).
Fire protection districts, rate reduction, §153A-309.2, (a), (b).
Fire protection district.
Annexation by chapter 69 district.
Fire protection tax, commissioners levying and collecting, §153A-304.2, (a), (b).
Annexation of all or part of district by municipality.
Fire protection tax, levy by commissioners, §153A-304.1, (b) to (c).
Publication.
Annexation of territory.
Notice of public hearing, §153A-303, (e).
Consolidation.
Notice of public hearing, §153A-304, (c).
Notice of public hearing before adopting resolution, §153A-302, (c).
Purposes, §143A-301, (a) to (d).
Research and production service districts, §153A-311.
Recreation.
Establishing district to provide, §143A-301, (a).
Removal of territory.
Research and production districts, §153A-314.1.
Report on establishing, §153A-302, (b).
Required provision or maintenance of services.
Consolidated district, §153A-305, (c).
Extended district, §153A-305, (b).
New districts, §153A-305, (a).
Research and production districts, §§153A-311 to 153A-317.
Sanitary districts within city limits.
Annexation, §153A-303, (c).
Sewage collection and disposal.
Establishing district to provide, §143A-301, (a).
Solid waste collection.
Establishing district to provide, §143A-301, (a).
Standards.
Considerations in establishing, §153A-302, (a).
Street maintenance.
Coastal area counties.
Establishing districts for, §143A-301, (b), (c).

COUNTY SERVICE DISTRICTS —Cont'd
Taxation.
Fire protection district.
Annexation by chapter 69 district.
Fire protection tax, commissioners levying and collecting, §153A-304.2, (a), (b).
Annexation of all or part of district by municipality.
Fire protection tax, levy by commissioners, §153A-304.1, (b) to (c).
Property taxes authorized, rate, §153A-307.
Ambulance and rescue district, rate reduction, §153A-310, (a), (b).
Fire protection districts, rate reduction, §153A-309.2, (a), (b).
Research and production service districts, §153A-317.
Water supply and water distribution.
Establishing district to provide, §143A-301, (a).

COUNTY STREETS AND HIGHWAYS.
Abandonment or change in secondary road.
Request by board of county commissioners, §136-63, (a).
Adopt-a-highway program, §136-140.1.
Appropriation to municipalities, §136-41.1, (a).
Allocation of funds, §136-41.1, (a) to (c).
Contracts for maintenance, etc., of streets, §136-41.3.
Eligible municipalities, §§136-41.1, (b), 136-41.2, (a) to (c).
Incorporated before January 1, 1945, §136-41.2A, (a), (b).
Incorporated since January 1, 1945, §136-41.2, (d).
Excess accumulation of funds, §136-41.3.
Nature of funds distributed, §136-41.1, (d).
Records and annual statement, §136-41.3.
Use of funds, §136-41.3.
Assigning street numbers in unincorporated areas, §153A-239.1, (a).
Bond issues.
Prohibition of local road bonds, §136-98, (a), (b).
Closing public roads or easements, §153A-241.
Coastal area counties.
Service districts.
Street maintenance provided, §153A-301, (b), (c).
Construction of roads by local authorities, §136-98, (a), (b).
Controlled-access facilities.
Authority of local units to consent, §136-89.54.
Coordinated street system.
Development of system, §136-66.2.
County containing protected mountain ridge.
Service districts.
Maintenance of public roads, §153A-301, (d).
County public roads incorporated into state highway system, §§136-51 to 136-64.1.
See STREETS AND HIGHWAYS.
Filing complaints with department of transportation, §136-64.
Fishing from bridges.
Regulation or prohibition, §153A-242.
Municipal street system.
Responsibility for streets inside municipalities, §136-66.1.
Naming roads and assigning street numbers in unincorporated areas, §153A-239.1, (a).
Public road.
Defined, §153A-238, (a).

COUNTY STREETS AND HIGHWAYS —Cont'd
Responsibility for streets inside municipalities, §136-66.1.
Responsibility of counties for upkeep, etc., terminated, §136-97, (a).
Rights of way.
Dedication of rights of way under local ordinances, §§136-66.10, 136-66.11.
Road equipment.
Department of transportation.
Authority to furnish, §136-34.
Rules and regulations.
Authority of municipalities, §136-66.4.
Secondary road construction programs by department of transportation.
Adoption of annual construction program for each county.
Board of transportation, §136-44.8, (e).
Department of transportation to follow, §136-44.8, (f).
Map showing tentative road paving projects.
Posting in county courthouse, §136-44.8, (a).
Notice of public meeting of board of county commissioners.
Deviations or priority of paving projects, §136-44.8, (d).
Presentation by department of annual program for county, §136-44.8, (b).
Public meeting on annual construction program for county, §136-44.8, (c).
Notice, §136-44.8, (b).
Public meeting on deviations or priority of paving projects, §136-44.8, (d).
Review of changes to which commissioners do not consent.
Petition by board, §136-44.8, (f).
Service districts for road maintenance.
Section not to prohibit, §136-98, (b).
Special assessments, §§153A-185 to 153A-206.
See SPECIAL ASSESSMENTS BY COUNTIES.
State highway system.
Maintenance of system by municipalities, §136-66.1.
Responsibility for streets inside municipalities, §136-66.1.
Taxation.
Prohibition of local road taxes, §136-98, (a), (b).

COUNTY SUBDIVISIONS, §§153A-331 to 153A-335.
Definitions, §153A-335.
Injunctions.
Penalties for transferring lots in unapproved subdivisions, §153A-334.
Ordinances.
Contents, §153A-331.
Procedure for plat approval, §153A-332.
Plat approval, §153A-332.
Requirements, §153A-331.
Regulations, §153A-330.
Plats.
Approval, §153A-332.
Effect on dedication, §153A-333.
Effect of plat approval on dedications, §153A-333.
Ordinance to contain procedure for plat approval, §153A-332.
Recommendations by certain agencies, §153A-332.
Recordation, §153A-332.
Statement by owner, §153A-332.

COUNTY SURVEYORS.
Appointment of county surveyor, §153A-441.
Bonds, surety generally, §§58-72-1 to 58-72-70.
See OFFICIAL BONDS OF COUNTY OFFICERS.
Coordinate system.
Assistance.
Board of county commissioners to apply for assistance, §102-16.
County projects eligible for assistance, §102-17.
Duties, failure to discharge, §14-230.
Employees of counties generally.
See COUNTY OFFICERS AND EMPLOYEES.
Fees.
Statement rendered by county officers compensated from fees, §128-13.
Penalty for failure to file statement, §128-13.
Oaths.
Administration of oaths.
When county surveyors may administer, §11-10.
Form of oath, §11-11.
Penalties.
Statement rendered by county officers compensated from fees.
Failure to file statement, §128-13.
Salaries.
Statement rendered by county officers compensated from fees, §128-13.
Penalty for failure to file statement, §128-13.

COUNTY TAXES.
Agricultural societies and fairs.
Exhibits exempt, §106-507.
Alcoholic beverages.
Excise tax on beer, wine and liquor.
Distribution of part of taxes, §105-113.82.
License tax.
Beer and wine retail licenses, §105-113.78.
Appraisals.
Reserve for octennial reappraisal, §153A-150.
Board of equalization and review, §105-322.
Collection of taxes.
Remedies for collecting taxes other than property taxes, §153A-147.
Community development, §153A-376, (e).
Continuing taxes, §153A-148.
Disclosure of certain information prohibited, §153A-148.1, (a).
Penalties, §153A-148.1, (b).
Economic development and training districts.
Property taxes.
County may levy within district, rate limitation, §153A-317.17.
Exemptions from tax, Const. N. C., art. V, §2.
Gross receipts tax on short-term vehicle leases or rentals, §153A-156, (a).
Collection of tax, §153A-156, (c), (d).
Definitions, §153A-156, (e).
Penalties and remedies, §153A-156, (f).
Provision noting in agreement, §153A-156, (b).
Income tax.
Levy prohibited, §105-247.
Inheritance tax.
Levy prohibited, §105-247.
Liability upon governing bodies of local units for failure to levy taxes.
Repeal of laws imposing, §105-270.
Licenses.
Privilege license taxes, §153A-152.
Low-level radioactive and hazardous waste facilities, §153A-152.1, (a) to (c).

COUNTY TAXES —Cont'd
Loan agencies, check cashing businesses and pawnbrokers.
Privilege tax.
Levy by counties authorized, §105-88, (e).
Low-level radioactive and hazardous waste facilities.
Privilege license taxes, §153A-152.1, (a) to (c).
Meals taxes.
Penalties, §153A-154.1, (a).
Scope of uniformity requirement, §153A-154.1, (b).
Motor vehicles.
Gross receipts tax on short-term vehicle leases or rentals, §153A-156.
Powers and duties.
Continuing taxes, §153A-48.
General power to impose taxes, §153A-146.
Remedies for collecting taxes other than property taxes, §153A-147.
Privilege license taxes, §153A-152, (a).
Animal taxes, §153A-153.
Cable television franchise taxes, §153A-154.
Low-level radioactive and hazardous waste facilities, §153A-152.1, (a) to (c).
Telecommunications restriction, §153A-152, (b).
Rates.
Property taxes.
Increase, §153A-149, (e).
Reappraisals.
Reserve for octennial reappraisals, §153A-150.
Remedies.
Collection of taxes other than property taxes, §153A-147.
Research and production service districts.
Authorized taxes, §153A-317.
Rate limitation, §153A-317.
Room occupancy tax, uniform provisions for counties authorized to levy.
Administered by taxing county, §153A-155, (d).
Charge for furnishing taxable accommodation, part of charge, §153A-155, (c).
Civil and criminal penalties.
Failure to file return or pay, §153A-155, (e).
Collection of tax by operator of business, §153A-155, (c).
Counties authorized to levy, applicability, §153A-155, (a), (g).
Disclosure of records, §153A-155, (d).
Discount allowed operator for collecting, §153A-155, (c).
Effective date, §153A-155, (b).
Levied only by resolution, §153A-155, (b).
Liability for tax attaching before repeal not affected, §153A-155, (f).
Passed on to purchaser, §153A-155, (c).
Public notice and public hearing on levy, §153A-155, (b).
Repeal or reduction by resolution, §153A-155, (f).
Return, §153A-155, (d).
Stated and charged separately, §153A-155, (c).
Waiver of penalties, §153A-155, (e).
When due and payable, §153A-155, (d).
Sales and use tax, §153A-151.
Service districts.
Research and production service districts, §153A-317.
Short-term vehicle leases or rentals.
Gross receipts tax on, §153A-156.
Special assessments, §§153A-185 to 153A-206.
See SPECIAL ASSESSMENTS BY COUNTIES.
Special tax areas, Const. N. C., art. V, §2.

COUNTY TAXES —Cont'd
Streets and highways.
Prohibition of local road taxes, §136-98, (a), (b).
Television.
Cable television franchises, §153A-154.

COUNTY TREASURERS.
Bonds, surety generally, §§58-72-1 to 58-72-70.
See OFFICIAL BONDS OF COUNTY OFFICERS.
Finance officer.
Fiscal control, §§159-24 to 159-38.
See LOCAL GOVERNMENT FINANCE.
Local government finance.
General provisions, §§159-1 to 159-188.
See LOCAL GOVERNMENT FINANCE.
Oaths.
Form of oath, §11-11.
Officers of counties generally.
See COUNTY OFFICERS AND EMPLOYEES.
Reports.
Misconduct in public office.
Swearing falsely to official reports, §14-232.

COUNTY WATER AND SEWER DISTRICTS, §§162A-86 to 162A-94.
Abolition, §162A-87.2.
Contracts for conveyance of land to city, §162A-87.2, (b).
Conveyance of land to a private person, §162A-87.2, (c).
Effective date of resolution, §162A-87.2, (d).
Public hearing, §162A-87.2, (a).
Assessments.
Special assessments authorized, §162A-92.
Assumption of indebtedness of district, §162A-101.
Board of county commissioners.
Creation of district, §§162A-86, 162A-87.
Defined, §162A-86, (a1).
Governing body of district, §162A-89, (a).
Bond issues.
Authorized, §162A-90.
Boundaries, initial.
Exclusion of areas, §162A-87.1A, (a).
Interpretation and construction, §162A-87.1A, (c).
Noncontiguous portions, §162A-87.1A, (b).
Consolidated city-county governing board.
Governing body of district, §162A-89, (b).
Contracts.
Contracts with private entities, §162A-88.1.
Validation of certain contracts, §162A-94.
Creation.
Authorized, §162A-86, (a).
Hearings, §162A-86, (b), (c).
Notice, §162A-86, (b).
Public hearing, §162A-86, (b1).
Resolution.
Findings required, §162A-87, (a).
Publication, §162A-87, (b).
Defined, §162A-86, (a1).
Eminent domain.
Power of district, §162A-89.1.
Extension.
Annexation by petition, §162A-87.1, (b).
Annexation of property within city or sanitary district, §162A-87.1, (c).
Effective date of resolution, §162A-87.1, (f).
Hearing, §162A-87.1, (e).
Notice.
Hearing, §162A-87.1, (e).
Report, §162A-87.1, (d).
Standards, §162A-87.1, (a).

COUNTY WATER AND SEWER DISTRICTS —Cont'd
Hearings.
Creation of district, §162A-86, (b), (c).
Notice, §162A-86, (b).
Public hearings, §162A-86, (b1).
Extension of districts, §162A-87.1, (e).
Limitation of actions.
Creation of district.
Action to set aside resolution, §162A-87, (b).
Municipal corporations.
Area annexed by city, §162A-93, (c), (d).
Duplicating water or sewer services provided by district, §162A-93, (a), (b).
Notice.
Creation of district.
Hearing, §162A-86, (b).
Resolution, §162A-87, (b).
Extension of district.
Hearing, §162A-87.1, (e).
Petitions.
Extension of districts.
Annexation by petition, §162A-87.1, (b).
Public hearings.
Creation of district, §162A-86, (b1).
Reports.
Extension of districts, §162A-87.1, (d).
Services outside district.
Authorized, §162A-87.3, (a).
Corporate limits of city or sanitary district.
Limitations, §162A-87.3, (c).
Customers lying within another county.
Limitations, §162A-87.3, (d).
Rates and charges.
Different schedule, §162A-87.3, (b).
Status, §162A-88.
Taxation.
Powers of district, §162A-91.
Tax anticipation notes.
Authorized, §162A-90.
Validation of certain contracts, §162A-94.

COUNTYWIDE BASE MAPS.
Financial assistance, §102-17.
Improvement of county land records program, §102-15.

COURIERS.
Private protective services generally, §§74C-1 to 74C-33.
See PRIVATE PROTECTIVE SERVICES.

COURSE OF DEALING.
Commercial code generally, §25-1-205.
Leases, UCC.
Course of performance control, §25-2A-207, (2).
Explaining or supplementing terms, §25-2A-202, (a).
Implied warranties may arise from, §25-2A-212, (3).
Sale of goods, UCC.
Implied warranties, §25-2-314, (3).
Exclusion or modification, §25-2-316, (3).
Used to explain terms of contracts, §25-2-202.

COURSE OF PERFORMANCE.
Leases, UCC.
Explaining or supplementing terms, §25-2A-202, (a).
Express terms.
Control course of performance, §25-2A-207, (2).
Relevance to determine meaning of lease agreement, §25-2A-207, (1).

COURSE OF PERFORMANCE —Cont'd
Leases, UCC —Cont'd
Relevant to show waiver or modification of term, §25-2A-207, (3).
Sale of goods, UCC, §25-2-208.
Used to explain terms of contract, §25-2-202.

COURT-APPOINTED COUNSEL.
Abused, neglected or dependent juvenile actions, §§7B-602, 7B-603.
Delinquent and undisciplined juvenile actions, §§7B-1906, (c), 7B-2000, 7B-2002.
Indigent defense services.
General provisions, §§7A-450 to 7A-458.
Indigent defense services act, §§7A-498 to 7A-498.8.
See INDIGENT DEFENSE SERVICES.
Indigent services rules, Rules 1.1 to 3.7.
See INDIGENT DEFENSE SERVICES.
Interstate compact on juvenile.
Return of escapees or absconders, §7B-2805, (c).
Mental health, developmental disability, substance abuse.
Involuntary commitment.
Substance abuser's commitment hearing, §122C-286, (d).
Termination of parental rights proceeding, §§7B-1101, 7B-1109, (b).

COURT INFORMATION TECHNOLOGY FUND, §7A-343.2.

COURT OF APPEALS, §§7A-16 to 7A-21.
Administration department.
Providing adequate quarters for court, §7A-19, (b).
Administrative agency decisions.
Appeal of right from certain administrative agencies, §7A-29, (a).
Appeals of right from superior courts.
Final judgments of superior court upon review of decision, §7A-27, (b).
Appeal of right from court of appeals, §7A-30; App. Proc. Rule 14.
Appeal bond, App. Proc. Rule 17, (a).
Briefs, App. Proc. Rule 14, (d).
Definition of appellant and appellee, App. Proc. Rule 16, (c).
Notice of appeal.
Contents, App. Proc. Rule 14, (b).
Filing and service, App. Proc. Rule 14, (a).
Record on appeal, App. Proc. Rule 14, (c).
Scope of review, App. Proc. Rule 16, (a), (b).
Appeals generally.
See APPEALS.
Arrest.
Warrant for arrest.
Judges may issue, §15A-304, (f).
Audits.
Clerk of court.
Financial accounts of clerk audited, §7A-20, (b).
Bonds, surety.
Clerk of court, §7A-20, (a).
Certification of appealed cases.
Appeal bonds, App. Proc. Rule 17, (b), (c).
Appellant and appellee defined, App. Proc. Rules 15, (i), 16, (c).
Briefs.
Filing and service, App. Proc. Rule 15, (g).
Interlocutory orders, App. Proc. Rule 15, (h).
Petition of party, App. Proc. Rule 15.
Record on appeal, App. Proc. Rule 15, (f).
Response to petition, App. Proc. Rule 15, (d).

COURT OF APPEALS —Cont'd
Certification of appealed cases —Cont'd
Scope of review, App. Proc. Rule 16, (a).
Certification of cause for review by supreme court, §7A-31, (a).
After determination by court of appeals, §7A-15, (c).
Before determination by court of appeals, §7A-15, (b).
Criminal cases, §7A-31, (a).
Exceptions, §7A-31, (a).
Procedure prescribed by supreme court, §7A-31, (d).
Transfer of cause to supreme court.
Effect of certification, §7A-31, (a).
Certiorari.
Issuance of remedial writs.
Power of court of appeals to issue, §7A-32, (b).
Chief judge.
Compensation of judges, §7A-18, (a).
Longevity pay, §7A-18, (b).
Designation, §7A-16.
Disability of chief judge, §7A-16.
Expenses.
Reimbursement for travel and subsistence expenses, §7A-18, (a).
Oath of office, §7A-16.
Panels.
Assignment of members to panels, §7A-16.
Sessions.
Scheduling sessions, §7A-19, (c).
Clerk of court.
Appointment of clerk, §7A-20, (a).
Assistants to clerk, §7A-20, (a).
Audit of financial accounts, §7A-20, (b).
Bond required, §7A-20, (a).
Fee bill for services, §7A-20, (b).
Oath of office, §7A-20, (a).
Salary of clerk, §7A-20, (a).
Seal of office, §7A-20, (a).
Composition, organization, etc., §7A-16; Const. N. C., art. IV, §7.
Cost.
New trials.
Discretion of court in awarding cost, §6-33.
Creation, §7A-16.
Delinquent and undisciplined juvenile actions.
Appeal of decision transferring jurisdiction of juvenile to superior court, §7B-2603, (d).
Waiver of right to raise transfer issue in court of appeals.
Failure to appeal transfer order to superior court, §7B-2603, (a).
Appeal of final order of court in review matter before court of appeals, §7B-2602.
Department of administration.
Providing adequate quarters for court, §7A-19, (b).
Depositions.
Reading deposition on the trial.
When witness is judge of court of appeals, §8-83.
Discretionary review by supreme court.
Certification of cause in court of appeals for review, §7A-31, (a) to (d).
District attorneys, removal from office.
Appeal to court of appeals, §7A-66.
District courts.
Appeals of right from district court.
Final judgments of district courts in civil actions, §7A-27, (c).

COURT OF APPEALS —Cont'd
District courts —Cont'd
Interlocutory orders or judgments of district court.
Appeals of right from district court to court of appeals, §7A-27, (d).
Elections.
Judges of court elected by qualified voters, §7A-16; Const. N. C., art. IV, §16.
Judicial voter guide.
Candidate information, §163-278.69, (b).
Disclaimer statement, §163-278.69, (c).
Publication by board, §163-278.69, (a).
Emergency judges, recall to active service.
Applicability of provisions.
Generally, §7A-39.12.
Article applicable to previously retired justices, §7A-39.10.
Commission, application to governor, §7A-39.6.
Compensation, §7A-39.3.
Emergency judge.
Defined, §7A-39.1.
Emergency recall judges, §7A-39.15.
Jurisdiction and authority, §7A-39.7.
Recall of judges reaching mandatory retirement age, §7A-39.13.
Retired judges recalled to active service, §7A-39.3.
Supreme court authorized to adopt rules, §7A-39.7.
Temporary incapacity of judge, §7A-39.5.
Temporary vacancies, §7A-39.14.
Termination of recall, §7A-39.9.
Evidence.
Review of errors, §8C-1, Rule 103, (d).
Fees.
Clerk of court.
Fee bill for services, §7A-20, (b).
Judges, Const. N. C., art. IV, §21.
Habeas corpus.
Issuance of remedial writs.
Power of court of appeals to issue, §7A-32, (a).
Health and human services department.
Appeals of right from department, §7A-29, (a).
Incompetence, determination of.
Appeal from order adjudicating incompetence, §35A-1115.
Industrial commission.
Appeals of right from industrial commission, §7A-29, (a).
Jurisdiction of court of appeals.
Power of court of appeals to issue remedial writs, §7A-32, (c).
Review of final orders, §7A-250, (b).
Insurance.
Commissioner of insurance.
Appeals of right from commissioner to court of appeals, §7A-29, (a).
Interlocutory orders.
Appeals of right from the courts of the trial divisions, §7A-27, (d).
Judges.
Age limit for service as justice or judge for general court of justice, §7A-4.20.
Appointments.
Temporary appointments, §7A-16.
Assignment of judges, Const. N. C., art. IV, §11.
Consolidated judicial retirement act, §§135-50 to 135-75.
See RETIREMENT SYSTEM FOR TEACHERS AND STATE EMPLOYEES.
Depositions.
Reading deposition on the trial.
When witness is judge of court of appeals, §8-83.

COURT OF APPEALS —Cont'd
Judges —Cont'd
Election, §7A-16; Const. N. C., art. IV, §16.
Emergency judges, recall to active service, §§7A-39.1 to 7A-39.15.
Expenses.
Reimbursement for travel and subsistence expenses, §7A-18, (a).
Habeas corpus, application for writ, §17-6.
Habeas corpus, issuance of writ, §17-8.
Increase in number of judges, §7A-16.
Judicial standards commission.
Chair of commission to be court of appeals judge, §7A-375, (a).
Jurisdiction.
Emergency judges, §7A-39.7.
Oaths.
Who may administer oaths of office, §11-7.1, (b).
Panels of judges, §7A-16.
Qualifications, Const. N. C., art. IV, §22.
Quorum constituted, §7A-16.
Recall of retired judges to active service, §§7A-39.1 to 7A-39.15.
Removal, Const. N. C., art. IV, §17.
Retirement, Const. N. C., art. IV, §§8, 21.
Age limit for service as justice or judge of general court of justice, §7A-4.20.
Consolidated judicial retirement act, §§135-50 to 135-75.
See RETIREMENT SYSTEM FOR TEACHERS AND STATE EMPLOYEES.
Salaries, fees and emoluments, §7A-18, (a); Const. N. C., art. IV, §21.
Longevity pay, §7A-18, (b).
Search warrants.
Issuance of warrant valid throughout state, §15A-243, (a).
Terms of office, §7A-16; Const. N. C., art. IV, §16.
Vacancies in office, Const. N. C., art. IV, §19.
Appointment by governor to fill, §163-9, (a), (c).
Term of appointee, §163-9, (a).
Judicial standards commission.
Chair of commission to be court of appeals judge, §7A-375, (a).
Jurisdiction, Const. N. C., art. IV, §12.
Administrative agencies.
Appeals of right from certain administrative agencies, §7A-29, (a).
Appellate jurisdiction, §7A-26.
Certiorari.
Power of court of appeals to issue remedial writs, §7A-32, (b).
Habeas corpus.
Power of court of appeals to issue remedial writs, §7A-32, (a).
Industrial commission.
Power of court of appeals to issue remedial writs, §7A-32, (c).
Judges.
Emergency judges, §7A-39.7.
Mandamus.
Power of court of appeals to issue remedial writs, §7A-32, (b).
Prohibition.
Power of court of appeals to issue remedial writs, §7A-32, (b).
Remedial writs.
Power of court of appeals to issue remedial writs, §7A-32.
Supersedeas.
Power of court of appeals to issue remedial writs, §7A-32, (b).

COURT OF APPEALS —Cont'd
Jurisdiction —Cont'd
Utilities commission.
Power of court of appeals to issue remedial writs, §7A-32, (c).
Locations.
Seats and sessions of court, §7A-19, (a).
Mandamus.
Issuance of remedial writs.
Power of court of appeals to issue, §7A-32, (b).
Marshal, §7A-21.
Motions.
Decisions on post trial motions for appropriate relief.
Finality, §7A-28, (a).
Decisions upon review of valuation of exempt property.
Finality, §7A-28, (b).
New trials.
Cost.
Discretion of appellate court, §6-33.
Oaths.
Clerk of court, §7A-20, (a).
Judges of court to take oath of office, §7A-16.
Organization, §7A-16.
Appellate division of general court of justice, §7A-5.
Powers.
Remedial writs.
Issuance of remedial writs by court of appeals, §7A-32.
Prohibition.
Issuance of remedial writs.
Power of court of appeals to issue, §7A-32, (b).
Property tax commission orders and decisions, appeal of.
Appeal from court of appeals to supreme court, §105-345.4.
Appeal to lie to, §105-345, (d).
Panels, assignment of hearing to, §105-345, (e).
Right of appeal from commission to court of appeals, §7A-29, (a).
Public utilities.
Jurisdiction of court of appeals.
Power to issue remedial writs in utilities commission proceedings, §7A-32, (c).
Quorum, §7A-16.
Recall, §§7A-39.1 to 7A-39.15.
Removal of causes.
Transfer of cause from court of appeals to supreme court.
Certification of appealed causes, §7A-31.
Reporters.
Appointment by supreme court for appellate division, §7A-6, (a).
Scope of review of decisions of court of appeals.
Appeals based solely upon dissent, App. Proc. Rule 16, (b).
How scope determined, App. Proc. Rule 16, (a).
Seal of office adoption, §7A-20, (a).
Search warrants.
Judges of court of appeals.
Issuance of search warrant valid throughout state, §15A-243, (a).
Sessions.
Scheduling of sessions by chief judge, §7A-19, (c).
Seats and sessions of court, §7A-19.
State auditor.
Clerk of the court.
Financial accounts of the clerk audited, §7A-20, (b).

COURT OF APPEALS —Cont'd
State bar.
Appeals of right from North Carolina state bar to court of appeals, §7A-29, (a).
State departments and agencies.
Decisions of agency.
Appeals of right from superior courts.
Final judgments upon review of decision, §7A-27, (b).
Superior courts.
Administrative agency decisions.
Final judgment of superior court upon review of decision, §7A-27, (b).
Appeals of right from superior courts, §7A-27.
Final judgments of superior court, §7A-27, (b).
Interlocutory orders or judgments of superior court.
Appeals of right from superior court to court of appeals, §7A-27, (d).
Statutory authorized appeals.
Direct appeal to court of appeals, §7A-27, (e).
Supersedeas.
Issuance of remedial writs.
Power of court of appeals to issue, §7A-32, (b).
Termination of parental rights adjudication or disposition.
Appeal to court of appeals, §7B-1113.
Terms and settings, App. Proc. Rule 29, (a).
Transfer of cause to supreme court.
Certification of cause for review by supreme court, §7A-31, (a) to (d).
Trial divisions.
Appeals of right from courts of the trial divisions, §7A-27.
Utilities commission.
Appeals of right from utilities commission to court of appeals, §7A-29, (a).
Jurisdiction of court of appeals.
Power of court of appeals to issue remedial writs, §7A-32, (c).
Review of final orders, §7A-250, (b).
Workers' compensation.
Appeals of right from industrial commission, §7A-29, (a).
Jurisdiction of court of appeals.
Issuing remedial writs, §7A-32, (c).
Writs.
Remedial writs.
Power of court of appeals to issue, §7A-32.

COURT REPORTERS.
Appellate division of general court of justice, §7A-6, (a).
Blind lawyers.
Lending North Carolina reports to blind lawyers, §111-29.
Copies of appellate division reports.
Administrative office of courts.
Distribution of copies, §7A-343.1.
Depositions.
Independent contractors.
Persons before whom deposition may be taken, §1A-1, Rule 28, (c).
District courts.
Appointment of reporter, §7A-198, (f).
Compensation and allowances, §7A-198, (f).
Civil trials, §7A-198.
Electronic or mechanical devices.
Inaccurate record produced, §7A-198, (g).
Operation of device while in progress, §7A-198, (c).

COURT REPORTERS —Cont'd
District courts —Cont'd
Electronic or mechanical devices —Cont'd
State of the art and techniques of recording testimony, §7A-198, (b).
Magistrates.
No provisions for reporting of trials before magistrates, §7A-198, (e).
Utilization of personnel for reporting civil trials, §7A-198, (a).
Waiver of reporting of trial by consent of parties, §7A-198, (d).
Perpetuation of testimony.
Certified transcript of court reporter, §8-85.
Superior courts.
Appointment of reporters, §7A-95, (e).
Availability of personnel, §7A-95, (a).
Compensation and allowances of reporters, §7A-95, (e).
Electronic or mechanical devices.
Operation of device while trial in progress, §7A-95, (c).
Use of in recording testimony, §7A-95, (b).
Sick leave.
Transfer of sick leave of court reporters earned as county or municipal employees, §7A-102.1, (a) to (c).
Testimony.
Investigating state of the art and techniques of recording testimony, §7A-95, (b).
Waiver of reporting by consent of party, §7A-95, (d).

COURTROOM COSTS.
Administration of estates, §7A-307, (a).
Civil actions in district or superior courts, §7A-305, (a).
Criminal actions in superior or district courts, §7A-304, (a).
Special proceedings in superior court, §7A-306, (a).

COURTROOM DECORUM.
Power of judge in maintaining order in courtroom, §§15A-1031 to 15A-1035.

COURTS.
Administration by general assembly, Const. N. C., art. IV, §14.
Administrative office of the courts, §§7A-340 to 7A-346.
See ADMINISTRATIVE OFFICE OF THE COURTS.
Appeals.
Cost on appeal, §6-33.
Court of appeals, §§7A-16 to 7A-21.
See COURT OF APPEALS.
General court of justice.
Appellate division, Const. N. C., art. IV, §5.
General provisions.
See APPEALS.
Supreme court, §§7A-5 to 7A-13.
See SUPREME COURT.
Appellate division reports.
Distribution of copies, §7A-343.1.
Child custody jurisdiction and enforcement.
Cooperation between courts, §50A-112.
Civil contempt, §§5A-21 to 5A-25.
See CONTEMPT.
Closed.
Day for doing act falls on, §103-5, (a), (b).

COURTS —Cont'd
Commission, §§7A-506 to 7A-510.
See COURTS COMMISSION.
Congress.
Power to constitute tribunals inferior to supreme court, Const. U. S., art. I, §8.
Contempt.
Civil contempt, §§5A-21 to 5A-25.
See CONTEMPT.
Criminal contempt, §§5A-11 to 5A-17.
See CONTEMPT.
Costs.
Courtrooms, §§7A-304 to 7A-307.
See COURTROOM COSTS.
General provisions, §§6-1 to 6-62.
See COSTS.
District courts.
See DISTRICT COURTS.
Drug treatment courts, §§7A-790 to 7A-801.
See DRUG TREATMENT COURTS.
Fiduciaries.
Investment of trust funds.
Power to deviate from terms of instrument, §36A-4.
General assembly.
Administration, Const. N. C., art. IV, §15.
General court of justice.
See GENERAL COURT OF JUSTICE.
Judges.
See JUDGES.
Judicial standards commission, §§7A-375 to 7A-377.
See JUDICIAL STANDARDS COMMISSION.
Jurisdiction generally, Const. N. C., art. IV, §12.
Open courts, Const. N. C., art. I, §18.
Orders.
See ORDERS.
Payment into court, §§1-508 to 1-510.
Records mutilation, larceny or destruction, §14-76.
Reporters.
See COURT REPORTERS.
Reports.
Administrative officer of the courts, §7A-6, (b).
Appellate division reports.
Distribution of copies, §7A-343.1.
Blind lawyers.
Lending North Carolina reports to blind lawyers, §111-29.
Designation of commercial reports as official reports, §7A-6, (b1).
Restriction of judicial power, Const. U. S., amd. XI.
Seals.
Governor to procure, §147-28.
New seals when necessary, §147-30.
Superior courts.
See SUPERIOR COURTS.
Supreme court, §§7A-5 to 7A-13.
See SUPREME COURT.
United States courts.
See UNITED STATES COURTS.
Weapons possession in courthouses, §14-269.4.

COURTS COMMISSION, §§7A-506 to 7A-510.
Administrative officer of the courts.
Ex officio members, §7A-507.
Appointment, §7A-506, (a).
Bar association.
Representative of association to be ex officio member, §7A-507.

COURTS COMMISSION —Cont'd
Chairman, §7A-509.
Compensation of members, §7A-509.
Composition, §7A-506, (b) to (e).
Creation, §7A-506, (a).
Duties, §7A-508.
Supporting services, §7A-510.
Ex officio members, §7A-507.
Meetings.
Designation of times and places of meetings by chairman, §7A-509.
Number of members, §7A-506, (a).
State bar council.
Representative of council to be ex officio member, §7A-507.
Supporting services, §7A-510.
Terms, §7A-506, (f).
Vacancies, §7A-506, (g).

COURTS-MARTIAL, NATIONAL GUARD, §§127A-47 to 127A-61.
Administrative procedure act.
Full exemption, §150B-1, (c).
Commitments, §127A-59.
Confinement.
Sentence of confinement, §127A-58.
Dismissals.
Sentence of dismissal, §127A-60.
Fines.
Disposition of fines, §127A-61.
General courts-martial, §127A-47.
Convening, §127A-48.
Powers, §127A-48.
Jurisdiction, §127A-52.
Manual for courts-martial, §127A-53.
Execution of processes and sentences, §127A-57.
Forms for courts-martial procedure, §127A-55.
Powers, §127A-56.
Procedure.
Forms for courts-martial procedure, §127A-55.
Processes.
Execution, §127A-57.
Sentences, §127A-54.
Execution, §127A-57.
Where executed, §127A-54.
Trials and proceedings.
Manual for courts-martial, §127A-53.
Military judges.
Appointment, §127A-50.1.
Qualifications, §127A-50.1.
Nonjudicial punishment, §127A-51.
No right to demand trial by special courts-martial, §127A-51.
Punishment.
Nonjudicial punishment, §127A-51.
No right to demand trial by special courts-martial, §127A-51.
Special courts-martial, §127A-47.
Appointment, §127A-49.
Authority, §127A-49.
No rights to demand trial by special courts-martial.
Nonjudicial punishment, §127A-51.
Summary courts-martial, §127A-50.
Power and authority, §127A-49.
Summary courts-martial, §127A-47.
Appointment, §127A-50.
Composition, §127A-50.
No right to demand trial by special courts-martial, §127A-50.
Powers, §127A-50.

COURTS OF THE UNITED STATES.
See UNITED STATES COURTS.

COVENANTS.
Contribution among joint tortfeasors.
Effect of release or covenant not to sue, §1B-4.
Conveyances generally.
See CONVEYANCES.
Covenant to stand seized to use.
Possession transferred to use in certain conveyances, §41-7.
Interest.
Default judgments.
Clerk to ascertain interest upon default judgment on covenant to pay money, §24-6.
Joint tortfeasor contributions.
Effect of release or covenant not to sue, §1B-4.
Life estates.
Warranties by life tenants deemed covenants, §41-8.
Probate and registration, §47-1.
Remainders, reversions and executory interests.
Grantees of reversion and assigns of lease have reciprocal rights under covenants, §42-8.
Unit ownership compliance with, §47A-10.

COVENTRY ACT.
Maiming, §§14-30, 14-30.1.

COVER.
Leases, UCC.
Cover by lessor, §25-2A-518.
Sale of goods, UCC.
Buyer's inability to effect cover.
Right to specific performance, §25-2-716.
Buyer's remedies, §§25-2-711, 25-2-712.
Merchant buyer's duties as to rightfully rejected goods, §25-2-603.

COVERED CLINICAL TRIALS.
Health benefit plan coverage, §58-3-255.

COVIN.
Suit for penalty.
Plaintiff's reply that former judgment obtained by, §1-59.

COWS.
Brands generally, §§80-45 to 80-66.
See LIVESTOCK BRANDS.
Brucellosis, §§106-388 to 106-398.
See BRUCELLOSIS.
Cattle tick, §§106-351 to 106-363.
See CATTLE TICK.
Compensation for killing diseased animals generally, §§106-323 to 106-335.
See LIVESTOCK DISEASES.
Control of livestock diseases generally, §§106-400 to 106-405.
See LIVESTOCK DISEASES.
Diseases generally, §§106-304 to 106-307.7.
See LIVESTOCK DISEASES.
Larceny, §14-81.
Livestock dealer licensing generally, §§106-418.8 to 106-418.16.
See LIVESTOCK DEALER LICENSING.
Livestock generally.
See LIVESTOCK.
Markets for livestock, §§106-406 to 106-418.
See LIVESTOCK MARKETS.
Meat inspections, §§106-549.15 to 106-549.39.
See MEAT INSPECTIONS.

COWS —Cont'd
Running at large generally, §§68-17 to 68-24.
See LIVESTOCK RUNNING AT LARGE.
Signs for protection of cattle, §136-33.1.

COYOTES.
Hunting preserves.
Controlled hunting preserve operator license, §113-273, (g).
Unlawfully transporting or breeding, §113-294, (o).

CPA'S.
See CERTIFIED PUBLIC ACCOUNTANTS.

CPR EDUCATION, §115C-81, (c).

CRAFTS.
Artwork on consignment, §§25C-1 to 25C-5.
Promotion of arts, §§143-403 to 143-407.1.
Sale of prints, §§25C-10 to 25C-16.

CRAPS.
Video craps.
Ban on new machines, regulation of existing machines, §14-306.1.

CRASHES.
Motor vehicle accidents generally.
See MOTOR VEHICLE ACCIDENTS.

CRASH PARTS.
Nonoriginal crash repair parts.
Definitions, §58-36-95, (a).
Disclosure to claimant by insurer.
Estimate of repair based on use, §58-36-95, (b).
Repair facility submitting invoice for original repair part, §58-36-90, (b).
Reporting fraud, §58-36-90, (c).
Original equipment manufactured crash parts, coverage specifying.
Development of policy endorsement permitting policyholders election, §58-36-41.

CRAVEN COUNTY.
Agricultural tenancies in certain counties.
Terms of, §42-23.
Ambulance service.
Attachment or garnishment and lien for, §§44-51.4 to 44-51.8.
Annexation, authority of municipality.
Inapplicability to municipality in county having population of less than 500 persons, §160A-34.
Condemnation or acquisition of land by local government unit outside county.
Consent of board of commissioners necessary, §153A-15.
Cropper or tenant refusing to perform terms of contract.
Forfeiture of right of possession to premises, §42-27.
Dog collars.
Unlawful removal of electronic dog collars, §14-401.17.
Forestland sales, distribution of funds, §113-38.
Game laws, local acts not repealed, §113-133.1, (e).
Global TransPark development zone, §§158-30 to 158-42.
See GLOBAL TRANSPARK DEVELOPMENT ZONE.
Grants in navigable waters, registration, §113-205, (a).

CRAVEN COUNTY —Cont'd
Low-income housing tax credits.
Qualified building eligible for credit, §105-129.41, (c).
Open fires, high hazard counties.
Applicability of provisions, §113-60.23, (a).
Ground clearing activities, special permit, §113-60.23, (c).
Woodland fires, permit required, §113-60.23, (b).
Private parking lots.
Removal of unauthorized vehicles, §20-219.2.
Room occupancy tax levied by county, uniform provision, §153A-155.
School property.
Acquisition and improvement, §153A-158.1.
Special school tax, election to abolish.
Petition required, §115C-505.

CREAMERY INSPECTIONS.
Generally, §§106-246 to 106-255.
See ICE CREAM PLANTS, CREAMERIES AND CHEESE FACTORIES.

CREATIVE WRITING.
Promotion of arts, §§143-403 to 143-407.1.

CREDIBILITY OF WITNESSES.
Impeachment generally.
See IMPEACHMENT OF WITNESSES.

CREDIT, Const. U. S., art. I, §10.
Cards.
See CREDIT CARDS.
Device fraud.
See CREDIT DEVICE FRAUD.
Instruments to secure equity lines of credit, §§45-81 to 45-84.
See MORTGAGES AND DEEDS OF TRUST.
Interest and service charges, §24-11, (b).
Letters of credit, §§25-5-101 to 25-5-117.
See LETTERS OF CREDIT.
Libraries.
Pledging of credit.
Political subdivisions to comply with pledging of credit, §125-13.
Married women.
Equal availability of credit for women, §25B-1, (a).
Repair services, §§66-220 to 66-226.
See CREDIT REPAIR SERVICES.
Retail installment sales, §§25A-1 to 25A-45.
See RETAIL INSTALLMENT SALES.
Secured transactions, §§25-9-101 to 25-9-710.
See SECURED TRANSACTIONS.
Women.
Actions.
Enforcement of article, §25B-3, (a).
Equal availability of credit for women.
Construction of term "credit," §25B-1, (c).
Married women, §25B-1, (a).
Unmarried women, §25B-1, (b).
Granting of credit not otherwise affected, §25B-4.
Injunctions.
Enforcement of article, §25B-3, (b).
Reporting agencies.
Separate credit histories to be maintained, §25B-2.
Unmarried women.
Equal availability of credit for women, §25B-1, (b).

CREDIT CARDS.
ABC stores.
Expansion of credit sales prohibited, §18B-800, (d).

CREDIT CARDS —Cont'd
Charges, §24-11.
Credit insurance on credit card balances, §58-57-105.
Premium rate allowed, §58-57-105, (b).
Solicitation or negotiation by credit card facilities, §58-57-105, (a).
Unsolicited telephone calls or facsimile transmissions.
Prohibited solicitation, §58-57-105, (a).
Disclosure requirements.
Applicability, §24-11.1, (a).
Charge cards, §24-11.2.
Construction and interpretation, §24-11.1, (f).
Federal requirements, §24-11.1, (c).
Generally, §24-11.1, (b).
Penalty for violation, §24-11.1, (d).
Severability of provisions, §24-11.1, (e).
Financial identity fraud.
Credit, charge, or debit card numbers on receipts, §14-113.24.
Generally, §§14-113.20 to 14-113.25.
Financial transaction cards, §§14-113.8 to 14-113.17.
See FINANCIAL TRANSACTION CARDS.
Fraud by generally.
See CREDIT DEVICE FRAUD.
Insurance.
Credit card guaranty or collateral.
Prohibited, §58-3-147.
Solicitation, negotiation or payment of premiums through credit card facilities.
Prohibited, §58-3-145.
Exceptions, §58-3-145.
Insurance institution, agent or support organization.
Sharing consumer's account number.
General prohibition, §58-39-76.
Interest.
Disclosure requirements.
Generally, §24-11.1.
Loans exempt from interest rate and fee limitations, §24-9, (d).
Loans exempt from interest rate and fee limitations, §24-9, (d).
Possession or manufacture of false or fraudulent identification cards, §14-100.1.
Retail installment sales.
General provisions, §§25A-1 to 25A-45.
See RETAIL INSTALLMENT SALES.
Savings and loan associations power to issue, §54B-77.
Savings banks.
Stock savings banks.
Powers as to, §54C-146, (a).
Statewide accounts receivable program.
Payment by, §147-86.22, (b).

CREDIT DEVICE FRAUD.
Actions.
Civil action for damages, §14-113.6, (c).
Applicability of article, §14-113.7A.
Construction of article.
Article not construed as repealing section 14-100, §14-113.7.
Electric companies, §§14-113.4, 14-113.5.
Financial transaction cards, §§14-113.8 to 14-113.17.
Knowledge.
Use of credit devices as prima facie evidence of knowledge, §14-113.3.

CREDIT DEVICE FRAUD —Cont'd
Multiple violations made felony, §14-113.6, (a).
Notice of revocation.
Definition of "notice," §14-113.2.
Prima facie evidence of receipt of notice, §14-113.2.
Use after notice, §14-113.1.
Repealing provision.
Article not construed as repealing section 14-100, §14-113.7.
Restitution or reparation.
Violation of provisions, §14-113.6, (b).
Revocation.
Use after notice of revocation, §14-113.1.
Telecommunication services.
Avoiding or attempting to avoid payment, §14-113.4.
Civil actions, §14-113.6, (c).
Concealment of existence, origin or destination of any telecommunication, §14-113.5.
Definitions, §14-113.5, (c).
Destination of telecommunication.
Concealment of destination, §14-113.5.
Existence of telecommunication.
Concealment of existence, §14-113.5.
Making, possessing or transferring device for theft of service, §14-113.5.
Origin of telecommunication.
Concealment of origin, §14-113.5.
Publication of information regarding schemes, devices, means or methods for theft, §14-113.5.
Venue of offenses, §14-113.6A, (b).
Theft of service.
Making, possessing or transferring device for theft, §14-113.5.
Publication of information regarding schemes, devices, means or methods for theft, §14-113.5.
Venue of offenses, §14-113.6A, (a).
Unauthorized use of another's credit device, §14-113.1.
Use of false or counterfeit credit device, §14-113.1.
Venue of offenses, §14-113.6A, (a), (b).
Violations made misdemeanor, §14-113.6, (a).

CREDIT INSURANCE, §§58-57-1 to 58-57-115.
Amount of insurance authorized.
Credit accident and health insurance, §58-57-15, (b).
Credit life insurance, §58-57-15, (a).
Credit unemployment insurance, §58-57-15, (b).
Appeals.
Orders of commissioner, §58-57-75.
Revocation or suspension of license, §58-57-80.
Applicability of provisions, §58-57-1.
Authorized, §58-7-15.
Automobile physical damage insurance.
Authorized, §58-57-100, (a).
Conditions, §58-57-100, (a).
Filing of documents with commissioner, §58-57-100, (b).
Choice of insurer, §58-57-65.
Claims.
Adjustment, §58-57-60, (c).
Payment, §58-57-60, (b).
Report to insurer, §58-57-60, (a).
Settlement, §58-57-60, (a).
Commissioner.
Orders, §58-57-70.
Judicial review, §58-57-75.
Revocation or suspension of licenses, §58-57-80.

CREDIT INSURANCE —Cont'd
Commissioner —Cont'd
Rules and regulations, §58-57-70.
Confidentiality of information.
Consumer and customer information.
Generally, §§58-39-1 to 58-39-165.
See INSURANCE CONSUMER AND CUSTOMER INFORMATION PRIVACY.
Credit card balances, §58-57-105.
Premium rate allowed, §58-57-105, (b).
Solicitation or negotiation by credit card facilities, §58-57-105, (a).
Unsolicited telephone calls or facsimile transmissions.
Prohibited solicitation, §58-57-105, (a).
Credit property insurance, §58-57-90.
Definitions.
Dual credit property, §58-57-90, (a).
Personal household property, §58-57-90, (a).
Single interest credit property, §58-57-90, (a).
Dual credit property.
Defined, §58-57-90, (a).
Premium, §58-57-90, (b).
Credit unemployment insurance.
Policy provisions, §58-57-110, (a) to (c).
Rate standards, §58-57-110, (a).
Definitions, §58-57-5.
Existing insurance.
Option of furnishing required insurance through, §58-57-65.
Family leave credit insurance, §58-57-115.
Coverage, §58-57-115, (b).
Definitions, §§58-57-5, 58-57-115, (a).
Eligibility for coverage, §58-57-115, (c).
Evidence of employer approval of qualified leave, §58-57-115, (h).
Exclusions from coverage, §58-57-115, (e).
Lump-sum payments, §58-57-115, (h).
Minimum monthly benefit amount, §58-57-115, (g).
Notice that benefits paid, §58-57-115, (f).
Premium rates, §58-57-115, (i).
Qualifying events for payment of benefits, §58-57-115, (d).
Refund of unearned premium, §58-57-115, (h).
Reports by insurers offering, §58-57-115, (j).
Waiting period for benefits, §58-57-115, (h).
Forms.
Disapproval by commissioner, §58-57-30, (b).
Notice, §58-57-30, (c).
Filing with commissioner, §58-57-30, (a).
Action by commissioner on, §58-57-30, (b).
Withdrawal of approval by commissioner, §58-57-30, (d), (e).
Licenses.
Revocation or suspension, §58-57-80.
Misdemeanors.
Requiring excessive insurance, §58-57-80.
Mortgages and deeds of trust.
Consumer home loans.
Financing credit insurance by lender, §24-10.2, (b).
Policies.
Amounts authorized, §58-57-15.
Contents, §58-57-25, (b).
Credit unemployment insurance.
Provisions, §58-57-110, (a) to (c).
Generally.
See INSURANCE POLICIES OR CONTRACTS.
Insurance to be evidenced by individual policy, §58-57-25, (a).

CREDIT INSURANCE —Cont'd
Policies —Cont'd
Issuance, §58-57-55.
Kinds of policies authorized, §58-57-10.
Notification when policy not delivered to debtor, §58-57-25, (e).
Prohibited provisions, §58-57-25, (d).
Required provisions, §58-57-25, (c).
Premiums.
Credit property insurance, §58-57-25, (b).
Credits, §58-57-50, (e).
Rate standards.
Credit accident and health insurance.
Applicability of rate standards, §58-57-45, (a).
Gainful employment debtor may be required, §58-57-45, (c).
Generally, §58-57-45, (d) to (g).
Joint accident and health coverage, §58-57-45, (h).
Restrictiveness of definition of "disability," §58-57-45, (b).
Credit life insurance.
Applicability of provisions, §58-57-40, (a).
Generally, §58-57-40, (c) to (h).
Joint life insurance coverage, §58-57-40, (d).
Level term life insurance, §58-57-40, (e).
More restrictive forms, §58-57-40, (b).
Credit unemployment insurance, §58-57-110, (a).
Generally, §58-57-35, (a), (b).
Determination according to age, §58-57-35, (c).
Refunds.
Generally, §58-57-50, (a) to (e).
Minimum amount, §58-57-50, (d).
Prompt payment of refund, §58-57-50, (b).
Reducing term insurance, §58-57-50, (b).
Rates.
Credit property insurance.
Premium rates, §58-57-90, (b).
Requiring excessive insurance, §58-57-80.
Rules and regulations.
Commissioner, §58-57-70.
Scope of provisions, §58-57-1.
Single interest credit property.
Defined, §58-57-90, (a).
Premium, §58-57-90, (b).
Termination prior to scheduled maturity, §58-57-20.
Term of insurance, §58-57-20.
Violations of provisions.
Penalties, §58-57-80.

CREDITORS.
Assignments for benefit of creditors.
See ASSIGNMENTS FOR BENEFIT OF CREDITORS.
Commercial code generally.
Defined, §25-1-201, (12).
Subordinated obligations, §25-1-209.
Community property rights at death, §31C-8.
Conveyances.
Intent to defraud, §§39-23.1 to 39-23.12.
See FRAUDULENT TRANSFERS.
Debts generally.
See DEBTS.
Decedents' estates.
Community property rights at death, §31C-8.
Limitation of actions.
Action against decedent's personal or real representative, §1-49.

CREDITORS —Cont'd
Decedents' estates —Cont'd
Notice for claims, §§28A-14-1 to 28A-14-3.
Sale, lease or mortgage of real property by heirs, §28A-17-12.
Executors and administrators.
When creditors may sue on claim, §28A-18-5.
Funds transfers.
Creditor process served on receiving bank, §25-4A-502.
Leases, UCC.
Creditors' special rights, §25-2A-308.
Lien creditors.
Lis pendens.
Notice of filing, §1-116, (d).
Limited liability companies.
Judgment creditors rights in members interest, §57C-5-03.
Nonprofit corporations.
Distribution of amounts due to unavailable creditors upon dissolution, §55A-14-40.
Powers of appointment.
Limitation against creditors and purchasers for value, §39-35.
Sale of goods, UCC.
Creditor's rights.
Consignment sales, §25-2-326.
Rights of seller's creditors against sold goods, §25-2-402.
Sale on approval, §25-2-326.
Sale or return, §25-2-326.
Supplemental proceedings to recover assets, §§1-352 to 1-368.
See SUPPLEMENTAL PROCEEDINGS.
Transfers.
Intent to defraud, §§39-23.1 to 39-23.12.
See FRAUDULENT TRANSFERS.
Uniform trusts act.
Bank account created to pay special debts.
Time limitation for presenting claim to bank for payment, §36A-61, (b).

CREDITORS BILLS.
Supplemental proceedings, §§1-352 to 1-368.
See SUPPLEMENTAL PROCEEDINGS.

CREDIT REPAIR SERVICES, §§66-220 to 66-226.
Acts prohibited, §66-223.
Applicability of chapter, §66-226.
Bonds, surety.
Required, §66-222.
Citation of article, §66-220.
Contracts.
Cancellation, §66-224.
Contents, §66-224.
Voiding.
Use of untrue or misleading statements, §66-225.
Definitions, §66-221.
Felonies.
Violation of provisions, §66-225.
Injunctions.
Violation of provisions, §66-225.
Prohibited acts, §66-223.
Purposes of article, §66-220.
Scope of article, §66-226.
Short title of article, §66-220.
Trust account.
Required, §66-222.
Violation of provisions, §66-225.
Waiver of provisions.
Void and unenforceable, §66-225.

CREDIT REPORTING AGENCIES.
Separate credit histories for married persons, responsibility to maintain, §25B-2.

CREDIT SALES, §§25A-1 to 25A-45.
See RETAIL INSTALLMENT SALES.

CREDIT SCORING.
Motor vehicle or property insurance, §58-36-90.

CREDITS UPON JUDGMENTS, §1-242.

CREDIT UNIONS, §§54-109.1 to 54-110.10.
Actions.
Power to sue and be sued, §54-109.21.
Administrator of credit unions.
Assistants, §54-109.10.
Confidential information, §54-109.105, (a).
Duties, §§54-109.11, 54-109.12.
Liquidation of credit unions, §54-109.13.
Removal of officers, §54-109.19.
Revocation of certificate of approval, §54-109.13.
Rules and regulations, §54-109.12.
Supervision of credit unions, §54-109.12.
Supervision of division, §54-109.10.
Suspension and conservation, §54-109.92.
Agents.
Personal agency accounts.
Generally, §54-109.63.
Age of members.
Minimum age to hold office, §54-109.31, (e).
Minimum age to vote at meetings, §54-109.31, (d).
Appeals.
Suspension and conservation.
Decisions of administrator, §54-109.92, (k).
Appraisal fees.
Loans secured by real property, §24-10, (h).
Articles of incorporation, §54-109.2, (b).
Amendment, §54-109.4, (a).
When effective, §54-109.4, (b).
Form, §54-109.3.
Assets.
Liquidation.
Voluntary liquidation.
Use of assets, §54-109.93, (g).
Associations.
Membership, §54-109.27.
Representation and voting at meetings, §54-109.31, (c).
Attorneys at law.
Selection of attorneys to handle loan-closing proceedings, §54-109.18.
Audits.
Supervisory committee, §54-109.49.
Bankruptcy and insolvency.
Suspension and conservation, §54-109.92.
Board of directors.
Conflicts of interest, §54-109.39.
Dividends.
Declaring, §54-109.54.
Duties, §54-109.44.
Election of directors, §54-109.35, (a).
Executive committee, §54-109.42.
Meetings, §54-109.43.
Number of members, §54-109.42.
Executive officers.
Election or employment, §54-109.40, (a), (d).
Expenses of directors, §54-109.38.
General direction of credit union, §54-109.41.
Loans.
Duties of directors as to, §54-109.44.
Meetings, §54-109.43.
Number of directors, §§54-109.2, (d), 54-109.35.

CREDIT UNIONS —Cont'd
Board of directors —Cont'd
Organization.
Selection, §54-109.2, (d).
Powers, §54-109.41.
Record of members, §54-109.36.
Removal of directors.
Grounds, §54-109.19, (a).
Hearing, §54-109.19, (b).
Notice, §54-109.19, (b).
Order of removal, §54-109.19, (b).
Power of administrator of credit unions, §54-109.19, (a).
Procedure, §54-109.19, (b).
Vacancies, §54-109.37.
Bonds, surety.
Blanket fidelity bond.
Purchase by board of directors, §54-109.44.
Generally, §54-109.11.
Borrowing money.
Powers of credit unions generally, §54-109.21.
Bylaws.
Amendment, §54-109.4, (a).
When effective, §54-109.4, (b).
Form, §54-109.3.
Preparation and adoption, §54-109.2, (c).
Capital.
Composition, §54-109.53, (a).
Changes in corporate status, §§54-109.92 to 54-109.95.
Child support enforcement.
Location of absent parents.
Information to be provided, §110-139, (d).
Commercial code.
Secured transactions.
Transfer of accounts excluded from provisions of article, §25-9-104, (l).
Commercial loan commitments to be in writing, §22-5.
Commission.
Created, §143B-439, (a).
Meetings, §143B-439, (a).
Members, §143B-439, (a).
Powers and duties, §143B-439, (c).
Quorum, §143B-439, (a).
Relationship between secretary of economic and community development and credit union commission, §143B-439, (b).
Terms, §143B-439, (a).
Confidentiality, §54-109.105.
Agencies of state, other states or United States.
Exchange of information permitted, §54-109.105, (d).
Application for new credit union.
Public information, §54-109.105, (c).
Disclosure.
Court of competent jurisdiction may order, §54-109.105, (b).
Liability for damages, §54-109.105.
Misdemeanors for violations, §54-109.105, (f).
Penalties for violation, §54-109.105, (e).
Records of information of credit union division, administrator or agents, §54-109.105, (a).
Conflicts of interest, §54-109.39.
Conservation.
Appeals from decisions of administrator, §54-109.92, (k).
Appointment of conservator, §54-109.92, (b), (e).
Costs, §54-109.92, (g).
Duration, §54-109.92, (i).
Duties of conservator, §54-109.92, (f).

CREDIT UNIONS —Cont'd
Conservation —Cont'd
Grounds, §54-109.92, (a).
Jurisdiction.
Suits during conservation, §54-109.92, (h).
Liquidating agent.
Appointment, §54-109.92, (j).
Liquidation.
Order of liquidation, §54-109.92, (j).
Merger.
Order of merger, §54-109.92, (j).
Order, §54-109.92, (b), (e).
Appeal from order, §54-109.92, (k).
Effect, §54-109.92, (c).
Reply to order, §54-109.92, (c).
Effect of failure to file, §54-109.92, (l).
Hearing, §54-109.92, (d).
Service, §54-109.92, (b).
Reports by conservator, §54-109.92, (f).
Consumer finance act.
Exemption of cooperative credit unions, §53-191.
Contracts.
Power to make contracts, §54-109.21.
Conversion of charter, §54-109.95.
Cooperative marketing arrangements.
Authorized, §54-109.77.
Corporate credit unions, §§54-110.1 to 54-110.10.
Applicability of article, §54-110.10.
Application form, §54-110.4, (a).
Articles of incorporation, §54-110.4, (b).
Bylaws, §54-110.4, (c).
Central financial system.
Participation in, §54-110.6.
Charter exclusive, §54-110.3.
Defined, §54-110.1, (a).
Directors.
Meetings, §54-110.5, (d).
Fees.
Operating fees, §54-110.8.
Liens.
Shares and deposit accounts, §54-110.7, (b).
Membership, §54-110.2, (a).
Name exclusive, §54-110.3.
Operating fees, §54-110.8.
Participation in central system, §54-110.6.
Powers, §54-110.5, (a), (b), (e).
Purposes, §54-110.1, (b).
Reserves, §54-110.9.
Security.
Loans, §54-110.7, (c).
Setoff.
Right of setoff, §54-110.7, (a).
Taxation.
Exemption, §54-110.5, (c).
Voting representatives.
Designation, §54-110.2, (b).
Credit committee.
Appointment, §54-109.35, (c).
Authority, §54-109.45.
Conflicts of interest, §54-109.39.
Dispensing with, §54-109.48.
Expenses of members, §54-109.38.
Loan officers in lieu of, §§54-109.35, (c), 54-109.48.
Loans.
Majority of committee must approve, §54-109.46.
Meetings, §54-109.46.
Number of members, §54-109.35, (c).
Powers, §54-109.45.
Record of members, §54-109.36.
Vacancies, §54-109.37.

CREDIT UNIONS —Cont'd
Definitions, §54-109.1.
Corporate credit unions, §54-110.1, (a).
Interest, §54-109.65.
"Membership," §54-109.26, (a).
Risk assets, §54-109.88.
Deposits.
Insurance.
Share and deposit insurance, §54-109.78, (a).
Prerequisite to granting of charter, §54-109.78, (b).
Lien on deposit, §54-109.59.
Savings accounts, §54-109.55.
Direction of affairs, §§54-109.35 to 54-109.49.
Dividends, §54-109.54.
Lien on accumulated dividends, §54-109.59.
Power to declare dividends, §54-109.21.
Division.
Administrator of credit unions. See within this heading, "Administrator of credit unions."
Creation, §54-109.10.
Supervision, §54-109.10.
Evidence.
Records.
Photostatic or photographic reproductions, §54-109.17, (c).
Examinations.
Administrator of credit unions.
Duties, §54-109.11.
Annual examinations required, §54-109.16.
Costs.
Payment, §54-109.16.
Fees, §54-109.14, (a).
Federal credit unions.
Conversion into state credit union, §54-109.95, (b).
Conversion of state credit union into, §54-109.95, (a).
Fees.
Disposition of moneys collected, §54-109.14, (b), (c).
Examination fees, §54-109.14, (a).
Organization, §54-109.2, (e).
Supervision fees, §54-109.14, (a).
Fiduciaries.
Power of credit unions generally, §54-109.21.
Financial records privacy generally, §§53B-1 to 53B-10.
See FINANCIAL RECORDS PRIVACY.
Foreign credit unions conducting business in state.
Approval.
Denial or revocation, §54-109.106, (c).
Prerequisites, §54-109.106, (a).
Required, §54-109.106, (a).
Requirements, §54-109.106, (a), (b).
Group purchasing.
Cooperative marketing arrangements authorized, §54-109.77.
Hearings.
Removal of officers, §54-109.19, (b).
Suspension and conservation.
Reply to order, §54-109.92, (d).
Installment loans, §54-109.69.
Insurance.
Members.
Cooperative marketing arrangements to facilitate members' purchase of, §54-109.75, (b).
Purchase of insurance for, §54-109.75, (a).
Officers.
Liability insurance for, §54-109.76.

CREDIT UNIONS —Cont'd
Insurance —Cont'd
Share and deposit insurance, §54-109.78, (a).
Prerequisite to granting of charter, §54-109.78, (b).
Insurance premium financing.
Exception to license requirement, §58-35-10, (a).
Interest, §54-109.65.
Investments, §54-109.82.
Authorized investments, §54-109.82.
Prudent person rule, §36A-2, (a).
Joint accounts.
Additions.
Effect, §54-109.58, (c).
Establishment, §54-109.58, (a).
Estate tax provisions not repealed, §54-109.58, (b).
Form of statement establishing, §54-109.58, (a).
Incidents of account, §54-109.58, (a).
Section deemed not exclusive, §54-109.58, (a1).
Withdrawals.
Effect, §54-109.58, (c).
Liens, §54-109.59.
Line of credit, §54-109.70.
Liquidation, voluntary.
Assets.
Use, §54-109.93, (g).
Authorized, §54-109.93, (a).
Certificate of dissolution, §54-109.93, (h).
Continuation of existence for certain purposes, §54-109.93, (f).
Notice.
Board of directors to notify administrator, §54-109.93, (c).
Meeting of members to consider question, §54-109.93, (e).
Records.
Retention, §54-109.93, (h).
Resolution, §54-109.93, (b).
Submission of question to members, §54-109.93, (b), (d), (e).
Loan officers.
Appointment, §54-109.47, (a).
Delegation of powers by credit committee, §54-109.47, (a).
In lieu of credit committee, §§54-109.35, (c), 54-109.48.
Review by credit committee of loan applications not approved by, §54-109.47, (b).
Loans, §§54-109.65 to 54-109.71.
Applications, §54-109.66.
Authorized investments generally, §54-109.82.
Boards of directors.
Duties of directors as to, §54-109.44.
Commercial loan commitments to be in writing, §22-5.
Conditional sales contracts of members.
Purchase, §54-109.71, (c).
Credit committee.
Majority of committee must approve, §54-109.46.
Guaranteed loan programs of federal and state governments.
Participation in, §54-109.71, (b).
Installments, §54-109.69.
Interest, §54-109.65.
Joint loans.
Participation in, §54-109.71, (a).
Limitations, §54-109.67.
Line of credit, §54-109.70.
Other credit unions.
Loans to as authorized investments, §54-109.82.
Powers of credit unions generally, §54-109.21.

CREDIT UNIONS —Cont'd
Loans —Cont'd
Purposes, §54-109.65.
Restrictions, §54-109.67.
Security, §54-109.68.
Terms, §54-109.65.
Written documents.
Loans to be evidenced by, §54-109.66.
Members, §§54-109.26 to 54-109.31.
Age.
Minimum age to hold office, §54-109.31, (e).
Minimum age to vote at meetings, §54-109.31, (d).
Associations, §54-109.27.
Representation and voting at meetings, §54-109.31, (c).
Expulsion.
Power of credit unions, §54-109.21.
Generally, §54-109.26.
Groups, §§54-109.26, (b), 54-109.27.
Representation and voting at meetings, §54-109.31, (c).
Insurance.
Cooperative marketing arrangements to facilitate members' purchase of, §54-109.75, (b).
Purchase of insurance for, §54-109.75, (a).
Leaving field of membership.
Retention of membership, §54-109.29.
Liquidation, voluntary.
Submission of question to members, §54-109.93, (b), (d), (e).
Meetings.
Election of directors, §54-109.35, (a).
Generally, §54-109.31, (a).
Voting, §54-109.31, (b).
Age.
Minimum age, §54-109.31, (d).
Societies, associations, copartnerships or corporations having membership, §54-109.31, (c).
Other credit unions, §54-109.28.
Proxy voting.
Prohibited, §54-109.31, (b).
Retention of membership on leaving field, §54-109.29.
Societies, §54-109.27.
Representation and voting at meetings, §54-109.31, (c).
Voting at meetings, §54-109.31, (b) to (d).
Withdrawal from membership, §54-109.21.
Merger, §54-109.94.
Minors as members.
Minimum age for holding office, §54-109.31, (e).
Minimum age for voting at meetings, §54-109.31, (d).
Names.
Articles of incorporation to state, §§54-109.2, (a), 54-109.3.
Exclusive use of name, §54-109.5.
Notice.
Liquidation.
Voluntary liquidation.
Board of directors to notify administrator, §54-109.93, (c).
Meeting of members to consider question, §54-109.93, (e).
Removal of officers, §54-109.19, (b).
Suspension of operations.
Notification to members of credit union commission, §54-109.92, (n).

CREDIT UNIONS —Cont'd
Office facilities.
Change of place of business, §54-109.6, (b).
Facilities at location other than main office, §54-109.6, (a).
Sharing office space with other credit unions, §54-109.6, (c).
Officers.
Age.
Minimum age to hold office, §54-109.31, (e).
Board of directors. See within this heading, "Board of directors."
Compensation, §54-109.38.
Conflicts of interest, §54-109.39.
Duties, §54-109.40, (c).
Enumerated, §54-109.40, (a), (d).
Executive officers.
Election by board, §54-109.40, (a).
Insurance.
Liability insurance for, §54-109.76.
Record of names and addresses, §54-109.36.
Removal.
Grounds, §54-109.19, (a).
Hearing, §54-109.19, (b).
Notice, §54-109.19, (b).
Order of removal, §54-109.19, (b).
Power of administrator of credit unions, §54-109.19, (a).
Procedure, §54-109.19, (b).
Terms of office, §54-109.40, (b).
Operating fees.
Corporate credit unions, §54-110.8.
Orders.
Confidential information.
Disclosure orders, §54-109.105, (b).
Conservation, §54-109.92.
Organization.
Applications for new credit unions.
Information contained in application to be public information, §54-109.105, (c).
Articles of incorporation, §54-109.2, (b).
Amendment, §54-109.4, (a).
When effective, §54-109.4, (b).
Form, §54-109.3.
Board of directors.
Selection, §54-109.2, (d).
Bylaws.
Preparation and adoption, §54-109.2, (c).
Certificate of approval, §54-109.2, (e).
Revocation, §54-109.13.
Charter members.
Number, §54-109.2, (a).
Fees, §54-109.2, (e).
Procedure, §54-109.2.
Supervisory committee.
Selection, §54-109.2, (d).
Other credit unions.
Joint loans with.
Participation in, §54-109.71, (a).
Loans to.
Authorized investments, §54-109.82.
Membership, §54-109.28.
Merger with, §54-109.94.
Out-of-state business, §54-109.7.
Payable on death (POD) accounts.
Additions, withdrawal, payment or change of beneficiary, effect, §54-109.57, (c).
Establishment, §54-109.57, (a).
Estate taxes, provisions not repealed or modified, §54-109.57, (d).
Form of statement creating, §54-109.57, (a).

CREDIT UNIONS —Cont'd
Payable on death (POD) accounts —Cont'd
Incidents of accounts, §54-109.57, (a).
Section not exclusive, §54-109.57, (a1).
Penalties.
Confidential information, §54-109.105.
Reports.
Neglect to make report, §54-109.15, (b).
Unlawful use of name containing words "credit union," §54-109.5.
Personal agency accounts.
Creation, §54-109.63, (a), (c).
Effect, §54-109.63, (d), (e).
Survivorship, §54-109.63, (b).
Place of business.
Change of place of business, §54-109.6, (b).
Facilities at locations other than main office, §54-109.6, (a).
Powers, §§54-109.21, 54-109.22.
Conducting business outside state, §54-109.7.
Generally, §54-109.21.
Incidental powers, §54-109.22.
Privacy of financial records generally, §§53B-1 to 53B-10.
See FINANCIAL RECORDS PRIVACY.
Prudent person rule.
Investments, §36A-2, (a).
Public officers and employees.
Members of state employee credit unions.
Deductions from salary or wages authorized, §143-3.3, (f).
Purposes, §54-109.1.
Incidental powers for, §54-109.22.
Records.
Board and committee members, §54-109.36.
Confidential information, §54-109.105, (a).
Destruction of records after expiration of retention time, §54-109.17, (b).
Generally, §54-109.17, (a).
Liquidation.
Voluntary liquidation.
Retention of records, §54-109.93, (h).
Photostatic or photographic reproductions.
Admissibility as evidence, §54-109.17, (c).
Privacy of financial records generally, §§53B-1 to 53B-10.
Reduction in shares, §54-109.61.
Regular reserve, §§54-109.86, 54-109.87.
Reports.
Conservation.
Reports by conservator, §54-109.92, (f).
Neglect to make report.
Penalty, §54-109.15, (b).
Revocation of certificate of approval, §54-109.13.
Required, §54-109.15, (a).
Reserves, §§54-109.86 to 54-109.88.
Corporate credit unions, §54-110.9.
Regular reserve.
Transfers to, §54-109.86, (a).
Increase or decrease of requirement, §54-109.86, (b).
Use, §54-109.87.
Requirements not to be construed as limiting, §54-109.86, (d).
Risk assets.
Defined, §54-109.88.
Special reserves, §54-109.86, (c).
Rules and regulations.
Administrator of credit unions, §54-109.12.
Savings accounts, §§54-109.53 to 54-109.63.
Deposits, §54-109.55.
Joint accounts, §54-109.58.

CREDIT UNIONS —Cont'd
Seals and sealed instruments.
Power to adopt and use seal, §54-109.21.
Secured transactions.
Transfer of accounts excluded from provisions of article, §25-9-104, (l).
Securities regulation.
Exempt securities, §78A-16.
Security for loans, §54-109.68.
Service of process.
Foreign credit unions.
Agent for service of process.
Required, §54-109.106, (b).
Suspension and conservation.
Order, §54-109.92, (b).
Shareholder liability, §54-109.30.
Small estates.
Collection of property by affidavit.
Transfer of rights by representation of affidavit, §28A-25-1, (c).
Social security.
Coverage under title II of social security act.
State employees' credit union.
Elections relating to membership, contributions and service, §135-27, (e).
State departments and agencies.
Information exchangers, §54-109.105, (d).
Stock and stockholders.
Articles of incorporation.
Information to be included, §§54-109.2, (b), 54-109.3.
Certificates.
Not required, §54-109.53, (c).
Insurance.
Share and deposit insurance, §54-109.78, (a).
Prerequisite to granting of charter, §54-109.78, (b).
Liability of shareholders, §54-109.30.
Lien on shares, §54-109.59.
Reduction in shares.
Conditions for, §54-109.61, (a).
Excess divided among members, §54-109.61, (b).
Majority vote of members at special meeting, §54-109.61, (a).
Subscriptions, §54-109.53, (b).
Transfer of shares, §54-109.53, (b).
Supervisory committee.
Appointment, §54-109.35, (b).
Audits, §54-109.49.
Clerical and auditing assistants in lieu of, §54-109.35, (b).
Conflicts of interest, §54-109.39.
Duties, §54-109.49.
Expenses of members, §54-109.38.
Number of members, §§54-109.2, (d), 54-109.35, (b).
Organization.
Selection, §54-109.2, (d).
Record of members, §54-109.36.
Removal or suspension of members, §54-109.35, (b).
Vacancies, §54-109.37.
Survivorship.
Personal agency accounts, §54-109.63, (b).
Trust accounts.
Governing provisions, §54-109.57.
Suspension of operations.
Appeals from decisions of administrator, §54-109.92, (k).
Extension of period of suspension, §54-109.92, (m).
Grounds, §54-109.92, (a).

CREDIT UNIONS —Cont'd
Suspension of operations —Cont'd
Notification of members of credit union committee, §54-109.92, (n).
Order, §54-109.92, (b).
Appeals, §54-109.92, (k).
Effect, §54-109.92, (c).
Reply to order, §54-109.92, (c).
Effect of failure to file, §54-109.92, (l).
Hearing on, §54-109.92, (d).
Taxation.
Exemptions, §54-109.99.
Restriction, §54-109.99.
Thrift accounts, §54-109.56.
Trust accounts.
Shares and deposits in trust, §54-109.59.
United States.
Exchange of information permitted, §54-109.105, (d).

CREEK OBSTRUCTIONS.
Free passage of boats, §77-12.
Natural drainage, §77-14.
Natural flow, §77-13.

CREMATION, §§90-210.40 to 90-210.54.
Access to crematory area.
Persons authorized, §90-210.49, (f).
Anatomical gifts.
Inapplicability of previsions to, §90-210.44, (d).
Authorization form.
Information required, §90-210.45, (a).
Liability for damages resulting from signing, §90-210.45, (b).
No liability of licensee for cremation pursuant to, §§90-210.45, (c), 90-210.51, (b).
Preneed basis, §90-210.45.
Required prior to cremation, §§90-210.49, (b), (c), 90-210.51, (b).
Revocation, §90-210.45, (d).
Standard form and procedures for execution.
Board may develop, §90-210.54, (a).
Truthfulness of facts set forth.
Authorizing agent signing warrants, §90-210.45, (b).
Authorization to cremate.
Required, §90-210.45, (a).
Revocation, §90-210.45, (d).
Vital statistics, §130A-113, (b).
Authorizing agent.
Defined, §90-210.41.
Liability for damages resulting from signing authorization form, §90-210.45, (b).
Persons authorized to serve as, §90-210.44, (a).
Responsibility for disposition of cremated remains, §90-210.50, (b).
Truthfulness of facts set forth in authorization form.
Agent warrants, §§90-210.45, (b), 90-210.51, (a).
Body parts.
Authorizing cremation of, §90-210.44, (c).
Burial-transit permit/cremation authorization form.
Required prior to cremation.
Deaths investigated by medical examiner, §90-210.49, (c).
Caskets.
Defined, §90-210.41.
Rules requiring remains be placed in or cremated in.
Licensee prohibited from making, §90-210.48, (a).

CREMATION —Cont'd
Certificate of cremations.
Issuance upon completion of cremation, §90-210.47, (e).
Citation of act.
Short title, §90-210.40.
Commingling with remains of another persons.
Disposition of cremated remains.
Prohibition, §90-210.50, (d).
Construction.
On or adjacent to cemetery or funeral establishment, §90-210.43, (b).
Cremating within 24 hours after death.
Restriction, §90-210.49, (e).
Crematory authority.
Appointment of members, §90-210.42, (b).
Composition, §90-210.42, (b).
Establishment, §90-210.42, (a).
Meetings, §90-210.42, (f).
Officers, §90-210.42, (e).
Per diem and travel expenses, §90-210.42, (d).
Quorum, §90-210.42, (f).
Terms of members, §90-210.42, (c).
Travel and subsistence expenses, §90-210.42, (d).
Crematory license.
Application, §90-210.43, (c).
Change of ownership, new application, §90-210.43, (e).
Change of ownership.
New application, §90-210.43, (e).
Expiration, §90-210.43, (e).
Fee schedule, §90-210.52, (a).
Issuance, §90-210.43, (c).
Probation, §90-210.43, (h).
Renewal, §90-210.43, (e).
Required, §90-210.43, (a), (f).
Suspension, revocation, refusal to renew, §90-210.43, (g).
Transfer, prohibition, §90-210.43, (e).
Crematory manager.
Identification by crematory licensee applicant, §90-210.43, (d).
Names and address, informing board, §90-210.43, (d).
Crematory operators.
Defined, §90-210.41.
Licenses.
Suspension or revocation.
Felony convictions, §15A-1331A.
Crematory technicians.
Employment required, number, §90-210.43, (d).
Identification by crematory licensee applicant, §90-210.43, (d).
Names and address, informing board, §90-210.43, (d).
Crime of violence in connection with death.
Cremation prohibited, §90-210.54, (d).
Criminal penalty for violations of article, §90-210.54, (c).
Death certificate.
Required before cremating, information required, §90-210.49, (a).
Definitions, §90-210.41.
Disposition of cremated remains.
Commingling with remains of another persons.
Prohibition, §90-210.50, (d).
Discharge from legal obligation or liability.
Final disposal of remains, §90-210.50, (b).
Licensee disposing of remains.
Authorizing agent's failure to specify, §90-210.50, (b).

CREMATION —Cont'd
Disposition of cremated remains —Cont'd
Placing remains of more than one persons in same container.
Restrictions, §90-210.50, (d).
Private property.
Disposal of remains on, §90-210.50, (c).
Release of cremated remains by licensee, §90-210.50, (e).
Responsibility of authorizing agent, §90-210.50, (b).
Scattering over uninhabited lands, public water ways or sea, §90-210.50, (f).
Statement provided by authorizing agent, §90-210.50, (a).
Disposition of remains of terminated pregnancies, §130A-131.10.
Dispute concerning cremation.
Refusal to accept body or perform cremation, §90-210.51, (d).
Dispute concerning release or disposition.
Refusal by licensee to release or dispose of remains, §90-210.51, (e).
Enclosed in container.
Required to cremate remains, §90-210.49, (g).
Fee schedule, §90-210.52, (a).
Funds collected part of general fund, §90-210.52, (b).
Felony convictions.
Forfeiture of license, §15A-1331A.
Funeral directors.
Conducting cremations exclusively through, §90-210.53, (c).
Hearings, §90-210.43, (i).
Holding and processing facility requirements, §90-210.49, (i).
Identification of bodies before, §90-210.29A.
Impossible or impractical cremations.
Not required, §90-210.49, (k).
Inspection of crematory, §90-210.43, (i).
Prior to licensing, §90-210.43, (c).
Medical examiners.
Postmortem medicolegal examinations and services.
When medical examiner's permission necessary before cremation, §130A-388, (a), (b).
Medical wastes.
Inapplicability of article to cremation of, §90-210.54, (b).
Other licenses or permits required by law.
Licensee required to obtain, §90-210.53, (b).
Pacemakers, defibrillators or other implants.
Cremating body containing prohibited, §90-210.49, (d).
Placement of cremated remains in container, §90-210.49, (l).
Remains of more than one persons in same container.
Restrictions, §90-210.50, (d).
Preneed cremation arrangements.
Cancellation of authorization form, §90-210.45, (a).
Disclosure required in authorization form, §90-210.46, (b).
Ensuring remains cremated, §90-210.46, (c).
Execution of authorization form, §90-210.45, (a).
Inapplicability to authorization executed prior to effective date of act, §90-210.46, (f).
Licensee required to cremate remains, §90-210.46, (d).
Release or disposal of remains, §90-210.46, (e).

CREMATION —Cont'd
Preneed cremation arrangements —Cont'd
Transfer of authorization form, §90-210.45, (a).
Private property.
Disposal of remains on, §90-210.50, (c).
Processing and pulverizing remains, standards, compliance, §90-210.49, (j).
Public, conducting cremation for or with, §90-210.53, (c).
Receipt furnished to person delivering remains, §90-210.47, (a).
Receipt furnished upon release of remains, §90-210.47, (b).
Record requirements, §90-210.47, (c), (d), (f).
Refusal to accept body or perform cremation.
Dispute concerning cremation, §90-210.51, (d).
Release of cremated remains by licensee, §90-210.50, (e).
Dispute concerning release or disposition.
Refusal by licensee to release or dispose of remains, §90-210.51, (e).
Residue of process, separating, §90-210.49, (g).
Responsibility for disposition of cremated remains, §90-210.50, (b).
Right to dispose of decedent's body.
Waiver, §90-210.44, (b).
Rules for carrying out and enforcement of provisions.
Adoption by board, §90-210.54, (a).
Rules for management and operation of crematory.
Licensee may adopt, §90-210.53, (a).
Scattering remains over uninhabited lands, public water ways or sea, §90-210.50, (f).
Shipping cremated remains, §90-210.49, (n).
Short title, §90-210.40.
Simultaneous cremation of more than one person.
Prohibition, §90-210.49, (h).
Storing or retaining cremated remains, §90-210.50, (a).
Temporary container.
Placement of cremated remains in, §90-210.49, (l) to (n).
Title of act.
Short title, §90-210.40.
Ultimate disposition of cremated remains.
Statement signed by authorizing agent, §90-210.50, (a).
Urn or receptacle.
Rules requiring remains be placed in or cremated in.
Licensee prohibited from making, §90-210.48, (b).
Valuables delivered to licensee.
Licensee not liable for, §90-210.51, (c).
Viewing chamber or holding and processing facility.
Restrictions, §90-210.49, (f).
Vital statistics.
Authorization for cremation, §130A-113, (b).
Waiver of right to dispose of decedent's body, §90-210.44, (b).

CRIME AGAINST NATURE, §14-177.

CRIME COMMISSION, §§143B-478 to 143B-480.
Adjunct committees.
Approval of actions, §143B-480, (e).
Composition, §143B-480, (b).
Creation, §143B-480, (a).
Powers and duties, §143B-480.

CRIME COMMISSION —Cont'd
Adjunct committees —Cont'd
Removal of members, §143B-480, (d).
Reports, §143B-480, (c).
Appointments, §143B-478, (c).
Creation, §143B-478, (a).
Directives.
Administered by director of crime control division, §143B-479, (b).
Meetings, §143B-478, (e).
Members, §143B-478, (b).
Powers and duties, §143B-479, (a).
Professional, clerical and staff services.
Crime control division to provide, §143B-477, (c).
Qualifications of members, §143B-478, (a).
Quorum, §143B-478, (e).
Removal of members, §143B-478, (d).
Terms, §143B-478, (c).
Transfer to department, §143A-244.
Vacancies, §143B-478, (c).

CRIME CONTROL AND PUBLIC SAFETY DEPARTMENT, §§143B-473 to 143B-499.7.
Alcoholic beverage control commission.
Transfer to department, §143A-243.
Alcohol law enforcement agents.
Appointment by secretary, §18B-500.
Alcohol law enforcement division.
Boxing.
Authority to regulate, rules, issuance, §143-652.1.
Defined, §18B-101.
Transfer of division to department, §§143A-243, 143B-475.
Butner public safety division, §122C-408.
Authorized, §122C-408, (a).
Camp Butner reservation, §122C-408.
Civil air patrol division.
Benefits, §143B-491, (b).
Established, §143B-490, (a).
Liability of state, §143B-492.
Personnel, §143B-491, (a).
Powers and duties, §143B-490, (b).
Transfer to department, §143A-241.
Civil preparedness agency.
Transfer of agency (emergency management division) to department, §§143A-240, 143B-475.
Creation, §143B-473.
Crime commission, §§143B-478 to 143B-480.
See CRIME COMMISSION.
Crime control division.
Established, §143B-477, (a).
Powers and duties, §143B-477, (b), (c).
Transfer to department, §143A-245.
Crime victims compensation commission.
Vested within department, §143B-475, (e).
Deferred prosecution, community service restitution and volunteer program.
Authority to conduct, §143B-262.4.
Boundaries of community service program districts, §143B-262.4, (e).
Coordinator.
Designation, §143B-262.4, (c).
Fees.
Payment of persons required to participate, §143B-262.4, (b).
Liability for damages for injury or loss sustained by individual performing community or reparation service, §143B-262.4, (d).

CRIME CONTROL AND PUBLIC SAFETY DEPARTMENT —Cont'd
Deferred prosecution, community service restitution and volunteer program —Cont'd
Significant violations of terms.
Community service staff to report, §143B-262.4, (f).
Duties, §§143B-474, 143B-475.
Emergency management division.
Transfer of civil preparedness agency (emergency management division) to department, §§143A-240, 143B-475.
Functions.
Assignment by governor, §143B-475, (b).
Transfer to department, §143B-475, (c).
Vesting in subunits, §143B-475, (a).
Head of department, §143B-476, (a).
Highway patrol.
Transfer to department, §143A-242.
Name, §143B-473.
National guard.
Transfer to department, §143A-239.
Powers and duties, §§143B-474, 143B-475.
Reports.
Vacancies on office, §120-12.1.
Secretary.
Assistance to state and local agencies, §143B-476, (b).
Center for missing persons, §§143B-497, 143B-498.
Head of department, §143B-476, (a).
National guard.
Tuition assistance, §§127A-190 to 127A-195.
Powers and duties, §143B-476, (a).
Emergencies and disasters, §143B-476, (c) to (g).
Report to legislative appropriations committees for review of proposed grant awards, §143B-476, (h).
Vacancies in office.
Report on long-term vacancies, §120-12.1.

CRIME VICTIMS.
Compensation, §§15B-1 to 15B-38.
See CRIME VICTIMS COMPENSATION.
DNA analysis, §§15A-266 to 15A-270.
See DNA DATABASE AND DATABANKS.
Financial recovery assistance act, §§15B-26 to 15B-38.
See CRIME VICTIMS FINANCIAL RECOVERY ASSISTANCE ACT.
Generally.
See VICTIMS OF CRIME.
Sexual offense victims assistance program, §§143B-480.1 to 143B-480.3.
See SEXUAL OFFENSES.

CRIME VICTIMS COMPENSATION, §§15B-1 to 15B-38.
Application for award.
Contents, §15B-7, (a).
False or fraudulent application, §15B-7, (b).
Filing, §15B-7, (a).
Procedure, §15B-8, (a).
Procedure.
Filing, §15B-8, (a).
Appropriations.
Compensation payable.
Available to extent that general assembly appropriates funds, §15B-25.
Attorney general.
Representation of state, §15B-5.

CRIME VICTIMS COMPENSATION —Cont'd
Availability of award.
Providing information to victim, §15B-20.
Award.
Claims exceeding $5,000 or involving future economic loss, §15B-10, (b).
Claims not exceeding $5,000 and not including future economic loss, §15B-10, (a).
Clerks of court.
Notice to, §15B-15.
Contested cases.
Claimants dissatisfied with decision, §15B-10, (d).
Economic loss.
Documentation establishing submitted to commission, §15B-10, (c).
Specific statements of loss.
Included in trial courts judgment.
Considered in making award, §15B-14, (c).
When compensation awarded, §15B-4.
Written statement of decision, §15B-10, (d).
Citation of chapter, §15B-1.
Clerks of court.
Notice.
Award made from crime victims compensation fund, §15B-15.
Commission.
Chairman, §15B-3, (d).
Compensation, §15B-3, (f).
Composition, §15B-3, (a).
Director, §15B-3, (g).
Established, §15B-3.
Powers, §15B-6, (a).
Quorum, §15B-3, (e).
Records.
Confidentiality, §15B-8.1, (b).
Reports.
Annual report, §15B-21.
Terms of office, §15B-3, (b).
Vacancies in office, §15B-3, (c).
Compensation payable.
Available to extent that general assembly appropriates funds, §15B-25.
Injury to or death of victim.
Maximum compensation payable, §15B-11, (g).
Work loss, replacement service loss or economic loss.
Maximum compensation per week, §15B-11, (f).
Construction and interpretation.
Right to receive compensation.
Act not construed to create, §15B-25.
Contested cases.
Commenced by claimants dissatisfied with decision, §15B-10, (d).
Evidence.
Exclusion of persons from hearings, §15B-12, (h).
Juvenile proceedings records, §15B-12, (g).
Law enforcement officers providing copies of information gathered in investigation, §15B-12, (d).
Medical or psychological reports, §15B-12, (e).
Mental or physical examination of claimants, §15B-12, (c).
Method of taking evidence, §15B-12, (a).
Official record open to public inspection, §15B-12, (i).
Privileges, §15B-12, (b).
Requesting evidence not admissible prohibited, §15B-12, (f).

CRIME VICTIMS COMPENSATION —Cont'd
Conviction of offender.
Effect, §15B-14, (a).
Crime victims financial recovery assistance act, §§15B-26 to 15B-38.
Definitions, §15B-2.
Denial of claim.
Contributory misconduct, §15B-11, (b).
Failure to cooperate with law enforcement agencies, §15B-11, (c).
Grounds, §15B-11, (a).
Reconsideration or reopening claim, §15B-11, (h).
Reimbursement from collateral sources, §15B-11, (d).
Director.
Powers, §15B-6, (b).
Disbursements, §15B-22.
Evidence.
Contested cases, §15B-12.
Execution.
Award not subject to, §15B-17, (b).
Fees.
Application for award.
Filing fee, §15B-7, (a).
Financial recovery assistance act.
See CRIME VICTIMS FINANCIAL RECOVERY ASSISTANCE ACT.
Fund.
Clerks of court.
Notified of awards made from, §15B-15.
Deposited with state treasurer, §15B-23.
Established, §15B-23.
Information provided to victims and dependents concerning existence, §15B-20.
Insufficient funds.
Payment delayed until sufficient funds available, §15B-22.
Investments by state treasurer, §15B-23.
Oversight of state auditor, §15B-23.
Surplus, §15B-23.
Hearings.
Contested cases.
Evidence, §15B-12.
Suspension.
Disposition of criminal prosecution, §15B-14, (b).
Investments.
Crime victims compensation fund.
Investments by state treasurer, §15B-23.
Notice.
Award made from crime victims compensation fund.
Clerks of court to be notified, §15B-15.
Payment.
Installments, §15B-16, (b).
Insufficient funds.
Delay until sufficient funds available, §15B-22.
Lump sum, §15B-16, (b).
Manner of payment, §15B-16, (a).
Negotiations with service providers.
Reduction of amount claimed by provider, §15B-16, (e).
Refunds, §15B-16, (d).
Privileges.
Applicability, §15B-8.1, (a).
Prosecution or conviction of offender.
Effect, §15B-14, (a).
Providing information to victims, §15B-20.
Publicity.
Information provided to victims and dependents of existence of crime victims compensation fund, §15B-20.

CRIME VICTIMS COMPENSATION —Cont'd
Reports.
Commission.
Annual report, §15B-21.
Restitution.
Requiring defendant to pay encouraged, §15B-24.
Right to receive compensation.
Act construed not to create, §15B-25.
Secured transactions.
Third parties.
Assignments.
Restrictions on assignments, §§25-9-406, (i), 25-9-408, (f).
Short title of chapter, §15B-1.
State auditor.
Crime victims compensation fund.
Oversight.
Responsibilities, §15B-23.
State treasurer.
Crime victims compensation fund.
Deposited with, §15B-23.
Investments by, §15B-23.
Subrogation.
Collateral sources, §15B-19.
State, §15B-18.
Taxation.
Exemption, §15B-17, (a).

CRIME VICTIMS FINANCIAL RECOVERY ASSISTANCE ACT, §§15B-26 to 15B-38.
Action to recover profits or funds, §15B-35, (a).
Commission, responsibilities of, §15B-35, (c).
Notice by eligible persons, §15B-35, (b).
Standing, §15B-35, (d).
Contract or agreement to pay an offender profit from crime or other funds.
Notice to commission, §15B-33, (a).
Notice to eligible persons, §15B-33, (b).
Conviction overturned or pardon issued, §15B-37.
Definitions, §15B-32.
Evasive action void, §15B-38.
Legislative intent, §15B-31.
Penalties.
Escrow account.
Establishment and notice, §15B-34, (d).
Satisfaction of judgment from, §15B-34, (e).
Unclaimed funds, return of, §15B-34, (f).
Failure to give notice, §15B-34, (a).
Failure to pay, §15B-34, (c).
Notice and opportunity to be heard required, §15B-34, (b).
Public policy, §15B-31.
Evasive action void, §15B-38.
Subrogation, §15B-36.

CRIMINAL CASE DOCKETING.
Superior courts, §7A-49.4.

CRIMINAL CONTEMPT, §§5A-11 to 5A-17.
See CONTEMPT.

CRIMINAL CONVERSATION.
Costs.
Allowance of costs to defendant, §6-19.
Allowance of costs to plaintiff, §6-18.
Limitation of actions, §1-52.
Parties as witnesses, §8-50, (a).

CRIMINAL HISTORY RECORD CHECKS, §§114-19.1 to 114-19.15.
Abuse, neglect or dependency of juvenile reports.
When juvenile removed from home.
Check of alleged abuser or abusers, §§7B-302, 7B-503, (b).

CRIMINAL HISTORY RECORD CHECKS
—Cont'd
Adoption.
Adoptive parents seeking to adopt minor in custody of county department of social services, §114-19.7.
Mandatory preplacement criminal checks, §48-3-309.
Agency placements.
Investigation required, §48-3-203, (d1).
Definition of "criminal history," §48-1-101.
Preplacement assessments, §48-3-303, (d).
Minor in custody or placement responsibility of county department of social services.
Mandatory preplacement criminal checks of prospective adoptive parents, §48-3-309.
Adult care home providers and employees, §§114-19.3, 114-19.10, 131D-40.
Adult care homes, §114-19.10.
Adult care homes employees, §131D-40.
Alarm systems licensing.
Persons applying for license, §74D-2, (c).
Area mental health, developmental disabilities, and substance abuse services authorities, §114-19.10.
Attorneys at law.
Applicants for admission to practice, §84-24.
Auctions and auctioneers.
Applicants for auctioneer, apprentice auctioneer or auction firm license, §114-19.8.
License applicants, §85B-3.2.
Charter schools, §115C-238.29K.
Child care providers, §114-19.5.
Mandatory checks, §110-90.2.
Compacts.
National crime prevention and privacy compact, §114-19.50.
Concealed handgun permit.
Fees, §14-415.19, (a).
Procedure for issuance of permit, §14-415.15, (a).
Dental hygienists.
Criminal records checks for license applicants, §90-224, (c).
Dentists.
Criminal records checks for license applicants, §90-30, (b).
Department of health and human services employees and applicants for employment, §114-19.6.
Department of juvenile justice and delinquency prevention employees and applicants for employment, §114-19.6.
Division of criminal statistics, §§114-10, 114-10.01.
Drug detection dog handlers, §90-102.1, (d).
Fees.
Conducted for purposes other than administration of criminal justice, §114-19.1, (a).
Fire departments, applicants, §114-19.12.
Foster parents, §§114-19.4, 131D-10.3A, (a) to (i).
Funeral service.
Criminal records checks for license applicants, §90-210.25, (a).
General assembly appointees, §§114-15, (a), 120-19.4, (a).
Home care agencies, §114-19.10.
Applicants for employment, §131E-265.
Insurance company incorporators and key persons, §58-7-37.
Interpreters and transliterators.
Criminal records checks for license applicants, §90D-7, (c).

CRIMINAL HISTORY RECORD CHECKS
—Cont'd
Locksmith licensing, §§74F-18, 114-19.15.
Requesting department of justice to conduct on applicants.
Power of board, §74F-6.
Manufactured home manufacturer, dealer, salesperson or set-up contractor.
Applicants for licensure as, §§114-19.13, 143-143.10A.
McGruff house program volunteers, §114-19.9.
Mental health, developmental disability, substance abuse.
Area authorities, §§114-19.3, 114-19.10, 122C-80.
Mortgage bankers and brokers, §53-243.16.
Authority of commissioner to require, §53-243.12, (l).
License application to contain consent to, §53-243.05, (a).
Licensee to furnish consent to, §53-243.06, (b1).
Municipal officers and employees, §160A-164.2.
Contents of application, §114-19.14.
National crime prevention and privacy compact, §114-19.50.
Nurses.
Registration as registered or licensed practical nurse, §114-19.11.
Nursing homes, §114-19.10.
Applicants for employment, §131E-265.
Pharmacists and pharmacies.
Criminal records checks for license applicants, §90-85.15, (c).
Physicians and surgeons.
Criminal records checks for license applicants, §90-11, (b).
Police information network, §114-10.1.
Precious metals dealers.
Applicants for permits.
Department of justice may provide law enforcement agency, §66-165, (c).
Priority in processing, §114-19.1, (c).
Private personnel services.
Criminal records checks for license applicants, §95-47.2, (d).
Private protective services.
Persons applying for license, §74C-8, (c).
Professional employer organizations.
Criminal history of license applicant furnished department upon request, §58-89A-60, (d).
Providers of treatment for or services to children, the elderly, mental health patients, the sick and the disabled.
Adoption.
Prospective adoptive parent, §114-19.3, (d).
Consent, §114-19.3, (b).
Fees, §114-19.3, (e).
Foster care.
Prospective foster care parent, §114-19.3, (d).
Generally, §114-19.3, (a).
Public utility employees, screening employment applications, §62-333.
Real estate appraisers and registered trainees, §93E-1-6, (c), (d).
Real estate brokers and salespersons.
Criminal records checks for license applicants, §93A-4, (b1).
Residential school personnel, §143B-146.16.
Respiratory care practitioners.
Applicants for license, §90-652, (a).
Rights to receive records of bureau.
Not enlarged, §114-19.1, (d).

CRIMINAL HISTORY RECORD CHECKS —Cont'd
School employees, §§114-19.2, 115C-332.
Charter schools, §115C-238.29K.
Residential schools, §143B-146.16.
Structural pest control.
Licenses, §106-65.26, (d), (e).
Volunteer fire departments, §114-19.12.

CRIMINAL INDEX RECORDS IN SUPERIOR COURTS.
Certified copies, admissibility, §8-35.2.

CRIMINAL INTELLIGENCE INFORMATION.
Withholding from public disclosure, §132-1.4, (d).
Defined, §132-1.4, (b).

CRIMINAL INVESTIGATION RECORDS.
Child abuse investigation records.
Law governing, §132-1.4, (l).
Complaining witness.
Temporarily withholding name or address by law enforcement, §132-1.4, (d).
Court records considered public record, §132-1.4, (k).
Definitions, §132-1.4, (b).
Deletion of information not public record.
Law enforcement to make clear deletion made, §132-1.4, (j).
Disclosure of records transmitted to prosecuting attorney.
Law governing, §132-1.4, (g).
Information considered public records, §132-1.4, (c).
Information not required to be disclosed, §132-1.4, (h).
911 or other communications.
Time required to maintain tape recordings, §132-1.4, (i).
Not public record, §132-1.4, (a).
Order of court preventing disclosure of information.
Law enforcement agency seeking, §132-1.4, (e).
Release by order of court, §132-1.4, (a).
Use of public record in custody of another public agency, §132-1.4, (f).

CRIMINAL JUSTICE EDUCATION AND TRAINING STANDARDS COMMISSION, §§17C-1 to 17C-13.
Ad hoc members.
Appointment, §17C-4, (b).
Appeals.
Denial, suspension or revocation of certification, §17C-11, (b).
Attorney general.
Chairman.
Designation, §17C-5, (a).
Custody of books, papers and other property, §17C-7, (b).
Staff assistance.
Attorney general to provide, §17C-7, (a).
Certification denied, suspended or revoked.
Appeal, §17C-11, (b).
Certification procedure.
Officers, §17C-10.
Powers of commission, §17C-6, (a).
Chairman.
Appointment, §17C-5, (a).
Compensation of members, §17C-4, (a).
Composition, §17C-3, (a).

CRIMINAL JUSTICE EDUCATION AND TRAINING STANDARDS COMMISSION —Cont'd
Concealed handgun permit.
Approved courses for firearms safety, §14-415.12, (a).
Certificate of completion of firearms safety course, §14-415.13, (a).
Filing of course description by instructor, §14-415.12, (a).
Contracts.
Power to enter into contracts, §17C-6, (a).
Criminal justice agencies.
Defined, §17C-2.
Criminal justice officers.
Defined, §17C-2.
Standards for, §17C-10, (b), (c).
Certificates evidencing satisfaction of requirements, §17C-10, (d).
Definitions, §17C-2.
Effect of standards, §17C-10, (a).
Electronic speed measuring device.
Minimum standards, §17C-6, (a).
Entry level.
Defined, §17C-2.
Standards for appointment at entry level, §17C-10, (b).
Established, §17C-3, (a).
Expenses of members, §17C-4, (a).
Grants.
Acceptance, §17C-12, (a).
Reimbursement by commission of political subdivisions, §17C-12, (b), (d).
Injunctions to prevent violations, §17C-11, (c).
Law enforcement officers.
Certification, §17C-10.
Legislative findings, §17C-1.
Meetings, §17C-5, (c).
Noncompliance by criminal justice officer.
Exercise of powers prohibited, enforcement, §17C-11, (a).
Injunctions against performing functions, §17C-11, (c).
Number of members, §17C-3, (a).
Officers.
Certification, §17C-10.
Pardons.
Denial, suspension or revocation of certification.
Persons granted an unconditional pardon.
Prohibited, §17C-13.
Policy of state, §17C-1.
Political subdivisions.
Reimbursement of funds, §17C-12.
Powers.
Advisory powers, §17C-6, (b).
Enforceable powers, §17C-6, (a).
Generally, §17C-6, (a).
Qualifications of members, §17C-3, (a).
Radar.
Establishing minimum standards, §17C-6, (a).
Recommendations.
Advisory powers, §17C-6, (b).
Records.
Personnel files.
Disclosure requirements, §17C-7, (c).
Reports, §17C-5, (d).
Advisory powers, §17C-6, (b).
Grant, §17C-12, (a).
Research.
Advisory powers, §17C-6, (b).

CRIMINAL JUSTICE EDUCATION AND TRAINING STANDARDS COMMISSION —Cont'd
Rules and regulations, §17C-6, (a).
Duration, §17C-6, (c).
Grant program, §17C-12, (c).
Powers enforceable through rules and regulations, §17C-6, (a).
Relation to federal standards, §17C-6, (d).
Speed-measuring instruments, §17C-6, (a).
Staff assistance.
Attorney general to provide, §17C-7, (a).
System.
Establishment of system, §17C-8.
Terms of members, §17C-3, (b).
Vice-chairman.
Selection, §17C-5, (b).

CRIMINAL JUSTICE INFORMATION NETWORK GOVERNING BOARD, §§143-660 to 143-664.
Appropriations, use, §143-663, (b).
Conflicts of interest, §143-661, (c).
Creation, §143-661, (a).
Definitions, §143-660.
Duties, §143-663, (a).
Expenses of members, §143-662.
Grants, use, §143-663, (b).
Meetings, §143-664, (a).
Members, §143-661, (b).
Officers, §143-664, (a).
Powers, §143-663, (a).
Staff, §143-664, (b).

CRIMINAL JUSTICE PARTNERSHIP ACT, §§143B-273 to 143B-273.19.
See STATE-COUNTY CRIMINAL JUSTICE PARTNERSHIP.

CRIMINAL JUSTICE STANDARDS DIVISION, §17C-9.

CRIMINAL LAW AND PROCEDURE.
Abduction, §§14-39 to 14-41.
Abortion.
General provisions, §§14-44 to 14-46.
See ABORTION.
Obstructing abortion clinics, §14-277.4, (c).
Parental consent to abortion violation, §90-21.10.
Abuse of children, §§14-318.2, 14-318.4.
Abuse of disabled or elder adults, §14-32.3, (a).
Abuse of patients.
Unlawful to physically abuse patient, §14-32.2, (a).
Criminal process, issuance, request of attorney general, §14-32.2, (g).
Defenses, §14-32.2, (f).
Definitions, §14-32.2, (c) to (e1).
Provisions not to supersede other offenses, §14-32.2, (h).
Punishment, §14-32.2, (b).
Accomplices and accessories, §§14-5.2, 14-7.
Acid or alkali, malicious throwing, §14-30.1.
Acting as officer before qualifying, §14-229.
Actions.
Damages arising out of a criminal act.
Civil actions seeking to recover.
Statutes of limitation and repose, §1-15.1.
Address confidentiality program, §§15C-1 to 15C-13.
See ADDRESS CONFIDENTIALITY PROGRAM.
Administration department.
Bribery.
Purchases and contracts to department.
Acceptance of bribes, §143-63.

CRIMINAL LAW AND PROCEDURE —Cont'd
Adoption.
Prohibited placement activities, §48-10-101.
Unauthorized disclosure of identifying information, §48-10-105.
Unlawful payments related to adoption, §48-10-102.
Adult care homes.
Criminal history record checks of employees.
Furnishing false information, §131D-40, (e).
Adult day care programs.
Harming or willfully neglecting person under care, §131D-6, (c1).
Adulterated or misbranded food, drugs or cosmetics.
Intent to cause serious injury or death, §14-34.4, (a).
Intent to extort, §14-34.4, (b).
Adultery, §14-184.
Adult establishments, §§14-202.10 to 14-202.12.
See ADULT ESTABLISHMENTS.
Adult protection.
Abuse of disabled or elder adults, §14-32.3, (a).
Exploitation of disabled or elder adult, §14-32.3, (c).
Neglect of disabled or elder adult, §14-32.3, (b).
Advertisements.
Defacing or destroying, §14-385.
Injuring advertisements, §14-384.
Affidavits.
Motion for appropriate relief.
Supporting affidavits, §15A-1420, (b).
Motion to suppress evidence.
Pretrial motion in superior court.
Affidavit supporting motion, §15A-977, (a).
Affrays.
Aggravated affrays.
Habitual misdemeanor assault, §14-33.2.
Punishment for misdemeanor affrays, §14-33, (b), (c).
Factors determining classification of offense, §14-33, (b), (c).
Self-defense.
Evidence of former threats upon plea of self-defense, §14-33.1.
Simple affray.
Punishment for misdemeanor affrays, §14-33, (a).
Air bags.
Unlawful installation or reinstallation, §20-136.2.
Albemarle Sound.
Lumbermen failing to remove obstructions, §76-42.
Alcoholic beverages.
County alcoholic beverage control act.
Defense of employees and officers in civil or criminal actions, §160A-167.
Forfeitures.
Disposition after trial, §18B-504, (e).
Owner unavailable for criminal trial, §18B-504, (i).
Return of property when no charge is made, §18B-504, (j).
Seizure of property, §18B-504, (c).
Imports and exports.
Unauthorized imports and exports, §18B-102, (b).
Interference with inspections, §18B-502, (b).
Law enforcement agents.
Subject-matter jurisdiction, §18B-500, (b).

CRIMINAL LAW AND PROCEDURE —Cont'd
Alcoholic beverages —Cont'd
Local ABC boards.
Embezzlement or malfeasance by members or employees, §18B-702, (f).
Local ABC officers.
Subject-matter jurisdiction, §18B-501, (b).
Territorial jurisdiction, §18B-501, (c).
Manufacturers.
Unauthorized manufacture, §18B-102, (b).
Second unlawful manufacturing offense, §18B-307, (c).
Minors.
Aiding and abetting sale to and purchase by underage persons, §18B-302, (c).
Fines and other penalties, §18B-302.1, (b), (c).
Purchase or possession, §18B-302, (b), (i).
Open container law, §20-138.7, (e).
Unlawful transportation, §18B-401, (a).
Poisonous beverages, trafficking in, transporting or possessing, §14-329.
Possession.
Unlawful possession, §18B-102, (b).
Sales.
Unauthorized sales, §18B-102, (b).
Searches and seizures.
Disposition after trial of seized alcoholic beverages, §18B-503, (c).
Holding seized alcoholic beverages for administrative hearings, §18B-503, (d).
Sale proceeds from disposition of seized alcoholic beverages, §18B-503, (f).
Transportation.
Open container violations, §18B-401, (a).
Unauthorized transportation, §18B-102, (b).
Alcoholic beverages tax.
Violations as misdemeanors, §105-113.73.
Alligator propagation and production.
Untagged or undocumented alligator possessed by operator of facility, §106-763.1, (c).
Alternative fuel, §105-449.139, (b).
Ambulances.
Making false ambulance request, §14-286.1.
Ambulatory surgical facility licensure.
Unlicensed operation, §131E-151.
American Legion emblem, §14-395.
Amusement device safety.
Death resulting from violation, §95-111.13, (i).
Analingus.
Sexual offenses generally.
See SEXUAL OFFENSES.
Animal auctions.
Public auctions.
Unlicensed operation, §19A-33.
Animal baiting, §14-362.1.
Dog baiting, §14-362.2.
Animal cruelty investigators.
Interference in performance of official duties, §19A-48.
Animal dealers.
Acting without license, §19A-34.
Cruelty to animals, §19A-35.
Animal fighting, §14-362.1.
Cockfighting, §14-362.
Dog fighting, §14-362.2.
Animal shelters.
Cruelty to animals, §19A-35.
Antifreeze solutions compounded with organic salts or petroleum distillates.
Manufacture or sale, §66-66.

CRIMINAL LAW AND PROCEDURE —Cont'd
Appeals.
Appellate division.
Certiorari, §15A-1444, (e), (g).
Correction of errors, §§15A-1441 to 15A-1453.
Burden of proof.
Prejudicial error, §15A-1443, (a).
Capital punishment.
Automatic review of judgment and sentence, §15A-2000, (d).
Direct appeal to supreme court.
Death sentences included in superior court judgments, §7A-27, (a).
New trial.
Notice of new trial, §15-193.
Prisoner taken to place of trial when new trial granted, §15-195.
Notice of appeals, §15-189.
Notice of reprieve or new trial, §15-193.
Certiorari, §15A-1444, (e), (g).
Correction of errors by appellate division, §15A-1448, (c).
Content of notice of appeal, App. Proc. Rule 4, (b).
Correction of errors by appellate division, §§15A-1441 to 15A-1453.
Affirmance of sentence, §15A-1447, (e).
Duties of clerk of superior court upon, §15A-1452, (b).
Ancillary actions during appeal, §15A-1453.
Authorized, §15A-1441.
Bail and recognizance.
Authority of court to act pending appeal, §15A-1453, (a).
Capital cases, §15A-1441.
Certiorari, §15A-1448, (c).
Compliance with directive of appellate court.
Duties of clerk of superior court, §15A-1452.
Double jeopardy.
When charges must be dismissed with prejudice, §15A-1447, (g).
Grounds, §15A-1442.
Jurisdiction, §15A-1448, (a).
Lack of jurisdiction on part of trial court.
Errors which may be reviewed even though no objection, exception or motion made, §15A-1446, (d).
Motion for appropriate relief, §15A-1453, (b).
New trial.
Duties of clerk of superior court upon order of new trial, §15A-1452, (c).
Relief available upon appeal, §15A-1447, (a).
Notice of appeal, §15A-1448, (b).
Time for, §15A-1448, (a).
Prejudice to defendant.
Burden of showing prejudice, §15A-1443, (a).
Grounds for correction of errors generally, §15A-1442.
No prejudice by granting of relief which defendant has sought, §15A-1443, (c).
When prejudice exists, §15A-1443, (a), (b).
Preservation of right to appeal, §15A-1446, (a).
Errors subject to review even though no objection, exception or motion made, §15A-1446, (d).
Waiver of right to assert error upon appeal.
Failure to make appropriate and timely motion or objection, §15A-1446, (b).
Procedures, §15A-1444, (d).
Relief available upon appeal, §15A-1447.
Reversal.
Relief available upon appeal, §15A-1447, (b), (c).

CRIMINAL LAW AND PROCEDURE —Cont'd
Appeals —Cont'd
Correction of errors by appellate division —Cont'd
Security for costs not required, §15A-1449.
Sentencing.
Relief available upon appeal, §15A-1447, (d), (f).
State may appeal, §15A-1445, (a).
Order granting motion to suppress, §15A-1445, (b).
Stays, §15A-1451, (a).
No stay when state appeals, §15A-1451, (b).
Time for entry of appeal, §15A-1448, (a).
Waiver of right to assert error upon appeal.
Failure to make appropriate and timely motion or objections, §15A-1446, (b).
Withdrawal of appeal, §15A-1450.
Order to be entered by clerk of superior court, §15A-1452, (a).
Right to appeal not waived, §15A-1448, (a).
Cost on appeal, §6-33.
Definitions, §15A-101.
Prejudicial error, §15A-1443, (a).
District courts, §7A-290.
Appeal by defendant from, §15A-1431, (b).
Compliance with judgment no bar, §15A-1431, (d).
Notice of appeal, §15A-1431, (c).
Appeal after compliance with judgment, §15A-1431, (d).
Pretrial release.
Order remains in effect pending appeal, §15A-1431, (e).
Procedure, §15A-1444, (c).
Stays, §15A-1431, (f).
Withdrawal of appeal, §15A-1431, (c), (g).
Appeal by state from, §15A-1432, (a).
Affirmance of judgment of district court, §15A-1432, (e).
Hearing on motion, §15A-1432, (c).
Motion, §15A-1432, (b).
Remand to district court for further proceedings, §15A-1432, (d).
Bail bond status, §7A-290.
Notice of appeal, §7A-290.
Appeal by defendant from district court, §15A-1431, (c), (d).
How and when taken, App. Proc. Rule 4.
Jurisdiction.
Correction of errors by appellate division.
Lack of jurisdiction on part of trial court.
Errors which may be reviewed even though no objection, motion or exception made, §15A-1446, (d).
Magistrates.
Appeal by defendant from, §15A-1431, (a).
Compliance with judgment no bar, §15A-1431, (d).
Notice of appeal, §15A-1431, (c).
Appeal after compliance with judgment, §15A-1431, (d).
Pretrial release.
Order remains in effect pending appeal, §15A-1431, (e).
Procedure, §15A-1444, (b).
Stays, §15A-1431, (f).
Withdrawal of appeal, §15A-1431, (c), (g).
Cost on appeal, §6-33.
Manner of taking, App. Proc. Rule 4, (a).
Motion for appropriate relief.
Correction of errors by appellate division.
Ancillary actions during appeal, §15A-1453, (b).

CRIMINAL LAW AND PROCEDURE —Cont'd
Appeals —Cont'd
Motion for appropriate relief —Cont'd
Denial of motion.
No effect on right to assert error upon appeal, §15A-1422, (e).
Finality of decision, §15A-1422, (f).
Making of motion not prerequisite to asserting error on appeal, §15A-1422, (a).
Motion in appellate division, §15A-1418.
Motion may be made and acted on regardless of notice of appeal, §15A-1414, (c).
Ruling of court subject to review, §15A-1444, (f).
Ruling on motion, §15A-1422, (b) to (d).
Motion to suppress evidence.
Order denying motion, §15A-979, (b).
Order granting motion, §15A-979, (c).
Notice of appeal, App. Proc. Rule 4, (b), (c).
Petition for rehearing not entertained, App. Proc. Rule 31, (g).
Plea bargaining.
Noncompliance with provisions.
Limitation on collateral attack on conviction, §15A-1027.
Prejudicial error.
Burden of proof, §15A-1443, (a).
Constitutional violations, §15A-1443, (b).
Defined, §15A-1443, (a).
Preservation of right to appeal.
Post-trial motions.
Not prerequisite to assertion of error on appeal, §15A-1446, (c).
Prosecutorial appeal, §15A-1445.
District courts.
Appeal by state from, §15A-1432.
Record on appeal, App. Proc. Rule 9, (b).
Relief from errors, §15A-1401.
Restitution to victims of crime.
Effect of appeal of conviction upon which order based, §15A-1340.38, (d).
Right of appeal, §15A-1444, (a).
Service of notice of appeal, App. Proc. Rule 4, (c).
State of North Carolina.
Correction of errors by appellate division.
Appeal by state, §15A-1445, (a).
Order granting motion to suppress, §15A-1445, (b).
Stays.
No stay when state appeals, §15A-1451, (b).
District courts.
Appeal by state from, §15A-1432.
Stays.
Correction of errors by appellate division, §15A-1451, (a).
No stay when state appeals, §15A-1451, (b).
Sufficiency of evidence.
Reviewable on appeal regardless of whether motion made during trial, §15A-1227, (d).
Time for taking appeal, App. Proc. Rule 4, (a).
To which appellate court addressed, App. Proc. Rule 4, (d).
Trial de novo, Const. N. C., art. IV, §12.
Appearances.
Bail and recognizance.
Failure to appear, §15A-543.
Closed-circuit television.
First appearance before district court judge, §15A-601.
Failure to appear.
Dismissal with leave when defendant fails to appear and cannot readily be found, §15A-932.

CRIMINAL LAW AND PROCEDURE —Cont'd
Appearances —Cont'd
Failure to appear —Cont'd
Penalties, §15A-543.
First appearance before district court judge.
Attorneys at law.
Determination whether defendant has retained or been assigned counsel.
Duty of judge, §15A-603, (a).
Indigent persons, §15A-603.
Probable cause hearing.
Defendant to be informed of right to counsel at probable cause hearing, §15A-606, (e).
Right to counsel.
Defendant to be informed by judge, §15A-603, (b), (d).
Waiver of representation by counsel, §15A-603, (e).
Charges.
Defendant to be informed of charges against him, §15A-605.
Sufficiency.
Determination, §15A-604, (a), (b).
Clerk of court.
When clerk may conduct appearance, §15A-601, (e).
Closed-circuit television, §15A-601.
Consolidation of proceedings, §15A-601, (b).
Continuance, §15A-601, (d).
Charges found to be insufficient, §15A-604, (b).
Generally, §15A-601, (a).
Information to be given defendant, §§15A-602, 15A-603, 15A-605.
Probable cause hearing, §15A-606.
Required, §15A-601, (a).
Self-incrimination.
Warning of right against self-incrimination, §15A-602.
Sufficiency of charge.
Determination, §15A-604, (a), (b).
Time for, §15A-601, (c).
Waiver not allowed, §15A-601, (d).
Infractions.
Appearance bonds, §15A-1113, (c).
Failure to appear to answer charge.
No order for arrest, §15A-1116, (b).
Initial appearance before magistrate, §15A-511.
Organizations.
Appearance by counsel or agent, §15A-773, (b).
Self-incrimination.
First appearance before district court judge.
Warning of right against self-incrimination, §15A-602.
Two-way audio and video transmissions, §15A-601, (a1), (a2).
Waiver.
Defendant may execute written waiver and plead not guilty, §15A-1011, (d), (e).
Apples.
Selling immature apples, §105-189.2, (b).
Appointment of counsel for indigent persons.
Generally, §§7A-450 to 7A-458.
See INDIGENT DEFENSE SERVICES.
Indigent defense services act, §§7A-498 to 7A-498.8.
See INDIGENT DEFENSE SERVICES.
Indigent services rules, Rules 1.1 to 3.7.
See INDIGENT DEFENSE SERVICES.

CRIMINAL LAW AND PROCEDURE —Cont'd
Aquatic weed control.
Violations as misdemeanors, §113A-226, (a).
Armed robbery, §14-87, (a).
Arraignment.
Attorneys at law.
Right to counsel, §15A-942.
Closed circuit television, §15A-941.
Generally, §15A-941.
Order of proceedings in jury trial, §15A-1221, (a).
Superior court.
Not guilty plea.
Effect, §15A-943, (b).
Optional calendaring, §15A-944.
Required calendaring, §15A-943, (a), (c).
Two-way audio and video transmissions, §15A-941, (b), (c).
Waiver, §15A-945.
Written request, §15A-941, (d).
Right to counsel, §15A-942.
Arrest.
Civil cases.
See ARREST IN CIVIL CASES.
General provisions.
See ARREST.
Arson, §§14-58 to 14-69.2.
See ARSON.
Assault and battery.
See ASSAULT AND BATTERY.
Assignments for benefit of creditors.
False swearing as to verified claims filed with clerk, §23-9.
Trustees violating duty, §23-12.
Assisted living administrators.
Practicing without certificate, §90-288.20.
Athlete agents, §78C-99.
Athletic contests.
Alcoholic beverages.
Publicly displaying fortified wine, spirituous liquor or mixed beverages at athletic contests, §18B-301, (f).
Bonuses.
Not forbidden, §14-379.
Bribery.
Acceptance of bribes by players, managers, etc., §14-374.
Completion of offenses, §14-375.
Completion of offenses, §14-375.
Definition of bribe, §14-376.
Elements of offense of bribery of players, managers, etc., §14-373.
Intentionally losing contests, §14-377.
Limiting margin of victory or defeat, §14-377.
Throwing, dropping, etc., objects at sporting events.
Offenses against the public safety, §14-281.1.
Venue.
Protection of athletic contests.
Proper venue of prosecutions under article, §14-378.
Atomic energy, radioactivity and ionizing radiation.
Disclosure of confidential information, §104E-29, (c).
Radiation protection violations, §104E-23, (a).
Attempts to commit crime.
Arson.
Burning or attempting to burn buildings not covered by other provisions, §14-67.1.
Bribery of horse show judges or officials, §14-380.2.

CRIMINAL LAW AND PROCEDURE —Cont'd
Attempts to commit crime —Cont'd
Controlled substances, §90-98.
Discharging certain barreled weapons or a firearm into occupied property, §14-34.1.
Explosives.
Malicious use of explosive or incendiary.
Property occupied by persons, §14-49.1.
Lesser included offenses.
Conviction for attempt, §15-170.
Robbery.
Common law robbery.
Punishment for attempted common law robbery, §14-87.1.
Firearms or other dangerous weapons.
Use of firearms or weapons in robbery, §14-87, (a).
Attorneys at law.
Abiding by client's decision, Prof. Cond. Rule 1.2.
Appearance.
Recordation.
Requirement that clerk record entry, §15A-142.
When entry of attorney in criminal proceeding occurs, §15A-141.
Appointment of counsel.
Indigent defendants in certain criminal cases.
See INDIGENT DEFENSE SERVICES.
Arraignment.
Right to counsel, §15A-942.
Conference between attorney and prisoner, secret listening, §§14-227.1, 14-227.3.
Contingent fees, charging prohibited, Prof. Cond. Rule 1.5.
Counsel for accused, Const. U. S., amd. VI.
Defendant representing himself.
Standby counsel, §15A-1243.
Entry of attorney in criminal proceeding.
General entry.
Attorney making general entry obligated to represent defendant at all subsequent stages, §15A-143.
Recordation.
Requirement that clerk record entry, §15A-142.
When entry of attorney occurs, §15A-141.
Meritorious claims and contentions, Prof Cond. Rule 3.1.
Motion for appropriate relief.
Appointment of counsel for indigent defendant, §15A-1421.
Pleas.
Aid of counsel, §15A-1012, (a).
Probable cause hearings.
Defendant to be advised of right to counsel, §15A-606, (e).
Determination whether right to counsel waived, §15A-611, (c).
Representation of state and defendant, §15A-611, (a).
Prosecutors, special responsibilities, Prof. Cond. Rule 3.8.
Right to counsel, §15-4; Const. N. C., art. I, §23; Const. U. S., amd. VI.
Arraignment, §15A-942.
Withdrawal of attorney with permission of court, §15A-144.
Attorneys specializing in criminal law.
Certification standards, Bar Rules & Regs., D, §§.2501 to .2507.

CRIMINAL LAW AND PROCEDURE —Cont'd
Bad checks.
Collection, program for.
Established in certain counties, §14-107.2.
Construing word "credit," §14-107, (c).
Credit defined, §14-107, (c).
Definitions.
Credit, §14-107, (c).
Drawing, making, uttering or issuing and delivering, unlawful, §14-107, (a).
Soliciting or aiding and abetting, §14-107, (b).
Identified check passer, §14-107.1, (d).
Obtaining property in return for worthless check, draft or order, §14-106.
Prima facie evidence in worthless check cases, §14-107.1.
Affidavit of employee of bank or depository, §14-107.1, (f).
Applicability of provisions, §14-107.1, (b), (c).
Definitions, §14-107.1, (a).
Dishonor of check or draft, §14-107.1, (e).
Identifying check passer, §14-107.1, (d).
Processing fees, payment, judge may order, §14-107, (e).
Punishment for worthless checks, §14-107, (d).
Restitution, judge may order, §14-107, (e).
Services charges, payment, judge may order, §14-107, (e).
Bail and recognizance.
See BAIL AND RECOGNIZANCE.
Bailments.
Embezzlement.
Receipt of property by bailee by virtue of office or employment, §14-90.
Hired property.
Conversion.
Bailees, lessees, tenants or attorneys in fact, §14-168.1.
Evidence of intent to convert property.
Prima facie evidence of intent, §14-168.3.
Definitions, §14-168.2.
Failure to return hired property, §14-167.
Hiring with intent to defraud, §14-168.
Malicious or willful injury to hired personal property, §14-165.
Protection of bailor against acts of bailee.
Violations made misdemeanors, §14-169.
Subletting hired property, §14-166.
Options to purchase.
Failing to return rented property on which there is purchase option, §14-168.4.
Subletting of hired property, §14-166.
Hiring with intent to defraud, §14-168.
Ballistic knives.
Possession and sale, §14-269.6, (a), (b).
Bankruptcy and insolvency.
Solicitation of claims of creditors in proceedings, §23-47.
Barrooms and billiard rooms, permitting minor to enter, §14-317.
Battleship commission.
Employees with interest, §143B-74.3.
Bawdy houses, §14-188.
Beacons.
Displaying false lights on seashore, §14-282.
Bicycles.
Child bicycle safety act violations, §20-171.9, (d).
Bids and bidding.
Public contracts, §§143-129, 143-129.1.
Bigamy, §14-183.

CRIMINAL LAW AND PROCEDURE —Cont'd
Billboards.
Streets and highways.
Obstructing view at entrance to building on public highway, §136-102.
Bill of particulars, §15A-925.
Bills of lading.
False bills.
Issuing false bills made felony, §21-42.
Violations of chapter made felony, §21-42.
Birth of child, concealing, §14-46.
Black bears.
Violation of protection provisions, §19A-13.
Blacklisting employees, §14-355.
Blood banks.
Supervision by licensed physician.
Violation of requirements, §90-220.12.
Blue Ridge Parkway.
Control of outdoor advertising.
Violations as misdemeanors, §113A-170.
Boating navigation rules violations, §75A-6.1, (c).
Body piercing.
Minors, without consent of parents, §14-400, (b).
Boilers.
Violations, §95-69.18.
Boll weevil eradication.
Violations of provisions, §106-65.78, (a), (b).
Bonds, surety.
Forfeitures.
When execution to issue, §1-305, (a).
Model payment and performance bonds.
Failure of official to require bond as misdemeanor, §44A-32.
Mortgage in lieu of bond.
Recognizance for appearance in criminal proceeding, §58-74-5.
Cancellation of mortgage in such proceedings, §58-74-10.
Security of costs or fine in criminal action, §58-74-5.
Cancellation of mortgage in such proceedings, §58-74-10.
Bottles and bottling.
Polluting bottles used for beverages.
Unlawful to pollute, §14-288.
Boxing, §143-658, (b).
Breaking and entering jail to injure prisoner, §14-221.
Breaking or entering, burglary.
Buildings, §14-54.
Capital punishment.
Aggravating circumstances.
Capital felony in commission of burglary, §15A-2000, (e).
Crimes punishable by death, Const. N. C., art. XI, §2.
Coin-operated machines.
Breaking into or forcibly opening, §14-56.1.
Damaging or destroying machine, §14-56.2.
Deadly force.
Use against an intruder, §14-51.1.
Dwelling houses.
Breaking out of dwelling house, §14-53.
Explosives.
Use of explosives in burglary, §14-57.
First degree burglary.
Defined, §14-51.
Punishment for burglary, §14-52.
Implements of housebreaking.
Preparation to commit burglary or other housebreakings, §14-55.

CRIMINAL LAW AND PROCEDURE —Cont'd
Breaking or entering, burglary —Cont'd
Murder during commission, §14-17.
Paper currency machines.
Breaking into machine, §14-56.3.
Preparation to commit burglary or other housebreakings, §14-55.
Railroad car, motor vehicle, aircraft, boat, etc., §14-56.
Retreat by occupant of home or residence.
Use of deadly force against an intruder, §14-51.1.
Second degree burglary.
Defined, §14-51.
Explosives used in burglary, §14-57.
Punishment for burglary, §14-52.
Sentencing.
Punishment for burglary, §14-52.
Slot machines.
Breaking into or forcibly opening, §14-56.1.
Breaking out of dwelling house, §14-53.
Bribery.
See BRIBERY.
Bridges.
Fastening vessels to bridges, §136-80.
Load limits for safe capacity.
Capacity violations, §136-72.
Budgets.
Diversion, use or expenditure of funds, §143-32, (b).
Noncompliance with article, §143-34.
Wrongful expenditures.
Prosecution, §143-32, (b).
Building code of state.
Representation of self as qualified code-enforcement official, §143-151.18.
Buoys, beacons and day marks.
Interfering with, §76-58.
Burden of proof.
Appeals.
Correction of errors by appellate division.
Prejudice to defendant.
Burden of showing prejudice, §15A-1443, (a).
Death penalty for mentally retarded defendants prohibited.
Defendant's burden, §15A-2005, (a), (c), (f).
Generally.
See BURDEN OF PROOF.
Securities regulation.
Exemptions, §78A-18, (b).
Bureau of investigation, §§114-12 to 114-20.1.
See BUREAU OF INVESTIGATION.
Burglary.
Breaking and entering into railroad car, motor vehicle, aircraft, boat, §14-56.
Breaking out of dwelling house, §14-53.
Capital punishment, §15A-2000, (e); Const. N. C., art. XI, §2.
Coin-operated machines generally.
Breaking into or forcibly opening, §14-56.1.
Damaging, §14-56.2.
Explosives used in burglary, §14-57.
First degree.
Defined, §14-51.
Punishment, §14-52.
Murder during, §14-17.
Paper currency machines, §14-56.3.
Possession of burglary tools, §14-55.
Punishment, §14-52.

CRIMINAL LAW AND PROCEDURE —Cont'd
Burglary —Cont'd
Second degree.
Defined, §14-51.
Punishment, §14-52.
Use of deadly force against intruders, §14-51.1.
Buying and selling offices, §14-228.
Calendar for criminal trial sessions.
Superior court, criminal case docketing, §7A-49.4.
Calendaring of actions for trial.
Calendaring by district attorney for administrative purposes, §15A-941, (e).
Capital punishment.
Generally.
See CAPITAL PUNISHMENT.
Mentally retarded defendants.
Death sentence prohibited, §15A-2005, (b).
Burden of proof on defendant, §15A-2005, (a), (c), (f).
Definitions, §15A-2005, (a).
Jury determination of aggravating or mitigating circumstance.
Consideration of evidence of retardation, §15A-2005, (g).
Legal defenses not precluded by pretrial determination, §15A-2005, (d).
Motion seeking appropriate relief.
Post conviction determination of mental retardation, §15A-2006.
Noncapital case, court declaration, §15A-2005, (c).
Other sentence not precluded, §15A-2005, (h).
Pretrial hearing to determine retardation, §15A-2005, (c).
Special issue submitted to jury.
Pretrial determination of retardation not found, §15A-2005, (e).
Carrying concealed weapons, §14-269.
Concealed handgun permit, §§14-415.10 to 14-415.24.
See CONCEALED HANDGUN PERMIT.
Castration, §§14-28, 14-29.
Cattle rustling, §14-81.
Cattle tick, §106-362.
Cave protection, §§14-159.20 to 14-159.23.
Definitions, §14-159.20.
Owners and agents.
Limitation of liability, §14-159.23.
Speleothems.
Defined, §14-159.20.
Sale.
Unlawful, §14-159.22.
Vandalism.
Prohibited acts, §14-159.21.
Certified public accountants.
Violations of provision, §93-13.
Change machines, burglary, §14-56.3.
Change of venue.
Motion, §15A-957.
Charitable solicitations by telephone, §14-401.12.
Check-cashing businesses, §53-287.
Checks, bad.
Collection, program for.
Established in certain counties, §14-107.2.
Construing word "credit," §14-107, (c).
Credit defined, §14-107, (c).
Definitions.
Credit, §14-107, (c).
Drawing, making, uttering or issuing and delivering, unlawful, §14-107, (a).
Soliciting or aiding and abetting, §14-107, (b).
Identified check passer, §14-107.1, (d).

CRIMINAL LAW AND PROCEDURE —Cont'd
Checks, bad —Cont'd
Obtaining property in return for worthless check, draft or order, §14-106.
Prima facie evidence in worthless check cases, §14-107.1.
Affidavit of employee of bank or depository, §14-107.1, (f).
Applicability of provisions, §14-107.1, (b), (c).
Definitions, §14-107.1, (a).
Dishonor of check or draft, §14-107.1, (e).
Identifying check passer, §14-107.1, (d).
Processing fees, payment, judge may order, §14-107, (e).
Punishment for worthless checks, §14-107, (d).
Restitution, judge may order, §14-107, (e).
Services charges, payment, judge may order, §14-107, (e).
Child abduction, §14-41, (a).
Child abuse, §§14-318.2, 14-318.4.
Child care facilities, §110-103.
Unauthorized administration of medicine, §110-102.1A, (c), (d).
Child custody orders.
Enforcement.
Criminal contempt, §50-13.3, (a).
Childhood vaccine-related injury compensation.
Diversion of certain vaccines, §130A-431.
Child placing agencies.
Unlicensed operation, §131D-10.7.
Children and minors.
Prosecution of juvenile as adult.
Commission of criminal offense after superior court conviction, §7B-1604, (b).
Commission of criminal offense on or after juvenile's sixteenth birthday, §7B-1604, (a).
Emancipated juveniles prosecuted as adult, §7B-1604, (a).
Transfer of jurisdiction of juvenile to superior court, §7B-2200.
Detention until transferred to department of correction, §7B-2204.
Fingerprinting juveniles, §7B-2201.
Pretrial release, §7B-2204.
Probable cause hearing, §7B-2202.
Transfer hearing, §7B-2203.
Children's health insurance program.
Fraud and misrepresentation, §108A-70.28.
Child support.
Enforcement of support.
Criminal contempt, §50-13.4, (f).
Failure to support, §14-322.
Chlamydia.
Testing for sexually transmitted infections, §15A-615, (a), (1).
Cigarettes and tobacco products.
Sale of certain packages of cigarettes, §14-401.18.
Sale or distribution to minors, §14-313.
Cigarette tax.
Violations as misdemeanors, §105-113.33.
Citation.
Contents, §15A-302, (c).
Criminal summons or warrant.
Citation no bar to, §15A-302, (f).
Defined, §15A-302, (a).
Dismissal by prosecutor, §15A-302, (e).
Form.
Preparation, §15A-302, (g).
Issuance, §15A-302, (b).
Service, §15A-302, (d).

CRIMINAL LAW AND PROCEDURE —Cont'd
Citation —Cont'd
Summons or warrant.
Citation no bar to, §15A-302, (f).
Civil rights restored to convicted persons, §§13-1 to 13-4.
Automatic restoration, §13-1.
Certificate or order of restoration.
Issuance and filing, §13-2.
Conditional pardon.
Endorsement of warrant, service and filing, §13-4.
Unconditional pardon.
Issuance, service and filing of warrant, §13-3.
Cleaning agents containing phosphorus.
Water and air resources.
Manufacturing, selling or distributing, §143-214.4, (f).
Clerks of court.
Superior court clerks.
Misapplying money received by virtue of office, §7A-112, (d).
Coal and petroleum suppliers.
Stocks of coals and petroleum fuel capacity.
Refusal to provide administration department, §143-345.14, (d).
Coastal area management.
Permits.
Violations as misdemeanors, §113A-126, (c).
Coast and shore lights.
Displaying false lights on seashore, §14-282.
Cockfighting, §14-362.
Coin-operated machines generally.
Burglary.
Breaking into or forcibly opening, §14-56.1.
Damaging or destroying machine, §14-56.2.
False pretenses and cheats.
Manufacture, sale or gift of devices for cheating slot machines, §14-109.
Obtaining property or services from machine by false coins or tokens, §14-108.
College curfews.
Violations, §116-213, (a).
College tuition.
Waiver for senior citizens.
Misrepresentation of eligibility, §115B-6.
Combinations and restraint of trade, §75-1.
Commercial bribery, §14-353.
Commercial drivers' licenses.
Driving while disqualified, §20-28, (d).
Commitments and preliminary examinations.
Generally, §15A-521, (a).
National guard.
Courts-martial, §127A-59.
Orders, §15A-521, (b).
Delivery, §15A-521, (c).
Modification, §15A-521, (b).
Receipt of prisoner, §15A-521, (c).
Witnesses, §15A-521, (d).
Commodities.
Violations of act, §78D-24, (a).
Referral for prosecution to attorney general or district attorney, §78D-24, (d).
Communications.
Magazines or periodicals.
Libelous matter communicated, §14-47.
Newspapers.
Libelous matter communicated to newspapers, §14-47.
Community corrections programs.
Sentencing services, §§7A-770 to 7A-777.
See SENTENCING SERVICES.

CRIMINAL LAW AND PROCEDURE —Cont'd
Compacts.
National crime prevention and privacy compact, §114-19.50.
Company police.
Violation of chapter, §74E-13.
Compensation to victims of crimes.
Financial recovery assistance act, §§15B-26 to 15B-38.
See CRIME VICTIMS FINANCIAL RECOVERY ASSISTANCE ACT.
Generally, §§15B-1 to 15B-38.
See CRIME VICTIMS COMPENSATION.
Computer related crimes, §§14-453 to 14-458.
Access.
Accessing or causing to be accessed.
Defined, §14-454, (c).
Defined, §14-453.
Felony offense of accessing computers, §14-454, (a).
Misdemeanor offense of accessing computers, §14-454, (b).
Computer trespass, §14-458.
Damaging computers and computer resources.
Application of provisions, §14-455, (b).
Unlawful acts, §14-455, (a), (a1).
Viruses.
Computer viruses, §14-454, (b).
Definitions, §14-453.
Denial of computer services to authorized user, §14-456, (a), (b).
Extortion, §14-457.
Solicitation of child by computer, §14-202.3, (c).
Concealed handgun permit, §§14-415.10 to 14-415.24.
See CONCEALED HANDGUN PERMIT.
Confidentiality.
Address confidentiality program, §§15C-1 to 15C-13.
See ADDRESS CONFIDENTIALITY PROGRAM.
Mental incapacity of defendant to proceed.
Reports to court, §15A-1002, (d).
Public officers and employees.
Misuse of confidential information, §14-234.1.
Consent searches, §§15A-222, 15A-223.
Defined, §15A-221, (b).
Contaminating food or drink to render one mentally incapacitated or physically helpless, §14-401.16.
Contempt.
Criminal contempt, §§5A-11 to 5A-17.
See CONTEMPT.
Continuances.
Superior or district court, §15A-952, (g).
Continuing care retirement communities.
Marketing by unlicensed providers, §58-64-5, (a).
Contributing to delinquency of minor, §14-316.1.
Controlled substances offenses.
Conditions of prescribed punishments and degree of offense, §90-95, (e).
Conspiracy to violate provision, §90-98.
Continuing criminal enterprise, §90-95.1, (a).
Counterfeit substance.
Prohibited acts, §90-95, (c).
Employing or intentionally using minor to commit drug law violations, §90-95.4, (a), (b).
Expunction of records, §90-96, (d) to (f).
Manufacture, §90-95, (b).
Enhanced sentencing in certain cases, §15A-1340.16D.

CRIMINAL LAW AND PROCEDURE —Cont'd
Controlled substances offenses —Cont'd
Participating in a drug violation by a minor, §90-95.7, (c).
Possession, §90-95, (d).
Precursor chemical.
Designation, §90-95, (d2).
Possession or distribution with intent to manufacture controlled substance or methamphetamine, §90-95, (d1), (d1a).
Prohibited acts generally, §90-108.
Promoting drug sales by a minor, §90-95.6, (c).
Sale, §90-95, (b).
Speedy disposition.
County appropriations for programs to protect the public, §153A-212.1.
Trafficking in, §90-95, (h).
Conspiracy, §90-95, (i).
Conversation.
Criminal conversation.
Allowance of costs, §§6-18, 6-19.
Conveyances.
Taxation.
Excise stamp tax.
Willful failure to pay as misdemeanor, §105-228.34.
Convict made goods.
Sale prohibited, §14-346, (a), (b).
Coram nobis.
Relief formerly available now available by motion for appropriate relief, §15A-1411, (c).
Corporations.
Defendants.
Appearance by counsel or agent, §15A-773, (b).
Securing attendance of organizations, §15A-773, (a).
Definition of "organization," §15A-773.
Nonprofit corporations.
Failure to answer interrogatories propounded by secretary.
Officers and directors, §55A-1-32, (b).
Cosmetic art, §88B-22, (f).
Costs.
Confession of judgment.
Bond given to secure fine and cost, §6-47.
Criminal actions in superior or district courts, §7A-304.
Defendant's liability in criminal actions.
Confession of judgment, §6-47.
Bond given to secure fine and cost, §6-47.
Nonpayment of costs.
Persons imprisoned for nonpayment released upon compliance with article, §23-24.
Prisoners.
Removal of trial from one county to another.
Liability of counties for cost, §6-40.
Trials.
Removal of trial from one county to another.
Liability of counties for cost, §6-40.
Counterfeiting.
Bills of lading, §21-42.
Coins.
Counterfeiting coin and uttering coin that is counterfeit, §14-13.
Issuing substitutes for money without authority, §14-15.
Possessing tools for counterfeiting, §14-14.
Receiving or passing unauthorized substitutes for money, §14-16.
Tools.
Possessing tools for counterfeiting, §14-14.

CRIMINAL LAW AND PROCEDURE —Cont'd
Counterfeiting —Cont'd
Trademarks.
Criminal use of counterfeit trademark, §80-11.1.
Deceptive or unfair trade practices, §80-12.
Infringement, §80-11.
Uttering.
Coin that is counterfeit, §14-13.
Counties.
Defense of employees and officers in criminal actions, §160A-167.
Inspection departments.
Certificates of compliance.
Violations as misdemeanor, §153A-363.
Defects in buildings.
Orders to take corrective action.
Failure to comply as misdemeanor, §153A-371.
Failure to perform duties as misdemeanor, §153A-356.
Notices.
Removing as misdemeanor, §153A-367.
Permits.
Violations as misdemeanors, §153A-357, (a).
Stop orders.
Violations as misdemeanor, §153A-361.
Public officers and employees.
Privacy of employee personnel records.
Violations, §153A-98, (f).
State-county criminal justice partnership, §§143B-273 to 143B-273.19.
See STATE-COUNTY CRIMINAL JUSTICE PARTNERSHIP.
Subdivisions.
Transferring lots in unapproved subdivisions, §153A-334.
Taxation.
Disclosure of certain information, §153A-148.1, (b).
Credit device fraud, §§14-113.1 to 14-113.7A.
Applicability of article, §14-113.7A.
Construction of article.
Article not construed as repealing section 14-100, §14-113.7.
Evidence.
Knowledge.
Use of credit device as prima facie evidence of knowledge, §14-113.3.
Notice of revocation.
Prima facie evidence of receipt of notice, §14-113.2.
Knowledge.
Use of credit devices as prima facie evidence of knowledge, §14-113.3.
Misdemeanors, §14-113.6, (a).
Multiple violations, felony, §14-113.6, (a).
Notice of revocation.
Definition of "notice," §14-113.2.
Prima facie evidence of receipt of notice, §14-113.2.
Use after notice, §14-113.1.
Repealing provision.
Article not construed as repealing section 14-100, §14-113.7.
Revocation.
Use after notice of revocation, §14-113.1.
Telecommunication services.
Avoiding or attempting to avoid payment, §14-113.4.
Concealment of existence, origin or destination of any telecommunication, §14-113.5.

CRIMINAL LAW AND PROCEDURE —Cont'd
Credit device fraud —Cont'd
Telecommunication services —Cont'd
Destination of telecommunication.
Concealment of destination, §14-113.5.
Existence of telecommunication.
Concealment of existence, §14-113.5.
Making, possessing or transferring device for theft of service, §14-113.5.
Origin of telecommunication.
Concealment of origin, §14-113.5.
Publication of information regarding schemes, devices, means or methods for theft, §14-113.5.
Venue of offenses, §14-113.6A, (b).
Theft of service.
Making, possessing or transferring device for theft, §14-113.5.
Publication of information regarding schemes, devices, means or methods for theft, §14-113.5.
Venue of offenses, §14-113.6A, (a).
Unauthorized use of another's credit device, §14-113.1.
Use of false or counterfeit credit device, §14-113.1.
Venue of offenses, §14-113.6A, (a), (b).
Violations made misdemeanor, §14-113.6, (a).
Credit repair service violations, §66-225, (f).
Credits on sentence, §§15-196.1 to 15-196.4.
Creeks, obstructing, §§77-12 to 77-14.
Cremation.
Violations of article, §90-210.54, (c).
Crime against nature, §14-177.
Crime victims compensation.
Financial recovery assistance act, §§15B-26 to 15B-38.
See CRIME VICTIMS FINANCIAL RECOVERY ASSISTANCE ACT.
Generally, §§15B-1 to 15B-38.
See CRIME VICTIMS COMPENSATION.
Criminal case docketing.
Superior courts, §7A-49.4.
Criminal contempt, §§5A-11 to 5A-17.
See CONTEMPT.
Criminal justice education and training standards.
See CRIMINAL JUSTICE EDUCATION AND TRAINING STANDARDS COMMISSION.
Criminologists.
State bureau of investigation.
Employment of criminologists, §114-16.
Crossbows.
Sale.
Dealer record violation, §14-408.
Cruel and unusual punishment, Const. U. S., amd. VIII.
Cruelty to animals.
Abandonment, §14-361.1.
Animal baiting, §14-362.1.
Dog baiting, §14-362.2.
Animal fights, §14-362.1.
Cockfighting, §14-362.
Dog fighting, §14-362.2.
Baby chicks.
Living baby chicks or other fowl under eight weeks of age.
Disposing of as pets or novelties forbidden, §14-363.1.
Cockfighting, §14-362.
Confiscation of cruelly treated animals, §14-363.2.
Construction and interpretation, §14-360.

CRIMINAL LAW AND PROCEDURE —Cont'd
Cruelty to animals —Cont'd
Conveying animals in cruel manner, §14-363.
Custody of confiscated animals, §14-363.2.
Definitions, §14-360, (c).
Dogs.
Restraining dogs in cruel manner, §14-362.3.
Exclusions, §14-360, (c).
Fowl.
Living baby chicks or other fowl under eight weeks of age.
Disposing of as pets or novelties forbidden, §14-363.1.
Instigating cruelty, §14-361.
Intentional cruelty, §14-360, (a).
Malicious cruelty, §14-360, (b).
Promoting cruelty, §14-361.
Rabbits.
Eight weeks of age or under rabbits.
Disposing of as pets or novelties forbidden, §14-363.1.
Currituck Sound, obstructing, §76-41.
Custodial interference.
Bail and recognizance, §15A-534.4.
Transporting child outside state intending to violate custody order, §14-320.1.
Cyberstalking, §14-196.3.
Dairy milk case or crate larceny, §14-72.4.
Damages.
Civil actions seeking to recover damages arising out of criminal act.
Statutes of limitation and repose, §1-15.1.
Dam safety, §143-215.36, (a).
Data processing, §§14-453 to 14-458.
Death.
Law-enforcement officers' death benefit act, §§143-166.1 to 143-166.7.
Death penalty.
General provisions.
See CAPITAL PUNISHMENT.
Debt adjusters.
Appointment of receiver for money and property employed, §14-425.
Definitions, §14-423.
Engaging, etc., in business of debt adjusting a misdemeanor, §14-424.
Persons not deemed debt adjusters, §14-426.
Practice of debt adjusting enjoined, §14-425.
Transactions not deemed debt adjustment, §14-426.
Defamation, §14-47.
Defendants.
Attendance.
Securing attendance of criminal defendants confined in institutions within state, §15A-711, (a) to (c).
Detainers, §15A-711, (d).
Civil commitment of defendants found not guilty by reason of insanity, §15A-1321.
DNA sample required for certain crimes, §15A-266.4.
Depositions, §8-74.
First appearance before district court judge, §§15A-601 to 15A-606.
Incapacity of defendant to proceed, §§15A-1001 to 15A-1009.
Insanity defense, §15A-959.
Joinder, §15A-926, (b).
Objection to joinder, §15A-927, (c).
Failure to prove grounds for joinder, §15A-927, (d).

CRIMINAL LAW AND PROCEDURE —Cont'd
Defendants —Cont'd
Physical restraint of defendant.
Maintenance of order in courtroom, §15A-1031.
Temporary restraint of mentally ill, §15A-1322.
Pleadings.
Each defendant to be charged with separate pleading, §15A-926, (b).
Pleas. See within this heading, "Pleas."
Prisons and prisoners.
Securing attendance of criminal defendants confined in institutions within state, §15A-711, (a) to (c).
Detainers, §15A-711, (d).
Probable cause hearings. See within this heading, "Hearings."
Removal of disruptive defendant.
Maintenance of order in courtroom, §15A-1032.
Representation of self at trial, §15A-1242.
Standby counsel, §15A-1243.
Restraint of defendant.
Maintenance of order in courtroom, §15A-1031.
Securing attendance.
Defendants confined in federal prisons, §15A-771, (a).
Certificate by superior court, §15A-771, (b).
Defendants who are outside United States.
Application by governor to secretary of state of United States, §15A-772, (b).
Application to governor, §15A-772, (a).
Extradition.
Applicability of provisions to, §15A-772, (c).
Organizations, §15A-773, (a).
Appearance by counsel or agent, §15A-773, (b).
Defined, §15A-773, (c).
Temporary restraint.
Mentally ill defendants, §15A-1322.
Defendant's rights.
First appearance before district court judge, §15A-601.
Indigent persons, §15A-603.
Information to be given defendant, §15A-605.
Right to counsel, §15A-603.
Warning against self-incrimination, §15A-602.
Defense of home or residence.
Use of deadly force against intruder, §14-51.1.
Defense of insanity notice.
Intent to introduce expert testimony, §15A-959, (b).
Pretrial determination of insanity, §15A-959, (c).
Pretrial hearing, §15A-959, (a).
Deferred prosecution, §15A-1341, (a1), (a2).
Community service restitution and volunteer program, §143B-262.4.
Dismissal with leave.
Pursuant to deferred prosecution agreement, §15A-932, (a1).
Reinstitution of proceedings if defendant fails to comply, §15A-932, (e).
Definitions, §15A-101.
Appeals.
Prejudicial error, §15A-1443, (a).
Bail and recognizance, §15A-531.
Citation, §15A-302, (a).
Criminal summons, §15A-303, (a).
Disposition of cases, §15A-1381.
Electronic technology in criminal process and procedure, §15A-101.1.
Grand jury, §15A-621.
Indictments, §15A-641, (a).

CRIMINAL LAW AND PROCEDURE —Cont'd
Definitions —Cont'd
Informations, §15A-641, (b).
Motion to suppress evidence, §15A-971.
Order for arrest, §15A-305, (a).
Presentments, §15A-641, (c).
Warrant for arrest, §15A-304, (a).
Witnesses.
Securing attendance.
Witnesses from without state, §15A-811.
Delinquent or undisciplined juvenile actions.
Willful violation of nontestimonial identification procedures, §7B-2109.
Demurrer to the evidence, §15-173.
Dental hygienists.
Violations of provision, §90-233.1.
Dentists.
Extraoral services performed for dentist, §90-29.2, (d), (e).
Practicing dentistry without license, §90-40.
Subpoenas of board of dental examiner.
Neglect or refusal to obey, §90-27.
Unauthorized practices, §90-40.
Violations of rules and regulations of board, §90-48.
Department of health and human services.
Buildings and grounds.
Rules governing department of persons in and suppression of nuisances and disorders, §143-116.6, (b).
Department of justice.
See JUSTICE DEPARTMENT.
Desertion and nonsupport.
Abandonment and failure to support spouse and children, §14-322.
Detainers.
Interstate agreement on detainers, §§15A-761 to 15A-767.
See DETAINERS.
Mandatory disposition of detainers, §§15-10.1 to 15-10.4.
See DETAINERS.
Detectives collecting claims, accounts, etc., §14-401.2.
Discovery, §§15A-901 to 15A-910.
Applicability of provisions, §15A-901.
Contempt.
Failure to comply with orders, §15A-910, (a).
Considerations of court before granting sanctions, §15A-910, (b).
Continuing duty to disclose, §15A-907.
Defendant.
Case files and expert witness information.
Disclosure by state, §15A-903, (a).
Disclosure of information by defendant, §15A-905.
Exemptions, §15A-906.
Notice to state of defenses and witnesses, §15A-905, (c), (d).
Statements of co-defendants.
Disclosure by state, §15A-903, (b).
Disclosure of information by defendant, §15A-905.
Documents.
Disclosure by defendant, §15A-905, (a).
Disclosure by state.
Certain information not subject to disclosure, §15A-904, (a).
Failure to comply with orders.
Sanctions, §15A-910, (a).
Considerations of court before granting, §15A-910, (b).

CRIMINAL LAW AND PROCEDURE —Cont'd
Discovery —Cont'd
Manner of discovery.
Motion for discovery, §15A-902.
Orders must specify, §15A-909.
Place of discovery.
Orders must specify, §15A-909.
Procedure, §15A-902.
Protective orders, §15A-908.
Reports of examinations and tests.
Disclosure by defendant, §15A-905, (b).
State.
Defendant's defenses and witnesses, §15-905, (c), (d).
State of North Carolina.
Disclosure of evidence by state, §15A-903.
Exemptions, §15A-904, (a), (b), (c).
Statements of state's witnesses, §15A-903.
Voluntary discovery.
Exemptions from required disclosure of evidence not to preclude voluntary disclosures or waiver of protections, §15A-904, (b).
Request by defendant for voluntary discovery from state, §15A-902, (d).
Request by state for voluntary discovery from defendant, §15A-902, (e).
Tangible objects.
Disclosure by defendant, §15A-905, (a).
Time of discovery.
Orders must specify, §15A-909.
Voluntary compliance with discovery request, §15A-902.
Discrimination against military personnel, §127B-15.
Dismissal, discontinuance and nonsuit.
Demurrer to the evidence, §15-173.
Dismissal with leave when defendant fails to appear and cannot be readily found, §15A-932, (a).
Effect, §15A-932, (b).
Entry of dismissal, §15A-932, (c).
Reinstitution of proceedings, §15A-932, (d).
Expungement of records when charges are dismissed, §15A-146.
Mental incapacity of defendant to proceed.
Dismissal of charges, §15A-1008.
Supplemental hearings, §15A-1007, (c).
Dismissal with leave, §15A-1009.
Motion for appropriate relief.
Relief available.
Dismissal of charges, §15A-1417, (a).
Motion for dismissal.
Death of defendant.
Dismissal required, §15A-954, (b).
Deferral of ruling on motion to dismiss when charge to be reinstituted, §15A-956.
Grounds, §15A-954, (a).
Motion to dismiss indictment, §15A-955.
Insufficiency of evidence.
Reviewable on appeal regardless of whether motion made during trial, §15A-1227, (d).
Ruling by judge on motion before trial may proceed, §15A-1227, (c).
Time for motion, §15A-1227, (a), (b).
Time for, §15A-954, (c).
Probable cause hearings.
Dispositional alternatives, §15A-612, (a).
Voluntary dismissal of criminal charges by state, §15A-931, (a), (a1).
Statute of limitations not tolled by charges dismissed, §15A-931, (b).

CRIMINAL LAW AND PROCEDURE —Cont'd
Disorderly conduct.
Administrative department.
Public buildings and grounds.
Disorderly conduct in and injury to, §143-345.2.
Airports, §14-275.1.
Bus stations, §14-275.1.
Militia.
Commander may prevent trespass and disorder, §127A-148.
Public buildings and facilities.
Trespasses to land and fixtures, §14-132.
Railroad stations, §14-275.1.
Disorderly houses, §14-188.
Disposition of cases.
Defined, §15A-1381.
Fingerprints.
Report of disposition of charges, §15A-1382, (a).
Plans for implementation of article, §15A-1383, (a).
Modification, §15A-1383, (c).
Not considered rules, §15A-1383, (d).
Punishment for failure to comply, §15A-1383, (b).
Reports, §15A-1382, (a).
Domestic violence to be indicated in report, §15A-1382.1, (a).
Felonies, §15A-1382, (b).
District attorneys.
General provisions.
See DISTRICT ATTORNEYS.
Prosecution of actions, Const. N. C., art. IV, §18.
District courts.
Appeal by defendant, §15A-1431.
Appeal by state, §15A-1432.
Costs in criminal actions, §7A-304.
General provisions.
See DISTRICT COURTS.
Prosecution in district court division, Const. N. C., art. IV, §18.
Seat of court in municipality with corporate limits extending into two or more contiguous counties.
Venue in criminal case, authority of judge, §7A-199, (c).
Division of criminal statistics, §§114-10, 114-10.01.
Divorce.
Alimony.
Willful disobedience of order for payment.
Enforcement of payment by criminal contempt, §50-16.7, (j).
DNA analysis.
General provisions, §§15A-266 to 15A-270.
See DNA DATABASE AND DATABANKS.
DNA evidence preservation.
Disposal of evidence before expiration of time period.
Conditions to be met, §15A-268, (b).
Notification to dispose of evidence.
Prior to expiration of time period, §15A-268, (b), (c).
Required to preserve.
Government agency collecting evidence, §15A-268, (a).
Time period evidence must be preserved, §15A-268, (a).
DNA records, expungement.
Charges dismissed, finding of not guilty or not responsible, §15A-146, (b1), (b2).

CRIMINAL LAW AND PROCEDURE —Cont'd
DNA records, expungement —Cont'd
Charges dismissed on appeal or pardon of innocence granted, §15A-149.
DNA samples from crime scene.
Defendant's access before trial, §15A-267, (a).
Costs of testing, defendant to bear, §15A-267, (d).
Ordering SBI to do DNA testing and database comparison, §15A-267, (c).
Statutes governing access, §15A-267, (b).
DNA testing after conviction.
Motion by defendant.
Appointment of counsel for indigent defendant, §15A-269, (c).
Conditions to be met, §15A-269, (a).
Costs of testing, defendant to bear, §15A-269, (d).
Delay of proceedings or execution of sentence pending testing.
Miscarriage of justice, §15A-269, (e).
Discharge of defendant, ordering on favorable results, §15A-270, (c).
Favorable results, order entered serving interest of justice, §15A-270, (c).
Granting motion, determinations required, §15A-269, (b).
Hearing to evaluate results, §15A-270, (a).
New trial, ordering on favorable results, §15A-270, (c).
Resentencing, ordering on favorable results, §15A-270, (c).
Time for testing order pursuant to motion, §15A-269, (e).
Unfavorable results, dismissal of motion, §15A-270, (b).
Vacating and setting aside judgment, ordering on favorable results, §15A-270, (c).
Dockets.
Superior courts.
Criminal case docketing, §7A-49.4.
Dogs.
Dangerous dogs.
Attacks by dangerous dogs, §67-4.3.
Precautions against attacks by dangerous dogs.
Violations by owners, §67-4.2, (c).
Electronic dog collars.
Unlawful removal, §14-401.17.
Larceny of dog, §14-81.
Mad dogs, failing to kill, §67-4.
Permitting bitch at large, §67-2.
Permitting to run at large at night, §67-12.
Restraining dogs in cruel manner, §14-362.3.
Sheep killing dogs.
Permitting dog to go at liberty, §67-3.
Dog wardens.
Animal welfare act violations, §19A-36.
Cruelty to animals, §19A-35.
Domestic criminal trespass, §14-134.3.
Domestic violence.
Disposition report, indication in, §15A-1382.1, (a).
Protective orders.
Violation of valid protective order, §50B-4.1.
Drainage.
Jurisdiction of county commissioners.
Refusal to comply with requirements, §156-33.
Refusal to serve on board, §156-32.
Obstructions, §§156-19, 156-24, 156-25.
Drainage districts.
Assessments.
Failure of sheriff to make settlements, §156-111.

CRIMINAL LAW AND PROCEDURE —Cont'd
Drainage districts —Cont'd
Assessments —Cont'd
Failure of treasurer to make payments, §156-112.
Conveyance of land.
Failure of chairman or board to act, §156-114, (e).
Injuring or damaging bridges, fences, ditches, etc., §156-92.
Reports.
Failure of commissioners to make reports, §156-132.
Drivers' licenses.
Motor vehicles. See within this heading, "Motor vehicles."
Driving by person less than 21 years old after consuming alcohol or drugs, §20-138.3, (a), (c).
Drug and alcohol screening tests.
Defrauding test, §14-401.20.
Drugs, controlled substances.
Conditions of prescribed punishments and degree of offense, §90-95, (e).
Conspiracy to violate provision, §90-98.
Continuing criminal enterprise, §90-95.1, (a).
Counterfeit substance.
Prohibited acts, §90-95, (c).
Employing or intentionally using minor to commit drug law violations, §90-95.4, (a), (b).
Expunction of records, §90-96, (d) to (f).
Manufacture, §90-95, (b).
Enhanced sentencing in certain cases, §15A-1340.16D.
Participating in a drug violation by a minor, §90-95.7, (c).
Possession, §90-95, (d).
Precursor chemical.
Designation, §90-95, (d2).
Possession or distribution with intent to manufacture controlled substance or methamphetamine, §90-95, (d1), (d1a).
Prohibited acts generally, §90-108.
Promoting drug sales by a minor, §90-95.6, (c).
Sale, §90-95, (b).
Trafficking in, §90-95, (h).
Conspiracy, §90-95, (i).
Drunkenness.
Aircraft.
Operation of aircraft while impaired, §63-27.
Boating safety.
Operation of boat or manipulation of water skis while intoxicated, §75A-10, (b), (b1).
Penalty, §75A-18, (b).
Impaired driving generally.
See IMPAIRED DRIVING.
Public intoxication.
Acquittal of defendant because of alcoholism.
Disposition of defendant, §14-446.
Defense of alcoholism, §14-445, (a).
Disposition of defendant acquitted because of alcoholism, §14-446.
Request for additional information, §14-445, (b).
Definitions, §14-443.
Elements of offense.
No prosecution for public intoxication, §14-447, (a).
Entering plea to charge, §14-445, (c).
Prehearing review of drinking history, §14-445, (d).

CRIMINAL LAW AND PROCEDURE —Cont'd
Drunkenness —Cont'd
Public intoxication —Cont'd
Shelter or health-care facility.
Transport and release of person to appropriate facility, §14-447, (b).
Ways of being intoxicated and disruptive in public, §14-444, (a).
Penalty for violation of provisions, §14-444, (b).
Dry-cleaning solvent cleanup, §143-215.104Q, (a) to (i).
Dune buggies used in violation of municipal ordinance, §160A-308.
Easements.
Streets and highways.
Regulation of scenic easements, §136-125.
Eavesdropping, §§14-227.1 to 14-227.3.
Egg promotion tax.
Handlers, §105-245.38.
Eggs.
Warnings in lieu of criminal prosecutions, §106-245.25.
Elections.
Absentee ballot violations, §§163-226.3, (a), 163-237.
County boards of elections, §163-236.
Appropriations from North Carolina political parties financing fund.
Violations of provisions, §163-278.44.
Certain acts declared felonies, §163-275.
Certain acts declared misdemeanors, §163-274.
Challenge of voters.
False swearing, §163-90.3.
Contributions and expenditures in political campaigns.
Disclosure before soliciting contributions violations, §163-278.20, (b).
Disclosure requirements for media advertisements.
Misrepresentation of authorization, §163-278.39, (c).
Fund-raising from lobbyists, §163-278.13, (a), (d).
Limitation on contribution violations, §163-278.13, (f).
Violations by business organizations and labor unions, §163-278.19, (a).
Violations generally, §163-278.27, (a).
Electioneering communications, §163-278.83.
Mass mailings and telephone banks, §163-278.93.
Interference with voters, §163-273.
Intimidation of voters by officers, §163-271.
Misdemeanor punishments, §163-272.1.
Offenses by voters, §163-273.
Signing name of another on petition, §163-221, (c).
Electrologists.
Violations of chapter, §88A-4, (b).
Electronic commerce in government, §66-58.8.
Electronic communications.
Cyberstalking, §14-196.3.
Electronic dog collars.
Unlawful removal, §14-401.17.
Electronic repository for criminal process.
Generally, §15A-301.1, (a) to (d).
Printing of process in paper form, §15A-301.1, (e), (f).
Service of process in, §15A-301.1, (g), (j), (k) to (n).
Tracking information, §15A-301.1, (h), (i), (m).

CRIMINAL LAW AND PROCEDURE —Cont'd
Electronic surveillance generally, §§15A-286 to 15A-298.
See ELECTRONIC SURVEILLANCE.
Electronic technology in criminal process and procedure.
Definitions, §15A-101.1.
Electronic repository for criminal process, §15A-301.1.
Elementary and secondary education.
Annual independent audit.
Interference with records, §115C-447.
Blind children.
Parents, etc., failing to enroll, §115C-383, (c).
Deaf children.
Parents, etc., failing to enroll, §115C-383, (b).
Employee health certificate.
Violations of provisions, §115C-323, (e).
Employees making false reports or records, §115C-317.
Fire prevention duties.
Failure to perform, §115C-525, (c).
Insurance.
Public school property.
Noncompliance with duties, §115C-534, (c).
Local boards of education.
Witness failing to appear, §115C-45, (b).
Principals or supervisors making false reports or records, §115C-288.
State board of education.
Disclosure of confidential records, §115C-13.
Student attendance.
School official's failure to carry out state board's instructions, §115C-379.
Violations of part, §115C-380.
Superintendent making false reports or records, §115C-276, (p).
Teachers making false reports or records, §115C-307, (g).
Elevator violations, §95-110.11.
E-mail.
Cyberstalking, §14-196.3.
Emancipated juvenile prosecuted as adult, §7B-1604, (a).
Embezzlement.
Banks.
Conservators.
Applicability of provisions, §53-157.
Prohibited acts, §53-129.
Charities.
Funds embezzled by public officers and trustees, §14-92.
Treasurers of charitable organizations, §14-93.
Indictments.
Description in bill for embezzlement of money, §15-150.
Insurance agents, brokers or administrators, §§58-2-162, 58-2-163.
Local government finance.
Penalty, §159-181, (b).
Medical assistance program.
Property of patients.
Prohibited acts, §108A-60, (a).
Motor carriers.
C.O.D. shipments, §62-273.
Partnerships.
Appropriation of partnership funds by partner to personal use, §14-97.
Surviving partner embezzling property, money or effects of partnership, §14-98.

CRIMINAL LAW AND PROCEDURE —Cont'd
Embezzlement —Cont'd
Preneed funeral contracts and funds, §90-210.70, (a), (c).
Public officers and employees.
Local officers and employees, §14-92.
Property of state embezzled by officers and employees, §14-91.
Taxes embezzled by officers, §14-99.
Railroads.
Officers of railroad companies, §14-94.
Receipt of property by virtue of office or employment, §14-90.
Religious societies.
Funds embezzled by public officers and trustees, §14-92.
Treasurers of religious organizations, §14-93.
Reports, §58-2-163.
State bureau of investigation.
Misuse of state property, §114-15.1.
Taxes.
Officers embezzling taxes, §14-99.
Emergency communication, interfering with, §14-286.2.
Emergency medical services.
EMS provider license.
Unlicensed operation, §131E-156, (e).
Regulation of emergency medical services.
Violations of article, §131E-161.
Employers and employees.
Duties owed employers.
Influencing employees to violate duties, §§14-353, 14-354.
Earnings of employees in interstate commerce.
Collection out of state to avoid exemption, §95-75.
Labor union violations by public employee, §95-99.
Payments to or for benefit of labor organization.
Violations, §95-104.
Employment security.
False statements or representation, §96-18, (a), (b).
Violations of chapter or rules or regulation, §96-18, (c).
Witness intimidation, §96-15.2.
Endangered plant species.
Unlawful acts, §106-202.19, (a), (a1).
Energy.
Crisis administration.
Violations as misdemeanors, §113B-24, (b).
Enhanced 911 wireless system for wireless communications.
Misuse of system, §62A-32.
Errors at trial.
Appropriate relief, §15A-1401.
Motion for appropriate relief, §§15A-1411 to 15A-1422. See within this heading, "Motion for appropriate relief."
Escape.
Allowing prisoners to escape, §14-239.
Burden of proof, §14-239.
District attorney to prosecute officer for escape, §14-240.
Arrest.
Persons escaped from penal institutions, §162-35.
Use of force in arrest, §15A-401, (d).
Assisting escape from state prison, §148-45.
Capital punishment.
Aggravating circumstances.
Capital felony committed for purpose of effecting escape, §15A-2000, (e).

CRIMINAL LAW AND PROCEDURE —Cont'd
Escape —Cont'd
Conveying messages and weapons to convicts and other prisoners, §14-258.
County confinement facilities or officers.
Prison breach and escape from facilities or officers, §14-256.
Definitions, §148-45, (g).
Felonies, §148-45, (b).
Guards.
Degree of protection against allowed, §148-46, (a), (b).
Harboring or aiding escaped prisoners, §14-259.
Misdemeanors, §148-45, (a), (d).
Municipal confinement facilities or officers.
Prison breach and escape from facilities or officers, §14-256.
Penalties, §148-45.
Prevention of escape.
Force.
Use of force in arrest, §15A-401, (d).
Private correction facilities, §14-256.1.
Recapture of escaped prisoners, §§148-40, 148-41.
State institutions.
Persuading inmates to escape, §§14-266, 14-268.
Treatment of convicted escapees, §148-45, (f).
Use of weapon in assisting prisoner to escape, §14-258.2, (b).
Working prisoners escaping from custody, §14-255.
Ethnic intimidation, §14-401.14, (a), (b).
Evasion of tax, §105-236.
Evidence.
Additional evidence.
Introduction at any time prior to verdict.
Discretion of judge, §15A-1226, (b).
Altering, destroying or stealing evidence of conduct.
Obstructing justice, §14-221.1.
Bawdy houses, keeping, §14-188, (a).
Demurrer to the evidence, §15-173.
Disorderly houses, keeping, §14-188, (a).
DNA samples and testing, §§15A-266 to 15A-270.
See DNA DATABASE AND DATABANKS.
Errors in admission or exclusion of evidence.
Correction of errors by appellate division, §15A-1442.
Forensic analysis.
Admissibility, §8-58.20, (a), (b).
Affidavit of analyst, §8-58.20, (c) to (f).
Service of report and affidavit on attorney of record for defendant, §8-58.20, (d), (e).
Hearsay.
Probable cause hearings, §15A-611, (b).
Insufficiency of evidence.
Grounds for correction of errors by appellate division, §15A-1442.
Jury.
Review of testimony, §15A-1233, (a).
Motion to suppress evidence, §8C-1, Rule 104, (c).
Appeals.
Order denying motion, §15A-979, (b).
Order granting motion, §15A-979, (c).
State may appeal, §15A-1445, (b).
Definitions, §15A-971.
During trial.
District court, §15A-973.
Hearing on motion.
Outside presence of jury, §15A-977, (e).
Superior court, §15A-975, (b).
Written or oral motion, §15A-977, (e).
Exclusive method of provisions, §15A-979, (d).

CRIMINAL LAW AND PROCEDURE —Cont'd
Evidence —Cont'd
Motion to suppress evidence —Cont'd
Findings of fact and conclusions of law.
Judgment set forth, §15A-977, (f).
Fruit of the poisonous tree doctrine, §15A-974.
Grounds for exclusion or suppression of unlawfully obtained evidence, §15A-974.
Order of suppression, §15A-979, (a).
Prior conviction obtained in violation of right to counsel, §15A-980, (b).
Burden of proof, §15A-980, (c).
When defendant has right to suppress, §15A-980, (a).
Prior to trial.
Affidavit supporting motion, §15A-977, (a).
Answer by state, §15A-977, (a).
District court, §15A-973.
Hearing on motion, §§15A-976, (c), 15A-977, (d).
Service of copies of motion, §15A-977, (a).
Superior court, §§15A-972, 15A-975, (a).
Time for motion, §15A-976, (a), (b).
Written motion required, §15A-977, (a).
Procedure, §15A-977.
Renewal of motion, §15A-975, (c).
Searches and seizures.
Challenge to probable cause supporting search warrant on grounds of truthfulness, §15A-978, (a).
Identity of informant to be disclosed, §15A-978, (b).
Challenge to truthfulness of testimony offered in support of search without warrant, §15A-978, (c).
Summary grant or denial of motion.
Grounds, §15A-977, (b), (c).
Pleadings not used in criminal prosecution against party as proof of fact admitted or alleged, §1-49.
Plea discussion and arrangement.
Inadmissible, §§8C-1, Rule 410, 15A-1025.
Probable cause hearings, §15A-611, (b).
Prostitution prosecution.
Reputation and prior convictions, admissibility, §14-206.
Rebuttal evidence, §15A-1226, (a).
Records.
Superior courts.
Criminal index maintained by clerk of court.
Records admissible in certain cases, §8-35.2.
Subpoena duces tecum, §15A-802.
Superior courts.
Clerks of court.
Criminal index.
Records admissible in certain cases, §8-35.2.
Suppression of evidence.
Motion to suppress evidence, §§15A-971 to 15A-980. See within this subheading, "Motion to suppress evidence."
Testimony by accused, §8C-1, Rule 104, (d).
Victims, impact of crime, §15A-833.
Examination question, tampering with, §14-401.1.
Excessive bail, Const. U. S., amd. VIII.
Exclusionary rule.
Motion to suppress evidence. See within this heading, "Evidence."

CRIMINAL LAW AND PROCEDURE —Cont'd
Execution on forfeiture of bonds.
Issuance, §1-305, (a).
Executions.
Capital punishment.
See CAPITAL PUNISHMENT.
Corporate agents, §1-324.5.
Supplemental proceedings.
Examination of parties and witnesses.
Incriminating answers not to be used in criminal proceedings, §1-357.
Exploitation of disabled or elder adult, §14-32.3, (c).
Explosives.
Attempts to commit crime.
Malicious use of explosive or incendiary.
Property occupied by persons, §14-49.1.
Bombs.
Exploding bombs, §14-283.
Burglary.
Use of explosives in burglary, §14-57.
Definitions.
Incendiary device or explosive or material, §14-50.1.
Powerful explosives, §14-284.1, (d).
Dynamite.
Exploding dynamite cartridges, §14-283.
Licenses.
Sale or selling explosives without license, §14-284.
Malicious use of explosive or incendiary, §14-49, (a), (b).
Churches and other buildings of worship, §14-49, (b1).
Government buildings, §14-49, (b2).
Punishment, §14-49.1.
Powerful explosives.
Defined, §14-284.1, (d).
Property occupied by persons.
Malicious damage by use of explosive or incendiary, §14-49.1.
Regulation of sale of explosives, §14-284.1.
Ex post facto laws.
Prohibited, Const. N. C., art. I, §16.
Expungement of records.
Dismissal of charges, finding of not guilty or not responsible.
Application to court, §15A-146, (a).
As result of identity fraud, §15A-147.
Confidential file containing names of persons granted expungement.
Administrative office of the courts to maintain, §15A-146, (c).
Costs taxed against petitioner, §15A-146, (b).
DNA records, application to expunge, §15A-146, (b1), (b2).
Failure to recite or acknowledge expunged records.
Not perjury or false statement, §15A-146, (a).
Hearing on application, §15A-146, (a).
Law enforcement agencies order to expunge records, §15A-146, (b).
Names of persons granted expungement.
Filed with administrative office of the courts, §15A-146, (c).
Order of court, §15A-146, (a), (b).
DNA records.
Charges dismissed, finding of not guilty or not responsible, §15A-146, (b1), (b2).
Charges dismissed on appeal or pardon of innocence granted, §15A-148, (a), (b).

CRIMINAL LAW AND PROCEDURE —Cont'd
Expungement of records —Cont'd
Drug offenses.
Expungement of juvenile records, §90-96.
First offenders under age of eighteen.
Clerks of court.
Duties, §15A-145, (d).
Orders of court, §15A-145, (b), (c).
Petition, §15A-145, (a).
Fee for filing, §15A-145, (e).
Identity fraud.
Dismissal of charges, finding of not guilty, another using identifying information.
Division of motor vehicles to expunge records, §15A-147, (c), (d).
Failure to acknowledge records not perjury, §15A-147, (b).
Hearing on petition or motion, court to hold, §15A-147, (a).
Insurance companies charging additional insurance points premium, refund, §15A-147, (f).
Law enforcement agencies and other agencies ordered to expunge, §15A-147, (c).
Order to expunge, §15A-147, (a).
Petition or motion, §15A-147, (a).
State or local agencies ordered to expunge, §15A-147, (c), (e).
Minors.
Controlled substances violations, §90-96, (b), (d).
First offenders under age of eighteen, §15A-145.
Juvenile records.
See JUVENILE RECORDS AND SOCIAL REPORTS.
Extension of session of court by trial judge, §15-167.
Extradition.
Uniform criminal extradition act, §§15A-721 to 15A-750.
See EXTRADITION.
Failure to appear, §15A-543.
Dismissal with leave when defendant fails to appear and cannot be found readily, §15A-932.
Failure to pay minor for certain work, §14-321.
False fire alarms.
Giving false fire alarms, §14-286.
Molesting fire alarm, §14-286.
False pretenses and cheats.
Ambulances.
Making false requests, §§14-111.3, 14-286.1.
Obtaining ambulance services without intending to pay, §§14-111.1, 14-111.2.
Animals.
Pedigree of animals.
Obtaining property by false representation of pedigree, §14-102.
Registration certificate of registration by false representation, §14-103.
Bad checks.
Obtaining property in return for worthless check, draft or order, §14-106.
Campgrounds.
Defrauding campground owner, §14-110.
Coin-operated machines.
Manufacture, sale or gift of devices for cheating slot machines, §14-109.
Obtaining property or services from machine by false coins or tokens, §14-108.
Credit cards and devices, §§14-113.1 to 14-113.7A.

CRIMINAL LAW AND PROCEDURE —Cont'd
False pretenses and cheats —Cont'd
Definitions.
Person, §14-100, (c).
Defrauding innkeeper, §14-110.
Filing false security agreements, §14-401.19.
Identification, false or fraudulent, §14-100.1.
Insurance consumer and customer information privacy.
Obtaining information under false pretenses, §58-39-115.
Nuclear, biological or chemical weapons.
Hoax or false report, §§14-288.23, 14-288.24.
Obtaining advances under promise to work, §14-104.
Written promise to pay therefore out of designated property, §14-105.
Obtaining merchandise on approval, §14-112.
Obtaining money by false representation or physical defect, §14-113.
Obtaining property by false pretenses, §14-100.
Elements of offense, §14-100, (a).
Establishing element of intent to defraud, §14-100, (b).
Obtaining signatures by false pretenses, §14-101.
Slot machines.
Manufacture, sale or gift of devices for cheating machines, §14-109.
Obtaining property or services from machines by false coins or tokens, §14-108.
Worthless check, draft or order, §14-107.
Obtaining property in return for worthless check, etc., §14-106.
Prima facie evidence in worthless check cases, §14-107.1.
False reports to law enforcement officers, §14-225.
Federal law enforcement officers.
Assistance in enforcing criminal laws in state.
Authority to assist, §15A-406, (b).
Federal tort claims act, applicability, §15A-406, (e).
Independent investigation into state law violations not authorized, §15A-406, (f).
List of federal law enforcement officers, §15A-406, (a).
Not considered officer, employee of state or local agency, §15A-406, (d).
Powers when assisting, §15A-406, (c).
Felonies.
See FELONIES.
Felonious restraint, §14-43.3.
Felony sentencing, §§15A-1340.13 to 15A-1340.17.
Ferries.
Chain guards or gates.
Safety violations, §136-89.
Financial identity fraud, §§14-113.20 to 14-113.25.
Expungement of criminal records.
Dismissal or finding of not guilty.
Crime committed by another using defendant's identifying information, §15A-147.
Financial transaction cards.
Credit cards and devices, §§14-113.1 to 14-113.7A.
Definitions, §14-113.8.
Felonies, §14-113.17, (b).
Forgery.
Devices.
Criminal possession of financial transaction card forgery devices, §14-113.14, (a), (b).

CRIMINAL LAW AND PROCEDURE —Cont'd
Financial transaction cards —Cont'd
Forgery —Cont'd
Elements of offense, §14-113.11, (a).
Embossing financial transaction card falsely, §14-113.11, (c).
Encoding financial transaction card falsely, §14-113.11, (d).
Making financial transaction card falsely, §14-113.11, (b).
Prima facie evidence of forgery, §14-113.12, (a), (b).
Fraud.
Application for financial transaction card.
False statements or reports on application, §14-113.13, (c).
Criminal factoring of records, §14-113.15A.
Elements of offense, §14-113.13, (a).
Furnisher of money, goods, services, etc.
Elements of financial transaction card fraud offense, §14-113.13, (b).
Goods and services.
Criminal receipt of goods and services fraudulently obtained, §14-113.15.
Presumption of criminal receipt, §14-113.16.
Notice of theft, loss, etc., of card.
False notice, §14-113.13, (d).
Prosecution for violation.
Occurrence of acts constituting crime, §14-113.13, (e).
Record of sale.
Fraudulent record, §14-113.13, (c1).
Report of theft, loss, etc., of card.
False report, §14-113.13, (d).
Revocation of financial transaction card.
Construing revocation, §14-113.13, (f).
Fire alarms.
False alarms, §14-286.
Firearms.
Sale of pistols.
Dealer record violation, §14-408.
Fire department.
Volunteer fire department.
Defense of employees and officers in civil or criminal actions, §160A-167.
Fires and fire protection.
Alarms.
Giving false fire alarms, §14-286.
Molesting fire alarm, §14-286.
Arson, §§14-58 to 14-69.2.
See ARSON.
Exposing minor to fire, §14-318.
Offenses against the public safety.
Molesting fire-detection or fire-extinguishing system, §14-286.
Fireworks.
Common carriers.
Not affected by fireworks provisions, §14-410, (a).
Definitions, §14-414.
Exhibitions.
Permitted fireworks at public exhibitions, §14-410, (a).
Use at public exhibitions requires permit, §14-413.
Manufacture of pyrotechnics.
Prohibited, §14-410, (a).
Possession.
Prima facie evidence of violations, §14-412.
Sale of pyrotechnics.
Deemed at site of delivery, §14-411.
Prohibited, §14-410, (a).

CRIMINAL LAW AND PROCEDURE —Cont'd
Fireworks —Cont'd
Sale of pyrotechnics —Cont'd
Sale to persons under age of 16, §14-410, (b).
Use of pyrotechnics.
Prohibited, §14-410, (a).
Violations of provisions made misdemeanor, §14-415.
Fish and fisheries resources.
Artificial reef marking devices.
Interference with as misdemeanor, §113-266.
Audits and auditing.
Promotion of coastal fisheries and seafood industry.
Violations as misdemeanors, §113-315.9, (b).
Buoys, nets, markers, stakes, etc.
Robbing or injuring as misdemeanor, §113-268, (a) to (d).
Coastal and estuarine commercial fishing licenses.
Spotter planes, §113-171.1, (d).
Coastal wetlands.
Orders to control activities.
Violations as misdemeanors, §113-230, (d).
Commercial fishing.
Violations as misdemeanors, §113-187, (a) to (d).
Dredging.
Permits.
Violations as misdemeanors, §113-229, (k).
Federal laws and regulations.
Legislative assent to specific federal acts.
Violations as misdemeanors, §113-307.1, (a).
Fees.
Acceptance by inspector of unauthorized fees as misdemeanors, §113-222.
Acceptance by protector of unauthorized fee as misdemeanor, §113-303.
Inland fishing licenses.
Administrative control.
Prohibited acts as misdemeanors, §113-276.2, (g), (i).
Prohibited acts as misdemeanors, §113-275, (j).
Licenses.
Suspension or revocation.
Prohibited acts during, §113-277, (b).
Robbing or injuring hatcheries and other aquaculture operations, §113-269, (e), (f).
Seafood.
Industrial park authority.
Traffic and parking.
Violations of rules as misdemeanors, §113-315.34, (c).
Seized property left with defendant.
Failure of defendant to keep property, §113-137, (f).
Spotter planes in commercial fishing operations.
Coastal and estuarine fishing licenses, §113-171.1, (d).
Taking fish by using poisons, drugs, explosives or electricity, §113-262, (a).
Unlawful sale or purchase of fish, §113-191, (a), (b).
Flag desecration, §14-381.
Flat trucks.
Violation of operation restriction, §20-120.
Floodplain regulation.
Violations, §143-215.58, (a), (b).
Food, drug and cosmetic act.
Advertising violations, §106-124.
Prosecution of violations, §106-126.
Food stamps.
Fraud, §108A-53.
Illegal possession or use, §108A-53.1.

CRIMINAL LAW AND PROCEDURE —Cont'd
Forensic analysis.
Admissibility in evidence, §8-58.20.
Forests and forestry.
Destruction of forestry notices, §113-58.
Hunting, fishing and trapping.
Violation of governor's proclamation as misdemeanor, §113-60.3.
Open fires.
Violations as misdemeanors, §113-60.29.
Posted notices.
Destruction as misdemeanor, §113-58.
Primary forest product assessment act.
Disclosure of confidential information as misdemeanor, §113A-195, (f).
Summons to assist in extinguishing fires.
Failure to comply as misdemeanor, §113-55, (a).
Forfeitures.
Alcoholic beverages.
Disposition after trial, §18B-504, (e).
Owner unavailable for criminal trial, §18B-504, (i).
Return of property when no charge is made, §18B-504, (j).
Seizure of property, §18B-504, (c).
Bonds in criminal cases.
When execution to issue, §1-305, (a).
Money or other property or interest acquired from felony, §14-2.3, (a).
Action to recover, statute of limitation, §14-2.3, (b).
Property traceable to owner or guardian, inapplicability of forfeiture, §14-2.3, (c).
Forgery, Const. U. S., art. I, §8.
Bills of exchange, §14-122.
Selling of certain forged securities, §14-121.
Bills of lading.
Felony, §21-42.
Bond issues, §14-122.
Selling of certain forged securities, §14-121.
Certificates of corporate stock forged, §14-124.
Checks, §14-119.
Controlled substances.
Acquiring or obtaining possession by, §90-108, (a).
Deeds, §14-122.
Diplomas, §14-122.1.
Elections.
Absentee ballots, §163-237, (c).
Excise stamp tax.
Reproduction of tax stamps, §105-228.36.
Financial transaction cards, §14-113.11.
Criminal possession of financial transaction card forgery devices, §14-113.14, (a), (b).
Prima facie evidence of forgery, §14-113.12, (a), (b).
Indictments.
Intent to defraud.
Sufficiency of allegation, §15-151.
Leases, §14-122.
Military discharges.
Forgery of discharge or certificate, §47-112.
Motor vehicle certificates of title, registration cards or applications, §20-71, (a).
Motor vehicle inspection stickers, §20-183.8, (c).
Notes, §14-119.
Connecting genuine parts of notes, §14-125.
Petitions, §14-123.
Promissory notes, §14-122.
Selling of certain forged securities, §14-121.

CRIMINAL LAW AND PROCEDURE —Cont'd
Forgery —Cont'd
Securities, §14-119.
Selling of certain forged securities, §14-121.
Uttering.
Elements of offense, §14-120.
Petitions forged, §14-123.
Wills, §14-122.
Forms of action, Const. N. C., art. IV, §13.
Fornication, §14-184.
Franchise tax.
Limited liability companies.
Controlled companies.
Underpayment, fraud to evade, penalty, §105-114.1, (h).
Fraud.
See FRAUD.
Fugitives from justice, Const. U. S., art. IV, §2.
Fundraising during legislative session, §163-278.13B, (e).
Funeral contracts and funds.
Violations generally, §90-210.70, (a), (b).
Funeral service.
Unlawful practices, §90-210.25, (f).
Futures.
Entering into or aiding, §16-4.
Opening office for sales, §16-5.
Gaming.
General provisions, §§14-289 to 14-300.
See GAMING.
Gasoline adulteration, §119-35.
Gasoline inspection violations, §119-39.
Gasoline inspectors.
Conflicts of interest, §119-25.
Failure or refusal to exhibit records to, §119-32.
Gasoline pumps.
Devices calculated to falsify measure, §119-33.
Display of grade rating, §119-27.
Gasoline tax.
Acts that are misdemeanors, §105-449.120.
Use of non-tax-paid fuel on highway, §105-449.117, (a).
General assembly.
Fundraising during legislative session, §163-278.13B, (e).
Geographically based field programs.
Limitations on eligible cases, §7A-474.3, (c).
Glue sniffing, §90-113.13.
Gonorrhea.
Testing for sexually transmitted infections, §15A-615, (a), (2).
Governor.
Emergency war powers.
Violations of orders, rules or regulations, §147-33.3.
Grand jury.
See GRAND JURY.
Gravestones, inscribing charging of crime, §14-401.3.
Greyhound racing, §14-309.20, (c).
Guarantees in criminal cases, Const. U. S., amds. V, VI.
Guilty pleas. See within this heading, "Pleas."
Habitual felons, §§14-7.1 to 14-7.6.
Charge of habitual felon, §14-7.3.
Defined, §14-7.1.
Evidence of prior convictions, §14-7.4.
Indictment, §14-7.2.
Charge of habitual felon, §14-7.3.
Judgment, §14-7.5.

CRIMINAL LAW AND PROCEDURE —Cont'd
Habitual felons —Cont'd
Prior convictions.
Evidence, §14-7.4.
Punishment, §14-7.2.
Sentencing, §§14-7.2, 14-7.6.
Structured sentencing.
Inapplicability to violent habitual felons, §15A-1340.10.
Verdict, §14-7.5.
Violent habitual felons.
Charge, §14-7.9.
Convicted defined, §14-7.7, (a).
Evidence of prior convictions, §14-7.10.
Persons declared to be, §14-7.7, (a).
Punishment, §14-7.8.
Sentencing, §14-7.12.
Verdict and judgment, §14-7.11.
Violent felony, crimes included in term, §14-7.7, (b).
Habitual misdemeanor assault, §14-33.2.
Halloween food, distributing certain food, §14-401.11.
Hazardous waste management.
Class I felonies, §130A-26.1, (f).
Class J felonies, §130A-26.1, (g).
False reporting, §130A-26.2.
Hazing, §§14-35 to 14-38.
Definitions, §14-35.
Indictments.
Self-incriminating testimony.
No indictment to be founded on self-incriminating testimony, §14-38.
Punishment for hazing, §14-35.
Witnesses in hazing trials, §14-38.
Health.
Violations of chapter or rules, §130A-25, (a).
Health care facility, obstruction, §14-277.4.
Hearings.
Interpreters generally.
See INTERPRETERS.
Mental incapacity of defendant to proceed.
Determination of incapacity, §15A-1002, (b).
Supplemental hearings, §15A-1007, (a).
Court's own determination, §15A-1007, (b).
Dismissal of charges, §15A-1007, (c).
Motion for appropriate relief, §15A-1420, (c).
Motion to suppress evidence.
Motion made during trial.
Hearing out of presence of jury, §15A-977, (e).
Pretrial motion, §§15A-976, (c), 15A-977, (d).
Pretrial motions.
Date for hearing, §15A-952, (f).
Motion to suppress evidence, §§15A-976, (c), 15A-977, (d).
Probable cause hearings.
Attorneys at law.
Defendant to be advised of right to counsel, §15A-606, (e).
Determination whether right to counsel waived, §15A-611, (c).
Representation of state and defendant, §15A-611, (a).
Continuances, §15A-606, (f).
Dispositional alternatives, §15A-612, (a).
Double jeopardy.
Findings at probable cause hearing not to preclude state from subsequent prosecution for same offense, §15A-612.
Evidence, §15A-611, (b).

CRIMINAL LAW AND PROCEDURE —Cont'd
Hearings —Cont'd
Probable cause hearings —Cont'd
First appearance before district court judge, §15A-606.
Guilty plea.
Acceptance, §15A-613.
Hearsay evidence, §15A-611, (b).
Informations.
Filing in superior court upon waiver of indictment.
Probable cause hearing may not be held, §15A-611, (d).
Pretrial release.
Review of eligibility for, §15A-614.
Procedure, §15A-611.
Scheduling, §15A-606, (a), (d).
Setting offense for trial in district court, §15A-613.
Review of eligibility for pretrial release, §15A-614.
Venue, §15A-131, (c).
Waiver, §15A-606, (a).
After first appearance before district court judge, §15A-606, (g).
Evidence of waiver not to be admitted at trial, §15A-606, (b).
Proceedings on, §15A-606, (c).
Witnesses, §15A-611, (a).
Hepatitis B.
Testing for sexually transmitted infections, §15A-615, (a), (3).
Hired property.
Conversion.
Bailees, lessees, tenants and attorneys in fact, §14-168.1.
Evidence of intent to convert property.
Prima facie evidence of intent, §14-168.3.
Definitions, §14-168.2.
Failure to return hired property, §14-167.
Fraud.
Hiring with intent to defraud, §14-168.
Malicious or willful injury to hired personal property, §14-165.
Protection of bailor against acts of bailee.
Violations made misdemeanors, §14-169.
Subletting hired property, §14-166.
Historical and cultural resources.
Violations of regulations, §121-4.
HIV.
Testing for sexually transmitted infections, §15A-615, (a), (4).
Home care agency licensure.
Unlicensed operation, §131E-141.1.
Home inspectors.
Violations as misdemeanors, §143-151.59.
Homicide.
Capital punishment crimes, Const. N. C., art. XI, §2.
Death by vehicle, §20-141.4.
First degree murder, §14-17.
Indictments.
Essentials of bill for homicide, §15-144.
Juveniles under 17 years of age.
First degree murder, §14-17.
Manslaughter.
Double jeopardy.
Death by vehicle.
Subsequent prosecutions prohibited, §20-141.4, (c).

CRIMINAL LAW AND PROCEDURE —Cont'd
Homicide —Cont'd
Manslaughter —Cont'd
Indictments.
Essentials of bill, §15-144.
Punishment for manslaughter, §14-18.
Motor vehicles.
Death by vehicle, §20-141.4.
Murder.
Indictments.
Essentials of bill, §15-144.
Juvenile committed for placement in youth development center.
Continued jurisdiction of juvenile court, §7B-1602, (a).
Juveniles under 17 years of age, §14-17.
Malice aforethought.
Allegation required in indictment, §15-144.
Murder in first and second degree, §14-17.
Punishment, §14-17.
Verdict for murder in first or second degree, §15-172.
Second degree murder, §14-17.
Suicide.
Crime of suicide abolished, §14-17.1.
Vehicular homicide.
Death by vehicle, §20-141.4.
Venue.
Assault in one county, death in another, §15-130.
Assault in this state, death in another, §15-131.
County where death occurs, §15-133.
Horse show officials or judges, bribery, §14-380.1.
Attempts at bribery to be reported, §14-380.2.
Definitions of "bribe," §14-380.3.
Printing provisions of article in horse show schedules, §14-380.4.
Hospice licensure.
Unauthorized disclosure of inspection information, §131E-207, (b).
Hospital discharged patient.
Failure or refusal to leave hospital, §131E-90.
Hospital employee personnel files.
Unlawful disclosure, §131E-257.2, (g).
Unlawful examination or use, §131E-257.2, (h).
Hospital inspections by department.
Disclosure of confidential or privileged information, §131E-80, (d).
Hospital licensure.
Disclosure of information, §131E-80, (d).
Unlicensed operation, §131E-81, (a).
Willful violations, §131E-81, (b).
Hotel admittance of pets, §72-7.1.
Hotel, false registration as husband and wife, §14-186.
Hotel room occupied by opposite sexes for immoral purposes, §14-186.
Houses of ill repute, §14-188.
Housing authorities and projects.
Fraudulent misrepresentation in obtaining housing assistance, §157-29.1, (a), (b).
Hunting and wildlife.
Criminal negligence.
Misdemeanors, §113-290.1, (a).
Violations resulting in death of another person.
Involuntary manslaughter, §113-290.1, (f).
Disabled sportsman.
Unlawful use of facilities provided for, §113-298.
Federal laws and regulations.
Legislative assent to specific federal acts.
Violations as misdemeanors, §113-307.1, (a).

CRIMINAL LAW AND PROCEDURE —Cont'd
Hunting and wildlife —Cont'd
Handicapped persons.
Vehicular access identification cards and permits.
Violations of rules restricting access to holders, §113-294, (n).
Hunting on Sunday, §103-2.
Hunting or fishing on registered property of another.
Hunting or fishing without entry permit as misdemeanor, §113-285, (c).
Posting of property.
Removal of signs after receipt of notice that tract has been deleted from registration.
Failure to remove as misdemeanor, §113-282, (h).
Removal, destruction or mutilation of posted notices, §113-286.
Licenses.
Agents.
Prohibited acts, §113-270.1, (d), (h).
False or misleading statements to secure, §113-294, (h).
Suspension or revocation.
Prohibited acts during, §113-277, (b).
Poisons and pesticides.
Violations as to use, §113-300.3, (b), (c).
Seized property left with defendant.
Failure of defendant to keep property, §113-137, (f).
Taking wildlife by using poisons, drugs, explosives or electricity, §113-262, (a).
Trapping.
Violations of provisions, §113-294, (i), (j).
Unlawful harassment of persons taking wildlife resources, §113-295, (a).
Unlawfully selling, possessing for sale or buying wildlife, §113-294, (a).
Bald eagle or golden eagle, §113-294, (l).
Bear, §113-294, (c1).
Beaver, §113-294, (f).
Cougar, §113-294, (c2).
Deer or wild turkey, §113-294, (b).
Unlawfully taking, possessing or transporting wildlife.
Bald eagle or golden eagle, §113-294, (l).
Bear, §113-294, (c1).
Beaver, §113-294, (f).
Black-tailed deer, §113-294, (p).
Cougar, §113-294, (c2).
Coyotes, §113-294, (o).
Deer, §113-294, (d), (e).
Fox, §113-294, (j).
Migratory game birds, §113-294, (m).
Mule deer, §113-294, (p).
Vessels with motors.
Taking from or with use of, §113-294, (g).
Wild turkey, §113-294, (c).
Weapons.
Possession of certain weapons, §113-291.1, (c).
Wildlife resources commission.
Property owned by commission.
Willful removal, damage or destruction as misdemeanor, §113-264, (b).
Husband and wife.
Competency as witnesses in criminal action, §8-57, (a) to (c).
Postnuptial crimes, §52-12.
Icebox abandonment, §14-318.1.

CRIMINAL LAW AND PROCEDURE —Cont'd
Identification.
DNA analysis, §§15A-266 to 15A-270.
See DNA DATABASE AND DATABANKS.
Nontestimonial identification, §§15A-271 to 15A-282. See within this heading, "Nontestimonial identification."
Identifying marks on machines or apparatus.
Removing, defacing, etc., §14-401.4.
Illegitimacy.
Nonsupport of illegitimate child by parents, §49-2.
Immunity of witnesses.
Evidence of grant of immunity may be fully developed, §15A-1055, (a).
Jury.
Argument to jury as to impact of immunity, §15A-1055, (b).
Order to testify or produce other information, §15A-1051, (a).
Application for.
Court proceedings, §15A-1052, (a), (b).
Grand jury proceedings, §15A-1053, (a), (b).
Court proceedings, §15A-1052, (a).
Definition of "other information," §15A-1051, (c).
Grand jury proceedings, §15A-1053, (a).
Application, §15A-1053, (a), (b).
Jury trial.
Judge to inform jury of grant of immunity, §15A-1052, (c).
When effective, §15A-1051, (b).
Self-incrimination, §15A-1051, (a).
Sentence concessions, §15A-1054, (a).
Evidence of testimonial arrangement may be fully developed, §15A-1055, (a).
Jury.
Argument to jury as to impact of agreement, §15A-1055, (b).
Notice of agreement, §15A-1054, (c).
Recommendations, §15A-1054, (b).
Impaired driving generally.
See IMPAIRED DRIVING.
Impersonation.
Emergency medical services personnel, §14-276.1.
Firemen, §14-276.1.
Law enforcement officers, §14-277, (a) to (d1).
Public officer or employee, §14-277, (e).
Incapacity of defendant to proceed, §§15A-1001 to 15A-1008. See within this heading, "Mental health, developmental disabilities, substance abuse."
Incest, §14-178.
Inciting riot, §14-288.2.
Indecent exposure, §14-190.9.
Indecent liberties between children, §14-202.2.
Indecent liberties with minor, §14-202.1.
Indictments.
See INDICTMENTS.
Indigent persons.
False material statements as to indigency.
Defendant seeking appointment of counsel, §7A-456, (a).
Guilty pleas.
Waiver of right to counsel, §7A-457, (b).
Representation of indigent persons.
Generally, §§7A-450 to 7A-458.
See INDIGENT DEFENSE SERVICES.
Indigent defense services act, §§7A-498 to 7A-498.8.
See INDIGENT DEFENSE SERVICES.
Indigent services rules, Rules 1.1 to 3.7.
See INDIGENT DEFENSE SERVICES.

CRIMINAL LAW AND PROCEDURE —Cont'd
Indigent persons —Cont'd
Representation of indigent persons —Cont'd
Motion for appropriate relief.
Appointment of counsel for indigent defendant, §15A-1421.
Informations.
Consolidation of charges, §15A-643.
Contents, §15A-644, (b).
Plea of guilty or no contest in district court, §15A-644.1.
Defined, §15A-641, (b).
Informality.
Bill or warrant not quashed for informality, §15-153.
Joinder.
Offenses and defendants, §15A-643.
Pleadings in felony cases and misdemeanor cases initiated in supreme court division.
Amendment, §15A-923, (d).
Form, §15A-923, (b).
Prosecution on information, §15A-923, (a).
Plea of guilty or no contest in district court, §15A-644.1.
Previous convictions.
Allegations, §15A-645.
Superior court.
Prosecutions originating in superior court to be upon indictment or information, §15A-642, (a).
Superseding informations, §15A-646.
Information technology procurement.
Office of information technology services.
Bribery, §147-33.99.
False certification that bid submitted without collusion, §147-33.100.
Financial interest of officers in sources of supply, §147-33.99.
Unauthorized use of procedures for private gain, §147-33.98, (c).
Insanity defense.
Notice.
Discovery generally, §15A-905, (c), (d).
Intent to introduce expert testimony, §15A-959, (b).
Pretrial hearing, §15A-959, (a).
Pretrial determination of insanity, §15A-959, (c).
Insolvent or imprisoned debtor.
False swearing, §23-43.
Inspections.
Alcoholic beverages.
Interference with inspections, §18B-502, (b).
Instructions to jury, §§15A-1231, 15A-1232.
Additional instructions, §15A-1234.
Appeals.
Failure to object not waiver of right to appeal, §15A-1231, (d).
Capital punishment.
Consequences of guilty verdict, §15-176.4.
Conference on instructions, §15A-1231, (b).
Deliberations.
Instructions as to, §15A-1235, (a), (b).
Error in instructions to prejudice of defendant.
Grounds for correction of errors by appellate division, §15A-1442.
Impaneling jury.
Instruction by clerk, §15A-1216.
Opinion.
Prohibited, §15A-1232.
Removal of disruptive defendant.
Instruction that removal not to be considered in deliberations, §15A-1032, (b).

CRIMINAL LAW AND PROCEDURE —Cont'd
Instructions to jury —Cont'd
Tender of instructions by parties, §15A-1231, (a).
Insurance.
Adjusters.
Acting for unauthorized company, §58-33-115.
Acting without license or violating insurance law generally, §§58-3-130, 58-33-120.
Agents.
Unauthorized insurers.
Soliciting, negotiating or selling insurance for, §58-33-95, (a).
Alien governments.
Companies owned or controlled by violations, §58-16-20, (c).
Books and papers.
Failure to exhibit or making false statements, §58-2-200.
Brokers.
Acting without license or violating insurance law generally, §58-3-130.
Unauthorized insurers.
Soliciting, negotiating or selling insurance for, §58-33-95, (a).
Commissioner.
False statements to, §58-2-180.
Credit insurance.
Requiring excessive insurance, §58-57-80.
Embezzlement by agents, brokers or administrators, §§58-2-162, 58-2-163.
False statement to procure or deny benefit of policy or certificate, §58-2-161, (b).
Fire insurance.
Unauthorized insurer violations, §58-28-45, (h).
Limited representatives.
Unauthorized insurers.
Soliciting, negotiating or selling insurance for, §58-33-95, (a).
Policy violations, §58-50-70.
Public officer and employee insurance committee, §58-31-60, (d).
Insurance consumer and customer information privacy.
False pretenses.
Obtaining information under, criminal penalty, §58-39-115.
Interfering with emergency communications, §14-286.2.
Internal improvements.
Report of railroad, canal, etc.
Failure to report, §124-3.
Interstate agreement on detainers, §§15A-761 to 15A-767.
See DETAINERS.
Interstate earnings of employee.
Collection out of state to avoid exemption, §95-75.
Intoxication.
Aircraft operation while impaired, §63-27.
Boating safety.
Operation of boat or manipulation of water skis while intoxicated, §75A-10, (b), (b1).
Penalty, §75A-18, (b).
County alcoholic beverage control board.
Defense of employees and officers in civil or criminal actions, §160A-167.
Definitions, §14-443.
Elements of offense.
No prosecution for public intoxication, §14-447, (a).
Entering plea to charge, §14-445, (c).

CRIMINAL LAW AND PROCEDURE —Cont'd
Intoxication —Cont'd
Definitions —Cont'd
Prehearing review of drinking history, §14-445, (d).
Shelter or health-care facility.
Transport and release of person to appropriate facility, §14-447, (b).
Ways of being intoxicated and disruptive in public, §14-444, (a).
Penalty for violation of provisions, §14-444, (b).
Impaired driving generally.
See IMPAIRED DRIVING.
Public conveyances.
Intoxicated person entering public conveyance after being forbidden by driver, §62-150.
Public intoxication.
Acquittal of defendant because of alcoholism.
Disposition of defendant, §14-446.
Defense of alcoholism, §14-445, (a).
Disposition of defendant acquitted because of alcoholism, §14-446.
Request for additional information, §14-445, (b).
Investment advisers.
Criminal penalties, §78C-39.
Involuntary servitude, §14-43.2.
Jail keepers causing injuries to prisoners, §162-55.
Jails.
See JAILS.
Joinder.
Defendants, §15A-926, (b).
Objection to joinder, §15A-927, (c).
Failure to prove grounds for joinder, §15A-927, (d).
Offenses, §15A-926, (a).
Failure to join related offenses, §15A-926, (c).
Venue.
Concurrent venue, §15A-132.
Journalist's qualified privilege against disclosure in any legal proceeding, §8-53.11, (b).
Definitions, §8-53.11, (a).
Eyewitness observation of criminal or tortuous conduct, no privilege, §8-53.11, (d).
Order to compel disclosure, notice to journalist and hearing, §8-53.11, (c).
Overcoming privilege, person seeking to compel disclosure, §8-53.11, (c).
Judges.
Admonitions to jurors, §15A-1236, (a).
Death, §15A-1224, (b).
Disability, §15A-1224, (a), (b).
Disqualification.
Motion of state or defendant, §15A-1223, (b), (c).
Time for filing, §15A-1223, (d).
Own motion, §15A-1223, (a).
Witness in case, §15A-1223, (e).
Opinion.
Expression of opinion in presence of jury prohibited, §15A-1222.
Verdict.
Comment on verdict.
Prohibited, §1-180.1.
Judicial comment on verdict, §15A-1239.
Judgments, entry of unauthorized judgment, §14-221.2.
Junk dealers.
Restrictions as to location of junkyards, §136-145.

CRIMINAL LAW AND PROCEDURE —Cont'd
Jurisdiction for appeals.
Correction of errors by appellate division, §15A-1448, (a).
Lack of jurisdiction on part of trial court.
Errors which may be reviewed even though no objection, exception or motion made, §15A-1446, (d).
Grounds for correction, §15A-1442.
Jury.
Admonitions to jurors, §15A-1236, (a).
Alternate jurors, §15A-1215, (a).
Capital cases, §15A-1215, (b).
Peremptory challenges.
One peremptory challenge for each alternate juror, §15A-1217, (c).
Argument to jury.
Capital punishment.
Consequences of guilty verdict, §15-176.5.
District attorney may argue for death penalty, §15-176.1.
Driver's license.
Loss.
Consequences of guilty verdict, §15-176.9.
Limitations on, §15A-1230.
Motor vehicle driver's license.
Loss.
Consequences of guilty verdict, §15-176.9.
Order of proceedings, §15A-1221, (a).
Bribery of juror, §14-220.
Capital punishment.
Alternate jurors in capital cases, §15A-1215, (b).
Arguments of counsel to jury.
Consequences of guilty verdict, §15-176.5.
District attorney may argue for death penalty, §15-176.1.
No limit as to number, §7A-97.
Informing potential jurors on consequences of guilty verdict, §15-176.3.
Instructions to jury on consequences of guilty verdict, §15-176.4.
Peremptory challenges.
Number in capital cases, §15A-1217, (a).
Questioning potential jurors on consequences of guilty verdict, §15-176.3.
Selection of jurors in capital cases.
Selection one at a time, §15A-1214, (j).
Sentencing proceedings.
Generally, §15A-2000, (a).
Recommendation by jury as to sentence, §15A-2000, (b).
Findings in support of sentence of death, §15A-2000, (c).
Sentencing upon, §15A-2002.
Challenges.
After juror accepted but before jury impaneled, §15A-1214, (g).
Challenge for cause.
Appeal on grounds that challenge for cause not allowed.
Prerequisites, §15A-1214, (h).
Grounds, §15A-1212.
Renewal of challenge for cause previously denied, §15A-1214, (i).
Challenge to the panel, §15A-1211, (c).
Judge to decide all challenges, §15A-1211, (b).
Peremptory challenges, §15A-1214, (d), (e).
Number of peremptory challenges, §15A-1217.
Communication with juror, §14-225.2.
Deadlocked jury, §15A-1235, (c), (d).

CRIMINAL LAW AND PROCEDURE —Cont'd
Jury —Cont'd
Deliberations.
Eavesdropping, §§14-227.2, 14-227.3.
Instructions as to, §15A-1235, (a), (b).
Evidence.
Review of testimony, §15A-1233, (a).
Use of evidence by jury, §15A-1233, (b).
Excusing jurors.
Power of judge, §15A-1211, (d).
Harassment of juror.
Generally, §14-225.2.
Hung jury, §15A-1235, (c), (d).
Impaneling jury, §15A-1216.
Indictment.
Reading of indictment to prospective jurors or to jury.
Prohibited, §15A-1221, (b).
Instructions, §§15A-1231, 15A-1232.
Additional instructions, §15A-1234, (a).
Given in open court, §15A-1234, (d).
Parties to be informed, §15A-1234, (c).
Record, §15A-1234, (d).
Repeating other instructions when additional instructions given, §15A-1234, (b).
Appeals.
Failure to object not waiver of right to appeal, §15A-1231, (d).
Capital punishment.
Consequences of guilty verdict, §15-176.4.
Conference on instructions, §15A-1231, (b).
Deliberations.
Instructions as to, §15A-1235, (a), (b).
Error in instructions to prejudice of defendant.
Grounds for correction of errors by appellate division, §15A-1442.
Impaneling jury.
Instruction by clerk, §15A-1216.
Opinion.
Prohibited, §15A-1232.
Record, §15A-1231, (d).
Additional instructions, §15A-1234, (d).
Removal of disruptive defendant.
Instruction that removal not to be considered in deliberations, §15A-1032, (b).
Tender of instructions by parties, §15A-1231, (a).
Notes by jury.
Authorized, §15A-1228.
Number of jurors, §15A-1201.
Opinion.
Argument to jury, §15A-1230, (a).
Expression of opinion by judge prohibited, §15A-1222.
Instructions.
Expression of opinion prohibited, §15A-1232.
Order of proceedings in jury trial, §15A-1221, (a).
Polling jury, §15A-1238.
Right to trial by jury, §15A-1201; Const. N. C., art. I, §24.
Selection of jurors, §15A-1211, (a).
Calling of jurors from panel, §15A-1214, (a).
Capital cases.
Selection of jurors one at a time, §15A-1214, (j).
Examination of prospective jurors, §15A-1214, (c) to (e).
Replacement jurors, §15A-1214, (f).
Informing prospective jurors of case, §§15A-1213, 15A-1214, (b).

CRIMINAL LAW AND PROCEDURE —Cont'd
Jury —Cont'd
Selection of jurors —Cont'd
Replacement jurors, §15A-1214, (d), (e).
Examination, §15A-1214, (f).
Sequestering jurors, §15A-1236, (b), (c).
Special venire from another county.
Motion for, §15A-958.
Verdict, §15A-1237.
Impeachment of verdict, §15A-1240, (b).
Testimony of juror, §15A-1240, (c).
Judicial comment on verdict, §15A-1239.
Mentally ill.
Finding that defendant not guilty on grounds of insanity at time of offense.
Verdict must so state, §15A-1237, (c).
Multiple defendants.
Separate verdict, §15A-1237, (d).
Multiple offenses, §15A-1237, (e).
Polling jury, §15A-1238.
Signing by foreman, §15A-1237, (a).
Unanimity, §§15A-1201, 15A-1237, (b).
Written verdict, §15A-1237, (a).
View by jury, §15A-1229, (a).
Witnesses.
Testimony at site of jury view, §15A-1229, (b).
Justice academy, §§17D-1 to 17D-4.
Justice department.
See JUSTICE DEPARTMENT.
Juvenile prosecuted as adult.
Commission of criminal offense after superior court conviction, §7B-1604, (b).
Commission of criminal offense on or after sixteenth birthday, §7B-1604, (a).
Emancipated juvenile prosecuted as adult, §7B-1604, (a).
Transfer of jurisdiction of juvenile to superior court, §7B-2200.
Court not transferring case to superior court, §7B-2203, (d).
Detention pending release, §7B-2204.
Detention pending transfer to department of correction, §7B-2204.
Fingerprinting juvenile transferred, §7B-2201.
Jurisdiction of superior court on transfer, §7B-2203, (c).
Pretrial release, §7B-2204.
Probable cause hearing.
Burden of state, §7B-2202, (c).
Conducted in felony cases, §7B-2202, (a).
Continuing for good cause, §7B-2202, (a).
Probable cause found and transferred to superior court not required, proceeding to transfer hearing, §7B-2202, (e).
Probable cause not found, §7B-2202, (f).
Prosecutor representing state, §7B-2202, (b).
Representation of juvenile by counsel, §7B-2202, (b).
Testimony and cross-examination, §7B-2202, (b).
Time for conducting, §7B-2202, (a).
Waiver of right and stipulating to finding of probable cause, §7B-2202, (d).
Transfer hearing, §7B-2203, (a).
Factors considered, §7B-2203, (b).
Transfer order, §7B-2203, (c).
Kaitlyn's law.
Child care facilities.
Unauthorized administration of medicine, §110-102.1A.

CRIMINAL LAW AND PROCEDURE —Cont'd
Kennels.
Cruelty to animals, §19A-35.
Unlicensed operation, §19A-33.
Kerosene.
Sale location prohibitions, §119-16.3.
Kerosene distributors, suppliers and terminal operators.
Bond or letter of credit.
Required for license, failure to comply, §119-15.3, (c).
Kidnapping and abduction, §§14-39 to 14-41.
Bail and recognizance, §15A-534.4.
Capital punishment.
Aggravating circumstances.
Capital felony in commission of kidnapping, §15A-2000, (e).
Child custody.
Transporting child outside state.
Intent to violate custody order, §14-320.1.
Corporations.
Punishment for firm or corporation convicted of kidnapping, §14-39, (c).
Elements of offense, §14-39, (a).
Employment of minors.
Enticing minors out of state for purpose of employment, §14-40.
Felonious restraint.
Lesser included offense of kidnapping, §14-43.3.
First degree kidnapping, §14-39, (b).
Murder during commission, §14-17.
Penalties for kidnapping, §14-39, (b).
Second degree kidnapping, §14-39, (b).
Labor.
Blacklisting employees, §14-355.
Duties owed employers.
Influencing employees to violate duties, §§14-353, 14-354.
Earnings of employees in interstate commerce.
Collection out of state to avoid exemption, §95-75.
Labor union violations by public employee, §95-99.
Medical examination as condition of employment, §14-357.1.
Payments to or for benefit of labor organization.
Violations, §95-104.
Lake lure marine commission.
Regulations applicable to lake and shoreline area.
Violations, §77-87, (b).
Landlord and tenant.
Lien on crops.
Tobacco marketing cards.
Failure of tenant to account for sales as misdemeanor, §42-22.1.
Unlawful seizure by landlord or removal by tenant, §42-22.
Sexual harassment in rental of residential property, §14-395.1, (a).
Willful destruction by tenant, §42-11.
Wrongful surrender to other landlord, §42-13.
Landscape architects.
Practice without registration or license, §89A-8, (a).
Larceny, §§14-70 to 14-86.1.
See LARCENY.
Laser devices.
Unlawful to intentionally point.
At head or face of another, §14-34.8, (b).
At law enforcement officer, §14-34.8, (b).
Inapplicability of provisions, §14-34.8, (d), (e).
Infraction, §14-34.8, (c).

CRIMINAL LAW AND PROCEDURE —Cont'd
Laser devices —Cont'd
Unlawful to intentionally point —Cont'd
Laser defined, §14-34.8, (a).
Law enforcement association publications.
Soliciting advertising, §14-401.10.
Leases.
Motor vehicles.
Sublease and loan assumption arranging, §20-106.2, (d), (e).
Legislators.
Bribery, §120-86, (a).
Extortion, §120-86, (b) to (e).
Letters.
Anonymous or threatening letters, §14-394.
Opening of sealed letters.
Unauthorized opening, §14-372.
Publishing of sealed letters.
Unauthorized publishing, §14-372.
Reading of sealed letters.
Unauthorized reading, §14-372.
Library books.
Failure to return, §125-11.
Library, museum, gallery, etc., theft or destruction of property, §14-398.
License taxes.
Application for license.
False statements, §105-33, (j).
Liens.
Docketing in violation of restrictions, §44A-12.1, (c).
Lighthouses.
Anchorage in range of, §76-43.
Displaying false lights on seashore, §14-282.
Lights.
Red or blue lights.
Operating vehicles resembling law enforcement vehicle, §20-137.2, (b).
Limitation of actions.
Civil actions seeking to recover damages arising out of criminal act, §1-15.1.
Dismissal of criminal charges.
Motion to dismiss.
Grounds, §15A-954, (a).
Voluntary dismissal by state.
Statute of limitations not tolled, §15A-931, (b).
Misdemeanors, §15-1.
Limited liability companies.
Franchise tax.
Controlled companies.
Underpayment, fraud to evade, penalty, §105-114.1, (h).
Interrogatories by secretary of state.
Manager's refusal or failure to answer, §57C-1-32, (b).
Liquefied petroleum gas dealers.
Violations, §119-59, (a).
Liquid fuels, lubricating oils, greases, etc.
Violations of article, §119-13.
Littering, §14-399.
Livestock.
Larceny, §14-81.
Livestock diseases.
Failure to destroy animal with glanders or farcy, §106-404.
Loans, usurious.
Household and kitchen furniture, §14-391.
Lobbying.
Violations of article, §120-47.9.

CRIMINAL LAW AND PROCEDURE —Cont'd
Local boards of education.
Defense of members in criminal action, §115C-43, (a) to (c).
Discipline of students.
Force, §115C-390.
Local government finance.
Fiscal control.
Annual independent audit.
Violations of requirements as misdemeanors, §159-34, (a).
Local governments.
Buildings unfit of human habitation.
Occupancy of buildings so posted, §160A-443.
Local officers government and employees.
Defense of criminal proceedings, §160A-167.
Locksmith licensing.
Unlicensed operation, §74F-3.
Long-term care ombudsman.
Unlawful disclosures, §143B-181.20, (a).
Willful interference, §143B-181.25.
Looting, §14-288.6, (b).
Lotteries, §§14-289 to 14-291.2.
Advertisements.
Misdemeanor offense of advertising lotteries, §14-289.
Agents.
Acting as agent for lotteries, §14-291.
Chain schemes.
Prohibited, §14-291.2.
Dealing in lotteries, §14-290.
"Numbers" tickets, §14-291.1.
Pyramid distribution plans.
Contracts void and unenforceable, §14-291.2, (d).
Definitions, §14-291.2, (b).
Enjoining continuation of scheme, §14-291.2, (c).
Prohibited, §14-291.2, (a).
Selling lottery tickets, §14-291.
Lubricating oils.
Violations of article, §§119-4, 119-13.
Machine guns.
Sale, use or possession, §14-409.
Magazines.
Communicating libelous matter to magazines, §14-47.
Magistrates.
Appeals, §15A-1431.
Powers of magistrates, §7A-273.
Arrest warrants.
Issuance of warrant, §7A-273.
Bail.
Granting of bail for noncapital offense, §7A-273.
Infraction cases, §7A-273.
Initial appearances.
Conduct of, §7A-273.
Judgments and decrees.
Entering judgments of chief district judge, §7A-273.
Misdemeanor cases, §7A-273.
Search warrants.
Issuance of warrant, §7A-273.
Written appearances.
Acceptance of, §7A-273.
Maiming.
Malicious maiming, §14-30.
Malfeasance.
Corporation officers and agents.
Misconduct in private office, §14-254.
Malicious conduct by prisoners, §14-258.4, (a).

CRIMINAL LAW AND PROCEDURE —Cont'd
Manslaughter.
Double jeopardy.
Death by vehicle.
Subsequent prosecutions prohibited, §20-141.4, (c).
Indictments.
Essentials of bill, §15-144.
Punishment for manslaughter, §14-18.
Manufactured homes.
Engaging in business without a license, §143-143.24.
Uniform standards.
Health and safety of purchaser threatened, §143-151, (b).
Marine fisheries commission rules violations, §113-135, (a) to (c).
Marine fisheries inspectors.
Refusal of person to stop in obedience to directions of, §113-136, (j).
Marriage.
Licenses.
Obtaining by false representation as misdemeanor, §51-15.
Solemnizing without license as misdemeanor, §51-7.
Massage and bodywork therapy.
Unlicensed acts, §90-634, (b).
Mass death and destruction weapons.
Manufacture, assembly, possession, etc., §14-288.8.
Nuclear, biological or chemical weapons.
False report or hoax, §§14-288.23, 14-288.24.
Manufacture, assembly, possession, etc., §14-288.21.
Use and delivery of weapons, §14-288.22.
Meat of diseased animal, selling, §14-342.
Medicaid.
Conflicts of interest, §108A-65, (b).
Fraud.
Providers, §108A-63, (c).
Recipients, §108A-64, (c).
Property of patients' violations, §108A-60, (b).
Withholding of information, §108A-57, (b).
Medical waste.
Depositing in navigable waters, §76-40, (a1).
Water and air resources.
Prohibited disposal, §143-214.2A, (a), (c).
Meetings of public bodies.
Disrupting, §143-318.17.
Mental health, developmental disabilities, substance abuse.
Advance instruction for mental health treatment.
Alteration, forgery, concealment or destruction of instrument, §122C-76.
Area authorities.
Unlawful access or disclosure of personnel records, §122C-158, (g), (h).
Camp Butner and community of Butner.
Violations of ordinances or rules, §122C-406.
Consumer advocacy program.
Confidentiality violations, §122C-17, (b).
Willful interference with consumer advocate, §122C-20.
Death penalty for mentally retarded defendants, §15A-2005, (b).
Burden of proof on defendant, §15A-2005, (a), (c), (f).
Definitions, §15A-2005, (a).
Jury determination of aggravating or mitigating circumstance.
Consideration of evidence of retardation, §15A-2005, (g).

CRIMINAL LAW AND PROCEDURE —Cont'd
Mental health, developmental disabilities, substance abuse —Cont'd
Death penalty for mentally retarded defendants —Cont'd
Legal defenses not precluded by pretrial determination, §15A-2005, (d).
Motion seeking appropriate relief.
Post conviction determination of mental retardation, §15A-2006.
Noncapital case, court declaration, §15A-2005, (c).
Other sentence not precluded, §15A-2005, (h).
Postconviction determination of mental retardation, §15A-2006.
Pretrial hearing to determine retardation, §15A-2005, (c).
Special issue submitted to jury.
Pretrial determination of retardation not found, §15A-2005, (e).
Defendant regains capacity for trial, §15A-1006.
Defendants incapable of proceeding, §15A-1005.
Defense of insanity.
Notice, §§15A-905, (c), (d), 15A-959, (a).
Intent to introduce expert testimony, §15A-959, (b).
Pretrial determination of insanity, §15A-959, (c).
Escape and commission of crime after escape or while resident of facility, §122C-254.
Furnishing false information, §122C-80, (f).
Incapacity of defendant to proceed.
Commitment.
Civil commitment, §15A-1003, (a), (b).
Evidence admissible at proceedings, §15A-1003, (c).
Institution of proceedings, §15A-1002, (b).
Observation and treatment, §15A-1002, (b).
Confidentiality of information.
Reports to court, §15A-1002, (d).
Determination of incapacity, §15A-1002, (b).
Dismissal of charges, §15A-1008.
Supplemental hearings, §15A-1007, (c).
Dismissal with leave, §15A-1009.
Hearings.
Supplemental hearings, §15A-1007, (a).
Court's own determination, §15A-1007, (b).
Dismissal of charges, §15A-1007, (c).
Motion, §15A-1002, (a).
No proceedings when defendant mentally incapacitated, §15A-1001, (a).
Exception as to motions which can be handled by counsel without assistance of defendant, §15A-1001, (b).
Orders for safeguarding defendant, §15A-1004, (a) to (c).
Amendment or supplementation, §15A-1004, (f).
Reports to court, §15A-1004, (d).
Return of defendant to stand trial, §15A-1004, (e).
Reports to court, §§15A-1002, (b), (b1), (d), 15A-1005.
Hospital or institution with custody of defendant, §15A-1002, (d).
Return of defendant for trial upon gaining capacity, §§15A-1004, (e), 15A-1006.
Temporary confinement of defendant, §15A-1002, (c).
Not guilty by reason of insanity.
Civil commitment of defendant, §15A-1321.
Temporary restraint of defendant, §15A-1322.

CRIMINAL LAW AND PROCEDURE —Cont'd
Mental health, developmental disabilities, substance abuse —Cont'd
Not guilty by reason of insanity —Cont'd
Verdict to state, §15A-1237, (c).
Operating a licensable facility without a license, §122C-28.
Quality assurance activities.
Unlawful disclosure of confidential information by secretary or his agent, §122C-192, (b).
Unlawful disclosure of confidential information generally, §122C-52, (e).
Unlawful disclosure of information gathered during inspections, §122C-25.
Violations of clients' rights, §§122C-62, 122C-65, (a), (b), 122C-66.
Methamphetamine watch program.
Immunity from civil and criminal liability.
Good faith actions, §114-43.
Migrant farm workers.
Motor carriers.
Violations of regulations, §20-215.4.
Military personnel.
Discrimination against, §127B-15.
Military property sales facilities.
Perjury.
Application for permit, §127B-5.
Violations of provisions by dealers, §127B-7.
Militia.
Composition of unauthorized militia.
Convicted felons excepted, §127A-7.
Conversion or destruction of military property, §127A-131.
Muster role.
Placing name wrongfully, §127A-152.
Organizing company without authority, §127A-151.
Milk case or crate larceny, §14-72.4.
Mines and minerals.
Notice of beginning business of manufacturing products from mineral resources of state.
Violations as misdemeanors, §113-25.
Miscarriage.
Injury to pregnant woman resulting in miscarriage or stillbirth, §14-18.2.
Use of instruments or drugs, §14-45.
Misconduct in private office.
Corporation officers and agents.
Malfeasance of officers and agents, §14-254, (a).
Definition of "person," §14-254.
Railroad officers.
Failure of certain officers to account with successors, §14-253.
Misconduct in public office, §§14-228 to 14-252.
Misdemeanors.
See MISDEMEANORS.
Missing persons center releasing information improperly, §143B-499.6.
Mistrial.
Deadlocked jury, §15A-1235, (d).
Disability of trial judge, §15A-1224, (a).
Finding of facts required, §15A-1064.
Grounds.
Hung jury, §15A-1063.
Impossibility of proceeding, §15A-1063.
Prejudice to defendant, §15A-1061.
Prejudice to state, §15A-1062.
Hung jury, §15A-1063.
Impossibility of proceeding, §15A-1063.
Prejudice to defendant, §15A-1061.
Prejudice to state, §15A-1062.

CRIMINAL LAW AND PROCEDURE —Cont'd
Mistrial —Cont'd
Procedure following mistrial, §15A-1065.
Modes of prosecution, Const. N. C., art. I, §23.
Money transmitters, §53-208.26.
Morality.
Public morality and decency.
Offenses against public morality and decency, §§14-177 to 14-202.2.
Mortgage bankers and brokers, §53-243.14.
Mortgages and deeds of trust.
Secondary or junior mortgages.
Willful or knowing violations, §24-17.
Motion for appropriate relief.
Action on, §15A-1420, (c), (d).
Actual prejudice to defendant, §15A-1419, (d).
Affidavits.
Supporting affidavits, §15A-1420, (b).
Amendment, §15A-1415, (g).
Appeals.
Correction of errors by appellate division.
Ancillary actions during appeal, §15A-1453, (b).
Denial of motion.
No effect on right to assert error on appeal, §15A-1422, (e).
Finality of decision, §15A-1422, (f).
Making of motion not prerequisite to asserting error on appeal, §15A-1422, (a).
Motion for appropriate relief in appellate division, §15A-1418.
Motion may be made and acted on regardless of notice of appeal, §15A-1414, (c).
Ruling of court subject to review, §15A-1444, (f).
Ruling on motion, §15A-1422, (b) to (d).
Appellate division.
Determination by appellate court on basis of materials before it, §15A-1418, (b).
Generally, §15A-1418, (a).
Remand, §15A-1418, (b), (c).
Authorized, §15A-1411, (a).
Capital cases, §15A-1415, (a).
Access to files, §15A-1415, (f).
Mental retardation, postconviction determination, §15A-2006.
Constitutional provisions.
Grounds which may be asserted without limitation as to time, §15A-1415, (b).
Coram nobis.
Relief formerly available now available by motion for appropriate relief, §15A-1411, (c).
Death sentence.
Mental retardation, postconviction determination, §15A-2006.
Denial.
Appeal from, §15A-1422, (b) to (d).
Burden of proof of defendant, §15A-1419, (b), (c).
Effect.
No effect on right to assert error on appeal, §15A-1422, (e).
Grounds, §15A-1419, (a).
Dismissal of charges.
Relief available, §15A-1417, (a).
Effect of provisions.
Procedural in nature, §15A-1412.
Filing, §15A-1420, (a).
Form, §15A-1420, (a).
Fundamental miscarriage of justice, §15A-1419, (e).

CRIMINAL LAW AND PROCEDURE —Cont'd
Motion for appropriate relief —Cont'd
Granting motion.
Appeal from, §15A-1422, (b), (c).
Court's own motion, §15A-1420, (d).
Generally, §15A-1420, (c).
Grounds, §§15A-1414 to 15A-1416.
Motion by state.
Motion within ten days of entry of judgment, §15A-1416, (a).
Motion without limitation as to time, §15A-1416, (b).
Motion within ten days from entry of judgment, §15A-1414, (b).
Motion without limitation of time, §15A-1415, (b).
Habeas corpus.
Availability of motion for appropriate relief not a bar, §15A-1411, (c).
Hearings, §15A-1420, (c).
Indigent defendants.
Appointment of counsel, §15A-1421.
Judges.
Power to act on motion.
Judge who did not hear case, §15A-1413, (c).
Trial judge, §15A-1413, (a), (b).
Lesser included offenses.
Plea of guilty to.
When court may accept, §15A-1417, (b).
Mental retardation, postconviction determination.
Persons convicted of first degree murder and sentenced to death, §15A-2006.
Motion for new trial.
Relief formerly available now available by motion for appropriate relief, §15A-1411, (c).
Motion in arrest of judgment.
Relief formerly available now available by motion for appropriate relief, §15A-1411, (c).
Motion in original cause and not new proceeding, §15A-1411, (b).
Motion to set aside verdict.
Relief formerly available now available by motion for appropriate relief, §15A-1411, (c).
Newly discovered evidence, §15A-1415, (c).
New trial.
Motion for new trial.
Relief formerly available now available by motion for appropriate relief, §15A-1411, (c).
Relief available, §15A-1417, (a).
Post-conviction proceedings.
Relief formerly available now available by motion for appropriate relief, §15A-1411, (c).
Procedural nature of provisions, §15A-1412.
Procedure on, §15A-1420.
Relief available, §15A-1417, (a).
Relief from errors committed in criminal trials and proceedings, §15A-1401.
Resentencing, §15A-1417, (c).
Service, §15A-1420, (a).
State of North Carolina.
Motion by state.
Motion within ten days of entry of judgment, §15A-1416, (a).
Motion without limitation as to time, §15A-1416, (b).

CRIMINAL LAW AND PROCEDURE —Cont'd
Motion for appropriate relief —Cont'd
Time for, §§15A-1414 to 15A-1416.
Extension of time, §15A-1415, (d).
Motion by state, §15A-1416, (a), (b).
No limitation of time for certain grounds, §15A-1415, (a), (b).
Ten days from entry of judgment, §15A-1414, (a), (b).
Trial judge.
Power to act on motion, §15A-1413, (a), (b).
Waiver of attorney-client privilege, §15A-1415, (e).
Motions.
Bill of particulars.
Motion for, §15A-925, (a), (b).
Change of venue, §§15A-133, (c), 15A-957.
Demurrer to the evidence, §15-173.
Denial of motions to prejudice of defendant.
Grounds for correction of errors by appellate division, §15A-1442.
Dismissal.
Death of defendant.
Dismissal required, §15A-954, (b).
Deferral of ruling on motion to dismiss when charge to be reinstituted, §15A-956.
Grounds, §15A-954, (a).
Motion to dismiss indictment, §15A-955.
Insufficiency of evidence.
Reviewable on appeal regardless of whether motion made during trial, §15A-1227, (d).
Ruling by judge on motion before trial may proceed, §15A-1227, (c).
Time for motion, §15A-1227, (a), (b).
Time for motion to dismiss, §15A-954, (c).
Disqualification of judge.
Motion of state or defendant, §15A-1223, (b), (c).
Time for filing, §15A-1223, (d).
Own motion, §15A-1223, (a).
District courts.
Motions practice, §15A-953.
Failure of pleadings to charge crime.
Motion by defendant to dismiss charges, §15A-924, (e).
Filing, §15A-951, (c).
Inflammatory or prejudicial surplusage in pleadings.
Motion of defendant to strike, §15A-924, (f).
Jury.
Special venire from another county, §15A-958.
Mental incapacity of defendant to proceed, §15A-1002, (a).
Notes by the jury, §15A-1228.
Post-trial motions.
Appeals.
Making of post-trial motions not prerequisite to assertion of error on appeal, §15A-1446, (c).
Denial of post-trial motion to which defendant entitled.
Grounds for correction of errors by appellate division, §15A-1442.
Motion for appropriate relief, §§15A-1411 to 15A-1422.
Motion for new trial.
Relief formerly available now available by motion for appropriate relief, §15A-1411, (c).
Motion in arrest of judgment.
Relief formerly available now available by motion for appropriate relief, §15A-1411, (c).

CRIMINAL LAW AND PROCEDURE —Cont'd
Motions —Cont'd
Post-trial motions —Cont'd
Motion to set aside verdict.
Relief formerly available now available by motion for appropriate relief, §15A-1411, (c).
Pretrial motions.
Hearing of motion.
Date, §15A-952, (f).
Scope, §15A-952, (a).
Time limits, §15A-952, (b), (c).
Exceptions, §15A-952, (d).
Failure to file within time required, §15A-952, (e).
Requirements, §15A-951, (a).
Service, §15A-951, (b).
Proof of service, §15A-951, (c).
Severance of offenses, §15A-927.
Suppression of evidence.
Motion to suppress evidence, §§15A-971 to 15A-980. See within this heading, "Evidence."
Motor carriers.
Embezzlement of COD shipments, §62-273.
Migrant farm workers.
Violations of regulations, §20-215.4.
Registration fees.
Carrying charge, §20-94.
Taxation.
Road tax on carriers using fuel purchased outside state.
Violations of provisions as misdemeanors, §105-449.51.
Motor carrier safety regulation unit.
Furnishing false information to division, §§20-396, 20-397.
Refusal to allow inspections, §20-390.
Unlawful motor carrier operations, §20-396.
Willful evasion of department of crime control and public safety regulations, §§20-396, 20-397.
Willful injury to property of motor carrier, §20-395.
Motor vehicle accident report violations, §20-166.1, (k).
False information, §20-279.31, (b).
Motor vehicles.
Accident report violations, §20-166.1, (k).
False information, §20-279.31, (b).
Accidents.
Failure to stop and give name, §20-166, (c), (c1).
Leaving scene of accident, §20-166, (a), (b).
Air bags.
Unlawful installation or reinstallation, §20-136.2.
Brake system.
Violations of sales restriction, §20-124, (h).
Certificates of title.
Altering or forging certificate of title, registration card or application, §20-71, (a).
Borrowing or lending, §20-111.
Reproducing or possessing blank title, §20-71, (b).
Satisfaction of liens.
Lienor refusal to surrender certificate, §20-59.
Transfer of title or interest.
Assignment of blank title.
Dealer or insurance company, §20-75.
Assignment with blank signature, §20-72, (b).
Failure of new owner to apply for new certificate, §20-73, (c).

CRIMINAL LAW AND PROCEDURE —Cont'd
Motor vehicles —Cont'd
Certificates of title —Cont'd
Transfer of title or interest —Cont'd
False statement in making an application, §20-74.
Conversion.
Bailees, lessees, tenants or attorneys in fact, §14-168.1.
Evidence of intent to convert property.
Prima facie evidence of intent, §14-168.3.
Damage to vehicle.
Failure to disclose when transferring, §20-71.4, (d).
Dealers.
License applications.
Violations of license provisions, §20-308.
Definitions, §14-168.2.
Division of motor vehicles.
Witness failure to obey summons, §20-47, (b).
Drivers' licenses.
Driving while license revoked, §20-28, (a).
Electronic information verification system.
Collecting and retaining information, §20-37.02, (c).
Failure to surrender, §20-45, (b).
False or fictitious name or address or other fraud, §20-30.
General penalty provision, §20-35, (a).
Learners' permits.
False or fictitious name or address or other fraud, §20-30.
Sale of reproduction, facsimile or simulation of license, §20-30.
Loss.
Informing jury of consequences of guilty verdict, §15-176.9.
Refusal to surrender license, §20-29.
Sale of reproduction, facsimile or simulation of license, §20-30.
Driver training schools.
Violations of licensing provisions, §20-327.
Driving by person less than 21 years old after consuming alcohol or drugs, §20-138.3, (a), (c).
Failure to return hired property, §14-167.
Felony death by vehicles, §20-141.4, (a1).
Punishment, §20-141.4, (b).
Felony violations.
Punished as class 1 felon, §20-177.
Financial responsibility, §20-279.31, (b) to (d).
False certification, §20-313.1, (a).
False information concerning another's responsibility, §20-313.1, (b).
Financial responsibility not in effect.
Revocation of registration.
Failure of owner to deliver certificate of registration and plates, §20-312.
Unlawful operation of motor vehicle, §20-313, (a).
Fraud.
Hiring with intent to defraud, §14-168.
Rental vehicles, §20-106.1.
Housemovers.
Article or rules violations, §20-371, (a).
Impaired driving.
Commercial vehicles.
Sentencing, §20-138.2, (e).
Sentencing, §20-138.1, (d).
Infractions or misdemeanors.
Penalty not specified, §20-176.
Injuring vehicle with intent to steal, §20-107, (b).

CRIMINAL LAW AND PROCEDURE —Cont'd
Motor vehicles —Cont'd
Insignia.
Operating vehicles resembling law enforcement vehicle, §20-137.2, (b).
Inspections, §20-183.8, (c).
Insurance.
Rental vehicle violations of insurance provisions, §20-284.
Leases.
Sublease and loan assumption arranging, §20-106.2, (d), (e).
License plates.
Alteration, disguise or concealment of numbers, §20-63, (g).
Borrowing or lending, §20-111.
Failure to surrender, §20-45, (b).
Manufacturer's and dealer's special plates.
Registration violations, §20-79, (e).
Neglect or refusal to clean plates, §20-63, (e).
Operating with false numbers, §20-63, (f).
Refusal to surrender illegible plates, §20-63, (a).
Lights.
Red or blue lights.
Violations of prohibition, §20-130.1, (e).
Malicious or willful injury to hired personal property, §14-165.
Manufacturers.
License applications.
Violations of license provisions, §20-308.
Manufacturer's certificate of origin.
Assignment with blank signature, §20-52.1, (c).
False sworn certification, §20-52.1, (d).
Manufacturer's serial or engine numbers.
Altering or changing numbers, §20-109, (a), (b).
Prohibitions as to vehicles without numbers, §20-108, (a).
Mechanic's or storage liens.
Failure to report unclaimed vehicles, §20-77, (d).
Misdemeanor death by vehicle, §20-141.4, (a2).
Punishment, §20-141.4, (b).
Nuclear fuel.
Transportation of spent nuclear fuel, §20-167.1, (d).
Odometers.
Prohibited acts, §20-350.
Unlawful change of mileage, §20-350.
Open container law, §20-138.7, (e).
Operating a commercial vehicle after consuming alcohol, §20-138.2A, (c).
Operating a school bus, school activity bus, or child care vehicle after consuming alcohol, §20-138.2B, (c).
Options to purchase.
Failing to return rented property on which there is purchase option, §14-168.4.
Ownership documents.
Failure to surrender, §20-45, (b).
Passing.
Driver of overtaken vehicle not giving way to right in favor of overtaking vehicle, §20-149, (b).
Peace officers.
Rights of misdemeanor arrestee, §20-114, (a).
Private lots.
Unauthorized vehicles, §20-219.2, (b).
Protection of bailor against acts of bailee.
Violations made misdemeanors, §14-169.
Racing on streets and highways, §20-141.3, (a) to (c).

CRIMINAL LAW AND PROCEDURE —Cont'd
Motor vehicles —Cont'd
Railroad grade crossing.
Vehicles required to stop, §20-142.3, (c).
Reckless driving, §20-140, (d).
Commercial motor vehicle carrying a load, §20-140, (f).
Registration application.
False or fictitious statement, §20-111.
Safety belt.
Violations of mandatory use provision, §20-135.2A, (e).
Salvage vehicles.
Certificate of title violations, §20-109.1, (f).
School buses.
Passing stopped school bus, §20-217.
Smoke screen.
Violations of prohibition, §20-136, (b).
Special identification card for nonoperators.
Fraud or misrepresentation in application, §20-37.7, (e).
Speed.
Commercial motor vehicle carrying a load, §20-141, (j3).
Stolen vehicles.
False report of theft or conversion, §20-102.1.
Subletting of hired property, §14-166.
Tampering with vehicle, §20-107, (a).
Tandem trailers and semitrailer.
Load limitation violations, §20-115.1, (i).
Total loss claim vehicle.
Removal of permanent marker affixed to vehicles doorjam, §20-71.4, (c).
Truck routes.
Designation violation, §20-116, (h).
Violations, §143-341.
Weighing or removing overloaded vehicle.
Refusal to permit law enforcement officer, §20-118.1.
Wrongful issuance of driver's license or special identification card, §20-34.1, (a).
Defenses precluded, §20-34.1, (b).
Motor vehicle titling.
Registration of security interest.
False filing, §20-58, (b).
Mountain ridge protection.
Violations subject to criminal sanctions, §113A-211, (a).
Municipal corporations.
Building inspection certificates of compliance.
Violations of provisions, §160A-423.
Building inspection department members.
Failure to perform duties, §160A-416.
Building inspector stop orders.
Violations, §160A-421, (b).
Building permit violations, §160A-417, (a).
Defense of employees and officers in criminal actions, §160A-167.
Notice of unsafe building.
Removal, §160A-427.
Personnel records.
Knowingly, willfully and with malice permitting access to, §160A-168, (e).
Removing or copying confidential personnel files, §160A-168, (f).
Subdivisions.
Transferring lots in unapproved subdivisions, §160A-375.
Swearing falsely at investigation by council, §160A-80, (b).

CRIMINAL LAW AND PROCEDURE —Cont'd
Municipal corporations —Cont'd
Taxation.
Disclosure of information, §160A-208.1, (b).
Vehicle used on foreshore, beach strand and barrier dune systems.
Violation of ordinance regulating, §160A-308.
Zoning boards of adjustment.
Swearing falsely before, §160A-388, (g).
Murder.
Indictments.
Essentials of bill, §15-144.
Juvenile committed for placement in youth development center.
Continued jurisdiction of juvenile court, §7B-1602, (a).
Juveniles under 17 years of age, §14-17.
Malice aforethought.
Allegation required in indictment, §15-144.
Murder in first and second degree, §14-17.
Punishment, §14-17.
Verdict for murder in first or second degree, §15-172.
Mutual burial associations.
Accepting application without collecting membership fee or assessment, §90-210.91.
False entries on books of association, §90-210.90.
False or fraudulent statement or representation, §90-210.97.
Free services, failure to assess, §90-210.93.
Operating without authority of board, §90-210.84.
Operation in noncompliance with bylaws, §90-210.88.
Wrongfully inducing change in membership, §90-210.89.
National crime prevention and privacy compact, §114-19.50.
Navigable waters.
Medical waste, depositing, §76-40, (a1).
Structures erected on floor of navigable waters, §76-40, (b).
Failure to remove abandoned structures, §76-40, (c).
Necessity.
Peace officers.
Non-law-enforcement actions when urgently necessary, §15A-285.
Neglect of disabled or elder adult, §14-32.3, (b).
Newspapers.
Libel and slander.
Communicating libelous matter to newspapers, §14-47.
New trial.
Appeals.
Correction of errors by appellate division.
Duties of clerk of superior court upon order of new trial, §15A-1452, (c).
Relief available upon appeal, §15A-1447, (a).
Motion for appropriate relief.
Motion for new trial.
Relief formerly available now available by motion for appropriate relief, §15A-1411, (c).
Relief available, §15A-1417, (a).
No contest pleas. See within this heading, "Pleas."
Nonprofit corporations.
Failure to answer interrogatories propounded by secretary.
Officers and directors, §55A-1-32, (b).
Nontestimonial identification, §§15A-271 to 15A-282.
Appearance.
Failure to appear, §15A-276.

CRIMINAL LAW AND PROCEDURE —Cont'd
Nontestimonial identification —Cont'd
Attorneys at law.
Copy of results.
Providing to person involved or his attorney, §15A-282.
Right to counsel, §15A-279, (d).
Bodily fluids.
Extraction.
Who may extract, §15A-279, (a).
Contempt.
Failure to appear, §15A-276.
Resistance to compliance, §15A-279, (e).
Copy of results.
Providing to person involved, §15A-282.
Defined, §15A-271.
Delinquent and undisciplined juvenile actions.
Willful violation of nontestimonial identification procedures, §7B-2109.
Destruction of products.
Motion by suspect, §15A-280.
Detention.
Length of detention, §15A-279, (c).
Failure to appear, §15A-276.
Force.
Unreasonable or unnecessary force not to be used, §15A-279, (b).
Investigations.
Additional investigative procedures not precluded, §15A-273.
Modification of order, §15A-275.
Order must state that person may request, §15A-278.
Order.
Application for.
Time for, §15A-272.
Contents, §15A-278.
Failure to obey order, §15A-276.
Grounds for issuance, §15A-273.
Implementation, §15A-279.
Issuance, §15A-274.
Grounds, §15A-273.
Who may issue, §15A-271.
Modification, §15A-275.
Order must state that person may request, §15A-278.
Previous order.
Effect, §15A-279, (f).
Request of defendant, §15A-281.
Return, §15A-280.
Service, §15A-277.
Time for, §15A-274.
Request by defendant for order, §15A-281.
Resistance.
Contempt, §15A-279, (e).
Evidentiary effect, §15A-279, (g).
Return, §15A-280.
Service of order, §15A-277.
Time for, §15A-274.
Time limit on procedure, §15A-279.
North Carolina state flag.
Desecration, §14-381.
Notaries public, §10A-12.
Not guilty pleas, §15A-1011.
Notice.
Appeals.
Correction of errors by appellate division.
Notice of appeal, §15A-1448, (b).
DNA evidence disposal.
Prior to expiration of time period for preserving, §15A-268, (b), (c).

CRIMINAL LAW AND PROCEDURE —Cont'd
Notice —Cont'd
Insanity defense.
Discovery generally, §15A-905, (c), (d).
Intent to introduce expert testimony, §15A-959, (b).
Pretrial hearing, §15A-959, (a).
Nursing home administrators.
Violations of provision, §90-288.
Nursing home licensure.
Inspection violations, §131E-109, (b).
Prohibited acts, §131E-109, (d).
Unlicensed operation, §131E-109, (a).
Nursing pools.
Unauthorized disclosure of inspection information, §131E-154.8, (b).
Obscenity, §§14-190.1 to 14-190.20.
Advertising obscene material, §14-190.1, (f).
Coercing acceptance of obscene articles or publications, §14-190.4.
Determination whether material obscene, §14-190.1, (b).
Displaying material harmful to minors, §14-190.14, (a).
Definitions for certain offenses concerning minors, §14-190.13.
Penalty, §14-190.14, (b).
Disseminating harmful material to minors, §14-190.15, (a).
Defenses, §14-190.15, (c).
Definitions for certain offenses concerning minors, §14-190.13.
Minors under the age of 13 years, §14-190.8.
Minors under the age of 16 years, §14-190.7.
Penalties, §14-190.15, (d).
Dissemination of obscene material.
Literature and exhibitions, §14-190.1.
Minors.
Under sixteen years of age, §14-190.7.
Under thirteen years of age, §14-190.8.
Employing or permitting minor to assist in offense under article, §14-190.6.
Indecent exposure, §14-190.9.
Issuance of search warrants, §14-190.20.
Local regulation, §14-190.1, (i).
Indecent exposure, §14-190.9, (c).
Motion pictures.
Preparation of obscene motion pictures, §14-190.5.
Preparation of obscene photographs, §14-190.5.
Promoting sale of obscene material, §14-190.1, (f).
Sexual conduct.
Defined, §14-190.1, (c).
Sexual exploitation of a minor, §§14-190.16, 14-190.17.
Sexually explicit nudity.
Defined, §14-190.13.
Standards for judging obscenity, §14-190.1, (d).
Summons and process.
Issuance of criminal process for violations, §14-190.20.
Telephones, §14-196.
Obstructing health care facilities, §14-277.4, (c).
Obstructing justice, §§14-221 to 14-227.
Altering court documents, §14-221.2.
Altering, destroying or stealing evidence of criminal conduct, §14-221.1.
Breaking or entering jails with intent to injure prisoners, §14-221.
Entering unauthorized judgments, §14-221.2.
Harassment of juror, §14-225.2.

CRIMINAL LAW AND PROCEDURE —Cont'd
Obstructing justice —Cont'd
Intimidating or interfering with witnesses, §14-226, (a).
Orders of court.
Violating orders of court, §14-226.1.
Parental rights.
Threatening witness in criminal proceeding with assertion or denial of parental rights, §14-226, (b).
Picketing or parading within certain distance of general court of justice, §14-225.1.
Reports to police radio broadcasting stations.
False, misleading or unfounded reports, §14-225.
Resisting officers, §14-223.
Witnesses before legislative committees.
Failing to attend as witness, §14-227.
Occupational safety and health.
Criminal penalties, §95-139.
Occupational therapists.
Violations of provision, §90-270.79.
Offering bribe, §14-218.
Office of information technology services.
Procurement of information technology.
Bribery, §147-33.99.
False certification that information technology bid submitted without collusion, §147-33.100.
Financial interest of officers in sources of supply, §147-33.99.
Unauthorized use of public purchase or contract procedures for private benefit, §147-33.98, (c).
Off-premises sales, failure to give right to cancel, §14-401.13.
Oil and gas conservation.
Violations as misdemeanors, §§113-380, 113-409.
Oil dispensing devices.
Falsification of measures, §119-33.
Oil inspection violations.
Generally, §119-39.
Oil inspectors.
Conflicts of interest, §119-25.
Failure or refusal to exhibit records to, §119-32.
Oil or hazardous substances discharges, §143-215.88B.
Oil refining facility permit violations, §143-215.102, (b).
Oils.
Lubricating oils.
Violations of article, §§119-4, 119-13.
Rerefined or reprocessed oil.
Violations of article, §119-13.3.
Oil terminal facilities.
Violations of provisions, §143-215.98.
Open container law, §20-138.7, (e).
Pleading and prosecutions, §20-138.7, (g).
Open fires violations, §113-60.29.
Opticians.
Allowing unlicensed person to use certificate or license, §90-251.
Sale of flammable frame, §90-255.1.
Unlicensed practice, §90-252.
Options to purchase rented property.
Failing to return.
Misdemeanor, §14-168.4, (a).
Presumptions from evidence.
Intent to commit crime, §14-168.4, (b).
Prosecution, §14-168.4, (c).

CRIMINAL LAW AND PROCEDURE —Cont'd
Optometrists.
Rules and regulations violation, §90-124.
Unauthorized practices, §90-118.11.
Orders.
Commitment order, §15A-1301.
Imprisonment.
Order of commitment, §15A-1301.
Suppression of evidence, §15A-979, (a).
Orders of court, violating, §14-226.1.
Ordinance violation, misdemeanor, §14-4, (a).
Osteopaths.
Prohibited acts.
Generally, §90-136.
Outdoor advertising.
Control act violations, §136-135.
Paper currency machine burglary, §14-56.3.
Parent and child.
Exclusion of witnesses.
Exception to provisions, §15A-1225.
Failure to support parent, §14-326.1.
Parking in private parking space, §14-401.9.
Parking on public grounds, §143-340.
Parking regulations of ports authority, §143B-461, (c).
Parks and recreation.
Concessions for operation of public service facilities in state forests and state parks, §113-35, (d).
Parole.
See PAROLE.
Partnerships.
Appearance by counsel or agent, §15A-773, (b).
Securing attendance of organizations, §15A-773, (a).
Definition of "organization," §15A-773, (c).
Party lines, refusal to relinquish, §14-401.8.
Patient abuse.
Unlawful to physically abuse patient, §14-32.2, (a).
Criminal process, issuance, request of attorney general, §14-32.2, (g).
Defenses, §14-32.2, (f).
Definitions, §14-32.2, (c) to (e1).
Provisions not to supersede other offenses, §14-32.2, (h).
Punishment, §14-32.2, (b).
Pawnbrokers.
Receiving stolen goods.
Criminal penalties, §91A-11, (b).
Violations, §91A-11, (a).
Peace officers.
Motor vehicles.
Rights of misdemeanor arrestee, §20-114, (a).
Peddlers, itinerant merchants and specialty markets.
Defenses to misdemeanor violations, §66-257, (d).
Misdemeanor violations, §66-257, (a) to (c).
Peeping into room occupied by another person, §14-202.
Pen registers and trap and trace devices, §§15A-260 to 15A-264.
Periodicals.
Communicating libelous matter to periodicals, §14-47.
Perjury, §§14-209 to 14-211.
Closing-out sales, §66-77, (d).
Drivers' licenses.
False affidavits, §20-31.
Elections.
Corruptly taking oath prescribed for voters, §163-275.

CRIMINAL LAW AND PROCEDURE —Cont'd
Perjury —Cont'd
Elements of offense, §14-209.
Fires and fire protection.
Investigations.
False swearing to attorney general, §58-79-10.
Indictments.
Form of bill for perjury, §15-145.
Subornation of perjury.
Sufficiency of bill, §15-146.
Legislative committees.
Willful and corrupt perjury offense, §14-211.
Military property sales facilities.
License applications, §127B-5.
Monopolies and restraint of trade.
False swearing by persons examined, §75-12.
Motor vehicle financial responsibility forms, §20-279.7A.
Precious metal dealers.
Application for permit or exemption, §66-167.
Public works.
Regulation of contractors, §133-31.
Punishment for perjury, §14-209.
Subornation of perjury, §14-210.
Racketeer influenced and corrupt organizations.
Examinations.
False testimony, §75D-7.
Subornation of perjury, §14-210.
Indictments.
Sufficiency of bill, §15-146.
Punishment for perjury, §14-210.
Wake county superior court.
Legislative committee perjury offense, §14-211.
Personnel system.
Political activities of employees.
Coercing employee to support or contribute to political candidate, committee or party, §§126-14, 126-14.1.
Restrictions, §126-13, (b).
Pesticide applicators and consultants.
Applying or combining prohibited substances, §143-458, (c) to (e).
Reporting of shipments and volumes of pesticides, §143-459.
Pesticide violations, §143-469, (a).
Applying or combining prohibited substances, §143-458, (c) to (e).
Petitions.
Review of criminal trials.
Generally, §15A-1420, (b1).
Pet shops.
Cruelty to animals, §19A-35.
Unlicensed shops, §19A-33.
Pharmacists and pharmacies.
Violations of article, §90-85.40, (h).
Phonograph records and tapes, §§14-432 to 14-437.
Civil action for damages by owner of recorded device, §14-436.
Definitions, §14-432.
Live concert recordings.
Unlawful in certain circumstances, §14-433, (a) to (c).
Retailers.
Unlawful retailing of certain recorded devices, §14-434.
Violation of article, §14-437, (a).
Physical therapists.
Unlicensed practice, §90-270.35.
Physicians and surgeons.
Limited license.
Holder practicing medicine beyond boundary of district laid down in license, §90-12, (a).

CRIMINAL LAW AND PROCEDURE —Cont'd
Physicians and surgeons —Cont'd
Limited volunteer licenses.
Practicing beyond scope of license, §90-12, (c).
Practicing without license, §90-18, (a).
Prosecution of violation, §90-21.
Picketing or parading within certain distance of general court of justice, §14-225.1.
Plastic yoke and ring type holding devices, §14-399.2.
Pleadings.
Bill of particulars, §15A-925.
Amendment, §15A-925, (e).
Effect, §15A-925, (e).
Filing, §15A-925, (d).
Motion for, §15A-925, (a), (b).
Order for, §15A-925, (a), (c).
Service, §15A-925, (d).
Contents, §15A-924, (a).
Defendants.
Each defendant to be charged in separate pleading, §15A-926, (b).
Duplicity, §15A-924, (b).
Enumerated, §15A-921.
Error in pleadings.
Correction of errors by appellate division, §15A-1442.
Failure to charge crime, §15A-924, (e).
Felony cases.
Indictment.
Amendment prohibited, §15A-923, (e).
Form, §15A-923, (b).
Prosecution on indictment, §15A-923, (a).
Waiver, §15A-923, (c).
Information.
Amendment, §15A-923, (d).
Form, §15A-923, (b).
Prosecution on information, §15A-923, (a).
Inflammatory or prejudicial surplusage.
Motion to strike, §15A-924, (f).
Misdemeanor cases.
Amendment of pleadings prior to or after final judgment, §15A-922, (f).
Citation, §15A-922, (a).
Objection to trial on citation, §15A-922, (c).
Criminal summons, §15A-922, (a).
Objection to sufficiency of criminal summons, §15A-922, (e).
Process as pleadings, §15A-922, (a).
Statement of charges, §15A-922, (b).
Determination of prosecutor, §15A-922, (d).
Superior courts.
Allegations in superior court of prior convictions, §15A-922, (h).
Prosecution initiated in superior court, §§15A-922, (g), 15A-923.
Previous convictions.
Alleging and proving, §§15A-924, (c), (d), 15A-928, (a), (b).
Grand jury.
State not relieved of obligation to prove prior conviction before grand jury, §15A-928, (e).
Rights of defendant as to, §15A-928, (c).
Misdemeanor tried de novo in superior court, §15A-928, (d).
Use of pleading as proof of fact admitted or alleged in it.
Prohibited in criminal prosecutions, §1-149.
Pleas.
Alternatives, §15A-1011, (a).

CRIMINAL LAW AND PROCEDURE —Cont'd
Pleas —Cont'd
Attorneys at law.
Aid of counsel, §15A-1012, (a).
Evidence.
Plea discussion and arrangement inadmissible, §§8C-1, Rule 410, 15A-1025.
Guilty pleas, §15A-1011, (a).
Acceptance.
District courts, §7A-272, (c), (d).
Prerequisites, §15A-1022, (a) to (c).
Capital offenses.
Death penalty or life imprisonment, §15A-2001.
Determinations by judge.
Required determination, §15A-1022, (a) to (c).
Factual basis for plea.
Judge must determine, §15A-1022, (c).
First degree murder.
Death penalty or life imprisonment, §15A-2001.
Improper pressure on defendant to plead guilty.
Determination by judge, §15A-1022, (b).
Prohibited, §15A-1021, (b).
Inadmissible in evidence, §8C-1, Rule 410.
Indigent persons.
Waiver of right to counsel, §7A-457, (b).
Information to be given defendant, §15A-1022, (a).
Informed choice.
Judge must determine, §15A-1022, (b).
Other crimes with which defendant charged, §15A-1011, (c).
Probable cause hearings.
Acceptance of guilty plea, §15A-613.
Record of proceedings, §§7A-191.1, 15A-1026.
Withdrawal.
Sentence not in accord with plea arrangement, §15A-1024.
No contest pleas, §15A-1011, (a).
Acceptance.
District courts, §7A-272, (c), (d).
Prerequisites, §15A-1022, (a) to (d).
Consent of prosecutor and presiding judge required, §15A-1011, (b).
Determinations by judge.
Required determinations, §15A-1022, (a) to (c).
Factual basis for plea.
Acceptance of plea even if defendant does not admit guilt, §15A-1022, (d).
Judge must determine, §15A-1022, (c).
Improper pressure on defendant to plead no contest.
Determination by judge, §15A-1022, (b).
Prohibited, §15A-1021, (b).
Inadmissible in evidence, §8C-1, Rule 410.
Information to be given defendant, §15A-1022, (a).
Informed choice.
Judge must determine, §15A-1022, (b).
Record of proceedings, §§7A-191.1, 15A-1026.
Not guilty pleas, §15A-1011, (a).
Waiver of appearance, §15A-1011, (d), (e).
Plea bargaining.
Agreement, §15A-1021, (c).
Appeals.
Noncompliance with provisions.
Limitation on collateral attack on conviction, §15A-1027.
Conference, §15A-1021, (a).

CRIMINAL LAW AND PROCEDURE —Cont'd
Pleas —Cont'd
Plea bargaining —Cont'd
Evidence.
Plea discussion and arrangement inadmissible, §§8C-1, Rule 410, 15A-1025.
Improper pressure on defendant.
Determination by judge, §15A-1022, (b).
Prohibited, §15A-1021, (b).
Judge.
Concurrence, §15A-1021, (c).
Determination whether plea bargaining took place.
Prerequisite to acceptance of plea of guilty or no contest, §15A-1022, (b).
Participation in discussions, §15A-1021, (a).
Sentencing.
Duties as to agreements relating to sentence, §15A-1023, (b), (c).
Record of proceedings, §§7A-191.1, 15A-1026.
Restitution or reparation, §15A-1021, (d).
Sentencing.
Disclosure of agreement relating to sentencing, §15A-1023, (a).
Duties of judge as to agreement relating to sentencing, §15A-1023, (b), (c).
Factual basis for plea.
Judge must determine, §15A-1023, (c).
Informed choice.
Judge must determine, §15A-1023, (c).
Withdrawal of guilty plea when sentence not in accord with plea arrangement, §15A-1024.
Withdrawal of guilty plea when sentence not in accord with plea arrangement, §15A-1024.
Received only from defendant in open court, §15A-1011, (a).
Exceptions, §15A-1011, (a).
Time for deliberation, §15A-1012, (b).
Poisons generally.
See POISONS.
Police dogs.
Injuring, maiming or killing, §14-163.1.
Pollution control.
Sedimentation pollution control act of 1973.
Violations as misdemeanors, §113A-64, (b).
Water pollution on lands used for dairy purposes, §14-382.
Portable smelters, §66-173.
Post conviction DNA testing.
Motion by defendant.
Appointment of counsel for indigent defendant, §15A-269, (c).
Conditions to be met, §15A-269, (a).
Costs of testing, defendant to bear, §15A-269, (d).
Delay of proceedings or execution of sentence pending testing.
Miscarriage of justice, §15A-269, (e).
Discharge of defendant, ordering on favorable results, §15A-270, (c).
Favorable results, order entered serving interest of justice, §15A-270, (c).
Granting motion, determinations required, §15A-269, (b).
Hearing to evaluate results, §15A-270, (a).
New trial, ordering on favorable results, §15A-270, (c).
Resentencing, ordering on favorable results, §15A-270, (c).

CRIMINAL LAW AND PROCEDURE —Cont'd
Post conviction DNA testing —Cont'd
Motion by defendant —Cont'd
Time for testing order pursuant to motion, §15A-269, (e).
Unfavorable results, dismissal of motion, §15A-270, (b).
Vacating and setting aside judgment, ordering on favorable results, §15A-270, (c).
Prayer for judgment continued.
Entry of PJC not considered entry of judgment, §15A-101.
Precious metal dealers, §66-172.
Pregnant women.
Abortion, §§14-44 to 14-46.
Injury to pregnant woman resulting in miscarriage or stillbirth, §14-18.2.
Use of instruments or drugs, §14-45.
Prejudicial error.
Appeals.
Burden of proof, §15A-1443, (a).
Definition of prejudicial error, §15A-1443, (a).
Preneed funeral contracts and funds.
Failure of person to obey subpoena, §90-210.69, (b).
Presentments.
Contents, §15A-644, (c).
Defined, §15A-641, (c).
Modes of prosecution, Const. N. C., art. I, §22.
Signatures.
Foreman of grand jury.
Signature attesting concurrence of twelve or more grand jurors, §15A-644, (c).
Venue.
Grand jury's venue.
To present or indict, §15A-631.
Pretrial conference in capital cases, Super. Ct. Rule 24.
Previous convictions.
Alleging, pleading and proving, §§15A-924, 15A-928.
Price tags, transfer, §14-72.1, (d).
Principals and accessories, §§14-5.2, 14-7.
Prisons and prisoners.
General provisions.
See PRISONS AND PRISONERS.
Private office.
Misconduct in private office.
Corporation officers and agents.
Malfeasance of officers and agents, §14-254, (a).
Definition of "person," §14-254, (b).
Railroad officers.
Failure of certain officers to account to successors, §14-253.
Private personnel services.
Operation without license, §95-47.9, (e).
Unlicensed operation, §95-47.9, (e).
Probable cause hearings.
Attorneys at law.
Defendant to be advised of right to counsel, §15A-606, (e).
Determination whether right to counsel waived, §15A-611, (c).
Representation of state and defendant, §15A-611, (a).
Continuances, §15A-606, (f).
Dispositional alternatives, §15A-612, (a).
Double jeopardy.
Findings at probable cause hearing not to preclude state from subsequent prosecution for same offense, §15A-612.

CRIMINAL LAW AND PROCEDURE —Cont'd
Probable cause hearings —Cont'd
Evidence, §15A-611, (b).
First appearance before district court judge, §15A-606.
Guilty plea.
Acceptance, §15A-613.
Hearsay evidence, §15A-611, (b).
Informations.
Filing in superior court upon waiver of indictment.
Probable cause hearing may not be held, §15A-611, (d).
Pretrial release.
Review of eligibility for, §15A-614.
Procedure, §15A-611.
Scheduling, §15A-606, (a), (d).
Setting offense for trial in district court, §15A-613.
Review of eligibility for pretrial release, §15A-614.
Venue, §15A-131, (c).
Waiver, §15A-606, (a).
After first appearance before district court judge, §15A-606, (g).
Evidence of waiver not to be admitted at trial, §15A-606, (b).
Proceedings on, §15A-606, (c).
Witnesses, §15A-611, (a).
Probate and registration.
Maps and plats.
Violations of certain provisions as misdemeanors, §47-32.2.
Registration of military discharges.
Forgery or alteration of discharge certificate as misdemeanor, §47-112.
Probation.
See PROBATION.
Process.
Failure to return or false return, §14-242.
Professional counselors.
Conviction of a crime.
Disciplinary action against licensee, §90-340.
Violation punishable as crime, §90-341.
Property taxes.
Abstracts.
False affirmation as misdemeanor, §105-310.
Attempting to evade or defeat taxes as misdemeanor, §105-308.
County assessor.
Disclosure of information as misdemeanor, §105-296, (h).
Subpoenas of county assessor.
Failure to appear as misdemeanor, §105-296, (g).
Liens.
Advertisement of lien.
Wrongful advertisement as misdemeanor, §105-369, (g).
Listing of property.
Failure to list as misdemeanor, §105-308.
Mobile homes.
Tax permit.
Violations as misdemeanors, §105-316.6, (a) to (c).
Payment of taxes.
Prepayments.
Chief accounting officer.
Failure to perform duties as misdemeanor, §105-359, (e).

CRIMINAL LAW AND PROCEDURE —Cont'd
Property taxes —Cont'd
Public utilities.
Reports.
False report as misdemeanor, §105-334, (b).
Receipts.
Delivery of tax receipts to tax collector.
Failure to meet prerequisites as misdemeanor, §105-352, (d).
Subpoenas of county board of equalization and review.
Willful failure to obey as misdemeanor, §105-322, (g).
Subpoenas of department of revenue.
Failure to appear as misdemeanor, §105-291, (c).
Subpoenas of property tax commission.
Failure to obey as misdemeanor, §105-290, (d).
Tax collectors.
Settlements.
Failure to make settlement as misdemeanor, §105-373, (f).
Wages.
Attachment and garnishment.
Prohibited acts as misdemeanors, §105-368, (i).
Proprietary schools.
Operating without license or bond, §115D-96.
Prostitution.
Acts declared unlawful, §14-204.
Assignation.
Defined, §14-203.
Definitions, §14-203.
Public place, §14-204.1.
Degrees of guilty, §14-207.
First degree prostitution, §14-207.
Punishment, §14-208.
In what courts violations may be prosecuted, §14-205.
Loitering for purpose of engaging in prostitution offense, §14-204.1.
Minors, §§14-190.18, 14-190.19.
Parole.
Venereal diseased persons.
Medical treatment insured, §14-208.
Prior convictions.
Admissibility as evidence, §14-206.
Probation.
Venereal diseased persons.
Medical treatment insured, §14-208.
Prosecutions for violation of provisions, §14-205.
Reputation of place, person, etc.
Admissibility as evidence, §14-206.
Second degree prostitution, §14-207.
Punishment, §14-208.
Psychologists.
Prohibited acts, §90-270.17.
Public buildings and grounds.
Disorderly conduct in and injury to, §143-345.2.
Motor vehicle regulations and parking, §143-340.
Violations of regulations, §143-345.1.
Public contracts.
Bids and bidding, §§143-129, 143-129.1.
Public intoxication.
Acquittal of defendant because of alcoholism.
Disposition of defendant, §14-446.
Defense of alcoholism, §14-445, (a).
Request for additional information, §14-445, (b).
Definitions, §14-443.
Elements of offense.
No prosecution for public intoxication, §14-447, (a).

CRIMINAL LAW AND PROCEDURE —Cont'd
Public intoxication —Cont'd
Entering plea to charge, §14-445, (c).
Prehearing review of drinking history, §14-445, (d).
Shelter or health-care facility.
Transport and release of person to appropriate facility, §14-447, (b).
Ways of being intoxicated and disruptive in public, §14-444, (a).
Penalty for violation of provisions, §14-444, (b).
Public lands.
Piers.
Erection on state lakes.
Violations of permits, §146-13.
Trees and timber.
Cutting before obtaining grant, §146-43.
Public morality and decency.
Offenses against public morality and decency, §§14-177 to 14-202.2.
Public officers and employees.
Bribery of officials, §14-217.
Insurance committee, §58-31-60, (d).
Misconduct in public office, §§14-228 to 14-252.
Acting as officer before qualifying as such, §14-229.
Buying and selling offices, §14-228.
Disposing of documents, §14-241.
Failing to file report of fines, §14-244.
Failing to make reports and discharge other duties, §14-231.
Failing to return process, §14-242.
Making false return, §14-242.
Motor vehicles.
Limitation of amount expended for vehicle.
Applicability of provisions to cities and towns, §14-252.
Violations made misdemeanors, §14-251.
Marking of publicly owned vehicle.
Applicability of provisions to cities and towns, §14-252.
Violations made misdemeanor, §14-251.
Obtaining repairs and supplies for private vehicle at expense of state, §14-248.
Applicability of provisions to cities and towns, §14-252.
Violations made misdemeanors, §14-251.
Private use of publicly owned vehicle, §14-247.
Applicability of provisions to cities and towns, §14-252.
Violations made misdemeanors, §14-251.
Refusing to deliver over documents to successor, §14-241.
Selling offices, §14-228.
Swearing falsely to official reports, §14-232.
Willfully failing to discharge duties, §14-230.
Political activities of employees.
Coercing employee to support or contribute to political candidate, committee or party, §§126-14, 126-14.1.
Restrictions, §126-13, (b).
Receiving compensation of subordinates for appointment or retention, §128-4.
Violations of law, §143-115.
Public peace.
Offenses against the public peace, §§14-269 to 14-277.1.
Public records.
Cultural resources department.
Disposition of records at end of official's term, §132-4.

CRIMINAL LAW AND PROCEDURE —Cont'd
Public records —Cont'd
Destruction, §121-5.
Unauthorized removal or destruction, §132-3.
Unlawful possession, §132-5.
Public safety.
Offenses against the public safety, §§14-278 to 14-288.
Public schools.
Contractors selling personally identifiable student information.
Criminal penalty, §115C-401.1, (c).
Criminal act on school property.
Policies of board regarding.
Report by principal, §115C-288, (g).
Public trial, Const. U. S., amd. VI.
Public utilities.
Allowing or accepting rebates, §62-318.
Property, willful damaging, §62-323.
Refusal to permit commission to inspect records, §62-313.
Public works.
Chapter violations, §133-4.
Contractor affidavits.
Perjury in affidavit, §133-31.
Contractor gifts and favors.
Public officers and employees, §133-32, (b).
Quarantine.
Rabies.
Dog or cat bites.
Owner's failure to confine pet, §130A-196.
Quo warranto.
Official papers.
Refusal to surrender by person against whom judgment rendered, §1-531.
Rabies.
Quarantine.
Dog or cat bites.
Owner's failure to confine pet, §130A-196.
Racing motor vehicles on streets and highways, §20-141.3, (a) to (c).
Railroads.
Cattle guards and crossings.
Failure to erect and maintain, §136-194.
Intoxicated person boarding train after being forbidden by conductor, §136-197.
Obstructing highways.
Failure to repair after notice, §136-192, (c).
Riding on train unlawfully, §§14-460, 62-319.
Switch-lock keys.
Unauthorized manufacture or sale, §§14-461, 62-322.
Rape, first degree, §14-27.2.
Juvenile committed for placement in youth development center.
Continued jurisdiction of juvenile court, §7B-1602, (a).
Rape, second degree, §14-27.3.
Rape shield law, §8C-1, Rule 412.
Real estate appraisers.
Practicing without license or certificate, §93E-1-13, (a).
Real property.
Furnishing false statements in connection with improvements as misdemeanor, §44A-24.
Rebellion, §14-10.
Punishment for rebellion, §14-8.
Rebirthing technique.
Practicing unlawful, §14-401.21.

CRIMINAL LAW AND PROCEDURE —Cont'd
Records.
Evidence.
Criminal index maintained by clerk of superior court.
Records admissible in certain cases, §8-35.2.
Expungement of records.
Dismissal of charges, finding of not guilty or not responsible, §15A-146.
Resulting from identity fraud, §15A-147.
DNA records.
Charges dismissed on appeal or pardon of innocence granted, §15A-148.
Drug violations.
Minors, §90-96, (b), (d).
First time offenders under age eighteen, §15A-145.
Minors.
Drug violations, §90-96, (b), (d).
Juvenile records, §§7B-3202, 90-96.
Plea bargaining.
Record of proceedings, §§7A-191.1, 15A-1026.
Subpoena duces tecum, §15A-802.
Trial, §15A-1241, (a), (b).
Objection to unrecorded statement, §15A-1241, (c).
Review of accuracy of record, §15A-1241, (d).
Refrigerator abandonment, §14-318.1.
Registers of deeds.
Failure to discharge duties, §161-27.
Rental vehicles.
Violations of insurance provisions, §20-284.
Reports.
Disposition of cases, §15A-1382, (a), (b).
Representation of indigent persons.
Generally, §§7A-450 to 7A-458.
See INDIGENT DEFENSE SERVICES.
Resisting officers, §14-223.
Respiratory care practitioners.
Regulatory violations, §90-662.
Restitution or reparation.
Parole.
Condition of parole, §§15A-1374, (b), 148-57.1.
Plea bargaining, §15A-1021, (d).
Probation.
Condition of probation, §§15A-1340.34, (b), 15A-1343, (d).
Restitution to law enforcement agencies, §90-95.3, (a), (c).
Sentencing, §§15A-1340.34 to 15A-1340.38.
See SENTENCING.
Stolen property.
Returned to owner, §15-8.
Victims of crime.
Sentencing, §§15A-1340.34 to 15A-1340.38.
See SENTENCING.
Restoration of citizenship rights to convicted persons, §§13-1 to 13-4.
Automatic restoration, §13-1.
Certificate or order of restoration.
Issuance and filing, §13-2.
Conditional pardon.
Endorsement of warrant, service and filing, §13-4.
Unconditional pardon.
Issuance, service and filing of warrant, §13-3.
Restraint.
Felonious restraint, §14-43.3.
Retirement system for counties, cities and towns, §§128-28, 128-32.
Confidentiality of information, §128-28, (q).

CRIMINAL LAW AND PROCEDURE —Cont'd
Retirement system for teachers and state employees.
Disclosure of confidential information concerning members, §135-6, (p).
False statements or falsified records, §135-10.
Review of criminal trials.
Petitions, §15A-1420, (b1).
Riding on train unlawfully, §§14-460, 62-319.
Rights of accused, Const. N. C., art. I, §23.
Right to counsel, §15-4; Const. N. C., art. I, §23; Const. U. S., amd. VI.
Riots and civil disorders, §§14-288.1 to 14-288.20.
See RIOTS AND CIVIL DISORDERS.
Rivers.
Obstructing natural drainage, §77-14.
Obstructing natural flow, §77-13.
Obstructing passage, §77-12.
Robbery.
Attempted common law robbery.
Punishment, §14-87.1.
Capital punishment.
Aggravating circumstances.
Capital felony in commission of robbery, §15A-2000, (e).
Firearms or other dangerous weapons, §14-87, (a).
Murder during commission, §14-17.
Restitution.
Stolen property returned to owner, §15-8.
Safecracking, §14-89.1.
Train robbery, §14-88.
Rules of procedure, Const. N. C., art. IV, §13.
Rustling cattle, §14-81.
Sales.
Convict made goods, §14-346, (a), (b).
Diseased animal meat, §14-342.
Railroad tickets, §14-343.
Scalping tickets, §14-344.
Sales and use tax.
Absorption of tax.
Advertisement to absorb tax as misdemeanor, §105-164.9.
Salvage of abandoned shipwrecks and other underwater archaeological sites.
Violations of article, §121-28.
Salvage vehicle certificate of title violations, §20-109.1, (f).
Sanitarians.
Violations, §90A-66.
Sanitary districts.
Noncompliance with board promulgated rules, §130A-55.
Sewer line or disposal plant.
Connection or reconnection without permit, §130A-65.
Scalping tickets, §14-344.
School buses.
Passing stopped school bus, §20-217.
Trespassing upon, damaging or impeding progress, §14-132.2.
School employees.
Defense of board of education members and employees, §115C-43, (a) to (c).
School of science and mathematics.
Nonattendance, §116-235, (b).
Traffic violations, §116-235, (e).
Searches and seizures.
See SEARCHES AND SEIZURES.
Secret listening, §§14-227.1 to 14-227.3.

CRIMINAL LAW AND PROCEDURE —Cont'd
Secret societies, §§14-12.1 to 14-12.15.
Administering oath for illegal purposes, §14-12.4.
Burning of flaming cross, §14-12.12.
Certain secret societies prohibited, §14-12.3.
Political and military organizations forbidden, §14-10.
Definitions, §14-12.2.
Entry, etc., upon premises of another while wearing masks or hood, §14-12.9.
Exemptions from provisions of article, §14-12.11.
Holding meetings while wearing masks, hoods, etc., §14-12.10.
Permitting, etc., meetings of prohibited secret societies, §14-12.5.
Placing exhibit while wearing mask or hood, §14-12.14.
Placing exhibit with intention of intimidating, §14-12.13.
Prohibited secret societies, §14-12.3.
Punishment for violation of article, §14-12.15.
Regulation of meeting places and meetings of secret societies, §14-12.6.
Use of disguises for illegal purposes, §14-12.4.
Use of grips for illegal purposes, §14-12.4.
Use of passwords for illegal purposes, §14-12.4.
Use of signs for illegal purposes, §14-12.4.
Wearing of masks, hoods, etc., on public property, §14-12.8.
Securities, §78A-57.
Dealing in securities on commission.
Taxed as private banker, §14-401.7.
Exemptions from securities regulation.
Burden of proof, §78A-18, (b).
Securities regulation.
Obstruction of investigation, §78A-58.
Security agreements.
Filing false security agreements, §14-401.19.
Seized property.
Disposition of unclaimed property, §§15-11 to 15-17.
See SEARCHES AND SEIZURES.
General provisions.
See SEARCHES AND SEIZURES.
Self-defense.
Affrays.
Evidence of former threats upon plea of self-defense, §14-33.1.
Assaulting law enforcement or assistance animals, §14-163.1, (f).
Defense of home or residence.
Use of deadly force against intruder, §14-51.1.
School employees.
Reasonable force, use to control certain behavior and self defense, §115C-391, (a).
Immunity from civil liability, §115C-391, (h).
Self-incrimination.
Generally.
See SELF-INCRIMINATION.
Sentencing.
Community corrections programs.
Sentencing services, §§7A-770 to 7A-777.
See SENTENCING SERVICES.
Death sentence.
See CAPITAL PUNISHMENT.
Felony sentencing, §§15A-1340.13 to 15A-1340.17.
See SENTENCING.
General provisions.
See SENTENCING.
Sentencing services act, §§7A-770 to 7A-777.
See SENTENCING SERVICES.

CRIMINAL LAW AND PROCEDURE —Cont'd
Service animals.
Prohibited acts, §168-4.5.
Service of process.
Citation, §15A-302, (d).
Criminal process generally, §15A-301, (c).
Electronic repository for criminal process.
Process in, §15A-301.1, (g), (j) to (n).
Motion for appropriate relief, §15A-1420, (a).
Motions, §15A-951, (b).
Proof of service, §15A-951, (c).
Recall of process, §15A-301, (g).
Severance of offenses.
Generally, §15A-927, (b).
Motion.
Motion of court, §15A-927, (e).
Renewal, §15A-927, (a).
Time for, §15A-927, (a).
Waiver, §15A-927, (a).
Sex offender and public protection registration.
General provisions, §§14-208.5 to 14-208.32.
See SEX OFFENDER AND PUBLIC PROTECTION REGISTRATION.
Sexual exploitation of minor, §§14-190.16 to 14-190.17A.
Sexual offenses.
Bail and recognizance, §15A-534.4.
Capital punishment.
Aggravating circumstances, §15A-2000, (e).
Crimes punishable by death, Const. N. C., art. XI, §2.
Castration, §§14-28, 14-29.
Definitions, §14-27.1.
Evidence, §8C-1, Rule 412.
Required evidence in prosecutions, §14-27.10.
First-degree rape, §14-27.2.
First-degree sexual offense, §14-27.4.
Generally.
See SEXUAL OFFENSES.
Hotels.
Falsely registering as husband and wife, §14-186.
Opposite sexes occupying same bedroom for immoral purposes, §14-186.
Husband and wife.
Victim is spouse of person committing act.
Defense that victim is spouse, §14-27.8.
Incest, §14-178.
Intercourse and sexual offenses with certain victims, §14-27.7, (a).
Indecent exposure, §14-190.9.
Indictments.
Essentials of bill, §15-144.2.
Juvenile committed for placement in youth development center.
Continued jurisdiction of juvenile court, §7B-1602, (a).
Mentally defective.
Defined, §14-27.1.
Mentally incapacitated.
Defined, §14-27.1.
Indictments.
Victim mentally defective or incapacitated, §15-144.2, (c).
Minors.
First degree offenses if committed by adult.
Commitment in youth development center, §7B-1602, (a).
Indecent liberties between children, §14-202.2.

CRIMINAL LAW AND PROCEDURE —Cont'd
Sexual offenses —Cont'd
Minors —Cont'd
Indictments.
Victim age 13 or less, §15-144.2, (b).
Intercourse and sexual offenses with certain victims, §14-27.7, (a).
Defendant at least six years older than victim, §14-27.7A, (a).
Defendant between four and six years older than victim, §14-27.7A, (b).
School personnel.
Acts with victim who is student, §14-27.7, (b).
Taking indecent liberties with children, §14-202.1.
Murder during commission, §14-17.
Physical incapacity.
No presumptions, §14-27.9.
Physically helpless.
Defined, §14-27.1.
Presumptions.
No presumption as to incapacity, §14-27.9.
Pretrial release, §15A-534.4.
Public morality and decency.
Offenses against public morality and decency, §§14-177 to 14-202.2.
Rape.
First-degree rape, §14-27.2.
Second-degree rape, §14-27.3.
Rape shield law, §8C-1, Rule 412.
Reputation or opinion.
Sexual behavior not proved by, §8C-1, Rule 412, (c).
Required evidence in prosecutions under article, §14-27.10.
School personnel.
Acts with victim who is student, §14-27.7, (b).
Second-degree sexual offense, §14-27.5.
Sexual act.
Defined, §14-27.1.
Sexual battery, §14-27.5A.
Sexual behavior.
Evidence, §8C-1, Rule 412.
Taking indecent liberties with children, §14-202.1.
Testing of persons for sexually transmitted infections, §15A-615.
Trial.
Bystanders.
Exclusion in trial for sex offenses, §15-166.
Venue, §15A-136.
Sharecroppers.
Landlord failing to make advance, §§14-358, 14-359.
Receiving advance with intent to defraud, §§14-358, 14-359.
Shellfish cultivation.
Clamming on posted oyster rocks as misdemeanor, §113-207, (b) to (d).
Leases.
Forms for determining amount of shellfish.
False statements as misdemeanors, §113-202, (o).
Polluted shellfish.
Taking or selling at night or with prior convictions as felony, §113-209, (d).
Ships and shipping.
Lights.
Displaying false lights on seashore, §14-282.
Shopping carts.
Removal from shopping premises, §14-72.3.

CRIMINAL LAW AND PROCEDURE —Cont'd
Slander.
Magazines or periodicals.
Libelous matter communicated, §14-47.
Newspapers.
Communicating libelous matter to newspapers, §14-47.
Slot machines, §§14-301 to 14-309.1.
Agreements with reference to slot machines or devices, §§14-305, 14-309.
Allowing illegal slot machines on premises, §14-297.
Antique slot machines.
Defense in prosecution for possession of slot machines or device, §14-309.1, (a), (b).
Breaking into or forcibly opening, §14-56.1.
Damaging or destroying machines, §14-56.2.
Declared a public nuisance, §14-308.
Violations made misdemeanors, §14-309.
Definitions, §§14-296, (a), 14-306.
Felony offenses, §14-309, (a), (b).
Issuance of license prohibited, §14-307.
Violations made misdemeanor, §14-309.
Keeping illegal slot machines, §14-295.
Manufacture, sale, etc., of slot machines and devices, §14-304.
Devices for cheating machine, §14-109.
Violations made misdemeanors, §14-309.
Obtaining property or services from machines by false coins or tokens, §14-108.
Operation.
Separate offenses, §§14-301, 14-302.
Violation made misdemeanor, §14-303.
Possession, §§14-301, 14-302.
Defense to possession, §14-309.1, (a).
Return of slot machine to defendant, §14-309.1, (b).
Misdemeanors, §14-303.
Separate offenses, §14-302.
Small business contractor act.
False statements and reports, §143B-472.97.
Snake handling, §§14-416 to 14-422.
Declared public nuisance, §14-416.
Destruction of reptiles, §14-419.
Examination of reptiles, §14-419.
Exemptions from provisions, §14-421.
Inducing others to handle, §14-418.
Regulation of ownership or use of poisonous reptiles, §14-417.
Return of reptiles, §14-419.
Seizure and examination of reptiles, §14-419.
Violation of provisions.
Arrest of persons violating, §14-420.
Investigation of suspected violations, §14-419.
Misdemeanor offenses, §14-422.
Social services.
Local confinement facilities.
Refusal to provide information, §131D-13.
Social workers.
Violations, §90B-12.
Soil and water conservation commission.
Refusing entry, resisting, delaying or obstructing employee or agent of commission, §143B-294, (c).
Soil scientists, §89F-22.
Solicitation of contributions.
Willful violations of chapter, §131F-22.
Solid waste management.
Disclosure of information received pursuant to article, §130A-304, (b).

CRIMINAL LAW AND PROCEDURE —Cont'd
Solid waste management —Cont'd
Used oil.
Disposal at landfills, §130A-309.15, (a).
Registration violations, §130A-309.17, (h).
Special prosecution division.
Duties, §114-11.6.
Established, §114-11.6.
Speech and language pathologists and audiologists.
Violations of provision, §90-306.
Speeding to elude arrest, §20-141.5.
Speedy trial, Const. U. S., amd. VI.
Denial.
Grounds for motion to dismiss, §15A-954, (a).
Felonies, §15-10.
Quo warranto, §1-521.
Treason, §15-10.
Sporting events, throwing, dropping, etc., objects at, §14-281.1.
Spring loaded projectile knives.
Possession and sale, §14-269.6, (a), (b).
Stalking, §14-277.3.
Cyberstalking, §14-196.3.
State auditor.
Obstruction of audit, §147-64.7A.
State bureau of investigation, §§114-12 to 114-20.1.
See BUREAU OF INVESTIGATION.
State-county criminal justice partnership, §§143B-273 to 143B-273.19.
State flag.
Desecration, §14-381.
State legislative building.
Removal of state-owned furniture, fixtures or equipment, §120-32.
Use and maintenance.
Violations of regulations, §120-32.1.
State of emergency.
County ordinance or proclamation dealing with, violation, §14-288.13, (d).
Extension of municipal restrictions into county, violation, §14-288.14, (e).
Governor's proclamation, violation, §§14-288.15, (e), 14-288.16, (e).
Municipal ordinance and proclamation, violation, §14-288.12, (e).
State personnel records.
Unlawful disclosure, §§126-27, 126-28.
State personnel system.
Compensation for assisting person in obtaining state employment, §126-18.
Political activity of employees, §§126-14, 126-14.1.
State treasurer.
Deposits.
Unauthorized depositories, §147-80.
Violations of provisions, §147-79, (c).
False entries in books, §147-76.
Statute of limitations.
Civil actions seeking to recover damages arising out of criminal act, §1-15.1.
Dismissal of criminal charges.
Motion to dismiss.
Grounds, §15A-954, (a).
Voluntary dismissal by state.
Statute of limitations not tolled, §15A-931, (b).
Misdemeanors, §15-1.
Stays.
Appeals.
Correction of errors by appellate division, §15A-1451, (a).
No stay when state appeals, §15A-1451, (b).

CRIMINAL LAW AND PROCEDURE —Cont'd
Stillbirth.
Injury to pregnant woman resulting in miscarriage or stillbirth, §14-18.2.
Use of instruments or drugs, §14-45.
Streets and highways.
Billboards.
Obstructing view at entrance to building on public highway, §136-102.
Controlled-access facilities.
Unlawful use, §136-89.58.
Easements.
Regulation of scenic easements, §136-125.
Highway construction or maintenance.
Injury to barriers, warning signs, etc., §136-26.
Obstructing highways and roads, §136-90.
Openings, structures, pipes or trees.
Permit violations, §136-93.
"Pull-over" areas, §136-18.4.
Rights of way.
Gates projecting over rights-of-way, §136-94.
Signs, signals or markers.
Blinding, deceptive or distracting lights, §136-32.2, (a).
Damaging or removing signs, §136-33, (b1).
Misleading signs, §136-32.1.
Unauthorized erection or maintenance, §136-32.
Subdivision streets.
Developer noncompliance with standards, §136-102.6.
Test drilling or boring upon right-of-way, §136-102.4.
Underpasses or overpasses.
Regulation of safety devices, §136-20, (e).
Subdivisions.
Streets and highways.
Developer noncompliance with standards, §136-102.6.
Submachine guns.
Sale, use or possession, §14-409.
Subornation of perjury, §14-210.
Subpoenas.
Documentary evidence, §15A-802.
General provisions.
See SUBPOENAS.
Witnesses, §15A-801.
Material witnesses.
Securing attendance, §15A-803, (g).
Subversion.
Activities aimed at overthrow of government, §14-11.
Certain subversive activities made unlawful, §14-12.1.
Punishment for violations, §14-12.
Summons and process.
Arrest.
Order for arrest, §15A-305.
Citation, §15A-302.
Copies, §15A-301, (e).
Criminal summons.
Contents, §15A-303, (b) to (d).
Defined, §15A-303, (a).
Enforcement, §15A-303, (e).
Issuance.
Who may issue, §15A-303, (f).
Order to appear, §15A-303, (d).
Probable cause.
Showing of probable cause, §15A-303, (c).
Statement of crime, §15A-303, (b).
Formal requirements, §15A-301, (a).

CRIMINAL LAW AND PROCEDURE —Cont'd
Summons and process —Cont'd
Liability.
Protection of process server executing process from liability, §15A-301, (f).
Public record, §132-1.4, (k).
Return, §15A-301, (d).
Sealing of summons to withhold public record, §132-1.4, (k).
Service, §15A-301, (c).
Citation, §15A-302, (d).
To whom process directed, §15A-301, (b).
Witnesses, securing attendance.
Other states, §15A-812.
Witnesses from without state, §§15A-812, 15A-813.
Definition of "summons," §15A-811.
Superior court costs, §7A-304.
Superior court procedure applicability, §15A-1101.
Support and maintenance.
Abandonment and failure to support spouse and children, §14-322.
Failure to support parent, §14-326.1.
Suppression of evidence.
Motion to suppress evidence, §§15A-971 to 15A-980. See within this heading, "Evidence."
Supreme court.
Discretionary review by the supreme court.
Certification of criminal cause after determination by court of appeals, §7A-31, (a).
Surveys and surveyors.
Coordinate system.
Damaging, defacing or destroying monuments, §102-4.
Swine kept near state institutions, §143-153.
Switch-lock keys used by railroads.
Unauthorized manufacture or sale, §§14-461, 62-322.
Syphilis.
Testing for sexually transmitted infections, §15A-615, (a), (5).
Taking indecent liberties with minor, §14-202.1.
Tattooing, §14-400, (a).
Taxation.
Attempt to evade or defeat tax as felony, §105-236.
Fraud.
Aid or assistance as felony, §105-236.
Officers, agents and employees.
Violations by as misdemeanors, §105-233.
Aiding or abetting violations, §105-234.
Tax information confidentiality, §105-259, (c).
Willful failure to collect, withhold or pay over tax as misdemeanor, §105-236.
Willful failure to file return, supply information or pay tax as misdemeanor, §105-236.
Tax preparers' unauthorized disclosure of tax information, §75-28.
Tear gas, unlawful possession, use, etc., §14-401.6.
Teflon-coated bullets.
Manufacture sale, purchase or possession unlawful, §14-34.3, (a).
Inapplicability of provisions, §14-34.3, (b).
Misdemeanor, §14-34.3, (c).
Telecommunications services, theft, §14-113.5.
Telegraphic and telephonic messages.
Delivery of message.
Failure to deliver promptly, §14-371.

CRIMINAL LAW AND PROCEDURE —Cont'd
Telegraphic and telephonic messages —Cont'd
Opening of sealed telegram.
Unauthorized opening, §14-372.
Publishing of sealed telegram.
Unauthorized publishing, §14-372.
Reading of sealed telegram.
Unauthorized reading, §14-372.
Transmission of message.
Failure to transmit promptly, §14-371.
Violating privacy of messages, §14-371.
Wrongfully obtaining or divulging knowledge of messages, §14-370.
Telephone party lines, refusal to relinquish, §14-401.8.
Telephone sales recovery services, §14-401.15.
Telephone threats, harassment, obscenity, etc., §14-196.
Testing of persons for sexually transmitted infections.
Agency to perform test, §15A-615, (c).
Petitions, §15A-615, (b).
Theft.
Elements of offense, §14-113.9, (a).
Larcenous conduct, §14-113.9, (b).
Prima facie evidence of theft, §14-113.10.
Threats.
Communicating, §14-277.1.
Telephones, §14-196.
Transmitting anonymous letters, §14-394.
Ticket scalping, §14-344.
Timber marks.
Altering timber trademark, §80-22.
Fraudulent use of mark, §80-20.
Possession of branded logs without consent, §80-23.
Time shares.
Registration of violations, §93A-40, (b).
Time share registrar violation, §93A-58.
Violations of provision, §93A-56.
Tobacco products.
Sale or distribution to minors, §14-313.
Toxic substances.
Disclosure of hazardous substance trade secret, §95-197.
Distribution or disclosure of emergency information, §95-194.
Dumping, §14-284.2.
Toxic vapors.
Violations of provision, §90-113.13.
Train surfing.
Riding on train unlawfully, §§14-460, 62-319.
Tramways.
Juvenile to be prosecuted as adult, §§7B-2200 to 7B-2204.
Operation of passenger route tramway without registration, §95-124.
Transportation board.
Malfeasance, §136-13, (c).
Profiting from proposed project, §136-14, (f).
Transportation department.
Airport landing area construction and alteration, §136-18.
Highway inspection reports.
Falsifying reports, §136-13.2, (a), (b).
Highway vending machines in rest areas, §136-18.
Ordinance violations, §136-18.
Utility lines and services, §136-18.
Tree cutting on town watershed.
Disposal violations, §14-383.

CRIMINAL LAW AND PROCEDURE —Cont'd
Trespass, §§14-127 to 14-165.
See TRESPASS.
Trial.
Access to courtroom.
Controlling, §15A-1034, (a).
Disqualification of judge.
Motion of state or defendant, §15A-1223, (b), (c).
Time for filing, §15A-1223, (d).
Own motion, §15A-1223, (a).
Witness in case, §15A-1223, (e).
District courts.
Procedure.
Applicability of superior court procedure, §15A-1101.
Errors in trials.
Relief, §15A-1401.
Extension of session of court by trial judge, §15-167.
Interpreters.
General provisions.
See INTERPRETERS.
Jury.
General provisions. See within this heading, "Jury."
Mistrial.
Deadlocked jury, §15A-1235, (d).
Disability of trial judge, §15A-1224, (a).
Finding of facts required, §15A-1064.
Grounds.
Hung jury, §15A-1063.
Impossibility of proceeding, §15A-1063.
Prejudice to defendant, §15A-1061.
Prejudice to state, §15A-1062.
Procedure following mistrial, §15A-1065.
New trial.
Appeals.
Correction of errors by appellate division.
Duties of clerk of superior court upon order of new trial, §15A-1452, (c).
Relief available upon appeal, §15A-1447, (a).
Motion for appropriate relief.
Motion for new trial.
Relief formerly available now available by motion for appropriate relief, §15A-1411, (c).
Relief available, §15A-1417, (a).
Order in courtroom.
Access to courtroom.
Controlling, §15A-1034, (a).
Contempt power of judge, §15A-1035.
Physical restraint of defendant or witness, §15A-1031.
Removal of disruptive defendant, §15A-1032.
Removal of disruptive witnesses and spectators, §15A-1033.
Restraint of defendant or witness, §15A-1031.
Searches of persons present, §15A-1034, (b).
Order of proceedings.
Jury trial, §15A-1221, (a).
Record of proceedings, §15A-1241, (a), (b).
Objections to unrecorded statement, §15A-1241, (c).
Review of accuracy of record, §15A-1241, (d).
Removal of trial from one county to another.
Liability of counties for cost, §6-40.
Setting offense for trial in district court, §15A-613.
Review of eligibility for pretrial release, §15A-614.

CRIMINAL LAW AND PROCEDURE —Cont'd
Trial —Cont'd
Speedy trial, Const. U. S., amd. VI.
Denial.
Grounds for motion to dismiss, §15A-954, (a).
Felonies, §15-10.
Quo warranto, §1-521.
Treason, §15-10.
Weapons.
Maintenance of order in courtroom.
Searching persons for weapons, §15A-1034, (b).
Trust companies.
Records violations, §53-355.
Reporting offenses or shortages, §53-358, (c).
Trust funds held by public officers.
Failure to keep separate, §128-12.
Unauthorized substances taxes.
Disclosure of confidential information, §105-113.112.
Underground petroleum storage tank leak cleanup.
Circumstantial evidence to prove actual knowledge, §143-215.94X, (e).
Defenses, affirmative defenses and bars to prosecution, applicability, §143-215.94X, (g).
Federal violations, conviction of, §143-215.94X, (d).
Knowingly and willfully committing offenses, §143-215.94X, (b), (c), (f).
Negligently committing offenses, §143-215.94X, (a).
Uniform criminal extradition act, §§15A-721 to 15A-750.
See EXTRADITION.
United States courts.
Solicitors.
Prosecution of cases removed to federal courts, §147-89.
United States flag.
Desecration, §14-381.
Used goods sold on consignment.
Recordkeeping violations, §66-67.2, (c).
Used oil.
Registration violations, §130A-309.17, (h).
Usurious loans.
Household and kitchen furniture, §14-391.
Vagrancy.
Counties.
Regulation of begging, §153A-126.
Municipal corporations.
Regulation of begging, §160A-179.
Vandalism.
Public utility property, willful injury, §62-323.
Venue.
Allegation of venue conclusive in absence of timely motion, §15A-135.
Assault in one county, death in another, §15-130.
Assault in this state, death in another, §15-131.
Athletic bribery prosecutions, §14-378.
Bigamy prosecutions, §14-183.
Change of venue, §15A-133, (c), (d).
Indictment may be returned in other county, §15A-133, (e).
Motion, §15A-957.
Concurrent venue, §15A-132.
Counties, §15A-131, (e).
Assault in one county, death in another, §15-130.
Concurrent venue, §15A-132.
County where death occurs, §15-133.

CRIMINAL LAW AND PROCEDURE —Cont'd
Venue —Cont'd
Counties —Cont'd
Waters dividing counties.
Offenses on, §15-129.
Dismissal for improper venue.
Motion, §15A-952, (b).
Allegation of venue conclusive in absence of timely motion, §15A-135.
District court proceedings, §15A-131, (a).
District courts.
Seat of court in municipality with corporate limits extending into two or more contiguous counties.
Venue in criminal case, authority of judge, §7A-199, (c).
Grand jury.
Presentment or indictment, §15A-631.
Homicide.
Assault in one county, death in another, §15-130.
Assault in this state, death in another, §15-131.
County where death occurs, §15-133.
Joinder.
Concurrent venue, §15A-132.
Offense occurring in part outside North Carolina, §15A-134.
Person in this state injuring one in another, §15-132.
Possessing stolen property prosecution, §14-71.1.
Pretrial proceedings, §15A-131, (a), (c), (f).
Receiving stolen property prosecutions, §14-71.
Sexual offenses, §15A-136.
Superior court proceedings, §15A-131, (b) to (d).
Waiver of venue, §15A-133, (a).
Waters dividing counties, §15-129.
Verdict.
General provisions.
See VERDICTS.
Jury. See within this heading, "Jury."
Veterans guardianship act.
Securities.
Investment by guardians in certain securities.
Violations as misdemeanors, §34-13.
Veterinarians.
Directing or permitting technician, intern or preceptee to commit practice violations, §90-187.6, (g).
Unauthorized practices, §90-187.12.
Veterinary technicians, student interns or student preceptees.
Practice violations, §90-187.6, (f).
Victims of crime.
Compensation.
See CRIME VICTIMS COMPENSATION.
Domestic violence victim assistance act, §§7A-474.16 to 7A-474.20.
Restitution or reparation.
Sentencing, §§15A-1340.34 to 15A-1340.38.
See SENTENCING.
Rights of victims.
Attendance by victim.
Court to permit, §15A-832, (e).
Commuted sentence.
Notice by governor's clemency office, §15A-838.
Custodial agency.
Defined, §15A-830, (a).
Notification to victim, §15A-836, (a).
Time for, §15A-836, (b).
Post trial responsibilities, §15A-835, (c).

CRIMINAL LAW AND PROCEDURE —Cont'd
Victims of crime —Cont'd
Rights of victims —Cont'd
Damages.
No claim for damages created by provisions, §15A-839.
Definitions, §§15A-824, 15A-830, (a).
District attorney's office.
Consultation by victim with.
Offering victim opportunity, §15A-832, (f).
Identifying information.
Submission of copy to court, §15A-832, (g).
Information to victim, §15A-832, (a), (b).
Notification to victim of trial proceedings, §15A-832, (c).
Post trial responsibilities, §15A-835, (a), (b).
Secure waiting area during court proceedings.
Providing for victims, §15A-832, (d).
Division of community corrections.
Notice to victim, responsibilities, §15A-837, (a).
Time period for notifying victim, §15A-837, (b).
Evidence of impact of crime.
District attorney or law enforcement officer may proffer evidence, §15A-833, (b).
No inference drawn from failure to offer evidence, §15A-833, (b).
Right of victim to offer admissible evidence, §15A-833, (a).
Victim not required to offer evidence, §15A-833, (b).
What evidence may be offered by victim, §15A-833, (a).
Grounds for relief.
Omissions not to be used as, §15A-840.
Identifying information.
Judicial officers issuing arrest warrants for misdemeanors, §15A-832.1.
Incompetent victim.
Exercise of rights by next of kin or legal guardian, §15A-841.
Judicial officials issuing arrest warrants for misdemeanors offenses.
Forwarding victim identifying information, §15A-832.1, (b).
Recording victim identifying information, §15A-832.1, (a).
Law enforcement agency.
Arresting law enforcement agency.
Defined, §15A-830, (a).
Responsibilities, §15A-831, (a), (c).
Investigating law enforcement agency.
Defined, §15A-830, (a).
Responsibilities, §15A-831, (b), (d).
Next of kin.
Defined, §15A-830, (a).
Entitled to rights of deceased victim, §15A-830, (b).
Pardon.
Notice by governor's clemency office, §15A-838.
Restitution, §15A-834.
Retrial or remand of case when conviction overturned.
Effect, §15A-835, (d).
Scope of provisions, §15A-827.
Treatment due victims, §15A-825.
Victim and witness assistants, §§7A-347, 7A-348, 15A-826.

CRIMINAL LAW AND PROCEDURE —Cont'd
Victims of crime —Cont'd
Victims of rape and sexual offenses.
Assistance program, §§143B-480.1 to 143B-480.3.
Office of coordinator of services for victims, §§143B-394.1 to 143B-394.3.
Violent habitual felons, §§14-7.7 to 14-7.12.
Vital statistics.
Birth certificates.
Registration outside.
Time period for filing, §130A-103.
Misdemeanors and felonies, §130A-26A, (a), (b).
Vocational rehabilitation services.
Withholding of information, §143-547, (f).
Wage and hour act.
Violations, §95-25.21, (c).
Waiver.
Appeals.
Correction of errors by appellate division.
Waiver of right to assert error upon appeal.
Failure to make appropriate and timely motion or objection, §15A-1446, (b).
Appearance.
Defendant may execute written waiver and plead not guilty, §15A-1011, (d), (e).
Arraignment, §15A-945.
Indictment, §15A-642, (b), (c).
Probable cause hearings, §15A-606, (a).
Evidence of waiver not to be admitted at trial, §15A-606, (b).
Proceedings upon waiver, §15A-606, (c).
Venue, §15A-133, (a).
Warehouse receipts.
Delivering goods without obtaining receipt, §27-58.
Deposit.
Fraudulent deposit and negotiation, §27-59.
Failure to obtain receipt.
Delivering goods without obtaining receipt, §27-58.
False statements.
Issuing receipt with false statement, §27-55.
Fraudulent deposit and negotiation, §27-59.
Fraudulent duplicates.
Issuance, §27-56.
Goods not stored.
Issuing receipt for goods not stored, §27-54.
Interest of warehouseman.
Failure to state in receipt the interest of warehouseman, §27-57.
Negotiation.
Fraudulent deposit and negotiation, §27-59.
Warrants.
Arrest.
See ARREST.
Searches and seizures.
See SEARCHES AND SEIZURES.
Water and air resources.
Air pollution control violations, §143-215.114B, (a) to (i).
Classifications, standards or limitations.
Violations, §143-215.6B, (f) to (i).
Cleaning agents containing phosphorus.
Manufacturing, selling or distributing, §143-214.4, (f).
Conservation and use of diverted waters within emergency areas.
Violations of regulations, §143-354.
Enforcement procedures.
Criminal penalties, §143-215.6B.

CRIMINAL LAW AND PROCEDURE —Cont'd
Water and air resources —Cont'd
Local air pollution control programs.
Violations, §143-215.112, (d).
Medical waste.
Prohibited disposal, §143-214.2A, (a), (c).
Reporting of quality.
Violations of part, §143-215.69, (a).
Violations of part regulating water usage, §143-215.17, (a).
Waters and watercourses.
Lake Wylie marine commission.
Jurisdiction.
Trial.
Criminal violations of regulations, §77-38, (c).
Natural and scenic rivers system.
Violations as misdemeanors, §113A-42, (b).
Water supply of public institutions.
Injuring, §143-152.
Weapons.
See WEAPONS.
Weight of vehicles and load.
Excessive size or weight.
Violations of special permit terms and condition, §20-119, (d).
Weights and measures offenses, §81A-29.
Well drilling, construction, etc., §143-355, (i).
Wells.
Leaving unused well open and exposed, §14-287.
Wildlife protectors.
Refusal of person to stop in obedience to directions of, §113-136, (j).
Wildlife resources commission rules violations, §§113-135, (a) to (c), 113-135.1, (a), (b).
Witnesses.
Arrest.
Material witnesses.
Order for arrest, §15A-803, (g).
Witnesses from without a state.
Exemption from arrest, §15A-814.
Competency of witnesses.
Defendant competent but not compelled to testify, §8-54.
Husband and wife, §8-57, (a) to (c).
Custody.
Arrest.
Order for arrest of material witness, §15A-803, (g).
Voluntary protective custody.
Material witness order.
Issuance not to preclude issuance of voluntary protective custody order, §15A-804, (c).
Order, §15A-804, (a).
Material witness order not precluded by issuance, §15A-804, (c).
Modification or vacation, §15A-804, (d).
Release of witness, §15A-804, (b).
Evidence of testimonial arrangement may be fully developed, §15A-1055, (a).
Exclusion of witnesses, §15A-1225.
Fees for attendance.
One fee for day's attendance, §6-60.
Husband and wife.
Competency of witnesses, §8-57, (a) to (c).
Immunity.
Evidence of grant of immunity may be fully developed, §15A-1055, (a).
Jury.
Argument to jury as to impact of immunity, §15A-1055, (b).

CRIMINAL LAW AND PROCEDURE —Cont'd
Witnesses —Cont'd
Immunity —Cont'd
Order to testify or produce other information.
Application for.
Court proceedings, §15A-1052, (a), (b).
Grand jury proceedings, §15A-1053, (a), (b).
Court proceedings, §15A-1052, (a).
Definition of "other information," §15A-1051, (c).
Grand jury proceedings, §15A-1053, (a).
Jury trial.
Judge to inform jury of grant of immunity, §15A-1052, (c).
When effective, §15A-1051, (b).
Self-incrimination, §15A-1051, (a).
Sentence concessions, §15A-1054, (a).
Evidence of testimonial arrangement may be fully developed, §15A-1055, (a).
Jury.
Argument to jury as to impact of agreement, §15A-1055, (b).
Notice of agreement, §15A-1054, (c).
Recommendations, §15A-1054, (b).
Insanity defense.
Notice of intent to introduce expert testimony, §15A-959, (b).
Intimidating or interfering with, §14-226, (a).
Jury view.
Testimony at site of jury view, §15A-1229, (b).
Material witnesses.
Arrest, §15A-803, (g).
Order for arrest, §15A-803, (g).
Order assuring attendance, §15A-803, (a), (e).
Modification, §15A-803, (f).
Period order effective, §15A-803, (c).
Procedure for obtaining, §15A-803, (d).
Vacation, §15A-803, (f).
Voluntary protective custody order not precluded, §15A-804, (c).
When issued, §15A-803, (b).
Subpoenas, §15A-803, (g).
Out-of-state witnesses.
Securing attendance.
Witnesses from without a state. See within this subheading, "Securing attendance."
Parental rights.
Threatening witness with assertion or denial of parental rights, §14-226, (b).
Perjury, §§14-209 to 14-211.
Physical restraint of witness.
Maintenance of order in courtroom, §15A-1031.
Prisoners.
Securing attendance, §§15A-821 to 15A-823.
Probable cause hearings, §15A-611, (a).
Protective custody.
Voluntary protective custody, §15A-804.
Removal of disruptive witnesses.
Maintenance of order in courtroom, §15A-1033.
Restraint of witness.
Maintenance of order in courtroom, §15A-1031.
Rights of victims and witnesses.
Assistants for administrative and victim and witness services, §15A-826.
Definitions, §15A-824.
Scope of article, §15A-827.
Treatment due witnesses, §15A-825.
Right to be confronted by witnesses, Const. U. S., amd. VI.
Securing attendance.
Material witnesses.
Order securing attendance, §15A-803.

CRIMINAL LAW AND PROCEDURE —Cont'd
Witnesses —Cont'd
Securing attendance —Cont'd
Prisoners in federal institutions as witnesses in proceedings in state.
Certificate, §15A-823, (a), (b).
Delivery to attorney general of United States, §15A-823, (c).
Prisoners in this state as witnesses in proceedings outside state, §15A-821, (a), (b).
Agreements, §15A-821, (c).
Prisoners outside state as witnesses in proceedings in state.
Certificate, §15A-822, (a), (b).
Delivery to court of other state, §15A-822, (c).
State institutions.
Witnesses confined in, §15A-805, (a), (b).
Cost of production of witness, §15A-805, (c).
Voluntary protective custody, §15A-804.
Witnesses from without a state.
Arrest.
Exemption from arrest, §15A-814.
Certificate of judge, §§15A-812, 15A-813.
Definitions, §15A-811.
Expenses of witnesses, §§15A-812, 15A-813.
Service of process.
Exemption, §15A-814.
Summons.
Defined, §15A-811.
Witness from another state summoned to testify in this state, §15A-813.
Witness in this state summoned to testify in another state, §15A-812.
Uniform act.
Construction and interpretation, §15A-815.
General provisions, §§15A-811 to 15A-816.
Title of act, §15A-816.
Witnesses in this state summoned to testify in another state, §15A-812.
Sentence concessions, §15A-1054, (a).
Jury.
Argument to jury as to impact of agreement, §15A-1055, (b).
Notice of agreement, §15A-1054, (c).
Recommendations, §15A-1054, (b).
Subpoenas, §15A-801.
Material witnesses.
Securing attendance, §15A-803, (g).
Voluntary protective custody, §15A-804.
Workers' compensation.
Coercing or attempting to coerce employee into agreeing to compensation.
Threatening employee with criminal prosecution, §97-88.2, (c).
False statements or representations, §97-88.2, (a).
Insurance carrier violation, §97-100, (g).
Insurance or proof of financial ability to pay benefit.
Refusal or neglect to secure compensation, §97-94, (c).
Receiving fee, other consideration or gratuity on account of services rendered, §97-90, (b).
Unlawful deduction by employers, §97-21.
Work first program fraud, §108A-39.
Worship places, obstructing way, §14-199.

CRIMINAL LAW SPECIALTY.
Certification standards, Bar Rules & Regs., D, §§.2501 to .2507.

CRIMINAL PENALTIES.
Crimes and offenses generally.
See CRIMINAL LAW AND PROCEDURE.
Felonies.
See FELONIES.
Fines.
See FINES.
Infractions.
See INFRACTIONS.
Misdemeanors.
See MISDEMEANORS.
Prison terms.
See PRISON TERMS.
Sentencing procedure for imposing punishment.
See SENTENCING.

CRIMINAL PROCESS.
Arrest warrants and orders for arrest.
Time for serving, §15A-301, (d).
To whom directed, §15A-301, (b).
Copy delivered to person arrested or served, §15A-301, (c).
Copy made and original transmitted to appropriate county.
Wrong venue, §15A-301, (e).
Copy of charges filed against defendant.
Furnishing defendant, §15A-301, (e).
Copy when original lost, §15A-301, (e).
Corporations.
Serving criminal summons on, §15A-301, (c).
Criminal summons.
Corporations, serving, §15A-301, (c).
Time for serving, §15A-301, (d).
To whom directed, delivery, service, §15A-301, (b).
Execution or service, §15A-301, (c).
Redelivery for further attempts at service, §15A-301, (d).
Time for serving, §15A-301, (d).
Failure to return.
Process not invalidated, §15A-301, (d).
Formal requirements, §15A-301, (a).
Immunity of server for due service, §15A-301, (f).
Lost original.
Copy when original lost, §15A-301, (e).
Protection of process server, §15A-301, (f).
Record of process issued maintained, §15A-301, (a).
Redelivery for further attempts at service, §15A-301, (d).
Return, §15A-301, (d).
Service or execution, §15A-301, (c).
Redelivery for further attempts at service, §15A-301, (d).
Time for serving, §15A-301, (d).
Signed and dated, requirement, §15A-301, (a).
Time for serving, §15A-301, (d).
To whom directed, §15A-301, (b).
Wrong venue.
Copy made and original transmitted to appropriate county, §15A-301, (e).

CRIMINAL RECORD CHECKS.
See CRIMINAL HISTORY RECORD CHECKS.

CRITICAL SCHOOL FACILITY NEEDS FUND, §§115C-489.1 to 115C-489.2.
Administration, §115C-489.1, (a).
Creation, §115C-489.1, (c).
Deposit, §115C-489.1, (b).
Grants, §115C-489.2, (a), (b).

CROATAN INDIANS.
Indians of Robeson county.
Rights and privileges, §71A-1.

CROPS.
Burning crops in the field.
Criminal trespass, §14-141.
Commodities.
General provisions, §§78D-1 to 78D-33.
See COMMODITIES.
Corn.
See CORN.
Damage to agricultural commodities or production systems.
Definitions, §1-539.2B, (c).
Double damage liability, §1-539.2B, (a).
Valuation, §1-539.2B, (b).
Decedents' estates.
Ungathered crops at death of decedent, §28A-15-1, (d).
Destroying crops in the field.
Criminal trespass, §14-141.
Execution not to be levied on growing crops until matured, §1-315, (c).
Exempt property from enforcement of claims of creditors, §1C-1601, (a).
Gleaned crops.
Income tax.
Individual income tax.
Credits, §105-151.14.
Grain adulteration, §§106-621 to 106-628.
See GRAIN ADULTERATION.
Grain dealers, §§106-601 to 106-615.
See GRAIN DEALERS.
Income tax credit for gleaned crops.
Corporation donating harvested crop to nonprofit organization, §105-130.37.
Landlord and tenant.
In lieu of emblements, farm lessee holds out year, with rents apportioned, §42-7.
Lien on crops, §§42-15 to 42-23.
Neglecting crops by tenant, §14-359.
Larceny.
Ungathered crops, §14-78.
Liens on crops, §§42-15 to 42-23.
Action to settle disputes between parties, §42-17.
Tenant's undertaking upon continuance or appeal, §42-18.
Advances, §42-15.
Appeals.
Tenant's undertaking on continuance or appeal, §42-18.
Assigns, §42-15.
Claim for delivery of personal property, §42-16.
Compliance with prices provided by agricultural liens, §42-15.
Delivery of crops to landlord on his undertaking, §42-19.
Enforcement, §§42-15, 42-15.1.
Executions.
Tenant's crop not subject to execution against landlord, §42-21.
Failure to make fair decision, §42-16.
Insurance.
Landlord's lien on crop insurance for rents, advances, etc., §42-15.1.
Priority, §42-15.
Removal of crops, §42-15.
Unlawful removal by tenant, §42-22.
Rents, §42-15.
Rights of tenant, §42-16.

CROPS —Cont'd
Liens on crops —Cont'd
Sale of crops if neither party gives undertaking, §42-20.
Seizures.
Unlawful seizure by landlord or removal by tenant misdemeanor, §42-22.
Terms of agricultural tenancies in certain counties, §42-23.
Tobacco.
Failure of tenant to account for sales under tobacco marketing cards, §42-22.1.
Wages.
Persons entitled to part of crop as wages.
Tenant's crop not subject to execution against landlord, §42-21.
Promotion of use and sale of agricultural products.
Generally, §§106-550 to 106-568.
See AGRICULTURAL PRODUCTS PROMOTION.
Sale of goods, UCC, §25-2-107, (2).
Definition of goods, §25-2-105, (1).
Identification of goods, §25-2-501, (1).
Secured transactions.
Priority of security interests in, §25-9-334, (i).
Production-money crops.
Defined, §25-9-102, (a).
Status of security interest in, §25-9-103.1, (a).
Production-money obligation.
Application of payments, §25-9-103.1, (b).
Defined, §25-9-102, (a).
Production-money security interests.
Priority, §25-9-324.1.
Status, §25-9-103.1, (a).
Burden of establishing, §25-9-103.1, (c).
Continuation of status, §25-9-103.1, (c).
Production of crops.
Defined, §25-9-102, (a).
Surety on crops.
Appeals, §§42-18 to 42-20.
Trespass.
Burning or otherwise destroying crops in the field.
Criminal trespass, §14-141.
Criminal trespass.
Injury to crops of another, §14-128.
Warehouse receipts.
Storage under government bond, §25-7-201, (2).

CROP SEED IMPROVEMENT BOARD, §§106-269 to 106-276.
See SEEDS.

CROSSBOWS.
Sale, §§14-402 to 14-408.
Collection.
Issuance of permit to nonresident, §14-404, (a).
Dealer records, requirements, §14-406.
Misdemeanor for violating, §14-408.
Definitions, §14-402, (c).
License or permit required, §14-402, (a).
Collection, issuance to nonresident, §14-404, (a).
Expiration date, §14-403.
Fee for sheriffs services, §14-404, (e).
Form, §14-403.
Inapplicability, §§14-402, (b), 14-404, (d).
Informing applicant as to action on issuance, §14-404, (f).
Issuance by sheriff, §14-403.
Records kept by sheriffs, §14-405.
Refusal to issue, grounds, appeal, §14-404, (b), (c).

CROSSBOWS —Cont'd
Sale —Cont'd
Mail or other parcel delivery.
Display of permit or license, §14-402, (a).

CROSS-CLAIMS.
Generally.
See COUNTERCLAIMS AND CROSS-CLAIMS.

CROSSES.
Burning or flaming crosses.
Placing on property of another or public street or highway, §14-12.12.
Placing with intent of intimidating, §§14-12.13, 14-12.14.

CROSS-EXAMINATION, Const. U. S., amd. V.
Criminal defendants competency, §8-54.
Depositions.
Oral examinations, §1A-1, Rule 30, (c).
Leading questions, §8C-1, Rule 611, (c).
Scope, §8C-1, Rule 611, (b).

CROSS-INDEX OF JUDGMENTS, §1-233.

CROSS-INDEX OF LIS PENDENS, §1-117.
Effect on subsequent purchasers, §1-118.

CROSSING OF UTILITY LINES AND RIGHTS OF WAY BY OTHER UTILITIES, §62-39.

CROSSINGS.
Controlled-access facilities.
Elimination of crossings, §§136-20, 136-89.53.
Public utilities.
Crossing of lines and rights of way, §62-39.
Railroad grade crossings, §§20-142.1 to 20-142.5.
See RAILROAD GRADE CROSSINGS.

CROSSWALKS.
Pedestrians.
Right of way, §§20-155, (c), 20-173, (a), (b).
Blind persons, §20-175.2.
When required to cross at crosswalk, §20-174, (c).
Stopping when traffic obstructed, §20-142.5.

CROWDERS MOUNTAIN STATE PARK.
Removal of land from state nature and historic preserve, §143-260.10G, (a).
Exchange of property by state, permitted purposes, §143-260.10G, (c).
Property deleted from state parks system, §143-260.10G, (b).

CRUELTY TO ANIMALS.
Abandonment, §14-361.1.
Baby chicks.
Living baby chicks or other fowl under eight weeks of age.
Disposing of as pets or novelties forbidden, §14-363.1.
Baiting, §14-362.1.
Dog baiting, §14-362.2.
Civil remedies for the protection of animals, §§19A-1 to 19A-4.
Definitions, §19A-1.
Exemptions from article, §19A-1.1.
Permanent injunction, §19A-4.
Preliminary injunction, §19A-3.
Purpose of article, §19A-2.
Real party in interest as defendant, §19A-2.
Real party in interest as plaintiff, §19A-2.
Termination of possession and right of ownership, §19A-4.
Cockfighting, §14-362.

CRUELTY TO ANIMALS —Cont'd
Confiscation of cruelly treated animals, §14-363.2.
Construction and interpretation, §14-360.
Conveying animals in cruel manner, §14-363.
Counties.
Regulation by local ordinance, §153A-127.
Custody of confiscated animals, §14-363.2.
Definitions, §§14-360, (c), 19A-1.
Dogs.
Dog fighting, §14-362.2.
Restraining dogs in cruel manner, §14-362.3.
Exclusions, §14-360, (c).
Fights, §14-362.1.
Cockfighting, §14-362.
Dog fighting, §14-362.2.
Fowl.
Living baby chicks or other fowl under eight weeks of age.
Disposing of as pets or novelties forbidden, §14-363.1.
Instigating cruelty, §14-361.
Intentional cruelty, §14-360, (a).
Investigators, §§19A-45 to 19A-49.
Malicious cruelty, §14-360, (b).
Municipal corporations.
Abuse of animals.
City may define and prohibit abuse of animals, §160A-182.
Promoting cruelty, §14-361.
Rabbits.
Eight weeks of age or under.
Disposing of as pets or novelties forbidden, §14-363.1.
Societies for the prevention of cruelty to animals.
Property used for charitable purposes, §105-278.6.

CRUELTY TO SPOUSE.
Divorce from bed and board, §50-7.

CRUISE VESSELS.
Alcoholic beverages for use on oceangoing ships, §18B-106.

CRUSTACEA.
Adulterated or misbranded crustacea.
Embargoes, §130A-21, (c).
Sanitation of shellfish and crustacea, §§130A-230, 130A-231.
Shellfish.
General provisions.
See SHELLFISH.

CRUTCHES.
Sales and use tax exemptions, §105-164.13.

CRYPTS.
Hearsay exception, engravings on, §8C-1, Rule 803.

CUCUMBERS.
Weights and measures, §81A-42.

CULTURAL RESOURCES DEPARTMENT.
Admission fees.
Museums owned by department, §121-7.3.
Appropriations.
Promotion of arts, §143-407.
Archival and historical agency of state, §121-3.
Artifacts owned by state and in custody of office of archives and history.
Selling, trading or placing on permanent loan, §121-7, (a).

CULTURAL RESOURCES DEPARTMENT —Cont'd
Archival and historical agency of state —Cont'd
Budget requests, procedure for preparing, §121-12.2.
Defined, §121-2.
Grants-in-aid.
Expending appropriation, §121-12.2.
Responsibility for administering appropriations, §121-12.1.
Museum of history, maintenance and administration by department, §121-7, (a).
Transfer of commission to department, §143B-51.
Tryon's Palace, §§121-14 to 121-21.
Commissions and divisions.
Organization of department, §143B-53.
Creation, §143B-49.
Definitions.
Arts, §143-403.
Executive Mansion.
Authority of department of administration not affected, §143-415.
Powers of department, §143-411.
Purpose of provisions, §143-410.
Functions of department, §143B-51, (a).
Transfer, §143B-51, (b).
Funds.
Promotion of arts, §143-407.
General assembly.
Retention of books, records, etc., by department, §120-37, (f).
Gifts.
Promotion of arts.
Acceptance of gifts by department, §143-407.
Head of department, §143B-52.
Historical markers.
Cooperation of department of transportation, §136-42.2.
Libraries.
State library agency, §§125-1 to 125-11.
See LIBRARIES AND LIBRARIANS.
Museums owned by department.
Admission fees, §121-7.3.
North Carolina register of historic places.
Power to establish, expand and maintain, §121-4.1, (a).
Organization of department, §143B-53.
Powers and duties, §§121-4, 143B-49, 143B-50.
Executive Mansion, §143-411.
Transfer, §143B-51, (b).
Promotion of arts.
Appropriations, §143-407.
Definitions, §143-403.
Duties of department, §143-406.
Funds, §143-407.
Gifts.
Acceptance, §143-407.
Reports.
Submission of biennial report to governor, §143-406.
Public records.
Administration of records management program by department, §132-8.1.
Assistance by and to department, §132-8.
Disposition of records at end of official's term, §132-4.
Register of historic places.
Power to establish, expand and maintain, §121-4.1, (a).
Reports.
Biennial report to governor.
Submission, §143-406.

CULTURAL RESOURCES DEPARTMENT —Cont'd
Roanoke Island commission, §§143B-131.1 to 143B-131.10.
Secretary.
Head of department, §143B-52.
Streets and highways.
Historical markers on highway.
Cooperation with department of transportation, §136-42.2.
Transportation department.
Historical markers on highway.
Cooperation with department of cultural resources, §136-42.2.
Veterans' memorial commission.
See VETERANS' MEMORIAL COMMISSION.

CUMBERLAND COUNTY.
Agricultural tenancies in certain counties.
Terms of, §42-23.
Ambulance service.
Attachment or garnishment and lien for, §§44-51.4 to 44-51.8.
Obtained without intending to pay, §14-111.2.
Board of county commissioners.
Filling vacancies on board, §153A-27.1.
Condemnation or acquisition of land by local government unit outside county.
Consent of board of commissioners necessary, §153A-15.
Counties generally.
See COUNTIES.
Cropper or tenant refusing to perform terms of contract.
Forfeiture of right of possession to premises, §42-27.
Dangerous firearm use by young children, permitting.
Air rifles, air pistols and BB guns not dangerous firearm, §14-316, (b).
Dog collars.
Unlawful removal of electronic dog collars, §14-401.17.
Game laws, local acts not repealed, §113-133.1, (e).
Probates and registration orders before clerks of inferior courts validated, §47-59.
Room occupancy tax levied by county, uniform provisions, §153A-155.
School property.
Acquisition and improvement, §153A-158.1.
Southeastern North Carolina regional economic development commission, §158-8.3.
Wild plants, taking of certain plants from land of another.
Inapplicability of provisions, §14-129.

CUNNILINGUS.
Rape.
See RAPE.
Sexual offenses generally.
See SEXUAL OFFENSES.

CURATIVE ACTS AND STATUTES.
Acknowledgments.
Banks.
Stockholders, officers or directors, §47-93.
Building and loan associations.
Officer or stockholder, §47-94.
Deeds.
Proof of execution, §47-100.

CURATIVE ACTS AND STATUTES —Cont'd
Acknowledgments —Cont'd
Failure of register of deeds to certify correctness of acknowledgment.
Registrations validated, §47-50.1.
Handwriting.
Probates on proof of handwriting of maker refusing to acknowledge, §47-57.
Married women.
Taken by officer who has grantor, §47-105.
Notary public.
Holding another office, §§47-104, 47-108.2.
Interested as trustee or holding other office, §47-95.
Officer in wrong capacity, §47-55.
Resident taking out-of-state, §47-78.
Savings and loan associations, §47-94.
Seals.
Omission of seal of acknowledging officer, §47-101.
Taking out-of-state by resident, §47-78.
Banks.
Acknowledgments taken by stockholders, officers, or directors, §47-93.
Nonresident banks.
Validation of certain deeds, §47-108.16.
Probate before stockholders and directors of banks, §47-92.
Building and loan associations.
Acknowledgment and registration by officer or stockholder, §47-94.
Certificate alleging examination of grantor instead of witness, §47-74.
Clerks of court.
Before clerks before year 1889, §47-58.
Before justices of the peace where clerk's certificate or order of registration defective, §47-56.
Deeds where clerk appointed himself to sell, §47-65.
Defective certification or adjudication of clerk, etc., admitting to registration, §47-49.
Deputy clerks of superior court, §47-108.6.
Inferior courts, §47-59.
Interested clerks.
Instruments in which clerk of court was party, §47-106.
Order of registration by interested clerk, §47-61.
Order of registration by judge where clerk party, §47-60.
Other states, §47-77.
Prior certificates.
Certificate failing to pass on all prior certificates, §47-48.
Seals.
Certificates of clerks without seal, §47-99.
Probate omitting seals, etc., §47-53.
Commissioners.
Validation of instruments acknowledged before United States commissioners, §47-108.12.
Commissioners of deeds.
Before commissioners, §47-81.
Commissioners of oaths, §47-81.1.
Consuls.
Probate of deeds before consular agents of the United States, §47-91.
Consuls general, §47-83.
Vice-consuls and vice-consuls general, §47-84.
Corporations.
By president and attested by treasurer under corporate seal, §47-70.

CURATIVE ACTS AND STATUTES —Cont'd
Corporations —Cont'd
By president and attested by witness before January 1, 1900, §47-71.
Deeds.
Error in acknowledgment or probate, §47-97.1.
Foreign corporations.
Validation of certain conveyances of foreign dissolved corporations, §47-108.6.
Mistake as to officer's name.
Validation of corporate deed, §47-97.
Name.
Corporate name not affixed, but signed otherwise prior to January, 1973, §47-72.
Oath of subscribing witness, §47-73.
Probates before officer of interested corporation, §47-63.
Proof of corporate articles before officer authorized to probate, §47-75.
Registration.
Validation of registration of certain corporate deeds, etc., §47-108.1.
Seal.
Corporate seal omitted prior to January 1, 1991, §47-71.1.
Validation of registration of certain corporate deeds, etc., §47-108.1.
Deeds.
Clerk's deeds where clerk appointed himself to sell, §47-65.
Corporate deeds.
Validation of certain deeds where admitted to record, §47-108.1.
Guardians.
Deeds by guardians omitting seal, prior to January 1, 1944, validated, §35A-1360.
Nonresident banks.
Validation of certain deeds, §47-108.16.
Official capacity not designated, §47-108.17.
Examinations.
Notaries holding other office, §47-108.2.
Foreign probates.
Commission of seal, §47-82.
Governor.
Sister state probates without governor's authentication, §47-80.
Guardians.
Deeds.
Guardians omitting seal, prior to January 1, 1944, validated, §35A-1360.
Validation of certain private sales, §35A-1361.
Handwriting.
Proof of handwriting of maker refusing to acknowledge, §47-57.
Husband and wife.
Before different officers, §47-68.
Different officers of deeds by husband and wife, §47-87.
Probates in wrong order, §47-67.
Instruments that were not acknowledged.
Validation of certain recorded instruments, §47-108.20.
Judges.
Before judges of supreme or superior courts or clerks before 1889, §47-58.
Jurisdiction.
Officer acting in wrong capacity or out of jurisdiction, §47-55.
Magistrates.
Clerk's certificate or order of registration defective, §47-56.

CURATIVE ACTS AND STATUTES —Cont'd
Maps and plats.
Register of deeds.
Acts in recording validated, §47-108.8.
Validation of certain maps and plats that cannot be copies, §47-108.19.
Validation of registration of plats upon probate in accordance with section 47-30, §47-108.10.
Married women.
Acknowledgment and private examination by officer who was grantor, §47-105.
Acknowledgments of instruments of married women made since February 7, 1945, §47-108.4.
Certificate of wife's "previous" examination, §47-66.
Wife free trader.
No examination or husband's assent, §47-69.
Masters in chancery.
Probate before masters in chancery, §§47-85, 47-85.1.
Military officers.
Instruments proved before officers of certain ranks, §47-81.2.
Name of grantor omitted from record, §47-107.
Notaries public.
Acknowledgments and examinations before notaries holding other office, §47-108.2.
Acknowledgments before notaries under age, §47-108.
Acknowledgments taken by notaries holding other office.
Validation, §47-90.
Acts prior to November 26, 1921, §47-108.3.
Interested parties.
Probates before interested notaries, §47-95.
Notary holding another office.
Acknowledgments, §47-104.
Other states, §47-77.
Probates before interested notaries, §47-62.
Seals.
Absence of notarial seal, §47-102.
Trustees.
Taking acknowledgments when interested as trustee, §47-95.
Validation of certain instruments containing notarial jurat, §47-108.18.
Oaths.
Before commissioner of oaths, §47-81.1.
Officer acting in wrong capacity or out of jurisdiction, §47-55.
Officers, stockholders or directors prior to January 1, 1945, §47-64.
Officials of wrong state, §47-76.
Order of registration.
Omitted, §47-50.
Registration without formal order validated, §§47-88, 47-89, 47-108.15.
Other states.
Certain deeds executed in other states where seal omitted, §47-108.5.
Defective probates beyond state, §47-98.
Notaries and clerks in other states, §47-77.
Officials of other states, §47-108.15.
Seal omitted, §§47-86, 47-108.5.
Sister state probates without governor's authentication, §47-80.
Public lands.
Conveyances of state-owned lands, §146-78.
Grants signed by deputy secretary of state.
Validation, §146-54.
Validation of irregular entries, §146-53.

CURATIVE ACTS AND STATUTES —Cont'd
Register of deeds.
Acts of register in recording plats and maps, §47-108.8.
Clerks or deputies.
Registration by register's deputies, assistants or clerks, §§47-54, 47-54.1.
Prior certificates.
Certificate failing to pass on all prior certificates, §47-48.
Registration.
Defective probates beyond state, §47-98.
Instruments registered prior to January 1, 1934.
Validation, §47-108.13.
Validation of instruments registered without probate, §47-96.
Sales.
Guardians.
Certain private sales validated, §35A-1361.
Savings and loan associations, §47-94.
Seals.
Clerks of court.
Certificates of clerks without seal, §47-99.
Foreign probate omitting seals, §47-82.
Notarial seal.
Absence, §47-102.
Omitted, §§47-51, 47-53.1, 47-101, 47-108.5.
Validation where seal omitted, §47-108.11.
Subscribing witnesses, §47-108.9.
Superior courts.
Before judges of superior court, §47-58.
Supreme court.
Before judges of supreme court, §47-58.
United States.
Conveyance acting by and through general services administration, §47-108.14.
Validation of certain recorded instruments that were not acknowledged, §47-108.20.
Veterans' guardianship act.
Validation of prior acts, §34-2.1.

CURATORS.
Powers of fiduciaries generally, §§32-25 to 32-28.
See FIDUCIARIES.
Prudent person rule.
Investment and deposit of funds, §36A-2, (a).
Uniform fiduciaries act, §§32-1 to 32-13.
See FIDUCIARIES.

CURBS.
Handicapped persons.
Curb ramps or curb cuts, §136-44.14.
Special assessments by counties, §§153A-185 to 153A-206.
See SPECIAL ASSESSMENTS BY COUNTIES.

CURFEW.
Cities.
Imposition of curfew on persons under 18, §160A-198.
Counties.
Imposition of curfew on persons under 18, §153A-142.
Delinquent juveniles, imposing, §7B-2506.
Frisk of curfew violators, §14-288.10.
Universities and colleges, §§116-212, 116-213.

CURRENCY.
Commodities.
General provisions, §§78D-1 to 78D-33.
See COMMODITIES.

CURRENCY —Cont'd
Counterfeiting, §§14-13 to 14-16.
See COUNTERFEITING.
European monetary union.
Continuity of contracts, §§53-295 to 53-300.
See EUROPEAN MONETARY UNION.
Foreign-money claims, §§1C-1820 to 1C-1834.
See FOREIGN-MONEY CLAIMS.
Money.
See MONEY.

CURRENT ACCOUNT ACTIONS.
Accrual of cause of action to recover balance due, §1-31.

CURRITUCK COUNTY.
Condemnation or acquisition of land by local government unit outside county.
Consent of board of commissioners necessary, §153A-15.
Cropper or tenant refusing to perform terms of contract.
Forfeiture of right of possession to premises, §42-27.
Game commission.
Regulatory authority not appealed or abridged, §113-133.1, (b).
Game laws, local acts not repealed, §113-133.1, (e).
Grants in navigable waters, registration, §113-205, (a).
Housing.
Tenant as commissioner, exemption from provision of law allowing, §157-5.
Northeastern North Carolina regional economic development commission, §158-8.2.
Officers compensated from fees.
Statement to be rendered, §128-13.
Open fires, high hazard counties.
Applicability of provisions, §113-60.23, (a).
Ground clearing activities, special permit, §113-60.23, (c).
Woodland fires, permit required, §113-60.23, (b).
Registration of deeds.
Tax certification, no delinquent taxes due, §161-31, (b).
Room occupancy tax levied by county, uniform provision, §153A-155.
School property.
Acquisition and improvement, §153A-158.1.
Special school tax, election to abolish.
Petition required, §115C-505.
Swimming, surfing and littering in Atlantic Ocean.
City ordinances effective, §160A-176.1.
Tax sales, notices by publication validated.
Inapplicability of provisions, §47-108.24.
Wastewater systems.
Innovative septic tank systems.
Ordinance billing fee as property tax, §130A-343.1, (c).
Wild plants, taking of certain plants from land of another.
Inapplicability of provisions, §14-129.

CURRITUCK SOUND.
Obstructing waters, §76-41.

CURSING.
See PROFANITY.

CURTESY.
Abolished, §§29-4, 41-4.

CURTESY —Cont'd
Renunciation by married person under age of 21, §39-13.2, (c).

CURVES.
Provisions marking of "pull off" areas, §136-18.4.

CUSTODIAL INTERFERENCE.
Abduction of child, §14-41, (a).
Bail and recognizance, §15A-534.4.
Transporting child outside state.
Intent to violate custody order, §14-320.1.

CUSTODIAL INTERROGATION OF JUVENILES.
Delinquent or undisciplined juveniles, §7B-2101.

CUSTODIAL TRUSTS, §§33B-1 to 33B-22.
Acceptance of custodial trust property.
Custodial trustee, §33B-4.
Accounting by trustee, §33B-15.
Applicability of provisions, §33B-19, (a).
Uniformity of application, §33B-20.
Beneficiaries.
Defined, §33B-1.
Directions of beneficiary.
Duty of trustee to follow, §33B-7, (b).
Incapacitated beneficiaries.
Administration of trust for incapacitated beneficiary.
Determination of incapacity by trustee, §33B-10, (c).
Requirements for, §33B-10, (a).
Determination by trustee, §33B-10, (b).
Administration of trust for incapacitated beneficiary, §33B-10, (c).
Trustee not liable for good faith determination, §33B-10, (f).
Effect of determination, §33B-10, (e).
Payment or expenditure for use and benefit of beneficiary, §33B-9, (b).
Petition for determination, §33B-10, (d).
Liability to third persons, §33B-12, (c), (d).
Payment or expenditure for use and benefit of beneficiary, §33B-9, (a).
Incapacitated beneficiaries, §33B-9, (b).
Separate custodial trust, §33B-6, (b).
Single beneficiary, §33B-6, (a).
Checking, savings or other accounts.
Establishment, withdrawal of funds, §33B-9, (c).
Citation of act.
Short title, §33B-21.
Conflict of laws, §33B-19, (b).
Construction and interpretation.
Other means of creating trusts not displaced or restricted, §33B-2, (h).
Uniformity of construction, §33B-20.
Contracts enter into by trustee during administration.
Asserting claim against trustee, §33B-12, (a).
Personal liability of beneficiary, §33B-12, (c).
Personal liability of trustee, §33B-12, (b).
Protection as insured by liability insurance, §33B-12, (d).
Creation of custodial trust, §33B-2, (a), (b).
Custodial trust to begin in the future, §33B-3, (a).
Customary methods of transferring or evidencing ownership of property, §33B-18, (b).
Forms, §33B-18, (a).
Custodial trustee.
Acceptance of custodial trust property.
Form of acceptance and receipt, §33B-4, (b).
Obligations arise upon, §33B-4, (a).

CUSTODIAL TRUSTS —Cont'd
Custodial trustee —Cont'd
Acceptance of custodial trust property —Cont'd
Statement provided by trustee, §33B-15, (a).
Subject to person jurisdiction of state upon, §33B-4, (c).
Accounting by trustee.
Instructions issued or review of actions.
Authority of court, §33B-15, (f).
Legal representative, account by, §33B-15, (d).
Petition, §33B-15, (b), (c).
Removal, §33B-15, (e).
Statements provided as to administration, §33B-15, (a).
Actions against.
Limitation of actions, §33B-16, (a).
Fraud, misrepresentation or concealment, §33B-16, (b).
When claims for relief not barred, §33B-16, (c).
Bond, §33B-14.
Checking, savings or other accounts.
Establishment, withdrawal of funds, §33B-9, (c).
Collect, manage, invest and reinvest trust property.
Duty, §33B-7, (c).
Control of trust property.
Duty to take, §33B-7, (c).
Custodial trust property.
Powers as to, §33B-8, (a).
Custodial trust to begin in the future, §33B-3, (b).
Dealing with trust property.
Prudent person standard of care, §33B-7, (b).
Declining to serve.
Notice, substitute, designation, §33B-13, (a).
Defined, §33B-1.
Directions of beneficiary.
Duty to follow, §33B-7, (b).
Duties, §33B-7.
Liability for violation, §33B-8, (b).
Expenses, §33B-14.
Incapacity of beneficiary.
Determination, §33B-10.
Ineligibility, death or incapacity.
Successor, §33B-13, (c).
Liability for violation of duties, §33B-8, (b).
Liability to third person, §33B-12, (b), (d).
Obligations.
Arise on acceptance of trust property, §33B-4, (a).
General duties, §33B-7.
Payment or expenditure for use and benefit of beneficiary, §33B-9, (a).
Incapacitated beneficiary, §33B-9, (b).
Personal jurisdiction of state.
Subject to, §33B-4, (c).
Powers, §33B-8.
Prudent person standard of care.
Dealing with trust property, §33B-7, (b).
Recordation or registration of instrument vesting title.
Duty of trustee if appropriate, §33B-7, (a).
Records of transactions.
Duty to keep, §33B-7, (e).
Removal.
Accounting by trustee, §33B-15, (e).
Petition for, §33B-13, (f).
Resignation.
Notice, successor, designation, §33B-13, (b).
Separate from other property.
Duty to keep, §33B-7, (d).

CUSTODIAL TRUSTS —Cont'd
Custodial trustee —Cont'd
Special skill or expertise.
Standard of care, §33B-7, (b).
Standard of care.
Dealing with trust property, §33B-7, (b).
Statements provided by trustee, §33B-15, (a).
Substitute trustee.
Designating.
Person originally designated declines to serve, §33B-13, (a).
Successor custodial trustee.
Designation, §33B-2, (g).
Successor trustee.
Accounting by predecessor.
Petition, §33B-15, (c).
Designating, §33B-13, (b) to (d).
Property and records, possession and control, §33B-13, (e).
Transfers to by fiduciary or obligor, §33B-5, (a), (b).
Exceptions, §33B-5, (c).
Custodial trust property.
Acceptance by trustee, §33B-4.
Augmentation of existing custodial trust property, §33B-2, (f).
Custodial trustee.
Powers as to property, §33B-8, (a).
Defined, §33B-1.
Limitation on value, §33B-22.
Recordation.
Adequate identification of property for record, §33B-7, (d).
Registration.
Adequate identification of property for record, §33B-7, (d).
Title, §33B-2, (c).
Custodial trust to begin in the future, §33B-3.
Definitions, §33B-1.
Durable power of attorney for incapacitated person.
Effective to terminate or direct administration or distribution of property.
Specific provision required, §33B-7, (f).
Forms.
Custodial trustee's receipt and acceptance, §33B-4, (b).
Declaration of trust under act, §33B-18, (a).
Transfer under act, §33B-18, (a).
Fraud.
Limitation of actions against custodial trustee, §33B-16, (b).
Incapacity of beneficiary.
Determination, §33B-10.
Limitation of actions against custodial trustee, §33B-16.
Notice.
Trustee declining to serve or resigning, §33B-13, (a), (b).
Obligations arising from ownership or control of property.
Asserting claim against trustee, §33B-12, (a).
Personal liability of beneficiary, §33B-12, (c).
Personal liability of trustee, §33B-12, (b).
Protection as insured by liability insurance, §33B-12, (d).
Payment or expenditure for use and benefit of beneficiary, §33B-9, (a), (b).
Petitions.
Accounting by trustee, §33B-15, (b), (c).

CUSTODIAL TRUSTS —Cont'd
Petitions —Cont'd
Incapacity of beneficiary, determination, §33B-10, (d).
Removal of trustee, §33B-13, (f).
Successor trustee, designation, §33B-13, (d).
Prudent person rule.
Trustee dealing with property.
Standard of care, §33B-7, (b).
Recordation.
Adequate identification of property for record, §33B-7, (d).
Duty of trustee to record instrument if appropriate, §33B-7, (a).
Records.
Transaction records, duty to keep, §33B-7, (d), (e).
Registration.
Adequate identification of trust property for registration, §33B-7, (d).
Termination of custodial trust, §33B-2, (d), (e).
Distribution on, §33B-17, (a), (d).
Death of beneficiary.
Effect, §33B-17, (c).
Incapacitated distributee, §33B-17, (b).
Third parties.
Liability to third person, §33B-12.
Third-party transactions, §33B-11.
Title of act.
Short title, §33B-21.
Title to custodial trust property, §33B-2, (c).
Tort committed in course of administering trust.
Asserting claim against trustee, §33B-12, (a).
Value of custodial trust property.
Limitation on, §33B-22.

CUSTODIANS.
Custodial trusts and trustees, §§33B-1 to 33B-22.
See CUSTODIAL TRUSTS.
Powers of fiduciaries generally, §§32-25 to 32-28.
See FIDUCIARIES.
Transfers to minors, §§33A-1 to 33A-24.
See TRANSFERS TO MINORS.
Uniform fiduciaries act, §§32-1 to 32-13.
See FIDUCIARIES.

CUSTODY.
Child custody generally.
See CHILD CUSTODY.

CUSTODY AND VISITATION MEDIATION PROGRAM, §§7A-494, 7A-495.

CUSTOMHOUSE LAND ACQUISITION, §§104-1, 104-7.
United States acquisition of land for public buildings, §104-7.

CUSTOMS OF THE ALCOHOLIC BEVERAGE TRADE, §18B-1116, (b).

CUSTOMS SERVICE OFFICERS' AUTHORITY, §15A-406.

CUTOUT MUFFLERS, §20-128, (b).
Motorboats, use of, §75A-9.

CUTTING TREES FOR TIMBER.
Damages for unlawful cutting, removal or burning, §1-539.1, (a).
Injunctions.
Insolvency of defendant need not be alleged, §1-486.
Trial of title to, §1-487.

CUTTING TREES FOR TIMBER —Cont'd
Injunctions —Cont'd
When timber may be cut, §1-488.
Timber of another, §14-135.

CYBERSTALKING, §14-193.3, (b).
Class 2 misdemeanor, §14-193.3, (d).
Constitutionally protected rights of speech, protest or assembly.
Section not to impair, §14-193.3, (e).
Definitions, §14-193.3, (a).
Peaceable, nonviolent or nonthreatening activity.
Inapplicability to, §14-193.3, (e).
Venue.
Offense committed by email or electronic communication, §14-193.3, (c).

CY PRES.
Management of institutional funds.
Applicability of doctrine to release of restrictions on use or investment, §36B-7, (d).

D

DAGGERS.
Carrying concealed, §14-269, (a), (b) to (d).
Educational property, §14-269.2.
Historic edged weapons defined, §14-409.12.
Weapons generally.
See WEAPONS.

DAIRIES AND DAIRY PRODUCTS.
Cooperative associations.
Authorized purposes, §§54-111, 54-124.
Ice cream plants, creameries and cheese factories.
Inspections generally, §§106-246 to 106-255.
See ICE CREAM PLANTS, CREAMERIES AND CHEESE FACTORIES.
Marketing associations, §§54-129 to 54-166.
See MARKETING ASSOCIATIONS.
Milk cases or crates.
Unauthorized taking or sale, §14-72.4.
Milk distributors and processors generally.
See MILK DISTRIBUTORS AND PROCESSORS.
Pollution control.
Water pollution on lands used for dairy purposes, §14-382.
Production, distribution, inspection, grading and testing generally, §§106-267 to 106-268.1.
See MILK AND MILK PRODUCTS.
Southern dairy compact, §§106-810, 106-811.

DALE EARNHARDT HIGHWAY, §136-18.5B.

DALLAS.
Satellite annexation.
Limitation on area of satellite corporate limits, inapplicability, §160A-58.1, (b).

DAMAGES.
Ad damnum clause, §1A-1, Rule 8, (a).
Adoption.
Failure to disclose nonidentifying information.
Civil action for monetary relief, §48-10-104.
Unauthorized disclosure of information.
Civil action for monetary relief, §48-10-105.
Aeronautics.
Forced landing, §63-13.
Agricultural commodities or production systems, injury to.
Definitions, §1-539.2B, (c).
Double damage liability, §1-539.2B, (a).

DAMAGES —Cont'd
Agricultural commodities or production systems, injury to —Cont'd
Valuation, §1-539.2B, (b).
Alcoholic beverages.
Beer franchises.
Transfer of wholesaler's business.
Disapproval or prevention of transfer, §18B-1307, (c).
Wrongful termination of agreement, §18B-1306, (b).
Sales to underage persons.
Compensation for injury caused by, limitation, §18B-123.
Anatomical gifts.
Persons acting with due care not liable, §130A-409, (c).
Appeal bond to stay execution on money judgment, §1-289, (a).
Cap in amount, noncompensatory damages of $25,000,000 or more, §1-289, (b), (c).
Arbitration.
Additional remedies, §1-569.21, (c).
Grounds for awarding, §1-569.21, (b).
Payment of arbitrator's expenses, §1-569.21.
Punitive damages, §1-569.21, (a), (e).
Athlete agents.
Action by education institution against agent or student-athlete, §78C-100, (b).
Attorneys at law.
Fraudulent practice.
Liability of attorney in double damages, §84-13.
Automobile dealers.
Punitive damages, §20-308.1, (b).
Bad checks.
Remedies for returned check, §6-21.3, (a), (d).
Baggage lost, damaged or destroyed by innkeeper's negligence, §72-2.
Bank deposits and collections, §25-4-103.
Banks.
Directors' liability, §53-82.
Betterments.
Assessment of damages.
Annual value of land and waste charged against defendant, §1-341.
Execution suspended for, §1-340.
Value of improvements estimated, §1-342.
Value of premises without improvements.
Estimate, §1-346.
Bills of lading.
Limitations of liability in bill of lading, §25-7-309.
Bonds, surety.
Actions on bonds.
Officer unlawfully detaining money liable for damages, §58-76-20.
Buildings.
Dismantling.
Joint owner dismantling portion of building, §1-539.2.
Business combinations unlawful.
Treble damages, §75E-4.
Business opportunity sales.
Remedy of purchaser, §66-100, (b).
Cable television franchises.
Civil penalties for theft of service, §14-118.5.
Campaign contributions and expenditures.
Disclosure requirements for media advertisements.
Television and radio advertisements supporting or opposing the nomination or election of one or more clearly identified candidates.
Legal remedy, §163-278.39A, (f).

DAMAGES —Cont'd
Cap on amount of appeal bond.
Staying execution on money judgment.
Noncompensatory damages of $25,000,000 or more, §1-289, (b), (c).
Cap on compensatory or consequential damages.
Employee theft, larceny, shoplifting, embezzlement or obtaining by false pretenses.
Civil liability, §1-538.2, (a), (b).
Cap on punitive damages, §1D-25, (b).
Exemption, DWI, injury or harm arising, §1D-26.
Not made known to trier of fact, §1D-25, (c).
Carriers.
Limitation of liability.
Carrier issuing bill of lading, §25-7-309, (2).
Checks.
Remedies for returned check, §6-21.3, (a), (d).
Childhood vaccine-related injury compensation.
Action by state against manufacturer, §130A-430, (b).
Actions by state against health care provider, §130A-430, (a).
Amount awarded against vaccine manufacturers.
Duplicate damages, prevention, §130A-423, (c).
Limitation on amount, §130A-423, (d).
Civil rights, interference with, §99D-1, (b), (b1).
Claims against state departments and agencies, §143-291, (a).
Collection agencies, §58-70-130, (a), (d).
Compromise and settlement.
Motor vehicles.
Property damage claims from collisions or accidents, §1-540.2.
Computer trespass.
Action by injured party, §14-458, (c).
Jurisdiction, §1-539.2A, (b).
Limitations period, §1-539.2A, (b).
Right to damages, §1-539.2A, (a).
Conditional offer of judgment, §1A-1, Rule 68, (b).
Contribution among joint tort-feasors, §§1B-1 to 1B-7.
Control share acquisitions unlawful.
Treble damages, §75E-4.
Credit rights for married women.
Actions to enforce articles, §25B-3, (a).
Crime victims' rights.
No claim for damages created, §15A-839.
Criminal law and procedure.
Civil actions seeking to recover damages arising out of criminal act.
Statutes of limitation and repose, §1-15.1.
Criminal trespass.
Gas companies.
Injuring fixtures and property of gas companies, §14-152.
Dam safety law.
Actions brought by state.
Liability for damages, §143-215.35.
Debt collectors.
Prohibited acts.
Restrictions on damages for, §75-56.
Discharge of employee called to jury duty, §9-32, (b).
Discount buying clubs.
Breach of contract.
Action against bond, §66-135, (c).
Action for damages, §66-136, (a).

DAMAGES —Cont'd
Discrimination against employees for lawful use of lawful products during nonworking hours.
Civil actions for violations, §95-28.2, (e).
Discrimination in business.
Actions by persons injured by violations, §75B-4.
Documents of title.
Limitation of liability in bill of lading, §25-7-309, (2).
Limitation of warehouseman's liability, §25-7-204, (1), (2).
Dogs.
Dangerous dogs.
Damages for injuries or property damage inflicted by dog.
Strict liability, §67-4.4.
Killing or injuring livestock.
Liability of owner, §67-1.
Mad dogs.
Failure to kill, §67-4.
Permitting dogs to run at large at night.
Liability of owner, §67-12.
Double damages.
Attorneys, fraudulent practice, §84-13.
Unlawful cutting, removal or burning of timber, §1-539.1, (a).
Drainage.
Assessments, §156-70.
Compensation for damage to lands.
Corporations, §156-48.
Petitions.
Agreement for construction.
Payment of damages, §156-27.
Railroads, §156-89.
Electronic surveillance.
Civil action for violation of article.
Actual damages, §15A-296, (a).
Embezzlement, civil liability.
Compensatory and punitive damages, §1-538.2, (a) to (d).
Eminent domain.
Compensation.
Generally.
See EMINENT DOMAIN.
Public condemnors.
Action in tort for damage to property.
Common law right not affected, §40A-51, (c).
Right of entry prior to condemnation.
Reimbursement to owner for damages resulting, §40A-11.
Employee theft, civil liability.
Compensatory and punitive damages, §1-538.2, (a) to (d).
Employer discrimination for lawful use of lawful products during nonworking hours.
Civil actions for violations, §95-28.2, (e).
Employment security.
Claims for benefits.
Discharge, demotion or intimidation of witnesses, §96-15.1, (b) to (d).
Excessive damages.
New trial, grounds for motion, §1A-1, Rule 59, (a).
Executors and administrators.
Wrongful death actions, §28A-18-2, (b).
Exemplary damages.
Civil rights, interference with, §99D-1, (b), (b1).
Motor fuel marketing violations, private actions, §75-86.
Trade secrets, willful and malicious misappropriations, §66-154, (c).

DAMAGES —Cont'd
False pretenses and cheats, civil liability.
Compensatory and punitive damages, §1-538.2, (a) to (d).
False report of nuclear, biological or chemical weapons, §14-288.23, (b).
Hoaxes, §14-288.24, (b).
Financial identity fraud.
Civil liability, §14-113.22, (b).
Financial records privacy.
Disclosures in violation of article, §53B-10, (a).
Funds transfers.
Improper execution or failure to execute payment order, §25-4A-305, (c).
Obligation of beneficiary's bank to pay and give notice to beneficiary.
Refusal to pay after demand and receipt of notice, §25-4A-404, (a).
Good funds settlement act.
Violation of chapter, §45A-7.
Habeas corpus.
Order of discharge.
Failure to comply, §17-23.
Health benefit plans.
Liability for negligent decision, §§90-21.50 to 90-21.56.
See HEALTH CARE LIABILITY.
Husband and wife.
Judgments against married persons for damages.
Levy and collection out of separate estate, §1-223.
Recovery by person suing alone, §52-4.
Tort actions arising out of acts occurring outside state, §52-5.1.
Torts between husband and wife, §52-5.
Identity fraud, §1-539.2C.
Inadequate damages.
New trial, grounds for motion, §1A-1, Rule 59, (a).
Injunctions.
Dissolution, §1A-1, Rule 65, (e).
Insurance.
Accident and health insurance.
Pharmacy of choice, §58-51-37, (h).
Insurance consumer and customer information privacy.
Action by individual for violations, §58-39-105, (b).
Jail keepers causing injuries to prisoners, §162-55.
Labor.
Discrimination for lawful use of lawful products during nonworking hours.
Civil actions for violations of section, §95-28.2, (e).
Retaliatory employment discrimination.
Relief in civil actions, §95-243, (c).
Right to work law.
Recovery of damages by persons denied employment, §95-83.
Landlord and tenant.
Accidental damages.
Liability of tenant, §42-10.
Military personnel.
Early termination of rental agreement.
Liquidated damages, liability for, §42-45, (b).
Summary ejectment.
Assessment to trial, §42-32.
Claims for damages, §42-28.
Disposition of tenant.
Damages to tenant for dispossession if proceedings quashed, §42-36.

DAMAGES —Cont'd
Landlord and tenant —Cont'd
Surrender by lessee where building destroyed or damaged, §42-12.
Wrongful surrender to other landlord misdemeanor, §42-13.
Willful destruction by tenant misdemeanor, §42-11.
Leases, UCC.
Consequential damages.
Limiting, altering or excluding, §25-2A-503, (3).
Cover by lessor, §25-2A-518.
Lessee's incidental and consequential damages, §25-2A-520.
Lessee's remedies for default by lessor, §25-2A-508, (1), (4).
Lessor's damages, §25-2A-523.
Incidental damages, §25-2A-530.
Liquidation, §25-2A-504.
Market rent, §25-2A-507.
Nonacceptance of goods.
Lessor's damages, §25-2A-528.
Nondelivery, repudiation, default and breach of warranty, §25-2A-519.
Lemon law, §§20-351.3, (a), 20-351.8.
Liens.
Enforcement of lien by sale.
Noncompliance, §44A-4, (g).
Recoveries for personal injuries.
Accounting for disbursements, §44-50.1, (a) to (c).
Limitation on damages.
Alcoholic beverage sales to underage persons, compensation for injury, §18B-123.
Littering.
Felony violations, §14-399, (e), (h).
Livestock impoundment.
Demand upon owner, §68-18.
Determination by selected landowners or by referee, §68-19.
Right of impounder to recover, §68-17.
Magistrates.
Dam, canal or ditch work.
Power of magistrate to assess contributions for damages or for work done, §7A-292.
Marketing associations.
Merger, consolidation or other fundamental changes.
Rights of objecting members.
Failure of association to mention provisions of section in notices, §54-166, (d).
Medicaid.
False claims submitted by providers, §108A-70.12, (b).
Membership camping, §66-247.
Mill construction.
Action for damages in superior court, §73-25.
Abatement of mill as nuisance when damages cannot be collected, §73-26.
Annual sum as damages, §73-27.
Cost, §73-28.
Execution, §73-28.
Judgment.
Annual sum as damages, §73-27.
Final judgment, §73-28.
Mines and minerals.
Trespass, §74-32.
Persons entitled to bring suit, §74-33.
Survey, §§74-34 to 74-36.
Application for, §74-34.
Costs, §74-36.

DAMAGES —Cont'd
Mines and minerals —Cont'd
Trespass —Cont'd
Survey —Cont'd
Free access to mine for, §74-35.
Order for, §74-34.
Water and drainage rights, §74-28.
Minors.
Malicious or willful destruction of property by minors.
Recovery of damages from parents, §1-538.1.
Negligent supervision of minor.
Right of educational entity to recover against parents, §1-538.3.
Monopolies and restraint of trade.
Treble damages, §75-16.
Mortgages and deeds of trust.
Reverse mortgages.
Actions by borrowers, §53-271, (d).
Motion pictures.
Fair competition.
Enforcement of provisions, §75C-5.
Motor fuel marketing violations, private actions, §75-86.
Motor vehicle repairs.
Remedies for violation of article, §20-354.9.
Motor vehicles.
First aid or emergency assistance at scene of accident, §20-166, (d).
Lemon law, §§20-351.3, (a), 20-351.8.
New motor vehicles warranties act, §§20-351.3, (a), 20-351.8.
Odometer violations, §20-348, (a), (b).
Repairs, remedies for violating article, §20-354.9.
Settlement of accident not to constitute admission of liability, §1-540.2.
Sublease and loan assumption arranging, §20-106.2, (f).
Mountain ridge protection.
Civil action against persons alleged in violation, §113A-211, (b).
Municipal corporations.
Rail transportation liability.
Liability limits, §160A-326, (d).
New motor vehicles warranties act, §20-351.8.
911 system.
Injuries, death or loss by act or omission of service suppliers.
Liability of service suppliers for damages in civil actions, §62A-10.
Nuisances.
Remedies, §1-539.
Offer of judgment.
Conditional offer of judgment for damages, §1A-1, Rule 68, (b).
Oil pollution and hazardous substances control.
Damage to public resources, §§143-215.90 to 143-215.94.
Contesting assessment of damages.
Time for filing petition, §143-215.90, (b).
Failure to pay, §143-215.90, (b).
Joint and several liability, §143-215.94.
Liability for damages caused, §143-215.94.
Offshore oil and gas activities.
Actions for damages, §143-215.94DD, (b).
Defined, §143-215.94BB.
Liability, §143-215.94CC, (a).
Exceptions, §143-215.94CC, (b).
Create no defense, §143-215.94DD, (b).

DAMAGES —Cont'd
Oil pollution and hazardous substances control —Cont'd
Offshore oil and gas activities —Cont'd
Liability —Cont'd
Personal injury.
Exclusions from liability, §143-215.94DD, (b).
Violations of part, §143-215.94FF, (a).
Removal of oil discharges.
Liability of responsible party for removal costs and damages, §143-215.93A, (c).
Limitation on liability of persons engaged in, §143-215.93A, (a).
Exceptions, §143-215.93A, (b).
Pain and suffering.
See PAIN AND SUFFERING.
Parent and child.
Malicious or willful destruction of property by minors.
Recovery of damages from parents, §1-538.1.
Negligent supervision of minor.
Right of educational entity to recover against parents, §1-538.3.
Party walls.
Dismantling portion of building, §1-539.2.
Personal property.
Interference with property rights, §99A-1.
Judgments in action for recovery of personal property, §1-230.
Pesticides.
Rules and regulations.
Prevention of damages, §143-458, (a), (b).
Pleadings.
Ad damnum clause, §1A-1, Rule 8.
Punitive damages, §1A-1, Rule 9, (k).
Special damage, §1A-1, Rule 9, (g).
Prepaid entertainment contracts.
Remedies of buyer, §66-125, (a).
Additional nature of remedies, §66-125, (b).
Property damage suits.
Attorneys' fees.
Allowance of counsel fees as part of costs, §6-21.1.
Psychotherapy patient/client sexual exploitation act, §90-21.43.
Public officers and employees.
Unconstitutional taxes.
Employee collecting or administering tax, §143-300.9.
Public safety telephone service.
Service suppliers.
Injuries, death or loss as result of act or omission.
Liability for damages in civil actions, §62A-10.
Public schools.
Liability of students and their parents or guardians for damages to buildings, furnishings or textbooks, §115C-398.
Negligent supervision of minor.
Right of educational entity to recover against parents, §1-538.3.
School buses, §115C-399.
Public works.
Regulation of contractors.
Civil damages, §133-28, (a), (b).
Relocation assistance.
Administrative payments, §133-17.
Punitive damages.
Aggravating factors, §1D-15, (a).
Burden of proof, §1D-15, (b).

DAMAGES —Cont'd
Punitive damages —Cont'd
Amount.
Considerations by trier of fact, §1D-35.
Trier of fact to determine amount, §1D-25, (a).
Appeal bond, staying execution on money judgment, §1-289, (a).
Cap on amount, noncompensatory damages of $25,000,000 or more, §1-289, (a).
Automobile dealers, §20-308.1, (b).
Bifurcated trial, §1D-30.
Breach of contract, §1D-15, (d).
Cap on amount awarded, §1D-25, (b).
Exemption, DWI, injury or harm arising, §1D-26.
Not made know to trier of fact, §1D-25, (c).
Cap on amount of appeal bond.
Staying execution on money judgment.
Noncompensatory damages of $25,000,000, §1-289, (b), (c).
Civil rights, interference with, §99D-1, (b), (b1).
Criminal actions, §99A-1.
Definitions, §1D-5.
Election of extracompensatory remedies, §1D-20.
Exemption from cap, §1D-26.
Family law arbitration, §50-51, (e).
Frivolous claims, §1D-45.
Judicial review of award, §1D-50.
Jury instructions, §1D-40.
Larceny, shoplifting, employee theft, embezzlement and obtaining by false pretenses.
Civil liability, §1-538.2, (a) to (d).
Limitation on amount of recovery, §1D-25, (b), (c).
Driving while impaired exemption, §1D-26.
Malicious claims, §1D-45.
Motor fuel marketing violations, private actions, §75-86.
Pleadings, stating demand for monetary relief, §1A-1, Rule 8, (a).
Special matters, §1A-1, Rule 9, (k).
Psychotherapy patient/client sexual exploitation act, §90-21.43.
Purpose of punitive damages, §1D-1.
Scope of chapter, §1D-10.
Separate determination, §§1D-25, (a), 1D-30.
Staying execution on money judgment.
Appeal bond, §1-289, (a).
Cap on amount, noncompensatory damages of $25,000,000 or more, §1-289, (b), (c).
Trade secrets, willful and malicious misappropriations, §66-154, (c).
Trier of fact to determine amount, §1D-25, (a).
Vicarious liability, §1D-15, (c).
Railroads.
Limitation of actions, §1-51.
Records and tapes.
Civil action for damages by owner of recorded device, §14-436.
Regional public transportation authority.
Rail transportation liability.
Liability limits, §160A-626, (d).
Registers of deeds.
Liability for damages.
Liability insurance coverage.
County decision not to provide insurance coverage, §161-4.2.
Rental referral agencies.
Action on bond, §66-145, (c).
Actions for damages, §66-146, (a).

DAMAGES —Cont'd
Restitution or reparation.
Civil actions seeking to recover damages arising out of criminal act.
Crediting of restitution against judgment, §1-15.1, (b).
Retail installment sales.
Action by buyer injured by violation, §25A-44.
Retaliatory employment discrimination, §95-243, (c).
RICO civil remedies.
Treble damages, §75D-8, (c).
Sale of goods, UCC.
Antecedent breach.
Effect of cancellation or rescission on claim, §25-2-720.
Buyer's damages, §§25-2-713 to 25-2-718.
Liquidation or limitation of damages, §§25-2-718, 25-2-719.
Proof of market price, §25-2-723.
Market price.
Admissibility of market quotations, §25-2-724.
Proof, §25-2-723.
Time and place, §25-2-723.
Seller's damages for repudiation, §25-2-708.
Seller's incidental damages, §25-2-710.
Third parties.
Who can sue third parties for injuries to goods, §25-2-722.
Sales.
Commissions.
Actions for damages, §66-192, (a).
Savings and loan associations.
Civil penalties.
Separate action for damages not precluded, §§54B-64, (d), 54B-65, (d).
Confidentiality of information, §54B-63, (e).
Savings banks.
Civil penalties.
Actions for damages not precluded, §§54C-77, (d), 54C-78, (d).
Confidentiality of information, §54C-60, (e).
School buses.
Public schools, §115C-399.
Secured transactions.
Remedies for noncompliance with article, §25-9-625, (b).
Consumer goods transactions.
Statutory damages, §25-9-625, (c).
Limitation of liability, §25-9-628.
Statutory damages.
Consumer goods transactions, §25-9-625, (c).
Generally, §25-9-625, (e).
Requests for accounting, collateral, etc., §25-9-625, (f).
Surplus or deficiency an issue.
Applicable rules, §25-9-626, (a).
Deficiency eliminated or reduced, §25-9-625, (d).
Nonconsumer transactions, §25-9-626, (b).
Securities regulation.
Civil liabilities generally, §78A-56.
Manipulation of market, §78A-56, (b1).
Seed law, claim of defective seeds.
Damages recoverable, §106-277.34, (b).
Shellfish.
Cultivation of oysters and clams.
Taking of property, §113-206, (e).
Shoplifting, civil liability.
Compensatory and punitive damages, §1-538.2, (a) to (d).

DAMAGES —Cont'd
Special damage, pleading, §1A-1, Rule 9, (g).
State institutions, damage of personal property.
Appeals, §143-127.6.
Negligence.
No reimbursement, §143-127.3.
Other remedies.
Good faith effort as prerequisite to reimbursement, §143-127.4.
Reimbursement.
Amount.
Restriction, §143-127.5.
Negligence.
No reimbursement, §143-127.3.
Other remedies.
Good faith effort required, §143-127.4.
Restriction on amount, §143-127.5.
Staying execution on money judgment.
Appeal bond, §1-289, (a).
Cap on amount of appeal bond.
Noncompensatory damages of $25,000,000 or more, §1-289, (b), (c).
Street and highway condemnation proceedings.
Determination of issues of damages, §136-109, (d).
Interest as part of just compensation, §136-113.
Measure of damages, §136-112.
Structured settlement agreements.
Violation of provisions, §1-543.15, (b).
Telephone service suppliers.
Public safety telephone service.
Injuries, death or loss as result of act or omission, §62A-10.
Telephone solicitations.
Action by subscriber for violation, §75-105, (b).
Torrens system registration.
Assurance fund.
Action for indemnity, §43-50.
Fund not liable for breach of trust, §43-54.
Trademarks.
Infringement, §§80-11, 80-12.
Trade secrets.
Misappropriation, §66-154, (b), (c).
Treble damages.
Business combinations or control share acquisitions unlawful, §75E-4.
Cable television systems theft, §14-118.5.
Littering, §14-399, (e), (h).
Monopolies and restraints of trade, private civil actions, §75-16.
New motor vehicles warranties act.
Manufacturer unreasonably refusing to comply, §20-351.8.
Retaliatory employment discrimination, §95-243, (c).
Returned checks, §6-21.3.
RICO civil remedies, §75D-8, (c).
Trespass to public lands, §14-130.
Vehicle mileage act violations, §20-348, (a).
Waste, §1-538.
Trees and timber.
Unlawful burning of timber, §1-539.1, (b).
Unlawful cutting or removal of timber, §1-539.1, (a).
Misrepresentation of property lines, §1-539.1, (c).
Trespass.
Personal property.
Interference with property rights, §99A-1.

DAMAGES —Cont'd
Trespass —Cont'd
Public lands.
Treble damages, §14-130.
Uniform contribution among tort-feasors, §§1B-1 to 1B-6.
Unit ownership.
Failure to comply with regulations and covenants, §47A-10.
Partition sale on resolution not to restore, §47A-25.
Vandalism by minors.
Recovery of damages from parents, §1-538.1.
Victims' rights.
No claim for damages created by provisions, §15A-839.
Waste, §1-533.
Treble damages and possession, §1-538.
Water and air resources.
Floodplain regulation.
Liability for damages in actions, §143-215.60.
Wrongful death, §28A-18-2.
Year 2000 liability and damages, §§66-295 to 66-298.

DAMS.
Fish and fisheries resources.
Inspecting plans and specifications of dams, §113-263.
Keeping open fishways in dams, §113-293, (c).
Obstructing rivers or creeks, §113-293.
Impounded water.
Right of withdrawal, §§143-215.44 to 143-215.50.
Inspections.
Plans and specifications of dams, §113-263.
Lowlands draining or damming.
Petitioner to pay costs, §6-22.
Magistrates.
Assessment of contribution for damages or for work done.
Power of magistrate, §7A-292.
Natural and scenic rivers system.
Restriction on project works, §113A-44.
Safety, §§143-215.23 to 143-215.37.
See DAM SAFETY.
Trespass.
Criminal trespass.
Injuries to dams of mills and factories, §14-142.

DAM SAFETY, §§143-215.23 to 143-215.37.
Alteration of dams, §143-215.27, (a), (b).
Appeals, §143-215.33.
Applications for construction.
Action by environmental management commission.
Approval or disapproval, §143-215.28, (a).
Commencement of construction, §143-215.28, (d).
Defective applications, §143-215.28, (b).
Return of disapproved applications with statement of objections, §143-215.28, (c).
Appeals, §143-215.33.
Fees, §143-215.28A, (a).
Dam safety account, §143-215.28A, (b).
Generally, §§143-215.26, 143-215.27.
Attorney general.
Civil penalties.
Institution of action to recover, §143-215.36, (b).
Injunctive relief, §143-215.36, (c).
Citation of part, §143-215.23.
Civil penalties, §143-215.36, (b).
Action to recover amount.
Failure to pay, §143-215.36, (b).
Remission, §143-215.36, (b).

DAM SAFETY —Cont'd
Construction of dams.
Applications, §143-215.28, (a) to (c).
Certification of final approval, §143-215.30, (c), (d).
Commencement, §143-215.28, (d).
Modification during work, §143-215.29, (c).
Notice of completion, §143-215.30, (a).
Repair, alteration or removal, §143-215.27, (a), (b).
Reports, §143-215.29, (b).
Requirements, §143-215.26, (a).
Applications, §143-215.26, (b).
Supervision by qualified engineers, §143-215.29, (a).
Contested cases.
Civil penalties.
Filing petitions, §143-215.36, (b).
Criminal law and procedure.
Violations of article, §143-215.36, (a).
Damages.
Liability, §143-215.35.
Declaration of purpose, §143-215.24.
Definitions, §143-215.25.
Employment of consultants, §143-215.34.
Enforcement procedures.
Generally, §143-215.36.
Enlargement.
Supplementary drawings and descriptive matter.
Applicability to new work only, §143-215.30, (b).
Exempt dams, §143-215.25A, (a).
Limited applicability, §143-215.25A, (b).
Fees.
Applications for construction, §143-215.28A.
Hearings.
Administrative hearing, §143-215.33.
Injunctions, §143-215.36, (c).
Inspections.
Authorization, §143-215.32, (a).
Dangerous or unsafe dams, §143-215.32, (c).
Orders to repair dams, §143-215.32, (b).
Service on owner, §143-215.32, (d).
Right of entry, §143-215.37.
Investigations, §143-215.34.
Right of entry, §143-215.37.
Judicial review, §143-215.33.
Legislative declaration, §143-215.24.
Liability for damages, §143-215.35.
Minimum streamflow, §143-215.31, (c) to (e).
Misdemeanors, §143-215.36, (a).
Notice.
Civil penalties.
Assessment, §143-215.36, (b).
Construction of dams.
Notice of completion, §143-215.30.
Petitions.
Civil penalties.
Contested cases, §143-215.36, (b).
Purpose, §143-215.24.
Repair of dams.
Applications, §143-215.27, (a).
Immediate work in emergency cases, §143-215.27, (b).
Reports.
Construction of dams, §143-215.29, (b).
Right of entry, §143-215.37.
Rules and regulations, §143-215.34.
Short title, §143-215.23.
Supervision by qualified engineers, §143-215.29.
Supervision over maintenance and operation of dams.
Commission to jurisdiction and supervision, §143-215.31, (a).

DAM SAFETY —Cont'd
Supervision over maintenance and operation of dams —Cont'd
Conditions or requirements in orders and written approvals, §143-215.31, (b).
Minimum streamflow, §143-215.31, (c) to (e).
Violations of part.
Civil penalties, §143-215.36, (b).

DANCE.
Admission fee charged.
License tax.
Cities may levy but counties may not, §105-37.1, (d).
Privilege tax on gross receipts, §105-37.1, (a).
Rate and payment, §105-37.1, (b).
Obscene exhibitions, §14-190.1.
Promotion of arts, §§143-403 to 143-407.1.

DANCE HALLS.
Counties.
Regulation of places of amusement, §153A-135.
Municipal corporations.
Regulation of dance halls, §160A-181.

DANCING LESSONS.
Prepaid entertainment contracts generally, §§66-118 to 66-125.
See PREPAID ENTERTAINMENT CONTRACTS.

DANGEROUS DOGS, §§67-4.1 to 67-4.5.
Applicability of provisions, §67-4.1, (b).
Attacks by dangerous dogs, §67-4.3.
Precautions against, §67-4.2.
Definitions, §67-4.1, (a).
Determination that dog is potentially dangerous, §67-4.1, (c).
Leaving dangerous dogs unattended, §67-4.2, (a).
Local programs for control of dangerous dogs, §67-4.5.
Permitting dangerous dogs to go beyond owner's real property, §67-4.2, (a).
Potentially dangerous dogs.
Defined, §67-4.1, (a).
Determination, §67-4.1, (c).
Precautions against attacks by dangerous dogs, §67-4.2.
Strict liability.
Damages for injuries or property damage inflicted by dangerous dog, §67-4.4.
Transfer of ownership or possession of dangerous dog.
Notice by owner, §67-4.2, (b).

DANGEROUS WEAPONS.
Deadly weapons generally.
See DEADLY WEAPONS.
Firearms generally.
See FIREARMS.
Weapons generally.
See WEAPONS.

DANIEL BOONE MEMORIAL COMMISSION, §143B-51.

DARE COUNTY.
Ambulance service.
Attachment or garnishment and lien for, §§44-51.4 to 44-51.8.
Blank or master forms of mortgages, deeds of trust, etc.
Indexing and recording, inapplicability of provisions, §47-21.

DARE COUNTY —Cont'd
Board of county commissioners.
Filling vacancies on board, §153A-27.1.
Eminent domain.
Exercise of power, purposes, modified provisions, §40A-3, (b1).
Game and wildlife commission, regulatory authority not appealed or abridged, §113-133.1, (b).
Game laws, local acts not repealed, §113-133.1, (e).
Grants in navigable waters, registration, §113-205, (a).
Housing authority commissioners.
Tenant as commissioner, exemption from provisions of law allowing, §157-5.
Low-income housing tax credits.
Qualified building eligible for credit, §105-129.41, (c).
Northeastern North Carolina regional economic development commission, §158-8.2.
Open fires, high hazard counties.
Applicability of provisions, §113-60.23, (a).
Woodland fires and ground clearing activities, permits, §113-60.23.
Private parking lots.
Removal of unauthorized vehicles, §20-219.2.
Room occupancy tax levied by county, uniform provisions, §153A-155.
School property.
Acquisition and improvement, §153A-158.1.
Swimming, surfing and littering in Atlantic Ocean.
City ordinances effective, §160A-176.1.
Wild plants, taking of certain plants from land of another.
Inapplicability of provisions, §14-129.

DARKENING WINDSHIELDS ON MOTOR VEHICLES, §20-127, (b) to (f).

DATA MATCH SYSTEMS.
Child support enforcement.
Agreements with financial institutions, §110-139.2.

DATA PROCESSING.
Child custody jurisdiction and enforcement.
Testimony of witnesses, §50A-111.
Computer related crime, §§14-453 to 14-458.
Electronic data-processing records, §132-6.1.
Jury lists.
Preparation of jury list.
Alternate procedure in certain counties, §9-2.1, (a).
Randomized list, §9-2.1, (b).
Medical care data, §§131E-214 to 131E-214.4.
See MEDICAL CARE DATA.
Office of information technology services.
Generally, §§147-33.75 to 147-33.103.
See INFORMATION TECHNOLOGY SERVICES.
Public school loan revolving fund, §115C-472.5.
Records.
Electronic data-processing records, §132-6.1.
Public records.
Copies of databases, §132-6.2, (c).
Geographical information systems databases, §132-10.
Sales and use tax.
Definitions, §105-164.3.
Software property tax exemption, §105-275.

DATA PROCESSING —Cont'd
Voter registration, §§163-82.11, 163-82.12.

DATA TRANSMISSION LINE ENVIRONMENTAL DOCUMENT, §113A-12.

DATE RAPE DRUG.
Gamma hydroxybutyric acid (GHB), §90-89.

DATING SERVICES.
Prepaid entertainment contracts generally, §§66-118 to 66-125.
See PREPAID ENTERTAINMENT CONTRACTS.

DAUGHTERS OF THE AMERICAN REVOLUTION.
Motor vehicle license plates.
Special plates, §§20-79.4, (b), 20-81.12, (b).

DAVIDSON COUNTY.
Ambulance service.
Attachment or garnishment and lien for, §§44-51.4 to 44-51.8.
Board of county commissioners.
Filling vacancies on board, §153A-27.1.
Condemnation or acquisition of land by local government unit outside county.
Consent of board of commissioners necessary, §153A-15.
Coroner elected as nominee of political party.
Filling vacancy in office, §152-1.
Counties generally.
See COUNTIES.
County boards of education elected on partisan basis.
Vacancies in office, §115C-37.1.
Cropper or tenant refusing to perform terms of contract.
Forfeiture of right of possession to premises, §42-27.
Dog collars.
Unlawful removal of electronic dog collars, §14-401.17.
Oil, gas and mineral interests separated from surface fee, extinguished, title in surface fee holder.
Interest not listed for tax purposes for 10 years prior to January 1, 1971.
Protection of surface interest from surface estate holder, §1-42.2, (d).
Registration of deeds.
Tax certification, no delinquent taxes due, §161-31, (b).
School property.
Acquisition and improvement, §153A-158.1.
Sheriff.
Vacancy, performance of duties until vacancy filled, §162-5.1.
Special school tax, election to abolish.
Petition required, §115C-505.

DAVIE COUNTY.
Ambulance service.
Attachment or garnishment and lien for, §§44-51.4 to 44-51.8.
Obtaining services without intending to pay, §14-111.2.
Requesting ambulance falsely, §14-111.3.
Board of county commissioners.
Filling vacancies on board, §153A-27.1.
Condemnation or acquisition of land by local government unit outside county.
Consent of board of commissioners necessary, §153A-15.

DAVIE COUNTY —Cont'd
Coroner elected as nominee of political party.
Filling vacancy in office, §152-1.
Counties generally.
See COUNTIES.
County boards of education elected on partisan basis.
Vacancies in office, §115C-37.1.
Game laws, local acts not repealed, §113-133.1, (e).
Room occupancy tax levied by county, uniform provision, §153A-155.
School property.
Acquisition and improvement, §153A-158.1.
Sheriff.
Vacancy, performance of duties until vacancy filled, §162-5.1.

DAY-CARE FACILITIES.
Generally, §§110-85 to 110-107.
See CHILD CARE FACILITIES.

DAY MARKS.
Interfering with, §76-58.
Rafts to exercise care in passing, §76-57.

DEA AUTHORITY.
U.S. department of justice, §15A-406.

DEAD ANIMALS.
See CARCASSES.

DEAD BODIES.
AIDS.
Handling and transportation of bodies, §130A-395, (a), (c).
Anatomical gifts, §§130A-402 to 130A-412.1.
See ANATOMICAL GIFTS.
Autopsies.
General provisions, §§130A-398 to 130A-401.
See AUTOPSIES.
Unclaimed bodies.
Consent of commission of anatomy, §130A-415, (d).
Burial.
General provisions.
See BURIAL.
Cemeteries.
General provisions, §§65-1 to 65-73.
See CEMETERIES.
Commission of anatomy, §§130A-33.30 to 130A-33.32.
Unclaimed bodies.
Adoption of rules, §130A-416.
Autopsies.
Consent of commission, §130A-415, (d).
Notification to commission, §130A-415, (a), (g), (i).
Cremation.
General provisions, §§90-210.40 to 90-210.54.
See CREMATION.
Disinterment.
Exhumations, §130A-390, (a) to (c).
Disposition of body or body parts.
Disposition of bodies as anatomical gifts.
Inapplicability of provisions, §130A-420, (d).
Persons authorized to determine method of disposition.
Decedent leaving no written authorization, §130A-420, (b).
Written authorization by decedent, §130A-420, (a), (c).
Exhumations, §130A-390, (a) to (c).

DEAD BODIES —Cont'd
Funeral service.
General provisions, §§90-210.18A to 90-210.29.
See FUNERAL SERVICE.
Handling.
Contagious diseases, §130A-395, (a) to (c).
Hepatitis.
Handling and transportation of bodies, §130A-395, (a), (c).
Identification before burial or cremation, §90-210.29A.
Medical examiners.
Unclaimed bodies.
Provisions inapplicable to bodies within jurisdiction of medical examiner, §130A-415, (h).
Minimum burial depth, §90-210.25A.
Orders.
Exhumation, §130A-390, (b).
Remains of terminated pregnancies.
Manner of disposition, §130A-131.10.
Rulemaking authority.
Unclaimed bodies.
Commission of anatomy, §130A-416.
Shielding from public view.
Unclaimed bodies, §130A-415, (e).
Smallpox.
Handling and transportation of bodies, §130A-395, (a), (b).
Transportation.
Contagious diseases, §130A-395, (a) to (c).
Unclaimed bodies.
Anatomical gifts.
Exemptions from provisions, §130A-415, (f).
Autopsies.
Consent of commission of anatomy, §130A-415, (d).
Commission of anatomy.
Adoption of rules, §130A-416.
Autopsies.
Consent of commission, §130A-415, (d).
Minors in custody of county at time of death.
Notification of commission, §130A-415, (g).
Definitions, §130A-415, (b).
Disposition, §130A-415, (a), (c).
Commission of anatomy declining to receive, §130A-415, (c).
Expenses for embalming and delivery, §130A-415, (b).
Medical examiners.
Provisions of part inapplicable to bodies within jurisdiction of medical examiner, §130A-415, (h).
Migrant farm workers and their dependents.
Delivery of bodies to commission of anatomy, §130A-418, (b).
Notification of commission of anatomy, §130A-415, (a).
Minors in custody of county at time of death, §130A-415, (g).
Rules and regulations.
Adoption by commission of anatomy, §130A-416.
Shielding from public view, §130A-415, (e).
Waters and watercourses.
Burial at sea, §§130A-113, (b), 130A-388, (b).

DEADLY FORCE.
Arrest by law enforcement officers, §15A-401.
Use against intruders, §14-51.1.

DEADLY WEAPONS.
Alcoholic beverages sold or consumed.
Carrying into establishments or assemblies, §14-269.3.

DEADLY WEAPONS —Cont'd
Arrest.
Use of deadly force, §15A-401.
Assault on handicapped persons, §14-32.1.
Assault upon emergency medical services personnel, §14-34.6, (b).
Assault upon government officials and employees, §14-34.2.
Electronic surveillance orders, §15A-290, (c4).
Ballistic knives.
Possession and sale, §14-269.6, (a), (b).
Burglary or housebreaking, preparation to commit, §14-55.
Carrying concealed weapon, §14-269, (a), (b) to (d).
Civil disorders, teaching or demonstrating use or assembling, §14-288.20.
Confiscation and disposition, §14-269.1.
Deadly force.
Use authorized during arrest, §15A-401.
Disasters.
Prohibitions and restrictions during state of emergency.
County powers, §14-288.13.
Municipal powers, §14-288.12.
Discharging weapon into occupied property, §14-34.1.
Emergencies.
Prohibitions and restrictions during state of emergency.
County powers, §14-288.13.
Municipal powers, §14-288.12.
Felonious assault with, §14-32.
Firearms generally.
See FIREARMS.
Furnishing to inmates of charitable, mental or penal institutions, §14-258.1.
Misdemeanor assaults, batteries or affrays, §14-33, (c).
Habitual misdemeanor assault, §14-33.2.
Warrantless arrest, §15A-401.
Parade, picket line, funeral procession, etc.
Possession while participating, §14-277.2.
Permitting young children to use dangerous firearm, §14-316.
Pointing gun, assault by, §14-34.
Habitual misdemeanor assault, §14-33.2.
Possessing or carrying on campus or other educational property, §14-269.2.
Possession of dangerous weapon in prison, §14-258.2.
Possession of handgun by minor, §14-269.7.
Riot or state of emergency existing.
Transporting dangerous weapon, §14-288.7.
Riots and civil disorders.
Prohibitions and restrictions during state of emergency.
County powers, §14-288.13.
Robbery.
Train robbery, §14-88.
Robbery with firearm or dangerous weapon, §14-87, (a).
Secret assault, §14-31.
Selling or giving weapons to minors, §14-315.
Spring loaded projectile knives.
Possession and sale, §14-269.6, (a), (b).
State of emergency.
Prohibitions and restrictions during.
County powers, §14-288.13.
Municipal powers, §14-288.12.

DEADLY WEAPONS —Cont'd
State property or courthouses, carrying or possessing, §14-269.4.
Storage of weapon to protect minor, §14-315.1.
Trains or passengers, shooting at, §14-280.
Warning upon sale or transfer of firearm to protect minor, §14-315.2.
Weapon of mass death and destruction.
Manufacture, assembly, possession, etc., §14-288.8.
Nuclear, biological or chemical weapons, §§14-288.21 to 14-288.24.
See WEAPONS OF MASS DEATH AND DESTRUCTION.
Weapons generally.
See WEAPONS.

DEAD MAN'S STATUTE, §8C-1, Rule 601, (c).

DEAF AND HEARING IMPAIRED.
See HEARING IMPAIRED.

DEALERS.
Animal dealers.
Defined, §19A-23.
Licenses.
Change in ownership, management or operation of business, §19A-31.
Fees, §19A-29.
Penalty for acting as dealer without license, §19A-34.
Refusal, suspension or revocation, §19A-30.
Appeals, §19A-32.
Required, §19A-29.
Transfer prohibited, §19A-31.
Art dealers.
Sale of fine prints, §§25C-10 to 25C-16.
Chick dealers.
Civil penalties, §106-549.01.
Compulsory testing for disease, §106-548.
Defined, §106-541.
False advertising, §106-545.
Fines, §106-549.01.
Misdemeanor offenses, §106-549.
Notice describing grade to be posted, §106-546.
Quarantine on premises, §106-548.
Records to be kept, §106-547.
Shipments from out of state, §106-544.
Violations of provisions a misdemeanor, §106-549.
Grain dealers, §§106-601 to 106-615.
See GRAIN DEALERS.
Liquefied petroleum gas, §119-56.
Livestock dealer licensing, §§106-418.8 to 106-418.16.
Application for license, §106-418.11, (a).
Information required, §106-418.11, (a).
Citation of act, §106-418.15.
Civil penalties, §106-418.16.
Definitions, §106-418.8.
Exemptions from provisions, §106-418.9.
Fines, §106-418.16.
Hearings required, §106-418.12.
Maintenance of records, §106-418.13.
Penalties, §§106-418.14, 106-418.16.
Prohibited conduct, §106-418.10.
Refusal to issue license, §106-418.11, (c), (d).
Renewal of licenses, §106-418.11, (a).
Revocation of license, §106-418.11, (b), (d).
Short title, §106-418.15.
Suspension of license, §106-418.11, (b), (d).
Unlawful acts, §106-418.10.

DEALERS —Cont'd
Motor vehicles.
See MOTOR VEHICLE DEALERS.
Pesticide dealer licensing, §§143-448 to 143-451.
Pesticides.
Dealer responsible for actions of employees, §143-450, (b).
Defined, §143-460.
Employer to list on license application, §143-450, (a).
Licenses, §§143-448 to 143-451.
Supervision of employees, agents, etc., to prevent making deceptive or misleading statements about pesticides, §143-442, (j).
Precious metal dealers, §§66-163 to 66-173.
See PRECIOUS METAL DEALERS.
Securities.
Bonds, surety, §78A-37, (d).
Defined, §78A-2.
Records.
Registered dealers, §78A-38, (a), (d).
Registration, §§78A-36 to 78A-40.
Reports.
Financial reports by registered dealers, §78A-38, (b).
Seeds.
Complaints by buyers, §106-277.30, (a).
Damages recoverable, §106-277.34, (b).
Evidence introduced in action, §106-277.34, (a).
Notice of procedure, §106-277.31.
Licensing of dealers, §106-277.18.
Revocation or refusal of license for cause, §106-277.19.
Referral of investigation to seed board, §106-277.30, (c).
Registration, §106-277.18.
Requesting investigation, §106-277.30, (b).
Weapons.
Fires and fire protection.
Door lock exemption permit, §§58-79-22, 143-143.4.

DEAL-MAKING BY PROSECUTION WITNESSES.
Immunity, charge reduction or sentence concessions, §§15A-1051 to 15A-1055.

DEATH.
Adoption.
Death of joint petitioner pending final decree, §48-2-204.
Adult care homes.
Reporting death of resident, §131D-34.1.
Advancements.
Death of advancee before intestate donor, §29-27.
Appeals.
Substitution of parties, App. Proc. Rule 38, (a).
Attachment.
Defendant.
Death after levy.
Effect, §1-440.34.
Attorneys at law.
Appointment to protect clients' interests, Bar Rules & Regs., B, §.0122.
Bail bondsman, §58-71-121.
Bank deposits and collections.
Death of customer.
Authority of payor or collecting bank, §25-4-405, (a), (b).
Controlling provisions, §25-4-405, (c).
Benefits act, §§143-166.1 to 143-166.7.

DEATH —Cont'd
Blind persons.
Aid to the blind.
Award and assistance check payable to decedents, §111-18.1, (a), (b).
Boating safety.
Collision or accident resulting in.
Duty of operator involved, §75A-11, (b).
Brain death, §90-323.
Burial at sea.
Certification and duties of medical examiners, §§130A-113, (b), 130A-388, (b).
Certificate of death.
Amendment fee, §130A-118, (d).
Child care facilities.
Report of death of child while in child care, §110-102.1, (b).
Child fatality or near fatality cases.
Disclosure of records, §7B-2902.
Child fatality prevention system, §§7B-1400 to 7B-1414.
See CHILD FATALITY PREVENTION SYSTEM.
Child fatality review team, §143B-150.20.
Child placing agencies.
Reporting death of resident, §131D-10.6B.
Community property rights, disposition at death, §§31C-1 to 31C-12.
See COMMUNITY PROPERTY RIGHTS, DISPOSITION AT DEATH.
Competency of witnesses.
Dying declarations, §8-51.1.
Conveyances.
Contingent limitations depending on death of person without heirs.
Limitations on failure of issue, §41-4.
Disclosure of death or illness of previous occupant, §39-50.
Coroners.
Conveyances of real property when not in office, §39-5.
Death benefits, §§143-166.1 to 143-166.7.
See DEATH BENEFITS.
Declarations.
Right to natural death.
Declaration of desire for natural death, §90-321.
Procedures in absence of declaration, §90-322.
Deeds.
Contingent limitations on death of person without heirs.
Limitations on failure of issue, §41-4.
Definitions.
Brain death, §90-323.
Right to natural death, §90-321, (a).
Depositions.
Reading deposition on trial.
When deposition may be read on trial, §8-83.
Determination that death has occurred, §90-323.
Disposition of body or body parts of decedent.
Decedent authorizing disposition in will, written statement, etc., §130A-420, (a).
Inapplicability of provisions to disposition of bodies as anatomical gifts, §130A-420, (d).
Persons authorized to determine method of disposition of decedent's body.
Decedent leaving no written authorization, §130A-420, (b).
Written authorization for disposition of body parts, §130A-420, (c).
Dying declarations, §8C-1, Rule 804, (b).
Competency of witnesses, §8-51.1.

DEATH —Cont'd
Executors and administrators.
Appointment of successor, §28A-6-3.
Powers and duties of successor, §28A-13-7.
Surviving personal representative.
Powers, §28A-13-9.
Extraordinary means of postponing.
Right to natural death, §§90-320 to 90-323.
Federal officers and employees.
Finding of presumed death, §8-37.1, (a), (b).
Authority to certify evidence, §8-37.3.
Deemed signed and issued pursuant to law, §8-37.3.
Report or record that person died, §8-37.2.
Certified copies deemed signed and issued pursuant to law, §8-37.3.
Authority to certify evidence, §8-37.3.
Fees.
Amendment of birth and death certificates, §130A-118, (d).
Felony death by vehicle, §20-141.4.
Fetal death registration.
Report of death, §130A-114, (a).
Preparation and filing of report, §130A-114, (c).
Required medical information, §130A-114, (b).
Gift tax.
Death of donor within three years.
Time for assessment, §105-194.
Guardians.
Appointment of successor guardian, §35A-1293.
Mortgages.
Powers passed to succeeding guardian, §45-19.
Health.
Communicable diseases.
Transportation of bodies of persons who have died of reportable diseases, §130A-146.
Health care powers of attorney, §§32A-15 to 32A-26.
See HEALTH CARE POWERS OF ATTORNEY.
Hearsay exception.
Family history, §8C-1, Rule 803.
Records of religious organizations, §8C-1, Rule 803.
Statements under belief of impending death, §§8-51.1, 8C-1, Rule 804, (b).
Highway patrol.
Badges and service sidearms of deceased members, §20-187.2, (a).
Joint tenants and tenants in common.
Ownership of corporate stock and investment securities, §41-2.2, (c).
Landlord and tenant.
Apportionment of rent.
Leases terminated by death, §42-5.
Right to payment terminated by death, §42-6.
Death, serious illness, or certain criminal convictions of previous occupant.
Deemed not a material fact in real property transactions, §42-14.2.
Leases.
Apportionment of rent where lease terminated by death, §42-5.
Death, serious illness, or certain criminal convictions of previous occupant.
Deemed not a material fact in real property transactions, §42-14.2.
Legislative retirement system.
Death benefits, §120-4.27.
Distributions, §120-4.26A.
Survivor's alternative benefit, §120-4.28.

DEATH —Cont'd
Limitation of actions.
Personal representative or collector.
Action by or against in event of death before limitation expires, §1-22.
Limited liability company member.
Cessation of membership, §57C-3-02.
Limited partnerships, revised act.
Exercise of partnership rights by legal representative, §59-705.
Living will.
Right to natural death, §§90-320 to 90-323.
Maltreatment of juvenile.
Disclosure of records in child fatality or near fatality cases, §7B-2902.
Report of death due to maltreatment, §7B-301.
Medical examiners.
Notification of certain deaths, §130A-383, (a).
Duties of medical examiners upon receipt of notice, §130A-385, (a).
Out of state bodies, §130A-384.
Postmortem medicolegal examinations and services, §§130A-377 to 130A-394.
See MEDICAL EXAMINERS.
Military affairs.
Absentees in military service.
Termination of receivership, §28B-8, (b).
Evidence.
Finding of presumed death, §8-37.1, (a), (b).
Powers of attorney.
Death of principal.
Affidavit of agent as to possessing no knowledge of death of principal, §165-40.
Provisions for revocation not affected, §165-42.
Report of "missing" not to constitute revocation, §165-41.
Validity of acts of agent, §165-39.
Militia.
Third party injuring or killing guard personnel.
Proceedings against third party, §127A-110.
Minors.
Child fatality or new fatality cases, disclosure of records, §7B-2902.
Child fatality prevention system, §§7B-1400 to 7B-1414.
See CHILD FATALITY PREVENTION SYSTEM.
Report of death due to maltreatment, §7B-301.
Misdemeanor death by vehicle, §20-141.4.
Missing persons.
Final finding and decree of absentee's death, §28C-11, (a).
Termination of receivership, §28C-12.
Monuments and memorials.
Not to be erected within 25 years of death of person, §100-8.
Mortgages and deeds of trust.
Guardians.
Powers passed to succeeding guardian, §45-19.
Representative succeeds on death of mortgagee or trustee in deeds of trust, §45-4.
Survivorship among donees of power of sale, §45-8.
Motor vehicle accidents.
Death as result of accident within twelve months after accident.
Supplemental report by investigating law enforcement officer, §20-166.1, (e).
Hospitals to notify medical examiner of death resulting from accidents, §20-166.1, (f).

DEATH —Cont'd
Motor vehicle accidents —Cont'd
Medical examiner to report death resulting from accident, §20-166.1, (f).
Vehicular homicide, §20-141.4.
Motor vehicle registration.
Death of owner of registered vehicle.
Continuation of registration, §20-64, (e).
National guard.
Mutual assistance compact.
Death benefits, §127A-177, (h).
Injury or death while going to or returning from duty, §127A-183.
Pensions for members of national guard.
Cessation of payments upon death of individual, §127A-40, (b).
Natural death.
Right to natural death, §§90-320 to 90-323.
Parties.
Substitution of parties, §1A-1, Rule 25, (a), (e), (f).
Partnerships.
Claims against partnership when one partner has died.
Failure to present claims in six months, §59-80.
Payment pro rata, §59-79.
Dissolution and winding up.
Continuation of business.
Rights of estate of deceased partner when business continued, §59-72.
Death of partner as cause of dissolution, §59-61.
Liability of individual property of deceased partner for obligations of partnership, §59-66, (d).
Fiduciary obligations of partner.
Applicability to representatives of deceased partner, §59-51, (b).
Surviving partners, §§59-74 to 59-84.1.
Physicians and surgeons.
Determination that person is dead, §90-323.
Police.
Badges and service side arms of deceased members, §20-187.2, (a).
Postmortem medicolegal examinations and services, §§130A-377 to 130A-394.
See MEDICAL EXAMINERS.
President of the United States.
Duty of congress, Const. U. S., art. II, §1.
President-elect.
Provision in case of, Const. U. S., amd. XX.
Succession upon death, Const. U. S., amd. XXV, §1.
Presumption, §28C-1.
Prisons and prisoners.
Investigations.
Death of convicts, §148-25.
Public schools.
School employees.
Payment of wages after death, §115C-324.
Real property.
Death, serious illness, or certain criminal convictions of previous occupant.
Deemed not a material fact in real property transactions, §42-14.2.
Rents.
Apportionment.
Lease terminated by death, §42-5.
Right to payment terminated by death, §42-6.
Retirement system for counties and cities.
Benefits.
Death benefit plan, §128-27, (l).

DEATH —Cont'd
Retirement system for teachers and state employees, §135-5.
Consolidated judicial retirement act.
Benefits on death after retirement, §135-64, (a) to (i).
Benefits on death before retirement, §135-63, (a) to (d).
Death benefit plan, §135-5, (l).
Survivor's alternate benefit, §135-5, (m).
Right to natural death, §§90-320 to 90-323.
See RIGHT TO NATURAL DEATH.
Sheriffs.
Deeds.
Official selling or empowered to sell property not in office, §39-5.
Pensions.
Sheriffs' supplemental pension fund act of 1985.
Cessation of benefits on death of pensioner, §143-166.85, (c).
Simultaneous death, §§28A-24-1 to 28A-24-7.
See SIMULTANEOUS DEATH.
Social services.
Checks payable to decedents, §108A-72.
State child fatality review team, §143B-150.20.
Substitution of parties, §1A-1, Rule 25, (a), (e), (f).
Superintendents of schools.
Vacancies in office, §115C-275.
Tax collectors.
Official selling real property not in office.
Execution by successor, §39-5.
Trusts and trustees.
Benefits, §§36A-100, 36A-101.
Contingent limitations on death of person without heirs.
Limitations on failure of issue, §41-4.
Cotrustees.
Powers, §36A-39.
Representative succeeds on death of trustee in deeds of trust, §45-4.
Successor trustee.
Appointment on clerk's own motion, §36A-33.
Vice-president, Const. U. S., art. II, §1.
Vital statistics generally, §§130A-90 to 130A-120.
See VITAL STATISTICS.
Wills.
Testator's death.
Construction of will, §31-41.
Witnesses.
Competency of witnesses.
Dying declarations, §8-51.1.
Workers' compensation.
See WORKERS' COMPENSATION.
Wrongful death.
See WRONGFUL DEATH.

DEATH BENEFITS, §§143-166.1 to 143-166.7.
Applicability of article, §143-166.7.
Awards.
Conclusiveness, §143-166.4.
Definitions.
Dependent child, §143-166.2, (a).
Dependent parent, §143-166.2, (b).
Generally, §143-166.2.
Killed in the line of duty, §143-166.2, (c).
Official duties, §143-166.2, (f).
Spouse, §143-166.2, (e).
Effect of payments on other benefits, §143-166.5.

DEATH BENEFITS —Cont'd
Industrial commission rules.
Abandonment of grounds for appeal.
Failure to include ground in statement, I.C. Death Benefits Rule IV.
Amendment of rules, I.C. Death Benefits Rule V.
Appeal to full commission, I.C. Death Benefits Rule IV.
Briefs on appeal, I.C. Death Benefits Rule IV.
Determination of claim, I.C. Death Benefits Rule III.
Grounds for appeal.
Statement, requirements, time for filing, I.C. Death Benefits Rule IV.
Guardian ad litem.
Appointment for infants and incompetents, I.C. Death Benefits Rule III.
Hearing on award.
Insufficient evidence or information, I.C. Death Benefits Rule III.
Insufficient evidence or information.
Hearing on award, I.C. Death Benefits Rule III.
Location of commission office, I.C. Death Benefits Rule I.
New evidence on appeal, prohibition, I.C. Death Benefits Rule IV.
New hearing to take additional evidence.
Motion, I.C. Death Benefits Rule IV.
Notice of appeal, I.C. Death Benefits Rule IV.
Oral argument on appeal, waiver, I.C. Death Benefits Rule IV.
Rehearing, ordering, I.C. Death Benefits Rule III.
Settlement for less than maximum amount.
Commission ordering or approving, I.C. Death Benefits Rule III.
Statement of facts and circumstances furnished by claimant.
Copy furnished opposing party, I.C. Death Benefits Rule III.
Statement of grounds for appeal.
Time for filing, I.C. Death Benefits Rule IV.
Sufficient evidence or information.
Award without hearing, I.C. Death Benefits Rule III.
Transacting business, continuous session, I.C. Death Benefits Rule II.
Legislative findings, §143-166.1.
Payments.
Amounts, §143-166.3, (b).
Awards exempt from taxes, §143-166.6.
Determination, §143-166.3, (a).
Other benefits not affected, §143-166.5.
Remainder of payments, §143-166.3, (c).
Service or merchandise payments.
Insurance company contracts, §58-3-55.
Subsequent ineligibility, §143-166.3, (c), (d).
Purpose, §143-166.1.
Renunciation of succession, §31B-1.
Source of funds, §143-166.4.
Taxation.
Awards exempt from taxes, §143-166.6.

DEATH BENEFITS, TRUST OF.
Applicability of article, §36A-101.
Construction of article, §36A-101.
Employee benefit plan.
Defined, §36A-100, (b).
Interest of trustee as beneficiary sufficient to support inter vivos or testamentary trust, §36A-100, (b).

DEATH BENEFITS, TRUST OF —Cont'd
Inter vivos or testamentary trust.
Interest of trustee as beneficiary of life insurance or other benefits sufficient, §36A-100, (a).
Life insurance policies.
Defined, §36A-100, (a).
Interest of trustee as beneficiary sufficient to support inter vivos or testamentary trust, §36A-100, (a).

DEATH BY VEHICLE.
Felony death by vehicle, §20-141.4, (a1).
Mandatory revocation of driver's license, §20-17, (a).
Permanent revocation, §20-19, (i).
Misdemeanor death by vehicle, §20-141.4, (a2).

DEATH CERTIFICATES.
Amendment by medical examiner, §130A-385, (c).
Amendment of death certificate, §130A-118, (a).
Contents of death certificate, §130A-116.
Cremation.
Authorization for cremation, §130A-113, (b).
Required before cremating, information required, §90-210.49, (a).
Duties of local registrars, §130A-97.
Duties of medical examiners, §130A-385.
Fee for registering or amending, copies, §161-10, (a).
Felonies and misdemeanors.
Generally, §130A-26A, (a), (b).
Filing of death certificate, §130A-115, (a).
Information to be obtained, §130A-115, (b).
Local registrar's duties, §130A-97.
Register of deeds.
Copies to be forwarded by local registrars, §130A-97.
Standard certificate of death.
Contents of death certificate, §130A-116.

DEATH OF A PARTY.
Substitution of party upon death, §1A-1, Rule 25, (a).

DEATH OF JUVENILE.
Child fatality prevention system, §§7B-1400 to 7B-1414.
See CHILD FATALITY PREVENTION SYSTEM.
Disclosure of records in child fatality or near fatality cases, §7B-2902.
Maltreatment, report, §7B-301.

DEATH PENALTY.
See CAPITAL PUNISHMENT.

DEATH PRESUMPTION.
Not presumed from mere absence, §28C-1, (a).
Specific peril exposure considered, §28C-1, (b).

DEATH WITH DIGNITY, §§90-320 to 90-323.
Advance health care directive registry, §§130A-465 to 130A-471.
Affirmative or deliberate ending of life not authorized, §90-320, (b).
Brain death.
Defined, §90-323.
Use as sole basis for determination of death, §90-323.
Cause of death.
Withholding or discontinuance of extraordinary means not to constitute, §§90-321, (h), 90-322, (d).
Comatose persons.
Procedures for natural death in absence of declaration, §90-322, (a), (b).

DEATH WITH DIGNITY —Cont'd
Declaration of desire, §90-321.
Absence of declaration.
Procedure for natural death, §90-322, (a), (b).
Health care power of attorney form.
Combination with or incorporation into, §§32A-26, 90-321, (j).
Definitions, §90-321, (a).
Determination of death, §90-323.
Form.
Declaration of desire for natural death, §90-321, (d).
Health care powers of attorney.
General provisions, §§32A-15 to 32A-26.
See HEALTH CARE POWERS OF ATTORNEY.
Insurance.
Signing of declaration not to be required as condition for becoming insured, §90-321, (g).
Legislative declaration, §90-320, (a).
Suicide.
Execution and consummation of declaration not to constitute, §90-321, (f).

DEBIT CARDS.
Financial identity fraud.
Generally, §§14-113.20 to 14-113.25.
See FINANCIAL IDENTITY FRAUD.
Financial transaction card crimes, §§14-113.8 to 14-113.17.
See FINANCIAL TRANSACTION CARDS.
Statewide accounts receivable program.
Payments by, authorized, §147-86.22, (b).

DEBT ADJUSTERS.
Definitions, §14-423.
Engaging, etc., in business of debt adjusting a misdemeanor, §14-424.
Injunctions.
Appointment of receiver for money and property employed, §14-425.
Practice of debt adjusting enjoined, §14-425.
Persons not deemed debt adjusters, §14-426.
Receivers.
Appointment of receiver for money and property employed, §14-425.
Transactions not deemed debt adjustment, §14-426.

DEBT COLLECTORS.
Arrests.
Representing that nonpayment may result in arrest, §75-51.
Coercion, §75-51.
Collection agencies.
General provisions, §§58-70-1 to 58-70-130.
See COLLECTION AGENCIES.
Prohibited acts by debt collectors.
Collection agencies exempted from provisions, §75-50.
Damages.
Restrictions on damages for prohibited acts, §75-56.
Deceptive representations, §75-54.
Definitions, §75-50.
Harassment, §75-52.
Obscenity.
Profane or obscene language, §75-52.
Penalties.
Civil penalties, §75-56.
Publication.
Unreasonable publication, §75-53.
Telephone harassment, §75-52.

DEBT COLLECTORS —Cont'd
Threats, §75-51.
Unconscionability, §75-55.

DEBT OF ANOTHER, PROMISE TO ANSWER.
Contract required to be in writing, §22-1.

DEBTOR LEAVING STATE.
Arrest, §1-355.

DEBTS.
Absentees in military service.
Receivers.
Collection and payment of debts, §28B-6.
Accounts and accounting.
Prisons and prisoners.
Trustee for estate of debtor, §23-20.
Adjusters, §§14-423 to 14-426.
See DEBT ADJUSTERS.
Adoption.
Debts and engagements contracted before, Const. U. S., art. VI.
Aid of rebellion, Const. U. S., amd. XIV.
Alimony.
Dependent spouse deemed creditor, §50-16.7, (h).
Arrest in civil cases.
Removal or disposition of property with intent to defraud creditors.
Cases in which arrest allowed, §1-410.
Art dealers.
Creditors of art dealer may not reach works of fine art on consignment with art dealer, §25C-4.
Assignments for benefit of creditors.
See ASSIGNMENTS FOR BENEFIT OF CREDITORS.
Attachment.
Intent to defraud creditors.
Grounds for attachment, §1-440.3.
Attorneys at law.
Appearance for creditor in insolvency and certain other proceedings.
Unlawful for anyone except attorney, §§84-9, 84-10.
Bonds, surety.
Actions on bonds.
Officer liable for negligence in collecting debt, §58-76-30.
Official bonds.
Justification of sureties.
Official bonds considered debts and liabilities, §58-72-40.
Collection agencies.
Debt collectors, §§75-51 to 75-56.
See DEBT COLLECTORS.
General provisions, §§58-70-1 to 58-70-130.
See COLLECTION AGENCIES.
Congress.
Powers of congress, Const. U. S., art. I, §8.
Consolidated city-county act.
Assumption of debt, §§160B-16 to 160B-21.
See CONSOLIDATED CITY-COUNTY ACT.
Limitation on indebtedness, §160B-15.
Contracts.
Promise to answer for debt of another.
Statute of frauds provisions, §22-1.
Costs.
Evidence of indebtedness.
Attorneys' fees in notes, etc., in addition to interest, §6-21.2.
Court process.
Collection of debt.
Simulation of court process in connection with collection, §14-118.1.

DEBTS —Cont'd
Credit repair services, §§66-220 to 66-226.
See CREDIT REPAIR SERVICES.
Debt collectors.
Collection agencies, §§58-70-1 to 58-70-130.
See COLLECTION AGENCIES.
General provisions, §§75-51 to 75-56.
See DEBT COLLECTORS.
Decedents' estates.
Debts and claims generally.
See DECEDENTS' ESTATES.
Notice to creditors, §§28A-14-1 to 28A-14-3.
Definitions.
Setoff debt collection act, §105A-2.
Electric membership corporations.
Contracting debt.
Specific grant of power, §117-18.
Executors and administrators.
Appointment of executor.
No discharge of debt due to decedent's estate, §28A-15-11.
Notice to creditors, §§28A-14-1 to 28A-14-3.
Satisfying debts or claims against decedent's estate, §28A-13-3, (a).
False swearing by imprisoned debtor, §23-43.
Fiduciaries.
Transfer of negotiable instruments.
Security for personal debt.
Liability of creditor or transferee, §32-5.
Fraud.
Court process in connection with collection of claim.
Simulation of court process, §14-118.1.
Garnishment.
Payment to defendant by garnishee, §1-440.31.
General assembly.
Indebtedness of state.
Requirements for passage of revenue bills, Const. N. C., art. II, §23.
Imprisonment for debt, Const. N. C., art. I, §28.
Joint and several debtors, §§1-113, 1-114.
Life insurance.
Exemption of benefits from claims of creditors except in case of fraud, §58-58-115.
Local government finance.
Authorized purposes, Const. N. C., art. V, §4.
Certain debts barred, Const. N. C., art. V, §4.
General provisions, §§159-1 to 159-188.
See LOCAL GOVERNMENT FINANCE.
Outstanding debt, Const. N. C., art. V, §4.
Regulation, Const. N. C., art. V, §4.
Two-thirds limitation in increase, Const. N. C., art. V, §4.
Missing persons.
Receivers.
Power to collect or pay, §28C-8.
Not to be questioned, Const. U. S., amd. XIV.
Oaths.
Prisons and prisoners.
Trustee for estate of debtor, §23-20.
Partition.
Petition by judgment creditor of cotenant, §46-5.
Personal property.
Exemptions from process, Const. N. C., art. X, §1.
Powers of appointment.
Limitation against creditors and purchasers for value.
Requisites, §39-35.
Powers of congress, Const. U. S., art. I, §8.
Prisons and prisoners.
Bankruptcy and insolvency, §§23-18 to 23-45.
See DISCHARGE OF INSOLVENT PRISONERS.

DEBTS —Cont'd
Prisons and prisoners —Cont'd
Bounds of jail.
Imprisoned debtor may take benefit of bounds, §23-45.
False swearing.
Perjury, §23-43.
Fees.
Creditor liable for jail fee, §23-42.
Fraud.
Superior or district court tries issue, §23-39.
Jail bounds.
Imprisoned debtor may take benefit of prison bounds, §23-45.
Perjury.
False swearing, §23-43.
Trustee for estate of debtor.
Accounting, §23-20.
Appointments.
Successor, §23-22.
Superior court appoints, §23-19.
Bonds, surety.
Release of insolvent upon giving bond, §23-40.
Surrender of principal.
Surety authorized to surrender, §23-41.
Copy of sentence to be produced, §23-19.
Court may appoint several trustees, §23-21.
Creditor liable for jail fees, §23-42.
Duties, §23-20.
False swearing.
Penalized as perjury, §23-43.
Fraud.
Superior or district court tries issue, §23-39.
Multiple trustees may be appointed, §23-21.
Oath, §23-20.
Persons who may apply for trustee, §23-18.
Powers, §23-44.
Removal, §23-22.
Superior court appoints, §23-19.
Probate and registration.
Conveyances.
Registration necessary to pass title as against creditors, §47-18.
Deeds of easements.
Registration necessary for validity as against creditors, §47-27.
Gifts.
Registration necessary for validity as against creditors and bona fide purchasers, §47-26.
Marriage settlements.
Registration necessary for validity as against creditors and bona fide purchasers, §47-25.
Proprietary schools.
Evidence of indebtedness with unlicensed schools null and void, §115D-97.
Retail installment sales generally, §§25A-1 to 25A-45.
See RETAIL INSTALLMENT SALES.
Secured transactions.
General provisions governing secured debt, §§25-9-101 to 25-9-710.
See SECURED TRANSACTIONS.
Small estates.
Debts of decedent, §§28A-25-1 to 28A-25-6.
See SMALL ESTATES.
State debt.
See STATE DEBT.
Statewide accounts receivable program, §§147-86.20 to 147-86.27.
See STATEWIDE ACCOUNTS RECEIVABLE PROGRAM.

DEBTS —Cont'd
Statute of frauds.
Promise to answer for debt of another.
Writing required, §22-1.
Revival of debt of bankrupt, §22-4.
Suretyship.
Joinder of debtor by surety, §26-12.
Notice to creditor to take action.
Effect of failure of creditor to take action.
Discharge, §26-9, (a).
Separate notice of co-sureties, co-indorsers or co-guarantors, §26-9, (c).
Waiver of defense provisions, §26-9, (b).
Evidence of notice, §26-8, (c).
Method of giving notice, §26-8, (a).
Service of notice returned, §26-8, (b).
Surety, indorser or guarantor may notify creditor to take action, §26-7, (a).
Applicability of section, §26-7, (d).
Extent of notice, §26-7, (b).
Holder or owner of obligation to disclose other sureties, indorsers or guarantors, §26-7, (c).
Tax debts.
Collection of tax debts.
Collection assistance fee, §105-243.1, (d).
Use of fee by department, §105-243.1, (e).
Contracting for collection, §105-243.1, (b).
Definitions, §105-243.1, (a).
Notice that debt submitted to contractor for collection, §105-243.1, (b).
Outsourcing collection, §105-243.1, (b).
Report by department, §105-243.1, (f).
Secrecy of collection.
Contract for collection conditioned on, §105-243.1, (c).
Termination of contract for collection.
Violation of secrecy requirement, §105-243.1, (c).
Status of tax as debt, §105-238.
Torrens system registration.
Method of transfer.
Land conveyed as security, §43-36.
Transfers to minors.
Obligor of debt owed to minor.
Transfer for benefit of minor, §33A-7.
Trusts and trustees.
Uniform trusts act.
Bank account to pay special debts, §36A-61, (a).
Venue.
Deficiency debtor, §1-76.1.
Workers' compensation.
Claims exempt from debt, §97-21.

DECEDENTS' ESTATES.
Absentees in military service, §§28B-1 to 28B-10.
See ABSENTEES IN MILITARY SERVICE.
Accounts and accounting.
Collectors.
Settlement of accounts, §28A-11-4, (b).
Executors and administrators, §§28A-21-1 to 28A-21-5.
See EXECUTORS AND ADMINISTRATORS.
Actions.
Powers of personal representatives or fiduciaries, §28A-13-3, (a).
Survival of actions, §28A-18-1.
Actions in favor of decedent which do not survive, §28A-18-1, (b).
Transfers or conveyances by decedent to defraud creditors.
Actions by personal representative to recover, §28A-15-10.

DECEDENTS' ESTATES —Cont'd
Administration of estates.
Costs of administration, §7A-307.
Additional costs assessable on appeal or upon transfer or cause, §7A-307, (d).
Amount of facilities fee, §7A-307, (b).
Assessment of costs, §7A-307, (a).
Completeness and exclusivity of costs, §7A-307, (c).
Courtroom and related judicial facilities.
Amount of facilities fee, §7A-307, (b).
Use of facilities, §7A-307, (a).
General court of justice.
Support of court, §7A-307, (a).
Liability of parties for costs, §7A-307, (e).
Miscellaneous fees, §7A-307, (b1).
Summary administration, §§28A-28-1 to 28A-28-7.
See within this heading, "Summary administration."
Administrators generally.
See EXECUTORS AND ADMINISTRATORS.
Adoption.
Inheritance rights of child subject to adoption.
Consequences of consent by parent to adoption, §48-3-607, (c).
Intestate succession, §29-17.
Share of after-adopted children, §28A-22-2.
Advancements, §§29-23 to 29-29.
Death of advancee before intestate donor, §29-27.
Effect, §29-25.
Generally, §29-23.
Gift inter vivos.
Presumption of gift, §29-24.
Inventory.
Failure to give inventory, §29-28.
Release by advancee, §29-29.
Taking into account and computation of estate, §29-23.
Valuation.
Determination, §29-26.
After-born children.
Shares, §28A-22-2.
Agriculture.
Continuation of farming operations, §§28A-13-3, 28A-13-4.
Crops of deceased persons, §28A-15-1.
Ancillary administration, §§28A-26-1 to 28A-26-9.
See EXECUTORS AND ADMINISTRATORS.
Annexation of wills.
Powers and duties of administrator with will annexed, §28A-13-8.
Annuities.
Killing decedents.
Additional liability for annuity company, §31A-11, (c).
Proceeds payable to slayer, §31A-11, (a).
Appeals.
Examination of persons or corporations believed to have possession of property, §28A-15-12, (b).
Appointment.
Annexation of will.
Powers and duties of administrator with will annexed, §28A-13-8.
Powers and duties of successor personal representative, §28A-13-7.
Appraisers.
Employment, §28A-20-4.
Arbitration and award.
Disputed claims, §28A-19-15.
Assets.
Abatement, §28A-15-5, (a).

DECEDENTS' ESTATES —Cont'd
Assets —Cont'd
Availability for discharge of debts and claims, §28A-15-1, (a).
Encumbered assets.
Payment of encumbrance by personal representative, §28A-15-4.
Joint deposit accounts.
Sources of assets to satisfy claims against estate, §28A-15-10, (a).
Order in which assets appropriated, §28A-15-5, (a).
Powers of personal representative, §28A-13-3.
Attachment.
Defendant's death after levy, §1-440.34.
Attorneys specializing in estate planning and probate law.
Certification standards, Bar Rules & Regs., D, §§.2301 to .2307.
Auctions and auctioneers.
Sales in settlement in decedents' estates.
Exemptions from auction provisions, §85B-2.
Bonds, surety.
Collectors, §28A-11-2.
Debts and claims.
Distribution of estate despite contingent or unliquidated claim.
Bond of heirs and devisees, §28A-19-5.
Examination of persons or corporations believed to have possession of property, §28A-15-12, (b).
Executors and administrators, §§28A-8-1 to 28A-8-6.
See EXECUTORS AND ADMINISTRATORS.
Cemeteries.
Perpetual care of cemetery lot, §28A-19-10.
Children born out of wedlock, intestate succession.
Descent and distribution upon intestacy, §29-20.
Legitimated children.
Succession, by, through and from, §29-18.
Person's illegitimate child entitled to take by, through and from, §29-19, (b).
Shares of others than surviving spouse, §29-22.
Succession by, through and from, §29-19, (a).
Surviving spouse.
Share of surviving spouse of illegitimate intestate, §29-21.
Shares of others than surviving spouse, §29-22.
Collectors.
Actions against collectors.
Service on or appearance of one binds all, §28A-18-4.
Appointment, §28A-11-1.
Termination.
Duties upon termination, §28A-11-4, (b).
Bond, §28A-11-2.
Commissions, §28A-23-3.
Collectors guilty of misconduct not entitled to commission, §28A-23-3, (e).
Computation, §28A-23-3, (f).
Construction of section, §28A-23-3, (d).
Determination of amount, §28A-23-3, (b).
Limitation on amount, §28A-23-3, (c).
Compensation, §28A-11-5.
Counsel fees.
Attorneys serving as collectors, §28A-23-4.
Defined, §28A-1-1, (1).
Duties, §28A-11-3.
Examination of accounts, §28A-11-4, (c).
Letters of collection, §28A-11-1.
Oaths, §28A-11-2.

DECEDENTS' ESTATES —Cont'd
Collectors —Cont'd
Personal property.
Court ordered sale or lease, §28A-16-2.
Powers, §28A-11-3.
When collectors' powers ceased, §28A-11-4, (a).
Qualifications, §28A-11-1.
Small estates.
Subsequently appointed collectors, §28A-25-5.
Community property rights, disposition at death, §§31C-1 to 31C-12.
See COMMUNITY PROPERTY RIGHTS, DISPOSITION AT DEATH.
Compromise and settlement.
Powers of personal representatives, §28A-13-3, (a).
Contracts.
Debts and claims.
Limitation on claims based on contract, §28A-19-3, (b).
Powers of personal representative, §28A-13-3, (a).
Costs.
Administration of estates, §7A-307.
Additional costs assessable on appeal or upon transfer of cause, §7A-307, (d).
Amount of facilities fee, §7A-307, (b).
Assessment of costs, §7A-307, (a).
Completeness and exclusivity of costs, §7A-307, (c).
Courtroom and related judicial facilities.
Amount of facilities fee, §7A-307, (b).
Use of facilities, §7A-306, (a).
General court of justice.
Support of court, §7A-307, (a).
Liability of parties for costs, §7A-307, (e).
Miscellaneous fees, §7A-307, (b1).
Reference of claim against deceased person.
Recovery of fees and other necessary disbursements, §6-31.
Creditors.
Notice to creditors, §§28A-14-1 to 28A-14-3.
Crops.
Ungathered crops at death of decedent, §28A-15-1, (d).
Death presumption, §28C-1.
Debts and claims.
Arbitration and award.
Referral of disputed claim, §28A-19-15.
Assets available for discharge of debts and claims, §28A-15-1.
Claims due representative not preferred, §28A-19-12.
Claims not due, §28A-19-14.
Classes of claims, §28A-19-6.
Preferences within class prohibited, §28A-19-13.
Contingent claims.
Payment of contingent or unliquidated claims, §28A-19-5.
Contracts.
Limitation on claims based on contract, §28A-19-3, (b).
Costs.
When costs against representative allowed, §28A-19-18.
Determination of property for discharge of debt, §28A-15-1, (b).
Disputed claims.
Claims not referred barred in three months, §28A-19-16.
Referral, §28A-19-15.
Equitable distribution.
Action for distribution.
Claimant may file, §28A-19-19, (c).

DECEDENTS' ESTATES —Cont'd
Debts and claims —Cont'd
Equitable distribution —Cont'd
Claims against estate, provisions inapplicable, §28A-19-19, (a).
Distribution, agreement by representative providing for, §28A-19-19, (b).
Fraudulent transfers or conveyances.
Actions by personal representative to recover, §28A-15-10, (b).
Limitation of actions.
Disputed claims not referred barred in three months, §28A-19-16.
Pleading statute of limitations, §28A-19-11.
Presentation of claims, §28A-19-3.
Marital or divisible property.
Action for distribution.
Claimant may file, §28A-19-19, (c).
Claims against estate, provisions inapplicable, §28A-19-19, (a).
Distribution, agreement by representative providing for, §28A-19-19, (b).
Mortgages.
Limitations on presentation of claims.
Exception as to enforcement of mortgage, §28A-19-3, (g).
Notice to creditors, §§28A-14-1 to 28A-14-3.
See EXECUTORS AND ADMINISTRATORS.
Order of payment, §28A-19-6.
Payment of claims and charges, §28A-19-4.
Preferences within class prohibited, §28A-19-13.
Presentation of claims.
Affidavit of claimant.
Right of personal representative or collector to require, §28A-19-2, (b).
Contents, §28A-19-1, (a).
Further information required by personal representative or collector, §28A-19-2, (a).
Limitations on presentation, §28A-19-3, (a) to (c).
Exceptions, §28A-19-3, (g) to (i).
Notice of claims.
Effect, §28A-19-3, (d) to (f).
Manner of presentation, §28A-19-1.
Method of presentation, §28A-19-1, (a).
Substitution of personal representatives, §28A-19-1, (c).
When commencement of action deemed presentation, §28A-19-1, (b).
Writing required, §28A-19-1, (a).
Rebate of interest on claims not due, §28A-19-14.
Reopening administration.
Assertion of claims already barred in opened administration, §28A-23-5.
Retaining property in satisfaction of representative claim, §28A-19-12.
Satisfaction of claims other than by payment, §28A-19-7.
Small estates.
Debts owed decedent, §§28A-25-1 to 28A-25-6.
See SMALL ESTATES.
Tentative trusts.
Sources of assets to satisfy claims, §28A-15-10, (a).
When charges and claims paid, §28A-19-4.
Wrongful death.
Application of recovery to payment of debts and claims against estate, §28A-15-10, (c).
Definitions, §28A-1-1.
Federal estate tax.
Apportionment, §28A-27-1.
Killing decedents, §31A-3.

DECEDENTS' ESTATES —Cont'd
Deposits.
Powers of personal representative or fiduciary, §28A-13-3, (a).
Devisees.
Defined, §28A-1-1, (1a).
Service of process, §28A-13-3.
Disbursement.
Scheme of distribution, §28A-22-1.
Discretion of executor or trustee over distributions, §28A-22-8.
Distribution.
After-born and after-adopted children.
Shares, §28A-22-2.
Discretion of executor or trustee, §28A-22-8.
Federal marital deduction.
Agreements with taxing authorities, §28A-22-6.
Guardians, §28A-22-7.
Inoperative trust, assets of, §28A-22-10.
Known but unlocated devisees or heirs, §28A-22-9.
Minors.
Guardian or parent of minor, §28A-22-7.
Nonresident trustees.
Appointment of process agent required, §28A-22-4, (a).
Parents, §28A-22-7.
Satisfaction of bequests and transfers.
Distribution of assets in kind, §28A-22-5, (a).
Requirements, §28A-22-5, (b).
Special proceeding against unknown heirs, §28A-22-3.
Unlocated devisees or heirs, §28A-22-9.
Elective life estate.
Marital interest in real property, §29-30.
Elective share of surviving spouse, §§30-3.1 to 30-3.6, 31-5.3.
Equitable distribution.
Action against surviving spouse.
Collaborative law proceedings, §50-79.
Limitation of actions, §50-20, (l).
Action for distribution.
Claimant may file, §28A-19-19, (c).
Claims against estate, provisions inapplicable, §28A-19-19, (a).
Distribution, agreement by representative providing for, §28A-19-19, (b).
Escheats.
Unclaimed personalty on settlements of decedents' estates to the escheat fund, §116B-3.
Estate taxes, §§105-32.1 to 105-32.8.
See ESTATE TAXES.
Evidence.
Killing decedent.
Record determining slayer admissible, §31A-13.
Examinations.
Persons or corporations believed to have possession of property of decedent, §28A-15-12.
Executions.
Defendant dying in execution.
Rights against property of defendant, §1-312.
Executors generally.
See EXECUTORS AND ADMINISTRATORS.
False imprisonment.
Rights of action not surviving decedent, §28A-18-1.
Farming.
Continuation of farming operations, §28A-13-4.
Federal estate tax apportionment.
Collection of uncollected taxes, §28A-27-4.
Credits, §28A-27-5, (b) to (d).

DECEDENTS' ESTATES —Cont'd
Federal estate tax apportionment —Cont'd
Definitions, §28A-27-1.
Determination.
Personal representative, §28A-27-3, (a).
Differences with federal estate tax law, §28A-27-8.
Distribution of property prior to final apportionment, §28A-27-7, (b).
Effective date of article, §28A-27-9.
Exemptions and deductions, §28A-27-5, (a).
Expenses, §28A-27-3, (c).
Generally, §28A-27-2, (a).
Inequitable apportionment, §28A-27-3, (b).
Method described in will, §28A-27-2, (b).
Personal representative.
Withholding amount of tax apportioned, §28A-27-7, (a).
Temporary and remainder interests.
No apportionment between, §28A-27-6.
Uncollected taxes.
Proceedings to recover, §28A-27-4.
Federal marital deduction.
Agreements with taxing authorities, §28A-22-6.
Fees.
Clerks of court.
Miscellaneous fees in administration of estates, §7A-307, (b1).
Fiduciaries.
Collection of rent, income, etc., §32-27.
Distribution in cash or kind.
Powers which may be incorporated by reference in trust instrument, §32-27.
General duties of representatives, §28A-13-2.
Incorporation by reference of certain powers.
Restriction on exercise of such powers, §32-26, (b), (c).
Foreign personal representatives.
Defined, §28A-1-1, (2).
Funerals.
Expenses.
Deemed obligation of estate, §28A-19-8, (a), (b).
Generation-skipping transfers.
Taxation, §105-32.1.
Gifts causa mortis.
Sources of assets to satisfy claims, §28A-15-10, (a).
Gravestones.
Providing gravestones authorized, §28A-19-9.
Guardian ad litem.
Unknown heirs.
Appointment of guardian ad litem, §28A-22-3.
Guardians.
Distribution to guardian of minor, §28A-22-7.
Heirs.
Construed to be "children" in certain limitations, §41-6.
Declaratory judgments.
Who may apply for declaration, §1-255.
Defined, §§28A-1-1, (3), 29-2.
Guardian ad litem.
Appointment for unknown heir, §28A-22-3.
Limitations on failure of issue, §41-4.
Renunciation of succession, right to renounce, §31B-1.
Sale, lease or mortgage of real property, §28A-17-12.
Service of process, §28A-13-3.
Unknown heirs.
Special proceedings prior to distribution, §28A-22-3.

DECEDENTS' ESTATES —Cont'd
Heirs —Cont'd
Waste.
Action by heirs, §1-537.
Wills.
See WILLS.
Homicide.
Killing decedent, §§31A-3 to 31A-15.
See SLAYER ACT.
Household effects.
Election of appropriate effects to be excluded from carry over basis, §28A-13-3, (a1).
Sales, §28A-16-3.
Husband and wife.
Spouse sole beneficiary.
Summary administration, §§28A-28-1 to 28A-28-7. See within this heading, "Summary administration."
Surviving spouses.
See SURVIVING SPOUSES.
Identity fraud.
Damages.
Recovery by estate, §1-539.2C, (b).
Illegitimate children, intestate succession.
Descent and distribution upon intestacy, §29-20.
Legitimated children.
Succession, by, through and from, §29-18.
Person's illegitimate child entitled to take by, through and from, §29-19, (b).
Succession by, through and from, §29-19, (a).
Surviving spouses.
Share of surviving spouse of illegitimate intestate, §29-21.
Shares of others than surviving spouse, §29-22.
Income.
Allocation of income.
Powers of personal representatives, §28A-13-3.
Inoperative trust.
Distribution of assets of, §28A-22-10.
Intestate succession.
General provisions, §§29-1 to 29-30.
See INTESTATE SUCCESSION.
Small estates, §§28A-25-1 to 28A-25-6.
See SMALL ESTATES.
Inventory.
Compelling inventory, §28A-20-2, (a).
Failure to file.
Liability for costs, §28A-20-2, (b).
Removal of representative, §28A-20-2, (a).
Required within three months, §28A-20-1.
Supplemental inventory.
Enforcement, §28A-20-3, (b).
Erroneous or misleading inventory, §28A-20-3, (a).
Investments.
Powers of personal representative or fiduciary, §28A-13-3, (a).
Joint tenants and tenants in common.
Descent and distribution of tenant's share, §41-2.
Jurisdiction.
Assistant clerk of superior court, §28A-2-2.
Clerk of superior court, §28A-2-1.
Jurisdiction where clerk interested, §28A-2-3.
Killing decedent, §§31A-3 to 31A-15.
See SLAYER ACT.
Kinship.
Degree computation, §§29-5, 104A-1.
Interpretation rule, §41-6.2.
Listing of personal property, §105-306.
Partnership rights, §59-55.
Renunciation of property interest, §31B-1.

DECEDENTS' ESTATES —Cont'd
Kinship —Cont'd
Wills, §41-6.1.
Probate of nuncupative, §31-18.3.
Workers' compensation, §97-10.1.
Order of compensation, §97-37.
Out-of-state accidents, §97-36.
Payments, §§97-38, 97-40.
Leases.
Abatement, §28A-15-5, (b).
Personal property.
Sale or lease, §§28A-16-1 to 28A-16-3.
Real property.
Personal representative leasing, §28A-17-11.
Void leases, §28A-17-12, (a).
Legitimation, effect, §49-11.
Mother married, legitimation when, §49-12.1.
Subsequent marriage, legitimation by, §49-12.
Letters testamentary.
Certified copy of record.
Admissibility as evidence, §8-36.
Libel and slander.
Rights of action not surviving defendant, §28A-18-1.
Liens.
Actions against personal representatives.
No lien created by suit, §28A-19-17.
Nonexoneration of encumbered property, §28A-15-3.
Payment of encumbered assets, §28A-15-4.
Limitation of actions.
Claims against the state.
Pleading statute of limitations, §28A-19-11.
Creditor of decedent against representative.
Seven-year limitation, §1-49.
Equitable distribution claim against surviving spouse, §50-20, (l).
Injury to incorporeal hereditament.
Six-year limitation, §1-50, (a).
Presentation of claims, §28A-19-3.
Limited liability companies.
Death of member, power of legal representative, §57C-5-05.
Loans.
Borrowing money.
Powers of personal representatives or fiduciaries, §28A-13-3, (a).
Marital or divisible property.
Action for distribution.
Claimant may file, §28A-19-19, (c).
Claims against estate, provisions inapplicable, §28A-19-19, (a).
Distribution, agreement by representative providing for, §28A-19-19, (b).
Medicaid.
Medicaid estate recovery plan, §108A-70.5.
Military affairs.
Absentees in military service, §§28B-1 to 28B-10.
See ABSENTEES IN MILITARY SERVICE.
Minors.
Distribution to parent or guardian of minor, §28A-22-7.
Missing persons, §§28C-1 to 28C-22.
See MISSING PERSONS.
Mortgages and deeds of trust.
Abatement, §28A-15-5, (b).
Debts and claims.
Limitations on presentation of claims.
Exception as to enforcement of mortgage, §28A-19-3, (g).

DECEDENTS' ESTATES —Cont'd
Mortgages and deeds of trust —Cont'd
Debts and claims —Cont'd
Mortgaging property for payment of debts, §28A-15-1, (c).
Defined, §28A-1-1, (4).
Encumbered assets.
Payment, §28A-15-4.
Nonexoneration of encumbered property, §28A-15-3.
Murder.
Killing decedent, §§31A-3 to 31A-15.
See SLAYER ACT.
Newly discovered property.
Reopening administration, §28A-23-5.
Oaths.
Collectors, §28A-11-2.
Parent and child.
Distribution to parent, §28A-22-7.
Parties.
Costs in administration of estates.
Liability for costs, §7A-307, (e).
Personal property.
Assets available for discharge of debts and claims, §28A-15-1.
Examination of persons or corporations believed to have possession, §28A-15-12, (a).
Nonexoneration of encumbered property, §28A-15-3.
Powers of personal representative, §28A-13-3.
Sale or lease.
Court ordered sale or lease, §28A-16-2.
Household furnishings, §28A-16-3.
Power of personal representative to sell or lease, §§28A-13-3, 28A-16-1, (a).
Special report not required, §28A-16-1, (b).
Title and right of possession, §28A-15-2, (a).
Personal representatives.
Defined, §28A-1-1, (5).
General provisions.
See EXECUTORS AND ADMINISTRATORS.
Persons interested in estate.
Relation to persons, §28A-13-2.
Phase II payments.
Tobacco growers and quota owner.
List of phase II distributees, §28A-21-3.1.
Property of distributees, §28A-15-9.1.
Powers of attorney.
Powers conferred by statutory short form, §32A-2.
Presumption of death, §28C-1.
Pretermitted children.
Shares, §28A-22-2.
Principal and income act.
Apportionment of receipts and disbursements when decedent dies, §37A-3-302, (a) to (c).
Determination of net income, §37A-2-201.
Distribution from estate during administration of trust, §37A-4-402.
Distribution of net income, §§37A-2-201, 37A-2-202.
General provisions, §§37A-1-101 to 37A-6-602.
See PRINCIPAL AND INCOME ACT.
Probate of wills, §§31-12 to 31-31.2.
See WILLS.
Public administrators, §§28A-12-1 to 28A-12-8.
See EXECUTORS AND ADMINISTRATORS.
Real property.
Abandoning or relinquishing rights in property.
Powers of personal representatives or fiduciaries, §28A-13-3, (a).

DECEDENTS' ESTATES —Cont'd
Real property —Cont'd
Assets available for discharge of debts and claims, §28A-15-1.
Examination of persons or corporations believed to have possession, §28A-15-12, (a).
Executors and administrators.
See EXECUTORS AND ADMINISTRATORS.
Nonexoneration of encumbered property, §28A-15-3.
Sale, lease or mortgage, §§28A-17-1 to 28A-17-13.
See EXECUTORS AND ADMINISTRATORS.
Summary administration.
Spouses as to real property.
Effect of clerks order, §28A-28-4, (b).
Title and possession, §28A-15-2, (b).
Record of administration.
Authenticated copy of record.
Admissibility as evidence, §8-36.
Reference of claim against deceased person.
Cost.
Recovery of fees and other necessary disbursements, §6-31.
Reopening administration, §28A-23-5.
Safe deposit boxes, §28A-15-3.
Clerk of court.
Presence not required, §28A-15-13, (c).
Presence required, §28A-15-13, (b).
Opening and inventorying, §28A-15-3.
Definitions, §28A-15-13, (a).
Release of contents by financial institution, §28A-15-13, (e).
Tax waiver, not required, §28A-15-13, (f).
Will or testamentary instrument in box, §28A-15-13, (d).
Secured transactions.
Financing statements.
Name of debtor and secured party, §25-9-503, (a).
Service of process.
Defined, §28A-1-1, (6).
Devisees and heirs made parties, §28A-13-3.
Distribution to nonresident trustees.
Appointment of process agent required, §28A-22-4.
Simultaneous death act, §§28A-24-1 to 28A-24-7.
See SIMULTANEOUS DEATH.
Slayer act, §31A-6.
Killing decedent generally, §§31A-3 to 31A-15.
See SLAYER ACT.
Small estates, §§28A-25-1 to 28A-25-6.
See SMALL ESTATES.
Stock and stockholders.
Powers of personal representative or fiduciary, §28A-13-3.
Selling or exercising stock subscription or conversion rights.
Powers of personal representatives or fiduciaries, §28A-13-3.
Summary administration, §§28A-28-1 to 28A-28-7.
Appointment of personal representative or collector.
Discharge of spouses liability, §28A-28-7, (b).
Clerks order, §§28A-28-3, 28A-28-4.
Spouses assumption of liabilities, §28A-28-6.
Order by clerk, §§28A-28-3, 28A-28-4.
Spouses assumption of liabilities, §28A-28-6.
Personal representative.
Discharge of spouses liability on appointment, §28A-28-7, (b).

DECEDENTS' ESTATES —Cont'd
Summary administration —Cont'd
Personal representative —Cont'd
Petition for appointment, §28A-28-7.
Petition by surviving spouse, §28A-28-1.
Contents, §28A-28-2, (a).
Filing, §28A-28-2, (b).
Signature, §28A-28-2, (a).
Real property.
Spouses as to real property.
Effect of clerks order, §28A-28-4, (b).
Spousal assumption of debt, §28A-28-6.
Transfer of property to surviving spouse.
Action to compel, §28A-28-5.
Effect, §28A-28-5.
Effect of clerks order, §28A-28-4, (a).
When authorized, §28A-28-1.
Superior courts.
Administration of decedents' estates.
Original jurisdiction in probate and administration of decedents' estates, §7A-241.
Transfer of civil causes, §7A-257.
Clerks, appeals of estate matters, §1-301.3.
Surviving spouses.
Elective share, §§30-3.1 to 30-3.6, 31-5.3.
Spouse as sole beneficiary.
Summary administration, §§28A-28-1 to 28A-28-7. See within this heading, "Summary administration."
Year's allowance, §§30-15 to 30-33.
See SURVIVING SPOUSES.
Taxation.
Carry over provisions.
Election of appropriate household effects, §28A-13-3, (a1).
Domicile of decedent.
Agreements with respect to, §105-240.1.
Estate taxes, §§105-32.1 to 105-32.8.
See ESTATE TAXES.
Excess funds, §28A-15-9.
Federal estate tax.
Apportionment, §§28A-27-1 to 28A-27-9.
Federal income tax refunds, §28A-15-6.
Separate returns, §28A-15-7.
Federal marital deduction.
Agreements with taxing authorities, §28A-22-6.
Generation-skipping transfers, §105-32.1.
Income tax.
Estates and trusts, §§105-160 to 105-160.8.
See INCOME TAX.
Joint returns.
Federal income tax refunds, §28A-15-6.
Powers of personal representatives or fiduciaries, §28A-13-3, (a).
Property taxes.
Preference accorded taxes in liquidation of debtors' estates, §105-365.
Separate returns.
Federal income tax refunds, §28A-15-7.
State income tax returns, §28A-15-8.
Title.
Personal property, §28A-15-2, (a).
Real property, §28A-15-2, (b).
Tobacco growers and quota owners.
Phase II payments.
List of distributees.
Definitions, §28A-21-3.1, (a).
Filing, conditions required, §28A-21-3.1, (b).
Information required, §28A-21-3.1, (c).
Payment to distributees, §28A-21-3.1, (e).

DECEDENTS' ESTATES —Cont'd
Tobacco growers and quota owners —Cont'd
Phase II payments —Cont'd
List of distributees —Cont'd
Reopening estate to file, §28A-21-3.1, (f).
Review by clerk, §28A-21-3.1, (d).
Payments while decedent alive.
Considered cash, §28A-21-3.1, (g).
Property of distributees, §28A-15-9.1.
Transfers to minors.
Authorized by will or trust, §33A-5.
Irrevocable transfer for benefit of minor.
Authority of personal representative or trustee to make as custodian, §33A-6, (a), (c).
Trusts and trustees.
Distribution to nonresident trustees.
Appointment of process agent required, §28A-22-4, (a).
Tentative trusts.
Sources of assets to satisfy claims against estate, §28A-15-10, (a).
Uniform simultaneous death act, §§28A-24-1 to 28A-24-7.
See SIMULTANEOUS DEATH.
Unknown heirs.
Special proceeding prior to distribution, §28A-22-3.
Wills.
General provisions, §§31-1 to 31-47.
See WILLS.
Witnesses.
Clerk of superior court.
Jurisdiction where clerk subscribing witness, §28A-2-3.
Wrongful death.
Application of recovery to payment of debts and claims, §28A-15-10, (c).
Killing decedent.
Acts barring property rights, §§31A-3 to 31A-15.
See SLAYER ACT.
Year's allowance, §§30-15 to 30-33.
See SURVIVING SPOUSES.

DECEPTIVE TRADE PRACTICES, §75-1.1.
Fruit handlers, §§106-496 to 106-501.
See FRUIT HANDLERS UNFAIR PRACTICES.
Insurance unfair trade practices, §§58-63-1 to 58-63-70.
See INSURANCE UNFAIR TRADE PRACTICES.
Monopolies and restraint of trade.
See MONOPOLIES AND RESTRAINT OF TRADE.
Motor vehicle rentals.
Advertising and sales practices, §66-206.
Notaries public, §10A-12, (g).
Price gouging during states of disaster.
Deceptive trade practice, §75-37.1, (a).
Determining whether price unreasonably excessive.
Considerations, §75-37.1, (a).
End of state of disaster, §75-37.1, (c).
Public policy, §75-37.
Statement that seller not in violation.
Issuance by attorney general, §75-37.1, (b).
Solicitation of contributions, §131F-21.
Vegetable handlers, §§106-496 to 106-501.
See VEGETABLE HANDLERS' UNFAIR PRACTICES.

DECLARATION OF INDEPENDENCE.
Basic education program, §115C-81, (g).

DECLARATION OF WAR.
Powers of congress, Const. U. S., art. I, §8.

DECLARATIONS.
Admissions.
See ADMISSIONS.
Confessions, §14-184.
Hearsay evidence.
See EVIDENCE.
Right to natural death.
Declaration of desire for natural death, §90-321.
Procedures in absence of declaration, §90-322.

DECLARATORY JUDGMENTS, §§1-253 to 1-267, 1A-1, Rule 57.
Administration of article.
Liberal administration, §1-264.
Administrative procedure.
Rulemaking procedure.
Temporary rules.
Rule returned to agency, §150B-21.1, (b2), (c1).
Affirmative or negative in form and effect, §1-253.
Appeals.
Review, §1-258.
Attorney general.
Party to proceedings involving constitutionality, §1-260.
Authorized, §1-253.
Automobile dealers associations, §20-308.1, (d).
Citation of act.
Short title, §1-267.
Construction and interpretation.
Liberal construction of provisions, §1-264.
"Person" defined, §1-265.
Uniformity of interpretation, §1-266.
Contracts.
Power of courts to construe, §1-254.
Costs, §1-263.
Deeds.
Power of courts to construe, §1-254.
Discretion of court, §1-257.
Effect, §1-253.
Establishment or disestablishment of statute, ordinance or regulation.
Superior court jurisdiction, §7A-245, (a).
Fiduciaries.
Who may apply for declaration, §1-255.
Forms.
Complaint for interpleader and declaratory relief, §1A-1, Rule 84.
Franchises.
Attorney general as party to proceedings involving constitutionality, §1-260.
Municipality as party to proceedings involving validity, §1-260.
Power of courts to construe, §1-254.
Guardian and ward.
Who may apply for declaration, §1-255.
Hearings.
Judge.
Hearing before judge where no issues of fact raised or jury trial waived, §1-262.
Heirs.
Who may apply for declaration, §1-255.
Hospital, medical and dental service corporations.
Protection or enforcement of rights of public, §58-65-132, (d).
Instruments.
Power of courts to construe, §1-254.

DECLARATORY JUDGMENTS —Cont'd
Jury.
Hearing before judge where no issues of fact raised or jury trial waived, §1-262.
Trial by jury, §1-261.
Waiver of jury trial.
Hearing before judge, §1-262.
Meetings violation.
Public bodies, §§143-318.16A to 143-318.16C.
Motor fuel marketing violations, §75-86.
Notice.
Hearing before judge, §1-262.
Ordinances.
Municipality as party to proceedings affecting validity, §1-260.
Power of courts to construe, §1-254.
Parties, §1-260.
Who may apply for declaration, §1-255.
Personal representatives.
Who may apply for declaration, §1-255.
Petitions.
Supplemental relief, §1-259.
Power of courts, §§1-253, 1-254.
Purpose of article, §1-264.
Refusal to render or enter.
Discretion of court, §1-257.
Removal of uncertainty by judgment or decree.
Enumeration of declarations not exclusive, §1-256.
Review, §1-258.
Rule adopted by administrative agency.
Emergency rules.
Standing to seek, §150B-21.1A, (c).
Temporary rules.
Standing to seek, §150B-21.1, (c).
Rulemaking procedure.
Temporary rules.
Rule returned to agency, §150B-21.1, (b2), (c1).
Scope.
Enumeration not exclusive, §1-256.
Power of courts to construe instruments, §1-254.
Who may apply for declaration, §1-255.
Statutes.
Attorney general as party to proceedings involving constitutionality, §1-260.
Power of courts to construe, §1-254.
Summary judgment, §1A-1, Rule 56.
Supplemental relief, §1-259.
Termination of controversy by judgment or decree.
Enumeration of declarations not exclusive, §1-256.
Title of act.
Short title, §1-267.
Trusts and trustees.
Modification and termination of irrevocable trusts.
Necessary parties to trust proceedings, §36A-125.11, (b).
Proceedings brought under act, §36A-125.11, (a).
Right of action for declaratory relief, §36A-23.1, (c).
Who may apply for declaration, §1-255.
Wills.
Power of courts to construe, §1-254.

DECLARATORY RULINGS.
Administrative procedure, §150B-4, (a).

DECODERS.
Cable television service theft, §14-118.5.

DECREES.
Divorce.
Alimony.
Enforcement, §50-16.7.

DECREES —Cont'd
Eastern band of the Cherokee Indians.
Full faith and credit for judgments, decrees, and orders of tribal court, §1E-1.
Emancipation of juveniles.
Final decree, §7B-3505.
Legal effect, §7B-3507.
Food, drugs and cosmetics.
Appeals.
Court of appeals.
Appeals of right from the courts of the trial divisions, §7A-27, (d).
Review on appeal from judgment, §1-278.
Supreme court review.
Discretionary review on certification, App. Proc. Rule 15, (h).
District courts.
Exercise of power to issue interlocutory orders, §7A-192.
Publication of reports of judgments, decrees and court orders, §106-142, (a).
Nonprofit corporations.
Judicial dissolution, §55A-14-33.
Real property.
Actions to quiet title, §41-10.
Title.
Actions to quiet title, §41-10.
Torrens system registration.
Effect, §43-12.
Entry of certificate of title and decree of registration construed as agreement running with land, §43-20.
Operation directly on land, §43-2.

DEDICATION.
Judicial sales.
Property subdivided for sale.
Dedicated to public, §1-339.9, (b).
State preserves, §§143-260.6 to 143-260.10F.
Streets and highways.
Abandonment of road or street for fifteen years, §136-96.
Partition, §46-17.1.
Special proceeding to declare right of way for public use, §136-96.1.

DEEDS.
Acknowledgments.
Certification of correctness.
Failure of register of deeds to certify.
Validation of registration, §47-50.1.
Defective acknowledgment on old deeds validated, §47-52.
Agents.
Execution of deed.
Dated before 1835.
Evidence of due execution, §8-13.
Torrens system registration.
Instruments describing party as agent not to operate as notice, §§43-63, 43-64.
Aliens.
Certified copies.
Registration allowed, §47-33.
Evidence.
Certified copies of deeds made by alien property custodians, §47-34.
Anson county.
Evidence.
Records of deeds in Anson, §8-26.
Assignment for benefit of creditors.
Generally, §§23-1 to 23-12.
See ASSIGNMENTS FOR BENEFIT OF CREDITORS.

DEEDS —Cont'd
Assignments.
Real property pledged as security, §47-17.2.
Attornment.
Unnecessary on conveyance of reversions, etc., §42-2.
Banks.
Attestation of conveyances by secretary of cashier, §47-42, (a).
Validation of deeds executed by nonresident bank, §47-108.16.
Validation of deeds executed prior to February 14, 1939, §47-42, (b).
Bargain and sale.
Possession transferred to use in certain conveyances, §41-7.
Business trusts.
Prior deeds validated, §39-47.
Cemeteries.
Validation of certain deeds for cemetery lots executed by suspended corporations, §65-73.
Charities.
Prior deeds validated, §39-27.
Clerks of court.
Probate and registration.
Where clerk appointed himself to sell, §47-65.
Contaminated site transferred.
Deed or other instrument of conveyance, contaminated property statement, §143B-279.10, (e).
Contingent limitations.
Failure of issue.
Limitations on failure, §41-4.
Contingent remainders.
Validation of transfer, §41-12.
Conveyances generally.
See CONVEYANCES.
Cooperative associations.
Prior deeds validated, §39-27.
Copies.
Certified copies.
Registration, §47-31, (a), (b).
Evidence.
Use as evidence, §47-31, (a), (b).
Coroners.
Official selling or empowered to sell not in office, §39-5.
Corporations.
Corporate seal.
Imprinting required, §47-41.1.
Forms of probate for deeds and other conveyances, §47-41.01.
Other forms of probate for corporate conveyances.
Generally, §47-41.02.
Probate and registration.
Error in acknowledgment of probate, §47-97.1.
Mistake as to officer's name, §47-97.
Probate of corporate deeds where corporation has ceased to exist, §47-16.
Covenants.
To stand seized to use.
Possession transferred to use in certain conveyances, §41-7.
Curative acts.
Before commissioners of deeds, §47-81.
Clerk's deeds where clerk appointed himself to sell, §47-65.
Corporate deeds.
Validation of certain deeds where admitted to record, §47-108.1.

DEEDS —Cont'd
Curative acts —Cont'd
Defective acknowledgment on old deeds, §47-52.
Guardians.
Deeds by guardians omitting seal, prior to January 1, 1944, validated, §35A-1360.
Nonresident banks.
Validation of certain deeds, §47-108.16.
Official capacity not designated, §47-108.17.
Death.
Contingent limitations on death of person without heirs.
Limitations on failure of issue, §41-4.
Declaratory judgments.
Power of court to construe declaratory judgment preceding, §1-254.
Defective acknowledgment on old deeds validated, §47-52.
Definitions.
Next of kin, §41-6.1.
Descriptions of land.
Vagueness not to invalidate, §39-2.
Drafters' errors in recorded deeds, §47-36.1.
Draftsman.
Registration.
Designation of draftsman on instrument required in certain counties, §47-17.1.
Drainage districts, §156-115.
Conveyance of land.
Warranty in deed runs to purchaser who pays assessment, §156-115.
Dry-cleaning solvent cleanup.
Notice of dry-cleaning solvent remediation.
Notice of restrictions in deed of sale, lease or conveyance, §143-215.104M, (d).
Easements.
Registration necessary for validity as against creditor, §47-27.
Errors in recorded deeds.
Correction, §47-36.1.
Evidence.
Anson county.
Records of deeds in Anson, §8-26.
Certified copies.
From other states, §8-32.
1835 or before.
Date on deed.
Execution of deed, §8-13.
Lost or destroyed deeds.
Presumed to be in due form, §8-21.
Registered instruments as evidence.
Certified copies of registered instruments, §8-18.
Lost or destroyed records.
Presumed to be in due form, §8-21.
Tax deeds.
Recitals in tax deeds in Haywood and Henderson counties, §8-22.
Richmond county, §8-22.1.
Tracts of land.
Common survey of contiguous tracts as evidence, §8-19.
Excise stamp tax on conveyances, §§105-228.28 to 105-228.37.
See EXCISE STAMP TAX ON CONVEYANCES.
Execution sales.
Real property sold, §1-339.68, (a).
Executors and administrators.
Contract for sale of real property by decedent.
Delivery of deed by personal representative, §28A-17-9.
Omitting seals, §47-51.

DEEDS —Cont'd
Failure of issue.
Limitations on failure, §41-4.
Forgery, §14-122.
Forms.
Register to fill in deeds on blank forms with lines, §47-35.
Fraternal orders.
Prior deeds validated, §39-27.
Fraudulent transfers, §§39-23.1 to 39-23.12.
See FRAUDULENT TRANSFERS.
Future interests.
Revocation of conveyances to persons not in esse, §39-6.
Validation of deeds, §39-6.1.
General assembly.
Giving effect to informal deeds.
Local, private and special legislation prohibited, Const. N. C., art. II, §24.
Gifts.
Registration required, §47-26.
Guardians.
Validation.
Deeds by guardians omitting seal, prior to January 1, 1944, §35A-1360.
Hearsay exception.
Records or documents or statements in documents affecting interest in property, §8C-1, Rule 803.
Heirs.
Construed to be "children" in certain limitations, §41-6.
Sale, lease or mortgage of real property, §28A-17-12.
Husband and wife.
Acknowledgments.
Absence of wife's acknowledgment not to affect deed as to husband, §39-9.
Different times and places, §39-8.
Conveyances under deed of separation, §39-13.4.
Fraud.
Certain conveyances not affected by fraud if acknowledgment or privy examination regular, §39-11.
Joint execution.
Married persons under 18 made competent as to certain transactions, §39-13.2, (a), (c).
Power to convey property without joinder, §39-7, (b).
Probates.
Different officers of deeds, §47-87.
Validation of deed executed by married women without private examination.
Deeds executed prior to Feb. 7, 1945, §39-13.1, (b).
Deeds executed since Nov. 7, 1944, §39-13.1, (a).
Validation of instruments not executed by husband, §39-7.1.
Informal deeds.
Giving effect to informal deeds.
Local, private and special legislation prohibited, Const. N. C., art. II, §24.
Judgments in which transfer of title declared regarded as deed of conveyance, §1-228.
Judicial sales.
Private sale of real property, §1-339.38, (a).
Public sale of real property, §1-339.29, (a), (b).
Lease and release.
Possession transferred to use in certain conveyances, §41-7.

DEEDS —Cont'd
Livery of seizin.
Probate and registration sufficient, §47-17.
Married women.
Private examination.
Repeal of laws requiring, §47-14.1.
Registration of instruments not executed by wife, §39-9.
Validation of deed executed by married women without private examination.
Deeds executed prior to Feb. 7, 1945, §39-13.1, (b).
Deeds executed since Nov. 7, 1944, §39-13.1, (a).
Validation of instruments not executed by husband, §39-7.1.
Mistake or error.
Correction of error in recorded instruments, §47-36.1.
Mortgages and deeds of trust.
Validation where no order or record of confirmation found, §45-21.42.
Municipal corporations.
Conveying property by, §160A-275.
Validation of certain deeds, §160A-18.
Next of kin.
Defined, §41-6.1.
Notary public.
Probate and registration.
Seal of notary not affixed.
Validation of deed, §47-103.
Notice.
Torrens system registration.
Instruments describing party as trustee or agent not to operate as notice, §§43-63, 43-64.
Partition sales.
Deed to purchaser, §46-30.
Effect of deed, §46-30.
Personal property.
Creation of interest or estate in, §39-6.2.
Presumptions and burden of proof.
Unborn infants.
When child presumed in esse, §41-5.
Probate and registration.
Before commissioners of deeds, §47-81.
Defective acknowledgment on old deeds validated, §47-52.
Easements.
Registration necessary for validity as against creditors, §47-27.
Gifts.
Deeds of gift.
Registration required, §47-26.
Livery of seizin.
Probate and registration sufficient without livery, §47-17.
Unregistered deeds prior to January, 1920.
Registration on affidavit, §47-19.
Public lands.
Execution, §146-75.
Failure to register.
Forfeiture of grants, §146-20.
Governor.
Signing of deeds, §146-75.
Swamplands.
Forfeiture for failure to register deeds, §146-20.
Public schools.
Custody of deeds to property, §115C-519.
Receivers.
Seals.
Omitting seals, §47-51.

DEEDS —Cont'd
Register of deeds, §§161-1 to 161-30.
See REGISTERS OF DEEDS.
Registration.
Judgment in which transfer of title declared, §1-228.
Certified registered copy evidence, §1-229.
Tax certification.
No delinquent taxes due.
Required to register, specified counties, §161-31.
Religious organizations.
Prior deeds validated, §39-27.
Remainders, reversions and executory interests.
Attornment unnecessary, §42-2.
Validation of sale or mortgage of contingent remainder, §41-12.
Scriveners' errors in recorded deeds, §47-36.1.
Seals and sealed instruments.
Guardians.
Deeds by guardians omitting seal, prior to January 1, 1944, validated, §35A-1360.
Official deeds omitting seals, §47-51.
Probates omitting official seals, §47-53.
Sheriffs.
Official selling or empowered to sell property not in office, §39-5.
Omitting seal, §47-51.
Simultaneous death.
Provision made for distribution of proceeds, §28A-24-5.
Stamp tax on conveyances, §§105-228.28 to 105-228.37.
See EXCISE STAMP TAX ON CONVEYANCES.
States.
Certified copies of deeds of other states, §8-32.
Statute of uses, §41-7.
Substitute for incompetent trustee appointed in special proceedings, §23-4.
Tax certification.
No delinquent taxes due.
Required to register, specified counties, §161-31.
Tax collectors.
Official selling or empowered to sell not in office, §39-5.
Tax deeds.
Hayward county, §8-22.
Henderson county, §8-22.
Richmond county, §8-22.1.
Trusts and trustees.
Charitable trusts.
Applicability of section, §36A-47.
Torrens system registration.
Instruments describing party as trustee not to operate as notice, §§43-63, 43-64.
Tryon's palace.
Execution of deeds, §121-14.
Unborn infants.
Taking by deed or writing, §41-5.
Unit ownership.
Conveying units, §47A-14.1, (a).
Validation of conveyances, §47A-14.1, (b).
Vagueness of description not to invalidate, §39-2.

DEEDS OF TRUST.
Assignments for benefit of creditors, §§23-1 to 23-12.
See ASSIGNMENTS FOR BENEFIT OF CREDITORS.

DEEDS OF TRUST —Cont'd
General provisions, §§45-4 to 45-80.
See MORTGAGES AND DEEDS OF TRUST.

DEEMER PROVISIONS.
Insurance policies or contracts.
Filing or contract deemed approved, §58-3-151.

DEER.
Black-tailed deer.
Unlawfully transporting or possessing, §113-294, (p).
Captivity licenses.
Issuance, §113-272.6, (d).
Regulations, §113-272.6, (a).
Violations, forfeitures, §113-272.6, (e).
Captivity permits.
Issuance, §113-272.6, (d).
Regulations, §113-272.6, (a).
Violations, forfeitures, §113-272.6, (e).
Dogs.
Injuring or killing deer on wildlife management area, killing, §67-14.1, (a).
Farmed deer.
Captivity licenses.
Issuance, §113-272.6, (d).
Regulations, §113-272.6, (a).
Violations, forfeitures, §113-272.6, (e).
Captivity permits.
Issuance, §113-272.6, (d).
Regulations, §113-272.6, (a).
Violations, forfeitures, §113-272.6, (e).
Possession and transportation of cervids.
Regulations, §113-272.6, (a).
Production and sale for commercial purposes, §§106-549.97, 106-549.98.
Regulation of farmed cervids, §106-549.97, (a).
Hunting.
Antlerless deer tags, §113-291.2, (e).
Dogs chasing deer.
Muzzle loading firearms season.
Dogs not used for hunting, §113-291.2, (a).
Regulation of use in hunting, limitation on regulations, §113-291.5, (a) to (b).
Muzzle loading firearms season.
Dogs not used for hunting, §113-291.2, (a).
Taking one antlerless deer, §113-291.2, (a).
Overpopulation of landowners land.
Survey to determine, special antlerless tags issued to owner, §113-291.2, (e).
Special antlerless deer tags, §113-291.2, (e).
Spotlighting.
Prima facie evidence, §113-302, (b).
Survey of deer population to determine overpopulation, §113-291.2, (e).
Sweeping area with lights at night, §113-291.1, (e1), (e2).
Unlawfully selling, possessing for sale or buying, §113-294, (b).
Unlawfully taking, possessing or transporting, §113-294, (d).
Night hunting with artificial lights, §113-294, (e).
Penalty, §113-294, (d).
Mule deer.
Unlawfully transporting or possessing, §113-294, (p).
Possession and transportation of cervids, §106-549.97, (b).
Captivity licenses.
Issuance, §113-272.6, (d).
Regulations, §113-272.6, (a).

DEER —Cont'd
Possession and transportation of cervids —Cont'd
Captivity licenses —Cont'd
Violations, forfeitures, §113-272.6, (e).
Captivity permits.
Issuance, §113-272.6, (d).
Regulations, §113-272.6, (a).
Violations, forfeitures, §113-272.6, (e).
Regulations, §113-272.6, (a).
Transportation permits.
Issuance, §113-272.6, (d).
Notice, compliance requirements, §113-272.6, (b).
Regulations, §113-272.6, (a).
Production and sale for commercial purposes, §§106-549.97, 106-549.98.
Defined terms, §106-549.97, (c).
Inspection fees, §106-549.98.
Possession and transportation of cervids, §106-549.97, (b).
Notice, compliance requirements, §113-272.6, (b).
Regulations, §113-272.6, (a).
Regulation of farmed cervids, §106-549.97, (a).
Regulations, §113-272.6, (c).
Transportation of cervids, §113-272.6.
Transportation permits.
Issuance, §113-272.6, (d).
Notice, compliance requirements, §113-272.6, (b).

DEFAMATION.
Allowance of costs, §§6-18, 6-19.
Answer alleging truth or mitigating circumstances, §1A-1, Rule 9, (i).
Banks.
Willfully and maliciously making derogatory reports, §53-128.
Congress.
Privilege of members of congress, Const. U. S., art. I, §6.
Decedents' estates.
Rights of action not surviving defendant, §28A-18-1.
Defenses.
Justification or truth as defense to libel, §15-168.
Elections.
False and derogatory reports as to candidates, §163-274.
Executors and administrators.
Actions in favor of decedent which do not survive, §28A-18-1.
Insurance.
Unfair trade practices, §58-63-15.
Insurance consumer and customer information privacy.
Immunity from suit.
Disclosure in accordance with article, §58-39-110.
Judicial standards commission proceedings.
Defamatory matter in proceedings, Jud. Stds. Comm. Rule 5.
Justification.
Defense to libel, §15-168.
Larceny, shoplifting, employee theft, embezzlement or false pretense.
Civil liability, demand letter for payment prior to action.
Qualified privilege of sender, §1-538.2, (c3).
Limitation of actions, §1-54.

DEFAMATION —Cont'd
Magazines.
Communicating libelous matter to magazines, §14-47.
Negligence.
Radio and television.
Negligence in permitting defamatory statements, §99-5.
Newspapers.
Anonymous publication, §99-3.
Communicating libelous matter to newspapers, §14-47.
Notice before action against newspaper, §99-1, (a).
Publication in good faith and retraction, §99-2, (a).
Notice.
Action against newspaper, §99-1, (a).
Action against radio or television station, §99-1, (b).
Periodicals.
Communicating libelous matter to periodicals, §14-47.
Pleading, §1A-1, Rule 9, (i).
Radio and television.
Anonymous communications, §99-3.
Broadcast in good faith and retraction, §99-2, (b).
Negligence in permitting defamatory statements, §99-5.
Notice before action against radio or television station, §99-1, (b).
Retraction.
Newspapers.
Publication in good faith and retraction, §99-2, (a).
Radio and television.
Broadcast in good faith and retraction, §99-2, (b).
Savings banks, §54C-64.
Truth as defense, §15-168.
Pleading affirmative defense, §1A-1, Rule 8, (c).

DEFAULTED STUDENT LOANS, EARNINGS WITHHOLDING, §§105B-1 to 105B-5.
Contested withholding, §105B-3, (e).
Definitions, §105B-1, (b).
Disposable earnings, §105B-3, (a).
Discharge from employment by payor, §105B-4, (b).
Election remedy in addition to and not substitution for other remedies, §105B-2.
Entering withholding order, §105B-3, (a).
Immunity of payor for withholding sum provided in notice or order, §105B-4, (c).
Inspection and copying of records by debtors, §105B-3, (c).
Motion for withholding order, §105B-3, (b).
Payor willfully refusing to comply with provisions, §105B-4, (a).
Purposes, §105B-1, (a).
Schedule for repayment.
Written agreement with state education assistance authority, §105B-3, (d).
Termination of withholding, §105B-5.
Transmittal of amount ordered to be withheld to clerk of superior court, §105B-3, (g).
Uncontested withholding, §105B-3, (f).
Verified motion for withholding order, §105B-3, (b).

DEFAULT JUDGMENTS, §1A-1, Rule 55, (b).
Adult publications.
Adjudication on potentially harmful materials, §19-16.

DEFAULT JUDGMENTS —Cont'd
Applicability of provisions of civil rule, §1A-1, Rule 55, (e).
Attorney disciplinary proceedings, Bar Rules & Regs., B, §.0114.
Bonds, surety.
Plaintiff, §1A-1, Rule 55, (c).
Civil no-contact orders.
Workplace violence prevention.
Failure of respondent to answer, §95-268, (c).
Clerks of superior courts authorized to enter, §§1-209, 7A-103.
Counterclaims.
Provisions of rule apply to parties pleading, §1A-1, Rule 55, (e).
Cross-claims.
Provisions of rule apply to party pleading, §1A-1, Rule 55, (e).
Demand for judgment, §1A-1, Rule 54, (c).
Divorce, §50-10, (e).
Entry of default, §1A-1, Rule 55, (a).
State of North Carolina or officers and officials.
No judgment by default entered against, §1A-1, Rule 55, (f).
Expedited evictions.
Failure to plead in accordance with time periods, §42-68.
Hearings or references as necessary and proper, §1A-1, Rule 55, (b2).
Interest.
Clerk to ascertain, §24-6.
Jury trial, §1A-1, Rule 55, (b2).
Minors.
Harmful materials, §19-16, (b).
Plaintiffs.
Provisions of rule applied to, §1A-1, Rule 55, (e).
Publication, service by.
Bond of plaintiff prior to entering, §1A-1, Rule 55, (c).
Quo warranto.
Judgment by default and inquiry on failure of defendant to give bond, §1-525.
Service by publication.
Bond of plaintiff prior to entering, §1A-1, Rule 55, (c).
Service of process.
Process or judgment by default not to be attacked on certain grounds, §1A-1, Rule 4, (j4).
Setting aside entry of default, §1A-1, Rule 55, (d).
Superior courts.
Authority of clerk to enter default judgment, §§1-209, 7A-103.
Third-party plaintiffs.
Provisions of rule applied to, §1A-1, Rule 55, (e).
Torrens system registration.
Prohibited, §43-11, (d).
Validation, §§1-217, 1-217.2.
Judgments by default to remove cloud from title to real estate, §1-217.2.
Workplace violence prevention.
Civil no-contact orders.
Failure of respondent to answer, §95-268, (c).

DEFAULT ON CRIMINAL FINES, §15A-1364.

DEFECTIVE IMPROVEMENT TO REAL PROPERTY.
Limitation of actions, §1-50, (a).

DEFENDANTS.
Arrest in civil cases.
See ARREST IN CIVIL CASES.

DEFENDANTS —Cont'd
Attendance.
Securing attendance of criminal defendants confined in institutions within state, §15A-711, (a) to (c).
Detainers, §15A-711, (d).
Civil procedure, §1-10.
Costs.
Allowance of costs, §6-19.
Discretion of court, §§6-20, 6-21.
Attorneys' fees.
Parties appealing or defending against agency decision, §6-19.1.
Bonds, surety.
Confession of judgment.
Bond given to secure fine and cost, §6-47.
Confession of judgment.
Bond given to secure fine and cost, §6-47.
Judgment confessed.
Bond given to secure fine and cost, §6-47.
Notice of no personal claim.
Payment of costs by defendant unreasonably defending after notice, §6-23.
Defined, §1-75.2.
Depositions.
Criminal actions, §8-74.
Discovery in criminal cases generally.
See CRIMINAL LAW AND PROCEDURE.
First appearance before district court judge.
See APPEARANCES.
Hearing impaired.
Interpreters, §8B-2.
Incapacity to proceed, §§15A-1001 to 15A-1009.
See CRIMINAL LAW AND PROCEDURE.
Interpreters.
Deaf or hearing impaired persons, §8B-2.
Joinder, §15A-926, (b).
Objections to joinder, §15A-927, (c).
Failure to prove grounds for joinder, §15A-927, (d).
Jurisdiction.
Defined, §1-75.2.
Jury challenges.
Civil cases having several defendants, §9-20.
Apportionment of challenges, §9-20.
Discretion of judge, §9-20.
Limitation of actions.
Out of state defendants.
When action begun or judgment enforced, §1-21.
Mentally ill.
Civil commitment of defendants found not guilty by reason of insanity, §15A-1321.
DNA sample required for certain crimes, §15A-266.4.
Incapacity of defendant to proceed, §§15A-1001 to 15A-1009.
See CRIMINAL LAW AND PROCEDURE.
Temporary restraint, §15A-1322.
Parties generally, §§1-57 to 1-72.
See PARTIES.
Physical restraint of defendant.
Maintenance of order in courtroom, §15A-1031.
Pleadings.
Each defendant to be charged with separate pleading, §15A-926, (b).
Pleas.
See PLEAS.
Prisons and prisoners.
Securing attendance of criminal defendants confined in institutions within state, §15A-711, (a) to (c).
Detainer, §15A-711, (d).

DEFENDANTS —Cont'd
Probable cause hearings.
See CRIMINAL LAW AND PROCEDURE.
Removal of disruptive defendant.
Maintenance of order in courtroom, §15A-1032.
Representation of self at trial, §15A-1242.
Standby counsel, §15A-1243.
Restraint of defendant.
Maintenance of order in courtroom, §15A-1031.
Securing attendance.
Defendants confined in federal prisons, §15A-771, (a).
Certificate by superior court, §15A-771, (b).
Defendants who are outside United States.
Application by governor to secretary of state of United States, §15A-772, (b).
Application to governor, §15A-772, (a).
Extradition.
Applicability of provisions to, §15A-772, (c).
Organizations, §15A-773, (a).
Appearance by counsel or agent, §15A-773, (b).
Defined, §15A-773, (c).
Small claim actions.
Answer of defendant, §7A-218.
Methods of subjecting persons of defendant to jurisdiction, §7A-217.
Temporary restraint.
Mentally ill defendants, §15A-1322.
Witnesses.
Criminal actions.
Defendant in criminal action competent but not compellable to testify, §8-54.

DEFENSE OF HOME OR RESIDENCE.
Use of deadly force against intruder.
Justification, §14-51.1, (a).
No duty to retreat, §14-51.1, (b).
Other defenses not repealed, expanded or limited, §14-51.1, (c).

DEFENSE OF PUBLIC SCHOOL EMPLOYEES, §§143-300.14 to 143-300.18.

DEFENSE OF STATE EMPLOYEES, §§143-300.2 to 143-300.18.
See PUBLIC OFFICERS AND EMPLOYEES.

DEFENSES.
Affirmative defenses, pleading, §1A-1, Rule 8, (c).
Affrays.
Plea of self-defense.
Evidence of former threats upon plea, §14-33.1.
Aircraft.
Operation while impaired.
Infliction of serious bodily injury.
Preclusion of defense, §63-28, (b).
Preclusion of defense, §63-27, (b).
Alcoholic beverages.
Minors.
Sales to.
Defense to violation of subsection, §18B-302, (d).
Assault and battery.
Plea of self-defense.
Evidence of former threats upon plea, §14-33.1.
Assaulting law enforcement or assistance animals, §14-163.1, (f).
Assignment of thing in action.
Action by assignee without prejudice to, §1-57.
Assumption of risk.
Controlled substances.
Employing or intentionally using minor to commit drug law violations, §90-95.5.

DEFENSES —Cont'd
Assumption of risk —Cont'd
Roller skaters and spectators, §§99E-13, 99E-14.
Bad checks.
Affirmative defense, §6-21.3, (c).
Bigamy.
Prosecutions for bigamy, §14-183.
Business necessity.
Fair housing violation, §41A-5, (a).
Charitable immunity.
Defense abolished, §1-539.9.
Checks.
Returned checks.
Affirmative defense, §6-21.3, (c).
Child prostitution.
Participating in prostitution of a minor.
Mistake of age not a defense, §14-190.19, (b).
Promoting prostitution of a minor.
Mistake of age not a defense, §14-190.18, (b).
Cigarettes and tobacco products.
Sale or distribution to minors.
Reliance upon proof of age, §14-313, (b).
Commodities trading.
Affirmative defenses, §78D-33.
Community colleges.
Tort actions against board of trustees, §115C-58.12, (c).
Consent to intercourse and sexual offense.
No defenses as to certain victims, §14-27.7, (a).
Consolidation of defenses in motion, §1A-1, Rule 12, (g).
Contributory negligence.
Bank deposits and collections.
Unauthorized signature or alteration, §25-4-406, (c), (d).
Burden of proof, §1-139.
Claims against state departments and agencies.
Doctrine a matter of defense, §143-299.1.
Controlled substances.
Employing or intentionally using minor to commit drug law violations.
Doctrine no defense to civil liability, §90-95.5.
Controlled substances.
Employing or intentionally using minor to commit drug law violations.
Assumption of risk, §90-95.5.
Contributory negligence, §90-95.5.
Mistake of age, §90-95.4, (c).
Participating in a drug violation by a minor.
Mistake of age not a defense, §90-95.7, (b).
Promoting drug sales by a minor.
Mistake of age, §90-95.6, (b).
Counties.
Public officers and employees.
Providing defenses for employees, §153A-97.
Criminal law and procedure.
Insanity defense.
Notice, §§15A-905, (c), (d), 15A-959, (a).
Intent to introduce expert testimony, §15A-959, (b).
Pretrial determination of insanity, §15A-959, (c).
Mistake of age.
Controlled substances.
Employing or intentionally using minor to commit drug law violations, §90-95.4, (c).
Participating in a drug violation by a minor, §90-95.7, (b).
Promoting drug sales by a minor, §90-95.6, (b).

DEFENSES —Cont'd
Disabled persons.
Protection act.
Employers.
Affirmative defenses, §168A-9.
Discovery.
Criminal law and procedure.
Notice to state of defenses and witnesses, §15A-905, (c), (d).
Drivers' licenses.
Failure to carry license, §20-35, (c).
Drugs.
Controlled substances.
Employing or intentionally using minor to commit drug law violations, §§90-95.4, (c), 90-95.5.
Participating in a drug violation by a minor.
Mistake of age not a defense, §90-95.7, (b).
Promoting drug sales by a minor.
Mistake of age, §90-95.6, (b).
Drunkenness.
Intoxicated and disruptive in public.
Alcoholism as defense, §14-445.
Electronic surveillance.
Actions for violation of article.
Good faith reliance, §15A-296, (b).
Expedited evictions.
Evidence of isolated or nonrecurring criminal activity.
Impermissible as defense, admissible as support of affirmative defenses, §42-67.
Fair housing.
Business necessity, §41A-5, (a).
Unlawful discriminatory housing practices.
Acting for another person no defense, §41A-5, (b).
Fire insurance.
Failure to render timely proof of loss, §58-44-50.
Flour, corn meal and grain.
Adulteration of grains.
Nonposting of sign not a defense, §106-626.
Foreign-money claims, §1C-1825, (b), (c).
Fraudulent transfers, §39-23.8.
Gaming.
Slot machines.
Possession of slot machine, §14-309.1, (a).
Return of slot machine to defendant, §14-309.1, (b).
Hazardous waste management.
Felonies, §130A-26.1, (e), (i).
Health care liability.
Actions for damages, §90-21.51, (c), (e).
How presented, §1A-1, Rule 12, (b).
Impaired driving.
Commercial vehicles.
Legal entitlement to use alcohol or drug, §20-138.2, (b).
Incest.
Child under age of sixteen, when other person at least four years older, §14-178, (c).
Insanity defense.
Notice, §15A-959, (a).
Discovery generally, §15A-905, (c), (d).
Intent to introduce expert testimony, §15A-959, (b).
Pretrial determination of insanity, §15A-959, (c).
Intercourse and sexual offenses with certain victims.
Consent no defense, §14-27.7, (a).
International commercial arbitration and conciliation.
Stating, requirements, §1-567.53, (a).
Amending or supplementing, §1-567.53, (b).

DEFENSES —Cont'd
International commercial arbitration and conciliation —Cont'd
Stating, requirements —Cont'd
More than two parties to arbitration, §1-567.53, (c).
Investment securities, §§25-8-202, 25-8-203.
Joint and several debtors.
Parties summoned after judgment, §1-114.
Judgments.
Foreign judgments.
Notice of defense.
Filing by judgment debtors, §1C-1705, (a).
Leases, UCC.
Unconscionability, §25-2A-108, (3).
Lemon law.
Affirmative defenses, §20-351.4.
Libel and slander.
Justification as defense to libel, §15-168.
Manufactured homes.
Conversion to another use.
Failure to give statutory notices, §42-14.3, (a).
Mental health, developmental disabilities and substance abuse.
Area authorities.
Defense of agents, employees and board members, §122C-153.
Minors.
Employing or intentionally using minor to commit drug law violations.
Assumption of risk, §90-95.5.
Contributory negligence, §90-95.5.
Mistake of age, §90-95.4, (c).
Intercourse and sexual offenses with certain victims.
Consent no defense, §14-27.7, (a).
Participating in a drug violation by a minor.
Mistake of age, §90-95.7, (b).
Promoting drug sales by a minor.
Mistake of age, §90-95.6, (b).
Prostitution.
Participating in prostitution of a minor.
Mistake of age not a defense, §14-190.19, (b).
Promoting prostitution of a minor.
Mistake of age not a defense, §14-190.18, (b).
Sexual exploitation of a minor.
Mistake of age not a defense, §§14-190.16, (c), 14-190.17, (c), 14-190.17A, (c).
Sexual offenses.
Intercourse and sexual offenses with certain victims.
Consent no defense, §14-27.7, (a).
Motions, defenses presented by, §1A-1, Rule 12, (b).
Motor vehicle equipment.
Window tinting, §20-127, (e).
Motor vehicle inspections.
Infractions, §20-183.8, (b).
Negotiable instruments.
Burden of establishing effectiveness of signature and holder in due course, §25-3-308.
Defenses generally, §25-3-305.
New motor vehicles warranties act.
Affirmative defenses, §20-351.4.
Obscenity.
Disseminating harmful material to minors, §14-190.15, (c).
Exhibiting harmful performances to minors, §14-190.15, (c).
Sexual exploitation of a minor.
Mistake of age not a defense, §§14-190.16, (c), 14-190.17, (c), 14-190.17A, (c).

DEFENSES —Cont'd
Oil pollution and hazardous substances control.
Offshore oil and gas activities.
Liability exceptions.
Exceptions constitute no defense, §143-215.94DD, (b).
Patient abuse and neglect, §14-32.2, (f).
Peddlers, itinerant merchants and specialty markets.
Misdemeanor violations, §66-257, (d).
Pleading, §1A-1, Rule 8, (b).
Affirmative defenses, §1A-1, Rule 8, (c).
How presented, §1A-1, Rule 12, (d).
Preliminary hearings, §1A-1, Rule 12, (d).
Products liability.
Breach of warranty, §99B-1.2.
Retail installment sales.
Preservation of consumers' claims and defenses, §25A-25, (a).
Compliance with federal trade commission requirements, §25A-25, (c).
Notice to be included in instrument, §25A-25, (b).
Roller skating rink safety and liability.
Assumption of risk of skaters and spectators, §§99E-13, 99E-14.
Seeds.
Use of disclaimers, nonwarranties and limited warranties, §106-277.11.
Sexual offenses.
Intercourse and sexual offenses with certain victims.
Consent no defense, §14-27.7, (a).
Minors.
Intercourse and sexual offenses with certain victims.
Consent no defense, §14-27.7, (a).
Spouse of person as victim.
Defense that victim is spouse of person committing act, §14-27.8.
Taking indecent liberties with a student.
Consent no defense, §14-202.4, (c).
Solid waste management.
Hazardous waste.
Felonies, §130A-26.1, (e), (i).
Spouse of person as victim.
Defense that victim is spouse of person committing act, §14-27.8.
Taking indecent liberties with a student.
Consent not a defense, §14-202.4, (c).
Ultra vires.
Business corporations, §55-3-04.
Nonprofit corporations, §55A-3-04.
Surety companies not to plead, §58-73-20.
Unclaimed property act.
Payment, satisfaction, discharge and want of consideration, §116B-58.
Underage drinking.
Sale to or purchase of alcoholic beverages by underage persons, §18B-302, (d).
Waiver or preservation of certain defenses, §1A-1, Rule 12, (h).
Warranties.
Products liability, §99B-1.2.
Water and air resources.
Criminal penalties.
Applicability of general defenses, affirmative defenses and other bars to prosecution, §143-215.6B, (e).

DEFENSES —Cont'd
Weapons.
Carrying concealed weapons, §14-269, (b1).
Window tinting of motor vehicles, §20-127, (e).

DEFERRED COMPENSATION PLANS.
Divorce.
Distribution of pension, retirement and deferred compensation benefits, §50-20.1.
Principal and income act.
Allocation of receipts normally apportioned during administration of trust, §37A-4-409.
Public employees, §143B-426.24.
Renunciation to succession, §31B-1.

DEFERRED INTEREST.
Home loan secured by first mortgages or first deeds of trust, §24-1.1A, (g).

DEFERRED PROSECUTION.
Community service restitution and volunteer program.
Boundaries of community service program districts, §143B-262.4, (e).
Coordinator to be secretary of department, §143B-262.4, (c).
Department of crime control and public safety may conduct, §143B-262.4, (a).
Fee paid for participating in program, §143B-262.4, (b).
Gross negligence or intentional wrongdoing.
Liability for injury or loss sustained by individual performing service, §143B-262.4, (d).
Significant violations reported by community service staff, §143B-262.4, (f).
Dismissal with leave pursuant to agreement, §15A-932.
Generally, §15A-1341, (a1), (a2).

DEFICIENCY JUDGMENTS, MORTGAGES AND DEEDS OF TRUST.
Abolished where more mortgage represents part of purchase price, §45-21.38.
Certain sections not applicable to tax suits, §45-21.37.
Tax foreclosures, §45-21.37.
Value of property.
Right of mortgagor to prove by way of defense, §45-21.36.

DEFINED TERMS
Abandoned.
Animals, §90-187.7, (c).
Child custody jurisdiction and enforcement, §50A-102.
Abandoned dry-cleaning facility site.
Dry-cleaning solvent cleanup act, §143-215.104B, (b).
Abandoned motor vehicle.
Defined, §20-137.7.
Removal and disposal, §153A-132, (b).
Street regulations, §160A-303.
Abandoned well.
Well construction, §87-85.
Abatement.
Asbestos hazard management, §130A-444.
Lead poisoning in children, §130A-131.7.
ABC commission.
Alcohol taxation, §105-113.68.
ABC law.
Alcoholic beverages, §18B-101.
Alcohol taxation, §105-113.68.

DEFINED TERMS —Cont'd
ABC permit.
Alcoholic beverages, §18B-101.
Alcohol taxation, §105-113.68.
ABC's program.
Education programs in residential schools, §143B-146.1, (b).
ABC system.
Alcoholic beverages, §18B-101.
Abode.
Tuition of active duty personnel in armed forces, §116-143.3, (a).
Abortion.
Parental or judicial consent to abortion, §90-21.6.
Absentee in military service.
Estates, §28B-1.
Absolute auction, §85B-1.
Abstract.
Elections, §163-182.
Property taxes, §105-273.
Abuse.
Adult care homes, §131D-2, (a).
Civil no-contact orders, §50C-1.
Patient abuse, §14-32.2, (e1).
Protection of disabled adults, §108A-101.
Abused juveniles.
Abused, neglected or dependent juveniles, §7B-101.
Academic year.
National Guard tuition assistance, §127A-192.
Academy.
Justice academy, §17D-1.
Academy property.
Justice academy, §17D-1.
Accept.
Educational personnel qualifications, §115C-350.
Letters of credit, §25-5-102, (b).
Private personnel services, §95-47.1.
Acceptance.
Commercial paper, §25-3-410.
Letters of credit, §25-5-102, (b).
Negotiable instruments, §25-3-409.
Accepted.
Limitation on fund-raising during legislative session, §163-278.13B, (a).
Acceptor.
Criminal law, §14-107.1.
Negotiable instruments, §25-3-103.
Accessing or causing to be accessed.
Computer related crime, §14-454, (c).
Accession.
Secured transactions, §25-9-102, (a).
Access or cause to be accessed.
Computer crimes, §14-453.
Government computers, §14-454.1, (d).
Accident.
Insurance, §58-3-30.
Medical service corporations, §58-65-80, (b).
Mines, §74-24.2.
Workers' compensation, §97-52.
Accidental injury.
Insurance, §58-3-30.
Medical service corporations, §58-65-80, (b).
Accidental means.
Insurance, §58-3-30.
Medical service corporations, §58-65-80, (b).
Accommodation bondsman.
Bail, §15A-531.
Bail bondsmen and runners, §58-71-1.
Account.
Banking, §25-4-104, (a).
Insurance guaranty association, §58-48-20.

DEFINED TERMS —Cont'd
Account —Cont'd
Secured transactions, §25-9-102, (a).
State-county criminal justice partnership, §143B-273.2.
Trust companies, §53-301, (a).
Accountant, §93-1.
Account debtor.
Secured transactions, §25-9-102, (a).
Accounting.
Incompetency, §35A-1202.
Secured transactions, §25-9-102, (a).
Accounting period.
Principal and income act, §37A-1-102.
Accounting system.
State auditor, §147-64.4.
State controller, §143B-426.35.
Account number.
Insurance information privacy, §56-39-76.
Accounts receivable.
Statewide accounts receivable program, §147-86.20.
Accredited college or university.
Speech and language pathologists and audiologists licensure, §90-293.
Accredited educational institution.
Pastoral counselors, §90-382.
Accredited school of veterinary medicine, §90-181.
Accredited sponsor.
Continuing legal education, rules governing administration, Bar Rules & Regs., D, §.1501.
Accredited state.
Producer-controlled property or casualty insurers, §58-3-165, (a).
Accumulated contributions.
Judicial retirement, §135-53.
Legislative retirement system, §120-4.8.
Retirement, §128-21.
State retirement system, §135-1.
Accused.
Crime victims' rights, §15A-830, (a).
Acknowledgment.
Impaired driving, §20-28.2, (a1).
Notaries, §10A-3.
Acquire.
Banking, §53-210.
Electric membership corporations, §117-7.
Regional reciprocal savings and loan acquisition act, §54B-48.2.
Acquired lands.
State lands, §146-64.
Acquiring persons statement.
Corporations, §75E-1.
Acquisition of a branch.
Interstate branch banking, §53-224.9.
Act as a fiduciary.
Trust companies, §53-301, (a).
Act as a mortgage broker.
Mortgage bankers and brokers, §53-243.01.
Act as a mortgage lender.
Mortgage bankers and brokers, §53-243.01.
Action.
Civil procedure, §1-2.
Foreign-money claims, §1C-1820.
Residential rental agreements, §42-40.
UCC, §25-1-201.
Active federal service.
Children of war veterans scholarships, §165-20.
Active ingredient.
Pesticide board, §143-460.

DEFINED TERMS —Cont'd
Actively engaged.
Athletic trainers, §90-530.
Active member.
Continuing legal education, rules governing administration, Bar Rules & Regs., D, §.1501.
Active punishment.
Structured sentencing, §15A-1340.11.
Actual address.
Address confidentiality program, §15C-2.
Actuarial certification.
Small employer group health coverage, §58-50-110.
Actuarial equivalent.
Judicial retirement, §135-53.
Legislative retirement system, §120-4.8.
Retirement, §128-21.
State retirement system, §135-1.
Acupuncture, §90-451.
Additional child fatality.
Child fatality prevention system, §7B-1401.
Address.
Address confidentiality program, §15C-2.
Address confidentiality program, §15C-2.
Addressing.
911 service, §62A-3.
Address of record.
Bail, §15A-531.
Adequate feed.
Protection of animals, §19A-23.
Adequate water.
Protection of animals, §19A-23.
Adjusted for inflation.
Tobacco reserve fund, §66-290.
Adjusted risk-based capital report.
Insurance companies, §58-12-2.
Adjuster.
Licensing, §58-33-10, (b).
Adjustment.
Weights and measures, §81A-9.
Administer.
Controlled substance, §90-87.
Pharmacy, §90-85.3, (a).
Administration.
National defense housing projects, §157-53.
Administration of criminal justice.
Background investigations, §114-19.1, (b).
Administrative area.
Community colleges, §115D-2.
Administrative charges.
Solid waste, §159I-3, (a).
Administrative committee.
Continuing legal education, Bar Rules & Regs., D, §.1501.
Administrative district.
Organization of schools, §115C-69.
Administrative law judge, §150B-2.
Administrator.
Adult care homes, §131D-2, (a).
Commodities act, §78D-1.
Drinking water, §130A-313.
Nursing homes, §131E-116.
Securities, §78A-2.
Administrator-in-training.
Assisted living administrators, §90-288.13.
Nursing home administrators, §90-276.
Admitted insurer.
Surplus lines, §58-21-10.
Admonition.
Discipline and disability rules of state bar, Bar Rules & Regs., B, §.0103.

DEFINED TERMS —Cont'd
Adopt.
Administrative procedure, §150B-2.
Adoptee, §48-1-101.
Adoption, §§48-1-101, 131D-10.2.
Workers' compensation, §97-2.
Adoption assistance state.
Interstate compact on adoption and medical assistance, §7B-3901.
Adoption facilitator, §48-1-101.
Adoptive home.
Child placing and care, §131D-10.2.
Adult.
Adoption, §48-1-101.
Custodial trusts, §33B-1.
Transfers to minors, §33A-1.
Adult bookstore, §14-202.10.
Adult care home, §131D-2, (a).
Bill of rights, §131D-20.
Certificates of need, §131E-176.
Facility licensure act, §131E-101.
Long-term care insurance, §58-55-35, (a).
Adult day care program.
Long-term care insurance, §58-55-35, (a).
Adulterated.
Meat inspection, §106-549.15.
Pesticide board, §143-460.
Poultry products inspection, §106-549.51.
Soil additives act, §106-50.30.
Adulterated grain, §106-621.
Adulteration.
Milk regulation, §106-268, (b).
Adult establishment, §14-202.10.
Adult live entertainment, §14-202.10.
Adult live entertainment business, §14-202.10.
Adult mini motion picture theater, §14-202.10.
Adult motion picture theater, §14-202.10.
Advance instruction.
Mental health treatment, §122C-72.
Power of attorney, §32A-16.
Advance instruction for mental health treatment.
Power of attorney, §32A-16.
Advancement.
Decedents' estates, §29-2.
Adverse action.
Credit scoring to rate motor vehicle and property insurance, §58-36-90, (a).
Nurse licensure compact, §90-171.82.
Adverse claim.
Investment securities, §25-8-102.
Adverse underwriting decision.
Insurance information and privacy protection act, §58-39-15.
Advertisement.
Antifreeze law, §106-579.3.
Campaign contributions and expenditures.
Disclosure requirements for media advertisements, §163-278.38Z.
Food, drugs and cosmetics, §106-121.
Funeral services, §90-210.20, (a).
Seed law, §106-277.2.
Advertising.
Viatical life insurance settlements, §58-58-205.
Advisers.
Letters of credit, §25-5-102, (a).
Advisory budget commission.
Executive budget act, §143-1.
Advisory committee.
Nursing home medication management advisory committee, §131E-128.1, (a).

DEFINED TERMS —Cont'd
Advisory organization.
Insurance rates, §58-40-5.
Aeronautical facilities, §63-79.
Aeronautics, §63-1.
Aeronautics instructor, §63-1.
Affected land.
Mining, §74-49.
Affiliate.
Banking, §53-104.1.
Brownfields property reuse act, §130A-310.31, (b).
Corporate franchise tax, §105-122, (b).
Dry-cleaning solvent cleanup act, §143-215.104B, (b).
Fraudulent transfers, §39-23.1.
Insurance guaranty association, §58-48-20.
Insurance holding companies, §58-19-5.
Insurance information and privacy protection act, §58-39-15.
Mining, §74-49.
Mortgages, high cost home loans, §24-1.1E, (a).
Motor fuel, §75-81.
Savings and loan associations, §54B-4.
Savings banks, §54C-4, (b).
Shareholder protection act, §55-9-01, (b).
Tax credit for qualified business investments, §105-163.010.
Telephone solicitations, §75-101.
Third party administrators, §58-56-2.
Tobacco reserve fund, §66-290.
Trust companies, §53-301, (a).
Trusts, §36A-60.
Underground storage tank cleanup, §143-215.94A.
Workers' compensation self-insurance.
Employer groups, §58-47-60.
Affiliated.
Insurance holding companies, §58-19-5.
Insurance information and privacy protection act, §58-39-15.
Affiliated group.
Corporate income tax.
Adjustment for expenses related to dividends, §105-130.6A, (a).
Franchise tax, §105-114.1, (a).
Affiliated provider.
Provider sponsored organizations, §131E-276.
Affiliate of a declarant.
Condominiums, §47C-1-103.
Affiliation period.
Health insurance portability and accountability.
Preexisting condition exclusions, §58-68-30, (g).
Affordable housing unit.
Housing trust, §122E-2.
African bee.
Bee and honey act, §106-635.
After-acquired property.
Probate and registration, §47-20.5.
After-acquired property clause.
Probate and registration, §47-20.5.
After-adopted.
Wills, §31-5.5, (c).
After-born.
Wills, §31-5.5, (c).
Aftercare.
Interstate compact on mental health, §122C-361.
Afternoon.
Banking, §25-4-104, (a).
Agencies of the United States.
Soil and water conservation districts, §139-3.
Agency.
Administration department, §143-336.
Administrative procedure, §150B-2.

DEFINED TERMS —Cont'd
Agency —Cont'd
Adoption, §48-1-101.
Archives and history, §121-2.
Coastal fisheries, §113-308.
Consultant service contracts, §143-64.20, (a).
Executive organization, §143B-3.
Fees and charges by state agencies, §12-3.1, (b).
Housing finance agency, §122A-3.
Housing trust, §122E-2.
Pollution control, §§159C-3, 159D-3.
Publications, §143-169.2, (b).
Public telecommunications, §143B-426.8.
Relocation assistance, §133-7.
Seaward boundary of coastal lands, §77-20, (c).
Solid waste, §159I-3, (a).
State government reorganization, §143A-3.
Surplus state property, §143-64.02.
Agency contract.
Athlete agents, §78C-86.
Agency identified adoption, §48-1-101.
Agency of North Carolina.
Address confidentiality program, §15C-2.
Agency of the state.
Service of process, §1A-1, Rule 4, (j).
Soil and water conservation districts, §139-3.
Agent.
Consent to health care of minor, §32A-29.
Controlled substances, §90-87.
Insurance information and privacy protection act, §58-39-15.
Licensing, §58-33-10, (a).
Mines, §74-24.2.
Nature of policies, §58-51-80, (d).
Privileged communications, rape crisis centers and domestic violence programs, §8-53.12.
Aggravated offense.
Sex offender and public protection registration, §14-208.6.
Aggregate withdrawal value of withdrawable accounts.
Savings and loan associations, §54B-4.
Aggrieved party.
Alcoholic beverages, §18B-120.
UCC, §25-1-201.
Aggrieved person.
Electronic surveillance, §15A-286.
Agreement.
Alcoholic beverages, §18B-1201.
City and town annexation agreements, §160A-58.22.
Electronic transactions, §66-312.
Farm machinery franchises, §66-180.
Job development investment grant program, §143B-437.51.
Membership camping, §66-232.
Sales, §25-2-106.
UCC, §25-1-201.
Uniform sales and use tax administration act, §105-164.42B.
Agreement for electronic presentment.
Banking, §25-4-110, (a).
Agreement materials.
Radiation protection, §104E-5.
Agreement state.
Radiation protection, §104E-5.
Agricultural commodities.
Double damage liability, §1-539.2B, (c).
Agricultural development, §106-581.1.
Agricultural employment.
Migrant housing, §95-223.

DEFINED TERMS —Cont'd
Agricultural land.
Taxation, §105-277.2.
Agricultural lien.
Secured transactions, §25-9-102, (a).
Agricultural loan, §122D-3.
Agricultural operation.
Nuisance liability of agriculture and forest operations, §106-701, (b).
Agricultural products.
Marketing associations, §54-130.
Agricultural seeds.
Seed law, §106-277.2.
Agriculture, §122D-3.
Development, §106-581.1.
Wage and hour act, §95-25.2.
AHERA.
Asbestos hazard management, §130A-444.
Air ambulance.
Certificate of need, §131E-176.
Air cleaning device.
Water and air resources, §143-213.
Air contaminant, §143-213.
Air contamination, §143-213.
Air contamination source, §143-213.
Air courier services.
Industrial development fund, §143B-437.01, (a1).
Tax incentives for new and expanding businesses, §105-129.2.
Aircraft.
Aeronautics, §63-1.
Global TransPark authority, §63A-2.
Littering, §14-399, (i).
Air instruction, §63-1.
Airline company.
Public service taxation, §105-333.
Airman, §63-1.
Air navigation, §63-1.
Air navigation facility, §63-1.
Air pollution, §143-213.
Air pollution control, §143-215.105.
Air pollution control facility, §159C-3.
North Carolina industrial and pollution control facilities financing act, §159D-3.
Airport, §§63-1, 63-65.
Airport hazard, §63-1.
Airport protection privileges, §63-1.
Air school, §63-1.
Alarm systems business, §74D-2.
Alcohol.
Motor vehicles, §20-4.01.
Alcohol concentration.
Motor vehicles, §20-4.01.
Alcoholic beverages, §18B-101.
Alcohol taxation, §105-113.68.
Open container law, §20-138.7, (f).
Alcoholism.
Public intoxication, §14-443.
ALE division.
Alcoholic beverages, §18B-101.
ALI.
E-911 system for wireless communications, §62A-21.
Alien company.
Insurance, §58-1-5.
Alien country.
Insurers supervision, §58-30-10.
Alien or foreign government.
Foreign insurers, §58-16-20, (a).
Alimony, §50-16.1A.

DEFINED TERMS —Cont'd
Allied mental health field.
Marriage and family therapists, §90-270.47.
Allocable share.
Tobacco reserve fund, §66-290.
Allocated interests.
Condominiums, §47C-1-103.
Planned community act, §47F-1-103.
Allowable expenses.
Victims compensation, §15B-2.
Alteration.
Negotiable instruments, §25-3-407.
Alternate standby guardian, §35A-1370.
Alternative fuel, §105-449.130.
Gasoline and oil inspection, §119-15.
Alternative fuel source.
Taxation, §105-151.6.
Alternative programs.
Nurse licensure compact, §90-171.82.
Amateur.
Boxing commission, §143-651.
Ambient temperature.
Protection of animals, §19A-23.
Ambulance.
Emergency medical services, §131E-155.
Motor vehicles, §20-4.01.
Ambulatory surgical facility, §131E-146.
Certificate of need, §131E-176.
Ambulatory surgical program, §131E-146.
Certificate of need, §131E-176.
Amenities.
Adult care homes, §131D-2, (a).
American vessel.
Unemployment insurance, §96-8.
Amount financed.
Installment sales, §25A-9.
Amount of the loan.
Banking, §53-165, (a).
Amusement device safety, §95-111.3, (a).
Amusement park.
Safety, §95-111.3, (b).
Ancillary state.
Insurers supervision, §58-30-10.
And official seal.
Corporate conveyance forms, §47-41.01, (d).
ANI.
E-911 system for wireless communications, §62A-21.
Animal clinic.
Veterinarians, §90-181.1, (b).
Animal control officer.
Rabies, §130A-134.
Animal dentistry, §90-181.
Animal feed.
Biological residues, §106-549.81.
Animal food manufacturer.
Meat inspection, §106-549.15.
Poultry products inspection, §106-549.51.
Animal health center.
Veterinarians, §90-181.1, (b).
Animal hospital, §90-181.1, (b).
Animal operation.
Animal waste management, §143-215.10B.
Animal produce.
Biological residues, §106-549.81.
Animals.
Biological residues, §106-549.81.
Biologics law, §106-708.
Conservation, §113-129.
Cruelty to animals, §14-360, (c).
Protection of animals, §§19A-1, 19A-23.

DEFINED TERMS —Cont'd
Animals —Cont'd
Structural pest control act, §106-65.24.
Veterinarians, §90-181.
Animal shelter.
Protection of animals, §19A-23.
Animal technician.
Veterinarians, §90-181.
Animal waste, §143-215.10B.
Animal waste management system operators, §90A-47.1.
Animal waste management system, §143-215.10B.
Annexation.
City and town agreements, §160A-58.22.
Announcer.
Boxing commission, §143-651.
Annual federal poverty guidelines.
Student loan collection, §105B-1.
Annual percentage rate.
Mortgages, high cost home loans, §24-1.1E, (a).
Annual statement filing.
Workers' compensation self-insurance.
Employer groups, §58-47-60.
Annuity.
Legislative retirement system, §120-4.8.
Retirement, §128-21.
State retirement system, §135-1.
Annuity issuer.
Structured settlement protection, §1-543.11.
Annuity reserve.
Legislative retirement system, §120-4.8.
Retirement, §128-21.
State retirement system, §135-1.
An offense involving assault.
Domestic violence in disposition report, §15A-1382.1, (c).
Anomalous endorsement.
Negotiable instruments, §25-3-205.
Antifreeze and summer coolant, §106-579.3.
Antimicrobial.
Pesticide board, §143-460.
Antique airplanes.
Property taxes, §105-277.12, (a).
Antique automobiles.
Property taxes, §105-330.9, (a).
Antique firearm, §14-409.11.
Sale of pistols and crossbows, §§14-402, (c), 14-409.11.
A period of war.
Employment preference for veterans, §128-15, (b).
Veteran's preference, §126-81.
Apiary.
Bee and honey act, §106-635.
Apparent owner.
Unclaimed property act, §116B-52.
Appeal.
Criminal procedure, §15A-101.
Appeals panel.
Mental health, developmental disability, substance abuse, §122C-151.4, (a).
Appellate division.
Discipline and disability rules of state bar, Bar Rules & Regs., B, §.0103.
Procedures for the authorized practice committee of the state bars, Bar Rules & Regs., D, §.0204.
Applicable state entity.
Drivers' licenses, lose control, lose license, §20-11, (n1).

DEFINED TERMS —Cont'd
Applicant.
Accredited sponsor.
Continuing legal education, Bar Rules & Regs., D, §.1902.
Auctions and auctioneers.
Criminal history record checks of applicants for license, §85B-3.2, (a).
Child support, §110-142.
CLE.
Specialization certification, Bar Rules & Regs., D, §.1902.
Clean water loans, §159G-3.
Client security fund of North Carolina state bar, rules governing, Bar Rules & Regs., D, §.1401.
Continuing legal education, Bar Rules & Regs., D, §.1902.
Fire departments, criminal history record checks, §114-19.12, (a).
Homeowner's recovery fund, §87-15.5.
Insurance information and privacy protection act, §58-39-15.
Letters of credit, §25-5-102, (a).
Locksmith licensing, §74F-18, (a).
Long-term care insurance, §58-55-20.
Manufactured homes.
Licensure of manufacturer, dealer, salesperson or set-up contractor, §143-143.10A, (a).
Medicare supplement insurance, §58-54-1.
Money transmitters, §53-208.2, (a).
Nurses, §90-171.48, (a).
Private personnel services, §95-47.1.
Professional employer organizations, §58-89A-5.
Public assistance program, §108A-24.
Refund anticipation loan act, §53-246.
Specialty field.
Continuing legal education, specialization certification, Bar Rules & Regs., D, §.1902.
Sponsor.
Continuing legal education, Bar Rules & Regs., D, §.1902.
Applicant for a certified applicator's identification card.
Structural pest control act, §106-65.24.
Applicant for a license.
Structural pest control act, §106-65.24.
Applicant for employment.
Employer and employee, §14-357.1.
Application.
Animal waste management system operators, §90A-47.1.
Savings and loan associations, §54B-4.
Application assistant.
Address confidentiality program, §15C-2.
Appointing authority.
Interpreters for hearing impaired, §8B-1.
Notice of public office appointments, §143-47.6.
Repayment of money owed to state, §143-555.
Apportionable income.
Corporate income tax, §105-130.4, (a).
Appraisal.
Property taxes, §105-273.
Real estate appraisers, §93E-1-4.
Relocation assistance, §133-7.
Appraisal assignment.
Real estate appraisers, §93E-1-4.
Appraisal foundation.
Real estate appraisals, §93E-1-4.
Appraisal report.
Real estate appraisers, §93E-1-4.

DEFINED TERMS —Cont'd
Appraised value.
Recreation and natural heritage, §113-77.6.
Apprentice, §94-6.
Cosmetic art, §88B-2.
Locksmiths, §74F-4.
Appropriate court.
Interstate agreement on detainers, §15A-762.
Appropriate evidence of appointment or incumbency.
Investment securities, §25-8-402, (c).
Approved activity.
Continuing legal education, rules governing administration, Bar Rules & Regs., D, §.1501.
Approved forest management plan.
Forest development act, §113A-178.
Approved laboratory.
Controlled substance examination regulation, §95-231.
Approved practices.
Forest development act, §113A-178.
Approved supervisor.
Substance abuse professional, §90-113.31.
Approving a site.
Counties.
Solid waste collection and disposal, §153A-136, (c).
Public enterprises, §160A-325, (a).
Aquaculture, §106-758.
Aquaculture facility, §106-758.
A qualified voter.
Soil and water conservation districts, §139-3.
Aquatic species.
Aquaculture development, §106-758.
Aquifer.
Well construction, §87-85.
Arbitral award.
Civil procedure, §1-567.32.
Arbitral tribunal.
Civil procedure, §1-567.32.
Arbitration.
Civil procedure, §1-567.32.
Arbitration agreement.
Civil procedure, §1-567.37.
Arbitration institution.
Family law arbitration, §50-45, (g).
Arbitration organization, §1-569.1.
Arbitrator, §1-569.1.
Archaeological investigation, §70-12.
Indian antiquities, §70-48.
Archaeological resource, §70-12.
Indian antiquities, §70-48.
Architect, §83A-1.
Area authority.
Mental health, §122C-3.
Mental health, developmental disabilities and substance abuse, §122C-80, (a).
Area board.
Mental health, §122C-3.
Area director.
Mental health, §122C-3.
Area facility.
Mental health, §122C-3.
Area of operation.
Urban redevelopment, §160A-503.
Area of the state.
Water and air resources, §143-212.
Areas developed for urban purposes.
City and town boundaries, §160A-48.
Areas of environmental concern.
Land policy act, §113A-152.

DEFINED TERMS —Cont'd
Armed forces.
Children of war veterans scholarships, §165-20.
Armed security guard, §74C-13.
Armed services.
Tuition of active duty personnel in armed forces, §116-143.3, (a).
Armory, §127A-161.
Armory car profession, §74C-3.
Armory site, §127A-161.
Arresting law enforcement agency.
Crime victims' rights, §15A-830, (a).
Arrest order.
Criminal process, §15A-305.
Arrest warrant.
Criminal process, §15A-304.
Arson.
Criminal law, §14-58.
Art dealer.
Sales, §25C-10.
Article.
Records, tapes and other recorded devices, §14-432.
State education assistance authority, §116-201.
Articles of dedication.
Nature preserves act, §113A-164.3.
Articles of incorporation.
Business corporations, §55-1-40.
Nonprofit corporations, §55A-1-40.
Articles of organization.
Limited liability companies, §57C-1-03.
Article 65 corporation.
Insurance company taxation, §105-228.3.
Artificial construction.
Floodplain regulations, §143-215.52, (a), (b).
Artist.
Minors, talent contracts, §48A-17.
Sales, §25C-10.
Artistic or creative services.
Minors, talent contracts, §48A-11.
Arts, §143-403.
Asbestos, §130A-444.
Asbestos containing material, §130A-444.
Asbestosis.
Workers' compensation, §97-62.
As-extracted collateral.
Secured transactions, §25-9-102, (a).
Assessment.
Property taxes, §105-273.
Assessment agreement.
Dry-cleaning solvent cleanup act, §143-215.104B, (b).
Assessment report.
License proposals, §120-149.2.
Asset-backed security.
Principal and income act, §37A-4-415, (a).
Assets, §58-13-15.
Fraudulent transfers, §39-23.1.
Assigned area.
Urban electrical service, §160A-331.
Assigned employee.
Interchange of governmental employees, §126-52.
Professional employer organizations, §58-89A-5.
Assigned supplier.
Urban electrical service, §160A-331.
Assignment.
Executive budget, §143-3.3, (a).
Assignment of leases, rents, issues or profits.
Probate and registration, §47-20.
Assistance animal.
Assaulting law enforcement or assistance animals, §14-163.1, (a).

DEFINED TERMS —Cont'd
Assisted living administrators, §90-288.13.
Assisted living residence.
Adult care homes, §131D-2, (a).
Adult care home's bill of rights, §131D-20.
Assisted living administrators, §90-288.13.
Associate.
Savings and loan associations, §54B-4.
Savings banks, §54C-4, (b).
Shareholder protection act, §55-9-01, (b).
Associate home inspector, §143-151.45.
Association.
Planned community act, §47F-1-103.
Savings and loan interstate branches, §54B-266.
Solicitation of contributions, §131F-2.
Association of unit owners, §47A-3.
Assorted chicks, §106-541.
Assuming insurer.
Reinsurance, §58-10-25, (a).
Assumption reinsurance agreement, §58-10-25, (a).
Athlete.
Athletic trainers, §90-523.
Athlete agent, §78C-86.
Athletic director.
Athlete agents, §78C-86.
Athletic trainer, §90-523.
Atomic energy.
Radiation protection, §104E-5.
Attack.
Local government during emergencies, §162B-7.
Attempted robbery.
Criminal law, §14-87.1.
Attempted telephone solicitation, §66-260.
Attending physician.
Advance instruction for mental health treatment, §122C-72.
Standby guardianship, §35A-1370.
Attending practitioner.
Adoption, §48-3-401.
Attending providers.
Drive-thru deliveries, §58-3-169, (a).
Attorney.
Client security fund, rules governing administration, Bar Rules & Regs., D, §.1401.
Procedures, Bar Rules & Regs., D, §.0101.
Reciprocal insurance, §58-15-5.
Attorney general.
Address confidentiality program, §15C-2.
Cooperative agreements.
Health care facilities, §131E-192.2.
Cooperative agreements among physicians or between physician, hospital or others, §90-21.25.
Electronic surveillance, §15A-286.
Medical assistance provider false claims act, §108A-70.11.
National crime prevention and privacy compact, §114-19.50.
RICO act, §75D-3.
Attorney of record.
Criminal procedure, §15A-101.
At will.
Leases, UCC, §25-2A-109, (1).
Auction, §85B-1.
Auctioneer, §85B-1.
Auction firm, §85B-1.
Audiologist.
Licensure, §90-293.
Audio-visual master.
Sales and use tax exemption, §105-164.13.

DEFINED TERMS —Cont'd
Audit.
State auditor, §147-64.4.
Audited financial report.
Workers' compensation self-insurance.
Employer groups, §58-47-75, (a).
Audited GAAP financial statement.
Professional employer organizations, §58-89A-5.
Aural transfer.
Electronic surveillance, §15A-286.
Authenticate.
Secured transactions, §25-9-102, (a).
Authentication.
Document authentication, §66-271.
Electronic medical records, §90-412, (b).
Authority.
Facility authorities, §160A-480.2.
Regional transit authority registration tax, §105-560.
Regional transit authority vehicle rental tax, §105-550.
Regional transportation authorities, §160A-631.
Small business contractor act, §143B-472.86.
Water and sewer, §162A-2.
Authority service area.
Public health authorities, §130A-45.01.
Authorization.
Computer crimes, §14-453.
Authorization to consent to health care for minor, §32A-29.
Authorized account.
Funds transfers, UCC, §25-4A-105, (a).
Authorized agent.
Weights and measures, §81A-9.
Authorized control event.
Risk based capital requirements, insurance companies, §58-12-21, (a).
Authorized control level risk-based capital.
Insurance companies, §58-12-2.
Authorized delegate.
Money transmitters, §53-208.2, (a).
Authorized investments.
State debt, §142-29.2.
Authorized lender.
Reverse mortgages, §53-257.
Authorized officer.
Public obligations, §159E-2.
Authorized representative.
Egg law, §106-245.14.
Meat inspection, §106-549.15.
Authorized shares.
Business corporations, §55-1-40.
Authorized trust institution.
Trust companies, §53-301, (a).
Authorizing agent.
Cremations, §90-210.41.
Autism.
Competency, §35A-1101.
Automated banking device.
Criminal law, §14-113.8.
Automated external defibrillator, §90-21.15, (b).
Automated transaction.
Electronic transactions, §66-312.
Automatic dialing and recorded message player.
Telephone solicitations, §75-101.
Automatic location identification.
E-911 system for wireless communications, §62A-21.
Automatic number identification.
E-911 system for wireless communications, §62A-21.

DEFINED TERMS —Cont'd
Automatic vending.
Aid to the blind, §111-49, (a).
Automobile graveyard.
Junkyard control, §136-143.
Average final compensation.
Judicial retirement, §135-53.
Retirement, §128-21.
State retirement system, §135-1.
Average weekly insured wage.
Unemployment insurance, §96-8.
Average weekly wages.
Workers' compensation, §97-2.
Axle group.
Motor vehicles, §20-118.
Bail agent, §15A-531.
Bail bond, §§15A-531, 58-71-1.
Bail bondsman, §58-71-1.
Bailee.
Oil and hazardous substance control, §143-215.77.
UCC, §25-7-102.
Bailment surcharge.
Alcoholic beverages, §18B-101.
Ballot.
Elections, §163-165.
Ballot item.
Elections, §163-165.
Ballot style.
Elections, §163-165.
Bank, §§32-2, 53-1.
Anatomical gifts, §130A-403.
Bank holding company act, §53-226.
Funds transfers, UCC, §25-4A-105, (a).
Good funds settlement act, §45A-3.
Interstate branch banking, §53-224.9.
Loans exempt from rate and fee limitations, §24-9, (a).
Reciprocal banking act, §53-210.
Secured transactions, §25-9-102, (a).
Trust companies, §53-301, (a).
UCC, §25-1-201.
Uniform fiduciaries act, §32-2, (a).
Bank acceptances, §53-56.
Bank holding company.
Bank holding company act, §53-226.
Corporate income tax.
Adjustment for expenses related to dividends, §105-130.6A, (a).
Interstate branch banking, §53-224.9.
Reciprocal banking act, §53-210.
Banking, §53-127, (a).
Banking business day.
Livestock prompt pay law, §106-418.3.
Banking day, §25-4-104, (a).
Banking entity, §53-127, (a).
Banking institution.
Rate of survivorship and joint deposits, §41-2.1, (e).
Banking office.
Reciprocal banking act, §53-210.
Bank of belowground crypts.
Cemeteries, §65-48.
Bank-offered spot rate.
Foreign-money claims, §1C-1820.
Bankrupt.
Limited liability companies, §57C-1-03.
Partnerships, §59-32.
Bankruptcy law specialty, Bar Rules & Regs., D, §.2202.
Bank supervisory agency.
Interstate branch banking, §53-224.9.
Trust companies, §53-301, (a).

DEFINED TERMS —Cont'd
Bar.
Procedures for ruling on questions of legal ethics, Bar Rules & Regs., D, §.0101.
Barrel.
Oil and hazardous substance control, §143-215.77.
Weights and measures, §81A-9.
Base flood.
Floodplain regulations, §143-215.52, (a).
Base floodplain.
Floodplain regulations, §143-215.52, (a).
Baseline reversion.
State employee incentive bonus program, §143-345.20.
Base period.
Unemployment insurance, §96-8.
Base premium rate.
Small employer group health coverage, §58-50-110.
Base rate of compensation.
Disability income plan, §135-101.
Base year exportation volume.
Tax credit for manufacturing cigarettes for exportation, §105-130.45, (a).
Base years.
Job development investment grant program, §143B-437.51.
Basic health care plan.
Small employer group health coverage, §58-50-110.
Basin.
Cooperative state-local coalition water quality protection plans, §143-214.14, (a).
Beach area.
Beach property insurance, §58-45-5.
Beach bingo games.
Lotteries and gaming, §14-309.6.
Beach nourishment.
Local government sales and use tax for beach nourishment, §105-527.
Bearer.
UCC, §25-1-201.
Bearer form.
Investment securities, §25-8-102.
Bed and breakfast inn.
Sanitation, §130A-247.
Bed capacity.
Certificate of need, §131E-176.
Bedding, §130A-261.
Bees, §106-635.
Bee yard.
Bee and honey act, §106-635.
Begin to construct.
Public utilities, §62-100.
Belowground crypts.
Cemeteries, §65-48.
Beneficial interest.
Asset-backed securities facilitation, §53-425.
RICO act, §75D-3.
Beneficial ownership.
Control share acquisitions, §55-9A-01, (b).
Beneficial shareholder.
Dissenters' rights, §55-13-01.
Beneficiary.
Community trust for persons with severe chronic disabilities, §36A-59.11.
Compensation of trustees and other fiduciaries, §32-53.
Custodial trusts, §33B-1.
Disability income plan, §135-101.
Funds transfers, UCC, §25-4A-103, (a).

DEFINED TERMS —Cont'd
Beneficiary —Cont'd
Judicial retirement, §135-53.
Letters of credit, §25-5-102, (a).
Local government law-enforcement retirement, §143-166.50, (a).
Modification and termination of irrevocable trusts, §36A-125.1.
Principal and income act, §37A-1-102.
Provider sponsored organizations, §131E-276.
Retirement, §128-21.
State law-enforcement retirement, §143-166.30, (a).
State retirement system, §135-1.
Trusts and trustees, §36A-22.1.
Beneficiary of the remainder interest.
Principal and income act, §37A-1-102.
Beneficiary's bank.
Funds transfers, UCC, §25-4A-103, (a).
Benefit booklet.
Readable insurance policies, §58-38-15.
Readable medical insurance, §58-66-15.
Benefit contract.
Fraternal benefit societies, §58-24-15, (a).
Benefit member.
Fraternal benefit societies, §58-24-15, (b).
Benefit plan.
Transfers to minors, §33A-1.
Benefits.
Direct access to obstetrician-gynecologist, §58-51-38, (a).
Disability income plan, §135-101.
Health benefit plan external review, §58-50-75, (c).
Unemployment insurance, §96-8.
Veterans, §34-2.
Best value.
Best value information technology procurements, §143-135.9.
Between merchants.
Sales, §25-2-104.
Bicycle, §136-71.7.
Child bicycle safety act, §20-171.8.
Motor vehicles, §20-171.1.
Bid.
Motion pictures, §75C-2.
Big game.
Conservation, §113-129.
Bikeway, §136-71.7.
Billing date.
Revolving credit charges, §24-11, (d).
Billing information.
Taxation, §132-1.1, (c).
Bill of lading.
UCC, §25-1-201.
Bingo game.
Lotteries and gaming, §14-309.6.
Biodiesel.
Gasoline tax, §105-449.60.
Biological agent.
Biological agents registry, §130A-479, (b).
Biological organism, §106-65.44.
Biological residue.
Animals, §106-549.81.
Biologics, §106-708.
Biomass equipment.
Tax credits for renewable energy equipment facility construction, §105-130.28, (b).
Bioprocessing.
Sales and use tax refunds, §105-164.14, (j).

DEFINED TERMS —Cont'd
Bioterrorism.
First responders vaccination program, §130A-485, (f).
Birds.
Conservation, §113-129.
Birth defect.
Monitoring program, §130A-131.16, (b).
Blanket accident and health insurance.
Nature of policies, §58-51-75.
Blanket encumbrance.
Membership camping, §66-232.
Blend.
Seed law, §106-277.2.
Blended fuel.
Gasoline tax, §105-449.60.
Blender.
Gasoline tax, §105-449.60.
Blighted area.
Urban redevelopment, §160A-503.
Blind bidding.
Motion pictures, §75C-2.
Blind person, §111-11.
Blind vendor.
Aid, §111-49, (b).
Blood.
Wholesale prescription drug distributors, §106-145.2.
Blood component.
Wholesale prescription drug distributors, §106-145.2.
Blue light.
Use of red or blue lights on vehicle, §20-130.1, (c).
Board.
Education, §115C-5, (a).
Interpreters and transliterators licensure act, §90D-3.
University of North Carolina, §116-2.
Board-approved school.
Massage and bodywork therapy, §90-622.
Boarding kennel.
Protection of animals, §19A-23.
Board of county commissioners.
County water and sewer districts, §162A-86, (a1).
Mental health, §122C-3.
Public hospitals, §131E-16.
Board of trade.
Commodities act, §78D-1.
Board of trustees.
Disability income plan, §135-101.
Judicial retirement, §135-53.
Regional natural gas districts, §160A-661, (b).
Regional public transportation, §160A-601.
Regional transit authority registration tax, §105-560.
Regional transportation authorities, §160A-631.
Saltwater fishing fund, §113-175.
Boat.
Coastal area management, §113A-103.
Boating and fishing access area.
Conservation, §113-129.
Body parts.
Cremation, §90-210.41.
Boiler.
Uniform act, §95-69.9, (b).
Boll weevil, §106-65.69.
Bolt.
Sale of pistols and crossbows, §14-402, (c).
Bona fide association.
Health insurance portability and accountability, §58-68-25, (a).

DEFINED TERMS —Cont'd
Bona fide loan discount points.
Mortgages, high cost home loans, §24-1.1E, (a).
Bona fide medical care provider.
Child care facilities, administration of medicine, §110-102.1A, (b).
Bona fide permanent employment.
Unemployment insurance, §96-8.
Bona fide title insurance agency, §58-27-5, (c).
Bona fide title insurance agent, §58-27-5, (c).
Bona fide title insurance company, §58-27-5, (c).
Bond documentation.
State debt, §142-29.2.
Bonded importer.
Gasoline tax, §105-449.66, (a).
Bonded indebtedness.
Capital facilities finance act, §142-82.
Bond rating.
Clean water loans, §159G-3.
Bond resolution.
State education assistance authority, §116-201.
Bonds.
Agricultural finance act, §122D-3.
City and town parking authorities, §160A-551.
Electric power, §159B-3.
Financing capital facilities, §116D-7.
Health facilities finance, §131A-3.
Higher education bonds, §116D-26, (f).
Housing authorities, §157-3.
Housing finance agency, §122A-3.
Pollution control, §§159C-3, 159D-3.
Private capital facilities finance act, §159D-37.
Public hospitals, §131E-16.
Solid waste, §159I-3, (a).
State debt, §142-29.2.
State education assistance authority, §116-201.
University of North Carolina, §116-41.1.
Urban redevelopment, §160A-503.
Bonds or notes.
Capital facilities finance act, §142-82.
Bone marrow transplantation services.
Certificate of need, §131E-176.
Books and records.
Workers' compensation.
Self-insurance.
Third-party administrators and service companies, §58-47-150.
Workers' compensation self-insurance.
Employer groups, §58-47-60.
Booth.
Cosmetic art, §88B-2.
Booth renter.
Cosmetic art, §88B-2.
Borrower.
Banking, §53-165, (b).
Good funds settlement act, §45A-3.
Reverse mortgages, §53-257.
Savings and loan associations, §54B-4.
Boxer, §143-651.
Boxing match, §143-651.
Brain death.
Natural death right, §90-323.
Branch.
Banking, §53-1.
Interstate branch banking, §53-224.9.
Savings and loan interstate branches, §54B-266.
Savings interstate branch banks, §54C-200.
Trust companies, §53-301, (a).
UCC, §25-1-201.
Branch manager.
Mortgage bankers and brokers, §53-243.01.

DEFINED TERMS —Cont'd
Branch office.
Mortgage bankers and brokers, §53-243.01.
Regional reciprocal savings and loan acquisition act, §54B-48.2.
Savings and loan associations, §54B-4.
Savings banks, §54C-4, (b).
Structural pest control act, §106-65.24.
Branch or district office.
Motor clubs and associations, §58-69-2.
Brand.
Livestock brands, §80-58.
Seed law, §106-277.2.
Brand family.
Tobacco escrow compliance, §66-292.
Brand name.
Commercial feed law, §106-284.33.
Commercial fertilizer, §106-657.
Brazilian bee.
Bee and honey act, §106-635.
Breach of the peace.
Public morals, §19-1.1.
Bribe.
Athletic contests, §§14-376, 14-380.3.
Bribery of officials, §14-217.
Broadcasting station.
Political campaigns, §163-278.6.
Broker.
Investment securities, §25-8-102.
Licensing, §58-33-10, (c).
Public utilities, §62-3.
Reinsurance intermediaries, §58-9-2, (a).
Transfers to minors, §33A-1.
Brokers-in-charge.
Real estate brokers and salespersons, §93A-2, (a1).
Brother.
Adoptee's new birth certificate, §48-9-107, (c).
Workers' compensation, §97-2.
Brownfields agreement, §130A-310.31, (b).
Brownfields property, §130A-310.31, (a).
Brownfields site, §130A-310.31, (b).
Brucellosis, §106-389.
Budget.
Local government finance, §159-7.
School budgets, §115C-423.
Budget ordinance.
Local government finance, §159-7.
Budget resolution.
School budgets, §115C-423.
Budget year.
Local government finance, §159-7.
School budgets, §115C-423.
Building, §47A-3.
Counties, §153A-350.
Criminal law, §§14-58.1, 14-159.11.
Criminal trespass, §14-132.
Building and loan association, §54B-4.
Building inspection official.
Volunteer architect during an emergency or disaster, §83A-13.1, (d).
Volunteer engineer during emergency or disaster, §89C-19.1, (d).
Building trades training.
Vocational and technical education, §115C-160.
Bulk.
Soil additives act, §106-50.30.
Bulk-end user.
Alternative fuel, §105-449.130.
Gasoline tax, §105-449.60.

DEFINED TERMS —Cont'd
Bulk fertilizer.
Commercial fertilizer, §106-657.
Bulk plant.
Gasoline tax, §105-449.60.
Bulk sale.
Weights and measures, §81A-9.
Bundled transactions.
Sales and use tax, §105-164.12B, (a).
Burden of establishing a fact.
UCC, §25-1-201.
Bureau.
Controlled substances, §90-87.
Veterans, §34-2.
Burglary.
Criminal law, §14-51.
Burial, §90-210.20, (c).
Burn intensive care services.
Certificate of need, §131E-176.
Bus company.
Public utilities, §62-3.
Bushel.
Conservation, §113-129.
Weights and measures, §81A-9.
Business.
Business discrimination, §75B-1.
Enterprise corporations, §53A-37.
Job development investment grant program, §143B-437.51.
Limited liability companies, §57C-1-03.
Partnerships, §§59-32, 59-102.
Relocation assistance, §133-7.
Sales and use tax, §105-164.3.
Tax credit for qualified business investments, §105-163.010.
Business agreement.
Tangible personal property, §105-304.
Business association.
Transportation board, §136-14, (h).
Unclaimed property act, §116B-52.
Business bankruptcy law, Bar Rules & Regs., D, §.2202.
Business combination.
Corporations, §75E-1.
Shareholder protection act, §55-9-01, (b).
Business day.
Invention development services, §66-209.
Legislative services commission enrolling clerk, §120-33, (d2).
Membership camping, §66-232.
Sales, §14-401.13.
State directory of new hires, §110-129.2, (j).
Business district.
Motor vehicles, §20-4.01.
Business entity.
Building codes, §143-143.4, (g).
Business corporations, §55-1-40.
Derivative transactions, insurance companies, §58-7-205, (a).
Insurance producers, §58-33-10.
Limited liability companies, §57C-1-03.
Partnerships, §59-102.
Conversion and merger, §59-73.1.
Political campaigns, §163-278.6.
Taxation, §105-277.2.
Business firm.
Engineering, §89C-3.
Business of viatical settlements.
Viatical life insurance settlements, §58-58-205.
Business opportunity.
Sales, §66-94.

DEFINED TERMS —Cont'd
Business or trade school.
National Guard tuition assistance, §127A-192.
Business paper.
Banking, §53-55.
Business premises.
Tangible personal property, §105-304.
Business property.
Business and energy tax credit, §105-129.15.
Business school.
Proprietary schools, §115D-87.
Business trust, §39-44.
Business with which associated.
Legislative ethics act, §120-85.
Bus line company.
Public service taxation, §105-333.
Butterfly ballot, §163-165.4B.
Buyer.
Manufactured housing, §143-143.9.
Pork promotion assessment, §106-792.
Sales, §25-2-103.
Seed law, §106-277.2.
Sublease of motor vehicle and loan assumption arranging, §20-106.2, (a).
Buyer in ordinary course of business.
Leases, UCC, §25-2A-103, (1).
UCC, §25-1-201.
Bylaws.
Nonprofit corporations, §55A-1-40.
By-product material.
Radiation protection, §104E-5.
Calendar quarter.
Unemployment insurance, §96-8.
Call-by-call basis.
Sales and use tax on telecommunications, §105-164.4C, (h).
Call center.
Sales and use tax on telecommunications, §105-164.4C, (h).
Camp Butner reservation.
Mental health, §122C-3.
Campgrounds.
Membership camping, §66-232.
Camping site.
Membership camping, §66-232.
Campus.
Certificate of need, §131E-176.
University of North Carolina, §116-44.3.
Cancellation.
Leases, UCC, §25-2A-103, (1).
Sales, §25-2-106.
Cancelled.
Motor vehicles, §20-4.01.
Candidate.
Campaign contributions and expenditures.
Disclosure requirements for media advertisements, §163-278.38Z.
Political campaigns, §163-278.6.
Public campaign financing fund, §163-278.62.
Candidate campaign committee.
Campaign contributions and expenditures.
Disclosure requirements for media advertisements, §163-278.38Z.
Candling and grading.
Egg law, §106-245.14.
Candy.
Sales and use tax, §105-164.3.
Canned pet food.
Commercial feed law, §106-284.33.
Canvass.
Elections, §163-182.5, (a).

DEFINED TERMS —Cont'd
Capable of use as human food.
Meat inspection, §106-549.15.
Poultry products inspection, §106-549.51.
Capital.
Banking, §53-62, (a).
Surplus lines, §58-21-10.
Capital costs.
Project development financing debt instruments, §159-103, (a).
Capital expenditure.
Certificate of need, §131E-176.
Capital expenditure project.
Certificate of need, §131E-176.
Capital facility.
Capital facilities finance act, §142-82.
Higher education bonds, §116D-1.
Capital improvement, §143-34.40.
Capital interest.
Franchise tax, §105-114.1, (a).
Capital project.
Local government finance, §159-13.2.
Capital stock.
Savings and loan associations, §54B-4.
Savings banks, §54C-4, (b).
Capitation arrangement.
Purchases and contracts through department of administration.
Medicaid program exemption, §143-48.1, (b).
Captive insurer.
Producer-controlled property or casualty insurers, §58-3-165, (a).
Card holder.
Criminal law, §14-113.8.
Cardiac angioplasty equipment.
Certificate of need, §131E-176.
Cardiac catheterization equipment.
Certificate of need, §131E-176.
Cardiac rehabilitation program, §131E-166.
Care.
Costs paid by persons admitted to institutions of department of health and human services, §143-117.1.
Career development; introductory.
Vocational and technical education, §115C-152.
Career employee.
Educational personnel, §115C-325, (a).
Career growth recognition award.
Personnel system.
Comprehensive compensation system, §126-7, (a2).
Career school administrator, §115C-325, (a).
Career state employee.
State personnel system, §126-1.1.
Career teacher.
Education personnel, §115C-325, (a).
Care for a term of years.
Health facilities finance, §131A-3.
Care for life.
Health facilities finance, §131A-3.
Caretaker.
Abused, neglected and dependent juveniles, §7B-101.
Abuse, neglect or exploitation of disabled or elder adults.
Criminal offense, §14-32.3, (d).
Protection of disabled adults, §108A-101.
Carnival area.
Safety, §95-111.3, (b1).
Carrier.
Health maintenance organizations, §58-67-5, (n).
Oil and hazardous substance control, §143-215.77.

DEFINED TERMS —Cont'd
Carrier —Cont'd
Small employer group health coverage, §58-50-110.
Carry a concealed handgun.
Concealed handgun permits, §14-415.10.
Case characteristics.
Small employer group health coverage, §58-50-110.
Case manager.
Educational personnel, §115C-325, (a).
Cash.
Banking, §53-51, (b).
Money transmitters, §53-208.2, (a).
Cash advance.
Banking, §53-165, (c).
Cash buyer.
Grain dealers, §106-601.
Cash dividend.
Life insurance solicitation, §58-60-10.
Cashier's check.
Good funds settlement act, §45A-3.
Cashing.
Check-cashing businesses, §53-275.
Cash price.
Installment sales, §25A-7.
Cash proceeds.
Secured transactions, §25-9-102, (a).
Casket.
Cremation, §90-210.41.
Casual sale of property.
Corporate income tax, §105-130.4, (a).
Cat, §130A-134.
Catastrophic conditions.
Civil actions, §7A-39, (c).
Catchment area.
Mental health, §122C-3.
Cave.
Criminal law and procedure, §14-159.20.
C corporation.
Taxation, §§105-130.2, 105-131.
Cede.
Vehicle reinsurance, §58-37-1.
Cemetery, §65-48.
Cemetery broker, §65-48.
Cemetery company, §65-48.
Cemetery management organization, §65-48.
Cemetery sales organization, §65-48.
Censure.
Discipline and disability rules of state bar, Bar Rules & Regs., B, §.0103.
Centennial campus, §116-198.33.
Center.
Privileged communications, rape crisis centers and domestic violence programs, §8-53.12.
Central administrative office.
Industrial development fund, §143B-437.01, (a1).
Central office or aircraft facility.
Tax incentives for new and expanding businesses, §105-129.2.
CERCLA/SARA.
Solid waste management, §§130A-290, (a), 130A-310.
Superfund program, §130A-310.20.
Cerebral palsy.
Competency, §35A-1101.
Certificate.
Boll weevil eradication, §106-65.69.
Drivers' licenses, lose control, lose license, §20-11, (n1).
Fraternal benefit societies, §58-24-15, (c).

DEFINED TERMS —Cont'd
Certificate —Cont'd
Long-term care insurance, §58-55-20.
Medicare supplement insurance, §58-54-1.
Public utilities, §62-3.
Certificated registered public obligation, §159E-2.
Certificated security.
Investment securities, §25-8-102.
Certificate holder.
Hospital, medical and dental service corporations.
Conversion, §58-65-131, (b).
Certificate of approval.
Savings and loan associations, §54B-4.
Certificate of conviction.
Discipline and disability rules of state bar, Bar Rules & Regs., B, §.0103.
Certificate of cremation, §90-210.41.
Certificate of deposit.
Negotiable instruments, §25-3-104.
Certificate of election.
Elections, §163-182.
Certificate of incorporation or charter.
Savings and loan associations, §54B-4.
Savings banks, §54C-4, (b).
Certificate of limited partnership, §59-102.
Certificate of need, §131E-176.
Certificate of registration.
Sanitarians, §90A-51.
Certificate of title.
Secured transactions, §25-9-102, (a).
Certificates of participation.
Capital facilities finance act, §142-82.
Energy conservation finance act, §142-61.
Lease or purchase of prison facilities constructed by private firm, §148-37.2, (b).
Certificates of participation indebtedness.
Capital facilities finance act, §142-82.
Certification.
Cardiac rehabilitation program, §131E-166.
Certification authority.
Electronic commerce in government, §66-58.2.
Certification of crop seeds.
Crop seed improvement board, §106-274.
Certified applicator.
Structural pest control act, §106-65.24.
Certified audit.
Workers' compensation self insurance, §97-165.
Certified automated system.
Uniform sales and use tax administration act, §105-164.42B.
Certified candidate.
Public campaign financing fund, §163-278.62.
Certified check.
Good funds settlement act, §45A-3.
Negotiable instruments, §25-3-409.
Certified clinical addictions specialist, §90-113.31.
Certified clinical supervisor, §90-113.31.
Certified copy.
Savings and loan associations, §54B-4.
Certified disaster service volunteer, §166A-31.
Certified employee assistance professionals, §90-500.
Certified historic structure.
Historic rehabilitation tax credit, §105-129.35, (c).
Certified industrial hygienist, §90-515.
Certified laboratory.
Drinking water, §130A-313.
Certified list.
Child support, §110-142.

DEFINED TERMS —Cont'd
Certified mail.
Public utilities, §62-3.
Certified master social worker, §90B-3.
Certified prescribed burner.
Prescribed burning of forestlands, §113-60.41.
Certified public accountant, §93-1.
Workers' compensation self insurance, §97-165.
Certified rabies vaccinator, §130A-134.
Certified rehabilitation.
Historic rehabilitation tax credit, §105-129.36, (b).
Certified residential facility director, §90-113.31.
Certified seeds.
Seed law, §106-277.2.
Certified service provider.
Uniform sales and use tax administration act, §105-164.42B.
Certified social worker, §90B-3.
Certified social work manager, §90B-3.
Certified substance abuse counselor, §90-113.31.
Certified substance abuse prevention consultant, §90-113.31.
Certified therapeutic recreation assistant, §90C-4, (b).
Certified therapeutic recreation specialist, §90C-4, (c).
Certified vegetable plants for transplanting.
Vegetable plant law, §106-284.16.
Cervid or cervidae.
Conservation, §113-129.
Deer, production and sale for commercial purposes, §106-549.97, (c).
Cession.
Vehicle reinsurance, §58-37-1.
CFTC rule.
Commodities act, §78D-1.
Chairlift.
Passenger tramway safety, §95-117.
Chairman.
Local government finance, §159-1.
Chairman of the board of county commissioners.
Civil disorders, §14-288.1.
Chairperson of the grievance committee.
Discipline and disability rules of state bar, Bar Rules & Regs., B, §.0103.
Chancellor.
University of North Carolina, §116-2.
Change in bed capacity.
Certificate of need, §131E-176.
Chapter 119 of the United States code.
Electronic surveillance, §15A-286.
Charge.
Liability of landowners associated with watershed improvement projects, §139-41.3.
Recreational trespass, §38A-2.
Exclusions from definition, §38A-3.
Charged.
Implied consent to chemical analysis, §20-16.2, (a1).
Charging officer.
Implied consent to chemical analysis, §20-16.2, (a1).
Motor vehicles, §20-16.5, (a).
Charitable.
Solicitation of contributions, §131F-2.
Trusts, §36A-53.
Charitable organization.
Civil procedure, §1-539.11.
Solicitation of contributions, §131F-2.

DEFINED TERMS —Cont'd
Charitable or religious corporations.
Nonprofit corporations, §55A-1-40.
Charitable purpose.
Property tax exemption, §§105-278.6, (b), 105-278.7, (f).
Solicitation, §14-401.12.
Taxation, §105-278.3.
Charitable remainder annuity trust, §36A-59.3.
Charitable remainder trust, §36A-59.3.
Charitable remainder unitrust, §36A-59.3.
Charitable sales promotion.
Solicitation of contributions, §131F-2.
Charter.
Cities and towns, §160A-1.
Marketing associations, §54-130.
Regional sports authorities, §160A-479.
Trust companies, §53-301, (a).
Charter operations.
Public utilities, §62-3.
Charter party.
Public utilities, §62-260.
Charter school.
Taxation, §105-228.90, (b).
Chattel paper.
Secured transactions, §25-9-102, (a).
Check.
Negotiable instruments, §§25-3-104, 25-3-312.
Check-cashing service, §53-275.
Check passer.
Bad checks, §14-107.2, (a).
Criminal law, §14-107.1.
Check taker, §14-107.2, (a).
Criminal law, §14-107.1.
Chemical analysis.
Motor vehicles, §20-4.01.
Chemical analyst.
Motor vehicles, §20-4.01.
Chemical dependency.
Accident and health insurance, §58-51-50, (a).
Health maintenance organizations, §58-67-70, (a).
Hospital, medical and dental service corporations, §58-65-75, (a).
State medical plan, §135-40.1.
Chemical dependency treatment beds.
Certificate of need, §131E-176.
Chemical dependency treatment facility.
Certificate of need, §131E-176.
Chemical manufacturer.
Toxic or hazardous substance identification, §95-174, (a).
Chemical name.
Toxic or hazardous substance identification, §95-174, (b).
Chemical or portable toilet.
Solid waste management, §130A-290, (a).
Chick dealer, §106-541.
Chief archaeologist.
Burial sites, §70-28.
Chief court counselor.
Delinquent and undisciplined juveniles, §7B-1501.
Department of juvenile justice and delinquency prevention, §143B-515.
Chief district court judge, §7A-200, (a).
Chief executive officer.
Annuities, §147-9.2.
Insurers supervision, §58-30-12.
Child.
Adoption, §48-1-101.
Child custody jurisdiction and enforcement, §50A-102.

DEFINED TERMS —Cont'd
Child —Cont'd
Child placing and care, §131D-10.2.
Children of war veterans scholarships, §165-20.
Support of illegitimate children, §49-2.
Workers' compensation, §97-2.
Child care, §110-86.
Mandatory child care provider criminal history checks, §110-90.2, (a).
Child care administrator, §110-86.
Child care center, §110-86.
Child care facility, §110-86.
Child care provider.
Mandatory criminal history checks, §110-90.2, (a).
Child care subsidy.
Fraudulent misrepresentation, §110-107, (c).
Child-custody determination.
Child custody jurisdiction and enforcement, §50A-102.
Child-custody proceeding.
Child custody jurisdiction and enforcement, §50A-102.
Child fatality.
Disclosure of records in child fatality or near fatality cases, §7B-2902, (a).
Child interstate family support, §52C-1-101.
Child-occupied facility.
Lead poisoning in children, §130A-131.7.
Child placing agency, §131D-10.2.
Children's camp.
Child placing and care, §131D-10.2.
Children with special needs.
Special education, §115C-109.
Child support case, §50-31.
Child support hearing officer, §50-31.
Child support obligation.
Unemployment insurance, §96-17, (d).
Child support order.
Interstate family support, §52C-1-101.
Child support payment.
Vesting of past due support, §50-13.10, (c).
Chiropractic, §90-143, (a).
Chlorofluorocarbon refrigerant.
Solid waste management, §130A-290.
Chore.
Long-term care insurance, §58-55-35, (a).
Chronically ill.
Viatical life insurance settlements, §58-58-205.
Chunking.
Motor vehicles, §20-122.1.
Church plan.
Health insurance portability and accountability.
Guaranteed availability of individual coverage to certain individuals with prior group coverage, §58-68-60, (h).
Cigar.
Taxation, §105-113.4.
Cigarette.
Taxation, §105-113.4.
Tobacco reserve fund, §66-290.
Citation.
Criminal process, §15A-302.
Motor vehicles, §20-4.18.
Citizens band radio equipment, §62-328.
City, §160A-1.
Annexation of noncontiguous areas, §160A-58.
Counties, §153A-1.
Housing authorities, §§157-3, 157-41.
Housing standards, §160A-442.
Insurance, §58-84-5.
Local government finance, §159-1.

DEFINED TERMS —Cont'd
City —Cont'd
Mental health, §122C-3.
Municipal campaign reporting, §163-278.40.
Parking authorities, §160A-551.
Public hospitals, §§131E-6, 131E-16.
Taxation, §105-228.90, (b).
Urban redevelopment, §160A-503.
Veterans' recreation, §165-25.
Water and sewer authorities, §162A-5.1, (a).
Zoning, §160A-385.1, (b).
City board of education, §115C-5, (b).
City clerk.
City and town parking authorities, §160A-551.
Housing authorities, §157-3.
Public hospitals, §131E-16.
Veterans' recreation, §165-25.
City council.
City and town parking authorities, §160A-551.
Metropolitan water districts, §162A-32, (a).
Public hospitals, §131E-16.
City employee, §160A-169.
Civil action.
Civil procedure, §1-6.
Civil aircraft.
Aeronautics, §63-1.
Civil air patrol members.
Death benefits, §143-166.2, (d).
Civil no-contact order, §50C-1.
Workplace violence prevention, §95-265.
Civil or criminal action or proceeding.
Legal defense of state employees, §143-300.2.
Civil proceeding.
RICO act, §75D-3.
Claim.
Counties.
Contracts with railroads to allocate financial responsibility, §153-279, (a).
Executive budget, §143-3.3, (a).
Fraudulent transfers, §39-23.1.
Medical assistance provider false claims act, §108A-70.11.
Rail transportation liability, §160A-326, (a).
Claimant agency.
Debt collection, §105A-2.
Claimants.
Asset protection, §58-13-15.
Bonds, §44A-25.
Insurance guaranty association, §58-48-20.
Negotiable instruments, §25-3-312.
Products liability, §99B-1.
Prompt claim payments under health benefit plans, §58-3-225, (a).
Punitive damages, §1D-5.
Vaccine-related injury, §130A-422.
Victims compensation, §15B-2.
Claim determination period.
State medical plan, §135-40.13, (b).
Claim submission policy.
Health plans, disclosure to providers, §58-3-227, (a).
Class A motor vehicle, §20-4.01.
Class B motor vehicle, §20-4.01.
Class C motor vehicle, §20-4.01.
Classified motor vehicle.
Taxation, §105-330.
Classified service.
Occupational safety and health, §95-127.
Class of business.
Small employer group health coverage, §58-50-110.

DEFINED TERMS —Cont'd
CLE, Bar Rules & Regs., D, §.1501.
Clean risk.
Vehicle reinsurance, §58-37-35, (l).
Clean water revolving loan and grant fund, §159G-3.
Clearing corporation.
Investment securities, §25-8-102.
Clearinghouse.
Banking, §25-4-104, (a).
Clerk.
Abused, neglected and dependent juveniles, §7B-101.
Counties, §153A-1.
Criminal procedure, §15A-101.
Delinquent and undisciplined juveniles, §7B-1501.
Incompetency, §§35A-1101, 35A-1202.
Insurance, §58-84-5.
Local government finance, §159-1.
Motor vehicles, §20-16.5, (a).
Clerk of superior court.
Judicial retirement, §135-53.
Client.
Mental health, §122C-3.
Mental health, developmental disability, substance abuse.
Appeals panel, §122C-151.4, (a).
Psychotherapy patient/client sexual exploitation act, §90-21.41.
Trust companies, §53-301, (a).
Client advocate.
Mental health, §122C-3.
Client company.
Professional employer organizations, §58-89A-5.
Client law enforcement client.
Peer support group counselor's privilege, §8-53.10, (a).
Clinical peer.
Accident and health insurance.
Utilization review, §58-50-61, (a).
Clinical pharmacist practitioners.
Pharmacy practice, §90-85.3, (b1).
Clinical review criteria.
Accident and health insurance.
Utilization review, §58-50-61, (a).
Clinical social work practice, §90B-3.
Clinical supervisor intern.
Substance abuse professionals, §90-113.31.
Clinical trials.
State medical plan, §135-40.1.
Clone.
Seed law, §106-277.2.
Closed block.
Insurance companies, conversion, §58-10-12, (a).
Closed formulary.
Health insurers maintaining, §58-3-221, (c).
Closing.
Good funds settlement act, §45A-3.
Closing funds.
Good funds settlement act, §45A-3.
Closing-out sale, §66-76.
Closure.
Solid waste management, §130A-290, (a).
Clothing.
Sales and use tax, §105-164.3.
Clothing accessories or equipment.
Sales and use tax, §105-164.3.
Club.
Commercial fisherman's hull insurance, §58-20-5.
CMRS.
E-911 system for wireless communications, §62A-21.

DEFINED TERMS —Cont'd
CMRS —Cont'd
Telecommunications relay service, §62-157, (a1).
CMRS connection.
E-911 system for wireless communications, §62A-21.
Telecommunications relay service, §62-157, (a1).
CMRS provider.
E-911 system for wireless communications, §62A-21.
Telecommunications relay service, §62-157, (a1).
Coal-fired generating unit.
Air pollution control, §143-215.107D, (a).
Environmental compliance costs, §62-133.6, (a).
Coalition plan.
Cooperative state-local coalition water quality protection plans, §143-214.14, (a).
Coastal area.
Beach property insurance, §58-45-5.
Coastal area management, §113A-103.
Coastal fisheries.
Conservation, §113-129.
Coastal fishing.
Conservation, §113-129.
Coastal fishing waters, §113-129.
Coastal sound, §113A-103.
Coastal wetlands.
Conservation, §113-230.
COBRA continuation provision.
Health insurance portability and accountability, §58-68-25, (a).
Code.
Elective share of surviving spouse, §30-3.2.
Gasoline tax, §105-449.60.
Manufactured housing, §143-143.9.
Officials qualification board, §143-151.8, (a).
Principal and income act, §37A-1-104.1.
Property taxes, §105-273.
Public obligations, §159E-2.
Taxation, §§105-33.1, 105-114, 105-130.2, 105-134.1, 105-228.90, (b).
Trusts, §36A-59.3.
Code book.
Locksmith licensing, §74F-4.
Code designation.
Seed law, §106-277.2.
Code enforcement.
Officials qualification board, §143-151.8, (a).
Codifier of rules.
Administrative procedure, §150B-2.
CODIS.
DNA database and databanks, §15A-266.2.
Coin or currency operated machine.
Criminal law, §14-56.1.
Collaborative law.
Divorce, §50-71.
Collaborative law agreement.
Divorce, §50-71.
Collaborative law procedures.
Divorce, §50-71.
Collaborative law settlement agreement.
Divorce, §50-71.
Collateral.
Secured transactions, §25-9-102, (a).
Collateral assignment.
Probate and registration, §47-20.
Collateral or bond.
Motor vehicles, §20-4.18.
Collateral source.
Victims compensation, §15B-2.

DEFINED TERMS —Cont'd
Collected funds.
Good funds settlement act, §45A-3.
Collecting bank, §25-4-105.1.
Banking, §25-4-105.
Collection agency, §58-70-15, (a), (b).
Prohibited collection practices, §58-70-90.
Collection site.
Scrap tire disposal, §130A-309.53.
Collector.
Decedents' estates, §28A-1-1.
Property taxes, §105-273.
Rendering plants, §106-168.1.
Collision damage waiver.
Rental cars, §66-201.
Colony.
Bee and honey act, §106-635.
Color.
Food, drugs and cosmetics, §106-121.
Color additive.
Food, drugs and cosmetics, §106-121.
Meat inspection, §106-549.15.
Poultry products inspection, §106-549.51.
Columbarium.
Cemeteries, §65-48.
Comb.
Bee and honey act, §106-635.
Combination home.
Facility licensure act, §131E-101.
Long-term care insurance, §58-55-35, (a).
Commencement.
Child custody jurisdiction and enforcement, §50A-102.
Commercial.
Solid waste management, §130A-290, (a).
Commercial aircraft.
Insurance, §58-1-5.
Commercial beekeeper.
Bee and honey act, §106-635.
Commercial cave.
Criminal law and procedure, §14-159.20.
Commercial detection service.
Controlled substances, §90-102.1, (a).
Commercial domicile.
Corporate income tax, §105-130.4, (a).
Commercial driver's license, §20-4.01.
Commercial driver training school, §20-320.
Commercial electronic mail.
Computer crimes, §14-453.
Commercial feed, §106-284.33.
Commercial fertilizer, §106-657.
Commercial fisherman, §58-20-5.
Commercial fishing boats, §75A-5.1.
Commercial fishing operation.
Coastal and estuarine commercial fishing licenses, §113-168.
Commercial fund.
Petroleum cleanup, §143-215.94A.
Commercial hazardous waste treatment facility, §130A-295.01, (a).
Commercial loan commitment.
Contracts to be in writing, §22-5.
Commercial mobile radio service.
E-911 system for wireless communications, §62A-21.
Commercial motor vehicle, §20-4.01.
Commercial paper.
Banking, §53-55.
Commercial production.
Strawberry assessment, §106-783.

DEFINED TERMS —Cont'd
Commercial purposes.
Littering, §14-399, (i).
Commercial tort claim.
Secured transactions, §25-9-102, (a).
Commercial underground storage tank.
Petroleum cleanup, §143-215.94A.
Commercial unit.
Leases, UCC, §25-2A-103, (1).
Sales, §25-2-105.
Commercial vehicle.
Motor vehicles, §20-4.2.
Commercial water pollution control system operating firm, §90A-46.
Commingled goods.
Secured transactions priority of security interests, §25-9-336, (a).
Commission chairperson.
Discipline and disability rules of state bar, Bar Rules & Regs., B, §.0103.
Commissioner of banks.
Regional reciprocal savings and loan acquisition act, §54B-48.2.
Commission for health services.
Clean water loans, §159G-3.
Committee.
Job development investment grant program, §143B-437.51.
Commodity, §78D-1.
Commodity account.
Secured transactions, §25-9-102, (a).
Commodity contract, §78D-1.
Secured transactions, §25-9-102, (a).
Commodity customer.
Secured transactions, §25-9-102, (a).
Commodity exchange act, §78D-1.
Commodity futures trading commission, §78D-1.
Commodity intermediary.
Secured transactions, §25-9-102, (a).
Commodity merchant, §78D-1.
Commodity option, §78D-1.
Common areas and facilities, §47A-3.
Common carrier.
Public utilities, §62-3.
Common carrier by motor vehicle.
Public utilities, §62-3.
Common carriers of passengers.
Motor vehicles, §20-4.01.
Common control.
Wholesale prescription drug distributors, §106-145.2.
Common elements.
Condominiums, §47C-1-103.
Planned community act, §47F-1-103.
Common expense liability.
Condominiums, §47C-1-103.
Planned community act, §47F-1-103.
Common expenses.
Condominiums, §47C-1-103.
Planned community act, §47F-1-103.
Unit ownership, §47A-3.
Common name.
Toxic or hazardous substance identification, §95-174, (c).
Common profits.
Unit ownership, §47A-3.
Common stock.
Shareholder protection act, §55-9-01, (b).
Communicable condition.
Public health, §130A-2.

DEFINED TERMS —Cont'd
Communicable disease.
Public health, §130A-2.
Communicate.
Investment securities, §25-8-102.
Secured transactions, §25-9-102, (a).
Communications common carrier.
Electronic surveillance, §15A-286.
Communications media.
Political campaigns, §163-278.6.
Community advisory committee.
Facility licensure act, §131E-101.
Community-based development organization.
Development zone project tax credit, §105-129.13, (b).
Community-based program.
Abused, neglected and dependent juveniles, §7B-101.
Delinquent and undisciplined juveniles, §7B-1501.
Department of juvenile justice and delinquency prevention, §143B-515.
Community college, §115D-2.
Construction contract claims, §143-135.6, (e).
Community college buildings.
Administration department, §143-336.
Community development corporation.
Development zone project tax credit, §105-129.13, (b).
Community development purpose.
Development zone project tax credit, §105-129.13, (b).
Community facilities.
Housing authorities, §157-3.
Community general hospital, §131E-6.
Public hospitals, §131E-16.
Community punishment.
Structured sentencing, §15A-1340.11.
Community schools advisory council.
Community schools act, §115C-205.
Community schools coordinator, §115C-205.
Community service.
Public assistance program, §108A-24.
Community theatre.
Alcoholic beverages, §18B-1000.
Community trust.
Persons with severe chronic disabilities, §36A-59.11.
Community water system, §143-355.
Drinking water, §130A-313.
Compact administrator.
Interstate compact on mental health, §122C-361.
Compact officer.
National crime prevention and privacy compact, §114-19.50.
Company.
Bank holding company act, §53-226.
Insurance, §58-1-5.
Insurance taxation, §105-228.8.
Regional reciprocal savings and loan acquisition act, §54B-48.2.
Trust companies, §53-301, (a).
Vehicle reinsurance, §58-37-1.
Company action level event.
Risk based capital requirements, insurance companies, §58-12-11, (a).
Company action level risk-based capital.
Insurance companies, §58-12-2.
Comparable replacement dwelling.
Relocation assistance, §133-7.
Comparative market analysis.
Real estate appraisers, §93E-1-4.

DEFINED TERMS —Cont'd
Compensation.
Corporate income tax, §105-130.4, (a).
Disability income plan, §135-101.
Home inspectors, §143-151.45.
Judicial retirement, §135-53.
Legislative retirement system, §120-4.8.
Lobbying, §120-47.1.
Lotteries, §14-291.2, (b).
Retirement, §128-21.
State retirement system, §135-1.
Tax withholding, §105-163.1.
Workers' compensation, §97-2.
Compensatory agent.
Adult care homes, §131D-2, (a).
Compensatory damages.
Punitive damages, §1D-5.
Compensatory mitigation.
Wetlands restoration program, §143-214.11, (a).
Compensatory programs.
Tobacco trust fund commission, §143-716.
Competent beneficiary.
Principal and income act, §37A-1-104.1.
Competent local attorneys.
Banking, §53-20, (w).
Competing local provider.
Public utilities, §62-3.
Competitor.
Skiing, §99C-1.
Complainant or complaining witness.
Discipline and disability rules of state bar, Bar Rules & Regs., B, §.0103.
Procedures for the authorized practice committee of the state bars, Bar Rules & Regs., D, §.0203.
Public records, §132-1.4.
Complaint.
Discipline and disability rules of state bar, Bar Rules & Regs., B, §.0103.
Private personnel services, §95-47.1.
Procedures for the authorized practice committee of the state bars, Bar Rules & Regs., D, §.0203.
Completed operations liability.
Liability risk retention, §58-22-10.
Complete eviction.
Expedited evictions, §42-59.
Complex sources.
Water and air resources, §143-213.
Compliance review documents.
Savings and loan associations, §54B-63.1, (a).
Savings banks, §54C-60.1, (a).
Compliance with an order for support.
Child support, §110-142.
Composite abstract.
Elections, §163-182.
Compounding.
Pharmacy practice, §90-85.3, (c).
Comprehensive health coverage.
Children's health insurance program, §108A-70.18.
Comprehensive planning.
Regional sewage disposal, §162A-27.
Comprehensive vocational and technical education, §115C-152.
Computer.
Computer crimes, §14-453.
Sales and use tax, §105-164.3.
Computer database.
Electronic data-processing records, §132-6.1, (d).

DEFINED TERMS —Cont'd
Computer hardware.
Electronic data-processing records, §132-6.1, (d).
Computer network.
Computer crimes, §14-453.
Computer program.
Computer crimes, §14-453.
Electronic data-processing records, §132-6.1, (d).
Electronic transactions, §66-312.
Computer services.
Computer crimes, §14-453.
Computer software.
Computer crimes, §14-453.
Electronic data-processing records, §132-6.1, (d).
Sales and use tax, §105-164.3.
Computer system.
Computer crimes, §14-453.
Tax incentives for new and expanding businesses, §105-129.2.
Computer system design and related services.
Tax incentives for new and expanding businesses, §105-129.2.
Condemnation.
Eminent domain, §40A-2.
Condemned equipment.
Weights and measures, §81A-9.
Condemnor.
Eminent domain, §40A-2.
Condominium, §§47A-3, 47C-1-103.
Planned community act, §47F-1-103.
Condominium unit, §47A-3.
Confidential information.
Legislative ethics act, §120-87, (b).
Mental health, §122C-3.
Confidential license plate.
Publicly owned vehicles, §20-39.1, (d).
Confirmed lead poisoning, §130A-131.7.
Confirmers.
Letters of credit, §25-5-102, (a).
Conflict of interest.
Savings and loan associations, §54B-4.
Savings banks, §54C-4, (b).
Conflict of interest transaction.
Nonprofit corporations, §55A-31, (a).
Conformed copy.
Partnerships, §59-102.
Savings and loan associations, §54B-4.
Conforming.
Leases, UCC, §25-2A-103, (1).
Conforming to contract.
Sales, §25-2-106.
Conformity.
Planning regionally significant transportation projects, §136-200.
Congressionally chartered veterans' organizations.
Alcoholic beverages, §18B-1000.
Consent.
Criminal procedure, §15A-221.
Conservation.
Endangered wildlife, §113-331.
Plant protection and conservation, §106-202.12.
Conservation agreement.
Historic preservation agreements, §121-35.
Conserve.
Endangered wildlife, §113-331.
Plant protection and conservation, §106-202.12.
Consideration.
Bail bondsman and runners, §58-71-1.
Consignee.
Secured transactions, §25-9-102, (a).
UCC, §25-7-102.

DEFINED TERMS —Cont'd
Consignment.
Secured transactions, §25-9-102, (a).
Consignor.
Secured transactions, §25-9-102, (a).
UCC, §25-7-102.
Consolidated city-county, §160B-2.
Consolidated county human services agency, §143B-139.7, (c).
Consolidated housing authorities, §157-39.5.
Consolidated human services board, §143B-139.7, (c).
Consolidated judicial retirement system, §135-53.
Consolidated metropolitan planning organization.
Planning regionally significant transportation projects, §136-200.
Consolidation of cases.
Discipline and disability rules of state bar, Bar Rules & Regs., B, §.0103.
Conspicuous.
Business corporation, §55-1-40.
Nonprofit corporations, §55A-1-40.
UCC, §25-1-201.
Conspiracy to commit bribery.
Public officers and employees, §14-217, (a).
Constituent institution.
University of North Carolina, §116-2.
Construction.
Mountain ridge protection, §113A-206.
Sewage systems, §130A-334.
Solid waste management, §130A-290, (a).
University of North Carolina, §116-41.1.
Construction contract.
Bonds, §44A-25.
Construction contract agreement.
Lease of purchase of prison facilities constructed by private firm, §148-37.2, (b).
Construction costs.
Clean water loans, §159G-3.
Construction loans.
Maximum fees on loans secured by real property, §24-10, (c).
Construction management at risk services, §143-128.1, (a).
Construction management services, §143-128.1, (a).
Construction manager at risk, §143-128.1, (a).
Construction of wells, §87-85.
Consulting forester, §89B-2.
Consult or consultation.
Employee assistance professionals, §90-500.
Consumer.
Credit repair business, §66-221.
Debt collectors, §75-50.
Egg law, §106-245.14.
MH/DD/SA consumer advocacy program, §122C-11.
Prohibited collection practices, §58-70-90.
Sales and use tax, §105-164.3.
Tanning equipment operators, §104E-9.1, (c).
Consumer advocate.
MH/DD/SA consumer advocacy program, §122C-15, (a).
Consumer bankruptcy law, Bar Rules & Regs., D, §.2202.
Consumer commodity.
Food, drugs and cosmetics, §106-121.
Consumer credit installment sale contract.
Installment sales, §25A-12.

DEFINED TERMS —Cont'd
Consumer credit protection act.
Installment sales, §25A-13.
Consumer credit sale.
Installment sales, §§25A-2, 25A-24.
Consumer debtor.
Secured transactions, §25-9-102, (a).
Consumer goods or services.
Sales, §14-401.13.
Secured transactions, §25-9-102, (a).
Consumer-goods transaction.
Secured transactions, §25-9-102, (a).
Consumer home loans.
Interest, consumer protection in home loans, §24-10.2, (a).
Consumer lease.
Leases, UCC, §25-2A-103, (1).
Consumer obligor.
Secured transactions, §25-9-102, (a).
Consumer report.
Insurance information and privacy protection act, §58-39-15.
Consumer reporting agency.
Insurance information and privacy protection act, §58-39-15.
Consumer service center.
Tax incentives for new and expanding businesses, §105-129.2.
Consumer transaction.
Electronic transactions, §66-312.
Secured transactions, §25-9-102, (a).
Consumptive use.
Water and air resources, §143-215.21.
Contact.
Inmates prohibited from contacting victims' family members, §148-10.2, (a), (b).
Container.
Egg law, §106-245.14.
Poultry products inspection, §106-549.51.
Contaminant.
Brownfields property reuse act, §130A-310.31, (b).
Drinking water, §130A-313.
Dry-cleaning solvent cleanup act, §143-215.104B, (b).
Contaminated with filth.
Food, drugs and cosmetics, §106-121.
Contaminating a public water system.
Criminal law, §14-159.1.
Contents.
Electronic surveillance, §15A-286.
Contest.
Boxing commission, §143-651.
Contestant.
Boxing commission, §143-651.
Contested case.
Administrative procedure, §150B-2.
Contested primary and contested general election.
Public campaign financing fund, §163-278.62.
Contiguous area.
City and town boundaries, §§160A-41, 160A-53.
Continually low-performing schools, §115C-105.37A, (a).
Continuation statement.
Secured transactions, §25-9-102, (a).
Continuing care, §58-64-1.
Health facilities finance, §131A-3.
Continuing director.
Shareholder protection act, §55-9-01, (b).
Continuing legal education, Bar Rules & Regs., D, §.1501.

DEFINED TERMS —Cont'd
Contract.
Athlete agents, §78C-86.
Electronic transactions, §66-312.
Housing authorities, §157-3.
Invention development services, §66-209.
Membership camping, §66-232.
Mental health, developmental disability, substance abuse.
Appeals panel, §122C-151.4, (a).
Private personnel services, §95-47.1.
Public hospitals, §131E-16.
Sales, §25-2-106.
UCC, §25-1-201.
Contract carrier of property vehicles.
Motor vehicles, §20-4.01.
Contract costs.
Membership camping, §66-232.
Contract feeder.
Commercial feed law, §106-284.33.
Contract for construction or repair work.
Community colleges, §143-135.6, (e).
Contract for sale.
Sales, §25-2-106.
Contracting body.
Bonds, §44A-25.
Contractor, §87-21.
Bonds, §44A-25.
Commercial fertilizer, §106-657.
Community college construction claims, §143-135.6, (e).
Liens, §44A-17.
Mental health, developmental disability, substance abuse.
Appeals panel, §122C-151.4, (a).
Property taxes, §105-273.
Public contracts.
Resolution and adjustment of state construction contract claim, §143-135.3, (a).
Subcontractors, §22C-1.
Tax withholding, §105-163.1.
Contract provider.
Accident and health insurance, §58-51-37, (b).
Pharmacy of choice, §58-51-37, (b).
Contract security company, §74C-13.
Contract term.
Small business contractor act, §143B-472.86.
Contractual control.
Year 2000 liability, §66-296.
Contractual obligation.
Insurance guaranty associations, §58-62-16.
Contribute.
Political campaigns, §163-278.6.
Contribution.
Lobbying, §120-47.1.
Partnerships, §59-102.
Public campaign financing fund, §163-278.62.
Solicitation, §§14-401.12, 131F-2.
Unemployment insurance, §96-8.
Contributions tax preparer.
Unemployment compensation, §96-18, (b1).
Control.
Bank holding company act, §53-226.
Banks, §53-42.1, (a).
Condominiums, §47C-1-103.
Development zone project tax credit, §105-129.13, (b).
Insurance guaranty association, §58-48-20.
Insurance holding companies, §58-19-5.
Insurance information and privacy protection act, §58-39-15.

DEFINED TERMS —Cont'd
Control —Cont'd
Interstate branch banking, §53-224.9.
Managing general agents, §58-34-2, (a).
Money transmitters, §53-208.2, (a).
Mortgage bankers and brokers, §53-243.01.
Producer-controlled property or casualty insurers, §58-3-165, (a).
Professional employer organizations, §58-89A-5.
Reciprocal banking act, §53-210.
Regional reciprocal savings and loan acquisition act, §54B-48.2.
Savings and loan associations, §54B-4.
Savings banks, §54C-4, (b).
Substances, §90-87.
Tax credit for qualified business investments, §105-163.010.
Trust companies, §53-301, (a).
Controlled-access facility, §136-89.49.
Controlled insurer.
Producer-controlled property or casualty insurers, §58-3-165, (a).
Controlled substance, §90-87.
Examination regulation, §95-231.
Unauthorized substances taxes, §105-113.106.
Controlled substance analogue, §90-87.
Controlling.
Insurance holding companies, §58-19-5.
Controlling capital stock.
Insurance holding companies, §58-19-17, (a).
Controlling person.
Money transmitters, §53-208.2, (a).
Reinsurance intermediaries, §58-9-2, (a).
Controlling producer.
Producer-controlled property or casualty insurers, §58-3-165, (a).
Control of the business enterprise.
Unemployment compensation, §96-9, (c).
Control share acquisition, §55-9A-01, (b).
Corporations, §75E-1.
Control shares, §55-9A-01, (b).
Control zone.
Protection of forest, §113-60.6.
Convention center.
Alcoholic beverages, §18B-1000.
Conversion.
Hospital, medical and dental service corporations, §58-65-131, (b).
Conversion building, §47A-34.
Condominiums, §47C-1-103.
Conversion date.
Foreign-money claims, §1C-1820.
Converted policy.
Group health insurance, §58-53-1.
Converting mutual.
Insurance companies, conversion, §58-10-12, (a).
Conveyance.
Partnerships, §59-32.
Convicted.
Crime victims financial recovery assistance act, §15B-32.
Conviction.
Alcoholic beverages, §18B-900, (b).
Firearms, §14-415.1.
Licenses and permits, §113-277.
North Carolina rate bureau, §58-36-65, (i).
Safe driver incentive program, §58-36-75, (g).
Cooking school.
Alcoholic beverages, §18B-1000.
Cooperative.
Planned community act, §47F-1-103.

DEFINED TERMS —Cont'd
Cooperative agreements.
Health care facilities, §131E-192.2.
Cooperative agreements among physicians or between physician, hospital or others, §90-21.25.
Coordinated licensure information system.
Nurse licensure compact, §90-171.82.
Copayment.
Accident and health insurance, §58-51-37, (b).
Pharmacy of choice, §58-51-37, (b).
Copy.
Criminal process and procedure.
Electronic technology, §15A-101.1.
Cord.
Motor vehicles, §20-122.1.
Weights and measures, §81A-9.
Core services.
Mental health, §122C-3.
Corporate certificate.
Architects, §83A-1.
Corporate credit unions, §54-110.1, (b).
Corporate practice of architecture.
Architects, §83A-1.
Corporate surety.
Workers' compensation self insurance, §97-165.
Corporation, Const. N. C., art. VIII, §2.
Business corporations, §§55-1-40, 55-8-50, (b).
Corporate conveyance forms, §47-41.01, (d).
Dissenters' rights, §55-13-01.
Electric membership corporations, §117-7.
Estimated income tax, §105-163.38.
Hospital, medical and dental service corporations.
Conversion, §58-65-131, (b).
Limited liability companies, §57C-1-03.
Medical service corporations, §58-65-166, (b).
Nonprofit corporations, §55A-1-40.
Political campaigns, §163-278.6.
Property taxes, §105-273.
Taxation, §§105-114, 105-130.2.
Corporation, foreign or domestic, authorized to do business in North Carolina.
Public hospitals, §§131E-6, 131E-16.
Correct.
Weights and measures, §81A-9.
Corrective order.
Insurance companies, §58-12-2.
Correspondence school.
Proprietary schools, §115D-87.
Cosmetic.
Food, drugs and cosmetics, §106-121.
Cosmetic art, §88B-2.
Cosmetic art school, §88B-2.
Cosmetic art shop, §88B-2.
Cosmetologist, §88B-2.
Cosmetology teacher, §88B-2.
Cost.
Bonds for student housing, §116-175.
Business and energy tax credit, §105-129.15.
Capital facilities finance act, §142-82.
Centennial campus and Horace William campus financing act, §116-198.33.
Electric power, §159B-3.
Energy conservation finance act, §142-61.
Health facilities finance, §131A-3.
Higher education bonds, §116D-1.
Higher education student housing, §116-189.
Metropolitan sewerage districts, §162A-65, (a).
Metropolitan water districts, §162A-32, (a).
Motor fuel, §75-81.
Pollution control, §§159C-3, 159D-3.

DEFINED TERMS —Cont'd
Cost —Cont'd
Private capital facilities finance act, §159D-37.
Solid waste, §159I-3, (a).
Tax incentives for new and expanding businesses, §105-129.2.
University of North Carolina, §116-41.1.
Water and sewer, §162A-2.
Cost-effective cleanup.
Petroleum cleanup, §143-215.94A.
Cost-of-living adjustment.
Personnel system.
Comprehensive compensation system, §126-7, (a2).
Cost of operation.
Education food service, §115C-264.
Cost price.
Tobacco taxation, §105-113.4.
Costs of collection.
Political campaign, §163-278.6.
Cotton.
Boll weevil eradication, §106-65.69.
Cotton gin, §106-451.40.
Cotton grower, §106-65.85.
Cotton merchant, §106-451.40.
Cotton warehouse, §106-451.40.
Counsel.
Discipline and disability rules of state bar, Bar Rules & Regs., B, §.0103.
Counselor.
Discipline and disability rules of state bar, Bar Rules & Regs., B, §.0103.
Reverse mortgages, §53-257.
Counterfeit.
Instruments, §14-119, (c).
Counterfeit controlled substance, §90-87.
Counterfeit drug.
Food, drugs and cosmetics, §106-121.
Counterfeit mark.
Trademarks, §80-11.1, (a).
Counterintelligence service profession, §74C-3.
Counterparty exposure.
Derivative transactions, insurance companies, §58-7-205, (a).
County, §153A-1.
Public health authorities, §130A-45.01.
Public hospitals, §131E-16.
Public utilities, §62-100.
Taxation, §105-228.90, (b).
Tribal lands, §153A-350.1.
County block grant.
Public assistance program, §108A-24.
County board of commissioners.
Public health authorities, §130A-45.01.
County board of education, §115C-5, (c).
County clerk.
Public hospitals, §131E-16.
County councils.
Department of juvenile justice and delinquency prevention, §143B-515.
County department of social services.
Public assistance program, §108A-24.
County employee.
Counties, §153A-99, (b).
County of residence.
Mental health, §122C-3.
County plan.
Public assistance program, §108A-24.
County program.
Mental health, §122C-3.

DEFINED TERMS —Cont'd
County registry.
Sex offender and public protection registration, §14-208.6.
County water and sewer district, §162A-86, (a1).
Courier service profession, §74C-3.
Court.
Abused, neglected and dependent juveniles, §7B-101.
Arbitration, §1-569.1.
Child custody jurisdiction and enforcement, §50A-102.
Civil procedure, §1-7.
Custodial trusts, §33B-1.
Delinquent and undisciplined juveniles, §7B-1501.
Department of juvenile justice and delinquency prevention, §143B-515.
Family law arbitration, §50-59.
Insurers supervision, §58-30-10.
Interstate compact on juveniles, §7B-2803.
Limited liability companies, §57C-1-03.
Partnerships, §59-32.
Transfers to minors, §33A-1.
Court competent jurisdiction.
Savings and loan associations, §54B-4.
Court officer.
Endangering officers, §14-16.10.
Court or courts of the state.
Discipline and disability rules of state bar, Bar Rules & Regs., B, §.0103.
Procedures for the authorized practice committee of the state bars, Bar Rules & Regs., D, §.0203.
Court order.
Child support, §110-129.
Coventurer.
Solicitation of contributions, §131F-2.
Coverage services.
State medical plan, §135-40.1.
Covered benefits.
Health benefit plan external review, §58-50-75, (c).
Covered claim.
Insurance guaranty association, §58-48-20.
Self-insurance guaranty association, §97-130.
Covered clinical trials.
Health benefit plan coverage, §58-3-255, (a).
Covered corporation.
Control share acquisitions, §55-9A-01, (b).
Covered equipment.
Overhead high-voltage line safety, §95-229.6.
Covered items.
Overhead high-voltage line safety, §95-229.6.
Covered multifamily dwellings, §41A-3.
Covered person.
Accident and health insurance.
Utilization review, §58-50-61, (a).
Criminal history record checks.
Employees of department of health and human services and department of juvenile justice and delinquency prevention, §114-19.6, (a).
Health benefit plan external review, §58-50-75, (c).
Covered policy.
Insurance guaranty associations, §58-62-16.
Covered services.
State medical plan, §135-40.13, (b).
Covered vaccine.
Vaccine-related injury, §130A-422.
CPA.
Workers' compensation self insurance, §97-165.

DEFINED TERMS —Cont'd
Crash.
Motor vehicles, §20-4.01.
Creation of a security interest.
Leases, UCC, §25-2A-303, (1).
Credentialing body.
Substance abuse professionals, §90-113.31.
Credit.
Equal availability of credit for women, §25B-1, (c).
Worthless checks, §14-107, (c).
Creditable service, §128-21.
Judicial retirement, §135-53.
Law-enforcement separation allowances, §143-166.41, (b).
Legislative retirement system, §120-4.12, (a).
State law-enforcement retirement, §143-166.30, (a).
State retirement system, §135-1.
Credit accident and health insurance, §58-57-5.
Credit card business.
Insurance, solicitation, negotiation or payment of premiums through, §58-3-155.
Credit facility.
Capital facilities finance act, §142-82.
Energy conservation finance act, §142-61.
Facility authorities, §160A-480.2.
Global TransPark authority, §63A-2.
Higher education bonds, §116D-1.
Local government bonds, §159-79, (c).
Solid waste, §159I-7.
Solid waste management loan program.
Special obligation bonds and notes of local governments, §159I-30, (g).
State debt, §142-29.2.
Credit hour.
Continuing legal education, Bar Rules & Regs., D, §.1501.
Credit insurance agent, §58-57-5.
Credit life insurance, §§58-57-5, 58-58-10.
Creditor.
Credit insurance, §58-57-5.
Fraudulent transfers, §39-23.1.
Insurers supervision, §58-30-10.
Refund anticipation loan act, §53-246.
UCC, §25-1-201.
Creditor process.
Funds transfers, UCC, §25-4A-502.
Credit repair business, §66-221.
Credit report.
Credit scoring to rate motor vehicle and property insurance, §58-36-90, (a).
Credit score.
Credit scoring to rate motor vehicle and property insurance, §58-36-90, (a).
Credit transaction.
Credit insurance, §58-57-5.
Credit unemployment insurance, §58-57-5.
Credit union, §54-109.1.
Cremated remains, §90-210.41.
Cremation, §90-210.41.
Cremation chamber, §90-210.41.
Cremation container, §90-210.41.
Cremation interment container, §90-210.41.
Crematorium, §90-210.41.
Crematory, §90-210.41.
Crematory licensee, §90-210.41.
Crematory manager, §90-210.41.
Crematory technician, §90-210.41.
Crest.
Mountain ridge protection, §113A-206.

DEFINED TERMS —Cont'd
Crime.
Victims and witnesses, §15A-824.
Crime insurance.
Beach property, §58-45-5.
Fair access to insurance requirements, §58-46-1, (c).
Crime memorabilia.
Crime victims financial recovery assistance act, §15B-32.
Criminal action.
Civil procedure, §1-5.
Criminal activity.
Expedited evictions, §42-59.
Criminal appellate practice.
Certification standards for criminal law specialty, Bar Rules & Regs., D, §.2502.
Criminal history.
Abused, neglected and dependent juveniles, §7B-101.
Adoption, §48-1-101.
Auctions and auctioneers.
Criminal history record checks of applicants for license, §85B-3.2, (a).
Charter schools, §115C-238.29K, (a).
Employees of department of health and human services and department of juvenile justice and delinquency prevention, §114-19.6, (a).
Fire departments, criminal history record checks, §114-19.12, (a).
Locksmith licensing, §74F-18, (a).
Mandatory child care provider criminal history checks, §110-90.2, (a).
Manufactured homes.
Licensure of manufacturer, dealer, salesperson or set-up contractor, §143-143.10A, (a).
Nurses, §90-171.48, (a).
Residential school personnel criminal history checks, §143B-146.16, (a).
School personnel, §115C-332, (a).
Criminal history record repository.
National crime prevention and privacy compact, §114-19.50.
Criminal history records.
National crime prevention and privacy compact, §114-19.50.
Criminal justice.
National crime prevention and privacy compact, §114-19.50.
Criminal justice agencies.
Criminal justice education, §17C-2.
Justice academy, §17D-1.
National crime prevention and privacy compact, §114-19.50.
Criminal justice officers.
Criminal justice education, §17C-2.
Criminal justice personnel.
Justice academy, §17D-1.
Criminal justice services.
National crime prevention and privacy compact, §114-19.50.
Criminal law specialty, Bar Rules & Regs., D, §.2502.
Criminally injurious conduct.
Victims compensation, §15B-2.
Criminal offense showing professional unfitness.
Discipline and disability rules of state bar, Bar Rules & Regs., B, §.0103.
Criminal proceeding.
RICO act, §75D-3.

DEFINED TERMS —Cont'd
Criminal street gang.
Aggravating factors in sentencing, §15A-1340.16, (d).
Criminal summons.
Criminal process, §15A-303.
Critical access hospital.
Hospital licensure, §131E-76.
Crossbow.
Sales, §14-402, (c).
Cruel treatment.
Protection of animals, §19A-1.
Cruelty.
Cruelty to animals, §14-360, (c).
Protection of animals, §19A-1.
Cruelty to animals.
Veterinarians, §90-181.
Crustaceans.
Conservation, §113-129.
Cued speech.
Interpreters and transliterators licensure act, §90D-3.
Culpably negligent.
Patient abuse, §14-32.2, (e).
Cultural purpose.
Taxation, §105-278.3.
Current assets.
Provider sponsored organizations, §131E-276.
Current liabilities.
Provider sponsored organizations, §131E-276.
Current model.
Farm machinery franchises, §66-180.
Current net price.
Farm machinery, §66-180.
Current ratio.
Provider sponsored organizations, §131E-276.
Current significant investigative information.
Nurse licensure compact, §90-171.82.
Current standards.
Dry-cleaning solvent cleanup act, §143-215.104B, (b).
Custodial accounts.
Livestock prompt pay law, §106-418.3.
Custodial agency.
Crime victims' rights, §15A-830, (a).
Custodial agent.
Managing general insurance agents, §58-34-2, (a).
Custodial parents.
Consent to health care for minor, §32A-29.
Custodial property.
Transfers to minors, §33A-1.
Custodial trustee, §33B-1.
Custodial trust property, §33B-1.
Custodian.
Abused, neglected and dependent juveniles, §7B-101.
Delinquent and undisciplined juveniles, §7B-1501.
Department of juvenile justice and delinquency prevention, §143B-515.
Transfers to minors, §33A-1.
Customer.
Banking, §25-4-104, (a).
Disposal of dyes, molds, forms and patterns, §66-67.3, (a).
Financial privacy, §53B-2.
Funds transfers, UCC, §25-4A-105, (a).
Insurance customer information safeguards, §58-39-140.
Invention development services, §66-209.
Motor vehicle repairs, §20-354.2.

DEFINED TERMS —Cont'd
Customer computer program.
Sales and use tax, §105-164.3.
Customer-formula feed.
Commercial feed law, §106-284.33.
Customer information.
Insurance customer information safeguards, §58-39-140.
Customer information systems.
Insurance customer information safeguards, §58-39-140.
Dairy case.
Criminal law, §14-72.4.
Dam.
Safety, §143-215.25.
Damage.
Contractors, §87-101.
Medical assistance provider false claims act, §108A-70.11.
Offshore oil and gas activities, §143-215.94B, (b).
Rental cars, §66-201.
Dangerous dog, §67-4.1.
Dangerous to himself or others.
Mental health, §122C-3.
Dangerous weapon or substance.
Civil disorders, §14-288.1.
Data.
Computer crimes, §14-453.
Data entry and preparation.
Tax incentives for new and expanding businesses, §105-129.2.
Data processing.
Industrial development fund, §143B-437.01, (a1).
Tax incentives for new and expanding businesses, §105-129.2.
Date of test.
Seed law, §106-277.2.
Day.
Education personnel, §115C-325, (a).
Local government finance, §159-2.
Migrant housing, §95-223.
Occupational safety and health, §95-127.
Political campaign, §163-278.6.
Day of adjournment.
Rulemaking procedure, §150B-21.3, (d).
Day-reporting center.
Structured sentencing, §15A-1340.11.
Dead human bodies, §90-210.20, (c1).
Deaf.
Health and human services division, §143B-216.30.
Deaf person.
Interpreters for hearing impaired, §8B-1.
Dealer.
Farm machinery, §66-180.
Firearms, §14-409.39.
Liquefied petroleum gases, §119-54, (a).
Manufactured housing, §143-143.9.
Motor vehicles, §20-4.01.
Precious metals, §66-164.
Protection of animals, §19A-23.
Securities, §78A-2.
Seed law, §106-277.2.
Unauthorized substances taxes, §105-113.106.
Wildlife dealer licenses, §113-273, (a).
Dealership facilities.
Motor vehicles, §20-286.
Dealing in furs.
Fur-dealer licenses, §113-273, (f).
Death.
Workers' compensation, §97-2.

DEFINED TERMS —Cont'd
Death taxes.
Elective share of surviving spouse, §30-3.2.
Debilitation.
Standby guardianship, §35A-1370.
Debris.
Solid waste management, §130A-290, (a).
Debt, Const. N. C., art. V, §§3, 4.
Debt collection, §105A-2.
Debt collectors, §75-50.
Fraudulent transfers, §39-23.1.
Prohibited collection practices, §58-70-90.
Debt adjuster, §14-423.
Debt adjusting, §14-423.
Debt collector, §75-50.
Debt instrument.
Clean water loans, §159G-3.
Solid waste, §159I-7.
Debtor.
Credit insurance, §58-57-5.
Debt adjusting, §14-423.
Debt collection, §105A-2.
Fraudulent transfers, §39-23.1.
Refund anticipation loan act, §53-246.
Secured transactions, §25-9-102, (a).
Statewide accounts receivable program, §147-86.20.
Student loan collections, §105B-1.
Debtor's correct name.
Secured transactions financing statements, §25-9-506, (d).
Debt security.
Trust companies, §53-301, (a).
Debt service.
Local government finance, §159-7.
Debt service reserve supplement requirement.
Revenue bonds, §159-97.
Decedent.
Anatomical gifts, §130A-403.
Decedents' estates, §31A-3.
Deceptive acts or practices.
Unfair trade practices, §58-63-15.
Declarant.
Condominiums, §47C-1-103.
Conversion building rental, §47A-34.
Evidence, §8C-1, Rule 801, (b).
Natural death right, §90-321, (a).
Planned community act, §47F-1-103.
Declaration.
Condominiums, §47C-1-103.
Planned community act, §47F-1-103.
Unit ownership, §47A-3.
Declaration of loss.
Negotiable instruments, §25-3-312.
Declared state of emergency.
Civil disorders, §14-288.1.
Declination of insurance coverage.
Insurance information and privacy protection act, §58-39-15.
Dedicate.
Nature preserves act, §113A-164.3.
Deductible.
State medical plan, §135-40.1.
Deed of trust.
Sales under power of sale, §45-21.1, (b).
Deemed status.
Substance abuse professionals, §90-113.31.
Deep water.
State lands, §146-64.
Deer.
Conservation, §113-129.

DEFINED TERMS —Cont'd
Defendant, §1-10.
Bail, §15A-531.
Civil procedure, §1-75.2.
Discipline and disability rules of state bar, Bar Rules & Regs., B, §.0103.
Procedures for the authorized practice committee of the state bars, Bar Rules & Regs., D, §.0203.
Punitive damages, §1D-5.
UCC, §25-1-201.
Defoliant.
Pesticide board, §143-460.
Degree.
Marriage and family therapists, §90-270.47.
Delegates.
Nonprofit corporations, §55A-1-40.
Delinquency proceeding.
Insurers supervision, §58-30-10.
Delinquent income tax debt.
Electrical contractors, §87-44.2, (a).
Engineers.
Licensing of nonresidents, §89C-18.1, (a).
General contractors.
Licensing of nonresidents, §87-10.1, (a).
Plumbing, heating and fire sprinkler contractors, §87-22.2, (a).
Delinquent insurer.
Insurance guaranty associations, §58-62-16.
Delinquent juvenile.
Delinquent and undisciplined juveniles, §7B-1501.
Department of juvenile justice and delinquency prevention, §143B-515.
Interstate compact on juveniles, §7B-2803.
Deliver.
Business corporations, §55-1-40.
Controlled substances, §90-87.
Nonprofit corporations, §55A-1-40.
Pharmacy practice, §90-85.3, (d).
Delivered electronically.
Sales and use tax, §105-164.3.
Delivery.
UCC, §25-1-201.
Delivery charges.
Sales and use tax, §105-164.3.
Delivery damages.
Motor vehicles, §20-305.1.
Delivery order.
UCC, §25-7-102.
Demand deposits.
Banking, §53-1.
Demolisher.
Motor vehicles, §20-137.7.
Demolition.
Solid waste management, §130A-290, (a).
Demote.
Educational personnel, §115C-325, (a).
De novo branch.
Interstate branch banking, §53-224.9.
Dental hygiene, §90-221, (a).
Dental hygienist, §90-221, (b).
Dental service plan, §58-65-1, (a).
Dentistry, §90-29.
Dependent.
Deceased migrant agricultural workers, §130A-417.
Small employer group health coverage, §58-50-110.
Tax withholding, §105-163.1.
Victims compensation, §15B-2.

DEFINED TERMS —Cont'd
Dependent child.
Child support, §110-129.
Death benefits, §143-166.2, (a).
Public assistance program, §108A-24.
State medical plan, §135-40.1.
Dependent juvenile.
Abused, neglected or dependent juveniles, §7B-101.
Dependent parent.
Death benefits, §143-166.2, (b).
Dependent's economic loss.
Victims compensation, §15B-2.
Dependent spouse.
Alimony, §50-16.1A.
Support and maintenance, §14-322, (a).
Dependent's replacement service loss.
Victims compensation, §15B-2.
Deposit account.
Right of survivorship in bank deposits, §41-2.1, (e).
Secured transactions, §25-9-102, (a).
Depositary bank.
Banking, §25-4-105.
Depository institution.
Savings banks, §54C-4, (b).
Trust companies, §53-301, (a).
Depository library, §125-11.6.
Deposits.
Regional reciprocal savings and loan acquisition act, §54B-48.2.
Depreciation.
Principal and income act, §37A-5-503, (a).
Deputy.
Opening and inventory of decedent's safe-deposit box, §28A-15-13, (a).
Deputy commissioner.
Banking, §53-165, (f).
Occupational safety and health, §95-127.
Derelict vehicle.
Motor vehicles, §20-137.7.
Derivative.
Principal and income act, §37A-4-414, (a).
Derivative instrument.
Derivative transactions, insurance companies, §58-7-205, (a).
Derivative proceedings, §55-7-40.1.
Derivative transaction.
Insurance companies, §58-7-205, (a).
Desiccant.
Pesticide board, §143-460.
Designated agency.
Incompetency, §§35A-1101, 35A-1202.
Designated family member.
Motor vehicles, §20-286.
Designated health care services.
Self-referrals by health care providers, §90-405.
Designated relative.
Private trust companies, §53-363, (a).
Designated representative.
Child support, §110-129.
Designated state official.
Educational personnel qualifications, §115C-350.
Designation.
Standby guardianship, §35A-1370.
Designator.
Standby guardianship, §35A-1370.
Destination state.
Gasoline tax, §105-449.60.
Detection of deception examiner.
Private protective services, §74C-3.

DEFINED TERMS —Cont'd
Detention.
Delinquent and undisciplined juveniles, §7B-1501.
Department of juvenile justice and delinquency prevention, §143B-515.
Detention facility.
Delinquent and undisciplined juveniles, §7B-1501.
Department of juvenile justice and delinquency prevention, §143B-515.
Determination date.
Urban electrical service, §160A-331.
Determination of debilitation.
Standby guardianship, §35A-1370.
Determination of incapacity.
Standby guardianship, §35A-1370.
Develop.
Certificate, §131E-176.
Developed losses.
Insurance rates, §58-36-100, (b).
Developer.
Time shares, §93A-41.
Development.
Coastal area management, §113A-103.
National defense housing projects, §157-53.
Developmental disability.
Council, §143B-178.
Mental health, §122C-3.
Developmentally disabled adult.
Adult care homes, §131D-2, (a).
Development project.
Local development, development financing, §158-7.3, (a).
Rural redevelopment authority, §143B-437.21.
Development rights.
Condominiums, §47C-1-103.
Development zone.
Tax incentives for new and expanding businesses, §105-129.2.
Development zone agency.
Development zone project tax credit, §105-129.13, (b).
Deviation.
Structural pest control act, §106-65.24.
Device.
Food, drugs and cosmetics, §106-121.
Pesticide board, §143-460.
Pharmacy practice, §90-85.3, (e).
Devisee.
Decedents' estates, §28A-1-1.
Wills, antilapse statute, §31-42, (d).
Diagnostic center.
Certificate of need, §131E-176.
Diamond.
Unfair trade practices, §§66-73, 66-74.
Diamond industry.
Unfair trade practices, §§66-73, 66-74.
Diamond Shamrock Litigation Funds.
Housing trust, §122E-2.
Diesel fuel.
Gasoline tax, §105-449.60.
Dietary supplement.
Sales and use tax, §105-164.3.
Dietetics/nutrition, §90-352.
Direct access.
National crime prevention and privacy compact, §114-19.50.
Direct mail.
Sales and use tax, §105-164.3.
Director.
Limited liability companies, §57C-1-03.

DEFINED TERMS —Cont'd
Director of the budget.
Executive budget act, §143-1.
Direct supervision.
Respiratory care practices act, §90-648.
Direct-to-home satellite services.
Sales and use tax, §105-164.3.
Disability income insurance policy, §58-51-130, (a).
Disabled adult.
Abuse, neglect or exploitation of disabled or elder adults.
Criminal offense, §14-32.3, (d).
Protection, §108A-101.
Disabled business enterprise.
Global TransPark authority, §63A-19.
Procurement, §143-48, (b).
Disabled or disability.
Discipline and disability rules of state bar, Bar Rules & Regs., B, §.0103.
Income plan, §135-101.
Workers' compensation, §§97-2, 97-55.
Disablement.
Workers' compensation, §97-54.
Disabling condition, §168A-3.
Disadvantaged business.
Roads and highways, §136-28.4, (c).
Disaster.
Emergency management, §166A-4.
Volunteer leave, §166A-31.
Disaster location.
First responders vaccination program, §130A-485, (f).
Discharge.
Liability for hazardous materials abatement, §143-215.103.
Oil and hazardous substance control, §143-215.77.
Discharge for misconduct with work.
Unemployment insurance, §96-14.
Discharge of waste, §143-213.
Disciplinary action.
Drivers' licenses, lose control, lose license, §20-11, (n1).
Disciplinary suspension.
Educational personnel, §115C-325, (a).
Disclosure date.
Electioneering communications, §§163-278.80, 163-278.90.
Discontinuance.
Health maintenance organizations, §58-67-5, (o).
Discount buying club, §66-131.
Discounted present value.
Structured settlement protection, §1-543.11.
Discovered property.
Property taxes, §105-273.
Discretionary trust.
Alienability of beneficiary's interest, §36A-115.
Discriminatory practice.
Persons with disabilities protection, §168A-3.
Disease.
Bee and honey act, §106-635.
Dishonest conduct.
Client security fund, rules governing administration, Bar Rules & Regs., D, §.1401.
Homeowner's recovery fund, §87-15.5.
Dishonor.
Letters of credit, §25-5-102, (a).
Disinterested directors.
Savings and loan associations, §54B-4.
Savings banks, §54C-4, (b).

DEFINED TERMS —Cont'd
Disinterested person.
Principal and income act, §37A-1-104.1.
Disinterested public agent.
Incompetency, §35A-1202.
Disorder.
Bee and honey act, §106-635.
Disorderly conduct.
Civil disorders, §14-288.1.
Dispense.
Controlled substances, §90-87.
Pharmacy practice, §90-85.3, (f).
Dispenser.
Controlled substances, §90-87.
Dispensing optician, §90-235.
Dispersement of settlement proceeds.
Good funds settlement act, §45A-3.
Displaced homemaker, §143B-394.4.
Displaced person.
Relocation assistance, §133-7.
Disposable earnings.
Child support, §110-136.
Debt collection, §105B-3.
Debts owed public hospitals, §131E-48.
Garnishment for enforcement of child-support obligations, §110-136, (a).
Disposable income.
Child support, §110-129.
Garnishment of wages to recoup fraudulent public assistance program payments, §108A-25.3, (a).
Disposal.
Dry-cleaning solvent cleanup act, §143-215.104B, (b).
Solid waste management, §130A-290, (a).
Disposal fee.
Scrap tire disposal, §130A-309.53.
Disposal system.
Water and air resources, §143-213.
Dispose.
Child support, §50-31.
Condominiums, §47C-1-103.
Conversion building rental, §47A-34.
Disposition.
Child support, §50-31.
Condominiums, §47C-1-103.
Conversion building rental, §47A-34.
Criminal procedure, §15A-1381.
Dispute.
Special education.
Mediation, §115C-116, (b).
Disqualification.
Motor vehicles, §20-4.01.
Disqualified person.
Professional corporations, §55B-2.
Dissenter.
Dissenters' rights, §55-13-01.
Dissolution.
Partnerships, §59-59.
Distillery.
Taxation, §105-151.6.
Distinguishing license plate.
Handicapped parking privileges, §20-37.5.
Distressed urban area.
E-NC authority, §143B-437.45.
Distress sale, §66-76.
Distributable system property.
Public service taxation, §105-333.
Distribute.
Antifreeze law, §106-579.3.
Commercial feed law, §106-284.33.

DEFINED TERMS —Cont'd
Distribute —Cont'd
Controlled substances, §90-87.
Seed law, §106-277.2.
Soil additives act, §106-50.30.
Youth access to tobacco products, §14-313, (a).
Distributed information technology assets.
Office of information technology services, §147-33.81.
Distribution.
Business corporations, §55-1-40.
Limited liability companies, §57C-1-03.
Nonprofit corporations, §55A-1-40.
Distribution proceeding.
Foreign-money claims, §1C-1820.
Distributive award.
Divorce, §50-20, (b).
Distributor.
Commercial feed law, §106-284.33.
Commercial fertilizer, §106-657.
Controlled substances, §90-87.
Egg law, §106-245.14.
Gasoline tax, §105-449.60.
Motion pictures, §75C-2.
Motor vehicles, §20-286.
Soil additives act, §106-50.30.
Tobacco taxation, §105-113.4.
Toxic or hazardous substance identification, §95-174, (d).
Distributor branch.
Motor vehicles, §20-286.
Distributor representative.
Motor vehicles, §20-286.
District.
Abused, neglected and dependent juveniles, §7B-101.
Aeronautics, §63-79.
Delinquent and undisciplined juveniles, §7B-1501.
Department of juvenile justice and delinquency prevention, §143B-515.
Metropolitan sewerage, §162A-65, (a).
Metropolitan water, §162A-32, (a).
Organization of schools, §115C-69.
Pollution control act, §113A-52.
Regional natural gas district, §160A-661, (b).
Soil and water conservation, §139-3.
District attorney.
Criminal procedure, §15A-101.
Judicial retirement, §135-53.
District bar.
Attorneys at law, §84-19.
District court.
Criminal procedure, §15A-101.
Protection of disabled adults, §108A-101.
Dividend credit.
Business corporations, §55-1-40.
Dividends.
Corporate income tax, §105-130.4, (f).
Adjustment for expenses related to dividends, §105-130.6A, (a).
Dividends on stock.
Savings and loan associations, §54B-4.
Savings banks, §54C-4, (b).
Dividends on withdrawable accounts.
Savings and loan associations, §54B-4.
Division of entomology.
Biological organism act, §106-65.44.
Division of environmental health.
Clean water loans, §159G-3.
DNA, §15A-266.2.
DNA record, §15A-266.2.

DEFINED TERMS —Cont'd
DNA sample, §15A-266.2.
Docket book.
Civil procedure, §1-208.1.
Doctor.
State medical plan, §135-40.1.
Doctor of veterinary medicine, §90-181.
Document.
Confidential legislative communications, §120-129.
Criminal process and procedure.
Electronic technology, §15A-101.1.
Letters of credit, §25-5-102, (a).
Property taxes, §105-273.
Secured transactions, §25-9-102, (a).
State depository library system, §125-11.6.
UCC, §25-7-102.
Documentary draft.
Banking, §25-4-104, (a).
Documentary material.
RICO act, §75D-3.
Document of title.
UCC, §25-1-201.
Dog, §130A-134.
Dog handler.
Controlled substances, §90-102.1, (a).
Doing business.
Insurers supervision, §58-30-10.
Taxation, §105-114.
Doing business in this state.
Telephone solicitations, §75-101.
Domestic.
Venue, §1-79, (b).
Domestic company.
Insurance, §58-1-5.
Domestic corporation.
Business corporations, §55-1-40.
Limited partnerships, §59-102.
Nonprofit corporations, §55A-1-40.
Partnerships, §59-32.
Taxation, §105-130.2.
Domestic guaranty association.
Insurers supervision, §58-30-10.
Domestic insurer.
Insurance companies, §58-12-2.
Protected cell companies, §58-10-80.
Domestic limited liability company.
Limited partnerships, §59-102.
Partnerships, §59-32.
Domestic limited partnership.
Partnerships, §59-32.
Domestic nonprofit corporation.
Limited partnerships, §59-102.
Partnerships, §59-32.
Domestic partnership.
Conversion and merger, §59-73.1.
Domestic setting.
Abuse, neglect or exploitation of disabled or elder adults, §14-32.3, (d).
Domestic violence, §50B-1, (a).
Domestic violence victim.
Domestic violence victim assistance act, §7A-474.17.
Privileged communications, rape crisis centers and domestic violence programs, §8-53.12.
Domicile.
Liability risk retention, §58-22-10.
Unclaimed property act, §116B-52.
Domiciliary state.
Insurers supervision, §58-30-10.
Donor.
Anatomical gifts, §130A-403.

DEFINED TERMS —Cont'd
Do not call registry.
Telephone solicitations, §75-101.
Downtown development project.
City and town planning, §160A-458.3.
Downtown revitalization project, §160A-536, (b).
Drawee.
Negotiable instruments, §25-3-103.
Drawer.
Negotiable instruments, §25-3-103.
Drilling wastes.
Offshore oil and gas activities, §143-215.94B, (b).
Drinking water rules, §130A-313.
Driver.
Motor vehicles, §20-4.01.
Drug.
Commercial feed law, §106-284.33.
Controlled substances, §90-87.
Food, drugs and cosmetics, §106-121.
Pharmacy practice, §90-85.3, (g).
Sales and use tax, §105-164.3.
Drug dependent person.
Controlled substances, §90-87.
Drug detection dog.
Controlled substances, §90-102.1, (a).
Drug sample.
Wholesale prescription drug distributors, §106-145.2.
Drug treatment court program.
Structured sentencing, §15A-1340.11.
Dry-cleaning facility.
Dry-cleaning solvent cleanup act, §143-215.104B, (b).
Dry-cleaning solvent tax, §105-187.30.
Dry-cleaning operation.
Dry-cleaning solvent cleanup act, §143-215.104B, (b).
Dry-cleaning solvent.
Dry-cleaning solvent cleanup act, §143-215.104B, (b).
Dry-cleaning solvent tax, §105-187.30.
Dry-cleaning solvent assessment agreement.
Dry-cleaning solvent cleanup act, §143-215.104B, (b).
Dry-cleaning solvent contamination.
Dry-cleaning solvent cleanup act, §143-215.104B, (b).
Dry-cleaning solvent remediation agreement.
Dry-cleaning solvent cleanup act, §143-215.104B, (b).
Dual credit property.
Credit property insurance, §58-57-90, (a).
Due notice.
Soil and water conservation districts, §139-3.
Due on sale clause.
Maximum fees on loans secured by real property, §24-10, (d).
Duly authorized representative of the state.
Home schools, §115C-563, (b).
Duly certified fee-based practicing pastoral counselor.
Health benefit plans, choosing services, §58-50-30, (c1).
Duly certified substance abuse professional.
Health benefit plans, choosing services, §58-50-30, (c2).
Duly licensed clinical social worker.
Health benefit plans, choosing services, §58-50-30, (c).
Duly licensed professional counselor.
Health benefit plans, choosing services, §58-50-30, (c3).

DEFINED TERMS —Cont'd
Duly licensed psychologist.
Health benefit plans, choosing services, §58-50-30, (b).
Dumbwaiter.
Elevator safety, §95-110.3, (c).
Duplicate.
Evidence, §8C-1, Rule 1001.
Duplicate record.
Workers' compensation self-insurance.
Employer groups, §58-47-75, (a).
Durable equipment.
Insurance companies, investments in chattel mortgages, §58-7-180, (b).
Insurance companies, investments in mortgage loans, §58-7-179, (b).
Durable medical equipment.
Sales and use tax, §105-164.3.
Durable medical supplies.
Sales and use tax, §105-164.3.
Durable power of attorney, §32A-8.
Duties.
Assault on school employees or volunteers, §14-33, (c).
Duty of support.
Interstate family support, §52C-1-101.
D. V. M., §90-181.
Dwelling.
Housing standards, §160A-442.
Dyed diesel fuel.
Gasoline tax, §105-449.60.
Early childhood, §143B-168.11.
Earnable compensation.
Retirement, §128-21.
State retirement system, §135-1.
Earned income.
Crime victims financial recovery assistance act, §15B-32.
Earnings.
Disability income plan, §135-101.
Eating establishment.
Alcoholic beverages, §18B-1000.
Economically distressed county.
Clean water loans, §159G-3.
Industrial development fund, §143B-437.01, (a), (a1).
Economically distressed units of local government.
Clean water management trust fund, §113A-252.
Economic development.
Fisherman, §113-315.17.
Economic distress.
Comprehensive strategic economic development, §143B-434.01, (a).
Economic interest.
Legislative ethics act, §120-85.
Economic life.
Energy in state buildings, §143-64.11.
Economic loss.
Victims compensation, §15B-2.
Educational institution, §105-134.1.
Charitable gift annuities, §58-3-6.
Gift taxes, §105-188.
Taxation, §105-278.4.
Educational interpreter or transliterator.
Interpreters and transliterators licensure act, §90D-3.
Educational personnel, §115C-350.
Educational property.
Negligent supervision of minor, §1-538.3.
Weapons on educational property, §14-269.2, (a).

DEFINED TERMS —Cont'd
Educational purpose.
Liability of landowners associated with watershed improvement projects, §139-41.3.
Property tax exemption.
Exemption of real and personal property used for, §105-278.7, (f).
Recreational trespass, §38A-2.
Taxation, §§105-278.3, 105-278.4.
Effective date of notice.
Business corporations, §55-1-40.
Effluent standards or limitations, §143-213.
Eggs, §106-245.14.
Elder adult.
Abuse, neglect or exploitation of disabled or elder adults, §14-32.3, (d).
Elderly person.
Roads and highways, §136-44.27, (b).
Electing county.
Public assistance program, §108A-24.
Election, §163-165.
Political campaigns, §163-278.6.
Electioneering communication, §§163-278.80, 163-278.90.
Elective supplier.
Gasoline tax, §105-449.60.
Electrical contracting, §87-43.
Electrical system.
Electric power, §159B-3.
Electric generating facility.
Boating safety, §75A-2.
Electric membership corporation.
Public service taxation, §105-333.
Electric personal assistive mobility device, §§20-4.01, 20-175.6, (a).
Electric power company.
Public service taxation, §105-333.
Electric power holding companies.
Corporate income tax.
Adjustment for expenses related to dividends, §105-130.6A, (a).
Electric supplier.
Public utilities, §62-110.2.
Electrologist, §88A-3.
Electrology, §88A-3.
Electrolysis, §88A-3.
Electronic.
Criminal process and procedure, §15A-101.1.
Electronic transactions, §66-312.
Sales and use tax, §105-164.3.
Electronic agent.
Electronic transactions, §66-312.
Electronic bidding.
Procurement of information technology, §147-33.95, (c).
Electronic chattel paper.
Secured transactions, §25-9-102, (a).
Electronic communication.
Cyberstalking, §14-196.3, (a).
Electronic surveillance, §15A-286.
Wiretaps, §15A-260.
Electronic communication service.
Electronic surveillance, §15A-286.
Electronic communication system.
Electronic surveillance, §15A-286.
Electronic data-processing system, §132-6.1, (d).
Electronic funds transfer.
Taxation, §105-228.90, (b).
Electronic instrument.
Money transmitters, §53-208.2, (a).

DEFINED TERMS —Cont'd
Electronic mail.
Computer related crime, §14-453.
Cyberstalking, §14-196.3, (a).
Electronic mail order house.
Tax incentives for new and expanding businesses, §105-129.2.
Electronic mail service provider.
Computer crimes, §14-453.
Electronic means.
Transportation contracts, §136-28.1, (k).
Electronic, mechanical or other device, §15A-286.
Electronic payment.
Statewide accounts receivable program, §147-86.20.
Electronic record.
Electronic transactions, §66-312.
Electronic repository.
Criminal process and procedure, §15A-101.1.
Electronic signature.
Criminal process and procedure, §15A-101.1.
Electronic commerce in government, §66-58.2.
Electronic transactions, §66-312.
Electronic storage.
Electronic surveillance, §15A-286.
Electronic surveillance, §15A-286.
Elementary school, §115C-75, (a).
Elevated blood lead level, §130A-131.7.
Elevator.
Safety, §95-110.3, (d).
Eligibility period.
Unemployment insurance, §96-12.01, (a).
Eligible assaultive and violent children.
Mental health, §122C-3.
Eligible client.
Judicial department, §7A-474.2.
Eligible employee.
Small employer group health coverage, §58-50-110.
Eligible entity.
Emergency management, §166A-4.
Eligible fireman.
Pension fund, §58-86-25.
Eligible individual.
Health insurance portability and accountability.
Guaranteed individual coverage for certain individuals with prior group coverage, §58-68-60, (b).
Eligible industry.
Industrial development fund, §143B-437.01, (a1).
Eligible infants and toddlers.
Mental health, §122C-3.
Eligible institution.
State education assistance authority, §116-201.
Eligible landowner.
Forest development act, §113A-178.
Eligible lands.
Forest development act, §113A-178.
Eligible major industry.
Tax incentives for new and expanding business, §105-129.2.
Eligible member.
Insurance companies, conversion, §58-10-12, (a).
Eligible person.
Crime victims financial recovery assistance act, §15B-32.
Eligible position.
Job development investment grant program, §143B-437.51.

DEFINED TERMS —Cont'd
Eligible projects.
Housing trust, §122E-6, (b).
Eligible PSAPs.
E-911 system for wireless communications, §62A-21.
Eligible psychologists.
Mental health, §122C-3.
Eligible rescue squad worker.
Pension fund, §58-86-30.
Eligible risk.
Vehicle reinsurance, §58-37-1.
Eligible surplus lines insurer, §58-21-10.
Eligible unit.
Workers' compensation fund for the benefit of volunteer safety workers, §58-87-10, (a).
Eligible veteran, §126-81.
Employment preference for veterans, §128-15, (b).
Emancipated minor.
Pharmacy practice, §90-85.3, (h).
Embalmer.
Funeral services, §90-210.20, (d).
Embalming.
Funeral services, §90-210.20, (e).
Emergency.
Medical plan for teachers and state employees.
Special benefits for chemical dependency and mental health care, §135-40.7B, (e).
National Guard compact, §127A-177.
Protection of disabled adults, §108A-101.
Radiation protection, §104E-5.
Telephones, §14-401.8.
Emergency circumstances.
Drinking water, §130A-323.
Emergency communication.
Offenses against public safety, §14-286.2, (b1).
Emergency facility.
Veterinarians, §90-181.1, (b).
Emergency interim successor.
Local government during emergencies, §162B-7.
Emergency judge.
Judicial department, §§7A-39.1, (b), 7A-50.
Emergency justice.
Judicial department, §7A-39.1, (b).
Emergency management, §166A-4.
Emergency management agency, §166A-4.
Emergency medical condition.
Accident and health insurance.
Utilization review, §58-50-61, (a).
Child care facilities, administration of medicine, §110-102.1A, (b).
Insurance coverage for emergency care, §58-3-190, (g).
Emergency medical dispatcher.
Emergency medical services, §131E-155.
Emergency medical services, §131E-155.
Emergency medical services-nurse practitioner, §131E-155.
Emergency medical services peer review committee, §131E-155.
Emergency medical services personnel, §131E-155.
Emergency medical services-physician assistant, §131E-155.
Emergency medical technician, §131E-155.
Emergency medical technician-intermediate, §131E-155.
Emergency medical technician-paramedic, §131E-155.
Emergency need.
Financial assistance for nursing students and inactive nurses, §90-171.51.

DEFINED TERMS —Cont'd
Emergency personnel.
Civil disorders, §14-288.9.
Emergency recall judge.
Judicial department, §7A-39.1, (b).
Emergency service employees.
Solicitation of contributions, §131F-2.
Emergency services.
Accident and health insurance.
Utilization review, §58-50-61, (a).
Insurance coverage for emergency care, §58-3-190, (g).
Protection of disabled adults, §108A-101.
Eminent domain, §40A-2.
Emission, §143-213.
Emissions county.
Motor vehicle inspections, §20-183.2, (c).
Employ.
Wage and hour act, §95-25.2.
Employed.
Sex offender and public protection registration, §14-208.6.
Employee.
Adult care homes, immunization, §131D-9, (g).
Annuities, §147-9.2.
Assault on school employees or volunteers, §14-33, (c).
Confidentiality of legislative communications, §120-131.1, (b).
Disability income plan, §135-101.
Group health insurance, §58-53-1.
Health insurance portability and accountability, §58-68-25, (a).
Health maintenance organizations, §58-67-85.
Legal defense by state, §143-300.2.
Mortgage bankers and brokers, §53-243.01.
Motor vehicle repairs, §20-354.2.
Nature of policies, §58-51-80, (c).
Negotiable instruments, §25-3-405.
Nursing homes, immunization, §131E-113, (g).
Occupational safety and health, §95-127.
Private personnel services, §95-47.1.
Public school employees.
Employment benefits, §115C-338, (a).
Repayment of money owed to state, §143-552.
Retirement, §128-21.
Safety and health, §95-250.
Social security eligibility, §135-20.
State directory of new hires, §110-129.2, (j).
State medical plan, §135-40.1.
State retirement system, §135-1.
Structural pest control act, §106-65.24.
Tax withholding, §105-163.1.
Toxic or hazardous substance identification, §95-174, (e).
Wage and hour act, §95-25.2.
Water and sewer authorities, §162A-6.1.
Weapons on educational property, §14-269.2, (a).
Workers' compensation, §97-2.
Employee assistance certification commission, §90-500.
Employee assistance professionals, §90-500.
Employee benefit plan.
Trusts of death benefits, §36A-100.
Employee life insurance, §58-58-150.
Employee on leave.
Governmental employees, §126-52.
Employee or officer.
Confidentiality of tax information, §105-259, (a).
Employer.
Annuities, §147-9.2.
Disability income plan, §135-101.

DEFINED TERMS —Cont'd
Employer —Cont'd
Employer and employee, §14-357.1.
Health insurance portability and accountability, §58-68-25, (a).
Industrial commission managed care organizations, I.C. Managed Care Orgs. R. II.
Local government law-enforcement retirement, §143-166.50, (a).
Motor vehicles, §20-4.01.
Nature of policies, §58-51-80, (c).
Occupational safety and health, §95-127.
Persons with disabilities protection, §168A-3.
Private personnel services, §95-47.1.
Retirement, §128-21.
State directory of new hires, §110-129.2, (j).
State law-enforcement retirement, §143-166.30, (a).
State retirement system, §135-1.
Tax withholding, §105-163.1.
Toxic or hazardous substance identification, §95-174, (f).
Tuition waiver for senior citizens, §115B-1.
Unemployment insurance, §96-8.
Wage and hour act, §95-25.2.
Workers' compensation, §97-2.
Workplace violence prevention, §95-265.
Employer network.
Industrial commission managed care organizations, I.C. Managed Care Orgs. R. II.
Employing entity.
Repayment of money owed to state, §§143-552, 143-555, 143-558.
Employing unit.
State medical plan, §135-40.1.
Unemployment insurance, §96-8.
Employment.
Legal defense of state employees, §143-300.2.
Private personnel services, §95-47.1.
Public assistance program, §108A-24.
Social security eligibility, §135-20.
Unemployment insurance, §96-8.
Workers' compensation, §97-2.
Employment agency.
Persons with disabilities protection, §168A-3.
Employment level.
Tax credit for manufacturing cigarettes for exportation, §105-130.46, (b).
Employment office.
Unemployment insurance, §96-8.
Employment security administration fund.
Unemployment insurance, §96-8.
Employment security law.
Unemployment insurance, §96-8.
EMS.
Rescue squad workers' relief fund, §58-86-40.
EMS provider.
Emergency medical services, §131E-155.
Encoded or scrambled signal.
Cable television theft, §14-118.5.
Encumbrance.
Secured transactions, §25-9-102, (a).
Endangered species, §113-331.
Plant protection and conservation, §106-202.12.
Endangered species act, §113-331.
Plant protection and conservation, §106-202.12.
End of state of disaster.
Price gouging during states of disaster, §75-37.1, (c).
Endorsement.
Investment securities, §25-8-102.

DEFINED TERMS —Cont'd
Endorsement contract.
Athlete agents, §78C-86.
Endowment fund.
Institution funds, §36B-1.
Energy conservation loan.
Housing finance agency, §122A-3.
Energy conservation measure.
Energy conservation finance act, §142-61.
Guaranteed energy savings contracts, §143-64.17.
Energy conservation property.
Energy conservation finance act, §142-61.
Energy-consuming system.
Energy policy and life-cycle cost analysis for state government, §143-64.11.
Energy-consumption analysis.
State buildings, §143-64.11.
Energy crisis, §113B-20, (a).
Energy savings.
Guaranteed energy savings contracts, §143-64.17.
Enforcement agency.
Structural pest control act, §106-65.24.
Enforcement costs.
Political campaign, §163-278.6.
Engaged in business.
Sales and use tax, §105-164.3.
Engage in an equine activity.
Equine activity liability, §99E-1.
Engineer, §89C-3.
Engineered barrier.
Radiation protection, §104E-5.
Engineering intern, §89C-3.
Enrolled.
Time shares, §93A-41.
Enrollee.
Health maintenance organizations, §58-67-5, (b).
Enrollment.
State medical plan, §135-40.1.
Entered.
Criminal process and procedure.
Electronic technology, §15A-101.1.
Enterprise.
RICO act, §75D-3.
Wage and hour act, §95-25.2.
Enterprise tier.
Job development investment grant program, §143B-437.51.
Tax incentives for new and expanding businesses, §105-129.2.
Entire premises.
Expedited evictions, §42-59.
Entitled after-born.
Wills, §31-5.5, (c).
Entitlement holder.
Investment securities, §25-8-102.
Entitlement order.
Investment securities, §25-8-102.
Entity.
Business corporations, §55-1-40.
Franchise tax, §105-114.1, (a).
Nonprofit corporations, §55A-1-40.
Principal and income act, §37A-4-401, (a).
Securities regulation, §78A-2.
Self-referrals by health care providers, §90-405.
Entrance fee.
Continuing care retirement communities, §58-64-1.
Entrance fee per withdrawable account.
Savings and loan associations, §54B-4.
Entry level.
Criminal justice education, §17C-2.

DEFINED TERMS —Cont'd
Entry of judgment.
Criminal procedure, §15A-101.
Entry permit.
Hunting and fishing on registered property of another, §113-281.
Enumerated student conduct.
Drivers' licenses, lose control, lose license, §20-11, (n1).
Environmental assessment, §113A-9.
Environmental compliance costs, §62-133.6, (a).
Environmental contamination.
Brownfields property reuse act, §130A-310.31, (b).
Environmental document, §113A-9.
Environmental impact statement, §113A-9.
Environmental law.
Fiduciaries, §32-27.
Powers of trustees under express trust, §36A-136.
Environmental management commission.
Clean water loans, §159G-3.
Soil and water conservation districts, §139-3.
Well construction, §87-85.
Epilepsy.
Incompetency, §35A-1101.
Equine.
Equine activity liability, §99E-1.
Equine activity.
Equine activity liability, §99E-1.
Equine activity sponsor.
Equine activity liability, §99E-1.
Equine infectious anemia.
Animal diseases, §106-405.15.
Equine professional.
Equine activity liability, §99E-1.
Equipment.
Pesticide board, §143-460.
Secured transactions, §25-9-102, (a).
Equity capital.
Trust companies, §53-301, (a).
Equity line of credit, §45-81.
Loans exempt from rate and fee limitations, §24-9, (a).
Equity security.
Domestic companies, §58-7-145, (f).
Enterprise corporations, §53A-37.
Tax credit for qualified business investments, §105-163.010.
Trust companies, §53-301, (a).
Equivalent drug product.
Pharmacy practice, §90-85.27.
Equivalent level annual dividend.
Life insurance solicitation, §58-60-10.
Equivalent level death benefit.
Life insurance solicitation, §58-60-10.
Erect.
Outdoor advertising control, §136-128.
Erosion.
Pollution control act, §113A-52.
Erosion control structures.
Coastal area management, erosion control structures, §113A-115.1, (a).
Escalator.
Elevator safety, §95-110.3, (e).
Escape.
State prisons, §148-45.
Escheated lands.
State lands, §146-64.
Escrow agreement.
Tobacco escrow compliance, §66-292.
Essential parts.
Motor vehicles, §20-4.01.

DEFINED TERMS —Cont'd
Essential property insurance.
Beach property insurance, §58-45-5.
Essential public health services, §130A-1.1, (b).
Essential services.
Protection of disabled adults, §108A-101.
Established business relationship.
Telephone solicitations, §75-101.
Established federal standard.
Migrant housing, §95-223.
Occupational safety and health, §95-127.
Established legal services program.
Domestic violence victim assistance act, §7A-474.17.
Established name.
Pharmacy practice, §90-85.27.
Established office.
Motor vehicles, §§20-4.01, 20-286.
Established salesroom.
Motor vehicles, §20-286.
Establishment.
Sanitation, §130A-247.
Tax incentives for new and expanding businesses, §105-129.2.
Wage and hour act, §95-25.2.
Establishment that prepares or serves drink.
Sanitation, §130A-247.
Establishment that prepares or serves food.
Sanitation, §130A-247.
Estate.
Decedents' estates, §29-2.
Federal estate tax, §28A-27-1.
Incompetency, §35A-1202.
Medicaid estate recovery plan, §108A-70.5, (b).
Veterans, §34-2.
Estate planning and probate law specialty, Bar Rules & Regs., D, §.2302.
Estate sale.
Auction and auctioneers, §85B-1.
Esthetician, §88B-2.
Esthetician teacher, §88B-2.
Estimated tax, §105-163.38.
Ethics advisory.
Procedures for ruling on questions of legal ethics, Bar Rules & Regs., D, §.0101.
Ethics decision.
Procedures for ruling on questions of legal ethics, Bar Rules & Regs., D, §.0101.
Euro.
European monetary union, §53-295.
European currency unit (ECU).
European monetary union, §53-295.
Euthanasia.
Protection of animals, §19A-23.
Event of withdrawal of a general partner.
Limited partnerships, §59-102.
Partnerships, §59-102.
Evidence.
Criminal procedure, §15A-971.
Obstruction of justice, §14-221.1.
Evidence of coverage.
Health maintenance organizations, §58-67-5, (c).
Exam.
Standards board for public school administration, §115C-290.2.
Examination and investigation.
Insurance commissioner, §58-2-131, (b).
Psychology practice act, §90-270.2.
Savings and loan associations, §54B-4.
Savings banks, §54C-4, (b).

DEFINED TERMS —Cont'd
Examinations and laboratory tests for the screening for the early detection of cervical cancer.
Accident and health insurance, §58-51-57, (a1).
Health maintenance organizations, §58-67-76, (a1).
Hospital, medical and dental services corporations, §58-65-92, (a1).
Examinee.
Controlled substance examination regulation, §95-231.
Examiner.
Controlled substance examination regulation, §95-231.
Insurance commissioner, §58-2-131, (b).
Excavation.
Contractors, §87-101.
Excepted benefits.
Health insurance portability and accountability, §58-68-25, (b).
Excess value of water.
Impounded water, §143-215.44, (c).
Exchange access facility.
911 service, §62A-3.
Telecommunications relay service, §62-157, (a1).
Exchange act.
Shareholder protection act, §55-9-01, (b).
Exchange company.
Time shares, §93A-41.
Exchange program.
Time shares, §93A-41.
Exchange teacher, §115C-325, (a).
Excluded corporation.
Corporate income tax, §105-130.4, (a).
Excursion passenger vehicles.
Motor vehicles, §20-4.01.
Executed.
Funds transfers, UCC, §25-4A-301, (a).
Execution date.
Funds transfers, UCC, §25-4A-301, (b).
Execution sale, §1-339.41, (a).
Executive.
Limited liability companies, §57C-1-03.
Executive authority.
Criminal extradition, §15A-721.
Executive board.
Condominiums, §47C-1-103.
Planned community act, §47F-1-103.
Executive budget act, §143-1.
Executive committee.
Pest control, §106-65.55.
Executive head.
Motor vehicles, §20-183.21.
Executive mortgage broker, §53-243.01.
Executive officer.
Endangering officers, §14-16.10.
Money transmitters, §53-208.2, (a).
Trust companies, §53-301, (a).
Executive order.
National crime prevention and privacy compact, §114-19.50.
Exempt for-hire vehicles.
Motor vehicles, §20-4.01.
Exempt loan.
Loans exempt from rate and fee limitations, §24-9, (a).
Exempt managerial position.
Personnel system, §126-5, (b).
Exempt organization.
Lotteries and gaming, §14-309.6.

DEFINED TERMS —Cont'd
Exempt person.
Mortgage bankers and brokers, §53-243.01.
Exempt policymaking position.
Personnel system, §126-5, (b).
Exempt position.
Personnel system, §126-5, (b).
Exhaustee.
Unemployment insurance, §96-12.01, (a).
Exhibit.
Motion pictures, §75C-2.
Exhibition.
Boxing commission, §143-651.
Exhibitor.
Motion pictures, §75C-2.
Existing facilities.
Centennial campus and Horace Williams campus financing act, §116-198.33.
Higher education bonds, §116D-22.
Higher education student housing, §116-189.
Existing sanitary landfill.
County solid waste disposal, §153A-136, (c).
Public enterprises, §160A-325, (a).
Exotic species.
Plant protection and conservation, §106-202.12.
Expedited process.
Child support, §50-31.
Expedited review.
Certificate of need, §131E-176.
Expenditure.
Lobbying, §120-47.1.
Political campaigns, §163-278.6.
Public campaign financing fund, §163-278.62.
Expense adjustment.
Corporate income tax.
Adjustment for expenses related to dividends, §105-130.6A, (a).
Expenses.
Business corporations, §55-8-50, (b).
Insurance rates, §58-36-100, (b).
Medical service corporations, §58-65-166, (b).
Workers' compensation self-insurance.
Employer groups.
Premium rates, §58-47-110, (a).
Experience.
Contractors, §87-21.
Experience rate modifier.
Safety and health, §95-250.
Experimental/investigational medical procedures.
State medical plan, §135-40.1.
Expiration date.
Prescription labels, §90-85.29.
Expired financial transaction card.
Criminal law, §14-113.8.
Explanation.
Secured transactions, disposition of collateral after default, §25-9-616, (a).
Exploitation.
Adult care homes, §131D-2, (a).
Adult care home's bill of rights, §131D-20.
Protection of disabled adults, §108A-101.
Exploration.
Offshore oil and gas activities, §143-215.94B, (b).
Exploration activity.
Mining, §74-76.
Explosive or incendiary device or substance.
Criminal law, §§14-50.1, 14-72.
Explosives.
Motor vehicles, §20-4.01.
Offenses against safety, §14-284.1.

DEFINED TERMS —Cont'd
Export.
Gasoline tax, §105-449.60.
Surplus lines, §58-21-10.
Exportation.
Tax credit for manufacturing cigarettes for exportation, §105-130.45, (a).
Increasing employment and utilizing state ports, §105-130.46, (b).
Exposed.
Bee and honey act, §106-635.
Express invitation or permission.
Telephone solicitations, §75-101.
Extended benefit period.
Unemployment insurance, §96-12.01, (a).
Extended benefits.
Unemployment insurance, §96-12.01, (a).
Extraordinary means.
Natural death right, §90-321, (a).
Extraordinary medical expenses.
State prisons, §148-32.1.
Facilitator.
Refund anticipation loan act, §53-246.
Facilities.
Armories, §127A-161.
Continuing care, §58-64-1.
Dry-cleaning solvent cleanup act, §143-215.104B, (b).
Egg law, §106-245.14.
Energy in state buildings, §143-64.11.
Membership camping, §66-232.
Mental health, §122C-3.
Nursing homes, §131E-116.
Toxic or hazardous substance identification, §95-174, (g).
Underground storage tank cleanup, §143-215.94A.
Vehicle reinsurance, §58-37-1.
Facsimile seal.
Public obligations, §159E-2.
Facsimile signature.
Public obligations, §159E-2.
Fact expert witness.
Medicolegal guidelines for attorney-physician relationship, MLG Rule 3.
Factory branch.
Motor vehicles, §20-286.
Factory representative.
Motor vehicles, §20-286.
Failure to list property.
Property taxes, §105-273.
Fair.
Supervision, §106-520.1.
Fair consideration.
Insurers supervision, §58-30-10.
Fair Labor Standards Act, §95-25.2.
Fair market value.
Self-referrals by health care providers, §90-405.
Fair value.
Dissenters' rights, §55-13-01.
Protected cell companies, §58-10-80.
Falconry.
Public activities, §113-130.
Familial status.
Fair housing act, §41A-3.
Family.
Debts owed public hospitals, §131E-48.
Fair housing act, §41A-3.
Public assistance program, §108A-24.
Student loan collections, §105B-1.
Family care home.
Adult care homes, §131D-2, (a).
Adult care home's bill of rights, §131D-20.

DEFINED TERMS —Cont'd
Family care home —Cont'd
Handicapped person, §168-21.
Long-term care insurance, §58-55-35, (a).
Family child care home, §110-86.
Family foster home.
Child placing and care, §131D-10.2.
Family income.
Children's health insurance program, §108A-70.18.
Student loan collections, §105B-1.
Family income of debtor.
Debts owed public hospitals, §131E-48.
Family law specialty, Bar Rules & Regs., D, §.2402.
Family leave credit insurance, §58-57-5.
Family member.
Farm machinery franchises, §66-180.
Private trust companies, §53-363, (a).
Victims and witnesses, §15A-824.
Family unit.
Mental health, developmental disabilities and substance abuse, voluntary admissions, §122C-211, (g).
Farmed cervid.
Conservation, §113-129.
Deer, production and sale for commercial purposes, §106-549.97, (c).
Farmer.
Property-hauling vehicle registration fees, §20-88, (b).
Farmers of low income.
Housing authorities, §157-3.
Farming activity.
Mediation of farm nuisance disputes, §7A-38.3, (a).
Farming operation.
Secured transactions, §25-9-102, (a).
Farm machinery.
Taxation, §105-151.21.
Farm nuisance dispute.
Prelitigation mediation, §7A-38.3, (a).
Farm operation.
Relocation assistance, §133-7.
Farm products.
Property-hauling vehicle registration fees, §20-88, (b).
Secured transactions, §25-9-102, (a).
Farm resident.
Mediation of farm nuisance disputes, §7A-38.3, (a).
Farm tractor.
Motor vehicles, §20-4.01.
Father.
Marriage proceedings, §51-2.2.
Fault.
Leases, UCC, §25-2A-103, (1).
UCC, §25-1-201.
FBI.
DNA database and databanks, §15A-266.2.
National crime prevention and privacy compact, §114-19.50.
FCC order.
E-911 system for wireless communications, §62A-21.
Feasibility study.
Liability risk retention, §58-22-10.
Federal act.
Drinking water, §130A-313.
Food, drugs and cosmetics, §106-121.
Occupational safety and health, §95-127.

DEFINED TERMS —Cont'd
Federal agency.
Drinking water, §130A-313.
Electric membership corporations, §117-7.
State auditor, §147-64.4.
Federal association.
Regional reciprocal savings and loan acquisition act, §54B-48.2.
Savings and loan associations, §54B-4.
Federal clean air act, §143-213.
Federal expedited process requirement.
Child support, §50-31.
Federal food, drug and cosmetic act.
Meat inspection, §106-549.15.
Poultry products inspection, §106-549.51.
Federal government.
Agricultural finance act, §122D-3.
Housing authorities, §157-3.
Interstate environmental compact, §113A-23.
National defense housing projects, §157-53.
Public health authorities, §130A-45.01.
Public hospitals, §131E-16.
Veterans' recreation, §165-25.
Federal installation.
Motor vehicle inspections, §20-183.2, (c).
Federal insurance contributions act.
Governmental employees and social security, §135-20.
Federal international banking institution.
International banking act, §53-232.2, (a).
Federally chartered savings institution.
Trust companies, §53-301, (a).
Federally guaranteed security.
Health facilities finance, §131A-3.
Federally insured mortgage note.
Health facilities finance, §131A-3.
Federally insured securities.
Housing finance agency, §122A-3.
Federal meat inspection act, §106-549.15.
Federal or state antitrust laws.
Cooperative agreements among physicians or between physician, hospital or others, §90-21.25.
Health care facilities.
Cooperative agreements, §131E-192.2.
Federal poultry products inspection act, §106-549.51.
Federal poverty level.
Children's health insurance program, §108A-70.18.
Federal reserve act, §53-61, (a).
Federal reserve banks, §53-61, (a).
Federal reserve board, §53-61, (a).
Federal retirement benefits.
Individual income tax, §105-151.20, (a).
Federal safety and hazardous material regulations.
Motor carriers, §20-376.
Federal TANF funds, §108A-24.
Federated fund-raising organization.
Solicitation of contributions, §131F-2.
Fee.
Mortgages, high cost home loans, §24-1.1E, (a).
Private personnel services, §95-47.1.
Fee-based pastoral counseling associate, §90-382.
Fee-based pastoral counselor, §90-382.
Fee-based practice of pastoral counseling, §90-382.
Fee-based professional pastoral counseling services, §90-382.

DEFINED TERMS —Cont'd
Feed ingredient.
Commercial feed law, §106-284.33.
Feedlot.
Animal waste management, §143-215.10B.
Felony.
Crime victims financial recovery assistance act, §15B-32.
Criminal law, §14-1.
Expedited evictions, §42-59.
Fertilizer coated seed.
Commercial fertilizer, §106-657.
Fertilizer material.
Commercial fertilizer, §106-657.
FICA.
Public assistance program, §108A-24.
Fiduciary, §32-25.
Federal estate tax, §28A-27-1.
Negotiable instruments, §25-3-307.
Principal and income act, §37A-1-102.
Trust, §36A-1, (a).
Trusts and trustees, §36A-22.1.
Uniform fiduciaries act, §32-2, (a).
Fiduciary record.
Trust companies, §53-301, (a).
Field.
Oil and gas conservation, §113-389.
Field of operation.
Urban redevelopment, §160A-503.
File number.
Secured transactions, §25-9-102, (a).
Filing.
Child support, §50-31.
Criminal process and procedure.
Electronic technology, §15A-101.1.
Judicial retirement, §135-53.
Legislative retirement system, §120-4.8.
Retirement, §128-21.
State retirement system, §135-1.
Filing office.
Secured transactions, §25-9-102, (a).
Filing-office rule.
Secured transactions, §25-9-102, (a).
Filing with the court.
Civil procedure, §1A-1, Rule 5.
Final compensation.
Judicial retirement, §135-53.
Final disposition.
Cremation, §90-210.41.
Finance charge.
Installment sales, §25A-8.
Finance lease.
Leases, UCC, §25-2A-103, (1).
Finance officer.
Local government bonds, §159-44.
Financial asset.
Asset-backed securities facilitation, §53-425.
Investment securities, §25-8-102.
Financial institution.
Commodities act, §78D-1.
Data match systems.
Child support enforcement, §110-139.2.
Fair housing act, §41A-3.
Financial privacy, §53B-2.
Forgery, §14-119, (c).
Funeral and burial trust funds, §90-210.60.
Rural redevelopment authority, §143B-437.21.
Savings and loan associations, §54B-4.
Tax credit for qualified business investments, §105-163.010.
Transfers to minors, §33A-1.

DEFINED TERMS —Cont'd
Financial instrument.
Computer crimes, §14-453.
Financial intermediary.
Public obligations, §159E-2.
Financial organization.
Unclaimed property act, §116B-52.
Financial record.
Financial privacy, §53B-2.
Financial report.
Incompetency, §35A-1202.
Financial responsibility.
Professional employer organizations, §58-89A-5.
Financial transaction card.
Criminal law, §14-113.8.
Financing agency.
Sales, §25-2-104.
Financing agreement.
Global TransPark authority, §63A-2.
Pollution control, §§159C-3, 159D-3.
Financing contract.
Capital facilities finance act, §142-82.
Energy conservation finance act, §142-61.
Financing contract indebtedness.
Capital facilities finance act, §142-82.
Financing entity.
Viatical life insurance settlements, §58-58-205.
Financing statement.
Secured transactions, §25-9-102, (a).
Finding of no significant impact.
Environmental policy act, §113A-9.
Findings and information.
Disclosure of records in child fatality or near fatality cases, §7B-2902, (a).
Fine print.
Sales, §25C-10.
Firearm, §14-409.39.
Criminal law, §14-72.
Fire chief.
Toxic or hazardous substance identification, §95-174, (h).
Fire department.
Toxic or hazardous substance identification, §95-174, (j).
Fire district.
Insurance, §58-84-5.
Firefighter, §113-60.32.
Tuition waiver for senior citizens, §115B-1.
Fireman.
Death benefits, §143-166.2, (e).
State medical plan, §135-40.1.
Fire protection.
Rural fire protection districts, §69-25.4, (b).
Fire sprinkler.
Contractors, §87-21.
Fire suppression duties, §113-60.32.
Firm.
Meat inspection, §106-549.15.
Rules of professional conduct, Prof. Cond. Rule 1.0.
First-degree murder.
Criminal law, §14-17.
First-degree rape.
Criminal law, §14-27.2.
First-degree sexual offense.
Criminal law, §14-27.4.
First responders.
Vaccination program, §130A-485, (f).
First stop employment assistance.
Public assistance program, §108A-24.

DEFINED TERMS —Cont'd
First-tier subcontractor, §143-128.1, (a).
Liens, §44A-17.
First-year licensee.
Bail bondsman and runners, §58-71-1.
Fiscal note.
Local government, §120-30.44.
Fiscal period.
Capital facilities finance act, §142-82.
Higher education bonds, §116D-1.
Fiscal year.
Capital facilities finance act, §142-82.
Estimated income tax, §105-163.38.
Higher education bonds, §116D-1.
Local government finance, §159-7.
School budgets, §115C-423.
State medical plan, §135-40.1.
Taxation, §§105-130.2, 105-134.1.
Fish.
Conservation, §113-129.
Sales and use tax exemptions, §105-164.13.
Fisheries director.
Conservation, §113-128.
Marine fisheries compact, §113-251.
Fisheries resources, §113-129.
Fisherman.
Fishermen's economic development, §113-315.17.
Fishing related industry.
Fishery resource grant program, §113-200, (b).
Fitting and selling hearing aids.
Dealers and board, §93D-1.
Five model years.
Failure to disclose damage to vehicle, §20-71.4, (a1).
Fixed.
Records, tapes and other recorded devices, §14-432.
Fixed location.
Dealing in regulated metals property, §66-11, (a).
Fixed route.
Public utilities, §62-3.
Fixture filing.
Secured transactions, §25-9-102, (a).
Fixtures.
Secured transactions, §25-9-102, (a).
Flesch scale analysis readability score.
Readable insurance policies, §58-38-15.
Readable medical insurance, §58-66-15.
Flight equipment.
Public service taxation, §105-333.
Flipping.
Interest, consumer protection in home loans, §24-10.2, (a).
Floating structure.
Coastal area management, §113A-103.
Flood hazard.
Floodplain regulations, §143-215.52, (a).
Flood vehicle.
Motor vehicles, §20-4.01.
Flour.
Weights and measures, §81A-9.
Fluid fertilizer.
Commercial fertilizer, §106-657.
Flying club.
Aeronautics, §63-1.
Focused growth institution.
Distinguished professors endowment trust fund, §116-41.13A.
Follow along services.
Community trust for persons with severe chronic disabilities, §36A-59.11.

DEFINED TERMS —Cont'd
Food.
Food, drugs and cosmetics, §106-121.
Sales and use tax, §105-164.3.
Food additive.
Food, drugs and cosmetics, §106-121.
Meat inspection, §106-549.15.
Poultry products inspection, §106-549.51.
Food business.
Alcoholic beverages, §18B-1000.
Food sold through vending machines.
Sales and use tax, §105-164.3.
Foreign bank.
Trust companies, §53-301, (a).
Foreign commerce.
Motor carriers, §20-376.
Public utilities, §62-3.
Foreign company.
Insurance, §58-1-5.
Foreign corporation.
Business corporations, §55-1-40.
Limited liability companies, §57C-1-03.
Limited partnerships, §59-102.
Nonprofit corporations, §55A-1-40.
Partnerships, §59-32.
Taxation, §105-130.2.
Foreign country.
Foreign legal consultants, §84A-1, (c).
International banking act, §53-232.2, (a).
Sales and use tax exemptions, §105-164.13.
Foreign entity.
Electrical contractors, §87-44.2, (a).
Engineers.
Licensing of nonresidents, §89C-18.1, (a).
General contractors, §87-10.1, (a).
Plumbing, heating and fire sprinkler contractors, §87-22.2, (a).
Foreign government.
Business discrimination, §75B-1.
Filing of agreements between North Carolina and foreign governments, §66-280, (c).
Foreign guaranty association.
Insurers supervision, §58-30-10.
Foreign insurer.
Insurance companies, §58-12-2.
Foreign judgment.
Judgments, §1C-1702.
Money judgments recognition, §1C-1801.
Foreign jurisdiction.
Document authentication, §66-271.
Foreign limited liability company, §57C-103.
Partnerships, §§59-32, 59-102.
Foreign limited liability partnership, §59-32.
Limited partnerships, §59-102.
Foreign limited partnership.
Limited liability companies, §57C-103.
Partnerships, §§59-32, 59-102.
Foreign money.
Foreign-money claims, §1C-1820.
Foreign nonprofit corporation.
Limited partnerships, §59-102.
Partnerships, §59-32.
Foreign official.
Document authentication, §66-271.
Foreign partnership.
Electrical contractors, §87-44.2, (a).
Engineers.
Licensing of nonresidents, §89C-18.1, (a).
General contractors, §87-10.1, (a).
Plumbing, heating and fire sprinkler contractors, §87-22.2, (a).

DEFINED TERMS —Cont'd
Foreign person.
Business discrimination, §75B-1.
Corporate income tax, §105-130.5, (b).
Foreign personal representative.
Decedents' estates, §28A-1-1.
Foreign state.
Foreign money judgments recognition, §1C-1801.
Foreign trade relationships.
Business discrimination, §75B-1.
Foreign trust institution.
Trust companies, §53-301, (a).
Foreign vehicle.
Motor vehicles, §20-4.01.
Forensic medical examination.
Assistance program for victims of rape and sex offenses, §143B-480.2, (b).
Forest development assessment.
Forest development act, §113A-178.
Forest development cost sharing payment.
Forest development act, §113A-178.
Forest development fund, §§113A-178, 113A-191.
Forester, §89B-2.
Forestland.
Protection of forest, §113-60.6.
Taxation, §105-277.2.
Forest laws, §113-53.1.
Forest operation.
Nuisance liability of agriculture and forest operations, §106-701, (b1).
Forest ranger.
Regulation of open fires, §113-60.22.
Forestry, §89B-2.
Forest trees, §113-60.6.
For-hire motor carrier, §20-4.01.
For hire passenger vehicles.
Motor vehicles, §20-4.01.
Formal delinquency proceeding.
Insurers supervision, §58-30-10.
Formal ethics opinion.
Procedures for ruling on questions of legal ethics, Bar Rules & Reg., D, §.0101.
Former Article 9 record.
Secured transactions filing office transition, §25-9-710, (a).
Former contractor.
Mental health, developmental disability, substance abuse.
Appeals panel, §122C-151.4, (a).
Former insurer.
Appointment of bondsmen, §58-71-141, (c).
Former mutual.
Insurance companies, conversion, §58-10-12, (a).
Form of identification, §14-100.1, (d).
Fortified mulch.
Commercial fertilizer, §106-657.
Fortified wine.
Alcoholic beverages, §18B-101.
Alcohol taxation, §105-113.68.
Foster care.
Children, §131D-10.2.
Foster child.
Family leave credit insurance, §58-57-115, (a).
Insurance, §58-51-30, (a).
Foster parent.
Child placing and care, §131D-10.2.
Foundation.
Hospital, medical and dental service corporations.
Conversion, §58-65-131, (b).
Foundation seeds.
Seed law, §106-277.2.

DEFINED TERMS —Cont'd
FPL.
Children's health insurance program, §108A-70.18.
Franchise.
Motor vehicles, §20-286.
Public utilities, §62-3.
Franchise accident and health insurance, §58-51-90.
Franchise motor vehicle dealer, §20-286.
Fraternal orders, §58-25-5.
Fraud or fraudulent.
Punitive damages, §1D-5.
Rules of professional conduct, Prof. Cond. Rule 1.0.
Securities, §78A-2.
Fraudulent endorsement.
Negotiable instruments, §25-3-405.
Fraudulent payment.
Garnishment of wages to recoup fraudulent public assistance program payments, §108A-25.3, (a).
Fraudulent viatical settlement act.
Viatical life insurance settlements, §58-58-205.
Free clinic.
Volunteer health care providers, §90-21.16, (c).
Free-flowing.
Natural and scenic rivers, §113A-33.
Freeholders in petition for special taxes.
Estates, §41-13.
Freestanding ambulatory surgical facility.
Medical care data, §131E-214.1.
Freight car line companies.
Taxation, §105-228.2.
Friable.
Asbestos hazard management, §130A-444.
Frontage road.
Controlled-access facilities, §136-89.49.
Fuel alcohol.
Gasoline tax, §105-449.60.
Fuel alcohol provider.
Gasoline tax, §105-449.60.
Full-screen.
Campaign contributions and expenditures.
Disclosure requirements for media advertisements, §163-278.38Z.
Full-time employee.
Job development investment grant program, §143B-437.51.
Full-time employment.
Public assistance program, §108A-24.
Full-time job.
Tax credit for manufacturing cigarettes for exportation.
Increasing employment and utilizing state ports, §105-130.46, (b).
Tax incentives for new and expanding businesses, §105-129.2.
Fully funded.
Protected cell companies, §58-10-80.
Fumigants.
Structural pest control act, §106-65.24.
Fund.
Armories, §127A-161.
Auction and auctioneers, §85B-1.
Client security fund, rules governing administration, Bar Rules & Regs., D, §.1401.
Dry-cleaning solvent cleanup act, §143-215.104B, (b).
Homeowner's recovery fund, §87-15.5.
Housing trust, §122E-2.

DEFINED TERMS —Cont'd
Fund —Cont'd
Local government finance, §159-7.
Recreation and natural heritage, §113-77.6.
Rescue squad workers' relief fund, §58-86-40.
Saltwater fishing fund, §113-175.
School budgets, §115C-423.
Self-insurance guaranty association, §97-130.
Unemployment insurance, §96-8.
Funding agreements.
Insurance, §58-7-16, (a).
Fund-raising consultant.
Solicitation of contributions, §131F-2.
Fund-raising cost.
Solicitation of contributions, §131F-2.
Funds of an offender.
Crime victims financial recovery assistance act, §15B-32.
Funds-transfer business day, §25-4A-105, (a).
Funds-transfers, §25-4A-104, (a).
Funds-transfer system, §25-4A-105, (a).
Funds-transfer system rule, §25-4A-501.
Funeral chapel, §90-210.20, (e1).
Funeral directing, §90-210.20, (f).
Funeral director, §90-210.20, (g).
Funeral establishment, §90-210.20, (h).
Funeral expenses.
Sales and use tax exemptions, §105-164.13.
Funeral processions, §20-157.1, (a).
Funeral service licensee, §90-210.20, (i).
Funeral service profession, §90-210.20, (j).
Fungi.
Structural pest control act, §106-65.24.
Fungible.
UCC, §25-1-201.
Fungicide.
Pesticide board, §143-460.
Fungus.
Pesticide board, §143-460.
Fur-bearing animals.
Conservation, §113-129.
Furniture requirements contracts, §143-57.1, (b).
Future goods.
Sales, §25-2-105.
GAAP financial statement.
Workers' compensation self insurance, §97-165.
Employer groups, §58-47-60.
Gallon.
Weights and measures, §81A-9.
Game.
Conservation, §113-129.
Game animals.
Conservation, §113-129.
Game birds.
Conservation, §113-129.
Game fish.
Conservation, §113-129.
Game lands.
Conservation, §113-129.
Gamma knife.
Certificate of need, §131E-176.
Garbage, §130A-290, (a).
Animal diseases, §106-405.1.
Garnishee, §1-440.21, (b).
Debts owed public hospitals, §131E-48.
Garnishment of wages to recoup fraudulent public assistance program payment, §108A-25.3, (a).
Gas.
Oil and gas conservation, §113-389.

DEFINED TERMS —Cont'd
Gas city.
Piped natural gas tax, §105-187.40.
Gas company.
Public service taxation, §105-333.
Gasohol.
Gasoline tax, §105-449.60.
Gasoline.
Gasoline and oil inspection, §119-15.
Taxation, §105-449.60.
Gas operators.
Public utilities, §62-50.
Gate.
Cave protection, §14-159.20.
General account.
Protected cell companies, §58-10-80.
General assets.
Insurers supervision, §58-30-10.
General contractor, §87-1.
Homeowner's recovery fund, §87-15.5.
General guardian.
Custodial trusts, §33B-1.
Incompetency, §35A-1202.
General intangible.
Secured transactions, §25-9-102, (a).
General laws, Const. N. C., art. XIV, §3.
Cities and towns, §160A-1.
Counties, §153A-1.
General license.
Radiation protection, §104E-5.
General obligation bonds.
Metropolitan sewerage districts, §162A-65, (a).
Metropolitan water districts, §162A-32, (a).
General partner.
Partnerships, §59-102.
General reserve.
Savings and loan associations, §54B-4.
General verdict, §1A-1, Rule 49, (a).
Generic name.
Life insurance solicitation, §58-60-10.
Genetic characteristic.
Discrimination in employment based on genetic information, §95-28.1A, (b).
Genetic information.
Discrimination in employment based on genetic information, §95-28.1A, (b).
Health insurance, §58-3-215, (a).
Genetic test.
Discrimination in employment based on genetic information, §95-28.1A, (b).
Genuine.
UCC, §25-1-201.
Geographically based field programs.
Judicial department, §7A-474.2.
Geologist, §89E-3.
Geologist-in-training, §89E-3.
Geology, §89E-3.
Germination.
Seed law, §106-277.2.
Gift instrument.
Institutional funds, §36B-1.
Gift or prize.
Telephonic sellers, §66-260.
Gleaning.
Tax credit for gleaned crop, §105-130.37, (b).
Global TransPark complex, §158-32.
Gold.
Precious metals, §66-164.
Gold Star parents.
State veterans home, §165-53.
Golf cart, §20-4.01.

DEFINED TERMS —Cont'd
Good cause.
Farm machinery franchises, §66-180.
Motor vehicles, §20-305.
Good faith.
Funds transfers, UCC, §25-4A-105, (a).
Investment securities, §25-8-102.
Letters of credit, §25-5-102, (a).
Motor vehicles, §20-286.
Negotiable instruments, §25-3-103.
Sales, §25-2-103.
Secured transactions, §25-9-102, (a).
UCC, §25-1-201.
Good manufacturing practice.
Pharmacy practice, §90-85.27.
Good moral character.
Architects, §83A-1.
Geologist, §89E-3.
Professional employer organizations, §58-89A-5.
Goods.
Installment sales, §25A-4.
Leases, UCC, §25-2A-103, (1).
Sales, §25-2-105.
Secured transactions, §25-9-102, (a).
UCC, §25-7-102.
Governing board.
Consolidated city-county, §160B-2.
Electric power, §159B-3.
Institutional funds, §36B-1.
Local government bonds, §159-44.
Pest control, §106-65.55.
Governing body, §162A-2.
Aeronautics, §63-79.
Bond sales, §159-120.
City and town transportation authorities, §160A-576.
Counties, §153A-217.
Hospital licensure, §131E-76.
Housing standards, §160A-442.
Metropolitan sewerage districts, §162A-65, (a).
Metropolitan water districts, §162A-32, (a).
Pollution control, §§159C-3, 159D-3.
Urban redevelopment, §160A-503.
Governing law.
Franchise tax, §105-114.1, (a).
Government.
Housing authorities, §157-3.
Interstate environmental compact, §113A-23.
Public health authorities, §130A-45.01.
Public hospitals, §131E-16.
Soil and water conservation districts, §139-3.
Urban redevelopment, §160A-503.
Veterans' recreation, §165-25.
Government agency.
Small business contractor act, §143B-472.86.
Governmental agency.
Contractors for public works, §133-23.
Electronic transactions, §66-312.
Housing finance agency, §122A-3.
Governmental entities.
Hazardous recreation activities, §99E-22.
Sales tax, §105-164.14.
Governmental plan.
Health insurance portability and accountability.
Guaranteed of availability of individual coverage to certain individuals with prior group coverage, §58-68-60, (h).
Governmental subdivision.
Business corporations, §55-1-40.
Nonprofit corporations, §55A-1-40.

DEFINED TERMS —Cont'd
Governmental unit.
Forgery, §14-119, (c).
Guaranteed energy savings contracts, §143-64.17.
Sale, lease, exchange and joint usae of governmental property, §160A-274, (a).
Secured transactions, §25-9-102, (a).
Swap agreements, §159-193.
Government authority.
Financial privacy, §53B-2.
Government computer.
Computer crimes, §14-453.
Government computer service.
Computer crimes, §14-456.1, (a).
Government inquiry.
Financial privacy, §53B-2.
Government-vendor partnership.
Best value information technology procurements, §143-135.9.
Governor.
Criminal extradition, §15A-721.
Interstate family support, §52C-8-801, (a).
Grade "A" milk, §130A-274.
Grades.
Commercial fertilizer, §106-657.
Egg law, §106-245.14.
Grain.
Adulteration, §106-621.
Dealers, §106-601.
Grain dealer, §106-601.
Adulteration of grain, §106-621.
Grandchild.
Workers' compensation, §97-2.
Grand jury.
Grand jury proceedings, §15A-621.
Grandparent.
Visitation rights, §50-13.2, (b1).
Grant.
Clean water loans, §159G-3.
Grantee.
Use of state funds by non-state entities, §143-6.2, (a).
Granting entity.
Tax credit for qualified business investments, §105-163.010.
Grantor.
Principal and income act, §37A-1-104.1.
Grant project.
Local government finance, §159-13.2.
Grave space.
Cemeteries, §65-48.
Grievance.
Accident and health insurance.
Utilization review, §58-50-61, (a).
Discipline and disability rules of state bar, Bar Rules & Regs., B, §.0103.
Grievance committee.
Discipline and disability rules of state bar, Bar Rules & Regs., B, §.0103.
Procedures for ruling on questions of legal ethics, Bar Rules & Regs., D, §.0101.
Gross earnings.
Freight line taxation, §105-228.2.
Minors, talent contracts, §48A-15, (h).
Gross gallons.
Gasoline tax, §105-449.60.
Gross income.
Taxation, §105-134.1.
Gross sales.
Sales and use tax, §105-164.3.

DEFINED TERMS —Cont'd
Gross tonnage of newsprint consumed.
Taxation, §105-102.6.
Gross vehicle weight rating.
Motor vehicles, §20-4.01.
Gross weight.
Motor vehicles, §20-118.
Grounds.
Legislative services commission, §120-32.2.
Group.
Workers' compensation self-insurance.
Employer groups, §58-47-60.
Group accident and health insurance.
Nature of policies, §58-51-80, (a).
Group annuity contracts, §58-58-145.
Group health insurance.
Providers of health benefits, §58-50-40, (a).
Group health plan.
Providers of health benefits, §58-50-40, (a).
Group life insurance, §58-58-135.
Group life insurance policy.
Trusts of death benefits, §36A-100.
Group long-term care insurance, §58-55-20.
Group policy, §58-53-1.
Group practice.
Self-referrals by health care providers, §90-405.
Grower.
Seed law, §106-277.2.
Swine integrator registration, §143-215.10H, (a).
Guaranteed.
Securities, §78A-2.
Guaranteed energy savings contract, §143-64.17.
Guarantee of the signature.
Investment securities, §25-8-402, (c).
Guaranty association.
Savings and loan associations, §54B-4.
Guard-dog service profession, §74C-3.
Guardian.
Adoption, §48-1-101.
Interstate compact on mental health, §122C-361.
Mental health, §122C-3.
Transfers to minors, §33A-1.
Veterans, §34-2.
Guardian ad litem.
Incompetency, §§35A-1101, 35A-1202.
Guardian of the estate.
Custodial trusts, §33B-1.
Incompetency, §35A-1202.
Guardian of the person.
Custodial trusts, §33B-1.
Incompetency, §35A-1202.
Guest.
Expedited evictions, §42-59.
Habilitation.
Mental health, §122C-3.
Habitual felons.
Criminal law, §14-7.1.
Handgun, §14-409.39.
Concealed handgun permits, §14-415.10.
Prohibitions on handguns for minors, §14-269.7, (c).
Handicapped.
Motor vehicles, §20-37.5.
Handicapped person, §168-1.
Assault on, §14-32.1.
Family care home, §168-21.
Handicapping condition, §41A-3.
Handler.
Egg promotion tax, §106-245.33, (b).

DEFINED TERMS —Cont'd
Handling.
Poisonous reptiles, §14-418.
Ports authority income tax, §105-130.41, (c).
Ports authority individual income tax, §105-151.22, (c).
Harasses or harassment.
Stalking, §14-277.3, (c).
Harassment of jurors.
Obstructing justice, §14-225.2.
Harass on the basis of sex.
Criminal law, §14-395.1.
Hard of hearing.
Health and human services division, §143B-216.30.
Hard seeds.
Seed law, §106-277.2.
Harmful material.
Public morals, §19-12.
Harmful noise.
Workers' compensation, §97-53.
Harmful to minors.
Offenses against morality, §14-190.13.
Public morals, §19-12.
Has a record of such an impairment.
Persons with disabilities protection, §168A-3.
Hatchery, §106-541.
Hatching egg dealer, §106-541.
Having control over oil or other hazardous substances, §143-215.77.
Hazardous chemical.
Toxic or hazardous substance identification, §95-174, (k).
Hazardous condition.
Trust companies, §53-301, (a).
Hazardous financial condition.
Continuing care retirement communities, §58-64-1.
Liability risk retention, §58-22-10.
Professional employer organizations, §58-89A-5.
Workers' compensation self insurance, §97-165.
Employer groups, §58-47-60.
Hazardous materials.
Emergency responses, §166A-21.
Liability for abatement, §143-215.103.
Motor vehicles, §20-4.01.
Hazardous materials emergency response team, §166A-21.
Hazardous materials incident.
Emergency responses, §166A-21.
Hazardous recreation activity, §99E-22.
Hazardous solvent.
Dry-cleaning equipment tax credit, §105-129.16C, (c).
Hazardous substance, §130A-310.
Control, §143-215.77.
Fiduciaries, §32-27.
Powers of trustees under express trust, §36A-136.
Hazardous substance list.
Toxic or hazardous substance identification, §95-174, (l).
Hazardous substance trade secret.
Toxic or hazardous substance identification, §95-174, (m).
Hazardous waste, §130A-290, (a).
Dry-cleaning solvent cleanup act, §143-215.104B, (b).
Hazardous waste disposal facility, §130A-290, (a).
Hazardous waste facility, §130A-290, (a).
Hazardous waste management, §130A-290, (a).

DEFINED TERMS —Cont'd
Hazardous waste management program, §130A-290, (a).
Hazing.
Criminal law, §14-35.
Hazmat team.
Hazardous materials emergency response, §166A-21.
HE.
Property taxes, §105-273.
Head of department.
Executive organization, §143B-3.
State government reorganization, §143A-2.
Head of household.
Taxation, §105-134.1.
Health benefit plan, §58-3-200, (a).
Applicability of acts of general assembly to health benefit plans, §58-3-167, (a).
Claims, §§58-3-171, (c), 58-3-172.
Closed formulary, health insurers maintaining, §58-3-221, (c).
Coordination of benefits with Medicaid, §58-51-115, (a).
Covered clinical trials, §58-3-255, (a).
Dental procedures performed in hospital or ambulatory surgical facility, §58-3-122, (b).
Diagnosis and evaluation of osteoporosis and low bone mass, §58-3-174.
Direct access to obstetrician-gynecologist, §58-51-38, (a).
Direct payment to government, §58-3-175, (a).
Drive-thru deliveries, §58-3-169, (a).
Emergency care coverage, §58-3-190, (g).
Employer obligations, §108A-69, (a).
Genetic information, §58-3-215, (a).
Health care liability, §90-21.50.
Insurance discrimination, §58-3-121, (a) to (c).
Lien on insurance settlement of child support obligor, §58-3-185, (b).
Managed care access to specialists, §58-3-223, (b).
Maternity coverage, §58-3-170, (b).
Pharmacy of choice, §58-51-37, (b).
Postmastectomy inpatient care coverage, §58-3-168, (b).
Prescription contraceptive drugs, devices and services covered by health benefit plan, §58-3-178, (c).
Prompt claim payments under health benefit plans, §58-3-225, (a).
Reporting and disclosure requirements, §58-3-191, (c).
Small employer group health coverage, §58-50-110.
Treatment discussions, §58-3-176.
Uniform prescription drug identification cards issued by health benefit plan, §58-3-177, (e).
Uniform provider credentialing, §58-3-230, (c).
Utilization review, §58-50-61, (a).
Health benefits representative.
State medical plan, §135-40.1.
Health care.
Consent to health care for minor, §32A-29.
Powers of attorney, §32A-16.
Health care agent.
Powers of attorney, §32A-16.
Health care decision.
Health care liability, §90-21.50.
Health care delivery assets.
Provider sponsored organizations, §131E-276.
Health care facilities, §131A-3.
Adoption, §48-3-401.
Cancer reporting, §130A-209, (c).

DEFINED TERMS —Cont'd
Health care facilities —Cont'd
Health plans, disclosure to providers, §58-3-227, (a).
Nursing pools, §131E-154.2.
Obstruction of health care facilities, §14-277.4, (f).
Patient abuse, §14-32.2, (c).
Prompt claim payments under health benefit plans, §58-3-225, (a).
Terrorist incident using nuclear, biological or chemical agents, §130A-476, (g).
Verification of nurse licensure status, §90-171.43A, (b).
Health-care-insurance receivable.
Secured transactions, §25-9-102, (a).
Health care operations.
Patient medical records, confidentiality of, §130A-12.
Health care plan.
Health maintenance organizations, §58-67-5, (d).
Health care power of attorney.
Powers of attorney, §32A-16.
Health care practitioners.
Identification, §90-640, (a).
Health care provider.
Accident and health insurance.
Utilization review, §58-50-61, (a).
Cancer reporting, §130A-209, (c).
Health care liability, §90-21.50.
Health plans, disclosure to providers, §58-3-227, (a).
Industrial commission managed care organizations, I.C. Managed Care Orgs. R. II.
Interim insurance claims payment, §58-2-235, (d).
Medical malpractice, §90-21.11.
Medical records, §90-410.
Nursing, §90-171.20.
Pharmacy practice, §90-85.3, (i).
Prompt claim payments under health benefit plans, §58-3-225, (a).
Provider sponsored organizations, §131E-276.
Referral fees and solicitation payments, §90-400.
Self-referrals, §90-405.
Temporary order by state health director to report health related information, §130A-141.1.
Terrorist incident using nuclear, biological or chemical agents, §130A-476, (g).
Workers' compensation, §97-2.
Health care services.
Accident and health insurance.
Utilization review, §58-50-61, (a).
Direct access to obstetrician-gynecologist, §58-51-38, (a).
Health care liability, §90-21.50.
Health maintenance organizations, §58-67-5, (e).
Obstruction of health care facilities, §14-277.4, (g).
Health certificate.
Bee and honey act, §106-635.
Health data.
Health statistics, §130A-372.
Health information.
Managed care patient assistance program, §143-730.
Health insurance.
Insurance guaranty associations, §58-62-16.
Health insurance coverage.
Health insurance portability and accountability, §58-68-25, (a).
Health insurance for the aged act, §58-54-1.
Health insurance plan.
Health insurance portability and accountability, §58-68-25, (a).

DEFINED TERMS —Cont'd
Health insurer, §58-12-2.
Coordination of benefits with Medicaid, §58-51-115, (a).
Employer obligations, §108A-69, (a).
Health insurance portability and accountability, §58-68-25, (a).
Health maintenance organization, §58-67-5, (f).
Certificate of need, §131E-176.
Health organization.
Risk based capital requirements, §58-12-2.
Health plan contract.
Provider sponsored organizations, §131E-276.
Health related services.
Continuing care retirement communities, §58-64-1.
Health service.
Certificate of need, §131E-176.
Psychology practice act, §90-270.2.
Health service facility.
Certificate of need, §131E-176.
Health service facility bed.
Certificate of need, §131E-176.
Health status-related factor.
Health insurance portability and accountability, §58-68-25, (a).
Hearing aid.
Dealers and board, §93D-1.
Hearing committee.
Discipline and disability rules of state bar, Bar Rules & Regs., B, §.0103.
Hearing officer.
Administrative procedure, §150B-2.
Child support, §50-31.
Hearsay.
Evidence, §8C-1, Rule 801, (c).
Heart-lung bypass machine.
Certificate of need, §131E-176.
Heating.
Contractors, §87-21.
Heating, group 1.
Contractors, §87-21.
Heating, group 2.
Contractors, §87-21.
Heating, group 3.
Contractors, §87-21.
Heating oil.
Petroleum cleanup, §143-215.94A.
Heir.
Decedents' estates, §§28A-1-1, 29-2.
Help America Vote act, §162-82.27.
Hemoglobin C trait, §58-58-25.
Labor discrimination, §95-28.1.
Herbicide.
Pesticide board, §143-460.
Hernia.
Workers' compensation, §97-2.
High-calcium foods and beverages.
School boards to give preference to, §115C-264.1, (a).
High cost home loans.
Mortgages, high cost home loans, §24-1.1E, (a).
Higher education.
Executive organization, §143B-3.
Highest annual salary.
Legislative retirement system, §120-4.8.
High Rock lake.
High Rock lake marine commission, §77-50.
High school, §115C-75, (a).
High-speed broadband internet access.
E-NC authority, §143B-437.45.

DEFINED TERMS —Cont'd
High unemployment period.
Unemployment insurance, §96-12.01, (a1).
High-voltage lines.
Overhead high-voltage line safety, §95-229.6.
Highway.
Alternative fuel, §105-449.130.
Contractors, §87-101.
Gasoline tax, §105-449.60.
Motor vehicles, §20-4.01.
Public utilities, §62-3.
Roads and highways, §136-91.
Highway vehicle.
Alternative fuel, §105-449.130.
Gasoline tax, §105-449.60.
Highway vending facilities.
Aid to the blind, §111-49, (c).
Highway work zone.
Speed limits, §20-141, (j2).
Hire.
Criminal law, §14-168.2.
Historic ABC establishment.
Alcoholic beverages, §18B-101.
Historically underutilized business.
Higher education bonds, §116D-1.
Historic district.
City and towns, §160A-400.3.
Historic dollar value.
Institutional funds, §36B-1.
Historic edged weapon.
Sale of pistols and crossbows, §§14-402, (c), 14-409.12.
Historic preservation.
Archives and history, §121-2.
Historic property, §121-2.
Hive.
Bee and honey act, §106-635.
HMO, §58-67-5, (f).
Holder.
Historic preservation agreements, §121-35.
UCC, §25-1-201.
Unclaimed property act, §116B-52.
Holder in due course.
Negotiable instruments, §25-3-302.
Holding and processing facility.
Cremation, §90-210.41.
Holding company.
Corporate income tax.
Adjustment for expenses related to dividends, §105-130.6A, (a).
Taxation, §105-120.2.
Holdover facility.
Delinquent and undisciplined juveniles, §7B-1501.
Home appliance.
Service agreement companies, §58-1-30, (b).
Home appliance service agreement.
Service agreement companies, §58-1-30, (b).
Home appliance service agreement company, §58-1-30, (b).
Home care agency, §131E-136.
Home care services, §131E-136.
Home consumer-sized package.
Antifreeze law, §106-579.3.
Home country.
Trust companies, §53-301, (a).
Home country regulator.
Trust companies, §53-301, (a).
Home health agency, §131E-136.
Certificate of need, §131E-176.
Home health aid.
State medical plan, §135-40.1.

DEFINED TERMS —Cont'd
Home healthcare agency.
State medical plan, §135-40.1.
Home healthcare coverage.
State medical plan, §135-40.1.
Home health services.
Certificate of need, §131E-176.
Long-term care insurance, §58-55-35, (a).
Home inspection, §143-151.45.
Home inspector, §143-151.45.
Homeless.
Assignment of student to particular school, §115C-366, (a2).
Student admission and assignment, §115C-366.
Home loan.
Contract rates on home loan secured by first mortgage or first deed of trust, §24-1.1A, (e).
Homemaker services.
Long-term care insurance, §58-55-35, (a).
Home office.
Structural pest control act, §106-65.24.
Home school, §115C-563, (a).
Home service business, §58-10-25, (a).
Home-solicitation sale.
Installment sales, §25A-38.
Home state.
Child custody jurisdiction and enforcement, §50A-102.
Insurance producers, §58-33-10.
Interstate branch banking, §53-224.9.
Interstate family support, §52C-1-101.
Nurse licensure compact, §90-171.82.
Savings and loan interstate branches, §54B-266.
Savings interstate branch banks, §54C-200.
Trust companies, §53-301, (a).
Home state action.
Nurse licensure compact, §90-171.82.
Home state regulator.
Trust companies, §53-301, (a).
Honey, §106-635.
Honeybees, §106-635.
Honeyflow, §106-635.
Honey plants, §106-635.
Honor.
Letters of credit, §25-5-102, (a).
UCC, §25-1-201.
Honorable military service.
Veterans cemeteries, §65-43.
Horace Williams campus, §116-198.33.
Horticultural land.
Taxation, §105-277.2.
Hospice, §131E-201.
Certificate of need, §131E-176.
Long-term care insurance, §58-55-35, (a).
Hospice inpatient facility.
Certificate of need, §131E-176.
Hospice licensure, §131E-201.
Hospice patient, §131E-201.
Hospice patient's family, §131E-201.
Hospice residential care facility.
Certificate of need, §131E-176.
Hospice licensure, §131E-201.
Hospice services.
Hospice licensure, §131E-201.
Hospice team, §131E-201.
Hospital.
Anatomical gifts, §130A-403.
Certificate of need, §131E-176.
Cooperative agreements.
Certificate of public advantage, §131E-192.2.

DEFINED TERMS —Cont'd
Hospital —Cont'd
Cooperative agreements among physicians or between physician, hospital or others, §90-21.25.
Licensure, §131E-76.
Medical care data, §131E-214.1.
State medical plan, §135-40.1.
Terrorist incident or communicable diseases, detection of, §130A-480, (d).
Hospital authority.
Public hospitals, §131E-16.
Hospital facilities, §131E-6.
Public hospitals, §131E-16.
Hospitalization.
Insurance, §58-51-105.
Hospital land, §131E-6.
Public hospitals, §131E-16.
Hospital medical records.
Evidence, §8-44.1.
Hospital service corporation, §58-65-1, (a).
Hospital service plan, §58-65-1, (a).
Hospital services.
Debts owed public hospitals, §131E-48.
Host.
Boll weevil eradication, §106-65.69.
Host state.
Interstate branch banking, §53-224.9.
Trust companies, §53-301, (a).
Hotel.
Alcoholic beverages, §18B-1000.
Hours worked.
Wage and hour act, §95-25.2.
House.
Criminal law, §14-58.1.
House arrest.
Delinquent and undisciplined juveniles, §7B-1501.
House arrest with electronic monitoring.
Structured sentencing, §15A-1340.11.
Household support loss.
Victim's compensation, §15B-2.
House trailer.
Motor vehicles, §20-4.01.
Housing accommodation, §41A-3.
Housing authority, §157-41.
National defense housing projects, §157-53.
Housing facility.
Protection of animals, §19A-23.
Housing finance agency.
Low-income housing tax credits, §105-129.40, (b).
Housing for older persons.
Fair housing, §41A-6, (e).
Housing project, §157-41.
Housing authorities, §157-3.
Hub.
Sales and use tax, §105-164.3.
Tax incentives for new and expanding businesses, §105-129.2.
HUD.
Uniform standards for manufactured homes act, §143-145.
Hull insurance and protection and indemnity, §58-20-5.
Human remains.
Cemeteries, §65-48.
Cremations, §90-210.41.
Human service agency.
Public utilities, §62-289.3.
Human services field.
Substance abuse professionals, §90-113.31.

DEFINED TERMS —Cont'd
Human service transportation.
Public utilities, §62-289.3.
Human skeletal remains.
Burial sites, §70-28.
Hybrid.
Seed law, §106-277.2.
Hydroelectric generator.
Business and energy tax credits, §105-129.15.
Hypothecation lender.
Membership camping, §66-246, (a).
Identifiable hospice administration.
Hospice licensure, §131E-201.
Identifying information.
Financial identity fraud, §14-113.20, (b).
Identifying number.
Condominiums, §47C-1-103.
III system.
National crime prevention and privacy compact, §114-19.50.
Illegal gas.
Oil and gas conservation, §113-389.
Illegal oil.
Oil and gas conservation, §113-389.
Illegal product.
Oil and gas conservation, §113-389.
Illegal signs.
Outdoor advertising control, §136-128.
Illegal slot machines.
Lotteries and gaming, §14-296.
Illicit drug.
Discipline and disability rules of state bar, Bar Rules & Regs., B, §.0103.
Illicit mixed beverage.
Unauthorized substances taxes, §105-113.106.
Illicit sexual behavior.
Alimony, §50-16.1A.
Illicit spirituous liquor.
Unauthorized substances taxes, §105-113.106.
Immediate container.
Food, drugs and cosmetics, §106-121.
Poultry products inspection, §106-549.51.
Immediate family.
Coastal and estuarine commercial fishing licenses, §113-168.
Custodial institutions, §14-259.
Peer support group counselor's privilege, §8-53.10, (a).
Savings and loan associations, §54B-4.
Savings banks, §54C-4, (b).
Transportation board, §136-14, (h).
Immediate family member.
Family leave credit insurance, §58-57-115, (a).
Self-referrals by health care providers, §90-405.
Voluntary shared leave program, §115C-12.2.
Immediate household.
Legislative ethics act, §120-85.
Immediate precursor.
Controlled substances, §90-87.
Imminent danger.
Mines, §74-24.2.
Occupational safety and health, §95-127.
Imminent hazard.
Dry-cleaning solvent cleanup act, §143-215.104B, (b).
Public health generally, §130A-2.
Impaired.
Insurers supervision, §58-30-12.
Impaired driving.
Motor vehicles, §20-138.1.

DEFINED TERMS —Cont'd
Impaired driving license revocation, §20-28.2, (a).
Impaired insurer.
Insurance guaranty associations, §58-62-16.
Small employer group health coverage, §58-50-110.
Impairing substance.
Motor vehicles, §20-4.01.
Implement of husbandry.
Motor vehicles, §20-4.01.
Implied-consent offense, §20-16.2, (a1).
Import.
Gasoline tax, §105-449.60.
Importer.
Alcohol taxation, §105-113.68.
Impound.
Impounded water, §143-215.44, (d).
Impracticable of fulfillment.
Charitable trusts, §36A-53.
Improve.
Statutory liens on real property, §44A-7.
Subcontractors, §22C-1.
Improvement project.
Development zone project tax credit, §105-129.13, (b).
Improvements.
Statutory liens on real property, §44A-7.
Subcontractors, §22C-1.
Water and sewer, §162A-2.
Inactive hazardous substance or waste disposal site, §130A-310.
Inactive licensee.
Engineering, §89C-3.
Inactive member.
Continuing legal education, Bar Rules & Regs., D, §.1501.
Inaugural period.
Ceremonies committee, §143-532.
Inaugural planning period.
Ceremonies committee, §143-532.
Inbred line.
Seed law, §106-277.2.
In bulk.
Seed law, §106-277.2.
Incapable.
Advance instruction for mental health treatment, §122C-72.
Incapacity or incapacitated.
Custodial trusts, §33B-1.
Discipline and disability rules of state bar, Bar Rules & Regs., B, §.0103.
Standby guardianship, §35A-1370.
Incapacity to proceed.
Criminal law and procedure, §15A-1001.
Inclined or vertical wheelchair lift.
Elevator safety, §95-110.3, (g).
Inclined stairway chair lift.
Elevator safety, §95-110.3, (f).
Includes.
Business corporations, §55-1-40.
Nonprofit corporations, §55A-1-40.
Income.
Interstate family support, §52C-1-101.
Principal and income act, §37A-1-102.
Property tax homestead exclusion, §105-277.1, (b).
Veterans, §34-2.
Income attributable to the state.
Taxation, §105-131.
Income beneficiary.
Principal and income act, §37A-1-102.

DEFINED TERMS —Cont'd
Income interest.
Principal and income act, §37A-1-102.
Income not attributable to the state.
Taxation, §105-131.
Income tax return preparer, §105-228.90.
Income-withholding order.
Interstate family support, §52C-1-101.
Income year.
Taxation, §§105-114, 105-130.2.
Incompetent adult.
Incompetency, §35A-1101.
Mental health, §122C-3.
Incompetent child.
Incompetency, §35A-1101.
Incompetent person.
Incompetency, §35A-1202.
In-county scrap tire, §130A-309.53.
Indebtedness.
Corporate franchise tax, §105-122, (b).
Credit insurance, §58-57-5.
Indemnity trigger.
Protected cell companies, §58-10-80.
Independent escrow agent.
Time shares, §93A-41.
Independent expenditure.
Political campaigns, §163-278.6.
Public campaign financing fund, §163-278.62.
Independent expert witness.
Medicolegal guidelines for attorney-physician relationship, MLG Rule 3.
Independent medical examination.
Medicolegal guidelines for attorney-physician relationship, MLG Rule 3.
Independent motor vehicle dealer, §20-286.
Independent professional advice.
Structured settlement protection, §1-543.11.
Independent review organization.
Health benefit plan external review, §58-50-75, (c).
Index rate.
Small employer group health coverage, §58-50-110.
Indictment, §15A-641.
Indigent.
Incompetency, §35A-1101.
Protection of disabled adults, §108A-101.
Indigent persons.
Judicial department, §7A-450.
Rules governing legal services provided by students, Bar Rules & Regs., C, §.0202.
Rules governing practical training of law students, Bar Rules & Regs., C, §.0202.
Indirect interest in transaction.
Nonprofit corporations, §55A-31, (b).
Individual.
Business corporations, §55-1-40.
Conservation, §113-130.
Insurance information and privacy protection act, §58-39-15.
Limited liability companies, §57C-1-03.
Nonprofit corporations, §55A-1-40.
Political campaigns, §163-278.6.
Respiratory care practices act, §90-648.
Taxation, §105-134.1.
Tax withholding, §105-163.1.
Individual health insurance coverage.
Health insurance portability and accountability, §58-68-25, (a).
Individually identifiable energy information.
Stocks of coal and petroleum fuels, §143-345.14, (f).

DEFINED TERMS —Cont'd
Individually owned.
Taxation, §105-277.2.
Individual market.
Health insurance portability and accountability, §58-68-25, (a).
Individual policy.
Group health insurance, §58-53-1.
Individual rental unit.
Expedited evictions, §42-59.
Indorsement.
Negotiable instruments, §25-3-204.
Industrial bank, §53-136.
Industrial hygiene, §90-515.
Industrial hygienist, §90-515.
Industrial hygienist in training, §90-515.
Industrial life insurance, §58-58-5.
Industrial plant.
Public utilities, §62-3.
Industrial project.
Pollution control, §159C-3.
Industrial-quality eye protective devices.
Vocational education, §115C-168.
Industrial sick benefit insurance.
Nature of policies, §58-51-65.
Industrial solid waste, §130A-290.
Industrial waste, §143-213.
Industry.
Passenger tramway safety, §95-117.
Inebriety.
Incompetency, §35A-1101.
Inert debris.
Solid waste management, §130A-290, (a).
Inert ingredient.
Pesticide board, §143-460.
Inert matter.
Seed law, §106-277.2.
Infected.
Bee and honey act, §106-635.
Infection.
Protection of forest, §113-60.6.
Infestation.
Protection of forest, §113-60.6.
Infested.
Bee and honey act, §106-635.
Boll weevil eradication, §106-65.69.
Infirmary.
Hospital licensure, §131E-76.
Informal bids.
Roads and highways, §136-28.1, (b).
Informal ethics advisory.
Procedures for ruling on questions of legal ethics, Bar Rules & Regs., D, §.0101.
Information, §15A-641.
Electronic transactions, §66-312.
Information center.
Outdoor advertising control, §136-128.
Information processing system.
Electronic transactions, §66-312.
Information technology.
Best value information technology procurements, §143-135.9.
Office of information technology services, §147-33.81.
Information technology enterprise management.
Office of information technology services, §147-33.81.
Information technology portfolio management.
Office of information technology services, §147-33.81.

DEFINED TERMS —Cont'd
Infraction.
Criminal law, §14-3.1.
In good faith.
Uniform fiduciaries act, §32-2, (b).
Ingredient statement.
Pesticide board, §143-460.
Inherent risk.
Hazardous recreation activities, §99E-22.
Inherent risks of equine activities.
Equine activity liability, §99E-1.
In-house continuing legal education, Bar Rules & Regs., D, §.1501.
Initial capital.
Trust companies, §53-301, (a).
Initial cost.
Energy policy for state government, §143-64.11.
Initial determination.
Child custody jurisdiction and enforcement, §50A-102.
Initial pledges for withdrawable accounts.
Savings and loan associations, §54B-4.
Initiating party.
Child support, §§50-31, 110-129.
Initiating state.
Interstate family support, §52C-1-101.
Initiating tribunal.
Interstate family support, §52C-1-101.
Injured party.
Offshore oil and gas activities, §143-215.94BB.
Injury.
Alcoholic beverages, §18B-120.
Workers' compensation, §97-2.
Inland fishing waters, §113-129.
Inland game fish.
Conservation, §113-129.
Inland marine insurance.
Insurance rates, §58-40-5.
Inmate.
State prisons, §148-120.
In need of protective services.
Protection of disabled adults, §108A-101.
Innocent owner.
Impaired driving, §20-28.2, (a1).
Inquiry.
Domestic violence in disposition report, §15A-1382.1, (c).
Insect.
Pesticide board, §143-460.
Structural pest control act, §106-65.24.
Insecticides.
Pesticide board, §143-460.
Structural pest control act, §106-65.24.
Insider.
Fraudulent transfers, §39-23.1.
Insolvency.
Banking, §53-1.
Health maintenance organizations, §58-67-5, (m).
Insurers supervision, §58-30-10.
Insolvency proceedings.
UCC, §25-1-201.
Insolvent.
Health maintenance organizations, §58-67-5, (m).
Insurers supervision, §§58-30-10, 58-30-12.
Trust companies, §53-301, (a).
UCC, §25-1-201.
Insolvent insurer.
Insurance guaranty association, §§58-48-20, 58-62-16.
Inspection certificate.
Boiler and pressure vessel regulation, §95-69.9, (e).

DEFINED TERMS —Cont'd
Inspection department.
Uniform standards for manufactured homes act, §143-145.
Inspection service.
Poultry products inspection, §106-549.51.
Inspector.
Conservation, §113-128.
Poultry products inspection, §106-549.51.
Inspector's commission.
Boiler and pressure vessel regulation, §95-69.9, (f).
Installation.
Weights and measures, §81A-9.
Installation of pumps and pumping equipment.
Well construction, §87-85.
Installment lease contract.
Leases, UCC, §25-2A-103, (1).
In-state-only supplier.
Gasoline tax, §105-449.60.
Institution.
Bonds for student housing, §116-175.
Centennial campus and Horace Williams campus financing act, §116-198.33.
Community colleges, §115D-2.
Decedents' estates, safe deposit boxes, §28A-15-13, (a).
Higher education bonds, §116D-22.
Higher education student housing, §116-189.
Institutional funds, §36B-1.
Interstate compact on mental health, §122C-361.
Mutual deposit guaranty associations, §54B-236.
Private educational institutions, §116-22.
State grants to students attending private universities or colleges, §116-43.5, (a).
State prisons, §148-120.
University of North Carolina, §§116-2, 116-15.
Institutional consumer.
Egg law, §106-245.14.
Institutional fund, §36B-1.
Institutional source.
Insurance information and privacy protection act, §58-39-15.
Institution for elementary and secondary education.
Private capital facilities finance act, §159D-37.
Institution of higher education.
Higher education tuition and fees, §116-143.1.
Private capital facilities finance act, §159D-37.
Psychology practice act, §90-270.2.
Sex offender and public protection registration, §14-208.6.
Instruction.
Investment securities, §25-8-102.
Instructional personnel.
Education programs in residential schools, §143B-146.1, (b).
Instructor.
Motor vehicles, §20-320.
Instrument.
Forgery, §14-119, (c).
Negotiable instruments, §25-3-104.
Registration by register of deeds, §161-14, (d).
Secured transactions, §25-9-102, (a).
Insurable interest.
Beach property insurance, §58-45-35, (a).
Insurable property.
Beach property insurance, §58-45-5.
Insurance.
Group health insurance, §58-53-1.
Insurance producers, §58-33-10.

DEFINED TERMS —Cont'd
Insurance —Cont'd
Liability risk retention, §58-22-10.
Third party administrators, §58-56-2.
Insurance company, §58-1-5.
Bail, §15A-531.
Funeral and burial trust funds, §90-210.60.
Impaired driving, §20-28.2, (a1).
Political campaigns, §163-278.6.
Regulatory charge, §58-6-25, (e).
Unclaimed property act, §116B-52.
Insurance fiduciary.
Providers of health benefits, §58-50-40, (a).
Insurance fund.
Pest control, §106-65.55.
Insurance holding company system, §58-19-5.
Insurance institution.
Insurance information and privacy protection act, §58-39-15.
Insurance of deposit accounts.
Savings banks, §54C-4, (b).
Insurance of withdrawable accounts.
Savings and loan associations, §54B-4.
Insurance policy or contract.
Readable insurance policies, §58-38-15.
Insurance premium finance agreement, §58-35-1.
Insurance premium finance company, §58-35-1.
Insurance proceeds.
Impaired driving, §20-28.2, (a1).
Insurance producer, §58-33-10.
Interagency consultation by insurance commissioner, §58-2-128, (d).
Insurance product.
Public officers and employees, §58-31-60, (a).
Insurance regulator, §58-2-131, (b).
Insurance guaranty associations, §58-62-16.
Insurance-support organization.
Insurance information and privacy protection act, §58-39-15.
Insurance transaction.
Insurance information and privacy protection act, §58-39-15.
Insured or enrollee.
Group health insurance, §58-53-1.
Health care liability, §90-21.50.
Insurer.
Accident and health insurance.
Pharmacy of choice, §58-51-37, (b).
Applicability of acts of general assembly to health benefit plans, §58-3-167, (a).
Bail bondsman and runners, §58-71-1.
Closed formulary, health insurers maintaining, §58-3-221, (c).
Dental procedures performed in hospital or ambulatory surgical facility, §58-3-122, (b).
Diagnosis and evaluation of osteoporosis and low bone mass, §58-3-174.
Drive-thru deliveries, §58-3-169, (a).
Elderly insurance, §58-52-1.
Emergency care coverage, §58-3-190, (g).
False statement to procure or deny benefit of policy or certificate, §58-2-161, (a).
Genetic information in health insurance, §58-3-215, (a).
Group health insurance, §58-53-1.
Health benefit plans, §58-3-200, (a).
Health care liability, §90-21.50.
Health plans, disclosure to providers, §58-3-227, (a).
Insurance, §58-1-5.

DEFINED TERMS —Cont'd
Insurer —Cont'd
Insurance company taxation, §105-228.3.
Insurance holding companies, §58-19-5.
Insurers supervision, §58-30-10.
Interim insurance claims payment, §58-2-235, (d).
Managed care access to specialists, §58-3-223, (b).
Managing general agents, §58-34-2, (a).
Medicare supplement insurance, §58-54-1.
Pharmacy of choice, §58-51-37, (b).
Preferred providers, §58-50-56, (a).
Prescription contraceptive drugs, devices and services covered by health benefit plan, §58-3-178, (c).
Producer-controlled property or casualty insurers, §58-3-165, (a).
Prompt claim payments under health benefit plans, §58-3-225, (a).
Rates, §58-36-100, (b).
Readable insurance policies, §58-38-15.
Regulatory charge, §58-6-25, (e).
Third party administrators, §58-56-2.
Treatment discussions, §58-3-176.
Uniform provider credentialing, §58-3-230, (c).
Use of nonoriginal crash parts, §58-36-95, (a).
Utilization review, §58-50-61, (a).
Workers' compensation, §97-2.
Intake.
Delinquent and undisciplined juveniles, §7B-1501.
Intangible personal property.
Property taxes, §105-273.
Integrative medicine, §90-2.1.
Intensive probation.
Structured sentencing, §15A-1340.11.
Intentional interference.
Interference with emergency communications, §14-286.2, (b1).
Interagency council.
Community schools act, §115C-205.
Intercept.
Electronic surveillance, §15A-286.
Intercollegiate sport.
Athlete agents, §78C-86.
Interconceptional care.
Midwifery practice, §90-178.2.
Interdisciplinary team, §131E-201.
Interest.
Dissenters' rights, §55-13-01.
Interested distributee.
Principal and income act, §37A-1-104.1.
Interested parties.
Structured settlement protection, §1-543.11.
Interested person.
Trusts and trustees, §36A-22.1.
Interested shares.
Control share acquisitions, §55-9A-01, (b).
Interested trustee.
Principal and income act, §37A-1-104.1.
Interest in real property.
Subordination agreements, §39-6.6, (a).
Interface.
Planning regionally significant transportation projects, §136-200.
Interim association.
Savings and loan associations, §54B-4.
Interim guardian.
Incompetency, §35A-1101.
Intermediary.
Reinsurance intermediaries, §58-9-2, (a).
Intermediary bank.
Banking, §25-4-105.
Funds transfers, UCC, §25-4A-104, (b).

DEFINED TERMS —Cont'd
Intermediate accident.
Safe driver incentive program, §58-36-75, (a).
Intermediate care facility.
Long-term care insurance, §58-55-35, (a).
Intermediate care facility for the mentally retarded.
Certificate of need, §131E-176.
Intermediate punishment.
Structured sentencing, §15A-1340.11.
Intermediate-term loan.
Rural redevelopment authority, §143B-437.21.
Internal revenue code.
Small business contractor act, §143B-472.86.
International bank agency.
International banking act, §53-232.2, (a).
International bank branch.
International banking act, §53-232.2, (a).
International banking corporation.
International banking act, §53-232.2, (a).
International banking facility.
Corporate income tax, §105-130.5, (b).
International organization.
Business discrimination, §75B-1.
International representative office.
International banking act, §53-232.2, (a).
International symbol of access.
Handicapped parking privileges, §20-37.5.
Interpreter.
Interpreters and transliterators licensure act, §90D-3.
Interpreting.
Interpreters and transliterators licensure act, §90D-3.
Intersection.
Motor vehicles, §20-4.01.
Intersection of highway.
Motor vehicles, §20-150.
Interstate air business.
Sales and use tax, §105-164.3.
Interstate air courier.
Tax incentives for new and expanding businesses, §105-129.2.
Interstate cases.
Child support income withholding procedures, §110-136.3, (b).
Interstate commerce.
Motor carriers, §20-376.
Public utilities, §62-3.
Interstate compact on juveniles, §7B-1501.
Interstate environment pollution.
Interstate environmental compact, §113A-23.
Interstate freight air carrier.
Sales and use tax, §105-164.3.
Interstate merger transaction.
Branch banking, §53-224.9.
Interstate motor carrier.
Motor carrier safety regulation unit, §20-376.
Interstate passenger air carrier.
Sales and use tax, §105-164.3.
Tax incentives for new and expanding businesses, §105-129.2.
Interstate system.
Junkyard control, §136-143.
Outdoor advertising control, §136-128.
Interview.
Private personnel services, §95-47.1.
In the presence of a minor.
Assault, §14-33, (d).
In this (the) state.
Sales and use tax, §105-164.3.

DEFINED TERMS —Cont'd
Intoxicated.
Mental health, §122C-3.
Public intoxication, §14-443.
Intoxication.
Toxic vapors act, §90-113.9.
Intrapartum care.
Midwifery practice, §90-178.2.
Intrastate commerce.
Meat inspection, §106-549.15.
Motor carriers, §20-376.
Poultry products inspection, §106-549.51.
Public utilities, §62-3.
Intrastate motor carrier.
Motor carrier safety regulation unit, §20-376.
Intrastate operations.
Public utilities, §62-3.
Intrastate system.
Highway trust fund, §136-175.
Introduction of the Euro.
European monetary union, §53-295.
Invention.
Invention development services, §66-209.
Invention developer, §66-209.
Invention development services, §66-209.
Inventory.
Farm machinery, §66-180.
Property taxes, §105-273.
Secured transactions, §25-9-102, (a).
Investigating law enforcement agency.
Crime victims' rights, §15A-830, (a).
Investigation.
Discipline and disability rules of state bar, Bar Rules & Regs., B, §.0103.
Procedures for the authorized practice committee of the state bars, Bar Rules & Regs., D, §.0203.
Investigative consumer report.
Insurance information and privacy protection act, §58-39-15.
Investigative or law enforcement officer.
Electronic surveillance, §15A-286.
Investigator.
Discipline and disability rules of state bar, Bar Rules & Regs., B, §.0103.
Procedures for the authorized practice committee of the state bars, Bar Rules & Regs., D, §.0203.
Investment adviser, §78C-2.
Investment adviser covered under federal law, §78C-2.
Investment adviser representative, §78C-2.
Investment advisers act of 1940, §78C-2.
Investment company security, §25-8-103.
Investment income.
Saltwater fishing fund, §113-175.
Investment interest.
Self-referrals by health care providers, §90-405.
Investment property.
Secured transactions, §25-9-102, (a).
Investor.
Self-referrals by health care providers, §90-405.
Investor-owned public utility.
Air pollution control, §143-215.107D, (a).
Environmental compliance costs, §62-133.6, (a).
Invitation to bid.
Motion pictures, §75C-2.
Involuntary servitude, §14-43.2.
Ionizing radiation.
Radiation protection, §104E-5.

DEFINED TERMS —Cont'd
Isolation authority.
Public health, §130A-2.
Isomer.
Controlled substances, §90-87.
Is regarded as having an impairment.
Persons with disabilities protection, §168A-3.
Issue.
Negotiable instruments, §25-3-105.
Occupational safety and health, §95-127.
Issued.
Criminal process and procedure.
Electronic technology, §15A-101.1.
Issuer.
Criminal law, §14-113.8.
Letters of credit, §25-5-102, (a).
Negotiable instruments, §25-3-105.
Public obligations, §159E-2.
Securities, §78A-2.
UCC, §25-7-102.
Issuer's jurisdiction.
Investment securities, §25-8-110.
Issuing court.
Child custody jurisdiction and enforcement, §50A-102.
Issuing state.
Child custody jurisdiction and enforcement, §50A-102.
Interstate family support, §52C-1-101.
Issuing tribunals.
Interstate family support, §52C-1-101.
Issuing unit.
Local government finance, §159-160.
Item.
Banking, §25-4-104, (a).
Telephonic sellers, §66-260.
Itinerant merchant, §66-250.
Itinerant vendor.
Bedding, §130A-261.
IV-D case child support, §110-129.
J bar, T bar or platter pull.
Passenger tramway safety, §95-117.
Jeopardized.
Trust companies, §53-301, (a).
Jobber, §106-541.
Job listing service, §95-47.19.
Job order.
Private personnel services, §95-47.1.
Job performance.
Employer disclosing information, §1-539.12, (b).
Joint accident and health coverage.
Credit insurance, §58-57-5.
Joint agency.
Electric power, §159B-3.
Joint fishing waters.
Conservation, §113-129.
Joint life coverage.
Credit insurance, §58-57-5.
Joint municipal assistance agency.
Electric power, §159B-3.
Joint ordinance.
High Rock lake marine commission, §77-50.
Lake Wylie marine commission, §77-30.
Joint resolution.
Mountain Island lake marine commission, §77-70.
Joint tenants.
Simultaneous death act, §28A-24-3, (b).
Journalist.
Journalist's qualified privilege, §8-53.11, (a).
Judge.
Abused, neglected and dependent juveniles, §7B-101.

DEFINED TERMS —Cont'd
Judge —Cont'd
Boxing commission, §143-651.
Civil procedure, §1A-1, Rule 30.
Condemnation, §136-115.
Delinquent and undisciplined juveniles, §7B-1501.
Department of juvenile justice and delinquency prevention, §143B-515.
Depositions upon oral examinations, §1A-1, Rule 30, (h).
Electronic surveillance, §15A-286.
Eminent domain, §40A-2.
Retirement, §135-53.
Judge of the court of appeals.
Judicial department, §7A-39.1, (a).
Judgment.
Civil procedure, §1A-1, Rule 54.
Motor vehicles, §20-279.1.
Judgment book.
Civil procedure, §1-208.1.
Judgment creditor.
Judgments, §1C-1702.
Judgment debtor.
Judgments, §1C-1702.
Judgment docket.
Civil procedure, §1-208.1.
Judicial district.
Abused, neglected and dependent juveniles, §7B-101.
Attorneys at law, §84-19.
Delinquent and undisciplined juveniles, §7B-1501.
Department of juvenile justice and delinquency prevention, §143B-515.
Judicial official.
Criminal procedure, §15A-101.
Motor vehicles, §20-16.5, (a).
Judicial review panel.
Electronic surveillance, §15A-286.
Judicial sale.
Civil procedure, §1-339.1, (a).
Junior high school, §115C-75, (a).
Junk.
Yard control, §136-143.
Junked motor vehicle, §153A-132, (b).
Street regulations, §160A-303.
Junk vehicle, §20-4.01.
Junkyard, §136-143.
Jurisdiction.
Motor vehicles, §20-4.2.
Psychology practice act, §90-270.2.
Jurisdiction of organization.
Secured transactions, §25-9-102, (a).
Juror.
Obstructing justice, §14-225.2.
Justice officer.
Sheriffs' education, §17E-2.
Justice of the supreme court.
Judicial department, §7A-39.1, (a).
Juvenile.
Abused, neglected and dependent juveniles, §7B-101.
Delinquent and undisciplined juveniles, §7B-1501.
Department of juvenile justice and delinquency prevention, §143B-515.
Juvenile court.
Delinquent and undisciplined juveniles, §7B-1501.
Department of juvenile justice and delinquency prevention, §143B-515.
Juvenile court counselor.
Delinquent and undisciplined juveniles, §7B-1501.

DEFINED TERMS —Cont'd
Juvenile court counselor —Cont'd
Department of juvenile justice and delinquency prevention, §143B-515.
Keeper.
Disorderly houses, §14-188.
Kerosene.
Gasoline and oil inspection, §119-15.
Kerosene distributor.
Gasoline and oil inspection, §119-15.
Kerosene supplier.
Gasoline and oil inspection, §119-15.
Key facilities.
Coastal area management, §113A-103.
Land policy act, §113A-152.
Key shareholder.
Money transmitters, §53-208.2, (a).
Kickboxer, §143-651.
Kickboxing match, §143-651.
Kidnapping.
Criminal law, §14-39.
Killed in the line of duty.
Death benefits, §143-166.2, (c).
Kind.
Seed law, §106-277.2.
Kinds of actions.
Civil procedure, §1-4.
Knowingly.
Medical assistance provider false claims act, §108A-70.11.
Rules of professional conduct, Prof. Cond. Rule 1.0.
Knowingly and willfully.
Public health generally, §130A-26.1, (d).
Underground petroleum storage tank leak cleanup, §143-215.94X, (b).
Knowledge.
Arbitration, §1-569.1.
Public morals, §19-1.1.
Knowledge of the minor's age.
Public morals, §19-12.
Knowledge of the nature of the material.
Public morals, §19-12.
Label.
Antifreeze law, §106-579.3.
Commercial feed law, §106-284.33.
Food, drugs and cosmetics, §106-121.
Meat inspection, §106-549.15.
Pesticide board, §143-460.
Pharmacy practice, §90-85.3, (j).
Poultry products inspection, §106-549.51.
Soil additives act, §106-50.30.
Structural pest control act, §106-65.24.
Toxic or hazardous substance identification, §95-174, (n).
Uniform standards for manufactured homes act, §143-145.
Labeling.
Antifreeze law, §106-579.3.
Commercial feed law, §106-284.33.
Food, drugs and cosmetics, §106-121.
Meat inspection, §106-549.15.
Pesticide board, §143-460.
Pharmacy practice, §90-85.3, (k).
Poultry products inspection, §106-549.51.
Seed law, §106-277.2.
Soil additives act, §106-50.30.
Structural pest control act, §106-65.24.
Labor organization.
Payment or benefits, §95-101.
Persons with disabilities protection, §168A-3.

DEFINED TERMS —Cont'd
Labor or materials.
Bonds, §44A-25.
Labor union.
Political campaigns, §163-278.6.
Lacks the capacity to consent.
Protection of disabled adults, §108A-101.
Lagoon.
Swine farms, §106-802.
Lake Lure.
Lake lure marine commission, §77-80.
Lake Wylie.
Lake Wylie marine commission, §77-30.
Land.
Clean water management trust fund, §113A-252.
Liability of landowners associated with watershed improvement projects, §139-41.3.
Mining, §§74-49, 74-76.
Pesticide board, §143-460.
Property taxes, §105-273.
Public utilities, §62-100.
Recreational trespass, §38A-2.
Recreation and natural heritage, §113-77.6.
State lands, §146-64.
Land adjoining.
Mining permits, §74-50, (b).
Land and loan associations, §54-45.
Land-clearing debris.
Solid waste management, §130A-290, (a).
Land-disturbing activity.
Pollution control act, §113A-52.
Landfill.
Solid waste management, §130A-290, (a).
Landholder.
Conservation, §113-130.
Landlord, §42-40.
Expedited evictions, §42-59.
Land occupier.
Soil and water conservation districts, §139-3.
Landowner.
City and town zoning, §160A-385.1, (b).
Counties, §153A-344.1.
Soil and water conservation districts, §139-3.
Landscape architect, §89A-1.
Landscape architecture, §89A-1.
Landscape contractor, §89D-2.
Land surveyor intern, §89C-3.
Large employer.
Health insurance portability and accountability, §58-68-25, (a).
Large group market.
Health insurance portability and accountability, §58-68-25, (a).
Large investment.
Tax incentives for new and expanding businesses, §105-129.2.
Large recycling facility.
Tax incentives for recycling facilities, §105-129.25.
Large-scale.
Certification of property mappers, §147-54.4.
Laser.
Criminal use of laser device, §14-34.8, (a).
Last known address.
Storage facilities, §44A-40.
Late enrollee.
Small employer group health coverage, §58-50-110.
Law.
Egg law, §106-245.14.
Electric membership corporations, §117-7.
Interstate family support, §52C-1-101.

DEFINED TERMS —Cont'd
Law enforcement agency.
Crime victims' rights, §15A-830, (a).
Law enforcement agency animal.
Assaulting law enforcement or assistance animals, §14-163.1, (a).
Law-enforcement officers.
Civil disorders, §14-288.1.
Collection of traffic law enforcement statistics, §114-10.01, (b).
Dealing in regulated metals property, §66-11, (a).
Death benefits, §143-166.2, (d).
Littering, §14-399, (i).
Local government retirement, §143-166.50, (a).
Mental health, §122C-3.
Retirement, §128-21.
Solicitation of contributions, §131F-2.
State retirement, §143-166.30, (a).
State retirement system, §135-1.
Tuition waiver for senior citizens, §115B-1.
Law-enforcement officers' retirement system, §143-166.30, (a).
Local government, §143-166.50, (a).
Law enforcement official.
Volunteer architect during an emergency or disaster, §83A-13.1, (d).
Volunteer engineer during emergency or disaster, §89C-19.1, (d).
Law practice assistance program.
Continuing legal education, Bar Rules & Regs., D, §.1501.
Law-related services.
Rules of professional conduct, Prof. Cond. Rule 5.7.
Laws.
Fraternal benefit societies, §58-24-15, (e).
Layaway contract.
Sales, §25-2-106.
Lead agency.
Relocation assistance, §133-7.
Lead-based paint hazard, §130A-131.7.
Lead poisoning hazard, §130A-131.7.
Lead regional organizations.
Coastal area management, §113A-103.
Lead-safe housing, §130A-131.7.
Lead teacher.
Child care facility, §110-86.
Lease.
Credit insurance, §58-57-5.
Criminal law, §14-168.2.
Leases, UCC, §25-2A-103, (1).
Sales and use tax, §105-164.3.
Sublease of motor vehicle and loan assumption arranging, §20-106.2, (a).
Lease agreement.
Leases, UCC, §25-2A-103, (1).
Lease contract.
Leases, UCC, §25-2A-103, (1).
Leased residential premises.
Expedited evictions, §42-59.
Leasehold condominium, §47C-1-103.
Leasehold interest.
Leases, UCC, §25-2A-103, (1).
Leasehold planned community, §47F-1-103.
Lease-purchase agreement.
Lease or purchase of prison facilities constructed by private firm, §148-37.2, (b).
Legal aid clinic.
Rules governing practical training of law students, Bar Rules & Regs., C, §.0202.

DEFINED TERMS —Cont'd
Legal assistance.
Domestic violence victim assistance act, §7A-474.17.
Judicial department, §7A-474.2.
Legal custody.
Adoption, §48-1-101.
Legal entity.
Liability of landowners associated with watershed improvement projects, §139-41.3.
Legal intern.
Rules governing legal services provided by students, Bar Rules & Regs., C, §.0202.
Legally responsible person.
Mental health, §122C-3.
Legal possessor.
Liens on personal property, §44A-1.
Legal proceeding.
Journalist's qualified privilege, §8-53.11, (a).
Legal representative.
Custodial trusts, §33B-1.
Transfers to minors, §33A-1.
Legal residence.
Higher education tuition and fees, §116-143.1.
Legal resident.
Veterans cemeteries, §65-43.
Legal services corporation.
Rules governing legal services provided by students, Bar Rules & Regs., C, §.0202.
Legislative action.
Lobbying, §120-47.1.
Legislative commission.
Confidential communications, §120-129.
Legislative day.
Rulemaking procedure, §150B-21.3, (d).
Legislative employee.
Confidential legislative communications, §120-129.
Legislative liaison personnel.
Lobbying, §120-47.1.
Legislative officer.
Endangering officers, §14-16.10.
Legislator.
Bribery and extortion, §120-86, (d).
Confidential communications, §120-129.
Lender.
Good funds settlement act, §45A-3.
Reverse mortgages, §53-257.
Lender is obligated, §45-81.
Lending institution.
Agricultural finance act, §122D-3.
Lessee.
Condominiums, §47C-1-103.
Criminal law, §14-395.1.
Leases, UCC, §25-2A-103, (1).
Motor vehicles, §20-341.
Planned community act, §47F-1-103.
Sublease of motor vehicle and loan assumption arranging, §20-106.2, (a).
Lessee in ordinary course of business.
Leases, UCC, §25-2A-103, (1).
Lessor.
Leases, UCC, §25-2A-103, (1).
Motor vehicles, §20-341.
Sublease of motor vehicle and loan assumption arranging, §20-106.2, (a).
Lessor's residual interest.
Leases, UCC, §25-2A-103, (1).
Letter of authority.
Decedents' estates, safe deposit boxes, §28A-15-13, (a).

DEFINED TERMS —Cont'd
Letter of caution.
Discipline and disability rules of state bar, Bar Rules & Regs., B, §.0103.
Procedures for the authorized practice committee of the state bars, Bar Rules & Regs., D, §.0203.
Letter-of-credit right.
Secured transactions, §25-9-102, (a).
Letter of notice.
Discipline and disability rules of state bar, Bar Rules & Regs., B, §.0103.
Procedures for the authorized practice committee of the state bars, Bar Rules & Regs., D, §.0203.
Letter of warning.
Discipline and disability rules of state bar, Bar Rules & Regs., B, §.0103.
Letters of credit, §25-5-102, (a).
Lever machine voting system, §163-165.4A, (a1).
Lewd matter.
Public morals, §19-1.1.
Lewdness.
Public morals, §19-1.1.
Liabilities, debts and obligations.
Limited liability companies, §57C-1-03.
Liability.
Business corporations, §55-8-50, (b).
Insurers supervision, §58-30-10.
Medical service corporations, §58-65-166, (b).
Risk retention, §58-22-10.
Library.
Records, §125-18.
Library agreement.
Interstate library compact, §125-12.
Library materials.
Counties, §153A-262.
Library record, §125-18.
Licensable facility.
Mental health, §122C-3.
License.
Administrative procedure, §150B-2.
Alcohol taxation, §105-113.68.
Architects, §83A-1.
Athletic trainers, §90-523.
Banking, §53-165, (g).
Child care facility, §110-86.
Child support, §110-142.
Dental hygiene, §90-221, (c).
Geologist, §89E-3.
Insurance companies.
Notifications to insurance commissioner, §58-2-69, (a).
Insurance customer information safeguards, §58-39-140.
Insurance producer, §58-33-10.
Interpreters and transliterators licensure act, §90D-3.
Locksmith licensing, §74F-4.
Manufactured housing, §143-143.9.
Motor vehicles, §20-4.01.
Nursing, §90-171.20.
Occupational boards, §93B-1.
Pharmacy practice, §90-85.3, (l).
Real estate appraisers, §93E-1-4.
Reciprocal insurance, §58-15-5.
Respiratory care practices act, §90-648.
Soil scientists, §89F-3.
Speech and language pathologists and audiologists, §90-293.
Trust companies, §53-301, (a).

DEFINED TERMS —Cont'd
License agreement.
Motion pictures, §75C-2.
Licensed clinical social workers, §90B-3.
Licensed dietitian/nutritionist, §90-352.
Licensed distributor.
Tobacco taxation, §105-113.4.
Licensed geologist, §89E-3.
Licensed marriage and family therapist, §90-270.47.
Licensed professional counselor, §90-330, (a).
Licensed psychological associate, §90-270.2.
Licensed psychologist, §90-270.2.
Licensed soil scientist, §89F-3.
Licensed veterinarian, §90-181.
Licensee.
Banking, §53-165, (h).
Boxing commission, §143-651.
Check-cashing service, §53-275.
Child support, §110-142.
Insurance companies.
Notifications to insurance commissioner, §58-2-69, (a).
Manufactured housing, §143-143.9.
Money transmitters, §53-208.2, (a).
Mortgage bankers and brokers, §53-243.01.
Motor clubs and associations, §58-69-2.
Nurse licensure compact, §90-171.82.
Private personnel services, §95-47.1.
Professional corporation, §55B-2.
Professional employer organizations, §58-89A-5.
Real estate appraisers, §93E-1-4.
Regulations for professional corporations and professional limited liability companies practicing law, Bar Rules & Regs., E, §.0101.
Respiratory care practices act, §90-648.
Street and highways, private pilot toll project, §136-89.172, (m).
Structural pest control act, §106-65.24.
Licensee in ordinary course of business.
Secured transactions priority of security interests, §25-9-321, (a).
License exempt organization.
Lotteries and gaming, §14-309.6.
License revenues.
Saltwater fishing fund, §113-175.
License year.
Coastal and estuarine commercial fishing licenses, §113-168.
Licensing.
Administrative procedure, §150B-2.
New occupations and professions, §120-149.2.
Licensing agency.
Forfeiture of licensing privilege after conviction of felony, §15A-1331A.
Licensing board.
Forfeiture of licensing privilege for non-payment of child support, §50-13.12, (a).
Nurse licensure compact, §90-171.82.
Professional corporations, §55B-2.
Licensing privilege.
Forfeiture after conviction of felony, §15A-1331A.
Forfeiture of licensing privilege for non-payment of child support, §50-13.12, (a).
Lien.
Fraudulent transfers, §39-23.1.
Leases, UCC, §25-2A-103, (1).
Motor vehicle titling, §20-58.8, (c).
Lien creditor.
Secured transactions, §25-9-102, (a).

DEFINED TERMS —Cont'd
Lienholder.
Impaired driving, §20-28.2, (a1).
Lienor.
Personal property, §44A-1.
Storage facilities, §44A-40.
Life care.
Health facilities finance, §131A-3.
Life-cycle cost analysis.
Energy policy and life-cycle cost analysis for state government, §143-64.11.
Life insurance.
Insurance information and privacy protection act, §58-39-15.
Life insurance cost indexes.
Life insurance solicitation, §58-60-10.
Life insurance policy.
Trusts of death benefits, §36A-100.
Life insurer, §58-12-2.
Life sustaining procedures.
Consent to health care for minor, §32A-29.
Powers of attorney, §32A-16.
Light-traffic roads.
Motor vehicles, §20-118.
Limited common areas and facilities.
Unit ownership, §47A-3.
Limited common element.
Condominiums, §47C-1-103.
Planned community act, §47F-1-103.
Limited contributee.
Limitation on fund-raising during legislative session, §163-278.13B, (a).
Limited contributor.
Limitation on fund-raising during legislative session, §163-278.13B, (a).
Limited driving privilege, §20-179.3, (a).
Limited food services establishment.
Sanitation, §130A-247.
Limited liability company, §57C-1-03.
Corporate income taxation, §105-130.2.
Individual income taxation, §105-134.1.
Limited liability limited partnership.
Limited partnerships, §59-102.
Limited license.
Physicians and surgeons, §90-12, (b).
Rental car companies selling insurance, §58-33-17, (a).
Limited licensee.
Self service storage renter's insurance, §58-33-18, (a).
Limited line credit insurance.
Insurance producer, §58-33-10.
Limited line credit insurance producer, §58-33-10.
Limited lines insurance.
Insurance producers, §58-33-10.
Limited obligation bond.
Capital facilities finance act, §142-82.
Limited partnership.
Limited liability company, §57C-1-03.
Limited representative.
Licensing, §58-33-10, (d).
Limited service facility.
Banking, §53-1.
Limited veterinary license, §90-181.
Limited volunteer license.
Physicians and surgeons, §90-12, (c).
Line.
Public utilities, §§62-100, 62-110.2.
Urban electrical service, §160A-331.

DEFINED TERMS —Cont'd
Lineal decedents.
Decedents' estates, §29-2.
Liquefied petroleum gas, §119-54, (a).
Liquidating asset.
Principal and income act, §37A-4-410, (a).
Liquidity fund.
Savings and loan associations, §54B-4.
Liquor.
Alcoholic beverages, §18B-101.
List.
Property taxes, §105-273.
Listed qualified individual.
Electrical contractors, §87-41.1.
Listing.
Property taxes, §105-273.
Literary purpose.
Property tax exemption, §105-278.7, (f).
Taxation, §105-278.3.
Lithotriptor.
Certificate of need, §131E-176.
Litter, §14-399, (i).
Live poultry or ratite dealer, §106-541.
Livestock, §68-15.
Dealer licensing, §106-418.8.
Livestock brands, §80-58.
Livestock dealer.
Licensing, §106-418.8.
Living unit.
Continuing care retirement communities, §58-64-1.
Llama.
Classification as livestock, §106-22.4.
Load and leave.
Sales and use tax, §105-164.3.
Loan, §66-106.
Loans exempt from rate and fee limitations, §24-9, (a).
Reverse mortgages, §53-257.
Solid waste, §159I-3, (a).
Loanable assets.
Banking, §53-165, (i).
Loan agreement.
Solid waste, §159I-3, (a).
Loan amount.
Loans exempt from rate and fee limitations, §24-9, (a).
Loan broker, §66-106.
Loan closing.
Good funds settlement act, §45A-3.
Loan documents.
Good funds settlement act, §45A-3.
Loan funds.
Good funds settlement act, §45A-3.
Petroleum cleanup, §143-215.94A.
Loan of credit.
State debt, Const. N. C., art. V, §§3, 4.
Loan officer.
Mortgage bankers and brokers, §53-243.01.
Loan production office.
Savings banks, §54C-4, (b).
Loan-related goods, products and services.
Interest rates, §24-8, (d).
Lobbying, §120-47.1.
Lobbyist, §120-47.1.
Lobbyist's principal.
Lobbying, §120-47.1.
Local act.
Cities and towns, §160A-1.
Counties, §153A-1.

DEFINED TERMS —Cont'd
Local agency.
Debt collection, §105A-2.
Local authorities.
Motor vehicles, §20-4.01.
Local board, §115C-5, (e).
Alcoholic beverages, §18B-101.
Local board of health.
Public health generally, §130A-2.
Local confinement facility.
Counties, §153A-217.
Local consumer advocacy program.
MH/DD/SA consumer advocacy program, §122C-11.
Local consumer advocate.
MH/DD/SA consumer advocacy program, §122C-11.
Local distribution company.
Piped natural gas tax, §105-187.40.
Local exchange carrier.
E-911 system for wireless communications, §62A-21.
Local exchange company.
Public utilities, §62-3.
Local funds.
Mental health, §122C-3.
Local governing body.
Dedication of property to nature and historic preserve, §143B-260.6, (a).
Local government.
Brownfields property reuse act, §130A-310.31, (b).
Certification of property mappers, §147-54.4.
Coastal area management, §113A-103.
Cooperative state-local coalition water quality protection plans, §143-214.14, (a).
Dedication of property to nature and historic preserves, §143B-260.6, (a).
Dry-cleaning solvent cleanup act, §143-215.104B, (b).
Floodplain regulations, §143-215.52, (a).
Land policy act, §113A-152.
Local sales and use tax, §105-521, (a).
911 service, §62A-3.
Pollution control act, §113A-52.
Risk pools, §58-23-1.
Smoking in public places, §143-596.
Local governmental employees' retirement system.
Law enforcement, §143-166.50, (a).
Local governmental entities.
Office of information technology services, §147-33.82, (b).
Local governmental unit.
Energy improvement loan program, §143-345.18, (e).
Guaranteed energy savings contracts, §143-64.17.
Local government commission.
Clean water loans, §159G-3.
Global TransPark authority, §63A-2.
Solid waste, §159I-3, (a).
Local government unit.
Clean water loans, §159G-3.
Local government user.
Criminal justice information network governing board, §143-660.
Local health department.
Public health generally, §130A-2.
Local health director.
Public health generally, §130A-2.
Local inspection department.
Code officials qualification board, §143-151.8, (a).

DEFINED TERMS —Cont'd
Local law enforcement agency.
Lotteries and gaming, §14-309.6.
Precious metals, §66-164.
Unauthorized substances tax, §105-113.106.
Locally assigned rolling stock.
Public service taxation, §105-333.
Local partnership.
Early childhood initiatives, §143B-168.11.
Local sales tax share.
Local sales and use tax, §105-521, (a).
Local school administrative unit.
Education, §115C-5, (f).
Local service provider.
Telecommunications relay service, §62-157, (a1).
Local tax district.
Organization of schools, §115C-69.
Local tax official.
Property taxes, §105-273.
Local team.
Child fatality prevention system, §7B-1401.
Location.
Sewage systems, §130A-334.
Location of underground utilities.
Contractors, §87-101.
Locksmith.
Locksmith licensing, §74F-4.
Locksmith services.
Locksmith licensing, §74F-4.
Locksmith tools.
Locksmith licensing, §74F-4.
Lodge.
Fraternal benefit societies, §58-24-15, (h).
Long term care facility.
Ombudsman program, §143B-181.16.
Temporary management, §131E-231.
Long-term care insurance, §58-55-20.
Long-term lease or rental.
Highway use tax, §105-187.1.
Regional transit authority vehicle rental tax, §105-550.
Loss trending.
Insurance rates, §58-36-100, (b).
Lot owner.
Planned community act, §47F-1-103.
Lots.
Egg law, §106-245.14.
Leases, UCC, §25-2A-103, (1).
Planned community act, §47F-1-103.
Sales, §25-2-105.
Seed law, §106-277.2.
Low dose screening mammography.
Accident and health insurance, §58-51-57, (a1).
Health maintenance organizations, §58-67-76, (b).
Hospital, medical and dental services corporations, §58-65-92, (b).
Lowest floor.
Floodplain regulations, §143-215.52, (a).
Low-income person.
Spay/neuter account, §19A-63, (b).
Low-level radioactive waste.
Radiation protection, §104E-5.
Low-speed vehicle, §20-4.01.
Low-street value drug.
Unauthorized substances taxes, §105-113.106.
Lubricating oil.
Regulation of rerefined or reprocessed oil, §119-13.1.
Machine guns, §14-409, (a).
Machinery and equipment.
Tax incentives for new and expanding businesses, §105-129.2.

DEFINED TERMS —Cont'd
Machinery and equipment —Cont'd
Tax incentives for recycling facilities, §105-129.25.
Machines and machinery.
Sales and use tax, §105-164.4A.
Made.
Limitation on fund-raising during legislative session, §163-278.13B, (a).
Magnetic resonance imaging scanner.
Certificate of need, §131E-176.
Mailed.
Business corporations, §55-1-40.
Mail order sale.
Sales and use tax, §105-164.3.
Main permanent campus.
Scholarship funds provided private colleges and universities, §116-22.
State grants to students attending private universities or colleges, §116-43.5, (a).
Maintain.
Forest development act, §113A-178.
Maintenance.
Sewage systems, §130A-334.
Weights and measures, §81A-9.
Maintenance standard.
Lead poisoning in children, §130A-131.7.
Major accident.
Safe driver incentive program, §58-36-75, (a).
Major development project.
Environmental policy act, §113A-9.
Major economic dislocation.
Industrial development fund, §143B-437.01, (a), (a1).
Major hypothecation loan.
Membership camping, §66-246, (a).
Majority.
Unit ownership, §47A-3.
Majority of unit owners, §47A-3.
Major life activities.
Persons with disabilities protection, §168A-3.
Major medical equipment.
Certificate of need, §131E-176.
Major recycling facility.
Sales and use tax, §105-164.3.
Tax incentives for recycling facilities, §105-129.25.
Make a mortgage loan.
Mortgage bankers and brokers, §53-243.01.
Maker.
Negotiable instruments, §25-3-103.
Malice.
Punitive damages, §1D-5.
Maliciously.
Cruelty to animals, §§14-360, (c), 14-362.3.
Malt beverage.
Alcoholic beverages, §18B-101.
Alcohol taxation, §105-113.68.
Managed care entity.
Health care liability, §90-21.50.
Managed care organization.
Industrial commission, I.C. Managed Care Orgs. R. II.
Workers' compensation, §97-2.
Managed care plan.
Utilization review, §58-50-61, (a).
Managed services.
Professional employer organizations, §58-89A-5.
Management.
Asbestos hazards, §130A-444.
Workers' compensation self insurance, §97-165.
Management contract.
Managing general insurance agents, §58-34-2, (a).

DEFINED TERMS —Cont'd
Management functions.
Executive reorganization act of 1971, §143A-6, (c).
Management of the affairs.
Limited liability companies, §57C-1-03.
Manager.
Boxing commission, §143-651.
County managers, §153A-81.
Limited liability companies, §57C-1-03.
Private personnel services, §95-47.1.
Reinsurance intermediaries, §58-9-2, (a).
Managing agent.
Lead poisoning in children, §130A-131.7.
Time shares, §93A-41.
Managing general agent, §58-34-2, (a).
Managing principal.
Mortgage bankers and brokers, §53-243.01.
Mandatory control level event.
Risk based capital requirements, insurance companies, §58-125, (a).
Mandatory control level risk-based capital.
Insurance companies, §58-12-2.
Mandatory income.
Principal and income act, §37A-1-102.
Manicuring, §88B-2.
Manicurist, §88B-2.
Manicurist teacher, §88B-2.
Manifest.
Solid waste management, §130A-290, (a).
Manipulated manures.
Commercial fertilizer, §106-657.
Manlift.
Elevator safety, §95-110.3, (h).
Manufacture.
Bedding, §130A-261.
Commercial feed law, §106-284.33.
Controlled substances, §90-87.
Manufactured home, §143-143.9.
Housing standards, §160A-442.
Sales and use tax, §105-164.3.
Secured transactions, §25-9-102, (a).
Uniform standards for manufactured homes act, §143-145.
Manufactured home dealer, §143-143.9.
Manufactured home manufacturer, §143-143.9.
Manufactured home salesman, §143-143.9.
Manufactured home salesperson, §143-143.9.
Manufactured home transaction.
Secured transactions, §25-9-102, (a).
Manufacture of an unlawful telecommunication device, §14-113.5.
Manufacturer.
Commercial fertilizer, §106-657.
Housing, §143-143.9.
Motor vehicles, §§20-4.01, 20-286.
Pesticide board, §143-460.
Pharmacy practice, §90-85.27.
Products liability, §99B-1.
Property taxes, §105-273.
Registration of prescription drug manufacturer, §106-140.1, (j).
Tobacco taxation, §105-113.4.
Wholesale prescription drug distributors, §106-145.2.
Manufacturer's certificate.
Motor vehicles, §20-4.01.
Manufacturing.
Industrial development fund, §143B-437.01, (a1).
Tax incentives for new and expanding businesses, §105-129.2.

DEFINED TERMS —Cont'd
Manufacturing facility.
Toxic or hazardous substance identification, §95-174, (o).
Map.
Probate and registration, §47-30.
Marijuana.
Controlled substances, §90-87.
Unauthorized substances taxes, §105-113.106.
Marine and estuarine resources.
Conservation, §113-129.
Offshore oil and gas activities, §143-215.94B, (b).
Marine fisheries commission.
Conservation, §113-128.
Marine fisheries inspector.
Conservation, §113-128.
Marital misconduct.
Alimony, §50-16.1A.
Marital property.
Divorce, §50-20, (b).
Market.
Egg law, §106-245.14.
Pork promotion assessment, §106-792.
Marketing of eggs.
Egg law, §106-245.14.
Market price.
Tax credit for gleaned crop, §105-130.37, (b).
Marriage and family therapy, §90-270.47.
Married individual.
Taxation, §105-134.1.
Mash.
Unauthorized substances taxes, §105-113.106.
Massage.
Adult establishments, §14-202.10.
Massage and bodywork therapist, §90-622.
Massage and bodywork therapy, §90-622.
Massage business.
Adult establishments, §14-202.10.
Mass gathering, §130A-252, (a).
Mass mailing.
Electioneering communications, §163-278.90.
Mastectomy.
Accident and health insurance, §58-51-62, (b).
Health maintenance organizations, §58-67-79, (b).
Hospital, medical and dental service corporations, §58-65-96, (b).
Postmastectomy inpatient care coverage, §58-3-168, (c).
Master association.
Condominiums, §47C-1-103.
Planned community act, §47F-1-103.
Master settlement agreement.
Tobacco reserve fund, §66-290.
Tobacco trust fund commission, §143-716.
Match.
Boxing commission, §143-651.
Matchmaker.
Boxing commission, §143-651.
Material.
Offenses against morality, §14-190.13.
Material litigation.
Money transmitters, §53-208.2, (a).
Material safety data sheet.
Pesticide board, §143-460.
Toxic or hazardous substance identification, §95-174, (p).
Matter.
Public morals, §19-1.1.
Mausoleum.
Cemeteries, §65-48.

DEFINED TERMS —Cont'd
Mausoleum section.
Cemeteries, §65-48.
Maximum contaminant level.
Drinking water, §130A-313.
Maximum imposed term.
Post-release supervision, §15A-1368, (a).
Maximum qualifying contribution.
Public campaign financing fund, §163-278.62.
Mayor.
Cities and towns, §160A-1.
Civil disorders, §14-288.1.
Housing authorities, §157-3.
Public hospitals, §131E-16.
Veterans' recreation, §165-25.
MCO.
Industrial commission managed care organizations, I.C. Managed Care Orgs. R. II.
Meal.
Weights and measures, §81A-9.
Meals tax.
Uniform penalties, §153A-154.1, (b).
Means.
Business corporations, §55-1-40.
Nonprofit corporations, §55A-1-40.
Meat broker.
Meat inspection, §106-549.15.
Meat food product.
Meat inspection, §106-549.15.
Meat inspection, §106-549.15.
Mediated settlement conference.
Administrative procedure, §150B-23.1, (b).
Superior court civil actions, §7A-38.1, (b).
Mediation.
Mediated settlement conferences, §7A-38.1, (b).
Special education, §115C-116, (b).
Mediator.
Administrative procedure, §150B-23.1, (b).
Farm nuisance dispute mediation, §7A-38.3, (a).
Mediated settlement conferences, §7A-38.1, (b).
Special education, §115C-116, (b).
Medical assistance.
Medicaid estate recovery plan, §108A-70.5, (b).
Medical assistance program.
Children's health insurance program, §108A-70.18.
Medical assistance provider false claims act, §108A-70.11.
Medical board.
Disability income plan, §135-101.
Judicial retirement, §135-53.
Legislative retirement system, §120-4.8.
Retirement, §128-21.
State retirement system, §135-1.
Medical care.
Health insurance portability and accountability, §58-68-25, (a).
Medical-care institution.
Insurance information and privacy protection act, §58-39-15.
Medical compensation.
Workers' compensation, §97-2.
Medical director.
Respiratory care practices act, §90-648.
Medical emergency.
Medical plan for teachers and state employees, §135-40.8, (e).
Medical equipment.
Pharmacy practice, §90-85.3, (l1).
Medical expense policy.
Narcotics and intoxicants, accident and health insurance, §58-51-16, (c).

DEFINED TERMS —Cont'd
Medically necessary services or supplies.
Accident and health insurance.
Utilization review, §58-50-61, (a).
Medical malpractice action, §90-21.11.
Medical professional.
Insurance information and privacy protection act, §58-39-15.
Medical-record information.
Insurance information and privacy protection act, §58-39-15.
Medical records, §90-410.
Health statistics, §130A-372.
Medicolegal guidelines for attorney-physician relationship, MLG Rule 3.
Medical rehabilitation.
Industrial commission utilization of rehabilitation professionals, I.C. Util. Rehab. Profs. I.
Medical report.
Medicolegal guidelines for attorney-physician relationship, MLG Rule 3.
Medical responder.
Emergency medical services, §131E-155.
Medical review committee, §90-21.22A, (a).
Facility licensure act, §131E-101.
Hospital licensure, §131E-76.
Medical service plan, §58-65-1, (a).
Medical waste.
Solid waste management, §130A-290, (a).
Medical witness.
Medicolegal guidelines for attorney-physician relationship, MLG Rule 3.
Medicare, §58-54-1.
Group health insurance, §58-53-1.
Health benefit plans.
Continuing care retirement community residents, §58-3-200, (f).
State medical plan, §135-40.1.
Medicare contract.
Provider sponsored organizations, §131E-276.
Medication-related error.
Nursing home medication management advisory committee, §131E-128.1, (a).
Member.
Disability income plan, §135-101.
Discipline and disability rules of state bar, Bar Rules & Regs., B, §.0103.
Facility authorities, §160A-480.2.
Group health insurance, §58-53-1.
Insurance companies, conversion, §58-10-12, (a).
Insurance rates, §58-40-5.
Judicial retirement, §135-53.
Limited liability companies, §57C-1-03.
Local government law-enforcement retirement, §143-166.50, (a).
Marketing associations, §54-130.
Nonprofit corporations, §55A-1-40.
Retirement, §128-21.
Savings and loan associations, §54B-4.
Savings banks, §54C-4, (b).
Self-insurance guaranty association, §97-130.
Self-insurer.
Self-insurance guaranty association, §97-130.
State law-enforcement retirement, §143-166.30, (a).
State retirement system, §135-1.
Taxation, §105-277.2.
Workers' compensation self-insurance.
Employer groups, §58-47-60.
Member bank, §53-61, (a).

DEFINED TERMS —Cont'd
Member in service.
Legislative retirement system, §120-4.8.
Member insurer.
Insurance guaranty association, §§58-48-20, 58-62-16.
Member of his or her own family.
Barbers, §86A-26.
Member of minor's family.
Transfers to minors, §33A-1.
Member of the beneficiary's family.
Custodial trusts, §33B-1.
Member of the diamond industry.
Unfair trade practices, §66-73.
Membership.
Credit unions, §54-109.26, (a).
Solicitation of contributions, §131F-2.
Membership camping agreements, §66-232.
Membership camping contracts, §66-232.
Membership camping operators, §66-232.
Membership interest.
Insurance companies, conversion, §58-10-12, (a).
Limited liability companies, §57C-1-03.
Membership service.
Disability income plan, §135-101.
Judicial retirement, §135-53.
Legislative retirement system, §120-4.12, (b).
Retirement, §§128-21, 135-1.
Member state.
Uniform sales and use tax administration act, §105-164.42B.
Mental abnormality.
Sex offender and public protection registration, §14-208.6.
Mental deficiency, §122C-361.
Mental health treatment.
Advance instruction, §122C-72.
Power of attorney, §32A-16.
Mental illness, §§122C-3, 122C-361.
Incompetency, §35A-1101.
Mentally defective.
Criminal law, §14-27.1.
Mentally incapacitated.
Criminal law, §14-27.1.
Mentally retarded.
Death sentence prohibited, mentally retarded defendants, §15A-2005, (a).
Mentally retarded with accompanying behavior disorder, §122C-3.
Mental retardation, §122C-3.
Incompetency, §35A-1101.
Merchant.
Sales, §25-2-104.
Merchant lessee.
Leases, UCC, §25-2A-103, (1).
Merger.
Business corporations, §55-1-40.
Metal tire.
Motor vehicles, §20-4.01.
Metropolitan planning organization.
Planning regionally significant transportation projects, §136-200.
MEWA.
Providers of health benefits, §58-49-30.
Mezzanine finance.
Enterprise corporations, §53A-37.
MGA, §58-34-2, (a).
MH/DD/SA.
Consumer advocacy program, §122C-11.
Middle school, §115C-75, (a).

DEFINED TERMS —Cont'd
Midnight deadline.
Banking, §25-4-104, (a).
Midwifery, §90-178.2.
Migrant, §95-223.
Migrant agricultural worker, §130A-417.
Migrant housing, §95-223.
Migratory birds.
Conservation, §113-129.
Migratory farm worker.
Motor vehicles, §20-215.1.
Migratory game birds, §113-129.
Migratory waterfowl, §113-129.
Mileage.
Motor vehicles, §20-341.
Military property, §127B-2.
Military property sales facility, §127B-1.
Milk or milk products, §130A-274.
Millennial campus, §116-198.33.
Mine, §74-24.2.
Miner, §74-24.2.
Mineral feed.
Commercial feed law, §106-284.33.
Mineral proceeds.
Unclaimed property act, §116B-52.
Minerals.
Mining, §74-49.
Unclaimed property act, §116B-52.
Minimal cost.
Public records, §132-1, (b).
Minimum amount of consideration.
Savings and loan associations, §54B-4.
Minimum amount on deposit in withdrawable accounts.
Savings and loan associations, §54B-4.
Minimum criteria.
Environmental policy act, §113A-9.
Minimum flows.
Dam safety, §143-215.25.
Minimum imposed term.
Post-release supervision, §15A-1368, (a).
Minimum stream flows.
Dam safety, §143-215.25.
Mining, §§74-37, 74-49.
Minister.
Pastoral counselors, §90-382.
Minor.
Adoption, §48-1-101.
Assault, §14-33, (d).
Consent to health care for minor, §32A-29.
Drug law violations, §90-95.4, (d).
Incompetency, §35A-1202.
Offenses against morality, §14-190.13.
Parental or judicial consent to abortion, §90-21.6.
Prohibition on handguns for minors, §14-269.7, (c).
Public morals, §19-12.
Storage of firearms to protect minors, §14-315.1, (d).
Transfers to minors, §33A-1.
Minor accident.
Safe driver incentive program, §58-36-75, (a).
Minor child.
Standby guardianship, §35A-1370.
Minority.
Roads and highways, §136-28.4, (c).
Minority business.
Public contracts, §143-128.2, (g).
Minority business enterprise.
Global TransPark authority, §63A-19.

DEFINED TERMS —Cont'd
Minority person.
Global TransPark authority, §63A-19.
Public contracts, §143-128.2, (g).
Misappropriation.
Trade secrets, §66-152.
Misbranded.
Meat inspection, §106-549.15.
Milk regulation, §106-268, (c).
Pesticide board, §143-460.
Poultry products inspection, §106-549.51.
Miscarriage.
Injury to pregnant woman resulting in miscarriage or stillbirth, §14-18.2, (a).
Miscellaneous payroll period.
Tax withholding, §105-163.1.
Misconduct connected with work.
Unemployment insurance, §96-14.
Misdemeanors.
Criminal law, §14-1.
Missing child.
Center, §143B-496.
Missing person.
Center, §143B-496.
Missing person report, §143B-496.
Mistake of fact.
Child support, §110-129.
Student loan collections, §105B-1.
Mixed beverage.
Alcoholic beverages, §18B-101.
Sales and use tax exemptions, §105-164.13.
Mixed chicks, §106-541.
Mixed fertilizers.
Commercial fertilizer, §106-657.
Mixture.
Seed law, §106-277.2.
Mobile facility.
Veterinarians, §90-181.1, (b).
Mobile home.
Housing standards, §160A-442.
Taxation, §105-316.7.
Tenancy by the entirety, §41-2.5, (c).
Mobile intensive care nurse.
Emergency medical services, §131E-155.
Mobile pharmacy, §90-85.3, (l2).
Mobile set telephone number.
E-911 system for wireless communications, §62A-21.
Mobile telecommunication center.
Sales and use tax on telecommunications, §105-164.4C, (h).
Mobile telecommunications service.
Sales and use tax, §105-164.3.
Modification.
Child custody jurisdiction and enforcement, §50A-102.
Modified permit.
Solid waste management, §130A-295.01, (a).
Modular home.
Sales and use tax, §105-164.3.
Modular homebuilder.
Sales and use tax, §105-164.3.
Molders.
Disposal of dyes, molds, forms and patterns, §66-67.3, (a).
Monetary compensation.
Regulation of nonconforming off-premises outdoor advertising, §153A-143, (e), §160A-199, (e).
Monetary transmission.
Money transmitters, §53-208.2, (a).

DEFINED TERMS —Cont'd
Monetary value.
Money transmitters, §53-208.2, (a).
Money.
Foreign-money claims, §1C-1820.
UCC, §25-1-201.
Money of the claim.
Foreign-money claims, §1C-1820.
Month.
Local government finance, §159-2.
Moody's corporate bond yield average.
Insurance guaranty associations, §58-62-16.
Moped.
Sales and use tax, §105-164.3.
Morehead city tariff, terminal tariff.
Ports authority income tax, §105-130.41, (c).
Ports authority individual income tax, §105-151.22, (c).
Mortgage.
Decedents' estates, §28A-1-1.
Housing authorities, §157-3.
Housing finance agency, §122A-3.
Sales under power of sale, §45-21.1, (b).
Secured transactions, §25-9-102, (a).
Mortgage banker.
Mortgage bankers and brokers, §53-243.01.
Mortgage broker.
Mortgage bankers and brokers, §53-243.01.
Mortgagee.
Sales under power of sale, §45-21.1, (b).
Mortgage guaranty insurers, §58-10-120.
Mortgage lenders.
Housing finance agency, §122A-3.
Mortgage loan.
Housing finance agency, §122A-3.
Mortgage bankers and brokers, §53-243.01.
Most qualified persons.
Personnel system, §126-14.2, (b).
Mother.
Marriage proceedings, §51-2.2.
Motion picture film.
Public morals, §19-1.1.
Motions.
Criminal procedure, §15A-951.
Motorboat.
Boating safety, §75A-2.
Motor carrier, §20-4.01.
Fuel taxes, §105-449.37, (a).
Public utilities, §62-3.
Motor carrier of migratory farm workers.
Motor vehicles, §20-215.1.
Motor club, §58-69-2.
Motorcycle.
Motor vehicles, §20-4.01.
Regional transit authority vehicle rental tax, §105-550.
Motor freight carrier company.
Public service taxation, §105-333.
Motor fuel, §75-81.
Alternative fuel, §105-449.130.
Gasoline and oil inspection, §119-15.
Gasoline tax, §105-449.60.
Larceny, §14-72.5, (b).
Motor fuel merchant, §75-81.
Motor fuel outlet, §75-81.
Motor fuel rate.
Alternative fuel, §105-449.130.
Gasoline tax, §105-449.60.
Motor fuel transporter.
Gasoline tax, §105-449.60.

DEFINED TERMS —Cont'd
Motor home.
Motor vehicles, §20-4.01.
Motorists services directional signs.
Exemption from removal, §136-140.7.
Motorized all terrain vehicle.
Trespass to land, §14-159.3, (b).
Motor vehicle, §§20-4.01, 20-286.
Counties, §153A-132, (b).
Fuel taxes, §105-449.37, (a).
Liens on personal property, §44A-1.
Motor vehicle repairs, §20-354.2.
Open container law, §20-138.7, (a3).
Public utilities, §62-3.
Sales and use tax, §105-164.3.
Vehicle reinsurance, §58-37-1.
Motor vehicle damage appraiser.
Licensing, §58-33-10, (e).
Motor vehicle dealer.
Motor vehicles, §20-286.
Motor vehicle insurance.
Vehicle reinsurance, §58-37-1.
Motor vehicle liability policy.
Motor vehicles, §20-279.21.
Motor vehicle owner.
Impaired driving, §20-28.2, (a1).
Motor vehicle repair, §20-354.2.
Motor vehicle repair shop, §20-354.2.
Motor vehicle salesman.
Motor vehicles, §20-286.
Motor vehicle service agreement.
Service agreement companies, §58-1-25, (b).
Motor vehicle service agreement company, §58-1-25, (b).
Mountain Island lake.
Marine commission, §77-70.
Movable frame hive.
Bee and honey act, §106-635.
Moving walk.
Elevator safety, §95-110.3, (i).
MSDS.
Pesticide board, §143-460.
Toxic or hazardous substance identification, §95-174, (p).
Mulch.
Commercial fertilizer, §106-657.
Multidisciplinary evaluation.
Competency, §35A-1202.
Incompetency, §35A-1101.
Multiple-county board.
State-county criminal justice partnership, §143B-273.2.
Multiple employer welfare arrangement.
Providers of health benefits, §58-49-30.
Multiplier.
Insurance rates, §58-36-100, (b).
Workers' compensation self-insurance.
Employer groups.
Premium rates, §58-47-110, (a).
Multispecialty ambulatory surgical program.
Certificate of need, §131E-176.
Multistate licensure privilege.
Nurse licensure compact, §90-171.82.
Municipal corporation.
Property taxes, §105-273.
Municipality.
Aeronautics, §63-1.
Armories, §127A-161.
Civil disorders, §14-288.1.
Electric power, §159B-3.
Housing authorities, §§157-3, 157-41.

DEFINED TERMS —Cont'd
Municipality —Cont'd
Local government finance, §159-160.
Property taxes, §105-273.
Public hospitals, §§131E-6, 131E-16.
Public utilities, §§62-3, 62-100.
Revenue bonds, §159-81.
Transportation authorities, §160A-576.
Urban redevelopment, §160A-503.
Well construction, §87-85.
Municipality's chief administrative official.
Parking authorities, §160A-576.
Municipal solid waste, §130A-290, (a).
Municipal solid waste management facility, §130A-290, (a).
Mutual association.
Savings and loan associations, §54B-4.
Mutual responsibility agreement (MRA).
Public assistance program, §108A-24.
Mutual savings bank, §54C-4, (b).
My commission expires.
Corporate conveyance forms, §47-41.01, (d).
NAIC.
Insurance, §58-1-5.
Tax incentives for new and expanding businesses, §105-129.2.
Narcotic drug.
Controlled substances, §90-87.
Narrow channel.
Personal watercraft, §75A-13.3, (f1).
Narrow therapeutic index drugs.
Pharmacy practice, §90-85.27.
National bank.
Trust companies, §53-301, (a).
National fingerprint file.
National crime prevention and privacy compact, §114-19.50.
National Guard members.
State medical plan, §135-40.1.
National identification index.
National crime prevention and privacy compact, §114-19.50.
National indices.
National crime prevention and privacy compact, §114-19.50.
National primary drinking water regulations, §130A-313.
National tobacco grower settlement trust.
Phase II payments and distributees, §28A-21-3.1, (a).
Tobacco trust fund commission, §143-716.
Natural area.
Nature preserves act, §113A-164.3.
Natural bait.
Fishing license exemptions, §113-276, (e).
Natural gas.
Offshore activities, §143-215.94B, (b).
Natural gas system.
Regional natural gas district, §160A-661, (b).
Natural obstruction.
Floodplain regulations, §143-215.52, (a).
Natural organic fertilizer.
Commercial fertilizer, §106-657.
Natural person.
Boxing commission, §143-651.
Natural resources, §130A-290, (a).
Offshore oil and gas activities, §143-215.94B, (b).
Natural shellfish bed.
Cultivation of shellfish, §113-201.1.
Nature preserve.
Nature preserves act, §113A-164.3.

DEFINED TERMS —Cont'd
Navigable air space.
Aeronautics, §63-1.
Navigable waters.
State lands, §146-64.
Near fatality.
Disclosure of records in child fatality or near fatality cases, §7B-2902, (a).
Near relative.
Absentee ballots, §163-230.1, (f).
Necessary information.
Accident and health insurance.
Utilization review, §58-50-61, (f), (g).
Negative.
Sales, §25C-10.
Negative trend.
Insurance companies, §58-12-2.
Neglect.
Adult care homes, §131D-2, (a).
Adult care home's bill of rights, §131D-20.
Protection of disabled adults, §108A-101.
Neglected juvenile.
Abused, neglected or dependent juveniles, §7B-101.
Negotiate.
Insurance producers, §58-33-10.
Negotiation.
Negotiable instruments, §25-3-201.
Neighboring.
Mining, §74-49.
Nematicide.
Pesticide board, §143-460.
Nematode.
Pesticide board, §143-460.
Neonatal intensive care services.
Certificate of need, §131E-176.
Nesting tobacco.
Leaf tobacco sales, §106-461.
Net cost.
Farm machinery, §66-180.
Net direct premiums.
Beach property insurance, §58-45-5.
Net direct written premiums.
Insurance guaranty association, §58-48-20.
Net disposable earnings.
Repayment of money owed to state, §143-552.
Net dividends.
Corporate income tax, §105-130.4, (f).
Net earnings.
Banking, §53-1.
Net economic loss.
Taxation, §105-130.8.
Net estate.
Decedents' estates, §29-2.
Net gallons.
Gasoline tax, §105-449.60.
Net income.
Principal and income act, §37A-1-102.
Net pension tax.
Individual income tax, §105-151.20, (a).
Net proceeds.
Land sales, §146-15.
Local government sales and use tax for beach nourishment, §105-527.
Net proceeds collected.
Debt collection, §105A-2.
Net taxable sales.
Sales and use tax, §105-164.3.
Net withdrawal value of withdrawable accounts.
Savings and loan associations, §54B-4.

DEFINED TERMS —Cont'd
Network.
Criminal justice information network, §143-660.
Network plan.
Health insurance portability and accountability, §58-68-25, (a).
Network user.
Criminal justice information network, §143-660.
Net worth.
Health maintenance organizations, §58-67-5, (i).
Savings and loan associations, §54B-4.
Savings banks, §54C-4, (b).
Neuropsychological.
Psychology practice, §90-270.2.
New applicant.
Alarm systems, §74D-30.
Private protective services, §74C-30.
New article.
Sales and use tax exemptions, §105-164.13.
New article 9.
1975 amendatory act, §25-11-101.1.
Newborn care.
Midwifery practice, §90-178.2.
New business premium rate.
Small employer group health coverage, §58-50-110.
New communities and large-scale developments.
Land policy act, §113A-152.
New debtor.
Secured transactions, §25-9-102, (a).
New drug.
Food, drugs and cosmetics, §106-121.
New employee.
Job development investment grant program, §143B-437.51.
New facility.
Solid waste management, §130A-295.01, (a).
New institutional health services.
Certificate of need, §131E-176.
New licensing board.
Occupations and professions, §120-149.2.
New location.
Sewage systems, §130A-334.
Newly admitted active member.
Continuing legal education, Bar Rules & Regs., D, §.1501.
New material.
Bedding, §130A-261.
New motor vehicle dealer.
Motor vehicles, §20-286.
New retail outlet.
Motor fuel, §75-81.
New sanitary landfill.
County solid waste disposal, §153A-136, (c).
Public enterprises, §160A-325, (a).
News medium.
Journalist's qualified privilege, §8-53.11, (a).
Newsprint.
Taxation, §105-102.6.
New value.
Secured transactions, §25-9-102, (a).
Next of kin.
Crime victims' rights, §15A-830, (a).
Mental health, §122C-3.
Workers' compensation, §97-40.
Niche.
Cremations, §90-210.41.
911 charge, §62A-3.
911 system, §62A-3.

DEFINED TERMS —Cont'd
Nominated person.
Letters of credit, §25-5-102, (a).
Nominating petition.
Soil and water conservation districts, §139-3.
Nonadmitted insurer.
Surplus lines, §58-21-10.
Nonadverse trustee.
Elective share of surviving spouse, §30-3.2.
Nonapportionable income.
Corporate income tax, §105-130.4, (a).
Nonattainment area, §143-213.
Nonbanking entity, §53-127, (a).
Non-business property.
Property taxes, §105-275.
Noncash proceeds.
Secured transactions, §25-9-102, (a).
Noncertification.
Accident and health insurance.
Utilization review, §58-50-61, (a).
Noncommercial fund.
Petroleum cleanup, §143-215.94A.
Noncommercial private passenger motor vehicle.
Credit scoring to rate motor vehicle and property insurance, §58-36-90, (a).
Noncommercial underground storage tank.
Petroleum cleanup, §143-215.94A.
Noncommunity water system.
Drinking water, §130A-313.
Noncompensatory damages.
Stay of execution on money judgment, §1-289, (b).
Nonconforming sign.
Outdoor advertising control, §136-128.
Nonconsensual.
Civil no-contact orders, §50C-1.
Nonconsumptive use.
Water and air resources, §143-215.21.
Noncriminal justice purposes.
National crime prevention and privacy compact, §114-19.50.
Nondistributable system property.
Public service taxation, §105-333.
Nondisturbance agreement.
Membership camping, §66-246, (a).
Noneconomic detriment.
Victims compensation, §15B-2.
Nonfleet.
Insurance rates, §58-40-10.
Nonfleet private passenger motor vehicle.
Limited driving privilege, §20-179.3, (l).
Motor vehicles, §§20-13.2, 20-16.1.
Nongame animals.
Conservation, §113-129.
Nongame fish.
Conservation, §113-129.
Nonindemnity trigger.
Protected cell companies, §58-10-80.
Nonionizing radiation.
Radiation protection, §104E-5.
Nonissuer.
Securities, §78A-2.
Non-IV-D case.
Child support, §110-129.
Nonmanufacturing facility.
Toxic or hazardous substance identification, §95-174, (q).
Nonoriginal crash repair part, §58-36-95, (a).
Nonparticipating candidate.
Public campaign financing fund, §163-278.62.

DEFINED TERMS —Cont'd
Nonparticipating manufacturer.
Tobacco escrow compliance, §66-292.
Nonparty state.
National crime prevention and privacy compact, §114-19.50.
Nonpotable mineralized water.
Well construction, §87-85.
Nonprofit.
Public utilities, §62-289.3.
Nonprofit agency.
Health facilities finance, §131A-3.
Nonprofit association.
Public hospitals, §131E-6.
Nonprofit corporation, §55A-1-40.
Nonprofit corporation or organization with which associated.
Legislative ethics act, §120-85.
Nonprofit organization.
Alcoholic beverage permits, §18B-1002, (a).
Energy improvement loan program, §143-345.18, (e).
Tax credit for gleaned crop, §105-130.37, (b).
Nonprofit tax exempt organizations.
Surplus state property agency, §143-64.02.
Nonprofit work center for the blind and the severely disabled, §143-48, (b).
Nonresident.
Higher education tuition and fees, §116-143.1.
Motor vehicles, §§20-4.01, 20-4.18.
Taxation, §105-134.5.
Nonresident entity.
Tax withholding, §105-163.1.
Nonresidential redevelopment area, §160A-503.
Nonresident individual.
Taxation, §105-134.1.
Nonresident retail or wholesale merchant.
Sales and use tax, §105-164.3.
Nonresident's operating privilege.
Motor vehicles, §20-279.1.
Nonresident student.
Sex offender and public protection registration, §14-208.6.
Nonresident worker.
Sex offender and public protection registration, §14-208.6.
Nonsmoking area, §143-596.
Non-state entity.
Use of state funds by non-state entities, §143-6.2, (a).
Nonsystem property.
Public service taxation, §105-333.
Nontax district.
Organization of schools, §115C-69.
Nontaxpaid alcoholic beverage.
Alcoholic beverages, §18B-101.
Nontestimonial identification.
Criminal law and procedure, §15A-271.
Delinquent or undisciplined juvenile actions, §7B-2103.
Non-U.S.A. vehicle.
Motor vehicles, §20-4.01.
Nonvested easement in gross, §41-28.
Nonvirgin newsprint.
Taxation, §105-102.6.
North Carolina association.
Regional reciprocal savings and loan acquisition act, §54B-48.2.
North Carolina bank.
Interstate branch banking, §53-224.9.
Reciprocal banking act, §53-210.

DEFINED TERMS —Cont'd
North Carolina bank holding company.
Reciprocal banking act, §53-210.
North Carolina coordinate system, §102-1.
North Carolina enterprise corporation.
Tax credit for qualified business investments, §105-163.010.
North Carolina Global TransPark, §158-32.
North Carolina museum of history, §121-2.
North Carolina public livestock market advisory board.
Livestock prompt pay law, §106-418.3.
North Carolina public school.
NBPTS certification, §115C-296.2, (b).
North Carolina resident.
Coastal and estuarine commercial fishing licenses, §113-168.
Salt water fishing license, §113-174.
North Carolina savings and loan holding company.
Regional reciprocal savings and loan acquisition act, §54B-48.2.
North Carolina school of the arts, §116-64.
North Carolina seed analysis tag.
Seed law, §106-277.2.
North Carolina state archives, §121-2.
North Carolina state bank.
Interstate branch banking, §53-224.9.
North Carolina state health coordinating council, §131E-176.
North Carolina taxable income, §§105-134.1, 105-134.5.
North Carolina university research expenses.
Research and development expenses tax credit, §105-129.50.
Notarial act, §10A-3.
Notary, §10A-3.
Notary public, §10A-3.
Document authentication, §66-271.
Notes.
Agricultural finance act, §122D-3.
Financing capital facilities, §116D-7.
Health facilities finance, §131A-3.
Housing finance agency, §122A-3.
Private capital facilities finance act, §159D-37.
Solid waste, §159I-3, (a).
State debt, §142-29.2.
Notice.
Business corporations, §55-1-40.
Conservation, §113-128.
Criminal law, §14-113.2.
UCC, §25-1-201.
Notification date.
Secured transactions disposition of collateral after default, §25-9-611, (a).
Noxious aquatic weed.
Aquatic weed control, §113A-221.
Noxious-weed seeds.
Seed law, §106-277.2.
Nuclear, biological or chemical weapon of mass destruction.
Weapons of mass death and destruction, §14-288.21, (c).
Nudity.
Public morals, §19-12.
Nuisance.
Mediation of farm nuisance disputes, §7A-38.3, (a).
Nuisance tire collection sites, §130A-309.60, (f).
Public morals, §19-1.

DEFINED TERMS —Cont'd
Nurses.
Nurse licensure compact, §90-171.82.
Nursing, §90-171.20.
Nursing care.
Certificate of need, §131E-176.
Nursing home.
Administrators, §90-276.
Facility licensure act, §131E-101.
Long-term care insurance, §58-55-35, (a).
Nursing home medication management advisory committee, §131E-128.1, (a).
Nursing home administrator, §90-276.
Nursing home facility.
Certificates of need, §131E-176.
Nursing pool, §131E-154.2.
Nursing program, §90-171.20.
Nutrition care services, §90-352.
Oath or affirmation.
Notaries, §10A-3.
Object or line item.
Budgets, §143-23, (f).
Obligated bank.
Negotiable instruments, §§25-3-312, 25-3-411.
Obligated resources.
Higher education bonds, §116D-22.
Obligations.
Housing finance agency, §122A-3.
Public obligations, §159E-2.
Swap agreements, §159-193.
Obligee.
Child support, §110-129.
Failure to pay child support, §50-13.12, (a).
Interstate family support, §52C-1-101.
Obligee of the authority.
Housing authorities, §157-3.
Obligee of the commission.
Urban redevelopment, §160A-503.
Obligor.
Bail, §15A-531.
Bail bondsman and runners, §58-71-1.
Child support, §§110-129, 110-142.
Failure to pay child support, §50-13.12, (a).
Global TransPark authority, §63A-2.
Interstate family support, §52C-1-101.
Liens, §44A-17.
Pollution control, §§159C-3, 159D-3.
Secured transactions, §25-9-102, (a).
Obscene matter.
Public morals, §19-1.1.
Occasional importer.
Gasoline tax, §105-449.66, (a).
Occupant.
Self service storage renter's insurance, §58-33-18, (a).
Storage facilities, §44A-40.
Occupational diseases.
Workers' compensation, §97-53.
Occupational license.
Administrative procedure, §150B-2.
Failure to pay child support, §50-13.12, (a).
Forfeiture of licensing privilege after conviction of felony, §15A-1331A.
Occupational licensing agency.
Administrative procedure, §150B-2.
Occupational licensing board, §93B-1.
Occupational loss of hearing.
Workers' compensation, §97-53.
Occupational safety and health, §95-127.
Occupational safety and health standards, §95-127.

DEFINED TERMS —Cont'd
Occupational skill development.
Vocational and technical education, §115C-152.
Occupational therapist, §90-270.67.
Occupational therapist assistant, §90-270.67.
Occupational therapy, §90-270.67.
Occupied residence.
Swine farms, §106-802.
Occupier of land.
Soil and water conservation districts, §139-3.
Ocean beaches.
Seaward boundary of coastal lands, §77-20, (e).
Oceangoing vessel.
Alcoholic beverages, §18B-106.
Ocean marine insurance.
Insurance guaranty association, §58-48-20.
Ocean shoreline.
Coastal area management, erosion control structures, §113A-115.1, (a).
Odometer.
Motor vehicles, §20-341.
Off-campus program.
Contracts with private institutions to aid North Carolina students, §116-19, (b).
Offender.
Crime victims financial recovery assistance act, §15B-32.
Offense.
Revocation of driver's license, §20-24.1, (e).
Offense against a minor.
Sex offender and public protection registration, §14-208.6.
Offense involving impaired driving.
Motor vehicles, §20-4.01.
Offer.
Certificate of need, §131E-176.
Commodities act, §78D-1.
Membership camping, §66-232.
Securities, §78A-2.
Offering.
Condominiums, §47C-1-103.
Conversion building rental, §47A-34.
Membership camping, §66-232.
Office.
Counties, §153A-230.1.
Delinquent or undisciplined juveniles, §7B-1501.
Local government during emergencies, §162B-7.
Public campaign financing fund, §163-278.62.
Sheriffs' education, §17E-2.
State controller, §143B-426.35.
Trust companies, §53-301, (a).
Veterinarians, §90-181.1, (b).
Office of the counsel.
Discipline and disability rules of state bar, Bar Rules & Regs., B, §.0103.
Procedures for the authorized practice committee of the state bars, Bar Rules & Regs., D, §.0203.
Office of the secretary.
Discipline and disability rules of state bar, Bar Rules & Regs., B, §.0103.
Procedures for the authorized practice committee of the state bars, Bar Rules & Regs., D, §.0203.
Officer.
Criminal procedure, §15A-101.
Death benefits, §143-166.2, (d).
Local government law-enforcement retirement, §143-166.50, (a).
Motor vehicles, §20-137.7.

DEFINED TERMS —Cont'd
Officer —Cont'd
State law-enforcement retirement, §143-166.30, (a).
Official.
Document authentication, §66-271.
Public obligations, §159E-2.
Official action.
Public obligations, §159E-2.
Transportation board, §136-14, (h).
Official ballot.
Elections, §163-165.
Official capacity.
Business corporations, §55-8-50, (b).
Medical service corporations, §58-65-166, (b).
Official certificate.
Meat inspection, §106-549.15.
Poultry products inspection, §106-549.51.
Official certifying agency.
Seed law, §106-277.2.
Official compendium.
Food, drugs and cosmetics, §106-121.
Official device.
Meat inspection, §106-549.15.
Poultry products inspection, §106-549.51.
Official duties.
Death benefits, §143-166.2, (f).
Official establishment.
Poultry products inspection, §106-549.51.
Official inspection legend.
Meat inspection, §106-549.15.
Poultry products inspection, §106-549.51.
Official in the executive branch of state government.
State officers, §147-16.2, (c).
Official mark.
Meat inspection, §106-549.15.
Poultry products inspection, §106-549.51.
Official meeting.
Public bodies, §143-318.10, (d).
Official misconduct.
Notaries, §10A-3.
Official record.
Administrative procedure, §150B-42.
Official sales.
Installment sales, §25A-10.
Official sample.
Commercial feed law, §106-284.33.
Commercial fertilizer, §106-657.
Off indicator.
Unemployment insurance, §96-12.01, (a).
Off-premises outdoor advertising.
Regulation of nonconforming off-premises outdoor advertising, §153A-143, (a), §160A-199, (a).
Off-premises sale.
Sales, §14-401.13.
Offshore waters.
Oil and gas activities, §143-215.94B, (b).
Oil.
Offshore activities, §143-215.94B, (b).
Oil and gas conservation, §113-389.
Pollution control, §143-215.77.
Oil terminal facility.
Oil and hazardous substance control, §143-215.77.
Old article 9.
1975 amendatory act, §25-11-101.1.
On-call emergency service.
Veterinarians, §90-181.1, (b).
Oncology treatment center.
Certificate of need, §131E-176.

DEFINED TERMS —Cont'd
On duty.
City and town personnel, §160A-169.
Counties, §153A-99, (b).
One bedding unit, §130A-269, (f).
100-year floodplain.
Floodplain regulations, §143-215.52, (a).
Ongoing special condition.
Health maintenance organizations, §58-67-88.
On indicator.
Unemployment insurance, §96-12.01, (a).
Open area.
Cities and towns, §160A-407, (a).
Open container.
Alcoholic beverages.
Ordinance regulating malt beverages and unfortified wine, §18B-300, (c).
Open container law, §20-138.7, (f).
Open dump, §130A-290, (a).
Open-end credit.
Credit insurance, §58-57-5.
Open-heart surgery services.
Certificate of need, §131E-176.
Open space.
Cities and towns, §160A-407, (b).
Open space land.
Cities and towns, §160A-407, (b).
Open space uses.
Cities and towns, §160A-407, (b).
Operate.
Boating safety, §75A-2.
Operating agreement.
Limited liability companies, §57C-1-03.
Operating costs.
Mental health, §122C-3.
Operating rights railroad.
Counties.
Contracts with railroads to allocate financial responsibility, §153A-279, (a).
Rail transportation liability, §§160A-326, (a), 160A-626, (a).
Operation of aircraft.
Aeronautics, §63-1.
Operation of wells.
Well construction, §87-85.
Operations.
Fuel taxes, §105-449.37, (a).
Operator.
Amusement device safety, §95-111.3, (e).
Child bicycle safety act, §20-171.8.
Child care facility, §110-86.
Dry-cleaning solvent cleanup act, §143-215.104B, (b).
Elevator safety, §95-110.3, (j).
Global TransPark authority, §63A-2.
Migrant housing, §95-223.
Mining, §74-49.
Motor vehicles, §20-4.01.
Oil and hazardous substance control, §143-215.77.
Passenger tramway safety, §95-117.
Petroleum cleanup, §143-215.94A.
Pollution control, §§159C-3, 159D-3.
Roller skating rink safety and liability, §99E-10.
Solid waste management, §§130A-290, (a), 130A-310.
Water pollution control system, §90A-46.
Water treatment facilities, §90A-20.1.
Operator in charge.
Animal waste management system operators, §90A-47.1.

DEFINED TERMS —Cont'd
Operator in responsible charge.
Water pollution control system, §90A-46.
Water treatment facilities, §90A-20.1.
Opiate.
Controlled substances, §90-87.
Opium poppy.
Controlled substances, §90-87.
Option in gross with respect to an interest in land, §41-28.
Optometry, §90-114.
Oral communication.
Electronic surveillance, §15A-286.
Order.
Negotiable instruments, §25-3-103.
Order for arrest.
Criminal process, §15A-305.
Order of forfeiture.
Impaired driving, §20-28.2, (a1).
Ordinary care.
Health care liability, §90-21.50.
Negotiable instruments, §25-3-103.
Ordinary pocket knife.
Concealed weapons, §14-269, (d).
Organic fertilizer.
Commercial fertilizer, §106-657.
Organization.
Securing attendance of organizations for criminal actions, §15A-773.
UCC, §25-1-201.
Organizer.
Limited liability companies, §57C-1-03.
Origin.
Seed law, §106-277.2.
Original.
Criminal process and procedure.
Electronic technology, §15A-101.1.
Evidence, §8C-1, Rule 1001.
Original debtor.
Secured transactions, §25-9-102, (a).
Original incorporators.
Savings and loan associations, §54B-4.
Savings banks, §54C-4, (b).
Original record.
Workers' compensation self-insurance.
Employer groups, §58-47-75, (a).
Originating state.
Educational personnel qualifications, §115C-350.
Originator.
Funds transfers, UCC, §25-4A-104, (c).
Originator's bank.
Funds transfers, UCC, §25-4A-104, (d).
OSHNC standard.
Toxic or hazardous substance identification, §95-174, (r).
Osteopathy, §90-129.
Other consideration to be received.
Shareholder protection act, §55-9-01, (b).
Other crop seeds.
Seed law, §106-277.2.
Other entity.
Shareholder protection act, §55-9-01, (b).
Other public right-of-way.
Child bicycle safety act, §20-171.8.
Other recipient.
Mental health, §122C-3.
Other valid coverage.
Nature of policies, §58-51-15, (b).
Other waste.
Water and air resources, §143-213.

DEFINED TERMS —Cont'd
Outbreak.
Public health, §130A-2.
Outdoor advertising.
Control, §136-128.
Outdoor recreational facility.
Swine farm, §106-802.
Outer banks of this state, §68-46.
Outlet.
Water and air resources, §143-213.
Out-of-counties scrap tire.
Scrap tire disposal, §130A-309.53.
Out-of-network services.
Provider sponsored organizations, §131E-276.
Out of service order.
Motor vehicles, §20-4.01.
Out-of-state.
Savings interstate branch banks, §54C-200.
Out-of-state association.
Savings and loan interstate branches, §54B-266.
Out-of-state bank.
Interstate branch banking, §53-224.9.
Out-of-state state bank.
Interstate branch banking, §53-224.9.
Out-of-state trust institution.
Trust companies, §53-301, (a).
Outpatient contraceptive services.
Prescription contraceptive drugs, devices and services covered by health benefit plan, §58-3-178, (c).
Outpatient treatment.
Mental health, §122C-3.
Outstanding balance.
Contempt, §6-21.2.
Reverse mortgages, §53-257.
Outstanding obligations.
State debt, §142-29.2.
Outstanding payment instrument.
Money transmitters, §53-208.2, (a).
Overburden.
Mining, §74-49.
Overdue tax debt.
Business tax incentives, §105-129.2.
Collection, §105-243.1, (a).
Job development investment grant program, §143B-437.51.
Overfished, §113-129.
Overfishing, §113-129.
Overhanging tobacco.
Leaf tobacco sales, §106-461.
Over-the-counter drug.
Sales and use tax, §105-164.3.
Owner.
Amusement device safety, §95-111.3, (f).
Auctions and auctioneers, §85B-1.
Cave protection, §14-159.20.
Condemnation, §136-115.
Conservation, §113-130.
Dangerous dogs, §67-4.1.
Elevator safety, §95-110.3, (k).
Eminent domain, §40A-2.
Housing standards, §160A-442.
Joyriding, §14-72.2.
Liability of landowners associated with watershed improvement projects, §139-41.3.
Liens on personal property, §44A-1.
Motor vehicles, §20-4.01.
Nature preserves act, §113A-164.3.
Oil and gas conservation, §113-389.
Petroleum cleanup, §143-215.94A.
Private personnel services, §95-47.1.

DEFINED TERMS —Cont'd
Owner —Cont'd
Property tax homestead exclusion, §105-277.1, (b).
Records, tapes and other recorded devices, §14-432.
Recreational trespass, §38A-2.
Residential property disclosure act, §47E-3.
Solicitation of contributions, §131F-2.
Solid waste management, §130A-310.
Statutory liens on real property, §44A-7.
Storage facilities, §44A-40.
Subcontractors, §22C-1.
Tax incentives for recycling facilities, §105-129.25.
Telephonic sellers, §66-260.
Unclaimed property act, §116B-52.
Owner-controlled or wrap-up insurance.
Public works projects, §58-31-65, (b).
Owner of land.
Soil and water conservation districts, §139-3.
Owners association.
Planned community act, §47F-1-103.
Owner's real property.
Dangerous dogs, §67-4.1.
Oyster rocks.
Cultivation of shellfish, §113-207.
Package.
Antifreeze law, §106-579.3.
Food, drugs and cosmetics, §106-121.
Poultry products inspection, §106-549.51.
Tobacco taxation, §105-113.4.
Weights and measures, §81A-9.
Packaged, labeled and released for shipment.
Pesticide board, §143-460.
Packer.
Egg law, §106-245.14.
Palliative care.
Hospice licensure, §131E-201.
PALS committee.
Discipline and disability rules of state bar, Bar Rules & Regs., B, §.0103.
Panel.
Public utilities, §62-3.
Parent.
Adoptee's new birth certificate, §48-9-107, (c).
Adoption, §48-1-102.
Brownfields property reuse act, §130A-310.31, (b).
Corporate franchise tax, §105-122, (b).
Dry-cleaning solvent cleanup act, §143-215.104B, (b).
Education assistance authority, §116-209.24.
Marriage proceedings, §51-2.2.
Mining, §74-49.
Public assistance program, §108A-24.
Special education.
Mediation, §115C-116, (b).
Underground storage tank cleanup, §143-215.94A.
Workers' compensation, §97-2.
Parental loans.
Education assistance authority, §116-209.24.
Parental obligations.
Education assistance authority, §116-209.24.
Parent company.
Insurance companies, conversion, §58-10-12, (a).
Parent of a sponsoring provider.
Provider sponsored organizations, §131E-276.
Parent organization.
Solicitation of contributions, §131F-2.
Par formula.
Capital facilities finance act, §142-82.
Facility authorities, §160A-480.2.
Global TransPark authority, §63A-2.

DEFINED TERMS —Cont'd
Par formula —Cont'd
Higher education bonds, §116D-1.
Local government bonds, §159-79, (c).
Solid waste management loan program.
Special obligation bonds and notes of local governments, §159I-30, (g).
State debt, §142-29.2.
Park.
State parks act, §113-44.9.
Parking project.
Parking authorities, §160A-551.
Parole.
Interstate compact on juveniles, §7B-2803.
Part.
Anatomical gifts, §130A-403.
Partial eviction.
Expedited evictions, §42-59.
Partial unemployment.
Insurance, §96-8.
Participant.
Boxing commission, §143-651.
Disability income plan, §135-101.
Equine activity liability, §99E-1.
Health insurance portability and accountability, §58-68-25, (a).
State law-enforcement retirement, §143-166.30, (a).
Participating agency.
State employee incentive bonus program, §143-345.20.
Participating candidate.
Public campaign financing fund, §163-278.62.
Participating city.
City and town annexation agreements, §160A-58.22.
Participating institution.
Private capital facilities finance act, §159D-37.
Participating manufacturer.
Tobacco escrow compliance, §66-292.
Participating provider.
Accident and health insurance.
Utilization review, §58-50-61, (a).
Health maintenance organizations, §58-67-5, (l).
Participating school.
Education programs in residential schools, §143B-146.1, (b).
Participatory CLE.
Continuing legal education, Bar Rules & Regs., D, §.1501.
Parties and interests.
Housing standards, §160A-442.
Partner.
Partnerships, §59-102.
Rules of professional conduct, Prof. Cond. Rule 1.0.
Partnership, §59-36.
Conversion and merger, §59-73.1.
Housing trust, §122E-2.
Individual income taxation, §105-134.1.
Partnership interest, §59-102.
Part-year residents.
Taxation, §105-134.5.
Party line.
Telephones, §14-401.8.
Party or parties.
Administrative procedure, §150B-2.
Adoption, §48-1-101.
Business corporations, §55-8-50, (b).
Civil procedure, §1-567.32.
Condemnation, §136-115.

DEFINED TERMS —Cont'd
Party or parties —Cont'd
Discipline and disability rules of state bar, Bar Rules & Regs., B, §.0103.
Good funds settlement act, §45A-3.
Industrial commission utilization of rehabilitation professionals, I.C. Util. Rehab. Profs. I.
Mediation of farm nuisance disputes, §7A-38.3, (a).
Medical service corporations, §58-65-166, (b).
Negotiable instruments, §25-3-103.
Procedures for the authorized practice committee of the state bars, Bar Rules & Regs., D, §.0203.
Special education.
Mediation, §115C-116, (b).
UCC, §25-1-201.
Party state.
National crime prevention and privacy compact, §114-19.50.
Nurse licensure compact, §90-171.82.
Passenger.
Child bicycle safety act, §20-171.8.
Skiing, §99C-1.
Passenger area of a motor vehicle.
Alcoholic beverages, §18B-401, (c).
Open container law, §20-138.7, (f).
Passenger motor vehicle.
Seat belt use mandatory, §20-135.2A, (b).
Passenger rail services.
Counties.
Contracts with railroads to allocate financial responsibility, §153-279, (a).
Rail transportation liability, §§160A-326, (a), 160A-626, (a).
Passenger tramway.
Safety, §95-117.
Skiing, §99C-1.
Passenger vehicles.
Motor vehicles, §20-4.01.
Pass-through entity.
Historic rehabilitation tax credit, §105-129.35, (c).
Low-income housing tax credits, §105-129.40, (b).
Taxation, §105-228.80, (b).
Tax credit for qualified business investments, §105-163.010.
Tax withholding, §105-163.1.
Past due.
Statewide accounts receivable program, §147-86.20.
Pastoral counseling, §90-382.
Pastoral psychotherapy.
Counseling, §90-382.
Patient.
Emergency medical services, §131E-155.
Interstate compact on mental health, §122C-361.
Nursing homes, §131E-116.
Patient counseling.
Hospital licensure, §131E-79.1, (b).
Patient data.
Medical care data, §131E-214.1.
Patient identifying information.
Medical care data, §131E-214.1.
Patient's representative.
Portable do not resuscitate orders, §90-21.17, (c).
Patterns of racketeering activity.
RICO act, §75D-3.
Pawn, §91A-3.
Pawnbroker, §91A-3.
Pawnshop, §91A-3.
Pawn transaction, §91A-3.

DEFINED TERMS —Cont'd
Payable at a definite time.
Negotiable instruments, §25-3-108.
Payable at bank, §25-4-105.1.
Payable in installments.
Installment sales, §25A-3.
Payable on demand.
Negotiable instruments, §25-3-108.
Payable through bank, §25-4-105.1.
Payday.
Wage and hour act, §95-25.2.
Payee.
Structured settlement protection, §1-543.11.
Payment.
Patient medical records, confidentiality of, §130A-12.
Principal and income act, §37A-4-409, (a).
Payment date.
Funds transfers, UCC, §25-4A-401.
Payment instrument.
Money transmitters, §53-208.2, (a).
Payment intangible.
Secured transactions, §25-9-102, (a).
Payment order.
Funds transfers, UCC, §25-4A-103, (a).
Payor.
Alimony, §50-16.1A.
Child support, §110-129.
Student loan collections, §105B-1.
Tax withholding, §105-163.1.
Payor bank.
Banking, §25-4-105.
Pay periods.
Wage and hour act, §95-25.2.
Payroll period.
Tax withholding, §105-163.1.
Peak.
Mining, §74-49.
Peddler, §66-250.
Peer counselor.
Peer support group counselor's privilege, §8-53.10, (a).
Peer review committee.
Facility licensure act, §131E-101.
Penal institution.
Sex offender and public protection registration, §14-208.6.
Pen register.
Wiretaps, §15A-260.
Pension.
Legislative retirement system, §120-4.8.
Retirement, §128-21.
State retirement system, §135-1.
Pension payer.
Tax withholding, §105-163.1.
Pension payment.
Tax withholding, §105-163.1.
Pension reserve.
Legislative retirement system, §120-4.8.
Retirement, §128-21.
State retirement, §135-1.
PEO agreement.
Professional employer organizations, §58-89A-5.
Percent.
Commercial feed law, §106-284.33.
Commercial fertilizer, §106-657.
Soil additives act, §106-50.30.
Percentage.
Commercial feed law, §106-284.33.
Soil additives act, §106-50.30.

DEFINED TERMS —Cont'd
Performance bonus.
Personnel system, §126-7, (a2).
Performed with due diligence.
Year 2000 liability, §66-296.
Period of measurement.
Research and development expenses tax credit, §105-129.50.
Period of war.
Children of war veterans scholarships, §165-20.
Permanent house guests.
Sanitation, §130A-247.
Permanently and totally disabled as a direct result of a traumatic injury sustained in the line of duty.
Tuition waiver for senior citizens, §115B-1.
Permanent residence.
Property tax homestead exclusion, §105-277.1, (b).
Permissible investments.
Money transmitters, §53-208.2, (a).
Permissive supplier.
Gasoline tax, §105-449.60.
Permit.
Bee and honey act, §106-635.
Boll weevil eradication, §106-65.69.
Concealed handgun permits, §14-415.10.
Pharmacy practice, §90-85.3, (m).
Wildlife permit, §113-274, (a).
Permit boundaries.
Mining permits, §74-50, (b).
Permitted analytical variation.
Commercial feed law, §106-284.33.
Permitted area.
Mining permits, §74-50, (b).
Persistent vegetative state.
Natural death right, §90-321, (a).
Person.
Address confidentiality program, §15C-2.
Administrative procedure, §150B-2.
Aeronautics, §63-1.
Agricultural finance act, §122D-3.
Alcoholic beverages, §18B-101.
Amusement device safety, §95-111.3, (g).
Animal diseases, §106-405.1.
Antifreeze law, §106-579.3.
Arbitration, §1-569.1.
Athlete agents, §78C-86.
Automated external defibrillator (AED), §90-21.15, (b).
Banking, §§53-42.1, (a), 53-99.1, (a), 53-165, (j).
Banks.
Total loans and extension of credit to one person, §53-48, (d).
Beach property insurance, §58-45-6.
Biological agents registry, §130A-479, (b).
Biological residues, §106-549.81.
Boating safety, §75A-2.
Boll weevil eradication, §106-65.69.
Boxing commission, §143-651.
Business corporations, §55-1-40.
Business discrimination, §75B-1.
Capital facilities finance act, §142-82.
Cave protection, §14-159.20.
Cemeteries, §65-48.
Certificate of need, §131E-176.
Check-cashing service, §53-275.
Child care facilities.
Fraudulent misrepresentation, §110-107, (c).
Child custody jurisdiction and enforcement, §50A-102.
Child placing and care, §131D-10.2.

DEFINED TERMS —Cont'd
Person —Cont'd
Children's health insurance program, §108A-70.28, (e).
Civil procedure, §1-75.2.
Coastal area management, §113A-103.
Commercial feed law, §106-284.33.
Commercial fertilizer, §106-657.
Commodities act, §78D-1.
Condemnation, §136-115.
Condominiums, §47C-1-103.
Conservation, §113-130.
Contractors, §87-101.
Contractors for public works, §133-23.
Controlled substances, §90-87.
Cooperative agreements among physicians or between physician, hospital or others, §90-21.25.
Corporations, §75E-1.
Cotton warehousing, §106-451.7.
Custodial trusts, §33B-1.
Debt adjusting, §14-423.
Decedents' estates, §28A-19-7.
Drinking water, §130A-313.
Dry-cleaning solvent cleanup.
Criminal penalties, §143-215.104Q, (i).
Egg law, §106-245.14.
Electric membership corporations, §117-7.
Electronic commerce in government, §66-58.2.
Electronic surveillance, §15A-286.
Electronic transactions, §66-312.
Elevator safety, §95-110.3, (l).
Eminent domain, §40A-2.
Energy conservation finance act, §142-61.
Engineering, §89C-3.
Fair access to insurance requirements, §58-46-2.
Fair housing act, §41A-3.
Federal estate tax, §28A-27-1.
Financial identity fraud, §14-113.24, (a).
Food, drugs and cosmetics, §106-121.
Foreign-money claims, §1C-1820.
Fraudulent transfers, §39-23.1.
Gasoline and oil inspection, §119-15.
Gasoline tax, §105-449.60.
Global TransPark authority, §63A-2.
Grain adulteration, §106-621.
Grain dealers, §106-601.
Health care facilities, §131E-1.
Certificate of public advantage, §131E-192.2.
Health maintenance organizations, §58-67-5, (g).
Insurance, §58-1-5.
Insurance commissioner examinations, §58-2-131, (b).
Insurance guaranty associations, §58-62-16.
Insurance holding companies, §58-19-5.
Insurance producers, §58-33-10.
Insurer supervision, rehabilitation and liquidation, §58-30-22, (a).
Investment advisers, §78C-2.
Liability for hazardous materials abatement, §143-215.103.
Limited liability companies, §57C-1-03.
Livestock brands, §80-58.
Livestock dealer licensing, §106-418.8.
Lobbying, §120-47.1.
Manufactured housing, §143-143.9.
Marketable title, §47B-8.
Marketing associations, §54-130.
Mediation of farm nuisance disputes, §7A-38.3, (a).
Membership camping, §66-232.

DEFINED TERMS —Cont'd
Person —Cont'd
Mental health, §122C-3.
Metropolitan sewerage districts, §162A-65, (a).
Metropolitan water districts, §162A-32, (a).
Migrant housing, §95-223.
Modification and termination of irrevocable trusts, §36A-125.1.
Money transmitters, §53-208.2, (a).
Mortgage bankers and brokers, §53-243.01.
Motion pictures, §75C-2.
Motor fuel, §75-81.
Motor vehicles, §§20-4.01, 20-286, 20-356.
Mountain ridge protection, §113A-206.
Nonprofit corporations, §55A-1-40.
Nursing program, §90-171.20.
Occupational safety and health, §95-127.
Occupational therapy, §90-270.67.
Oil and gas conservation, §113-389.
Oil and hazardous substance control, §143-215.77.
Overhead high-voltage line safety, §95-229.6.
Partnerships, §§59-32, 59-102.
Patient abuse, §14-32.2, (d).
Pawnbrokers, §91A-3.
Peddlers, itinerant merchants and specialty markets, §66-250.
Persons with disabilities protection, §168A-3.
Pesticide board, §143-460.
Pharmacy practice, §90-85.3, (n).
Planned community act, §47F-1-103.
Political campaigns, §163-278.6.
Pollution control act, §113A-52.
Pork promotion assessment, §106-792.
Poultry products inspection, §106-549.51.
Principal and income act, §37A-1-102.
Private personnel services, §95-47.1.
Professional employer organizations, §58-89A-5.
Property taxes, §105-273.
Proprietary schools, §115D-87.
Protection of animals, §§19A-1, 19A-23.
Public health generally, §§130A-2, 130A-26.1, (a).
Public morals, §§19-1.1, 19-12.
Public utilities, §§62-3, 62-289.3.
Radiation protection, §104E-5.
Readable insurance policies, §58-38-15.
Reciprocal insurance, §58-15-5.
Refund anticipation loan act, §53-246.
Regulation of open fires, §113-60.22.
Relocation assistance, §133-7.
Rendering plants, §106-168.1.
Rental cars, §66-201.
Respiratory care practices act, §90-648.
Retaliatory work discrimination, §95-240.
Sales, §§25C-10, 66-76.
Sales and use tax, §105-164.3.
Sales representatives, §66-190.
Savings and loan associations, §54B-63.1, (a).
Savings banks, §54C-60.1, (a).
Securities, §78A-2.
Seed law, §106-277.2.
Soil additives act, §106-50.30.
Solid waste management, §130A-290, (a).
Speech and language pathologists and audiologists licensure, §90-293.
Sport shooting range protection, §14-409.45.
Statewide accounts receivable program, §147-86.20.
Street and highways, private pilot toll project, §136-89.172, (m).
Structural pest control act, §106-65.24.

DEFINED TERMS —Cont'd
Person —Cont'd
Sublease of motor vehicle and loan assumption arranging, §20-106.2, (a).
Taxation, §§105-33.1, 105-134.1, 105-228.90, (b).
Telephone solicitations, §75-101.
Telephonic sellers, §66-260.
Therapeutic recreation personnel certification, §90C-4, (d).
Time shares, §93A-41.
Trade secrets, §66-152.
Transfers to minors, §33A-1.
Trust companies, §53-301, (a).
Trusts, §§36A-1, (b), 36A-60.
Trusts and trustees, §36A-22.1.
UCC, §25-1-201.
Unauthorized substances taxes, §105-113.106.
Unclaimed property act, §116B-52.
Unfair trade practices, §58-63-5.
Uniform fiduciaries act, §32-2, (a).
Uniform sales and use tax administration act, §105-164.42B.
Unit ownership, §47A-3.
Vehicle reinsurance, §58-37-1.
Veterans, §34-2.
Veterinarians, §90-181.
Wage and hour act, §95-25.2.
Water and air resources, §§143-212, 143-215.6B, (a).
Water and sewer, §162A-2.
Weights and measures, §81A-9.
Well construction, §87-85.
Well contractor certification, §87-98.2.
Wholesale prescription drug distributors, §106-145.2.
Work first program fraud, §108A-39, (c).
Year 2000 liability, §66-296.
Person acting as a parent.
Child custody jurisdiction and enforcement, §50A-102.
Person aggrieved.
Administrative procedure, §150B-2.
Personal care services.
Adult care homes, §131D-2, (a).
Personal household property.
Credit property insurance, §58-57-90, (a).
Personal identification code.
Criminal law, §14-113.8.
Personal information.
Insurance information and privacy protection act, §58-39-15.
Personality disorder.
Sex offender and public protection registration, §14-208.6.
Personal knowledge of identity.
Notaries, §10A-3.
Personal property.
Storage facilities, §44A-40.
Personal recognizance.
Motor vehicles, §20-4.18.
Personal relationship.
Domestic violence, §50B-1, (b).
Domestic violence in disposition report, §15A-1382.1, (c).
Personal representative.
Custodial trusts, §33B-1.
Decedents' estates, §28A-1-1.
Estate taxes, §105-32.1.
Joint personal representatives, §28A-13-6.
Transfers to minors, §33A-1.
Personal risk liability, §58-22-10.

DEFINED TERMS —Cont'd
Personal watercraft, §75A-13.3, (a).
Person financially responsible.
Contractors, §87-101.
Person having custody of prisoner.
Approval of education and other training programs, §162-59.1.
Person in loco parentis.
Pharmacy practice, §90-85.3, (o).
Person interested in the estate.
Federal estate tax, §28A-27-1.
Person in the position of a seller.
Sales, §25-2-707.
Personnel.
School-based management and accountability program, §115C-105.36, (a).
Personnel hoist.
Elevator safety, §95-110.3, (m).
Personnel placement services.
Professional employer organizations, §58-89A-5.
Personnel professional.
Personnel system, §126-5, (b).
Person related to, individual.
Secured transactions, §25-9-102, (a).
Person related to, organization.
Secured transactions, §25-9-102, (a).
Person responsible for the work to be done.
Overhead high-voltage line safety, §95-229.6.
Persons admitted.
Costs paid by persons admitted to institutions of department of health and human services, §143-117.1.
Persons and families of lower income.
Housing finance agency, §122A-3.
Persons and families of moderate income.
Housing finance agency, §122A-5.4.
Persons engaged in national defense activities.
National defense housing projects, §157-53.
Persons of low income.
Housing authorities, §157-3.
National defense housing projects, §157-53.
Persons of moderate income.
Housing authorities, §157-3.
Person with a disability, §168A-3.
Pest.
Pest control, §106-65.55.
Pesticide board, §143-460.
Structural pest control act, §106-65.24.
Pest control consultant.
Pesticide board, §143-460.
Pesticide.
Board, §143-460.
Structural pest control act, §106-65.24.
Pesticide applicator, §143-460.
Pesticide board, §143-460.
Pesticide chemical.
Food, drugs and cosmetics, §106-121.
Meat inspection, §106-549.15.
Poultry products inspection, §106-549.51.
Pesticide classified for restricted use, §143-460.
Pesticide dealer.
Board, §143-460.
Pet.
Commercial feed law, §106-284.33.
Pet food.
Commercial feed law, §106-284.33.
Petition.
Soil and water conservation districts, §139-3.
Petitioner.
Abused, neglected or dependent juveniles, §7B-101.

DEFINED TERMS —Cont'd
Petitioner —Cont'd
Child custody jurisdiction and enforcement, §50A-301.
Delinquent and undisciplined juveniles, §7B-1501.
Standby guardianship, §35A-1370.
Petroleum.
Oil or hazardous substances discharge, §143-215.85, (b).
Underground storage tank cleanup, §143-215.94A.
Petroleum product.
Underground storage tank cleanup, §143-215.94A.
Pet shop.
Protection of animals, §19A-23.
Pharmaceutical and medicine manufacture and distribution.
Sales and use tax refunds, §105-164.14, (j).
Pharmacist, §90-85.3, (p).
Pharmacy, §90-85.3, (q).
Pharmacy of choice, §58-51-37, (b).
Phased development plan.
Counties, §153A-344.1.
Phased development planning.
City and town zoning, §160A-385.1, (b).
Phase II payments.
Phase II payments and distributees, §28A-21-3.1, (a).
Photograph.
Evidence, §8C-1, Rule 1001.
Sales, §25C-10.
Photographic image.
Peeping into room occupied by another person, §14-202, (b).
Physical custody.
Adoption, §48-1-101.
Child custody jurisdiction and enforcement, §50A-102.
Physical harm.
Assaulting law enforcement or assistance animals, §14-163.1, (a).
Physically helpless.
Criminal law, §14-27.1.
Physical or mental impairment.
Persons with disabilities protection, §168A-3.
Physical therapist, §90-270.24.
Physical therapist assistant, §90-270.24.
Physical therapy, §90-270.24.
Physical therapy aide, §90-270.24.
Physician.
Accident and health insurance.
Diabetes treatment coverage, §58-51-61, (b).
Anatomical gifts, §130A-403.
Boxing commission, §143-651.
Cooperative agreements among physicians or between physician, hospital or others, §90-21.25.
Health care liability, §90-21.50.
Health maintenance organizations.
Diabetes treatment coverage, §58-67-74, (b).
Hospital, medical and dental service corporations.
Diabetes treatment coverage, §58-65-91, (b).
Industrial commission utilization of rehabilitation professionals, I.C. Util. Rehab. Profs. I.
Medicolegal guidelines for attorney-physician relationship, MLG Rule 3.
Mental health, §122C-3.
Natural death right, §90-321, (a).
Respiratory care practices act, §90-648.
Pipeline.
Oil and hazardous substance control, §143-215.77.

DEFINED TERMS —Cont'd
Pipeline company.
Public service taxation, §105-333.
Place.
Public morals, §19-1.1.
Placed for adoption.
Health insurance portability and accountability, §58-68-25, (a).
Placement.
Adoption, §48-1-101.
Placement in the foster home.
Family leave credit insurance, §58-57-115, (a).
Insurance, §58-51-30, (a).
Place of business.
Sales, §14-401.13.
Secured transactions debtor's location, §25-9-307, (a).
Sewage systems, §130A-334.
Place of primary use.
Sales and use tax, §§105-163.3, 105-164.3.
Telecommunications, §105-164.4C, (h).
Place of public accommodations.
Persons with disabilities protection, §168A-3.
Place of public assembly.
Sewage systems, §130A-334.
Plaintiff, §1-10.
Civil procedure, §1-75.2.
Discipline and disability rules of state bar, Bar Rules & Regs., B, §.0103.
Procedures for the authorized practice committee of the state bar, Bar Rules & Regs., D, §.0203.
Plan.
Annuities, §147-9.2.
Disability income, §135-101.
Self-insurance guaranty association, §97-130.
Separate insurance benefits for law enforcement, §143-166.60, (a).
State medical coverage, §§135-40.1, 135-40.13, (b).
State parks act, §113-44.9.
Planned community, §47F-1-103.
Planning commission.
Urban redevelopment, §160A-503.
Plan of conversion.
Insurance companies, conversion, §58-10-12, (a).
Savings and loan associations, §54B-4.
Savings banks, §54C-4, (b).
Plan of operation.
Beach area essential property insurance, §58-45-30, (f).
Beach property insurance, §58-45-5.
Liability risk retention, §58-22-10.
Vehicle reinsurance, §58-37-1.
Plant.
Plant protection and conservation, §106-202.12.
Plant pest, §106-419.
Plant regulator.
Pesticide board, §143-460.
Plat.
Probate and registration, §47-30.
Plate.
Sales, §25C-10.
Platinum.
Precious metals, §66-164.
Pledged goods.
Pawnbrokers, §91A-3.
Plumbing.
Contractors, §87-21.
Pneumatic tire.
Motor vehicles, §20-4.01.
Podiatry, §90-202.2, (a).

DEFINED TERMS —Cont'd
Points and fees.
Mortgages, high cost home loans, §24-1.1E, (a).
Point source, §143-213.
Policy.
Insurance guaranty associations, §58-62-16.
Long-term care insurance, §58-55-20.
Medicare supplement insurance, §58-54-1.
Readable insurance policies, §58-38-15.
Viatical life insurance settlements, §58-58-205.
Policyholder.
Assumption reinsurance, §58-10-25, (a).
Insurance guaranty association, §58-48-20.
Insurance information and privacy protection act, §58-39-15.
Policyholder-related liabilities.
Asset protection, §58-13-15.
Policyholders position.
Mortgage guaranty insurers, §58-10-120.
Policyholders surplus.
Mortgage guaranty insurers, §58-10-120.
Policy summary.
Life insurance solicitation, §58-60-10.
Political action committee.
Campaign contributions and expenditures.
Disclosure requirements for media advertisements, §163-278.38Z.
Political committee.
Campaigns, §163-278.6.
Candidates' financing fund, §163-278.45.
Public campaign financing fund, §163-278.62.
Political organization.
Alcoholic beverage permits, §18B-1002, (a).
Political party, §163-96, (a).
Campaigns, §163-278.6.
Political party organization.
Campaign contributions and expenditures.
Disclosure requirements for media advertisements, §163-278.38Z.
Political subdivision.
Emergency management, §166A-4.
Governmental employees and social security, §135-20.
Local government during emergencies, §162B-7.
Metropolitan sewerage districts, §162A-65, (a).
Metropolitan water districts, §162A-32, (a).
North Carolina trail system, §113A-85.
Pollution control, §§159C-3, 159D-3.
Water and sewer, §162A-2.
Polluted water.
Well construction, §87-85.
Pollution.
Pollution control, §§159C-3, 159D-3.
Pollution control project, §159C-3.
Pool.
Oil and gas conservation, §113-389.
Small employer group health coverage, §58-50-110.
Poppy straw.
Controlled substances, §90-87.
Population.
Regional public transportation, §160A-601.
Regional transportation authorities, §160A-631.
Porcine animal.
Pork promotion assessment, §106-792.
Pork producer.
Promotion assessment for pork, §106-792.
Position holder.
Gasoline tax, §105-449.60.
Positive identification.
National crime prevention and privacy compact, §114-19.50.

DEFINED TERMS —Cont'd
Positron emission tomography scanner.
Certificate of need, §131E-176.
Possessory liens.
Secured transactions priority of security interests, §25-9-333, (a).
Postconsumer recovered paper.
Newspaper taxation, §105-102.6.
Post-consumer waste material.
Tax incentives for recycling facilities, §105-129.25.
Posted property, §113-281.
Postpaid calling service.
Sales and use tax on telecommunications, §105-164.4C, (h).
Postpartum care.
Midwifery practice, §90-178.2.
Post-release program.
Department of juvenile justice and delinquency prevention, §143B-515.
Post-release supervision, §15A-1368, (a).
Delinquent and undisciplined juveniles, §7B-1501.
Post-secondary degree.
University of North Carolina, §116-15.
Post-secondary degree activity.
University of North Carolina, §116-15.
Post-termination transition period.
Taxation, §105-131.
Potentially dangerous dog, §67-4.1.
Potentially responsible party.
Brownfields property reuse act, §130A-310.31, (b).
Dry-cleaning solvent cleanup act, §143-215.104B, (b).
Potential medication-related error.
Nursing home medication management advisory committee, §131E-128.1, (a).
Potential testimony.
Criminal procedure, §15A-971.
Poultry.
Product inspection, §106-549.51.
Regulation, §106-541.
Poultry composting facility.
Poultry products inspection, §106-549.51.
Poultry product.
Inspection, §106-549.51.
Poultry products broker.
Poultry products inspection, §106-549.51.
Pound.
Weights and measures, §81A-9.
Practical banker, §53-1.
Practical examination.
Emergency medical services, §131E-155.
Practice law.
Attorneys at law, §84-2.1.
Practice of acupuncture, §90-451.
Practice of architecture, §83A-1.
Practice of audiology.
Licensure, §90-293.
Practice of counseling.
Licensed professional counselors, §90-330, (a).
Practice of engineering, §89C-3.
Practice of forestry, §89B-2.
Practice of funeral service, §90-210.20, (k).
Practice of land surveying, §89C-3.
Practice of marriage and family therapy, §90-270.47.
Practice of massage and bodywork therapy, §90-622.
Practice of nursing by a licensed practical nurse, §90-171.20.
Practice of nursing by a registered nurse, §90-171.20.

DEFINED TERMS —Cont'd
Practice of pharmacy, §90-85.3, (r).
Practice of psychology, §90-270.2.
Practice of respiratory care.
Respiratory care practices act, §90-648.
Practice of social work, §90B-3.
Practice of soil science, §89F-3.
Practice of veterinary medicine, §90-181.
Practicing.
Medicine, §90-18, (b).
Practitioner.
Controlled substances, §90-87.
Food, drugs and cosmetics, §106-121.
Prearrangement insurance policy.
Funeral and burial trust funds, §90-210.60.
Preceptor.
Assisted living administrators, §90-288.13.
Nursing home administrators, §90-276.
Precious metal, §66-164.
Commodities act, §78D-1.
Predecessor plan.
State medical coverage, §135-40.1.
Preeffective-date financing statement.
Secured transactions transitional provisions regarding financing statements, §25-9-707, (a).
Preemptive right in the nature of a right to first refusal in gross with respect to an interest in land, §41-28.
Preexisting condition.
Health maintenance organizations, §58-67-85.
Long-term care insurance, §58-55-30, (c).
Medical service corporations, §58-65-60.
Nature of policies, §58-51-80, (b).
State medical plan, §135-40.1.
Preexisting condition exclusion.
Health insurance portability and accountability, §58-68-30, (b).
Preexisting-conditions provision.
Small employer group health coverage, §58-50-110.
Preferred claim.
Insurers supervision, §58-30-10.
Preferred provider, §§58-50-56, (a), 58-65-1, (a).
Preferred provider benefit plan, §58-50-56, (a).
Preferred provider contracts or networks.
Medical plan for teachers and state employees, §135-40.4, (b).
Preferred provider organization, §58-50-56, (a).
Pregnancy.
State medical plan, §135-40.1.
Preliminary damage assessment.
Emergency management, §166A-4.
Preliminary hearing.
Discipline and disability rules of state bar, Bar Rules & Regs., B, §.0103.
Procedures for the authorized practice committee of the state bars, Bar Rules & Regs., D, §.0203.
Premarital agreement, §52B-2.
Premises, §42-40.
Larceny of shopping carts, §14-72.3.
Piped natural gas tax, §105-187.40.
Public utilities, §62-110.2.
Urban electrical service, §160A-331.
Premium.
Fraternal benefit societies, §58-24-15, (d).
Group health insurance, §58-53-1.
Insurance guaranty associations, §58-62-16.
Providers of health benefits, §58-50-40, (a).

DEFINED TERMS —Cont'd
Premium —Cont'd
Small employer group health coverage, §58-50-110.
Prenatal care.
Midwifery practice, §90-178.2.
Preneed funeral contract, §90-210.60.
Preneed funeral contract beneficiary, §90-210.60.
Preneed funeral funds, §90-210.60.
Preneed funeral planning, §90-210.60.
Preneed licensee.
Funeral and burial trust funds, §90-210.60.
Prepaid entertainment contract, §66-118.
Prepaid health services.
Medicaid program exemption, §143-48.1, (b).
Prepaid legal services plan or group services plan.
Rules of professional conduct, Prof. Cond. Rule 7.3.
Prepaid telephone calling arrangement.
Sales and use tax, §105-164.3.
Prepaid telephone calling service.
Sales and use tax on telecommunications, §105-164.4C, (h).
Preparation for advanced education.
Vocational and technical education, §115C-152.
Prepared.
Meat inspection, §106-549.15.
Prepared food.
Sales and use tax, §105-164.3.
Preplacement assessment.
Adoption, §48-1-101.
Preschool handicapped children.
Special education, §115C-146.1.
Prescribed burning, §113-60.41.
Prescriber.
Pharmacy practice, §90-85.27.
Prescription.
Controlled substances, §90-87.
Prescribed burning of forestlands, §113-60.41.
Sales and use tax, §105-164.3.
Prescription contraceptive drugs and devices.
Prescription contraceptive drugs, devices and services covered by health benefit plan, §58-3-178, (c).
Prescription drug.
Pharmacy practice, §90-85.3, (s).
Registration of prescription drug wholesalers, manufacturers or repackagers, §106-140.1, (j).
Wholesale prescription drug distributors, §106-145.2.
Prescription order.
Pharmacy practice, §90-85.3, (t).
Presentation.
Letters of credit, §25-5-102, (a).
Presenters.
Letters of credit, §25-5-102, (a).
Presenting.
Criminal law, §14-113.8.
Presenting bank.
Banking, §25-4-105.
Present member of the general assembly.
Legislative retirement system, §120-4.8.
Presentment, §15A-641.
Negotiable instruments, §25-3-501.
Present sale.
Sales, §25-2-106.
Present-use value.
Taxation, §105-277.2.

DEFINED TERMS —Cont'd
Present value.
Leases, UCC, §25-2A-103, (1).
UCC, §25-1-201.
Preservation agreement, §121-35.
Preserving the status quo.
Public morals, §19-1.1.
President.
University of North Carolina, §116-2.
Pressure vessel.
Uniform act, §95-69.9, (g).
Presumption.
UCC, §25-1-201.
Pretext interview.
Insurance information and privacy protection act, §58-39-15.
Pretreatment.
Sewage systems, §130A-334.
Pretreatment facility, §143-213.
Pretreatment standards, §143-213.
Prevention.
Substance abuse professionals, §90-113.31.
Prevention of significant deterioration.
Water and air resources, §143-213.
Previously used material.
Bedding, §130A-261.
Previous system.
Judicial retirement, §135-53.
Prewritten computer software.
Sales and use tax, §105-164.3.
Primarily educational institution.
Child placing and care, §131D-10.2.
Primary corporate limits.
City and town annexation of noncontiguous areas, §160A-58.
Primary enclosure.
Protection of animals, §19A-23.
Primary forest product, §113A-191.
Primary standards.
Weights and measures, §81A-9.
Primary system.
Junkyard control, §136-143.
Outdoor advertising control, §136-128.
Prime suppliers.
Stocks of coal and petroleum fuels, §143-345.14, (b).
Urban electrical service, §160A-331.
Principal.
Advance instruction for mental health treatment, §122C-72.
Bail, §15A-531.
Bail bondsman and runners, §58-71-1.
Education, §115C-5, (g).
Lobbying, §120-47.1.
Powers of attorney, §32A-16.
Principal and income act, §37A-1-102.
Sales representatives, §66-190.
Telephonic sellers, §66-260.
Uniform fiduciaries act, §32-2, (a).
Principal amount.
Interest, §24-13.
Principal office.
Business corporations, §55-1-40.
Limited liability companies, §57C-1-03.
Limited partnerships, §59-102.
Nonprofit corporations, §55A-1-40.
Savings and loan associations, §54B-4.
Savings banks, §54C-4, (b).
Trust companies, §53-301, (a).
Principal officer.
Land policy act, §113A-152.

DEFINED TERMS —Cont'd
Principal place of business.
Reciprocal banking act, §53-210.
Regional reciprocal savings and loan acquisition act, §54B-48.2.
Principal shareholder.
Trust companies, §53-301, (a).
Principal state department.
Executive organization, §143B-3.
Principle display panel.
Food, drugs and cosmetics, §106-121.
Print.
Sales, §25C-10.
Print media.
Campaign contributions and expenditures.
Disclosure requirements for media advertisements, §163-278.38Z.
Prior conviction.
Structured sentencing, §15A-1340.11.
Priority.
Priority in employment assistance for United States armed forces veteran, §165-44.3.
Prior rehabilitation.
Disability income plan, §135-101.
Prior service.
Judicial retirement, §135-53.
Legislative retirement system, §120-4.12, (c).
Retirement, §128-21.
State retirement system, §135-1.
Prisoner.
Counties, §153A-217.
State prisons, §148-118.4.
Private act.
Cities and towns, §160A-1.
Private carrier.
Public utilities, §62-3.
Private club.
Alcoholic beverages, §§18B-1000, 18B-1006.
Sanitation, §130A-247.
Private detectives and investigators, §74C-3.
Private educational institution.
Children of war veterans scholarships, §165-20.
National Guard tuition assistance, §127A-192.
Private facility.
Mental health, §122C-3.
Private hauler vehicles.
Motor vehicles, §20-4.01.
Private institution.
State education assistance authority, §116-201.
Private library agency.
Interstate library compact, §125-12.
Private license plate.
Publicly owned vehicles, §20-39.1, (d).
Private motor carrier, §20-4.01.
Private nonprofit utilities.
Emergency management, §166A-4.
Private passenger automobile, §20-135.4.
Private passenger motor vehicle.
Credit scoring to rate motor vehicle and property insurance, §58-36-90, (a).
Insurance rates, §58-40-10.
Private passenger vehicles.
Motor vehicles, §20-4.01.
Private personnel service, §§95-47.1, 95-47.19.
Private pond, §113-129.
Private protective services, §74C-3.
Private real estate school, §93A-32.
Private road or driveway.
Motor vehicles, §20-4.01.
Private telecommunication service.
Sales and use tax on telecommunications, §105-164.4C, (h).

DEFINED TERMS —Cont'd
Private trust company.
Trust companies, §53-301, (a).
Privilege communication.
Peer support group counselor's privilege, §8-53.10, (a).
Privileged information.
Insurance information and privacy protection act, §58-39-15.
Probable cause.
Discipline and disability rules of state bar, Bar Rules & Regs., B, §.0103.
Procedures for the authorized practice committee of the state bars, Bar Rules & Regs., D, §.0203.
Probation.
Delinquent and undisciplined juveniles, §7B-1501.
Department of juvenile justice and delinquency prevention, §143B-515.
Interstate compact on juveniles, §7B-2803.
Probationary state employee.
State personnel system, §126-15.1.
Probationary teacher.
Education personnel, §115C-325, (a).
Proceeding.
Business corporations, §§55-1-40, 55-8-50, (b).
Medical service corporations, §58-65-166, (b).
Nonprofit corporations, §55A-1-40.
Proceeds.
Secured transactions, §25-9-102, (a).
Processed.
Poultry products inspection, §106-549.51.
Processing.
Cremation, §90-210.41.
Seed law, §106-277.2.
Solid waste management, §130A-290, (a).
Processing site.
Scrap tire disposal, §130A-309.53.
Processor.
Forest product assessment act, §113A-191.
Producer.
Cotton warehousing, §106-451.7.
Grain dealers, §106-601.
Oil and gas conservation, §113-389.
Producer-controlled property or casualty insurers, §58-3-165, (a).
Reinsurance intermediaries, §58-9-2, (a).
Sweet potato assessment, §106-564.4, (d).
Producing broker.
Surplus lines, §58-21-10.
Product.
Oil and gas conservation, §113-389.
Weights and measures, §81A-51.
Production.
Controlled substances, §90-87.
Production company.
Film industry development account, §143B-434.4, (c).
Sales and use tax, §105-164.3.
Exemption of audio-visual master, §105-164.13.
Production-money crops.
Secured transactions, §25-9-102, (a).
Production-money obligation.
Secured transactions, §25-9-102, (a).
Production of crops.
Secured transactions, §25-9-102, (a).
Production systems.
Double damage liability for damage to agricultural systems, §1-539.2B, (c).
Production work.
Vocational and technical education, §115C-160.

DEFINED TERMS —Cont'd
Product liability.
Liability risk retention, §58-22-10.
Product liability action, §99B-1.
Product name.
Commercial feed law, §106-284.33.
Soil additives act, §106-50.30.
Professional.
Boxing commission, §143-651.
Professional archaeologists.
Burial sites, §70-28.
Professional association.
Political campaigns, §163-278.6.
Professional bondsman.
Bail, §15A-531.
Bail bondsman and runners, §58-71-1.
Professional corporations, §55B-2.
Regulations for practicing law, Bar Rules & Regs., E, §.0101.
Professional discipline.
Substance abuse professionals, §90-113.31.
Professional employer organization, §58-89A-5.
Professional employer organization group, §58-89A-5.
Professional employer services, §58-89A-5.
Professional engineer, §89C-3.
Professional engineer, retired, §89C-3.
Professional fund-raising counsel.
Solicitation, §14-401.12.
Professionalism.
Continuing legal education, Bar Rules & Regs., D, §.1501.
Professional land surveyor, §89C-3.
Professional limited liability company or companies.
Regulations for practicing law, Bar Rules & Regs., E, §.0101.
Professional responsibility.
Continuing legal education, Bar Rules & Regs., D, §.1501.
Professional service.
Professional corporations, §55B-2.
Professional solicitor.
Solicitation, §14-401.12.
Professional-sports-services contract.
Athlete agents, §78C-86.
Profit.
Transportation board, §136-14, (h).
Profit from crime.
Crime victims financial recovery assistance act, §15B-32.
Program.
Bicycle and bikeway act, §136-71.7.
Birth defects monitoring program, §130A-131.16, (b).
Child support, §110-129.
Indian antiquities, §70-48.
Relocation assistance, §133-7.
Program director.
Mental health, §122C-3.
Program evaluation.
Commission on governmental operations, §120-72.
Program participant.
Address confidentiality program, §15C-2.
Prohibited noxious-weed seeds.
Seed law, §106-277.2.
Prohibited source.
Electioneering communication, §§163-278.80, 163-278.90.
Project.
Bonds for student housing, §116-175.

DEFINED TERMS —Cont'd
Project —Cont'd
Centennial campus and Horace Williams campus financing act, §116-198.33.
Certificate of need, §131E-176.
Electric power, §159B-3.
Global TransPark authority, §63A-2.
Higher education student housing, §116-189.
Lease or purchase of prison facilities constructed by private firm, §148-37.2, (b).
Pollution control, §§159C-3, 159D-3.
Private capital facilities finance act, §159D-37.
Relocation assistance, §133-7.
Solid waste, §159I-3, (a).
Street and highways, private pilot toll project, §136-89.172, (m).
University of North Carolina, §116-41.1.
Project broker.
Time shares, §93A-41.
Project of regional impact.
Land policy act, §113A-152.
Promise.
Negotiable instruments, §25-3-103.
Promissory note.
Secured transactions, §25-9-102, (a).
Promoter.
Boxing commission, §143-651.
Prompt payment discounts.
Motor fuel, §75-81.
Proof of age.
Youth access to tobacco products, §14-313, (a).
Proof of financial responsibility.
Motor vehicles, §§20-279.1, 20-280.
Properly payable.
Banking, §25-4-104, (a).
Property, §47A-3.
City and town zoning, §160A-385.1, (b).
Computer crimes, §14-453.
Counties, §153A-344.1.
Decedents' estates, §31A-3.
Dedication of property to nature and historic preserves, §143B-260.6, (a).
Eminent domain, §40A-2.
Fraudulent transfers, §39-23.1.
Premarital agreements, §52B-2.
Sales under power of sale, §45-21.1, (b).
Unclaimed property act, §116B-52.
Property-hauling vehicles.
Motor vehicles, §20-4.01.
Property mappers.
Certification of local government property mappers, §147-54.4.
Property or casualty insurer, §58-12-2.
Property passing to surviving spouse.
Elective share of surviving spouse, §30-3.3, (a).
Property registered.
Motor vehicles, §20-4.2.
Property subsequently acquired.
Probate and registration, §47-20.5.
Property taxes, §§105-151.21, 105-163.2.
Proposal.
Secured transactions, §25-9-102, (a).
Proposed association.
Savings and loan associations, §54B-4.
Proposed savings bank, §54C-4, (b).
Proprietary business school, §115D-87.
Proprietary information.
E-911 system for wireless communications, §62A-21.
Proprietary security organization, §74C-13.
Proprietary technical institute, §115D-87.

DEFINED TERMS —Cont'd
Proprietary technical school, §115D-87.
Proprietary trade school, §115D-87.
Pro rata share.
Taxation, §105-131.
Prosecutor.
Abused, neglected or dependent juveniles, §7B-101.
Criminal procedure, §15A-101.
Delinquent and undisciplined juveniles, §7B-1501.
Prosecutorial districts.
Judicial department, §7A-60.
Prospective client.
Rules of professional conduct, Prof. Cond. Rule 1.18.
Prospective developer.
Brownfields property reuse act, §130A-310.31, (b).
Prospective lessee.
Criminal law, §14-395.1.
Prospective loss costs.
Insurance rates, §58-36-100, (b).
Workers' compensation self-insurance.
Employer groups.
Premium rates, §58-47-110, (a).
Prospective purchaser.
Telephonic sellers, §66-260.
Prostate-specific antigen (PSA) tests or equivalent test for the presence of prostate cancer, §58-51-58.
Health maintenance organizations, §58-67-77, (b).
Hospital, medical and dental service corporations, §58-65-93, (b).
Prosthetic device.
Sales and use tax, §105-164.3.
Prostitution.
Criminal law, §14-203.
Offenses against morality, §14-190.13.
Public morals, §19-1.1.
Protected animal.
Endangered wildlife, §113-331.
Protected animal list, §113-331.
Protected cell.
Protected cell companies, §58-10-80.
Protected cell account.
Protected cell companies, §58-10-80.
Protected cell assets.
Protected cell companies, §58-10-80.
Protected cell company, §58-10-80.
Protected cell company insurance, §58-10-80.
Protected cell liabilities.
Protected cell companies, §58-10-80.
Protected mountain ridges, §113A-206.
Protected plant.
Plant protection and conservation, §106-202.12.
Protective bicycle helmet.
Child bicycle safety act, §20-171.8.
Protective custody.
Department of juvenile justice and delinquency prevention, §143B-515.
Protective equipment.
Sales and use tax, §105-164.3.
Protective order.
Domestic violence, §50B-1, (c).
Protective services.
Protection of disabled adults, §108A-101.
Protective supervision.
Delinquent and undisciplined juveniles, §7B-1501.
Protective trust.
Alienability of beneficiary's interest, §36A-115.
Protector.
Conservation, §113-128.

DEFINED TERMS —Cont'd
Protest.
Elections, §163-182.
Prove.
Funds transfers, UCC, §25-4A-105, (a).
Negotiable instruments, §25-3-103.
Provider.
Accident and health insurance.
Utilization review, §58-50-61, (a).
Continuing care retirement communities, §58-64-1.
Health maintenance organizations, §58-67-5, (h).
Industrial commission managed care organizations, I.C. Managed Care Orgs. R. II.
Provider sponsored organizations, §131E-276.
Provider of alternative fuel, §105-449.130.
Provider of support services.
Mental health, §122C-3.
Provider sponsored organization, §131E-276.
Provisional license.
Child placing and care, §131D-10.2.
Interpreters and transliterators licensure act, §90D-3.
Provisional licensee.
Motor vehicles, §20-4.01.
Provisionally approved septic tank or innovative septic tank system, §130A-343.1, (a).
Provisional official ballot.
Elections, §163-165.
PSAP.
E-911 system for wireless communications, §62A-21.
Pseudo-ANI.
E-911 system for wireless communications, §62A-21.
Pseudoautomatic number identification.
E-911 system for wireless communications, §62A-21.
Psychiatric facility, §131E-176.
Psychologist, §§90-270.2, 122C-3.
Psychotherapist.
Psychotherapy patient/client sexual exploitation act, §90-21.41.
Public agency.
Disclosure of records in child fatality or near fatality cases, §7B-2902, (a).
Electronic commerce in government, §66-58.2.
Health facilities finance, §131A-3.
911 service, §62A-3.
Public aircraft.
Aeronautics, §63-1.
Public area.
Asbestos hazard management, §130A-444.
Public assistance program.
Garnishment of wages to recoup fraudulent public assistance program payment, §108A-25.3, (a).
Publication.
Counties, §153A-1.
Local government finance, §159-1.
Public morals, §19-1.1.
Public auction.
Protection of animals, §19A-23.
Public authority.
Housing standards, §160A-442.
Local government finance, §159-7.
Use of state funds by non-state entities, §143-6.2, (a).
Public bicycle path.
Child bicycle safety act, §20-171.8.

DEFINED TERMS —Cont'd
Public body.
Meetings, §143-318.10, (b), (c).
Public building or facility.
Criminal trespass, §14-132.
Public buildings and grounds.
Administration department, §143-336.
Public corporation.
Business corporations, §55-1-40.
Foreign trade zones, §55C-2.
Public disturbance.
Civil disorders, §14-288.1.
Public document.
Publications, §143-169.2, (a).
Public enterprise, §160A-311.
Counties, §153A-274.
Public entity.
Public obligations, §159E-2.
Public-finance transaction.
Secured transactions, §25-9-102, (a).
Public fishing waters, §113-129.
Public health.
Dry-cleaning solvent cleanup act, §143-215.104B, (b).
Public health authority, §130A-45.01.
Public health facility.
Public health authorities, §130A-45.01.
Public health threat.
Terrorist incident using nuclear, biological or chemical agents, §130A-475, (d).
Public hospital.
Debts owed public hospitals, §131E-48.
Donation of surplus equipment, §131E-250, (a).
Public hospital personnel act, §131E-257, (e).
Public hunting grounds.
Conservation, §113-129.
Public land.
Environmental policy act, §113A-9.
Public law enforcement agencies.
Public records, §132-1.4.
Public library agency.
Interstate library compact, §125-12.
Public livestock market.
Livestock prompt pay law, §106-418.3.
Public-local act.
Cities and towns, §160A-1.
Publicly registered name.
University of North Carolina, §116-15.
Public meetings.
Smoking in public places, §143-596.
Public mills, §73-1.
Public mountain trout waters.
Special license for fishing mountain trout waters, §113-272, (c).
Public office.
Notice of appointments, §143-47.6.
Political campaigns, §163-278.6.
Repayment of money owed to state, §143-555.
Public officer.
Housing standards, §160A-442.
Public contracts, §14-234, (a1).
Public official.
Repayment of money owed to state, §143-555.
Volunteer architect during an emergency or disaster, §83A-13.1, (d).
Volunteer engineer during emergency or disaster, §89C-19.1, (d).
Public operator.
Pesticide board, §143-460.
Public or community sewage systems, §130A-334.

DEFINED TERMS —Cont'd
Public place.
Public intoxication, §14-443.
Public practice of accountancy, §93-1.
Public practice of geology.
Geologist, §89E-3.
Public record, §132-1, (a).
Address confidentiality program, §15C-2.
Archives and history, §121-2.
Public road.
Counties, §153A-238, (a).
Public roadway.
Child bicycle safety act, §20-171.8.
Public safety agency.
911 service, §62A-3.
Public safety answering point.
E-911 system for wireless communications, §62A-21.
Public safety official.
Volunteer architect during an emergency or disaster, §83A-13.1, (d).
Volunteer engineer during emergency or disaster, §89C-19.1.
Public school.
Child care facilities, §110-86.
State retirement system, §135-1.
Public school buildings.
Public school building capital fund, §115C-546.2.
Public school employee, §143-300.13.
Public school facility.
Community schools act, §115C-205.
Public service company.
Public service taxation, §105-333.
Public services.
Mental health, §122C-3.
Public spaces.
Contractors, §87-101.
Public transportation.
Cities and towns, §160A-576.
Regional authority, §160A-601.
Regional transportation authorities, §160A-631.
Public transportation system.
Cities and towns, §160A-576.
Regional authority, §160A-601.
Regional transit authority registration tax, §105-560.
Regional transit authority vehicle rental tax, §105-550.
Regional transportation authorities, §160A-631.
Public trust resources.
Beach access program, §113A-134.2, (b).
Jurisdiction of conservation agencies, §113-131, (e).
Public trust rights.
Beach access program, §113A-134.2, (b).
No adverse possession of property subject to, §1-45.1.
Public use and enjoyment.
City and town open space, §160A-407, (b).
Public used oil collection center.
Solid waste management, §130A-290, (b).
Public utility, §§62-3, 62-100.
Corporate income tax, §105-130.4, (a).
Public vehicular area.
Motor vehicles, §20-4.01.
Roads and highways, §136-91.
Public waters.
Conservation, §113-129.
Public water system.
Drinking water, §130A-313.
Water treatment facility operators, §90A-20.1.

DEFINED TERMS —Cont'd
Public weighmaster.
Weights and measures, §81A-51.
Publish.
Cities and towns, §160A-1.
Local development, development financing, §158-7.3, (a).
Unlawful telecommunications devices, §14-113.5.
Published.
Procedures for ruling on questions of legal ethics, Bar Rules & Regs., D, §.0101.
Published monthly average.
Life insurance loan interest rates, §58-61-5.
Publisher.
Newspaper taxation, §105-102.6.
Pulverization.
Cremation, §90-210.41.
Pumps, §87-85.
Punchboards.
Lotteries and gaming, §14-296.
Punitive damages, §1D-5.
Purchase.
Business and energy tax credit, §105-129.15.
Leases, UCC, §25-2A-103, (1).
Pawnbrokers, §91A-3.
Sales and use tax, §105-164.3.
Tax incentives for new and expanding businesses, §105-129.2.
Tax incentives for recycling facilities, §105-129.25.
UCC, §25-1-201.
Purchase agreement.
Lease or purchase of prison facilities constructed by private firm, §148-37.2, (b).
Purchase money.
Membership camping, §66-232.
Purchase-money collateral.
Secured transactions, §25-9-103, (a).
Purchase-money obligation.
Secured transactions, §25-9-103, (a).
Purchase price.
Sales, §14-401.13.
Sales and use tax, §105-164.3.
Purchaser.
Condominiums, §47C-1-103.
Membership camping, §66-232.
Planned community act, §47F-1-103.
Residential property disclosure act, §47E-3.
Telephonic sellers, §66-260.
Time shares, §93A-41.
UCC, §25-1-201.
Purchasing group.
Liability risk retention, §58-22-10.
Pure seed.
Seed law, §106-277.2.
Purity.
Seed law, §106-277.2.
Purpose or program.
Budgets, §143-23, (f).
Pursuant to commitment.
Secured transactions, §25-9-102, (a).
Pyramid distribution plan.
Lotteries, §14-291.2, (b).
Pyrotechnics.
Sale of pyrotechnics, §14-414.
Qualifications.
Personnel system.
Priority given employee separated due to reduction in force, §126-7.1, (d).
Qualified actuary.
Counties, §153A-93.
Managing general agents, §58-34-2, (a).

DEFINED TERMS —Cont'd
Qualified actuary —Cont'd
Workers' compensation self insurance, §97-165.
Employer groups, §58-47-60.
Qualified agricultural programs.
Tobacco trust fund commission, §143-716.
Qualified allocation plan.
Low-income housing tax credits.
Federal credit allocation on or after January 1, 2003, §105-129.42, (a).
Qualified assignment agreement.
Structured settlement protection, §1-543.11.
Qualified business.
Tax credit for qualified business investments, §105-163.010.
Qualified business venture.
Tax credit for qualified business investments, §105-163.010.
Qualified charitable organization.
Executive budget, §143-3.3, (a).
Qualified clearinghouse.
Derivative transaction, insurance companies, §58-7-205, (a).
Qualified code-enforcement official.
Board, §143-151.8, (a).
Qualified contingency.
Trusts, §36A-59.3.
Qualified dry-cleaning equipment.
Dry-cleaning equipment tax credit, §105-129.16C, (c).
Qualified escrow fund.
Tobacco reserve fund, §66-290.
Qualified exchange.
Derivative transaction, insurance companies, §58-7-205, (a).
Qualified foreign exchange.
Derivative transaction, insurance companies, §58-7-205, (a).
Qualified former sworn law enforcement officer.
Concealed handgun permits, §14-415.10.
Qualified geologist, §89E-3.
Qualified grantee business.
Tax credit for qualified business investments, §105-163.010.
Qualified individual.
Anatomical gifts, §130A-403.
Diagnosis and evaluation of osteoporosis and low bone mass, §58-3-174.
Electrical contractors, §87-41.1.
Qualified interpreter.
Interpreters for hearing impaired, §8B-1.
Qualified lender.
Mortgage bankers and brokers, §53-243.01.
Qualified licensee business.
Tax credit for qualified business investments, §105-163.010.
Qualified North Carolina business.
Enterprise corporations, §53A-37.
Qualified North Carolina low-income building.
Low-income housing tax credits, §105-129.41, (c).
Federal credit allocation on or after January 1, 2003, §105-129.42, (a).
Qualified North Carolina research expenses.
Research and development expenses tax credit, §105-129.50.
Qualified person.
Decedents' estates, safe deposit boxes, §28A-15-13, (a).
Mortgage bankers and brokers, §53-243.01.
Qualified person with a disability, §168A-3.

DEFINED TERMS —Cont'd
Qualified professional.
Mental health, §122C-3.
Qualified provider.
Guaranteed energy savings contracts, §143-64.17.
Qualified rehabilitation expenditures.
Historic rehabilitation tax credit, §105-129.35, (c).
Qualified residential unit.
Low-income housing tax credits.
Federal credit allocation on or after January 1, 2003, §105-129.42, (a).
Qualified sworn law enforcement officer.
Concealed handgun permits, §14-415.10.
Qualified United States financial institution.
Domestic companies, §58-7-26, (b).
Reinsurance intermediaries, §58-9-2, (a).
Qualified uses.
Taxation, §105-151.6.
Qualified veteran.
Veterans cemeteries, §65-43.
Qualified witness.
Advance instruction for mental health treatment, §122C-72.
Powers of attorney, §32A-16.
Qualifying contribution.
Public campaign financing fund, §163-278.62.
Qualifying improvements.
Property taxes on Brownfields properties, §105-277.13, (b).
Qualifying period.
Public campaign financing fund, §163-278.62.
Quality assurance committee, §90-21.22A, (a).
Facility licensure act, §131E-101.
Nursing home medication management advisory committee, §131E-128.1, (a).
Quarantine authority.
Public health, §130A-2.
Rabies vaccine, §130A-184.
Racketeering activity.
RICO act, §75D-3.
Radiation, §104E-5.
Radiation machine, §104E-5.
Radio.
Campaign contributions and expenditures.
Disclosure requirements for media advertisements, §163-278.38Z.
Radioactive material.
Radiation protection, §104E-5.
Radiology.
Practice of medicine, §90-18, (c).
Railroad.
Counties.
Contracts with railroads to allocate financial responsibility, §153-279, (a).
Rail transportation liability, §§160A-326, (a), 160A-626, (a).
Railroad company.
Public service taxation, §105-333.
Railroad operating revenue.
Corporate income tax, §105-130.4, (m).
Rape crisis center.
Privileged communications, rape crisis centers and domestic violence programs, §8-53.12.
Raptor.
Conservation, §113-129.
Rate.
Insurance, §58-36-100, (b).
Public utilities, §62-3.
Workers' compensation self-insurance.
Employer groups, §58-47-60.

DEFINED TERMS —Cont'd
Rate of exchange.
Foreign-money claims, §1C-1820.
Rate of insured unemployment.
Unemployment insurance, §96-12.01, (a).
Rating organization.
Insurance rates, §58-40-5.
Rating period.
Small employer group health coverage, §58-50-110.
Ratite.
Meat inspection, §106-549.15.
Regulation of dealers, §106-541.
Raw agricultural commodity.
Food, drugs and cosmetics, §106-121.
Meat inspection, §106-549.15.
Poultry products inspection, §106-549.51.
Raw material.
Rendering plants, §106-168.1.
RCGL.
Coastal and estuarine commercial fishing licenses, §113-168.
RCRA.
Solid waste management, §130A-290, (a).
Readily accessible lead-bearing substance, §130A-131.7.
Readily accessible to the general public.
Electronic surveillance, §15A-286.
Real estate.
Appraisers, §93E-1-4.
Condominiums, §47C-1-103.
Planned community act, §47F-1-103.
Property taxes, §105-273.
Real estate appraisal, §93E-1-4.
Real estate appraiser, §93E-1-4.
Real estate appraising, §93E-1-4.
Real estate broker or salespersons, §93A-2, (a), (b).
Fair housing act, §41A-3.
Real estate contract.
Residential property disclosure act, §47E-3.
Real-estate related business.
Tax credit for qualified business investments, §105-163.010.
Real estate transaction, §41A-3.
Real property, §41A-3.
Appraisers, §93E-1-4.
City and town parking authorities, §160A-551.
Housing authorities, §157-3.
Mortgages and deeds of trust.
Sales under power of sale, §45-21.1, (b).
Partnerships, §59-32.
Property taxes, §105-273.
Public health authorities, §130A-45.01.
Public hospitals, §131E-16.
Residential property disclosure act, §47E-3.
RICO act, §75D-3.
Statutory liens, §44A-7.
Subcontractors, §22C-1.
Urban redevelopment, §160A-503.
Veterans' recreation, §165-25.
Real property law-business, commercial and industrial transactions, Bar Rules & Regs., D, §.2102.
Real property law-residential transactions, Bar Rules & Regs., D, §.2102.
Real property law specialty, Bar Rules & Regs., D, §.2102.
Reasonable.
Rules of professional conduct, Prof. Cond. Rule 1.0.

DEFINED TERMS —Cont'd
Reasonable accommodations.
Persons with disabilities protection, §168A-3.
Reasonable and customary.
Group health insurance, §58-53-1.
Reasonable attorneys' fees.
Planned community act, §47F-1-103.
Reasonable belief.
Rules of professional conduct, Prof. Cond. Rule 1.0.
Reasonable efforts.
Abused, neglected or dependent juveniles, §7B-101.
Reasonably should know.
Rules of professional conduct, Prof. Cond. Rule 1.0.
Receipt.
Cotton warehousing, §106-451.7.
Research and development expenses tax credit, §105-129.50.
Sales, §25-2-103.
Receiver.
Insurers supervision, §58-30-10.
Receives.
Criminal law, §14-113.8.
Receiving agency.
Clean water loans, §159G-3.
Interchange of governmental employees, §126-52.
Receiving bank.
Funds transfers, UCC, §25-4A-103, (a).
Receiving state.
Educational personnel qualifications, §115C-350.
Interstate agreement on detainers, §15A-761.
Interstate compact on mental health, §122C-361.
State prisons, §148-120.
Recidivist.
Sex offender and public protection registration, §14-208.6.
Recipient.
Public assistance program, §108A-24.
Reciprocal.
Reciprocal insurance, §58-15-5.
Reciprocal insurance, §58-15-5.
Reciprocal program.
Membership camping, §66-232.
Reciprocal state.
Insurers supervision, §58-30-10.
Reciprocating state.
Motor vehicles, §20-4.18.
Reckless driving.
Motor vehicles, §20-140.
Reclaiming.
Solid waste management, §130A-290, (b).
Reclamation.
Mining, §74-49.
Reclamation plan.
Mining, §74-49.
Recognized educational institution.
Marriage and family therapists, §90-270.47.
Recognized hybrid designation.
Seed law, §106-277.2.
Recognized variety name.
Seed law, §106-277.2.
Reconstructed vehicle.
Motor vehicles, §20-4.01.
Reconstructive breast surgery.
Accident and health insurance, §58-51-62, (b).
Health maintenance organizations, §58-67-79, (b).
Hospital, medical and dental service corporations, §58-65-96, (b).

DEFINED TERMS —Cont'd
Record.
Adoption, §48-9-101.
Arbitration, §1-569.1.
Athlete agents, §78C-86.
Child custody jurisdiction and enforcement, §50A-110.
Electronic transactions, §66-312.
Indian antiquities, §70-48.
Letters of credit, §25-5-102, (a).
Secured transactions, §25-9-102, (a).
Unclaimed property act, §116B-52.
Recordation.
Unit ownership, §47A-3.
Record center.
Archives and history, §121-2.
Record date.
Business corporations, §55-1-40.
Nonprofit corporations, §55A-1-40.
Recordings.
Evidence, §8C-1, Rule 1001.
Record shareholder.
Dissenters' rights, §55-13-01.
Records of criminal intelligence information.
Public records, §132-1.4.
Records of criminal investigations.
Public records, §132-1.4.
Recovered materials.
Solid waste management, §130A-290, (a).
Recreation.
Cities and towns, §160A-352.
Local affairs, §143-320.
Recreational fishing.
Salt water fishing license, §113-174.
Recreational purpose.
Liability of landowners associated with watershed improvement projects, §139-41.3.
Recreational trespass, §38A-2.
Recreational vehicle, §20-4.01.
Highway use tax, §105-187.1.
Recreation authority.
Veterans, §165-25.
Recreation district.
Alcoholic beverage permits, §18B-1006, (j).
Recyclable material, §130A-290, (a).
Surplus state property, §143-64.02.
Recycled content percentage.
Taxation, §105-102.6.
Recycled content tonnage.
Taxation, §105-102.6.
Recycled oil, §119-13.1.
Recycling, §130A-290, (a), (b).
Newspaper taxation, §105-102.6.
Recycling tonnage.
Newspaper taxation, §105-102.6.
Redeveloper.
Urban redevelopment, §160A-503.
Redevelopment, §160A-503.
Redevelopment area, §160A-503.
Redevelopment commission, §160A-503.
Redevelopment contract, §160A-503.
Redevelopment plan, §160A-503.
Redevelopment project, §160A-503.
Redevelopment proposal, §160A-503.
Red light.
Use of red light or blue lights on motor vehicles, §20-130.1, (a).
Reemployment services.
Unemployment insurance, §96-8.
Refer.
Private personnel services, §95-47.1.

DEFINED TERMS —Cont'd
Referee.
Boxing commission, §143-651.
Referendum.
Elections, §163-165.
Political campaigns, §163-278.6.
Referendum committee.
Political campaigns, §163-278.6.
Public campaign financing fund, §163-278.62.
Referral.
Self-referrals by health care providers, §90-405.
Refiner.
Motor fuel, §75-81.
Refrigeration contractor, §87-58.
Refrigeration trade or business.
Refrigeration contractors, §87-58.
Refund.
Debt collection, §105A-2.
Refund anticipation loan.
Refund anticipation loan act, §53-246.
Refund anticipation loan fee.
Refund anticipation loan act, §53-246.
Refunding obligations.
State debt, §142-29.2.
Refuse.
Mining, §74-49.
Solid waste management, §130A-290, (a).
Refuse-derived fuel.
Solid waste management, §130A-290, (a).
Region.
Land policy act, §113A-152.
Reciprocal banking act, §53-210.
Regional bank.
Reciprocal banking act, §53-210.
Regional bank holding company.
Reciprocal banking act, §53-210.
Regional facility.
Facility authorities, §160A-480.2.
Regional institution.
Community colleges, §115D-2.
Regionally significant project.
Planning regionally significant transportation projects, §136-200.
Regional natural gas district, §160A-661, (b).
Regional ombudsman.
Long-term care program, §143B-181.16.
Regional partnership.
E-NC authority, §143B-437.45.
Rural redevelopment authority, §143B-437.21.
Regional public transportation authority, §160A-601.
Territorial jurisdiction, §160A-602.
Regional response team.
Hazardous materials emergency response, §166A-21.
Regional sewage disposal system, §162A-27.
Regional transportation authority, §160A-631.
Regional travel demand model.
Planning regionally significant transportation projects, §136-200.
Regional water system, §162A-22.
Register.
Interstate family support, §52C-1-101.
Registered agent.
Savings and loan associations, §54B-4.
Savings banks, §54C-4, (b).
Registered forester, §89B-2.
Registered form.
Investment securities, §25-8-102.
Registered handler.
Egg promotion tax, §106-245.33, (b).

DEFINED TERMS —Cont'd
Registered limited liability partnerships.
Partnerships, §59-32.
Registered organization.
Secured transactions, §25-9-102, (a).
Registered owner.
Impaired driving, §20-28.2, (a1).
Registered pesticide.
Structural pest control act, §106-65.24.
Registered property.
Hunting and fishing on registered property of another, §113-281.
Registered public obligation, §159E-2.
Registered sanitarian, §90A-51.
Registered seeds.
Seed law, §106-277.2.
Registered technician.
Structural pest control act, §106-65.24.
Registered trainee.
Real estate appraisers, §93E-1-4.
Registering tribunal.
Interstate family support, §52C-1-101.
Registrant.
Controlled substances, §90-87.
Hunting and fishing on registered property of another, §113-281.
Pesticide board, §143-460.
Refund anticipation loan act, §53-246.
Soil additives act, §106-50.30.
Substance abuse professional, §90-113.31.
Registration.
Adult care homes, §131D-2, (a).
Athlete agents, §78C-86.
Nature preserves act, §113A-164.3.
Registration as a trainee.
Real estate appraisers, §93E-1-4.
Regular accumulated contributions.
State law-enforcement retirement, §143-166.30, (a).
Regular benefits.
Unemployment insurance, §96-12.01, (a).
Regular boarder.
Sanitation, §130A-247.
Regular driver's license.
Motor vehicles, §20-4.01.
Regular interest, §128-21.
Legislative retirement system, §120-4.8.
State retirement system, §135-1.
Regularly visits.
Lead poisoning in children, §130A-131.7.
Regular resident superior court judge of the district or set of districts.
Judicial department, §7A-41.1, (a).
Regular session.
Limitation on fund-raising during legislative session, §163-278.13B, (a).
Lobbying, §120-47.1.
Regular vending facility.
Aid to the blind, §111-42, (a).
Regulated article.
Bee and honey act, §106-635.
Boll weevil eradication, §106-65.69.
Regulated entity.
Year 2000 liability, §66-296.
Regulated metals property.
Dealing in, §66-11, (a).
Regulated substance.
Brownfields property reuse act, §130A-310.31, (b).
Dry-cleaning solvent cleanup act, §143-215.104B, (b).

DEFINED TERMS —Cont'd
Regulatory action level event.
Risk based capital requirements, insurance companies, §58-12-11, (a).
Regulatory action level risk-based capital.
Insurance companies, §58-12-2.
Rehabilitation.
Housing finance agency, §122A-3.
Rehabilitation, conservation and reconditioning area.
Urban redevelopment, §160A-503.
Rehabilitation expenses.
Historic rehabilitation tax credit, §105-129.36, (b).
Rehabilitation facility, §131E-176.
Reimbursable loss.
Client security fund, rules governing administration, Bar Rules & Regs., D, §.1401.
Homeowner's recovery fund, §87-15.5.
Reimbursement policy.
Health plans, disclosure to providers, §58-3-227, (a).
Reinsurance intermediaries, §58-9-2, (a).
Reinsurer.
Reinsurance intermediaries, §58-9-2, (a).
Reinsuring carrier.
Small employer group health coverage, §58-50-110.
Rejected equipment.
Weights and measures, §81A-9.
Related member.
Job development investment grant program, §143B-437.51.
Related or subordinate party.
Principal and income act, §37A-1-104.1.
Related party.
Small business contractor act, §143B-472.86.
Related person.
Research and development expenses tax credit, §105-129.50.
Related provider trust.
Viatical life insurance settlements, §58-58-205.
Related services.
Special education, §115C-108.
Relative.
Fraudulent transfers, §39-23.1.
Taxation, §105-277.2.
Trusts, §36A-60.
Release.
Decedents' estates, §28A-19-7.
Dry-cleaning solvent cleanup act, §143-215.104B, (b).
Sex offender and public protection registration, §14-208.6.
Solid waste management, §130A-310.
Released claims.
Tobacco reserve fund, §66-290.
Releasing parties.
Tobacco reserve fund, §66-290.
Relevant evidence.
Evidence, §8C-1, Rule 401.
Relevant market area or trade area.
Motor vehicles, §20-286.
Relevant offense.
Mental health, developmental disabilities and substance abuse, §122C-80, (e).
Relevant time after driving.
Motor vehicles, §20-4.01.
Religious assembly.
Governing body of assembly authorized to adopt regulations, §61-7, (f).
Religious societies, §61-7.

DEFINED TERMS —Cont'd
Religious institution.
Solicitation of contributions, §131F-2.
Religious purpose.
Taxation, §105-278.3.
Religious sponsored child care facilities, §110-106.
Relinquishment.
Adoption, §48-1-101.
Relocation officer, §133-7.
Remainder beneficiary.
Principal and income act, §37A-1-102.
Remedial action.
Solid waste management, §130A-310.
Remedial program.
Brownfields property reuse act, §130A-310.31, (b).
Dry-cleaning solvent cleanup act, §143-215.104B, (b).
Remediation.
Brownfields property reuse act, §130A-310.31, (b).
Dry-cleaning solvent cleanup act, §143-215.104B, (b).
Lead poisoning in children, §130A-131.7.
Remedy.
Civil procedure, §1-1.
Solid waste management, §130A-310.
UCC, §25-1-201.
Remit.
Money transmitters, §53-208.2, (a).
Remitter.
Negotiable instruments, §25-3-103.
Remitting bank.
Banking, §25-4-105.
Remote state action.
Nurse licensure compact, §90-171.82.
Remote states.
Nurse licensure compact, §90-171.82.
Removable windshield placard.
Handicapped parking privileges, §20-37.5.
Removal.
Asbestos hazard management, §130A-444.
Gasoline tax, §105-449.60.
Remove.
Solid waste management, §130A-310.
Renderer.
Meat inspection, §106-549.15.
Poultry products inspection, §106-549.51.
Rendering operation, §106-168.1.
Rendering plant, §106-168.1.
Renewable biomass resources.
Business and energy tax credits, §105-129.15.
Renewable energy equipment.
Tax credits for renewable energy equipment facility construction, §105-130.28, (b).
Renewable energy property.
Business and energy tax credits, §105-129.15.
Renewable fuel.
Business and energy tax credits, §105-129.15.
Renewal certificate, §90-221, (d).
Renovate.
Bedding, §130A-261.
Rent.
Corporate income tax, §105-130.4.
Rental agreement.
Rental car companies selling insurance, §58-33-17, (a).
Rental cars, §66-201.
Self service storage renter's insurance, §58-33-18, (a).
Storage facilities, §44A-40.

DEFINED TERMS —Cont'd
Rental car company, §66-201.
Rental car companies selling insurance, §58-33-17, (a).
Rental referral agency, §66-142.
Rental vehicle.
Motor vehicles, §20-84.2.
Renter.
Rental car companies selling insurance, §58-33-17, (a).
Rental cars, §66-201.
Self service storage renter's insurance, §58-33-18, (a).
Rents, issues or profits.
Criminal law, §14-168.2.
Probate and registration, §47-20.
Repackager.
Registration of prescription drug repackager, §106-140.1, (j).
Repair.
Motor vehicles, §20-341.
Sewage systems, §130A-334.
Weights and measures, §81A-9.
Well construction, §87-85.
Repealed reimbursement amount.
Local sales and use tax, §105-521, (a).
Repeated violation.
Mines, §74-24.2.
Repellents.
Structural pest control act, §106-65.24.
Replacement equipment.
Certificate of need, §131E-176.
Replacement services loss.
Victims compensation, §15B-2.
Replication transaction.
Derivative transaction, insurance companies, §58-7-205, (a).
Report.
False reports concerning destructive devices, §14-69.1, (e).
Weapons of mass death and destruction, §14-288.23, (c).
Reportable conviction.
Sex offender and public protection registration, §14-208.6.
Reportable crash.
Motor vehicles, §20-4.01.
Report to the court.
Adoption, §48-1-101.
Representative.
Compensation of trustees and other fiduciaries, §32-53.
UCC, §25-1-201.
Representative payee.
Nursing homes, §131E-116.
Representative trust office.
Trust companies, §53-301, (a).
Represented person.
Negotiable instruments, §25-3-307.
Reprimand.
Discipline and disability rules of state bar, Bar Rules & Regs., B, §.0103.
Reproduction.
Sales, §25C-10.
Request for an accounting.
Secured transactions, §25-9-210, (a).
Requesting state.
National Guard compact, §127A-177.
Pest control, §106-65.55.
Request regarding a list of collateral.
Secured transactions, §25-9-210, (a).

DEFINED TERMS —Cont'd
Request regarding a statement of account.
Secured transactions, §25-9-210, (a).
Requests.
Secured transactions, information as to collateral, §25-9-210, (a).
Requests for proposals.
Guaranteed energy savings contracts, §143-64.17.
Requisites of contract, §58-58-1.
Rerefined oil, §119-13.1.
Rerefining, §130A-290, (b).
Resale.
Mortgages and deeds of trust.
Sales under power of sale, §45-21.1, (a).
Rescue, §58-87-5, (c).
Rescue squad.
Highway use tax, §105-187.1.
Insurance, volunteer rescue/ems fund and safety workers assistance, §58-87-5, (c).
Rescue squad worker.
Death benefits, §143-166.2, (d).
State medical plan, §135-40.1.
Tuition waiver for senior citizens, §115B-1.
Rescue unit, §58-87-5, (c).
Research and production service district.
Counties, §153A-312.
Research facility.
Protection of animals, §19A-23.
Research university.
Research and development expenses tax credit, §105-129.50.
Reservation deposit, §116B-54, (b).
Reserve.
Banking, §§53-51, (a), 53-84.
Reserve assets.
Asset protection, §58-13-15.
Reserve trust fund.
State education assistance authority, §116-201.
Residence.
Administrative procedure, §150B-2.
Asbestos hazard management, §130A-444.
Continuing care retirement communities, §58-64-1.
False advertising, §58-29-5.
Insurance guaranty associations, §58-62-16.
Interstate compact on juveniles, §7B-2803.
Sewage systems, §130A-334.
Voting, §163-57.
Residence state.
Interstate compact on adoption and medical assistance, §7B-3901.
Residency.
Municipal voting, §163-282.
Resident.
Adult care homes, §131D-2, (a).
Adult care home's bill of rights, §131D-20.
Conservation, §113-130.
Expedited evictions, §42-59.
Higher education tuition and fees, §116-143.1.
Insurance guaranty association, §58-48-20.
Long-term care ombudsman program, §143B-181.16.
Motor vehicles, §20-4.01.
Public assistance program, §108A-24.
Taxation, §105-134.1.
Temporary management of long-term care facilities, §131E-231.
Resident for tuition purposes.
Higher education tuition and fees, §116-143.1.
Residential building.
Home inspectors, §143-151.45.

DEFINED TERMS —Cont'd
Residential care facility.
Patient abuse, §14-32.2, (c1).
Residential child-care facility, §131D-10.2.
Residential district.
Motor vehicles, §20-4.01.
Residential facility.
Mental health, §122C-3.
Residential housing.
Housing finance agency, §122A-3.
Residential manufactured home.
Installment sales, §25A-15.
Residential private club.
Alcoholic beverages, §18B-1000.
Residential program.
Structured sentencing, §15A-1340.11.
Residential property.
Credit scoring to rate motor vehicle and property insurance, §58-36-90, (a).
Vacation rentals, §42A-4.
Residential purposes.
Condominiums, §47C-1-103.
Conversion building rental, §47A-34.
Residential real estate.
Real estate appraisers, §93E-1-4.
Residential real property.
Mortgage bankers and brokers, §53-243.01.
Residential school personnel.
Criminal history checks, §143B-146.16, (a).
Resident plant or resident species.
Plant protection and conservation, §106-202.12.
Resident trainee.
Funeral services, §90-210.20, (l).
Resident training license.
Physician and surgeons, §90-12, (b).
Residual market mechanism.
Insurance information and privacy protection act, §58-39-15.
Resolution.
State education assistance authority, §116-201.
Resource.
Computer crimes, §14-453.
Resource recovery.
Solid waste management, §130A-290, (a).
Respiratory care.
Respiratory care practices act, §90-648.
Respiratory care practitioner, §90-648.
Respite care, institutional.
Long-term care insurance, §58-55-35, (a).
Respite care, noninstitutional.
Long-term care insurance, §58-55-35, (a).
Respondent.
Child custody jurisdiction and enforcement, §50A-301.
Discipline and disability rules of state bar, Bar Rules & Regs., B, §.0103.
Incompetency, §35A-1101.
Temporary management of long-term care facilities, §131E-231.
Vaccine-related injury, §130A-422.
Responding state, §127A-177.
Interstate family support, §52C-1-101.
Pest control, §106-65.55.
Responding tribunal.
Interstate family support, §52C-1-101.
Response costs.
Dry-cleaning solvent cleanup act, §143-215.104B, (b).
Responsibility.
Negotiable instruments, §25-3-405.

DEFINED TERMS —Cont'd
Responsibility for streets.
Municipal streets and highways, §136-66.1.
Responsible administrative authority.
Structured settlement protection, §1-543.11.
Responsible charge.
Engineering, §89C-3.
Responsible charge of work.
Geologist, §89E-3.
Soil scientists, §89F-3.
Responsible parent.
Child support, §110-129.
Responsible party.
Manufactured housing, §143-143.9.
Solid waste management, §130A-310.
Responsible person.
Offshore oil and gas activities, §143-215.94B, (b).
Responsible professional.
Mental health, §122C-3.
Restaurant.
Alcoholic beverages, §18B-1000.
Smoking in public places, §143-596.
Restoration.
Oil and hazardous substance control, §143-215.77.
Restraining seat.
Child bicycle safety act, §20-171.8.
Restricted access drug and device.
Health insurers maintaining, §58-3-221, (c).
Restricted area.
Aeronautics, §63-1.
Restricted noxious-weed seeds.
Seed law, §106-277.2.
Restricted use pesticide.
Pesticide board, §143-460.
Structural pest control act, §106-65.24.
Resulting bank.
Interstate branch banking, §53-224.9.
Resumption of marital relation, §52-10.2.
Retail business.
Alcoholic beverages, §18B-1000.
Retail dealer.
Tobacco taxation, §105-113.4.
Retailer.
Alternative fuel, §105-449.130.
Commercial fertilizer, §106-657.
Egg law, §106-245.14.
Gasoline tax, §105-449.60.
Highway use tax, §105-187.1.
Sales and use tax, §105-164.3.
Retail installment sale.
Motor vehicles, §20-286.
Retail merchant.
Property taxes, §105-273.
Retail sale or sale at retail.
Sales and use tax, §105-164.3.
Retail sales value.
Counterfeit trademarks, §80-11.1, (a).
Retained expert witness.
Medicolegal guidelines for attorney-physician relationship, MLG Rule 3.
Retaliatory action.
Employment discrimination, §95-240.
Retired employee.
State medical plan, §135-40.1.
Retired teacher.
Educational personnel, §115C-325, (a).
Retiree.
State medical plan, §135-40.1.
Retirement, §128-21.
Disability income plan, §135-101.
Judiciary, §135-53.

DEFINED TERMS —Cont'd
Retirement —Cont'd
Legislature, §120-4.8.
State retirement, §135-1.
Retirement allowance, §128-21.
Judiciary, §135-53.
State law-enforcement, §143-166.30, (a).
State retirement, §135-1.
Retirement benefits.
Taxation, §105-134.1.
Retirement system, §128-21.
Disability income plan, §135-101.
Judiciary, §135-53.
State retirement, §135-1.
Retrospective compensation agreements.
General insurance agents, §58-34-5, (b).
Return to work.
Industrial commission utilization of rehabilitation professionals, I.C. Util. Rehab. Profs. I.
Reuse, §130A-290, (a).
Revenue bond project, §§159-81, 159-97.
Revenue bonds, §159-81.
Metropolitan sewerage districts, §162A-65, (a).
Metropolitan water districts, §162A-32, (a).
State education assistance authority, §116-201.
University of North Carolina, §116-41.1.
Revenue-neutral property tax rate.
Local budgets, §159-11, (e).
Revenues.
Centennial campus and Horace Williams campus financing act, §116-198.33.
Global TransPark authority, §63A-2.
Higher education student housing, §116-189.
Metropolitan sewerage districts, §162A-65, (a).
Metropolitan water districts, §162A-32, (a).
Pollution control, §§159C-3, 159D-3.
Revenue bonds, §159-81.
Rural redevelopment authority, §143B-437.21.
Solid waste, §159I-3, (a).
University of North Carolina, §116-41.1.
Water and sewer, §162A-2.
Reverse auction.
Procurement of information technology, §147-33.95, (c).
Public contracts, §143-129.9, (a).
Reverse mortgage loan, §53-257.
Revised rules of professional conduct.
Discipline and disability rules of state bar, Bar Rules & Regs., B, §.0103.
Procedures for ruling on questions of legal ethics, Bar Rules & Regs., D, §.0101.
Revocation or suspension.
Motor vehicles, §20-4.01.
Revocation report.
Motor vehicles, §20-16.5, (a).
Revoked financial transaction card.
Criminal law, §14-113.8.
Revolving charge account contract.
Installment sales, §25A-11.
Revolving construction loan.
Clean water loans, §159G-3.
Revolving emergency loan.
Clean water loans, §159G-3.
Revolving loan.
Clean water loans, §159G-3.
Ridge.
Mining, §74-49.
Mountain ridge protection, §113A-206.
Right of withdrawal.
Impounded water, §143-215.44, (b).

DEFINED TERMS —Cont'd
Rights.
UCC, §25-1-201.
Ring official.
Boxing commission, §143-651.
Ring signaling device.
Deaf and the hard of hearing, §143B-216.30.
Riot, §14-288.2, (a).
Civil disorders, §14-288.1.
Riparian owner.
Cultivation of shellfish, §113-201.1.
Risk assets.
Cooperative organizations' reserve allocations, §54-109.88.
Risk-assuming carrier.
Small employer group health coverage, §58-50-110.
Risk-based.
Contamination of site, §143B-279.9, (d).
Risk-based capital level.
Insurance companies, §58-12-2.
Risk retention group, §58-22-10.
River.
Natural and scenic rivers, §113A-33.
River basin, §77-110.
Water withdrawals and transfers, §143-215.22G.
Road.
Natural and scenic rivers, §113A-33.
Road construction.
Contractors, §87-101.
Road maintenance.
Contractors, §87-101.
Road tractors.
Motor vehicles, §20-4.01.
Roadway.
Motor vehicles, §20-4.01.
Roanoke river basin.
Roanoke river basin commission, §77-90.
Robbery.
Criminal law, §14-87.1.
Rodenticides.
Pesticide board, §143-460.
Structural pest control act, §106-65.24.
Roller skater.
Roller skating rink safety and liability, §99E-10.
Roller skating rink.
Roller skating rink safety and liability, §99E-10.
Rolling stock.
Public service taxation, §105-333.
Room.
Peeping into room occupied by another person, §14-202, (b).
Room operator.
Telephonic sellers, §66-260.
Route.
Public utilities, §62-3.
Royalties.
Corporate income tax, §105-130.4.
RSCFL.
Coastal and estuarine commercial fishing licenses, §113-168.
Rules.
Fraternal benefit societies, §58-24-15, (f).
Rules and regulations.
Administrative procedure, §150B-2.
Continuing legal education, Bar Rules & Regs., D, §.1501.
Fees and charges by state agencies, §12-3.1, (b).
Savings and loan associations, §54B-4.
Rules of professional conduct.
Discipline and disability rules of state bar, Bar Rules & Regs., B, §.0103.

DEFINED TERMS —Cont'd
Run.
Motion pictures, §75C-2.
Runner.
Bail bondsman and runners, §58-71-1.
Rural areas.
Enterprise corporations, §53A-37.
Rural county.
E-NC authority, §143B-437.45.
Rural redevelopment authority, §143B-437.21.
Rural fire department.
Cities and towns, §160A-1.
Rural hospital network.
Hospital licensure, §131E-76.
Rural transportation planning organizations.
Transportation department, §136-210.
Sadomasochistic abuse.
Public morals, §19-12.
Safe home.
Abused, neglected or dependent juveniles, §7B-101.
Safekeeping property.
Rules of professional conduct, Prof. Cond. Rule 1.15-1.
Safety glass.
Motor vehicles, §20-135, (b).
Safety rest area.
Outdoor advertising control, §136-128.
Safety zone.
Motor vehicles, §20-4.01.
Sale.
Alcoholic beverages, §18B-101.
Alcohol taxation, §105-113.68.
Bedding, §130A-261.
Civil procedure, §1-339.41, (b).
Commercial fertilizer, §106-657.
Corporate income tax, §105-130.4, (a).
Judicial sales, §1-339.1, (b).
Motor fuel, §75-81.
Public morals, §19-1.1.
Sales, §25-2-106.
Sales and use tax, §105-164.3.
Sales under power of sale, §45-21.1, (a).
Securities, §78A-2.
Soil additives act, §106-50.30.
Weights and measures, §81A-9.
White goods disposal tax, §105-187.20.
Sale of obscene or lewd matter.
Public morals, §19-1.1.
Sales customer.
Piped natural gas tax, §105-187.40.
Salesman.
Manufactured housing, §143-143.9.
Securities, §78A-2.
Salespersons.
Membership camping, §66-232.
Telephonic sellers, §66-260.
Sales price.
Sales and use tax, §105-164.3.
Sales representative, §66-190.
Sales tax.
Uniform sales and use tax administration act, §105-164.42B.
Sales territory.
Alcoholic beverages, §18B-1201.
Salvage motor vehicle, §20-4.01.
Salvage rebuilt vehicle.
Motor vehicles, §20-4.01.
Salvage yard.
Motor vehicles, §20-137.7.

DEFINED TERMS —Cont'd
Sample.
Youth access to tobacco products, §14-313, (a).
Sanctioned amateur.
Boxing commission, §143-651.
Sanctioned amateur match.
Boxing commission, §143-651.
Sanitarian, §90A-51.
Sanitarian intern, §90A-51.
Sanitary landfill, §130A-290, (a).
Sanitary sewage systems, §130A-334.
Sanitize.
Bedding, §130A-261.
Protection of animals, §19A-23.
Satellite corporate limits.
City and town annexation of noncontiguous areas, §160A-58.
Satellite jail/work release unit.
Counties, §153A-230.1.
Satisfactory evidence of identity.
Notaries, §10A-3.
Savings and loan association, §§54B-4, 54C-4, (a).
Savings and loan holding company.
Regional reciprocal savings and loan acquisition act, §54B-48.2.
Savings association.
Trust companies, §53-301, (a).
Savings bank, §54C-4, (b).
Savings interstate branch banks, §54C-200.
Savings institution, §54C-4, (b).
SBI.
DNA database and databanks, §15A-266.2.
Scale technician.
Weights and measures, §81A-9.
Scan line.
Campaign contributions and expenditures.
Disclosure requirements for media advertisements, §163-278.38Z.
Scanning device.
Financial transaction cards, §14-113.8.
Scattering area.
Cremations, §90-210.41.
Scenic easement.
Natural and scenic rivers, §113A-33.
North Carolina trail system, §113A-85.
SCFL.
Coastal and estuarine commercial fishing licenses, §113-168.
Schedule of fees.
Health plans, disclosure to providers, §58-3-227, (a).
School.
Attendance, §115C-378.
Drivers' licenses, lose control, lose license, §20-11, (n1).
Leave for parent involvement in schools, §95-28.3, (a).
Taking indecent liberties with a student, §14-202.4, (d).
Weapons on educational property, §14-269.2, (a).
School activity bus, §20-4.01.
School administrator, §115C-325, (a).
Drivers' licenses, lose control, lose license, §20-11, (n1).
Standards board for public school administration, §115C-290.2.
School bus, §20-4.01.
School district.
Funding bonds, §115C-481.

DEFINED TERMS —Cont'd
School personnel.
Charter schools.
Criminal history checks, §115C-238.29K, (a).
Criminal history records checks, §115C-332, (a).
Taking indecent liberties with a student, §14-202.4, (d).
School property.
Drivers' licenses, lose control, lose license, §20-11, (n1).
Education programs at residential schools.
Duty to report certain acts to law enforcement, §143B-146.15.
Principals to report certain acts to law enforcement, §115C-288, (g).
School safety officer.
Taking indecent liberties with a student, §14-202.4, (d).
School system.
Organization of schools, §115C-74.
Scientific committee.
Plant protection and conservation, §106-202.12.
Scientific council.
Endangered wildlife, §113-331.
Scientific purposes.
Property tax exemption, §105-278.7, (f).
Taxation, §105-278.3.
Scope of therapeutic recreation.
Personnel certification, §90C-4, (e).
S corporations and partnerships.
Taxation, §§105-130.2, 105-131, 105-134.1, 105-134.5.
Scrap fishing, §113-185, (b).
Scrap tire, §130A-309.53.
Tire disposal tax, §105-187.15.
Screened.
Rules of professional conduct, Prof. Cond. Rule 1.0.
Screening.
Controlled substance examination regulation, §95-231.
Seed law, §106-277.2.
Sealed record information.
National crime prevention and privacy compact, §114-19.50.
Sealed with its corporate seal.
Corporate conveyance forms, §47-41.01, (d).
Search warrant, §15A-241.
Seasonal food service establishment.
Wage and hour act, §95-25.2.
Seasonal or religious nonprofit educational conference center or a seasonal amusement or recreational establishment.
Wage and hour act, §95-25.2.
Second.
Boxing commission, §143-651.
Secondary metals recycler.
Dealing in regulated metals property, §66-11, (a).
Secondary obligor.
Secured transactions, §25-9-102, (a).
Secondary standards.
Weights and measures, §81A-9.
Secondary supplier.
Urban electrical service, §160A-331.
Second-degree murder.
Criminal law, §14-17.
Second-degree rape.
Criminal law, §14-27.3.
Second-degree sexual offense.
Criminal law, §14-27.5.
Secondhand bedding, §130A-261.

DEFINED TERMS —Cont'd
Second tier subcontractor.
Liens, §44A-17.
Secretary.
Business corporations, §55-1-40.
Nonprofit corporations, §55A-1-40.
Secretary of health, education and welfare.
Governmental employees and social security, §135-20.
Secretary-treasurer.
Rescue squad workers' relief fund, §58-86-40.
Secret military society.
Criminal law, §14-12.2.
Secret political society.
Criminal law, §14-12.2.
Secret society.
Criminal law, §14-12.2.
Secured claim.
Insurers supervision, §58-30-10.
Secured party, §44A-1.
Secured transactions, §25-9-102, (a).
Sublease of motor vehicle and loan assumption arranging, §20-106.2, (a).
Securities intermediary.
Investment securities, §25-8-102.
Securitization.
Asset-backed securities facilitation, §53-425.
Security, §78A-2.
Enterprise corporations, §53A-37.
Investment securities, §25-8-102.
Public utilities, §62-3.
Tax credit for qualified business investments, §105-163.010.
Security agreement.
Motor vehicles, §20-4.01.
Secured transactions, §25-9-102, (a).
Security certificate.
Investment securities, §25-8-102.
Security document.
Global TransPark authority, §63A-2.
Pollution control, §§159C-3, 159D-3.
Security entitlement.
Investment securities, §25-8-102.
Security guard and patrol profession, §74C-3.
Security holder.
Insurance holding companies, §58-19-5.
Security instrument, §45-67.
Security interest, §44A-1.
Motor vehicles, §20-4.01.
Sublease of motor vehicle and loan assumption arranging, §20-106.2, (a).
UCC, §25-1-201.
Security procedure.
Electronic transactions, §66-312.
Funds transfers, UCC, §25-4A-201.
Sediment.
Pollution control act, §113A-52.
Seed offered for sale, §106-277.2.
SEIBP.
State employee incentive bonus program, §143-345.20.
Seizure.
Seed law, §106-277.2.
Selected contractors.
Lease or purchase of prison facilities constructed by private firm, §148-37.2, (b).
Self-insurer.
Insurance company taxation, §105-228.3.
Self-insurance guaranty association, §97-130.
Workers' compensation.
Third-party administrators and service companies, §58-47-150.

DEFINED TERMS —Cont'd
Self-insurer —Cont'd
Workers' compensation self insurance, §97-165.
Self-propelled pole carrier, §20-116, (f).
Self-service storage company.
Self service storage renter's insurance, §58-33-18, (a).
Self-service storage facility, §44A-40.
Self-supporting agencies.
State-owned office space.
Fees for use by, §143-342.1.
Sell.
Commercial fertilizer, §106-657.
Insurance producers, §58-33-10.
Soil additives act, §106-50.30.
Seller.
Installment sales, §25A-6.
Products liability, §99B-1.
Sales, §§14-401.13, 25-2-103.
Selling or leasing at retail.
Tax credit for qualified business investments, §105-163.010.
Semitrailers.
Motor vehicles, §20-4.01.
Send.
Secured transactions, §25-9-102, (a).
UCC, §25-1-201.
Sender.
Funds transfers, UCC, §§25-4A-103, (a), 25-4A-202, (d).
Sending agency.
Interchange of governmental employees, §126-52.
Sending state.
Interstate agreement on detainers, §15A-761.
Interstate compact on mental health, §122C-361.
State prisons, §148-120.
Senior high school, §115C-75, (a).
Sentencing plan.
Sentencing services act, §7A-771.
Sentencing services program, §7A-771.
Separate property.
Divorce, §50-20, (b).
Septage.
Solid waste management, §130A-290, (a).
Septage management firm.
Solid waste management, §130A-290, (a).
Septic tank system.
Sewage systems, §130A-334.
Serious bodily injury.
Assault, §14-32.4, (a).
Child abuse, §14-318.4, (a3).
Failure to yield right of way, §20-160.1, (b).
Serious or chronic degenerative, disabling or life-threatening disease or condition.
Managed care access to specialists, §58-3-223, (b).
Serious physical harm.
Assaulting law enforcement or assistance animals, §14-163.1, (a).
Serious traffic violation.
Motor vehicles, §20-4.01.
Serious violation.
Commercial drivers' licenses, disqualification, §20-17.4, (d).
Occupational safety and health, §95-127.
Service.
Computer crimes, §14-453.
Decedents' estates, §28A-1-1.
Disability income plan, §135-101.
District attorneys, §7A-65, (c), (d).
Installment sales, §25A-5.

DEFINED TERMS —Cont'd
Service —Cont'd
Privileged communications, rape crisis centers and domestic violence programs, §8-53.12.
Public utilities, §62-3.
Retirement, §128-21.
State retirement, §135-1.
Weights and measures, §81A-9.
Service agreement, §58-1-35, (b).
Service agreement company, §58-1-35, (b).
Service area.
Certificate of need, §131E-176.
Costs for solid waste management, determining, §130A-309.08, (c).
Service certificate.
Weights and measures, §81A-73.
Service charges.
University of North Carolina, §116-41.1.
Service company.
Workers' compensation.
Self-insurance, §58-47-150.
Employer groups, §58-47-60.
Service corporation.
Regional reciprocal savings and loan acquisition act, §54B-48.2.
Savings and loan associations, §54B-4.
Savings banks, §54C-4, (b).
Service provider.
Insurance customer information safeguards, §58-39-140.
Service-related industry.
Tax credit for qualified business investments, §105-163.010.
Services rendered.
Sales and use tax exemptions, §105-164.13.
Service supplier.
E-911 system for wireless communications, §62A-21.
911 service, §62A-3.
Service taxes.
Sales and use tax, §105-164.12B, (e).
Set of districts.
District court districts, §7A-200, (a).
Judicial department, §7A-41.1, (a).
Settle.
Banking, §25-4-104, (a).
Settled claim.
Structured settlement protection, §1-543.11.
Settlement.
Good funds settlement act, §45A-3.
Settlement agent.
Good funds settlement act, §45A-3.
Setup.
Manufactured housing, §143-143.9.
Set-up contractor.
Manufactured housing, §143-143.9.
7Q10 conditions.
Solid waste management, §130A-295.01, (a).
Severe and persistent mental illness, §122C-3.
Severe chronic disability.
Community trusts, §36A-59.11.
Severe injury.
Dangerous dogs, §67-4.1.
Sewage, §§130A-334, 143-213, 162A-2.
Metropolitan districts, §162A-65, (a).
Sewage disposal system, §162A-2.
Metropolitan districts, §162A-65, (a).
Sewerage system.
Metropolitan districts, §162A-65, (a).
Metropolitan water districts, §162A-32, (a).

DEFINED TERMS —Cont'd
Sewers, §162A-2.
Metropolitan districts, §162A-65, (a).
Metropolitan water districts, §162A-32, (a).
Sewer system, §§143-213, 162A-2.
Sexual act.
Criminal law, §14-27.1.
Sexual activity.
Offenses against morality, §14-190.13.
Sexual assault.
Assistance program for victims of rape and sex offenses, §143B-480.2, (a).
Privileged communications, rape crisis centers and domestic violence programs, §8-53.12.
Sexual assault victim.
Privileged communications, rape crisis centers and domestic violence programs, §8-53.12.
Sexual behavior.
Rape shield law, §8C-1, Rule 412.
Sexual conduct.
Civil no-contact orders, §50C-1.
Obscene literature, §14-190.1.
Public morals, §19-12.
Sexual contact.
Sex offenses, §14-27.1.
Sexual excitement.
Public morals, §19-12.
Sexual exploitation.
Psychotherapy patient/client sexual exploitation act, §90-21.41.
Sexual history.
Psychotherapy patient/client sexual exploitation act, §90-21.41.
Sexually explicit nudity.
Offenses against morality, §14-190.13.
Sexually oriented devices.
Adult establishments, §14-202.10.
Sexually violent offense.
Sex offender and public protection registration, §14-208.6.
Sexually violent predator.
Sex offender and public protection registration, §14-208.6.
Sexual penetration.
Civil no-contact orders, §50C-1.
Sexual relations with clients.
Rules of professional conduct, Prof Cond. Rule 1.19.
SFL.
Salt water fishing license, §113-174.
Shallow land burial.
Radiation protection, §104E-5.
Shampooing, §88B-2.
Shared appreciation.
Reverse mortgages, §53-257.
Shared value.
Reverse mortgages, §53-257.
Shareholder.
Business corporations, §55-1-40.
Derivative actions, §55-7-40.1.
Dissenters' rights, §55-13-01.
Shares.
Business corporations, §55-1-40.
Decedents' estates, §29-2.
Shellfish, §113-201.1.
Conservation, §113-129.
Shellfish lease.
Conservation, §113-269.
Shelter care.
Abused, neglected or dependent juveniles, §7B-101.

DEFINED TERMS —Cont'd
Sheriff.
Civil procedure, §1-339.41, (b).
Sex offender and public protection registration, §14-208.6.
Shingling tobacco.
Leaf tobacco sales, §106-461.
Shipping container.
Poultry products inspection, §106-549.51.
Shopping cart.
Larceny, §14-72.3.
Shoreline area.
High Rock lake marine commission, §77-50.
Lake lure marine commission, §77-80.
Lake Wylie marine commission, §77-30.
Short-term lease or rental.
Highway use tax, §105-187.1.
Regional transit authority vehicle rental tax, §105-550.
Sickle cell trait.
Labor discrimination, §95-28.1.
Signator.
Interstate environmental compact, §113A-23.
Signature.
Criminal process and procedure.
Electronic technology, §15A-101.1.
Signed.
UCC, §25-1-201.
Signed print.
Sales, §25C-10.
Significant limitations in adaptive functioning.
Death sentence prohibited, mentally retarded defendants, §15A-2005, (a).
Significantly subaverage general intellectual functioning.
Death sentence prohibited, mentally retarded defendants, §15A-2005, (a).
Silicosis.
Workers' compensation, §97-62.
Silver.
Precious metals, §66-164.
Simultaneous conversion/merger.
Mutual and stock associations, §54B-37.1, (a).
Single-axle weight.
Motor vehicles, §20-118.
Single-family residential dwelling unit.
Homeowner's recovery fund, §87-15.5.
Single family unit.
Cultivation of shellfish, §113-201.1.
Single interest credit property.
Credit property insurance, §58-57-90, (a).
Singular.
Workers' compensation, §97-2.
Sinking fund.
Local government bonds, §159-44.
Local government finance, §159-7.
Sister.
Adoptee's new birth certificate, §48-9-107, (c).
Workers' compensation, §97-2.
Site.
Solid waste management, §130A-310.
Specific development plan.
Counties, §153A-344.1.
Site development, §143B-437.02, (c).
Site evaluation.
Swine farms, §106-802.
Site plan.
Sewage systems, §130A-334.
Site specific development plan.
City and town zoning, §160A-385.1, (b).

DEFINED TERMS —Cont'd
Situated.
Tangible personal property, §105-304.
Size or weight class.
Egg law, §106-245.14.
Skeletal analyst.
Burial sites, §70-28.
Ski area, §99C-1.
Ski area operator, §99C-1.
Skier, §99C-1.
Skilled care.
State medical plan, §135-40.1.
Skilled nursing facility.
Long-term care insurance, §58-55-35, (a).
State medical plan, §135-40.1.
Skimobile.
Passenger tramway safety, §95-117.
Slayer.
Decedents' estates, §31A-3.
Slot device.
Lotteries and gaming, §14-306, (a).
Slot machine.
Lotteries and gaming, §14-306, (a).
Sludge.
Solid waste management, §130A-290, (a).
Small business.
Research and development expenses tax credit, §105-129.50.
Small business investment company.
Rural redevelopment authority, §143B-437.21.
Small claim action.
Judicial department, §7A-210.
Small employer.
Health insurance portability and accountability, §58-68-25, (a).
Small employer group health coverage, §58-50-110.
Small employer carrier.
Small employer group health coverage, §58-50-110.
Small group market.
Health insurance portability and accountability, §58-68-25, (a).
Small power producer.
Public utilities, §62-3.
Smoking, §143-596.
Socially and economically disadvantaged individual.
Public contracts, §143-128.2, (g).
Social security act.
Governmental employees, §135-20.
Social security breakpoint.
State retirement system, §135-1.
Social worker.
Certification, §90B-3.
Society.
Fraternal benefit societies, §58-24-15, (g).
Socioeconomic and demographic data.
County solid waste disposal, §153A-136, (c).
Public enterprises, §160A-325, (a).
Soft drink.
Sales and use tax, §105-164.3.
Software.
Secured transactions, §25-9-102, (a).
Soil.
Soil scientists, §89F-3.
Soil additive, §106-50.30.
Soil and water conservation commission, §139-3.
Soil and water conservation district, §139-3.
Soil science, §89F-3.

DEFINED TERMS —Cont'd
Soil scientist, §89F-3.
Soil scientist-in-training, §89F-3.
Solar electric or thermal equipment.
Tax credits for renewable energy equipment facility construction, §105-130.28, (b).
Sold.
Bedding, §130A-261.
Sole beneficiary.
Modification and termination of irrevocable trusts, §36A-125.1.
Solicit.
Insurance producers, §58-33-10.
Solicitation, §14-401.12.
Solicitation.
Civil procedure, §1-75.2.
Solicitation of contributions, §131F-2.
Solicitor.
Solicitation of contributions, §131F-2.
Solid organ transplantation service.
Certificate of need, §131E-176.
Solid tire.
Motor vehicles, §20-4.01.
Solid waste, §130A-290, (a).
Counties, §§153A-136, (d), 153A-294, 153A-421.
Pollution control, §§159C-3, 159D-3.
Public enterprises, §160A-325, (b).
Solid waste disposal facility, §159C-3.
Pollution control, §159D-3.
Solid waste disposal site, §130A-290, (a).
Solid waste generation, §130A-290, (a).
Solid waste management, §130A-290, (a).
Solid waste management facility, §130A-290, (a).
Solution-based solicitation.
Best value information technology procurements, §143-135.9.
Sound-amplifying equipment.
Disruption of state-owned campuses, §116-213.
Sound management program.
Taxation, §105-277.2.
Source material.
Radiation protection, §104E-5.
Southern region association.
Regional reciprocal savings and loan acquisition act, §54B-48.2.
Southern region savings and loan holding company.
Regional reciprocal savings and loan acquisition act, §54B-48.2.
Southern region states.
Regional reciprocal savings and loan acquisition act, §54B-48.2.
Special ABC area.
Alcoholic beverages, §18B-101.
Special act.
Cities and towns, §160A-1.
Special annuity account accumulated contributions.
State law-enforcement retirement, §143-166.30, (a).
Special annuity accounts.
State law-enforcement retirement, §143-166.30, (a).
Special care service.
Adult day care programs.
Alzheimer's disease, §131D-6, (b4).
Special care unit.
Adult care homes, §131D-4.6, (a).
Nursing homes, §131E-114, (e).
Special concern species.
Endangered wildlife, §113-331.
Plant protection and conservation, §106-202.12.

DEFINED TERMS —Cont'd
Special corporation.
Capital facilities finance act, §142-82.
Energy conservation finance act, §142-61.
Special declarant rights.
Condominiums, §47C-1-103.
Planned community act, §47F-1-103.
Special deposit claim.
Insurers supervision, §58-30-10.
Special deputy.
Sheriffs' education, §17E-2.
Special district.
County board of elections conducting, §163-285, (c).
Local government finance, §159-7.
Special education, §115C-108.
Special equipment.
Elevator safety, §95-110.3, (n).
Special fund for individual schools, §115C-448, (c).
Special funds for individual institutions.
University of North Carolina constituent institutions, §116-36.2, (b).
Special indebtedness.
Capital facilities finance act, §142-82.
Special limited guard and patrol profession, §74C-3.
Specially constructed vehicles.
Motor vehicles, §20-4.01.
Special mobile equipment.
Sales and use tax, §105-164.3.
Special needs institution.
Distinguished professors endowment trust fund, §116-41.13A.
Special nonprofit corporation.
Lease or purchase of prison facilities constructed by private firm, §148-37.2, (b).
Special nuclear material.
Radiation protection, §104E-5.
Special obligation bond project.
Higher education bonds, §116D-22.
Special proceedings.
Civil procedure, §1-3.
Special purpose entity.
Asset-backed securities facilitation, §53-425.
Viatical life insurance settlements, §58-58-205.
Special purpose institution.
Private capital facilities finance act, §159D-37.
Special purpose project.
Pollution control, §159C-3.
Special-purpose unit of government.
Environmental policy act, §113A-9.
Specialty ambulatory surgical program.
Certificate of need, §131E-176.
Specialty fertilizer.
Commercial fertilizer, §106-657.
Specialty market, §66-250.
Specialty market operator, §66-250.
Specialty market vendor, §66-250.
Specialty pet.
Commercial feed law, §106-284.33.
Specialty pet food.
Commercial feed law, §106-284.33.
Specialty services.
Mental health, §122C-3.
Specialty vehicles, §20-4.01.
Special user project.
Global TransPark authority, §63A-2.
Special verdict, §1A-1, Rule 49, (a).
Special wastes.
Solid waste management, §130A-290, (a).

DEFINED TERMS —Cont'd
Specifications.
Refined or reprocessed oil, §119-13.1.
Specific contracted work site.
Owner-controlled or wrap-up insurance, §58-31-65, (b).
Specific license.
Radiation protection, §104E-5.
Specific reserve account.
Savings and loan associations, §54B-4.
Specified anatomical areas.
Adult establishments, §14-202.10.
Specified sexual activities.
Adult establishments, §14-202.10.
Specimen.
Document authentication, §66-271.
Spectator.
Roller skating rink safety and liability, §99E-10.
Speech and language pathologist.
Licensure, §90-293.
Speech impaired.
Health and human services division, §143B-216.30.
Speleothem.
Cave protection act, §14-159.20.
Spirituous liquor.
Alcoholic beverages, §18B-101.
Alcohol taxation, §105-113.68.
Sales and use tax exemptions, §105-164.13.
Spoil bank.
Mining, §74-49.
Sponsor.
Campaign contributions and expenditures.
Disclosure requirements for media advertisements, §163-278.38Z.
Continuing legal education, Bar Rules & Regs., D, §.1501.
Solicitation of contributions, §131F-2.
Sponsoring providers.
Provider sponsored organizations, §131E-276.
Sponsor purpose.
Solicitation of contributions, §131F-2.
Sponsor sales promotion.
Solicitation of contributions, §131F-2.
Sport or recreational equipment.
Sales and use tax, §105-164.3.
Sports club.
Alcoholic beverages, §18B-1000.
Sports events.
Assault and battery, §14-33.
Sport shooting range, §14-409.45.
Sports officials.
Assault and battery, §14-33.
Spot rate.
Foreign-money claims, §1C-1820.
Spotter plane.
Coastal and estuarine commercial fishing licenses, §113-171.1, (a).
Spousal-support order.
Interstate family support, §52C-1-101.
Spouse.
Death benefits, §143-166.2, (e).
Taxation, §105-277.2.
Stabilize.
Accident and health insurance.
Utilization review, §58-50-61, (a).
Stafford act.
Emergency management, §166A-4.
Stalking.
Civil no-contact orders, §50C-1.

DEFINED TERMS —Cont'd
Standard health care plan.
Small employer group health coverage, §58-50-110.
Standard program county.
Public assistance program, §108A-24.
Standards.
Vegetable plant law, §106-284.16.
Water and air resources, §143-213.
Standards for quality.
Egg law, §106-245.14.
Standard transportation practices.
Joint rate agreements, §62-152.2, (a).
Standard work first program.
Public assistance program, §108A-24.
Standard working hours.
Limited driving privilege, §20-179.3, (f1).
Standby guardian, §35A-1370.
State.
Aeronautics, §63-1.
Agricultural finance act, §122D-3.
Anatomical gifts, §130A-403.
Biological residues, §106-549.81.
Business corporations, §55-1-40.
Capital facilities finance act, §142-82.
Child custody jurisdiction and enforcement, §50A-102.
Clean water loans, §159G-3.
Controlled substances, §90-87.
Criminal extradition, §15A-721.
Criminal procedure, §15A-101.
Custodial trusts, §33B-1.
Disability income plan, §135-101.
Educational personnel qualifications, §115C-350.
Electric power, §159B-3.
Electronic transactions, §66-312.
Executive budget, §143-3.3, (a).
Foreign-money claims, §1C-1820.
Health facilities finance, §131A-3.
Housing authorities, §157-3.
Housing finance agency, §122A-3.
Insurance taxation, §105-228.8.
Interstate agreement on detainers, §15A-761.
Interstate branch banking, §53-224.9.
Interstate compact on adoption and medical assistance, §7B-3901.
Interstate compact on education, §115C-104.
Interstate compact on juveniles, §7B-2803.
Interstate compact on mental health, §122C-361.
Interstate environmental compact, §113A-23.
Interstate family support, §52C-1-101.
Law-enforcement retirement, §143-166.30, (a).
Legal defense of employees, §143-300.2.
Limited liability companies, §57C-1-03.
Local government law-enforcement retirement, §143-166.50, (a).
Mines, §§74-24.2, 74-37.
Motor vehicles, §20-4.01.
National crime prevention and privacy compact, §114-19.50.
Nonprofit corporations, §55A-1-40.
Nurse licensure compact, §90-171.82.
Occupational safety and health, §95-127.
Partnerships, §59-102.
Pest control, §106-65.55.
Public health authorities, §130A-45.01.
Public hospitals, §131E-16.
Public utilities, §62-3.
Reciprocal banking act, §53-210.
Regional reciprocal savings and loan acquisition act, §54B-48.2.

DEFINED TERMS —Cont'd
State —Cont'd
Secured transactions, §25-9-102, (a).
Securities, §78A-2.
Soil and water conservation districts, §139-3.
State prisons, §148-120.
Transfers to minors, §33A-1.
Unclaimed property act, §116B-52.
Unemployment insurance, §96-8.
Uniform sales and use tax administration act, §105-164.42B.
Veterans' recreation, §165-25.
Witnesses, §15A-811.
State acquisition and relocation fund.
Emergency management, §166A-4.
State action.
Dentist peer review organizations, §90-48.2, (f).
State agency, §143-34.40.
Aid to the blind, §111-42, (b).
Capital facilities finance act, §142-82.
Criminal justice information network, §143-660.
Debt collection, §105A-2.
Depository library system, §125-11.6.
Disaster service volunteer leave, §166A-31.
Employees and social security, §135-20.
Energy in state buildings, §143-64.11.
Environmental policy act, §113A-9.
Office of information technology services, §147-33.81.
Office of the controller, §143B-426.35.
Sales and use tax, §105-164.3.
State auditor, §147-64.4.
State lands, §146-64.
State officers, §147-86.11.
Statewide accounts receivable program, §147-86.20.
State airway.
Aeronautics, §63-1.
State archaeologist.
Indian antiquities, §70-48.
State-assisted state facility.
Energy in state buildings, §143-64.11.
State association.
Regional reciprocal savings and loan acquisition act, §54B-48.2.
Savings and loan associations, §54B-4.
Savings and loan interstate branches, §54B-266.
State bank.
Trust companies, §53-301, (a).
State bar.
Client security fund, rules governing administration, Bar Rules & Regs., D, §.1401.
State board.
Community colleges, §115D-2.
Education, §115C-5, (a).
State building.
Administration department, §143-336.
Aid to the blind, §111-42, (c).
Sales and use tax exemptions, §105-164.13.
State capital improvement project.
State building commission, §143-135.27.
State-certified general real estate appraiser, §93E-1-4.
State-certified historic structure.
Historic rehabilitation tax credit, §105-129.36, (b).
State-certified residential real estate appraiser, §93E-1-4.
State consumer advocate.
MH/DD/SA consumer advocacy program, §122C-11.
State corporate income tax, §105-130.4, (a).

DEFINED TERMS —Cont'd
State council.
Department of juvenile justice and delinquency prevention, §143B-515.
State criminal law.
Certification standards for criminal law specialty, Bar Rules & Regs., D, §.2502.
State DNA databank, §15A-266.2.
State DNA database, §15A-266.2.
State educational institution.
Children of war veterans scholarships, §165-20.
National Guard tuition assistance, §127A-192.
State education assistance authority loan fund, §116-201.
State employee.
State employee incentive bonus program, §143-345.20.
State employee credit union.
Executive budget, §143-3.3, (a).
State environmental management commission.
Soil and water conservation districts, §139-3.
State facility.
Energy in state buildings, §143-64.11.
Mental health, §122C-3.
State funds.
Executive budget act, §143-1.
Office of the controller, §143B-426.35.
State government.
Smoking in public places, §143-596.
State governmental unit.
Guaranteed energy savings contract, §143-64.17B.
State historic preservation officer.
Historic rehabilitation tax credit, §105-129.36, (b).
Historic structure rehabilitation tax credit, §105-129.35, (c).
State historic site, §121-2.
State lands, §146-64.
Archaeology, §70-12.
State law.
Outdoor advertising control, §136-128.
Unemployment insurance, §96-12.01, (a).
State law enforcement agency.
Unauthorized substances tax, §105-113.106.
State legislative buildings and grounds, §120-32.1, (d).
State library agency.
Interstate library compact, §125-14.
State-licensed residential real estate appraiser, §93E-1-4.
State medical facilities plan.
Certificate of need, §131E-176.
Statement.
Evidence, §8C-1, Rule 801, (a).
False statement to procure or deny benefit of policy or certificate, §58-2-161, (a).
State net income.
Taxation, §105-130.2.
State of emergency.
Alcoholic beverages, §18B-110.
Civil disorders, §14-288.1.
State official.
Environmental policy act, §113A-9.
State ombudsman.
Long-term care program, §143B-181.16.
State or local child support enforcement agency.
Unemployment insurance, §96-17, (d).
State or local consumer advocate.
Mental health, §122C-3.
State-owned passenger motor vehicle.
Assignment of vehicles by department of administration, §143-341.

DEFINED TERMS —Cont'd
State parks and forest road system.
Motor vehicle laws applicable to, §143-116.8.
State parks system, §113-44.9.
State plan.
Children's health insurance program, §108A-70.18.
Mental health, §122C-3.
Public assistance program, §108A-24.
State practice laws.
Nurse licensure compact, §90-171.82.
State property.
Aid to the blind, §111-42, (c).
State publication.
Depository library system, §125-11.6.
State public body.
National defense housing projects, §157-53.
State public health veterinarian.
Rabies, §130A-184.
State public work project.
State prisons, §148-26.1.
State recreation trails.
North Carolina trail system, §113A-86.
State resources.
Mental health, §122C-3.
State retirement system.
Law-enforcement, §143-166.30, (a).
State savings association.
Trust companies, §53-301, (a).
State savings bank, §54C-4, (b).
Savings interstate branch banks, §54C-200.
State scenic trails.
North Carolina trail system, §113A-86.
State team.
Child fatality prevention system, §7B-1401.
State trails system.
North Carolina trail system, §113A-85.
State treasurer.
Clean water loans, §159G-3.
State trust company.
Trust companies, §53-301, (a).
State trust company facility, §53-340, (b).
Trust companies, §53-301, (a).
State trust institution.
Trust companies, §53-301, (a).
Statewide data processor.
Medical care data, §131E-214.1.
Statewide registry.
Sex offender and public protection registration, §14-208.6.
Status report.
Incompetency, §35A-1202.
Stepparent.
Adoption, §48-1-101.
Stillbirth.
Injury to pregnant woman resulting in miscarriage or stillbirth, §14-18.2, (a).
Stock association.
Savings and loan associations, §54B-4.
Stock savings bank, §54C-4, (b).
Stop-sale.
Seed law, §106-277.2.
Storage.
Sales and use tax, §105-164.3.
Storage and container.
Solid waste management, §130A-290, (a).
Toxic or hazardous substance identification, §95-174, (s).
Storage media.
Sales and use tax, §105-164.3.

DEFINED TERMS —Cont'd
Storage unit.
Self service storage renter's insurance, §58-33-18, (a).
Stored value.
Money transmitters, §53-208.2, (a).
Stormwater, §143-213.
Strawberry plant seller, §106-783.
Stream.
Floodplain regulations, §143-215.52, (a).
Street.
Contractors, §87-101.
Motor vehicles, §20-4.01.
Roads and highways, §136-41.1.
Street address.
Telephonic sellers, §66-262, (b).
Strike.
Public employees and unions, §95-98.2.
Stripper Well Litigation Funds.
Housing trust, §122E-2.
Structural pest control, §106-65.24.
Structural pest control act, §106-65.24.
Structure.
Floodplain regulations, §143-215.52, (a), (b).
Structured settlement, §1-543.11.
Structured settlement agreement, §1-543.11.
Structured settlement obligor, §1-543.11.
Structured settlement payment rights, §1-543.11.
Student.
Drivers' licenses, lose control, lose license, §20-11, (n1).
Private educational institutions, §116-22.
Sex offender and public protection registration, §14-208.6.
State education assistance authority, §116-201.
State grants to students attending private universities or colleges, §116-43.5, (a).
Taking indecent liberties with a student, §14-202.4, (d).
Weapons on educational property, §14-269.2, (a).
Student-athlete.
Athlete agents, §78C-86.
Student loans.
Education assistance authority, §116-209.24.
State education assistance authority, §116-201.
Student loan collections, §105B-1.
Student obligations.
State education assistance authority, §116-201.
Student teacher, §115C-309, (a).
Student teaching, §115C-309, (a).
Subcontractor, §22C-1.
Bonds, §44A-25.
Subdivision.
City and town planning, §160A-376.
Counties, §153A-335.
Subgrantee.
Use of state funds by non-state entities, §143-6.2, (a).
Sublease.
Leases, UCC, §25-2A-103, (1).
Motor vehicle and loan assumption arranging, §20-106.2, (a).
Sublease arranger.
Motor vehicle and loan assumption arranging, §20-106.2, (a).
Submachine gun, §14-409, (a).
Submerged lands.
State lands, §146-64.
Subordinate.
Geologist, §89E-3.
Soil scientists, §89F-3.

DEFINED TERMS —Cont'd
Subordinated debt.
Enterprise corporations, §53A-37.
Tax credit for qualified business investments, §105-163.010.
Subscriber.
Business corporations, §55-1-40.
Health maintenance organizations, §58-67-5, (k).
Insurance rates, §58-40-5.
Reciprocal insurance, §58-15-5.
Subscriptions.
Savings and loan associations, §54B-4.
Subsidiary.
Bank holding company act, §53-226.
Brownfields property reuse act, §130A-310.31, (b).
Corporate franchise tax, §105-122, (b).
Dry-cleaning solvent cleanup act, §143-215.104B, (b).
Insurance holding companies, §58-19-5.
Mining, §74-49.
Reciprocal banking act, §53-210.
Regional reciprocal savings and loan acquisition act, §54B-48.2.
Trust companies, §53-301, (a).
Underground storage tank cleanup, §143-215.94A.
Substance abuse.
Mental health, §122C-3.
Substance abuse counseling, §90-113.31.
Substance abuse counselor intern.
Substance abuse professionals, §90-113.31.
Substance abuse professional, §90-113.31.
Substance abuser, §122C-3.
Substandard unit.
Housing trust, §122E-2.
Substantial.
Rules of professional conduct, Prof. Cond. Rule 1.0.
Substantial change in use.
Sport shooting range protection, §14-409.45.
Substantial completion.
Civil procedure, §1-50, (a).
Substantial defect.
Manufactured housing, §143-143.9.
Substantial economic impact.
Rulemaking procedure, §150B-21.4, (b1).
Substantial evidence.
Administrative procedure, §150B-2.
Victims compensation, §15B-2.
Substantial fault.
Unemployment insurance, §96-14.
Substantial injury.
Partition sales of real property, §46-22, (b).
Substantially equivalent.
State personnel system, §126-11.
Substantial plurality.
Primary elections, §163-111, (a).
Substantial proportion of the services.
Provider sponsored organizations, §131E-276.
Substantial understatement.
Property tax, §105-273.
Substantive violation.
Migrant housing, §95-223.
Substitute address.
Address confidentiality program, §15C-2.
Successor external review process.
Health care liability, §90-21.50.
Successor in business.
Tax credit for manufacturing cigarettes for exportation, §105-130.45, (a).
Increasing employment and utilizing state ports, §105-130.46, (b).

DEFINED TERMS —Cont'd
Successors of a beneficiary.
Letters of credit, §25-5-102, (a).
Sui juris.
Modification and termination of irrevocable trusts, §36A-125.1.
Suitable employment.
Industrial commission utilization of rehabilitation professionals, I.C. Util. Rehab. Profs. I.
Unemployment insurance, §96-14.
Suitable transportation.
Assignment of suitable transportation to state employee or agency by department of administration, §143-341.
Suitable work.
Unemployment insurance, §96-12.
Summons.
Witnesses, §15A-811.
Superintendent.
Education, §115C-5, (h).
Superior court.
Civil procedure, §1-567.32.
Criminal procedure, §15A-101.
Superior court district.
Sentencing services act, §7A-771.
Superior court judge.
Criminal procedure, §15A-101.
Superseded part.
Farm machinery franchises, §66-180.
Supervised living facility of developmentally disabled adults.
Long-term care insurance, §58-55-35, (a).
Supervisee.
Post-release supervision, §15A-1368, (a).
Supervising attorney.
Rules governing legal services provided by students, Bar Rules & Regs., C, §.0202.
Supervising bail bondsman, §58-71-1.
Supervision.
Dental hygiene, §90-221, (f).
Supervisor.
Education, §115C-5, (i).
Licensed professional counselors, §90-330, (a).
Savings and loan interstate branches, §54B-266.
Savings interstate branch banks, §54C-200.
Soil and water conservation districts, §139-3.
Supervisory agency.
Financial privacy, §53B-2.
Supplemental address.
Lead poisoning in children, §130A-131.7.
Supplemental retirement income plan.
State law-enforcement, §143-166.30, (a).
Supplementary rating information.
Insurance, §58-36-100, (b).
Workers' compensation self-insurance.
Employer groups.
Premium rates, §58-47-110, (a).
Supplementary report.
License proposals, §120-149.2.
Supplier.
Beer franchises, §18B-1301.
Farm machinery, §66-180.
Gasoline tax, §105-449.60.
Leases, UCC, §25-2A-103, (1).
Manufactured housing, §143-143.9.
Supplier of water.
Drinking water, §130A-313.
Supply contract.
Leases, UCC, §25-2A-103, (1).
Support activities.
Respiratory care practices act, §90-648.

DEFINED TERMS —Cont'd
Support enforcement agency.
Interstate family support, §52C-1-101.
Supporting obligation.
Secured transactions, §25-9-102, (a).
Supporting spouse.
Alimony, §50-16.1A.
Support and maintenance, §14-322, (a).
Support order.
Interstate family support, §52C-1-101.
Support our students.
School-aged children, §143B-152.2.
Support trust.
Alienability of beneficiary's interest, §36A-115.
Supreme court.
Client security fund, rules governing administration, Bar Rules & Regs., D, §.1401.
Discipline and disability rules of state bar, Bar Rules & Regs., B, §.0103.
Procedures for the authorized practice committee of the state bars, Bar Rules & Regs., D, §.0203.
Supreme court orders.
Client security fund, rules governing administration, Bar Rules & Regs., D, §.1401.
Surety.
Bail, §15A-531.
Bail bondmen and runners, §58-71-1.
UCC, §25-1-201.
Surety bondsman.
Bail bondsman and runners, §58-71-1.
Surface water.
Water withdrawals and transfers, §143-215.22G.
Surgeon.
Anatomical gifts, §130A-403.
Surplus.
Banking, §53-1.
Surplus lines, §58-21-10.
Surplus funds.
Drainage, §156-82.1, (c).
Surplus lines insurance, §58-21-10.
Surplus lines licensee, §58-21-15.
Surplus trust funds.
Community trust for persons with severe chronic disabilities, §36A-59.11.
Surrender of a driver's license.
Motor vehicles, §20-16.5, (a).
Surveying and platting.
Limitations of actions, §1-47.
Survivor.
Tuition waiver for senior citizens, §115B-1.
Survivorship in joint tenancies.
Estates, §41-2.
Suspends payments.
Banking, §25-4-104, (a).
Suspension.
Motor vehicles, §20-4.01.
Sustainable harvests.
Conservation, §113-129.
Swamplands.
State lands, §146-64.
Swap agreement, §159-193.
Swine farm, §106-802.
Swine integrator registration, §143-215.10H, (a).
Swine house, §106-802.
Swine operation integrator, §143-215.10H, (a).
Switchblade knife.
Weapons on educational property, §14-269.2, (a).
Symptomless carrier.
Bee and honey act, §106-635.

DEFINED TERMS —Cont'd
System.
State parks act, §113-44.9.
System of registration.
Public obligations, §159E-2.
System property.
Public service taxation, §105-333.
System transfer.
Gasoline tax, §105-449.60.
Table funding.
Mortgage bankers and brokers, §53-243.01.
Tag.
Motor vehicles, §20-137.7.
Talent agency.
Minors, talent contracts, §48A-17.
Tall buildings or structures.
Mountain ridge protection, §113A-206.
Tandem-axle weight.
Motor vehicles, §20-118.
Tangible chattel paper.
Secured transactions, §25-9-102, (a).
Tangible personal property.
Property taxes, §105-273.
Sales and use tax, §105-164.3.
Tank wagon.
Gasoline tax, §105-449.60.
Tank wagon importer.
Gasoline tax, §105-449.66, (a).
Tanning equipment, §104E-9.1, (c).
Tanning facility, §104E-9.1, (c).
Targeted population.
Mental health, §122C-3.
Targeted to the relevant electorate.
Electioneering communication, §§163-278.80, 163-278.90.
Task force.
Child fatality prevention system, §7B-1401.
Tattooing, §130A-283, (a).
Tax, §105-228.90, (b).
Federal estate tax, §28A-27-1.
Fiduciaries, §32-26.
Gasoline tax, §105-449.60.
Local government finance, §159-7.
Property taxes, §105-273.
Taxable income, §105-134.1.
Taxable period.
Taxation, §105-131.
Taxable year, §§105-130.2, 105-134.1, 105-163.2.
Estimated income tax, §105-163.38.
Tax withholding, §105-163.1.
Tax collector.
Property taxes, §105-273.
Tax debt.
Collection, §105-243.1, (a).
Taxicab.
Motor vehicles, §20-87.
Tax information.
Confidentiality, §105-259, (a).
Taxing unit, §§105-151.21, 105-163.2.
Property taxes, §105-273.
Tax-levying authority.
Community colleges, §115D-2.
Education, §115C-5, (j).
Taxpayer, §§105-130.2, 105-134.1, 105-163.2, 105-228.90, (b).
Property taxes, §105-273.
Sales and use tax, §105-164.3.
Tax year.
Individual income tax, §105-151.20, (a).
TDD.
Deaf and the hard of hearing, §143B-216.30.

DEFINED TERMS —Cont'd
Teacher.
Disability income plan, §135-101.
Education personnel, §115C-325, (a).
NBPTS certification, §115C-296.2, (b).
State retirement system, §135-1.
Team coordinator.
Child fatality prevention system, §7B-1401.
Technical institute.
Proprietary schools, §115D-87.
Technical school.
Proprietary schools, §115D-87.
Technical specialist.
Animal waste management, §143-215.10B.
Technician-level entry capability.
Hazardous materials emergency response, §166A-21.
Teen court program.
Delinquent and undisciplined juveniles, §7B-1501.
Telecommunications.
Public agency, §143B-426.8.
Telecommunications device.
Deaf and the hard of hearing, §143B-216.30.
Electronic surveillance, §14-113.5.
Telecommunication service.
Sales and use tax on telecommunications, §§105-164.3, 105-164.4C, (h).
Unlawful telecommunications devices, §14-113.5.
Telecommunication service provider.
Unlawful telecommunications devices, §14-113.5.
Telegram.
UCC, §25-1-201.
Telegraph company.
Public service taxation, §105-333.
Telemarketing sales rule.
Telephone solicitations, §75-101.
Telephone bank.
Electioneering communications, §163-278.90.
Telephone company.
Public service taxation, §105-333.
Telephone room.
Securities regulation, §78A-11.
Telephone solicitation, §75-101.
Telephone solicitor, §75-101.
Telephone subscriber.
911 service, §62A-3.
Telephone solicitations, §75-101.
Telephonic communications.
Criminal law and procedure, §14-196.
Telephonic seller, §66-260.
Television.
Campaign contributions and expenditures.
Disclosure requirements for media advertisements, §163-278.38Z.
Teller's check.
Good funds settlement act, §45A-3.
Negotiable instruments, §25-3-104.
Temporarily.
Hospitals, §131E-83.
Temporary.
Public assistance program, §108A-24.
Temporary appraiser licensure or certification.
Real estate appraisers, §93E-1-4.
Temporary container.
Cremation, §90-210.41.
Temporary employees.
Professional employer organizations, §58-89A-5.
Tenant.
Expedited evictions, §42-59.
Tenant year.
Agricultural leases, §42-23.

DEFINED TERMS —Cont'd
Tender.
Oil and gas conservation, §113-389.
Term.
UCC, §25-1-201.
Terminal.
Gasoline and oil inspection, §119-15.
Gasoline tax, §105-449.60.
Terminally ill.
Viatical life insurance settlements, §58-58-205.
Terminal operator.
Gasoline and oil inspection, §119-15.
Gasoline tax, §105-449.60.
Terminal supplier.
Motor fuel, §75-81.
Terminal transfer system.
Gasoline tax, §105-449.60.
Terminate.
Insurance producers, §58-33-10.
Sales representative commissions, §66-190.
Termination.
Farm machinery, §66-180.
Health maintenance organizations, §58-67-88.
Leases, UCC, §25-2A-103, (1).
Sales, §25-2-106.
Termination of insurance coverage.
Insurance information and privacy protection act, §58-39-15.
Termination of mining, §74-49.
Termination statement.
Secured transactions, §25-9-102, (a).
Term of a trust.
Principal and income act, §37A-1-102.
Terms of the structured settlement, §1-543.11.
Territory.
Alcoholic beverages, §18B-1201.
Territory of the United States.
Trust companies, §53-301, (a).
Testimony of witness unavailable.
Probate of attested written will, §31-18.1, (c).
Theatre.
Motion pictures, §75C-2.
Therapeutic deception.
Psychotherapy patient/client sexual exploitation act, §90-21.41.
Therapeutic foster home, §131D-10.2.
Therapeutic recreation.
Personnel certification, §90C-4, (f).
Third party.
Sublease of motor vehicle and loan assumption arranging, §20-106.2, (a).
Year 2000 liability, §66-296.
Third party administrator, §58-56-2.
Interim insurance claims payment, §58-2-235, (d).
Workers' compensation.
Self-insurance, §58-47-150.
Workers' compensation self-insurance.
Employer groups, §58-47-60.
Third-party expert.
Divorce, §50-71.
Third tier subcontractor.
Liens, §44A-17.
This state.
Savings and loan associations, §54B-4.
Taxation, §105-134.1.
Threatened species.
Endangered wildlife, §113-331.
Plant protection and conservation, §106-202.12.
Three counties.
Lake Wylie marine commission, §77-30.

DEFINED TERMS —Cont'd
Thresholds.
Mortgages, high cost home loans, §24-1.1E, (a).
Throughput.
Ports authority income tax, §105-130.41, (c).
Ports authority individual income tax, §105-151.22, (c).
Time deposits, §53-1.
Timekeeper.
Boxing commission, §143-651.
Timely postdelivery care.
Drive-thru deliveries, §58-3-169, (e).
Time share, §93A-41.
Condominiums, §47C-1-103.
Time share instrument, §93A-41.
Time share program, §93A-41.
Time share project, §93A-41.
Time share registrar, §93A-41.
Time share salesmen, §93A-41.
Time share unit, §93A-41.
Tip.
Wage and hour act, §95-25.2.
Tipped employee.
Wage and hour act, §95-25.2.
Tire.
Scrap tire disposal, §130A-309.53.
Tire disposal tax, §105-187.15.
Tire collector.
Scrap tire disposal, §130A-309.53.
Tire-derived fuel.
Solid waste management, §130A-290, (a).
Tire hauler.
Scrap tire disposal, §130A-309.53.
Tire processor.
Scrap tire disposal, §130A-309.53.
Tire retailer.
Scrap tire disposal, §130A-309.53.
Tissue banks.
Anatomical gifts, §130A-403.
Title II.
Water and air resources, §143-213.
Title III.
Water and air resources, §143-213.
Title IV.
Water and air resources, §143-213.
Title IV-A.
Public assistance program, §108A-24.
Title transaction.
Marketable title, §47B-8.
Title V.
Water and air resources, §143-213.
Title V account.
Water and air resources, §143-213.
Title XXI.
Children's health insurance program, §108A-70.18.
Tobacco product.
Taxation, §105-113.4.
Youth access to tobacco products, §14-313, (a).
Tobacco product component business.
Tobacco trust fund commission, §143-716.
Tobacco product manufacturer.
Tobacco reserve fund, §66-290.
Tobacco-related business.
Tobacco trust fund commission, §143-716.
Tobacco-related employment.
Tobacco trust fund commission, §143-716.
To buy.
Public activities, §113-130.
To discover property.
Property taxes, §105-273.

DEFINED TERMS —Cont'd
TODS.
Tourist-oriented directional sign program, §136-140.15, (b).
To fish.
Public activities, §113-130.
To hunt.
Public activities, §113-130.
Ton.
Commercial feed law, §106-284.33.
Commercial fertilizer, §106-657.
Weights and measures, §81A-9.
Torment.
Cruelty to animals, §14-360, (c).
Torture.
Cruelty to animals, §14-360, (c).
To sell.
Public activities, §113-130.
To stabilize.
Emergency care coverage, §58-3-190, (g).
To take.
Public activities, §113-130.
Total actual investment in tangible property.
Corporate franchise tax, §105-122, (d).
Total assets.
Savings and loan associations, §54B-4.
Total loan amount.
Mortgages, high cost home loans, §24-1.1E, (a).
Totally and permanently disabled.
Property tax homestead exclusion, §105-277.1, (b).
Total net assets.
Elective share of surviving spouse, §30-3.2.
Total operating revenues.
Hospital authorities, §131E-32, (e).
Total return intrust.
Principal and income act, §37A-1-104.1.
Total unemployment.
Insurance, §96-8.
To trap.
Public activities, §113-130.
Touching.
Sex offenses, §14-27.1.
Tough man contestant, §143-651.
Tough man event, §143-651.
Tourism ABC establishment, §18B-101.
Tourism resort.
Alcoholic beverages, §18B-101.
Tourist-oriented business.
Tourist-oriented directional sign program, §136-140.15, (b).
Tourist-oriented facility.
Tourist-oriented directional sign program, §136-140.15, (b).
To use any pesticide in a manner inconsistent with its labeling.
Pesticide board, §143-460.
Tow.
Motor vehicles, §20-219.9.
Tower.
Motor vehicles, §20-219.9.
Towing fee.
Motor vehicles, §20-219.9.
Town.
Insurance, §58-84-5.
Public hospitals, §131E-6.
Public utilities, §62-3.
Toxic waste, §143-213.
TPA.
Third party administrators, §58-56-2.
Workers' compensation self-insurance, §58-47-150.
Employer groups, §58-47-60.

DEFINED TERMS —Cont'd
Tract.
Pollution control act, §113A-52.
Trade acceptance.
Banks, §53-55.
Trade school.
Proprietary schools, §115D-87.
Trade screening.
Motion pictures, §75C-2.
Trade secret, §66-152.
Traditional financial institutions.
Enterprise corporations, §53A-37.
Trail.
North Carolina trail system, §113A-85.
Trailers.
Motor vehicles, §20-4.01.
Trainee.
Real estate appraisers, §93E-1-4.
Trainee registration.
Real estate appraisers, §93E-1-4.
Training.
Automated external defibrillator (AED), §90-21.15, (b).
Transact business with the general public.
Private trust companies, §53-363, (a).
Transaction.
Electronic commerce in government, §66-58.2.
Electronic transactions, §66-312.
Transaction account.
Insurance information privacy, §56-39-76.
Transfer.
Fraudulent transfers, §39-23.1.
Insurers supervision, §58-30-10.
Motor vehicles, §20-341.
Oil and hazardous substance control, §143-215.77.
Structured settlement protection, §1-543.11.
Sublease of motor vehicle and loan assumption arranging, §20-106.2, (a).
Transfers to minors, §33A-1.
Water, §143-215.22G.
Transferability.
Sales, §25-2-105.
Transferable record.
Electronic transactions, §66-326, (a).
Transfer agreement.
Structured settlement protection, §1-543.11.
Transferee.
Motor vehicles, §20-341.
Transferor.
Asset-backed securities facilitation, §53-425.
Custodial trusts, §33B-1.
Motor vehicles, §20-341.
Transfers to minors, §33A-1.
Transferred.
Solid waste, §153A-421.
Transferring insurer.
Assumption reinsurance, §58-10-25, (a).
Transfer statement.
Secured transactions title transfers upon default, §25-9-619, (a).
Transliterating.
Interpreters and transliterators licensure act, §90D-3.
Transliterator.
Interpreters and transliterators licensure act, §90D-3.
Transmission line.
Public utilities, §62-100.
Transmitting utility.
Secured transactions, §25-9-102, (a).

DEFINED TERMS —Cont'd
Transmix.
Gasoline tax, §105-449.60.
Transportation customer.
Piped natural gas tax, §105-187.40.
Transportation equipment.
Sales and use tax, §105-164.4B, (c).
Transportation improvement program.
Highway trust fund, §136-175.
Transport truck.
Gasoline tax, §105-449.60.
Trap and trace device.
Wiretaps, §15A-260.
Trash fishing, §113-185, (b).
Trauma.
Nursing pools, §131E-154.2.
Traveler's check.
Negotiable instruments, §25-3-104.
Tread.
Motor vehicles, §20-122.1.
Tread depth.
Motor vehicles, §20-122.1.
Treasurer.
Housing trust, §122E-2.
Political campaigns, §163-278.6.
Unclaimed property act, §116B-52.
Treated.
Seed law, §106-277.2.
Treatment.
Dry-cleaning solvent cleanup act, §143-215.104B, (b).
Medical care of minors, §§90-21.2, 90-21.3.
Patient medical records, confidentiality of, §130A-12.
Solid waste management, §130A-290, (a).
Treatment facility.
Incompetency, §35A-1101.
Treatment technique requirement.
Drinking water, §130A-313.
Treatment works, §143-213.
Trial division.
Involuntary commitment, §122C-268.1, (g).
Mental health, §122C-268.1.
Tribe.
Child custody jurisdiction and enforcement, §50A-102.
Tribunal.
Interstate family support, §52C-1-101.
Rules of professional conduct, Prof. Cond. Rule 1.0.
Tricycle.
Child bicycle safety act, §20-171.8.
Triggering event.
Standby guardianship, §35A-1370.
Trigger or rescue funds.
Public campaign financing fund, §163-278.62.
Truck tractors.
Motor vehicles, §20-4.01.
True lease.
Global TransPark authority, §63A-2.
True mileage, §20-342.
Truncated coverage.
Credit insurance, §58-57-5.
Trust, §36A-22.1.
Compensation of trustees and other fiduciaries, §32-53.
Modification and termination of irrevocable trusts, §36A-125.1.
Uniform trust act, §36A-60.
Trust business.
Trust companies, §53-301, (a).

DEFINED TERMS —Cont'd
Trust company, §53-301, (a).
Custodial trusts, §33B-1.
Transfers to minors, §33A-1.
Trustee, §36A-22.1.
Community trust for persons with severe chronic disabilities, §36A-59.11.
Gasoline tax, §105-449.60.
Medical service corporations, §58-65-166, (b).
Modification and termination of irrevocable trusts, §36A-125.1.
Mortgages and deeds of trust.
Sales under power of sale, §45-21.1, (b).
Principal and income act, §§37A-1-102, 37A-1-104.1.
Recreation and natural heritage, §113-77.6.
RICO act, §75D-3.
Uniform trust act, §36A-60.
Trust fund.
Highways, §136-175.
Trust indenture.
Housing authorities, §157-3.
Trust institution.
Trust companies, §53-301, (a).
Trust marketing.
Trust companies, §53-301, (a).
Trust office.
Trust companies, §53-301, (a).
Tuition.
Tuition waiver for senior citizens, §115B-1.
Tuition assistance.
Tuition of active duty personnel in armed forces, §116-143.3, (a).
Turnpike authority, §136-89.181.
Turnpike project, §136-89.181.
Turnpike system, §136-89.181.
24-hour facility.
Mental health, §122C-3.
Two-car aerial passenger tramway.
Safety, §95-117.
Two-cent sales taxes.
Local sales and use tax, §105-521, (a).
Two counties.
High Rock lake marine commission, §77-50.
Two-party exchange.
Gasoline tax, §105-449.60.
Type A violation.
Mental health, development disability, substance abuse, §122C-24.1, (a).
Type B violation.
Mental health, development disability, substance abuse, §122C-24.1, (a).
UCR.
State medical plan, §135-40.1.
U-drive-it passenger vehicle, §20-4.01.
Regional transit authority vehicle rental tax, §105-551.
U-drive-it vehicles, §20-4.01.
Ultimate user.
Controlled substances, §90-87.
Ultimate warrior match, §143-651.
Unallocated annuity contract.
Insurance guaranty associations, §58-62-16.
Unauthorized.
UCC, §25-1-201.
Unauthorized insurer.
Insurance information and privacy protection act, §58-39-15.
Unauthorized substance.
Unauthorized substances taxes, §105-113.106.

DEFINED TERMS —Cont'd
Unauthorized trust activity.
Trust companies, §53-301, (a).
Unavailability as a witness.
Evidence, §8C-1, Rule 804, (a).
Unavailable.
Local government during emergencies, §162B-7.
Unavoidably unsafe.
Products liability for prescription drugs, §99B-6.
Uncertificated registered public obligation, §159E-2.
Uncertificated security.
Investment securities, §25-8-102.
Uncovered expenditures.
Health maintenance organizations, §58-67-5, (p).
Underage person.
Alcoholic beverages, §18B-120.
Underground utility.
Contractors, §87-101.
Undertaking.
City and town cooperation, §160A-460.
Under the direct supervision of a certified applicator.
Structural pest control act, §106-65.24.
Under the influence of an impairing substance.
Motor vehicles, §20-4.01.
Underwrite.
Managing general agents, §58-34-2, (a).
Underwriting.
Third party administrators, §58-56-2.
Workers' compensation.
Self-insurance.
Employer groups, §58-47-60.
Third-party administrator and service companies, §58-47-150.
Undisciplined juvenile.
Delinquent or undisciplined juveniles, §7B-1501.
Department of juvenile justice and delinquency prevention, §143B-515.
Undistributed income.
Principal and income act, §37A-3-303, (a).
Undivided profits.
Banking, §53-1.
Undue family hardship.
Unemployment insurance, §96-8.
Unemancipated minor.
Parental or judicial consent to abortion, §90-21.6.
Unemployment.
Insurance, §96-8.
Unemployment compensation, §96-17, (d).
Unemployment insurance, §96-8.
Unethical acts.
Speech and language pathologists and audiologists licensure, §90-301A.
Unethical conduct.
Chiropractic, §90-154.2.
Unethical practices.
Speech and language pathologists and audiologists licensure, §90-301A.
Unfair methods of competition.
Unfair trade practices, §58-63-15.
Unfair trade practice act.
False advertising, §58-29-5.
Unfair trade practices, §66-73.
Unfortified wine.
Alcoholic beverages, §18B-101.
Alcohol taxation, §105-113.68.
Uniform application.
Insurance producers, §58-33-10.
Uniform business entity application.
Insurance producers, §58-33-10.

DEFINED TERMS —Cont'd
Uniformed services voter.
Military absentee voting, §163-246.
Uniform manual.
Roads and highways, §136-30, (d).
Uniform portal process.
Mental health, §122C-3.
Unimpaired capital fund.
Banking, §53-1.
Unincorporated entity.
Business corporations, §55-1-40.
Nonprofit corporations, §55A-1-40.
Uninsured.
Children's health insurance program, §108A-70.18.
Union school, §115C-75, (a).
Unit, §47A-3.
Aeronautics, §63-79.
Armories, §127A-161.
City and town cooperation, §160A-460.
Condominiums, §47C-1-103.
Counties, §153A-217.
Local government bonds, §159-44.
Local government finance, §§159-7, 159-160.
Property taxes, §105-277.2.
Time shares, §93A-41.
Unit designation, §47A-3.
Unit dose medication system.
Pharmacy practice, §90-85.3, (u).
United States.
Business corporations, §55-1-40.
Nonprofit corporations, §55A-1-40.
Soil and water conservation districts, §139-3.
Unit of local government.
City and town cooperation, §160A-460.
Counties, §153A-421.
Global TransPark development zone act, §158-32.
Local government finance, §159-160.
Local government fiscal information, §120-30.42.
Project development financing debt instruments, §159-102.
Public health generally, §130A-2.
Regional councils, §160A-470.
Regional natural gas district, §160A-661, (b).
Regional public transportation, §160A-601.
Regional sports authorities, §160A-479.
Regional transportation authorities, §160A-631.
Septic tank systems, §130A-343.1, (b).
Solid waste, §159I-3, (a).
Solid waste management, §130A-290, (a).
Use of state funds by non-state entities, §143-6.2, (a).
Water treatment facility operators, §90A-20.1.
Unit of local government's chief administrative official.
Regional natural gas district, §160A-661, (b).
Regional public transportation, §160A-601.
Regional transportation authorities, §160A-631.
Unit owner, §47A-3.
Condominiums, §47C-1-103.
Unit owners' associations.
Condominiums, §47C-1-103.
Unitrust amount.
Principal and income act, §37A-1-104.1.
Units sold.
Tobacco reserve fund, §66-290.
University.
Higher education bonds, §116D-1.
University of North Carolina, §116-41.1.
University enterprises.
University of North Carolina, §116-41.1.

DEFINED TERMS —Cont'd
University property.
University of North Carolina, §116-44.3.
Unlawful conduct.
Civil no-contact orders, §50C-1.
Workplace violence prevention, §95-265.
Unlawful telecommunications device, §14-113.5.
Unmanipulated manures.
Commercial fertilizer, §106-657.
Unmarked human burial.
Burial sites, §70-28.
Unobscured.
Campaign contributions and expenditures.
Disclosure requirements for media advertisements, §163-278.38Z.
Unreserved credit balance.
Budget, general fund, §143-15.2, (a).
Unrestricted use standards.
Brownfields property reuse tax, §130A-310.31, (b).
Contamination of site, §143B-279.9, (d).
Unsolicited.
Computer crimes, §14-453.
Unsolicited telephone call.
Telephone solicitations, §75-101.
Unwithdrawn deposit.
Right of survivorship in bank deposits, §41-2.1, (e).
Unzoned area.
Junkyard control, §136-143.
Outdoor advertising control, §136-128.
Upgrading supplement requirement.
Revenue bonds, §159-97.
Upland game birds.
Conservation, §113-129.
Urban area.
Outdoor advertising control, §136-128.
Urban area revitalization project, §160A-536, (c).
Urban forester, §89B-2.
Urban service districts.
Consolidated city-county, §§160B-3 to 160B-6.
Urn.
Cremation, §90-210.41.
Use.
Sales and use tax, §105-164.3.
Tobacco taxation, §105-113.4.
Used for profit.
Public morals, §19-1.1.
Used motor vehicle dealer.
Motor vehicles, §20-286.
Used oil.
Regulation of rerefined or reprocessed oil, §119-13.1.
Solid waste management, §130A-290, (b).
Used oil recycling facility.
Solid waste management, §130A-290, (b).
Use of public land.
Environmental policy act, §113A-9.
User.
Criminal justice information network, §143-660.
Electronic surveillance, §15A-286.
Use tax.
Sales and use tax, §105-164.3.
Uniform sales and use tax administration act, §105-164.42B.
Usual, customary and reasonable.
State medical plan, §135-40.1.
Utility.
Road construction, §136-102.6, (e).
Unclaimed property act, §116B-52.

DEFINED TERMS —Cont'd
Utility or public service enterprise.
Local government bonds, §159-44.
Utility owner.
Contractors, §87-101.
Utility vehicles, §20-4.01.
Utilization review, §58-50-61, (a).
Utilization review organization, §58-50-61, (a).
Vacant and unappropriated lands.
State lands, §146-64.
Vacation rental, §42A-4.
Vacation rental agreement, §42A-4.
Vaccination.
Rabies, §130A-184.
Vaccine-related injury, §130A-422.
Valid lien.
Fraudulent transfers, §39-23.1.
Valuation.
Property taxes, §105-273.
Value.
Exempt property from enforcement of claims of creditors, §1C-1601, (b).
Judgments, §1C-1601.
Letters of credit, §25-5-102, (b).
Secured transactions third party assignees, §25-9-403, (a).
UCC, §25-1-201.
Variety.
Seed law, §106-277.2.
Vault.
Cemeteries, §65-48.
Vegetable plants, §106-284.16.
Vegetable seeds, §106-277.2.
Vehicle, §§14-399, (i), 20-4.01, (49).
Alcoholic beverages, §18B-120.
Criminal procedure, §15A-101.
Gross receipts tax on short-term leases or rentals, §153A-156, (e).
Motor vehicles, §§20-4.01, 20-137.7, 20-138.1.
Rental car companies selling insurance, §58-33-17, (a).
Rental cars, §66-201.
Vehicle recycling.
Motor vehicles, §20-137.7.
Vending facilities.
Aid to the blind, §111-42, (d).
Budgets, vending facilities, §143-12.1, (h).
Community colleges, §115D-2.
Local government finance, §159-7.
School budgets, §115C-423.
University of North Carolina, §116-2.
Vendor.
Seed law, §106-277.2.
Verification or proof.
Notaries, §10A-3.
Vessel.
Boating safety, §75A-2.
Conservation, §113-130.
Liens on personal property, §44A-1.
Oil and hazardous substance control, §143-215.77.
Vested right.
City and town zoning, §160A-385.1, (b).
Counties, §153A-344.1.
Vested trust.
Legislative ethics act, §120-85.
Veteran, §§126-81, 165-3.
Children of war veterans scholarships, §165-20.
Employment preference for veterans, §128-15, (b).
Minor spouses of veterans, §165-17.
Minor veterans, §165-13.

DEFINED TERMS —Cont'd
Veteran —Cont'd
Priority in employment assistance for United States armed forces veterans, §165-44.2.
Recreation, §165-25.
Veterans' organization, §165-3.
Veterans' recreation project, §165-25.
Veterinarian, §90-181.
Veterinary clinic, §90-181.1, (b).
Veterinary hospital, §90-181.1, (b).
Veterinary license, §90-181.
Veterinary medicine, §90-181.
Veterinary student intern, §90-181.
Veterinary student preceptee, §90-181.
Veterinary technician, §90-181.
Viatical settlement broker.
Viatical life insurance settlements, §58-58-205.
Viatical settlement contract.
Viatical life insurance settlements, §58-58-205.
Viatical settlement provider.
Viatical life insurance settlements, §58-58-205.
Viatical settlement purchase agreement.
Viatical life insurance settlements, §58-58-205.
Viatical settlement purchaser.
Viatical life insurance settlements, §58-58-205.
Viaticated policy.
Viatical life insurance settlements, §58-58-205.
Viator.
Viatical life insurance settlements, §58-58-205.
Victim.
Crime victims, §§15A-824, 15A-830, (a).
Crime victims financial recovery assistance act, §15B-32.
Restitution, §15A-1340.34.
Victims compensation, §15B-2.
Victim of a sexual offense.
Address confidentiality program, §15C-2.
Victim of domestic violence.
Address confidentiality program, §15C-2.
Victim of stalking.
Address confidentiality program, §15C-2.
Video gaming machine, §14-306.1, (c).
Village.
Public hospitals, §131E-6.
Violations of the law.
Public records, §132-1.4.
Virgin newsprint.
Newspaper taxation, §105-102.6.
Virulent hog-cholera virus, §106-316.2.
Visible.
Junkyard control, §136-143.
Outdoor advertising control, §136-128.
Visually impaired person, §111-11.
Vital records.
Public health generally, §130A-2.
Vocational rehabilitation.
Industrial commission utilization of rehabilitation professionals, I.C. Util. Rehab. Profs. I.
Volatile substances capable of producing toxic effect.
Household cleaners, §66-85.
Volume control handset.
Deaf and the hard of hearing, §143B-216.30.
Voluntary dissolution.
Savings and loan associations, §54B-4.
Savings banks, §54C-4, (b).
Volunteer.
Assault on school employees or volunteers, §14-33, (c).
Civil procedure, §1-539.11.

DEFINED TERMS —Cont'd
Volunteer firefighter.
Tuition waiver for senior citizens, §115B-1.
Volunteer transportation.
Public utilities, §62-289.3.
Vote.
Nonprofit corporations, §55A-1-40.
Voting booth.
Elections, §163-165.
Voting enclosure.
Elections, §163-165.
Voting group.
Business corporations, §55-1-40.
Voting place.
Elections, §163-165.
Voting security.
Insurance holding companies, §58-19-5.
Voting shares.
Shareholder protection act, §55-9-01, (b).
Voting system.
Elections, §163-165.
Wage.
Child support, §110-129.
Governmental employees and social security, §135-20.
Tax withholding, §105-163.1.
Unemployment insurance, §96-8.
Wage and hour act, §95-25.2.
Ward.
Incompetency, §§35A-1101, 35A-1202.
Veterans, §34-2.
Warehouse.
Cotton warehousing, §106-451.7.
Warehouseman.
Cotton warehousing, §106-451.7.
UCC, §25-7-102.
Warehouse receipt.
UCC, §25-1-201.
Warehousing and distribution.
Tax incentives for new and expanding businesses, §105-129.2.
Warehousing and wholesale trade.
Industrial development fund, §143B-437.01, (a1).
Warning sign.
Overhead high-voltage line safety, §95-229.6.
Warrant.
Child custody jurisdiction and enforcement, §50A-102.
Warrant for arrest.
Criminal process, §15A-304.
Wartime.
Children of war veterans scholarships, §165-20.
Waste.
Oil and gas conservation, §113-389.
Solid waste management, §130A-290, (a).
Water and air resources, §143-213.
Water pollution control system operators, §90A-46.
Waste treatment management practice, §143-213.
Wastewater accounts.
Clean water loans, §159G-3.
Wastewater collection system.
Clean water loans, §159G-3.
Wastewater treatment works.
Clean water loans, §159G-3.
Water column.
Cultivation of shellfish, §113-201.1.
Watercraft, §75A-33.
Littering, §14-399, (i).
Water distribution system.
Metropolitan water districts, §162A-32, (a).
Water pollution, §143-213.

DEFINED TERMS —Cont'd
Water pollution control facility.
Pollution control, §§159C-3, 159D-3.
Water pollution control system.
Operators, §90A-46.
Water quality protection.
Cooperative state-local coalition water quality protection plans, §143-214.14, (a).
Waters.
Dry-cleaning solvent cleanup act, §143-215.104B, (b).
Oil and hazardous substance control, §143-215.77.
Water and air resources, §143-212.
Watershed, §143-213.
Watershed improvement project.
Soil and water conservation, §139-3.
Watershed improvement work.
Soil and water conservation, §139-3.
Waterslide.
Safety, §95-111.3, (h).
Waters of this state.
Aquatic weed control, §113A-221.
Boating safety, §75A-2.
Water supply accounts.
Clean water loans, §159G-3.
Water supply system.
Clean water loans, §159G-3.
Water supply well.
Well construction, §87-85.
Water system, §162A-2.
Metropolitan water districts, §162A-32, (a).
Water treatment facility.
Operators, §90A-20.1.
Water treatment or purification plant.
Metropolitan water districts, §162A-32, (a).
Weapon of like kind.
Deadly weapons, §14-269.1.
Weapon of mass death and destruction.
Civil disorders, §14-288.8.
Weapons.
Educational property, §14-269.2, (a).
Weed.
Pesticide board, §143-460.
Weed seeds.
Seed law, §106-277.2.
Weekly benefit amount.
Unemployment insurance, §96-8.
Weigh.
Weights and measures, §81A-51.
Weight.
Weights and measures, §§81A-9, 81A-51.
Well.
Well construction, §87-85.
Well contractor.
Certification, §87-98.2.
Well contractor activity.
Well contractor certification, §87-98.2.
Well driller.
Well construction, §87-85.
Well seal.
Well construction, §87-85.
Wet marine and transportation insurance.
Surplus lines, §58-21-10.
Wharfage.
Ports authority income tax, §105-130.41, (c).
Ports authority individual income tax, §105-151.22, (c).
When he deems himself insecure.
Leases, UCC.
Option to accelerate at will, §25-2A-109, (1).

DEFINED TERMS —Cont'd
White goods.
Solid waste management, §130A-290, (a).
White-tailed deer.
Deer, production and sale for commercial purposes, §106-549.97, (c).
Wholesale dealer.
Tobacco taxation, §105-113.4.
Wholesale distribution.
Wholesale prescription drug distributors, §106-145.2.
Wholesale distribution facility.
Dry-cleaning solvent cleanup act, §143-215.104B, (b).
Wholesale distributor, §106-145.2.
Dry-cleaning solvent cleanup act, §143-215.104B, (b).
Wholesale merchant.
Property taxes, §105-273.
Sales and use tax, §105-164.3.
Wholesaler.
Alcohol taxation, §105-113.68.
Beer franchises, §18B-1301.
Commercial fertilizer, §106-657.
Motor vehicles, §20-286.
Registration of prescription drug wholesalers, §106-140.1, (j).
Seed law, §106-277.2.
Wholesale sale.
Sales and use tax, §105-164.3.
Wholesale trade.
Tax incentives for new and expanding businesses, §105-129.2.
Widow.
Workers' compensation, §97-2.
Widower.
Workers' compensation, §97-2.
Wild animals.
Conservation, §113-129.
Endangered wildlife, §113-331.
Wild birds.
Conservation, §113-129.
Wilderness program.
Delinquent and undisciplined juveniles, §7B-1501.
Wildlife.
Conservation, §113-129.
Pesticide board, §143-460.
Resources commission, §143-238.
Wildlife commission.
High Rock lake marine commission, §77-50.
Lake lure marine commission, §77-80.
Lake Wylie marine commission, §77-30.
Wildlife protector.
Conservation, §113-128.
Wildlife refuge.
Conservation, §113-129.
Wildlife resources.
Commission, §143-238.
Conservation, §113-129.
Offshore oil and gas activities, §143-215.94B, (b).
Wildlife resources commission, §113-128.
Will.
Discipline and disability rules of state bar, Bar Rules & Regs., B, §.0103.
Willful.
Insurance rates, §58-40-5.
Willful or wanton conduct.
Punitive damages, §1D-5.
Wilmington tariff, terminal tariff.
Ports authority income tax, §105-130.41, (c).

DEFINED TERMS —Cont'd
Wilmington tariff, terminal tariff —Cont'd
Ports authority individual income tax, §105-151.22, (c).
Wind energy equipment.
Tax credits for renewable energy equipment facility construction, §105-130.28, (b).
Wine.
Alcohol taxation, §105-113.68.
Wine producer, §18B-1000.
Winery.
Alcoholic beverages, §18B-1201.
Wine shipper permittee.
Alcoholic beverages tax, §105-113.68.
Wine wholesaler.
Alcoholic beverages, §18B-1201.
Wire communication.
Electronic surveillance, §15A-286.
Wireless enhanced 911 system.
E-911 system for wireless communications, §62A-21.
Wireless fund.
E-911 system for wireless communications, §62A-21.
Wireless 911 system.
E-911 system for wireless communications, §62A-21.
Withdrawable accounts.
Savings and loan associations, §54B-4.
Withholding agent.
Tax withholding, §105-163.1.
Withholdings.
Job development investment grant program, §143B-437.51.
Without authority.
Computer trespass, §14-458, (a).
Witness.
Victims and witnesses, §15A-824.
Witnesses, §15A-811.
Women's business enterprise.
Global TransPark authority, §63A-19.
Woodland, §113-57.
Regulation of open fires, §113-60.22.
Setting fire to woodlands, §14-138.1.
Work.
Public assistance program, §108A-24.
Unemployment insurance, §96-8.
Work day.
Contractors, §87-101.
Workers' compensation, §97-2.
Disability income plan, §135-101.
Workers' compensation act.
Industrial commission managed care organizations, I.C. Managed Care Orgs. R. II.
Work first diversion assistance.
Public assistance program, §108A-24.
Work first family assistance.
Public assistance program, §108A-24.
Work first program.
Public assistance program, §108A-24.
Work first program assistance.
Public assistance program, §108A-24.
Work first services.
Public assistance program, §108A-24.
Working capital, §58-67-5, (j).
Working days.
Pollution control act, §113A-52.
Work loss.
Victims compensation, §15B-2.
Work of art.
Sales, §25C-10.
Sales and use tax exemptions, §105-164.13.

DEFINED TERMS —Cont'd
Work of art —Cont'd
State monuments, §100-2.
Workplace.
City and town personnel, §160A-169.
Counties, §153A-99, (b).
Worksite.
Safety and health, §95-250.
Work week.
Wage and hour act, §95-25.2.
Wreckers.
Motor vehicles, §20-4.01.
Property-hauling vehicle registration fees, §20-88, (b).
Write-off.
Statewide accounts receivable program, §147-86.20.
Writings.
Evidence, §8C-1, Rule 1001.
UCC, §25-1-201.
Written.
UCC, §25-1-201.
Yard trash.
Solid waste management, §130A-290, (a).
Year.
Continuing legal education, Bar Rules & Regs., D, §.1501.
Educational personnel, §115C-325, (a).
Judicial retirement, §135-53.
Legislative retirement system, §120-4.8.
Local government finance, §159-2.
Retirement, §128-21.
State retirement system, §135-1.
Year 2000 processing, §66-296.
Youth development center.
Delinquent and undisciplined juveniles, §7B-1501.
Department of juvenile justice and delinquency prevention, §143B-515.
Zone.
Global TransPark development zone, §158-32.

DEFORMED CHILDREN.
Prohibited exhibition, §110-20.1.

DEGREES OF KINSHIP.
Computation, §§29-5, 104A-1.
Intestate succession, §29-7.

DELINQUENCY HISTORY LEVELS, §§7B-2507, 7B-2508, (b).
Disposition chart, §7B-2508, (f).
Level one to level three dispositions, §7B-2508, (b) to (e).

DELINQUENCY PROCEEDINGS, INSURERS.
Generally, §§58-30-1 to 58-30-310.
See INSURER SUPERVISION, REHABILITATION AND LIQUIDATION.

DELINQUENT AND UNDISCIPLINED JUVENILES, §§7B-1500 to 7B-2827.
Absconding juveniles.
Returning from one state to another.
Interstate compact on juveniles generally, §§7B-2800 to 7B-2827.
See INTERSTATE COMPACT ON JUVENILES.
Taking juvenile into temporary custody, §7B-1900.
Transporting to nearest secure facility, §7B-1901, (c).
Adjudication of juvenile, §7B-2411.
Delinquent adjudication not considered conviction of criminal offense nor cause for forfeiture of citizenship rights, §7B-2412.

DELINQUENT AND UNDISCIPLINED JUVENILES —Cont'd
Adjudicatory hearing.
Admissibility of statement made by juvenile to juvenile court counselor during preliminary inquiry, §7B-2408.
Admissions by juvenile, when accepted by court, §7B-2407.
Clear and convincing evidence, petition alleging undisciplined behavior, §7B-2409.
Conduct of hearing, §7B-2405.
Continuance, §7B-2406.
Due process rights protected, §7B-2405.
Jeopardy attaches, §7B-2414.
Rights of juvenile and parent, guardian or custodian protected to assure due process, §7B-2405.
Rules of evidence, §7B-2408.
Time and place for holding, §7B-2403.
Admissions by juvenile, when accepted by court.
Duties of court before accepting, §7B-2407, (a).
Factual basis for admission determination, §7B-2407, (c).
Product of informed choice determination by court, §7B-2407, (b).
Statement made to juvenile court counselor during preliminary inquiry, §7B-2408.
Adoption.
Bringing juvenile delinquents into state for placement or adoption, §§7B-3700 to 7B-3705.
See CHILD PLACEMENT.
Sending child out of state for purposes of placement, §§7B-3702 to 7B-3705.
Adult, prosecution of juvenile as.
Commission of offense after superior court conviction, §7B-1604, (b).
Emancipated juvenile prosecuted as adult for commission of criminal offense, §7B-1604, (a).
Juvenile committing criminal offense on or after sixteenth birthday, §7B-1604, (a).
Transfer of jurisdiction to superior court, §§7B-2200 to 7B-2204.
Appeal, §7B-2603.
Age governs for purposes of determining jurisdiction.
Jurisdiction over delinquent juveniles, §7B-1601, (a).
Jurisdiction over undisciplined juvenile, §7B-1600, (a).
Alcohol rehabilitation center.
Taking absconding juvenile into temporary custody, §7B-1900.
Duties of persons taking juvenile into temporary custody, §7B-1901, (a).
Transporting to approved secure custody facility, §7B-1901, (c).
Allowing family opportunity to meet needs of juvenile, §7B-2501, (d).
Alternative dispositions for delinquent juveniles, §7B-2506.
Alternative dispositions for undisciplined juvenile, §7B-2503.
Amendment of petition, §7B-2400.
Appeal of final order of court.
County appeals, limitations, §7B-2604, (c).
Modification or alteration of original order upon affirmation of order by appellate court, §7B-2606.
Notice of appeal, §7B-2602.
Parties, §7B-2604, (a).

DELINQUENT AND UNDISCIPLINED JUVENILES —Cont'd
Appeal of final order of court —Cont'd
Release of juvenile pending disposition of appeal, §7B-2605.
Review of final order before court of appeals, §7B-2602.
Right to appeal, §7B-2602.
Transfer decision, §7B-2603.
State appeal, limitations, §7B-2604, (b).
Temporary order affecting custody or placement pending disposition, §7B-2605.
Time for filing notice, §7B-2602.
Transfer of jurisdiction of juvenile to superior court for prosecution as adult.
Abuse of discretion, review by superior court, §7B-2603, (a).
Appeal to court of appeals, §7B-2603, (d).
Appeal to superior court for hearing on record, §7B-2603, (a).
Interlocutory order, order of superior court considered, §7B-2603, (d).
Notice of appeal, §7B-2603, (a).
Pretrial release of juvenile, §7B-2603, (b).
Probable cause or underlying offense findings, superior court not to review, §7B-2603, (a).
Remanding case to juvenile court, §7B-2603, (c).
Transfer of case to superior court docket, §7B-2603, (a).
Waiver of right to raise issue of transfer before court of appeals, §7B-2603, (a).
Who may take appeal, §7B-2604.
Appearance of parent, guardian or custodian.
Contempt, failure to appear, §§7B-1805, (c), 7B-1806.
Excusing appearance, §7B-2700.
Requirement as to attending hearings, §7B-2700.
Appointment of counsel for indigent parent, guardian or custodian.
Summons to notify of right, §7B-1805, (b).
Appointment of counsel for juvenile, §7B-2000, (a).
Conclusive presumption of indigence, §7B-2000, (b).
Payment, §§7B-2002, 7B-2704.
Secure or nonsecure custody hearing, §7B-1906, (c).
Audio and video transmission, continued custody hearing conducted by, §7B-1906, (h).
Authority over parents of juveniles adjudicated delinquent or undisciplined.
Appearance at hearings required, §7B-2700.
Compliance with orders, §7B-2703, (a).
Contempt for failure to comply with provisions, §7B-2706.
Cooperation with and assisting juvenile in complying with terms and conditions of probation or orders, §7B-2703, (b).
Court-appointed attorneys' fees, ordering payment, §7B-2704.
Employment discrimination unlawful for compliance with provisions of articles, §7B-2705.
Excusing appearance of parent, §7B-2700.
Insurance coverage to cover medical costs while juvenile in out-of-home custody, ordering, §7B-2704.
Medical, surgical, psychiatric, psychological or other evaluation or treatment ordered, §7B-2702.

DELINQUENT AND UNDISCIPLINED JUVENILES —Cont'd
Authority over parents of juveniles adjudicated delinquent or undisciplined —Cont'd
Parental responsibility classes, ordering parent to attend, §7B-2701.
Probation supervision fees or residential facility costs, ordering payment, §7B-2704.
Support of juvenile, payment ordered, §7B-2704.
Transportation for juvenile to keep appointment with juvenile court counselor, court ordering, §7B-2703, (a).
Beyond reasonable doubt quantum of proof.
Petition alleging juvenile delinquent, §7B-2409.
Black Mountain center.
Juvenile absconders, taking into temporary custody, §7B-1900.
Duties of persons taking juvenile into temporary custody, §7B-1901, (a).
Blood specimens.
Grounds for obtaining, §7B-2105, (b).
Nontestimonial identification order procedures, §§7B-2103 to 7B-2109.
Books, papers, documents, etc.
Disclosure by juvenile, §7B-2301, (b).
Disclosure by petitioner, §7B-2300, (c).
Bringing juvenile delinquents into state for placement or adoption, §§7B-3700 to 7B-3705.
See CHILD PLACEMENT.
Burden at adjudicatory hearing, §7B-2409.
Burden at secure or nonsecure custody hearing, §7B-1906, (d).
Chart of dispositions of delinquent juveniles.
Class of offense in delinquency history level, §7B-2508, (f).
Chief court counselor.
Defined, §7B-1501.
Delegation of court's authority to issue secure and nonsecure custody orders to, §7B-1902.
Establishment of intake services, §7B-1700.
Maintenance or records, confidentiality, §7B-3001, (a).
Citizenship rights, forfeiture.
Delinquent adjudication not cause for, §7B-2412.
Classification of offenses, §7B-2508, (a).
Consolidation of offenses, §7B-2508, (h).
Delinquency history levels, §§7B-2507, 7B-2508, (b).
Disposition chart, §7B-2508, (f).
Levels one to three dispositions, §7B-2508, (c) to (e).
Clear and convincing evidence.
Petition alleging undisciplined behavior, §7B-2409.
Secure or nonsecure custody hearing, §7B-1906, (d).
Clerk to maintain complete records, §7B-3001, (a).
Closure of hearing, §7B-2402.
Commencement of action by filing petition, §7B-1804, (a).
Commencement of proceeding in district other than that of juvenile's residence, §7B-1800, (a).
Commitment of delinquent juvenile to department of juvenile justice and delinquency prevention.
Commitment services in a program not located in a youth development center or detention facility, §7B-2513, (e).

DELINQUENT AND UNDISCIPLINED JUVENILES —Cont'd
Commitment of delinquent juvenile to department of juvenile justice and delinquency prevention —Cont'd
Placement in youth development center, §7B-2513.
Extended commitment, §7B-2515.
Post-release supervision, §§7B-2514, 7B-2516, (c).
Community service, juveniles ordered to perform, §7B-2506.
Complaint filed as petition, §7B-1803.
Juvenile court counselor determination, §7B-1702.
Juvenile court counselor's findings as to commission of certain nondivertible offenses, §7B-1702.
Notice to complainant on determination that petition should not be filed, §7B-1703, (c).
Time for filing after juvenile court counselor determination, §7B-1703, (b).
Compulsory school attendance law, excusing juvenile.
Delinquent juveniles, §7B-2506.
Undisciplined juveniles, §7B-2503.
Conditions of protective supervision.
Undisciplined juvenile placed under, §7B-2504.
Confidentiality of records and social reports, §7B-3000, (b).
Chief court counselor's records, §7B-3001, (a).
Department of juvenile justice and delinquency prevention records and files, §7B-3001, (c).
Law enforcement records and files, §7B-3001, (b).
Sealing of records, §7B-3000, (c).
Sharing of information between designated local agencies, §7B-3100.
Confinement in detention facility.
Alternative disposition for delinquent juvenile, §7B-2506.
Contempt of court for undisciplined juvenile, §7B-2505.
Consent of department of health and human services for purposes of placement of juvenile.
Bringing or sending juvenile into state or sending juvenile out of state, §§7B-3700 to 7B-3705.
Contempt.
Failure of parent, guardian or custodian to appear.
Show cause order for contempt, §7B-1806.
Summons to notify parent, guardian or custodian, §7B-1805, (c).
Undisciplined juveniles, failure to comply with disposition order, §7B-2505.
Continuance of adjudicatory hearing, §7B-2406.
Continued jurisdiction of court to modify or vacate order, §7B-2600, (c).
Continued jurisdiction until terminated by court order or emancipation of juvenile.
Jurisdiction over delinquent juveniles, §7B-1601, (a).
Jurisdiction over undisciplined juveniles, §7B-1600, (b).
Juvenile placed in youth development center for committing certain offenses, §7B-1602.
Continued secure or nonsecure custody hearing, §7B-1906.
Contributing to delinquency, §14-316.1.
Conviction of criminal offense, delinquent adjudication not considered, §7B-2412.
County appeals, limitations, §7B-2604, (c).

DELINQUENT AND UNDISCIPLINED JUVENILES —Cont'd
County or unit of government operating juvenile detention facility.
Required standards and rules, §7B-1905, (b).
Criminal process, provisions applicable to juvenile process, §7B-1806.
Criminal prosecution of juvenile as adult.
Commission of offense after superior court conviction, §7B-1604, (b).
Commission of offense by juvenile on or after sixteenth birthday, §7B-1604, (a).
Emancipated juvenile prosecuted as, §7B-1604, (a).
Transfer of jurisdiction of juvenile to superior court, §7B-2200.
Appeal of transfer order, §7B-2603, (a).
Appeal of superior court decision to court of appeals, §7B-2603, (d).
Appeal to superior court for hearing on record, §7B-2603, (a).
Authority of superior court on review, §7B-2603, (a).
Interlocutory order, superior court order considered, §7B-2603, (d).
Notice of appeal, §7B-2603, (a).
Pretrial release of juvenile, §7B-2603, (b).
Remanding case to juvenile court for adjudication or upholding transfer order, §7B-2603, (c).
Waiver of right to raise issue of transfer before court of appeal.
Failing to appeal transfer order to superior court, §7B-2603, (a).
Case not transferred, §7B-2203, (d).
Detention pending pretrial release, §7B-2204.
Detention pending transfer to department of correction, §7B-2204.
Fingerprinting juvenile transferred, §7B-2201.
Pretrial release, right once order entered, §7B-2204.
Probable cause found and transfer to superior court not required, §7B-2202, (e).
Probable cause hearing.
Burden of state, §7B-2202, (c).
Conducting, §7B-2202, (a).
Representation of state, juvenile, testimony and cross-examination of witnesses, §7B-2202, (b).
Time for conducting, §7B-2202, (a).
Waiver of right and stipulating to finding, §7B-2202, (d).
Probable cause not found, §7B-2202, (f).
Transfer hearing, §7B-2203, (a).
Factors considered for transfer, §7B-2203, (b).
Transfer order, §7B-2203, (c).
Curfew, imposition on delinquent juvenile, §7B-2506.
Custodial interrogation procedures.
Admissibility of in-custody admission or confession, §7B-2101, (b).
Admission into evidence of statement resulting from interrogation, court findings required, §7B-2101, (d).
Advising juvenile of rights, §7B-2101, (a).
Ceasing questioning when juvenile indicates a wish not to be questioned, §7B-2101, (c).
Custody of juvenile.
Administrative order, delegation of court's authority, §7B-1902.

DELINQUENT AND UNDISCIPLINED JUVENILES —Cont'd
Custody of juvenile —Cont'd
Authority of court to issue custody orders, §7B-1902.
Delegation of court's authority to chief court counselor or chief court counselor's counseling staff, §7B-1902.
Law enforcement procedures after juvenile taken into custody, §§7B-2100 to 7B-2109.
Secure or nonsecure custody, §§7B-1903 to 7B-1906.
Taking into temporary custody, §§7B-1900, 7B-1901.
Law enforcement, roles and permitted actions, §7B-2100.
Telephone communications, notices, orders, authorizations and requests, §7B-1907.
Day programs, disposition of delinquent juvenile, §7B-2506.
Definitions, §7B-1501.
Nontestimonial identification, §7B-2103.
Delinquency history levels.
Calculating, §7B-2507, (a).
Classification of offenses, §7B-2508.
Classification of prior adjudication from other jurisdictions, §7B-2507, (e).
Classification of prior offense, §7B-2507, (c).
Consolidation of offenses for disposition.
Adjudication of more than one offense during session, §7B-2508, (h).
Determination, §7B-2508, (b).
Dispositional chart, §7B-2508, (f).
Juvenile adjudicated delinquent for more than one offense in single session of district court, §7B-2507, (d).
Level one, community disposition, §7B-2508, (c).
Level two, intermediate disposition, §7B-2508, (d).
Level three, commitment, §7B-2508, (e).
Low, medium, high, §7B-2507, (c).
Minor offense, committed to level three disposition, §7B-2508, (g).
Points, assignments, §7B-2507, (b).
Prior adjudications.
Classification when from other jurisdiction, §7B-2507, (e).
Methods for proving, §7B-2507, (f).
Multiple adjudications obtained in one court session, §7B-2507, (d).
Delinquent juvenile.
Defined, §7B-1501.
Delivery of notification to school, §7B-3101, (a).
Department of juvenile justice and delinquency prevention, §§143B-511 to 143B-557.
See JUVENILE JUSTICE AND DELINQUENCY PREVENTION DEPARTMENT.
Determination of incapacity to proceed.
Cases in which juvenile alleged to be delinquent, §7B-2401.
Disclosure of evidence by petitioner or juvenile, §§7B-2300 to 7B-2303.
Disclosure of information by local agencies, §7B-3100.
Discovery and disclosure of evidence.
Continuing duty to disclose, §7B-2303.
Denying, restricting or deferring discovery or inspection, §7B-2302, (a).
Supporting affidavits or statements for in camera inspection, §7B-2302, (b).

DELINQUENT AND UNDISCIPLINED JUVENILES —Cont'd
Discovery and disclosure of evidence —Cont'd
Disclosure by juvenile.
Books, papers, documents, etc., inspection and copying by petitioner, §7B-2301, (b).
Names of persons to be called as witnesses, §7B-2301, (a).
Physical or mental examinations or tests, inspecting and copying, §7B-2301, (c).
Tests, measurements or experiments, inspection and copying, §7B-2301, (c).
Disclosure by petitioner.
Books, papers, documents, etc., inspection and copying by juvenile, §7B-2300, (c).
Furnishing names of persons to be called as witnesses, §7B-2300, (b).
Internal documents, records or memoranda not subject to disclosure, §7B-2300, (e).
Oral statements, divulging in written or recorded form, §7B-2300, (a).
Physical evidence, inspecting, examining and testing by juvenile, §7B-2300, (d).
Physical or mental examinations, juvenile to inspect and copy, §7B-2300, (d).
Record of witnesses under age of sixteen, copy furnished juvenile, §7B-2300, (b).
Tests, measurements or experiments, inspection and copying by juvenile, §7B-2300, (d).
Voluntary disclosures not prohibited, §7B-2300, (f).
Work product not subject to disclosure, §7B-2300, (e).
Written or recorded statements by juvenile, §7B-2300, (a).
Dismissal of petition with prejudice.
Allegations not proved, §7B-2411.
Dispositional hearing, §7B-2501, (a).
Court to proceed to hearing upon receipt of predisposition report, §7B-2413.
Opportunity to present evidence and advise court as to disposition in best interest of juvenile, §7B-2501, (b).
Dispositional order, §7B-2512.
Disposition chart, delinquent juveniles, §7B-2508, (f).
Dispositions in juvenile actions.
Allowing family opportunity to meet needs of juvenile, §7B-2501, (d).
Alternatives for delinquent juvenile, §7B-2506.
Alternatives for undisciplined juveniles, §7B-2503.
Appeals, §§7B-2603 to 7B-2606.
Commitment of delinquent to office of juvenile justice, §7B-2513.
Notification of extended commitment, plan of treatment, §7B-2515.
Consideration by court in developing, §7B-2500.
Considerations of court in selecting disposition, §7B-2501, (c).
Contempt of court for undisciplined juveniles, §7B-2505.
Delinquency history levels, §7B-2507.
Limitations, §7B-2508.
Evaluation and treatment of juveniles, §7B-2502.
Hearing, §7B-2501, (a).
Opportunity to present evidence and advise court as to disposition in best interest of juvenile, §7B-2501, (b).
Limits for each class of offense and delinquency history level, §7B-2508.

DELINQUENT AND UNDISCIPLINED JUVENILES —Cont'd
Dispositions in juvenile actions —Cont'd
Modification or vacation of disposition, §7B-2600.
Request of modification for lack of suitable services, §7B-2601.
Most appropriate disposition, court to select, §7B-2501, (c).
Order, §7B-2512.
Post-release supervision, §7B-2514.
Revocation, §7B-2516, (a) to (c).
Probation, §7B-2510.
Probation termination, §7B-2511.
Protective supervision for undisciplined juveniles, conditions, §7B-2504.
Purposes, §7B-2500.
Transfer of juvenile by governor from jail or penal facility to residential facility, §7B-2517.
District court jurisdiction, §§7B-1600 to 7B-1604.
Diversion contract with juvenile and parent, guardian or custodian, §7B-1706, (b).
Compliance determination by juvenile court counselor, §7B-1706, (e).
Destruction of contract when juvenile reaches age of eighteen years or no longer under jurisdiction of court, §7B-1706, (d).
Maintenance of contract to determine whether complaint previously diverted, §7B-1706, (d).
Not public records, §7B-1706, (d).
Diversion of juvenile pursuant to diversion plan, §7B-1706, (a).
Compliance determination by juvenile court counselor, §7B-1706, (e).
Destruction of plans when juvenile reaches age of eighteen years or no longer under jurisdiction of court, §7B-1706, (d).
Maintenance of plans to determine whether complaint previously diverted, §7B-1706, (d).
Plans not public records, §7B-1706, (d).
Emancipated juvenile prosecuted as adult, §7B-1604, (a).
Escaped delinquent juveniles, returning from one state to another.
Interstate compact on juveniles, §§7B-2800 to 7B-2827.
See INTERSTATE COMPACT ON JUVENILES.
Evaluation of complaint, §7B-1702.
Notice to complainant on determination that petition should not be filed, §7B-1703, (c).
Time for completing by juvenile court counselor, §7B-1703, (a).
Time for filing complaint as petition after juvenile court counselor determination, §7B-1703, (b).
Evaluation of progress of juvenile.
Periodic evaluation by office of juvenile justice, §7B-2514, (a).
Evidence, §§7B-2300 to 7B-2303.
Adjudicatory hearings, §7B-2408.
Dispositional hearings, §7B-2501, (a).
Rebutting predisposition report, opportunity to juvenile, §7B-2413.
Examination and copying of evidence.
Discovery and disclosure of evidence generally, §§7B-2300 to 7B-2303.
Exclusive original jurisdiction over delinquent juveniles, §7B-1601, (a).
Exclusive original jurisdiction over undisciplined juvenile, §7B-1600, (a).
Expunction of juvenile records.
Effect of expunction, §7B-3101.

DELINQUENT AND UNDISCIPLINED JUVENILES —Cont'd
Expunction of juvenile records —Cont'd
Failure to recite or acknowledge record or response after expunction.
Person not guilty of perjury or giving false statements, §7B-3201, (a).
Notice of expunction, §7B-3202.
Person adjudicated, undisciplined or delinquent.
Ordering and directing expungement, §7B-3200, (d), (e).
Petition filed by person adjudicated delinquent, §7B-3200, (b), (c).
Petition filed by person adjudicated undisciplined, §7B-3200, (a), (c).
Retention or disposal of records maintained by juvenile court counselor or intake officer, §7B-3200, (f).
Retention or disposition of records maintained by residential facility, §7B-3200, (g).
Service of petition, §7B-3200, (c).
Person alleged to be delinquent or undisciplined.
Hearing on objection to petition, §7B-3200, (h).
Petition, §7B-3200, (h).
Service of petition, §7B-3200, (h).
Report clerk of superior court of names persons granted expunction, §7B-3200, (i).
Testimony with respect of whether juvenile adjudicated delinquent.
Juvenile defendant in choosing to testify or juvenile called as witness, §7B-3201, (b).
Extended jurisdiction of juvenile court, §§7B-1601, (f), 7B-1602.
Failure of parent, guardian or custodian to appear.
Show cause order for contempt, §7B-1806.
Summons to notify parent, guardian or custodian, §7B-1805, (c).
Filing of petition.
Time for filing after determination that complaint should be filed as petition, §7B-1703, (b).
Fines, delinquent juveniles, §7B-2506.
Fingerprinting and photographing juveniles.
Destruction of records, §7B-2102, (e).
Escape of juvenile from facility or law enforcement.
Release of photograph to public, §7B-2102, (d1).
Juvenile adjudicated delinquent, §7B-2102, (b).
Nondivertible offense, juvenile in custody for, §7B-2102, (a).
Nontestimonial identification order procedures, §§7B-2103 to 7B-2109.
Not public records, §7B-2102, (d).
Escape of juvenile from facility or law enforcement.
Release of photograph to public, §7B-2102, (d1).
Proper format for transfer to state bureau of investigation and federal bureau of investigation, §7B-2102, (c).
First appearance for felony cases.
Continuance to time certain for good cause, §7B-1808, (a).
Duty of court to inform juveniles, §7B-1808, (b).
Place of hearing when juvenile in secure or nonsecure custody, §7B-1808.
Time for juvenile's appearance, §7B-1808, (a).
Footprinting juvenile.
Nontestimonial identification order procedures, §§7B-2103 to 7B-2109.

DELINQUENT AND UNDISCIPLINED JUVENILES —Cont'd
Forfeiture of citizenship rights.
Delinquent adjudication not cause for, §7B-2412.
Governor.
Transferring juvenile from jail or penal facility to residential facility, §7B-2517.
Guardian appointed for juvenile, §7B-2001.
Hair samples.
Nontestimonial identification order procedures, §§7B-2103 to 7B-2109.
Handling of notice by principal, §7B-3101, (c).
Handwriting exemplars.
Nontestimonial identification order procedures, §§7B-2103 to 7B-2109.
Hearings to be open to public unless court closes hearing, §7B-2402.
Holdover facilities.
Defined, §7B-1501.
Retaining juvenile allegedly committing Class A, B1, B2, C, D or E felony, §7B-1905, (c).
House arrest of delinquent juvenile, §7B-2506.
Identification procedures, nontestimonial, §§7B-2103 to 7B-2109.
Identifying information not to be disclosed or shared, §7B-3100, (b).
Incapacity to proceed, determination.
Cases in which juvenile alleged to be delinquent, §7B-2401.
Inspection and copying of evidence.
Discovery and disclosure of evidence generally, §§7B-2300 to 7B-2303.
Inspection of predisposition report by juvenile, §7B-2413.
Intake counselor.
Defined, §7B-1501.
Referral of juvenile to teen court program, §7B-1706, (c).
Intake process, steps included, §7B-1702.
Intake services.
Establishment by chief court counselor, §7B-1700.
Juvenile court counselors.
Field investigations, prohibition from engaging in, §7B-1700.
Purposes, §7B-1700.
Interpretation and construction of subchapter to implement purposes and policies, §7B-1500.
Interrogation procedures when juvenile in custody.
Admission into evidence of statement resulting from interrogation, court findings required, §7B-2101, (d).
Admission or confession resulting from interrogation, admissibility into evidence, §7B-2101, (b).
Advising juvenile of rights, §7B-2101, (a).
Ceasing questioning when juvenile indicates a wish not to be questioned further, §7B-2101, (c).
Interstate compact on juveniles, §§7B-2800 to 7B-2827.
See INTERSTATE COMPACT ON JUVENILES.
Interstate compact on the placement of children, §§7B-3800 to 7B-3806.
Interviews with complainant, victim, juvenile, etc.
Intake process to include, §7B-1702.
Jeopardy attaches in adjudicatory hearing, §7B-2414.

DELINQUENT AND UNDISCIPLINED JUVENILES —Cont'd
Jurisdiction of court to modify order.
Continued jurisdiction, §7B-2600, (b).
Jurisdiction over delinquent juveniles.
Age governs for determining jurisdiction, §7B-1601, (a).
Continued jurisdiction of juvenile court.
Juvenile committed to youth development center.
Class B1, B2, C, D OR E felony, §7B-1602, (b).
First-degree murder, first-degree rape or first-degree sexual offense, §7B-1602, (a).
Continued jurisdiction until terminated by court order or emancipation of juvenile, §7B-1601, (b).
Exclusive original jurisdiction of district court, §7B-1601, (a).
Extended jurisdiction of juvenile court, §7B-1601, (f).
Parent, guardian or custodian, jurisdiction over, §7B-1601, (g).
Preliminary inquiry.
Personal jurisdiction, §7B-1701.
Probable cause hearing and transfer hearing, §7B-1601, (c), (d).
Retention of jurisdiction for purposes of probable cause hearing and transfer hearing.
Delinquent proceedings not concluded before juvenile reaches age of 18 years, §7B-1601, (c).
Violation of terms of juvenile's post-release supervision, §7B-1601, (e).
Jurisdiction over parent, guardian or custodian.
Authority of court generally, §§7B-2700 to 7B-2706.
Court having jurisdiction over delinquent juvenile, §7B-1601, (g).
Court having jurisdiction over undisciplined juvenile, §7B-1600, (c).
Summons to advise, §7B-1805, (c).
Jurisdiction over undisciplined juveniles.
Age governs for determining jurisdiction, §7B-1600, (a).
Continued jurisdiction until terminated by court order or emancipation of juvenile, §7B-1600, (b).
Exclusive original jurisdiction of district court, §7B-1600, (a).
Parent, guardian or custodian, jurisdiction over, §7B-1600, (c).
Juvenile court counselors.
Defined, §7B-1706, (b).
Diversion contract with juvenile and parent, guardian or custodian, §7B-1706, (b).
Compliance determination by juvenile court counselor, §7B-1706, (e).
Diversion of juvenile pursuant to diversion plan, §7B-1706, (a).
Compliance determination by juvenile court counselor, §7B-1706, (e).
Evaluation of complaint, §7B-1702.
Notice to complainant on determination that petition should not be filed, §7B-1703, (c).
Time for completing, §7B-1703, (a).
Time for filing complaint as petition after determination, §7B-1703, (b).
Intake services.
Field investigations, prohibition from engaging in, §7B-1700.

DELINQUENT AND UNDISCIPLINED JUVENILES —Cont'd
Juvenile court counselors —Cont'd
Petition drawn by counselor, §7B-1803, (a).
Preliminary determination upon receipt of complaint, §7B-1702.
Referral of juvenile to teen court program, §7B-1706, (c).
Taking juvenile into temporary custody without court order, §7B-1900.
Duties, §7B-1901, (a).
Juvenile court jurisdiction, §§7B-1600 to 7B-1604.
Juvenile court defined as district court exercising jurisdiction, §7B-1501.
Juvenile detention facility operated by county or unit of government.
Standards and rules required, §7B-1905, (b).
Lack of suitable services, request for modification, §7B-2601.
Law enforcement officers taking juvenile into temporary custody, §7B-1900.
Duties, §7B-1901, (a).
Selecting appropriate course of action, permitted action, §7B-2100.
Law enforcement records and files.
Kept separate from records and files of adults, confidentiality, §7B-3001, (b).
Level one disposition, delinquent juveniles, §7B-2508, (c).
Level two disposition, delinquent juveniles, §7B-2508, (d).
Level three disposition, delinquent juveniles, §7B-2508, (e).
Liberty restrictions on release from secure custody, §7B-1906, (f).
Lineups.
Nontestimonial identification order procedures, §§7B-2103 to 7B-2109.
Local agencies.
Designated to share information, §7B-3100.
Magistrates drawing and verifying petition, §7B-1804, (b).
Mail service of summons.
Parent, guardian or custodian not found, §7B-1806.
Malicious conduct by prisoners, §14-258.4, (a).
Measurements taken from juvenile.
Nontestimonial identification order procedures, §§7B-2103 to 7B-2109.
Medical, surgical, psychiatric or psychological evaluation, examination or treatment.
Court ordering examination, §7B-2502, (a).
Direct involvement of parent in evaluation or treatment, court ordering, §7B-2702, (b).
Disclosure of examination results by juvenile, §7B-2301, (c).
Disclosure of examination results by petitioner, §7B-2300, (d).
Hearing to determine whether juvenile in need of evaluation or treatment, §7B-2502, (b).
Ordering parent to undergo evaluation or treatment, §7B-2702, (c), (d).
Payment of costs of treatment or care by parent or other responsible party, court ordering, §7B-2702, (a).
Mental illness or developmental disability, court presented with evidence to effect.
Institutionalization of juvenile, requirements, §7B-2502, (c).

DELINQUENT AND UNDISCIPLINED JUVENILES —Cont'd
Mental illness or developmental disability, court presented with evidence to effect —Cont'd
Referral of juvenile to area mental health, developmental disabilities and substance abuse services director, §7B-2502, (c).
Minor offenses.
Commission to level three disposition, §7B-2508, (g).
Delinquency history levels, §§7B-2507, 7B-2508, (b).
Disposition chart, §7B-2508, (f).
Levels one to three disposition, §7B-2508, (c) to (e).
Offense classification, §7B-2508, (a).
Modification or vacation of order.
Authority of court to modify or alter order after affirmation by appellate court, §7B-2606.
Changes in circumstances or needs of juvenile, §7B-2600, (a).
Continued jurisdiction of court to modify order, §7B-2600, (c).
Duration of disposition of delinquent, reduction, §7B-2600, (b).
Lack of suitable services, request for modification, §7B-2601.
Nature of disposition of delinquent, reduction, §7B-2600, (b).
Reduction of delinquent's nature or duration of disposition, §7B-2600, (b).
Review hearing to determine, §7B-2600, (a).
Multipurpose group homes, residential placement of delinquent juvenile, §7B-2506.
Nontestimonial identification orders where juvenile alleged to be delinquent, §§7B-2103 to 7B-2109.
Affidavit required for issuance of order, §7B-2105.
Authority to issue order, §7B-2103.
Blood specimen to be obtained, grounds, §7B-2105, (b).
Destruction of records, §7B-2108.
Grounds, §7B-2105, (a).
Blood specimen to be obtained, §7B-2105, (b).
Juvenile requesting order, §7B-2107.
Misdemeanor for willful violation of procedures, §7B-2109.
Nontestimonial identification defined, §7B-2103.
Procedure for issuance of order upon showing grounds, §7B-2106.
Request for order by juvenile, §7B-2107.
Request for order made prior to taking juvenile into custody or after custody and prior to adjudicatory hearing, §7B-2104.
Retention of records in court file, §7B-2108.
Notice of date and time of scheduled hearings to parent and juvenile, §7B-1807.
Notice requirements of summons, §7B-1805, (b), (c).
Notice that petition should not be filed.
Juvenile court counselor determination, §7B-1703, (c).
Notice to juvenile's parent, guardian or custodian.
Person taking juvenile into temporary custody without court order, §7B-1901, (a).
Notification of principals of schools when juvenile alleged or found to be delinquent, §7B-3101.

DELINQUENT AND UNDISCIPLINED JUVENILES —Cont'd
Offense classification, §7B-2508, (a).
Consolidation of offenses, §7B-2508, (h).
Dispositional chart, §7B-2508, (f).
Level one disposition, community disposition, §7B-2508, (c).
Level two disposition, intermediate disposition, §7B-2508, (d).
Level three disposition, commitment, §7B-2508, (e).
Minor offense, commission to level three disposition, §7B-2508, (g).
Open hearings, §7B-2402.
Palm printing juvenile.
Nontestimonial identification order procedures, §§7B-2103 to 7B-2109.
Parties to appeal, §7B-2604, (a).
Payment of support or other expenses, parent ordered to pay, §7B-2704.
Contempt.
Parent's failure to comply with orders, §7B-2706.
Discrimination in employment for complying with provisions, §7B-2705.
Employer discharging, demoting or denying promotion to employee complying with provisions of article.
Prohibition, §7B-2705.
Insurance coverage to cover medical costs of juvenile while in detention.
Parent ordered to assign private insurance coverage, §7B-2704.
Probation.
Parent ordered to pay fee for supervision, §7B-2704.
Support of juvenile, parent ordered to pay, §7B-2704.
Personal service of summons, §7B-1806.
Petition alleging delinquency or undiscipline, §7B-1802.
Amendment, §7B-2400.
Commencement of action by filing, §7B-1804, (a).
Complaint filed as petition, §7B-1803.
Time for filing, §7B-1703, (b).
Copy attached to summons, §7B-1805.
Law enforcement officer seeking upon taking custody of juvenile, §7B-2100.
Magistrate drawing and verifying petition, §7B-1804, (b).
Person taking juvenile into temporary custody requesting, §7B-1901, (a).
Pleading in juvenile action by petition, §7B-1801.
Petition should not be filed.
Notice to complainant, juvenile court counselor determination, §7B-1703, (c).
Review by prosecutor of juvenile court counselor's decision, §7B-1705.
Request, §7B-1704.
Photographing and fingerprinting juveniles.
At time juvenile adjudicated delinquent, §7B-2102, (b).
Destruction of records, §7B-2102, (e).
Escape of juvenile from facility or law enforcement.
Release of photograph to public, §7B-2102, (d1).
Nondivertible offense, juvenile in custody for, §7B-2102, (a).
Nontestimonial identification order procedures, §§7B-2103 to 7B-2109.

DELINQUENT AND UNDISCIPLINED JUVENILES —Cont'd
Photographing and fingerprinting juveniles —Cont'd
Not public records, §7B-2102, (d).
Escape of juvenile from facility or law enforcement.
Release of photograph to public, §7B-2102, (d1).
Proper format for transfer to state bureau of investigation and federal bureau of investigation, §7B-2102, (c).
Placement of juvenile.
Alternative disposition for delinquent juvenile, §7B-2506.
Alternative disposition for undisciplined juveniles, §7B-2503.
Bringing delinquents into state for placement or adoption, §§7B-3700 to 7B-3705.
See CHILD PLACEMENT.
Interstate compact on the placement of children, §§7B-3800 to 7B-3806.
Secure or nonsecure custody orders, §§7B-1902 to 7B-1906.
Sending child out of state for purposes of placement, §§7B-3702 to 7B-3705.
Pleading in juvenile action by petition, §7B-1801.
Points, assignment.
Delinquency history levels, §7B-2507, (b).
Post-release supervision.
Credit for definite term for time juvenile spends on supervision, §7B-2514, (f).
Defined, §7B-1501.
Hearing on violation of terms.
Rights of juvenile, §7B-2516, (a).
Hearing to review progress, §7B-2516, (a).
Indefinite commitment, period to be served before release, §7B-2514, (e).
Initiation of planning process, §7B-2514.
Jurisdiction of district court for determining whether juvenile violated terms, §7B-1601, (e).
Length of supervision, §7B-2514, (b).
Notification before releasing juvenile, §7B-2514, (d).
Planning process, what included, §7B-2514, (a).
Revocation, §7B-2516, (b), (c).
Secure custody for juvenile violating conditions, §7B-1903, (d).
Supervision by juvenile court counselor, §7B-2514, (g).
Termination of supervision order, §7B-2514, (g).
Time for releasing juvenile, §7B-2514, (c).
Violation of terms, revocation, §7B-2516, (a), (b).
Predisposition investigation and report, §7B-2413.
Preliminary determination as to whether court has jurisdiction.
Juvenile court counselor to make determination upon receipt of complaint, §7B-1702.
Pretrial release of juvenile.
Appeal of order transferring jurisdiction to superior court, §7B-2603, (b).
Release of juvenile once transfer order entered, §7B-2204.
Principals of schools notified when juvenile alleged or found to be delinquent, §7B-3101.
Use of information, §115C-404.

DELINQUENT AND UNDISCIPLINED JUVENILES —Cont'd
Prior adjudication of delinquent juvenile.
Delinquency history levels.
Adjudications from other jurisdiction, §7B-2507, (e).
Methods of proving, §7B-2507, (f).
Multiple adjudications obtained in one court session, §7B-2507, (d).
Probable cause hearing.
Transfer of jurisdiction of juvenile to superior court, §7B-2202.
Probation.
Alternative disposition for delinquent juvenile, §7B-2506.
Conditions, §7B-2510, (a).
Additional conditions, §7B-2510, (b).
Extension of order for additional period, §7B-2510, (c).
Length order to remain in force, §7B-2510, (c).
Level three disposition for violation of conditions not to be ordered by court.
Juvenile adjudicated delinquent for minor offense, §7B-2510, (f).
Modification of conditions or duration, §7B-2510, (d).
Review of progress of juvenile, §7B-2510, (d).
Secure custody for juvenile violating conditions, §7B-1903, (d).
Termination by written order, §7B-2511.
Violation of conditions, authority of court on finding, §7B-2510, (e).
Visitation by juvenile court counselor of juvenile in home, §7B-2510, (a).
Production of books, records, documents, etc., for inspection and copying.
Disclosure by juvenile, §7B-2301, (b).
Disclosure by petitioner, §7B-2300, (d).
Prosecution review of intake counselor's decision not approving filing of petition, §§7B-1705, 7B-1803, (b).
Prosecution review of juvenile court counselor's decision not to approve filing of petition, §§7B-1705, 7B-1803, (b).
Request for review, §7B-1704.
Prosecutor to represent state, §7B-2404.
Protective orders.
Regulation of discovery, §7B-2302.
Protective supervision by juvenile court counselor.
Placing undisciplined juveniles under, §7B-2503.
Conditions, §7B-2504.
Public access to hearings, §7B-2402.
Publication service of summons.
Parent, guardian or custodian not found, §7B-1806.
Purposes of subchapter, §7B-1500.
Recidivism rates, computation.
Chief court counselor to forward to department of juvenile justice and delinquency prevention relevant information, §7B-3300, (b).
Department of juvenile justice and delinquency prevention to compute, §7B-3300, (a).
Recording adjudicatory and dispositional hearings and hearings on probable cause and transfer, §7B-2410.
Records and social reports in juvenile cases.
Chief court counselor to maintain records of cases, §7B-3001, (a).
Clerk to maintain complete set of records, §7B-3000, (a).

DELINQUENT AND UNDISCIPLINED JUVENILES —Cont'd
Records and social reports in juvenile cases —Cont'd
Confidentiality generally, §7B-3000, (b).
Confidentiality of chief court counselor's records, §7B-3001, (a).
Confidentiality of information shared among local agencies, §7B-3100, (a).
Confidentiality of law enforcement records and files, §7B-3001, (b).
Confidentiality of records and files maintained by office of juvenile justice, §7B-3001, (c).
Designation of local agencies to share information, §7B-3100, (a).
Destruction of juvenile records, §7B-3000, (g).
Expunction of juvenile records, §§7B-3200 to 7B-3202.
Family background information to be contained in chief court counselor's records, §7B-3001, (a).
Identifying information not be disclosed by local agency, §7B-3100, (b).
Law enforcement records and files kept separate from records and files of adults, §7B-3001, (b).
Local agencies authorized to share information, §7B-3100, (a).
Person who may exam juvenile records, §7B-3000, (b).
Prosecutor sharing information with law enforcement officers, §7B-3000, (b).
School notified when juvenile alleged or found to be delinquent.
Actions requiring notification, §7B-3101, (a).
Delivery of notifications, §7B-3101, (a).
Handling of notification by principals, §7B-3101, (c).
Juvenile transferring to another school, §7B-3101, (b).
School defined, §7B-3101, (d).
Time for delivering notice, §7B-3101, (a).
Use of information by schools.
Burning, shredding or destroying documents to protect confidentiality, §115C-404, (a).
Confidentiality of records, §115C-404, (a).
Dismissal of employee for failure to maintain confidentiality, §115C-404, (b).
Maintaining documents in safe, locked storage, §115C-404, (a).
Return of documents to juvenile court counselor, §115C-404, (c).
Suspension or expelling student on basis of documents, prohibition, §115C-404, (b).
Sealing juveniles' record, §7B-3000, (c).
Transcribing electronic or mechanical recording of hearing upon filing notice of appeal, §7B-3000, (d).
Use of record of adjudication of delinquency for offense that would be felony if committed by adult, §7B-3000, (e), (f).
Reduction of nature or duration of delinquent's disposition, §7B-2600, (b).
Referral to teen court program, §7B-1706, (c).
Regimented training program.
Delinquent juvenile ordered to participate in, §7B-2506.
Registration of juvenile for certain sexual offenses, §7B-2509.
Relative willing and able to provide care and supervision.
Placing juvenile in nonsecure custody, §7B-1905, (a).

DELINQUENT AND UNDISCIPLINED JUVENILES —Cont'd
Release from secure or nonsecure custody.
Allegations in petition not proved, §7B-2411.
Restrictions on liberty, §7B-1906, (f).
Release of juvenile pending disposition of appeal, §7B-2605.
Release of juvenile to juvenile's parent, guardian or custodian.
Action by law enforcement officer after taking juvenile into custody, §7B-2100.
Person taking juvenile into temporary custody without court order, §7B-1901, (a).
Restitution, delinquent juveniles, §7B-2506.
Returning from one state to another of delinquent juveniles escaping or absconding.
Interstate compact on juveniles generally, §§7B-2800 to 7B-2827.
See INTERSTATE COMPACT ON JUVENILES.
Review by prosecutor of juvenile court counselor's decision not to approve filing of petition, §§7B-1704, 7B-1705, 7B-1803, (b).
Review hearing as to modification or vacation of order, §7B-2600, (a).
Right to counsel, §7B-2000, (a).
Summons to contain notice of parent's guardian's or custodian's right, §7B-1805, (b).
Risk and needs assessment.
Included in predisposition report, §7B-2413.
Rules of evidence.
Adjudicatory hearings, §7B-2408.
Dispositional hearings, §7B-2501, (a).
Saliva samples.
Nontestimonial identification order procedures, §§7B-2103 to 7B-2109.
School defined, §7B-3101, (b).
School notification when juvenile alleged or found to be delinquent, §7B-3101.
Actions requiring notification, §7B-3101, (a).
Delivery of notification, §7B-3101, (a).
Handling of notification by principal, §7B-3101, (c).
Juvenile transferring to another school, §7B-3101, (b).
Use of juvenile court information by school.
Burning, shredding or destroying documents to protect confidentiality, §115C-404, (a).
Confidential records, §115C-404, (a).
Dismissal of employee for failure to maintain confidentiality, §115C-404, (b).
Maintaining documents in safe, locked storage, §115C-404, (a).
Returning documents to juvenile court counselor, §115C-404, (c).
Suspending or expelling student solely on basis of information, prohibition, §115C-404, (b).
Sealing of juvenile's records, §7B-3000, (c).
Secure or nonsecure custody.
Administrative order issued by chief court counselor, §7B-1902.
Appointment of counsel for juvenile, §7B-1906, (c).
Assignment of counsel, court to determine, §7B-1906, (c).
Audio and video transmission, continued custody hearings, §7B-1906, (h).
Authority of court to issue custody order, §7B-1902.
Burden at custody hearing, §7B-1906, (d).
Circumstances required to exist for ordering secure custody, §7B-1903, (b).

DELINQUENT AND UNDISCIPLINED JUVENILES —Cont'd
Secure or nonsecure custody —Cont'd
Clear and convincing evidence standard at custody hearing, §7B-1906, (d).
Confidential communications with attorney during hearing, §7B-1906, (h).
Continuance or waiver of custody hearing prohibited, §7B-1906, (a).
Continued custody hearings, §7B-1906, (b).
Audio and video transmission, hearing conducted by, §7B-1906, (h).
Criteria in determining whether continued custody warranted, §7B-1906, (e).
Order for continued custody, issuance, §7B-1906, (g).
Testimony and opportunity to introduce evidence, §7B-1906, (d).
County or unit of government operating juvenile detention facility, standards, §7B-1905, (b).
Delegation of court's authority to issue orders, §7B-1902.
Department of social services, placing juvenile in nonsecure custody, §7B-1905, (a).
Execution of order for custody, §7B-1904.
Hearings, §7B-1906.
Holdover facility, placing juvenile in secure custody.
Juvenile committing offense classified as Class A, B1, B2, C, D or E felony, §7B-1905, (c).
Law enforcement procedure after taking juvenile into custody, §§7B-2100 to 7B-2109.
Order directing officer or authorized person to assume custody, secure custody, §7B-1903, (e).
Pending dispositional hearing or placement, ordering secure custody, §7B-1903, (c).
Placing juvenile in nonsecure custody, §7B-1905, (a).
Reasonable factual basis to believe juvenile committed offense alleged.
Required for order for nonsecure custody, §7B-1903, (b).
Reasonable factual basis to believe matters alleged true.
Required for order for nonsecure custody, §7B-1903, (a).
Relative of juvenile willing and able to provide care and supervision, nonsecure custody, §7B-1905, (a).
Release of juvenile to juvenile's parent, guardian, custodian or other responsible adult.
First consideration of court on request for nonsecure custody, §7B-1903, (a).
Request made for nonsecure custody, §7B-1903, (a).
Request made for secure custody, §7B-1903, (b).
Requirements for order for secure or nonsecure custody, §7B-1904.
Restrictions on liberty of juvenile released from secured custody, §7B-1906, (f).
Retention of counsel, court to determine, §7B-1906, (c).
Telephone communications, notices, orders, etc., §7B-1907.
Temporary detention in approved detention facility, §7B-1905, (b).
Temporary residential placement, nonsecure custody, §7B-1905, (a).
Time for holding custody hearing, §7B-1906, (a).
Continued custody hearing, §7B-1906, (b).

DELINQUENT AND UNDISCIPLINED JUVENILES —Cont'd
Secure or nonsecure custody —Cont'd
Violation of conditions of probation or post-release supervision, ordering secure custody, §7B-1903, (d).
Secure or nonsecure custody hearings, §7B-1906.
Selecting most appropriate disposition.
Considerations by court, §7B-2501, (c).
Sending delinquent juvenile out of state for purposes of placement, §§7B-3702 to 7B-3705.
Serious offenses.
Delinquency history levels, §§7B-2507, 7B-2508, (b).
Disposition chart, §7B-2508, (f).
Levels one to three disposition, §7B-2508, (c) to (e).
Offense classification, §7B-2508, (a).
Service of summons, §7B-1806.
Criminal contempt for failure to appear, notice, §7B-1805, (c).
Criminal process applicable to juvenile process, §7B-1806.
Delivered to person authorized to serve process, §7B-1805, (d).
Directed to person summoned to appear, §7B-1805, (d).
Form and notice requirements, §7B-1805, (b).
Issuance of summons after petition filed, §7B-1805, (a).
Jurisdiction over parent, guardian or custodian, notice, §7B-1805, (c).
Mail or publication, parent, guardian or custodian not found, §7B-1806.
Personal service, §7B-1806.
Process is summons, §7B-1801.
Show cause order for contempt.
Failure of parent, guardian or custodian to appear, §7B-1806.
Time for service, §7B-1806.
Sex offender registration.
Juveniles adjudicated delinquent for committing certain offenses generally, §§14-208.26 to 14-208.32.
See SEX OFFENDER AND PUBLIC PROTECTION REGISTRATION.
Requirement generally, §7B-2509.
Sharing of information by local agencies, §7B-3100.
State appeals, limitations, §7B-2604, (b).
Statements made by juvenile.
Disclosure by petitioner, §7B-2300, (a).
State represented by prosecutor, §7B-2404.
Summons.
Copy of petition attached to summons, §7B-1805, (a).
Criminal contempt for failure of parent, guardian or custodian to appear.
Notice in summons, §7B-1805, (c).
Delivered to person authorized to serve process, §7B-1805, (d).
Directed to person summoned to appear, §7B-1805, (d).
Form and content requirements, §7B-1805, (b).
Issuance after petition filed, §7B-1805, (a).
Jurisdiction over parent, guardian or custodian upon service, §7B-1805, (c).
Process in juvenile action by, §7B-1801.
Service, §7B-1806.

DELINQUENT AND UNDISCIPLINED JUVENILES —Cont'd
Superior court, transfer of jurisdiction of juvenile, §§7B-2200 to 7B-2204.
Appeal of transfer decision, §7B-2603.
Suspension of imposition of disposition.
Delinquent juvenile, §7B-2506.
Taking juvenile into temporary custody, §§7B-1900, 7B-1901.
Law enforcement officers role, permitted actions, §7B-2100.
Teen court program.
Defined, §7B-1501.
Referral of juvenile to, §7B-1706, (c).
Temporary custody of juvenile without court order.
Authority of court to issue orders, §7B-1902.
Circumstances allowing, §7B-1900.
Delegation of court's authority to issue orders, §7B-1902.
Duties of persons taking juvenile into custody, §7B-1901, (a).
Law enforcement officers role, permitted actions, §7B-2100.
Law enforcement procedures after taking juvenile into custody, §§7B-2100 to 7B-2109.
Notice to juvenile's parent, guardian or custodian.
Duty of persons taking juvenile into custody, §7B-1901, (a).
Release of juvenile to juvenile's parent, guardian or custodian, §7B-1901, (a).
Requesting that petition be drawn if juvenile not released, §7B-1901, (a).
Telephone communications, notices, orders, etc., §7B-1907.
Temporary custody defined, §7B-1900.
Time limitation on holding juvenile, §7B-1901, (b).
Transporting absconders to nearest facility providing secure custody, §7B-1901, (c).
Temporary detention in approved detention facility, §7B-1905, (b).
Tests, measurements or experiments made in connection with case.
Disclosure by juvenile, §7B-2301, (c).
Disclosure by petitioner, §7B-2300, (d).
Time for completing evaluation of complaint, §7B-1703, (a).
Time for holding secure or nonsecure custody hearing, §7B-1906, (a).
Continued custody hearing, §7B-1906, (b).
Time for notice of date and time of scheduled hearings, §7B-1807.
Time for service of summons, §7B-1806.
Time limit on holding juvenile in temporary custody, §7B-1901, (a).
Transcripts.
Reducing recording of proceeding when notice of appeal filed, §7B-3000, (d).
Transfer hearing.
Transfer of jurisdiction of juvenile to superior court, §7B-2203.
Transfer of jurisdiction of juvenile to superior court, §7B-2200.
Appeal of transfer decision to superior court for hearing on record, §7B-2603.
Appealing transfer issue to court of appeals, §7B-2603, (d).
Waiver of right for failure to appeal order to superior court, §7B-2603, (a).
Authority of superior court on review, §7B-2603, (a).

DELINQUENT AND UNDISCIPLINED JUVENILES —Cont'd
Transfer of jurisdiction of juvenile to superior court —Cont'd
Appeal of transfer decision to superior court for hearing on record —Cont'd
Interlocutory order, superior court order considered, §7B-2603, (d).
Notice of appeal, §7B-2603, (a).
Pretrial release of juvenile, §7B-2603, (b).
Remanding case to juvenile court for adjudication or upholding transfer order, §7B-2603, (c).
Waiver of right to raise issue on appeal to court of appeals.
Failure to appeal transfer order to superior court, §7B-2603, (a).
Commission of offense by juvenile after superior court conviction.
Prosecution as adult, §7B-1604, (a).
Court not transferring case, §7B-2203, (d).
Detention pending pretrial release, §7B-2204.
Detention pending transfer to department of correction, §7B-2204.
Fingerprinting juvenile, §7B-2201.
Pretrial release, right once order of transfer entered, §7B-2204.
Probable cause found and transfer not required, §7B-2202, (e).
Probable cause hearing.
Burden of state, §7B-2202, (c).
Conducting, §7B-2202, (a).
Jurisdiction of district court for purposes of conducting, §7B-1601, (c), (d).
Representation of state and juvenile, testimony and cross-examination, §7B-2202, (b).
Time for conducting, §7B-2202, (a).
Waiver and stipulation to finding, §7B-2202, (d).
Probable cause not found, §7B-2202, (f).
Transfer hearing, §7B-2203, (a).
Factors considered for transfer, §7B-2203, (b).
Jurisdiction of district court for purposes of conducting, §7B-1601, (c), (d).
Transfer order, §7B-2203, (c).
Transfer of juvenile from jail or penal facility to residential facility.
Governor's authority to order, §7B-2517.
Transfer of proceeding to court in district where juvenile resides, §7B-1800, (b).
Undisciplined juvenile.
Defined, §7B-1501.
Urine specimens.
Nontestimonial identification order procedures, §§7B-2103 to 7B-2109.
Venue of proceedings, §7B-1800.
Victim-offender reconciliation program, delinquent juvenile participation, §7B-2506.
Violent offenses.
Delinquency history levels, §§7B-2507, 7B-2508, (b).
Disposition chart, §7B-2508, (f).
Levels one to three disposition, §7B-2508, (c) to (e).
Offense classifications, §7B-2508, (a).
Voice samples.
Nontestimonial identification order procedures, §§7B-2103 to 7B-2109.
Wilderness program.
Defined, §7B-1501.
Delinquent juvenile ordered to cooperate with placement in, §7B-2506.

DELINQUENT AND UNDISCIPLINED JUVENILES —Cont'd
Witnesses, names of persons to be called.
Disclosure by juvenile, §7B-2301, (a).
Disclosure by petitioner, §7B-2300, (b).
Work product.
Disclosure of reports, memoranda or other internal documents made in connection with investigation or prosecution.
Disclosure by petitioner not required, §7B-2300, (e).
Youth development center.
Commitment of delinquent juvenile to department of juvenile justice and delinquency prevention for placement, §7B-2513, (a).
Commitment of delinquent juvenile to department of juvenile justice for placement.
Plan for care or treatment, department to prepare, §7B-2513, (f).
Commitment of delinquent juvenile to office of juvenile justice for placement.
Age limit for commitment for placement in youth development center, §7B-2513, (a).
Commitment order to be forwarded to department, §7B-2513, (e).
Continued commitment beyond maximum commitment period.
Notice, §7B-2515, (a).
Review by court, §7B-2515, (c).
Continuing jurisdiction over juvenile and parent not terminated by placement, §7B-2513, (g).
Controlled substance or alcohol testing of juvenile, §7B-2513, (i).
Extended commitment, notification, review, §7B-2515.
Housing delinquent juvenile in holdover facility pending placement, §7B-2513, (h).
Indefinite term of at least six months, §7B-2513, (a).
Modification of plan of care or treatment, §7B-2515, (b).
Notice of intention to continue commitment beyond maximum commitment period, §7B-2515, (a).
Post-release supervision planning process, §7B-2514, (a).
Credit for definite term for time juvenile spends, §7B-2514, (f).
Notification prior to release of juvenile, §7B-2514, (d).
Release of juvenile under indefinite commitment, §7B-2514, (e).
Release of juvenile under plan, §7B-2514, (c).
Revocation of post-release supervision, §7B-2516, (c).
Supervision by juvenile court counselor, §7B-2514, (g).
Termination of release by court order, §7B-2514, (g).
Time for completing, §7B-2514, (b).
Previous adjudication for two or more felony offenses and previous commitment to youth development center.
Length of term, §7B-2513, (b).
Progress evaluation by department, §7B-2514, (a).
Records requested to accompany juvenile, §7B-2513, (d).
Review by court of decision to extend commitment, §7B-2515, (c).
Term time limitation, §7B-2513, (a).

DELINQUENT AND UNDISCIPLINED JUVENILES —Cont'd
Youth development center —Cont'd
Commitment of delinquent juvenile to office of juvenile justice for placement —Cont'd
Transporting juvenile to youth development center, §7B-2513, (c).
Victim and members of victim's immediate family notified of placement, §7B-2513, (j).
Continued jurisdiction of court, §7B-1602.
Placement of delinquent juveniles in, §7B-2506.
Youth services generally.
See YOUTH SERVICES.

DELIVERY.
Claim and delivery, §§1-472 to 1-484.1.
See CLAIM AND DELIVERY.
Commercial code generally.
Defined, §25-1-201, (14).
Commercial paper.
Defined, §25-1-201, (14).
Documents of title.
See DOCUMENTS OF TITLE.
Sale of goods, UCC.
See SALE OF GOODS, UCC.

DEMAND DEPOSITS, BANKS, §53-65.

DEMAND FOR JUDGMENT, §1A-1, Rule 54, (c).

DEMAND FOR JURY TRIAL, §1A-1, Rule 38, (b).
Small claims actions.
Appeals, §7A-230.
Specification of issues, §1A-1, Rule 38, (c).

DEMAND LETTER.
Bad checks.
Form, §6-21.3, (a2).
Civil liability for larceny, shoplifting, employee theft, embezzlement or false pretense.
Seeking damages prior to action, §1-538.2, (c2) to (c4).

DEMANDS FOR SERVICE, §1A-1, Rule 5, (a).

DEMOLISHER STATEMENTS.
Purchase or acquisition of abandoned or derelict vehicles.
Statement under oath that vehicle shredded or recycled, §20-137.11.

DEMOLITION.
Construction indemnity agreements invalid, §22B-1.

DEMONSTRATIONS.
Private health care facilities.
Possession of weapon, §14-277.2.
Riots and civil disorders, §§14-288.1 to 14-288.19.
See RIOTS AND CIVIL DISORDERS.
Secret societies.
Masks, hoods or disguises.
Holding demonstrations while wearing masks, hoods, etc., §14-12.10.
Permitting, etc., demonstrations of prohibited secret societies, §14-12.5.
Weapons, possession, §14-277.2.

DEMURRER.
Abolished, §1A-1, Rule 7, (c).
Evidence.
Criminal law and procedure, §15-173.

DENATURED ALCOHOL.
Exemption from alcoholic beverage provisions, §18B-103.

DE NOVO TRIALS.
Abortion.
Parental or judicial consent to abortion.
Waiver of parental consent requirement, appeal by minor, §90-21.8, (h).
Appeals.
District courts, §15A-1431.
Magistrates, §15A-1431.
Small claims actions, §§7A-228, 7A-229.
Criminal contempt appeals, §5A-17.
District courts.
Appeals, §15A-1431.
Superior court, §7A-196, (b).
Impaired driving.
Chemical analysis of impairing substances in blood.
Revocation of license in event of refusal, §20-16.2, (d).
Incompetence, determination of.
Appeal from order adjudicating incompetence, §35A-1115.
Incompetence, restoration.
Appeal from clerk's order denying petition, §35A-1130, (f).
Judgment of magistrate in civil action improperly assigned or not assigned.
Appeal to district court judge, §7A-212.
Magistrates.
Appeals, §15A-1431.
Small claim action appeals, §§7A-228, 7A-229.
Jury trial, §7A-230.
Special proceedings.
Clerk ordering survey, appeal, §1-408.1.

DENTAL HEALTH PROGRAM.
Children's health insurance program.
Dental coverage, §108A-70.21, (b).
Establishment, §130A-366, (a).
Problem access areas.
Dental providers for, §130A-367.
Rules and regulations, §130A-366, (b).

DENTAL HYGIENISTS, §§90-221 to 90-233.1.
Administration of provisions.
Board of dental examiners, §90-222.
Board of dental examiners.
Administration of provisions, §90-222.
Definition of "board," §90-221, (e).
Duties, §90-223, (c), (d).
Impaired dental hygienist programs, authority to provide, §90-223, (e).
Powers, §90-223, (a), (b).
Disciplinary measures, §90-229, (a).
Records, §90-223, (c).
Rules and regulations, §90-223, (b).
Examinations, §90-224, (b).
Renewal certificates, §90-227, (b).
Subpoenas.
Power to issue, §90-231, (c).
Child support enforcement.
Forfeiture of licensing privilege, §50-13.12.
Continuing education, §90-225.1.
Criminal law and procedure.
Violations of provision, §90-233.1.
Definitions, §90-221.
Disciplinary proceedings.
Definition of "licensee," §90-229, (b).
Grounds, §90-229, (a).
Hearings.
Conduct of hearings, §90-231, (c).
Consent order in lieu of, §90-231, (b).
Right to hearing, §90-231, (a).

DENTAL HYGIENISTS —Cont'd
Disciplinary proceedings —Cont'd
Powers of board, §90-229, (a).
Provisional licensees subject to, §90-226, (e).
Drugs.
Chronic or persistent use as grounds for disciplinary measures, §90-229, (a).
Drunkenness.
Grounds for disciplinary measures, §90-229, (a).
Employment of two dental hygienists by dentists, §90-233, (b).
Fees.
Generally, §90-232.
Felony convictions.
Forfeiture of license, §15A-1331A.
Grounds for disciplinary measures, §90-229, (a).
Fraud.
Grounds for disciplinary measures, §90-229, (a).
Hearings.
Disciplinary proceedings, §90-231.
Impaired dental hygienist programs.
Annual renewal fee to finance, §90-232.
Board's authority to provide, §90-223, (e).
Peer review organizations for impaired dentists.
Inclusion of dental hygienists in programs, §90-48.3.
Licenses.
Certificate upon transfer to another state, §90-230.
Credentials, license by, §90-224.1, (a) to (e).
Fees, §90-232.
Criminal records checks for license applicants, §90-224, (c).
Defined, §90-221, (c).
Display.
Place for display to be determined by board, §90-225, (b).
Examinations.
Credentials, license by, §90-224.1, (a), (c), (d).
Fee, §90-232.
Notification of successful candidates.
Board to determine method and time, §90-225, (b).
Power of board to conduct examinations, §90-223, (a).
Rules and regulations of board as to, §90-224, (b).
Fees, §90-232.
Issuance, §90-225, (a).
Practice of dental hygiene.
Required, §90-233, (c).
Provisional license, §90-226.
Applications, §90-226, (d).
Disciplinary proceedings.
Provisional licensee subject to, §90-226, (e).
Eligibility for, §90-226, (a), (c).
Fee, §90-232.
Issuance, §90-226, (a).
Term, §90-226, (b).
Qualifications of applicants, §90-224, (a).
Credentials, license by, §90-224.1, (a) to (c).
Renewal certificates.
Defined, §90-221, (d).
Fee, §90-232.
Issuance, §90-227, (a).
Power of board, §90-223, (a).
Renewal of license of dental hygienists who fails to obtain renewal certificate, §90-228.
Rules and regulations as to, §90-227, (b).
Revocation or suspension.
Felony convictions, §15A-1331A.

DENTAL HYGIENISTS —Cont'd
Misdemeanors.
Violations, §90-233.1.
Peer review organizations for impaired dentists.
Inclusion of dental hygienists in programs, §90-48.3.
Practice of dental hygiene.
Acts and practices which do not constitute, §90-233, (c).
Definition of "dental hygiene," §90-221, (a).
Licenses.
Required, §90-233, (c).
Supervision by dentists required, §90-233, (a).
Definition of "supervision," §90-221, (f).
Records.
Board of dental examiners, §90-223, (c).
Criminal records checks for license applicants, §90-224, (c).
Referral fees and solicitation payments, §§90-400 to 90-402.
Health care provider defined, §90-400.
Prohibited, §90-401.
Sanctions, §90-402.
Removal from state.
Certificate upon transfer to another state, §90-230.
Rules and regulations.
Board of dental examiners, §90-223, (b).
Examinations, §90-224, (b).
Renewal certificates, §90-227, (b).
Subpoenas.
Hearings.
Power of board to issue, §90-231, (c).
Supervision by licensed dentist, §90-233, (a).
Definition of "supervision," §90-221.
Violations of provisions.
Misdemeanors, §90-233.1.

DENTISTS, §§90-22 to 90-48.2.
Actions.
Injunctions.
Unauthorized practice.
Action for injunction, §90-40.1.
Alcoholic beverages.
Exemption from chapter, §18B-103.
Anesthesia and parenteral sedation.
Practice of dentistry, §90-29, (b).
Standards for general anesthesia and parenteral sedation.
Board of dental examiners to establish by regulation, §90-30.1.
Board of dental examiners.
Agreements with special peer review organizations for impaired dentist, §90-48.2.
Anesthesia and parenteral sedation.
Standards for general anesthesia and parenteral sedation.
Board to establish by regulation, §90-30.1.
Bylaws, §90-28.
Compensation of members, §§90-22, (d), 90-43.
Composition, §90-22, (b).
Disciplinary action, §90-41.
Hearings, §90-41.1.
Election of members, §90-22, (c).
Expenses of members, §§90-22, (d), 90-43.
Hearings.
Disciplinary proceedings, §90-41.1.
Meetings.
Adjourned meetings.
Effect, §90-24.
Annual meetings, §90-26.

DENTISTS —Cont'd
Board of dental examiners —Cont'd
Meetings —Cont'd
Notice, §90-26.
Special meetings, §90-26.
Nominations of members, §90-22, (c).
Number of members, §90-22, (b).
Oaths.
Power to administer, §90-27.
Officers, §90-23.
Qualifications of members, §90-22, (b).
Quorum, §90-24.
Records, §90-25.
Reports.
Annual report, §90-44.
Rules and regulations, §§90-28, 90-48.
Seal, §90-23.
Secretary, §90-22, (e).
Subpoenas.
Powers, §90-27.
Terms of members, §90-22, (b).
Vacancies, §90-22, (b).
Child support enforcement.
Forfeiture of licensing privilege, §50-13.12.
Confidentiality of information.
Criminal records checks for license applicants, §90-30, (b).
Peer review committees.
Proceedings and records, §90-48.10.
Consent to health care for minors.
Reliance on agent's authorization, §32A-33.
Construction and interpretation.
Liberal construction of provisions, §90-22, (a).
Continuing education, §90-31.1.
Limited volunteer dental licenses, §90-36, (f).
Corporations.
Dental service corporations generally, §§58-65-1 to 58-66-40.
See HOSPITAL, MEDICAL AND DENTAL SERVICE CORPORATIONS.
Professional corporations generally, §§55B-1 to 55B-16.
See PROFESSIONAL CORPORATIONS.
Criminal law and procedure.
Extraoral services performed for dentist, §90-29.2, (d), (e).
Practicing dentistry without license, §90-40.
Subpoenas of board of dental examiner.
Neglect or refusal to obey, §90-27.
Unauthorized practice, §90-40.
Limited volunteer dental licenses, §90-36, (g).
Violations of rules and regulations of board, §90-48.
Dental health program.
Problem access areas.
Dental providers for, §130A-367.
Dental hygienists.
See DENTAL HYGIENISTS.
Dental service corporations generally, §§58-65-1 to 58-66-40.
See HOSPITAL, MEDICAL AND DENTAL SERVICE CORPORATIONS.
Disciplinary action, §90-41.
Attorneys at law.
Employment of legal counsel by board, §90-41, (e).
Definition of "licensee," §90-41, (f).
Grounds, §90-41, (a).
Hearings.
Consent orders, §90-41.1, (b).
Rights of parties, §90-41.1, (c).

DENTISTS —Cont'd
Disciplinary action —Cont'd
Hearings —Cont'd
Right to hearing, §90-41.1, (a).
Initiation of proceedings by board, §90-41, (c).
Intern permit.
Holder subject to, §90-29.4.
Investigators.
Appointment by board, §90-41, (d).
Powers of board, §90-41, (a).
Provisional licensee subject to, §90-29.3, (e).
Records.
Confidentiality of information, §90-41, (g).
Public records.
Access to records, §90-41, (g).
Revocation or suspension of license, §90-41, (a).
Practice while license suspended, §90-41, (b).
Restoration of revoked license, §90-42.
Drugs.
Chronic or persistent use.
Grounds for disciplinary action, §90-41, (a).
Prescriptions, §90-46.
Elections.
Board of dental examiners.
Nominations and elections of members, §90-22, (c).
Evidence.
Medical charges at issue.
Injured party as witness.
Competency to give evidence regarding amount of charges, §8-58.1.
Rebuttable presumption of reasonableness of charges.
Testimony of person establishing, §8-58.1.
Examinations.
Licenses, §90-30, (a).
Extraoral services performed for dentists, §90-29.1.
Prohibited acts, §90-29.2, (d), (e).
Work orders.
Copies.
Retention, §90-29.2, (b).
Subwork orders, §90-29.2, (c).
Written work orders required, §90-29.2, (a).
Fees.
Anesthesia and parenteral sedation.
Standards for general anesthesia and parenteral sedation.
Board of dental examiners to establish by regulation, §90-30.1.
Examination and inspection.
Dental offices, §90-30.1.
Intern permits, §90-39.
Licenses, §90-39.
Duplicate licenses, §90-35.
Renewal, §§90-31, 90-39.
Felony convictions.
Forfeiture of license, §15A-1331A.
Grounds for disciplinary action, §90-41, (a).
Fines.
Subpoenas of board of medical examiner.
Neglect or refusal to obey, §90-27.
Unauthorized practice, §90-40.
Violations of rules and regulations of board, §90-48.
Fraud.
Grounds for disciplinary action, §90-41, (a).
Licenses.
Obtained through fraud void, §90-30, (a).
Free choice by patient, §90-48.1.

DENTISTS —Cont'd
Health benefit plans.
Right of subscriber to choose service, payment, §58-50-30.
Hearings.
Disciplinary proceedings, §90-41.1.
Identification badges required, §90-640.
Immunity.
Peer review committees.
Members, §90-48.8.
Witnesses, §90-48.9.
Injunctions.
Unauthorized practice, §90-40.1.
Action for injunction, §90-40.1, (a).
Plaintiff entitled to examination of adverse party and witnesses, §90-40.1, (d).
Venue, §90-40.1, (c).
Judgment.
Effect, §90-40.1, (b).
Venue for actions, §90-40.1, (c).
Instructors.
Licenses, §90-29.5.
Fee, §90-39.
Intern permits, §90-29.4.
Fee, §90-39.
Legislative declaration, §90-22, (a).
Licenses.
Applications, §90-29.3, (d).
Limited volunteer dental licenses, §90-36, (e).
Certificate issued to dentist moving out of state, §90-37.
Fee, §90-39.
Contents of original license, §90-32.
Credentials, license by, §90-36, (a) to (e).
Fees, §90-39.
Criminal records checks for license applicants, §90-30, (b).
Denial.
Grounds, §90-30, (a).
Display, §90-33.
Duplicate licenses, §90-35.
Fee, §90-35.
Eligibility, §90-29.3, (a), (c).
Examinations, §90-30, (a).
Limited volunteer dental licenses, §90-36, (b), (d), (e).
Fees, §90-39.
Duplicate licenses, §90-35.
Renewal, §§90-31, 90-39.
Former dentists who have moved back into state or resumed practice, §90-38.
Fraud or false representation.
License obtained through.
Void, §90-30, (a).
Instructors, §§90-29, (c), 90-29.5.
Fee, §90-39.
Intern permits, §90-29.4.
Fee, §90-39.
Limited volunteer dental licenses, §90-36, (a) to (i).
Fees, §90-39.
Provisional licenses, §90-29.3.
Authorized, §90-29.3, (a).
Disciplinary action.
Provisional licensee subject to, §90-29.3, (e).
Fee, §90-39.
Qualifications, §90-30, (a).
Limited volunteer dental licenses, §90-36, (a) to (d).
Reciprocity, §90-36.
Fees, §90-39.

DENTISTS —Cont'd
Licenses —Cont'd
Renewal, §90-31.
Certificate of renewal, §90-31.
Display, §90-33.
Fees, §90-39.
Additional late fee, §90-31.
Refusal to grant, §90-34.
Required, §90-29, (a).
Revocation or suspension, §90-41, (a).
Felony convictions, §15A-1331A.
Practicing while license suspended, §90-41, (b).
Restoration of revoked license, §90-42.
Taxation.
Professional licenses generally, §105-41.
Term, §90-29.3, (d).
Unlicensed practice.
Injunction, §90-40.1.
Misdemeanor, §90-40.
Liens, recoveries for personal injuries, §44-49.
Attorneys' fees, §44-50.
Charges, §44-50.
Disputed claims to be settled before payment, §44-51.
Evidence, §44-50.
Limit on recovery, §44-50.
Receiving person charged with duty of retaining funds, §44-50.
Limited volunteer dental licenses, §90-36, (a) to (i).
Fees, §90-39.
Nonprofit health care facilities list, §90-36, (h).
Malpractice.
Actions generally, §§90-21.11 to 90-21.14.
See MEDICAL MALPRACTICE.
Grounds for disciplinary action, §90-41, (a).
Pleading special matters, §1A-1, Rule 9, (j).
Medical records, §§90-410, 90-411.
Electronic medical records, §90-412.
Misdemeanors.
Extraoral services performed for dentists.
Prohibited acts, §90-29.2, (d), (e).
Rules and regulations.
Violations, §90-48.
Subpoenas of board of dental examiners.
Neglect or refusal to obey, §90-27.
Unauthorized practice, §90-40.
Limited volunteer dental licenses, §90-36, (g).
Negligence.
Grounds for disciplinary action, §90-41, (a).
Notice.
Board of dental examiners.
Meetings, §90-26.
Oaths.
Board of dental examiners.
Power to administer oaths, §90-24.
Peer review committees.
Citation of act.
Short title, §90-48.7.
Confidentiality of proceedings and records, §90-48.10.
Immunity of members, §90-48.8.
Immunity of witnesses, §90-48.9.
Previous privileges and immunities not limited, §90-48.11.
Savings clause.
No limitation on previous privileges and immunities, §90-48.11.
Title of act.
Short title, §90-48.7.

DENTISTS —Cont'd
Peer review committees —Cont'd
Witnesses.
Immunity, §90-48.9.
Peer review organizations for impaired dentists.
Board agreements, §90-48.2.
Composition and activities, §90-48.2, (a).
Confidentiality, §90-48.2, (e).
Dental hygienists, inclusion, §90-48.3.
Immunity from liability, §90-48.2, (f).
Powers, §90-48.2, (b).
Programs, §90-48.2, (c).
Reporting requirements, §90-48.2, (d).
Penalties.
Rules and regulations.
Violations, §90-48.
Practice of dentistry.
License required, §90-29, (a).
Unauthorized practice.
Injunction, §90-40.1.
Limited volunteer dental licenses, §90-36, (g).
Misdemeanor, §90-40.
What constitutes, §90-29, (b).
What does not constitute, §90-29, (c).
Extraoral services performed for dentists, §90-29.1.
Prescriptions, §90-46.
Presumptions.
Medical charges at issue.
Injured party as witness.
Rebuttable presumption of reasonableness.
Testimony of person establishing, §8-58.1.
Prison terms.
Subpoenas of board of medical examiner.
Neglect or refusal to obey, §90-27.
Unauthorized practice, §90-40.
Violations of rules and regulations of board, §90-48.
Privileges to practice in hospitals, §131E-85.
Professional corporations generally, §§55B-1 to 55B-16.
See PROFESSIONAL CORPORATIONS.
Reciprocity.
Licenses, §90-36.
Fees, §90-39.
Records.
Board of dental examiners, §90-25.
Disciplinary action.
Confidentiality of information, §90-41, (g).
Public records.
Access to records, §90-41, (g).
Peer review committees.
Confidentiality of records, §90-48.10.
Referral fees and solicitation payments, §§90-400 to 90-402.
Health care provider defined, §90-400.
Prohibited, §90-401.
Sanctions, §90-402.
Removal from state.
Certificate of license issued to dentist moving out of state, §90-37.
Fee, §90-39.
Licensing former dentists who have moved back into state, §90-38.
Reports.
Board of dental examiners.
Annual report, §90-44.
Residency programs.
Establishment of public health programs, §130A-11.

DENTISTS —Cont'd
Residency programs established in public health, §130A-11.
Rules and regulations.
Anesthesia and parenteral sedation.
Standards for general anesthesia and parenteral sedation.
Board of dental examiners to establish by regulation, §90-30.1.
Board of dental examiners, §§90-28, 90-48.
Limited volunteer dental licenses, §90-36, (i).
Seals and sealed instruments.
Board of dental examiners, §90-23.
Sedation standards, §90-30.1.
Self-referrals, §§90-405 to 90-408.
Solicitation.
Direct solicitation prohibited, §90-401.1.
Grounds for disciplinary action, §90-41, (a).
Payment prohibitions, §90-401.
Sanctions for violating prohibitions, §90-402.
Subpoenas.
Board of dental examiners.
Powers, §90-27.
Venue.
Injunctions.
Unauthorized practice.
Actions for injunctions, §90-40.1, (c).
Volunteers.
Limited volunteer dental licenses, §90-36, (a) to (i).
Nonprofit health care facilities list, §90-36, (h).
Witnesses.
Medical charges at issue.
Injured party as witness.
Competency to give evidence regarding amount, §8-58.1.
Rebuttable presumption of reasonableness.
Testimony of person establishing, §8-58.1.
Peer review committees.
Immunity of witnesses, §90-48.9.

DEPARTMENT OF ADMINISTRATION.
Generally.
See ADMINISTRATION DEPARTMENT.

DEPARTMENT OF AGRICULTURE AND CONSUMER SERVICES, §§143A-56 to 143A-65.
See AGRICULTURE AND CONSUMER SERVICES DEPARTMENT.

DEPARTMENT OF CORRECTIONS, §§143B-260 to 143B-271.
See CORRECTION DEPARTMENT.

DEPARTMENT OF CRIME CONTROL AND PUBLIC SAFETY, §§143A-239 to 143A-245, 143B-473 to 143B-492.
See CRIME CONTROL AND PUBLIC SAFETY DEPARTMENT.

DEPARTMENT OF CULTURAL RESOURCES, §§143B-49 to 143B-133.1.
See CULTURAL RESOURCES DEPARTMENT.

DEPARTMENT OF ENVIRONMENT AND NATURAL RESOURCES, §§143B-279.1 to 143B-336.1.
See ENVIRONMENT AND NATURAL RESOURCES DEPARTMENT.

DEPARTMENT OF HEALTH AND HUMAN SERVICES.
Generally, §§143B-136.1 to 143B-216.34.
See HEALTH AND HUMAN SERVICES DEPARTMENT.

DEPARTMENT OF INSURANCE.
See INSURANCE DEPARTMENT.

DEPARTMENT OF JUSTICE, §§143A-49 to 143A-55.1.
See JUSTICE DEPARTMENT.

DEPARTMENT OF JUVENILE JUSTICE AND DELINQUENCY PREVENTION.
Generally, §§143B-511 to 143B-557.
See JUVENILE JUSTICE AND DELINQUENCY PREVENTION DEPARTMENT.

DEPARTMENT OF LABOR, §§143A-67 to 143A-72.
See LABOR DEPARTMENT.

DEPARTMENT OF PUBLIC INSTRUCTION.
See EDUCATION.

DEPARTMENT OF REVENUE, §§143B-217 to 143B-220.
See REVENUE DEPARTMENT.

DEPARTMENT OF SECRETARY OF STATE, §§143A-19 to 143A-23.
See SECRETARY OF STATE.

DEPARTMENT OF STATE AUDITOR, §§143A-24 to 143A-29.
See STATE AUDITOR.

DEPARTMENT OF STATE TREASURER, §§143A-30 to 143A-38.1.
See STATE TREASURER.

DEPARTMENT OF TRANSPORTATION, §§143B-345 to 143B-360.
See TRANSPORTATION DEPARTMENT.

DEPENDENT JUVENILES.
Abused, neglected or dependent juveniles.
Generally, §§7B-100 to 7B-1414.
See CHILD ABUSE, NEGLECT OR DEPENDENCY.
Defined, §7B-101.

DEPOSIT IN LIEU OF BAIL.
Arrest in civil cases, §1-426.
Application of deposit to plaintiff's judgment, §1-429.
Bail substituted for deposit, §1-428.

DEPOSIT IN LIEU OF PROSECUTION BOND.
Plaintiffs, for cost, §1-109.

DEPOSIT INSURANCE.
Banks, §53-9.1.

DEPOSITIONS.
Administrative procedure.
Hearings, §§150B-28, (a), 150B-39, (a).
Subpoenas.
Witnesses.
Fees, §150B-39, (c).
Appeals.
Pending appeal, §1A-1, Rule 27, (b).
Arbitration.
Discovery permitted, §1-569.17, (b).
Before action, §1A-1, Rule 27, (a).
Change of venue.
Removal for fair trial.
Taking after cause directed to be removed, §1-87, (b).
Commissioners.
Allowance of costs to either party or apportioned in discretion of court, §6-21.
Witnesses.
Attendance before commissioner enforced, §8-79.

DEPOSITIONS —Cont'd
Commissioners —Cont'd
Witnesses —Cont'd
Attendance before commissioner enforced —Cont'd
Defaulting witness before commissioner.
Remedies against defaulting witness, §8-80.
Enforcement of attendance before commissioner, §8-79.
Power to subpoena witnesses, §8-78.
Punishment for contempt, §8-78.
Conflicts of interest.
Persons before whom depositions may be taken.
Disqualification for interest, §1A-1, Rule 28, (c).
Congress.
Reading deposition on trial, §8-83.
Contempt.
Commissioner may punish for contempt, §8-78.
Costs.
Compensation of referees and commissioners.
Allowance of costs to either party or apportioned in discretion of court, §6-21.
Court of appeals.
Reading deposition on trial.
When witness is judge of court of appeals, §8-83.
Court reporters.
Perpetuation of testimony.
Certified transcription of court reporter, §8-85.
Criminal actions.
Defendant's deposition in criminal actions, §8-74.
Death.
Reading deposition on trial.
When deposition may be read, §8-83.
Defendants.
Criminal actions, §8-74.
Discovery generally.
See DISCOVERY.
District attorneys.
Reading deposition on trial.
When deposition may be read, §8-83.
Employment security.
Commission.
Power to take depositions, §96-4, (h).
Errors or irregularities in depositions.
Effect, §1A-1, Rule 32, (d).
Failure of party to attend at own deposition, §1A-1, Rule 37, (d).
Fee of magistrate, §7A-309.
Filing, §1A-1, Rule 5, (d).
Foreign countries.
Reading deposition on trial.
When deposition may be read, §8-83.
General assembly.
Contested elections, §120-11.
Governor.
Reading deposition on trial.
When deposition may be read, §8-83.
Interrogatories.
See INTERROGATORIES.
Judges.
Reading deposition on trial.
When deposition may be read, §8-83.
Larceny.
Mutilation, larceny or destruction of public records and papers, §14-76.
Leaving county or country.
Deposition upon oral examination, leave of court not required, §1A-1, Rule 30, (b).

DEPOSITIONS —Cont'd
Magistrates.
Authority to take depositions.
Power of magistrates, §7A-292.
Fee for taking deposition, §7A-309.
Reading deposition on trial.
When deposition may be read, §8-83.
Mentally ill.
Reading deposition on trial.
When deposition may be read, §8-83.
Municipal corporations.
Taking deposition before municipal authorities, §8-76.
Nonresidents.
Reading deposition on trial.
When deposition may be read, §8-83.
Notice, §1A-1, Rule 27, (a), (b).
Oral examination, §1A-1, Rule 30, (b).
Written questions, §1A-1, Rule 31, (a).
Filing of deposition, §1A-1, Rule 31, (c).
Objections to admissibility, §1A-1, Rule 32, (b).
Occupational safety and health.
Board, §95-135, (d).
Oral examination.
Certification of deposition by officer, §1A-1, Rule 30, (f).
Cross-examination, §1A-1, Rule 30, (c).
Failure to attend or serve subpoenas.
Expenses, §1A-1, Rule 30, (g).
Filing of deposition by officer, §1A-1, Rule 30, (f).
General requirements, §1A-1, Rule 30, (b).
"Judge" defined, §1A-1, Rule 30, (h).
Leave of court not required.
Circumstances, §1A-1, Rule 30, (b).
Leaving county or country.
Leave of court not required, §1A-1, Rule 30, (b).
Limitation of examination.
Motion, §1A-1, Rule 30, (d).
Notice, §1A-1, Rule 30, (b).
Oath, §1A-1, Rule 30, (c).
Objections, §1A-1, Rule 30, (c).
Organizations, §1A-1, Rule 30, (b).
Record of examination, §1A-1, Rule 30, (c).
Signing of deposition by deponent, §1A-1, Rule 30, (e).
Submission of deposition to deponent, §1A-1, Rule 30, (e).
Termination of examination.
Motion, §1A-1, Rule 30, (d).
Voyage to sea.
Leave of court not required, §1A-1, Rule 30, (b).
When depositions may be taken, §1A-1, Rule 30, (a).
Orders, §1A-1, Rule 27, (a), (b).
Pending appeal, §1A-1, Rule 27, (b).
Perjury.
Punishment for perjury, §14-209.
Perpetuation of testimony, §1A-1, Rule 27, (a).
Pending appeal, §1A-1, Rule 27, (b).
Perpetuation by action, §1A-1, Rule 27, (c).
Persons before whom depositions may be taken.
Conflicts of interest.
Disqualification for interest, §1A-1, Rule 28, (c).
Depositions to be used outside state, §1A-1, Rule 28, (d).
In foreign countries, §1A-1, Rule 28, (b).
In United States, §1A-1, Rule 28, (a).
Petitions, §1A-1, Rule 27, (a), (b).
Physicians and surgeons.
Hearings before board, §90-14.5.

DEPOSITIONS —Cont'd
Physicians and surgeons —Cont'd
Reading deposition on trial.
When deposition may be read, §8-83.
President of the United States.
Reading deposition on trial.
When deposition may be read, §8-83.
Prisons and prisoners.
Reading deposition on trial.
When deposition may be read, §8-83.
Production of documents and things.
Oral examination.
Service of subpoena duces tecum, §1A-1, Rule 30, (b).
Public officers and employees.
Reading deposition on trial.
When deposition may be read, §8-83.
Public utilities.
Utilities commission, §62-66.
Quashing deposition.
Trial.
Deposition not quashed after trial begun, §8-82.
Referees.
Compensation of referees.
Allowance of costs to either party or apportioned in discretion of court, §6-21.
Remedies.
Witnesses before commissioner.
Remedies against defaulting witness, §8-80.
Removal for fair trial, §1-87, (b).
Sealing.
Protective orders, §1A-1, Rule 26, (c).
Service of process, §1A-1, Rule 27, (a), (b).
Oral examination notice, §1A-1, Rule 30, (b).
Written questions, §1A-1, Rule 31, (a).
State auditor.
Authority to take depositions, §147-64.7, (c).
State departments and agencies.
Reading deposition on trial.
When deposition may be read, §8-83.
Stipulations regarding discovery procedure, §1A-1, Rule 29.
Subpoena duces tecum.
Oral examination.
Service of subpoena, §1A-1, Rule 30, (b).
Subpoenas, §1A-1, Rule 45, (d).
Commissioner may subpoena witnesses, §8-78.
Summary judgment.
Affidavit supplemented or opposed by, §1A-1, Rule 56, (e).
Supreme court.
Reading deposition on trial.
When witness is justice of supreme court, §8-83.
Trial.
Objection to deposition before trial, §8-81.
Quashing deposition after trial begun, §8-82.
Reading deposition on trial.
When deposition may be read, §8-83.
When deposition may be read on trial, §8-83.
University of North Carolina, president.
Reading deposition on trial, §8-83.
Use of depositions, §1A-1, Rule 27, (a), (b).
Court proceedings, §1A-1, Rule 32, (a).
Effect of taking or using depositions, §1A-1, Rule 32, (c).
Objections to admissibility, §1A-1, Rule 32, (b).
Voyages to sea.
Deposition upon oral examination, leave of court not required, §1A-1, Rule 30, (b).
Wage and hour act.
Power of commissioner of labor to take depositions, §95-25.16, (b).

DEPOSITIONS —Cont'd
Witnesses.
Commissioner to take depositions.
Attendance before commissioner enforced, §8-79.
Punishment for contempt, §8-78.
Remedies against defaulting witness before commissioner, §8-80.
Reading deposition on trial.
When deposition may be read, §8-83.
Workers' compensation.
Contested cases, I.C. Rule 612.
Industrial commission, §97-80, (d).
Written questions.
Cross questions, service, §1A-1, Rule 31, (a).
Notice, §1A-1, Rule 31, (a).
Filing of deposition, §1A-1, Rule 31, (c).
Person to take responses and prepare record, §1A-1, Rule 31, (b).
Service of questions, §1A-1, Rule 31, (a).

DEPOSIT MADE TO SECURE JUDGMENT.
Supersedeas to suspend execution.
Filing for judgment sought to be vacated, §1-269.

DEPOSITS.
Bail and recognizance.
Deposit in lieu of bail.
Civil cases, §§1-426 to 1-429.
Bail bondsmen and runners.
Deposit of securities, §§58-71-135 to 58-71-160.
Bank deposits.
See BANKS.
Bank deposits and collections, §§25-4-101 to 25-4-504.
See BANK DEPOSITS AND COLLECTIONS.
Bonds, surety.
State funds, §147-79.
Budget.
State employees.
Deposit of payroll deductions, §143-34.6.
Certificate of deposit.
Negotiable instruments.
General provisions, §§25-3-101 to 25-3-605.
See NEGOTIABLE INSTRUMENTS.
Clerks of court.
Superior court.
Money held by clerk of superior court, §7A-112.1.
Fees, §7A-308.1.
Collection agencies.
Remittance trust account, §58-70-65, (a) to (c).
Community college investments.
Daily deposits, §115D-58.9.
Form, §115D-58.6, (b), (c).
Generally, §115D-58.6, (a).
Securing deposits, §115D-58.7, (b).
Selection of depository, §115D-58.7, (a).
Credit unions.
Insurance.
Share and deposit insurance, §54-109.78, (a).
Prerequisite to granting of charter, §54-109.78, (b).
Lien on deposit, §54-109.59.
Savings accounts, §54-109.55.
Decedents' estates.
Powers of personal representative or fiduciary, §28A-13-3, (a).
Drainage districts.
Bond issues.
Receipt of bonds as deposits, §156-102.
Economic development commissions, §158-12.1.

DEPOSITS —Cont'd
Electrologists.
Fees payable to board of electrologist examiners, §88A-7.
Eminent domain.
Public condemnors.
Complaints.
Deposit of estimated compensation to accompany complaint
Estates.
Survivorship in bank deposit created by written agreement, §41-2.1.
Fiduciaries.
Banking deposits in name of fiduciary, §32-8.
Investment and deposit of trust funds, §§36A-1 to 36A-7.
Personal account of fiduciary, §32-10.
Principal.
Deposit in name of principal, §32-9.
Trustees.
Deposits in name of two or more trustees, §32-11.
Foreign or alien insurance companies.
Generally, §§58-5-5 to 58-5-40.
See FOREIGN OR ALIEN INSURANCE COMPANIES.
Home inspector licensure board.
Moneys received by, §143-151.63, (b).
Housing authorities and projects.
National defense housing projects.
Security for public deposits, §157-57.
Security for funds deposited, §157-24.
Insurance.
Banks.
Requirements as to deposit insurance, §53-9.1.
Foreign or alien insurance companies, §§58-5-5 to 58-5-40.
See FOREIGN OR ALIEN INSURANCE COMPANIES.
Liens.
Discharge of liens, §44-48.
Local government finance.
Fiscal control.
Daily deposits.
Required, §159-32.
Selection of depository, §159-31.
Mortgages and deeds of trust.
Sales under power of sale.
Failure of bidder to cash deposit, §45-21.30, (a).
Requirement of cash deposit at sale, §45-21.10.
Nurses.
Board of nursing.
Funds, §90-171.25.
Parking authorities.
Moneys of authority, §160A-559.
Payment into court, §§1-508 to 1-510.
Powers of attorney.
Powers conferred by statutory short form, §32A-2.
Prisons and prisoners.
Canteens.
Revenue from prison canteens, §148-2, (c).
Prison enterprises fund, §148-2, (b).
Provider sponsored organizations.
See PROVIDER SPONSORED ORGANIZATIONS.
Public officers and employees.
Daily deposit of funds to credit of state treasurer, §147-77.
Report of daily deposits to state treasurer, §147-84.
Rental referral agencies, §66-143, (b).

DEPOSITS —Cont'd
Savings banks.
Deposit accounts.
See SAVINGS BANKS.
Security deposits of tenants, §§42-50 to 42-56.
Application of article, §42-56.
Deposit in trust accounts, §42-50.
Deposits from tenant, §42-50.
Landlord may furnish bond from insurance company, §42-50.
Landlord to notify tenant of bank holding deposit, §42-50.
Obligations of landlord, §42-52.
Permitted uses of deposit, §42-51.
Pet deposits, §42-53.
Recovery of deposit, §42-55.
Remedies, §42-55.
Rent.
Use for deposit, §42-51.
Transfer of dwelling units, §42-54.
Withholding of deposit.
Normal wear and tear, §42-52.
State departments and agencies.
Daily deposit of funds to credit of state treasurer, §147-77.
Report of daily deposits to state treasurer, §147-84.
State treasurer.
Contracts, §147-81.
Daily deposit of funds to credit of treasurer, §147-77.
Good faith deposits.
Master trust, §147-78.1.
Interest.
Contracts as to interest, §147-81.
Number of depositories, §147-81.
Office declared office of deposit and disbursement, §147-74.
Receipts from federal government and gifts not affected, §147-83.
Reports of depositories, §147-79.
Security for deposits, §147-79.
Selection.
Treasurer to select depositories, §147-78.
State funds.
Deposits of state funds in banks and savings and loans regulated, §147-69.
Streets and highways.
Condemnation proceedings.
Disbursement of deposit, §136-105.
Serving copy of disbursing order, §136-105.
Refund of deposit, §136-121.
Superior courts.
Clerks of court.
Money held by clerk, §7A-112.1.
Fees, §7A-308.1.
Taxation.
Collection of taxes.
Bank deposits subject to attachment or garnishment, §105-242, (b).
Tenant security deposits, §§42-50 to 42-56.
Trust companies.
Financial holding companies.
Trust funds, §53-366, (f).
Multistate trust institutions, §53-309.
Seizure by commissioner.
Deposit of funds collected, §53-390.
Trusts and trustees.
Deposit in name of two or more trustees, §32-11.
Funds held by corporation exercising fiduciary powers awaiting investment or distribution.
Deposits in bank, §36A-63, (b).

DEPOSITS —Cont'd
Trusts and trustees —Cont'd
Investment and deposit of trust funds, §§36A-1 to 36A-7.
Powers of trustees under express trust, §36A-136.
Unclaimed property generally, §§116B-51 to 116B-80.
See UNCLAIMED PROPERTY.
University of North Carolina.
Trust funds, §116-36.1, (b), (c).
Official depositories, §116-36.1, (h).
Wages.
Payroll deductions.
State employees, §143-34.6.
Warehouse receipts.
Fraudulent deposit and negotiation, §27-59.

DEPOSITS INTO COURT.
Arrest in civil cases.
Application of deposit to plaintiff's judgment, §1-429.
Bail substituted for deposit, §1-428.
Deposit in lieu of bail.
Paid into court, §1-427.
Discharge of defendants, §1-419.
Interpleader.
Funds to competing claims by parties, §1A-1, Rule 22, (b).
Order paid into court, §1-508.
Orders seized by sheriff, §1-509.
Staying execution on money judgment, §1-289, (a).

DEPOTS.
No title by possession of real estate condemned by railroad, plank road, etc., for, §1-44.

DEPRECIATION.
Corporate income tax.
Recapture of depreciation required under internal revenue code.
Inclusion in state net income, §105-130.5, (e).
Public utilities.
Depreciation charges, §62-35, (c).

DEPRESSANTS.
Schedule I controlled substances, §90-89.
Schedule II controlled substances, §90-90.
Schedule IV controlled substances, §90-92, (a).
Exemption of compounds, mixtures or preparations, §90-92, (b).
Unauthorized substances taxes, §§105-113.105 to 105-113.113.
See UNAUTHORIZED SUBSTANCES TAXES.

DEPUTY SHERIFFS.
Allowing prisoners to escape, §14-239.
District attorney to prosecute officer for escape, §14-240.
Compensation, §153A-103.
Vacancy in office of sheriff.
Performance of duties, §162-5.
Workers' compensation benefits, §160A-282, (c).

DERELICT MOTOR VEHICLES.
Generally, §§20-137.6 to 20-137.14.
See ABANDONED AND DERELICT MOTOR VEHICLES.

DERIVATIVE ACTIONS, §1A-1, Rule 23, (b).
Attorneys' fees.
Payment, §55-7-46.
Costs and expenses.
Payment, §55-7-46.
Definitions, §55-7-40.1.

DERIVATIVE ACTIONS —Cont'd
Demand requirement, §55-7-42.
Discontinuance or settlement, §55-7-45.
Dismissal, §55-7-44.
Foreign corporations.
Applicability, §55-7-47.
Jurisdiction, §55-7-40.
Limited liability companies, §57C-8-01.
Limited partners, §§59-1001 to 59-1006.
Nonprofit corporations.
Members and directors, §55A-7-40.
Privileged communications, §55-7-49.
Standing, §55-7-41.
Stays, §55-7-43.

DESCENT AND DISTRIBUTION.
Decedents' estates.
Distribution, §§28A-22-1 to 28A-22-10.
See DECEDENTS' ESTATES.
Degrees of kinship.
How computed, §104A-1.
Executors and administrators.
See EXECUTORS AND ADMINISTRATORS.
Intestate succession, §§29-1 to 29-30.
See INTESTATE SUCCESSION.

DESCRAMBLERS.
Cable television service theft, §14-118.5.

DESECRATION OF FLAG, §14-381.

DESERTION AND NONSUPPORT.
Child support enforcement program generally, §§110-128 to 110-142.2.
See CHILD SUPPORT.
Compelling disclosure of information respecting parent, §110-131.
Illegitimate children, §49-2.
Support and maintenance.
General provisions.
See SUPPORT AND MAINTENANCE.
Willful abandonment and failure to support spouse and children, §14-322, (b), (c).
Child support, payment order, determining, §14-322, (e).
Definitions, §14-322, (a).
Dependent spouse defined, §14-322, (a).
First offense, penalty, §14-322, (f).
Parents, §14-322, (d).
Second or subsequent offense, §14-322, (f).
Supporting spouse defined, §14-322, (a).
Supporting spouse living with dependent spouse, §14-322, (c).

DESTRUCTION OF INSTRUMENTS AND RECORDS.
Deeds.
Evidence.
Presumed to be in due form, §8-21.
Grants.
Burke county, §8-10.
Public records, destruction regulated, §132-3.
Wills, §31-5.1.
Evidence.
Proved and lost before recorded, §8-31.

DESTRUCTION OF WILL, §31-5.1.
Evidence.
Proved and lost before recorded, §8-31.

DETAINERS.
Continuance, §15-10.2, (a).
Definitions.
Interstate agreement on detainers, §15A-761.
"Appropriate court" defined, §15A-762.

DETAINERS —Cont'd
Disposition, §§15-10.2 to 15-10.4.
Mandatory disposition of detainers, §§15-10.1 to 15-10.4.
Mentally ill.
Exception as to prisoners who are mentally ill, §15-10.4.
Information to be furnished prisoner, §15-10.2, (b).
Interstate agreement on detainers, §§15A-761 to 15A-767.
Administrator, §15A-766.
Designation of central administrator, §15A-766.
Appropriate court.
Defined, §15A-762.
Cooperation in enforcement, §15A-763.
Copies of provisions.
Distribution, §15A-767.
Courts.
Cooperation in enforcement, §15A-763.
Definitions, §15A-761.
"Appropriate court," §15A-762.
Designation of enforcement officer, §15A-766.
Distribution of copies of provisions, §15A-767.
Enactment, §15A-761.
Escape from temporary custody, §15A-764.
General provisions, §15A-761.
Information agent, §15A-761.
Designation, §15A-766.
Penal or correctional institutions.
Officials in charge.
Authority and duty, §15A-765.
Public officers and employees.
Cooperation in enforcement, §15A-763.
Set forth, §15A-761.
State departments and agencies.
Cooperation in enforcement, §15A-763.
Temporary custody, §15A-761.
Escape from temporary custody, §15A-764.
Text of agreement, §15A-761.
Warden's, etc., duties, §15A-765.
Mandatory disposition of detainers, §§15-10.1 to 15-10.4.
Continuance, §15-10.2.
Information to be furnished prisoner, §15-10.2.
Mentally ill.
Exception as to prisoners who are mentally ill, §15-10.4.
Procedure, §15-10.3.
Request for final disposition of charges, §15-10.2.
Return of prisoner after trial, §15-10.3.
Manner of use, §15-10.1.
Mentally ill persons.
Mandatory disposition of detainer.
Exceptions as to mentally ill prisoners, §15-10.4.
Purpose, §15-10.1.
Request for final disposition of charges, §15-10.2, (a).
Securing attendance of criminal defendants confined in institutions within state, §15A-711, (d).

DETECTIVES.
Misdemeanor for detective to collect claims, accounts, etc., §14-401.2.
Private protective services generally, §§74C-1 to 74C-33.
See PRIVATE PROTECTIVE SERVICES.
State departments and agencies.
Use of private investigators limited, §114-15.2.

DETINUE.
Claim and delivery, §§1-472 to 1-480.

DETOURS.
Road repair, §136-25.

DEVELOPMENT.
Armories.
Fostering development of armories and facilities.
Authority to foster, §127A-162.
Authorities, borrowing, §159-188.
Balanced growth policy act, §§143-506.6 to 143-506.14.
See BALANCED GROWTH POLICY ACT.
Economic development commissions, §§158-8 to 158-15.
See ECONOMIC DEVELOPMENT COMMISSIONS.
Environmental impact statements.
Ordinances requiring statements for major development projects, §113A-8, (a) to (c).
Industrial development, §§158-16 to 158-24.
See INDUSTRIAL DEVELOPMENT.
Local development generally.
See LOCAL DEVELOPMENT.
Multi-county water conservation and infrastructure district, §158-15.1.
Subdivisions.
Control corners in real estate developments, §§39-32.1 to 39-32.4.
Streets and highways.
Minimum standards of board of transportation.
Compliance with standards required of developers, §136-102.6.

DEVELOPMENTAL DISABILITIES.
Adult care homes.
Generally.
See ADULT CARE HOMES.
Generally.
See MENTAL HEALTH, DEVELOPMENTAL DISABILITY, SUBSTANCE ABUSE.
Incompetence, determination of, §§35A-1101 to 35A-1116.
See INCOMPETENCE.
Joint committee on mental health, developmental disabilities, and substance abuse services, §§120-240 to 120-242.

DEVELOPMENT FINANCING DISTRICTS.
Annexation of district established by county, §159-107, (e).
Base valuation in development finance district.
Adjustments during lifetime of district, §159-107, (b).
Determination by tax assessor, §159-107, (a).
Duration, §159-107, (g).
Project development financing debt instruments, §§159-101 to 159-113.
See LOCAL GOVERNMENT FINANCE.
Property taxes.
Assessment of property.
District subject to agreement, §§105-277.11, 105-284, (d).
Levy within development financing district, §159-107, (d).
Revenue increment fund, §159-107, (c).
Use of money, §159-107, (f).

DEVELOPMENT ZONES.
Tax credit, §105-129.13.
Business tax incentives.
Zone designation, §105-129.3A.
Zone project credit, §105-129.13.

DEVISAVIT VEL NON, §31-35.

DEVISEES' RIGHT TO RENOUNCE, §31B-1.

DEVISES.
Wills generally.
See WILLS.

DIABETES.
Accident and health insurance.
Coverage for certain treatment, §58-51-61, (a).
Definition of "physician," §58-51-61, (b).
Food, drug or cosmetic act.
Drug or device, false advertising, §106-138, (b).
Health maintenance organizations.
Coverage for certain treatment, §58-67-74, (a).
Definition of "physician," §58-67-74.
Hospital, medical and dental service corporations.
Coverage for certain treatment, §58-65-91, (a).
Definition of "physician," §58-65-91, (b).
Jail prisoner unconscious or semiconscious.
Duty of custodial personnel.
Reasonable effort to determine if prisoner wearing emergency alert symbol, §153A-225.1, (a) to (c).
Police assistance to persons arrested while unconscious or semiconscious, §15A-503.
Program establishment, §130A-221, (a), (b).

DIAGNOSTIC CENTERS.
Certificates of need, §§131E-175 to 131E-190.
See HEALTH CARE FACILITIES.

DIAMOND INDUSTRY TRADE PRACTICES.
Definitions, §66-73.
Violations of provisions.
Penalty, §66-75.
What constitutes unfair trade practice, §66-74.

DIESEL FUEL TAX.
Gasoline tax generally, §§105-449.60 to 105-449.127.
See GASOLINE TAX.

DIESEL-POWERED MOTOR VEHICLE EMISSIONS, §20-128.1, (a).

DIETARY SUPPLEMENTS.
Sales and use tax.
Defined, §105-164.3.
Subject to tax, §105-164.13B, (a).

DIETITIANS AND NUTRITIONISTS, §§90-350 to 90-369.
Applicability of provisions.
Persons and practices not affected, §90-368.
Board of dietetics/nutrition.
Appointment of members, §90-354, (a).
Compensation, §90-354, (f).
Composition, §90-353, (a).
Professional members, §90-353, (b).
Public at large members.
Professions excluded from appointment, §90-353, (c).
Creation, §90-353, (a).
Defined as "board," §90-352.
Meetings, §90-355, (b).
Officers.
Election of, §90-355, (a).
Powers and duties, §90-356.
Quorum, §90-355, (b).
Removal of members, §90-354, (d).
Responsibilities, §90-356.
Terms of members, §90-354, (b).
Limitation, §90-354, (c).
Vacancies, §90-354, (e).

DIETITIANS AND NUTRITIONISTS —Cont'd
Child support enforcement.
Forfeiture of licensing privilege, §50-13.12.
Citation of title.
Dietetics/nutrition practice act, §90-350.
Criminal law and procedure.
Violations of provision, §90-366.
Definitions, §90-352.
Disciplinary actions, §90-363.
Grounds.
Prohibited conduct, §90-363.
Prohibited conduct.
Grounds for disciplinary action, §90-363.
Education.
License requirements, §90-357.
Examinations.
Fee for examination or reexamination, §90-364.
Fees.
Schedule of fees, §90-364.
Felony convictions.
Forfeiture of license, §15A-1331A.
Fines.
Violations of provision, §90-366.
Inapplicability of provisions, §90-368.
Injunctions.
Violation of provisions, §90-367.
Legislative declaration.
Purpose of provisions, §90-351.
Letters.
"LD" "LN" or "LDN."
Use of letters or any facsimile or combination.
License required, §90-365.
Licensed dietitian/nutritionist.
Defined, §90-352.
Use of words.
License required, §90-365.
Licenses.
Application, §90-357.
Evaluation.
Notification of applicant, §90-358.
Initial application fee, §90-364.
Display requirement, §90-362, (b).
Evaluation of application.
Notification of applicant, §90-358.
Examinations, §90-359.
Administration, §90-359.
Granting license without examination, §90-360.
Fees, §90-357.
Granting license without examination, §90-360.
Inactive status.
Application for active status, §90-362, (g).
Request by licensee, §90-362, (g).
Issuance.
Fee, §90-364.
Late renewal.
Fee, §90-364.
Notification requirements, §90-362, (c).
Practice of dietetics/nutrition.
Requirement of license, §90-365.
Property of board.
License as constituting, §90-362, (a).
Provisional licenses, §90-361.
Fee, §90-364.
Renewal, §90-362, (d).
Board notification, §90-362, (e).
Fee, §90-364.
Late renewal, §90-362, (f).
Requirements, §90-357.
Revocation or suspension.
Felony convictions, §15A-1331A.

DIETITIANS AND NUTRITIONISTS —Cont'd
Misdemeanors.
Violation of provisions, §90-366.
Nutrition care services.
Defined, §90-352.
"Nutritionist" or "licensed nutritionist."
Use of words.
License required, §90-365.
Prison terms.
Violations of provision, §90-366.
Purpose of provisions, §90-351.
Referral fees and solicitation payments, §§90-400 to 90-402.
Health care provider defined, §90-400.
Prohibited, §90-401.
Sanctions, §90-402.
Rules and licensure standards.
Copy fees, §90-364.
Rules and regulations.
Board of dietetics/nutrition.
Licensure standards and rules.
Copy fees, §90-364.
Rulemaking authority, §90-356.
Short title.
Dietetics/nutrition practice act, §90-350.
Third-party reimbursement, §90-369.
Limitation on modifications, §90-369.
Title.
Use of title "dietitian/nutritionist."
License required, §90-365.
Title of act.
Dietetics/nutrition practice act, §90-350.
Unlawful use of title, words or letters, §90-365.
Words.
"Dietitian" or "licensed dietitian."
Use of words.
License required, §90-365.

DIGGING.
Underground damage prevention, §§87-100 to 87-114.
See UNDERGROUND DAMAGE PREVENTION.

DIGITAL SIGNATURES.
Electronic medical records, authorization, §90-412, (b).
Financial identity fraud.
Generally, §§14-113.20 to 14-113.25.
Public agency transactions, §§66-58.1 to 66-58.12.
See ELECTRONIC COMMERCE IN GOVERNMENT.

DILATORY PLEADINGS, §1A-1, Rule 11, (a).

DIMMING HEADLIGHTS, §20-131, (a).
Failure to dim, §20-181.

DIPHTHERIA.
Childhood vaccine-related compensation, §§130A-422 to 130A-434.
Drug or device, false advertising, §106-138, (b).
Immunization, §§130A-152 to 130A-158.

DIPLOMAS.
Forgery, §14-122.1.
Obtaining by fraudulent means, §14-118.2.
World War II veterans.
Special high school diplomas.
Powers of board of education, §115C-12.

DIPLOMATS.
Foreign diplomat.
Holder of driver's license issued by United States department of state.
Notice to department of state.
Violation of state or local traffic law, revocation order, §20-37.20.

DIRECT CRIMINAL CONTEMPT, §5A-13.
Summary proceedings, §5A-14.

DIRECTED VERDICT MOTIONS, §1A-1, Rule 50, (a).
Judgment notwithstanding verdict, §1A-1, Rule 50, (b) to (d).

DIRECTING, CONTROLLING OR REGULATING TRAFFIC.
Willful failure to obey law-enforcement or traffic-control officer, §20-114.1.

DIRECTIONAL FLOW PEAK TRAFFIC LANES, §20-146.2, (c).

DIRECTIONAL SIGNALS ON MOTOR VEHICLES.
Motorcycles.
Provisions not applicable, §20-125.1, (d).
Requirements generally, §20-125.1, (a), (b).
Safety inspections, scope, §20-183.3, (a).
Trailers.
When not required, §20-125.1, (c).

DIRECT MAIL MARKETING.
Insurance consumer's or customer's account number.
Insurance institution, agent or support organization sharing.
General prohibition, §58-39-76.

DIRECT MAIL SALES.
Sales and use tax.
Direct mail defined, §105-164.3.
Sourcing sale of product.
Inapplicability of principles, §105-164.3, (d).

DIRECTOR OF THE BUDGET.
See BUDGETS.

DIRECTORY ASSISTANCE.
Sales and use tax on telecommunications services.
Gross receipts determination, §105-164.4C, (b), (c).

DIRECTORY LISTINGS.
Sales and use tax on telecommunications services.
Gross receipts determination, §105-164.4C, (b), (c).

DIRECTORY OF NEW HIRES, §110-129.2.

DIRECT-TO-HOME SATELLITE SERVICES.
Sales and use tax.
Defined, §105-164.3.
Rate of tax on gross receipts derived from, §105-164.4, (a).

DIRKS.
Carrying concealed, §14-269, (a), (b) to (d).
Carrying or possessing on educational property, §14-269.2.
Sale to minors, §14-315.
Weapons generally.
See WEAPONS.

DIRT ROADS.
Driving farm tractors on dirt roads from farm to farm, §20-122, (d).
Natural and scenic rivers system.
Road defined, §113A-33.

DISABILITY INCOME INSURANCE.
Policy standards, §58-51-130.
Applicability of provisions, §58-51-130, (b).
Definitions, §58-51-130, (a).
Disclosure standards, §58-51-130, (c).

DISABILITY INCOME INSURANCE —Cont'd
Policy standards —Cont'd
Exceptions, §58-51-130, (e).
Other income sources, §58-51-130, (h).
Other provisions applicable, §58-51-130, (g).
Preexisting conditions, when denial of claim prohibited, §58-51-130, (d).
Required provisions, §58-51-130, (f).

DISABILITY INCOME PLAN, §§135-100 to 135-114.
Amendment of provisions.
Reservation of power, §135-113.
Benefits.
Adjustments.
Post disability benefit adjustments, §135-108.
Defined, §135-101.
Long-term disability benefits.
Amount, §135-106, (b), (c).
Generally, §135-106, (a).
Medical review.
Annual medical review, §135-106, (a).
Post disability benefit adjustments, §135-108.
Short-term disability benefits.
Administration of provisions, §135-105, (d).
Amount, §135-105, (c).
Commencement, §135-105, (b).
Determination of eligibility, §135-105, (f).
Extension, §135-105, (g).
Generally, §135-105, (a).
Return to service for trial rehabilitation, §135-105, (e).
Status.
Not part of an employment contract, §135-113.
Waiting period, §135-104, (a).
Return to service for trial rehabilitation, §135-104, (b).
Salary continuation, §135-104, (a).
Board of trustees.
Administration of provisions, §135-102, (a).
Defined, §135-101.
Powers, §135-102, (c), (e).
Rules and regulations, §135-102, (c).
Trust fund.
Board as trustee of fund, §135-110, (a).
Citation of article.
Short title, §135-100, (a).
Compensation.
Base rate of compensation.
Defined, §135-101.
Defined, §135-101.
Consolidated judicial retirement system.
Reciprocity of membership service, §135-114.
Contributions.
Employers, §135-110, (b), (c).
Definitions, §135-101.
Disability salary continuation plan.
Transition provisions.
Benefit recipients under former disability salary continuation plan, §135-112, (b), (c).
Earnings.
Defined, §135-101.
Reports of earnings, §135-109.
Employers.
Contributions, §135-110, (b), (c).
Defined, §135-101.
Exemptions.
Applicability of provisions to plan, §135-111.
Investigations.
Medical board, §135-102, (d).

DISABILITY INCOME PLAN —Cont'd
Investments.
Trust fund.
Assets of fund, §135-110, (d).
Legislative retirement system.
Reciprocity of membership service, §135-114.
Medical board, §135-102, (d).
Composition, §135-102, (d).
Defined, §135-101.
Duties, §135-102, (d).
Modification of provisions.
Reservation of power, §135-113.
Optional retirement program, §135-107.
Other pension laws.
Applicability, §135-111.
Participants.
Cessation of participation, §135-103, (b).
Defined, §135-101.
Eligible participants, §135-103, (a).
Powers of plan, §135-102, (b).
Purpose of article, §135-100, (b).
Repeal of provisions.
Reservation of power, §135-113.
Reports.
Earnings, §135-109.
Retirement.
Defined, §135-101.
Optional retirement program, §135-107.
Rules and regulations, §135-102, (c).
Short title of article, §135-100, (a).
State treasurer.
Administration of provisions, §135-102, (a).
Powers, §135-102, (c), (e).
Rules and regulations, §135-102, (c).
Trust fund.
Custodian of fund, §135-110, (d).
Teachers.
Defined, §135-101.
Eligible participants, §135-103, (a).
Title of article.
Short title, §135-100, (a).
Transition provisions.
Disability salary continuation plan.
Benefit recipients under former disability salary continuation plan, §135-112, (b), (c).
Generally, §135-112, (a).
Trust fund, §135-110, (a).
Board of trustees.
Board as trustee of fund, §135-110, (a).
Investment of assets, §135-110, (d).
State treasurer.
Custodian of fund, §135-110, (d).

DISABILITY OF ATTORNEYS.
Disability proceedings generally, Bar Rules & Regs., B, §§.0101 to .0217.
See ATTORNEYS AT LAW.

DISABILITY OF JUDGE, §1A-1, Rule 63.

DISABILITY OF MARRIAGE.
Adverse possession, §1-18.

DISABLED ADULT PROTECTION ACT, §§108A-99 to 108A-111.
See ABUSED, NEGLECTED OR EXPLOITED DISABLED ADULTS.

DISABLED AMERICAN VETERANS.
Property tax exclusion, §105-275.

DISABLED PERSONS.
Access to and use of public places, §168-2.

DISABLED PERSONS —Cont'd
Actions.
Protection act.
Civil actions for discriminatory practices, §§168A-11, 168A-12.
Adult protection.
Protection of abused, neglected or exploited adults, §§108A-99 to 108A-111.
See ABUSED, NEGLECTED OR EXPLOITED DISABLED ADULTS.
Alcoholic beverages.
Refusal to sell not to be discriminatory, §18B-305, (c).
Amusements.
Right to use of places of public amusement, §168-3.
Animals.
Service animals, §§168-4.2 to 168-4.6.
Assault and battery.
Aggravated assault, §14-32.1, (e).
Assaults upon handicapped persons, §14-32.1.
Punishments, §14-32.1.
Definition of handicapped person, §14-32.1, (a).
DNA analysis.
Blood sample required upon conviction, §15A-266.4.
Simple assault, §14-32.1, (f).
Assistance dogs.
See ASSISTANCE DOGS.
Attorney general.
Designation of attorney specializing in law of the handicapped, §114-4.2F.
Attorneys, CLE substitute program, Bar Rules & Regs., D, §.1607.
Aviation.
Right to use of public conveyances, §168-3.
Betterments.
Procedure where plaintiff is under disability, §1-349.
Blind persons.
General provisions, §§111-4 to 111-47.
See BLIND PERSONS.
Boats.
Right to use of public conveyances, §168-3.
Buses.
Right to use of public conveyances, §168-3.
Carriers.
Right to use of public conveyances, §168-3.
Charities.
Governor's council on employment of the handicapped.
Council to be nonpartisan and nonprofit, §143-283.8.
Child custody.
Persons incapable of self-support upon reaching majority.
Rights same as minor child for custody purposes, §50-13.8.
Commission for the blind.
Consumer and advocacy advisory committee for the blind, §§143B-163, 143B-164.
General provisions, §§143B-157 to 143B-160.
See BLIND PERSONS.
Professional advisory committee, §§143B-161, 143B-162.
Commission to study the care of the aged and handicapped, §§143-279 to 143-283.
See AGED PERSONS.
Community trust for persons with severe chronic disabilities, §§36A-59.10 to 36A-59.20.
See COMMUNITY TRUST FOR PERSONS WITH SEVERE CHRONIC DISABILITIES.

DISABLED PERSONS —Cont'd
Contractors.
Public building contracts.
Small, minority, physically handicapped and women contractors.
Cooperation in promoting use, §143-135.5.
Council on developmental disabilities, §§143B-177 to 143B-179.
See MENTAL HEALTH, DEVELOPMENTAL DISABILITY, SUBSTANCE ABUSE.
Curb ramps or curb cuts.
Minimum requirements, §136-44.14.
Custody.
Persons incapable of self-support upon reaching majority.
Rights same as minor child for custody purposes, §50-13.8.
Defenses.
Protection act.
Employers.
Affirmative defenses, §168A-9.
Definitions, §168-1.
Council on developmental disabilities, §143B-178.
Protection act, §168A-3.
Developmental disabilities.
General provisions.
See MENTAL HEALTH, DEVELOPMENTAL DISABILITY, SUBSTANCE ABUSE.
Protection act.
General provisions, §§168A-1 to 168A-12. See within this heading, "Protection act."
Discrimination.
Protection act, §§168A-1 to 168A-12. See within this heading, "Protection act."
Divorce.
Custody.
Persons incapable of self-support upon reaching majority, §50-13.8.
Dogs.
Assistance dogs.
See ASSISTANCE DOGS.
Drivers' licenses.
Persons not to be licensed, §20-9, (e).
When persons may be licensed, §20-9, (g).
Education.
Preschool handicapped children.
Special education, §§115C-146.1 to 115C-146.4.
See SPECIAL EDUCATION.
Right to habilitation and rehabilitation services, §168-8.
Special education.
See SPECIAL EDUCATION.
Elections.
Accessible polling places, §163-131.
Assistance to voters, §163-166.8.
Curbside voting, §163-166.9.
Satellite voting places for disabled voters, §163-130.
Employment.
Governor's council on employment of the handicapped, §§143-283.1 to 143-283.8. See within this heading, "Governor's council on employment of the handicapped."
Employment security.
Disability benefits.
Eligibility conditions, §96-14.
Fair housing, §§41A-1 to 41A-10.
See FAIR HOUSING.
False pretenses and cheats.
Money.
Obtaining money by false representation of physical defect, §14-113.

DISABLED PERSONS —Cont'd
False representation as to physical defect to obtain money, §14-113.
Family care homes.
Definitions, §168-21.
"Handicapped persons" defined, §168-21.
Private agreements.
Certain agreements void, §168-23.
Public policy, §168-20.
Zoning.
Deemed residential use of property, §168-22.
Permits not required, §168-22.
Firemen's pension fund.
Monthly pensions upon retirement.
Totally and permanently disabled members, §58-86-55.
Global TransPark authority.
Goals for participation by, §63A-19.
Governor's advocacy council for persons with disabilities.
Appointment, §143B-403.2, (a).
Chair.
Designation, §143B-403.2, (d).
Clerical and other services, §143B-403.2, (d).
Composition, §143B-403.2, (b).
Creation, §143B-403.1.
Duties, §143B-403.1.
Expenses, §143B-403.2, (d).
Members generally, §143B-403.2, (a).
Number of members, §143B-403.2, (a).
Powers and duties, §143B-403.1.
Qualifications, §143B-403.2, (b).
Quorum, §143B-403.2, (d).
Removal, §143B-403.2, (d).
Terms, §143B-403.2, (c), (d).
Vacancies, §143B-403.2, (c), (d).
Governor's council on employment of the handicapped, §§143-283.1 to 143-283.8.
Celebration of National Employ the Physically Handicapped Week, §143-283.3.
Charitable organization, §143-283.8.
Citation of article, §143-283.1.
Cooperation with president's committee, §143-283.2.
National Employ the Physically Handicapped Week.
Celebration, §143-283.3.
Nature of council, §143-283.8.
Nonpartisan organization, §143-283.8.
Nonprofit organization, §143-283.8.
Purpose of article, §143-283.2.
Short title, §143-283.1.
Title of article, §143-283.1.
Hearing impaired.
See HEARING IMPAIRED.
Highways.
Right of access to and use of public places, §168-2.
Holidays.
National Employ the Physically Handicapped Week.
Celebration, §143-283.3.
Homestead exclusion.
Property taxes, §105-277.1.
Notice on abstract, §105-309, (f).
Hotels, inns and other transient lodging places.
Right to use of public accommodations, §168-3.
Housing.
Fair housing, §§41A-1 to 41A-10.
See FAIR HOUSING.
Right to housing, §168-9.

DISABLED PERSONS —Cont'd
Human service and volunteer transportation, §§62-289.1 to 62-289.7.
See HUMAN SERVICE AND VOLUNTEER TRANSPORTATION.
Hunting and fishing.
Disabled sportsman program, §113-296.
Income tax credits, §105-151.18.
Construction of dwelling units for, §105-151.1.
Definitions, §105-151.18, (c).
Disabled dependent, §105-151.18, (b).
Disabled taxpayer, §105-151.18, (a).
Limitations, §105-151.18, (d).
Injunctions.
Protection act.
Relief available, §168A-11, (b).
Insurance.
Discrimination.
Prohibited, §168-10.
Proceeds belonging to incapacitated adults.
Payment to and receipt by clerks of superior courts or public guardians, §7A-111, (b), (d).
Jurisdiction.
Protection act.
Civil actions, §168A-11, (c).
Legislative declaration, §168-1.
Legislative retirement system.
Disability retirement benefits, §120-4.22.
Reexamination for disability retirement allowance, §120-4.23.
Limitation of actions.
Protection act.
Civil actions for discriminatory practices, §168A-12.
Mattresses and bedding.
Exemptions for bedding manufactured, sanitized or renovated by nonprofit agency for the blind or severely handicapped, §130A-272, (a).
Mentally ill.
General provisions.
See MENTAL HEALTH, DEVELOPMENTAL DISABILITY, SUBSTANCE ABUSE.
Minors.
Interagency coordinating council for children from birth to five with disabilities and their families.
Agency cooperation, §143B-179.6.
Compensation, §143B-179.5, (e).
Composition, §143B-179.5, (b).
Duties, §143B-179.5, (d).
Agency cooperation, §143B-179.6.
Establishment, §143B-179.5, (a).
Organization, §143B-179.5, (c).
Clerical and support services, §143B-179.5, (f).
Regional councils.
Annual report, §143B-179.5A, (f).
Cochairs, §143B-179.5A, (d).
Composition, §143B-179.5A, (c).
Early intervention plan, development, §143B-179.5A, (e).
Established, number, §143B-179.5A, (a).
Meetings, quorum, §143B-179.5A, (d).
Members, appointment, number, term, removal, vacancy, §143B-179.5A, (b).
Reporting, §143B-179.5, (f).
Money belonging to incapacitated adults.
Payment to and receipt by clerks of superior courts or public guardians, §7A-111, (b), (d).
Motor carriers.
Right to use of public conveyances, §168-3.

DISABLED PERSONS —Cont'd
Motorized wheelchairs.
Registration and certificate of title.
Exemption from requirements, §20-51.
Nonprofit work centers for the blind and severely disabled.
Public contracts.
Purchases from, §143-129.5.
Purchases through department of administration.
Agency procurement of goods directly from center, §143-48.2, (a).
Agency procurement of services directly from center, §143-48.2, (b).
Bids and making offers by center, §143-48.2, (c).
Parking.
Designation of parking places, §20-37.6, (d).
Enforcement of handicapped parking privileges, §20-37.6, (e).
License plates.
Distinguishing license plates, §20-37.6, (b), (c1).
Out-of-state plates, §20-37.6A.
Penalties for violations, §20-37.6, (f).
Placards.
Out-of-state placards, §20-37.6A.
Windshield placards, §20-37.6, (c) to (c2).
Privileges generally, §20-37.6, (a).
Definitions, §20-37.5.
Public vehicular areas.
Signs differing from uniform signs, §136-30, (c).
Violations of provisions.
Penalties, §20-37.6, (f).
Prohibited acts, §20-37.6, (e).
Personnel system.
Discrimination against handicapped prohibited, §128-15.3.
Recruitment, etc., of handicapped persons, §128-15.3.
Property taxes.
Homestead exclusion, §105-277.1.
Notice on abstract, §105-309, (f).
Reduced valuation of permanent residence.
Abstract notice, §105-309, (f).
Protection act.
Actions.
Attorneys' fees.
Award, §168A-11, (d).
Jurisdiction, §168A-11, (c).
Limitation of actions, §168A-12.
Relief, §168A-11, (b).
Right of action, §168A-11, (a).
Citation.
Short title, §168A-1.
Defenses.
Employers.
Affirmative defenses, §168A-9.
Definitions, §168A-3.
Discriminatory practices.
Defined, §168A-3.
Employment, §168A-5, (a).
Exemptions, §168A-5, (b).
Public accommodations, §168A-6.
Public service, §168A-7.
Public transportation, §168A-8.
Transportation.
Public transportation, §168A-8.
Employers.
Defenses.
Affirmative defenses, §168A-9.
Defined, §168A-3.
Discriminatory practices, §168A-5.

DISABLED PERSONS —Cont'd
Protection act —Cont'd
Employers —Cont'd
Retaliation.
Prohibited, §168A-10.
Employment agencies.
Defined, §168A-3.
Discriminatory practices, §168A-5.
Retaliation.
Prohibited, §168A-10.
Injunctions.
Relief available, §168A-11, (b).
Jurisdiction.
Civil actions, §168A-11, (c).
Legislative findings, §168A-2, (b).
Limitation of actions, §168A-12.
Public accommodations.
Definition of "place of public accommodations," §168A-3.
Discriminatory practices, §168A-6.
Public service.
Discriminatory practices, §168A-7.
Public transportation.
Discriminatory practices, §168A-8.
Purpose of act, §168A-2, (a).
Qualified person with a disability.
Defined, §168A-3.
Reasonable accommodations.
Defined, §168A-3.
Duties as to, §168A-4.
Investigation of whether there are reasonable accommodations that can be made, §168A-4, (b).
Request for.
Duties of qualified handicapped person, §168A-4, (a).
Retaliation.
Prohibited, §168A-10.
Short title, §168A-1.
Title.
Short title, §168A-1.
Transportation.
Discrimination in public transportation, §168A-8.
Protection of abused, neglected or exploited adult, §§108A-99 to 108A-111.
See ABUSED, NEGLECTED OR EXPLOITED DISABLED ADULTS.
Public buildings.
Right of access to and use of public places, §168-2.
Public contracts.
Nonprofit work centers for the blind and severely disabled.
Purchases from, §143-129.5.
Public transportation.
Elderly and disabled transportation assistance program.
General provisions, §136-44.27.
Purchases through department of administration.
Cooperation in promoting use of small contractors, minority contractors, physically disabled contractors and women contractors, §143-48.
Purposes of provisions, §168-1.
Railroads.
Right to use of public conveyances, §168-3.
Ramps.
Curb ramps or curb cuts.
Minimum requirements, §136-44.14.
Rape.
Indictments.
Essentials of bill.
Victim physically helpless, §15-144.1, (c).

DISABLED PERSONS —Cont'd
Retirement system for counties and cities.
Benefits.
Allowance on disability retirement, §128-27, (d).
Disability retirement benefits, §128-27, (c).
Restriction of benefits, municipal officers and employees, §160A-163, (g).
Increase in benefits.
Those persons on disability retirement who were retired prior to July 1, 1971, §128-27, (p), (t).
Reexamination of beneficiaries retired on account of disability, §128-27, (e).
Retirement system for superior court judges.
Total and permanent disability, §§7A-55, 7A-56.
Retirement system for teachers and state employees.
Disability retirement, §135-5.
Consolidated judicial retirement act, §§135-59, 135-60.
Rights.
Generally, §§168-1 to 168-10.
School buses.
Authority to expend funds for transportation of students with special needs, §115C-250.
Schools.
Employment of handicapped, §115C-330.
Medicaid for students with disabilities.
Collaboration of agencies to ensure maximum funding, §108A-55.2.
Special education.
See SPECIAL EDUCATION.
Service animals, §§168-4.2 to 168-4.6.
Service of process.
Personal jurisdiction.
Manner of service to exercise, §1A-1, Rule 4, (j).
Sexual offenses.
Indictments.
Essentials of bill.
Victim physically helpless, §15-144.2, (c).
Special education.
See SPECIAL EDUCATION.
Streets and highways.
Condemnation proceedings.
Appointment of guardian ad litem for person with disability, §136-110.
Curb ramps or curb cuts for handicapped, §136-44.14.
Right of access to and use of public places, §168-2.
Sundays, holidays and special days.
National Employ the Physically Handicapped Week.
Celebration, §143-283.3.
Taxation on property.
Abstracts.
Information on tax relief for, §105-309, (f).
Failure to give required information, §105-309, (g).
Visually handicapped, §§111-4 to 111-47.
See BLIND PERSONS.
Voting.
Accessible voting places, §163-131.
Assistance to voters, §163-166.8.
Curbside voting, §163-166.9.
Satellite voting places for disabled voters, §163-130.
Wage and hour act.
Minimum wage established by commissioner, §95-25.3, (c).

DISABLED SPORTSMAN PROGRAM, §113-296.

DISABLED VEHICLES.
Abandoned and derelict motor vehicles generally, §§20-137.6 to 20-137.14.
See ABANDONED AND DERELICT MOTOR VEHICLES.
Unattended motor vehicles standing on public highway or public vehicular area.
Stopping engine, setting brake, etc., §20-163.

DISAFFIRMANCE OF MINOR'S CONTRACT.
Artistic and creative services contracts, §48A-12, (a) to (d).
Talent agency contracts, §48A-18.
Determining applicable period of time, §48A-3.

DISASTER RELIEF.
Disaster service volunteer leave, §§166A-30 to 166A-32.
Emergency management.
General provisions, §§166A-1 to 166A-16.
See EMERGENCY MANAGEMENT.
Emergency management assistance compact, §§166A-40 to 166A-53.
Hazardous materials emergency response, §§166A-20 to 166A-28.
See HAZARDOUS MATERIALS EMERGENCY RESPONSE.
Low-income housing tax credits.
Hurricane damage or hurricane disaster.
Qualified North Carolina low-income building, §105-129.41, (c).
Nuclear, biological or chemical agents.
Terrorist incident using, §§130A-475 to 130A-479.
See TERRORIST INCIDENT USING NUCLEAR, BIOLOGICAL OR CHEMICAL AGENTS.
State of emergency.
Government powers and proclamations generally, §§14-288.12 to 14-288.18.
See STATE OF EMERGENCY.

DISASTER RELIEF VEHICLES.
Motor vehicle license plates.
Permanent license plates for privately owned vehicles dedicated to support of disaster relief, §20-84, (b).

DISASTER RESPONSE PLAN OF THE STATE BAR, Bar Rules & Regs., D, §§.0301 to .0303.

DISASTERS.
Alcoholic beverage tax.
Exemptions, §105-113.81, (a).
Architects.
Qualified immunity for volunteers during emergency or disaster, §83A-13.1.
Emergencies.
See EMERGENCIES.
Emergency management.
See EMERGENCY MANAGEMENT.
Engineers.
Qualified immunity for volunteers during emergency or disaster, §89C-19.1.
Limitation of actions, extension.
Catastrophic conditions in one or more counties.
Authority of chief justice, §7A-39, (b).
Militia.
Unorganized militia.
Ordered out for service, §127A-87.
Physicians and surgeons.
Waiver of provisions, §90-12.2.
Presidentially declared disaster.
Tax penalties not assessed, §105-249.2, (b).

DISASTERS —Cont'd
Price gouging during states of disaster.
Deceptive trade practice, §75-37.1, (a).
Determining whether price unreasonably excessive.
Considerations, §75-37.1, (a).
End of state of disaster, §75-37.1, (c).
Public policy, §75-37.
Statement that seller not in violation.
Issuance by attorney general, §75-37.1, (b).
Public safety.
Department of crime control and public safety.
Secretary.
Powers and duties as to emergencies and disasters, §143B-476, (c) to (g).
Riots and civil disorders, §§14-288.1 to 14-288.20.
See RIOTS AND CIVIL DISORDERS.
State of disaster.
Declaration by governor or general assembly, powers, §166A-6.
Price gouging during state of disaster, §§75-37, 75-37.1.
State of disaster assistance funds, §166A-6.01.
State of emergency.
Government powers and proclamations generally, §§14-288.12 to 14-288.18.
See STATE OF EMERGENCY.
Statute of limitations, extension.
Catastrophic conditions in one or more counties.
Authority of chief justice, §7A-39, (b).
Tax penalties during presidentially declared disaster.
Not assessed, §105-249.2, (b).
Trespass during emergencies, §14-288.6.
Unemployment compensation.
Waiting period credit not required or waived, §96-13, (c).
Waiting period for benefit year not required, §96-13, (c1).
Volunteers, qualified immunity.
Architects, §83A-13.1.
Engineers, §89C-19.1.
Warnings regarding personal safety issued during disaster.
Civil liability for cost of rescue when willfully ignoring, §166A-15.1.

DISASTER SERVICE VOLUNTEER LEAVE, §§166A-30 to 166A-32.
Certified disaster service volunteer.
Defined, §166A-31.
Citation of provisions, §166A-30.
Disaster.
Defined, §166A-31.
Personnel called into service, §166A-17.
Persons eligible for leave, §166A-32.
Requests for leave, §166A-32.
Short title, §166A-30.
State agency.
Defined, §166A-31.
Workers' compensation, §166A-32.

DISBARMENT OF ATTORNEYS, §84-28, (c).
Consent to disbarment, Bar Rules & Regs., B, §.0117.
Disciplinary and disability rules of state bar generally, Bar Rules & Regs., B, §§.0101 to .0217.
See ATTORNEYS AT LAW.
Employing as legal clerk or assistant, Prof. Cond. Rule 5.5.

DISBARMENT OF ATTORNEYS —Cont'd
Forfeiture of license for felony conviction, §15A-1331, (a).
Imposition of discipline, Bar Rules & Regs., B, §.0123.
Obligations of disbarred or suspended attorneys, Bar Rules & Regs., B, §.0124.
Reinstatement, Bar Rules & Regs., B, §.0125.
Resignation while under investigation, order disbarring member, Bar Rules & Regs., B, §.0117.

DISCHARGE AND RELEASE.
Generally.
See RELEASES.
Mortgages and deeds of trust, §§45-36.2 to 45-42.1.
See MORTGAGES AND DEEDS OF TRUST.
Unclaimed property act, affirmative defense, §116B-58.

DISCHARGE FROM CIVIL ARREST, §1-419.

DISCHARGE OF ATTACHMENT.
Giving bond, §1-440.39.

DISCHARGE OF CLAIMS OR MONEY DEMANDS.
Advance payments to person claiming bodily injury, §1-540.3.
By agreement receipt of less sum is discharged, §1-540.
Motor vehicle accident settlements, §1-540.2.

DISCHARGE OF INSOLVENT PRISONERS, §§23-18 to 23-45.
Arrests, §23-29.
Bail and recognizance, §23-29.
Bonds, surety.
Release of insolvent upon giving bond, §23-40.
Surrender of principal, §23-41.
Continuance granted for cause, §§23-35, 23-45.
Creditor liable for jail fees, §23-42.
Executions, §23-29.
False swearing punished as perjury, §23-43.
Fraud.
Absent suggestion of fraud, discharge granted, §23-34.
Imprisonment for fraud, §23-37.
Suggestion of fraud, §23-28.
Superior or district court tries issue of fraud, §§23-29, 23-39.
Trial required before discharge, §23-36.
Who may suggest, §23-33.
Nonpayment of costs in criminal cases, §23-24.
Notice, §23-32.
Petition, §23-25.
Oath, §23-23.
Order of discharge, §23-38.
Persons taken in arrest and bail proceedings or in execution, §23-29.
Petition.
Before whom made, §23-25.
Contents, §23-31.
Notice, §23-25.
Proceeding on application, §23-27.
Verification, §23-31.
When filed, §23-30.
Proceeding on application, §23-27.
Provisional release, §23-30.1.
Release, §23-30.1.
Service of notice, §23-25.
Warrant issued for prisoner, §23-26.

DISCHARGE OF RECEIVERS.
Corporate receivers, debts provided for, §1-507.10.

DISCHARGES FROM MILITARY.
Concealed handgun permit eligibility.
Discharged other than honorably, §14-415.12, (b).
Registration, §§47-109 to 47-114.
Book for record of discharges in office of register of deeds, §47-109.
Certified copies of registration, §47-113.
Expenses.
Payment of expenses incurred, §47-114.
Fees.
Lost certificates.
Certificate of lost discharge, §47-110.
Oath of applicant, §47-111.
Recordation without charge, §47-110.
Forgery, §47-112.
Operation, §47-112.
Register of deeds.
Inquiry by register, §47-111.
Specifications, §47-109.
Removal or review of discharge paper.
Restricting access to military discharge documents, §47-113.2.
Restricting access to military discharge documents.
Construction of terms, §47-113.2, (l).
Copies, availability of, §47-113.2, (d), (h).
Cost of compliance with provision, §47-113.2, (j).
Filing fees authorized, §47-113.2, (i).
Filing requirements, §47-113.2, (c).
Good faith immunity, §47-113.2, (k).
Indexing and document images, §47-113.2, (f).
Parties authorized access, §47-113.2, (b).
Preservation of prior records, §47-113.2, (g).
Public records with restricted access, §47-113.2, (a).
Refusal of filing officer to accept, §47-113.2, (c1).
Rulemaking authority, §47-113.2, (e).

DISCHARGES OF OIL OR HAZARDOUS SUBSTANCES.
Dry-cleaning solvent cleanup, §§143-215.104A to 143-215.104U.
See DRY-CLEANING SOLVENT CLEANUP.
Generally, §§143-215.83 to 143-215.94.
See OIL OR HAZARDOUS SUBSTANCES DISCHARGES.
Offshore oil and gas activities, §§143-215.94AA to 143-215.94JJ.
See OFFSHORE OIL AND GAS ACTIVITIES.
Underground petroleum storage tank leak cleanup, §§143-215.94A to 143-215.94Y.
See UNDERGROUND PETROLEUM STORAGE TANK LEAK CLEANUP.

DISCHARGING WEAPON INTO OCCUPIED PROPERTY, §14-34.1.

DISCIPLINE OF ATTORNEYS.
Disciplinary rules of state bar generally, Bar Rules & Regs., B, §§.0101 to .0217.
See ATTORNEYS AT LAW.

DISCIPLINE OF STUDENTS.
Appeals, §115C-392.
Assault on teacher or other employee or other student.
Removal to alternative educational setting, §115C-391, (d2).
Corporal punishment, §115C-391, (a).
Immunity from civil liability when use consistent with state and local laws, §115C-391, (h).

DISCIPLINE OF STUDENTS —Cont'd
Corporal punishment —Cont'd
Reasonable force may be used, §115C-390.
English second language of parent or guardian.
Notice of students rights, §115C-391, (d5).
Expulsion of students.
English second language of parent or guardian.
Notice of students rights, §115C-391, (d5).
Notice to parent or guardian.
Students rights, §115C-391, (d5).
Student's conduct threat to safety of other students or employees, §115C-391, (d).
Alternative program offered, consideration prior to expulsion, §115C-391, (d).
Readmission of student, §115C-391, (d).
Request by student to board to reconsider decision, §115C-391, (d).
Students rights.
Notice to parent or guardian, §115C-391, (d5).
Force.
Reasonable force may be used, §115C-390.
Local boards of education.
Use of force may not be prohibited, §115C-390.
Lose control, lose license, §20-11, (n1).
Management and placement of disruptive students, §115C-397.1.
Notice to parent or guardian.
Students rights, §115C-391, (d5).
Powers and duties of principal, §115C-288, (e).
Principals.
Powers and duties of principal, §115C-288, (e).
Reasonable force may be used, §115C-390.
Reasonable force.
Immunity from civil liability when use consistent with state and local laws, §115C-391, (h).
School personnel may use, §115C-390.
Use to control certain behavior and self defense, §115C-391, (a).
Removal to alternative educational setting.
Student physically assaulting teacher or other employee, §115C-391, (d2).
School committees.
Use of force may not be prohibited, §115C-390.
Students rights.
Notice to parent or guardian, §115C-391, (d5).
Suspension.
Appeal to local board of education, §115C-391, (e).
Assault on teacher or other employee or other student.
Alternative educational setting not available, §115C-391, (d2).
English second language of parent or guardian.
Notice of students rights, §115C-391, (d5).
False threats to destroy or damage property by explosion, blasting or burning, §115C-391, (d3).
Judicial review of local board of education decision, §115C-391, (e).
Notice to parent or guardian.
Students rights, §115C-391, (d5).
Periods in excess of ten days, authority of principal, §115C-391, (c).
Principal, authority, §115C-391, (b), (c).
Students rights.
Notice to parent or guardian, §115C-391, (d5).
Ten day suspension, authority of principal, §115C-391, (b).
Weapons, bringing onto educational property, §115C-391, (d1).

DISCIPLINE OF STUDENTS —Cont'd
Teachers.
Duties of teachers, §115C-307, (a).
Reasonable force may be used, §115C-390.

DISCLAIMER.
Intestate succession renunciation, §§31B-1 to 31B-7.
See INTESTATE SUCCESSION.
Seeds.
Use of disclaimer as defense in prosecution or proceedings, §106-277.11.
Torrens system registration.
Deemed admission of allegations, §43-9.
Will renunciation, §§31B-1 to 31B-7.
See WILLS.

DISCLOSURE OF INFORMATION.
See CONFIDENTIALITY.

DISCLOSURE OF MILEAGE ON MOTOR VEHICLE TRANSFERS, §20-347.

DISCLOSURE OF PERSONAL INFORMATION IN MOTOR VEHICLE RECORDS, §20-43.1.

DISCLOSURE REQUIREMENTS FOR CREDIT CARDS, §§24-11.1, 24-11.2.

DISCLOSURES IN RESIDENTIAL PROPERTY SALES, §§47E-1 to 47E-10.
See RESIDENTIAL PROPERTY DISCLOSURE ACT.

DISCLOSURES ON SALE OF PRINTS BY ART DEALERS, §25C-14.

DISCLOSURE STATEMENT OF MEMBERSHIP CAMPING OPERATOR, §66-238.

DISCLOSURE STATEMENTS REQUIRED OF LOAN BROKERS, §66-107.

DISCONTINUANCE.
Generally.
See DISMISSAL, DISCONTINUANCE AND NONSUIT.

DISCOUNT BUYING CLUBS.
Bonds, surety, §66-135, (a).
Actions on bond, §66-135, (c).
Violation of requirement.
Felony, §66-135, (d).
Contracts.
Breach.
Action against bond, §66-135, (c).
Cancellation.
Business days.
Defined, §66-133, (e).
Customer's right to cancel, §66-133, (a).
Statement of right to be included in contract, §66-132, (a).
Notice, §66-133, (b) to (d).
When cancellation occurs, §66-133, (b).
Contents, §66-132, (a).
Waiver of certain formalities.
Requirements for waiver, §66-132, (b).
Formalities.
Waiver of certain formalities.
Requirements for waiver, §66-132, (b).
Written contracts required, §66-132, (a).
Damages.
Breach of contract.
Action against bond, §66-135, (c).
Violations of provisions.
Action against bond, §66-135, (c).
Action for damages, §66-136, (a).

DISCOUNT BUYING CLUBS —Cont'd
Defined, §66-131.
Felonies.
Bond and trust account requirements.
Violations, §66-135, (d).
Mail.
Cancellation of contract by customer.
Notice of cancellation, §66-133, (c).
Notice.
Cancellation of contract by customer, §66-133, (b) to (d).
Prohibited acts, §66-134.
Sales and use tax, §66-137.
Taxation, §66-137.
Trust account.
Required, §66-135, (b).
Exceptions, §66-135, (b).
Violation of requirement.
Felony, §66-135, (d).
Violations of provisions.
Bond and trust account requirements.
Felonies, §66-135, (d).
Damages.
Action against bond, §66-135, (c).
Action for damages, §66-136, (a).
Prohibited acts, §66-134.
Remedies, §66-136, (a), (b).
Additional nature of remedies, §66-136, (c).
Unfair acts and practices.
Violations to constitute, §66-136, (b).

DISCOUNT FEES.
Loans secured by real property, §24-10, (a).
Revolving credit charges, §24-11, (a2).
Structured settlement transfers, §1-543.12.

DISCOUNT POINTS.
Home loan secured by first mortgage or first deed of trust, §24-1.1A, (c).

DISCOVERED PROPERTY.
Property taxes, listing assessing and taxing, §105-312.

DISCOVERING ASSETS OF JUDGMENT DEBTOR.
Supplemental proceedings, §§1-352 to 1-368.
See EXECUTIONS.

DISCOVERY.
Abused, neglected or dependent juvenile actions, §7B-700.
Administrative procedure.
Hearings, §§150B-28, (b), 150B-39, (b).
Subpoenas.
Witnesses.
Fees, §150B-39, (c).
Admissions.
See ADMISSIONS.
Adult care homes.
Quality assurance, medical, or peer review committee information, immunity from discovery, §131D-21.2, (b).
Amendment of responses, §1A-1, Rule 26, (e).
Arbitration.
Grounds for permitting, §1-569.17, (c).
Issuance of process, §1-569.17, (d).
Attorney disciplinary proceedings, Bar Rules & Regs., B, §.0114.
Attorneys at law.
Frivolous discovery, Prof Cond. Rule 3.4.
Bank compliance review documents.
Undiscoverable matter, §53-99.1, (b).

DISCOVERY —Cont'd
Bills of lading.
Actions by or against common or connecting carriers.
Bills of lading as evidence, §8-41.
Child fatality prevention system.
Confidential information and records created by local teams, prohibition, §7B-1413, (c).
Compromise and settlement.
Mediated settlement conferences in superior court civil actions, §7A-38.1, (l).
Conference, §1A-1, Rule 26, (f).
Failure to participate in framing of discovery plan, §1A-1, Rule 37, (g).
Medical malpractice, §1A-1, Rule 26, (f1).
Contempt.
Criminal law and procedure.
Failure to comply with orders, §15A-910, (a).
Considerations of court before granting sanctions, §15A-910, (b).
Order compelling discovery.
Failure to comply, §1A-1, Rule 37, (b).
Criminal procedure.
Applicability of provisions, §15A-901.
Contempt.
Failure to comply with orders, §15A-910, (a).
Considerations of court before granting sanctions, §15A-910, (b).
Continuing duty to disclose, §15A-907.
Defendant.
Case files and expert witness information.
Disclosure by state, §15A-903, (a).
Disclosure of information by defendant.
Documents, §15A-905, (a).
Exemptions, §15A-906.
Reports of examinations and tests, §15A-905, (b).
Tangible objects, §15A-905, (a).
Notice to state of defenses and witnesses, §15A-905, (c), (d).
Documents.
Disclosure by defendant, §15A-905, (a).
Disclosure by state.
Certain information not subject to disclosure, §15A-904, (a).
Duty to disclose.
Continuing duty, §15A-907.
Failure to comply with orders.
Sanctions, §15A-910, (a).
Considerations of court before granting, §15A-910, (b).
Manner of discovery.
Orders must specify, §15A-909.
Motion for discovery, §15A-902, (a), (f).
Hearing before superior court judge, §15A-902, (c).
Physical and mental examinations.
Disclosure of results by defendant, §15A-905.
Place of discovery.
Orders must specify, §15A-909.
Procedure, §15A-902.
Protective orders, §15A-908, (a).
Supporting affidavits or statements.
Submission to court for in camera inspection, §15A-908, (b).
Reports of examinations and tests.
Disclosure by defendant, §15A-905, (b).
State of North Carolina.
Defendant's defenses and witnesses, §15-905, (c), (d).

DISCOVERY —Cont'd
Criminal procedure —Cont'd
State of North Carolina —Cont'd
Disclosure of evidence by state.
Case files and expert witness information, §15A-903, (a).
Defendant's defenses and witnesses, §15-905, (c), (d).
Exemptions, §15A-904, (a), (b), (c).
Statement of co-defendant, §15A-903, (b).
Voluntary discovery.
Exemptions from required disclosure of evidence not to preclude voluntary disclosures or waiver of protections, §15A-904, (b).
Request by defendant for voluntary discovery from state, §15A-902, (d).
Request by state for voluntary discovery from defendant, §15A-902, (e).
Tangible objects.
Disclosure by defendant, §15A-905, (a).
Time of discovery.
Orders must specify, §15A-909.
Voluntary compliance with discovery request.
Effect, §15A-902, (b).
Request for or written agreement required, §15A-902, (a).
Scope of disclosure, §15A-903, (b).
State of North Carolina.
Request for voluntary discovery from defendant, §15A-902, (e).
Request for voluntary discovery from state, §15A-902, (d).
Delinquent and undisciplined juvenile actions.
Continuing duty to disclose, §7B-2303.
Denying, restricting or deferring discovery, §7B-2302, (a).
Submission of supporting affidavits or statements for court in camera inspection, §7B-2302, (b).
Disclosure of evidence by juvenile.
Inspection and copying of books, papers, documents, etc., §7B-2301, (b).
Names of persons to be called as witnesses, §7B-2301, (a).
Physical or mental examination or test results, §7B-2301, (c).
Tests, measurements or experiments made in connection with case, §7B-2301, (c).
Disclosure of evidence by petitioner.
Books, papers, documents, etc., §7B-2300, (c).
Names of persons to be called as witness, §7B-2300, (b).
Oral statements of juvenile, §7B-2300, (a).
Physical or mental examination or test results, §7B-2300, (d).
Tests, measurements or experiments made in connection with case, §7B-2300, (d).
Voluntary disclosures permitted, §7B-2300, (f).
Work product of petitioner, law enforcement officers or other persons.
Production of reports, memoranda or other internal documents in connection with investigation not required to be disclosed, §7B-2300, (e).
Written or recorded statements of juvenile, §7B-2300, (b).
Protective orders, §7B-2302.
Depositions.
See DEPOSITIONS.

DISCOVERY —Cont'd
Discipline of attorneys, Bar Rules & Regs., B, §.0114.
District courts, Super. Ct. Rule 8.
Civil actions.
Fee on filing verified petition, §7A-305.1.
Divorce.
Distribution by court of marital and divisible property.
Equitable distribution.
Discovery and scheduling conference, §50-21, (d).
Procedures in actions, §50-21, (a).
Sanctions for delay, §50-21, (e).
Entry on land for inspection and other purposes, §1A-1, Rules 26, (a); 34.
Executions.
Assets of judgment debtor.
Generally, §1-352.2.
Interrogatories, §1-352.1.
Expedited evictions.
Authority to conduct discovery generally, §42-70, (a).
Injunction against illegal activity pending completion of discovery, §42-70, (e).
Interrogatories.
Time for response, §42-70, (d).
Request for admissions.
Time for response, §42-70, (d).
Request for production of documents.
Time for response, §42-70, (d).
Time for initiation by defendant, §42-70, (b).
Time for initiation by plaintiff, §42-70, (c).
Experts.
Trial preparation, scope of discovery, §1A-1, Rule 26, (b).
Frequency or extent of use of discovery methods.
Limitation by court, §1A-1, Rule 26, (b).
Frivolous discovery.
Attorneys at law, Prof Cond. Rule 3.4.
Health care liability.
Separate discovery on claims, §90-21.53.
Insurance agreements.
Scope of discovery, §1A-1, Rule 26, (b).
International commercial arbitration and conciliation.
Assistance of superior court in obtaining, request, §1-567.57, (a).
Tribunal conducting proceeding, §1-567.49, (b).
Interrogatories.
See INTERROGATORIES.
Interstate family support.
Tribunal requesting assistance with, §52C-3-317.
Managed care entities, claims involving.
Separate discovery and trial, §1A-1, Rule 42, (b).
Mediated settlement conferences in superior court civil actions, §7A-38.1, (l).
Mediated settlement conferences or other settlement procedures in district court.
Actions involving equitable distribution, alimony or support.
Evidence of statements made and conduct occurring in proceeding not subject to discovery, §7A-38.4A, (j).
Medical malpractice.
Discovery conference, §1A-1, Rule 26, (f1).
Methods of discovery, §1A-1, Rule 26, (a).
Motions.
Order compelling discovery.
Motion for, §1A-1, Rule 37, (a).

DISCOVERY —Cont'd
Notice.
Discovery conference, service, §1A-1, Rule 26, (f).
Order compelling discovery.
Failure to comply with order.
Sanctions, §1A-1, Rule 37, (b).
Motion for, §1A-1, Rule 37, (a).
Physical and mental examination of persons, §1A-1, Rules 26, (a); 35.
Production of documents and things, §1A-1, Rules 26, (a); 34.
Protective orders, §1A-1, Rule 26, (c).
Abused, neglected or dependent juvenile actions, §7B-700.
Criminal procedure, §15A-908.
Delinquent and undisciplined juvenile actions, §7B-2302.
Trade secrets, actions for misappropriation, §66-156.
Psychotherapy patient/client sexual exploitation act.
Clients conduct.
Specific information or examples, §90-21.44, (b).
Sexual history of client, §90-21.44, (a).
Savings and loan associations.
Compliance review documents, §54B-63.1, (b).
Scope of discovery, §1A-1, Rule 26, (b).
Sealing deposition.
Protective orders, §1A-1, Rule 26, (c).
Sequence and timing of discovery, §1A-1, Rule 26, (d).
Service of process.
Notice of motion for discovery conference, §1A-1, Rule 26, (f).
Papers relating to discovery, §1A-1, Rule 5, (a).
Subpoenas for production of documentary evidence, §8-61.
Signing of discovery requests, responses and objections, §1A-1, Rule 26, (g).
Stipulations regarding discovery procedure, §1A-1, Rule 29.
Superior courts, Super. Ct. Rule 8.
Civil actions.
Fee on filing verified petition, §7A-305.1.
Criminal procedure, §§15A-901 to 15A-910. See within this heading, "Criminal procedure."
Supplementation of responses, §1A-1, Rule 26, (e).
Trade secrets.
Protective orders, §1A-1, Rule 26, (c).
Trial preparation.
Scope of discovery, §1A-1, Rule 26, (b).
University of North Carolina.
Mediation of personnel matters.
Not subject to discovery, §116-3.3, (a).
Wage and hour act.
Files and other records relating to investigations and enforcement proceedings, §95-25.20.
Workers' compensation.
Contested cases, I.C. Rules 605, 606.
Industrial commission.
Power to limit discovery, §97-80, (f).
Work product.
Health care facility certificate of public advantage.
Actions on issuing or remaining in effect.
Department's or attorney general's work product, §131E-192.10, (d).
Trial preparation, scope of discovery, §1A-1, Rule 26, (b).

DISCOVERY CONFERENCE, §1A-1, Rule 26, (f).
Failure to participate, §1A-1, Rule 37, (g).
Medical malpractice, §1A-1, Rule 26, (f1).

DISCOVERY OF INJURY, LOSS, DEFECT OR DAMAGE.
Malpractice action.
Time limitation for commencing action, §1-15, (c).

DISCOVERY OF JUDGMENT DEBTOR ASSETS.
Supplemental proceedings generally, §§1-352 to 1-368.
See SUPPLEMENTAL PROCEEDINGS.

DISCRETIONARY REVIEW BY SUPREME COURT.
Certification of cause in court of appeals for review, §7A-31, (a) to (d).

DISCRETIONARY TRUSTS IN FINANCIAL INSTITUTIONS.
Credit unions, §36A-80.
Interest or estate of beneficiary not alienable, §36A-115, (b).

DISCRIMINATION.
Actions.
Discrimination in business.
Enforcement of provisions, §75B-4.
Agricultural marketing authority.
Prohibition on discrimination, §106-531.
Alcoholic beverages.
Refusal to sell not to be discriminatory, §18B-305, (c).
Alternative dispute resolution.
Persons with disabilities.
Public service discrimination cases, §168A-10.1.
Attorney general.
Discrimination in business.
Enforcement of provisions.
Actions, §75B-4.
Burial without regard to race or color, §65-72, (a).
Violations of provisions.
Misdemeanors, §65-72, (b).
Business.
Actions.
Enforcement of provisions, §75B-4.
Attorney general.
Enforcement of provisions.
Actions, §75B-4.
Construction and interpretation.
Provisions not exclusive, §75B-7.
Contracts.
Prohibited contracts, §75B-2.
Void contracts, §75B-6.
Cumulative nature of remedies, §75B-5.
Damages.
Actions for.
Persons injured by violations, §75B-4.
Definitions, §75B-1.
Enforcement of provisions, §75B-4.
Cumulative nature of remedies, §75B-5.
Injunctions.
Enforcement of provisions, §75B-4.
Prohibited acts, §75B-2.
Actions not prohibited, §75B-3.
Carriers.
Connecting lines.
Discrimination between connecting lines prohibited, §62-210.
Cemeteries.
Burial without regard to race or color, §65-72, (a).
Violations of provisions.
Misdemeanors, §65-72, (b).

DISCRIMINATION —Cont'd
Community colleges.
Nondiscrimination policy, §115D-77.
Constitution of North Carolina.
Jury service, Const. N. C., art. I, §26.
Constitution of the United States, Const. U. S., amds. XIV, XV.
Consumer finance act.
Prohibited acts, §53-180, (d).
Contracts.
Discrimination in business.
Prohibited contracts, §75B-2.
Void contracts, §75B-6.
Damages.
Discrimination in business.
Actions by persons injured by violations, §75B-4.
Definitions.
Discrimination in business, §75B-1.
Disabled persons.
Protection act.
General provisions, §§168A-1 to 168A-12.
See DISABLED PERSONS.
Elections.
Voting rights act of 1965.
Submission of charges to United States attorney general, §§120-30.9A to 120-30.9H.
See ELECTIONS.
Electric membership corporations.
Prohibition on discrimination, §117-16.1.
Emergency management.
Prohibited, §166A-12.
Employment.
Equal employment practices, §§143-422.1 to 143-422.3.
Citation of article, §143-422.1.
Human relations council.
Charges of discrimination.
Receipt, §143-422.3.
Conciliations, §143-422.3.
Investigations, §143-422.3.
Legislative declaration, §143-422.2.
Purpose of article, §143-422.2.
Short title, §143-422.1.
Lawful use of lawful products during nonworking hours, §95-28.2.
Personnel system.
Assistance in obtaining state employment, §§126-16 to 126-18.
Retaliatory employment discrimination, §§95-240 to 95-245.
Civil action by employees, §95-243, (a).
Civil action filed by commissioner or employee, §95-242, (b).
Complaint, §95-242, (a).
Conciliation, §95-242, (a), (b).
Confidential information, §95-242, (d), (e).
Informal procedures, §95-242, (b).
Definitions, §95-240.
Discrimination prohibited, §95-241, (a).
Effect of article on other rights, §95-244.
Exception to violation of article, §95-241, (b).
Investigation, §95-242, (a).
Jury trial in civil actions, §95-243, (d).
Other rights afforded employee.
Effect of article on, §95-244.
Relief in civil actions, §95-243, (c).
Required for employee to bring actions, §95-243, (e).
Right-to-sue letter, §95-242, (a) to (c).
Subpoenas, §95-242, (f).

DISCRIMINATION —Cont'd
Employment —Cont'd
Retaliatory employment discrimination —Cont'd
Time for commencing civil actions, §95-243, (b).
Use of leave for parent involvement in schools, §95-28.3, (b), (c).
Venue of civil action by employees, §95-243, (a).
Sickle cell trait or hemoglobin C trait.
Discrimination against persons possessing, §95-28.1.
Equal employment practices, §§143-422.1 to 143-422.3.
Ethnic intimidation.
Assaulting person or damaging or defacing property, §14-401.14, (a).
Teaching techniques, §14-401.14, (b).
Fair housing, §§41A-1 to 41A-10.
See FAIR HOUSING.
Felonies.
Offenses committed because of victim's race, etc., §14-3, (c).
Firemen's relief fund.
No discrimination on account of race, §58-84-55.
Genetic testing, information or counseling.
Employment discrimination.
Based on person's genetic information, §95-28.1A, (a).
Genetic characteristic defined, §95-28.1A, (b).
Genetic information defined, §95-28.1A, (b).
Genetic test defined, §95-28.1A, (b).
Person requesting genetic test or counseling, §95-28.1A, (a).
Health maintenance organizations.
Mentally ill and chemically dependent.
Applicability of section, §58-67-75, (d).
Coverage, §58-67-75, (b1), (c).
Prohibited acts, §58-67-75, (b).
Prohibited acts, §58-67-65, (f).
Hospital, medical and dental service corporations.
Mentally ill and chemically dependent.
Applicability of section, §58-65-90, (d).
Coverage, §58-65-90, (b1), (c).
Definitions, §58-65-90, (a).
Prohibited acts, §58-65-90, (b).
Exceptions, §58-65-90, (c).
Prohibited practices, §58-65-85.
Housing.
Fair housing, §§41A-1 to 41A-10.
See FAIR HOUSING.
Handicapped persons.
Right to housing, §168-9.
Human relations council, §§143-422.1 to 143-422.3.
Injunctions.
Discrimination in business.
Enforcement of provisions, §75B-4.
Insurance.
Accident and health insurance.
Coverage of bones and joints, §58-3-121, (a) to (c).
Group accident and health insurance.
Mentally ill and chemically dependent.
Applicability, §58-51-55, (d).
Coverage, §58-51-55, (b1), (c).
Definitions, §58-51-55, (a).
Prohibited acts, §58-51-55, (b), (c).
Bones, coverage of, §58-3-121, (a) to (c).
Employer discrimination against lawful use of lawful products during nonworking hours.
Health, disability or life insurance policies distinguishing between employees, §95-28.2, (b).

DISCRIMINATION —Cont'd
Insurance —Cont'd
Handicapped persons.
Prohibited, §168-10.
Joints, coverage of, §58-3-121, (a) to (c).
Life insurance.
Prohibited acts, §58-58-35.
Motor vehicles.
Prohibited practices, §58-3-25.
Race, color or national or ethnic origin.
Prohibited acts, §58-3-25, (c).
Rates not to be unfairly discriminatory, §58-40-20, (a), (e).
Method of rate making, §58-36-10.
Unfair trade practices.
Prohibited acts, §58-63-15.
Insurance companies.
Between individuals of same class, prohibition, §58-3-120, (b).
In favor of any person, prohibition, §58-3-120, (a).
Lawful use of lawful products by employees during nonworking hours, §95-28.2.
Military personnel, discrimination against.
Employer discrimination prohibited, §127B-14.
Misdemeanors, §127B-15.
Penalties.
Violations of article, §127B-15.
Private discrimination prohibited, §127B-11.
Public discrimination prohibited, §127B-12.
Purpose of article, §127B-10.
Refusing entrance prohibited, §127B-13.
Violation of article.
Penalties, §127B-15.
Misdemeanors.
Offenses committed because of victim's race, etc., §14-3, (c).
Motor carriers.
Penalty, §62-325, (a).
Motor vehicle manufacturers.
Discriminating among dealers, §20-305.6.
Nursing home administrators.
Grounds for revocation or suspension of license, §90-285.1.
Occupational safety and health.
Prohibited, §95-151.
Personnel system.
Equal employment opportunity.
Assistance in obtaining state employment, §§126-16 to 126-18.
Compensation for assisting person barred, §126-18.
Equal employment opportunity institute.
Training, §126-16.1.
Local political subdivisions, §126-16.
Retaliation against protecting employees, §126-17.
Newly appointed managers and supervisors.
Training, §126-16.1.
State departments and agencies, §126-16.
Retaliation against protecting employees, §126-17.
Training, §126-16.1.
Grounds for filing contested case, §126-34.1, (a).
Denial of equal opportunity, §126-34.1, (b).
Handicapped persons.
Prohibited discrimination against, §128-15.3.
Persons with disabilities.
Alternative dispute resolutions.
Public service discrimination cases, §168A-10.1.
Provider sponsored organizations.
Prohibited acts, §131E-290, (c).

DISCRIMINATION —Cont'd
Public schools.
Assignment on certain basis prohibited, §115C-367.
Public utilities.
Prohibited, §62-140, (a), (c).
Rules and regulations to prevent, §62-140, (b).
Retaliatory employment discrimination, §§95-240 to 95-245.
Whistleblower protection.
Retaliatory employment discrimination, §§95-240 to 95-245.
Wine distribution agreements.
Inducement, coercion or discrimination prohibited, §18B-1202.
Intent of article to prohibit unlawful discrimination, §18B-1215.
Notice of intent to terminate, §18B-1205, (a).
Wholesalers, §18B-1211.

DISCS.
Compact discs.
Record and tape piracy generally.
See RECORD AND TAPE PIRACY.

DISEASES.
AIDS.
See AIDS.
Alzheimer's subcommittee, §120-186.1.
Bee and honey industry.
Authority of commissioner to protect industry from diseases, §106-640.
Giving false information to commissioner, §106-641.
Defined, §106-635.
Minimum standards for disease tolerance levels, §106-638.
Moveable frame hives, §106-641.
Regulations for control and prevention, §106-639.
Bioterrorism.
Nuclear, biological or chemical agents.
Terrorist incident using, §§130A-475 to 130A-479.
See TERRORIST INCIDENT USING NUCLEAR, BIOLOGICAL OR CHEMICAL AGENTS.
Blood banks.
Selection of donors.
Risk of diseased transmission to be minimized, §90-220.13.
Cancer.
See CANCER.
Child care operators.
Communicable diseases.
Reports, §130A-136.
Chiropractors.
Control of contagious and infectious diseases.
Chiropractors subject to state and municipal regulations as to, §90-157.
Communicable diseases generally, §§130A-134 to 130A-148.
See COMMUNICABLE DISEASES.
Conveyances.
Disclosure of death or illness of previous occupant, §39-50.
Dead bodies.
Contagious diseases.
Handling and transportation of bodies, §130A-395, (a) to (c).

DISEASES —Cont'd
Health emergency.
Nuclear, biological or chemical agents.
Terrorist incident using, §§130A-475 to 130A-479.
See TERRORIST INCIDENT USING NUCLEAR, BIOLOGICAL OR CHEMICAL AGENTS.
Hearing aid dealers and fitters.
Freedom from contagious or infectious diseases.
Prerequisite to issuance of license, §93D-5, (a).
Heart disease and stroke.
Justus-Warren heart disease and stroke prevention task force, §143B-216.60.
Immunization, §§130A-152 to 130A-158.
Certificate of immunization, §130A-154.
Adults attending school, §130A-155, (d).
Child care facilities, §130A-155, (a) to (c).
Information to be contained, §130A-154, (a).
Maintenance of record, §130A-155, (b).
School authorities, §130A-155, (a), (c).
State other than North Carolina, §130A-154, (b).
Submission of certificate to child care facility, preschool and school authorities, §130A-155, (a).
Universities and colleges, §130A-155.1.
Charge for obtaining immunization, §130A-153, (a).
Childhood vaccine-related injury compensation, §§130A-422 to 130A-434.
See CHILDHOOD VACCINE-RELATED INJURY COMPENSATION.
Commission for health services.
Promulgation of rules concerning implementation of program, §130A-152, (c).
Enforcement of article.
Rules and regulations, §130A-152, (c).
Fees.
Adoption of rules establishing, §130A-152, (c1).
Implementation of article.
Rules and regulations, §130A-152, (c).
Implementation of program.
Promulgation and enforcement of rules concerning implementation, §130A-152, (c).
Medical exemption, §130A-156.
Minors, §130A-153, (d).
Obtaining immunization, §130A-153, (a).
Records.
Access to records, §130A-153, (c).
Certificate of immunization.
Maintenance of record.
By child care facility and school authorities, §130A-155, (b).
By college or university, §130A-155.1, (b).
Religious exemption, §130A-157.
Reports, §130A-153, (b).
Certificate of immunization.
Filing of report.
By child care facility and school authorities, §130A-155, (c).
By college or university, §130A-155.1, (c).
Required, §130A-152, (a).
Additional immunization, §130A-152, (e).
Requirements that can be placed on child or parent.
Adoption of rules, §130A-152, (c1).
Rules and regulations, §130A-152, (c).
Standards of vaccine preparations used, §130A-152, (d).
Vaccine preparations, §130A-152, (d).

DISEASES —Cont'd
Kidneys.
Chronic renal disease program, §130A-220, (a), (b).
Livestock.
Bang's disease, §§106-388 to 106-398.
See BRUCELLOSIS.
Brucellosis, §§106-388 to 106-398.
See BRUCELLOSIS.
Cattle tick, §§106-351 to 106-363.
See CATTLE TICK.
Compensation for killing diseased animals, §§106-323 to 106-335.
See LIVESTOCK DISEASES.
Control of livestock diseases generally, §§106-400 to 106-405.
See LIVESTOCK DISEASES.
Equine infectious anemia, §§106-405.15 to 106-405.20.
Generally, §§106-304 to 106-307.7.
See LIVESTOCK DISEASES.
Hog cholera, §§106-310 to 106-322.3.
See HOG CHOLERA.
Tuberculosis, §§106-336 to 106-350.
See TUBERCULOSIS IN LIVESTOCK.
Meat and meat products.
Regulation, §14-342.
Rendering operations.
Disposal of diseased animals, §106-168.10.
Meningococcal disease vaccination information.
Universities and colleges.
Providing students information, §116-260.
Occupational diseases generally.
Workers' compensation.
See WORKERS' COMPENSATION.
Occupational diseases, reportable.
Avoidance of duplication of reports, §130A-455.
Department of labor.
Reports to, §130A-460.
Immunity of persons who report, §130A-459.
Laboratories, §130A-458.
Medical facilities, §130A-457.
Physicians and surgeons, §130A-456.
Rules and regulations, §130A-455.
Osteopaths subject to state and municipal regulations relating to, §90-134.
Physicians and surgeons.
Reports of diseases, §130A-135.
Rabies, §§130A-184 to 130A-201.
See RABIES.
Schools.
Communicable diseases.
Report by school principals, §130A-136.
Sickle cell trait.
Accident and health insurance.
Policies to be issued to persons possessing sickle cell trait or hemoglobin C trait, §58-51-45.
Council, §§130A-131 to 130A-131.2.
Employers.
Discrimination against persons possessing sickle cell trait, §95-28.1.
Hospital, medical and dental service corporations.
Contracts to cover persons possessing sickle cell trait, §58-65-70.
Life insurance.
Policies not to be denied to person possessing sickle cell trait or hemoglobin C trait, §58-58-25.
Local health departments.
Duties, §130A-130.
Sickle cell program, §130A-129.

DISEASES —Cont'd
Terrorism.
Nuclear, biological or chemical agents.
Terrorist incident using, §§130A-475 to 130A-479.
See TERRORIST INCIDENT USING NUCLEAR, BIOLOGICAL OR CHEMICAL AGENTS.
Tuberculosis.
See TUBERCULOSIS.
Venereal diseases.
See VENEREAL DISEASES.

DISGUISES OF SECRET SOCIETIES.
Entry, etc., upon premises of another while wearing disguises, §14-12.9.
Exemptions from provisions of article, §14-12.11.
Exhibit with intention of intimidating, etc., another.
Placing exhibit while wearing disguise, §14-12.14.
Holding meetings while wearing disguise, §14-12.10.
Use of disguises for illegal purposes, §14-12.4.
Wearing of masks, hoods, etc., on public ways, §14-12.7.

DISHWASHING DETERGENT.
Containing phosphorus.
Manufacture, storage or sale.
Prohibition, exceptions, penalties, §143-214.4, (a) to (g).

DISINTERMENT, §130A-390, (a) to (c).
Cemeteries.
Disinterment and reinterment, §65-13.
Permits.
Disinterment and reinterment, §130A-113, (c).
Veterans.
Disinterment of, §65-43.4.

DISMISSAL, DISCONTINUANCE AND NONSUIT.
Abused, neglected or dependent juvenile actions.
Court finding allegations not proven, §7B-807, (a).
Adoption.
Petition to adopt minor, §48-2-604, (a), (b).
Brief in support or opposition to motion to dismiss.
Service, §1A-1, Rule 5, (a1).
Business corporations.
Derivative proceedings, §55-7-45.
Dismissal of proceedings, §55-7-44.
Child custody.
Action or proceeding for custody or visitation.
Dismissal on prejudicial grounds, §50-13.1, (d).
Class actions, §1A-1, Rule 23, (c).
Cost, §1A-1, Rule 41, (d).
Counterclaims and cross-claims, §1A-1, Rule 41, (c).
Dismissal as to plaintiff's claim.
Effect on counterclaim, §1-183.1.
Criminal procedure.
Deferred prosecution agreement.
Dismissal with leave, §15A-932, (a1).
Reinstitution of proceedings for failure to comply, §15A-932, (e).
Demurrer to the evidence, §15-173.
Dismissal with leave when defendant fails to appear and cannot be readily found, §15A-932, (a).
Effect, §15A-932, (b).
Entry of dismissal, §15A-932, (c).

DISMISSAL, DISCONTINUANCE AND NONSUIT —Cont'd
Criminal procedure —Cont'd
Dismissal with leave when defendant fails to appear and cannot be readily found —Cont'd
Reinstitution of proceedings, §15A-932, (d).
Mental incapacity of defendant to proceed.
Dismissal of charges, §15A-1008.
Supplemental hearings, §15A-1007, (c).
Dismissal with leave, §15A-1009.
Motion for appropriate relief.
Relief available.
Dismissal of charges, §15A-1417, (a).
Motion for dismissal.
Death of defendant.
Dismissal required, §15A-954, (b).
Deferral of ruling on motion to dismiss when charge to be reinstituted, §15A-956.
Grounds, §15A-954, (a).
Motion to dismiss indictment, §15A-955.
Insanity of defendant, §15A-959.
Insufficiency of evidence.
Reviewable on appeal regardless of whether motion made during trial, §15A-1227, (d).
Ruling by judge on motion before trial may proceed, §15A-1227, (c).
Time for motion, §15A-1227, (a), (b).
Time for, §15A-954, (c).
Probable cause hearings.
Dispositional alternatives, §15A-612, (a).
Voluntary dismissal of criminal charges by state, §15A-931, (a), (a1).
Statute of limitations not tolled by charges dismissed, §15A-931, (b).
Deferred prosecution agreement.
Dismissal with leave pursuant to, §15A-932.
Derivative proceedings.
Business corporations, §55-7-45.
Dismissal of proceedings, §55-7-44.
Dismissal with leave for nonappearance, §15A-932.
Double jeopardy.
Motion to dismiss.
Grounds, §15A-954, (a).
Eminent domain.
Abandonment of condemnation proceedings by petitioner.
Petitioner taxed with fee for respondent's attorney, §1-209.1.
Voluntary nonsuit authorized, §1-209.2.
Voluntary nonsuit by petitioner in condemnation proceedings, §1-209.2.
Petitioner taxed with fee for respondent's attorney, §1-209.1.
Frivolous complaints by prisoners, §1-110, (b).
Impaired driving charge.
Explanation by prosecutor, §20-138.4.
Incompetence, determination of.
Finding that respondent not incompetent, §35A-1112, (c).
Voluntary dismissal, §35A-1112, (g).
Appointment of interim guardian, §35A-1114, (f).
Indictments.
Grounds for motion to dismiss, §15A-955.
Involuntary dismissal, §1A-1, Rule 41, (b).
Effect, §1A-1, Rule 41, (b).
Limitation of actions.
Motion to dismiss.
Grounds, §15A-954, (a).

DISMISSAL, DISCONTINUANCE AND NONSUIT —Cont'd
Limited liability companies.
Derivative actions by members, §57C-8-01, (b).
New action after voluntary dismissal.
Time for commencing, §1A-1, Rule 41, (a).
Quo warranto.
Failure to bring action within requisite time, §1-522.
Small claims actions.
Dismissal of appeal for failure to pay costs, §7A-228, (b).
Summons and process.
No endorsement of summons nor issuance of alias or pluries.
Summons within time specified.
Action discontinued, §1A-1, Rule 4, (e).
Superior courts.
Judgments of voluntary nonsuit.
Clerk of court may enter, §1-209.
Termination of parental rights proceedings, §7B-1110, (b), (c).
Third-party practice, §1A-1, Rule 41, (c).
Trusts and trustees.
Foreign trusts.
Dismissal of matters concerning, §36A-25.1.
Voluntary dismissal, §1A-1, Rule 41, (a).
Effect, §1A-1, Rule 41, (a).
Voluntary nonsuit.
Clerks of superior courts.
Authorized to enter judgment, §1-209.
Petitioner in condemnation proceeding, §1-209.2.
Workers' compensation.
Contested cases, I.C. Rule 613.

DISMISSAL WITHOUT PREJUDICE.
Involuntary dismissal, §1A-1, Rule 41, (b).
Voluntary dismissal, §1A-1, Rule 41, (a).

DISORDERLY CONDUCT, §14-288.4.
Administrative department.
Public buildings and grounds.
Disorderly conduct in and injury to, §143-345.2.
Airports, §14-275.1.
Alcoholic beverage permittees.
Unlawful conduct on premises, §18B-1005, (a).
Buildings.
Public buildings and facilities.
Trespasses to land and fixtures, §14-132.
Bus stations, §14-275.1.
Conduct constituting, §14-288.4, (a).
Court orders abating disorderly conduct.
Violation of court orders, §14-226.1.
Failure to disperse when commanded, §14-288.5.
Militia.
Commander may prevent trespass and disorder, §127A-148.
Public intoxication, §§14-443 to 14-447.
Punishment, §14-288.4, (b).
Railroad stations, §14-275.1.
Riots and civil disorders generally, §§14-288.1 to 14-288.20.
See RIOTS AND CIVIL DISORDERS.

DISORDERLY HOUSES, §14-188.
Evidence of reputation or character of house admissible, §14-188, (a).
Prostitution generally, §§14-203 to 14-208.
See PROSTITUTION.

DISPATCHERS OF EMERGENCY COMMUNICATIONS.
Interfering with, §14-286.2.

DISPENSING OPTICIANS.
See OPTICIANS.

DISPLACED HOMEMAKERS.
Center.
Establishment, §143B-394.5.
Evaluation of programs, §143B-394.9, (b).
Funding, §143B-394.7.
Location, §143B-394.5.
Services to be provided, §143B-394.8, (a), (b).
Staff, §143B-394.6.
Definitions, §143B-394.4.
Establishment of center, §143B-394.5.
Evaluation of program, §143B-394.9, (b).
Funding, §143B-394.7.
Location of center, §143B-394.5.
North Carolina fund for displaced homemakers, §143B-394.10, (a).
Rules to implement, §143B-394.10, (b).
Rules and regulations.
Promulgation by department, §143B-394.9, (a).
Staff for center, §143B-394.6.

DISPLACED PERSONS.
Public works relocation assistance, §§133-5 to 133-18.
See RELOCATION ASSISTANCE.

DISPOSAL OF PROPERTY WITH INTENT TO DEFRAUD CREDITORS.
Arrest in civil cases, §1-410.

DISPOSITION OF DECEDENT'S BODY OR BODY PARTS, §130A-420.

DISPOSITION OF JUVENILE.
Abused, neglected or dependent juvenile actions, §§7B-900 to 7B-1004.
See CHILD ABUSE, NEGLECT OR DEPENDENCY.
Delinquent or undisciplined juveniles, §§7B-2500 to 7B-2606.
See DELINQUENT AND UNDISCIPLINED JUVENILES.

DISPOSITION OF SEIZED, CONFISCATED OR UNCLAIMED PROPERTY, §§15-11 to 15-17.
See SEARCHES AND SEIZURES.

DISPOSITION OF UNCLAIMED PROPERTY.
Generally, §§116B-51 to 116B-80.
See UNCLAIMED PROPERTY.

DISPUTE RESOLUTION.
Arbitration.
Generally.
See ARBITRATION.
Revised uniform arbitration act, §§1-569.1 to 1-569.31.
See ARBITRATION.
Community mediation centers, §7A-38.5.
Negotiation not discoverable or admissible in evidence, §8-110.
Custody and visitation mediation program, §§7A-494, 7A-495.
Labor disputes.
Conciliation service and mediation of disputes generally, §§95-32 to 95-36.
See LABOR DISPUTES.
Voluntary arbitration, §§95-36.1 to 95-36.9.
See LABOR DISPUTES.
Mediated settlement conferences in superior court civil actions, §7A-38.1.
Regulation of mediators, §7A-38.2.

DISPUTE RESOLUTION —Cont'd
Mediation generally.
See MEDIATION.
New motor vehicles warranties act.
Utilization of informal settlement procedure.
Manufacturer requiring, §20-351.7.
Nurse licensure compact, §90-171.92.
Office of information technology services.
Services, fees and charges.
Dispute resolution panel, §147-33.93.
Public contracts, §143-128, (g).

DISPUTE RESOLUTION CENTERS, §7A-38.1.
Negotiation not discoverable or admissible in evidence, §8-110.

DISPUTE RESOLUTION COMMISSION, §7A-38.2, (b), (c).

DISSECTION PRIVILEGES.
Schools for teaching mortuary science, §90-210.23, (g).

DISSENTING FROM A WILL.
Acts bearing rights of spouse, §31A-1, (b).

DISSENTING SHAREHOLDERS, §§55-13-01 to 55-13-31.
See CORPORATIONS.
Trust companies.
Merger or share exchange, §53-362.

DISSOLUTION.
Attachment orders.
Jury trial, §1-440.36, (c).
Motion for, §1-440.36, (a).
Hearing of motion, §1-440.36, (b), (c).
Remedies of third person claiming attached property or interest therein, §1-440.43.
Service of process.
Noncompliance with time limit, §1-440.7, (b).
Stay of order dissolving order of attachment, §1-440.38.
Banks.
See BANKS.
Bridge authority, §136-89.167.
Community trust for persons with severe chronic disabilities, §36A-59.20.
Corporations.
Generally, §§55-14-01 to 55-14-40.
See CORPORATIONS.
Nonprofit corporations, §§55A-14-01 to 55A-14-40.
See NONPROFIT CORPORATIONS.
District health department, §130A-38.
Facility authorities.
Dissolution of authority by general assembly, §160A-480.5.
Limited liability companies, §§57C-6-01 to 57C-6-09.
See LIMITED LIABILITY COMPANIES.
Mosquito control districts.
Procedure for dissolution of certain mosquito control districts, §130A-358.
Mutual burial associations.
Request for voluntary dissolution, §90-210.107, (h) to (k).
Partnerships, §§59-59 to 59-73.
See PARTNERSHIPS.
Property.
Possession upon dissolution, §136-89.167.
Public health authorities, §130A-45.2.
Real property.
Vesting upon dissolution, §136-89.167.

DISSOLUTION —Cont'd
Sanitary districts.
See SANITARY DISTRICTS.
Title.
Vesting on dissolution, §136-89.167.
Trust companies.
Foreign offices.
Change in control, transactions causing, §53-328.
Out-of-state institutions.
Notice of change in control, §53-322.
Voluntary dissolution, §§53-372 to 53-376.

DISTILLERY PERMITS, §18B-1105, (a), (b).

DISTINGUISHED FLYING CROSS.
Motor vehicle license plates.
Special plates for recipients, §20-79.4, (b).

DISTINGUISHED PROFESSORS ENDOWMENT TRUST FUND, §§116-41.13 to 116-41.19.
See UNIVERSITY OF NORTH CAROLINA.

DISTINGUISHED SERVICE CROSS.
Special registration plates issued to recipient, §20-79.4, (b).

DISTRAINT, §42-25.7.

DISTRESS, REMEDY, §42-25.7.

DISTRESS SALES.
Closing-out sales, §§66-76 to 66-83.
See CLOSING-OUT SALES.

DISTRESS SIGNALS.
Interception of radio communications not unlawful, §15A-287, (b).

DISTRIBUTION AGREEMENTS, WINE, §§18B-1200 to 18B-1216.
See WINE DISTRIBUTION AGREEMENTS.

DISTRIBUTION BUSINESSES.
Tax incentives for new and expanding businesses generally, §§105-129.2 to 105-129.13.
See TAX INCENTIVES FOR NEW AND EXPANDING BUSINESSES.

DISTRIBUTION OF APPELLATE REPORTS, §7A-343.1.

DISTRIBUTION OF DECEDENTS' ESTATES.
Executors and administrators.
See EXECUTORS AND ADMINISTRATORS.
General provisions, §§28A-22-1 to 28A-22-10.
See DECEDENTS' ESTATES.
Intestate succession, §§29-1 to 29-30.
See INTESTATE SUCCESSION.

DISTRIBUTION OF MARITAL AND DIVISIBLE PROPERTY, §50-20.
Absolute divorce, effects, §50-11, (e), (f).
Procedures, §50-21.

DISTRIBUTORS, DISTRIBUTOR BRANCHES, DISTRIBUTOR REPRESENTATIVES.
Motor vehicles.
Automobile dealers licensing act.
Generally, §§20-285 to 20-308.2.
See MOTOR VEHICLE DEALERS.

DISTRIBUTORS OF MILK AND MILK PRODUCTS.
Generally.
See MILK DISTRIBUTORS AND PROCESSORS.

DISTRICT ATTORNEYS.
Abuse, neglect or dependency of juveniles.
Report by director on finding evidence of abuse, §7B-307, (a).
Review of director's decision that petition not be filed, §§7B-306, 7B-403, (b).
Request for review, §7B-305.
Acting district attorneys, §7A-62.
Administrative and victim and witness services assistants.
Allocation to offices, §7A-347.
Administrative assistants.
Appointment, §7A-68, (a).
Duties, §7A-68, (b).
Expenses.
Entitled to reimbursement, §7A-68, (c).
Advance sheets.
Furnishing advance sheets without charge, §7A-6, (c).
Aid to families with dependent children.
Reports to district attorneys, §§15-155.1 to 15-155.3.
Allowances, §7A-65, (a).
Service.
What constitutes, §7A-65, (c).
Antifreeze.
Violations of article.
Institution and prosecution of proceedings, §106-579.12, (c).
Assistant district attorneys.
Allowances, §7A-65, (a).
Appointment, §7A-63.
Compensation, §7A-65, (a).
Duties, §7A-63.
Number of full-time assistants in prosecutorial districts, §7A-60, (a1).
Oath of office, §7A-63.
Vacancies in office, §7A-63.
Attorney general.
Consulting and advising prosecutors.
Duties of attorney general, §114-2.
Bad checks cases.
Establishment of collection program, §14-107.2, (b).
Biologics.
Prosecution of violations.
Concurrent jurisdiction with attorney general, §106-714, (a).
Calendaring of criminal cases in superior court.
Criminal case docketing plan, §7A-49.4, (a).
Order in which case called for trial, announcing, §7A-49.4, (f).
Publication of trial calendar, §7A-49.4, (e).
Capital punishment.
Argument for death penalty, §15-176.1.
Duties on sentence of death, §15-189.
Child support.
Duty to assist in enforcing support, §110-138.1.
Reports to district attorneys of aid to dependent children and illegitimate births, §§15-155.1 to 15-155.3.
Commercial feed.
Prosecution of violations of article, §106-284.44, (c).
Compensation, §7A-65, (a).
Longevity pay, §7A-65, (c), (d).
Service.
What constitutes, §7A-65, (c).
Conference of district attorneys.
Bylaws, §7A-412, (d).
Clerical support, §7A-414.

DISTRICT ATTORNEYS —Cont'd
Conference of district attorneys —Cont'd
Establishment, §7A-411.
Executive committee, §7A-412, (c).
Executive secretary, §7A-414.
Meetings.
Annual meetings, §7A-412, (a).
Attendance.
Duty to attend, §7A-412, (e).
Calling of meetings, §7A-412, (e).
Officers.
Election, §7A-412, (b).
Organization, §7A-412, (d).
Powers.
Adoption of rules, §7A-413, (b).
Generally, §7A-413, (a).
Purposes, §7A-411.
Confidentiality of information.
Child support.
Reports to district attorneys of aid to dependent children and illegitimate births, §15-155.3.
Corruption.
Elections.
Investigation and prosecution of violations, §163-278.
Criminal case records to identify attorney representing state, §7A-109.2.
Criminal investigation and intelligence information.
Disclosure of records transmitted to district attorneys, §132-1.4, (g).
Criminal law and procedure.
Prosecution of actions, Const. N. C., art. IV, §18.
Defined, §15A-101.
Delinquent and undisciplined juvenile actions.
Representation of state, §7B-2404.
Review of juvenile court counselor's decision not to approve filing of petition, §§7B-1705, 7B-1803, (b).
Request for review, §7B-1704.
Depositions.
Reading deposition on the trial.
When deposition may be read, §8-83.
District court division, §7A-132.
District court prosecutors.
Advance sheets.
Furnishing advance sheets without charge, §7A-6, (c).
Dockets.
Preparation of trial dockets, §7A-61.
Duties.
Dockets.
Preparation of trial dockets, §7A-61.
Generally, §147-89.
Juvenile cases.
Representation of state in cases in which juvenile represented by attorney, §7A-61.
Elections, §7A-60, (b).
Corruption.
Investigation and prosecution of violations, §163-278.
Prosecutorial districts, §7A-60, (b).
Vacancies in office.
Election to fill, §163-10.
Employment security.
Prosecution of violations, §96-7, (b).
Escape.
Allowing prisoners to escape.
Prosecution of sheriffs or other officers for escape, §14-240.

DISTRICT ATTORNEYS —Cont'd
Federal courts.
Prosecution of cases removed to federal courts, §147-89.
Food, drugs and cosmetics.
Prosecution of violations of article, §106-126.
General assembly.
Appointment of district attorneys, Const. N. C., art. IV, §18.
Habeas corpus.
Notice, §17-30.
Illegitimacy.
Child support.
Reports to district attorneys of aid to dependent children and illegitimate births, §§15-155.1 to 15-155.3.
Infractions.
Hearing procedure.
Duties, §15A-1114, (e).
Preparation of trial dockets, §7A-61.
Interchangeable use of terms "solicitor" and "district attorney," §7A-66.1, (a).
Authorized in proceedings, documents and quotations, §7A-66.1, (c).
Investigatorial assistants, §7A-69.
Juvenile courts.
Duties of district attorney.
Representation of state and juvenile cases in which juvenile represented by attorney, §7A-61.
License plates, §20-79.4, (a).
Milk and milk products.
Ice cream plants, creameries and cheese factories.
Closure of plants for violation of article.
Certificate to district attorney, §106-252.
Monopolies and restraint of trade.
Prosecution of violations.
Assistants to attorney general, §75-13.
Motor vehicles.
Antifreeze.
Violations of article.
Institution and prosecution of proceedings, §106-579.12, (c).
Motor vehicle special license plates, §20-79.4, (a).
Nuisances against public morals, action to abate, §19-2.1.
Oaths.
Acting district attorneys, §7A-62.
Assistant district attorneys, §7A-63.
Form of oaths of office, §11-11.
Obscenity offenses.
Issuance of search warrant or criminal process, §14-190.20.
Offenses against.
Aggravating factor in sentencing, §15A-1340.16.
Patient abuse.
Issuance of criminal process only upon request of, §14-32.2, (g).
Physicians and surgeons.
Practicing without license, §90-21.
Powers.
Generally, §147-89.
Practice of law.
Prohibition on private practice of law, §§7A-61, 84-2.
Prosecutorial districts, Const. N. C., art. IV, §18.
Allocation of office and term of district attorney from prosecutorial district 12, §7A-60, (c).
Division of state into districts, §7A-60, (a), (a1).
Election of district attorney, §7A-60, (b).

DISTRICT ATTORNEYS —Cont'd
Prosecutorial districts —Cont'd
Full-time assistant district attorneys.
Number, §7A-60, (a1).
Public lands.
Trees and timber.
Cutting before obtaining grant.
Prosecution, §146-43.
Removal from office, §7A-66.
Removal of causes.
United States courts.
Prosecution of cases removed to federal courts, §147-89.
Search warrants for obscenity offenses.
Issuance upon request of prosecutors, §14-190.20.
Secretaries.
Sick leave.
Transfer of earned leave as county or municipal employees, §7A-102.1, (a) to (c).
Solicitors.
Denomination of office of solicitor as office of district attorney, §7A-66.1, (a).
Special responsibilities, Prof Cond. Rule 3.8.
Subpoenas.
Witnesses proving single material fact.
No more than two witnesses may be subpoenaed, §6-60.
Suspension, §7A-66.
Temporary assistance to district attorneys.
Application to director of administrative office of the courts, §7A-64, (a).
Length of service and compensation to temporary appointee, §7A-64, (c).
Required showing in order to provide assistance, §7A-64, (b).
Term of office, §7A-60, (b).
United States courts.
Prosecution of cases removed to federal courts, §147-89.
Vacancies in office.
Filling, §§7A-60, (a), 163-10.
Witnesses.
Discharge of state's witnesses.
Announcement of discharge by district attorney, §6-62.
Subpoenaing witnesses to prove single material fact.
No more than two witnesses may be subpoenaed, §6-60.

DISTRICT BOARDS OF HEALTH.
Adjudicatory bodies, §130A-37, (a).
Appointment of members, §130A-37, (b), (c).
Attorney at law.
Contracting for services, §130A-37, (k).
Chairperson, §130A-37, (f).
Compensation of board members, §130A-37, (i).
Composition, §130A-37, (a), (b).
Dissolution of board, §130A-37, (d).
Expenses, §130A-37, (i).
Fees.
Power to impose for services rendered by local department, §130A-39, (g).
Liability insurance contracts, §130A-37, (k).
Meetings, §130A-37, (j).
Policy-making body, §130A-37, (a).
Quorum, §130A-37, (g).
Removal of board members, §130A-37, (h).
Rules, §130A-37, (a).
Authority to adopt, §130A-39, (a).

DISTRICT BOARDS OF HEALTH —Cont'd
Rules —Cont'd
Code, standard, rule or regulation.
Adoption by reference to, §130A-39, (f).
Copies, filing, §130A-39, (e).
More stringent rules, power to adopt, §130A-39, (b).
Municipalities, applicability to, §130A-39, (c).
Notice prior to adoption, repeal or amendment, §130A-39, (d).
Secretary, §130A-37, (f).
Terms of office, §130A-37, (c).
Vacancies, §130A-37, (e).

DISTRICT COURT DIVISION OF GENERAL COURT OF JUSTICE.
Age.
Official actions of twenty-fifth judicial district judges.
Validation of actions after mandatory retirement age, §7A-4.21.
Composition, §7A-130.
Creation, §7A-130.
Districts.
Composition of split districts, §7A-133, (b), (b1).
Number of judges by districts, §7A-133, (a).
Organization into territorial districts, §7A-130.
Establishment of district courts, §7A-131.
Transfer of pending cases when present inferior court replaced by district courts, §7A-135.
Inferior courts replaced by district courts.
Transfer of pending cases, §7A-135.
Judges, §7A-132.
Mandatory retirement age.
Official actions of twenty-fifth judicial district judges.
Validation of actions performed after mandatory retirement age, §7A-4.21.
Number of judges by districts, §7A-133, (a).
Judicial districts.
Trial court administrators, §7A-355.
Duties, §7A-356.
Magistrates, §7A-132.
Number of magistrates for each county, §7A-133, (c).
Number of judges by districts, §7A-133, (a).
Organization into territorial districts, §7A-130.
Schedule of establishment of district courts, §7A-131.
Seats of court, §7A-130.
Additional seats, §7A-133, (c).
Appointment of judges, §7A-133, (a).
Solicitors, §7A-132.
Transfer of pending cases.
When present inferior courts replaced by district courts, §7A-135.
Trial court administrators.
Duties, §7A-356.
Judicial districts having administrator, §7A-355.

DISTRICT COURT JUDGES.
Age.
Limit for service as judge, §7A-4.20.
Official actions of judges of twenty-fifth judicial district.
Validation of actions after mandatory retirement age, §7A-4.21.
Assignment of judges, Const. N. C., art. IV, §11.
Assignment of judge to another district or specialized duty, §7A-141.
Chambers.
Hearings and orders in chambers, §7A-191.
Interlocutory orders in chambers, §7A-192.

DISTRICT COURT JUDGES —Cont'd
Chief judge.
Administrative authority, §7A-146.
Annual conference of chief district judges.
Purposes of conference, §7A-148, (a).
Designation of chief judge, §7A-141; Const. N. C., art. IV, §10.
Duties, §7A-146.
Multicopy uniform traffic ticket and complaint, §7A-148, (b).
Powers, §7A-146.
Compensation, §7A-144, (a); Const. N. C., art. IV, §21.
Longevity pay, §7A-144, (b).
Depositions.
Judge defined, §1A-1, Rule 30, (h).
Disability of judge.
Performance of duties, §1A-1, Rule 63.
Election, §§7A-140, 163-132, 163-335.
Applicability of provisions, §163-321.
Ballots.
Counting, §163-334.
Furnished by county boards, §163-332, (b).
Official ballots, printing, names of candidates, §163-332, (a).
Certificate that candidate registered voter.
Filing with notice of candidacy, §163-323, (d).
Certification of candidate.
Acknowledgment of receipt, §163-326, (c).
To local boards of elections, §163-326, (b).
To secretary of state, §163-326, (a).
Date of election, §163-1, (a).
Death, disqualification or resignation of candidate.
After election, §163-327, (b).
Before election, §163-328, (b), (c).
Before primary election, §163-327, (a).
Fees.
Petition in lieu of payment of fees, §163-325.
Refund, §163-324, (b).
Schedule, §163-324, (a).
Insufficient number of candidates, §163-328, (a).
Nonpartisan primary election.
Date, §163-331.
Determination of election winners, §163-322, (c).
Determination of nominees, §163-322, (b).
Generally, §163-322, (a).
Voting, §163-330.
Notice of candidacy.
Certification, §163-326.
Form, §163-323, (a).
For more than one office, prohibition, §163-323, (e).
Indicating vacancy, §163-323, (f).
Specialized judgeship, §163-323, (f).
Time for filing, §163-323, (b).
Withdrawal, §163-323, (c).
Other rules, §163-335.
Petition in lieu of payment of fees, §163-325, (a).
Requirements, deadline for filing, §163-325, (b).
Emergency judges, recall to active service.
Commission, application to governor, §7A-53.
Compensation for emergency judges on recall, §7A-52, (b).
Jurisdiction of emergency district court judges, §7A-53.1.
Recall of judges who have reached mandatory retirement age, §7A-57.
Retired judge may become emergency judge subject to recall, §7A-52, (a).
Interlocutory orders.
By whom power to enter orders exercised, §7A-192.

DISTRICT COURT JUDGES —Cont'd
Judicial sales, §§1-339.1 to 1-339.40.
See JUDICIAL SALES.
Jurisdiction, §7A-149, (a).
License plates, §20-79.6, (c).
Marriage.
Solemnization, §51-1.
Number of judges, §7A-140.
Oaths.
Administration of oaths, §7A-291.
Oath of office, §7A-140.
Orders in chambers, §7A-191.
Powers, §7A-291.
Practice of law.
Prohibition on practice of law, §7A-140.
Qualifications, §7A-140; Const. N. C., art. IV, §22.
Residence in district for which elected.
Requirement, Const. N. C., art. IV, §10.
Retirement.
Age limit for service as judge, §7A-4.20.
Consolidated judicial retirement, §§135-50 to 135-75.
See RETIREMENT SYSTEM FOR TEACHERS AND STATE EMPLOYEES.
Recall to active service, §7A-52, (a).
Compensation for emergency judges on recall, §7A-52, (b).
Limitation upon compensation, §7A-52, (b).
Validation of actions performed after mandatory retirement age, §7A-4.21.
Salary, §7A-144, (a); Const. N. C., art. IV, §21.
Longevity pay, §7A-144, (b).
Specialized judgeships.
Designation of specialty, §7A-147, (a).
Filling of positions, §7A-147, (a).
Juvenile cases, §7A-147, (c).
Powers of specialized judge, §7A-147, (b).
Sessions for trial of specialized cases, §7A-147, (b).
Subpoenas.
Issuance, §1A-1, Rule 45, (b).
Temporary or specialized duty.
Assignment of judge to another district, §7A-141.
Term of office, §§7A-140, 163-1, (a); Const. N. C., art. IV, §10.
Vacancies in office, Const. N. C., art. IV, §§10, 19.
Appointment by governor to fill.
Nominations submitted by district bar, §7A-142.
Filling, §§7A-142, 163-9, (d).

DISTRICT COURTS, Const. N. C., art. IV, §10.
Abortion.
Parental or judicial consent to abortion.
Jurisdiction over proceedings, §7B-200, (a).
Absence of party or counsel during trial.
Civil actions, Super. Ct. Rule 13.
Accounts and accounting.
Small claim actions.
Form of complaint on account, §7A-232.
Additional seats of court authorized.
Clerical functions furnished by clerk of superior court, §7A-182, (a), (b).
Administrative office of the courts, §§7A-340 to 7A-346.
See ADMINISTRATIVE OFFICE OF THE COURTS.
Advance sheets.
Furnishing advance sheets without charge, §7A-6, (c).
Age.
Twenty-fifth judicial district judges.
Validation of official acts performed after mandatory retirement age, §7A-4.21.

DISTRICT COURTS —Cont'd
Alimony.
Mediated settlement conferences or other settlement procedures in actions involving, §7A-38.4A.
Amount in controversy.
Determination of proper division for trial of civil actions, §7A-243.
Annulment of marriage.
Proper division for trial of civil actions, §7A-244.
Appeals.
Appeal from judge, §1-277, (a).
Clerk to judge, §7A-251, (b).
Costs in civil actions.
Collection of advance court costs, §7A-305, (c).
Cumulative nature of costs, §7A-305, (b).
Costs in criminal actions, §7A-304, (b).
Criminal law and procedure.
Appeals by defendant, §15A-1431.
Appeals by state, §15A-1432.
Final judgment of district court in civil actions.
Direct appeal to court of appeals, §7A-27, (c).
Game commission rulings.
Heard in district court division, §7A-250, (a).
Interlocutory orders.
Direct appeal to court of appeals, §7A-27, (d).
Liens.
Possessory liens on personal property.
Action to regain possession of motor vehicle or vessel.
Appeal to district court for trial de novo, §44A-6.1, (b).
Procedure after determination of appeal, §1-298.
Settling record on appeal.
Power of trial judge, §1-283.
Small claim actions.
Indigent persons, §7A-228, (b1).
Jury trial on appeal, §7A-230.
Priority of judgment when appeal taken, §7A-226.
Stay of execution on appeal, §7A-227.
Trial de novo, §7A-228, (a).
Dismissal of appeal, §7A-228, (c).
Oral notice of appeal, §7A-228, (a).
Perfection of appeal, §7A-228, (b).
Procedure generally, §7A-229.
Trial tribunals.
Inclusion within term, App. Proc. Rule 1, (c).
Appearances.
Attorneys at law.
Withdrawal of appearance, Super. Ct. Rule 16.
First appearance before district court judge, §§15A-601 to 15A-606.
See APPEARANCES.
Applicability of rules of practice and procedure, Super. Ct. Rule 1.
Arguments.
Opening and concluding arguments, Super. Ct. Rule 10.
Arrest.
Costs in criminal actions, §7A-304, (a).
Warrant for arrest.
Judges may issue, §15A-304, (f).
Attorneys at law.
Courtroom decorum, Super. Ct. Rule 12.
Scheduling conflicts.
Guidelines for resolving, Super. Ct. Rule 3.1.
Withdrawal of appearance, Super. Ct. Rule 16.
Bail and recognizance.
Criminal actions.
Status of bail bond, §7A-290.

DISTRICT COURTS —Cont'd
Bail and recognizance —Cont'd
Judges of district court.
Power to set bail, §7A-291.
Boats.
Possessory liens on personal property.
Action to regain possession of vessel.
Involuntary relinquishment of possession by lienor.
Appeal to district court for trial de novo, §44A-6.1, (b).
Calendars.
Civil cases, Super. Ct. Rule 2.
Certificate of readiness.
Form, Super. Ct. Rule 24.
Chambers of judge.
Hearings and orders in chambers, §7A-191.
Interlocutory orders in chambers, §7A-192.
Chief court counselors, §143B-535.
Chief judge.
Administrative authority, §7A-146.
Annual conference of chief district judges.
Purposes of conference, §7A-148, (a).
Designation of, §7A-141.
Duties, §§7A-146, 7A-200, (b).
Multicopy uniform traffic ticket and complaint, §7A-148, (b).
Powers, §7A-146.
Child abuse, neglect or dependency.
Generally, §§7B-100 to 7B-1414.
See CHILD ABUSE, NEGLECT OR DEPENDENCY.
Child custody.
Action or proceeding for custody or visitation.
Denial of parental visitation rights.
Written findings of fact, §50-13.5, (i).
Proper division for trial of civil actions, §7A-244.
Child support.
Proper division for trial of civil actions, §7A-244.
Civil actions.
Absence of party or counsel during trial, Super. Ct. Rule 13.
Applicability of civil procedure generally, §7A-193.
Calendaring of civil cases, Super. Ct. Rule 2.
Costs in civil actions.
Appeal costs.
Collection of advance court costs, §7A-305, (c).
Cumulative nature of costs, §7A-305, (b).
Assessment of costs, §7A-305, (a).
Completeness and exclusivity of costs, §7A-305, (d).
Courtroom and related judicial facilities.
Use of facilities, §7A-305, (a).
General court of justice.
Support of court, §7A-305, (a).
Liability of parties for costs, §7A-305, (e).
Cover sheets.
Subsequent filings.
Cover sheets unnecessary if certain requirements met, §7A-34.1.
Designation of case or group of cases as exceptional, Super. Ct. Rule 2.1.
Discovery procedures.
Fee on filing verified petition, §7A-305.1.
Fees.
Uniform civil process fees, §7A-311.
Amount, §7A-311, (a).
Collection of fees in advance, §7A-311, (b).
Completeness and exclusivity of fees and commissions, §7A-311, (c).
Jury trials, §7A-196, (a).

DISTRICT COURTS —Cont'd
Civil actions —Cont'd
Motions, Super. Ct. Rule 6.
Reporting of civil trials.
Appointment of reporters, §7A-198, (f).
Compensation and allowances of reporters, §7A-198, (f).
Electronic or mechanical devices.
Inaccurate record produced, §7A-198, (g).
Operation of device while trial in progress, §7A-198, (c).
State of the art and techniques of recording testimony, §7A-198, (b).
Magistrates.
No provisions for reporting of trial before magistrates, §7A-198, (e).
Utilization of court-reporting personnel, §7A-198, (a).
Waiver of reporting of trial by consent of party, §7A-198, (d).
Clerks of court.
Additional seats of court authorized.
Clerical functions furnished by clerk of superior court, §7A-182, (a), (b).
Appeal of clerk to judge, §7A-251, (b).
Equipment and supplies in clerk's office, §7A-303.
Jurisdiction, §7A-149, (c).
Complex business cases.
Designation, Super. Ct. Rule 2.1.
Superior court judges.
Designation of special superior court judge for, Super. Ct. Rule 2.2.
Construction and interpretation, Super. Ct. Rule 1.
Contempt.
Civil contempt.
Proceedings for civil contempt, §5A-23.
Judges of district courts.
Power to punish for contempt, §7A-291.
Continuances, Super. Ct. Rule 3.
Conversion.
Small claim actions.
Form of complaint for conversion, §7A-232.
Costs.
Civil actions, §7A-305.
Criminal actions, §7A-304.
Determination and disbursement after date court established.
Administration of estates, §7A-318, (b).
Assessment of matter pending in general court of justice, §7A-318, (a).
Disbursement according to prior law, §7A-318, (d), (e).
General court of justice fee and facilities fee remission to state, §7A-318, (c).
Fees are exclusive, §7A-320.
Uniform costs and fees in trial divisions, §§7A-304 to 7A-318.
Counterclaims and cross-claims.
Small claim actions.
Impermissible counterclaims and cross-claims, §7A-219.
Counties.
Facilities and courtrooms.
Responsibility of county for physical facilities, §7A-302.
Unincorporated seats of court.
Disposition of fees in counties, §7A-317.1.
Court of appeals.
Appeals of right from district court.
Final judgments of district courts in civil actions, §7A-27, (c).

DISTRICT COURTS —Cont'd
Court of appeals —Cont'd
Interlocutory orders or judgments of district court.
Appeals of right from district court, §7A-27, (d).
Court reporters.
Appointment of reporter, §7A-198, (f).
Compensation and allowances, §7A-198, (f).
Civil trials, §7A-198.
Electronic or mechanical devices.
Inaccurate record produced, §7A-198, (g).
Operation of device while in progress, §7A-198, (c).
State of the art and techniques of recording testimony, §7A-198, (b).
Magistrates.
No provisions for reporting of trials before magistrates, §7A-198, (e).
Utilization of personnel for reporting civil trials, §7A-198, (a).
Waiver of reporting of trial by consent of parties, §7A-198, (d).
Courtroom decorum, Super. Ct. Rule 12.
Cover sheets.
Subsequent filings in civil actions.
Cover sheets unnecessary if certain requirements met, §7A-34.1.
Criminal law and procedure.
Appeals.
Appeals by defendant, §15A-1431.
Appeals by state, §15A-1432.
Costs in criminal actions, §7A-304.
Appeal costs, §7A-304, (b).
Arrest or personal service of criminal process, §7A-304, (a).
Assessment of costs, §7A-304, (a).
Collection of costs, §7A-304, (a).
Completeness and exclusivity of costs, §7A-304, (c).
Courtroom and related judicial facilities.
Use of facilities, §7A-304, (a).
Determination, §7A-304, (d).
General court of justice.
Support of general court of justice, §7A-304, (a).
Law-enforcement officers' benefit and retirement fund.
Assessment and collection of costs, §7A-304, (a).
Personal service of criminal process, §7A-304, (a).
Felony guilty or no contest pleas.
Transfer of case from superior court to district court, §15A-1029.1, (a).
Infractions.
Procedure for hearing and disposition, §§15A-1111 to 15A-1118.
See INFRACTIONS.
Judge.
Finder of fact, §15A-1201.
Jurisdiction of district court, §7A-270.
Accepting guilty plea or no contest plea to certain felonies, §7A-272, (c), (d).
Petty offenses triable by court, §7A-272, (a).
Preliminary examinations.
Conduct of examinations, §7A-272, (b).
Prosecution in district court division, Const. N. C., art. IV, §18.
Record of proceeding.
Guilty or no contest plea to certain felonies, §7A-191.1.

DISTRICT COURTS —Cont'd
Criminal law and procedure —Cont'd
Seat of court in municipality with corporate limits extending into two or more contiguous counties.
Venue in criminal case, authority of judge, §7A-199, (c).
Trial procedure.
Applicability of superior court procedure, §15A-1101.
Definitions.
Chief district court judge, §7A-200, (a).
Set of districts, §7A-200, (a).
Small claim actions, §7A-210.
Delinquent and undisciplined juveniles.
Generally, §§7B-1500 to 7B-2827.
See DELINQUENT AND UNDISCIPLINED JUVENILES.
Jurisdiction over delinquent juveniles.
Age governs for purposes of determining jurisdiction, §7B-1601, (a).
Continued jurisdiction of juvenile court.
Placement in youth development center for offense classified as class B1, B2, C, D OR E felony, §7B-1602, (b).
Placement in youth development center for offense of first-degree murder, first-degree rape or first-degree sexual offense, §7B-1602, (a).
Until terminated by court order or emancipation of juvenile, §7B-1601, (b).
Exclusive original jurisdiction, §7B-1601, (a).
Extended jurisdiction of juvenile court.
Persons 18 years of age or older.
Under extended jurisdiction, §7B-1601, (f).
Parent, guardian or custodian of juvenile, jurisdiction over, §7B-1601, (g).
Retention of jurisdiction when proceedings not concluded before juvenile reaches age of 18 years, §7B-1601, (c).
Violation of terms of post-release supervision, §7B-1601, (e).
When court has not obtained jurisdiction over juvenile before juvenile reaches age of 18.
Jurisdiction over felony and related misdemeanors committed by juvenile after thirteenth and prior to sixteenth birthday, §7B-1601, (d).
Jurisdiction over undisciplined juveniles.
Age governs for purposes of determining jurisdiction, §7B-1600, (a).
Continued jurisdiction until terminated by court order or emancipation of juvenile, §7B-1600, (b).
Exclusive original jurisdiction, §7B-1600, (a).
Parent, guardian or custodian of juvenile, jurisdiction over, §7B-1600, (c).
Limitations on juvenile court jurisdiction.
Emancipated juveniles prosecuted as adult, §7B-1604, (a).
Juvenile committing criminal offense after superior court conviction as adult, §7B-1604, (b).
Juvenile committing criminal offense on or after sixteenth birthday subject to prosecution as adult, §7B-1604, (a).
Designation of case or group of cases as exceptional.
Civil actions, Super. Ct. Rule 2.1.
Discovery, Super. Ct. Rule 8.
Civil actions.
Fee on filing verified petition, §7A-305.1.

DISTRICT COURTS —Cont'd
Districts.
Composition of split districts, §7A-133, (b), (b1).
Divorce and alimony.
Cost of final action for absolute divorce, §7A-305, (a2).
Mediated settlement conference or other settlement procedures.
Actions involving equitable distribution, alimony and support.
Administrative fee, §7A-38.4A, (l).
Appointment of mediator by district court judge.
Failure of parties to designate mediator, §7A-38.4A, (f).
Attendance at settlement conference, parties required to attend, §7A-38.4A, (d).
Authority of chief district court judge to order, §7A-38.4A, (c).
Costs, born by parties, §7A-38.4A, (i).
Definitions applicable to section, §7A-38.4A, (b).
Designation of mediators, §7A-38.4A, (f).
Design, implementation and evaluation of pilot program, purpose of section, §7A-38.4A, (a).
Evidence of statements in conduct not subject to discovery and inadmissible in action or other actions, §7A-38.4A, (j).
Failure of persons required to attend, monetary sanctions, §7A-38.4A, (e).
Fees of mediators, payment, §7A-38.4A, (i).
Immunity of mediators and neutrals acting pursuant to section, §7A-38.4A, (h).
Jury trial, right not restricted, §7A-38.4A, (n).
Mediator or neutral not to be compelled to testify or produce evidence, §7A-38.4A, (j).
Monetary sanctions.
On person failing to attend, §7A-38.4A, (e).
Neutrals, selection and compensation.
Other settlement procedures authorized, §7A-38.4A, (g).
Order to attend and participate in other settlement procedure, §7A-38.4A, (f).
Purpose of section, §7A-38.4A, (a).
Report of statistical data about settlement procedures by judges, §7A-38.4A, (m).
Rules to implement section, supreme court may adopt, §7A-38.4A, (o).
Standards for certification and conduct of mediators and neutrals, supreme court may adopt, §7A-38.4A, (k).
Proper division for trial of civil actions, §7A-244.
Domestic relations.
Proper division for trial of civil actions, §7A-244.
Emancipation of juvenile.
Jurisdiction over proceedings to determine, §§7B-200, (a), 7B-1603.
Emergency medical treatment of juveniles, authorization, §7B-3600.
Jurisdiction over proceedings involving judicial consent, §§7B-200, (a), 7B-1603.
Entries on records, Super. Ct. Rule 17.
Equitable distribution.
Mediated settlement conferences or other settlement procedures in actions involving, §7A-38.4A.
Evidence.
Custody and disposition, Super. Ct. Rule 14.
Judges of district court.
Power to compel production of evidence, §7A-291.

DISTRICT COURTS —Cont'd
Exceptional civil case.
Designation, Super. Ct. Rule 2.1.
Facilities.
Costs in civil actions.
Use of courtroom and related judicial facilities, §7A-305, (a).
Costs in criminal actions.
Use of courtroom and related judicial facilities, §7A-304, (a).
Responsibility for physical facilities.
Counties and municipalities responsible, §7A-302.
Fees.
Civil process.
Uniform civil process fees, §7A-311.
Amount, §7A-311, (a).
Collection of fees in advance, §7A-311, (b).
Completeness and exclusivity of fees and commissions, §7A-311, (c).
Costs are exclusive, §7A-320.
Discovery procedures.
Filing of verified petition, §7A-305.1.
Judges, Const. N. C., art. IV, §21.
Uniform costs and fees in trial divisions, §§7A-304 to 7A-318.
Unincorporated seats of court.
Disposition of fees in counties, §7A-317.1.
Felony offenses, guilty or no contest pleas.
Appeals, §15A-1029.1, (b).
Record of proceedings, §7A-191.1.
Transfer of case from superior court to district court, §15A-1029.1, (a).
Foster care placement of juvenile.
Jurisdiction over proceedings to review, §7B-200, (a).
Game commission rulings.
Appeals heard in district court division, §7A-250, (a).
General assembly.
Organization and establishment of district courts, Const. N. C., art. IV, §10.
Guardian ad litem.
Appointment for minors, Super. Ct. Rule 7.1.
Guardian ad litem program.
Providing services to abused, neglected or dependent juveniles, §§7B-1200 to 7B-1204.
Hearings.
Chambers.
Hearings and orders in chambers, §7A-191.
Interlocutory orders in chambers, §7A-192.
Conduct of hearings, §7A-191.
Infractions.
Cost in criminal actions.
Applicability of section to infractions disposed of in district courts, §7A-304, (e).
Hearings conducted in open court, §7A-191.
Jurisdiction for adjudication and disposition, §7A-253.
No right to trial by jury in adjudicatory hearings, §7A-196, (c).
Procedure for hearing and disposition, §§15A-1111 to 15A-1118.
See INFRACTIONS.
Reporting not provided in hearings to adjudicate, §7A-198, (e).
Injunctions.
Extension, modification or vacation.
Applications.
Before whom heard, §1-498.
Jurisdiction of judge, §1-493.

DISTRICT COURTS —Cont'd
Injunctions —Cont'd
Return, §1-494.
Statutes.
Enforcement or invalidation of statutes.
Grounds for transfer, §7A-245, (b).
Interlocutory orders.
Appeals of right from district courts to court of appeals, §7A-27, (d).
Exercise of power to enter interlocutory orders, §7A-192.
Interstate compact on the placement of children.
Jurisdiction of court, §§7B-200, (a), 7B-1603.
Judges.
See DISTRICT COURT JUDGES.
Selection of nominees, Bar Rules & Regs., A, §.1013.
Judgments.
Appeals of right from district courts to court of appeals.
Direct appeal to court of appeals, §7A-27, (d).
Final judgments of district courts in civil action, §7A-27, (c).
Small claim actions.
Lien and execution of judgment, §7A-225.
Priority of judgment when appeal taken, §7A-226.
Rendition and entry of judgment, §7A-224.
Judicial districts.
Trial court administrators, §7A-355.
Jurisdiction, Const. N. C., art. IV, §12.
Abused, neglected or dependent juveniles, §7B-200.
Accepting guilty plea or no contest plea to certain felonies, §7A-272, (c), (d).
Clerks, §7A-149, (c).
Concurrently held original jurisdiction.
Allocation between trial divisions, §7A-242.
Criminal actions.
General jurisdiction for trial of criminal actions, §7A-270.
Petty misdemeanors triable by court, §7A-272, (a).
Preliminary examinations.
Conduct of examinations, §7A-272, (b).
Delinquent and undisciplined juveniles.
Extended jurisdiction over delinquent juvenile, §7B-1602.
Jurisdiction over delinquent juveniles, §7B-1601.
Jurisdiction over undisciplined juveniles, §7B-1600.
Limitations on juvenile court jurisdiction, §7B-1604.
Emancipation of juvenile, proceeding to determine, §§7B-200, (a), 7B-1603.
Emergency medical or surgical treatment for juvenile, judicial consent proceedings, §§7B-200, (a), 7B-1603.
Foster care placement, proceedings to review, §7B-200, (a).
Infractions, §7A-253.
Interstate compact on the placement of children, proceedings under, §§7B-200, (a), 7B-1603.
Judges, §7A-149, (a).
Marriage by underage parties, §7B-200, (a).
Original civil jurisdiction.
Alimony proceedings, §7A-244.
Amount in controversy.
Proper division for trial of civil actions generally determined by amount in controversy, §7A-243.

DISTRICT COURTS —Cont'd
Jurisdiction —Cont'd
Original civil jurisdiction —Cont'd
Annulment of marriage proceedings, §7A-244.
Child custody proceedings, §7A-244.
Child support proceedings, §7A-244.
Concurrently held original jurisdiction allocated between trial divisions, §7A-242.
Divorce proceedings, §7A-244.
Domestic relations, §7A-244.
Generally, §7A-240.
Parental or judicial consent to abortion proceedings, §7B-200, (a).
Parent, guardian or custodian of juvenile, §7B-200, (b).
Parent or guardian of juvenile adjudicated abused, neglected or dependent, §7B-200, (b).
Retention of jurisdiction until terminated by court or emancipation, §7B-201.
Small claim actions.
Defendants.
Methods of subjecting person of defendant to jurisdiction, §7A-217.
Objections to jurisdiction over person, §7A-221.
Termination of parental rights proceedings, §§7B-200, (a), 7B-1101.
Jury.
Jury instruction conference, Super. Ct. Rule 21.
Petit jurors.
Applicability of provisions, §7A-197.
Seat of court in municipality with corporate limits extending into two or more contiguous counties.
Summoning jury, challenges, §7A-199, (b).
Summary jury trial, Super. Ct. Rule 23.
Trial by jury.
No right to jury trial in criminal cases, §7A-196, (b).
Right to trial by jury in conformity with rules of civil procedure, §7A-196, (a).
Juvenile code.
Specialized judgeships, §7A-147, (c).
Juvenile court counselors, §143B-536.
Chief court counselors, §143B-535.
Juvenile court services.
Chief court counselors, §143B-535.
Juvenile court counselors, §143B-536.
Landlord and tenant.
Summary ejectment.
Appeals to district court, §42-32.
Liens.
Possessory liens on personal property.
Action to regain possession of motor vehicle or vessel.
Involuntary relinquishment of possession by lienor.
Appeal to district court for trial de novo, §44A-6.1.
Small claim actions.
Enforcement of motor vehicle mechanic and storage liens, §7A-211.1.
Execution and lien of judgment, §7A-225.
Local court rules, Super. Ct. Rule 22.
Magistrates.
Assignment of small claim actions to magistrates, §7A-211.
Judgment of magistrate in civil action improperly assigned or not assigned, §7A-212.
Number of magistrates for each county, §7A-133, (c).

DISTRICT COURTS —Cont'd
Magistrates —Cont'd
Reporting of civil trials.
No provision for reporting before magistrates, §7A-198, (e).
Small claim actions.
Assignment of small claim actions to magistrates.
Request for and notice of assignment, §7A-213.
Form of magistrate summons, §7A-232.
New trial before magistrate, §7A-228, (a).
Stay of execution on appeal, §7A-227.
Mediated settlement conferences or other settlement procedures.
Actions involving equitable distribution, alimony and support, §7A-38.4A.
Administrative fees, §7A-38.4A, (l).
Appointment of mediator by judge, parties failure to designate, §7A-38.4A, (f).
Attendance at mediated settlement conference.
Failure to attend, monetary sanctions, §7A-38.4A, (e).
Parties required to attend, §7A-38.4A, (d).
Attendance at settlement procedure in lieu of attending mediated settlement conference, §7A-38.4A, (g).
Compelling mediator or neutral to testify, prohibition, §7A-38.4A, (j).
Costs of mediated settlement conference, §7A-38.4A, (i).
Definitions applying to section, §7A-38.4A, (b).
Designation of mediator by parties, §7A-38.4A, (f).
Design, implementation and evaluation of pilot program, purposes of section, §7A-38.4A, (a).
Discovery of statements made and conduct occurring in settlement proceeding, prohibition, §7A-38.4A, (j).
Evidence of statements made and conduct occurring in settlement proceeding, in admissibility, §7A-38.4A, (j).
Fees of mediators, payment, §7A-38.4A, (i).
Immunity of mediators and neutrals, §7A-38.4A, (h).
Neutrals acting at settlement procedure, selection and compensation, §7A-38.4A, (g).
Report as to statistical data, §7A-38.4A, (m).
Right to jury trial not limited, §7A-38.4A, (n).
Rules to implement section, supreme court may adopt, §7A-38.4A, (o).
Sanctions for failure to attend conference, §7A-38.4A, (e).
Standards for certification and conduct of mediators and neutrals, adoption by supreme court, §7A-38.4A, (k).
Divorce and alimony.
Actions involving equitable distribution, alimony and support.
Authority of chief district court judge to order, §7A-38.4A, (c).
Mediation.
Civil district court action, judge to encourage, §7A-38.5, (d).
Criminal district court action, judge to encourage, §7A-38.5, (c).
Motions.
Civil actions, Super. Ct. Rule 6.
Motor vehicle mechanic and storage liens.
Small claim actions.
Enforcement of liens, §7A-211.1.

DISTRICT COURTS —Cont'd
Motor vehicles.
Chief district judges.
Multicopy uniform traffic ticket and complaint.
Judges to prescribe, §7A-148, (b).
Possessory liens on personal property.
Action to regain possession.
Involuntary relinquishment of possession by lienor.
Appeal to district court for trial de novo, §44A-6.1, (b).
Motor vehicle special registration plates.
Judges, §20-79.6, (c).
Municipal corporations.
Facilities and courtrooms.
Responsibility of municipalities for physical facilities, §7A-302.
Seat of court in municipality with corporate limits extending into two or more contiguous counties.
Venue, special rules, place for recording judgments, §7A-199, (a) to (d).
No contest plea to felony.
Record of proceeding, §7A-191.1.
Notice.
Criminal actions.
Notice of appeal, §7A-290.
Small claim actions.
Appeal for trial de novo.
Oral notice of appeal, §7A-228, (a).
Assignment of actions.
Form of notice, §7A-232.
Number of judges by districts, §7A-133, (a).
Oaths.
Judges of district court.
Administration of oaths, §7A-291.
Oath of office, §7A-140.
Open.
Court always open, §7A-190.
Opening statements, Super. Ct. Rule 9.
Orders in chambers, §7A-191.
Interlocutory orders, §7A-192.
Parental or judicial consent to abortion.
Jurisdiction over proceedings, §7B-200, (a).
Personal injury.
Small claim actions.
Form of complaint for injury to person, §7A-232.
Photography and photostating.
Photographs or reproduction of court proceedings, Super. Ct. Rule 15.
Place court to sit, Const. N. C., art. IV, §10.
Pleadings.
Form, Super. Ct. Rule 5.
Small claim actions.
No required pleadings other than complaint, §7A-220.
Presence of counsel during jury deliberations.
Criminal actions, Super. Ct. Rule 13.
Pre-trial procedure, Super. Ct. Rule 7.
Conferences in capital cases, Super. Ct. Rule 24.
Order on final pre-trial conference.
Form, Super. Ct. Forms.
Promissory notes.
Small claim actions.
Form of complaint on promissory note, §7A-232.
Property.
Small claim actions.
Form of complaint for injury to property, §7A-232.
Receivers.
Appointment of receivers.
Jurisdiction of judges, §1-501.

DISTRICT COURTS —Cont'd
Remedies.
Small claim actions.
Provisional and incidental remedies, §7A-231.
Removal for fair trial, §1-84.
Affidavits on hearing, §1-85.
Depositions, §1-87, (b).
Subsequent proceedings, §1-87, (a).
Transcripts, §1-87, (a).
Reporting of civil trials.
Appointment of reporters, §7A-198, (f).
Compensation and allowances of reporters, §7A-198, (f).
Electronic or mechanical devices.
Inaccurate record produced, §7A-198, (g).
Operation of device while trial in progress, §7A-198, (c).
State of art and techniques of recording testimony, §7A-198, (b).
Infractions.
No reporting of hearings to adjudicate and dispose of, §7A-198, (e).
Magistrates.
No provisions for reporting trials before magistrate, §7A-198, (e).
Utilization of court-reporting personnel, §7A-198, (a).
Waiver of reporting of trial by consent of party, §7A-198, (d).
Retirement system for teachers and state employees.
Consolidated judicial retirement act, §§135-50 to 135-75.
See RETIREMENT SYSTEM FOR TEACHERS AND STATE EMPLOYEES.
Rules of civil procedure govern procedure, §1A-1, Rule 1.
Scheduling conflicts.
Guidelines for resolving, Super. Ct. Rule 3.1.
Search warrants.
Judges of district courts.
Issuance of search warrant, §15A-243, (b).
Seat of court.
Additional seat, §7A-133, (c).
Appointment of judges, §7A-133, (a).
Clerical functions furnished by clerk of superior court, §7A-182, (a), (b).
Unincorporated seats of court.
Disposition of fees in counties, §7A-317.1.
Unincorporated seats of court.
Disposition of fees in counties, §7A-317.1.
Venue.
Special venue rule when court sits without jury and seat of court lies in more than one county, §7A-199, (a) to (d).
Sessions, §7A-149, (b).
Settlement procedures and mediated settlement conferences.
Actions involving equitable distribution, alimony and support, §7A-38.4A.
Small claims actions, §§7A-210 to 7A-232.
See SMALL CLAIM ACTIONS.
Statutes.
Injunctive and declaratory relief.
Enforcement or invalidation of statutes.
Grounds for transfer, §7A-245, (b).
Stays.
Small claim actions.
Execution on appeal, §7A-227.
Subpoenas.
Issuance by judge, §1A-1, Rule 45, (b).
Summary jury trial, Super. Ct. Rule 23.

DISTRICT COURTS —Cont'd
Summons and process.
Fees.
Uniform civil process fees, §7A-311.
Judges of district court.
Power to issue process and orders, §7A-291.
Superior court clerks.
Additional seats of district court.
Clerical functions at additional seats, §7A-182.
Assistant clerks.
Functions of assistant clerks in district court matters, §7A-181.
Deputy clerks.
Functions of deputy clerks in district court matters, §7A-181.
Functions of clerk in district court matters, §7A-180.
Support and maintenance.
Mediated settlement conferences or other settlement procedures in actions involving support, §7A-38.4A.
Supreme court.
Rules of practice and procedure in trial courts.
Power of supreme court to prescribe, §7A-34.
Sureties, Super. Ct. Rule 20.
Termination of parental rights.
Generally, §§7B-1101 to 7B-1113.
See TERMINATION OF PARENTAL RIGHTS.
Jurisdiction over proceedings, §§7B-200, (a), 7B-1101.
Third party practice.
Small claim actions.
Impermissible third party claims, §7A-219.
Time.
Enlargement of time, Super. Ct. Rule 4.
Traffic ticket and complaint.
Chief judge.
Prescribing multicopy uniform traffic ticket and complaint, §7A-148, (b).
Transfer of cases.
Felony guilty or no contest pleas, §15A-1029.1, (a).
Judge's own motion, §7A-259, (b).
Review of matters, §7A-260.
Trial court administrators.
Duties, §7A-356.
Trials.
Chambers.
Hearings and orders in chambers, §7A-191.
Interlocutory orders in chambers, §7A-192.
Conducted in open court, §7A-191.
Jury trials.
No right to jury trial on criminal cases, §7A-196, (b).
Right to trial by jury in conformity with the rules of civil procedure, §7A-196, (a).
On merits conducted at regularly scheduled trial sessions, §7A-190.
Undisciplined juveniles.
Generally, §§7B-1500 to 7B-2827.
See DELINQUENT AND UNDISCIPLINED JUVENILES.
Jurisdiction over, §7B-1600.
Venue.
Seat of court in municipality with corporate limits extending into two or more contiguous counties.
Civil jury actions, summoning jurors, challenges, §7A-199, (b).
Criminal cases, §7A-199, (c).
Nonjury civil or juvenile matters, §7A-199, (a).
Recording judgment, place for, §7A-199, (d).

DISTRICT COURTS —Cont'd
Venue —Cont'd
Small claim actions.
Objections to venue, §7A-221.
Vessels.
Possessory liens on personal property.
Action to regain possession.
Involuntary relinquishment of possession by lienor.
Appeal to district court for trial de novo, §44A-6.1, (b).
Warrants.
Judges of district court.
Power to issue arrest and search warrants, §7A-291.
Witnesses.
Examination, Super. Ct. Rule 11.
Judges of district court.
Power to compel attendance of witnesses, §7A-291.

DISTRICT OF COLUMBIA, Const. U. S., art. I, §8.

DISTRICTS.
Airports.
Special airport districts, §§63-78 to 63-89.
See AIRPORTS.
Congress.
Congressional districts specified, §163-201, (a).
General assembly apportionment act.
Compliance with federal law, §163-201.2, (c).
Limitation on number of divisions, §163-201.2, (b).
Restriction, §163-201.2, (a).
Names and boundaries, §163-201, (b).
Additions or modifications, §163-201, (c).
Change of precinct boundary, no effect on district, §163-201, (d).
Severability of congressional apportionment acts, §163-201.1.
Unassigned districts, §163-163, (e).
Consolidated city-county act.
Urban service districts.
See CONSOLIDATED CITY-COUNTY ACT.
Constitution of North Carolina.
General assembly.
House of representatives, Const. N. C., art. II, §5.
Senate, Const. N. C., art. II, §3.
Superior court districts, Const. N. C., art. IV, §9.
Counties.
Economic development and training districts, §§153A-317.11 to 153A-317.17.
See ECONOMIC DEVELOPMENT AND TRAINING DISTRICTS.
Mosquito control districts, §§130A-352 to 130A-358.
See MOSQUITO CONTROL DISTRICTS.
Research and production service districts, §§153A-311 to 153A-317.
See COUNTY RESEARCH AND PRODUCTION SERVICE DISTRICTS.
Water and sewer districts, §§162A-86 to 162A-94.
See COUNTY WATER AND SEWER DISTRICTS.
County service districts.
Economic development and training districts, §§153A-317.11 to 153A-317.17.
See ECONOMIC DEVELOPMENT AND TRAINING DISTRICTS.

DISTRICTS —Cont'd
County service districts —Cont'd
Generally, §§153A-300 to 153A-310.
See COUNTY SERVICE DISTRICTS.
Research and production service districts, §§153A-311 to 153A-317.
See COUNTY RESEARCH AND PRODUCTION SERVICE DISTRICTS.
Drainage districts, §§156-54 to 156-138.4.
See DRAINAGE DISTRICTS.
Eminent domain power, §40A-3, (c).
Fire protection districts.
Rural fire protection districts, §§69-25.1 to 69-25.17.
See RURAL FIRE PROTECTION DISTRICTS.
General assembly.
Dividing precincts in apportionment acts, §120-2.2.
Representative districts, §120-2, (a) to (c); Const. N. C., art. II, §5.
Senatorial districts, §120-1, (a) to (c); Const. N. C., art. II, §3.
Severability of apportionment acts, §120-2.1.
Historic districts generally, §§160A-400.1 to 160A-400.14.
See HISTORIC DISTRICTS AND LANDMARKS.
Hospital districts.
See HOSPITAL DISTRICTS.
Judicial department.
District court division.
Composition of split districts, §7A-133, (b), (b1).
Number of judges by districts, §7A-133, (a).
Organization into territorial district, §7A-130.
Libraries.
Interstate library districts, §125-12, art. III.
Governing board, §125-12, art. IV.
State and federal aid to districts, §125-15.
Local government finance.
General provisions, §§159-1 to 159-188.
See LOCAL GOVERNMENT FINANCE.
Metropolitan sewerage districts, §§162A-64 to 162A-81.
See METROPOLITAN SEWERAGE DISTRICTS.
Metropolitan water districts, §§162A-31 to 162A-58.
See METROPOLITAN WATER DISTRICTS.
Mosquito control districts, §§130A-352 to 130A-358.
See MOSQUITO CONTROL DISTRICTS.
Municipal service districts, §§160A-535 to 160A-544.
See MUNICIPAL SERVICE DISTRICTS.
Public school districts.
Generally.
See SCHOOL DISTRICTS AND ADMINISTRATIVE UNITS.
Regional natural gas districts, §§160A-660 to 160A-676.
See REGIONAL NATURAL GAS DISTRICTS.
Sale, lease or exchange of property between governmental units.
Action taken by governmental unit, §160A-274, (c).
Authority, §160A-274, (b).
Governmental unit defined, §160A-274, (a).
Sanitary districts, §§130A-47 to 130A-85.
See SANITARY DISTRICTS.
School districts.
See SCHOOL DISTRICTS AND ADMINISTRATIVE UNITS.

DISTRICTS —Cont'd
Soil and water conservation districts, §§139-1 to 139-57.
See SOIL AND WATER CONSERVATION DISTRICTS.
Superior courts, Const. N. C., art. IV, §9.
Transportation department.
Administrative districts.
Establishment, §136-15.
Water supply and waterworks.
County water and sewer districts, §§162A-86 to 162A-94.
See COUNTY WATER AND SEWER DISTRICTS.
Metropolitan water districts, §§162A-31 to 162A-58.
See METROPOLITAN WATER DISTRICTS.

DISTRICT SCHOOL COMMITTEES DISCIPLINING STUDENTS, §115C-390.

DISTURBING OFFICIAL MEETINGS, §143-318.17.

DISTURBING THE PEACE.
Disorderly conduct.
See DISORDERLY CONDUCT.
Public intoxication, §§14-443 to 14-447.
Riots and civil disorders, §§14-288.1 to 14-288.20.
See RIOTS AND CIVIL DISORDERS.

DITCHES.
Drainage.
Open drains within thirty feet of ditch, §156-9.
Magistrates.
Assessment or contribution for damages or for work done on ditch.
Power of magistrate to assess, §7A-292.
Streets and highways.
Diverting water from public road by ditch or drain, §136-95.

DIVER'S FLAGS.
Skin and scuba divers, §75A-13.1.

DIVERSION OF DELINQUENT OR UNDISCIPLINED JUVENILES, §7B-1706.

DIVIDENDS.
Bank holding companies.
Income tax.
Adjustment to expenses related to, §105-130.6A, (c), (e), (f), (h).
Banks, §53-87.
Dissolution and liquidation, §§53-18, 53-20, (m).
Preferred stock, §53-155.
Use of surplus, §53-88.
Cooperative associations, §54-126.
Time for, §54-127.
Corporations.
Distributions to shareholders generally, §55-6-40.
Income tax.
Adjustment to for expenses related to, §105-130.6A.
Information filed with secretary of revenue.
Persons receiving dividends, §105-130.21, (b).
S corporations.
Distributions to shareholders, §105-131.6.
Information filed with secretary of revenue.
Resident taxpayers receiving dividends, §105-130.21, (b).
Nonprofit corporations.
Unlawful distributions by directors, §55A-8-33.

DIVIDENDS —Cont'd
Credit unions, §54-109.54.
Lien on accumulated dividends, §54-109.59.
Power to declare dividends, §54-109.21.
Electric power holding companies.
Income tax.
Adjustment for expenses related to, §105-130.6A, (d), (g), (h).
Income tax.
Bank holding companies.
Adjustment to for expenses related to, §105-130.6A, (c), (e), (f), (h).
Corporations.
Adjustment to for expenses related to, §105-130.6A.
Information filed with secretary of revenue.
Persons receiving dividends, §105-130.21, (b).
S corporations.
Distributions to shareholders, §105-131.6.
Electric power holding companies.
Adjustment to for expenses related to, §105-130.6A, (d), (g), (h).
Insurance companies.
Conversion of stock corporations into mutual corporations.
Repayment of dividends to corporation for beneficiaries, §58-10-5.
Impairment of capital.
Dividends not payable when capital impaired, §58-7-125.
Liability of stockholders for unlawful stockholders, §58-7-125.
Rate bureau.
Payment of dividends not prohibited or regulated by rate bureau division, §58-36-60.
Restrictions, requirements for declaring, §58-7-130.
Insurance holding companies.
Extraordinary dividends, §58-19-30, (c).
Reporting of dividends by registered insurers, §58-19-25, (d).
Limitation of actions.
Actions on account of, §1-50, (a).
Mutual insurance companies.
Dividends to policyholders, §58-8-25, (a), (b).
Nonprofit corporations.
Unlawful distributions by directors, §55A-8-33.
Partition, §§46-10, 46-11.
Savings and loan associations.
Approval by commissioner required, §54B-43.
Withdrawable accounts, §§54B-122, 54B-123.
Forced retirement.
Effect, §54B-126, (b), (c).
Savings banks.
Stock dividends, §54C-44.
Share dividends.
Generally, §55-6-23, (a), (b).
Record date for shareholders entitled to share dividend, §55-6-23, (c).
Trust companies.
Seizure by commissioner.
Dividends to shareholders and claimants, §53-389.
Unclaimed dividends, §53-392.
Unclaimed property generally, §§116B-51 to 116B-80.
See UNCLAIMED PROPERTY.

DIVISION OF MOTOR VEHICLES.
See MOTOR VEHICLES DIVISION.

DIVORCE, §§50-2 to 50-22.
Abandonment.
Grounds for divorce, §50-7.
Absolute divorce.
Cost of final action filed in district court, §7A-305, (a2).
Effect of decree on certificate failing to comply with former section 52-6, §52-9.
Effects, §50-11.
Incompetent spouses, §50-22.
Incurable insanity, §50-5.1.
Separation of one year, §50-6.
Summary judgment, §50-10, (d).
Accident and health insurance.
Coverage of children, §58-51-120, (c).
Actions.
Competency of witnesses.
Communications between marital counselor and parties, §8-53.6.
Acts barring rights of spouse, §31A-1, (a).
Adoption.
Visitation of adopted grandchild.
Action by biological grandparent, §50-13.2A.
Adultery.
Grounds for divorce, §50-7.
Alcohol abuse.
Grounds for divorce, §50-7.
Alimony.
Absolute divorce.
Effects, §50-11, (c).
Divorce obtained outside state in which jurisdiction over dependent spouse not obtained.
Right to alimony not impaired or destroyed, §50-11, (d).
Actions.
Independent actions.
Maintenance of certain actions as independent actions permissible, §50-19, (a).
Separate action prosecuted during pendency, §50-19, (b).
Maintenance of certain actions as independent actions permissible, §50-19, (a).
Without action, §50-16.10.
Amount, §50-16.3A, (b).
Determination of amount, §50-16.3A.
Arrest.
Remedy available, §50-16.7, (d).
Attachments.
Remedy available, §50-16.7, (e).
Attorney at law.
Fees.
Action for alimony, §50-16.4.
Attorneys' fees, §50-16.4.
Bail.
Remedy available, §50-16.7, (d).
Barred by separation agreement or premarital agreement provisions, §50-16.6, (b).
Bonds, surety.
Bond for costs unnecessary, §50-2.
Change in circumstances.
Modification.
Family law arbitration act, §50-56.
Cohabitation of dependent spouse.
Termination of alimony, §50-16.9, (b).
Confession of judgment, §1A-1, Rule 68.1, (e).
Costs.
Bond for costs unnecessary, §50-2.
Debtors and creditors.
Dependent spouse deemed creditor, §50-16.7, (h).

DIVORCE —Cont'd
Alimony —Cont'd
Decree.
Enforcement, §50-16.7.
Definitions, §50-16.1A.
Dependent spouse.
Deemed creditor, §50-16.7, (h).
Defined, §50-16.1A.
Distribution by court of marital and divisible property.
Equitable distribution.
Without regard to alimony, §50-20, (f).
Duration, §50-16.3A, (b).
Effects of absolute divorce, §50-11, (c).
Divorce obtained outside state in which jurisdiction over dependent spouse not obtained.
Right to alimony not impaired or destroyed, §50-11, (d).
Entitlement, §50-16.3A, (a).
Equitable distribution.
Hearing claim for alimony prior to, effect, §50-16.3A, (a).
Execution, execution sales and supplemental proceedings.
Remedies available, §50-16.7, (k).
Execution of judgment.
Time limitation as to execution not to apply, §1-306.
Exempt property from enforcement of claims of creditors.
Exception, §1C-1601, (e).
Findings of fact, §50-16.3A, (c).
Garnishment.
Remedy available, §50-16.7, (e).
Grounds for alimony, §50-16.3A.
Guardians.
Incompetent spouses.
General guardian may commence, defend or maintain actions, §50-22.
Illicit sexual behavior.
Defined, §50-16.1A.
Dependent or supporting spouse participating in, §50-16.3A, (a).
Income withholding.
Application to court by dependent spouse, §50-16.7, (l1).
Limitation on amount withheld, §110-136.6, (b1).
Incompetent spouse.
Actions on behalf of, §50-22.
Independent actions.
Maintenance of certain actions as independent actions permissible, §50-19, (a).
Separate action prosecuted during pendency, §50-19, (b).
Injunctions.
Remedy available, §50-16.7, (f).
Judgments.
Not lien against real property, §50-16.7, (i).
Jury trial, §50-16.3A, (c).
Liens.
Judgment not lien, §50-16.7, (i).
Local, private and special legislation prohibited, Const. N. C., art. II, §24.
Lump sum payments, §50-16.7, (a).
Marital misconduct.
Defined, §50-16.1A.
Mediated settlement conferences or other settlement procedures.
District court actions, §7A-38.4A.

DIVORCE —Cont'd
Alimony —Cont'd
Military affairs.
Residence of military personnel, §50-18.
Modification.
Change in circumstances.
Family law arbitration act, §50-56.
Mortgages and deeds of trust.
Securing payments, §50-16.7, (b).
Orders.
Modification, §50-16.9, (a).
Payment.
How paid, §50-16.7.
Willful disobedience of order for payment, §50-16.7, (j).
Contempt to enforce payment, §50-16.7, (j).
Personal property.
Transfer as part of order, §50-16.7, (c).
Postseparation support. See within this heading, "Postseparation support."
Preliminary injunction enjoining spouse from interfering with threatening or molesting plaintiff during pendency of suit.
Bond not required, §1A-1, Rule 65, (c).
Real property.
Transfer as part of order, §50-16.7, (c).
Writ of possession issued, §50-17.
Receivers.
Appointment, §50-16.7, (g).
Reference by consent, §1A-1, Rule 53, (a).
Remarriage of dependent spouse.
Termination of alimony, §50-16.9, (b).
Remedies supplemental, §50-16.7, (l).
Removal of action, §50-3.
Supporting spouse.
Defined, §50-16.1A.
Temporary restraining order enjoining spouse from interfering with threatening or molesting plaintiff during pendency of suit.
Bond not required, §1A-1, Rule 65, (c).
Termination, §50-16.9, (b).
Travel expenses of defendant.
Payment, §50-18.
Without action, §50-16.10.
A mensa et thoro.
Bed and board.
Grounds for divorce, §50-7.
Annulment of marriage.
General provisions.
See ANNULMENT OF MARRIAGE.
Appearances.
Failure of defendant to appear in action.
Notice of trial not required, §50-10, (b).
Arbitration.
Family law arbitration generally, §§50-41 to 50-62.
See FAMILY LAW ARBITRATION.
Arrest.
Remedy available, §50-16.7, (d).
Attorneys' fees.
Action for alimony, §50-16.4.
Barred by separation agreement or premarital agreement provisions, §50-16.6, (b).
Custody and support of minor children.
Counsel fees in actions for, §50-13.6.
Attorneys specializing in family law, Bar Rules & Regs., D, §§.2401 to .2407.
A vinculo.
Effects of absolute divorce, §50-11.
Grounds for absolute divorce.
Separation of one year, §50-6.
Incompetent spouses, §50-22.

DIVORCE —Cont'd
A vinculo —Cont'd
Summary judgment.
Applicability of provisions, §50-10, (d).
Bed and board divorce grounds, §50-7.
Bonds, surety.
Bond for costs unnecessary, §50-2.
Change of venue, §1-83.
Child custody.
Action or proceeding for child custody or visitation, §50-13.1.
Procedure, §50-13.5.
Enforcement of order, §50-13.3.
General provisions.
See CHILD CUSTODY.
Grandparents' visitation, §50-13.2, (b1).
Adopted grandchild.
Action by biological grandparent, §50-13.2A.
Independent actions permissible, §50-19.
Judgment provisions pertaining to custody, §50-11.2.
Change in conditions.
Jurisdiction requirements, §50-11.2.
Modification upon substantial change, §50-11.2.
Mediation program, §§7A-494, 7A-495.
Modification of orders, §50-13.7.
Persons entitled, §50-13.2, (a), (b).
Persons incapable of self-support upon reaching majority, §50-13.8.
Taking child outside state, §50-13.2, (c).
Child support.
Action for support of minor child, §50-13.4.
Procedure, §50-13.5.
Distribution by court of marital and divisible property.
Equitable distribution without regard to child support, §50-20, (f).
General provisions.
See CHILD SUPPORT.
Independent actions permissible, §50-19.
Judgment provisions pertaining to care, tuition and maintenance, §50-11.2.
Change of conditions.
Modification upon substantial change, §50-11.2.
Modification of orders, §50-13.7.
Past due child support, §50-13.10.
Procedure to insure payment, §50-13.9.
Collaborative law proceedings, §§50-70 to 50-79.
See COLLABORATIVE LAW PROCEEDINGS.
Community property.
Equitable distribution of marital property generally, §§50-11, 50-20 to 50-22.
Cross-actions, jurisdiction, §7A-244.
Decedents' estates.
Claim for distribution of marital or divisible property, §28A-19-19.
Mediated settlement conferences, district courts, §7A-38.4A.
Complaint.
Contents of complaint, §50-8.
Material facts deemed denied by defendant, §50-10, (a).
Resumption of maiden name or adoption of name of prior deceased or living husband.
Incorporation for petition of resumption or use in complaint for divorce, §50-12, (d).
Verification, §50-8.
Confession of judgment.
Alimony.
Alimony without action, §50-16.10.

DIVORCE —Cont'd
Contempt.
Alimony.
Payment.
Willful disobedience of order for payment.
Enforcement of payment by contempt, §50-16.7, (j).
Order for custody of minor child.
Enforcement, §50-13.3, (a).
Costs.
Allowance of costs to either party or apportioned in discretion of court, §6-21.
Bond for costs unnecessary, §50-2.
Counterclaims and cross-claims.
Resumption of maiden name or adoption of name of prior deceased or prior living husband.
Incorporation of petition for resumption or use of name in complaint or counterclaim for divorce, §50-12, (d).
Cruel or barbarous treatment endangering life of the other.
Grounds for divorce, §50-7.
Decrees.
Alimony.
Enforcement, §50-16.7.
Default judgments, §50-10, (e).
Deferred compensation plans.
Distribution of pension, retirement and deferred compensation benefits, §50-20.1.
Definitions, §50-16.1A.
Distribution by court of marital and divisible property.
Equitable distribution, §50-20, (b).
Discovery.
Distribution by court of marital and divisible property.
Equitable distribution.
Discovery and scheduling conference, §50-21, (d).
Procedures in actions, §50-21, (a).
Prejudicial delays.
Sanctions for, §50-21, (e).
Distribution by court of marital and divisible property.
Absolute divorce.
Equitable distribution.
Effects of absolute divorce, §50-11, (e), (f).
Cross action for equitable distribution.
Jurisdiction.
District court division, §7A-244.
Decedents' estates.
Claim for distribution of marital or divisible property, §28A-19-19.
Equitable distribution, §50-20.
Absolute divorce.
Effects of absolute divorce, §50-11, (e), (f).
Agreements providing for equitable distribution, §50-20, (d).
Alimony.
Equitable distribution without regard to, §50-20, (f).
Hearing claim prior to distribution, §50-16.3A, (a).
Child support.
Equitable distribution without regard to, §50-20, (f).
Death of party, §50-20, (c), (l).
Definitions, §50-20, (b).
Discovery, §50-20, (a).
Discovery and scheduling conference, §50-21, (d).

DIVORCE —Cont'd
Distribution by court of marital and divisible property —Cont'd
Equitable distribution —Cont'd
Discovery —Cont'd
Prejudicial delay sanctions, §50-21, (e).
Distributive award.
Defined, §50-20, (b).
Duties of court, §50-20, (a).
Equal division.
By using net value of marital property, §50-20, (b), (c).
Equity between parties.
Distributive award in order to achieve, §50-20, (e).
Filing of claims, §50-21, (a).
Incompetent spouse.
Ordering equitable distribution on behalf of, §50-22.
Injunctive relief, §50-20, (i).
Interim distribution.
Partial distribution, §50-20, (i1).
Judgments.
Entry, §50-21, (a).
Jury trial.
Section not to restrict or extend right, §50-21, (c).
Lis pendens, §50-20, (h).
Marital property.
Defined, §50-20, (b).
Mediated settlement conference or other settlement procedures.
District court actions, §7A-38.4A.
Rules implementing procedures, Settle. Proc. Equitable distribution Rules 1-15.
See MEDIATED SETTLEMENT CONFERENCES.
Net value of marital property.
Equal division, §50-20, (c).
Partial distribution, §50-20, (i1).
Pensions, retirement and deferred compensation benefits, §50-20.1.
Distributive award, §50-20, (b).
Personal property.
Located outside of state.
Subject to equitable distribution, §50-21, (a).
Order transferring title, §50-20, (g).
Pretrial conference, §50-21, (d).
Procedures, §50-21.
Qualified domestic relations order.
Distributive award, §50-20, (b).
Real property.
Located outside of state.
Subject to equitable distribution, §50-21, (a).
Order transferring title, §50-20, (g).
Rights of parties.
Species of common ownership, §50-20, (k).
Second or subsequent spouse.
Interest in marital or divisible property, §50-20, (c1).
Separate property.
Defined, §50-20, (b).
Transfer of title, §50-20, (g).
Valuation of marital property.
Date, §50-21, (b).
Vesting of rights, §50-20, (k).
Waste or destruction of marital or separate property.
Temporary orders preventing, §50-21, (a).

DIVORCE —Cont'd
Distribution by court of marital and divisible property —Cont'd
Equitable distribution —Cont'd
Written findings of fact.
Requirement, §50-20, (j).
Pension or retirement benefits.
Actual receipt of benefits.
Payment upon, §50-20.1, (c).
Applicability of provisions, §50-20.1, (h).
Basis of award, §50-20.1, (d).
Death of person receiving award.
Passing of unpaid balance, §50-20.1, (f).
Determination of award, §50-20.1, (d).
Maximum percentage of benefits received, §50-20.1, (e).
Nonvested benefits, §50-20.1, (b).
Qualified domestic relations order.
Distribution by, §50-20.1, (g).
Vested benefits, §50-20.1, (a).
Presumption of marital property, §50-20, (b).
Second or subsequent spouse.
Interest in marital or divisible property, §50-20, (c1).
District courts.
Proper division for trial of civil actions, §7A-244.
Drugs.
Grounds for divorce, §50-7.
Equitable distribution, §§50-20 to 50-22.
Alimony claim.
Hearing claim prior to distribution, §50-16.3A, (a).
Mediated settlement conferences or other settlement procedures.
District court actions, §7A-38.4A.
Rules implementing procedures, Settle. Proc. Equitable distribution Rules 1-15.
See MEDIATED SETTLEMENT CONFERENCES.
Family law arbitration generally, §§50-41 to 50-62.
See FAMILY LAW ARBITRATION.
General assembly.
Local, private and special legislation prohibited, Const. N. C., art. II, §24.
Grandparent visitation, §§50-13.2, (b1), 50-13.5, (j).
Adopted grandchild.
Action by biological grandparent, §50-13.2A.
Grounds.
Abandonment.
Bed and board, §50-7.
Adultery.
Bed and board, §50-7.
Alcohol or drugs.
Excessive use.
Bed and board, §50-7.
Bed and board, §50-7.
Bonds of matrimony.
Insanity of spouse, §50-5.1.
Separation of one year, §50-6.
Cruelty.
Bed and board, §50-7.
Insanity of spouse.
Bonds of matrimony, §50-5.1.
Maliciously turning other out of doors.
Bed and board, §50-7.
Separation of one year.
Bonds of matrimony, §50-6.

DIVORCE —Cont'd
Guardians.
Incompetent spouses.
Actions on behalf of.
General guardian may commence, defend or maintain, §50-22.
Handicapped persons.
Custody.
Persons incapable of self-support upon reaching majority.
Physically incapable of self-support, §50-13.8.
Health insurance.
Coverage of children, §58-51-120, (c).
Hearsay exception.
Statement of personal or family history, §8C-1, Rules 803, 804.
Illegitimacy.
Effects of absolute divorce.
No judgment to render children illegitimate, §50-11, (b).
Voidable marriages.
Children born legitimate, §50-11.1.
Incompetent spouses.
Actions on behalf of, §50-22.
Independent actions.
Maintenance of certain actions as independent actions permissible, §50-19, (a).
Separate action prosecuted during pendency of independent action, §50-19, (b).
Injunctions.
Distribution by court of marital and divisible property.
Equitable distribution, §50-20, (i).
Order for custody of minor child.
Enforcement, §50-13.3, (b).
Judges.
Jury trial or trial before judge without jury.
Determination, §50-10, (c).
Material facts found by judge or jury.
Judgment not given in favor of plaintiff until, §50-10, (a).
Judgments.
Collaborative law agreement.
Entry of judgment to effectuate, §50-75.
Default judgments, §50-10, (e).
Distribution by court of marital and divisible property.
Equitable distribution.
Entry of judgment, §50-21, (a).
Material facts found by judge or jury.
Judgment in favor of plaintiff not given until, §50-10, (a).
Provisions pertaining to care, custody, tuition and maintenance of minor children, §50-11.2.
Validation of certain judgments entered prior to January 1, 1981, §50-11.3.
Validation of certain judgments entered prior to October 1, 1983, §50-11.4.
Jurisdiction.
Child custody or child support actions, §50-13.5, (c).
In rem or quasi in rem jurisdiction.
Grounds, §1-75.8.
Personal jurisdiction based on marital relationship, §1-75.4.
Jury.
Distribution by court of marital and divisible property.
Equitable distribution.
Jury trial.
Nothing in section to restrict or extend right, §50-21, (c).

DIVORCE —Cont'd
Jury —Cont'd
Jury trial or trial before judge without jury.
Determination, §50-10, (c).
Material facts found by judge or jury.
Judgment not given in favor of plaintiff until, §50-10, (a).
Lis pendens.
Distribution by court of marital and divisible property.
Equitable distributions, §50-20, (h).
Local, private and special legislation prohibited, Const. N. C., art. II, §24.
Maiden or premarriage surname.
Resumption, §50-12, (a).
Application, §50-12, (b).
Man applying to change surname to premarriage surname, §50-12, (a1).
Incorporation of petition for resumption in complaint or counterclaim for divorce, §50-12, (d).
Man applying to change surname to premarriage surname, §50-12, (a1).
Validation of previous resumptions, §50-12, (c).
Maliciously turning out of doors.
Grounds for divorce, §50-7.
Marital property.
Decedents' estates.
Claim for distribution of marital or divisible property, §28A-19-19.
Defined, §50-20, (b).
Equitable distribution, §§50-20 to 50-22.
Presumptions, §50-20, (b).
Marriage.
See MARRIAGE PROCEEDINGS.
Material facts found by judge or jury.
Genuine issue of material fact.
Determination, §50-10, (d).
Judgment not given in favor of plaintiff until, §50-10, (a).
Material facts in complaint deemed denied by defendant, §50-10, (a).
Mediated settlement conference and other settlement procedures.
District court actions involving equitable distribution, alimony or support, §7A-38.4A.
Equitable distribution and other family financial cases.
Rules implementing, Settle. Proc. Equitable Distribution Rules 1 to 15.
See MEDIATED SETTLEMENT CONFERENCES.
Rules.
Agreement of parties.
Finalizing settlement, Rule 4.B.
Selection of mediator, Rule 2.A.
Selection of neutrals, Rule 10.C.(10).
Appointment of mediator by court, Rule 2.B.
Attendance at settlement conference, Rule 4.A.
Other settlement procedures, Rule 10.C.(8).
Sanction for failure to attend, Rule 10.C.(9).
Sanction for failure to attend, Rule 5.
Authority of mediators, Rule 6.
Authorizing procedures other than mediated settlement conference, Rule 1.C.(3).
Bias.
Disclosure by mediator, Rule 6.B.(2).
Disclosure by neutral, Rule 10.C.(13).
Certification of mediators, Rule 8.
Certification of mediator training programs, Rule 9.

DIVORCE —Cont'd
Mediated settlement conference and other settlement procedures —Cont'd
Rules —Cont'd
Certified family financial mediator.
Selection, Rule 2.
Child custody and visitation.
Including in settlement proceedings, Rule 1.C.(2).
Compelling mediator or neutral to testify.
Prohibition, Rule 10.C.(5).
Compensation of mediator.
Generally, Rule 7.
Paid by parties, Rules 4.C, 7.C.
Compensation of neutral, Rule 10.C.(8), (12).
Computation of time limits, Rule 15.
Confidentiality.
Judicial settlement conference, Rule 12.C.
Counsel consultations with clients and opposing counsel.
Duty, Rule 1.B.
Court appointment of mediator, Rule 2.B.
Decertification of mediators, Rule 8.
Definitions.
AOC forms, Rule 14.B.
Court, Rule 14.A.
Family financial case, Rule 14.C.
Delay of other proceedings.
Mediated settlement conference.
Not cause for, Rule 3.E.
Other settlement procedures.
Not cause for delay, Rule 10.C.(4).
Designation of mediator by agreement.
Filing with court, Rule 2.A.
Dispensing with settlement.
Motion, Rule 1.C.(6).
Disqualification of mediator, Rule 2.D.
Disqualification of neutral, Rule 10.C.(11).
Duties of mediators, Rule 6.B.
Equitable distribution actions.
Requirement for settlement procedures.
Scheduling order to include, Rule 1.C.(1).
Evidence of statements and conduct at settlement proceeding.
Inadmissibility, Rule 10.C.(5).
Executing final agreement.
Time, Rule 4.B.
Ex parte communication.
By mediators, Rule 6.A.(2).
Fee of mediator.
Generally, Rule 7.
Paid by parties, Rules 4.C, 7.C.
Fee of neutral, Rule 10.C.(8), (12).
Finalizing settlement agreement, Rule 4.B.
Impasse.
Mediator declaring, Rule 6.A.(3).
Inability to pay.
Failure to move court promptly for determination.
Sanctions, Rule 7.F.
Indigent status.
Failure to move court promptly for indigency determination.
Sanctions, Rule 7.F.
Judicial settlement conference.
Authorized settlement procedures, Rule 10.B.(2).
Conduct of conference.
By district court judge, Rule 12.A.
Discretion of judge, Rule 12.B.
Confidentiality, Rule 12.C.

DIVORCE —Cont'd
Mediated settlement conference and other settlement procedures —Cont'd
Rules —Cont'd
Judicial settlement conference —Cont'd
Disqualification of settlement judge to hear action, Rule 12.A.
Imposition of settlement prohibited, Rule 12.B.
Report by judge, Rule 12.C.
Selection of settlement judge, Rule 12.A.
Local rule making, Rule 13.
Mediated settlement conference.
Attendance.
Excused or modified attendance, Rule 4.A.(2).
Persons required to attend, Rule 4.A.(1).
Phone, attendance by, Rule 4.A.(2).
Sanction for failure to attend, Rule 5.
Authority of mediators, Rule 6.
Deadline for completion, Rule 3.B.
Request to extend, Rule 3.C.
Delay of other proceedings prohibited, Rule 3.E.
Duties of mediators, Rule 6.B.
Postponement of conference, Rule 7.E.
Recesses, Rule 3.D.
When held, Rule 3.B.
Where held, Rule 3.A.
Mediator directory, Rule 2.C.
Mediators.
Authority, Rule 6.A.
Brochure.
Distributing before conference, Rule 6.B.(6).
Certification, Rule 8.
Compelling mediator or neutral to testify.
Prohibition, Rule 10.C.(5).
Compensation, Rule 7.B.
Agreement of parties to compensation, Rule 7.A.
Court order, Rule 7.B.
Duty of parties to pay, Rule 4.C.
Inability of party to pay full share, Rule 7.D.
Payment by parties, Rule 7.C.
Postponement fee, Rule 7.E.
Sanctions for failure to pay mediator's fee, Rule 7.F.
Control of conference, Rule 6.A.(1).
Disclosures, Rule 6.A.(1).
Bias, prejudice or partiality, Rule 6.A.(2).
Disqualification, Rule 2.D.
Duties, Rule 6.B.
Evaluation forms.
Distributing at conference, Rule 6.B.(7).
Fee.
Compensation generally, Rule 7.
Payment, Rules 4.C, 7.C.
Impasse, declaring, Rule 6.A.(3).
Other settlement procedures.
General rules, Rule 10.C.
Postponement fee, Rule 7.E.
Private communications with participant during conference, Rule 6.A.(2).
Report of results of conference, Rule 6.B.(4).
Revocation of mediator certification, Rule 8.
Scheduling and holding conference, Rule 6.B.(5).
Selection.
Agreement of parties, Rule 2.A.

DIVORCE —Cont'd
Mediated settlement conference and other settlement procedures —Cont'd
Rules —Cont'd
Mediators —Cont'd
Selection —Cont'd
Certified family financial mediator, Rules 2.A, 2.B.
Designation of mediator by agreement, Rule 2.A.
Nomination of non-certified family financial mediator, Rule 2.A.
Training and experience.
Certification, Rule 8.
Certification of mediator training programs, Rule 9.
Mediators' fee.
Compensation generally, Rule 7.
Payment, Rule 4.C.
Mediator training programs.
Certification.
Administrators' fees, payment to complete certification, Rule 9.D.
Before attendance at program, Rule 9.C.
Curriculum, Rules 9.A, 9.B.
Minimum hours of instruction, Rules 9.A, 9.B.
Programs attended prior to rules, Rule 9.C.
Motions.
Court appointment of mediator, Rule 2.B.
Dispensing with settlement, Rule 1.C.(6).
Disqualification of mediator, Rule 2.D.
Extension of time to complete settlement conference, Rule 3.C.
Inability to pay share of mediator's fee, Rule 7.D.
Sanction for failure to attend conference, Rule 5.
Settlement procedures in other family financial cases, Rule 1.C.(5).
Use of settlement procedures other than mediated settlement conference, Rule 1.C.(3).
Neutral evaluation.
Abbreviated presentation of facts and issues, Rule 11.A.
Authorized settlement procedures, Rule 10.B.(1).
Conference procedure, Rule 11.E.
Modification, Rule 11.F.
Neutral evaluator.
Assistance to parties in settlement discussions, Rule 11.H.
Duties, Rule 11.G.
Opening statements, Rule 11.G.(1).
Report to court, Rule 11.G.(3).
Report to parties, Rule 11.G.(2).
Responsibilities, Rule 11.A.
Pre-conference submissions, Rule 11.C.
Replies, Rule 11.D.
Time.
Pre-conference submissions, Rule 11.C.
When conference held, Rule 11.B.
Neutrals.
Agreement of parties.
Selection of neutrals, Rule 10.C.(10).
Authority and duties, Rule 10.C.(13).
Bias, prejudice or partiality, disclosure, Rule 10.C.(13).
Compensation, Rule 10.C.(8), (12).
Control of proceeding, Rule 10.C.(13).

DIVORCE —Cont'd
Mediated settlement conference and other settlement procedures —Cont'd
Rules —Cont'd
Neutrals —Cont'd
Disclosures, Rule 10.C.(13).
Disqualification, Rule 10.C.(11).
Fee, Rule 10.C.(8), (12).
Holding proceeding, Rule 10.C.(13).
Reporting results, Rule 10.C.(13).
Scheduling proceeding, Rule 10.C.(13).
Selection of neutrals, Rule 10.C.(10).
Nomination of non-certified family mediator.
Selecting mediator by agreement.
Filing with court, Rule 2.A.
Notarized agreement.
Finalizing settlement agreement, Rule 4.B.
Ordering settlement procedures, Rule 1.C.
Contents of order, Rule 1.C.(4).
Other family financial cases, Rule 1.C.(5).
Other settlement procedures, Rule 10.A.
Other settlement procedures.
Attendance, Rule 10.C.(8).
Sanctions for failure to attend, Rule 10.C.(9).
Delay of other proceedings.
Prohibited, Rule 10.C.(4).
Duties of parties, Rule 10.C.(8).
Finalizing agreement, Rule 10.C.(8).
General rules, Rule 10.C.
Inadmissibility of proceedings, Rule 10.C.(5).
Neutrals.
Selection, disqualification, compensation, authority, duties, Rule 10.C.
Neutral's fee.
Payment, Rule 10.C.(8).
Order authorizing, Rule 10.A.
Procedures authorized by rules, Rule 10.B.
Record not made, Rule 10.C.(6).
Time for conducting, Rule 10.C.(1).
Extension, Rule 10.C.(2).
When proceeding conducted, Rule 10.C.(1).
Where conducted, Rule 10.C.(3).
Partiality.
Disclosure by mediator, Rule 6.B.(2).
Disclosure by neutral, Rule 10.C.(13).
Phone.
Attendance at settlement conference by, Rule 4.A.(2).
Postponement fee.
Mediators, Rule 7.E.
Postponement of conference, Rule 7.E.
Prejudice.
Disclosure by mediator, Rule 6.B.(2).
Disclosure by neutral, Rule 10.C.(13).
Private communication.
By mediators, Rule 6.A.(2).
Purpose of mandatory settlement procedures, Rule 1.A.
Recesses.
Mediated settlement conference, Rule 3.D.
Report by mediator.
Results of conference, Rule 6.B.(4).
Report by neutral, Rule 10.C.(13).
Report by neutral evaluator.
To court, Rule 11.G.(3).
To parties, Rule 11.G.(2).
Report by settlement judge, Rule 12.C.
Revocation of mediator certification, Rule 8.
Sanctions.
Failure to attend settlement conference, Rule 5.

DIVORCE —Cont'd
Mediated settlement conference and other settlement procedures —Cont'd
Rules —Cont'd
Sanctions —Cont'd
Failure to attend settlement proceeding, Rule 10.C.(9).
Failure to pay mediator's fee, Rule 7.F.
Scheduling conference.
Equitable distribution action.
Scheduling order requiring settlement procedure, Rule 1.C.(1).
Selection of mediator, Rule 2.
Scheduling order.
Order requiring settlement procedures, Rule 1.C.
Contents of order, Rule 1.C.(4).
Other family financial cases, Rule 1.C.(5).
Scope of settlement proceedings, Rule 1.C.(2).
Selection of certified family financial mediator.
Appointment by court, Rule 2.B.
By agreement of parties, Rule 2.A.
Mediator directory, Rule 2.C.
Selection of non-certified family financial mediator.
By agreement.
Filing nomination of non-certified family financial mediator, Rule 2.A.
Settlement conference.
Authority of mediators, Rule 6.
Duties of mediators, Rule 6.B.
Duties of parties attorneys and participants, Rule 4.
Generally, Rule 3.
Judicial settlement conference.
Authorized settlement procedures, Rule 10.B.(2).
Other settlement procedures, Rule 10.
Postponement of conference, Rule 7.E.
Sanctions for failure to attend, Rule 5.
Summary memorandum.
Essential terms of settlement agreement reduced to, Rule 4.B.
Telephone.
Attendance at settlement conference by, Rule 4.A.(2).
Time.
Completion of settlement conference, Rule 3.B.
Extension of time, Rule 3.C.
Computation of limits, Rule 15.
Executed final agreement, Rule 4.B.
Neutral evaluation pre-conference submission, Rule 11.C.
Replies, Rule 11.D.
Neutral evaluator's report to court, Rule 11.G.(3).
Other settlement procedures, Rule 10.C.(1).
Extension, Rule 10.C.(2).
Report by mediator on results of conference, Rule 6.B.(4).
Waiver or extension of limits allowed, Rule 15.
Training and experience.
Certification of mediators, Rule 8.
Training programs for mediators.
Certification, Rule 9.
Mediation.
Child custody and visitation.
Action or proceeding for custody or visitation, §50-13.1.

DIVORCE —Cont'd
Mediation —Cont'd
Custody and visitation mediation program, §§7A-494, 7A-495.
Mental health, developmental disabilities and substance abuse.
Custody.
Persons incapable of self-support upon reaching majority.
Mentally incapable of self-support, §50-13.8.
Incurable insanity.
Grounds for absolute divorce, §50-5.1.
Names.
Adoption of prior deceased husband's name, §50-12, (a).
Application, §50-12, (b).
Incorporation of petition for adoption in complaint or counterclaim for divorce, §50-12, (d).
Validation of use, §50-12, (c).
Resumption of maiden or premarriage surname, §50-12, (a).
Application, §50-12, (b).
Man applying to change surname to premarriage surname, §50-12, (a1).
Incorporation of petition for resumption in complaint or counterclaim for divorce, §50-12, (d).
Man applying to change surname to premarriage surname, §50-12, (a1).
Validation of use of name, §50-12, (c).
Use of surname of prior living husband, §50-12, (a).
Application, §50-12, (b).
Incorporation of petition for use of name in complaint or counterclaim for divorce, §50-12, (d).
Validation of use, §50-12, (c).
No-fault divorce.
Separation of one year, §50-6.
Nonresidents.
Venue and service on, §50-8.
Notice.
Child custody or child support actions, §50-13.5, (d), (e).
Failure of defendant to appear in action.
Notice of trial not required, §50-10, (b).
Offering indignities causing intolerable and burdensome conditions.
Grounds for divorce, §50-7.
Pensions and retirement benefits.
Distribution, §§50-20, (b), 50-20.1.
Personal jurisdiction based on marital relationship, §1-75.4.
Personal property distribution by court.
Equitable distribution.
Generally, §§50-20, 50-21.
Orders transferring title, §50-20, (g).
Personal property located outside of state, §50-21, (a).
Pleadings.
Verification.
When verification required, §50-8.
Postseparation support.
Attorneys' fees, §50-16.4.
Barred by separation agreement or premarital agreement provisions, §50-16.6, (b).
Basis of award, §50-16.2A, (b).
Change in circumstances.
Modification.
Family law arbitration act, §50-56.

DIVORCE —Cont'd
Postseparation support —Cont'd
Considerations in awarding support, §50-16.2A, (b).
Marital misconduct of dependent spouse, §50-16.2A, (d), (e).
Court's duty, §50-16.8.
Defined, §50-16.1A.
Either party may move for, §50-16.2A, (a).
Enforcement of decree, §50-16.7.
Entitlement of dependent spouse to award, §50-16.2A, (c).
How paid, §50-16.7.
Income withholding.
Limitation on amount withheld, §110-136.6, (b1).
Maintenance of certain actions as independent actions permissible, §50-19.
Marital misconduct of dependent spouse.
Considering, §50-16.2A, (d), (e).
Modification, §50-16.9.
Change in circumstances.
Family law arbitration act, §50-56.
Procedure, §50-16.8.
Verified pleading, motion or affidavit.
Requirements, §50-16.2A, (a).
Preliminary injunction enjoining spouse from interfering with, threatening or molesting plaintiff during pendency of suit.
Bond not required, §1A-1, Rule 65, (c).
Premarital agreements generally, §§52B-1 to 52B-11.
See PREMARITAL AGREEMENTS.
Presumptions.
Marital property, §50-20, (b).
Qualified domestic relations orders.
Distribution by court of marital and divisible property, §§50-20, (b), 50-20.1, (g).
Real property distribution by court.
Equitable distribution.
Generally, §§50-20, 50-21.
Lis pendens, §50-20, (h).
Orders transferring title, §50-20, (g).
Real property located outside of state, §50-21, (a).
Reference by consent, §1A-1, Rule 53, (a).
Removal of action, §50-3.
Retirement property distribution by court, §50-20, (b).
Rights arising out of marriage.
Effects of absolute divorce, §50-11, (a).
Separate property.
Defined, §50-20, (b).
Separation.
One year separation on application of either party, §50-6.
Separation agreements, §52-10.1.
Service of process.
Absolute divorce for incurable insanity, §50-5.1.
Child custody or child support actions, §50-13.5, (d).
Nonresidents, §50-8.
Validation where summons answered, §50-9.
Summary judgment.
When summary judgment provisions applicable, §50-10, (d).
Support and maintenance.
Child support.
General provisions.
See CHILD SUPPORT.

DIVORCE —Cont'd
Support and maintenance —Cont'd
General provisions.
See SUPPORT AND MAINTENANCE.
Mediated settlement conferences or other settlement procedures.
District court actions, §7A-38.4A.
Postseparation support, §50-16.2A.
Attorneys' fees, §50-16.4.
Barred by separation agreement or premarital agreement provisions, §50-16.6, (b).
Basis of award, §50-16.2A, (b).
Change in circumstances.
Modification.
Family law arbitration act, §50-56.
Considerations in awarding support, §50-16.2A, (b).
Marital misconduct of dependent spouse, §50-16.2A, (d), (e).
Court's duty, §50-16.8.
Defined, §50-16.1A.
Either party may move for, §50-16.2A, (a).
Enforcement of decree, §50-16.7.
Entitlement of dependent spouse to award, §50-16.2A, (c).
How paid, §50-16.7.
Maintenance of certain actions as independent actions permissible, §50-19.
Marital misconduct of dependent spouse.
Considering, §50-16.2A, (d), (e).
Modification, §50-16.9.
Change in circumstances.
Family law arbitration act, §50-56.
Procedure, §50-16.8.
Verified pleading, motion or affidavit.
Requirements, §50-16.2A, (a).
Temporary restraining order enjoining spouse from interfering with, threatening or molesting plaintiff.
Bond not required, §1A-1, Rule 65, (c).
Title.
Distribution by court of marital and divisible property.
Personal or real property.
Orders transferring title, §50-20, (g).
Trial.
Jury trial or trial before judge without jury.
Determination, §50-10, (c).
Notice of trial.
Failure of defendant to appear in action.
Notice not required, §50-10, (b).
Validation.
Judgments entered prior to January 1, 1981, §50-11.3.
Judgments entered prior to October 1, 1983, §50-11.4.
Prior judgments or decrees, §§50-8, 50-9.
Venue, §50-3.
Change of venue, §1-83.
Child custody or child support actions, §50-13.5, (f).
Nonresidents, §50-8.
Verification.
Complaint verified, §50-8.
Pleadings.
When verifications required, §50-8.
Visitation.
Action or proceeding for child custody or visitation, §50-13.1.
Denial of parental visitation rights.
Written findings of fact, §50-13.5, (i).

DIVORCE —Cont'd
Visitation —Cont'd
Grandparents, §§50-13.2, (b1), 50-13.5, (j).
Adopted grandchild.
Action by biological grandparent, §50-13.2A.
Mediation, §§7A-494, 7A-495.
Vital statistics.
Registration of divorce, §130A-111.
Void ab initio.
What marriages may be declared void upon application of either party, §50-4.
Voidable marriage.
Children born legitimate, §50-11.1.
Waste.
Temporary orders preventing, §50-21, (a).
Will revocation and revival, §31-5.4.

DIVORCE FROM BED AND BOARD.
Acts barring rights of spouse, §31A-1, (a).
Divorce generally.
See DIVORCE.
Grounds, §50-7.
Reference by consent, §1A-1, Rule 53, (a).

DIVORCE FROM BONDS OF MATRIMONY.
Acts barring rights of spouse, §31A-1, (a).
Divorce generally.
See DIVORCE.
Effect of answer of summons by defendant, §50-9.
Effects of absolute divorce, §50-11.
Equitable distribution judgment not entered prior to decree, §50-21, (a).
Former section 52-6, effect of decree or certificate not complying with, §52-9.
Incurable insanity, §50-5.1.
Judgments entered prior to January 1, 1981 validated, §50-11.3.
Maiden or premarriage surname.
Resumption by woman or man, §50-12.
Separation for one year, §50-6.
Summary judgment.
Applicability of provisions, §50-10, (d).

DNA ANALYSIS, §§15A-266 to 15A-270.
See DNA DATABASE AND DATABANKS.

DNA DATABASE AND DATABANKS, §§15A-266 to 15A-270.
Access by defendant to crime scene samples.
Before trial, §15A-267.
Analysis upon conviction or finding of not guilty by reason of insanity.
Blood samples, §15A-266.4.
Blood samples.
Conducting DNA analysis, §15A-266.7.
Convictions requiring samples, §15A-266.4, (a), (b).
Procedure for withdrawal, §15A-266.6, (a) to (c).
Tests to be performed, §15A-266.5.
Cancellation of authority to exchange records, §15A-266.9.
Citation of provisions, §15A-266.
CODIS.
Defined, §15A-266.2.
Conducting analysis of blood samples, §15A-266.7.
Confidentiality of records, §15A-266.12, (a).
Crimes listed.
Blood samples required on conviction, §15A-266.4, (b).
Database exchange, §15A-266.8.

DNA DATABASE AND DATABANKS —Cont'd
Defendant's access to crime scene samples.
Pretrial access, §15A-267, (a).
Costs of further testing, defendant to bear, §15A-267, (d).
Statutes governing access, §15A-267, (b).
Definitions, §15A-266.2.
Disclosing individually identifiable information, §15A-266.11, (a).
DNA.
Defined, §15A-266.2.
DNA record.
Defined, §15A-266.2.
DNA samples and testing.
Collection and storage of samples and records, §15A-266.12.
Post conviction DNA testing.
Motion by defendant.
Appointment of counsel for indigent defendant, §15A-269, (c).
Conditions to be met, §15A-269, (a).
Costs of testing, defendant to bear, §15A-269, (d).
Delay of proceedings or execution of sentence pending testing.
Miscarriage of justice, §15A-269, (e).
Discharge of defendant, ordering on favorable results, §15A-270, (c).
Favorable results, order entered serving interest of justice, §15A-270, (c).
Granting motion, determinations required, §15A-269, (b).
Hearing to evaluate results, §15A-270, (a).
New trial, ordering on favorable results, §15A-270, (c).
Resentencing, ordering on favorable results, §15A-270, (c).
Time for testing order pursuant to motion, §15A-269, (e).
Unfavorable results, dismissal of motion, §15A-270, (b).
Vacating and setting aside judgment, ordering on favorable results, §15A-270, (c).
Sample defined, §15A-266.2.
Exchange of information, §15A-266.8.
Cancellation of authority, §15A-266.9.
Expungement of DNA records.
Dismissal of charges or person found not guilty or not responsible, §15A-146, (b1), (b2).
FBI.
Defined, §15A-266.2.
Procedural compatibility, §15A-266.3.
Identification of persons.
Policy of state, §15A-266.1.
Individually identifiable information.
Disclosure, §15A-266.11, (a).
Obtaining, §15A-266.11, (b).
Insanity defense.
Blood sample required upon finding of not guilty by reason of insanity of certain crimes, §15A-266.4.
Listed crimes.
Blood samples required on conviction, §15A-266.4, (b).
Not guilty by reason of insanity.
Blood sample required upon finding of not guilty by reason of insanity of certain crimes, §15A-266.4.
Penalties, §15A-266.11.
Policy, §15A-266.1.

DNA DATABASE AND DATABANKS —Cont'd
Post conviction DNA testing.
Motion by defendant.
Appointment of counsel for indigent defendant, §15A-269, (c).
Conditions to be met, §15A-269, (a).
Costs of testing, defendant to bear, §15A-269, (d).
Delay of proceedings or execution of sentence pending testing.
Miscarriage of justice, §15A-269, (e).
Discharge of defendant, ordering on favorable results, §15A-270, (c).
Favorable results, order entered serving interest of justice, §15A-270, (c).
Granting motion, determinations required, §15A-269, (b).
Hearing to evaluate results, §15A-270, (a).
New trial, ordering on favorable results, §15A-270, (c).
Resentencing, ordering on favorable results, §15A-270, (c).
Time for testing order pursuant to motion, §15A-269, (e).
Unfavorable results, dismissal of motion, §15A-270, (b).
Vacating and setting aside judgment, ordering on favorable results, §15A-270, (c).
Preservation of DNA evidence.
Disposal of evidence before expiration of time period.
Conditions to be met, §15A-268, (b).
Notification to dispose of evidence.
Prior to expiration of time period, §15A-268, (b), (c).
Required to preserve.
Government agency collecting evidence, §15A-268, (a).
Time period evidence must be preserved, §15A-268, (a).
Pretrial access by defendant to crime scene samples, §15A-267.
Procedural compatibility with the FBI, §15A-266.3.
Records.
Cancellation of authority to exchange, §15A-266.9.
Collection and storage, §15A-266.12, (b).
Confidentiality, §15A-266.12, (a).
SBI.
Defined, §15A-266.2.
Materials and supplies, provision of, §15A-266.6, (c).
Short title, §15A-266.
State DNA databank.
Defined, §15A-266.2.
State DNA database.
Defined, §15A-266.2.
Tests to be performed on blood samples, §15A-266.5.
Unauthorized use of databank, §15A-266.11.
Withdrawal of blood samples, §15A-266.6, (a) to (c).

DNA EVIDENCE PRESERVATION.
Disposal of evidence before expiration of time period.
Conditions to be met, §15A-268, (b).
Notification to dispose of evidence.
Prior to expiration of time period, §15A-268, (b), (c).

DNA EVIDENCE PRESERVATION —Cont'd
Required to preserve.
Government agency collecting evidence, §15A-268, (a).
Time period evidence must be preserved, §15A-268, (a).

DNA SAMPLES AND TESTING.
Database and databank, §§15A-266 to 15A-266.12.
Post conviction DNA testing.
Motion by defendant.
Appointment of counsel for indigent defendant, §15A-269, (c).
Conditions to be met, §15A-269, (a).
Costs of testing, defendant to bear, §15A-269, (d).
Delay of proceedings or execution of sentence pending testing.
Miscarriage of justice, §15A-269, (e).
Discharge of defendant, ordering on favorable results, §15A-270, (c).
Favorable results, order entered serving interest of justice, §15A-270, (c).
Granting motion, determinations required, §15A-269, (b).
Hearing to evaluate results, §15A-270, (a).
New trial, ordering on favorable results, §15A-270, (c).
Resentencing, ordering on favorable results, §15A-270, (c).
Time for testing order pursuant to motion, §15A-269, (e).
Unfavorable results, dismissal of motion, §15A-270, (b).
Vacating and setting aside judgment, ordering on favorable results, §15A-270, (c).
Pretrial access by defendant of samples, §15A-267, (a).
Costs of further testing, defendant to bear, §15A-267, (d).
Ordering SBI to conduct testing and database comparison, §15A-267, (c).
Statutes governing access, §15A-267, (b).

DOCKET BOOK.
Appeals.
Clerks of court, App. Proc. Rule 39, (b).
Defined, §1-208.1.
Judgments.
Cancellation, assignment, etc., of judgments, §1-239.1.

DOCKETS.
Appeals, App. Proc. Rule 12, (b).
Clerks of court.
Docket book, App. Proc. Rule 39, (b).
Judgment docket, App. Proc. Rule 39, (b).
Stays.
Docket entry of stay, §1-293.
Attachment.
Levy on real property, §1-440.17.
Criminal case docketing.
Superior courts, §7A-49.4.
District attorneys.
Preparation of trial dockets, §7A-61.
Docket book.
See DOCKET BOOK.
Executions.
County to which execution to be issued.
Docketing in as prerequisite to issuance, §1-308.

DOCKETS —Cont'd
Executions —Cont'd
Returns.
Entry on judgment docket, §1-321.
Judgment docket and judgment in docket book.
Defined, §1-208.1.
Judgments, §§1-233, 1-234.
Assignment of judgment.
Entry on judgment docket, §1-246.
Deemed rendered and docketed on first day of session, §1-233.
Federal court judgments, §1-237.
Foreign judgments, §1C-1703, (b).
Judgment of appellate division docketed in superior court, §1-235.
Modification of judgment on appeal, §1-242.
Payment to clerk.
Docket credited, §1-239, (a).
Entry of payment on docket, §1-239, (c).
Liens.
Restrictions on docketing, §44A-12.1.
Magistrates to keep, §7A-175.
Stays.
Appeals.
Docket entry of stay, §1-293.
Summons, §1A-1, Rule 4, (g).
Superior courts.
Clerks, record-keeping procedures, §7A-109, (a) to (e).
Criminal case docketing, §7A-49.4.
Torrens system registration.
Liens on registered lands.
Docketed judgments, §43-45.
Wills.
Caveat to will.
Transfer of cause to trial docket, §31-33.

DOCTOR-PATIENT PRIVILEGE.
Communications between doctor and patient, §8-53.
Alimony and divorce actions, §8-53.6.
Waiver of privilege in child abuse cases, §8-53.1.
Medical review committee.
Testimony of members of committees, §131E-95, (b), (c).
Workers' compensation.
Medical examinations, facts not privileges, §97-27, (a).

DOCTORS.
Chiropractors, §§90-139 to 90-157.3.
See CHIROPRACTORS.
Dentists, §§90-22 to 90-48.11.
See DENTISTS.
Generally.
See PHYSICIANS AND SURGEONS.
Optometrists, §§90-114 to 90-127.3.
See OPTOMETRISTS.
Osteopaths, §§90-129 to 90-138.
See OSTEOPATHS.
Podiatrists, §§90-202.2 to 90-202.14.
See PODIATRISTS.
Psychologists, §§90-270.1 to 90-270.21.
See PSYCHOLOGISTS.
Veterinarians, §§90-179 to 90-187.13.
See VETERINARIANS.

DOCTRINE OF WORTHIER TITLE.
Abolished, §41-6.2, (a).
Applicable to revocable trusts, §41-6.2.

DOCUMENTARY DRAFTS.
Negotiable instruments generally.
See NEGOTIABLE INSTRUMENTS.

DOCUMENTARY EVIDENCE.
Accounts and accounting.
Itemized and verified accounts, §8-45.
Bills of lading in evidence, §8-41.
Book accounts.
Copies of accounts in evidence, §8-44.
Executors and administrators.
Approving book accounts by personal representative, §8-43.
Under $60, §8-42.
Carriers.
Actions by or against common or connecting carriers.
Bills of lading in evidence, §8-41.
Contract actions.
Book accounts under $60, §8-42.
Copies of book accounts in evidence, §8-44.
Executors and administrators.
Book accounts approved by personal representative, §8-43.
Hospital records.
Copies of medical records, §8-44.1.
Itemized and verified accounts, §8-45.
Meat inspection.
Production of documentary evidence, §106-549.36, (b), (c).
Medical records.
Copies of medical records, §8-44.1.
Parol evidence.
Identifying land described, §8-39.
Real property.
Parol evidence to identify land described, §8-39.
Remainder of or related writings or recorded statements, §8C-1, Rule 106.
Subpoena for production, §§1A-1, Rule 45, (c), 8-61.

DOCUMENT AUTHENTICATION.
Certificates of authentication.
Authority of secretary of state, §66-270.
Definitions, §66-271.
Issuance of certificate, §66-272.
Limitation on authority of secretary, §66-274, (c).
Non-certifiable documents, §66-274, (b).
Other methods of authentication, §66-275.
Prerequisites to authentication, §66-273.
Purpose of certificate precluding issuance, §66-274, (a).

DOCUMENTS OF TITLE, §§25-7-101 to 25-7-603.
Alteration of instruments.
Bills of lading, §25-7-306.
Warehouse receipts, §25-7-208.
Applicability of chapter, §25-7-103.
Attachment of goods covered by a negotiable document, §25-7-602.
Bailee.
Defined, §25-7-102.
Bills of lading.
Altered bills, §25-7-306.
Attachment of goods covered by a negotiable document, §25-7-602.
Care.
Contractual limitation of carrier's liability, §25-7-309, (2).
Duty of care, §25-7-309, (1).
Change of instructions, §25-7-303, (1).

DOCUMENTS OF TITLE —Cont'd
Bills of lading —Cont'd
Claims.
Time and manner of presentation, §25-7-309, (3).
Damages.
Limitation of liability, §25-7-309, (2).
Defined, §25-1-201, (6).
Destination bills, §25-7-305, (1).
Substitute bills, §25-7-305, (2).
Diversion, §25-7-303, (1).
Duty of carrier, §25-7-309, (1).
Evidence.
Actions by or against common or connecting carriers, §8-41.
Handling.
Proper handling, §25-7-301, (1).
In a set, §25-7-304.
Instructions.
Change of instructions, §25-7-303, (1).
Liability for non-receipt or misdescription.
"Said to contain," §25-7-301, (1).
"Shipper's weight, load and count," §25-7-301, (1), (2).
Liability of carrier.
Contractual limitation of liability of carrier, §25-7-309, (2).
Duty of carrier, §25-7-309, (1).
Lien of carrier, §25-7-307, (1), (2).
Enforcement, §25-7-308.
Limitation of actions.
Limitations in bill of lading or tariff, §25-7-309, (1).
Misdescription.
Liability for misdescription, §25-7-301, (5).
Negotiability, §25-7-104, (1).
Negotiation. See within this heading, "Negotiation."
Non-negotiable bills of lading, §25-7-104, (2).
Non-receipt.
Liability for non-receipt, §25-7-301, (1), (5).
Original terms.
Holding to original terms, §25-7-303, (2).
Overseas shipment.
Form of bill, §25-2-323.
Reconsignment, §25-7-303, (1).
"Said to contain," §25-7-301, (1).
Sets.
Bills of lading in a set, §25-7-304.
"Shipper's weight, load and count," §25-7-301, (1), (3).
Substitute bills, §25-7-305, (2).
Third party documents.
Prima facie evidence, §25-1-202.
Through bills of lading and similar documents, §25-7-302, (1), (2).
Issuers, §25-7-302, (3).
Citation of chapter.
Short title, §25-7-101.
Claims.
Conflicting claims, §25-7-603.
Consignee.
Defined, §25-7-102.
Consignor.
Defined, §25-7-102.
Construction and interpretation, §25-7-105.
Damages.
Limitation of liability in bill of lading, §25-7-309, (2).
Limitation of warehouseman's liability, §25-7-204, (1), (2).

DOCUMENTS OF TITLE —Cont'd
Defeated.
Document of title to goods defeated in certain cases, §25-7-503.
Definitions, §§25-1-201, (15), 25-7-102.
Bailees, §25-7-102.
Bills of lading, §25-1-201, (6).
Consignee, §25-7-102.
Consignor, §25-7-102.
Delivery order, §25-7-102.
Documents, §25-7-102.
Goods, §25-7-102.
Index of definitions, §25-7-102.
Issuer, §25-7-102.
Warehouseman, §25-7-102.
Warehouse receipts, §25-1-201, (45).
Delivery.
Excuse, §25-7-403, (1).
Good faith delivery.
No liability for good faith delivery pursuant to receipt or bill, §25-7-404.
Liens.
Satisfaction before delivery, §25-7-403, (2).
No liability for good faith delivery pursuant to receipt or bill, §25-7-404.
Obligation of warehouseman or carrier to deliver, §25-7-403, (1).
Seller's stoppage of delivery, §25-7-504, (4).
Without indorsement, §25-7-506.
Delivery order.
Defined, §25-7-102.
Destroyed documents, §25-7-601, (1).
Delivery by bailee, §25-7-601, (2).
Due negotiation.
Absence of due negotiation.
Rights acquired in absence, §25-7-504, (1), (2).
Duplicates, §25-7-402.
Evidence.
Prima facie evidence by third party documents, §25-1-202.
Executions.
Lien on goods covered by a negotiable document, §25-7-602.
Fungible goods.
Buyer in the ordinary course of business.
Delivery by warehouseman, §25-7-205.
Goods.
Defined, §25-7-102.
Guaranty.
Indorser not guarantor for other parties, §25-7-505.
Indorsement, §25-7-501, (1).
Compelling indorsement.
Right to compel, §25-7-506.
Delivery to compel indorsement, §25-7-506.
Indorser not guarantor for other parties, §25-7-505.
Power to compel indorsement, §25-7-506.
Requirements of due negotiation, §25-7-501.
Injunctions.
Enjoining negotiations of document, §25-7-602.
Interpleader and intervention, §25-7-603.
Irregularities in issue or conduct of issuer, §25-7-401.
Issuance.
Irregularities in issue, §25-7-401.
Overissue, §25-7-402.
Issuer.
Conduct.
Irregularities in conduct of issuer, §25-7-401.
Defined, §25-7-102.

DOCUMENTS OF TITLE —Cont'd
Issuer —Cont'd
Irregularities in conduct of issuer, §25-7-401.
Liability.
No liability for good faith delivery pursuant to receipt or bill, §25-7-404.
Liens.
Satisfaction before delivery, §25-7-403, (2).
Warehouseman, §25-7-209, (1).
Enforcement of lien, §25-7-210.
Limitation of actions.
Bill of lading or tariff, §25-7-309, (3).
Warehouse receipt or tariff, §25-7-204, (3).
Lost instruments and records, §25-7-601, (1).
Delivery by bailee, §25-7-601, (2).
Missing documents, §25-7-601, (1).
Delivery by bailee, §25-7-601, (2).
Negative implication.
Construction against, §25-7-105.
Negotiation.
Absence of due negotiation.
Rights acquired in the absence of due negotiation, §25-7-504, (1), (2).
Attachment of goods covered by a negotiable document, §25-7-602.
Contract.
When adequate compliance with commercial contract, §25-7-509.
Defeated.
Document of title to goods defeated in certain cases, §25-7-503.
Delivery.
Seller's stoppage of delivery, §25-7-504, (1).
Without indorsement, §25-7-506.
Diversion.
Change of shipping instructions, §25-7-504, (3).
Effect of diversion, §25-7-504, (3).
Due negotiation.
Rights acquired by due negotiation, §25-7-502, (1), (2).
Rights acquired in the absence of due negotiation, §25-7-504, (1), (2).
Enjoining negotiation of document, §25-7-602.
Form of negotiation, §25-7-501.
Indorsement.
Compelling indorsement, §25-7-506.
Delivery without indorsement, §25-7-506.
Due negotiation, §25-7-501, (1).
Form of negotiation, §25-7-501.
Indorser not guarantor for other parties, §25-7-505.
Non-negotiable document, §25-7-501, (1), (5).
Power to compel, §25-7-506.
Right to compel, §25-7-506.
Negotiability, §25-7-104.
Warranties, §25-7-507.
Collecting bank.
Warranties of collecting bank as to documents, §25-7-508.
Non-negotiable documents, §25-7-104, (2).
Indorsement, §25-7-501, (1), (5).
Rights acquired by due negotiation, §25-7-502, (1), (2).
Warranties.
Collecting bank, §25-7-508.
Negotiation or transfer of receipt or bill, §25-7-507.
When adequate compliance with commercial contract, §25-7-509.
Obligation of warehouseman or carrier to deliver, §25-7-403, (1).

DOCUMENTS OF TITLE —Cont'd
Overissue, §25-7-402.
Relation of chapter to treaties, statutes, tariffs, etc., §25-7-103.
Retail installment sales.
Payment.
Return of title documents upon full payment, §25A-22, (b).
Sale of goods, UCC.
Bill of lading required in overseas shipment, §25-2-323.
When deliverable on acceptance and when on payment, §25-2-514.
Secured transactions.
Priority of security interests, §25-9-331.
Short title of chapter, §25-7-101.
Stolen documents, §25-7-601, (1).
Delivery by bailee, §25-7-601, (2).
Storage.
Termination of storage at warehouseman's option, §25-7-206.
Suretyship.
Indorser not guarantor for other parties, §25-7-505.
Tariffs.
Relation of chapter to tariffs, §25-7-103.
Transfer.
Warranties, §25-7-507.
Treaties.
Relation of chapter to treaty, §25-7-103.
United States statutes.
Relation of chapter to statute, §25-7-103.
Warehouseman.
Defined, §25-7-102.
Warehouse receipts.
Agricultural commodities stored under government bond, §25-7-201, (2).
Alcoholic beverages.
Distilled spirits stored under government bond, §25-7-201, (2).
Altered warehouse receipts, §25-7-208.
Contractual limitation of warehouseman's liability, §25-7-204, (4).
Crops.
Storage under government bond, §25-7-201, (2).
Defined, §§25-1-201, (45), 25-7-201, (2).
Distilled spirits.
Storage under government bond, §25-7-201, (2).
Duty of care, §25-7-204, (1).
Forms, §25-7-202, (1).
Fungible goods, §25-7-207, (2).
Title of buyer in ordinary course of business, §25-7-205.
Goods must be kept separate, §§25-7-204, 25-7-207.
Issuance.
Who may issue, §25-7-201, (1).
Liability for non-receipt or misdescription, §25-7-203.
Contractual limitation of warehouseman's liability, §25-7-204, (4).
Lien of warehouseman, §25-7-209, (1), (2).
Enforcement, §25-7-210.
Limitation of actions.
Contractual limitation of warehouseman's liability, §25-7-204, (3), (4).
Misdescription.
Liability for, §25-7-203.
Non-negotiable warehouse receipts, §25-7-104, (2).
Non-receipt.
Liability for, §25-7-203.

DOCUMENTS OF TITLE —Cont'd
Warehouse receipts —Cont'd
Storage.
Under government bond, §25-7-201, (2).
Termination of storage at warehouseman's option, §25-7-206.
Terms.
Essential terms, §25-7-202, (1), (2).
Optional terms, §25-7-202, (3).
Title under warehouse receipt defeated in certain cases, §25-7-205.
Who may issue, §25-7-201, (1).
Warranties.
Collecting banks.
Warranties of collecting bank as to documents, §25-7-508.
Negotiation, §25-7-507.

DOG BAITING, §14-362.2.

DOG FIGHTING, §14-362.2.

DOGS.
Applicability of provisions, §67-18.
Assistance dogs.
Assaulting law enforcement or assistance animals, §14-163.1.
Blind pedestrians rights and privileges without guide dog, §20-175.3.
Common carrier fares for blind person accompanied by, §62-144, (b).
Right of way at crossings, intersections and traffic control signal points.
Guide dog to serve as signal for the blind, §20-175.2.
Running at large.
Dangerous dogs.
Permitting dangerous dog to go beyond owner's real property unless leashed and muzzled.
Unlawful, §67-4.2, (a).
Female dogs in heat.
Penalty for permitting to run at large, §67-2.
Nighttime.
Permitting to run at large at night.
Penalty, §67-12.
Sheep-killing dogs.
Penalty for permitting such dog to run at large, §67-3.
Wildlife management areas.
Unmuzzled dogs running at large.
Impoundment, §67-14.1, (b) to (e).
Spay/neuter program, §§19A-60 to 19A-65.
State dog.
Plott hound, §145-13.
Superior courts.
Dangerous dogs.
Determination that dog is potentially dangerous dog.
Appeals to superior court of final decisions, §67-4.1, (c).
Taxation.
Property taxes.
Exemption, §105-275.
Venue.
Dangerous dogs.
Determination that dog is potentially dangerous dog.
Appeals to superior court of final decisions, §67-4.1, (c).
Vicious animals.
Confinement or leashing of vicious animals, §130A-200.

DOGS —Cont'd
Assistance dogs —Cont'd
Vicious animals —Cont'd
Dangerous dogs. See within this heading, "Dangerous dogs."
Wildlife management areas.
Killing or injuring deer or bear.
Dog may be killed without liability, §67-14.1, (a).
Running at large.
Unmuzzled dogs running at large.
Impoundment, §67-14.1, (b) to (e).
Beagles.
Field trials for beagles.
Hunting license exemption, §113-276, (k).
Counties.
Annual license tax.
Power to levy, §153A-153.
Dangerous dogs.
Local ordinances for control of dangerous dogs.
Article not to prevent, §67-4.5.
Potentially dangerous dogs.
Persons or board responsible for determining.
Designation, §67-4.1, (c).
Dog wardens.
Appointment of animal control officers, §67-30.
Duties, §67-31.
Powers, §67-31.
Rabies control officers.
Dog warden as assistant, §67-31.
Provisions as to dogs applicable to all counties, §67-18.
Supplemental nature of provisions, §67-36.
Criminal law and procedure.
Assistance dogs.
Assaulting law enforcement or assistance animals, §14-163.1.
Cruelty to animals.
Restraining dogs in cruel manner, §14-362.3.
Dangerous dogs.
Attacks by dangerous dogs, §67-4.3.
Precautions against.
Violations by owners, §67-4.2, (c).
Cruelty to animals.
Restraining dogs in cruel manner, §14-362.3.
Damages.
Dangerous dogs.
Damages for injuries or property damage inflicted by dog.
Strict liability, §67-4.4.
Killing or injuring livestock.
Liability of owner, §67-1.
Mad dogs.
Failure to kill, §67-4.
Permitting dogs to run at large at night.
Liability of owner, §67-12.
Dangerous dogs, §§67-4.1 to 67-4.5.
Actions.
Strict liability.
Damages for injuries or property damage inflicted by dangerous dog, §67-4.4.
Appeals.
Determination that dog is potentially dangerous, §67-4.1, (c).
Applicability of provisions, §67-4.1, (b).
Assault, torment or abuse of dog.
Injury inflicted by dog.
Inapplicability of provisions, §67-4.1, (b).
Attacks by dangerous dogs.
Misdemeanors, §67-4.3.
Precautions against, §67-4.2.

DOGS —Cont'd
Dangerous dogs —Cont'd
Counties.
Adopting or enforcing programs for control of dangerous dogs.
Article not construed to prevent, §67-4.5.
Potentially dangerous dogs.
Persons or board responsible for determining designation, §67-4.1, (c).
Damages.
Strict liability for injuries or property damage by dangerous dog, §67-4.4.
Definitions, §67-4.1, (a).
Determination that dog is potentially dangerous, §67-4.1, (c).
Appeals from final decisions, §67-4.1, (c).
Hearings.
Determination that dog is potentially dangerous, §67-4.1, (c).
Herding dogs.
Inapplicability of provisions, §67-4.1, (b).
Hunting.
Dogs being used in lawful hunt.
Inapplicability of provisions, §67-4.1, (b).
Law enforcement officers.
Dogs being used by.
Inapplicability of provisions, §67-4.1, (b).
Leaving dangerous dogs unattended.
Unlawful, §67-4.2, (a).
Local programs for control of dangerous dogs.
Article not construed to prevent, §67-4.5.
Misdemeanors.
Attacks by dangerous dogs, §67-4.3.
Precautions against.
Violations of section, §67-4.2, (c).
Municipal corporations.
Adopting or enforcing programs for control of dangerous dogs.
Article not construed to prevent, §67-4.5.
Potentially dangerous dogs.
Person or board responsible for determining designation, §67-4.1, (c).
Notice.
Determination that dog is potentially dangerous, §67-4.1, (c).
Appeals to superior court, §67-4.1, (c).
Transfer of ownership or possession of dangerous dog, §67-4.2, (b).
Ordinances.
Local programs for control of dangerous dogs.
Article not construed to prevent, §67-4.5.
Owners.
Defined, §67-4.1, (a).
Leaving dangerous dog unattended on owner's real property.
Unlawful, §67-4.2, (a).
Permitting dangerous dog to go beyond owner's real property.
Unlawful, §67-4.2, (a).
Penalty for attacks by dangerous dogs, §67-4.3.
Petitions.
Determination that dog is potentially dangerous.
Appeals to superior court from final decisions, §67-4.1, (c).
Potentially dangerous dogs.
Defined, §67-4.1, (a).
Determination, §67-4.1, (c).
Precautions against attacks by dangerous dogs, §67-4.2.

DOGS —Cont'd
Dangerous dogs —Cont'd
Predator control dogs.
Inapplicability of provisions, §67-4.1, (b).
Real property.
Owner's real property.
Defined, §67-4.1, (a).
Strict liability.
Damages for injuries or property damage inflicted by dangerous dog, §67-4.4.
Torts.
Injury inflicted on person committing tort.
Inapplicability of provisions, §67-4.1, (b).
Transfer of ownership or possession of dangerous dog.
Notice by owner, §67-4.2, (b).
Trespass.
Injury inflicted by dog on person committing willful trespass.
Inapplicability of provisions, §67-4.1, (b).
Venue.
Determination that dog is potentially dangerous.
Appeals to superior court, §67-4.1, (c).
Definitions.
Dangerous dogs, §67-4.1, (a).
Drug detection dogs.
Handlers, commercial detection services, §90-102.1.
Electronic dog collars.
Applicable counties, §14-401.17, (d).
Enforcement, §14-401.17, (c).
Jurisdiction, §14-401.17, (c).
Penalties, §14-401.17, (b).
Unlawful removal, §14-401.17, (a).
Field trials for beagles.
Hunting license exemption, §113-276, (k).
Foxes.
Taking with dogs at night or day or year-round basis, §113-291.4, (b).
Greyhound racing, §14-309.20.
Guide dogs.
Assaulting law enforcement or assistance animals, §14-163.1.
Blind pedestrians rights and privileges without guide dog, §20-175.3.
Common carrier fares for blind person accompanied by, §62-144, (b).
Right of way at crossings, intersections and traffic control signal points.
Guide dog to serve as signal for the blind, §20-175.2.
Hearings.
Dangerous dogs.
Determination that dog is potentially dangerous dog, §67-4.1, (c).
Hotel rooms, admittance of pets, §72-7.1.
Hunting and wildlife.
Dangerous dogs.
Dogs used in lawful hunt.
Inapplicability of provisions of article to, §67-4.1, (b).
Field trials with dogs, §113-291.1, (d).
Foxes, §113-291.4, (b).
Muzzle loading firearm deer season.
Using dogs to hunt deer prohibited, §113-291.2, (a).
Raccoon and opossum hunting at night, §113-291.1, (e).
Regulation of use, §113-291.5.
Limitations on authority, §113-291.5.
Training during closed season, §113-291.1, (d1).

DOGS —Cont'd
Hunting and wildlife —Cont'd
Use in taking wildlife, §113-291.1, (a).
Impoundment.
Wildlife management areas.
Unmuzzled dogs running at large, §67-14.1, (b) to (e).
Larceny.
Felony, §14-81, (a1).
Probation, conditions required, §14-81, (b).
Sentencing to active sentence.
Judge's authority not limited, §14-81, (b).
Taking dogs for temporary purpose, §14-82.
Law enforcement dogs.
Assaulting law enforcement or assistance animals, §14-163.1.
Dangerous dogs.
Inapplicability of article to dogs used by, §67-4.1, (b).
Injuring, maiming or killing, §14-163.1.
Liability of owners.
Dangerous dogs.
Attacks by dangerous dogs, §67-4.3.
Precautions against.
Violations of section by owners, §67-4.2, (c).
Strict liability in civil damages for injuries, §67-4.4.
Killing or injuring livestock or fowl, §67-1.
Liability to discharge duties imposed under provision.
Penalty, §67-16.
Mad dogs.
Failure of owner to kill, §67-4.
Permitting dogs to run at large at night.
Liability for damages, §67-12.
Licenses.
Counties.
Power to levy tax, §153A-153.
Livestock.
Dangerous dogs.
Herding dogs.
Inapplicability of provisions of article to, §67-4.1, (b).
Killing or injuring livestock.
Damages.
Liability of owner, §67-1.
Liability of owner, §67-1.
Sheep-killing dogs.
Any person may kill, §67-14.
Refusal to kill.
Penalty, §67-3.
Mad dogs.
Killing.
Any person may kill, §67-14.
Failure to kill.
Liability of owner, §67-4.
Misdemeanors.
Dangerous dogs.
Attacks by dangerous dogs, §67-4.3.
Precautions against.
Violations by owners, §67-4.2, (c).
Failure to discharge duties imposed under provisions, §67-16.
Mad dogs.
Failure to kill, §67-4.
Permitting dogs to run at large at night, §67-12.
Sheep-killing dogs.
Permitting to go at large, §67-3.
Motor vehicles.
Duties of drivers approaching person using guide dog, §168-5.

DOGS —Cont'd
Municipal corporations.
Dangerous dogs.
Local ordinances for control of dangerous dogs.
Article not to prevent, §67-4.5.
Potentially dangerous dogs.
Person or board responsible for determining.
Designation, §67-4.1, (c).
Regulation of domestic animals, §160A-186.
Nighttime.
Permitting dogs to run at large at night.
Penalty, §67-12.
Notice.
Dangerous dogs.
Determination dog potentially dangerous.
Appeals to superior court, §67-4.1, (c).
Notice to owner, §67-4.1, (c).
Transfer of ownership or possession of dangerous dog.
Notice by owner, §67-4.2, (b).
Wildlife management areas.
Unmuzzled dogs running at large.
Impoundment, §67-14.1, (c).
Ordinances.
Dangerous dogs.
Local enforcement programs for control of dangerous dogs.
Article not to prevent, §67-4.5.
Persons bitten by dogs.
Confinement of all biting dogs and cats, §130A-196.
Notice to local health director, §130A-196.
Rabies.
General provisions, §§130A-184 to 130A-201.
See RABIES.
Reports by physicians, §130A-196.
Plott hound.
State dog, §145-13.
Police dogs, injuring, maiming or killing, §14-163.1.
Rabies, §§130A-184 to 130A-201.
See RABIES.
Racing, greyhounds, §14-309.20.
Service animals.
Prohibited acts as to, §168-4.5.
Registration, §168-4.3.
Responsibility for, §168-4.4.
Right to be accompanied by, §168-4.2.
Penalty for depriving of right, §168-4.5.
Tags, §168-4.2.
Training, §168-4.3.
Donation for training, §168-4.6.
Torts.
Dangerous dogs.
Persons committing torts.
Injuries inflicted by dogs.
Inapplicability of article to, §67-4.1, (b).
Trespass.
Dangerous dogs.
Persons committing willful trespass.
Injuries inflicted by dogs.
Inapplicability of provisions of article, §67-4.1, (b).

DOG SHOWS.
License tax, §105-37.1, (d).
Privilege tax on gross receipts, §105-37.1, (a).
Advance report when bringing show from outside to state, §105-37.1, (c).
Rate and payment, §105-37.1, (b).

DOG WARDENS.
Appointment of animal control officer by county, §67-30.
Powers and duties, §67-31.

DOGWOOD.
State flower, §145-1.
Trespass.
Taking, etc., of flowering dogwood from land of another, §14-129.

DOLPHIN PROTECTION, §113-189, (b).

DOMESTICATED ANIMALS.
Animals generally.
See ANIMALS.
Animal welfare act generally, §§19A-20 to 19A-40.
See ANIMAL WELFARE.
Cats.
See CATS.
Dead animals.
Disposition of, §106-403.
Dogs generally.
See DOGS.
Rabbits.
Poultry products inspection.
Applicability of article to domesticated rabbits, §106-549.51A.

DOMESTIC CRIMINAL TRESPASS, §14-134.3.
Arrest without warrant, §15A-401.
Deadly weapons.
Trespass on property of safe house, §14-134.3, (b).
Defined, §14-134.3, (a).
Evidence that couple living apart, §14-134.3, (a).
Safe houses.
Trespass with a deadly weapon, §14-134.3, (b).

DOMESTIC RECIPROCALS.
Generally, §§58-15-100 to 58-15-150.
See RECIPROCAL INSURANCE.

DOMESTIC RELATIONS.
Alimony.
See DIVORCE.
Annulment of marriage.
See ANNULMENT OF MARRIAGE.
Attorneys specializing in family law.
Certification standards, Bar Rules & Regs., D, §§.2401 to .2407.
Child custody.
See CHILD CUSTODY.
Child support.
See CHILD SUPPORT.
District courts.
Proper division for trial of civil actions, §7A-244.
Divorce.
See DIVORCE.
Domestic violence, §§50B-1 to 50B-9.
See DOMESTIC VIOLENCE.
Husband and wife.
See HUSBAND AND WIFE.
Marriage.
See MARRIAGE PROCEEDINGS.
Married women.
See MARRIED WOMEN.
Minors.
See MINORS.
Parent and child.
See PARENT AND CHILD.
Trespass.
Criminal trespass, §14-134.3.
Arrest without warrant, §15A-401.

DOMESTIC RELATIONS —Cont'd
Violence, §§50B-1 to 50B-9.
See DOMESTIC VIOLENCE.

DOMESTIC SERVANTS.
Workers' compensation.
Exceptions to provisions, §97-13, (b).

DOMESTIC VIOLENCE.
Actions.
Institution of civil action, §50B-2, (a).
Who may institute, §50B-2, (a).
Adultery.
Effect upon prosecution for violation of section 14-184 or other offense against public morals, §50B-8.
Agreements.
Contents, §50B-3, (a).
Arrest.
Violation of order, §50B-4, (b).
Attorneys' fees, §50B-3, (a).
Attorneys specializing in family law.
Certification standards, Bar Rules & Regs., D, §§.2401 to .2407.
Bail and recognizance, §15A-534.1, (a).
Retention of defendant in custody without action, time limitation, §15A-534.1, (b).
Centers for victims of domestic violence.
Domestic violence center fund.
Purposes, §50B-9.
Child custody.
Award of temporary custody, §§50B-2, (c1), (c2), 50B-3, (a), (a1).
Emergency relief ex parte orders, §50B-2, (c) to (c2).
Child support, §50B-3, (a).
Commission, §§143B-394.15, 143B-394.16.
See DOMESTIC VIOLENCE COMMISSION.
Community punishment.
Special probation conditions in addition to, §15A-1382.1, (b).
Concealed handgun permit.
Suspension as part of orders issued by court, §14-415.18, (b).
Construction and interpretation.
Construction of chapter, §50B-6.
Contempt.
Enforcement of orders, §50B-4.
Copies.
Issuance of copy of order to parties, §50B-3, (c).
Counties.
Appropriations. for programs to protect the public, §153A-212.1.
Defined, §50B-1.
Disposition report, indication on, §15A-1382.1, (a).
Domestic violence commission, §§143B-394.15, 143B-394.16.
Domestic violence treatment program.
Establishment by department of correction, §143B-262, (e).
Inmates with record of domestic violence.
Completion of program, §143B-262, (e).
Emergency assistance, §50B-5, (a).
Who may request, §50B-5, (a).
Emergency relief.
Custody ex parte orders, §50B-2, (c) to (c2).
Enforcement of orders.
Generally, §50B-4.
Ex parte orders, §50B-2, (c).
Authorized magistrates, §50B-2, (c1), (c2).

DOMESTIC VIOLENCE —Cont'd
Emergency relief —Cont'd
Ex parte orders —Cont'd
Firearms.
Surrender required, §50B-3.1, (a), (d).
Disposal, §50B-3.1, (h).
Retrieval, §50B-3.1, (e).
Motion, §50B-2, (b).
Pro se forms, §50B-2, (d).
Relief authorized.
Generally, §50B-3.
Employment discrimination.
Persons seeking relief under provisions.
Prohibited acts by employers, §50B-5.5, (a).
Enforcement, §50B-5.5, (b).
Eviction.
Orders for relief, §50B-3, (a).
Firearms.
Emergency or ex parte orders.
Surrender of firearms required, §50B-3.1, (a), (d).
Additional relief, §50B-3.1, (l).
Disposal, §50B-3.1, (h).
Exemptions for official use, §50B-3.1, (k).
Hearings, §50B-3.1, (b), (c).
Motions for return of firearms, §50B-3.1, (f), (g).
Retrieval of firearms, §50B-3.1, (e).
Violations, §50B-3.1, (i), (j).
Forms.
Pro se forms, §50B-2, (d).
Fornication.
Effect upon prosecution for violation of section 14-184 or other offense against public morals, §50B-8.
Funds.
Domestic violence center fund, §50B-9.
Geographically based field programs.
Eligible cases for legal assistance, §7A-474.3, (b).
Grants.
Domestic violence center fund, §50B-9.
Harassment.
Orders for relief, §50B-3, (a).
Hearings.
Emergency relief, §50B-2, (b).
Firearms.
Inquiry as to defendants' access to firearms, §50B-3.1, (b), (c).
Housing.
Orders for relief, §50B-3, (a).
Trespass on property of safe house with a deadly weapon, §14-134.3, (b).
Jurisdiction.
District court to have original jurisdiction, §50B-2, (a).
Law enforcement officers.
Emergency assistance, §50B-5, (a).
Who may request, §50B-5, (a).
Liability, §50B-5, (b).
Magistrates.
Emergency relief ex parte orders, §50B-2, (c1), (c2).
Motions.
Contempt, §50B-4, (a).
Emergency relief, §50B-2, (b).
Who may move, §50B-2, (b).
Firearms, return of, §50B-3.1, (f), (g).
North Carolina Coalition Against Domestic Violence, Inc.
Domestic violence center fund.
Purposes, §50B-9.

DOMESTIC VIOLENCE —Cont'd
Notice.
Emergency relief hearings, §50B-2, (b).
Orders.
Arrest for violation, §50B-4, (b).
Copies.
Issuance to parties, §50B-3, (c).
Enforcement, §50B-4, (a), (b).
Full faith and credit, §50B-4, (d).
Out-of-state orders, §50B-4, (e).
Who may seek enforcement, §50B-4, (b).
Without further order, §50B-4, (c).
Entry into information registry, §50B-3, (d).
Ex parte orders, §50B-2, (c).
Firearms.
Surrender required, §50B-3.1, (a), (d).
Disposal, §50B-3.1, (h).
Retrieval, §50B-3.1, (e).
False statement regarding, §50B-4.2.
Protective orders, §50B-3, (a).
Period of time, §50B-3, (b).
Purchase or possession of firearms by person subject to order prohibited, §14-269.8.
Temporary orders.
Ex parte orders, §50B-2, (c).
Violation of valid protective order as felony, §50B-4.1, (d), (f).
Violation of valid protective order as misdemeanor, §50B-4.1, (a).
Warrantless arrest by law enforcement officer, §50B-4.1, (b), (c).
Pregnant women.
Injury to pregnant woman resulting in miscarriage or stillbirth, §14-18.2, (c).
Programs for victims.
Privileged communications.
Definitions, §8-53.12, (a).
Duty in cases of abuse or neglect, §8-53.12, (c).
Generally, §8-53.12, (b).
Pro se forms, §50B-2, (d).
Protective orders, §50B-3, (a).
Defined, §50B-1, (c).
Enforcement, §50B-4.
Firearms, surrender and disposal.
Emergency or ex parte orders, §50B-3.1.
Period of time, §50B-3, (b).
Relief.
Generally, §50B-3, (a).
Remedies not exclusive, §50B-7.
Safe houses.
Trespass with a deadly weapon, §14-134.3, (b).
Spousal assault.
Competency of spouse as witness, §8-57, (b).
Victim assistance act, §§7A-474.16 to 7A-474.20.
Victims programs.
Privileged communications.
Definitions, §8-53.12, (a).
Duty in cases of abuse or neglect, §8-53.12, (c).
Generally, §8-53.12, (b).

DOMESTIC VIOLENCE COMMISSION, §§143B-394.15, 143B-394.16.
Chair, §143B-394.15, (e).
Established, §143B-394.15, (a).
Located within department of administration, §143B-394.15, (a).
Meetings, §143B-394.15, (i).
Membership, §143B-394.15, (c).
Office space provided by department of administration, §143B-394.15, (k).

DOMESTIC VIOLENCE COMMISSION —Cont'd
Per diem, subsistence and travel allowances, §143B-394.15, (g).
Powers and duties, §143B-394.16, (a).
Purpose, §143B-394.15, (b).
Quorum, §143B-394.15, (j).
Removal, §143B-394.15, (h).
Report on findings and recommendations, §143B-394.16, (b).
Staffing, §143B-394.15, (l).
Terms, §143B-394.15, (d).
Vacancies, §143B-394.15, (f).

DOMESTIC VIOLENCE VICTIM ASSISTANCE ACT, §§7A-474.16 to 7A-474.20.
Definitions, §7A-474.17.
Eligible activities, §7A-474.18, (a).
Eligible cases, §7A-474.18, (b).
Funding, §7A-474.19.
Legislative declaration, §7A-474.16.
Prohibited purposes for funds, §7A-474.18, (c).
Records, §7A-474.20.
Reports, §7A-474.20.

DOMESTIC WORKERS.
Wage and hour act exemptions, §95-25.14, (a).

DOMICILIARY HOMES.
Adult care homes.
Generally.
See ADULT CARE HOMES.
Sales and use tax refunds for nonprofits, §105-164.14, (b).

DONATIONS.
Bees and honey.
Authority of board to accept, §106-637.
Food.
Food bank information and referral service.
Maintenance of information by department of agriculture and consumer services, §106-21.2.
Immunity for, §99B-10.
Inspections by department of agriculture and consumer services, §106-141.1.
Hospitals.
Surplus medical equipment, §131E-250, (a), (b).
Housing authorities and projects.
Municipal cooperation and aid.
Advances and donations by city and municipality, §157-43.
Justice department.
Justice academy, §17D-3.
Nonprofit corporations.
Acceptance after mergers, §55A-11-07.
Public schools.
Powers of local boards of education, §115C-47.
Secretary of state.
International relations, authority to accept, §147-54.6, (b).
Sheriffs' education and training standards commission, §17E-10.

DONKEYS.
Equine activity liability, §§99E-1 to 99E-3.
Equine infectious anemia, §§106-405.15 to 106-405.20.
See EQUINE INFECTIOUS ANEMIA.

DO NOT CALL LAW, §§75-100 to 75-103.
Notification to telephone subscribers.
Opportunity to object to telephone solicitation, §62-54.

DO NOT RESUSCITATE ORDERS, §90-21.17.
Immunity from liability, §90-21.17, (d).
Issuance, §90-21.17, (b).
Official form, §90-21.17, (c).
Public policy, §90-21.17, (a).
Reciprocal acceptance, §90-21.17, (e).

DOOR CLOSING ACT.
Deficiency judgments, §45-21.38.

DOOR LOCK EXEMPTION PERMITS, §143-143.4.

DOOR-TO-DOOR SALES.
Buyer's right.
Limitation on buyer's right, §25A-39, (e).
Notice, §25A-39, (b) to (d).
Restoration of down payment, §25A-41, (a).
Goods as down payment, §25A-41, (b).
Retention of goods, §25A-41, (d).
Return and care of goods, §25A-42, (a).
Cancellation.
Buyer's right, §25A-39, (a).
Delay of seller, §25A-39, (f).
No compensation for services of seller prior to cancellation, §25A-42, (c).
Care of goods by buyer, §25A-42, (b).
Defined, §25A-38.
Failure to give right to cancel in off premises sales, §14-401.13.
Form of agreement or offer, §25A-40.
Negotiation or transfer of note, contract or other evidence of indebtedness.
Compensation, §25A-42, (b).
Time limitation, §25A-42, (d).
Statement of buyer's rights, §25A-40.

DORMITORY FIRE SAFETY, §§116-44.6 to 116-44.8.

DORMITORY TELEPHONE SERVICE, §62-110, (d).

DOROTHEA DIX HOSPITAL JOINT SECURITY FORCE, §122C-430.20.

DOUBLE BOTTOM TRAILERS.
Department of transportation not authorized to permit to operate over state highways, §20-119, (a).

DOUBLE DAMAGES.
Attorneys, fraudulent practice, §84-13.
Unlawful cutting, removal or burning of timber, §1-539.1, (a).

DOUBLE JEOPARDY, Const. U. S., amd. V.
Appeals.
Correction of errors by appellate division.
When charges must be dismissed with prejudice, §15A-1447, (g).
Death by vehicle.
Manslaughter.
Subsequent prosecutions prohibited, §20-141.4, (c).
Dismissal motions, §15A-954, (a).
Manslaughter.
Death by vehicle.
Subsequent prosecutions prohibited, §20-141.4, (c).
Probable cause hearings.
Findings by judge not to preclude subsequent prosecution for same offense, §15A-612, (b).
Subsequent prosecution for same offense not barred, §15A-612.

DOVES.
Hunting and wildlife generally.
See HUNTING AND WILDLIFE.

DOWER.
Abolished, §29-4.
Renunciation by married person under age of 21, §39-13.2, (c).

DOWNTOWN REVITALIZATION PROJECTS.
Municipal service districts.
See MUNICIPAL SERVICE DISTRICTS.

DRAFT ANIMALS.
Passing horses or other draft animals, §20-216.

DRAFTS.
Checks.
See CHECKS.
False pretenses and cheats.
Worthless checks, draft or order.
Obtaining property in return for worthless check, etc., §14-106.
Negotiable instruments generally, §§25-3-101 to 25-3-605.
See NEGOTIABLE INSTRUMENTS.
Powers of attorney.
Powers conferred by statutory short form, §32A-2.
Unclaimed property generally, §§116B-51 to 116B-80.
See UNCLAIMED PROPERTY.

DRAG RACING.
Racing on streets and highways generally, §20-141.3.

DRAINAGE, §§156-1 to 156-53.
Appeals.
Canals.
Right to drain into canal, §156-10.
Petitions.
Agreement for construction, §156-29.
Apportionment.
Expenses for repairs, §156-11.
Assessments.
Deficiencies.
Supplemental assessments to make up deficiencies, §156-22.
Jurors.
Vacancy appointments of assessment jurors, §156-22.
Liens.
Drainage assessments declared liens, §156-21.
Petitions.
Agreement for construction.
Viewers, §156-28.
Subsequent owners bound, §156-14.
Supplemental assessment to make up deficiencies, §156-22.
Vacancy appointments of assessment jurors, §156-22.
Bond issues.
Payment of bonds authorized, §156-53.
Bonds, surety.
Petitions.
Agreement for construction, §156-26, (d).
Canals.
Earth from canal removed or leveled, §156-8.
Maintenance for seven years presumed a necessity, §156-21.
Necessity that canals be maintained for seven years, §156-21.
Protection of canals, ditches and natural drains, §156-25.

DRAINAGE —Cont'd
Canals —Cont'd
Right to drain into canal, §156-10.
Commissioners.
Appointments, §156-2.
Corporations, §§156-38, 156-40, 156-43.
Duties.
Generally, §156-3.
Examination of lands and making reports, §156-17.
Jurisdiction in county commissioners. See within this heading, "Jurisdiction in county commissioners."
Liens, §156-21.
Powers, §156-3.
Reports, §156-4.
Confirmation, §156-4.
Examination of lands and making reports, §156-17.
Vacancy appointments, §156-22.
Contributions.
Amount of contribution for repair ascertained, §156-15.
Subsequent owners bound, §156-14.
Corporations, §§156-37 to 156-53.
See DRAINAGE BY CORPORATION.
Costs.
Allowance of costs to either party or apportioned in discretion of court, §6-21.
Amount of contribution for repair ascertained, §156-15.
Lowlands draining or damming.
Petitioner to pay costs, §6-22.
Repairs enforced by judgment, §156-18.
Damages.
Compensation for damage to lands.
Corporations, §156-48.
Petitions.
Agreement for construction.
Payment of damages, §156-27.
Dams.
Earth for construction of, §156-7.
Default.
Judgment against owner in default, §156-13.
Districts, §§156-54 to 156-138.4.
See DRAINAGE DISTRICTS.
Ditches.
Open drains within thirty feet of, §156-9.
Easements.
Acquisition, §156-4.
Petition by servient owner against dominant owner, §156-16.
Repairs.
Right of dominant owner to repair, §156-20.
Surrender of drainage easements, §156-23.
Width of right of way for repairs, §156-5.
Eminent domain.
Powers of local public condemnors, §40A-3, (b).
Supplemental proceeding, §156-1.
Fences.
Right of owner, §156-6.
Hearings.
Petitions.
Agreement for construction, §156-26, (c).
Judgments.
Corporations, §156-42.
Cost of repairs enforced by judgment, §156-18.
Default.
Judgment against owner in default, §156-13.
Expenses of repairs, §156-11.
Owners in default, §156-13.

DRAINAGE —Cont'd
Judgments —Cont'd
Repairs.
Cost of repairs enforced by judgment, §156-18.
Subsequent owners bound, §156-14.
Jurisdiction in county commissioners.
Board.
Appointment, §156-32.
Chairman, §156-32.
Compensation, §156-36.
Compliance with requirements, §156-33.
Composition, §156-32.
Duties, §156-33.
Meetings, §156-33.
Notice to landowners, §156-32.
Penalties.
Refusal to comply with requirements, §156-33.
Refusal to serve, §156-32.
Powers, §156-33.
Qualifications of members, §156-32.
Refusal to serve, §156-32.
Reports.
Filing, §156-34.
Ditches.
Owners to keep open, §156-35.
Obstructions.
Keeping ditch open, §156-35.
Penalties.
Board.
Refusal to comply with requirements, §156-33.
Jury.
Assessment jurors.
Vacancy appointments, §156-22.
Petitions.
Agreement for construction.
Trial by jury, §156-29.
Liens.
Default judgments, §156-13.
Drainage assessment declared liens, §156-21.
Judgments against owners in default, §156-13.
Laborer's lien for work on canal, §156-50.
Subsequent owners bound, §156-14.
Magistrates.
Contributions for repairs.
Amount ascertained, §156-15.
Mechanic liens.
Laborer's lien for work on canal, §156-50.
Misdemeanors.
Obstructions in drainage ditches, §77-14.
Municipal service districts.
Authorized purposes of districts, §160A-536, (a).
Notice.
Easements.
Surrender of drainage easements, §156-23.
Petitions.
Agreement for construction, §156-26.
Landowners, §156-28.
Repairs, §156-12.
Obstructions.
Canals, ditches and natural drains, §156-25.
Canals or ditches dug under agreement, §156-19.
Drainage districts.
Penalty, §77-14.
Drains cut by consent, §156-24.
Keeping ditches open, §156-35.
Protection of canals, ditches and natural drains, §156-25.
Open drains.
No open drains within thirty feet, §156-9.

DRAINAGE —Cont'd
Owners.
Right of dominant owner to repair, §156-20.
Subsequent owners bound, §156-14.
Petitions.
Agreement for construction.
Appeals, §156-29.
Assessments made by viewers, §156-28.
Benefits.
Recovery, §156-27.
Bonds, surety, §156-26, (d).
Confirmation of reports, §156-30.
Construction authorized, §156-26, (e).
Damages.
Payment, §156-27.
Hearings, §156-26, (c).
Installment payments, §156-31.
Jury trials, §156-29.
Names filed, §156-26, (a).
Notice, §156-26, (b).
Landowners, §156-28.
Payment in installments, §156-31.
Payment of damages, §156-27.
Procedure upon agreement, §156-26.
Recovery for benefits, §156-27.
Reports, §156-26, (d).
Confirmation, §156-30.
Filing, §156-29.
Viewers, §156-26, (c).
Assessments, §156-28.
Contents, §156-2.
Corporations.
Filing in superior court, §156-37.
Filing, §156-2.
Repairs.
Amount of contribution for repair ascertained, §156-15.
Cost of repairs enforced by judgment, §156-18.
Entry for repairs, §156-6.
Judgments against owners in default, §156-13.
Notice, §156-12.
Right of dominant owner to repair, §156-20.
Right of way for repairs, §156-5.
Subsequent owners bound, §156-14.
Width of right of way, §156-5.
Reports.
Canals already constructed, §156-43.
Commissioners, §156-4.
Examination of land, §156-17.
Confirmation, §156-4.
Corporations.
Commissioners, §156-38.
Confirmation, §156-40.
Jurisdiction in county commissioners.
Board appointed by county commissioners, §156-34.
Petitions.
Agreement for construction, §156-26, (d).
Confirmation of report, §156-30.
Filing of reports, §156-29.
Right of entry.
Repairs, §156-6.
Rights of way.
Widths, §156-5.
Special proceedings.
Dissolution of corporations, §156-49.
Streets and highways.
Application to court, §136-21.
Appointment of commissioners, §136-21.
Judgment of commissioners, §136-22.
Right to appeal, §136-23.

DRAINAGE —Cont'd
Streets and highways —Cont'd
Obstructing highway drains misdemeanor, §136-92.
Special proceedings.
Rights of parties, §136-24.
Summons and process, §136-21.
View by commissioners, §136-22.
Report, §136-22.
Water must be diverted from public road by ditch or drain, §136-95.
Summons and process.
Petition by servient owner against dominant owner, §156-16.
Surveys and surveyors.
Corporations.
Employment of surveyors, §156-39.
County surveyor as chairman of board, §156-32.

DRAINAGE BY CORPORATION.
Actions.
Payment of bonds enforced, §156-53.
Assessments, §156-42.
Canal already constructed, §156-43.
Payment of dues entitles to use of canal, §156-46.
Penalty for nonpayment of assessments, §156-51.
Shareholders to pay assessments, §156-45.
Board of directors, §156-42.
Bond issues, §§156-52, 156-53.
Actions to enforce payment, §156-53.
Payment of bonds enforced, §156-53.
Canals.
Payment of dues entitles to use, §156-46.
Capital stock.
Amount, §156-41.
Commissioners.
Appointment, §156-38.
Canals already constructed, §156-43.
Duties.
Generally, §156-38.
Reports, §156-38.
Confirmation, §156-40.
Corporate name, §156-42.
Damages.
Compensation for damage to lands, §156-48.
Dissolution of corporations, §156-49.
Eminent domain, §156-48.
Infants.
Rights of infant owners protected, §156-47.
Judgments.
Assessments, §156-42.
Liens.
Assessments, §156-42.
Bond issues constitute liens, §156-52.
Laborer's lien for work on canal, §156-50.
Minors.
Rights of infant owners protected, §156-47.
Name, §156-42.
Officers, §156-42.
Organization, §156-42.
Payment.
Entitles to use of canal, §156-46.
Petitions.
Filing in superior court, §156-37.
Powers.
Generally, §156-42.
Proprietors become a corporation, §156-41.
Reports.
Canals already constructed, §156-43.
Confirmation, §156-40.
Contents, §156-38.

DRAINAGE BY CORPORATION —Cont'd
Shares of stock annexed to land, §156-44.
Stock.
Amount of capital stock, §156-41.
Shareholders to pay assessments, §156-45.
Shares of stock annexed to land, §156-44.
Surveyors' employees, §156-39.

DRAINAGE DISTRICTS.
Accounts and accounting.
Expenses.
Filing account of expenses, §156-77.
Actions.
Bond issues.
Holder's remedy, §156-99.
Amendments, §156-104.
Anticipation notes, issuing, §156-93.1, (g).
Appeals.
Acquiring title for purpose of easements or rights-of-way, §156-70.1.
Bonds, surety, §156-66.
Construction of drainage law, §156-135.
Easements, §156-70.1.
Hearings.
Final hearings, §156-75.
Improvement, renovation, enlargement and extension of canals, structures and boundaries, §§156-93.2, 156-93.3.
Notice, §156-70.1.
Publication in case of unknown owners, §156-58.
Public or private ways.
Maintenance of drainage across, §156-88.
Railroads.
Drainage across railroads, §156-90.
Right of appeal, §156-66.
Rights of way, §156-70.1.
Applicability of provisions.
Local drainage laws not affected, §156-137.
Appointments.
Commissioners.
Amended act, §156-81.
Method of appointment, §156-81, (a).
Failure to appoint, §156-81, (e).
Original act, §156-79.
Statutory appointment of elected commissioners, §156-82.2.
Validation of election of members of drainage commission, §156-82.
Statutory appointment of elected drainage commissioners, §156-82.2.
Curative statutes.
Validation of election of members of drainage commission, §156-82.
Statutory appointment of elected drainage commissioners, §156-82.2.
Validation of prior actions of members of drainage commission, §156-82.3, (a), (b).
Assessments.
Adjustment of delinquent assessments.
Amount of assessments limited, §156-129.
Approval of adjustment by local government commission, §156-128.
Authorized, §156-125.
Distribution of collections, §156-127.
Extension, §156-126.
Fund.
Distribution of collections, §156-127.
Special fund set up, §156-127.
Limitation on amount of assessments, §156-129.
Local government commission.
Approval of adjustments, §156-128.
Reassessments regulated, §156-129.

DRAINAGE DISTRICTS —Cont'd
Assessments —Cont'd
Advancement of funds and repayment from assessments, §156-61.
Amendment or reformation of proceedings, §156-104.
Application of amendatory provisions of certain sections, §156-104.
Arrears.
Authority to collect arrears, §156-110.
Benefits.
Classification, §156-71.
Collection.
Authority to collect arrears, §156-110.
Fees, §156-113.
Installments, §156-95.
Not collectible out of other property of delinquent, §156-106.
Procedure generally, §§156-105, 156-106.
Construction of drainage law, §156-135.
Conveyance of land.
Change in assessment rolls, §156-114.
Costs.
Total cost of improvement.
Ascertained for three years, §156-94.
Rate per acre, §156-95.
Damages, §156-70.
Default.
Authority to collect arrears, §156-110.
Delinquent assessments, §156-105.
Adjustment, §§156-125 to 156-129.
Authority to collect arrears, §156-110.
Eminent domain.
Damages, §156-70.
Estimates, §156-61.
Excess assessments, §156-98.
Extension of adjusted installments, §156-126.
Fees.
Collection fees, §156-113.
Improvements.
Renovation, enlargement and extension of canals, structures and boundaries, §156-93.5.
Judgments, §156-103.
Levy.
No assessments to be levied on property when once paid in full, §156-124.
Liens, §§156-61, 156-105.
Payment of assessments which become liens after original bond issue, §156-100.2.
Maintenance, §§156-92, 156-93.1, (a), (e).
Modification of assessments.
Additional bonds issued, §156-116, (e).
Insufficient funds, §156-116, (d).
Manner of issue, §156-116, (f).
Relevy, §156-116, (a).
Surplus funds, §156-116, (c).
Upon sale of land for assessments, §156-116, (b).
Not collectible out of other property of delinquent, §156-106.
Notice, §156-95.
Requirements generally, §156-138.3.
Payment, §156-61.
Assessments may not be levied on property when once paid in full, §156-124.
Assessments which become liens after original bond issue, §156-100.2.
Time of payment, §156-95.
Warranty in deed runs to purchaser who pays assessment, §156-115.

DRAINAGE DISTRICTS —Cont'd
Assessments —Cont'd
Power to assess, §156-54.
Public or private ways.
Maintenance of drainage across, §156-88.
Railroads.
Drainage across railroads, §156-89.
Receipt book.
Land in two or more counties, §156-109.
Preparation, §156-108.
Rolls.
Change in assessment rolls.
Effect, §156-114.
Procedure, §156-114.
Contents, §156-103.
Copies, §156-103.
Preparation, §156-103.
Recording, §156-103.
Sale of land.
Delinquent assessments, §156-105.
Sheriff in good faith selling property for assessment not liable for irregularity, §156-107.
Sheriffs.
Authority to collect arrears, §156-110.
Collection, §156-105.
Fees, §156-113.
Liability for good faith selling of property, §156-107.
Monthly settlements to be made, §156-111.
Penalty for failure to make, §156-111.
Subdistricts.
Formation of subdistricts, §156-117.
Surplus assessments, §156-98.
Treasurer.
Duty of treasurer to make payments, §156-112.
Waiver.
Defense to assessment waived, §156-96.
Warranty in deed runs to purchaser who pays assessment, §156-115.
Attorneys at law.
Petitions, §156-60.
Payment of petitioners attorney, §156-61.
Auditor.
Appointment, §156-133.
Compensation, §156-133.
Duties, §§156-133, 156-134.
Removal, §156-136.
Reports.
Duties of auditor, §§156-133, 156-134.
Benefits.
Assessments.
Classification, §156-71.
Railroads.
Assessment benefits, §156-89.
Bids and bidding.
Construction of improvements.
Regulations, §156-84.
Bond issues.
Actions.
Holder's remedy, §156-99.
Amendment or reformation of proceedings, §156-104.
Amount, §156-97.
Anticipation notes, §156-97.
Force and effect of bonds, §156-97.1.
Form, §156-98.
Interest rate, §156-97.1.
Issuance, §156-97.1.
Sale, §156-100.1.
Sinking fund, §156-100.3.

DRAINAGE DISTRICTS —Cont'd
Bond issues —Cont'd
Application of amendatory provisions of certain sections, §156-104.
Application of funds, §156-99.
Collection.
Holder's remedy, §156-99.
Commissioners.
Powers and duties of board, §156-82.1, (a).
Consent to issuance.
Failure to pay deemed consent to bond issue, §156-96.
Construction of drainage law, §156-135.
Construction of improvements.
Destruction of work.
Assessments, §156-116.
Conveyance of land.
Assessments.
Modification of assessments, §156-116.
Cost.
Total cost for three years ascertained, §156-94.
Default.
Holder's remedy, §156-99.
Deposits.
Drainage bonds received as deposits, §156-102.
Excess assessments, §156-98.
Extinguishing debt, §156-122.
Form, §156-98.
Improvements and maintenance.
Increase to extinguish debt, §156-122.
Proceedings as for original bond issue, §156-123.
Redress to dissatisfied landowners, §156-121.
Renovation, enlargement and extension of canals, structures and boundaries, §156-93.5.
Increase to extinguish debt, §156-122.
Installments, §156-97.
Interest, §§156-95, 156-97.
Collection, §156-97.
Payment.
Duty of treasurer, §156-112.
Rate, §156-97.
Issuance.
Additional bonds, §156-116.
Modification of assessments, §156-116.
Failure to pay deemed consent to bond issue, §156-96.
Generally, §156-97.
Maintenance anticipation notes, §156-93.1, (g).
Modification of assessments, §156-116.
Notice, §156-95.
Sale of bonds, §156-100.
Payments.
Enforcement, §156-99.
Installments, §156-97.
Time, §156-97.
Procedure.
Generally, §156-97.
Recreational facilities, §156-82.1, (g).
Redress to dissatisfied landowners, §156-121.
Refunding bonds.
General provisions, §156-101.
Increase to extinguish debt, §156-122.
Proceedings as for original bond issue, §156-123.
Requirements.
Generally, §156-97.
Sale of bonds, §§156-99, 156-100.
Sinking fund, §156-100.3.

DRAINAGE DISTRICTS —Cont'd
Bonds, surety.
Amount of penalty, §156-57.
Appeals, §156-66.
Construction of improvements.
Contractors, §156-84.
Penalties.
Amount of penalty, §156-57.
Petitions.
Filing with petition, §156-57.
Treasurer, §156-81.1.
Boundaries.
Establishment, §156-65.
Existing districts may act together to extend boundaries, §156-93.7.
Extension, §156-93.3.
Existing districts may act together, §156-93.7.
Bridges.
Control and repairs by commissioners, §156-92.
Public or private ways.
Maintenance of drainage across, §156-88.
Canals.
Improvement, renovation, enlargement and extension.
Procedures generally, §§156-93.2, 156-93.3.
Public or private ways.
Maintenance of drainage across, §156-88.
Channelization.
Procedures to be followed, §156-138.4.
Rules and regulations, §156-138.4.
Classification.
Lands and benefits, §156-71.
Redress to dissatisfied landowners, §156-121.
Commissioners.
Amendment or reformation of proceedings, §156-104.
Application of amendatory provisions of certain sections, §156-104.
Application of section, §156-81, (h).
Appointments.
Amended act, §156-81.
Failure to appoint, §156-81, (e).
Method of appointment, §156-81, (a).
Original act, §156-79.
Statutory appointment of elected commissioners, §156-82.2.
Validation of election of members of drainage commission, §156-82.
Statutory appointment of elected drainage commissioners, §156-82.2.
Chairman, §§156-79, 156-81, (b).
Compensation, §156-81, (g).
Construction of improvements.
Control and repairs by commissioners, §156-92.
Control and repairs by commissioners, §156-92.
Duties, §156-82.1, (a) to (i).
Elected commissioners.
Statutory appointment, §156-82.2.
Meetings, §156-81, (f).
Names of districts, §156-80.
Organization, §156-81, (b).
Original act, §156-79.
Powers, §§156-79, 156-82.1, (a) to (i).
Prior actions.
Validation of prior actions of members of drainage commission, §156-82.3, (a), (b).
Removal, §156-136.
Repairs, §156-92.
Reports.
Annual reports, §156-131.
Penalty for failure to make, §156-132.

DRAINAGE DISTRICTS —Cont'd
Commissioners —Cont'd
Reports —Cont'd
Statements to be made, §156-130.
Subdistricts.
Powers and authority, §156-117.
Superintendent of construction.
Appointment, §156-83.
Term of office, §156-81, (c).
Treasurer.
Appointment, §156-81.1.
Elected treasurer.
Statutory appointment, §156-82.2.
Statutory appointment of elected treasurer, §156-82.2.
Vacancies, §§156-79, 156-81, (d).
Compensation of viewers, §156-76.
Condemnation of land, §156-67.
Consolidation of services and equipment.
Board, setting up, §156-93.1, (d).
Construction and interpretation.
Construction of drainage law, §156-135.
Local drainage laws not affected, §156-137.
Construction of improvements.
Bids and bidding.
Regulations, §156-84.
Bonds, surety.
Contractors, §156-84.
Commissioners.
Control and repairs by commissioners, §156-92.
Contracts.
Bids and bidding, §156-84.
Failure of contractors, §156-86.
Letting contracts, §156-84.
Monthly estimates for work and payments thereon, §156-85.
Payment, §156-85.
Reletting contract, §156-86.
Improvement, renovation, enlargement and extension of canals, structures and boundaries.
Assessments, §156-93.5.
Bond issues, §156-93.5.
Coordination of proceedings, §156-93.4.
Easements, §156-93.6.
Existing districts may act together, §156-93.7.
Extension of boundaries, §156-93.3.
Procedures.
Coordination of proceedings, §156-93.4.
Generally, §§156-93.2, 156-93.3.
Rights of way, §156-93.6.
Lateral drains, §156-93.
Notice.
Letting contracts, §156-84.
Payments.
Final payments, §156-85.
Monthly estimates for work and payments thereon, §156-85.
Publication.
Letting contracts, §156-84.
Public or private ways.
Maintenance of drainage across, §156-88.
Railroads.
Appeals, §156-90.
Construction across railroads, §156-91, (a) to (d).
Drainage across railroads, §156-89.
Reports.
Contracts, §156-84.
Right of entry, §156-87.

DRAINAGE DISTRICTS —Cont'd
Construction of improvements —Cont'd
Superintendent of construction.
Appointment, §156-83.
Duties, §156-83.
Estimates.
Monthly estimates for work and payments thereon, §156-85.
Powers, §156-83.
Removal, §156-136.
Trees and timber.
Removal of timber, §156-87.
Contracts.
Construction of improvements.
Bids and bidding, §156-84.
Failure of contractors, §156-86.
Letting contracts, §156-84.
Monthly estimates for work and payments thereon, §156-85.
Payment, §156-85.
Reletting contract, §156-86.
Conveyance of land.
Application of section, §156-114, (l).
Assessments.
Change in assessment rolls, §156-114.
Rolls.
Costs.
Determined, §156-114, (j).
Effect in change of assessment roll, §156-114, (g).
Number of copies, §156-114, (i).
Preparation of new rolls by clerk, §156-114, (h).
Chairman.
Represents board, §156-114, (k).
Costs.
Determination of costs, §156-114, (j).
Deeds.
Warranty in deed runs to purchaser who pays assessment, §156-115.
Delinquent assessments.
Collection, §156-105.
Duty of chairman of commissioners, §156-114, (d).
Establishment of districts.
Conveyance afterwards, §156-114, (c).
Failure of chairman or board to act, §156-114, (e).
Lease to or from federal or state government or agency thereof, §156-138.1.
Petition, §156-114, (f).
Reports.
Before final report, §156-114, (b).
Conveyance before final report, §156-114, (b).
Sale of land.
Delinquent assessments, §156-105.
Status of land fixed, §156-114, (a).
When owner may file petition with clerk, §156-114, (f).
Costs.
Assessments.
Total cost of improvements.
Ascertained for three years, §156-94.
Rate per acre, §156-95.
Bond issues.
Total cost for three years ascertained, §156-94.
Conveyance of land.
Determination of costs, §156-114, (j).
Payment by petitioners, §156-74.
Counties.
Article applicable to certain counties only, §156-141.

DRAINAGE DISTRICTS —Cont'd
Counties —Cont'd
Cleaning and draining of streams under supervision of governmental agencies, §156-139.
Drainage by certain counties.
Article applicable to certain counties only, §156-141.
Cleaning and draining of streams, §156-139.
Tax levy, §156-140.
Taxation.
Levy of tax, §156-140.
Curative statutes.
Appointments.
Validation of election of members of drainage commission, §156-82.
Statutory appointment of elected drainage commissioners, §156-82.2.
Prior actions.
Validation of prior actions of members of drainage commission, §156-82.3, (a), (b).
Damages.
Assessments, §156-70.
Railroads.
Drainage across railroads, §156-89.
Deeds.
Conveyance of land.
Warranty in deed runs to purchaser who pays assessment, §156-115.
Definitions.
Majority of resident landowners, §156-138.2.
Owners of three fifths of land area, §156-138.2.
Deposits.
Bond issues.
Drainage bonds received as deposits, §156-102.
Disposing of equipment, §156-93.1, (c).
Disposition of lands, §156-138.1.
Ditches.
Control and repairs by commissioners, §156-92.
Easements, §156-70.1.
Improvements.
Renovation, enlargement and extension of canals, structures and boundaries, §156-93.6.
Elections.
Commissioners.
Elected commissioners.
Statutory appointment, §156-82.2.
Eminent domain.
Acquisition and disposition of lands.
Generally, §156-138.1.
Assessments.
Damages, §156-70.
Compensation of landowners.
When title deemed acquired for purpose of easements or rights of way, §156-70.1.
Condemnation of land, §156-67.
Employing engineering assistance, equipment, superintendents and equipment operators, §156-93.1, (a), (b).
Equipment.
Consolidation of services and equipment.
Board, setting up, §156-93.1, (d).
Disposing of equipment, §156-93.1, (c).
Duty of commissioners to maintain, §156-82.1, (b).
Employing engineering assistance, equipment, superintendents and equipment operators, §156-93.1, (a), (b).
Establishment.
Adjudication upon final report, §156-74.

DRAINAGE DISTRICTS —Cont'd
Establishment —Cont'd
Conveyance of land after district established, §156-114, (c).
Jurisdiction, §156-54.
Special proceedings, §156-55.
Survey, plan and specifications, §§156-68, 156-69.
Venue, §156-55.
Expenses.
Account of expenses filed, §156-77.
Advancement of funds and repayment from assessments, §156-61.
Estimate of expense and manner of payment, §156-61.
Fees, §156-113.
Fish and fisheries resources.
Conservation and replacement of fish and wildlife habitat, §156-69.
Forms.
Receipt books, §§156-108, 156-109.
Funds.
Advancement of funds.
Repayment from assessments, §156-61.
Investment of surplus funds, §156-135.1.
Sinking fund, §156-100.3.
Surplus funds.
Investment, §156-135.1.
Good faith.
Sheriffs.
Liability for good faith selling of property, §156-107.
Governmental agencies, contracting with, §156-82.1, (d).
Hearings.
Appeals.
Final hearings, §156-75.
Final hearings.
Adjudication upon final report, §156-74.
Appeals, §156-75.
Notice, §156-73.
First hearing of preliminary report, §156-63.
Further hearings.
District established, §156-65.
Generally, §156-65.
Improvement, renovation, enlargement and extension of canals, structures and boundaries, §§156-93.2, 156-93.3.
Notice.
Final hearings, §156-73.
Further hearing, §§156-64, 156-73.
Reports.
First hearing of preliminary report, §156-63.
Highways.
Public or private ways.
Maintenance of drainage across, §156-88.
Hunting and wildlife.
Conservation and replacement, §156-69.
Improvements.
Assessments.
Renovation, enlargement and extension of canals, structures and boundaries, §156-93.5.
Canals, structures and boundaries.
Renovation, enlargement and extension.
Procedures generally, §§156-93.2, 156-93.3.
Construction of improvements. See within this heading, "Construction of improvements."
Easements.
Renovation, enlargement and extension of canals, structures and boundaries, §156-93.6.

DRAINAGE DISTRICTS —Cont'd
Interest.
Bond issues, §§156-95, 156-97.
Anticipation notes, §156-97.1.
Payment.
Duty of treasurer, §156-112.
Investments.
Surplus funds, §156-135.1.
Joint use of facility for impoundment or storage of water.
Contracts for, §156-82.1, (h).
Judgments.
Adjudication upon final report, §156-74.
Assessments, §156-103.
Establishment of district, §156-65.
Jurisdiction.
Establishment of districts, §156-54.
Lateral drains.
Construction, §156-93.
Leases.
Acquisition and disposition of lands, §156-138.1.
Liens.
Assessment liens, §§156-61, 156-105.
Payment of assessments which become liens after original bond issue, §156-100.2.
Local government finance generally, §§159-1 to 159-188.
See LOCAL GOVERNMENT FINANCE.
Maintenance assessments, §§156-92, 156-93.1, (a), (e).
Majority of resident landowners.
Defined, §156-138.2.
Maps and plats.
Contents, §156-69.
Copies kept by clerk, §156-78.
Municipal corporations.
Classification of lands and benefits, §156-71.
Contribution of funds, §156-78.1, (b).
Necessary expenses, §156-78.1, (c).
Participation in works or projects, §156-78.1, (a).
Permissive nature of applicable section, §156-78.1, (d).
Names, §156-80.
Notice.
Acquisition of title for purpose of easements or rights of way, §156-70.1.
Appeals, §156-70.1.
Assessments, §156-95.
Bond issues, §156-95.
Sale of bonds, §156-100.
Construction of improvements.
Letting contracts, §156-84.
Hearings.
Final hearings, §156-73.
Further hearings, §§156-64, 156-73.
Improvement, renovation, enlargement and extension of canals, structures and boundaries, §§156-93.2, 156-93.3.
Maintenance assessment, meeting to determine levy, §156-93.1, (a).
Publication in case of unknown owners, §§156-57, 156-58.
Railroads.
Drainage across railroads, §§156-89, 156-90.
Requirements generally, §156-138.3.
Obstructions.
Penalty, §77-14.
Officers.
Removal, §156-136.
Owners of three fifths of land area.
Defined, §156-138.2.

DRAINAGE DISTRICTS —Cont'd
Parties.
Unknown owners.
Publication in case of unknown owners, §156-58.
Petitions.
Adjudication upon final report, §156-74.
Amendments, §156-65.
Attorneys for petitioners, §156-60.
Payment, §156-61.
Bonds, surety.
Filing with petition, §156-57.
Contents, §156-56.
Conveyance of land, §156-114, (f).
Costs.
Payment by petitioners, §156-74.
Filing, §156-56.
Hearings.
First hearing of preliminary report, §156-63.
Improvement, renovation, enlargement and extension of canals, structures and boundaries, §§156-93.2, 156-93.3.
Prosecution bonds.
Institution of actions without being required to give, §1-109.
Public or private ways, §156-88.
Purchasing, selling or leasing equipment, §156-93.1, (c).
Railroads.
Appeals.
Drainage across railroads, §156-90.
Assessments.
Drainage across railroads, §156-89.
Benefits.
Assessment benefits, §156-89.
Construction across.
Agreement as to exact time work to be done, §156-91, (a).
Utilities commission to settle disagreements, §156-91, (b).
Duty of railroad, §156-91, (a).
Expenses for railroad opening tracks.
Bill for, payment, §156-91, (d).
Penalty for delay of construction, §156-91, (c).
Removal of rails, ties and other obstructions.
Duty of railroad, §156-91, (b).
Penalty for delay, §156-91, (c).
Construction of improvements.
Appeals, §156-90.
Drainage across railroads, §156-89.
Damages.
Drainage across railroads, §156-89.
Notice.
Drainage across railroads, §§156-89, 156-90.
Receipt books.
Land in two or more counties, §156-109.
Preparation, §156-108.
Records.
Assessments.
Rolls, §156-103.
Bond issue recorded, §156-99.
Drainage record.
Certificate of assessment recorded, §156-95.
Clerk to keep book, §156-78.
Recreational facilities.
Contracts for operating, authority, §156-82.1, (g).
Issuance of revenue bonds or notes, §156-82.1, (g).
Recreational purpose.
Use of stored or impounded water for, authorizing, §156-82.1, (g).
Redress to dissatisfied landowners, §156-121.

DRAINAGE DISTRICTS —Cont'd
Refunding bonds, §§156-101, 156-122, 156-123.
Release of areas taken for rights-of way, §156-82.1, (e).
Reports.
Auditor.
Duties of auditor, §§156-133, 156-134.
Commissioners.
Annual reports, §156-131.
Penalty for failure to make, §156-132.
Statements to be made, §156-130.
Construction of improvements.
Contracts, §156-84.
Conveyance of land.
After final report, §156-114, (c).
Before final report, §156-114, (b).
Extension of time for reports, §156-72.
Final reports.
Adjudication upon final report, §156-74.
Filing, §156-73.
Hearings.
First hearing of preliminary report, §156-63.
Improvement, renovation, enlargement and extension of canals, structures and boundaries, §§156-93.2, 156-93.3.
Penalties.
Failure of commissioners to make reports, §156-132.
Preliminary report of viewers, §156-62.
First hearing of preliminary report, §156-63.
Right of entry.
Construction of improvements.
Entry upon lands, §156-87.
Rights of way.
Appeals, §156-70.1.
Improvement, renovation, enlargement and extension of canals, structures and boundaries, §156-93.6.
When title deemed acquired for purpose of easements or rights of way.
Claim for compensation, §156-70.1.
Notice to landowner, §156-70.1.
Rules and regulations.
Channelization, §156-138.4.
Sales.
Assessments.
Delinquent assessments.
Sale of land, §156-105.
Bond issues, §§156-99, 156-100.
Anticipation notes, §156-100.1.
Sheriffs.
Assessments.
Authority to collect arrears, §156-110.
Collection of assessments, §156-105.
Fees, §156-113.
Good faith.
Liability for good faith selling of property, §156-107.
Monthly settlements to be made, §156-111.
Penalty for failure to make, §156-111.
Sale of land.
Delinquent assessments, §156-105.
Liability for good faith selling of property, §156-107.
Sinking fund.
Bond issues, §156-100.3.
Special proceedings.
Establishment of districts, §156-55.
Storage of water, §156-69.
Streets and highways.
Public or private ways.
Drainage across public or private ways, §156-88.
Subdistricts, §156-117.

DRAINAGE DISTRICTS —Cont'd
Summons and process.
Issuance, §156-57.
Unknown owners, §156-58.
Surplus funds, use, §156-82.1, (c).
Surveys and surveyors.
Classification of lands and benefits, §156-71.
Complete survey ordered, §156-68.
Expenses.
Account of expenses filed, §156-77.
Nature of survey, §156-69.
Taxation.
Power to levy taxes, §156-54.
Treasurer.
Appointment, §156-81.1.
Assessments.
Duty of treasurer to make payments, §156-112.
Penalty for failure to make, §156-112.
Bonds, surety, §156-81.1.
Elected treasurer.
Statutory appointment, §156-82.2.
Fees.
Collection and disbursement of funds, §156-113.
Jurisdiction where lands in two or more counties, §156-109.
Qualifications, §156-81.1.
Removal, §156-136.
Statutory appointment of elected treasurer, §156-82.2.
Term of office, §156-81.1.
Trees and timber.
Construction of improvements.
Removal of timber, §156-87.
Venue.
Establishment of districts, §156-55.
Viewers.
Appointment, §156-59.
Classification of lands and benefits, §156-71.
Compensation, §156-76.
Duties.
Generally, §156-59.
Examination of lands, §156-62.
Expenses.
Account of expenses filed, §156-77.
Qualifications, §156-59.
Removal, §156-136.
Reports.
Adjudication upon final report, §156-74.
Correction and modification by commissioners, §156-84.
Extension of time for reports, §156-72.
Final reports.
Filing, §156-73.
Hearings.
First hearing of preliminary report, §156-63.
Preliminary reports, §156-62.
Violations.
Penalties generally, §156-138.
Waiver.
Assessments.
Defense to assessment waived, §156-96.
Warranties.
Deed runs to purchaser who pays assessment, §156-115.
Water-retardant structures.
Maintaining and operating, §156-93.1, (f).
Waters and watercourses.
Control of water, §156-69.
Injuring or damaging, §156-92.
Storage of water, §156-69.

DRAINAGE DITCH OBSTRUCTIONS, §77-14.

DRAINAGE PROJECTS.
Special assessments by counties, §§153A-185 to 153A-206.
See SPECIAL ASSESSMENTS BY COUNTIES.

DRAMA.
Promotion of arts, §§143-403 to 143-407.1.

DRAM SHOP LIABILITY.
Discretion for seller, §18B-305, (b).
Discriminatory refusals prohibited, §18B-305, (c).
Intoxicated persons, §18B-305, (a).
Refusal to sell.
Discretion for seller, §18B-305, (b).
Discriminatory refusals prohibited, §18B-305, (c).

DRAWINGS.
Artwork on consignment, §§25C-1 to 25C-5.

DREDGING PERMITS.
Appeals, §113-229, (f), (g).
Applicability of section, §113-229, (m).
Applications, §113-229, (b).
Beach-quality sand, §113-229, (h1), (h2), (i).
Civil actions, §113-229, (l).
Coastal wetlands.
Orders to control activities.
Powers and duties of department as to permits not repealed by section, §113-230, (h).
Conditions, §113-229, (e).
Construction of terms, §113-229, (n).
Coordination, §113-229, (e).
Definitions, §113-229, (n).
Denial of applications, §113-229, (e).
Emergency dredging, §113-229, (d), (e1).
Federal laws, compliance with requirements, §113-229, (j).
Issuance, §113-229, (c).
Major or minor development.
General or blanket permits issued, §113-229, (c1).
Objections.
Circulating among agencies for opportunity to raise objections, §113-229, (e).
Required, §113-229, (a).
Rules.
General permits issued as, §113-229, (c2).
Time for action on application, §113-229, (e).
Violations, §113-229, (k).

DRIED APPLES.
Standard weights and measures, §81A-42.

DRILLING FOR OIL AND GAS.
Applications.
Punishment for making false entries, §113-409.
Residence address of applicant to be included, §113-408.
Bond, surety.
Required, §113-378.
Development of lands.
Cooperative development not in restraint of trade, §113-393, (c).
Variation from vertical, §113-393, (d).
When each owner may drill, §113-393, (b).
Filing log of drilling and development of each well, §113-379.
Keeping under control.
Required, §113-396.
Location of wells, §113-392, (c).
Notice and payment of fee to department, §113-395.

DRILLING FOR OIL AND GAS —Cont'd
Offshore oil and gas activities, §§143-215.94AA to 143-215.94JJ.
See OFFSHORE OIL AND GAS ACTIVITIES.
Pools.
Units in pools, §113-392, (b).
Test drilling or boring.
Filing record of results, §136-102.3.
Penalty for violations of provisions, §136-102.4.
Right of way.
Authorization required, §136-102.2.
Filing record of results, §136-102.2.
Variation from vertical, §113-393, (d).
When each owner may drill, §113-393, (b).

DRINKING WATER.
Community water systems.
Local water supply plans, §143-355.
Permits.
Fees, §130A-328, (b).
Required, §130A-328, (a).
Enforcement of provisions, §130A-327.
Interpretation of article.
Construction of provisions, §130A-327.
Penalties.
Prohibited acts, §130A-22, (b).
Prohibited acts.
Administrative penalties, §130A-22, (b).
Regulation of public water systems supplying drinking water, §§130A-311 to 130A-328.
See WATER SUPPLY AND WATERWORKS.
Violations of provisions.
Administrative penalties, §130A-22, (b).

DRIVE BY SHOOTINGS.
Discharging weapon into occupied property, §14-34.1.

DRIVER EDUCATION.
Availability, §20-88.1, (a).
Contracts to provide programs, §20-88.1, (b1).
Expenses.
Payment out of highway fund, §20-88.1, (c).
Instructors.
Qualifications, §20-88.1, (b1).
Salary range, §20-88.1, (b).
Organization and administration of program, §20-88.1, (a).
Public schools, §§115C-215, 115C-216.
School-based management and accountability program, §115C-105.25, (b).
Training school licensing, §§20-320 to 20-328.
See DRIVER TRAINING SCHOOL LICENSING.

DRIVER IMPROVEMENT CLINICS.
Fee, §20-16, (e).
Points deducted for attending, §20-16, (c).

DRIVER'S LICENSE COMPACT, §§20-4.21 to 20-4.30.
Administration of information, §20-4.28.
Commissioner.
Authority to make reciprocity agreements, arrangements or declarations, §20-4.22.
Construction and severability, §20-4.30.
Conviction reports, §20-4.24.
Convictions to be reported, §20-4.24, (a).
Effect, §20-4.24, (b).
Effect on laws or agreements, §20-4.26.
Effect on other state driver's license laws, §20-4.27.
Exchange of information, §20-4.28.
Findings of legislature, §20-4.23.

DRIVER'S LICENSE COMPACT —Cont'd
License status in other states.
Review upon application for license in member state, §20-4.25.
Policy of state, §20-4.23.
Title of article, §20-4.21.
Withdrawal from compact, §20-4.29.

DRIVERS' LICENSES, §§20-5 to 20-37.
Accidents.
Failure to report reportable accident.
Suspension of license, §20-279.31, (a).
Failure to stop and render assistance.
Revocation or suspension, §20-166, (e).
Mandatory revocation, §20-17, (a).
Affidavits.
False affidavits.
Perjury, §20-31.
Age, §20-9, (a).
Alcohol and drug education traffic (ADED) school.
Restoration of license after impaired driving conviction or conviction for driving while less than 21 years old after consuming alcohol or drugs.
Obtaining certificate of completion, §20-17.6, (c).
Alcoholic beverages.
Issuance of drivers' licenses to habitual drunkards.
Prohibited, §20-9, (c).
Minors.
Sale to or purchase by underage persons.
Allowing use of identification, §18B-302, (f).
Defense, §18B-302.
Fraudulent use of identification, §18B-302, (e).
Use of fraudulent license, §18B-302.
Revocation or suspension.
Mental incompetents, alcoholics and habitual users of narcotic drugs, §20-17.1.
Appeals.
Denial, cancellation, suspension or revocation, §20-25.
Applications, §20-7, (b).
Contents, disclosures and other information, §20-7, (b1).
False statements or information.
Prohibited, §20-30.
Fraud or incorrect information.
Grounds for cancellation of license, §20-15, (a).
Minors.
Signatures, §20-11, (i).
Armed forces members.
Eye exam exemption.
Renewing by mail, §20-7, (r).
Military designation.
Issuance, renewal by mail, §20-7, (q).
Authorization of license, §20-7, (a).
Bomb scares.
Revocation or suspension of license.
Minors, §20-13.2, (c2).
Issuance of license during revocation or suspension, §20-9, (b1).
Cancellation, §20-15, (a).
Appeals, §20-25.
Commercial drivers' licenses.
Driving during cancellation.
Prohibited, §20-37.12, (b).
Notice of cancellation, §20-37.18, (c).
Surrender of license, §20-15, (b).

DRIVERS' LICENSES —Cont'd
Carrying license while driving.
Required, §20-7, (a).
Change of address.
Application for duplicate license, §20-7.1, (a).
Change of name.
Application for duplicate license, §20-7.1, (b).
Child support.
Access to information or data storage and retrieval system maintained by department of transportation.
Powers of department of health and human services, §110-129.1, (a).
Forfeiture of licensing privilege for failure to pay, §50-13.12.
Suspension or revocation.
Delinquent obligors or individuals not in compliance with orders, §§110-142, 110-142.2.
Mandatory revocation, §20-17, (b).
Classes of motor vehicles allowed to be driven, §20-7, (a).
Classes of regular drivers' licenses, §20-7, (a).
Color photocopies or color reproductions.
Prohibition, §20-30.
Color photograph, §20-7, (n).
Commercial drivers' licenses, §§20-37.10 to 20-37.23.
See COMMERCIAL DRIVERS' LICENSES.
Community service.
Mandatory revocation for noncompliance with community service obligations, §20-17, (b).
Compact, §§20-4.21 to 20-4.30.
See DRIVER'S LICENSE COMPACT.
Confidentiality of photographic image or signature recorded in format, §20-43, (a).
Convictions.
Forwarding record of conviction to division, §20-24, (b).
Substituting period of probation for revocation or disqualification, failure to receive record, §20-24, (b1).
Special information required, §20-24, (e).
Counterfeiting.
Prohibited, §20-30.
Defect or disease affecting operation of vehicle.
Certificate of applicant's condition.
Requirement, §20-7, (e).
Defenses.
Failure to carry license, §20-35, (c).
Defined, §20-4.01.
Denial.
Appeals, §20-25.
Disclosure of impairments, §20-9.1.
Drivers license technology fund, §20-37.01.
Driving eligibility certificate.
Minors, §20-11, (n).
Charter school's designee, duties, §115C-238.29F, (j).
Duty of state board of education to develop rules for issuance, §115C-12.
Principals of schools, duties, §115C-288, (k).
Private and home schools, duties, §115C-566.
School disciplinary actions.
Effect on eligibility for certificate, §20-11, (n1).
Provisional license revocation, §20-13.2, (c1).
State board of community colleges, adoption of rules, §115D-5, (a3).

DRIVERS' LICENSES —Cont'd
Drugs.
Issuance of driver's license to habitual user.
Prohibited, §20-9, (c).
Revocation or suspension.
Mental incompetents, alcoholics and habitual users of narcotic drugs, §20-17.1.
Drunkenness.
Issuance of license to habitual drunkard.
Prohibited, §20-9, (c).
Revocation or suspension.
Mental incompetents, alcoholics and habitual users of narcotic drugs, §20-17.1.
Duplicate licenses, §20-14.
Change of address.
Application for duplicate license, §20-7.1, (a).
Change of name.
Application for duplicate license, §20-7.1, (b).
Commercial drivers' licenses, §20-37.15, (b).
Fees, §20-7.1, (c).
Electronic system to verify information.
Collection or retention of information prohibited, §20-37.02, (c).
Costs of equipment and communications lines.
Retailers responsibility, §20-37.02, (d).
Division to establish and operate, §20-37.02, (a).
Fictitious identification.
System used to prevent, §20-37.02, (a).
Funding, §20-37.02, (e).
Verification of information.
Retailers and ABC permit holders, §20-37.02, (b).
Endorsement required to drive vehicle, §20-7, (a).
Motorcycle endorsement, §20-7, (a1).
Fee, §20-7, (i).
Requirements for obtaining, §20-7, (b).
Examinations, §20-7, (c).
Exclusive nature of provisions, §20-37.
Reexamination.
Commissioner may require, §20-29.1.
Exclusive nature of provisions, §20-37.
Exemptions, §20-8.
Mopeds, §20-8.
Expiration, §20-7, (f).
Explosives.
Revocation or suspension of license.
Minors, §20-13.2, (c2).
Issuance of license during revocation or suspension, §20-9, (b1).
Eye exam, §20-7, (f).
Exemption when renewing by mail.
Armed forces members, national guard members and reservists, §20-7, (r).
Fake IDs.
Electronic system to verify information, §20-37.02.
Presenting license with fake name in commission of felony, §20-30.
Violations of license or learner's permit provisions, §20-30.
Wrongful issuance of drivers' licenses, §20-34.1.
Farm tractors.
Exemption from driver's license requirement, §20-8.
Fees, §20-7, (i).
Duplicate licenses, §20-14.
Highway fund, placing in, §20-7, (j).
Learners' permits, §20-7, (l).
Minors, expanding privileges, §20-11, (j).
Records.
Copies.
Furnishing, §20-26, (c).

DRIVERS' LICENSES —Cont'd
Fees —Cont'd
Records —Cont'd
Copies —Cont'd
Not subject to provisions of chapter 132, §20-26, (d).
Refund in event of mistake on part of person ordering, §20-26, (e).
Restoration fee.
Person whose license has been revoked, §20-7, (i1).
Fictitious names.
Electronic system to verify information, §20-37.02.
Presenting license with fake name in commission of felony, §20-30.
Financial identity fraud.
Generally, §§14-113.20 to 14-113.25.
Financial responsibility.
Proof required for issuance, forms of proof, §20-7, (c1).
Revocation.
Appeals, §20-279.2.
Surrender of license, §20-279.30.
Misdemeanor for failure to surrender, §20-279.31, (c).
Suspension, §20-279.5, (b).
Duration, §20-279.7.
Licenses in other states, §20-279.8, (c).
Nonpayment of judgments, §20-279.13, (a).
Continuation of suspension until judgment satisfied, §20-279.14.
Default on installment payment, §20-279.16, (c).
Exceptions, §20-279.13, (b), (c).
Surrender of license, §20-279.30.
First driver's license.
Expiration, §20-7, (f).
Foreign licenses.
No operation under during suspension or revocation in state, §20-21.
Forfeited privileges.
Revocation when privileges forfeited, §20-15.1.
Forfeiture of licensing privilege after conviction of felony, §15A-1331A.
Limited driving privilege.
Eligibility of persons whose license revoked, §20-179.3, (b).
Forfeiture of licensing privilege for failure to pay child support, §50-13.12.
Format, §20-7, (n).
Full provisional license, §20-11, (f), (g).
Handbook.
Copies given to clerks of superior courts, §20-7, (p).
Highway fund.
Placing fees in, §20-7, (j).
Hospitals for mentally disordered.
Persons not to be licensed, §20-9, (d), (e).
Ignition interlock devises.
Impaired driving conviction.
Restoration of license conditioned on use.
Vehicles subject to requirement, §20-17.8, (c1).
Ignition interlock system.
Impaired driving conviction.
Restoration of license conditioned on use of interlock.
Duration of condition, §20-17.8, (c).
Limited driving privilege, effect, §20-17.8, (d).
Notice of requirement, §20-17.8, (e).
Scope, §20-17.8, (a).

DRIVERS' LICENSES —Cont'd
Ignition interlock system —Cont'd
Impaired driving conviction —Cont'd
Restoration of license conditioned on use of interlock —Cont'd
Violation as driving while license revoked, §20-17.8, (f), (g).
Commencement of revocation, §20-17.8, (h).
Hearings, §20-17.8, (j).
Notification of revocation, §20-17.8, (i).
Restoration after revocation for violating this section, §20-17.8, (k).
When required, §20-17.8, (b).
Limited driving privileges.
When allowed, §20-179.3, (g3).
When required as condition, §20-179.3, (g5).
Immediate civil license revocation.
Implied consent violations.
Civil actions, §20-16.5, (o).
Costs, §20-16.5, (j).
Definitions, §20-16.5, (a).
Effect of revocation, §20-16.5, (i).
Exceptions, §20-16.5, (n).
Hearing, contesting validity, §20-16.5, (g).
Limited driving privilege, §20-16.5, (p).
Modification of order, §20-16.5, (m).
Persons charged with violations, §20-16.5, (b).
Precharge test results basis for revocation, §20-16.5, (b1).
Refusal to submit to chemical analysis, §20-16.5, (b).
Report to division, §20-16.5, (k).
Report to judicial officials.
Duty of charging officers, §20-16.5, (c).
Judicial officer with whom report filed, §20-16.5, (d).
Person not present, procedure for filing, §20-16.5, (f).
Person present, procedure for filing, §20-16.5, (e).
Restoration fee, person with no license, §20-16.5, (l).
Return of license, §20-16.5, (h).
Impaired driving.
Immediate civil license revocation, §20-16.5.
Mandatory revocation, §20-17, (a).
Period of suspension or revocation, §20-19, (c1) to (e).
Permanent revocation.
Habitual impaired driving, §20-138.5, (d).
Refusal of chemical analyses, §20-16.5, (b).
Restoration after conviction, §20-17.6.
Ignition interlock as condition.
Duration of condition, §20-17.8, (c).
Limited driving privilege, effect, §20-17.8, (d).
Notice of requirement, §20-17.8, (e).
Scope, §20-17.8, (a).
Vehicles subject to requirement, §20-17.8, (c1).
Violation as driving while license revoked, §20-17.8, (f), (g).
Commencement of revocation, §20-17.8, (h).
Hearings, §20-17.8, (j).
Notification of revocation, §20-17.8, (i).
Restoration after revocation for violating this section, §20-17.8, (k).
When required, §20-17.8, (b).
Revocation for refusal of chemical analysis, §20-16.2, (d).
Hearing in superior court, §20-16.2, (e).
Limited driving privilege after six months, §20-16.2, (e1).

DRIVERS' LICENSES —Cont'd
Impaired driving —Cont'd
Revocation for refusal of chemical analysis —Cont'd
Nonresidents, notice to other states, §20-16.2, (f).
Revocation or suspension, provisional licenses, §20-13.2, (b), (c).
Implements of husbandry.
Exemption from driver's license requirement, §20-8.
Incendiaries.
Revocation or suspension of license.
Minors, §20-13.2, (c2).
Issuance of license during revocation or suspension, §20-9, (b1).
Information, §20-7, (n).
Instruction.
Licensed drivers.
Giving instructions while under influence of impairing substances, §20-12.1.
Instruction permit, §20-7, (m).
Insurance points.
Offenses for which points charged, §58-36-75.
Issuance, §20-7, (c1).
During period of revocation or suspension, §20-9, (b), (f).
Explosives offenses by minors, §20-9, (b1).
Habitual user of drugs or alcohol, §20-9, (c).
Handicapped persons.
Persons not to be licensed, §20-9, (e).
When license may be issued, §20-9, (g).
Mentally ill.
Persons not to be licensed, §20-9, (d), (e).
When license may be issued, §20-9, (g).
What persons should not be licensed, §20-9.
Wrongful issuance, §20-34.1, (a).
Jury commissions.
Current list of licensed drivers.
Providing to commission, §20-43.4.
Larceny of motor fuel.
Second or subsequent conviction.
Limited driving privilege.
Allowed person whose license revoked, §20-16, (e2).
Mandatory revocation of driver's license, §20-17, (a).
Period of revocation of driver's license, §20-19, (g2).
Learners' permits, §20-7, (l).
Age for obtaining, §20-7, (l).
Applications, §20-7, (b).
Color photocopies or color reproductions.
Prohibition, §20-30.
Expiration, §20-7, (l).
Fees, §20-7, (l).
Motorcycle learner's permit, §20-7, (a2).
Prohibited acts as to, §20-30.
Renewal, §20-7, (l).
Resident of state.
Proof required for issuance, documents evidencing, §20-7, (b2), (b3), (b4).
Social security number or tax payer identification number.
Providing required for issuance of license, §20-7, (b1).
Limited driving privileges, §§20-16, (e1), 20-16.1, (b1).
After six months.
Driver's license revoked for refusal to submit to chemical analysis of blood, §20-16.2, (e1).

DRIVERS' LICENSES —Cont'd
Limited driving privileges —Cont'd
Application for, §20-179.3, (d).
Conviction for excessive speeding.
Limited driving permits for first offenders.
Proof of financial responsibility, §20-16.1, (g).
Conviction of motor fuel larceny.
Allowed person whose license revoked on second conviction, §20-16, (e2).
Copy of privilege to division, §20-179.3, (k).
Court-ordered revocation, privilege not effective until after compliance, §20-179.3, (c).
Definition of limited driving privilege, §20-179.3, (a).
Driving by person less than 21 years old after consuming alcohol or drugs, §20-138.3, (d).
Driving for other than work-related purposes, §20-179.3, (g2).
Driving for work-related purposes.
Nonstandard hours, §20-179.3, (g1).
Standard working hours, §20-179.3, (g).
Eligibility of persons whose license revoked for privilege, §20-179.3, (b).
Exception to restriction set forth, §20-179.3, (g4).
Hearings.
Scheduling of subsequent hearings, §20-179.3, (d).
Ignition interlock system.
When allowed, §20-179.3, (g3).
When required as condition, §20-179.3, (g5).
Impaired driving.
Indefinite revocation for refusal to submit to chemical analysis, §20-16.5, (p).
Insurance verification, §20-179.3, (l).
Invalidity of privilege, action taken, §20-179.3, (k).
Limited basis for and effect of privilege, §20-179.3, (e).
Modification or revocation of privilege, §20-179.3, (i).
Nonfleet private passenger motor vehicle.
Defined, §20-179.3, (l).
Open container law violations, §20-138.7, (g).
Other mandatory and permissive conditions or restrictions, §20-179.3, (h).
Proof of financial responsibility, §20-179.3, (l).
Restoration of license after impaired driving conviction or conviction for driving while less than 21 years old after consuming alcohol or drugs.
Persons subject to section not eligible for, §20-17.6, (e).
Standard working hours.
Defined, §20-179.3, (f1).
Use of privilege, overall provisions, §20-179.3, (f).
Violations of restrictions, effect, §20-179.3, (j).
Limited learner's permit, §20-11, (b), (c).
Limited licenses.
Issuance, §20-29.1.
Limited provisional license, §20-11, (d), (e).
Lose control, lose license, §20-11, (n1).
Mail renewal, §20-7, (f).
Military designation, §20-7, (q).
Mental health, developmental disabilities and substance abuse.
Persons not to be licensed, §20-9, (d), (e).
Retention of motor vehicle driver's license by clients, §122C-62, (b).
Military affairs.
Exemption, §20-8.
Eye exam exemption.
Renewal by mail, §20-7, (r).

DRIVERS' LICENSES —Cont'd
Military affairs —Cont'd
Military designation.
Issuance, renewal by mail, §20-7, (q).
Selective service system registration requirements, §20-9.2.
Military designation.
Issuance, renewal, §20-7, (q).
Minors.
Driving eligibility certificate, §20-11, (n).
Charter school's designee, duties, §115C-238.29F, (j).
Duty of state board of education to develop rules for issuance, §115C-12.
Principals of schools, duties, §115C-288, (k).
Private and home schools, duties, §115C-566.
School disciplinary actions.
Effect on eligibility for certificate, §20-11, (n1).
Provisional license revocation, §20-13.2, (c1).
State board of community colleges, adoption of rules, §115D-5, (a3).
Grounds for revoking provisional license.
Driving by provisional licensee after consuming alcohol or drugs, §20-13.2, (a).
Driving eligibility certificate not maintained, §20-13.2, (c1).
Explosives offenses, §20-13.2, (c2).
Impaired driving conviction, §20-13.2, (b).
Issuance of license during revocation or suspension, §20-9, (b1).
Length of revocation, §20-13.2, (d).
Restoration of license, proof of financial responsibility, §20-13.2, (e).
Willful refusal to submit to chemical analysis, §20-13.2, (c).
Insurance, §20-11, (m).
Length of suspension, §20-13, (b).
Lose control, lose license, §20-11, (n1).
Motor vehicle moving violation defined, §20-13, (a).
Nonresidents, §20-11, (h) to (h2).
Federally issued licenses, §20-11, (h3).
Permitting unlicensed minor to drive motor vehicle.
Prohibited, §20-32.
Probation, placing licensee on, §20-13, (b).
Process for expanding privileges, §20-11, (a).
Provisional licensee defined, §20-4.01, (31a).
Restoration of license on probationary status, hearing request, §20-13, (b).
Retention of license until hearing held, §20-13, (a).
Rules for issuance of driving eligibility certificates.
Duty of state board of education to develop, §115C-12.
Suspending license of provisional licensee, §20-13, (a).
Suspension in addition to other remedies, §20-13, (d).
Two or more offenses committed on single occasion, §20-13, (c).
Underage purchase of alcohol.
Revocation, §20-17.3.
Violations, §20-11, (l).
Mopeds.
Driver's license not required, §20-8.
Motorcycles, §20-7, (a1).
Motor vehicle accidents.
Suspension of license for failure to report reportable accident, §20-279.31, (a).

DRIVERS' LICENSES —Cont'd
National guard.
Eye exam exemption.
Renewing by mail, §20-7, (r).
New residents of state.
Time for obtaining license after becoming resident, §20-7, (a).
Nonresidents.
Minors, §20-11, (h) to (h2).
Federally issued licenses, §20-11, (h3).
Surrender of license issued by other jurisdiction.
Prerequisite to issuance of driver's license, §20-9, (h).
Open container law violations.
Limited driving privileges, §20-138.7, (h).
Operating privileges of persons not holding licenses.
Suspending or revoking, §20-23.1.
Oral test, §20-7, (c).
Organ, eye and tissue donor cards.
Availability at division offices issuing drivers' licenses, §20-7.3.
Perjury.
False affidavits, §20-31.
Permanent revocation.
Habitual impaired driving, §20-138.5, (d).
Photographic image or signature recorded in format.
Confidentiality, §20-43, (a).
Photostating or otherwise reproducing.
Prohibited, §20-30.
Physicians and psychologists disclosing impairments.
Authority to disclose, §20-9.1, (a).
Immunity of disclosing person, §20-9.1, (c).
Use of information, §20-9.1, (b).
Points.
Suspension, §20-16, (c).
Probation.
Substituted for revocation or disqualification.
Failure of division to receive record of conviction, §20-24, (b1).
Surrender of drivers' license, §15A-1343, (b1).
Prohibited acts, §20-30.
False affidavits, §20-31.
Permitting unlicensed minor to drive motor vehicle, §20-32.
Permitting violations of provisions, §20-34.
Proof of financial responsibility.
Required for issuance, forms of proof, §20-7, (c1).
Provisional licensees.
Defined, §20-4.01, (31a).
Driving by licensee after consuming alcohol or drugs.
Restoration after conviction, §20-17.6.
Revocation of operator's license, §20-13.2.
Suspension of operator's license, §20-13.
Provisional license revocation.
Driving after consuming alcohol or drugs, §20-13.2, (a).
Driving eligibility certificate not maintained, §20-13.2, (c1).
Grounds for revoking provisional license.
Explosives offenses, §20-13.2, (c2).
Issuance of license during revocation or suspension, §20-9, (b1).
Impaired driving conviction, §20-13.2, (b).
Length of revocation, §20-13.2, (d).
Restoration of license, proof of financial responsibility, §20-13.2, (e).

DRIVERS' LICENSES —Cont'd
Provisional license revocation —Cont'd
Willful refusing to submit to chemical analysis, §20-13.2, (c).
Provisional license suspension, §20-13, (a).
Length of suspension, §20-13, (b).
Motor vehicle moving violation defined, §20-13, (a).
Probation, placing licensee on, §20-13, (b).
Restoration of license on probationary status, request for hearing, §20-13, (b).
Retention of license until hearing held, §20-13, (a).
Suspension in addition to other remedies, §20-13, (d).
Two or more motor vehicle moving offenses committed on single occasion, §20-13, (c).
Pump and run.
Second or subsequent conviction.
Limited driving privilege.
Allowed person whose license revoked, §20-16, (e2).
Mandatory revocation of driver's license, §20-17, (a).
Period of revocation, §20-19, (g2).
Racing vehicles on streets and highways.
Revocation or suspension, §20-141.3, (d) to (f).
Records.
Availability, §20-27, (a).
Issuance.
Prior record check requirement, §20-37.17.
Convictions.
Forwarding of record of conviction to division, §20-24, (b).
Substituting period of probation for revocation, failure to receive record, §20-24, (b1).
Copies, §20-26, (b).
Furnishing, §20-26, (c).
Charges not subject to provisions of chapter 132, §20-26, (d).
Division to furnish to insurance agents, insurance companies and to insurance support organizations, §20-26, (f).
Fees, §20-26, (c).
Refund of fee in event of mistake on part of person ordering, §20-26, (e).
Generally, §20-26, (a).
Inspection, §20-27, (a).
Weight of vehicles.
Evidentiary effect of records, §20-26, (b1).
Renewal.
Application, §20-7, (f).
Expiration of license, §20-7, (f).
Learners' permits, §20-7, (l).
Mail renewal, §20-7, (f).
Military designation, mail, §20-7, (q).
Proof of financial responsibility.
Furnishing not required, §20-7, (c1).
Road test, when required, §20-7, (c).
Temporary license.
Mail renewal, §20-7, (f).
Time period during which person may apply, §20-7, (f).
Rental vehicles.
Insurance sales or solicitation.
Rental car company representatives.
Agent license required, §66-205.
Required, §20-17.6.
Certificate of completion.
Required for restoration, §20-17.6, (b).
Requirements for obtaining, §20-17.6, (c).

DRIVERS' LICENSES —Cont'd
Required —Cont'd
Limited driving privileges.
Person subject to section not eligible for, §20-17.6, (e).
Notice of requirements of section, §20-17.6, (d).
Requirements for restoring license, §20-17.6, (b).
Scope of sections, §20-17.6, (a).
Required to drive, §20-7, (a).
Resident of state.
Proof required for issuance, documents evidencing, §20-7, (b2), (b3), (b4).
Restoration fee.
Person whose license has been revoked, §20-7, (i1).
Restricted instruction permit, §20-7, (m).
Restricted licenses, §20-7, (e).
Issuance, §20-29.1.
Operating vehicle without complying with restriction.
Deemed operating vehicle without license, §20-7, (e).
Restrictions, imposing, §20-7, (e).
Revocation or suspension, §20-16, (d).
Accidents.
Failure to report reportable accidplying with restriction
Failure to stop and render assistance, §20-166, (e).
Mandatory revocation, §20-17, (a).
Suspension of license until reported, §20-279.31, (a).
Alcoholic beverages.
Underage purchasers of alcohol, §20-17.3.
Appeals, §20-25.
No suspension pending appeal of conviction, §20-16, (b).
Article governs revocation and disqualification, §20-24, (b).
Assault with motor vehicle.
Mandatory revocation, §20-17, (a).
Authority of division to suspend license, §20-16, (e).
Child support scofflaws.
Mandatory revocation, §§20-17, (b), 110-142, 110-142.2.
Community service noncompliance, §20-17, (b).
Convictions.
Criminal convictions.
Limited driving privilege.
Eligibility of persons whose driver's license revoked, §20-179.3, (b).
Forwarding record of conviction to division, §20-24, (b).
Substituting probation for revocation, failure to receive record, §20-24, (b1).
Impaired driving in federal court, §20-23.2.
In another state.
Suspending resident's license upon, §20-23.
Special information required, §20-24, (e).
Ten-year-old convictions not considered, §20-36.
Death by vehicle.
Mandatory revocation, §20-17, (a).
Period of suspension, §20-19, (a).
Defined, §20-4.01.
Driving by person less than 21 years old after consuming alcohol or drugs.
Limited driving privilege, §20-138.3, (d).
Driving while license suspended or revoked.
Application for new license after license revoked, §20-28, (c).

DRIVERS' LICENSES —Cont'd
Revocation or suspension —Cont'd
Driving while license suspended or revoked —Cont'd
Impaired driving.
Aggravating factor to be weighed, §20-179, (d).
Grossly aggravating factors, §20-179, (c).
Imprisonment for misdemeanor violation.
Restriction, §20-176, (c1).
Moving offense during.
Additional period of revocation, §20-28.1, (a), (b).
New license, §20-28.1, (c).
Prohibited, §20-28, (a).
When treated as driving without a license, §20-28, (a1).
Explosives offenses by minors, §20-13.2, (c2).
Issuance of license during revocation or suspension, §20-9, (b1).
Failure to appear or pay fines, penalties or costs, §20-24.1, (a).
Duration of revocation, §20-24.1, (b).
"Offense" defined, §20-24.1, (e).
Reports to DMV, §20-24.2, (a).
Section not applicable to offenses in which order of forfeiture of cash bond entered and reported to division, §20-24.2, (b).
Restoration of license, §20-24.1, (c).
Copy of notice of compliance given person, §20-24.1, (d).
Trial or hearing afforded within reasonable time of defendant's appearance, §20-24.1, (b1).
Failure to stop and render aid, §20-17, (a).
False or fictitious name or address in application.
Mandatory revocation, §20-17, (a).
Federal traffic conviction, §20-23.2.
Fee upon restoration of license.
Person whose license has been revoked, §20-7, (i1).
Felony convictions, §15A-1331A.
Felony in commission of which motor vehicle used.
Mandatory revocation, §20-17, (a).
Financial responsibility.
Misdemeanor for refusal to surrender, §20-279.31, (c).
Foreign license.
No operation under during suspension or revocation in state, §20-21.
Forfeiture of licensing privileges.
Revocation when privilege forfeited, §20-15.1.
Grounds.
Suspension, §20-16, (a).
Headlamps.
Failure to dim or low beam headlamps not grounds for revocation or suspension, §20-18.
Hearings, §20-16, (d).
Immediate civil license revocation, §20-16.5.
Impaired driving, §20-19, (c1) to (e).
Amended revocation orders, §20-19, (j).
Conviction in federal court, §20-23.2.
Court-ordered revocations, §20-17.2.
Habitual impaired driving.
Permanent revocation, §20-138.5, (d).
Immediate revocation of person's driving privilege, §20-16.2, (a).
Implied consent, §20-16.2.
Mandatory revocation, §20-17, (a).
Period of suspension, §20-19, (c1) to (e).

DRIVERS' LICENSES —Cont'd
Revocation or suspension —Cont'd
Impaired driving —Cont'd
Mental incompetents, alcoholics and habitual users of narcotic drugs, §20-17.1.
Period of suspension or revocation, §20-19, (c1) to (e).
Permanent revocation, §§20-19, (i), 20-138.5, (d).
Restoration after conviction, §20-17.6.
Ignition interlock as condition, §20-17.8, (a), (b).
Duration of condition, §20-17.8, (c).
Limited driving privilege, effect, §20-17.8, (d).
Notice of requirement, §20-17.8, (e).
Restoration after revocation for violating this section, §20-17.8, (k).
Vehicles subject to requirement, §20-17.8, (c1).
Violation results in revocation, §20-17.8, (f) to (j).
Implied consent offenses, §20-16.2.
Immediate civil license revocation, §20-16.5.
Issuance of license during period of revocation or suspension.
Prohibited, §20-9, (b), (f).
Larceny of motor fuel, §14-72.5, (c).
Larceny of motor vehicle, second or subsequent conviction.
Limited driving privilege may be allowed by judge, §20-16, (e2).
Mandatory revocation of driver's license, §20-17, (a).
Period of revocation, §20-19, (g2).
Limitation of actions.
Ten-year-old convictions not considered, §20-36.
Limited driving privilege, §§20-16, (e1), 20-179.3.
Driving by person less than 21 years old after consuming alcohol or drugs, §20-138.3, (d).
Open container law violations, §20-138.7, (h).
Violations of restrictions, effect, §20-179.3, (j).
Mandatory revocation.
Grounds, §20-17, (a).
Manslaughter or negligent homicide.
Mandatory revocation, §20-17, (a).
Mental incompetents, alcoholics and habitual users of narcotic drugs.
Adjudication.
Copy of abstract to commissioner, §20-17.1, (b).
Generally, §20-17.1, (a).
Institutions.
Agreements for care and treatment, §20-17.1, (d).
Information to be furnished, §20-17.1, (e).
Legislative intent, §20-17.1, (d).
Review of revocation, §20-17.1, (f).
Motor fuel larceny conviction.
Limited driving privilege may be allowed by judge, §20-16, (e2).
Mandatory revocation of driver's license.
Second or subsequent conviction, §20-17, (a).
Period of revocation, §20-19, (g2).
Nonresidents.
Suspending privileges of nonresidents, §20-22, (a).
Notice, §20-16, (d).
Open container law violations.
Limited driving privilege, §20-138.7, (h).

DRIVERS' LICENSES —Cont'd
Revocation or suspension —Cont'd
Open container law violations —Cont'd
Second or subsequent conviction, mandatory revocation, §20-17, (a).
Operating privilege of person not holding license, §20-23.1.
Period of suspension or revocation.
Death by vehicle, §20-19, (a).
Driving under the influence, §20-19, (c1) to (e).
Financial responsibility.
Proof required on seeking to have license restored, §20-19, (k).
Generally, §20-19, (c), (f), (g).
Provisional license revoked, §20-13.2, (b).
Restoration.
Proof of financial responsibility required, §20-19, (k).
Speeding, §20-19, (a), (b).
Perjury or false affidavit or statement under oath to division.
Mandatory revocation, §20-17, (a).
Permanent revocation.
Habitual impaired driving, §20-138.5, (d).
Points.
Child restraint systems, failure to use, §20-137.1, (d).
Generally, §20-16, (c).
Schedule of point values, §20-16, (c).
Probation.
Condition, §15A-1343, (b1).
Substituted for revocation.
Failure to receive record of conviction, §20-24, (b1).
Provisional licensees.
Financial responsibility.
Proof required prior to restoration, §20-13.2, (e).
Impaired driving, §20-13.2, (b).
Period of revocation, §20-13.2, (d).
Receipt of record of conviction, §20-13.2, (a).
Refusal to submit to chemical analysis, §20-13.2, (c).
Suspension upon moving violation conviction, §20-13, (a).
Length of suspension, §20-13, (b).
Motor vehicle moving violation defined, §20-13, (a).
Probation, placing licensee on, §20-13, (b).
Restoration of license on probationary status, hearing request, §20-13, (b).
Retention of license until hearing, §20-13, (a).
Suspension in addition to other remedies, §20-13, (d).
Two or more offenses committed on single occasion, §20-13, (c).
Provisional licenses.
Driving after consuming alcohol or drugs, §20-13.2, (a).
Driving eligibility certificate not maintained, §20-13.2, (c1).
Impaired driving conviction, §20-13.2, (b).
Length of revocation, §20-13.2, (d).
Restoration, proof of financial responsibility, §20-13.2, (e).
Willful refusing to submit chemical analysis, §20-13.2, (c).
Racing vehicles on streets and highways, §20-141.3, (d) to (f).
Reckless driving.
Two charges within 12 month period or transportation of illegal intoxicants.
Mandatory revocation, §20-17, (a).

DRIVERS' LICENSES —Cont'd
Revocation or suspension —Cont'd
Record of conviction, forwarding to division, §20-24, (b).
Probation substituted for revocation, failure to receive record, §20-24, (b1).
Restoration, conditions upon, §20-19, (c3).
Violation of conditions.
Hearing, §20-19, (c5).
Procedure, §20-19, (c4).
Review of division's decision, §20-19, (c6).
Restoration fee.
Person whose license has been revoked, §20-7, (i1).
Restoration of license after conviction of driving while impaired or driving less than 21 years old after consuming alcohol or drugs, §20-17.6.
Speeding.
Mandatory revocation for excessive speeding, §20-17, (a).
Mandatory suspension for excessive speeding, §20-16.1, (a).
Limited driving permits for first offenders, §20-16.1, (b1).
Longer period of suspension authorized, §20-16.1, (e).
Reckless driving on same occasion as speeding offense, §20-16.1, (d).
Second or subsequent offense, §20-16.1, (c).
Period of suspension, §20-19, (a), (b).
Surrender of license to court or child support enforcement agency, §20-24, (a).
Road test, §20-7, (c).
Safe driver incentive plan.
Offenses for which insurance points charged, §58-36-75.
Sale.
Reproduction or facsimile or simulation of driver's license.
Prohibited, §20-30.
School bus drivers.
Requirements, §20-218, (a).
Selective service system registration requirements, §20-9.2, (a).
Forwarding of information to selective service system, §20-9.2, (b).
Social security number or tax payer identification number.
Providing required for issuance of license, §20-7, (b1).
Special identification cards for nonoperators, §§20-37.7, 20-37.8.
Application, §20-7, (b).
Confidentiality of photographic image or signature recorded, §20-43, (a).
Resident of state.
Proof required for issuance, documents evidencing, §20-7, (b2), (b3), (b4).
Social security number or tax payer identification number.
Providing required for issuance of license, §20-7, (b1).
Speeding.
Revocation or suspension, §20-17, (a).
Period of suspension, §20-19, (a), (b).
Substance abuse assessment.
Restoration of license after impaired driving conviction or conviction for driving while less than 21 years old after consuming alcohol or drugs.
Obtaining certificate of completion, §20-17.6, (c).

DRIVERS' LICENSES —Cont'd
Supervising driver for minor, §20-11, (k).
Impaired supervision or instruction, §20-12.1.
Surrender of license.
Conviction of offense requiring revocation, §20-24, (a).
Financial responsibility.
Misdemeanor for failure to surrender, §20-279.31, (c).
Generally, §20-29.
Suspension.
Speeding to elude arrest convictions, §20-141.5, (d).
Tamperproof, §20-7, (n).
Taxicabs.
Cities and towns.
Power to regulate, §20-37.
Tax lien, §20-98.
Temporary license.
Mail renewal, §20-7, (f).
Tests of physical and mental ability, §20-7, (c).
Time for obtaining license after becoming resident, §20-7, (a).
Title of act, §20-5.
Uniform driver's license act.
Citation of provisions, §20-5.
Violations of provisions.
Failure to carry license.
When person may not be convicted of, §20-35, (c).
False affidavits, §20-31.
General penalty provision, §20-35, (a).
Permitting unlicensed minor to drive motor vehicle, §20-32.
Permitting violations of provisions, §20-34.
Prohibited acts, §20-30.
Vision test, §20-7, (c).
Exemption when renewing by mail.
Armed forces members, national guard members and reservists, §20-7, (r).
Written test for literate applicants, §20-7, (c).
Wrongful issuance, §20-34.1.

DRIVER'S LICENSE TECHNOLOGY FUND, §20-37.01.

DRIVER'S PRIVACY PROTECTION ACT.
Disclosure of personal information in motor vehicle records, §20-43.1.

DRIVER TRAINING SCHOOL LICENSING, §§20-320 to 20-328.
Cancellation of licenses, §20-325.
Commissioner of motor vehicles.
Administration and enforcement of provisions, §20-321, (b).
Powers, §20-321, (a).
Regulations as to requirements, §§20-322, (b), 20-323, (b).
Definitions, §20-320.
Denial of licenses, §20-325.
Division of motor vehicles.
Administration of provisions, §20-328.
Employers and employees.
Exemptions from provisions, §20-326.
Examining of applications.
Duty of commissioner or authorized representative, §20-321, (a).
Exemptions from provisions, §20-326.
Expiration of licenses, §20-324, (a).
Fees, §20-324, (b).

DRIVER TRAINING SCHOOL LICENSING —Cont'd
Inspecting school facilities, records and equipment.
Duty of commissioner or authorized representative, §20-321, (a).
Instructors.
Defined, §20-320.
Licenses required, §20-323, (a).
Renewal of licenses, §20-324, (a).
Refusal to renew, §20-325.
Requirements.
Licenses for instructors, §20-323, (a).
Licenses for schools, §20-322, (a).
Regulations as to requirements, §§20-322, (b), 20-323, (b).
Rules and regulations.
Commissioner of motor vehicles, §§20-321, (a), 20-322, (b), 20-323, (b).
Penalty for violation, §20-327.
Suspension or revocation of licenses, §20-325.
Violations of provisions or regulations, §20-327.

DRIVE-THRU DELIVERIES, §58-3-169.

DRIVEWAYS.
Driver emerging from or entering to yield right of way to pedestrian, §20-173, (c).
Environmental document not required for construction of driveway connecting public roadway, §113A-12.
Parking in front of private driveway, §20-162, (a).
Right of way of vehicle about to enter or cross, §20-156, (a).
Subcontractors, payments to, §§22C-1 to 22C-6.

DRIVING BY PERSON LESS THAN 21 YEARS OLD AFTER CONSUMING ALCOHOL OR DRUGS.
Implied consent law, offense subject to, §20-138.3, (b).

DRIVING BY PROVISIONAL LICENSEE AFTER CONSUMING ALCOHOL OR DRUGS.
Restoration of license after conviction, §20-17.6.

DRIVING ELIGIBILITY CERTIFICATE, §20-11, (n).
Charter school's designee, duties, §115C-238.29F, (j).
Principals of schools, duties, §115C-288, (k).
Private or home schools, duties, §115C-366.
School disciplinary actions.
Effect on eligibility, §20-11, (n1).
Revocation of provisional license, §20-13.2, (c1).
State board of community colleges, rules, duty to adopt, §115D-5, (a3).
State board of education, rules, duty to develop, §115C-12.

DRIVING ON RIGHT SIDE OF HIGHWAY, §20-146.

DRIVING UNDER THE INFLUENCE.
Generally.
See IMPAIRED DRIVING.

DRIVING WHILE DISQUALIFIED, §20-28, (d).

DRIVING WHILE INTOXICATED.
Generally.
See IMPAIRED DRIVING.

DRIVING WHILE LICENSE REVOKED, §20-28, (a).
Impaired driving.
Aggravating factor to be weighed, §20-179, (d).
Grossly aggravating factors, §20-179, (c).
Seizure and forfeiture of vehicle, §20-28.3.
Imprisonment for misdemeanor violation.
Restrictions, §20-176, (c1).
Moving offense during.
Additional period of revocation, §20-28.1, (a), (b).
New license, §20-28.1, (c).
When treated as driving without a license, §20-28, (a1).

DRIVING WITHOUT LICENSE.
Defenses, §20-35, (c).
License revoked as result of prior impaired driving offenses.
Seizure and forfeiture of vehicle, §20-28.3.
Restricted licenses.
Operating vehicle without complying with restriction.
Deemed operating vehicle without license, §20-7, (e).

DROPOUT RATES.
Reporting, reducing.
Powers and duties of state board of education, §115C-12.

DROPSY.
Drug or device, false advertising, §106-138, (b).

DROUGHT ADVISORIES.
Issuance by drought management advisory council, §143-355.1, (e).
Considerations before issuing, §143-355.1, (f).

DROUGHT MANAGEMENT ADVISORY COUNCIL.
Chair.
Employee of department designated as, §143-355.1, (d).
Drought advisory, issuance, §143-355.1, (e).
Considerations before issuing, §143-355.1, (f).
Established by department of environment and natural resources, §143-355.1, (a).
Meetings, §143-355.1, (d).
Purpose, §143-355.1, (a).
Report, §143-355.1, (g).
Representatives to serve on council.
Organizations to designate, §143-355.1, (b), (c).

DROUGHTS.
Closing of forests and woodlands to hunting, fishing and trapping, §§113-60.1 to 113-60.3.
Fire patrols, designated during season of drought, §113-55, (a).
Open burning prohibited statewide during periods of hazardous forest fire conditions, §113-60.25.

DRUG ADDICTION.
Chemical dependency.
See CHEMICAL DEPENDENCY.
Chiropractors.
Grounds for disciplinary action, §90-154, (b).
Drug treatment courts, §§7A-790 to 7A-801.
See DRUG TREATMENT COURTS.
Generally.
See MENTAL HEALTH, DEVELOPMENTAL DISABILITY, SUBSTANCE ABUSE.
Incompetence, determination of, §§35A-1101 to 35A-1116.
See INCOMPETENCE.

DRUG ADDICTION —Cont'd
Lawyers and judges impaired by substance abuse or addiction.
Lawyer assistance program, Bar Rules & Regs., D, §§.0601 to .0623.
See LAWYERS ASSISTANCE PROGRAM.
Physicians and surgeons.
Ground for denial, revocation or suspension of license, §90-14, (a).
Referral of physician to state medical society physician health and effectiveness committee, §90-14, (b).
Work first program recipients of assistance.
Treatment required, drug testing, §108A-29.1.

DRUG ALCOHOL RECOVERY TREATMENT PROGRAM.
Probation.
Special condition.
Screening and assessing for chemical dependency, §15A-1343, (b3).

DRUG DETECTION DOG HANDLERS.
Registration, acquisition of controlled substances, disclosure of dog alert, §90-102.1.

DRUG DETECTION DOGS.
Commercial detection services utilizing.
Certification of dogs, §90-102.1, (h).
Confidentiality of client records, exception, §90-102.1, (h).
Defined, §90-102.1, (a).
Disclosure of dog alert or discovery, §90-102.1, (h).
Defined, §90-102.1, (a).
Handlers.
Acquisition of controlled substances for training, §90-102.1, (e).
Record keeping, inventory maintenance, §90-102.1, (f).
Complaints against handlers.
Investigation, §90-102.1, (j).
Defined, §90-102.1, (a).
Dog alert or discovery of controlled substances.
Notifying and informing law enforcement, §90-102.1, (g).
Commercial detection services, §90-102.1, (h).
Disclosure of requirement in contracts, §90-102.1, (i).
Inapplicability to law enforcement agencies, §90-102.1, (k).
Registration if controlled substances used in training, §90-102.1, (b).
Criminal record check, §90-102.1, (d).
Denial, revocation or suspension, §90-102.1, (j).
Prerequisites, §90-102.1, (c).

DRUG ENFORCEMENT ADMINISTRATION AGENTS' AUTHORITY, §15A-406.

DRUG EXAMINATION AND SCREENING OF EMPLOYEES, §§95-230 to 95-235.
Action to recover amount of civil penalty, §95-234, (b).
Approved labs, §95-232, (c).
Chain of custody, §95-232, (e).
Civil penalty for violation, §95-234.
Collection of samples, §95-232, (b).
Compliance with procedural requirements, §95-232, (a).
Confirmation of samples, §95-232, (c1).
Definitions, §95-231.
Defrauding drug and alcohol screening tests.
Penalties, §14-401.20, (c).
Unlawful acts, §14-401.20, (a), (b).

DRUG EXAMINATION AND SCREENING OF EMPLOYEES —Cont'd
Determination of whether violation occurred, §95-234, (a).
Disposition of civil penalties collected, §95-234, (c).
Duty of examiners to conduct examinations.
No duty to examine, §95-233.
Exemption.
Certain federal agencies, §95-235.
Federal agencies.
Certain ones exempted, §95-235.
Intent of general assembly, §95-230.
No duty to examine, §95-233.
On-site training for prospective employees, §95-232, (c).
Procedural requirements, §95-232.
Purposes, §95-230.
Requirements, §95-232.
Retention of samples, §95-232, (d).
Retesting of positive samples, §95-232, (f).
Statute of limitations on assessment of penalties, §95-234, (d).
Violations, §95-234.

DRUGGISTS, §§90-85.2 to 90-85.41.
See PHARMACISTS AND PHARMACIES.

DRUG PARAPHERNALIA.
Advertisements.
Penalties, §90-113.24, (b).
Prohibited acts, §90-113.24, (a).
Citation of act.
Short title, §90-113.20.
Defined, §90-113.21, (a).
Delivery, §90-113.23.
To minors, §90-113.23, (c).
Enumerated, §90-113.21, (a).
Evidence.
Determination where object is drug paraphernalia.
What may be considered, §90-113.21, (b).
Manufacture.
Penalty, §90-113.23, (c).
Prohibited acts, §90-113.23, (a), (b).
Minors.
Delivery of drug paraphernalia to certain younger persons.
Felony, §90-113.23, (c).
Possession.
Penalty, §90-113.22, (b).
Prohibited, §90-113.22, (a).
Prohibited acts as to, §§90-113.22 to 90-113.24.
Short title of act, §90-113.20.

DRUG PRODUCT SELECTION.
Definitions, §90-85.27.
Equivalent drug product.
Defined, §90-85.27.
Price.
Limitation on selected drugs, §90-85.28, (c).
Selection by pharmacist, §90-85.28, (a).
Liability of prescriber and pharmacist not extended, §90-85.31.
Prescriber may permit or prohibit, §90-85.28, (b).
Liability of prescriber and pharmacist not extended, §90-85.31.
Prescriptions.
Label, §90-85.29.
Record, §90-85.30.

DRUGS.
Abortion.
Destroying unborn child.
Using drugs or instruments to destroy, §14-44.
Injuring pregnant woman.
Using drugs to injure, §14-45.
Miscarriages.
Using drugs to produce miscarriage, §14-45.
Actions.
Civil actions.
Minors.
Employing or intentionally using minor to commit drug law violations, §90-95.5.
Aircraft.
Forfeiture of conveyances used in controlled substances violations.
Generally, §§90-112, 90-112.1.
Operation of aircraft while impaired.
Chemical analysis, §63-27, (d).
Defense precluded, §63-27, (b).
Infliction of serious bodily injury.
Defense precluded, §63-28, (b).
Felony, §63-28, (d).
Offense, §63-28, (a).
Pleading, §63-28, (c).
Misdemeanor, §63-27, (e).
Offense, §63-27, (a).
Penalty, §63-27, (e).
Pleading, §63-27, (c).
Alcoholic beverage permittees.
Certain conduct unlawful on premises, §18B-1005, (a).
Amusement device operators.
Operating device equipment under the influence.
Prohibition, §95-111.11, (b).
Attorney disciplinary amnesty in elicit drug use cases, Bar Rules & Regs., B, §.0130.
Boating safety.
Operation of boat or manipulation of water skis while under influence of drugs, §75A-10, (b), (b1).
Penalty, §75A-18, (b).
Capital punishment.
Manner of execution, §15-187.
Chemical analysis of impairing substances in blood generally.
See IMPAIRED DRIVING.
Child care facilities.
Unauthorized administration of medicine, §110-102.1A.
Chiropractors.
Addiction or severe dependency.
Grounds for disciplinary action, §90-154, (b).
Prescriptions.
Prohibited, §90-151.
Commercial drivers' licenses.
Disqualification.
Use of commercial motor vehicle in felony involving controlled substances.
Lifetime disqualification, §20-17.4, (c).
Commission for mental health, developmental disabilities and substance abuse services, §§143B-147 to 143B-150.
Construction and interpretation.
Wholesale prescription drug distributors, §106-145.1.
Application of other laws, §106-145.10.
Controlled substances generally, §§90-86 to 90-113.8.
See CONTROLLED SUBSTANCES.

DRUGS —Cont'd
Corrections.
Substance abuse program, §§143B-262, 143B-262.1.
Courts.
Drug treatment courts, §§7A-790 to 7A-801.
See DRUG TREATMENT COURTS.
Dental hygienists.
Chronic or persistent use as grounds for disciplinary measures, §90-229, (a).
Dentists.
Chronic or persistent use.
Grounds for disciplinary action, §90-41, (a).
Prescriptions, §90-46.
Discrimination by employer for lawful use of lawful products during nonworking hours, §95-28.2.
Divorce grounds, §50-7.
Drivers' licenses.
Instruction by licensed drivers.
Giving instructions while under the influence of impairing substances, §20-12.1.
Issuance of driver's license to habitual user.
Prohibited, §20-9, (c).
Revocation or suspension.
Mental incompetents, alcoholics and habitual users of narcotic drugs, §20-17.1.
Driving by person less than 21 years old after consuming, §20-138.3.
Driving by provisional licensee after consuming.
Restoration of license after conviction, §20-17.6.
Driving under the influence generally.
See IMPAIRED DRIVING.
Drug use review program.
Rules implementing, §108A-68.
Education.
Children with chemical dependency.
Drug addicted children.
Appropriate education provided for.
Policy of state to insure, §115C-149.
Children with special needs.
Drug addicted children excluded from article, §115C-149.
Policy of state, §115C-149.
State board of education to adopt rules, §115C-150.
Employee examination and screening for controlled substances, §§95-230 to 95-235.
Employer discrimination for lawful use of lawful products during nonworking hours, §95-28.2.
Eviction of drug traffickers and other criminals, §§42-59 to 42-76.
See EXPEDITED EVICTIONS.
Fees.
Expunction of records, §90-96, (f).
Wholesale prescription drug distributors.
License application fees, §106-145.4, (b).
Fish or wildlife taken by use of, §113-262, (a), (b).
Permit authorizing, §113-261, (b).
Food, drug and cosmetic act, §§106-120 to 106-145.
See FOOD, DRUG AND COSMETIC ACT.
Forfeitures.
Conveyances used in violations of controlled substances provisions.
Generally, §§90-112, 90-112.1.
Vehicles and other personal property used in controlled substances offenses, §90-112.
Applicability of article, §90-113.7.
Mitigation or remission of forfeitures, §90-112.1.

DRUGS —Cont'd
Hospitals.
Licensed chiropractors may practice in public hospitals, §90-153.
Hypodermic syringes and needles generally.
See DRUG PARAPHERNALIA.
Impaired driving generally.
See IMPAIRED DRIVING.
Labor.
Lawful use of lawful products during nonworking hours by employees.
Discrimination against prohibited, §95-28.2.
Licenses.
Wholesale prescription drug distributors, §§106-145.3 to 106-145.6.
Liens.
Medical attention to injured persons, §44-49.
Charges, §44-50.
Evidence, §44-50.
Funds for purpose.
Duty of receiving person, §44-50.
Limit on recovery, §44-50.
Settlement.
Disputed claims to be settled before payment, §44-51.
Medicaid.
Prior authorization requirement.
Exemptions, §108A-68.1.
Medical plan for teachers and state employees.
Prescription drugs, §135-40.5, (g).
Mental health, developmental disabilities and substance abuse.
General provisions.
See MENTAL HEALTH, DEVELOPMENTAL DISABILITY, SUBSTANCE ABUSE.
Methamphetamines.
Precursor chemicals.
Possession or distribution with intent to manufacture, §90-95, (d1).
List of chemicals to which subsection applies, §90-95, (d2).
Trafficking in, §90-95, (h).
Methamphetamine watch program.
Immunity from civil and criminal liability.
Good faith actions, §114-43.
Minors.
Driving after consuming drugs.
Restoration of license after conviction, §20-17.6.
Driving by person less than 21 years old after consuming alcohol or drugs, §20-138.3.
Municipal corporations.
Drug abuse programs, §160A-494.
New drugs.
Regulations for sale of, §106-135.
Nuisances.
Abatement.
Offenses against public morals.
See NUISANCES.
Nurses.
Use of drugs as grounds for revocation, suspension or denial of license, §90-171.37.
Optometrists.
Prescriptions, §90-118, (e).
Copy of prescription.
Furnished on request, §90-127.3.
Filling, §90-127.2.
Osteopaths.
Habitual addiction as grounds for refusal, suspension or revocation of license, §90-136.
Outdated prescription drugs.
Wholesale prescription drug distributors.
Duties, §106-145.7, (e).

DRUGS —Cont'd
Over-the-counter drugs.
Sales and use tax.
Defined, §105-164.3.
Paraphernalia, §§90-113.20 to 90-113.24.
See DRUG PARAPHERNALIA.
Pharmacists and pharmacies generally, §§90-85.2 to 90-85.41.
See PHARMACISTS AND PHARMACIES.
Physicians and surgeons.
Optometry provisions not to apply, §90-127.
Post-release supervision.
Controlling conditions, nonuse, §15A-1364.4, (e).
Prescription drugs.
Sales and use tax.
Defined, §105-164.3.
Exemption, §105-164.13.
Prescriptions.
See PRESCRIPTIONS.
Public schools.
Basic education program.
Alcohol and drug education program, §115C-81, (a3).
Instruction in dangers of harmful or illegal drugs, §115C-81, (c).
Children with chemical dependency.
Drug addicted children.
Appropriate education provided for.
Policy of state to insure, §115C-149.
Children with special needs.
Excluded from provisions of article, §115C-149.
Policy of state, §115C-149.
State board of education to adopt rules, §115C-150.
Records.
Prescription drugs.
Wholesale distributors.
Duties, §106-145.8.
Returned prescription drugs.
Wholesale prescription drug distributors.
Duties, §106-145.7, (e).
Sales and use tax.
Defined, §105-164.3.
Exemptions, §105-164.13.
Over-the-counter drugs.
Defined, §105-164.3.
Exemption, §105-164.13.
Prescription drugs.
Defined, §105-164.3.
Exemption, §105-164.13.
Special education.
Children with chemical dependency.
Drug addicted children excluded from provisions of article, §115C-149.
Statements obtained from person under the influence of drugs.
Presumption of fraud, §8-45.5.
State prison system.
Employees.
Use of intoxicants, narcotic drugs or profanity.
Prohibited, §148-23.
Storage.
Prescription drugs.
Wholesale distributors, §106-145.7.
Substance abuse generally.
See MENTAL HEALTH, DEVELOPMENTAL DISABILITY, SUBSTANCE ABUSE.
Substance abuse professionals, §§90-113.30 to 90-113.46.
See SUBSTANCE ABUSE PROFESSIONALS.

DRUGS —Cont'd
Taxation.
Unauthorized substances taxes, §§105-113.105 to 105-113.113.
See UNAUTHORIZED SUBSTANCES TAXES.
Wholesale prescription drug distributors generally, §§106-145.1 to 106-145.12.
See WHOLESALE PRESCRIPTION DRUG DISTRIBUTORS.
Workers' compensation.
Injury or death caused by employee being under influence.
No compensation payable, §97-12.
Zero tolerance law.
Driving by person less than 21 years old after consuming alcohol or drugs, §20-138.3.

DRUGSTORES.
Alcoholic beverage permits.
Food business defined to include, §18B-1000.
Off-premises fortified wine permit.
Kind of permit that may be issued, §18B-1001.
Off-premises malt beverage permit.
Kind of permit that may be issued, §18B-1001.
On-premises malt beverage permit.
Kind of permit that may be issued, §18B-1001.
On-premises unfortified wine permit.
Kind of permit that may be issued, §18B-1001.
Special occasion permit.
Kind of permit that may be issued, §18B-1001.
Generally.
See PHARMACISTS AND PHARMACIES.

DRUG THERAPY MANAGEMENT.
Clinical pharmacist practitioners generally.
See PHARMACISTS AND PHARMACIES.
Practicing medicine without a license.
Exception, §90-18, (c).

DRUG TRAFFICKING, §90-95, (h).
Children or minors.
Delivery of drug paraphernalia to certain youths, §90-113.23.
Employing or intentionally using minors to commit drug law violations, §90-95.4, (a), (b).
Civil liability, §90-95.5.
"Minor" defined, §90-95.4, (d).
Mistake of age, §90-96, (b), (d).
Conspiracy, §90-95, (i).
Electronic surveillance.
Issuance of orders for surveillance, §15A-290, (a1).
Landlord and tenant.
Eviction of drug traffickers and other criminals, §§42-59 to 42-76.
See EXPEDITED EVICTIONS.

DRUG TREATMENT COURTS, §§7A-790 to 7A-801.
Advisory committee, §7A-795.
Applications for grants, §7A-798, (a), (b).
Awarding of grants, §7A-798, (a).
Citation of act, §7A-790.
Costs of treatment program, §7A-800.
Eligibility guidelines, §7A-797.
Establishment of programs, §7A-793.
Evaluation plans and reports, §7A-801.
Fund administration, §7A-794.
Goals of programs, §7A-792.
Guidelines for court operation, §7A-797.
Local drug treatment court management committees, §7A-796.
Local program directors, §7A-798, (b).
Plans for evaluation, §7A-801.

DRUG TREATMENT COURTS —Cont'd
Purpose of act, §7A-791.
Right to treatment not conferred, §7A-799.
Short title, §7A-790.
State drug treatment court advisory committee, §7A-795.
Treatment not guaranteed, §7A-799.

DRUNK DRIVING.
Generally.
See IMPAIRED DRIVING.

DRUNKENNESS.
Generally.
See INTOXICATION.

DRY CLEANERS.
Generally.
See LAUNDRIES AND DRY CLEANING ESTABLISHMENTS.

DRY-CLEANING EQUIPMENT TAX CREDIT.
Equipment not using hazardous substances, §105-129.16C, (a) to (c).

DRY-CLEANING SOLVENT CLEANUP, §§143-215.104A to 143-215.104U.
Action for reimbursement cost.
Remediation of uncertified site, §143-215.104O, (a), (b).
Administrative functions of commission, §143-215.104D, (a).
Appeals, §143-215.104S.
Assessment agreements.
Costs for reimbursement equals or exceeds money in fund.
Notice, further agreement prohibited, §143-215.104N, (d).
Determination no remediation or further action required, §143-215.104H, (f).
Determination of risk to public health acceptable, §143-215.104H, (e).
Generally, §143-215.104H, (a).
Liability protection of potentially responsible persons, §143-215.104K.
Obligation to reimburse response cost.
Expressed in agreement, §143-215.104N, (d).
Petition generally, §143-215.104H, (a).
Refusal of commission to enter into, §143-215.104H, (c), (d).
Renegotiation or termination generally, §143-215.104J.
Requirements for petitioning for, §143-215.104F.
Terms and conditions, §143-215.104H, (b).
Brownfields notice.
Notice of dry-cleaning solvent remediation in lieu of notice, §143-215.104M, (g).
Certification of facilities and abandoned sites, §143-215.104, (a).
Assessment or remediation of contamination by person with access to property, §143-215.104G, (d).
Changing initial priority ranking, §143-215.104G, (b).
Costs not reimbursed from fund, §143-215.104F, (c1).
Decertification generally, §143-215.104J.
Information provided by potentially responsible party, §143-215.104G, (c).
Requirements for petitioning, §143-215.104F.
Citation of act, §143-215.104A.
Civil penalties.
Amounts, §143-215.104P, (a), (b).
Assessment by secretary, §143-215.104P, (a).

DRY-CLEANING SOLVENT CLEANUP —Cont'd
Civil penalties —Cont'd
Civil action for unpaid penalty, §143-215.104P, (f).
Considerations in determining, §143-215.104P, (c).
Notice of assessment, §143-215.104P, (d).
Remission, request for, §143-215.104P, (e).
Construction of provisions, §143-215.104T, (a).
Cost of assessment and remediation activities.
Reimbursement generally, §143-215.104N.
Criminal penalties and prosecutions.
Applicability of general defenses, affirmative defenses and bars to prosecution, §143-215.104Q, (g), (h).
Circumstantial evidence, §143-215.104Q, (e).
Knowingly and willfully committing offense, §143-215.104Q, (b).
Person in imminent danger of death or serious bodily injury, §143-215.104Q, (c).
Knowingly and willfully or knowingly, proving state of mind, §143-215.104Q, (f).
Negligently committing offense, §143-215.104Q, (a).
Person defined, §143-215.104Q, (i).
Previous conviction of federal violation based upon same facts, §143-215.104Q, (d).
Decertification of facility, renegotiation or termination of assessment agreement or remediation agreement, §143-215.104J, (a).
Notice of opportunity for hearing, §143-215.104J, (b).
Rights of other petitioners not affected, §143-215.104J, (c).
Definitions, §143-215.104B, (b).
Applicability, §143-215.104B, (a).
Delegation of functions of commission to contractors, §143-215.104D, (a).
Delegation of rights, duties and responsibilities to department, §143-215.104D, (d).
Dry-cleaning solvent cleanup fund.
Established, §143-215.104C, (a).
Payment of claims filed from money in fund, §143-215.104C, (c).
Sources of revenue, §143-215.104C, (b).
Transfer of sales and use taxes to fund, §105-164.44E.
Financial responsibility for certification of facility, assessment agreement or remediation agreement, §143-215.104F, (f).
Immunity of state, agencies, officers, etc., §143-215.104T.
Injunctions, §143-215.104R.
Intention of provisions, §143-215.104T.
Land-use restrictions.
Notice of dry-cleaning solvent remediation, §143-215.104M.
Liability protection when entering into assessment or remediation agreement.
Persons conducting environmental assessment or transaction screen, §143-215.104K, (b).
Potentially responsible parties, §143-215.104K, (a).
Violations of land-use restrictions, §143-215.104K, (c).
Notice of dry-cleaning solvent remediation, §143-215.104M, (a).
Cancellation, §143-215.104M, (e).
Enforcement of restrictions on current or future use of property, §143-215.104M, (f).
Notice in lieu.
Brownfields notice, §143-215.104M, (g).
Recordation, §143-215.104M, (c).

DRY-CLEANING SOLVENT CLEANUP —Cont'd
Notice of dry-cleaning solvent remediation —Cont'd
Restrictions contained in notice, §143-215.104M, (b).
Sale, lease, conveyance or transfer of property.
Notice in deed, §143-215.104M, (d).
Notice of intent to remediate, §143-215.104L, (a), (b).
Petition for certification of facility, assessment agreement or remediation agreement.
Assessment agreements generally, §143-215.104H.
Certification of facilities generally, §143-215.104G.
Financial responsibility requirement, §143-215.104F, (f).
Grounds for rejecting petition, §143-215.104F, (d), (e).
Potentially responsible persons, requirements generally, §143-215.104F, (b).
Property owners, requirements, §143-215.104F, (c).
Public meetings on proposed agreement, §143-215.104L, (c).
Refusal to enter into, §143-215.104I, (d) to (f).
Rejection of petition not to effect rights of other petitioners, §143-215.104G, (e).
Remediation agreements generally, §143-215.104I.
Renegotiation or termination generally, §143-215.104J.
Requirements for petitioning for, §143-215.104F.
Requirements generally, §143-215.104F, (a).
Terms and conditions, §143-215.104I, (g).
Publication of notice of intent to remediate, §143-215.104L, (b).
Public meeting on proposed remediation agreement, §143-215.104L, (c).
Reimbursement for assessment and remediation agreements, §§143-215.104M, (a), 143-215.104N, (a).
Cost equaling or exceeding money in fund.
Notice of determination, §143-215.104N, (d).
Exhaustion of financial resources by petitioner required, §143-215.104N, (c).
Express statement as to reimbursement obligation in agreements.
Contingent on money in fund, §143-215.104N, (d).
Limitations, §§143-215.104M, (b), 143-215.104N, (b).
Reimbursable response cost, §143-215.104N, (e).
Remediation agreements.
Costs for reimbursement equals or exceeds money in fund.
Notice, further agreement prohibited, §143-215.104N, (d).
Description of site and statement required, §143-215.104I, (c).
Failure to comply, violation of provisions, §143-215.104I, (h).
Future uses, refusal to accept limitations on, §143-215.104I, (e).
Generally, §143-215.104I, (a).
Land-use restrictions, reliance on when negotiating, §143-215.104I, (b).
Liability protection of potentially responsible persons, §143-215.104K.
Notice of intent to remediate, §143-215.104L, (a), (b).
Obligation to reimburse response cost.
Expressed in agreement, §143-215.104N, (d).

DRY-CLEANING SOLVENT CLEANUP —Cont'd
Remediation agreements —Cont'd
Petition for certification of facility. See within this heading, "Petition for certification of facility, assessment agreement or remediation agreement."
Remediation of uncertified site.
Civil action to secure reimbursement of cost, §143-215.104O, (b), (c).
Renegotiating assessment agreement or remediation agreement.
Generally, §143-215.104J.
Report by secretary, §143-215.104U, (a).
Time for reporting, §143-215.104U, (b).
Response cost.
Reimbursement generally, §143-215.104N.
Rulemaking, §143-215.104D, (b).
Applicability to dry-cleaning facilities, wholesale distribution facilities and abandoned dry-cleaning facilities, §143-215.104D, (c).
Termination of assessment agreement or remediation agreement.
Generally, §143-215.104J.
Uncertified site, remediation, §143-215.104O.

DRY-CLEANING SOLVENT TAX, §§105-187.30 to 105-187.34.
Collected and administered in same manner as sales and use tax, §105-187.32.
Credit of taxes to dry-cleaning solvent cleanup funds, §105-187.34.
Definitions, §105-187.30.
Excise tax imposed on dry-cleaning solvent purchased outside state, §105-187.31.
Exemptions not to apply, §105-187.33.
Privilege tax imposed on dry-cleaning solvent retailers, §105-187.31.
Rate of privilege tax and excise tax, §105-187.31.
Refunds to apply, §105-187.33.

DRYERS.
Service agreements, §§58-1-25 to 58-1-42.

DUAL OFFICEHOLDING, Const. N. C., art. VI, §9.
"Elective office" defined, §128-1.1, (d).
Ex officio service by county and city representatives and officials, §128-1.2.
No person shall hold more than one office, §128-1.
When allowed, §128-1.1, (a) to (c).

DUCK BLINDS.
Hunting, fishing or trapping on posted property, §§14-159.6 to 14-159.10.

DUCKS.
Baby ducklings.
Disposing of as pets or novelties.
Cruelty to animals, §14-363.1.
Hunting and wildlife generally.
See HUNTING AND WILDLIFE.

DUCKS UNLIMITED.
License plates.
Special registration plates, §§20-79.4, (b), 20-81.12, (b13).

DUE ON SALE CLAUSE FEES.
Mortgages or deeds of trust, §24-10, (d).

DUE PROCESS, Const. N. C., art. I, §19; Const. U. S., amds. V, XIV.
Abused, neglected or dependent juvenile actions.
Adjudicatory hearing, §7B-802.

DUE PROCESS —Cont'd
Banking.
Administrative orders of commissioner.
Hearings, §53-107.1.
Delinquent and undisciplined juvenile actions.
Adjudicatory hearing.
Protection of due process rights, §7B-2405.
Interstate family support.
Issuance of support orders, §52C-4-401.
Trust companies.
Administrative enforcement, §53-370.
Foreign offices.
Emergency enforcement, waiver of due process, §53-327, (c).
Out-of-state institutions, offices.
Violation of provisions.
Waiver of due process in emergency, §53-321, (c).

DUI.
Generally.
See IMPAIRED DRIVING.

DUKE MEDICAL SCHOOL.
Scholarships.
Financial aid for North Carolina students.
Appropriation of funds, §116-21.5, (a).
Board of Governors' powers and duties, §116-21.5, (d), (e).
Disbursement to Duke, §116-21.5, (c).
Transfer of unused funds from other programs, §116-21.5, (e).

DUMBWAITERS.
Elevator safety act generally, §§95-110.1 to 95-110.15.
See ELEVATORS.
Inspection fees.
Assessment and collection, §95-107.
Disposition, §95-108.

DUMPING LITTER, §14-399.

DUMPING OF RADIOACTIVE MATERIALS OR TOXIC SUBSTANCES, §14-284.2.

DUNE BUGGIES.
Municipal corporations.
Regulation, §160A-308.
Utility easements.
Operating vehicle upon after being forbidden to do so, §14-134.2.

DUNKERS.
Affirmations in lieu of oaths, §11-4.

DUPLIN COUNTY.
Acquisition of property, power, §153A-158.1, (a).
Agricultural tendencies in certain counties.
Terms of, §42-23.
Ambulance service, attachment or garnishment and lien for, §§44-51.4 to 44-51.8.
Ambulances requested falsely, §14-111.3.
Condemnation or acquisition of land by local government unit outside county.
Consent of board of commissioners necessary, §153A-15.
Counties generally.
See COUNTIES.
Cropper or tenant refusing to perform terms of contract.
Forfeiture of right of possession to premises, §42-27.

DUPLIN COUNTY —Cont'd
Evidence.
Partition of real estate in Duplin.
Records of partition, §8-24.
Wills in Duplin.
Records of wills, §8-25.
Game laws, local acts not repealed, §113-133.1, (e).
Global TransPark development zone, §§158-30 to 158-42.
Housing authority commissioners.
Tenant as commissioner, exemption from provision of law allowing, §157-5.
Low-income housing tax credits.
Qualified building eligible for credit, §105-129.41, (c).
Officers compensated from fees.
Statement to be rendered, §128-13.
On-premises unfortified wine licenses.
Discretion to decline to issue, §105-113.71, (b).
Open fires, §113-60.23.
Applicability of provisions, §113-60.23, (a).
Ground clearing activities, special permit, §113-60.23, (c).
Woodland fires, permit required, §113-60.23, (b).
Partition.
Evidence.
Records of partition in Duplin, §8-24.
Probates and registration orders before clerks of inferior courts validated, §47-59.
Records.
Partition of real estate in Duplin.
Evidence of records of partition, §8-24.
Wills in Duplin.
Evidence, §8-25.
School property.
Acquisition and improvement, §153A-158.1.
Special school tax, election to abolish.
Petition required, §115C-505.
Wild plants, taking of certain plants from land of another.
Inapplicability of provisions, §14-129.
Wills.
Evidence.
Records of wills in Duplin, §8-25.

DURABLE POWER OF ATTORNEY, §§32A-8 to 32A-14.
Accounts.
Filing.
Incapacity or incompetence of principal, §32A-11, (b).
Acknowledgment of substitution, §32A-12, (b).
Appointment, §32A-12, (a).
Attorney-in-fact.
Relations to court-appointed fiduciary, §32A-10.
Compensation of attorney-in-fact.
Incapacity or incompetence of principal, §32A-11, (c).
Trustees and other fiduciaries generally, §§32-53 to 32-62.
See FIDUCIARIES.
Copy of power.
Filing.
Incapacity or incompetence of principal, §32A-11, (a).
Custodial trusts.
Effective to terminate or direct administration or distribution of property.
Specific provision required in power, §33B-7, (f).

DURABLE POWER OF ATTORNEY —Cont'd
Death of attorney-in-fact.
Substitution, §32A-12, (b).
Definition, §32A-8.
Execution of power prior to October 1, 1988 pursuant to G.S. 47-115.1.
Deemed durable power, §32A-14, (a).
Fiduciaries.
Relation of attorney-in-fact to court-appointed fiduciary, §32A-10.
Good faith dealing with attorney-in-fact.
Incapacity or incompetence of principal, §32A-9, (c).
Health care powers of attorney, §§32A-14 to 32A-26.
See HEALTH CARE POWERS OF ATTORNEY.
Incapacity of attorney-in-fact to act.
Substitution, §32A-12, (b).
Incapacity or mental incompetence of principal.
Commissions attorney-in-fact to receive, §32A-11, (c).
Custodial trust, terminating or directing distribution.
Specific provision required in power, §33B-7, (f).
Filing copy of power with clerk, §32A-11, (a).
Inventories and accounts, filing, §32A-11, (b).
Records of transactions, attorney-in-fact to keep, §32A-11, (a).
Substitution of attorney-in-fact.
Recordation, §32A-12, (b).
Validity of acts done by attorney-in-fact, §32A-9, (a).
Protection of person dealing in good faith with attorney-in-fact, §32A-9, (c).
Registration of power required, §32A-9, (b).
Inventories.
Filing.
Incapacity or incompetence of principal, §32A-11, (b).
Notice of substitution, §32A-12, (b).
Reference to chapter 32B.
Authority to refer to chapter 32B, §32A-14, (b).
Registration.
Incapacity or incompetence of principal, §32A-9, (b).
Removal, §32A-12, (a).
Resignation, §32A-12, (a).
Revocation, §32A-13, (a), (b).
Affidavit of attorney-in-fact, §32A-13, (c).
Rights, powers, duties and responsibilities, §32A-12, (a).
Substitution, §32A-12, (a), (b).

DURESS.
Adoption proceedings.
Waiver of notice, §48-2-406, (c).
Affirmative defense, pleading, §1A-1, Rule 8, (c).
Capital punishment.
Mitigating circumstances, §15A-2000, (f).
Criminal procedure.
Notice to state of defenses, §15A-905, (c), (d).
Evidence.
Statements, releases, etc., obtained from persons in shock or under the influence of drugs.
Presumption of fraud, §8-45.5.
Husband and wife.
Conveyances.
Certain conveyances not affected by fraud or duress, §39-11.

DURESS —Cont'd
Insurance.
Statements, releases, etc., obtained from persons in shock or under the influence of drugs.
Presumption of fraud, §8-45.5.
Private personnel services contracts, §95-47.4, (d).
Special matters, pleading, §1A-1, Rule 9, (b).

DURHAM, CITY OF.
Condemnation of unsafe buildings, §§160A-425.1, 160A-426, (d), 160A-432, (a1).
Private parking lots, removal of unauthorized vehicles, §20-219.2.
Traffic control photographic systems, §160A-300.1, (d).

DURHAM COUNTY.
Ambulance service.
Attachment or garnishment and lien for, §§44-51.4 to 44-51.8.
Condemnation or acquisition of land by local government unit outside county.
Consent of board of commissioners necessary, §153A-15.
Counties generally.
See COUNTIES.
Dangerous firearm use by young children, permitting.
Air rifles, air pistols and BB guns not dangerous firearm, §14-316, (b).
Durham-Orange historical commission.
Transfer of commission to department, §143B-51.
Motor vehicle emission inspections.
Counties inspections required to be performed in, §143-215.107A, (c).
Oil, gas and mineral interests separated from surface fee, extinguished, title in surface fee holder.
Failure to list interest for tax purposes for 10 years prior to January 1, 1965.
Protection of subsurface interest from surface fee holder, §1-42.1, (d).
Failure to list interest for tax purposes for 10 years prior to January 1, 1971.
Protection of surface interest from surface estate holder, §1-42.2, (d).
School property.
Acquisition and improvement, §153A-158.1.
Special police officers for territory of Camp Butner reservation.
Jurisdiction, §122C-408.
Water and sewer systems within Camp Butner reservation, §122C-407, (b).

DUTCHMAN'S BREECHES.
Taking, etc., of certain wild plants from land of another, §14-129.

DUTY FREE PERIOD.
Teachers, §115C-301.1.

DUTY TO RETREAT.
Use of deadly physical force against an intruder, §14-51.1.

DWI.
Generally.
See IMPAIRED DRIVING.

DYES, MOLDS, FORMS AND PATTERNS, §66-67.3.
Definitions, §66-67.3, (a).
Ownership and transfer, §66-67.3, (b).
Procedure for transfer, §66-67.3, (c).
Use upon transfer, §66-67.3, (d).

DYES, MOLDS, FORMS AND PATTERNS —Cont'd
Rights under state and federal laws, §66-67.3, (e).

DYING DECLARATIONS, §8C-1, Rule 804, (b).
Admissibility, §8-51.1.
Wrongful death, §28A-18-2.

DYNAMITE.
Burglary using explosives, §14-57.
Exploding cartridges, §14-283.
Explosives generally.
See EXPLOSIVES.
Keeping for sale or selling without license, §14-284.

E

EAGLES.
Unlawfully taking, possessing, transporting, etc., §113-294, (l).

EAGLE SCOUTS.
Motor vehicle license plates.
Special plates, §20-79.4, (b).

EARLY CHILDHOOD ADMINISTRATION CREDENTIAL.
Child center administrators.
Requirements, §110-91.

EARLY CHILDHOOD INITIATIVES.
Consent.
Home-centered services, §143B-168.16.
Definitions, §143B-168.11, (b).
Findings of legislature, §143B-168.10.
Home-centered services, §143B-168.16.
Legislative findings, §143B-168.10.
Local partnerships.
Audit and review by state auditor, §143B-168.14, (b).
Capital projects, funding guidelines, §143B-168.12, (e).
Conditions for receiving state funds, §143B-168.14, (a).
Contractors.
Requirements as to, §143B-168.12, (c).
Defined, §143B-168.11, (b).
Long-term plans, §143B-168.15, (c).
Needs improvement rating.
Annual audit, §143B-168.14, (b).
Qualifying expenses.
Monitoring, §143B-168.12, (f).
State funds.
Conditions for receiving, §143B-168.14, (a).
County expenditures.
State funds not to supplant, §143B-168.15, (e).
Expansion of child care subsidies, §143B-168.15, (g).
Start-up and related activities, §143B-168.15, (d).
Use, §143B-168.15, (a).
Direct services, §143B-168.15, (b).
Superior or satisfactory rating.
Biennial audit, §143B-168.14, (b).
Technical and administrative assistance, §143B-168.13, (a).
North Carolina Partnership for Children, Inc.
Audit and review by state auditor, §143B-168.12, (b).

EARLY CHILDHOOD INITIATIVES —Cont'd
North Carolina Partnership for Children, Inc —Cont'd
Board of directors, §143B-168.12, (a).
Defined, §143B-168.11, (b).
Conditions for receiving state funds, §143B-168.12, (a).
Definition of "North Carolina partnership," §143B-168.11, (b).
Local partnerships.
Capital projects, funding guidelines, §143B-168.12, (e).
Qualifying expenses.
Uniform guidelines and reporting format, establishment.
Documentation of qualifying expenses, §143B-168.12, (f).
Reports, §143B-168.12, (a), (d).
Uniform guidelines and reporting format, establishment.
Documentation of qualifying expenses, §143B-168.12, (f).
Purpose of provisions, §143B-168.11, (a).
Records.
Home-centered services.
Parents to have access to records, §143B-168.16.
Rules to implement part, adoption, §143B-168.13, (a).
Statewide needs and resource assessment, §143B-168.13.

EARLY PERIODIC SCREENING, DIAGNOSIS AND TREATMENT PROGRAM.
Child care facilities.
Health assessments, §110-91.

EARNED TIME CREDIT.
Good behavior, §15A-1355, (c).
Impaired drivers, §15A-1355, (c).
Mentally and physically unfit inmates, §15A-1355, (d).
Misdemeanors, §15A-1340.20, (d).

EARNINGS.
Garnishment.
See GARNISHMENT.
Salaries.
See SALARIES.
Wages.
See WAGES.

EASEMENTS.
Abandonment of railroad easement.
Presumptive ownership, §1-44.2, (a), (b).
Agricultural conservation easements.
Purchase, §106-744.
Airports.
Municipal airports.
Acquisition of easements, §63-49, (c).
Cartways, etc.
Abandonment or discontinuance, §§136-68, 136-70.
Alteration, §§136-68, 136-70.
Establishment, §§136-68, 136-69, (a) to (c).
Procedure for laying out, §136-69, (a) to (c).
Condominiums.
Encroachments, §47C-2-114, (a), (b).
Conservation easements, §§106-744, 113A-230 to 113A-235.
Creation, §39-6.4, (a).
Doctrine of merger, §39-6.4, (b).
Drainage.
Acquisition, §156-4.

EASEMENTS —Cont'd
Drainage —Cont'd
Petition by servient owner against dominant owner, §156-16.
Repairs.
Right of dominant owner to repair, §156-20.
Surrender of drainage easements, §156-23.
Width of right of way for repairs, §156-5.
Drainage districts, §156-70.1.
Improvements.
Renovation, enlargement and extension of canals, structures and boundaries, §156-93.6.
Metropolitan sewerage districts.
Streets and highways, §162A-74.
Metropolitan water districts.
Streets and highways, §162A-54.
Mosquito control districts.
Acquisition and holding of easements, §130A-355.
Municipal corporations.
Grant of easements, §160A-273.
Natural resources easement fund, §146-14.1.
Navigation.
Filling navigable water.
Application for easement, §146-6, (c).
Nonvested easement in gross.
Defined, §41-28.
Time limit, §41-31.
Presumptive ownership of abandoned railroad easement, §1-44.2, (a), (b).
Public lands.
Allocated state lands.
Exemptions, §146-32.
Filling navigable water.
Application for easements, §146-6, (c).
Granting, §146-11.
Lands covered by water, §146-12, (a) to (n).
Natural resources easement fund, §146-14.1.
Public schools.
Granting, §115C-518, (b).
Public utilities.
Lines laid out on petition.
Procedure, §136-71.
Trespass.
Motor vehicles.
Operating vehicle upon easements after being forbidden to do so, §14-134.2.
Utility easement at William B. Umstead State Park, §143-260.10E, (a) to (c).
Railroads.
Presumptive ownership of abandoned easement, §1-44.2, (a), (b).
Sanitary districts.
Acquisition and holding of easements.
Corporate powers of sanitary district board, §130A-55.
Power to purchase and condemn property, §130A-57.
Streets and highways.
Neighborhood roads, cartways, church roads, etc.
General provisions, §§136-67 to 136-71.
Public utility lines laid out on petition.
Procedure, §136-71.
Scenic beauty of areas along highways.
Regulation of scenic easements, §136-125.
Trails.
North Carolina trails system.
Scenic easements within right of way, §113A-90.
Trespass.
Motor vehicles.
Operating vehicle upon utility easements after being forbidden to do so, §14-134.2.

EASEMENTS —Cont'd
Unit ownership.
Unit owners not to impair easements, §47A-11.
Waters and watercourses.
Natural and scenic rivers system.
Charitable deductions.
Claim and allowance for contribution or gift of easement, §113A-39.
New river.
Acquisition of land and easement, §113A-35.1, (a).

EAST CAROLINA UNIVERSITY.
Constituent institution of University of North Carolina, §116-4.
Medical faculty practice plan.
Clinical programs and facilities, operating, §116-40.6, (a).
Construction and renovation of buildings, facilities and other property, §116-40.6, (e).
Division of school of medicine, §116-40.6, (a).
Open-end design agreements, using, §116-40.6, (e).
Personnel, §116-40.6, (b).
Property, acquiring or disposing of, §116-40.6, (d).
Purchases, §116-40.6, (c).
School of medicine.
Accrediting agencies.
Meeting requirements of, §116-40.4.
Medical faculty practice plan, §116-40.6.

EASTERN NORTH CAROLINA AGRICULTURAL CENTER FUND, §106-6.2, (a).

EASTERN NORTH CAROLINA HOSPITAL.
Department of environment and natural resources.
Control of certain hospitals transferred to department, §131E-67.
Power of secretary to regulate, §131E-67.

EASTERN NORTH CAROLINA SCHOOL FOR THE DEAF AT WILSON.
Education programs in residential schools generally, §§143B-146.1 to 143B-146.21.
See EDUCATION.
Schools for the deaf generally, §§143B-216.40 to 143B-216.44.
See HEARING IMPAIRED.

EAVESDROPPING.
Conference between prisoner and his attorney, §14-227.1, (a).
Admissibility as evidence, §14-227.1, (b).
Violations made misdemeanors, §14-227.3.
Deliberations of grand or petit jury, §14-227.2.
Violations made misdemeanors, §14-227.3.
Electronic surveillance generally, §§15A-286 to 15A-298.
See ELECTRONIC SURVEILLANCE.
Telephones and telegraphs.
Unauthorized connections, §14-155.

ECCLESIASTICAL OFFICERS.
Property of church or religious sect, society or denomination.
Power to acquire, hold and transfer, §61-5.

ECOLOGICAL PROTECTION.
Air pollution control.
See AIR POLLUTION CONTROL.
Balanced growth policy act generally, §§143-506.6 to 143-506.14.
See BALANCED GROWTH POLICY ACT.

ECOLOGICAL PROTECTION —Cont'd
Biological organism act generally, §§106-65.42 to 106-65.49.
See BIOLOGICAL ORGANISM ACT.
Department of environment and natural resources.
See ENVIRONMENT AND NATURAL RESOURCES DEPARTMENT.
Discharges of oil or hazardous substances.
Generally, §§143-215.83 to 143-215.94.
See OIL OR HAZARDOUS SUBSTANCES DISCHARGES.
Offshore oil and gas activities, §§143-215.94AA to 143-215.94JJ.
See OFFSHORE OIL AND GAS ACTIVITIES.
Dry-cleaning solvent cleanup, §§143-215.104A to 143-215.104U.
See DRY-CLEANING SOLVENT CLEANUP.
Environmental compact, §§113A-21 to 113A-23.
Environmental impact statements, §§113A-8 to 113A-13.
See ENVIRONMENTAL IMPACT STATEMENTS.
Environmental management commission, §§143B-282 to 143B-285.
See ENVIRONMENTAL MANAGEMENT COMMISSION.
Environmental policy act, §§113A-1 to 113A-13.
See ENVIRONMENTAL POLICY ACT.
Environmental review commission, §§120-70.41 to 120-70.47.
See ENVIRONMENTAL REVIEW COMMISSION.
Floodplain regulation, §§143-215.51 to 143-215.61.
See FLOODPLAIN REGULATION.
Industrial and pollution control facilities financing.
Industrial and pollution control facilities financing act, §§159C-1 to 159C-27.
See INDUSTRIAL AND POLLUTION CONTROL FACILITIES FINANCING.
North Carolina capital facilities financing act.
North Carolina industrial and pollution control facilities financing act, §§159D-1 to 159D-27.
See INDUSTRIAL AND POLLUTION CONTROL FACILITIES FINANCING.
Leaking petroleum underground storage tank cleanup, §§143-215.94A to 143-215.94Y.
See UNDERGROUND PETROLEUM STORAGE TANK LEAK CLEANUP.
Office of environmental education, §§143B-285.20 to 143B-285.25.
See ENVIRONMENTAL EDUCATION, OFFICE OF.
Pesticides generally.
See PESTICIDES.
Pollution control generally.
See POLLUTION CONTROL.
Sedimentation control commission, §§113A-50 to 113A-67.
See SEDIMENTATION CONTROL COMMISSION.
Stream watch program, §§143-215.74F to 143-215.74I.
Water and air quality reporting, §§143-215.63 to 143-215.69.
See WATER AND AIR QUALITY REPORTING.
Water and air resources.
See WATER AND AIR RESOURCES.
Water resources development projects.
Federal projects, §§143-215.38 to 143-215.43.
See WATER RESOURCES DEVELOPMENT PROJECTS.

ECOLOGICAL PROTECTION —Cont'd
Water resources development projects —Cont'd
Generally, §§143-215.70 to 143-215.73A.
See WATER RESOURCES DEVELOPMENT PROJECTS.
Water supply watershed protection, §§143-214.5 to 143-214.7.
Wetlands restoration program, §§143-214.8 to 143-214.13.
See WETLANDS RESTORATION PROGRAM.

ECONOMICALLY DISADVANTAGED.
Indigent persons.
See INDIGENT PERSONS.
Minimum wage, subminimum wage, §95-25.3, (d).

ECONOMIC AND COMMUNITY DEVELOPMENT.
Commerce department generally, §§143B-427 to 143B-472.81.
See COMMERCE DEPARTMENT.

ECONOMIC DEVELOPMENT AND TRAINING DISTRICTS, §§153A-317.11 to 153A-317.17.
Abolition, §153A-317.16.
Advisory committee for district.
Creation in resolution establishing district, §153A-317.13, (a).
Membership, §153A-317.13, (b).
Recommendations.
Prior to establishing budget and levying tax, §153A-317.13, (c).
Annexation of territory to district.
Effective date of resolution, §153A-317.14, (d).
Findings required, §153A-317.14, (a).
Notice of public hearing, §153A-317.14, (c).
Public hearing, §153A-317.14, (c).
Report by board prior to public hearing, §153A-317.14, (b).
Resolution of board of commissioners, §153A-317.14, (a).
Establishment.
Effective date of resolution creating, §153A-317.12, (e).
Findings required to establish, §153A-317.12, (b).
Notice of public hearing, §153A-317.12, (d).
Public hearing, §153A-317.12, (d).
Report by board of commissioners.
Prior to public hearing on establishing, §153A-317.12, (c).
Resolution of board of commissioners, §153A-317.12, (a).
Standards for area or areas of county where established, §153A-317.12, (a).
Petition requesting abolition, §153A-317.16.
Property taxes.
County may levy within district, rate limitation, §153A-317.17.
Purposes for which created, §153A-317.11.
Skills training center.
Additions to.
Required when district extended, §153A-317.15, (b).
Providing for and maintaining.
Required when creating new district, §153A-317.15, (a).
Purposes for creating district, §153A-317.11.

ECONOMIC DEVELOPMENT COMMISSIONS, §§158-8 to 158-15.
Appropriations.
Localities, §158-12.

ECONOMIC DEVELOPMENT COMMISSIONS —Cont'd
Committees.
Appointment, §158-9.
Composition, §158-8.
Contracts.
Service contracts, §158-10.
Counties.
Regional planning and economic development commissions.
Authorized, §158-14.
Creation.
Authorized, §158-8.
Deposits, §158-12.1.
Duties.
General provisions, §158-13.
Equipment.
Lease or purchase, §158-11.
Federal aid.
Acceptance, §158-12.
Meetings, §158-9.
Northeastern North Carolina regional economic development commission.
Counties served, §158-8.2, (a).
Created, §158-8.2, (a).
Director of economic development, §158-8.2, (g).
Director of tourism, §158-8.2, (g).
Economic development advisory board, §158-8.2, (e).
Meetings.
Initial meeting, §158-8.2, (d1).
Members, §158-8.2, (b).
Office space, §158-8.2, (g).
Per diem and travel expenses, §158-8.2, (h).
Personnel, §158-8.2, (g).
Powers and duties, §158-8.2, (f).
Removal of members, §158-8.4.
Reports to general assembly, §158-8.2, (f).
Terms of members, §158-8.2, (c).
Vacancies, §158-8.2, (d).
Offices.
Lease or rent of space, §158-11.
Organization, §158-9.
Powers.
General provisions, §158-13.
Supplementary, §158-15.
Regional commissions.
Authorized, §158-14.
Joining, §158-8.
Withdrawal from commission, §158-8.
Rules and regulations.
Adoption, §158-9.
Sales and use tax.
Refunds, §105-164.14, (c).
Southeastern North Carolina regional economic development commission.
Contracts, §158-8.3, (f).
Counties served, §158-8.3, (a).
Created, §158-8.3, (a).
Meetings.
Initial meeting, §158-8.3, (c1).
Members, §158-8.3, (b).
Per diem and travel expenses, §158-8.3, (d).
Personnel, §158-8.3, (f).
Powers and duties, §158-8.3, (e).
Removal of members, §158-8.4.
Report to general assembly, §158-8.3, (e).
Terms, §158-8.3, (c).
Vacancies, §158-8.3, (c).
Staff, §158-10.

ECONOMIC DEVELOPMENT COMMISSIONS —Cont'd
Western North Carolina regional economic development commission.
Counties served, §158-8.1, (a).
Created, §158-8.1, (a).
Meetings.
Initial meeting, §158-8.1, (c1).
Members, §158-8.1, (b).
Per diem and travel expenses, §158-8.1, (d).
Powers and duties, §158-8.1, (e).
Removal of members, §158-8.4.
Terms of members, §158-8.1, (c).
Vacancies, §158-8.1, (c).

ECONOMIC INTEREST STATEMENTS.
General assembly, §§120-89 to 120-98.
See GENERAL ASSEMBLY.

ECONOMIC OR MONETARY LOSS.
Action to recover damages for defective or unsafe condition of improvement to real property.
Limitation of actions, §1-50, (a).
Retaliatory employment discrimination civil actions.
Award to employee, §95-243, (c).
Trade secrets, action for misappropriation.
Actual damages recovered measured by, §66-154, (b).

ECONOMIC PROGRESS.
Balanced growth policy act, §§143-506.6 to 143-506.14.

EDDIE BRIDGES FUND, §143-250.1, (a) to (h).

EDENTON HISTORICAL COMMISSION.
Appointments, §143B-98.
Compensation of members, §143B-98.
Creation, §143B-95.
Department of cultural resources.
Transfer of commission to department, §143B-51.
Duties, §143B-95.
Exemption from provisions, §143B-96.
Members, §143B-98.
Powers and duties, §143B-95.
Quorum, §143B-98.
Reports, §143B-97.
Selection of members, §143B-98.
Status, §143B-96.

EDGECOMBE COUNTY.
Agricultural tendencies in certain counties.
Terms of, §42-23.
Ambulance service.
Attachment or garnishment and lien for, §§44-51.4 to 44-51.8.
Condemnation or acquisition of land by local government unit outside county.
Consent of board of commissioners necessary, §153A-15.
Cropper or tenant refusing to perform terms of contract.
Forfeiture of right of possession to premises, §42-27.
Game laws, local acts not repealed, §113-133.1, (e).
Global TransPark development zone, §§158-30 to 158-42.
See GLOBAL TRANSPARK DEVELOPMENT ZONE.
Housing authority commissioners.
Tenant as commissioner, exemption from provision of law allowing, §157-5.

EDGECOMBE COUNTY —Cont'd
Industrial development.
Tax elections, §§158-16 to 158-24.
See INDUSTRIAL DEVELOPMENT.
Low-income housing tax credits.
Qualified building eligible for credit, §105-129.41, (c).
Probate and registration orders before clerks of inferior courts validated, §47-59.
Registration of deeds.
Tax certification, no delinquent taxes due, §161-31, (b).
School property.
Acquisition and improvement, §153A-158.1.
Sheriff.
Vacancy, performance of duties until vacancy filled, §162-5.1.
Tax elections for industrial development purposes, §§158-16 to 158-24.
Taxicabs.
Certificates of necessity and convenience, §20-87.
Wild plants, taking of certain plants from land of another.
Inapplicability of provisions, §14-129.

EDUCATION.
Academic credit.
Fraudulent means in obtaining credit, §14-118.2, (b).
Accountants, §93-12.
Actions.
Local boards of education.
Actions by and against boards, §115C-44, (a), (b).
Defense of members and employees, §115C-43, (a) to (d).
Tort or negligence action against board, §115C-42.
Administrative procedure, §115C-2.
Adult education.
Entitlement to attend, §115C-231, (c).
Free tuition.
Persons 18 years of age or older not having completed high school, §115C-231, (b).
Organization and administration of program, §115C-231, (a).
Removal or prohibiting enrollment.
Persons having attained age of 21 years, §115C-231, (c).
Aged persons.
Senior citizen tuition waiver, §§115B-1 to 115B-6.
Alcohol addicted children.
Appropriate education provided for.
Policy of state to insure, §115C-149.
Children with special needs.
Alcohol addicted children excluded from article, §115C-149.
Policy of state, §115C-149.
State board of education to adopt rules, §115C-150.
Appeals.
Budget dispute between board of education and board of county commissioners.
Procedure for resolution, §115C-431, (c) to (e).
Employees.
Repayment of money owed to state.
Delinquent employees, §143-554, (a).
Local boards of education.
Appeals to local boards, §115C-45, (c).
Appeals to superior court, §115C-45, (c).

EDUCATION —Cont'd
Appropriations.
Additional to receipts, §143-27.
Arts.
North Carolina School of the Arts, §§116-63 to 116-69.
See UNIVERSITY OF NORTH CAROLINA.
At-risk students.
Extended service programs, §§115C-238.30 to 115C-238.33.
See AT-RISK STUDENTS.
Attorneys at law.
Continuing legal education, CLE Rules 1 to 27.
See CONTINUING LEGAL EDUCATION.
Bail bondsmen and runners.
Approval of courses, §58-71-71, (d).
Continuing education, §58-71-71, (b), (c).
Failure to comply with requirements, §58-71-71, (e).
Instructor's qualifications, §58-71-72, (a), (b).
Qualifications of instructors, §58-71-72, (a), (b).
Requirements, §58-71-71, (a), (b).
Exemptions, §58-71-71, (c).
Rules and regulations, §58-71-71, (f).
Basic education program, §115C-81.
Bequests.
State board of education.
Power to accept bequests, §115C-410.
Black Mountain Advancement Center for Women.
Educational and vocational training for inmates, §143B-269, (f).
Blind children.
Governor Morehead school, §§143B-164.10 to 143B-164.17.
See GOVERNOR MOREHEAD SCHOOL.
Boards of education.
Local boards, §§115C-35 to 115C-50.
See LOCAL BOARDS OF EDUCATION.
State board of education.
See STATE BOARD OF EDUCATION.
Bond issues.
State debt, §§142-1 to 142-29.7.
See STATE DEBT.
Budgets.
Public schools generally, §§115C-425 to 115C-434.
See SCHOOL DISTRICTS AND ADMINISTRATIVE UNITS.
Buildings.
Generally, §§115C-517 to 115C-528.
See SCHOOL BUILDINGS AND PROPERTY.
Buses.
School buses.
See SCHOOL BUSES.
Business and education technology alliance, §115C-102.15.
Cabinet, §116C-1.
Capital facilities finance.
Private capital facilities finance act.
Institutions for higher education and elementary and secondary education, §§159D-35 to 159D-57.
See CAPITAL FACILITIES FINANCE AGENCY.
Charitable gift annuities.
Generally, §58-3-6.
Charter schools, §§115C-238.29A to 115C-238.29K.
See CHARTER SCHOOLS.
Cheating.
Academic credit obtained by fraudulent means, §14-118.2.

EDUCATION —Cont'd
Children with chemical dependency.
Appropriate education provided drug and alcohol addicted children.
Policy of state to insure, §115C-149.
Policy of state, §115C-149.
Rules and regulations.
State board to adopt rules, §115C-150.
Special education.
Children with special needs.
Drugs and alcohol addicted children excluded from article, §115C-149.
State board of education.
Adoption of rules, §115C-150.
Chiropractors.
Requirements for licensure, §90-143, (b).
Church schools and schools of religious charter, §§115C-547 to 115C-554.
See CHURCH SCHOOLS AND SCHOOLS OF RELIGIOUS CHARTER.
Committees.
School committees.
Discipline of students.
Use of force may not be prohibited, §115C-390.
Community colleges, §§115D-1 to 115D-97.
See COMMUNITY COLLEGES.
Community schools act, §§115C-203 to 115C-209.
See COMMUNITY SCHOOLS ACT.
Compulsory attendance law, §§115C-378 to 115C-383.
See COMPULSORY SCHOOL ATTENDANCE.
Confidentiality.
Contractors prohibited from selling personally identifiable student information, §115C-401.1.
Penalty for disclosure of certain information, §115C-13.
State board of education.
Duty to maintain confidentiality of certain information, §115C-13.
Statewide testing program.
Public records exemption, §115C-174.13.
Student records, §115C-402.
Consolidation of administrative units and school districts, §§115C-68 to 115C-72.
Contempt.
Local boards of education.
Power to punish for contempt, §115C-45, (a).
Continuum of education programs.
Strategic design to be developed by education cabinet, §116C-3.
Council on educational services for exceptional children, §115C-121.
Criminal justice education and training standards, §§17C-1 to 17C-12.
See CRIMINAL JUSTICE EDUCATION AND TRAINING STANDARDS COMMISSION.
Criminal record checks of school personnel, §114-19.2.
Definitions, §115C-5.
Children with special needs, §115C-109.
Employees.
Repayment of money owed to state, §143-552.
Senior citizens.
Tuition waiver, §115B-1.
Special education, §115C-108.
Vocational and technical education, §115C-152.
Department of public instruction.
Confidentiality.
Duty to maintain confidentiality of certain records, §115C-13.

EDUCATION —Cont'd
Department of public instruction —Cont'd
Confidentiality of certain records.
Disclosure by member, officer or employee, §115C-13.
Created, §143A-44.1.
Head of department.
State board of education, §143A-44.1.
Impaired driving.
Forfeiture of motor vehicles.
Contracts for services to tow, store, process, maintain, and sell seized vehicles.
Authorized, §20-28.9, (a).
Fees, §20-28.9, (b), (c).
Interstate compact for education.
Rights, duties and privileges, §143A-45.
Office of environmental education.
Liaison between office and department, §143B-285.25.
Office of superintendent of public instruction.
Transferred to department of public instruction, §143A-44.3.
Records.
Duty to maintain confidentiality of certain records, §115C-13.
Salaries for employees injured during an episode of violence, §115C-338.
State board of education.
Head of department, §143A-44.1.
Transfer of powers and duties to state board, §143A-44.2.
Superintendent of public instruction to be secretary and chief administrative officer of state board of education, §143A-44.3.
Textbook commission.
Transfer to department of public instruction, §143A-48.
Transfer of powers and duties to state board of education, §143A-44.2.
Transferred to department of public instruction, §143A-44.3.
Dietitians and nutritionists.
License requirements, §90-357.
Discipline of students.
See DISCIPLINE OF STUDENTS.
Districts.
Local government finance generally, §§159-1 to 159-188.
See LOCAL GOVERNMENT FINANCE.
School districts.
See SCHOOL DISTRICTS AND ADMINISTRATIVE UNITS.
Driver education, §§20-88.1, 115C-215, 115C-216.
Driver training school licensing, §§20-320 to 20-328.
See DRIVER TRAINING SCHOOL LICENSING.
Dropout rates.
Reporting, reducing.
Powers and duties of state board of education, §115C-12.
Drug addicted children.
Appropriate education provided for.
Policy of state to insure, §115C-149.
Children with special needs.
Drug addicted children excluded from article, §115C-149.
Conditions governing prescribed punishments and degree of offenses, §90-95, (e).
Policy of state, §115C-149.
State board of education to adopt rules, §115C-150.

EDUCATION —Cont'd
Early childhood initiatives, §§143B-168.10 to 143B-168.16.
See EARLY CHILDHOOD INITIATIVES.
Education assistance authority, §§116-201 to 116-209.35.
See EDUCATION ASSISTANCE AUTHORITY.
Education commission, §§143-261 to 143-266.
See EDUCATION COMMISSION.
Elections.
Local boards of education, §115C-37.
State education commission officers, §143-262.
Electrologists.
Continuing education.
License renewal.
Requirements, §88A-13.
Embezzlement.
Funds embezzled by public officers and trustees, §14-92.
Emergency paramedical program.
Duty of state board of education to provide for, §115C-12.
Encouragement of education, Const. N. C., art. IX, §1.
Endowment funds, §§115C-490 to 115C-494.
Engineers and land surveyors.
Requirements for licensure generally, §89C-13.
Environmental education, office of, §§143B-285.20 to 143B-285.25.
See ENVIRONMENTAL EDUCATION, OFFICE OF.
Evaluation of certified employees, §§115C-333 to 115C-335.
Exceptional children.
Council on educational services for exceptional children, §115C-121.
Special education.
See SPECIAL EDUCATION.
Eye protection devices, §§115C-166 to 115C-169.
See VOCATIONAL AND TECHNICAL EDUCATION.
Federal aid.
State board of education.
Power to accept federal funds and aid, §115C-409, (a), (b).
First in America innovative education act.
Annual report, §116C-4, (c).
Cooperative efforts.
Secondary schools and institutions of higher education, §116C-4, (a).
Funding, §116C-4, (b).
Fiscal control of public schools, §§115C-435 to 115C-452.
See SCHOOL DISTRICTS AND ADMINISTRATIVE UNITS.
Forgery.
Diplomas, §14-122.1.
Transcripts, §14-122.1.
Fraud.
Academic credit by fraudulent means.
Assisting, etc., in obtaining credit, §14-118.2, (a), (b).
Senior citizens.
Tuition waiver.
Misrepresentation of eligibility, §115B-6.
Funds.
Apportionment by state board, §115C-12.
Capital outlay fund, §115C-426, (c), (f).
Computer loan revolving fund, §115C-472.5.
County school fund.
Composition of fund, Const. N. C., art. IX, §7.

EDUCATION —Cont'd
Funds —Cont'd
Critical school facility needs fund, §§115C-489.1, 115C-489.2.
Endowment funds, §§115C-490 to 115C-494.
Local current expense fund, §115C-426, (c), (e).
Management of institutional funds, §§36B-1 to 36B-10.
See MANAGEMENT OF INSTITUTIONAL FUNDS.
Public school building capital fund, §§115C-546.1, 115C-546.2.
Public school insurance fund, §§115C-536, 115C-539, 115C-541.
Scholarship loan fund for prospective teachers, §§115C-468 to 115C-472.1.
See TEACHERS.
State fund.
Penalties, fines and forfeitures collected by state agencies (effective upon approval), Const. N. C., art. IX, §7.
State literary fund, §§115C-458 to 115C-467.
See STATE LITERARY FUND.
State public school fund, §115C-426, (c), (d).
State school fund.
Composition of fund, Const. N. C., art. IX, §6.
General and uniform system of schools, §115C-1; Const. N. C., art. IX, §2.
General assembly.
Joint legislative education oversight committee, §§120-70.80 to 120-70.83.
Local government fiscal information act, §§120-30.41 to 120-30.49.
Geologists.
Licenses.
Minimum qualifications, §89E-9.
Gifts.
Charitable gift annuities, §58-3-6.
State board of education.
Power to accept gifts, §115C-410.
Governor Morehead School.
Education programs in residential schools generally, §§143B-146.1 to 143B-146 .21. See within this heading, "Residential schools."
State school for sight impaired children, §§143B-164.10 to 143B-164.17.
See GOVERNOR MOREHEAD SCHOOL.
Grants.
State board of education.
Power to accept grants, §115C-410.
Handicapped persons.
Preschool handicapped children.
Special education, §§115C-146.1 to 115C-146.4.
See SPECIAL EDUCATION.
Right to habilitation and rehabilitation services, §168-8.
Special education.
See SPECIAL EDUCATION.
State school for hearing-impaired children, §§143B-216.40 to 143B-216.44.
See HEARING IMPAIRED.
Hearing aid dealers and fitters.
Occupational instruction courses.
Board may require as prerequisite to license renewal, §93D-11.
Qualifications for licenses, §93D-5, (a).
Hearing-impaired children.
Schools for the deaf generally, §§143B-216.40 to 143B-216.44.
See HEARING IMPAIRED.

EDUCATION —Cont'd
Higher education.
Benefits of public institutions to the people of state free of expense, Const. N. C., art. IX, §9.
Community colleges, §§115D-1 to 115D-97.
See COMMUNITY COLLEGES.
Maintenance of public system of higher education, Const. N. C., art. IX, §8.
North Carolina school of the arts, §§116-63 to 116-69.
See UNIVERSITY OF NORTH CAROLINA.
Students.
Escheats.
Disposition of escheats after June 30, 1971, Const. N. C., art. IX, §10.
Universities and colleges.
See UNIVERSITIES AND COLLEGES.
University of North Carolina, §§116-1 to 116-44.5.
See UNIVERSITY OF NORTH CAROLINA.
Home schools, §§115C-563 to 115C-565.
Hospitals.
Health education facilities.
Sale or lease, §131E-8.1.
Immunity.
Local boards of education, §115C-42.
Income withholding.
Local board of education employees.
Charitable organization approved by local board.
Deduction of contribution from salary or wage, §143-3.3, (i).
Indians.
State advisory council on Indian education, §§115C-210 to 115C-210.4.
See INDIANS.
Information.
Access to information and public records, §115C-3.
Infractions.
Motor vehicles.
Powers of local boards of education to regulate parking, §115C-46, (a).
Institutional fund management, §§36B-1 to 36B-10.
See MANAGEMENT OF INSTITUTIONAL FUNDS.
Insurance.
Continuing education program for licensees, §§58-33-130, 58-33-135.
Local boards of education.
Liability insurance, §115C-42.
State insurance of public school property, §§115C-533 to 115C-543.
See SCHOOL BUILDINGS AND PROPERTY.
Interstate agreement on qualifications of educational personnel, §§115C-349 to 115C-358.
See SCHOOL EMPLOYEES.
Interstate compact for education.
Department of public education.
Rights, duties and privileges, §143A-45.
Enactment of compact, §115C-104.
State superintendent of public instruction.
Rights, duties and privileges, §143A-45.
Text of compact, §115C-104.
Investments.
State board of education.
Authority to invest school funds, §115C-411.
Joint legislative education oversight committee, §§120-70.80 to 120-70.83.
Justice academy, §§17D-1 to 17D-4.

EDUCATION —Cont'd
Local boards of education, §§115C-35 to 115C-50.
See LOCAL BOARDS OF EDUCATION.
Local government finance.
Budget and fiscal control.
Application of article to school administrative units, §159-7, (d).
Local government fiscal information act, §§120-30.41 to 120-30.49.
See GENERAL ASSEMBLY.
Management of institutional funds, §§36B-1 to 36B-10.
See MANAGEMENT OF INSTITUTIONAL FUNDS.
Marriage and family therapists.
Continuing education requirements, §90-270.58C.
Licensing requirements, §90-270.54.
Recognized educational institution.
Defined, §90-270.47.
Massage and bodywork therapy.
Approval of schools.
Rules of board, §90-631.
Continuing education.
License renewal, §90-632.
Qualifications for licensure, §90-629.
Meetings.
Open meetings law, §115C-4.
Merger of administrative units and school districts, §§115C-68 to 115C-72.
Militia.
Commissions for commandants and officers at qualified educational institutions, §127A-23.
Misdemeanors.
Confidentiality of certain records.
Disclosure, §115C-13.
Negligence.
Local boards of education.
Action against board, §115C-42.
Nonprofit corporations.
Certain associations deemed incorporated, §55A-17-02.
Notice.
State board of education.
Special meetings, §115C-11, (c).
Nurses.
Baccalaureate in nursing candidate credits, §90-171.41.
Continuing education.
Approval of programs by board, §90-171.42, (a).
Advanced skills, §90-171.42, (b).
Emergency financial assistance fund.
Established, §90-171.51.
Licensing exam follow-up assistance, §90-171.52.
Local health directors.
Nurse pilot program, §130A-40.1, (a) to (c).
Need-based nursing scholarships fund.
Establishment, §90-171.65.
Publicity program.
Salary levels, job opportunities, refresher courses and license renewal requirements.
Developing publicity on, §90-171.53.
Scholarship and loan information.
Consolidation, §90-171.50.
Nursing scholars program, §§90-171.60 to 90-171.62.
Nursing home administrators.
Continuing education.
Powers of board as to, §90-286.
Qualifications for licenses, §90-278.
Oaths.
Chairman of the board of education.
Administration of oaths by chairman, §11-9.

EDUCATION —Cont'd
Oaths —Cont'd
Local boards of education.
Oath of office, §115C-37, (d).
Occupational safety and health.
Commissioner of labor.
Powers and duties, §95-147, (a), (b).
Open meetings law, §115C-4.
Opticians.
Qualifications, §90-237.
Optometrists.
Continuing education courses required, §90-123.1.
Osteopaths.
Requirements, §90-131.
Parking violations, §115C-46, (a).
Parochial schools generally, §§115C-547 to 115C-554.
See CHURCH SCHOOLS AND SCHOOLS OF RELIGIOUS CHARTER.
Payroll deductions.
Local board of education employee.
Charitable organization approved by local board.
Deduction of contribution from salary or wages, §143-3.3, (i).
Personnel evaluation of certified school employees, §§115C-333 to 115C-335.
Podiatrists.
Continuing education courses required, §90-202.11.
Qualifications for examination, §90-202.5.
Principals, §§115C-284 to 115C-289.
See PRINCIPALS OF SCHOOLS.
Prisons and prisoners.
Facilities and programs for selected inmates, §148-22.1, (a), (b).
Private capital facilities finance act.
Institutions for higher education and elementary and secondary education, §§159D-35 to 159D-57.
See CAPITAL FACILITIES FINANCE AGENCY.
Private schools.
See PRIVATE SCHOOLS.
Property taxes.
Supplementary taxes for school purposes, §§115C-500 to 115C-513.
See SCHOOL DISTRICTS AND ADMINISTRATIVE UNITS.
Use for, §§105-278.4 to 105-278.7.
Proprietary schools, §§115D-87 to 115D-97.
See PROPRIETARY SCHOOLS.
Public instruction department. See within this heading, "Department of public instruction."
Public lands.
State board of education.
Notice to board of sales, §146-4.
Public records.
Access to information and public records, §115C-3.
Student records not public, §115C-402.
Public school buildings and property generally, §§115C-517 to 115C-528.
See SCHOOL BUILDINGS AND PROPERTY.
Public school employees.
Administrator qualifications and standards, §§115C-290.1 to 115C-290.9.
See SCHOOL ADMINISTRATOR QUALIFICATIONS AND STANDARDS.
Evaluation of certified employees, §§115C-333 to 115C-335.

EDUCATION —Cont'd
Public school employees —Cont'd
Generally.
See SCHOOL EMPLOYEES.
Principals, §§115C-284 to 115C-289.
See PRINCIPALS OF SCHOOLS.
Superintendents of schools, §§115C-271 to 115C-278.
See SUPERINTENDENTS OF SCHOOLS.
Supervisors, §§115C-284 to 115C-289.
See SUPERVISORS OF SCHOOLS.
Teachers, §§115C-295 to 115C-309.
See TEACHERS.
Public schools generally.
See PUBLIC SCHOOLS.
Records.
Access to information and public records, §115C-3.
Confidentiality of certain records.
State board of education or department of public education.
Duty to maintain, §115C-13.
State board of education.
Record of proceedings, §115C-11, (g).
Statewide testing program.
Public records exemption, §115C-174.13.
Student records.
Maintenance, contents and confidentiality, §115C-402.
Recreational trespass.
Definition of "educational purpose," §38A-2.
Generally, §§38A-1 to 38A-4.
Regional organization of schools, §115C-65.
Research.
Local boards of education.
Authorization to conduct, §115C-230.
Powers to sponsor or conduct, §115C-47.
Special projects.
Local boards authorized to sponsor or conduct, §115C-230.
State board of education.
Power to conduct education research, §115C-12.
Residence.
Local school boards.
Requirements for members, §115C-35, (b).
Residential schools.
ABC's program.
Annual performance goals, §143B-146.3.
Decision making and parental involvement, §143B-146.2, (c).
Defined, §143B-146.1, (b).
Participation in program, §143B-146.2, (a).
Flexibility in use of funds, §143B-146.2, (d).
Guidelines, §143B-146.2, (b).
Appeals from decisions of school personnel to secretary, §143B-146.14.
Calendars, §143B-146.11.
Criminal acts.
Duty to report to law enforcement, §143B-146.15.
Criminal history checks of school personnel.
Definitions, §143B-146.16, (a).
Department of justice.
Duties, §143B-146.16, (c).
Fingerprints.
Applicant not to be required to pay for being fingerprinted, §143B-146.16, (c).
Negligence.
Immunity from liability, §143B-146.16, (g).
Privileged information, §143B-146.16, (f).
Review by state board of education, §143B-146.16, (e).

EDUCATION —Cont'd
Residential schools —Cont'd
Criminal history checks of school personnel —Cont'd
Review of criminal history by secretary, §143B-146.16, (d).
Secretary to require, §143B-146.16, (b).
Definitions, §143B-146.1, (b).
Criminal history checks of school personnel, §143B-146.16, (a).
School property, §143B-146.15.
Dispute resolution, §143B-146.14.
Duties of secretary of health and human services, §143B-146.21, (a), (b).
Independent living facilities.
Policies to ensure that students are given priority to residing in, §143B-146.21, (d).
Low-performing schools.
Annual review of progress, §143B-146.6, (d).
Assessment teams, §143B-146.9.
Duties, §143B-146.9.
Assistance teams, §143B-146.6, (a), (b).
Recommendations, §143B-146.6, (c).
Certificated personnel.
Action plans, §143B-146.8, (b).
Annual evaluations, §143B-146.8, (a).
Reevaluation, §143B-146.8, (c).
Standards and criteria for, §143B-146.10.
Assessment teams, §143B-146.9.
Consequences of identification as low-performing school for, §143B-146.7, (b) to (d).
Dismissal.
State board notification, §143B-146.8, (d).
Negligence in action taken under provisions.
Civil immunity, §143B-146.8, (e).
Performance standards and criteria for, §143B-146.10.
Contracts of school administrators.
Termination if dismissed, §143B-146.7, (e).
Identification, §143B-146.5, (a), (b).
Written notification to parents, §143B-146.5, (c).
Superintendents.
Consequences of identification as low-performing school for superintendent, §143B-146.7, (a).
Evaluation, §143B-146.8, (f).
Mission of schools, §143B-146.1, (a).
Performance recognition, §143B-146.4, (a).
Allocation of funds for awards, §143B-146.4, (b).
Professional development opportunities.
Availability to be offered and communicated, §143B-146.21, (c).
School calendar, §143B-146.11.
School improvement plans, §143B-146.12, (a).
Action by secretary on, §143B-146.12, (e).
Availability and accessibility to parents and school community.
Secretary to ensure, §143B-146.12, (i).
Duration, §143B-146.12, (f).
Recommendation of strategies by secretary, §143B-146.12, (h).
Review and vote by instructional personnel, §143B-146.12, (d).
Strategies for improving student performance, §143B-146.12, (c).
Use of funds made available, §143B-146.12, (g).
School improvement teams, §143B-146.12, (a), (b).
School technology plan, §143B-146.13, (a).
Use of funds, §143B-146.13, (b).

EDUCATION —Cont'd
Rules and regulations.
Drug and alcohol addicted children.
State board of education to adopt rules, §115C-150.
Educational institutions.
Sanitation regulated by commission for health services, §§130A-235, 130A-236.
Motor vehicles.
Powers of local boards of education to regulate parking, §115C-46, (a).
Private educational institutions.
Sanitation regulated by commission for health services, §§130A-235, 130A-236.
Senior citizens.
Tuition waiver.
Promulgation, §115B-3.
State board of education, §115C-11, (h).
Safe and orderly schools.
Local plans for maintaining, §§115C-105.45 to 115C-105.47.
Salaries.
Commission.
Executive secretary, §143-265.
Local board of education employees.
Deductions from salaries.
Charitable organization approved by local board.
Contributions, §143-3.3, (i).
Sanitarians continuing education, §90A-63, (c).
School administrative units.
Generally.
See SCHOOL DISTRICTS AND ADMINISTRATIVE UNITS.
School administrator qualifications and standards, §§115C-290.1 to 115C-290.9.
See SCHOOL ADMINISTRATOR QUALIFICATIONS AND STANDARDS.
School-based management and accountability program.
Generally, §§115C-105.20 to 115C-105.41.
See PUBLIC SCHOOLS.
Residential schools.
ABC's program, §§143B-146.1 to 143B-146.21.
See within this heading, "Residential schools."
School boards.
Local boards of education, §§115C-35 to 115C-50.
See LOCAL BOARDS OF EDUCATION.
State board of education.
See STATE BOARD OF EDUCATION.
School budget and fiscal control act.
Generally, §§115C-422 to 115C-452.
See SCHOOL DISTRICTS AND ADMINISTRATIVE UNITS.
School buildings and property, §§115C-517 to 115C-528.
See SCHOOL BUILDINGS AND PROPERTY.
School buses.
See SCHOOL BUSES.
School committees.
Discipline of students.
Use of force may not be prohibited, §115C-390.
School districts.
See SCHOOL DISTRICTS AND ADMINISTRATIVE UNITS.
School employees.
See SCHOOL EMPLOYEES.
School for sight impaired children.
Governor Morehead school, §§143B-164.10 to 143B-164.17.
See GOVERNOR MOREHEAD SCHOOL.

EDUCATION —Cont'd
Schools for the deaf.
Education programs in residential schools generally, §§143B-146.1 to 143B-146.21. See within this heading, "Residential schools."
Generally, §§143B-216.40 to 143B-216.44.
See HEARING IMPAIRED.
Science and mathematics school of the University of North Carolina, §§116-230.1 to 116-238.1.
See UNIVERSITY OF NORTH CAROLINA.
Searches and seizures.
Disposition of seized, confiscated or unclaimed property.
Sale proceeds to county boards of education, §15-15.
Senior citizens tuition waiver, §§115B-1 to 115B-6.
Authorization, §115B-2.
Credit for scholarship value, §115B-5A.
Definition, §115B-1.
Eligibility, §115B-2, (a).
Misrepresentation, §115B-6.
Proof, §115B-5, (a), (b).
Enrollment computation for funding purposes, §115B-4.
Misrepresentation of eligibility, §115B-6.
Proof of eligibility, §115B-5, (a), (b).
Rules and regulations.
Promulgation, §115B-3.
Space available basis, §115B-2, (b).
Standards, §115B-2, (b).
Sheriffs' education and training standards commission, §§17E-1 to 17E-12.
See SHERIFFS' EDUCATION AND TRAINING STANDARDS COMMISSION.
Special education.
See SPECIAL EDUCATION.
Speech and language pathologists and audiologists.
Qualifications of applicants for licensure, §90-295.
Sports medicine.
State board of education.
Duty to provide for, §115C-12.
State board of education.
See STATE BOARD OF EDUCATION.
State education assistance authority, §§116-201 to 116-209.35.
See EDUCATION ASSISTANCE AUTHORITY.
State education commission, §§143-261 to 143-266.
See EDUCATION COMMISSION.
State literary fund, §§115C-458 to 115C-467.
See STATE LITERARY FUND.
State school for sight impaired children.
Governor Morehead school, §§143B-164.10 to 143B-164.17.
See GOVERNOR MOREHEAD SCHOOL.
State schools for hearing-impaired children.
Schools for the deaf generally, §§143B-216.40 to 143B-216.44.
See HEARING IMPAIRED.
State superintendent of public instruction.
See SUPERINTENDENT OF PUBLIC INSTRUCTION.
Statewide testing program, §§115C-174.10 to 115C-174.14.
See PUBLIC SCHOOLS.
Subpoenas.
Local boards of education.
Power to subpoena, §115C-45, (a).

EDUCATION —Cont'd
Summer schools.
Local financing, §115C-232.
Operation, §115C-233.
Sunshine act.
Open meetings law, §115C-4.
Superintendent of public instruction.
See SUPERINTENDENT OF PUBLIC INSTRUCTION.
Superintendents of schools, §§115C-271 to 115C-278.
See SUPERINTENDENTS OF SCHOOLS.
Superior courts.
Local boards of education.
Appeals to superior court, §115C-45, (c).
Supervisors of schools, §§115C-284 to 115C-289.
See SUPERVISORS OF SCHOOLS.
Supplementary taxes for school purposes, §§115C-500 to 115C-513.
See SCHOOL DISTRICTS AND ADMINISTRATIVE UNITS.
Taking indecent liberties with a student, §14-202.4.
Taxation.
Supplementary taxes for school purposes, §§115C-500 to 115C-513.
See SCHOOL DISTRICTS AND ADMINISTRATIVE UNITS.
Teacher enhancement program.
Teaching fellows commission, §§115C-363.22, 115C-363.23.
Teaching fellows program, §115C-363.23A.
Teachers.
Generally, §§115C-295 to 115C-309.
See TEACHERS.
Retirement system for teachers and state employees.
See RETIREMENT SYSTEM FOR TEACHERS AND STATE EMPLOYEES.
Technical education generally.
See VOCATIONAL AND TECHNICAL EDUCATION.
Technology.
Business and education technology alliance, §115C-102.15.
School technology commission, §§115C-102.5 to 115C-102.7.
School technology plan, §§115C-102.6A to 115C-102.6D.
Statewide testing program, §§115C-174.10 to 115C-174.14.
See PUBLIC SCHOOLS.
Technology alliance, §115C-102.15.
Textbooks generally, §§115C-85 to 115C-102.
See TEXTBOOKS.
Trespass.
Recreational trespass.
Definition of "educational purpose," §38A-2.
Generally, §§38A-1 to 38A-4.
See RECREATIONAL TRESPASS.
Tuition.
Senior citizen tuition waiver, §§115B-1 to 115B-6.
Uniform system of schools, §115C-1; Const. N. C., art. IX, §2.
Universities and colleges.
See UNIVERSITIES AND COLLEGES.
University of North Carolina, §§116-1 to 116-44.5.
See UNIVERSITY OF NORTH CAROLINA.
Veterinarians.
Continuing education.
Powers of board as to, §90-186.

EDUCATION —Cont'd
Violence.
Salaries for employees injured during an episode of violence, §115C-338.
Vocational education generally.
See VOCATIONAL AND TECHNICAL EDUCATION.
Voted tax supplements for school purposes, §§115C-500 to 115C-513.
See SCHOOL DISTRICTS AND ADMINISTRATIVE UNITS.
Wastewater treatment.
Certification of water pollution control system operators.
Powers of certification commission, §90A-43.
Water treatment facility operators.
Powers of board as to, §90A-28.
Qualifications for certificates.
Establishment, §90A-24.
Witnesses.
Local boards of education.
Failure to appear, §115C-45, (b).

EDUCATIONAL ASSOCIATIONS.
Sales and use tax refunds.
Educational institutions not operated for profit, §105-164.14, (b).
Solicitation of contributions, §§131F-1 to 131F-24.
See CHARITABLE SOLICITATION.

EDUCATIONAL DISTRICTS ENUMERATED, §115C-65.

EDUCATIONAL PERSONNEL QUALIFICATIONS.
Administrator qualifications and standards, §§115C-290.1 to 115C-290.9.
See SCHOOL ADMINISTRATOR QUALIFICATIONS AND STANDARDS.
Interstate agreement, §§115C-349 to 115C-358.
See SCHOOL EMPLOYEES.
Personnel evaluation of certified employees, §§115C-333 to 115C-335.

EDUCATIONAL TELEVISION.
Agency for public telecommunications, §§143B-426.8 to 143B-426.20.
See PUBLIC TELECOMMUNICATIONS, AGENCY FOR.

EDUCATION ASSISTANCE AUTHORITY, §§116-201 to 116-209.35.
Acquisition of obligations, §§116-206, 116-207.
Acts or undertakings.
Defined, §116-201, (b).
Fees.
Powers as to, §116-204.
Limited to revenues, §116-202.
Board of directors, §116-203.
Board of governors of University of North Carolina.
Cooperation, §116-209.21.
Bond issues.
Authorized, §116-209.4.
Bond holder remedies, §116-209.8.
Credit of state not pledged, §116-209.12.
Definitions, §116-201, (b).
Investments.
Eligibility for investment, §116-209.10.
Issuance of bonds, §116-209.4.
Maturity of bonds, §§116-209.4.
Negotiability of bonds, §116-209.9.

EDUCATION ASSISTANCE AUTHORITY —Cont'd
Bond issues —Cont'd
Parental loans.
Power of authority to issue bonds, §116-209.24, (e).
Refunding bonds, §116-209.4.
Remedies of bondholders, §116-209.8.
Reserves, §116-209.2.
Resolution, §116-209.5.
Revenues.
Sufficiency to pay bonds, §116-209.6.
Security of bonds.
Additional pledge, §116-209.11.
Credit of state not pledged, §116-209.12.
Reserve trust fund.
Pledge of security interest for payment of bonds, §116-209.
Trust agreement, §116-209.5.
Remedies of bond holders, §116-209.8.
Tax exemption, §116-209.13.
Terms and conditions of bonds, §116-209.4.
Trust agreement, §116-209.5.
Remedies of bond holders, §116-209.8.
Trust funds, §116-209.7.
Merger, §116-209.15.
United States funds.
Pledge for security of bonds, §116-209.11.
Collection of loan repayments.
Scholarship loan fund for prospective teachers, §§115C-472.1, 116-204.
Teaching fellows program, §§115C-363.23A, (g), 116-204.
Conflict of laws.
Inconsistent laws inapplicable, §116-209.23.
Repeal of certain provisions to extent of conflict, §116-209.1.
Construction and interpretation.
Liberal construction of provisions, §116-208.
Severability of provisions, §116-209.22.
Creation, §116-203.
Definitions, §116-201, (b).
Expenditures.
Public purpose, §116-209.20.
Grants to students, §116-209.19.
Legislative declaration, §116-201, (a).
Loan fund, §116-209.3.
Obligations.
Acquisition, §116-206.
Terms of acquisitions, §116-207.
Defined, §116-201, (b).
Power to buy and sell students obligations, §116-202.
Offices, §116-205, (c).
Parental loans.
Assistance to parents.
Powers of authority, §116-209.24, (c).
Bond issues.
Power of authority to issue, §116-209.24, (e).
Buying and selling parental obligations.
Power of authority, §116-209.24, (d).
Definitions, §116-209.24, (b).
Purpose, §116-209.24, (a).
Powers.
Generally, §§116-204, 116-209.3, 116-209.16.
Student assistance program, §§116-209.16 to 116-209.18.
Property.
Powers as to, §116-204.
State property.
Consent to use, §116-205, (b).

EDUCATION ASSISTANCE AUTHORITY —Cont'd
Property —Cont'd
Title to property in name of authority, §116-205, (a).
Purposes, §116-201, (a).
Expenditures to be for public purpose, §116-209.20.
Reports.
Annual report, §116-209.14.
Reserves, §116-209.2.
Revenues, §116-209.6.
Undertakings of authority limited to revenues, §116-202.
Severability of provisions, §116-209.22.
Status, §116-203.
Student assistance program.
Powers as to, §116-209.16.
Administration of program, §116-209.18.
Establishment of program, §116-209.17.
Students.
Defined, §116-201, (b).
Grants to students, §116-209.19.
Obligations.
Acquisition, §§116-206, 116-207.
Defined, §116-201, (b).
Power to buy and sell, §116-202.
Taxation.
Exemptions, §116-209.13.
Teacher assistant scholarship fund, §116-209.35.
Trust funds.
Generally, §116-209.7.
Merger, §116-209.15.
Reserve trust fund.
Creation, §116-209.
Escheat fund.
Transfer, §116-209.

EDUCATION CABINET.
Created, §116C-1, (a).
Duties, §116C-1, (c).
First in America innovative education act.
Annual report, §116C-4, (c).
Funding, §116C-4, (b).
Members, §116C-1, (b).
Staff, §116C-1, (d).
Strategic design for continuum of education programs, §116C-3.

EDUCATION COMMISSION, §§116C-2, 143-261 to 143-266.
Appointments, §143-261.
Compensation, §143-264.
Duties, §§116C-2, 143-261.
Elections.
Officers, §143-262.
Executive secretary.
Powers, §143-266.
Salary, §143-265.
Expenses, §143-264.
Members, §116C-2.
Status, §143-262.
Membership, §143-261.
Officers.
Election, §143-262.
Organization meeting, §143-262.
Per diem expenses, §143-264.
Powers of executive secretary, §143-266.
Purpose, §143-261.
Comprehensive study of education problems, §143-263.

EDUCATION COMMISSION —Cont'd
Salaries.
Executive secretary, §143-265.
Status of members, §143-262.
Studies.
Commission to make comprehensive studies of educational problems, §143-263.
Travel allowances, §143-264.

EFFECTIVE DATES OF STATUTES AND ACTS, §§120-20, 164-8.

EFFLUENT STANDARDS AND LIMITATIONS.
Contents of standards and limitations, §143-215, (b).
Powers of commission, §143-215, (a).

EGG PROMOTION TAX, §§106-245.30 to 106-245.39.
Amount, §106-245.32.
Collection.
Delinquent taxes, §106-245.36.
Definitions, §106-245.31.
Effect on Article 50 of Chapter 106, §106-245.39.
Exemptions, §106-245.34.
Eggs assessed under agricultural marketing agreement act of 1937, §106-245.34A.
Funds.
North Carolina egg fund, §106-245.37.
Handlers.
Defined, §106-245.33, (b).
Exemptions, §106-245.34.
False reports or records, failure to record.
Criminal penalty, §106-245.38, (a).
Functions, §106-245.33, (b).
Payment by handler, §106-245.33, (a).
Records, §106-245.35.
Registration, §106-245.33, (b).
Failure, criminal penalty, §106-245.38, (b).
Report of tax, §106-245.33, (a).
Interest.
Delinquent taxes, §106-245.36.
Legislative findings, §106-245.30.
Levy of tax, §106-245.32.
Purpose of article, §106-245.30.
Records, §106-245.35.
Return of tax.
Taxes paid on exempt eggs or processed eggs, §106-245.34.
Rules and regulations.
Promulgation, §106-245.32.

EGGS, §§106-245.13 to 106-245.28.
Advertisements.
Designation in block letters, §106-245.20.
Agents.
Act of agent as that of principal, §106-245.28.
Aiding and abetting.
Violations of egg act.
Persons punishable as principals, §106-245.27, (a), (b).
Citation of act, §106-245.13.
Commissioner of agriculture.
Defined, §106-245.14.
Power of commissioner, §106-245.23.
Sanitary conditions.
Approval of methods by commissioner, §106-245.22, (a).
Construction and interpretation.
Rule of construction, §106-245.13.
Containers.
Defined, §106-245.14.

EGGS —Cont'd
Containers —Cont'd
Grades.
Designation of grade and class on containers required, §106-245.15.
Conformity with designation, §106-245.15.
Exemption, §106-245.15.
Labeling on containers, §106-245.18, (a).
Descriptive terms, §106-245.18, (b).
Size or weight class.
Designation of grade and class on containers required, §106-245.15.
Conformity with designation, §106-245.15.
Exemption, §106-245.15.
Criminal law and procedure.
Warnings in lieu of criminal prosecutions, §106-245.25.
Definitions, §106-245.14.
Grades.
Containers, designation of grade and class on, §106-245.15.
Defined, §106-245.14.
Establishment and promulgation of grades, §106-245.16.
Injunctions.
Granting temporary or permanent injunction, §106-245.24, (b).
Invoices.
Copy of invoice to be filed, §106-245.19, (b).
Furnishing to purchaser at time of delivery, §106-245.19, (a).
Labels.
Container labeling, §106-245.18, (a).
Descriptive terms, §106-245.18, (b).
Misdemeanors.
Violations of egg law, §106-245.24.
Orders.
Stop-sale orders, §106-245.17.
Penalties.
Violations of the egg law, §106-245.24.
Principal and agent.
Act of agent as that of principal, §106-245.28.
Promotion of use and sale of agricultural products.
Generally, §§106-550 to 106-568.
See AGRICULTURAL PRODUCTS PROMOTION.
Promotion tax, §§106-245.30 to 106-245.39.
See EGG PROMOTION TAX.
Publications.
Rules and regulations to be published, §106-245.21.
Remedies.
Cumulative nature of remedies, §106-245.26.
Rules and regulations.
Publication and copies, §106-245.21.
Rules of construction, §106-245.13.
Sanitation.
Approval of methods by commissioner of agriculture, §106-245.22, (a).
Scope of article, §106-245.13.
Short title, §106-245.13.
Size or weight classes.
Containers, designation of grade and class, §106-245.15.
Defined, §106-245.14.
Establishment and promulgation of classes, §106-245.16.
Standards for quality.
Defined, §106-245.14.

EGGS —Cont'd
Standards for quality —Cont'd
Establishment and promulgation of standards, §106-245.16.
Stop-sale orders.
Violations of article, §106-245.17.
Taxation.
Promotion tax, §§106-245.30 to 106-245.39.
See EGG PROMOTION TAX.
Title of article, §106-245.13.
Venue.
Proceedings for violations of article, §106-245.24, (c).
Violations of article.
Penalties, §106-245.24, (a).
Persons punishable as principals, §106-245.27, (a), (b).
Stop-sale orders, §106-245.17.
Venue of proceedings, §106-245.24, (c).

EIGHT LINER.
Video gaming machines.
Ban on new machines, regulation of existing machines, §14-306.1.

82ND AIRBORNE DIVISION ASSOCIATION.
License plates.
Special registration plates, §20-79.4, (b).

EJECTMENT.
Expedited evictions of drug traffickers and other criminals, §§42-59 to 42-76.
See EXPEDITED EVICTIONS.
Landlord and tenant.
Residential tenants, §§42-25.6 to 42-25.9.
See LANDLORD AND TENANT.
Retaliatory eviction, §§42-37.1 to 42-37.3.
Summary ejectment, §§42-26 to 42-36.2.
See LANDLORD AND TENANT.
Small claim actions.
Form of complaint, §7A-232.
Practice and procedure in actions for summary ejectment, §7A-223.
Summary ejectment.
Defendant's bond for costs and damages in land actions.
Not required in summary ejectment action, §1-112, (b).
Generally, §§42-26 to 42-36.2.
See LANDLORD AND TENANT.
Practice and procedure in actions for, §7A-223.

ELBOW PADS.
Skateboard parks.
Wearing required, §99E-23.

ELDERLY PERSONS.
See AGED PERSONS.

ELECTIONEERING COMMUNICATIONS.
Disclosures, prohibited sources, §§163-278.80 to 163-278.83.
Mass mailings and telephone banks, §§163-278.90 to 163-278.93.

ELECTION OFFICERS.
Accepting bribes, §163-275.
County boards of elections generally.
See COUNTY BOARDS OF ELECTIONS.
Precinct election officials, §§163-41 to 163-48.
See PRECINCT ELECTION OFFICIALS.
State board of elections generally.
See STATE BOARD OF ELECTIONS.

ELECTION OF RIGHTS AND REMEDIES.
Betterments.
Election by plaintiff that defendant take premises, §1-347.

ELECTION OF RIGHTS AND REMEDIES —Cont'd
Bonds, surety.
Actions on bonds.
Suing officer individually, §58-76-10.
Judges.
Consolidated judicial retirement act.
Transfer of members to another system, §135-70.
Retirement system for teachers and state employees.
Consolidated judicial retirement act.
Optional allowance election, §135-61.
Transfer of members to another system, §135-70.
State institutions of higher education.
Optional retirement program, §135-5.1, (b).
Social security.
Coverage of governmental employees under title II of social security act.
Local governmental employees' retirement system.
Transfer of members to employment covered by retirement system, §135-28.
Transfers from state to certain association service, §135-27.
Uniform judicial retirement system.
Transfer of members to employment covered by retirement system, §135-28.1.

ELECTION OF TAX AGAINST WHICH CREDIT CLAIMED.
Business tax credit, §105-129.17, (a).
Tax incentives for new and expanding businesses, §105-129.5, (a).

ELECTIONS, §§163-1 to 163-306.
Absentee ballots.
Generally, §§163-226 to 163-239.
See ABSENTEE BALLOTS.
Military absentee voting, §§163-245 to 163-257.
See ABSENTEE BALLOTS.
Abstracts.
Composite abstracts, §163-182.6, (b).
Forms, §163-182.6, (d).
Preparation by county board, §163-182.6, (a).
Secretary of state, duties, §163-182.6, (c).
Actions.
State board of elections.
Authority to assist in litigation, §163-25.
Address confidentiality program.
Substitute address.
Use by boards of elections, §15C-8, (e).
Administrative procedure.
Precinct boundaries.
Exemption of state board of elections, §163-132.5B.
Advertisements.
Charges by media, §163-278.18, (a), (b).
Disclosure requirements for media advertisements, §§163-278.39 to 163-278.39C.
Age.
Persons eighteen years of age, Const. U. S., amd. XXVI.
Qualifications of voters.
Minimum age, §163-55.
Right to vote not to be abridged on account of age, Const. U. S., amd. XXVI.
Aged persons.
Accessible polling places, §163-131.
Curbside voting, §163-166.9.
Satellite voting places, §163-130.

ELECTIONS —Cont'd
Agriculture.
Commissioner of agriculture, §106-10.
Airports.
Special airport districts.
Bond elections, §63-87.
Creation, §63-80, (c).
Alcoholic beverages.
See LOCAL OPTION ELECTIONS.
Appeals.
Contributions and expenditures in political campaigns.
State board of elections.
Appeals from board, §163-278.26.
Protest of election.
Appeal of decision to state board, §163-182.11.
Appeal of decision to superior court, §163-182.14.
Public campaign financing fund.
Adverse agency decisions, §163-278.68, (c).
Arrest.
County boards of elections.
Power to maintain order, §163-34.
Interference with voters.
Election officers to cause violators to be arrested, §163-273, (b).
Offenses by voters.
Election officers to cause violators to be arrested, §163-273, (b).
Precinct election officials.
Power to maintain order, §163-48.
State board of elections.
Power to maintain order, §163-24.
Assistance to voters.
Admission of person rendering assistance to voting booth, §163-166.8, (c).
Generally, §163-166.8, (a).
Request for, §163-166.8, (b).
Assistants at polls, §163-42.
Compensation, §163-46.
Student election assistants, §163-42.1.
Attorney general.
Date of election, §163-1, (a).
Elective officers, Const. N. C., art. III, §7.
Vacancy in office.
Election to fill, §163-8.
Ballot boxes.
State board of elections.
Access to ballot boxes, §163-22, (j).
Ballot counters, §163-43.
Ballots.
Absentee ballots generally, §§163-226 to 163-239.
See ABSENTEE BALLOTS.
Arrangement of official ballots, §163-165.6.
Butterfly ballots.
Use prohibited, §163-165.4B.
Candidate ballot items.
Order of precedence, §163-165.6, (a) to (d).
Changes.
Late changes in ballots, §163-165.3, (c).
Characteristics for official ballots, §163-165.4.
Confidentiality of voted ballots, §163-165.1, (e).
Contents of official ballots, §163-165.5.
Counting ballots. See within this heading, "Counting ballots."
Counting of votes, §§163-182 to 163-182.5.
County boards of elections.
Preparation and production of official ballots and instructions, §163-165.3, (b).
Documents resembling official ballot.
Disclaimer, §163-165.2, (b).
Headings of official ballots, §163-165.5.

ELECTIONS —Cont'd
Ballots —Cont'd
Instructions to voters.
English and Spanish, §163-165.5A.
Posting of voter information, §163-166.7A.
Preparation and production by county boards, §163-165.3, (b).
Lever machines, use of, §163-165.4A, (a1).
Effective date of provision, §163-165.4A, (b).
New elections.
Candidates on ballot, §163-182.13, (e).
Other uses prohibited, §163-165.1, (d).
Persons previously registered by mail who have not voted for federal office.
Exemptions, §163-166.12, (d).
Identification proof submitted by voter.
County board to note, §163-166.12, (b1).
In-person voting, §163-166.12, (a).
Mail-in absentee voting, §163-166.12, (b).
Provisional voting, §163-166.12, (c).
Primary elections.
Order of candidates, §163-165.6, (c).
Provisional ballots.
Persons previously registered by mail, §163-166.12, (c).
Posting of voter information, §163-166.7A, (a).
Procedures generally, §163-166.11.
Voting after hours, §163-166.01.
Punch-card ballots.
Use prohibited, §163-165.4A, (a).
Effective date, §163-165.4A, (b).
Referendum questions.
Order of precedence, §163-165.6, (g).
Requirements, §163-165.1, (b).
Compliance with provisions, §163-165.1, (c).
Return and accounting of ballots.
Procedures after close of voting, §163-166.10.
Sample ballots, §163-165.2, (a).
Posting of voter information, §163-166.7A, (a).
Scope of provisions, §163-165.1, (a).
Special ballots, §163-165.3, (d).
Standards for official ballots, §163-165.4.
State board of elections.
Responsibilities in connection with official ballots, §§163-165.3, (a), (c), (d).
Straight-party voting, §163-165.6, (e).
Voted ballots.
Confidentiality and disclosure, §163-165.1, (e).
Voting procedures.
Distribution of official ballots, §163-166.7, (b).
Write-in voting, §163-165.6, (f).
Blind persons.
Assistance to voters, §163-166.8.
Boards of elections.
County boards of elections, §§163-30 to 163-37.
See COUNTY BOARDS OF ELECTIONS.
Municipal boards of elections, §163-280.
Abolished, exception, §163-280.1.
Political activities by board members, §§163-38 to 163-40.1.
Applicability of provisions, §163-38.
Definitions and proof of terms used, provision applicable, §163-40.1.
Limitation on activities, §163-39.
Removal, violation grounds for, §163-40.
State board of elections, §§163-19 to 163-28.
See STATE BOARD OF ELECTIONS.
Boundaries.
Precincts, §§163-132.3 to 163-132.5F.

ELECTIONS —Cont'd
Bribery.
Officers of elections.
Accepting bribes.
Felony, §163-275.
Butner advisory council, §122C-413, (a) to (d1).
Butterfly ballot.
Use prohibited, §163-165.4B.
Campaign contributions and expenditures.
Generally, §§163-278.5 to 163-278.38.
See CAMPAIGN CONTRIBUTIONS AND EXPENDITURES.
Municipal campaign reporting, §§163-278.40 to 163-278.40I.
See CAMPAIGN CONTRIBUTIONS AND EXPENDITURES.
Public campaign financing fund, §§163-278.61 to 163-278.70.
Candidates.
Municipal elections generally.
See MUNICIPAL ELECTIONS.
Political parties.
Certificate of party affiliation, §163-106, (f).
Primary elections.
Certificate of registration, §163-106, (f).
Death of candidate before primary.
Filling vacancy, §163-112.
Nomination determined by substantial plurality, §163-111, (a).
Nominee's right to withdraw as candidate, §163-113.
Notice of candidacy, §163-106, (a).
Certification, §163-108, (a) to (c).
Acknowledgment, §163-108, (d).
Eligibility to file, §163-106, (b).
Filing fees, §163-107, (a).
Petition in lieu of payment of fee, §163-107.1.
Refund, §163-107, (b).
Filing for more than one office, §163-106, (h).
Inspection of registration records upon receipt of notice, §163-106, (g).
Petition in lieu of payment of filing fee.
County, municipal and district primaries, §163-107.1, (c).
Generally, §163-107.1, (a), (b).
Nonpartisan primaries and elections, §163-107.1, (d).
Time for filing, §163-106, (c).
Vacancies in office.
Notice of candidacy for certain offices to indicate vacancy, §163-106, (d).
Withdrawal, §163-106, (e).
Presidential preference primary.
Names to appear on ballot or voting machine, §163-213.7.
Nomination by petition, §§163-213.5, 163-213.6.
Nomination by state board of elections, §§163-213.4, 163-213.6.
Notification of nomination, §163-213.6.
Sole candidate declared nominee, §163-110.
Unaffiliated voters, §163-119.
Withdrawal.
Nominee's right to withdraw as candidate, §163-113.
State board of elections.
Certifying names of candidates to county board, §163-22, (h).
Unaffiliated candidate.
Nomination by petition, §163-122, (a).
Form, §163-122, (b).
Inapplicability of provisions, §163-122, (c).

ELECTIONS —Cont'd
Candidates —Cont'd
Write-in candidates.
Counting and recording of votes, §163-123, (f).
Declaration of intent, §163-123, (b).
Defeated primary candidate, §163-123, (e).
Municipal and nonpartisan elections excluded, §163-123, (g).
Petitions, §163-123, (c).
Forms, §163-123, (d).
Procedure for qualifying as, §163-123, (a).
Candidates' financing fund.
Contribution of individual income tax refund to, §105-269.6.
Canvassing votes.
County board, §163-182.5, (b).
Definitions of canvass, §163-182.5, (a).
State board, §163-182.5, (c).
Capitation tax prohibited, Const. N. C., art. V, §1.
Census data by precinct, §163-132.5F.
Certain acts declared misdemeanors, §163-274.
Certificate of election.
Appeal of decision to superior court.
Stay of certificate, §163-182.14.
Contributions and expenditures in political campaigns.
Filing of statements as prerequisite, §163-278.25.
Copy to secretary of state, §163-182.15, (c).
Governor to issue commission upon certification of election.
Certain offices, §163-182.16.
Municipal elections.
Chairman of election to furnish certificate, §163-301.
When county board to issue, §163-182.15, (a).
When state board to issue, §163-182.15, (b).
Certificate of nomination.
Copy to secretary of state, §163-182.15, (c).
When county board to issue, §163-182.15, (a).
When state board to issue, §163-182.15, (b).
Challenge of voters.
Absentee ballots.
Burden of proof, §163-89, (c).
Hearing, §163-89, (e).
Separate challenge to each ballot, §163-89, (c).
Signing of challenge, §163-89, (c).
Time for challenge, §163-89, (a).
To whom challenge addressed, §163-89, (d).
Who may challenge, §163-89, (b).
Burden of proof, §163-90.1, (b).
Challenge to absentee ballots, §163-89, (c).
Day of primary or election.
Authorized, §163-87.
Grounds, §163-87.
Hearing, §163-88.
Oath of challenged registrant, §163-88.
Request for challenged ballot, §163-88.1, (a), (b).
Preservation of such ballots, §163-88.1, (c).
Felonies.
Answer to challenge as felon not to be used on prosecution, §163-90.
Hearings.
Challenge on day of primary or election, §163-88.
Challenge other than on day of primary or election, §163-86.
Challenge to absentee ballots, §163-89, (e).
Municipal elections, §163-289.

ELECTIONS —Cont'd
Challenge of voters —Cont'd
Notice.
Challenge on other than day of primary or election, §163-86, (d).
Oaths.
Challenge on day of primary or election.
Challenged registrant, §163-88.
Challenge other than on day of primary or election.
Challenged registrant, §163-86, (c).
False swearing.
Felony, §163-90.3.
Other than on day of primary or election.
Action by county board of elections on challenge, §163-85, (b).
Grounds, §163-85, (c).
Challenge to specify, §163-85, (b).
Hearing, §163-86, (a).
Appearance by challenged registrant, §163-86, (d).
Notice, §163-86, (b).
Scheduling, §163-85, (d).
Notice of challenge, §163-86, (b).
Oath of challenged registrant, §163-86, (c).
Time for challenge, §163-84.
Voter no longer residing in precinct, prima facie evidence, §163-85, (e).
Who may challenge, §163-85, (a).
Overruled or dismissed challenge.
Action by board on, §163-90.2, (c).
Appeals, §163-90.2, (d).
Reasonable belief by challenger required, §163-90.1, (a).
Sustained challenge.
Action by board on, §163-90.2, (a), (b).
Appeals, §163-90.2, (d).
Changes affecting voting.
Voting rights act of 1965.
Submissions to attorney general of United States, §§120-30.9A to 120-30.9I.
Citizenship.
Presidential elections.
Residence period for presidential elections, Const. N. C., art. VI, §2.
State elections.
Residence period for state elections, Const. N. C., art. VI, §2.
Closing voting places.
Hours for voting, §163-166.01.
Community colleges.
Financial support.
Elections on questions of appropriations.
See COMMUNITY COLLEGES.
Composite abstracts, §163-182.6, (b).
Confidentiality.
Address confidentiality program.
Substitute address.
Use by boards of elections, §15C-8, (e).
Voted ballots, §163-165.1, (e).
Congress.
Contributions and expenditures in political campaigns.
Candidates for federal office to file information report, §163-278.30.
Date of elections, §163-1, (a).
Districts.
Congressional districts specified, §163-201, (a).
General assembly apportionment act.
Compliance with federal law, §163-201.2, (c).

ELECTIONS —Cont'd
Congress —Cont'd
Districts —Cont'd
General assembly apportionment act —Cont'd
Limitation on number of divisions, §163-201.2, (b).
Restriction, §163-201.2, (a).
Names and boundaries, §163-201, (b).
Additions or modifications, §163-201, (c).
Change of precinct boundary, no effect on district, §163-201, (d).
Severability of congressional apportionment acts, §163-201.1.
Unassigned districts, §163-163, (e).
House of representatives.
Districts.
Congressional districts specified, §163-201, (a).
Reapportionment.
Election after reapportionment, §163-202.
Senate.
Vacancy in office, §§163-12, 163-115, (e).
Severability of congressional apportionment acts, §163-201.1.
Vacancies in office.
Filling.
House of representatives, §§163-13, 163-115, (b).
Senate, §§163-12, 163-115, (e).
Consolidated city-county act.
Bond issues, §160B-14.
Contests.
Executive branch.
Joint ballot of both houses of general assembly.
General assembly to determine, Const. N. C., art. VI, §5.
Continuation in office, Const. N. C., art. VI, §10.
Contributions and expenditures in political campaigns.
Generally, §§163-278.5 to 163-278.38.
See CAMPAIGN CONTRIBUTIONS AND EXPENDITURES.
Municipal campaign reporting, §§163-278.40 to 163-278.40I.
See CAMPAIGN CONTRIBUTIONS AND EXPENDITURES.
Convention of the people.
Procedure for calling, Const. N. C., art. XIII, §1.
Coroners, §152-1.
Date of election, §163-1, (a).
Corruption.
Convicted officials.
Disqualification from voting, §163-276.
Removal from office, §163-276.
District attorneys.
Investigation and prosecution of violations, §163-278.
Felonies.
Certain acts declared felonies, §163-275.
Fraud.
Felonies, §163-275.
Interference with voters.
Duties of election officers upon, §163-273, (b).
Prohibited acts, §163-273, (a).
Intimidation of voters by officers, §163-271.
Misdemeanors.
Generally, §§163-271 to 163-274.
Offenses of voters, §163-273, (a).
Duties of election officers upon, §163-273, (b).
Penalties.
Felonies, §163-275.

ELECTIONS —Cont'd
Corruption —Cont'd
State board of elections.
Investigation of violations, §163-278.
Witnesses.
Self-incrimination.
Immunity from prosecution, §163-277.
Subpoenas, §§163-277, 163-278.
Powers of district attorneys, §163-278.
Counties.
Alcoholic beverages.
See LOCAL OPTION ELECTIONS.
Boards of commissioners, §153A-34.
Altering mode of elections, §153A-58.
Modification of structures of boards, §§153A-61 to 153A-64.
Voting systems.
Powers and duties as to, §163-165.8.
Consolidation.
Plans proposed by governmental study commissions, §153A-405, (a) to (e).
Electoral districts, §153A-22.
Map of districts, §153A-20.
Industrial development.
Tax elections, §§158-16 to 158-19.
Sales and use tax.
Local government sales and use tax.
Election on adoption.
First one-cent tax, §105-465.
Sheriffs, Const. N. C., art. VII, §2.
Structure of boards of commissioners.
Alteration.
Effective date, §153A-62.
Initiation of alterations by resolution.
Filing copy, §153A-63.
Submission of proposition to voters, §153A-61.
Filing results of election, §153A-64.
Taxation.
Property taxes, §153A-149.
Time generally, §163-1, (a).
Watershed improvement programs, §§139-39, 139-40.
Counting ballots.
Chief judge of precinct, duties, §163-182.3.
County boards of elections.
Duties as to, §163-33.
Definitions, §163-182.
Elections by people to be by ballot, Const. N. C., art. VI, §5.
General principles, §163-182.1, (a).
Initial ballot count.
General principles, §163-182.2, (a).
Rules promulgation, §163-182.2, (b).
Jurisdiction.
County board, §163-182.4, (a).
Duties of those having jurisdiction, §163-182.4, (c).
State board, §163-182.4, (b).
Military voting absentee, §§163-245 to 163-257.
See ABSENTEE BALLOTS.
Official ballots only, §163-182.1, (a).
Political parties.
New political party, §163-98.
Presidential elections.
Electors.
Names not printed on ballots, §163-209.
Presidential preference primaries, §163-213.7.
Presidential preference primaries, §163-213.7.
Primary elections, §163-109, (a).
County boards of elections.
Furnishing, §163-109, (c).
Names of candidates, §163-137, (c).

ELECTIONS —Cont'd
Counting ballots —Cont'd
Primary elections —Cont'd
Presidential preference primaries, §163-213.7.
State board of elections.
Furnishing, §163-109, (b).
Printing and distribution.
Time for, §163-137, (b).
Promulgation of rules, §163-182.1, (b).
Protest filed with county board, §163-182.9.
Standards and procedures, adoption, §163-182.1, (b).
State board of elections.
Duties as to, §163-22, (e), (f).
Write-in votes, §163-182.1, (a).
County boards of elections, §§163-30 to 163-37.
See COUNTY BOARDS OF ELECTIONS.
Court of appeals.
Judges of court elected by qualified voters, §7A-16; Const. N. C., art. IV, §16.
Judicial voter guide.
Candidate information, §163-278.69, (b).
Disclaimer statement, §163-278.69, (c).
Publication by board, §163-278.69, (a).
Public campaign financing fund, §§163-278.61 to 163-278.70.
Criminal law and procedure.
Absentee ballot violations, §§163-226.3, (a), 163-237.
County boards of elections, §163-236.
Appropriations from North Carolina political parties financing fund.
Violations of provisions, §163-278.44.
Certain acts declared felonies, §163-275.
Certain acts declared misdemeanors, §163-274.
Challenge of voters.
False swearing, §163-90.3.
Contributions and expenditures in political campaigns.
Disclosure before soliciting contributions violations, §163-278.20, (b).
Disclosure requirements for media advertisements.
Misrepresentation of authorization, §163-278.39, (c).
Fund-raising from lobbyists, §163-278.13, (a), (d).
Limitation on contribution violations, §163-278.13, (f).
Violations by business organizations and labor unions, §163-278.19, (a).
Violations generally, §163-278.27, (a).
Electioneering communications, §163-278.83.
Mass mailings and telephone banks, §163-278.93.
Interference with voters, §163-273.
Intimidation of voters by officers, §163-271.
Misdemeanor punishments, §163-272.1.
Offenses by voters, §163-273.
Signing name of another on petition, §163-221, (c).
Curbside voting, §163-166.9.
Death of candidate before primary.
Filling vacancy, §163-112.
Definitions, §163-165.
Butterfly ballot, §163-165.4B.
Contributions and expenditures in political campaigns, §163-278.6.
Election, §§163-278.6, 163-278.13, (d).
Political party, §§163-278.6, 163-278.13, (e).
Counting ballots, canvassing votes, etc., §163-182.

ELECTIONS —Cont'd
Definitions —Cont'd
Electioneering communications, §§163-278.80, 163-278.90.
Funds.
Appropriations from North Carolina political parties financing fund, §163-278.45.
Political parties, §§163-96, (a), 163-278.6, 163-278.13, (e).
Residence, §163-57.
Dental examiners board, §90-22, (c).
Disabled voters.
Assistance to voters, §163-166.8.
Curbside voting, §163-166.9.
Discrimination.
Voting rights act of 1965.
Submission of charges to United States attorney general, §§120-30.9A to 120-30.9I. See within this heading, "Voting rights act of 1965."
Disqualifications for office, Const. N. C., art. VI, §8.
District attorneys.
Corruption.
Investigation and prosecution of violations, §163-278.
Prosecutorial districts, §7A-60, (a).
Vacancies in office.
Election to fill, §163-10.
District courts.
Judges of district courts, §7A-140.
Generally, §§163-321 to 163-335.
See DISTRICT COURT JUDGES.
Dual office holding, Const. N. C., art. VI, §9.
Education.
Commission.
Officers, §143-262.
Local boards of education, §§115C-35, (a), 115C-37.
Elected officers, Const. N. C., art. III, §7.
Electioneering communications, §§163-278.80 to 163-278.93.
Definitions, §§163-278.80, 163-278.90.
Disclosures
Mass mailings and telephone banks.
Statement required, §163-278.91, (a).
Contents, §163-278.91, (b).
Criminal and civil penalties for violations, §163-278.93.
Statement required, §163-278.81, (a).
Contents, §163-278.81, (b).
Criminal civil penalties for violations, §163-278.83.
Prohibited sources.
Corporate or labor disbursements for communications, §163-278.82, (a), (b).
Criminal civil penalties for violations, §163-278.83.
Mass mailings and telephone banks, §§163-278.92, (a), (b).
Criminal and civil penalties for violations, §§163-278.93.
Eligibility to elective office, Const. N. C., art. VI, §6.
Eligibility to vote, Const. N. C., art. VI, §1.
Executive branch.
Contested elections.
Joint ballot of both houses of general assembly.
General assembly to determine, Const. N. C., art. VI, §5.

ELECTIONS —Cont'd
Expenses.
Primary elections.
Payment, §163-105.
Faithless elector statute.
Failure of presidential elector to attend and vote, §163-212.
Felonies.
Absentee ballots.
Prohibited act, §163-226.3, (a).
Challenge of voters.
Answer to challenge as felon not to be used on prosecution, §163-90.
False swearing, §163-90.3.
Corruption.
Certain acts declared felonies, §163-275.
Disqualification from office, Const. N. C., art. VI, §8.
Disqualification from voting, §163-55; Const. N. C., art. VI, §2.
Fines.
Penalties for misdemeanors, §163-272.1.
Fire district elections.
Absentee voting not permitted, §163-226, (b).
Fish and fisheries.
Coastal fisheries and seafood industry promotion referenda, §§113-312 to 113-315.7.
Forgery.
Absentee ballots, §163-237, (c).
Fraud.
Absentee ballots.
Misdemeanors, §163-237, (c).
Felonies, §163-275.
Registration of voters.
Felonies, §163-275.
State bureau of investigation.
Authority to make investigations, §114-15, (a).
Free elections, Const. N. C., art. I, §10.
Frequent elections required, Const. N. C., art. I, §9.
Full-time election offices.
County boards of elections.
Modified full-time offices, §163-36.
Funds.
Political parties financing fund, §§163-278.41 to 163-278.45.
Gambling.
Bet or wager on election.
Misdemeanor, §163-274.
General assembly, Const. N. C., art. II, §8.
Apportionment act.
Congressional districts, §§163-201 to 163-201.2.
Contests.
Depositions taken, §120-11.
Notice of contest, §120-10.
Witnesses, §120-11.
Corrupt practices in election.
Expulsion for corrupt practices, §120-8.
Date of election, §163-1, (a).
Elections by general assembly to be by viva voce, Const. N. C., art. VI, §5.
House of representatives.
Nomination of candidates, §163-108.1.
Lobbying.
Prohibited election influence, §120-47.5, (b).
Primaries moved from date provided.
Holding on same day, §163-1, (d).
Governor, Const. N. C., art. III, §2.
Commission of certain offices issued upon certification of election, §163-182.16.
Date of election, §163-1, (a).

ELECTIONS —Cont'd
Governor —Cont'd
Governor-elect and lieutenant governor-elect.
Office space and expenses, §147-31.1.
Summary of duties.
Counting votes, canvassing, abstracts and protests, §163-182.17, (f).
Vacancy in office.
Election to fill, §163-8.
Hand counting of ballots, §163-182.1, (a).
Handicapped persons.
Accessible polling places, §163-131.
Satellite voting places for disabled voters, §163-130.
Hearings.
Challenge of voters.
Challenge on day of primary or election, §163-88.
Challenge other than on day of primary or election, §163-86.
Challenge to absentee ballots, §163-89, (e).
Help America Vote act compliance.
Complaint procedure.
Administrative procedure act exemptions, §163-91, (b), (c).
Establishment, §163-91, (a).
Proposed plan, §163-91, (b).
Computerized voter registration, §163-82.11, (c).
Drivers' license offices, duties, §163-82.19, (b).
Election fund established, §163-82.28.
Generally, §162-82.27.
Posting of voter information, §163-166.7A, (b).
Holidays.
Election day as public holiday, §103-4, (a).
Hospital districts.
Referendum on repeal of tax levy, §131E-46, (a) to (d).
Hours for voting, §163-166.01.
Husband and wife.
Precinct election officials.
Certain relatives prohibited from serving together, §163-41.1.
Residence.
Eligibility to establish separate domicile, §163-57.
Inaugural ceremonies committee, §§143-532 to 143-539.
Income tax.
Individual income tax refund.
Contribution to candidates' financing fund, §105-269.6.
Industrial development.
Tax elections for industrial development purposes, §§158-16 to 158-19.
Injunctions.
Contributions and expenditures in political campaigns.
Violations of provisions, §163-278.28, (a).
Insurance commissioner, §58-2-5.
Interference with voters, §163-273.
Intimidation.
Officers of election.
Felony, §163-275.
Voters.
Intimidation by officers, §163-271.
Misdemeanor, §163-274.
Investigations.
County boards of elections, §163-33.
State board of elections, §163-22, (d).
Judges of election.
Appointment, §163-41, (a).
Chief judge, §163-47.

ELECTIONS —Cont'd
Judges of election —Cont'd
Compensation, §163-46.
Counting ballots.
Chief judge of precinct, duties, §163-182.3.
Duties, §163-47.
Jurisdiction.
Counting ballots, §163-182.4.
Labor.
Commissioner of labor, §95-2.
Date of election, §163-1.
Lawyer candidate for judicial office.
Compliance with Code of Judicial Conduct, Prof. Cond. Rule 8.2.
Libel and slander.
False and derogatory reports as to candidates.
Misdemeanors, §163-274.
Libraries and librarians.
Registration of voters.
Designation of library employees to register voters, §153A-272.
Lieutenant governor, Const. N. C., art. III, §2.
Date of election, §163-1, (a).
Vacancy in office.
Election to fill, §163-8.
Literacy.
Qualifications of voters, Const. N. C., art. VI, §4.
Littering.
County boards of elections.
Littering notification, §163-33.3.
State board of elections.
Littering notification, §163-22.3.
Livestock.
Tuberculosis.
Appropriations by counties for eradication of tuberculosis, §§106-343, 106-344.
Local boards of education.
Election of members, §§115C-35, (a), 115C-37.
Local development.
Industrial development taxation, §§158-16 to 158-19.
Married women.
Residence.
Eligibility to establish separate domicile, §163-57.
Metropolitan sewerage districts.
Assumption of sewerage system indebtedness of political subdivision by district, §162A-77.
Inclusion of additional political subdivision or unincorporated areas, §162A-68, (d).
Merger of metropolitan sewerage districts into cities or towns, §162A-77.1.
Metropolitan water districts.
Inclusion of unincorporated area, §162A-35.
Misdemeanors.
Electioneering communications, §163-278.83.
Mass mailings and telephone banks, §163-278.93.
Mosquito control districts.
Formation of districts.
Procedure for forming, §130A-353, (b) to (g).
Mountain ridge protection.
Exemption from coverage, binding referendum, §113A-214, (a).
Municipal elections, §§163-279 to 163-306.
See MUNICIPAL ELECTIONS.
Nepotism.
Precinct election officials.
Certain relatives prohibited from serving together, §163-41.1.

ELECTIONS —Cont'd
New elections.
Candidates on ballot, §163-182.13, (e).
Jurisdiction, §163-182.13, (d).
Procedures set by state board, §163-182.13, (b).
Tie votes, §163-182.13, (f).
Voter eligibility, §163-182.13, (c).
When ordered, §163-182.13, (a).
911 system charges.
Special elections.
Adoption of ordinance imposing, §62A-4.
Nonpartisan elections.
County board of elections.
Notice of candidacy, §163-106, (a).
Local boards of education, §115C-37, (a), (h).
Municipal elections generally.
See MUNICIPAL ELECTIONS.
Sanitary districts, board members, §139-6.
Write-in candidates.
Municipal and nonpartisan elections excluded, §163-123, (g).
Notice.
Challenge of voters.
Challenge on other than day of primary or election, §163-86, (d).
County boards of elections.
Duties of boards, §163-33.
Municipal campaign reporting.
Notice of reports due, §163-278.40H.
Precinct boundaries.
Alterations to approved precinct boundaries.
Disapproval, §163-132.3, (c).
Presidential preference primaries.
National committees of political parties to be notified of provisions, §163-213.9.
Nomination.
Notification to candidates, §163-213.6.
Primary elections.
Candidacy, §163-106, (a).
Certification of notice of candidacy, §163-108, (a) to (c).
Acknowledgment, §163-108, (d).
Filing fees, §163-107, (a).
Petition in lieu of payment of fee, §163-107.1.
Refund, §163-107, (b).
Petition in lieu of payment of filing fee, §163-107.1, (a), (b).
County, municipal and district primaries, §163-107.1, (c).
Nonpartisan primaries and elections, §163-107.1, (d).
Time for filing, §163-106, (c).
Vacancies in office.
Notice of candidacy for certain offices to indicate vacancy, §163-106, (d).
Withdrawal of notice of candidacy, §163-106, (e).
Protest filed with county board.
Appeal of decision to state board, §163-182.11, (a).
Notice of hearing, §163-182.10, (b).
Oaths.
Challenge of voters.
Challenge on day of primary or election.
Challenged registrant, §163-88.
Challenge other than on day of primary or election.
Challenged registrant, §163-86, (c).
False swearing, §163-90.3.

ELECTIONS —Cont'd
Oaths —Cont'd
County boards of elections.
Oath of office of members, §163-30.
Power of chairman to administer, §163-33.1.
False swearing.
Felony, §163-275.
Precinct election officials.
Oaths of office.
Assistants at polls, §163-42.
Ballot counters, §163-43.
Judges of election and registrars, §163-41, (a).
State board of elections.
Oath of office of members, §163-19.
Offenses by voters, §163-273.
Officers of elections.
Bribery.
Accepting bribes, §163-275.
County boards of elections generally.
See COUNTY BOARDS OF ELECTIONS.
Delegation of tasks among, §163-166.6.
Intimidation of officers.
Felony, §163-275.
Municipal precinct election officials, §§163-280, 163-281.
Precinct election officials, §§163-41 to 163-48.
See PRECINCT ELECTION OFFICIALS.
State board of elections generally.
See STATE BOARD OF ELECTIONS.
One stop voting.
Procedure, §163-227.2.
Opening voting places.
Hours for voting, §163-166.01.
Ordinances.
Ballots.
Submission of proposition to voters, §160A-105.
Out-out-precinct voting places, §163-130.1.
Overvotes.
Counting ballots, §163-182.1, (a).
Parent and child.
Precinct election officials.
Certain relatives prohibited from serving together, §163-41.1.
Perjury.
Corruptly taking oath prescribed for voters, §163-275.
Personnel system.
Interchange of governmental employees.
Authority to interchange employees.
Participation of elected officials in program, §126-53, (d).
Petitions.
Limitation on petitions, §163-219.
Petition circulated prior to July 1, 1957, §163-220.
Notice of circulation of petition.
Registration, §163-218.
Petition void after one year from registration, §163-219.
Political parties.
New political party.
Petition for formation, §163-96, (b).
Presidential preference primaries.
Nomination by petition, §§163-213.5, 163-213.6.
Notification to candidates, §163-213.6.
Primary elections.
Notice of candidacy.
Petition in lieu of payment of filing fee, §163-107.1.
Signing name of another.
Penalty, §163-221, (c).
Prohibited, §163-221, (a), (b).

ELECTIONS —Cont'd
Petitions —Cont'd
Unaffiliated candidate.
Nomination by petition, §163-122.
Political activities of government employees, §§126-13 to 126-15.1.
See POLITICAL ACTIVITIES OF GOVERNMENT EMPLOYEES.
Political campaign contributions and expenditures.
Generally, §§163-278.6 to 163-278.38.
See CAMPAIGN CONTRIBUTIONS AND EXPENDITURES.
Municipal campaign reporting, §§163-278.40 to 163-278.40I.
See CAMPAIGN CONTRIBUTIONS AND EXPENDITURES.
Political parties.
Ballots.
New political party, §163-98.
Defined, §§163-96, (a), 163-278.6, 163-278.13, (e).
New political party.
General election participation by, §163-98.
Petition for formation, §163-96, (b).
Observers, §163-45.
Placement of available funds in fund, §163-278.41, (c).
Political parties financing fund, §§163-278.41 to 163-278.45.
Public buildings.
Use for political meetings, §163-99.
Registration of voters.
Change of party affiliation, §163-82.17.
Voters affiliated with expired political party, §163-97.1.
Schools.
Use for political meetings, §163-99.
Termination of status as political party, §163-97.
Voters affiliated with expired political party, §163-97.1.
Political parties financing fund, §§163-278.41 to 163-278.45.
Administration and enforcement ,rules, adoption, §163-278.43, (c1).
Contributions, receipts reported as, §163-278.43, (c2).
Criminal penalty for violations, §163-278.44.
Definitions, §163-278.45.
Disbursement of deposited funds.
Application for, §163-278.41, (a) to (c).
Disbursement of funds by state chairman, §163-278.42, (a) to (f).
Eligibility to receive funds.
Review and certification of applications, §163-278.43, (c1).
Expenditures, disbursement reported as, §163-278.43, (c2).
Payment of funds held by state treasurer, §163-278.41, (b), (c).
Placement of available funds in fund, §163-278.41, (c).
Records of parties receipts, expenditures and disbursements, §163-278.43, (a).
Report on parties receipts, expenditures and disbursements, §163-278.43, (b).
Unlawful use of fund, §163-278.42, (g).
Poll tax.
Failure to pay poll or other tax.
Denial or abridgement of right to vote by reason of failure prohibited, Const. U. S., amd. XXIV.

ELECTIONS —Cont'd
Poll tax —Cont'd
Prohibited, Const. N. C., art. V, §1.
Precinct election officials, §§163-41 to 163-48.
Assistants at polls, §163-42.
Student election assistants, §163-42.1.
Ballot counters, §163-43.
Compensation, §163-46.
Initial ballot count.
General principles, §163-182.2, (a).
Judges of election.
Appointment, §163-41, (a).
Chief judge, §163-47.
Duties, §163-47.
Oath of office, §163-41, (a).
Municipal corporations, §§163-280, 163-281.
Municipal precinct election officials, §163-281.
Observers, §163-45.
Power to maintain order of place of registration voting, §163-48.
Publication of names, §163-41, (c).
Relatives prohibited from serving together, §163-41.1.
Special registration commissioners, §163-41, (b).
Student election assistants, §163-42.1.
Summary of duties.
Counting votes, canvassing, abstracts and protests, §163-182.17, (b).
Precincts.
Alteration to precinct name, §163-132.3A.
Boundaries.
Administrative procedure act.
State board exempt from act, §163-132.5B.
Alterations to approved precinct boundaries.
Approval of maps and written descriptions, §163-132.3, (b).
Disapproval of precinct boundaries, §163-132.3, (c).
Examination of maps of proposed new or altered precincts, §163-132.3, (b).
Methods of alteration, §163-132.3, (a).
Notice of disapproval, §163-132.3, (c).
Report of boundary changes, §163-132.3, (a).
Submission of certain alterations to United States attorney general.
State board of elections, §120-30.9B, (a).
Census data by precinct, §163-132.5F.
Cooperation of state and local agencies, §163-132.5.
Crossing township lines, §163-132.5C, (b).
Directives, §163-132.4.
Local act, §163-132.5C, (a).
Maps.
Retention of precinct maps, §163-132.5D.
Municipal and township boundaries, §163-132.1, (e).
Retention of precinct maps, §163-132.5D.
Census data by precinct.
State to request, §163-132.5F.
Census redistricting data program.
Block boundary suggestion program, §163-132.1, (b).
Freezing of precincts, §163-132.1, (d).
Phase I, §163-132.1, (b).
Phase II, §163-132.1, (c).
Postponement of effective date of precincts, §163-132.1, (d1), (d2).
Purpose, §163-132.1, (a).
Rules and regulations, §163-132.1, (f).
Cooperation of state and local agencies.
Establishment of boundaries, §163-132.5.

ELECTIONS —Cont'd
Precincts —Cont'd
County boards of elections.
Map of precinct boundaries.
Duty to prepare, §163-128, (b).
Powers as to precincts, §163-128, (a).
Directives.
Boundaries, §163-132.4.
Division of counties into precincts, §163-128, (a).
Freezing of precinct boundaries, §163-132.1, (d).
Maps.
Maps of counties showing precinct boundaries.
County boards of elections to prepare, §163-128, (b).
Retention, §163-132.5D.
Municipal and township boundaries, §163-132.1, (e).
Name.
Alteration, §163-132.3A.
Prima facie evidence.
Voter no longer living in precinct, §163-85, (e).
Two voting places for certain precincts.
Temporary designation, §163-130.2.
Voting data maintained by, §163-132.5G.
Preclearance pursuant to voting rights act.
Submissions to attorney general of United States, §§120-30.9A to 120-30.9I. See within this heading, "Voting rights act of 1965."
Presidential elections.
Generally.
See PRESIDENTIAL ELECTIONS.
Preference primary, §§163-213.1 to 163-213.9.
See PRESIDENTIAL PREFERENCE PRIMARY.
Presidential election year candidates fund, §§163-278.41 to 163-278.45.
Administration and enforcement ,rules, adoption, §163-278.43, (c1).
Contributions, receipts reported as, §163-278.43, (c2).
Criminal penalty for violations, §163-278.44.
Definitions, §163-278.45.
Eligibility to receive funds.
Review and certification of applications, §163-278.43, (c1).
Expenditures, disbursement reported as, §163-278.43, (c2).
Payment of funds held by state treasurer, §163-278.41, (b).
Placement of available funds in fund, §163-278.41, (c).
Records of parties receipts, expenditures and disbursements, §163-278.43, (a).
Report on parties receipts, expenditures and disbursements, §163-278.43, (b).
Unlawful use of fund, §163-278.42, (g).
Primary elections.
Generally, §§163-1, 163-104 to 163-119.
See PRIMARY ELECTIONS.
Municipal elections generally.
See MUNICIPAL ELECTIONS.
Presidential preference primary, §§163-213.1 to 163-213.9.
See PRESIDENTIAL PREFERENCE PRIMARY.
Prison terms.
Penalties for misdemeanors, §163-272.1.
Property qualifications prohibited, Const. N. C., art. I, §11.
Protest filed with county board.
Appeal of decision to state board.
Consideration of appeal, §163-182.11, (b).
Decision, §163-182.11, (b).

ELECTIONS —Cont'd
Protest filed with county board —Cont'd
Appeal of decision to state board —Cont'd
Filing, §163-182.11, (a).
Notice, §163-182.11, (a).
Who may appeal, §163-182.11, (a).
Appeal of decision to superior court, §163-182.14.
Conduct of hearing, §163-182.10, (c).
Contents, §163-182.9, (b).
Effect on canvass, §163-182.10, (a2).
Findings of fact and conclusions of law, §163-182.10, (d).
Forms, §163-182.9, (c).
Initial consideration, §163-182.10, (a).
Notice of hearing, §163-182.10, (b).
Order, §163-182.10, (c), (d).
Promulgation of rules, §163-182.10, (e).
Time for filing, §163-182.9, (b).
Who may file, §163-182.9, (a).
Protest initiated by state board, §163-182.12.
Appeal of decision to superior court, §163-182.14.
Provisional ballots.
Persons previously registered by mail, §163-166.12, (c).
Posting of voter information, §163-166.7A, (a).
Procedures generally, §163-166.11.
Voting after hours, §163-166.01.
Provisional official ballots.
Initial count, §163-182.2, (a).
Public campaign financing fund, §§163-278.61 to 163-278.70.
Administration of article, §163-278.67.
Advisory council.
Establishment, §163-278.68, (b).
Reporting requirements, §163-278.68, (e).
Amount of fund distributions, §163-278.65, (b).
Appeal of adverse agency decisions, §163-278.68, (c).
Attorneys at law.
Opportunity to contribute, §105-41, (a).
Availability of rescue funds, §163-278.67, (a).
Certification of candidates, §163-278.64, (c).
Civil penalty, §163-278.70.
Declaration on intent to participate, §163-278.64, (a).
Definitions, §163-278.62.
Demonstration of support of candidacy, §163-278.64, (b).
Determination of fund amount, §163-278.63, (c).
Distributions from the fund, §163-278.65.
Enforcement of article, §163-278.67.
Establishment, §163-278.63, (a).
Individual income taxpayer.
Allocation to fund by individual, §105-159.2, (a).
Instructions for individual to designate allocation, §105-159.2, (c).
Returns to give individual opportunity to designate allocation, §105-159.2, (b).
Judicial voter guide, §163-278.69.
Legislative intent, §163-278.61.
Limit on rescue funds.
Contested general election, §163-278.67, (c).
Contested primary, §163-278.67, (b).
Method of fund distributions, §163-278.65, (c).
Noncertified candidates and independent expenditure entities.
Reporting requirements, §163-278.66, (a).
Participating and certified candidates.
Reporting requirements, §163-278.66, (b).
Restrictions on contributions and expenditures, §163-278.64, (d).

ELECTIONS —Cont'd
Public campaign financing fund —Cont'd
Public policy, §163-278.61.
Reporting requirements, §163-278.66.
Advisory council, §163-278.68, (e).
Rescue funds, §163-278.67.
Revocation of decision to participate, §163-278.64, (e).
Source of funding, §163-278.63, (b).
Timing of fund distributions, §163-278.65, (a).
Public officers and employees.
Continuation in office, Const. N. C., art. VI, §10.
Disqualifications for office, Const. N. C., art. VI, §8.
Dual office holding, Const. N. C., art. VI, §9.
Eligibility to elective office, Const. N. C., art. VI, §6.
Felonies.
Disqualifications from holding office, Const. N. C., art. VI, §8.
Oaths, Const. N. C., art. VI, §7.
Officers of state institutions.
Generally, §§143-108 to 143-116.
See STATE DEPARTMENTS AND AGENCIES.
Public schools, supplementary taxes for.
Districts created from portions of contiguous counties, §115C-510.
Effective date of action after election, §115C-508, (b).
Frequency of elections, §115C-502, (b).
Petitions.
Action of counties or municipalities, §115C-506.
Boards of education must consider, §115C-505.
Necessary information, §115C-504.
Who may petition for election, §115C-503.
Purposes for which elections may be called, §115C-501.
Rules governing, §115C-507.
Public witness of ballot count, §163-182.2, (a).
Qualifications of voters.
Absentee ballots.
Who may vote absentee ballot.
Primary elections, §163-226.1.
Convicted persons.
Restoration of citizenship rights, §§13-1 to 13-4.
Generally, §163-55; Const. N. C., art. VI, §2; Const. U. S., amd. XXVI.
Municipal elections, §§163-282, 163-283.
Presidential preference primaries, §163-213.2.
Independent voters not to participate, §163-213.7.
Primary elections, §163-59.
Municipal elections, §163-283.
Registration a prerequisite to voting, §163-54.
Primary elections, §163-59.
Residence requirements, §163-55.
Racial minorities, Const. U. S., amd. XV.
Radio.
Campaign contributions and expenditures
Disclosure requirements for media advertisements, §§163-278.39 to 163-278.39C.
Recounts.
Demand, §163-182.7, (b), (c).
Discretionary recounts, §163-182.7, (a).
Mandatory recounts.
County board jurisdiction, §163-182.7, (b).
State board jurisdiction, §163-182.7, (c).
Rules of conducting, §163-182.7, (d).
Referenda.
See REFERENDUM.
Registers of deeds, §§161-1, 161-2.

ELECTIONS —Cont'd
Registration of voters, §§163-82.1 to 163-91.
See REGISTRATION OF VOTERS.
Reports.
Contributions and expenditures in political campaigns.
Declaration of nomination or certificate of election.
Filing of statements as prerequisite, §163-278.25.
Elected officials to report funds, §163-278.36.
Examination of statements within four months, §163-278.24.
Federal officers.
Candidates to file information reports, §163-278.30.
Inactive candidate or committee, §163-278.10.
Preservation, §163-278.35.
County boards of elections to preserve reports, §163-278.37.
Violations of provisions.
Board to report to prosecuting authorities, §163-278.27, (b).
County boards of elections.
State board of elections may require reports from county boards, §163-22, (c).
Residence.
Married women.
Establishment of separate domicile, §163-57.
Presidential elections.
Period for presidential elections, Const. N. C., art. VI, §2.
Qualifications to vote, §163-55.
Definition of residence, §163-57.
State election.
Period for state elections, Const. N. C., art. VI, §2.
Returns.
Abstract of returns.
Municipal elections.
Disposition of duplicate abstracts, §163-300.
Abstracts, §163-182.6.
Canvassing votes, §163-182.5.
Counting ballots, §§163-182 to 163-182.5.
False or fraudulent returns.
Felony, §163-275.
New election ordered, §163-182.13.
Presidential elections, §163-208.
Presidential preference primaries, §163-213.3.
Primary elections.
Presidential preference primaries, §163-213.3.
Protest of election, §163-182.9.
Recounts, §163-182.7.
Primary elections.
Rules and regulations.
Issuance, §163-22, (m).
Rules and regulations.
Issuance, §163-22, (m).
Tie votes, §163-182.8.
Right to vote, Const. U. S., amds. XIV, XIX, XXVI.
Rules and regulations.
Absentee ballots.
Military absentee voting.
State board of elections, §§163-246, 163-256.
Contributions and expenditures in political campaigns.
State board of elections, §163-278.21.
County boards of elections, §163-33.
State board of elections, §163-22, (a).
Power to promulgate temporary rules and regulations, §163-22.2.

ELECTIONS —Cont'd
Rules and regulations —Cont'd
State board of elections —Cont'd
Publication, §163-22, (b).
Temporary rules and regulations, §163-22.2.
Rural fire protection districts.
Abolition, §69-25.10.
Tax question, §§69-25.1 to 69-25.4.
Sales and use tax.
Local government sales and use tax.
Election on adoption of tax.
First one-cent tax, §105-465.
Second one-half cent tax, ballot question, form, §105-499, (a).
Election on repeal of levy.
First one-cent tax, §105-473, (a), (b).
Second one-half cent tax, ballot question, form, §105-499, (b).
Sanitary districts, §§130A-52.1, 130A-53.
Board members, §130A-50, (b), (c).
County with no incorporated city, §130A-50, (b2).
Meetings for purpose of election, §130A-50, (a).
Multi-county districts, §130A-50, (b1).
Results of election certified, §130A-50, (d).
Validation of election of members of district boards, §130A-79, (a), (b).
Extension of district.
Procedure for extension, §130A-69.
Removal of member of board, §130A-66.
Returns of elections, §130A-68.
Special election if election not held in November of 1981, §130A-52, (a) to (d).
Two contiguous sanitary districts merger, §130A-83.
Satellite voting places, §163-130.
School elections.
Merger of administrative units.
Units in adjoining counties, §115C-68, (c).
Supplementary taxes for school purposes, §§115C-500 to 115C-511.
See SCHOOL DISTRICTS AND ADMINISTRATIVE UNITS.
Secretary of state.
Abstracts, duties, §163-182.6, (c).
Date of election, §163-1, (a).
Elective officers, Const. N. C., art. III, §7.
Summary of duties.
Counting votes, canvassing, abstracts and protests, §163-182.17, (e).
Vacancy in office.
Election to fill, §163-8.
Sheriffs, §162-1.
County sheriffs, Const. N. C., art. VII, §2.
Date of election, §163-1, (a).
Soil and water conservation districts.
Watershed improvement works or projects.
Alternative method of financing watershed improvement programs by special county tax, §139-39.
Conduct of election, §139-40, (a).
Appointment of judges and election officials, §139-40, (c).
Conduct of elections, §139-40, (a).
Form of question, §139-40, (b).
Majority vote, §139-40, (d).
Split-ticket votes.
Counting ballots, §163-182.1, (a).
State auditor.
Date of election, §163-1, (a).
Elective officers, Const. N. C., art. III, §7.

ELECTIONS —Cont'd
State auditor —Cont'd
Vacancy in office.
Election to fill, §163-8.
State board of elections, §§163-19 to 163-28.
See STATE BOARD OF ELECTIONS.
State departments and agencies.
Influencing election or political activities.
Removal by governor, §143B-16.
State superintendent of public instruction, §115C-18.
State treasurer.
Date of election, §163-1, (a).
Elective officers, Const. N. C., art. III, §7.
Vacancy in office.
Election to fill, §163-8.
Stay of certificate.
Appeal of decision to superior court, §163-182.14.
Straight-party tickets.
Ballots, §163-165.6, (e).
Counting, §163-182.1, (a).
Student election assistants, §163-42.1.
Subpoenas.
Corruption.
Witnesses, §§163-277, 163-278.
State board of elections.
Powers of chairman, §163-23.
Suffrage, Const. U. S., amds. XV, XIX.
Summary of officials' duties, §163-182.17, (a).
Superintendent of public instruction, §115C-18.
Superior courts.
Clerks of court, §7A-100, (a).
Date of election, §163-1, (a).
Vacancy or people failing to elect, §163-115, (a).
Judges, §7A-41.2; Const. N. C., art. IV, §16.
Date of election, §163-1, (a).
Generally, §§163-321 to 163-335.
See SUPERIOR COURT JUDGES.
Supreme court justices, Const. N. C., art. IV, §16.
Judicial voter guide.
Candidate information, §163-278.69, (b).
Disclaimer statement, §163-278.69, (c).
Publication by board, §163-278.69, (a).
Qualified electors of state to elect justices, §7A-10, (a).
Taxation.
Denial or abridgment of right to vote.
Failure to pay poll or other tax, Const. U. S., amd. XXIV.
Poll tax.
Prohibited, Const. N. C., art. V, §1.
Television.
Campaign contributions and expenditures.
Disclosure requirements for media advertisements, §§163-278.39 to 163-278.39C.
Tie vote.
New elections, §163-182.13, (f).
Resolution, §163-182.8.
Time.
Generally, §163-1, (a).
Municipal elections, §163-279.
Presidential elections, §163-1, (c).
Primary elections, §163-1, (b), (d).
Modification of time schedule.
Power of state board of elections, §163-104.
Presidential preference primaries, §163-213.2.
Training for election officials, §163-82.24, (a).
Certification, §163-82.24, (b).
Transportation board.
Use of position to influence elections or political action, §136-13.1.

ELECTIONS —Cont'd
Transportation department.
Use of position to influence elections or political action, §136-13.1.
Treason.
Disqualifications from office, Const. N. C., art. VI, §8.
Unaffiliated candidate.
Nomination by petition, §163-122, (a).
Form, §163-122, (b).
Inapplicability of provisions, §163-122, (c).
Vacancies in office.
County boards of elections.
Filling, §163-30.
Elections to fill.
Congress.
House of representatives.
Nominating procedures, §163-13, (b).
Special election, §§163-13, (a), 163-115, (b).
Senate, §163-12.
District attorneys, §163-10.
State executive offices, §163-8.
Primary elections.
Death of candidate before primary.
Filling vacancy, §163-112.
Nominees.
Filling vacancies among party nominees occurring after nomination and before election, §163-114.
Notice of candidacy for certain offices to indicate vacancy, §163-106, (d).
Special provisions for obtaining nominations when vacancies occur in certain offices, §163-115, (a) to (e).
State board of elections.
Filling, §163-19.
State or district office other than U.S. house of representatives, §163-115, (c).
Vote-buying, §163-275.
Voters.
Age.
Minimum age, §163-55.
Persons eighteen years of age, Const. U. S., amd. XXVI.
Right to vote not to be abridged on account of age, Const. U. S., amd. XXVI.
Aged voters.
Curbside voting, §163-166.9.
Assistance to voters, §163-166.8.
Blind voters.
Assistance to voters, §163-166.8.
Challenge of voters.
Absentee ballots, §163-89.
Answer to challenge as felon not to be used on prosecution, §163-90.
Burden of proof, §163-90.1, (b).
Challenge to absentee ballots, §163-89, (c).
Day of primary or election, §§163-87 to 163-88.1.
False swearing.
Felony, §163-90.3.
Municipal elections, §163-289.
Other than on day of primary or election, §§163-85, 163-86.
Overruled or dismissed challenge.
Action by board on, §163-90.2, (c).
Appeals, §163-90.2, (d).
Reasonable belief by challenger required, §163-90.1, (a).
Sustained challenge.
Action by board on, §163-90.2, (a), (b).
Appeals, §163-90.2, (d).

ELECTIONS —Cont'd
Voters —Cont'd
Disabled voters.
Assistance to voters, §163-166.8.
Curbside voting, §163-166.9.
Eligibility to vote, Const. N. C., art. VI, §1.
Felons, restoration of citizenship after conviction.
Persons who become qualified to register and vote, §163-82.6, (e).
Intimidation of voters.
Misdemeanors, §163-274.
Officers, §163-271.
Naturalized citizens.
Persons who become qualified to register and vote, §163-82.6, (e).
No longer living in precinct.
Prima facie evidence, §163-85, (e).
Party primaries.
Right to participate or vote in, §163-59.
Municipal elections, §163-283.
Persons eighteen years of age, Const. U. S., amd. XXVI.
Persons who become qualified to register and vote, §163-82.6, (e).
Preventing from voting or other irregularities.
New elections, §163-182.13, (a).
Voter eligibility, §163-182.13, (c).
Prima facie evidence.
Voter no longer living in precinct, §163-85, (e).
Qualifications of voters.
Absentee ballots.
Who may vote absentee ballot.
Primary elections, §163-226.1.
Convicted persons.
Restoration of citizenship rights, §§13-1 to 13-4.
Generally, §163-55; Const. N. C., art. VI, §2; Const. U. S., amd. XXVI.
Municipal elections, §§163-282, 163-283.
Presidential preference primaries, §163-213.2.
Independent voters not to participate, §163-213.7.
Primary elections, §163-59.
Municipal elections, §163-283.
Registration a prerequisite to voting, §163-54.
Primary elections, §163-59.
Residence requirements, §163-55.
Registration of voters, §§163-82.1 to 163-91.
See REGISTRATION OF VOTERS.
Voting places.
Accessible polling places, §163-131, (a).
Definitions, §163-131, (b).
Access to voting enclosure.
Limiting, §163-166.3.
Activity in voting place and buffer zone around it.
Limitations on, §163-166.4.
Agreements for election-related activity, §163-166.4, (b).
Arrangement of voting enclosure, §163-166.2.
Assistance to voters, §163-166.8.
Buffer zones and adjacent areas, §163-166.4, (a).
Agreements for election-related activity, §163-166.4, (b).
Notice to public, §163-166.4, (c).
Closing voting places.
Hours for voting, §163-166.01.
Procedures after close of voting, §163-166.10.
Contents of voting enclosure, §163-166.2.
County boards of elections.
Duties, §163-166.1.
Duties as to, §163-129.

ELECTIONS —Cont'd
Voting places —Cont'd
Curbside voting, §163-166.9.
Electioneering.
Limitations on activity in voting place and buffer zone around it, §163-166.4.
Hours for voting, §163-166.01.
Limiting access to voting enclosure, §163-166.3.
Marking off limits, §163-129.
Opening voting places.
Hours for voting, §163-166.01.
Out-of-precinct voting places, §163-130.1.
Political activity.
Limitations on activity in voting place and buffer zone around it, §163-166.4.
Posting of voter information, §163-166.7A, (a).
Intent, §163-166.7A, (b).
Procedure for voting, §163-166.7.
Procedures after close of voting, §163-166.10.
Procedures before voting begins, §163-166.5.
Satellite voting places, §163-130.
Setting up voting place.
Procedures before voting begins, §163-166.5.
Structures at, §163-129.
Two voting places for certain precincts.
Temporary designation, §163-130.2.
Voting rights act of 1965.
Submission of acts to United States attorney general, §§120-30.9A to 120-30.9I.
Constitutional amendments.
Secretary of state, §120-30.9D.
Counties.
Alternate submission authority, §120-30.9I.
County attorney, §120-30.9E.
Judicial system.
Administrative office of the court, §120-30.9C.
Municipalities.
Municipality attorney, §120-30.9F.
North Carolina register.
Decision letters of U. S. attorney general.
Published in North Carolina register, §120-30.9H.
Publication of decision letters of U. S. attorney general in North Carolina register, §120-30.9H.
Purpose of article, §120-30.9A.
School administrative units.
Alternate submission authority, §120-30.9I.
Boards of education attorney, §120-30.9G, (b).
State board of education, §120-30.9G, (a).
Statewide statutes.
State board of elections, §120-30.9B, (a), (b).
Voting systems.
Boards of county commissioners.
Powers and duties, §163-165.8.
County boards of elections.
Powers and duties, §§163-165.9, 163-165.10.
Examination by county board of elections, §163-33.2.
Lever machines or punch cards, use of, §163-165.4A, (a1).
Effective date of provision, §163-165.4A, (b).
State board of elections.
Access to voting machines, §163-22, (j).
Powers and duties, §163-165.7.
Watershed improvement programs.
Generally, §§139-39, 139-40.
Wildlife resource commission offices, §143-243.
Witnesses.
Contributions and expenditures in political campaigns.
Self-incrimination.
Immunity from prosecution, §163-278.29.

ELECTIONS —Cont'd
Witnesses —Cont'd
Corruption.
Self-incrimination.
Immunity from prosecution, §163-277.
Subpoenas, §§163-277, 163-278.
Power of district attorneys, §163-278.
State board of elections.
Powers of chairman as to witnesses, §163-23.
Woman suffrage, Const. U. S., amd. XIX.
Write-in votes.
Ballots, §163-165.6, (f).
Counting ballots, §163-182.1, (a).

ELECTIVE LIFE ESTATE.
Marital interest in real property, §29-30.
Waiver, §39-7, (a), (c).

ELECTIVE SHARE OF SURVIVING SPOUSE, §§30-3.1 to 30-3.6, 31-5.3.
Appeal from decision of clerk to superior court, §30-3.4, (g).
Claim.
Petition prior to marriage, §31-5.3.
Time for making, §30-3.4, (b).
Death taxes, §30-3.1, (c).
Preparation of tax form, §30-3.4, (d).
Property passing to surviving spouse.
Reduction of value, §30-3.3, (b).
Definitions, §§30-3.2, 30-3.3, (a).
Exercise of right only during lifetime, §30-3.4, (a).
Generally, §30-3.1, (a).
Hearing.
Findings and conclusions, §30-3.4, (f).
Time for, §30-3.4, (c).
Personal representative.
Recovery of assets by, §30-3.5.
Property passing to surviving spouse, §30-3.3, (a).
Death taxes.
Reduction of value of property passing to surviving spouse, §30-3.3, (b).
Duplication prohibited, §30-3.3, (c).
Recovery of assets by personal representative, §30-3.5, (a).
Bond, §30-3.5, (e).
Expenses, §30-3.5, (d).
Satisfaction of liability, §30-3.5, (c).
Standstill order, §30-3.5, (b).
Reduction of applicable share, §30-3.1, (b).
Valuation of interests in property, §30-3.4, (e).
Waiver of rights, §30-3.6, (a).
Estates of decedents dying on or before December 31, 2000.
Waiver effective, §30-3.6, (c).
When not enforceable, §30-3.6, (b).

ELECTRICAL APPLIANCE AND EQUIPMENT SALES, §§66-23 to 66-27.
Actions.
Enforcement of provisions, §66-27.01.
Compliance with provisions required, §66-23.
Evidence.
Acceptable listings as to safety of goods, §66-25.
Identification marks, §66-24.
Installation.
Legal responsibility for proper installation unaffected, §66-26.
Liability.
Effect of provisions, §66-26.

ELECTRICAL APPLIANCE AND EQUIPMENT SALES —Cont'd
Merchantability.
Acceptable listings as to safety of goods, §66-25.
Misdemeanors.
Violations of provisions, §66-27.
Safety.
Acceptable listings as to safety of goods, §66-25.
Testing.
Acceptable listings as to safety of goods, §66-25.

ELECTRICAL CONTRACTORS, §§87-39 to 87-51.
Applicability of provisions.
Exceptions, §87-43.1.
Board of examiners.
Appointment of members, §87-39.
Classification of licenses.
Standards for, §87-43.3.
Composition, §87-39.
Disciplinary proceedings.
Generally, §87-47.
Duties, §87-42.
Meetings, §87-39.
Oath of office of members, §87-39.
Office.
Principal office, §87-39.
Officers, §87-39.
Powers, §87-42.
Public awareness program, §87-50.1.
Quorum, §87-39.
Seal, §87-41.
Secretary-treasurer, §87-40.
Terms of members, §87-39.
Vacancies, §87-39.
Child support enforcement.
Forfeiture of licensing privilege, §50-13.12.
Complaints against licensees.
Records, §87-47, (c).
Continuing education requirements, §87-44.1.
Corporations.
Licenses, §87-43.2.
Definitions, §87-41.1.
Electrical contracting, §87-43.
Education.
Continuing education requirements, §87-44.1.
Examinations.
No examination required of licensed contractors, §87-49.
Exceptions to provisions, §87-43.1.
Fees.
Licenses, §87-44.
Use of funds collected, §87-45.
Injunctions.
Violations of provisions, §87-48, (b).
Licenses.
Classification of licenses, §87-43.3.
Corporations, §87-43.2.
Disciplinary actions, §87-47, (a1) to (a3).
Display, §87-43.
Examinations.
No examination required of licensed contractors, §87-49.
Fees, §87-44.
Use of funds collected, §87-45.
Issuance, §87-43.2.
Nonresidents.
Definitions, §87-44.2, (a).
Delinquents, §87-44.2, (d).
Information, §87-44.2, (c).
Prerequisites to issuance of license, §87-44.2, (b).

ELECTRICAL CONTRACTORS —Cont'd
Licenses —Cont'd
Partnerships, §87-43.2.
Reciprocity, §87-50.
Registry of licenses, §87-43.
Renewal, §87-44.
Residential dwelling license, §87-43.4.
Responsibilities of licensees, §87-46.
Revocation or suspension.
Felony convictions, §15A-1331, (a).
Reissuance, §87-47, (d).
Rules governing, §87-47, (b).
Signing, §87-43.
Term, §87-44.
Negligence.
Immunity of board for negligent acts of license holders, §87-46.
Nonresidents.
Licensing of nonresidents, §87-44.2.
Partnerships.
Licenses, §87-43.2.
Public awareness program, §87-50.1.
Residential dwelling license, §87-43.4.
Severability of provisions, §87-51.
Violations of provisions.
Injunctions, §87-48, (b).
Penalty, §87-48, (a).

ELECTRICAL INSPECTORS.
County inspection departments generally, §§153A-350 to 153A-375.
See COUNTY INSPECTION DEPARTMENTS.

ELECTRIC CHAIR, DEATH BY.
Abolished, §15-187.

ELECTRIC COMPANIES.
Bills to show reading or meter, §66-9.
Child support enforcement.
Location of absent parents.
Information to be provided, §110-139, (d).
Coal-fired generating units.
Emissions of oxides of nitrogen and sulfur dioxide by investor-owned utilities, §143-215.107D.
Environmental compliance costs recovery, §62-133.6.
Costs of petitions for condemnation of land, §6-22.
Eminent domain.
By whom right may be exercised, §40A-3, (a).
Dwelling house, yard, kitchen, etc., of owner taken under certain cases, §62-184.
Exercise of right, parties interest only taken, §62-185.
Grant, §62-183.
Petition costs, §6-22.
Powers granted corporations exercisable by persons, firms or copartnerships, §62-189.
Proceedings as under eminent domain, §62-187.
Use or occupancy of public highway, §62-181.
Environmental compliance costs recovery.
Coal-fired generating units, §62-133.6.
Franchise or privilege tax.
Additional tax imposed by county or city.
Companies not subject to, §105-116, (e1).
Annual tax imposed, §105-116, (a).
City not to impose or collect greater tax, §105-116, (e).
County or city imposing additional tax.
Companies not subject to, §105-116, (e1).
Distribution to cities, §105-116, (d).
City's share, §105-116.1, (b).
Definitions, §105-116.1, (a).

ELECTRIC COMPANIES —Cont'd
Franchise or privilege tax —Cont'd
Distribution to cities —Cont'd
Hold-back amount for 1995-96 fiscal year, §105-116.1, (c) to (d).
Municipality incorporated on or after January 1, 2000, §105-116.1, (e).
Payment, return, report, §105-116, (b).
Rate of tax, §105-116, (a).
Generating facilities, §§62-82, 62-110.1.
Joint municipal electric power and energy, §§159B-1 to 159B-52.
See JOINT MUNICIPAL ELECTRIC POWER AND ENERGY ACT.
Membership corporations, §§117-6 to 117-26.
See ELECTRIC MEMBERSHIP CORPORATIONS.
Meters.
Electric light bills to show reading of meter, §66-9.
Master electrical meters, §143-151.42.
Municipal corporations.
Electric service in urban areas, §§160A-331 to 160A-338.
See ELECTRIC SERVICE IN URBAN AREAS.
Electric service outside of municipalities, §62-110.2.
Joint municipal electric power and energy, §§159B-1 to 159B-52.
See JOINT MUNICIPAL ELECTRIC POWER AND ENERGY ACT.
Joint ownership of generation and transmission facilities, Const. N. C., art. V, §10.
Public enterprises generally, §§160A-311 to 160A-326.
See MUNICIPAL UTILITIES.
Nuclear facilities producing electricity, fees, §166A-6.1.
Overhead high-voltage line safety, §§95-229.5 to 95-229.13.
See OVERHEAD HIGH-VOLTAGE LINE SAFETY.
Property taxes.
Public service corporations.
Generally, §§105-333 to 105-344.
See PROPERTY TAXES.
Public utilities generally, §§62-1 to 62-333.
See PUBLIC UTILITIES.
Rates for electric power.
Conservation of energy.
Change of rates.
Application to be accompanied by report of probable effect, §62-155, (e).
Generally, §62-155, (b) to (d).
Policy of state, §62-155.
Exemption of certain electric utilities, §62-134, (d).
Fuel charge adjustment, §62-133.2.
Hearing, §62-134, (b), (c).
Increase notices, §62-81, (b).
Small power producers.
Power sales to public utilities, §62-156, (a).
Determinations by commission, §62-156, (b).
Surplus power rates, §62-154.
Rates for public utilities generally, §§62-130 to 62-159.
See PUBLIC UTILITY RATES.
Right-of-way.
Acquisition by contract, §62-182.
Grant of eminent domain, §62-183.
Rural electrification authority, §§117-1 to 117-5.
See RURAL ELECTRIFICATION AUTHORITY.

ELECTRIC COMPANIES —Cont'd
Transmission line construction, §§62-180, 113A-12.
Transmission line siting, §§62-100 to 62-107.
See ELECTRIC TRANSMISSION LINE SITING.
Trespass.
Criminal trespass.
Damaging wires and other fixtures, §§14-154, 14-156.
Felling trees onto electric-power wires, §14-157.
Interfering with electric appliances, §14-151.
Underground damage prevention, §§87-100 to 87-114.
See UNDERGROUND DAMAGE PREVENTION.
Wastewater systems.
Limitation on electrical service, §130A-339.
Temporary electrical service, §130A-339.

ELECTRIC FENCES.
Electronic dog collars, unlawful removal, §14-401.17.

ELECTRICITY.
Actions.
Sale of electrical materials, devices, appliances and equipment.
Enforcement of provisions, §66-27.01.
Building codes.
Certificates for occupancy, §143-139.2, (b).
Applicability of provisions, §143-139.2, (c).
Insulation requirements, §143-139.2, (a), (b).
Applicability of provisions, §143-139.2, (c).
Wiring of houses, buildings and structures.
Requirements, §143-143.2.
Coal-fired generating units.
Emissions of oxides of nitrogen and sulfur dioxide by investor-owned utilities, §143-215.107D.
Environmental compliance costs recovery, §62-133.6.
Cogenerating power plants.
Income tax credit.
Corporation or partnership constructing in state, §105-130.25, (a).
Application for credit, §105-130.25, (d).
Ceiling on credit, §105-130.25, (e).
Cogenerating power plant defined, §105-130.25, (b).
Cost paid during earlier year, alternative method, §105-130.25, (c).
Companies.
See ELECTRIC COMPANIES.
Contractors, §§87-39 to 87-51.
See ELECTRICAL CONTRACTORS.
Cooperative associations.
Authorized purposes, §§54-111, 54-124.
Electric membership corporations, §§117-6 to 117-26.
See ELECTRIC MEMBERSHIP CORPORATIONS.
Environmental compliance costs recovery.
Coal-fired generating units, §62-133.6.
Sales and use tax.
Payment, return, §105-164.16, (c).
Rate, §105-164.4, (a).
Sale reported on accrual basis, §105-164.20.

ELECTRIC MEMBERSHIP CORPORATIONS, §§117-6 to 117-26.
Amendments.
Certificate of incorporation, §117-25.
Assessments, §117-19.

ELECTRIC MEMBERSHIP CORPORATIONS —Cont'd
Board of directors.
Bylaws.
Power of board to adopt and amend, §117-14.
Compensation, §117-13.
Election, §117-13.
Indemnification of directors, §117-46.
Powers.
Adoption and amendment of bylaws, §117-14.
Delegation of powers, §117-14.
Enumerated, §117-14.
President, §117-13.
Rules and regulations.
Powers of board, §117-14.
Secretary, §117-13.
Bond issues, §117-21.
Agreements for security of bonds, §117-22.
Cancellation of bonds, §117-23.
Covenants or agreements for security of bonds, §117-22.
Purchase and cancellation of bonds, §117-23.
Specific grant of power, §117-18.
Borrowing money.
Specific grant of power, §117-18.
Bylaws.
Power of board of directors to adopt and amend, §117-14.
Certificate of dissolution, §117-24.
Certificate of incorporation.
Amendment of certificate, §117-25.
Authorized formation, §117-10.
Contents, §117-11.
Execution of certificate by residents of territory served, §117-12.
Filing of certificate by residents of territory served, §117-12.
Formation authorized, §117-10.
Permissible provisions, §117-11, (b).
Required provisions, §117-11, (a).
Certificates of membership, §117-15.
Citation of act, §117-6.
Conditions of membership, §117-16.
Consolidation.
Articles of consolidation, §117-41, (c).
Filing and recording of articles, §117-43.
Recording of articles, §117-43.
Compliance with provisions, §117-41, (a).
Effect of consolidation, §117-44.
Procedure, §117-41, (c).
Proposition for consolidation, §117-41, (b).
Validation, §117-45.
Contracts.
Specific grant of power, §117-18.
Corporate purpose, §117-16.
General grant of powers, §117-17.
Debts.
Contracting debt.
Specific grant of power, §117-18.
Definitions, §117-7.
Discrimination prohibited, §117-16.1.
Dissolution.
Certificate of dissolution, §117-24.
Federal aid.
Acceptance of gifts or grants, §117-18.
Application for grant or loan from governmental agency, §117-26.
Fees.
Applicability, §62-300, (e).
Regulatory fee, §117-3.1.
Rate, §62-302, (b1).

ELECTRIC MEMBERSHIP CORPORATIONS —Cont'd
Foreign corporations, §117-28.
Domestication, §117-28.
Privileges, §117-28.
Rights and privileges, §117-28.
Formation in unserved communities, §117-8.
Application.
Filed with rural electrification authority, §117-8.
Issuance of privilege for formation of such corporation, §117-9.
Authorized, §117-10.
Privilege for formation of such corporation.
Issuance of privilege, §117-9.
Franchises.
Eligibility to receive franchise, §117-10.1.
Restriction on municipal service, §117-10.2.
Grants.
Application for grant or loan from governmental agency, §117-26.
Indemnification.
Directors, officers, employees and agents, §117-46.
Loans.
Application for grant or loan from governmental agency, §117-26.
Membership.
Certificates of membership, §117-15.
Conditions of membership, §117-16.
Terms of membership, §117-16.
Merger.
Articles of merger, §117-42, (c).
Filing and recording of articles, §117-43.
Recording of articles, §117-43.
Compliance with provisions, §117-42, (a).
Effect of merger, §117-44.
Procedure, §117-42, (c).
Proposition for merger, §117-42, (b).
Validation, §117-45.
Municipal franchises.
Eligibility to receive franchise, §117-10.1.
Restriction on municipal service, §117-10.2.
Political subdivision.
No corporation to be or have rights of political subdivision of state, §117-19, (a).
Powers.
General grant of powers, §117-17.
Specific grant of powers, §117-18.
Property.
Acquiring, holding and disposing of property.
Specific grant of power, §117-18.
Disposal of property, §117-20.
Encumbrance of property, §117-20.
Property taxes.
Public service corporations.
Generally, §§105-333 to 105-344.
See PROPERTY TAXES.
Public agency.
No corporation to be public agency, §117-19, (a).
Purpose.
Corporate purpose, §§117-16, 117-17.
General grant of powers, §117-17.
Rates.
Discrimination prohibited, §117-16.1.
Regulatory fee.
Due date, §117-3.1, (c).
Imposition, purpose, use, §117-3.1, (a).
North Carolina rural electrification authority fund.
Creation, proceeds deposited in, §117-3.1, (d).
Rate, §117-3.1, (b).

ELECTRIC MEMBERSHIP CORPORATIONS —Cont'd
Rural electric membership corporations.
Sale of merchandise by governmental units.
Exception to prohibition, §66-58, (b).
Sale of merchandise by governmental units.
Exception to provisions, §66-58, (b).
Seal.
Specific grant of powers, §117-18.
Subsidiary business activities, §117-18.1, (a).
Employment of director or spouse, §117-18.1, (c).
Prohibited activities, §117-18.1, (b).
Taxes and assessments.
Subject to certain taxes, §117-19, (b).
Telephone corporations.
Applicability of provisions, §117-30, (a).
Terms and conditions of membership, §117-16.
Title of article, §117-6.
Utilities commission.
Regulation by commission, §62-53.

ELECTRIC PERSONAL ASSISTIVE MOBILITY DEVICES.
Defined, §§20-4.01, 20-175.6, (a).
Municipal regulation, §20-175.6, (d).
Registration and certificate of title.
Exemption, §§20-51, 20-175.6, (b).
Use, §20-175.6, (c).

ELECTRIC POWER AND ENERGY ACT, §§159B-1 to 159B-52.
See JOINT MUNICIPAL ELECTRIC POWER AND ENERGY ACT.

ELECTRIC POWER HOLDING COMPANIES.
Dividends.
Income tax.
Adjustment for expenses related to, §105-130.6A, (d), (g), (h).

ELECTRIC POWER RATES.
Conservation of energy.
Change of rates.
Application to be accompanied by report of probable effect, §62-155, (e).
Generally, §62-155, (b) to (d).
Policy of state, §62-155.
Exemption of certain electric utilities, §62-134, (d).
Fuel charge adjustment, §62-133.2.
Hearing, §62-134, (b), (c).
Notice of rate increase, §62-81, (b).
Small power procedures.
Power sales to public utilities, §62-156, (a).
Determinations by commission, §62-156, (b).
Surplus power rates, §62-154.

ELECTRIC SERVICE IN URBAN AREAS, §§160A-331 to 160A-338.
City facilities, §160A-336.
Contracts, §160A-322.
Definitions, §160A-331.
Load management, §160A-323.
Peak load pricing, §160A-323.
Police powers, §160A-338.
Rates, §160A-323.
Suppliers.
Assigned supplier.
Defined, §160A-331.
Police power, §160A-338.
Primary supplier.
Defined, §160A-331.
Effect of provisions, §160A-337.

ELECTRIC SERVICE IN URBAN AREAS —Cont'd
Suppliers —Cont'd
Primary supplier —Cont'd
Furnishing electric service for city facilities, §160A-336.
Rights and restrictions, §160A-332, (a).
Cities incorporated after April 20, 1965, §160A-332, (b).
Secondary supplier.
Defined, §160A-331.
Discontinuance of service and transfer of facilities by, §160A-335.
Temporary electric service, §160A-333.
Temporary electric service, §160A-333.
Utilities commission.
Authority and jurisdiction, §160A-334.
Discontinuance of service and transfer of facilities by secondary supplier, §160A-335.
Orders, §160A-334.

ELECTRIC TRANSMISSION LINE CONSTRUCTION.
Environmental document.
Not required when constructing, maintaining or removing lines across right of way of street or highway, §113A-12.
Rights of persons operating to construct and maintain along highways and railroads, §62-180.

ELECTRIC TRANSMISSION LINE SITING.
Construction certificate.
Application.
Amendment of certificate, §62-102, (e).
Contents, §62-102, (a).
Inadvertent failure of service on or notice to, §62-102, (d).
Notice, §62-102, (c).
Service of copies, §62-102, (b).
Burden of proof, §62-105.
Compliance with certificate, §62-101, (b).
Conditions, §62-105.
Effect of local ordinances, §62-106.
Exemptions, §62-101, (c).
Hearing or making complaint, §§62-101, (f), 62-104.
Initial construction without certificate, §62-101, (e).
Intervention in proceedings, §62-103, (b).
Parties to proceedings, §62-103, (a).
Required, §62-101, (a).
Rules and regulations, §62-107.
Waiver of notice and hearing requirement, §62-101, (d).
Definition, §62-100.
Underground damage prevention, §§87-100 to 87-114.
See UNDERGROUND DAMAGE PREVENTION.

ELECTRIC VEHICLES.
Low speed vehicle defined, §20-4.01.
Operation on certain roadways, restrictions, equipment, registration, insurance, §20-121.1.
Registration fees, §20-87.

ELECTROCUTION, CAPITAL PUNISHMENT.
Abolished, §15-187.

ELECTROLOGISTS, §§88A-1 to 88A-23.
Actions.
Reports of violations of chapter.
Immunity from suit, §88A-23.

ELECTROLOGISTS —Cont'd
Actions —Cont'd
Venue for actions brought under chapter, §88A-22, (b).
Advertisement.
Board of electrologist examiners.
Powers to regulate, §88A-6.
Disseminating false, deceptive or misleading advertising.
Grounds for disciplinary action, §88A-21, (a).
Board of electrologist examiners.
Appointment of members, §88A-5, (a), (b).
"Board" defined, §88A-3.
Compensation, §88A-5, (f).
Composition, §88A-5, (a).
Created, §88A-5, (a).
Custody and use of funds, §88A-7.
Disciplinary authority, §88A-21.
Duties.
Generally, §88A-6.
Expenses.
Reimbursement, §88A-5, (f).
Grants, contributions, devises, etc.
Accepted, §88A-8.
Meetings, §88A-5, (h).
Number of members, §88A-5, (a).
Officers.
Elections, §88A-5, (g).
Powers.
Generally, §88A-6.
Quorum, §88A-5, (h).
Removal of members, §88A-5, (e).
Terms of members, §88A-5, (c).
Vacancies.
Filling, §88A-5, (d).
Bribery.
Grounds for disciplinary actions, §88A-21, (a).
Calls outside office, §88A-16, (d).
Change of address, §88A-16, (b).
Citation of chapter.
Short title, §88A-1.
Continuing education.
License renewal requirement, §88A-13.
Conviction of crime.
Grounds for disciplinary actions, §88A-21, (a).
Criminal law and procedure.
Violations of chapter, §88A-4, (b).
Definitions, §88A-3.
Deposits.
Fees payable to board of electrologist examiners, §88A-7.
Disciplinary actions.
Certification, §88A-21, (b).
Grounds, §88A-21, (a).
Licenses.
Reinstatement of revoked license or removal of restrictions, §88A-21, (c).
Restrictions, revocation or suspension, §88A-21, (b), (c).
Remedial education.
Requiring, §88A-21, (b).
Reprimands.
Letters of reprimand, §88A-21, (b).
Education.
Continuing education.
License renewal.
Requirements, §88A-13.
Electrology.
Defined, §88A-3.

ELECTROLOGISTS —Cont'd
Electrology instructors.
Certification.
Examinations, §88A-17, (b).
Failure to renew, §88A-18.
Issuance of certificate, §88A-17, (b).
Renewal.
Annual renewal, §88A-18.
Failure to renew.
Examination, §88A-18.
Requirements, §88A-17, (a).
Electrolysis.
Defined, §88A-3.
Examinations.
Certification of electrology instructors, §88A-17, (b).
Failure to renew certificate, §88A-18.
Licenses, §88A-10, (b).
Without examination, §88A-11.
Expenses, §88A-9, (a).
Fees.
Board of electrologist examiners.
Duties to collect, §88A-6.
Deposits, §88A-7.
Salaries, compensation and expenses incurred paid from, §88A-9, (a).
Schedule, §88A-9, (b).
Felony convictions.
Forfeiture of license, §15A-1331A.
Financial obligations binding upon state.
Prohibited, §88A-9, (a).
Forfeitures.
Schools of electrology.
Failure to renew certification, §88A-20.
Fraud.
Grounds for disciplinary actions, §88A-21, (a).
Gifts.
Acceptance by board of electrologist examiners, §88A-8.
Grants.
Acceptance by board of electrologist examiners, §88A-8.
Hearings.
Reports of violations of chapter.
Notice of administrative hearing, §88A-23.
Immunity.
Reports of violations of chapter, §88A-23.
Injunctions, §88A-22, (a).
Intent of chapter, §88A-2.
Investigations.
Board of electrologist examiners.
Powers, §88A-6.
Licenses.
Board of electrologist examiners.
Powers, §88A-6.
Continuing education.
License renewal requirements, §88A-13.
Display in conspicuous place, §88A-16, (c).
Education.
Continuing education requirements, §88A-13.
Examinations, §88A-10, (b).
Licensure without examination, §88A-11.
Exemptions from licensure, §88A-15.
Fees.
Schedule, §88A-9, (b).
Inactive status, §88A-14.
Issuance, §88A-10, (c).
Nonresidents.
Licensure without examination, §88A-11.
Statement of intent to practice, §88A-10, (d).

ELECTROLOGISTS —Cont'd
Licenses —Cont'd
Practice of electrolysis without license.
Unlawful practice, §88A-4, (a).
Proof to be furnished board, §88A-10, (a1).
Records.
Continuing education.
Records of educational course work, §88A-13, (c).
Renewal.
Annual renewal, §88A-12, (a).
Continuing education.
Approval of program, §88A-13, (b).
Hours and subject matter, §88A-13, (a).
Maintenance and distribution of appropriate records of educational course work, §88A-13, (c).
Failure to renew.
Reinstatement, §88A-12, (b).
Inactive status.
Removal from inactive status, §88A-14.
Late renewal, §88A-12, (a).
Requirements, §88A-10, (a).
Restrictions, revocation or suspension.
Disciplinary actions, §88A-21, (b).
Reinstatement of revoked license or removal of restrictions, §88A-21, (c).
Felony convictions, §15A-1331A.
Temporary license.
Issuance, §88A-10.1.
Malpractice.
Grounds for disciplinary actions, §88A-21, (a).
Mental health, developmental disabilities and substance abuse.
Judicial determination of mental incompetency.
Grounds for disciplinary actions, §88A-21, (a).
Misdemeanors.
Violations of chapter, §88A-4, (b).
Nonresidents.
Licensure without examination, §88A-11.
Statement of intent to practice, §88A-10, (d).
Notice.
Change of address or opening of new office, §88A-16, (b).
Reports of violations of chapter.
Notice of administrative hearing, §88A-23.
Opening of new offices.
Notice, §88A-16, (b).
Permanent establishments.
Required, §88A-16, (a).
Physicians and surgeons.
Exemptions from licensure, §88A-15.
Place of business.
Calls outside office, §88A-16, (d).
Change of address or opening of new office.
Notice, §88A-16, (b).
Permanent establishment.
Required, §88A-16, (a).
Practice of electrolysis.
Unlawful practice, §88A-4, (a).
Purposes of chapter, §88A-2.
Records.
Board of electrologist examiners.
Duty to maintain records of proceedings, §88A-6.
Continuing education requirements.
Records of educational course work, §88A-13, (c).
Reports.
Violations of chapter, §88A-23.
Immunity from suit, §88A-23.

ELECTROLOGISTS —Cont'd
Reprimands.
Disciplinary actions.
Letters of reprimand, §88A-21, (b).
Rules and regulations.
Board of electrologist examiners.
Powers to adopt, §88A-6.
Salaries, §88A-9, (a).
Schools of electrology.
Certification.
Display, §88A-19, (e).
Forfeiture.
Failure to renew, §88A-20.
Issuance of certificate, §88A-19, (b).
Renewal.
Annual renewal, §88A-20.
Failure to renew.
Forfeiture, §88A-20.
Requirements, §88A-19, (a).
Transferability of certificates, §88A-19, (d).
Valid for location named in application only, §88A-19, (c).
Epilators.
Used in school.
Approval by food and drug administration of United States government, §88A-19, (f).
Renewal.
Failure to renew.
Examination, §88A-18.
Seals and sealed instruments.
Board of electrologist examiners.
Powers to adopt, §88A-6.
Short title, §88A-1.
Superior courts.
Venue for actions brought under chapter, §88A-22, (b).
Temporary license.
Issuance, §88A-10.1.
Title of chapter.
Short title, §88A-1.
Unprofessional conduct.
Grounds for disciplinary actions, §88A-21, (a).
Venue.
Actions brought under chapter, §88A-22, (b).
Violations of chapter.
Injunctions, §88A-22.
Misdemeanors, §88A-4, (b).
Reports, §88A-23.
Immunity from suit, §88A-23.

ELECTROMAGNETIC RADIATION.
Radiation protection act generally, §§104E-1 to 104E-29.
See RADIATION PROTECTION.

ELECTRONIC ACCESS TO STATE SERVICES.
Electronic and digital transactions.
Access to services through.
Agencies encouraged to maximize, §66-58.12, (a).
Fees, §66-58.12, (b), (c).
Judicial department exempt from provisions, §66-58.12, (d).
Webportal system.
Agency links, §66-58.20, (b).
Development and implementation, §66-58.20, (a).

ELECTRONIC AUCTION SERVICE.
Disposition of seized, confiscated or unclaimed property, §15-14.1.
State surplus property.
Sale or disposal using, §143-64.03, (d).

ELECTRONIC BULLETIN BOARD SERVICE.
Sales and use tax on telecommunications services.
Excluded from gross receipts, §105-164.4C, (c).

ELECTRONIC CHATTEL PAPER.
Secured transactions.
Control, §25-9-105.
Perfection by control, §25-9-314, (a).

ELECTRONIC COMMERCE IN GOVERNMENT, §§66-58.1 to 66-58.12.
Access to services through electronic and digital transactions.
Agencies encouraged to maximize, §66-58.12, (a).
Fees, §66-58.12, (b), (c).
Judicial department exempt from provisions, §66-58.12, (d).
Certification authorities.
Licensing, §66-58.3.
Civil penalties for violations, §66-58.7.
Conflict of other rights, §66-58.6, (d).
Criminal penalties for violations, §66-58.8, (a).
Definitions, §66-58.2.
Deposit of fees, §66-58.10, (c).
Electronic signatures.
Acceptance and use by public agencies, §66-58.4.
Enforceability of transactions, §66-58.5, (b).
Presumptions and burden of proof not effected, §66-58.5, (c).
Validity, §66-58.5, (a).
Enforcement of provisions, §66-58.6, (a).
Evidence of criminal violations, §66-58.8, (b).
Exemptions from article, §66-58.9.
Jurisdiction over transactions, §66-58.6, (b).
Legislative purpose, §66-58.1.
Limitation of authority for criminal punishment, §66-58.8, (c).
Non-applicability of article, §66-58.9.
Purpose of article, §66-58.1.
Reciprocal agreements, §66-58.11.
Representation by Attorney General, §66-58.6, (c).
Rulemaking.
Procedures, §66-58.10, (a).
Temporary rules, §66-58.10, (b).

ELECTRONIC DOG COLLARS.
Applicable counties, §14-401.17, (d).
Enforcement, §14-401.17, (c).
Jurisdiction, §14-401.17, (c).
Penalties, §14-401.17, (b).
Unlawful removal, §14-401.17, (a).

ELECTRONIC FUNDS TRANSFERS.
Funds transfers generally, §§25-4A-101 to 25-4A-507.
See FUNDS TRANSFERS.
Local government finance.
Acceptance of electronic payments, §159-32.1.
Public hospitals, §159-39, (i), (i1).
Statewide accounts receivable program.
Payments by, authorized, §147-86.22, (b).
Taxes.
Payment by, §105-241, (b).
Penalty for bad transfer, §105-236.

ELECTRONIC MAIL.
Cyberstalking, §14-196.3.
Electronic records and signatures.
Uniform electronic transactions act, §§66-311 to 66-330.
See ELECTRONIC TRANSACTIONS.

ELECTRONIC MAIL —Cont'd
Sales and use tax on telecommunications services.
Excluded from gross receipts, §105-164.4C, (c).
Spam.
Damage recovery, §1-539.2A.
Personal jurisdiction for actions regarding, §1-75.4.
Stalking, §14-277.3.

ELECTRONIC MEDICAL RECORDS, §90-412.

ELECTRONIC MONITORING DEVICES, §15A-1343, (b1).
Costs, §148-10.3.
House arrest with electronic monitoring, defined, §15A-1340.11.

ELECTRONIC RECORDS AND SIGNATURES.
Uniform electronic transactions act, §§66-311 to 66-330.
See ELECTRONIC TRANSACTIONS.

ELECTRONIC SPEED-MEASURING INSTRUMENTS.
Admissibility of results, §8-50.2.
Calibration and testing standards, §8-50.2, (c).

ELECTRONIC SURVEILLANCE.
Actions.
Civil cause of action for violation of article.
Damages authorized, §15A-296.
Administrative subpoena to compel production of business records, §15A-298.
Advertisement for surveillance devices.
Felony, §15A-288, (a2).
Aggrieved person.
Defined, §15A-286.
Appeals.
Order granting motion to suppress, §15A-294, (h).
Attorneys' fees.
Civil action for violation of article, §15A-296, (a).
Aural transfers.
Defined, §15A-286.
Bugging devices.
Advertisements for, §15A-288, (a2).
Confiscation of, §15A-289.
Manufacture, §15A-288.
Citizens band radio communications.
Interception not unlawful, §15A-287, (b2).
Civil action for violation of article.
Damages authorized, §15A-296.
Civil defense signals.
Interception not unlawful, §15A-287, (b2).
Communications common carriers.
Defined, §15A-286.
Permissible manufacture, assembly, possession, purchase or sale of surveillance devices, §15A-288, (b1).
Confiscation of electronic surveillance devices, §15A-289.
Conformity to federal law, §15A-297.
Conspiracy to commit certain crimes.
Issuance of orders for surveillance, §15A-290, (a2).
Continuing criminal enterprise.
Issuance of orders for electronic surveillance, §15A-290, (a1).
Costs.
Civil action for violation of article, §15A-296, (a).
Damages.
Civil action for violation of article.
Actual damages, §15A-296, (a).
Defenses.
Actions for violation of article.
Good faith reliance, complete defense, §15A-296, (b).

ELECTRONIC SURVEILLANCE —Cont'd
Definitions.
Generally, §15A-286.
Disclosure of communications.
Discretion of judicial review panel to disclose to party or counsel, §15A-294, (e).
Evidence.
Copy of order and application must be furnished to parties, §15A-294, (f).
Law enforcement officers in performance of duty, §15A-294, (a), (b).
Testifying under oath, §15A-294, (c).
Distress or public use signals.
Interception not unlawful, §15A-287, (b2).
Drug-trafficking violations.
Issuance of orders for surveillance, §15A-290, (a1).
Electronic communications.
Authorized interception by law enforcement personnel, §15A-290, (d).
Defined, §15A-286.
Disclosure by law enforcement officer in performance of duty, §15A-294, (a).
Use of contents by law enforcement officer in performance of duty, §15A-294, (b).
Willful disclosure, felony, §15A-287, (a3).
Willful interception, felony, §15A-287, (a1).
Electronic communication services.
Administrative subpoena to compel production of business records, §15A-298.
Defined, §15A-286.
Interception by agent of providers.
Not unlawful if necessary to services, §15A-287, (c).
Electronic communication systems.
Defined, §15A-286.
Electronic storage.
Defined, §15A-286.
Evidence.
Admissibility of contents of communications.
Copy of order and application must be furnished to parties, §15A-294, (f).
Disclosure of communications.
Copy of order and application must be furnished to parties, §15A-294, (f).
Motion to suppress contents of communications, §15A-294, (g).
Appeal of order granting motion, §15A-294, (h).
Extortion.
Electronic surveillance orders, §15A-290, (b).
Federal communications commission officers.
Interception in discharge of monitoring responsibilities.
Not unlawful, §15A-287, (d).
Federal law, legislative intent of conformity, §15A-297.
Felony offenses, surveillance orders to be issued.
Adulteration of food, drugs or cosmetics, §15A-290, (c5).
Assault or threats against executive or legislative officers, §15A-290, (c4).
Assault with deadly weapon of government officers, §15A-290, (c4).
Intimidation or harassment of jurors or witnesses, §15A-290, (c3).
Mass death or destruction weapons.
Manufacture, assembly, etc., §15A-290, (c5).
Murder, kidnapping, robbery, etc., §15A-290, (b).
Obstructing criminal investigations, §15A-290, (c2).
Offenses against minors, §15A-290, (c1).

ELECTRONIC SURVEILLANCE —Cont'd
Forfeiture of electronic surveillance devices, §15A-289.
Good faith reliance.
Complete defense to actions for violation of article, §15A-296, (b).
Ham radio communications.
Interception not unlawful, §15A-287, (b2).
Judicial review panels.
Applications for electronic surveillance orders, §§15A-291, (a), 15A-292, (a).
Contents, §15A-291, (d).
Compliance with federal statute, §15A-291, (b).
Composition, §15A-291, (a).
Contents of application for surveillance order, §15A-291, (d).
Defined, §15A-286.
Determination of probable cause for orders, §15A-291, (e).
Disclosure of recorded material.
Discretion to disclose to party or counsel, §15A-294, (e).
Emergency applications for surveillance orders.
Compliance with federal statute, §15A-291, (b).
Examination of applicant under oath, §15A-291, (e).
Interception of communications by law enforcement personnel.
Felonies other than those specified, §15A-290, (d).
Judge may preside over trial resulting from surveillance order, §15A-291, (c).
Orders for surveillance.
Application and granting, §15A-292, (a).
Applications sealed by panel, §15A-293, (d2).
Contents of order, §15A-293, (b).
Custody of applications for orders, §15A-293, (d2).
Denial, §15A-294, (h).
Destruction of orders, §15A-293, (d2).
Determinations necessary for issuance, §15A-293, (a).
Inventory of parties upon issuance of order, §15A-294, (d).
Notice to parties upon issuance of order, §15A-294, (d), (d1).
Reports, §15A-293, (d).
Probable cause for surveillance orders, determination of, §15A-291, (e).
Recorded material.
Custody of recordings, §15A-293, (d).
Discretion to disclose portion of material to party or counsel, §15A-294, (e).
Report to supreme court regarding surveillance orders, §15A-292, (c).
Trials resulting from electronic surveillance order.
Member of panel may not preside, §15A-291, (c).
Law enforcement communications available to general public.
Interception not unlawful, §15A-287, (b2).
Manufacture of surveillance devices.
Felony, §15A-288, (a1).
Law enforcement use, permissible manufacture, §15A-288, (c).
Mobile radio communications.
Interception not unlawful, §15A-287, (b2).
Notice.
Orders for surveillance.
Application and granting of order, §15A-292, (a).
Oral communications.
Defined, §15A-286.

ELECTRONIC SURVEILLANCE —Cont'd
Oral communications —Cont'd
Disclosure by law enforcement officer in performance of duty, §15A-294, (a).
Lawful interception by law enforcement personnel, §15A-290, (d).
Use of contents by law enforcement officer in performance of duty, §15A-294, (b).
Willful disclosure, felony, §15A-287, (a3).
Willful interception, felony, §15A-287, (a1).
Order denying application for surveillance order, §15A-294, (h).
Orders for surveillance.
Appeal of order denying application, §15A-294, (h).
Application, §15A-292, (a).
Application by attorney general independent of law enforcement agencies, §15A-292, (b).
Authorized duration of order, §15A-293, (c).
Contents required, §15A-293, (b).
Custody of applications and orders, §15A-293, (d2).
Destruction of applications or orders, §15A-293, (d2).
Determinations by judicial review panel, §15A-293, (a).
Duration of order, §15A-293, (c).
Implementation generally, §15A-293.
Notice of application and granting, §15A-292, (a).
Notice to parties of issuance, §15A-294.
Obstruction of investigation or prosecution of surveillance subject matter.
Grossly negligent disclosure, misdemeanor, §15A-287, (f).
Willful disclosure, felony, §15A-287, (e).
Offenses for which orders may be granted, §15A-290.
Progress reports to judicial review panel required in order, §15A-293, (d).
Reports to supreme court, §15A-292, (c).
Request of attorney general for applications, §15A-292, (a).
Sealed by judicial review panel, §15A-293, (d2).
Time period authorized, §15A-293, (c).
Possession of surveillance devices.
Felony, §15A-288, (a1).
Law enforcement use, §15A-288, (c).
Privileged character of communications, §15A-290, (e).
Public officers and employees.
Obstruction of investigation or prosecution of subject matter of surveillance.
Removal from office, §15A-287, (g).
Permissible manufacture, possession, purchase or sale of devices for surveillance, §15A-288, (b2).
Punitive damages.
Civil action for violation of article, §15A-296, (a).
Purchase of surveillance devices.
Felony, §15A-288, (a1).
Law enforcement use, §15A-288, (c).
Radio communications.
Interception not unlawful, §15A-287, (b2).
Readily accessible to the general public.
Defined, §15A-286.
Interception of or access to electronic communications.
Not unlawful, §15A-287, (b1).
Recorded material.
Custody of recordings, §15A-293, (d).
Destruction of recordings, §15A-293, (d).

ELECTRONIC SURVEILLANCE —Cont'd
Recorded material —Cont'd
Disclosure by law enforcement officers in performance of duties, §15A-294, (a).
Disclosure of contents in testimony under oath, §15A-294, (c).
Duplicate recordings, §15A-293, (d).
Judicial review panels.
Discretion to disclose portion of material to party or counsel, §15A-294, (e).
Use of contents by law enforcement officer in performance of duty, §15A-294, (b).
Recording equipment.
Procedures for use established by attorney general, §15A-293, (f).
State bureau of investigation to own and operate equipment, §15A-293, (e).
Recording of communications, procedure, §15A-293, (d).
Records of business.
Subpoena duces tecum, §15A-298.
Reports.
Attorney general report to administrative office of United States court, §15A-295.
Copy of attorney general's report filed with administrative office of courts of North Carolina, §15A-295.
Orders for surveillance, report to supreme court, §15A-292, (c).
Progress reports on orders for surveillance, §15A-293, (d).
Sale of surveillance devices.
Felony, §15A-288, (a1).
Law enforcement use, §15A-288, (c).
Service of process.
Issuance of surveillance order.
Inventory served on parties, §15A-294, (d).
State bureau of investigation.
Operation of recording equipment, §15A-293, (e).
Subpoenas.
Issuance to communications carriers or services for production of business records, §15A-298.
Suppression of evidence.
Appeal of order granting motion, §15A-294, (h).
Motion to suppress contents of communications, §15A-294, (g).
Switchboard operators.
Interception or disclosure of communications in normal course of employment.
Not unlawful, §15A-287, (c).
Training of law enforcement officers for surveillance.
Attorney general, §15A-293, (f).
Users.
Defined, §15A-286.
Willful use of contents of wire or oral communications, felony, §15A-287, (a4).
Willful use of devices to intercept oral communications, felony, §15A-287, (a2).
Wire communications.
Defined, §15A-286.
Disclosure by law enforcement officer in performance of duty, §15A-294, (a).
Lawful interception by law enforcement personnel, §15A-290, (d).
Use of contents by law enforcement officer in performance of duty, §15A-294, (b).
Willful disclosure, felony, §15A-287, (a3).
Willful interception, felony, §15A-287, (a1).

ELECTRONIC SURVEILLANCE ORDERS, §15A-290, (b).

ELECTRONIC TRANSACTIONS, §§66-311 to 66-327.
Agreements.
Defined, §66-312.
Effect, §66-315, (b), (c).
Waiver of provisions by agreement, §66-315, (d).
Applicability of act, §§66-313, (a), (c), 66-315, (b), 66-316.
Exceptions, §66-313, (b), (e).
Prospective application, §66-314.
Athlete agents and agency contracts.
Law governing electronic records and signatures, §78C-103.
Automated transactions, §66-324.
Citation of act, §66-311.
Computer information agreement.
Choice of law, §66-329.
Construction of provisions, §66-316.
Severability, §66-330.
Consumer transactions.
Consent to electronic records, §66-327, (c).
Entered into in state, §66-327, (f).
Federal law compliance, §66-328.
Written copy of contract, §66-327, (d).
Contracts.
Automated transactions, §66-324.
Consumer transactions.
Written copy of contract, §66-327, (d).
Defined, §66-312.
Corporations.
Agreement to conduct, §55-1-50.
Criminal process and procedure.
Definitions relating to electronic technology, §15A-101.1.
Electronic repository for criminal process, §15A-301.1.
Definitions, §66-312.
Transferable record, §66-326, (a).
Electronic records.
Acknowledgment, §66-321.
Attribution, §66-319, (a).
Change.
Effect, §66-320.
Consumer transactions.
Consent to electronic records, §66-327, (c).
Defined, §66-312.
Effect, §66-319, (b).
Error.
Effect, §66-320.
Evidence.
Admissibility, §66-323.
Inhibiting of ability of recipient to store or print by sender.
Record not enforceable against recipient, §66-318, (c), (d).
Legal consequences.
Determination, §66-315, (e).
Legal effect, §66-317, (a) to (c).
Notarization, §66-321.
Posting or display, §66-318, (b), (d).
Receipt.
Effect, §66-325, (f), (g).
What constitutes, §66-325, (b) to (e).
Retention, §66-322, (a) to (d), (f).
Additional requirements by governmental agencies, §66-322, (g).
Checks, §66-322, (e).
Sending.
What constitutes, §66-325, (a), (d).
Transferable records.
Control, §66-326, (b) to (d), (f).
Defined, §66-326, (a).

ELECTRONIC TRANSACTIONS —Cont'd
Electronic records —Cont'd
Transferable records —Cont'd
Obligor's rights and defenses, §66-326, (e).
Proof of control, §66-326, (f).
Use not required by provisions, §66-315, (a).
Electronic signatures.
Acknowledgment, §66-321.
Athlete agents and agency contracts.
Law governing, §78C-103.
Attribution, §66-319, (a).
Criminal process and procedure.
Definitions relating to electronic technology, §15A-101.1.
Defined, §66-312.
Effect, §66-319, (b).
Evidence.
Admissibility, §66-323.
Legal consequences.
Determination, §66-315, (e).
Legal effect, §66-317, (a), (d).
Notarization, §66-321.
Public agencies.
Acceptance and use, §66-58.4.
Validity.
Transactions between person and agency, §66-58.5.
Use not required by provisions, §66-315, (a).
Evidence.
Admissibility of electronic signatures and records, §66-323.
Oral communications, §66-327, (e).
Other applicable laws, §66-313, (d).
Determination of legal consequences of electronic record or signature, §66-315, (e).
Prospective application of act, §66-314.
Public agencies.
Electronic signatures.
Acceptance and use, §66-58.4.
Validity.
Transactions between person and agency, §66-58.5.
Retention of electronic records, §66-322, (a) to (d), (f).
Additional requirements by governmental agencies, §66-322, (g).
Checks, §66-322, (e).
Severability of provisions, §66-330.
Title of act, §66-311.
Writing.
Consumer transactions.
Written copy of contract, §66-327, (d).
Provision of information in writing, §66-318, (a), (d).

ELECTRONS.
Radiation protection act generally, §§104E-1 to 104E-29.
See RADIATION PROTECTION.

ELEMENTARY EDUCATION.
Public schools.
See PUBLIC SCHOOLS.

ELEVATING HEIGHT OF PASSENGER MOTOR VEHICLE, §20-135.4, (d).

ELEVATOR INSURANCE, §58-7-15.
Mandatory or voluntary risk sharing plans.
See MANDATORY OR VOLUNTARY RISK SHARING PLANS.

ELEVATORS, §§95-110.1 to 95-110.15.
Accidents.
Investigations, §95-110.9, (b).
Operating after accident, §95-110.9, (c).

ELEVATORS —Cont'd
Accidents —Cont'd
Removal of damaged equipment, §95-110.9, (d).
Reports.
Required, §95-110.9, (a).
Appeals.
Violations of article, §95-110.10.
Applicability of article, §95-110.2.
Attorney general.
Representing department of labor, §95-110.12.
Building codes.
Enforcement, §143-139, (d).
Special safety to life requirements applicable to existing high-rise buildings.
Class I buildings, §143-138, (i).
Class II buildings, §143-138, (i).
Class III buildings, §143-138, (i).
Certificate of operation.
Required, §95-110.7, (a).
Suspension, revocation or refusal to issue or renew.
Operation after commissioner has refused to issue or has revoked, §95-110.7, (c).
Violations of article, §95-110.6, (b).
Commissioner of labor.
Powers and duties.
Generally, §95-110.5.
Compliance with article, §95-110.7, (b).
Confidentiality.
Trade secrets, §95-110.14.
Construction of article, §95-110.15.
Criminal law and procedure, §95-110.11.
Definitions, §95-110.3.
Elevator and amusement device division, §95-110.4.
Exemptions from article, §95-110.2.
Federal law.
Agreements for enforcement, §95-110.13.
Fines, §95-110.11.
Misdemeanors.
Violations, §95-110.11.
Noncomplying devices and equipment.
Appeals, §95-110.6, (c).
Stopping or limiting use, §95-110.6, (a).
Penalties, §95-110.10.
Prison terms, §95-110.11.
Purpose of general assembly, §95-110.1.
Rules and regulations.
Adoption, §95-110.5.
Construction, §95-110.15.
Scope of article, §95-110.2.
Severability of article, §95-110.15.
Short title of article, §95-110.1.
Smoking in, §143-599.
Trade secrets.
Confidentiality, §95-110.14.
Unsafe device or equipment.
Operation, §95-110.8.
Violation of article.
Appeals, §95-110.10.
Certificate of operation.
Suspension, revocation or refusal to issue or renew, §95-110.6, (b).
Civil penalties, §95-110.10.
Criminal penalties, §95-110.11.

ELIZABETH CITY STATE UNIVERSITY.
Constituent institution of University of North Carolina, §116-4.
Generally.
See UNIVERSITY OF NORTH CAROLINA.

ELIZABETH CITY STATE UNIVERSITY —Cont'd
Distinguished professors endowment trust fund.
Focused growth institutions.
Allocation, §116-41.15, (b).
Contributions, matching, §116-41.16, (b).
Defined, §116-41.13A.

ELUDING ARREST OR APPREHENSION.
Impaired driving.
Aggravating factor to be weighed, §20-179, (d).
Police chases, speed limits not applicable, §20-145.
State parks and forest road system, §143-116.8, (b).

E-MAIL.
Cyberstalking, §14-196.3.
Electronic records and signatures.
Uniform electronic transactions act, §§66-311 to 66-330.
See ELECTRONIC TRANSACTIONS.
General assembly commissions, committees or subcommittees meeting.
Notice, §143-318.14A, (b).
Sales and use tax on telecommunications services.
Excluded from gross receipts, §105-164.4C, (c).
Spam.
Damage recovery, §1-539.2A.
Personal jurisdiction for actions regarding, §1-75.4.
Stalking, §14-277.3.

EMANCIPATION, §§7B-3500 to 7B-3509.
Age of minor, §48A-2.
Answer, time for filing, §7B-3502.
Appeals, §7B-3508.
Burden of showing emancipation in petitioner's best interest, §7B-3503.
Child support.
Termination of support, §50-13.4, (c).
Common law.
Provisions superseded by provisions of chapter, §7B-3509.
Considerations in determining best interest of petitioner, §7B-3504.
Continuing hearing and ordering investigation by juvenile court counselor, §7B-3503.
Contracting as adult, right of emancipated juvenile, §7B-3507.
Conveyances as adult, legal effect of final decree, §7B-3507.
Costs of proceeding, taxing, §7B-3506.
Criminal prosecution of emancipated juvenile as adult, §7B-1604, (a).
Custody.
Persons incapable of self-support upon reaching majority, §50-13.8.
District court jurisdiction, §§7B-200, (a), 7B-1603.
Entry of final decree of emancipation, §7B-3505.
Examination of juvenile by psychiatrist, psychologist or physician.
Court ordering, §7B-3503.
Final decree of emancipation, §7B-3505.
Hearing by court without jury, §7B-3503.
Husband-wife privilege, inapplicability, §7B-3503.
Irrevocability of decree, §7B-3507.

EMANCIPATION —Cont'd
Legal effect of final decree, §7B-3507.
Married juvenile emancipated by provisions of article, §7B-3509.
Married persons, §52-2.
Notice of appeal, §7B-3508.
Parent relieved of legal duties and obligations, §7B-3507.
Petition.
Juveniles sixteen years or older filing, §7B-3500.
Signing and verifying, content requirements, §7B-3501.
Physician-patient privilege, inapplicability, §7B-3503.
Service of summons, §7B-3502.
Summons, §7B-3502.
Temporary order pending disposition of appeal, §7B-3508.
Transacting business as adult, legal effect of final decree, §7B-3507.

EMBALMERS.
Defined, §90-210.20, (d).
Embalming defined, §90-210.20, (e).
License qualifications, §90-210.25, (a).
Medical examiner's permission necessary before embalming, §130A-388, (a), (b).

EMBARGOES.
Authority of department of agriculture and consumer services.
Not limited, §130A-21, (d).
Construing adulterated and misbranded, §130A-21, (e).
Detention of product or article suspected of being misbranded or adulterated, §106-125.
Exercise of authority, §130A-21, (a).
Grade A milk, §130A-21, (b).
Milk and milk products, §130A-21, (b).
Scallops, shellfish or crustacea, §130A-21, (c).
Secretary or local health director.
Exercise of authority, §130A-21, (a).

EMBEZZLEMENT.
Agents.
Property.
Receipt of property by virtue of office or employment, §14-90.
Arrest in civil cases.
Cases in which arrest allowed, §1-410.
Bailments.
Property.
Receipt of property by bailee by virtue of office or employment, §14-90.
Banks.
Conservators.
Applicability of provisions, §53-157.
Prohibited acts, §53-129.
Charities.
Funds embezzled by public officers and trustees, §14-92.
Treasurers of charitable organizations, §14-93.
Civil liability for damages, §1-538.2, (a).
Action brought regardless of criminal action, §1-538.2, (c).
Consequential and punitive damages and attorneys' fees.
Additional recovery allowed, §1-538.2, (a).
Amount of damages, cap, §1-538.2, (a).
Parent or legal guardian liable for acts of minor, §1-538.2, (b).

EMBEZZLEMENT —Cont'd
Civil liability for damages —Cont'd
Consequential and punitive damages and attorneys' fees —Cont'd
Consequential damages, included in, §1-538.2, (c1).
Demand letter, seeking damages prior to action, §1-538.2, (c2).
Payment of money demanded, no further action, §1-538.2, (c4).
Demand letter, seeking damages prior to action, §1-538.2, (c2).
Payment of money demanded, no further action, §1-538.2, (c4).
Qualified privilege of sender, §1-538.2, (c3).
Libel and slander.
Demand letter, seeking damages prior to action.
Qualified privilege of sender, §1-538.2, (c3).
Other theories of law, recovery under, §1-538.2, (d).
Parent or legal guardian liable for acts of minor, §1-538.2, (b).
Recovery of value of goods and merchandise, §1-538.2, (a).
Consignees.
Property.
Receipt of property by virtue of office or employment, §14-90.
Corporations.
Officers or agents of corporation.
Receipt of property by virtue of office or employment, §14-90.
Counties.
Funds embezzled by public officers and trustees, §14-92.
Drugs.
Controlled substances, §90-108, (a).
Education.
Funds embezzled by public officers and trustees, §14-92.
Employees.
Property.
Receipt of property by virtue of office or employment, §14-90.
Executors and administrators.
Liability, §28A-13-10.
Property.
Receipt of property by virtue of office or employment, §14-90.
Fiduciaries.
Property.
Receipt of property by virtue of office or employment, §14-90.
Fraternal benefit societies.
Treasurers of benevolent organizations, §14-93.
Guardians.
Property.
Receipt of property by virtue of office or employment, §14-90.
Indictments.
Description in bill for embezzlement of money, §15-150.
Insurance agents, brokers or administrators, §§58-2-162, 58-2-163.
Labor.
Receipt of property by virtue of office or employment, §14-90.
Larceny by servant or employee, §14-74.
Limited partnerships.
Appropriation of partnership funds by partner to personal use, §14-97.

EMBEZZLEMENT —Cont'd
Limited partnerships —Cont'd
Surviving partner embezzling property, money or effects of partnership, §14-98.
Local government finance.
Penalty, §159-181, (b).
Motor carriers.
C.O.D. shipments, §62-273.
Municipal corporations.
Funds embezzled by public officers and trustees, §14-92.
Partnerships.
Appropriation of partnership funds by partner to personal use, §14-97.
Surviving partner embezzling property, money or effects of partnership, §14-98.
Preneed funeral contracts and funds, §90-210.70, (a), (c).
Prisons and prisoners.
Funds embezzled by public officers and trustees, §14-92.
Property.
Receipt of property by virtue of office or employment, §14-90.
Public officers and employees.
Property of state embezzled by officers and employees, §14-91.
Taxes embezzled by officers, §14-99.
Railroads.
Officers of railroad companies, §14-94.
Receivers.
Property.
Receipt of property by virtue of office or employment, §14-90.
Religious societies.
Funds embezzled by public officers and trustees, §14-92.
Treasurers of religious organizations, §14-93.
Seized items under warrant, §15A-242.
Social services.
Medical assistance program.
Property of patients.
Prohibited acts, §108A-60, (a).
State bureau of investigation.
Misuse of state property, §114-15.1.
State of North Carolina.
Property of state.
Public officers and employees of embezzling state property, §14-91.
Taxation.
Officers embezzling taxes, §14-99.
Trusts and trustees.
Funds embezzled by public officers and trustees, §14-92.
Property.
Receipt of property by virtue of office or employment, §14-90.
Universities and colleges.
Funds embezzled by public officers and trustees, §14-92.

EMBLEMENTS.
Crops.
See CROPS.

EMBLEMS.
Insurance companies, §58-3-50.
Motor clubs and associations.
Approval by commissioner of insurance, §58-69-20.
Tryon's Palace, §121-21.

EMERALD.
State stone, §145-8.

EMERALD ISLE.
Eminent domain.
Exercise of power, purposes, modified provisions, §40A-3, (b1).
Vesting of title and right to possession, §40A-42, (a).
Ordinances to regulate and control swimming, personal watercraft operation, surfing and littering in Atlantic Ocean, §160A-176.2.

EMERGENCIES.
Abortion.
Parental consent requirement waiver, §90-21.9.
Adult care homes.
Waiver of rules for certain homes providing shelter or service during disaster or emergency, §131D-7, (a).
Alcoholic beverages.
State of emergency.
Powers of governor, §18B-110.
Ambulances.
See AMBULANCES.
Archives and history.
Historic properties.
Acquisition where funds not immediately available, §121-9, (f).
Banks.
Suspension of business.
Authorization, §53-77.3, (b).
Construction and interpretation, §53-77.3, (d).
Definitions, §53-77.3, (a).
Legal holiday for certain purposes, §53-77.3, (c).
Bees and honey.
Action by commissioner, §106-642.
Bioterrorism.
Nuclear, biological or chemical agents.
Terrorist incident using, §§130A-475 to 130A-479.
See TERRORIST INCIDENT USING NUCLEAR, BIOLOGICAL OR CHEMICAL AGENTS.
Civil preparedness, §§166A-1 to 166A-16.
See EMERGENCY MANAGEMENT.
Concealed handgun permit.
Temporary permit issuance, §14-415.15, (b).
Contracts.
Purchases and contracts through department of administration.
Purchase of articles in certain emergencies, §143-57.
Corporations.
Business corporations.
Emergency bylaws, §55-2-07.
Emergency powers, §55-3-03.
Criminal law and procedure.
Interfering with emergency communication, §14-286.2.
Definitions.
Emergency communication, §14-286.2, (b).
Drinking water, public water system supplying.
Definition of emergency circumstances, §130A-323, (b).
Plan for provision of drinking water under emergency circumstances, §130A-323, (a).
Emergency management, §§166A-1 to 166A-16.
See EMERGENCY MANAGEMENT.
Emergency management assistance compact, §§166A-40 to 166A-53.
Emergency medical services, §§143-507 to 143-519.
See EMERGENCY MEDICAL SERVICES.

EMERGENCIES —Cont'd
Emergency war powers act, §§147-33.1 to 147-33.6.
See GOVERNOR.
Energy crisis administration, §§113B-20 to 113B-24.
Energy program, §113B-9.
Engineers.
Qualified immunity for volunteers during emergency or disaster, §89C-19.1.
Evacuation of public building.
Power of governor to order evacuation.
Willful refusal to leave building, §14-288.19, (b).
Governor.
Emergency management.
Mutual aid agreements.
Power to establish, §166A-10, (a).
Emergency war powers, §§147-33.1 to 147-33.6.
See GOVERNOR.
Evacuation of public buildings.
Power of governor to order evacuation, §14-288.19, (a).
Penalty for willful refusal to leave building, §14-288.19, (b).
Succession to office of governor, §147-11.1, (a) to (f).
Guns.
Concealed handgun permit, §14-415.15, (b).
Hazardous materials emergency response, §§166A-20 to 166A-28.
See HAZARDOUS MATERIALS EMERGENCY RESPONSE.
Health care facilities.
Temporary shelter or temporary services during disaster or emergency.
Waiver of rules for facilities that provide, §131E-112, (a).
Ignoring warning regarding personal safety during disaster.
Civil liability for cost of rescue effort, §166A-15.1.
Interfering with emergency communication.
Definitions, §14-286.2, (b1).
Penalties, §14-286.2, (a).
Prohibited, §14-286.2, (a).
Livestock diseases.
Threat imminent.
Warrantless inspection, §106-399.5.
Loans.
State debt, §§142-16 to 142-19.
State treasurer.
Short-term notes in emergencies, §147-70.
Management, §§166A-1 to 166A-16.
See EMERGENCY MANAGEMENT.
Medical emergencies.
Parental consent requirement for abortion, waiver, §90-21.9.
Mental health, developmental disabilities and substance abuse.
Involuntary commitment.
Special emergency procedure for individuals needing immediate hospitalization, §122C-262.
Substance abusers, §122C-282.
Militia.
Arrest power in certain emergencies, §127A-149.
Unorganized militia.
Ordered out for service, §127A-87.
Misdemeanors.
Interfering with emergency communication, §14-286.2, (a).

EMERGENCIES —Cont'd
Motor carriers.
Grant of emergency operating authority, §62-265.
Motor vehicle license plates.
Emergency use, §20-64.2.
Municipal corporations.
Vehicles in riot areas or approaching municipalities during emergencies.
Warrants to inspect vehicles, §14-288.11.
Municipal elections.
Emergency administration, §163-304, (b), (c).
National guard.
Mutual assistance compact, §§127A-175 to 127A-184.
See NATIONAL GUARD.
Natural resources.
Emergency conservation work.
Reimbursement of government for expense, §113-28.
911 system.
Enhanced 911 system for wireless communications, §§62A-21 to 62A-32.
See 911 SYSTEM.
General provisions, §§62A-1 to 62A-12.
See 911 SYSTEM.
Nurses.
Assistance by person in case of emergency.
Not prohibited, §90-171.43.
Parking on highway, §20-161, (a).
Peace officers.
Urgent necessity.
Non-law-enforcement actions authorized, §15A-285.
Permits for concealed handguns, §14-415.15, (b).
Personnel.
Assault on emergency personnel, §14-288.9.
Pesticides.
Registration.
Emergency suspension, §143-447, (a).
Pharmacists and pharmacies.
Declaration of disaster or state of emergency by governor.
Waiver of certain requirements, §90-85.25, (a).
Price gouging during states of disaster.
Deceptive trade practice, §75-37.1, (a).
Determining whether price unreasonably excessive.
Considerations, §75-37.1, (a).
End of state of disaster, §75-37.1, (c).
Public policy, §75-37.
Statement that seller not in violation.
Issuance by attorney general, §75-37.1, (b).
Public safety.
Department of crime control and public safety.
Powers and duties as to emergencies and disasters, §143B-476, (c) to (g).
Public schools.
Loans from state literary fund.
Loans not granted in accordance with section 115C-458, §115C-466.
Rabies emergencies, §130A-201.
Radiation protection.
See ATOMIC ENERGY, RADIOACTIVITY AND IONIZING RADIATION.
Retirement system for teachers and state employees.
Provision for emergency expenses of integration of system, §135-18.5.
Riots and civil disorders.
Assault on emergency personnel, §14-288.9, (a).
Definition of term "emergency personnel," §14-288.9, (b).

EMERGENCIES —Cont'd
Riots and civil disorders —Cont'd
Assault on emergency personnel —Cont'd
Penalties for violations of provisions, §14-288.9, (c).
Dangerous weapon or substance.
Transporting weapon or substance during emergency, §14-288.7.
Exceptions, §14-288.7, (b).
Penalty for violation of provisions, §14-288.7, (c).
Declared state of emergency defined, §14-288.1.
Definitions.
Declared state of emergency, §14-288.1.
Savings and loan associations.
Withdrawable accounts.
Limitations on amounts withdrawable or payable, §54B-125.
Savings banks.
Powers of commissioner of banks.
Imposition of limitation, §54C-87.
State bar disaster response plan, Bar Rules & Regs., D, §§.0301 to .0303.
State board of elections.
Executive director.
Emergency powers, §163-27.1.
State debt.
Borrowing in emergencies, §§142-16 to 142-19.
State literary fund.
Loans not granted in accordance with section 115C-458, §115C-466.
State of emergency.
Government powers and proclamations generally, §§14-288.12 to 14-288.18.
See STATE OF EMERGENCY.
State treasurer.
Short-term notes in emergencies.
Authorization to make, §147-70.
Telephones.
False statement of emergencies.
Securing use of party telephone line by false statement, §14-401.8.
Refusing to relinquish party telephone line in emergency, §14-401.8.
Securing use of party telephone line.
False statement of emergency, §14-401.8.
Terrorism.
Nuclear, biological or chemical agents.
Terrorist incident using, §§130A-475 to 130A-479.
See TERRORIST INCIDENT USING NUCLEAR, BIOLOGICAL OR CHEMICAL AGENTS.
Trespass during, §14-288.6, (a).
Warnings regarding personal safety during disaster.
Civil liability for cost of rescue when willfully ignoring, §166A-15.1.
War powers act, §§147-33.1 to 147-33.6.
See GOVERNOR.
Water and air resources.
Water emergencies, §143-354.
Weapons.
Temporary concealed handgun permit, §14-415.15, (b).

EMERGENCY CARE INSURANCE COVERAGE.
Definitions, §58-3-190, (g).
Information to covered persons, §58-3-190, (f).
Requirements, §58-3-190, (a) to (e).

EMERGENCY COMMUNICATION INTERFERENCE, §14-286.2.

EMERGENCY ENERGY PROGRAM.
Contents, §113B-9, (f).
Contingency plans, §113B-9, (d).
Cooperative and joint plans, §113B-9, (c).
Emergency curtailment plan.
Electric and gas utilities to submit proposed plan, §113B-9, (b).
Governor.
Authority to accept and enforce federal programs, §113B-9, (k).
Duties, §113B-9, (i).
Hearings.
Council to hold public hearing, §113B-9, (e).
Investigations.
Council to carry out investigations and studies, §113B-9, (g).
National supply curtailment.
Oil producers to submit, §113B-9, (b).
Preparation, §113B-9, (a).
Recommendations, §113B-9, (h).
State departments and agencies.
Council to collect contingency plans, §113B-9, (d).
Updating program, §113B-9, (j).

EMERGENCY JUSTICE OR JUDGE.
Applicability of provisions, §7A-39.12.
Commission as, application to governor, §7A-39.6.
Court of appeals emergency recall judges, §7A-39.15.
Decisions regarding recall.
Final, §7A-39.9, (a).
Defined, §7A-39.1, (b).
District courts.
Commission, application to governor, §7A-53.
Compensation, §7A-52, (b).
Jurisdiction, §7A-53.1.
Recall of judges reaching mandatory retirement age, §7A-57.
Retired judges may become emergency judges, §7A-52, (a).
Emergency recall judges of the court of appeals, §7A-39.15.
Emergency special judges of superior court.
Jurisdiction, §7A-48.
Jurisdiction and authority, §7A-39.7.
Recall for temporary vacancy, §7A-39.14.
Recall of judges reaching mandatory retirement age, §7A-39.13.
Superior court, §7A-57.
Recall upon temporary incapacity of justice or judge, §7A-39.5.
Retired justices and judges may become, §7A-39.3.
Superior court, §7A-52, (a).
Special judges of superior court, §7A-45.2.
Superior court.
Commission, application to governor, §7A-53.
Compensation, §7A-52, (b).
Emergency judge.
Defined, §7A-50.
Recall of active and emergency trial judges reaching mandatory retirement age, §7A-57.
Retired judge may become emergency judge, §7A-52, (a).
Supreme court authorized to adopt rules, §7A-39.8.
Termination of recall by chief justice or chief judge, §7A-39.9, (b).

EMERGENCY MANAGEMENT, §§166A-1 to 166A-16.
Bioterrorism.
Nuclear, biological or chemical agents.
Terrorist incident using, §§130A-475 to 130A-479.
See TERRORIST INCIDENT USING NUCLEAR, BIOLOGICAL OR CHEMICAL AGENTS.
Citation of act.
Short title, §166A-1.
Communist party.
Members of Communist party ineligible as emergency management personnel, §166A-13, (a).
Compensation for taking of property, §166A-11.
Construction and interpretation.
Limitations on, §166A-3.
Counties, §166A-7, (a).
Appropriations, §166A-7, (c), (d).
Gifts and grants.
Acceptance, §166A-9.
Local state of emergency.
Declaration, §166A-8.
Mutual aid agreements, §166A-10, (b), (c).
Powers, §166A-7, (d).
State financial assistance, §166A-7, (e).
Definitions, §166A-4.
Department of crime control and public safety.
Civil preparedness agency (emergency management division).
Transfer to department, §§143A-240, 143B-475.
Secretary.
Powers and duties, §166A-5.
Disasters.
Defined, §166A-4.
First responders.
Vaccination program, §130-485.
State of disaster.
Declaring, powers, §166A-6.
Price gouging during state of disaster, §§75-37, 75-37.1.
State of disaster assistance funds, §166A-6.01.
Discrimination.
Prohibited, §166A-12.
Emergency management assistance compact, §§166A-40 to 166A-53.
Eminent domain.
Compensation for taking of property, §166A-11.
Federal aid.
Acceptance, §166A-9.
First responders.
Vaccination program, §130-485.
Functions of program, §166A-5.
General assembly.
State of disaster.
Declaring, §166A-6.
Governmental immunity, §166A-14, (a).
Governor.
Mutual aid agreements.
Power to establish, §166A-10, (a).
Powers, §166A-5.
State of disaster.
Declaring, powers, §166A-6.
State of disaster assistance funds, §166A-6.01.
Hazardous materials emergency response, §§166A-20 to 166A-28.
See HAZARDOUS MATERIALS EMERGENCY RESPONSE.
Ignoring warning in disaster.
Civil liability for cost of rescue, §166A-15.1.
Immunity, §§166A-14, 166A-15.

EMERGENCY MANAGEMENT —Cont'd
Leave options for emergency service personnel.
Definition of disaster or emergency, §166A-17, (c).
Enforcement of provisions, §166A-17, (d).
Right to leave without pay, §166A-17, (a).
Written request required, §166A-17, (b).
Legislative declaration.
Purposes of act, §166A-2.
Licenses.
Exemptions from requirements of professional licenses, §166A-14, (c).
Municipal corporations, §166A-7, (b).
Appropriations, §166A-7, (c), (d).
Gifts and grants.
Acceptance, §166A-9.
Local state of emergency.
Declaration, §166A-8.
Mutual aid agreements, §166A-10, (b), (c).
Powers, §166A-7, (d).
Mutual aid agreements.
Establishment, §166A-10.
Governor.
Power to enter into, §166A-10, (a).
Political subdivisions, §166A-10, (b), (c).
Scope, §166A-10, (d).
National guard training.
State of disaster.
Use of funds in preparation for, §166A-6, (d).
Nuclear facilities.
Fees, §166A-6.1, (a), (b).
Oaths.
Personnel, §166A-13, (a).
Personnel.
Definition of "emergency management worker," §166A-14, (d).
Disqualifications, §166A-13, (a).
Oath, §166A-13, (a).
Positions not deemed offices, §166A-13, (b).
Privileges and immunities, §166A-14, (b), (c), (e).
Purposes of act, §166A-2.
Rescue of individuals ignoring warning in disaster.
Civil liability for cost, §166A-15.1.
Secretary of crime control and public safety.
Powers and duties, §166A-5.
Sedition.
Certain persons ineligible as emergency management personnel, §166A-13, (a).
Severability of provisions, §166A-16.
Smallpox vaccination for first responders.
Sick leave and salary policy, time off due to adverse reaction, §160A-164.1.
State of disaster.
Governor or general assembly declaring, §166A-6, (a).
Governor's powers, §166A-6, (b).
Concurrence of council of state, §166A-6, (c).
National guard training.
Use of funds in preparation for, §166A-6, (d).
Preliminary damage assessment.
Providing governor and general assembly, §166A-6, (a1).
Price gouging during state of disaster, §§75-37, 75-37.1.
State of disaster assistance funds.
Governor to make available, §166A-6.01, (a).
Type I disaster, §166A-6.01, (b).
Type II disaster, §166A-6.01, (c).
Type III disaster, §166A-6.01, (d).

EMERGENCY MANAGEMENT —Cont'd
State of disaster —Cont'd
Termination.
Proclamation or governor or resolution of general assembly, §166A-6, (a2).
Type I disaster.
Declaring, expiration, §166A-6, (a1).
State of disaster assistance funds, §166A-6.01, (b).
Type II disaster.
Declaring, expiration, §166A-6, (a1).
State of disaster assistance funds, §166A-6.01, (c).
Type III disaster.
Declaring, expiration, §166A-6, (a1).
State of disaster assistance funds, §166A-6.01, (d).
State of emergency.
Government powers and proclamations generally, §§14-288.12 to 14-288.18.
See STATE OF EMERGENCY.
Terrorism.
Nuclear, biological or chemical agents.
Terrorist incident using, §§130A-475 to 130A-479.
See TERRORIST INCIDENT USING NUCLEAR, BIOLOGICAL OR CHEMICAL AGENTS.
Title of act.
Short title, §166A-1.
Volunteer leave, §§166A-30 to 166A-32.
Personnel called into service, §166A-17.
Warnings regarding personal safety during disaster.
Civil liability for cost of rescue on willfully ignoring warning, §166A-15.1.
Workers' compensation.
Right to receive benefits not affected by performance of functions, §166A-14, (b).

EMERGENCY MANAGEMENT ASSISTANCE COMPACT, §§166A-40 to 166A-53.
Action by party state requested to render mutual aid, §166A-44, (a).
Additional provisions, §166A-53.
Compensation and death benefits to injured members of emergency forces, §166A-48.
Consultation between state officials, §166A-43, (c).
Deposit of authenticated copies with party state, §166A-51.
Effective date, §166A-51, (a).
Entering into compact, §166A-40, (b).
Evacuation and interstate recession of portions of civilian population, §166A-50.
Formulation of appropriate interstate mutual aid plans and procedures.
Official responsible, §166A-42, (c).
Liability of officers or employees of party state rendering aid, §166A-46.
Mutual cooperation, §166A-41, (b).
Powers, duties, rights and privileges of forces of party state.
Rendering mutual aid, §166A-44, (b).
Principle of articles of compact, §166A-42, (b).
Purposes, §166A-41, (a).
Recognition by party state, §166A-42, (a).
Recognition of licenses and permits issued by party state, §166A-45.
Reimbursement of party state rendering aid in another state, §166A-49.

EMERGENCY MANAGEMENT ASSISTANCE COMPACT —Cont'd
Requesting assistance of other party states, §166A-43, (b).
Responsibility of party states, §166A-43, (a).
Supplementary agreement, §166A-47.
Title of provisions, §166A-40, (a).
Validity, §166A-52.
Withdrawal from compact, §166A-51, (b).

EMERGENCY MEDICAL OR SURGICAL TREATMENT OF JUVENILE.
Judicial consent, §7B-3600.
District court jurisdiction over proceedings, §7B-1603.

EMERGENCY MEDICAL SERVICES, §§143-507 to 143-519.
Advisory council.
Appointments of members, §143-510, (a).
Chairperson and vice-chairperson.
Election annually, §143-510, (f).
Composition, §143-510, (a).
Created, §143-510, (a).
Duties.
Generally, §143-511.
Expenses, §143-510, (d).
Members, §143-510, (a).
Per diem and travel expenses, §143-510, (d).
Powers.
Generally, §143-511.
Quorum to transact business, §143-510, (e).
Terms of office, §143-510, (b).
Vacancies, §143-510, (c).
Ambulance permit.
Application, §131E-156, (b).
Equipment, failure to meet standards on inspection.
Revocation of permit, §131E-157, (c).
Inspection of records, §131E-156, (d).
Required, §131E-156, (a).
Temporary permits, §131E-156, (c).
Ambulance support for citizens, §143-517.
Arson.
Burning of rescue-squad building, §14-61.
Assault or affray while discharging official duties, §14-34.6, (a).
Infliction of bodily injury, §14-34.6, (b).
Use of deadly weapon other than firearms, §14-34.6, (b).
Use of firearms, §14-34.6, (c).
Assault with deadly weapon, §14-34.6, (b).
Electronic surveillance orders, §15A-290, (c4).
Personnel assaulted with deadly weapon, §14-34.2.
Automated external defibrillator (AED), §90-21.15.
Buildings.
Burning of rescue-squad building, §14-61.
Communicable diseases.
Emergency departments, surveillance by state health director, reporting requirements, §130A-480, (a), (b).
Confidentiality of patient information, §143-518.
Consolidation of state functions relating to services, §143-508.
County fire protection district.
EMS services in, §153A-309, (a), (b).
Credentialed personnel.
Minimum standard, §131E-158, (a).
Rules for exemptions, §131E-158, (b).

EMERGENCY MEDICAL SERVICES —Cont'd
Credentialed personnel —Cont'd
Scope of practice, §143-514.
Credentialing requirements.
Application, §131E-159, (a).
Disciplinary actions, §131E-159, (f).
Dispatchers, waiver of examination, §131E-159, (d).
Duration of credentials, §131E-159, (a).
EMT-waiver of examination, §131E-159, (c).
Examination, §131E-159, (a).
Rules of commission, §131E-159, (b).
Temporary credentials, §131E-159, (e).
Crossing median of divided highway.
When permitted, §20-140.3.
Definitions, §§131E-155, 143-507, (d).
Department of health and human services.
Regional demonstration plans, §143-512.
Designation of regions, §143-515.
Disciplinary committee.
Chairperson and vice-chairperson.
Election annually, §143-519, (f).
Members, §143-519, (b).
Purpose and creation, §143-519, (a).
Quorum to transact business, §143-519, (e).
Staggered terms, §143-519, (c).
Vacancy appointments, §143-519, (d).
Duties of secretary of department of health and human services, §143-509.
Effect of article upon, §143-517.
Emergency support vehicles.
Horns and warning devices, §20-125, (b).
Red lights.
Exception to prohibition, §20-130.1, (b).
EMS provider license.
Application, §131E-155.1, (b).
Denial, suspension or revocation, §131E-155.1, (d).
Qualification rules, §131E-155.1, (c).
Required, §131E-155.1, (a).
Unlicensed operation, §131E-155.1, (e).
Equipment sanitation, supply and design.
Failure to comply, §131E-157, (c).
Inspection of ambulance for compliance, §131E-157, (b).
Rules and standards, §131E-157, (a).
Establishment and maintenance of program for improving and upgrading services, §143-508, (a).
Establishment of program, §143-507, (a).
Exempt vehicles, §131E-160.
Federal emergency medical services legislation enacted.
Department of health and human services to assist in development of plans and programs, §143-516.
Grants-in-aid.
Regional demonstration plans, §143-512.
Impersonation of firemen or emergency medical services personnel, §14-276.1.
Insect sting reactions.
Training individuals to administer life-saving treatment to person suffering, §143-509.
Leave options for personnel in disaster or emergency, §166A-17.
Medical care commission.
Adoption of rules and regulations, §143-508, (b) to (d).
Patient medical records.
Confidentiality, §143-518.
Financial data, no release, §143-518, (b).

EMERGENCY MEDICAL SERVICES —Cont'd
Patient medical records —Cont'd
Patient identifiable data.
Conditions for release, §143-518, (a).
Powers of secretary of department of health and human services, §143-509.
Programs.
Establishment, §143-507, (a).
Public health threats, reports by emergency departments to state health director, §130A-480, (a), (b).
Purpose of article, §143-507, (c).
Regional demonstration plans, §143-512.
Regional emergency medical services councils.
Establishment by secretary of department of health and human services, §143-513.
Regions.
Establishment, §143-515.
Regulation of emergency medical services, §§131E-155 to 131E-161.
Reports by emergency departments to state health director, detection of public health threats, §130A-480, (a), (b).
Sanitary districts.
Corporate powers of sanitary district boards, §130A-55.
Scope of practice for personnel, §143-514.
Scope of system, §143-507, (b), (d).
Smallpox vaccination for first responders.
Sick leave and salary policy, time off due to adverse reaction, §160A-164.1.
Standards and criteria, §143-508, (d).
Terrorist incident using nuclear, biological or chemical agents.
Emergency departments, surveillance by state health director, reporting requirements, §130A-480, (a), (b).
Traffic lights.
Preempting.
Local authority to permit, §20-169.
Trauma system, establishment, §143-509.
Vehicles exempt, §131E-160.
Violations of article, §131E-161.
Wage and hour act.
Exemptions, §95-25.14, (b1).

EMERGENCY MEDICAL TECHNICIANS.
Arson or other unlawful burning.
Serious injury to emergency medical technician, §14-69.3.
Automated external defibrillator (AED), §90-21.15.
Offenses against.
Aggravating factor in sentencing, §15A-1340.16.
Regulation of emergency medical services, §§131E-155 to 131E-161.
See EMERGENCY MEDICAL SERVICES.

EMERGENCY ROAD SERVICE.
Motor clubs and associations, §58-69-2.

EMERGENCY TELEPHONE SYSTEM.
Enhanced 911 system for wireless communications, §§62A-21 to 62A-32.
See 911 SYSTEM.
General provisions, §§62A-1 to 62A-12.
See 911 SYSTEM.

EMERGENCY WAR POWERS ACT, §§147-33.1 to 147-33.6.
See GOVERNOR.

EMINENT DOMAIN.
Abandonment of condemnation proceeding.
Petitioner abandoning taxed with fee for respondent's attorney, §1-209.1.

EMINENT DOMAIN —Cont'd
Airports.
Municipal airports, §§63-5, 63-6, 63-49, (b).
Joint operation of airports, §63-56, (h).
Special airport districts.
Powers of districts, §63-83.
Zoning.
Acquisition of air rights, §63-36.
Answers.
Private condemnors.
Petitions.
Answer to petition, §40A-25.
Public condemnors, §40A-45, (a).
Determination of issues raised, §40A-42, (d).
Failure to answer, §40A-46.
Reply to answer, §40A-45, (b).
Service of answer, §40A-45, (b).
Time for filing answer, §40A-46.
Appeals, §40A-13.
Private condemnors, §40A-28, (c).
Jury trial, §40A-29.
Appraisals, right of entry to make, §40A-11.
Archives and history.
Historic properties.
Power to acquire property by condemnation, §121-9, (g).
Attorneys at law.
Abandonment of condemnation proceedings by petitioner.
Petitioner taxed with fee for respondent's attorney, §1-209.1.
Attorneys' fees.
Petitioner abandoning proceeding taxed with fee for respondent's attorney, §1-209.1.
Right of entry prior to condemnation.
Recovery for damages resulting, §40A-11.
Authorities.
Power of eminent domain, §40A-3, (c).
Blue Ridge parkway.
Control of outdoor advertising.
Condemnation procedure, §113A-169.
Borings, right of entry to make, §40A-11.
Bridges.
By whom right may be exercised, §40A-3, (a).
Buildings.
Removal of structures on condemned land, §40A-9.
Bus stations.
By whom right may be exercised, §40A-3, (a).
Canals.
By whom right may be exercised, §40A-3, (a).
Cemeteries.
Powers of local public condemnors, §40A-3, (b).
Coastal area management.
Commission order not applicable to certain land.
Acquisition of fee or lessor interest in land, §113A-123, (c).
Commercial feed.
Detained commercial feeds, §106-284.43, (b).
Commissioners.
Private condemnors.
Appointment, §40A-25.
Meetings.
Notice, §40A-26.
New commissioners.
Appointment, §40A-32, (b).
Oath of office, §40A-26.
Powers, §40A-26.
Qualifications, §40A-25.
Report of assessed compensation, §40A-26.
Exceptions to, §40A-28, (a).
Form, §40A-27.

EMINENT DOMAIN —Cont'd
Commissioners —Cont'd
Private condemnors —Cont'd
Subpoenas.
Power to issue, §40A-26.
Public condemnors.
Appointment, §40A-48, (a).
Community colleges.
Board of trustees, §40A-3, (c).
Compensation.
Applicability of principles, §40A-62.
Date of valuation.
Day of filing of petition or complaint, §40A-63.
Determination of amount, §40A-63.
Effect of condemnation procedure on value, §40A-65, (a), (c).
Project expanded or changed to require taking of additional property, §40A-65, (b).
Entire tract, §40A-67.
Fair market value, §40A-64, (a).
Project as planned.
Compensation to reflect, §40A-66.
Removal of timber, buildings or other permanent improvements or fixtures.
Value not included, §40A-64, (c).
Taking of less than entire tract.
Measure of compensation, §40A-64, (b).
Entire tract.
Determination of amount, §40A-67.
Fair market value.
Measure of amount, §40A-64, (a).
Lien.
Acquisition of property subject to lien, §40A-68.
Life tenancy.
Taking of property subject to, §40A-69.
Measure of compensation, §40A-64, (a), (b).
Principles governing, §40A-62.
Private condemnors.
Ascertainment and determination by commissioners, §40A-26.
Deposit by condemnor with clerk of superior court, §40A-28, (d).
Failure to pay.
Effect, §40A-28, (f).
Rights of claimants of fund.
Determination, §40A-31.
Project as planned.
Compensation to reflect, §40A-66.
Public condemnors.
Deposit of estimated compensation to accompany complaint, §40A-41.
Disbursement of deposit, §40A-44.
Refund of deposit, §40A-56.
Interest as part of just compensation, §40A-53.
Measure of compensation, §40A-52.
Payment of compensation, §40A-55.
Refund of deposit, §40A-56.
Remedy where no declaration of taking filed, §40A-51, (a).
Remainder, value of.
Tacking of less than entire track, §40A-66, (a), (b).
Tacking of less than entire track.
Value of remainder, §40A-66, (a), (b).
Value of remainder.
Tacking of less than entire track, §40A-66, (a), (b).
Complaints of public condemnors.
Contents, §40A-41.
Deposit of estimated compensation to accompany complaint, §40A-41.
Disbursement of deposits, §40A-44.
Refund of deposit, §40A-56.

EMINENT DOMAIN —Cont'd
Complaints of public condemnors —Cont'd
Filing, §40A-41.
Memorandum of action, §40A-43.
Recordation, §40A-51, (b).
Condemnors.
Defined, §40A-2.
Private condemnors. See within this heading, "Private condemnors."
Public condemnors. See within this heading, "Public condemnors."
Condominiums.
Awards, §47C-1-107, (a).
Common elements, §47C-1-107, (c).
Partial taking, §47C-1-107, (d).
Recording of court decree, §47C-1-107, (d).
Conflict of laws.
Exclusive nature of provisions, §40A-1.
Constitution of the United States, Const. U. S., amd. V.
Constructive notice.
Filing of notice of proceedings, §40A-21.
Continuances.
Public condemnors.
Power of judge, §40A-50.
Conveyances.
Private condemnors.
Change of ownership pending proceedings, §40A-33.
Corporations.
By whom right may be exercised, §40A-3, (a).
Costs, §40A-13.
Award of costs, §40A-8, (a), (b).
Action against condemnor, §40A-8, (c).
Condemnation action denied or abandoned, §40A-8, (b).
Petitioner to pay costs in certain cases, §6-22.
Streets and highways, §136-119.
Streets and highways.
Condemnation proceedings, §136-119.
Counties.
Federal water resources projects.
Acquisition of lands, §143-215.42, (a) to (h).
Local government unit outside county.
City property within corporate limits, inapplicability of section, §153A-15, (d).
Consent of board required, §153A-15, (a), (b).
Applicability of requirement, §153A-15, (c).
Power to exercise, purposes, §§40A-3, (b), (b1), 153A-158.
Public condemnors generally. See within this heading, "Public condemnors."
Public lands.
Acquisition or condemnation.
Local government unit outside county.
Consent of board required, §153A-15.
Solid waste facility.
Purchasing site by condemnation, §153A-292, (c).
State psychiatric hospital.
Selection of county as site for.
Acquisition by county, conveyance to state, §153A-178.
Water and sewer districts.
Power of district, §162A-89.1.
Damages.
Compensation.
Generally. See within this heading, "Compensation."
Public condemnors.
Action in tort for damage to property.
Common law right not affected, §40A-51, (c).
Definitions, §40A-2.

EMINENT DOMAIN —Cont'd
Department of environment and natural resources.
Power to acquire lands as state forests and parks, §113-34, (a).
Deposit of estimated compensation to accompany complaint, §40A-41.
Disbursement, §40A-44.
Refund, §40A-56.
Dismissal, discontinuance and nonsuit.
Abandonment of condemnation proceedings by petitioner.
Petitioner taxed with fee for respondent's attorney, §1-209.1.
Voluntary nonsuit authorized, §1-209.2.
Voluntary nonsuit by petitioner in condemnation proceedings, §1-209.2.
Petitioner taxed with fee for respondent's attorney, §1-209.1.
Disposition of land condemned, §40A-10.
Districts.
Power of eminent domain, §40A-3, (c).
Drainage.
Corporations, §156-48.
Powers of local public condemnors, §40A-3, (b).
Supplemental proceeding, §156-1.
Drainage districts.
Acquisition and disposition of lands.
Generally, §156-138.1.
Assessments.
Damages, §156-70.
Compensation of landowners.
When title deemed acquired for purpose of easements or rights of way, §156-70.1.
Condemnation of land, §156-67.
Electric companies.
By whom right may be exercised, §40A-3, (a).
Costs of petitions for condemnation of land.
Petitioner to pay costs in certain cases, §6-22.
Dwelling house of owner taken under certain cases, §62-184.
Exercise of right, parties interest only taken, §62-185.
Grant of eminent domain, §62-183.
Powers granted corporations exercisable by persons, firms or copartnerships, §62-189.
Proceedings as under eminent domain, §62-187.
Use or occupancy of public highway, §62-181.
Emergency management.
Compensation for taking of property, §166A-11.
Entry.
Right to enter prior to condemnation, §40A-11.
Environment and natural resources department.
Marine and estuarine resources.
Powers as to, §113-226, (a).
Examinations, right of entry to make, §40A-11.
Exclusive nature of provisions, §40A-1.
Fire stations.
Powers of local public condemnors, §40A-3, (b).
Fish and fisheries resources.
Coastal wetlands, orders to control activities.
Taking fee of land order inapplicable to, §113-230, (g).
Seafood industrial park authority, §113-315.32.
Fixtures.
Removal of fixtures on condemned land, §40A-9.
Flumes.
Flume companies exercising right to become common carriers, §62-191.

EMINENT DOMAIN —Cont'd
Forests and forestry.
Acquisition of and for purposes of establishing and developing state forests, state parks and other areas, §113-34, (a).
Forms.
Private condemnors.
Commissioners.
Report of assessed compensation, §40A-27.
Public condemnors.
Commissioners.
Report of assessed compensation, §40A-48, (c).
Global TransPark authority.
Powers, §63A-6, (b).
Guardian ad litem.
Public condemnors.
Appointment for infants and incompetents, §40A-50.
Guardians.
Private condemnors.
Acquisition of title of infants, incompetents, inebriates or trustees without power of sale.
Power of court to appoint guardian, §40A-30.
Historic districts and landmarks.
Powers of local public condemnors, §40A-3, (b).
Hospital authorities, §131E-10.
Power of eminent domain, §§40A-3, (c), 131E-24, (a).
Certificate of public convenience and necessity.
Prerequisite to exercise of power, §131E-24, (c).
Restrictions, §131E-24, (b).
Hospitals.
Municipal hospitals, §131E-10.
Powers of local public condemnors, §40A-3, (b).
Housing authorities and projects.
Certificate of convenience and necessity.
Required, §157-28.
Declaration of necessity, §157-48.
Exercise of right, §157-50.
Finding and declaration of necessity, §157-48.
Housing project.
Defined, §157-49.
Municipal cooperation and aid.
Restrictions on exercise of right, §157-45.
Power of eminent domain, §§40A-3, (c), 157-11, 157-50.
Restrictions on right, §157-28.
Hydraulic power corporations.
Use or occupancy of public highway, §62-181.
Injunctions.
Private condemnors.
Provisions not to preclude injunctive relief, §40A-28, (g).
Public condemnors.
Remedy not precluded by provisions, §40A-42, (f).
Interest.
Public condemnors.
Compensation.
Interest as part of just compensation, §40A-53.
Inverse condemnation, §40A-51.
Judges.
Power to make additional orders and rules of procedure, §40A-12.
Judgments.
Private condemnors, §40A-28, (b).
Powers of judge to carry into effect, §40A-28, (e).

EMINENT DOMAIN —Cont'd
Judgments —Cont'd
Public condemnors.
Final judgments, §40A-54.
Junkyard control, §136-150.
Jury.
Private condemnors.
Appeals.
Provision for jury trial, §40A-29.
Right to trial by jury granted to parties in condemnation proceedings, §1A-1, Rule 38, (e).
View by jury, §1-181.1.
Land policy act.
Taking of property without compensation.
Protection of rights, §113A-158.
Legislative declaration, §40A-1.
Libraries.
Powers of local public condemnors, §40A-3, (b).
Liens.
Compensation.
Acquisition of property subject to lien, §40A-68.
Removal of structures on condemned land, §40A-9.
Life estates.
Taking of property subject to life tenancy.
Compensation, §40A-69.
Limitation of actions.
Inverse condemnation, §40A-51, (a).
Lis pendens.
Filing of notice of proceedings, §40A-21.
Local governments.
Federal water resources projects.
Acquisition of lands, §143-215.42, (a) to (h).
Powers, §40A-3, (b), (b1).
Public condemnors generally. See within this heading, "Public condemnors."
Maps and plats.
Public condemnors.
Filing of plat, §40A-45, (c).
Metropolitan sewerage districts.
Powers of districts, §162A-69.
Metropolitan water districts.
Powers of districts, §162A-36, (a).
Mining, water and drainage rights.
Appraisers.
Appointment, §74-27.
Duties, §74-27.
Number, §74-27.
Report, §74-27.
Confirmation, §74-28.
Registration, §74-29.
Fee, §74-29.
Damages.
Payment, §74-28.
Obstructing mining drains.
Misdemeanor, §74-30.
Petition for, §74-25.
Contents, §74-26.
Waste.
Disposition, §74-31.
Minors.
Private condemnors.
Acquisition of title of infant.
Powers of court upon, §40A-30.
Mosquito control districts.
Powers of boards of commissioners, §§40A-3, (c), 130A-355.
Motor carriers.
By whom right may be exercised, §40A-3, (a).
Municipal corporations.
Cemeteries.
Authority to condemn cemeteries, §160A-345.

EMINENT DOMAIN —Cont'd
Municipal corporations —Cont'd
Cemeteries —Cont'd
Authority to condemn easements for perpetual care, §160A-346.
Trustees, §160A-349.10.
Costs.
Petitions for condemnation of land.
Petitioner to pay costs in certain cases, §6-22.
Federal water resources projects.
Acquisition of lands, §143-215.42, (a) to (h).
Joint municipal electric power and energy act, §159B-33.
Powers, §§40A-3, (b), (b1), 160A-240.1.
Procedures for exercise of power, §160A-240.1.
Public condemnors generally. See within this heading, "Public condemnors."
Streets and alleys.
Acquiring land, §160A-296, (a).
Extraterritorial planning jurisdiction, exercising power in, §160A-296, (a1).
Notice.
Private condemnors.
Meeting of commissioners, §40A-26.
Proceedings by, §40A-21.
Public condemnors.
Determination of issues other than damages, §40A-47.
Intent to institute action to condemn property, §40A-40.
Right of entry.
Notice to owner of entry prior to condemnation, §40A-11.
Orders.
Power of judges to effectuate provisions, §40A-12.
Public condemnors.
Power of judge to enter orders, §40A-42, (e).
Outdoor advertising, §136-132.
Parking authorities.
Acquisition of real property, §§160A-556, 160A-557, (d).
Parks and recreation.
Powers of local public condemnors, §40A-3, (b).
Perfection of title.
Private condemnation proceedings, §40A-34.
Persons under legal disabilities.
Private condemnation proceedings.
Procedure, §40A-30.
Petitions.
Private condemnors, §§40A-20, 40A-25.
Answer to petition, §40A-25.
Contents, §40A-20.
Filing, §40A-20.
Pipelines.
By whom right may be exercised, §40A-3, (a).
Right conferred on pipeline companies, §62-190.
Planned community act.
Common elements, §47F-1-107, (d).
Compensation of lot owner, §47F-1-107, (a), (b).
Decree.
Recordation, §47F-1-107, (e).
Reallocation of interests, §47F-1-107, (a), (b).
Amendment to declaration reflecting, §47F-1-107, (c).
Pollution control.
Industrial and pollution control facilities financing act.
No power of eminent domain, §159C-20.
Ports authority.
Power of eminent domain, §143B-457.

EMINENT DOMAIN —Cont'd
Poultry and poultry products.
Inspections.
Seizure or condemnation proceedings, §106-549.66.
Principal and income act.
Allocation of receipts not normally apportioned during administration of trust, §37A-4-404.
Prior purchase offer.
Not necessary, §40A-4.
Private condemnors.
Amendments of proceedings.
Power of clerk or judge, §40A-32, (b).
Appeals, §40A-28, (c).
Jury trial, §40A-29.
Commissioners.
Appointment, §40A-25.
Meetings.
Notice, §40A-26.
New commissioners.
Appointment, §40A-32, (b).
Oath of office, §40A-26.
Powers, §40A-26.
Qualifications, §40A-25.
Report of assessed compensation, §40A-26.
Exceptions to report, §40A-28, (a).
Form, §40A-27.
Subpoenas.
Power to issue, §40A-26.
Compensation.
Ascertainment and determination by commissioners, §40A-26.
Deposit by condemnor with clerk of superior court, §40A-28, (d).
Failure to pay.
Effect, §40A-28, (f).
Rights of claimants of fund.
Determination, §40A-31.
Condemnation proceedings by, §§40A-19 to 40A-34.
Conveyances.
Change of ownership pending proceeding, §40A-33.
Defective title.
How cured, §40A-34.
Guardians.
Acquisition of title of infants, incompetents, inebriates or trustees without power of sale.
Power of court to appoint guardian, §40A-30.
Incompetent persons.
Acquisition of title of.
Powers of court upon, §40A-30.
Infants.
Acquisition of title of.
Powers of court upon, §40A-30.
Injunctions.
Provisions not to preclude, §40A-28, (g).
Judgments, §40A-28, (b).
Powers of judge to carry into effect, §40A-28, (e).
Jury.
Appeals.
Provision for jury trial on appeal, §40A-29.
Notice.
Meeting of commissioners, §40A-26.
Proceedings by, §40A-21.
Petitions.
Answer to petition, §40A-25.
Contents, §40A-20.
Filing, §40A-20.

EMINENT DOMAIN —Cont'd
Private condemnors —Cont'd
Proceedings for condemnation by, §§40A-19 to 40A-34.
Right of eminent domain, §§40A-3, (a), 40A-19.
Service of process, §40A-22.
Special proceedings.
Service as in special proceedings in absence of other provisions, §40A-24.
Unknown parties, §40A-23.
Title.
Defective title.
How cured, §40A-34.
Transfer of property pending proceedings, §40A-33.
Trustees.
Acquisition of title of trustees without power of sale.
Powers of court upon, §40A-30.
Unknown parties.
Attorney for unknown parties.
Appointment, §40A-32, (a).
Service where parties unknown, §40A-23.
Property tax reimbursement, §40A-6, (a).
Deferred taxes paid by owner, §40A-6, (b).
Public condemnors.
Answers, §40A-45, (a).
Determination of issues raised, §40A-42, (d).
Failure to answer, §40A-46.
Reply, §40A-45, (b).
Service, §40A-45, (b).
Time for filing, §40A-46.
Commissioners.
Appointment, §40A-48, (a).
Compensation.
Deposit of estimated compensation to accompany complaint, §40A-41.
Disbursement of deposit, §40A-44.
Refund of deposit, §40A-56.
Interest as part of just compensation, §40A-53.
Measure of compensation, §40A-52.
Payment of compensation, §40A-55.
Refund of deposit, §40A-56.
Remedy where no declaration of taking filed, §40A-51, (a).
Transfer of case to civil docket, §40A-49.
Complaints.
Contents, §40A-41.
Deposit of estimated compensation to accompany complaint, §40A-41.
Disbursement of deposit, §40A-44.
Refund of deposit, §40A-56.
Filing, §40A-41.
Memorandum of action, §40A-43.
Recordation, §40A-51, (b).
Condemnation proceedings by, §§40A-40 to 40A-56.
Continuances.
Power of judge, §40A-50.
Damages.
Action in tort for damaged property.
Common law right not affected, §40A-51, (c).
Guardian ad litem.
Appointment for infants or incompetents, §40A-50.
Injunctions.
Remedy not precluded, §40A-42, (f).
Interest.
Compensation.
Part of just compensation, §40A-53.

EMINENT DOMAIN —Cont'd
Public condemnors —Cont'd
Issues other than damages.
Determination, §40A-47.
Judgments.
Final judgments, §40A-54.
Local public condemnors.
Power to exercise, purposes.
Modified provision for certain localities, §40A-3, (b1).
Standard provision, §40A-3, (b).
Memorandum of action, §40A-43.
Recordation, §40A-51, (b).
Notice.
Determination of issues other than damages, §40A-47.
Intent to institute action to condemn property, §40A-40, (a).
Vesting of title and right of possession, §40A-40, (b).
Time for filing, manner of serving owners, §40A-40, (a).
Number, §40A-48, (a).
Orders.
Power of judge to enter orders, §40A-42, (e).
Plat.
Filing, §40A-45, (c).
Powers, §40A-48, (b).
Proceedings for condemnation by, §§40A-40 to 40A-56.
Qualifications, §40A-48, (a).
Report of assessed compensation, §40A-48, (b).
Exceptions to, §40A-48, (d).
Form, §40A-48, (c).
Service on parties, §40A-48, (d).
Request for appointment, §40A-48, (a).
Procedure when no request, §40A-49.
Return of condemned property, §40A-70.
Right of eminent domain, §40A-3, (b), (c).
Service of process.
Answer, §40A-45, (b).
Report of commissioners.
Service of copies on parties, §40A-48, (d).
Title.
Vesting of title, §40A-42, (a) to (c).
Torts.
Action in tort for damages to property.
Common law right not affected, §40A-51, (c).
Unknown parties.
Appointment of attorney for, §40A-50.
Public institutions.
Costs of petitions for condemnation of land.
Petitioner to pay costs in certain cases, §6-22.
Public lands.
Consent of state to taking, §40A-5, (a).
Public schools.
Acquisition of school sites, §115C-517.
Powers of local boards of education, §40A-3, (b).
Public utilities.
Burial grounds, §62-184.
By whom right may be exercised.
Private condemnors, §40A-3, (a).
Costs of petitions for condemnation of land.
Petitioner to pay costs in certain cases, §6-22.
Dwelling houses, §62-184.
Exercise of power by persons, firms or copartnerships, §62-189.
Exercise of right under general eminent domain provisions, §62-185.
Flume companies exercising right become common carriers, §62-191.

EMINENT DOMAIN —Cont'd
Public utilities —Cont'd
Grant of eminent domain, §62-183.
Dwelling houses, etc., §62-184.
Exceptions, §62-183.
Powers granted to be exercisable by persons, firms or copartnerships, §62-189.
Highways.
Use of highways generally, §§62-180, 62-181.
Pipeline companies.
Right of eminent domain conferred upon, §62-190.
Proceedings as under eminent domain, §62-187.
Surveys.
No survey required, §62-185.
Public water systems, §130A-319.
Public works relocation assistance, §§133-5 to 133-18.
See RELOCATION ASSISTANCE.
Purposes.
Local public condemnors.
Modified provisions for certain localities, §40A-3, (b1).
Standard provisions, §40A-3, (b).
Other public condemnors, §40A-3, (c).
Railroads.
By whom right may be exercised, §40A-3, (a).
Costs.
Petitions for condemnation of land.
Petitioner to pay costs in certain cases, §6-22.
Fee simple condemnations, §40A-3, (a).
Intersection with highways, §136-191.
Limitation of actions.
Damages or compensation for railroad right of way, §1-51.
Powers of railroad corporations, §136-190.
Right of eminent domain.
Consent of state required, §40A-5, (a).
Regional natural gas districts.
Continuing power, §160A-674, (a).
Procedure when exercising power, §160A-674, (b).
Regional transportation authorities.
Continuing power, §160A-649, (a).
Procedures when exercising powers, §160A-649, (b).
Right of eminent domain, §40A-3, (c).
Relocation assistance, §§133-5 to 133-18.
See RELOCATION ASSISTANCE.
Remainder of track.
Less than entire tract taken.
Value of, §40A-66, (a), (b).
Removal of structures on condemned land, §40A-9.
Reports of assessed compensation.
Private condemnors.
Commissioners, §40A-26.
Exceptions to report, §40A-28, (a).
Form of report, §40A-27.
Public condemnors.
Commissioners, §40A-48, (b) to (d).
Residential property disclosure act.
Applicability of act, §47E-2.
Return of condemned property.
Public condemnors, §40A-70.
Right of eminent domain.
No prior purchase offer necessary, §40A-4.
Private condemnors, §§40A-3, (a), 40A-19.
Property owned by other condemnors, §40A-5, (b).
Public condemnors, §40A-3, (b), (c).
Railroads, state owned.
Consent of state requires, §40A-5, (a).

EMINENT DOMAIN —Cont'd
Right of eminent domain —Cont'd
State property.
Consent of state required, §40A-5, (a).
Who may exercise right, §40A-3.
Right of entry prior to condemnation, §40A-11.
Sales.
Disposition of land condemned, §40A-10.
Sanitary districts.
Power of boards, §§40A-3, (c), 130A-57.
Schools.
Acquisition of school sites, §115C-517.
By whom right may be exercised.
Private condemnor, §40A-3, (a).
Powers of local boards of education, §40A-3, (b).
Seafood industry park authorities, §113-315.32.
Service of process.
Private condemnors, §40A-22.
Special proceedings.
Service as in special proceedings in absence of other provisions, §40A-24.
Unknown parties, §40A-23.
Public condemnors.
Answer, §40A-45, (b).
Report of commissioners.
Service of copies on parties, §40A-48, (d).
Sewers.
Powers of local public condemnors, §40A-3, (b).
Public sewerage systems.
Private condemnors, §40A-3, (a).
Soil and water conservation districts.
Watershed improvement districts.
Power of eminent domain, §40A-3, (c).
State lands.
Acquiring allocated lands.
Administration department.
Powers generally, §146-24.1.
Procedure to obtain, §146-24, (c).
State of North Carolina.
Taking of state lands.
Consent of state required, §40A-5, (a).
Statute of limitations.
Inverse condemnation, §40A-51, (a).
Street railways.
Costs of petitions for condemnation of land.
Petitioner to pay costs in certain cases, §6-22.
Streets and highways.
Cartways, church roads or mill roads.
Special proceeding for establishment, alteration or discontinuance, §136-68.
Condemnation, §§136-103 to 136-121.1.
See STREETS AND HIGHWAYS.
Powers of local public condemnors, §40A-3, (b).
Subpoenas.
Private condemnors.
Commissioners.
Power to issue, §40A-26.
Summons and process.
Private condemnors, §40A-22.
Unknown parties, §40A-23.
Superior courts.
Proper division for trial of actions and proceedings, §7A-248.
Surveys, right of entry to make, §40A-11.
Taxation.
Reimbursement of owner for taxes paid on condemned property, §40A-6, (a).
Deferred taxes paid, §40A-6, (b).
Telephone and telegraph companies, §§62-183 to 62-189.
By whom may be exercised, §40A-3, (a).
Petition costs, §6-22.

EMINENT DOMAIN —Cont'd
Title.
Private condemnation proceedings.
Curing of defective title, §40A-34.
Torts.
Public condemnors.
Action in tort for damage to property.
Common law right not affected, §40A-51, (c).
Tramways.
By whom right may be exercised, §40A-3, (a).
Transportation department.
Powers of department, §§136-18, 136-19.
Trespass.
Right of entry prior to condemnation not deemed, §40A-11.
Trusts and trustees.
Private condemnors.
Acquisition of title of trustee without power of sale.
Powers of court upon, §40A-30.
Tryon's Palace restoration, §121-16.
Turnpike authority.
Power, §136-89.184, (a).
Procedure, §136-89.184, (b).
Urban redevelopment, §160A-515.
Powers of redevelopment commissions generally, §160A-512.
Vesting of title and right to possession, §40A-42, (b).
Modified provision for certain localities, §40A-42, (a).
Property owned by private condemnor, §40A-42, (c).
Standard provision, §40A-42, (a).
Voluntary nonsuit, §1-209.2.
Petitioner taxed with fee for respondent's attorney, §1-209.1.
Water and air resources.
Federal water resources development projects, §143-215.42, (a) to (h).
Water and sewer authorities.
Power of authority, §162A-6, (a), (c).
Waters and watercourses.
Natural and scenic rivers system.
Acquisition of land by administration department, §113A-38, (b).
Watershed improvement works or projects.
Certification of copies of findings to applicant district, §139-44, (b).
Interest in land acquired pursuant to section, §139-44, (e).
Power conferred on county, §139-44, (a).
Procedure, §139-44, (d).
Repeal of inconsistent provisions, §139-44, (f).
Words construed, §139-44, (c).
Water supply and waterworks.
By whom right may be exercised, §40A-3, (a).
Public water systems supplying drinking water, §130A-319.
Wetlands mitigation.
Condemnor seeking to acquire land for purposes of.
Payment to county where land located by condemnor, §153A-15.1, (a), (b).
Applicability of provisions, §153A-15.1, (e).
Estimated amount of ad valorem taxes that would have accrued for next 20 years defined, §153A-15.1, (c).
Exception, §153A-15.1, (d).
Wharves.
Powers of local public condemnors, §40A-3, (b).

EMINENT DOMAIN —Cont'd
Whole parcel or building.
Acquisition.
Generally, §40A-7, (a), (c).
Sale or disposal of residues required under provisions, §40A-7, (b).

EMISSIONS FROM MOTOR VEHICLES, §§20-128.1, 20-128.2.
Commissioner of motor vehicles.
Rules and regulations, §20-39.
Control devices, §20-128, (c).
Exception for pollution reduction modifications, §20-128, (d).
Safety inspections, scope, §20-183.3, (a).
Enforcement of provisions, §20-128.1, (c).
Inspections.
Counties, inspections performed in, §143-215.107A, (c).
Additional counties, requiring tests in, §143-215.107A, (c).
Decentralized network of test and repair stations.
Performing inspections, §143-215.107A, (a).
Emission mechanic license.
Required of persons performing, §§20-183.4A, 143-215.107A, (a).
Emissions program account, §20-183.7, (d).
General provisions, §143-215.107A, (a).
License to perform emissions inspection.
Mechanic qualifications, §20-183.4A, (c).
Required, §§20-183.4A, 143-215.107A, (a).
Self-inspector qualifications, §20-183.4A, (d).
Station qualifications, §20-183.4A, (b).
Scope, §20-183.3, (b), (b1).
Ten day temporary permit.
Vehicle failing inspection, §20-143.4C, (b).
Two-mode acceleration simulation mode (ASM) test, §143-215.107A, (b).
Vehicle subject to, §20-183.2, (b).
Waiver after failing inspection.
Missing emission control devices.
Expiration of inspection sticker received after waiver, §20-183.5A, (d).
Procedure for obtaining, §20-183.5A, (b).
Repairs equaling or exceeding waiver amount.
Repairs and costs not considered in determining, §20-183.5A, (c).
Requirements for waiver, §20-183.5A, (a).
Procedure, §20-183.5, (b).
Repairs, §20-183.5, (c).
Requirements, §20-183.5, (a).
Sticker expiration, §20-183.5, (d).
When vehicle must be inspected, §20-183.4C, (a).
Municipal regulations, §160A-185.
Requirements generally, §§20-128, (a), 20-128.1, (a).
Standards.
Rules and regulations, §20-128.2, (a).
State plans to reduce emissions from job-related travel.
Alternative-fueled or low emission vehicles, purchase by state, §143-215.107C, (a) to (c).
Plan for private sector employees, §143-215.107C, (e).
Plan for state employees, §143-215.107C, (d).
Violations of provisions.
Penalty, §20-128.1, (d).
Time for bringing vehicle into conformity with standards, §20-128.1, (b).

EMOTIONAL CONDITION, HEARSAY EXCEPTION, §8C-1, Rule 803.

EMOTIONAL DISTRESS.
Childhood vaccine injury compensation.
Commission awards, §130A-427, (a).
Ejectment of residential tenants.
Damages in action by tenant not to include, §42-25.9, (a).
Stalking, §14-277.3.

EMPLOYEE ASSISTANCE PROFESSIONALS, §§90-500 to 90-511.
Advertising.
Representation as licensed professional, §90-508.
Board.
Chair, §90-501, (j).
Compensation, §90-501, (i).
Composition, §90-501, (b).
Creation, §90-501, (a).
Diversity, §90-501, (h).
Duties, §90-502.
Independence, §90-501, (l).
List of nominees, §90-501, (e).
Meetings, §90-501, (k).
Powers, §90-502.
Prerequisites, §90-501, (d).
Qualifications, §90-501, (c).
Removal of members, §90-501, (f).
Secretary, §90-501, (j).
Vacancies, §90-501, (g).
Definitions, §90-500.
Enforcement of article, §90-506.
Considerations, §90-506, (b).
Enforcement options, §90-506, (a).
Hearings, §90-507.
Fees.
License application fee, §90-503.
Hearings.
Enforcement or disciplinary actions, §90-507.
Identification badges required, §90-640.
Immunities.
Good faith report of violations, §90-510.
Investigations.
Violations of provisions, §90-510.
Licenses.
Denial, suspension or revocation, §90-509.
Duration, §90-503.
Qualifications, §90-503.
Renewals, §90-504.
Misrepresentation.
Prohibited, §90-509.
Representation as licensed professional, §90-508.
Nonresidents.
Requirements for persons licensed out-of-state, §90-505.
Practice by members of other professional groups, §90-511.
Prohibited activities, §90-509.
Reciprocity, §90-505.
Representation as licensed professional, §90-508.
Violations of article, §90-506.

EMPLOYEE BENEFIT PLAN SUCCESSION RENUNCIATION, §31B-1.

EMPLOYEE SAFETY AND HEALTH PROGRAMS, §§95-250 to 95-256.
Additional rights, §95-253.
Amount of civil penalties, §95-256, (a).
Appeals of civil penalty, §95-256, (c).
Certification that employer meets requirement, §95-255, (b).
Civil penalties, §95-256.

EMPLOYEE SAFETY AND HEALTH PROGRAMS —Cont'd
Committees.
Composition, §95-252, (d).
Establishment, §95-252, (a).
Requirements, §95-252, (c).
Selection, §95-252, (d).
Temporary help services not counted as employee, §95-252, (b).
Definitions, §95-250.
Determination of amount of civil penalties, §95-256, (b).
Employee assistance professionals, §§90-500 to 90-511.
See EMPLOYEE ASSISTANCE PROFESSIONALS.
Establishment of program, §95-251, (a).
Experience rate modifiers.
Defined, §95-250.
Goals of program, §95-254, (a).
Notice that employer to comply with provision, §95-255, (a), (c).
Technical assistance, §95-255.1.
Pay during time employees participating.
No loss of pay, §95-251, (c).
Payment of civil penalties into general fund, §95-256, (d).
Reports, §95-255.
Requirements of program, §95-251, (b).
Rights additional to other rights, §95-253.
Rules, §95-254, (b).
Worksite.
Defined, §95-250.

EMPLOYEE THEFT.
Civil liability for damages, §1-538.2, (a).
Action brought regardless of criminal action, §1-538.2, (c).
Consequential and punitive damages and attorneys' fees.
Additional recovery allowed, §1-538.2, (a).
Amount of damages, cap, §1-538.2, (a).
Parent or legal guardian liable for acts of minor, §1-538.2, (b).
Consequential damages, included in, §1-538.2, (c1).
Demand letter, seeking damages prior to action, §1-538.2, (c2).
Payment of money demanded, no further action, §1-538.2, (c4).
Demand letter, seeking damages prior to action, §1-538.2, (c2).
Payment of money demanded, no further action, §1-538.2, (c4).
Qualified privilege of sender, §1-538.2, (c3).
Libel and slander.
Demand letter, seeking damages prior to action.
Qualified privilege of sender, §1-538.2, (c3).
Other theories of law, recovery under, §1-538.2, (d).
Parent or legal guardian liable for acts of minor, §1-538.2, (b).
Recovery of value of goods and merchandise, §1-538.2, (a).
Embezzlement.
See EMBEZZLEMENT.

EMPLOYER REPORTS TO DIRECTORY OF NEW HIRES, §110-129.2, (b) to (e).

EMPLOYERS AND EMPLOYEES.
Arbitration of labor disputes.
Conciliation service and mediation, §§95-32 to 95-36.
See LABOR DISPUTES.

EMPLOYERS AND EMPLOYEES —Cont'd
Arbitration of labor disputes —Cont'd
Voluntary arbitration, §§95-36.1 to 95-36.9.
See LABOR DISPUTES.
Child labor.
See CHILD LABOR.
Child support.
Directory of new hires.
Employer reporting, §110-129.2, (b) to (e).
Employee verification form.
Establishing obligor's gross income, §110-139, (c1).
Location of parent, employer information, providing, §110-139, (c).
Withholding of income.
Generally, §§110-136.3 to 110-136.14.
See CHILD SUPPORT.
Interstate family support act, §§52C-5-501 to 52C-5-507.
See INTERSTATE FAMILY SUPPORT.
Cigarettes and tobacco products.
Distribution to minor employee in performance of duties, §14-313, (b).
Civil no-contact orders.
Workplace violence prevention, §§95-265 to 95-276.
See WORKPLACE VIOLENCE PREVENTION.
Commissioner of labor.
See LABOR COMMISSIONER.
Conciliation and mediation of labor disputes, §§95-32 to 95-36.
See LABOR DISPUTES.
Controlled substances, examination and screening of employees, §§95-230 to 95-235.
Criminal law and procedure.
Victims or witnesses.
Employer intercession services, §15A-825.
Department of labor.
See LABOR DEPARTMENT.
Discharge of employee called to jury duty.
Prohibition, §9-32, (a).
Action for damages, §9-32, (b), (c).
Disclosure of information by employer.
Employee's job performance or job history.
Immunity, §1-539.12, (a) to (d).
Discrimination.
Equal employment practices, §§143-422.1 to 143-422.3.
Genetic testing, information or counseling, §95-28.1A.
Lawful use of lawful products during nonworking hours by employees, §95-28.2.
Retaliatory employment discrimination, §§95-240 to 95-245.
See RETALIATORY EMPLOYMENT DISCRIMINATION.
Drug examination and screening of employees for controlled substances, §§95-230 to 95-235.
Duties owed employer.
Influencing employees to violate duties, §§14-353, 14-354.
Embezzlement.
See EMBEZZLEMENT.
Employee assistance professionals, §§90-500 to 90-511.
See EMPLOYEE ASSISTANCE PROFESSIONALS.
Employee examination and screening for controlled substances, §§95-230 to 95-235.

EMPLOYERS AND EMPLOYEES —Cont'd
Employee's job history or performance.
Immunity, employer disclosing information, §1-539.12, (a) to (d).
Employment agencies.
Job listing services, §§95-47.19 to 95-47.32.
See JOB LISTING SERVICES.
Private personnel services, §§95-47.1 to 95-47.15.
See PRIVATE PERSONNEL SERVICES.
Professional employer organization act, §§58-89A-1 to 58-89A-180.
See PROFESSIONAL EMPLOYER ORGANIZATIONS.
Employment security, §§96-1 to 96-29.
See UNEMPLOYMENT COMPENSATION.
Equal employment practices, §§143-422.1 to 143-422.3.
Family leave credit insurance, §58-57-115.
General provisions.
See LABOR.
Genetic testing, information or counseling.
Discrimination against persons based on, §95-28.1A.
Handicapped persons.
Governor's council on employment of the handicapped, §§143-283.1 to 143-283.8.
Harassment.
Workplace violence prevention.
Civil no-contact orders, §§95-265 to 95-276.
See WORKPLACE VIOLENCE PREVENTION.
Health programs generally, §§95-250 to 95-256.
See EMPLOYEE SAFETY AND HEALTH PROGRAMS.
Hospital employees.
Public hospital personnel act, §§131E-257 to 131E-257.2.
Hours of labor.
Wage and hour act.
General provisions, §§95-25.1 to 95-25.25.
See WAGE AND HOUR ACT.
Immunity of employer.
Disclosure of information.
Employee's job history or performance, §1-539.12, (a) to (d).
Income withholding.
Child support.
Generally, §§110-136.3 to 110-136.14.
See CHILD SUPPORT.
Interstate family support act, §§52C-5-501 to 52C-5-507.
See INTERSTATE FAMILY SUPPORT.
Influencing employees in violating duties owed employers, §§14-353, 14-354.
Interstate commerce.
Earnings of employees in interstate commerce.
Collections out of state to avoid exemptions, §§95-73 to 95-77.
Invention development by employees, §§66-57.1, 66-57.2.
Job listing services, §§95-47.19 to 95-47.32.
See JOB LISTING SERVICES.
Job performance or job history.
Disclosure of information by employer.
Immunity, §1-539.12, (a) to (d).
Job training, education and placement information management, §§96-30 to 96-35.
See JOB TRAINING, EDUCATION AND PLACEMENT INFORMATION MANAGEMENT.

EMPLOYERS AND EMPLOYEES —Cont'd
Jury duty.
Discharge of employee called to jury duty.
Damages suffered by employee, employer liable for, §9-32, (b).
Burden of proof on employee, §9-32, (b).
Statute of limitation, §9-32, (c).
Prohibition, §9-32, (a).
Kidnapping and abduction.
Enticing minors out of state for employment purposes, §14-40.
Labor organizations.
Unions generally.
See LABOR UNIONS.
Larceny by servant or employee, §14-74.
Managed care organizations, I.C. Managed Care Orgs. R. I to X.
See INDUSTRIAL COMMISSION.
Minimum wage.
Wage and hour act, §§95-25.1 to 95-25.25.
See WAGE AND HOUR ACT.
National guard.
Reemployment rights, §§127A-201 to 127A-203.
No-contact orders.
Workplace violence prevention.
Civil no-contact orders, §§95-265 to 95-276.
See WORKPLACE VIOLENCE PREVENTION.
Occupational safety and health.
General provisions, §§95-126 to 95-155.
See OCCUPATIONAL SAFETY AND HEALTH.
Safety and health programs, §§95-250 to 95-256.
See EMPLOYEE SAFETY AND HEALTH PROGRAMS.
Personnel system.
See PERSONNEL SYSTEM.
Precinct election officials.
Discharge or demotion of employee because of appointment as, §163-41.2.
Priority in employment assistance for United States armed forces veterans, §§165-44.1 to 165-44.6.
Private personnel services, §§95-47.1 to 95-47.15.
See PRIVATE PERSONNEL SERVICES.
Private protective services, §74C-11.
Professional employer organization act, §§58-89A-1 to 58-89A-180.
See PROFESSIONAL EMPLOYER ORGANIZATIONS.
Proprietary schools.
Schools maintained or classes conducted by employers for employees.
Exemptions from article, §115D-88.
Public hospital personnel act, §§131E-257 to 131E-257.2.
Public officers and employees.
See PUBLIC OFFICERS AND EMPLOYEES.
Reports.
Directory of new hires.
Employer reporting, §110-129.2, (b) to (e).
Retaliatory employment discrimination, §§95-240 to 95-245.
See RETALIATORY EMPLOYMENT DISCRIMINATION.
Retirement system for teachers and state employees.
See RETIREMENT SYSTEM FOR TEACHERS AND STATE EMPLOYEES.
Right to work law, §§95-78 to 95-84.
See LABOR.

EMPLOYERS AND EMPLOYEES —Cont'd
Safety programs generally, §§95-250 to 95-256.
See EMPLOYEE SAFETY AND HEALTH PROGRAMS.
Salaries.
See SALARIES.
Screening employees for controlled substances, §§95-230 to 95-235.
State employees.
General provisions.
See PUBLIC OFFICERS AND EMPLOYEES.
Retirement system for teachers and state employees.
General provisions.
See RETIREMENT SYSTEM FOR TEACHERS AND STATE EMPLOYEES.
State personnel system.
See PERSONNEL SYSTEM.
Support and maintenance.
Child support.
Income withholding.
Generally, §§110-136.3 to 110-136.14.
See CHILD SUPPORT.
Interstate family support act, §§52C-5-501 to 52C-5-507.
See INTERSTATE FAMILY SUPPORT.
Theft by employees, civil liability, §1-538.2, (a) to (d).
Threats.
Workplace violence prevention.
Civil no-contact orders, §§95-265 to 95-276.
See WORKPLACE VIOLENCE PREVENTION.
Tobacco products.
Distribution to minor employee, §14-313, (b).
Unemployment compensation, §§96-1 to 96-29.
See UNEMPLOYMENT COMPENSATION.
Unions generally.
See LABOR UNIONS.
Veterans priority in employment assistance, §§165-44.1 to 165-44.6.
Violence in the workplace.
Prevention.
Civil no-contact orders, §§95-265 to 95-276.
See WORKPLACE VIOLENCE PREVENTION.
Wage and hour act.
General provisions, §§95-25.1 to 95-25.25.
See WAGE AND HOUR ACT.
Wages generally.
See WAGES.
Whistleblower protection.
Retaliatory employment discrimination, §§95-240 to 95-245.
See RETALIATORY EMPLOYMENT DISCRIMINATION.
Withholding of income.
Child support.
Generally, §§110-136.3 to 110-136.14.
See CHILD SUPPORT.
Interstate family support act, §§52C-5-501 to 52C-5-507.
See INTERSTATE FAMILY SUPPORT.
Workforce development, §§143B-438.10 to 143B-438.13.
Workplace violence prevention.
Civil no-contact orders, §§95-265 to 95-276.
See WORKPLACE VIOLENCE PREVENTION.
Youth employment.
General provisions.
See CHILD LABOR.

EMPLOYMENT AGENCIES.
Immunity of employer for disclosure of information.
Employee's job performance or job history.
Employer includes job placement service, §1-539.12, (c).
Job listing services, §§95-47.19 to 95-47.32.
See JOB LISTING SERVICES.
Private personnel services, §§95-47.1 to 95-47.15.
See PRIVATE PERSONNEL SERVICES.
Professional employer organization act, §§58-89A-1 to 58-89A-180.
See PROFESSIONAL EMPLOYER ORGANIZATIONS.

EMPLOYMENT AND TRAINING GRANT PROGRAM.
Workforce development, §143B-438.13.

EMPLOYMENT DISCRIMINATION.
Domestic violence.
Persons seeking relief under provisions.
Prohibited acts by employers, §50B-5.5, (a).
Enforcement, §50B-5.5, (b).
Equal employment practices, §§143-422.1 to 143-422.3.
Genetic information, testing or counseling services.
Basis of genetic information, §95-28.1A, (a).
Genetic characteristic defined, §95-28.1A, (b).
Genetic information defined, §95-28.1A, (b).
Genetic test defined, §95-28.1A, (b).
Person having requested genetic tests or counseling, §95-28.1A, (a).
Lawful use of lawful products during non-working hours by employees, §95-28.2.
Persons possessing sickle cell trait or hemoglobin C trait, §95-28.1.
Whistleblower protection.
Retaliatory employment discrimination, §§95-240 to 95-245.
See RETALIATORY EMPLOYMENT DISCRIMINATION.

EMPLOYMENT PREFERENCE ACT, VETERANS, §128-15, (a) to (d).
Preferences generally.
See PERSONNEL SYSTEM.
Priority in employment assistance for United States armed forces veterans, §§165-44.1 to 165-44.6.

EMPLOYMENT SECURITY COMMISSION.
Administrative procedure act.
Full exemption, §150B-1, (c).
Child support enforcement.
Directory of new hires.
Access to information, §110-129.2, (g).
Destruction of records, §132-3, (c).
Evidence.
Computer records.
Reproduction of records stored on permanent computer-readable media, §8-45.3, (b).
First stop employment assistance program, §108A-29.
Job training, education and placement information management, §§96-30 to 96-35.
See JOB TRAINING, EDUCATION AND PLACEMENT INFORMATION MANAGEMENT.
Records.
Destruction of records, §132-3, (c).
Photographic reproduction, §8-45.3, (a1).

EMPLOYMENT SECURITY COMMISSION —Cont'd
Unemployment compensation, §§96-1 to 96-29.
See UNEMPLOYMENT COMPENSATION.

E-NC AUTHORITY, §§143B-437.44 to 143B-437.47.
Commission.
Appointment of members, number, §143B-437.46, (b).
Chair, §143B-437.46, (e).
Conflicts of interest, §143B-437.46, (j).
Expenses, §143B-437.46, (h).
Governing body, §143B-437.46, (b).
Oath of office, §143B-437.46, (c).
Removal, §143B-437.46, (g).
Staff, §143B-437.46, (i).
Terms, §143B-437.46, (d).
Vacancies, §143B-437.46, (f).
Created within department of commerce, §143B-437.46, (a).
Definitions, §143B-437.45.
Duties, §143B-437.47, (b).
Eminent domain, no power of, §143B-437.47, (d).
Intent of authority.
Continue and conclude work of rural internet access authority, §143B-437.44.
Legislative findings, §143B-437.44.
Powers, §143B-437.47, (a).
Limitations, §143B-437.47, (d).
Purpose, §143B-437.46, (a).
Report, §143B-437.47, (e).
Taxing or charging telecommunications.
No power, §143B-437.47, (d).

ENCROACHMENT UPON PUBLIC WAY.
No title by possession, §1-45.

ENDANGERED PLANT SPECIES.
Board, §§106-202.14, 106-202.15.
Criteria and procedures for placing on list, §106-202.16.
Declaration of policy, §106-202.13.
Definitions, §106-202.12.
Enforcement of article, §106-202.19, (b).
Ginseng dealers.
Permits, §106-202.21.
Illegally possessed plants.
Forfeiture and disposition, §106-202.20.
Injunctive relief.
Violations of article, §106-202.19, (c).
Legislative findings, §106-202.13.
Permits.
Denial, suspension or revocation, §106-202.22.
Ginseng dealers, §106-202.21.
Policy of state, Const. N. C., art. XIV, §5.
Declaration, §106-202.13.
Right of entry.
Enforcement of article, §106-202.19, (b).
Scientific committee, §§106-202.17, 106-202.18.
Unlawful acts, §106-202.19, (a).
Civil penalties, §106-202.19, (a2).
Criminal penalties, §106-202.19, (a1).

ENDANGERED WILDLIFE SPECIES.
Declaration of policy, §113-332.
Definitions, §113-331.
Federal list species.
Same status on state list, §113-334, (a).
Nongame wildlife advisory committee, §§113-335, 113-336.
Placing on protected lists.
Examination of relevant scientific and economic data.
Commission finding probable merit in proposal, §113-334, (c).

ENDANGERED WILDLIFE SPECIES —Cont'd
Placing on protected lists —Cont'd
Federal list species.
Same status on state list, §113-334, (a).
Notice of proposed rulemaking, publication, §113-334, (d).
Resolution proposing adding or removing species.
Advisory committee proposing to commission, §113-334, (b).
Tentative determine on regulatory action, §113-334, (d).
Policy of state, §113-332.
Unlawful acts, §113-337, (a).
Misdemeanors, §113-337, (b).
Wildlife resources commission.
Conservation plan, §113-333, (b), (c).
Powers and duties, §113-333, (a).

ENDANGERING EXECUTIVE, LEGISLATIVE OR COURT OFFICERS, §§14-16.6 to 14-16.10.
Electronic surveillance orders, §15A-290, (c4).

ENDORSEMENTS.
Commercial code.
Unauthorized indorsements defined, §25-1-201, (43).
Documents of title, §25-7-501, (1).
Compelling endorsement.
Right to compel, §25-7-506.
Delivery to compel endorsement, §25-7-506.
Endorser not guarantor for other parties, §25-7-505.
Power to compel endorsement, §25-7-506.
Requirements of due negotiation, §25-7-501.
Investment securities.
Assurance that indorsements are effective, §25-8-402.
Negotiable instruments generally.
See NEGOTIABLE INSTRUMENTS.
Uttering instrument containing forged endorsement, §14-120.

ENDOWMENT FUNDS.
Management of institutional funds.
See MANAGEMENT OF INSTITUTIONAL FUNDS.
Public schools, §§115C-490 to 115C-494.

ENERGY.
Coal and petroleum suppliers.
Reporting petroleum fuel capacity, §§143-345.13, 143-345.14.
Conservation loan authority, §§122A-5.3, 122A-6.1.
Crisis administration, §§113B-20 to 113B-24.
See ENERGY CRISIS ADMINISTRATION.
Emergency energy program, §113B-9.
Energy efficiency program, §113B-7.
Energy improvement loan program, §§143-345.16 to 143-345.18.
Energy savings contracts.
Guaranteed energy savings contracts, §§143-64.17 to 143-64.17K, 143-129.4.
Guaranteed energy savings contracts, §§143-64.17 to 143-64.17K, 143-129.4.
Local governmental units.
Installment and lease purchase contracts, §143-64.17I.
State governmental units.
Financing by, §143-64.17J.
Inspection and compliance certification for, §143-64.17K.

ENERGY —Cont'd
Guaranteed energy savings contracts —Cont'd
State governmental units —Cont'd
Reports, §§143-64.17G, 143-64.17H.
Use of contracts when feasible, rules, recommendation, §143-64.17F.
Management plan, §113B-8.
Nuclear facility fees.
Carried forward amount of fees, §166A-6.1, (c).
Oil and gas conservation, §§113-378 to 113-415.
See OIL AND GAS CONSERVATION.
Policy council, §§113B-1 to 113B-12.
See ENERGY POLICY COUNCIL.
Public buildings and grounds.
Energy policy and life-cycle cost analysis for state government, §§143-64.10 to 143-64.16.
Guaranteed energy savings contracts, §§143-64.17 to 143-64.17K, 143-129.4.
Research and development program, §113B-10.
Southern states energy compact, §§104D-1 to 104D-5.
State energy conservation finance act, §§142-60 to 142-70.
See ENERGY CONSERVATION FINANCE ACT.

ENERGY CONSERVATION FINANCE ACT, §§142-60 to 142-70.
Certificates of participation.
Defined, §142-61.
Interest, §142-67, (b).
Investment eligibility, §142-70.
Other agreements authorized, §142-69.
Powers of state treasurer, §142-67, (a).
Sale, §142-67, (b).
Tax exemption, §142-68.
Trust agreement, §142-67, (c).
Citation of act, §142-60.
Credit facility.
Defined, §142-61.
Security for payments under financing contract, §142-65, (g).
Definitions, §142-61.
Financing contract.
Authorization, §142-63.
Breach.
Deficiency judgment not to be rendered against state in action for, §142-65, (b).
Defined, §142-61.
Entry into.
Certification of availability of funds to make payments due under, §142-64, (d).
Conditions, §142-64, (b).
Factors in determining whether to approve, §142-64, (c).
Request for approval, §142-64, (a).
Faith and credit of state not pledged, §142-66.
Interest component of installment payments under.
Calculation, §142-65, (f).
Investment eligibility, §142-70.
Nonsubstitution clauses prohibited, §142-65, (c).
Other agreements authorized, §142-69.
Payments under, §142-66.
Provisions authorized, §142-65, (d), (e).
Security for performance of state's obligations under.
Credit facility, §142-65, (g).
Lien on conservation property, §142-65, (a).
Tax exemption, §142-68.

ENERGY CONSERVATION FINANCE ACT —Cont'd
Liens.
Security for performance of state's obligations under financing contract.
Lien on conservation property, §142-65, (a).
Title of act, §142-60.

ENERGY CRISIS ADMINISTRATION, §§113B-20 to 113B-24.
Attorney general enforcement, §113B-24, (a).
Declaration of crisis.
Energy policy council.
Emergency energy coordinating body.
Council to become upon declaration of energy crisis, §113B-23, (a).
Implementation and enforcement of emergency energy program, §113B-23, (b).
Power of governor, §§113B-20, (b), 113B-23, (c).
Definitions, §113B-20, (a).
Emergency energy coordinating body.
Declaration of energy crisis.
Energy policy council, §113B-23, (a).
Emergency proposals.
Consultation by governor with committee, §113B-22, (b).
Contents, §113B-22, (d).
Duration, §113B-22, (c).
Effective date, §113B-22, (b).
Procedure for adoption, §113B-22, (a).
Energy policy council.
Declaration of energy crisis.
Emergency energy coordinating body, §113B-23, (a).
Duties, §113B-23, (a).
Enforcement.
Powers and duties of attorney general, §113B-24, (a).
Governor.
Declaration of crisis, §113B-20, (b).
Powers, §113B-23, (c).
Implementation and enforcement of emergency energy programs.
Declaration of energy crisis, §113B-23, (b).
Injunctions.
Enforcement of article, §113B-24, (c).
Legislative committee.
Composition, §113B-21, (a).
Created, §113B-21, (a).
Governor to consult with, §113B-22, (b).
Meetings, §113B-21, (b).
Reimbursement of members, §113B-21, (c).
Penalties, §113B-24, (b).
Violations.
Injunctions, §113B-24, (c).
Penalty, §113B-24, (b).

ENERGY EFFICIENCY PROGRAM.
Attorney general.
Assignment of attorney for program, §114-4.2D.
Contents, §113B-7, (c).
Initial plan.
Completion, §113B-7, (a).
Preparation by council, §113B-7, (a).
Purpose of plan, §113B-7, (b).
Recommendations of council, §113B-7, (c), (d).
Review of plan, §113B-7, (g).
Transmission to governor, §113B-7, (e).
Transmission to legislature, §113B-7, (f).

ENERGY IMPROVEMENT LOAN PROGRAM, §§143-345.16 to 143-345.18.
Administrative expenses.
Applicability of stripper well settlement, §143-345.18, (d).

ENERGY IMPROVEMENT LOAN PROGRAM —Cont'd
Definitions, §143-345.18, (e).
Interest rates, §143-345.18, (c1).
Lead agency, §143-345.18, (a).
Powers and duties, §143-345.18, (b).
Public policy, §143-345.17.
Revolving fund.
Annual interest rate charged for use, §143-345.18, (c).
Establishment, §143-345.18, (b).
Short title, §143-345.16.

ENERGY MANAGEMENT PLAN.
Components of plan, §113B-8, (b).
Contents, §113B-8, (c).
Governor.
Authority, §113B-8, (g), (h).
Preparation, §113B-8, (a).
Purpose of plan, §113B-8, (b).
Recommendations, §113B-8, (d).
Transmission to governor and legislature, §113B-8, (e).
Updating plan by council, §113B-8, (f).

ENERGY POLICY COUNCIL, §§113B-1 to 113B-12.
Advisory committees.
Authority to create, §113B-5, (c).
Attorney general.
Assignment of attorney for council, §114-4.2D.
Chairman, §113B-4, (a).
Composition, §113B-3, (a).
Creation, §113B-2, (a).
Declaration of energy crisis.
Emergency energy coordinating body, §113B-23, (a).
Duties, §113B-23, (a).
Duties, §§113B-2, (b), 113B-6.
Emergency energy program.
Preparation, §113B-9, (a).
Energy efficiency program.
Administrative responsibility.
Assignment by governor, §113B-7, (e).
Attorney general.
Assignment of attorney for program, §114-4.2D.
Distribution, §113B-7, (d).
Governor.
Transmission to senate, §113B-7, (f).
Preparation, §113B-7, (a).
Purpose of plan, §113B-7, (b).
Recommendations of council, §113B-7, (c), (d).
Review by council, §113B-7, (g).
Transmission to governor for approval or disapproval, §113B-7, (e).
Funds.
Authority to allocate and dispense, §113B-11, (d).
Grants.
Authority of council to apply and utilize, §113B-11, (c).
Information.
Authority of council to secure, §113B-11, (a).
Initial appointments, §113B-3, (b).
Legislative findings, §113B-1.
Management plan.
Governor.
Authority, §113B-8, (g), (h).
Procedures, §113B-8, (e).
Preparation, §113B-8, (a).
Purpose of plan, §113B-8, (b).
Recommendations, §113B-8, (d).
Updating by council, §113B-8, (f).

ENERGY POLICY COUNCIL —Cont'd
Organization, §113B-5, (a).
Powers, duties and functions, §§113B-2, (b), 113B-6.
Purpose of article, §113B-1.
Purpose of council, §113B-2, (c).
Qualifications, §113B-3, (c).
Reimbursement of members, §113B-4, (c).
Reports, §113B-12, (a), (b).
Annual report, §113B-11, (a).
Council may require filing, §113B-11, (b).
Research and development program, §113B-10.
Rules of procedure.
Adoption, §113B-5, (b).
Staff, §113B-11, (e).
Terms of members, §113B-3, (b).
Vacancies, §113B-4, (b).

ENERGY RESEARCH AND DEVELOPMENT PROGRAM.
Central repository, §113B-10, (c).
Council to encourage, §113B-10, (a).
Interagency cooperation, §113B-10, (e).
Review and coordination of state agency research and planning.
Duties of council, §113B-10, (d).
Statewide program of research and development, §113B-10, (b).

ENERGY SAVINGS CONTRACTS.
Guaranteed energy savings contracts, §§143-64.17 to 143-64.17K, 143-129.4.
Local governmental units.
Installment and lease purchase contracts, §143-64.17I.
State governmental units.
Financing by, §143-64.17J.
Inspection and compliance certification for, §143-64.17K.
Reports, §§143-64.17G, 143-64.17H.
Use of contracts when feasible, rules, recommendations, §143-64.17F.

ENFORCEMENT OF CHILD SUPPORT PROGRAM.
Generally, §§110-128 to 110-142.2.
See CHILD SUPPORT.

ENFORCEMENT OF FOREIGN JUDGMENTS, §§1C-1701 to 1C-1708.
See FOREIGN JUDGMENTS, ENFORCEMENT.

ENGINEERS.
Air pollution control.
Expedited review of applications certified by professional engineer, §143-215.108, (h).
Appeals.
Disciplinary action.
Judicial review, §89C-22, (d).
Applicability of provisions.
Limitations, §89C-25.
Architects.
Exemption of architectural work incidental to engineering project, §83A-13, (a).
Attorney general.
Legal adviser to board, §89C-23.
Board of examiners.
Appointment of members, §89C-4.
Compensation of members, §89C-6.
Composition, §89C-4.
Continuing professional competency activities.
Licensing of sponsors, §89C-10, (h).
Creation, §89C-4.

ENGINEERS —Cont'd
Board of examiners —Cont'd
Executive director, §89C-9.
Bond, surety, §89C-9.
Expenses of members, §89C-6.
Funds, §89C-11.
Injunctions.
Power to seek, §89C-10, (c).
Instructional programs.
Powers as to, §89C-10, (g).
Licensure by discipline.
Submission of program, §89C-25.2.
Meetings, §89C-8.
Number of members, §89C-4.
Officers, §89C-8.
Powers.
Generally, §89C-10.
Qualifications of members, §§89C-4, 89C-5.
Quorum, §89C-8.
Real property, powers, §89C-10, (i).
Records, §89C-12.
Removal of members, §89C-7.
Reports.
Annual report to governor, §89C-12.
Residence requirements for membership, §89C-5.
Rules and regulations, §89C-10, (a).
Rules of professional conduct.
Promulgation, §89C-20.
Seal, §89C-10, (b).
Secretary.
Duties, §89C-11.
Election, §89C-8.
Terms of members, §89C-4.
Vacancies, §§89C-4, 89C-7.
Bonds, surety.
Board of examiners.
Executive director, §89C-9.
Child support enforcement.
Forfeiture of licensing privilege, §50-13.12.
Citation of act.
Short title, §89C-1.
Conflicts of interest.
Public works.
Employment of engineers when interest in use of materials prohibited, §133-1.
Construction of act.
Citation of title, §89C-1.
Exemptions from act's provisions, §89C-25.
Limitations on act's applicability, §89C-25.
Public policy, §89C-2.
Severability of provisions, §89C-27.
Continuing education.
Sponsors of continuing professional competency activities.
Licensing, §89C-10, (h).
Corporations.
Practice of engineering or land surveying, §89C-24.
Definitions, §89C-3.
Disciplinary action, §89C-22.
Appeals.
Judicial review, §89C-22, (d).
Certificate of authorization of corporation.
Revocation or suspension, §89C-21, (b).
Reissuance, §89C-22, (e).
Charges, §89C-22, (a).
Hearing, §89C-22, (b).
Grounds, §89C-21, (a).
Penalties.
Civil penalties, §89C-21, (c), (d).

ENGINEERS —Cont'd
Disciplinary action —Cont'd
Revocation or suspension of certificate, §89C-21, (a).
Reissuance, §89C-22, (e).
Education.
Continuing education.
Licensing of sponsors of professional competency activities, §89C-10, (h).
Requirements for licensure generally, §89C-13.
Emergency or disaster.
Qualified immunity for volunteers, §89C-19.1.
Engineering interns.
Licenses.
Qualifications, §89C-13, (a).
Evidence.
Licenses.
Certificates of licensure.
Evidentiary effect, §89C-16, (b).
Examinations, §89C-15.
Power of board, §89C-10, (d).
Reexamination, §89C-14, (e).
Requirements for licensure generally, §89C-13.
Scope, §89C-15, (b).
Time and place, §89C-15, (a).
Exemptions from provisions, §89C-25.
Fees.
Continuing professional competency activities.
Sponsors' licenses, §89C-10, (h).
Felony convictions.
Forfeiture of license, §15A-1331A.
Injunctions, §89C-10, (c).
Instructional programs.
Board of examiners.
Powers as to, §89C-10, (g).
Investigations.
Duties of board, §89C-10, (f).
Land surveyor interns.
Licenses.
Qualifications, §89C-13, (b).
Land surveyors.
Soil scientists.
Unlawful acts as to land surveying, §89F-19, (e).
Legislative declaration, §89C-2.
Licenses.
Applications, §89C-14, (a).
Certificates of licensure.
Evidentiary effect, §89C-16, (b).
Expiration, §89C-17.
Issuance, §89C-16, (a).
Power of board, §89C-10, (e).
Lost or destroyed certificates.
Duplicate certificate, §89C-18.
Renewal, §89C-17.
Comity or indorsement.
Requirements for licensure by.
Professional engineer, §89C-13, (a).
Professional land surveyor, §89C-13, (b).
Corporations and business firms, §89C-24.
Engineering interns.
Qualifications, §89C-13, (a).
Examinations, §89C-15.
Reexamination, §89C-14, (e).
Requirements for licensure generally, §89C-13.
Scope, §89C-15, (b).
Time and place, §89C-15, (a).
Existing licensure not affected, §89C-28.
Expiration of certificates, §89C-17.
Fees, §89C-14, (b), (c).
Corporations and business firms, §89C-24.
Duplicate certificates, §89C-18.

ENGINEERS —Cont'd
Licenses —Cont'd
Fees —Cont'd
Renewal of certificate, §89C-17.
Return on denial of certificate, §89C-14, (d).
Issuance of certificate of licensure.
Power of board, §89C-10, (e).
Land surveyor interns.
Qualifications, §89C-13, (b).
Nonresidents.
Definitions, §89C-18.1, (a).
Delinquents, §89C-18.1, (d).
Generally, §89C-18.1, (b).
Information, §89C-18.1, (d).
Professional engineers.
Qualifications, §89C-13, (a).
Professional land surveyors.
Qualifications, §89C-13, (b).
Qualifications, §89C-13.
Renewal of certificate, §89C-17.
Required, §89C-2.
Revocation or suspension.
Disciplinary action generally, §§89C-21, 89C-22.
Felony convictions, §15A-1331A.
Saving clause, §89C-28.
Supervision of unlicensed individuals by licensed person, §89C-25.1.
License tax.
Professional licenses generally, §105-41.
Licensure by discipline.
Board to submit program, §89C-25.2.
Limitation of actions.
Real property improvements.
Recovery of damages for defective or unsafe conditions.
Six-year limitation, §1-50, (a).
Nonresidents.
Licensing of nonresidents, §89C-18.1.
Penalties.
Violations of provisions, §89C-23.
Practice of engineering.
Corporations and business firms, §89C-24.
Practice of land surveying.
Corporations and business firms, §89C-24.
Professional corporations, §55B-14, (b).
Professional engineers.
Licenses.
Qualifications, §89C-13, (a).
Professional land surveyors.
Licenses.
Qualifications, §89C-13, (b).
Public buildings and grounds.
Bids and bidding.
Architectural, engineering and surveying services, §§143-64.31 to 143-64.34.
See PUBLIC CONTRACTS.
Certain buildings involving public funds to be designed, etc., by engineer, §133-1.1.
Public works.
Bids and bidding.
Architectural, engineering and surveying services, §§143-64.31 to 143-64.34.
See PUBLIC CONTRACTS.
Buildings involving expenditure of public funds.
Certain buildings involving public funds to be designed, etc., by engineer, §133-1.1.
Employment of engineers when interest in use of materials prohibited, §133-1.
Requirements, §89C-19.
Records.
Board of examiners, §89C-12.

ENGINEERS —Cont'd
Reports.
Board of examiners.
Annual report to governor, §89C-12.
Rules and regulations of board of examiners, §89C-10, (a).
Rules of professional conduct, §89C-20.
Safety professionals, §§90-671 to 90-674.
Sanitary districts.
Employment of engineers.
Corporate powers of sanitary district board, §130A-55.
Plan for accomplishment of objects of district.
Engineers to provide plans and supervise work, §130A-63, (a), (c).
Report on problems of sanitary district, §130A-59.
Consideration of reports and adoption of plan, §130A-60, (a), (b).
Seals and sealed instruments, §89C-16, (c).
Board of examiners, §89C-10, (b).
Severability of provisions, §89C-27.
Soil scientists.
Unlawful acts by soil scientists as to engineering, §89F-19, (f).
Streets and highways.
Right-of-way acquisitions.
Preliminary engineering annual report, §136-44.11, (a).
Subcontractors, payments to for improvements upon real property, §§22C-1 to 22C-6.
Supervision of unlicensed individuals by licensed person, §89C-25.1.
Title of act.
Short title, §89C-1.
Transportation department.
Division engineer to manage personnel department, §136-14.2.
Unit ownership.
Plans of buildings.
Certificate of engineer, §47A-15, (a).
Violations of provisions.
Injunctions, §89C-10, (c).
Penalties, §89C-23.
Prohibited act, §89C-23.

ENGINE NUMBERS.
Altering or changing.
Prohibited acts, §20-109, (a).
Intent to conceal or misrepresent true identity of vehicle, §20-109, (b).
New.
Division to be notified on installation, §20-70, (a).
Surrender of certificate of title and registration card on installation, §20-70, (b).
Removal or obliteration.
New engine number, §20-69.
Surrender of registration card and certificate of title, §20-70, (b).
Vehicles without manufacturer's numbers.
Prohibitions as to, §20-108.

ENGINE TAMPERING, §14-153.

ENGLISH LANGUAGE.
Public schools.
Basic education program.
Classes to be conducted in English, §115C-81, (c).
State language, §145-12.

ENGRAVINGS.
Sale of prints, §§25C-10 to 25C-16.

ENLARGEMENT OF TIME, §§1-593, 1A-1, Rule 6, (b).

ENTERPRISE CORPORATIONS, §§53A-35 to 53A-47.
See NORTH CAROLINA ENTERPRISE CORPORATIONS.

ENTERPRISE TIER.
Tax incentives for new and expanding businesses.
Defined, assignment and rankings of counties, §105-129.3.
Development zone designation.
Relationship with enterprise tiers, §105-129.3A, (c).

ENTERTAINMENT CONTRACTS.
See PREPAID ENTERTAINMENT CONTRACTS.

ENTERTAINMENT TAX.
License tax by city but not county, §105-37.1, (d).
Privilege tax on gross receipts, admission fee charged, §105-37.1, (a).
Rate and payment, §105-37.1, (b).

ENTICING MINOR OUT OF STATE FOR EMPLOYMENT PURPOSES, §14-40.

ENTRAPMENT.
Criminal law and procedure.
Notice to state of defenses, §15A-905, (c), (d).

ENTRY OF JUDGMENT, §1A-1, Rule 58.
Confession of judgment, §1A-1, Rule 68.1, (d).
Default, §1A-1, Rule 55, (a), (b).
Setting aside, §1A-1, Rule 55, (d).
Judgment by confession, §1A-1, Rule 68.1.
Multiple claims or parties, §1A-1, Rule 54, (b).
Small claims actions, §7A-224.

ENTRY, RIGHT OF.
See RIGHT OF ENTRY.

ENVIRONMENTAL COMPACT, §§113A-21 to 113A-23.
Citation of article, §113A-21.
Compact provisions, §113A-23.
Legislative findings, §113A-22.
Provisions generally, §113A-23.
Purposes, §113A-22.
Short title, §113A-21.

ENVIRONMENTAL COMPLIANCE COSTS.
Accelerated costs recovery.
Coal-fired investor-owned generating units, §62-133.6, (b).
Adjustments or reductions in rate base, §62-133.6, (e), (f).
Amortization, §62-133.6, (b).
Compliance plans, filing, §62-133.6, (c).
Defined, §62-133.6, (a).
Emissions limitations, statement by utilities subject to, §62-133.6, (i), (j).
Enforcement of utility compliance, §62-133.6, (h).
Final agency action not subject to review, §62-133.6, (k).
Hearing to review compliance costs, §62-133.6, (d).
Market based rates and services, authority to implement, §62-133.6, (g).
Rate base to remain unchanged, §62-133.6, (e).

ENVIRONMENTAL CONTAMINATION.
Brownfields property reuse act of 1997, §§130A-310.30 to 130A-310.40.
See BROWNFIELDS PROPERTY REUSE.

ENVIRONMENTAL EDUCATION, OFFICE OF, §§143B-285.20 to 143B-285.25.
Awards.
Objectives, §143B-285.24.
Citation of act.
Short title, §143B-285.20.
Creation, §143B-285.22.
Department of public instruction.
Liaison with, §143B-285.25.
Grants.
Objectives, §143B-285.24.
Legislative declaration, §143B-285.21.
Powers and duties, §143B-285.23.
Purpose of act, §143B-285.21.
Secretary.
Powers and duties, §143B-285.23.
Title of act.
Short title, §143B-285.20.

ENVIRONMENTAL ENFORCEMENT OFFICERS.
Municipal corporations.
Enforcing restrictions on illegal disposal of solid waste, §160A-185.

ENVIRONMENTAL IMPACT STATEMENTS, §§113A-8 to 113A-13.
Environmental documents.
Defined, §113A-9.
Review, §113A-13.
Where not required, §§113A-12, 113A-13.
Major development projects in counties, cities or towns.
Ordinance requiring statement of impact, §113A-8, (a) to (c).
Provisions supplemental, §113A-10.
Rules adoption, §113A-11.

ENVIRONMENTAL MANAGEMENT COMMISSION, §§143B-282 to 143B-285.
Air pollution control, §§143-215.105 to 143-215.114C.
See AIR POLLUTION CONTROL.
Appointments, §143B-283, (a).
Conflicts of interest, §143B-283, (c).
General assembly appointments, §143B-283, (d).
Officers, §143B-284.
Chairman, §143B-284.
Committee on civil penalty remissions.
Appointment of members, §143B-282.1, (c).
Civil actions.
Institution for civil penalty remissions, §143B-282.1, (e).
Clerical and other services, §143B-283, (b4).
Coastal habitat protection plans, §143B-279.8.
Committee on civil penalty remissions.
Appointment by chairman, §143B-282.1, (c).
Conditions for remission, §143B-282.1, (d).
Institution of civil action.
When allowed, §143B-282.1, (e).
Conflicts of interest, §143B-283, (c).
Contested cases.
Final agency decision.
Procedures, §143B-282.1, (b).
Creation, §143B-282, (a).
Within department of natural resources and community development, §143B-282, (a).
Discharges of oil or hazardous substances, §§143-215.83 to 143-215.94.
See OIL OR HAZARDOUS SUBSTANCES DISCHARGES.

ENVIRONMENTAL MANAGEMENT COMMISSION —Cont'd
Dry-cleaning solvent cleanup act, §§143-215.104A to 143-215.104U.
See DRY-CLEANING SOLVENT CLEANUP.
Duties, §143B-282, (a).
Geographic representation on, §143B-282, (e).
Impaired waters.
Identifying and prioritizing, §143B-282, (c).
Meetings, §143B-285.
Members, §143B-283, (a).
Conflicts of interest, §143B-283, (c).
General assembly appointments, §143B-283, (d).
Officers, §143B-284.
Oil or hazardous substances discharges, §§143-215.83 to 143-215.94.
See OIL OR HAZARDOUS SUBSTANCES DISCHARGES.
Per diem and travel and subsistence expenses, §143B-283, (b2).
Powers and duties, §143B-282, (a).
Procedures.
Contested cases, §143B-282.1, (b).
Quasi-judicial powers, §143B-282.1, (a).
Quorum, §143B-283, (b), (b3).
Removal of members, §143B-283, (b1).
Reports, §143B-282, (b).
Secretary.
Defined, §143B-282.1, (f).
Special meetings, §143B-285.
Terms, §143B-283, (b).
Use of water resource regulation, §§143-215.11 to 143-215.22B.
See WATER RESOURCE USE REGULATION.
Vice-chairman, §143B-284.
Water and air resources.
See WATER AND AIR RESOURCES.
Water quality of coastal fishing waters.
Monitoring quality, §§130A-233, 130A-233.1, (b).
Removal or destruction of signs, §130A-233.2.
Water quality standards.
Adopting rules setting out strategies necessary for assuring, §143B-282, (d).

ENVIRONMENTAL NOTICES.
Recording, §47-29.1.

ENVIRONMENTAL ORGANIZATIONS.
Solicitation of contributions, §§131F-1 to 131F-24.
See CHARITABLE SOLICITATION.

ENVIRONMENTAL PERMITS.
Department of environment and natural resources.
One-stop permit application assistance and tracking system.
Duties of department upon submission of application, §143B-279.12, (a).
Establishment, §143B-279.12, (a).
Timely processing by department.
Automatic granting of permit.
Failure of department to act in timely manner, §143B-279.12, (c).
Date of final decision on application.
Estimate provided by department, §143B-279.12, (b).
Report on application taking longer than ninety days to process, §143B-279.12, (e).
Rules to implement provision, adoption, §143B-279.12, (f).

ENVIRONMENTAL PERMITS —Cont'd
Department of environment and natural resources —Cont'd
Timely processing by department —Cont'd
Time required to process applications.
Department to track and compare, §143B-279.12, (d).

ENVIRONMENTAL POLICY ACT, §§113A-1 to 113A-13.
Actions.
Review of agency actions involving major adverse changes or conflicts, §113A-5.
Administrative procedures.
Conformity to state environmental policy, §113A-6.
Agencies.
Cooperation, §113A-4.
Statutory obligations of agencies, §113A-7.
Appeals.
Review of agency actions involving major adverse changes or conflicts, §113A-5.
Availability of information, §113A-4.
Bridges.
Replacement program for bridges.
Applicability of act to replacement program, §136-76.1, (b).
Citation, §113A-1.
Conformity of administrative procedures to state environmental policy, §113A-6.
Other statutory obligations of agencies, §113A-7.
Cooperation of agencies, §113A-4.
Declaration of state environmental policy, §113A-3.
Definitions, §113A-9.
Driveway connections to public roadways.
Environmental document not required, §113A-12.
Environmental documents.
Defined, §113A-9.
Review.
Administrative and judicial review, §113A-13.
When not required, §§113A-12, 113A-13.
Information.
Availability, §113A-4.
Legislative declaration, §§113A-2, 113A-3.
Major development projects, §113A-8, (a) to (c).
Policy.
Declaration of state environmental policy, §113A-3.
Projects.
Major development projects, §113A-8, (a) to (c).
Provisions supplemental, §113A-10.
Purposes, §113A-2.
Release or permit granted by state agency.
Environmental document not required, §113A-12.
Reports.
Submission, §113A-4.
Review of actions.
Agency actions involving major adverse changes or conflicts, §113A-5.
Rules and regulations.
Adoption by department of administration, §113A-11, (a).
Adoption by state agencies to establish minimum criteria, §113A-11, (b).
State agencies.
Establishment of minimum criteria, §113A-11, (b).
Short title, §113A-1.
Statutes.
Other statutory obligations of agencies, §113A-7.
Supplemental provisions, §113A-10.

ENVIRONMENTAL POLICY ACT —Cont'd
Surface water transfers.
Environmental assessment, §113A-8.1.
Title, §113A-1.
Utility line construction, etc.
Environmental document not required, §113A-12.

ENVIRONMENTAL PROTECTION.
Air pollution control.
See AIR POLLUTION CONTROL.
Balanced growth policy act, §§143-506.6 to 143-506.14.
See BALANCED GROWTH POLICY ACT.
Biological organism act.
General provisions, §§106-65.42 to 106-65.49.
See BIOLOGICAL ORGANISM ACT.
Corporate franchise tax.
Deducted reserves, §105-122, (d).
Deductible liabilities, §105-122, (b).
Discharges of oil or hazardous substances.
Generally, §§143-215.83 to 143-215.94.
See OIL OR HAZARDOUS SUBSTANCES DISCHARGES.
Offshore oil and gas activities, §§143-215.94AA to 143-215.94JJ.
See OFFSHORE OIL AND GAS ACTIVITIES.
Dry-cleaning equipment not using hazardous substances.
Business and energy tax credits, §105-129.16C, (a) to (c).
Dry-cleaning solvent cleanup, §§143-215.104A to 143-215.104U.
See DRY-CLEANING SOLVENT CLEANUP.
Environmental policy act, §§113A-1 to 113A-13.
See ENVIRONMENTAL POLICY ACT.
Floodplain regulation, §§143-215.51 to 143-215.61.
See FLOODPLAIN REGULATION.
Hazardous substances.
Discharges generally, §§143-215.83 to 143-215.94.
See OIL OR HAZARDOUS SUBSTANCES DISCHARGES.
Oil pollution and hazardous substances control generally, §§143-215.75 to 143-215.82.
See OIL POLLUTION AND HAZARDOUS SUBSTANCES CONTROL.
Industrial and pollution control facilities financing.
Industrial and pollution control facilities financing act, §§159C-1 to 159C-27.
See INDUSTRIAL AND POLLUTION CONTROL FACILITIES FINANCING.
North Carolina capital facilities financing act.
North Carolina industrial and pollution control facilities financing act, §§159D-1 to 159D-27.
See INDUSTRIAL AND POLLUTION CONTROL FACILITIES FINANCING.
Leaking petroleum underground storage tank cleanup, §§143-215.94A to 143-215.94Y.
See UNDERGROUND PETROLEUM STORAGE TANK LEAK CLEANUP.
Offshore oil and gas activities, §§143-215.94AA to 143-215.94JJ.
See OFFSHORE OIL AND GAS ACTIVITIES.
Oil or hazardous substances discharges, §§143-215.83 to 143-215.94.
See OIL OR HAZARDOUS SUBSTANCES DISCHARGES.
Oil pollution and hazardous substances control generally, §§143-215.75 to 143-215.82.
See OIL POLLUTION AND HAZARDOUS SUBSTANCES CONTROL.

ENVIRONMENTAL PROTECTION —Cont'd
Pesticide applicators, §§143-452 to 143-459.
See PESTICIDE APPLICATORS.
Pesticide board.
See PESTICIDE BOARD.
Pesticide consultants, §§143-455, 143-456.
Pesticide dealers and manufacturers licenses, §§143-448 to 143-451.
Pesticide registration.
See PESTICIDE REGISTRATION.
Pesticides generally.
See PESTICIDES.
Pollution control.
Air pollution control.
See AIR POLLUTION CONTROL.
Generally.
See POLLUTION CONTROL.
Water and air resources.
See WATER AND AIR RESOURCES.
Powers of fiduciaries to comply with, §32-27.
Sedimentation control commission, §§113A-50 to 113A-67.
See SEDIMENTATION CONTROL COMMISSION.
Stream watch program, §§143-215.74F to 143-215.74I.
Trusts and trustees.
Powers of trustees under express trust, §36A-136.
Water and air quality reporting, §§143-215.63 to 143-215.69.
See WATER AND AIR QUALITY REPORTING.
Water and air resources.
See WATER AND AIR RESOURCES.
Water resources development projects.
Federal projects, §§143-215.38 to 143-215.43.
See WATER RESOURCES DEVELOPMENT PROJECTS.
Generally, §§143-215.70 to 143-215.73A.
See WATER RESOURCES DEVELOPMENT PROJECTS.
Water supply watershed protection, §§143-214.5 to 143-214.7.
Wetlands restoration program, §§143-214.8 to 143-214.13.
See WETLANDS RESTORATION PROGRAM.

ENVIRONMENTAL REVIEW COMMISSION, §§120-70.41 to 120-70.47.
Allocation of money to fund commission, §120-70.47.
Clerical staff, §120-70.46.
Cochairs, §120-70.42, (b).
Compensation, §120-70.45.
Consolidation and reorganization of environmental agency.
Study, §120-70.43, (b).
Created, §120-70.41.
Department of environment and natural resources.
Report to commission on well drilling activities, §143-355, (n).
Duties, §120-70.43, (a) to (c).
Established, §120-70.41.
Expenses, §120-70.45.
Clerical staff, §120-70.46.
Funding, §120-70.47.
Hazardous waste management.
Powers and duties, §120-70.43, (c).
Meetings, §120-70.44.
Membership, §120-70.42, (a).

ENVIRONMENTAL REVIEW COMMISSION —Cont'd
Powers, §120-70.43, (a) to (c).
Additional powers, §120-70.44.
Quorum, §120-70.42, (d).
Recommendations as to studies or reports.
Proposed legislation.
Introduction and consideration, §120-70.44.
Staffing, §120-70.46.
Term, vacancy, §120-70.42, (c).

ENVIRONMENTAL SAFETY.
Safety professionals, §§90-671 to 90-674.

ENVIRONMENT AND NATURAL RESOURCES DEPARTMENT.
Administrative penalties, §130A-22.
Advertisements.
Blue Ridge parkway.
Control of outdoor advertising, §§113A-165 to 113A-170.
Agreements with federal agencies, §113-17.
Air pollution control program administration, §143-215.106.
Air quality compliance advisory council, §§143B-317 to 143B-319.
Appalachian trail system, §§113A-72 to 113A-77.
Applicability of certain provisions, §143B-279.1, (b).
Arrest.
Special peace officers.
Arrest powers, §113-28.2.
Balanced growth policy act, §§143-506.6 to 143-506.14.
See BALANCED GROWTH POLICY ACT.
Biennial state of environment report.
Cooperation in preparing report, §143B-279.5, (b).
Included in report, §143B-279.5, (a).
Time secretary to report, §143B-279.5, (a).
Blue Ridge parkway.
Control of outdoor advertising, §§113A-165 to 113A-170.
Brownfields property reuse act of 1997, §§130A-310.30 to 130A-310.40.
See BROWNFIELDS PROPERTY REUSE.
Bureau of mines.
Establishment, §113-26.1.
Coastal area management.
General provisions, §§113A-100 to 113A-128.
See COASTAL AREA MANAGEMENT.
Coastal habitat protection plans.
Actions of commission to be consistent with protection plan, §143B-279.8, (c).
Explanation of inconsistent actions by commission, §143B-279.8, (d).
Preparation and goal of plans, §143B-279.8, (a).
Reports, §143B-279.8, (e), (f).
Review commission, §143B-279.8, (b).
Coastal wetlands.
Orders controlling activities in, §113-230.
Community development council, §§143B-437.1 to 143B-437.3.
See COMMUNITY DEVELOPMENT COUNCIL.
Compacts.
Marine fisheries compact, §§113-251 to 113-257.
Southeastern interstate forest fire protection compact, §§113-60.11 to 113-60.15.
Conferences with federal agencies, §113-17.
Conservation as policy of state, Const. N. C., art. XIV, §5.
Conservation easements, §§113A-230 to 113A-235.

ENVIRONMENT AND NATURAL RESOURCES DEPARTMENT —Cont'd
Contamination at site.
Deed or other instrument of conveyance, contaminated property statement, §143B-279.10, (e).
Land-use restrictions to reduce danger to public health, §143B-279.9.
Authority to impose, §143B-279.9, (a).
Definitions, §§143B-279.9, (d), 143B-279.10, (d), (h).
Obligations and liabilities imposed by other laws, §143B-279.9, (c).
Remedial action plan, §143B-279.9, (b).
Notice of contamination.
Cancellation after contamination eliminated, owner's request, §143B-279.10, (f).
Exceptions, §143B-279.10, (g).
Filing copy in register of deeds office, §143B-279.10, (b).
Recording copy, §143B-279.10, (c).
Secretary may prepare and file, owner's failure, §143B-279.10, (d).
Survey plat submitted by owner, §143B-279.10, (a).
Cooperation with agencies of federal government, §113-16.
Cooperation with counties and municipal corporations, §113-20.
Water resource surveys, §113-21.
Cooperation with other state departments, §113-19.
Corporations for protection and development of forest, §§113-61 to 113-77.
See FOREST PROTECTION AND DEVELOPMENT CORPORATIONS.
Counties.
Cooperation with counties and municipal corporations, §113-20.
Demonstration forests.
Use of lands acquired by counties through tax foreclosures.
County commissioners turning over to department title to tax-delinquent lands, §113-30.
Forests and forestry.
Department.
Cooperation between counties and state in forest protection and development, §113-59.
Soil and water conservation work.
Promotion, §153A-440.
Water resource surveys.
Cooperation of counties with state in making, §113-21.
Creation, §143B-279.1, (a).
Crime control division.
Transfer to department of crime control and public safety, §143A-245.
Dam safety law, §§143-215.23 to 143-215.37.
See DAM SAFETY.
Definitions.
Meaning of terms, §113-1.
Discharges of oil or hazardous substances.
Generally, §§143-215.83 to 143-215.94.
See OIL OR HAZARDOUS SUBSTANCES DISCHARGES.
Leaking petroleum underground storage tank cleanup, §§143-215.94A to 143-215.94Y.
See UNDERGROUND PETROLEUM STORAGE TANK LEAK CLEANUP.

ENVIRONMENT AND NATURAL RESOURCES DEPARTMENT —Cont'd
Discharges of oil or hazardous substances —Cont'd
Offshore oil and gas activities, §§143-215.94AA to 143-215.94JJ.
See OFFSHORE OIL AND GAS ACTIVITIES.
Division of North Carolina aquariums, §§143B-289.40, 143B-289.41.
Divisions created within department, §143B-279.3, (c).
Drainage districts, §§156-54 to 156-138.4.
See DRAINAGE DISTRICTS.
Drinking water.
Regulation of public water systems supplying, §§130A-311 to 130A-328.
See WATER SUPPLY AND WATERWORKS.
Drought management advisory council, §143-355.1.
Dry-cleaning solvent cleanup, §§143-215.104A to 143-215.104U.
See DRY-CLEANING SOLVENT CLEANUP.
Emergency conservation work.
Reimbursement of government for expense, §113-28.
Eminent domain, §113-34, (a).
Marine and estuarine resources.
Powers as to, §113-226, (a).
Environmental health division.
Created within department, §143B-279.3, (c).
Environmental management commission, §§143B-282 to 143B-285.
Environmental permits.
One-stop permit application assistance and tracking system.
Duties of department upon submission of application, §143B-279.12, (a).
Establishment, §143B-279.12, (a).
Timely processing by department.
Automatic granting of permit.
Failure of department to act in timely manner, §143B-279.12, (c).
Date of final decision on application.
Estimate provided by department, §143B-279.12, (b).
Report on application taking longer than ninety days to process, §143B-279.12, (e).
Rules to implement provision, adoption, §143B-279.12, (f).
Time required to process applications.
Department to track and compare, §143B-279.12, (d).
Environmental policy act generally, §§113A-1 to 113A-13.
See ENVIRONMENTAL POLICY ACT.
Federal agencies.
Agreements, negotiations and conferences with, §113-17.
Cooperation with agencies, §113-16.
Federal power commission.
Department authorized to receive funds from, §113-18.
Fish and fisheries resources.
Administrative authority, §113-226.
Cooperative agreements.
Authority to enter into, §113-224.
License fees.
Government owned property unaffected, §113-39.
Fish kill response protocols.
Development by department, §143B-279.7, (a).

ENVIRONMENT AND NATURAL RESOURCES DEPARTMENT —Cont'd
Fish kill response protocols —Cont'd
Necessary and appropriate steps to carry out purposes, §143B-279.7, (b).
Report, §143B-279.7, (c).
Floodplain regulation, §§143-215.51 to 143-215.61.
See FLOODPLAIN REGULATION.
Forest fires.
Powers and duties, §113-51, (a), (b).
Forestry council, §§143B-308 to 143B-310.
Forestry services and advice for owners and operators of forestlands, §§113-81.1 to 113-81.3.
Forests and forestry.
See FORESTS AND FORESTRY.
Funds.
Federal power commission.
Department authorized to receive funds, §113-18.
Trees and timber.
Sales of state timber.
Bladen lakes state forest fund, §113-36, (d).
Forest seedling nursery program fund, §113-36, (c).
Tree cone and seed purchase fund.
Application of proceeds, §113-36, (b).
Health.
Powers of secretary generally.
See HEALTH.
Highway construction projects.
Permits issued by department for.
Modification and cancellation, restrictions, §136-44.7B.
Hotels or tourist inns in parks over which department has jurisdiction.
Department not to construct, maintain, operate or lease, §66-58, (b).
Hunting and wildlife.
General provisions.
See HUNTING AND WILDLIFE.
License fees.
Government owned property unaffected, §113-39.
Interstate compacts.
Marine fisheries compacts, §§113-251 to 113-257.
Southeastern interstate forest fire protection compact, §§113-60.11 to 113-60.15.
Land policy act, §§113A-150 to 113A-159.
See LAND POLICY ACT.
Leaking petroleum underground storage tank cleanup, §§143-215.94A to 143-215.94Y.
See UNDERGROUND PETROLEUM STORAGE TANK LEAK CLEANUP.
Local affairs, §§143-320 to 143-326.
See LOCAL AFFAIRS.
Marine fisheries commission, §§143B-289.50 to 143B-289.61.
See MARINE FISHERIES COMMISSION.
Marine fisheries compact, §§113-251 to 113-257.
Maritime museum.
Selling or exchanging objects from collections, §143B-344.22.
Mattresses and bedding.
Enforcement of part, §130A-271, (a).
Meaning of terms, §113-1.
Milk and milk product sanitation, §130A-277.
Mineral museum.
Establishment, §113-26.1.

ENVIRONMENT AND NATURAL RESOURCES DEPARTMENT —Cont'd
Mines and minerals.
Beginning business of manufacturing products from mineral resources.
Notice to department, §113-25.
Bureau of mines.
Established as part of department, §113-26.1.
Mineral museum.
Established as part of department, §113-26.1.
Mining commission, §§143B-290 to 143B-293.
Monuments, memorials and parks.
Control of Mount Mitchell park and other state parks.
Department to have control, §113-23.
Mosquito and vector control program, §§130A-346 to 130A-349.
See MOSQUITO AND VECTOR CONTROL.
Motor vehicle laws applicable to state parks and forest road system, §143-116.8.
Mount Mitchell park.
Control of park, §§100-11, 113-23.
Fees.
Powers as to, §100-13.
Powers, §§100-11 to 100-13.
Protection of property, §100-12.
Rules and regulations, §100-13.
Municipal corporations.
Cooperation with counties and municipal corporations, §113-20.
Museum of natural sciences.
Selling or exchanging objects from collection, §143B-344.22.
National park, parkway and forest development council, §§143B-324.1 to 143B-324.3.
Natural and scenic rivers system.
Administrative agency, §113A-36, (a).
Nature preserves, §§113A-164.1 to 113A-164.11.
See NATURAL HERITAGE AREAS REGISTRY.
North Carolina aquarium division.
Created in department, §143B-289.40.
Organization, §143B-289.41, (a).
Powers and duties, §143B-289.41, (a).
Rules and procedures, §143B-289.41, (b).
Notice.
Mines and mining.
Beginning business of manufacturing products from mineral resources of state, §113-25.
Nutbush conservation area, §§143-286.1, 143-289.
Oaths.
Special peace officers.
Required, §113-28.4.
Office of environmental education, §§143B-285.20 to 143B-285.25.
Offshore oil and gas activities, §§143-215.94AA to 143-215.94JJ.
See OFFSHORE OIL AND GAS ACTIVITIES.
Oil and gas conservation, §§113-397, 113-398.
Actions by department, §113-399.
Appeals, §113-401.
Effect of pendency of judicial review, §113-406.
Bonds, surety.
Stay of proceedings, §113-407.
Drilling wells.
Applications to include residence address, §113-408.
False entries.
Penalties, §113-409.

ENVIRONMENT AND NATURAL RESOURCES DEPARTMENT —Cont'd
Oil and gas conservation —Cont'd
Hearings.
Contested cases, §113-402.
Costs, §113-400.
Parties, §113-401.
Stay of proceedings, §113-406.
Bond, §113-407.
Injunctions, §113-408.
Jurisdiction and authority, §113-391.
Misrepresentation.
Punishment, §113-409.
Orders, §113-391.
Parties to hearings, §113-401.
Penalties.
Violations, §§113-409, 113-410.
Rules and regulations, §113-391.
Service of process, §113-408.
Stay of proceedings, §113-406.
Bond, §113-407.
Suits by department, §113-399.
Violations.
Penalties, §§113-409, 113-410.
Oil or hazardous substances discharges, §§143-215.83 to 143-215.94.
See OIL OR HAZARDOUS SUBSTANCES DISCHARGES.
Oil pollution and hazardous substance control generally, §§143-215.75 to 143-215.82.
See OIL POLLUTION AND HAZARDOUS SUBSTANCES CONTROL.
Outer continental shelf task force.
Administration, §143B-279.2.
Parks.
Control of Mount Mitchell park and other state parks, §113-23.
Power to acquire lands, §113-34.
Parks and recreation authority.
Administered by department, §143B-313.1.
Peace officers.
Special peace officers, §§113-28.1 to 113-28.4.
Penalties.
Administrative penalties, §130A-22.
Pollution control.
Generally.
See POLLUTION CONTROL.
Offshore oil and gas activities generally, §§143-215.94AA to 143-215.94JJ.
See OFFSHORE OIL AND GAS ACTIVITIES.
Pollution prevention pays programs.
Established within department, §113-8.01.
Pollution prevention pays programs, §113-8.01.
Powers and duties, §§113-3, (a), 113-8, 143B-279.1, (a), 143B-279.2.
Additional powers and duties.
Solid waste management, §130A-309.06, (a).
Forest fires, §113-51, (a), (b).
Generally, §§113-8, 143B-279.3, (d).
Promotion of seashore industry and recreation, §113-14.1, (b).
Transferred to and vested in department, §§143-355, 143B-279.3, (a), (b).
Prisons and prisoners.
Supervision of sanitary and health conditions of prisoners, §148-10.
Property of department.
Regulatory power over property, §113-264.
Removal, damage or destruction, §113-264, (b).
Protection and development of forest corporations, §§113-61 to 113-77.
See FOREST PROTECTION AND DEVELOPMENT CORPORATIONS.

ENVIRONMENT AND NATURAL RESOURCES DEPARTMENT —Cont'd
Publications.
Resources material, §113-14.3.
Public lands.
Disposition of mineral deposits in state lands under water, §146-8.
Radiation protection act generally, §§104E-1 to 104E-29.
See RADIATION PROTECTION.
Recreation and natural heritage trusts, §§113-77.6 to 113-77.9.
See NATURAL HERITAGE TRUST FUND.
Reports.
Biennial state of environment report, §143B-279.5.
Coastal habitat protection plan, §143B-279.8, (f).
Environmental permits taking longer than ninety days to process, §143B-279.12, (e).
Fish kill response protocols, §143B-279.7, (c).
Publication, §113-14.3.
Sedimentation pollution control act.
Annual report by department, §113A-67.
Sale of merchandise by governmental units.
Exception to prohibition, §66-58, (b).
Sanitation program, §130A-227.
Scientific advisory council on water resources and coastal fisheries management, §143-215.22J.
Seashore industry and recreation.
Promotion, §113-14.1, (b).
Secretary.
Biennial state of the environment report, §143B-279.5.
Deputy secretaries, §143B-279.4, (b).
Forest rangers.
Appointment, §113-52.
Head of department, §143B-279.4, (a).
Health.
Powers of secretary generally.
See HEALTH.
Natural history museum.
Advisory commission.
Member of commission, §143B-344.18.
Office of environmental education.
Powers and duties of secretary, §143B-285.23.
Protection and development of forests.
Corporations for.
Secretary defined, §113-61, (a).
Recreation and natural heritage trusts, §§113-77.6 to 113-77.9.
See NATURAL HERITAGE TRUST FUND.
State forests.
Department and secretary to have full control, §113-22.
Streets and highways.
Test drilling or boring upon public land.
Filing record of results with secretary, §136-102.3.
Sedimentation control commission, §§143B-298, 143B-299.
Sedimentation pollution control act of 1973, §§113A-50 to 113A-67.
See SEDIMENTATION CONTROL COMMISSION.
Shellfish generally.
See SHELLFISH.
Soil and water conservation account, §143B-297.1.
Soil and water conservation commission, §§143B-294 to 143B-297.

ENVIRONMENT AND NATURAL RESOURCES DEPARTMENT —Cont'd
Soil and water conservation districts, §§139-1 to 139-57.
See SOIL AND WATER CONSERVATION DISTRICTS.
Solid waste management.
Authority in establishing program, §130A-294, (a).
Division of waste management.
Legislative declaration, §130A-291, (a), (b).
Permits.
Refusal.
Prior violations, §130A-309.06, (b).
Powers and duties.
Additional powers and duties, §130A-309.06.
Reports.
Annual report, §130A-309.06, (c).
Septage.
Duties and septage management program, §130A-291.1.
Single agency designation, §130A-299.
Southeastern interstate forest fire protection compact, §§113-60.11 to 113-60.15.
Special peace officers, §§113-28.1 to 113-28.4.
Arrest powers, §113-28.2.
Commissioned as special peace officers.
Designated employees commissioned special peace officers by governor, §113-28.1.
Cooperation between law enforcement agencies, §113-28.2A.
Designated employees commissioned special officers by governor, §113-28.1.
Governor.
Designated employees commissioned special officers by, §113-28.1.
Oaths.
Required, §113-28.4.
Powers.
Arrest, §113-28.2.
State departments and agencies.
Cooperation with other state departments, §113-19.
State forests.
Control of state forests, §113-22.
Power to acquire lands, §113-34.
State parks system.
Control of Mount Mitchell park and other parks in, §113-23.
State prison.
Supervision of sanitary and health conditions of prisoners, §148-10.
Statutes.
Repeal of certain public, public-local, special and private acts, §113-377.8.
Streets and highways.
Test drilling or boring upon public land.
Filing record of results with secretary, §136-102.3.
Surveys and surveyors.
Cooperation of counties with state in making water resources surveys, §113-21.
Terms.
Meaning, §113-1.
Traffic laws applicable to state parks and forest road system, §143-116.8.
Trails.
See TRAILS.
Trails committee, §§143B-333, 143B-334.
Transfer of functions, powers, duties and obligations to department, §§143-355, 143B-279.3, (a), (b).

ENVIRONMENT AND NATURAL RESOURCES DEPARTMENT —Cont'd
Trees and timber.
Disposition of lands acquired and revenues received, §113-42.
Disposition of products from lands, §113-41.
Sales.
Application of proceeds, §113-36, (a).
Bladen lakes state forest fund, §113-36, (d).
Forest seedling nursery program fund, §113-36, (c).
Tree cone and seed purchase fund, §113-36, (b).
Unused state lands.
Growing timber on authorized, §113-29.1.
Trespass.
Land under option by federal government, §14-131.
Underground petroleum storage tank leak cleanup, §§143-215.94A to 143-215.94Y.
See UNDERGROUND PETROLEUM STORAGE TANK LEAK CLEANUP.
Waste management division, §130A-291, (a), (b).
Created within department, §143B-279.3, (c).
Wastewater systems, §§130A-333 to 130A-343.
See WASTEWATER SYSTEMS.
Water and air quality reporting, §§143-215.63 to 143-215.69.
See WATER AND AIR QUALITY REPORTING.
Water and air resources.
Research functions, §143-215.3, (b).
Water pollution control system operators.
Certification commission, §§143B-300, 143B-301.
Water resources development projects.
Federal projects, §§143-215.38 to 143-215.43.
See WATER RESOURCES DEVELOPMENT PROJECTS.
Generally, §§143-215.70 to 143-215.73A.
See WATER RESOURCES DEVELOPMENT PROJECTS.
Well contractor certification, §§87-98.1 to 87-98.13.
See WELL CONTRACTORS.
Well contractor certification commission, §§143B-301.10 to 143B-301.12.
Wetlands.
Coastal wetlands.
Orders controlling activities in, §113-230.
Wildlife generally.
See HUNTING AND WILDLIFE.
Wildlife resources commission.
Transfer to department, §143B-281.1.
Zoological park council, §§143B-335, 143B-336.

EPILEPSY.
Arrest.
Police assistance to persons arrested while unconscious or semiconscious, §15A-503.
Defined, §35A-1101.
Determination of incompetence, §§35A-1101 to 35A-1116.
See INCOMPETENCE.
Jail prisoner unconscious or semiconscious.
Duty of custodial personnel.
Reasonable effort to determine if prisoner wearing emergency alert symbol, §153A-225.1, (a) to (c).

E-PROCUREMENT SERVICE.
Purchases through department of administration.
Electronic procurement, §143-48.3.

EQUAL AVAILABILITY OF CREDIT FOR WOMEN, §25B-1.

EQUAL EMPLOYMENT OPPORTUNITY.
Citation of article, §143-422.1.
Conciliations.
Human relations council to use good offices, §143-422.3.
Human relations council.
Charges of discrimination.
Receipt, §143-422.3.
Conciliations, §143-422.3.
Investigations, §143-422.3.
Legislative declaration, §143-422.2.
Personnel system.
Assistance in obtaining state employment.
Compensation for assisting person barred, §126-18.
Exception, §126-18.
Equal employment opportunity institute.
Training, §126-16.1.
Local political subdivisions, §126-16.
Retaliation against protesting employees, §126-17.
Managers.
Newly appointed managers.
Training, §126-16.1.
State departments and agencies, §126-16.
Retaliation against protesting employees, §126-17.
Supervisors.
Newly appointed supervisor.
Training, §126-16.1.
Training, §126-16.1.
Plans.
Development and submission by certain agencies, §126-19, (a).
Reports, §126-19, (b).
State personnel director.
Maintenance of services by, §126-19, (c).
Purpose of article, §143-422.2.
Short title, §143-422.1.

EQUAL PROTECTION, Const. N. C., art. I, §19; Const. U. S., amd. XIV.

EQUINE ACTIVITY LIABILITY, §§99E-1 to 99E-3.
Acts not preventing or limiting liability, §99E-2, (b).
Definitions, §99E-1.
Immunity of liability generally for injury or death of participant, §99E-2, (a).
Products liability law.
Liability not prevented or limited for violation, §99E-2, (c).
Warning notice.
Contents, §99E-3, (b).
Failure to comply, §99E-3, (c).
Posting requirement, §99E-3, (a).

EQUINE INFECTIOUS ANEMIA, §§106-405.15 to 106-405.20.
Control and eradication program.
Implementation of program, §106-405.18.
Defined, §106-405.15.
Fine, §106-405.20.
Implementation of control and eradication program, §106-405.18.
Penalties, §106-405.20.
Quarantine of infected or exposed animals, §106-405.16.

EQUINE INFECTIOUS ANEMIA —Cont'd
Rules and regulations.
Authority to promulgate and enforce, §106-405.17.
Violation made misdemeanor, §106-405.19.

EQUIPMENT IDENTIFICATION OR MARKS, §14-401.4.

EQUITABLE DISTRIBUTION OF MARITAL PROPERTY, §50-20.
Absolute divorce, effects, §50-11, (e), (f).
Collaborative law proceedings, §§50-70 to 50-79.
See COLLABORATIVE LAW PROCEEDINGS.
Decedents' estates.
Claim for distribution of marital or divisible property, §28A-19-19.
Mediated settlement conferences or other settlement procedures.
District court actions, §7A-38.4A.
Rules implementing procedures, Settle. Proc. Equitable Distribution Rules 1 to 15.
See MEDIATED SETTLEMENT CONFERENCES.
Pensions, retirement and deferred compensation benefits, §50-20.1.
Procedures, §50-21.

EQUITY.
Divorce.
Distribution by court of marital and divisible property, §50-20.
Absolute divorce, effect, §50-11.
Mediated settlement conference, §7A-38.4A.
Procedure, §50-21.
Mortgages and deeds of trust.
Injunctions.
Enjoining sales on equitable grounds, §45-21.34.
Nuisances.
See NUISANCES.
Ordinances.
Enforcement of ordinance by appropriate equitable remedies, §160A-175, (d).

EQUITY LINES OF CREDIT.
Instruments to secure equity lines of credit.
Advances and future obligations.
Extension, §45-82.1.
Future advances statute not to apply, §45-83.
Applicability of provisions.
Article not exclusive, §45-84.
Future advances statute not to apply, §45-83.
Article not exclusive, §45-84.
Definitions, §45-81.
Equity line of credit.
Defined, §45-81, (a).
Extension of period for advances, §45-82.1, (a).
Certificate of extension, §45-82.1, (c).
Form, §45-82.1, (d).
Priority of security instrument, §45-82.1, (b).
Future advances statute not to apply, §45-83.
Lender is obligated.
Defined, §45-81, (b).
Payment and satisfaction of interest.
Lender to make written entry upon security instrument to that effect, §45-81, (c).
Priority of security instrument, §45-82.
Security instrument.
Priority of security instrument, §45-82.
Interest rates.
Adjustable or variable interest, §24-1.2A, (a).
Contract in writing, §24-1.2A, (a).
Fees for modification, renewal, extension, §24-1.2A, (b).

EQUITY LINES OF CREDIT —Cont'd
Interest rates —Cont'd
Loans exempt from interest rate and fee limitations, §24-9, (c).
Loans exempt from interest rate and fee limitations, §24-9, (c).

EQUITY OF REDEMPTION.
Execution sales.
Sheriff's deed on sale of equity of redemption, §1-317.

EQUIVALENT DRUG PRODUCT.
Defined, §90-85.27.
Liability of prescriber and pharmacist not extended, §90-85.31.
Prescriptions.
Label, §90-85.29.
Record, §90-85.30.
Price.
Limitation on selected drugs, §90-85.28, (c).
Selection by pharmacist, §90-85.28, (a).
Liability of prescriber and pharmacist not extended, §90-85.31.
Prescriber may permit or prohibit, §90-85.28, (b).

EROSION.
County equipment.
Authority to provide farmers with erosion equipment, §106-532.
Municipal corporations.
Control of erosion and sedimentation, §160A-458.
Sedimentation control commission, §§113A-50 to 113A-67.
See SEDIMENTATION CONTROL COMMISSION.
Transportation department.
Control of erosion.
Powers of department, §136-18.

ERROR.
Generally.
See MISTAKE OR ERROR.

ESCALATORS.
Inspection fees.
Assessment and collection, §95-107.
Disposition, §95-108.
Safety, §§95-110.1 to 95-110.15.

ESCAPE.
Accomplices and accessories.
Assisting escape from state prison, §148-45.
Allowing prisoners to escape.
Burden of proof on officers to show escape not by consent, §14-239.
Arrest.
Peace officers.
Prevention of escape.
Use of force in arrest, §15A-401, (d).
Persons escaped from penal institutions, §162-35.
Burden of proof.
Allowing prisoners to escape.
Burden of proof upon sheriff or other officer, §14-239.
Capital punishment.
Aggravating circumstances.
Capital felony committed for purpose of effecting escape, §15A-2000, (e).
Coroners allowing prisoners to escape, §14-239.
District attorney to prosecute officer for escape, §14-240.
Counties.
Confinement facilities or officers.
Prison breach and escape from facilities or officers, §14-256.

ESCAPE —Cont'd
Definitions, §148-45, (g).
Delinquent and undisciplined juveniles.
Absconding juveniles, taking into temporary custody, §7B-1900.
Transporting to nearest secure custody facility, §7B-1901, (c).
Detainers.
Escape from temporary custody, §15A-764.
District attorney.
Prosecution of officers for allowing prisoners to escape, §14-240.
Felonies, §148-45, (b).
Guards.
Degree of protection against allowed, §148-46, (a), (b).
Harboring or aiding escaped prisoners, §14-259.
Interstate compact on juveniles, §§7B-2800 to 7B-2827.
See INTERSTATE COMPACT ON JUVENILES.
Jails.
Allowing prisoners to escape.
Burden of proof upon jailer to show that escape was not by consent or negligence, §14-239.
District attorney to prosecute jailer for escape, §14-240.
Reduction of sentence for work, education or training programs.
Forfeiture of reduction, §162-60, (c).
Juvenile escapees.
Delinquent and undisciplined juveniles, §§7B-1900, 7B-1901.
Photographs of escaped juveniles, release to public, §7B-2102, (d1).
Limitation of actions.
Public officers.
Actions against for escape of prisoner arrested or imprisoned on civil process, §1-54.
Mental health, developmental disabilities and substance abuse.
Assisting client to leave facility without authority, §122C-65, (a), (b).
Discharge of clients who escape or breach conditions of release, §122C-205.1, (a), (b), (d).
Notice, §122C-205.1, (c).
Involuntary commitment.
Commission of criminal offense, §122C-254, (a) to (d).
Denial of pretrial release, §122C-254, (a).
Notice of discharge of clients who escape or breach conditions of release, §122C-205.1, (c).
Notice of escape or breach of conditional release, §122C-205, (d).
Return of clients to 24-hour facilities, §122C-205, (a) to (c).
Messages.
Conveying messages to convicts and other prisoners, §14-258.
Misdemeanors, §148-45, (a), (d).
Municipal corporations.
Confinement facilities or officers.
Prison breach and escape from facilities or officers, §14-256.
Peace officers.
Prevention of escape.
Force.
Use of force in arrest, §15A-401, (d).
Penalties, §148-45.
Private correction facilities, §14-256.1.

ESCAPE —Cont'd
Recapture of escaped prisoners, §§148-40, 148-41.
Rewards.
Governor may offer rewards, §15-53.
Sentencing.
Aggravating factor, §15A-1340.16.
Treatment of convicted escapees, §148-45, (f).
Sheriffs allowing prisoners to escape, §14-239.
District attorney to prosecute officer for escape, §14-240.
Solicitor.
Allowing prisoners to escape.
Prosecution of sheriffs or other officers for escape, §14-240.
State institutions.
Persuading inmates to escape, §§14-266, 14-268.
Temporary custody.
Interstate agreement on detainers, §15A-764.
Juvenile escapees.
Delinquent and undisciplined juveniles, §§7B-1900, 7B-1901.
Weapons.
Conveying messages and weapons to convicts and other prisoners, §14-258.
Use in assisting prisoner to escape, §14-258.2, (b).
Working prisoners escaping from custody, §14-255.

ESCHEAT FUND, §§116B-5 to 116B-7.

ESCHEATS, §§116B-1 to 116B-4.
Attorney to perform title search, employment, §116B-8.
Claim for, §116B-4.
Consultants, real estate managers and others with specialized skills.
Employment, §116B-8.
Disposition of, Const. N. C., art. IX, §10.
Escheat fund, §§116B-5 to 116B-7.
Distribution, §116B-7, (a), (b).
Escheat account.
Excess funds, §116B-6, (e).
Investments, §116B-6, (b).
Limitation on amount of secured obligation, §116B-6, (d).
Placement of funds, §116B-6, (a).
Security interest, §116B-6, (c).
Expenditures from fund, §116B-6, (h).
Payments into, §116B-1.
Property paid into fund, §116B-5.
Records, §116B-6, (i).
Refund reserve, §116B-6, (f).
Refunds, additional funds, §116B-6, (g).
Report by secretary of revenue, §105-256, (d).
Personal property, §116B-2.
Decedents' estates, §116B-3.
Real property, §116B-2.
Unclaimed property generally, §§116B-51 to 116B-80.
See UNCLAIMED PROPERTY.

ESCORT VEHICLES ACCOMPANYING OVERSIZE OR OVERWEIGHT LOADS.
Escort driver training and certification program, §20-119, (f).

ESCROW ACCOUNTS IN PREPAID ENTERTAINMENT CONTRACTS, §66-124.

ESCROW OF FUNDS BY TOBACCO MANUFACTURERS.
Tobacco reserve fund, §§66-290, 66-291.
Escrow compliance, §§66-292 to 66-294.1.

ESPIONAGE, INDUSTRIAL.
Larceny of secret technical processes, §14-75.1.

ESTATE PLANNING AND PROBATE LAW SPECIALTY.
Certification standards, Bar Rules & Regs., D, §§.2301 to .2307.

ESTATES.
Absentees in military service, §§28B-1 to 28B-10.
See ABSENTEES IN MILITARY SERVICE.
Contingent limitations.
Death of person without heirs.
Limitations on failure, §41-4.
Conversion of fee tail into fee simple, §41-1.
Conveyances.
General provisions.
See CONVEYANCES.
Decedents' estates.
See DECEDENTS' ESTATES.
Deeds.
General provisions.
See DEEDS.
Definitions.
Freeholders in petition for special taxes, §41-13.
Time limits on options in gross and certain other interests in land, §41-28.
Deposits.
Survivorship in bank deposit created by written agreement, §41-2.1.
Devise presumed to be in fee, §31-38.
Doctrine of worthier title.
Abolished, §41-6.2, (a).
Executions.
Execution sales.
Leasehold estates.
Liability to sale under execution, §1-315, (a).
Trust estates.
Title of purchaser, §1-316.
Executors and administrators.
See EXECUTORS AND ADMINISTRATORS.
Failure of issue.
Limitations on failure, §41-4.
Freeholders.
Taxation.
Freeholders in petition for special taxes.
Defined, §41-13.
Income tax on estates and trusts.
Amount, §105-160.2.
Changes, §105-160.8.
Corrections, §105-160.8.
Credits, §105-160.3, (a).
Credits not allowed, §105-160.3, (b).
Income taxes paid to other states, §105-160.4.
Definitions, §105-160.1.
Imposition of tax, §105-160.2.
Payment.
Place of payment, §105-160.7, (a).
Returns, §105-160.5.
Place of filing, §105-160.6.
Time of filing, §105-160.6.
Taxable income, §105-160.2.
Inheritance tax generally.
See INHERITANCE TAX.
Issue.
Limitations on failure of issue, §41-4.
Joint tenants and tenants in common.
See JOINT TENANTS AND TENANTS IN COMMON.
Landlord and tenant.
See LANDLORD AND TENANT.

ESTATES —Cont'd
Life estates.
See LIFE ESTATES.
Military service.
Absentees in military service, §§28B-1 to 28B-10.
See ABSENTEES IN MILITARY SERVICE.
Missing persons, §§28C-1 to 28C-22.
See MISSING PERSONS.
Next of kin.
Defined, §41-6.1.
Possession.
Transferred to use in certain conveyances, §41-7.
Possibility of reverter.
Time limits, §41-32.
Powers of attorney.
Powers conferred by statutory short form, §32A-2.
Presumptions and burden of proof.
Fee presumed though word heirs omitted, §39-1.
Unborn infants.
Presumed in esse, §41-5.
Probate of wills.
General provisions, §§31-12 to 31-31.2.
See WILLS.
Quieting title.
Actions, §41-10.
Rule in Shelley's case.
Abolished, §41-6.3.
Small estates, §§28A-25-1 to 28A-25-6.
See SMALL ESTATES.
State.
Trying title to land where state claims interest, §41-10.1.
Time limits on certain interests in land, §§41-28 to 41-33.
Applicability of provisions.
Prospective application, §41-33.
Definitions, §41-28.
Leases to commence in the future, §41-30.
Nonvested easement in gross, §41-31.
Defined, §41-28.
Option in gross with respect to an interest in land, §41-29.
Defined, §41-28.
Possibility of reverter, §41-32.
Preemptive right, §41-29.
Defined, §41-28.
Prospective application to divisions, §41-33.
Title.
See TITLE.
Unborn infants.
Taking by deed or writing, §41-5.
Waste, §§1-533 to 1-538.
See WASTE.
Wills.
General provisions, §§31-1 to 31-47.
See WILLS.

ESTATE TAXES, §§105-32.1 to 105-32.8.
Administration, §105-32.4, (e).
Amount, §105-32.2, (b).
Federal determination which changes, §105-32.8.
Assets of estates.
Payable from, §105-32.3, (a).
Sale to obtain money due, §105-32.4, (d).
Clerk of court.
Liability for tax.
Allowing personal representative to make final settlement without presenting affirmation or certificate, §105-32.3, (c).
Correct amount of tax payable, return reflecting.
Federal determination changing amount payable, §105-32.8.

ESTATE TAXES —Cont'd
Definitions, §105-32.1.
Due date, §105-32.4, (a).
Generation-skipping transfer, §105-32.7, (c).
Federal determination changing amount of tax, §105-32.8.
Federal estate tax apportionment, §§28A-27-1 to 28A-27-9.
Credits, §28A-27-5, (b) to (d).
Deductions, §28A-27-5, (a).
Definitions, §28A-27-1.
Determining apportionment.
Personal representative to determine, §28A-27-3, (a).
Basis for determining, §28A-27-3, (b).
Expenses for apportionment to be apportioned, §28A-27-3, (c).
Distribution before final apportionment.
Personal representative may require bond for tax liability, §28A-27-7, (b).
Effective date of provisions, §28A-27-9.
Exemptions, §28A-27-5, (a).
Computations, §28A-27-5, (d).
Federal tax law to determine liabilities imposed, §28A-27-8.
Method of apportionment, §28A-27-2, (a).
Choosing method, §28A-27-2, (b).
Rights and duties of personal representative, §28A-27-7, (a).
Temporary and remainder interests need not be apportioned, §28A-27-6.
Uncollected taxes, §28A-27-4.
Generation-skipping transfer.
Amount, §105-32.7, (b).
Correct amount of tax payable, return reflecting.
Federal determination changing amount payable, §105-32.8.
Due date, §105-32.7, (c).
Imposition of tax, §105-32.7, (a).
Net value of property located in state, §105-32.7, (b).
Payment, §105-32.7, (c).
Return, §105-32.7, (c).
State percentage of tax, §105-32.7, (b).
Imposition on estate of decedent, §105-32.2, (a).
Inheritance tax.
See INHERITANCE TAX.
Installment payments, §105-32.5.
Intestate succession.
Descent and distribution subject to payment, §29-13.
Liability for tax.
Clerk of court.
Allowing personal representative to make final settlement without presenting affirmation or certificate, §105-32.3, (c).
Generation-skipping transfer, §105-32.7, (c).
Personal representative.
Tax not paid within 2 years after tax due, §105-32.3, (b).
Person who receives property, §105-32.3, (a).
Liens, §105-32.6.
Payment of tax.
Due date, §105-32.4, (a).
Filing return, §105-32.4, (b), (c).
Generation-skipping transfer, §105-32.7, (c).
Installment payments, §105-32.5.
Selling assets to obtain money due, §105-32.4, (d).
Personal representative.
Liability for tax.
Tax not paid within 2 years after tax due, §105-32.3, (b).

ESTATE TAXES —Cont'd
Renunciation of property and fiduciary powers, §31B-1, (b).
Return.
Due date, §105-32.4, (a).
Filing, §105-32.4, (b).
Extension of time, §105-32.4, (c).
Generation-skipping transfer, §105-32.7, (c).
Sale of assets of estates.
Obtaining money due, §105-32.4, (d).
Wills.
Federal estate tax apportionment.
Method described in will, §28A-27-2, (b).

ESTHETICIANS.
Cosmetic art generally, §§88B-1 to 88B-29.
See COSMETIC ART.

ESTOPPEL.
Affirmative defense, pleading, §1A-1, Rule 8, (c).
Limited liability companies.
Applicability of law under chapter, §57C-10-03, (b).
Medicaid.
False claims by providers.
Final judgment rendered in favor of state in criminal proceeding, §108A-70.13, (d).
Partnerships.
Applicability of law of estoppel, §59-34, (b).
Partner by estoppel.
Agent of persons consenting to representation, §59-46, (b).
Liability, §59-46, (a).
RICO criminal convictions, §75D-8, (e).
Small claims actions, §7A-219.

ESTRAYS.
Dogs running at large.
Dangerous dogs.
Permitting dangerous dog to go beyond owner's real property unless leashed and muzzled.
Unlawful, §67-4.2, (a).
Female dogs in heat.
Penalty, §67-2.
Nighttime.
Permitting to run at large at night.
Penalty, §67-12.
Sheep-killing dogs.
Penalty for permitting such dog to run at large, §67-3.
Wildlife management areas.
Unmuzzled dogs running at large.
Impoundment, §67-14.1, (b) to (e).
Livestock running at large.
Allowing livestock to run at large prohibited, §68-16.
Diseased livestock, §106-307.7.
Fowl, killing by permit, §68-25.
Outer Banks.
Impoundment.
Applicability of general provisions, §68-45.
Penalty, §68-44.
Prohibited, §68-42.
Protection of livestock running at large, §14-366.
Molesting, §14-366.

ESTUARINE WATER BEACHES.
Coastal area management generally, §§113A-100 to 113A-128.
See COASTAL AREA MANAGEMENT.

ETCHINGS.
Artwork on consignment, §§25C-1 to 25C-5.
Sale of fine prints, §§25C-10 to 25C-16.

ETHANOL.
Renewable fuel facility construction tax credit, §105-129.16D.

ETHICS.
Arbitration.
Canons of ethics for arbitrators.
Integrity of arbitration process.
Upholding, CEA Rule 1.
Confidentiality of information.
See CONFIDENTIALITY.
Conflicts of interest.
See CONFLICTS OF INTEREST.
Judicial standards commission, §§7A-375 to 7A-377.
See JUDICIAL STANDARDS COMMISSION.
Legal ethics, procedures for ruling on questions of, Bar Rules & Regs., D, §§.0101 to .0104.
Definitions, Bar Rules & Regs., D, §.0101.
Ethics advisories, Bar Rules & Regs., D, §.0103.
Requests for, Bar Rules & Regs., D, §.0102.
Ethics decisions, Bar Rules & Regs., D, §.0104.
Formal ethics opinion, Bar Rules & Regs., D, §.0104.
General provisions, Bar Rules & Regs., D, §.0102.
Informal ethics advisories, Bar Rules & Regs., D, §.0103.
Requests for, Bar Rules & Regs., D, §.0102.
Legislative ethics, §§120-85 to 120-106.
See LEGISLATIVE ETHICS.
Privileged communications.
See PRIVILEGED COMMUNICATIONS.
Soil scientists.
Code of professional conduct, §89F-17.
Speech and language pathologists and audiologists.
Unethical acts and practices, §90-301A.
Transportation board.
Disclosures, §143B-350, (i) to (l).
Education program on ethics, §143B-350, (m).
Ethics policy, §143B-350, (k).

ETHNIC ANIMOSITY.
Punishment of offenses committed with, §14-3, (c).

ETHNIC INTIMIDATION.
Assaulting person or damaging or defacing property, §14-401.14, (a).
Teaching techniques, §14-401.14, (b).

ETHYL ALCOHOL.
Exemption from alcoholic beverage provisions, §18B-103.

EUROPEAN MONETARY UNION.
Application of provisions, §53-299.
Other currency alterations, §53-300.
Continuity of contracts, §§53-295 to 53-300.
Currency alterations generally.
Application of provisions, §53-300.
Currency substitutions.
Commercially reasonable substitutes, §53-296, (a), (b).
Designated by contract, §53-296, (c).
Effect, §53-297.
Definitions, §53-295.
References to ECU in contracts, §53-298, (a), (b).

EVACUATION OF PUBLIC BUILDINGS, §143-341.1.
Power of governor to order, §14-288.19.
State legislative building, §120-32.1A.

EVALUATION OF CERTIFIED SCHOOL EMPLOYEES, §§115C-333 to 115C-335.

EVASION OF TAX, §105-236.

EVICTION.
Betterments.
Defendant evicted may recover from plaintiff, §1-350.
Criminals, expedited evictions, §§42-59 to 42-76.
See EXPEDITED EVICTIONS.
Domestic violence.
Orders for relief, §50B-3, (a).
Ejectment of residential tenants, §§42-25.6 to 42-25.9.
Abandoned personal property of tenant.
Determination of abandonment, §42-25.9, (e).
Disposition, §42-25.9, (d).
Liability of recipient, §42-25.9, (f).
Contrary lease provisions.
Void, §42-25.8.
Damages.
Remedies, §42-25.9, (a), (b).
Distraint.
Prohibited, §42-25.7.
Distress.
Prohibited, §42-25.7.
Execution of writ of possession.
Personal property valued at less than $100.
Disposition, §42-25.9, (h).
Notice to tenant of sale of personal property left on premises, §42-25.9, (g).
Seizure of personal property of tenant prohibited, §42-25.7.
Exclusive nature of provisions, §42-25.6.
Lease provisions.
Contrary lease provisions void, §42-25.8.
Manner of ejectment, §42-25.6.
Personal property of tenant abandoned.
Delivery of property into custody of nonprofit organization, §42-25.9, (d).
No liability to owner of property for disposition of such property, §42-25.9, (f).
Determination of abandonment, §42-25.9, (e).
Policy of state, §42-25.6.
Remedies, §42-25.9, (a), (b).
Supplementary nature, §42-25.9, (c).
Expedited eviction of drug traffickers and other criminals, §§42-59 to 42-76.
See EXPEDITED EVICTIONS.
Retaliatory eviction, §§42-37.1 to 42-37.3.
Actions for summary ejectment.
Tenant may raise affirmative defense of retaliatory evictions, §42-37.1, (b).
Activities protected by law, §42-37.1, (a).
Complaints.
Good faith complaints.
Activities protected by law, §42-37.1, (a).
Health or safety laws.
Good faith complaints to government agencies.
Activities protected by law, §42-37.1, (a).
Public policy estate, §42-37.1, (a).
Remedies.
Court may deny request for judgment, §42-37.2, (a).
Generally, §42-37.2, (a), (b).
Supplementary to existing common law and statutory rights and remedies, §42-37.2, (b).
Repairs.
Good faith or request to repairs.
Activities protected by law, §42-37.1, (a).

EVICTION —Cont'd
Retaliatory eviction —Cont'd
Summary ejectment.
When landlord may prevail in action, §42-37.1, (c).
Tenant unions.
Activities protected by law, §42-37.1, (a).
Waiver of rights, §42-37.3.
Sale of abandoned personal property, §42-25.9.
Summary ejectment, §§42-26 to 42-36.2.
See LANDLORD AND TENANT.
Vacation rentals.
Expedited eviction proceedings, §§42A-23 to 42A-27.

EVIDENCE, §8C-1, Rule 412.
Absentees in military service.
Transfer of property.
Court order authorizing transfer, §§28B-9, (c), 28B-10, (f).
Absolute divorce for incurable insanity, §50-5.1.
Abstracts of grants, certified copies, §§8-6, 8-7.
Recording of certified copies, §8-8.
Validation, §8-9.
Abused, neglected or dependent juvenile actions.
Adjudicatory hearing, applicability of rules of evidence, §7B-804.
Dispositional hearings, §7B-901.
No privilege except attorney-client grounds for failing to report or excluding evidence, §7B-310.
Permanency planning hearings, §7B-907, (b).
Placement review, parental rights terminated, §7B-908, (a).
Review hearings, §7B-906, (c).
Accident reports by motor carriers.
Inadmissibility, §62-274.
Accident reports involving public utilities not admissible, §62-41.
Accounts and accounting.
Book accounts.
Copies of book accounts in documentary evidence, §8-44.
Documentary evidence of book accounts under $60, §8-42.
Executors and administrators to approve book accounts, §8-43.
Documentary evidence.
Itemized and verified accounts, §8-45.
Accused's character.
Admissibility of evidence of pertinent trait, §8C-1, Rule 404, (a).
Acts of the general assembly.
Certified copies as evidence, §8-1.
Administrative procedure.
Appeals.
New evidence, §150B-49.
Dying declarations, §8-51.1.
Hearings, §150B-41, (a), (b).
Opportunity to present evidence, §§150B-25, (c), 150B-40, (a).
Rules of evidence, §150B-29, (a), (b).
Subpoenas, §§150B-27, 150B-39, (c).
Admissibility.
Character evidence.
Not admissible to prove conduct, §8C-1, Rule 404, (a).
Collaborative law proceedings.
Privileged and inadmissible evidence, §50-77, (a), (b).

EVIDENCE —Cont'd
Admissibility —Cont'd
Compromises and offers to compromise, §8C-1, Rule 408.
Dying declarations, §8-51.1.
Evidence of other crimes, wrongs or acts, §8C-1, Rule 404.
Irrelevant evidence.
Inadmissible, §8C-1, Rule 402.
Limited admissibility, §8C-1, Rule 105.
Medical, hospital or other expenses.
Evidence of furnishing or offering or promising to pay.
Inadmissible to prove liability for injury, §8C-1, Rule 409.
Pleas, plea discussions and related statements.
Inadmissibility, §8C-1, Rule 410.
Questions of admissibility generally, §8C-1, Rule 104, (a).
Relevant evidence, §8C-1, Rule 402.
Exclusions.
Prejudice, confusion or waste of time, §8C-1, Rule 403.
Rulings on, §1A-1, Rule 46, (a).
Subsequent remedial measures, §8C-1, Rule 407.
Adult care homes.
Temporary management.
Hearing on petition for appointment of temporary manager, §131E-233, (b).
Adverse possession.
Seven years possession under color of title, §1-38, (b).
Affrays.
Plea of self-defense.
Evidence of former threats upon plea, §14-33.1.
Agriculture.
Marketing and branding farm products.
Certificate of grade or classifications of farm product prima facie evidence, §106-192.
Seed law, claim of defective seeds, §106-277.34, (a).
Alcoholic beverages.
Compensation for injury caused by sales to underage persons.
Admissibility, §18B-122.
Open container law.
Alcohol screening test, §20-138.7, (d).
Odor, sufficiency to determine whether alcohol remains in driver's body, §20-138.7, (c).
Possession for purpose of sale.
Prima facie evidence.
Possession by person not permitted to possess, §18B-304, (b).
Aliens.
Real property.
Certified copies of deeds made by alien property custodians.
Admissible in evidence, §47-34.
Altering, destroying, etc., evidence of criminal conduct, §14-221.1.
Amendment of pleading to conform to evidence, §1A-1, Rule 15, (b).
Annuities.
Mortality tables.
Worth of annuities.
Establishing present worth, §8-47.
Antifreeze.
Enforcement of article.
Copy of analysis administered as evidence, §106-579.10, (c).

EVIDENCE —Cont'd
Appeals.
Exceptions, §1-186, (b).
Applicability of rules, §8C-1, Rule 1101, (a).
Arbitration.
Compelling attendance of witnesses, §1-569.17, (a).
Depositions permitted, §1-569.17, (b).
Discovery.
Grounds for permitting, §1-569.17, (c).
Issuance of process, §1-569.17, (d).
Presentation of case, §1-569.7, (c).
Rules of evidence.
Applicability to proceedings, §1-569.7, (f).
Arbitration and award.
Rules for court-ordered arbitration.
Exhibits.
Copies admissible, Arbitration Rule 3.
Law of evidence used as guide, Arbitration Rule 3.
Trial de novo.
No evidence of arbitration admissible, Arbitration Rule 5.
Assault and battery.
Plea of self-defense.
Evidence of former threats upon plea, §14-33.1.
Assumed names.
Business under assumed name.
Copy of certificate prima facie evidence, §66-69.1.
Attorneys at law.
Altering, destroying or concealing, Prof Cond. Rule 3.4.
Appearances.
Attorney-client relationship.
Filing or producing if requested, §84-11.
Disciplinary proceedings.
Formal hearings, Bar Rules & Regs., B, §.0114.
Preservation of evidence, Bar Rules & Regs., B, §.0118.
False evidence offered, Prof Cond. Rule 3.3.
Obstructing party's access to, Prof Cond. Rule 3.4.
Prohibited acts as to opposing party and counsel, Prof Cond. Rule 3.4.
Attorneys' fees in nonjustifiable cases, §6-21.5.
Authentication and identification.
General provisions, §8C-1, Rule 901, (a).
Illustration of examples, §8C-1, Rule 901, (b).
Self-authentication, §8C-1, Rule 902.
Subscribing witness.
Testimony not necessary to authenticate, §8C-1, Rule 903.
Bad checks.
Prima facie evidence in worthless check cases, §14-107.1.
Bail bondsmen and runners.
Commissioners' actions, §58-71-5, (b).
Bailments.
Conversion.
Prima facie evidence of intent to convert property, §14-168.3.
Options to purchase.
Failing to return rented property on which there is purchase option.
Intent to commit crime.
Presumptions from evidence, §14-168.4, (b).
Banks.
Records.
Certified copies, §53-113.
Bawdy houses, keeping, §14-188, (a).

EVIDENCE —Cont'd
Best evidence.
Contents of writings, recordings and photographs, §8C-1, Rules 1001 to 1008.
Bills of lading.
Actions by or against common or connecting carriers, §8-41.
Birth certificate as evidence, §130A-109.
Bladen county.
Records in Bladen.
Copies of lost records, §8-33.
Blind persons.
Aid to the blind.
Personal representatives for certain recipients of aid.
Findings not competent as evidence in other proceedings, §111-32.
Blood tests and samples.
Competency of blood tests.
Civil actions, §8-50.1, (b1).
Jury charge, §8-50.1, (b1).
Taxing of expenses as cost, §8-50.1, (b1).
Cost.
Taxing of expenses as cost, §8-50.1.
Criminal actions, §8-50.1, (a).
Jury charge, §8-50.1, (a).
Taxing of expenses as cost, §8-50.1, (a).
Jury charge, §8-50.1.
Impaired driving chemical analysis.
Admissibility of results, §20-139.1, (a).
Alcohol screening tests, §20-16.3, (d).
Refusal to submit to analysis, §20-139.1, (f).
Qualification of person withdrawing blood, §20-139.1, (c).
Boating safety.
Proof of ownership of motorboat, §75A-10.2.
Boats.
Certificate of title.
Prima facie evidence of ownership, §75A-37, (a).
Bonds, surety.
Actions on bonds.
Evidence against principal admissible against sureties, §58-76-25.
Model payment and performance bond.
Certified copies of bonds.
Prima facie evidence, §44A-31, (b).
Brunswick county.
Wills in Brunswick.
Records of wills, §8-27.
Burden of proof.
See BURDEN OF PROOF.
Bureau of investigation.
Availability to district attorneys, §114-15, (c).
Burke county.
Grants.
Copies of grants in Burke.
Admission into evidence, §8-10.
Business corporation document filing.
Certificate of existence.
Evidentiary effect, §55-1-28, (c).
Evidentiary, §55D-17.
Calendar.
Proof of dates.
Clark's calendar may be used, §8-48, (a).
Campaign contributions and expenditures.
Communications are "to support or oppose the nomination or election of one or more clearly identified candidates," §163-278.14A, (a).
Carriers.
Actions by or against common or connecting carriers.
Bills of lading in evidence, §8-41.

EVIDENCE —Cont'd
Chain of custody.
Courier service and contract carriers, §8-103.
Character evidence.
Accused's character, §8C-1, Rule 404, (a).
Credibility of witness, §8C-1, Rule 608.
Juvenile's character.
Other crimes, wrongs or acts, §8C-1, Rule 404, (b).
Methods of proving character, §8C-1, Rule 405.
Not admissible to prove conduct.
Exceptions, §8C-1, Rule 404, (a).
Opinion, §8C-1, Rule 405, (a).
Other crimes, wrongs or acts, §8C-1, Rule 404, (b).
Juveniles, §8C-1, Rule 404, (b).
Reputation, §8C-1, Rule 405, (a).
Specific instances of conduct, §8C-1, Rule 405, (b).
Victim's character, §8C-1, Rule 404, (a).
Witness's character, §8C-1, Rule 404, (a).
Cherokee Indians.
Maps of Cherokee lands.
Certified copies of maps, §8-14.
Child care facilities.
Prima facie evidence of existence, §110-98.1.
Child custody jurisdiction and enforcement.
Testimony, §50A-111.
Child support.
Agency payment records as admissible evidence, §50-13.9, (b).
Employee verification form, §110-139, (c1).
Citation of rules of evidence, §8C-1, Rule 1102.
Clergymen.
Communications between clergymen and communicants, §8-53.2.
Code, §8C-1, Rules 101 to 1102.
Collaborative law proceedings.
Privileged and inadmissible evidence, §50-77, (a), (b).
Commercial code generally.
Prima facie evidence of third party documents, §25-1-202.
Usage of trade, §25-1-205.
Commercial vehicles.
Operation after consuming alcohol.
Odor of alcohol, §20-138.2A, (b1).
Common carriers.
Actions by or against common carriers.
Bills of lading, §8-41.
Common law.
Laws of foreign countries or states.
Proof by oral evidence, §8-3, (a).
Competency of witnesses.
See COMPETENCY OF WITNESSES.
Completeness rule, §8C-1, Rule 106.
Compromise and settlement.
Mediated settlement conferences in superior court civil actions.
Inadmissibility of negotiations, §7A-38.1, (l).
Offering or accepting.
Admissibility, §8C-1, Rule 408.
Conduct of witness.
Credibility, §8C-1, Rule 608.
Construction and interpretation.
Photographing and photostating public records.
Uniformity of interpretation, §8-45.2.
Rules of evidence, §8C-1, Rule 102, (a).
Contractors.
General contractors license certificate, §87-12.
Controlled substances.
Chain of custody, §90-95, (g1).

EVIDENCE —Cont'd
Conviction of crime.
Impeachment, §8C-1, Rule 609.
Copies.
Use of registered copies as evidence, §47-31, (a), (b).
Coroners.
Bonds, surety.
Certified copies evidence, §152-4.
Corporations.
Business corporation documents filing.
Certificate of existence.
Evidentiary effect, §55-1-28, (c).
Evidentiary effect of copy of filed document, §55D-17.
Probate and registration.
Execution of corporate instruments.
Instruments executed bearing seal.
Prima facie evidence seal duly adopted, §47-18.3, (b).
Cost.
Blood tests.
Competency of blood tests.
Taxing of expenses as cost, §8-50.1.
Counselors.
Privileged communications, §8-53.8.
Court reporters.
Perpetuation of testimony.
Certified transcription of court reporter, §8-85.
Credit cards and devices fraud, §14-113.3.
Credit unions.
Records.
Photostatic or photographic reproductions, §54-109.17, (c).
Crime victims compensation.
Contested cases, §15B-12.
Criminal law and procedure.
Additional evidence.
Introduction at any time prior to verdict.
Discretion of judge, §15A-1226, (b).
Altering, destroying or stealing evidence of conduct.
Obstructing justice, §14-221.1.
Bawdy houses, keeping.
Reputation or character of house admissible, §14-188, (a).
Demurrer to the evidence, §15-173.
DNA samples and testing, §§15A-266 to 15A-270.
See DNA DATABASE AND DATABANKS.
Errors in admission or exclusion of evidence.
Correction of errors by appellate division, §15A-1442.
Forensic analysis.
Admissibility, §8-58.20, (a), (b).
Affidavit of analyst, §8-58.20, (c) to (f).
Service of report and affidavit on attorney of record for defendant, §8-58.20, (d), (e).
Fruit of the poisonous tree doctrine, §15A-974.
Hearsay.
Probable cause hearings, §15A-611, (b).
Insufficiency of evidence.
Grounds for correction of errors by appellate division, §15A-1442.
Jury.
Review of testimony, §15A-1233, (a).
Motion to suppress evidence.
Appeals.
Order denying motion, §15A-979, (b).
Order granting motion, §15A-979, (c).
State may appeal, §15A-1445, (b).
Definitions, §15A-971.

EVIDENCE —Cont'd
Criminal law and procedure —Cont'd
Motion to suppress evidence —Cont'd
During trial.
District court, §15A-973.
Hearing on motion.
Outside presence of jury, §15A-977, (e).
Superior court, §15A-975, (b).
Written or oral motion, §15A-977, (e).
Exclusive method of provisions, §15A-979, (d).
Findings of fact and conclusions of law.
Judgment set forth, §15A-977, (f).
Grounds for exclusion or suppression of unlawfully obtained evidence, §15A-974.
Hearing of jury, §8C-1, Rule 104, (c).
Order of suppression, §15A-979, (a).
Prior to trial.
Affidavit supporting motion, §15A-977, (a).
Answer by state, §15A-977, (a).
District court, §15A-973.
Hearing on motion, §§15A-976, (c), 15A-977, (d).
Service of copies of motion, §15A-977, (a).
Superior court, §§15A-972, 15A-975, (a).
Time for motion, §15A-976, (a), (b).
Written motion required, §15A-977, (a).
Procedure, §15A-977.
Renewal of motion, §15A-975, (c).
Searches and seizures.
Challenge to probable cause supporting search warrant on grounds of truthfulness, §15A-978, (a).
Identity of informant to be disclosed, §15A-978, (b).
Challenge to truthfulness of testimony offered in support of search without warrant, §15A-978, (c).
Summary grant or denial of motion.
Grounds, §15A-977, (b), (c).
Pleadings used in criminal prosecution as proof of fact admitted or alleged, §1-49.
Plea discussion and arrangement.
Inadmissible, §15A-1025.
Probable cause hearings, §15A-611, (b).
Prostitution prosecution.
Reputation and prior convictions, admissibility, §14-206.
Rebuttal evidence, §15A-1226, (a).
Records.
Superior courts.
Criminal index maintained by clerk of court.
Records admissible in certain cases, §8-35.2.
Subpoena duces tecum, §15A-802.
Superior courts.
Clerks of court.
Criminal index.
Records admissible in certain cases, §8-35.2.
Suppression of evidence.
Motion to suppress evidence, §§15A-971 to 15A-980.
Testimony by accused, §8C-1, Rule 104, (d).
Victims, impact of crime, §15A-833.
Custody.
Chain of custody.
Courier service and contract carriers, §8-103.
Dead man's statute, §8C-1, Rule 601, (c).
Death.
Competency of witnesses.
Dying declarations, §8-51.1.

EVIDENCE —Cont'd
Death —Cont'd
Federal officers and employees.
Finding of presumed death, §8-37.1, (a), (b).
Authority to certify evidence, §8-37.3.
Deemed signed and issued pursuant to law, §8-37.3.
Report or record that person died, §8-37.2.
Certified copies deemed signed and issued pursuant to law, §8-37.3.
Authority to certify evidence, §8-37.3.
Death presumption.
Federal officers and employees, §§8-37.1, 8-37.3.
Specific peril exposure, §28C-1, (b).
Decedents' estates.
Killing decedent.
Record determining slayer admissible, §31A-13.
Deeds.
Anson county.
Records of deeds in Anson, §8-26.
Certified copies.
From other states, §8-32.
1835 or before.
Date on deed.
Execution of deed, §8-13.
Execution of deed.
Dated before 1835.
Evidence of due execution, §8-13.
Lost or destroyed deeds.
Presumed to be in due form, §8-21.
Registered instruments as evidence.
Certified copies of registered instruments, §8-18.
Lost or destroyed records.
Presumed to be in due form, §8-21.
Tax deeds.
Recitals in tax deeds in Haywood and Henderson counties, §8-22.
Richmond county, §8-22.1.
Tracts of land.
Common survey of contiguous tracts as evidence, §8-19.
Deer hunting.
Spotlighting.
Prima facie evidence, §113-302, (b).
Definitions.
Hearsay, §8C-1, Rule 801, (a) to (c).
Relevant evidence, §8C-1, Rule 401.
Writings, recordings and photographs, §8C-1, Rule 1001.
Delinquent and undisciplined juvenile actions.
Court acceptance of admission by juvenile, §7B-2407.
Custodial interrogation of juvenile.
In-custody admission, confession or other statement, §7B-2101, (b), (c).
Dispositional hearings, §7B-2501, (a).
Rules of evidence at hearing, §7B-2408.
Dentists.
Medical charges at issue.
Injured party as witness.
Competency to give evidence regarding amount of charges, §8-58.1.
Rebuttable presumption of reasonableness of charges.
Testimony of person establishing, §8-58.1.
Department of health and human services actions to recover costs of care.
Prima facie evidence, §143-121, (c).
Depositions, §§8-74 to 8-83.
Use in court proceedings, §1A-1, Rule 32.

EVIDENCE —Cont'd
Disability of attorney proceedings.
Preservation, Bar Rules & Regs., B, §.0118.
Discipline of attorneys.
Formal hearings, Bar Rules & Regs., B, §.0114.
Disorderly conduct.
Remaining at scene after command to disperse, §14-288.5, (c).
Disorderly houses, keeping, §14-188, (a).
District courts.
Custody and disposition, Super. Ct. Rule 14.
Judges of district court.
Power to compel production of evidence, §7A-291.
Divorce.
Absolute divorce for incurable insanity, §50-5.1.
DNA samples and testing, §§15A-266 to 15A-270.
See DNA DATABASE AND DATABANKS.
Doctor-patient privilege, §8-53.
Waiver of privilege in child abuse cases, §8-53.1.
Documentary evidence.
Accounts and accounting.
Itemized and verified accounts, §8-45.
Bills of lading in evidence, §8-41.
Book accounts.
Copies of accounts in evidence, §8-44.
Executors and administrators.
Approving book accounts by personal representative, §8-43.
Under $60, §8-42.
Carriers.
Actions by or against common or connecting carriers.
Bills of lading in evidence, §8-41.
Contract actions.
Book accounts under $60, §8-42.
Copies of book accounts in evidence, §8-44.
Executors and administrators.
Book accounts approved by personal representative, §8-43.
Hospital records.
Copies of medical records, §8-44.1.
Itemized and verified accounts, §8-45.
Meat inspection.
Production of documentary evidence, §106-549.36, (b), (c).
Medical records.
Copies of medical records, §8-44.1.
Parol evidence.
Identifying land described, §8-39.
Real property.
Parol evidence to identify land described, §8-39.
Remainder of or related writings or recorded statements, §8C-1, Rule 106.
Subpoena for production, §§1A-1, Rule 45, (c), 8-61.
Documents of title.
Prima facie evidence by third party documents, §25-1-202.
Drug paraphernalia.
Determination where object is drug paraphernalia.
What may be considered, §90-113.21, (b).
Drugs.
Controlled substances.
Reports of analysis, §90-95, (g).
Duplin county.
Partition of real estate in Duplin.
Records of partition, §8-24.
Wills in Duplin.
Records of wills, §8-25.

EVIDENCE —Cont'd
Duress.
Statements, releases, etc., obtained from persons in shock or under the influence of drugs.
Presumption of fraud, §8-45.5.
Dying declarations.
Admissibility, §8-51.1.
Wrongful death actions.
Admissibility, §28A-18-2, (d).
Elections.
Challenge to voter.
Voter no longer living in precinct, prima facie evidence, §163-85, (e).
Protest filed with county board.
Conduct of hearing, §163-182.10, (c).
Electronic surveillance.
Admissibility of contents of communications.
Copy of order and application must be furnished to parties, §15A-294, (f).
Motion to suppress contents of communications, §15A-294, (g).
Appeal of order granting motion, §15A-294, (h).
Electronic transactions.
Admissibility of electronic signatures and records, §66-323.
Employment security.
Hearings by commission.
Rules of evidence, §96-4, (p).
Employment security commission.
Reproduction of records stored on permanent computer-readable media, §8-45.3, (b).
Engineer licensure certificates, §89C-16, (b).
Exceptions, §1A-1, Rule 46, (a), (b).
Exceptions to decisions of court, §1-186.
Excluded evidence.
Penalty for failure to comply with discovery order, §15A-910, (a).
Considerations of court before granting, §15A-910, (b).
Record, §1A-1, Rule 43, (c).
Executors and administrators.
Book accounts proved by personal representative, §8-43.
Medical, hospital or other charges at issue.
Competency to give evidence regarding amount, §8-58.1.
Testimony establishing rebuttable presumption of reasonableness, §8-58.1.
Vouchers.
Presumptive evidence of disbursement, §28A-21-5.
Wrongful death actions.
Evidence establishing elements of damages, §28A-18-2, (c).
Expert witnesses.
See EXPERT WITNESSES.
Fair housing.
Intent to discriminate, establishing, §41A-5, (a).
Fairs.
County societies.
Records may be read in evidence, §106-511.
False pretenses and cheats.
Worthless check cases.
Prima facie evidence in cases, §14-107.1.
Family law arbitration, §50-49.
Financial transaction cards.
Forgery of transaction card.
Prima facie evidence of forgery, §14-113.12, (a), (b).
Theft of financial transaction card.
Prima facie evidence of theft, §14-113.10.

EVIDENCE —Cont'd
Fireworks.
Possession prima facie evidence of violation, §14-412.
Fish and fisheries resources.
Possession of illegally killed fish as evidence, §113-262, (b).
Replacement costs of resources, §113-267.
Unlawful possession of game fish, §113-302, (a).
Warning tickets not to constitute evidence of commission of offense, §113-140, (g).
Foreign country laws.
Admission into evidence, §8-3, (a).
Exhibiting copy of law from printed volume, §8-3, (b).
Judicial notice of laws, §8-4.
Form, §1A-1, Rule 43, (a).
Francis X. Martin.
Collection of Martin's private acts, §8-2.
Fraud.
Statements, releases, etc., obtained from persons in shock or under the influence of drugs.
Presumption of fraud, §8-45.5.
Frivolous actions.
Attorneys' fees in nonjustifiable cases, §6-21.5.
Funeral charges at issue.
Competency to give evidence regarding amount of charges, §8-58.1.
Rebuttable presumption of reasonableness, §8-58.1.
Futures contracts.
Prosecutions under provisions, §16-6.
Gasoline and oil inspection.
Certified copies of official tests admissible in evidence, §119-36.
General statutes.
Printed statutes and certified copies as evidence, §8-1.
Supplements.
Prima facie evidence of laws, §164-11, (a).
Cumulative supplements, §164-11.1.
Global TransPark development zone.
Certificate of incorporation as conclusive evidence on zone creation and establishment, §158-33, (d).
Grants.
Abstracts of grants.
Certified copies, §8-7.
Recording of certified copies, §8-8.
Secretary of state or state archivist to certify, §8-6.
Burke county.
Copies of grants in Burke.
Admission into evidence, §8-10.
Certified copies, §8-7.
Recording of certified copies, §8-8.
Validation by clerk of secretary of state, §8-9.
H.E. McCulloch grants.
Evidence of title under grants, §8-16.
Conveyances, §8-17.
Moore county.
Copies of grants in Moore, §8-11.
Onslow county.
Copies of grants in Onslow.
Admission into evidence, §8-12.
Secretary of state.
Validation of copies of grants certified by clerk of secretary, §8-9.
Guardians.
Ancillary guardian appointed for nonresident ward with property in state.
Certified or exemplified copy of appointment, §35A-1280, (c).

EVIDENCE —Cont'd
Guardians —Cont'd
Medical, hospital or other charges at issue.
Competency to give evidence regarding amount, §8-58.1.
Rebuttable presumption of reasonableness.
Testimony establishing, §8-58.1.
Habeas corpus ad testificandum, §§17-41 to 17-46.
See HABEAS CORPUS AD TESTIFICANDUM.
Habits of person.
Relevant to prove conduct of person, §8C-1, Rule 406.
Habitual felons.
Prior convictions, §14-7.4.
Violent habitual felons, §14-7.10.
Violent habitual felons, §14-7.10.
Harmless error, §1A-1, Rule 61.
Haywood county.
Tax deeds in Haywood.
Recitals in tax deeds, §8-22.
Hazardous waste management.
Felonies.
Circumstantial evidence of defendant's possession of actual knowledge, §130A-26.1, (c).
Health care liability.
Admissibility of evidence, §90-21.55, (b).
Hearing impaired.
Statement taken under custody without interpreter present.
Admissibility, §8B-2.
Hearing of jury, §8C-1, Rule 104, (c).
Hearsay.
Attacking credibility of declarant, §8C-1, Rule 806.
Credibility of declarant.
Attacking and supporting, §8C-1, Rule 806.
Definitions, §8C-1, Rule 801, (a) to (c).
Exceptions.
Admissions by party-opponent, §8C-1, Rule 801, (d).
Availability of declarant immaterial, §8C-1, Rule 803.
Declarant unavailable, §8C-1, Rule 804.
Enumeration, §8C-1, Rule 803.
Hearsay within hearsay, §8C-1, Rule 805.
Probable cause hearings, §15A-611, (b).
Rule generally, §8C-1, Rule 802.
Supporting credibility of declarant, §8C-1, Rule 806.
H.E. McCulloch grants.
Title under grants, §8-16.
Conveyances, §8-17.
Henderson county.
Tax deeds in Henderson.
Recitals in tax deeds, §8-22.
Homicide.
Killing decedents.
Record determining slayer admissible in evidence, §31A-13.
Hospital authorities.
Certificate of incorporation.
Copy of certificate admissible in evidence, §131E-19.
Hospitals.
Medical records.
Copies of medical records as documentary evidence, §8-44.1.
Medical review committee.
Introduction of records into evidence, §131E-95, (b), (c).

EVIDENCE —Cont'd
Hospitals —Cont'd
Medical review committee —Cont'd
Testimony of members of committees, §131E-95, (b), (c).
Hunting and wildlife.
Possession of illegally killed wildlife as evidence, §113-262, (b).
Spotlighting deer.
Prima facie evidence, §113-302, (b).
Warning tickets not to constitute evidence of commission of offense, §113-140, (g).
Husband and wife.
Competency of witnesses.
Paternity proceedings, §8-57.2.
Privilege.
Child abuse cases, §8-57.1.
Civil actions, §8-56.
Criminal actions, §8-57, (a) to (c).
Illustrative evidence.
Photographs as substantive or illustrative evidence, §8-97.
Impaired driving.
Chemical analysis of impairing substances in blood.
Admissibility of results, §20-139.1, (a).
Alcohol screening tests, §20-16.3, (d).
Refusal to submit to analysis, §20-139.1, (f).
Qualification of person withdrawing blood, §20-139.1, (c).
Sentencing hearing.
Prior convictions, §20-179, (o).
Standards, §20-179, (o).
Impoundment.
Property impounded for evidence, §15-11.1.
Inapplicability of rules, §8C-1, Rule 1101, (b).
Insufficiency of evidence.
New trial.
Grounds, §1A-1, Rule 59, (a).
Insurance.
Documents executed by commissioner.
Certificate as evidence of authority to do business, §58-2-115.
Originals and certified copies, §58-2-110.
Liability insurance.
Evidence of existence of insurance inadmissible, §8C-1, Rule 411.
Existence inadmissible.
Mental health area authorities, §122C-152, (f).
Tort action against community college trustees, §115D-58.12, (d).
Motor vehicle accident reports, §20-279.11.
International commercial arbitration and conciliation.
Admissions and documents, §1-567.81.
Documentary evidence, translation, tribunal ordering, §1-567.52, (b).
Tribunal conducting proceeding.
Not limited to rules of evidence, §1-567.49, (b).
Interstate commerce.
Earnings of employees in interstate commerce.
Collections out of state to avoid exemptions.
Evidence of intent to violate provisions, §95-76.
Investment securities.
Certificated securities, §25-8-114.
Journalist's qualified privilege against disclosure in any legal proceeding, §8-53.11, (b).
Definitions, §8-53.11, (a).

EVIDENCE —Cont'd
Journalist's qualified privilege against disclosure in any legal proceeding —Cont'd
Eyewitness observation of criminal or tortuous conduct, no privilege, §8-53.11, (d).
Order to compel disclosure, notice to journalist and hearing, §8-53.11, (c).
Overcoming privilege, person seeking to compel disclosure, §8-53.11, (c).
Judgments, §1-229.
Judicial notice.
Adjudicative facts.
Instructing jury, §8C-1, Rule 201, (g).
Kinds of facts, §8C-1, Rule 201, (b).
Opportunity to be heard, §8C-1, Rule 201, (e).
Scope of rule, §8C-1, Rule 201, (a).
Time of taking notice, §8C-1, Rule 201, (f).
When discretionary, §8C-1, Rule 201, (c).
When mandatory, §8C-1, Rule 201, (d).
Laws of United States, other states and foreign countries, §8-4.
Photographic speed-measuring instruments.
Admissibility as evidence.
Judicial notice of rules and procedures, §8-50.3, (d).
Speed-measuring instruments.
Admissibility as evidence.
Judicial notice taken of use of certain models and types, §8-50.2, (d).
Photographic speed-measuring instruments.
Judicial notice of rules and procedures, §8-50.3, (d).
Judicial standards commission, Jud. Stds. Comm. Rule 15.
Jurisdiction.
Proof of jurisdiction.
Judgment against nonappearing defendant, §1-75.11.
Jury.
Blood tests.
Competency of blood tests.
Charge to jury, §8-50.1.
Juvenile code.
Character.
Other crimes, wrongs or acts, §8C-1, Rule 404, (b).
Conviction of crime.
Impeachment in juvenile adjudication, §8C-1, Rule 609, (d).
Labor.
Interstate commerce.
Earnings of employees in interstate commerce.
Collections out of state to avoid exemptions.
Evidence of intent to violate, §95-76.
Land surveyors' licensure certificate, §89C-16, (b).
Land tracts.
Contiguous tracts as evidence.
Common survey of contiguous tracts, §8-19.
Larceny.
Concealment of merchandise in mercantile establishments.
Prima facie evidence of willful concealment, §14-72.1, (a).
Laser speed enforcement instrument.
Admissibility of result, §8-50.2.
Leases, UCC.
Extrinsic evidence, §25-2A-202.
Proof of market rent, §25-2A-507.
Unconscionability.
Parties afforded reasonable opportunity to present, §25-2A-108, (3).

EVIDENCE —Cont'd
Legal notices.
Newspapers.
Proof of publication of notice in newspaper.
Prima facie evidence, §1-600, (b).
Qualification.
Sworn statement prima facie evidence of qualification, §1-598.
Letters testamentary.
Certified copies, §8-36.
Liability insurance.
Evidence of existence of insurance inadmissible, §8C-1, Rule 411.
Existence inadmissible, §8C-1, Rule 411.
Mental health area authorities, §122C-152, (f).
Tort action against community college trustees, §115D-58.12, (d).
Liens.
Physicians and surgeons.
Recoveries for personal injuries, §44-50.
Life tables.
Annuities.
Present worth of annuities, §8-47.
Establishing expectancy of continued life of person, §8-46.
Limited liability companies.
Certificate of existence or authorization, §57C-1-28, (c).
Filing of articles of organization, §57C-2-20, (b).
Limiting instruction on admissibility, §8C-1, Rule 105.
Lost instruments and records.
Bladen county.
Copies of lost records in Bladen, §8-33.
Copies, §98-1.
Wills, §98-5.
Court records.
Conveyances reciting court records.
Prima facie evidence thereof, §§98-16, 98-17.
Proof of destroyed instruments set out therein, §98-12.
Deeds and records thereof lost.
Presumed to be in due form, §8-21.
Mortgages and deeds of trust.
Affidavit of lost instrument, §47-46.3.
Wills.
Copy of lost will, §98-5.
Lotteries.
"Numbers" tickets.
Possession prima facie evidence of violation, §14-291.1.
Possession, §14-290.
Malpractice.
Medical malpractice.
Standard of health care, §90-21.12.
Statements by health care provider to ameliorate or mitigate adverse outcomes, §8C-1, Rule 413.
Maps and plats.
Certified copies of maps, §8-14.
Copies of plats.
Certification, §8-6.
Tennessee.
Certified copies of certain surveys and maps obtained from state of Tennessee, §8-15.
Market value.
Sale of goods, UCC, §§25-2-723, 25-2-724.
Marriage and family therapists privilege.
Alimony and divorce actions, §8-53.6.
Communications between therapists and clients, generally, §8-53.5.

EVIDENCE —Cont'd
Marriage certificate registration, §130A-110, (b).
Marriage proceedings.
Underage pregnant females.
Action for judicial authorization to marry, §51-2.1, (f).
Material facts.
Proof of single material fact.
No more than two witnesses may be subpoenaed to prove, §6-60.
Meat and meat product inspections, §106-549.36, (c).
Mediated settlement conferences in district court.
Equitable distribution, alimony or support actions.
Statements made and conduct occurring in settlement proceeding, §7A-38.4A, (j).
Mediated settlement conferences in superior court civil actions.
Inadmissibility of negotiations, §7A-38.1, (l).
Medical examiners.
Postmortem medicolegal examinations and services.
Reports and records received as evidence, §130A-392.
Medical, hospital or other expenses.
Evidence of furnishing or offering or promising to pay.
Inadmissible to prove liability for injury, §8C-1, Rule 409.
Injured as witness when medical charges an issue.
Competency to give evidence regarding amount, §8-58.1.
Reasonableness of amount of charges.
Rebuttable presumption, §8-58.1.
Mental health, developmental disabilities and substance abuse.
Involuntary commitment.
District court hearing.
Admissible evidence, §122C-268, (f).
Hearing following automatic commitment, §122C-268.1, (f), (h), (i).
Substance abuser's commitment hearing, §122C-286, (c).
Microfilm.
Admissible photographic reproductions, §8-45.1.
Citation of act, §8-45.4.
Uniformity of interpretation, §8-45.2.
Department of revenue.
Reproductions of records, §8-45.3, (a).
Employment security commission.
Reproduction of records, §8-45.3, (a1).
Military affairs.
Death.
Finding of presumed death, §8-37.1, (a), (b).
Missing in action.
Report or record that person is missing in action.
Prima facie evidence, §8-37.2.
Missing persons records and reports.
Certified copies deemed signed and issued pursuant to law, §8-37.3.
Prima facie evidence, §8-37.2.
Mode and order of presenting evidence.
Control of court, §8C-1, Rule 611, (a).
Moore county.
Grants.
Copies of grants in Moore, §8-11.
Mortality tables.
Annuities.
Present worth of annuities, §8-47.

EVIDENCE —Cont'd
Mortality tables —Cont'd
Establishing expectancy of continued life of person, §8-46.
Mortgages and deeds of trust.
Registered instruments as evidence.
Certified copies of registered instruments, §8-18.
Sales under power of sale.
Requests for copies of notice, §45-21.17A, (e).
Motions.
Evidence on motions, §1A-1, Rule 43, (e).
Suppression of evidence.
Motion to suppress evidence, §§15A-971 to 15A-980.
Motor carrier accident reports, §62-274.
Motor vehicle accidents.
Reports, §20-166.1, (i).
Information on financial responsibility contained in accident report, §20-279.11.
Settlements, §1-540.2.
Motor vehicle financial responsibility.
Matters not to be evidence in civil suit, §20-279.11.
Operation of vehicle without, §20-313, (b).
Motor vehicle license plates.
Ownership, §8-37.
Motor vehicle radar.
Radio microwave or other speed-measuring instruments.
Admissible as evidence, §8-50.2.
Motor vehicle registration.
Ownership evidence, §20-71.1, (b).
Motor vehicles.
Altering to increase potential speed.
Prima facie rule of evidence as to operation, §20-141.2.
Antifreeze.
Enforcement of article.
Copy of analysis administered as evidence, §106-579.10, (c).
Impaired driving.
Records of division of motor vehicles.
Admissibility of records as prima facie evidence of convictions, §8-35.1.
Open container law.
Alcohol screening test, §20-138.7, (d).
Odor, sufficiency to determine whether alcohol remains in driver's body, §20-138.7, (c).
Ownership.
Certificate of commissioner as to ownership, §8-37.
Evidence of defendant's responsibility for conduct of operation, §20-71.1, (a).
Photographic speed-measuring instruments.
Admissibility of result, §8-50.3.
Radar use.
Admissibility of results, §8-50.2.
Speed-measuring instrument.
Admissibility of result, §8-50.2.
Speed-measuring instruments.
Admissibility of result.
Photographic speed-measuring instruments, §8-50.3.
Motor vehicles commissioner.
Certified copies of documents issued by, §20-42, (b).
Proceedings before, §20-279.2.
Motor vehicle size, weight and loads.
Registered or declared weight.
Prima facie evidence, §20-26, (b1).

EVIDENCE —Cont'd
Municipal corporations.
Compelling the production of evidence.
Powers of council, §160A-80, (a).
Ordinances, §160A-79.
Negligence.
Liability insurance.
Admissibility, §8C-1, Rule 411.
Subsequent remedial measures.
Admissibility, §8C-1, Rule 407.
Negotiable instruments.
Dishonor.
Evidence of dishonor, §25-3-505.
Negotiations.
Mediated settlement conferences, §7A-38.1, (l).
Newly discovered evidence.
New trial.
Grounds, §1A-1, Rule 59, (a).
Relief from judgment or order, §1A-1, Rule 60, (b).
Nonprofit corporations.
Articles of incorporation, §55A-2-03, (b).
Certificates of existence or authorization.
Conclusive evidence of existence or authority, §55A-1-28, (c).
Nuisances.
Abatement.
Offenses against public morals, §19-3, (b), (c).
Nurses.
Privileged communications, §8-53.13.
Nursing homes.
Temporary management.
Hearing on petition for appointment of temporary manager, §131E-233, (b).
Objections, §§1A-1, Rule 46, (a), (b), 8C-1, Rule 103, (a).
Admissibility of evidence, §1A-1, Rule 46, (a).
Matters other than admissibility of evidence, §1A-1, Rule 46, (b).
Obscenity.
Literature and exhibitions.
Dissemination of obscene material, §14-190.1, (d).
Obstructing justice.
Altering, destroying or stealing evidence of criminal conduct, §14-221.1.
Offer of judgment.
Withdrawn offer, §1A-1, Rule 68, (a).
Offer of proof, §8C-1, Rule 103, (a), (b).
Offer to compromise, §8C-1, Rule 408.
Oil pollution and hazardous substances control.
Offshore oil and gas activities.
Removal of prohibited discharges.
Actions taken not to be construed as admission of liability for discharge, §143-215.94EE, (d).
Onslow county grants, copies of, §8-12.
Open container law.
Alcohol screening test, §20-138.7, (d).
Odor on driver's breath as determining whether alcohol remains in driver's body, §20-138.7, (c).
Options.
Failing to return rented property on which there is purchase option.
Intent to commit crime.
Presumptions from evidence, §14-168.4, (b).
Optometrists.
Privileged communications, §8-53.9.
Rules and regulations.
Certified copies, §90-124.

EVIDENCE —Cont'd
Ordinances.
Certified under seal by city clerk, §160A-79, (b).
Code of ordinances, §160A-79, (b).
Map book.
Copies, §160A-79, (b).
Proving city ordinances, §160A-79, (c).
Uniform law, §160A-79, (e).
Town ordinances certified.
Prima facie evidence of existence of ordinance, §8-5.
Osteopaths.
Records of board, §90-130.
Other crimes, wrongs or acts, §8C-1, Rule 404, (b).
Parking violations.
Prima facie rule of evidence, §20-162.1.
Parol evidence.
Documentary evidence.
Identifying land described by parol evidence, §8-39.
Leases.
Recovery for use and occupation, §42-4.
Leases, UCC, §25-2A-202.
Sale of goods, UCC.
Contracts, §25-2-202.
Statute of frauds, §§22-1 to 22-4.
See STATUTE OF FRAUDS.
Partition.
Duplin county.
Records of partition in Duplin, §8-24.
Partition sales.
Order confirming sale.
Evidence required of purchasers, §46-28.1, (c).
Revocation of confirmation order.
Proof required of purchaser, §46-28.1, (c).
Partnerships.
Admission of partner, §59-41.
Continuation of partnership beyond fixed term.
Continuation of business as prima facie evidence, §59-53, (b).
Paternity actions.
Action brought more than three years after birth of child.
Required evidence, §49-14, (d).
Blood or genetic marker tests, §49-14, (d).
Invoices for services rendered, §49-14, (g).
Proof of paternity beyond reasonable doubt, §49-14, (b).
Temporary order of child support.
Clear, cogent and convincing evidence, §49-14, (f).
Perpetuation of testimony.
Deposition before action, §1A-1, Rule 27, (a).
Deposition pending appeal, §1A-1, Rule 27, (b).
Perpetuation by action, §1A-1, Rule 27, (c).
Personal knowledge, §8C-1, Rule 602.
Personal property.
Impoundment, §15-11.1.
Return to victim as soon as possible, §15A-825.
Photographic speed-measuring instruments.
Results of use.
Admissibility as evidence, §8-50.3, (a), (b).
Judicial notice, §8-50.3, (d).
Testing accuracy of instruments, §8-50.3, (c).
Photography and photostating.
Admissibility of other evidence of contents, §8C-1, Rule 1004.
Admissible photographic reproductions, §8-45.1, (a).
Destruction of originals, §8-45.1, (a).

EVIDENCE —Cont'd
Photography and photostating —Cont'd
Admissible photographic reproductions —Cont'd
Records stored on permanent, computer-readable media, §8-45.1, (b).
Citation of act, §8-45.4.
Construction and interpretation.
Uniformity of interpretation, §8-45.2.
Definitions, §8C-1, Rule 1001.
Department of revenue.
Reproductions of records, §8-45.3, (a).
Records stored on computer readable media, §8-45.3, (b).
Destruction of originals, §8-45.1, (a).
Duplicates.
Admissibility, §8C-1, Rule 1003.
Employment security commission.
Reproduction of records, §8-45.3, (a1).
Records stored on computer readable media, §8-45.3, (b).
Functions of court and jury, §8C-1, Rule 1008.
Original.
Requirement, §8C-1, Rule 1002.
Revenue department.
Reproduction of records, §8-45.3, (a).
Records stored on computer readable media, §8-45.3, (b).
Substantive or illustrative evidence, §8-97.
Summaries, §8C-1, Rule 1006.
Testimony or written admission of party, §8C-1, Rule 1007.
Title of article, §8-45.4.
Physicians and surgeons.
Charges.
Evidence of furnishing or offering or promising to pay.
Inadmissible to prove liability for injuring, §8C-1, Rule 409.
Injured party as witness when medical charges at issue.
Competency to give evidence regarding amount, §8-58.1.
Reasonableness of amount of charges.
Testimony of injured party.
Rebuttable presumption established, §8-58.1.
Communications between physician and patient.
Confidentiality of information, §8-53.
Alimony and divorce actions, §8-53.6.
Waiver of privilege in child abuse cases, §8-53.1.
Hearings before board, §90-14.6, (a) to (c).
Records of board.
Transcript, §90-16.
Treatment of patient who has not consented to public disclosure.
Receipt of evidence concerning, §90-16.
Plats.
Copies of plats.
Certification by secretary of state or state archivist, §8-6.
Pleas.
Inadmissibility of pleas, plea discussions and related statements, §8C-1, Rule 410.
Poultry and poultry products.
Inspections.
Receiving evidence, §106-549.68, (b).
Powers of attorney.
Registered instruments as evidence.
Certified copies of registered instruments, §8-18.

EVIDENCE —Cont'd
Preliminary questions, §8C-1, Rule 104.
Admissibility, §8C-1, Rule 104, (a).
Relevancy.
Conditions on fact, §8C-1, Rule 104, (b).
Presumption of death.
Specific peril exposure, §28C-1, (b).
Presumptions.
See PRESUMPTIONS.
Prima facie evidence.
Bad checks, §14-107.1.
Baggage or property lost, damaged or destroyed by innkeeper's negligence.
Proof of loss, §72-2.
Child care facility existence, §110-98.1.
Conveyances reciting destroyed court records.
Prima facie evidence of records, §98-17.
Devisavit vel non.
Affidavit of witness to will, §31-35.
Elections.
Challenge to voter.
Voter no longer living in precinct, §163-85, (e).
Fraternal benefit society license.
Copy or duplicate, §58-24-130.
Motor carriers embezzlement of COD shipments, §62-273.
Motor vehicle operated so as to increase potential speed, §20-141.2.
Parking violations, §20-162.1.
Surety, indorser or guarantor notifying creditor to take action, §26-8, (c).
Unclaimed property act.
Record of issuance of check, draft or similar instrument, §116B-58.
Watercraft titling, ownership, §75A-49.
Year 2000 liability.
Performance with due diligence, §66-297, (c).
Printed statutes.
Admission into evidence, §8-1.
Prior crimes, wrongs or acts, §8C-1, Rule 404, (b).
Prior statements of witness, §8C-1, Rule 613.
Prisoners of war.
Report or record that person is beleaguered, besieged or captured by enemy.
Prima facie evidence, §8-37.2.
Prisons and prisoners.
Compensation to persons erroneously convicted of felonies, §148-84.
Habeas corpus ad testificandum, §§17-41 to 17-46.
See HABEAS CORPUS AD TESTIFICANDUM.
Private protective services.
License suspension or revocation.
Prima facie evidence, §74C-12, (a).
Privileges.
General rule, §8C-1, Rule 501.
Proof of official records.
Copies, authentication, §1A-1, Rule 44, (a).
Lack of record, §1A-1, Rule 44, (b).
Other proof, §1A-1, Rule 44, (c).
Prostitution.
Reputation and prior conviction admissible as evidence, §14-206.
Psychologist-patient privilege.
Disclosure of information, §8-53.3.
Alimony and divorce actions, §8-53.6.
Psychotherapy patient/client sexual exploitation act.
Sexual history.
Admissibility of evidence, §90-21.45, (a), (b).
Reputation or opinion evidence, §90-21.45, (c).

EVIDENCE —Cont'd
Public lands.
Record of surveys, §146-42.
Public utility accident reports.
Not admissible in evidence, §62-41.
Public utility rate schedules, §62-143.
Punitive damages.
Bifurcated trial, §1D-30.
Radar, §8-50.2.
Rape shield law, §8C-1, Rule 412.
Real property.
Identifying land described.
Parol evidence to identify, §8-39.
Record chain of title, §1-42.
Rebuttal.
Deposition evidence, §1A-1, Rule 32, (c).
Records.
Administration of decedents' estates.
Record of administration.
Authenticated copy of record, §8-36.
Admissibility of other evidence of contents, §8C-1, Rule 1004.
Admission of remainder of or related writings or recorded instruments, §8C-1, Rule 106.
Anson county.
Deeds and wills in Anson, §8-26.
Bladen county.
Records in Bladen.
Copies of lost records, §8-33.
Brunswick county.
Wills in Brunswick, §8-27.
Criminal index of clerk of superior court.
Records admissible in certain cases, §8-35.2.
Death of federal officers and employees.
Certified record deemed signed and issued pursuant to law, §8-37.3.
Authority to certify evidence, §8-37.3.
Prima facie evidence that person is dead, §8-37.2.
Deeds and records thereof lost.
Presumed to be in due form, §8-21.
Definitions, §8C-1, Rule 1001.
Duplicates.
Admissibility, §8C-1, Rule 1003.
Duplin county.
Partition of real estate in Duplin, §8-24.
Wills in Duplin, §8-25.
Functions of court and jury, §8C-1, Rule 1008.
Grants and abstracts.
Certified copies of grants and abstracts to be recorded, §8-8.
Internment in neutral country.
Certified record deemed signed and issued pursuant to law, §8-37.3.
Authority to certify evidence, §8-37.3.
Prima facie evidence that person is interned, §8-37.2.
Lost instruments and records.
See LOST INSTRUMENTS AND RECORDS.
Medical records.
Copies of medical records as documentary evidence, §8-44.1.
Missing in action.
Prima facie evidence that person is missing in action, §8-37.2.
Missing persons.
Certified record deemed signed and issued pursuant to law, §8-37.3.
Authority to certify evidence, §8-37.3.
Prima facie evidence that person is missing, §8-37.2.

EVIDENCE —Cont'd
Records —Cont'd
Motor vehicles.
Driving under the influence.
Convictions.
Admissibility of records of division as prima facie evidence, §8-35.1.
Ownership.
Certificate of commissioner as to ownership, §8-37.
Original.
Requirement of original, §8C-1, Rule 1002.
Prisoners of war.
Certified record deemed signed and issued pursuant to law, §8-37.3.
Authority to certify evidence, §8-37.3.
Prima facie evidence that person is beleaguered, besieged or captured by enemy, §8-37.2.
Proof of official record.
Authentication of copy, §1A-1, Rule 44, (a).
Generally, §1A-1, Rule 44, (c).
Proof of lack of record, §1A-1, Rule 44, (b).
Public records, §8C-1, Rule 1005.
Reproduction of county records.
Admissibility in evidence, §153A-436, (e).
Summaries, §8C-1, Rule 1006.
Superior courts.
Clerks of court.
Criminal index.
Records admissible in certain cases, §8-35.2.
Testimony or written admission of party, §8C-1, Rule 1007.
Tyrrell county.
Copies of records from Tyrrell, §8-23.
Refreshing memory.
Writing or object used, §8C-1, Rule 612.
Relevancy.
Conditions on fact, §8C-1, Rule 104, (b).
Habits of a person, §8C-1, Rule 406.
Irrelevant evidence.
Inadmissible, §8C-1, Rule 402.
Relevant evidence.
Admissibility, §8C-1, Rule 402.
Defined, §8C-1, Rule 401.
Exclusion.
Prejudice, confusion or waste of time, §8C-1, Rule 403.
Routine practice.
Organizations, §8C-1, Rule 406.
Sexual behavior, §8C-1, Rule 412.
Subsequent remedial measures, §8C-1, Rule 407.
Religious beliefs or opinions, §8C-1, Rule 610.
Reports.
Death of federal officers and employees.
Certified report deemed signed and issued pursuant to law, §8-37.3.
Authority to certify evidence, §8-37.3.
Finding of presumed death, §8-37.1, (a), (b).
Authority to certify evidence, §8-37.3.
Deemed signed and issued pursuant to law, §8-37.3.
Prima facie evidence that person is dead, §8-37.2.
Internment in neutral country.
Certified report deemed signed and issued pursuant to law, §8-37.3.
Authority to certify evidence, §8-37.3.
Prima facie evidence that person is interned, §8-37.2.

EVIDENCE —Cont'd
Reports —Cont'd
Missing in action.
Prima facie evidence that person is missing in action, §8-37.2.
Missing persons.
Certified report deemed signed and issued pursuant to law, §8-37.3.
Prima facie evidence that person is missing, §8-37.2.
Prisoners of war.
Certified report deemed signed and issued pursuant to law, §8-37.3.
Authority to certify evidence, §8-37.3.
Prima facie evidence that person is beleaguered, besieged or captured by enemy, §8-37.2.
Required evidence in prosecutions under article, §14-27.10.
Retail installment sales.
Unconscionability, §25A-43, (b).
Richmond county tax deeds, §8-22.1.
Riots and civil disorders.
Command to disperse.
Failure to disperse when commanded.
Prima facie evidence, §14-288.5, (c).
Remaining at scene after command to disperse, §14-288.2, (c).
Routine practice of organization.
Relevant to prove conformity with routine practice, §8C-1, Rule 406.
Rule of completeness, §8C-1, Rule 106.
Rules review commission.
Failure of commission to object to rule, §143B-30.4.
Rulings on evidence, §1A-1, Rule 46, (a), (b).
Erroneous rulings.
Effect, §8C-1, Rule 103, (a).
Review where justice requires, §8C-1, Rule 103, (d).
Hearing of jury, §8C-1, Rule 103, (c).
Objections, §8C-1, Rule 103, (a).
Offer of proof, §8C-1, Rule 103, (a).
Record, §8C-1, Rule 103, (b).
Record, §8C-1, Rule 103, (b).
Safety belts.
Failure to wear, §20-135.2A, (d).
Sale of evidence.
Proceeds.
Use for public school fund, §15-15.
Sale of goods, UCC.
Extrinsic evidence, §25-2-202.
Parol evidence, §25-2-202.
Preserving evidence of goods in dispute, §25-2-515.
Remedies.
Market quotations.
Admissibility, §25-2-724.
Price.
Proof of market price, §25-2-723.
Savings and loan associations.
Certificate of incorporation, §54B-14, (d).
Compliance review documents, §54B-63.1, (b).
Records.
Reproductions, §54B-55, (e).
School buses.
Operating a school bus, school activity bus, or child care vehicle after consuming alcohol.
Odor of alcohol, §20-138.2B, (b1).
School counselor-student privilege, §§8-53.4, 115C-401.
Scope of evidence rules, §8C-1, Rule 101.

EVIDENCE —Cont'd
Searches and seizures.
Item subject to seizure under search warrant, §15A-242.
Seat belts.
Failure to wear, §20-135.2A, (d).
Secret listening.
Conference between prisoner and his attorney.
Admissibility as evidence, §14-227.1, (b).
Seized property, §15-11.1.
Self-incrimination.
See SELF-INCRIMINATION.
Sentencing hearings.
Rules of evidence, inapplicability, §§8C-1, Rule 1101, (b), 15A-1334, (b).
Seven years possession under color of title, §1-38, (b).
Sexual offenses.
Rape shield law, §8C-1, Rule 412.
Records of in camera hearings.
Inspection, §8C-1, Rule 412, (e).
Required evidence and prosecutions of article, §14-27.10.
Sexual behavior.
Defined, §8C-1, Rule 412, (a).
Introduction of evidence, §8C-1, Rule 412, (d).
Not proved by reputation or opinion, §8C-1, Rule 412, (c).
Relevancy, §8C-1, Rule 412, (b).
Shop-book rule, §§8-42 to 8-44.
Shoplifting, §14-72.1, (a).
Short title.
Rules of evidence, §8C-1, Rule 1102.
Small claims actions.
Rules of evidence generally observed, §7A-222.
Social workers.
Privileged communications, §8-53.7.
Solid waste management.
Hazardous waste.
Felonies.
Circumstantial evidence concerning defendant's possession actual knowledge, §130A-26.1, (c).
Speed-measuring instruments.
Results of use.
Admissibility as evidence, §8-50.2, (a), (b).
Judicial notice taken of use of certain models and types, §8-50.2, (d).
Photographic speed-measuring instruments, §8-50.3.
Testing accuracy of instruments, §8-50.2, (c).
State child fatality review team findings and records.
Inadmissible, §143B-150.20, (b), (f).
State departments and agencies.
Rules review commission.
Failure of commission to object to rules, §143B-30.4.
States.
Deeds from other states.
Certified copies of deeds, §8-32.
Laws of other states.
Admission into evidence, §8-3, (a).
Exhibition of copy of law from printed volume, §8-3, (b).
Judicial notice of laws, §8-4.
Wills from other states.
Certified copies of wills, §8-32.
Statutes.
Foreign countries.
Laws of foreign countries, §8-3.

EVIDENCE —Cont'd
Statutes —Cont'd
Printed statutes.
Admission into evidence, §8-1.
States.
Laws of other states, §§8-3, 8-4.
Stolen property.
Return to victim as soon as possible, §15A-825.
Subdivisions.
Control corners.
Use of corners to fix distances and boundaries, prima facie evidence of correct method, §39-32.4.
Subdivisions of rules of evidence, §8C-1, Rule 102, (b).
Subpoenas.
Documentary evidence.
Production of documentary evidence, §§1A-1, Rule 45, (c), 8-61.
Subsequent remedial measures, §8C-1, Rule 407.
Substantive evidence.
Photographs as substantive or illustrative evidence, §8-97.
Summons.
Issuance.
Date.
Prima facie evidence, §1A-1, Rule 4, (a).
Superior courts.
Custody and disposition, Super. Ct. Rule 14.
Suppression of evidence.
Motion to suppress evidence, §§15A-971 to 15A-980.
Surveys and surveyors.
Certificates of survey.
Copies of certificates.
Certification by secretary of state or state archivist, §8-6.
Contiguous tracts of land.
Common survey of contiguous tracts as evidence, §8-19.
Tennessee.
Certified copies of certain surveys and maps obtained from state of Tennessee, §8-15.
Tax deeds.
Haywood county.
Recitals in tax deeds in Haywood, §8-22.
Henderson county.
Recitals in tax deeds in Henderson, §8-22.
Richmond county, §8-22.1.
Tennessee.
Surveys and maps obtained from state of Tennessee.
Certified copies of certain surveys and maps, §8-15.
Testimony.
By accused, §8C-1, Rule 104, (d).
Expert witnesses.
See EXPERT WITNESSES.
Time.
Proof of dates.
Clark's calendar may be used, §8-48, (a).
Torrens system registration.
Decree.
Conclusive evidence that person or corporation is owner of land, §43-12.
Powers of examiner to take and call for evidence, §43-11, (d).
Town ordinances.
Certification of ordinances.
Prima facie evidence of existence of ordinance, §8-5.

EVIDENCE —Cont'd
Trademarks.
Registration.
Certificate of registration, §80-4.
Timber marks.
Evidence of ownership, §80-19.
Trees and timber.
Trademark on timber evidence of ownership, §80-19.
Trespass.
Marketable title.
Actions for recovery of real property.
Quieting title, etc.
Prima facie evidence of title ownership, §47B-2, (d).
Prima facie evidence of title ownership, §47B-2, (d).
Tyrrell county.
Records from Tyrrell.
Copies of records, §8-23.
Undue influence.
Statements, releases, etc., obtained from persons in shock or under the influence of drugs.
Presumption of fraud, §8-45.5.
United States.
Laws of United States.
Judicial notice of laws, §8-4.
University of North Carolina.
Mediation of personnel matters.
Inadmissible, §116-3.3, (a).
Usage of trade, §25-1-205.
Utilities commission hearings.
Affidavits, §62-68.
Depositions, §62-66.
Rules of evidence, §62-65, (a).
Vacation rentals.
Expedited evictions, §42A-24, (c).
Veterans' guardianship act.
Certificate as evidence in regard to guardianship of mentally incompetent wards, §34-7.
Certificate of director.
Prima facie evidence of necessity for appointment of guardian, §34-6.
Victim's character.
Evidence of pertinent trait, §8C-1, Rule 404, (a).
Victims, impact of crime, §15A-833.
Victims of crime.
Return of stolen or personal property, §15A-825.
Videotape.
Substantive or illustrative evidence, §8-97.
Violent habitual felons.
Prior convictions, §14-7.10.
Vital statistics.
Marriage certificates.
Copies as evidence, §130A-110, (b).
Water and air resources.
Criminal penalties.
Enforcement procedures.
Use of circumstantial evidence, §143-215.6B, (c).
Judicial notice.
Commission.
Judicial notice of official studies, reports and statistical data.
Authority as to, §143-215.4, (d).
Weights and measures.
Official certificate as prima facie evidence, §25-1-202.
Regular use of devices.
Presumptive evidence, §81A-31.

EVIDENCE —Cont'd
Wills.
Affidavit of witnesses as evidence, §31-35.
Anson county.
Records of wills in Anson, §8-26.
Brunswick county.
Records of wills in Brunswick, §8-27.
Copies of wills, §8-28.
From other states, §8-32.
Lost wills, §98-5.
Proved and lost before recorded, §8-31.
Recording of wills.
Proved and lost before recorded, §8-31.
Wrong county, §8-30.
Secretary of state's office to contain copies, §8-29.
Counties.
Copies of wills recorded in wrong county, §8-30.
Duplin county.
Records, §8-25.
Lost wills.
Copy of lost will, §98-5.
Recording of wills.
Lost before recorded.
Copy of will proved and lost before recorded, §8-31.
Wrong county.
Copies of wills recorded in wrong county, §8-30.
Witnesses.
Character and conduct of witnesses, §8C-1, Rules 404, (a), 608.
Competency of witnesses.
See WITNESSES.
Expert witnesses.
See EXPERT WITNESSES.
General provisions, §§8-49 to 8-64.
See WITNESSES.
Proof of single material fact.
No more than two witnesses may be subpoenaed, §6-60.
Wills.
Affidavit of witness as evidence, §31-35.
Workers' compensation.
Electronically transmitted or recorded documents, §97-92, (f).
Work first program.
Mismanagement of assistance, appointment of personal representative.
Use of evidence in other proceedings prohibited, §108A-37, (d).
Writings.
Admissibility of other evidence of contents, §8C-1, Rule 1004.
Definitions, §8C-1, Rule 1001.
Documentary evidence. See within this heading, "Documentary evidence."
Duplicates.
Admissibility, §8C-1, Rule 1003.
Functions of court and jury, §8C-1, Rule 1008.
Original.
Requirement of original, §8C-1, Rule 1002.
Probate of wills.
Proof and examination in writing, §31-17.
Summaries, §8C-1, Rule 1006.
Testimony or written admission of party, §8C-1, Rule 1007.
Wrongful death.
Dying declarations.
Admissibility, §28A-18-2, (c).

EVIDENCE —Cont'd
X rays.
Photographs as substantive or illustrative evidence, §8-97.
Year 2000 liability.
Performance with due diligence.
Prima facie evidence, §66-297, (c).

EXAMINATION QUESTION TAMPERING, §14-401.1.

EXAMINATIONS.
Accountants.
Powers and duties of board as to, §93-12.
Qualifications of applicants, §93-12.
New requirements.
Effect, §93-12.1.
Alarm systems licensing.
Oral or written examinations.
Board may require, §74D-2, (e).
Anatomical gifts.
Gift authorizes examinations, §130A-404, (e).
Animal waste management system operators, §90A-47.3, (b).
Architects.
Licensing by examination, §83A-7, (a).
Qualification requirements, §83A-7, (a).
Bail bondsmen and runners.
Commissioner of insurance, §58-71-170.
Educational requirements for taking, §58-71-71, (a).
Licenses, §58-71-70.
Fees, §58-71-70.
Bank examiners, §§53-117 to 53-123.
See BANK EXAMINERS.
Barbers.
Applications, §86A-8.
Apprenticeship, §86A-24, (a).
Retaking.
Requirement, §86A-24, (c).
Fees, §86A-25.
Payment required, §86A-8.
Frequency, §86A-9.
Instructors, §86A-23, (a).
Applications for, §86A-23, (b).
Qualifications for certificate of registration, §86A-3.
Times and places, §86A-9.
Blind persons.
Eye examinations.
Aid to the blind.
Application for aid, §111-14.
Arranging for examination of eyes, §111-8.
Medical and surgical treatment, §111-8.
Bonds, surety.
Annual examination of official bonds, §58-72-20.
Budget.
Agencies and officers, §143-3.
Surveys, studies and examinations of departments and institutions, §143-22.
Cosmetic art.
Licensure, §88B-18.
Fees, §88B-20, (a).
Credit unions.
Administrator of credit unions.
Duties, §54-109.11.
Annual examinations required, §54-109.16.
Costs.
Payment, §54-109.16.
Fees, §54-109.14, (a).
Decedents' estates.
Persons or corporations believed to have possession of property of decedent, §28A-15-12.

EXAMINATIONS —Cont'd
Dental hygienists.
Credentials, license by, §90-224.1, (a), (c), (d).
Fee, §90-232.
Notification of successful candidates.
Board to determine method and time, §90-225, (b).
Power of board to conduct examinations, §90-223, (a).
Rules and regulations of board as to, §90-224, (b).
Dentists.
Licenses, §90-30, (a).
Discovery methods, §1A-1, Rule 26, (a).
Electrologists.
Certification of electrology instructors, §88A-17, (b).
Failure to renew certificate, §88A-18.
Licenses, §88A-10, (b).
Without examination, §88A-11.
Emergency medical services.
Credentialing requirements, §131E-159, (a).
Waiver of examination, §131E-159, (c), (d).
Engineers, §89C-15.
Power of board, §89C-10, (d).
Reexamination, §89C-14, (e).
Requirements for licensure generally, §89C-13.
Scope, §89C-15, (b).
Time and place, §89C-15, (a).
Executors and administrators.
Persons or corporations believed to have possession of property of decedent, §28A-15-12, (a).
Food, drugs and cosmetics.
Conduct of examinations, §106-141, (b).
Foresters.
Fees, §89B-12.
Registration, §89B-12.
Fraternal benefit societies, §58-24-135, (a).
Agents, §58-24-160, (a).
Geologists, §89E-10.
Confidentiality of results, §89E-14, (c).
Qualifications for license, §89E-9.
Health maintenance organizations.
Powers of commissioner, §58-67-100, (a).
Report in lieu of, §58-67-100, (d).
Hearing aid dealers and fitters, §93D-8, (a).
Scope, §93D-8, (a).
Successfully passing examination required, §93D-5, (b).
Home inspectors.
Failure of examination.
Subsequent application.
Additional application fee not required, §143-151.57, (b).
Knowledge gained through experience to be emphasized, §143-151.49, (b).
Passing examination required, §143-151.51.
Associate home inspectors, §143-151.52.
Husband and wife.
Conveyances.
Certain conveyances not affected by fraud if acknowledgment or privy examination regular, §39-11.
Insurance commissioner generally.
See INSURANCE COMMISSIONER.
Laboratories.
State laboratory of public health, §130A-88, (a).
Landscape contractors.
Certificates of registration, §89D-5, (b).
Exemptions, §§89D-8, 89D-9.

EXAMINATIONS —Cont'd
Marriage and family therapists.
Failure.
Subsequent examination, §90-270.55.
Frequency, §90-270.55.
Licensing requirement, §90-270.54.
Scope, §90-270.55.
Married women.
Certificate of wife's "previous" examination, §47-66.
Repeal of laws requiring private examination, §47-14.1.
Massage and bodywork therapy.
Licensure, §90-629.
Medical examiners.
Postmortem medicolegal examinations and services, §§130A-377 to 130A-394.
See MEDICAL EXAMINERS.
Mental health, developmental disabilities and substance abuse.
Involuntary commitment, §122C-263.
Mobile homes and trailer park licenses, §143-143.24.
Nurses.
Follow-up assistance.
Nursing licensing exam follow-up assistance, §90-171.52.
Frequency, §90-171.30.
Generally, §90-171.30.
Licensure by examination, §90-171.30.
Notice, §90-171.30.
Qualifications of applicant, §90-171.29.
Reexamination, §90-171.31.
Occupational licensing board.
Disclosure of questions or answers.
Restrictions, §93B-8, (d).
Failure to pass.
Review of examination, §93B-8, (c).
Identification of applicants by number only, §93B-8, (b).
Written examinations, §93B-8, (a).
Occupational therapists.
Applications, §90-270.71, (a).
Contents, §90-270.71, (b).
Fees, §90-270.77.
Scores.
Obtaining by applicant, §90-270.71, (d).
Time and place, §90-270.71, (c).
Waiver of requirements, §90-270.72, (a).
Reciprocity, §90-270.72, (b).
Opticians.
Fee, §90-246.
Frequency, §90-240, (c).
National examinations.
Board may include, §90-240, (e).
Notice, §90-240, (c).
Qualifications for taking examination, §90-240, (a).
Scope, §90-240, (b).
Scores.
Applicant may receive upon request, §90-240, (d).
Waiver of examination requirements, §90-241, (a), (b).
Application, §90-241, (c).
Physical and mental examination of persons, §1A-1, Rule 26, (a).
Order for examination, §1A-1, Rule 35, (a).
Report of examining physician, §1A-1, Rule 35, (b).

EXAMINATIONS —Cont'd
Physician and surgeon licenses, §90-9.
Licensure without examination, §§90-10, 90-13.
Rules and regulations governing, §90-6, (a).
Podiatrists.
Clinical residency requirements, §90-202.5, (a).
Failure to pass.
Reexamination, §90-202.6, (c).
Fee, §§90-202.5, (a), 90-202.9.
Reexamination, §90-202.6, (c).
Frequency, §90-202.6, (a).
Postgraduate clinical program requirements, §90-202.5, (a).
Qualifications of applicants, §90-202.5, (a).
Reexamination, §90-202.6, (c).
Scope, §90-202.6, (a).
Waiver of examination, §90-202.6, (b).
Postmortem medicolegal examinations and services, §§130A-377 to 130A-394.
See MEDICAL EXAMINERS.
Provider sponsored organizations, §131E-296.
Racketeer influenced and corrupt organizations.
False testimony, §75D-7.
Power to compel examination, §75D-6.
Real estate brokers and salespersons.
Licenses, §93A-4, (b).
Records.
Public records, §132-6.
Refrigeration contractors, §87-58, (d).
Fees, §87-64.
Licenses granted without examination, §87-58, (f).
Retirement system for teachers and state employees.
Consolidated judicial retirement act.
Disability retirement benefits.
Medical examination required, §135-60, (b).
Sales and use tax.
Examination of records, §§105-164.30, 105-164.31.
Savings and loan associations.
See SAVINGS AND LOAN ASSOCIATIONS.
Savings banks.
Administrator of savings institution division, §54C-54, (a).
Confidentiality of information, §54C-60.
Costs.
Extended audit, examination or reevaluation, §54C-56, (b).
Payment when person not employed by administrator's office appointed to make, §54C-55, (c).
Extended audit, examination or reevaluation, §54C-56, (a).
Payment of expenses, §54C-56, (b).
Fees, §54C-55, (a), (b).
Powers in connection with examinations.
Misdemeanors, §54C-54, (c), (d).
Report, §54C-54, (a), (b).
Service corporations, §54C-144, (c).
Soil scientists.
Licenses, §89F-11.
Passing examination as qualification, §89F-10, (a).
Speech and language pathologists and audiologists, §§90-295, 90-296.
American Speech and Hearing Association.
Certificate of clinical competence.
Examination not required of person who holds certificate, §90-296, (c).
Fee, §90-305.
Frequency, §90-296, (b).

EXAMINATIONS —Cont'd
Speech and language pathologists and audiologists —Cont'd
Required, §90-296, (a).
Exceptions, §90-296, (c).
State departments and agencies.
Special investigations, §143-158.
Conduct, §143-160.
Stenographic record of proceedings, §143-161.
Subjects, §143-159.
Statewide testing program, §§115C-174.10 to 115C-174.14.
See PUBLIC SCHOOLS.
Structural pest control.
Applicants for certified applicator's identification card, §106-65.27.
Substance abuse professionals, §90-113.41.
Applications, §90-113.41, (a).
Criteria for examinations, §90-113.41, (b).
Obtaining and reviewing scores, §90-113.41, (d).
Time and place, §90-113.41, (c).
Tampering with examination questions a misdemeanor, §14-401.1.
Teachers.
Certification requirements, §115C-296, (a), (a1).
Torrens system registration.
Title, §43-11, (d).
Trust companies.
Conservatorship.
Oversight by commissioner, §53-402.
Foreign offices, §53-326, (a).
Out-of-state institutions, offices, §53-320, (a).
Voluntary dissolution, §53-375.
Unit ownership.
Availability of records for examinations, §47A-20.
Veterinarians.
Applications.
Time for, §90-187.1.
Frequency, §90-187.1.
Licensure without examination, §§90-187, (d), 90-187.3, (a), (b).
Oral or practical examination of person qualifying, §90-187.3, (c).
Notification of results, §90-187.1.
Viatical life insurance settlements.
Conducted in accordance with examination law, §58-58-230, (b).
Examiners and costs of examiners, §58-58-230, (d).
Foreign or alien persons, §58-58-230, (c).
Frequency of examination by commissioner, §58-58-230, (a).
Wastewater treatment plant operators, §90A-39.

EXAMINERS OF BANKS, §§53-117 to 53-123.
See BANK EXAMINERS.

EXCAVATION.
Construction indemnity agreements invalid, §22B-1.
Subcontractors, payments to, §§22C-1 to 22C-6.
Underground damage prevention, §§87-100 to 87-114.
See UNDERGROUND DAMAGE PREVENTION.

EXCEPTIONAL CHILDREN.
Council on educational services for exceptional children, §115C-121.
Special education.
See SPECIAL EDUCATION.

EXCEPTIONS FOR INSUFFICIENCY, §1A-1, Rule 7, (c).

EXCEPTIONS TO DECISIONS OF COURT, §1-186.

EXCEPTIONS TO RULINGS ON EVIDENCE, §1A-1, Rule 46, (a), (b).

EXCISE STAMP TAX ON CONVEYANCES, §§105-228.28 to 105-228.37.
Actions.
Taxes recoverable by action, §105-228.33.
Administrative provisions.
Applicability, §105-228.35.
Applicability of provisions, §§105-228.28, 105-228.35.
Collection of tax before instrument recorded, §105-228.32.
Consideration not due or paid, exempted transfer, §105-228.29.
County registers of deeds.
Remittance of net proceeds to county finance officer, §105-228.30, (b).
Exempted transfers, §105-228.29.
Failure to pay tax.
Recovery of tax by action, §105-228.33.
Willful failure.
Penalty, §105-228.34.
Forgery.
Reproduction of tax stamps, §105-228.36.
Gift, transfer by exempted, §105-228.29.
Imposition of tax, §105-228.30, (a).
Intestacy, transfer by exempted, §105-228.29.
Issuance of tax stamp, §105-228.31.
Lease for term of years, exempted transfer, §105-228.29.
Marking instrument indicating tax paid.
Before recording of instrument, §105-228.32.
Merger, conversion, consolidation, exempted transfer, §105-228.29.
Operation of law, transfers by, exemption, §105-228.29.
Payment of tax.
County finance officer.
Who to pay, §105-228.30, (b).
Recovery of tax by action, §105-228.33.
Who to pay, §105-228.30, (b).
Willful failure to pay.
Penalty, §105-228.34.
Penalties.
Willful failure to pay tax, §105-228.34.
Rate of tax, §105-228.30, (a).
Recovery of unpaid taxes by action, §105-228.33.
Refunds for overpayment of tax.
Hearing by county, §105-228.37, (b).
Interest, §105-228.37, (f).
Judicial review, §105-228.37, (d).
Recording correct deed, §105-228.37, (e).
Request for refund, §105-228.37, (a).
Review by Secretary, §105-228.37, (c).
Remittance of net proceeds, §105-228.30, (b).
Report of amount of tax due.
Presentation for registration, §105-228.32.
Securing indebtedness, instrument exempted, §105-228.29.
Stamps, §105-228.31.
Forgery, §105-228.36.
Issuance, §105-228.31.
Reproduction.
Prohibited, §105-228.36.
Wills, transfers by, exempted, §105-228.29.

EXCISE TAXES.
Dry-cleaning solvent tax, §§105-187.30 to 105-187.34.

EXCISE TAXES —Cont'd
Piped natural gas tax, §§105-187.40 to 105-187.46.
See PIPED NATURAL GAS TAX.

EXCITED UTTERANCE, §8C-1, Rule 803.

EXCLUDED EVIDENCE OR TESTIMONY RECORD, §1A-1, Rule 43, (c).

EXCLUSIONARY RULE.
Motion to suppress evidence, §§15A-971 to 15A-980.

EXCLUSION OF WITNESSES, §8C-1, Rule 615.

EXCLUSIVE OUTLETS.
Alcoholic beverage manufacturers, bottlers or wholesalers.
Acquiring prohibited, §18B-1116.

EXCUSABLE NEGLECT.
Enlargement of time, §§1-593, 1A-1, Rule 6, (b).
Relief from judgment or order, §1A-1, Rule 60, (b).
Small claims actions.
Setting aside order or judgment, §7A-228, (a).

EXECUTION OF POWER OF APPOINTMENT BY WILL, §31-4.

EXECUTION OF WILLS.
Attestation, §31-3.3.
Compliance required, §31-3.1.
Establishment of due execution, §31-18.1, (b).
Holographic will, §31-3.4.
Noncupative, §31-3.5.
Power of appointment, §31-4.
Revival of revoked will, §31-5.8.
Seal not required, §31-3.6.
Self-proved will, §31-11.6.
Signature of testator, §31-3.3, (b), (c).
Who may make, §31-1.

EXECUTIONS, §§1-302 to 1-368.
Absconders.
Debtor leaving state or concealing self.
Arrest, §1-355.
Against property, §1-303.
Forms, §1-313.
Against the person, §§1-303, 1-311.
Findings of fact required, §1-311.
Form, §1-313.
Indigent defendants.
Appointment of counsel, §1-311.
Contents of execution, §1-313.
Alimony.
Time limitation for enforcing execution not to apply, §1-306.
Alimony, remedies available, §50-16.7, (k).
Appeals.
Costs.
Collection of costs in appellate courts, App. Proc. Rule 35, (d).
Procedure after determination, §1-298.
Arrest.
Debtor leaving state or concealing self, §1-355.
Assets of judgment debtor.
Discovery.
Generally, §1-352.2.
Interrogatories, §1-352.1.
Unsatisfied execution.
Debtor ordered to answer concerning his property, §1-352.
Withholding of property from execution.
Proceedings for application of property, §1-353.

EXECUTIONS —Cont'd
Attorney general.
Execution sales.
Notification of attorney general, §1-339.55.
Attorneys at law, §47-43.1.
Execution against the person.
Indigent defendants.
Appointment of counsel, §1-311.
Bail bond forfeiture.
Final judgment, §15A-544.7, (c), (d).
Bank deposits and collections.
When item subject to legal process, §25-4-303, (a).
Betterments.
Suspension of execution for assessment, §1-340.
Bills of lading.
Lien on goods covered by a negotiable document, §25-7-602.
Blind persons.
Aid to the blind.
Payment of awards.
Exemption from execution, §111-18.
Bona fide purchasers.
Execution against property of judgment debtor not lien on personal property as against, §1-313.
Bonds, surety.
Debtor leaving state or concealing self, §1-355.
Execution sales.
Special proceedings to determine ownership of surplus.
Transfer of proceedings to civil issue docket of superior court, §1-339.71, (c).
Upset bid on real property.
Compliance bond, §1-339.64, (b).
Forthcoming bond for personal property.
Generally, §1-318.
Procedure on giving bond, §1-319.
Subsequent levies, §1-319.
Summary remedy on bond, §1-320.
Staying personal property, §1-290.
Stay in judgment for real property, §1-292.
Stay of execution on money judgment, §1-289, (a).
Cap on amount, noncompensatory damages of $25,000,000 or more awarded, §1-289, (b), (c).
Breaking and entering.
When executing officer may break and enter premises or vehicle, §15A-251.
Child support.
Enforcement of support, §50-13.4, (f).
Choses in action.
Execution sales.
Property liable to sale under execution, §1-315, (a).
Clerks of court.
Directing execution to clerk in counties which office of coroner abolished, §1-313.
Execution sales.
Procedural details.
Authority to fix, §1-339.42.
Issuance.
Duties, §1-305, (a).
Time for, §1-305, (a).
Violations of provisions.
Penalty, §1-305, (a).
When clerk may not issue, §1-305, (b).
Returns.
Entry on judgment docket, §1-321.
Violations of provisions.
Penalty, §1-321.
Subscribed by clerk, §1-303.

EXECUTIONS —Cont'd
Commercial code.
Bank deposits and collections.
When items subject to legal process, §25-4-303, (a).
Documents of title.
Lien on goods covered by a negotiable document, §25-7-602.
Confession of judgment.
Issuance and enforcement, §1A-1, Rule 68.1, (e).
Contempt.
Debtor leaving state or concealing self, §1-355.
Discovery of assets of judgment debtor.
Disobedience of orders of court, §§1-352.1, 1-352.2.
Interrogatories to discover assets.
Disobedience of order of court, §1-352.1.
Orders of court.
Disobedience, §1-368.
Contents, §1-313.
Conveyance directed by judgment.
Stay, §1-291.
Coroners.
Directed to coroner where sheriff is party or interested in action, §1-313.
Corporations.
Agents of corporations.
Duties, §§1-324.2 to 1-324.4.
Penalty for violations, §1-324.5.
Books and records.
Nonresident custodian, §§1-324.6, 1-324.7.
Debts due corporations.
Subject to execution, §1-324.4.
Information as to corporate officers and property.
Duty of agents to furnish, §1-324.2.
Information as to corporate shares.
Duty of agents to furnish, §1-324.3.
Information as to debts due corporation.
Duty of agents to furnish, §1-324.4.
Judgment against corporation.
Property subject to execution, §1-324.1.
Nonresident custodian of corporate books.
Duties, §1-324.7.
Liability, §1-324.7.
Notice to, §1-324.6.
Proceedings, §1-324.6.
Stock and stockholders.
Shares subject to execution, §1-324.3.
Costs.
Issuance of execution for unpaid costs, §6-4.
Livestock.
Cost of keeping.
Officer's account, §1-322.
Crime victims compensation.
Award not subject to, §15B-17, (b).
Criminal law and procedure.
Supplemental proceedings.
Examination of parties and witnesses.
Incriminating answers not to be used in criminal proceedings, §1-357.
Crops.
Execution not to be levied on growing crops until matured, §1-315, (c).
Dating.
When dated, §1-310.
Death of defendant in execution.
Rights against property of defendant, §1-312.
Debtors and creditors.
Debtor leaving state or concealing self.
Bonds, surety, §1-355.

EXECUTIONS —Cont'd
Debtors and creditors —Cont'd
Debtors of judgment debtor.
Execution on property of debtors, §1-360.1.
Receivers.
Actions by receiver against, §1-366.
Satisfaction of execution, §1-359.
Summoning, §1-360.
Rights against property of defendant dying in execution, §1-312.
Decedents' estates.
Defendant dying in execution.
Rights against property of defendant, §1-312.
Defective title.
Remedy of purchaser against defendant, §1-323.
Definitions.
Execution sales, §1-339.41, (a).
Delivery of possession of real or personal property, §1-303.
Form of execution, §1-313.
Discovery.
Assets of judgment debtor.
Generally, §1-352.2.
Interrogatories, §1-352.1.
Docket entry of stay, §1-293.
Dockets.
County to which execution to be issued.
Docketing in as prerequisite to issuance, §1-308.
Returns.
Entry on judgment docket, §1-321.
Documents of title.
Lien on goods covered by a negotiable document, §25-7-602.
Enforcement as of course, §1-306.
Enforcement of judgments by execution, §1-302.
Secreting property to hinder enforcement of lien after judgment, §14-115.
Equity of redemption.
Execution sales.
Sheriff's deed on sale of equity of redemption, §1-317.
Estates.
Execution sales.
Trust estates.
Title of purchaser, §1-316.
Execution sales, §§1-339.41 to 1-339.71.
See EXECUTION SALES.
Executors and administrators.
Action by creditors.
When execution to issue, §28A-18-5.
Defendant dying in execution.
Rights against property of defendant, §1-312.
Form of execution against property in hands of personal representative, §1-313.
Successors in office, §28A-18-7.
Exemptions, §§1C-1601 to 1C-1604; Const. N. C., art. X, §§2 to 4.
Limitation of wage garnishment, §1-362.
Mechanics' and materialmen's liens.
Inapplicability of exemption, Const. N. C., art. X, §3.
Fee of magistrate for proof of execution, §7A-309.
Fines.
Docketed judgments for fines, §15A-1365.
Payment as authorized condition of parole, §15A-1374, (b).
Forfeiture of bonds in criminal cases.
When execution to issue, §1-305, (a).
Forms, §1-313.

EXECUTIONS —Cont'd
Garnishment.
Issuance of execution against garnishee, §1-440.32, (a).
Bonds, surety.
Garnishee retaining possession, §1-440.32, (b).
Governor.
Execution sales.
Notification of governor, §1-339.55.
Habeas corpus.
Party held in execution not to be discharged, §17-36.
Homestead exemptions, §§1C-1601 to 1C-1604; Const. N. C., art. X, §2.
Time limitation not to apply to enforcing lien of judgment upon, §1-306.
Housing authorities and projects.
Exemptions of property from execution, §157-21.
Husband and wife.
Married women.
Levy and collection from separate property, §1-304.
Indigent persons.
Execution against the person.
Appointment of counsel, §1-311.
Contents of execution, §1-313.
Injunctions.
Execution sales.
Dissolution of order restraining or enjoining sale.
Procedure upon, §1-339.59, (a), (b).
Insurance.
Life insurance.
Group insurance.
Exemptions from execution, §58-58-165.
Supervision, rehabilitation and liquidation of insurers.
Levy of execution prohibited during pendency of liquidation proceeding, §58-30-295.
Interrogatories.
Discovery of assets of judgment debtor, §1-352.1.
Issuance.
Clerks of court.
Duties, failure to issue, when not to issue, §1-305, (a), (b).
Court of rendition.
Issuance from, §1-307.
Time limits, §1-306.
To what counties issued, §1-308.
Joint debtors.
Supplemental proceedings against, §1-354.
Judgment directing payment of money.
Appeal bond, stay, §1-289, (a).
Cap on amount, noncompensatory damages of $25,000,000 or more, §1-289, (b), (c).
Judicial sales.
See JUDICIAL SALES.
Kinds of executions, §1-303.
Laborers' liens.
Exemptions from process.
Inapplicability, Const. N. C., art. X, §3.
Landlord and tenant.
Lien on crops.
Tenant's crop not subject to execution against landlord, §42-21.
Leasehold estates.
Liability to sale under execution, §1-315, (a).
Liens.
Execution sales.
Real property.
Property remains subject to liens, §1-339.68, (b).

EXECUTIONS —Cont'd
Liens —Cont'd
Mechanics, laborers and materialmen dealing with owner.
Sale of property in satisfaction of judgment.
Execution sale, §44A-14, (a).
Secreting property to hinder enforcement after judgment, §14-115.
Limitation of actions.
Issuance of executions requiring payment of money or recovery of personal property, §1-306.
Livestock.
Cost of keeping.
Officer's account, §1-322.
Married women.
Execution against, §1-304.
Money.
Execution sales.
Sale to be made for cash, §1-339.47.
Judgment for payment of money.
Enforcement by execution, §1-302.
Time limit on issuance of execution, §1-306.
Motor vehicles.
Delinquent taxes.
Remedies for collection, §20-99.
Nonresidents.
Corporations.
Nonresident custodian of corporate books, §§1-324.6, 1-324.7.
Orders of court.
Contempt.
Disobedience of orders, §1-368.
Debtors of judgment debtor.
Summoning, §1-360.
Discovery of assets, §§1-352.1, 1-352.2.
Disposition of property.
Order forbidden, §1-358.
Property withheld from execution.
Application of property, §1-353.
Receivers.
Appointment, §§1-363 to 1-365.
Sale of debtor's property, §1-362.
Unsatisfied execution.
Order for debtor to answer, §1-352.
Where proceedings instituted and defendant examined, §1-361.
Parties.
Supplemental proceedings.
Contempt.
Disobedience of orders, §1-368.
Examination of parties and witnesses, §1-356.
Incriminating answers not privileged, §1-357.
Partition.
Right of judgment creditor to sue execution on judgment, §46-5.
Penalties.
Clerks of court.
Issuance.
Violations of provisions, §1-305, (a).
Corporations.
Agents.
Violations of duties, §1-324.5.
Execution sales.
Sheriffs.
Return of no sale for want of bidders.
Failure to make required statement, §1-339.50.
Selling contrary to law, §1-339.49.
Returns.
Entry on judgment docket.
Violations of provisions by clerk, §1-321.

EXECUTIONS —Cont'd
Person.
Execution against person, §1-303.
Personal property.
Bonds, surety.
Forthcoming bond for personal property, §§1-318 to 1-320.
Execution for delivery of possession of personal property, §1-303.
Execution sales.
Bids.
Defaulting bidder, §1-339.69, (a).
Bill of sale, §1-339.62.
Defective title.
Remedy of purchaser against defendant, §1-323.
Delivery of property, §1-339.62.
Description of property.
Notice of sale to contain, §1-339.51.
Report of sale to contain, §1-339.63, (b).
Exemptions from process, Const. N. C., art. X, §1.
Notice of sale.
Posting, §1-339.53.
Place of sale, §1-339.44, (c).
Posting of notice, §1-339.53.
Presence of property at sale required, §1-339.45.
Property liable to sale under execution, §1-315, (a).
Judgment for delivery of personal property.
Enforcement by execution, §1-302.
Time limit on issuance of execution, §1-306.
Stay of judgment, §1-290.
Prisons and prisoners.
Debtor and creditor.
Discharge of insolvent prisoners.
Persons taken in execution, §23-29.
Property of debtor of judgment debtor, §1-360.1.
Property of judgment debtor, §1-303.
Purchase money of land.
Form of execution, §1-313.
Real property.
Execution for delivery of possession of real property, §1-303.
Execution sales, §1-309.
Bids.
Defaulting bidder, §1-339.69, (b).
Confirmation of sale, §1-339.67.
Deed, §1-339.68, (a).
Defective title.
Remedy of purchaser against defendant, §1-323.
Description of property.
Notice of sale to contain, §1-339.51.
Report of sale to contain, §1-339.63, (b).
Liens.
Property remains subject to, §1-339.68, (b).
Notice of sale.
Judgment debtor, §1-339.54.
Posting, §1-339.52, (a), (c).
Publication, §1-339.52, (a) to (c).
Orders for possession, §1-339.68, (c), (d).
Place of sale, §1-339.44, (a), (b).
Posting of notice, §1-339.52, (a), (c).
Property liable to sale under execution, §1-315, (a).
Sale as a whole or in parts, §1-339.46.
Judgment for delivery of real property.
Enforcement by execution, §1-302.
Stays, §1-292.

EXECUTIONS —Cont'd
Receivers.
Actions.
Receiver to sue debtors of judgment debtor, §1-366.
Appointment, §1-363.
Filing, §1-364.
Record, §1-364.
Where order of appointment recorded, §1-365.
Debtors of judgment debtor.
Actions by receiver against, §1-366.
Title.
Vesting of property in receiver, §1-364.
Reports.
Execution sales.
Contents, §1-339.63, (b).
Required, §1-339.63, (a).
Retirement system for counties and cities.
Exemptions from execution, §128-31.
Retirement system for teachers and state employees.
Exemption from execution, §135-9.
Return.
Clerks of superior court.
Return to clerk, §1-210.
Court of rendition.
Return to, §1-307.
Judgment docket.
Entry of returns on, §1-321.
No sale for want of bidders, §1-339.50.
Unsatisfied execution.
Order for debtor to answer, §1-352.
Proceedings against joint debtors, §1-354.
When returnable, §1-310.
Sales.
Execution sales, §§1-339.41 to 1-339.71.
See EXECUTION SALES.
Judicial sales, §§1-339.1 to 1-339.40.
See JUDICIAL SALES.
Seals and sealed instruments.
Executions running out of county.
Seal of court required, §1-303.
Self-incrimination.
Supplemental proceedings.
Examination of parties and witnesses.
Incriminating answers not privileged, §1-357.
Service of process.
Discovery of assets of judgment debtor.
Interrogatories, §1-352.1.
Notice of motion, §1-352.2.
Interrogatories to discover assets, §1-352.1.
Sheriffs.
Conflicts of interest.
Directed to coroner where sheriff interested in action, §1-313.
Costs.
Levy of execution for unpaid costs, §6-4.
County where judgment docketed.
Issuance to sheriff of such county, §1-308.
Directed to sheriff, §1-313.
Execution sales.
See EXECUTION SALES.
Forthcoming bond for personal property, §§1-318 to 1-320.
Livestock.
Cost of keeping.
Officer's account, §1-322.
Payment of money collected on execution, §162-18.
Return of execution.
Clerk of superior court, §1-210.
Small claims actions, §7A-225.

EXECUTIONS —Cont'd
Stays, §1A-1, Rule 62.
Docket entry, §1-293.
Execution on money judgment.
Appeal bond, §1-289, (a).
Cap on amount, noncompensatory damages of $25,000,000 or more awarded, §1-289, (b), (c).
Judgment directing conveyance, §1-291.
Judgment for real property, §1-292.
Personal property judgment, §1-290.
Stock and stockholders.
Corporate shares subject to execution, §1-324.3.
Sundays.
Execution sales.
Holding on Sunday prohibited, §1-339.43.
Superior court clerks, §1-210.
Supplemental proceedings.
Contempt.
Disobedience of orders, §1-368.
Debtor leaving state or concealing self, §1-355.
Debtors of judgment debtor.
Satisfaction of execution, §1-359.
Summoning, §1-360.
Discovery of assets.
Generally, §1-352.2.
Interrogatories, §1-352.1.
Disposition of property.
Order forbidden, §1-358.
Examination of parties and witnesses, §1-356.
Incriminating answers not privileged, §1-357.
Inspection and copying of designated documents, papers, books, etc., of judgment debtor, §1-352.2.
Joint debtors.
Proceedings against, §1-354.
Parties.
Contempt.
Disobedience of orders, §1-368.
Examination, §1-356.
Incriminating answers not privileged, §1-357.
Receivers, §§1-363 to 1-366.
Referees.
Appointment, §1-367.
Examination of parties and witnesses, §1-356.
Reference to, §1-367.
Sale of debtor's property, §1-362.
Statute of limitations.
Additional method of discovering assets, §1-352.2.
Unsatisfied execution.
Debtor ordered to answer, §1-352.
Proceedings against joint debtors, §1-354.
Where proceedings instituted and defendant examined, §1-361.
Witnesses.
Contempt.
Disobedience of orders, §1-368.
Examination, §1-356.
Incriminating answers not privileged, §1-357.
Suretyship.
Principal and surety distinguished in judgment and execution, §26-1.
Principal liable on execution before surety, §26-2.
Stay of execution.
Dissenting surety not liable to surety on stay of execution, §26-6.
Surviving spouses.
Exemption from execution, §30-15.
Taxation.
Collection of taxes, §105-242, (a).

EXECUTIONS —Cont'd
Torrens system registration.
Conveyance as security for debts.
Sale under lien, §43-36, (f).
Trust estate sales, §1-316.
Unincorporated associations, organizations or societies.
Findings of fact, §1-69.1.
Variance between judgment and execution.
Effect, §1-314.
Venue.
Against the person, §1-311.
Sale of land under execution, §1-309.
To what counties issued, §1-308.
Where proceedings instituted and defendant examined, §1-361.
Waiver.
Homestead exemption, §1C-1601, (c).
Warehouse receipts.
Lien on goods covered by a negotiable document, §25-7-602.
Witnesses.
Supplemental proceedings.
Contempt.
Disobedience of orders, §1-368.
Examination of parties and witnesses, §1-356.
Incriminating answers not privileged, §1-357.

EXECUTIONS AGAINST THE PERSON, §§1-303, 1-311.
Form, §1-313.

EXECUTION SALES, §§1-339.41 to 1-339.71.
Alimony, remedies available, §50-16.7, (k).
Attorneys' fees.
Special proceeding to determine ownership of surplus, §1-339.71, (d).
Bill of sale, §1-315, (b).
Bonds, surety.
Special proceedings to determine ownership of surplus.
Transfer of proceedings to civil issue docket of superior court, §1-339.71, (c).
Upset bid on real property.
Compliance bond, §1-339.64, (b) to (d).
Cash.
Sale to be made for cash, §1-339.47.
Clerks of court.
Procedural details.
Authority to fix, §1-339.42.
Commencement.
Time for, §1-339.60, (a), (b).
When sale commenced, §1-339.48.
Confirmation.
Sale of real property, §1-339.67.
Validation.
Certain sales confirmed prior to time prescribed by law, §1-339.77.
Continuance of sale, §1-339.60, (c).
Uncompleted sale, §1-339.61.
Validation of certain sales continued beyond time prescribed by law, §1-339.75.
Days on which sale may be held, §1-339.43.
Validation of sales held on other days, §§1-339.73, 1-339.74.
Defaulting bidder.
Liability on bid, §1-339.69, (c).
Other remedies against defaulting bidders unimpaired, §1-339.69, (d).
Personal property, §1-339.69, (a).
Real property, §1-339.69, (b).

EXECUTION SALES —Cont'd
Defective title.
Remedy of purchaser against defendant, §1-323.
Deferred payments.
More than two years.
Validation of sale, §1-339.76.
Definitions, §1-339.41, (a), (b).
Equity of redemption.
Sheriff's deed on sale, §1-317.
Exemptions.
Mechanics' and materialmen's liens, Const. N. C., art. X, §3.
Fees.
Uniform civil process fees, §7A-311, (a).
Homestead exemption, Const. N. C., art. X, §§2, 3.
Injunctions.
Dissolution of order restraining or enjoining sale.
Procedure upon, §1-339.59, (a), (b).
Leasehold estates.
Liability to sale under execution, §1-315, (a).
Liens.
Real property remains subject to liens, §1-339.68, (b).
Motor vehicles, §20-77.
Notice.
Attorney general, §1-339.55.
Contents of notice of sale, §1-339.51.
Exception as to perishable property, §1-339.56.
Governor.
Notice to, §1-339.55.
Judgment debtor of sale of real property, §1-339.54.
Posting and publishing sale of real property, §1-339.52, (a) to (c).
Posting sale of personal property, §1-339.53.
Postponement of sale, §1-339.58, (b), (c).
Real property.
Judgment debtor.
Notice to, §1-339.54.
Validation of certain sales as to publication of notice, §1-339.72.
Payment deferred more than two years.
Validation of sale, §1-339.76.
Payment of judgment.
Application of proceeds to, §1-339.70, (b).
Penalties.
Sheriffs.
Return of no sale for want of bidders.
Failure to make required statement, §1-339.50.
Selling contrary to law, §1-339.49.
Perishable property, §1-339.56.
Personal property.
Bids.
Defaulting bidder, §1-339.69, (a).
Bill of sale, §1-339.62.
Defective title.
Remedy of purchaser against defendant, §1-323.
Delivery of property, §1-339.62.
Description of property.
Notice of sale to contain, §1-339.51.
Report of sale to contain, §1-339.63, (b).
Exemptions from process, Const. N. C., art. X, §1.
Notice of sale.
Posting, §1-339.53.
Place of sale, §1-339.44, (c).
Posting of notice, §1-339.53.
Presence of property at sale required, §1-339.45.
Property liable to sale under execution, §1-315, (a).

EXECUTION SALES —Cont'd
Place of sale, §1-339.44.
Posting and publishing notice.
Exception as to perishable property, §1-339.56.
Sale of personal property, §1-339.53.
Sale of real property, §1-339.52, (a) to (c).
Postponement.
Grounds, §1-339.58, (a).
Notice, §1-339.58, (b), (c).
Proceeds.
Disposition, §1-339.70, (a) to (c).
Surplus.
Disposition, §1-339.70, (c).
Special proceedings to determine ownership of surplus, §1-339.71, (a) to (d).
Property liable to sale under execution, §1-315, (a).
Real property.
Confirmation, §1-339.67.
Deed, §1-339.68, (a).
Defaulting bidder, §1-339.69.
Failure of bidder to comply with bid, §1-339.69.
Liens effective prior to lien of judgment property sold remains subject to, §1-339.68, (b).
Notice of sale.
Notice to judgment debtor, §1-339.54.
Posting and publishing, §1-339.52, (a) to (c).
Order for possession, §1-339.68, (c).
Resale.
Failure of bidder to comply with bid, §1-339.69.
Upset bid on real property, §1-339.64, (a).
Binding terms of original notice, §1-339.64, (h).
Compliance bonds, §1-339.64, (b).
Notice, §1-339.64, (e), (f).
Orders of clerk of court, §1-339.64, (i).
Release of last bidder, §1-339.64, (g).
Resale order, §1-339.66A.
Separate upset bids when real property sold in parts, §1-339.65.
Receipt for proceeds.
Clerk to furnish sheriff, §1-339.70, (a).
Reports.
Contents, §1-339.63, (b).
Required, §1-339.63, (a).
Residential property disclosure act.
Applicability of act, §47E-2.
Return of no sale for want of bidders, §1-339.50.
Satisfaction of judgment before sale completed, §1-339.57.
Secured transactions.
Default.
Effect, §25-9-601, (e).
Sheriffs.
Defined, §1-339.41, (b).
Equity of redemption.
Sheriff's deed on sale, §1-317.
Fees.
Uniform civil process fees, §7A-311, (a).
Penalties.
Return of no sale for want of bidders.
Failure to make required statement, §1-339.50.
Selling contrary to law, §1-339.49.
Real property, §1-309.
Special proceeding to determine ownership of surplus.
Attorneys' fees, §1-339.71, (d).
Defendants in proceeding, §1-339.71, (b).
Instituted by person claiming money, §1-339.71, (a).

EXECUTION SALES —Cont'd
Special proceeding to determine ownership of surplus —Cont'd
Transfer of proceeding to civil case docket.
Issues of fact as to ownership, §1-339.71, (c).
Sundays.
Sale may not be held on Sunday, §1-339.43.
Supplemental proceedings.
Debtor's property ordered sold, §1-362.
Time for sale, §1-339.60.
Commencement of sale, §1-339.60, (a), (b).
Continuance of sale, §§1-339.60, (c), 1-339.61.
Failure to hold sale by time fixed, §1-339.58, (d).
Trust estates.
Title of purchaser, §1-316.
Upset bid.
Binding terms of original notice, §1-339.64, (h).
Bonds, surety.
Compliance bond, §1-339.64, (b).
Generally, §1-339.64, (a).
Notice, §1-339.64, (e), (f).
Orders of clerk of court, §1-339.64, (i).
Release of last prior bidder, §1-339.64, (g).
Resale order, §1-339.66A.
Separate upset bids when real property sold in parts, §1-339.65.
Validation.
Confirmation of sales prior to time prescribed by law, §1-339.77.
Continuation of sale for longer period than prescribed by law, §1-339.75.
Notice.
Validation of certain sales as to publication of notice, §1-339.72.
Payment deferred more than two years, §1-339.76.
Payment deferred over two years, §1-339.76.
Sales held on days other than day required by statute, §§1-339.73, 1-339.74.
Variance between judgment and execution.
Title of purchaser not invalidated, §1-314.
Venue.
Place of sale, §1-339.44.
When sale may be held, §1-339.43.

EXECUTIVE BUDGET ACT, §§143-1 to 143-34.7.
See BUDGETS.

EXECUTIVE MANSION.
Department of cultural resources.
Authority of administration department not affected, §143-415.
Powers of department, §143-411.
Purposes, §143-410.
Secretary.
Executive mansion fine arts committee.
Committee to give aid and advice, §143B-79.
Fine arts committee, §§143B-79, 143B-80.
See EXECUTIVE MANSION FINE ARTS COMMITTEE.

EXECUTIVE MANSION FINE ARTS COMMITTEE.
Appointments, §143B-80.
Compensation of members, §143B-80.
Creation, §143B-79.
Department of cultural resources.
Transfer of commission to department, §143B-51.
Duties, §143B-79.
Members, §143B-80.
Powers and duties, §143B-79.
Quorum, §143B-80.
Selection of members, §143B-80.

EXECUTIVE ORGANIZATION ACT OF 1971.
State departments and agencies.
See STATE DEPARTMENTS AND AGENCIES.

EXECUTIVE ORGANIZATION ACT OF 1973.
State departments and agencies.
See STATE DEPARTMENTS AND AGENCIES.

EXECUTORS AND ADMINISTRATORS.
Abatement, revival and survival of actions.
Death before limitation expires.
Action by or against personal representative or collector, §1-22.
Presentation of claims.
Substitution of personal representative to constitute, §28A-19-1, (c).
Rights of action not surviving decedent, §28A-18-1.
Wrongful death, §28A-18-2.
Absence.
Service by publication on executor without bond, §28A-18-6.
Absentees in military service, §§28B-1 to 28B-10.
See ABSENTEES IN MILITARY SERVICE.
Accounts and accounting.
Annual accounts.
Filing required, §28A-21-1.
Book accounts.
Proved by personal representative, §8-43.
Certification of final account, §28A-21-2, (a).
Clerk may order account, §28A-21-4.
Contents of accounts, §28A-21-3.
Evidence.
Vouchers presumptive evidence, §28A-21-5.
Examination by clerk, §28A-21-1.
Failure to make account, §28A-21-4.
Final accounts, §28A-21-2, (b).
Time for filing, §28A-21-2, (a).
Grounds for summary revocation of letters testamentary, §28A-9-2.
Improper appointment.
Filing accounting with clerk of superior court, §28A-3-3.
Presumptions.
Vouchers presumptive evidence, §28A-21-5.
Public administrator.
Procedure after removal from office, §28A-12-7.
Resignation.
Statement of account, §28A-10-3.
Revocation of letters.
Filing accounting, §28A-9-3.
Tobacco grower and quota owner payments.
Phase II payments.
List of phase II distributees, filing, §28A-21-3.1.
Vouchers.
Lost vouchers, §28A-21-5.
Presumptive evidence of disbursement, §28A-21-5.
What accounts must contain, §28A-21-3.
Actions.
Actions brought by or against in representative capacity, §28A-18-3.
Bonds, surety.
Action against obligors on bond, §28A-8-6.
Costs.
When costs against representative allowed, §28A-19-18.
Creditors.
When creditors may sue on claim, §28A-18-5.
False imprisonment.
Rights of action not surviving decedent, §28A-18-1.

EXECUTORS AND ADMINISTRATORS —Cont'd
Actions —Cont'd
Libel and slander.
Rights of actions which do not survive, §28A-18-1.
Liens.
Commencement of actions against personal representatives not lien, §28A-19-17.
Representative capacity.
To sue or defend in representative capacity, §28A-18-3.
Revocation of letters.
Actions to continue, §28A-18-8.
Service on or appearance of one binds all, §28A-18-4.
Survival of actions, §28A-18-1.
Actions which do not survive, §28A-18-1, (b).
Venue of actions against executors and administrators, §1-78.
Wrongful death.
Power to maintain actions, §28A-13-3, (a).
Age.
Persons disqualified to serve, §28A-4-2.
Agriculture.
Continuation of farming operations, §28A-13-4.
Powers of personal representative, §28A-13-3, (a).
Crops.
Ungathered at death of deceased person, §28A-15-1, (d).
Ancillary administration, §§28A-26-1 to 28A-26-9.
Assets.
Assets in jurisdiction outside state subject to ancillary administration, §28A-26-1.
Nonresident decedents.
Assets subject to claims, allowances, etc., §28A-26-8, (a).
Remission of surplus assets, §28A-26-9.
Authority of domiciliary.
Personal representative for nonresident decedent, §28A-26-5.
Bonds, surety.
Personal representatives granted ancillary letters, §28A-26-4, (a).
Claims.
Certain claims binding, §28A-26-8, (b).
Limitation on presentation, §28A-26-8, (c).
Payment, §28A-26-8, (d).
Duties of personal representatives in ancillary administration, §28A-26-8.
Foreign corporations.
Authority to act as ancillary personal representative, §28A-26-3, (a).
General provisions, §28A-26-1.
Granting ancillary letters, §28A-26-3, (a).
Bond for personal representative, §28A-26-4.
Nonexistence of domiciliary personal representative, §28A-26-3, (b).
Jurisdiction.
Domiciliary personal representative of nonresident decedent.
Invoking or submission to jurisdiction of state courts, §28A-26-6.
Nonresident decedents.
Personal jurisdiction by service of process, §28A-26-7.
No ancillary administrator within ninety days.
Payment of debt and delivery of property to nonresident domiciliary, §28A-26-2, (c).
Nonresident decedents.
Assets subject to claims, etc., §28A-26-8, (a).

EXECUTORS AND ADMINISTRATORS —Cont'd
Ancillary administration —Cont'd
Payment of debt and delivery of property without ancillary administration in state, §28A-26-2.
Appeals.
Resignation, §28A-10-6.
Revocation of letters, §28A-9-4.
Stay of further proceedings in court below.
Security limited for fiduciaries, §1-294.
Appearances.
Actions against personal representatives or collectors.
Service on or appearance of one binds all, §28A-18-4.
Appointment.
Carrying out powers and duties prior to appointment, §28A-13-1.
Delay in appointment, §28A-6-1, (b).
Discharge of debt due, §28A-15-11.
Improper appointment.
Liability of personal representative appointed in improper county, §28A-3-4.
Procedure after determination, §28A-3-3.
Powers and duties accrue upon appointment, §28A-13-1.
Reopening administration, §28A-23-5.
Resignation.
Rights and duties devolve on successor, §28A-10-7.
When appointment of successor not required, §28A-10-8.
Revocation of letters, §28A-9-6.
Rights and duties devolve on successor, §28A-9-7.
Right to contest appointment, §28A-6-4.
Successors, §28A-6-3.
Appraisers.
Employment, §28A-20-4.
Arbitration and award.
Referral of disputed claim, §28A-19-15.
Assets.
Ancillary administration.
Jurisdiction outside of state, §28A-26-1.
Nonresident decedents, §28A-26-8, (a).
Remission of surplus assets, §28A-26-9.
Encumbered assets.
Payment by personal representative, §28A-15-4.
Improper appointment.
Surrender of assets, §28A-3-3.
Nonresident decedents.
Assets subject to claims, allowances, etc., §28A-26-8, (a).
Retaining in satisfaction of representative claim, §28A-19-12.
Revocation of letters.
Surrender of assets, §28A-9-3.
Sources of assets to satisfy claims against estate.
Tentative trusts, §28A-15-10, (a).
Surplus assets.
Remission by ancillary representatives, §28A-26-9.
Attachment.
Death of defendant after levy.
Judgment against real property enforced through defendant's personal representative, §1-440.34, (b).
Service on personal representative for levy to remain in force, §1-440.34, (a).
Attorneys at law.
Counsel fees allowable to attorneys serving as representatives, §28A-23-4.

EXECUTORS AND ADMINISTRATORS —Cont'd
Attorneys at law —Cont'd
Employing attorneys.
Powers of personal representatives and fiduciaries, §28A-13-3, (a).
Audits and auditors.
Employment of auditors.
Powers of personal representatives, §28A-13-3, (a).
Banks.
Acting as executor or administrator authorized, §53-159.
Fiduciaries generally.
See BANKS.
Stock and stockholders.
Executors and administrators not personally liable, §53-40.
Blind persons.
Aid to the blind.
Personal representatives for certain recipients of aid, §§111-30 to 111-33.
Bonds, surety.
Actions.
Right of action against obligor on bond of personal representative, §28A-8-6.
Amount, §28A-8-2.
Ancillary administration.
Personal representatives granted ancillary letters, §28A-26-4.
Appeal perfected staying further proceedings in court below.
Security limited for fiduciaries, §1-294.
Breach of bond.
Action against obligors, §28A-8-6.
Deposited money.
Exclusion from computation of bond, §28A-8-1.1.
Failure to give additional bond, §28A-8-4.
Increase of bond or security in case of inadequacy or insufficiency, §28A-8-3, (a).
Increase of bond upon sale of real estate, §28A-8-3, (b).
Judicial sales.
Person holding sale, §1-339.10, (b), (c).
Limitation of action against surety, §1-52.
Manner of security, §28A-8-2.
Mortgages and deeds of trust.
Bonds secured by mortgage or deed of trust, §28A-8-3.
Provisions of bond, §28A-8-2.
Public administrator, §28A-12-3.
Reduction, §28A-8-3, (c).
Required prior to issuance of letters, §28A-8-1, (a).
Rights of surety in danger of loss, §28A-8-5.
Service of process on executor without bond, §28A-18-6.
Substitution of security, §28A-8-3, (d).
When bond not required, §28A-8-1, (b).
Book accounts proved by personal representative.
Evidence, §8-43.
Breach of duty, §28A-13-10, (c).
Burial.
Carrying out burial arrangements prior to appointment, §28A-13-1.
Cemeteries.
Perpetual care of cemetery lot.
Authorized, §28A-19-10.
Claims against estate.
General provisions, §§28A-19-1 to 28A-19-18.
See DECEDENTS' ESTATES.

EXECUTORS AND ADMINISTRATORS —Cont'd
Claims against estate —Cont'd
Notice for claims, §28A-14-1.
Delivery or mailing, §28A-14-1, (b), (c).
Personal notice to creditors, §28A-14-3.
Proof of notice, §28A-14-2.
Publication, §28A-14-1, (a).
Validation of certain notices, §28A-14-1.1.
Collateral attack.
Letters not subject to attack, §28A-6-5.
Collectors, §§28A-11-1 to 28A-11-5.
See DECEDENTS' ESTATES.
Commercial code.
Representative defined, §25-1-201, (35).
Commingling of estates.
Liability, §28A-13-10, (c).
Commissions, §28A-23-3, (a).
Computation, §28A-23-3, (f).
Construction of section, §28A-23-3, (d).
Determination of amount, §28A-23-3, (b).
Limitation on amount, §28A-23-3, (c).
Personal representatives guilty of misconduct not entitled to commission, §28A-23-3, (e).
Compensation of trustees and other fiduciaries, §§32-53 to 32-62.
See FIDUCIARIES.
Compromise and settlement.
Wrongful death actions, §28A-13-3, (a).
Contests.
Right to contest appointment, §28A-6-4.
Continuation of businesses or ventures.
Powers of personal representative and fiduciary, §28A-13-3, (a).
Contracts.
Exoneration from personal liability.
Powers of personal representative, §28A-13-3, (a).
Sale of real property.
Death of vendor under contract.
Delivery of deed by executor, §28A-17-9.
Conveyances.
Contract for sale of real property by decedent.
Delivery of deed by personal representative, §28A-17-9.
Real property conveyed to personal representative, §28A-17-10.
Convicted felons.
Persons disqualified to serve, §28A-4-2.
Corporations.
Disqualifications for service.
Not authorized as personal representative, §28A-4-2.
Incorporation of businesses or ventures.
Power of personal representative or fiduciary, §28A-13-3, (a).
Costs.
Administration of estates, §7A-307.
Recovery of costs when executor or administrator a party, §6-31.
When chargeable to estate, §6-31.
Creditors.
Notice to creditors. See within this heading, "Notice."
When creditors may sue on claim, §28A-18-5.
Damages.
Wrongful death actions, §28A-18-2, (b).
Death.
Appointment of successor, §28A-6-3.
Powers and duties of successor, §28A-13-7.
Surviving personal representative.
Powers, §28A-13-9.

EXECUTORS AND ADMINISTRATORS —Cont'd
Debts and claims.
Discharge of debt by appointment, §28A-15-11.
Notice to creditors, §§28A-14-1 to 28A-14-3.
Satisfying debts or claims against decedent's estate, §28A-13-3, (a).
Declaratory judgments.
Who may apply for declaration, §1-255.
Deeds.
Contract for sale of real property by decedent.
Delivery of deed by personal representative, §28A-17-9.
Omitting seals, §47-51.
Definitions, §28A-1-1.
Deposits.
Estate funds deposited in bank, §28A-13-3, (a).
Designation.
Successors.
When appointment of successor not required, §28A-10-8.
Devisees.
Defined, §28A-1-1, (1a).
Service of process, §28A-13-3.
Disqualifications, §28A-4-2.
Distribution, §§28A-22-1 to 28A-22-10.
See DECEDENTS' ESTATES.
Domiciliary administration.
Foreign corporations.
Authority to act as ancillary personal representative, §28A-26-3, (a).
Jurisdiction, §28A-26-1.
Nonresident decedents.
Invoking jurisdiction, §28A-26-6, (a).
Personal jurisdiction by service of process, §28A-26-7.
No ancillary administrator qualifying within ninety days.
Payment of debt or delivery of property, §28A-26-2, (c).
Nonexistence of domiciliary personal representative.
Issuance of ancillary letters, §28A-26-3, (b).
Nonresidents.
Authority of domiciliary personal representative, §28A-26-5.
Jurisdiction.
Invoking jurisdiction of state, §28A-26-6, (a).
Personal jurisdiction by service of process, §28A-26-7.
Submission to jurisdiction of state courts, §28A-26-6, (b).
Payment of debt and delivery of property without ancillary administration, §28A-26-2, (a).
Release of debt, §28A-26-2, (b).
Remission of surplus assets, §28A-26-9.
Taxation.
Right and duty to pay off federal and state taxes, §28A-26-1.
Duties.
Annexation of will.
Powers and duties of administrator with will annexed, §28A-13-8.
General duties, §28A-13-2.
Settlement of estate, §28A-13-2.
Successors, §28A-13-7.
Time of accrual of duties, §28A-13-1.
Embezzlement.
Liability, §28A-13-10.
Property.
Receipt of property by virtue of office or employment, §14-90.

EXECUTORS AND ADMINISTRATORS —Cont'd
Employment of persons to assist in performance of duties.
Powers of personal representatives, §28A-13-3, (a).
Estate taxes.
Liability of personal representative.
Tax not paid within 2 years after due, §105-32.3, (b).
Evidence.
Book accounts proved by personal representative, §8-43.
Medical, hospital or other charges at issue.
Competency to give evidence regarding amount, §8-58.1.
Testimony establishing rebuttable presumption of reasonableness, §8-58.1.
Vouchers.
Presumptive evidence of disbursement, §28A-21-5.
Wrongful death actions.
Evidence establishing elements of damages, §28A-18-2, (c).
Examinations.
Persons or corporations believed to have possession of property of decedent, §28A-15-12, (a).
Executions.
Action by creditors.
When execution to issue, §28A-18-5.
Defendant dying in capital offense execution.
Rights against property of defendant, §1-312.
Form of execution against property in hands of personal representative, §1-313.
Successors in office, §28A-18-7.
False imprisonment.
Rights of action which do not survive, §28A-18-1.
Farming.
Continuation of farming operations, §28A-13-3, (a).
Federal estate tax apportionment.
Personal representative to determine apportionment, §28A-27-3.
Fiduciaries generally, §§32-1 to 32-13.
See FIDUCIARIES.
Foreclosures.
Validation, §45-5.
Foreign personal representatives.
Ancillary administration, §§28A-26-1 to 28A-26-9.
Defined, §28A-1-1, (2).
Fraud.
Sales of real property.
Conveyance by deceased in fraud of creditors.
Property subject to sale, §28A-17-5.
Transfers or conveyances by decedent to defraud creditors.
Action by personal representative to recover, §28A-15-10.
Funerals.
Carrying out funeral arrangements prior to appointment, §28A-13-1.
Gravestones.
Authorized, §28A-19-9.
Hearings.
Contesting appointments, §28A-6-4.
Letters testamentary and of administration.
Revocation, §28A-9-1.
Resignation.
Hearing on petition, §28A-10-4.
Heirs.
Defined, §28A-1-1, (3).
Parties to proceeding, §28A-13-3.

EXECUTORS AND ADMINISTRATORS —Cont'd
Heirs —Cont'd
Service of process, §28A-13-3.
Household furnishings.
Sales, §28A-16-3.
Illiterates.
Persons disqualified to serve, §28A-4-2.
Improper appointment.
Liability of personal representative appointed in improper county, §28A-3-4.
Procedure after determination, §28A-3-3.
Income.
Allocation of state income.
Powers of personal representatives, §28A-13-3.
Incorporation of businesses or ventures.
Powers of personal representative or fiduciary, §28A-13-3.
Inheritance tax.
See INHERITANCE TAX.
Inventory, §§28A-20-1 to 28A-20-4.
See DECEDENTS' ESTATES.
Joint personal representatives.
Exercise of powers by one or more than one, §28A-13-6.
Joint tenants and tenants in common.
Personal representatives to hold in joint tenancy, §28A-13-5.
Property to descend to heirs, executors and administrators, etc., §41-2.
Judgments and decrees.
Execution by successor in office, §28A-18-7.
Judicial sales.
Authority to hold sale, §1-339.4.
Bond of person holding sale, §1-339.10, (b), (c).
Jurisdiction.
Clerk of superior court.
Jurisdiction for administration of estates, §28A-2-1.
Nonresident decedents.
Invoking jurisdiction by domiciliary personal representative, §28A-26-6.
Personal jurisdiction by service of process, §28A-26-7.
Personal jurisdiction.
Grounds, §1-75.4.
Leases.
Authority to lease real property, §28A-17-11.
Certain leases void as to creditors and personal representatives, §28A-17-12, (a).
Leasing property for payment of debts, §28A-15-1.
Personal property.
Sale or lease, §§28A-16-1 to 28A-16-3.
Real property, §28A-17-11.
Letters of collection, §28A-11-1.
Letters testamentary and of administration.
Actions.
Continuation though letters revoked, §28A-18-4.
Ancillary administration.
Granting ancillary letters, §28A-26-3, (a).
Application.
Form, §28A-6-1, (a).
Recording, §28A-6-1, (a).
Clerks of superior courts.
Authority of clerk to grant and revoke letters, §7A-103.
Collateral attack.
Validity of letters not subject to, §28A-6-5.
Contesting appointment, §28A-6-4.
Delaying of appointment, §28A-6-1, (b).
Equally entitled applicants, §28A-4-1.

EXECUTORS AND ADMINISTRATORS —Cont'd
Letters testamentary and of administration —Cont'd
Issuance, §28A-6-1, (b).
Oath required prior to issuance, §28A-7-1.
Without notice, §28A-6-2.
Jurisdiction.
Assistant clerk of superior court, §28A-2-2.
Clerk of superior court, §28A-2-1.
Limitation of actions.
Time during controversy on granting letters, §1-24.
Notice.
Issuance without notice, §28A-6-2.
Oaths.
Required prior to issuance, §28A-7-1.
Order of persons qualified to serve, §28A-4-1.
Public administrator.
Revocation for false representation, §28A-12-6.
When administrator to apply for letters, §28A-12-4.
Renunciation.
Express renunciation, §28A-5-2, (a).
Implied renunciation, §28A-5-2, (b).
Nomination by person renouncing, §28A-5-2, (c).
Revocation.
Accounting.
Required, §28A-9-3.
Actions.
Continuation of actions though letters revoked, §28A-18-8.
Appeals, §28A-9-4.
Appointment of successor, §§28A-6-3, 28A-9-6.
Effect, §28A-9-3.
Failure to give additional bond, §28A-8-4.
Grounds, §28A-9-1, (a).
Summary revocation, §28A-9-2, (a).
Hearing, §28A-9-1.
Interlocutory orders, §28A-9-5.
Procedure, §28A-9-1, (b).
Summary revocation, §28A-9-2, (b).
Rights and duties devolve on successor, §28A-9-7.
Stays, §28A-9-4.
Summary revocation.
Grounds, §28A-9-2, (a).
Procedure, §28A-9-2, (b).
Surrender of assets upon revocation, §28A-9-3.
Time pleaded as bar to action.
Controversy on granting letters, §1-24.
Validity.
Collateral attack on validity, §28A-6-5.
Liability.
Property not part of estate, §28A-13-10, (b).
Property of estate, §28A-13-10, (a).
Libel and slander.
Actions in favor of decedent which do not survive, §28A-18-1.
Liens.
Actions against personal representatives.
No lien by suit, §28A-19-17.
Payment of encumbered assets, §28A-15-4.
Limitation of actions.
Ancillary administration.
Presentation of claims, §28A-26-8, (c).
Bonds, surety, §1-50, (a).
Action against surety, §1-52.
Claims against the state, §28A-19-3, (a).
Creditor against personal representative, §1-49.
Death before limitation expires.
Action by or against personal representative or collector, §1-22.

EXECUTORS AND ADMINISTRATORS —Cont'd
Limitation of actions —Cont'd
Time during controversy on granting of letters, §1-24.
Limited liability companies.
Death of member, powers upon, §57C-5-05.
Mentally ill.
Persons disqualified to serve, §28A-4-2.
Military affairs.
Estates of absentees in military service, §§28B-1 to 28B-10.
See ABSENTEES IN MILITARY SERVICE.
Minors.
Persons disqualified to serve as personal representative, §28A-4-2.
Settlement.
Payment into court of fund due minor, §28A-23-2.
Missing persons.
Estates of missing persons, §§28C-1 to 28C-22.
See MISSING PERSONS.
Mortgages and deeds of trust.
Authority to mortgage real property, §28A-17-11.
Bonds secured by mortgage, §28A-8-3, (d).
Certain mortgages void as to creditors and personal representatives, §28A-17-12.
Debts and claims.
Mortgaging property for payment of debts, §28A-15-1.
Definition of "mortgage," §28A-1-1, (4).
Foreclosures.
Validation, §45-5.
Payment of encumbered assets, §28A-15-4.
Renunciation by representative, §45-6.
Newly discovered property.
Reopening administration, §28A-23-5.
Nonresidents.
Domiciliary administration.
Authority of domiciliary personal representative for nonresident decedent, §28A-26-5.
Personal jurisdiction by service of process, §28A-26-7.
Submission to jurisdiction of court, §28A-26-6, (b).
Persons disqualified to serve, §28A-4-2.
Service of process.
Service on personal representative, §28A-26-7.
Notice.
Letters testamentary and of administration.
Issuance without notice, §28A-6-2.
Notice to creditors, §28A-14-1.
Delivery or mailing, §28A-14-1, (b), (c).
Personal notice to creditors, §28A-14-3.
Proof of notice, §28A-14-2.
Publication, §28A-14-1, (a).
Real property.
Sale, lease or mortgage by heirs or devisees.
Certain transactions void as to creditors and personal representatives, §28A-17-12.
Validation of certain notices, §28A-14-1.1.
Resignation.
Petition, §28A-10-2.
Oaths.
Form of oaths of office, §11-11.
Letters testamentary and of administration.
Oath required before issuance, §28A-7-1.
Public administrator, §28A-12-2.
Order of persons qualified to serve.
Letters of administration, §28A-4-1, (b).
Letters testamentary, §28A-4-1, (a).

EXECUTORS AND ADMINISTRATORS —Cont'd
Parent and child.
Acts barring rights of parents, §31A-2.
Parties, §1A-1, Rule 17, (a).
Sales of real property.
Adverse claimant to be heard, §28A-17-6.
Heirs and devisees necessary parties, §28A-17-4.
Partition.
Petitions by personal representative of cotenant, §46-3.
Partnerships.
Continuing partnerships.
Powers of personal representatives, §28A-13-3, (a).
Fiduciary obligations of partners.
Applicability to representatives of deceased partner, §59-51, (b).
Personal property.
Sale or lease, §§28A-16-1 to 28A-16-3.
Personal representatives defined, §28A-1-1, (5).
Petitions.
Resignation of office, §28A-10-2.
Phase II distributees.
Tobacco growers and quota owners.
List of distributees, filing, §28A-21-3.1.
Powers.
Annexation of will.
Powers and duties of administrator with will annexed, §28A-13-8.
Carrying out powers and duties prior to appointment, §28A-13-1.
Performance in reasonable and prudent manner, §28A-13-3, (a).
Powers of fiduciaries generally, §§32-25 to 32-28.
Successors, §28A-13-7.
Surviving personal representative, §28A-13-9.
Time of accrual of powers, §28A-13-1.
Presumptions.
Medical, hospital or other charges at issue.
Reasonableness of amount.
Testimony establishing rebuttable presumption, §8-58.1.
Principal and income act.
General provisions, §§37A-1-101 to 37A-6-602.
See PRINCIPAL AND INCOME ACT.
Probate of wills.
Application for probate, §31-12.
Substitution of consolidated bank as executor or trustee, §31-19.
Prudent person rule.
Investment and deposit of funds, §36A-2, (a).
Liability for loss to the estate, §28A-13-10, (c).
Public administrators.
Accounts and accounting.
Procedure after removal from office, §28A-12-7.
Appointment, §28A-12-1.
Bonds, surety, §28A-12-3, (a).
Commissions, §28A-23-3, (a).
Computation, §28A-23-3, (f).
Construction of section, §28A-23-3, (d).
Determination of amount, §28A-23-3, (b).
Limitation on amount, §28A-23-3, (c).
Public administrator guilty of misconduct not entitled to commission, §28A-23-3, (e).
Compensation, §28A-12-8.
Counsel fees.
Attorney serving as representatives, §28A-23-4.
Duties, §28A-12-5, (a).
Letters testamentary and of administration.
Revocation, §28A-12-6.

EXECUTORS AND ADMINISTRATORS —Cont'd
Public administrators —Cont'd
Letters testamentary and of administration —Cont'd
When administrator to apply for letters, §28A-12-4.
Missing persons.
Appointment of public administrator as receiver, §28C-17.
Nonresidents.
Removal from office upon becoming nonresident, §28A-12-6.
Oath of office, §28A-12-2.
Permanent bond, §28A-12-3, (b).
Powers, §28A-12-5, (a).
Removal from office, §28A-12-6.
Procedure after removal, §28A-12-7.
Term, §28A-12-1.
Expiration.
Administering estates upon expiration, §28A-12-5, (b).
Qualifications.
Age, §28A-4-2.
Convicted felons, §28A-4-2.
Equally entitled applicants, §28A-4-1.
Illiterates, §28A-4-2.
Incompetents, §28A-4-2.
Mentally ill, §28A-4-2.
Nonresidents, §28A-4-2.
Order of persons qualified to serve.
Letters of administration, §28A-4-1, (b).
Letters testamentary, §28A-4-1, (a).
Persons disqualified to serve, §28A-4-2.
Real estate brokers and salespersons.
Exemptions from provisions, §93A-2, (c).
Real property.
Assets available for discharge of debts and claims, §28A-15-1.
Conveyance to personal representative.
Title in personal representative for estate, §28A-17-10.
Damages to property.
Actions to recover damages, §28A-13-3, (a).
Death of vendor under contract.
Delivery of deed by personal representative, §28A-17-9.
Deeds.
Death of vendor under contract.
Delivery of deed by personal representative, §28A-17-9.
Warranties.
Death of vendor under contract, §28A-17-9.
Fraud.
Property subject to sale.
Conveyance by deceased in fraud of creditors, §28A-17-5.
Leases.
Certain leases void as to creditors and personal representatives, §28A-17-12, (a).
Personal representative may lease, §28A-17-11.
Mortgages and deeds of trust. See within this heading, "Mortgages and deeds of trust."
Order authorizing possession, custody or control.
Petition to clerk of court, §28A-13-3, (c).
Partition.
Petition for partition, §28A-17-3.
Power to sell or lease, §28A-13-3, (a).
Prior validating acts, §28A-17-13.
Purchase of property belonging to decedent's estate.
Powers of personal representative, §28A-13-3, (a).

EXECUTORS AND ADMINISTRATORS —Cont'd
Real property —Cont'd
Sales, §§28A-17-1 to 28A-17-13.
Adverse claimants.
Making party to proceeding, §28A-17-6.
Application to clerk, §28A-17-1.
Certain sales void as to creditors and personal representatives, §28A-17-12.
Conveyance by deceased in fraud of creditors.
Property subject to sale, §28A-17-5.
Guardian ad litem.
Appointment for heirs and devisees, §28A-17-4.
Heirs or devisees.
Necessary parties, §28A-17-4.
Void sales, etc., §28A-17-12.
Increase of bond, §28A-8-3, (b).
Joinder of issues of law or fact, §28A-17-6.
Partition.
Petition for partition, §28A-17-3.
Petitions, §28A-17-1.
Contents of petition for sale, §28A-17-2.
Partition, §28A-17-3.
Private sales, §28A-17-7.
Property recovered from fraudulent alienee subject to sale, §28A-17-5.
Property subject to sale, §28A-17-5.
Summary orders, §28A-17-7.
Wills.
Public or private sales, §28A-17-8.
Title.
Actions to determine title.
Powers of personal representative, §28A-13-3, (a).
Renunciation.
Express renunciation by executor, §28A-5-1, (a).
Implied renunciation by executor, §28A-5-1, (b).
Letters of administration.
Express renunciation, §28A-5-2, (a).
Implied renunciation, §28A-5-2, (b).
Nomination by person renouncing, §28A-5-2, (c).
Persons disqualified to serve, §28A-4-2.
Procedure upon renunciation, §28A-5-1, (c).
Right to renounce succession, §31B-1, (a).
Reopening administration, §28A-23-5.
Resignation.
Accounting to successor.
When resignation becomes effective, §28A-10-5.
Appeals, §28A-10-6.
Appointment of successor, §28A-6-3.
Clerk's power to accept, §28A-10-1.
Petition.
Contents, §28A-10-2, (a).
Hearing on petition, §28A-10-4.
Notice of petition, §28A-10-2, (b).
Powers and duties of successor, §28A-13-7.
Statement of account, §28A-10-3.
Stays, §28A-10-6.
Successors.
Rights and duties devolve on successor, §28A-10-7.
When appointment of successor not required, §28A-10-8.
When resignation becomes effective, §28A-10-5.
Revocation of letters, §§28A-9-1 to 28A-9-7.
Sales.
Personal property.
Sale or lease, §§28A-16-1 to 28A-16-3.
Seals and sealed instruments.
Deeds.
Official deeds omitting seals, §47-51.

EXECUTORS AND ADMINISTRATORS —Cont'd
Securities regulation.
Exempt transactions, §78A-17.
Self-dealing.
Losses to estate through self-dealing.
Liability of personal representative, §28A-13-10, (c).
Service of process.
Actions against personal representatives or collectors.
Service on or appearance of one binds all, §28A-18-4.
Defined, §28A-1-1, (6).
Devisees and heirs made parties by service, §28A-13-3.
Executors without bond, §28A-18-6.
Nonresident decedents.
Nonresident drivers.
Personal representatives of deceased nonresident drivers, §1-105.
Service on personal representative, §28A-26-7.
Settlement, §28A-13-2.
After final account filed, §28A-23-1.
Discharge of personal representative from liability, §28A-23-1.
Investments.
Funds due minor, §28A-23-2.
Minor.
Payment into court of fund due minor, §28A-23-2.
Small estates.
Subsequently appointed personal representative or collector, §28A-25-5.
Statute of frauds.
Contracts charging representative personally, §22-1.
Stays.
Resignation, §28A-10-6.
Revocation of letters, §28A-9-4.
Security limited for fiduciaries, §1-294.
Stock and stockholders.
Powers of personal representatives, §28A-13-3.
Summary administration of estates.
Appointment of personal representative.
Discharge of spouses liability, §28A-28-7, (b).
Petition, §28A-28-7, (a).
Surviving spouses.
Right to administer estate of other spouse.
Acts barring rights of spouse, §31A-1, (b).
Taxation.
Carry-over basis provision.
Election of excluded items, §28A-13-3, (a1).
Domiciliary representative to pay off federal and state taxes, §28A-26-1.
Marital deduction.
Power of personal representative to secure benefit of marital deduction, §28A-13-3, (a).
Power to enter agreements with taxing authorities, §28A-13-3, (a).
Property taxes.
Payment of taxes by fiduciaries, §105-383.
Title.
Actions to determine title.
Powers of personal representative, §28A-13-3.
Tobacco growers and quota owners.
Phase II distributees.
List of distributees, filing, §28A-21-3.1.
Transfers to minors.
Authority to make transfer, §33A-5, (a).
Designation of custodians by personal representative, §33A-5, (c).

EXECUTORS AND ADMINISTRATORS —Cont'd
Transfers to minors —Cont'd
Irrevocable transfer for benefit of minor.
Authority to make as custodian, §33A-6, (a), (c).
Uniform fiduciaries act, §§32-1 to 32-13.
See FIDUCIARIES.
Validation.
Notice to creditors, §28A-14-1.1.
Venue.
Actions against executors and administrators, §1-78.
Improper appointment.
Liability of personal representative appointed in improper county, §28A-3-4.
Procedure after determination, §28A-3-3.
Priority of venue, §28A-3-5.
Proceedings commenced in more than one county, §28A-3-2, (a).
Proceedings to determine venue, §28A-3-2.
Proper county, §28A-3-1.
Waiver, §28A-3-5.
When proceeding deemed commenced, §28A-3-2, (b).
Waiver.
Venue, §28A-3-5.
Wills.
Appointment of successor to personal representative required by will, §28A-6-3.
Bonds, surety.
Execution without giving bond, §28A-26-4, (b).
Executor competent witness, §31-9.
Probate of wills generally.
See WILLS.
Qualification of trustee named in will, §36A-107, (a).
Testamentary trust created under will, §36A-107, (b).
Witnesses.
Medical, hospital or other charges at issue.
Competency to give evidence regarding amount, §8-58.1.
Rebuttable presumption of reasonableness.
Testimony establishing, §8-58.1.
Wills.
Executor competent witness, §31-9.
Wrongful death.
Damages recoverable by personal representative, §28A-18-2, (b).
Distribution of sums recovered from wrongful death.
Powers of personal representative, §28A-13-3, (a).
Dying declarations.
Admissibility, §28A-18-2, (d).
Evidence establishing elements of damages, §28A-18-2, (c).
Maintaining action for wrongful death.
Powers of personal representative and fiduciary, §28A-13-3, (a).
Survival of actions, §28A-18-2, (a).
Authority of personal representative or collector to pay reasonable and necessary expenses from assets of estate, §28A-18-2, (a).

EXECUTORY INTERESTS.
General provisions.
See REMAINDERS, REVERSIONS AND EXECUTORY INTERESTS.

EXEMPLARY DAMAGES.
Civil rights, interference with, §99D-1, (b), (b1).

EXEMPLARY DAMAGES —Cont'd
Motor fuel marketing violations, private actions, §75-86.
Trade secrets, willful and malicious misappropriations, §66-154, (c).

EXEMPTION OF PROPERTY FROM CREDITOR CLAIMS.
Alternative exemptions, §1C-1602.
Bankruptcy.
Federal bankruptcy act.
Exemptions not applicable to residents of state, §1C-1601, (f).
Conveyances.
Effect of exemption of property.
Conveyance of exempt property, §1C-1604, (a).
Homestead, Const. N. C., art. X, §2.
Disability income plan.
Applicability of provisions to plan, §135-111.
Effect of exemption of property, §1C-1604, (a).
Executions, §§1C-1601 to 1C-1604; Const. N. C., art. X, §§2 to 4.
Limitation of wage garnishment, §1-362.
Mechanics' and materialmen's liens.
Inapplicability of exemption, Const. N. C., art. X, §3.
Federal bankruptcy act.
Exemptions not applicable to residents of state, §1C-1601, (f).
Forms.
Setting aside exempt property.
Statement by debtor, §1C-1603, (c).
Furniture.
Exempt property, §1C-1601, (a).
Recent purchases, §1C-1601, (d).
Household goods and furnishings, §1C-1601, (g).
Gifts.
Continuation of exemption of property, §1C-1604, (b).
Homestead.
See HOMESTEAD EXEMPTIONS.
Household goods and furnishings, §1C-1601, (g).
Husband and wife.
Property of married women secured to them, Const. N. C., art. X, §4.
Property passing by bequest, devise, intestate succession or gift to dependent spouse.
Continuation of exemption, §1C-1604, (b).
Individual retirement accounts (IRA's), §1C-1601, (a).
Intestate succession.
Continuation of exemption of property, §1C-1604, (b).
Laborers' liens, Const. N. C., art. X, §3.
Life insurance, §1C-1601, (a).
Proceeds of life policy exempt from process of predators, Const. N. C., art. X, §5.
Limitation of actions.
Effect of exemption of property, §1C-1604, (a1).
Married women.
Property of married women secured to them, Const. N. C., art. X, §4.
Mechanics' and materialmen's liens, Const. N. C., art. X, §3.
Minors.
Homestead exemption.
Exemption for benefit of children, Const. N. C., art. X, §2.
Motions.
Setting aside exempt property, §1C-1603, (a), (b).

EXEMPTION OF PROPERTY FROM CREDITOR CLAIMS —Cont'd
Motor vehicles.
Exempt property, §1C-1601, (a).
Recent purchases, §1C-1601, (d).
Notice.
Setting aside exempt property.
Notice to persons affected, §1C-1603, (d).
Partition.
Assignment of homestead, §46-5.
Personal property.
Exemption of personal property from execution or other process, Const. N. C., art. X, §1.
Laborers' liens.
Inapplicability of exemption provisions, Const. N. C., art. X, §3.
Mechanics' and materialmen's liens.
Inapplicability of exemption from process, Const. N. C., art. X, §3.
Personnel system, §126-5.
Petitions.
Setting aside exempt property, §1C-1603, (a), (b).
Physical therapists, §§90-270.34, 90-270.39.
Private protective services, §74C-3, (b).
Restitution.
Criminal restitution orders docketed as civil judgments, §1C-1601.
Securities regulation, §§78A-16 to 78A-18.
Setting aside exempt property.
Modification, §1C-1603, (g).
Motion, §1C-1603, (a).
Contents, §1C-1603, (b).
Notation of order on motion docket, §1C-1603, (f).
Notice to persons affected, §1C-1603, (d).
Petition, §1C-1603, (a).
Contents, §1C-1603, (b).
Procedure, §1C-1603, (e).
Statement by debtor, §1C-1603, (c).
Surviving spouse.
Homestead exemption.
Exemption for benefit of surviving spouse, Const. N. C., art. X, §2.
Wage and hour act, §95-25.14.
Wages.
Limitation on wage garnishment, §1-362.
Waiver.
Homestead exemption, §1C-1601, (c).
Women.
Married women.
Property of married women secured to them, Const. N. C., art. X, §4.

EXHAUST SYSTEMS.
Motor vehicle inspections generally, §§20-183.2 to 20-183.8G.
See MOTOR VEHICLE INSPECTIONS.

EXHIBITION OF CHILDREN.
Prohibited exhibition, §110-20.1.

EXHIBITIONS.
Fireworks.
Permitted fireworks at public exhibitions, §14-410, (a).
Use at public exhibitions requires permit, §14-413.
License tax, §105-37.1, (d).
Obscenity, §§14-190.1 to 14-190.20.
See OBSCENITY.
Privilege tax on gross receipts, §105-37.1, (a).
Advance report when bringing show from outside to state, §105-37.1, (c).

EXHIBITIONS —Cont'd
Privilege tax on gross receipts —Cont'd
Rate and payment, §105-37.1, (b).
Secret societies.
Placing exhibit with intention of intimidating, §14-12.13.
Wearing of disguise, §14-12.14.
Theft.
Destruction or theft of property of exhibition, §14-398.

EXHIBITS.
Part of pleading, §1A-1, Rule 10, (c).

EXHUMATIONS, §130A-390, (a) to (c).

EX MERO MOTU.
Findings of fact and conclusions of law necessary, §1A-1, Rule 52, (a).
Removal for fair trial, §1-84.

EXONERATION.
Contribution among joint tort-feasors, §§1B-1 to 1B-7.
Decedents' estates.
Nonexoneration of encumbered property, §28A-15-3.

EXONERATION OF BAIL.
Arrest in civil cases, §1-433.
Surrender of defendant, §1-434.

EXPANDING BUSINESSES.
Tax incentives for new and expanding businesses generally, §§105-129.2 to 105-129.13.
See TAX INCENTIVES FOR NEW AND EXPANDING BUSINESSES.

EX PARTE PROCEEDINGS.
Discovery.
Protective orders, §15A-908, (a).
Guardians.
Motions in the cause, §35A-1207, (d).
Referees meetings.
Failure of party to appear, §1A-1, Rule 53, (f).
Special proceedings, §§1-400 to 1-402.

EXPEDITED EVICTIONS, §§42-59 to 42-76.
Actions.
Nature of cause of action of landlord, §42-60.
Parties.
Defendants to action, §42-62, (b).
Who may bring action, §42-62, (a).
Standard of proof, §42-61.
Adjudication of delinquency.
Conclusive proof in civil action, §42-69, (b).
Effect in civil action, §42-69, (a).
Admissions.
Request for, §42-70, (d).
Affirmative defenses.
Complete evictions, §42-64, (a).
Evidence of isolated or nonrecurring incidents.
May be offered only to support affirmative defense, §42-67.
Subsequent actions, availability of affirmative defense, §42-64, (b).
Answers.
Time for filing, §42-68.
Applicability of provisions, §42-59.1.
Applicability of rules of civil procedure, §42-68.
Availability of law enforcement resources to plaintiffs, §42-72.
Burden of proof.
Affirmative defense to subsequent action for complete eviction, §42-64, (b).

EXPEDITED EVICTIONS —Cont'd
Burden of proof —Cont'd
Civil causes of action, §42-61.
Exemption from complete eviction where grounds established, §42-64, (c).
Civil immunity from liability, §42-76.
Civil procedure rules.
Applicability, §42-68.
Collection of rent by landlord not waiver of default, §42-73.
Complaints.
Service of complaint on defendant, §42-62, (c).
Complete evictions.
Affirmative defenses, §42-64, (a).
Subsequent action, availability of defense, §42-64, (b).
Defined, §42-59.
Exemption, §42-64, (c).
Grounds, §42-63, (a).
Conditional evictions.
Order against tenant.
Removal order issued against person other than tenant, §42-63, (b), (c).
Contempt.
Violation of injunction or preliminary relief, §42-74.
Continuances.
Procedure in standards for continuances, §42-68.
Conviction of criminal activity.
Conclusive proof in civil action, §42-69, (b).
Effect in civil action, §42-69, (a).
Counterclaims.
Time for filing reply to counterclaim, §42-68.
Criminal activity.
Conviction as proof in civil action, §42-69, (b).
Defined, §42-59.
Criminal proceedings.
Adjudication of delinquency.
Conclusive proof in civil action, §42-69, (b).
Pendency of proceedings not to preclude civil action, §42-69, (a).
Admissibility of sealed records in civil action, §42-69, (d).
Admissibility of trial recordings or transcripts in civil action, §42-69, (c).
Conviction of criminal activity.
Conclusive proof in civil action, §42-69, (b).
Pendency of criminal proceedings not to preclude civil action, §42-69, (a).
Cumulative remedies, §42-75.
Default judgments.
Failure to plead in accordance with time periods, §42-68.
Defenses.
Affirmative defenses. See within this heading, "Affirmative defenses."
Evidence of isolated or nonrecurring criminal activity.
Impermissible as defense, admissible as support of affirmative defenses, §42-67.
Definitions, §42-59.
Discovery.
Authority to conduct discovery generally, §42-70, (a).
Injunction against illegal activity pending complete of discovery, §42-70, (e).
Interrogatories.
Time for response, §42-70, (d).
Request for admissions.
Time for response, §42-70, (d).

EXPEDITED EVICTIONS —Cont'd
Discovery —Cont'd
Request for production of documents.
Time for response, §42-70, (d).
Time for initiation by defendant, §42-70, (b).
Time for initiation by plaintiff, §42-70, (c).
Entire premises.
Defined, §42-59.
Evidence.
Criminal proceeding sealed records.
Admissibility in civil actions, §42-69.
Isolated or nonrecurring criminal activities, §42-67.
Exemption from complete eviction where grounds established, §42-64, (c).
Felonies.
Defined, §42-59.
Grounds for complete eviction, §42-63, (a).
Grounds for partial eviction and issuance of removal order, §42-63, (b).
Guests.
Defined, §42-59.
Hearings.
Procedure for expedited hearing, §42-68.
Immunities.
Civil liability, §42-76.
Individual rental units.
Defined, §42-59.
Injunctions.
Preliminary injunction against illegal activity pending completion of discovery, §42-70, (e).
Preliminary injunction in emergency situation, §42-74.
Intent of provisions, §42-59.1.
Interrogatories.
Time for response, §42-70, (d).
Landlords.
Defined, §42-59.
Law enforcement resources.
Availability of police or lab reports to plaintiffs, §42-72.
Leased residential premises.
Defined, §42-59.
Mandatory evictions, §42-66, (b).
Motions.
Enforcement of eviction and removal orders.
Expedited hearings, §42-66, (a).
Notice.
Service of complaint, §42-62, (c).
Obstructing execution or enforcement of removal or eviction order, §42-65.
Orders for eviction.
Mandatory eviction, §42-66, (b).
Motion to enforce, §42-66, (a).
Obstruction of execution or enforcement, §42-65.
Partial evictions.
Defined, §42-59.
Grounds, §42-63, (b).
Parties.
Defendants, §42-62, (b).
Who may bring action, §42-62, (a).
Preliminary or emergency relief, §42-74.
Protection of threatened witnesses or affiants, §42-71.
Public policy statement, §42-59.1.
Records.
Admissibility of sealed criminal proceeding records in civil action, §42-69, (d).
Remedies, cumulative nature, §42-75.

EXPEDITED EVICTIONS —Cont'd
Removal orders.
Grounds to remove from premises person other than tenant, §42-63, (b).
Conditional eviction order against tenant, §42-63, (c).
Motion to enforce, §42-66, (a).
Obstruction of execution or enforcement, §42-65.
Rents.
Collection of rent by landlord does not constitute waiver, §42-73.
Reports.
Availability of police or lab reports to plaintiffs, §42-72.
Residents.
Defined, §42-59.
Rules of civil procedure, applicability, §42-68.
Service of process.
Complaint, §42-62, (c).
Small claim actions.
Applicability of expedited process for summary ejectment, §42-68.
Nature of actions, §42-60.
Standard of proof, §42-61.
Subpoena duces tecum, §42-70, (d).
Temporary restraining orders.
Preliminary or emergency relief, §42-74.
Tenants.
Defined, §42-59.
Threats against witnesses.
Protection by court, §42-71.
Time for filing.
Extensions of time, §42-68.
Transcripts.
Admissibility of criminal trial recordings or transcripts in civil action, §42-69, (c).
Vacation rentals, §§42A-23 to 42A-27.
Violation of injunctions or preliminary relief.
Civil or criminal contempt, §42-74.
Violations of orders.
Mandatory eviction, §42-66, (b).
Witnesses.
Protection of threatened witnesses, §42-71.

EXPEDITED PROCESS FOR CHILD SUPPORT, §§50-30 to 50-39.
See CHILD SUPPORT.

EXPEDITED REFEREES PROCEEDINGS, §1A-1, Rule 53, (f).

EXPENSES OF LITIGATION.
See COSTS.

EXPERIENCE AND CAREER EXPLORATION PROGRAMS.
Hours of work per week of enrollees, §95-25.5, (c).

EXPERTS IN CAPITAL CASES.
Indigent defense services.
Appointment and compensation, other expenses, IDS Rules 2D.1 to 2D.5.

EXPERT WITNESSES.
Basis of opinion testimony, §8C-1, Rule 703.
Court appointed experts, §8C-1, Rule 706.
Disclosure of facts and data underlying opinion, §8C-1, Rule 705.
Fees.
Uniform fees for witnesses, §7A-314, (d).
Indigent defense services.
Fees paid by state, §7A-454.

EXPERT WITNESSES —Cont'd
Insanity defense.
Notice required, §15A-959.
International commercial arbitration and conciliation, §1-567.56.
Limitation of number, pre-trial conference, §1A-1, Rule 16, (a).
Medical malpractice actions.
Contingency fee testimony prohibited, §8C-1, Rule 702, (f).
Qualifications of expert.
General provisions, §8C-1, Rule 702, (b).
Testimony against general practitioner, §8C-1, Rule 702, (c).
Testimony regarding administrative or other nonclinical issues, §8C-1, Rule 702, (h).
Testimony regarding medical support staff, §8C-1, Rule 702, (d).
Waiver of requirements by resident judge, §8C-1, Rule 702, (e).
Trial court disqualification of expert.
Power not limited by section, §8C-1, Rule 702, (g).
Medical malpractice discovery conference, §1A-1, Rule 26, (f1).
Medicolegal guidelines for attorney-physician relationship, MLG Rules 1 to 6.
Notice to defense of intent to call, §15A-903, (a).
Notice to state of intent to call, §15A-905, (c), (d).
Physicians and surgeons.
Hearing before medical board.
Right of licensee to call, §90-14.6, (b).
Specialized knowledge, §8C-1, Rule 702, (a).
Testimony generally, §8C-1, Rule 702, (a).
Ultimate issue to be decided by trier of fact, §8C-1, Rule 704.

EXPLOITED, ABUSED OR NEGLECTED DISABLED ADULTS, §§108A-99 to 108A-111.
See ABUSED, NEGLECTED OR EXPLOITED DISABLED ADULTS.

EXPLORATION FOR OIL AND GAS OFFSHORE, §§143-215.94AA to 143-215.94JJ.
See OFFSHORE OIL AND GAS ACTIVITIES.

EXPLOSIVES.
Attempts to commit crime.
Malicious use of explosive or incendiary.
Property occupied by persons, §14-49.1.
Punishment, §14-49.1.
Bombs.
Exploding bombs, §14-283.
License.
Keeping for sale or selling explosives without license, §14-284.
Burglary.
Use of explosives in burglary, §14-57.
Campus or other education property, possessing or carrying unlawful.
Class 1 felony, §14-269.2, (b1).
Class 1 misdemeanors, §14-269.2, (f).
Definitions, §14-269.2, (a).
Exceptions, §14-269.2, (g), (h).
Minors, aiding to possess or carry.
Class 1 felony, §14-269.2, (c1).
Civil disorders, §14-288.20.
Construction and interpretation.
Regulation of sale of explosives, §14-284.1, (g).
Counties.
Regulation, §153A-128.

EXPLOSIVES —Cont'd
Definitions.
Incendiary device or explosive or material, §14-50.1.
Drivers' licenses.
Revocation or suspension of license.
Minors, §20-13.2, (c2).
Dynamite.
Exploding dynamite cartridges, §14-283.
License.
Keeping for sale or selling explosives without license, §14-284.
Failure of town or city officer to inspect incendiary fires, §14-69.
False reports concerning destructive device.
Destructive device located in any building or vehicle, §14-69.1, (a).
Destructive device located in public building, §14-69.1, (c).
Report defined, §14-69.1, (d).
Restitution, costs and consequential damages, ordering, §14-69.1, (d).
Fireworks, §§14-410 to 14-415.
Fish or wildlife taken by use of.
Permit authorizing, §113-261, (b).
Hoax by use of false bomb or other device, §14-69.2, (a).
Public buildings, §14-69.2, (c).
Restitution, costs and consequential damages, ordering, §14-69.2, (d).
Larceny.
Felony larceny.
When value of property in question irrelevant, §14-72.
Licenses.
Sale or selling explosives without license, §14-284.
Malicious use of explosive or incendiary, §14-49, (a), (b).
Churches and other buildings of worship, §14-49, (b1).
Government buildings, §14-49, (b2).
Punishment, §14-49.1.
Mass death and destruction weapons.
Manufacture, assembly, etc., §14-288.8.
Minors detonating in schools.
Parental liability for damages, §1-538.3.
Motor vehicles transporting, §20-167.
Municipal corporations.
Regulation of explosive substances, §160A-183.
Penalties.
Regulation of sale of explosives, §14-284.1, (f).
Possessing or carrying on campus or other educational property, §14-269.2.
Powerful explosives.
Defined, §14-284.1, (d).
Property occupied by persons.
Malicious damage by use of explosive or incendiary, §14-49.1.
Attempt to commit crime, §14-49.1.
Punishment for malicious use of explosive or incendiary.
Attempt to commit crime.
Property occupied by persons, §14-49.1.
Occupied property damaged.
Punishment, §14-49.1.
Records.
Regulation of sale of explosives, §14-284.1, (b).
Safecracking, §14-89.1.
Sales.
License.
Keeping for sale or selling explosives without license, §14-284.

EXPLOSIVES —Cont'd
Sales —Cont'd
Regulation of sale of explosives, §14-284.1.
Applicability of provisions, §14-284.1, (f).
Application of person or agent of person purchasing or receiving explosive, §14-284.1, (a).
Construing provisions, §14-284.1, (g).
Definition of term "powerful explosives," §14-284.1, (d).
Exceptions, §14-284.1, (f).
Identifying purchaser, §14-284.1, (a).
Penalties for violation of provisions, §14-284.1, (e).
Powerful explosives.
Defined, §14-284.1, (d).
Record of sales or deliveries, §14-284.1, (b).
Storage of explosives, §14-284.1, (c).
School, community college, college or university.
Possessing or carrying on campus or educational property, §14-269.2.
Storage.
Regulation of sale of explosives, §14-284.1, (c).
Transporting, §20-167.
Weapons generally.
See WEAPONS.

EXPORTS.
Generally.
See IMPORTS AND EXPORTS.

EX POST FACTO LAWS, Const. N. C., art. I, §16; Const. U. S., art. I, §§9, 10.

EXPRESS WARRANTIES.
Leases, UCC, §25-2A-210.
Displacement of inconsistent implied warranties, §25-2A-215, (c).
Third-party beneficiaries, §25-2A-216.
New motor vehicles warranties act, §§20-351 to 20-351.10.
See LEMON LAW.
Sale of goods, UCC, §25-2-313.
Cumulation and conflict, §25-2-317.
Third party beneficiaries, §25-2-318.

EXPULSION OF STUDENTS.
Student's conduct threat to safety of other students or employees, §115C-391, (d).
Alternative program offered, consideration prior to expulsion, §115C-391, (d).
Readmission of student, §115C-391, (d).
Request by student to board to reconsider decision, §115C-391, (d).

EXPUNGEMENT OF RECORDS.
Dismissal of charges, finding of not guilty or not responsible.
Application to court, §15A-146, (a).
As result of identity fraud, §15A-147.
Confidential file containing names of persons granted expungement.
Administrative office of the courts to maintain, §15A-146, (c).
Costs taxed against petitioner, §15A-146, (b).
DNA records, application to expunge, §15A-146, (b1), (b2).
Failure to recite or acknowledge expunged records.
Not perjury or false statement, §15A-146, (a).
Hearing on application, §15A-146, (a).
Law enforcement agencies order to expunge records, §15A-146, (b).

EXPUNGEMENT OF RECORDS —Cont'd
Dismissal of charges, finding of not guilty or not responsible —Cont'd
Names of persons granted expungement.
Filed with administrative office of the courts, §15A-146, (c).
Order of court, §15A-146, (a), (b).
DNA records.
Charges dismissed, finding of not guilty or not responsible, §15A-146, (b1), (b2).
Charges dismissed on appeal or pardon of innocence granted, §15A-148, (a), (b).
Drug offenses, §90-96.
First offenders under age of eighteen.
Clerks of court, duties, §15A-145, (d).
Orders of court, §15A-145, (b), (c).
Petition, §15A-145, (a).
Fee for filing, §15A-145, (e).
Identity fraud.
Dismissal of charges, finding of not guilty, another using identifying information.
Division of motor vehicles to expunge records, §15A-147, (c), (d).
Failure to acknowledge records not perjury, §15A-147, (b).
Hearing on petition or motion, court to hold, §15A-147, (a).
Insurance companies charging additional insurance points premium, refund, §15A-147, (f).
Law enforcement agencies and other agencies ordered to expunge, §15A-147, (c).
Order to expunge, §15A-147, (a).
Petition or motion, §15A-147, (a).
State or local agencies ordered to expunge, §15A-147, (c), (e).
Juveniles alleged or adjudicated delinquent.
Effect of expunction, §7B-3201.
Notice of expunction, §7B-3202.
Ordering and directing expungement, §7B-3200, (d), (e).
Petition filed by person adjudicated delinquent or undisciplined, §7B-3200, (a), (c).
Petition filed by person alleged delinquent or undisciplined, §7B-3200, (h).
Report by clerk of superior court of names of persons granted expunction, §7B-3200, (i).
Retention or disposition of records.
Juvenile court counselor, §7B-3200, (f).
Residential facility, §7B-3200, (g).
Minors.
Drug offenses, §90-96.
First offense, §15A-145.
Juveniles alleged or adjudicated delinquent, §§7B-3200 to 7B-3202.
Nurse licensure compact.
Coordinated licensure information system, §90-171.88, (f).
Presentence reports, §15A-1333.
Special education.
Right of student or parents, §115C-114, (c).
Student records, §115C-402, (b).

EXTENSION OF MUNICIPAL CORPORATION LIMITS, §§160A-29 to 160A-58.28.
See ANNEXATION.

EXTENSION OF TIME FOR FILING TAX REPORTS OR RETURNS, §105-263.

EXTENSION SERVICE.
Agricultural development generally, §§106-580 to 106-587.
See AGRICULTURAL DEVELOPMENT.

EXTORTION.
Adulterated or misbranded food, drugs or cosmetics.
Intent to extort, §14-34.4, (b).
Computer-related crime, §14-457.
County inspectors of articles of commerce, §66-7.
Electronic surveillance orders, §15A-290, (b).
Elements of offense, §14-118.4.
General assembly.
Legislative ethics act, §120-86, (b) to (e).
Police.
Removal of unfit officers, §128-16.
Sheriffs.
Removal of unfit officers, §128-16.

EXTRADITION, §§15A-721 to 15A-750; Const. U. S., art. II, §2; art. IV, §2.
Assisting arresting officer.
Refusing assistance, §15A-729.
Asylum.
No right of asylum, §15A-748.
Citation of act.
Short title, §15A-750.
Construction and interpretation, §15A-749.
Definitions, §15A-721.
Evidence, rules of, §8C-1, Rule 1101, (b).
Fugitives from other states, §§15A-728, 15A-729.
Arrest by officers from other states, §15A-403.
Arrest prior to requisition, §15A-733.
Bail and recognizance.
Conditions of bond, §15A-736.
Forfeiture of bail, §15A-738.
Generally, §§15A-735, 15A-736.
Recovery on bond, §15A-738.
Commitment to await requisition, §15A-735.
Extension of time of commitment, §15A-737.
Confinement in jail when necessary, §15A-732.
Criminal charges pending in this state, §15A-739.
Demand for extradition.
Contents, §15A-723.
Form, §15A-723.
Investigation.
Governor may cause investigation to be made, §15A-724.
Governor.
Duty as to, §15A-722.
Investigation.
Governor may cause investigation to be made, §15A-724.
Warrant of arrest, §§15A-727 to 15A-729.
Guilt or innocence of accused.
When inquired into, §15A-740.
Habeas corpus.
Application for, §15A-730.
Imprisoned or awaiting trial in another state, §15A-725.
Intent of fugitive irrelevant, §15A-725.
Jail.
Commitment to await requisition, §15A-735.
Extension of time of commitment, §15A-737.
Confinement in jail when necessary, §15A-732.
Commitment to await requisition, §15A-735.
Officers or agents passing through state.
Confinement of prisoner in local jails, §15A-732.
Persons imprisoned or awaiting trial in another state or who have left the demanding state under compulsion, §15A-725.
Persons not present in demanding state at time of commission of crime, §15A-726.

EXTRADITION —Cont'd
Fugitives from other states —Cont'd
Persons under criminal prosecution in this state at time of requisition, §15A-739.
Persons who left state under compulsion, §15A-725.
Presence in demanding state not required, §15A-726.
Rights of accused person, §§15A-730, 15A-731.
Violation, §15A-731.
Warrantless arrest, §15A-734.
Warrant of arrest.
Alias.
Issuance, §15A-741.
Execution of warrant.
Commanding aid, §§15A-728, 15A-729.
Time and place, §15A-728.
Issuance, §15A-727.
Recall of warrant, §15A-741.
Recitals, §15A-727.
Fugitives from this state.
Costs, §15A-744.
Demand, §15A-742.
Expenses, §15A-744.
Governor.
Duty, §15A-742.
Immunity from civil process, §15A-745.
Requisition.
Application for issuance, §15A-743, (a), (b).
Contents, §15A-743, (c).
Service of process.
Immunity from service of process in certain civil actions, §15A-745.
Fugitives in other countries.
Securing attendance, §15A-772.
Guilt or innocence of accused.
Fugitives from other states, §15A-740.
Immunities.
No immunity from other criminal prosecution while in this state, §15A-748.
International fugitives.
Procedure for extraditing fugitives in other countries, §15A-772.
Interstate compact on juveniles, §§7B-2800 to 7B-2827.
See INTERSTATE COMPACT ON JUVENILES.
Interstate family support.
Interstate rendition, §§52C-8-801, 52C-8-802.
Minors.
Harmful materials.
Contempt.
Persons guilty of contempt, §19-20, (c).
Multiple jurisdiction.
Fugitives from other states awaiting prosecution in this state, §15A-739.
Probation.
Secretary of correction.
Duties, §15-203.
Rules of evidence.
Inapplicability, §8C-1, Rule 1101, (b).
Title of act.
Short title, §15A-750.
Waiver.
Nonwaiver by this state, §15A-747.
Written waiver of extradition proceedings, §15A-746.

EXTRAJUDICIAL STATEMENTS.
Attorneys at law, Prof Cond. Rule 3.6.

EXTRAORDINARY REMEDIES.
Appeals, App. Proc. Rule 24.

EXTRAORDINARY REMEDIES —Cont'd
Habeas corpus, §§17-1 to 17-46.
See HABEAS CORPUS.
Mandamus.
See MANDAMUS.
Prohibition, §7A-32, (b); App. Proc. Rule 22.
Quo warranto, §§1-514 to 1-532.
See QUO WARRANTO.
Receivers.
General provisions.
See RECEIVERS.
Waste, §§1-533 to 1-538.
See WASTE.

EYE DONOR CARDS.
Availability at division of motor vehicles offices, §20-7.3.

EYEGLASSES.
Contact lenses.
Prescriptions.
Requirements for filling, §90-236.1.
Eye protection devices.
Schools, §§115C-166 to 115C-169.
See EYE PROTECTION DEVICES IN SCHOOLS.
Opticians.
General provisions, §§90-234 to 90-255.1.
See OPTICIANS.
Optometrists.
General provisions, §§90-114 to 90-127.3.
See OPTOMETRISTS.
Safety glasses.
Schools, §§115C-166 to 115C-169.
See EYE PROTECTION DEVICES IN SCHOOLS.
Sales.
Flammable frames.
Prohibited, §90-255.1.
Opticians.
Requirements, §90-250.
Sales and use tax.
Exemption, §105-164.13.

EYE PROTECTION DEVICES IN SCHOOLS, §§115C-166 to 115C-169.
Corrective protective devices, §115C-169.
Industrial quality eye protective devices.
Defined, §115C-168.
Required in certain courses, §115C-166.
Visitors to wear, §115C-167.

EYES.
Anatomical gifts.
Manner of making gift of eye, §130A-406, (e).
Children's health insurance program.
Vision benefits, §108A-70.21, (b).
Corneal tissue removal.
Authorization, §130A-391, (a).
Conditions for removal, §130A-391, (a).
Immunity from liability, §130A-391, (b).
Glaucoma.
Department of environment and natural resources.
Establishment of program, §130A-221, (a), (b).
Opticians generally, §§90-234 to 90-255.1.
See OPTICIANS.
Optometrists generally, §§90-114 to 90-127.3.
See OPTOMETRISTS.
Protection devices.
Schools, §§115C-166 to 115C-169.
See EYE PROTECTION DEVICES IN SCHOOLS.

EYEWITNESS OBSERVATIONS.
Journalist's qualified privilege.
Eyewitness observation of criminal or tortuous conduct, no privilege, §8-53.11, (d).

F

FACE BONES AND JOINTS.
Insurance discrimination, §58-3-121, (a) to (c).

FACILITY AUTHORITIES, §§160A-480.1 to 160A-480.15.
Accounts and accounting.
Fiscal accountability, §160A-480.3, (f).
Actions.
Powers of authority, §160A-480.4.
Arenas.
Seating at regional facility arena, §160A-480.7.
Bids and bidding.
Construction contracts, §160A-480.6.
Bond issues.
Approval, §160A-480.8, (g).
Basis of investment, §160A-480.8, (k).
Certification of approval, §160A-480.8, (g).
Details of bonds or notes, §160A-480.8, (j).
Faith and credit of state not pledged, §160A-480.11.
Investment basis, §160A-480.8, (k).
Investment securities, §160A-480.8, (i).
Issuance generally, §160A-480.8, (f).
Liability, §160A-480.15.
Pledge of state, §160A-480.8, (h).
Powers of authority, §160A-480.4.
Proceeds from bonds deemed trust funds, §160A-480.10.
Proceeds, use, §160A-480.8, (b).
Refunding bonds, §160A-480.12.
Revenue, §160A-480.8, (d).
Securities eligible for investment, §160A-480.13.
Security interest, §160A-480.8, (e).
Security of bonds, §160A-480.8, (c).
State pledge, §160A-480.8, (h).
Tax exemption, §160A-480.14.
Terms of bonds, §160A-480.8, (a).
Trust agreements securing bonds, §160A-480.9.
Use of proceeds, §160A-480.8, (b).
Bylaws, §160A-480.3, (d).
Powers of authority to adopt, §160A-480.4.
Charter, §160A-480.3, (d).
Citation of act.
Short title, §160A-480.1.
Conflicts of interest.
Members, officers or employees.
Disclosure to authority, §160A-480.3, (g).
Construction contracts, §160A-480.6.
Consultants, employment.
Powers of authority, §160A-480.4.
Contracts.
Conflicts of interest.
Disclosure to authority, §160A-480.3, (g).
Construction contracts, §160A-480.6.
Investment of bonds, §160A-480.8, (k).
Powers of authority, §160A-480.4.
Creation of authority, §160A-480.3, (a).
Credit facilities.
Defined, §160A-480.2.
Definitions, §160A-480.2.
Dissolution.
Dissolution of authority by general assembly, §160A-480.5.

FACILITY AUTHORITIES —Cont'd
Fees.
Powers of authority, §160A-480.4.
Fiscal accountability, §160A-480.3, (f).
Grants.
Powers of authority, §160A-480.4.
Investment securities.
Bond issues, §160A-480.8, (i).
Bond issues made securities eligible for investment, §160A-480.13.
Jurisdiction.
Territorial jurisdiction of authority, §160A-480.3, (a).
Liability of members or officers, §160A-480.15.
Loans.
Powers of authority, §160A-480.4.
Meetings, §160A-480.3, (e).
Members.
Appointment, §160A-480.3, (b).
Defined, §160A-480.2.
Disclosure of conflicts of interest to authority, §160A-480.3, (g).
Liability for bond issues, §160A-480.15.
Terms, §160A-480.3, (b).
Par formulas.
Defined, §160A-480.2.
Personal property.
Powers of authority, §160A-480.4.
Powers generally, §160A-480.4.
Purpose of authority, §160A-480.3, (c).
Real property.
Powers of authority, §160A-480.4.
Refunding bonds, §160A-480.12.
Regional facilities.
Construction and operation, powers of authority, §160A-480.4.
Defined, §160A-480.2.
Seating at arenas, §160A-480.7.
Sales and use tax refunds, §105-164.14, (c).
Seals and sealed instruments.
Power of authority to adopt official seal, §160A-480.4.
Security interest.
Bond issues, §160A-480.8, (e).
Short title, §160A-480.1.
State debt not created by bond issues, §160A-480.11.
Surveys and surveyors.
Powers of authority, §160A-480.4.
Taxation.
Bond issues exempt from taxation, §160A-480.14.
Trusts and trustees.
Receipt of proceeds from sale of bonds deemed trust funds, §160A-480.10.
Trust agreement or resolution securing bond issues, §160A-480.9.
University of North Carolina.
Athletic events at regional facility arena.
Student seating, §160A-480.7.

FACSIMILE FILING AND SERVICE OF PLEADINGS AND PAPERS, §1A-1, Rule 5, (b), (e).

FACSIMILE SIGNATURES.
Blind or visually handicapped persons.
Use of signature facsimile by visually handicapped person, §22A-1.
Electronic records and signatures.
Uniform electronic transactions act, §§66-311 to 66-330.
See ELECTRONIC TRANSACTIONS.

FACSIMILE SIGNATURES —Cont'd
State controller.
Warrants for payment of money.
Issuance of warrants upon state treasurer.
Use of facsimile signature machine, §143-3.2, (a).

FACSIMILE SOLICITATION.
Credit insurance on credit card balances.
Unsolicited facsimile transmission prohibited, §58-57-105, (a).

FACSIMILE TRANSMISSIONS.
Electronic records and signatures.
Uniform electronic transactions act, §§66-311 to 66-330.
See ELECTRONIC TRANSACTIONS.
Facsimile signatures.
See FACSIMILE SIGNATURES.
Filing of pleadings and papers, §1A-1, Rule 5, (e).
Interstate family support.
Admissibility as evidence, §52C-3-315, (e).
Military absentee voting.
Facsimile, electronic mail or scanned transmission of election materials, §163-257.
Nonprofit corporations.
Notice communicated by, §55A-1-41, (b).
Service and filing of pleadings and papers, §1A-1, Rule 5, (b), (e).

FACTORS.
Agents generally.
See AGENTS.
Brokers generally.
See BROKERS.
Disclosure of real parties.
Person trading as "factor" to disclose, §66-72.
Sale of goods, UCC.
Consignment sales, §25-2-326.
Power to transfer title, §25-2-403.
Sale on approval or return, §25-2-326.
Trader or merchant transacting business with addition of words factor.
Disclosure of name of principal or partner by sign placed conspicuously in place of business, §66-72.

FACTORY BRANCHES AND FACTORY REPRESENTATIVES.
Motor vehicles.
Automobile manufacturers licensing act.
Generally, §§20-285 to 20-308.2.
See MOTOR VEHICLE MANUFACTURERS.

FAILURE OF CONSIDERATION.
Affirmative defense, pleading, §1A-1, Rule 8, (c).

FAILURE TO APPEAR.
Abused, neglected or dependent juvenile actions, §7B-407.
Delinquent and undisciplined juvenile actions.
Contempt for parent's guardian's or custodian's failure to appear, §§7B-1805, (b), (c), 7B-1806.
Dismissal with leave when defendant fails to appear and cannot readily be found, §15A-932.
Divorce or annulment.
Notice of trial not required, §50-10, (b).
Garnishees, §1-440.27.
Motor vehicle offenses.
Court to report failure to appear, §20-24.2.
Revocation of driver's license, §20-24.1.

FAILURE TO APPEAR —Cont'd
Pretrial release, conditions imposed.
Prior failure to appear and answer charges, §15A-534, (d1).
Referees meetings, §1A-1, Rule 53, (f).
Service of pleadings and other papers on party in default not required, §1A-1, Rule 5, (a).
Small claims actions.
Appeals, §7A-228, (c).

FAILURE TO DIM HEADLIGHTS, §20-181.

FAILURE TO DISPERSE WHEN COMMANDED, §14-288.5.

FAILURE TO JOIN PARTY.
Defense by pretrial motion, §1A-1, Rule 12, (b).

FAILURE TO SHOW RIGHT TO RELIEF.
Involuntary dismissal, §1A-1, Rule 41, (b).

FAILURE TO STATE CLAIM.
Defense by pretrial motion, §1A-1, Rule 12, (b).
Involuntary dismissal, plaintiff failed to show right to relief, §1A-1, Rule 41, (b).

FAILURE TO YIELD RIGHT-OF-WAY.
Interstate or defense highways or controlled-access highways, §20-140.3.
Point schedule, §20-16, (c).

FAIR ACCESS TO INSURANCE, §§58-46-1 to 58-46-60.
See PROPERTY INSURANCE.

FAIR HOUSING, §§41A-1 to 41A-10.
Actions.
Commission may bring to obtain relief, §41A-7, (h).
Complaints.
Judicial review.
Final agency decision, §41A-7, (m).
Jury trial, §41A-7, (k).
Right-to-sue letter.
Issuance, §41A-7, (h).
Time for issuing, §41A-7, (i).
Superior courts.
Filing of certified copy of commission's final order.
Clerk of court to enter order enforcing council's final order, §41A-7, (n).
Venue, §41A-10.
Appeals.
Final agency decisions, §41A-7, (m).
Building code provisions applicable to handicapped.
Exemption from chapter, §41A-6, (d).
Business necessity.
Not violation, §41A-5, (a).
Certification.
Commission certification by federal department prerequisite to acceptance of complaints, §41A-7, (a).
Citation of chapter, §41A-1.
Coercion, intimidation, threats or interference, §41A-4, (e).
Commercial real estate.
Exemption from chapter, §41A-6, (a).
Complaints.
Actions.
Commission issuance of notice of conciliation failure.
Actions of council when civil action not elected, §41A-7, (l).
Issuance of right-to-sue letter, §41A-7.

FAIR HOUSING —Cont'd
Complaints —Cont'd
Actions —Cont'd
Judicial review.
Final agency decision, §41A-7, (m).
Right-to-sue letter.
Time for issuance, §41A-7, (i).
Answers.
Filing, §41A-7, (b).
Appeals.
Final agency decisions, §41A-7, (m).
Assignment of administrative law judges, §41A-7, (l).
Certification.
Commission certification by federal department prerequisite to acceptance of complaints, §41A-7, (a).
Conciliation.
Agreements.
Commission to approve, §41A-7, (g).
Public disclosure, §41A-7, (g).
Commission to seek to informally resolve complaint, §41A-7, (g).
Failure of conciliation.
Actions of commission, §41A-7, (h).
Notice of conciliation failure, §41A-7, (k).
Resolution by conciliation, §41A-7, (d).
Conference.
Commission to seek to bring about informal resolution through conference, §41A-7.
Resolution by informal conference, §41A-7, (d).
Dismissal, §41A-7, (f).
Filing, §41A-7, (a), (b).
Final decision.
Commission's panel composition, §41A-7, (l).
Final administrative disposition.
Time in which commission shall make, §41A-7, (b).
Judicial review, §41A-7, (m).
Penalties of commission, §41A-7, (l).
Remedies of commission, §41A-7, (l).
Form, §41A-7, (a).
Grounds for belief of occurrences.
Unlawful discriminatory housing practices.
Steps council to take, §41A-7, (g).
Injunction, §41A-7, (j).
Investigations, §41A-7, (e).
Jurisdiction, §41A-7, (c).
Notice, §41A-7, (a).
Persuasion.
Commission to seek informal resolution through persuasion, §41A-7, (g).
Resolution of complaint by persuasion, §41A-7, (d).
Relief.
Commission may grant appropriate relief, §41A-7, (j).
Resolution.
Failure to resolve.
Actions of commission, §41A-7, (h).
Informal resolution, §41A-7, (d).
Commission to attempt to bring about, §41A-7, (g).
Respondent.
Notice of procedural rights and obligations, §41A-7, (a).
Serving of complaint, §41A-7, (a).
Right-to-sue letter.
Council issuance of notice of conciliation failure.
Actions of commission when letter not requested, §41A-7, (l).

FAIR HOUSING —Cont'd
Complaints —Cont'd
Time for determination, §41A-7, (e).
Damages.
Actual and punitive damages, §41A-7, (j).
Defenses.
Business necessity, §41A-5, (a).
Unlawful discriminatory housing practices.
Acting for another no defense, §41A-5, (b).
Definitions, §41A-3.
Residential real estate related transactions, §41A-4, (b1).
Disclosures.
Conciliation agreements, §41A-7, (g).
Evidence.
Intent to discriminate, establishing, §41A-5, (a).
Exemptions.
Building code provisions, §41A-6, (d).
Familial status.
Inapplicability to housing for older persons, §41A-6, (e).
Generally, §41A-6, (a).
Maximum number of occupants.
Local or state restrictions, §41A-6, (c).
Threat to health or safety.
Tenancy constituting, §41A-6, (b).
Familial status provisions contained in chapter.
Inapplicability to housing for older persons, §41A-6, (e).
Financial institutions.
Unlawful discriminatory housing practices, §41A-4, (b).
Four families or less, accommodations for.
Exemption from chapter, §41A-6, (a).
Housing for older persons.
Inapplicability of famial status provisions, §41A-6, (e).
Injunctions.
Appropriateness of relief, §41A-7, (j).
Intent of chapter, §41A-2.
Intent to discriminate.
Establishing, §41A-5, (a).
Investigations, §41A-8, (a).
Complaints, §41A-7, (e).
Maximum number of occupants.
Local or state restrictions.
Exemption from chapter, §41A-6, (c).
Notice.
Complaints, §41A-7, (a).
Respondent.
Notice of procedural rights and obligations, §41A-7, (a).
Conciliation.
Notice of conciliation failure, §41A-7, (k).
Orders, §41A-7.
Commission.
Final decision orders, §41A-7, (l).
Superior courts.
Clerk of court to enter order enforcing commission's final orders, §41A-7, (n).
Penalties.
Complaints.
Commission's final decisions, §41A-7, (l).
Private clubs.
Exemption from chapter, §41A-6, (a).
Private house, rental of room or rooms.
Exemption from chapter, §41A-6, (a).
Purpose of chapter, §41A-2.
Real estate brokers.
Unlawful discriminatory housing practices, §41A-4, (d).

FAIR HOUSING —Cont'd
Real estate transactions.
Unlawful discriminatory housing practices, §41A-4, (c).
Religious institutions.
Exemption from chapter, §41A-6, (a).
Remedies.
Complaints.
Commission's final decisions, §41A-7, (l).
Residential real estate related transactions.
Defined, §41A-4, (b1).
Single sex dormitory.
Exemption from chapter, §41A-6, (a).
Subpoenas.
Issuance, §41A-8, (b).
Refusal to obey, §41A-8, (d).
Respondent, entitlement to issuance, §41A-8, (c).
Superior courts.
Filing of certified copy of council's final order.
Clerk of court to enter order enforcing commission's final order, §41A-7, (n).
Threat to health or safety.
Exemption from chapter, §41A-6, (b).
Title of chapter, §41A-1.
Unlawful discriminatory housing practices.
Acting for another no defense, §41A-5, (b).
Enumeration, §41A-4.
Generally, §41A-4, (a).
Proof of violation, §41A-5, (a).
Steps commission to take, §41A-7, (g).
Violations.
Proof of violation, §41A-5, (a).
Venue.
Civil actions, §41A-10.

FAIR LABOR STANDARDS ACT OF 1938.
Enforcement, §95-14.
Limitation of actions, §1-52.

FAIR MARKET VALUE.
Eminent domain.
Compensation for taking, §40A-64.

FAIRS.
Agricultural exhibits.
Local aid, §106-520.
Animal exhibits.
Local aid, §106-520.
Commissioner of agriculture.
Supervision of fairs, §106-520.3.
County commissioners.
Application for license to commissioners, §106-517.
Penalty for violation of provisions, §106-518.
Refusal to license shows within five miles, §106-519.
County societies.
Evidence.
Records may be read in evidence, §106-511.
Exhibits exempt from state and county taxes, §106-507.
Funds to be used in paying premiums, §106-508.
Incorporation, §106-505.
New members, §106-506.
Officers, §106-506.
Organization, §106-506.
Powers, §106-505.
Premiums awarded by societies.
Funds to be used in paying premiums, §106-508.
Publication of statements required, §106-510.

FAIRS —Cont'd
County societies —Cont'd
Records to be kept, §106-511.
May be read in evidence, §106-511.
Statements.
Annual statements to state treasurer, §106-509.
Publication required, §106-510.
State treasurer.
Annual statement to treasurer, §106-509.
Taxation.
Exhibits exempt from state and county taxes, §106-507.
Term of existence, §106-505.
Definitions.
Supervision of fairs, §106-520.1.
Exhibitors' license to be paid if near fairs, §106-516.
Unlicensed exhibiting a misdemeanor, §106-518.
General assembly.
Land set apart for state fair.
Repossession of land at will of general assembly, §106-504.
Licenses.
Application for license to county commissioners, §106-517.
Penalty for violation of provisions, §106-518.
Refusal to license shows within five miles, §106-519.
Exhibitors near fairs to pay license, §106-516.
Protection and regulation of fairs.
Lien against licensees' property to secure charge, §106-512.
Notice of sale to owner, §106-513.
Refusal to license shows within five miles, §106-519.
Vendors near fairs to pay license, §106-516.
Liens.
Protection and regulation of fairs.
Lien against licensees' property to secure charge, §106-512.
Notice of sale to owner, §106-513.
Local aid to agricultural, animal and poultry exhibits, §106-520.
Supervision of fairs, §106-520.4.
Permits.
Carnivals and similar amusements not to operate without permit, §106-516.1.
Poultry exhibits.
Local aid, §106-520.
Property.
Theft or destruction of property of fairs, §14-398.
State fair.
Admission to fair grounds.
Fees or charges.
Establishment by regulations, §106-503.
Board of agriculture.
Constructing and financing facilities and improvements for fair, §106-503.1.
Operation of fair, §106-503, (a).
Bond issues, §106-503.1, (a).
Borrowing money, §106-503.1, (a).
Constructing facilities and improvements of fair, §106-503.1.
Contracts and leases, §106-503.1, (b).
Dedication of land, §106-502.
Repossession of land at will of general assembly, §106-504.
Endowments, §106-503.1, (c).
Fees or charges.
Admission to fair grounds.
Establishment by regulations, §106-503, (b).

FAIRS —Cont'd
State fair —Cont'd
Financing facilities and improvements for fair, §106-503.1.
Gate receipts.
Pledge of receipts, §106-503.1, (b).
General assembly.
Land dedicated by state may be repossessed at will, §106-504.
Gifts and endowments, §106-503.1, (c).
Land set apart, §106-502.
Leases, §106-503.1, (b).
Operation of fair, §106-503, (a).
Pledge of gate receipts, etc., §106-503.1, (b).
Recycling bins.
Providing and maintaining, §106-503, (d).
Rental rates.
Establishment of schedule, §106-503, (c).
Rules and regulations.
Fees for admission to fair grounds, §106-503, (b).
Sale of merchandise by governmental units.
Exception to prohibition, §66-58, (b).
State lands.
Land set aside for state fair, §106-502.
Repossession of land at will of general assembly, §106-504.
State lands.
Land set apart for state fair, §106-502.
Repossession of land at will of general assembly, §106-504.
Supervision of fairs.
Commissioner of agricultural to regulate, §106-520.3.
Definition of fair, §106-520.1.
Local supervision of fairs, §106-520.4.
Misdemeanors, §106-520.7.
Name of exhibition.
Use of "fair" in name, §106-520.2.
Premiums and premium lists supplemented, §106-520.6.
Reports, §106-520.5.
Supplementing premiums and premium lists, §106-520.6.
Use of "fair" in name of exhibition, §106-520.2.
Violations made misdemeanor, §106-520.7.
Theft.
Destruction or theft of property of fair, §14-398.
Unlawful entry on grounds.
Assisting unlawful entry a misdemeanor, §106-515.
Misdemeanor offenses, §§106-514, 106-515.
Vendors' licenses to be paid if near fairs, §106-516.
Unlicensed vending a misdemeanor, §106-518.

FAIR TRADE.
Monopolies and restraint of trade.
See MONOPOLIES AND RESTRAINT OF TRADE.

FAITHLESS ELECTOR STATUTE.
Failure of presidential elector to attend and vote, §163-212.

FAKE ID'S.
Alcoholic beverage sales to or purchases by underage persons.
Fraudulent use of identification, §18B-302, (e).
Driver's license information verification system, §20-37.02.
Possession or manufacture, §14-100.1.

FAKE ID'S —Cont'd
Violations of driver's license or learner's permit provisions, §20-30.
Wrongful issuance of drivers' licenses or special identification cards, §20-34.1.

FALCONRY.
Licenses, §113-270.3, (b).
Method of taking wild animals or wild birds, §113-291.1, (a).

FALLOW DEER.
Meat inspections.
Generally, §§106-549.15 to 106-549.39.
See MEAT INSPECTIONS.

FALSE ADVERTISING ACT, §§66-76 to 66-83.
See CLOSING-OUT SALES.

FALSE ADVERTISING BY UNAUTHORIZED INSURERS.
Unauthorized insurers false advertising process act, §§58-29-1 to 58-29-25.
See UNAUTHORIZED INSURERS.

FALSE ALARMS.
Students communicating false threats of harm, §115C-391, (d4).

FALSE AMBULANCE REQUESTS, §14-286.1.

FALSE BILLS OF LADING.
Issuing, §21-42.

FALSE CLAIMS BY MEDICAL ASSISTANCE PROVIDERS, §§108A-70.10 to 108A-70.16.
See MEDICAID.

FALSE COINS OR TOKENS.
Counterfeiting and uttering, §14-13.
Manufacture, sale or gift, §14-109.
Obtaining property or services by use of, §14-108.

FALSE FIRE ALARMS.
Giving false fire alarms, §14-286.
Molesting fire-alarm, §14-286.

FALSE IMPERSONATION.
Emergency medical services personnel, §14-276.1.
Firemen, §14-276.1.
Law enforcement officers, §14-277, (a) to (d1).
Public officers and employees, §14-277, (e).
Public weighmasters.
Prohibited, §81A-55, (b).

FALSE IMPRISONMENT.
Allowance of costs to defendant, §6-19.
Allowance of costs to plaintiff, §6-18.
Limitation of actions, §1-52.
Rights of action not surviving decedent, §28A-18-1.
Shoplifting.
Detention or arrest of suspects.
Liability for false imprisonment, §§14-72, (d), 14-72.1, (c).

FALSE NAMES.
Drivers' licenses.
Presenting license with fake name in commission of felony, §20-30.
Identification cards.
Presenting identification card with fake name in commission of felony, §20-37.8, (b).

FALSE PRETENSES AND CHEATS, §§14-100 to 14-113.
Absentees in military service.
Receiver appointment obtained by false representation, §28B-7.

FALSE PRETENSES AND CHEATS —Cont'd
Advances under promise to work and pay for same.
Obtaining advances, §14-104.
Property.
Written promise to pay therefor out of designated property, §14-105.
Ambulances.
Obtaining ambulance services without intending to pay, §§14-111.1, 14-111.2.
Animal pedigree.
Obtaining property by false representation of pedigree, §14-102.
Animal registration.
Obtaining certificate of registration by false representation, §14-103.
Bad checks, §14-107.
Obtaining property in return for worthless check, draft or order, §14-106.
Prima facie evidence in worthless check cases, §14-107.1.
Bed and breakfast establishments.
Defrauding innkeeper, §14-110.
Bounced checks.
Obtaining property in return for worthless check, draft or order, §14-106.
Worthless check, draft or order, §14-107.
Prima facie evidence in worthless check cases, §14-107.1.
Campgrounds.
Defrauding campground owner, §14-110.
Checks.
Worthless check, draft or order, §14-107.
Obtaining property in return for worthless check, etc., §14-106.
Prima facie evidence in worthless check cases, §14-107.1.
Choses in action.
Obtaining property by false pretenses, §14-100.
Civil liability for damages, §1-538.2, (a).
Action brought regardless of criminal action, §1-538.2, (c).
Consequential and punitive damages and attorneys' fees.
Additional recovery allowed, §1-538.2, (a).
Amount of damages, cap, §1-538.2, (a).
Parent or legal guardian liable for acts of minor, §1-538.2, (b).
Consequential damages, included in, §1-538.2, (c1).
Demand letter, seeking damages prior to action, §1-538.2, (c2).
Payment of money demanded, no further action, §1-538.2, (c4).
Demand letter, seeking damages prior to action, §1-538.2, (c2).
Payment of money demanded, no further action, §1-538.2, (c4).
Qualified privilege of sender, §1-538.2, (c3).
Libel and slander.
Demand letter, seeking damages prior to action.
Qualified privilege of sender, §1-538.2, (c3).
Other theories of law, recovery under, §1-538.2, (d).
Parent or legal guardian liable for acts of minor, §1-538.2, (b).
Recovery of value of goods and merchandise, §1-538.2, (a).
Coin-operated machines.
Manufacture, sale, or gift of devices for cheating slot machines, §14-109.

FALSE PRETENSES AND CHEATS —Cont'd
Coin-operated machines —Cont'd
Obtaining property or services from machine by false coins or tokens, §14-108.
Contracts.
Advance payments under promise to work and pay for same, §14-104.
Nonfulfillment of contract obligation, §14-100.
Credit cards, §§14-113.1 to 14-113.7A.
See CREDIT CARDS.
Definitions.
Person, §14-100, (c).
Disabled persons.
Obtaining money by false representation of physical defect, §14-113.
Drafts.
Worthless check, draft or order, §14-107.
Obtaining property in return for worthless check, etc., §14-106.
Prima facie evidence in worthless check cases, §14-107.1.
Forgery.
Generally.
See FORGERY.
Obtaining signatures by false pretenses, §14-101.
Fraud.
See FRAUD.
Handicapped persons.
Obtaining money by false representation of physical defect, §14-113.
Hotels.
Defrauding innkeeper, §14-110.
Identification, false or fraudulent, §14-100.1.
Insurance consumer and customer information privacy.
Obtaining information under false pretenses, §58-39-115.
Kennel clubs.
Animal registration certificate obtained by false representation, §14-103.
Letters testamentary and of administration.
Grounds for revocation, §28A-9-1.
Marriage license obtained by false pretenses, §51-15.
Merchants.
Obtaining merchandise on approval, §14-112.
Money.
Counterfeiting generally, §§14-13 to 14-16.
See COUNTERFEITING.
Physical defects.
Obtaining money by false representation of physical defect, §14-113.
Nuclear, biological or chemical weapons.
Hoax or false report, §§14-288.23, 14-288.24.
Person.
Defined, §14-100, (c).
Physically disabled persons.
Obtaining money by false representation of physical defect, §14-113.
Promises to work and pay for same.
Obtaining advances under promise to work, §14-104.
Written promise to pay therefor out of designated property, §14-105.
Property.
Advances under promise to work and pay for same.
Obtaining advances under written promise therefor out of designated property, §14-105.
Definition of "person," §14-100, (c).

FALSE PRETENSES AND CHEATS —Cont'd
Property —Cont'd
Obtaining property by false pretenses, §14-100.
Elements of offense, §14-100, (a).
Establishing element of intent to defraud, §14-100, (b).
Restaurants.
Failure to pay for services, §14-110.
Security agreements.
Filing false security agreements, §14-401.19.
Signatures.
Obtaining signatures by false pretenses, §14-101.
Slot machines.
Manufacture, sale, or gift of devices for cheating machines, §14-109.
Obtaining property or services from machines by false coins or tokens, §14-108.
Telecommunications.
Concealment of destination of telecommunications, §14-113.5.
Payment for telecommunication services.
Avoiding or attempting to avoid payment, §14-113.4.
Telephones.
Obtaining property or services by false or fraudulent use, §14-113.6A.

FALSE REPORTS CONCERNING DESTRUCTIVE DEVICE.
Destructive device located in any building or vehicle, §14-69.1, (a).
Destructive device located in public building, §14-69.1, (c).
Report defined, §14-69.1, (d).
Restitution, costs and consequential damages, ordering, §14-69.1, (d).

FALSE REPORTS TO LAW ENFORCEMENT OFFICERS, §14-225.

FALSE RETURN OF PROCESS, §14-242.

FALSE STATEMENT TO PROCURE OR DENY INSURANCE BENEFIT, §58-2-161.

FALSE SWEARING.
Perjury generally.
See PERJURY.

FALSE TEETH.
Sales and use tax.
Exemptions, §105-164.13.

FALSE THREATS TO DESTROY OR DAMAGE PROPERTY.
Suspension of school student making, §115C-391, (d3).

FAMILY AND MARRIAGE THERAPY LICENSURE ACT, §§90-270.45 to 90-270.62.
See MARRIAGE AND FAMILY THERAPISTS.

FAMILY CARE HOMES, §§168-20 to 168-23.
Definitions, §168-21.
"Handicapped persons" defined, §168-21.
Private agreements.
Certain agreements void, §168-23.
Public policy, §168-20.
Zoning.
Deemed residential use of property, §168-22.
Permits not required, §168-22.

FAMILY CHILD CARE HOMES.
Capacity, §110-91.
Child care facilities generally, §§110-85 to 110-107.
See CHILD CARE FACILITIES.
Defined, §110-86.

FAMILY FOSTER HOMES.
Regulation of agencies receiving or placing children, §§131D-10.1 to 131D-10.9.
See CHILD PLACING AGENCIES.

FAMILY HISTORY.
Hearsay exceptions, §8C-1, Rules 803, 804.

FAMILY LAW.
Alimony.
See ALIMONY.
Annulment of marriage.
See ANNULMENT OF MARRIAGE.
Attorneys specializing in.
Certification standards, Bar Rules & Regs., D, §§.2401 to .2407.
Child custody.
General provisions.
See CHILD CUSTODY.
Jurisdiction and enforcement, §§50A-101 to 50A-317.
See CHILD CUSTODY JURISDICTION AND ENFORCEMENT.
Child support.
See CHILD SUPPORT.
Divorce.
See DIVORCE.
Domestic violence, §§50B-1 to 50B-9.
See DOMESTIC VIOLENCE.
Husband and wife.
See HUSBAND AND WIFE.
Marriage, §§51-1 to 51-21.
See MARRIAGE PROCEEDINGS.
Minors.
See MINORS.
Parent and child.
See PARENT AND CHILD.

FAMILY LAW ARBITRATION, §§50-41 to 50-62.
Appeals, §50-60.
Application of law by arbitrator, §50-60, (b).
Generally, §50-60, (a).
Manner of appeals, §50-60, (c).
Application of provisions.
Enforcement, §50-42, (b).
Applications, §50-43, (c).
Motions, §50-58.
Appointment of arbitrators, §50-45.
Court appointment, §50-45, (d).
Method, §50-45, (b).
Arbitrators.
Appointment, §50-45.
Change award, §50-52.
Hearings, §50-47.
Liability, §50-45, (f).
Majority action, §50-46.
Number of arbitrators, §50-45, (a).
Powers, §§50-45, (c), 50-49, (a), (b).
Majority action, §50-46.
Awards, §50-51.
Change award, §50-52.
Confirmation, §50-53.
Correction, §50-55.
Interest, §50-51, (c).
Modification, §§50-55, 50-56.
Orders or judgments on award, §50-57.
Punitive damages, §50-51, (e).
Reasons upon which based, §50-51, (b).
Requirements, §50-51, (a).
Specific performance, §50-51, (d).
Vacating, §50-54.
Child abuse or neglect, §50-44, (h).

FAMILY LAW ARBITRATION —Cont'd
Collaborative law proceedings.
Alternative dispute resolution permitted, §50-78.
Consolidation, §50-50, (a), (b).
Construction of provisions, §50-62.
Costs.
Awards, §50-51, (f), (g).
Modification or correction of awards, §50-55, (d).
Rules for conducting arbitration, §50-45, (h).
Definitions.
Appointment of arbitrators, §50-45, (g).
Court, §50-59.
Enforcement, §50-42, (a).
Evidence, §50-49, (d).
Hearings, §50-47.
Attorneys at law, §50-48.
Interest.
Awards, §50-51, (c).
Interim relief, §50-44.
Applicable law, §50-44, (a).
Findings of fact, §50-44, (e).
Jurisdiction, §50-44, (f).
Remedies, §50-44, (c).
Request for, §50-44, (i).
Right to seek, §50-44, (b).
Interpretation of provisions, §50-61.
Uniformity of interpretation, §50-62.
Jurisdiction, §50-59.
Modification or correction of award, §§50-55, 50-56.
Alimony, postseparation support, child custody or child support.
Change in circumstances, §50-56.
Application, §50-55, (a).
Vacating award, §50-55, (c).
Change in circumstances.
Applicability of G.S. 50-55, §50-56, (f).
Authority of court or arbitrators to modify, §50-56, (a).
Child support or child custody, §50-56, (c).
Post separation support or alimony, §50-56, (b).
Confirmation of award.
Matters submitted to arbitrators, §50-56, (d), (e).
Confirmation, §50-55, (b).
Costs, §50-55, (d).
Orders, §50-43, (d).
Interim relief, §50-44, (d).
Refusal to grant, §50-43, (e).
Proceedings to compel, §50-43, (a).
Punitive damages, §50-51, (e).
Purpose, §50-41, (a).
Refusal to grant order or stay, §50-43, (e).
Retroactive application, §50-61.
Rules for arbitration, §50-45, (e).
Short title, §50-41, (b).
Specific performance, §50-51, (d).
Stays, §50-43, (b).
Orders, §50-43, (d).
Refusal to grant, §50-43, (e).
Subpoenas.
Powers of arbitrators, §50-49, (a), (c), (e).
Vacating awards.
Application to vacate, §50-54, (a), (b).
Denial, §50-54, (d).
Grounds, §50-54, (c).
Modification or correction of awards, §50-55, (c).
Validity of arbitration agreements, §50-42, (a).

FAMILY LAW SPECIALTY.
Certification standards, Bar Rules & Regs., D, §§.2401 to .2407.

FAMILY LEAVE.
Public schools.
School employees.
Parental leave, §115C-336.1.
Teachers.
Parental leave, §115C-302.1, (j).

FAMILY LEAVE CREDIT INSURANCE.
Defined, §58-57-5.
Policy standards and provisions, §58-57-115.
Coverage, §58-57-115, (b).
Definitions, §58-57-115, (a).
Eligibility for coverage, §58-57-115, (c).
Evidence of employer approval of qualified leave, §58-57-115, (h).
Exclusions from coverage, §58-57-115, (e).
Lump-sum payments, §58-57-115, (h).
Minimum monthly benefit amount, §58-57-115, (g).
Notice that benefits paid, §58-57-115, (f).
Premium rates, §58-57-115, (i).
Qualifying events for payment of benefits, §58-57-115, (d).
Refund of unearned premium, §58-57-115, (h).
Reports by insurers offering, §58-57-115, (j).
Waiting period for benefits, §58-57-115, (h).

FAMILY MEDICINE.
Primary care physicians, medical education, §143-613.

FAMILY PRESERVATION, §§143B-150.5, 143B-150.6.
Cooperation of state agencies, §143B-150.5, (d).
Development and implementation of family preservation services program, §143B-150.5, (a).
Eligible families for services, §143B-150.6, (b).
Services delivered to, §143B-150.6, (c).
Establishment of family preservation services program, §143B-150.5, (a).
Financing family preservation services.
Grants, §143B-150.5, (c).
Grants.
Awarding to local agencies, §143B-150.6, (d).
Financing family preservation services, §143B-150.5, (c).
Purposes of family preservation services program, §143B-150.5, (b).
Services delivered to eligible families, §143B-150.6, (c).
Services provided under family preservation services program, §143B-150.6, (a).
Use of funds available to divisions to support program, §143B-150.6, (e).

FAMILY PURPOSE DOCTRINE.
Boating safety.
Applicability of doctrine, §75A-10.1.
Strict liability for damage to person or property by minors, §1-538.1.

FAMILY RECORDS.
Hearsay exception, §8C-1, Rule 803.

FAMILY RESOURCE CENTER GRANT PROGRAM, §§143B-152.10 to 143B-152.15.

FAMILY THERAPY, §§90-270.45 to 90-270.62.
See MARRIAGE AND FAMILY THERAPISTS.

FARM AND HOME DEVELOPMENT PROGRAM.
Agricultural development generally, §§106-580 to 106-587.
See AGRICULTURAL DEVELOPMENT.

FARM CONTAINERS.
Sales and use tax.
Rate on sales to farmers, §105-164.4A.

FARM CREDIT ADMINISTRATION.
Banks.
Investment in farm loan bonds, §53-60.
Obligations of agencies supervised by.
Investments in, §53-44.1.
Securities for deposit of public funds, §53-43.1.

FARM EQUIPMENT.
Age for operation, §20-10.
Certificate of title exemptions, §20-51.
Defined, §20-4.01.
Driver's license requirement exemptions, §20-8.
Identification marks, removing, defacing, etc., §14-401.4.
Inside rearview mirror requirement exempt from provisions, §20-126, (a).
Mechanical breakdown service agreement, §58-1-42.
Motor vehicle repairs.
Applicability of provisions to farm vehicles, §20-354.1.
Registration exemptions, §20-51.
Sales and use tax.
Rate of tax on farm machines and machinery, §105-164.4A.

FARMERS MARKETS.
Sale of merchandise by governmental units.
Department of agriculture and consumer services operated markets, exception in provisions, §66-58, (b).

FARM FORECLOSURES.
Geographically based field programs.
Eligible cases, §7A-474.3, (b).

FARMING OUT CONVICTS, §§148-66 to 148-70.
See PRISONER LABOR.

FARMLAND PRESERVATION, §§106-735 to 106-743.
Agricultural advisory board, §106-739.
Authorization of programs, §106-736.
Citation of act.
Short title, §106-735, (a).
Condemnation of farmland.
Hearings, §106-740.
Conservation agreements.
Qualifying farmland, §106-737.
Revocation, §106-737.1.
Hearings.
Condemnation of farmland, §106-740.
Notice.
Record notice of proximity to farmlands, §106-741, (a).
Immunities from liability in connection with, §106-741, (b), (c).
Ordinances.
Agricultural advisory board.
Ordinance to provide for, §106-739.
Commissioner of agriculture.
Consultation with before adopting ordinance, §106-743.
Establishment of programs, §106-736.
Voluntary agricultural districts.
Ordinance to provide for, §106-738, (a).
Water and sewer assessments.
Waiver, §106-742, (a), (b), (d).
Purpose of act, §106-735, (b).
Qualifying farmland, §106-737.

FARMLAND PRESERVATION —Cont'd
Reports.
Counties to report to commissioner of agriculture, §106-743.
Revocation of conservation agreements, §106-737.1.
Short title of act, §106-735, (a).
Voluntary agricultural districts.
Ordinance to provide for, §106-738, (a).
Purpose, §106-738, (b).
Water and sewer assessments.
Authority of counties to hold assessments in abeyance not diminished, §106-742, (e).
Limitation of actions.
Suspension during time assessment held in abeyance, §106-742, (c).
Ordinance, §106-742, (d).
Waiver.
Ordinance, §106-742, (a), (b).

FARMLAND PRESERVATION TRUST FUND, §106-744, (c) to (c2).

FARM MACHINERY FRANCHISES.
Commercial practices.
Uniformity, §66-186.
Definitions, §66-180.
Usage of trade, §66-181.
Notice.
Termination by dealer.
Contents requirements, §66-182, (c).
Required, §66-182, (b).
Termination by supplier.
Contents requirements, §66-182, (c).
Required, time limit, §66-182, (a).
Prohibited acts, §66-187.1.
Repurchase.
Cost of shipping and handling, §66-184, (d).
Death of dealer or majority stockholder.
Exercise of heir's options, §66-184, (g).
Supplier's duty, §66-183, (b).
Exceptions to repurchase requirements, §66-185.
Full payment, time for, §66-184, (e).
New agreement to operate dealership, §66-184, (h).
Payments to dealer, §66-184, (b).
Succession agreement, §66-184, (i).
Supplier's duty to repurchase, §66-183.
Failure to repurchase, §66-188.
Termination by death or incompetence of dealer, §66-183, (b).
Termination by either party, §66-183, (a).
Terms, §66-184.
Time for, §66-184, (a).
Transfer of title, §66-184, (f).
Termination.
Supplier's duty to repurchase, §66-183.
Exceptions, §66-185.
Failure to repurchase, §66-188.
Repurchase terms, §66-184.
Termination by dealer.
Notice.
Contents requirements, §66-182, (c).
Required, §66-182, (b).
Termination by supplier.
Cure of deficiency.
Notice void, §66-182, (a).
Good cause.
Notice not required, §66-182, (a1).
Notice.
Contents requirements, §66-182, (c).
Required, time limit, §66-182, (a).

FARM MACHINERY FRANCHISES —Cont'd
Termination by supplier —Cont'd
Right-to-cure deficiency.
Required to provide dealer, §66-182, (a).
Uniform commercial practice, §66-186.
Effect on security interests, §66-186, (a).
Representatives to inspect parts, §66-186, (c).
Warranties.
Claim for work prior to termination, §66-187, (c).
Errors, adjustment for, §66-187, (h).
Expenses excluded under warranty, §66-187, (f).
Indemnification, §66-187, (a), (b).
Interest on unpaid claims, §66-187, (d).
Obligations, §66-187.
Payment for parts, §66-187, (g).
Reasonable and customary rates, §66-187, (e).
Reimbursement in lieu of warranty provisions, §66-187, (i).

FARM MACHINERY TAX CREDIT.
Property taxes paid on, §105-151.21.

FARM NAME REGISTRATION, §§80-34 to 80-39.
Application for registry, §80-36.
Hearing on, §80-36.
Publication, §80-36.
Authorized, §80-33.
Cancellation of registry, §80-39.
Fee, §80-39.
Continuation of name.
When transfer of farm carries name, §80-38.
Distinctive name required, §80-35.
Effect, §80-34.
Fees, §80-37.
Cancellation of registry, §80-39.
Hearing on application, §80-36.
Non-confusing name required, §80-35.
Similar names not to be registered after registry, §80-34.
Transfer of farm.
When transfer carries name, §80-38.

FARM NUISANCE DISPUTES.
Prelitigation mediation, §7A-38.3.
Certification that mediation concluded, Farm Med. Rule 8.
Compensation of mediator, Farm Med. Rule 6.
Completion, Farm Med. Rule 4.
Conclusion.
Certification, Farm Med. Rule 8.
Certification training programs, Farm Med. Rule 10.
Compensation, Farm Med. Rule 8.
Selection, Farm Med. Rule 3.
Submission of dispute, Farm Med. Rule 1.
Waiver, Farm Med. Rule 7.

FARM OPERATIONS COMMISSION.
Exception to prohibition of merchandise sales by state agencies, §66-58, (b).

FARM PRODUCTS MARKETING AND BRANDING, §§106-185 to 106-196.
Agents.
Power to employ, §106-186.
Aggregate state service credit for graders, §106-190.1.
Appeal from classification of farm products, §106-191.
Apple grade standards.
Requirements for maturity, adoption, §106-189.2, (a).
Criminal penalty for violating, §106-189.2, (b).

FARM PRODUCTS MARKETING AND BRANDING —Cont'd
Assistants.
Power to employ assistants, §106-186.
Board of agriculture.
Investigating marketing of farm products, §106-187.
Classification of farm products.
Appeal from classification, §106-191.
Prima facie evidence, §106-192.
Unwholesome products not classified, §106-193.
Conformity to requirements of article.
Sale and receptacles of standardized products must conform, §106-189.
Construction of term "farm products," §106-185, (a).
Employment of agents and assistants, §106-186.
Evidence.
Certificate of grade or classification of farm product prima facie evidence, §106-192.
Federal-state cooperation, §106-185, (b).
Grades.
Aggregate state service credit for graders, §106-190.1.
Authorized graders, §106-190.
Certificate of grade.
Prima facie evidence, §106-192.
Establishment and maintenance of standard grades, §§106-185, (a), 106-188.
Health officer.
Notification in cases of unwholesome products, §106-193.
Immature apples.
Apple grade standards including requirements for maturity, adoption, §106-189.2, (a).
Criminal penalty for violating, §106-189.2, (b).
Inspections.
Authorized farm products, §106-194.
Farm product inspection account, §106-194.1.
Inspectors.
Authorized, §106-190.
Investigations.
Board of agriculture to investigate marketing of farm products, §106-187.
Licenses.
Revocation of license, §106-190.
Misdemeanors.
Violation of article or regulations a misdemeanor, §106-196.
Packages.
Establishment and maintenance of standard packages, §106-185, (a).
Prescribing rules and regulations, §106-195.
Promotion of use and sale of agricultural products.
Generally, §§106-550 to 106-568.
See AGRICULTURAL PRODUCTS PROMOTION.
Purpose of article, §106-185, (a).
Receptacles of standardized products.
Conforming as to requirements, §106-189.
Establishment and promulgation of standards for opened and closed receptacles, §106-188.
Marks, brands and labels, §106-188.
Requirements of article.
Sale and receptacles of standardized products must conform, §106-189.
Rules and regulations.
How prescribed, §106-195.
Misdemeanor offenses, §106-196.

FARM PRODUCTS MARKETING AND BRANDING —Cont'd
Sampling of farm products.
Authorized, §106-194.
Standardized products.
Conforming to requirements, §106-189.
State service credit.
Aggregate credit for graders, §106-190.1.
Unwholesome products.
Classification of farm products, §106-193.
Notification of health officer, §106-193.
Violations of article.
Misdemeanor offenses, §106-196.

FARMS AND FARMERS.
Adulteration of grain, §§106-621 to 106-628.
See GRAIN ADULTERATION.
Agriculture generally.
See AGRICULTURE.
Animals generally.
See ANIMALS.
Animal waste management, §§143-215.10A to 143-215.10H.
See ANIMAL WASTE MANAGEMENT.
Aquaculture development, §§106-756 to 106-760.
Auction of livestock.
Livestock markets.
Generally, §§106-406 to 106-418.
See LIVESTOCK MARKETS.
Bees and honey.
See BEES AND HONEY.
Biological organism act, §§106-65.42 to 106-65.49.
Biologics, §§106-707 to 106-715.
Board of agriculture.
See AGRICULTURE BOARD.
Boll weevil eradication, §§106-65.67 to 106-65.78.
Cigarettes and tobacco products generally.
See CIGARETTES AND TOBACCO PRODUCTS.
Commercial feed, §§106-284.30 to 106-284.46.
See FEED.
Commercial fertilizers, §§106-655 to 106-677.
See FERTILIZERS.
Commissioner of agriculture.
See AGRICULTURE COMMISSIONER.
Commission on agriculture and forestry awareness, §§120-150 to 120-154.
Commodities generally, §§78D-1 to 78D-33.
See COMMODITIES.
Cotton.
Generally.
See COTTON.
Cotton grower's association, §§106-65.84 to 106-451.28.
See COTTON WAREHOUSES.
Crops generally.
See CROPS.
Dairies and dairy products.
Generally.
See MILK AND MILK PRODUCTS.
Ice cream plants, creameries and cheese factories generally, §§106-246 to 106-255.
See ICE CREAM PLANTS, CREAMERIES AND CHEESE FACTORIES.
Department of agriculture and consumer services.
See AGRICULTURE AND CONSUMER SERVICES DEPARTMENT.
Development act generally, §§106-580 to 106-587.

FARMS AND FARMERS —Cont'd
Drainage, §§156-1 to 156-41.
See DRAINAGE.
Drainage districts, §§156-54 to 156-138.4.
See DRAINAGE DISTRICTS.
Eggs, §§106-245.13 to 106-245.28.
Extension service.
Agriculture development generally, §§106-580 to 106-587.
Farm machinery franchises, §§66-180 to 66-188.
Farm name registration, §§80-33 to 80-39.
Farm nuisance dispute mediation, §7A-38.3; Farm Med. Rules 1 to 10.
Farm worker council, §§143B-426.25, 143B-426.26.
Feed generally, §§106-284.30 to 106-284.46.
See FEED.
Fees and taxes generally.
See AGRICULTURAL FEES AND TAXES.
Fertilizers.
Generally, §§106-655 to 106-677.
See FERTILIZERS.
Soil additives act, §§106-50.28 to 106-50.41.
See SOIL ADDITIVES ACT.
Finance authority, §§122D-1 to 122D-23.
See AGRICULTURAL FINANCE AUTHORITY.
Food, drug and cosmetic act, §§106-120 to 106-145.
See FOOD, DRUG AND COSMETIC ACT.
Fruit handlers unfair practices, §§106-496 to 106-501.
Grain dealers, §§106-601 to 106-615.
See GRAIN DEALERS.
Grape growers' council, §§106-750, 106-751.
Hall of fame, §§106-568.13 to 106-568.17.
Ice cream plants, creameries and cheese factories, §§106-246 to 106-255.
See ICE CREAM PLANTS, CREAMERIES AND CHEESE FACTORIES.
Limestone, marl and landplaster, §§106-92.1 to 106-92.17.
See LIMESTONE, MARL AND LANDPLASTER.
Livestock brands, §§80-45 to 80-66.
See LIVESTOCK BRANDS.
Livestock dealer licensing, §§106-418.8 to 106-418.16.
Livestock diseases.
Brucellosis, §§106-388 to 106-398.
See BRUCELLOSIS.
Cattle tick, §§106-351 to 106-363.
See CATTLE TICK.
Compensation for killing diseased animals, §§106-323 to 106-335.
See LIVESTOCK DISEASES.
Equine infectious anemia, §§106-405.15 to 106-405.20.
Generally, §§106-304 to 106-307, 106-400 to 106-405.
See LIVESTOCK DISEASES.
Hog cholera, §§106-310 to 106-322.3.
See HOG CHOLERA.
Tuberculosis, §§106-336 to 106-350.
See TUBERCULOSIS IN LIVESTOCK.
Livestock generally.
See LIVESTOCK.
Livestock markets.
Generally, §§106-406 to 106-418.
See LIVESTOCK MARKETS.
Prompt payment, §§106-418.1 to 106-418.7A.
See LIVESTOCK MARKETS.

FARMS AND FARMERS —Cont'd
Marketing and branding farm products, §§106-185 to 106-196.
See FARM PRODUCTS MARKETING AND BRANDING.
Marketing associations generally, §§54-129 to 54-166.
See MARKETING ASSOCIATIONS.
Marketing authority, §§106-528 to 106-534.
Meat inspections, §§106-549.15 to 106-549.39.
See MEAT INSPECTIONS.
Migrant farm workers.
See MIGRANT FARM WORKERS.
Milk and milk products.
Generally, §§106-267 to 106-268.1.
See MILK AND MILK PRODUCTS.
Ice cream plants, creameries and cheese factories, §§106-246 to 106-255.
See ICE CREAM PLANTS, CREAMERIES AND CHEESE FACTORIES.
Milk distributors and processors generally.
See MILK DISTRIBUTORS AND PROCESSORS.
Nuisance liability of agricultural and forestry operations, §§106-700, 106-701.
Farm nuisance dispute mediation, §7A-38.3; Farm Med. Rules 1 to 10.
Pest control.
Biological organism act, §§106-65.42 to 106-65.49.
Boll weevil eradication, §§106-65.67 to 106-65.78.
Compact, §§106-65.55 to 106-65.61.
Plant pests, §§106-419 to 106-423.1.
Structural pest control, §§106-65.22 to 106-65.41.
Plant protection and conservation, §§106-202.12 to 106-202.22.
See PLANT PROTECTION AND CONSERVATION.
Poultry generally.
See POULTRY AND POULTRY PRODUCTS.
Poultry products inspections, §§106-549.49 to 106-549.69.
See POULTRY PRODUCTS INSPECTIONS.
Preservation of farmland, §§106-735 to 106-743.
Promotion of agricultural products, §§106-550 to 106-568.
See AGRICULTURAL PRODUCTS PROMOTION.
Prompt pay law, §§106-418.1 to 106-418.7A.
See LIVESTOCK MARKETS.
Property taxes.
Agricultural, horticultural and forestland, §§105-277.2 to 105-277.7.
See PROPERTY TAXES.
Rendering plants and rendering operations, §§106-168.1 to 106-168.16.
See RENDERING PLANTS AND RENDERING OPERATIONS.
Research, §§106-568.1 to 106-568.12.
See AGRICULTURAL RESEARCH.
Seeds, §§106-269 to 106-284.22.
See SEEDS.
Slaughterhouses generally.
See SLAUGHTERHOUSES.
Soil additives act, §§106-50.28 to 106-50.41.
See SOIL ADDITIVES ACT.
Soil and water conservation districts, §§139-1 to 139-57.
See SOIL AND WATER CONSERVATION DISTRICTS.
Structural pest control, §§106-65.22 to 106-65.41.
See STRUCTURAL PEST CONTROL.
Swine farms, §§106-800 to 106-803.
See HOGS.

FARMS AND FARMERS —Cont'd
Tenant farmers.
See SHARECROPPING.
Tobacco products generally.
See CIGARETTES AND TOBACCO PRODUCTS.
Vegetable handlers unfair practices, §§106-496 to 106-501.
Vegetable plant law, §§106-284.14 to 106-284.22.
See VEGETABLE PLANT LAW.

FARM STORAGE FACILITIES.
Sales and use tax.
Rate on sale and of grain, feed or soybean storage facilities, §105-164.4A.

FARM TRACTORS.
Age for operation, §20-10.
Certificates of title exemptions, §20-51.
Defined, §20-4.01.
Driver's license exemptions, §20-8.
Identification marks.
Removing.
Defacing, etc., §14-401.4.
Motor vehicle repairs.
Applicability of provisions to farm vehicles, §20-354.1.
Registration exemptions, §20-51.
Tires.
Driving on dirt roads from farm to farm, §20-122, (d).
Movable tracks.
Special permits, §20-122, (c).

FARMWORKER COUNCIL, §§143B-426.25, 143B-426.26.
Administrative services, §143B-426.25, (h).
Annual report, §143B-426.26, (b).
Appointments, §143B-426.25, (d).
Clerical equipment and administrative services, §143B-426.25, (h).
Composition, §143B-426.25, (b).
Creation, §143B-426.25, (a).
Duties, §143B-426.26, (a).
Established, §143B-426.25, (a).
Meetings, §143B-426.25, (f).
Members, §143B-426.25, (b).
Quorum, §143B-426.25, (e).
Subsistence and travel allowances, §143B-426.25, (g).
Vacancies, §143B-426.25, (c).

FARO BANKS AND TABLES.
Gaming.
Opening, establishing, etc., bank or table, §14-294.
Illegal operation.
Testimony enforced in certain criminal investigations.
Immunity of witness, §8-55.

FAST-FOOD BUSINESSES, ALCOHOLIC BEVERAGE PERMITS, §18B-1001.

FAX.
Electronic records and signatures.
Uniform electronic transactions act, §§66-311 to 66-330.
See ELECTRONIC TRANSACTIONS.
Facsimile signatures.
See FACSIMILE SIGNATURES.
Filing of pleadings and papers, §1A-1, Rule 5, (e).
Interstate family support.
Admissibility as evidence, §52C-3-315, (e).

FAX —Cont'd
Military absentee voting.
Facsimile, electronic mail or scanned transmission of election materials, §163-257.
Nonprofit corporations.
Notice communicated by, §55A-1-41, (b).
Service and filing of pleadings and papers, §1A-1, Rule 5, (b), (e).

FAYETTEVILLE, CITY OF.
Condemnation of unsafe buildings, §§160A-425.1, 160A-426, (d), 160A-432, (a1).
Private parking lots.
Removal of unauthorized vehicles, §20-219.2.
Traffic control photographic systems, §160A-300.1, (d).

FAYETTEVILLE STATE UNIVERSITY.
Constituent institution of University of North Carolina, §116-4.
Generally.
See UNIVERSITY OF NORTH CAROLINA.
Distinguished professors endowment trust fund.
Focused growth institutions.
Allocation, §116-41.15, (b).
Contributions, matching, §116-41.16, (b).
Defined, §116-41.13A.

FBI.
Agents authorized to enforce criminal laws, §15A-406.
DNA database and databanks.
FBI defined, §15A-266.2.
Procedural compatibility, §15A-266.3.
Expungement of criminal records.
Charges dismissed or person found not guilty or not responsible.
Law enforcement agencies ordered to expunge records, §15A-146, (b).
As result of identity fraud, §15A-147, (c).

FDIC.
Banks.
Deposit insurance, §53-9.1.
Public contracts.
Deposit of cash in bank or trust company insured by FDIC.
Proposal not considered or accepted unless deposit made, §143-129, (b).

FEDERAL AID.
Airports.
Acceptance, §§63-70, 63-71, (a).
Department of transportation.
Powers as to, §63-71.
Municipal airports, §63-54.
Acceptance, §63-54, (a).
Compliance with federal regulations, §63-54, (b), (c).
Archives and history.
Historic preservation program.
Cooperation with federal government, §121-8, (d).
Blind persons.
Aid to the blind.
Acceptance of aid, §111-25.
Authority of department of health and human services to receive, §111-28.
Grants affording maximum aid, §111-29.
Grants from federal government, §111-24.
Matching federal funds, §111-6.
Termination of aid, §111-26.

FEDERAL AID —Cont'd
Blind persons —Cont'd
Aid to the blind —Cont'd
Use of aid, §111-25.
Private contributions for particular facilities.
Treating contributions as state funds to match federal funds, §111-12.2.
Rehabilitation center for the blind and visually impaired.
Authority to receive federal grants-in-aid, §111-6.1.
Budget.
Expenditure and reporting of federal funds, §143-16.1, (a), (b).
Child support.
Conformity with federal requirements, §110-140, (a).
Community colleges.
Budgets, §115D-58.1.
State board of community colleges.
Authority to accept, receive, use or reallocate federal funds or aid, §115D-31, (b).
Counties.
Public health or mental health grants.
Recovery of indirect costs on certain grants by counties, §130A-8, (a).
Exception, §130A-8, (b).
Drinking water.
Receipt of financial and technical assistance, §130A-326.
Education.
State board of education.
Power to accept federal funds and aid, §115C-409, (a), (b).
Electric membership corporations.
Acceptance of gifts or grants, §117-18.
Application for grant or loan from governmental agency, §117-26.
Emergency management.
Acceptance, §166A-9.
Employment security.
Employment service division, §96-24.
Method of handling funds, §96-27.
Governor.
Highway safety act of 1966.
Contracts with United States government, §147-12, (a).
Health.
Public health or mental health grants.
Counties to recover indirect costs on certain grants, §130A-8, (a).
Exception, §130A-8, (b).
Hospital authorities.
Contracts with federal government, §131E-27.
Hospitals.
Construction and enlargement of local hospitals, §131E-70, (c), (e).
Unallocated federal sums or balances, §131E-70, (g).
Municipal hospitals, §131E-11.
Housing authorities and projects.
Authority to secure federal aid, §157-23.
Contracts.
Agreement to sell as security for obligations, §157-39.8.
Housing finance agency.
Participation in federally assisted lease program for housing for persons of lower income.
General power of agency, §122A-5.
Junkyard control.
Availability of federal aid funds, §136-155.

FEDERAL AID —Cont'd
Libraries.
Authority to accept and administer funds from federal government and other agencies.
Department of cultural resources authorized to accept and administer, §125-8.
Interstate library districts, §125-15.
Local development.
Economic development commissions.
Acceptance, §158-12.
Metropolitan water districts.
Power to receive and accept, §162A-36, (a).
Militia.
Support of militia.
Requisition for federal funds, §127A-137.
Outdoor advertising.
Control act.
Availability of federal aid funds, §136-140.
Parking authorities.
Power to accept, §160A-556.
Personnel system.
Application to local employees, §126-1.
Public officers and employees.
Repayment of money owed to state.
Preservation of federal funds, §143-561.
Public schools.
Powers of local boards of education, §115C-47.
Public works.
Relocation assistance.
Real property furnished to federal government, §133-16.
Railroads.
Revitalization programs, §§136-44.35 to 136-44.38.
Social services.
Acceptance of grants-in-aid authorized, §108A-71.
Solid waste management.
Receipt and distribution of funds, §130A-297.
Special education.
Allocation of federal funds, §115C-145.
State departments and agencies.
Acceptance of federal loans and grants.
Permitted, §143-164.
Receipt from federal government and gift not affected, §147-83.
State treasurer.
Receipts from federal government and gifts not affected, §147-83.
Streets and highways.
Historical marker program, §136-42.3.
Scenic beauty of areas along highways.
Availability of federal aid funds, §136-124.
Telephone membership corporations.
Grants or loans from federal agencies, §117-32.
Transportation department.
Compliance with federal aid acts.
Powers of department, §136-18.
University of North Carolina.
Acceptance by board of governors, §116-40.
Veterans' recreation authorities.
Acceptance, §165-37.
Vocational and technical education.
Acceptance of benefits of federal vocational act, §115C-155.
Division of federal funds, §115C-158.
Vocational rehabilitation services.
Federal funds provided under rehabilitation act of 1973, §143-546.1, (b).
Water resources development projects, §§143-215.38 to 143-215.43.
Waters and watercourses.
Natural and scenic rivers system.
Acceptance of federal grants, §113A-36, (b).

FEDERAL BUREAU OF INVESTIGATION.
See FBI.

FEDERAL COURTS.
General provisions.
See UNITED STATES COURTS.

FEDERAL CREDIT UNIONS.
Conversion into state credit union, §54-109.95, (b).
Conversion of state credit union, §54-109.95, (a).

FEDERAL DEPOSIT INSURANCE CORPORATION.
Banks.
Deposit insurance, §53-9.1.
Public contracts.
Deposit of cash in bank or trust company insured by FDIC.
Proposal not considered or accepted unless deposit made, §143-129, (b).

FEDERAL ESTATE TAX APPORTIONMENT, §§28A-27-1 to 28A-27-9.
Credits, §28A-27-5, (b) to (d).
Deductions, §28A-27-5, (a).
Computations, §28A-27-5, (d).
Definitions, §28A-27-1.
Determining apportionment.
Personal representative to determine, §28A-27-3, (a).
Basis for determining, §28A-27-3, (b).
Expenses for apportionment to be apportioned, §28A-27-3, (c).
Distribution before final apportionment.
Personal representative may require bond for tax liability, §28A-27-7, (b).
Effective date of provisions, §28A-27-9.
Exemptions, §28A-27-5, (a).
Computations, §28A-27-5, (d).
Federal tax law to determine liabilities imposed, §28A-27-8.
Method of apportionment, §28A-27-2, (a).
Choosing method, §28A-27-2, (b).
Rights and duties of personal representative, §28A-27-7, (a).
Temporary and remainder interests need not be apportioned, §28A-27-6.
Uncollected taxes, §28A-27-4.
Wills.
Method described in will, §28A-27-2, (b).

FEDERAL GOVERNMENT.
General provisions.
See UNITED STATES.

FEDERAL GOVERNMENT WORKERS INCOME TAX CREDIT OR REFUND.
Credit or partial refund for tax paid on certain federal government benefits, §105-151.20.

FEDERAL HOME LOAN BANK BOARD.
Investment in obligations of agencies supervised by, §53-44.2.
Obligations of agencies supervised by.
Securities for deposit of public funds, §53-43.2.

FEDERAL HOUSING ADMINISTRATION.
Investments in and loans of securities approved by.
Financial institutions, insurance companies, mortgage and loan correspondents and fiduciaries, §53-45.

FEDERALIST PAPERS.
Basic education program, §115C-81, (g).

FEDERAL LAW ENFORCEMENT OFFICERS.
Assistance in enforcing criminal laws in state.
Authority to assist, §15A-406, (b).
Federal tort claims act, applicability, §15A-406, (e).
Independent investigation into state law violations not authorized, §15A-406, (f).
List of federal law enforcement officers, §15A-406, (a).
Not considered officer, employee of state or local agency, §15A-406, (d).
Powers when assisting, §15A-406, (c).

FEDERAL LIEN REGISTRATION, §§44-68.10 to 44-68.17.
Application of provisions.
Uniformity required, §44-68.16.
Attachment.
Certificate of nonattachment.
Filing officer.
Duties, §44-68.14, (b), (c).
August 1, 1990.
Liens filed before, §44-68.17.
Certificates.
August 1, 1990.
Certificates filed before, §44-68.17.
Discharge of lien.
Filing officer.
Duties, §44-68.14, (b), (c).
Execution, §44-68.13.
Fees, §44-68.14, (d).
Filing and indexing, §44-68.15, (a), (b).
Filing officer.
Duties, §44-68.14.
Nonattachment of lien.
Filing officer.
Duties, §44-68.14, (b), (c).
Notices.
Revocation of certificate.
Filing officer.
Duties, §44-68.14, (a).
Release of lien.
Filing officer.
Duties, §44-68.14, (b), (c).
Revocation.
Notice.
Filing officer.
Duties, §44-68.14, (a).
Subordination of lien.
Filing officer.
Duties, §44-68.14, (b), (c).
Citation of act.
Short title, §44-68.10.
Construction and interpretation.
Scope of article, §44-68.11.
Uniformity of application and construction, §44-68.16.
Discharge.
Certificates.
Filing officer.
Duties, §44-68.14, (b), (c).
Fees.
Billing of officials, §44-68.15, (c).
Certificates, §44-68.14, (d).
Filing and indexing, §44-68.15, (a), (b).
Notices, §44-68.14, (d).
Filing and indexing, §44-68.15, (a), (b).
Notices.
Execution, §44-68.13.
Fees, §44-68.14, (d).
Filing and indexing, §44-68.15, (a), (b).

FEDERAL LIEN REGISTRATION —Cont'd
Notices —Cont'd
Filing.
August 1, 1990.
Notices filed before, §44-68.17.
Duties of filing officer, §44-68.14.
Fee, §44-68.15, (a), (b).
Generally, §44-68.12, (a).
Personal property liens, §44-68.12, (c).
Real property liens, §44-68.12, (a).
Refiling.
August 1, 1990.
Refilings filed before, §44-68.17.
Duties of filing officer, §44-68.14, (a), (b).
Revocation of certificate.
Duties of filing officer, §44-68.14, (a).
Personal property.
Notice of filing lien, §44-68.12, (c).
Real property.
Notice of filing lien, §44-68.12, (b).
Releases.
August 1, 1990.
Releases filed before, §44-68.17.
Certificate of release.
Filing officer.
Duties, §44-68.14, (b), (c).
Scope of article, §44-68.11.
Subordination.
Certificates.
Filing officer.
Duties, §44-68.14, (b), (c).
Title of act.
Short title, §44-68.10.

FEDERAL MANDATES.
Certification of legislation required by federal law, §120-36.8.
Local government fiscal information.
Complying federal mandate report, §120-30.49.

FEDERAL PARENT LOCATOR SERVICE.
Access by department of health and human services, §110-139.1.

FEDERAL PARKS.
Construction of federal parkways and entrance roads to parks.
Powers of department of transportation, §136-19, (g).
Property tentatively designated as federal parkway, §136-19, (i).
National park system, §§104-31 to 104-33.

FEDERAL POWER COMMISSION.
Environment and natural resources.
Department authorized to receive funds from commission, §113-18.

FEDERAL REMEDY RESTORATION ACT.
State employee suits against state, §143-300.35.

FEDERAL RESERVE SYSTEM.
Banks, §§53-50, 53-61, 54C-177.
Definitions, §53-61, (a).
Funds transfers, UCC.
Reserve regulations and operating circulars.
Inconsistent provisions superseded, §25-4A-107.
Membership in federal reserve bank, §53-61, (b).
Compliance with reserve requirements required, §53-61, (d).
Powers vested by federal act, §53-61, (c).
Supervision and examination of bank, §53-61, (e).

FEDERAL RESERVE SYSTEM —Cont'd
Reserve requirements.
Compliance, §53-61, (d).
Members of system, §53-50, (b).
Savings banks.
Authority to join federal reserve bank, §54C-177.

FEDERAL SURPLUS PROPERTY.
Surplus property of state.
State agency, §§143-64.1 to 143-64.5.
See SURPLUS PROPERTY.

FEDERAL WATER RESOURCES DEVELOPMENT PROJECTS, §§143-215.38 to 143-215.43.

FEE-BASED PRACTICING PASTORAL COUNSELORS.
Certification of fee-based practicing pastoral counselors, §§90-380 to 90-395.
See PASTORAL COUNSELORS.
Professional counselors.
General provisions, §§90-329 to 90-344.
See PROFESSIONAL COUNSELORS.

FEED, §§106-284.30 to 106-284.46.
Acts.
Prohibited acts, §106-284.39.
Administration of article.
Commissioner of agriculture to administer, §106-284.32.
Adulteration.
Deemed to be adulterated, §106-284.38.
Analysis.
Deficiencies in commercial feed of any component, §106-284.42, (g).
Penalties for multiple deficiencies, §106-284.42, (k).
Deviation from guaranteed analysis, §106-284.42, (h).
Penalty for deviation, §106-284.42, (i).
Penalties.
Collection and assessment of penalties, §106-284.42, (l).
Deficiencies in commercial feed or any component, §106-284.42, (k).
Deviation from guaranteed analysis, §106-284.42, (i).
Permitted analytical variation deviation, §106-284.42, (j).
Permitted analytical variation, §106-284.42, (h).
Schedule of penalties, §106-284.42, (j).
Results of analysis, §106-284.42, (f).
Sampling and analysis.
Conduct of, §106-284.42, (e).
Appeals.
Judicial review of act, orders or rulings, §106-284.44, (e).
Bag weights.
Prescribed standard-weight bags or packages, §106-284.36.
Canned pet food.
Defined, §106-284.33.
Inspection fees, §106-284.40, (a).
Commissioner of agriculture.
Enforcement of article, §106-284.32.
Condemnation.
Detained commercial feeds, §106-284.43, (b).
Confidentiality.
Information obtained to be confidential, §106-284.44, (f).
Customer-formula feed.
Defined, §106-284.33.
Labeling, §106-284.35.

FEED —Cont'd
Definitions, §106-284.33.
Detained commercial feed.
Condemnation and confiscation, §106-284.43, (b).
Withdrawal from distribution orders, §106-284.43, (a).
District attorneys.
Prosecution of violations of article, §106-284.44, (c).
Enforcement of article.
Inspections authorized, §106-284.42, (a).
Right of entry, §106-284.42, (a).
Enforcing official, §106-284.32.
Feed advisory service.
Operated by department of agriculture and consumer services, §106-21.1.
Fees.
Inspection fees, §106-284.40.
Registration fee.
Delinquent fee, §106-284.34, (e).
Injunctions.
Relief from violations of article, §106-284.44, (d).
Inspections.
Canned pet food.
Fees for inspection, §106-284.40, (a).
Court order, §106-284.42, (d).
Description of samples obtained, §106-284.42, (c).
Enforcement of article, §106-284.42, (a).
Fees.
Canned pet food, §106-284.40.
Liability for payment, §106-284.40, (c).
Rate of inspection fee, §106-284.40, (a), (b).
Liability for payment of inspection fees, §106-284.40, (c).
Presentation of appropriate credentials, §106-284.42, (b).
Refusing admission of commissioner or agent, §106-284.42, (d).
Sampling and analysis.
Description of samples obtained, §106-284.42, (c).
Labels.
Customer-formula feed, §106-284.35.
Defined, §106-284.33.
Information required, §106-284.35.
Liability.
Inspection fees.
Payment of fee, §106-284.40, (c).
Misbranding.
Deemed to be misbranded, §106-284.37.
Misdemeanors.
Violations of article, §106-284.44, (a).
Notice.
Violations of article.
Warning notice in writing, §106-284.44, (b).
Orders.
Detained commercial feeds.
Withdrawal from distribution orders, §106-284.43, (a).
Penalties.
Sampling and analysis.
Assessment and collection of penalties, §106-284.42, (l).
Deficiencies in commercial feed of any component, §106-284.42, (k).
Deviation from guaranteed analysis, §106-284.42, (i).
Permitted analytical variation, §106-284.42, (j).
Violations of article, §106-284.44.
Permits.
Registration procedure, §106-284.34.

FEED —Cont'd
Permitted analytical variation, §106-284.42, (h).
Penalties, §106-284.42, (j).
Prohibited act, §106-284.39.
Publications.
Information to be published, §106-284.46.
Purpose of article, §106-284.31.
Registration.
Application for permit, §106-284.34, (a).
Application for registration.
Manner of submission, §106-284.34, (c).
Cancellation of registration, §106-284.34, (d).
Delinquent registration fee, §106-284.34, (e).
Expiration of registration, §106-284.34, (c).
Fees, §106-284.34, (c).
Delinquent registration fee, §106-284.34, (e).
Filing requirements, §106-284.34, (a).
Issuance, §106-284.34, (c).
Permits.
Application for permit, §106-284.34, (a).
Issuance, §106-284.34, (b).
Use of permits, §106-284.34, (b).
Refusal of registration, §106-284.34, (d).
Reports.
Inspection fees and reports, §106-284.40.
Right of entry.
Purposes of enforcement of article, §106-284.42, (a).
Rules and regulations.
Authority to promulgate, §106-284.41, (a).
Issuance, amendment or repeal of rule or regulation, §106-284.41, (b).
Sampling and analysis.
Conduct of sampling and analysis, §106-284.42, (e).
Deficiencies in commercial feed of any component, §106-284.42, (g).
Penalties for multiple deficiencies, §106-284.42, (k).
Deviation from guaranteed analysis, §106-284.42, (a).
Penalty for deviation, §106-284.42, (i).
Inspections.
Description of samples obtained, §106-284.42, (c).
Penalties.
Assessment and collection of penalties, §106-284.42, (l).
Deficiencies in commercial feed of any component, §106-284.42, (k).
Deviation from guaranteed analysis, §106-284.42, (i).
Permitted analytical variation deviation, §106-284.42, (j).
Permitted analytical variation.
Penalty schedule, §106-284.42, (j).
Results of analysis, §106-284.42, (f).
Short title, §106-284.30.
State departments and agencies.
Corporation with other entities, §106-284.45.
Statement of purpose, §106-284.31.
Title of article, §106-284.30.
United States.
Corporation with other entities, §106-284.45.
Unlawful acts, §106-284.39.
Violations of article.
Injunctive relief, §106-284.44, (d).
Misdemeanor offenses, §106-284.44, (a).
Prosecution of violations, §106-284.44, (c).
Warning notice in writing, §106-284.44, (b).

FEED —Cont'd
Warnings.
Notice of violations of article, §106-284.44, (b).
Weights and measures.
Bag weights, §106-284.36.

FEED ADVISORY SERVICE.
Operation by department of agriculture and consumer services, §106-21.1.

FEEDING GARBAGE TO SWINE, §§106-405.1 to 106-405.9.
Application for permit, §106-405.3.
Cooking or other treatment, §106-405.6.
Definitions, §106-405.1.
Enforcement of article, §106-405.8.
Fees.
Permit for feeding garbage to swine.
Application for permit, §106-405.3, (b), (c).
Inspecting conditions, §106-405.7, (a).
Investigating conditions, §106-405.7, (a).
Penalties for violation of provisions, §106-405.9.
Permit for feeding garbage to swine.
Applicability of provisions, §106-405.2, (c), (d).
Application for permit, §106-405.3, (a).
Fees, §106-405.3, (b), (c).
Federal permits.
Exemption of holders from provisions, §106-405.2, (d).
Issuance, §106-405.2, (a).
Prohibiting local regulations, §106-405.2, (b).
Revocation of permits, §106-405.4.
Records to be maintained, §106-405.7, (b).
Removal of garbage from premises, §106-405.7, (c).
Revocation of permits for feeding garbage to swine, §106-405.4.
Rules and regulations, §106-405.8.
Sanitary conditions, §106-405.5.
Treatment of garbage fed to swine, §106-405.6.

FEEDING MANAGEMENT SERVICE TO ANIMAL PRODUCERS.
Feed advisory service operated by department of agriculture and consumer services, §106-21.1.

FEEDLOTS.
Animal waste management, §§143-215.10A to 143-215.10H.
See ANIMAL WASTE MANAGEMENT.

FEES.
Accountants.
Board of examiners, §93-12.
Acupuncture, §90-457.
Administration department.
Use of state-owned office space by self-supporting agencies, §143-342.1.
Administrative code, §150B-21.25.
Administrative procedure.
Subpoenas.
Witness fees, §150B-39, (c).
Adoption.
Agency placements.
Schedule of fees included in statement of services, §48-3-203, (b).
Dispositional hearing on petition.
Disclosure of fees and charges, §48-2-602.
Lawful payments related to adoption, §48-10-103.
Payments related to adoption.
Agency fees and charges, §48-10-103, (e).
Preplacement assessments, §48-3-304.

FEES —Cont'd
Adoption —Cont'd
Report to court, §48-2-504.
Unlawful payments related to adoption, §48-10-102, (a).
Advance health care directive registry.
Fee for filing, §§130A-466, 130A-470.
Agriculture.
See AGRICULTURAL FEES AND TAXES.
Air pollution control.
Title V program.
Assessment of implementation fees, §143-215.106A.
Alarm systems licensing, §74D-7, (e).
Transfer of certain fees, §74D-13.
Alcoholic beverages.
Permits, §18B-902, (d).
Combined applications, §18B-902, (e).
Disposition, §18B-902, (g).
Lost permits.
Issuance of duplicate, §18B-903, (f).
Name change.
Issuance of new permit, §18B-903, (g).
Nonrefundable, §18B-902, (f).
Registration of persons holding permits, §18B-903, (b1).
Renewal, §18B-903, (b).
Wine shipper permit, §18B-902, (d).
Animal waste management, §143-215.10G, (a) to (c).
Animal waste management system operators.
Certification, §90A-47.4, (a).
Renewal fee, §90A-47.4, (b).
Arbitration.
Witnesses fees, §1-569.17, (f).
Arbitration and award.
Arbitrators.
Rules for court-ordered arbitration, Arbitration Rule 2.
Rules for court-ordered arbitration.
Arbitrators, Arbitration Rule 2.
Trial de novo.
Filing fee, Arbitration Rule 5.
Statewide court-ordered nonbinding arbitration in certain civil actions, §7A-37.1, (c1).
Architects.
Board, §83A-4.
Asbestos hazard management.
Accreditation fees, §130A-448, (a), (b).
Removal permits, §130A-450.
Athlete agents.
Registration, §78C-93.
Athletic fees.
Schools for the deaf, §143B-216.44.
Atomic energy.
Radiation protection.
Department of environment and natural resources, §104E-19, (a).
Attorneys at law.
Continuing legal education, Bar Rules & Regs., D, §.1606.
Attendee's fees.
Source of funding, CLE Rule 12.
Fiscal responsibility, CLE Rule 13.
Sponsors.
Source of funding, CLE Rule 12.
Organization of judicial district bars, Bar Rules & Regs., A, §§.0902, .0903.
Attorneys' fees.
See ATTORNEYS' FEES.

FEES —Cont'd
Auctions and auctioneers.
Auctioneer recovery fund.
Fee to be included in fund, §85B-4.1, (a).
Licenses, §85B-6.
Autopsies.
Medical examiners, §130A-389, (a).
Bail bondsmen and runners.
Disposition, §58-71-180.
Licenses, §58-71-55.
Examinations, §58-71-70.
Renewal, §58-71-75.
Dual license holding, §58-71-82.
Banks.
Branch banks.
Interstate banking.
Application fees, §53-224.11, (b).
Checks.
Remittance covering checks.
No fees to be charged, §53-70.
Directors.
Acceptance prohibited, §53-86.
Fiduciaries.
Licensed to do business, §53-160.
Officers.
Acceptance prohibited, §53-86.
Banks and consumer finance licensees.
Operating and maintaining office of commissioner of banks, §53-122, (a), (e), (f).
Barbers.
Examinations, §86A-25.
Payment required, §86A-8.
Generally, §86A-25.
Biologics.
Licenses.
Production licenses, §106-710, (d).
Birth certificates.
New birth certificates, §130A-118, (d).
Boards and commissions.
Rules and regulations.
Agencies establishing fees and charges by rule, §12-3.1, (a), (c).
Definitions, §12-3.1, (b).
Boxing licenses and permits, §143-655, (a), (d).
Bridge authority, §136-89.160.
Brownfields property reuse.
Credit to Brownfields property reuse act implementation account, §130A-310.39, (b).
Failure to pay fees, §130A-310.39, (c).
Schedule of fees to be collected, §130A-310.39, (a).
Building code.
Code officials qualification board.
Certificates for code enforcement officials, §143-151.16.
Disposition, §143-151.21.
Door lock exemptions.
Conditions for permit, §143-143.4, (b).
Business corporations.
Expedited filings, §55D-11.
Filing, service and copying fees, §55-1-22.
Capital punishment.
Execution fee, §15-190.
Cemeteries.
Change of control of cemetery company.
Application.
Filing fee, §65-59.
Commission, §65-54.
Licenses.
Cemetery companies.
Application.
Filing fee, §65-55, (c).
Sale of preneed grave space, etc., §65-58, (c).

FEES —Cont'd
Cemeteries —Cont'd
Licenses —Cont'd
Sales organizations, management organizations and brokers.
Application.
Filing fee, §65-57, (c).
Charitable solicitations.
Licensing.
Fund-raising consultants, §131F-15, (c), (f).
Solicitor's license, §131F-16, (c).
Charitable solicitation sponsors.
License fees, §131F-8, (a) to (d).
Check-cashing business.
License applications, §53-278, (c).
Service fees, §53-280, (a).
Notice of fees charged, posting, §53-280, (c).
Checks.
Remittances covering checks.
Banks and trust companies not to charge fees, §53-70.
Childhood vaccine-related injury compensation.
Covered vaccines.
Providing, §130A-433.
Children's health insurance program.
Enrollment, §108A-70.21, (c).
Chiropractors.
Collection of certain fees prohibited, §90-154.1.
Diagnostic imaging technicians, §90-143.2, (b).
Licenses.
Application fee, §90-149.
Renewal, §90-155.
CLE, Bar Rules & Regs., D, §.1606; CLE Rules 12, 13.
Clerks of court.
Court of appeals.
Fee bill for services, §7A-20, (b).
Limitation of actions for fees, §1-52.
Superior court clerks, Const. N. C., art. IV, §21.
Accounting for fees and other receipts, §7A-108.
Annual audit, §7A-108.
Deposits of money held by clerk, §7A-308.1.
Investment of funds in clerk's hands, §7A-308.1.
Statement rendered by county officer compensated from fees, §128-13.
Penalty for failure to file statement, §128-13.
Closing-out sales.
License fee, §66-77, (b).
Coastal area management.
Permits, §113A-119.1, (a), (b).
Applications.
Submitted with application, §113A-119, (a).
Collection agencies.
Permit fees, §§58-70-35, (a), 58-70-45.
Commercial drivers' licenses.
Applications for commercial drivers' licenses, §20-37.15, (a1).
Issuance, §20-37.16, (d).
Commercial feed.
Inspection fees and reports, §106-284.40.
Registration fees, §106-284.34.
Commissioner of motor vehicles.
Service upon nonresident drivers and personal representatives of deceased nonresident drivers, §1-105.
Verification of equipment to be used on vehicles, §20-39, (f).
Commissioners.
Action in which clerk may allow, §1-408.

FEES —Cont'd
Community colleges.
Extension courses.
Schedule of uniform registration fees, §115D-5, (b).
Waiver of registration fees, §115D-5, (b).
Community services.
Impaired driving alternative punishment, §20-179.4, (c), (d).
Concealed handgun permit, §14-415.13, (a).
Criminal records checks, §14-415.19, (a).
Fingerprint processing, §14-415.19, (b).
Retired sworn law enforcement officer, §14-415.19, (a1).
Schedule of fees, §14-415.19, (a).
Consumer finance act.
Commissioner of banks.
Payment for expenses of supervision, §53-167.
Processing fee.
Maximum fee, §§53-173, (a1), 53-176, (b).
Recording fees, §53-177.
Continuing care retirement communities.
Disclosure statements.
Annual revised disclosure statement.
Filing fee, §58-64-30, (b).
Return of entrance fee held in escrow, §58-64-35, (d).
Licenses.
Application fee, §58-64-5, (b).
Nursing beds and adult care home beds.
Licensure fees, §131E-138.1.
Continuing legal education, Bar Rules & Regs., D, §.1606; CLE Rules 12, 13.
Cooperative agreements among physicians or between physician, hospital or other person.
Application for certificate of public advantage or filing of periodic reports, §90-21.34.
Cooperative associations.
Incorporation, §54-115.
Coroners.
Generally, §152-5.
Statement rendered by county officers compensated from fees, §128-13.
Cosmetic art.
Board of cosmetic art.
Collection by executive director, §88B-6, (e).
Licensure, §88B-20.
Costs.
Court costs generally.
See COSTS.
Uniform costs and fees in trial division, §§7A-304 to 7A-318, 7A-320.
Councils.
Rules and regulations.
Agencies establishing fees and charges by rule, §12-3.1, (a), (c).
Definitions, §12-3.1, (b).
Counties.
Boards of commissioners.
Commissioners to fix fees, §153A-102.
Inspectors of articles of commerce, §§66-3, 66-7.
Payment, §138-2.
Uniform fees in trial divisions.
Requirement to advance certain fees, §7A-317.
County surveyors.
Statements rendered by county officers compensated from fees, §128-13.
Court of appeals.
Clerk of court.
Fee bill for services, §7A-20, (b).
Judges, Const. N. C., art. IV, §21.

FEES —Cont'd
Credit unions.
Disposition of moneys collected, §54-109.14, (b), (c).
Examination fees, §54-109.14, (a).
Organization, §54-109.2, (e).
Supervision fees, §54-109.14, (a).
Cremation.
Schedule of fees, §90-210.52, (a).
Dams.
Dam safety law.
Applications for construction.
Application fees, §143-215.28A.
Death.
Amendment of birth and death certificates, §130A-118, (d).
Decedents' estates.
Clerks of court.
Miscellaneous fees in administration of estates, §7A-307, (b1).
Dental hygienists.
Generally, §90-232.
Dentists.
Anesthesia and parenteral sedation.
Standards for general anesthesia and parenteral sedation.
Board of dental examiners to establish by regulation, §90-30.1.
Examination and inspection.
Dental offices, §90-30.1.
Intern permits, §90-39.
Licenses, §90-39.
Duplicate licenses, §90-35.
Renewal, §§90-31, 90-39.
Dietitians and nutritionists.
Schedule of fees, §90-364.
District courts.
Civil process.
Uniform civil process fees, §7A-311.
Amount, §7A-311, (a).
Collection of fees in advance, §7A-311, (b).
Completeness and exclusivity of fees and commissions, §7A-311, (c).
Costs are exclusive, §7A-320.
Discovery procedures.
Filing of verified petition, §7A-305.1.
Judges, Const. N. C., art. IV, §21.
Uniform costs and fees in trial divisions, §§7A-304 to 7A-318.
Unincorporated seats of court.
Disposition of fees in counties, §7A-317.1.
Division of motor vehicles.
Acknowledgment of signatures, §20-42, (a).
Certified copies, §20-42, (b).
Drainage districts.
Collection of assessments and disbursements, §156-113.
Drinking water, public water systems supplying.
Community water system operating permit, §130A-328, (b).
Laboratory certification, §130A-326.
Laboratory costs, recovery, §130A-326.
Drivers' licenses, §20-7, (i).
Commercial drivers' licenses.
Application fee, §20-37.15, (a1).
Issuance, §20-37.16, (d).
Duplicate licenses, §20-14.
Highway fund, placing in, §20-7, (j).
Learners' permits, §20-7, (l).
Minors, expanding privileges, §20-11, (j).

FEES —Cont'd
Drivers' licenses —Cont'd
Records.
Copies.
Furnishing, §20-26, (c).
Refund in event of mistake of person ordering, §20-26, (e).
Restoration fee.
Person whose license has been revoked, §20-7, (i1).
Drugs.
Expunction of records, §90-96, (f).
Wholesale prescription drug distributors.
License application fees, §106-145.4, (b).
Electrical contractors.
Licenses, §87-44.
Use of funds collected, §87-45.
Electric membership corporations.
Regulatory fee, §117-3.1.
Electrologists.
Board of electrologist examiners.
Duties to collect, §88A-6.
Deposits, §88A-7.
Salaries, compensation and expenses incurred paid from, §88A-9, (a).
Schedule, §88A-9, (b).
Employee assistance professionals.
License application fee, §90-503.
Engineers.
Continuing professional competency activities.
Sponsors' licenses, §89C-10, (h).
Engineers' licensure, §89C-14, (b), (c).
Corporations and business firms, §89C-24.
Duplicate certificates, §89C-18.
Renewal of certificate, §89C-17.
Return on denial of certificate, §89C-14, (d).
Enhanced 911 wireless system for wireless communications.
Administrative fee for fund management, §62A-26.
Executions.
Execution sales.
Uniform civil process fees, §7A-311, (a).
Expert witnesses.
Indigent defense services.
Fees paid by state, §7A-454.
Uniform fees, §7A-314, (d).
Expungement of records.
First offenders under age eighteen.
Filing of petition, §15A-145, (e).
Facility authorities.
Powers of authority, §160A-480.4.
Family court programs, §7A-314.1, (a).
Reduction, procedure for application for, §7A-314.1, (b).
Farm names.
Registration, §80-37.
Cancellation of registry, §80-39.
Farm nuisance disputes.
Prelitigation mediation.
Mediator fees, Farm Med. Rule 6.
Federal liens.
Billing of officials, §44-68.15, (c).
Certificates, §44-68.14, (d).
Filing and indexing, §44-68.15, (a), (b).
Notices, §44-68.14, (d).
Filing and indexing, §44-68.15, (a), (b).
Fishing.
Arrest, §§113-222, 113-303.
Inland fishing licenses, §113-271, (d).

FEES —Cont'd
Fishing —Cont'd
Licenses.
Collection licenses, §113-272.4, (c).
Combination hunting and fishing licenses, §113-270.1C, (b).
Disposition of license funds, §113-306.
Fishing guides, §113-270.4.
Government-owned property.
Collecting fees for licenses for fishing on, §113-39.
Inland fishing licenses, §113-271, (d).
Lifetime licenses.
Administrative fee for issuing, §113-272.3, (d).
Salt water fishing license, §113-174.2, (c).
Special device license, §113-272.2, (c).
Special trout license, §113-272, (d).
Service of process, §§113-222, 113-303.
State forests and parks.
Collection of reasonable fees by department of environment and natural resources, §113-35, (b).
Witnesses, §§113-222, 113-303.
Food establishments, §130A-248, (d).
Foreign legal consultants.
Certificate of registration, §84A-2, (c).
Foreign or alien insurance companies.
Redomestication, §58-7-155.
Retaliatory laws, §58-16-25.
Foresters.
Registration, §§89B-10, (a), 89B-11, (a).
Examinations, §89B-12.
Gasoline and oil inspection.
Collection of fees by department of revenue, §119-23.
Payment of fees into state treasury, §119-23.
General assembly.
Lobbying.
Contingency lobbying fees, §120-47.5, (a).
Witness fees and expenses.
Committee activity, §120-19.3.
General contractors.
Licenses, §87-10, (a).
Geologists.
Board.
Establishing and collecting, §89E-5, (g).
Examinations, §89E-10, (b).
Grain dealers.
License fees, §§106-604, 106-607, 106-608.
Grand jury.
Uniform fees for jurors, §7A-312.
Guardians.
Determination of incompetence.
Payment of fees, §35A-1116, (c).
Health.
County boards of health, §130A-39, (g).
District boards of health, §130A-39, (g).
Industrial hygiene consultation services and occupational consultation services, §130A-5.
Health care facilities.
Certificate of public advantage, §131E-192.11.
Review of application, §131E-192.11, (b).
Certificates of need, §131E-182, (c).
Finance act, §§131A-13, 131A-14.
Health and human services department.
Certification fee for abortion facilities, §131E-269.
Review of construction projects and plans, §131E-267.
Health maintenance organizations, §58-67-160.

FEES —Cont'd
Hearing aid dealers and fitters.
Licenses.
Application fee, §93D-5, (a).
Issuance of license certificate, §93D-8, (b).
Reciprocity, §93D-6.
Reissuance of suspended license, §93D-13, (b).
Renewal fees, §93D-11.
Hearing impaired.
Interpreters for hearing impaired.
Licenses, §90D-10, (b).
Service fee, §8B-10.
Training and licensing preparation program fee, §8B-10.
Home inspectors.
Deposit of moneys received by board, §143-151.63, (b).
Licenses, §143-151.57.
Hospital, medical and dental service corporations.
Certificate of authority or license, §58-65-55, (b).
Hotels, inns and other transient lodging places, §130A-248, (d).
Housing finance agency.
Mortgage insurance authority.
Application fee prescribed, §122A-5.2, (c).
Hunting.
Arrest, §113-303.
Licenses, §113-270.2.
Captivity license, §113-272.5, (b).
Collection licenses, §113-272.4, (c).
Combination fishing and hunting licenses, §113-270.1C, (b).
Controlled hunting preserve hunting license, §113-270.2, (c).
Controlled hunting preserve operators, §113-273, (g).
Disposition of license funds, §113-306, (b).
Furbearer propagation, §113-273, (h).
Fur-dealers, §113-273, (f).
Fur-dealer stations, §113-273, (f).
Game bird propagation, §113-273, (h).
Government-owned property.
Collecting fees for hunting on government-owned property, §113-39.
Guides, §113-270.4, (b).
Lifetime licenses.
Administrative fee for issuing, §113-272.3, (d).
Lifetime resident comprehensive hunting license, §113-270.2, (a), (c).
New license to replace lost or destroyed license, §113-275, (c1).
Nonresident license fee increase, §113-275, (a1).
Nonresident state hunting license, §113-270.2, (a), (c), (d).
Resident annual comprehensive hunting license, §113-270.2, (a), (c).
Resident county hunting license, §113-270.2, (a), (c).
Resident state hunting license, §113-270.2, (a), (c).
Special activity licenses, §113-270.3, (b).
Sportsmen licenses.
Annual license, §113-270.1D, (a).
Disabled resident sportsman license, §113-270.1D, (b).
Lifetime license, §113-270.1D, (b).
Taxidermy, §113-273, (k).
Trapping licenses, §113-270.5, (b).
Service of process, §113-303.

FEES —Cont'd
Hunting —Cont'd
State forests.
Collection of reasonable fees for privileges by department of environment and natural resources, §113-35, (b).
Witnesses, §113-303.
Identification cards for nonoperators.
Issuance and reissuance, §20-37.7, (d).
Immunization.
Administering covered vaccines, §130A-433, (b).
Impaired driving.
Community service alternative punishment, §20-179.4, (c), (d).
Substance abuse services, §122C-142.1, (f).
Indigent defense services.
Appointment fee in criminal cases, §7A-455.1.
Expert witnesses.
Fees paid by state, §7A-454.
Representation of indigent persons, §7A-452, (b).
Supporting services.
Fees and expenses paid by state, §7A-454.
Industrial commission mediated settlement and neutral evaluation conferences.
Payment of mediator's fee, I.C. Mediated Settlmt. Conf. R. 4(e).
In forma pauperis appeals.
Clerks' fees, §1-288.
Insurance commissioner.
Report and payment monthly by commissioner of fees received, §58-6-1.
Schedule of fees and charges, §58-6-5.
Insurance companies.
Consolidation, §58-7-150.
License fees.
Annual continuation fee, §58-6-7, (a), (b).
Defined, §58-6-15.
When submitted, §58-6-15.
Insurance premium financing.
Disposition, §58-35-95.
Excessive finance charges, §58-35-35.
Licenses, §58-35-5, (d), (e).
Nonrefundable, §58-35-100.
Insurer supervision, rehabilitation and liquidation.
Exemption from filing fees, §58-30-310.
Interpreters for hearing impaired.
Licenses, §90D-10, (b).
Interstate and international law firm registration, Bar Rules & Regs., E, §.0203.
Interstate compact for the supervision of adult offenders.
Supervision fee, §148-65.7.
Interstate family support, §52C-3-312.
Jails.
Uniform jail fees, §7A-313.
Job development investment grant program.
Applications, §143B-437.55, (b).
Records of recipient, §143B-437.58, (a).
Job listing services.
Receipt, §95-47.27.
Judgments.
Foreign judgments.
Enforcement, §1C-1706.
Judicial department.
Indigent persons.
Representation of indigent persons, §7A-452, (b).
Revenues and expenses, Const. N. C., art. IV, §20.
Uniform costs and fees in trial divisions, §§7A-304 to 7A-318.

FEES —Cont'd
Judicial officers, Const. N. C., art. IV, §21.
Judicial sales.
Uniform civil process fees, §7A-311, (a).
Junkyard control.
Permits, §136-149.
Jury.
Uniform fees for jurors, §7A-312.
Justice department.
Bureau of investigation.
Performance of certain background investigations, §114-19.1, (a).
Landlord and tenant.
Late rent payment fees, §42-46.
Landscape architects, §89A-6.
Landscape contractors.
Certificates of registration.
Application fee, §89D-5, (a).
Duplicate certificates, §89D-5, (c).
Examination fee, §89D-5, (b).
Renewal fee, §89D-5, (c).
Examinations, §89D-5, (b).
Lead-based paint abatement permit, §130A-453.09, (b).
Learners' permits, §20-7, (l).
License taxes.
General provisions, §§105-33 to 105-109.
See LICENSE TAXES.
Life insurance.
Registration of policies, §58-59-30.
Limestone, marl and landplaster.
Sale of agricultural liming materials and landplaster.
Registration and tonnage fees, §§106-92.7, (a), 106-92.8.
Limitation of actions.
Action for fee due officer, §1-52.
Limited liability companies.
Filing, service and copying fees, §57C-1-22.
Limited partnerships, revised act.
Schedule, §59-1106.
Liquefied petroleum gas.
Tank data plates.
Replacements, §119-61.
Livestock.
Brands.
Registration, §80-62.
Livestock market operation fee, §106-408.1.
Loans.
Conveyance of property other than collateral in consideration for loan, §24-8, (c).
Insurance proceeds to lender, §24-8, (e).
Loan amount $300,000 or less, §24-8, (a).
Loan-related goods, products and services.
Collection of payment for, §24-8, (d).
Small business investment companies.
Applicability of provisions, §24-8, (f).
Lobbyists.
Registration fee, §120-47.3.
Locksmith licensing, §74F-9.
Magistrates, Const. N. C., art. IV, §21.
Special fees collected by magistrate, §7A-309.
Marketing associations.
Filing fees, §54-144.
Marriage and family therapists.
Disposition of funds, §90-270.59.
Licenses, §90-270.57.
Reinstatement after expiration, §90-270.58A.
Renewal, §90-270.58.
Inactive status, §90-270.58B.

FEES —Cont'd
Massage and bodywork therapy.
Board of massage and bodywork therapy, §§90-627, 90-628.
Mass gatherings.
Additional services, §130A-254, (e).
Mattresses and bedding.
Licenses, §130A-269, (c) to (d1), (e), (f).
Deposit of fees, §130A-270.
Meat inspection.
Bison, §106-549.39, (b).
Deer.
Production and sale for commercial purposes, §106-549.98.
Hours of inspection, §106-549.39, (a).
Ostriches and other ratites, §106-549.39, (b).
Overtime work, §106-549.39, (a).
Mediated settlement conferences.
Court ordered conferences in superior court civil actions.
Compensation of mediator, Super. Ct. Mediated Settlmt. Conf. R. 7(D).
Payment of mediator's fee by parties, Super. Ct. Mediated Settlmt. Conf. R. 4(D).
Training programs, Super. Ct. Mediated Settlmt. Conf. R. 9(C).
Mediation.
Certification of mediators and mediation training programs, §7A-38.2, (d).
Community mediation centers.
Dispute resolution fee, §7A-38.7, (a).
Medical examiners.
Postmortem medicolegal examinations and services, §130A-387.
Autopsies, §130A-389, (a).
Cremation or burial at sea certification and duties, §130A-388, (b).
Medical records.
Searching, handling, copying and mailing, §90-411.
Medicolegal guidelines for attorney-physician relationship.
Witnesses, MLG Rule 5.
Membership camping.
Registration, §66-236.
Midwives.
Approval, §90-178.4, (b).
Report to state treasurer, §90-178.4, (d).
Milk and milk products.
Inspection fees, §§106-254, 106-267.1.
Mobile homes and trailer parks.
Registration of house trailers, §20-87.
Uniform standards code.
Licenses.
Supplemental licenses, §143-143.11, (f).
Money transmitters, §53-208.9.
Mortgage bankers and brokers.
Continuing education courses.
Filing of information regarding course materials, §53-243.07, (c).
License filing fee, §53-243.05, (e).
License renewal, §53-243.06.
Prohibited acts, §53-243.11.
Mortgages and deeds of trust.
Appraisal by financial institution employee.
Fee charge authorized, §24-10, (h).
High cost home loans.
Definition of points and fees, §24-1.1E, (a).
Financing points, fees, prepayments, etc., §24-1.1E, (e).
Modification and deferral fees, §24-1.1E, (b).

FEES —Cont'd
Mortgages and deeds of trust —Cont'd
Sales under power of sale.
Trustee's fees, §45-21.15.
Motor carriers.
Registration, §20-87.
Utilities commission, §62-300.
Motor clubs and associations.
License fees, §58-69-10.
Disposition, §58-69-40.
Motorcycles.
Registration.
Private motorcycles, §20-87.
Motor vehicle certificates of title.
Permanent registration plate holders.
No fee, §20-85, (c).
Schedule of fees, §20-85.
Motor vehicle inspections, §20-183.7, (a).
Display of information by inspection stations, §20-183.7, (f), (h).
Distribution of fees, §20-183.7, (c).
Emissions program account, §20-183.7, (d).
Self-inspectors, §20-183.7, (b).
Telecommunications account, §20-183.7, (d1).
Motor vehicle license plates.
Dealers plates.
Temporary plates or markers, §20-79.1, (a).
Disposition of fees collected, §20-85, (b).
Permanent license plates, §20-84, (a).
Schedule of fees, §20-85, (a).
Special plates, §§20-79.4, (b), 20-79.7.
Special registration plates, §20-79.7.
Motor vehicle manufacturers.
License fees, §20-289.
Motor vehicle registration.
Actions.
Recovery of taxes, §20-91.1.
Additional local taxes, §20-97, (e).
Carriers.
Property-hauling vehicles, §20-88.
Records.
Failure, common neglect or refusal to keep, §20-91, (c).
Reports.
Failure, common neglect or refusal to make, §20-91, (c).
Carrying charge.
Partial payment, §20-94.
Collection of delinquent taxes.
Remedies, §20-99.
Common carriers of passengers, §20-87.
Contract carriers, §20-87.
Copies of registration card, §20-57, (b).
Dealers, §20-87.
Destroyed vehicles.
Credit, §20-100.
Disposition of fees collected, §20-85, (b).
Driveaway companies, §20-87.
House trailers, §20-87.
International registration plan, §20-86.1, (a).
Junked vehicles.
Credit, §20-100.
Lien of taxes, §20-98.
Limousine vehicles, §20-87.
Manufacturers, §20-87.
Motorcycles.
Private motorcycles, §20-87.
Municipal corporations.
Taxi tax, §20-97, (d).
Vehicle taxes, §20-97, (b), (c).

FEES —Cont'd
Motor vehicle registration —Cont'd
Operation of vehicles without registration plates subject to civil penalty, §20-118.3.
Overpayment.
Refund with interest, §20-91.2.
Partial payments, §20-94.
Passenger carrier vehicles.
Except for-hire passenger carrier vehicles, §20-87.
Passenger vehicles, §§20-87, 20-87.1.
Property-hauling vehicles, §20-88.
Prorated fee for license plate issued for other than a year, §20-95, (a).
Exceptions to provisions, §20-95, (b).
Plate with renewal sticker, §20-95, (a1).
Protest.
Payment under protest, §20-91.1.
Refund.
Overpayment to be refunded with interest, §20-91.2.
Schedule of fees, §20-85, (a).
Special mobile equipment, §20-87.
Taxes credited to highway fund, §20-97, (a).
Taxicabs, §20-87.
Temporary registration marker, §20-50, (b).
U-drive-it vehicles, §20-87.
Motor vehicle titling.
Registration.
Security interest.
Notation of security interest, §20-58, (b).
Municipal corporations.
Solid waste disposal facilities, §160A-314.1.
Uniform fees in trial divisions.
Requirement to advance certain fees, §7A-317.
Mutual burial associations.
Membership, §90-210.81.
Negotiable instruments.
Collection of processing fee for returned checks, §25-3-506.
911 system.
Administrative fees, §62A-6.
Nonprofit corporations, §55A-1-22.
North Carolina register, §150B-21.25.
Notaries public, §10A-10.
Commission application, §10A-4, (b).
Ex officio notaries, §10A-14, (d).
Instructor's certification, §10A-7, (a).
Renewal, §10A-7, (b).
Posting of notice that notary is not an attorney in fee schedule, §10A-9, (g), (j).
Structured settlement transfers, §1-543.12.
Nuclear facilities, §166A-6.1, (a), (b).
Carried forward amount of fees, §166A-6.1, (c).
Nursing board.
Expenses payable from fees collected, §90-171.27, (a).
Powers as to.
Generally, §90-171.23, (b).
Refunds.
Prohibited, §90-171.27, (c).
Schedule of fees, §90-171.27, (b).
Nursing home administrators' licenses, §90-280, (b).
Application fee, §90-280, (a).
Disposition of fees collected, §90-281.
Duplicate license, §90-280, (d).
Inactive list, §90-280, (e).
Renewal, §90-280, (b).
Temporary license, §90-280, (f).

FEES —Cont'd
Nursing home administrators' licenses —Cont'd
Training and continuing education courses, §90-280, (g).
Occupational licensing boards.
Payment by members of armed forces, §93B-15.
Occupational therapists.
Licenses and examinations, §90-270.77.
Oil and gas conservation.
Notice and payment of fee to department before drilling or abandoning well, §113-395.
Opticians.
Licenses, §90-246.
Collection of fees, §90-245.
Examination, §90-246.
Reinstatement of expired license, §90-244, (b).
Optometrists.
Licenses.
Generally, §90-123.
Persons in practice before passage of statute.
Certificate of registration without examination, §90-119.
Renewal, §90-123.
Additional late renewal fee, §90-118.10.
Osteopaths.
Board of osteopathic examination and registration.
Payment in advance, §90-133.
Licenses.
Application fee, §90-131.
Reciprocity, §90-132.
Registration.
Annual registration, §90-132.
Parks and recreation.
State parks system.
Use of fees, §100-14.
Parole.
Supervision fee.
Condition of parole, §15A-1374, (c).
Partnerships.
Filing of documents, §59-35.2.
Pastoral counselors.
Certification of fee-based practicing pastoral counselors.
Disposition of fees, §90-392.
Duplicate and replacement certificates, §90-394.
Issuance of certificate, §90-387.
Refusal, suspension or revocation of certificate, §90-390.
Renewal of certificate, §90-389.
Pawnbrokers, §91A-8.
Licenses.
Municipal or county authority to regulate, §91A-12.
Pesticides.
Board.
Disposition of fees, §143-468, (a).
Pesticide environmental trust fund, §143-468, (b).
Consultants.
Applications.
Non-refundable annual fee, §143-455, (a).
Dealers and manufacturers.
Licenses.
Applications, §143-448, (b).
Non-refundable fee, §143-452, (b).
Inspection fees, §143-452, (b).
Registration, §143-442, (b).
Pharmacists and pharmacies.
Board of pharmacy.
Fees collectible by board, §90-85.24.

FEES —Cont'd
Pharmacists and pharmacies —Cont'd
Out-of-state pharmacies.
Shipping, mailing or delivering dispensed legend drugs in state.
Registration, §90-85.21A, (c).
Physical therapists.
Licenses.
Applications, §§90-270.29, 90-270.33.
Disposition of fees collected, §90-270.28.
Renewal, §§90-270.32, (a), 90-270.33.
Schedule of fees, §90-270.33.
Physicians and surgeons.
Licenses, §§90-6, 90-15.
Registration, §90-15.1.
Plumbing, heating and fire sprinkler contractors.
Licenses, §§87-22, 87-22.1.
Payable in advance, §87-27.
Podiatrists.
Licenses.
Examination fee, §§90-202.5, (a), 90-202.9.
Reexamination, §90-202.6, (c).
Issuance of license, §90-202.9.
Renewal, §90-202.10.
Pollution control.
Sedimentation pollution control act of 1973.
Erosion control plans.
Approval fees, §113A-54.2, (a), (b), (d).
Ports authority.
Establishment or increase of fee.
Report to joint legislative commission on governmental operations, §12-3.1, (d).
Post-assessment insurance guaranty association.
Exemption, §58-48-70.
Post-release supervision fee, §15A-1368.4, (f).
Precious metal dealers.
Employees.
Certificate of compliance, §66-165, (b).
Permits, §66-165, (a).
Exemptions.
Application for exemption, §66-166.
Special occasion permit, §66-165, (c).
Prepaid legal services plans.
Registration fee, Bar Rules & Regs., E, §.0306.
Private personnel services.
Defined, §95-47.1.
Overstated earnings expectations.
Reimbursements from employers due to, §95-47.3A.
Prohibited acts as to, §95-47.6.
Schedule of fees.
License applicant to file with commissioner, §95-47.3, (a).
Private protective services.
Licenses, §74C-9, (e).
Recovery fund.
Fees to be deposited into fund, §74C-30, (c).
Special limited guard and patrol license fee, §74C-9, (f).
Privilege taxes.
General provisions, §§105-33 to 105-109.
See LICENSE TAXES.
Probate and registration.
Clerks of court.
Miscellaneous fees in administration of estates, §7A-307, (b1).
Register of deeds.
Generally, §161-10.

FEES —Cont'd
Probation.
Supervision fee, §15A-1343, (c1).
Professional corporations.
Filing fees, Bar Rules & Regs., E, §.0105.
Registration with licensing board, §55B-10; Bar Rules & Regs., E, §.0103.
Renewal of certificate of registration, §55B-11.
Professional counselors.
Professional disclosure statement, §90-343.
Schedule of fees, §90-334, (f).
Professional employer organizations, §58-89A-65.
Change of names, §58-89A-80, (b).
Professional limited liability company practicing law.
Filing fees, Bar Rules & Regs., E, §.0105.
Registration, Bar Rules & Regs., E, §.0103.
Proprietary schools.
Licenses.
Authority to establish fees, §115D-92.
Psychologists.
Licenses.
Disposition of fees, §90-270.18.
Schedule of fees, §90-270.18.
Temporary licenses, §90-270.5, (e).
Public livestock market operation fees, §106-408.1.
Public officers and employees.
County officers.
Statement rendered by officers compensated from fees, §128-13.
Penalty for failure to file, §128-13.
Payment, §138-2.
When to be paid in advance, §138-2.
Rules and regulations.
Agencies establishing fees and charges by rule, §12-3.1, (a), (c).
Definitions, §12-3.1, (b).
Public records, §132-6.2.
Public schools, §115C-103.
Collection, §115C-103.
Powers of local boards of education, §115C-47.
Student fees, §115C-384, (a).
Refund upon transfer of pupils, §115C-384, (b).
Textbooks.
Damage fees authorized, §§115C-100, 115C-384, (c).
Rental fees prohibited, §§115C-100, 115C-384, (c).
Public utilities.
State bureau of investigation.
Criminal history record information, §62-333.
Utilities commission, §62-300, (a).
Exemptions from certain fees, §62-300, (d).
Payment, §62-300, (b).
Into treasury, §62-18, (b).
Prerequisites to filings, §62-300, (c).
Public vehicular area, registering, §20-219.4, (c).
Rabies.
Vaccination at county rabies vaccination clinics, §130A-188.
Real estate appraisers.
License or certificate of registered trainee renewal fees, §93E-1-7, (a).
License or certificate of registered trainee replacement fees, §93E-1-7, (d).
License or certificate of registered trainee renewal fees,
Late filing fees, §93E-1-7, (c).

FEES —Cont'd
Real estate appraisers —Cont'd
Licenses or certificates for registration as trainee, §93E-1-6, (b).
Schools or course sponsors, §93E-1-8, (b), (d).
Temporary licensure or certification for nonresidents, §93E-1-9, (c).
Real estate brokers and salespersons.
Continuing education, §93A-4A, (d).
License fees, §93-4.
Referees.
Reference of claim against deceased person.
Recovery of referee's fees, §6-31.
Refrigeration contractors.
Licenses, §87-64.
Payable in advance, §87-63.
Registers of deeds.
Collection prior to rendition of service, §161-10, (c).
Exclusive nature of fees, §161-10, (b).
Marriages.
Licenses.
Portion of fee for children's trust fund, §161-11.1, (a).
Portion of fee for domestic violence centers, §161-11.2.
Salary in counties where fees formerly allowed, §161-4.1.
Schedule of fees, §161-10, (a).
Statement rendered by county officers compensated from fees, §128-13.
Penalty for failure to file statement, §128-13.
Uniform fees, §161-10.
Veterans.
Exemption of armed service discharge documents and certain other records needed in support of claims for veterans benefits, §161-10.1.
Rental referral agencies.
Deposits to be applied toward fees, §66-143, (b).
Failure to obtain housing, §66-143, (c).
Refunds.
Application for refund, §66-143, (d).
Restrictions on, §66-143, (a).
Rents.
Late rent payment fees, §42-46.
Residential property disclosure act.
Forms prepared by real estate commission, §47E-10.
Respiratory care practitioners.
Schedule of license fees, §90-660, (b).
Restaurants, §130A-248, (d).
Retail installment sales.
Attorneys' fees.
Provisions includable, §25A-21.
Collateral.
Substitution, §25A-26.
Official fees.
Defined, §25A-10.
Substitution of collateral, §25A-26.
Transfer of equity.
Transfer fee, §25A-16.
Salvage vehicle certificate of title, §20-109.1, (g).
Savings and loan associations.
Examination and investigation.
Deposit of funds collected, §54B-57, (b).
Licenses.
Annual license fees, §54B-74.
Out-of-state branch offices.
Supervisory and examination fees, §54B-273, (d).

FEES —Cont'd
Savings and loan associations —Cont'd
Statement filed by association, §54B-75.
Supervision and examination fees.
Deposit of funds collected, §54B-57, (a), (b).
Taxation.
Credit for supervisory fees, §105-130.43.
Savings banks.
Administrator of savings institution division.
Supervision and examination fees, §54C-55, (a).
Use of funds collected, §54C-55, (b).
Examinations by commissioner of banks, §54C-55, (a).
Use of funds collected, §54C-55, (b).
Interstate branch banks.
Regulatory and supervisory oversight, §54C-207, (d).
Licenses.
Annual license fees, §54C-61.
Statements filed by savings banks.
Filing fee, §54C-62.
Schools for the deaf.
Athletic fees, §143B-216.44.
Scrap tire disposal.
Taxation generally, §§105-187.15 to 105-187.19.
Secretary of state.
Copying and certifying documents, §147-37.
Corporations.
Filing, service and copying fees, collection, §55-1-22.
Secured transactions.
Filing office fees, §25-9-525.
Information requests.
Response charges, §25-9-210, (f).
Securities regulation.
Collection and payment over, §78A-45, (c).
"No action" letter, §78A-50, (e).
Registration.
Amendment of registration statements, §78A-28, (j).
Dealers and salesmen.
Application fee, §78A-37, (b).
Securities.
Filing fee, §78A-28, (b).
Seeds.
Licenses and inspections, §106-277.28.
Service of process.
Uniform civil process fees, §7A-311.
Setoff debt collection.
Assistance fees, §105A-13.
Shellfish.
Cultivation of shellfish.
Leases.
Application, §113-202, (d1).
Renewal, §113-202, (j).
Sheriffs.
Civil process.
Uniform civil process fees, §7A-311.
License or permit to sell crossbows or pistols.
Services provided, §14-404, (e).
Limitation of actions for, §1-52.
Statement rendered by county officers compensated from fees, §128-13.
Penalty for failure to file statement, §128-13.
Social services.
County boards of social services, §108A-10.
Social workers.
Certification and licensure, §90B-6.2, (a), (b).
Soil additives act.
Registration of additives, §106-50.31.
Soil scientists, §89F-25.

FEES —Cont'd
Solicitors of contributions.
License, §131F-16, (c).
Solid waste management.
Hazardous waste generators, transporters and facilities, §130A-294.1.
Landfills, §130A-309.27, (c).
Septage management firms, §130A-291.1, (e) to (e2).
Solid waste disposal, §130A-309.08.
Special proceedings.
Commissioners, §1-408.
Surveyors' fees, §1-408.1.
Uniform civil process fees, §7A-311.
Witness fees.
Not entitled to fees in advance, §6-51.
Speech and language pathologists and audiologists.
Licenses, §90-305.
State departments and agencies.
Statutory construction, §12-3.1.
State institutions.
Rules and regulations.
Agencies establishing fees and charges by rule, §12-3.1, (a), (c).
Definitions, §12-3.1, (b).
Streets and highways.
Controlled access facilities.
Commercial enterprises.
Logo sign installation and maintenance, §136-89.56.
Structural pest control.
Applicants for certified applicator's identification card or license.
Examinations of applicants, §106-65.27, (a), (b).
Identification cards.
Certified applicators, §106-65.31, (a).
Employees, §106-65.31, (b1).
Licenses.
Issuance and renewal, §106-65.31, (b).
Substance abuse professionals.
Certification.
Written verification of certification, §90-113.38.
Disposition of funds, §90-113.35.
Examinations, §90-113.41.
Maximums, §90-113.38.
Renewal of certification, §90-113.37, (a).
Superior courts.
Accounting for fees and other receipts, §7A-108.
Civil process.
Uniform civil process fees, §7A-311.
Amount, §7A-311, (a).
Collection of fees in advance, §7A-311, (b).
Completeness and exclusivity of fees and costs, §7A-311, (c).
Clerks of court, Const. N. C., art. IV, §21.
Accounting for fees and other receipts, §7A-108.
Annual audit, §7A-108.
Deposits of money held by clerk, §7A-308.1.
Investment of funds in clerk's hands, §7A-308.1.
Statement rendered by county officer compensated from fees, §128-13.
Costs are exclusive, §7A-320.
Deposits of money held by clerk, §7A-308.1.
Discovery procedures.
Filing of verified petition, §7A-305.1.
Investment of funds in clerk's hands, §7A-308.1.
Judges, Const. N. C., art. IV, §21.
Uniform costs and fees in trial division, §§7A-304 to 7A-318.

FEES —Cont'd
Supreme court.
Clerk of the supreme court, §7A-11.
Justices, Const. N. C., art. IV, §21.
Librarian of supreme court.
Copying service fees, §7A-13, (f).
Fees for copying service, §7A-13, (f).
Surplus lines insurance.
Eligibility, applying for, §58-21-20, (c).
Licenses.
Agents and brokers, §58-21-65, (b).
Surveyors' fees.
In civil actions involving sale of land, §1-408.1.
Taxicabs.
Registration, §20-87.
Tax incentives for new and expanding business, §105-129.6, (a), (a1).
Teacher certification, §115C-296, (a2).
Telephone membership corporations.
Regulatory fee, §117-3.1.
Telephonic sellers.
Registration, §66-261, (a), (c).
Therapeutic recreation personnel.
Certification, §90C-10.
Deposit for fees, §90C-7.
Time shares.
Registration of time share projects.
Application fee, §93A-52, (a).
Renewal fee, §93A-52, (d).
Title insurance.
Licenses.
Companies.
Collateral loan certificate, §58-27-10.
Torrens system registration, §43-5.
Trademarks.
Registration.
Renewal fee, §80-5.
Underground storage tanks.
Leaking petroleum cleanup, §143-215.94C.
Uniform civil process fees, §7A-311.
Uniform costs and fees in trial division, §§7A-304 to 7A-318.
Uniform trusts act.
Funds held by corporation exercising fiduciary powers awaiting investment or distribution.
Fee for temporary investment, §36A-63, (d).
Veterinarians.
Licenses.
Renewal.
Additional late renewal fee, §90-187.5.
Veterinary student interns.
Special registration, §90-186.
Veterinary technicians.
Special registration, §90-186.
Viatical life insurance settlements.
Offer or sale of contract, costs of filing, §78A-17.
Viatical settlement brokers and providers.
Licenses, §58-58-210, (b).
Renewal fee, §58-58-210, (c).
Vital statistics.
Abandoned children.
Establishing facts relating to birth, §130A-107, (d).
Establishing fact of birth by person without certificate, §130A-106, (b).
State registrar.
Providing copies or searching vital records, §§130A-93, (i), 130A-93.1, (a).
Refund of overpayments, §130A-92, (b).
Unknown parentage.
Establishing facts relating to birth, §130A-107, (d).

FEES —Cont'd
Warrants for payment of money.
Issuance of warrants upon state treasurer.
Overdrafts against disbursing accounts, §143-3.2, (b).
Wastewater systems.
On-site subsurface systems.
Review fee, §130A-343, (k).
Wastewater treatment.
Certification of water pollution control system operator.
Fee schedule, §90A-42, (a).
Water and air resources.
Applications.
Disposition of fees, §143-215.3, (a).
Use of application and permit fees, §143-215.3A.
Water treatment facility operators.
Certificates, §90A-27.
Weights and measures.
Testing and certifying, §81A-11.
Well contractor certification, §87-98.9.
Wetlands restoration program.
Fund payments, §143-214.12, (b).
Witnesses.
Action for fees, §6-53.
Advance receipt of fees.
Not entitled to fees in advance, §6-51.
Attendance.
Compulsion to attend more than one day, §6-51.
One fee for day's attendance, §6-60.
Proof of attendance, §6-53.
Commissioner of banks.
Employees of office used as witnesses, §53-122, (c).
Criminal actions.
Payment of witness fees in criminal actions, §7A-316.
When defendant not liable.
Liability of state for witness fees, §7A-315.
Disbursement of expenses, §7A-301.
Expert witnesses.
Indigent defense services.
Fees paid by state, §7A-454.
Uniform fees, §7A-314, (d).
Interpreters.
Uniform fees, §7A-314, (f).
Legislative committees.
Expenses and fees of witness, §120-19.3.
Not entitled to fees in advance, §6-51.
Poultry products inspection.
Mileage and fees of witnesses, §106-549.68, (b).
Proof of single material fact.
Liability for fees of such witnesses, §6-60.
Reference of claim against deceased person.
Recovery of fees of witnesses, §6-31.
State of North Carolina.
Criminal cases when defendant not liable.
Liability of state for witness fees, §7A-315.
Uniform fees for witnesses, §7A-314, (a).
Expert witness, §7A-314, (d).
Language interpreters, §7A-314, (f).
Limit on number, §7A-314, (e).
Mileage rate of reimbursement, §7A-314, (c).
Out-of-state witnesses, §7A-314, (c).
Reimbursement for travel expenses, §7A-314, (b).
Workers' compensation.
Expert witnesses, §97-26.1.
Medical records and reports, §97-26.1.
Medical treatment, fees allowed, §97-26.

FEES —Cont'd
Workers' compensation —Cont'd
Occupational disease.
Medical examinations.
Asbestosis and silicosis.
Schedule of fees for examinations and reports, §97-73.
Wreckers.
Removal of unauthorized vehicles from private lots.
Applicability of provisions, §20-219.2, (c).
Zoological authority.
Establishment of admission fees, §143-177.3, (b).

FEE SIMPLE.
Condemnation.
State owned railroad companies, §40A-3, (a).
Conversion of fee tail to fee simple, §41-1.
Conveyances.
Presumption of fee though word heirs omitted, §39-1.
Possibility of reverter, right of entry or executory interest.
Time limit, §41-32.
Wills.
Devise presumed to be in fee, §31-38.

FEET.
Podiatrists.
See PODIATRISTS.

FEE TAIL.
Conversion into fee simple, §41-1.

FELLATIO.
Sexual offenses generally.
See SEXUAL OFFENSES.

FELONIES.
Abortion, §§14-44 to 14-46.
Destruction of unborn child.
Use of drugs or instruments, §14-44.
Accomplices and accessories.
Before the fact accessories.
Accessory before fact punishable as principal felon, §14-5.2.
Administration department.
Bribery.
Purchases and contracts to department.
Acceptance of bribes, §143-63.
Adoption.
Unlawful payments related to adoption.
Subsequent violations, §48-10-102, (b).
Adulterated or misbranded food, drugs or cosmetics.
Intent to cause serious injury or death, §14-34.4, (a).
Intent to extort, §14-34.4, (b).
Adult protection.
Abuse of disabled or elder adults, §14-32.3, (a).
Exploitation of disabled or elder adult, §14-32.3, (c).
Neglect of disabled or elder adult, §14-32.3, (b).
Aircraft.
Infliction of serious bodily injury by operation of aircraft while impaired, §63-28.
Alcoholic beverages.
Beer franchise agreements.
Felony conviction affecting goodwill, §18B-1305.
Commission.
Felony conviction as grounds for removal from office, §18B-202.
Direct shipment into state, §18B-102.1, (e).

FELONIES —Cont'd
Alcoholic beverages —Cont'd
Employee discharge.
Felony conviction as grounds for discharge from employment, §18B-202.
Local ABC boards.
Embezzlement or malfeasance by members or employees, §18B-702, (f).
Manufacturers.
Second unlawful manufacturing offense, §18B-307, (c).
Permit issuance.
Felony conviction as disqualification for permit, §§18B-900, (a), 18B-1003, (c).
Alligator propagation and production.
Untagged or undocumented alligator possessed by operator of facility, §106-763.1, (c).
Animals.
Injuring, maiming or killing law enforcement agency animal, §14-163.1.
Interference with animal research, §14-159.2, (c).
Animal shelters.
Certificates of registration.
Felony conviction as grounds for denial of certificate, §19A-30.
Appearances.
Failure to appear, §15A-543.
Arrest.
Duty of arresting officer to provide information to state, §15A-501.
Without warrant, §15A-401.
Arson generally.
See ARSON.
Assault.
Habitual misdemeanor assault, §14-33.2.
Lesser included offense, §15-169.
Secret assault, §14-31.
Serious bodily injury.
Assault inflicting, §14-32.4, (a).
Strangulation.
Assault inflicting, §14-32.4, (b).
Assault with deadly weapon.
Intent to kill or inflicting serious injury, §14-32.
Athlete agents, §78C-99.
Athletic contests generally, §§14-373 to 14-379.
Attempt to commit felony.
Punishment for, §14-2.5.
Bail and recognizance.
Failure to appear, §15A-543, (b).
Bail bondsmen and runners.
Conviction of felony.
Grounds for denial, suspension, revocation or refusal to renew license, §58-71-80, (a), (b).
Monthly report.
Knowingly and willfully falsifying, §58-71-165.
Bailments.
Conversion, §14-168.1.
Banks.
Bank examiners.
False reports, §53-124.
Keeping or accepting bribe or gratuity, §53-124.
Deposits.
Insolvent banks.
Receiving deposits, §53-132.
Embezzlement or misapplication of funds, §53-129.
False certification of check, §53-131.
False entries in banking accounts, §53-130.
Misrepresenting assets and liabilities of banks, §53-130.

FELONIES —Cont'd
Barbers.
Conviction.
Disqualifications for certificates or permits, §86A-18.
Battery.
Habitual misdemeanor assault, §14-33.2.
Bigamy.
Constitutes a felony, §14-183.
Bills of lading.
Issuing false bills, §21-42.
Birth of child.
Concealment, §14-46.
Bomb scares, §§14-69.1, 14-69.2.
Breaking and entering.
Generally, §14-54.
Prevention of felonies.
All persons authorized to break open and enter house, §15-43.
Breaking out of dwelling house, §14-53.
Bribery.
Athletic contests, §§14-373 to 14-376.
See ATHLETIC CONTESTS.
Buildings.
Breaking or entering buildings.
Generally, §14-54.
Burglary, §§14-51 to 14-57.
See BURGLARY.
Burial.
Unmarked human burial and human skeletal remains protection.
Certain prohibited acts, §70-40, (b).
Carrying concealed weapons.
Second or subsequent offense, §14-269, (c).
Castration, §§14-28, 14-29.
Cemeteries.
Defacing or desecrating grave sites.
Plowing over or covering up graves, §14-149.
Violations of North Carolina cemetery act, §65-71, (a).
Check-cashing businesses, §53-287.
Child abuse or neglect, §14-318.4.
Child care facilities.
Fraudulent misrepresentation, §110-107, (b).
Subsequent offenses, §110-103, (d).
Unauthorized administration of medicine, §110-102.1A, (c).
Violation causing serious injury to a child, §110-103, (c).
Willful violations, §110-103, (b).
Childhood vaccine-related injury compensation.
Certain vaccine diversions, §130A-431.
Children's health insurance program.
Fraud and misrepresentation, §108A-70.28.
Classification.
Default classification, §15A-1340.17.
Sentencing commission, §164-41.
Coin-operated machines.
Burglary, §§14-56.1, 14-56.2.
Collection agencies.
Doing business without permit, §58-70-1.
Commodities.
Violations of act, §78D-24, (a).
Compensation to persons erroneously convicted of felonies, §§148-82 to 148-84.
Amount of compensation, §148-84.
Forms, §148-83.
Hearings, §148-83.
Payment of compensation, §148-84.
Petitions, §148-83.

FELONIES —Cont'd
Compensation to persons erroneously convicted of felonies —Cont'd
Provision for compensation, §148-82.
Computer related crime.
Accessing computers, §14-454, (a).
Computer trespass, §14-458, (b).
Damaging computers and computer resources, §14-455, (a), (a1).
Government computers.
Accessing, §14-454.1, (a), (b).
Altering, damaging or destroying, §14-455, (a1).
Denial of government computer services to an authorized user, §14-456.1, (a).
Solicitation of child by computer, §14-202.3, (c).
Computer trespass, §14-458, (b).
Concealing birth of child, §14-46.
Conspiracy.
Punishment for conspiracy to commit a felony, §14-2.4, (a).
Contaminating food or drink to render one mentally incapacitated or physically helpless, §14-401.16, (c).
Contempt.
Criminal contempt.
Circumstances for final imprisonment, §5A-12.
Continuing criminal enterprise, §14-7.20.
Contracts through department of administration.
False certification that bids were submitted without collusion, §143-54.
Controlled substances.
Amphetamines.
Trafficking in amphetamines, §90-95, (h).
Conditions of prescribed punishments and degree of offenses, §90-95, (e).
Conspiracy to violate provision, §90-98.
Continuing criminal enterprise, §90-95.1, (a).
Counterfeit substances.
Prohibited acts as to, §90-95, (c).
Heroin.
Trafficking in heroin, §90-95, (h).
Manufacture, §90-95, (b).
Marijuana.
Trafficking in marijuana, §90-95, (h).
Methamphetamines.
Trafficking in methamphetamines, §90-95, (h).
Methaqualone.
Trafficking in methaqualone, §90-95, (h).
Minors.
Delivery of drug paraphernalia to, §90-113.23, (c).
Employing or intentionally using minor to commit drug law violations, §90-95.4, (a), (b).
Participating in a drug violation by a minor, §90-95.7, (c).
Promoting drug sales by a minor, §90-95.6, (c).
Opium.
Trafficking in opium, §90-95, (h).
Possession, §90-95, (d).
Precursor chemicals.
Designation, §90-95, (d2).
Prohibited acts as to, §90-95, (d1), (d1a).
Prohibited acts.
Violations committed intentionally, §90-108, (b).
Sales, §90-95, (b).
Wholesale prescription drug distributors, §106-145.6, (b).
Conversion.
Bailments, §14-168.1.

FELONIES —Cont'd
Corruption.
Elections, §163-275.
Counterfeiting, §14-13.
Bills of lading, §21-42.
Instruments, §14-119, (a), (b).
Possessing tools for counterfeiting, §14-14.
Credit cards and devices.
False or fraudulent use of credit device.
Multiple violations, §14-113.6, (a).
Credit repair services, §66-225.
Crime against nature, §14-177.
Crops.
Burning crops in the field.
Criminal trespass, §14-141.
Cruelty to animals.
Animal fights and baiting, §14-362.1, (d).
Dog fighting and baiting, §14-362.2, (b), (c).
Default classification, §15A-1340.17.
Definitions, §14-1.
Habitual felons, §14-7.1.
Delinquent and undisciplined juvenile actions.
First appearance of juvenile for felony cases, §7B-1808.
Dental hygienists.
Conviction as grounds for disciplinary measures, §90-229, (a).
Dentists.
Conviction.
Grounds for disciplinary action, §90-41, (a).
Desecrating, plowing over or covering up graves, §14-149.
Destroying unborn child.
Use of drugs or instruments, §14-44.
Detention facilities.
Assault on person employed at state or local detention facility, §14-34.7, (b).
Assault with firearm upon, in performance of duties, §14-34.5, (b).
Disability income plan.
Disability or disabled.
Defined as incapacity not resulting from felonious conduct, §135-101.
Discount buying clubs.
Bond and trust account requirements.
Violations, §66-135, (d).
Discrimination.
Offenses committed because of victim's race, etc., §14-3, (c).
DNA analysis.
Blood sample required upon conviction of certain crimes, §15A-266.4.
Domestic criminal trespass, §14-134.3, (b).
Domestic violence.
Protective orders.
Firearms violations, §50B-3.1, (j).
Violation of valid protective order, §50B-4.1, (d), (f).
Drivers' licenses.
Commercial driver's license disqualification, §20-17.4, (a).
Forfeiture of licensing privilege, §15A-1331A.
Limited driving privilege, eligibility, §20-179.3, (b).
Sale of reproduction, facsimile or simulation of license, §20-30.
Use of motor vehicle in commission of felony, §20-17, (a).
Wrongful issuance, §20-34.1, (a).
Drug and alcohol screening tests.
Defrauding test.
Second or subsequent offense, §14-401.20, (c).

FELONIES —Cont'd
Drug paraphernalia.
Minors.
Delivery of drug paraphernalia to certain younger persons, §90-113.23, (c).
Drugs.
Amphetamines.
Trafficking in, §90-95, (h).
Conditions of prescribed punishments and degree of offenses, §90-95, (e).
Conspiracy to violate provision, §90-98.
Continuing criminal enterprise, §90-95.1, (a).
Counterfeit substances.
Prohibited acts as to, §90-95, (c).
Heroin.
Trafficking in, §90-95, (h).
Manufacturers, §90-95, (b).
Enhanced sentencing in certain cases, §15A-1340.16D.
Marijuana.
Trafficking in, §90-95, (h).
Methamphetamines.
Trafficking in methamphetamines, §90-95, (h).
Methaqualone.
Trafficking in, §90-95, (h).
Minors.
Delivery of drug paraphernalia to certain youths, §90-113.23, (c).
Employing or intentionally using minor to commit drug law violations, §90-95.4, (a), (b).
Participating in a drug violation by a minor, §90-95.7, (c).
Promoting drug sales by a minor, §90-95.6, (c).
Opium.
Trafficking in, §90-95, (h).
Possession, §90-95, (d).
Precursor chemicals.
Designation, §90-95, (d2).
Prohibited acts as to, §90-95, (d1), (d1a).
Prohibited acts.
Violations committed intentionally, §90-108, (b).
Sale, §90-95, (b).
Wholesale prescription drug distributors, §106-145.6, (b).
Dry-cleaning solvent cleanup, §143-215.104Q, (b), (c).
Elections.
Absentee ballot violations, §163-226.3, (a).
Challenge of voters.
Answer to challenge as felon not to be used on prosecution, §163-90.
False swearing, §163-90.3.
Corruption.
Certain acts declared felonies, §163-275.
Disqualification from voting, §163-55; Const. N. C., art. VI, §2.
Disqualifications from office, Const. N. C., art. VI, §8.
Electronic commerce in government, §66-58.8.
Electronic surveillance.
Advertisement of surveillance devices, §15A-288, (a2).
Manufacture, possession, purchase or sale of devices, §15A-288, (a1).
Willful interception or disclosure of wire, oral or electronic communications, §15A-287, (a1) to (a4).
Embezzlement generally.
See EMBEZZLEMENT.

FELONIES —Cont'd
Emergency medical services personnel.
Assault or affray upon while discharging duties, §14-34.6.
Assault with dangerous weapon or substance, §14-288.9, (c).
Endangering executive, legislative or court officers, §§14-16.6 to 14-16.10.
Escape, §148-45, (b).
Private correction facilities, §14-256.1.
Ethnic animosity.
Offenses committed because of victim's nationality, §14-3, (c).
Evasion of tax, §105-236.
Explosives.
Malicious use of explosive or incendiary, §14-49.
Property occupied by persons, §14-49.1.
Used in burglary, §14-57.
Extortion, §14-118.4.
Failure to appear, §15A-543.
False names.
Identification card for nondrivers presented with fake name in commission of felony, §20-37.8, (b).
False pretenses and cheats generally.
See FALSE PRETENSES AND CHEATS.
Fictitious names.
Presenting identification card with fake name in commission of felony, §20-37.8, (b).
Financial identity fraud, §§14-113.20, (a), 14-113.22, (a), (a1).
Trafficking in stolen identities, §14-113.20A, (b).
Financial transaction cards, §14-113.17, (b).
Firearms.
Discharging firearm into occupied property, §14-34.1.
Possession of firearms, etc., by felon prohibited, §14-415.1, (a).
Indictment charging with violations of provisions, §14-415.1, (c).
Person charged with felony acquitted by reason of insanity, §14-415.3, (a), (b).
Person charged with felony found incompetent to stand trial, §14-415.3, (a), (b).
Prior convictions causing disentitlement, §14-415.1, (b).
Use or display during commission of felony.
Enhanced sentence, §15A-1340.16A.
Fishing licenses.
Forfeiture of licensing privilege after conviction of felony, §15A-1331A.
Food.
Distribution of harmful substances at Halloween and other times, §14-401.11.
Food stamps.
Fraud, §108A-53, (a).
Illegal possession or use, §108A-53.1.
Forfeitures.
Licensing privilege after conviction of felony, §15A-1331A.
Money or other property or interest acquired, §14-2.3, (a).
Action to recover, statute of limitation, §14-2.3, (b).
Property traceable to owner or guardian, inapplicability of forfeiture, §14-2.3, (c).
Forgery generally.
See FORGERY.
Franchise tax.
Limited liability companies.
Controlled companies.
Underpayment, fraud to evade, penalty, §105-114.1, (h).

FELONIES —Cont'd
Franchise tax —Cont'd
Limited liability companies —Cont'd
Income, assets, liabilities and equity.
Failure to included in member corporation's computation of tax, §105-114, (c).
Fraternal benefit societies.
False statements under oath, §58-24-180, (e).
Mergers and consolidation.
Violations of provisions of section, §58-24-180, (d).
Fraud.
Rental vehicles, §20-106.1.
Work first program, §108A-39, (b).
General assembly.
Restoring rights of citizenship of convicts.
Local, special and private legislation prohibited, Const. N. C., art. II, §24.
Threats to influence legislator in discharge of duties, §120-86, (e).
Ginseng.
Larceny, §14-79.
Habitual felons, §§14-7.1 to 14-7.12, 15A-1340.10.
Charge of habitual felon, §14-7.3.
Defined, §14-7.1.
Evidence of prior convictions, §14-7.4.
Indictment, §14-7.2.
Charge of habitual felon, §14-7.3.
Judgment, §14-7.5.
Prior convictions.
Evidence, §14-7.4.
Punishment, §14-7.2.
Sentencing, §§14-7.2, 14-7.6.
Structured sentencing.
Inapplicability to violent habitual felons, §15A-1340.10.
Verdict, §14-7.5.
Violent habitual felons.
Charge, §14-7.9.
Convicted defined, §14-7.7, (a).
Evidence of prior convictions, §14-7.10.
Persons declared to be, §14-7.7, (a).
Punishment, §14-7.8.
Sentencing, §14-7.12.
Verdict and judgment, §14-7.11.
Violent felony, crimes included in term, §14-7.7, (b).
Habitual misdemeanor assault, §14-33.2.
Handguns.
Sale to minors, §14-315.
Hazardous waste management, §130A-26.1.
Class I felonies, §130A-26.1, (f).
Class J felonies, §130A-26.1, (g).
"Knowingly and willingly" defined, §130A-26.1, (d).
Highway patrol.
Crossing median of divided highway.
Apprehension of felon, §20-140.3.
Conditions under which authorized, §136-89.58.
Homicide generally.
See HOMICIDE.
Housing authorities and projects.
Fraudulent misrepresentation in obtaining housing assistance, §157-29.1, (b).
Hunting licenses.
Forfeiture of licensing privilege after conviction of felony, §15A-1331A.
Identification cards for nondrivers.
False or fictitious names.
Presenting identification card with fake name in commission of felony, §20-37.8, (b).

FELONIES —Cont'd
Impeachment.
Causes for impeachment, §123-5.
Impersonation.
Law enforcement or other public officer, §14-277, (d1).
Incest, §14-178, (b).
Indigent persons.
False material statements as to indigency.
Defendant seeking appointment of counsel, §7A-456, (a).
Insolvent or imprisoned debtor.
False swearing, §23-43.
Insurance agents, broker or limited representatives.
Unauthorized insurers.
Soliciting, negotiating or selling insurance for, §58-33-95, (a).
Insurance commissioner, false statements to, §58-2-180.
Insurance fraud.
False statement to procure or deny benefit of policy or certificate, §58-2-161, (b).
Investment advisers, §78C-39, (a) to (a4).
Involuntary servitude, §14-43.2.
Juvenile proceedings.
Committed to youth development center for offense classified as class B1, B2, C, D or E felony.
Continued jurisdiction of juvenile court, §7B-1602, (b).
Delinquent and undisciplined juvenile actions.
First appearance of juvenile for felony case, §7B-1808.
Kidnapping and abduction.
Abduction of children, §14-41, (a).
Punishment for kidnapping, §14-39, (b).
Larceny generally.
See LARCENY.
Law enforcement officers.
Assault upon, in performance of duties, §14-34.7.
Assault with firearm upon, in performance of duties, §14-34.5, (a).
Impersonation, §14-277, (a1).
Leases.
Motor vehicles.
Sublease and loan assumption arranging, §20-106.2, (d), (e).
Legislators.
Bribery, §120-86, (e).
Extortion, §120-86.
Licensing privileges.
Forfeiture after conviction of felony.
Automatic forfeiture, §15A-1331A, (b).
Definitions, §15A-1331A, (a).
Judge to make findings and judgment, §15A-1331A, (c).
Limited driving privilege, §15A-1331A, (d).
Lights.
Displaying false lights on seashore, §14-282.
Limited liability companies.
Franchise tax.
Controlled companies.
Underpayment, fraud to evade, penalty, §105-114.1, (h).
Income, assets, liabilities and equity.
Failure to included in member corporation's computation of tax, §105-114, (c).
Littering, §14-399.
Livestock.
Cattle tick.
Damaging dipping vats, §106-363.
Poisoning livestock, §14-163.

FELONIES —Cont'd
Livestock —Cont'd
Pursuing or injuring with intent to steal, §14-85.
Tuberculosis.
Sale of tubercular animal a felony, §106-350.
Looting, §14-288.6.
Machine guns.
Sale, use or possession, §14-409.
Maiming.
Castration, §§14-28, 14-29.
Malicious maiming, §14-30.
Malicious throwing of acid or alkali, §14-30.1.
Malicious castration, §14-28.
Malicious conduct by prisoners, §14-258.4, (a).
Manslaughter, §14-18.
Manufactured homes uniform standards.
Health and safety of purchaser threatened, §143-151, (b).
Marriage and family therapists.
Conviction as grounds for disciplinary action, §90-270.60, (a).
Meat inspections, §106-549.35, (a).
Medicaid.
Fraud of providers, §108A-63, (c).
Property of patients violations, §108A-60, (b).
Medical waste.
Depositing in navigable waters, §76-40, (a1).
Water and air resources.
Prohibited disposal of waste, §143-214.2A, (c).
Militia.
Composition of unauthorized militia.
Convicted felons excepted, §127A-7.
Minors.
Controlled substances.
Delivery of drug paraphernalia to certain youths, §90-113.23, (c).
Employing minor to commit drug law violations, §90-95.4, (a), (b).
Participating in a drug violation by a minor, §90-95.7, (c).
Promoting drug sales by a minor, §90-95.6, (c).
Juvenile proceedings. See within this heading, "Juvenile proceedings."
Prostitution.
Participating in prostitution of a minor, §14-190.19, (c).
Promoting prostitution of a minor, §14-190.18, (c).
Sexual exploitation of a minor.
First degree, §14-190.16, (d).
Second degree, §14-190.17, (d).
Solicitation of child by computer, §14-202.3, (c).
Taking indecent liberties with children, §14-202.1.
Miscarriage or injury to pregnant woman.
Use of drugs or instruments to produce, §14-45.
Monopolies and restraint of trade.
Contracts, combinations and conspiracies, §75-1.
Mortgage bankers and brokers, §53-243.14.
Motor carriers embezzling COD shipments, §62-273.
Motor vehicle financial responsibility.
False affidavit or knowingly swearing or affirming falsely, §20-279.31, (c1).
Motor vehicles.
Accidents.
Leaving scene of accident, §20-166, (a), (b).
Certificates of title.
Altering or forging certificate of title, registration card or application, §20-71, (a).
Reproducing or possessing blank title, §20-71, (b).

FELONIES —Cont'd
Motor vehicles —Cont'd
Commercial drivers' licenses.
Forfeiture of driving privilege after conviction of felony, §15A-1331A.
Lifetime disqualification.
Use of commercial vehicle in commission of felony, §20-17.4, (c).
Use of commercial vehicle in commission of felony, §20-17.4, (a).
Lifetime disqualification, §20-17.4, (c).
Dealers.
License applications.
Felony conviction as grounds for denial, §20-294.
Drivers' licenses.
Commercial driver's license disqualification, §20-17.4, (a).
Forfeiture of licensing privilege after conviction of felony, §15A-1331A.
Limited driving privilege, eligibility, §20-179.3, (b).
Learners' permits.
Sale of reproduction, facsimile or simulation of license, §20-30.
Sale of reproduction, facsimile or simulation of license, §20-30.
Use of motor vehicle in commission of felony, §20-17, (a).
Wrongful issuance, §20-34.1, (a).
Engine numbers.
Altering or changing, §20-109, (a).
Intent to conceal or misrepresent true identity of vehicle, §20-109, (b).
Felony death by vehicles, §20-141.4, (a1).
Punishment, §20-141.4, (b).
Felony violations punished as class 1 felon, §20-177.
Fraud.
Rental vehicles, §20-106.1.
Impaired driving.
Habitual impaired driving, §20-138.5, (b).
Inspections, §20-183.8, (c).
Leases.
Sublease and loan assumption arranging, §20-106.2, (d), (e).
Licenses.
Commercial drivers' licenses.
Disqualification.
Using commercial vehicle in commission of felony, §20-17.4, (a).
Sale of reproduction or facsimile or simulation of driver's license, §20-30.
Manufacturer's certificate of origin.
False sworn certification, §20-52.1, (d).
Odometers.
Unlawful change of mileage, §20-350.
Registration.
Altering or forging registration card, §20-71, (a).
Security interest, registration.
False filing, §20-58, (b).
Serial numbers.
Altering or changing, §20-109, (a).
Intent to conceal or misrepresent true identity of vehicle, §20-109, (b).
Smoke screen violations, §20-136, (b).
Special identification card.
Wrongful issuance, §20-34.1, (a).
Stolen vehicles.
Receiving or transferring stolen vehicles, §20-106.

FELONIES —Cont'd
Motor vehicles —Cont'd
Sublease and loan assumption arranging, §20-106.2, (d).
Total loss claim vehicle.
Removal of permanent marker affixed to vehicles doorjam, §20-71.4, (c).
Use of motor vehicle in commission of felony.
Mandatory revocation of license, §20-17, (a).
Murder, §14-17.
Navigable waters.
Medical waste, depositing, §76-40, (a1).
Neglect of disabled or elder adult, §14-32.3, (b).
Notaries public.
False or fraudulent acknowledgments or verifications, §10A-12, (c).
Nuclear, biological or chemical weapons.
False report or hoax, §§14-288.23, (a), 14-288.24.
Manufacture, assembly, possession, etc., §14-288.21.
Use and delivery of weapons, §14-288.22.
Obscenity.
Dissemination to minors under the age of 16 years, §14-190.7.
Sexual exploitation of a minor.
First degree, §14-190.16, (d).
Second degree, §14-190.17, (d).
Obstructing justice generally.
See OBSTRUCTING JUSTICE.
Obstruction of health care facilities.
Habitual offenders, §14-277.4, (c).
Occupational licenses.
Forfeiture of licensing privilege after conviction of felony, §15A-1331A.
Office of information technology services.
Procurement of information technology.
Bribery, §147-33.99.
False certification that information technology bid submitted without collusion, §147-33.100.
Financial interest of officers in sources of supply, §147-33.99.
Oil or hazardous substances discharges, §143-215.88B, (e), (f), (h).
Optometrists.
Conviction as grounds for disciplinary action, §90-121.2, (a).
Osteopaths.
Conviction as grounds for refusal, revocation or suspension of license, §90-136.
Paper currency machines, §14-56.3.
Parole of felons.
Automatic parole under certain conditions, §15A-1371, (g).
Patient abuse, §14-32.2, (b).
Pederasty.
Taking indecent liberties with children, §14-202.1.
Peeping Toms.
Secretly peeping into room occupied by another person, §14-202, (d) to (i).
Perjury generally.
See PERJURY.
Physical therapists.
Conviction as grounds for disciplinary action, §90-270.36.
Pine needles or pine straw.
Larceny, §14-79.1.
Poisoning livestock, §14-163.
Police.
Conviction of felony.
Removal of unfit officers, §128-16.
Possession of burglary tools, §14-55.

FELONIES —Cont'd
Poultry products inspections, §106-549.59, (a).
Pregnant women.
Injury to pregnant woman resulting in miscarriage or stillbirth, §14-18.2, (b).
Using drugs or instruments to injure, §14-45.
Preneed funeral contracts and funds, §90-210.70, (a).
Prescriptions.
Wholesale prescription drug distributors, §106-145.6, (b).
Prevention.
Breaking and entering of a house.
Authorization, §15-43.
Probation or parole officers.
Assault upon, in performance of duties, §14-34.7, (a).
Assault with firearm upon in performance of duties, §14-34.5, (a).
Prostitution.
Minors.
Participating in prostitution of a minor, §14-190.19, (c).
Promoting prostitution of a minor, §14-190.18, (c).
Public officers and employees.
Assault with a deadly weapon, §14-34.2.
Disqualifications from holding office, Const. N. C., art. VI, §8.
Misconduct in office, §§14-228 to 14-252.
See MISCONDUCT IN PUBLIC OFFICE.
Public works.
Contractor affidavits.
Perjury in affidavit, §133-31.
Racial minorities.
Offenses committed because of victim's race, §14-3, (c).
Railroads.
Injury to property of railroads, §§14-278, 14-279.
Officers.
Misconduct in private office, §14-253.
Shooting or throwing at trains or passengers, §14-280.
Rape, §§14-27.2, 14-27.3.
Rebellion, §14-8.
Rebirthing technique.
Practicing.
Second or subsequent offense, §14-401.21, (b).
Religious discrimination.
Offenses committed because of victim's religion, §14-3, (c).
Restoration of felon's citizenship rights, §§13-1 to 13-4.
Restraint.
Felonious restraint, §14-43.3.
Riots and civil disorders.
Engaging to riot, §14-288.2.
Robbery.
Armed robbery, §14-87, (a).
Common law robbery, §14-87.1.
Train robbery, §14-88.
Safecracking, §14-89.1.
School personnel.
Sexual acts with victim who is student, §14-27.7, (b).
Seashore.
Displaying false lights on seashore, §14-282.
Secret societies.
Violation of article, §14-12.15.
Securities regulation.
Obstruction of investigation, §78A-58.
Securities regulation violations, §78A-57.

FELONIES —Cont'd
Sentencing.
Commitment to department of correction, §15A-1352, (b).
Enhanced sentence.
Bullet-proof vests.
Defendant wearing or having in possession during commission of felony, §15A-1340.16C, (a).
Burden of proof, §15A-1340.16C, (d).
Exceptions, §15A-1340.16C, (b), (e).
Indictments or informations, §15A-1340.16C, (c).
Firearm used or displayed during commission of felony, §15A-1340.16A, (c).
Burden of proof, §15A-1340.16A, (e).
Circumstances in which provisions do not apply, §15A-1340.16A, (f).
Indictments or informations, §15A-1340.16A, (d).
Methamphetamine manufacture.
Serious injury inflicted on law or emergency personnel, §15A-1340.16D, (a).
Applicability, §15A-1340.16D, (d).
Burden of proof, §15A-1340.16D, (c).
Indictment allegations, §15A-1340.16D, (b).
Forfeiture of licensing privilege after conviction of felony, §15A-1331A.
Habitual felons, §§14-7.2, 14-7.6.
Inapplicability of structured sentencing to violent habitual felons, §15A-1340.10.
Violent habitual felons, §14-7.12.
Licensing privileges.
Forfeiture after conviction.
Automatic forfeiture, §15A-1331A, (b).
Definitions, §15A-1331A, (a).
Judge to make findings and judgment, §15A-1331A, (c).
Limited driving privilege, §15A-1331A, (d).
Structured sentencing, §§15A-1340.13 to 15A-1340.17.
Violent habitual felons, §14-7.12.
Sex offender and public protection registration.
Failure to register, subsequent violations, §14-208.11, (a).
Sexual offenses.
Crime against nature, §14-177.
Generally.
See SEXUAL OFFENSES.
Shellfish.
Polluted shellfish.
Taking or selling at night or with prior convictions, §113-209, (d).
Sheriffs.
Conviction of felony.
Removal of unfit officers, §128-16.
Slot machines, §14-309, (a), (b).
Social services.
Food stamps.
Fraudulent misrepresentation, §108A-53, (a).
Medical assistance program.
Fraud.
Providers of medical assistance, §108A-63, (c).
Recipients, §108A-64, (c).
Property of patients.
Certain violations as to, §108A-60, (b).
Solicitation to commit felony.
Punishment for, §14-2.6, (a).
Solid waste management.
Hazardous waste, §130A-26.1.
Speeding to elude arrest, §20-141.5, (b).

FELONIES —Cont'd
Speedy trial, §15-10.
Stalking, §14-277.3.
Statutory rape, §§14-27.2, 14-27.4.
First-degree sexual offense, §14-27.4.
Strangulation.
Assault inflicting, §14-32.4, (b).
Submachine guns.
Sale, use or possession, §14-409.
Subversion.
Punishment for violations, §14-12.
Taking indecent liberties with a student, §14-202.4, (a).
Taxation, §105-236.
Tax evasion, §105-236.
Telephone sales recovery services, §14-401.15, (c).
Time shares.
Registration.
Violation of requirement, §93A-40, (b).
Time share registrar.
Violations as to, §93A-58, (b).
Toxic substances.
Disclosure of hazardous substance trade secret, §95-197.
Dumping of toxic substances, §14-284.2.
Trademarks.
Criminal use of counterfeit trademark, §80-11.1, (b), (c).
Transportation board.
Conflicts of interest, §136-14, (i).
Malfeasance, §136-13, (c).
Profiting from proposed project, §136-14, (f).
Transportation department.
Highway inspection reports.
Falsifying reports, §136-13.2, (a), (b).
Trespass.
Crops.
Burning or destroying crops in the field, §14-141.
Trial.
Speedy trial, §15-10.
Trust companies.
Records violations, §53-355.
Underground petroleum storage tank leak cleanup, §143-215.94X, (b), (c).
Uttering, §14-120.
Bills of lading, §21-42.
Viatical life insurance settlements.
Fraudulent viatical settlement act, §58-58-265, (a).
Violent habitual felons, §§14-7.7 to 14-7.12.
Charge, §14-7.9.
Convicted defined, §14-7.7, (a).
Evidence of prior convictions, §14-7.10.
Persons declared to be, §14-7.7, (a).
Punishment, §14-7.8.
Sentencing, §14-7.12.
Verdict in judgment, §14-7.11.
Violent felony, crimes included in term, §14-7.7, (b).
Vital statistics, §130A-26A, (b).
Water and air resources.
Air pollution control violations, §143-215.114B, (a) to (i).
Classifications, standards or limitations.
Knowing and willful violations, §143-215.6B.
Medical waste.
Prohibited disposal, §143-214.2A, (c).
Water supply and waterworks.
Contamination of public water system, §14-159.1.

FELONIES —Cont'd
Weapons.
Mass death and destruction.
Manufacture, assembly, possession, etc., §14-288.8.
Nuclear, biological or chemical weapons.
False report or hoax, §§14-288.23, (a), 14-288.24.
Manufacture, assembly, possession, etc., §14-288.21.
Use and delivery of weapons, §14-288.22.
Sale of handguns to minors, §14-315, (a1).
Wholesale prescription drug distributors, §106-145.6, (b).
Workers' compensation.
Insurance or proof of financial ability to pay benefits.
Refusal or neglect to secure compensation, §97-94, (c).
Willfully fails to bring employer into compliance, §97-94, (d).
Work first program fraud, §108A-39, (b).
Worthless checks, §14-107, (d).

FELONIOUS ASSAULT WITH DEADLY WEAPON, §14-32.

FELONIOUS RESTRAINT, §14-43.3.

FELONIOUS VEHICULAR HOMICIDE, §20-141.4, (a1).
Mandatory revocation of driver's license, §§20-17, (a), 20-19, (i).

FELONS.
Alcoholic beverage permittee.
Certain employees prohibited, §18B-1003, (c).
Compensation to persons erroneously convicted of felonies.
Amount of compensation, §148-84.
Hearings, §148-83.
Provision for compensation, §148-82.
Firearms possession, §14-415.1.
Persons charged with felony acquitted by reason of insanity, §14-415.3, (a), (b).
Persons charged with felony found incompetent to stand trial, §14-415.3, (a), (b).
Physicians and surgeons.
Automatic revocation of license for felony conviction, §90-14, (c).

FELONY MURDER, §14-17.

FENCES.
Cemeteries.
Criminal trespass.
Destruction or removal of fence enclosing cemeteries, §14-148.
Drainage.
Right to owner, §156-6.
Housing authorities and projects.
Electrified fences, spikes or barbed wire prohibited, §157-9, (d).
Invisible fences.
Unlawful removal of electronic dog collars, §14-401.17.
Mount Mitchell park.
Powers of department of environment and natural resources, §100-12.
Trespass.
Criminal trespass.
Injuring fences, §§14-144, 14-159.

FENCING OF STOLEN PROPERTY.
Art objects, §14-398.

FENCING OF STOLEN PROPERTY —Cont'd
Possessing stolen property, §14-71.1.
Degree of punishment depending on value of property, §14-72.
Felony without regard to value of property, §14-72, (c).
Receiving stolen property, §14-71.
Degree of punishment depending on value of property, §14-72.
Felony without regard to value of property, §14-72, (c).
Jurisdiction in superior courts, §14-73.

FERRIES.
Arson.
Burning of ferries, §14-63.
Costs.
Application for establishment, alteration or discontinuance.
Allowance of costs to either party or apportioned in discretion of court, §6-21.
County commissioners.
Authority of county commissioners with regard to ferries, §136-88.
Department of transportation.
Letting contracts to bidders after advertisement, §136-28.1, (a) to (k).
Construction, maintenance and repair of ferry deemed highway construction, §136-28.1, (c).
Ferry repair facilities.
Contracts with electricity generators, §136-28.1, (i).
Establishment.
Department of transportation to establish, §136-82.
General assembly.
Local, private and special legislation prohibited, Const. N. C., art. II, §24.
Guard chains or gates.
Safety measures, §136-89.
Liability.
Owners of ferries not under supervision of department of transportation.
Rights and liabilities of owners, §136-88.
Maintenance.
Department of transportation to maintain, §136-82.
Owners of ferries not under supervision of department of transportation.
Rights and liabilities of owners, §136-88.
Purchase in transportation improvement program.
Board of transportation approval, considerations, §143B-350, (f2).
Safety, §136-89.
Transportation department.
Establishment and maintenance of ferries, §136-82.

FERRIS WHEELS.
Amusement device safety generally, §§95-111.1 to 95-111.18.
See AMUSEMENT DEVICE SAFETY.

FERTILIZERS, §§106-655 to 106-677.
Administration of article, §106-658.
Analysis of commercial fertilizers.
Duty of commissioner to make analysis, §106-662, (a).
Methods of analysis, §106-662, (c).
Result of official analysis, §106-662, (d).

FERTILIZERS —Cont'd
Analysis of commercial fertilizers —Cont'd
Rules and regulations, §106-662, (e).
Anhydrous ammonia.
Installation, §106-660, (g).
Appeals.
Assessments of penalties for other final orders or rulings, §106-670.
Board of agriculture.
Authority to make rules and regulations, §106-673.
Brand names.
Defined, §106-657.
False or misleading statements, §106-663.
Commercial values, §106-664.
Commissioner of agriculture, §106-658.
Analyzing, inspection, sampling and testing commercial fertilizers, §106-662, (a).
Condemnation of commercial fertilizer, §106-667.
Declaration of policy, §106-672.
Definitions, §106-657.
Distributors.
Defined, §106-657.
Registration requirements, §106-660, (b).
Enforcing official, §106-658.
False or misleading statements, §106-663.
Fees.
Inspection fees, §106-671, (a).
Reporting system, §106-671, (b).
Registration of brands, §106-660, (a).
Fluid fertilizers.
Defined, §106-657.
Method of transfer of custody, §106-660, (e).
Grade-tonnage reports, §106-677.
Imports.
Sales or exchanges between imports, §106-676.
Information concerning fertilizers.
Publication of information, §106-675.
Inspections.
Duty of commissioner to inspect, §106-662, (a).
Fees, §106-671, (a).
Reporting system, §106-671, (b).
Labeling.
Accompanying delivery, §106-661, (b).
Data required, §106-661, (a).
Identical guarantees for each product, §106-661, (d).
Mixed fertilizer sold in bags weighing more than 100 pounds, §106-661, (c).
Supplied to purchaser, §106-661, (b).
Legislative findings and declarations, §106-672.
Licenses.
Fertilizer manufacturers and distributors to be licensed, §106-660, (d).
Revocation or suspension of license, §§106-663, 106-669, 106-677.
Manufacturers.
Defined, §106-657.
Licensing of fertilizer manufacturers and distributors, §106-660, (d).
Revocation or suspension of licenses, §§106-663, 106-669, 106-677.
Sales or exchanges between manufacturers, §106-676.
Minimum plant food requirement, §106-659.
Misleading statements, §106-663.
Misrepresentations, §106-663.
Mixed fertilizers.
Defined, §106-657.

FERTILIZERS —Cont'd
Mixed fertilizers —Cont'd
Sale in bags weighing more than 100 pounds.
Labeling requirements, §106-661, (c).
Penalties.
Appeals from assessment of penalty, §106-670.
Deficiency in plant food, §106-665, (b), (c).
Determination and publication of commercial values, §106-664.
"Stop sale, use or removal" orders, §106-666, (a), (b).
Violations of article, §106-668.
Plant food.
Deficiency in plant food, §106-665, (a).
Assessment of penalties, §106-665, (b), (c).
Minimum plant food requirement, §106-659.
Policy declaration, §106-672.
Publications.
Commercial values, §106-664.
Information concerning fertilizers, §106-675.
Purpose of article, §106-656.
Registration of brands.
Application, §106-660, (a).
Cancellation of registration, §106-669.
Distributor not required to register, §106-660, (b).
Fee, §106-660, (a).
Guaranteed analysis changed, §106-660, (c).
Material changes, §106-660, (c).
Refusal of registration, §106-669.
Sources of materials changed, §106-660, (c).
Reporting system.
Inspection fees, §106-671, (b).
Reports.
Grade-tonnage reports, §106-677.
Rules and regulations.
Authority of board of agriculture to make, §106-673.
Sampling analysis, §106-662, (e).
Sales and use tax.
Exemption, §105-164.13.
Sampling.
Duty of commissioner to sample, §106-662, (a).
Methods of sampling, §106-662, (b).
Rules and regulations, §106-662, (e).
Seizure of commercial fertilizer, §106-667.
Short title, §106-655.
Short weight, §106-674.
Soil additives act, §§106-50.28 to 106-50.41.
See SOIL ADDITIVES ACT.
Statement of purpose, §106-656.
"Stop sale, use or removal" order.
Appeals from final order or ruling, §106-670.
Issuance and enforcement, §106-666, (a), (b).
Testing.
Duty of commissioner to test, §106-662, (a).
Title of article, §106-655.
Trademarks.
Misleading or deceptive trademark, §106-663.
Violations of article.
Determination and publication of commercial values, §106-664.
Plant food deficiencies, §106-665, (b), (c).
Punishment for violations, §106-668.
Seizure of commercial fertilizer, §106-667.
"Stop sale, use or removal" orders, §106-666, (a), (b).
Weights and measures.
Short weight, §106-674.

FETAL DEATH REGISTRATION.
Information.
Required medical information, §130A-114, (b).

FETAL DEATH REGISTRATION —Cont'd
Report of death, §130A-114, (a).
Preparation and filing of report, §130A-114, (c).
Required medical information, §130A-114, (b).

FETUS.
Abortion generally.
See ABORTION.
Remains of terminated pregnancies.
Manner of disposition.
Disposal by burial or cremation, §130A-131.10, (b).
Liability or additional duty not imposed on medical waste treatment facility, §130A-131.10, (d).
Relief from obligation to dispose by burial or cremation.
Sending remains to medical or research laboratory or facility, §130A-131.10, (c).
Rules to ensure disposition by burial or cremation, §130A-131.10, (a).
Using drugs or instruments to destroy unborn child, §14-44.

FFA.
Special registration plates, §20-79.4, (b).

FICTITIOUS NAMES.
Boxing under fictitious or assumed name, §143-654, (b).
Business names, §§66-68 to 66-81.
See ASSUMED NAMES.
Drivers' licenses.
Presenting license with fake name in commission of felony, §20-30.
Identification cards.
Presenting identification card with fake name in commission of felony, §20-37.8, (b).
Professional employer organizations.
Conducting business under, §58-89A-80, (a).

FIDELITY AND SURETY INSURANCE, §58-7-15.
Foreign or alien insurance companies.
Deposits required, §58-5-10.
Mandatory or voluntary risk sharing plans, §§58-42-1 to 58-42-50.
See MANDATORY OR VOLUNTARY RISK SHARING PLANS.
Mutual insurance companies.
Organization of companies, §58-7-75.

FIDUCIARIES.
Accountants.
Employment and compensation.
Powers which may be incorporated by reference in trust instrument, §32-27.
Accounts and accounting.
Personal accounts.
Deposit in fiduciary's personal account, §32-10.
Actions.
Claims against estate or trust.
Powers which may be incorporated by reference in trust instrument, §32-27.
Administrators.
See EXECUTORS AND ADMINISTRATORS.
Adult care homes.
Bill of rights.
Transfer of management responsibilities, §131D-22.
Agents generally.
See AGENTS.
Appeals.
Stay of further proceedings in court.
Security limited for fiduciaries, §1-294.
Application of payments, §32-3.

FIDUCIARIES —Cont'd
Attorneys at law.
Counsel fees allowed attorney serving as fiduciary, §32-61.
Employment and compensation.
Powers which may be incorporated by reference in trust instrument, §32-27.
Banks.
Acting in fiduciary capacity, §53-159.
Bank holding companies.
Retaining stock.
Fiduciary authorized to retain, §36A-3, (b).
Clearing corporations.
Deposit of securities in, §53-159.1.
Deposit in name of fiduciary.
Bank authorized to pay amount of deposit, §32-8.
License to do business.
Generally, §53-160.
Notification of clerk of superior court, §53-163.
Revocation, §53-163.
Merger or consolidation.
Fiduciary powers and liabilities of banks or trust companies merging or transferring assets and liabilities, §53-17.
Securities.
Deposit in clearing corporation, §53-159.1.
Solvency.
Certificate of solvency, §53-162.
Stock and stockholders.
Fiduciaries not personally liable, §53-40.
Trusts and trustees.
See BANKS.
Bonds, surety.
Appeal perfected staying further proceedings in court below.
Security limited for fiduciaries, §1-294.
Removal of fiduciary funds.
Local fiduciaries appointed to receive property administered in another state, §36A-15.
Surety companies.
Expense of fiduciary bond charged to fund, §58-73-35.
Capacity to sue in representative capacity.
Affirmative averment in pleading, §1A-1, Rule 9, (a).
Cases not provided for in article, §32-12.
Checks.
Checks drawn payable to third persons, §32-6.
Payable to fiduciary, §32-7.
Compensation of trustees and other fiduciaries, §§32-53 to 32-62.
Attorneys serving as fiduciaries.
Counsel fees allowed, §32-61.
Compensation in amount provided by law.
Instrument providing, §32-60.
Definitions, §32-53.
Effective date of provision, §32-62.
Maximum amount provided by law.
Instrument providing, §32-60.
Other fiduciaries, §32-59.
Reasonable compensation.
Entitlement, §32-59.
Service without compensation.
Instrument providing, §32-60.
Trustees.
Excessive compensation received.
Refund on clerk's determination, §32-57, (b).
Expense reimbursement, entitlement, §32-58.
Notice of proposed payment, §32-55, (a).
Alternative notice, §32-55, (b).
Beneficiary under legal disability, §32-55, (c).

FIDUCIARIES —Cont'd
Compensation of trustees and other fiduciaries —Cont'd
Trustees —Cont'd
Notice of proposed payment —Cont'd
When deemed given, §32-55, (d).
Payment without prior approval of clerk of superior court, §32-56.
Reasonable compensation.
Entitlement, compensation not specified, §32-54, (a).
Factors considered in determining, §32-54, (b).
Refunds.
Clerk's determination excessive compensation received, §32-57, (b).
Review of reasonableness, approval or denial of payment, §32-57, (a).
Condominium owners' associations.
Executive board, §47C-3-103, (a).
Conservatorship.
Banks, §§53-148 to 53-158.
See BANKS.
Credit unions.
Conservation generally, §54-109.92.
Limited liability companies.
Incompetence of member, powers upon, §57C-5-05.
Prudent person rule.
Investment and deposit of funds, §36A-2, (a).
Securities regulation.
Appointment of conservator for defendant's assets, §78A-47, (a).
Exempt transactions, §78A-17.
Construction and interpretation.
Uniform fiduciaries act.
Uniformity of interpretation, §32-13.
Contribution.
Joint tort-feasors.
Provisions not to apply to breaches of trust or of other fiduciary obligations, §1B-1, (g).
Corporations.
Foreign corporations.
Restrictions on fiduciary powers.
Business corporations, §55-15-05, (a).
Oaths, §11-5.
Participation in reorganizations.
Powers which may be incorporated by reference in trust instrument, §32-27.
Courts.
Investment of trust funds.
Power to deviate from terms of instrument, §36A-4.
Credit unions.
Power of credit unions generally, §54-109.21.
Custodial trusts and trustees, §§33B-1 to 33B-22.
See CUSTODIAL TRUSTS.
Debts.
Transfer of negotiable instruments.
Security for personal debt.
Liability of creditor or transferee, §32-5.
Decedents' estates.
Collection of rent, income, etc., §32-27.
Federal estate tax apportionment.
Distribution of property before final apportionment, §28A-27-7.
Incorporation by reference of certain powers.
Restriction on exercise of such powers, §32-26, (b), (c).
Declaratory judgments.
Who may apply for declaration, §1-255.

FIDUCIARIES —Cont'd
Definitions.
Investment and deposit of trust funds, §36A-1.
Powers of fiduciaries, §32-25.
Uniform fiduciary act, §32-2.
Deposits.
Banking deposits in name of fiduciary, §32-8.
Personal account of fiduciary, §32-10.
Principal.
Deposit in name of principal, §32-9.
Trustees.
Deposits in name of two or more trustees, §32-11.
Discharge of resident fiduciary.
Removal of fiduciary funds, §36A-14.
Durable power of attorney.
Attorney-in-fact accountable to court appointed fiduciary, §32A-10, (a).
Nomination of fiduciary by durable power of attorney for consideration by court, §32A-10, (b).
Embezzlement.
Property.
Receipt of property by virtue of office or employment, §14-90.
Executors and administrators.
See EXECUTORS AND ADMINISTRATORS.
Funds.
Removal.
Applicability of article, §36A-16.
Appointment of local fiduciary, §36A-15.
Authorized, §36A-13.
Bonds, surety.
When required, §36A-15.
Discharge of resident fiduciary, §36A-14.
Petition, §36A-13.
To this state, §36A-15.
Guardians.
General provisions.
See GUARDIANS.
Payments to or for minors or incompetents.
Powers which may be incorporated by reference in trust instrument, §32-27.
Health maintenance organizations.
Responsibilities of directors, officers and partners, §58-67-45.
Hearings.
Removal of fiduciary funds to nonresident fiduciary, §36A-13.
Housing authorities and projects.
Bond issues.
Legal investments, §157-25.
Income tax.
Individual income tax.
Filing returns, §105-152, (b).
Indorsements.
Negotiable instruments.
Transfer, §32-5.
In good faith.
Thing done in, §32-2, (b).
Institutional funds.
Management of institutional funds, §§36B-1 to 36B-10.
See MANAGEMENT OF INSTITUTIONAL FUNDS.
Investments.
Housing authorities and projects.
Bond issues of authority, §157-25.
Powers which may be incorporated by reference in trust instrument, §32-27.

FIDUCIARIES —Cont'd
Investments —Cont'd
Securities approved by secretary of housing and urban development, federal housing administration and veterans administration, §53-45.
Trust funds.
Applicability of provisions, §§36A-5, 36A-7.
Authority to acquire and retain certain kinds of property, §36A-2, (b).
Definition, §36A-1.
Departure from express terms of instrument, §36A-3, (a).
Power of court not restricted, §36A-4.
Employee trusts.
Validity, §36A-6.
Excluded fiduciary or co-fiduciary not liable, §36A-3, (d).
Power of court not restricted, §36A-4.
Prudent person rule, §36A-2, (a).
Retaining stock of bank holding companies, §36A-3, (b).
Rule against perpetuities.
Instruments not invalid as violating rule, §36A-6.
Standard of judgment and care.
Observation by fiduciary, §36A-2, (a).
Terms of creating instrument, §36A-3, (a).
United States government obligations.
Scope of authority of fiduciary to invest in obligations, §36A-3, (c).
Judgments and decrees.
Defense after judgment set aside.
No liability for prior distribution of fund, §1-108.
Judicial sales.
Bond of person holding sale, §1-339.10, (b), (c).
Law merchant.
Applicability, §32-12.
Letters testamentary and of administration.
Grounds for revocation.
Violation of fiduciary duty, §28A-9-1.
Limitation of actions.
Bonds, surety, §1-50, (a).
Action against surety, §1-52.
Loans.
Insured or guaranteed loans.
Securities approved by secretary of housing and urban development, federal housing administration and veterans administration, §53-45.
Management of institutional funds, §§36B-1 to 36B-10.
See MANAGEMENT OF INSTITUTIONAL FUNDS.
Marital deduction.
Incorporation by reference of certain powers, §32-26.
Mentally ill.
Payments to or for incompetents, §32-27.
Negotiable instruments.
Breach of fiduciary duty, §25-3-307.
Defined, §25-3-307.
Transfer, §32-5.
Notice.
Removal of fiduciary funds to nonresident fiduciary, §36A-13.
Nursing homes.
Patients' bill of rights.
Transfer of management responsibilities, §131E-118.

FIDUCIARIES —Cont'd
Orders.
Investment of trust funds.
Applicability of provisions, §36A-5.
Partnerships.
Partner accountable as fiduciary, §59-51, (a).
Applicability to representatives of deceased partner, §59-51, (b).
Personal property.
Retaining original property.
Powers which may be incorporated by reference in trust instrument, §32-27.
Petitions.
Removal of fiduciary funds to nonresident fiduciary, §36A-13.
Powers.
Definition, §32-25.
Exercise of powers for fiduciary's benefit.
Definitions, §32-34, (a).
Restrictions on power, §32-34, (b).
Applicability of provisions, §32-34, (d).
Incorporation by reference of certain powers, §32-26, (a).
Restriction on exercise of certain powers, §32-26, (b), (c).
Trust powers, §32-27.
Trust instruments.
Powers which may be incorporated by reference, §32-27.
Powers of appointment.
Method of release or limitation of power, §39-33.
Not exclusive, §39-34.
Notice.
Necessity for actual notice of release to bind, §39-36.
Principal and income act.
General provisions, §§37A-1-101 to 37A-6-602.
See PRINCIPAL AND INCOME ACT.
Prudent person rule.
Investment and deposit of trust funds, §36A-2, (a).
Management of institutional funds.
Standard of care, §36B-6.
Transfers to minors.
Care of custodial property, §33A-12, (b).
Removal of fiduciary funds, §§36A-13 to 36A-16.
Renunciation of fiduciary powers.
Effect of renunciation, §31B-3, (a).
Exclusiveness of remedy, §31B-5.
Instrument of renunciation.
Contents, §31B-1A, (b).
Right to renounce, §31B-1A, (a).
Waiver of bar.
Application for appointment or assumption of duties as fiduciary.
Not deemed to waive or bar right to renounce fiduciary powers, §31B-4, (c).
Renunciation of trustees.
See TRUSTS AND TRUSTEES.
Rule against perpetuities.
Investment of trust funds.
Employee trusts not invalid as violating rule, §36A-6.
Rules of law and equity.
Applicability, §32-12.
Savings and loan associations.
Officers and directors to act in fiduciary capacity toward association, §54B-103.
Power of state associations to act in fiduciary capacity, §54B-77.
Savings banks.
Directors and officers to act in fiduciary capacity, §54C-103.

FIDUCIARIES —Cont'd
Savings bonds, United States.
Investment of trust funds, §36A-3, (c).
Stays.
Security limited, §1-294.
Stock and stockholders.
Investments and reinvestments.
Powers which may be incorporated by reference in trust instrument, §32-27.
Retaining stock of bank holding companies, §36A-3, (b).
Superior courts.
Clerks of court.
Authority of clerk to audit accounts of fiduciaries, §7A-103.
Taxation.
Failure to file fiduciary informational return, §105-236.
Incorporation by reference of certain powers.
Depriving trust or estate of tax exemptions, deductions or credits, §32-26.
Property taxes.
Payment of taxes by fiduciaries, §105-383.
Reserves.
Establishing and maintaining.
Powers which may be incorporated by reference in trust instrument, §32-27.
Security transfers
Settlement of fiduciary's account.
Prerequisites, §105-240.
Third persons.
Check drawn payable to third person, §32-6.
Title.
Right or title acquired from fiduciary.
Validity, §32-3.
Transfers of money or property.
Responsibility for proper application by fiduciary, §32-3.
Transfers to minors, §§33A-1 to 33A-24.
See TRANSFERS TO MINORS.
Treasury bonds, United States.
Investment of trust funds, §36A-3, (c).
Trust companies.
Fiduciary records, §53-357.
Powers of state trust company, §53-331, (b).
Trusts and trustees.
See TRUSTS AND TRUSTEES.
Uniform fiduciaries act.
Short title, §32-1.
Uniformity of interpretation, §32-13.
Uniform management of institutional funds act, §§36B-1 to 36B-10.
See MANAGEMENT OF INSTITUTIONAL FUNDS.
United States.
Investments.
Trust funds.
Scope of authority of fiduciary to invest in United States government obligations, §36A-3, (c).
Wills.
Incorporation by reference of certain powers, §32-26, (a).
Investment of trust funds.
Applicability of provisions, §36A-5.

FIELDS.
Setting fire to fields, §14-137.

FIELD TRIALS.
Beagles.
Hunting license exemption, §113-276, (k).
Hunting on Sunday exceptions, §103-2.

FIERI FACIAS.
Executions generally.
See EXECUTIONS.

FIFTH WHEEL TRAILER.
Recreational vehicle, §20-4.01.

FIGHTING.
Alcoholic beverage permittees.
Unlawful conduct on premises, §18B-1005, (a).
Animal fighting, §14-362.1.
Cockfighting, §14-362.
Dog fighting, §14-362.2.
Assault and battery, §14-33.
Evidence of threats upon plea of self-defense, §14-33.1.
Cock fighting, §14-362.
Disorderly conduct, §14-288.4.
Dog fighting, §14-362.2.

FILING OF CORPORATE DOCUMENTS.
Generally.
See CORPORATIONS.
Nonprofit corporations, §§55A-1-20 to 55A-1-22.
See NONPROFIT CORPORATIONS.

FILING OF PLEADINGS AND OTHER PAPERS, §1A-1, Rule 5.
Filing with court defined, §1A-1, Rule 5, (e).

FILLING STATIONS.
Self-service stations.
Advertising price, §14-117.2.
Unauthorized vehicles, §20-219.3.

FILM.
Children and minors.
Artistic and creative services and talent agency contracts, §§48A-11 to 48A-18.
Film industry development account, §143B-434.4.
Production companies.
Use of public property by, §143-162.2.
Public property.
Film production companies.
Use of public property by, §143-162.2.
Record and tape piracy generally.
See RECORD AND TAPE PIRACY.

FILM INDUSTRY DEVELOPMENT ACCOUNT.
Administration of program, requirements, §143B-434.4, (b).
Created in department of commerce, §143B-434.4, (b).
Legislative findings and purposes, §143B-434.4, (a).
Obscene material in production.
Limitation on eligiblity, §143B-434.4, (d).
Production company defined, §143B-434.4, (c).
Report by department, §143B-434.4, (e).

FINANCE.
Agricultural finance authority, §§122D-1 to 122D-23.
See AGRICULTURAL FINANCE AUTHORITY.
Bond issues.
See BOND ISSUES.
Budgets.
See BUDGETS.
Cash management.
Community colleges, §147-86.13.
Failure of employees to follow policy.
Dismissal, §147-86.11, (i).
General court of justice, §147-86.14.
Highway fund, §147-86.15.

FINANCE —Cont'd
Cash management —Cont'd
Highway trust fund, §147-86.15.
Investments.
Net earnings on invested funds.
Payment to beneficial owners of funds, §147-86.11, (d).
Legislative declaration.
Policy of state, §147-86.10.
Plan.
Disbursements, §147-86.11, (f).
Earnings on trust funds, §147-86.11, (d).
Elements, §147-86.11, (e).
Interest, §147-86.11, (g).
New technologies and procedures, §147-86.11, (h).
Uniform statewide plan, §147-86.11, (a).
Policy of state, §147-86.10.
Reports.
State treasurer.
Quarterly report, §147-86.11, (c).
School administration units, §147-86.12.
State auditor.
Monitoring agency compliance with provisions, §147-86.11, (b).
State treasurer.
Reports.
Quarterly report, §147-86.11, (c).
Community colleges and technical institutes.
Cash management for community colleges, §147-86.13.
Constitution of North Carolina, Const. N. C., art. V, §§1 to 10.
Funds.
See FUNDS.
Industrial and pollution control facilities financing.
Industrial and pollution control facilities financing act, §§159C-1 to 159C-27.
See INDUSTRIAL AND POLLUTION CONTROL FACILITIES FINANCING.
North Carolina capital facilities financing act.
North Carolina industrial and pollution control facilities financing act, §§159D-1 to 159D-27.
See INDUSTRIAL AND POLLUTION CONTROL FACILITIES FINANCING.
Local government finance, §§159-1 to 159-188.
See LOCAL GOVERNMENT FINANCE.
Parking authorities, §160A-559.
Pest control.
Compact.
Financial assets of insurance fund, §106-65.55.
Private capital facilities finance act.
Institutions for higher education and elementary and secondary education, §§159D-35 to 159D-57.
See CAPITAL FACILITIES FINANCE AGENCY.
Public transportation authorities, §160A-583.
Fiscal accountability, §160A-582.
Registered public obligations, §§159E-1 to 159E-15.
See REGISTERED PUBLIC OBLIGATIONS.
Schools.
Cash management for school administration units, §147-86.12.
Social services, §§108A-86 to 108A-93.
See SOCIAL SERVICES.
Taxation.
See TAXATION.

FINANCE —Cont'd
Veterans' recreation authorities.
Exemption from local government and county fiscal control acts, §165-35.

FINANCE CHARGES.
Attorneys' fees and notes, etc., in addition to legal rate of finance charges, §6-21.2.
Contract rates and fees, §24-1.1.
Disclosure requirements for credit cards, §24-11.1, (b).
Equity lines of credit.
Fees for modification, extension, renewal, etc., §24-1.2A, (b).
Home loans secured by first mortgage or first deed of trust, §24-1.1A, (c).
Insurance premium financing.
Excessive charges, §58-35-35.
Interest generally.
See INTEREST.
Late fees, §24-10.1.
Loans secured by real property, maximum fees, §24-10.
Manufactured home loans.
Unearned finance charge credits.
Prepayment of mobile home loans, §25A-32.1.
Motor vehicle retail installment sales.
Consumer credit installment sale contracts.
Finance charge rates for used cars, §25A-15, (c).
Seller to deliver written statement to buyer, §20-303, (b).
Written instruments, §20-303, (a).
Retail installment sales.
Consolidation and refinancing, §25A-31, (c).
Consumer credit installment sale contracts.
Division of simple transaction into two or more sales to avoid limitations prohibited, §25A-15, (e).
Rates, §25A-15, (a).
Determination, §25A-15, (b).
Residential manufactured homes.
Sale secured by first lien, §25A-15, (f).
Security interest.
Rates chargeable, §25A-15, (d).
Used cars.
Rate chargeable, §25A-15, (c).
Defined, §25A-8, (a).
Exclusions from definition, §25A-8, (b).
Refinancing, §25A-31, (c).
Remedies and penalties, §25A-44.
Revolving charge account contracts.
Default or deferral charges, §25A-14, (c).
Insurance.
Additional charges for insurance, §25A-17, (b).
Rates, §25A-14, (a).
Security interest.
Rates, §25A-14, (b).
Security interest.
Transactions in which seller acquires security interest, §25A-8, (c).
Unearned finance charge credits.
Prepayment of real property and mobile home loans, §25A-32.1.
Revolving credit charges, §24-11.

FINANCE COMPANIES.
Annual tax on privilege of doing business, §105-88, (a).
Applicability of provisions, §105-88, (b).
City or county levying license tax, §105-88, (e).
Loan not collectable unless tax paid, §105-88, (d).
Statement to borrower, §105-88, (c).

FINANCE COMPANIES —Cont'd
Consumer finance act, §§53-164 to 53-191.
See CONSUMER FINANCE ACT.
Housing finance agency, §§122A-1 to 122A-23.
See HOUSING FINANCE AGENCY.

FINANCE LEASES.
Defined, §25-2A-103.
Delay or nondelivery.
Notice, §25-2A-405, (c).
Effect of acceptance, §25-2A-516, (2).
Fitness for particular purpose.
Implied warranties, §25-2A-213.
Infringement.
Warranty against, §25-2A-211.
Irrevocable promises, §25-2A-407.
Leases, UCC generally, §§25-2A-101 to 25-2A-532.
See LEASES, UCC.
Losses.
Casualty to identified goods, §25-2A-221.
Risk of loss, §25-2A-219.
Merchantability.
Implied warranties, §25-2A-212.
Notice.
Delay or nondelivery, §25-2A-405, (c).
Supply contracts.
Lessee under finance lease as beneficiary, §25-2A-209.

FINANCIAL IDENTITY FRAUD, §§14-113.20 to 14-113.25.
Additional crimes.
Court records to reflect, §14-113.22, (c).
Attorney General.
Investigation of complaints, §14-113.23.
Cash registers and other receipt printing machines.
Sale of, §14-113.25.
Credit, charge, or debit card numbers on receipts, §14-113.24.
Damages.
Civil liability, §14-113.22, (b).
Definition of "identifying information," §14-113.20, (b).
Exceptions, §14-113.20, (c).
Felonies, §§14-113.20, (a), 14-113.22, (a), (a1).
Trafficking in stolen identities, §14-113.20A, (b).
Investigations.
Attorney General, §14-113.23.
Obtaining credit information lawfully.
Not violation, §14-113.20, (c).
Security interest or offset, good faith exercise.
Not violation, §14-113.20, (c).
Trafficking in stolen identities, §14-113.20A, (a).
Felony, §14-113.20A, (b).
Venue.
Criminal proceedings, §14-113.21.
Warrant or court order, good faith compliance with.
Not violation, §14-113.20, (c).

FINANCIAL INSTITUTIONS.
Bank examiners generally, §§53-117 to 53-123.
See BANK EXAMINERS.
Bank holding companies generally, §§53-225 to 53-232.
See BANK HOLDING COMPANIES.
Banks.
See BANKS.
Child support enforcement.
Data match systems.
Agreements with financial institutions, §110-139.2.

FINANCIAL INSTITUTIONS —Cont'd
Commissioner of banks.
Generally, §§53-92 to 53-116.
See BANKS COMMISSIONER.
Commodities.
General provisions, §§78D-1 to 78D-33.
See COMMODITIES.
Credit unions.
See CREDIT UNIONS.
Financial records privacy, §§53B-1 to 53B-10.
See FINANCIAL RECORDS PRIVACY.
Gramm-Leach-Bililey act.
Affiliations between depository institutions and insurers, §58-19-2.
Industrial banks generally, §§53-136 to 53-145.
See INDUSTRIAL BANKS.
International banking, §§53-232.1 to 53-232.17.
See INTERNATIONAL BANKING.
Lead-based paint presence on property or other health-related issues.
Providing financial assistance, §130A-131.9F.
Reciprocal interstate banking, §§53-209 to 53-218.
See RECIPROCAL INTERSTATE BANKING.
Savings and loan associations.
See SAVINGS AND LOAN ASSOCIATIONS.
Savings banks, §§54C-1 to 54C-141.
See SAVINGS BANKS.
Trust companies and interstate trust business, §§53-301 to 53-415.
See TRUST COMPANIES.
Unclaimed property generally, §§116B-51 to 116B-80.
See UNCLAIMED PROPERTY.

FINANCIAL PRIVACY ACT, §§53B-1 to 53B-10.
See FINANCIAL RECORDS PRIVACY.

FINANCIAL RECORDS PRIVACY, §§53B-1 to 53B-10.
Access to financial records.
Authorization of customer, §53B-4.
Customer challenge, §53B-7, (a).
Delayed notice, §53B-6.
Disclosure of financial records, §53B-8.
Duty of financial institution to locate and make available, §53B-9, (a).
Fees, §53B-9, (b).
Generally, §53B-4.
Government authority requesting.
Financial institution's right to challenge, §53B-7, (b).
Limitation of liability, §53B-9, (c).
Notice, §53B-5.
Delayed notice, §53B-6.
Penalty, §53B-10.
Service on customer certification, §53B-5.
Child support enforcement.
Location of absent parents.
Information to be provided, §110-139, (d).
Citation of chapter, §53B-1.
Customer challenge.
Access to financial records, §53B-7, (a).
Damages.
Disclosures in violation of article, §53B-10, (a).
Definitions, §53B-2.
Disclosure of financial records, §53B-8.
Penalty, §53B-10.
Duty of financial institution, §53B-9.
Government participating or inducing violation.
Liability to customer, §53B-10, (b).

FINANCIAL RECORDS PRIVACY —Cont'd
Government requesting access to records.
Financial institution's right to challenge, §53B-7, (b).
Immunity.
Disclosure of financial records by financial institution, §53B-9, (c).
Public policy, §53B-3.
Real estate commission.
Exemption, §93A-6.1, (b).
Service on customer certification, §53B-5.
Short title, §53B-1.
State policy, §53B-3.
Violations of article.
Penalties, §53B-10.

FINANCIAL RESPONSIBILITY.
Alcoholic beverage permittees, §18B-1003, (b).
Motor vehicles.
Act of 1957 generally, §§20-309 to 20-319.
See MOTOR VEHICLE FINANCIAL RESPONSIBILITY.
Drivers' licenses.
Proof required for issuance, forms of proof, §20-7, (c1).
Generally, §§20-279.1 to 20-284.
See MOTOR VEHICLE FINANCIAL RESPONSIBILITY.
Structural pest control.
Conditions, limitations and requirements, §106-65.37, (b).
Indemnifying persons, §106-65.37, (a).

FINANCIAL TRANSACTION CARDS, §§14-113.8 to 14-113.17.
Credit cards.
Fraud by credit devices.
See CREDIT DEVICE FRAUD.
General provisions.
See CREDIT CARDS.
Definitions, §14-113.8.
Evidence.
Forgery of transaction card.
Prima facie evidence of forgery, §14-113.12, (a), (b).
Theft of financial transaction card.
Prima evidence of theft, §14-113.10.
Felonies, §14-113.17, (b).
Forgery.
Elements of offense, §14-113.11, (a).
Embossing financial transaction card falsely, §14-113.11, (c).
Encoding financial transaction card falsely, §14-113.11, (d).
Making financial transaction card falsely, §14-113.11, (b).
Prima facie evidence of forgery, §14-113.12, (a), (b).
Two or more cards, possession.
Prima facies evidence, §14-113.12, (a), (b).
Forgery devices.
Criminal possession, §14-113.14, (a).
Incomplete cards, §14-113.14, (b).
Punishment, §14-113.14, (b).
Fraud.
Application for financial transaction card.
False statements or reports on application, §14-113.13, (c).
Credit devices.
See CREDIT DEVICE FRAUD.
Criminal factoring of records, §14-113.15A.
Elements of offense, §14-113.13, (a).

FINANCIAL TRANSACTION CARDS —Cont'd
Fraud —Cont'd
Furnisher of money, goods, services, etc.
Elements of financial transaction card fraud offense, §14-113.13, (b).
Goods and services.
Criminal receipt of goods and services fraudulently obtained, §14-113.15.
Presumption of criminal receipt, §14-113.16.
Notice of theft, loss, etc., of card.
False notice, §14-113.13, (d).
Prosecution for violation.
Occurrence of acts constituting crime, §14-113.13, (e).
Record of sale.
Fraudulent record, §14-113.13, (c1).
Report of theft, loss, etc., of card.
False report, §14-113.13, (d).
Revocation of financial transaction card.
Construing revocation, §14-113.13, (f).
Goods.
Fraudulently obtained goods.
Criminal receipt of goods, §14-113.15.
Presumption of criminal receipt, §14-113.16.
Larceny.
Theft of financial transaction card.
Conduct defined is larceny, §14-113.9, (b).
Misdemeanors, §14-113.17, (a).
Notice.
Fraud.
Theft, loss, disappearance, etc., of card falsely noted, §14-113.13, (d).
Penalties.
Crime act of punishment and penalties, §14-113.17.
Presumptions.
Goods and services fraudulently obtained.
When criminal receipt presumed, §14-113.16.
Records.
Criminal factoring of records, §14-113.15A.
Reports.
Fraud.
Theft, loss, disappearance of card falsely reported, §14-113.13, (d).
Theft.
Elements of offense, §14-113.9, (a).
Larcenous conduct, §14-113.9, (b).
Prima facie evidence of theft, §14-113.10.

FINANCING AGREEMENTS.
General provisions, §§159-148 to 159-152.
See LOCAL GOVERNMENT FINANCE.

FINANCING CONTRACT INDEBTEDNESS.
State capital facilities finance act.
Special indebtedness generally, §§142-80 to 142-101.
See CAPITAL FACILITIES FINANCE ACT.

FINANCING HEALTH CARE FACILITIES, §§131A-1 to 131A-25.
See HEALTH CARE FACILITY FINANCING.

FINDINGS BY COURT, §1A-1, Rule 52, (a).
Amendment, §1A-1, Rule 52, (b).
Review on appeal, §1A-1, Rule 52, (c).

FINE PRINT SALES.
Applicability of article, §25C-16.
Art dealers.
Disclosures, §25C-11, (b).
Catalogs, §25C-11, (a).
Consignments, §25C-12, (b).

FINE PRINT SALES —Cont'd
Definitions, §25C-10.
Disclosure.
Disclaimer of art dealer, §25C-14, (d).
Limited additions, §25C-14, (c).
Mechanical, photomechanical or photographic copies, §25C-14, (b).
Requirements, §25C-14, (a).
Exemptions from article, §25C-16.
General prohibitions, §25C-11.
Rights and liabilities created by article.
Not inclusive, §25C-15, (d).
Sale by artist, §25C-12, (a).
Violation of article.
Repayment of purchaser's consideration, §25C-15, (a).
Wrongful refusal to repay, §25C-15, (b).
Willful violation, §25C-15, (c).
Warranties.
Evidence, §25C-13, (c).
Express warranties, §25C-13, (a), (b).
FINES.
Address confidentiality program.
Disclosure of address.
Prohibited acts, §15C-9, (f).
Falsifying application information.
Civil penalty, §15C-6.
Administration department.
Bribery.
Purchases and contracts to department, §143-63.
Adoption.
Unlawful payments related to adoption, §48-10-102, (b).
Adult care homes.
Bill of rights, §131D-34.
Aiding and abetting.
Alcoholic beverages.
Sale to or purchase by underage persons, §18B-302, (c).
Requirements for punishment, §18B-302.1, (b), (c).
Alcoholic beverages.
Aiding and abetting.
Sale to or purchase by underage persons, §18B-302, (c).
Requirements for punishment, §18B-302.1, (b), (c).
Direct shipment into state, §18B-102.1, (e).
Imports and exports.
Unauthorized imports and exports, §18B-102, (b).
Interference with inspections, §18B-502, (b).
Manufacturers.
Unauthorized manufacture, §18B-102, (b).
Minors.
Aiding and abetting sale to or purchase by underage persons, §18B-302, (c).
Purchase or possession by 19 or 20 year olds, §18B-302, (i).
Open container law, §20-138.7, (e).
Unlawful transportation, §18B-401, (a).
Possession.
By 19 or 20 year old, §18B-203.
Unauthorized possession, §18B-102, (b).
Purchase by 19 or 20 year old, §18B-203.
Sales.
Unauthorized sales, §18B-102, (b).
Transportation.
Open container violations, §18B-401, (a).
Unauthorized transportation, §18B-102, (b).
FINES —Cont'd
Ambulatory surgical facility licensure.
Unlicensed operation, §131E-151.
Amusement device safety.
Death resulting from violation, §95-111.13, (i).
Animal auctions.
Public auctions.
Unlicensed operation, §19A-33.
Animal cruelty investigators.
Interference with performance of official duties, §19A-48.
Animal dealers.
Acting without license, §19A-34.
Cruelty to animals, §19A-35.
Animal shelters.
Cruelty to animals, §19A-35.
Animal waste management system operators.
Willful violations, §90A-47.5, (b).
Apportionment to school administrative units, §115C-452.
Aquatic weed control, §113A-226, (a).
Arrest in civil cases, §1-410.
Arson.
Failure of officers to investigate fires, §14-69.
Failure of property owner to comply with orders of authorities, §14-68.
Atomic energy, radioactivity and ionizing radiation.
Confidentiality of information, §104E-29, (c).
Auctions and auctioneers.
Civil penalties.
Imposition by commission, §85B-3.1, (b).
Authorized fines, §15A-1361.
Banks.
Administrative orders of commissioner.
Violations, §53-107.2.
Commissioner of banks.
Failure to make report to commissioner, §53-107.
Battleship commission.
Employees with interest, §143B-74.3.
Billboards.
Streets and highways.
Obstructing view at entrance to building on public highway, §136-102.
Blacklisting employees, §14-355.
Boating navigation rules violations, §75A-6.1, (c).
Boilers, §95-69.18.
Bonds, surety.
Mortgage in lieu of bond.
Security of costs or fine in criminal action, §58-74-5.
Cancellation of mortgage in such proceedings, §58-74-10.
Bottles and bottling.
Polluting bottles used for beverages, §14-288.
Bribery.
Administration department.
Purchases and contracts to department, §143-63.
Budgets.
Diversion, use or expenditure of funds, §143-32, (b).
Noncompliance with article, §143-34.
Building codes.
Door lock exemptions.
Penalty for violation of provisions, §143-143.4, (h).
Buying or selling untaxed motor fuel, §105-449.118.

FINES —Cont'd
Cable television franchises.
Theft of services, §14-118.5.
Certified public accountants, §93-13.
Childhood vaccine-related injury compensation.
Diversion of certain vaccines, §130A-431.
Child placing agencies.
Unlicensed operation, §131D-10.7.
Chiropractors.
Unlicensed practice, §90-147.
Cleaning agents containing phosphorus.
Water and air resources.
Manufacturing, selling or distributing agents, §143-214.4, (f).
Coastal area management.
Permit violations, §113A-126, (c).
College tuition.
Waiver for senior citizens.
Misrepresentation of eligibility, §115B-6.
Commercial vehicles.
Out of service fines, §20-17.7.
Commodities.
Power of court to grant injunctive relief.
Imposition of civil penalty, §78D-23.
Violations of chapter.
When allowed, §78D-24, (b), (c).
Commodity violations, §78D-24, (b).
Community colleges.
Traffic regulations, §115D-21, (b), (c).
Constitution of North Carolina.
Enumeration of permissible punishments, Const. N. C., art. XI, §1.
Constitution of the United States.
Excessive fines, Const. U. S., amd. VIII.
Contempt.
Criminal contempt, §5A-12, (a).
Contracts.
Unauthorized use of public purchase or contract procedures for private benefit, §143-58.1, (c).
Conveyances.
Taxation.
Excise stamp tax.
Willful failure to pay, §105-228.34.
Counterfeiting.
Issuing substitutes for money without authority, §14-15.
Receiving or passing unauthorized substitutes for money, §14-16.
Counties.
Public officers and employees.
Privacy of employee personnel records, §153A-98, (f).
Crime victims financial recovery assistance act.
Escrow account.
Establishment and notice, §15B-34, (d).
Satisfaction of judgment from, §15B-34, (e).
Unclaimed funds, return of, §15B-34, (f).
Failure to give notice, §15B-34, (a).
Failure to pay, §15B-34, (c).
Notice and opportunity to be heard required, §15B-34, (b).
Remittance of proceeds from civil penalty, §15B-34, (g).
Criminal offenses.
Authorized fines, §15A-1361.
Dam safety law.
Violations of article, §143-215.36, (a).
Default.
Imprisonment.
Show cause orders, §§15A-1362, (c), 15A-1364, (a).

FINES —Cont'd
Defendant's liability in criminal actions.
Confession of judgment.
Bond given to secure fine and cost, §6-47.
Delinquent juveniles.
Alternative dispositions, imposition, §7B-2506.
Dentists.
Subpoenas of board of medical examiner.
Neglect or refusal to obey, §90-27.
Unauthorized practices, §90-40.
Violations of rules and regulations of board, §90-48.
Dietitians and nutritionists, §90-366.
Disbursement of proceeds.
School administrative units, §115C-452.
Discrimination.
Against military personnel, §127B-15.
Dog wardens.
Animal welfare act violations, §19A-36.
Cruelty to animals, §19A-35.
Drainage.
Jurisdiction of county commissioners.
Refusal to comply with requirements, §156-33.
Refusal to serve on board, §156-32.
Obstructions, §§156-19, 156-24, 156-25.
Drainage districts.
Injuring or damaging bridges, fences, ditches, etc., §156-92.
Drug paraphernalia.
Advertisement, §90-113.24, (b).
Manufacture or deliveries, §90-113.23, (c).
Possession, §90-113.22, (b).
Drugs.
Controlled substance.
Conspiracy to violate provision, §90-98.
Violations generally, §90-95.
Elections, §163-272.1.
Public campaign financing fund.
Regulator violations, §163-278.70.
Electronic commerce in government, §66-58.7.
Elementary and secondary education.
Annual independent audit.
Interference with records, §115C-447.
Blind children.
Parents, etc., failing to send, §115C-383, (c).
Deaf children.
Parents, etc., failing to enroll, §115C-383.
Employee health certificate, §115C-323, (e).
Employees making false reports or records, §115C-317.
Fire prevention duties.
Failure to perform, §115C-525, (c).
Insurance of public school property.
Noncompliance with provisions, §115C-534, (c).
Local boards of education.
Witness failing to appear, §115C-45, (b).
Principals or supervisors making false reports or records, §115C-288, (b).
State board of education.
Disclosure of confidential records, §115C-13.
Student attendance, §115C-380.
Superintendents making false reports or records, §115C-276, (p).
Teachers making false reports or records, §115C-307, (g).
Elevators, §95-110.11.
Employee assistance professionals.
Failure to be licensed.
Civil penalty, §90-506, (a), (c).
Employment security.
Witness intimidation, §96-15.2.

FINES —Cont'd
Endangered plant species.
Unlawful acts, §106-202.19, (a), (a1).
Executions.
Docketed judgments for fines, §15A-1365.
Payment as authorized condition of parole, §15A-1374, (b).
Fish and fisheries resources.
Buoys, nets, markers, stakes, etc.
Robbing or injuring, §113-268, (d).
Coastal and estuarine commercial fishing licenses.
Fraud or deception as to licenses, permits or records, §113-170.2, (b).
Coastal wetlands.
Orders to control activities, §113-230, (d).
Commercial fishing, §113-187, (d).
Dredging.
Permit violations.
Violations, §113-229, (k).
Refusal to stop in obedience to directions of inspector or director, §113-136, (j).
Robbing or injuring hatcheries and other aquaculture operations, §113-269, (e), (f).
Seafood.
Industrial park authority.
Traffic and parking violations, §113-315.34, (c).
Taking fish by illegal means, §113-262, (a).
Food, drug and cosmetic act.
Violations of article.
Civil penalties, §106-124.1.
Remission of proceeds, §106-124.1, (d).
Forests and forestry.
Open fires provisions, §113-60.29.
Posted notices.
Destruction, §113-58.
Primary forest product assessment act.
Disclosure of confidential information, §113A-195, (f).
Funeral service.
Unlawful practices, §90-210.25, (f).
Gaming.
Allowing illegal slot machines or punchboards on premises, §14-297.
Gas conservation, §§113-380, 113-409.
Gasoline adulteration, §119-35.
Gasoline inspection violations, §119-39.
Prosecution of offenders, §119-38.
Gasoline inspectors.
Conflicts of interest, §119-25.
Gasoline pumps.
Devices calculated to falsify measures, §119-33.
Display of grade rating, §119-27.
Gasoline tax.
Buying or selling non-tax-paid motor fuel, §105-449.118.
Failure to report deduction of exempt sale, §105-449.94, (e).
Shipping documents, §105-449.115, (f).
Geologists.
Civil penalty for license violations, §89E-19, (c).
Civil action to recover, §89E-19, (d).
Habeas corpus.
Disobedience to writ, §17-26.
Judges.
Refusal to grant precept to bring up party detained, §17-20.
Refusal to grant writ of attachment, §17-17.
Refusal or neglect to make return, §17-26.
Unlawful refusal to grant writ, §17-10.

FINES —Cont'd
Handicapped persons.
Parking violations, §20-37.6, (f).
Hazardous waste management.
Class I felonies, §130A-26.1, (f).
Class J felonies, §130A-26.1, (g).
Historical and cultural resources, §121-4.
Home care agency licensure.
Unlicensed operation, §131E-141.1.
Hospice licensure.
Unauthorized disclosure of inspection information, §131E-207, (b).
Hospital discharged patient.
Discharge from hospital.
Failure or refusal to leave hospital, §131E-90.
Hospital employee personnel files.
Unlawful disclosure, §131E-257.2, (g).
Unlawful examination or use, §131E-257.2, (h).
Hospital inspections by department.
Disclosure of confidential or privileged information, §131E-80, (d).
Hospital licensure.
Disclosure of information, §131E-80, (d).
Unlicensed operation, §131E-81, (a).
Willful violations, §131E-81, (b).
Housemovers.
Article or rules violations, §20-371, (a).
Hunting and wildlife.
Handicapped persons.
Special vehicular access identification card and permit, §113-294, (n).
Hunter orange material, §113-291.8, (b).
Hunting on Sunday, §103-2.
License agent.
Termination of appointment, §113-270.1, (h).
Limitation upon penalty for offense creating by rules of wildlife resources commission, §113-135.1, (a), (b).
Poisons and pesticides, §113-300.3, (c).
Refusal to stop in obedience to directions of protector, §113-136, (j).
Taking fish by illegal means, §113-262, (a).
Trapping.
Violation of provisions, §113-294, (i), (j).
Unlawful harassment of persons taking wildlife resources, §113-295, (a).
Unlawfully selling, possessing for sale or buying wildlife, §113-294, (a).
Bald eagle or golden eagle, §113-294, (l).
Bear, §113-294, (c1).
Beaver, §113-294, (f).
Cougar, §113-294, (c2).
Deer or wild turkey, §113-294, (b).
Unlawfully taking, possessing or transporting wildlife.
Bald eagle or golden eagle, §113-294, (l).
Bear, §113-294, (c1).
Beaver, §113-294, (f).
Cougar, §113-294, (c2).
Deer, §113-294, (d), (e).
Fox, §113-294, (j).
Migratory game birds, §113-294, (m).
Vessel equipped with motor.
Taking from or with use of, §113-294, (g).
Wild turkey, §113-294, (c).
Impaired driving.
Level one punishment, §20-179, (g).
Level two punishment, §20-179, (h).
Level three punishment, §20-179, (i).
Level four punishment, §20-179, (j).
Level five punishment, §20-179, (k).

FINES —Cont'd
Infractions, §15A-1361.
Enforcement of sanctions.
Use of fine collection procedures, §15A-1116, (a).
Inspections.
Alcoholic beverages.
Interference with inspections, §18B-502, (b).
Insurance commissioner, false statements to, §58-2-180.
Interstate earnings of employee.
Collection out of state to avoid exemption, §95-75.
Kennels.
Boarding kennels, §19A-33.
Kidnapping and abduction.
Corporations, §14-39.
Labor.
Earnings of employees in interstate commerce.
Collection out of state to avoid exemption, §95-75.
Payments to or for benefit of labor organization, §95-104.
Larceny.
Horses, mules, swine, cattle or dogs, §14-81.
Library books.
Failure to return, §125-11.
Liens.
Docketed judgments for fines, §15A-1365.
Payments as authorized condition of parole, §15A-1374, (b).
Liquid fuels, lubricating oils, greases, etc.
Violations of article, §119-13.
Littering, §14-399, (c), (d), (e).
Livestock diseases.
Quarantine.
Hiding or concealing animal subject to, §106-405, (c).
Lobbying, §120-47.9.
Local government finance.
Fiscal control.
Annual independent audit, §159-34, (a).
Manufactured homes.
Licenses.
Obtaining by false representation, §51-15.
Meat and meat products.
Rendering plants and rendering operations, §106-168.16.
Medical waste.
Water and air resources.
Prohibited disposal of waste, §143-214.2A, (c).
Meetings of public bodies.
Disrupting, §143-318.17.
Mental health, developmental disabilities and substance abuse.
Area authorities.
Unlawful access or disclosure of personnel records, §122C-158, (g), (h).
Camp Butner and community of Butner, §122C-406.
Facility licensing.
Regulatory violations, §122C-24.1.
Operating a licensable facility without a license, §122C-28.
Quality assurance activities.
Unlawful disclosure of confidential information.
Secretary or designee, §122C-192, (b).
Unlawful disclosure of confidential information, §122C-52, (e).
Gathered during inspections, §122C-25.
Midwives, §90-178.7, (b).
Migrant farm workers.
Motor carrier violations, §20-215.4.

FINES —Cont'd
Military personnel.
Discrimination against, §127B-15.
Military property sales facilities.
Dealer violations, §127B-7.
Milk sanitation.
Administrative penalties, §130A-22, (a).
Mines and minerals.
Notice of beginning business of manufacturing products from mineral resources of state, §113-25.
Minors.
Alcoholic beverages.
Aiding and abetting sale to or purchase by underage persons, §18B-302, (c).
Purchase or possession by 19 or 20 year olds, §18B-302, (i).
Missing persons center.
Improper release of information, §143B-499.6.
Money transmitters, §53-208.24, (a).
Mopeds, §20-140.4, (c).
Mortgage bankers and brokers.
Disciplinary action, §53-243.12, (c), (d).
Exempt persons.
Filing requirement.
Penalty for failure to file, §53-243.15, (b).
Motor carriers.
Migrant farm workers, §20-215.4.
Road tax on carriers using fuel purchased outside state.
Failure to file report, §105-449.45, (d).
Safety regulation unit.
Furnishing false information to department of crime control and public safety, §§20-396, 20-397.
Refusal to allow inspections, §20-390.
Unlawful motor carrier operations, §20-396.
Willful evasion of department of crime control and public safety regulations, §§20-396, 20-397.
Taxation.
Road tax on carriers using fuel purchased outside state.
Violations of provisions, §105-449.51.
Motorcycles, §20-140.4, (c).
Motor vehicle insurance.
Rental vehicle violations of insurance provisions, §20-284.
Motor vehicles.
Accidents.
Failure to stop and give name, §20-166, (c), (c1).
Leaving scene of accident, §20-166, (a), (b).
Certificates of title.
Satisfaction of liens.
Lienor refusal to surrender certificate, §20-59.
Transfer of title or interest.
Failure of new owner to apply for new title, §20-73, (c).
False statement in making an application, §20-74.
Commercial drivers' licenses.
Driving without license, §20-37.21, (a).
Violation of employer responsibilities, §20-37.21, (c).
Violations of driver notice requirements, §20-37.21, (b).
Commercial vehicles.
Impaired driving, §20-138.2, (e).
Operating a commercial vehicle after consuming alcohol, §20-138.2A, (c).

FINES —Cont'd
Motor vehicles —Cont'd
Dealers.
License applications.
Violations of licensing provisions, §20-308.
Driver's license.
Driving while license revoked, §20-28, (a).
Driver training schools.
Violations of licensing provisions, §20-327.
Felony death by vehicles, §20-141.4, (b).
Financial responsibility.
False certification, §20-313.1, (a).
False information concerning another's responsibility, §20-313.1, (b).
Fire department vehicles.
Motorist approach violation, §20-157, (a).
Flat trucks.
Violations of operation restriction, §20-120.
Handicapped persons.
Parking violations, §20-37.6, (f).
Housemovers.
Article or rules violations, §20-371, (a).
Injuring vehicle with intent to steal, §20-107, (b).
License plates.
Borrowing or lending, §20-111.
Manufacturer's and dealer's special plates.
Registration violations, §20-79, (e).
Lights.
Requirement violations, §20-129, (a).
Manufacturer's serial or engine numbers.
Altering or changing numbers, §20-109, (a), (b).
Prohibitions as to vehicles without numbers, §20-108, (a).
Mechanic's or storage liens.
Failure to report unclaimed vehicles, §20-77, (d).
Misdemeanor death by vehicle, §20-141.4, (b).
Nuclear fuel.
Transportation of spent nuclear fuel, §20-167.1, (d).
Open container law violations, §20-138.7, (e).
Private lots.
Unauthorized vehicles, §20-219.2, (b).
Railroad grade crossing.
Crossing gate violation, §20-142.1, (d).
Moving heavy equipment, §20-142.4, (f).
Obstructing traffic and pedestrian walkway, §20-142.5.
Stop sign violation, §20-142.2.
Reckless driving, §20-140, (d).
School buses.
Operating after consuming alcohol, §20-138.2B, (c).
Passing stopped school bus, §20-217.
Seat belt.
Violations of mandatory use provision, §20-135.2A, (e).
Special identification card for nonoperators.
Fraud or misrepresentation in application, §20-37.7, (e).
Speedometer.
Requirement violations, §20-123.2, (b).
Stopping.
Obstructing traffic and pedestrian walkway, §20-142.5.
Tampering with vehicle, §20-107, (a).
Tandem trailers and subtrailer.
Load limitation violations, §20-115.1, (h), (i).
Weight of vehicles and load.
Excessive size or weight.
Violations of special permit terms and condition, §20-119, (d).

FINES —Cont'd
Motor vehicles —Cont'd
Window tinting.
Medical exception, failure to display sticker, §20-127, (f).
Municipal corporations.
Personnel records.
Knowingly, willfully and with malice permitting access to, §160A-168, (e).
Removing or copying confidential personnel files, §160A-168, (f).
Vehicle used on foreshore, beach strand and barrier dune systems, §160A-308.
Violation of ordinances, §§160A-175, (a), 160A-308.
National guard.
Courts-martial.
Disposition of fines, §127A-61.
Negligence.
Reckless driving, §20-140, (d).
Nonpayment.
Arrest for nonpayment, §6-48.
Docketed judgments for fines, §15A-1365.
Imprisonment.
Commitment to department of correction or local confinement facility, §15A-1352, (c).
Criteria, §15A-1364, (b).
Order to defendant to show cause why he should not be imprisoned, §§15A-1362, (c), 15A-1364, (a).
Release upon payment, §23-24.
Lien.
Docketed judgments for fine, §15A-1365.
Modification of fine or cost, §15A-1364, (c).
Order to defendant to show cause why he should not be imprisoned, §§15A-1362, (c), 15A-1364, (a).
Nursing home administrators, §90-288.
Nursing home licensure.
Inspection violations, §131E-109, (b).
Prohibited acts, §131E-109, (d).
Unlicensed operation, §131E-109, (a).
Nursing pools.
Unauthorized disclosure of inspection information, §131E-154.8, (b).
Obstructing justice.
Violating orders of court, §14-226.1.
Occupational safety and health, §95-130.
Occupational therapists, §90-270.79.
Oil or hazardous substances discharges, §143-215.88B, (e), (f), (h).
Oil refining facility permit violations, §143-215.102, (b).
Oils.
Conservation, §§113-380, 113-409.
Dispensing devices.
Falsification of measures, §119-33.
Inspection violations.
Generally, §119-39.
Inspectors.
Conflicts of interest, §119-25.
Lubricating oils, §§119-4, 119-13.
Terminal facilities, §143-215.98.
Open container law violations, §20-138.7, (e).
Opticians.
Allowing unlicensed person to use certificate or license, §90-251.
Sale of flammable frame, §90-255.1.
Unlicensed practice, §90-252.
Optometrists.
Subpoenas of board of examiner.
Neglect or refusal to obey, §90-117.4.
Unauthorized practices, §90-118.11.

FINES —Cont'd
Optometrists —Cont'd
Violations of rules and regulations, §90-124.
Organizations.
Payment of fines, §15A-1364, (d).
Osteopaths.
Prohibited acts, §90-136.
Parking regulations of ports authority, §143B-461, (c).
Pawnbrokers, §91A-11, (a).
Payment.
Determination of method of payment.
Criteria, §15A-1362, (a).
Installment or delayed payments, §15A-1362, (b).
Nonpayment. See within this heading, "Nonpayment."
Organizations, §15A-1364, (d).
Pet shops.
Cruelty to animals, §19A-35.
Unlicensed shops, §19A-33.
Physical therapists.
Unlicensed practice, §90-270.35.
Physicians and surgeons.
Limited licensee practicing beyond boundaries of district laid down in license, §90-12, (a).
Limited volunteer licenses.
Practicing beyond scope of license, §90-12, (c).
Podiatrists.
Unlawful practices, §90-202.3.
Pollution control.
Sedimentation pollution control act of 1973, §113A-64, (b).
Preneed funeral contracts and funds, §90-210.70, (b).
Determining penalty amount, §90-210.69, (f).
Private personnel services.
Unlicensed operation, §95-47.9, (e).
Probate and registration.
Maps and plats, §47-32.2.
Property taxes.
Abstracts.
False affirmation, §105-310.
Attempting to evade or defeat taxes, §105-308.
County assessor.
Disclosure of information, §105-296, (h).
Liens.
Advertisement of lien.
Wrongful advertisement, §105-369, (g).
Listing of property.
Failure to list, §105-308.
Mobile homes.
Tax permit violations, §105-316.6, (a) to (c).
Public utilities.
Reports.
False reports, §105-334, (b).
Proprietary schools.
Operating without license or bond, §115D-96.
Psychologists.
Prohibited acts, §90-270.17.
Public lands.
Piers.
Erection on state lakes, §146-13.
Public officers and employees.
Misconduct in public office.
Failing to file report of fines, §14-244.
Public records.
Cultural resources department.
Disposition of records at end of official's term, §132-4.
Unauthorized removal or destruction, §132-3.
Unlawful possession, §132-5.

FINES —Cont'd
Public schools.
Apportionment to school administrative units, §115C-452.
Contractors selling personally identifiable student information.
Criminal penalty, §115C-401.1, (c).
Public utilities.
Refusal to permit commission to inspect records, §62-313.
Public works.
Chapter violations, §133-4.
Quarantine.
Dog or cat bites.
Owner's failure to confine pet, §130A-196.
Quo warranto.
Judgment in actions, §1-527.
Rabies.
Quarantine of pets.
Owner's failure to confine pet, §130A-196.
Real estate brokers and salespersons, §93A-8.
Remission or revocation of fine or cost, §§15A-1363, 15A-1364, (c).
Rental vehicles.
Violations of insurance provisions, §20-284.
Retirement system for counties, cities and towns, §§128-28, 128-32.
Retirement system for teachers and state employees.
Disclosure of confidential information concerning members, §135-6, (p).
False statements or falsified records, §135-10.
School buses.
Passing stopped school bus, §20-217.
School of science and mathematics.
Nonattendance, §116-235, (b).
Traffic violations, §116-235, (e).
Service animals, §168-4.5.
Shellfish.
Cultivation of shellfish.
Polluted shellfish.
Taking or selling at night or with prior convictions, §113-209, (d).
Privately leased, franchised or deeded shellfish bottom areas.
Taking without permission, §113-208, (a).
Social workers, §90B-12.
Solid waste management.
Disclosure of information received pursuant to article, §130A-304, (b).
Landfill fees.
Failure to collect or report revenue, §130A-309.27, (c).
Speech and language pathologists and audiologists, §90-306.
Stalking, §14-277.3.
State personnel records.
Unlawful disclosure, §§126-27, 126-28.
State personnel system.
Compensation for assisting person in obtaining state employment, §126-18.
Political activities of employees, §§126-14, 126-14.1.
State treasurer.
False entries in books, §147-76.
Streets and highways.
Billboards.
Obstructing view at entrance to building on public highway, §136-102.
Controlled-access facilities.
Unlawful use, §136-89.58.
Obstructing highway drains, §136-92.

FINES —Cont'd
Streets and highways —Cont'd
Obstructing highways and roads, §136-90.
"Pull-over" areas, §136-18.4.
Rights of way.
Gates projecting over rights-of-way, §136-94.
Signs, signals or markers.
Blinding, deceptive or distracting lights, §136-32.2, (a).
Damaging or removing signs, §136-33, (b1).
Misleading signs, §136-32.1.
Underpasses or overpasses.
Regulation of safety devices, §136-20, (e).
Swine near state institutions.
Keeping, §143-153.
Taking certain wild plants from land of another, §14-129.
Taking sea oats from land of another, §14-129.2, (b).
Taxation.
Attempt to evade or defeat tax, §105-236.
Fraud.
Aid or assistance in fraud, §105-236.
Officers, agents and employees, §§105-233, 105-234.
Time shares, §93A-56.
Disciplinary action by real estate commission, §93A-54, (a), (a1).
Toxic substances.
Dumping of toxic substances, §14-284.2.
Tramways.
Operation of passenger tramway without registration, §95-124.
Transportation board.
Conflicts of interest, §136-14, (i).
Malfeasance, §136-13, (c).
Trust companies.
Administrative enforcement, §53-369, (b).
Underground petroleum storage tank leak cleanup.
Criminal penalties, §143-215.94X, (a) to (c).
Wage and hour act, §95-25.21, (c).
Recordkeeping requirements, §95-25.23A.
Civil penalty collection, §95-25.23B.
Water and air resources.
Air pollution control violations, §143-215.114B, (a) to (i).
Classifications, standards or limitations, §143-215.6B, (f) to (i).
Cleaning agents containing phosphorus.
Manufacturing, selling or distributing agents, §143-214.4, (f).
Conservation and use of diverted waters within emergency areas, §143-354.
Medical waste.
Civil penalties.
Prohibited disposal, §143-214.2A, (b).
Criminal penalties.
Prohibited disposal, §143-214.2A, (c).
Prohibited disposal of waste, §143-214.2A, (c).
Reporting of quality.
Violations of part, §143-215.69, (a).
Violations of part regulating water usage, §143-215.17, (a).
Waters and watercourses.
Natural and scenic rivers system, §113A-42, (b).
Water supply of public institutions.
Injuring, §143-152.
Well drilling, construction, etc., §143-355, (i).
Witnesses.
Depositions.
Default before commissioner, §8-80.
Failure to appear upon subpoena, §8-79.

FINES —Cont'd
Witnesses —Cont'd
Failure to attend until discharged, §8-63.
Workers' compensation.
Insurance carrier violation, §97-100, (g).
Receiving fee, other consideration or gratuity on account of services rendered, §97-90, (b).
Unlawful deduction by employers, §97-21.

FINGERPRINTING.
Alarm systems licensees employees, §74D-8, (a).
Arrest.
Person arrested, §15A-502, (a).
Exceptions, §15A-502, (b), (c).
Law enforcement agencies.
Forwarding of fingerprints to, §15A-502, (e).
Attorneys at law.
Applicants for admission to practice, §84-24.
Automated fingerprint identification system.
Delinquent or undisciplined juveniles fingerprints to be placed in, §7B-2102, (c).
Bail bondsmen and runners.
License application.
Fingerprints and photograph of applicant, §58-71-50, (a).
Child care providers.
Criminal history record check, §110-90.2.
Concealed handgun permit.
Fees for processing, §14-415.19, (b).
Renewal of permit, new set of fingerprints, §14-415.16.
Submitted to state bureau of investigation for record check, §14-415.13, (b).
Submitted with application, §14-415.13, (a).
Criminal law and procedure.
Report of disposition of charges, §15A-1382.
Dental hygienists.
Criminal records checks for license applicants, §90-224, (c).
Dentists.
Criminal records checks for license applicants, §90-30, (b).
Funeral service.
Criminal records checks for license applicants, §90-210.25, (a).
Insurance company incorporators and key persons, §58-7-37.
Interpreters and transliterators.
Criminal records checks for license applicants, §90D-7, (c).
Juvenile actions.
Fingerprinting and photographing delinquent or undisciplined juveniles, §7B-2102.
Nontestimonial identification order procedures, §§7B-2103 to 7B-2109.
Transfer of jurisdiction to superior court for prosecution as adult, §7B-2201.
Nontestimonial identification, §§15A-271 to 15A-282.
See IDENTIFICATION.
Pharmacists and pharmacies.
Criminal records checks for license applicants, §90-85.15, (c).
Physicians and surgeons.
Criminal records checks for license applicants, §90-11, (b).
Precious metals dealers.
Applicants for permits to provide, §66-165, (a), (c).
Private personnel services.
Criminal records checks for license applicants, §95-47.2, (d).

FINGERPRINTING —Cont'd
Professional employer organizations.
Furnished by license applicant, §58-89A-60, (d).
Real estate brokers and salespersons.
Criminal records checks for license applicants, §93A-4, (b1).
Reports.
Criminal law and procedure.
Disposition of cases, §15A-1382.
Respiratory care practitioners.
Applicants for license, §90-652, (a).
Sex offender and public protection registration.
Fingerprints of offender taken at registration, §14-208.7, (b).
State bureau of investigation.
Rules and regulations.
Authority to make, §114-18.

FINGERS.
Workers' compensation.
Loss of fingers.
Computation rate compensation, I.C. Rule 405.

FIRE ALARM SYSTEMS.
Building codes.
Special safety to life requirements applicable to existing high-rise buildings.
Requirements for class I buildings, §143-138, (i).
Requirements for class II buildings.
Manual fire alarm, §143-138, (i).

FIRE AND RESCUE COMMISSION, §§58-78-1 to 58-78-20.
Compensation of members, §58-78-1, (f).
Created, §58-78-1, (a).
Duties, §58-78-5, (a).
Executive director, §58-78-15, (a).
Fiscal affairs, §58-78-20.
Funds.
Appropriation, §58-78-20.
Meetings, §58-78-10, (c).
Members, §58-78-1, (a) to (f).
Organization, §58-78-10, (a).
Powers, §58-78-5, (a).
Rules and regulations.
Adoption and promulgation, §58-78-10, (b).
Staff, §58-78-15, (b).
State agencies to furnish information, §58-78-5, (b).
Terms, §58-78-1, (b).
Vacancies, §58-78-1, (c).

FIREARMS.
Acquittal by reason of insanity.
Possession by persons so acquitted of felony prohibited, §14-415.3, (a), (b).
Administration department.
Sale to local government, law enforcement agency or state, §143-63.1, (b).
Destruction of unsold weapons, §143-63.1, (c).
Alcoholic beverages sold or consumed.
Carrying into establishments or assemblies, §14-269.3.
Antique firearm.
Defined, §14-409.11.
Permit or license to sell pistols.
Inapplicability of provisions to, §14-402, (b).
Armed private security officers.
Firearm registration permits.
Application, §74C-13, (c).
Denial, §74C-13, (g).

FIREARMS —Cont'd
Armed private security officers —Cont'd
Firearm registration permits —Cont'd
Fees.
Expenditure, §74C-13, (k).
Form, §74C-13, (d).
Issuance.
Prerequisites, §74C-13, (i).
Renewal, §74C-13, (d).
Required, §74C-13, (a), (b).
Rules and regulations, §74C-13, (j).
Suspension or revocation, §74C-13, (g).
Temporary employment, §74C-13, (f).
Termination of employment.
Expiration and return of permit, §74C-13, (e).
Assault and battery, §14-34.2.
Detention facility personnel and probation or parole officers, §14-34.5.
Habitual misdemeanor assault, §14-33.2.
Pointing gun at person, §14-34.
Blank cartridge pistols.
Sale, §14-407.1.
Boats.
Discharging firearm into occupied property, §14-34.1.
Buildings.
Discharging firearm into occupied property, §14-34.1.
Attempt, §14-34.1.
Bullets.
Teflon-coated bullets.
Manufacture, sale, purchase or possession prohibited, §14-34.3.
Bureau of investigation.
Surplus weapons.
Sale, trade or disposal, §143-63.1, (d).
Campus or other education property, possessing or carrying unlawful.
Class 1 felony, §14-269.2, (b).
Class 1 misdemeanors, §14-269.2, (f).
Definitions, §14-269.2, (a).
Exceptions, §14-269.2, (g), (h).
Minors, aiding to possess or carry.
Class 1 felony, §14-269.2, (c).
Carrying concealed pistol or gun.
Burden of proving defense, §14-269, (c).
Defenses to prosecution, §14-269, (c).
Persons to which prohibition inapplicable, §14-269, (b).
Unlawful to carry, exceptions, §14-269, (a1).
Class 1 felony, second or subsequent offense, §14-269, (c).
Class 2 misdemeanor, §14-269, (c).
Charities.
Cartridges or ammunition for firearms.
Furnishing to inmates of charitable institutions, §14-258.1, (a).
Civil disorders, teaching or demonstrating use or assembling, §14-288.20.
Concealed handgun permit, §§14-415.10 to 14-415.24.
See CONCEALED HANDGUN PERMIT.
Confiscation and disposition of deadly weapon, §14-269.1.
Counties.
Confinement facilities.
Furnishing cartridges or ammunition for firearms to inmates, §14-258.1.
Regulation of firearms by counties, §153A-129.
Statewide uniformity of local regulation, §14-409.40.

FIREARMS —Cont'd
Dealer.
Defined, §14-409.39.
Definitions, §14-409.39.
Antique firearm, §14-409.11.
Historic edged weapons, §14-409.12.
Disasters.
Prohibitions and restrictions during state of emergency.
County powers, §14-288.13.
Municipal powers, §14-288.12.
Discharging firearm, §14-34.1.
Display during commission of felony.
Enhanced sentence, §15A-1340.16A.
Domestic violence.
Emergency or ex parte orders.
Surrender of firearms required, §50B-3.1, (a), (d).
Additional relief, §50B-3.1, (l).
Disposal, §50B-3.1, (h).
Exemptions for official use, §50B-3.1, (k).
Hearings, §50B-3.1, (b), (c).
Motions for return of firearms, §50B-3.1, (f), (g).
Retrieval of firearms, §50B-3.1, (e).
Violations, §50B-3.1, (i), (j).
Emergencies.
Prohibitions and restrictions during state of emergency.
County powers, §14-288.13.
Municipal powers, §14-288.12.
Emergency medical services personnel.
Assault with firearm upon personnel discharging official duties, §14-34.6, (c).
Enhanced sentence.
Use or display during commission of felony, §15A-1340.16A, (c).
Burden of proof, §15A-1340.16A, (e).
Circumstances in which provisions do not apply, §15A-1340.16A, (f).
Indictments or informations, §15A-1340.16A, (d).
Felonies.
Discharging firearm into occupied property, §14-34.1.
Possession of firearms, etc., by felon prohibited, §14-415.1, (a).
Indictment charging with violations of provisions, §14-415.1, (c).
Prior convictions causing disentitlement, §14-415.1, (b).
Use or display during commission of felony.
Enhanced sentence, §15A-1340.16A.
Felons possessing firearm or handgun.
Persons charged with felony acquitted by reason of insanity, §14-415, (a), (b).
Persons charged with felony found incompetent to stand trial, §14-415, (a), (b).
Prohibited, §14-415.1, (a).
Indictment charging defendant, §14-415.1, (c).
Prior convictions causing disentitlement, §14-415.1, (b).
Handguns.
Concealed handgun permit, §§14-415.10 to 14-415.24.
See CONCEALED HANDGUN PERMIT.
Defined, §14-409.39.
Highway patrol.
Surplus weapons.
Sale, trade or disposal, §143-63.1, (d).

FIREARMS —Cont'd
Historic edged weapons.
Defined, §14-409.12.
Identification marks.
Alteration, destruction, etc., §14-160.1.
Incompetency to stand trial.
Possession by incompetent persons charged with felony prohibited, §14-415.3, (a), (b).
Indictments.
Enhanced sentence.
Use or display of firearm during commission of felony, §15A-1340.16A, (d).
Felony firearms act.
Possession of firearms, etc., by felon prohibited, §14-415.1, (c).
Larceny.
Felony larceny.
When value of property in question irrelevant, §14-72.
Law enforcement officers.
Assault with firearm upon law enforcement officer, §§14-34.2, 14-34.5, (a).
Licenses.
Sale of pistols, §§14-402 to 14-408.
Machine guns.
Defined, §14-409, (a).
Unlawful to sell, give away, use or possess, exceptions, §14-409, (b).
Punishment, §14-409, (c).
Mass death and destruction weapons.
Manufacture, assembly, etc., §14-288.8.
Mentally ill.
Cartridges or ammunition for firearms.
Furnishing to inmates of mental institutions, §14-258.1, (a).
Minors.
Permitting young children to use dangerous firearms, §14-316, (a).
Air rifles, air pistols and BB guns not deemed dangerous firearms, §14-316, (b).
Schools, bringing weapons in.
Action against parent for negligent supervision of minor, §1-538.3.
Motor vehicles.
Discharging firearm into occupied property, §14-34.1.
Attempt, §14-34.1.
Municipal corporations.
Confinement facilities.
Furnishing cartridges or ammunition for firearms to inmates, §14-258.1.
Regulation, §160A-189.
Statewide uniformity of local regulation, §14-409.40.
Parade, picket line, funeral procession, etc.
Possession while participating, §14-277.2.
Peace officers.
Assault with firearm upon law enforcement officer, §§14-34.2, 14-34.5, (a).
Permits.
Concealed handgun permit, §§14-415.10 to 14-415.24.
See CONCEALED HANDGUN PERMIT.
Sale of pistols, §§14-402 to 14-408.
Permitting young children to use dangerous firearm, §14-316.
Persons subject to domestic violence orders.
Purchase or possession of firearms prohibited, §14-269.8, (a), (b).
Pointing gun at person.
Assault and battery, §14-34.
Habitual misdemeanor assault, §14-33.2.

FIREARMS —Cont'd
Possessing or carrying on campus or other educational property, §14-269.2.
Possession of handgun by minor, §14-269.7.
Post-release supervision.
Controlling conditions, possession prohibited, §15A-1364.4, (e).
Prisons and prisoners.
Cartridges or ammunition for firearms.
Furnishing to inmates, §14-258.1, (a).
Products liability.
Firearms or ammunition.
Burden of proof, §99B-11, (b).
Defect in design, §99B-11, (a).
Public schools.
Discipline of students.
Driving eligibility certificate.
Effect of disciplinary action for enumerated student conduct, §20-11, (n1).
Purchases out of state, §14-409.10.
Regulation by counties, §153A-129.
Reports.
Wounds.
Physicians and hospitals to report certain wounds, §90-21.20.
Rifles.
Purchase of rifles out of state, §14-409.10.
Riots and civil disorders.
Certain weapons, §14-288.20.
Prohibitions and restrictions during state of emergency.
County powers, §14-288.13.
Robbery.
Train robbery, §14-88.
Use of firearms or other dangerous weapons in robbery, §14-87, (a).
Rules and regulations.
Statewide uniformity of local regulation.
County or municipality regulations, §14-409.40, (b).
Legislative declarations, §14-409.40, (a), (a1).
Local government employees, §14-409.40, (e).
Preemption by state, §14-409.40, (a), (g).
Public buildings and areas, §14-409.40, (f).
Shows, §14-409.40, (d).
Zoning, §14-409.40, (c), (d).
Safety and training course.
Concealed handgun permits, §14-415.12, (a).
Qualified sworn law enforcement officers.
Exemption for, §14-415.12A.
Sale of pistols, §§14-402 to 14-408.
Blank cartridge pistols, §14-407.1.
Collection.
Issuance of permit to nonresident, §14-404, (a).
Dealer records, requirements, §14-406.
Misdemeanor for violating, §14-408.
Definitions, §14-402, (c).
License or permit required, §14-402, (a).
Collection, issuance to nonresident, §14-404, (a).
Expiration date, §14-403.
Fee for sheriffs services, §14-404, (e).
Form, §14-403.
Inapplicability, §§14-402, (b), 14-404, (d).
Informing applicant as to action on issuance, §14-404, (f).
Issuance by sheriff, §14-403.
Records kept by sheriffs, §14-405.
Refusal to issue, grounds, appeal, §14-404, (b), (c).
Mail or other parcel delivery.
Display of permit or license, §14-402, (a).

FIREARMS —Cont'd
Schools.
Discipline of students.
Driving eligibility certificate.
Effect of disciplinary action for enumerated student conduct, §20-11, (n1).
Minors bringing to school.
Action against parent for negligent supervision of minor, §1-538.3.
Possessing or carrying on campus or educational property, §14-269.2.
Seizure.
Disposition of seized firearms, §15-11.1, (b1).
Selling or giving weapons to minors, §14-315.
Sentencing.
Enhanced sentence.
Use or display during commission of felony, §15A-1340.16A.
Serial numbers.
Alteration, destruction, etc., §14-160.1.
Shotguns.
Purchase of shotguns out of state, §14-409.10.
Sport shooting range protection, §§14-409.45 to 14-409.47.
State of emergency.
Prohibitions and restrictions during.
County powers, §14-288.13.
Municipal powers, §14-288.12.
State officers, officials and employees.
Unlawful to dispose of, §143-63.1, (a).
State property or courthouses, carrying or possessing, §14-269.4.
Storage of weapon to protect minor, §14-315.1.
Submachine guns.
Defined, §14-409, (a).
Unlawful to sell, give away, use or possess, exceptions, §14-409, (b).
Punishment, §14-409, (c).
Teflon-coated bullets.
Manufacture, sale, purchase or possession prohibited, §14-34.3.
Trains or passengers, shooting at, §14-280.
Uniformity of rules and regulations.
County or municipality regulations, §14-409.40, (b).
Legislative declarations, §14-409.40, (a), (a1).
Local government employees, §14-409.40, (e).
Preemption by state, §14-409.40, (a), (g).
Public buildings and areas, §14-409.40, (f).
Shows, §14-409.40, (d).
Zoning, §14-409.40, (c), (d).
Use during commission of felony.
Enhanced sentence, §15A-1340.16A.
Warning upon sale or transfer of firearm to protect minor, §14-315.2.
Watercraft.
Discharging firearm into occupied property, §14-34.1.
Weapons generally.
See WEAPONS.
Wounds.
Reports.
Physicians and hospitals to report certain wounds, §90-21.20.

FIRE DEPARTMENTS.
Assault on emergency personnel, §14-288.9.
Aggravating factor in sentencing, §15A-1340.16.
Authority of firemen, §58-82-1.
Burning of fire house, §14-61.

FIRE DEPARTMENTS —Cont'd
Contracts.
Purchases and contracts through department of administration, §143-49.1.
Criminal history record checks, §114-19.12.
Conditional offer pending check, §114-19.12, (f).
Confidentiality of information, §114-19.12, (b).
Releases of information, §114-19.12, (c).
Convictions, effect, §114-19.12, (d).
Defined terms, §114-19.12, (a).
Denial of application, factors, §114-19.12, (d).
Denial of application, refusal to consent, §114-19.12, (e).
Local homeland security directory to provide when requested, §114-19.12, (b).
Refusal to consent, §114-19.12, (e).
Releases of information, §114-19.12, (c).
Death benefits, §§143-166.1 to 143-166.7.
See DEATH BENEFITS.
Deceased or retiring county firefighters.
Honoring, awarding helmet, §153A-236.
Failure of owner of property to comply with orders of chief, §14-68.
Firearms.
Assault with firearm upon firemen, §14-34.2.
Firemen as traffic officers, §20-114.1, (b).
Hazardous substance list provided by employer by fire chiefs, §95-194.
Highway use tax.
Exemption, §105-187.6, (a).
Impersonation of firemen or emergency medical services personnel, §14-276.1.
Interference with firemen.
Penalty for willful interference, §58-82-1.
Leave options for personnel in disaster or emergency, §166A-17.
Light-traffic road weight and load limitations.
Exceptions to firefighting vehicles, §20-118, (c).
Misdemeanors.
Willful interference with firemen, §58-82-1.
Motor vehicle license plates.
Permanent license plates for rural fire department vehicles, §20-84, (b).
Special plates, §20-79.4, (b).
Municipal corporations, §§160A-291 to 160A-294.
Annexation.
Loss of rural fire employment.
Actions of city, §160A-294, (a), (b).
Employment of firefighters, §160A-291.
Fire chief.
Appointment, §160A-291.
Duties, §160A-292.
Reports, §160A-292.
Fire protection outside city limits, §160A-293.
Helmet of deceased firefighter awarded to surviving relative, §160A-294.1.
Powers of cities as to, §160A-291.
Rural fire departments in annexed area.
Assumption of department debts, §§160A-37.2, (a), (b), 160A-49.2, (a), (b).
Contracts with.
Appeal to local government commission, no good faith offer, §§160A-37.1, (g) to (i), 160A-49.1, (g) to (i).
Good faith effort to negotiate 5 year contract, §§160A-37.1, (a), 160A-49.1, (a).
Good faith offers, §§160A-37.1, (b) to (e), 160A-49.1, (b) to (e).
No obligation to enter into contract, §§160A-37.1, (f), 160A-49.1, (f).

FIRE DEPARTMENTS —Cont'd
Municipal corporations —Cont'd
Smallpox vaccination of first responders.
Policies for time off due to adverse reaction, §160A-164.1.
State volunteer fire department.
Acceptance of provisions, §58-80-15.
Dispatching firemen and apparatus from municipalities, §58-80-25.
Municipalities not to be unprotected, §58-80-40.
Local appropriations, §58-80-55.
Withdrawal from participation, §58-80-20.
Mutual aid between fire departments, §58-83-1.
Offenses against firemen.
Aggravating factor in sentencing, §15A-1340.16.
Parking in front of entrance to fire station, §20-162, (a).
Rural fire departments.
Annexation of district by city.
Assumption of departments debts, §§160A-37.2, (a), (b), 160A-49.2, (a), (b).
Contract with department to provide protection, §§160A-37.1, (a) to (i), 160A-49.1, (a) to (i).
Defined, §58-82-5, (a).
Liability.
Limited, §58-82-5, (b).
Acts or omissions relating to direction of traffic or enforcement of traffic laws, §20-114.1, (b1).
Motor vehicle license plates.
Permanent license plates for department vehicles, §20-84, (b).
State volunteer fire department, §§58-80-1 to 58-80-60.
See VOLUNTEER FIRE DEPARTMENTS.
Traffic officers.
Firemen as, §20-114.1, (b).
Trucks and vehicles generally.
See FIRE TRUCKS AND VEHICLES.
Volunteer fire departments.
Generally.
See VOLUNTEER FIRE DEPARTMENTS.
State volunteer fire department, §§58-80-1 to 58-80-60.
See VOLUNTEER FIRE DEPARTMENTS.
Weapons.
Assault with deadly weapon upon firemen, §14-34.2.

FIRE DRILLS.
Public schools.
Powers and duties of principal, §115C-288, (d).

FIRE EXTINGUISHERS.
Boating safety.
Requirements, §75A-6, (g), (h).
Misuse or damage of system, §14-286.
Roller skating rinks.
Duties of operator, §99E-11.

FIREFIGHTERS ASSOCIATION OF STATE.
Members, §58-85-20.
Departments, §58-84-50.
Treasurer.
Payment of fund to treasurer by commissioner, §58-84-25.
State appropriation, §58-85-10.
Volunteer firefighters association, §58-85-30.

FIRE HOSES.
Driving over prohibited, §20-157, (d).

FIRE HYDRANTS.
Blocking prohibited, §20-157, (b).
Parking in front of, §20-162, (a).

FIRE INSURANCE, §§58-31-1 to 58-31-50.
Authorized, §58-7-15.
Beach area property essential property insurance, §§58-45-1 to 58-45-90.
See BEACH AREA ESSENTIAL PROPERTY INSURANCE.
Community college buildings and contents, §115D-58.11, (a) to (c).
Contracts.
Devices.
Performance of contracts as to devices not prohibited, §58-43-1.
Indemnity contracts for difference in actual value and cost of replacement, §58-43-5.
Extended coverage, §58-31-15.
Firemen's relief fund, §§58-84-1 to 58-84-55.
See FIREMEN'S RELIEF FUND.
Foreign or alien insurance companies.
Deposits.
Required, §58-5-5.
Forms.
Standard fire insurance policy, §58-44-15, (c).
State property fire insurance fund.
Policy forms, §58-31-12.
Funds.
Firemen's relief fund, §§58-84-1 to 58-84-55.
See FIREMEN'S RELIEF FUND.
Husband and wife.
Policy issued to husband or wife on joint property, §58-44-45.
Information to be furnished by insurance companies, §58-79-40, (a), (b).
Confidentiality of information, §58-79-40, (d).
Immunity from liability, §58-79-40, (c).
Testimony by officials as to information, §58-79-40, (e).
Inspections of state property, §58-31-40, (a).
Limitation of actions.
Claim for loss covered by insurance policy.
Standard fire insurance policy for North Carolina, §1-52.
Limitation of fire insurance risk, §58-43-25.
Limitation of liability on total lost, §58-43-10.
Mandatory or voluntary risk sharing plans, §§58-42-1 to 58-42-50.
See MANDATORY OR VOLUNTARY RISK SHARING PLANS.
Misdemeanors.
Unauthorized insurers.
Violations of provisions, §58-28-45, (h).
Mortgages and deeds of trust.
Policies for benefit of mortgagees, §58-43-15.
Mutual insurance companies.
Surplus.
Requirements, §58-7-75.
Nuclear reaction, nuclear radiation or radioactive contamination.
Optional policy provisions as to loss or damage from, §58-44-25.
Penalties.
Unauthorized insurers, §58-28-45, (h).
Policies.
Amount.
Limitation, §58-43-5.
Conditions of insurance to be stated, §58-44-1.
Devices.
Performance of contracts as to devices not prohibited, §58-43-1.

FIRE INSURANCE —Cont'd
Policies —Cont'd
Encumbrances.
Notice to encumbrance.
Effect of failure to give, §58-44-40.
Functional replacement, §58-43-5.
Husband and wife.
Policy issued to husband or wife on point property, §58-44-45.
Indemnity contracts for difference in actual value and cost of replacement, §58-43-5.
Items to be stated in policies, §58-44-5.
Mortgagees.
Policies for benefit of, §58-43-15.
Standard fire insurance policy, §58-44-15, (a), (b).
Form, §58-44-15, (c).
Increase of hazard, unoccupancy and other insurance.
Notice by insured or agent as, §58-44-30.
Nuclear reaction, nuclear radiation or radioactive contamination.
Optional provisions as to loss or damage from, §58-44-25.
Permissible variations, §58-44-20.
Umpire.
Judge to select, §58-44-35.
Term.
Limitation, §58-43-5.
Premiums.
Excess over actual cash value of property.
Reimbursement, §58-43-10.
Proof of loss.
Failure to render timely proof of loss.
Bar to defense, §58-44-50.
Reports.
Fire incident reports, §58-79-45, (a) to (c).
Risks.
Limitation of fire insurance risks, §58-43-25.
Service of process.
Unauthorized insurers, §58-28-45, (e).
State property fire insurance fund, §§58-31-1 to 58-31-50.
Appropriations, §58-31-5.
Commissioner.
Information furnished commissioner by officers in charge, §58-31-35.
Inspection of state property, §58-31-40, (a).
Reports to governor, §58-31-45.
Rules and regulations, §58-31-10, (b).
Creation, §58-31-1.
Expenses.
Administrative expenses, §58-31-5.
Extended coverage insurance, §58-31-15.
Hazardous conditions in state-owned buildings, §58-31-13.
Motor vehicles.
Liability insurance required for state-owned vehicles, §58-31-50.
Officers in charge of state property.
Furnishing information to commissioner, §58-31-35.
Payment of losses, §58-31-10, (a).
Plans for erection of building.
Review of plan by commissioner, §58-31-40, (c).
Submitting to commissioner, §58-31-40, (b).
Policy forms, §58-31-12.
Rules and regulations.
Promulgation by commissioner, §58-31-10, (b).
Sprinkler leakage insurance, §58-31-10, (c).
State-owned buildings.
Hazardous conditions in, §58-31-13.

FIRE INSURANCE —Cont'd
State property fire insurance fund —Cont'd
State treasurer.
Custodian of fund, §58-31-1.
Transfers to fund, §58-31-10, (a).
Unauthorized insurers.
Actions.
Prerequisites to instituting or filing, §58-28-45, (f), (g).
Citation of act, §58-28-45, (j).
Construction and interpretation, §58-28-45, (i).
Prohibited acts, §58-28-45, (a) to (c).
Exceptions, §58-28-45, (d).
Service of process, §58-28-45, (e).
Violations of provisions.
Penalties, §58-28-45, (h).
Use and occupancy and business interruption insurance, §58-31-20.

FIRE INVESTIGATIONS AND INSPECTION OF PREMISES, §§58-79-1 to 58-79-45.
See FIRES AND FIRE PROTECTION.

FIRE LANES.
Parking prohibited, §20-162, (b).

FIREMEN'S AND RESCUE SQUAD WORKERS' PENSION FUND, §§58-86-1 to 58-86-91.
Administration of fund.
Appropriations for administrative expenses, §58-86-20.
Board of trustees to administer, §58-86-1.
Annexation.
Firemen whose residence is annexed by a city.
Monthly pensions upon retirement, §58-86-55.
Appropriations.
Administrative expenses of fund, §58-86-20.
Benefits.
Attachment.
Exemption of pensions from attachment, §58-86-90.
Deductions for payments to certain employees' or retirees' associations, §58-86-91.
Disabled members.
Totally and permanently disabled members entitled to monthly benefit, §58-86-55.
Garnishment.
Exemption of pensions from garnishment, §58-86-90.
Judgments.
Exemption of pensions from judgments, §58-86-90.
Lump-sum payments, §58-86-60.
Monthly pensions upon retirement, §58-86-55.
Nonassignable, §58-86-90.
Pro rata reduction of benefits.
When fund insufficient to pay in full, §58-86-65.
Board of trustees.
Administration of fund, §58-86-1.
Compensation, §58-86-5.
Creation, §58-86-5.
Duties, §58-86-10.
Lump-sum payments, §58-86-60.
Membership, §58-86-5.
Powers, §58-86-10.
Rules and regulations, §58-86-1.
Contributions to fund, §58-86-20.
Creditable service.
Determination, §58-86-75.
Information furnished by applicants for membership, §58-86-75.

FIREMEN'S AND RESCUE SQUAD WORKERS' PENSION FUND —Cont'd
Creditable service —Cont'd
Service in more than one department or squad.
Length of service not affected, §58-86-80.
Transfer from one department or squad to another, §58-86-80.
Custodian of fund.
State treasurer to be custodian, §58-86-20.
Deductions for payments to certain employees' or retirees' associations, §58-86-91.
Definitions, §58-84-5.
Eligible firemen, §58-86-25.
Eligible rescue squad worker, §58-86-30.
Office created, §58-86-15.
Director.
Office created, §58-86-15.
Disabled members.
Totally and permanently disabled member.
Monthly benefit, §58-86-55.
Eligible firemen, §58-86-25.
Eligible rescue squad worker, §58-86-30.
Establishment of fund, §58-86-1.
Expenditures, §58-86-20.
Legislative change.
Provisions subject to future legislative change, §58-86-70.
Lump-sum payments.
Board of trustees to direct payment and lump-sums in certain cases, §58-86-60.
Membership.
Additional retroactive membership, §58-86-45, (a) to (b).
Application for membership in fund, §§58-86-35, 58-86-40.
Information furnished by applicants for membership.
Determination of creditable service, §58-86-75.
Monthly payments by members, §§58-86-35, 58-86-40.
Rejoining fund.
Administrative fee, §58-86-50.
Retroactive membership.
Additional retroactive membership, §58-86-45, (a) to (b).
Monthly pensions upon retirement, §58-86-55.
Municipal corporations.
Council may provide for enrolling city employees, §160A-163, (a).
Firemen whose residence is annexed by a city, §58-86-55.
Payments by members.
Crediting payments to separate accounts of members, §§58-86-35, 58-86-40.
Delinquent payments.
Effect of member being six months delinquent, §58-86-85.
Monthly payments, §§58-86-35, 58-86-40.
Effect of member being six months delinquent, §58-86-85.
Rejoining fund.
Administrative fee, §58-86-50.
Pro rata reduction of benefits.
When fund insufficient to pay in full, §58-86-65.
Provisions subject to future legislative change, §58-86-70.
Retirement.
Monthly pensions upon retirement, §58-86-55.
Rules and regulations.
Board of trustees to make necessary rules and regulations, §58-86-1.

FIREMEN'S AND RESCUE SQUAD WORKERS' PENSION FUND —Cont'd
Secured transactions.
Third parties.
Assignments.
Restrictions on assignments, §§25-9-406, (i), 25-9-408, (f).
State auditor.
Transfer to department of state auditor, §143A-27.1.
State treasurer.
Custodian of fund, §58-86-20.
Volunteer firemen, §58-86-25.

FIREMEN'S RELIEF FUND, §§58-84-1 to 58-84-55.
Accounts and accounting.
Disbursement of funds by trustees.
Account of moneys received and disbursed to be kept, §58-84-40, (a) to (d).
Application of fund.
State appropriation, §58-85-1.
Appropriation by state.
Applicability of provisions, §58-85-25.
Application of fund, §58-85-1.
Applied to members of regular fire company, §58-85-25.
Treasurer of state firemen's association, §58-85-10.
Who shall participate, §58-85-15.
Bonds, surety.
Treasurer of state firemen's association.
State appropriation.
Bond to be given by treasurer, §58-85-10.
Trustees.
Treasurer of board of trustees, §58-84-30.
Certificate of eligibility, §58-84-46.
Definitions, §58-84-5.
Disbursement of funds.
Board of trustees to disburse, §58-84-35.
Account of moneys received and disbursed to be kept, §58-84-40, (a) to (d).
Discrimination.
No discrimination on account of race, §58-84-55.
Fire companies.
State appropriation.
Applied to members of regular fire company, §58-85-25.
State firemen's association.
Departments to be members of association, §58-84-50.
Firemen's and rescue squad workers' pension fund, §§58-86-1 to 58-86-91.
See FIREMEN'S AND RESCUE SQUAD WORKERS' PENSION FUND.
Insurance commissioner.
Certificate of eligibility, §58-84-46.
Treasurer of state firemen's association.
Payment of fund to treasurer by commissioner, §58-84-25.
Trustees.
Payment of fund to treasurer of local board of trustees, §58-84-25.
Participation in fund.
State appropriation.
Who shall participate, §58-85-15.
Reports.
Disbursement of funds by trustees.
Report of moneys received and disbursed to be filed, §58-84-40, (a) to (d).
Premiums collected and received from fire and lightning insurance business, §58-84-1.

FIREMEN'S RELIEF FUND —Cont'd
Reports —Cont'd
Treasurer of state firemen's association.
State appropriation.
Filing of report by treasurer, §58-85-10.
State appropriation.
Applicability of provisions, §58-85-25.
Application of fund, §58-85-1.
Fire companies.
Applied to members of regular fire company, §58-85-25.
Participation in fund.
Who shall participate, §58-85-15.
Treasurer of state firemen's association, §58-85-10.
State firemen's association.
Fire companies.
Departments to be members of association, §58-84-50.
Members, §58-85-20.
Treasurer.
Payment of fund to treasurer by commissioner, §58-84-25.
State appropriation.
Bond to be given by treasurer, §58-85-10.
Filing of report by treasurer, §58-85-10.
Volunteer firemen's association.
Payment of fund by treasurer to volunteer firemen's association, §58-85-30.
Taxation.
Payment and crediting of tax, §58-84-1.
Treasurer of state firemen's association.
Insurance commissioner.
Payment of fund to treasurer by commissioner, §58-84-25.
Trustees, §58-84-30.
Disbursement of funds, §58-84-35.
Account of moneys received and disbursed to be kept, §58-84-40, (a) to (d).
Insurance commissioner.
Payment of fund to treasurer of local board of trustees, §58-84-25.
Volunteer firemen's association, §58-85-30.

FIRE PATROLS.
Designated during season of drought, §113-55, (a).

FIRE PREVENTION INSPECTORS.
County inspection departments.
Generally, §§153A-350 to 153A-375.
See COUNTY INSPECTION DEPARTMENTS.

FIRE PROTECTION DISTRICTS.
County service districts.
Generally, §§153A-300 to 153A-310.
See COUNTY SERVICE DISTRICTS.
Rural fire protection districts.
Generally, §§69-25.1 to 69-25.17.
See RURAL FIRE PROTECTION DISTRICTS.

FIRE PROTECTION GRANT FUND.
Appropriations, §58-85A-1, (c).
Creation, §58-85A-1, (a).
Distributions, §58-85A-1, (b).

FIRE SALES, §§66-76 to 66-83.
See CLOSING-OUT SALES.

FIRES AND FIRE PROTECTION.
Alarms.
Giving false fire alarms, §14-286.
Molesting fire alarm, §14-286.
Annexation.
Rural fire protection districts.
Annexation by municipality furnishing fire protection, §69-25.15.

FIRES AND FIRE PROTECTION —Cont'd
Arrest.
Arson.
Power of attorney general, §58-79-1.
Arson, §§14-58 to 14-69.2.
See ARSON.
Assault with deadly weapon.
Firemen assaulted with deadly weapon, §14-34.2.
Boundaries.
Rural fire protection districts.
Changes in area of district, §69-25.11.
Brushlands.
Setting fire to grass, brushlands and woodlands, §§14-136 to 14-140.1.
Building codes.
Generally.
See BUILDING CODES.
Special safety to life requirements applicable to existing high-rise buildings, §143-138, (i).
Camp Butner hospital.
Contracts for fire protection, §122C-411.
Certain fires to be guarded by watchman, §14-140.1.
Child care facilities.
Mandatory standards for licensing, §110-91.
Visitation and inspection of centers, §110-92.
Commissioner of insurance.
Education.
Duties as to, §58-79-35.
Inspection of premises, §58-79-20.
Confidentiality of information.
Insurance.
Information furnished by insurance companies, §58-79-40, (d).
Contempt.
Investigations.
Failure to comply with summons or subpoena, §58-79-15.
Counties.
Fire fighting and prevention services, §153A-233.
Fire marshal.
Appointment, §153A-234.
Firemen's association.
Membership, §58-58-20.
Investigations.
County officers, §58-79-1.
Regulation of explosive, corrosive, inflammable or radioactive substances, §153A-128.
Rural fire protection districts, §§69-25.1 to 69-25.17.
Service districts generally, §§153A-300 to 153A-310.
Door lock provision of building code.
Exemption permit, §§58-79-22, 143-143.4.
Dormitory fire safety, §§116-44.6 to 116-44.8.
Education, §58-79-35.
Explosives.
See EXPLOSIVES.
Fire and rescue commission, §§58-78-1 to 58-78-20.
See FIRE AND RESCUE COMMISSION.
Fire departments.
See FIRE DEPARTMENTS.
Fire-detection systems.
Molesting systems, §14-286.
Fire-extinguishing systems.
Molesting systems, §14-286.
Fire hoses.
Driving over, §20-157, (d).
Fire hydrants.
Blocking prohibited, §20-157, (b).

FIRES AND FIRE PROTECTION —Cont'd
Fire lanes.
Parking prohibited, §20-162, (b).
Fire trucks and vehicles generally.
See FIRE TRUCKS AND VEHICLES.
Fireworks, §§14-410 to 14-414.
Forest fires.
Generally.
See FOREST FIRES.
Fraternities.
Supplemental fire safety protection system, §§116-44.6 to 116-44.8.
General assembly.
Evacuation of state legislative buildings and grounds, §120-32.1A.
Grass.
Setting fire to grass, §§14-136 to 14-140.1.
Hotels and other transient lodging places, §§58-81-5 to 58-81-15.
Building inspectors.
Powers and duties not limited, §58-81-15.
Careless or negligent setting of fires, §58-81-5.
Loss by fire.
Liability, §72-4.
Negligent or careless setting of fires, §58-81-5.
Noncompliance with provisions.
Penalty, §58-81-10.
Powers and duties of fire chiefs and building inspectors not limited, §58-81-15.
House trailers.
Two door requirement, §66-27.5.
Investigations, §§58-79-1 to 58-79-45.
Attorney general.
Authorized investigations, §58-79-1.
Forest fires.
Deputy investigators, §58-79-25.
Powers of attorney general, §§58-79-5, 58-79-10.
Right of entry, §58-79-10.
Subpoenas, §58-79-10.
Failure to comply.
Contempt, §58-79-15.
Witnesses.
Powers as to, §58-79-10.
Authorized, §58-79-1.
Combustible materials or flammable conditions, §58-79-20.
Contempt.
Failure to comply with summons or subpoena, §58-79-15.
County officers, §58-79-1.
Perjury.
False swearing, §58-79-10.
Police.
Chiefs of police, §58-79-1.
Preliminary investigation, §58-79-1.
Reports, §58-79-1.
Right of entry.
Attorney general, §58-79-10.
State bureau of investigation.
Attorney general acting through bureau, §58-79-1.
Subpoenas.
Failure to comply.
Contempt, §58-79-15.
Powers of attorney general, §58-79-10.
Witnesses.
Powers of attorney general as to, §58-79-10.
Landlord and tenant.
Agreements to rebuild.
Construction in case of fire, §42-9.
Willful destruction by tenant, §42-11.

FIRES AND FIRE PROTECTION —Cont'd
Leases.
Agreements to build.
Construction in case of fire, §42-9.
Matches, §§66-12 to 66-16.
Minors.
Exposing children to fire, §14-318.
Municipal corporations.
Fire limits, §§160A-435 to 160A-438.
Open fires regulation, §§113-60.21 to 113-60.31.
See OPEN FIRES.
Perjury.
Investigations.
False swearing to attorney general, §58-79-10.
Police.
Inspection of premises.
Chiefs of police, §58-79-20.
Investigations.
Chiefs of police, §58-79-1.
Public schools.
Course of study on fire prevention, §58-79-35.
Duty of principals, §115C-525, (a), (c).
Fire drills, §115C-288, (d).
Fire prevention day, §58-79-35.
Inspection of schools, §§115C-288, (d), 115C-525, (b).
Removal of hazards, §115C-525, (b).
Reports.
Commissioner of insurance.
Inspection of premises, §58-79-20.
Investigations, §58-79-1.
Right of entry.
Attorney general.
Investigations, §58-79-10.
Inspection of premises, §58-79-20.
Rural fire protection districts, §§69-25.1 to 69-25.17.
See RURAL FIRE PROTECTION DISTRICTS.
Safety professionals, §§90-671 to 90-674.
Sanitary districts.
Establishment of fire department, §130A-55.
Sororities.
Supplemental fire safety protection system, §§116-44.6 to 116-44.8.
State bureau of investigation.
Investigations.
Attorney general acting through bureau, §58-79-1.
State fire and rescue commission, §§58-78-1 to 58-78-20.
See FIRE AND RESCUE COMMISSION.
State volunteer fire department, §§58-80-1 to 58-80-60.
See VOLUNTEER FIRE DEPARTMENTS.
Streets and highways.
Pavement of driveways from state-maintained roads to rural fire district firehouses.
Powers of department of transportation, §136-18.
Subpoenas.
Investigations.
Failure to comply.
Contempt, §58-79-15.
Powers of attorney general, §58-79-10.
Transportation department.
Pavement of driveways from state-maintained roads to rural fire district firehouses.
Powers of department, §136-18.
Trees and timber.
Damages.
Unlawful setting on fire of timber, §1-539.1, (b).

FIRES AND FIRE PROTECTION —Cont'd
Trespass.
Crops.
Burning crops in the field, §14-141.
Setting fire to grass, brushlands and woodlands, §14-136.
Willfully or negligently setting fire to woods and fields, §14-137.
Universities and colleges.
Fraternities, sororities and residence halls.
Supplemental fire safety protection systems, §§116-44.6 to 116-44.8.
Volunteer fire department fund, §58-87-1.
Volunteer fire departments.
See VOLUNTEER FIRE DEPARTMENTS.
Weapons.
Assault with deadly weapon upon firemen, §14-34.2.
Witnesses.
Investigations.
Powers of attorney general, §58-79-10.
Woodland.
Setting fire to grass, brushlands and woodlands, §§14-136 to 14-140.1.

FIRE SPRINKLER CONTRACTORS.
Generally, §§87-16 to 87-27.1.
See PLUMBING, HEATING AND FIRE SPRINKLER CONTRACTORS.

FIRE TRUCKS AND VEHICLES.
Duty to drive with due regard for safety of others, §20-156, (b).
Following too closely, §20-157, (b), (c).
Highways.
Crossing median of divided highway.
When permitted, §20-140.3.
Horns and warning devices, §20-125, (b).
Siren must be audible within 1,000 feet, §§20-156, (b), 20-157, (a).
Siren necessary for right of way, §20-157, (a).
Lights.
Electronically modulated headlamps, §20-130, (d).
Red lights.
Exception to prohibition, §20-130.1, (b).
Parked or standing on roadway and giving warning signal.
Duties of driver approaching, §20-157, (f).
Right of way, §§20-156, (b), 20-157, (a).
Speed, §20-145.
Duty to drive with due regard for safety of others, §20-156, (b).
Traffic lights.
Preempting.
Local authority to permit, §20-169.

FIREWORKS.
Common carriers.
Not affected by fireworks provisions, §14-410, (a).
Definitions, §14-414.
Exceptions to definition of pyrotechnics, §14-414.
Delivery site.
Sale deemed made at site, §14-411.
Evidence.
Possession prima facie evidence of violation, §14-412.
Exhibitions.
Permitted fireworks at public exhibitions, §14-410, (a).
Use at public exhibitions requires permit, §14-413.

FIREWORKS —Cont'd
Manufacture of pyrotechnics.
Prohibited, §14-410, (a).
Minors.
Sale of pyrotechnics to minors, §14-410, (b).
Misdemeanor violations, §14-415.
Possession.
Prima facie evidence of violations, §14-412.
Public exhibitions.
Permits for use at public exhibitions, §14-413, (a).
Indoor use, §14-413, (b).
Permitted, §14-410, (a).
Sale of pyrotechnics.
Deemed at site of delivery, §14-411.
Prohibited, §14-410, (a).
Sale to minors prohibited, §14-410, (b).
State parks.
Special-use permit authorizing use of pyrotechnics in state parks, §113-35, (a1).
Use of pyrotechnics.
Prohibited, §14-410, (a).

FIRING EMPLOYEES.
Retaliatory employment discrimination, §§95-240 to 95-245.
See RETALIATORY EMPLOYMENT DISCRIMINATION.

FIRM OFFERS.
Leases, UCC, §25-2A-205.
Sale of goods, UCC, §25-2-205.

FIRST AID.
First aid or emergency treatment.
Limitation of liability, §90-21.14, (b).
Good Samaritan statutes.
Nonliability, §90-21.14, (a), (b).
Conflict of laws, §90-21.14, (c).
Mine safety and health.
Safety standards, §74-24.4, (b).
Motor vehicle accidents.
Non-liability in civil damages, §20-166, (d).

FIRST DEGREE ARSON, §14-58.

FIRST DEGREE BURGLARY, §§14-51, 14-52.

FIRST DEGREE CRIMINAL TRESPASS, §14-159.12.

FIRST DEGREE KIDNAPPING, §14-39, (b).

FIRST DEGREE MURDER, §14-17.
Capital punishment.
See CAPITAL PUNISHMENT.
Guilty plea.
Death penalty or life imprisonment, §15A-2001.

FIRST DEGREE PROSTITUTION, §§14-207, 14-208.

FIRST-DEGREE RAPE, §14-27.2.
Elements of offense, §14-27.2, (a).
Punishment, §14-27.2, (b).

FIRST-DEGREE SEXUAL EXPLOITATION OF MINOR, §14-190.16.
Electronic surveillance orders, §15A-290.

FIRST-DEGREE SEXUAL OFFENSE, §14-27.4.
Bail and recognizance, §15A-534.4.
Elements of offense, §14-27.4, (a).
Punishment, §14-27.4, (b).

FIRST FLIGHT CENTENNIAL COMMISSION.
Chair, §143-640, (e).
Commemoration activities, §143-641, (b).
Contracts, §143-641, (c).

FIRST FLIGHT CENTENNIAL COMMISSION —Cont'd
Duties, §143-641, (a).
Established, §143-640, (a).
Meetings, §143-640, (i).
Members, §143-640, (c).
Compensation, §143-640, (g).
Quorum, §143-640, (j).
Removal, §143-640, (h).
Terms, §143-640, (d).
Vacancies, §143-640, (f).
Office space, §143-642, (b).
Powers, §143-641, (a).
Contracts, §143-641, (c).
Property.
Assignment of property to commission, §143-642, (a).
Purpose, §143-640, (b).
Quorum, §143-640, (j).
Reports.
Annual report, §143-643, (a).
Final report, §143-643, (b).
Termination, §143-640, (k).
Vacancies, §143-640, (f).

FIRST IN AMERICA INNOVATIVE EDUCATION ACT, §116C-4.

FIRST IN FLIGHT LICENSE PLATES, §20-63, (b).

FIRST RESPONDERS.
Smallpox vaccination.
Sick leave and salary policy, time off due to adverse reaction, §160A-164.1.
Vaccination program.
Definitions, §130-485, (f).
Infectious disease exposure, §130-485, (a).
Medical waiver, §130-485, (c).
Notice requirements, §130-485, (e).
Priority in case of shortage, §130-485, (d).
Voluntary participation, §130-485, (b).

FIRST STOP EMPLOYMENT ASSISTANCE PROGRAM, §108A-29.

FISCAL CONTROL ACT.
Local government finance, §§159-1 to 159-188.
See LOCAL GOVERNMENT FINANCE.

FISCAL INFORMATION ON BILLS, RESOLUTIONS, OR RULES.
Local government fiscal information act, §§120-30.41 to 120-30.49.

FISCAL NOTES ON RULES.
Content, §150B-21.4, (b2).
Erroneous note, §150B-21.4, (c).
Local funds, §150B-21.4, (b).
State funds, §150B-21.4, (a).
Substantial economic impact, §150B-21.4, (b1).

FISCAL YEAR.
Agricultural.
Marketing authority, §106-532.
State fiscal year, §147-85.
Taxation.
Period of taxes, §105-241, (c).

FISH AND FISHING.
Accounts and accounting.
Marine fisheries commission.
Examination of accounts and books by state auditor, §113-257.
Actions.
Civil actions.
Dredging permits, §113-229.

FISH AND FISHING —Cont'd
Adverse possession of property subject to public trust rights.
No adverse possession, §1-45.1.
Appeals.
Dredging permits, §113-229.
Aquaculture development, §§106-756 to 106-760.
Aquariums.
North Carolina aquariums, §§143B-289.40 to 143B-289.44.
See NORTH CAROLINA AQUARIUMS.
Arrest.
Fees, §§113-222, 113-303.
Inspectors.
Arrest without warrant, §113-136, (d).
Search on arrest, §113-137, (a).
Service of arrest warrant, §113-136, (e).
Artificial reef marking devices.
Interference with, §113-266.
Assessments.
Promotion of coastal fisheries and seafood industry.
Alternative method for collection, §113-315.5.
Amount and basis, §113-314.
Collection, §§113-315.4, 113-315.5.
Levy and collection, §113-315.4.
Maximum assessment, §113-315.
Public interest, §113-311.
Refunds, §113-315.8.
Refusal to pay, §113-315.8.
Subsequent referenda where assessments adopted, §113-315.7.
Subsequent referenda where assessments defeated, §113-315.6.
Use of proceeds and other funds, §113-315.4.
Atlantic states marine fisheries compact, §§113-251 to 113-258.
Attorney general.
Legal counsel for agencies, §113-131, (d).
Audits and auditing.
Promotion of coastal fisheries and seafood industry, §113-315.9.
Seafood industrial park authority.
Oversight of state auditor, §113-315.35.
Bond issues.
Seafood industrial park authority, §113-315.31.
Bonds, surety.
Promotion of coastal fisheries and seafood industry.
Financial officers, §113-315.9, (a), (b).
Bridges.
Fishing from bridges.
Power to prohibit or regulate, §160A-302.1.
Buoys.
Damaging or injuring, §113-267.
Child support enforcement.
Forfeiture of licensing privilege, §50-13.12.
Closing forests and woodlands to fishing.
Authority of governor, §113-60.1.
Publication of proclamation, §113-60.2.
Violation of proclamation as misdemeanor, §113-60.3.
Coastal and estuarine commercial fishing licenses, §§113-168 to 113-173.
Advance sale of licenses, §113-168.1, (j).
Cancellation, §113-168.1, (i).
Definitions, §113-168.
Spotter plane, §113-171.1, (a).
Duration of licenses and endorsements, §113-168.1, (a).

FISH AND FISHING —Cont'd
Coastal and estuarine commercial fishing licenses —Cont'd
Exportation of fish and equipment.
Rules governing, §113-170.
False information, §113-168.1, (i).
Fees.
Fish dealers license, §113-169.3, (e), (f).
Land or sell license for vessel fishing beyond territorial waters, §113-169.5, (b).
Menhaden license for nonresidents not eligible for SCFL, §113-169.
Ocean fishing piers, §113-169.4, (c).
Payment of full annual license fee, §113-168.1, (a).
Recreational commercial gear license, §113-173, (e), (f).
Recreational fishing tournament license, §113-168.4, (c).
Retired standard commercial fishing license, §113-168.3, (b).
Spotter plane license, §113-171.1, (b).
Standard commercial fishing licenses, §113-168.2, (e).
Fish dealers license.
Application, §113-169.3, (b).
Replacement license, §113-169.3, (h).
Bait operations, §113-169.3, (f1).
Eligibility, §113-169.3, (a).
Fees, §113-169.3, (e), (f).
Finfish dealer license, §113-169.3, (f1).
Purchase and sale of fish, §113-169.3, (i).
Replacement license, §113-169.3, (h).
Requirement, §113-169.3, (c).
Exceptions, §113-169.3, (d).
Transfer prohibited, §113-169.3, (j).
Format, §113-168.1, (e).
Fraud or deception as to licenses, permits or records, §113-170.2, (a).
Fines, §113-170.2, (b).
Importation of fish and equipment.
Rules governing, §113-170.
Ineligibility, §113-168.1, (g).
Inspection.
Availability of licenses and endorsements for, §113-168.1, (c).
Issuance, §113-168.1, (f).
Land or sell license for vessel fishing beyond territorial waters, §113-169.5, (a).
Fees, §113-169.5, (b).
Licensed agents, §113-172, (a).
Compensation.
Surcharge, §113-172, (b).
Menhaden endorsements, §113-168.5, (c).
Menhaden license for nonresidents, §113-169.
Nonresidents.
Reciprocal agreements, §113-170.1.
Ocean fishing piers.
Fees, §113-169.4, (c).
Manager who secures license, §113-169.4, (d).
Required, §113-169.4, (a), (b).
Permits for gear, equipment and other specialized activities, §113-169.1.
Possession of fisheries resources.
Rules as to, §113-170.5.
Violations as to, §113-170.5.
Primary situs of vessel in state, §113-168.6, (a).
Prohibited acts with respect to, §113-170.5.
Reciprocity, §113-170.1.
Recordkeeping.
Confidentiality of records, §113-170.3, (c).
Fraud or deception as to records, §113-170.2.

FISH AND FISHING —Cont'd
Coastal and estuarine commercial fishing licenses —Cont'd
Recordkeeping —Cont'd
Refusal or neglect to keep records and accounts, §113-170.3, (b).
Requirements, §113-170.3, (a).
Recreational commercial gear license.
Assignment prohibited, §113-173, (h).
Authorized commercial gear, §113-173, (c).
Availability for inspection, §113-173, (g).
Exemptions, §113-173, (j).
Fees, §113-173, (e), (f).
Purchase, §113-173, (d).
Renewal, §113-173, (d).
Replacement license, §113-173, (e).
Reporting requirements, §113-173, (i).
Required, §113-173, (a).
Sale of fish prohibited, §113-173, (b).
Transfer prohibited, §113-173, (h).
Recreational fishing tournament license, §113-168.4, (c).
Registration of vessels with division, §113-168.6, (b).
Annual fee, §113-168.6, (c).
Expiration, §113-168.6, (d).
Place of registration, §113-168.6, (d).
Replacement, §113-168.6, (e).
Unlawful to use unregistered vessel, §113-168.6, (b).
Vessels with primary situs in state, §113-168.6, (a).
Renewal, §113-168.1, (f).
Replacement, §113-168.1, (h).
Required, §113-168.1, (b).
Fish dealers license, §113-169.3, (c), (d).
Recreational commercial gear license, §113-173, (a).
Standard commercial fishing licenses, §113-168.2, (a).
Residence.
No dual residency, §113-168.1, (d).
Retired standard commercial fishing license.
Applicability of SCFL provisions, §113-168.3, (a).
Assignment prohibited, §113-168.3, (d).
Eligibility, §113-168.3, (b).
Fees, §113-168.3, (b).
Transfer, §113-168.3, (c).
Rules as to possession, transportation and disposition, §113-170.4.
Sale of fish.
Nonprofit recreational fishing tournament.
Fish taken in connection with, §113-168.4, (c).
Requirements, §113-168.4, (a), (b).
Shellfish endorsement, §113-168.5, (d).
Shellfish license for North Carolina residents without SCFL.
Change in name or address, §113-169.2, (f).
Exempt persons, §113-169.2, (h).
Fee, §113-169.2, (c).
Inspection, availability, §113-169.2, (d).
Personal use, taking shellfish without license for, §113-169.2, (i).
Transfer prohibited, §113-169.2, (g).
Unlawful to take shellfish without license, §113-169.2, (a).
Shellfish taken without license for personal use, §113-169.2, (i).
Specialized activities.
Permits, §113-169.1.

FISH AND FISHING —Cont'd
Coastal and estuarine commercial fishing licenses —Cont'd
Spotter planes, §113-171.1, (b).
Defined, §113-171.1, (a).
Unlawful activities, §113-171.1, (c), (d).
Standard commercial fishing license.
Assignment, §113-168.2, (f).
Fees, §113-168.2, (e).
Identification as commercial fishermen, §113-168.2, (h).
Identification, license to serve as, §113-168.2, (h).
One vessel only to be in use, §113-168.2, (a1).
Recordkeeping by fish dealers, §113-168.2, (i).
Recordkeeping requirements, §113-168.2, (i).
Requirement, §113-168.2, (a).
Transfers, §113-168.2, (g).
Surrender of cancelled license, §113-168.1, (i).
Suspension or revocation, §113-171, (a), (b).
Administrative review, §113-171, (e).
Contested case, §113-171, (f).
Convictions which may not be considered, §113-171, (h).
Individuals in responsible positions of control.
Disclosure of identity, §113-171, (g).
Notice, §113-171, (d).
Reissuance, §113-171, (c).
Transportation of fisheries resources.
Prohibited acts as to, §113-170.5.
Rules as to, §113-170.5.
Coastal fisheries.
Monitoring water quality, §§130A-233, 130A-233.1, (a), (b).
Promotion of coastal fisheries and seafood industry, §§113-308 to 113-315.9.
See SEAFOOD INDUSTRY AND COASTAL FISHERIES PROMOTION.
Coastal habitat protection plans.
Department of environment and natural resources, §143B-279.8.
Coastal reserves, §113A-129.2, (a).
Coastal wetlands.
Orders to control activities, §113-230, (a), (b).
Dredging permits.
Powers and duties of department not repealed by section, §113-230, (h).
Eminent domain.
Taking fee of land order inapplicable to, §113-230, (g).
Recording copy, §113-230, (c).
Restraining violations, §113-230, (e).
Unreasonable exercise of police power, §113-230, (f).
Violations, §113-230, (b).
Commercial fishing.
Generally.
See COMMERCIAL FISHING.
Licenses.
Coastal and estuarine commercial fishing licenses, §§113-168 to 113-173.
Confiscation.
Proofs and instrumentalities of offenses in question, §113-137, (i).
Conflicts of interest.
Inspectors, §113-225.
Cooperative agreements.
Department of environment and natural resources.
Authority to enter into, §113-224.
Wildlife resources commission, §113-305.

FISH AND FISHING —Cont'd
Costs.
Replacement costs of resources, §113-267.
Councils.
Mid-Atlantic fishery management council.
North Carolina members, §113-260.
South Atlantic fishery management council.
North Carolina members, §113-259.
Counties.
Bridges.
Prohibition or regulation of fishing from bridges, §153A-242.
Creel limits.
Authority of commission to regulate, §113-292, (a).
Cultivation of shellfish, §§113-201 to 113-210.
See SHELLFISH.
Currituck county game commission.
Authority not repealed or abridged by limitation upon local regulations, §113-133.1, (d).
Dams.
Inspecting plans and specifications of dams, §113-263.
Keeping open fishways in dams, §113-293, (c).
Obstructing rivers or creeks.
Unlawful, §113-293.
Dare county game and wildlife commission.
Authority not repealed or abridged by limitation upon local regulations, §113-133.1, (d).
Definitions, §§113-127 to 113-130.
Activities of public, §113-130.
Agencies, §113-128.
Powers, §113-128.
Application of article, §113-127.
Coastal and estuarine commercial fishing licenses, §113-168.
Spotter plane, §113-171.1, (a).
Dredging.
Permits, §113-229, (n).
Fishermen's economic development program, §113-315.17.
Marine, estuarine and wildlife resources, §113-129.
Marine fisheries compact, §113-251.
Promotion of coastal fisheries and seafood industry, §113-308.
Public activities, §113-130.
Public trust resources, §113-131, (e).
Resources, §113-129.
Department of environment and natural resources.
Administrative authority, §113-226, (a).
Adoption of federal regulations, §113-228.
Cooperative agreements, §113-224.
Duties.
Generally, §113-181, (a).
Requirement to carry out duties, §113-181, (b).
Fishery management plans, §113-182.1.
Powers, §§113-131, (b), 113-226, (a).
Generally, §113-181, (a).
Proclamations, §113-221.1.
Rules and regulations, §113-221.
Taking fish in manner prohibited.
Authority, §113-261, (c).
Disabled sportsman program, §113-296.
Discharge of oil or hazardous substances.
Damage to fish, liability, §143-215.90, (a) to (c).
Dolphins.
Protection of porpoises, §113-189, (b).
Drainage districts.
Conservation and replacement of fish and wildlife habitat, §156-69.

FISH AND FISHING —Cont'd
Dredging permits, §113-229.
Drugs.
Taking fish by drugs.
Permits issued by department and commission authorizing, §113-261, (b).
Prohibited, §113-262, (a), (b).
Eastern Band of the Cherokee Indians.
Inapplicability of license provisions, §113-276, (l).
Electricity.
Taking fish by electricity.
Permits issued by department and commission authorizing, §113-261, (b).
Prohibited, §113-262, (a), (b).
Eminent domain.
Coastal wetlands, orders to control activities.
Taking fee of land order inapplicable to, §113-230, (g).
Seafood industrial park authority, §113-315.32.
Enjoyment of marine and estuarine resources, §113-133.
Equipment.
Authority of commission to regulate, §113-292, (a).
Evidence.
Possession of illegally killed fish as evidence, §113-262, (b).
Replacement costs of resources, §113-267.
Unlawful possession of game fish, §113-302, (a).
Warning tickets not to constitute evidence of commission of offense, §113-140, (g).
Executive budget act.
Atlantic states marine fisheries commission.
Applicability of provisions, §113-258.
Explosives.
Taking fish by explosives.
Permits issued by department and commission authorizing, §113-261, (b).
Prohibited, §113-262, (a), (b).
Federal laws and regulations.
Adoption by wildlife resources commission, §113-307.
Legislative assent to specific federal acts, §113-307.1.
Fees.
Arrest, §§113-222, 113-303.
Coastal and estuarine commercial fishing licenses.
Fish dealer's license, §113-169.3, (e), (f).
Land or sell license for vessel fishing beyond territorial waters, §113-169.5, (b).
Menhaden license for nonresidents not eligible for SCFL, §113-169.
Ocean fishing piers, §113-169.4, (c).
Payment of full annual license fee, §113-168.1, (a).
Recreational commercial gear license, §113-173, (e), (f).
Recreational fishing tournament license, §113-168.4, (c).
Retired standard commercial fishing license, §113-168.3, (b).
Spotter plane license, §113-171.1, (b).
Standard commercial fishing licenses, §113-168.2, (e).
Inland fishing licenses, §113-271, (d).
Licenses.
Combination hunting and fishing licenses, §113-270.1C, (b).
Disposition of license funds, §113-306.
Fishing guides, §113-270.4.
Government-owned property.
Collecting fees for licenses for fishing on, §113-39.

FISH AND FISHING —Cont'd
Fees —Cont'd
Licenses —Cont'd
Inland fishing licenses, §113-271, (d).
Service of process, §§113-222, 113-303.
State forests and parks.
Collection of reasonable fees by department of environment and natural resources, §113-35, (b).
Witnesses, §§113-222, 113-303.
Felony convictions.
Forfeiture of licensing privilege after conviction of felony, §15A-1331A.
Fines.
Coastal and estuarine commercial fishing licenses.
Fraud or deception as to licenses, permits or records, §113-170.2, (b).
Refusal to stop in obedience to directions of inspector or director, §113-136, (j).
Fish-cultural stations.
U.S. acquisition of land for, §104-1.
Fishermen's economic development program, §§113-315.15 to 113-315.19.
Fishery management plans.
Achieving sustainable harvest under plan, §113-182.1, (g).
Advisory council, §113-182.1, (c).
Consultation with regional advisory committees regarding preparation, §113-182.1, (c1).
Generally, §113-182.1, (a), (b).
Limiting participation in fishery, recommending to general assemblies, §113-182.1, (g).
Monitoring of progress, §113-182.1, (e).
Revision, §113-182.1, (d).
Rules to implement, §113-182.1, (f).
Fishery resource grant program.
Application for grant, §113-200, (d).
Award process, §113-200, (f).
Creation, §113-200, (a).
Grants committee, §113-200, (e1).
Priorities, §113-200, (b).
Reports, §113-200, (h), (i).
Restrictions on grants, §113-200, (g).
Review process, §113-200, (e).
Soliciting proposals, procedure, §113-200, (c).
Fishing guide licenses.
Fees, §113-270.4, (b).
Nonresidents, §113-270.4, (a).
Qualifications and duties, §113-270.4, (c).
Required, §113-270.4, (a).
Fish inspectors and protectors.
See FISH INSPECTORS AND PROTECTORS.
Fish kills.
Discharge of oil or hazardous substances.
Liability, §143-215.90, (a) to (c).
Fish restoration and management projects.
Legislative assent to federal acts, §113-307.1, (c).
Fishways.
Keeping open fishways in dams, §113-293, (c).
Forests and forestry.
Governor.
Authority of governor to close forests and woodlands to hunting, fishing and trapping, §113-60.1.
Publication of proclamation, §113-60.2.
Annulment thereof, §113-60.2.
Violation of proclamation a misdemeanor, §113-60.3.
Forfeiture of licensing privilege after conviction of felony, §15A-1331A.

FISH AND FISHING —Cont'd
Forfeiture of licensing privilege for failure to pay child support, §50-13.12.
Fraud.
Coastal and estuarine commercial fishing licenses, §113-170.2.
Free fishing day.
July fourth, §113-276, (m).
Funds.
Administration of funds, §113-226, (b), (c).
General assembly.
Joint legislative commission on seafood and aquaculture, §§120-70.60 to 120-70.66.
Guides.
Licenses, §113-270.4.
Harassment.
Unlawful harassment of persons taking wildlife resources, §113-295.
Hatchery or other aquaculture operation.
Obstructing or polluting flow of water into hatcheries, §113-265, (a).
Robbing or injuring.
Destroying or injuring aquaculture facility, §113-269, (d).
Misdemeanors, §113-269, (e), (f).
Notarized written authorization for taking, §113-269, (h).
Receiving or possessing fish or aquatic species stolen from aquaculture facility, §113-269, (c).
Restitution to victim, §113-269, (g).
Shellfish lease defined, §113-269, (a).
Taking fish or aquatic species being cultivated or reared by owner, §113-269, (b).
Hearings.
Coastal wetlands.
Orders to control activities, §113-230, (b).
Dredging permits, §113-229.
Hook-and-line licenses, §113-271.
Hull insurance, protection and indemnity clubs, §§58-20-1 to 58-20-40.
See HULL INSURANCE, PROTECTION AND INDEMNITY CLUBS.
Income tax credit.
Donations of real property for fish and wildlife conservation, §105-151.12.
Injunctions.
Buoys, nets, markers, stakes, etc.
Robbing or injuring, §113-268, (e).
Encroachment upon, usurpation or otherwise violating public trust rights of people, §113-131, (c).
Interference with taking of wildlife resources, §113-295, (b).
Inland fishing licenses.
Generally.
See FISHING LICENSES.
Inspections.
Jurisdiction of fisheries agencies generally.
Seafood industrial park authority, §113-315.34.
Licensed or commercial premises, §113-302.1.
Inspectors and protectors.
See FISH INSPECTORS AND PROTECTORS.
Insurance.
Hull insurance, protection and indemnity clubs.
See HULL INSURANCE, PROTECTION AND INDEMNITY CLUBS.
July fourth.
Free fishing day, §113-276, (m).
Jurisdiction of fisheries agencies.
Seafood industrial park authority, §113-315.34.

FISH AND FISHING —Cont'd
Jurisdiction of marine fisheries commission.
Marine resources in Atlantic Ocean, §113-134.1.
Jurisdiction of marine fisheries inspectors, §113-136, (b).
Law enforcement officers.
Jurisdiction of fishing agencies not limitation on officers authority, §113-132, (f).
Licenses.
Commercial fishing.
Coastal and estuarine commercial fishing licenses, §§113-168 to 113-173.
Generally.
See FISHING LICENSES.
Local coastal laws.
Abolition, §113-133.
Local regulation of wildlife resources.
Abolition of local coastal fishing laws, §113-133.
Limitations upon, §113-133.1, (c).
Repeal generally.
Of special, local and private acts, §113-133.1, (b).
Repeal specifically of local acts, §113-133.1, (g).
Retention of specific local acts or portions of local acts, §113-133.1, (e).
Review by wildlife resources commission of local acts, §113-133.1, (f).
Magistrates.
Powers in cases involving fishing offenses, §7A-273.
Marine and estuarine resources belong to people of state, §113-131, (a).
Marine fisheries commission.
Generally, §§143B-289.50 to 143B-289.61.
See MARINE FISHERIES COMMISSION.
Marine fisheries compact, §§113-251 to 113-257.
Marine fisheries endowment fund, §143B-289.58.
Mid-Atlantic fishery management council.
North Carolina members.
Number of members from state, §113-260, (a).
Principal state official with marine fishery management responsibility, first council member, §113-260, (b).
Selection of other members from state, §113-260, (c).
Migrant farm workers.
Resident privileges, §113-276, (j).
Misdemeanors.
Buoys, nets, markers, stakes, etc.
Robbing or injuring, §113-268, (b).
Coastal wetlands.
Orders to control activities, §113-230, (d).
Seized property left with defendant.
Willful failure or inexcusable neglect, §113-137, (f).
Violations of provisions or rules of marine fisheries commission, §113-135, (a) to (c).
Monitoring water quality of coastal fishing waters, §§130A-233, 130A-233.1, (a), (b).
Motor vehicles.
Temporary stops by inspectors or protectors, §113-136, (f), (g), (j).
Nets.
Bow nets.
Use by other than licensee, §113-276, (g).
Destroying or damaging, §113-268, (b) to (e).
Landing nets.
Special device license not required, §113-276, (f).
Obstructing rivers or creeks.
Unlawful, §113-293.

FISH AND FISHING —Cont'd
Nets —Cont'd
Taking fish from nets to use as bait without owner's permission, §113-268, (a), (d), (e).
Nonresidents.
Coastal and estuarine commercial fishing licenses.
Reciprocal agreements, §113-170.1.
Fishing guide licenses, §113-270.4, (a).
North Carolina aquariums, §§143B-289.40 to 143B-289.44.
See NORTH CAROLINA AQUARIUMS.
Notice.
Coastal wetlands.
Orders to control activities, §113-230.
Promotion of coastal fisheries and seafood industry.
Referenda, §113-314.
Nuisance zoological or botanical species.
Authority of commission to regulate, §113-292, (d).
Nurseries.
Obstructing or polluting flow of water into nurseries, §113-265, (a).
Obstructing rivers or creeks, §113-293.
Ocean fishing piers.
Fishing near piers, §113-185, (a).
Opening and closing seasons.
Authority of commission to regulate, §113-292, (b).
Orders.
Coastal wetlands.
Control of activities, §113-230, (a), (b).
Oysters and clams generally.
See SHELLFISH.
Peace officers.
Inspectors granted powers of, §113-136, (a).
Penalties.
Coastal wetlands.
Orders to control activities, §113-230.
Dredging permits.
Violations, §113-229.
Taking fish by illegal means, §113-262, (a), (b).
Unlawful possession, transportation and sale of fish, §113-183, (a), (b).
Permits.
Administrative control of permittees, §113-276.2.
Dredging, §113-229.
Drugs, electricity, explosives or poisons.
Authorizing fish to be taken by use of, §113-261, (b).
Major and minor developments.
Issuance, §113-229, (c1).
Suspension or revocation by courts, §113-277.
Pesticide use, §113-300.1.
Petitions.
Coastal wetlands, orders to control activities.
Order constituting equivalent of taking without compensation, §113-230, (f).
Piers.
Fishing near piers, §113-185, (a).
Poisons and pesticides.
Taking fish by poisons.
Permits issued by department and commission authorizing, §113-261, (b).
Prohibited, §113-262, (a), (b).
Use, §113-300.1.
Pollution control.
Hatcheries.
Obstructing or polluting flow of water into hatcheries, §113-265, (a).
Throwing fish offal into waters, §113-265, (b).
Porpoises.
Protection of porpoises, §113-189, (b).

FISH AND FISHING —Cont'd
Posted property.
Trespassing upon posted property, §§14-159.6 to 14-159.10.
See TRESPASS.
Private ponds.
Regulation of fish in connection with.
Authority of commission, §113-292, (c).
Property of another.
Hunting and fishing on registered property of another, §§113-281 to 113-287.
Hunting, fishing or trapping on posted property, §§14-159.6 to 14-159.10.
Protectors of fish.
See FISH INSPECTORS AND PROTECTORS.
Public lands.
Fishing licenses.
Fees.
Collecting fees for licenses for fishing on government-owned property, §113-39.
Nonresidents of counties in which state lakes are situated, §146-19.
Public trust resources.
Defined, §113-131, (e).
Public trust rights, no adverse possession, §1-45.1.
Real property.
Seafood industrial park authority.
Approval of acquisition and disposition, §113-315.30.
Exchange of property, §113-315.33.
Reciprocity.
Agreements generally, §113-223.
Coastal and estuarine commercial fishing licenses, §113-170.1.
Licenses, §113-304.
Recordation.
Coastal wetlands, orders to control activities.
Copies of order, §113-230, (c).
Records.
Coastal and estuarine commercial fishing licenses, §§113-170.2, 113-170.3.
Referenda.
Promotion of coastal fisheries and seafood industry.
Agency to determine time and place, §113-314.
Application to marine fisheries commission for authority to conduct, §113-312.
Action of commission on application, §113-313.
Arrangements for and management of referenda, §113-315.1.
Ballots.
Mail ballot or box ballot, §113-315.2.
Preparation and distribution, §113-315.3.
Canvass and declaration of results, §113-315.3.
Conduct, §113-315.3.
Expenses, §113-315.1.
Mail ballot or box ballot, §113-315.2.
Notice, §113-314.
Preparation and distribution of ballots, §113-315.3.
Public interest, §113-311.
Subsequent referenda where assessments adopted, §113-315.7.
Subsequent referenda where assessments defeated, §113-315.6.
Voting, §113-315.2.
Refunds.
Promotion of coastal fisheries and seafood industry.
Assessments, §113-315.8.

FISH AND FISHING —Cont'd
Reports.
Marine fisheries commission, §113-257.
Recommendations for legislative action, §113-257.
Restitution.
Robbing or injuring hatcheries and other aquaculture operation, §113-269, (g).
Restraint of trade.
Promotion of coastal fisheries and seafood industry.
Certain activities not to be deemed illegal or in restraint of trade, §113-310.
Restrictions, new rules, adopting.
Notification to public, §113-301.1, (c), (d).
Revisions of subchapter.
General statement of purpose and effect, §113-316.
Rules and regulations.
Adoption, §§113-221, (a), 113-228.
Affected persons to keep themselves informed, §113-221, (f).
Copies, §113-221, (b).
Effective dates, §113-221, (d).
Federal laws and regulations.
Adoption, §113-307.
Legislative assent to specific federal acts, §113-307.1.
Judicial notice of codification of regulations, §113-221, (g).
Notification to members of general public.
New laws and rules affecting public, §113-301.1.
Penalties for violations, §113-187.
Publication, §113-221, (c).
Wildlife resources commission.
Violations as misdemeanors, §113-135, (a) to (c).
Sales and use tax.
Commercial fishermen.
Exemptions, §105-164.13.
Wildlife resources fund.
Transfer of taxes on hunting and fishing supplies and equipment, §105-164.44B.
Sales of fish.
See FISH SALES.
Saltwater fishing fund, §§113-175 to 113-175.4.
Administrative and operating expenses.
Percentage or amount allocated to, §113-175.3, (c).
Applicants for money from fund.
Eligibility, §113-175.3, (b).
Board of trustees.
Chair.
Appointment by governor, §113-175.2, (c).
Established, §113-175.2, (a).
Investment income disbursed upon board direction, §113-175.3, (a).
Locations for purchase and renewal of saltwater fishing licenses.
Designation by board, §113-175.3, (f).
Meetings, §113-175.2, (f).
Membership, qualifications, §113-175.2, (b).
Per diem and expenses, §113-175.2, (g).
Real property.
Acquisition, §113-175.3, (d).
Management, §113-175.3, (e).
Report to joint legislative committee on seafood and aquaculture.
Submission by chair, §113-175.4.
Rules, adoption, §113-175.3, (g).
Terms of members, §113-175.2, (d).
Vacancies, §113-175.2, (e).

FISH AND FISHING —Cont'd
Saltwater fishing fund —Cont'd
Board of trustees —Cont'd
Vice-chair.
Election by members, term, §113-175.2, (c).
Definitions, §113-175.
Disbursement of investment income, §113-175.3, (a).
Established as nonreverting fund, §113-175.1.
Held separate and apart, §113-175.1.
Investment of assets, §113-175.1.
Locations for purchase and renewal of saltwater fishing licenses.
Designation by board, §113-175.3, (f).
Purpose, §113-175.1.
Real property.
Acquisition, §113-175.3, (d).
Management, §113-175.3, (e).
Revenues included in fund, §113-175.1.
Salt water fishing license, §§113-174 to 113-174.2.
Scrap fishing.
Measures for fish scrap and oil, §113-186.
Prohibited, §113-185, (b).
Seafood.
Promotion of coastal fisheries and seafood industry, §§113-308 to 113-315.9.
Shellfish generally.
See SHELLFISH.
Seafood industry promotion.
Generally, §§113-308 to 113-315.9.
See SEAFOOD INDUSTRY AND COASTAL FISHERIES PROMOTION.
Searches and seizures.
Exhibiting upon request by inspector of items required to be carried, §113-136, (k).
Search on arrest by inspector or protector, §113-137, (a).
Seizure of lawfully discovered evidence by inspectors or protectors, §113-137, (b), (c).
Leaving property in possession of defendant, §113-137, (f).
Return to owner, §113-137, (h).
Safeguarding pending trial, §113-137, (a).
Sale of perishable or seasonable fish prior to trial, §113-137, (g).
Sale of seized property, §113-137, (i) to (k).
Summary disposition of live or perishable fish or wildlife, §113-137, (d).
Service of search warrants by inspectors and protectors, §113-136, (e).
Temporary stops by inspectors or protectors, §113-136, (f), (g), (j).
Unreasonable searches and seizures prohibited, §113-136, (l).
Seasons.
Authority of commission to regulate, §113-292, (a), (b).
Sea turtles.
Protection of sea turtles, §113-189, (a).
Service of process.
Fees, §§113-222, 113-303.
Service by inspectors and protectors.
Arrest warrants, search warrants, orders for arrest, etc., §113-136, (e).
Shellfish.
General provisions.
See SHELLFISH.
Size limits.
Authority of commission to regulate, §113-292, (a).
South Atlantic fishery management council.
North Carolina members.
Number of members from state, §113-259, (a).

FISH AND FISHING —Cont'd
South Atlantic fishery management council —Cont'd
North Carolina members —Cont'd
Principal state official with marine fishery management responsibility, first council member, §113-259, (b).
Selection of other members from state, §113-259, (c).
Special conservation officers.
Jurisdiction and powers generally, §113-138, (d).
Law enforcement powers, §113-138, (a).
Limitation on exercise of authority, §113-138, (b).
Specification of particular officers or class of officers upon whom powers conferred, §113-138, (c).
Standard weight and measure, §81A-42.
State auditor.
Marine fisheries commission.
Examination of accounts and books by auditor, §113-257.
State fish.
Channel bass, §145-6.
State forests and parks.
Collection of reasonable fees by department of environment and natural resources, §113-35, (b).
Statutes.
Repeal of certain public, public-local, special and private acts, §113-377.8.
Striped bass.
Suspending or extending hook and line season.
Authority of commission, §113-292, (c1).
Subpoenas.
Service by inspectors or protectors, §113-136, (e).
Taking of land without compensation.
Coastal wetlands, orders to control activities, §113-230, (f).
Taxation.
Seafood industrial park authority.
Exemptions from taxation, §§113-315.31, 113-315.39.
Transitional provisions.
Purpose of effect of revisions, §113-316.
Transportation of fish.
Unlawful transportation, §113-183, (a), (b).
Trash fishing.
Prohibited, §113-185, (b).
Trespass.
Hunting, fishing or trapping on "posted" property, §§14-159.6 to 14-159.10.
Trout licenses.
Public mountain trout waters, §113-272, (a) to (d).
Turtles.
Protection of sea turtles, §113-189, (a).
United States agencies.
Taking fish in manner prohibited.
Authority, §113-261, (c).
Unlawful possession of game fish.
Prima facies evidence possession for purposes of resale, §113-302, (a).
Unlawful possession, transportation and sale of fish, §113-183, (a), (b).
U.S. fish and wildlife service officers.
Authorized to enforce criminal laws, §15A-406.
Venue.
Buoys, nets, markers, stakes, etc.
Robbing or injuring.
Injunctive relief to restrain, §113-268, (e).
Violations.
Commercial fishing violations, §113-187.

FISH AND FISHING —Cont'd
Violations —Cont'd
Unlawful possession, transportation and sale of fish, §113-183, (a), (b).
Warning tickets.
Accounting for and recording of tickets, §113-140, (e).
Conditions for issuance, §113-140, (c).
Evidence of commission of offense.
Tickets not to constitute, §113-140, (g).
Inappropriate issuance, §113-140, (d).
Issuance by inspectors or protectors, §113-140, (a).
Powers of inspectors, protectors or law enforcement officers not restricted, §113-140, (f).
Standards for issuance, §113-140, (b).
Water and air resources, §§143-211 to 143-215.9B.
See WATER AND AIR RESOURCES.
Water quality of coastal fishing waters.
Monitoring water quality, §§130A-233, 130A-233.1, (a), (b).
Watersheds of navigable streams, protection of.
Legislative assent to specific federal acts, §113-307.1, (a).
Weights and measures.
Fish scrap and oil, §113-186.
Wildlife protectors.
Enforcement authority generally, §113-136.
Jurisdiction, §113-136, (c).
Wildlife resources commission.
Administrative authority, §113-306, (a).
Authority in regulating inland fishing, §113-292, (a) to (e).
Cooperative agreements, §113-305.
Delegation of powers, §113-306, (c).
Federal laws and regulations.
Adoption, §113-307.
Jurisdiction, §113-132.
Notification to public affected by laws and rules, §113-301.1.
Poisons and pesticides.
Use, §113-300.1.
Powers, §113-131, (b).
Reciprocal agreements, §113-304.
Rules and regulations.
Violations as misdemeanors, §113-135, (a) to (c).
Taking fish in manner prohibited.
Authority, §113-261, (c).
Wildlife resources fund.
Sales and use taxes.
Transfer of taxes on hunting and fishing supplies and equipment, §105-164.44B.
Wildlife restoration projects.
Legislative assent to specific federal acts, §113-307.1, (b).
Witnesses.
Fees, §§113-222, 113-303.

FISHERMEN'S ECONOMIC DEVELOPMENT PROGRAM, §§113-315.15 to 113-315.19.
Authorization to establish, §113-315.18.
Citation of article, §113-315.15.
Definitions, §113-315.17.
Establishment authorized, §113-315.18.
Legislative findings, §113-315.16.
Personnel needs, §113-315.19.
Purpose of article, §113-315.16.
Short title, §113-315.15.

FISHING GUIDES.
Licenses, §113-270.4.

FISHING LICENSES.
Child support enforcement.
Forfeiture of privilege, §50-13.12.
Suspension or revocation of fishing licenses.
Delinquent obligors or individuals not in compliance with orders, §§110-142, 110-142.2.
Coastal and estuarine commercial fishing licenses, §§113-168 to 113-173.
Collection licenses.
Issuance by wildlife resources commission, §113-272.4, (a).
Assistants in taking, utilization by licensees, authorization, §113-272.4, (e).
Authority delegated to executive director, §113-272.4, (b).
Duration period, §113-272.4, (c).
Fee, §113-272.4, (c).
Restrictions imposed, §113-272.4, (d).
Combination hunting and fishing licenses, §113-270.1C, (a), (b).
Commercial fishing.
Coastal and estuarine commercial fishing licenses, §§113-168 to 113-173.
Duration of validity, §113-270.1B, (b).
Eastern Band of the Cherokee Indians.
Inapplicability of license provisions to, §113-276, (l).
Exemptions and exceptions, §113-276, (c) to (m).
Fees.
Collection licenses, §113-272.4, (c).
Combination hunting and fishing licenses, §113-270.1C, (b).
Disposition of license funds, §113-306.
Fishing guides, §113-270.4.
Government-owned property.
Collecting fees for licenses for fishing on, §113-39.
Inland fishing licenses, §113-271, (d).
Lifetime licenses.
Administrative fee for issuing, §113-272.3, (d).
Salt water fishing license, §113-174.2, (c).
Special device license, §113-272.2, (c).
Special trout license, §113-272, (d).
Felony convictions.
Forfeiture of privilege after conviction, §15A-1331A.
Free fishing day.
Fourth day of July, §113-276, (m).
Guides, §113-270.4.
Hook-and-line license, §113-271.
Inland fishing licenses.
Administrative control over licensees and permittees.
Applicability of section, §113-276.2, (a).
Investigations of person subject to administrative control, §113-276.2, (i).
Notice upon refusing to issue or reissue, §113-276.2, (d).
Orders placing restrictions on licensees or permittees, §113-276.2. (j).
Reapplication after refusal of issuance or reissuance, §113-276.2, (h).
Refusal to issue, §113-276.2, (b).
Reissuance review, §113-276.2, (c).
Return upon revocation, §113-276.2, (g).
Revocation, §113-276.2, (e).

FISHING LICENSES —Cont'd
Inland fishing licenses —Cont'd
Bow nets.
Use by other than licensee, §113-276, (g).
Collection licenses, §113-272.4.
Conviction of suspension offense.
Mandatory suspension of license or permit, §113-276.3.
Discretionary revocation or suspension of license or permit by court, §113-277, (a), (a1).
Concurrent or consecutive suspension, §113-277, (a2).
Conviction defined, §113-277, (a3).
Criminal offenses during period of suspension or revocation, §113-277, (b).
Surrender of license or permit, §113-277, (a4).
Exemptions and exceptions, §113-276, (c) to (m).
Fees, §113-271, (d).
Felony convictions.
Forfeiture of privilege after conviction, §15A-1331A.
General provisions respecting licenses and permits issued by wildlife resources commission, §113-275.
Hook-and-line licenses.
Fees, §113-271, (d).
Requirements generally, §113-271, (a).
Landing nets, §113-272.3, (b).
Special device license not required, §113-276, (f).
Lawfully authorized techniques, §113-272.3, (a).
Lifetime licenses, §113-272.3, (c), (d).
Mandatory suspension of license or permit.
Conviction of suspension offense, §113-276.3, (a).
Beginning of period of suspension, §113-276.3, (a).
Discretionary court suspension supersedes section's provisions, §113-276.3, (e).
Offenses requiring suspension, §113-276.3, (d).
Period of suspension, §113-276.3, (d).
Reporting convictions and suspensions, §113-276.3, (c).
Surrender of licenses and permits, §113-276.3, (b).
Permits.
Suspension or revocation.
Discretionary revocation or suspension by court, §113-277.
Mandatory suspension for offenses, §113-276.3.
Regulatory authority of commission as to requirements and exemptions, §113-276.1.
Requirements generally, §113-271, (a).
Revocation or suspension of license or permit.
Discretionary revocation or suspension by court, §113-277.
Mandatory suspension for conviction of offense, §113-276.3.
Special device licenses, §113-272.2, (a), (c).
Special trout licenses, §113-272, (a) to (d).
Trout licenses.
Mountain trouts waters, §113-272, (a) to (d).
July fourth.
Free fishing day, §113-276, (m).
License agents.
Informational materials prepared by commission.
Distribution to agents, §113-301.1, (a).
Mail, issuance by.
Information on laws and regulations applicable to type of license.
Furnishing licensee, §113-301.1, (b).

FISHING LICENSES —Cont'd
Marine fisheries commission.
Authority generally, §113-182, (a), (b).
Migrant farm workers.
Resident privileges, §113-276, (j).
Natural bait users.
Exemption from license requirement, §113-276, (e).
Probation.
Purchase of certain licenses as condition, §15A-1343, (b1).
Required, §113-270.1B, (a).
Salt water fishing license, §§113-174 to 113-174.2.
Assignment or transfer of license.
Prohibition, §113-174.1, (c).
Biological sampling and survey programs.
Licensed person to comply, §113-174.1, (g).
Cancellation, §113-174.1, (f).
Definitions, §113-174.
Designated offices.
Purchase or renewal at, §113-174.2, (b).
Locations designated by saltwater fishing fund board of trustees, §113-175.3, (f).
Fees, types of licenses, §113-174.2, (c).
Individuals on charterboat or headboat engaged in recreational fishing.
License required, §113-174.1, (e).
Name and address, providing.
Request from inspector or law enforcement, §113-174.1, (d).
Persons 18 or younger enrolled in school.
Exemption, §113-174.2, (d).
Required for recreational fishing in coastal waters, §§113-174.1, (a), 113-174.2, (a).
Recreational fishing defined, §113-174.
Sale of fish caught.
License does not authorize, §113-174.1, (b).
Separation of revenues.
Precondition for receiving funds under cooperative program, §113-307.1, (d).
Special device licenses.
Inland fishing licenses, §113-272.2, (a), (c).
Suspension, revocation and reissuance.
Conviction of suspension offense, §113-276.3.
Discretionary revocation or suspension by court, §113-277.
Mandatory suspension, §113-276.3.
Trout licenses.
Mountain trout waters, §113-272, (a) to (d).

FISH INSPECTORS AND PROTECTORS.
Arrest warrants, search warrants, orders for arrest.
Service by inspectors, §113-136, (e).
Arrest without warrant, §113-136, (b).
Conflicts of interest, §113-225.
Exhibiting upon request items required to be carried, §113-136, (k).
Jurisdiction, §113-136, (b).
Peace officer powers, §113-136, (a).
Searches within cartilage or living quarters of vessel.
Unreasonable searches and seizures prohibited, §113-136, (l).
Search on arrest, §113-137, (a).
Seizure of lawfully discovered evidence, §113-137, (b), (c).
Leaving in possession of defendant, §113-137, (f).
Return of property to owner, §113-137, (h).
Safeguarding pending trial, §113-137, (e).
Sale of perishable fish prior to trial, §113-137, (g).

FISH INSPECTORS AND PROTECTORS —Cont'd
Seizure of lawfully discovered evidence —Cont'd
Summary disposition of live or perishable fish or wildlife, §113-137, (d).
Stopping temporarily persons or motor vehicles, §113-136, (f), (g), (j).
Warning tickets, §113-140.
Warrantless arrests, §113-136, (a).

FISH KILLS.
Discharge of oil or hazardous substances.
Liability, §143-215.90, (a) to (c).

FISH KILLS RESPONSE PROTOCOLS, §143B-279.7.
Development of protocols, §143B-279.7, (a).
Reports, §143B-279.7, (c).
Secretary of department of environment and natural resources to take necessary steps to carry out provisions, §143B-279.7, (b).

FISH SALES.
Civil penalties, §113-191, (c) to (g).
Criminal penalties, §113-191, (a), (b).
Seized or confiscated property, §113-137, (i).
Seized perishable or seasonable fish, §113-137, (g).
Unlawful sale of fish, §113-183, (a), (b).

FITNESS FOR PARTICULAR PURPOSE.
Leases, UCC.
Implied warranties, §25-2A-213.
Exclusion or modification, §25-2A-214, (2).
Express warranty not to displace inconsistent implied warranty of fitness, §25-2A-215, (c).
Sale of goods, UCC.
Implied warranty, §25-2-315.

511 TRAVELER INFORMATION SYSTEM.
Operated by department of transportation.
Telephone menu requirements, §143-162.1, (d).

FIXING ATHLETIC CONTESTS, §§14-373 to 14-379.

FIXTURES.
Eminent domain.
Removal by owner of fixtures from property taken.
Determination of just compensation, §40A-64, (c).
Removal of fixtures on condemned land, §40A-9.
Leases, UCC.
Defined, §§25-2A-103, (1), 25-2A-309.
Lessor's and lessee's rights when goods become fixtures, §25-2A-309.
Secured transactions.
Defaults.
Procedure when fixtures involved, §25-9-604, (b).
Removal of fixtures, §25-9-604, (c).
Injury from removal, §25-9-604, (d).
Priority of security interests in, §25-9-334, (a).
Consent, disclaimer, or right to remove fixture.
Effect on priority, §25-9-334, (f).
Construction mortgage, §25-9-334, (h).
Continuation of interest, §25-9-334, (g).
Purchase money priority, §25-9-334, (d).
Real property, interests in, §25-9-334, (e).
Real property law security interests, §25-9-334, (b).
Subordination, §25-9-334, (c).
Trade fixtures.
Possessory lien.
Persons entitled to, §44A-2, (e).

FLAG DESECRATION, §14-381.

FLAGS.
Boating safety.
Diver's flag, §75A-13.1.
Violations of provisions.
Penalty, §75A-18, (c).
Load of motor vehicle extending beyond rear or body, §20-117.
Parks and recreation.
Display of flags, §100-18.
Flagpoles.
Donation, §100-19.
Erection in each state park, §100-17.
Sale of state flags by department of administration to citizens, §66-58, (c).
State flag.
Colors of flag, §144-6.
Conformity of flags to law, §144-5.
County courthouses.
Display of flags, §144-4.
Description, §144-1.
Desecration of state flag, §14-381.
Display of flags, §20-117.
County courthouses, §144-4.
Public buildings and institutions, §144-3.
Generally, §144-1.
Motto.
Appearance on flag, §144-2.
Official "prisoner of war/missing in action" flag.
State capitol.
Department of administration authorized to fly on certain holidays, §143-345.9.
Public buildings and institutions.
Display of flags, §144-3.
Sale by department of administration to citizens, §66-58, (c).
United States flag.
Desecration of United States flag, §14-381.

FLANAGAN ACT.
Slot machines, §§14-304 to 14-309.1.
See GAMING.

FLANGES.
Tires not to have, §20-122, (b).

FLASHING.
Indecent exposure, §14-190.9.

FLASHING RED OR YELLOW LIGHTS.
Traffic lights generally, §20-158.

FLATBED TRUCKS.
Loads of logs, cotton bales, boxes, etc.
Load required to be securely fastened, §20-120.

FLAVORS OR FLAVOR EXTRACTS.
Alcoholic beverages.
Exemption from alcoholic beverage provisions, §18B-103.

FLAXSEED.
Standard weight and measure, §81A-42.

FLEA MARKETS.
County regulation, §153A-125.
Municipal regulation, §160A-178.

FLEAS.
Mosquito and vector control program, §§130A-346 to 130A-349.
See MOSQUITO AND VECTOR CONTROL.

FLEEING OR ATTEMPTING TO ELUDE ARREST OR APPREHENSION.
Impaired driving.
Aggravating factor to be weighed, §20-179, (d).

FLEEING OR ATTEMPTING TO ELUDE ARREST OR APPREHENSION —Cont'd
Police chases, speed limits not applicable, §20-145.
Speeding, §20-141.5.
State parks and forest road system, §143-116.8, (b).

FLEXIBLE WORK HOURS.
Work options program for state employees, §§126-74 to 126-79.
See WORK OPTIONS FOR STATE EMPLOYEES.

FLIES.
Mosquito and vector control program, §§130A-346 to 130A-349.
See MOSQUITO AND VECTOR CONTROL.

FLIPPING LOANS.
Consumer home loans, §24-10.2, (c).

FLOOD CONTROL.
Dam safety law, §§143-215.23 to 143-215.37.
See DAM SAFETY.
Special assessments by counties, §§153A-185 to 153A-206.
See SPECIAL ASSESSMENTS BY COUNTIES.

FLOODPLAIN REGULATION, §§143-215.51 to 143-215.61.
Artificial obstructions.
Existing obstructions, §143-215.55.
Other approvals required, §143-215.59.
Violations, §143-215.58, (b).
Criminal penalty for violation, §143-215.58, (a).
Damages.
Liability, §143-215.60.
Definitions, §143-215.52, (a), (b).
Delineation of floodplain hazard area.
Department providing advice and assistance, §143-215.56, (b).
Methods locality may use, §143-215.56, (c).
Technical assistance, locality requesting, §143-215.56, (a).
Utilization of reports and data supplied by state and federal governments, §143-215.56, (a).
Educational program of floodplain management measures.
Department of environment and natural resources directed to pursue, §143-355, (b1).
Enjoining violation, §143-215.58, (c).
Existing artificial obstructions, §143-215.55.
Flood hazard areas.
New waste disposal facilities, §143-215.54, (c).
Ordinances regulating, §143-215.54, (a).
Permissible uses, §143-215.54, (b).
Flood hazard prevention ordinances.
Minimum standards, §143-215.54A, (a).
Variances, criteria, §143-215.54A, (b).
Floodplain management, §143-215.61.
Legislative declaration, §143-215.51.
Liability for damages, §143-215.60.
Management, §143-215.61.
Map identifying 100-year floodplain and base flood elevations.
Conditions for department to prepare, §143-215.56, (d).
Copies provided locality, §143-215.56, (f).
Incorporation into local ordinance, §143-215.56, (g).
Notification to localities prior to preparing, §143-215.56, (e).
Submission to federal emergency management agency, §143-215.56, (f).

FLOODPLAIN REGULATION —Cont'd
Obstructions.
Existing artificial obstructions, §143-215.55.
Other approvals required, §143-215.59.
Violations, §143-215.58, (b).
Permits.
Issuance, §143-215.57, (a), (b).
Other approvals required, §143-215.59, (a), (b).
Procedures in issuing, §143-215.57, (a).
Rules and regulations, §143-215.57, (c).
Standards and requirements, §143-215.57, (b).
Purpose of part, §143-215.51.
Remedies for enforcing ordinance, §143-215.58, (a1).
Rules and regulations.
Adoption and promulgation, §143-215.57, (c).
Violations, §143-215.58, (a) to (c).

FLOODS.
Dam safety law, §§143-215.23 to 143-215.37.
See DAM SAFETY.
Floodplain regulation, §§143-215.51 to 143-215.61.
See FLOODPLAIN REGULATION.
Hurricanes.
Flood protection and beach erosion control project revolving fund.
Conditions, §143-215.62, (b).
Established, §143-215.62, (a).
Procedures, §143-215.62, (c).
Municipal corporations.
Assessments.
Authority to make assessments for flood and hurricane protection works, §160A-238.
Floodway regulations ordinances authorized, §160A-458.1.
Property.
Removal of property deposited by flood, §104B-1.
Protection works.
Special assessments by counties, §§153A-185 to 153A-206.
See SPECIAL ASSESSMENTS BY COUNTIES.
Secondary roads within watershed improvement district.
Closing roads within watershed improvement district, §136-64.1, (a) to (d).

FLOODWAYS.
Swine farms.
Constructing component of liquid animal waste management system within 100-year floodway, §106-803, (a2).

FLOWER OF STATE.
Dogwood, §145-1.

FLOWERS.
Promotion of use and sale of agricultural products.
Generally, §§106-550 to 106-568.
See AGRICULTURAL PRODUCTS PROMOTION.

FLU.
Charter school students parents or guardians.
Information provided, §115C-238.29F, (a).
Church schools and schools of religious charter.
Information provided parents and guardians of students, §115C-548.
Home schools.
Information provided, §115C-565.
Local boards of education.
Information provided parents and guardians, §115C-47.

FLUME COMPANIES.
Eminent domain.
Flume companies exercising right become common carriers, §62-191.

FLU VACCINATION INFORMATION.
Charter schools.
Information provided, §115C-238.29F, (a).
Church schools and schools of religious charter.
Information provided, §115C-548.
Home schools.
Information provided, §115C-565.
Local boards of education.
Information provided parents and guardians, §115C-47.

F.O.B.
Sale of goods, UCC, §25-2-319.
Form of bill of lading required in overseas shipment, §25-2-323.

FOLKMOOT USA.
State international festival, §145-19.

FOLLOWING TOO CLOSELY, §20-152.
Fire apparatus, §20-157, (b), (c).
Points.
Schedule of point values, §20-16, (c).

FOOD.
Amateur athletic events.
Limited food establishments.
Preparing and serving food in conjunction with.
Permits, issuance, §130A-248, (a4).
Sanitation, adoption of rules, §130A-248, (a4).
Bed and breakfast establishments.
Exemption from certain sanitation requirements, §130A-250.
Child care facilities.
Mandatory standards for licensing, §110-91.
Contaminating food or drink to render one mentally incapacitated or physically helpless.
Exceptions, §14-401.16, (d).
Felony, §14-401.16, (c).
Prohibited acts, §14-401.16, (a), (b).
Donated food.
Immunity for, §99B-10.
Embargoes.
Adulterated or misbranded foods, §130A-21, (a) to (e).
Fees.
Establishment preparing and selling food, §130A-248, (d).
Food, drug and cosmetic act.
See FOOD, DRUG AND COSMETIC ACT.
Fruit.
Unfair practices by handlers, §§106-496 to 106-501.
Halloween.
Distribution of certain food prohibited, §14-401.11, (a), (b).
Health.
Adulterated or misbranded foods.
Embargoes, §130A-21, (a) to (e).
High-calcium foods and beverages.
Local boards of education.
Preference in purchasing contracts, §115C-264.1, (a), (b).
Implied warranty of merchantability.
Sale of goods, UCC, §25-2-314.

FOOD —Cont'd
Limited food establishments.
Amateur athletic events.
Preparing and serving food in conjunction with.
Permits, issuance, §130A-248, (a4).
Sanitation, adoption of rules, §130A-248, (a4).
Meat inspections, §§106-549.15 to 106-549.39.
See MEAT INSPECTIONS.
Merchantability, implied warranty.
Sale of goods, UCC, §25-2-314.
Permits or transitional permits.
Establishment preparing and selling food, §130A-248, (b) to (c).
Polystyrene foam products used in conjunction with food.
Recycling, §130A-309.10, (d).
Poultry generally.
See POULTRY AND POULTRY PRODUCTS.
Poultry products inspections, §§106-549.49 to 106-549.69.
See POULTRY PRODUCTS INSPECTIONS.
Prepared food.
Sales and use tax.
Defined, §105-164.3.
Subject to tax, exception, §105-164.13B, (a).
Products liability.
Donated food.
Immunity, §99B-10, (a).
Liability of donee that uses or distributes food, §99B-10, (b).
Public schools.
Food services, §§115C-263, 115C-264.
High-calcium food and beverages.
Preference to when purchasing, §115C-264.1, (a), (b).
Push carts and mobile food units.
Sanitation, rules governing, §130A-248, (c1).
Sale of goods, UCC.
Implied warranty of merchantability, §25-2-314.
Sales and use tax.
Administration of local taxes imposed on food, §105-164.13B, (b).
Defined, §105-164.3.
Exempt from tax, items subject to tax, §105-164.13B, (a).
Local government sales and use tax.
First one-cent tax.
Administration tax levied on, distribution, allocation, §105-469, (a).
Rate of tax.
First one-cent tax, §105-467.
Prepared food.
Defined, §105-164.3.
Prepared food and drink.
Defined, §105-164.3.
Sanitation of food and lodging establishments, §§130A-247 to 130A-250.
Warranties.
Implied warranty of merchantability, §25-2-314.

FOOD ADDITIVES.
Food, drug and cosmetic act.
Additives deemed unsafe, §106-132.
Foods deemed to be adulterated, §106-129.

FOOD AND LODGING ESTABLISHMENT SANITATION, §§130A-247 to 130A-250.

FOOD BANK INFORMATION AND REFERRAL SERVICE.
Maintenance of information by department of agriculture and consumer services, §106-21.2.

FOOD DONATIONS.
Food bank information and referral service.
Maintenance of information by department of agriculture and consumer services, §106-21.2.
Inspections of donated food, §106-141.1.

FOOD, DRUG AND COSMETIC ACT, §§106-120 to 106-145.
Acts.
Certain acts prohibited, §106-122.
Additives deemed unsafe.
What constitutes unsafe additives, §106-132.
Adulteration.
Cosmetics deemed adulterated, §106-136.
Detention of product or article suspected of being adulterated, §106-125, (a).
Declaration of nuisance, §106-125, (d).
Delegation of authority, §106-141, (c).
Destruction of article, §106-125, (c).
Expenses taxed against claimant of article, §106-125, (c).
Order for condemnation of article, §106-125, (b).
Drugs deemed to be adulterated, §106-133.
Electronic surveillance orders, §15A-290, (c5).
Felonies.
Intent to cause serious injury or death, §14-34.4, (a).
Intent to extort, §14-34.4, (b).
Foods deemed to be adulterated, §106-129.
Advertisements.
Definitions and general consideration, §106-121.
Dissemination of advertisement.
Violations made misdemeanor, §106-124, (c).
False advertising, §106-138, (a).
Exceptions, §106-138, (b).
Board of agriculture.
Regulations of board, §106-139.
Standards of quality.
Establishment of reasonable standards, §106-128.
Certain acts prohibited, §106-122.
Citation of act, §106-120.
Color.
Defined, §106-121.
Color additive.
Defined, §106-121.
Commissioner of agriculture.
Enforcement of article, §106-140.
Reports.
Minor violations of article to be reported, §106-127.
Violations of article.
Report of minor violations in discretion of commissioner, §106-127.
Construction and interpretation.
Supplementary construction of article, §106-143.
Consumer commodity.
Defined, §106-121.
Consumer goods.
Declaration of net quantity of contents, §106-139.1.
Regulations by board of agriculture, §106-139, (c).
Exemption from certain labeling requirements, §106-139, (b).
Consumer protection.
Dissemination of certain information, §106-142, (b).
Contaminated with filth.
Defined, §106-121.
Contamination with microorganisms.
Manufacture of foods.
Permits governing manufacture of foods subject to contamination, §106-131.

FOOD, DRUG AND COSMETIC ACT —Cont'd
Cosmetic.
Defined, §106-121.
Counterfeit drug.
Defined, §106-121.
Decrees.
Publication of reports of judgments, decrees and court orders, §106-142, (a).
Definitions, §106-121.
Device.
Defined, §106-121.
District attorneys.
Prosecutions of violations of article, §106-126.
Donated food.
Inspections of food.
Applicability of provisions, §106-141.1, (c).
Authorized, §106-141.1, (a).
Compliance with provisions, §106-141.1, (a).
Injunctive relief restraining violations, §106-141.1, (b).
Drug.
Defined, §106-121.
Effective date of article, §106-145.
Enforcement of article.
Commissioner of agriculture.
Further powers of commissioner, §106-140.
Regulations by board of agriculture, §106-139, (a).
Entry of establishment.
Power of commissioner, §106-140, (a).
Examinations.
Conduct of examinations, §106-141, (b).
Samples, §106-140, (d).
Exemptions from provisions, §106-144.
False advertising, §106-138, (a).
Exceptions, §106-138, (b).
Federal act.
Defined, §106-121.
Food.
Defined, §106-121.
Food additive.
Defined, §106-121.
General considerations, §106-121.
Hearings.
Procedures, §106-139, (d).
Immediate container.
Defined, §106-121.
Injunctions.
Inspections of donated food.
Restraining violations of article, §106-141.1, (b).
Restraining violations of provisions, §106-123.
Inspections.
Additives deemed unsafe, §106-132.
Donated food, §106-141.1.
Manufacture of foods subject to contamination with microorganisms.
Permits governing manufacture, §106-131, (c).
Power of commissioner, §106-140, (a) to (c).
Investigations.
Conduct of investigations, §106-141, (b).
Judgments.
Publication of reports of judgments, decrees and court orders, §106-142, (a).
Labels.
Declaration of net quantity of contents.
Commercial distribution, §106-139.1, (c).
Conformity with requirements, §106-139.1, (a).
Distributing in commerce, §106-139.1, (c).
Statement of net quantity per serving, §106-139.1, (b).
Defined, §106-121.

FOOD, DRUG AND COSMETIC ACT —Cont'd
Labels —Cont'd
Prescription drugs.
Requirements for labeling, §106-134.1, (b), (d).
Regulations by board of agriculture.
Exemption of certain consumer commodities, §106-139, (b).
Manufacture of foods.
Contamination with microorganisms.
Permits governing manufacture of foods subject to contamination, §106-131.
Meat and meat products.
Exemptions from provisions, §106-144.
Misbranding.
Cosmetics deemed misbranded, §106-137.
Detention of product or article suspected of being misbranded, §106-125, (a).
Declaration of nuisance, §106-125, (d).
Delegation of authority, §106-141, (c).
Destruction of article, §106-125, (c).
Expenses taxed against claimant of article, §106-125, (c).
Order for condemnation of article, §106-125, (b).
Drugs deemed misbranded, §106-134.
Prescription provisions, §106-134.1, (d).
Foods deemed misbranded, §106-130.
Prescriptions.
Drugs deemed misbranded, §106-134.1, (d).
Misdemeanors, §106-124.
New drugs.
Defined, §106-121.
Regulations for sale.
Applicability of provisions, §106-135, (g).
Application, §106-135, (a).
Effectiveness, §106-135, (b).
Order refusing to permit effectiveness of application, §106-135, (c).
Revocation of application, §106-135, (f).
Effectiveness of application, §106-135, (b).
Order refusing to permit, §106-135, (c).
Exemptions from provisions, §106-135, (d), (g).
Order refusing to permit effectiveness of application, §106-135, (c).
Records required, §106-135, (e).
Reports required, §106-135, (e).
Revocation of application, §106-135, (f).
Notice.
Civil penalties.
Notice prior to assessment, §106-124.1, (b).
Nuisances.
Adulterated or misbranded product or article.
Detention of suspected product or article.
Declaration of nuisance, §106-125, (d).
Official compendium.
Defined, §106-121.
Orders.
Publication of reports of judgments, decrees and court orders, §106-142, (a).
Regulations for sale of new drugs.
Refusal to commit effectiveness of application, §106-135, (c).
Package.
Defined, §106-121.
Partitioner.
Defined, §106-121.
Permits.
Manufacture of foods subject to contamination with microorganisms.
Conditions attached, §106-131, (a).
Inspections, §106-131, (c).
Suspension of permit, §106-131, (b).

FOOD, DRUG AND COSMETIC ACT —Cont'd
Person.
Defined, §106-121.
Pesticide chemical.
Defined, §106-121.
Poisons.
Adulteration.
Foods deemed to be adulterated, §106-129.
Putting poisonous foodstuffs, etc., in certain public places prohibited, §14-401.
Poultry and poultry products.
Exemptions from provisions, §106-144.
Prescription medicine wholesalers, manufacturers or repackagers.
Registration, §106-140.1, (a), (b).
Additional establishment, §106-140.1, (c).
Assignment of number, §106-140.1, (d).
Definition, §106-140.1, (j).
Exemptions from registration requirement, §106-140.1, (f).
Fee, §106-140.1, (h).
Inspection of establishments registered, §106-140.1, (g).
Inspection of registration, §106-140.1, (e).
Name to include partnership or corporation name, §106-140.1, (i).
Rules to implement registration, adoption, §106-140.1, (h).
Prescriptions.
Applicability of provisions, §106-134.1, (e).
Label requirements, §106-134.1, (b), (d).
Misbranding.
Drugs deemed misbranded, §106-134.1, (d).
Removal of certain drugs from requirements of section, §106-134.1, (b), (c).
Required, §106-134.1, (a).
Principal display panel.
Defined, §106-121.
Prohibited acts, §106-122.
Publications.
Reports of judgments, decrees and court orders to be published, §106-142, (a).
Purpose of article, §106-121.
Quality standards.
Board of agriculture.
Establishment of reasonable standards, §106-128.
Raw agricultural commodity.
Defined, §106-121.
Records.
Carriers in commerce.
Access, copying, power of commissioner, §106-140, (a).
Regulations for sale of new drugs, §106-135, (e).
Registration.
Prescription drug wholesalers, manufacturers or repackagers, §106-140.1.
Reports.
Following inspection, §106-140, (b).
Minor violations to be reported, §106-127.
Publication of reports of judgments, decrees and court orders, §106-142, (a).
Regulations for sale of new drugs, §106-135, (e).
Restraining orders.
Injunctions restraining violations, §106-123.
Inspections of donated food, §106-141.1, (b).
Rules and regulations.
Board of agriculture to promulgate regulations, §106-139.
Sale of new drugs, §106-135.

FOOD, DRUG AND COSMETIC ACT —Cont'd
Samples acquired during inspection.
Examination, §106-140, (d).
Payment for, §106-140, (e).
Short title, §106-120.
Solicitors.
Prosecutions of violations of article, §106-126.
Standards of quality.
Board of agriculture.
Establishment of reasonable standards, §106-128.
Superior courts.
Injunctions restraining violations of provisions, §106-123.
Title of article, §106-120.
Training and management practices.
Violations of article.
Civil penalties.
Mitigating factors, §106-124.1, (c).
Violations of article.
Certain acts prohibited, §106-122.
Civil penalties, §106-124.1.
Assessment, §106-124.1, (a).
Mitigating factors, §106-124.1, (c).
Notice prior to assessment, §106-124.1, (b).
Remission of proceeds, §106-124.1, (d).
Commissioner of agriculture.
Report of minor violations in discretion of commissioner, §106-127.
Dissemination of advertisement, §106-124, (c).
Guaranty or undertaking established, §106-124, (b).
Injunctions restraining violations, §106-123.
Misdemeanor offenses, §106-124, (a).
Mitigating factors.
Civil penalties, §106-124.1, (c).
Notice prior to assessment.
Civil penalties, §106-124.1, (b).
Prohibited acts, §106-122.
Prosecutions of violations, §106-126.

FOOD STAMPS, §§108A-51 to 108A-53.1.
Administration of program, §108A-51.
Appeals, §108A-79, (h).
Authorization of program, §108A-51.
Controlled substance felony offense conviction.
Eligibility to participate in program, §108A-25.2.
Creation of program, §108A-25, (a).
Eligibility determination, §108A-52.
Financial assistance and in-kind goods or services received not considered in determining amount of assistance, §108A-26.
Fraud, §108A-53.
Garnishment of wages to recoup, §108A-25.3.
Illegal possession or use.
Buying, selling, distributing or possessing in manner contrary to authorization or regulation, §108A-53.1, (a).
Using, transferring, acquiring, etc., in manner contrary to authorization, §108A-53.1, (b).
Setoff debt collection, §§105A-1 to 105A-16.
See SETOFF DEBT COLLECTION.

FOOT AND MOUTH DISEASE.
Appropriation to combat disease, §§106-308, 106-309.

FOOTBALL.
Protection of athletic contests.
See ATHLETIC CONTESTS.

FOOTPRINTS.
Nontestimonial identification.
Delinquent or undisciplined juvenile actions, §§7B-2103 to 7B-2109.
Generally, §§15A-271 to 15A-282.
See IDENTIFICATION.

FORCE.
Detaining intoxicated person.
Use of reasonable force by law enforcement officers, §122C-301, (b).
Seizure and impoundment of motor vehicles.
Impaired driving arrest, §20-28.3, (c1).
Use of deadly force against intruders, §14-51.1.

FORCED OUT SALES, §§66-76 to 66-83.
See CLOSING-OUT SALES.

FOREBEARANCES.
Contract rates and fees, §24-1.1.
Savings and loan association interest rates, §24-1.4.

FORECLOSURES.
Alcoholic beverage ownership or possession acquired by.
Special one-time permit issued, §18B-1002, (a).
Banks.
Foreclosures and execution of deeds by commissioner, validation, §53-35.
Condominiums.
Lien for assessment, §47C-116, (a).
Lien or encumbrance, §47C-2-118, (i), (j).
Special declarant rights, §47C-3-104, (c), (d).
Executors and administrators.
Validation, §45-5.
Fiduciaries.
Powers which may be incorporated by reference in trust instrument, §32-27.
Guardian's powers in administering incompetent's estate, §35A-1251.
Guardian's powers in administering minor ward's estate, §35A-1252.
Judicial sales.
General provisions.
See JUDICIAL SALES.
Limitation of actions.
Mortgages and deeds of trust, §1-47.
Attacking certain foreclosures.
On ground trustee was agent, etc., of owner of debt, §45-21.39.
Deficiency judgments after foreclosure, §1-54.
Taxation, §1-54.
Mortgages and deeds of trust.
Attorneys at law.
Fee for conducting foreclosure.
Prohibited to all except licensed attorneys, §84-6.
Corporate mortgages.
Receivers and trustees of corporate mortgages or grantees, §1-507.4.
Default judgment by clerk, §1A-1, Rule 55, (a).
Deficiency judgments, §§45-21.36 to 45-21.38.
Fee for conducting foreclosure.
Prohibited to all except licensed attorneys, §84-6.
Fiduciaries.
Powers which may be incorporated by reference in trust instrument, §32-27.
Guardian's powers in administering incompetent's estate, §35A-1251.
Guardian's powers in administering minor ward's estate, §35A-1252.

FORECLOSURES —Cont'd
Mortgages and deeds of trust —Cont'd
In rem or quasi in rem jurisdiction, §1-75.8.
Judicial sales.
Who may hold sale, §1-339.4.
Limitation of actions, §1-47.
Attacks on certain foreclosures on grounds trustee was agent, etc., of owner of debt, §45-21.39.
Deficiency judgment following foreclosure, §1-54.
Redemption of mortgage, §1-47.
Sales under power of sale.
Application of statute to serial notes, §45-21.11.
Lis pendens, §1-116.
Notice.
Recording, §45-38.
Receivers and trustees of corporate mortgages or grantees, §1-507.4.
Receivers of corporations.
Powers, §§1-507.2, 1-507.4.
Recording, §45-38.
Reverse mortgages.
Initiation of foreclosure.
Time for, §53-268.
Sales under power of sale.
Article not applicable to foreclosure by court action, §45-21.2.
Barred when foreclosure barred, §45-21.12.
Orders signed on days other than first and third Mondays validated, §45-21.41.
Simultaneous foreclosure of two or more instruments, §45-21.9A.
Superior courts.
Clerks of court authorized to order foreclosure, §1-209.
Trustee officer of owner of debt.
Validation of foreclosure sale, §45-21.47.
Validation.
Foreclosures by representatives validated, §45-5.
Sales where posting and publication not complied with, §§45-21.46, (a), 45-21.48.
Foreclosure commenced on or after June 1, 1983 and consummated prior to April 1, 1985, §45-21.46, (b).
When trustee is officer of owner of debt, §45-21.47.
Venue, §1-76.
Property taxes.
Foreclosure of tax lien, §§105-374 to 105-376.
Residential property disclosure act.
Applicability of act, §47E-2.
Secured transactions.
Default.
Enforcement after default, §25-9-601, (a).
Execution sale, security interest foreclosed, §25-9-601, (f).
Tax liens.
Limitation of actions, §1-54.
Property taxes, §§105-374 to 105-376.
Torrens system registration.
Method of transfer.
Land conveyed as security.
Sale under lien, §43-36, (f).
Transfer of proceedings to superior court.
Exceptions, §1-301.2, (g).
Trusts and trustees.
Powers of trustees under express trust, §36A-136.

FORECLOSURES —Cont'd
Venue.
Mortgages, §1-76.

FOREIGN BANKING CORPORATIONS.
International banking generally, §§53-232.1 to 53-232.17.
See INTERNATIONAL BANKING.

FOREIGN BIRTH.
Certificate of identification for individual of foreign birth, §130A-108, (a).
Readoption in state, §130A-108, (b).

FOREIGN CORPORATIONS.
Attachment.
Grounds for attachment, §1-440.3.
Derivative actions.
Applicability, §55-7-47.
Franchise tax generally, §§105-114 to 105-129.
See FRANCHISE TAX.
Garnishment.
To whom process delivered when garnishee corporations, §1-440.26, (b).
Generally, §§55-15-01 to 55-15-33.
See CORPORATIONS.
Mergers.
Nonprofit corporations, §55-11-09.
Nonprofit corporations, §§55A-1-01 to 55A-17-05.
See NONPROFIT CORPORATIONS.
Professional corporations, §55B-16.
Service of process.
Personal jurisdiction, manner of serving, §1A-1, Rule 4, (j).
Venue of actions against, §1-80.

FOREIGN COUNTRIES.
Depositions.
Persons before whom taken, §1A-1, Rule 28, (b).
Reading deposition on the trial.
When deposition may be read, §8-83.
Evidence.
Laws of foreign countries.
Admission into evidence, §8-3, (a).
Exhibiting copy of law from printed volume, §8-3, (b).
Judicial notice of laws, §8-4.
Missing persons.
Provisions applicable, §28C-20.
Service of process, §1A-1, Rule 4, (j3).
Wills.
Certified copies proved in another country, §31-22.

FOREIGN CURRENCY.
Commodities generally, §§78D-1 to 78D-33.
See COMMODITIES.

FOREIGN DIPLOMATS.
Holders of driver's license issued by United States department of state.
Notice to department of state.
Violation of state or local traffic law, revocation order, §20-37.20.

FOREIGN GOVERNMENTS.
Agreements between North Carolina and foreign governments.
Filing of copies, §66-280, (a), (b).
Definition of "foreign government," §66-280, (c).
Business discrimination.
Persons doing business in state entering into agreement with foreign governments, §§75B-1 to 75B-7.

FOREIGN JUDGMENTS, ENFORCEMENT, §§1C-1701 to 1C-1708.
Actions to enforce.
Creditor's judgment.
Article not construed to impair, §1C-1707.
Affidavit that judgment final and unsatisfied.
Filing, §1C-1703, (a).
Burden of proof.
Motion for enforcement of judgment, §1C-1705, (b).
Citation of act.
Short title, §1C-1701.
Construction and interpretation.
Actions to enforce creditor's judgment.
Article not construed to impair, §1C-1707.
Costs, §1C-1706.
Defenses.
Final judgments subject to same defenses as judgments of state, §1C-1703, (c).
Notice of defense.
Filing, §1C-1705, (a).
Definitions, §1C-1702.
Docketing, §1C-1703, (b).
Eastern band of the Cherokee Indians.
Judgments, decrees, and orders of Tribal Court.
Considered foreign judgments by state, §1E-1, (b).
Effect, §1C-1703, (c).
Fees, §1C-1706.
Filing in office of clerk of superior court, §1C-1703, (a).
Notice of filing.
Content, §1C-1704, (b).
Service and proof of service, §1C-1704, (a).
Hearings.
Motion for enforcement of foreign judgment, §1C-1705, (b).
Indexing, §1C-1703, (b).
Judgments against public policy.
Provisions not to apply to, §1C-1708.
Limitation of actions.
Ten-year limitation, §1-47.
Money judgment recognition, §§1C-1800 to 1C-1808.
See FOREIGN MONEY JUDGMENTS RECOGNITION.
Motions.
Enforcement of foreign judgments, §1C-1705, (b).
Relief from foreign judgments, §1C-1705, (a).
Notice of defense.
Filing notice of defense, §1C-1705, (a).
Notice of filing.
Contents, §1C-1704, (b).
Service and proof of service of notice, §1C-1704, (a).
Optional procedure, §1C-1707.
Public policy.
Judgments against.
Provisions of article not to apply to, §1C-1708.
Relief from foreign judgments.
Motion for, §1C-1705, (a).
Service of process.
Notice of filing.
Service and proof of service of notice, §1C-1704, (a).
Short title, §1C-1701.
Status.
Same effect and subject to same defenses as judgments of state, §1C-1703, (c).
Stays, §1C-1705, (a).

FOREIGN JUDGMENTS, ENFORCEMENT —Cont'd
Title of act.
Short title, §1C-1701.

FOREIGN LAW.
Determination of foreign law, §1A-1, Rule 44.1.

FOREIGN LEGAL CONSULTANTS, §§84A-1 to 84A-8; Bar Rules & Regs., F, §§.0101 to .0113.
Administrative committee recommendations, Bar Rules & Regs., F, §.0107.
Adoption of rules, §84A-8.
Appeals, Bar Rules & Regs., F, §.0108.
Applications, Bar Rules & Regs., F, §.0101.
Denial, Bar Rules & Regs., F, §.0113.
Fees, Bar Rules & Regs., F, §.0111.
Forms, Bar Rules & Regs., F, §.0102.
Audits, §84A-5.
Board of law examiners.
Delegation of duties by state bar, §84A-7.
Certificate of registration, §84A-2.
Application, §84A-2, (a).
Accompanying documents, §84A-2, (d).
Fee, §84A-2, (c).
Photograph of applicant, §84A-2, (b).
Evidence of applicant's application, qualifications, etc., §84A-2, (e).
Good moral character of applicant, §84A-3, (c).
Issuance of certificate, §84A-3, (b).
Failure to satisfy all provisions, §84A-3, (d).
Review by North Carolina state bar, §84A-3, (a).
Committee recommendations, Bar Rules & Regs., F, §.0107.
Delegation of duties by state bar, §84A-7.
Duties, §84A-5.
Failure to disclose, Bar Rules & Regs., F, §.0105.
Fees.
Certificate of registration, §84A-2, (c).
Duties of consultant, §84A-5.
Foreign country.
Defined, §84A-1.
Good moral character of applicant.
Certificate of registration, §84A-3, (c).
Hearings, Bar Rules & Regs., F, §.0109.
Investigations, Bar Rules & Regs., F, §.0106.
Licenses, §84A-1.
Examinations, §84A-1, (b).
Issuance, §84A-1, (a).
Moral character and general fitness.
Burden of proof, Bar Rules & Regs., F, §.0104.
Permanent record, Bar Rules & Regs., F, §.0112.
Prohibited activities, §84A-4, (b).
Public records, §84A-2, (f).
Reciprocity, §84A-2, (g).
Requirements for applicants, Bar Rules & Regs., F, §.0103.
Review and order of council, Bar Rules & Regs., F, §.0110.
Rules and regulations.
Adoption of rules, §84A-8.
Scope of practice, §84A-4.
Service of process, §84A-6.
Written legal advice.
Jurisdiction other than admitted to practice in, §84A-4, (c).

FOREIGN LIMITED LIABILITY COMPANIES.
See LIMITED LIABILITY COMPANIES.

FOREIGN LIMITED LIABILITY PARTNERSHIPS, §§59-90 to 59-94.
See LIMITED LIABILITY PARTNERSHIPS.

FOREIGN LIMITED PARTNERSHIPS.
See LIMITED PARTNERSHIPS.

FOREIGN-MONEY CLAIMS, §§1C-1820 to 1C-1834.
Agreements by parties, §1C-1822, (a), (b).
Amount of money.
Distribution proceedings, §1C-1827.
Judgments and awards, §1C-1826, (g).
Measurement by exchange rate, §1C-1824, (b).
Measurement by specified amounts, §1C-1824, (a), (c).
Applicability of article, §1C-1821, (a), (b).
Uniformity of application and construction, §1C-1833.
Asserting claims, §1C-1825, (a).
Citation of article, §1C-1834.
Clerks of court.
Powers and liabilities, §1C-1826, (j).
Conflict of laws.
Interest rates, §1C-1828, (a).
Scope of article, §1C-1821, (b).
Costs.
Assessment of cost in U. S. dollars, §1C-1826, (c).
Counterclaims, §1C-1825, (c).
Currency revalorization, §1C-1831, (a), (b).
Defending claims, §1C-1825, (b), (c).
Definitions, §1C-1820.
Determining proper money of claim, §1C-1824.
Agreement by parties, §1C-1823, (a).
No agreement by parties, §1C-1823, (b).
Question of law, §1C-1825, (d).
Distribution proceedings.
Conversions of foreign money, §1C-1827.
Docketing of judgments.
Foreign judgments, §1C-1829.
Enforcement of judgments.
Affidavit or certificate stating rate of exchange, §1C-1826, (i).
Foreign judgments, §1C-1829.
Seizure or restraint of assets, §1C-1830, (a) to (d).
Form of judgment, §1C-1826, (f).
General principles of law.
Supplement to provisions of article, §1C-1832.
Interest.
Increase or decrease, §1C-1828, (b).
Rate of interest, §1C-1828, (a), (c).
Judgments and awards.
Amendment following substitute of new money, §1C-1831, (b).
Amount of money, §1C-1826, (g).
Clerk's powers and liabilities, §1C-1826, (j).
Cost assessed in U. S. dollars, §1C-1826, (c).
Discharge of judgment by payment, §1C-1826, (h).
Docketing judgment, §1C-1826, (h).
Effect of judgments, §1C-1826, (h).
Enforcement of judgments.
Affidavit or certificate stating rate of exchange, §1C-1826, (i).
Foreign judgments, §1C-1829.
Seizure or restraint of assets, §1C-1830, (a) to (d).
Filing of judgment, §1C-1826, (h).
Foreign judgment enforcement, §1C-1829.
Form, §1C-1826, (f).
Indexing of judgment, §1C-1826, (h).
Interest, §1C-1828, (a) to (c).
Netting of certain awards, §1C-1826, (e).
Payable in foreign money or equivalent, §1C-1826, (b), (d).

FOREIGN-MONEY CLAIMS —Cont'd
Judgments and awards —Cont'd
Stating in amount of money of claim, §1C-1826, (a).
Payment of awards, §1C-1826, (b), (d).
Scope of article, §1C-1821, (a), (b).
Uniformity of application and construction, §1C-1833.
Seizure or restraint of assets, §1C-1830, (a) to (d).
Setoffs, §1C-1825, (c).
Short title, §1C-1834.
Substitution of currency, §1C-1831, (a), (b).
Supplementary general principals of law, §1C-1832.
Uniformity of application and construction, §1C-1833.
United States dollar value of assets to be seized.
Determining, §1C-1830, (a) to (d).
Variation by agreement, §1C-1822, (a), (b).

FOREIGN MONEY JUDGMENTS RECOGNITION, §§1C-1800 to 1C-1808.
Appeals, §1C-1806.
Applicability of provisions, §1C-1802.
Basis for personal jurisdiction, §1C-1805, (a).
Recognition of other bases by courts of state, §1C-1805, (b).
Citation of act, §1C-1800.
Conclusiveness of judgments.
Grounds for nonrecognition, §1C-1804, (a).
Court recognition of bases of jurisdiction, §1C-1805, (b).
Enforcement of provisions, §1C-1803.
Final and conclusive judgments, §1C-1802.
Foreign judgment.
Defined, §1C-1801.
Foreign state.
Defined, §1C-1801.
Fraud.
Grounds for nonrecognition of judgment, §1C-1804, (b).
Interpretation of provisions, §§1C-1807, 1C-1808.
Notice.
Grounds for nonrecognition of judgment, §1C-1804, (b).
Personal jurisdiction, §1C-1805, (a).
Purpose of provisions.
Uniformity of interpretation, §1C-1808.
Recognition of judgments, §1C-1803.
Grounds for nonrecognition.
Foreign judgment not conclusive, §1C-1804, (a).
Fraud, §1C-1804, (b).
General grounds for nonrecognition, §1C-1804, (b).
Notice, §1C-1804, (b).
Short title, §1C-1800.
Situations not covered by article, §1C-1807.
Stay pending appeal, §1C-1806.

FOREIGN OBJECT LEFT IN BODY.
Medical malpractice actions, time limitation for commencing, §1-15, (c).

FOREIGN OR ALIEN INSURANCE COMPANIES.
Admission to do business, §58-16-1.
Deposit requirements, §58-5-15.
Kinds of insurance.
Limitations as to, §58-16-10.
Requirements, §58-16-15.

FOREIGN OR ALIEN INSURANCE COMPANIES —Cont'd
Alien governments.
Companies owned or controlled by.
Exceptions to provisions, §58-16-20, (d).
Licenses.
Issuance prohibited, §58-16-20, (b).
Prohibited from doing business, §58-16-20, (a).
Violations as crimes, §58-16-20, (c).
Amendments to documents, §58-16-55.
Approval as domestic insurer, §58-7-60.
Attorney general.
Actions to enforce compliance with provisions, §58-16-50.
Casualty insurance.
Deposits.
Required, §58-5-10.
Charters.
Amendments to documents, §58-16-55.
Deposit of copy with commissioner, §58-16-5.
Commissioner.
Service of process, §58-16-30.
Appointment of commissioner as attorney for service.
Condition for admission to do business, §58-16-5.
Notification of company of service or acceptance of process, §58-16-45.
Unauthorized insurers process act, §58-16-35, (b).
Conditions of licensure, §58-16-5.
Conversion to foreign insurer, §58-7-65.
Definitions, §58-1-5.
Deposits.
Alien companies generally, §§58-5-100, 58-5-105.
Approval of commissioner, §58-5-95.
Bond in lieu of deposit, §58-5-110.
Depreciation of securities.
Replacements upon, §58-5-25.
Domestic companies may be required to maintain deposits.
Composition of deposit, §58-5-55, (c).
Mutual insurance companies, §58-5-55, (b).
Stock insurance companies, §58-5-55, (a).
Examination by commissioner, §58-5-95.
Faith of state pledged for securities, §58-5-35.
Increase of deposit.
Authority of commissioner, §58-5-40.
Interest, §58-5-63, (a).
Lien of policyholders on deposits, §58-5-70.
Subordination, §58-5-71.
Life insurance companies, §58-5-50.
Companies not chartered in United States, §58-5-105.
Liquidation for liabilities, §58-5-63, (b).
Companies subject of supervision or rehabilitation, §58-5-63, (c).
Power of attorney as to securities deposited.
Delivery to commissioner by company, §58-5-30.
Registration of bonds deposited in name of treasurer or commissioner, §58-5-110.
Costs, §58-5-120.
Expenses, §58-5-120.
Notation of registration, §58-5-115.
Release from registration, §58-5-115.
Requirements.
Alien companies generally, §§58-5-100, 58-5-105.
Depreciation of securities.
Replacements upon depreciation, §58-5-25.

FOREIGN OR ALIEN INSURANCE COMPANIES —Cont'd
Deposits —Cont'd
Requirements —Cont'd
Fidelity, surety and casualty insurance companies, §58-5-10.
Fire and/or marine insurance companies, §58-5-5.
Increase of deposit.
Authority of commissioner, §58-5-40.
Minimum deposit required upon admission, §58-5-15.
Power of attorney as to securities.
Company to deliver to commissioner, §58-5-30.
Type of deposit, §58-5-20.
Return of deposits, §58-5-80.
Substitution of securities paid, §58-5-75.
Taxation.
Exemption of securities deposited, §58-5-35.
Treasurer of state to hold securities, §58-5-35.
Trusts and trustees.
Deposits held in trust by commissioner or treasurer, §58-5-90, (a), (b).
Action to enforce or terminate trust, §58-5-90, (c).
Type of deposits, §58-5-20.
Domestic insurers.
Approval as, §58-7-60.
Conversion to foreign insurer, §58-7-65.
Effect of redomestication, §58-7-70.
Enforcement of provisions.
Actions to enforce compliance, §58-16-50.
Fees.
Redomestication, §58-7-155.
Retaliatory laws, §58-16-25.
Fidelity and surety insurance.
Deposits.
Required, §58-5-10.
Fire insurance.
Deposits.
Required, §58-5-5.
Licenses.
Conditions of continuance, §58-16-6.
Conditions of licensure, §58-16-8.
Restricting license.
Prohibiting or limiting kinds or amount of insurance, §58-3-100, (e).
Retaliatory laws, §58-16-25.
Revocation, suspension or refusal to renew.
Notice to agents in state, writing new business prohibited, §58-3-100.
Life insurance company deposits, §58-5-50.
Limitations upon kinds of insurance, §58-16-10.
Liquidation of deposits for liabilities, §58-5-63, (b).
Companies subject of supervision or rehabilitation, §58-5-63, (c).
Marine insurance.
Deposits.
Required, §58-5-5.
Misdemeanors.
Alien governments.
Companies owned or controlled by governments, §58-16-20, (c).
Reciprocal insurance.
Attorneys.
Domicile, §58-15-45.
Certification of foreign and alien reciprocals, §58-15-40.

FOREIGN OR ALIEN INSURANCE COMPANIES —Cont'd
Redomestication.
Effect of, §58-7-70.
Fees, §58-7-155.
Requirements upon admission, §58-16-15.
Retaliatory laws, §58-16-25.
Risk based capital requirements, §58-12-45.
Security substitution upon payment, §58-5-75.
Service of process.
Alternative service of process, §58-16-40.
Appointment of commissioner as attorney for service.
Condition for admission to do business, §58-16-5.
Commissioner of insurance, §58-16-30.
Notification of company of service or acceptance of service of process, §58-16-45.
Unauthorized insurers process act, §58-16-35, (b).
Supervision, rehabilitation and liquidation generally, §§58-30-1 to 58-30-310.
See INSURER SUPERVISION, REHABILITATION AND LIQUIDATION.
Unauthorized insurers.
Generally, §§58-28-1 to 58-28-45.
See UNAUTHORIZED INSURERS.

FOREIGN PERSONAL REPRESENTATIVES.
Ancillary administration, §§28A-26-1 to 28A-26-9.
See EXECUTORS AND ADMINISTRATORS.

FOREIGN PERSONS.
Aliens.
See ALIENS.

FOREIGN TRADE ZONES, §§55C-1 to 55C-4.
Definitions.
"Public corporation," §55C-2.
Federal law.
Corporations establishing foreign trade zone to be governed by, §55C-4.
Private corporations.
Application for privilege for establishing foreign trade zone.
Authorized, §55C-3.
Federal law.
Private corporation establishing foreign trade zone to be governed by, §55C-4.
Public corporations.
Application for privilege of establishing foreign trade zone.
Authorized, §55C-1.
Defined, §55C-2.
Federal law.
Public corporation establishing foreign trade zone to be governed by, §55C-4.

FOREST DEVELOPMENT ACT, §§113A-176 to 113A-183.
Administration of cost sharing.
Authority of secretary, §113A-180.
Approved forest management plan.
Defined, §113A-178.
Approved practices.
Defined, §113A-178.
Cost-share agreements.
Agreement with department as requirement to receive payments, §113A-180.1, (a).
Repayment to fund for failure to maintain practices, §113A-180.1, (b).
Voluntary relinquishment of control or title by landowner, §113A-180.1, (c).

FOREST DEVELOPMENT ACT —Cont'd
Definitions, §113A-178.
Department.
Defined, §113A-178.
Disbursing agency, §113A-179, (b).
Eligible landowners.
Defined, §113A-178.
Eligible lands.
Defined, §113A-178.
Equipment.
Authority of secretary to purchase, §113A-179, (d).
Funds used for purchase.
Limited to appropriations from general fund, §113A-183, (e).
Federal cost sharing programs.
Eligible landowners may not use state funds, §113A-181, (c).
Forest development assessments.
Defined, §113A-178.
Forest development fund.
Created, §113A-183, (a).
Defined, §113A-178.
Depository, §113A-183, (b).
Equipment.
Funds used for purchase, §113A-183, (e).
Expenditures.
Limitation, §113A-183, (e).
Percentage of funds used for program support, §113A-183, (d).
Funds.
Forest development fund, §113A-183.
Defined, §113A-178.
Intention of act, §113A-177, (c).
Legislative purpose, §113A-177, (a), (b).
Participation by government political subdivisions, §113A-182.
Payments.
Funds from federal cost sharing programs, §113A-181, (c).
Limitation of payments, §113A-181, (a).
Maximum amount, §113A-181, (b).
Political subdivisions.
Participation, §113A-182.
Secretary.
Administration of cost sharing.
Authority of secretary, §113A-180.
Defined, §113A-178.
Equipment.
Authority to purchase, §113A-179, (d).
Powers and duties, §113A-179, (a).
Staff, §113A-179, (c).
Title of act, §113A-176.

FORESTERS, §§89B-1 to 89B-15.
Affidavits.
Consulting foresters.
Affidavit of compliance with provisions, §89B-14, (b).
Board of registration.
Appointment of members, §89B-3, (a).
Compensation of members, §89B-4.
Composition, §89B-3, (a).
Creation, §89B-3, (a).
Expenses of members, §89B-4.
Hearings.
Charges against registrants, §89B-13.
Meetings, §89B-5.
Number of members, §89B-3, (a).
Oaths.
Members may administer, §89B-6.
Officers, §89B-3, (d).

FORESTERS —Cont'd
Board of registration —Cont'd
Qualifications of members, §89B-3, (a), (b).
Quorum, §89B-3, (d).
Records, §89B-8.
Reports, §89B-8.
Roster of registered foresters, §89B-14, (a).
Rules and regulations, §89B-6.
Seal, §89B-6.
Special meetings, §89B-5.
Terms of members, §89B-3, (a).
Vacancies, §89B-3, (c).
Bonds, surety.
Board of registration.
Secretary, §89B-7.
Child support enforcement.
Forfeiture of licensing privilege, §50-13.12.
Continuing education.
Registration renewal, §89B-11, (b).
Corporations.
Professional corporations generally, §§55B-1 to 55B-16.
See PROFESSIONAL CORPORATIONS.
Registration.
Prohibited, §89B-9, (b).
Criminal laws.
Enforcement by United States forest service officers, §15A-406.
Definitions, §89B-2.
Examinations.
Fees, §89B-12.
Registration, §89B-12.
Fees.
Registration, §§89B-10, (a), 89B-11, (a).
Examinations, §89B-12.
Felony convictions.
Forfeiture of license, §15A-1331A.
Hearings.
Charges against registrants, §89B-13.
Legislative declaration.
Intention of chapter, §89B-1, (b).
Misdemeanors.
Violations of provisions, §89B-15.
Oaths.
Board of registration.
Members may administer, §89B-6.
Partnerships.
Registration.
Prohibited, §89B-9, (b).
Professional corporations generally, §§55B-1 to 55B-16.
See PROFESSIONAL CORPORATIONS.
Reciprocity.
Registration, §89B-9, (d).
Records.
Board of registration, §89B-8.
Registration.
Applications, §89B-10, (a).
Board. See within this heading, "Board of registration."
Examinations, §89B-12.
False or forged information.
Providing to board in obtaining certificate of registration, §89B-10, (b).
Fees, §§89B-10, (a), 89B-11, (a).
Examinations, §89B-12.
Forester-in-training certificate, §89B-9, (b1).
Individual persons only, §89B-9, (b).
Nonresidents, §89B-9, (c) to (e).
Qualifications, §89B-9, (a).
Reciprocity, §89B-9, (d).

FORESTERS —Cont'd
Registration —Cont'd
Renewal, §89B-11.
Required, §89B-1, (a).
Revocation or suspension, §89B-13.
Felony convictions, §15A-1331A.
Reissuance, §89B-13.
Roster of registered foresters, §89B-14, (a).
Reports.
Board of registration, §89B-8.
Rules and regulations.
Board of registration, §89B-6.
Seals and sealed instruments.
Board of registration, §89B-6.
Funds.
Receipts and disbursements, §89B-7.
United States forest service.
Officers authorized to enforce criminal laws, §15A-406.
Violations of provisions.
Misdemeanors, §89B-15.

FOREST FIRES.
Attorney general.
Investigations.
Deputy investigators, §58-79-25.
Cooperation between counties and state in forest protection and development, §113-59.
Department of environment and natural resources.
Powers, §113-51, (a), (b).
Destruction of posted forestry notices.
Misdemeanor, §113-58.
Firefighters on standby duty.
Definitions, §113-60.32.
Distance from duty station, §113-60.33, (a).
Exceptions, §113-60.33, (b).
Electronic paging devices, §113-60.33, (a).
Generally, §113-60.33, (a).
Fire patrol designated during season of drought, §113-55, (a).
Forest rangers.
Overtime compensation for forest firefighting, §113-56.1.
Powers to prevent and extinguish fires, §113-55, (a).
Overtime compensation for forest firefighting, §113-56.1.
Prescribed burning of forestland, §§113-60.40 to 113-60.45.
Setting fire to woodland.
Criminal trespass, §14-136.
Willfully or negligently setting fire to woods, §14-137.
Southeastern interstate forest fire protection compact, §§113-60.11 to 113-60.15.
Summoning residents to assist in extinguishing.
Powers of forest rangers, §113-55, (a).
Woodland defined, §113-57.

FOREST INSECT INFESTATION AND DISEASE PROTECTION, §§113-60.4 to 113-60.10.
Actions against insects and diseases, §113-60.7.
Agreements.
Cooperative agreements, §113-60.9.
Annulment of control zone, §113-60.10.
Authority of department of environment and natural resources, §113-60.5.
Authority of secretary of environment and natural resources, §113-60.8.

FOREST INSECT INFESTATION AND DISEASE PROTECTION —Cont'd
Control zone.
Annulment, §113-60.10.
Cooperative agreements, §113-60.9.
Definitions, §113-60.6.
Department of environment and natural resources.
Authority, §113-60.5.
Secretary.
Actions against insects and diseases, §113-60.7.
Authority, §113-60.8.
Intent of article, §113-60.4, (a), (b).
Legislative findings, §113-60.4, (a), (b).
Purpose and intent, §113-60.4, (a), (b).
Right of entry.
Secretary of environment and natural resources, §113-60.8.
Secretary of environment and natural resources.
Authority, §113-60.8.

FOREST LAW-ENFORCEMENT OFFICERS, §113-55.1.

FOREST OF STATE.
Generally.
See STATE FORESTS.

FOREST PRACTICE GUIDELINES RELATED TO WATER QUALITY, §113A-52.1.

FOREST PRODUCTS ASSESSMENT, §§113A-189 to 113A-196.
Collection of assessment.
Assessments levied against processors of primary forest products, §113A-195, (a).
Enforcement of collection, §113A-196.
Suspension, §113A-192, (c).
Carry forward from previous years, §113A-192, (d).
Ending of suspension, §113A-192, (e).
Definitions, §113A-191.
Disclosure of confidential information, §113A-195, (f).
Enforcement of collection, §113A-196.
Forest development fund.
Defined, §113A-191.
Levy of assessment, §113A-195, (a).
Method of payment, §113A-195, (c).
Operation of system.
Levy of general assembly, §113A-192, (a).
Primary forest product.
Defined, §113A-191.
Processors.
Defined, §113A-191.
Purpose of article, §113A-190, (a).
Purposes of assessments levied, §113A-190, (b).
Rate of assessment, §113A-194, (b).
Records of processor, §113A-195, (d).
Reports.
Production reports of processors, §113A-195, (e).
Rights of assessment, §113A-192, (b).
Standards, §113A-194, (a).
Secretary of department of environment and natural resources.
Duties, §113A-193, (b).
Secretary of department of revenue.
Duties, §113A-193, (a).
Reimbursement for expenditures, §113A-193, (c).
Short title, §113A-189.
Title.
Short title, §113A-189.
When assessments payable, §113A-195, (b).

FOREST PROTECTION AND DEVELOPMENT CORPORATIONS, §§113-61 to 113-77.
Appeals.
Provision for appeal by corporations to governor, §113-66.
Application of corporate income, §113-76.
Borrowing money.
Power limited, §113-74.
Bounties.
Limitation on bounties to stockholders, §113-69.
Cutting and sale of timber, §113-72.
Consent required, §113-73.
Department of environment and natural resources.
Department defined, §113-61, (a).
Development plans.
Secretary to approve, §113-75.
Directors, §113-63.
Dissolution of corporations, §113-71.
Dividends.
Earnings above dividend requirements payable to state, §113-70.
Limitations, §113-67.
Formation.
Manner of organizing, §113-62.
Private limited dividend corporations, §113-61, (b).
Income.
Application of corporate income, §113-76.
Injunctions.
Secretary of environment and natural resources.
Power to apply for injunctions, §113-65.
Interest rates.
Maximum rates allowable, §113-73.
Issuance of securities.
Restricted, §113-68.
Limitations as to dividends, §113-67.
Loans.
Power to borrow money limited, §113-74.
Mandamus.
Secretary of environment and natural resources.
Power to petition for writ of mandamus, §113-65.
Mortgaging property.
Consent required, §113-73.
Number of directors, §113-63.
Organization.
Manner of organizing, §113-62.
Private limited dividend corporations.
Formation, §113-61, (b).
Manner of organizing, §113-62.
Provision for appeal by corporations to governor, §113-66.
Reorganization of corporations, §113-77.
Sale of property, §§113-72, 113-73.
Consent required, §113-73.
Secretary of environment and natural resources.
Approval of development plans, §113-75.
Director, §113-63.
Duties.
Supervisory duties, §113-64.
Powers, §113-65.
Supervisory duties, §113-64.
Secretary defined, §113-61, (a).
Supervisory duties, §113-64.
Stock and stockholders.
Earnings above dividend requirements payable to state, §113-70.
Issuance of securities restricted, §113-68.
Limitation on bounties to stockholders, §113-69.
Limitations as to dividends, §113-67.

FOREST RANGERS.
Appointment.
Secretary of environment and natural resources, §113-52.
Citations.
Authority to issue, §113-55, (b).
Compensation, §113-56.
Duties.
Generally, §113-54.
Expenses.
Payment by state and counties, §113-54.
Forest fires.
Overtime compensation for forest fire fighting, §113-56.1.
Power to prevent and extinguish fires, §113-55, (a).
Instructions on forest preservation and development, §113-60, (a), (b).
Powers.
Forest fires.
Prevention and extinguishing, §113-55, (a).
Generally, §113-55.1.
Warning tickets and citations.
Authority to issue, §113-55, (b).
Warning tickets.
Authority to issue, §113-55, (b).

FOREST RESERVE.
United States acquisition of land for national forest reserve, §104-5.

FOREST ROAD SYSTEM.
Motor vehicle laws applicable to state parks and forest road system, §143-116.8.

FORESTRY COUNCIL, §§143B-308 to 143B-310.
Appointments, §143B-309.
Clerical services, §143B-309, (h).
Creation, §143B-308.
Meetings, §143B-310.
Members.
Categories, §143B-309, (a).
Chairperson, §143B-309, (c).
Designation from categories, §143B-309, (b).
Expenses, §143B-309, (f).
Quorum, §143B-309, (g).
Removal of members, §143B-309, (e).
Terms, §143B-309, (d).
Powers and duties, §143B-308.
Special meetings, §143B-310.

FORESTRY DEVELOPMENT ACT.
Primary forest product assessment act, §§113A-189 to 113A-196.
See FOREST PRODUCTS ASSESSMENT.

FORESTRY NOTICES.
Penalty to destroy, §113-58.

FORESTRY OPERATION NUISANCE LIABILITY, §§106-700, 106-701.

FORESTRY SERVICES FOR OWNERS AND OPERATORS OF FORESTLAND.
Administration of provisions.
Under direction of secretary, §113-81.2, (a).
Deposits of receipts with state treasury, §113-81.3.
Expenses for services and advice, §113-81.2, (b), (c).
Scientific forestry services, §113-81.1, (a), (b).

FORESTS AND FORESTRY.
Acquisition of lands.
Disposition of lands acquired.
Department of environment and natural resources, §113-44.

FORESTS AND FORESTRY —Cont'd
Acquisition of lands —Cont'd
Disposition of revenues received.
Department of environment and natural resources, §113-42.
State not obligated for debts created hereunder, §113-43.
Appeals.
Protection and development corporations, §113-66.
Appropriations.
Forest management appropriation, §113-33.
Arrest.
Forest law-enforcement officers.
Powers, §113-55.1.
Assessment of primary forest products, §§113A-189 to 113A-196.
See FOREST PRODUCTS ASSESSMENT.
Burning.
Prescribed burning of forestlands, §§113-60.40 to 113-60.45.
Citations.
Forest rangers.
Authority to issue, §113-55, (b).
Closing forests and woodlands to hunting, fishing and trapping, §113-60.1.
Publication of proclamation, §113-60.2.
Annulment thereof, §113-60.2.
Violation of proclamation a misdemeanor, §113-60.3.
Commission on agriculture and forestry awareness, §§120-150 to 120-154.
Cooperative agreements.
Insect infestation and disease, §113-60.9.
Cooperative associations.
Authorized purposes, §§54-111, 54-124.
Corporations for protection in development of forest, §§113-61 to 113-77.
See FOREST PROTECTION AND DEVELOPMENT CORPORATIONS.
Counties.
Cooperation between counties and state in forest protection and development, §113-59.
Demonstration forests.
Use of lands acquired by counties through tax foreclosures, §113-30.
Procedure for acquisition of delinquent tax lands from counties, §113-31.
Taxation.
Procedure for acquisition of delinquent tax lands from counties, §113-31.
Definitions.
Forest fires.
Firefighters on standby duty, §113-60.32.
Forest laws, §113-53.1.
Insect infestation and disease, §113-60.6.
Open fires, §113-60.22.
Owners and operators of forest land, §113-81.1, (a).
Primary forest product assessment act, §113A-191.
Protection and development of forests, §113-61, (a).
Woodlands, §113-57.
Demonstration forests.
Purchase of lands for use, §113-32.
Use of lands acquired by counties through tax foreclosures, §113-30.
Procedure for acquisition of delinquent tax lands from counties, §113-31.
Department of environment and natural resources.
Acquisition and control of state forests.
Department defined, §113-29, (a).

FORESTS AND FORESTRY —Cont'd
Department of environment and natural resources —Cont'd
Acquisition and control of state forests —Cont'd
Policy and plan to be inaugurated by department, §113-29, (b).
Power to acquire, §113-34, (a), (b).
Acquisition of lands.
Disposition of lands acquired, §113-44.
State not obligated for debts created hereunder, §113-43.
Control of state forest.
Department and secretary to have full control, §113-22.
Cooperation between counties and state in forest protection and development, §113-59.
Corporations for protection and development of forests.
Department defined, §113-61, (a).
Secretary defined, §113-61, (a).
Counties.
Demonstration forests.
Use of lands acquired by counties through tax foreclosures.
Procedure for acquisition of delinquent tax lands from counties, §113-31.
Demonstration forests.
Purchase of lands for use, §§113-31, 113-32.
Use of lands acquired by counties through tax foreclosures, §113-30.
Procedure for acquisition of tax-delinquent lands from counties, §113-31.
Disposition of revenues received from lands acquired, §113-42.
Donations of property for forestry or park purposes, §113-40.
Expenditure of funds for development, §113-41.
Rules and regulations, §113-41.
Eminent domain.
Land for purposes of establishing or developing state forests, state parks and other areas, §113-34, (a).
Forest fires.
Powers, §113-51, (a), (b).
Forest rangers.
Appointment by secretary, §113-52.
Compensation, §113-56.
Gifts of land.
Acceptance, §113-34, (a), (b).
Insect infestation and disease, §§113-60.4 to 113-60.10.
See FOREST INSECT INFESTATION AND DISEASE PROTECTION.
Leases of lands and waters, §113-34, (c).
Owners and operators of forestland.
Forestry service and advice for.
Department defined, §113-81.1, (a).
Secretary defined, §113-81.1, (a).
Protection and development of forests.
Corporations for.
Department defined, §113-61, (a).
Secretary defined, §113-61, (a).
Purchase of lands.
Legislative authority necessary for payment, §113-37.
Sale of forestlands.
Distribution of funds, §113-38.
Secretary.
Insect infestation and disease.
Authority of secretary, §113-60.8.

FORESTS AND FORESTRY —Cont'd
Department of environment and natural resources —Cont'd
State forests, parks, lakes and recreation areas.
Acquisition of land, power, §113-34, (a), (b), (f).
Authority of department generally, §113-35, (e).
Concessions for operation of public service facilities, §113-35, (b).
Control of state forest, §113-22.
Hunting and fishing privileges.
Collection of reasonable fees, §113-35, (b).
Leases of lands and waters for, §113-34, (c).
Public service facilities and conveniences.
Construction, operation and collection of reasonable fees, §113-35, (b).
Selling, cutting and removing timber and other products, §113-35, (a).
Selling seedlings from nurseries and orchards, §113-35, (a).
Tree nurseries and tree seed orchards, §113-35, (a).
Eminent domain.
Acquisition of and for purposes of establishing and developing state forests, state parks and other areas, §113-34, (a).
Forest development act, §§113A-176 to 113A-183.
See FOREST DEVELOPMENT ACT.
Foresters, §§89B-1 to 89B-15.
See FORESTERS.
Forest fires.
Generally.
See FOREST FIRES.
Forest laws.
Defined, §113-53.1.
Forest rangers.
Generally.
See FOREST RANGERS.
Forestry council, §§143B-308 to 143B-310.
Gifts.
Acceptance of gifts of forest and submarginal farm land acquired by federal government, §113-34, (b).
Acceptance of gifts of land to state to be used as state forest, §113-34, (a).
Donations of property for forestry or park purposes, §113-40.
Governor.
Acceptance of gifts of land for state forests purposes, §113-34, (a).
Authority to close forests and woodlands to hunting, fishing and trapping, §§113-60.1 to 113-60.3.
Immunities.
Prescribed burning of forestlands, §113-60.42, (b), (c).
Insect infestation and disease protection, §§113-60.4 to 113-60.10.
See FOREST INSECT INFESTATION AND DISEASE PROTECTION.
Law enforcement officers, §113-55.1.
Littering state forests, §14-399.
Loans.
Protection and development corporations.
Power to borrow money limited, §113-74.
Marketing associations, §§54-129 to 54-166.
See MARKETING ASSOCIATIONS.
National park, parkway and forest development council, §§143B-324.1 to 143B-324.3.
North Carolina museum of forestry.
Satellite museum of state museum of natural sciences, §143B-344.23.

FORESTS AND FORESTRY —Cont'd
Notice.
Destruction of posted forestry notices, §113-58.
Nuisances.
Liability of agricultural and forestry operations, §§106-700, 106-701.
Prescribed burning of forestlands.
Not to constitute public or private nuisance, §113-60.42, (a).
Open fires regulation, §§113-60.21 to 113-60.31.
See OPEN FIRES.
Overtime compensation for forest firefighting, §113-56.1.
Owners and operators of forestland.
Department of environment and natural resources.
Department defined, §113-81.1.
Expenses of services.
Deposit of receipts with state treasury, §113-81.3.
Scientific forestry services, §113-81.1, (a), (b).
Secretary of environment and natural resources.
Secretary defined, §113-81.1.
Services and advice.
Administration of provisions.
Under direction of secretary, §113-81.2, (a).
Expenses, §113-81.2, (b), (c).
Pollution control.
Forest practice guidelines related to water quality.
Best management practices, §113A-52.1.
Prescribed burning of forestlands, §§113-60.40 to 113-60.45.
Conduct, §113-60.43, (b).
Definitions, §113-60.41.
Division of forest resources.
Rules, §113-60.44.
Exemptions, §113-60.45.
Immunities, §113-60.42, (b), (c).
Legislative findings, §113-60.40.
Nuisances.
Not to constitute, §113-60.42, (a).
Open-burning permit, §113-60.43, (c).
Prescription, §113-60.43, (a).
Rules, §113-60.44.
Primary forest product assessment act, §§113A-189 to 113A-196.
See FOREST PRODUCTS ASSESSMENT.
Prisons and prisoners.
Employment of prisoners, §148-26, (c).
Property taxes.
Agricultural, horticultural and forestland, §§105-277.2 to 105-277.7.
Protection and development.
Cooperation between counties and state, §113-59.
Corporations, §§113-61 to 113-77.
See FOREST PROTECTION AND DEVELOPMENT CORPORATIONS.
Instructions on forest preservation and development, §113-60, (a), (b).
Purchase of lands.
Legislative authority necessary for payment, §113-37.
Real property.
Donations of property for forestry or park purposes, §113-40.
Sales.
Distribution of funds from sale, §113-38.
State forests.
Seedlings from forest nurseries and forest seed orchards.
Authority of department of environment and natural resources, §113-35, (a).

FORESTS AND FORESTRY —Cont'd
Sales —Cont'd
State forests —Cont'd
Selling, cutting and removing timber and other products.
Authority of department of environment and natural resources, §113-35, (a).
Scientific forestry services.
Authority to render, §113-81.1, (a), (b).
Sedimentation pollution control act of 1973.
Forest practice guidelines related to water quality.
Best management practices, §113A-52.1.
Southeastern interstate forest fire protection compact, §§113-60.11 to 113-60.15.
State forest.
Generally.
See STATE FORESTS.
Taxation.
Counties.
Procedure for acquisition of delinquent tax lands from counties, §113-31.
Demonstration forests.
Use of lands acquired by counties through tax foreclosures, §113-30.
Procedure for acquisition of delinquent tax lands from counties, §113-31.
Property taxes.
Agricultural, horticultural and forestland, §§105-277.2 to 105-277.7.
See PROPERTY TAXES.
Trees and timber.
See TREES AND TIMBER.
United States.
Donations of property for forestry or park purposes.
Agreements with federal government or agencies for acquisition, §113-40.
Forest development act.
Federal cost sharing programs.
Eligible landowners may not use state funds if funds from federal program received, §113A-181, (c).
Forest reserve in North Carolina.
Acquisition of land for, §104-5.
Authorized, §104-5.
Warning tickets.
Issuance, §113-55.2, (a).
Authority to issue, §113-55, (b).
Conditions, §113-55.2, (b).
No right to be issued, §113-55.2, (d).
Previously issued tickets, §113-55.2, (c).
Water and air resources.
Sedimentation pollution control act of 1973.
Forest practice guidelines related to water quality.
Best management practices, §113A-52.1.
Western North Carolina arboretum, §§116-240 to 116-244.

FORFEITURE OF OFFICE.
Quo warranto action by attorney general, §1-515.

FORFEITURES.
Accident and health insurance.
Final payment of premium.
Notice required before forfeiture, §58-50-35.
Actions to recover.
Repeal of statute not to affect actions, §12-2.
Alcoholic beverages, §18B-504.

FORFEITURES —Cont'd
Apportionment to school administrative units, §115C-452.
Archaeological resources protection.
Violations of provisions, §70-17.
Bail bond forfeiture, §§15A-544.1 to 15A-544.8.
See BAIL AND RECOGNIZANCE.
Bail bondsmen and runners, §58-71-35.
Bonds, surety.
Failure of surety companies to pay judgment is forfeiture, §58-73-25.
Child support enforcement.
Licensing privileges, §50-13.12.
Civil penalty and forfeiture fund, §§115C-457.1 to 115C-457.3.
Commercial drivers' licenses.
Child support enforcement, §50-13.12.
Conviction of felony, automatic forfeiture, §15A-1331A.
Constitution of North Carolina.
Local, private and special legislation prohibited, Const. N. C., art. II, §24.
Continuing criminal enterprise.
Forfeiture of profits, §14-7.20, (b).
Disbursement of proceeds.
School administrative units, §115C-452.
Drivers' licenses.
Child support enforcement, §50-13.12.
Conviction of felony, automatic forfeiture, §15A-1331A.
Limited driving privilege, eligibility, §20-179.3, (b).
Drugs.
Controlled substances, §§90-112, 90-112.1.
Vehicles and other personal property used in controlled substances offenses, §90-112.
Applicability of article, §90-113.7.
Mitigation or remission of forfeitures, §90-112.1.
Electrologists.
Schools of electrology.
Failure to renew certification, §88A-20.
Electronic surveillance devices, §15A-289.
Felonies.
Licensing privilege after conviction of felony, §15A-1331A.
Money or other property or interest acquired, §14-2.3, (a).
Action to recover, statute of limitation, §14-2.3, (b).
Property traceable to owner or guardian, inapplicability of forfeiture, §14-2.3, (c).
Fishing licenses.
Child support enforcement, §50-13.12.
Conviction of felony, automatic forfeiture, §15A-1331A.
General assembly.
Local, private and special legislation prohibited, Const. N. C., art. II, §24.
Health.
Money or property unlawfully acquired, §130A-27.
Hunting licenses.
Child support enforcement, §50-13.12.
Conviction of felony, automatic forfeiture, §15A-1331A.
Impaired driving offenses, §§20-28.2 to 20-28.9.
Landlord and tenant.
Term forfeited for nonpayment of rent, §42-3.
Larceny, conveyances used in committing, §14-86.1.
Lewd matter, §19-6.

FORFEITURES —Cont'd
Licensing privileges.
Child support enforcement, §50-13.12.
Conviction of felony, automatic forfeiture, §15A-1331A.
Limitation of action, §1-54.
Littering.
Vehicles or machines involved in disposal of certain amount of litter, §14-399, (g).
Lubricating oils.
Person violating or allowing employee to violate article, §119-5.
Motor vehicles.
Controlled substances.
Conveyances used in violations of provisions, §§90-112, 90-112.1.
Forfeitures of personal property used in controlled substances offenses, §90-112.
Applicability of article, §90-113.7.
Mitigation or remission of forfeiture, §90-112.1.
Impaired driving offenses, §§20-28.2 to 20-28.9.
Habitual impaired driving, §20-138.5, (e).
Nuisances against public morals, abatement, §19-6.
Occupational licenses.
Child support enforcement, §50-13.12.
Conviction of felony, automatic forfeiture, §15A-1331A.
Pawnbrokers.
Pawn transactions, §91A-9.
Personal property.
Controlled substances offenses, §90-112.
Applicability of article, §90-113.7.
Mitigation or remission of forfeiture, §90-112.1.
Plant protection and conservation.
Illegally possessed plants, §106-202.20.
Public schools.
Apportionment to school administrative units, §115C-452.
Racketeer influenced and corrupt organizations.
Forfeiture of property.
See RACKETEER INFLUENCED AND CORRUPT ORGANIZATIONS.
Record and tape piracy.
Infringing articles, implements, devices and equipment, §14-437, (b).
Rents.
Term forfeited for nonpayment of rent, §42-3.
Tax credit for qualified business investments, §105-163.014.
Usury, §24-2.
Venue.
Action of recovery of penalty or forfeiture, §1-77.
Vessels.
Controlled substances.
Conveyances used in violations of provisions.
Generally, §§90-112, 90-112.1.
Weapons.
Confiscation of deadly weapons generally, §14-269.1.

FORGERY.
Bank deposits and collections.
Customer's duty to discover and report, §25-4-406.
Banks.
Notes, checks and other securities, §14-119.
Connecting genuine parts, §14-125.
Bills of exchange, §14-122.
Selling of certain forged securities, §14-121.

FORGERY —Cont'd
Bills of lading.
Felony, §21-42.
Bond issues, §14-122.
Selling of certain forged securities, §14-121.
Checks, §14-119.
Constitution of the United States, Const. U. S., art. I, §8.
Conveyances.
Excise stamp tax.
Reproduction of tax stamps, §105-228.36.
Corporations.
Certificates of corporate stock forged, §14-124.
Counterfeit money, §§14-13 to 14-16.
See COUNTERFEITING.
Deeds, §14-122.
Diplomas, §14-122.1.
Drugs.
Controlled substances.
Acquiring or obtaining possession by, §90-108, (a).
Education.
Diplomas, §14-122.1.
Documents issued by educational institutions.
Governmental agency, §14-122.1, (b).
Making or using, §14-122.1, (a).
Misdemeanors, §14-122.1, (c).
Postsecondary educational institution, §14-122.1, (b).
Secondary school, §14-122.1, (b).
Transcripts, §14-122.1.
Elections.
Absentee ballots, §163-237, (c).
False pretenses and cheats.
Obtaining signatures by false pretenses, §14-101.
Financial transaction cards.
Criminal possession of financial transaction card forgery devices, §14-113.14, (a), (b).
Elements of offense, §14-113.11, (a).
Embossing financial transaction card falsely, §14-113.11, (c).
Encoding financial transaction card falsely, §14-113.11, (d).
Making financial transaction card falsely, §14-113.11, (b).
Prima facie evidence of forgery, §14-113.12, (a), (b).
Indictments.
Intent to defraud.
Sufficiency of allegation, §15-151.
Leases, §14-122.
Letters of credit.
Basis for dishonor, §25-5-108, (d).
Injunction on honoring, §25-5-109, (b).
Issuer allowed to honor despite, §25-5-109, (a).
Military affairs.
Registration of military discharges.
Forgery of discharge or certificate, §47-112.
Motor vehicle certificates of title, registration cards or applications, §20-71, (a).
Motor vehicle inspection stickers, §20-183.8, (c).
Negotiable instruments.
Bank notes, checks and other securities, §14-119.
Connecting genuine parts, §14-125.
Uttering instrument containing forged endorsement, §14-120.
Notes, §14-119.
Connecting genuine parts of notes, §14-125.
Petitions, §14-123.
Probate and registration.
Military discharge registration, §47-112.

FORGERY —Cont'd
Promissory notes, §14-122.
Selling of certain forged securities, §14-121.
Securities, §14-119.
Selling of certain forged securities, §14-121.
Universities and colleges.
Transcripts and diplomas, §14-122.1.
Uttering.
Elements of offense, §14-120.
Petitions forged, §14-123.
Wills, §14-122.

FOR-HIRE PASSENGER VEHICLES.
Window tinting exceptions, §20-127, (c).

FORMA PAUPERIS.
See IN FORMA PAUPERIS.

FORMER TESTIMONY.
Hearsay exception, §8C-1, Rule 804, (b).

FORMS.
Absentees in military service.
Transfer of property valued at less than five thousand dollars.
Procedure without receivership, §28B-9, (a).
Acknowledgments.
Acknowledgment by grantor, §47-38.
Certificate of acknowledgment of instrument executed by attorney-in-fact, §47-43.
Advance instruction for mental health treatment, §122C-77.
Answers, §1A-1, Rule 84.
Appeals, App. Proc., Appx. D.
Briefs, App. Proc., Appx. E.
Entries, App. Proc., Appx. D.
Petition for discretionary review, App. Proc., Appx. D.
Petition for writ of supersedeas and motion for temporary stay, App. Proc., Appx. D.
Appointment to public office.
Notice, §143-47.7, (c).
Arbitration and award.
Rules for court-ordered arbitration, Arbitration Rule 8.
Attorney disciplinary proceedings.
Form letters, district grievance committees.
Letter of notice to respondent attorney, Bar Rules & Regs., B, §.0216.
Letter to complainant acknowledging grievance, Bar Rules & Regs., B, §.0213.
Letter to complainant from investigating attorney, Bar Rules & Regs., B, §.0215.
Letter to complainant/respondent where district committee recommends finding of no probable cause, Bar Rules & Regs., B, §.0210.
Letter to complainant where district committee recommends finding of probable cause, Bar Rules & Regs., B, §.0212.
Letter to complainant where local grievance alleges fee dispute and other violations, Bar Rules & Regs., B, §.0209.
Letter to complainant where local grievance alleges fee dispute only, Bar Rules & Regs., B, §.0208.
Letter to investigating attorney assigning grievance, Bar Rules & Regs., B, §.0214.
Letter to respondent where district committee recommends finding of probable cause, Bar Rules & Regs., B, §.0211.
Letter transmitting completed file to North Carolina state bar, Bar Rules & Regs., B, §.0217.

FORMS —Cont'd
Bad checks.
Letters of notification and demand, §6-21.3, (a1), (a2).
Bonds, surety.
Model payment and performance bonds, §44A-33.
Summary ejectment.
Bond to stay execution.
Form of undertaking, §42-34, (d).
Budget.
Itemized statements and forms, §143-7, (a).
Account codes, §143-7, (b).
Limit on number of state employees, §143-10.2.
Certiorari.
Petition for writ, App. Proc., Appx. D.
Child care provider criminal history record check.
Statement furnished to child care provider, §110-90.2, (c).
Childhood vaccine-related injury compensation.
Official forms of the industrial commission, Childhood Vac. Rule 103.
Civil actions, §1A-1, Rule 84.
Claim and delivery.
Notice of hearing, §1-474.1, (c).
Waiver of hearing, §1-474.1, (c).
Commodities.
Adoption or modification.
Approval of administrator required, §78D-27, (b).
Publication authority of administrator, §78D-27, (c).
Complaints, §1A-1, Rule 84.
Concealed handgun permit.
Application form provided by sheriff, §14-415.13, (a).
Contents of form, §14-415.14.
Consent to health care for minor.
Authorization, §32A-34.
Corporations.
Conveyances.
Probate for deeds and other conveyances, §47-41.01, (b), (c).
Instrument executed by president or presiding member or trustee, §47-41.02, (b) to (d).
Other forms not excluded, §47-41.01, (a).
Other forms of probate for corporate conveyances.
Contracts in writing for purchase of personal property, §47-41.02, (f).
Other forms not excluded, §47-41.02, (a).
Validation of deeds and other conveyances executed on or before April 12, 1974, §47-41.02, (g).
Validation of conveyances probated and recorded prior to February 14, 1939, §47-41.02, (e).
Criminal history record checks.
Child care providers.
Statement furnished to child care provider, §110-90.2, (c).
Custodial trusts.
Custodial trustees receipt and acceptance, §33B-4, (b).
Declaration of trust under act, §33B-18, (a).
Transfer under act, §33B-18, (a).
Deeds.
Register to fill in deeds on blank forms with lines, §47-35.

FORMS —Cont'd
Domestic violence.
Pro se forms, §50B-2, (d).
Drainage districts.
Receipt books, §§156-108, 156-109.
Eminent domain.
Private condemnors.
Commissioners.
Report of assessment of compensation, §40A-27.
Public condemnors.
Commissioners.
Report of assessment of compensation, §40A-48, (c).
Executions, §1-313.
Exemptions.
Setting aside exempt property.
Statement by debtor, §1C-1603, (c).
Exempt property from claims of creditors.
Notice, §1C-1603, (a).
Exempt property from enforcement of claims of creditors.
Statement of debtor, §1C-1603, (c).
Foreign-money claims.
Judgments, §1C-1826, (f).
Garnishment.
Notice of levy, §1-440.24.
Summons to garnishee, §1-440.23.
General assembly.
Approval of bills, §120-29.1.
Reconvened sessions.
Request that session not be held, §120-6.1, (b).
Health.
Communicable diseases.
Form and content of reports, §130A-141.
Temporary order to report health related information, §130A-141.1.
Health care powers of attorney.
Statutory form, §32A-25.
Husband and wife.
Acknowledgments.
Husband's and wife's acknowledgment before same officer, §47-40.
Indictments.
Defects which do not vitiate, §15-155.
Informality.
Bill or warrant not quashed for informality, §15-153.
Perjury.
Bill for perjury, §15-145.
Insurance.
Accident and health insurance.
Approval by commissioner, §§58-3-150, (b), 58-51-95, (a).
Group or blanket accident and health insurance, §58-51-85.
Policies, §58-51-5, (a).
Approval of forms by commissioner, §58-51-1.
Other states, §58-51-5, (b).
Approval of policy forms by commissioner of insurance, §58-3-150, (a).
Credit insurance.
Disapproval by commissioner, §58-57-30, (b).
Notice, §58-57-30, (c).
Filing with commissioner, §58-57-30, (a).
Action by commissioner on, §58-57-30, (b).
Withdrawal of approval by commissioner, §58-57-30, (d), (e).
Existing policy forms, §58-40-115.
Fire insurance.
Standard fire insurance policy, §58-44-15, (c).

FORMS —Cont'd
Insurance —Cont'd
Fire insurance —Cont'd
State property fire insurance fund.
Policy forms, §58-31-12.
Life insurance.
Group life insurance policies, §58-3-150, (b).
Proof of lost forms.
Insurance companies to furnish, §58-3-40.
Uniform claim forms for health benefit plans, §58-3-171.
Joint accounts.
Credit unions.
Statement establishing, §54-109.58, (a).
Savings and loan associations.
Statement establishing, §54B-129, (a).
Joint deposits.
Right of survivorship, §41-2.1, (g).
Judgments.
Cancellation, assignment, etc., of judgments.
Docket or record book, §1-239.1.
Landlord and tenant.
Summary ejectment.
Undertaking and order to stay execution of judgment, §42-34, (d).
Law students providing legal services.
Withdrawal of dean's certificate, Bar Rules & Regs., C, §.0210.
Leases.
Registration of leases, §47-118.
Libraries.
Interstate library compact.
Articles of compact, §125-12.
Loan broker disclosure statements, §66-107.
Marriage.
Licenses, §51-16.
Registration of marriage certificates, §130A-110, (a).
Membership camping contracts, notice of cancellations, §66-240.
Mental health, developmental disability, substance abuse.
Advance instruction for mental health treatment, §122C-77.
Mortgages and deeds of trust.
Affidavit of lost note, §47-46.3.
Probate and registration.
Blank and master forms of mortgages, §47-21.
Sales under power of sale.
Requests for notice, §45-21.17A, (a).
Satisfaction of deeds of trust and mortgages, §47-46.2.
Motions, §1A-1, Rule 84.
Motor vehicles.
Commissioner of motor vehicles to provide, §20-41.
Municipal corporations.
Annexation by petition.
Form of petition, §160A-31, (b).
Negligence.
Complaints for negligence, §1A-1, Rule 84.
Notice.
Service of process by publication, §1A-1, Rule 4, (j).
Notice of appointment to public office, §143-47.7, (c).
Notice of open dumps, §130A-301, (f).
Oaths, §11-11.
Open dump notice, §130A-301, (f).
Payment bond, §44A-33, (a).

FORMS —Cont'd
Payment on death accounts.
Form of statement to be signed and executed, §53-146.2, (a).
Savings and loan associations.
Statement establishing, §54B-130, (a).
Performance bond, §44A-33, (a).
Personal agency accounts.
Credit unions.
Statement establishing, §54-109.63, (a).
Physicians dispensing prescription drugs.
Registration forms, §90-85.21, (b).
Pleadings, §1A-1, Rule 84.
POD accounts.
Form of statement to be signed and executed, §53-146.2, (a).
Savings and loan associations.
Statement establishing, §54B-130, (a).
Powers of attorney.
Certificate of acknowledgment of instrument executed by attorney-in-fact, §47-43.
Statutory short form, §§32A-1 to 32A-3.
Prisons and prisoners.
Compensation to persons erroneously convicted of felonies, §148-83.
Probate and registration.
Acknowledgment by grantor, §47-38.
Adjudication and order of registration, §47-37, (b).
Blank and master forms of mortgages.
Embodiment by reference in instruments later filed, §47-21.
Certificate of acknowledgment of instrument executed by attorney-in-fact, §47-43.
Certificate of registration, §47-37, (a).
Corporate conveyances, §47-41.01, (b), (c).
Other forms not excluded, §47-41.01, (a).
Other forms of probate for corporate conveyances.
Contracts in writing for purchase of personal property, §47-41.02, (f).
Instrument executed by president or presiding member or trustee, §47-41.02, (b) to (d).
Other forms not excluded, §47-41.01, (a).
Validation of certain forms.
Prior to February 14, 1939, §47-41.02, (e).
Validation of deeds and conveyances executed on or before April 12, 1974, §47-41.02, (g).
Leases.
Registration of lease, §47-118.
Magistrates.
Clerk's certificate upon probate by magistrate, §47-44.
Master forms of deeds, mortgages and deeds of trust, §47-21.
Military officers, §47-2.
Notice of satisfaction of deed of trust or other instrument, §47-46.1.
Officer's certificate upon proof of instrument by proof of signature of subscribing witness, §§47-43.3, 47-43.4.
Options.
Memorandum of options, §47-117.
Probate by nonresident official without seal.
Clerk's certificate, §47-45.
Register of deeds.
Register to fill in deeds on blank forms with lines, §47-35.
Subscribing witnesses.
Officer's certificate upon proof of instrument by witness, §47-43.2.

FORMS —Cont'd
Probate and registration —Cont'd
Verification by register of deeds.
Form of entry, §47-46.
Professional corporation or professional limited liability company practicing law, Bar Rules & Regs., E, §.0106.
Publication.
Notice of service of process by publication, §1A-1, Rule 4, (j).
Termination of parental rights proceedings.
Unknown parent, §7B-1105, (d).
Real property.
Options to purchase real property, §47-119.
Reconvening of legislature.
Request that session not be held, §120-6.1, (b).
Register of deeds.
Filling in deeds on blank forms with lines, §47-35.
Notice of satisfaction of deed of trust or other instrument, §47-46.1.
Verification of instruments.
Form of entry, §47-46.
Residential property disclosure act.
North Carolina real estate commission to prepare forms, §47E-10.
Restricted driving judgment, §20-16.1, (b1).
Retail installment sales.
Consumer credit installment sale contracts, §25A-28.
Home-solicitation sale.
Agreement or offer, §25A-40.
Rules of civil procedure, §1A-1, Rule 84.
Sale of crossbows or pistols.
License or permit, §14-403.
Sales and use tax.
Duties of secretary as to, §105-164.15.
Secured transactions.
Defaults.
Disposition of collateral after.
Consumer goods transactions.
Notification, §25-9-614.
Notification, §25-9-613.
Financing statements.
Amendment form, §25-9-521, (b).
Initial financing statement form, §25-9-521, (a).
Service of process.
Notice of service by publication, §1A-1, Rule 4, (j).
Small claim actions, §7A-232.
Specific performance.
Complaint for specific performance, §1A-1, Rule 84.
State treasurer.
Furnished by auditor, §147-84.
Taxation.
Furnished by secretary of revenue, §105-254.
Property taxes.
Department of revenue.
Prescribing forms, §105-318.
Mobile homes.
Tax permit, §105-316.5.
Order of collection, §105-321, (b).
Release of lien, §105-242, (c), (c1).
Termination of parental rights proceedings.
Publication, unknown parent, §7B-1105, (d).
Third-party practice.
Motion to bring in third-party defendant, §1A-1, Rule 84.
Third-party complaint, §1A-1, Rule 84.
Torrens system registration.
Attorney general to prescribe, §43-3.
Certificate of title, §43-15.

FORMS —Cont'd
Torrens system registration —Cont'd
Method of transfer.
Conveyance as security for debt, §43-36.
Release from registration, §43-25.
Transfers to minors.
Creating custodial property and effecting transfer, §33A-9, (a), (b).
Manner of creating custodial property and effecting transfer, §33A-9.
Viatical settlements.
License application, §58-58-210, (d).
Warehouse receipts, §25-7-202, (1).
Workers' compensation.
Compromise settlement agreements, I.C. Forms IIa to IIIb.
Official forms, I.C. Rule 103.
Tort claims rules, Tort Claim Rule T103.
Third party recovery.
Order directing distribution of, I.C. Form I.

FORMULAS.
Larceny of secret technical processes, §14-75.1.

FORNICATION, §§14-184, 50B-8.
Domestic violence.
Effect upon prosecution for public morals offenses, §50B-8.
Elements of offense, §14-184.
Hotels and inns.
Man and woman occupying same bedroom for immoral purposes, §14-186.
Sexual offenses generally.
See SEXUAL OFFENSES.

FORSYTH COUNTY.
Acquisition of property, power, §153A-158.1, (a).
Ambulance service.
Attachment or garnishment and lien for, §§44-51.4 to 44-51.8.
False pretenses and cheats.
Obtaining ambulance services without intending to pay, §14-111.2.
Board of county commissioners.
Filling vacancies on board, §153A-27.1.
Condemnation or acquisition of land by local government unit outside county.
Consent of board of commissioners necessary, §153A-15.
Counties generally.
See COUNTIES.
County boards of education elected on partisan basis.
Vacancies in office, §115C-37.1.
Cropper or tenant refusing to perform terms of contract.
Forfeiture of right of possession to premises, §42-27.
Dangerous firearm use by young children, permitting.
Air rifles, air pistols and BB guns not dangerous firearm, §14-316, (b).
Motor vehicle emission inspections.
Counties inspections required to be performed in, §143-215.107A, (c).
Private parking lots.
Removal of unauthorized vehicles, §20-219.2.
Real estate mortgage loans.
Interest, commissions and repayment, §45-43.
Registration of deeds.
Tax certification, no delinquent taxes due, §161-31, (b).

FORSYTH COUNTY —Cont'd
School property.
Acquisition and improvement, §153A-158.1.
Sheriff.
Vacancy, performance of duties until vacancy filled, §162-5.1.

FORT FISHER RECREATION AREA.
Twenty-four hour access from Sept. 15 through March 15.
Persons paying fees, §113-35, (b1).

FORTHCOMING BOND FOR PERSONAL PROPERTY, §1-318.
Procedure on giving bond, §1-319.
Subsequent levies, §1-319.
Summary remedy, §1-320.

FORTIFIED WINE.
Consumption, §18B-301, (d).
Definition of fortified wine, §18B-101.
Possession, §18B-301.

FORUM NON CONVENIENS.
Change of venue, §1-83.
Child custody jurisdiction and enforcement, §§50A-206, (a), 50A-207.
Stay of proceeding to permit trial in foreign jurisdiction, §1-75.12.

FORUM SELECTION.
Contracts to improve real property.
Subject to laws of another state.
Void and against public policy, §22B-2.
Contracts with forum selection provisions.
Invalid and against public policy, §22B-3.
Leases, UCC.
Commercial leases.
Limitation on power of parties to choose applicable law and judicial forum, §25-2A-106.

FOSTER CARE AND ADOPTION ASSISTANCE, §§108A-48 to 108A-50.
Adoption assistance payments.
Granting, rules, §108A-49, (b).
Benefits for certain adoptive children.
Authorization of program, §108A-50, (a).
Eligibility, §108A-50, (c).
When assistance not to be provided, §108A-50, (d).
Purpose of program, §108A-50, (b).
Special needs adoption incentive fund, §108A-50.1.
Creation of program, §108A-25, (a).
Foster care benefits program.
Authorized, §108A-48, (a).
Eligibility, §108A-48, (b).
Granting assistance, rules, §108A-49, (a).
Purposes, §108A-48, (a).
Use of available federal payments, §108A-49, (c).
Special needs adoption incentive fund, §108A-50.1.
Using federal payments, §108A-49, (c).

FOSTER HOMES.
Abused, neglected or dependent juvenile actions.
Dispositional order placing juvenile, requirements, §7B-905, (c).
Review by court of voluntary foster care placements, §7B-910.
Additional hearings, §7B-909, (c).
Authority of court upon making findings, §7B-909, (b).

FOSTER HOMES —Cont'd
Abused, neglected or dependent juvenile actions —Cont'd
Review by court of voluntary foster care placements —Cont'd
Findings to be made, §7B-909, (a).
Notice of hearings, §7B-909, (c).
Time for holding hearings, §7B-909, (c).
Child placement.
Control over child caring facilities, §§110-45 to 110-48.
Foster care and adoption assistance, §§108A-48 to 108A-50.
Criminal record checks, §114-19.4.
Educating children with special needs placed in home.
Costs borne by local board of education, §115C-140.1, (a).
Actual cost of service, department to determine, §115C-140.1, (c).
Reserve fund to reimburse board, §115C-140.1, (b).
Public schools.
Children living in foster homes.
Assignments to school, §115C-366, (a1).
Regulation of agencies receiving or placing children, §§131D-10.1 to 131D-10.9.
See CHILD PLACING AGENCIES.

FOSTER PARENTS.
Criminal history records checks.
Annual check, §131D-10.3A, (b).
Confidential and privileged information, §131D-10.3A, (f), (g).
Department of justice to provide information, §131D-10.3A, (d).
Destruction of information, §131D-10.3A, (g).
Fee for check, §131D-10.3A, (i).
Hearing, request by foster parent, §131D-10.3A, (f).
Immunity for action taken in carrying out provision, §131D-10.3A, (h).
Mandatory checks, §131D-10.3A, (a).
Notice of mandatory checks.
Placement on application, §131D-10.3A, (e).
Prohibiting person from providing foster care, §131D-10.3A, (c).
Review of information, right of individual, §131D-10.3A, (f).
Providing foster care.
Regulation generally, §§131D-10.1 to 131D-10.9.
See CHILD PLACING AGENCIES.
Register of applicants.
Division to maintain, §131D-10.6C.
Contents, §131D-10.6C, (a).
Training, §131D-10.6A, (a).

FOXES.
Calling devices.
Taking with electronic calling devices, §113-291.4, (d).
Closed seasons.
Hunting foxes with dogs harmful to turkey restoration, §113-291.4, (h).
Contagious diseases.
Population control measures, §113-291.4, (i).
Dogs.
Taking with dogs at night or day on year-round basis, §113-291.4, (b).
Firearms.
Taking foxes with, §113-291.4, (c).

FOXES —Cont'd
Hunting and wildlife generally.
See HUNTING AND WILDLIFE.
Open seasons for taking foxes with firearms, §113-291.4A, (a), (b).
Rabies emergencies.
Plan to reduce threat of rabies exposure to humans and domestic animals, §130A-201.
Rabies emergency for particular county.
Plan to reduce exposure to humans and domestic animals, §113-291.2, (a1).
Regulatory powers of wildlife resources commission.
Applicability to foxes, §113-291.4, (a).
Sale of parts prohibited, §113-291.3, (b).
Sales.
Foxes lawfully taken in areas of open seasons, §113-291.4, (g).
Seasons for taking foxes with weapons and trapping.
Continuance of seasons, §113-291.4, (f1).
Studies of fox and fur-bearer populations.
Wildlife resources commission to improve capabilities, §113-291.4, (e).
Tagging foxes and fox furs, §113-291.4, (g).
Trapping, §113-291.4, (f), (f1).
Unlawful trapping with electronic calling device, §113-294, (j).
Weapons.
Taking foxes with firearms, §113-291.4, (c).

FOX HUNTING.
Equine activity liability, §§99E-1 to 99E-3.

FOX HUNTING PRESERVES.
Controlled hunting preserve operator license, §113-273, (g).

FRAGILE RECORDS.
Inspection of public records, §132-6, (f).

FRANCHISE CARRIERS.
Junked or destroyed vehicles, §20-100.
Licenses for less than one year, §20-95.
Liens.
Taxation, §20-98.
Partial payments, §20-94.
Taxation.
Compensatory nature, §20-97.
Liens, §20-98.
Overpayment, §20-91.2.
Remedies for collection, §20-99, (a).

FRANCHISES.
Ambulances.
County ambulance services, §153A-250.
Beer franchises, §§18B-1300 to 18B-1308.
See BEER FRANCHISES.
Business opportunity sales, §§66-94 to 66-100.
See BUSINESS OPPORTUNITY SALES.
Cable television.
Counties, §153A-137.
Tax levy, §153A-154.
Municipal corporations, §160A-319.
Franchise tax, §160A-212.
Theft of cable television services, §14-118.5.
Carriers.
See FRANCHISE CARRIERS.
Cooperative associations.
Taxes, §54-118.2.
Counties.
Ambulance services, §153A-250.
Cable television franchises, §153A-137.
Taxation.
Power to levy annual taxes, §153A-154.
Ordinances, §153A-46.

FRANCHISES —Cont'd
Declaratory judgments.
Attorney general as party to proceedings involving constitutionality, §1-260.
Municipality as party to proceedings involving validity, §1-260.
Power of courts to construe, §1-254.
Electric membership corporations.
Municipal franchises, §§117-10.1, 117-10.2.
Farm machinery, §§66-180 to 66-188.
Gas and gas companies.
Natural gas.
Local distribution companies, §§62-36A, 62-36B.
Landfills.
Obtaining franchise to operate from local government, §130A-294, (b1).
Marketing associations, §54-143.1.
Motor carriers, §§62-111 to 62-113.
Motor vehicle dealers, §§20-305, 20-305.5, 20-307, 20-307.1.
Municipal corporations.
Cable television system, §160A-319, (b).
Ordinances, §160A-76, (a).
Public utilities, §160A-319, (a).
Taxicabs, §160A-304.
Natural gas.
Local distribution companies, §§62-36A, 62-36B.
Obscene articles or publications.
Denial of franchise for refusal to accept, §14-190.4.
Ordinances.
Grant, renewal, extension or amendment by ordinance.
Procedure, §160A-76, (a).
Public transportation authorities.
Effect of provisions on existing franchises and operations, §160A-584.
Power to grant franchises and enter into franchise agreements, §160A-579.
Public utilities.
Bus companies.
Application of provisions, §62-112, (d).
Certificates of convenience and necessity.
Generating facilities, §§62-82, 62-110.1.
Required, §62-110.
Conditions, §62-113, (a).
Defined, §62-3.
Effective date, §62-112, (a).
Emergency operating authority, §62-116, (b).
Motor carriers, §§62-111 to 62-113.
Partnership franchises, §62-115.
Same or similar names, §62-117.
Suspension or revocation, §62-112, (b).
Temporary authority to operate, §62-116, (a).
Terms, §62-113, (a).
Transfer, §62-111, (a).
Motor carriers, §62-111, (b), (c), (e).
Obtaining franchise for purpose of transferring same.
Prohibited, §62-111, (d).
Quo warranto.
Several claims to same franchise.
Tried in one action, §1-520.
Usurpation.
Action by attorney general, §1-515.
Shellfish.
Cultivation of shellfish.
Claims based upon perpetual franchise for shellfish cultivation, §113-206, (a1).
Leases.
Perpetual franchises, §113-202.2.

FRANCHISES —Cont'd
Solid waste management.
Obtaining franchise to operate landfill from local government, §130A-294, (b1).
Taxation, §§105-114 to 105-129.
See FRANCHISE TAX.

FRANCHISE TAX, §§105-114 to 105-129.
Burial.
Mutual burial associations, §105-121.1.
Business and energy tax credits, §§105-129.15 to 105-129.19.
Condition for doing business in state.
Payment, §105-114, (a2).
Corporations.
Additional nature of tax, §105-122, (f).
Allocation and apportionment of net income for income tax purposes, §105-122, (c).
Appraised value of tangible property, §105-122, (d).
Computing total actual investment in tangible personal property, §105-122, (d).
Credits, §105-122, (d1).
Deductible liabilities, §105-122, (b).
Defined, §105-114, (b).
Dissolved domestic corporations, §105-127, (f).
Exemptions, §105-125.
Formula for allocation, §105-122, (c).
Holding companies, §105-120.2.
Indebtedness owed to parent, subsidiary or affiliate, §105-122, (b).
Limited liability companies.
Controlled companies, §105-114.1.
Local taxation prohibited, §105-122, (g).
Minimum tax, §105-122, (d).
Nature of tax upon, §105-114, (a).
Nonprofit corporations.
Exemptions, §105-125.
Payment of tax, §105-122, (d).
Annual payment, §105-127, (a).
Pollution abatement equipment.
Deducted reserves, §105-122, (d).
Deductible liabilities, §105-122, (b).
Privilege of carrying on, doing business and/or continuance of articles of incorporation, §105-122, (d).
Rate of tax, §105-122, (d).
Reports, §105-122, (a).
Returns, §105-122, (a).
Change of income year, §105-122, (e).
Stock, surplus and undivided profits.
Determination of total amount, §105-122, (b).
Treasurers.
Duties, §105-127, (c).
Credit.
Low-income housing tax credits, §§105-129.40 to 105-129.45.
Research and development credit, §§105-129.50 to 105-129.55.
Tax incentives for new and expanding businesses generally, §§105-129.2 to 105-129.13.
See TAX INCENTIVES FOR NEW AND EXPANDING BUSINESSES.
Definitions, §105-114, (b).
Holding companies, §105-120.2, (c).
Electric companies.
Additional tax imposed by county or city.
Companies not subject to, §105-116, (e1).
Annual tax imposed, §105-116, (a).
City not to impose or collect greater tax, §105-116, (e).

FRANCHISE TAX —Cont'd
Electric companies —Cont'd
County or city imposing additional tax.
Companies not subject to, §105-116, (e1).
Distribution to cities, §105-116, (d).
City's share, §105-116.1, (b).
Definitions, §105-116.1, (a).
Hold-back amount for 1995-96 fiscal year, §105-116.1, (c) to (d).
Municipality incorporated on or after January 1, 2000, §105-116.1, (e).
Payment, return, report, §105-116, (b).
Rate of tax, §105-116, (a).
Exemptions, §105-125.
Holding companies, §105-120.2.
Defined, §105-120.2, (c).
Local taxation prohibited, §105-120.2, (e).
Rate of tax, §105-120.2, (b).
Reports, §105-120.2, (a).
Investment companies.
Exemption, §105-125, (b).
Joint municipal electric power and energy act.
Payments in lieu of taxes, §159B-27, (b).
Limited liability companies.
Controlled companies.
Constructive ownership rules.
Ownership of capital interest determined by, §105-114.1, (c).
Definitions, §105-114.1, (a).
Percentage included in tax base, §105-114.1, (b).
Exemption, §105-114.1, (f).
Owner of capital interests affiliated group of corporations, §105-114.1, (e).
Time ownership of capital interests determined, §105-114.1, (g).
Underpayment, fraud to evade, penalty, §105-114.1, (h).
Income, assets, liabilities and equity.
Included in member corporation's computation of tax, §105-114, (c).
Low-income housing tax credits, §§105-129.40 to 105-129.45.
Mutual burial associations, §105-121.1.
Nature of taxes, §105-114, (a).
New and expanding businesses.
Tax incentives generally, §§105-129.2 to 105-129.13.
See TAX INCENTIVES FOR NEW AND EXPANDING BUSINESSES.
No double taxation, §105-114, (a4).
Payment.
Condition for doing business in state, §105-114, (a2).
Power of attorney.
Secretary of revenue, §105-128.
Privilege or excise taxes, §105-114, (a1).
Real estate investment trust.
Exemption, §105-125, (b).
Recycling facilities.
Tax credit for large or major recycling facility investment, §§105-129.25 to 105-129.28.
Regulated investment companies.
Exemption, §105-125, (b).
Reports.
Corporations, §105-122, (a).
Research and development tax credit, §§105-129.50 to 105-129.55.
Returns.
Corporations, §105-122, (a).
Change of income year, §105-122, (e).
Extension of time for filing, §105-129.

FRANCHISE TAX —Cont'd
Scope of tax, §105-114, (a1).
Secretary of revenue.
Extension of time for filing returns, §105-129.
Power of attorney, §105-128.
Sewerage companies.
Annual tax imposed, §105-116, (a).
City not to impose or collect greater tax, §105-116, (e).
Distribution to cities, §105-116, (d).
Payment, return, report, §105-116, (b).
Rate of tax, §105-116, (a).
Tax incentives for new and expanding businesses generally, §§105-129.2 to 105-129.13.
See TAX INCENTIVES FOR NEW AND EXPANDING BUSINESSES.
Tax year, §105-114, (a3).
Telephone companies.
Distribution of gross receipts taxes to cities, §105-116.1.
Definitions, §105-116.1, (a).
Water companies.
Annual tax imposed, §105-116, (a).
City not to impose or collect greater tax, §105-116, (e).
Distribution to cities, §105-116, (d).
Payment, return, report, §105-116, (b).
Rate of tax, §105-116, (a).

FRANCIS X. MARTIN.
Evidence.
Collection of Martin's private acts, §8-2.

FRANKLIN COUNTY.
Acquisition of property, §153A-158.1, (a).
Ambulance service.
Attachment or garnishment and lien for, §§44-51.4 to 44-51.8.
Condemnation or acquisition of land by local government unit outside county.
Consent of board of commissioners necessary, §153A-15.
Counties generally.
See COUNTIES.
Cropper or tenant refusing to perform terms of contract.
Forfeiture of right of possession to premises, §42-27.
Housing authority commissioners.
Tenant as commissioner, exemption from provision of law allowing, §157-5.
Maps in special proceedings, recording of photographic copies, §§47-32, 47-32.2.
Oil, gas and mineral interests separated from surface fee, extinguished, title in surface fee holder.
Failure to list interest for tax purposes 10 years prior to January 1, 1965.
Protection of subsurface interest from surface fee holder, §1-42.1, (d).
Failure to list interest for tax purposes for 10 years prior to January 1, 1971.
Protection of surface interest from surface estate holder, §1-42.2, (d).
School property.
Acquisition and improvement, §153A-158.1.
Special school tax, election to abolish.
Petition required, §115C-505.
Tax elections for industrial development purposes, §§158-16 to 158-24.

FRANKLIN COUNTY —Cont'd
Wild plants, taking of certain plants from land of another.
Inapplicability of provisions, §14-129.

FRANKLIN, TOWN OF.
Condemnation of unsafe buildings, §§160A-425.1, 160A-426, (d), 160A-432, (a1).
Room occupancy taxes.
Uniform provisions, §160A-215.

FRATERNAL BENEFIT SOCIETIES, §§58-24-1 to 58-24-190.
Administrative procedure act.
Commissioner.
Review of decisions and findings, §58-24-175.
Affidavits.
Consolidations and mergers.
Evidence of furnishing notice or document, §58-24-65, (d).
Agents, §58-24-160, (a).
Alcoholic beverage permits.
Special one-time permits, §18B-1002, (a).
Amendments to laws of society.
Approval by commissioner, §58-24-50, (b).
Benefit contracts, §58-24-90, (b).
Evidence of adoption.
Printed copies, §58-24-50, (e).
Filing with commissioner, §58-24-50, (d).
Furnishing to members, §58-24-50, (c).
Meetings, §58-24-50, (a).
Referendums, §58-24-50, (a).
Annual statements, §58-24-30, (c).
Applicability of article.
Exemption of certain societies, §58-24-185, (a) to (f).
Articles of incorporation.
Filing, §58-24-45, (b).
Attachment.
Benefits.
Not subject to attachment, §58-24-85.
Beneficiaries, §58-24-80, (a).
Benefits.
Attachment.
Not subject to attachment, §58-24-85.
Cash surrender values, certificate loans and other options.
Calculation of amount by date of issuance, §58-24-95, (a), (b).
Certificates.
Valuation.
By date of issuance, §58-24-120, (a), (b).
Commissioner's discretion, §58-24-120, (c).
Excess reserves, §58-24-120, (d).
Filing of annual valuation, §58-24-125, (b).
Standard of valuation, §58-24-120.
Contract, §58-24-90, (a) to (h).
Issuance on variable basis, §58-24-105, (c).
Death benefits.
Payment to personal representative, §58-24-80, (c).
Eligibility for benefits, §58-24-75, (b).
Funeral benefits.
Payment, §58-24-80, (b).
Garnishment.
Not subject to garnishment, §58-24-85.
Minors.
Life insurance, §58-24-75, (b).
Nonforfeiture benefits.
Calculation of amount by date of issuance, §58-24-95, (a), (b).
Types of benefits, §58-24-75, (a).

FRATERNAL BENEFIT SOCIETIES —Cont'd
Bonds, surety.
Filing with articles of incorporation, §58-24-45, (b).
Cemeteries.
Exemptions from North Carolina cemetery act, §65-47, (b).
Commissioner, §58-24-175.
Communications to members, §58-24-30, (b).
Consolidations and mergers.
Affidavits.
Evidence of furnishing notice or document, §58-24-65, (d).
Approval by commissioner, §58-24-65, (b).
Evidence of furnishing notice or document, §58-24-65, (d).
Felonies.
Violation of provisions of section, §58-24-180, (d).
Filing with commissioner, §58-24-65, (a).
Insurance.
Reinsurance upon consolidation or merger, §58-24-60, (b).
Procedure generally, §58-24-65, (a) to (e).
Vesting, §58-24-65, (c).
Construction and interpretation.
Severability of provisions of article, §58-24-190.
Contracts.
Benefit contract.
Amendments to laws of society, §58-24-90, (b).
Assignment by society of terms and conditions, §58-24-90, (h).
Attaining age of majority, §58-24-90, (c).
Certificate of benefits, §58-24-90, (a).
Certified copies.
Evidence of terms and conditions, §58-24-90, (e).
Evidence of terms and conditions.
Certified copies, §58-24-90, (e).
Filing and approval by commissioner, §58-24-90, (f).
Impairment of certificates, §58-24-90, (d).
Issuance on variable basis, §58-24-105, (c).
Transfer of control of ownership, §58-24-90, (g).
Conveyances.
Authorized, §39-25.
Effect as to conveyances by trustees, §39-26.
Prior deeds validated, §39-27.
Deeds.
Prior deeds validated, §39-27.
Deficiencies, §58-24-145, (a).
Action not recognized unless brought by attorney general, §58-24-145, (e).
Commencement of action to enjoin, §58-24-145, (b).
Correction, time period, §58-24-145, (a).
Enjoining society, §58-24-145, (c).
Liquidating society, §58-24-145, (d).
Notice by commissioner, §58-24-145, (a).
Receiver appointed, commissioner appointed as receiver, §58-24-145, (e).
Voluntary discontinuance of business, applicability of provisions, §58-24-145, (f).
Definitions, §§58-24-1 to 58-24-15.
Directors.
Powers of society to purchase and maintain insurance for, §58-24-35, (c).
Embezzlement.
Treasurers of benevolent organizations, §14-93.
Employees.
Powers of society to purchase and maintain insurance, §58-24-35, (c).

FRATERNAL BENEFIT SOCIETIES —Cont'd
Examinations, §58-24-135, (a).
Agents, §58-24-160, (a).
Exemption from examination requirement, §58-24-160, (b).
Exemptions from article.
Benefit certificates for death or disability benefits, §58-24-185, (b).
Compensation for procuring new members, §58-24-185, (c).
Death or disability solely from accident, §58-24-185, (d).
General insurance laws of state, also exempt from, §§58-24-110, 58-24-185, (f).
Generally, §58-24-185, (a).
Information to commissioner to determine exemption, §58-24-185, (e).
Other provisions of insurance law, §§58-24-110, 58-24-185, (f).
Fees.
Financial statements.
Filing annual statements, §58-24-125, (a).
Felonies.
Consolidations and mergers.
Violation of provisions of section, §58-24-180, (d).
False statements under oath, §58-24-180, (e).
Mergers and consolidation.
Violations of provisions of section, §58-24-180, (d).
Financial statements.
Annual statements.
Filing, §58-24-125.
Filing annual statements, §58-24-125, (a).
Penalties, §58-24-125, (c).
Fines.
Filing annual statements, §58-24-125, (c).
Not specified violations, §58-24-180, (c).
Solicitation or procurement of membership.
Unauthorized, §58-24-180, (b).
Foreign or alien societies, §58-24-140.
Continuation of authorized contracts, §58-24-150, (b).
Licenses.
Continuation of authorized contracts, §58-24-150, (b).
Refusal to issue, §58-24-150, (a).
Required, §58-24-140.
Suspension or revocation, §58-24-150, (a).
Formation.
Structure of organization, §58-24-45, (a).
Funds.
Establishment, §58-24-105, (b).
Generally, §58-24-105, (a).
Investments, §58-24-100.
Separate accounts, §58-24-105, (c).
Garnishment.
Benefits.
Not subject to garnishment, §58-24-85.
Grievance or complaint procedures, §58-24-30, (d).
Immunities.
Officers.
Civil liability for monetary damages, §58-24-35, (d).
Indemnification.
Officers, directors, employees or agents, §58-24-35, (b).
Injunctions.
Application or petition for.
Attorney general upon request of commissioner, §58-24-155.

FRATERNAL BENEFIT SOCIETIES —Cont'd
Institutions, §58-24-55.
Insurance.
Directors, officers, employees or agents.
Powers of society to purchase and maintain insurance, §58-24-35, (c).
Exemptions from general insurance laws, §58-24-110.
Mutual life insurance companies.
Conversion of society into company, §58-24-70.
Reinsurance, §58-24-60, (a).
Consolidation or merger, §58-24-60, (b).
Investments.
Funds, §58-24-100.
Laws of society.
Amendments.
Approval by commissioner, §58-24-50, (b).
Benefit contracts, §58-24-90, (b).
Evidence of adoption.
Printed copies, §58-24-50, (e).
Filing with commissioner, §58-24-50, (d).
Furnishing to members, §58-24-50, (c).
Meetings, §58-24-50, (a).
Referendums, §58-24-50, (a).
Liability.
Officers and members.
Not personally liable for benefits provided by society, §58-24-35, (a).
Licenses, §58-24-45, (e).
Agents, §58-24-160, (a).
Annual license continuation fee, §58-24-130.
Copy or duplicate.
Prima facie evidence, §58-24-130.
Exemption from licensing requirement, §58-24-160, (b).
Foreign or alien societies.
Continuation of authorized contracts, §58-24-150, (b).
Refusal to issue, §58-24-150, (a).
Required, §58-24-140.
Suspension or revocation, §58-24-150, (a).
Perpetual licensing, §58-24-130.
Preliminary licenses, §58-24-45, (c), (d).
Lodge system.
Defined, §58-24-5, (a).
Minors.
Organization and operation of lodges for children, §58-24-5, (b).
Long-term care insurance, §§58-55-1 to 58-55-50.
See LONG-TERM CARE INSURANCE.
Meetings.
Generally, §58-24-30, (a).
Members.
Liability.
Not personally liable for benefits provided by society, §58-24-35, (a).
Qualifications for membership, §58-24-25, (a).
Rights of membership not assignable, §58-24-25, (c).
Social members, §58-24-25, (b).
Mergers and consolidations.
Affidavits.
Evidence of furnishing notice or document, §58-24-65, (d).
Approval by commissioner, §58-24-65, (b).
Evidence of furnishing notice or document, §58-24-65, (d).
Felonies.
Violations of provisions of section, §58-24-180, (d).
Filing with commissioner, §58-24-65, (a).

FRATERNAL BENEFIT SOCIETIES —Cont'd
Mergers and consolidations —Cont'd
Procedure generally, §58-24-65, (a) to (e).
Reinsurance upon consolidation or merger, §58-24-60, (b).
Vesting, §58-24-65, (c).
Minors.
Life insurance, §58-24-75, (b).
Lodge systems.
Organization and operation of lodges for children, §58-24-5, (b).
Misdemeanors.
False or fraudulent statements, §58-24-180, (a).
Not specified violations, §58-24-180, (c).
Solicitation or procurement of membership.
Unauthorized, §58-24-180, (b).
Mutual life insurance companies.
Conversion of society into company, §58-24-70.
Officers.
Immunities.
Civil liability for monetary damages, §58-24-35, (d).
Indemnification, §58-24-35, (b).
Insurance.
Power of society to purchase and maintain insurance, §58-24-35, (c).
Liability.
Not personally liable for benefits provided by society, §58-24-35, (a).
Offices.
Location of principal office, §58-24-30, (a).
Organization, §58-24-45, (a) to (f).
Bonds, surety.
Filing with articles of incorporation, §58-24-45, (b).
Filing articles of incorporation, §58-24-45, (b).
Licenses, §58-24-45, (e).
Preliminary licenses, §58-24-45, (c), (d).
Reincorporation, §58-24-45, (f).
Structure, §58-24-45, (a).
Penalties.
False or fraudulent statements, §58-24-180, (a).
Under oath, §58-24-180, (e).
Felonies.
False statements under oath, §58-24-180, (e).
Mergers and consolidation.
Violations of provisions of section, §58-24-180, (d).
Filing financial statements, §58-24-125, (c).
Mergers and consolidations.
Felonies.
Violations of provisions of section, §58-24-180, (d).
Not specified violations, §58-24-180, (c).
Solicitation or procurement of membership.
Unauthorized, §58-24-180, (b).
Violation of article, §58-24-180.
Powers.
Generally, §58-24-20, (b).
Purposes, §58-24-20, (a).
Real property.
Authority to acquire and hold, §39-24.
Conveyances.
Authorized, §39-25.
Effect as to conveyances by trustees, §39-26.
Prior deeds validated, §39-27.
Probate, §39-25.
Trustees.
Effect as to conveyance by trustees, §39-26.
Vesting title, §39-25.

FRATERNAL BENEFIT SOCIETIES —Cont'd
Referendums.
Amendments to laws of society, §58-24-50, (a).
Reincorporation, §58-24-45, (f).
Reinsurance, §58-24-60, (a).
Consolidation or merger, §58-24-60, (b).
Reports.
Annual reports required, §58-24-125, (a).
Filing financial statements, §58-24-125, (a).
Penalties, §58-24-125, (c).
Valuation, §58-24-125, (b).
Representative form of government.
Defined, §58-24-10.
Reserves.
Excess reserves.
Establishment and maintenance, §58-24-120, (d).
Impairment.
Apportionment of deficiency among owners, §58-24-90.
Secret societies and activities, §§14-12.2 to 14-12.15.
See SECRET SOCIETIES.
Securities regulation.
Exempt securities, §78A-16.
Service of process.
Appointment of commissioner, §58-24-170, (a).
Procedure, §58-24-170, (b).
Severability of provisions of article, §58-24-190.
Taxation.
Exemptions, §58-24-115.
Unfair and deceptive acts and practices, §58-24-165.
Waiver.
Laws of society.
Not authorized, §58-24-40.

FRATERNAL ORDERS, §§58-25-1 to 58-25-70.
Admission to state.
Conditions precedent to doing business, §58-25-25.
Agents.
Collector or receiver of assessments and dues, §58-25-15.
Licenses, §58-25-25.
Applicability of article.
Certain lodge systems exempt, §58-25-30.
Assessments.
Collection, §58-25-15.
Funds derived from, §58-25-10.
Badges.
Unauthorized wearing, §58-25-70.
Conditions precedent to doing business, §58-25-25.
Conveyances.
Authorized, §39-25.
Effect as to conveyances by trustees, §39-26.
Prior deeds validated, §39-27.
Criminal law and procedure.
Securing attendance of organizations as defendants, §15A-773.
Deeds.
Prior deeds validated, §39-27.
Defined, §58-25-5.
Dues.
Collection, §58-25-15.
Funds derived from, §58-25-10.
Exemptions from article, §58-25-30.
Financial statements.
Annual report, §58-25-50.
Funds.
Assessments and dues, §58-25-10.
Payments to expense or general fund, §58-25-55.

FRATERNAL ORDERS —Cont'd
Funds —Cont'd
Separation of funds.
Annual financial statement, §58-25-50.
General insurance law not applicable, §58-25-1.
Hazing, §§14-35 to 14-38.
Licenses.
Agents, §58-25-25.
Meetings.
Governing body, §58-25-20.
Minors.
Insurance, §58-25-35.
Certificates and contributions, §58-25-40.
Continuation of certificate, §58-25-60.
Exchange of certificate, §58-25-45.
Medical examination, §58-25-40.
Reserve fund, §58-25-45.
Offices.
Principal office, §58-25-20.
Payments to expense or general fund, §58-25-55.
Penalties.
Badges.
Unauthorized wearing, §58-25-70.
Real property.
Authority to acquire and hold, §39-24.
Conveyances.
Authorized, §39-25.
Effect as to conveyances by trustees, §39-26.
Prior deeds validated, §39-27.
Probate, §39-25.
Trustees.
Effect as to conveyance by trustees, §39-26.
Vesting title, §39-25.
Reports.
Annual financial statement.
Separation of funds, §58-25-45.
Secret societies and activities, §§14-12.2 to 14-12.15.
Trusts and trustees.
Appointment of trustees to hold property, §58-25-65.
Conveyances.
Effect as to conveyance by trustees, §39-26.

FRATERNITIES.
Hazing, §§14-35 to 14-38.
Supplemental fire safety protection system, §§116-44.6 to 116-44.8.

FRAUD.
Academic credit.
Assisting, etc., in obtaining credit by fraudulent means, §14-118.2, (a).
Penalty for violations of provisions, §14-118.2, (b).
Accounts and accounting.
Accrual of action for relief on ground of, §1-52.
Court process in connection with collection of account.
Simulation of court process, §14-118.1.
Adoption proceedings.
Waiver of notice, §48-2-406, (c).
Advertisements.
Deceptive and fraudulent advertising, §14-117.
Gasoline price advertisements.
Purchaser himself drawing or pumping fuel, §14-117.2.
Affirmative defense, pleading, §1A-1, Rule 8, (c).
Alarm systems licensing.
Conviction of crime involving fraud.
Grounds for denial of license, §74D-6.

FRAUD —Cont'd
Alcoholic beverage purchases by minors.
Use of fraudulent identification, §18B-302, (e).
Allowing use of identification, §18B-302, (f).
Arrest in civil cases.
Cases in which arrest allowed, §1-410.
Arson.
Dwelling houses fraudulently set fire to, §14-65.
Assignments for benefit of creditors.
Judgment of fraud by opposing creditor, §23-17.
Superior or district court to try issue, §23-39.
Attorneys at law.
Client engaging in fraudulent conduct, remedial measures, Prof Cond. Rule 3.3.
Defined, Prof. Cond. Rule 1.0.
Lawyer not to counsel client to engage in fraudulent conduct, Prof. Cond. Rule 1.2.
Liability for fraudulent practice.
Double damages, §84-13.
Bail bondsmen and runners.
Grounds for denial, suspension, revocation or refusal to renew license, §58-71-80, (a).
Bailments.
Hired property, §14-168.
Barbers.
Prohibited acts, §86A-20.
Blackmail.
Elements of offense, §14-118.
Blind persons.
Aid to the blind.
Misrepresentation or fraud in obtaining assistance, §111-23.
Campgrounds.
Defrauding campground owner, §14-110.
Child care facilities.
Fraudulent misrepresentation, §110-107, (a), (b).
Children's health insurance program, §108A-70.28.
Chiropractors.
Grounds for disciplinary action, §90-154, (b).
Collection agencies.
Court process in connection with collection of claim.
Simulation of court process, §14-118.1.
Deceptive representation.
Prohibited acts, §58-70-110.
Commodities.
Fraudulent conduct, §78D-6.
Complaints.
Form, §1A-1, Rule 84.
Concealed handgun permit.
Revocation or suspension of permit for fraud in obtaining permit, §14-415.18, (a).
Consumer finance act.
False or misleading statements.
Prohibited acts, §53-183.
Contractors.
Improvements to real property.
Furnishing false statements.
Misdemeanor, §44A-24.
Custodial trusts.
Limitation of actions against custodial trustee, §33B-16, (b).
Debts and claims.
Court process in connection with collection of claim.
Simulation of court process, §14-118.1.
Demands.
Court process in connection with collection of demand.
Simulation of court process, §14-118.1.

FRAUD —Cont'd
Dental hygienists.
Grounds for disciplinary measures, §90-229, (a).
Dentists.
Grounds for disciplinary action, §90-41, (a).
Licenses.
License obtained through fraud void, §90-30, (a).
Diamonds.
Unfair trade practices in diamond industry.
What constitutes unfair trade practice, §66-74.
Drug and alcohol screening tests.
Defrauding test, §14-401.20.
Drugs.
Controlled substances.
Prohibited acts, §90-108, (a).
Education.
Academic credit by fraudulent means.
Assisting, etc., in obtaining credit, §14-118.2, (a).
Penalty for violation of provisions, §14-118.2, (b).
Senior citizens.
Tuition waiver.
Misrepresentation of eligibility, §115B-6.
Elections.
Absentee ballots.
Misdemeanors, §163-237, (c).
Felonies, §163-275.
Registration of voters.
Felonies, §163-275.
State bureau of investigation.
Authority to make investigations, §114-15, (a).
Electrologists.
Grounds for disciplinary actions, §88A-21, (a).
Executors and administrators.
Referral of disputed claims.
Evidence in action for fraud, §28A-19-15.
Sales of real property.
Conveyance by deceased in fraud of creditors.
Property subject to sale, §28A-17-5.
Transfers or conveyances by decedent to defraud creditors.
Action by personal representative to recover, §28A-15-10.
False pretenses and cheats, §§14-100 to 14-113.
See FALSE PRETENSES AND CHEATS.
Financial identity fraud, §§14-113.20 to 14-113.25.
Expungement of criminal records.
Dismissal or finding of not guilty.
Crime committed by another using defendant's identifying information, §15A-147.
Financial transaction cards.
Application for financial transaction card.
False statements or reports on application, §14-113.13, (c).
Elements of offense, §14-113.13, (a).
Furnisher of money, goods, services, etc.
Elements of financial transaction card fraud offense, §14-113.13, (b).
Goods and services.
Criminal receipt of goods and services fraudulently obtained, §14-113.15.
Presumption of criminal receipt, §14-113.16.
Notice of theft, loss, etc., of card.
False notice, §14-113.13, (d).
Prosecution for violation.
Occurrence of acts constituting crime, §14-113.13, (e).

FRAUD —Cont'd
Financial transaction cards —Cont'd
Report of theft, loss, etc., of card.
False report, §14-113.13, (d).
Revocation of financial transaction card.
Construing revocation, §14-113.13, (f).
Fish and fishing.
Coastal and estuarine commercial fishing licenses, §113-170.2.
Food stamps, §108A-53.
Foreign money judgments recognition, §1C-1804, (b).
Gasoline.
Price advertisements.
Purchaser himself drawing or pumping fuel, §14-117.2.
Hospitals.
Information obtained from patients.
Acquisition and use of information for fraudulent purposes, §14-118.3.
Housemovers.
Licenses.
Obtaining license or permit by fraud, §20-367.
Housing authorities and projects.
Misrepresentation.
Fraudulent misrepresentation in obtaining housing assistance, §157-29.1.
Husband and wife.
Conveyances.
Certain conveyances not affected by fraud, §39-11.
Identification.
Alcoholic beverage purchases by minors, §18B-302, (e).
Allowing use of identification, §18B-302, (f).
False or fraudulent, §14-100.1.
Financial identity fraud, §§14-113.20 to 14-113.25.
Expungement of criminal records.
Dismissal or finding of not guilty.
Crime committed by another using defendant's identifying information, §15A-147.
Identity fraud.
See IDENTITY FRAUD.
Imprisonment for debt, Const. N. C., art. I, §28.
Indictments.
Intent to defraud.
Sufficiency of allegation, §15-151.
Injunctions.
Removal or disposition of property with intent to defraud plaintiff.
Issuance of preliminary injunction when threatened, §1-485.
Insurance.
Arson, §14-65.
Burning of personal property, §14-66.
Dwelling house fraudulently set fire to, §14-65.
False statement to procure or deny benefit of policy or certificate, §58-2-161.
Immunity from liability for reporting fraud, §58-2-160, (a), (b).
Life insurance.
Creditors deprived of benefits of policies except in cases of fraud, §58-58-115.
Misrepresentation of policies prohibited, §58-58-40.
Personal property set fire to, §14-66.
Reinsurance.
Reporting and investigation of, §58-2-160, (a), (b).

FRAUD —Cont'd
Insurance —Cont'd
Statements, releases, etc., obtained from persons in shock or under the influence of drugs.
Presumption of fraud, §8-45.5.
"Twisting," §58-3-115.
Interpreters and transliterators.
Licenses.
Revocation, suspension or denials of licenses, §90D-12.
Judgments.
Relief from judgment or order, §1A-1, Rule 60, (b).
Leases, UCC.
Effect on rights and remedies, §25-2A-505, (4).
Letters of credit.
Basis for dishonor, §25-5-108, (d).
Injunction on honoring, §25-5-109, (b).
Issuer allowed to honor despite, §25-5-109, (a).
Liens.
Real property.
Furnishing false statements in connection with improvements, §44A-24.
Limitation of actions, §1-52.
Marriage and family therapists.
Grounds for disciplinary action, §90-270.60, (a).
Marriage licenses.
Minors procuring license by, §51-2, (c).
Obtaining license by false representation, §51-15.
Procuring license by fraud or misrepresentation, §51-2, (c).
Massage and bodywork therapy.
Disciplinary action.
Grounds, §90-633.
Medicaid.
Medical assistance provider false claims act, §§108A-70.10 to 108A-70.16.
See MEDICAID.
Providers, §108A-63.
Recipients, §108A-64.
Misdemeanors.
Offenses committed with deceit and intent to defraud, §14-3, (b).
Security interest on personal property.
Fraudulent disposal of property, §14-114, (a).
Money transmitters.
Criminal penalty, §53-208.26, (b).
Delegates.
False statements by delegate, §53-208.20, (a).
Mortgage bankers and brokers.
Prohibited acts, §53-243.11.
Mortgages and deeds of trust.
Disposal of property.
Intent to commit crime, §14-114, (b).
Refusal to turn over property without judgment or order, §14-114, (a).
Reverse mortgages.
Prohibited acts by lenders, §53-270.
Motor vehicle repairs.
Altering estimate, bill, etc., §20-354.8.
Remedies for violation, §20-354.9.
Deceptive statements, etc., §20-354.8.
Remedies for violation, §20-354.9.
Motor vehicles.
Rental of motor vehicles, §20-106.1.
Rescission and cancellation of registration.
Grounds.
False or fraudulent statement in application, §20-110, (h).
Mutual burial associations.
False entries on books of association, §90-210.90.

FRAUD —Cont'd
Mutual burial associations —Cont'd
False or fraudulent statement or representation, §90-210.97.
Inducing change in membership, §90-210.89.
Negotiable instruments.
Indorsements.
Responsibility of employer for fraudulent indorsement by employee, §25-3-405.
Nurses.
Prohibited acts, §90-171.44.
Oil and gas conservation.
Drilling wells.
Applications, §113-409.
Optometrists.
Grounds for disciplinary action, §90-121.2, (a).
License obtained through fraud void, §90-118, (d).
Partition.
Report of commissioners.
Impeachment of report for fraud, §46-19, (a).
Penalties.
Academic credit by fraudulent means.
Assisting, etc., in obtaining credit, §14-118.2, (b).
Plaintiff may reply fraud to plea of release, §1-59.
Personal property.
Refusal to turn over without judgment or order, §14-114, (a).
Security interests.
Fraudulent disposal of property, §14-114.
Personnel system.
Application for state employment.
Fraudulent disclosure and willful nondisclosure, §126-30, (a).
Rules and regulations, §126-30, (c).
Verification of accuracy of statements, §126-30, (b).
Physical therapists.
Grounds for disciplinary action, §90-270.36.
Preneed funeral contracts and funds, §90-210.70, (a), (c).
Refusal to issue or renew, suspension or revocation of licenses, §90-210.69, (c).
Presumptions.
Security interest on personal property.
Fraudulent disposal of property, §14-114, (b).
Prisons and prisoners.
Debtor and creditor.
Discharge of insolvent prisoners.
Absent suggestion of fraud, discharge granted, §23-34.
Imprisonment of if fraud found, §23-37.
Suggestion of fraud, §23-28.
Trial required where fraud in issue, §23-36.
Who may suggest fraud, §23-33.
Private personnel services.
Contracts, §95-47.4, (d).
Prohibited acts, §95-47.6.
Professional counselors.
Disciplinary action against licensee, §90-340.
Violation punishable as crime, §90-341.
Public assistance program payments.
Garnishment of wages to recoup fraudulent payments, §108A-25.3.
Real estate brokers and salespersons.
Grounds for revocation or suspension of licenses, §93A-6, (a).
Respiratory care practitioners.
License application, §90-659.
Retirement system for counties and cities.
Protection of records against fraud, §128-32.

FRAUD —Cont'd
Retirement system for teachers and state employees.
Protection against fraud, §135-10.
Sale of goods, UCC.
Misrepresentation of buyer's solvency.
Seller's remedies, §25-2-702.
Remedies for fraud, §25-2-721.
Rights of seller's creditors against sold goods, §25-2-402.
Transfer of title obtained by fraud, §25-2-403, (1).
Securities regulation, §§78A-8 to 78A-10.
Security interest.
Fraudulent disposal of personal property.
Intent, §14-114, (b).
Refusal to turn over property without judgment or order, §14-114, (a).
Social security.
Bureau of investigation, investigations by, §114-15, (a).
Special matters, pleading, §1A-1, Rule 9, (b).
Speech and language pathologists and audiologists.
Grounds for suspension or revocation of license, §90-301.
Obtaining fee by fraud or misrepresentation.
Unethical acts and practices, §90-301A.
State treasurer.
False entries in books, §147-76.
Tax penalties, §105-236.
Trademarks.
Counterfeit trademarks, §§80-11, 80-11.1.
Deceptive or unfair trade practices, §80-12.
Fraudulent registration, §80-10.
Timber marks.
Fraudulent use, §80-20.
Transfers.
Fraudulent transfers, §§39-23.1 to 39-23.12.
See FRAUDULENT TRANSFERS.
Unemployment compensation benefits.
False statements, §96-18.
Universities and colleges.
Academic credit by fraudulent means.
Assisting, etc., in obtaining credit, §14-118.2, (a).
Penalty for violation of provisions, §14-118.2, (b).
Viatical life insurance settlements.
Felony offense for fraudulent viatical settlement act, §58-58-265, (a).
Investigations of fraudulent acts, §58-58-240.
Warehouse receipts.
Fraudulent deposit and negotiation, §27-59.
Issuing fraudulent duplicates, §27-56.
Workers' compensation.
False statements or representations, §97-88.2, (a).
Health care providers, §97-88.3, (a).
Hospital liability.
Reliance on written order of physician, §97-88.3, (f).
Reporting information relating to possible violations, §97-88.3, (e).
Insurance carriers, §97-100, (g).
Investigation, §97-88.2, (b).
Report to general assembly, §97-88.2, (e).
Referral of suspected fraud cases, §97-88.2, (b).
Liability of commission, §97-88.2, (d).
Work first program, §108A-39.

FRAUDS, STATUTE OF.
See STATUTE OF FRAUDS.

FRAUDULENT TRANSFERS, §§39-23.1 to 39-23.12.
Applicability of provisions.
Uniformity of application, §39-23.11.
Assignments for benefit of creditors.
Trustee to recover property conveyed fraudulently, §23-3.
Child support.
Enforcement of support.
Minor child creditor within meaning of chapter, §50-13.4, (f).
Citation of article, §39-23.12.
Construction and interpretation.
Uniformity, §39-23.11.
Definitions, §39-23.1.
Good faith taker for reasonably equivalent value.
Entitlement notwithstanding voidablity of transfer, §39-23.8, (d).
Transfer not voidable as to, §39-23.8, (a).
Insider giving new value.
Transfers not voidable, §39-23.8, (f).
Insolvent.
Assets, §39-23.2, (d).
Debts, §39-23.2, (e).
Elements, §39-23.2, (a).
Partnerships, §39-23.2, (c).
Presumption, §39-23.2, (b).
Intent, §39-23.4, (b).
Joinder of remedies, §1A-1, Rule 18, (b).
Judgments.
Execution, §39-23.7, (b).
For value of asset transfer.
Recovery by creditor where transfer voidable, §39-23.8, (b), (c).
Leases.
Termination upon default.
Transfers not voidable, §39-23.8, (e).
Leases, UCC.
Special rights of creditors, §25-2A-308.
Levy of execution, §39-23.7, (b).
Limitation of actions, §39-23.9.
Ordinary course of business.
Transfers not voidable, §39-23.8, (f).
Present and future creditors, §§39-23.4, (a), 39-23.5, (a).
Voidable transfers, §39-23.5, (b).
Provisions supplementary, §39-23.10.
Rehabilitation of debtor.
Transfers not voidable, §39-23.8, (f).
Remedies of creditors, §39-23.7, (a).
Secured transactions.
Enforcement of security interest in compliance with UCC secured transactions article.
Transfers not voidable, §39-23.8, (e).
Statute of limitations, §39-23.9.
Supplementary provisions, §39-23.10.
Time.
When transfer made, §39-23.6.
Title of article, §39-23.12.
Transfer not voidable, §39-23.8, (e), (f).
Value, §39-23.3, (a).
Present value, §§39-23.2, (c), 39-23.3, (c).
Reasonably equivalent value, §39-23.3, (b).
When transfer made or obligation incurred, §39-23.6.

FREAK SHOWS.
Exhibition of mentally ill, retarded or deformed children prohibited, §110-20.1.

FREEDOM OF INFORMATION.
Access to records, §132-9.
Bank compliance review documents.
Unavailability, §53-99.1, (b).
Certified copies of records, §132-7.
Confidential communications.
Enumeration, §132-1.2.
Legal counsel's advice to public board or agency, §132-1.1.
Cooperative agreements among physicians or between physician, hospital or other person.
Files of department of health and human services public record, §90-21.30.
Work product of attorney general in suit to cancel agreement not public record, §90-21.33, (d).
Criminal investigation or intelligence records or information, §132-1.4.
Cultural resources department.
Assistance by and to, §132-8.
Records management program, §132-8.1.
Selection and preservation of records considered essential, §132-8.2.
Custodian designated, §132-2.
Demanding custody, §132-5.
Destruction of records.
Employment security commission, §132-3, (c).
Prohibition, §132-3, (a).
Revenue records after copies made, §132-3, (b).
Discharge papers.
Restricting access to military discharge documents.
Public records with restricted access, §47-113.2.
Disposition of records at end of official's term, §132-4.
Financial records privacy, §§53B-1 to 53B-10.
See FINANCIAL RECORDS PRIVACY.
Foster parents.
Register of applicants.
Exemption for FOIA, §131D-10.6C, (b).
Industrial commission managed care organizations, I.C. Managed Care Orgs. R. VII.
Inspection and examination of records, §132-6.
Keeping records in safe places, §132-7.
Motor vehicle accident reports.
Reports by persons not law enforcement officers or medical examiners not public records, §20-166.1, (i).
Physicians and surgeons.
Disciplinary matters, inquiries or interviews not public record, §90-16.
Privacy of financial records, §§53B-1 to 53B-10.
See FINANCIAL RECORDS PRIVACY.
Public records.
Definitions, §132-1.
911 database not public record, §132-1.5.
Public security information, §132-1.7, (a) to (c).
Regaining custody, §132-5.1.
Civil remedies, §132-5.1.
Savings and loan associations.
Compliance review documents, §54B-63.1, (b).
Tax information secrecy, §105-259.

FREE ENTERPRISE SYSTEM.
Basic education program, §115C-81, (c).

FREE FISHING DAY.
July fourth, §113-276, (m).

FREESTYLE BICYCLING.
Assumption of inherent risk, §99E-24, (a).

FREESTYLE BICYCLING —Cont'd
Governmental entities.
Limitation of liability, §99E-25, (b).
Duty of care not created, §99E-25, (d).
Exceptions, §99E-25, (c).
Independent concessionaires or other persons or organizations.
Liability not limited by section, §99E-25, (e).
Insurance carried by entity.
Not waiver of liability limits, §99E-25, (f).
Sovereign immunity not waived, §99E-25, (d).
Specifically designated areas for activities.
Required to participate on property owner or controlled by entity, §99E-25, (a).
Responsibilities of participants, §99E-24, (b).

FREE TRADER AGREEMENTS, §52-10.

FREE TRANSPORTATION OFFERED BY COMMON CARRIERS, §62-144.

FREEZER LOCKER PLANTS.
Sales and use tax.
Rate on sales of machinery, §105-164.4A.

FREEZERS.
Chlorofluorocarbon refrigerants, §§130A-309.80 to 130A-309.87.

FREIGHT.
Bills of lading.
Issuance, §62-203, (a).
Careful handling required, §62-202.
Carriers, §§62-200 to 62-204.
Unclaimed freight, §62-209.
Emergency operating authority granted to owner of duly licensed vehicles to transport, §62-265.
Line company gross earnings tax.
See FREIGHT LINE COMPANY GROSS EARNINGS TAX.
Lost or damaged goods and property.
Additional nature of provisions, §62-203, (g).
Causes of action may be united, §62-203, (f).
Claims.
Notice, §62-204.
Time for adjustment and payment, §62-203, (b).
Penalty for failure to adjust and pay claim during time, §62-203, (c).
Liability for, §62-203, (a), (c).
Limitation of actions, §62-204.
Motor carriers.
Exemptions from provisions, §62-203, (h).
Rates.
Charges to be at legal rates, §62-201.
Damages for failure or refusal to comply with provisions, §62-201.
Reasonable time for transportation, §62-200, (a), (b).
Motor carriers of passengers.
Provisions not applicable, §62-200, (d).
Violations of provisions.
Forfeiture, §62-200, (b).
Taxation.
Freight line company gross earnings tax.
See FREIGHT LINE COMPANY GROSS EARNINGS TAX.
Unclaimed freight.
Sale, §62-209.
Motor carriers of passengers.
Exemption from provisions, §62-209, (d).
Notice, §62-209, (a).
Record, §62-209, (c).

FREIGHT LINE COMPANY GROSS EARNINGS TAX.
Effective date of provisions, §105-228.2, (j).
Enforcement of payment of taxes, §105-228.2, (i).
Failure to pay tax, §105-228.2, (i).
"Gross earning received from all sources by such freight line companies within state."
Defined, §105-228.2, (e).
In lieu of ad valorem taxes, §§105-228.1, 105-228.2, (a).
Purpose of provisions, §105-228.1.
Rate of tax, §105-228.2, (d).
Reports, §105-228.2, (f) to (h).
Situs of cars in state, §105-228.2, (c).
What constitutes freight line company, §105-228.2, (b).

FREON, §§130A-309.80 to 130A-309.87.

FRESH PURSUIT.
Campus police officers, §15A-402, (f).
Company police, §74E-6.
County and city officers, §15A-402, (d).
Officers from other states, §15A-403.

FRIED FOODS.
Child care centers frying foods.
Use of commercial hoods, §110-91.

FRINGE TREE.
Trespass.
Taking, etc., of certain wild plants from land of another, §14-129.

FRISKING.
Persons present on premises or in vehicle to be searched, §15A-255.
Riots and civil disorders.
Curfew violators, §14-288.10, (b).
Grounds for frisk of persons during violent disorders, §14-288.10, (a).

FRIVOLOUS ACTIONS.
Attorneys' fees.
Cases involving principals or teachers, §6-21.4.
Child custody or support, §50-13.6.
Interference with civil rights, §99D-1, (b).
Nonjustifiable cases, §6-21.5.
Punitive damages, §1D-45.
Retaliatory employment discrimination, §95-243, (c).
Defendant unreasonable defending after notice of no personal claim to pay costs, §6-23.
Inmates presenting frivolous complaints.
Court determination, dismissal, §1-110, (b).
Limited liability company derivative actions by members.
Actions brought by without reasonable cause, §57C-8-01, (f).
Mortgages and deeds of trust.
Consumer home loans.
Attorneys' fees for prevailing party, §24-10.2, (f).
Punitive damages.
Attorneys' fees, §1D-45.
Sales representatives.
Action against principal for commission, §66-192, (b).

FRIVOLOUS APPEALS, App. Proc. Rule 34.

FRIVOLOUS CLAIMS AND CONTENTIONS.
Attorneys at law, Prof Cond. Rule 3.1.

FRIVOLOUS COMPLAINTS IN JUDICIAL STANDARDS COMMISSION PROCEEDINGS, Jud. Stds. Comm. Rule 6.

FRIVOLOUS DISCOVERY.
Attorneys at law, Prof Cond. Rule 3.4.

FRIVOLOUS PLEADINGS, §1A-1, Rule 11, (a).

FRIVOLOUS PROSECUTION.
Imprisonment of prosecuting witness for willful nonpayment of costs, §6-50.
Prosecuting witness liable for costs, §6-49.

FROZEN FOOD.
Ice cream plants, creameries and cheese factories.
Inspections generally, §§106-246 to 106-255.
See ICE CREAM PLANTS, CREAMERIES AND CHEESE FACTORIES.
Trade names.
Regulating trade or brand names of frozen or semifrozen desserts, §106-253.

FRUIT.
Damage to agricultural commodities or production systems.
Definitions, §1-539.2B, (c).
Double damage liability, §1-539.2B, (a).
Valuation, §1-539.2B, (b).
Definition of handler, §106-496.
Food, drug and cosmetic act.
Condemnation or destruction of articles found to be unsound, filthy, etc., §106-125, (d).
Larceny.
Ungathered crops, §14-78.
Liens.
Effective period for liens on fruit, §44-69.2.
Promotion of use and sale of agricultural products.
Generally, §§106-550 to 106-568.
See AGRICULTURAL PRODUCTS PROMOTION.
State fruit, §145-18, (a).
Unfair practices by handlers, §§106-496 to 106-501.
See FRUIT HANDLERS UNFAIR PRACTICES.
Weights and measures.
Standard weights and measures, §81A-42.

FRUIT HANDLERS UNFAIR PRACTICES, §§106-496 to 106-501.
Bond required, §106-498.
Commissioner of agriculture.
Contracts between handlers and producers.
Approval of commissioner, §106-499.
Enforcement of article, §106-500.
Powers of commissioner, §106-500.
Contracts between handlers and producers, §106-499.
Definition of handler, §106-496.
Enforcement of article.
Commissioner of agriculture to enforce, §106-500.
Penalties, §106-501.
Permits required, §106-497.
Protection against unfair trade practices, §106-496.

FRUIT OF THE POISONOUS TREE DOCTRINE, §15A-974.

FRYING PAN LIGHTSHIP MARINE MUSEUM COMMISSION.
Department of cultural resources.
Transfer of commission to department, §143B-51.

FUEL ALCOHOL.
Distilleries.
Permits, §18B-1105, (b).

FUELS.
Alternative fuel generally, §§105-449.130 to 105-449.139.
See ALTERNATIVE FUEL.
Commodities.
General provisions, §§78D-1 to 78D-33.
See COMMODITIES.
Gasoline and oil inspection.
See GASOLINE AND OIL INSPECTION.
Gasoline tax, §§105-449.60 to 105-449.127.
See GASOLINE TAX.
Liquid fuels, §§119-7 to 119-13.
Motor fuels.
Marketing, §§75-80 to 75-89.
Sales and use tax exemption, §105-164.13.
Road tax on carriers using fuel purchased outside state, §§105-449.37 to 105-449.57.
See MOTOR CARRIERS.
Sales and use tax.
Rate, §105-164.4, (a).

FUELS TAX.
Administrative provisions.
Applicability of general provisions, §105-269.3.
Alternative fuel, §§105-449.130 to 105-449.139.
See ALTERNATIVE FUEL.
Gasoline tax, §§105-449.60 to 105-449.127.
See GASOLINE TAX.
Road tax on carriers using fuel purchased outside state, §§105-449.37 to 105-449.57.
See MOTOR CARRIERS.

FUEL TANKS ON VEHICLES.
Tank not to project beyond sides of vehicle, §20-117.1, (b).

FUGITIVE HUSBANDS.
Interstate family support, §§52C-1-100 to 52C-9-902.
See INTERSTATE FAMILY SUPPORT.

FUGITIVES FROM JUSTICE.
Concealed handgun permit.
Grounds for denial of permit, §14-415.12, (b).
Extradition.
Fugitives from other states.
See EXTRADITION.
Jails.
Harboring or aiding escaped prisoners, §14-259.
Rewards.
Governor may offer rewards, §15-53.
Information leading to arrest and conviction, §15-53.1.
Officer entitled to reward, §15-54.
State institutions.
Harboring fugitives, §§14-267, 14-268.

FULL FAITH AND CREDIT, Const. U. S., art. IV, §1.
Child support.
Past due child support judgment, §50-13.10, (b).
Paternity determination by another state, §110-132.1.
Eastern Band of Cherokee Indians.
Judgments, decrees, and orders, §1E-1.
Subject to certain provisions, §1E-1, (b).
Tribal Court.
Subject to full faith and credit of Tribal Court, §1E-1, (a).

FULL FAITH AND CREDIT —Cont'd
Limited liability companies.
Intent of general assembly, §57C-10-07.
Paternity determination by another state, §110-132.1.
Public records.
Certified and authenticated, §8-35.

FULLY HALOGENATED CHLOROFLUOROCARBONS (CFC).
Containers manufactured with, restrictions, §130A-309.10, (b).

FUNDRAISING.
Alcoholic beverage permits issued to nonprofit organization.
Special one-time permit, §18B-1002, (a).
Charitable solicitation generally, §§131F-1 to 131F-24.
See CHARITABLE SOLICITATION.
Winery special event permit authorization, §18B-1114.1.

FUNDS.
Administration department.
Contingency and emergency fund.
Use for construction and repair of public buildings, §143-345.3.
Adoption.
Special needs adoption incentive fund, §108A-50.1.
Adult care home specialist fund, §131D-4.7.
Agriculture.
Eastern North Carolina agricultural center fund, §106-6.2, (a).
Farmland preservation trust fund, §106-744, (c) to (c2).
Southeastern North Carolina agricultural center fund, §106-6.2, (b).
Alarm systems recovery fund, §§74D-30 to 74D-33.
Appellate courts printing and computer operations fund, §7A-343.3.
Assurance fund, §§43-49 to 43-55.
Atomic energy.
Nonreverting radiation protection fund, §§104E-16 to 104E-18.
Auctioneer recovery fund, §§85B-4.1 to 85B-4.11.
Automation enhancement and preservation fund.
Register of deeds, §161-11.3.
Bad checks.
Collection of worthless checks fund, §7A-308, (c).
Bladen lakes state forest fund, §113-36, (d).
Boards and commissions.
Settlement of affairs of certain inoperative boards and agencies, §§143-267 to 143-272.
See BOARDS AND COMMISSIONS.
Budget.
Building and permanent improvement funds, §143-31.
Maintenance funds.
All funds for itemized purposes, §143-23, (a).
Savings reserve account.
Established as special fund in state treasury, §143-15.3, (a).
Reserving to account unreserved credit balance remaining in general fund, §143-15.3, (a1).
Building and permanent improvement fund, §143-31.1.
Child health insurance fund, §135-39.6, (d).
Children's trust fund, §7B-1302, (a), (b).

FUNDS —Cont'd
Child vaccine injury compensation fund, §130A-434.
Civil penalty and forfeiture fund, §§115C-457.1 to 115C-457.3.
Clean water management trust fund, §§113A-251 to 113A-259, 143-15.3B.
See WATERS AND WATERCOURSES.
Clean water revolving loan and grant fund, §159G-5.
Community colleges instructional fund, §115D-42.
Court information technology fund, §7A-343.2.
Crime victims' compensation.
Crime victims' compensation fund.
Clerks of court.
Notified of awards made from, §15B-15.
Deposited with state treasurer, §15B-23.
Established, §15B-23.
Information provided to victims and dependents concerning existence, §15B-20.
Insufficient funds.
Payment delayed until sufficient funds available, §15B-22.
Investments by state treasurer, §15B-23.
Oversight of state auditor, §15B-23.
Surplus, §15B-23.
Displaced homemakers.
North Carolina fund for displaced homemakers, §143B-394.10.
Distinguished professors endowment trust fund, §§116-41.13 to 116-41.19.
See UNIVERSITY OF NORTH CAROLINA.
Domestic violence center fund, §50B-9.
Drivers license technology fund, §20-37.01.
Drug treatment court program fund, §7A-794.
Dry-cleaning solvent cleanup fund, §143-215.104C.
Eastern North Carolina agricultural center fund, §106-6.2, (a).
Economic and community development department.
Industrial development fund, §143B-437.01.
Main street financial incentive fund, §143B-472.35.
Eddie Bridges fund, §143-250.1, (a) to (h).
Education.
County school fund.
Composition of fund, Const. N. C., art. IX, §7.
State fund.
Penalties, fines and forfeitures collected by state agencies (effective upon approval), Const. N. C., art. IX, §7.
State school fund.
Composition of fund, Const. N. C., art. IX, §6.
Egg fund, §106-245.37.
Emergency response fund, §130A-306.
Emergency telephone system fund, §§62A-7, 62A-8.
Endowment funds.
Public schools, §§115C-490 to 115C-494.
Environment and natural resources.
Bladen lakes state forest fund, §113-36, (d).
Forest seedling nursery program fund, §113-36, (c).
Tree cone and seed purchase fund.
Application of proceeds, §113-36, (b).
Escheat fund, §§116B-5 to 116B-7.
Farmland preservation trust fund, §106-744, (c) to (c2).

FUNDS —Cont'd
Fire insurance.
State property fire insurance fund, §§58-31-1 to 58-31-50.
See FIRE INSURANCE.
Firemen's and rescue squad workers' pension fund, §§58-86-1 to 58-86-91.
See FIREMEN'S AND RESCUE SQUAD WORKERS' PENSION FUND.
Firemen's relief fund, §§58-84-1 to 58-84-55.
See FIREMEN'S RELIEF FUND.
Fire protection grant fund, §58-85A-1.
Fire safety loan fund.
Universities and colleges, §116-44.8.
Forests and forestry.
Development fund, §113A-183.
Forest seedling nursery program fund, §113-36, (c).
Foster care and adoption assistance.
Special needs adoption incentive fund, §108A-50.1.
HAVA election fund, §163-82.28.
Hazardous materials emergency response fund, §166A-28.
Hazardous waste site remedial fund, §130A-306.
Inactive hazardous sites cleanup fund, §130A-310.11.
Health and wellness trust fund, §§147-86.30 to 147-86.36.
See HEALTH AND WELLNESS TRUST FUND.
Health benefit reserve fund, §135-39.6, (a).
Help America Vote act, election fund, §163-82.28.
Highway fund, §§136-41.1 to 136-41.3.
Fees from drivers' licenses, placing fees in, §20-7, (j).
Highway trust fund, §§136-175 to 136-184.
See STREETS AND HIGHWAYS.
Homeownership assistance fund, §122A-5.7.
Homeowners' recovery fund, §§87-15.5 to 87-15.9.
Housing finance agency.
Adult care home, group home and nursing home fire protection fund, §122A-5.13.
Housing trust fund, §§122E-1 to 122E-9.
Hurricane flood protection and beach erosion control project revolving fund, §143-215.62.
Industrial development fund, §143B-437.01.
Information technology fund, §147-33.72H.
Institutional funds.
Management of institutional funds, §§36B-1 to 36B-10.
See MANAGEMENT OF INSTITUTIONAL FUNDS.
Insurance.
Consumer protection fund, §58-2-215.
State property fire insurance fund, §§58-31-1 to 58-31-50.
See FIRE INSURANCE.
Investor protection and education trust fund, §147-54.5, (a) to (f).
JDIG reserve fund, §143-15.3E.
Legislative retirement system.
Annuity savings fund, §120-4.17, (b).
Accumulated contributions paid from fund, §120-4.17, (b).
Assets credited to, §120-4.17, (a).
Management of fund, §120-4.18.
Transfer of accumulated contributions to pension accumulation fund upon retirement, §120-4.17, (c).

FUNDS —Cont'd
Legislative retirement system —Cont'd
Annuity savings fund —Cont'd
Transfer of interest from pension accumulation fund to annuity savings fund, §120-4.17, (e).
Pension accumulation fund, §120-4.17, (d).
Assets credited to, §120-4.17, (a).
Management of fund, §120-4.18.
Transfer of accumulated contributions from annuity savings fund to pension accumulation fund upon retirement, §120-4.17, (c).
Transfer of interest to annuity savings fund, §120-4.17, (e).
Loan fund for prospective college teachers, §§116-71 to 116-74.
Long-term rural development fund, §143B-437.28.
Main street financial incentive fund, §143B-472.35.
Management of institutional funds, §§36B-1 to 36B-10.
See MANAGEMENT OF INSTITUTIONAL FUNDS.
Marine fisheries endowment fund, §143B-289.58.
Mental health, developmental disabilities and substance abuse services and bridge funding needs.
Trust for, §143-15.3D.
Militia.
State defense militia, §127A-80.
Missing persons.
Absentee insurance fund, §28C-19.
Mosquito control funds, §130A-347.
Motor vehicle special registration plate funds, §20-79.7.
Natural gas expansion fund, §62-158.
Natural resources easement fund, §146-14.1.
Need-based nursing scholarships fund, §90-171.65.
Nonreverting radiation protection fund, §§104E-16 to 104E-18.
North Carolina aquariums fund, §143B-289.44, (b), (c).
Food and vending services proceeds credited to, §111-47.1, (a).
North Carolina community colleges instructional fund, §115D-42.
North Carolina rural electrification authority fund.
Electric and telephone membership corporation regulatory fees, §117-3.1, (d).
North Carolina youth advocacy and involvement fund, §143B-387.1.
Nurses.
Emergency financial assistance fund, §90-171.51.
Need-based nursing scholarships fund, §90-171.65.
Oil pollution protection fund, §143-215.87.
One North Carolina fund, §§143B-437.70 to 143B-437.74.
Parental savings trust fund, §116-209.25.
Parks and recreation trust fund, §113-44.15.
Pest control.
Insurance fund.
Articles of pest control compact, §106-65.55.
Cooperation of state agencies, §106-65.56.
Request for assistance.
Pest control compact, §106-65.59.
Pesticide environmental trust fund, §143-468, (b).

FUNDS —Cont'd
Political parties financing fund, §§163-278.41 to 163-278.45.
Post-war reserve fund, §§143-191 to 143-194.
Presidential election year candidates fund, §§163-278.41 to 163-278.45.
Prisons and prisoners.
Correction inmate welfare fund, §148-2, (c).
Prison enterprises fund, §148-2, (b).
Private protective services recovery fund, §§74C-30 to 74C-33.
Public employee health benefit fund, §135-39.6, (a), (b).
Public employee long-term care benefit fund, §135-39.6, (c).
Public lands, §§146-71 to 146-73.
Public schools.
Capital outlay fund, §115C-426, (c), (f).
Computer load revolving fund, §115C-472.5.
County school fund, Const. N. C., art. IX, §7.
Critical school facility needs fund, §§115C-489.1 to 115C-489.2.
Endowment funds, §§115C-490 to 115C-494.
Fund for the reduction of class size, §115C-472.10.
Local current expense fund, §115C-426, (c), (e).
Public school building capital fund, §§115C-546.1, 115C-546.2.
Public school insurance fund, §115C-536.
Scholarship loan fund for prospective teachers, §§115C-468 to 115C-472.1.
State fund.
Penalties, fines and forfeitures collected by state agencies (effective upon approval), Const. N. C., art. IX, §7.
State public school fund, §115C-426, (c), (d); Const. N. C., art. IX, §6.
Radiation protection, nonreverting fund, §§104E-16 to 104E-18.
Real estate recovery fund, §§93A-16 to 93A-26.
Recreation and natural heritage trust fund, §§113-77.6 to 113-77.9.
Regional water supply planning.
Revolving fund, §162A-24.
Rescue squad workers' relief fund, §§58-88-1 to 58-88-30.
See RESCUE SQUAD WORKERS' RELIEF FUND.
Retirement system for counties and cities, §§128-29, 128-30.
Retirement system for teachers and state employees.
Annuity reserve fund, §135-8, (c).
Annuity savings fund, §135-8, (b).
Pension accumulation fund, §135-8, (d).
Pension reserve fund, §135-8, (g).
Retiree health benefit fund, §135-7, (f).
Riparian buffer restoration fund, §143-214.22.
Roanoke Island commission endowment fund, §143B-131.8, (b).
Roanoke Island commission fund, §143B-131.8, (a).
Rural investment fund, §143B-437.27.
Saltwater fishing fund, §§113-175 to 113-175.4.
Savings reserve account.
Established as special fund in state treasury, §143-15.3, (a).
Reserving to account unreserved credit balance remaining in general fund, §143-15.3, (a1).
Transfer of funds from unreserved credit balance to savings reserve account, §143-15.2, (b).

FUNDS —Cont'd
Settlement reserve fund.
Cigarette and tobacco products, §143-16.4.
Sinking funds.
Inviolability, Const. N. C., art. V, §6.
Site infrastructure development fund, §143B-437.02, (b).
Small business contract financing fund, §143B-472.89.
Small business surety bond fund, §143B-472.91.
Social services.
Special needs adoption incentive fund, §108A-50.1.
Social workers' education loan fund, §116-209.30.
Solid waste management.
Emergency response fund, §130A-306.
Hazardous waste fund, §130A-298.
Loan fund, §159I-7.
Trust fund, §130A-309.12.
Southeastern North Carolina agricultural center fund, §106-6.2, (b).
Special zoo fund, §143B-336.1.
State fire protection grant fund, §58-85A-1.
State literary fund.
See STATE LITERARY FUND.
Stonewall Jackson memorial fund.
Department of cultural resources.
Transfer of commission to department, §143B-51.
Teachers.
Scholarship loan fund for prospective teachers.
See TEACHERS.
Teacher assistant scholarship fund, §116-209.35.
Tobacco reserve fund, §§66-290, 66-291.
Tobacco trust fund.
General provisions, §§143-715 to 143-723.
See TOBACCO TRUST FUND COMMISSION.
Torrens system registration.
Assurance fund, §§43-49 to 43-55.
Trade jobs for success fund, §143B-438.16, (b).
Tree cone and seed purchase fund, §113-36, (b).
Underground petroleum storage tank leak cleanup.
Commercial leaking petroleum underground storage tank cleanup fund, §143-215.94B, (a) to (f).
Noncommercial leaking petroleum underground storage tank cleanup fund, §143-215.94D.
Underground storage tanks.
Leaking petroleum cleanup.
Groundwater protection loan fund, §143-215.94P.
Petroleum underground storage tank funds council, §143-215.94O.
Unemployment compensation.
Administration fund, §96-5.
Unemployment insurance fund, §96-6.
Uniform management of institutional funds act, §§36B-1 to 36B-10.
See MANAGEMENT OF INSTITUTIONAL FUNDS.
Universities and colleges.
Parental savings trust fund, §116-209.25.
University of North Carolina.
Centennial campus trust fund, §116-36.5.
Endowment funds generally, §116-36.
Land scrip fund, §116-40.1.
School of arts endowment fund, §116-68.
School of science and mathematics endowment fund, §116-238.

FUNDS —Cont'd
University of North Carolina —Cont'd
University improvement bonds fund.
Financing capital facilities, §116D-11, (g).
Vital records automation fund, §130A-93.1, (b).
Volunteer fire department fund, §58-87-1.
Volunteer rescue/EMS fund, §58-87-5, (a) to (c).
Wastewater treatment works emergency maintenance, operation and repair fund, §143-215.3B.
Well construction fund, §87-98.9.
Wetlands restoration fund, §143-214.12.
Wildlife endowment fund, §143-250.1, (a) to (h).
Wildlife resources fund, §143-250.
Hunting and fishing license fees placed in, §113-306, (b).
Wireless fund.
Enhanced 911 system for wireless communications, §62A-22, (c), (d).
Workers' compensation.
Second injury fund, §97-40.1.
Volunteer safety workers, §58-87-10, (a) to (e).
Work first reserve fund, §143-15.3C.
Worthless checks.
Collection of worthless checks fund, §7A-308, (c).
Zoological authority.
Sources of funds, §143-177.3, (a).
Zoological park fund, §143-177.1.
Zoological park.
Special zoo fund, §143B-336.1.

FUNDS TRANSFERS, §§25-4A-101 to 25-4A-507.
Applicability of article, §25-4A-102.
Exclusion of consumer transactions governed by federal law, §25-4A-108.
Attachment and garnishment.
Creditor process served on receiving bank, §25-4A-502.
Attorneys' fees.
Improper execution or failure to execute payment order, §25-4A-305, (e).
Beneficiary.
Defined, §25-4A-103.
Payment order misdescription, §25-4A-207.
Beneficiary's bank.
Defined, §25-4A-103.
Payment order misdescription, §25-4A-208.
Payment orders.
Obligation to pay and give notice to beneficiary, §25-4A-404.
Payment to beneficiary, §25-4A-405.
Set-off by, §25-4A-502.
Choice of law, §25-4A-507.
Citation of title, §25-4A-101.
Conflict of laws.
Choice of law, §25-4A-507.
Exclusion of consumer transactions governed by federal law, §25-4A-108.
Federal reserve regulations and operating circulars, §25-4A-107.
Consumer transactions governed by federal law.
Exclusion, §25-4A-108.
Creditor process served on receiving bank, §25-4A-502.
Damages.
Improper execution or failure to execute payment order, §25-4A-305, (c).
Obligation of beneficiary's bank to pay and give notice to beneficiary.
Refusal to pay after demand and receipt of notice, §25-4A-404, (a).

FUNDS TRANSFERS —Cont'd
Definitions.
Authorized account, §25-4A-105.
Bank, §25-4A-105.
Beneficiary, §25-4A-103.
Beneficiary's bank, §25-4A-103.
Creditor process, §25-4A-502.
Customer, §25-4A-105.
Executed, §25-4A-301.
Execution date, §25-4A-301.
Funds-transfer business day, §25-4A-105.
Funds-transfer system, §25-4A-105.
Funds-transfer system rule, §25-4A-501.
Good faith, §25-4A-105.
Index of definitions, §25-4A-105.
Intermediary bank, §25-4A-104.
Originator, §25-4A-104.
Originator's bank, §25-4A-104.
Payment date, §25-4A-401.
Payment order, §25-4A-103.
Prove, §25-4A-105.
Receiving bank, §25-4A-103.
Security procedure, §25-4A-201.
Sender, §25-4A-103.
Authorized and verified payment orders, §25-4A-202, (d).
Federal reserve regulations and operating circulars, §25-4A-107.
Funds-transfer system rule.
Defined, §25-4A-501.
Effect of, §25-4A-501.
Variation by agreement, §25-4A-501.
Injunctive relief, §25-4A-503.
Interest.
Rate of interest, §25-4A-506.
Intermediary bank.
Defined, §25-4A-104.
Payment order misdescription, §25-4A-208.
Limitation of actions.
Objection to debit of customer's account, §25-4A-505.
Notice.
Cancellation and amendment of payment orders, §25-4A-211.
Payment orders.
Obligation of beneficiary's bank to give notice to beneficiary, §25-4A-404.
Rejection, §25-4A-210.
Payment orders.
Acceptance, §25-4A-209.
Amendment, §25-4A-211.
Authorized payment orders, §25-4A-202.
Cancellation, §25-4A-211.
Cut-off time, §25-4A-106.
Defined, §25-4A-103.
Discharge of underlying obligation, §25-4A-406.
Erroneous payment orders, §25-4A-205.
Execution by receiving bank.
Erroneous execution, §25-4A-303.
Duty of sender to report, §25-4A-304.
"Executed" defined, §25-4A-301.
"Execution date" defined, §25-4A-301.
Failure to execute.
Liability for, §25-4A-305.
Improper execution.
Liability for, §25-4A-305.
Late execution.
Liability for, §25-4A-305.
Obligations of receiving bank, §25-4A-302.
Misdescription.
Beneficiary, §25-4A-207.
Beneficiary's bank, §25-4A-208.

FUNDS TRANSFERS —Cont'd
Payment orders —Cont'd
Misdescription —Cont'd
Intermediary bank, §25-4A-208.
Objection to debit of customer's account.
Preclusion of objection, §25-2A-505.
Obligation of beneficiary's bank, §25-2A-404.
Obligation of sender to pay receiving bank, §25-2A-402.
Order in which payment orders may be charged to account, §25-2A-504.
Order of withdrawals from account, §25-2A-504.
Payment by beneficiary's bank to beneficiary, §25-2A-405.
Payment by originator to beneficiary, §25-4A-406.
Payment by sender to receiving bank, §25-4A-403.
Payment date.
Defined, §25-4A-401.
Preclusion of objection to debit of customer's account, §25-4A-505.
Rejection, §25-4A-210.
Liability and duty of receiving bank regarding unaccepted payment order, §25-4A-212.
Security procedure.
Commercial reasonableness, §25-4A-202, (c).
Defined, §25-4A-201.
Time of acceptance, §25-4A-209.
Time received, §25-4A-106.
Transmission through communications system, §25-4A-206.
Transmission through funds-transfer system, §25-4A-206.
Unauthorized payment orders.
Duty of customer to report, §25-4A-204.
Refund of payment, §25-4A-204.
Verified payment orders, §25-4A-202.
Unenforceability of, §25-4A-203.
Refunds.
Beneficiary's bank making payment that is provisional under system rule, §25-4A-405, (b).
Payment of unauthorized payment orders, §25-4A-204.
Sender paying payment order and not obligated to pay, §25-4A-402.
Scope of article, §25-4A-102.
Exclusion of consumer transactions governed by federal law, §25-4A-108.
Service of process.
Creditor process on receiving bank, §25-4A-502.
Setoff by beneficiary's bank, §25-4A-502.
Short title, §25-4A-101.
Statute of limitations.
Objection to debit of customer's account, §25-4A-505.
Title of article, §25-4A-101.

FUNERAL CONTRACTS AND FUNDS.
Preneed contracts and funds generally, §§90-210.60 to 90-210.73.
See PRENEED FUNERAL CONTRACTS AND FUNDS.

FUNERAL PROCESSIONS.
Defined, §20-157.1, (a).
Following vehicles.
Close but safe distance, §20-157.1, (d).
Non-compliance with traffic control signals, §20-157.1, (c).
Headlights to be illuminated, §20-157.1, (b).
Lead vehicle.
Compliance with traffic-control signals, §20-157.1, (c).

FUNERAL PROCESSIONS —Cont'd
Local authorities.
Regulating use of highways by processions, §20-169.
Mingling into procession, §20-157.1, (i).
Moving violations.
Violations of provisions do not constitute, §20-157.1, (m).
Negligence per se.
Violations of provisions do not constitute, §20-157.1, (k).
Opposite direction vehicles.
Yielding to procession, §20-157.1, (g).
Ordinances conflicting with provisions, §20-157.1, (l).
Passing procession, §20-157.1, (h).
Police escort, §20-157.1, (j).
Regulation by local authorities, §20-169.
Right side of roadway operation, §20-157.1, (d).
Same direction vehicles.
Mingling into procession, §20-157.1, (i).
Yielding to procession, §20-157.1, (h).
Speed, §20-157.1, (f).
Weapons, possession, §14-277.2.
Yielding to law enforcement, emergency, etc., vehicles, §20-157.1, (e).

FUNERAL SERVICE.
Advertisements.
Defined, §90-210.20, (a).
Affidavits.
Good moral character of license applicant, §90-210.26.
Age.
Qualifications for licenses, §90-210.25, (a).
Board.
Created, §90-120.18A, (b).
Definition of "board," §90-210.20, (b).
Expenses of members, §90-210.23, (c).
Inspection and regulation of funeral establishments, §90-210.23, (e).
Inspectors.
Appointment, §90-210.24, (a).
Identification cards, §90-210.24, (c).
Inspection form, §90-210.24, (d).
Powers, §90-210.24, (b).
Legal counsel, clerical and technical assistance, employment, §90-210.23, (h2).
Meetings, §90-210.22.
Members, §90-120.18A, (b).
Mutual burial associations.
Generally, §§90-210.80 to 90-210.107.
See MUTUAL BURIAL ASSOCIATIONS.
Oath of office of members, §90-210.19.
Officers, §90-210.23, (b).
Powers generally, §90-210.23, (i).
Quorum, §90-210.22.
Real property, powers, §90-210.23, (h1).
Removal, §90-120.18A, (d).
Resident trainees.
Furnishing information to board, §90-210.23, (d).
Powers as to programs for, §90-210.23, (f).
Rules and regulations, §90-210.23, (a).
Seal, §90-210.23, (h).
Vacancies, §90-120.18A, (c).
Burial.
Defined, §90-210.20, (c).
Burial depth, minimum depth, §90-210.25A.
Child support enforcement.
Forfeiture of licensing privilege, §50-13.12.

FUNERAL SERVICE —Cont'd
Cremation.
General provisions, §§90-210.40 to 90-210.54.
See CREMATION.
Criminal law and procedure.
Unlawful practices, §90-210.25, (f).
Dead human bodies.
Defined, §90-210.20, (c1).
Death certificates.
Entitlement of funeral director or funeral service licensee to certified copy upon request, §130A-93, (c1).
Decedents' estates.
Funeral expenses deemed obligation of estate, §28A-19-8, (a), (b).
Definitions, §90-210.20.
Dissection.
Schools for teaching mortuary science.
Privileges as to use of bodies for dissection, §90-210.23, (g).
Embalmers.
Defined, §90-210.20, (d).
Licenses.
Qualifications, §90-210.25, (a).
Revocation or suspension.
Felony convictions, §15A-1331A.
Embalming.
Defined, §90-210.20, (e).
Evidence.
Funeral charges at issue, §8-58.1.
Executors and administrators.
Carrying out funeral arrangements prior to appointment, §28A-13-1.
Wrongful death.
Damages recoverable by personal representative, §28A-18-2, (b).
Fees.
Establishment permits, §90-210.28.
Licenses, §90-210.28.
Schedule of fees, §90-210.28.
Felony convictions.
Forfeiture of licenses, §15A-1331A.
Fines.
Unlawful practices, §90-210.25, (f).
Funeral chapels.
Defined, §90-210.20, (e1).
Registration.
Fee, §90-210.28.
Required, §90-210.27A, (g).
Funeral contracts and funds.
Preneed funeral contracts and funds generally, §§90-210.60 to 90-210.73.
See PRENEED FUNERAL CONTRACTS AND FUNDS.
Funeral directing.
Defined, §90-210.20, (f).
Funeral directors.
Defined, §90-210.20, (g).
Identification of bodies before burial or cremation, §90-210.29A.
Licenses, §§90-210.25, 90-210.26.
Criminal records checks for license applicants, §90-210.25, (a).
Revocation or suspension.
Felony convictions, §15A-1331A.
Funeral establishments.
Defined, §90-210.20, (h).
Funeral chapels.
Defined, §90-210.20, (e1).
Registration.
Fees, §90-210.28.
Required, §90-210.27A, (g).

FUNERAL SERVICE —Cont'd
Funeral establishments —Cont'd
Inspection, §90-210.23, (e).
Licenses.
Owners, §90-210.27A, (e).
Person under whose name funeral establishment does business, §90-210.27A, (f).
Misleading or unregistered name.
Use prohibited, §90-210.27A, (i).
Ownerships.
Restrictions, §90-210.27A, (e).
Permits, §90-210.25, (d).
Fees, §90-210.28.
Preparation room.
Persons allowed in, §90-210.27A, (b).
Requirements as to, §90-210.27A, (a).
Registered name, use required, §90-210.27A, (j).
Reposing room.
Requirements as to, §90-210.27A, (c).
Identification of bodies before burial or cremation, §90-210.29A.
Injunctions.
Power of board to seek injunction, §90-210.25, (f).
Inspectors, §90-210.24.
Legislative declaration, §90-120.18A, (a).
Liberal construction of article, §90-120.18A, (a).
Licenses.
Criminal records checks for license applicants, §90-210.25, (a).
Embalmers.
Qualifications, §90-210.25, (a).
Fees, §90-210.28.
Funeral establishments.
Owners, §90-210.27A, (e).
Person under whose name funeral establishment does business, §90-210.27A, (f).
"Funeral service licensee" defined, §90-210.20, (i).
Qualifications, §90-210.25, (a).
Good moral character.
Affidavits as to, §90-210.26.
Reciprocity, §90-210.25, (b).
Registration, §90-210.25, (c).
Revocation or suspension, §90-210.25, (e).
Felony convictions, §15A-1331A.
Penalty in compromise, §90-210.25, (e).
Unlicensed practice.
Penalty, §90-210.25, (f).
Minimum burial depth, §90-210.25A.
Misdemeanors.
Unlawful practice, §90-210.25, (f).
Oaths.
Board members.
Oath of office of members, §90-210.19.
Penalties.
Revocation or suspension of license.
Payment of penalty in compromise, §90-210.25, (e).
Unlawful practice, §90-210.25, (f).
Permits.
Funeral establishments, §90-210.25, (d).
Fees, §90-210.28.
Student permits, §90-210.29, (b).
Practice of funeral service.
Defined, §90-210.20, (k).
Unlawful practice, §90-210.25, (f).
Preneed funeral contracts and funds generally, §§90-210.60 to 90-210.73.
See PRENEED FUNERAL CONTRACTS AND FUNDS.

FUNERAL SERVICE —Cont'd
Presumptions.
Funeral charges at issue.
Rebuttable presumption of reasonableness, §8-58.1.
Prison terms.
Unlawful practices, §90-210.25, (f).
Reciprocity.
Licenses, §90-210.25, (b).
Reports.
Resident trainees, §90-210.25, (a).
Resident trainees.
Certificate of resident traineeship, §90-210.25, (a).
Fees, §90-210.28.
Defined, §90-210.20, (l).
Information.
Furnishing to board, §90-210.23, (d).
Powers of board, §90-210.23, (f).
Qualifications, §90-210.25, (a).
Reports, §90-210.25, (a).
Seals and sealed instruments.
Board, §90-210.23, (h).
Students.
Authorized practices, §90-210.29, (a).
Permits, §90-210.29, (b).
Venue.
Injunctions.
Actions by board to enjoin violations, §90-210.25, (f).
Witnesses.
Funeral charges at issue.
Injured party or guardian, administrator or executor.
Competency to give evidence regarding amount of charges, §8-58.1.

FUNGIBLE GOODS.
Duplicate receipt or bill.
Rights conferred, §25-7-402.
Warehousemen.
Duty to keep goods separate, §25-7-207, (1).
Liability for commingling goods, §25-7-207, (2).

FUNGICIDES.
Pesticide applicators, §§143-452 to 143-459.
See PESTICIDE APPLICATORS.
Pesticide board generally.
See PESTICIDE BOARD.
Pesticide consultants, §§143-455, 143-456.
Pesticide dealers and manufacturers licenses, §§143-448 to 143-451.
Pesticide registration.
See PESTICIDE REGISTRATION.
Pesticides generally, §§143-434 to 143-470.1.
See PESTICIDES.

FURBEARER PROPAGATION.
Licenses, §113-273, (i).

FUR-DEALER LICENSES, §113-273, (f).

FURNITURE.
Child care facilities.
Mandatory standards for licensing, §110-91.
Exempt property from enforcement of claims of creditors, §1C-1601, (a).
Household goods and furnishings, §1C-1601, (g).
Recent purchases, §1C-1601, (d).
Liens.
Possessory liens on personal property.
Persons entitled to lien, §44A-2, (e).
Loans.
Household and kitchen furniture.
Usurious loans on furniture, §14-391.

FURNITURE —Cont'd
Property taxes.
Exclusion of non-business property.
Household furnishings, §105-275.
Purchases through department of administration.
Furniture requirements contracts, §143-57.1.
Sales and use.
Tax holiday, inapplicability, §105-164.13C, (b).

FUTURE ADVANCEMENTS, §§29-23 to 29-29.

FUTURE ADVANCES.
Secured transactions.
Priority of security interests.
Buyers of goods, ordinary course of business, §25-9-323, (d).
Commitment, advances pursuant to, §25-9-323, (e).
Buyers of receivables holding interest, §25-9-323, (c).
Lessees of goods, §25-9-323, (f).
Commitment, advances pursuant to, §25-9-323, (g).
Lien creditors, §25-9-323, (b).
Time of advance basis, §25-9-323, (a).
Security interest in, §25-9-204, (c).

FUTURE FARMERS OF AMERICA.
Special license plates, §20-79.4, (b).

FUTURE INTERESTS.
Conveyances.
Inter vivos and testamentary conveyances of future interests permitted, §39-6.3, (a) to (c).
Revocation of conveyances to persons not in esse, §§39-6, 39-6.1.
Validation of deed, §39-6.1.
Killing decedent.
Contingent remainders and executory interests, §31A-8.
Mortgages and deeds of trust.
Advances and future obligations, §§45-68 to 45-74.
Property passed by will, §31-40.
Remainders, reversions and executory interests generally.
See REMAINDERS, REVERSIONS AND EXECUTORY INTERESTS.
Renunciation.
Effect, §31B-3, (a).
Succession, §31B-1.
Time for filing, §31B-2, (b).
Wills.
What property passes by will, §31-40.

FUTURE OF THE NORTH CAROLINA RAILROAD STUDY COMMISSION, §§120-245 to 120-255.
Cochairs, §120-249.
Consultants, hiring, §120-253.
Duties, §120-247.
Established, §120-245.
Meeting space, location, §120-254.
Membership, §120-246.
Per diem, subsistence and travel expenses, §120-251.
Quorum, §120-250.
Report, §120-255.
Staff, §120-252.
Vacancies, §120-248.

FUTURES CONTRACTS.
Commodities as which contracts void, §16-3.

FUTURES CONTRACTS —Cont'd
Evidence.
Prosecutions under provisions, §16-6.
Misdemeanors.
Entering into or aiding futures contract, §16-4.
Opening office for sales of futures, §16-5.
Voidability, §16-3.
Witnesses.
Prosecutions under provisions, §16-6.

FUTURES TRADING.
Commodities.
General provisions, §§78D-1 to 78D-33.
See COMMODITIES.

G

GAG ORDERS.
Open court proceedings or reports of public records, §7A-276.1.

GAIN FROM FELONY.
Forfeiture, §14-2.3.

GALLERIES.
Destruction of property of gallery, §14-398.

GALLSTONES.
Food, drug and cosmetic act.
Drug or device, false advertising, §106-138, (b).

GAMBLING.
Alcoholic beverage permittees.
Conduct unlawful on premises, §18B-1005, (a).
Elections.
Bet or wager on election, §163-274.
Futures contracts, §§16-3 to 16-6.
Gaming, §§14-289 to 14-309.15.
See GAMING.

GAME BIRD PROPAGATION.
Licenses, §113-273, (h).

GAME LAWS.
Fish and fishing generally.
See FISH AND FISHING.
Hunting and wildlife.
See HUNTING AND WILDLIFE.

GAMING, §§14-289 to 14-309.15.
Bureau of investigation.
Investigation of gaming law violations, §114-15, (a).
Contracts.
Futures contracts, §§16-3 to 16-6.
Void, §16-1.
Witnesses.
Players and betters competent witnesses, §16-2.
Definitions.
Illegal slot machines, §14-296.
Punchboards, §14-296.
Slot machines, §14-306, (a).
Destruction of gaming devices, police.
Opposing destruction, §14-300.
Elements of offense, §14-292.
False coins or tokens.
Obtaining property or services from slot machines, vending machines, etc., by false coins or tokens, §14-108.
Faro banks and tables.
Opening, establishing, etc., bank or table, §14-294.
Greyhound racing, §14-309.20.
Houses of public entertainment, §14-293.
Indians.
Authorization for federally recognized tribes, §71A-8.

GAMING —Cont'd
Lotteries.
Acting as agent for lotteries, §14-291.
Advertising lotteries, §14-289.
Dealing in lotteries, §14-290.
"Numbers" tickets, §14-291.1.
Selling lottery tickets, §14-291.
Police.
Destruction of gaming devices.
Opposing destruction, §14-300.
Public entertainment, §14-293.
Punchboards.
Allowing illegal punchboards on premises, §14-297.
Definition of illegal punchboards, §14-296.
Keeping illegal punchboards, §14-295.
Operation of punchboard, §§14-302, 14-303.
Criminal violation, §14-303.
Racing, greyhounds, §14-309.20.
Raffles.
Bingo.
Raffles not to be conducted in conjunction with bingo, §14-309.15, (e).
Defined, §14-309.15, (b).
Nonprofit organization or association.
Conduct authorized, §14-309.15, (a).
Number per year, §14-309.15, (c).
Prizes.
Maximum cash prizes, §14-309.15, (d).
Proceeds.
Disposition, §14-309.15, (f).
Seizure of property exhibited by gamblers and illegal gaming items, §§14-298, 14-299.
Disposition of property, §14-299.
Opposing seizure of property, §14-300.
Slot machines.
Agreements with reference to slot machines or devices made unlawful, §§14-305, 14-309.
Criminal violation, §14-309.
Allowing illegal slot machines on premises, §14-297.
Antique slot machines.
Defense in prosecution for possession of slot machine or device, §14-309.1, (a).
Return of slot machine to defendant, §14-309.1, (b).
Burglary.
Breaking into or forcibly opening, §14-56.1.
Damaging or destroying machines, §14-56.2.
Defined, §14-306, (a).
Illegal slot machines, §14-296.
Devices not considered slot machines, §14-306, (b).
Criminal offense to make unlawful payout, §14-306, (d).
Paying more than allowed by law.
Warning sticker or message as to criminal penalty affixed to machine, §14-306, (c).
Pay off in cash, exception inapplicable, §14-306, (d).
Repurchase of prize for cash or reward in cash, inapplicability of exception, §14-306, (d).
False pretenses and cheats.
Manufacture, sale or gift of devices for cheating slot machines, §14-109.
Obtaining property or services from machine by false coins or tokens, §14-108.
Felony offenses, §14-309, (a), (b).
Keeping illegal slot machines, §14-295.
License.
Issuance of license prohibited, §§14-307, 14-309.
Criminal violation, §14-309.

GAMING —Cont'd
Slot machines —Cont'd
Manufacture, sale, etc., of slot machines and devices, §§14-304, 14-309.
Criminal violation, §14-309.
Manufacture, sale or gift of devices for cheating machine, §14-106.
Nuisance.
Declared a public nuisance, §§14-308, 14-309.
Criminal violation, §14-309.
Operation of slot machine, §§14-301 to 14-303.
Criminal violation, §14-303.
Possession of slot machine, §§14-301, 14-302.
Criminal violation, §14-303.
Defense to possession, §14-309.1, (a).
Return of slot machine to defendant, §14-309.1, (b).
Separate offenses, §§14-302, 14-303.
Tables.
Allowing gaming tables on premises, §14-297.
Destruction of gaming tables by police officers.
Opposing destruction of gaming tables, §14-300.
Faro tables, §14-294.
Keeping gaming tables, §14-295.
Video gaming machines.
ABC law violations, §14-306.2.
Advertising prohibited, §14-306.1, (g).
Age requirements, §14-306.1, (d).
Ban on warehousing, §14-306.1, (m).
Convicted persons, §14-306.1, (p).
Costs of enforcement and registration efforts.
Report to joint legislative commission on governmental operations, §14-306.1, (k).
Criminal offense to make unlawful payout, §14-306, (d).
Definitions, §14-306.1, (c).
Devices not considered slot machines, §14-306, (b).
Exemptions of section, §14-306.1, (l).
Hours of operation, §14-306.1, (e).
Illustrations of prohibited games, §14-306.1, (c).
Indian gaming regulatory act.
Exemptions under, §14-306.1, (n).
Local preemptions, §14-306.1, (o).
Minimum distance from other location operating machines, §14-306.1, (h).
More than three existing machines at one location.
Prohibition, §14-306.1, (b).
New machines, ban on, date of ban, §14-306.1, (a).
Paying more than allowed by law.
Warning sticker or message as to criminal penalty affixed to machine, §14-306, (c).
Pay off in cash.
Exception to slot machine definition inapplicable, §14-306, (d).
Permanent buildings required, §14-306.1, (h).
Plan view of persons visiting premises.
Requirement, §14-306.1, (f).
Receipts, prizes and merchandise awarded.
Reports on, §14-306.1, (j).
Registration with sheriff.
Required, §14-306.1, (i).
Repurchase of prize for cash or reward in cash.
Inapplicability of exception to slot machine definition, §14-306, (d).
Unlawful activity not legalized, §14-306.1, (q).
Witnesses.
Testimony enforced in certain criminal investigations, §8-55.
Immunity of witness, §8-55.

GAMMA HYDROXYBUTYRIC ACID (GHB).
Date rape drug, §90-89.
Scheduled I controlled substance, §90-89.
Schedule III controlled substance, §90-91, (l).
Schedule IV controlled substance, §90-92.

GAMMA RAYS.
Radiation protection act generally, §§104E-1 to 104E-29.
See RADIATION PROTECTION.

GANG RAPE.
Venue, §15A-136.

GARAGES.
Motor vehicle mechanic and storage liens.
Assignment of actions to enforce to magistrates, §7A-211.1.
Repair of motor vehicles, §§20-354 to 20-354.9.
See MOTOR VEHICLE REPAIRS.

GARBAGE AND TRASH.
Boating safety.
Depositing or discharging litter, §75A-10, (c).
Medical waste, §§75A-10, (d), 75A-18, (d).
Counties.
Areas outside corporate limits.
Establishing and operating facilities, §153A-292, (a).
Collection of fees, §153A-293.
Cooperation between department of transportation and counties, §153A-291.
Costs of providing and operating facility.
Determining for imposition of fees, §153A-292, (b).
County collection and disposal, §153A-292, (a) to (f).
Definitions, §§153A-136, (c), (d), 153A-294.
Disposal and removal of trash and garbage.
Boards of commissioners to provide for, §153A-132.1.
Equipment.
Agreement with department of transportation to make available, §153A-291.
Fees.
Collection, use of facility and availability of facility.
Authority to impose, determining amount, §153A-292, (b).
Property taxes, billing and collecting in same manner, §153A-293.
Gate across highway leading to facility.
Erecting, §153A-292, (c).
Highway rights-of-way, containers on.
Misdemeanor for placing garbage on right-of-way, inapplicability, §136-18.3, (b).
Permits, issuance by department of transportation, §136-18.3, (a).
Removal or change of location, order of department, §136-18.3, (d).
Written permission of owner of underlying fee, required, §136-18.3, (c).
Landfills.
Selection and approval of site, §153A-136, (c).
Low-income persons, providing aid to, §153A-292, (f).
Ordinances, §153A-136, (b).
Prison and other labor.
Agreement with department of transportation to make available, §153A-291.
Regulation of disposal facilities, nature of disposal and method of disposal, §153A-292, (a).
Regulation of solid wastes, §153A-136.

GARBAGE AND TRASH —Cont'd
Counties —Cont'd
Regulation of storage, collection, transportation and use, §153A-136, (a).
Removal and disposal of trash and garbage.
Boards of commissioners to provide for, §153A-132.1.
Service districts, §§153A-300 to 153A-310.
Site for facility.
Acquiring by purchase or condemnation, §153A-292, (c).
Use of suitable vacant land, §153A-292, (c).
Highway rights-of-way.
Location of collection containers on.
Counties and municipalities, §136-18.3, (a) to (d).
Hogs.
Feeding garbage to swine, §§106-405.1 to 106-405.8.
Light-traffic road weight and load limitations.
Garbage collection exception, §20-118, (c).
Littering.
Prohibited, §14-399.
Litter prevention.
Special license plates, §§20-79.4, (b), 20-81.12, (b15).
Municipal corporations.
Accidental spilling during loading of garbage truck.
Inapplicability of littering statute, §14-399, (a2).
Annexation of area where private solid waste collection firm providing services, §160A-324.
Collection and disposal by city.
Fee for collection, imposing, §160A-317, (c).
Participation in service provided by city.
Requiring property owner, §160A-317, (b).
Placing waste in specific places or receptacles.
Authority to require property owners, §160A-317, (b).
Separation of materials before collection.
Requiring property owner, §160A-317, (b).
Extension of corporate limits.
Population less than five thousand.
Contract with private solid waste collection firms, §160A-37.3.
Population of five thousand or more.
Contract with private solid waste collection firms, §160A-49.3.
Highway rights-of-way, containers on.
Misdemeanor for placing garbage on right-of-way, inapplicability, §136-18.3, (b).
Permits, issuance by department of transportation, §136-18.3, (a).
Removal or change of location, order of department, §136-18.3, (d).
Written permission of owner of underlying fee, required, §136-18.3, (c).
Littering statute, inapplicability.
Accidental spilling during loading of garbage truck, §14-399, (a2).
Recycling program.
Requiring property owner's participation, §160A-317, (b).
Regulation of placing of garbage and trash within municipal limits, §160A-303.1.
Navigation and pilotage.
Commissioners of navigation to designate place for, §76-55.
Navigable waters.
Deposit prohibited, §76-40, (a).

GARBAGE AND TRASH —Cont'd
Public lands.
Dumping rights, §146-11.
Regional solid waste management authorities, §§153A-421 to 153A-432.
See REGIONAL SOLID WASTE MANAGEMENT AUTHORITIES.
Sanitary districts.
Collection and disposal.
Corporate powers of sanitary district board, §130A-55.
Solid waste management.
General provisions, §§130A-290 to 130A-305.
See SOLID WASTE MANAGEMENT.
Street and highways.
Litter prevention account, §§136-125.1, 136-125.2.

GARNER.
Condemnation of unsafe buildings, §§160A-425.1, 160A-426, (d), 160A-432, (a1).

GARNISHMENT.
Admission by garnishee.
Debt or personal property due defendant payable at future date.
Denial of allegation by plaintiff, §1-440.28, (e).
Indebted to defendant.
Judgment entered by clerk, amount, §1-440.28, (a).
Not in possession of property belonging to defendant at time of answer, value of property determined, §1-440.28, (c).
Judgment entered by clerk, amount, §1-440.28, (d).
Possession of personal property belonging to defendant.
Judgment entered by clerk, delivery of property to sheriff, §1-440.28, (b).
Agriculture.
Delinquent fees and taxes.
Collection of delinquent fees and taxes, §106-9.4, (b).
Alimony.
Remedy available, §50-16.7, (e).
Ambulances.
County or city ambulance service, §§44-51.4 to 44-51.8.
Ancillary proceeding, §1-440.21, (a).
Answer by garnishee.
Admissions in answer, §1-440.28, (a) to (e).
Lien or other valid claim asserted, §1-440.28, (g).
Setoff, right asserted, §1-440.28, (f).
Attachment.
General provisions.
See ATTACHMENT.
Blind persons.
Aid to the blind.
Exemption from garnishment, §111-18.
Bonds, surety.
Garnishee retaining possession, §1-440.32, (b).
Child support, §110-136.
Corporations.
Summons and process.
Delivery of garnishment process to corporate garnishee, §1-440.26.
Debtors and creditors.
Payment to defendant by garnishee, §1-440.31.
Denials by garnishee, §1-440.29, (a).
Jury trial, §§1-440.28, (e), 1-440.29, (b).
Executions.
Issuance of execution against garnishee, §1-440.32, (a).
Bonds, surety.
Garnishee retaining possession, §1-440.32, (b).

GARNISHMENT —Cont'd
Exemptions.
Limitation on wage garnishment, §1-362.
Failure of garnishee to appear.
Generally, §1-440.27, (a).
Notice requiring appearance, §1-440.27, (b).
Family law arbitration, §50-44, (c).
Firemen's and rescue squad workers' pension fund.
Exemption of pensions from garnishment, §58-86-90.
Forms.
Notice of levy, §1-440.24.
Summons to garnishee, §1-440.23.
Fraternal benefit societies.
Benefits.
Not subject to garnishment, §58-24-85.
Fraudulent public assistance program payments.
Recoupment of fraudulent payments, §108A-25.3.
Funds transfers, UCC.
Creditor process served on receiving bank, §25-4A-502.
Garnishee defined, §1-440.21, (b).
Hospitals.
Debts owed public hospitals, §§131E-48 to 131E-51.
Insurer supervision, rehabilitation and liquidation.
Garnishment prohibited during pendency of liquidation proceeding, §58-30-295.
Jury.
Denials by garnishee.
Jury trial, §§1-440.28, (e), 1-440.29, (b).
Time of jury trial, §1-440.30.
Legislative retirement system.
Exemption from garnishment, §120-4.29.
Levy.
How made, §1-440.25.
Notice.
Delivery to garnishee, §1-440.25.
Corporate garnishee, §1-440.26.
Form, §1-440.24.
Liens.
County or city ambulance service, §§44-51.4 to 44-51.8.
Garnishee may assert lien, §1-440.28, (g).
Levy on defendant's personal property in hands of garnishee, §1-440.33, (c).
More than one order served on garnishee.
Determination of questions of priority, §1-440.33, (g).
Limitation on wage garnishment, §1-362.
More than one order served on garnishee.
Determination of questions of priority, §1-440.33, (g).
Motor vehicles.
Delinquent taxes.
Remedies for collection, §20-99.
Municipal corporations.
Taxation.
Remedies for collecting taxes, §160A-207.
Nature of garnishment, §1-440.21, (a), (b).
Notice.
Failure of garnishee to appear.
Notice requiring appearance, §1-440.27, (b).
Levy.
Delivery to garnishee, §§1-440.25, 1-440.26.
Form, §1-440.24.
Purpose, §1-440.21, (a).

GARNISHMENT —Cont'd
Retirement system for teachers and state employees.
Exemption from garnishment, §135-9.
Return where garnishee process issued, §1-440.16, (b).
Service of process.
Issuance of summons to garnishee, §1-440.22, (a), (b).
Setoff.
Garnishee may assert right of setoff, §1-440.28, (f).
Sheriff's return.
Where garnishee process issued, §1-440.16, (b).
Summons to garnishee.
Delivery to garnishee, §1-440.25.
Corporate garnishee, §1-440.26, (a).
Foreign corporation, §1-440.26, (b).
Local agent, §1-440.26, (a), (c).
Form, §1-440.23.
Issuance, §1-440.22, (a), (b).
Supplemental retirement income act.
Exemption from garnishment, §135-95.
Support and maintenance.
Child support, §110-136.
Taxation.
Collection of taxes, §105-242, (b).
Exempt property, §105-242, (e).
Wages.
Fraudulent public assistance program payments, §108A-25.3.
Limitation on wage garnishment, §1-362.

GAS AND GAS COMPANIES.
Bills to show reading of meter, §66-9.
Discharges of oil or hazardous substances, §§143-215.83 to 143-215.94.
See OIL OR HAZARDOUS SUBSTANCES DISCHARGES.
Franchised natural gas local distribution companies.
Natural gas planning.
Reports detailing plans for providing gas service in areas of franchise territory, §62-36A.
Natural gas service agreements.
Interstate or intrastate pipeline companies.
Orders directing distribution companies to enter into service agreements within reasonable time, §62-36B.
Funds.
Natural gas expansion fund, §62-158.
Additional funds, §62-159.
Leaking petroleum underground storage tank cleanup, §§143-215.94A to 143-215.94Y.
See UNDERGROUND PETROLEUM STORAGE TANK LEAK CLEANUP.
Meters.
Master and natural gas meters, §143-151.42.
Municipal corporations.
Lease or purchase of natural gas fields, reserves and supplies.
Authority to operate, §160A-312, (c).
Natural gas expansion fund, §62-158.
Construction of facilities, §62-159, (a).
Determination of economic feasibility, §62-159, (b).
Exclusive franchises, §62-159. (c).
Rules promulgated by commission, §62-159, (d).
Natural gas planning, §62-36A.
Natural gas service agreements.
Regulation of, §62-36B.

GAS AND GAS COMPANIES —Cont'd
Offshore oil and gas activities, §§143-215.94AA to 143-215.94JJ.
See OFFSHORE OIL AND GAS ACTIVITIES.
Oil and gas conservation.
General provisions, §§113-378 to 113-415.
See OIL AND GAS CONSERVATION.
Property taxes.
Public service corporations.
Generally, §§105-333 to 105-344.
See PROPERTY TAXES.
Reports.
Franchised natural gas local distribution companies.
Natural gas planning.
Reports detailing plans for providing natural gas service in areas of franchise territory, §62-36A.
Trespass.
Criminal trespass, §14-152.
Interfering with gas appliances, §14-151.

GAS CHAMBER.
Capital punishment generally.
See CAPITAL PUNISHMENT.

GAS CONSERVATION, §§113-378 to 113-415.
See OIL AND GAS CONSERVATION.

GAS COST ADJUSTMENT FOR NATURAL GAS LOCAL DISTRIBUTION COMPANIES, §62-133.4.

GASOLINE.
Advertisements.
Price advertisements.
Drawing or pumping fuel by purchaser himself, §14-117.2, (a), (b).
Commodities.
General provisions, §§78D-1 to 78D-33.
See COMMODITIES.
Fraud.
Price advertisements.
Purchaser himself drawing or pumping fuel, §14-117.2.
Inspection, §§119-14 to 119-47.
See GASOLINE AND OIL INSPECTION.
Larceny of motor fuels, §14-72.5.
Driver's license, second or subsequent conviction.
Limited driving privilege.
Allowed person whose license revoked, §20-16, (e2).
Mandatory revocation of driver's license, §20-17, (a).
Period driver's license revoked, §20-19, (g2).
Sulfur content standards, §119-26.2.

GASOLINE AND OIL INSPECTION, §§119-14 to 119-47.
Administration of provisions.
Commissioner of agriculture to administer, §119-23.
Inspection tax proceeds.
Allotment for administration expenses, §119-18, (b).
Inspectors, clerks and assistants.
Appoint and employ, §119-25.
Adoption of certain laws as part of article, §119-45.
Adulteration.
Products offered for sale, §119-35.
Analysis of inspected products.
Charges for analysis of samples, §119-46.
Establishment of laboratory for analysis, §119-30.

GASOLINE AND OIL INSPECTION —Cont'd
Analysis of inspected products —Cont'd
Evidence.
Certified copies of official tests admissible in evidence, §119-36.
Assistants.
Appoint and employ, §119-25.
Bill of sale.
Persons engaged in transporting.
Required to have in possession bill of sale, §119-42.
Bills of lading.
Transporters.
Required to have in possession an invoice, bill of sale or bill of lading, §119-42.
Board, §119-26.
Rules and regulations.
Availability to interested parties, §119-29.
Transfer to department of agriculture and consumer services, §143A-62.
Bonds, surety.
Cancellation of license, §119-19.
Inspectors to be bonded, §119-25.
Carriers.
Invoice, bill of sale or bill of lading.
Required to be in possession of transporters, §119-42.
Certain laws adopted as part of article, §119-45.
Charges for analysis of samples, §119-46.
Citation of act, §119-14.
Clerks.
Appointment and employ, §119-25.
Commissioner of agriculture.
Administration of provisions, §119-23.
Delegation of duties.
Oxygen content standards and reformulated gasoline, §119-26.1, (d).
Conflicts of interest.
Inspectors, §119-25.
Containers.
Display required on containers used in making deliveries, §119-43.
Definitions, §119-15.
Department of revenue.
Fees.
Collection of fees by department, §119-23.
Enforcement of provisions.
Inspectors, clerks and assistants.
Appoint and employ, §119-25.
Equipment for measuring liquid petroleum products, §119-33.
Evidence.
Certified copies of official tests admissible in evidence, §119-36.
Fees.
Collection of fees by department of revenue, §119-23.
Payment of fees into state treasury, §119-23.
Fines.
Prosecution of offenders, §119-38.
Gasoline.
Inspection of gasoline, §119-17.
Renaming, etc., of gasoline.
Filing of notice of intention to rename, etc., with board, §119-26.
Grade rating on pumps, etc., §119-27.
Inspectors.
Appointment and employ, §119-25.
Authority of inspectors, §119-32.
Bond to be given, §119-25.
Conflicts of interest, §119-25.

GASOLINE AND OIL INSPECTION —Cont'd
Inspectors —Cont'd
Equipment for measuring liquid petroleum products, §119-33.
Oath of office, §119-25.
Powers, §119-32.
Samples taken for inspection purposes.
Payment for samples, §119-31.
Invoices.
Persons engaged in transporting.
Required to have in possession an invoice, §119-42.
Kerosene.
Certain kerosene sales prohibited, §119-16.3.
Inspection of kerosene, §119-17.
Sales in proximity to gasoline or gasohol, §119-16.3.
Kerosene distributors.
Deferred payment of inspection tax, §119-18, (a1).
Defined, §119-15.
License.
Application, §119-15.2.
Bond or letter of credit required for obtaining and keeping, §119-15.3, (a).
Adjustment, §119-15.3, (b).
Failure to comply, criminal penalty, §119-15.3, (c).
Required, §119-15.1, (a), (b).
Kerosene suppliers.
Defined, §119-15.
License.
Application, §119-15.2.
Bond or letter of credit required for obtaining and keeping, §119-15.3, (a).
Adjustment, §119-15.3, (b).
Failure to comply, criminal penalty, §119-15.3, (c).
Required, exception, §119-15.1, (a), (b).
Kerosene terminal operators.
License.
Application, §119-15.2.
Bond or letter of credit required for obtaining and keeping, §119-15.3, (a).
Adjustment, §119-15.3, (b).
Failure to comply, criminal penalty, §119-15.3, (c).
Required, exception, §119-15.1, (a), (b).
Labels.
Display of grade rating on pumps, etc., §119-27.
Laboratories.
Analysis of inspected products.
Establishment of laboratory for analysis, §119-30.
Licenses.
Cancellation of license, §119-19.
Persons required to have, §§119-15.1 to 119-15.3.
Liquefied petroleum gases, §§119-54 to 119-61.
See LIQUEFIED PETROLEUM GAS.
Measuring equipment, §119-33.
Misdemeanors, §119-39.
Offshore oil and gas activities, §§143-215.94AA to 143-215.94JJ.
See OFFSHORE OIL AND GAS ACTIVITIES.
Oxygen content standards, §119-26.1.
Penalties.
Civil penalties, §119-39.1.
Oxygen content standards and reformulated gasoline, §119-26.1, (c), (c1).
Prosecution of offenders, §§119-38, 119-39.
Petroleum products.
Inspection of kerosene, gasoline and other petroleum products provided for, §119-17.

GASOLINE AND OIL INSPECTION —Cont'd
Pumps or other dispensing devices, §119-27.
Self-service gasoline pumps.
Display of owner's or operator's name, address and telephone number, §119-27.1, (a).
Enforcement of provisions, §119-27.1, (b).
Reformulated gasoline, §119-26.1.
Retailers.
Delivery tickets.
Required to keep copies of delivery tickets, §119-37.
Invoices.
Required to keep copies of invoices, §119-37.
Responsibility of retailers for quality of products, §119-34.
Rules and regulations.
Availability of rules and regulations of board to interested parties, §119-29.
Oxygen content standards and reformulated gasoline, §119-26.1, (a), (b).
Violations, civil penalties, §119-26.1, (c).
Sales.
Adulteration of products offered for sale, §119-35.
Bill of sale.
Persons engaged in transporting required to have in possession bill of sale, §119-42.
Display of grade rating, etc.
Not labeled pumps or devices, §119-27.
Standards indicated on label not met, §119-27.
Substitutes for or motor fuel improvers.
Regulations for sale of substitutes, §119-28.
Samples taken for inspection.
Charges for analysis of samples, §119-46.
Payment for samples, §119-31.
Secretary of revenue.
Failure to report or pay tax.
Determination of tax liability by secretary, §119-21.
Self-service gasoline pumps.
Display of owner's or operator's name, address and telephone number, §119-27.1, (a).
Enforcement of provisions, §119-27.1, (b).
State of North Carolina.
Fuels used by state to be inspected, §119-47.
State treasurer.
Disposition of moneys by state treasurer, §119-23.
Substitutes for or motor fuel improvers.
Regulations for sale of substitutes, §119-28.
Sulfur content standards for gasoline, §119-26.2, (a).
Rules to implement, adoption, §119-26.2, (b).
Taxation.
Deferred payment, §119-18, (a1).
Failure to report or pay tax.
Cancellation of license, §119-19.
Secretary of revenue to determine tax liability, §119-21.
Local tax prohibited, §119-18, (c).
Proceeds of inspection tax, §119-18, (b).
Rate of taxation, §119-18, (a).
Time of payment, §119-18, (a).
Title of article, §119-14.

GASOLINE SERVICE STATIONS.
Leaking petroleum underground storage tank cleanup, §§143-215.94A to 143-215.94Y.
See UNDERGROUND PETROLEUM STORAGE TANK LEAK CLEANUP.
Low-cost selling of motor fuels, §75-82, (a).
Self-service stations.
Price advertisements.
Drawing or pumping fuel by purchaser himself, §14-117.2.

GASOLINE SERVICE STATIONS —Cont'd
Unauthorized vehicles.
Notice of violations, §20-219.3, (b).
Prohibited acts, §20-219.3, (a).
Remedies of owner or operator of station, §20-219.3, (c), (d).
Removal, §20-219.3, (c).

GASOLINE TAX, §§105-449.60 to 105-449.127.
Accidental mix refund, §105-449.105, (c).
Account number on return, §105-449.104.
Administration of chapter, §105-449.61, (c).
Alternative fuels generally, §§105-449.130 to 105-449.139.
See ALTERNATIVE FUEL.
Amount of fuel sold or used in state.
Failure to disclose correct amount, §105-449.120, (a).
Audit of records, §105-449.121, (b).
Backup tax on certain fuels, §105-449.87, (a).
Liability, §105-449.87, (b).
Behind-the-rack transfers.
Excise tax, §105-449.81.
Liability, §105-449.84A.
Blended fuel.
Defined, §105-449.60.
Excise tax, §105-449.81.
Motor fuel excise tax liability, §105-449.84.
Blender.
Defined, §105-449.60.
License required, §105-449.65, (a).
Motor fuel excise tax liability, §105-449.84, (a).
Separate licenses as motor fuel transporter, §105-449.65, (b).
Bonded importer, §105-449.66, (a).
Bonds, surety.
Failure to file replacement bond or additional bond, §105-449.120, (a).
Required as condition of obtaining and keeping certain licenses, §105-449.72.
Bulk-end user.
Defined, §105-449.60.
Removals by out-of-state users, §105-449.89.
Bulk plant operator.
Reliance on shipping documents, §105-449.115, (c).
Bulk plants.
Defined, §105-449.60.
Return by distributor showing exports from, §105-449.102, (a).
Contents, §105-449.102, (b).
Cherokee Indians.
Eastern band. See within this heading, "Eastern band of Cherokee Indians."
Civil penalties.
Refusing to allow samples of motor fuel, §105-449.118A.
Unlawful use of dyed diesel fuel, §105-449.117, (b).
Unlawful use of non-tax-paid fuel, §105-449.117, (b).
Code.
Defined, §105-449.60.
Collection by supplier of tax on out-of-state removals.
Permissive suppliers, §105-449.71.
Credit card companies.
Bond when company applies for refund, §105-449.72, (e).
Credit card or access code enabling person to remove fuel without paying tax.
Buying fuel at retail, §105-449.88A, (b).
Cardholder liability, §105-449.88A, (c).

GASOLINE TAX —Cont'd
Credit card or access code enabling person to remove fuel without paying tax —Cont'd
Deduction of amount of tax imposed on fuel purchase with exempt card or code, §105-449.97, (d).
Licensed distributor or licensed importer removing fuel from terminal, §105-449.88A, (a).
Deduction for exempt sales, §105-449.93.
Deductions allowed supplier when filing return, §105-449.97.
Defense to violation.
State exemption not defense, §105-449.117, (c).
Deferred payments.
Refusing to allow, §105-449.120, (a).
Definitions, §105-449.60.
Types of importer, §105-449.66, (a).
Designated to be paid by person consuming fuel, §105-449.62.
Destination state.
Defined, §105-449.60.
Destination state tax collected on exported motor fuel.
Payment by supplier, §105-449.90A.
Diesel fuel.
Defined, §105-449.60.
Discounts.
Importers, §105-449.99, (b).
Percentage discounts.
Quarterly calculation per distributors, §105-449.95, (a).
Refund to distributors, §105-449.95, (b).
Refusing to allow, §105-449.120, (a).
Suppliers, allowed when filing return, §105-449.97.
Dispensing non-tax-paid motor fuel, §105-449.120, (b).
Distribution of revenues, §105-449.125.
Distributors.
Cancellation or reissuance after cancellation of license.
Notice to suppliers, §105-449.92.
Defined, §105-449.60.
Exempt sale deduction, §105-449.93, (a).
Percentage discount, §105-449.93, (b).
Nonpayment of tax due.
Notice by suppliers to department, §105-449.98, (c).
Notice by supplier to distributor of taxable gallons received during reporting period, §105-449.98, (b).
Persons who may obtain license, §105-449.67.
Quarterly hold harmless for licensed distributors, §105-449.95.
Remittance of tax to suppliers, §105-449.91, (a).
Method, §105-449.91, (d).
Return showing exports from bulk plant, §105-449.102.
Separate license as importer for motor fuel transporter, §105-449.65, (b).
Diverted fuel.
Liability, §105-449.87, (c).
Double tax prohibited, §105-449.61, (b).
Dyed diesel fuel.
Defined, §105-449.60.
Listed on shipping document.
Joint and several liability where fuel not dyed diesel fuel, §105-449.82, (c).
Motor fuel excise tax.
Liability, §105-449.86, (b).
Rate, §105-449.86, (a).

GASOLINE TAX —Cont'd
Dyed diesel fuel —Cont'd
Motor fuel excise tax liability, §105-449.86.
Unlawful for highway use, §105-449.117, (a) to (c).
Dyed motor fuel.
Marking requirements for dyed motor fuel storage facilities, §105-449.123, (a).
Exception to facility containing fuel used in heating, dying crops or manufacturing process, §105-449.123, (b).
Eastern band of Cherokee Indians.
Refund of motor fuels or special fuel taxes.
Definitions applicable, §105-449.114, (b).
Memorandum of understanding or agreement, §105-449.114, (c).
Recognition as possessing sovereign legal rights, §105-449.114, (a).
Election by supplier to collect tax on out-of-state removals, §105-449.70.
Permissive suppliers, §105-449.71.
Elective supplier.
Defined, §105-449.60.
Examination of books and records by secretary.
Refusal to allow, §105-449.120, (a).
Excise tax on motor fuel, §105-449.81.
Blended fuel.
Liability, §105-449.84.
Dyed diesel fuel.
Tax and liability, §105-449.86.
Exemptions, §105-449.88.
Imports.
Liability for tax, §105-449.83.
Liability for fuel grade ethanol tax, §105-449.83A.
Liability on removal.
Refineries, §105-449.82, (a).
Terminal racks, §105-449.82, (c).
Terminal systems, §105-449.82, (b).
Unaccounted for motor fuel losses, §105-449.85.
Exempt card or exempt access code.
Persons removing fuel without paying tax.
Buying fuel at retail, §105-449.88A, (b).
Deduction of amount of excise tax imposed on fuel purchased with card or code, §105-449.97, (d).
Liability of cardholder, §105-449.88A, (c).
Licensed distributor or licensed importer removing fuel from terminal, §105-449.88A, (a).
Exempt fuel refund, §105-449.105, (a).
Exemptions from excise tax, §105-449.88.
Exempt sales deduction, §105-449.93, (a).
Failure to report, §105-449.94, (e).
Payment of tax on difference at motor fuel rate, §105-449.94, (b).
Percentage discount, §105-449.93, (b).
Quarterly reconciling return, §105-449.94, (a).
Refund, §105-449.94, (c).
Exported motor fuel, destination state tax.
Payment by supplier of tax collected on, §105-449.90A.
Exporters.
Application for license, §105-449.69, (e).
Cancellation or reissuance after cancellation of license.
Notice to suppliers, §105-449.92.
License required, §105-449.65, (a).
Nonpayment of tax due.
Notice by suppliers to department, §105-449.98, (c).

GASOLINE TAX —Cont'd
Exporters —Cont'd
Notice by supplier of taxable gallons received during reporting period, §105-449.98, (b).
Remittance of tax to suppliers, §105-449.91, (b).
Method, §105-449.91, (d).
Exports.
Defined, §105-449.60.
False statements, §105-449.120, (a).
Federal certificate of registry.
Required for applicants for licenses, §105-449.69, (c).
Federal excise tax, §105-449.81.
Fiduciary duty of supplier on remitting tax to secretary, §105-449.98, (a).
Fines.
Buying or selling untaxed motor fuel, §105-449.118.
Credited to the highway fund, §105-449.127.
Shipping documents, §105-449.115, (f).
Fuel alcohol.
Defined, §105-449.60.
Fuel alcohol or biodiesel.
Excise tax, §105-449.81.
Fuel alcohol provider.
Defined, §105-449.60.
Fuel grade ethanol.
Liability for tax on, §105-449.83A.
Gasohol.
Defined, §105-449.60.
Gasoline.
Defined, §105-449.60.
Gross gallons.
Defined, §105-449.60.
Hearings.
Assessment of civil penalty, §105-449.119.
Highway.
Defined, §105-449.60.
Highway fund.
Part revenues distributed to wildlife resources fund, §105-449.126.
Receipt of civil penalties collected under this article, §105-449.127.
Highway vehicle.
Defined, §105-449.60.
Importers.
Application for license, §105-449.69, (d).
Blended fuel.
Motor fuel excise tax, §105-449.84, (b).
Cancellation or reissuance after cancellation of license.
Notice to suppliers, §105-449.92.
Discounts, §105-449.99, (b).
Exempt sale deduction, §105-449.93, (a).
Percentage discount, §105-449.93, (b).
License required, §105-449.65, (a).
Quarterly hold harmless, §105-449.95.
Remittance of tax to suppliers, §105-449.91, (c).
Method, §105-449.91, (d).
Restrictions, §105-449.66, (b).
Returns, §105-449.99, (a).
Separate licenses distributor, §105-449.65, (b).
Types, §105-449.66, (a).
Imports.
Defined, §105-449.60.
Motor fuel excise tax, §105-449.83.
Informational returns.
Distributor showing exports from bulk plant, §105-449.102.
Motor fuel transporters showing deliveries of imported or exported fuel, §105-449.101.

GASOLINE TAX —Cont'd
Informational returns —Cont'd
Terminal operators.
Changes in amount of motor fuel at terminal, §105-449.100.
In-state-only supplier.
Defined, §105-449.60.
Investigations to identify violations.
Power of secretary, §105-449.117, (c).
Letters of credit.
Required as condition of obtaining and keeping certain licenses, §105-449.72.
Liability.
Backup tax on certain fuels, §105-449.87, (b).
Diverted fuel, §105-449.87, (c).
Liability for tax on behind-the-rack transfers, §105-449.84A.
Liability for tax on fuel grade ethanol, §105-449.83A.
Liability for tax on removals from refinery or terminal, §105-449.82.
Licenses, §§105-449.65 to 105-449.77.
Applications.
Approval, §105-449.74.
Denial, §105-449.73.
Export activity, §105-449.69, (e).
Federal certificate, §105-449.69, (c).
Generally, §105-449.69, (a).
Specific requirements, §105-449.69, (b).
Bond of applicant required for license.
Adjustment, §105-449.72, (b).
Additional bond, filing, §105-449.72, (c).
Credit card companies.
Company applying for refund, §105-449.72, (e).
Initial bond, §105-449.72, (a).
Multiple activities by applicants, §105-449.72, (a1).
Replacement for previously filed bond, §105-449.72, (d).
Bond, surety.
Cancellation of license, §105-449.76.
Cancellation, §105-449.76.
Notice to suppliers, §105-449.92, (a).
Effect of notice, §105-449.92, (b).
Cancellation or reissuance after cancellation of license.
Joint and several liability for selling fuel after notice, §105-449.92, (b).
Notice to suppliers, §105-449.92, (a).
Credit card companies.
Bond when company applies for refund, §105-449.72, (e).
Denial, §105-449.73.
Discontinuance of business.
Notification to secretary, §105-449.75.
Display required, §105-449.74.
Distributors.
Restrictions, §105-449.68.
Failing to obtain license required, §105-449.120, (a).
Failure to pay tax.
Cancellation of license, §105-449.76.
False statements, §105-449.120, (a).
Federal certificate of registry required for applicant, §105-449.69, (c).
Grounds for denial of application, §105-449.73.
Hearings.
Cancellation of license, §105-449.76.
Import activity, §105-449.69, (d).

GASOLINE TAX —Cont'd
Licenses —Cont'd
Importers.
Types, §105-449.66, (a).
Issuance, §105-449.74.
Denial, §105-449.73.
Letter of credit required by applicant for license.
Adjustment, §105-449.72, (b).
Initial letter, §105-449.72, (a).
Replacement for previously filed letter, §105-449.72, (d).
List of persons who must have license, §105-449.65, (a).
Multiple activities, §105-449.65, (b).
Bond required of applicant, §105-449.72, (a1).
Non-transferable, §105-449.74.
Persons who may obtain license, §105-449.67.
Records kept by secretary, §105-449.77, (a).
Reissuance of certain licenses.
Notice to suppliers, §105-449.92, (a).
Effect of notice, §105-449.92, (b).
Requirements for applications.
Specific requirements, §105-449.69, (b).
Restrictions.
Distributors, §105-449.68.
Revocation, §105-449.76.
Separate tax for person engaged in multiple activities, §105-449.65, (b).
Supplier election to collect tax on out-of-state removals, §105-449.70.
Permissive suppliers, §105-449.71.
Lists.
License holders, §105-449.77, (b).
Persons who must have license, §105-449.65, (a).
Local taxation prohibited, §105-449.61, (a).
Losses of motor fuel at terminal.
Compensating tax on and liability for unaccounted, §105-449.85.
Lost fuel refund, §105-449.105, (b).
Metered pumps.
Required, §105-449.122, (a).
Misdemeanors.
Class 1 misdemeanors, §105-449.120, (a).
Class 2 misdemeanors, §105-449.120, (b).
Use of dyed diesel fuel on highway, §105-449.117, (a).
Use of non-tax-paid fuel on highway, §105-449.117, (a).
Motor fuel.
Defined, §105-449.60.
Motor fuel excise tax, §105-449.81.
Blender fuel.
Liability, §105-449.84.
Dyed diesel fuel.
Tax and liability, §105-449.86.
Exemptions, §105-449.88.
Imports.
Liability for tax, §105-449.83.
Liability for tax.
Refinery removals, §105-449.82, (a).
Terminal rack removals, §105-449.82, (c).
Terminal system removals, §105-449.82, (b).
Unaccounted for motor fuel losses, §105-449.85.
Motor fuel rate.
Defined, §105-449.60.
Motor fuel transporters.
Defined, §105-449.60.
Informational returns showing deliveries of imported or exported motor fuel.
Contents, §105-449.101, (b).
Requirement, §105-449.101, (a).

GASOLINE TAX —Cont'd
Motor fuel transporters —Cont'd
License required, §105-449.65, (a).
Name on return, §105-449.104.
Nature of tax, §105-449.62.
Net gallons.
Defined, §105-449.60.
Non-tax-paid fuel.
Dispensing, §105-449.120, (b).
Unlawful use, §105-449.117, (a) to (c).
Notice.
Distributors or exporters not paying tax due.
Department notification by supplier, §105-449.98.
Taxable gallons received by supplier during reporting period.
Distributors or exporters notice, §105-449.98, (b).
Tax rate, §105-449.80, (c).
Occasional importer, §105-449.66, (a).
Out-of-state bulk-end users, removals, §105-449.89.
Out-of-state bulk plant.
Motor fuel excise tax liability, §105-449.83, (c).
Out-of-state removals.
Election of supplier to collect tax on, §105-449.70.
Permissive suppliers, §105-449.71.
Out-of-state terminal.
Motor fuel excise tax liability, §105-449.83, (b).
Part of cost of fuel, §105-449.62.
Payment of tax.
Application of payments by supplier received from distributors or exporters, §105-449.98, (d).
Deferred payments.
Refusing to allow, §105-449.120, (a).
Destination state tax collected on exported motor fuel, §105-449.90A.
Distributors or exporters not paying tax due.
Notice by suppliers to department, §105-449.98, (c).
Failing to pay, §105-449.120, (a).
Payable when return due, §105-449.90, (a).
Permissive suppliers.
Defined, §105-449.60.
Election to collect tax on out-of-state removals, §105-449.71.
Person.
Defined, §105-449.60.
Position holder.
Defined, §105-449.60.
Rack.
Defined, §105-449.60.
Railroad tank cars.
Shipping documents required, §105-449.115.
Rate of tax, §105-449.80, (a).
Rebates, §§105-449.105 to 105-449.110. See within this heading, "Refunds or rebates."
Recordkeeping requirements, §105-449.121, (a).
Records.
License holders and license applicants, §105-449.77, (a).
Records, failure to keep, §105-449.120, (a).
Records, inspections, §105-449.121, (b).
Records kept by secretary, §105-449.77, (a).
Refineries.
Excise tax motor fuel, §105-449.81.
Removals.
Motor fuel excise tax liability, §105-449.82.
Refiners.
License required, §105-449.65, (a).

GASOLINE TAX —Cont'd
Refunds or rebates, §§105-449.105 to 105-449.110.
Accidental mixes, §105-449.105, (c).
Amount of refund, §105-449.105, (e).
Applications.
Due date, §105-449.108, (a).
Requirements, §105-449.108, (b).
Review, §105-449.110, (a).
Bulk feed vehicles, §105-449.107, (b).
Bulk fertilizer vehicles, §105-449.107, (b).
Certain vehicles with power attachments, §105-449.107, (b).
Commercial vehicle delivering and spreading mulch, soils, composts, etc., §105-449.107, (b).
Credit card companies.
Bond when company applies for refund, §105-449.72, (e).
Dump trucks.
Farm use, §105-449.107, (b).
Exempt fuel, §105-449.105, (a).
Exempt sales, §105-449.94, (c).
False statements, §105-449.120, (a).
Garbage trucks, §105-449.107, (b).
Interest, §105-449.110, (b).
Kerosene, §105-449.105A.
Liability for overpayment, §105-449.105A, (b).
Late application, §105-449.108, (d).
Liability for overpayment.
Kerosene, §105-449.105A, (b).
Local government entities.
Quarterly refunds, §105-449.106, (a).
Lost fuel, §105-449.105, (b).
Nonprofit organizations.
Quarterly refunds, §105-449.106, (a).
Off-highway use.
Licensed highway vehicles, §105-449.107, (a).
Percentage discounts to suppliers.
Quarterly refunds to distributors, §105-449.95, (b).
Review of applications, §105-449.110, (a).
Special mobile equipment operated off-highway, §105-449.106, (c).
Tank wagons, §105-449.107, (b).
Taxis.
Quarterly refunds, §105-449.106, (b).
Remittance of tax by supplier to secretary.
Fiduciary duty, §105-449.98, (a).
Remittance of tax to suppliers, §105-449.91.
Method of remittance, §105-449.91, (d).
Removal.
Defined, §105-449.60.
Restrictions, §105-449.61, (a), (b).
Retailer.
Defined, §105-449.60.
Returns.
Annual filers, §105-449.90, (b).
Distributor showing exports from bulk plant, §105-449.102.
Exempt sales.
Quarterly reconciling return, §105-449.94, (a).
Failing to file, §105-449.120, (a).
False statements, §105-449.120, (a).
Filing period, §105-449.90, (a).
Importers, §105-449.99, (a).
Informational return.
Distributor showing exports from bulk plant, §105-449.102.
Motor fuel transporters, deliveries of imported or exported motor fuel, §105-449.101.
Terminal operators, changes in amount of motor fuel at terminal, §105-449.100.

GASOLINE TAX —Cont'd
Returns —Cont'd
Monthly filers, §105-449.90, (d), (e).
Motor fuel transporters.
Informational return showing deliveries of imported or exported fuel, §105-449.101.
Name and account number, §105-449.104.
Quarterly filers, §105-449.90, (c).
Suppliers.
Administrative discounts, §105-449.97, (b).
Deductions and discounts allowed, §105-449.97.
Information required, §105-449.96.
Percentage discount, §105-449.97, (c).
Taxes not remitted by distributors, §105-449.97, (a).
Revenues.
Distribution, §105-449.125.
Road tax on carriers using fuel purchased outside state, §§105-449.37 to 105-449.57.
See MOTOR CARRIERS.
Samples of motor fuel, §105-449.121, (b).
Refusing to allow, §105-449.118A.
Secretary.
Defined, §105-449.60.
Determination of wholesale price, §105-449.80, (b).
Shipping documents.
Contents, §105-449.115, (b).
Duties of person receiving shipment, §105-449.115, (e).
Duties of transporter, §105-449.115, (d).
Failure to show or give documents required, §105-449.120, (a).
Issuance, §105-449.115, (a).
Reliance by terminal operator or bulk plant operator, §105-449.115, (c).
Sanctions, §105-449.115, (f).
Tank wagon, transporting fuel by, §105-449.115A.
Stopping vehicles for purposes of taking sample, §105-449.121, (b).
Suppliers.
Application of payments received from distributors or exporters, §105-449.98, (d).
Cancellation or reissuance of license to distributor, exporter or importer.
Notice to suppliers, §105-449.92, (a).
Joint and several liability for selling fuel after notice, §105-449.92, (b).
Deductions and discounts allowed when filing return, §105-449.97.
Defined, §105-449.60.
Destination state tax collected on exported motor fuel.
Payment by supplier, §105-449.90A.
Distributors or exporters not paying tax due.
Notice to department, §105-449.98.
Duties.
Application of payments, §105-449.98, (d).
Election to collect tax on out-of-state removals, §§105-449.70, (a), 105-449.71.
Effect of election, §105-449.70, (b).
Permissive suppliers, §105-449.71, (a).
Effect of election, §105-449.71, (b).
Submission to jurisdiction of state for administration of provisions, §105-449.71, (c).
Submission to jurisdiction of state for administration of provisions, §105-449.70, (c).
Fiduciary duty on remitting tax to secretary, §105-449.98, (a).
License required, §105-449.65, (a).

GASOLINE TAX —Cont'd
Suppliers —Cont'd
Permissive suppliers.
Persons who may obtain license, §105-449.67.
Remittance of tax to, §105-449.91.
Method of remittance, §105-449.91, (d).
Remittance to secretary by supplier.
Fiduciary duty, §105-449.98, (a).
Returns.
Deductions and discounts allowed, §105-449.97.
Information required, §105-449.96.
Separate license for other activity, §105-449.65, (b).
System transfer.
Defined, §105-449.60.
Excise tax motor fuel, §105-449.81.
Motor fuel excise tax liability, §105-449.83, (a).
Tank trucks.
Connections between cargo tank and fuel supply tank prohibited, §105-449.122, (b).
Tank wagon.
Defined, §105-449.60.
Shipping document required for transporting fuel by.
Duties of transporter to whom document issued, §105-449.115A, (b).
Issuance, requirements for, §105-449.115A, (a).
Sanctions, transporting without document, §105-449.115A, (c).
Tank wagon importer, §105-449.66, (a).
Taxable gallons received during reporting period.
Notice by supplier to distributor or exporter, §105-449.98, (b).
Terminal operators.
Changes in amount of motor fuel at terminal.
Informational return, §105-449.100.
Defined, §105-449.60.
Informational return showing changes in amount of motor fuel at terminal, §105-449.100.
License required, §105-449.65, (a).
Reliance on shipping documents, §105-449.115, (c).
Terminal racks.
Behind-the-rack transfers.
Excise tax, §105-449.81.
Liability, §105-449.84A.
Exempt card or exempt access code.
Removal by licensed distributor or licensed importer, §105-449.88A, (a).
Removals.
Motor fuel excise tax liability, §105-449.82, (c).
Behind-the-rack transfer, §105-449.84A.
Terminals.
Blended fuel.
Motor fuel excise tax liability, §105-449.84, (c).
Defined, §105-449.60.
Excise tax motor fuel, §105-449.81.
Unaccounted for motor fuel losses.
Liability, §105-449.85, (b).
Tax, §105-449.85, (a).
Terminal transfer systems.
Defined, §105-449.60.
Removals.
Motor fuel excise tax liability, §105-449.82.
Transmix.
Defined, §105-449.60.
Transporter.
Shipping documents, duties, §105-449.115, (d).
Transporting fuel by tank wagon, §105-449.115A, (b).

GASOLINE TAX —Cont'd
Transport trucks.
Defined, §105-449.60.
Shipping documents, §105-449.115.
Trustee.
Defined, §105-449.60.
Two-party exchange.
Defined, §105-449.60.
Understatement of liability, §105-236.
Wholesale price.
Determination, §105-449.80, (b).
Wildlife resources fund.
Allocation from part of the highway fund, §105-449.126.

GAS PIPELINE FACILITIES.
Underground damage prevention, §§87-100 to 87-114.
See UNDERGROUND DAMAGE PREVENTION.

GAS PIPELINE SAFETY, §62-50.
Agreements with federal agencies.
Powers of utilities commission, §62-50, (b), (c).
Civil penalty, §62-50, (d), (e).
Gas operators.
Defined, §62-50, (g).
Utilities commission.
Powers, §62-50, (a) to (c).

GAS STATIONS.
Self-service stations.
Price advertisements, §14-117.2.
Unauthorized vehicles, §20-219.3.

GASTON COUNTY.
Agricultural tendencies in certain counties.
Terms of, §42-23.
Ambulances.
Attachment or garnishment and lien for, §§44-51.4 to 44-51.8.
False pretenses and cheats.
Obtaining ambulance services without intending to pay, §14-111.2.
Condemnation or acquisition of land by local government unit outside county.
Consent of board of commissioners necessary, §153A-15.
Counties generally.
See COUNTIES.
Cropper or tenant refusing to perform terms of contract.
Forfeiture of right of possession to premises, §42-27.
Dangerous firearm use by young children, permitting.
Air rifles, air pistols and BB guns not dangerous firearm, §14-316, (b).
False pretenses and cheats.
Ambulance services.
Obtaining services without intending to pay, §14-111.2.
Lake Wylie, regulations for lake and shoreline.
Copy of regulations promulgated sent to clerk of superior court of county, §77-37, (d).
Motor vehicle emission inspections.
Counties inspections required to be performed in, §143-215.107A, (c).
Oil, gas or mineral interest separated from surface interest, extinguished, title in surface fee holder.
Failure to list interest for tax purposes for 10 years prior to January 1, 1974.
Protection of interest from surface estate, §1-42.3, (d).

GASTON COUNTY —Cont'd
Private parking lots.
Removal of unauthorized vehicles, §20-219.2.
Real estate mortgage loans.
Interest, commissions and repayment, §45-43.
Registration of deeds.
Tax certification, no delinquent taxes due, §161-31, (b).
School property.
Acquisition and improvement, §153A-158.1.
Sheriff.
Vacancy, performance of duties until vacancy filled, §162-5.1.
Wild plants, taking of certain plants from land of another.
Inapplicability of provisions, §14-129.

GAS WARS.
Below-cost selling of motor fuels, §75-82, (a).

GATES.
Housing authorities and projects.
Electrified gates, spikes or barbed wire prohibited, §157-9, (d).
Housing authority commissioners.
Tenant as commissioner, exemption from provision of law allowing, §157-5.
Rights of way.
Projection of gates over rights of way prohibited, §136-94.

GATES COUNTY.
Blank or master forms of mortgages, deeds of trust, etc.
Indexing and recording, inapplicability of provisions, §47-21.
Counties generally.
See COUNTIES.
Cropper or tenant refusing to perform terms of contract.
Forfeiture of right of possession to premises, §42-27.
Game laws, local acts not repealed, §113-133.1, (e).
Grants in navigable waters, registration, §113-205, (a).
Northeastern North Carolina regional economic development commission, §158-8.2.
Oil, gas or mineral interest separated from surface interest, extinguished, title in surface fee holder.
Failure to list interest for tax purposes for 10 years prior to January 1, 1974.
Protection of interest from surface estate, §1-42.3, (d).
Open fires, high hazard counties.
Applicability of provisions, §113-60.23, (a).
Ground clearing activities, special permit, §113-60.23, (c).
Woodland fires, permit required, §113-60.23, (b).
School property.
Acquisition and improvement, §153A-158.1.
Special school tax, election to abolish.
Petition required, §115C-505.
Wastewater systems.
Innovative septic tank systems.
Ordinance billing fee as property tax, §130A-343.1, (c).

GED.
Jail prisoner's participation.
Person having custody to approve, revocation of approval, §162-59.1.

GED —Cont'd
Jail prisoner's participation —Cont'd
Reduction in sentence for participation, §162-60, (b).
Escape, forfeiture of reduction, §162-60, (c).
Person in custody judge of faithful participation, §162-60, (c).
Post-release supervision.
Reintegrative conditions, §15A-1364.4, (d).

GEESE.
Hunting and wildlife generally.
See HUNTING AND WILDLIFE.

GEMS AND GEMSTONES.
Commodities.
General provisions, §§78D-1 to 78D-33.
See COMMODITIES.
Diamonds.
Unfair trade practices in diamond industry, §§66-73 to 66-75.

GEM, STATE.
Emerald, §145-8.

GENDER.
Construction and interpretation of statutes, §12-3.

GENDER BASED APPOINTMENTS.
Appointing members to statutorily created decision making or regulatory entities.
Appointments to reflect proportion that gender represents in population of state, §143-157.1, (a).
Report by appointing authority of number appointments of each gender, §143-157.1, (b).

GENDER DISCRIMINATION.
Discrimination generally.
See DISCRIMINATION.
Fair housing, §§41A-1 to 41A-10.
See FAIR HOUSING.

GENEALOGIES.
Hearsay exception, family records, §8C-1, Rule 803.

GENERAL ASSEMBLY.
Acts.
Coded bill drafting, §120-20.1.
Style of the acts, Const. N. C., art. II, §21.
When acts take effect, §120-20.
Actuarial note act, §§120-112 to 120-114.
Adult care homes.
Residents' bill of rights.
Legislative intent, §131D-19.
Aged persons.
Study commission on aging.
General provisions, §§120-180 to 120-188.
See AGED PERSONS.
Alimony.
Local, private and special legislation prohibited, Const. N. C., art. II, §24.
Appeals.
Investigating committees.
Appeal from denial of right to be heard, §120-18.
Apportionment, §§120-1, 120-2.
Approval of act amending, deleting, adding to, modifying or repealing plan.
Attorney general to seek, §120-30.9B, (b).
Challenge to plan.
Action, §§1-81.1, 1-267.1, 120-2.3 to 120-2.5.
Three-judge panel, §1-267.1.

GENERAL ASSEMBLY —Cont'd
Apportionment —Cont'd
Dividing precincts.
Compliance with federal law, §120-2.2, (c).
Prohibited, §120-2.2, (a).
Rejection based upon federal law, §120-2.2, (a), (b).
House of representatives, §120-2, (a) to (c); Const. N. C., art. II, §5.
Senate, §120-1, (a) to (c); Const. N. C., art. II, §3.
Severability of apportionment acts, §120-2.1.
Appropriations.
Budgets.
Reduction, §143-15.
Reports to or of appropriations committees, etc.
Effect, §143-15.
Committees.
Transportation department.
Reports to committees, §136-44.2B.
Current operations appropriations act.
Enactment, §143-15.1, (a).
General fund credit balance.
Appropriation of anticipated credit balance not expected to be reserved.
Capital improvements or other one-time expenditures only, §143-15.2, (e).
General fund financial model, §143-15.1, (b).
Legislative research commission.
Payment of expenses from appropriations, §120-30.18.
No expenditures for purposes for which general assembly has considered but not enacted appropriation, §143-16.3.
Savings reserve account, §143-15.4, (a).
Approval of bills, §120-29.1.
Aquaculture and seafood.
Joint legislative commission on seafood and aquaculture, §§120-70.60 to 120-70.66.
Archives and history division.
Retention of books, records, etc.
Ultimate retention or disposition by division, §120-37, (f).
Arrest.
Duty and privilege of members.
Protection from arrest, §120-9.
Arson.
Burning of certain public buildings, §14-59.
Attorney general.
Lobbying.
Enforcement of article by attorney general, §120-47.10.
Opinion on questions of law.
Duties of attorney general, §114-2.
Attorneys at law.
Committee activity.
Examination of witnesses, §120-19.1.
Bicycles.
Legislative findings.
Bicycles and bikeway act, §136-71.8.
Bills.
Actions on bills, Const. N. C., art. II, §22.
Approval of bills, §120-29.1.
Action by governor, §120-29.1, (a).
Calculation of time for approval, §120-29.1, (d).
Failure of governor to take action, §120-29.1, (b).
Objections of governor, §120-29.1, (c).
Calculation of time for approval, §120-29.1, (d).
Coded bill drafting.
Effective date of provisions, §120-20.1, (d).
Generally, §120-20.1, (a) to (b2).

GENERAL ASSEMBLY —Cont'd
Bills —Cont'd
Coded bill drafting —Cont'd
Resolutions.
Included in terms "act" and "law," §120-20.1, (c).
Enrolling clerk.
Deposit of original bills and resolutions enrolled for application, §120-33, (f).
Duties, §120-33.
Presenting true ratified copies, §120-33, (d) to (d2).
Proofreading bills, §120-33, (c).
Ratification of enrolled bills, §120-33, (a).
Substituting corresponding Arabic numerals for written words, §120-33, (b).
Typewritten bills, §120-33, (c).
Governor's approval, §120-29.1, (a).
Governor's failure to take action, §120-29.1, (b).
Governor's veto, Const. N. C., art. II, §22.
Legislative services commission.
Duties of enrolling clerk, §120-33.
Local government fiscal information act, §§120-30.41 to 120-30.49.
Objections by governor, §120-29.1, (c).
Principal clerk.
Retention of bills and resolutions in office for certain period, §120-37, (f).
Reconvening of legislature, Const. N. C., art. II, §22; art. III, §5.
Request that session not be held, §120-6.1, (a), (b).
Revenue bills.
Requirements for passage, Const. N. C., art. II, §23.
Veto by governor, Const. N. C., art. II, §22.
Voting rights act of 1965.
Submission of changes to United States attorney general, §§120-30.9A to 120-30.9H.
Board service by members of general assembly, §120-123.
Bomb scares.
Evacuation of state legislative buildings and grounds, §120-32.1A.
Bond issues.
Requirements for passage of revenue bills, Const. N. C., art. II, §23.
Bribery.
Legislative ethics act.
Code of legislative ethics, §120-86, (a).
Bridges.
Local, private and special legislation prohibited, Const. N. C., art. II, §24.
Budget.
Advisory budget commission.
Appointment of members, §143-4, (a).
Participation by legislative officers, §143-34.7.
Appropriations, §143-15.
Bills containing proposed appropriations, §143-12, (a).
Current operations appropriations act.
Enactment, §143-15.1, (a).
Expenditures.
Reporting as to legislative and judicial expenditures and finances, §143-8.
General fund credit balance.
Priority of uses, §143-15.2.
General fund financial model, §143-15.1, (b).
General fund operating budget size limit.
Research division.
Tentative estimate, §143-15.4, (c).

GENERAL ASSEMBLY —Cont'd
Budget —Cont'd
House of representatives.
Transfer between objects and line items in budget of, §143-23, (d).
Joint meetings of committees, §143-14.
No expenditures for purposes for which general assembly has considered but not enacted appropriation, §143-16.3.
Other than senate or house.
Transfer between objects and line items in budget of, §143-23, (e).
Savings reserve account.
Appropriations, §143-15.4, (a).
Senate.
Transfer between objects and line items in budget of, §143-23, (c).
Buildings.
State legislative building.
Official name, §129-12.1.
Bureau of investigation.
Background investigation of person who must be confirmed by legislative action.
Requests to bureau of investigation, §120-19.4A.
Capital improvements.
Joint legislative oversight committee on capital improvements, §§120-258 to 120-260.
Cemeteries.
Local, private and special legislation prohibited, Const. N. C., art. II, §24.
Children.
Legislative study commission on children and youth, §§120-215 to 120-220.
CLE exemption, Bar Rules & Regs., D, §.1517.
Clerks.
Approval of bills, §120-29.1.
Journals.
Indexing of journals by clerks, §120-28.
Preparation and filing by clerks, §120-27.
Legislative services commission.
Duties of enrolling clerk, §120-33.
Principal clerk.
Bills and resolutions.
Retention in office for certain periods, §120-37, (f).
Duties.
Assignment of additional duties, §120-37, (d).
Election, §120-37, (a).
Employing temporary assistance, §120-37, (e).
Retention of books, records, etc., §120-37, (f).
Salary, §120-37, (c).
Staff employees of office.
Additional full-time employees, §120-37, (d).
Term, §120-37, (a).
Reading clerk.
Election, §120-37, (a).
Salary, §120-37, (b).
Term, §120-37, (a).
Code of legislative ethics, §§120-85 to 120-88.
Commissions.
Appointments, §120-121.
Consultants.
Contracting for consultant services, §120-32.02, (a) to (c).
Contributions.
Applying for, receiving or accepting, §120-32.03, (a), (b).
Employees.
Contracting for employment, §120-32.02, (a) to (c).

GENERAL ASSEMBLY —Cont'd
Commissions —Cont'd
Environmental review commission, §§120-70.41 to 120-70.47.
Grants.
Applying for, receiving or accepting, §120-32.03, (a), (b).
Historical commission.
Recommendations to legislative committees, §121-12, (d).
Joint legislative commission on governmental operations, §§120-71 to 120-79.
Joint legislative commission on seafood and aquaculture, §§120-70.60 to 120-70.66.
Legislative appointments to boards and commissions, §§120-121 to 120-123.
Legislative research commission, §§120-30.10 to 120-30.18.
Legislative services commission, §§120-31 to 120-36.
Legislative study commission on children and youth, §§120-215 to 120-220.
Legislative study commission on mental health, developmental disabilities and substance abuse services, §§120-204 to 120-207.
Loans.
Applying for, receiving or accepting, §120-32.03, (a), (b).
Meetings.
Official meetings of commissions, committees and standing subcommittees, §143-318.14A.
Public health study commission, §§120-195 to 120-203.
Reports for state institutions and departments, §120-12.
Service by general assembly members, §120-123.
Vacancies, §120-122.
Committees.
Appropriations.
Transportation department.
Reports to committees, §136-44.2B.
Attorneys at law.
Examination of witnesses, §120-19.1, (f).
Bureau of investigation.
Background investigation of person who must be confirmed by legislative action.
Requests to bureau of investigation, §120-19.4A.
Capital improvements.
Joint legislative oversight committee, §§120-258 to 120-260.
Chairmen.
Oaths.
Who may administer oaths of office, §11-7.1, (a).
Consultants.
Contracting for consultant services, §120-32.02, (a) to (c).
Contempt, §120-19.4.
Contributions.
Applying for, receiving or accepting, §120-32.03, (a), (b).
Education.
Joint legislative education oversight committee, §§120-70.80 to 120-70.83.
Employees contracting for employment, §120-32.02, (a) to (c).
Ethics.
Legislative ethics committee, §§120-99 to 120-106.
Finance committees, §122A-16.

GENERAL ASSEMBLY —Cont'd
Committees —Cont'd
Grants.
Applying for, receiving or accepting, §120-32.03, (a), (b).
Hearings.
Examination of witnesses, §§120-19.1, 120-19.2, (b).
Counsel, §120-19.1, (f).
Fees and expenses of witness, §120-19.3.
Members questions directed to chairman or presiding officer, §120-19.1, (c).
Notice of hearing, §120-19.2, (d).
Objections to propriety of questions, §120-19.1, (d).
Transcript, §120-19.1, (e).
Under oath, §120-19.1, (b).
Holding separate or joint hearings, §120-19.1, (a).
Oaths.
Examination of witnesses, §120-19.1, (b).
Transcript of proceedings, §120-19.1, (e).
When hearings and examinations held, §120-19.2, (b).
Highways.
Joint legislative transportation oversight committee, §§120-70.50 to 120-70.52.
Local acts affecting state highway system.
Consideration by transportation committees, §120-19.9.
Historical commission.
Recommendations to legislative committees, §121-12, (d).
Interim committee activity.
Applicability of provisions, §120-19.8.
Investigating committees, §§120-14 to 120-19.
Joint legislative administrative procedure oversight committee, §§120-70.100 to 120-70.103.
Joint legislative corrections, crime control, and juvenile justice oversight committee, §§120-70.93 to 120-70.95.
Joint legislative growth strategies oversight committee, §§120-70.120 to 120-70.122.
Joint legislative health care oversight committee, §§120-70.110 to 120-70.112.
Joint legislative oversight committee on capital improvements, §§120-258 to 120-260.
Joint legislative oversight committee on information technology, §§120-230 to 120-235.
Joint legislative utility review committee, §§120-70.1 to 120-70.6.
Joint select committee on low-level radioactive waste, §§120-70.31 to 120-70.37.
Legislative services officer.
Authority to assign committee staff assistance, §120-19.5.
Loans.
Applying for, receiving or accepting, §120-32.03, (a), (b).
Meetings.
Official meetings of commissions, committees and standing subcommittees, §143-318.14A.
Occupational licensing boards.
New boards.
Legislative committee on new licensing boards, §120-149.6.
Public officers and employees.
Furnishing data and information to legislative committees, §120-19.

GENERAL ASSEMBLY —Cont'd
Committees —Cont'd
Retirement system for general assembly.
Committees on pensions and retirement, §§120-111.1 to 120-111.4.
Revenue laws study committee, §§120-70.105 to 120-70.108.
Seafood and aquaculture.
Joint legislative commission, §§120-70.60 to 120-70.66.
Staff assistance, §120-19.5.
Applicability of provisions, §120-19.8.
Limitation by resolution of either house, §120-19.8.
Standing committee.
Staff assistance, §120-19.5.
State departments and agencies.
Furnishing data and information to legislative committees, §120-19.
Subcommittees, §120-19.7.
Subpoenas.
Failure to respond to subpoena punishable as contempt, §120-19.4, (a).
Filing of complaint, §120-19.4, (b).
Form of subpoena, §120-19.2, (e).
Issuance of subpoena to obtain testimony, §120-19.2, (c).
Return of subpoena, §120-19.2, (f).
Witnesses.
Examination of witnesses, §§120-19.1, 120-19.2, (b).
Members questions directed to chairman or presiding officer, §120-19.1, (c).
Notice of hearing, §120-19.2, (d).
Objections to propriety of questions, §120-19.1, (d).
Under oath, §120-19.1, (b).
Failing to attend as witness before committee, §14-227.
Fees and expenses of witness, §120-19.3.
Invitations to witnesses, §120-19.2, (a).
Perjury before committees, §14-211.
Refusal to testify punishable as contempt, §120-19.4, (a).
Filing of complaint, §120-19.4, (b).
Compensation and allowances of member, Const. N. C., art. II, §16.
Comprehensive major medical plan, §§135-39 to 135-40.14.
See MEDICAL PLAN FOR TEACHERS AND STATE EMPLOYEES.
Confidentiality.
Code of legislative ethics.
Disclosure of confidential information, §120-87, (a), (b).
Legislative communications, §§120-129 to 120-134.
Definitions, §120-129.
Documents prepared by legislative employees, §120-131, (a).
When dissemination of information or language not prohibited, §120-131, (c).
When documents become available to public, §120-131, (b).
Drafting requests, §120-130, (a).
Not public records, §120-130, (d).
Revelation of legislator's identity restricted, §120-130, (a).
Supporting documents, §120-130, (c).
Fiscal note preparation requests, §120-131.1.
Information requests, §120-130, (b).
Not public records, §120-130, (d).
Supporting documents, §120-130, (c).

GENERAL ASSEMBLY —Cont'd
Confidentiality —Cont'd
Legislative communications —Cont'd
Penalty, §§120-131.1, (c), 120-134.
Redistricting communications, §120-133.
Testimony by legislative employees, §120-132.
Conflicts of interest.
Service by members of general assembly on certain boards and commissions, §120-123.
Consolidated city-county act.
Local government to be provided for by general assembly, Const. N. C., art. VII, §1.
Consultants.
Legislative commissions and committees.
Contracting for consultant services, §120-32.02, (a) to (c).
Contempt, §120-19.4.
Legislative services commission.
Subpoena and contempt powers, §120-32.4.
Continuances.
Obligation of services member, §1A-1, Rule 40, (b).
Continuing legal education exemption, Bar Rules & Regs., D, §.1517.
Contracts.
Public building contracts.
Exemption from certain purchasing requirements, §143-129.3.
Convening.
Members to convene at appointed time and place, §120-6.
Reconvened sessions.
Request that session not be held, §120-6.1, (a), (b).
Corporations.
Reservation of power.
Business corporations.
Amendment or repeal of provisions, §55-1-02.
Counties.
Governmental consolidation.
Action by assembly after referendum, §153A-405, (d).
House of representatives.
Apportionment, §120-2.
Local government to be provided for by general assembly, Const. N. C., art. VII, §1.
Senatorial districts.
Established, §120-1.
Number of senators, §120-1.
Courts.
Administration, Const. N. C., art. IV, §15.
Cultural resources department.
Retention of books, records, etc.
Ultimate retention or disposition by department, §120-37, (f).
Debts.
Indebtedness of state.
Requirements for passage of revenue bills, Const. N. C., art. II, §23.
Deeds.
Giving effect to informal deeds.
Local, private and special legislation prohibited, Const. N. C., art. II, §24.
Definitions.
Confidentiality of legislative communications, §120-129.
Ethics.
Code of legislative ethics, §120-85.
Joint legislative commission on governmental operations.
Program evaluation, §120-72.
Lobbying, §120-47.1.

GENERAL ASSEMBLY —Cont'd
Definitions —Cont'd
Local government fiscal information act.
Fiscal note, §120-30.44.
Unit of local government, §120-30.42.
Repayment of money owed to state by legislators, §143-558.
Depositions.
Contested elections, §120-11.
Directory.
Published by division of publications, §147-54.1.
Disasters.
State of disaster, declaring, §166A-6.
District attorneys.
Appointment of district attorneys, Const. N. C., art. IV, §18.
District courts.
Organization and establishment of district courts, Const. N. C., art. IV, §10.
Districts.
Representative districts, §120-2, (a) to (c); Const. N. C., art. II, §5.
Senatorial districts, §120-1, (a) to (c); Const. N. C., art. II, §3.
Dividing precincts in apportionment acts, §120-2.2.
Division of publications.
Generally, §147-54.1.
Divorce.
Local, private and special legislation prohibited, Const. N. C., art. II, §24.
Economic interest statement, §§120-89 to 120-98.
Appointment of person to legislative seat.
Failure to file, notification, §120-98, (c).
Filing required, §120-92.1.
Candidates for nomination or election.
Filing required, §120-89, (a).
Not nominated in primary elections.
Filing by candidates, §120-92.
Certification, §120-93.1.
Contents of statement, §120-96, (a).
County boards of elections.
Forwarding to board, §120-93.1.
Notifying candidates of economic-interest-statement requirements, §120-93.
Filing, §120-89, (b).
Candidates not nominated in primary elections, §120-92.
Penalty for failure to file, §120-98, (a).
Persons appointed to legislative seats, §120-92.1.
Required, §120-89, (a).
Form of statement, §120-96, (a).
Information to be current, §120-96, (b).
Notice.
Requirements of economic-interest-statements.
County board of elections to notify candidates, §120-93.
Penalty for failure to file, §120-98, (a).
Public records, §120-94.
Education.
Joint legislative education oversight committee, §§120-70.80 to 120-70.83.
Elections, Const. N. C., art. II, §8.
Contests.
Depositions taken, §120-11.
Notice of contest, §120-10.
Witnesses, §120-11.
Corrupt practices in election.
Expulsion for corrupt practices, §120-8.
Date of election, §163-1, (a).

GENERAL ASSEMBLY —Cont'd
Elections —Cont'd
Elections by general assembly to be by viva voce, Const. N. C., art. VI, §5.
House of representatives.
Nomination of candidates, §163-108.1.
Lobbying.
Prohibited election influence, §120-47.5, (b).
Primaries moved from date provided.
Holding on same day, §163-1, (d).
Electronic voting apparatus.
Installation and use of apparatus, §120-11.2.
Emergency management.
State of disaster, declaring, §166A-6.
Employees.
Confidentiality of legislative communications.
Disciplinary actions, §§120-131.1, (c), 120-134.
Legislative commissions and committees.
Contracting for employment, §120-32.02, (a) to (c).
Endangering executive, legislative or court officers, §§14-16.6 to 14-16.10.
Electronic surveillance orders, §15A-290, (c4).
Environmental review commission, §§120-70.41 to 120-70.47.
Ethics, §§120-85 to 120-106.
See LEGISLATIVE ETHICS.
Evidence.
Printed statutes and certified copies as evidence, §8-1.
Expenses.
Committee activity.
Witness fees and expenses, §120-19.3.
Joint operation of general assembly.
Payment for expenses, §120-35.
Legislative ethics committee, §120-101.
Legislative research commission.
Payments from appropriations, §120-30.18.
Lobbying.
Legislative agent's lobbying expenses.
Statements required, §120-47.6, (a).
Form and contents, §120-47.6, (b), (c).
Noncompliance with provisions, §120-47.6, (d).
Open to public inspection, §120-47.6, (c).
Lobbyist's principal.
Statements of expenses.
Noncompliance with provisions, §120-47.7, (d).
Open to public inspection, §120-47.7, (c).
Required, §120-47.7, (a).
Members, §120-3, (a) to (c).
Officers, §120-3, (a) to (c).
Extortion.
Legislative ethics act, §120-86, (b) to (e).
Fairs.
Land set apart for state fair.
Repossession of land at will of General Assembly, §106-504.
Federal mandates.
Certification of legislation required by federal law.
Attachment of certification, §120-36.8, (c), (d).
Contents, §120-36.8, (a).
Duties of research division, §120-36.8, (b).
Required, §120-36.8, (a).
Local government fiscal information.
Annual report on federal mandates, §120-30.49.
Fees and charges by state agencies, §12-3.1, (a).
Felonies.
Restoring rights of citizenship of convicts.
Local, special and private legislation prohibited, Const. N. C., art. II, §24.

GENERAL ASSEMBLY —Cont'd
Felonies —Cont'd
Threats to influence legislator in discharge of duties, §120-86, (e).
Ferries.
Local, private and special legislation prohibited, Const. N. C., art. II, §24.
Fertilizers.
Commercial fertilizers.
Legislative findings and declarations, §106-672.
Fires and fire protection.
Evacuation of state legislative buildings and grounds, §120-32.1A.
Fiscal information act, §§120-30.41 to 120-30.49.
Forfeitures.
Local, private and special legislation prohibited, Const. N. C., art. II, §24.
Forms.
Approval of bills, §120-29.1.
Reconvened sessions.
Request that session not be held, §120-6.1, (b).
Freedom of speech.
Duty and privilege of members, §120-9.
Fundraising during legislative session, limitation, §163-278.13B.
Funds.
Legislative retirement fund.
Repealed, §120-4.2.
Governmental operations.
Joint legislative commission on governmental operations, §§120-71 to 120-79.
Governor.
Approval of bills, §120-29.1.
Books to be produced for general assembly, §147-14.
Calculation of time for approval of bills, §120-29.1, (d).
Executive officer's report to governor.
Reports transmitted to general assembly, §147-5.
Failure to take action on bills, §120-29.1, (b).
Objections to bills, §120-29.1, (c).
Grants.
Legislative commissions and committees.
Applying for, receiving or accepting, §120-32.03, (a), (b).
Health.
Human tissue donation program.
Legislative findings and purpose, §130A-413, (a).
Local, private and special legislation prohibited, Const. N. C., art. II, §24.
Health care facilities.
Certificate of need law.
Legislative findings of fact, §131E-175.
Finance act.
Legislative findings and declarations, §131A-2.
Hearings.
Legislative ethics committee.
Possible violations of provisions, §120-103, (b).
Highways.
Controlled-access facilities.
Legislative findings and declarations, §136-89.48.
Joint legislative transportation oversight committee, §§120-70.50 to 120-70.52.
Local acts affecting state highway system.
Consideration by transportation committees, §120-19.9.
Local, private and special legislation prohibited, Const. N. C., art. II, §24.

GENERAL ASSEMBLY —Cont'd
Highways —Cont'd
Reports to appropriations committees of general assembly, §136-44.2B.
Scenic beauty of areas along highways.
Legislative findings and declaration of policy, §136-122.
Historical commission.
Legislative committees.
Furnishing recommendations to committees, §121-12, (d).
Holiday leave.
Temporary employees, §120-32.5.
House of representatives.
Apportionment, §120-2, (a) to (c); Const. N. C., art. II, §5.
Dividing precincts restricted, §120-2.2.
Severability of acts, §120-2.1.
Arrest.
Protection from arrest, §120-9.
Depositions.
Contested elections, §120-11.
Districts, §§120-1, 120-2, (a); Const. N. C., art. II, §5.
Areas not specifically assigned to, §120-2, (e).
Boundaries, §120-2, (b), (c).
Change, §120-2, (d).
Duties.
Penalty for failure to discharge duty, §120-7.
Elections.
Contests.
Depositions taken, §120-11.
Notice of contest, §120-10.
Witnesses, §120-11.
Corrupt practices in election.
Expulsion for corrupt practices, §120-8.
Electronic voting apparatus.
Installation and use of apparatus, §120-11.2.
Expense allowance, §120-3, (a) to (c).
Failure to discharge duty.
Penalty for failure, §120-7.
Freedom of speech, §120-9.
Impeachment.
Court of impeachment, §§123-1 to 123-5.
Effect of impeachment, §§123-12, 123-13.
Power to bring, Const. N. C., art. IV, §4.
Procedure in impeachment, §§123-6 to 123-11.
See IMPEACHMENT.
Journals.
Deposited with secretary of state, §120-29.
Indexed by clerks, §120-28.
Preparation and filing by clerks, §120-27.
Majority leader.
Salary and expenses, §120-3, (a), (c).
Meetings.
Convening at appointed time and place, §120-6.
Time of meeting, §120-11.1.
Minority leader.
Salary and expenses, §120-3, (a), (c).
Number of representatives, Const. N. C., art. II, §4.
Oaths.
Presiding officers may administer oaths, §120-5.
Officers of house, Const. N. C., art. II, §15.
Elected officers.
Salary and expenses, §120-37, (a) to (c).
Pay of members and officers, §120-3, (a) to (c).
Penalties.
Failure to discharge duty, §120-7.
Qualifications for representative, Const. N. C., art. II, §7.

GENERAL ASSEMBLY —Cont'd
House of representatives —Cont'd
Salaries, §120-3, (a) to (c).
Sessions.
Time of meeting, §120-11.1.
Speaker, Const. N. C., art. II, §15.
Council on educational services for exceptional children.
Appointment of members, §115C-121, (b).
Expense allowance, §120-3, (a), (c).
Legislative research commission.
Ex officio member, §120-30.10, (a).
Legislative services commission.
Chairman of commission, §120-31, (b).
Member of commission, §120-31, (a).
Oaths.
Administration of oaths for qualification of officers of house and members, §120-5.
Public health study commission members.
Appointment, §120-197, (a).
Salary, §120-3, (a), (c).
School health advisory committee.
Appointment of member, §115C-81, (e).
Succession to office of governor, §147-11.1, (b).
Speaker pro tempore.
Salary, §120-3, (a), (c).
Subsistence and travel allowances, §120-3.1, (a).
Payment of allowances, §120-3.1, (b).
When general assembly not in session, §120-3.1, (c).
Term of office, Const. N. C., art. II, §9.
Travel allowances, §120-3.1, (a).
Payment of allowances, §120-3.1, (b).
When general assembly not in session, §120-3.1, (c).
Vacancies, Const. N. C., art. II, §10.
Voting.
Electronic voting apparatus.
Amendment providing for installation and use, §120-11.2, (b).
Installation and use of apparatus, §120-11.2, (a).
Working plans for installation, §120-11.2, (c).
Witnesses.
Contested elections, §120-11.
Housing finance agency.
Finance committees of general assembly.
Oversight by committees, §122A-16.
Legislative findings and purposes, §122A-2.
Moderate income persons and families.
Legislative findings and determinations, §122A-5.4, (a).
Impeachment, §§123-1 to 123-13.
See IMPEACHMENT.
Indexes.
Journals indexed by clerks, §120-28.
Local legislation.
Published by division of publications, §147-54.1.
Session laws, §120-34, (a), (b).
Information technology.
Joint legislative oversight committee, §§120-230 to 120-235.
Interim committee activity.
Authority to meet in interim period, §120-19.6, (a).
Limitation of activities, §120-19.6, (c).
Creation of interim committees, §120-19.6, (a1).
Limitation by resolution of either house, §120-19.8.
Rules, §120-19.6, (b).

GENERAL ASSEMBLY —Cont'd
Interns.
Legislative intern program council, §120-56.
Plan for use of legislative intern, §120-57.
Investigating committees.
Appeal from denial of right to be heard, §120-18.
Appearance before committee, §120-17.
Appeal from denial of right to be heard, §120-18.
Application, §120-17.
Chairman may administer oaths, §120-15.
Oaths.
Chairman may administer oaths, §120-15.
Power of committees, §120-14.
Production of papers, §120-14.
Public officers and employees.
Furnishing data and information to legislative committees, §120-19.
State departments and agencies.
Furnishing data and information to legislative committees, §120-19.
Witnesses, §120-14.
Pay of witnesses, §120-16.
Joint committee on mental health, developmental disabilities, and substance abuse services, §§120-240 to 120-242.
Establishment, §120-240, (a).
Membership, §120-240, (b).
Organization, §120-242.
Employees and consultants, §120-242, (c).
Meetings, §120-242, (a).
Quorum, §120-242, (b).
Purpose, §120-241.
Quality and delivery of services.
Purpose, §120-241.
Vacancies, §120-240, (c).
Joint legislative administrative procedure oversight committee.
Co-chairs, §120-70.102, (a).
Composition, §120-70.100, (a).
Established, §120-70.100, (a).
Expenses, §120-70.102, (c).
Notebook maintenance, §120-70.103.
Organization of committee, §120-70.102.
Place of meetings, §120-70.102, (c).
Powers and duties, §120-70.101.
Delegation of duty to maintain notebook, §120-70.103.
Quorum, §120-70.102, (b).
Staff and employees, §120-70.102, (c).
Term of members, §120-70.100, (b).
Time of meetings, §120-70.102, (a).
Vacancies, §120-70.100, (b).
Joint legislative commission on future strategies for North Carolina.
Appointment, §120-84.7.
Co-chairpersons.
Election, §120-84.7.
Compensation, §120-84.11.
Duties generally, §120-84.8.
Establishment, §120-84.6.
Expenses, §120-84.11.
Membership, §120-84.7.
Powers generally, §120-84.8.
Additional powers, §120-84.10.
Purpose, §120-84.6.
Reports, §120-84.9.
Staff, §120-84.12, (a), (b).
Terms of members, §120-84.7.
Vacancies.
Filling, §120-84.7.

GENERAL ASSEMBLY —Cont'd
Joint legislative commission on governmental operations.
Access to papers and documents, §120-77.
Appointment of members, §120-74.
Co-chairman, §120-75.
Compelling attendance before commission, §120-77.
Compensation of commission members, §120-78.
Composition, §120-74.
Definition.
Program evaluation, §120-72.
Duties.
Enumerated, §120-76.
Studies to be conducted, §120-73.
Established, §120-73.
Expenses of commission members, §120-78.
Organization of commission, §120-75.
Powers, §120-76.
Additional powers, §120-77.
Program evaluation.
Defined, §120-72.
Purpose, §120-71.
Removal from membership, §120-74.
Resignation or removal from membership, §120-74.
Salaries.
Employees of commission, §120-79, (b).
Staff.
Assignment and direction of activities of employees, §120-79, (a).
Availability of funds, §120-79, (d).
Salaries, §120-79, (b).
Subsistence and travel allowances, §120-79, (b).
Use of other employees, §120-79, (c).
Studies to be conducted, §120-73.
Subsistence and travel expenses, §120-78.
Staff of commission, §120-79, (b).
Taxpayer services.
Reporting by department of revenue, §105-256, (a).
Terms of office, §120-74.
Travel expenses, §120-78.
Vacancies.
Filling of vacancy, §120-74.
Joint legislative commission on municipal incorporations, §§120-158 to 120-174.
See MUNICIPAL CORPORATIONS.
Joint legislative commission on seafood and aquaculture.
Appointment of members, §120-70.61.
Co-chairpersons, §120-70.61.
Compensation of members, §120-70.64.
Composition, §120-70.61.
Duties generally, §120-70.62.
Employment of personnel, §120-70.65.
Established, §120-70.60.
Expenses of members, §120-70.64.
Funding, §120-70.66.
Meetings, §120-70.63.
Personnel, §120-70.65.
Powers generally, §120-70.62.
Additional powers, §120-70.63.
Quorum, §120-70.61.
Vacancies, §120-70.61.
Joint legislative corrections, crime control, and juvenile justice oversight committee.
Co-chairs, §120-70.95, (a).
Creation, §120-70.93.
Expenses, §120-70.95, (c).
Membership, §120-70.93.

GENERAL ASSEMBLY —Cont'd
Joint legislative corrections, crime control, and juvenile justice oversight committee —Cont'd
Organization, §120-70.95.
Powers, §120-70.94, (a).
Purpose, §120-70.94.
Quorum, §120-70.95, (b).
Reports, §120-70.94, (b).
Staff, §120-70.95, (c).
Joint legislative education oversight committee.
Additional powers, §120-70.83.
Appointment, §120-70.80.
Co-chairs, §120-70.82, (a).
Creation, §120-70.80.
Expenses.
Subsistence and travel expenses, §120-70.82, (c).
Meetings, §120-70.82, (a).
Membership, §120-70.80.
Powers generally, §120-70.81, (a).
Additional powers, §120-70.83.
Quorum, §120-70.82, (b).
Reports to general assembly, §120-70.81, (b).
Resignation or removal of members, §120-70.80.
Terms of members, §120-70.80.
Vacancies, §120-70.80.
Joint legislative growth strategies oversight committee, §§120-70.120 to 120-70.122.
Assistance, §120-70.122, (c).
Co-chairs, §120-70.122, (a).
Creation, §120-70.120.
Expenses of members, §120-70.122, (d).
Membership, §120-70.120.
Powers, §120-70.121, (a).
Quorum, §120-70.122, (b).
Reports, §120-70.121, (b).
Staff, §120-70.122, (d).
Joint legislative health care oversight committee, §§120-70.110 to 120-70.112.
Co-chairs, §120-70.112, (a).
Creation, §120-70.110.
Expenses, §120-70.112, (c).
Health insurance program for children.
Oversight and review, §120-70.111, (c).
Members, §120-70.110.
Ongoing review, §120-70.111, (a).
Organization, §120-70.112.
Powers, §120-70.111, (a).
Purpose, §120-70.111.
Quorum, §120-70.112, (b).
Reports, §120-70.111, (b).
Staff, §120-70.112, (c).
Joint legislative oversight committee on capital improvements, §§120-258 to 120-260.
Access to papers and documents, compelling attendance, §120-259, (c).
Capital improvements planning act.
Oversight over implementation, §120-259, (b).
Cochairs, §120-260, (a).
Created, §120-258.
Interim reports, §120-259, (d).
Membership, §120-258.
Purpose, §120-259, (a).
Quorum, §120-260, (b).
Subsistence and travel expenses, §120-260, (c).
Terms, §120-258.
Vacancy, §120-258.
Joint legislative oversight committee on information technology, §§120-230 to 120-235.

GENERAL ASSEMBLY —Cont'd
Joint legislative oversight committee on information technology —Cont'd
Assistance to committee, §120-233, (a).
Authority to obtain information and data, §120-234.
Cochair, §120-232, (e).
Consultation with information resource management commission, §120-231, (b).
Duties, §120-231, (a).
Established, §120-230.
Goals and objectives, §120-230.
Meetings, §120-232, (d).
Membership, §120-232, (a).
Per diem, subsistence and travel allowances, §120-233, (b).
Proceeding, provision applicable, §120-234.
Reimbursement of costs in providing information to committee, §120-234.
Report, §120-231, (c).
Service until successor appointed, §120-232, (f).
Subcommittees, §120-235.
Terms, §120-232, (b).
Elected members completing term of service, §120-232, (c).
Joint legislative oversight committee on mental health, developmental disabilities and substance abuse services.
Division of mental health, developmental disabilities and substance abuse services.
Reports to committee, §120-243.
Joint legislative transportation oversight committee, §§120-70.50 to 120-70.52.
Co-chairpersons, §120-70.52, (a).
Composition, §120-70.50.
Employment of personnel, §120-70.52, (c).
Established, §120-70.50.
Expenses.
Subsistence and travel expenses, §120-70.52, (c).
Funding, §120-70.52, (c).
Meetings, §120-70.52, (a).
Powers generally, §120-70.51, (a).
Quorum, §120-70.52, (b).
Reports to general assembly, §120-70.51, (b).
Resignation or removal of members, §120-70.50.
Terms of members, §120-70.50.
Vacancies.
Filling, §120-70.50.
Joint legislative utility review committee.
Appointment, §120-70.2.
Compensation, §120-70.5.
Composition, §120-70.2.
Duties.
Generally, §120-70.3.
Established, §120-70.1.
Expenses, §120-70.5.
Meetings, §120-70.4.
Organization, §120-70.2.
Powers and duties.
Additional powers, §120-70.4.
Generally, §120-70.3.
Staff, §120-70.6.
Vacancies in office, §120-70.2.
Joint select committee on low-level radioactive waste, §§120-70.31 to 120-70.37.
Allocation of money to fund committee, §120-70.37.
Appointment of members, §120-70.32.
Clerical staff, §120-70.36.
Co-chairman.
Appointment, §120-70.32.
Compensation, §120-70.35.

GENERAL ASSEMBLY —Cont'd
Joint select committee on low-level radioactive waste —Cont'd
Composition, §120-70.32.
Definition of joint select committee, §120-70.31.
Duties, §120-70.33.
Established, §120-70.31.
Expenses, §120-70.35.
Clerical staff, §120-70.36.
Funding, §120-70.37.
Meetings, §120-70.34.
Membership, §120-70.32.
Powers, §120-70.33.
Additional powers, §120-70.34.
Quorum, §120-70.32.
Staffing, §120-70.36.
Vacancies, §120-70.32.
Journals, Const. N. C., art. II, §17.
Clerks.
Indexing of journals by clerks, §120-28.
Deposited with secretary of state, §120-29.
Disposition of damaged and unsaleable publications, §147-49.
Filing by clerks of houses, §120-27.
Preparation and filing by clerks of houses, §120-27.
Printing of session laws.
Legislative services commission, §120-34.
Record votes, Const. N. C., art. II, §19.
Sale, §147-48.
Judges.
Removal, Const. N. C., art. IV, §17.
Junkyard control.
Legislative findings and declarations, §136-142.
Jury.
Pay of jurors.
Local, private and special legislation prohibited, Const. N. C., art. II, §24.
Labor.
Local, private and special legislation prohibited, Const. N. C., art. II, §24.
Land protection and conservation.
Legislative findings, §106-202.13.
Legislative actuarial note act, §§120-112 to 120-114.
Legislative appointments to boards and commissions, §120-121, (d).
Bill enactment required, §120-121, (a).
Conflicts of interest.
Service by members of general assembly on certain boards and commissions, §120-123.
Contents of bills, §120-121, (c).
Multiple appointments, §120-121, (b).
Service by members of general assembly on certain boards and commissions, §120-123.
Vacancies in appointments, §120-122.
Legislative building.
Burning of certain public buildings, §14-59.
Legislative intern program council, §120-56.
Plan for use of legislative interns, §120-57.
Legislative power, Const. N. C., art. II, §1.
Legislative research commission, §§120-30.10 to 120-30.18.
See LEGISLATIVE RESEARCH COMMISSION.
Legislative retirement fund.
Repealed, §120-4.2, (a).
Continuation of authority and duties for administration of certain benefits, §120-4.2, (c).
Entitlement to further benefits, §120-4.2, (b).

GENERAL ASSEMBLY —Cont'd
Legislative retirement fund —Cont'd
Transfer of membership and benefits from retirement fund to legislative retirement system, §120-4.13, (a).
Legislative retirement system.
General provisions, §§120-4.8 to 120-4.32.
See LEGISLATIVE RETIREMENT SYSTEM.
Legislative services commission, §§120-31 to 120-36.
See LEGISLATIVE SERVICES COMMISSION.
Legislative services officer.
Appointment, §120-36, (a).
Committee staff assistance.
Authority to assign, §120-19.5.
Compensation, §120-36, (a).
Duties, §120-36, (b).
Legislative study commission on children and youth, §§120-215 to 120-220.
Administration, §120-218.
Authority, §120-220.
Composition, §120-217.
Creation, §120-215.
Duties, §120-216.
Hearings, §120-218, (b).
Meetings, §120-218, (a).
Members, §120-217, (a).
Compensation, §120-217, (c).
Expenses, §120-217, (c).
Terms, §120-217, (b).
Vacancies, §120-217, (b).
Powers, §120-220.
Purpose, §120-215.
Duties, §120-216.
Reports, §120-219.
Staff, §120-218, (c).
Studies, evaluations or assessments.
Duties, §120-216.
Legislative study commission on mental health, developmental disabilities and substance abuse services, §§120-204 to 120-207.
Legitimation.
Local, private and special legislation prohibited, Const. N. C., art. II, §24.
Lieutenant governor.
President of the senate, Const. N. C., art. II, §13.
Limestone, marl and landplaster.
Sale of agricultural liming materials and landplaster.
Legislative findings and declarations, §106-92.15.
Limitation on fundraising during legislative session.
Definitions, §163-278.13B, (a).
Exceptions, §163-278.13B, (d).
Misdemeanor for violating provisions, §163-278.13B, (e).
Prohibited contributions by limited contributor, §163-278.13B, (c).
Prohibited solicitations by limited contributee, §163-278.13B, (b).
Limited liability companies.
Reservation of power to amend or repeal, §57C-1-02.
Loans.
Legislative commissions and committees.
Applying for, receiving or accepting, §120-32.03, (a), (b).
Lobbying, §§120-47.1 to 120-47.12.
See LOBBYING.

GENERAL ASSEMBLY —Cont'd
Local government.
Provision for local government by general assembly, Const. N. C., art. VII, §1.
Local government fiscal information.
Administrative rules.
Fiscal impact, §120-30.48.
Citation of act, §120-30.41.
Definitions.
Fiscal note, §120-30.44.
Unit of local government, §120-30.42.
Federal mandate report.
Assistance in preparation of report, §120-30.49, (b).
Contents, §120-30.49, (a).
Copies provided, §120-30.49, (c).
Fiscal note.
Attachment to bill, §120-30.45, (a), (c), (d).
Confidentiality of requests for assistance in preparation, §120-131.1, (a).
Contents, §120-30.45, (a).
Copies to be furnished, §120-30.45, (f).
Defined, §120-30.44.
Introduction of legislation by request, §120-30.47.
Preparation of note, §120-30.45, (e).
Research division duties, §120-30.45, (b).
Introduction of legislation by request, §120-30.47.
Legislation introduced by request, §120-30.47.
Purposes of article, §120-30.43.
Short title, §120-30.41.
State appropriations.
Fiscal information related to requests, §120-30.46.
Unit of local government.
Defined, §120-30.42.
Local, private and special legislation.
Limitations, Const. N. C., art. II, §24.
Prohibited subjects, Const. N. C., art. II, §24.
Manual.
Published by division of publications, §147-54.1.
Manufacturing.
Local, private and special legislation prohibited, Const. N. C., art. II, §24.
Mass gatherings.
Exceptions to provisions, §143-318.18.
Legislative intent and purpose, §130A-251.
Legislative research commission, §120-30.14.
Members to convene at appointed time and place, §120-6.
Official meetings of commissions, committees and standing subcommittees.
Code sections.
Applicable to meetings of, §143-318.14A, (e).
Enumerated, §143-318.14A, (a).
Final action only in open meeting, §143-318.14A, (c).
Notice, §143-318.14A, (b).
Open sessions, §143-318.14A, (a).
Violation of section.
Punishable as prescribed by rules of house or senate, §143-318.14A, (d).
Public bodies, §§143-318.9 to 143-318.18.
Time of meeting, §120-11.1.
Medical plan for teachers and state employees, §§135-39 to 135-40.14.
See MEDICAL PLAN FOR TEACHERS AND STATE EMPLOYEES.
Mental health, developmental disabilities and substance abuse.
Legislative study commission on mental health, developmental disabilities and substance abuse services, §§120-204 to 120-207.

GENERAL ASSEMBLY —Cont'd
Mental health, developmental disabilities and substance abuse —Cont'd
State facilities.
Ex officio visitors of facilities, §122C-186.
Mines and minerals.
Local, private and special legislation prohibited, Const. N. C., art. II, §24.
Minors.
Legislative study commission on children and youth, §§120-215 to 120-220.
Motor vehicle special license plates, §20-79.4, (a).
Municipal corporations.
Joint legislative commission on municipal incorporations, §§120-158 to 120-174.
See MUNICIPAL CORPORATIONS.
Joint municipal electric power and energy act.
Legislative findings and purposes, §159B-2.
Local government to be provided for by general assembly, Const. N. C., art. VII, §1.
Local, private and special legislation prohibited, Const. N. C., art. II, §24.
Names.
Altering name of person.
Local, private and special legislation prohibited, Const. N. C., art. II, §24.
Notice.
Committee activity.
Examination of witnesses, §120-19.2, (d).
Contested elections, §120-10.
Legislative ethics committee.
Possible violations of provisions, §120-103, (b).
Meetings of commissions, committees and standing subcommittees.
Official meetings, §143-318.14A, (b).
Repayment of money owed to state by legislators.
Legislative ethics committee to be notified, §143-559.
Statement of economic interest.
County boards of elections to notify candidates of economic-interest-statement requirements, §120-93.
Nuisances.
Abatement of nuisances.
Local, private and special legislation prohibited, Const. N. C., art. II, §24.
Oaths, Const. N. C., art. II, §12.
Chairman of committees.
Who may administer oaths of office, §11-7.1, (a).
Committee activity.
Examination of witnesses, §120-19.1, (b).
Investigating committees.
Chairman may administer oaths, §120-15.
Police.
State legislative building special police, §120-32.3.
Presiding officers may administer oaths, §120-5.
Supporting constitutions, §11-7; Const. N. C., art. II, §12.
Obstructing justice.
Witnesses before legislative committees.
Failing to attend as witness, §14-227.
Occupational licensing boards.
New boards.
Legislative committee on new licensing boards, §120-149.6.
Officers.
Elected officers, §120-37.
Expense allowances, §120-3.

GENERAL ASSEMBLY —Cont'd
Officers —Cont'd
Legislative ethics committee.
Article applicable to presiding officers, §120-106.
Salaries, §120-3.
Parking.
State legislative building.
Authority to regulate parking, §120-32.1, (c).
Penalties.
Confidentiality of legislative communications.
Disciplinary actions, §§120-131.1, (c), 120-134.
Duty and privilege of members.
Failure to discharge duty, §120-7.
Legislative ethics committee.
Disposition of violators, §120-103, (d1).
Inquisitorial proceedings, §120-103, (b), (c).
Possible violations of provisions, §120-103, (a).
Lobbying.
Punishment for violation, §120-47.9.
Local, private and special legislation prohibited, Const. N. C., art. II, §24.
Statement of economic interest, §120-98, (a).
Pensions.
Committees on pensions and retirement, §§120-111.1 to 120-111.4.
Perjury before legislative committees, §14-211.
Personnel system.
Exemption of officers and employees, §126-5, (c1).
Police.
State legislative building special police, §§120-32.2, 120-32.3.
Evacuation of buildings and grounds during emergencies, §120-32.1A.
Post-war reserve fund.
Direction of use of fund, §143-193.
Reports, §143-194.
Powers of general assembly, Const. N. C., art. II, §20.
Presidential elections.
Appointment of electors, §163-213, (a).
Printing of session laws.
Delivery to secretary of state, §120-34, (c).
Index references, §120-34, (b).
Number of volumes printed, §120-34, (c).
Requirements, §120-34, (a).
Property tax subcommittee.
Revenue laws study committee, §120-70.108.
Protests, Const. N. C., art. II, §18.
Public buildings and grounds.
Legislative services commission.
Use and maintenance of buildings and grounds, §120-32.1.
Public health study commission, §§120-195 to 120-203.
Authority, §120-201.
Creation and purpose, §120-195.
Duties, §120-196.
Meetings, §120-198.
Membership, vacancies, terms, §120-197.
Reimbursement for expenses, §120-199.
Reports, §120-202.
Staff, meeting place, §120-203.
Subcommittees, §120-200.
Public officers and employees.
Communications with members of the general assembly, §126-90.
Legislative committees and commissions.
Furnishing data and information to, §120-19.
Legislative research commission.
Cooperation with commission, §120-30.16.

GENERAL ASSEMBLY —Cont'd
Public utilities.
Joint legislative utility review committee, §§120-70.1 to 120-70.6.
Radioactive waste.
Low-level radioactive waste.
Joint select committee, §§120-70.31 to 120-70.37. See within this heading, "Joint select committee on low-level radioactive waste."
Railroads.
Revitalization programs, §§136-44.35 to 136-44.38.
Reconvening of legislature, Const. N. C., art. II, §22; art. III, §5.
Request that session not be held, §120-6.1, (a), (b).
Record votes.
Keeping in journal, Const. N. C., art. II, §19.
Regional public transportation authority.
Authority recommendation of additional revenue sources, §160A-624.
Approval by legislature required, §160A-624.
Reports to general assembly, §160A-625.
Repayment of money owed to state by legislators.
Applicability of statute of limitations, §143-562.
Confidentiality exemption, §143-560.
Definition of employing entity, §143-558.
Investigations, §143-559.
Notice.
Legislative ethics committee to be notified of delinquent legislators, §143-559.
Preservation of federal funds, §143-561.
Repeals.
Local, private and special legislation.
Partial repeal not to affect local, private or special act, Const. N. C., art. II, §24.
Reports.
Appropriations.
Reports to committees.
Effect, §143-15.
Executive officer's reports to governor.
Transmitted to general assembly by governor, §147-5.
State agency reports to general assembly.
Copies, who receives, electronic copy available, informing members, §120-29.5.
Research division of legislative services commission, §§120-36.1 to 120-36.7.
See LEGISLATIVE SERVICES COMMISSION.
Resolutions.
Actions on resolutions, Const. N. C., art. II, §22.
Binding original statutes, resolutions and documents, §147-42.
Disposition of damaged and unsaleable publications, §147-49.
Secretary of state to be custodian, §147-39.
Retaliatory actions.
Personnel-related actions, §120-86.1.
Retirement fund.
Legislative retirement fund.
Repealed, §120-4.2.
Retirement system for counties and cities.
Reservation of power to change, §128-38.
Retirement system for general assembly.
Actuarial note act, §§120-112 to 120-114.
See RETIREMENT SYSTEM FOR GENERAL ASSEMBLY.
Committees on pensions and retirement, §§120-111.1 to 120-111.4.
See RETIREMENT SYSTEM FOR GENERAL ASSEMBLY.

GENERAL ASSEMBLY —Cont'd
Retirement system for general assembly —Cont'd
Legislative retirement system, §§120-4.8 to 120-4.32.
See LEGISLATIVE RETIREMENT SYSTEM.
Retirement system for teachers and state employees.
Creditable service.
Including service rendered as member or officer, §135-4, (j).
Purchase of creditable service, §135-4, (j1).
Legislative retirement fund.
Transfer to department of state treasurer, §143A-37.
Reservation of power to change, §135-18.4.
Revenue bills.
Requirements for passage, Const. N. C., art. II, §23.
Revenue laws study committee, §§120-70.105 to 120-70.108.
Co-chairs, §120-70.107, (a).
Creation, §120-70.105.
Expenses, §120-70.107, (c).
Funding, §120-70.107, (c).
Members, §120-70.105, (a).
Organization, §120-70.107.
Powers, §§120-70.106, (a), 120-70.107, (b).
Property tax subcommittee.
Duties, §120-70.108, (b).
Membership, §120-70.108, (a).
Report on recommendations, §120-70.108, (c).
Quorum, §120-70.107, (b).
Reports, §120-70.106, (b).
Staff, §120-70.107, (c).
Terms of office, §120-70.105, (b).
Rules and regulations.
Legislative services commission.
Adoption of rules, §120-31, (d).
Use and maintenance of building, §120-32.1, (a).
Posting of rules and regulations, §120-32.1, (b).
Salaries.
Clerks.
Principal clerk, §120-37, (c).
Reading clerk, §120-37, (b).
Elected officers, §120-37.
Joint legislative commission on governmental operations.
Staff of commission, §120-79, (b).
Members, §120-3, (a) to (c).
Officers, §120-3, (a) to (c).
Research division.
Director of fiscal research, §120-36.2, (c).
Professional and clerical employees, §120-36.2, (c).
Sergeant-at-arms, §120-37, (b).
Sanitation.
Local, private and special legislation prohibited, Const. N. C., art. II, §24.
School districts.
Local, private and special legislation prohibited, Const. N. C., art. II, §24.
Seafood and aquaculture.
Joint legislative commission, §§120-70.60 to 120-70.66.
Secretary of state.
Attendance at sessions of legislature, §147-36.
Binding original statutes, resolutions and documents, §147-42.
Custodian of statutes, resolutions, etc., §147-39.

GENERAL ASSEMBLY —Cont'd
Secretary of state —Cont'd
Journals.
Deposited with secretary of state, §120-29.
Disposition of damaged and unsaleable publications, §147-49.
Sale, §147-48.
Legislative services commission.
Printing of session laws, §120-34.
Lobbying.
Provisions.
Authority of secretary, §120-47.11.
Printing of session laws.
Delivery to secretary for distribution, §120-34, (c).
Senate.
Apportionment, §120-1, (a) to (c); Const. N. C., art. II, §3.
Dividing precincts restricted, §120-2.2.
Severability of acts, §120-2.1.
Arrest.
Protection from arrest, §120-9.
Depositions.
Contested elections, §120-11.
Deputy president pro tempore.
Salary, §120-3, (a), (c).
Districts, §120-1, (a) to (c); Const. N. C., art. II, §3.
Areas not specifically assigned to, §120-1, (d).
Boundaries, §120-1, (b), (c).
Change, §120-1, (e).
Establishment of senatorial districts, §120-1, (a).
Duties.
Penalty for failure to discharge duty, §120-7.
Elections.
Contests.
Depositions taken, §120-11.
Notice of contest, §120-10.
Witnesses, §120-11.
Corrupt practices in election.
Expulsion for corrupt practices, §120-8.
Electronic voting apparatus.
Installation and use of apparatus, §120-11.2.
Expense allowance, §120-3, (a), (c).
Failure to discharge duty.
Penalty for failure, §120-7.
Freedom of speech, §120-9.
Impeachment, §§123-1 to 123-13.
See IMPEACHMENT.
Journals.
Deposited with secretary of state, §120-29.
Indexed by clerks, §120-28.
Preparation and filing by clerk, §120-27.
Majority leader, §120-3, (a), (c).
Meetings.
Convening at appointed time and place, §120-6.
Time of meeting, §120-11.1.
Minority leader, §120-3, (a), (c).
Number of senators, Const. N. C., art. II, §2.
Oaths.
Presiding officers may administer oaths, §120-5.
Officers, Const. N. C., art. II, §14.
Elected officers, §120-37.
Pay of members and officers, §120-3, (a) to (c).
Penalties.
Failure to discharge duty, §120-7.
President.
Lieutenant governor to preside, Const. N. C., art. II, §13.

GENERAL ASSEMBLY —Cont'd
Senate —Cont'd
President —Cont'd
Oaths.
Administration of oaths for qualification of senators and officers of senate, §120-5.
School health advisory committee.
Appointment of member, §115C-81, (e).
Succession to office of governor, §147-11.1, (b).
President pro tempore.
Expense allowance, §120-3, (a), (c).
Legislative research commission.
Ex officio member, §120-30.10, (a).
Legislative services commission.
Chairman of commission, §120-31, (b).
Member of commission, §120-31, (a).
Public health study commission members.
Appointment, §120-197, (a).
Salary, §120-3, (a), (c).
Succession to presidency, Const. N. C., art. II, §14.
Temporary succession, Const. N. C., art. II, §14.
Qualifications for senator, Const. N. C., art. II, §6.
Salaries, §120-3, (a) to (c).
Sessions.
Time of meeting, §120-11.1.
Subsistence and travel allowances, §120-3.1, (a).
Payment of allowances, §120-3.1, (b).
When general assembly not in session, §120-3.1, (c).
Terms of office, Const. N. C., art. II, §9.
Travel allowances, §120-3.1, (a).
Payment of allowances, §120-3.1, (b).
When general assembly not in session, §120-3.1, (c).
Vacancies, Const. N. C., art. II, §10.
Voting.
Electronic voting apparatus.
Amendment providing for installation and use, §120-11.2, (b).
Installation and use of apparatus, §120-11.2, (a).
Working plans for installation, §120-11.2, (c).
Witnesses.
Contested elections, §120-11.
Sergeant-at-arms.
Election, §120-37, (a).
Employing temporary assistance, §120-37, (e).
Salary, §120-37, (b).
Term, §120-37, (a).
Session laws.
Printing of session laws.
Legislative services commission, §120-34.
Sessions.
Extra sessions on legislative call, Const. N. C., art. II, §11.
Reconvened sessions.
Request that session not be held, §120-6.1, (a), (b).
Regular sessions, Const. N. C., art. II, §11.
Time of meeting, §120-11.1.
Severability of apportionment acts, §120-2.1.
Sick leave.
Temporary employees, §120-32.5.
Southern growth policies agreement, §§143-490 to 143-506.
See SOUTHERN GROWTH POLICIES AGREEMENT.
Special education.
Findings, §115C-107.
Policy of state, §115C-106, (a), (b).

GENERAL ASSEMBLY —Cont'd
Special police.
State legislative building.
Evacuation of legislative buildings and grounds during emergencies, §120-32.1A.
Powers of policemen, §120-32.2.
State departments and agencies.
Legislative committees and commissions.
Furnishing data and information to, §120-19.
Legislative research commission.
Cooperation with commission, §120-30.16.
Lobbying.
Restrictions on principal state departments, §120-47.12.
Reports.
Certain institutions to report to general assembly, §143-156.
Report from chief officer to general assembly, §120-12.
State agency reports to general assembly.
Copies, who receives, electronic copy available, informing members, §120-29.5.
Vacancies in offices of some departments, §120-12.1.
State institutions.
Legislative research commission.
Cooperation with commission, §120-30.16.
Reports from state institutions and departments, §120-12.
State legislative building.
Defined, §120-32.1, (d).
Designation, §129-12.1.
Evacuation in emergencies, §120-32.1A.
Legislative research commission.
Availability of facilities to the commission, §120-30.18.
Official name, §129-12.1.
Parking regulations, §120-32.1, (c).
Research division.
Office space and equipment in state legislative building, §120-36.5.
Rules and regulations.
Use and maintenance of buildings, §120-32.1, (a), (b).
Special police, §120-32.2.
Evacuation of buildings and grounds during emergencies, §120-32.1A.
Use and maintenance of building, §120-32.1, (a).
Rules and regulations, §120-32.1, (a).
Posting, §120-32.1, (b).
State literary fund.
Report by state board of education on operation, §115C-414.
State of disaster, declaring, §166A-6.
State treasurer.
Legislative retirement fund.
Transfer to department of state treasurer, §143A-37.
Structural pest control.
Legislative findings, §106-65.22.
Subpoenas.
Committee activity.
Failure to respond to subpoena punishable as contempt, §120-19.4.
Form of subpoena, §120-19.2, (e).
Issuance of subpoena to obtain testimony, §120-19.2, (c).
Return of subpoena, §120-19.2, (f).
Legislative ethics committee.
Possible violations of provisions, §120-103, (c).

GENERAL ASSEMBLY —Cont'd
Subpoenas —Cont'd
Legislative services commission.
Subpoena and contempt powers, §120-32.4.
Subsistence and travel allowances.
Joint legislative commission on governmental operations, §120-78.
Staff of commission, §120-79, (b).
Legislative ethics committee, §120-101.
Legislative research commission, §120-30.18.
Legislative services commission.
Reimbursement for allowance, §120-31, (e).
Members of general assembly, §120-3.1.
Subsistence expenses.
Members also members of state board or commission, §138-5, (f).
Supreme court.
Claims against the state.
Original jurisdiction of the supreme court, §7A-25.
Taxation.
Amendment or repeal of subchapter.
Power of general assembly, §105-1.1.
Local, private and special legislation prohibited, Const. N. C., art. II, §24.
Power of taxation vested in general assembly, §105-1.1.
Requirements for passage of revenue bills, Const. N. C., art. II, §23.
Temporary employees.
Leave for temporary employees, §120-32.5.
Terms of office, Const. N. C., art. II, §9.
Threats.
Code of legislative ethics.
Intent to influence legislator in discharge of duties, §120-86, (b) to (e).
Personnel-related actions, §120-86.1.
Intent to influence legislator in discharge of duties.
Compelling threatened person to attempt to influence legislator, §120-86, (b1).
Legislator defined, §120-86, (d).
Legislator to threaten other legislator, §120-86, (c).
Penalties, §120-86, (e).
Threats to legislator by partner, client, customer or employer, §120-86, (b).
Towns.
Local government to be provided by general assembly, Const. N. C., art. VII, §1.
Townships.
Local, private and special legislation prohibited, Const. N. C., art. II, §24.
Trade.
Local, private and special legislation prohibited, Const. N. C., art. II, §24.
Transportation department.
Data report to general assembly, §136-12, (a).
Reports to appropriations committees of general assembly, §136-44.2B.
Travel allowances.
Joint legislative commission on governmental operations, §120-78.
Staff of commission, §120-79, (b).
Legislative ethics committee, §120-101.
Legislative research commission, §120-30.18.
Legislative services commission.
Reimbursement for subsistence in travel allowance, §120-31, (e).
Members of general assembly, §120-3.1.

GENERAL ASSEMBLY —Cont'd
Travel expenses.
Members also members of state board or commission, §138-5, (f).
Underground storage tanks.
Leaking petroleum cleanup.
Implementation of provisions of part.
Part not construed to obligate to make appropriation, §143-215.94J, (b).
Vacancies.
Appointment by governor to fill, §§163-11, (a).
County executive committee of political party of vacating member.
Recommendation, §§163-11, (b), (c).
House or senate district committee.
Recommendation, §§163-11, (d).
Filling vacancies, Const. N. C., art. II, §10.
Legislative appointments, §120-122.
Vacation leave.
Temporary employees, §120-32.5.
Veto by governor, Const. N. C., art. II, §22; art. III, §5.
Voting.
Electronic voting apparatus.
Installation and use of apparatus, §120-11.2.
Wage and hour act.
Pages in general assembly.
Exemptions, §95-25.14, (a).
Waters and watercourses.
Nonnavigable streams.
Local, private and special legislation prohibited, Const. N. C., art. II, §24.
Wills.
Giving effect to informal wills.
Local, private and special legislation prohibited, Const. N. C., art. II, §24.
Witnesses.
Committee activity.
Examination of witnesses, §§120-19.1, 120-19.2, (b).
Notice of hearing, §120-19.2, (d).
Failing to attend as witness before committees, §14-227.
Fees and expenses of witness, §120-19.3.
Invitations to witnesses, §120-19.2, (a).
Perjury, §14-211.
Refusal to testify punishable as contempt, §120-19.4.
Contested elections, §120-11.
Investigating committees, §120-14.
Pay of witnesses, §120-16.
Legislative research commission.
Powers and duties, §120-30.17.

GENERAL CONTRACTORS, §§87-1 to 87-15.3.
Bidding.
Copy of provisions to be included in specifications, §87-15.
Licenses.
Bid not considered unless contractor licensed, §87-15.
Board.
Appointment of members, §87-2.
Composition, §87-2.
Creation, §87-2.
Employees, §87-4.
Equipment and supplies, authority to purchase, §87-9.1, (b).
Funds.
Disposition, §87-7.

GENERAL CONTRACTORS —Cont'd
Board —Cont'd
Liability insurance, authority to purchase, §87-9.1, (b).
Meetings, §87-6.
First meeting, §87-4.
Notice, §87-6.
Number of members, §87-2.
Oath of office of members, §87-3.
Officers, §87-4.
Public awareness program, §87-15.2.
Purchasing authority.
Equipment and supplies, §87-9.1, (b).
Real property, §87-9.1, (a).
Qualifications of members, §87-2.
Quorum, §87-6.
Real property, authority to acquire and own, §87-9.1, (a).
Records, §§87-7, 87-8.
Complaints against licensees, §87-11, (c).
Removal of members, §87-2.
Reports.
Annual report to governor, §87-8.
Seal, §87-5.
Terms of members, §87-2.
Vacancies, §87-2.
Building permits.
Regulations as to issuance, §87-14.
Child support enforcement.
Forfeiture of licensing privilege, §50-13.12.
Complaints against licensees, §87-11, (a1).
Confidentiality of complaining party, §87-15.3.
Confidentiality of complaining party.
Complaints against licensees or unlicensed contractors, §87-15.3.
Defined, §87-1.
Evidence.
Licenses.
Certificate evidence of license, §87-12.
Federal highway act.
Compliance by department of transportation not prevented, §87-9.
Fees.
Licenses, §87-10, (a).
Fire service mains, §87-10, (b1).
Highways.
Federal requirements.
Compliance not prevented, §87-9.
Homeowners recovery fund.
Administration, §87-15.6, (a).
Definitions, §87-15.5.
Establishment, §87-15.6, (a).
Fees.
Building permits.
Collection, §87-15.6, (b).
Purposes, §87-15.6, (a).
Reimbursements.
Application, §87-15.8, (a).
Investigation, §87-15.8, (a).
Determination of procedures, §87-15.7, (a).
Eligibility, §87-15.8, (a).
Payment, §87-15.8, (b).
Subrogation, §87-15.9.
Rules and regulations.
Adoption, §87-15.6, (c).
Subrogation.
Reimbursements, §87-15.9.
Use of funds, §87-15.7, (b).
Impersonating contractor, §87-13.
Injunctions.
Power of board to seek, §87-13.1.

GENERAL CONTRACTORS —Cont'd

Insurance.
Board.
Liability insurance, authority to purchase, §87-9.1, (b).

Licenses.
Applications, §87-10, (a).
Bidding.
Bid not considered unless contractor licensed, §87-15.
Certificates, §87-10, (e).
Evidence of license, §87-12.
False certificate, §87-13.
Lost or destroyed certificates.
Replacement, §87-11, (d).
Complaints against licensees, §87-11, (a1).
Examinations, §87-10, (b), (c).
Exception.
Public building project owner, bidding and contracting with, §87-1.1.
Fees, §87-10, (a).
Nonresidents.
Definitions, §87-10.1, (a).
Reciprocity, §87-15.1.
Reexaminations, §87-10, (d).
Renewal, §87-10, (e).
Revocation.
Felony conviction, §15A-1331, (a).
Grounds, §87-11, (a).
Reissuance, §87-11, (d).
Rules and regulations governing, §87-11, (b).

Misdemeanors.
Building permits.
Issuance violations, §87-14.
Prohibited acts, §87-13.

Nonresidents.
Licenses, §87-10.1.

Penalties, §87-13.
Building permits.
Issuance violations, §87-14.

Prohibited acts, §87-13.

Public awareness program, §87-15.2.

Public building project owners.
Bidding and contracting directly with.
License exception, §87-1.1.

Public utilities contractors.
Water service or sewer lines.
Line terminations and fire service mains, §87-10, (b1).

Reciprocity.
Licenses, §87-15.1.

Records.
Board, §§87-7, 87-8.
Complaints against licensees, §87-11, (c).

Roster of licensed contractors, §87-8.

Subcontractors.
Payments to subcontractors.
Inapplicability of provisions of chapter to residential contractors, §22C-6.

Unauthorized practice of contracting, §87-13.

Water or wastewater systems.
Contracts, §87-9.
Public utilities contractors.
Line terminations and fire service mains, §87-10, (b1).

GENERAL COURT OF JUSTICE.

Administration, §7A-2.
Unified judicial system for purposes of administration, §7A-4.

GENERAL COURT OF JUSTICE —Cont'd

Advance sheets.
Furnishing advance sheets without charge, §7A-6, (c).

Age limit for service as justice or judge, §7A-4.20.

Appeals.
Cost on appeal, §6-33.

Appellate division, §§7A-5 to 7A-7; Const. N. C., art. IV, §5.
Court of appeals.
See COURT OF APPEALS.
Organization, §7A-5.
Utilities commission.
Parties on appeal, §62-92.
Relief pending review on appeal, §62-95.
Right of appeals from utilities commission, §62-90, (d).

Cancellation of court sessions.
Adverse weather conditions, §7A-39, (a).

Cash management, §147-86.14.

Clerks of court.
Practice of law.
Prohibited, §84-2.

Closing court offices, §7A-39, (a).
Adverse weather conditions, §7A-39, (a).

Costs.
Civil actions, §7A-305, (a).
Criminal actions.
Assessment and collection of costs, §§7A-2, 7A-304, (a).
Recovery of cost on appeal, §6-33.

Court of appeals.
See COURT OF APPEALS.

Court reporters.
Appellate division of general court of justice, §7A-6, (a).

District courts.
See DISTRICT COURTS.

Divisions.
Enumeration, Const. N. C., art. IV, §2.

Financial support of judicial department, §7A-2.

Inclement weather.
Cancellation of court sessions, §7A-39, (a).
Chambers or ex parte jurisdiction, §7A-39, (c).

Judicial conduct.
Authority of supreme court to prescribe standards, §7A-10.1.

Judicial department.
See JUDICIAL DEPARTMENT.

Judicial power, §7A-3.
Vesting, Const. N. C., art. IV, §1.

Jurisdiction.
Chambers or ex parte jurisdiction.
Inclement weather conditions, §7A-39, (c).
Divisions, §7A-2.
Enforcement of judgments, §7A-3.
Unified judicial system for purposes of jurisdiction, §7A-4.

Meetings of public bodies.
Exception to provisions, §143-318.18.

Oaths.
Form of oath, §11-11.
Who may administer oaths of office, §11-7.1, (a).

Obstructing justice.
Picketing or parading within certain distance of court, §14-225.1.

Operation.
Unified judicial system for purposes of operation, §7A-4.

GENERAL COURT OF JUSTICE —Cont'd
Organization of divisions, §§7A-2, 7A-4.
Picketing or parading within certain distance of court.
Obstructing justice, §14-225.1.
Pleadings.
Verification.
Judges or clerks competent to take affidavits, §1-148.
Powers.
Judicial power, §7A-3.
Vesting, Const. N. C., art. IV, §1.
Public utilities commission.
Parties on appeal, §62-92.
Relief pending review on appeal, §62-95.
Right of appeal, §62-90, (d).
Purposes of chapter, §7A-2.
Retirement.
Age limit for service as justice or judge, §7A-4.20.
Consolidated judicial retirement act, §§135-50 to 135-75.
See RETIREMENT SYSTEM FOR TEACHERS AND STATE EMPLOYEES.
Small claim actions in district courts, §§7A-210 to 7A-232.
See SMALL CLAIM ACTIONS.
Superior courts.
See SUPERIOR COURTS.
Support of court.
Administration of estates.
Facilities fee as part of costs in administration of estates, §7A-307, (a), (b).
Costs in civil actions, §7A-305, (a).
Costs in criminal actions, §7A-304, (a).
Supreme court.
See SUPREME COURT.
Transfer of civil causes.
Motion to transfer.
Consent of parties required, §7A-258, (a).
Contents, §7A-258, (d).
Effectiveness when order of transfer filed, §7A-258, (h).
Filing of motion, §7A-258, (b).
Parties other than plaintiff, §7A-258, (c).
In writing requirement, §7A-258, (d).
Notice required, §7A-258, (e).
Sole method for seeking transfer, §7A-258, (g).
Stay of proceedings, §7A-258, (f).
Venue determination, §7A-258, (f).
Waiver of objection to jurisdiction where motion filed, §7A-258, (f).
When second transfer not authorized, §7A-258, (i).
Retention and docketing of causes in originally designated trial division until transferred, §7A-256.
Review of transfer matters, §7A-260.
Waiver of proper division, §7A-257.
Exceptions, §7A-257.
Transition provisions, §7A-3.
Vesting of judicial power, Const. N. C., art. IV, §1.

GENERAL EDUCATION DEVELOPMENT DEGREE.
Jail prisoner's participation.
Person having custody to approve, revocation of approval, §162-59.1.
Reduction in sentence for participation, §162-60, (b).
Escape, forfeiture of reduction, §162-60, (c).

GENERAL EDUCATION DEVELOPMENT DEGREE —Cont'd
Jail prisoner's participation —Cont'd
Reduction in sentence for participation —Cont'd
Person in custody judge of faithful participation, §162-60, (c).
Post-release supervision.
Reintegrative conditions, §15A-1364.4, (d).

GENERAL STATUTES.
Adoption.
Replacement volume 1A, §164-11.9, (a).
Replacement volume 1B, §164-11.9, (b).
Replacement volumes 1C and 1D, §164-11.8, (a), (d).
Replacement volume 2A, §164-11.8, (b), (d).
Replacement volume 2B, §164-11.6, (a), (c).
Replacement volumes 2B, 2C and 2D, §164-11.7, (a), (c).
Replacement volume 2C, §164-11.5, (a), (c).
Replacement volume 3A, §§164-11.6, (b), (c), 164-11.8, (c), (d).
Replacement volume 3B, §164-11.5, (b), (c).
Replacement volumes 3B, 3C and 3D, §164-11.7, (b), (c).
Volumes 1A, 1B and 1C, §164-11.4.
Volumes 2A, 2B and 2C, §164-11.2.
Volumes 3A, 3B and 3C, §164-11.3.
Citation of revision, §164-1.
Commission.
General statutes commission, §§164-12 to 164-19.
See GENERAL STATUTES COMMISSION.
Definitions, Const. N. C., art. XIV, §3.
Division of legislative drafting and codification of statutes.
Completion of general statutes by, §164-9.
Duties and powers generally, §164-10.
Supplements to general statutes, §164-10.
Effect.
Repeal of other statutes, §164-2.
Offenses, penalties and liabilities not affected, §164-4.
Pending actions and proceedings not affected, §164-5.
Persons holding office, §164-6.
Rights accrued or suits commenced not affected, §164-3.
Statutes not repealed, §164-7.
When acts take effect, §120-20.
Effective date, §164-8.
When acts take effect, §120-20.
Evidence.
Supplements.
Prima facie evidence of laws, §164-11, (a).
Cumulative supplements, §164-11.1.
Penalties.
Repeals not to affect, §164-4.
Repeal of other statutes, §164-2.
Offenses, penalties and liabilities not affected, §164-4.
Pending actions and proceedings not affected, §164-5.
Persons holding office.
Effect of repeal on, §164-6.
Rights accrued or suits commenced not affected, §164-3.
Statutes not repealed, §164-7.
Supplements, §164-10.
Citation, §164-11, (b).
Cumulative supplements.
Prima facie evidence of laws, §164-11.1.

GENERAL STATUTES —Cont'd
Supplements —Cont'd
Prima facie statement of laws, §164-11, (a).
Cumulative supplements, §164-11.1.
Title of revision, §164-1.

GENERAL STATUTES COMMISSION, §§164-12 to 164-19.
Appointment of members, §164-14, (a).
Reported to secretary of commission, §164-14, (e).
Committees, §164-17.
Compensation of members, §164-19.
Composition, §164-14, (a).
Creation, §164-12.
Department of justice.
Transfer to department, §143A-53.
Duties, §164-13, (a).
Funds.
Use of funds, §164-13, (b).
Meetings, §164-15.
Name, §164-12.
Number of members, §164-14, (a).
Officers, §164-16.
Election, §164-16.
Terms of office, §164-16.
Quorum, §164-15.
Reports, §164-18.
Rules and regulations, §164-17.
Secretary.
Revisor of statutes as ex officio secretary, §164-16.
Terms of members, §164-14, (b), (c), (f).
Travel allowances of members, §164-19.
Vacancies.
Filling, §164-14, (d).

GENERATING FACILITIES.
Certificates for construction.
Analysis for needs for expansion of facilities, §62-110.1, (c).
Appeal from award order, §62-82, (b).
Application.
Factors in action, §62-110.1, (d).
Hearing, §62-82, (a).
Notice, §62-82, (a).
Electric membership corporations.
Inclusion in definition "public utility," §62-110.1, (b).
Estimate of construction costs.
Condition for receiving certificate, §62-110.1, (e).
Required, §62-110.1, (a).
Exceptions, §62-110.1, (g).
Review of construction.
Ongoing review by commission, §62-110.1, (f).

GENERATION-SKIPPING TRANSFER TAX.
Amount, §105-32.7, (b).
Correct amount of tax payable, return reflecting.
Federal determination changing amount payable, §105-32.8.
Due date, §105-32.7, (c).
Imposition of tax, §105-32.7, (a).
Net value of property located in state, §105-32.7, (b).
Payment, §105-32.7, (c).
Return, §105-32.7, (c).
State percentage of tax, §105-32.7, (b).

GENERATORS.
Mechanical breakdown service agreement, §58-1-42.

GENERIC DRUGS.
Drug product selection.
Definitions, §90-85.27.

GENERIC DRUGS —Cont'd
Drug product selection —Cont'd
Equivalent drug product.
Defined, §90-85.27.
Price.
Limitation on selected drugs, §90-85.28, (c).
Selection by pharmacist, §90-85.28, (a).
Liability of prescriber and pharmacist not extended, §90-85.31.
Prescriber may permit or prohibit, §90-85.28, (b).
Liability of prescriber and pharmacist not extended, §90-85.31.
Prescriptions.
Label, §90-85.29.
Record, §90-85.30.

GENETIC IDENTIFICATION, §§15A-266 to 15A-270.
See DNA DATABASE AND DATABANKS.

GENETIC INFORMATION.
Employment discrimination based on, §95-28.1A.
Health insurance, §58-3-215.

GENETIC MARKERS.
Paternity, actions to establish, §49-14, (d).
Competency of tests, §8-50.1.

GENETIC TESTING.
Employment discrimination based on, §95-28.1A.
Paternity.
Expedited procedures to establish paternity in IV-D cases, §110-132.2.

GENTIANS.
Trespass.
Taking, etc., of certain wild plants from land of another, §14-129.

GEOGRAPHICALLY BASED FIELD PROGRAMS, §§7A-474.1 to 7A-474.5.
Access to civil justice act.
Definitions, §7A-474.2.
Eligible activities, §7A-474.3, (a).
Limitations, §7A-474.3, (c).
Eligible cases, §7A-474.3, (b).
Limitations, §7A-474.3, (c).
Eligible clients.
Defined, §7A-474.2.
Findings of general assembly, §7A-474.1.
Funding, §7A-474.4.
Legal assistants.
Defined, §7A-474.2.
Legal representation for indigent persons in certain civil matters.
Purposes, §7A-474.1.
Limitations on activities in cases, §7A-474.3, (c).
North Carolina state bar.
Funds authorized by law, §7A-474.4.
Purposes, §7A-474.1.
Records, §7A-474.5.
Reports, §7A-474.5.
Defined, §7A-474.2.

GEOGRAPHIC INFORMATION COORDINATING COUNCIL, §§143-725 to 143-727.
Center for geographic information and analysis.
Role, §143-725, (b).
Compensation of members, §143-727.

GEOGRAPHIC INFORMATION COORDINATING COUNCIL —Cont'd
Established, §143-725, (a).
Expenses of members, §143-727.
Meetings, §143-726, (e).
Members, §143-726, (a), (d).
Compensation, §143-727.
General assembly appointments, §143-726, (c).
Governor appointments, §143-726, (b).
Offensive geographic place-names.
Abrogation, §147-54.7.
Reports, §143-726, (g).
Scope of responsibility, §143-725, (a).
Secretary, §143-726, (f).
Staff support, §143-726, (f).
Standing committees, §143-726, (h).
Workgroups, §143-726, (h).

GEOLOGISTS, §§89E-1 to 89E-24.
Appeals.
Judicial review of final agency decision, §89E-20, (c).
Applicability of chapter, §89E-6.
Exemptions, §§89E-6, 89E-7, (b).
Attorney general.
Legal advisor to board, §89E-24.
Board for licensing of geologists.
Administration of chapter, §§89E-4, (a), 89E-5, (a).
Appointment of members, §89E-4, (b).
Attorney general.
Legal advisor of board, §89E-24.
Compensation, §89E-4, (g).
Composition, §89E-4, (d).
Enforcement of chapter, §89E-5, (a).
Expenditures.
Authorization, §89E-5, (e).
Payment, §89E-5, (e).
Expenses.
Reimbursement, §89E-4, (g).
Fees.
Establishment and collection, §89E-5, (g).
Governor.
Appointment of members, §89E-4, (b).
Removal of members, §89E-4, (b).
Meetings, §89E-5, (f).
Number of members, §89E-4, (b).
Officers, §89E-5, (b).
Personnel.
Authority to hire, §89E-4, (h).
Powers and duties.
Generally, §89E-5, (h).
Qualifications of members, §89E-4, (c).
Quorum, §89E-5, (b).
Records.
Maintaining, §89E-14, (a).
Register of applications for licensing.
Contents, §89E-14, (b).
Maintenance, §89E-14, (a).
Removal of members, §89E-4, (b).
Rules and regulations.
Adoption, §89E-5, (b).
Seal.
Adoption, §89E-5, (d).
State geologist.
Ex officio member, §89E-4, (b).
Terms of office, §89E-4, (e).
Expiration, §89E-4, (f).
Child support enforcement.
Forfeiture of licensing privilege, §50-13.12.
Citation of chapter, §89E-1.

GEOLOGISTS —Cont'd
Code of professional conduct.
Adoption, §89E-16.
Comity.
Licenses, §89E-11.
Complaints, §89E-17, (a).
Confidentiality.
Examination test scores, applications, etc., §89E-14, (c).
Corporations, §89E-7, (a).
Definitions, §89E-3.
Disciplinary procedures, §89E-19.
Civil penalty for violations, §89E-19, (c).
Civil action to recover, §89E-19, (d).
Grounds, §89E-19, (a).
Hearings, §89E-20.
Professional incompetence, §89E-19, (b).
Education.
Licenses.
Minimum qualifications, §89E-9.
Examinations.
Conducted by board, §89E-10, (a).
Fees, §89E-10, (b).
Professional competence, §89E-19, (b).
Qualifications for license, §89E-9.
Results.
Confidential, §89E-14, (c).
Fees.
Board.
Establishing and collecting, §89E-5, (g).
Examinations, §89E-10, (b).
Felony convictions.
Forfeiture of license, §15A-1331A.
Fines.
Civil penalty for license violations, §89E-19, (c).
Civil action to recover, §89E-19, (d).
Governor.
Board for licensing of geologists.
Appointment and removal of members, §89E-4, (b).
Grounds for discipline, §89E-19, (a).
Hearings.
Code of professional conduct.
Revision and amendment to code, §89E-16.
Disciplinary procedures, §89E-20, (a).
Incompetence, §89E-19, (b).
Injunctions.
Violation of chapter, §89E-23.
Investigations, §89E-17, (b).
Confidentiality of proceedings, §89E-17, (c).
Licenses.
Applications.
Contents, §89E-8.
Fees, §89E-8.
Register of applications, §89E-14, (b).
Comity, §89E-11.
Education.
Minimum qualifications, §89E-9.
Examination.
Qualifications of applicants, §89E-9.
Experience requirements, §89E-9.
Expiration, §89E-12, (b).
Issuance, §89E-12, (a).
Board, §89E-5, (c).
Lost, destroyed or mutilated.
Issuance and replacement of license, §89E-12, (c).
Qualifications of applicant.
Board to examine and pass on, §89E-5, (c).
Minimum qualifications, §89E-9.
Reciprocity, §89E-11.

GEOLOGISTS —Cont'd
Licenses —Cont'd
Renewal, §89E-12, (b).
Standards for licensing and renewal.
Establishment by board, §89E-5, (i).
Suspension or revocation.
Disciplinary procedures, §89E-19.
Felony convictions, §15A-1331A.
Reissuance, §89E-21.
Limitation of actions.
Real property improvements.
Recovery of damages for defective or unsafe conditions.
Six-year limitation, §1-50, (a).
Partnerships, §89E-7, (a).
Penalties.
Violation of chapter, §89E-22.
Petitions.
Hearings, §89E-20, (b).
Professional associations, §89E-7, (a).
Professional corporations, §55B-14, (b).
Prohibited acts, §89E-18.
Public policy, §89E-2.
Purpose of chapter, §89E-2.
Reciprocity.
Licenses, §89E-11.
Roster of licensed geologists, §89E-15.
Seals.
Board for licensing of geologists.
Adoption of seal, §89E-5, (b).
Design, §89E-13.
Required, §89E-13.
Use, §89E-13.
Short title of chapter, §89E-1.
State geologist.
Board for licensing of geologists.
Ex officio member, §89E-4, (b).
Unlawful acts, §89E-18.
Violation of chapter.
Injunctions, §89E-23.
Penalties, §89E-22.

GEORGIA HOME BOY.
Gamma hydroxybutyric acid (GHB).
Date rape drug, §90-89.

GETAWAY CARS.
Seizure and forfeiture of conveyances used in committing larceny and similar crimes, §14-86.1.

GHOST IN THE ATTIC, §39-50.

GIFT CERTIFICATES.
Unclaimed property generally, §§116B-51 to 116B-80.
See UNCLAIMED PROPERTY.

GIFTED CHILDREN.
Special education.
See SPECIAL EDUCATION.

GIFTS.
Agriculture.
Hall of fame.
Acceptance of gifts, §106-568.17.
Anatomical gifts, §§130A-402 to 130A-412.1.
See ANATOMICAL GIFTS.
Art.
Promotion of arts.
Acceptance of gifts by cultural resources department, §143-407.
Bees and honey.
Authority of board to accept, §106-637.

GIFTS —Cont'd
Community trust for persons with severe chronic disabilities.
Acceptance, §36A-59.15.
Constitution of the United States.
Foreign presents to United States officials, Const. U. S., art. I, §9.
Cultural resources department.
Promotion of arts.
Acceptance of gifts by department, §143-407.
Deeds.
Registration required, §47-26.
Donated food.
Inspections by department of agriculture and consumer services, §106-141.1.
Education.
Charitable gift annuities, §58-3-6.
State board of education.
Power to accept gifts, §115C-410.
Electrologists.
Acceptance by board of electrologist examiners, §88A-8.
Employment security.
Employment service division.
Acceptance and use of donations, §96-25.
Excise stamp tax on conveyances.
Exempted transfers, §105-228.29.
Exemptions.
Continuation of exemption of property, §1C-1604, (b).
Fairs.
State fair.
Constructing and financing facilities and improvements, §106-503.1, (c).
Foreign presents to United States officials, Const. U. S., art. I, §9.
Forests and forestry.
Acceptance of gifts of forest and submarginal farm land acquired by federal government, §113-34, (b).
Acceptance of gifts of land to state to be used as state forest, §113-34, (a).
Donations of property for forestry or park purposes, §113-40.
Agreements with federal government for agencies for acquisition, §113-40.
Governor.
Executive Mansion.
Department of cultural resources, §143-411.
Guardians.
Declaring revocable trust irrevocable and making gift of incompetent's life interest.
Approval of judge of superior court.
Authorized, §35A-1335.
Fact that incompetent had not previously made similar gifts, §35A-1337.
Prerequisites to approval, §§35A-1336, 35A-1336.1.
Hospitals.
Donation of surplus medical equipment, §131E-250, (a), (b).
Housing finance agency.
Receipt, administration and compliance with conditions and requirements of gift.
General power of agency, §122A-5.
Inter vivos.
Presumed absolute gift and not advancement, §29-24.
Intestate succession.
Advancements.
Gift inter vivos presumed absolute gift, §29-24.

GIFTS —Cont'd
Libraries.
Acceptance of gifts, bequests and endowments.
Powers and duties of department of cultural resources, §125-2.
Local government finance.
Regulation, Const. N. C., art. V, §4.
Management of institutional funds.
Gift instruments.
Construction and interpretation.
Rules of construction, §36B-3.
Defined, §36B-1.
Mentally ill.
Declaring trust irrevocable and making gift of life interest.
Approval of judge of superior court, §35A-1350.
Prerequisites, §35A-1351.
Authorization of declaration and gift, §35A-1350.
Legatees and devisees.
Who deemed specific and residuary legatees and devisees of incompetent, §35A-1352.
Minors.
Notice to minors, §35A-1353.
Objections to proposed declaration and gift, §35A-1354.
Prerequisites to approval of gift, §35A-1351.
Previously made gifts, §35A-1354.
State departments and agencies, §35A-1350.
Validity of declaration and gift, §§35A-1338, 35A-1355.
From income for certain purposes.
Approval of judge of superior court, §35A-1335.
Fact that incompetent had not previously made similar gifts, §35A-1337.
Prerequisites to approval, §§35A-1336, 35A-1336.1.
State departments and agencies.
Gifts from income of incompetent to departments and agencies, §35A-1335.
Validity of gift, §35A-1338.
From principal for certain purposes.
Approval of judge of superior court.
Fact that incompetent had previously made similar gifts, §35A-1344.
Prerequisites to approval, §§35A-1341, 35A-1341.1.
Legatees and devisees.
Fact that incompetent had previously made similar gifts, §35A-1337.
Notice to minors and incompetents, §35A-1343.
Objections to proposed gift, §35A-1344.
Who deemed specific and residuary legatees and devisees of incompetent, §35A-1342.
Validity of gift, §35A-1345.
Minors.
Transfers to minors.
General provisions, §§33A-1 to 33A-24.
See TRANSFERS TO MINORS.
Monuments and memorials.
Acceptance of commemorative funds for useful work, §100-8.
Mosquito control districts.
Acceptance of gifts or endowments.
Corporate powers of board of commissioners, §130A-355.
Municipal corporations.
Cemetery trustees.
Acceptance, §160A-349.12.

GIFTS —Cont'd
Nonprofit corporations.
Acceptance after mergers, §55A-11-07.
North Carolina museum of art.
Exemption from taxation, §140-5.16, (b).
Special fund, §140-5.16, (a).
North Carolina symphony society.
Counties and municipalities authorized to make contributions, §140-10.
Nurses.
Board of nursing.
Acceptance, §90-171.26.
Nutbush conservation area.
Authorization, §143-289.
Opticians.
Prohibited acts, §90-255.
Parks and recreation.
Acceptance of land for state forests, state parks, etc., §113-34, (a), (b).
Donation of property for park purposes, §113-40.
Pesticides.
Board.
Acceptance of gifts, §143-437.
Powers of attorney.
Authority of attorney-in-fact to make gifts, §32A-14.1.
Court order authorizing gift, §32A-14.10.
Appeal, §32A-14.11.
Costs and fees, §32A-14.12.
Statutory short form.
Powers conferred by, §32A-2.
Presumption of abandonment, time, §116B-53, (c).
Prisons and prisoners.
Acquisition of property, §148-3, (b).
Probate and registration.
Deeds of gift.
Registration required, §47-26.
Public lands.
Allocated state lands, §146-26.
Administration department, §146-27, (a).
Public officers and employees.
Benefiting from public contracts, §14-234, (a).
Public works.
Contractors.
Regulation of gifts and favors, §133-32, (a) to (d).
Public schools.
Endowment funds, §115C-492.
Riparian buffer protection program.
Acceptance of donated property, §143-214.22.
Roanoke Island historical association.
Authorization to accept, §143-202.
Sanitary districts.
Acceptance of gifts for nonprofit cemetery.
Corporate powers of sanitary district board, §130A-55.
Secretary of state.
International relations, authority to accept, §147-54.6, (b).
Southern growth policies agreement.
Board.
Acceptance of gifts, §143-496, (h).
State debt.
Regulation, Const. N. C., art. V, §3.
State departments and agencies.
Mentally ill.
Declaring revocable trust irrevocable and making of incompetent's life interest, §35A-1350.
Gifts from income of incompetents, §35A-1335.

GIFTS —Cont'd
State departments and agencies —Cont'd
Receipts from federal government and gifts not affected, §147-83.
State forests.
Governor authorized to accept gifts of land to state, §113-34, (a).
State treasurer.
Receipts from federal government and gifts not affected, §147-83.
State veterans home, §165-49, (b).
Tobacco trust fund commission.
Authority to accept, §143-718.
Transfers to minors.
General provisions, §§33A-1 to 33A-24.
See TRANSFERS TO MINORS.
Tryon's palace.
Restoration.
Acceptance and administration of gifts for restoration, §121-14.
Unclaimed property generally, §§116B-51 to 116B-80.
See UNCLAIMED PROPERTY.
Uniform transfers to minors act, §§33A-1 to 33A-24.
See TRANSFERS TO MINORS.
United States.
Foreign presents to United States officials, Const. U. S., art. I, §9.
University of North Carolina.
Board of governors.
Acceptance, §116-40.
Unsolicited merchandise.
When deemed gift to recipient, §75-27.
Utilities commission.
Members, commission employees or public staff.
Receiving or accepting, §62-327.
Western North Carolina arboretum.
Acceptance, §116-242.
Wildlife resources commission.
Commission may accept, §143-247.1.
Wills.
General gifts by will.
Execution of power of appointment, §31-43.
Zoological authority.
Cities and counties, §143-177.2.
Right to receive, §143-177.
Tax exemption, §143-177.1.

GIFTS TO MINORS.
General provisions, §§33A-1 to 33A-24.
See TRANSFERS TO MINORS.

GIFT TAX, §§105-188 to 105-197.1.
Annuities.
Manner of determining value, §105-195.
Applicability, §105-188, (b) to (d).
Minimum value, §105-188, (d).
Bond issues.
Port authority bonds.
Gain from transfer not exempt, §143B-456, (g).
Refunding obligations issued by state.
Gain from transfer not exempt from taxation, §142-29.6, (f).
State bonds, act authorizing not addressing exemption from taxation.
Not exempt from tax on gain from transfer, §142-12.
Charities.
Exemptions, §105-188, (h).
Collection of tax, §105-193.
Computation of tax, §105-188, (e).

GIFT TAX —Cont'd
Consideration.
Transfer for less than adequate and full consideration, §105-189.
Corrections and changes, §105-197.1.
Death.
Death of donor within three years.
Time for assessment, §105-194.
Exclusion.
Ten thousand dollar exclusion, §105-188, (d).
Exemptions, §105-188, (g), (h), (i).
Port authority bonds.
Gain from transfer not exempt, §143B-456.
Refunding obligations issued by state.
Gain from transfer not exempt from tax, §142-29.6, (f).
State bonds, act authorizing not addressing exemption from taxation.
Not exempt from tax on gain from transfer, §142-12.
Interest in land.
Value of interest less than absolute interest.
Manner of determining, §105-195.
Levy of taxes, §105-188, (a).
Liens, §105-193.
Life estates.
Manner of determining value, §105-195.
Nonresidents.
Applicability to gift made by nonresident, §105-188, (b).
Port authority bonds.
Gain from transfer not exempt, §143B-456, (g).
Powers of appointment.
General power of appointment.
Defined, §105-188.1, (a).
Holder deemed owner of interest, §105-188.1, (b).
Special power of appointment.
Computation of tax, §105-188.1, (d).
Exercise or relinquishment not deemed to constitute gift, §105-188.1, (c).
Property.
Fair market value of property, §105-190.
Qualified terminable interest property.
Inapplicability of tax to, §105-188, (j).
Qualified tuition programs, §105-188, (k).
Rates of tax, §105-188, (f).
Refunds.
Corrections and changes, §105-197.1.
Renunciation of property and fiduciary powers, §31B-1, (b).
Reports.
Changes, §105-197.1.
Returns.
Due date, §105-197, (b).
When return required, §105-197, (a).
State bonds, act authorizing not addressing exemption from taxation.
Not exempt from tax on gain from transfer, §142-12.
State refunding obligations.
Gain from transfer not exempt from tax, §142-29.6, (f).
Trusts and trustees.
Applicability of tax to gift in trust, §105-188, (b), (c).
Value of gift.
Actual value of property.
Tax to be assessed upon, §105-195.
Annuities.
Manner of determining value, §105-195.
Fair market value of property, §105-190.

GIFT TAX —Cont'd
Value of gift —Cont'd
Interest less than absolute interest.
Manner of determining value, §105-195.
Life estates.
Manner of determining value, §105-195.
Minimum value, §105-188, (d).

GINHOUSES.
Arson, §14-64.

GINSENG.
Larceny, §14-79.

GINSENG DEALERS.
Permits, §106-202.21.
Applications, §106-202.21, (b).
Expiration, §106-202.21, (b).
Issuance, §106-202.21, (e).
Notice of change of address, §106-202.21, (d).
Renewal, §106-202.21, (c).
Requirement of permit, §106-202.21, (a).

GIRL SCOUT GOLD AWARD.
Motor vehicle license plates.
Special plates for recipients, §20-79.4, (b).

GLANDERS.
Compensation for killing diseased animals.
Appraisal of animals affected with glanders, §106-325.
Control of livestock diseases.
Animals affected with glanders to be killed, §106-404.

GLASS.
Houses.
Amusement device safety generally, §§95-111.1 to 95-111.18.
See AMUSEMENT DEVICE SAFETY.
Insurance, §58-7-15.
Placing glass, etc., or injurious obstructions in road, §136-91.
Repair of motor vehicles, §§20-354 to 20-354.9.
See MOTOR VEHICLE REPAIRS.
Scrap, salvage or surplus dealers.
Failure to keep purchase records, §66-10, (b).

GLASSES.
Eyeglasses.
See EYEGLASSES.

GLASSHOUSES.
Amusement device safety generally, §§95-111.1 to 95-111.18.
See AMUSEMENT DEVICE SAFETY.

GLASS INSURANCE.
Authorized, §58-7-15.
Mandatory or voluntary risk sharing plans, §§58-42-1 to 58-42-50.
See MANDATORY OR VOLUNTARY RISK SHARING PLANS.

GLEANING.
Agriculture.
Exemption from civil liability for farmers permitting, §106-706.

GLOBAL TRANSPARK AUTHORITY, §§63A-1 to 63A-25.
Applicability of general laws, §63A-24.
Board of directors.
Appointment, §63A-3, (b).
Selection criteria, §63A-3, (c).
Bylaws, §63A-3, (h).
Compensation, §63A-3, (i).

GLOBAL TRANSPARK AUTHORITY —Cont'd
Board of directors —Cont'd
Composition, §63A-3, (b).
Dissolution of authority, §63A-25.
Office, §63A-3, (l).
Officers, §63A-3, (e).
Ordinances.
Adoption, §63A-7, (a).
Organization, §63A-3, (h).
Quorum, §63A-3, (h).
Removal of members, §63A-3, (g).
Terms of office, §63A-3, (d).
Treasurer, §63A-3, (j).
Vacancies, §63A-3, (f).
Bond issues.
Conditions, §63A-9, (b).
Financing agreements, §63A-13.
Hearings.
Conduct, §63A-12.
Interest, §63A-9, (a).
Interim receipts or temporary bonds, §63A-9, (i).
Investments.
Authorized investments, §63A-9, (o).
Issuance, §63A-9, (a).
Approval.
Certification, §63A-9, (g).
Local government commission, §63A-9, (f).
Resolution, §63A-9, (k).
Maturity, §63A-9, (c).
Officers.
Immunity, §63A-20.
Pledge of faith in credit of state.
Not to constitute debt secured by, §63A-9, (m).
Pledges to holders of bonds, §63A-9, (n).
Proceeds.
Investment, §63A-9, (k).
Use, §63A-9, (h).
Refunding bonds or notes, §63A-10.
Registration, §63A-9, (e).
Rights of holders, §63A-16.
Security, §63A-9, (j).
Security documents, §63A-14.
Signatures, §63A-9, (d).
Special user projects, §63A-11.
Taxation, §63A-9, (l).
Uniform commercial code.
Status under, §63A-17.
Commercial code.
Bond issues.
Status under code, §63A-17.
Conflicts of interest.
Members, officers or employees, §63A-21.
Counties.
Agreements to make payments to authority, §63A-15.
Creation, §63A-3, (a).
Definitions, §63A-2.
Dissolution, §63A-25.
Eminent domain.
Powers, §63A-6, (b).
Enforcement of chapter.
Rights of bondholders, §63A-16.
Executive director, §63A-3, (k).
Funds.
Deposits, §63A-8.
Expenditures, §63A-8.
General laws.
Applicability to authority, §63A-24.
Handicapped persons.
Goals for participation by, §63A-19.

GLOBAL TRANSPARK AUTHORITY —Cont'd
Hearings.
Bond issues, §63A-12.
Immunity.
Officers.
Issuance of bonds and notes, §63A-20.
Intent of chapter, §63A-1.
Interest.
Bond issues, §63A-9, (a).
Officers.
Conflicts of interest, §63A-21.
Immunity.
Issuance of bonds and notes, §63A-20.
Ordinances.
Adoption, §63A-7, (a).
Personnel system.
Exemption of employees, §126-5, (c1).
Police.
Special police officers.
Designation, §63A-7, (b).
Policies.
Determination, §63A-4, (b).
Powers.
General provisions, §63A-4, (a).
Police powers, §63A-7.
Racial minorities.
Goals for participation by, §63A-19.
Real property.
Acquisition.
Approval, §63A-6, (a).
Eminent domain, §63A-6, (b).
Eminent domain, §63A-6, (b).
Exchange, §63A-6, (c).
Site selection, §63A-6, (b).
Refunding bonds or notes, §63A-10.
Reports.
Annual and quarterly reports, §63A-23.
Sale of merchandise by governmental units.
Exception to provisions, §66-58, (b).
Short title of chapter, §63A-1.
Site selection, §63A-6, (b).
Special user projects.
Bond issues.
Financing agreements, §63A-13.
Security documents, §63A-14.
Bonds or notes, §63A-11.
Authorized, §63A-11, (a).
Contracts with private parties, §63A-11, (d).
Security for payment, §63A-11, (c).
Where payable from, §63A-11, (b).
Defined, §63A-2.
Financing agreements, §63A-13.
Security documents, §63A-14.
State departments and agencies.
Cooperation by, §63A-22.
Tax exemptions, §§63A-5, 63A-9, (l).
Women.
Goals for participation by, §63A-19.
Zoning.
Powers of authority, §63A-18.

GLOBAL TRANSPARK DEVELOPMENT ZONE, §§158-30 to 158-42.
Addition of counties to zone.
Amendment of certificate, §158-33.1, (e).
Application, §158-33.1, (b).
Approval, §158-33.1, (c).
Authority, §158-33.1, (a).
Commission resolution, §158-33.1, (d).
Payments in lieu of taxes, §158-33.1, (f).

GLOBAL TRANSPARK DEVELOPMENT ZONE —Cont'd
Certificate of incorporation.
Amendment.
Addition of counties to zone, §158-33.1, (e).
Effect, §158-33, (d).
Issuance by secretary of state, §158-33, (c).
Citation of article, §158-30.
Commission.
Compensation, travel, subsistence and reasonable per diem expenses, §158-35, (f).
Dual office holding, §158-35, (d).
Governing body of zone, §158-35, (a).
Majority vote to transact business, §158-36.
Members, §158-35, (a).
Officers, §158-35, (e).
Quorum, §158-36.
Removal, §158-35, (c).
Terms, §158-35, (b).
Vacancies, §158-35, (c).
Voting, §158-36.
Creation of zone, §158-33.
Definitions, §158-32.
Dissolution of zone and termination of existence, §158-41, (b).
Economic development powers of zone, §158-37, (b).
Evidence.
Certificate of incorporation as conclusive evidence on zone creation and establishment, §158-33, (d).
Exemption from taxation, §158-40.
Fiscal accountability, §158-38.
Funding of zone, §158-39.
Grants.
Authority to apply for, §158-39.
Hearings.
Public hearing on creation of zone, §158-33, (b).
Incorporation of zone, §158-33, (c).
Effect of incorporation, §158-33, (d).
Jurisdiction.
Territorial jurisdiction of zone, §158-34.
Local government finance.
Zone subject to provisions of chapter, §158-38.
Motor vehicles.
Registration tax on motor vehicles with tax situs within zone.
Administration of tax, §158-42, (d).
Amount, §158-42, (a).
Applicability of tax, §158-42, (a).
Distribution of proceeds, §158-42, (e).
Effective date, §158-42, (b).
Expiration, §158-42, (b).
Repeal of tax, §158-42, (c).
Use of tax proceeds, §158-42, (f).
Notice.
Public hearing on creation of zone, §158-33, (b).
Powers of zone, §158-37, (a).
Economic development power, §158-37, (b).
Property taxes.
Exemptions, §158-40.
Public hearing on creation of zone, §158-33, (b).
Public purpose.
Establishment and operation of zone constitutes, §158-39.
Purposes of article, §158-31.
Purposes of zone, §158-31.
Recordation.
Certificate of incorporation, §158-33, (c).
Resolution to create zone, §158-33, (a).
Resolution withdrawing from zone, §158-41, (a).

GLOBAL TRANSPARK DEVELOPMENT ZONE —Cont'd
Secretary of state.
Incorporation of zone, §158-33, (c).
Tax exemption, §158-40.
Tax on motor vehicles with tax situs within zone.
Registration tax, §158-42.
Termination of zone existence, §158-41, (b).
Territorial jurisdiction of zone, §158-34.
Title of article, §158-30.
Withdrawal of county from zone, §158-41, (a).

GLOVE COMPARTMENT OF MOTOR VEHICLE.
Open container law.
Passenger area of motor vehicle defined as including, §20-138.7, (f).

GLUE SNIFFING.
Toxic vapors generally, §§90-113.8A to 90-113.14.

GOATS.
Compensation for killing diseased animals generally, §§106-323 to 106-335.
See LIVESTOCK DISEASES.
Control of livestock diseases generally, §§106-400 to 106-405.
See LIVESTOCK DISEASES.
Dealer licensing generally, §§106-418.8 to 106-418.16.
See LIVESTOCK DEALER LICENSING.
Diseases generally.
See LIVESTOCK DISEASES.
Dogs killing goats.
Any person may kill, §67-14.
Meat inspections.
Generally, §§106-549.15 to 106-549.39.
See MEAT INSPECTIONS.
Pursuing or injuring with intent to steal, §14-85.
Quarantine of diseased animals generally.
See LIVESTOCK DISEASES.

GODWIN.
Satellite annexation.
Limitation on area of satellite corporate limits, inapplicability, §160A-58.1, (b).

GOING OUT OF BUSINESS SALES.
Closing-out sales, §§66-76 to 66-83.
See CLOSING-OUT SALES.

GOLD.
Brands and marks, §80-40.
Articles of gold plate, §80-42.
Violations of provisions.
Misdemeanors, §80-44.
Leases for digging gold required to be in writing, §22-2.
Precious metal dealers.
General provisions, §§66-163 to 66-173.
See PRECIOUS METAL DEALERS.

GOLDEN EAGLES.
Unlawfully taking, possessing, etc., §113-294, (l).

GOLDSBORO.
Condemnation of unsafe buildings, §§160A-425.1, 160A-426, (d), 160A-432, (a1).
Room occupancy tax.
Uniform provisions for municipalities authorized to levy, §160A-215.

GOLF CARTS.
Defined, §20-4.01.

GOLF CARTS —Cont'd
Division refusal of registration or issuance of certificate title, §20-54.
Sales and use tax.
Electric golf cart and battery charger.
Considered single article, §105-164.12A.

GOLF COURSES.
Alcoholic beverage permits.
Residential sports club permit, §18B-1006, (k).
Sports club defined to include, §18B-1000.
University of North Carolina and constituent institutions.
Information supplied legislative commission on government operations.
Prior to issuing debt or executing contract, §66-58, (h).

GONORRHEA.
Sexually transmitted diseases.
See VENEREAL DISEASES.

GOOD BEHAVIOR.
Prisoners.
Earned time credit, §15A-1355, (c).

GOOD CAUSE.
Continuance granting, §1A-1, Rule 40, (b).

GOOD CHARACTER, PROOF.
Change of name.
Filing with application, §101-4.

GOOD FAITH.
Abused, neglected or dependent juvenile reports or investigations.
Presumption in proceeding involving liability or person reporting, §7B-309.
Discharge papers.
Restricting access to military discharge documents.
Good faith immunity, §47-113.2, (k).
Durable power of attorney.
Incapacity or incompetence of principal.
Protection of person dealing in good faith with attorney-in-fact, §32A-9, (c).
Fiduciaries.
Thing done in good faith, §32-2, (b).
Nonprofit corporations.
Directors, discharging duties, §55A-8-30, (a).
Officers, §55A-8-42, (a).
Physicians and surgeons.
Fitness to practice reported or investigated.
Good faith immunity, §90-14, (f).
Principal and income act.
Conversion to uniturst.
Good faith immunity, §37A-1-104.8.
Sale of goods, UCC.
Definition of good faith, §25-2-103, (1).
Purchase of goods, §25-2-103.
Securities regulation.
Effect, §78A-49, (f).

GOOD FRIDAY.
Public holiday, §103-4, (a).

GOOD FUNDS SETTLEMENT ACT.
Applicability of chapter, §45A-2.
Citation of chapter, §45A-1.
Damages.
Violation of chapter, §45A-7.
Deeds.
Validity, §45A-6.
Definitions, §45A-3.
Dispersement of settlement proceeds, §45A-4.

GOOD FUNDS SETTLEMENT ACT —Cont'd
Lender.
Duties, §45A-5.
Loan documents.
Validity, §45A-6.
Purchaser.
Duties, §45A-5.
Scope of chapter, §45A-2.
Seller.
Duties, §45A-5.
Settlement agents.
Duties, §45A-4.
Short title, §45A-1.
Violations.
Penalties, §45A-7.

GOOD NEIGHBOR COUNCIL ACT, §§143B-391, 143B-392.

GOOD SAMARITAN STATUTES.
First aid or emergency treatment.
Nonliability, §90-21.14, (a), (b).
Conflict of laws, §90-21.14, (c).
Motor vehicle accidents, §20-166, (d).
Non-profit community health centers, §90-21.14, (a), (b).
Volunteer health care providers, §90-21.16.
Oil pollution and hazardous substances control.
Removal of oil discharges.
Limitation on liability of persons engaged in, §143-215.93A, (a).
Volunteer immunity, §§1-539.10, 1-539.11.

GOOD TIME CREDITS.
Prisons and prisoners.
Allowance of time and privileges, §148-13.

GOODWILL INDUSTRIES.
Property taxes.
Exclusion, §105-275.

GOOSEBERRIES.
Standard weight and measure, §81A-42.

GOVERNMENTAL IMMUNITY.
Agricultural finance authority, §122D-23.
Boards of education, local, §115C-42.
Claims against the state.
Affidavit of claimant, §143-297.
Settlement of claims, §143-295, (b).
Amateur sports, §143-299.3, (b).
Appeals.
Costs, §143-291.1.
Court of appeals, §143-293.
Supersedeas, §143-294.
Full commission, §143-292.
Transcript costs, §143-291.1.
Supersedeas.
Appeal to court of appeals to act as supersedeas, §143-294.
Attorney general.
Duties, §§143-298, 147-17, (b).
Employment of counsel in cases where state is interested, §147-17, (a).
Expenses, §143-298.
Burden of proof, §143-299.1.
Contributory negligence, §143-299.1.
Costs, §143-291.1.
Taxing, §143-291.2, (a).
Counterclaims by state, §143-291.3.
Court of appeals.
Appeals to, §143-293.
Supersedeas, §143-294.

GOVERNMENTAL IMMUNITY —Cont'd
Claims against the state —Cont'd
Damages, §143-291, (a), (a1).
Defenses, §143-299.1.
Determination of claim.
Notice, §143-292.
Docketing, §143-297.
Evidence.
Burden of proof, §143-299.1.
Fee assessments, §143-291.2, (b).
Hearings.
Industrial commission constitutes a court to hear and determine claims, §143-291, (a).
Notice, §143-297.
High School Athletic Association, Incorporated, §143-291, (c).
Industrial commission.
Constituted court to hear and determine claims, §143-291, (a).
Deputies, §143-296.
Evidence, §143-300.
Hearings, §143-297.
Limitations, §143-299.
Powers, §143-296.
Records, §143-300.
Rules and regulations, §143-300.
Rules of procedure, §143-300.
School buses, §143-300.1, (a).
Settlement of claims, §143-295.
School bus accidents, §143-300.1, (a).
Venue, §143-297.
Insurance purchases, §143-291, (b).
Limitation of actions, §143-299.
Maximum amount of payment, §143-299.2, (a), (b).
Motor vehicle title transfers, §143-295, (c).
Negligence.
Contributory negligence as defense, §143-299.1.
Notice.
Determination of claim, §143-292.
Hearings, §143-297.
Payment.
Maximum amount, §143-299.2, (a), (b).
Payment of state excess liability, §143-299.4.
Record destruction, §143-300.
School bus accidents, §143-300.1.
Defense of claim by attorney general, §143-300.1, (d).
Duties of attorney general, §143-300.1, (b).
Jurisdiction, §143-300.1, (a).
Payment of damages, §143-300.1, (c).
Procedure, §143-300.1, (a).
Settlement, §143-295.
Affidavit of complainant, §143-295, (b).
Maximum amount, §143-295, (a).
Smallpox vaccinations of state employees.
Claims arising from, §143-300.1A.
Subpoenas.
Issuance, §143-298.
Supersedeas.
Court of appeals to act as, §143-294.
Venue, §143-297.
Community colleges.
Negligence of agents and employees of institutions.
Waiver of governmental immunity by act obtaining liability insurance, §115D-24.
Counties.
Waiver of liability insurance.
Evidentiary effect, §153A-435, (b).
Emergency management, §166A-14, (a).

GOVERNMENTAL IMMUNITY —Cont'd
Federal remedy restoration act.
State employee suits against state.
Damage limitation, §143-300.35, (b).
Waiver of sovereign immunity, §143-300.35, (a).
Guardsmen, §127A-150, (a) to (c).
Medical examiners.
Corneal tissue removal, §130A-391, (b).
Mental health, developmental disabilities and substance abuse.
Area authorities.
Waiver of immunity as to torts of agents, employees and board members, §122C-152, (a) to (f).
Militiamen, §127A-150, (a) to (c).
Municipal corporations, §160A-11.
Exercise of corporate powers, §160A-12.
Tort liability.
Waiver of immunity through insurance purchase, §160A-485.
Rescue squads, volunteer, §90-21.14, (a), (b).
School bus drivers, §115C-255.
University of North Carolina.
Insurance.
Provisions not deemed to waive sovereign immunity of state, §116-221.

GOVERNMENT EMPLOYEES INTERCHANGE PROGRAM, §§126-51 to 126-58.
See PERSONNEL SYSTEM.

GOVERNOR.
Absence from state.
Acting governor, §147-11.1, (a), (c).
Acting governor, §147-11.1, (a), (b).
Actions against government.
Employment of counsel in cases where state is interested, §147-17, (a).
Payment of counsel, §147-17, (c).
Advocacy council on children and youth, §§143B-414 to 143B-416.
Alcoholic beverages.
State of emergency.
Powers of governor, §18B-110.
Archives and history.
Historical publications.
Editing and publishing of official messages and other papers of governor, §121-6, (b).
Security of historic properties.
Designated employees commissioned special peace officers by governor, §121-10, (a).
Attorneys at law.
Impracticability of representing state entity.
Advice to governor to employ outside counsel, §147-17.
Balanced growth policy act.
Citizen participation.
Governor to establish process, §143-506.11.
Designation of growth centers, §143-506.10.
Banks.
Holidays.
Power to proclaim banking holidays, §53-77.
Board of therapeutic recreation certification.
Appointment of members, §90C-5, (b).
Bond issues.
Council of state.
Duties performed by other officers, §142-9.
Books and papers.
General assembly.
Production before, §147-14.
Bounty hunters.
Authorized to employ, §15-53.

GOVERNOR —Cont'd
Budget.
Advisory budget commission.
Appointment of members, §143-4, (a).
Calling of meetings, §143-4, (c).
Borrowing money, §143-24.
Dismissals from office, §143-34.
Transfer between objects and line items in budget of, §143-23, (e1).
Child and youth advocacy council, §§143B-414 to 143B-416.
CLE exemption, Bar Rules & Regs., D, §.1517.
Closing forests and woodlands to fishing, hunting and trapping.
Authority of governor, §113-60.1.
Publication of proclamation, §113-60.2.
Violation of proclamation as misdemeanor, §113-60.3.
Commander in chief, Const. N. C., art. XII, §1.
Commissioner of banks.
Appointment, §53-92.
Compensation, §147-11.
Surviving spouses of governors, §147-32.
Composer-laureate for state.
Appointment, §143-407.1, (a).
Consolidation of state agencies.
Authority to direct agencies to consolidate, §147-13.1, (c).
Studies as to consolidation of agencies.
Authority to conduct, expenditure of funds, §147-13.1, (a), (b).
Continuing legal education exemption, Bar Rules & Regs., D, §.1517.
Contractors.
Plumbing, heating and fire sprinkler contractors.
Board of examiners.
Appointment of members, §87-16.
Contracts to obtain consultant services.
Approval required, §143-64.20, (b).
Findings to be made by governor, §143-64.21.
Council of state.
General provisions.
See COUNCIL OF STATE.
Council on educational services for exceptional children.
Appointment of members, §115C-121, (b).
Crime commission, §§143A-244, 143B-478 to 143B-480.
Transfer to department of crime control and public safety, §143A-244.
Delinquent and undisciplined juveniles.
Transferring juvenile from jail or penal facility to residential facility, §7B-2517.
Depositions.
Reading deposition on trial.
When deposition may be read on the trial, §8-83.
Detainers.
Designation of central administrator, §15A-766.
Disasters.
State of disaster.
Declaring, powers, §166A-6.
State of disaster assistance funds, §166A-6.01.
District court judges.
Vacancy in office.
Appointment from nominations submitted from district bar, §7A-142.
Duties.
Generally, §147-12, (a).
Elections, Const. N. C., art. III, §2.
Date of election, §163-1, (a).

GOVERNOR —Cont'd
Elections —Cont'd
Governor-elect and lieutenant governor-elect.
Office space and expenses, §147-31.1.
Summary of duties.
Counting votes, canvassing, abstracts and protests, §163-182.17, (f).
Vacancy in office.
Election to fill, §163-8.
Emergencies.
Energy crisis administration, §§113B-20 to 113B-24.
Evacuation of public buildings.
Power of governor to order evacuation, §14-288.19, (a).
Penalty for willful refusal to leave building, §14-288.19, (b).
State of emergency.
Alcoholic beverages.
Powers of governor, §18B-110.
Succession to office of governor, §147-11.1, (a) to (f).
Emergency management.
Mutual aid agreements.
Power to establish, §166A-10, (a).
Powers, §166A-5.
State of disaster.
Declaring, powers, §166A-6.
State of disaster assistance funds, §166A-6.01.
Emergency war powers.
Citation of article, §147-33.1.
Construction of article, §147-33.6.
Description of powers, §147-33.2.
Federal action controlling, §147-33.5.
Immunities granted, §147-33.4.
Orders, §147-33.3.
Powers.
Description, §147-33.2.
Rules and regulations, §147-33.3.
Short title, §147-33.1.
Endangering executive, legislative or court officers, §§14-16.6 to 14-16.10.
Electronic surveillance orders, §15A-290, (c4).
Energy crisis administration, §§113B-20 to 113B-24.
Execution sales.
Notification of governor, §1-339.55.
Executive Mansion.
Department of cultural resources.
Authority of department of administration not affected, §143-415.
Powers, §143-411.
Purposes, §143-410.
Generally, §147-10.
Western governor's mansion, §143-345.7.
Executive mansion fine arts committee.
Appointments, §143B-80.
Compensation of members, §143B-80.
Creation, §143B-79.
Meetings.
Regular and special meetings, §143B-80.1.
Members, §143B-80.
Powers and duties, §143B-79.
Quorum, §143B-80.
Regular and special meetings, §143B-80.1.
Selection of members, §143B-80.
Executive orders.
Orders creating boards, committees, councils or commissions.
Expiration of order, §147-16.2, (a).
Publication, §147-16.1.

GOVERNOR —Cont'd
Executive organization act of 1971.
See STATE DEPARTMENTS AND AGENCIES.
Executive organization act of 1973.
See STATE DEPARTMENTS AND AGENCIES.
Expenses.
Allowance, §147-11.
Lieutenant governor, §147-33.
Governor-elect and lieutenant governor-elect, §147-31.1.
Representation of governor's office.
Allowance to designated person, §147-11.
Extradition.
Duty, §15A-742.
Fugitives from other states.
Duty as to, §15A-722.
Investigation.
Governor may cause investigation to be made, §15A-724.
Generally, §§15A-721 to 15A-750.
See EXTRADITION.
Federal aid.
Highway safety act of 1966.
Contracts with United States government, §147-12, (a).
Forests and forestry.
Acceptance of gifts of land for state forests purposes, §113-34, (a).
Authority to close forests and woodlands to hunting, fishing and trapping, §§113-60.1 to 113-60.3.
General assembly.
Approval of bills, §120-29.1, (a).
Calculation of time for approval, §120-29.1, (d).
Failure to take action, §120-29.1, (b).
Objections of governor, §120-29.1, (c).
Books to be produced for general assembly, §147-14.
Executive officer's report to governor.
Reports transmitted to general assembly, §147-5.
Reconvening of legislature, Const. N. C., art. II, §22; art. III, §5.
Request that session not be held, §120-6.1, (a), (b).
Veto, Const. N. C., art. II, §22.
Geologists.
Board for licensing of geologists.
Appointment and removal of members, §89E-4, (b).
Gifts.
Executive Mansion.
Department of cultural resources, §143-411.
Land to be administered as state forests.
Authorization to accept, §113-34, (a).
Governor's administrative rules review commission.
Executive organization act of 1973.
Administrative services to commissions.
Provisions inapplicable to governor's administrative rules review commission, §143B-14.
Review of rules, §143B-2.
Governor's management council, §§143B-426.22, 143B-426.23.
Highway patrol.
Appointment of commanding officer, §20-185, (a).
Patrolmen assigned to governor's office, §20-189.
Housing authorities and projects.
Indian housing authority.
Powers of governor, §157-67.

GOVERNOR —Cont'd
Housing coordination and policy council, §§122A-5.10 to 122A-5.12.
Impeachment, Const. N. C., art. III, §3.
Chief justice.
Presiding officer, §123-2.
Inaugural ceremonies committee, §§143-532 to 143-539.
Indians.
Designation of Indian day, §147-18.
Institute of medicine.
Appointment of members, §90-470.
Internal improvements.
Control of internal improvements, §124-1.
Investigation of corporations.
Power of investigation, §124-7.
Proxies.
Appointment of proxies, etc., §124-6, (a).
Interstate compact for the supervision of adult offenders.
Execution of compact, §148-65.5.
Executive orders for implementation, §148-65.6, (f).
Interstate compact on the placement of children.
Appointment of compact administrator, §7B-3806.
Management council, §§143B-426.22, 143B-426.23.
Mentally ill.
Succession to office of governor, §147-11.1, (c).
Military affairs.
Commander in chief, Const. N. C., art. III, §5; art. XII, §1.
Militia.
Commander in chief of militia, §127A-16, (a).
Regulations prescribed, §127A-17.
Personal staff of governor, §127A-18.
State active duty status.
Power to place in, §127A-16, (b).
State defense militia.
Authority to organize and maintain state defense militia, §127A-80.
Cadre, §127A-81.
Motor vehicles.
Furnished with driver, §147-10.
Municipal corporations.
Council.
Filling vacancies on council, §160A-63.
National guard.
Distinguished service medal by governor, §127A-42.
Natural History Museum.
Advisory commission.
Appointment of members, §143B-344.18.
Nomination of officers.
Timely nominations required where legislative body must confirm, §147-16.3.
Notaries, §143A-23.
Office.
Space and expenses for governor-elect and lieutenant governor-elect, §147-31.1.
Office of the information technology services.
General provisions, §§147-33.75 to 147-33.103.
See INFORMATION TECHNOLOGY SERVICES.
Official correspondence.
Preservation, §147-14.
Oil pollution and hazardous substances control.
Offshore oil and gas activities, §143-215.94II.

GOVERNOR —Cont'd
Pardons.
Application made to governor in writing, §147-21.
Conditional pardon, §147-23.
Duties of governor when conditions of pardon violated, §147-24.
Duties, Const. N. C., art. III, §5.
Return to governor's office, §147-25.
Parks and recreation.
Gifts of land for state forests.
Acceptance by governor, §113-34, (a).
Pensions.
Surviving spouses, §147-32.
Personnel.
Appointment, §147-12, (a).
Competitive service.
Determination of competitive service by governor, §126-12.
Personnel system.
Exemption of employees of office of governor, §126-5, (c1).
Exempt policymaking positions, §126-5, (d).
Pest control.
Compact.
Executive head means governor, §106-65.61.
Pesticides.
Appointment of board, §143-436, (b).
Portraits.
Acquisition of portrait of governor during term of office, §121-13.
Presidential elections.
Appointment of electors, §163-213, (b), (c).
Prisons and prisoners.
Transfer of convicted foreign citizens under treaty.
Consent by governor, §148-122.
Transfer of property.
Governor to have final authority, §148-3, (a).
Private secretary.
Appointment, §147-14.
Salary, §147-15.
Probate and registration.
Sister state probates without governor's authentication, §47-80.
Publication of executive orders, §147-16.1.
Public health study commission.
Appointment of member, §120-197, (a).
Public lands.
Conveyances.
Approval, §146-74.
Deeds.
Signing of deeds, §146-75.
Employment of personnel, §146-67.
United States.
Acquisitions for and conveyances to federal government, §146-36.
Public officers and employees.
Appointments, §147-12, (a).
Public utilities.
Utilities commission.
Executive director, §62-15, (a).
Reconvening of legislature, Const. N. C., art. II, §22; art. III, §5.
Request that session not be held, §120-6.1, (a), (b).
Records, §147-16, (a).
Official government records.
Preservation, §147-14.
Reports.
State departments and agencies.
Certain institutions to report to governor, §143-156.

GOVERNOR —Cont'd
Residence, §147-10.
Western residence of the governor.
Repair and reconstruction, §143-345.7.
Retirement system for appellate division.
Emergency justices or judges.
Application to the governor, §7A-39.6.
Rewards.
Fugitives from justice.
Power to offer rewards, §§15-53, 15-53.1.
Richard Caswell memorial commission.
Department of cultural resources.
Transfer of commission to department, §143B-51.
Riots and civil disorders.
Evacuation of public buildings.
Penalty for willful refusal to leave building, §14-288.19, (b).
Power of governor to order evacuation, §14-288.19, (a).
Rules and regulations.
Emergency war powers, §147-33.3.
Salary, §147-11.
Administrative officers.
Governor to set salaries, §138-4.
Exceptions, §138-4.
Longevity pay, §138-4.
Lieutenant governor, §147-33.
Private secretary, §147-15.
School buses.
Use by state guard or national guard.
Request by governor, §115C-254.
School health advisory committee.
Appointment of members, §115C-81, (e).
Seals.
Affixing great seal, §147-27.
Courts.
Procuring seals for departments and courts, §147-28.
Custody of great seal of state, §147-12, (a).
Description.
Great seal, §147-26.
Great seal.
Affixing great seal, §147-27.
Dates appearing upon seal, §147-26.
Description, §147-26.
Destruction of old seal, §147-30.
Procuring great seal of state, §147-26.
New seals when necessary, §147-30.
Old seals.
Destruction, §147-30.
Procuring great seal of state, §147-26.
Secretary of state.
Seal of department of state.
Description, §147-29.
Secretary of state.
Duties.
Transfer of duties to department of secretary of state, §143A-23.
Powers.
Transfer to department of secretary of state, §143A-23.
Receiving documents from governor, §147-36.
Staff.
Appointment, §147-12, (a).
State banking commission.
Appointment of members, §53-92.
State board of education.
Appointment of members, §115C-10.
State boundaries.
Establishment of boundaries, §141-1.

GOVERNOR —Cont'd
State boundaries —Cont'd
Jurisdiction over territory within state, §141-6, (c).
Protection of boundaries, §141-1.
State debt.
Duties performed by other officers, §142-9.
Emergencies.
Borrowing on notes in emergencies, §142-16.
Signing certificates and bonds, §142-9.
State departments and agencies.
Bond issues.
Approval by governor, §143-165.
Consolidation of state agencies.
Powers of governor, §147-13.1, (a) to (c).
Executive organization act of 1973.
Continuation of powers and duties, §143B-5.
Policy-making authority and administrative powers of governor, §143B-4.
Powers and duties, §§143B-4, 143B-5.
Investigations.
Authority to direct, §143-159.
Conduct, §143-160.
Reports.
Certain institutions to report to governor, §143-156.
State of disaster.
Declaring, powers, §166A-6.
State of disaster assistance funds, §166A-6.01.
State treasurer.
Additional clerical assistance authorized, §147-86.
Succession to office, §147-11.1; Const. N. C., art. III, §3.
Acting governor generally, §147-11.1, (c) to (f).
Lieutenant governor, §147-11.1, (a).
President of senate, speaker of house or other officers, §147-11.1, (b).
Surviving spouse of governors.
Compensation, §147-32.
Term of office, §163-1, (a).
Thanksgiving day.
Designation, §147-19.
Transportation department.
Annual reports to governor, §136-11.
United States.
Highway safety act of 1966.
Contracts with United States government, §147-12, (a).
University of North Carolina.
Board of governors.
Member emeritus, serving on board after serving as governor, §116-6, (g).
Vacancy in office.
Filling, §163-8.
Veto, Const. N. C., art. II, §22.
War powers act, §§147-33.1 to 147-33.6.
Work first program.
Duty to sign state plan and submit to federal officials, §108A-27.10, (c).

GOVERNOR MOREHEAD SCHOOL, §§143B-164.10 to 143B-164.17.
ABC's program.
Annual performance goals, §143B-146.3.
Defined, §143B-146.1, (b).
Participation, §143B-146.2.
Admission of pupils, §143B-164.13.
Nonresidents, §143B-164.14.
Age.
Compulsory attendance, §115C-383, (a).

GOVERNOR MOREHEAD SCHOOL —Cont'd
Board of directors.
Chairman, §143B-164.12, (b).
Clerical and other assistants provided by secretary of department, §143B-164.12, (e).
Created, §143B-164.11, (a).
Expense reimbursement, §143B-164.12, (d).
Meetings, §143B-164.12, (c).
Membership, §143B-164.12, (a).
Powers and duties, §143B-164.11, (a).
Private nonprofit corporations to support institution.
Encouragement, §143B-164.11, (c).
Quorum, §143B-164.12, (c).
Rulemaking, §143B-164.11, (a), (b).
Vice-chairman, §143B-164.12, (b).
Calendars, §143B-146.11.
Clothing or traveling expenses.
Counties paying for, §143B-164.17.
Compulsory attendance, §115C-383, (a).
Criminal history checks of personnel, §143B-146.16.
Diplomas or marks of achievement.
Conferring upon graduates, §143B-164.15.
Dispute resolution, §143B-146.15.
Education programs in residential schools.
Generally, §§143B-146.1 to 143B-146.21.
See EDUCATION.
Incorporation, §143B-164.10.
Low-performing residential schools, §§143B-146.5 to 143B-146.9.
Dismissal of administrators and teachers at residential schools identified as low-performing, §115C-325, (p1).
Managed by department of health and human services and director of school, §143B-164.10.
Minimum attendance, §115C-383, (a).
Mission, §143B-146.1.
Name, §143B-164.10.
Nonresidents.
Admission of pupils from other states, §143B-164.14.
Parent, guardian or custodian.
Failure to enroll child, §115C-383, (b).
Failure to send child to school, §115C-383, (c).
Private nonprofit corporations to support institution.
Encouragement by board of directors, §143B-164.11, (c).
Establishment, §143B-164.18.
Reports on blind children.
Local school superintendents, §115C-383, (d).
School improvement plans, §143B-146.12.
School technology plans, §143B-146.13.
Treasurer of institution.
State treasurer ex officio treasurer, §143B-164.16.

GOVERNOR RICHARD CASWELL MEMORIAL COMMISSION.
Department of cultural resources.
Transfer of commission to department, §143B-51.

GOVERNOR'S ADVISORY COUNCIL ON AGING, §§143B-180, 143B-181.

GOVERNOR'S ADVOCACY COUNCIL ON CHILDREN AND YOUTH, §§143B-414 to 143B-416.

GOVERNOR'S COUNCIL ON PHYSICAL FITNESS AND HEALTH, §§130A-33.40, 130A-33.41.

GOVERNOR'S CRIME COMMISSION, §§143B-478 to 143B-480.
Transfer to department of crime control and public safety, §143A-244.

GOVERNOR'S MANAGEMENT COUNCIL, §§143B-426.22, 143B-426.23.

GRADE CROSSINGS.
Controlled-access facilities.
Elimination of grade crossings, §136-89.53.
Elimination or safeguarding of crossings, §136-20.
Railroad grade crossings.
Motor vehicle traffic regulation generally, §§20-142.1 to 20-142.5.
See RAILROAD GRADE CROSSINGS.

GRADES AND GRADING.
Eggs, §§106-245.14 to 106-245.16.
Farm products marketing and branding.
Aggregate state service credit for graders, §106-190.1.
Authorized graders, §106-190.
Certificate of grade.
Prima facie evidence, §106-192.
Establishment and maintenance of standard grades, §§106-185, (a), 106-188.
Milk, §§106-267, 106-268, 106-268.1.
Poultry and poultry products, §106-546.

GRAHAM COUNTY.
Ambulances.
Attachment or garnishment and lien for, §§44-51.4 to 44-51.8.
Obtaining ambulance services without intending to pay, §14-111.2.
Requesting ambulances falsely, §14-111.3.
Board of county commissioners.
Filling vacancies on board, §153A-27.1.
Condemnation or acquisition of land by local government unit outside county.
Consent of board of commissioners necessary, §153A-15.
Coroner elected as nominee of political party.
Filling vacancy in office, §152-1.
Counties generally.
See COUNTIES.
County boards of education elected on partisan basis.
Vacancies in office, §115C-37.1.
Dog collars.
Unlawful removal of electronic dog collars, §14-401.17.
Foxes, open seasons for taking.
Wildlife resources commission authorized to continue from year to year, §113-291.4, (f1).
Oil, gas or mineral interest separated from surface interest, extinguished, title in surface fee holder.
Failure to list interest for tax purposes for 10 years prior to January 1, 1974.
Protection of interest from surface estate, §1-42.3, (d).
Registration of deeds.
Tax certification, no delinquent taxes due, §161-31, (b).
School property.
Acquisition and improvement, §153A-158.1.
Sheriff.
Vacancy, performance of duties until vacancy filled, §162-5.1.

GRAHAM COUNTY —Cont'd
Western North Carolina Development Association, Inc.
Appropriation of funds to, §153A-447, (a), (b).
Western North Carolina regional economic development commission, §158-8.1.

GRAIN.
Adulteration, §§106-621 to 106-628.
See GRAIN ADULTERATION.
Commodities.
General provisions, §§78D-1 to 78D-33.
See COMMODITIES.
Larceny.
Ungathered crops, §14-78.
Liens.
Effective period, §44-69.1.

GRAIN ADULTERATION.
Applicability of article, §106-628.
Commissioner.
Defined, §106-621.
Sign furnished by commissioner, §106-624.
Defenses.
Nonposting not a defense, §106-626.
Definitions, §106-621.
Determination of adulteration, §106-627.
Sampling and analysis, §106-627.
Penalties, §106-623.
Posting of sign, §106-625.
Nonposting not a defense, §106-626.
Prohibited acts, §106-622.
Sampling and analysis.
Determination of adulteration, §106-627.
Signs.
Furnished by commissioner, §106-624.
Nonposting not a defense, §106-626.
Posting of sign, §106-625.
Terms of article, §106-628.
Unlawful acts, §106-622.

GRAIN ALCOHOL.
Use for compounding, mixing or preserving medicines or medical preparations.
Exemptions from alcoholic beverage control regulations, §18B-103.

GRAIN DEALERS, §§106-601 to 106-615.
Bond.
Application for license, §106-604.
Action on bond, §106-605, (b).
Execution of bond, §106-605, (a).
Exemption, §106-604.
Form of bond, §106-605, (a).
Terms of bond, §106-605, (a).
Commissioner.
Authority to investigate, §106-612.
Defined, §106-601, (b).
Decal on truck or tractor-trailer unit, §106-606.
Definitions.
Cash buyer, §106-601, (a).
Commissioner, §106-601, (b).
Department, §106-601, (c).
Grain, §106-601, (d).
Grain dealer, §106-601, (e).
Person, §106-601, (f).
Producer, §106-601, (g).
Injunction for violations of article, §106-615.
Investigations.
Authority to investigate, §106-612.
Licenses.
Application for license, §106-603.
Bond required, §106-604.
Action on bond, §106-605, (b).

GRAIN DEALERS —Cont'd
Licenses —Cont'd
Application for license —Cont'd
Bond required —Cont'd
Execution, terms and form of bond, §106-605, (a).
Exemption, §106-604.
Fee, §106-604.
Bond required, §106-604.
Action on bond, §106-605, (b).
Execution, terms and form of bond, §106-605, (a).
Exemption, §106-604.
Decal on truck or tractor-trailer unit, §106-606.
Denial.
Procedure, §106-611, (a).
Fees, §106-604.
Disposition of fees, §106-608.
Renewal of license, §106-607.
Grounds for refusal, suspension or revocation of license, §106-610.
Operation without license unlawful, §106-615.
Injunction for violation, §106-615.
Posting of license, §106-606.
Refusal of license.
Grounds for refusal, §106-610.
Renewal of license, §§106-603, 106-607.
Fees, §106-607.
Disposition of fees, §106-608.
Required, §106-602.
Revocation of license.
Grounds for revocation, §106-610.
Obtaining another license, time period, §106-611, (b).
Procedure, §106-611, (a).
Suspension of license.
Grounds for suspension, §106-610.
Procedure, §106-611, (a).
Time limit, §106-611, (b).
Misdemeanors, §106-614.
Recorders to be kept by dealers, §106-609.
Rules and regulations.
Adoption, §106-613.
Uniform scale ticket.
Board may prescribe form, §106-609.
Injunction, §106-615.

GRAIN MILLS.
Mills generally, §§73-1 to 73-28.
See MILLS.

GRAIN STORAGE FACILITIES.
Sales and use tax.
Rate on sales, §105-164.4A.

GRAMM-LEACH-BLILEY ACT.
Affiliations between depository institutions and insurers, §58-19-2.

GRANARIES.
Arson, §14-62.

GRANDCHILDREN.
Adoption, §50-13.2A.
Biological grandparent, §50-13.2A.
Child custody and visitation.
Grandparents visitation rights, §§50-13.2, (b1), 50-13.5, (j).
Incest, §14-178.

GRAND JURY.
Challenges to panel.
Provisions governing, §15A-622, (a).

GRAND JURY —Cont'd
Confidentiality of information.
Bill of indictment, §15A-623, (f).
Disclosure of information.
Contempt, §15A-623, (g).
Secrecy of proceedings, §15A-623, (e).
Constitution of the United States, Const. U. S., amd. V.
Contempt.
Confidentiality of information.
Unauthorized disclosures, §15A-623, (g).
Continuing criminal enterprise.
Examination of witnesses by prosecutor, §15A-623, (h).
Petition for convening of grand jury, §15A-622.
Defined, §15A-621.
Deliberations, secret listening, §§14-227.2, 14-227.3.
Discharge of grand jurors, §15A-622, (c).
Drugs.
Controlled substances.
Examination of witnesses by prosecutor, §15A-623, (h).
Petition for convening of grand jury, §15A-622.
Duties, §15A-628, (a).
Evidence, rules of.
Inapplicability, §8C-1, Rule 1101, (b).
Excusing grand juror from service, §15A-622, (d).
Facts.
Exclusive judge of fact, §15A-624, (a).
Fees.
Uniform fees for jurors, §7A-312.
Foreman.
Appointment, §15A-622, (e).
Duties, §15A-623, (b), (c).
Oaths.
Form of oath, §11-11.
Signature.
Indictments.
Signature attesting concurrence of twelve or more grand jurors, §15A-644, (a).
Presentments.
Signature of foreman attesting concurrence of twelve or more grand jurors, §15A-644, (c).
Impaneling, §15A-622, (b).
Provisions governing, §15A-622, (a).
Second grand jury, §15A-622, (b).
Indictments.
Confidentiality of information.
Bill of indictment, §15A-623, (f).
Foreman.
Signature, §15A-644, (a).
Notice.
True bill of indictment.
Notice to defendant, §15A-630.
Number of members required to concur, §15A-623, (a).
Return of bill of indictment, §15A-628, (a), (c).
Not true bill, §15A-628, (a).
Institution of new charge, §15A-629, (b).
Procedure upon finding of not true bill, §15A-629, (a).
True bill, §15A-628, (a).
Notice to defendant, §15A-630.
Submission of bill of indictment by prosecutor, §15A-627, (a).
Offenses within original jurisdiction of superior court, §15A-627, (b).

GRAND JURY —Cont'd
Indictments —Cont'd
True bill.
Return as not true bill, §15A-628, (a).
Institution of new charge, §15A-629, (b).
Procedure upon, §15A-629, (a).
Return as true bill, §15A-628, (a).
Notice to defendant, §15A-630.
Validity inquiry.
Testimony of jurors, §8C-1, Rule 606.
Instructions to grand jurors, §15A-622, (f).
Interpreters.
Permitted in grand jury room during proceedings, §15A-623, (d).
Investigations.
Powers, §15A-628, (a).
Journalist's qualified privilege, §8-53.11.
Judges.
Presiding or convening judge as legal advisor, §15A-624, (b).
Judicial department.
Superior court division.
Sessions of court in cities other than county seats, §7A-42, (e).
Meetings.
Meetings of public bodies.
Exceptions to provisions, §143-318.18.
Notice.
Indictments.
Notice to defendant of true bill of indictment, §15A-630.
Number of grand jurors, §15A-621.
Actions or decisions.
Number required to concur, §15A-623, (a).
Oaths.
Foreman and other grand jurors, §15A-622, (f).
Form of oath, §11-11.
Persons permitted in grand jury room.
Oath of secrecy, §15A-623, (d).
Officers.
Oaths.
Form of oath, §11-11.
Persons permitted in grand jury room during proceedings, §15A-623, (d).
Powers, §15A-628, (a), (b).
Reconvening, §15A-622, (g).
Records.
Matters returned by grand jury to judge.
Clerk to keep, §15A-628, (d).
Rules of evidence.
Inapplicability, §8C-1, Rule 1101, (b).
Secrecy, §15A-623.
Selection of grand jurors, §15A-622, (b).
Provisions governing, §15A-622, (a).
Shortening term of grand jury, §15A-622, (b).
Subpoenas.
Witnesses, §15A-626, (e).
Superior court division of judicial department.
Sessions of court in cities other than county seats, §7A-42, (e).
Venue.
Indictment or presentment, §15A-631.
War.
Presentment as dispensable in certain cases, Const. U. S., amd. IV.
Witnesses, §15A-626.
Deposing before grand jury.
Form of oath of witness, §11-11.
Immunity, §15A-1053.
Members of grand jury, §15A-626, (c).
Prosecution witnesses, §15A-626, (b).

GRAND JURY —Cont'd
Witnesses —Cont'd
Right to call witness or appear as witness, §15A-626, (a), (d).
Subpoenas, §15A-626, (e).

GRAND LARCENY.
Larceny generally, §§14-70 to 14-86.1.
See LARCENY.

GRAND LODGE OF ANCIENT, FREE AND ACCEPTED MASONS OF NORTH CAROLINA.
Property tax exclusion, §105-275.

GRANDPARENTS.
Abortion.
Parental consent to abortion.
Consent of grandparent when minor living with required, §90-21.7, (a).
Adoption.
Action by biological grandparents, §50-13.2A.
Visitation rights of biological grandparents of adoptee, §48-1-106, (f).
Child custody and visitation.
Adoption proceedings, §50-13.2A.
Grandparent defined, §50-13.5, (j).
Visitation rights, §§50-13.2, (b1), 50-13.5, (j).
Incest, §14-178.

GRANITE.
State rock, §145-10.

GRANITE FALLS.
Board of election not abolished, §163-280.1.
Elections.
Conducted by town, request that county board of elections conduct, §163-285, (a).

GRANTS.
Alcoholism.
Research authority.
Applications for grants, §122C-433.
Archives and history.
Department of cultural resources, §121-12.1.
Responsibility for administering appropriations for grants-in-aid, §121-12.1.
Expending appropriations for grants-in-aid, §121-12.2.
Bees and honey.
Authority of board to accept, §106-637.
Blind persons.
Aid to the blind.
Affording maximum federal aid, §111-29.
Federal aid, §111-24.
Rehabilitation center for the blind and visually impaired.
Authority to receive federal grants-in-aid, §111-6.1.
Block grants.
Block grant plans.
Submission by agency receiving federal grants, §143-16.1, (b).
Department of administration duties and powers, §143-341.
Burke county.
Copies of grant.
Admission into evidence, §8-10.
Children's health insurance program.
Outreach efforts, §108A-70.26, (b).
Clean water revolving loans and grants, §§159G-1 to 159G-18.
Coastal area management.
Planning grants, §113A-112.

GRANTS —Cont'd
Community colleges.
Federal contracts and grants, §115D-58.1.
Counties.
Contracts.
Acceptance of grants and loans from other governments, §153A-14.
Public health or mental health grants from federal government.
Recovery of indirect costs on certain grants by counties, §130A-8, (a).
Exception, §130A-8, (b).
Criminal justice education and training standards.
Authority to accept, §17C-12.
Domestic violence.
Domestic violence center fund, §50B-9.
Economic and community development department.
Block grants, §143B-437.04.
Main street financial incentive fund.
Application for grants and loans, §143B-472.35, (c), (d), (e).
Power to apply for and accept, §143B-431, (d).
Education.
State board of education.
Power to accept grants, §115C-410.
Electric membership corporations.
Application for grant or loan from governmental agency, §117-26.
Electrologists.
Acceptance by board of electrologist examiners, §88A-8.
Employment and training grant program.
Workforce development, §143B-438.13.
Energy.
Policy act of 1975.
Council.
Authority to apply and utilize, §113B-11, (c).
Evidence.
See EVIDENCE.
Facility authorities.
Powers of authority, §160A-480.4.
Family preservation.
Awarding to local agencies, §143B-150.6, (d).
Financing family preservation services, §143B-150.5, (c).
Fishery resource grant program, §113-200.
General assembly.
Legislative commissions and committees.
Applying for, receiving or accepting, §120-32.03, (a), (b).
Global TransPark development zone.
Authority to apply for, §158-39.
Health.
Federal public health or mental health grants.
Counties to recover indirect costs, §130A-8, (a).
Applicability of section, §130A-8, (b).
Grants-in-aid, §130A-7.
Public health or mental health grants from federal government.
Counties to recover indirect costs on certain grants, §130A-8, (a).
Health and human services department.
Requests for grants by head of department, §143B-139.2.
Hospital authorities.
Contracts with federal government, §131E-27.
Hospitals.
Construction and enlargement of local hospitals, §131E-70, (c), (e).

GRANTS —Cont'd
Housing finance agency.
Receipt, administration and compliance with conditions and requirements of grant.
General power of agency, §122A-5.
Job development investment grant program, §§143B-437.50 to 143B-437.63.
Justice department.
Justice academy, §17D-3.
Local government finance.
Anticipation notes, §§159-171, 159-172.
Defined, §159-13.2, (a).
Ordinances, §§159-13.2, 159-17.
Mental health, developmental disability, substance abuse.
Area authorities.
Appropriations.
Allocation of funds, §122C-147.1, (d).
Moore county.
Copies of grants.
Admission into evidence, §8-11.
Mosquito control districts.
Receipt of federal and state grants.
Corporate powers of board of commissioners, §130A-355.
Municipal corporations.
Joint municipal electric power and energy act.
Government grants, §159B-32.
Urban development action grants, §160A-457.1.
Non-state entities receiving state funds.
Accounting of receipts and expenditures.
Annual filing required of grantee, §143-6.1, (c).
Audit oversight, state auditor, §143-6.1, (f).
Audit reports.
Annual filing by grantee, §143-6.1, (d).
Description of activities and accomplishments.
Annual filing by grantee, §143-6.1, (d).
Disbursement of funds, §143-6.1, (a).
Failure of grantee to comply.
Report on, §143-6.1, (d3).
Federal reporting requirements, §143-6.1, (e).
Financial statement.
Annual filing by grantee, §143-6.1, (d).
Grantee defined, §143-6.1, (a).
Grantee responsibilities, §143-6.1, (b1).
Receipt and expenditure reports.
Annual filing required of grantee, §143-6.1, (c).
State agency responsibilities, §143-6.1, (b).
State auditor's responsibilities, §143-6.1, (d1).
Unauthorized expenditures.
Action by director of budget, §143-6.1, (a1).
Use or expenditure of funds, §143-6.1, (a).
Verification of compliance with report requirements.
Prior to disbursement, §143-6.1, (d2).
Non-state entities receiving state funds (eff 7/1/2005).
Actions to recover state funds, §143-6.2, (k).
Audit oversight, §143-6.2, (h).
Definitions, §143-6.2, (a), (b).
Disbursement and use of state funds, §143-6.2, (a).
List submitted by grantor state agencies, §143-6.2, (j).
Non-state entity defined, §143-6.2, (a).
Report, §143-6.2, (i).
Rules to ensure uniform administration.
Adoption, §143-6.2, (d) to (f).
Suspension of disbursement, §143-6.2, (g).
Unauthorized use or expenditure.
Action by director of budget, §143-6.2, (c).

GRANTS —Cont'd
Nutbush conservation area.
Authorized, §143-289.
Onslow county.
Copies of grants.
Admission into evidence, §8-12.
Pollution control.
Sedimentation pollution control act of 1973.
Commission authorized to receive financial and other assistance, §113A-63.
Public lands.
See PUBLIC LANDS.
Roanoke Island historical association.
Authorization to accept, §143-202.
Secretary of state.
Certified copies.
Admission into evidence of copies certified by secretary, §8-6.
Validation of copies of grants certified by clerk, §8-9.
Shellfish.
Cultivation of shellfish.
Leases, §§113-202, 113-206.
Registration of grants in navigable waters, §113-205, (a).
Sheriffs' education and training standards commission, §17E-10.
Site development, §143B-437.02.
Small business contractor act, §§143B-472.85 to 143B-472.97.
Solid waste management.
Used oil.
Grants to local governments, §130A-309.22, (a) to (d).
Telephone membership corporations.
Loans or grants from federal agencies, §117-32.
Urban redevelopment.
Action grants, §160A-457.1.
White goods management account.
Grants to local government, use of account for, §130A-309.83, (b) to (d).
Workforce development.
Employment and training grant program, §143B-438.13.
Zoological authority.
Cities and counties, §143-177.2.
Right to receive, §143-177.
Taxation.
Exemption, §143-177.1.

GRANVILLE COUNTY.
Ambulance service.
Attachment or garnishment and lien for, §§44-51.4 to 44-51.8.
Blank or master forms of mortgages, deeds of trust, etc.
Indexing and recording, inapplicability of provisions, §47-21.
Condemnation or acquisition of land by local government unit outside county.
Consent of board of commissioners necessary, §153A-15.
Game laws, local acts not repealed, §113-133.1, (e).
Maps in special proceedings, recording of photographic copies, §§47-32, 47-32.2.
Multi-county water conservation and infrastructure district.
Generally, §158-15.1.

GRANVILLE COUNTY —Cont'd
Nutbush conservation area.
Annual contributions to department of environment and natural resources, §143-289.
On-premises unfortified wine licenses.
Discretion to decline to issue, §105-113.71, (b).
Probates and registration orders before clerks of inferior courts validated, §47-59.
Registration of deeds.
Tax certification, no delinquent taxes due, §161-31, (b).
Room occupancy tax levied by county, uniform provision, §153A-155.
Special police force for territory of Camp Butner reservation.
Jurisdiction, §122C-408.
Water and sewer system within Camp Butner reservation, §122C-407, (b).
Wild plants, taking of certain plants from land of another.
Inapplicability of provisions, §14-129.

GRAPE GROWERS COUNCIL, §§106-750, 106-751.
Appointment of members, §106-751, (a).
Chairman, §106-751, (d).
Clerical and other services, §106-751, (c).
Compensation of members, §106-751, (b).
Composition, §106-751, (a).
Creation, §106-750.
Duties, §106-750.
Expenses of members, §106-751, (b).
Meetings, §106-751, (f).
Per diem of members, §106-751, (b).
Powers, §106-750.
Qualifications of members, §106-751, (a).
Quorum, §106-751, (g).
Secretary, §106-751, (e).
Terms of members, §106-751, (a).
Vacancies.
Filling, §106-751, (a).

GRAPES.
Growers council, §§106-750, 106-751.
Weights and measures.
Standard weights and measures, §81A-42.

GRAPHIC ART.
Artwork on consignment, §§25C-1 to 25C-5.
Sale of prints, §§25C-10 to 25C-16.

GRASS.
Criminal trespass.
Setting fire to grass, §14-136.
Fire.
Setting grass on fire, §§14-136 to 14-140.1.
Criminal trespass, §14-136.
Marijuana.
See MARIJUANA.
Seed.
Weights and measures, §81A-42.
Setting fire to grass, brushlands and woodlands, §§14-136 to 14-140.1.

GRASSROOTS ARTS PROGRAM, §§143B-121 to 143B-125.
Adoption of procedures and rules, §143B-123.
Agents, §143B-124.
Counties.
Distribution of funds for counties without organizations meeting department standards, §143B-125.
Distribution of funds, §§143B-122, 143B-125.

GRASSROOTS ARTS PROGRAM —Cont'd
Establishment, §143B-121.
Funds.
Designation of organization as official distributing agent, §143B-124.
Disposition of funds for counties without organizations meeting department standards, §143B-125.
Distribution, §143B-122.
Standards for qualification, §143B-123.
Procedures.
Adoption, §143B-123.
Standards for qualification for funds, §143B-123.

GRASS SEED.
Weights and measures.
Standard weights and measures, §81A-42.

GRAVESTONES.
Decedents' estates.
Authorized expense of estate, §28A-19-9.
Inscription charging crime, §14-401.3.

GRAVEYARDS.
Cemeteries generally.
See CEMETERIES.
Monuments and memorials, §§100-2 to 100-19.
See MONUMENTS AND MEMORIALS.

GREASES.
Brands and marks.
Juggling mark prohibited, §119-10.
Mixing different brands for sale under standard trade name prohibited, §119-11.
Lubricating oils.
See LUBRICATING OILS.
Penalties.
Aiding and assisting in violation of article, §119-12.
Misdemeanor offenses, §119-13.
Sales.
Advertised name.
Prohibited sale of lubricants different from advertised name, §119-8.
Brands for sale.
Mixing different brands for sale under standard trade name prohibited, §119-11.
Deceptive sale of lubricants as to quality, etc., prohibited, §119-7.
Trademarks.
Juggling trademarks prohibited, §119-10.
Trade names.
Juggling trade names prohibited, §119-10.
Mixing different brands for sale under standard trade name prohibited, §119-11.

GREAT SMOKY MOUNTAINS NATIONAL PARK.
National park, parkway and forest development council, §§143B-324.1 to 143B-324.3.

GREEK INDEPENDENCE DAY.
Public holiday, §103-4, (a).

GREENBELT LAW.
Agricultural, horticultural and forestland, §§105-277.2 to 105-277.7.
See PROPERTY TAXES.

GREENE COUNTY.
Agricultural tendencies in certain counties.
Terms of, §42-23.

GREENE COUNTY —Cont'd
Ambulances.
Attachment or garnishment and lien for, §§44-51.4 to 44-51.8.
False pretenses and cheats.
Requesting ambulance falsely, §14-111.3.
Condemnation or acquisition of land by local government unit outside county.
Consent of board of commissioners necessary, §153A-15.
Cropper or tenant refusing to perform terms of contract.
Forfeiture of right of possession to premises, §42-27.
Game laws, local acts not repealed, §113-133.1, (e).
Global TransPark development zone, §§158-30 to 158-42.
See GLOBAL TRANSPARK DEVELOPMENT ZONE.
Low-income housing tax credits.
Qualified building eligible for credit, §105-129.41, (c).
Maps in special proceedings, recording of photographic copies, §§47-32, 47-32.2.
On-premises unfortified wine licenses.
Discretion to decline to issue, §105-113.71, (b).
Probates and registration orders before clerks of inferior courts validated, §47-59.
School property.
Acquisition and improvement, §153A-158.1.
Special school tax, election to abolish.
Petition required, §115C-505.

GREENSBORO.
Traffic control photographic systems, §160A-300.1, (d).

GREENVILLE.
Traffic control photographic systems, §160A-300.1, (d).

GRENADES.
Civil disorders.
Certain weapons at civil disorders, §14-288.20.
Mass death and destruction weapons.
Manufacture, assembly, etc., §14-288.8.
Weapons generally.
See WEAPONS.

GREYHOUND RACING, §14-309.20.
Conducting in state prohibited, §14-309.20, (a).
Interstate or intrastate simulcasting prohibited, §14-309.20, (b).
Penalty, §14-309.20, (c).

GRIEVANCE PROCEDURES FOR HEALTH INSURERS, §58-50-62.

GRIEVANCES OF ATTORNEYS.
Attorneys at law.
Disciplinary rules of state bar generally, Bar Rules & Regs., B, §§.0101 to .0217.
See ATTORNEYS AT LAW.

GRIEVANCES OF PRISONERS.
Procedure generally, §§148-118.1 to 148-118.9.
See PRISONER'S GRIEVANCE PROCEDURE.

GRILLS.
Alcoholic beverage permits, §18B-1000.
Restaurants generally.
See RESTAURANTS.

GRIPS.
Secret societies.
Use of grips for illegal purposes, §14-12.4.

GRIST MILLS.
Generally, §§73-1 to 73-28.
See MILLS.

GROCERY STORES.
Alcoholic beverage permits, §18B-1001.

GROSS RECEIPTS TAX.
Amusement or entertainment not otherwise taxed, §105-37.1.
Athletic contest for which admission fee charged, §105-37.1.
Dance for which admission fee charge, §105-37.1.
Performance, show or exhibition not otherwise taxed, §105-37.1.
Regional transit authority vehicle rental tax, §§105-550 to 105-555.
See REGIONAL TRANSIT AUTHORITY VEHICLE RENTAL TAX.
Short-term leases and rentals of vehicles.
Cities levying, §160A-215.1.

GROUND CEDAR.
Trespass.
Taking, etc., of certain wild plants from land of another, §14-129.

GROUND PINE.
Trespass.
Taking, etc., of certain wild plants from land of another, §14-129.

GROUNDWATER RIGHTS.
Construction of water wells, §§87-83 to 87-96.
See WATER WELL CONSTRUCTION.
Underground storage tanks.
Leaking petroleum cleanup.
Groundwater protection loan fund, §143-215.94P.
Use of water resources.
Regulation generally, §§143-215.11 to 143-215.22B.
See WATER RESOURCE USE REGULATION.

GROUP HOMES FOR THE HANDICAPPED, §§168-20 to 168-23.
Defined terms, §168-21.
Educating special needs children placed in group homes.
Costs borne by local board of education, §115C-140.1, (a).
Actual cost of service, department to determine, §115C-140.1, (c).
Reserve fund to reimburse board, §115C-140.1, (b).
Private agreements, §168-23.
Public policy, §168-20.
Zoning, §168-22.

GROWERS AND PRODUCERS ASSOCIATIONS.
Cotton grower's organization, §§106-65.84 to 106-65.91.
Promotion of use and sale of agricultural products.
Generally, §§106-550 to 106-568.
See AGRICULTURAL PRODUCTS PROMOTION.

GROWTH HORMONES.
Biological residues in animals, §§106-549.81 to 106-549.89.
See BIOLOGICAL RESIDUES IN ANIMALS.

GUANACOS.
Llamas classified as livestock.
Definition of llama as including, §106-22.4.

GUARANTEED ARREST BOND CERTIFICATES.
Issuance by motor clubs.
Acceptance in lieu of cash bail or other bond, §58-69-55, (a).
Forfeiture and enforcement, applicable provisions, §58-69-55, (b).
Surety company becoming surety with respect to.
Filing undertaking, amount, §58-69-50, (a).
Form of undertaking, §58-69-50, (b).

GUARANTEED ENERGY SAVINGS CONTRACTS, §§143-64.17 to 143-64.17K, 143-129.4.
Bonds, surety, §143-64.17B, (c), (d).
Continuance of contract, §143-64.17D.
Definitions, §143-64.17.
Duration of contract, §143-64.17D.
Evaluation of sealed proposals, §143-64.17A, (b).
Evaluation of use by state agencies, §143-64.17F, (a).
Rule for evaluation, adoption, §143-64.17F, (b).
Exclusive nature of provisions, §143-129.4.
Installment and lease purchase contracts, §143-64.17I.
Interpretation and construction.
Provisions not to limit certain powers of local governmental units, §143-64.17A, (e).
Investment grade audit.
Qualified provider to conduct, §143-64.17B, (f).
Maintenance contracts or other maintenance agreements from qualified provider.
Contract may not require local governmental unit to purchase, §143-64.17B, (e).
Notice.
Entry into contract, §143-64.17B, (b).
Requests for proposals, §143-64.17A, (a).
Opening of sealed proposals, §143-64.17A, (c), (c1).
Payments under contract, §143-64.17E.
Recommendations as to savings.
State energy office, §143-64.17F, (c).
Reconciliation statement.
Provided annually by qualified provider, §143-64.17B, (g).
Reports, §§143-64.17G, 143-64.17H.
Requests for proposals, §143-64.17A, (a).
Requirements, §143-64.17B, (a).
Selection of qualified provider.
Factors, §143-64.17A, (d).
Shortfalls in savings.
Provider to pay, §143-64.17B, (g).
Solicitation, §143-64.17A.
State appropriations not to be reduced as result of savings, §143-64.17E.
State governmental units.
Financing by, §143-64.17J.
Inspection and compliance certification for, §143-64.17K.
Termination project.
Investment grade audit.
Results not within guaranteed savings, §143-64.17B, (f).
Use when feasible.
State agencies, §143-64.17F, (a).

GUARANTORS.
Joinder of debtor by surety.
Surety defined to include, §26-12, (a).
Notice to creditors to take action, §26-7.
Failure of creditor to take action, §26-9.
How given, prima facie evidence, §26-8.

GUARANTORS —Cont'd
Surety's recovery on obligation paid.
Surety defined to include, §26-3.1, (b).

GUARANTY ASSOCIATION ACT.
Life and health insurance guaranty association generally, §§58-62-2 to 58-62-95.
See LIFE AND HEALTH INSURANCE GUARANTY ASSOCIATION.

GUARDIAN AD LITEM, §1A-1, Rule 17, (b).
Abortion.
Parental consent to abortion.
Petition by guardian ad litem on behalf of pregnant minor for waiver of parental consent requirement.
Assistance of court in preparing and filing petitions, §90-21.8, (b).
Proceedings for waiver of parental consent requirement.
Participation by guardian ad litem on minor's behalf, §90-21.8, (c).
Absentees in military service.
Appointment of guardian ad litem by court, §28B-3, (c).
Petition for transfer of property valued at more than five thousand dollars, §28B-10, (d).
Abused, neglected or dependent juvenile actions, §§7B-1200 to 7B-1204.
Advisory committee, §7B-1201, (b).
Appointment, duties, §7B-601.
Local programs.
Administration and establishment, §7B-1201, (a).
Alternative plans, §7B-1203.
Conflicts of interest, appointment, §7B-1202.
Office of guardian ad litem services, §7B-1200.
Payment, §7B-603, (a) to (c).
Periodic review hearings, placement of juvenile.
Termination of parental rights, §7B-908, (b).
Petition alleging abuse, neglect or dependency.
Copy of petition to be provided to guardian ad litem office, §7B-408.
Volunteers.
Civil liability, §7B-1204.
Administrative office of the courts.
Guardian ad litem program.
Providing services to abused, neglected or dependent juveniles, §§7B-1200 to 7B-1204.
Adoption.
Adoption of incompetent adults.
Investigation and report to court, §48-5-103, (c).
Consent execution for incompetent parents, §48-3-602.
Representation of adoptee, §48-2-201, (b).
Appointment procedure, §1A-1, Rule 17, (d).
Discharge and appointment, §35A-1107, (a), (b).
Child abuse, neglect or dependency actions.
Parents.
Appointed for parents when incapable or underage, §7B-602, (b).
Childhood vaccine-related injury compensation.
Filing of claims on behalf of minors or incompetent persons, §130A-429, (a).
Corporations, trusts or other entities not in existence, §1A-1, Rule 17, (b), (d).
Costs.
Responsibility of guardian for costs against infant plaintiff, §6-30.
Decedents' estates.
Unknown heirs and devisees.
Appointment of guardian ad litem, §28A-22-3.
Sale of real property, §28A-17-4.

GUARDIAN AD LITEM —Cont'd
Determination of incompetence.
Attorney as guardian ad litem, §35A-1107, (b).
Discharge and appointment, §35A-1107, (a), (c).
Domestic relations actions.
When guardian ad litem not required, §1A-1, Rule 17, (b).
Duties, §1A-1, Rule 17, (e).
Eminent domain.
Public condemnors.
Appointment for infants and incompetents, §40A-50.
Fees, responsibility for payment, §7A-450.1.
Determination of persons responsible, §§7A-450.2, 7A-450.3.
Generally, §1A-1, Rule 17, (b).
General or testamentary guardian.
Appointment of guardian ad litem notwithstanding, §1A-1, Rule 17, (b).
Incompetence, determination.
Fees, payments, §35A-1116, (c).
Right to an appointment of court-appointed guardian ad litem, §35A-1107, (a), (b).
Incompetence, restoration.
Appointment, §35A-1130, (c).
Incompetent persons, §1A-1, Rule 17, (b).
Appointment procedure, §1A-1, Rule 17, (c).
Indigent persons.
Marriage proceedings.
Guardian ad litem for underage parties, §§7A-451, (f), 51-2.1.
Interstate compact on juvenile.
Return of escapees or absconders.
Appointment for juvenile, §7B-2805, (c).
Judgments and decrees.
Effect where party represented by guardian ad litem, §1A-1, Rule 17, (e).
Legitimation of illegitimate children.
Appointment in legitimation proceeding where mother married, §49-12.1, (a).
Marriage proceedings.
Guardian ad litem for underage parties, §§7A-451, (f), 51-2.1.
Mentally ill, §1A-1, Rule 17, (b).
Appointment procedure, §1A-1, Rule 17, (c).
Highway projects.
Condemnation proceedings.
Appointment of guardian ad litem, §136-110.
Minors.
Abused, neglected or dependent juvenile actions. See within this heading, "Abused, neglected or dependent juvenile actions."
Appointment of guardian, §1A-1, Rule 17, (b), (c); Super. Ct. Rule 7.1.
Standby guardians for minor children, §35A-1379.
Termination of parental rights proceedings. See within this heading, "Termination of parental rights proceedings."
Missing persons.
Action for receiver.
Filing of answer on behalf of absentee, §28C-2, (c).
Office of guardian ad litem services.
Services to abused, neglected or dependent juveniles, §§7B-1200 to 7B-1204.
Searches and seizures.
Unknown or absent defendants, §15-11.1, (b).
Service of process.
Appointment of unborn persons, §1A-1, Rule 17, (b).

GUARDIAN AD LITEM —Cont'd
Service of process —Cont'd
Manner of service on minor to exercise personal jurisdiction.
No parent, guardian or other person having care and control of child, §1A-1, Rule 4, (j).
Standby guardians for minor children.
Appointment of guardian ad litem, §35A-1379, (a).
Duties of guardian ad litem, §35A-1379, (b).
Investigation of fitness of intended standby guardian, §35A-1379, (c).
Substitution of parties.
Insanity or incompetency, §1A-1, Rule 25, (b).
Talent contracts entered into by minors.
Proceeding for court approval, §48A-12, (d).
Termination of parental rights proceedings.
Answer denying allegations, appointment, §7B-908, (b), (d).
Appointment, §7B-1101.
Answer denying allegations of petition, §7B-1108, (b), (d).
Discretion of court, assistance in determining best interests of juvenile, §7B-1108, (c).
Attorney appointed to assist nonattorney guardian ad litem, §7B-1108, (b).
Discretion of court to appoint, assistance in determining best interests, §7B-1108, (c).
Persons who may file petition or motion, intervention, right, §7B-1103, (a), (b).
Placement review hearing, §7B-908, (b).
Search for unknown parent, appointment, §7B-1105, (b).
Service of copy of order terminating rights on, §7B-1110, (d).
Torrens system registration.
Representation of persons under disability, §43-9.
Unborn persons, §1A-1, Rule 17, (b).
Appointment procedure, §1A-1, Rule 17, (d).
Workers' compensation.
Contested cases, I.C. Rule 604.

GUARDIAN AD LITEM ADVISORY COMMITTEE.
Guardian ad litem program to provide services to abused, neglected or dependent juveniles, §7B-1201, (b).

GUARDIANS.
Abandoned incompetent spouse's estate.
Sale of spouse's separate property by guardian, §35A-1306.
Abortion.
Parental consent to abortion.
Consent by legal guardian or legal custodian required, §90-21.7, (a).
Absentees in military service.
Appointment of guardian ad litem, §28B-3, (c).
Abused, neglected or dependent juvenile actions.
Appointment, authority, §7B-600, (a).
Court's inquiry into person's qualifications to act as guardian, §7B-600, (c).
Periodic review hearings, placement of juvenile.
Court's inquiry into person's qualifications to act as guardian, §7B-906, (g).
Custody removed from parent, appointment after findings, §7B-906, (d).
Termination of guardianship, criteria, §7B-600, (b).
Accounts and accounting.
Annual accounts.
Approval, §35A-1264.

GUARDIANS —Cont'd
Accounts and accounting —Cont'd
Annual accounts —Cont'd
Compelling accounting, §35A-1265, (a).
Contempt, §35A-1265, (a).
Corporation as guardian, §35A-1265, (b).
Costs of proceedings, §35A-1265, (a).
Required, §35A-1264.
Applicability of article, §35A-1260.
Commissions, §35A-1269.
Exhibition of investments and bank statements, §35A-1268.
Expenses and disbursements.
Chargeable in annual account, §35A-1267.
Final account and discharge of guardian, §35A-1266.
Responsibility of guardian for accounting until discharged, §35A-1295, (b).
Restoration to competence, §35A-1130, (e).
Inventory or account required within three months, §35A-1261.
Compelling inventory or account, §35A-1262, (a).
Contempt, §35A-1262, (a).
Costs of proceedings.
Personal liability of guardian, §35A-1262, (b).
Supplemental inventory, §35A-1263.1.
Removal or resignation of guardian or guardian stopped serving, §35A-1294, (a).
Restoration to competence.
Final accounts, §35A-1130, (e).
Standby guardians for minor children, §35A-1380.
Ad litem.
See GUARDIAN AD LITEM.
Adoption.
Appointment for minor child.
Consent not required from parent, §48-3-603, (a).
Execution of consent, time, §48-3-604, (c).
Incompetent adults.
Consent, §48-5-103, (a), (b).
Adult care homes.
Bill of rights.
Transfer of management responsibilities, §131D-22.
Advancements.
Guardian party to proceeding, §35A-1324.
Alimony.
Incompetent spouses.
General guardian may commence, defend or maintain actions, §50-22.
Anatomical gifts.
Manner of making anatomical gifts, §130A-406, (f).
Persons who may execute anatomical gift, §130A-404, (c).
Ancillary guardians.
Appointment for nonresident ward with property in state, §35A-1280, (a).
Certified or exemplified copy, evidence of, §35A-1280, (c).
Notice to appropriate court of ward's residence, §35A-1280, (d).
Venue, §35A-1204, (c).
Powers, duties and responsibilities with respect to nonresident ward's property, §35A-1280, (b).
Annulment of marriage.
Incompetent spouses.
General guardian may commence, defend or maintain actions, §50-22.

GUARDIANS —Cont'd
Appeals.
Determination of incompetence.
Order of clerk, §35A-1115.
Appointment.
Ancillary guardians.
Nonresident ward having property in state, §35A-1280.
Clerks of superior court.
Jurisdiction.
Standby guardians for minor children, §35A-1371.
Determination of incompetence, §35A-1120.
Interim guardians, §35A-1114.
Incompetent person, guardian for, §§35A-1210 to 35A-1216.
Jurisdiction.
Clerks of superior courts, §35A-1203, (a), (e).
Standby guardians for minor children, §35A-1371.
Letters of appointment, §35A-1206.
Minors, guardian for, §§35A-1220 to 35A-1228.
Standby guardians for minor children.
Jurisdiction, §35A-1371.
Petition, §35A-1373.
Written designation, §35A-1374.
Successor guardians, §35A-1293.
Resignation of guardian, §35A-1292.
Venue, §35A-1204.
Transfer to different county, §35A-1205.
Attorneys at law.
Determination of incompetence.
Right to counsel, §35A-1107, (a), (b).
Attorneys' fees.
Procedure to compel accounting, §35A-1265, (a).
Banks.
Acting as guardian authorized, §53-159.
Deposit of ward's money held by applicant for letters, §35A-1232, (b) to (d).
Stock and stockholders.
Personal liability of guardians, §53-40.
Bond of guardian.
Action on bond.
Persons injured by breach of condition, §35A-1234.
Relief of endangered guardians, §35A-1237.
Several wards with estate in common, §35A-1235.
Adjusting guardians bond.
Authority of clerks of superior court, §35A-1203, (c).
Approval, §35A-1230.
Breach of condition.
Action on bond by person issued by, §35A-1234.
Clerk.
Approval, §35A-1230.
Liability.
Taking insufficient bond, §35A-1238, (a).
Willfully or negligently does prohibited act, §35A-1238, (b).
Recording, §35A-1231, (a).
Reduced penalty, §35A-1233.
Renewal of bond.
Duties of clerk upon failure to renew, §35A-1236.
Common wards for one guardian, §35A-1235.
Conditions of bond, §35A-1231, (a).
Deposited or invested money, ward's estate including.
Excluded from computation of amount of bond, §35A-1232.

GUARDIANS —Cont'd
Bond of guardian —Cont'd
Disinterested public agents.
Health and human services bond, §35A-1239.
Health and human services bond, §35A-1239.
Increase on sale of realty or personal property, §35A-1231, (b).
Insufficient bond.
Liability of clerk, §35A-1238, (a).
Judicial sale, holding, §1-339.10, (b), (c).
Limitation of action against surety, §1-52.
Nonresident guardian, §35A-1230.
Penalty.
Reduction by clerk, §35A-1233.
Public guardian, §35A-1271.
Real property.
Increase on sale of realty, §35A-1231, (b).
Recording, §35A-1231, (a).
Renewal, §35A-1236.
Failure to renew, §35A-1236.
Required, §35A-1230.
Standby guardians for minor children, §35A-1380.
Sureties.
Relief of endangered sureties, §35A-1237.
Terms of bond, §35A-1231, (a).
Care, comfort and maintenance.
Guardian of person, duty to provide, §35A-1241, (a).
Childhood vaccine-related injury compensation.
Filing of claims on behalf of minors or incompetent persons, §130A-429, (a).
Clerk of superior court.
Authority of clerk.
Standby guardians for minor children, §35A-1371.
Bond of guardian.
Approval, §35A-1230.
Liability.
Taking insufficient bond, §35A-1238, (a).
Willfully or negligently does prohibited act, §35A-1238, (b).
Recording in clerk's office, §35A-1231.
Reduction of penalty, §35A-1233.
Renewal of bond.
Duties of clerk upon failure to renew, §35A-1236.
Interlocutory order on revocation, §35A-1291.
Jurisdiction and authority.
Adjusting guardians bond, §35A-1203, (c).
Appointment of guardian, §35A-1203, (e).
Original jurisdiction, §35A-1203, (a).
Disputes between guardians, determining, §35A-1203, (c).
Original jurisdiction to appoint, §35A-1203, (a).
Petition to exercise clerk's authority, §35A-1203, (d).
Retention of jurisdiction following appointment, §35A-1203, (b).
Standby guardians for minor children, §35A-1371.
Receiver for ward's estates.
Acting as or appointing, estate without guardian, §35A-1294, (b).
Removal of guardian.
Causes for removal, §35A-1290, (b), (c).
Emergency removal without hearing, §35A-1291.
Power and authority, §35A-1290, (a).
Transfer of matter to different county, §35A-1205.

GUARDIANS —Cont'd
Clothing, furniture, vehicles and other personal effects.
Guardian of person, duty to take care of, §35A-1241, (a).
Commissions.
Allowable, §35A-1269.
Community trust for persons with severe chronic disabilities.
Acceptance of appointment as guardian by community trust, §36A-59.13, (f).
Compensation of trustees and other fiduciaries, §§32-53 to 32-62.
See FIDUCIARIES.
Compound interest.
Obligation due guardians, §24-4.
Confidentiality.
Status report for incompetent wards.
Restrictions on person with access to information, §35A-1242, (c).
Consent.
Guardian of the person.
Power to give for ward, §35A-1241, (a).
Construction and interpretation.
Accounts and accounting.
Applicability of article, §35A-1260.
Powers and duties of guardian of the estate, §35A-1250, (b).
Powers and duties of guardian of the person.
Applicability of article, §35A-1240.
Contempt.
Accounts and accounting.
Annual accounts.
Compelling accounting, §35A-1265, (a).
Inventory or account required within three months.
Compelling inventory or account, §35A-1262, (a).
Corporations.
Accounting, procedure to compel.
Persons proceeded against, §35A-1265, (a).
Appointment as guardian for incompetent, §35A-1213, (c).
Priorities for appointment, §35A-1214.
Status reports for incompetent guardians.
Procedure to compel, §35A-1244.
Costs.
Accounts and accounting.
Annual accounts.
Compelling accounting, §35A-1265, (a).
Inventory or account required within three months.
Compelling inventory or account.
Personal liability of guardian for costs of proceedings, §35A-1262, (b).
Determination of incompetence.
Taxing of costs, §35A-1116, (a).
Responsibility of guardian for costs against infant plaintiff, §6-30.
Criminal law and procedure.
Victims' rights.
Exercise of incompetent victims rights by guardian, §15A-841.
Curative acts.
Deeds.
Guardians omitting seal, prior to January 1, 1944, validated, §35A-1360.
Validation of certain private sales, §35A-1361, (a).
Custody of the person.
Guardian of person entitled to, §35A-1241, (a).

GUARDIANS —Cont'd
Damages.
Guardian of the person.
When not liable for damages, §35A-1241, (c).
Death.
Appointment of successor guardian, §35A-1293.
Mortgages.
Powers passed to succeeding guardian, §45-19.
Decedents' estates.
Distribution to guardian of minor, §28A-22-7.
Unborn heirs.
Appointment of guardian ad litem, §28A-22-3.
Declaratory judgments.
Who may apply for declaration, §1-255.
Deeds.
Validation.
Deeds by guardians omitting seal, prior to January 1, 1944, §35A-1360.
Definitions, §35A-1202.
Determination of incompetence, §35A-1101.
Standby guardians for minor children, §35A-1370.
Delinquent and undisciplined juvenile actions.
Appointment, authority, §7B-2001.
Deposit of ward's money by applicant for letters, §35A-1232, (b).
Account in an insured savings and loan association.
Defined, §35A-1232, (c).
Money defined, §35A-1232, (d).
Exclusion of money in computing amount of bond, §35A-1232, (a).
Determination of incompetence.
Adjudication order, §35A-1112.
Appeals.
Orders of clerk, §35A-1115.
Appointment, §35A-1120.
Interim guardians, §35A-1114.
Attorneys at law.
Right to counsel, §35A-1107, (a).
Clerk of superior court.
Multidisciplinary evaluation.
Order of clerk, §35A-1111.
Order of clerk, §35A-1112, (d).
Appeal from clerk's order, §35A-1115.
Multidisciplinary evaluation, §35A-1111.
Restoration to competency.
Proceedings before clerk, §35A-1130.
Costs.
Taxing of costs, §35A-1116, (a).
Definitions, §35A-1101.
Exclusive procedure, §35A-1102.
Guardian ad litem.
Attorney as guardian ad litem, §35A-1107, (a), (b).
Hearings.
Appointment of interim guardian, §35A-1114, (c).
Generally, §35A-1112.
Incompetence determined in another state, §35A-1113.
Multidisciplinary evaluation.
Extension of time for hearing, §35A-1108, (b).
Notice, §35A-1108, (a).
Service, §35A-1109.
Interim guardians.
Appointment.
Motion for appointment.
Contents, §35A-1114, (b).
Filing, §35A-1114, (a).
Hearing, §35A-1114, (c).

GUARDIANS —Cont'd
Determination of incompetence —Cont'd
Interim guardians —Cont'd
Appointment —Cont'd
Motion for appointment —Cont'd
When petition may be dismissed, §35A-1114, (f).
Orders, §35A-1114, (d).
Contents, §35A-1114, (e).
Defined, §35A-1101.
Jurisdiction, §35A-1103.
Jury.
Right to jury, §35A-1110.
Minors, §35A-1225, (b).
Multidisciplinary evaluation.
Defined, §35A-1101.
Designated agency, §35A-1111.
Order of clerk, §35A-1111.
Notice.
Hearing, §35A-1108, (a).
Orders.
Adjudication orders, §35A-1112.
Petitions.
Contents, §35A-1106.
Filing, §35A-1105.
Service, §35A-1109.
Who may file, §35A-1105.
Procedure exclusive, §35A-1102.
Restoration to competency.
Proceedings before clerk, §35A-1130.
Service of process.
Notice and petition, §35A-1109.
Venue, §35A-1103.
Change of venue, §35A-1104.
Discharge of guardian.
Final account and discharge of guardian, §35A-1266.
Responsibility of guardian for accounting until discharged, §35A-1295, (b).
Restoration to competence, §35A-1130, (e).
Disinterested public agent.
Appointment as guardian for incompetent, §35A-1213, (d).
Priority for appointments, §35A-1214.
Rule-making power of secretary, §35A-1216.
Defined, §35A-1202.
Status reports for incompetent wards.
Procedure to compel, §35A-1244.
Disputes between guardians.
Authority of clerks of superior court to determine, §35A-1203, (c).
Divorce.
Incompetent spouses.
Actions on behalf of.
General guardian may commence, defend or maintain, §50-22.
Domicile.
Establishing ward's place of abode within or without state.
Power of guardian of the person, §35A-1241, (a).
Durable power of attorney.
Attorney-in-fact accountable to court appointed guardian, §32A-10, (a).
Nomination of guardian by durable power of attorney for consideration by court, §32A-10, (b).
Embezzlement.
Property.
Receipt of property by virtue of office or employment, §14-90.

GUARDIANS —Cont'd
Eminent domain.
Private condemnors.
Acquisition of title of infants, incompetents, inebriates or trustees without power of sale.
Power of court to appoint guardian, §40A-30.
Evidence.
Ancillary guardian appointed for nonresident ward with property in state.
Certified or exemplified copy of appointment, §35A-1280, (c).
Medical, hospital or other charges at issue.
Competency to give evidence regarding amount, §8-58.1.
Rebuttable presumption of reasonableness.
Testimony establishing, §8-58.1.
Exercising authority of clerk of superior court.
Petitions, §35A-1203, (d).
Ex parte order, entry by clerk, §35A-1207, (d).
Expenses.
Reimbursement of reasonable and proper expenditures.
Guardian of the person, §35A-1241, (b).
Fiduciaries.
General provisions.
See FIDUCIARIES.
Payments to or for minors or incompetents.
Powers which may be incorporated by reference in trust instrument, §32-27.
Findings of general assembly, §35A-1201, (a).
Gifts.
Declaring revocable trust irrevocable and making gift of incompetent's life interest
From income for certain purposes.
Approval of judge of superior court.
Authorized, §35A-1335.
Fact that incompetent had not previously made similar gifts, §35A-1337.
Prerequisites to approval, §§35A-1336, 35A-1336.1.
Validity of gift, §35A-1338.
Health care powers of attorney.
Appointment of guardian.
Effect on power of attorney, §32A-22, (a).
Nomination of guardian by health care power of attorney, §32A-22, (b).
Hearings.
Appointment of guardians.
Incompetent persons, §35A-1212.
Minors, §35A-1223.
Determination of incompetence.
Appointment of interim guardian, §35A-1114, (c).
Generally, §35A-1112.
Incompetence determined in another state, §35A-1113.
Notice, §35A-1108, (a).
Service of notice, §35A-1109.
Husband and wife.
Abandoned incompetent spouse's estate.
Sale of spouse's separate property by guardian, §35A-1306.
Mortgage or sale of estates held by the entireties, §§35A-1310 to 35A-1314.
See HUSBAND AND WIFE.
Sale of ward's estate.
Spouse entitled to special proceedings for sale of real property, §35A-1307.
Immunities.
Guardian of the person.
Acting within limits imposed by powers and duties or order of appointment, §35A-1241, (c).

GUARDIANS —Cont'd
Incompetent persons.
Abandoned incompetent spouse's estate.
Sale of spouse's separate property by guardian, §35A-1306.
Appointment.
Application, §35A-1210.
Contents, §35A-1210.
Service, §35A-1211, (a).
Application for appointment joined with petition for adjudication of incompetence, §35A-1211, (b).
Corporations as guardian, §35A-1213.
Designated agency, clerk naming, §35A-1212, (d).
Disinterested public agents, §35A-1213.
When may be appointed, §35A-1214.
Employee of treatment facilities, §35A-1213.
Evidence, receipt by clerk, §35A-1212, (a).
Inquiry by clerk, §35A-1212, (a).
Legal rights and privileges retained by ward.
Clerk ordering, §35A-1215, (b).
Letters of appointment.
Issuance, §35A-1215, (c).
Motions.
Service, §35A-1211, (a).
Multidisciplinary evaluation.
Order for, §35A-1212, (b).
Notice.
Service, §35A-1211, (a).
Orders of clerk.
Contents, §35A-1215, (a).
Entering of order, §35A-1215, (a).
Priorities for appointment, §35A-1214.
Qualifications of guardians, §35A-1213.
Rules and regulations.
Issuance, §35A-1216.
Suitability of prospective guardian.
Report to evaluate, §35A-1212, (c).
Venue, §35A-1204, (a).
Determination of incompetence, §§35A-1101 to 35A-1115.
Guardian of the estate.
Powers in administering estate, §35A-1251.
Hearings before clerk.
Appointment, §35A-1212.
Insurance proceeds received as beneficiary on death of insured.
Payment to and receipt by public guardian, §7A-111, (b), (d).
Legal rights and privileges retained by ward.
Clerk ordering, §35A-1215, (b).
Modification of guardianship, program or plan.
Petition by designated agency requesting, §35A-1243, (b) to (d).
Money belonging to incapacitated adult without guardian.
Payment to and receipt by public guardian, §7A-111, (b), (d).
Performance of duties imposed on guardian.
Petition by designated agency requiring guardian to perform, §35A-1243, (b) to (d).
Petitions.
Designated agency requesting certain actions against guardian of incompetent, §35A-1243, (b) to (d).
Removal of guardian.
Petition by designated agency requesting, §35A-1243, (b) to (d).
Restoration to competency.
Petition by designated agency requesting, §35A-1243, (b) to (d).

GUARDIANS —Cont'd
Incompetent persons —Cont'd
Sale, lease or exchange of ward's estate, §35A-1251.
Status reports.
Filing by guardian of the person, §35A-1242.
Compelling, procedure, §35A-1244.
Duties of designated agency after receipt, §35A-1243.
Sterilization of mentally ill or retarded ward.
Consent or approval of guardian of person, prohibition to give, §35A-1241, (a).
Termination of guardianship.
Adjudication of restoration to competency, §35A-1295, (a).
Treatment facility employee.
Ineligibility to serve as guardian for patient at facility, §35A-1213, (e).
Venue.
Appointment, §35A-1204, (a).
Inebriates.
Guardian of the estate.
Powers in administering estate, §35A-1251.
Interest.
Compound interest.
Obligations due guardians to bear compound interest, §24-4.
Interim guardian.
Incompetence, determination of.
Appointments, §35A-1114.
Inventories.
Accounts and accounting.
Inventory or account required within three months, §§35A-1261 to 35A-1263.1.
Procedure to compel inventory, §35A-1262.
Supplemental inventory, §35A-1263.1.
Judicial sales.
Authority of guardian to hold sale, §1-339.4.
Bond of person holding sale, §1-339.10, (b), (c).
Juries.
Determination of incompetence.
Right to jury, §35A-1110.
Jurisdiction.
Clerk of superior court.
Standby guardians for minor children, §35A-1371.
Determination of incompetence, §35A-1103.
Standby guardians for minor children, §35A-1371.
Juvenile facilities.
Home visits, §143B-528, (b).
Visitation, §143B-528, (a).
Larceny.
Concealment of merchandise in mercantile establishments.
Detention of minors by merchants.
Notice to guardian during period of detention, §§14-72, (d), 14-72.1, (c).
Leases.
Power to lease real estate.
Administration of incompetent ward's estate, §35A-1251.
Administration of minor ward's estate, §35A-1252.
Special proceedings to sell, exchange, mortgage or lease ward's real estate, §35A-1301.
Letters of guardianship.
Public guardians, §35A-1273.
Revocation.
Interlocutory orders upon revocation, §35A-1291.

GUARDIANS —Cont'd
Liability.
Public guardians, §35A-1272.
Limited liability companies.
Incompetence of members, powers of guardian, §57C-5-05.
Medical, legal, psychological and other professional care.
Consent or approval, power of guardian of person, §35A-1241, (a).
Mental health, developmental disabilities and substance abuse.
Abandoned incompetent spouse's estate.
Sale of spouse's separate property by guardian, §35A-1306.
Adults adjudicated incompetents.
Mental health officials and employees as public guardians, §122C-122.
Appointment for incompetent, §§35A-1210 to 35A-1216.
Venue, §35A-1204, (a).
Appointment for mentally ill, §1A-1, Rule 17, (b).
Guardianship of incompetent adults.
Guardian of the estate.
Powers in administering estate, §35A-1251.
Mental health officials and employees as public guardians, §122C-122.
Modification of terms of guardianship of incompetent.
Petition by designated agency requesting, §35A-1243, (b) to (d).
Mortgage or sale of estates held by the entireties, §§35A-1310 to 35A-1314.
Performance of guardian's duties.
Petition by designated agency requiring, §35A-1243, (b) to (d).
Petition by designated agency requesting certain actions, §35A-1243, (b) to (d).
Remainders, reversions and executory interests.
Sale, lease or mortgages in case of remainders.
Appointment of guardian ad litem, §41-11.
Removal of guardian of incompetent.
Petition by designated agency requesting, §35A-1243, (b) to (d).
Restoration to competency.
Petition by designated agency requesting, §35A-1243, (b) to (d).
Status reports.
Filing by guardian of the person, §35A-1242.
Sterilization of mentally ill or retarded ward.
Consent or approval of guardian of person, prohibition to give, §35A-1241, (a).
Medical necessity, procedure to permit, §35A-1245.
Torrens system registration.
Persons under disability may sue by guardian, §43-8.
Venue.
Appointment of guardian for incompetent, §35A-1204, (a).
Military affairs.
Children of servicemen.
Temporary guardian to receive and disburse allotments and allowances, §35A-1228.
Veterans' guardianship act, §§34-1 to 34-18.
See VETERANS' GUARDIANSHIP ACT.
Minors, §1A-1, Rule 17, (b).
Abused, neglected or dependent juvenile actions.
Appointment, §7B-600, (a) to (c).
Court's inquiry into person's qualifications to act as guardian, §7B-600, (c).

GUARDIANS —Cont'd
Minors —Cont'd
Abused, neglected or dependent juvenile actions —Cont'd
Periodic review hearings, placement of juvenile, §7B-906, (d).
Court's inquiry into person's qualifications to act as guardian, §7B-906, (g).
Appointment, §§35A-1220 to 35A-1226.
Absence of natural guardian.
County social services director to be guardian, §35A-1220.
Application for appointment.
Contents, §35A-1221.
Service, §35A-1222.
Who may make, §35A-1221.
Corporations, §35A-1224, (c).
Employee of treatment facilities, §35A-1224, (e).
Guardian of the estate, §35A-1224, (a).
Guardian of the person or general guardian only for minor who has no natural guardian, §35A-1224, (a).
Hearings, §35A-1223.
Notice.
Service, §35A-1222.
Incompetent minors.
Petition for adjudication of incompetence and appointment of guardian, §35A-1225.
Letters of appointment.
Issuance, §35A-1226.
Orders of clerk, §35A-1226.
Qualifications, §35A-1224, (b), (c).
Social services director of county.
To be guardian in absence of natural guardian, §35A-1220.
Testamentary recommendations of parents.
Effect, §35A-1224, (d).
Presumptions, §35A-1225, (a).
Venue, §35A-1204, (b).
Delinquent and undisciplined juvenile actions.
Appointment, authority, §7B-2001.
Devise or legacy of personal property.
Distribution, §35A-1227, (b).
Funds owed to minors.
Disposition, §35A-1227, (a).
Guardian of the estate.
Powers in administering estate, §35A-1252.
Insurance proceeds owed to minors.
Disposition, §35A-1227, (a).
Insurance proceeds received by minors on death of insured.
Payment over to and receipt by public guardian, §7A-111, (a), (c).
Military service.
Children of servicemen.
Allotments and allowances, §35A-1228.
Money for minor for whom there is no guardian.
Payment over to public guardian, §7A-111, (a), (c).
Property due minor.
Disposition, §35A-1227, (c).
Remainders, reversions and executory interests.
Sale, lease or mortgage in case of remainders.
Appointment of guardian ad litem, §41-11.
Sale, lease or exchange of ward's estate, §35A-1252.
Standby guardians, §§35A-1370 to 35A-1382. See within this heading, "Standby guardians for minor children."
Termination of guardianship.
Ward ceasing to be minor, §35A-1295, (a).

GUARDIANS —Cont'd
Minors —Cont'd
Testamentary recommendation by parent, §35A-1224, (d).
Guardian for incompetent minor, §35A-1225.
Torrens system registration.
Infants may sue by guardian, §43-8.
Transfers to minors.
Disposition, §35A-1227, (d).
Irrevocable transfer for benefit of minor.
Authority to make as custodian, §33A-6, (b), (c).
Venue.
Appointment, §35A-1204, (b).
Mortgages and deeds of trust.
Sales under power of sale.
Powers passed to succeeding guardian upon death, §45-19.
Special proceedings to sell, exchange, mortgage or lease ward's real estate, §35A-1301.
Substitution of trustees.
Powers pass to succeeding guardian, §45-19.
Motions in the cause.
All requests treated as motions in the cause, §35A-1207, (b).
Ex parte order, entry by clerk, §35A-1207, (d).
Filing, place for, §35A-1207, (a).
Hearing, time, date and place, movant to obtain, §35A-1207, (c).
Service or motion and notice of hearing, §35A-1207, (c).
Multidisciplinary evaluations.
Appointment of guardians.
Incompetent persons, §35A-1212, (b).
Nonresidents.
Ancillary guardian for nonresident ward having property in state, §35A-1280.
Venue for appointment, §35A-1204, (c).
Qualifications for appointment as guardian for incompetent, §35A-1213, (b).
Removal of nonresident ward's personalty from state.
Banking institution guardian.
Removal without finding as to sureties, §35A-1281, (c).
Copy of appointment, guardian to show court, §35A-1281, (c).
Party defendant, persons who may be made, §35A-1281, (c).
Personal estate defined, §35A-1281, (a).
Petition for removal, §35A-1281, (b).
Venue for filing petition, §35A-1281, (b).
Notice.
Ancillary guardian appointed for nonresident ward with property in state, §35A-1280, (d).
Appointment of guardian.
Minors.
Service, §35A-1222.
Determination of incompetence.
Hearings, §35A-1108, (a).
Service of notice, §35A-1109.
Motions in the cause.
Service of motion and notice of hearing, §35A-1207, (c).
Sale of ward's estate.
Abandoned incompetent spouse's separate property.
Service of notice on abandoning spouse, §35A-13-6, (b).
Standby guardians.
Appointment by written designation.
Service of petition and notice of hearing, §35A-1374, (g).

GUARDIANS —Cont'd
Nursing homes.
Patients' bill of rights.
Transfer of management responsibilities, §131E-118.
Oaths.
Public guardians, §35A-1270.
Status report for incompetent wards.
Filed under guardians oath or affirmation, §35A-1242, (b).
Orders.
Letters of guardianship.
Interlocutory orders upon revocation, §35A-1291.
Special proceedings involving infants.
Approval of clerk's order by judge, §1-402.
Parties, §1A-1, Rule 17, (a).
Persons under legal disability.
Torrens system registration.
Guardians may sue, §43-8.
Petitions.
Designated agency requesting certain actions against guardian of incompetent, §35A-1243, (b) to (d).
Determination of incompetence.
Contents, §35A-1106.
Filing, §35A-1105.
Service, §35A-1109.
Who may file, §35A-1105.
Exercising authority of clerk of superior court, §35A-1203, (d).
Mentally ill.
Gifts from income of incompetents, §35A-1335.
Removal of nonresident ward's personalty from state, §35A-1281, (b).
Sale of ward's estate.
Special proceedings to sell, exchange, mortgage or lease real estate, §35A-1301, (b), (d).
Standby guardians for minor children.
Appointment by petition, §35A-1373.
Appointment by written designation, §35A-1374.
Place of abode.
Establishing ward's place of abode within or without state.
Power of guardian of the person, §35A-1241, (a).
Powers and duties.
Ancillary guardian for nonresident ward with property in state, §35A-1280, (b).
Fiduciaries generally, §§32-25 to 32-28.
Guardian of the estate.
Administration of incompetent ward's estate, §35A-1251.
Administration of minor ward's estate, §35A-1252.
Applicability of article, construction, §35A-1250, (a), (b).
Specific duties of guardian of the estate, §35A-1253.
Guardian of the person.
Applicability of article, §35A-1240.
Generally, §35A-1241, (a).
Status reports for incompetent wards, §35A-1242.
Compelling status reports.
Procedure, §35A-1244.
Public guardians, §35A-1272.
Standby guardians for minor children, §35A-1377.
Presumptions.
Medical, hospital or other charges at issue.
Rebuttable presumption of reasonableness.
Testimony establishing, §8-58.1.

GUARDIANS —Cont'd
Prudent person rule.
Investment and deposit of funds, §36A-2, (a).
Public guardians.
Appointment, §35A-1270.
Bond, §35A-1271.
Compensation, §35A-1272.
Letters of guardianship.
Issuance, §35A-1273.
Liability, §35A-1272.
Oaths, §35A-1270.
Powers and duties, §35A-1272.
Terms of office, §35A-1270.
Purpose of provisions, §35A-1201, (b).
Real estate brokers and salespersons.
Exemption of guardian from provisions, §93A-2, (c).
Receiver for estate without guardian.
Accounts, return, audit and settlement, §35A-1294, (b).
Clerk acting as or appointing, §35A-1294, (b).
Compensation for, §35A-1294, (b).
Continuation until other guardian appointed, §35A-1294, (b).
Payment over to newly appointed guardian, §35A-1294, (c).
Remedy of ward upon emancipation, §35A-1294, (c).
Remainders, reversions and executory interests.
Sale, lease or mortgage in case of remainders.
Appointment of guardian ad litem for minors and persons under disability, §41-11.
Removal of guardian.
Appointment of successor guardian, §35A-1293.
Bond of guardian.
Failure to renew bond, §35A-1236.
Causes for removal.
Clerk removing, §35A-1290, (b), (c).
Clerk of superior court.
Causes for removal, §35A-1290, (b), (c).
Emergency removal without hearing, §35A-1291.
Interlocutory orders on revocation, §35A-1291.
Power and authority, §35A-1290, (a).
Guardian for incompetent.
Petition by designated agency, §35A-1243, (b) to (d).
Receiver appointed.
Estate without guardian, §35A-1294.
Removal of nonresident ward's personalty from state, §35A-1281.
Renunciation.
Right to renounce, §31B-1.
Reports.
Status reports.
Compelling status reports.
Procedure to compel, §35A-1244.
Filing by guardian of the person, §35A-1242.
Duties of designated agency after receipt, §35A-1243.
Resignation of guardian.
Application in writing, §35A-1292, (a).
Appointment of successor, §35A-1293.
Liability after discharge, §35A-1292, (a).
Partial resignation, §35A-1292, (b).
Partial resignation as guardian of estate.
Remaining guardian of the person, §35A-1292, (b).
Receiver appointed.
Estate without guardian, §35A-1294.

GUARDIANS —Cont'd
Rules and regulations.
Appointment of guardians.
Incompetent persons, §35A-1216.
Sale of ward's estate.
Abandoned incompetent spouse's separate property.
Bar to abandoning spouse in property, §35A-1306, (c).
Initiation of special proceeding requesting, §35A-1306, (a).
Issuance of order, required findings, §35A-1306, (c).
Service of notice on ward's spouse, §35A-1306, (b).
Authority of guardian to hold sale, §1-339.4.
Conversion and reconversion, §35A-1303.
Curative acts and statutes.
Certain private sales validated, §35A-1361.
Estate in another county.
Procedure when property lies in county in which guardian does not reside, §35A-1302.
Funds from sale.
Character of estate sold and subject to same trust, §35A-1303.
Husband and wife.
Incompetent spouses.
Mortgage or sale of estates held by the entireties, §§35A-1310 to 35A-1314.
Spouse entitled to special proceedings for sale of real property, §35A-1307.
Incompetent wards, §35A-1251.
Minor wards, §35A-1252.
Petitions.
Special proceedings to sell, exchange, mortgage or lease real estate, §35A-1301, (b), (d).
Procedure for sale.
Property lying in county in which guardian does not reside, §35A-1302.
Special proceedings to sell, exchange, mortgage or lease real estate.
Construction of word "guardian," §35A-1301, (a).
Minor ward.
Special requirements, §35A-1301, (c).
Order by clerk, §35A-1301, (b).
Petition, §35A-1301, (b).
Filing, §35A-1301, (d).
Private sales.
Courts not divested of power to order, §35A-1301, (f).
Procedure for sale, §35A-1301, (e).
Validity of sales, §35A-1301, (g).
Timber.
When timber may be sold, §35A-1305.
Savings and loan associations.
Deposit of ward's money held by applicant for letters, §35A-1232, (b) to (d).
Seals and sealed instruments.
Deeds by guardians omitting seal, prior to January 1, 1944, validated, §35A-1360.
Securities regulation.
Exempt transactions, §78A-17.
Service of process.
Appointment of guardian.
Incompetent persons.
Service of application, motions and notices, §35A-1211.
Minors.
Service of application and notices, §35A-1222.
Determination of incompetence.
Service of notice and petition, §35A-1109.

GUARDIANS —Cont'd
Service of process —Cont'd
Motions in the cause.
Motion and notice of hearing, §35A-1207, (c).
Natural persons under disabilities, §1A-1, Rule 4, (j).
Nonresident appointed guardian for incompetent.
Appointment of agent to accept service, §35A-1213, (b).
Sale of ward's estate.
Abandoned incompetent spouse's separate property, §35A-13-6, (b).
Standby guardians for minor children.
Appointment by written designation.
Service of petition and notice of hearing, §35A-1374, (g).
Petition of appointment, §35A-1373, (c), (d).
Shoplifting.
Concealment of merchandise in mercantile establishments.
Detention of minors by merchants.
Notice to guardian during period of detention, §§14-72, (d), 14-72.1, (c).
Social services.
County directors of social services.
Director and assistant directors as public guardians, §108A-15.
Special proceedings.
Order of clerk.
Approval of judge required, §1-402.
Standby guardians for minor children, §§35A-1370 to 35A-1382.
Accounting by guardian, §35A-1382.
Applicability of provisions, §35A-1372.
Appointment.
Jurisdiction, §35A-1371.
Petition, §35A-1373.
Written designation, §35A-1374.
Bond of guardian, §35A-1380.
Definitions, §35A-1370.
Designation.
Appointment by written designation.
Alternate standby guardian.
Commencement of proceeding for appointment, §35A-1374, (d).
Commencement of authority of standby guardian, §35A-1374, (c).
Contents of designation, §35A-1374, (b).
Custody of minor child.
Claim by parent, §35A-1374, (h).
Generally, §35A-1374, (a).
Hearing, §35A-1373, (i).
Petition by standby guardian to be appointed, §35A-1374, (d) to (g).
Revocation of standby guardianship, §35A-1374, (j).
Complaint for custody, stay of proceedings, §35A-1374, (h).
Defined, §35A-1370.
Hearing and order for appointment, §35A-1374, (i).
Service of petition, §35A-1374, (g).
Time for filing petition, §35A-1374, (e).
Determination of debilitation, §35A-1375, (a), (b).
Commencement of standby guardian's authority as result of.
Informing petitioner or designator, §35A-1375, (d).
Copy to be supplied to standby guardian, §35A-1375, (c).
Defined, §35A-1370.

GUARDIANS —Cont'd
Standby guardians for minor children —Cont'd
Determination of incapacity, §35A-1375, (a), (b).
Commencement of standby guardian's authority as result of.
Informing petitioner or designator, §35A-1375, (d).
Copy to be supplied to standby guardian, §35A-1375, (c).
Defined, §35A-1370.
Guardian ad litem.
Appointment, §35A-1379, (a).
Duties, §35A-1379, (b).
Investigation of fitness of intended standby guardian, §35A-1379, (c).
Jurisdiction, §35A-1371.
Parental rights.
Authority concurrent to, §35A-1377.
Petition for appointment.
Commencement of standby guardian, §35A-1373, (i) to (l).
Contents, §35A-1373, (b).
Filing, §35A-1373, (a).
Hearing on, §35A-1373, (e), (f), (h).
Letters of appointment, §35A-1373, (g).
Renunciation of appointment, §35A-1373, (n).
Revocation of standby guardianship, §35A-1373, (m).
Service, §35A-1373, (c), (d).
Powers and duties, §35A-1378.
Restoration of capacity or ability.
Suspension of guardianship, §35A-1376.
Revocation of standby guardianship.
Appointment by petition, §35A-1373, (m).
Appointment by written designation, §35A-1374, (j).
Termination of standby guardianship generally, §35A-1382.
Suspension of guardianship.
Restoration of capacity or ability, §35A-1376.
Termination of standby guardianship, §35A-1382.
Unwillingness or inability of standby guardian to serve, §35A-1372.
State departments and agencies.
Gifts from income of incompetents, §35A-1335.
Status reports for incompetent wards.
Designated agencies.
Actions agency may take after receipt, §35A-1243, (b).
Certification that report reviewed, mailing copy to guardian, §35A-1243, (a).
Petitions requesting certain actions, §35A-1243, (b) to (d).
Filing by guardian of the person.
Compelling, procedure, §35A-1244.
Guardian of the person.
Confidentiality, access by persons or agencies, §35A-1242, (c).
Duty to file, §35A-1242, (a).
Oath or affirmation, filed under, §35A-1242, (b).
Second report, filing, time, §35A-1242, (a).
Time for filing after appointment, §35A-1242, (a).
Sterilization of mentally ill or retarded ward.
Consent or approval of guardian, §35A-1241, (a).
Duty to obtain order permitting guardian to consent, §90-275.
Medical necessity.
Procedure to permit, §35A-1245.
Mental necessity, procedure to permit, §35A-1245.
Appeal of clerk's order, §35A-1245, (f).
Consent requirements, §35A-1245, (a).

GUARDIANS —Cont'd
Sterilization of mentally ill or retarded ward —Cont'd
Mental necessity, procedure to permit —Cont'd
Court petition for consent, §35A-1245, (b).
Entry order, §35A-1245, (e).
Hearing on petition, §35A-1245, (d).
Service of petition, §35A-1245, (c).
Successor guardian.
Accounting by predecessor.
Compelling, §35A-1294, (a).
Appointment by clerk.
Resignation of guardian, §35A-1292.
Surplus income and advancements.
Parties to proceeding for advancements, §35A-1324.
Taxation.
Property taxes.
Payment of taxes by fiduciaries, §105-383.
Termination of guardianship, §35A-1295, (a).
Termination of parental rights proceedings.
Persons who may file petition or motion, intervention, right, §7B-1103, (a), (b).
Testamentary recommendation by parent for appointment of guardian of minor, §35A-1224, (d).
Guardian for incompetent minor, §35A-1225.
Torrens system registration.
Infants and persons under disability may sue by guardian, §43-8.
Training, education, employment, rehabilitation or habitation.
Guardian of person, duty to arrange for, §35A-1241, (a).
Transfer to minors.
Irrevocable transfer for benefit of minor.
Authority to make as custodian, §33A-6, (b), (c).
Trees and timber.
Sale of ward's estate.
When timber may be sold, §35A-1305.
Uniform fiduciaries act, §§32-1 to 32-13.
See FIDUCIARIES.
Validation.
Deeds by guardians omitting seal, prior to January 1, 1944, §35A-1360.
Sales.
Certain private sales validated, §35A-1361.
Venue.
Appointment, §35A-1204.
Determination of incompetence, §35A-1103.
Change of venue, §35A-1103.
Transfer to different county, §35A-1205.
Veterans' guardianship act, §§34-1 to 34-18.
See VETERANS' GUARDIANSHIP ACT.
Waste.
For and against whom action lies, §1-534.
Witnesses.
Medical, hospital or other charges at issue.
Competency to give evidence regarding amount, §8-58.1.
Rebuttable presumption of reasonableness.
Testimony establishing, §8-58.1.
Year's allowance for child.
Application, §30-20.
Superior court, §30-27.

GUARDRAILS.
Reports as to damage, §20-166, (c1).

GUARDS.
Prison guards.
Protection against violence.
Degree of protection allowed, §148-13, (a), (b).

GUARDS —Cont'd
Private protective services, §§74C-1 to 74C-33.
See PRIVATE PROTECTIVE SERVICES.

GUIDANCE COUNSELORS.
Communication between counselors and students, §§8-53.4, 115C-401.

GUIDE DOGS, §§168-4.2 to 168-4.6.
Blind pedestrians' rights and privileges without guide dog, §20-175.3.
Common carrier fares for blind person accompanied by, §62-144, (b).
Donation of service animal for training, §168-4.6.
Drivers duties approaching person using guide dog, §168-5.
Mobility impaired persons.
Defined, §168-4.2.
Pedestrian's rights and privileges without guide dog, §20-175.3.
Registration of service animal, §168-4.3.
Responsibility for service animals, §168-4.4.
Right of way at crossings, intersections and traffic control signal points.
Guide dog to serve as signal for the blind, §20-175.2.
Right to be accompanied by service animal, §168-4.2.
Penalty for depriving of right, §168-4.5.
Signal for blind persons crossing street, §20-175.2.
Tags, §168-4.2.
Training of service animal, §168-4.3.
Donation, §168-4.6.

GUIDES.
Hunting or fishing guides.
License, §113-270.4.

GUILFORD COUNTY.
Ambulances.
Attachment or garnishment and lien for, §§44-51.4 to 44-51.8.
False pretenses and cheats.
Obtaining ambulance services without intending to pay, §14-111.2.
Bicentennial commission.
Department of cultural resources.
Transfer of commission to department, §143B-51.
Blank or master forms of mortgages, deeds of trust, etc.
Indexing and recording, inapplicability of provisions, §47-21.
Board of county commissioners.
Filling vacancies on board, §153A-27.1.
Condemnation or acquisition of land by local government unit outside county.
Consent of board of commissioners necessary, §153A-15.
Coroner elected as nominee of political party.
Filling vacancy in office, §152-1.
Counties generally.
See COUNTIES.
County boards of education elected on partisan basis.
Vacancies in office, §115C-37.1.
Cropper or tenant refusing to perform terms of contract.
Forfeiture of right of possession to premises, §42-27.

GUILFORD COUNTY —Cont'd
Department of cultural resources.
Bicentennial commission.
Transfer of commission to department, §143B-51.
Dogs used in hunting.
Regulation by wildlife resources commission, §113-291.5, (a).
False pretenses and cheats.
Ambulance services.
Obtaining services without intending to pay, §14-111.2.
Motor vehicle emission inspections.
Counties inspections required to be performed in, §143-215.107A, (c).
Oil, gas and mineral interests separated from surface fee, extinguished, title in surface fee holder.
Failure to list interest for tax purposes 10 years prior to January 1, 1965.
Protection of subsurface interest from surface fee holder, §1-42.1, (d).
Failure to list interest for tax purposes for 10 years prior to January 1, 1971.
Protection of surface interest from surface estate holder, §1-42.2, (d).
Private parking lots.
Removal of unauthorized vehicles, §20-219.2.
School property.
Acquisition and improvement, §153A-158.1.
Sheriff.
Vacancy, performance of duties until vacancy filled, §162-5.1.

GUILTY PLEAS, §15A-1011, (a).
Acceptance.
District courts, §7A-272, (c), (d).
Prerequisites, §15A-1022, (a) to (c).
Capital offenses.
Death penalty or life imprisonment, §15A-2001.
Determinations by judge.
Required determination, §15A-1022, (a) to (c).
Factual basis for plea.
Judge must determine, §15A-1022, (c).
Felony cases transferred to district court.
Appeals, §15A-1029.1, (b).
Consent of parties, §15A-1029.1, (a).
Filing of information, §15A-644.1.
First degree murder.
Death penalty or life imprisonment, §15A-2001.
Impaired driving charge.
Acceptance by prosecutor, explanation, §20-138.4.
Improper pressure on defendant to plead guilty.
Determination by judge, §15A-1022, (b).
Prohibited, §15A-1021, (b).
Inadmissible in evidence, §8C-1, Rule 410.
Information, filing when plea of guilty or no contest in district court, §15A-644.1.
Information to be given defendant, §15A-1022, (a).
Informed choice.
Judge must determine, §15A-1022, (b).
Other crimes with which defendant charged, §15A-1011, (c).
Probable cause hearings.
Acceptance of guilty plea, §15A-613.
Record of proceedings, §§7A-191.1, 15A-1026.
Withdrawal.
Sentence not in accord with plea arrangement, §15A-1024.

GUNS.
Firearms generally.
See FIREARMS.
Weapons generally.
See WEAPONS.

GUNSHOT WOUNDS.
Reports.
Physicians and hospitals to report, §90-21.20.

GUTTERS.
Special assessments by counties, §§153A-185 to 153A-206.
See SPECIAL ASSESSMENTS BY COUNTIES.

GYNECOLOGISTS, DIRECT INSURANCE ACCESS, §58-51-38, (a).

GYNECOLOGY.
Primary care physicians, medical education, §143-613.

H

HABEAS CORPUS, §§17-1 to 17-46.
Absentees.
Party ill or infirm.
Cause determined in his absence, §17-37.
Ad prosequendum, §15-10.3.
Alternative in formal procedure, §15A-711.
Mentally ill prisoners, §15-10.4.
Ad testificandum, §§17-41 to 17-46.
Application for writ.
Contents, §17-7.
Denial, §17-4.
Habeas corpus ad testificandum.
Bond of applicant, §17-44.
Contents of application, §17-42.
Expenses, §17-44.
Verification, §17-42.
Issuance of writ without application, §17-8.
Judges to whom directed, §17-6.
Parties.
By whom application made, §17-5.
Signature of applicant, §17-6.
Statements required in applications, §17-7.
Verification by oath of applicant, §17-7.
Who may apply, §17-3.
Written application, §17-6.
Arrest in civil cases.
Party held in execution not to be discharged, §17-36.
Attachment.
County may be called on to aid execution, §17-22.
Failure to obey writ, §17-16.
Refusal of attachment.
Liability of judge refusing attachment, §17-17.
Sheriffs.
Attachment against sheriff to be directed to coroner, §17-18.
Order of discharge.
Compelling obedience, §17-23.
Bail and recognizance.
Right of habeas corpus not abridged, §15A-547.
When party bailed or remanded, §17-35.
Capital punishment.
Procedure when considering application, Super. Ct. Rule 25.
Concealing party entitled to writ, §17-28.
Constitution of North Carolina.
Inquiry into restraints on liberty, Const. N. C., art. I, §21.

HABEAS CORPUS —Cont'd
Constitution of North Carolina —Cont'd
Remedy without delay for restraint of liberty, §17-1.
Suspension of habeas corpus, §17-2.
Constitution of the United States.
Habeas corpus not to be suspended, Const. U. S., art. I, §9.
Contempt.
Remand of party in custody for contempt, §17-34.
Coroners.
Hearings by coroner, §152-10.
Costs.
Allowance of costs to either party or apportioned in discretion of court, §6-21.
Court of appeals.
Issuance of remedial writs, §7A-32, (a).
Damages.
Order of discharge.
Failure to comply, §17-23.
Defects of form immaterial, §17-11.
Denial of writ, §17-4.
Discharge of party.
Bail and recognizance.
When party bailed or remanded, §17-35.
Executions.
Party held in execution not to be discharged, §17-36.
Grounds, §17-33.
Judgment or order of discharge.
Enforcement, §17-23.
No civil liability for obedience, §17-24.
Jurisdiction of court or officer exceeded, §17-33.
Recommittal after discharge, §17-25.
Remand, §§17-34, 17-35.
Second committal after discharge, §17-38.
When discharged, §17-33.
Executions.
Party held in execution not to be discharged, §17-36.
Extradition.
Fugitives from other states.
Application for writ, §15A-730.
Form of writ.
Defects of form immaterial, §17-11.
Habeas corpus ad testificandum, §§17-41 to 17-46.
Hearings.
Summary hearing of issues, §17-32.
Illness or infirmity of party.
Cause determined in his absence, §17-37.
Industrial commission.
Issuance of writs, §97-101.1.
Issuance of writ.
Grant of writ without delay, §17-9.
Penalty for refusal to grant, §17-10.
Without application, §17-8.
Judges.
Attachment for failure to obey writ, §§17-16, 17-17.
Granting of writ without delay, §17-9.
Penalty for refusal to grant, §17-10.
Impeachment.
Attachment for failure to obey writ.
Judge refusing attachment, §17-17.
Insufficient return.
Liability of judge conniving at, §17-21.
Precept to bring up party detained.
Judge refusing precept, §17-20.
Insufficient return.
Liability of judge conniving at, §17-21.

HABEAS CORPUS —Cont'd
Judges —Cont'd
Precept to bring up party detained, §17-19.
Liability of judge refusing precept, §17-20.
Jurisdiction of court or officer exceeded.
Discharge of party, §17-33.
Laches.
Willful neglect to apply for writ.
Grounds for denial of application, §17-4.
Mental health, developmental disabilities and substance abuse.
Involuntary inpatient commitment.
Availability of relief to respondent, §122C-268.1, (j).
Misdemeanors.
Concealing party entitled to writ, §17-28.
False returns, §17-27.
Recommittal after discharge, §17-25.
Motion for appropriate relief.
Availability not a bar to habeas corpus, §15A-1411, (c).
Notice.
District attorney, §17-30.
Interested parties, §17-29.
Oaths and affirmations.
Application for writ.
Verification by oath of applicant, §17-7.
Return of writ.
Verification by oath, §17-14.
Obedience to order of discharge.
No civil liability, §17-24.
Parties.
Application for writ.
By whom application made, §17-5.
Penalties.
Attachment for failure to obey writ.
Liability of judge refusing attachment, §17-17.
Disobedience to writ, §17-26.
Insufficient return.
Liability of judge conniving at, §17-21.
Order of discharge.
Failure to comply, §17-23.
Precept to bring up party detained.
Refusal of precept.
Liability of judge refusing, §17-20.
Refusal to grant writ, §17-10.
Return.
Refusal or neglect to make return, §17-26.
Second committal after discharge, §17-38.
Precept to bring up party detained, §17-19.
County may be called on to aid execution, §17-22.
Refusal of precept.
Liability of judge refusing precept, §17-20.
Production of body if required, §17-15.
Precept to bring up party detained, §17-19.
Refusal of precept.
Liability of judge refusing, §17-20.
Time for, §17-13.
Recommittal after discharge, §17-25.
Remand of party.
Executions.
Party held in execution not to be discharged, §17-36.
When party remanded, §§17-34, 17-35.
Return of writ.
Contents of return, §17-14.
False return, §17-27.
Insufficient return.
Judge conniving at, §17-21.
Proceedings on return, §17-32.

HABEAS CORPUS —Cont'd
Return of writ —Cont'd
Production of body if required, §17-15.
Time for, §17-13.
Refusal or neglect to make return, §17-26.
Time for, §17-13.
Verification by oath, §17-14.
Written return, §17-14.
Right to remedy, §17-1.
Granting of writ without delay, §17-9.
Penalty for refusal to grant, §17-10.
Who may prosecute writ, §17-3.
Service of writ, §17-12.
County may be called on to aid service, §17-22.
Habeas corpus ad testificandum, §17-43.
Applicant to pay expenses and give bond to return, §17-44.
Duty of officer to whom writ delivered or on whom served, §17-45.
Subpoenas.
Witnesses in habeas corpus proceedings, §17-31.
Sufficiency of writ, §17-11.
Supreme court.
Issuance of remedial writs, §7A-32, (a).
Suspension.
Prohibited, §17-2; Const. U. S., art. I, §9.
United States courts.
Persons committed or detained by.
When application denied, §17-4.
Remand of party.
When party remanded, §17-34.
Verification.
Application for habeas corpus ad testificandum, §17-42.
Return of writ.
Verification by oath, §17-14.
Witnesses.
Habeas corpus ad testificandum, §§17-41 to 17-46.
Subpoenas in habeas corpus proceedings, §17-31.

HABEAS CORPUS AD TESTIFICANDUM, §§17-41 to 17-46.
Application for writ.
Bond of applicant, §17-44.
Contents of application, §17-42.
Expenses.
Applicant to pay, §17-44.
Verification, §17-42.
Bond of applicant, §17-44.
Clerks of superior court.
Power to issue writ, §17-41.
Courts of record.
Power to issue writ, §17-41.
Issuance of writ.
Authority to issue, §17-41.
Magistrates.
Power to issue writs, §17-41.
Remand of party, §17-46.
Service of writ, §17-43.
Applicant to pay expenses and give bond to return, §17-44.
Duty of officer to whom writ delivered or on whom served, §17-45.

HABITS.
Relevancy to prove conduct of person, §8C-1, Rule 406.

HABITUAL FELONS, §§14-7.1 to 14-7.12.
Charge of habitual felon, §14-7.3.
Defined, §14-7.1.
Evidence of prior convictions, §14-7.4.

HABITUAL FELONS —Cont'd
Indictment, §14-7.2.
Charge of habitual felon, §14-7.3.
Judgment, §14-7.5.
Prior convictions.
Evidence, §14-7.4.
Punishment, §14-7.2.
Sentencing, §§14-7.2, 14-7.6.
Structured sentencing.
Inapplicability to violent habitual felons, §15A-1340.10.
Verdict, §14-7.5.
Violent habitual felons.
Charge, §14-7.9.
Convicted defined, §14-7.7, (a).
Evidence of prior convictions, §14-7.10.
Persons declared to be, §14-7.7, (a).
Punishment, §14-7.8.
Sentencing, §14-7.12.
Verdict and judgment, §14-7.11.
Violent felony, crimes included in term, §14-7.7, (b).

HAGUE CONVENTION.
Child custody jurisdiction and enforcement, §50A-302.
Prosecutor or public official, role of, §50A-315.

HAIL INSURANCE.
Beach area essential property insurance, §58-45-35, (e).
Property insurance generally.
See PROPERTY INSURANCE.

HAIR DYE.
Food, drug and cosmetic act.
Cautionary statement required, §106-136.

HAIR SAMPLES.
Nontestimonial identification.
Delinquent or undisciplined juvenile actions, §§7B-2103 to 7B-2109.
Generally, §§15A-271 to 15A-282.
See IDENTIFICATION.

HALF-WAY HOUSES.
Post-release supervision, §§15A-1368 to 15A-1368.6.
See POST-RELEASE SUPERVISION.

HALIFAX COUNTY.
Ambulance service.
Attachment or garnishment and lien for, §§44-51.4 to 44-51.8.
Obtaining ambulance services without intending to pay, §14-111.2.
Requesting ambulance falsely, §14-111.3.
Blank or master forms of mortgages, deeds of trust, etc.
Indexing and recording, inapplicability of provisions, §47-21.
Condemnation or acquisition of land by local government unit outside county.
Consent of board of commissioners necessary, §153A-15.
Cropper or tenant refusing to perform terms of contract.
Forfeiture of right of possession to premises, §42-27.
Game laws, local acts not repealed, §113-133.1, (e).
Grants in navigable waters, registration, §113-205, (a).

HALIFAX COUNTY —Cont'd
Housing authority commissioners.
Tenant as commissioner, exemption from provision of law allowing, §157-5.
Low-income housing tax credits.
Qualified building eligible for credit, §105-129.41, (c).
Multi-county water conservation and infrastructure district.
Generally, §158-15.1.
Northeastern North Carolina regional economic development commission, §158-8.2.
Officers compensated from fees.
Statement to be rendered, §128-13.
Oil, gas or mineral interest separated from surface interest, extinguished, title in surface fee holder.
Failure to list interest for tax purposes for 10 years prior to January 1, 1974.
Protection of interest from surface estate, §1-42.3, (d).
Probates and registration orders before clerks of inferior courts validated, §47-59.
Registration of deeds.
Tax certification, no delinquent taxes due, §161-31, (b).
School property.
Acquisition and improvement, §153A-158.1.
Tax sales, notices by publication validated.
Inapplicability of provisions, §47-108.24.

HALIFAX DAY.
Public holiday, §103-4, (a).

HALIWA SAPONI TRIBE.
Rights, privileges, immunities, obligations and duties, §71A-5.

HALLOWEEN.
Distribution of certain food at Halloween and all other times prohibited, §14-401.11, (a), (b).

HALLS OF FAME.
Agriculture, §§106-568.13 to 106-568.17.
See AGRICULTURAL HALL OF FAME.

HALLUCINOGENIC SUBSTANCES.
Schedule I controlled substances, §90-89.
Schedule II controlled substances, §90-90.
Unauthorized substances taxes, §§105-113.105 to 105-113.113.
See UNAUTHORIZED SUBSTANCES TAXES.

HAMMOCKS BEACH STATE PARK.
Removal from state nature and historic preserve, §143-260.10D.

HAM RADIO OPERATORS.
Interception of radio communications not unlawful, §15A-287, (b).
Special license plates, §20-79.4, (a).

HAND AND ARM SIGNALS.
Operators of motor vehicles, §20-154, (b).

HANDGUNS.
Concealed handgun permit, §§14-415.10 to 14-415.24.
See CONCEALED HANDGUN PERMIT.
Firearms generally.
See FIREARMS.
Weapons generally.
See WEAPONS.

HANDICAPPED PERSONS.

Abused, neglected or exploited disabled adults, §§108A-99 to 108A-111.
See ABUSED, NEGLECTED OR EXPLOITED DISABLED ADULTS.

Alcoholic beverages.
Refusal to sell not to be discriminatory, §18B-305, (c).

Animals.
Service animals, §§168-4.2 to 168-4.6.

Blind persons generally, §§111-4 to 111-47.
See BLIND PERSONS.

Commission for the blind, §§143B-157 to 143B-160.
Consumer and advocacy advisory committee for the blind, §§143B-163, 143B-164.
Professional advisory committee, §§143B-161, 143B-162.

Commission to study the care of the aged and handicapped, §§143-279 to 143-283.

Community trust for persons with severe chronic disabilities, §§36A-59.10 to 36A-59.20.
See COMMUNITY TRUST FOR PERSONS WITH SEVERE CHRONIC DISABILITIES.

Consumer and advocacy advisory committee for the blind, §§143B-163, 143B-164.

Council on developmental disabilities, §§143B-177 to 143B-179.

Developmental disabilities generally.
See MENTAL HEALTH, DEVELOPMENTAL DISABILITY, SUBSTANCE ABUSE.

Disabled persons generally.
See DISABLED PERSONS.

Fair housing generally, §§41A-1 to 41A-10.
See FAIR HOUSING.

Generally.
See DISABLED PERSONS.

Governor's advocacy council for persons with disability, §§143B-403.1, 143B-403.2.

Governor's council on employment of the handicapped, §§143-283.1 to 143-283.8.

Hearing impaired generally.
See HEARING IMPAIRED.

Human service and volunteer transportation, §§62-289.1 to 62-289.7.
See HUMAN SERVICE AND VOLUNTEER TRANSPORTATION.

Hunting and fishing.
Disabled sportsman program, §113-296.
Special vehicular access identification card and permit.
Violation of rules restricting access to holders, §113-294, (n).

Indictments.
Essentials of bill.
Victim physically helpless, §15-144.2, (c).

Interagency coordinating council for children from birth to five with disabilities and their families, §§143B-179.5, 143B-179.6.
Regional councils, §143B-179.5A.

Mentally ill generally.
See MENTAL HEALTH, DEVELOPMENTAL DISABILITY, SUBSTANCE ABUSE.

Parking, §§20-37.6, 20-37.6, (a).
Definitions, §20-37.5.
Public vehicular areas.
Signs differing from uniform signs, §136-30, (c).

Service animals, §§168-4.2 to 168-4.6.

Special education.
See SPECIAL EDUCATION.

HANDLERS OF FRUIT OR VEGETABLES.

Unfair practices by handlers, §§106-496 to 106-501.
Bond required, §106-498.
Contracts between handlers and producers, §106-499.
Definition of handler, §106-496.
Enforcement of article.
Commissioner of agriculture to enforce, §106-500.
Permits required, §106-497.
Powers of commissioner, §106-500.
Protection against unfair trade practices, §106-496.
Violations of article or rules made misdemeanor, §106-501.

HANDS.

Workers' compensation.
Loss of hands.
Rates of compensation, I.C. Rule 405.

HANDSHAKES.

Secret societies' use of grips for illegal purposes, §14-12.4.

HANDWRITING.

Acknowledgments.
Proof of handwriting of maker refusing to acknowledge, §47-57.

Authentication and identification of evidence, §8C-1, Rule 901, (b).

Holographic wills, §31-3.4.

Nontestimonial identification.
Delinquent and undisciplined juveniles, §§7B-2103 to 7B-2109.
Generally, §§15A-271 to 15A-282.
See IDENTIFICATION.

Probates on proof of handwriting of maker refusing to acknowledge, §47-57.

Proof of attested instrument by proof of handwriting, §47-12.1, (a).
Section not to affect certain requirements, §47-12.1, (b).

Proof of unattested writing, §47-13.

HARASSMENT.

Assaulting law enforcement or assistance animals, §14-163.1, (d).

Civil rights, interference with, §99D-1.

Collection agencies.
Prohibited practices, §58-70-100.

Debt collectors.
Prohibited acts, §75-52.

Domestic violence.
Orders for relief, §50B-3, (a).

Fish and fisheries resources.
Unlawful harassment of persons taking wildlife resources, §113-295.

Hunting and wildlife.
Unlawful harassment of persons taking wildlife resources, §113-295.

Jury.
Definition of "juror," §14-225.2, (b).
Elements of offense, §14-225.2, (a).
Penalties, §14-225.2, (c).

Public schools.
Conflict resolution and mediation models, §115C-81, (a4).

Sexual harassment.
Equal employment practices, §§143-422.1 to 143-422.3.

HARASSMENT —Cont'd
Sexual harassment —Cont'd
Rental of residential property.
Definitions, §14-395.1, (b).
Offense, §14-395.1, (a).
School employees, §115C-335.5.
Stalking.
See STALKING.
Telephones, §14-196.
Threats.
See THREATS.
Workplace violence prevention.
Civil no-contact orders, §§95-265 to 95-276.
See WORKPLACE VIOLENCE PREVENTION.

HARBORING OR AIDING ESCAPEE, §14-259.
State institution, §14-267.

HARBOR MASTERS.
How appointed, §76-53.
No board of navigation, §76-56.

HARBORS.
Municipal corporations.
Property taxes.
Authorized purposes, §160A-209, (c).
Ports authority.
See PORTS AUTHORITY.
United States acquisition of land for harbor improvements, §104-6.

HARMLESS ERROR, §1A-1, Rule 61.

HARNETT COUNTY.
Acquisition of property, power, §153A-158.1, (a).
Ambulance service.
Attachment or garnishment and lien for, §§44-51.4 to 44-51.8.
Condemnation or acquisition of land by local government unit outside county.
Consent of board of commissioners necessary, §153A-15.
Cropper or tenant refusing to perform terms of contract.
Forfeiture of right of possession to premises, §42-27.
Dangerous firearm use by young children, permitting.
Air rifles, air pistols and BB guns not dangerous firearm, §14-316, (b).
Game laws, local acts not repealed, §113-133.1, (e).
Maps in special proceedings, recording of photographic copies, §47-32.
Violation as misdemeanor, inapplicability of provisions, §47-32.2.
Officers compensated from fees.
Statement to be rendered, §128-13.
Registration of deeds.
Tax certification, no delinquent taxes due, §161-31, (b).
School property.
Acquisition and improvement, §153A-158.1.
Tax elections for industrial development purposes, §§158-16 to 158-24.
Tax sales, notices by publication validated.
Inapplicability of provisions, §47-108.24.

HATCHBACKS.
Open container law.
Definition of passenger area of motor vehicle, §20-138.7, (f).

HATCHERIES.
Fish.
Obstructing or polluting flow of water into hatcheries, §113-265, (a).

HATCHERIES —Cont'd
Fish —Cont'd
Robbing or injuring, §113-269.
Poultry.
Compulsory testing for disease, §106-548.
Defined, §106-541.
Fines, §106-549.01.
Grade of chicks.
Posting of notice describing grade, §106-546.
License needed to operate, §106-542.
Misdemeanor offenses, §106-549.
Penalties.
Civil penalties, §106-549.01.
Quarantine on premises, §106-548.
Records to be kept, §106-547.
Rules and regulations, §106-540.
Shipments from out of state, §106-544.

HATE CRIMES.
Ethnic intimidation, §14-401.14, (a), (b).
Misdemeanors.
Punishment, §14-3, (c).
Secret societies and activities generally, §§14-12.2 to 14-12.15.
See SECRET SOCIETIES.

HAUNTED HOUSES.
Amusement device safety generally, §§95-111.1 to 95-111.18.
See AMUSEMENT DEVICE SAFETY.
Real estate sales disclosures, §39-50.

HAYWOOD COUNTY.
Acquisition of property, power, §153A-158.1, (a).
Ambulance service.
Attachment or garnishment and lien for, §§44-51.4 to 44-51.8.
Obtaining ambulance services without intending to pay, §§14-111.1, 14-111.2.
Requesting ambulance falsely, §14-111.3.
Board of county commissioners.
Filling vacancies on board, §153A-27.1.
Condemnation or acquisition of land by local government unit outside county.
Consent of board of commissioners necessary, §153A-15.
Coroner elected as nominee of political party.
Filling vacancy in office, §152-1.
Counties generally.
See COUNTIES.
County boards of education elected on partisan basis.
Vacancies in office, §115C-37.1.
Dangerous firearm use by young children, permitting.
Air rifles, air pistols and BB guns not dangerous firearm, §14-316, (b).
Dog collars.
Unlawful removal of electronic dog collars, §14-401.17.
Forestland sales, distribution of funds, §113-38.
Game laws, local acts not repealed, §113-133.1, (e).
Housing authority commissioners.
Tenant as commissioner, exemption from provision of law allowing, §157-5.
Officers compensated from fees.
Statement to be rendered, §128-13.
Oil, gas and mineral interests separated from surface fee, extinguished, title in surface fee holder.
Interest not listed for tax purposes for 10 years prior to January 1, 1971.
Protection of surface interest from surface estate holder, §1-42.2, (d).

HAYWOOD COUNTY —Cont'd
On-premises unfortified wine licenses.
Discretion to decline to issue, §105-113.71, (b).
Registration of deeds.
Tax certification, no delinquent taxes due, §161-31, (b).
School property.
Acquisition and improvement, §153A-158.1.
Sheriff.
Vacancy, performance of duties until vacancy filled, §162-5.1.
Tax deeds in Haywood.
Recitals in tax deeds, §8-22.
Tax elections for industrial development purposes, §§158-16 to 158-24.
Western North Carolina Development Association, Inc.
Appropriation of funds to, §153A-447, (a), (b).
Western North Carolina regional economic development commission, §158-8.1.

HAZARDOUS CHEMICALS RIGHT TO KNOW ACT, §§95-173 to 95-218.
See TOXIC SUBSTANCES.

HAZARDOUS MATERIALS EMERGENCY RESPONSE, §§166A-20 to 166A-25.
Contracts with local governments, §166A-23.
Costs for responses, recovery, §166A-24.
Definitions, §166A-21.
Equipment loans, §166A-23.
Fund, §166A-28.
Immunity from liability.
Regional response team personnel, §166A-24.
Program established, §166A-22.
Purpose of act, §166A-20.
Regional response team advisory committee, §166A-26.
Created, §166A-26, (a).
Duties, §166A-26, (d).
Meetings, §166A-26, (b).
Membership, §166A-26, (a).
Reimbursement for expenses, §166A-26, (c).
Regional response team personnel.
Immunity from liability, §166A-24.
Right of entry.
Emergency response team personnel, §166A-25.
Standards, §166A-22.
Title of act, §166A-20.

HAZARDOUS RECREATION ACTIVITIES, §§99E-21 to 99E-25.
Assumption of inherent risks, §99E-24, (a).
Definitions, §99E-22.
Governmental entities.
Limitation of liability, §99E-25, (b).
Duty of care not created, §99E-25, (d).
Exceptions, §99E-25, (c).
Independent concessionaires or other persons or organizations.
Liability not limited by section, §99E-25, (e).
Insurance carried by entity.
Not waiver of liability limits, §99E-25, (f).
Sovereign immunity not waived, §99E-25, (d).
Operating unsupervised skateboard park.
Wearing of helmet, elbow pads and kneepads.
Satisfaction of requirement, §99E-23, (b).
Specifically designated areas for activities.
Required to participate on property owner or controlled by entity, §99E-25, (a).

HAZARDOUS RECREATION ACTIVITIES —Cont'd
Helmet, elbow pads and kneepads.
Skateboard parks.
Wearing required, §99E-21, (a).
Governmental entity operating park not supervised on regular basis.
Satisfaction of requirement, §99E-21, (b).
Inherent risk.
Assumption, §99E-24, (a).
Negligence.
Responsibilities of participants.
Failure to comply, §99E-24, (c).
Observers.
Assumption of inherent risks, §99E-24, (a).
Participants.
Assumption of inherent risks, §99E-24, (a).
Purpose of article, §99E-21.
Responsibilities of participants, §99E-24, (b).
Negligence, failure to comply, §99E-24, (c).
Skateboard parks.
Helmet, elbow pads and kneepads.
Wearing required, §99E-21, (a).
Governmental entity operating park not supervised on regular basis.
Satisfaction of requirement, §99E-21, (b).

HAZARDOUS SUBSTANCES.
Brownfields property reuse act of 1997, §§130A-310.30 to 130A-310.40.
See BROWNFIELDS PROPERTY REUSE.
Chlorofluorocarbons refrigerants.
Management of discarded white goods, §§130A-309.80 to 130A-309.87.
See WHITE GOODS.
Commercial drivers' licenses.
Disqualification.
Offenses while transporting hazardous materials, §20-17.4, (e).
Contamination at site.
Deed or other instrument of conveyance, contaminated property statement, §143B-279.10, (e).
Land use restrictions imposed by secretary of environment and natural resources.
Reduction of danger to public health, §143B-279.9.
Notice of contamination, survey plat identifying designated area submitted by owner of site, §143B-279.10, (a).
Cancellation after contamination eliminated, owner's request, §143B-279.10, (f).
Filing copy in register of deeds office, §143B-279.10, (b).
Recording copy, §143B-279.10, (c).
Secretary may prepare and file, owner's failure, §143B-279.10, (d).
Control generally, §§143-215.75 to 143-215.82.
See OIL POLLUTION AND HAZARDOUS SUBSTANCES CONTROL.
Discharges, §§143-215.83 to 143-215.94.
See OIL OR HAZARDOUS SUBSTANCES DISCHARGES.
Dry-cleaning solvent cleanup, §§143-215.104A to 143-215.104U.
See DRY-CLEANING SOLVENT CLEANUP.
Dumping, §14-284.2.
Highway patrol.
Oversized and hazardous shipment escort fee, §20-196.4.

HAZARDOUS SUBSTANCES —Cont'd
Identification of toxic or hazardous substances, §§95-173 to 95-218.
See TOXIC SUBSTANCES.
Land-use restrictions at contaminated site.
Imposed by secretary of environment and natural resources.
Reduction of danger to public health, §143B-279.9.
Lead-based paint hazard management program, §§130A-453.01 to 130A-453.11.
See LEAD-BASED PAINT.
Leaking petroleum underground storage tank cleanup, §§143-215.94A to 143-215.94Y.
See UNDERGROUND PETROLEUM STORAGE TANK LEAK CLEANUP.
Notice of contamination, survey plat submitted by owner of site, §143B-279.10.
Offshore oil and gas activities, §§143-215.94AA to 143-215.94JJ.
See OFFSHORE OIL AND GAS ACTIVITIES.
Pesticide applicators, §§143-452 to 143-459.
See PESTICIDE APPLICATORS.
Pesticide board generally.
See PESTICIDE BOARD.
Pesticide consultants, §§143-455, 143-456.
Pesticide dealers and manufacturers licenses, §§143-448 to 143-451.
Pesticide registration.
See PESTICIDE REGISTRATION.
Poisons.
See POISONS.
Toxic substances.
See TOXIC SUBSTANCES.
White goods.
Management of discarded white goods, §§130A-309.80 to 130A-309.87.
See WHITE GOODS.

HAZARDOUS WASTE, LITTERING, §14-399, (e).

HAZARDOUS WASTE MANAGEMENT, §§130A-291 to 130A-310.23.
Abandoned, idle or unused property.
Brownfields property reuse act of 1997, §§130A-310.30 to 130A-310.40.
See BROWNFIELDS PROPERTY REUSE.
Appeals.
Hazardous waste facilities.
Preempting local ordinance, §130A-293, (e).
Bond issues.
Solid waste management loans and local government special obligation bonds.
Generally, §§159I-1 to 159I-30.
See SOLID WASTE MANAGEMENT LOANS AND SPECIAL OBLIGATION BONDS.
Brownfields property reuse act of 1997.
Generally, §§130A-310.30 to 130A-310.40.
See BROWNFIELDS PROPERTY REUSE.
Chemical storage facilities.
New facilities in flood hazard areas, §143-215.54, (c).
Chlorofluorocarbons refrigerants.
Management of discarded white goods, §§103A-309.80 to 130A-309.87.
See WHITE GOODS.
Commission.
Personnel system.
Exemption of employees, §126-5, (c1).
Comprehensive waste treatment facility.
Defined, §130A-290.
Containers, §130A-295.03.

HAZARDOUS WASTE MANAGEMENT —Cont'd
Contamination at site.
Deed or other instrument of conveyance, contaminated property statement, §143B-279.10, (e).
Exceptions to recordation provisions, §143B-279.10, (g).
Land use restrictions imposed by secretary of environment and natural resources.
Reduction of danger to public health, §143B-279.9.
Notice of contamination, survey plat identifying designated area submitted by owner of site, §143B-279.10, (a).
Cancellation after contamination eliminated, owner's request, §143B-279.10, (f).
Filing copy in register of deeds office, §143B-279.10, (b).
Recording copy, §143B-279.10, (c).
Secretary may prepare and file, owner's failure, §143B-279.10, (d).
Conveyances.
Hazardous waste landfill facility.
Land used for facility conveyed to state, §130A-292.
Counties.
Local ordinances prohibiting facilities invalid, §130A-293.
Defenses.
Felonies, §130A-26.1, (e), (i).
Definitions, §130A-290.
Hazardous waste treatment facility, §130A-290.
Inactive hazardous sites, §130A-310.
Long-term retrievable storage, §130A-290.
Superfund program, §130A-310.20.
Emergency response fund, §130A-306.
Eminent hazard.
Elimination of hazard, §130A-303, (b).
Existence of eminent hazard, §130A-303, (a).
Environmental review commission.
Powers and duties, §120-70.43, (c).
Evidence.
Circumstantial evidence of defendant's possession of actual knowledge, §130A-26.1, (c).
Facilities.
Commercial hazardous waste treatment facilities.
Definitions, §130A-295.01, (a).
Inspectors.
Resident inspectors, §130A-295.02.
Requirements for permits, §130A-295.01, (b).
Resident inspectors, §130A-295.02.
Containers.
Use, §130A-295.03.
Continuing releases at permitted facilities.
Corrective actions beyond facility boundary, §130A-309.
Conveyance of land used for facility to state.
Consideration for conveyance, §130A-292, (a).
Liability of lessee, §130A-292, (b).
Termination of lease, §130A-292, (c), (d).
Criteria and standards to be considered in location, §130A-294, (g).
Defined, §130A-290.
Disposal of solid waste in or upon water, §130A-294, (l).
Fees, §130A-294.1, (k), (l).
Permit for facility, §130A-294.1, (m), (n).
Resident inspectors at commercial hazardous waste facilities.
Costs of employment and assignment, §130A-295.02, (h).

HAZARDOUS WASTE MANAGEMENT —Cont'd
Facilities —Cont'd
Financially qualified, §130A-295, (b).
Hearings.
Permit for facility, §130A-294, (f).
Inspectors.
Resident inspectors at commercial hazardous waste facilities, §130A-295.02.
License tax.
Counties, §153A-152.1, (a) to (c).
Rates applied by localities to.
Review upon appeal, §130A-294, (r).
Local ordinances prohibiting facilities invalid, §130A-293, (a).
Petition to preempt local ordinance, §130A-293, (b) to (f).
Monitoring and regulating generators, §130A-294, (i).
Permit for facility.
Conduct of public hearing, §130A-294, (f).
Criteria and standards to be considered, §130A-294, (g).
Fees, §130A-294.1, (m), (n).
Need for facility, §130A-295, (c).
Requirements.
Additional requirements for facilities, §130A-295, (a).
Commercial hazardous waste treatment facilities, §130A-295.01, (b).
Public education and involvement in decision-making process, §130A-294, (o).
Releases.
Continuing releases at permitted facilities.
Corrective actions beyond facility boundary, §130A-309.
Corrective action.
Request for determination that corrective action completed, §130A-308, (b).
Required, §130A-308, (a).
Requirements.
Additional requirements for facility, §130A-295, (a).
Resident inspectors at commercial hazardous waste facilities.
Access to operation areas, §130A-295.02, (d).
Costs of employment and assignment, §130A-295.02, (h).
Duration of assignment, §130A-295.02, (i).
Employment, §130A-295.02, (a).
Facilities, §130A-295.02, (b), (c).
Maintenance or repair.
Presence of inspector required, §130A-295.02, (e).
Peace officers.
Commissioning inspectors as special peace officers, §130A-295.02, (g).
Powers, §130A-295.02, (a).
Purpose of provisions, §130A-295.02, (f).
Qualifications.
Division to establish requirements, §130A-295.02, (b).
Special purpose commercial hazardous waste facilities, §130A-295.02, (j).
Testing or calibration.
Presence of inspector required, §130A-295.02, (e).
Right of entry by department, §130A-294, (s).
Rules and regulations, §130A-294, (b), (h).
Volume and quantity or toxicity of waste.
Description of program to minimize or reduce, §130A-294, (k).

HAZARDOUS WASTE MANAGEMENT —Cont'd
False reports.
Penalty, §130A-26.2.
Fees.
Hazardous waste generators, transporters and facilities.
Deposit of fees collected, §130A-294.1, (d).
Facilities, §130A-294.1, (k), (l).
Permits, §130A-294.1, (m), (n).
Generators of hazardous waste, §130A-294.1, (e) to (i).
Legislative intent, §130A-294.1, (a), (c).
Reports by department.
Cost of program, §130A-294.1, (p).
Transporters of hazardous waste, §130A-294.1, (j).
Use of funds collected, §130A-294.1, (b).
When fees due, §130A-294.1, (o).
Felonies.
Classification, §130A-26.1, (f), (g), (i).
Defenses, §130A-26.1, (e), (i).
Definition of "person," §130A-26.1, (a).
Federal violation based on same set of facts.
Conviction as bar to proceedings, §130A-26.1, (b).
"Knowingly and willingly."
Circumstantial evidence of defendant's possession of actual knowledge, §130A-26.1, (c).
Meaning of term, §130A-26.1, (h).
Restrictions on findings concerning defendant's state of mind, §130A-26.1, (d).
Second or subsequent conviction, §130A-26.1, (i), (j).
Flood hazard areas.
New facilities in, §143-215.54, (c).
Funds.
Emergency response fund, §130A-306.
Establishment of hazardous waste fund, §130A-298.
Hazardous waste fund, §130A-298.
Inactive hazardous sites cleanup fund, §130A-310.11.
Superfund program, §§130A-310.20 to 130A-310.23.
Governor's award of excellence, §130A-294, (p).
Hazardous waste long-term storage facility, §130A-290.
Hearings.
Hazardous waste facilities.
Conduct of public hearing.
Prior to issuance of permit, §130A-294, (f).
Petition to preempt local ordinance, §130A-293, (c).
Impoundments.
Locating, cataloging and monitoring, §130A-294, (i).
Inactive hazardous sites, §§130A-310 to 130A-310.13.
Access to site, right of secretary, §130A-310.1, (i).
Administrative procedure.
Applicability to provisions, §130A-310.12, (a).
Administrative search and inspection warrant.
Refusal to grant access to site, §130A-310.1, (i).
Citation of part, §130A-310.13.
Clean drinking water fund, §130A-310.11.
Cleanup fund, §130A-310.11.
Costs.
Actions taken by secretary, §130A-310.1, (e).
Declaration that site endangers public health or environment, §130A-310.3, (a).

HAZARDOUS WASTE MANAGEMENT —Cont'd
Inactive hazardous sites —Cont'd
Definitions, §130A-310.
Determination that site remediated to current standards, request, §130A-310.7, (c).
Drinking water.
Clean drinking water fund, §130A-310.11.
Furnishing information, documents or records to secretary, §130A-310.1, (f).
Groundwater flow.
Migrating waste to property.
Waiver of recordation of notice of sites, §130A-310.8, (h).
Imminent hazard.
Action taken by secretary, §130A-310.5, (a).
Cost, §130A-310.5, (c).
Orders by secretary, §130A-310.5, (a).
Injunctions, §130A-310.5, (b).
Implementation of remedial action.
Limitation on liability, §130A-310.9, (a).
Voluntary remedial action program, §130A-310.9, (b), (c).
Injunctions.
Failure to submit data or comply with orders, §130A-310.1, (d).
Imminent hazard orders, §130A-310.5, (b).
Inspection and copying information, documents and records, §130A-310.1, (g).
Inventory, §130A-310.1, (a).
Land-use restrictions imposed by owner, operator, etc., §130A-310.3, (f).
Limitation of liability for implementing remedial action program, §130A-310.9, (a).
List.
Priority list, §130A-310.2.
Notice.
Copies of proposed plan.
Availability for inspection and copying, §130A-310.4, (b).
Imminent hazard.
Orders, §130A-310.5, (a).
Local health director.
Involvement in development of plan, §130A-310.4, (a).
Orders.
Monitoring, testing, analysis and reporting, §130A-310.1, (c).
Remedial action, §130A-310.3, (c).
Recordation of sites generally, §130A-310.8.
Remedial action.
Form and content of notices, §130A-310.4, (g).
Orders, §130A-310.3, (c).
Proposed plan, §130A-310.4, (c).
Hearing on, §130A-310.4, (f).
Operator.
Data to be submitted by, §130A-310.1, (b).
Failure to submit data.
Injunction, §130A-310.1, (d).
Defined, §130A-310.
Orders.
Imminent hazard, §130A-310.5, (a), (b).
Monitoring, testing, analysis and reporting, §130A-310.1, (c).
Injunction, §130A-310.1, (d).
Remedial action, §130A-310.3, (c).
Owner.
Data to be submitted by, §130A-310.1, (b).
Failure to submit data, §130A-310.1, (b).
Defined, §130A-310.
Priority list, §130A-310.2.

HAZARDOUS WASTE MANAGEMENT —Cont'd
Inactive hazardous sites —Cont'd
Recordation of notice of sites.
Applicability of provisions, §130A-310.8, (g).
Cancellation when hazards eliminated, §130A-310.8, (f).
Filing, §130A-310.8, (b) to (d).
Groundwater migrating waste to property.
Waiver of recordation, §130A-310.8, (h).
Sale, lease, conveyance or transfer of site, §130A-310.8, (e).
Submission to department, §130A-310.8, (a).
Waiver of recordation.
Residential real property contaminated by waste migration, §130A-310.8, (h).
Remedial action.
Defined, §130A-310.
Federal approval of programs, §130A-310.3, (d).
Notice, §§130A-310.3, (c), 130A-310.4, (c), (f), (g).
Orders, §130A-310.3, (c).
Permits, §130A-310.3, (e).
Powers and duties of secretary, §130A-310.3, (a) to (c).
Proposed plan.
Copies, §130A-310.4, (b).
Hearings on, §130A-310.4, (e), (f).
Notice, §130A-310.4, (c).
Public meeting to explain, §130A-310.4, (d).
Restrictions on current or future use of real property, §130A-310.3, (f).
Voluntary remedial action program, §130A-310.9, (b), (c).
Reports.
Annual report by secretary, §130A-310.10, (a), (b).
Requests for determination that site remediated to current standards, §130A-310.7, (c).
Responsible party.
Default of responsible party, §130A-310.6, (a).
Defined, §130A-310.
Generally, §130A-310.7, (a).
Inability to locate responsible party, §130A-310.6, (b).
Liability, §130A-310.7, (a).
Exceptions, §130A-310.7, (b).
Restrictions on current or future use of real property comprising.
Owner, operator or other responsible party authorized to impose, §130A-310.3, (f).
Rules and regulations, §130A-310.12, (b).
Short title of part, §130A-310.13.
Subpoenas by secretary to collect information, §130A-310.1, (h).
Voluntary remedial action program.
Agreement with owner, operator or other responsible party for implementation, §130A-310.9, (b).
Approving private environmental consulting engineering firm to implement, §130A-310.9, (c).
Information on handling and disposing, §130A-294, (n).
Interstate agreements.
Assistance with negotiation by secretary, §130A-294, (q).
Land-use restrictions at contaminated site.
Imposed by secretary of environment and natural resources.
Reduction of danger to public health, §143B-279.9.

HAZARDOUS WASTE MANAGEMENT —Cont'd
License tax on facilities.
Counties, §153A-152.1, (a) to (c).
Littering, §14-399, (e).
Loans.
Solid waste management loans and local government special obligation bonds.
Generally, §§159I-1 to 159I-30.
See SOLID WASTE MANAGEMENT LOANS AND SPECIAL OBLIGATION BONDS.
Municipal corporations.
Local ordinances prohibited facilities invalid, §130A-293.
Navigable waters.
Deposit prohibited, §76-40, (a1).
Notice of contamination, survey plat by owner of contaminated site, §143B-279.10.
Oil.
Used oil.
See USED OIL.
Ordinances.
Hazardous waste facilities.
Local ordinances prohibited facilities invalid, §130A-293.
Permits.
Hazardous waste facilities, §130A-294.
Fees, §130A-294.1, (m), (n).
Petitions.
Hazardous waste facilities.
Preempting local ordinance, §130A-293, (b) to (f).
Privilege license tax on facilities.
Counties, §153A-152.1, (a) to (c).
Recordation.
Contaminated site, notice of, §47-29.1, (f).
Dry-cleaning solvent remediation.
Notice, §47-29.1, (e).
Inactive hazardous substance or waste disposal site, §47-29.1, (b).
Oil or hazardous substance discharge site.
Notice, §47-29.1, (d).
Residual petroleum.
Notice, §47-29.1, (g).
Waste disposal permit, §47-29.1, (a).
Releases at facilities.
Corrective action.
Request for determination that corrective action completed, §130A-308, (b).
Required, §130A-308, (a).
Research and development on handling and disposing, §130A-294, (n).
Right of entry by department, §130A-294, (s).
Rules concerning management of waste, §130A-294, (c).
State of North Carolina.
Conveyance of land used for hazardous waste landfill facility, §130A-292.
Superfund program, §§130A-310.20 to 130A-310.23.
Administration, §130A-310.21.
Appropriations.
Not obligated, §130A-310.22, (c).
Assurances required by federal law, §130A-310.22, (b).
Contracts.
Authorized, §130A-310.22, (a).
Definitions, §130A-310.20.
Notices of superfund liens.
Filing, §130A-310.23.
Program administration, §130A-310.21.

HAZARDOUS WASTE MANAGEMENT —Cont'd
Used oil.
Regulation of used oil as hazardous waste, §130A-309.18.
White goods.
Management of discarded white goods, §§130A-309.80 to 130A-309.87.
See WHITE GOODS.

HAZING.
Definitions, §14-35.
Punishment for hazing, §14-35.
Self-incrimination.
No indictment to be founded on self-incriminating testimony, §14-38.
Trials for offense of hazing, §14-38.

HAZMAT TEAMS.
General provisions, §§166A-20 to 166A-28.
See HAZARDOUS MATERIALS EMERGENCY RESPONSE.

HEAD BONES AND JOINTS.
Insurance discrimination, §58-3-121, (a) to (c).

HEADLIGHTS.
Bicycles, §20-129, (e).
Motorcycles, §20-129, (c).
Motor vehicles, §20-129, (b).
Requirements, §20-131.

HEALTH.
Abatement of nuisances.
Imminent hazards, §130A-20.
Public health nuisances, §130A-19.
Actions.
Forfeiture of money or property unlawfully acquired, §130A-28.
Recovery of money or property, §130A-27.
Administration of chapter, §130A-4, (a).
Administrative penalties, §130A-22.
Asbestos hazard management violations, §130A-22, (b1), (b2).
Civil actions to recover penalty, §130A-22, (g).
Civil penalty and forfeiture fund.
Remittance of clear proceeds to, §130A-22, (i).
Continuing violations, §130A-22, (g).
Drinking water, §130A-22, (b).
Factors considered in determining amount of penalty, §130A-22, (d).
Lead-based paint hazard management violations, §130A-22, (b3).
Milk sanitation, §130A-22, (a), (a1).
Persons contesting penalty.
Administrative hearing and judicial review, §130A-22, (e).
Rules and regulations, §130A-22, (f).
Sanitary sewage systems, §130A-22, (c), (h).
Administrative search and inspection warrant.
Consent to right of entry not given, §130A-17, (a).
Adult health.
Commission for health services.
Adoption of rules, §130A-223, (b).
Department of health and human services.
Establishment and administration of program, §130A-223, (a).
Advance instruction for mental health treatment, §§122C-71 to 122C-77.
See MENTAL HEALTH, DEVELOPMENTAL DISABILITY, SUBSTANCE ABUSE.
Agencies.
Budget.
Submission of appropriation requests, §143-31.3.

HEALTH —Cont'd
Ambulatory surgical facilities.
Licenses, §§131E-145 to 131E-152.
See AMBULATORY SURGICAL FACILITIES.
Anatomical gifts, §§130A-402 to 130A-412.1.
See ANATOMICAL GIFTS.
Appeals, §130A-24.
Applicability of provisions to actions taken by department of environment and natural resources, §130A-24, (e).
Decisions of local boards of health, §130A-24, (c), (d).
Interpretation and enforcement of rules.
Adopted by commission, §130A-24, (a).
Adopted by local board of health, §130A-24, (b).
Petition for contested case, §130A-24, (a1).
Arthritis program, §130A-222, (a).
Rules and regulations.
Implementation of program, §130A-222, (b).
Asbestos hazard management, §§130A-444 to 130A-451.
See ASBESTOS HAZARD MANAGEMENT.
Assignment to state of rights to third party benefits.
Applying for financial eligiblity for medical payment program, §130A-13, (a).
Attorneys retained by recipient, compensation, §130A-13, (a).
Liability for reimbursement, determining, §130A-13, (d).
Rules, adoption, §130A-13, (c).
Shares in recovery, federal and state government, §130A-13, (a).
Third party resources collection unit.
Department to establish, §130A-13, (b).
Attorneys at law.
District boards of health.
Contracting for services of attorney, §130A-37, (b).
Authorities.
Public health authorities, §§130A-45 to 130A-45.12.
See PUBLIC HEALTH AUTHORITIES.
Autopsies.
General provisions, §§130A-398 to 130A-401.
See AUTOPSIES.
Bail and recognizance.
Detention to protect public health, §15A-534.5.
Basic education program.
School health education program, §115C-81, (e).
Bedding.
General provisions, §§130A-261 to 130A-273.
See MATTRESSES AND BEDDING.
Blood banks, §§90-220.12 to 90-220.14.
See BLOOD BANKS.
Cancer.
Control program.
Duties of department of health and human services, §130A-214.
General provisions, §§130A-205 to 130A-215.
See CANCER.
Secretary of health and human services.
Reports by secretary, §130A-215.
Cardiac rehabilitation certification program, §§131E-165 to 131E-170.
Center for health statistics, §§130A-371 to 130A-374.
Certificates of need.
General provisions, §§131E-175 to 131E-190.
See HEALTH CARE FACILITIES.

HEALTH —Cont'd
Child care facilities.
Immunization.
Certificate of immunization, §130A-155, (b).
Report of communicable diseases, §130A-136.
Standards for licensing, §110-91.
Childhood vaccine-related injury compensation, §§130A-422 to 130A-434.
See CHILDHOOD VACCINE-RELATED INJURY COMPENSATION.
Chiropractors, §§90-139 to 90-157.3.
See CHIROPRACTORS.
Chronic disease.
Cancer, §§130A-205 to 130A-215.
See CANCER.
Chronic renal disease.
Establishment of program, §130A-220, (a), (b).
Church schools and schools of religious charter.
Sanitation, §§130A-235 to 130A-237.
Coastal fishing waters.
Monitoring water quality, §§130A-233, 130A-233.1, (a), (b).
Commission for health services generally.
See HEALTH SERVICES COMMISSION.
Committees.
Advisory committees, §130A-10.
Communicable diseases generally, §§130A-134 to 130A-148.
See COMMUNICABLE DISEASES.
Constitution of North Carolina.
Local, private and special legislation prohibited, Const. N. C., art. II, §24.
Corneal tissue removal, §130A-391, (a), (b).
Counties.
Boards of health, §130A-35.
Powers and duties, §130A-39.
Consolidated human services agencies, boards and directors.
See CONSOLIDATED HUMAN SERVICES AGENCY.
Health services, §§153A-247 to 153A-250.
Nuisances.
Abatement of public health nuisances, §153A-140.
Public health or mental health grants for federal government.
Recovery of indirect costs on certain grants by county, §130A-8, (a).
Exception, §130A-8, (b).
Crustacea.
Adulterated or misbranded crustacea.
Embargoes, §130A-21, (c).
Sanitation of scallops, shellfish and crustacea, §§130A-230, 130A-231.
Definitions, §130A-2.
Essential public health services, §130A-1.1, (b).
State center for health statistics, §130A-372.
Delegation of authority, §130A-6.
Dental health program.
Adoption by commission for health services, §130A-366, (b).
Department of health and human services.
Establishment and administration of program, §130A-366, (a).
Problem access areas.
Dental providers for, §130A-367.
Dental hygienists.
General provisions, §§90-221 to 90-233.1.
See DENTAL HYGIENISTS.

HEALTH —Cont'd
Dentists.
General provisions.
See DENTISTS.
Department of environment and natural resources.
Abatement of imminent hazard, §130A-20, (b).
Abatement of public health nuisance, §130A-19, (b).
Actions to recover money, §130A-27.
Administrative penalties, §130A-22.
Appeals procedure.
Applicability of provisions to department, §130A-24, (e).
Sanitation program, §130A-227.
Secretary.
Abatement of imminent hazard, §130A-20, (b).
Abatement of public health nuisance, §130A-19, (b).
Administrative penalties, §130A-22.
Embargo, §130A-21.
Injunctive relief.
Powers to seek, §130A-18, (b).
Provisions administered and enforced by secretary, §130A-4, (c).
Right of entry.
Powers to enforce provisions, §130A-17, (b).
Suspension and revocation of permits and program participation, §130A-23, (e).
Suspension and revocation of permits and program participation, §130A-23, (e).
Department of health and human services.
Abatement of imminent hazard, §130A-20, (a).
Abatement of public health nuisance, §130A-19, (a).
Adult health.
Establishment of program, §130A-223, (a).
Bedding.
General provisions, §§130A-261 to 130A-273.
See MATTRESSES AND BEDDING.
Cancer control program.
Duties of department, §130A-214.
General provisions, §§130A-205 to 130A-215.
Chronic renal disease.
Establishment of program, §130A-220, (a), (b).
Dental health.
Establishment and administration of program, §130A-366, (a).
Dentists.
Residency program in public health field established, §130A-11.
Diabetes.
Establishment of program, §130A-221.
Duties of department, §130A-214.
Nutrition program, §130A-361, (a).
Examinations.
Postmortem medicolegal examinations and services, §§130A-377 to 130A-394.
See MEDICAL EXAMINERS.
Glaucoma.
Establishment of program, §130A-221, (a).
Immunization.
Enforcement of rules concerning implementation of program, §130A-152, (c).
Mattresses and bedding.
General provisions, §§130A-261 to 130A-273.
See MATTRESSES AND BEDDING.
Medical examiners.
Postmortem medicolegal examinations and services, §§130A-377 to 130A-394.
See MEDICAL EXAMINERS.

HEALTH —Cont'd
Department of health and human services —Cont'd
Mosquito control districts, §§130A-352 to 130A-358.
See MOSQUITO CONTROL DISTRICTS.
Nutrition program, §130A-361, (a).
Patient health records.
Confidentiality, §130A-12.
Postmortem medicolegal examinations and services, §§130A-377 to 130A-394.
See MEDICAL EXAMINERS.
Private nonprofit foundations.
Department may assist, §130A-14, (a).
Right of entry.
Power of secretary to enforce provisions, §130A-17.
Sanitation.
Schools.
Inspections and reports by department, §130A-236.
Secretary.
Abatement of imminent hazard, §130A-20, (a).
Abatement of public health nuisance, §130A-19, (a).
Administration of chapter, §130A-4, (a).
Appointment of state health director, §130A-3.
Arthritis program.
Administration of program, §130A-222, (a).
Cancer control program.
Reports by secretary, §130A-215.
Injunctive relief.
Powers to seek, §130A-18, (a).
Powers and duties, §130A-5.
Rights of entry, §130A-17.
Vital statistics, §§130A-90 to 130A-120.
See VITAL STATISTICS.
Solid waste management.
General provisions, §§130A-290 to 130A-305.
See SOLID WASTE MANAGEMENT.
State center for health statistics.
Established within department, §130A-371.
Vital statistics, §§130A-90 to 130A-120.
See VITAL STATISTICS.
Diabetes.
Establishment of program, §130A-221, (a), (b).
Rules and regulations, §130A-221.
Dietitians and nutritionists.
Dietetics/nutrition practice act, §§90-350 to 90-369.
See DIETITIANS AND NUTRITIONISTS.
Disposition of decedent's body or body parts, §130A-420.
District boards of health, §130A-37.
Powers and duties, §130A-39.
District health departments, §§130A-36 to 130A-38.
Drinking water.
Regulation of public water systems supplying drinking water, §§130A-311 to 130A-328.
See WATER SUPPLY AND WATERWORKS.
Embargoes, §130A-21.
Emergency medical services.
Regulation of emergency medical services, §§131E-155 to 131E-161.
See EMERGENCY MEDICAL SERVICES.
Employee safety and health programs, §§95-250 to 95-256.
See EMPLOYEE SAFETY AND HEALTH PROGRAMS.

HEALTH —Cont'd
Employment security.
Medical condition.
Eligibility conditions, §96-14.
Essential public health services.
Defined, §130A-1.1, (b).
List of services not to limit or restrict powers and duties of department, §130A-1.1, (d).
Nonessential services, §130A-1.1, (c).
Examinations.
Postmortem medicolegal examinations and services, §§130A-377 to 130A-394.
See MEDICAL EXAMINERS.
State laboratory of public health to make examinations, §130A-88, (a).
Federal public health or mental health grants.
Counties to recover indirect costs on certain grants, §130A-8, (a).
Exception, §130A-8, (b).
Fees.
County and district boards of health, §130A-39, (g).
Industrial hygiene consultation services and occupational consultation services, §130A-5.
Forfeitures.
Money or property unlawfully acquired, §130A-27.
General assembly.
Establishment of program, §130A-221, (a), (b).
Human tissue donation program.
Legislative findings and purpose, §130A-413, (a).
Implementation of provisions, §130A-221, (b).
Local, private and special legislation prohibited, Const. N. C., art. II, §24.
Rules and regulations, §130A-221, (b).
Grants.
Federal public health or mental health grants.
Counties to recover indirect costs, §130A-8, (a).
Applicability of section, §130A-8, (b).
Grants-in-aid, §130A-7.
Liberal construction of chapter, §130A-7.
Health care facilities.
Certificates of need, §§131E-175 to 131E-190.
See HEALTH CARE FACILITIES.
General provisions.
See HEALTH CARE FACILITIES.
Health care powers of attorney.
Advance instruction for mental health treatment, §§122C-71 to 122C-77.
See MENTAL HEALTH, DEVELOPMENTAL DISABILITY, SUBSTANCE ABUSE.
Generally, §§32A-15 to 32A-26.
See HEALTH CARE POWERS OF ATTORNEY.
Health care providers, self-referrals, §§90-405 to 90-408.
Health promotion services.
Appropriations, §130A-4.2.
Health systems agencies.
Certificates of need generally, §§131E-175 to 131E-190.
See HEALTH CARE FACILITIES.
Hearings.
Suspension or revocation of permits and program participation, §130A-23, (c), (d).
Heart disease and stroke.
Justus-Warren heart disease and stroke prevention task force, §143B-216.60.
Home care agencies.
Home care agencies licensing, §§131E-135 to 131E-142.
See HEALTH CARE FACILITIES.

HEALTH —Cont'd
Hospitals.
Certificates of need, §§131E-175 to 131E-190.
See HEALTH CARE FACILITIES.
Communicable diseases.
Emergency departments, reports to state health director, §130A-480, (a), (b).
Medical facilities may report, §130A-137.
Emergency departments, reports to state health director of public health threats, §130A-480, (a), (b).
Generally.
See HOSPITALS.
Sanitation, §130A-235.
Hotels, inns and other transient lodging places.
Sanitation of food and lodging establishments, §§130A-247 to 130A-250.
Human tissue donation program, §130A-413.
Imminent hazards.
Abatement.
Secretary of environment and natural resources or local health directors, §130A-20, (b).
Secretary of health and human services or local health directors, §130A-20, (a).
Suspension or revocation of permits and program participation, §130A-23, (d).
Immunity from liability.
Communicable disease investigations.
Immunity of persons who report, §130A-142.
Persons permitting access to medical records, §130A-144, (c).
Local health departments, §90-21.16, (a), (b).
Non-profit community health centers, §90-21.16, (a), (b).
Immunization, §§130A-152 to 130A-158.
See IMMUNIZATION.
Infants.
Perinatal health care, §130A-127.
Injunctions.
Secretary of environment and natural resources or local health directors, §130A-18, (b).
Secretary of health and human services or local health directors, §130A-18, (a).
Institute of medicine, §90-470.
Insurance.
District health departments.
Board of health.
Authority to provide liability insurance, §130A-37, (k).
Generally.
See ACCIDENT AND HEALTH INSURANCE.
Jails.
Commitment to another jail when county jail unhealthy, §15-126.
Supervision by department of health and human services, §148-10.
Joint legislative health care oversight committee, §§120-70.110 to 120-70.112.
Juvenile facilities.
Surgical operations on inmates of state institutions, §143B-526.
Kindergartens.
Health assessments for kindergarten children in public schools, §§130A-440 to 130A-443.
Labor.
Occupational safety and health, §§95-126 to 95-155.
See OCCUPATIONAL SAFETY AND HEALTH.
Landlord and tenant.
Good faith complaints.
Health or safety law violations, §42-37.1.

HEALTH —Cont'd
Lead-based paint hazard management program, §§130A-453.01 to 130A-453.11.
See LEAD-BASED PAINT.
Lead poisoning in children, §§130A-131.5 to 130A-131.9H.
See LEAD POISONING IN CHILDREN.
Local boards of health.
Powers and duties, §130A-39.
Local health departments, §§130A-34 to 130A-42.
See LOCAL HEALTH DEPARTMENTS.
Maintenance organizations, §§58-67-1 to 58-67-185.
See HEALTH MAINTENANCE ORGANIZATIONS.
Managed care patient assistance program, §143-730.
Mass gatherings.
Commission for health services.
Rules and regulations of commission, §130A-257.
Maternal and child health services, §130A-124, (a) to (c).
County appropriations.
Local health departments not to reduce, §130A-4.1, (a).
Income earned by local health departments.
Departments required to budget and expend, §130A-4.1, (b).
Mattresses and bedding.
General provisions, §§130A-261 to 130A-273.
See MATTRESSES AND BEDDING.
Medical education in primary care, §143-613.
Medical payments programs administered under chapter 130A.
Assignment to state of rights to third party benefits, §130A-13, (a).
Attorneys retained by recipient, compensation, §130A-13, (a).
Liability for reimbursement, determining, §130A-13, (d).
Rules, adoption, §130A-13, (c).
Shares in recovery, federal and state government, §130A-13, (a).
Third party resources collection unit.
Department to establish, §130A-13, (b).
Mental health, developmental disability, substance abuse.
See MENTAL HEALTH, DEVELOPMENTAL DISABILITY, SUBSTANCE ABUSE.
Metabolic and other hereditary and congenital disorders.
Screening of newborns, §130A-125.
Metropolitan water districts.
Commission for health services.
Authorized to create, §130A-29, (d).
Milk and milk products.
Embargoes, §130A-21, (b).
Minority health advisory council, §§130A-33.43, 130A-33.44.
Misdemeanors.
Violations of chapter or rules, §130A-25, (a).
Imprisonment for certain violations, §130A-25, (b).
Discharge, §130A-25, (c).
Mosquito control districts.
Commission for health services.
Authorized to create mosquito control districts, §130A-29, (d).
General provisions, §§130A-352 to 130A-358.
See MOSQUITO CONTROL DISTRICTS.

HEALTH —Cont'd
Municipal corporations.
Abatement of public health nuisances, §160A-193.
North Carolina traumatic brain injury advisory council, §§143B-216.65, 143B-216.66.
Notice.
Suspension and revocation of permits and program participation, §130A-23, (c), (d).
Nuisances.
Abatement of imminent hazard, §130A-20.
Abatement of public health nuisances.
Secretary of environment and natural resources and local health directors, §130A-19, (b).
Secretary of health and human services and local health directors, §130A-19, (a).
Nurses.
General provisions, §§90-171.19 to 90-171.48.
See NURSES.
Nursing home administrators.
General provisions, §§90-275.1 to 90-288.
See NURSING HOME ADMINISTRATORS.
Nursing homes.
General provisions.
See NURSING HOMES.
Patients' bill of rights, §§131E-115 to 131E-131.
See NURSING HOMES.
Nutritionists.
Dietetics/nutrition practice act, §§90-350 to 90-369.
See DIETITIANS AND NUTRITIONISTS.
Nutrition program.
Department of health and human services.
Establishment of program, §130A-361, (a), (b).
Powers and duties relative to nutrition program, §130A-361, (a).
Powers and duties relative to nutrition program, §130A-361, (a).
Rules and regulations, §130A-361, (b).
Violations, §130A-22, (c1).
Occupational safety and health, §§95-126 to 95-155.
See OCCUPATIONAL SAFETY AND HEALTH.
Office of women's health, §130A-131.25.
Optometrists, §§90-114 to 90-127.3.
See OPTOMETRISTS.
Osteopaths, §§90-127 to 90-138.
See OSTEOPATHS.
Participation in programs under chapter 130A.
Suspension or revocation, §130-23, (b).
Patient medical records.
Confidentiality, §130A-12.
Perinatal health care, §130A-127.
Establishment of program, §130A-127, (a).
Rules and regulations.
Adoption, §130A-127, (b).
Permits.
Suspension or revocation of permit issued under chapter, §130A-23, (a), (c), (d).
Findings, §130A-23, (a).
Imminent hazard, §130A-23, (d).
Notice, §130A-23, (c), (d).
Powers of secretary of environment and natural resources, §130A-23, (e).
Personnel.
District health departments.
Personnel records, §130A-42.
Pharmacists and pharmacies, §§90-85.2 to 90-85.41.
See PHARMACISTS AND PHARMACIES.
Physical fitness and health council, §§130A-33.40, 130A-33.41.

HEALTH —Cont'd
Physical therapists, §§90-270 24 to 90-270.39.
See PHYSICAL THERAPISTS.
Physicians and surgeons.
See PHYSICIANS AND SURGEONS.
Podiatrists, §§90-202.2 to 90-202.14.
See PODIATRISTS.
Postmortem medicolegal examinations and services, §§130A-377 to 130A-394.
See MEDICAL EXAMINERS.
Principals of schools.
Reports of communicable diseases, §130A-136.
Prisons and prisoners.
Health services generally, §148-19, (a) to (d).
Sanitary and health conditions of prisoners.
Department of health and human services to supervise, §148-10.
Self-inflicted injuries.
Treatment of injuries upon prisoners, §148-46.2.
Procedure when consent is refused by prisoner, §148-46.2.
Surgical operations on inmates of state institutions.
Juveniles in juvenile facilities, §143B-526.
Procedure when surgical operations necessary, §148-22.2.
Private nonprofit foundations.
Department may assist, §130A-14, (a).
Annual audit of accounts required, §130A-14.
Psychologists, §§90-270.1 to 90-270.21.
See PSYCHOLOGISTS.
Public health authorities, §§130A-45 to 130A-45.12.
See PUBLIC HEALTH AUTHORITIES.
Public health law of North Carolina.
Mission of public health system, §130A-1.1, (a).
Title of chapter, §130A-1.
Public health services.
County health departments.
Provision of public health services, §130A-34, (a).
Public health study commission, §§120-195 to 120-203.
Authority, §120-201.
Created, §120-195.
Duties, §120-196.
Meetings, §120-198.
Place, §120-203.
Membership, §120-197, (a).
Purpose, §120-195.
Reports, §120-202.
Staff, §120-203.
Subcommittees, §120-200.
Subsistence and travel expenses, §120-199.
Terms, §120-197, (c).
Vacancies, §120-197, (b).
Public officers and employees.
Delegation of authority, §130A-6.
Public schools.
Development and administration of school health education program, §115C-81, (e).
Employee health certificate, §115C-323.
Form, §115C-323, (d).
Nonresident physicians, §115C-323, (c).
Requirements, §115C-323, (a).
Who may prepare, §115C-323, (b).
Kindergartens.
Health assessments for kindergarten children in public schools, §§130A-440 to 130A-443.
Sanitation, §§130A-235 to 130A-237.

HEALTH —Cont'd
Public schools —Cont'd
State-funded school health coordinator.
Qualifications, §115C-81, (e).
State school health advisory committee, §115C-81, (e).
Recovery of property.
Wrongfully paid or transferred to person under program, §130A-27.
Renal disease.
Chronic renal disease.
Department of health and human services.
Establishment of program, §130A-220, (a), (b).
Respiratory care practitioners.
General provisions, §§90-646 to 90-666.
See RESPIRATORY CARE PRACTITIONERS.
Restaurants.
Sanitation of food and lodging establishments, §§130A-247 to 130A-250.
Restitution.
Recovery of money or property wrongfully disbursed, §130A-27.
Retirement system for counties and cities.
District health departments.
Membership of employees, §128-37.
Public health authorities.
Membership of employees, §128-37.
Right of entry to enforce provisions.
Administrative search and inspection warrant.
Obtaining if consent not given, §130A-17, (a).
Imminent hazard existing.
No warrant required for entry, §130A-17, (a).
Powers of secretary and local health directors, §130A-17, (a).
Powers of secretary of department of environment and natural resources and local health directors, §130A-17, (b).
Rules and regulations.
Appeals procedure.
Interpretation and enforcement of rules.
Adopted by commission, §130A-24, (a).
Adopted by local boards of health, §130A-24, (b).
Petition for contested case, §130A-24.
Sanitarians.
General provisions, §§90A-50 to 90A-66.
See SANITARIANS.
Sanitary districts.
Commission for health services.
Authorized to create sanitary districts, §130A-29, (d).
General provisions, §§130A-47 to 130A-85.
See SANITARY DISTRICTS.
Sanitation.
Church schools and schools of religious charter, §§130A-235 to 130A-237.
Crustacea, §§130A-230, 130A-231.
Definitions, §130A-227, (b).
Establishment of program, §130A-227, (a).
Hospitals, §130A-235.
Mass gatherings generally, §§130A-251 to 130A-258.
Milk and milk products, §§130A-274 to 130A-279.
Private schools, §§130A-235 to 130A-237.
Public schools, §§130A-235 to 130A-237.
Sanitation of food and lodging establishments, §§130A-247 to 130A-250.
Shellfish, §§130A-230, 130A-231.
Scallops.
Sanitation of scallops, shellfish and crustacea, §§130A-230, 130A-231.

HEALTH —Cont'd
School health advisory committee, §115C-81, (e).
Schools, sanitation, §§130A-235 to 130A-237.
Searches and seizures.
Administrative search and inspection warrants, §130A-17.
Self-referrals by health care providers, §§90-405 to 90-408.
Shellfish.
Sanitation of scallops, shellfish and crustacea, §§130A-230, 130A-231.
Sickle cell program, §130A-129.
Sickle cell trait.
See SICKLE CELL TRAIT.
Solid waste management.
General provisions, §§130A-290 to 130A-305.
See SOLID WASTE MANAGEMENT.
Standards.
Commission authorized to establish, §130A-9.
State health standards, §130A-5.1.
State center for health statistics, §§130A-371 to 130A-374.
State health director, §130A-3.
Terrorist incident using nuclear, biological or chemical agents.
Powers and duties, §§130A-475 to 130A-477.
State health planning and development agency.
Department of health and human services designated state agency, §131E-177.
State health standards, §130A-5.1.
Adoption, §130A-5.1, (a).
Assistance of other entities, §130A-5.1, (b).
State institutions.
Surgical operations on inmates of state institutions.
Juveniles in juvenile facilities, §143B-526.
Procedure when surgical operations necessary, §148-22.2.
State laboratory of public health.
Established, §130A-88, (a).
Rules and regulations, §130A-88, (b).
Sterilization, §§90-271 to 90-275.
Mentally ill or mentally retarded wards.
Medical necessity cases, §35A-1245.
Substance abuse professionals, §§90-113.30 to 90-113.46.
See SUBSTANCE ABUSE PROFESSIONALS.
Suspension or revocation of participation in health programs, §130-23, (b).
Teen pregnancy prevention.
Establishment of program, §130A-131.15A.
Third party resources collection unit.
Department to establish, §130A-13, (b).
Title of chapter.
Public health law of North Carolina, §130A-1.
Tourist camps and homes.
Sanitation of food and lodging establishments, §§130A-247 to 130A-250.
Toxic vapors.
General provisions, §§90-113.8A to 90-113.14.
See TOXIC VAPORS.
Traumatic brain injury advisory council, §§143B-216.65, 143B-216.66.
Veterinarians.
General provisions, §§90-179 to 90-187.13.
See VETERINARIANS.
Vital statistics.
General provisions, §§130A-90 to 130A-120.
See VITAL STATISTICS.

HEALTH —Cont'd
Wastewater systems, §§130A-333 to 130A-343.
See WASTEWATER SYSTEMS.
Water and air resources, §§143-211 to 143-215.9B.
See WATER AND AIR RESOURCES.
Women's health, office of, §130A-131.25.

HEALTH AND HUMAN SERVICES DEPARTMENT.
Abortion.
Statistical summary reports concerning medical and demographic characteristics of abortions, §14-45.1, (c).
Abuse, neglect or dependency of juveniles, child fatalities.
Central registry.
Duty of department to maintain, §7B-311.
Report by director of social services where maltreatment involved, §7B-307, (c).
Report by director of social services to department.
Finding evidence of abuse or neglect in child care facility, §7B-307, (b), (c).
Adult care homes.
Compliance history provider file, §131D-41.
Joint training.
Division facility services consultants and county DDS adult care home specialists and providers, §143B-139.5B.
Share of costs with counties, §143B-139.5.
Adult day care programs, §131D-6.
Advisory committee on cancer coordination and control, §§130A-33.50, 130A-33.51.
Ambulatory surgical facilities.
Licenses, §§131E-145 to 131E-152.
See AMBULATORY SURGICAL FACILITIES.
Appeals of right, court of appeals, §7A-29, (a).
Arthritis.
Administration of arthritis program, §130A-222, (a).
Rules and regulations.
Implementation of program, §130A-222, (b).
Audits.
Office of internal auditor, §§143B-216.50, 143B-216.51.
Blind persons.
Aid to the blind, §§111-13 to 111-35.
See BLIND PERSONS.
Blind or visually handicapped employees.
Enrollment in retirement system for teachers and state employees, §135-16.1, (a) to (c).
General provisions, §§111-4 to 111-12.6.
See BLIND PERSONS.
Operation of highway vending facilities, §§111-48 to 111-52.
See BLIND PERSONS.
Operation of vending facilities on state property, §§111-41 to 111-47.
See BLIND PERSONS.
Certificates of need.
Health care facilities generally, §§131E-175 to 131E-190.
See HEALTH CARE FACILITIES.
Child care commission, §§143B-168.3 to 143B-168.5.
Child care facilities.
Generally, §§110-85 to 110-107.
See CHILD CARE FACILITIES.
Child fatality review team, §143B-150.20.

HEALTH AND HUMAN SERVICES DEPARTMENT —Cont'd
Childhood vaccine-related injury compensation, §§130A-422 to 130A-434.
See CHILDHOOD VACCINE-RELATED INJURY COMPENSATION.
Child support enforcement.
Generally, §§110-128 to 110-142.2.
See CHILD SUPPORT.
State directory of new hires, §110-129.2.
Child welfare services delivery.
Action by secretary to ensure delivery.
Cooperation with county board of commissioners, county board of social services, etc., §108A-74, (g).
County funding of services to continue, §108A-74, (f).
Definitions, §108A-74, (a).
Directive plan of action to be developed and implemented, §108A-74, (e).
Divestiture of county director of social services upon assumption of service by secretary, §108A-74, (d).
Intervention in particular service or services provided by county department of social services, §108A-74, (b).
Withholding funding for services provided by county boards of social services, §108A-74, (c).
Commission for mental health, developmental disabilities and substance abuse services, §§143B-147 to 143B-150.
Commission for the blind, §§143B-157 to 143B-160.
Commission of anatomy, §§130A-33.30 to 130A-33.32.
Confidentiality of privileged patient medical records, §143B-139.6.
Consolidated county human services.
Adoption of rules, §143B-139.7, (a), (b).
Allocation of funds, §143B-139.7, (a).
Definitions, §143B-139.7, (c).
Consumer and advocacy advisory committee for the blind, §§143B-163, 143B-164.
Contracts.
Authority of department to contract with other entities, §143B-139.3, (a), (b).
Recovery of county funded financial assistance program expenditures.
Contracts and intermediary status authorized between federal agency and county, §143B-139.3, (b).
Costs paid by persons admitted to institutions of department, §§143-117 to 143-127.1.
Action to accrue for costs in favor of state, §143-121, (a).
Actual cost of care to be paid.
Secretary to determine and fix, §143-118, (a).
Attorney general to prosecute suits at request of institution, §143-124.
Compromise of accounts, §143-118, (e).
Death of person admitted leaving costs unpaid.
Lien on decedent's property, §143-126, (a).
Cancellation of lien upon payment of unpaid balance, §143-126, (e).
Filing verified statement of account, §143-126, (b).
Limitation of actions, §143-126, (d).
Notice, §143-126, (c).
Definitions, §143-117.1.

HEALTH AND HUMAN SERVICES DEPARTMENT —Cont'd
Costs paid by persons admitted to institutions of department —Cont'd
Discharge from institution of person refusing to pay, §143-119, (e).
Financial ability to pay, secretary to ascertain, §143-118, (d).
General rate of charge, authority of secretary to fix, §143-118, (a).
Included institutions, §143-117.
Indigent persons.
Authority to provide care not limited, §143-123, (a).
Collection of costs of indigent succeeding to inheritance or acquiring property, §143-123, (b).
Judgment not barred by statute of limitations, §143-125.
Lien on property for unpaid balance due institution, §143-126.1, (a).
Admission of person after judgment or settlement of claim, §143-126.1, (g).
Applicability to both real and personal property, §143-126.1, (b).
Cancellation upon payment of unpaid balance, §143-126.1, (f).
Death of person admitted leaving costs unpaid, §143-126.
Filing of verified statement of account, §143-126.1, (c).
Limitation of action to enforce, §143-126.1, (e).
Notice, §143-126.1, (d).
Priority, §143-126.1, (e).
List of unpaid accounts for audit, §143-119, (d).
Long-term patients.
Defined, §143-127.1, (c).
Parental liability, §143-127.1, (a), (b).
No statute of limitation on action for costs, §143-122.
Notification of amount due, §143-119, (b).
Payment into state treasury, §143-127.
Payment of portion of costs, §143-119, (c).
Payments by person admitted or person legally responsible for payments, §143-119, (a).
Prima facie evidence in action for costs, §143-121, (c).
Provisions directory and not mandatory, §143-121, (d).
Ratification of past acts, §143-121.1.
Reduction of rates for persons admitted to facility for mentally ill research purposes, §143-118, (f).
Statute of limitations not to bar judgment, §143-125.
Venue for action for costs, §143-121, (b).
Venue of action to collect costs.
Right of institution to select, §143-124.
Council for the deaf and the hard of hearing, §§143B-216.30 to 143B-216.34.
Council on developmental disabilities, §§143B-177 to 143B-179.
Created, §143B-136.1.
Criminal history record checks of employees and applicants for employment.
Conditional offer of employment pending results of record checks, §114-19.6, (f).
Conviction revealed by verified criminal history record check.
Just cause for not selecting person or dismissing person, §114-19.6, (d).

HEALTH AND HUMAN SERVICES DEPARTMENT —Cont'd
Criminal history record checks of employees and applicants for employment —Cont'd
Definitions, §114-19.6, (a).
Department of justice to provide information, §114-19.6, (b).
Just cause for not selecting person for employment or dismissing person.
Record check revealing conviction, §114-19.6, (d).
National criminal record checks, §114-19.6, (b).
Privileged information, §114-19.6, (c).
Refusal to consent to record check.
Denial of employment or dismissal, §114-19.6, (e).
Damage of personal property by clients.
Repair or replacement, §143-127.2.
Deportment of persons in buildings and grounds of institutions under jurisdiction of department.
Adoption of rules governing, §143-116.6, (a).
Misdemeanor for violation, §143-116.6, (b).
Directory of new hires, §110-129.2.
Division of aging, §§143B-181.1 to 143B-181.1, (b).
Division of services for the deaf and hard of hearing, §§143B-216.30 to 143B-216.34.
Drug treatment by nonprofessional organizations.
Responsibility for issuing license, §90-109.
Duties, §§143B-137.1, 143B-138.1, (a) to (e).
Early childhood initiatives, §§143B-168.10 to 143B-168.16.
See EARLY CHILDHOOD INITIATIVES.
Early intervention services.
Responsibilities of secretary regarding availability, §143B-139.6A.
Eastern North Carolina hospital.
Control of certain hospitals transferred to department of health and human services, §131E-67.
Power of secretary to regulate, §131E-67.
Education.
Residential schools under control of secretary.
Education programs in, §§143B-146.1 to 143B-146.21.
See EDUCATION.
Emergency medical services, §§143-507 to 143-519.
See EMERGENCY MEDICAL SERVICES.
Emergency rules.
When agency may adopt, §150B-21.1A, (a).
Established, §143B-136.1.
Family preservation act, §§143B-150.5, 143B-150.6.
First responders.
Vaccination program, §130-485.
Food stamps.
Generally, §§108A-51 to 108A-53.1.
Fraudulent public assistance program payments.
Garnishment of wages to recoup, §108A-25.3.
Functions, powers, duties and obligations generally, §143B-138.1, (a) to (e).
Governor Morehead school, §§143B-164.10 to 143B-164.17.
See GOVERNOR MOREHEAD SCHOOL.
Governor's advisory council on aging, §§143B-180, 143B-181.
Governor's council on physical fitness and health, §§130A-33.40, 130A-33.41.

HEALTH AND HUMAN SERVICES DEPARTMENT —Cont'd
Grants-in-aid for programs of public assistance.
Acceptance, §108A-25, (c).
Grants-in-aid from non-state agencies.
Requests submitted through secretary, §143B-139.2.
Head of department, §143B-139.
Health.
Powers generally.
See HEALTH.
Hospitals.
Construction and enlargement of local hospitals, §131E-70.
Eastern North Carolina hospital.
Control of certain hospitals transferred to department of health and human services, §131E-67.
Power of secretary to regulate, §131E-67.
Program of hospital care, §131E-70.
Specialty hospitals.
Control of certain hospitals transferred to department of health and human services, §131E-67.
Power of secretary to regulate, §131E-67.
Indian child welfare.
Division of social services.
Collaboration with commission of Indian affairs, §143B-139.5A.
Insect sting reactions.
Training individuals to administer life-saving treatment to persons suffering, §143-509.
Interagency coordinating council for children from birth to five with developmental disabilities and their families, §§143B-179.5, 143B-179.6.
Interagency coordinating council for children from birth to five with disabilities and their families.
Regional councils, §143B-179.5A.
Internal auditor, §§143B-216.50, 143B-216.51.
Local health and human services agencies.
Adoption of rules by secretary, §143B-139.1.
Long-term care ombudsman program, §§143B-181.15 to 143B-181.24.
See LONG-TERM CARE OMBUDSMAN.
Lost, destruction or damage.
Property of resident of department institution.
Direct payment or replacement by institution, §143-295.1.
Maternity homes.
Licensing, §131D-1.
Medical assistance program generally, §§108A-54 to 108A-70.5.
See MEDICAID.
Medical care commission, §§143B-165 to 143B-168.
Medical records.
Confidentiality of privileged patient medical records, §143B-139.6.
Mental health, developmental disabilities and substance abuse.
Administration and enforcement of chapter, §122C-111.
Application of funds belonging to facilities, §122C-185.
Cooperation with other agencies, §122C-113, (a) to (b1), (c).
Facility licensing, §122C-27.

HEALTH AND HUMAN SERVICES DEPARTMENT —Cont'd
Mental health, developmental disabilities and substance abuse —Cont'd
Powers and duties of secretary, §122C-112.1, (a), (b).
State plan, §122C-102.
Minority health advisory council, §§130A-33.43, 130A-33.44.
Motor vehicle operation on grounds of institutions operated by department.
Adoption of rules by secretary, §143-116.7, (b).
Civil penalty for violations, §143-116.7, (e).
General fund budget code of institution.
Deposit of fees or civil penalties, §143-116.7, (h).
General laws relating to use of highways of state and operation of vehicles applicable, §143-116.7, (a).
Infractions, §143-116.7, (g).
Parking, §143-116.7, (c), (d).
Removal of illegally parked vehicle, §143-116.7, (f).
Negligent lost, destruction or damage of property.
Property of resident of department institution.
Direct payment or replacement by institution, §143-295.1.
North Carolina traumatic brain injury advisory council, §§143B-216.65, 143B-216.66.
Nursing homes.
Medication error quality initiative.
Development and implementation, §131E-128.5, (a).
Office of internal auditor.
Access to records, data or other information of department, §143B-216.50, (e).
Appointment by secretary, §143B-216.50, (c).
Auditing duties and responsibilities, §143B-216.51, (b).
Auditing standards, §143B-216.51, (c).
Duties and responsibilities of internal auditor, §143B-216.50, (b).
Established, §143B-216.50, (a).
Final reports submitted to secretary, §143B-216.51, (e).
Implementation of department's response to audit.
Internal auditor to monitor, §143B-216.51, (g).
Independent reviews and analyses of various functions and programs, §143B-216.50, (a).
Long-term and annual audit plans, development, §143B-216.51, (h).
Official designated by secretary, report to, §143B-216.30, (d).
Political affiliation not considered in appointing, §143B-216.50, (c).
Qualifications, §143B-216.51, (a).
Reports.
Final report to secretary, §143B-216.51, (e).
Retention of audit report information, §143B-216.51, (d).
Retention of file of audit reports and information, §143B-216.51, (d).
State auditor considering work of internal auditor, §143B-216.51, (f).
Office of rural health and resource development.
In-kind watch to nonprofit organizations establishing health programs.
Assignment of office employees, §143B-139.4, (c).
Office of women's health, §130A-131.25.

HEALTH AND HUMAN SERVICES DEPARTMENT —Cont'd
Parking of vehicles on grounds of institutions under department's jurisdiction.
Providing for registration and parking of vehicles, fee, §143-116.7, (d).
Regulating parking and establishing parking areas, §143-116.7, (c).
Removal of illegally parked vehicles, §143-116.7, (f).
Paternity, establishing.
Additional powers and duties of department, §110-129.1, (a).
Patient medical records.
Confidentiality of privileged records, §143B-139.6.
Perinatal health care, §130A-127.
Personal property damaged or stolen by clients.
Repair or replacement, §143-127.2.
Powers and duties generally, §143B-138.1, (a) to (e).
Private nonprofit organizations working with department services or programs.
Annual audit reports, §143B-139.4, (b).
Employees allowed to provide services to organizations, §143B-139.4, (a).
Office of rural health and resources development employees.
Assignment to serve as in-kind watch to organization establishing health programs, §143B-139.4, (c).
Renal disease.
Chronic renal disease.
Department to establish program, §130A-220, (a), (b).
Residential schools under control of secretary.
Education programs in, §§143B-146.1 to 143B-146.21.
See EDUCATION.
Retirement system for teachers and state employees.
Blind or visually handicapped employees, §135-16.1, (a) to (c).
Rulemaking procedure.
Emergency rules.
When agency may adopt, §150B-21.1A, (a).
Temporary rules.
When agency may adopt, §150A-21.1, (a).
Sale of merchandise by governmental units.
Exception to prohibition, §66-58, (b).
Schools.
Criminal record checks of personnel, §114-19.2, (c1).
Residential schools under control of secretary.
Education programs in, §§143B-146.1 to 143B-146.21.
See EDUCATION.
Secretary.
Early intervention services.
Responsibilities regarding availability, §143B-139.6A.
Grants-in-aid from non-state agencies.
Requests through secretary, §143B-139.2.
Head of department, §143B-139.
Hospitals.
Power of secretary to regulate certain hospitals, §131E-67.
Rulemaking authority.
Rules applicable to local health and human services agencies, §143B-139.1.

HEALTH AND HUMAN SERVICES DEPARTMENT —Cont'd
Secretary —Cont'd
Vaccines.
Contracts for purchase of covered vaccines.
Authority of secretary of health and human services, §130A-433, (a).
Senior tarheel legislature, §143B-181.55.
Setoff debt collection, §§105A-1 to 105A-16.
See SETOFF DEBT COLLECTION.
Small claims against institutions of department.
Settlement.
Direct payment or replacement by institution, §143-295.1.
Social services commission, §§143B-153 to 143B-156.
State child fatality review team, §143B-150.20.
State-county special assistance for adults, §§108A-40 to 108A-47.
See SOCIAL SERVICES.
State directory of new hires, §110-129.2.
Subrogation.
Vocational rehabilitation services.
Rights of department, §143-547.
Suppression of nuisances and disorders in buildings and grounds of institutions under department's jurisdiction.
Adoption of rules governing, §143-116.6, (a).
Misdemeanor for violating, §143-116.6, (b).
Temporary rules.
When agency may adopt, §150A-21.1, (a).
Theft of personal property by clients.
Repair or replacement, §143-127.2.
Towing of illegally parked vehicles on grounds of institutions under department's jurisdiction, §143-116.7, (f).
Traffic regulation on grounds of buildings under department's jurisdiction.
Adoption of rules by secretary, §143-116.7, (b).
Applicability of general laws relating to use of highways and operation of vehicles, §143-116.7, (a).
Civil penalty for violations, §143-116.7, (e).
General fund budget code of institution.
Deposit of fees or civil penalties collected, §143-116.7, (h).
Infractions, §143-116.7, (g).
Parking.
Fee for registration and parking of vehicles, §143-116.7, (d).
Regulating parking and establishing parking area, §143-116.7, (c).
Removal of illegally parked vehicles, §143-116.7, (f).
Transfer of functions, powers, duties, etc., by type I transfer, §143B-138.1, (a), (c).
Transfer of funds to department.
Contributed funds subject to department control, §143-23.2, (b).
Political subdivisions, other public agencies and private agencies, §143-23.2, (a).
Transfer of functions, powers, duties, etc., by type II transfer, §143B-138.1, (b), (d).
Traumatic brain injury advisory council, §§143B-216.65, 143B-216.66.
Vaccination program.
First responders, §130-485.
Vocational rehabilitation services.
Duties of secretary, §143-546.1, (a).
Services provided by department, §143-545.1, (b).

HEALTH AND HUMAN SERVICES DEPARTMENT —Cont'd
Vocational rehabilitation services —Cont'd
Subrogation, §143-547.
Women's health, office of, §130A-131.25.
Work first program, §§108A-27 to 108A-39.
See WORK FIRST PROGRAM.

HEALTH AND WELLNESS TRUST FUND, §§147-86.30 to 147-86.36.
Advisory council, §147-86.34.
Commission.
Advisory council, §147-86.34.
Duties, §147-86.33, (a).
Established, §147-86.32, (a).
Meetings, §147-86.32, (e) to (g).
Open meeting requirements, §147-86.36.
Members, §147-86.32, (b), (c).
Conflicts of interest, §147-86.32, (i).
Per diem and expenses, §147-86.32, (h).
Officers, §147-86.32, (c).
Powers, §147-86.33, (b), (c).
Reports by chair, §147-86.35, (a).
Vacancies, §147-86.32, (d).
Debt service paid during fiscal year, §147-86.30, (c).
Established, §147-86.30, (a).
Expenses.
Limit on operating and administrative expenses, §147-86.30, (f).
Grants.
Eligible applicants, §147-86.31, (a).
Reports from non-state agency recipients, §§147-86.31, (b), 147-86.35, (b).
Open meeting requirements, §147-86.36.
Public records requirements, §147-86.36.
Purposes, §147-86.30, (e).
Reports.
Chair of commission, §147-86.35, (a).
Grant or financial assistance recipients that are not state agencies, §§147-86.31, (b), 147-86.35, (b).
State treasurer.
Custodian of fund, §147-86.30, (b).
Use of funds after payment of debt service, §147-86.30, (d).

HEALTH ASSESSMENTS.
Child care facilities, §110-91.

HEALTH AUTHORITIES.
Public health authorities generally, §§130A-45 to 130A-45.12.
See PUBLIC HEALTH AUTHORITIES.

HEALTH BENEFIT PLANS.
External review, §§58-50-75 to 58-50-95.
See ACCIDENT AND HEALTH INSURANCE.
Generally, §§58-3-167 to 58-3-178, 58-3-190 to 58-3-265.
See ACCIDENT AND HEALTH INSURANCE.
Managed care patient assistance program, §143-730.

HEALTH BOARDS, DISTRICT, §130A-37.
Powers and duties, §130A-39.

HEALTH CARE BENEFITS PROVIDERS.
Health benefit plans.
External review, §§58-50-75 to 58-50-95.
Generally, §§58-3-167 to 58-3-178, 58-3-190 to 58-3-265.
See ACCIDENT AND HEALTH INSURANCE.

HEALTH CARE BENEFITS PROVIDERS —Cont'd
Health benefit plans —Cont'd
Managed care patient assistance program, §143-730.
Insurance companies generally.
See INSURANCE COMPANIES.
Jurisdiction over providers, §§58-49-1 to 58-49-25.
Authority of commissioner, §58-49-5.
Commissioner, §58-49-5.
Examination by, §58-49-15.
Conflict of laws, §58-49-20.
Disclosure, §58-49-25, (a), (b).
Establishment, §58-49-10.
Examination by commissioner, §58-49-15.
How to show jurisdiction, §58-49-10.
Purpose of article, §58-49-1.
Stop-loss insurance.
Disclosure of amount, §58-49-25, (b).
Subject to state laws, §58-49-20.
Medicaid, §§108A-54 to 108A-70.5.
See MEDICAID.
Multiple employer welfare arrangements, §§58-49-30 to 58-49-65.
Acknowledgment of claims, §58-3-100, (c).
Failure to acknowledge after receiving notice.
Civil penalty, §58-3-100, (c).
Actuarial certification, §58-49-60, (c).
Applicability of other provisions of law, §58-49-55, (a).
Claims.
Acknowledgment of claims, §58-3-100, (c).
Failure to acknowledge after receiving notice.
Civil penalty, §58-3-100, (c).
Contracts.
Filing with commissioner, §58-49-40, (f).
Defined, §58-49-30, (a).
Examinations, §58-49-55, (b).
Excess insurance.
Maintenance, §58-49-40, (c).
Exemptions, §58-49-35, (b).
Financial statements, §58-49-60, (d).
Impairment or insolvency.
Corrective action plan, §58-49-65, (c).
Information provided commissioner, §58-49-30, (c).
Licenses.
Application, §58-49-50.
Denial, suspension or revocation.
Grounds, §§58-49-40, (e), (g), 58-49-65, (a), (b).
Qualifications of applicant, §58-49-40, (a).
Required, §58-49-35, (a).
Loss reserves, §58-49-40, (d).
Names.
Certain words prohibited in name, §58-49-45.
Policies.
Insurance policies and contracts generally.
See INSURANCE POLICIES OR CONTRACTS.
Issuance, §58-49-40, (b).
Reports.
Additional information required by commissioner, §58-49-60, (b).
Annual reports, §58-49-60, (a).
Failure to file, §58-49-60, (e).
Suspension of authority to enroll new insured, §58-49-65, (d).
Trustees, managers or administrators.
Qualifications, §58-49-40, (e).

HEALTH CARE FACILITIES.
Abused juveniles brought for medial diagnosis or treatment.
Obtaining judicial authority to retain physical custody of juvenile when abuse suspected, §7B-308.
Abuse of patients, §14-32.2.
Ambulatory surgical facilities.
Licenses, §§131E-145 to 131E-152.
See AMBULATORY SURGICAL FACILITIES.
Bomb scares, §§14-69.1, 14-69.2.
Bond issues.
Authority to finance by bond, Const. N. C., art. V, §8.
Cardiac rehabilitation certification program, §§131E-165 to 131E-170.
See CARDIAC REHABILITATION CERTIFICATION PROGRAM.
Certificate of public advantage, §§131E-192.1 to 131E-192.13.
Actions on decision to issue or remain in effect, §131E-192.10, (a) to (d).
Applications, §§131E-192.3, 131E-192.11, (a).
Review of applications, §131E-192.11, (b).
Definitions, §131E-192.2.
Effects of certificate, §131E-192.13, (a) to (c).
Fees, §131E-192.11, (a).
Applications.
Review of application, §131E-192.11, (b).
Findings of general assembly, §131E-192.1.
Issuance, §131E-192.5.
Review after issuance, §131E-192.8.
Judicial review.
Decision to allow certificate to remain in effect or make changes, §131E-192.10, (b).
Attorney general action, §131E-192.10, (c).
Decision to issue or not issue, §131E-192.10, (a).
Work product of department, attorney general.
Not discoverable or admissible, §131E-192.10, (d).
Objection by attorney general, §131E-192.6.
Procedure for review, §131E-192.4, (a).
Records, §131E-192.7.
Report of activities pursuant to cooperative agreement.
Attorney general, copy submitted to, §131E-192.9, (a).
Content requirements, §131E-192.9, (a).
Failure to file or give information.
Revocation of certificate, §131E-192.9, (b).
Filed every 2 years, §131E-192.9, (a).
Notice of receipt, North Carolina register, §131E-192.9, (a).
Public comment after notice of receipt, time, §131E-192.9, (a).
Review by department, §131E-192.9, (c).
Required, §131E-192.3, (a).
Rules and regulations.
Authority of department and attorney general, §131E-192.12.
Standards for review, §131E-192.4, (b).
Certificates of need, §§131E-175 to 131E-190.
Activities requiring certificates, §131E-178.
Capital expenditure obligations, §131E-178, (c) to (e).
Predevelopment activities, §131E-178, (e).
Administrative review, §131E-188, (a), (a1).
Affected persons.
Defined, §131E-188, (c).
Issuance of certificate.
Contested case hearing.
Withdrawal of request for or final agency decision following, §131E-187, (b).

HEALTH CARE FACILITIES —Cont'd
Certificates of need —Cont'd
Appeals.
Affected persons.
Defined, §131E-188, (c).
Bond, surety, §131E-188, (b1).
Rights of appeal, §131E-188, (b).
Application for certificate.
Capital expenditure amount.
Adjustment, §131E-181, (c).
Compliance with representations in application.
Enforcement, §131E-190, (i).
Required, §131E-181, (b).
Decision on application, §131E-186, (a).
Notice, §131E-186, (b).
Fees, §131E-182, (c).
Forms, §131E-182, (b).
Information to be contained, §131E-182, (b).
Review criteria, §131E-183, (a).
Complete for review, §131E-185, (c).
Expedited review, §131E-185, (a2).
Extension of review period, §131E-185, (c).
Particular types of applications, §131E-183, (b).
Process for review, §131E-185, (a1).
Time limit for review of project, §131E-185, (a1).
Schedules for submission and review of applications, §131E-182, (a).
Approval of certificate.
Required approvals, §131E-184, (a), (b).
Exemptions, §131E-184, (c).
Assignability, §131E-181, (a).
Capital expenditure.
Activities requiring certificates, §131E-178, (c) to (e).
Defined, §131E-176.
Required approvals, §131E-184, (a).
Certified cost estimates.
Defined, §131E-176.
Charges of facility, §131E-179, (b).
Civil penalties, §131E-190, (f).
Violations of article, §131E-190, (f).
Completion of project, §131E-181.
Conditional issuance.
Withdrawal of issuance, §131E-189, (b).
Definitions, §131E-176.
Affected persons, §131E-188, (c).
Department.
Defined, §131E-176.
Exemption for substance abuse contractors in correctional facilities, §131E-184, (d).
Fees, §131E-182, (c).
Findings of fact, §131E-175.
Health care facilities.
Charges of facility, §131E-179, (b).
Defined, §131E-176.
Health maintenance organizations, §131E-180.
Defined, §131E-176.
Injunctions.
Noncompliance with representations in application for certificate, §131E-190, (i).
Violations of article generally, §131E-190, (h).
Issuance.
Conditional issuance.
Withdrawal of certificate, §131E-189, (b).
Time for, §131E-187, (a).
Contested case hearing.
Withdrawal of request for or final agency decision on, §131E-187, (b).

HEALTH CARE FACILITIES —Cont'd
Certificates of need —Cont'd
Judicial review, §131E-188, (b).
Affected persons defined, §131E-188, (c).
Legislative findings of fact, §131E-175.
Nature of certificate, §131E-181, (a).
New institutional health services.
Activities requiring certificates, §131E-178, (a).
Acquisition of service, §131E-178, (b).
Defined, §131E-176.
Development, §131E-190, (a).
Financing, construction or acquisition commitments, §131E-190, (b).
No formal commitments made until certificate granted, §131E-190, (b).
Offering, §131E-190, (a).
Financing, construction or acquisition commitments, §131E-190, (b).
Penalties for violation of provisions, §131E-190, (d), (e).
Nursing care, §131E-176.
Offering or developing services without certificate, §131E-190, (d), (e).
Research activities, §131E-179, (c).
Not requiring certificate, §131E-179, (a).
Penalties.
Civil penalty, §131E-190, (f).
Injunctive relief, §131E-190, (h).
Offering or developing services without certificate, §131E-190, (d), (e).
Powers and duties of department, §131E-177.
Required approvals, §131E-184, (a), (b).
Exemptions, §131E-184, (c).
Research activities, §131E-179, (c).
Not requiring certificate, §131E-179, (a).
Revocation of certificate.
Reasons, §131E-189.
Rights of appeal, §131E-188, (b).
State departments and agencies.
Prohibition on assisting entities in violation of article, §131E-190, (g).
State health planning and development agency.
Designation, §131E-177.
Timetable to be followed.
Withdrawal of certificate, §131E-189, (a).
Transferability, §131E-181, (a).
Withdrawal of certificate, §131E-189, (c).
Withdrawal of certificate, §131E-189.
Confidentiality of information.
Competitive health care information, §131E-97.3.
Elected officials, access to, §131E-97.3, (c).
Request for disclosure, §131E-97.3, (b).
What is public record, §131E-97.3, (a).
Credentialing information, §131E-97.2.
Health care contracts, §131E-99.
Hospices, §131E-207, (a) to (c).
Patient information, §131E-97, (a), (b).
Personnel files, §131E-97.1, (a).
Cooperative agreements.
Certificate of public advantage, §§131E-192.1 to 131E-192.13.
Applications, §131E-192.3, (b).
Procedure for review, §131E-192.4, (a).
Definitions, §131E-192.2.
Effects of certificate, §131E-192.13, (a) to (c).
Findings of general assembly, §131E-192.1.
Issuance, §131E-192.5.
Review after issuance, §131E-192.8.
Judicial review, §131E-192.10, (a) to (d).
Objection by attorney general, §131E-192.6.
Records, §131E-192.7.

HEALTH CARE FACILITIES —Cont'd
Cooperative agreements —Cont'd
Certificate of public advantage —Cont'd
Report of activities while certificate in effect, §131E-192.9, (a) to (c).
Required, §131E-192.3, (a).
Rules and regulations.
Authority of department and attorney general, §131E-192.12.
Standards for review, §131E-192.4, (b).
Criminal record checks of personnel, §114-19.3.
Dangerous weapons at demonstration at health care facility, §14-277.2.
Definitions, §131E-1.
Cardiac rehabilitation certification program, §131E-166.
Certificate of public advantage, §131E-192.2.
Certificates of need, §131E-176.
Finance act, §131A-3.
Home care agencies, §131E-136.
Licenses, §131E-136.
Hospices, §131E-201.
Demonstration at private health care facilities.
Possession of weapon, §14-277.2.
Designation of state health planning and development agency, §131E-177.
Donation of medical equipment no longer needed.
Public or state hospital, §131E-250, (a), (b).
Emergencies.
Temporary shelter or temporary services during disaster or emergency.
Waiver of rules for facilities that provide, §131E-112, (a).
Definition of "emergency management agency," §131E-112, (b).
Emergency medical services.
Regulation of emergency medical services, §§131E-155 to 131E-161.
See EMERGENCY MEDICAL SERVICES.
Employee personnel files.
Confidentiality, §131E-97.1, (a).
Fees.
Certificate of public advantage, §131E-192.11.
Review of application, §131E-192.11, (b).
Health and human services department.
Certification fee for abortion facilities, §131E-269.
Review of construction projects and plans, §131E-267.
Financing, §§131A-1 to 131A-25.
See HEALTH CARE FACILITY FINANCING.
Firearm at demonstration at health care facility, §14-277.2.
Health and human services department.
Abortion facilities.
Department certification fee authorized, §131E-269.
Construction projects and plans.
Fee for department review, §131E-267.
Health care personnel registry.
Administrative hearings, §131E-256, (d).
Contents, §131E-256, (a).
Contest of placement of certain information.
Procedure, §131E-256, (d1), (d2).
Disputed entries, statement in registry, §131E-256, (a1).
Establishment, §131E-256.
"Health care facility" defined, §131E-256, (b).
"Health care personnel" defined, §131E-256, (c).
Immunity, §131E-256, (f).

HEALTH CARE FACILITIES —Cont'd
Health care personnel registry —Cont'd
Information furnished to employer, §131E-256, (e).
Removal from registry in certain cases of neglect, §131E-256, (i).
Reports of disciplinary actions, §131E-256, (g).
Rules, §131E-256, (h).
Hiring nurses.
Verification of licensure status, §90-171.43A, (a), (b).
Home care agencies licensing, §§131E-135 to 131E-142.
Adverse action on licenses, §131E-139, (a), (b).
Definitions, §131E-136.
Enforcement of rules, §131E-140, (b).
Establishment of licensing requirements.
Purpose of part, §131E-135, (b).
Injunctions, §131E-142, (a) to (c).
Inspections, §131E-141, (a), (b).
Penalties.
Violation of provisions, §131E-141.1.
Purpose of act, §131E-135, (b).
Requirements, §131E-138, (a) to (g).
Rules and regulations, §131E-140, (a), (a1).
Services provided in all counties, §131E-137, (a) to (c).
Title of part.
Home health agency licensing act, §131E-135, (a).
Violation of provisions.
Penalties, §131E-141.1.
Hospices.
Care to be available at all times, §131E-203, (c).
Certificates of need.
Definitions, §131E-176.
Citation of article, §131E-200.
Confidentiality of information, §131E-207, (a) to (c).
Definitions, §131E-201.
Injunctions.
Violations of article, §131E-206, (a) to (c).
Inspections, §131E-204.
Confidentiality of information, §131E-207, (a) to (c).
Licenses, §§131E-200 to 131E-207.
Applications.
Department to provide, §131E-202, (b).
Display, §131E-202, (b).
Exemptions, §131E-203, (b).
Issuance, §131E-202, (b).
Nontransferable, §131E-202, (b).
Purpose of article, §131E-200.
Renewal, §131E-202, (c).
Required, §131E-203, (a).
Rules and regulations.
Adoption by commission, §131E-202, (a).
Suspension or revocation.
Grounds, §131E-205, (a).
Procedure, §131E-205, (b).
Title of article, §131E-200.
Hospital authorities, §§131E-15 to 131E-34.
See HOSPITAL AUTHORITIES.
Hospitals.
See HOSPITALS.
Independent contractors.
Confidential information, information public record, §131E-97.1, (c).
Malpractice actions generally, §§90-21.11 to 90-21.14.
See MEDICAL MALPRACTICE.

HEALTH CARE FACILITIES —Cont'd
Managed care patient assistance program, §143-730.
Medical care commission, §§143B-166 to 143B-168.
Municipal hospitals, §§131E-5 to 131E-14.2.
See MUNICIPAL HOSPITALS.
Nurses, hiring.
Verification of licensure status, §90-171.43A, (a), (b).
Nursing homes.
Licenses, §§131E-100 to 131E-110.
See NURSING HOMES.
Patients' bill of rights, §§131E-115 to 131E-131.
See NURSING HOMES.
Nursing pools.
General provisions, §§131E-154.1 to 131E-154.8.
See NURSES.
Obstruction of health care facility, §14-277.4.
Patient information.
Confidentiality.
Financial records, §131E-97, (b).
Medical records, §131E-97, (a).
Personnel files.
Confidentiality, §131E-97.1, (a).
Planning and development agency, §§131E-140, 131E-177.
Provider sponsored organizations.
General provisions, §§131E-275 to 131E-314.
See PROVIDER SPONSORED ORGANIZATIONS.
Sales and use tax.
Refunds.
Certain nonprofit organizations, §105-164.14, (b).
Specialty hospitals.
Other programs controlled by department, §131E-67.
Alcohol detoxification program, §131E-65.
Surplus medical equipment.
Donation by public or state hospital, §131E-250, (a), (b).
Suspension, cancellation or amendment of license, §131E-256.1, (a), (b).
Trauma.
Statewide trauma system, §131E-162.
Weapons at demonstration at health care facility, §14-277.2.

HEALTH CARE FACILITY FINANCING, §§131A-1 to 131A-25.
Additional and alternative method for doing authorized things, §131A-23.
Applicability of provisions.
Inconsistent laws inapplicable, §131A-25.
Audit of books and accounts, §131A-19.
Bonds and notes.
Application requesting approval of issuance, §131A-11.
Authentication, §131A-11.
Authorized, §§131A-11, 131A-18.
Defined, §131A-3.
Eligibility for investment, §131A-17.
Exemption from taxation, §131A-21.
Interest, §131A-11.
Interim receipts, §131A-11.
Investment securities, §131A-16.
Issuance, §131A-11.
Application requesting approval, §131A-11.
Liability of officers, §131A-20.

HEALTH CARE FACILITY FINANCING —Cont'd
Bonds and notes —Cont'd
Limiting or altering rights of holders of bonds or notes, §131A-13, (d).
Maturity, §131A-11.
Mutilated, destroyed or lost bonds or notes, §131A-11.
Officers not liable, §131A-20.
Principal and interest, §131A-11.
Redemption, §131A-11.
Refunding bonds or notes, §131A-18.
Remedies of holders of bonds or notes, §131A-15.
Replacement of mutilated, destroyed or lost bonds or notes, §131A-11.
Sale of bonds or notes, §131A-11.
Proceeds of sale, §131A-11.
Supplemental and additional conferred powers, §131A-23.
Tax exemption, §131A-21.
Temporary bonds, §131A-11.
Trust agreement or resolution, §131A-12.
Citation, §131A-1.
Commission.
Defined, §131A-3.
Powers.
Additional powers, §131A-4.
Conflicts of interest, §131A-22.
Construction contracts, §131A-9.
Construction of chapter.
Liberal construction, §131A-24.
Contracts.
Construction contracts, §131A-9.
Conveyance of interest in health care facilities, §131A-8.
Credit of state not pledged, §131A-10.
Criteria and requirements, §131A-5.
Procedural requirements, §131A-7.
Definitions, §131A-3.
Fees.
Fixing and collecting fees, §131A-13, (a).
Providing fund sufficient, §131A-13, (b).
Trust funds, §131A-14.
Inconsistent laws inapplicable, §131A-25.
Investments.
Bonds and notes, §131A-16.
Eligibility for investment, §131A-17.
Lease agreements, §131A-8.
Legislative findings and declarations, §131A-2.
Loan agreements, §131A-8.
Repayments of loan, §131A-13, (a).
Trust funds, §131A-14.
Operation of health care facilities, §131A-8.
Pledges of revenues, §131A-13, (c).
Powers.
Additional powers of commission, §131A-4.
Additional powers of public agencies, §131A-6.
Supplemental and additional conferred powers, §131A-23.
Procedural requirements of chapter, §131A-7.
Public agencies.
Defined, §131A-3.
Powers.
Additional powers, §131A-6.
Purchase price payments.
Fixing and collecting, §131A-13, (a).
Providing fund sufficient, §131A-13, (b).
Trust funds, §131A-14.
Purpose of act, §131A-2.
Remedies.
Holders of bonds or notes, §131A-15.

HEALTH CARE FACILITY FINANCING —Cont'd
Rents and charges.
Fixing and collecting, §131A-13, (a).
Providing fund sufficient, §131A-13, (b).
Trust funds, §131A-14.
Reports.
Annual report, §131A-19.
Requirements of chapter, §131A-5.
Procedural requirements, §131A-7.
Revenues.
Pledges of revenues, §131A-13, (c).
Sales.
Agreements of sale, §131A-8.
Short title, §131A-1.
Trust agreement or resolution.
Security for bonds or notes, §131A-12.
Trust funds, §131A-14.

HEALTH CARE FOR MINORS, CONSENT TO, §§32A-28 to 32A-34.
Authorization.
Duration, §32A-32.
Form, §32A-34.
Good faith reliance on, §32A-33.
Reliance on authorization, §32A-33.
Revocation, §32A-32.
Statutory form, §32A-34.
Who may make an authorization, §32A-30.
Custodial parents.
Authority, §32A-30.
Definitions, §32A-29.
Extent and limitations of authority, §32A-31.
Public policy, §32A-28, (a).
Purpose of article, §32A-28, (b).
Treatment by physician.
Consent of minor sufficient, §90-21.5, (a).
Consent of parent or guardian.
When not required, §90-21.1.
Who may make an authorization to consent, §32A-30.

HEALTH CARE LIABILITY, §§90-21.50 to 90-21.56.
Admissibility of evidence, §90-21.55, (b).
Corporate practice of medicine defense, §90-21.51, (e).
Covered benefits, §90-21.51, (g).
Damages.
Actions for recovery of, §90-21.51, (c), (e).
Contribution and indemnity, §90-21.52, (c).
Hold harmless contracts, §90-21.51, (f).
Joint liability, §90-21.51, (f).
Liability for damages, §90-21.51, (b).
Limitation on recovery of damages, §90-21.56, (b).
Recovery of damages, §90-21.56, (a).
Waiver of right to recovery, §90-21.56, (c).
Defense to actions, §90-21.51, (c), (e).
Definitions, §90-21.50.
Employer liability, §90-21.52, (a).
Exhaustion of administrative remedies and appeals, §90-21.54.
External review decisions, §90-21.55, (a), (b).
Hold harmless contracts, §90-21.51, (f).
Ordinary care, duty to exercise, §90-21.51, (a).
Proof of agency, §90-21.51, (d).
Separate trial and discovery on claims, §90-21.53.

HEALTH CARE PERSONNEL REGISTRY.
Administrative hearings, §131E-256, (d).
Contents, §131E-256, (a).

HEALTH CARE PERSONNEL REGISTRY —Cont'd
Contesting placement of certain information.
Procedure, §131E-256, (d1), (d2).
Disputed entries, statement in registry, §131E-256, (a1).
Establishment, §131E-256.
"Health care facility" defined, §131E-256, (b).
"Health care personnel" defined, §131E-256, (c).
Immunity, §131E-256, (f).
Information furnished to employer, §131E-256, (e).
Removal from registry in certain cases of neglect, §131E-256, (i).
Reports of disciplinary actions, §131E-256, (g).
Rules, §131E-256, (h).

HEALTH CARE POWERS OF ATTORNEY, §§32A-15 to 32A-26.
Advance health care directive registry, §§130A-465 to 130A-471.
Attorney-in-fact.
Combination with general power of attorney, §32A-22, (d).
Eligibility to act as, §32A-18.
General power of attorney.
Effect of health care power of attorney, §32A-22, (c).
Who may act as, §32A-18.
Children.
Consent to health care for minors.
Parent authorizing agent to consent, §§32A-28 to 32A-34.
Declaration of desire for natural death.
Combined with or incorporated into, §32A-26.
Definitions, §32A-16.
Disposition of decedent's body or body parts, §130A-420, (a).
Durable power.
Chapter 32A, Article 2 not applicable, §32A-23.
Eligibility to make health care power of attorney, §32A-17.
Execution prior to effective date of act.
Effect of act, §32A-19, (f).
Forms.
Statutory form, §32A-25.
Guardians.
Appointment.
Effect, §32A-22, (a).
Nomination by health care power of attorney, §32A-22, (b).
Health care agents.
Appointment, §32A-21, (a).
Authority.
Extent, §32A-19, (a), (c).
Limitations, §32A-19, (d), (e).
Spouse of principal.
Revocation upon divorce or separation, §32A-20, (c).
Decisions, §32A-24, (b).
Defenses, §32A-24, (c).
Defined, §32A-16.
Reliance on authority, §32A-24, (a).
Removal, §32A-21, (a).
Resignation, §32A-21, (a).
Substitution, §32A-21, (a).
Intent and construction of article, §32A-15, (c), (d).
Involuntary commitment to mental health facility.
Effect of advance instruction, §32A-19, (a1).

HEALTH CARE POWERS OF ATTORNEY —Cont'd
Mental health advance instructions.
Generally, §§122C-71 to 122C-77.
See MENTAL HEALTH, DEVELOPMENTAL DISABILITY, SUBSTANCE ABUSE.
Incorporation into health care power of attorney, §32A-19, (b).
Involuntary commitment to mental health facility.
Effect of advance instruction, §32A-19, (a1).
Minors.
Consent to health care for minors.
Parent authorizing agent to consent, §§32A-28 to 32A-34.
Physicians.
Determinations by, §32A-20, (a).
Health care agents' reliance on, §32A-24, (a).
Principal.
Defined, §32A-16.
Grant of authority, §32A-19, (a).
Public policy, statement, §32A-15, (a).
Purpose of article, §32A-15, (b).
Revocation, §32A-20, (d).
Generally, §32A-20, (b).
Health care agents.
Death, §32A-21.
Failure or refusal to act, §32A-21, (b).
Spouse of principal.
Revoked by divorce or separation, §32A-20, (c).
Suicide.
Actions under not considered suicide, §32A-24.
Who may make, §32A-17.
Withholding or discontinuing life sustaining procedures.
Specific authority given, no declaration as to present condition executed, §32A-15, (c).

HEALTH CARE PROVIDER REFERRAL FEES AND PAYMENTS FOR SOLICITATIONS, §§90-400 to 90-402.
Health care provider defined, §90-400.
Prohibited, §90-401.
Sanctions, §90-402.

HEALTH CARE PROVIDERS' IMMUNITY.
Nonprofit medical or health care facilities, §90-21.16.

HEALTH CARE PROVIDERS' SELF-REFERRALS, §§90-405 to 90-408.
Claim for payment, §90-406, (b), (c).
Cross-referral arrangements, §90-406, (d).
Penalties, §90-407, (c), (d).
Definitions, §90-405.
Disciplinary actions.
Grounds, §90-407, (a).
Exceptions for underserved areas.
Disclosure of investment interests by provider, §90-408, (c).
Generally, §90-408, (a).
Regulations governing applications for exemptions, §90-408, (b).
General prohibition, §90-406, (a).
Invoices, §90-406, (b), (c).
Penalties for designated misconduct, §90-407, (b), (d).
Underserved areas.
Exceptions, §90-408.

HEALTH CARE RECORDS.
See MEDICAL RECORDS.

HEALTH CARE RESEARCH FACILITIES.
Financing health care facility generally, §§131A-1 to 131A-25.
See HEALTH CARE FACILITY FINANCING.

HEALTH CLUBS.
Prepaid entertainment contracts.
General provisions, §§66-118 to 66-125.
See PREPAID ENTERTAINMENT CONTRACTS.

HEALTH DEPARTMENTS, LOCAL, §§130A-34 to 130A-42.
See LOCAL HEALTH DEPARTMENTS.

HEALTH DIRECTOR OF STATE, §138-3.

HEALTH EMERGENCY.
Nuclear, biological or chemical agents.
Terrorist incident using, §§130A-475 to 130A-479.
See TERRORIST INCIDENT USING NUCLEAR, BIOLOGICAL OR CHEMICAL AGENTS.

HEALTH INSURANCE.
Children.
Health insurance program, §§108A-70.18 to 108A-70.28.
See CHILDREN'S HEALTH INSURANCE PROGRAM.
Joint legislative health care oversight committee.
Powers and duties, §120-70.111, (c).
Child support, medical support orders and agreements, §50-13.11.
National medical support notice, §§110-136.11 to 110-136.14.
Confidentiality of consumer and customer information.
Generally, §§58-39-1 to 58-39-165.
See INSURANCE CONSUMER AND CUSTOMER INFORMATION PRIVACY.
Credit insurance.
Generally, §§58-57-1 to 58-57-115.
See CREDIT INSURANCE.
Determination of jurisdiction over health care benefits providers.
Generally, §§58-49-1 to 58-49-25.
See HEALTH CARE BENEFITS PROVIDERS.
External review of health benefit plan, §§58-50-75 to 58-50-95.
See ACCIDENT AND HEALTH INSURANCE.
Generally.
See ACCIDENT AND HEALTH INSURANCE.
Health insurance innovations commission, §§58-90-1 to 58-90-25.
Health maintenance organizations, §§58-67-1 to 58-67-185.
See HEALTH MAINTENANCE ORGANIZATIONS.
Hospital, medical and dental service corporations, §§58-65-1 to 58-66-40.
See HOSPITAL, MEDICAL AND DENTAL SERVICE CORPORATIONS.
Law enforcement officers.
Separate insurance benefits plan for state and local officers, §143-166.60, (a) to (h).
Life and health insurance guaranty association, §§58-62-2 to 58-62-95.
See LIFE AND HEALTH INSURANCE GUARANTY ASSOCIATION.
Long-term care insurance, §§58-55-1 to 58-55-50.
See LONG-TERM CARE INSURANCE.
Managed care patient assistance program, §143-730.

HEALTH INSURANCE —Cont'd
Medicaid, §§108A-54 to 108A-70.5.
See MEDICAID.
Medical support orders and agreements for children, §50-13.11.
Medicare supplement insurance, §§58-54-1 to 58-54-50.
See MEDICARE.
Multiple employer welfare arrangements regulation generally, §§58-49-30 to 58-49-65.
See HEALTH CARE BENEFITS PROVIDERS.
Portability and accountability, §§58-68-25 to 58-68-75.
See HEALTH INSURANCE PORTABILITY AND ACCOUNTABILITY.
Small employer group health coverage, §§58-50-105 to 58-50-150.
See SMALL EMPLOYER GROUP HEALTH COVERAGE.
Teachers and state employees.
Comprehensive major medical plan, §§135-39 to 135-40.14.
See MEDICAL PLAN FOR TEACHERS AND STATE EMPLOYEES.
Third party administrators, §§58-56-2 to 58-56-66.
See THIRD PARTY ADMINISTRATORS.

HEALTH INSURANCE INNOVATIONS COMMISSION, §§58-90-1 to 58-90-30.
Deposit of funds, §§58-90-25.
Duties and responsibilities, §§58-90-10.
Established, §§58-90-5.
Funding, §§58-90-15.
Issues and strategies, §§58-90-10.
Meetings, §§58-90-15.
Members, §§58-90-5.
Purposes, §§58-90-1.
Staff, §§58-90-15.
Temporary rules to allow implementation, §§58-90-20.

HEALTH INSURANCE PORTABILITY AND ACCOUNTABILITY, §§58-68-25 to 58-68-75.
Definitions, §58-68-25, (a), (b).
Guaranteed availability of individual coverage to certain individuals with prior group coverage, §58-68-60, (b), (h).
Preexisting condition exclusion, §58-68-30, (b).
Group market reforms, §§58-68-25 to 58-68-55.
Disclosure of information by health insurers, §58-68-50, (a).
Description of information, §58-68-50, (b).
Discrimination against individual participants and beneficiaries based on health status.
Eligibility to enroll, §58-68-35, (a).
Premium contributions, §58-68-35, (b).
Excepted benefits.
Conditions, §58-68-55, (b).
Exclusion of certain plans.
Excepted benefits, §58-68-55, (a).
Preexisting condition exclusions.
Increase portability through limitation on, §58-68-30.
Renewability coverage.
Guaranteed renewability for employers in group market.
Associations.
Application to coverage offered only through, §58-68-45, (e).
Exceptions, §58-68-45, (b).
Uniform modification of coverage, §58-68-45, (d).

HEALTH INSURANCE PORTABILITY AND ACCOUNTABILITY —Cont'd
Group market reforms —Cont'd
Renewability coverage —Cont'd
Guaranteed renewability for employers in group market —Cont'd
Generally, §58-68-45, (a).
Termination of coverage.
Requirements for uniform termination, §58-68-45, (c).
Size of employer.
Application of certain rules in determining, §58-68-25, (c).
Small group market.
Guaranteed availability of coverage for employers in.
Exceptions, §58-68-40, (d), (e).
Financial capacity limits.
Applications, §58-68-40, (c).
Issuance of coverage, §58-68-40, (a).
Network plans.
Special rules for, §58-68-40, (b).
Health maintenance organizations.
Preexisting condition exclusion.
Use of affiliation period as alternative to exclusion, §58-68-30, (g).
Individual market reforms, §§58-68-60 to 58-68-75.
Excepted benefits, §58-68-75, (a).
Certain conditions met, §58-68-75, (b).
Guaranteed availability of individual coverage to certain individuals with prior group coverage, §58-68-60.
Guaranteed renewability of individual coverage.
Associations.
Application to coverage offered only through, §58-68-65, (e).
Exceptions, §58-68-65, (b), (d).
Generally, §58-68-65, (a).
Termination of coverage.
Requirements for uniform termination, §58-68-65, (c).
Preexisting condition exclusions.
Certification of coverage, §58-68-70.
Prior group coverage.
Guaranteed availability of individual coverage to certain individuals with, §58-68-60.
Renewability of individual coverage.
Guaranteed renewability, §58-68-65.
Preexisting condition exclusions.
Certifications and disclosure of coverage, §58-68-30, (e).
Crediting previous coverage, §58-68-30, (a), (c).
Definitions, §58-68-30, (b).
Exceptions, §58-68-30, (d).
Health maintenance organizations.
Use of affiliation period as alternative to exclusion, §58-68-30, (g).
Individual market reforms.
Certification of coverage, §58-68-70.
Limitation on exclusion period, §58-68-30, (a).
Special enrollment periods, §58-68-30, (f).
Prior group coverage.
Guaranteed availability of individual coverage to certain individuals with.
Alternative coverage permitted, §58-68-60, (c).
Construction and interpretation, §58-68-60, (g).
Definitions, §58-68-60, (b), (h).
Financial capacity limits.
Application, §58-68-60, (e).
Generally, §58-68-60, (a).

HEALTH INSURANCE PORTABILITY AND ACCOUNTABILITY —Cont'd
Prior group coverage —Cont'd
Guaranteed availability of individual coverage to certain individuals with —Cont'd
Market requirements, §58-68-60, (f).
Network plans.
Special rules for, §58-68-60, (d).

HEALTH MAINTENANCE ORGANIZATIONS, §§58-67-1 to 58-67-185.
Abortion.
Lawful abortions.
Requiring health care institution to perform abortion, §14-45.1, (f).
Acknowledgment of claims, §58-3-100, (c).
Failure to acknowledge after receiving notice.
Civil penalty, §58-3-100, (c).
Action for negligent decisions.
Health care liability, §§90-21.50 to 90-21.56.
See HEALTH CARE LIABILITY.
Additional coverage mandates prohibited, §58-50-63, (a).
Employer not prohibited from expanding coverage, §58-50-63, (b).
Insurer and health benefit plan defined, §58-50-63, (c).
Administrative penalty in addition to or in lieu of suspension or revocation of certificate of authority, §58-67-165, (a).
Administrative procedures, §58-67-155.
Advance practice registered nurse.
Payment or reimbursement, §58-50-30, (d).
Right to choose services, §58-50-30, (a1) to (a3), (g), (h).
Advertising.
False or misleading advertising, §58-67-65, (a).
Solicitation of enrollees.
Not deemed validation of law relating to advertising by health professionals, §58-67-170, (b).
Agents.
Licensing, §58-67-90.
Applicability of other laws, §58-67-171.
Breast cancer.
Mammograms, coverage, §58-67-76.
Cancer treatment.
Cervical cancer screening, coverage, §58-67-76.
Colorectal cancer examinations, laboratory tests and screening.
Coverage required of all health benefit plans, §58-3-179, (a).
Limitations applicable to services, §58-3-179, (b).
Coverage of certain prescribed drugs for, §58-67-78, (a).
Exceptions, §58-67-78, (b), (c).
Mammograms, coverage, §58-67-76.
Carrier defined, §58-67-5, (n).
Cease and desist orders, §58-67-165, (c), (d).
Certificates of need.
Applications.
Granting certificate, §131E-180, (e).
Reviewing certificate of need applications, §131E-180, (d).
Definition of health maintenance organization, §131E-176.
Fee-for-service component.
Qualification for exemption, §131E-180, (c).
General provisions, §§131E-175 to 131E-190.
See HEALTH CARE FACILITIES.

HEALTH MAINTENANCE ORGANIZATIONS —Cont'd
Certificates of need —Cont'd
New institutional health services.
Offering or developing services, §131E-180, (a).
Applicability of provisions, §131E-180, (b).
Cervical cancer.
Screening for early detection.
Coverage requirements, §58-67-76, (a), (e).
Defined, §58-67-76, (a1).
Chemical dependency.
Contracts to cover treatment, §58-67-70, (a) to (f).
Coverage not required, §58-67-75, (c).
Defined, §58-67-75, (a).
Discrimination.
Applicability of section, §58-67-75, (d).
Prohibited acts, §58-67-75, (b).
Chiropractors.
Right to choose services, §58-50-30, (a1) to (a3), (g), (h).
Choice of service providers, §58-50-30, (a1) to (a3).
Pediatrician for minors, §58-3-240.
Provider directories, §58-3-245.
Specialist selected as primary care provider, §58-3-235.
Uniform provider credentialing, §58-3-230.
Citation of act.
Short title, §58-67-1.
Claims.
Acknowledgment of claims, §58-3-100, (c).
Failure to acknowledge after receiving notice.
Civil penalty, §58-3-100, (c).
Incurred by not reported claims, §58-67-135, (a).
Computation of liabilities, §58-67-135, (b).
Notice of claim denied, §58-3-172, (a).
Health benefit plan defined, §58-3-172, (b).
Uniform claim forms, §58-3-171, (a).
Health benefit plan defined, §58-3-171, (c).
Workers' compensation as health benefit plan, §58-3-171, (b).
Clinical social workers.
Defined, §58-50-30, (c).
Right to choose services, §58-50-30, (a1) to (a3), (g), (h).
Clinical trials, coverage, §58-3-255, (b).
Costs not required to be covered, §58-3-255, (d).
Covered clinical trials defined, §58-3-255, (a).
Definitions, §58-3-255, (a).
Medical necessary costs covered, §58-3-255, (c).
Closed formularies or restricted access to prescription drugs, §58-3-221.
Collaboration with local health departments, §58-67-66.
Colorectal cancer examinations, laboratory tests and screening.
Coverage required of every health benefit plan, §58-3-179, (a).
Limitations applicable to services, §58-3-179, (b).
Commissioner of insurance.
Administrative procedures, §58-67-155.
Cease and desist orders, §58-67-165, (c), (d).
Definition of "commissioner," §58-67-5, (a).
Deposits.
Administration, §58-67-25, (c).
Commissioner must require minimum deposit, §58-67-25, (b).
Protection of enrollees, §58-67-25, (a).
Examinations, §58-67-100.
Hazardous financial condition.
Authority as to, §58-67-105.

HEALTH MAINTENANCE ORGANIZATIONS —Cont'd
Commissioner of insurance —Cont'd
Hazardous financial condition —Cont'd
Rules and regulations.
Authority as to, §58-67-105, (b).
Steps reasonably necessary to rectify situation.
Enumerated, §58-67-105, (a).
Insolvency.
Protection against insolvency.
Adequacy of plan, §58-67-110, (e).
Commissioner to require deposit, §58-67-110, (a).
Rehabilitation, liquidation or conservation of health maintenance organizations, §58-67-145.
Reports.
Annual reports to commissioner, §58-67-55.
Rules and regulations, §58-67-150.
Confidentiality of information, §58-67-180.
Construction and interpretation, §58-67-170.
Continuation of benefits, §58-67-120, (a).
Plan for, §58-67-120, (a).
Continuing care retirement community residents, §58-3-200, (f).
Continuity of care.
Conditions of coverage, §58-67-88, (h).
Construction of provision, §58-67-88, (i).
Definitions, §58-67-88, (a).
Disclosure of right to transition, §58-67-88, (j).
Length of transitional period, §58-67-88, (d).
Pregnancy, §58-67-88, (f).
Scheduled inpatient treatment, §58-67-88, (e).
Terminal illness, §58-67-88, (g).
Newly covered insured, transition coverage, §58-67-88, (c).
Termination of contract.
Election to continue, §58-67-88, (b).
Contraceptive drugs or devices and outpatient contraceptive services.
Coverage by insurer providing health benefit plan, §58-3-178, (a), (b).
Definitions, §58-3-178, (c).
Prohibited acts, §58-3-178, (d).
Religious employer requesting exclusion of coverage, §58-3-178, (e).
Contracts.
Certain words prohibited, §58-67-65, (d).
Chemical dependency.
Contracts to cover treatment, §58-67-70, (a) to (f).
Custodial agreements.
Exclusivity prohibited, §58-67-30, (a).
Grounds for disapproval, §58-67-30, (b).
Insurers and hospital and medical service corporations.
Contracts with health maintenance organizations, §58-67-95, (b).
Management agreements.
Exclusivity prohibited, §58-67-30, (a).
Grounds for disapproval, §58-67-30, (b).
Master group contracts, §58-67-85.
Powers of organizations generally, §58-67-35, (a).
Credentialing providers.
Health benefit plan and insurer defined, §58-3-230, (c).
Process requirements, §58-3-230, (a).
Time limit on processing applications, §58-3-230, (a).
Uniform provider credentialing application form.
Commissioner to adopt by rule, §58-3-230, (b).

HEALTH MAINTENANCE ORGANIZATIONS —Cont'd
Definitions, §58-67-5, (a) to (p).
Accident, accidental injury and accidental means, §58-67-80, (b).
Applicability of definitions, §58-67-80, (a).
Certificate of need law, §131E-176.
Mastectomy.
Coverage for reconstructive breast surgery following, §58-67-79, (b).
Mental illness and chemical dependency, §58-67-75, (a).
Dental procedures performed in hospital or ambulatory surgical facility.
Children under age nine, persons with serious mental and physical condition and persons with significant behavior problems.
Definitions, §58-3-122, (b).
Health benefit plans to provide coverage for payment of anesthesia and facility charges, §58-3-122, (a).
Dentists.
Right to choose services, §58-50-30, (a1) to (a3), (g), (h).
Deposits.
Administration, §58-67-25, (c).
Commissioner must require minimum deposit, §58-67-25, (b).
Protection of enrollees, §58-67-25, (a).
Determinations as to coverage, §58-3-200, (c).
Diabetes.
Coverage for certain treatment, §58-67-74, (a).
Definition of "physician," §58-67-74.
Directories of providers, §58-3-245.
Direct payment to government agency, §58-3-175, (b).
Health benefit plan defined, §58-3-175, (a).
Inapplicability of provisions, §58-3-175, (c).
When not required, §58-3-175, (d).
Disclosure requirements for health benefit plans, §58-3-191, (b).
Discontinuance defined, §58-67-5, (o).
Discrimination.
Mentally ill and chemically dependent.
Applicability of section, §58-67-75, (d).
Coverage, §58-67-75, (b1), (c).
Prohibited acts, §58-67-75, (b).
Prohibited acts, §58-67-65, (f).
Drive-thru deliveries, §58-3-169.
Electronic or on-line system for up-to-date network information.
Plan to provide, §58-3-245, (a).
Emergency care.
Coverage required, §58-3-190.
Enrollees.
Defined, §58-67-5, (b).
Deterioration of health.
Cancellation or nonrenewal because of, §58-67-65, (c).
Evidence of coverage.
Enrollees entitled to, §58-67-50, (a).
Unable to arrange adequate services.
Refusal to enroll, §58-67-65, (e).
Enrollment period, §58-67-125, (a).
Group contracts, §58-67-125, (b).
Nongroup enrollees, §58-67-125, (c).
Evidence of coverage.
Content, §58-67-50, (a).
Defined, §58-67-5, (c).
Enrollees entitled to, §58-67-50, (a).

HEALTH MAINTENANCE ORGANIZATIONS —Cont'd
Evidence of coverage —Cont'd
Forms.
Approval by commissioner, §58-67-50, (c).
Copies to be filed with commissioner, §58-67-50, (a).
Disapproval by commissioner.
Notice, §58-67-50, (c).
Information needed for determination by commissioner.
Power to require, §58-67-50, (d).
Information regarding coverage and premiums.
Provision to group subscribers when requested, §58-67-50, (e).
Notice, expenses may exceed covered amount, §58-3-250, (b).
Payment obligations, explanation by insurer, §58-3-250, (a).
Examinations.
Powers of commissioner, §58-67-100, (a).
Report in lieu of, §58-67-100, (d).
Exemptions from provisions, §58-67-10, (b).
External review of health benefit plan, §§58-50-75 to 58-50-95.
See ACCIDENT AND HEALTH INSURANCE.
Fee based pastoral counselor.
Defined, §58-50-30, (c1).
Right to choose services, §58-50-30, (a1) to (a3), (g), (h).
Fees.
License application and annual continuation fees, §58-67-160.
Fiduciaries.
Responsibilities of directors, officers and partners, §58-67-45.
Financial incentives to delay, deny or reduce coverage.
Plan prohibited from offering provider, §58-3-265.
Foreign corporations.
Qualifications to do business in state, §58-67-10, (a).
Genetic information in health insurance, §58-3-215.
Grandfather clause, §58-67-10, (b).
Grievance procedures for insurers, §58-50-62.
External review of decision, §§58-50-75 to 58-50-95.
Hazardous financial condition.
Authority of commissioner, §58-67-105.
Rules and regulations, §58-67-105, (b).
Steps reasonably necessary to rectify situation, §58-67-105, (a).
Health benefit plans generally, §§58-3-167 to 58-3-178.
See ACCIDENT AND HEALTH INSURANCE.
Health care plans.
Defined, §58-67-5, (d).
Health care services.
Defined, §58-67-5, (e).
Health insurance portability and accountability.
Preexisting condition exclusion.
Use of affiliation period as alternative to exclusion, §58-68-30, (g).
Transition of care after provider contract terminated, §58-67-88.
High-risk populations.
Nondiscrimination against, §58-3-200, (e).
HMO defined, §58-67-5, (f).

HEALTH MAINTENANCE ORGANIZATIONS —Cont'd
Hold harmless agreements, §58-67-115, (a).
Special deposit in lieu of, §58-67-115, (b).
Hospital, medical and dental service corporations.
Contracts with health maintenance organizations, §58-67-95, (b).
Power to organize and operate health maintenance organization, §58-67-95, (a).
Provisions not applicable to health maintenance organizations, §58-67-170, (a).
Incentives to delay, deny or reduce coverage.
Plan prohibited from offering provider, §58-3-265.
Injunctions, §58-67-165, (e).
Insolvency.
Defined, §58-67-5, (m).
Hold harmless agreements, §58-67-115, (a).
Insolvent defined, §58-67-5, (m).
Protection against insolvency.
Adequacy of plan, §58-67-110, (e).
Deposit, §58-67-110, (a).
Minimum net worth, §58-67-110, (b).
Insurance companies.
Contracts with health maintenance organizations, §58-67-95, (b).
General provisions.
See INSURANCE COMPANIES.
Power to organize and operate health maintenance organizations, §58-67-95, (a).
Provisions not applicable to health maintenance organizations, §58-67-170, (a).
Investments, §58-67-60.
Licenses.
Agents, §58-67-90.
Application, §58-67-10, (c).
Additional information, §58-67-11, (a).
Changes, notification, §58-67-11, (b).
Denial, §58-67-20, (c).
Fees.
Application and annual continuation fees, §58-67-160.
Issuance.
Determinations required, §58-67-20, (a).
Factors which may be considered, §58-67-20, (b).
Monetary penalty for violations, §58-2-70, (c), (d), (g).
Required, §58-67-10, (a).
Restitution for violations, §58-2-70, (e) to (g).
Surrender, §58-2-65.
Suspension or revocation.
Administrative penalty in addition to or in lieu of, §58-67-165, (a).
Applicable provisions, §58-2-70, (h).
Criminal convictions, §58-2-60, (b).
Grounds, §58-67-140, (a).
Hearings.
Action following, §58-67-155, (b).
Notice, §58-67-155, (a).
Notice and hearing, §58-2-70, (b).
Procedure, §§58-67-140, (b) to (d), 58-67-155.
Liquidation, §58-67-145.
Local health departments.
Collaboration with, §58-67-66.
Long-term care insurance, §§58-55-1 to 58-55-50.
See LONG-TERM CARE INSURANCE.
Malpractice actions generally, §§90-21.11 to 90-21.14.
See MEDICAL MALPRACTICE.

HEALTH MAINTENANCE ORGANIZATIONS —Cont'd
Mammograms.
Coverage requirements, §58-67-76, (a), (c).
Low dose mammography defined, §58-67-76, (b).
Reimbursement, §58-67-76, (d).
Managed care patient assistance program, §143-730.
Marriage and family therapists.
Defined, §58-50-30, (c4).
Right to choose services, §58-50-30, (a1) to (a3).
Mastectomy.
Coverage for reconstructive breast surgery following, §58-67-79, (a).
Definitions, §58-67-79, (b).
Notice of available coverage, §58-67-79, (d).
Prohibited act, §58-67-79, (c).
Master group contracts.
Adding employees to coverage.
Time for, §58-67-85, (d).
Authorized, §58-67-85, (a).
Successor corporations.
Liability, §58-67-85, (e).
Maternity coverage requirements, §58-3-170, (a).
Health benefit plans defined, §58-3-170, (b).
Minimum hospital stay following birth, §58-3-169.
Medical necessity.
Requirements for health benefit plans that limit coverage to medically necessary services and supplies, §58-3-200, (b).
Mental health area facilities.
Contracts with health maintenance organizations, §122C-141, (c).
Misdemeanors, §58-67-165, (b).
Modifications of operations.
Notice to commissioner, §58-67-10, (d).
Names.
Prohibited words, §58-67-65, (d).
Negligent decisions of plan providers.
Health care liability, §§90-21.50 to 90-21.56.
See HEALTH CARE LIABILITY.
Net worth.
Defined, §58-67-5, (i).
Risk based capital requirement, §58-12-70.
Newborn hearing screening.
Coverage required, §58-3-260, (b).
Health benefit plan and insurer defined, §58-3-260, (a).
Notice.
Claim denied, §58-3-172, (a).
Health benefit plan defined, §58-3-172, (b).
Exercise of powers, §58-67-35, (b).
Modification of operations, §58-67-10, (d).
Obstruction of health care facility, §14-277.4.
Offset or reversal of payment, §58-50-57, (a).
Contract with provider not to contain provision authorizing, §58-50-57, (b).
Optometrists.
Right to choose services, §58-50-30, (a1) to (a3), (g), (h).
Osteoporosis or low bone mass.
Bone mass measurement for diagnosis and evaluation.
Health benefit plan to provide coverage, §58-3-174, (a).
Definitions, §58-3-174, (d).
Frequency of coverage, §58-3-174, (b).
Screening for nonqualified individuals not covered, §58-3-174, (c).
Participating provider defined, §58-67-5, (l).

HEALTH MAINTENANCE ORGANIZATIONS —Cont'd
Payment obligations for covered services.
Explanation by insurer, §58-3-250, (a).
Notice that actual expenses may exceed covered amount, §58-3-250, (b).
Payment to government agency.
Direct payment, §58-3-175.
Pediatrician.
Direct access for minors, §58-3-240.
Pharmacist.
Payment or reimbursement, §58-50-30, (e).
Right to choose services, §58-50-30, (a1) to (a3), (g), (h).
Physician assistant.
Payment or reimbursement, §58-50-30, (f).
Right to choose services, §58-50-30, (a1) to (a3), (g), (h).
Physicians and surgeons.
Disciplinary action by health care institutions.
Reports, §90-14.13.
Plan summaries.
Notice, expenses may exceed covered amount, §58-3-250, (b).
Payment obligations, explanation by insurer, §58-3-250, (a).
Podiatrists.
Right to choose services, §58-50-30, (a1) to (a3), (g), (h).
Policies and contracts.
Insurance policies and contracts generally.
See INSURANCE POLICIES OR CONTRACTS.
Powers, §58-67-35, (a).
Notice of exercise of powers, §58-67-35, (b).
Practice of medicine or dentistry.
Health maintenance organizations not deemed to be practicing medicine or dentistry, §58-67-170, (c).
Premiums.
Information regarding premiums and coverage.
Providing to group subscribers when requested, §58-67-50, (e).
Schedule.
Approval by commissioner, §58-67-50, (c).
Disapproval by commissioner.
Notice, §58-67-50, (c).
Establishment of premiums, §58-67-50, (b).
Filing of copy with commissioner, §58-67-50, (b).
Information needed for determination by commissioner.
Power to require, §58-67-50, (d).
Prescription drug identification cards.
Plan issuing prescription drug cards to issue uniform identification cards, §58-3-177, (a).
Definitions, §58-3-177, (e).
Electronic verification of claim, §58-3-177, (d).
Exceptions, §58-3-177, (f).
Information contained in card, §58-3-177, (a), (b).
Issued annually if change in coverage, §58-3-177, (c).
Prescription drugs.
Closed formularies or restricted access to perspiration drugs or devices.
Definitions, §58-3-221, (c).
Medically necessary nonformulary or restricted access drug or device prescribed.
Voiding or refusing to renew contract prohibited, §58-3-221, (b).
Payment for drugs or devices specifically excluded from coverage not required, §58-3-221, (d).

HEALTH MAINTENANCE ORGANIZATIONS —Cont'd
Prescription drugs —Cont'd
Closed formularies or restricted access to perspiration drugs or devices —Cont'd
Requirements of insurers maintaining, §58-3-221, (a).
Contraceptive drugs or devices.
Coverage by insurer providing health benefit plan, §58-3-178.
Primary care provider, specialist selected.
Insured diagnosed with serious or chronic degenerative, disabling or life threatening disease, §58-3-235, (a).
Care authorized by specialist, §58-3-235, (b).
Denial of access by insurer, §58-3-235, (a).
Treatment plan approved by insurer, selection under, §58-3-235, (b).
Privileged communications.
Confidentiality of medical information, §58-67-180.
Professional counselor.
Defined, §58-50-30, (c3).
Right to choose services, §58-50-30, (a1) to (a3), (g), (h).
Prohibited practices, §58-67-65, (a) to (f).
Prostate-specific antigen (PSA) tests.
Coverage, §58-67-77, (a), (c).
Defined, §58-67-77, (b).
Provider credentialing.
Health benefit plan and insurer defined, §58-3-230, (c).
Process requirements, §58-3-230, (a).
Time limit on processing applications, §58-3-230, (a).
Uniform provider credentialing application form.
Commissioner to adopt by rule, §58-3-230, (b).
Provider defined, §58-67-5, (h).
Provider directories.
Allied health professionals, listing, §58-3-245, (c).
Information included in directory listing, §58-3-245, (b).
Plan required to provide, §58-3-245, (a).
Provider networks.
Services outside networks, §58-3-200, (d).
Psychologists.
Defined, §58-50-30, (b).
Right to choose services, §58-50-30, (a1) to (a3), (g), (h).
Public documents.
Filings and reports as, §58-67-175.
Racial minorities.
Discrimination, §58-67-65, (f).
Reciprocity.
Organizations of bordering states may be admitted to do business, §58-67-15.
Reconstructive breast surgery.
Coverage following mastectomy, §58-67-79.
Rehabilitation, liquidation or conservation, §58-67-145.
Replacement coverage, §58-67-130, (a).
Exceptions, §58-67-130, (b).
Reports.
Examinations.
Report in lieu of examination, §58-67-100, (d).
Health benefit plan reporting requirements, §58-3-191, (a).
Access to reports, §58-3-191, (b1).
Public documents, §58-67-175.
Risk based capital requirements.
Insurance companies, §§58-12-2 to 58-12-70.
See INSURANCE COMPANIES.

HEALTH MAINTENANCE ORGANIZATIONS —Cont'd
Rules and regulations, §58-67-150.
Hazardous financial condition, §58-67-105.
Severability of provisions, §58-67-185.
Specialist care referral.
In-plan specialists.
Definitions, §58-3-223, (b).
Duties of insurer providing health benefit plan, §58-3-223, (a).
Specialist selected as primary care provider.
Insured diagnosed with serious or chronic degenerative, disabling or life threatening disease, §58-3-235, (a).
Care authorized by specialist, §58-3-235, (b).
Denial of access by insurer, §58-3-235, (a).
Treatment plan approved by insurer, selection under, §58-3-235, (b).
Subscriber defined, §58-67-5, (k).
Substance abuse professional.
Defined, §58-50-30, (c2).
Right to choose services, §58-50-30, (a1) to (a3), (g), (h).
Telephone system for up-to-date network information.
Plan to provide, §58-3-245, (a).
Title of act.
Short title, §58-67-1.
Transition of care after provider contract terminated, §58-67-88.
Treatment discussions.
Limiting prohibited, §58-3-176.
Uncovered expenditures defined, §58-67-5, (p).
Unfair trade practices, applicable provisions, §58-67-65, (b).
Uniform claim forms, §58-3-171.
Uniform prescription drug identification cards, §58-3-177.
Uniform provider credentialing, §58-3-230.
Utilization review.
External review, §§58-50-75 to 58-50-95.
Generally, §58-50-61, (a) to (o).
Violations of provisions generally, §58-67-165, (b).
Working capital.
Defined, §58-67-5, (j).

HEALTH ORGANIZATIONS.
Provider sponsored organizations, §§131E-275 to 131E-314.
See PROVIDER SPONSORED ORGANIZATIONS.
Solicitation of contributions, §§131F-1 to 131F-24.
See CHARITABLE SOLICITATION.

HEALTH RECORDS.
Generally.
See MEDICAL RECORDS.

HEALTH SERVICES COMMISSION.
Adult health.
Adoption of rules, §130A-223, (b).
Appointments, §130A-30, (a), (b).
Officers, §130A-31.
Arthritis.
Adoption of rules, §130A-222, (b).
Chronic renal disease.
Adoption of rules, §130A-220, (b).
Communicable diseases.
Establishing lists of communicable diseases and conditions to be reported, §130A-134.
Rules of commission, §130A-147.

HEALTH SERVICES COMMISSION —Cont'd
Compensation, §130A-30, (e).
Creation, §130A-29, (a).
Crustacea.
Sanitation of scallops, shellfish and crustacea.
Rules relating to sanitation, §130A-230.
Defined, §130A-2.
Dental health program.
Adoption of rules by commission, §130A-366, (b).
Diabetes.
Adoption of rules, §130A-221, (b).
Duties, §130A-29, (a) to (d).
Educational institutions.
Regulation of sanitation by commission, §§130A-235, 130A-236.
Election meetings, §130A-32.
Glaucoma.
Adoption of rules, §130A-221, (b).
Hospitals.
Regulation of sanitation by commission, §130A-235.
Immunization.
Promulgation of rules concerning implementation of program, §130A-152, (c).
Mass gatherings.
Rules and regulations of commission, §130A-257.
Meetings.
Election meetings, §130A-32.
Regular and special meetings, §130A-33.
Members, §130A-30, (a).
Metropolitan water districts.
Commission authorized to create, §130A-29, (d).
Mosquito control districts.
Commission authorized to create, §130A-29, (d).
Officers, §130A-31.
Powers, §130A-29, (a) to (d).
Private educational institutions.
Regulation of sanitation by commission, §§130A-235, 130A-236.
Private hospitals.
Regulation of sanitation by commission, §130A-235.
Quorum, §130A-30, (d).
Removal of members, §130A-30, (c).
Rules and regulations, §130A-29, (b) to (e).
Mass gatherings, §130A-257.
Sanitary districts.
Commission authorized to create, §130A-29, (d).
Sanitation.
Regulation of sanitation by commission, §§130A-235, 130A-236.
Scallops.
Rules relating to sanitation, §130A-230.
Schools.
Regulation of sanitation by commission, §§130A-235, 130A-236.
Shellfish.
Rules relating to sanitation, §130A-230.
Special meetings, §130A-33.
Standards.
Establishment by commission authorized, §130A-9.

HEALTH SPAS.
Child care facilities.
Drop-in or short-term child care offered.
Not included in term child care, §110-86.
Prepaid entertainment contracts generally, §§66-118 to 66-125.
See PREPAID ENTERTAINMENT CONTRACTS.

HEALTH STATISTICS, STATE CENTER, §§130A-371 to 130A-374.
Analysis and indexing, §130A-373, (e).
Authority and duties, §130A-373.
Collection, maintenance and analyses of health data.
Authority and duties, §130A-373, (a) to (c).
Confidentiality.
Security of health data, §130A-374, (a), (b).
Coordination of health data activities within state, §130A-373, (f).
Definitions, §130A-372.
Department of health and human services.
Center established within department, §130A-371.
Duties, §130A-373.
Established within department, §130A-371.
Governmental organizations.
Collecting data on behalf of, §130A-373, (b).
Health data.
Defined, §130A-372.
Mandatory reporting of health data, §130A-373, (c).
Medical records.
Defined, §130A-372.
Nonprofit organizations.
Collecting data on behalf of, §130A-373, (b).
Powers and duties, §130A-373.
Publishing, availability and dissemination of statistics, §130A-373, (e).
Quality, timely and comprehensive statistics, §130A-373, (e).
Security of health data, §130A-374, (a), (b).
Sharing health data with other entities, §130A-373, (d).
Voluntary basis for collecting data, §130A-373, (c).

HEARING AID DEALERS AND FITTERS, §§93D-1 to 93D-16.
Age.
Qualifications for license, §93D-5, (a).
Apprenticeship registration.
Applications, §93D-9, (a).
Fee, §93D-9, (b).
Display of apprenticeship registration, §93D-12.
Holding apprenticeship license for one year as prerequisite to issuance of license, §93D-5, (c).
Issuance, §93D-9, (b).
Renewal, §93D-9, (d), (e).
Fees, §93D-9, (e).
Supervision and training by licensee.
Prerequisite to issuance, §93D-9, (c).
Board.
Appointment of members, §93D-3, (a).
Composition, §93D-3, (a).
Creation, §93D-3, (a).
Defined, §93D-1.
Disciplinary action, §93D-13.
Duties, §93D-3, (c).
Executive secretary, §93D-3, (b).
Expenses of members, §93D-3, (d).
Injunctions.
Actions for, §93D-4.
Meetings, §93D-3, (b).
Number of members, §93D-3, (a).
Officers, §93D-3, (b).
Qualifications of members, §93D-3, (a).
Quorum, §93D-3, (b).
Records, §93D-3, (b).
Reports.
Annual report to governor, §93D-3, (d).

HEARING AID DEALERS AND FITTERS —Cont'd
Board —Cont'd
Secretary-treasurer, §93D-3, (d).
Bond, surety, §93D-3, (d).
Terms of members, §93D-3, (a).
Vacancies.
Filling, §93D-3, (a).
Child support enforcement.
Forfeiture of licensing privilege, §50-13.12.
Definitions, §93D-1.
Disciplinary proceedings, §93D-13.
Diseases.
Freedom from contagious or infectious diseases.
Prerequisite to issuance of license, §93D-5, (a).
Education.
Occupational instruction courses, §93D-11.
Qualifications for licenses, §93D-5, (a).
Examinations.
Licenses, §93D-8, (a).
Successfully passing examination required, §93D-5, (b).
Exemptions from provisions, §93D-14.
Fees.
Licenses.
Application fee, §93D-5, (a).
Issuance of license certificate, §93D-8, (b).
Reciprocity, §93D-6.
Reissuance of suspended license, §93D-13, (b).
Renewal fees, §93D-11.
Felony convictions.
Forfeiture of license, §15A-1331A.
Fitting and selling hearing aids.
Defined, §93D-1.
License required, §§93D-2, 93D-5, (a).
Statements of sale, §93D-7.
Injunctions, §93D-4.
Licenses.
Applications, §93D-5, (a).
Apprenticeship licenses.
Holding for one year as prerequisite to issuance of license, §93D-5, (c).
Display, §93D-12.
Duties of board as to, §93D-3, (c).
Examinations, §93D-8, (a).
Scope, §93D-8, (a).
Successfully passing examination required, §93D-5, (b).
Fees.
Application fee, §93D-5, (a).
Issuance of license certificate, §93D-8, (b).
Reciprocity, §93D-6.
Reissuance of suspended license, §93D-13, (b).
Renewal fees, §93D-11.
Issuance, §93D-8, (b).
Qualifications, §93D-5, (a).
Reciprocity, §93D-6.
Renewal, §93D-11.
Required, §§93D-2, 93D-5, (a).
Revocation or suspension.
Felony convictions, §15A-1331A.
Grounds, §93D-13, (a).
Procedure, §93D-13, (b).
Reissuance of suspended license, §93D-13, (b).
Misdemeanors.
Violations of provisions, §93D-15.
Notice.
Mailing of notices to licensees, §93D-10.
Physicians and surgeons.
Exemption of physicians and surgeons from provisions, §93D-14.

HEARING AID DEALERS AND FITTERS —Cont'd
Reciprocity.
Licenses, §93D-6.
Registration.
Apprentices, §§93D-9, 93D-10.
Licensees, §93D-10.
Reports.
Board.
Annual report to governor, §93D-3, (d).
Rules and regulations.
Board, §93D-3, (c).
Sales and use tax.
Exemption, §105-164.13.
Severability of provisions, §93D-16.
Speech and language pathologists and audiologists.
Exemption of practice of fitting and selling hearing aids, §90-294, (e).
Statements of sale, §93D-7.
Subpoenas.
Powers of board, §93D-3, (c).
Venue.
Injunctions.
Actions by board to enjoin illegal practices, §93D-4.
Violations of provisions.
Penalties, §93D-15.

HEARING IMPAIRED.
Assault and battery.
Assault upon handicapped persons, §14-32.1.
DNA analysis.
Blood sample required upon conviction, §15A-266.4.
Commission to study the care of the aged and handicapped, §§143-279 to 143-283.
Council for the deaf and hard of hearing.
Appointment of members, §143B-216.32, (a).
Chairman, §143B-216.32, (c).
Clerical assistance, §143B-216.32, (f).
Composition, §143B-216.32, (a).
Creation, §143B-216.31.
Definitions, §143B-216.30.
Duties, §143B-216.31.
Expenses of members.
Reimbursement, §143B-216.32, (e).
Meetings, §143B-216.32, (d).
Quorum, §143B-216.32, (d).
Terms of members, §143B-216.32, (b).
Definitions.
Council for the deaf and hard of hearing, §143B-216.30.
Division of services for the deaf and hard of hearing, §143B-216.30.
Interpreters for hearing impaired, §§8B-1, 90D-3.
Division of services for the deaf and hard of hearing.
Communication services program.
Established, §143B-216.34, (a).
Creation, §143B-216.33, (a).
Definitions, §143B-216.30.
Division under authority of department of health and human services, §143B-216.33, (b).
Duties, §143B-216.33, (a), (b).
Funding, §143B-216.33, (c).
Powers, §143B-216.33, (a).
Rules, §§143B-216.33, (d), 143B-216.34, (b).
Sheriffs.
Central communications office of county sheriff's department, §143B-216.34, (c).

HEARING IMPAIRED —Cont'd
Division of services for the deaf and hard of hearing —Cont'd
TDD equipment, §143B-216.34, (c), (d).
Educational agency employed interpreters and transliterators.
Annual job related training, number of hours, §115C-110, (n).
Evidence.
Statement taken under custody without interpreter present.
Admissibility, §8B-2.
False representation as to physical defect to obtain money, §14-113.
Fees.
Interpreters for hearing impaired.
Licenses, §90D-10, (b).
Service fee, §8B-10.
Training and licensing preparation program fee, §8B-10.
Governor's council on employment of the handicapped, §§143-283.1 to 143-283.8.
Insurance on motor vehicles.
Discriminatory practices prohibited, §58-3-25, (b).
Interpreters.
Administrative proceedings.
Appointment if deaf person party or witness before, §8B-2, (c).
Appointment, §§8B-1, 8B-2, (a) to (g).
Compensation, §8B-8.
Waiver of appointed interpreter, §8B-3, (a), (b).
Arrest of deaf person.
Arresting officer to procure, §8B-2, (d).
Civil, criminal or juvenile proceedings.
Appointment if deaf person party or witness, §8B-2, (a).
Compensation, fees and expenses.
Administrative agencies.
Payment for services before, §8B-8, (e).
City or county administrative proceedings.
Payment for services, §8B-8, (f).
Civil cases and special proceedings.
Payment for services, §8B-8, (c).
Criminal and juvenile proceedings.
Payment for services, §8B-8, (b).
Fixed by appointing authority, §8B-8, (a).
Legislative bodies.
Payment for services before, §8B-8, (d).
Reasonable fee for services, entitlement, included in, §8B-8, (a).
Travel and subsistence expenses, §8B-8, (a).
Competence.
Determination, §8B-1.
Confidentiality.
Privileged communications, §8B-5.
Coordination of interpreter services, §8B-6.
Definitions, §8B-1.
Determination of competence, §8B-1.
Educational agency employed interpreters and transliterators.
Annual job related training, number of hours, §115C-110, (n).
Fees.
Licenses, §90D-10, (b).
Training and licensing preparation program fee, §8B-10.
Funds.
Responsibility for payment to implement chapter, §8B-9.
Legislative committees.
Appointment if deaf person witness before, §8B-2, (b).

HEARING IMPAIRED —Cont'd
Interpreters —Cont'd
Licenses, §§90D-1 to 90D-13.
See INTERPRETERS.
Lists of interpreters, §8B-6.
Notice.
Need for interpreter, §8B-4.
Oath, §8B-7.
Parent of juvenile brought before court deaf.
Appointment for parent, §8B-2, (e).
Preliminary determination for appointment, §8B-2, (f).
Privileged communications, §8B-5.
Proof of deafness, §8B-4.
Removal, §8B-2, (g).
Responsibility for payment of funds to implement chapter, §8B-9.
Right to interpreter, §8B-1.
Training and licensing preparation program fee, §8B-10.
Waiver of appointed interpreter, §8B-3, (a), (b).
Motor vehicle insurance.
Discriminatory practices prohibited, §58-3-25, (b).
Parent and child.
Failure to enroll deaf child in school, §115C-383, (b).
Schools for the deaf, §§143B-216.40 to 143B-216.44.
ABC's program.
Annual performance goals, §143B-146.3.
Defined, §143B-146.1, (b).
Participation, §143B-146.2.
Age limits, §115C-383, (a).
Age of students, §115C-383, (a).
Agreements with local governing authorities, §143B-216.43.
Athletic fees, §143B-216.44.
Board of directors.
Duties, §143B-216.40.
Calendars, §143B-146.11.
Classroom equipment, §143B-216.41, (c).
Compulsory attendance of children, §115C-383, (a).
Courses of study, §143B-216.41, (c).
Criminal history checks of personnel, §143B-146.16.
Criteria for admission, §143B-216.41, (a).
Dispute resolution, §143B-146.15.
Education programs in residential schools generally, §§143B-146.1 to 143B-146.21.
See EDUCATION.
Establishment of schools, §143B-216.40.
Failure of parent, guardian or custodian to enroll child in school, §115C-383, (b).
Failure of parent, guardian or custodian to send child to school, §115C-383, (c).
Free textbooks, §143B-216.42.
Institutions of higher education.
Collaborative relationship with, maintaining, §143B-216.41, (d).
Low-performing residential schools, §§143B-146.5 to 143B-146.9.
Dismissal of administrators and teachers in schools identified as low-performing, §115C-325, (p1).
Minimum attendance, §115C-383, (a).
Mission, §143B-146.1.
Nonresidents.
Admission to schools, §143B-216.41, (b).
Operation and maintenance of schools.
Department of health and human services responsible for, §143B-216.40.

HEARING IMPAIRED —Cont'd
Schools for the deaf —Cont'd
Parents.
Failure to enroll child in school, §115C-383, (b).
Purchase and rental system operated by state, §143B-216.42.
Report of deaf children in school.
Local superintendent, §115C-383, (d).
Sale of merchandise by governmental units.
Exception to prohibition, §66-58, (b).
School improvement plans, §143B-146.12.
School technology plans, §143B-146.13.
Service animals, §§168-4.2 to 168-4.6.
Donation for training, §168-4.6.
Prohibited acts, §168-4.5.
Registration and training, §168-4.3.
Responsibility for, §168-4.4.
Right to be accompanied by, §168-4.2.
Penalty for depriving of right, §168-4.5.
Tags, §168-4.2.
Special education.
See SPECIAL EDUCATION.
Telecommunications relay service, §62-157.
Vocational rehabilitation, §168-14.
Witnesses.
Interpreters for deaf parties or witnesses, §8B-2, (a) to (g).
Workers' compensation.
Loss of hearing.
Rates of compensation, §97-31.
Occupational diseases.
Loss of hearing caused by harmful noise in employment, §97-53.

HEARING LOSS.
Children's health insurance program.
Hearing tests, §108A-70.21, (b).
Newborn hearing screening.
Health benefit plan coverage, §58-3-260.
Rules to include in newborn screening program, §130A-125, (b), (b1).
Occupational diseases.
Hearing loss caused by harmful noise in employment, §97-53.
Workers' compensation, §97-31.

HEARINGS.
Abortion.
Parental or judicial consent to abortion.
Waiver of parental consent requirement proceedings, §90-21.8, (b).
Absentees in military service.
Action to appoint receiver, §28B-3.
Transfer of property valued at more than five thousand dollars, §28B-10, (c).
Abused, neglected or dependent juvenile actions.
Adjudicatory hearing, §§7B-801 to 7B-807.
Cease obstruction or interference with investigation, §7B-303, (c).
Dispositional hearing, §7B-901.
Nonsecure custody, §7B-506.
Periodic review hearings as to placement.
Custody removed from parent, §7B-906.
Surrender of child for adoption, agency plan for placement, §7B-909.
Termination of parental rights, §7B-908.
Voluntary foster care placement, §7B-910.
Permanency planning hearing, custody removed from parent, §7B-906, (e).
Administrative procedure, §§150B-22 to 150B-42.
See ADMINISTRATIVE PROCEDURE.

HEARINGS —Cont'd
Adoption.
Confidentiality of hearings, §48-2-203.
Dispositional hearing on uncontested petition, §48-2-601.
Petition for adoption.
Continuance of hearing on court's motion, §48-2-603, (c).
Procedure generally, §48-2-603.
Sanctions for violations of chapter, §48-2-603, (b).
Standard of proof, §48-2-603, (a).
Petition to adopt adult.
Appearance of parties, §48-2-605, (a).
Burden of proof, §48-2-605, (b).
Procedure generally, §48-2-605, (b).
Aged persons.
Study commission on aging, §120-185.
Agriculture.
Assessment of fees and taxes.
Procedure for assessment, §106-9.3, (c).
Aid to the blind.
Denial of application for aid, §111-16.
Air pollution control.
Local air pollution control programs.
Situations under which commission may hold, §143-215.112, (e).
Alarm systems licensing.
Board, §74D-5, (b).
Alcoholic beverage permits.
Local government official designated to make recommendations.
Testimony at hearing, §18B-904, (f).
Location, §18B-906, (b).
Annexation.
Population less than five thousand, §160A-37.
Attorney disability proceedings, Bar Rules & Regs., B, §.0118.
Attorney discipline.
Formal hearings, Bar Rules & Regs., B, §.0114.
Attorneys CLE hearings, Bar Rules & Regs., D, §§.1001 to .1011.
Attorney specialization.
Denial of certification or continued certification, Bar Rules & Regs., D, §§.1801 to .1806.
Auctions and auctioneers.
Commission, §85B-8, (e).
Bail bondsmen and runners.
Denial, suspension, revocation or refusal to renew license, §58-71-85, (b).
Boundaries.
Special proceeding to establish boundaries, §38-3, (a).
Building code enforcement agencies.
Questions under building code, §143-140.
Bus companies discontinuing or reducing service.
Permission granted with or without public hearing, §62-262.2, (b).
Check-cashing businesses.
Licensing.
Denial of license, §53-279, (b).
Child custody.
Action or proceeding for custody or visitation.
Heard without jury by judge, §50-13.5, (h).
Child support.
Action for support of minor child.
Heard by judge without jury, §50-13.5, (h).
Amount of support payments.
Request of party, §50-13.4, (c).

HEARINGS —Cont'd
Child support —Cont'd
Expedited process.
Appeal from orders of child support hearing officer.
De novo hearing, §50-38, (a).
Procedure to insure payment.
Cases heard for enforcement.
Informing district court judge, §50-13.9, (f).
Delinquency in non-IV-D cases.
Enforcement order, §50-13.9, (d).
City councils.
Conduct of public hearings, §160A-81.
Claim and delivery, §1-474.1, (a).
Clean water revolving loans and grants, §159G-8, (c).
Coastal area management.
Areas of environmental concern, §113A-115.
Land-use plans, §113A-110.
Coastal wetland activities.
Orders to control activities, §113-230, (b).
Collection agencies.
Denial of permit, §58-70-30.
Commodities.
Commencement of administrative proceedings, §78D-30.
Investigations, §78D-21.
Community service for impaired driving violations, §20-179.4, (e).
Consolidated city-county act.
Urban service districts.
Abolition of districts, §160B-10.
Consolidation of district, §160B-8, (c).
Establishment of district, §160B-6, (c).
Extension of district, §160B-7, (d).
Consumer finance act.
License applications, §53-168, (b).
Contempt.
Civil contempt.
Proceedings for civil contempt, §5A-23.
Criminal contempt.
Plenary proceedings for contempt.
Show cause hearings, §5A-15.
Cooperative agreements among physicians or between physician, hospital or other person.
Public hearing on issuance of certificate of public advantage, §90-21.27, (a).
Coroners.
Preliminary hearings.
Duties of coroners, §152-7.
Hearings by coroner in lieu of other preliminary hearing, §152-10.
County boards of adjustment, §153A-345, (b).
County boards of commissioners.
Conduct, §153A-52.
County inspection departments, §153A-361.
County planning and zoning.
Public hearing.
Adoption or amendment of ordinance, §153A-323, (a).
County research and production service districts.
Abolition, §153A-316.
Establishment, §153A-312, (b).
Extension, §153A-314, (c).
Removal of territory.
Public hearing, §153A-314.1, (c).
County service districts.
Abolition, §153A-306.
Annexation of territory, §153A-303, (e).

HEARINGS —Cont'd
County service districts —Cont'd
Before adopting resolution, §153A-302, (c).
Consolidation or extensions, §§153A-303, (c), (e), 153A-304, (c).
Establishments, §153A-302, (c).
County special assessments.
Preliminary assessment roll, §153A-195.
Preliminary resolutions, §153A-192.
County water and sewer districts.
Abolition of districts, §162A-87.2, (a).
Creation of district, §162A-86, (b), (c).
Extension of districts, §162A-87.1, (e).
Credit unions.
Removal of officers, §54-109.19, (b).
Suspension and conservation.
Reply to order, §54-109.92, (d).
Crematory licensees, §90-210.43, (i).
Criminal procedure.
See CRIMINAL LAW AND PROCEDURE.
Dangerous dog determination, §67-4.1, (c).
Declaratory judgments.
Hearing before judge where no issues of fact raised or jury trial waived, §1-262.
Delinquent and undisciplined juvenile actions.
Adjudicatory hearing.
Conduct generally, §7B-2405.
Due process rights protected, §7B-2405.
Quantum of proof, §7B-2409.
Time and place for holding, §7B-2403.
Admissions by juveniles, when accepted by court, §7B-2407.
Closure of hearings for good cause, §7B-2402.
Continuances, §7B-2406.
Dispositional hearing, §7B-2501.
Medical, surgical, psychiatric, psychological or other evaluation or treatment, determination by court, §7B-2502, (b).
Open hearing, §7B-2402.
Post-release supervision, progress review, violation of terms, §7B-2516, (a).
Prosecutor to represent state at hearings, §7B-2404.
Record of proceedings, §7B-2411.
Rules of evidence, §7B-2408.
Secure or nonsecure custody hearings, §7B-1906.
Transfer of jurisdiction of juvenile to superior court.
Probable cause hearing, §7B-2202.
Transfer hearing, §7B-2203.
Dental hygienists.
Disciplinary proceedings, §90-231.
Dentists.
Disciplinary proceedings, §90-41.1.
Disability of attorney, Bar Rules & Regs., B, §.0118.
Discipline of attorneys.
Formal hearings, Bar Rules & Regs., B, §.0114.
Discovery motions, §15A-902, (c).
District attorneys, removal from office, §7A-66.
District courts.
Conduct of hearings, §7A-191.
Domestic violence.
Emergency relief, §50B-2, (b).
Firearms.
Inquiry as to defendants' access to firearms, §50B-3.1, (b).
Drainage districts.
See DRAINAGE DISTRICTS.
Drainage petitions.
Agreement for construction, §156-26, (c).

HEARINGS —Cont'd
Drivers' licenses.
Revocation or suspension, §20-16, (d).
Economic development and training districts.
Annexation of territory to district.
Public hearing, §153A-317.14, (c).
Establishment by county.
Public hearing, §153A-317.12, (d).
Elections.
Challenge of voters.
Challenge on day of primary or election, §163-88.
Challenge other than on day of primary or election, §163-86.
Challenge to absentee ballots, §163-89, (e).
Protest filed with county board, §163-182.10.
Electrologists.
Reports of violations of chapter.
Notice of administrative hearing, §88A-23.
Emancipation of juvenile, §7B-3503.
Employee assistance professionals.
Enforcement or disciplinary actions, §90-507.
Employment security.
Commission, §96-4, (m) to (r).
Excise stamp tax on conveyances.
Refunds for overpayment of tax.
Hearing by county, §105-228.37, (b).
Executors and administrators.
Contested appointments, §28A-6-4.
Letters testamentary and of administration.
Revocation, §28A-9-1.
Resignation.
Hearing on petition, §28A-10-4.
Expedited evictions.
Procedure for expedited hearing, §42-68.
Extradition.
Fugitives from other states.
Writ of habeas corpus, §15A-730.
Family law arbitration, §50-47.
Attorneys at law, §50-48.
Farm name registration applications, §80-36.
Fiduciaries.
Removal of fiduciary funds to nonresident fiduciary, §36A-13.
Food, drug and cosmetic act.
Procedures, §106-139, (d).
Foreign judgments.
Motion for enforcement of foreign judgment, §1C-1705, (b).
Foresters.
Charges against registrants, §89B-13.
Gasoline and oil inspection.
Cancellation of license, §119-19.
Gasoline tax.
Assessment of civil penalty, §105-449.119.
Licenses.
Cancellation of license, §105-449.76.
General assembly.
Committees.
Examination of witnesses, §§120-19.1, 120-19.2.
Fees and expenses of witness, §120-19.3.
Legislative ethics committee.
Possible violations of provisions, §120-103, (b).
Geologists.
Code of professional conduct.
Revision and amendment to code, §89E-16.
Disciplinary procedures, §89E-20, (a).
Global TransPark authority.
Bond issues, §63A-12.
Global TransPark development zone.
Public hearing on creation of zone, §158-33, (b).

HEARINGS —Cont'd
Grade crossings.
Elimination or safeguarding of crossings, §136-20, (b).
Guardians.
Appointment of guardians.
Incompetent persons, §35A-1212.
Minors, §35A-1223.
Motions in the cause, §35A-1207, (c).
Sterilization of mentally ill or retarded ward.
Mental necessity, petition for consent, §35A-1245, (d).
Habeas corpus.
Summary hearing of issues, §17-32.
Hazardous waste facilities.
Conduct of public hearing prior to issuance of permit, §130A-294, (f).
Petition to preempt local ordinance, §130A-293, (c).
Health permits and program participation.
Suspension or revocation, §130A-23, (c), (d).
Hospital districts.
Petition for formation of hospital district, §131E-42.
Hospitals.
Administrative procedure.
Contested case hearing petition time limit, §131E-2.
Licenses, §131E-78, (b).
Rate schedules, §58-65-45.
Housing authorities and projects.
Creation of authority, §157-4.
Counties, §157-33.
Regional housing authority.
Creation of authority, §157-39.4.
Decreasing area of operation, §157-39.3.
Increasing area of operation, §157-39.2.
Hunting license agents.
Suspension, revocation or nonrenewal of appointment, §113-270.1, (f).
Impaired driving.
Chemical analysis of impairing substances in blood.
Mandatory revocation of license in event of refusal, §20-16.2, (d), (e).
Sentencing hearing, §20-179, (a), (c) to (f), (o).
Impaired driving sentencing hearing.
Aggravating factors to be weighed, §20-179, (d).
Evidentiary standards, §20-179, (o).
Grossly aggravating factors, determining existence, §20-179, (c).
Mitigating factors to be weighed, §20-179, (e).
Prior convictions, proof of, §20-179, (o).
Required, §20-179, (a).
Weighing aggravating and mitigating factors, §20-179, (f).
Income tax refunds.
Anticipation loans, §53-248, (d).
Incompetence, determination of.
Incompetence determined in another state, §35A-1113.
Interim guardian, appointment, §35A-1114, (c), (d).
Place of hearing, §35A-1112, (a).
Rights of petitioner and respondents, §35A-1112, (b).
Time for holding, §35A-1108, (a).
Multidisciplinary evaluation ordered, extension of time, §35A-1108, (b).
Incompetence, restoration, §35A-1130, (b), (c).

HEARINGS —Cont'd
Infractions.
Procedure for hearing and disposition, §§15A-1111 to 15A-1118.
See INFRACTIONS.
Injunctions, §§1-494, 1-495.
Extension, modification or vacation.
Applications, §1-498.
Temporary restraining order, §1A-1, Rule 65, (b).
Insurance commissioner, §58-2-20.
Accident and health insurance.
Withdrawal of approval of forms, §58-51-95, (e).
Appeals.
Rules for hearing of, §58-2-52, (a), (c).
Filing of approvals and disapprovals.
Agency decision for certain purposes, §58-2-53.
Hearing officers, designating, §58-2-55.
Rates, §58-40-105, (a).
Applicable procedural provisions, §58-2-52, (b).
Imposition of penalties or suspension of licenses, §58-40-110, (c).
Unfair trade practices, §58-63-25.
Insurance companies.
Refusal to approve formation or initial license, §58-7-37, (d).
Risk based capital requirements.
Confidential hearing on commissioner's determination, §58-12-30.
Insurance information privacy violations, §58-39-80, (b).
Insurance rates, §58-40-105, (a).
Rate bureau.
Disapproval of rates, §58-36-20, (a).
Violations of provisions.
Imposition of penalty or suspension of license, §58-40-110, (c).
Insurance supervision, rehabilitation and liquidation.
Claims denial, §58-30-205, (b).
Confidentiality of hearings, §58-30-70.
Seizure order by court.
Hearing and review, §58-30-65, (e), (f).
Insurance unfair trade practices, §58-63-25, (b), (c).
Commissioner's powers and duties as to, §58-63-25, (d).
Immunity from prosecution, §58-63-60.
Notice, §58-63-25, (a).
Service, §58-63-25, (e).
Powers and duties of commissioner as to, §58-63-25, (d).
Undefined practices, §58-63-40, (a).
Witnesses.
Immunity from prosecution, §58-63-60.
Powers of commissioner as to, §58-63-25, (d).
International commercial arbitration and conciliation.
Closing at conclusion of evidence, §1-567, (f).
Confidentiality of matters, §1-567, (d).
Experts.
Participation in, §1-567.56, (b).
Held at appropriate stage of proceedings, §1-567, (a).
In camera, held in, §1-567, (d).
Notice for purposes of inspection of property or documents, §1-567, (b).
Record or transcript, agreement on, §1-567, (e).
Service of statements, documents or other information, §1-567, (c).
Tribunal to decide whether to hold, §1-567, (a).

HEARINGS —Cont'd
Interpreters.
Hearing impaired.
Appointment authorized, §8B-2.
Interrogatories to discover assets of judgment debtors.
Hearing before court or judge to answer oral questions concerning property, §1-352.1.
Investment advisers.
Public hearing, §78C-30.
Judicial standards commission.
Censure or removal of justice, §7A-378, (b).
Complaint concerning qualifications or conduct of judges.
Procedures governing hearing, §7A-377, (a).
Formal hearings, Jud. Stds. Comm. Rule 11.
Rights of respondent, Jud. Stds. Comm. Rule 14.
Juvenile hearings.
See JUVENILE HEARINGS.
Lake lure marine commission.
Public hearing on creation, §77-81.
Regulations applicable to lake and shoreline area.
Public hearing required, §77-87, (a).
Land policy act.
Council, §113A-153, (d).
Liens.
Possessory liens on personal property.
Enforcement by sale.
Motor vehicles, §44A-4, (b), (1), (2).
Limited driving privileges, §20-179.3, (d).
Livestock dealer licensing, §106-418.12.
Livestock market permits, §106-406.
Local government finance.
Bond issues.
Application to commission for approval, §159-52, (b).
Bond order, §159-57.
Budget hearings, §159-12, (b).
Magistrates.
Suspension of magistrate, §7A-173, (c).
Medical and dental service corporations.
Rate schedule.
Revision of existing schedule or establishment of new schedule, §58-65-45.
Mental health, developmental disability, substance abuse.
Imposition of civil penalty on licensed facility.
Contesting, §122C-24.1, (f).
Involuntary commitment.
See MENTAL HEALTH, DEVELOPMENTAL DISABILITY, SUBSTANCE ABUSE.
Suspension of new admissions to licensed facility.
Contesting, §122C-23, (g).
Metropolitan sewerage districts.
Creation of district, §162A-66.
Inclusion of additional political subdivision or unincorporated area, §162A-68, (b).
Metropolitan water districts.
Creation of district, §162A-33.
Inclusion of additional political subdivision or unincorporated area, §162A-35.
Milk and milk products.
Testing dairy products.
Revocation of license, §106-267.3.
Mine safety and health.
Accident investigations, §74-24.7, (c).
Modification of safety and health standards, §74-24.5.
Missing persons.
Action for appointment of permanent receiver, §28C-6.

HEARINGS —Cont'd
Mobile homes and trailers.
Uniform standards code.
Suspension, revocation or denial of license, §143-143.14, (b).
Mortgages and deeds of trust.
Foreclosure sales.
Validation where hearing not provided, §45-21.45.
Motion for appropriate relief, §15A-1420, (c).
Motor clubs and associations.
Denial of license.
Notice of right to hearing, §58-69-15.
Right to hearing, §58-69-25.
Motor vehicle dealer licensing.
Denial, §§20-295, 20-296.
Notice, §20-305.3.
Powers of commissioner, §20-301, (c).
Suspension or revocation, §20-296.
Motor vehicle manufacturer licensing.
Denial, §§20-295, 20-296.
Notice, §20-305.3.
Powers of commissioner, §20-301, (c).
Suspension or revocation, §20-296.
Municipal assessments.
Preliminary assessment rule, §§160A-227, 160A-228.
Preliminary resolution, §§160A-224, 160A-225.
Municipal charter amendment, §160A-102.
Municipal personnel board, §160A-165.
Municipal service district.
Abolition of district, §160A-541.
Consolidation of districts, §160A-539, (c).
Establishment, §160A-537, (c).
Extension of district, §160A-538, (d).
Reduction of district, §160A-538.1, (a).
Municipal zoning.
Procedure for adopting or amending ordinance, §160A-364, (a).
Mutual burial associations.
Dispute over liability for benefits, §90-210.102.
Nonprofit corporations.
Receiver appointment in judicial dissolution, §55A-14-32, (a).
Occupational licensing boards.
New boards.
Assessment report, §120-149.5, (a).
Oil and gas conservation.
See OIL AND GAS CONSERVATION.
Optometrists.
Disciplinary proceedings, §90-121.3.
Ordinances.
Public hearing by council.
Amendment of charter by ordinance, §160A-102.
Sunday-closing ordinances.
Limitations on enactment, §160A-191.
Parental authority over juvenile.
Order directing juvenile to appear before court, §7B-3404.
Parking authorities.
Creation of authority, §160A-552.
Parole.
See PAROLE.
Personnel system.
Grievances and disciplinary action, §126-37, (a).
Records.
Privacy of state employee personnel records.
Access to material in file for agency hearing, §126-29.
Pesticide board.
Public hearings, §143-461.

HEARINGS —Cont'd
Physicians and surgeons.
Evidence, §90-14.6, (a) to (c).
Licenses.
Denial of license, §90-14.1.
Depositions, §90-14.5.
Failure to appear for hearing.
Procedure upon, §90-14.7.
Revocation or suspension of license, §90-14.2.
Place of hearing, §90-14.4.
Trial examiner, §90-14.5.
Record of proceeding required to be made, §90-14.6, (a).
Police.
Removal of unfit officers.
Suspension pending hearing, §128-19.
Post-release supervision, §15A-1368.6.
Preneed funeral contracts and funds, §90-210.69, (e).
Prisons and prisoners.
Compensation to persons erroneously convicted of felonies.
Nature of hearing, §148-83.
Private personnel services.
Complaints, §95-47.9, (c).
Private protective services recovery fund, §74C-31, (b), (e).
Probation, §15A-1345.
Property taxes.
Public utilities.
Review of appraisal and apportionment, §105-342, (b) to (d).
Public schools.
Reassignment of students, §115C-369.
School budget.
Public hearing by board of education, §115C-428, (b).
Teachers.
Career teachers.
Dismissal or demotion, §115C-325.
Public utilities.
Bus companies.
Discontinuance or reduction in service, §62-262.2, (b).
Rates.
Change of rates, §62-134, (b), (c).
Price flexibility or detariffing of services, §62-134, (i).
Scope of rate hearings, §62-137.
Rate bureau.
Disapproval of rates, §58-36-20, (a).
Real estate brokers and salespersons.
Real estate recovery fund.
Applications for payment from, §93A-18.
Retailers and wholesale merchants.
Certificates of registration.
Sales and use tax.
Revocations of certificates, §105-164.29, (d).
Rural fire protection districts.
Changes in area of district, §69-25.11.
Sales and use tax.
Certificates of registration.
Wholesale merchants and retailers.
Revocations of certificates, §105-164.29, (d).
Sanitary districts.
Dissolution of certain sanitary districts.
No outstanding indebtedness districts, §130A-72.
Extension of district.
Procedure for extension, §130A-69.

HEARINGS —Cont'd
Savings and loan associations.
Applicable law, §54B-6.
Incorporation, §54B-13, (b), (d).
Notice, §54B-13, (c).
Supervisory control by commissioner.
Time for, procedure, §54B-68, (a).
Savings banks.
Conduct of hearings.
Applicable law, §54C-6.
Removal of directors, officers and employees, §54C-82, (a).
Supervisory control, §54C-81, (a).
Securities regulation.
Cease and desist orders, §78A-47, (b).
Public hearings, §78A-49, (g).
Seeds.
Notice of violations of article, §106-277.23.
Revocation or refusal of license for cause, §106-277.19.
Sentence and punishment.
Proceedings at sentencing hearing, §15A-1334, (b).
Sentence hearing in other district, §15A-1334, (c).
Time of sentencing hearing, §15A-1334, (a).
Setoff debt collection.
Appeals from, §105A-9.
Contest by debtor of setoff by local agency, §105A-5, (c), (d).
Contested claim of state agency, §105A-8, (b), (c).
Sheriffs.
Removal of unfit officers.
Suspension pending hearing, §128-19.
Social security.
Coverage of governmental employees under Title II of social security act.
Plans for coverage of employees of political subdivisions, §135-23, (b).
Soil and water conservation districts.
Adoption of land-use regulations, §139-9.
Creation of districts, §139-5, (c).
Discontinuance of districts, §139-13.
Payment of expenses, §139-5, (b).
Solid waste management.
Application for permit, public hearing, §130A-294, (b1).
Special education.
Administrative review.
Closed hearing, §115C-116, (g).
Venue of hearing, §115C-116, (f).
State department and agency personnel file access.
Access to material in file for agency hearing, §126-29.
Streets and highways.
County public roads incorporated into state highway system.
Filing of complaints, §136-64.
Sunday-closing ordinances.
Limitations on enactment, §160A-191.
Tax review board.
Administrative review, §105-241.2, (b) to (b2).
Temporary restraining order, §1A-1, Rule 65, (b).
Termination of parental rights proceedings.
Adjudicatory hearing, §7B-1109.
Permanent placement review, §7B-908.
Special hearing to determine issues raised by petition and answer, §7B-1106, (b).
Torrens system registration.
Certificate.
Hearing by clerk of superior court, §43-17.4.

HEARINGS —Cont'd
Torrens system registration —Cont'd
Referral of petition in answer to examiner, §43-11, (a).
Removal of land from system, §43-56.
Tramways.
Passenger tramways.
Commissioner of labor, §95-120.
Transfer of juvenile to superior court for prosecution as adult.
Probable cause hearing, §7B-2202.
Transfer hearing, §7B-2203.
Urban redevelopment.
Powers of redevelopment commissions generally, §160A-512.
Project financing.
Development financing plan.
Public hearing on adoption, §160A-515.1, (g).
Redevelopment plans.
Commission, §160A-513, (e).
Governing body, §160A-513, (h).
Veterans' guardianship act.
Accounts, §34-10.
Water and air resources, §§143-215.4, 143-215.5.
Civil penalties.
Assessment by local government, §143-215.6A, (k).
Proposed adoption and assignment of classifications, §143-214.1.
Revision to water quality standards, §143-214.3, (a).
Water resource use.
Capacity use areas, §143-215.15.
Well construction.
Appeals, §87-92.
Wholesale merchants and retailers.
Certificates of registration.
Sales and use tax.
Revocations of certificates, §105-164.29, (d).
Workers' compensation.
See WORKERS' COMPENSATION.
Work first program.
Mismanagement of assistance, appointment of personal representative, §108A-37, (b).

HEARSAY.
Attacking creditability of declarant, §8C-1, Rule 806.
Civil no-contact orders.
Prior sexual activity of victim inadmissible.
Hearsay exception, §50C-4.
Definitions, §8C-1, Rule 801, (a) to (c).
Exceptions.
Admissions by party-opponent, §8C-1, Rule 801, (d).
Availability of declarant immaterial, §8C-1, Rule 803.
Declarant unavailable, §8C-1, Rule 804.
Hearsay within hearsay, §8C-1, Rule 805.
Probable cause hearings, §15A-611, (b).
Rule generally, §8C-1, Rule 802.
Supporting creditability of declarant, §8C-1, Rule 806.

HEART DISEASE.
Automated external defibrillator (AED), §90-21.15.
Food, drug and cosmetic act.
Drug or device, false advertising, §106-138, (b).
Jail prisoner unconscious or semiconscious.
Duty of custodial personnel.
Reasonable effort to determine if prisoner wearing emergency alert symbol, §153A-225.1, (a) to (c).

HEART DISEASE —Cont'd
Justus-Warren heart disease and stroke prevention task force, §143B-216.60.

HEATERS.
Public assistance.
Weatherization assistance program, §108A-70.30.
Service agreements, §§58-1-25 to 58-1-42.

HEATING CONTRACTORS.
Generally, §§87-16 to 87-27.1.
See PLUMBING, HEATING AND FIRE SPRINKLER CONTRACTORS.

HEATING INSPECTORS.
County inspection departments, §§153A-350 to 153A-375.
See COUNTY INSPECTION DEPARTMENTS.

HEATING OIL.
Leaking petroleum underground storage tank cleanup, §§143-215.94A to 143-215.94Y.
See UNDERGROUND PETROLEUM STORAGE TANK LEAK CLEANUP.
Light-traffic road weight and load limitations.
Exceptions to vehicles transporting for on-premises use, §20-118, (c).

HEATING SYSTEMS.
Dwelling unit leased as rental property.
City or county requirements, §160A-443.1.

HEDGING TRANSACTION.
Insurance companies.
Authority to enter into, §58-7-205, (d).

HEIMLICH MANEUVER.
Basic education program, §115C-81, (c).

HEIRS.
Construed to be "children" in certain limitations, §41-6.
Declaratory judgments, §1-255.
Defined, §§28A-1-1, (3), 29-2.
Guardian ad litem.
Appointment for unknown heir, §28A-22-3.
Limitations on failure of issue, §41-4.
Renunciation of succession, right to renounce, §31B-1.
Sale, lease or mortgage of real property, §28A-17-12.
Service of process, §28A-13-3.
Unknown heirs.
Special proceedings prior to distribution, §28A-22-3.
Waste.
Action by heirs, §1-537.
Wills generally.
See WILLS.

HELMETS.
Child bicycle safety act, §§20-171.6 to 20-171.9.
Safety helmets required while riding motorcycles or mopeds, §20-140.4.
Skateboard parks.
Wearing required, §99E-23.

H.E. MCCULLOCH GRANTS.
Evidence.
Title under grants, §8-16.

HEMLOCK.
Taking, etc., of certain wild plants from land of another, §14-129.

HEMLOCK BLUFFS STATE NATURAL AREA.
Removal of land from state nature and historic preserve, §143-260.10C.

HEMODIALYSIS UNITS.
Certificates of need generally, §§131E-175 to 131E-190.
See HEALTH CARE FACILITIES.

HEMOGLOBIN C TRAIT.
Employment discrimination against persons possessing hemoglobin C trait, §95-28.1.
Life insurance policies not to be denied solely on grounds of, §58-58-25.

HEMP SEED.
Standard weight and measure, §81A-42.

HENDERSON COUNTY.
Ambulances.
Obtaining ambulance services without intending to pay, §14-111.2.
Ambulance service.
Attachment or garnishment and lien for, §§44-51.4 to 44-51.8.
Board of county commissioners.
Filling vacancies on board, §153A-27.1.
Condemnation or acquisition of land by local government unit outside county.
Consent of board of commissioners necessary, §153A-15.
Coroner elected as nominee of political party.
Filling vacancy in office, §152-1.
Counties generally.
See COUNTIES.
County boards of education elected on partisan basis.
Vacancies in office, §115C-37.1.
Dog collars.
Unlawful removal of electronic dog collars, §14-401.17.
Forestland sales, distribution of funds, §113-38.
Foxes, open seasons for taking.
Wildlife resources commission authorized to continue from year to year, §113-291.4, (f1).
Game laws, local acts not repealed, §113-133.1, (e).
Housing authority commissioners.
Tenant as commissioner, exemption from provision of law allowing, §157-5.
Oil, gas or mineral interest separated from surface interest, extinguished, title in surface fee holder.
Failure to list interest for tax purposes 10 for 10 years prior to January 1, 1974.
Protection of interest from surface estate, §1-42.3, (d).
Real estate mortgage loans.
Interest, commissions and repayment, §45-43.
School property.
Acquisition and improvement, §153A-158.1.
Sheriff.
Vacancy, performance of duties until vacancy filled, §162-5.1.
Small city mixed beverage elections.
Inapplicability of provisions to, §18B-600, (e1).
Special school tax, election to abolish.
Petition required, §115C-505.
Tax deeds in Henderson.
Recitals in tax deeds, §8-22.
Tax sales, notices by publication validated.
Inapplicability of provisions, §47-108.24.
Western North Carolina Development Association, Inc.
Appropriation of funds to, §153A-447, (a), (b).

HENDERSON COUNTY —Cont'd
Western North Carolina regional economic development commission, §158-8.1.

HENRY MCCULLOCH.
Evidence.
Title under grants.
Conveyances, §8-17.

HEPATICA.
Taking, etc., of certain wild plants from land of another, §14-129.

HEPATITIS.
Arrest.
Detention of defendant for testing, §15A-534.3.
Blood banks.
Selection of donors.
Risk of transmission of agents that may cause hepatitis to be minimized, §90-220.13.
Handling of dead body of person infected with hepatitis B.
Notification to persons handling, §130A-395, (a), (c).
Testing of persons for sexually transmitted infections, §15A-615, (a), (3).

HEROIN.
Controlled substances generally, §§90-86 to 90-113.8.
See CONTROLLED SUBSTANCES.
Food, drug and cosmetic act.
Drugs deemed misbranded, §106-134.
Schedule I controlled substance, §90-89.
Trafficking in, §90-95, (h), (i).

HERTFORD COUNTY.
Ambulance service.
Attachment or garnishment and lien for, §§44-51.4 to 44-51.8.
Cropper or tenant refusing to perform terms of contract.
Forfeiture of right of possession to premises, §42-27.
Game laws, local acts not repealed, §113-133.1, (e).
Grants in navigable waters, registration, §113-205, (a).
Housing authority commissioners.
Tenant as commissioner, exemption from provision of law allowing, §157-5.
Low-income housing tax credits.
Qualified building eligible for credit, §105-129.41, (c).
Maps in special proceedings, recording of photographic copies, §47-32.
Violation as misdemeanor, inapplicability of provisions, §47-32.2.
Northeastern North Carolina regional economic development commission, §158-8.2.
Officers compensated from fees.
Statement to be rendered, §128-13.
Probates and registration orders before clerks of inferior courts validated, §47-59.
Tax elections for industrial development purposes, §§158-16 to 158-24.
Tax sales, notices by publication validated.
Inapplicability of provisions, §47-108.24.
Wastewater systems.
Innovative septic tank systems.
Ordinance billing fee as property tax, §130A-343.1, (c).

HERTFORD COUNTY —Cont'd
Watermelon festival.
Adoption as official Northeastern North Carolina watermelon festival, §145-16, (a).
Wild plants, taking of certain plants from land of another.
Inapplicability of provisions, §14-129.

HETEROLOGOUS.
Artificial insemination.
Status of child born, §49A-1.

HICKORY NUTS.
Standard weight and measure, §81A-42.

HIGH BLOOD PRESSURE.
Food, drug and cosmetic act.
Drug or device, false advertising, §106-138, (b).

HIGH COST HOME LOANS, §24-1.1E.

HIGHER EDUCATION.
Bonds, §§116D-1 to 116D-49.
Capital facilities finance.
Private capital facilities finance act.
Institutions for higher education and elementary and secondary education, §§159D-35 to 159D-57.
See CAPITAL FACILITIES FINANCE AGENCY.
Community colleges.
See COMMUNITY COLLEGES.
Education cabinet, §116C-1.
Education commission, §§143-261 to 143-266.
See EDUCATION COMMISSION.
General provisions.
See UNIVERSITIES AND COLLEGES.
North Carolina school of the arts, §§116-63 to 116-69.
See NORTH CAROLINA SCHOOL OF THE ARTS.
Private capital facilities finance act.
Institutions for higher education and elementary and secondary education, §§159D-35 to 159D-57.
See CAPITAL FACILITIES FINANCE AGENCY.
University of North Carolina.
See UNIVERSITY OF NORTH CAROLINA.

HIGHER EDUCATION BONDS, §§116D-1 to 116D-49.
Committee, §116D-5.
Creation, §116D-5, (a).
Duties, §116D-5, (c).
Expiration, §116D-5, (h).
Funding, §116D-5, (f).
Organization, §116D-5, (e).
Reports, §116D-5, (d).
Staff, §116D-5, (g).
Terms, §116D-5, (b).
Community colleges facilities finance, §§116D-41 to 116D-49.
Authorization, §116D-43.
Definitions, §116D-42.
Designation of capital facilities, §116D-44.
Faith and credit, §116D-45.
Issuance, §116D-46.
Application of proceeds, §116D-46, (d).
Community college bonds fund, §116D-46, (g).
Manner of sale, §116D-46, (c).
Refunding bonds and notes, §116D-46, (f).
Repayment of notes, §116D-46, (e).
Signatures, §116D-46, (b).

HIGHER EDUCATION BONDS —Cont'd
Community colleges facilities finance —Cont'd
Issuance —Cont'd
Terms and conditions, §116D-46, (a).
Other agreements, §116D-48.
Procurement of capital facilities, §116D-49.
Short title, §116D-41.
Variable rate demand bonds and notes, §116D-47.
Amount, §116D-47, (b).
Generally, §116D-47, (a).
Definitions, §116D-1.
Financing capital facilities, §§116D-6 to 116D-13.
Authorization of bonds and notes, §116D-8.
Definitions, §116D-7.
Designation of facilities, §116D-9.
Faith and credit, §116D-10.
Issuance, §116D-11.
Application of proceeds, §116D-11, (d).
Expenses, §116D-11, (c).
Form and denomination, §116D-11, (b).
Manner of sale, §116D-11, (c).
Notes, §116D-11, (e).
Refunding bonds and notes, §116D-11, (f).
Registration, §116D-11, (b).
Repayment, §116D-11, (e).
Signatures, §116D-11, (b).
Terms and conditions, §116D-11, (a).
University improvement bonds fund, §116D-11, (g).
Other agreements, §116D-13.
Short title, §116D-6.
Variable rate bonds and notes, §116D-12, (a), (b).
General provisions, §116D-2.
Improvements to facilities, §§116D-21 to 116D-31.
Additional and alternative method of doing things authorized, §116D-31.
Board of governors, §116D-24.
Consultation with joint legislative commission on governmental operations, §116D-25.
Credit and taxing power of state, §116D-23.
Definitions, §116D-22.
Issuance, §116D-26.
Approval, §116D-26, (b).
Authority, §116D-26, (a).
Generally, §116D-26, (f).
Proceeds, §116D-26, (d).
Temporary bonds, §116D-26, (e).
Term, §116D-26, (c).
Obligated resources, §116D-28.
State pledge, §116D-28, (b).
Sufficient resources, §116D-28, (a).
Powers of board of governors, §116D-24.
Purpose, §116D-21.
Refunding bonds, §116D-30.
Trust agreement, §116D-27.
Insurance, §116D-27, (c).
Remedies, §116D-27, (d).
Securing bonds, §116D-27, (a).
Trust funds, §116D-27, (b).
Vesting powers in committee, §116D-29.
Inconsistent laws.
Inapplicability to chapter, §116D-2, (d).
Investment eligibility, §116D-2, (c).
Minority and historically underutilized businesses, §116D-4.
Compliance, §116D-4, (a).
Contracting opportunities, §116D-4, (b).
Reports, §116D-3.
Board of governors, §116D-3, (a).
Community colleges, §116D-3, (c).

HIGHER EDUCATION BONDS —Cont'd
Reports —Cont'd
Treasurer, §116D-3, (b).
Signatures, §116D-2, (a).
Financing capital facilities.
Issuance of bonds, §116D-11, (b).
Tax exemption, §116D-2, (b).

HIGHER EDUCATION, STATE BOARD OF, §116-158.

HIGHLAND SCHOOL IN MACON COUNTY.
Sale of merchandise by governmental units.
Exceptions to provisions, §66-58, (b).

HIGH OCCUPANCY VEHICLE LANES, §20-146.2.

HIGH POINT.
Condemnation of unsafe buildings, §§160A-425.1, 160A-426, (d), 160A-432, (a1).
Hospital authorities.
Applicability of provisions to city of High Point, §131E-34.
Room occupancy tax.
Uniform provisions for municipalities authorized to levy, §160A-215.
Traffic control photographic systems, §160A-300.1, (d).

HIGH-RISE BUILDINGS.
Special safety to life requirements applicable, §143-138, (i).

HIGH ROCK LAKE MARINE COMMISSION, §§77-50 to 77-58.
Administrative provisions, §77-55.
Budgetary and accounting procedures, §77-53.
Commissioners.
Appointment, §77-52.
Compensation, §77-53.
Election of officers, §77-54.
Terms, §77-52.
Creation, §77-51.
Definitions, §77-50.
Law enforcement officers.
Authority, §77-58.
Meetings, §77-54.
Officers.
Election by commissioners, §77-54.
Ordinances.
Creation of commission, §77-51.
Effective date, §77-56, (b).
Evidence.
Admissibility in court, §77-56, (b).
Filing requirements, §77-56, (a).
Peace officers.
Authority, §77-58.
Powers, §77-55.
Rules and regulations, §77-57.
Shoreline areas.
Rules and regulations, §77-57.

HIGH SCHOOL APPRENTICESHIP ENROLLEES.
Number of hours of work per week, §95-25.5, (c).

HIGH SCHOOL ATHLETIC ASSOCIATION.
Tort claims against state departments and agencies, §§143-291 to 143-300.1A.
See TORT CLAIMS AGAINST STATE DEPARTMENTS AND AGENCIES.

HIGH SCHOOLS.
Adult education.
Entitlement to attend, §115C-231, (c).

HIGH SCHOOLS —Cont'd
Adult education —Cont'd
Free tuition.
Persons 18 years of age or older not having completed high school, §115C-231, (b).
Organization and administration of program, §115C-231, (a).
Removal or prohibiting enrollment.
Persons having attained age of 21 years, §115C-231, (c).
Classification.
Recommended school classification, §115C-75, (a), (b).
Closing schools and transferring students, §115C-72, (a), (b).
Consolidation, §115C-72, (a), (b).
Cooperative innovative high school programs.
Established by local boards and community college board of trustees, §§115C-238.50 to 115C-238.55.
See COOPERATIVE INNOVATIVE HIGH SCHOOL PROGRAMS.
Defined, §115C-75, (a).
Driver education.
State board and local boards of education required to provide, §115C-216, (a).
First in America innovative education act, §116C-4.
Junior high schools.
Classification.
Recommended school classification, §115C-75, (a), (b).
Defined, §115C-75, (a).
Senior high schools.
Classification.
Recommended school classification, §115C-75, (a), (b).
Defined, §115C-75, (a).
Statewide testing program.
Alternative means and standards, adoption, §115C-174.11, (b).
Annual testing program, §115C-174.11, (a), (c).
Church schools and schools of religious charter, §§115C-549, 115C-551.
Competency testing program, §115C-174.11, (b).
Confidentiality of scores.
Public records exemption, §115C-174.13.
Failure to pass.
Ninth grade students, §115C-174.11, (b).
Students with disabilities, §115C-174.11, (b).
Field tests administered at schools.
Superintendent to notify schools, §115C-174.12, (b1).
Local boards of education.
Responsibilities, §115C-174.12, (c).
Nonpublic schools.
Provisions for, §115C-174.14.
Preliminary scholastic aptitude test (PSAT).
Opportunity to take, §115C-174.18.
Private schools, §§115C-557, 115C-559.
Public records exemption, §115C-174.13.
Purposes, §115C-174.10.
Standardized tests, adoption, §115C-174.11, (b).
Superintendent of public instruction.
Responsibilities, §115C-174.12, (b).
Student councils.
Encouraged to have elected councils, §115C-81, (g2).
Vocational and technical education generally, §§115C-151 to 115C-169.
See VOCATIONAL AND TECHNICAL EDUCATION.

HIGH-SPEED RAIL TRANSPORTATION.
Virginia-North Carolina interstate high-speed rail compact, §§136-220 to 136-222.

HIGH WATER MARK.
Seaward boundary of private property adjoining ocean, §77-20, (a) to (c).

HIGHWAY PATROL, §§20-184 to 20-196.4.
Added positions.
Filling, §20-185, (i).
Aircraft.
Use of aircraft to discover certain motor vehicle violations, §20-196.2.
Appointment of members, §20-185, (a).
Arrest powers, §§20-49, 20-188.
Assault with deadly weapon.
Law enforcement officer assaulted with deadly weapon, §14-34.2.
Awards.
Certificates of award, §20-187.1, (c).
Committee.
Appointment of members, §20-187.1, (a).
Composition, §20-187.1, (a).
Duties, §20-187.1, (d).
Meetings, §20-187.1, (a).
Recommendations, §20-187.1, (d).
Term of members, §20-187.1, (a).
Qualifications, §20-187.1, (b).
Recommendations, §20-187.1, (d), (e).
Rules and regulations, §20-187.1, (f).
Badges and service sidearms of deceased members, §20-187.2, (a).
Commanding officer.
Appointment by governor, §20-185, (a).
Awards.
Committee.
Appointment of members, §20-187.1, (a).
Rules and regulations, §20-187.1, (f).
Composition, §20-185, (a).
Death benefits act, §§143-166.1 to 143-166.7.
See DEATH BENEFITS.
Defense of members and other state law enforcement officers in civil action, §20-194, (b).
Department of crime control and public safety.
Arms.
Furnishing, §20-190.
Expenses of highway patrol.
Providing for, §20-190.
Highway patrol division.
Establishment in department, §20-184.
Motor vehicles.
Furnishing, §20-190.
Transfer to department, §143A-242.
Uniforms.
Adoption and furnishing, §20-190.
Duties, §20-188.
Election abstracts.
Delivery to state board of elections, §163-182.6, (a).
Excess coverage over commercial liability insurance up to limit of tort claims act, §20-194, (c).
Expenses.
Department of crime control and public safety to provide for, §20-190.
Expenses incurred in carrying out provisions of article, §20-194, (c).
Firearms.
Assault with firearm upon law enforcement officer, §14-34.2.

HIGHWAY PATROL —Cont'd
Firearms —Cont'd
Change of type of firearm by active member, §20-187.2, (b).
Deceased or retiring members entitled to service sidearms, §20-187.2, (a).
Furnished by department, §20-190.
Surplus weapons.
Sale, trade or disposal, §143-63.1, (d).
Governor.
Appointment of commanding officer, §20-185, (a).
Patrolmen assigned to governor's office, §20-189.
Highways.
Powers and duties as to patrolling of highways, §20-188.
Judgments rendered as result of civil action against member.
Payment as expense of administration up to limit provided in tort claims act, §20-194, (b).
Local officers.
Cooperation, §20-195.
Motor carrier enforcement officers.
Supplemental authority, §20-49.2.
Motor vehicle accidents.
Notice of reportable accident to highway patrol.
Accident occurring outside city or town, §20-166.1, (a).
Motor vehicle license plates.
Retired highway patrol.
Special plates, §20-79.4, (b).
Special license plates, §20-79.4, (b).
Motor vehicles.
Assignment of new highway patrol cars, §20-190.3.
Color, §20-190.
Furnishing to members, §20-190.
Horns and warning devices, §20-125, (b).
New highway patrol cars.
Assignment, §20-190.3.
Percentage of marked vehicles, §20-190.
Signs showing highways patrolled by, §20-190.2.
Red lights, §20-130.1, (b).
Sirens, §20-190.1.
Oath of office of members, §20-186.
Offenses against.
Aggravating factor in sentencing, §15A-1340.16.
Office space.
Use, §20-191.
Oversized and hazardous shipment escort fee, §20-196.4, (a) to (c).
Escort fee account, §20-196.4, (d), (e).
Police authority of members, §20-49.
Powers, §20-188.
Radio system, §20-196.
Retirement.
Badges and service sidearms of retiring members, §20-187.2, (a).
General provisions.
See LAW-ENFORCEMENT OFFICERS' RETIREMENT SYSTEM.
Motor vehicle license plates.
Retired highway patrol.
Special plates, §20-79.4, (b).
Special license plates, §20-79.4, (b).
Rules and regulations.
Awards, §20-187.1, (f).
Secretary of crime control and public safety, §20-187.
Salaries, §20-185, (a).
Salary continuation plan, §§143-166.13 to 143-166.20.
See PEACE OFFICERS.

HIGHWAY PATROL —Cont'd
Sale of merchandise by governmental units.
Inapplicability of prohibition, §66-58, (b).
Secretary of crime control and public safety.
Cooperation between patrol and local officers.
Encouraging, §20-195.
Orders, §20-187.
Rules and regulations, §20-187.
Supervision, direction and control of highway patrol, §20-184.
Shifting of patrolmen from one district to another, §20-192.
Sick leave.
Replacement of officer on final sick leave, §126-8.2.
State bureau of investigation.
Cooperation of local enforcement officers, §114-17.
Supervisory personnel.
Percentage of total, §20-185, (a).
Telephone line use in emergencies, §20-196.
Who may hold supervisory positions over sworn members of patrol, §20-196.3.
Traffic citations.
Quotas prohibited, §20-187.3, (a).
Transfer of personnel, §20-192.
Transfer to department of crime control and public safety, §143A-242.
Uniforms, §20-190.
Unmarked highway patrol vehicles.
Percentage of marked vehicles, §20-190.
Sign showing highways patrolled by, §20-190.2.
Use of facilities, §20-191.
Weapons.
Active members.
Change of type, §20-187.2, (b).
Deceased or retiring members.
Service sidearms, §20-187.2, (a).
Furnishing to members, §20-190.
Surplus weapons.
Sale, trade or disposal, §143-63.1, (d).
Workers' compensation.
Total incapacity, §97-29.

HIGHWAYS.
Blind persons.
Operation of highway vending facilities, §§111-48 to 111-52.
See BLIND PERSONS.
Bridges.
See BRIDGES.
Condemnation.
Generally, §§136-103 to 136-121.1.
See STREETS AND HIGHWAYS.
Relocation assistance, §§133-5 to 133-18.
See RELOCATION ASSISTANCE.
General assembly.
Joint legislative transportation oversight committee, §§120-70.50 to 120-70.52.
See GENERAL ASSEMBLY.
Littering, §14-399.
Relocation assistance, §§133-5 to 133-18.
See RELOCATION ASSISTANCE.
Streets and highways.
See STREETS AND HIGHWAYS.
Traffic laws.
See TRAFFIC LAWS.

HIGHWAY TRUST FUND, §§136-175 to 136-184.
See STREETS AND HIGHWAYS.

HIGHWAY USE TAX, §§105-187.1 to 105-187.11.
Additional to all other taxes and fees, §105-187.2.

HIGHWAY USE TAX —Cont'd
Amount.
Maximum tax, §105-187.3, (a).
Appeals, §105-187.10, (c).
Credits.
Tax paid in another state, §105-187.7, (a).
Vehicle previously registered in another state, §105-187.7, (b).
Definitions, §105-187.1.
Exemptions.
Full exemption, §105-187.6, (a).
Out-of-state vehicles, §105-187.6, (c).
Partial exemption, §105-187.6, (b).
General fund.
Credit of taxes collected to, §105-187.9, (a).
Highway trust fund.
Credit of taxes collected to, §105-187.9, (a).
Transfer of taxes deposited, §105-187.9, (b).
Imposition, §105-187.2.
Levy, §105-187.2.
Maximum tax, §105-187.3, (a).
Motor vehicles.
Renting or leasing.
Alternate tax, §105-187.5.
Transition from sales tax to highway use tax, §105-187.11.
Retail value, §105-187.3, (b).
Return of purchased vehicle.
Refund of tax, §105-187.8.
Payment.
Methods, §105-187.4, (a).
Sale by retailer, §105-187.4, (b).
Penalties, §105-187.10, (a).
Refunds.
Return of purchased motor vehicle, §105-187.8.
Renting or leasing of motor vehicles.
Alternate tax.
Election, §105-187.5, (a).
Methods, §105-187.5, (c).
Rate, §105-187.5, (b).
Reporting, §105-187.5, (d).
Transition from sales tax to highway use tax, §105-187.11.
Retail value.
Motor vehicles, §105-187.3, (b).
Return of purchased motor vehicle.
Refund of tax, §105-187.8.
Sales and use tax.
Renting or leasing of motor vehicles.
Transition from sales tax to highway use tax, §105-187.11.
Schedules, §105-187.3, (c).
Tax paid in another state.
Credits, §105-187.7, (a).
Unpaid taxes, §105-187.10, (b).
Vehicle previously registered in another state.
Credit, §105-187.7, (b).

HIGHWAY WORK ZONES.
Speed limit, §20-141, (j2).

HILLSBOROUGH HISTORICAL COMMISSION, §§143B-103 to 143B-106.
Appointments, §143B-106.
Compensation of members, §143B-106.
Creation, §143B-103.
Department of cultural resources.
Transfer of commission to department, §143B-51.
Duties, §143B-103.
Exemption from provisions, §143B-104.
Members, §143B-106.
Powers and duties, §143B-103.

HILLSBOROUGH HISTORICAL COMMISSION —Cont'd
Quorum, §143B-106.
Reports.
Submission of annual report, §143B-105.
Selection of members, §143B-106.
Status, §143B-104.

HINNIES.
Equine activity liability, §§99E-1 to 99E-3.

HIRED GUN.
Sentencing.
Aggravating factor, §15A-1340.16.

HIRED PERSONAL PROPERTY.
Vehicles and draft animals, protection of bailor against bailee's act, §§14-165 to 14-169.
Borrowing with intent to default, §14-168.
Conversion by bailees, lessees, tenants or attorneys-in-fact, §14-168.1.
Prima facie evidence of intent to convert, §14-168.3.
Definitions, §14-168.2.
Failure to return hired property, §14-167.
Malicious or willful injury to hired personal property, §14-165.
Options to purchase.
Failure to return rented property on which there is purchase option, §14-168.4.
Subletting hired property, §14-166.
Violations made misdemeanor, §14-169.

HISTORICAL ASSOCIATIONS.
Counties.
Assistance to, §153A-437, (a) to (c).
Property taxes.
Exemption of real and personal property, §105-278.7.
Roanoke Island historical association, §§143-199 to 143-202.
See ROANOKE ISLAND HISTORICAL ASSOCIATION.

HISTORICAL ATTRACTION SPECIAL REGISTRATION PLATES, §§20-79.4, (b), 20-81.12, (b).
Application, §20-81.12, (c).

HISTORICAL COMMISSION.
Appointments, §143B-63.
Officers, §143B-64.
Approval before acceptance by state, §100-2.
Bridges and other structures, §100-3.
Disqualification to vote, §100-6.
Works of art, §100-2.
Disqualification to vote, §100-6.
Governor to accept works of art approved by commission, §100-4.
Archaeological resources protection.
Rules and regulations, §70-14.
Budget.
Allotment and expenditure of funds, §143-31.2.
Compensation of members, §143B-63.
Creation, §143B-62.
Defined, §121-2.
Department of cultural resources.
Transfer of commission functions to department, §143B-51.
Duties, §143B-62.
Executive mansion fine arts committee, §143B-79.
Action approval, §143B-79.

HISTORICAL COMMISSION —Cont'd
Historical museums.
State aid.
Criteria for state aid to historical museums, §121-12, (c1).
Historic properties.
Criteria for state aid to historic properties, §121-12, (c).
Criteria for state historic properties, §121-12, (b).
Historic structure rehabilitation tax credit.
Certification process.
Fees, adoption of schedule, §105-129.36A, (b).
Rules, adoption, §105-129.36A, (a).
Legislative committees.
Furnishing recommendations to committees, §121-12, (d).
Meetings.
Regular and special meetings, §143B-65.
Members, §143B-63.
National register.
Protection of properties on register, §121-12, (a).
North Carolina register of historic places.
Criteria for inclusion, establishment, §121-4.1, (b).
Time for owners to concur or object to property inclusion.
Rules and regulations to include, §121-4.1, (c).
Officers, §143B-64.
Powers and duties, §143B-62.
Protection of properties on national register, §121-12, (a).
Public buildings.
Duties as to buildings erected or remodeled by state, §100-5.
Quorum, §143B-63.
Recommendations to legislative committees, §121-12, (d).
Regulation of existing memorials, §100-2.
Reports.
Expenditure of funds, §143-31.2.
Selection of members, §143B-63.
Special meetings, §143B-65.
State aid.
Historical museums.
Criteria for state aid to historical museums, §121-12, (c1).
Historic properties.
Criteria for state aid to historic properties, §121-12, (c).
Works of art.
Approval before acceptance by state, §100-2.
Disqualification to vote, §100-6.
Governor to accept works of art approved by commission, §100-4.

HISTORICAL DRAMAS.
Outdoor historical dramas.
Allotments to outdoor historical dramas, §143-204.8.
Amusement tax exemption, §105-40.
Wage and hour act exemptions, §95-25.14, (a).
Youth employment, §95-25.5, (h).

HISTORICAL MARKERS.
Cooperation with department of cultural resources, §136-42.2.
Correction of historical markers.
Procedure for correction, §136-43.1.
Establishment of program, §136-42.3.
Federal highway fund expenditures, §136-42.3.
Procedure for correction and relocation of markers, §136-43.1.

HISTORICAL MARKERS —Cont'd
Purchase by department of transportation, §136-42.3.
Relocation of historical markers.
Procedure for relocation, §136-43.1.

HISTORICAL PRESERVES.
Dedication of state conservation and historical preserves, §§143-260.6 to 143-260.10F.
Registry of natural heritage areas, §§113A-164.1 to 113A-164.11.

HISTORICAL PUBLICATIONS.
Alkaline (acid-free) paper.
Printing state publications of historical value on, §§125-11.13, (a) to (c), 143-170.5.
Colonial North Carolina records, §121-6, (c).
Editing and publishing of official messages and other papers of governor, §121-6, (b).
Generally, §121-6, (a).

HISTORIC AND NATURE PRESERVE DEDICATIONS, §§143-260.6 to 143-260.10F.
See NATURE AND HISTORIC PRESERVES.

HISTORIC DISTRICTS AND LANDMARKS, §§160A-400.1 to 160A-400.14.
Advertising.
Outdoor advertising adjacent to districts.
Limitations, §136-129.2, (a) to (c).
Appropriations, §160A-400.12.
Buildings.
Demolition of buildings and landmarks.
Delay, §160A-400.14.
Certificate of appropriateness.
Required for changes in historic properties, §160A-400.9.
Changes in historic properties.
Certain changes not prohibited, §160A-400.13.
Certificate of appropriateness required, §160A-400.9.
Conflict of laws, §160A-400.10.
Counties.
Exercise of same powers as cities, §160A-400.2.
Demolition of buildings and landmarks within district.
Delay, §160A-400.14.
Districts.
Character of historic district, §160A-400.3.
Designation, §160A-400.4.
Establishment.
Criteria, §160A-400.3.
Zoning ordinance, §160A-400.4.
Eminent domain.
Powers of local public condemnors, §40A-3, (b).
Findings of legislature, §160A-400.1.
Historic preservation commission.
Appropriations, §160A-400.12.
Duties, §160A-400.8.
Establishment, §160A-400.7.
Joint commission, §160A-400.7.
Number of members, §160A-400.7.
Powers and duties, §160A-400.8.
Qualifications of members, §160A-400.7.
Terms of members, §160A-400.7.
Injunctions.
Violations of part, §160A-400.11.
Landmark designation.
Authority, §160A-400.5.
Criteria, §160A-400.5.
Inventory of significant properties, §160A-400.6.
Ordinance, §160A-400.5.
Procedures, §160A-400.6.
Legislative findings, §160A-400.1.

HISTORIC DISTRICTS AND LANDMARKS —Cont'd
North Carolina register of historic places.
Criteria for inclusion in register.
North Carolina historical commission to establish, §121-4.1, (b).
Department of cultural resources.
Power to establish, expand and maintain, §121-4.1, (a).
Objection by owner of property for inclusion, §121-4.1, (c).
Owners given time to concur or object to inclusion, §121-4.1, (c).
Outdoor advertising adjacent to districts.
Limitations, §136-129.2, (a) to (c).
Swine houses, lagoons and land areas.
Siting near historic places, §106-803, (a), (b).
Violations of part.
Remedies, §160A-400.11.

HISTORIC PRESERVATION.
Abandoned cemeteries, §121-8, (g).
Advisory council.
Department of cultural resources.
Transfer of council to department, §143B-51.
Continuing programs, §121-8, (f).
Cooperation with federal government, §121-8, (d).
Cooperation with local governments, §121-8, (e).
Defined, §121-2.
Designation of historic preservation agency, §121-8, (a).
Statewide historic preservation plan, §121-8, (c).
Surveys of historic properties, §121-8, (b).
Tax credit for rehabilitation expenditures for historic structures, §§105-129.35 to 105-129.37.

HISTORIC PRESERVATION AND CONSERVATION AGREEMENTS, §§121-34 to 121-42.
Acquisition of agreements, §§121-37, 121-38, (b).
Applicability of article, §121-36, (a).
Approval of agreements, §121-37.
Assessment of land or improvements subject to agreement, §121-40.
Citation of act, §§121-34, 121-42.
Construction and interpretation, §121-36, (b), (c).
Definitions, §121-35.
Duration of agreements, §121-38, (c).
Effectiveness of agreements, §121-38, (c).
Enforceability of agreements, §121-38, (a).
Right of entry, §121-39, (b).
Who may enforce, §121-39, (a).
Holders.
Defined, §121-35.
Enforceability of agreements, §121-39, (a).
Public recording of agreements, §121-41.
Register of deeds.
Public recording of agreements, §121-41, (a).
Releases or terminations of agreements, §121-41, (b).
Right of entry.
Enforceability of agreements, §121-39, (b).
Short title, §121-34.
Taxation.
Assessment of land or improvements subject to agreement, §121-40.

HISTORIC PRESERVATION AND CONSERVATION AGREEMENTS —Cont'd
Validity of agreements, §121-38.
Imposition of continuing obligations, §121-38, (d).

HISTORIC PROPERTIES.
Acquisition of historic properties, §121-9, (b).
Administration of properties acquired by state, §121-9, (a).
Capitol of the state, §121-9, (h).
Emergency acquisition where funds not immediately available, §121-9, (f).
Interests which may be acquired, §121-9, (c).
Power to acquire property by condemnation, §121-9, (g).
Procedures where assistance extended to cities, counties and other agencies or individuals, §121-11.
Reports, §121-9, (b1).
Use of properties so acquired, §121-9, (e).
Administration of properties acquired by state, §121-9, (a).
Allotment and expenditure of funds, §143-31.2.
Capitol of the state, §121-9, (h).
Condemnation.
Power to acquire property by condemnation, §121-9, (g).
Conveyance of property for preservation purposes, §121-9, (d).
Counties.
Acquisition, maintenance, etc., of property.
Procedures where assistance extended, §121-11.
Defined, §121-2.
Development of historic properties.
Procedures where assistance extended to cities, counties and other agencies or individuals, §121-11.
Emergency acquisition where funds not immediately available, §121-9, (f).
Historical commission.
Criteria for state aid, §121-12, (c).
Criteria for state historical properties, §121-12, (b).
Interests which may be acquired, §121-8, (c).
Maintenance of historical properties.
Procedures where assistance extended to cities, counties and other agencies or individuals, §121-11.
North Carolina register of historic places.
Criteria for inclusion in register.
North Carolina historical commission to establish, §121-4.1, (b).
Department of cultural resources.
Power to establish, expand and maintain, §121-4.1, (a).
Objection by owner of property for inclusion, §121-4.1, (c).
Owners given time to concur or object to inclusion, §121-4.1, (c).
Power to acquire property by condemnation, §121-9, (g).
Procedures where assistance extended to cities, counties and other agencies or individuals, §121-11.
Special peace officers.
Arrest powers, §121-10, (b).
Bond, §121-10, (c).
Designated employees commissioned special peace officers by governor, §121-10, (a).
Oaths, §121-10, (d).

HISTORIC PROPERTIES —Cont'd
State acquired properties.
Administration, §121-9, (a).
State aid.
Criteria for state aid to historic properties, §121-12, (c).
Surveys of historic properties.
Historic preservation program, §121-8, (b).
Swine houses, lagoons and land areas.
Siting near historic places, §106-803, (a), (b).
Tax credit for rehabilitation expenditures for historic structures, §§105-129.35 to 105-129.37.
Use of property so acquired, §121-9, (e).

HISTORIC PUBLICATIONS, §121-6.

HISTORIC STRUCTURE REHABILITATION TAX CREDIT, §§105-129.35 to 105-129.37.
Allocation of credit among owners, §105-129.35, (b).
Amount of credit, §105-129.35, (a).
Carryforward, §105-129.37, (b).
Certification process.
Fees, adoption of schedule, §105-129.36A, (b).
Rules needed to administer, adoption, §105-129.36A, (a).
Death of owner, exemption from forfeiture, §105-129.37, (e).
Definitions, §105-129.35, (c).
Forfeiture, §105-129.37, (c), (d).
Exemptions, §105-129.37, (e).
Liability, §105-129.37, (f).
Income tax credited, §105-129.37, (a).
Installment payments, taking credit in, §105-129.37, (b).
Nonincome producing structure.
Amount of credit, §105-129.36, (a).
Definitions, §105-129.36, (b).

HIT AND RUN DRIVING, §20-166.
Commercial driver license disqualification, §20-17.4, (a).
Commercial vehicles.
Special information in judgment for conviction, §20-24, (e).
Mandatory revocation of driver's license.
Failure to stop and render aid, §20-17, (a).
Points.
Schedule of point values, §20-16, (c).
Special information in judgment in conviction, §20-24, (e).

HITCHHIKING.
Prohibited, §20-175, (a).

HITMEN.
Sentencing.
Aggravating factor, §15A-1340.16.

HIVES.
Bees and honey generally, §§106-634 to 106-644.
See BEES AND HONEY.

H.M.O., §§58-67-1 to 58-67-185.
See HEALTH MAINTENANCE ORGANIZATIONS.

HOAXES.
False bomb or other device, §14-69.2, (a).
Minors causing bomb scares or threats.
Parental liability for disruption, §1-538.3.
Nuclear, biological or chemical weapons, §14-288.24.
Perpetrating hoax by use of bomb or device, §14-69.2.

HOAXES —Cont'd
False bomb or other device —Cont'd
Public buildings, §14-69.2, (c).
Restitution, costs and consequential damages, ordering, §14-69.2, (d).
Students communicating false threats of harm, §115C-391, (d4).

HOBOS.
Train surfing.
Riding on train unlawfully, §§14-460, 62-319.

HOG CHOLERA, §§106-310 to 106-322.3.
Burial.
Hogs and other livestock dying in transit, §106-319.
Hogs dying natural death, §106-310.
Compensation for killing diseased animals generally, §§106-323 to 106-335.
See LIVESTOCK DISEASES.
Confinement of hogs affected with cholera, §106-311.
Control of livestock diseases generally, §§106-400 to 106-405.
See LIVESTOCK DISEASES.
Cooperative agreements between state and federal government, §106-322.1.
Counties.
Authorized to purchase and supply serums, §106-316.
Destruction of swine affected with or exposed to hog cholera, §106-322.2.
Indemnity payments, §106-322.2.
When indemnity payments not to be made, §106-322.3.
Effect of sections, §106-322.
Eradication areas.
Establishment of areas, §106-322.1.
Health certificates.
Issuance for swine and livestock, §106-318.
Importation of hogs and other livestock into state.
Regulation of transportation or importation, §106-317.
Indemnity.
Destruction of swine affected with or exposed to hog cholera, §106-322.2.
When indemnity payments not to be made, §106-322.3.
Inspections required, §106-318.
Livestock diseases generally, §§106-304 to 106-307.7.
See LIVESTOCK DISEASES.
Manufacture and use of serum and virus restricted, §106-314.
Natural death.
Burial of hogs dying natural death required, §106-310.
Penalties for violation of provisions, §§106-316.4, 106-321.
Prevention of spread of hog cholera.
Purpose of article, §106-316.1.
Price of serum to be fixed, §106-313.
Purpose of article.
Prevention of spread of hog cholera, §106-316.1.
Regulation of transportation or importation of hogs and other livestock into state, §106-317.
Segregation of hogs affected with cholera, §106-311.
Serum.
Counties authorized to purchase and supply serum, §106-316.

HOG CHOLERA —Cont'd
Serum —Cont'd
Manufacture and use of serum restricted, §106-314.
Price of serum to be fixed, §106-313.
Shipping hogs from cholera-infected territory, §106-312.
State-federal hog-cholera cooperative agreements, §106-322.1.
Transportation or importation of hogs and other livestock into state.
Burial of hogs and other livestock dying in transit, §106-319.
Regulation of transportation or importation, §106-317.
United States.
State-federal hog-cholera cooperative agreements, §106-322.1.
Veterinarian.
Sale, use or distribution of hog-cholera virus or organisms.
Written permission from state veterinarian, §106-315.
Violation of provisions.
Penalties, §§106-316.4, 106-321.
Virus.
Definition of virulent hog-cholera virus, §106-316.2.
Importing hogs inoculated with virulent virus, §106-316.3.
Manufacture and use of serum restricted, §106-314.
Modified live virus vaccines, §106-316.2.
Use of virulent hog-cholera virus prohibited without permit, §106-316.2.

HOGS.
Allowance to officers for keeping and maintaining hogs taken into custody under legal process, §1-322.
Animal waste management, §§143-215.10A to 143-215.10H.
See ANIMAL WASTE MANAGEMENT.
Certificate of registration obtained by false representation, §14-103.
Compensation for killing diseased animals, §§106-323 to 106-335.
See LIVESTOCK DISEASES.
Control of livestock diseases generally, §§106-400 to 106-405.
See LIVESTOCK DISEASES.
Dealer licensing generally, §§106-418.8 to 106-418.15.
See LIVESTOCK DEALER LICENSING.
Diseases generally, §§106-304 to 106-307.7.
See LIVESTOCK DISEASES.
Dogs killing hogs.
Any person may kill, §67-14.
Feeding garbage to swine, §§106-405.1 to 106-405.9.
Application for permit, §106-405.3.
Cooking or other treatment, §106-405.6.
Definitions, §106-405.1.
Enforcement of article, §106-405.8.
Fees.
Permit for feeding garbage to swine.
Application for permit, §106-405.3, (b), (c).
Inspecting conditions, §106-405.7, (a).
Investigating conditions, §106-405.7, (a).
Penalties for violation of provisions, §106-405.9.

HOGS —Cont'd
Feeding garbage to swine —Cont'd
Permit for feeding garbage to swine.
Applicability of provisions, §106-405.2, (c), (d).
Application for permit, §106-405.3, (a).
Fees, §106-405.3, (b), (c).
Federal permits.
Exemption of holders from provisions, §106-405.2, (d).
Issuance, §106-405.2, (a).
Prohibiting local regulations, §106-405.2, (b).
Revocation of permits, §106-405.4.
Records to be maintained, §106-405.7, (b).
Removal of garbage from premises, §106-405.7, (c).
Revocation of permits for feeding garbage to swine, §106-405.4.
Rules and regulations, §106-405.8.
Sanitary conditions, §106-405.5.
Treatment of garbage fed to swine, §106-405.6.
Hog cholera, §§106-310 to 106-322.3.
See HOG CHOLERA.
Larceny, §14-81.
Livestock markets.
Removal of swine from market for slaughter and nonslaughter purposes, §106-410.
Regulation of use of swine removed from market, §106-411.
Meat inspections.
Generally, §§106-549.15 to 106-549.39.
See MEAT INSPECTIONS.
Poisoning of livestock, §14-163.
Pork promotion assessments, §§106-790 to 106-796.
Pursuing or injuring with intent to steal, §14-85.
Quarantine of diseased animals generally.
See LIVESTOCK DISEASES.
State institutions.
Keeping swine near state institutions, §143-153.
Swine farm siting, §§106-800 to 106-805.
Awarding costs, §106-804, (c).
Definitions, §106-802.
Floodway.
Constructing liquid animal waste management system component within 100-year floodway, §106-803, (a2).
Location requirements for swine house or lagoon, §106-803, (a).
Notice.
Written notice, §106-805.
Outdoor perimeter, location requirements, §106-803, (a1).
Permission to locate swine house or lagoon closer to residence, school, etc., §106-803, (b).
Persons directly affected by siting requirements, §106-804, (b).
Purpose, §106-801.
Restriction of other rights persons have, §106-804, (d).
Title of act, §106-800.
Violation points system applicable to permits for animal waste management systems for swine farms, §143-215.6E.

HOGSHEADS.
Truck on which leaf tobacco in hogsheads.
Load to be securely fastened, §20-120.

HOKE COUNTY.
Agricultural tendencies in certain counties.
Terms of, §42-23.

HOKE COUNTY —Cont'd
Ambulances.
Attachment or garnishment and lien for ambulance service, §§44-51.4 to 44-51.8.
Obtaining ambulance services without intending to pay, §14-111.2.
Requesting ambulance falsely, §14-111.3.
Condemnation or acquisition of land by local government unit outside county.
Consent of board of commissioners necessary, §153A-15.
Cropper or tenant refusing to perform terms of contract.
Forfeiture of right of possession to premises, §42-27.
Game laws, local acts not repealed, §113-133.1, (e).
Housing authority commissioners.
Tenant as commissioner, exemption from provision of law allowing, §157-5.
Maps in special proceedings, recording of photographic copies, §47-32.
Violation as misdemeanor, inapplicability of provisions, §47-32.2.
Oil, gas and mineral interests separated from surface fee, extinguished, title in surface fee holder.
Failure to list interest for tax purposes ten years prior to January 1, 1965.
Protection of subsurface interest from surface fee holder, §1-42.1, (d).
Interest not listed for tax purposes for 10 years prior to January 1, 1971.
Protection of surface interest from surface estate holder, §1-42.2, (d).
School property.
Acquisition and improvement, §153A-158.1.
Southeastern North Carolina regional economic development commission, §158-8.3.
Special school tax, election to abolish.
Petition required, §115C-505.

HOLDEN BEACH.
Eminent domain.
Exercise of power, purposes, modified provisions, §40A-3, (b1).
Vesting of title and right to possession, §40A-42, (a).
Ordinances to regulate and control swimming, personal watercraft operation, surfing and littering in Atlantic Ocean, §160A-176.2.

HOLDER IN DUE COURSE.
Commercial paper.
Value.
When bank gives value for purposes of holder in due course, §25-4-209.
Holder defined, §25-1-201.

HOLD HARMLESS PROMISES OR AGREEMENTS.
Construction indemnity agreements invalid, §22B-1.
Farm machinery franchises.
Supplier to hold harmless and indemnify dealer against judgment, §66-187, (b).
Leases, UCC.
Lessees furnishing specifications to lessor or supplier, §25-2A-211, (3).

HOLDING COMPANIES.
Bank holding companies.
Generally, §§53-225 to 53-232.
See BANK HOLDING COMPANIES.

HOLDING COMPANIES —Cont'd
Bank holding companies —Cont'd
Reciprocal interstate banking act generally, §§53-209 to 53-218.
See RECIPROCAL INTERSTATE BANKING.
Franchise tax, §105-120.2.
Credits, §105-120.2, (f).
Defined, §105-120.2, (c).
Local taxation prohibited, §105-120.2, (e).
Rate of tax, §105-120.2, (b).
Reports, §105-120.2, (a).
Insurance holding companies, §§58-19-1 to 58-19-70.
See INSURANCE HOLDING COMPANIES.
Savings and loan holding companies, §§54B-261, 54B-262.
Savings banks, §§54C-178, 54C-195, 54C-196.

HOLDING OVER.
Landlord and tenant.
Summary ejectment, §§42-26 to 42-36.2.
Tenant holding over may be dispossessed in certain cases, §42-26, (a).

HOLIDAY FESTIVALS.
Winery special event permit authorization, §18B-1114.1.

HOLIDAYS.
Act to be done falls on holiday, §103-5, (a), (b).
American family day, §103-7.
America's four hundredth anniversary committee.
Compensation of members, §143B-86.
Creation, §143B-85.
Members, §143B-86.
Powers and duties, §143B-85.
Quorum, §143B-86.
Selection of members, §143B-86.
Arbor week, §103-6.
Banks.
Emergency suspension of business.
Legal holiday for certain purposes, §53-77.3, (c).
Governor empowered to proclaim banking holidays, §53-77.
Opening for transactions on holidays not required, §53-54.
Savings banks, §54C-175.
Civil no-contact orders.
Workplace violence prevention.
Orders expiring on, extension, §95-272, (d).
Computation of time, §§1-593, 1A-1, Rule 6, (a).
County officers and employees, §153A-94, (b).
Enumeration of legal holidays, §103-4, (a).
Halloween.
Food distribution.
Certain foods prohibited at Halloween and all other times, §14-401.11.
Indian day.
Designation, §147-18.
Indian solidarity week, §103-8.
National Employ the Physically Handicapped Week.
Celebration, §143-283.3.
Pearl Harbor remembrance day, §103-10.
Prisoners of war recognition day, §103-9.
Public schools.
Number during school calendar, §115C-84.2, (a).
Savings and loan associations, §54B-110.
Sundays.
General provisions.
See SUNDAYS.

HOLIDAYS —Cont'd
Sundays —Cont'd
Public holiday falling on Sunday.
Monday following to be public holiday, §103-4, (b).
Thanksgiving day, §103-4, (a).
Veterans.
Pearl Harbor remembrance day, §103-10.
Prisoner of war recognition day, §103-9.
Workplace violence prevention.
Civil no-contact orders.
Orders expiring on, extension, §95-272, (d).

HOLOCAUST.
North Carolina council on the Holocaust, §143A-48.1.
Appointment of members, §143A-48.1, (b).
Assistance, §143A-48.1, (d).
Clerical or other assistance, §143A-48.1, (d).
Composition, §143A-48.1, (b).
Creation, §143A-48.1, (a).
Expenses of members.
Reimbursement, §143A-48.1, (c).
Purpose, §143A-48.1, (a).
Quorum, §143A-48.1, (b).
Terms of members, §143A-48.1, (b).

HOLOGRAPHIC WILLS.
Beneficiaries.
Competency as witness, §31-10, (b).
Contents, §31-3.4.
Personal property and real property may be devised by, §31-3.2, (a).
Probate, §31-18.2.
Wills generally.
See WILLS.

HOME APPLIANCES.
Service agreements, §§58-1-25 to 58-1-42.

HOME APPLIANCE SERVICE AGREEMENT COMPANIES, §§58-1-25 to 58-1-42.
Applicability of provisions, §§58-1-30, (a), 58-1-35, (a).
Authority restricted, §58-1-30, (a).
Cancellation of agreement, §58-1-35, (e).
Contents of agreement.
Prohibited contents, §58-1-35, (d).
Required contents, §58-1-35, (e).
Definitions, §§58-1-30, 58-1-35, (b).
Disclosures.
Required disclosures, §58-1-35, (c).
Document and other materials submitted to department.
Paper size, stapling and binding, §58-1-35, (m).
Financial statements, §58-1-30, (a).
Fronting company, §58-1-35, (h).
Funds, §58-1-35, (i).
Insurance.
Requirements, §58-1-36.
Name, §58-1-35, (l).
Records, §58-1-35, (f).
Registration.
Required, §58-1-35, (j).
Transacting business, §58-1-30, (a).

HOME CARE AGENCY LICENSING.
Adverse action on licenses, §131E-139, (a), (b).
Application for license, §131E-138, (c).
Criminal history record checks of applicants for employment.
Conditional employment, §131E-265, (f).
Confidentiality, §131E-265, (a).

HOME CARE AGENCY LICENSING —Cont'd
Criminal history record checks of applicants for employment —Cont'd
Contract agency offering employment, §131E-265, (a1).
Factors in determining whether to hire applicant.
Record check revealing one or more convictions of relevant offense, §131E-265, (b).
Immunity, §131E-265, (c), (g).
Penalty for furnishing false information, §131E-265, (e).
Refusal to consent to check, §131E-265, (a).
Relevant offense defined, §131E-265, (d).
Requirement as condition of employment, §131E-265, (a).
Contract agency offering employment, §131E-265, (a1).
Submission of request to department of justice, §131E-265, (a).
Criminal record checks of providers of treatment for or services to children, elderly, mental health patients, etc., §114-19.3.
Definitions, §131E-136.
Enforcement of rules, §131E-140, (b).
Establishment of licensing requirements.
Purpose of part, §131E-135, (b).
Injunctions.
Hindering secretary's performance of duties, §131E-142, (b).
Operation without license, §131E-142, (a).
Procedure, §131E-142, (c).
Inspections, §131E-141, (a), (b).
License required to operate, §131E-138, (a).
Posting in conspicuous place, §131E-138, (f).
Purpose of act, §131E-135, (b).
Renewal of license, §131E-138, (d).
Rules, adoption, §131E-138, (g).
Rules and regulations, §131E-140, (a), (a1).
Services provided in all counties, §131E-137, (a) to (c).
Title of part.
Home health agency licensure act, §131E-135, (a).
Transfer or assignment, restriction, §131E-138, (e).
Violation of provisions, §131E-141.1.

HOME EXERCISE AND FITNESS EQUIPMENT.
Service agreements, §§58-1-25 to 58-1-42.

HOME FOR AGED AND INFIRM.
Domiciliary homes.
General provisions.
See DOMICILIARY HOMES.
Nursing homes.
General provisions.
See NURSING HOMES.
Nursing pools.
General provisions, §§131E-154.1 to 131E-154.8.
See NURSES.

HOME HEALTH AGENCY LICENSING.
Criminal history records checks of employees, §114-19.10.

HOME HEALTH AGENCY OFFICES.
Certificates of need, §§131E-175 to 131E-190.
See HEALTH CARE FACILITIES.

HOME HEALTH CARE EQUIPMENT.
Service agreements, §§58-1-25 to 58-1-42.

HOME IMPROVEMENTS.
High cost home loans, use of proceeds, §24-1.1E, (c).

HOME INSPECTORS, §§143-151.43 to 143-151.63.
Applicability of provisions.
Exceptions, §143-151.62.
Associate home inspectors.
Defined, §143-151.45.
Licenses.
Exceptions to requirement that applicant for licensure first have license as associate home inspector, §143-151.61.
Qualifications, §143-151.52.
Bond required, §143-151.58, (b).
Citation of act.
Short title, §143-151.43.
Continuing education for licensees, §143-151.64, (a).
Credit for unapproved course, §143-151.64, (c).
Extension of time to comply, §143-151.64, (d).
Fees, §143-151.64, (b).
Rules, §143-151.64, (e).
Definitions, §143-151.45.
Division of engineering and building code.
Duties, §143-151.63, (a).
Examinations, §§143-151.51, 143-151.52.
Exceptions to provisions, §143-151.62.
Fees.
Deposit of moneys received by board, §143-151.63, (b).
Licenses, §143-151.57.
Injunctions, §143-151.60.
Legislative declaration, §143-151.44.
Licenses.
Applications.
Notification of applicant following evaluation of application, §143-151.53.
Submission, §143-151.51.
Associate home inspectors, §143-151.52.
Associate home inspectors.
Exceptions to requirement that applicant for licensure first have license as associate home inspector, §143-151.61.
Qualifications, §143-151.52.
Change of address by license holder.
Report to board, §143-151.54.
Continuing education, §143-151.64.
Denial.
Grounds, §143-151.56, (a).
Hearing, §143-151.56, (b).
Examinations.
Failure of examination.
Subsequent application.
Additional application fee not required, §143-151.57, (b).
Knowledge gained through experience to be emphasized, §143-151.49, (b).
Passing examination required, §143-151.51.
Associate home inspectors, §143-151.52.
Fees.
Maximum fees, §143-151.57, (a).
Inactive licenses, §143-151.55, (c).
Individuals only to be licensed, §143-151.50, (b).
Lapsed license, §143-151.55, (d).
Notification of applicant following evaluation of application, §143-151.53.
Probationary conditions.
Grounds, §143-151.56, (a).
Hearing, §143-151.56, (b).
Property of board.
License as, §143-151.54.
Qualifications for licensure, §143-151.51.
Associate home inspector, §143-151.52.

HOME INSPECTORS —Cont'd
Licenses —Cont'd
Renewal, §143-151.55, (a).
Late renewal, §143-151.55, (b).
Refusal to renew.
Grounds, §143-151.56, (a).
Hearing, §143-151.56, (b).
Required, §143-151.50, (a).
Revocation or suspension.
Grounds, §143-151.56, (a).
Hearing, §143-151.56, (b).
Reinstatement of revoked license.
Application for, §143-151.56, (b).
Surrender of license to board, §143-151.54.
Licensure board.
Books and records.
Oversight of state auditor, §143-151.63, (c).
Compensation of members, §143-151.47.
Definition of "board," §143-151.45.
Deposit of moneys received by board, §143-151.63, (b).
Meetings, §143-151.48, (b).
Members, §143-151.46, (a).
Officers, §143-151.48, (a).
Powers, §143-151.49, (a).
Terms of members, §143-151.46, (b).
Vacancies, §143-151.46, (c).
Misdemeanors, §143-151.59.
Purpose of act, §143-151.44.
Records, §143-151.58, (d).
Licensure board.
Books and records subject to oversight of state auditor, §143-151.63, (c).
Report to person for whom inspection perform, §143-151.58, (a).
Supervision of licensed associate, §143-151.58, (c).
Title of act.
Short title, §143-151.43.

HOMELESS PERSONS.
Housing finance authority.
Powers, §122A-5.
Public schools.
Assignments of homeless children to schools, §115C-366, (a2).
Special identification cards for nondrivers.
Fee, inapplicability to homeless, §20-37.7.

HOME LOANS.
Contract rates on loans secured by first mortgages or first deeds of trust, §24-1.1A.
Generally.
See MORTGAGES AND DEEDS OF TRUST.
Late payment charges, §24-10.1.

HOMEMAKERS.
Displaced homemakers, §§143B-394.4 to 143B-394.10.
See DISPLACED HOMEMAKERS.

HOMEOPATHIC DRUGS.
Food, drug and cosmetic act.
Drugs deemed adulterated, §106-133.
Drugs deemed misbranded, §106-134.

HOMEOWNERS' ASSOCIATIONS.
Franchise tax.
Exemption, §105-125, (a).

HOMEOWNERS' INSURANCE.
Beach area essential property insurance.
Issuance of policy, §58-45-35, (b1).

HOMEOWNERS' INSURANCE —Cont'd
Beach area essential property insurance —Cont'd
Special surcharges, schedule, adoption, §58-45-45, (c).
Claim closed without payment.
Termination or refusal to issue or renew residential real property insurance.
Prohibition, §58-36-115.
Inquiry as to policy provisions not resulting in claim.
Termination or refusal to issue or renew residential real property insurance.
Prohibition, §58-36-115.
Rate bureau.
Generally, §§58-36-1 to 58-36-110.
See RATE BUREAU.

HOMEOWNERS OR PROPERTY OWNERS ASSOCIATIONS.
Alcoholic beverage permits.
Special one-time permits, §18B-1002, (a).

HOMEOWNERS RECOVERY FUND, §§87-15.5 to 87-15.9.
Administration, §87-15.6, (a).
Building permit fees.
Collection, §87-15.6, (b).
Definitions, §87-15.5.
Establishment, §87-15.6, (a).
Purposes, §87-15.6, (a).
Reimbursements.
Application, §87-15.8, (a).
Determination of procedures, §87-15.7, (a).
Eligibility, §87-15.8, (a).
Payment, §87-15.8, (b).
Subrogation, §87-15.9.
Rules and regulations.
Adoption, §87-15.6, (c).
Subrogation.
Reimbursements, §87-15.9.
Use of funds, §87-15.7, (b).

HOME SCHOOLS.
Definitions, §115C-563, (a), (b).
Driving eligibility certificates.
Adoption of procedures to meet requirements, §115C-566, (a).
Form for parent's consent, §115C-366, (b).
Obtaining parent's consent, §115C-366, (c).
Flu and meningitis and vaccines.
Information provided, §115C-565.
Qualifications, §115C-564.
Requirements.
Exclusivity, §115C-565.
Generally, §115C-564.

HOME-SOLICITATION SALES.
Cancellation.
Buyer's right to cancel, §25A-39, (a).
Limitation, §25A-39, (e).
Delay of seller, §25A-39, (f).
No compensation for services of seller prior to cancellation, §25A-42, (c).
Notice of cancellation, §25A-39, (b), (c).
Form, §25A-39, (d).
Restoration of down payment, §25A-41, (a).
Goods as down payment, §25A-41, (b).
Return and care of goods, §25A-42, (a).
Care of goods by buyer, §25A-42, (b).
Defined, §25A-38.
Failure to give right to cancel in off premises sales, §14-401.13.

HOME-SOLICITATION SALES —Cont'd
Form of agreement or offer, §25A-40.
Negotiation or transfer of note, contract or other evidence of indebtedness.
Compensation, §25A-42, (d).
Time limitation, §25A-42, (d).
Statement of buyer's rights, §25A-40.

HOMESTEAD EXEMPTIONS.
Acts barring rights of spouse.
Rights lost, §31A-1, (b).
Aged persons.
Property tax exclusion, §105-277.1.
Notice on abstract, §105-309, (f).
Alternative exemptions, §1C-1602.
Appraisal costs.
Laying off homestead and exemption, §6-28.
Reassessment of homestead, §6-29.
Children.
Exemption for benefit of children, Const. N. C., art. X, §2.
Conveyance of homestead, Const. N. C., art. X, §2.
Costs.
Appraising costs and expenses, §6-28.
Laying off homestead and exemption, §6-28.
Reallotment of homestead for increase in value.
Allowance of costs to either party or apportioned in discretion of court, §6-21.
Reassessment of homestead, §6-29.
Disabled persons.
Property tax exclusion, §105-277.1.
Notice on abstract, §105-309, (f).
Effect of exemptions, §1C-1604, (a).
Exceptions, §1C-1601, (e).
Execution sales, Const. N. C., art. X, §2.
Exemption from sale, Const. N. C., art. X, §2.
Mechanics' and materialmen's liens.
Inapplicability of exemption, Const. N. C., art. X, §3.
Federal bankruptcy act.
Exemptions not applicable to resident of state, §1C-1601, (f).
Judgment enforcing lien upon homestead.
Limitation as to execution and not to apply, §1-306.
Laborers' liens.
Inapplicability of exemption, Const. N. C., art. X, §3.
Mechanics' and materialmen's liens.
Inapplicability of exemption, Const. N. C., art. X, §3.
Minors.
Exemption for benefit of children, Const. N. C., art. X, §2.
Property exempt, §1C-1601, (a).
Property tax exclusion.
Elderly and disabled, §105-277.1.
Notice on abstract, §105-309, (f).
Recent purchases, §1C-1601, (d).
Setting aside exempt property.
Modification, §1C-1603, (g).
Motion, §1C-1603, (a).
Contents, §1C-1603, (b).
Notation of order on judgment docket, §1C-1603, (f).
Notice to persons affected, §1C-1603, (d).
Petition, §1C-1603, (a).
Contents, §1C-1603, (b).
Procedure, §1C-1603, (e).
Statement by debtor, §1C-1603, (c).

HOMESTEAD EXEMPTIONS —Cont'd
Surviving spouse.
Exemption for benefit of surviving spouse, Const. N. C., art. X, §2.
Value.
Defined, §1C-1601, (b).
Waiver, §1C-1601, (c).

HOMICIDE.
Autopsies, §15-7.
Capital punishment.
Crimes punishable by death, Const. N. C., art. XI, §2.
Generally.
See CAPITAL PUNISHMENT.
Death by vehicle, §20-141.4.
Mandatory revocation of license, §20-17, (a).
Permanent revocation, §20-19, (i).
Decedents' estates.
Slayer act, §31A-6.
Definitions, §14-17.
First degree murder, §14-17.
Guilty plea.
Death penalty or life imprisonment, §15A-2001.
Impaired driving.
Special information if conviction of homicide involves, §20-24, (e).
Indictments.
Essentials of bill for homicide, §15-144.
Indigent persons.
Representation of indigent persons.
Appointment of assistant counsel, §7A-450, (b1).
Juveniles under 17 years of age.
First degree murder, §14-17.
Killing decedent, §§31A-3 to 31A-15.
See SLAYER ACT.
Malice aforethought.
Allegation required in indictment, §15-144.
Manslaughter.
Double jeopardy.
Death by vehicle.
Subsequent prosecutions prohibited, §20-141.4, (c).
Indictments.
Essentials of bill, §15-144.
Motor vehicles.
Revocation or suspension of license.
Mandatory revocation, §20-17, (a).
Permanent revocation, §20-19, (i).
Punishment for manslaughter, §14-18.
Motor vehicles.
Death by vehicle, §20-141.4.
Mandatory revocation of license, §20-17, (a).
Permanent revocation, §20-19, (i).
Manslaughter.
Revocation or suspension of license.
Mandatory revocation, §20-17, (a).
Permanent revocation, §20-19, (i).
Murder.
Definitions.
Murder in first and second degree, §14-17.
Degrees, §14-17.
Verdict for murder in first or second degree, §15-172.
First degree.
Juveniles under 17 years of age, §14-17.
Indictments.
Essentials of bill, §15-144.
Indigent persons.
Representation of indigent persons.
Appointment of assistant counsel, §7A-450, (b1).

HOMICIDE —Cont'd
Murder —Cont'd
Juvenile committed for placement in youth development center for offense of first degree if committed by adult.
Continued jurisdiction of juvenile court, §7B-1602, (a).
Malice aforethought.
Allegation required in indictment, §15-144.
Punishment, §14-17.
Verdict.
First or second degree, §15-172.
Postmortem examinations, §15-7.
Second degree murder, §14-17.
Slayer act.
Decedents' estates, §31A-6.
Killing decedent generally, §§31A-3 to 31A-15.
See SLAYER ACT.
Suicide.
Crime of suicide abolished, §14-17.1.
Vehicular homicide.
Death by vehicle, §20-141.4.
Mandatory revocation of driver's license, §20-17, (a).
Permanent revocation, §20-19, (i).
Venue.
Assault in one county, death in another, §15-130.
Assault in this state, death in another, §15-131.
County where death occurs, §15-133.
Verdict.
Murder.
First or second degree, §15-172.
Wills.
Lapse.
Property passes according to lapse statute, §31A-10, (a).
Workers' compensation.
Injury or death caused by willful intention of employee to injure or kill another.
No compensation payable, §97-12.

HOMINY.
Standard weight, §81A-42.

HOMOSEXUAL MARRIAGES, §51-1.2.

HONEY.
Generally, §§106-634 to 106-644.
See BEES AND HONEY.

HONEYBEE.
Generally, §§106-634 to 106-644.
See BEES AND HONEY.
State insect, §145-7.

HONORARY COUNSELOR CORPS.
Special registration plates, §20-79.4, (b).

HONORARY TRUSTS, §36A-145.

HOOF AND MOUTH DISEASE.
Livestock diseases.
Emergency measures when threat imminent.
Warrantless inspection, §106-399.5.
Generally, §§106-400 to 106-405.

HOPE MILLS.
Condemnation of unsafe buildings, §§160A-425.1, 160A-426, (d), 160A-432, (a1).

HORIZONTAL PROPERTY, §§47A-1 to 47A-28.
See UNIT OWNERSHIP.

HORMONES.
Biological residues in animals, §§106-549.81 to 106-549.89.
See BIOLOGICAL RESIDUES IN ANIMALS.

HORNS AND WARNING DEVICES ON MOTOR VEHICLES.
Ambulances, §§20-156, (b), 20-157, (a).
Disabled trucks and trailers, §20-161, (c).
Fire department vehicles.
Siren must be audible within 1,000 feet, §20-157, (a).
Siren necessary for right of way, §20-156, (b).
Overtaking and passing.
Duty of driver of overtaking vehicle to give audible warning, §20-149, (b).
Pedestrians.
Signal to pedestrian by horn or warning device, §20-154, (a).
Police department vehicles.
Siren must be audible within 1,000 feet, §20-157, (a).
Siren necessary for right of way, §20-156, (b).
Requirements generally, §20-125, (a).
Safety inspections.
Scope of inspection, §20-183.3, (a).
Siren must be audible within 1,000 feet, §§20-156, (b), 20-157, (a).
Siren necessary for right of way, §20-157, (a).
Special horns on vehicles, §20-125, (b).
Turning, §20-154.

HORSEBACK RIDING.
Equine activity liability, §§99E-1 to 99E-3.

HORSE INDUSTRY PROMOTION, §§106-820 to 106-825.
Assessment, §§106-823 to 106-825.
Definitions, §106-822.
Purpose, §106-821.
Short title, §106-820.

HORSEPASTURE RIVER.
Natural and scenic rivers system.
Additional component of system, §113A-35.2.

HORSERADISH.
Standard weight and measure, §81A-42.

HORSES.
Allowance to officers for keeping and maintaining horses taken into custody under legal process, §1-322.
Bailments.
Vehicles and draft animals, protection of bailor against bailee's act, §§14-165 to 14-169.
See BAILMENTS.
Bribery of horse show judges or officials, §14-380.1.
Attempts at bribery to be reported, §14-380.2.
Definition of "bribe," §14-380.3.
Printing provisions of article in horse show schedules, §14-380.4.
Carcasses.
Slaughter, sale and transportation of carcasses, §106-549.25.
Cattle tick, §§106-351 to 106-363.
See CATTLE TICK.
Certificate of registration obtained by false representation, §14-103.
Compensation for killing diseased animals, §§106-323 to 106-335.
See LIVESTOCK DISEASES.
Control of livestock diseases generally, §§106-400 to 106-405.
See LIVESTOCK DISEASES.
Dealer licensing generally, §§106-418.8 to 106-418.16.
See LIVESTOCK DEALER LICENSING.

HORSES —Cont'd
Diseases generally, §§106-304 to 106-307.7.
See LIVESTOCK DISEASES.
Equine activity liability, §§99E-1 to 99E-3.
Equine infectious anemia, §§106-405.15 to 106-405.20.
Civil penalties, §106-405.20.
Control and eradication program.
Implementation of program, §106-405.18.
Defined, §106-405.15.
Fine, §106-405.20.
Implementation of control and eradication program, §106-405.18.
Quarantine of infected or exposed animals, §106-405.16.
Rules and regulations.
Authority to promulgate and enforce, §106-405.17.
Violation made misdemeanor, §106-405.19.
Larceny.
Felony, §14-81, (a).
Probation, conditions required, §14-81, (b).
Sentencing to active sentence.
Judge's authority not limited, §14-81, (b).
Taking horses for temporary purposes, §14-82.
Livestock brands generally, §§80-45 to 80-66.
See LIVESTOCK BRANDS.
Meat inspection.
Equine carcasses.
Slaughter, sale and transportation of carcasses, §106-549.25.
Motor vehicles.
Passing horses or other draft animals.
Reasonable care, §20-216.
Poisoning of horses, §14-163.
Ponies.
Outer Banks, §§68-42 to 68-46.
Removal or confinement of ponies on Ocracoke Island and Shackleford Banks, §68-43.
Running at large.
Exceptions to prohibition, §68-42.
Promotion of horse industry.
Assessment.
Amount required on referendum ballot, §106-823, (c).
Applicability, §106-824, (a).
Approval by majority, §106-824, (a).
Council determinations required, §106-823, (b).
Notice and eligibility for voting, §106-823, (d).
Referendum request, §106-823, (a).
Refund, §106-825, (b).
Unpaid assessment collection, §106-824, (b).
Use of funds collected, §106-825, (a).
Definitions, §106-822.
Legislative purpose, §106-821.
Short title of article, §106-820.
Protection of horse shows.
Bribery of horse show judges or officials, §14-380.1.
Attempts at bribery to be reported, §14-380.2.
Definition of "bribe," §14-380.3.
Printing provisions of article in horse show schedules, §14-380.4.
Pursuing or injuring with intent to steal, §14-85.
Quarantine of diseased animals generally.
See LIVESTOCK DISEASES.
Sales and use tax.
Rate of tax, §105-164.4, (a).
Stables.
Arson, §14-62.
Traffic laws apply to riding animals, §20-171.

HORSE SHOWS.
Bribery of judges or officials, §§14-380.1 to 14-380.4.
Equine activity liability, §§99E-1 to 99E-3.

HORSE TRAILERS.
Weigh stations in state.
Trailers not required to stop at, §20-118.1.

HOSPICES, §§131E-200 to 131E-207.
Care to be available at all times, §131E-203, (c).
Certificates of need.
Definitions, §131E-176.
Generally, §§131E-175 to 131E-190.
See HEALTH CARE FACILITIES.
Citation of article, §131E-200.
Confidentiality of information, §131E-207, (a) to (c).
Criminal record checks of providers of treatment for or services to children, elderly, mental health patients, etc., §114-19.3.
Definitions, §131E-201.
Health care personnel registry, §131E-256.
Injunctions.
Hindering department's performance of duties, §131E-206, (c).
Operation without license, §131E-206, (a).
Substantial noncompliance, §131E-206, (b).
Inspections, §131E-204.
Confidentiality of information, §131E-207, (a) to (c).
Licenses.
Applications.
Department to provide, §131E-202, (b).
Display, §131E-202, (b).
Exemptions, §131E-203, (b).
Issuance, §131E-202, (b).
Nontransferable, §131E-202, (b).
Renewal, §131E-202, (c).
Required, §131E-203, (a).
Rules and regulations.
Adoption by commission, §131E-202, (a).
Suspension or revocation.
Grounds, §131E-205, (a).
Procedure, §131E-205, (b).
Purpose of article, §131E-200.
Title of article, §131E-200.

HOSPITAL AUTHORITIES, §§131E-15 to 131E-34.
Agents.
Powers of authority.
Corporate agents, §131E-23, (b).
Exercise of powers through agents, §131E-23, (b).
Applicability of provisions.
Controlling provisions, §131E-33.
High Point city, §131E-34.
Appropriations, §131E-30.
Audits and auditing.
Reports to be filed, §131E-29.
Bond issues.
Definition of bonds, §131E-16.
Exemption from taxation, §131E-28, (c).
Local government finance, §§159-1 to 159-188.
See LOCAL GOVERNMENT FINANCE.
Revenue bonds and notes, §131E-26, (a), (b).
Borrowing money.
Contracts with federal government, §131E-27.
Boundaries.
Creation of authority, §131E-20, (a), (b).

HOSPITAL AUTHORITIES —Cont'd
Buildings.
Subject to building laws, ordinances and regulations, §131E-25.
Certificate of incorporation.
Admissibility in evidence of copy of certificate, §131E-19.
Creation of authority, §131E-19.
Change of name, §131E-19, (c).
Charges against commissioners.
Removal of commissioners, §131E-22, (a) to (d).
Citation of act, §131E-5, (a).
Commissioners.
Appointment, §§131E-17, (b), 131E-18, (a), (b).
After resolution creating authority, §131E-17, (b).
Certificate of appointment or reappointment, §131E-18, (e).
Counties with population less than 75,000, §131E-18, (g).
Right to name commissioners, §131E-31, (b).
Chairman, §131E-18, (c).
Charges against.
Removal, §131E-22, (a) to (d).
Compensation, §131E-18, (f).
Conflicts of interest, §131E-21.
Counties with population less than 75,000.
Appointment of members, §131E-18, (g).
Defined, §131E-16.
Expenses, §131E-18, (f).
Number of commissioners, §131E-18, (a).
Quorum, §131E-18, (h).
Removal.
Authority willfully violated law or contract, §131E-22, (b).
Grounds, §131E-22, (a).
Mailing charges to commissioner's home, §131E-22, (c).
Notice and opportunity for hearing, §131E-22, (a).
Preparation for hearing, time for, §131E-22, (a).
Record of proceedings, filing, §131E-22, (d).
Right to name commissioners, §131E-31, (b).
Terms of office, §131E-18, (a).
Vacancies filled, §131E-18, (b), (d).
Vice-chairman, §131E-18, (c).
Willful violation of law or contract by authority.
Removal of commissioner, §131E-22, (b).
Conflicts of interest, §131E-21.
Construction and interpretation.
Controlling provisions, §131E-33.
Contracts.
Federal government contracts, §131E-27.
Controlling provisions, §131E-33.
Conveyance or transfers of property to authority, §131E-31, (a), (b).
Counties.
Appropriations by city, town or county, §131E-30.
Creation, §131E-19.
By resolution, §131E-17, (a).
Definitions, §131E-16.
Eminent domain, §131E-10.
Power of eminent domain, §§40A-3, (c), 131E-24, (a).
Certificate of public convenience and necessity.
Prerequisite to exercise of power, §131E-24, (c).
Restrictions, §131E-24, (b).
Evidence.
Certificate of incorporation.
Copy of certificate admissible in evidence, §131E-19.

HOSPITAL AUTHORITIES —Cont'd
Exemption from taxes and fees, §131E-28, (a).
Bonds, notes, debentures, §131E-28, (c).
Property of authority, §131E-28, (b).
Federal aid.
Contracts with federal government, §131E-27.
Finance.
Local government finance, §§159-1 to 159-188.
See LOCAL GOVERNMENT FINANCE.
Financial interests in facilities.
Disclosures, §131E-21, (c).
Exemptions from provision, §131E-21, (d), (e).
Restrictions, §131E-21, (a).
Stock ownership, effect, §131E-21, (b).
Void contracts due to, §131E-21, (f).
Grants.
Contracts with federal government, §131E-27.
High Point.
Applicability of provisions to city of High Point, §131E-34.
Incorporation, §131E-19.
Applications for incorporation, §131E-19, (a).
Examination by secretary of state, §131E-19, (b).
Change of name, §131E-19, (c).
Copy of certificate of incorporation, §131E-19, (d).
Lease of property to authority, §131E-31, (a), (b).
Lease, sale or conveyance of hospital facility, §131E-13, (a).
Bonds outstanding at time of lease, §131E-13, (c).
Bonds outstanding at time of sale or conveyance, §131E-13, (b).
Development, construction and operation of medical office buildings, §131E-13, (e).
Inapplicability of other provisions, §131E-13, (g).
Length of lease, determination, §131E-13, (c).
Nonprofit corporations.
Lease of facilities to, §131E-14.
Pledge of hospital land or leasehold estate, §131E-13, (f).
Procedures before leasing, selling or conveying, §131E-13, (d).
Sublease or assignment of lease, §131E-13, (c).
Mortgages and deeds of trust.
Purchase money security interests, §131E-32, (a) to (e).
Municipal corporations.
Appropriations by city, town or county, §131E-30.
Planning laws, ordinances and regulations, §131E-25.
Powers.
Agents.
Corporate agents, §131E-23, (b).
Exercise of powers through agents, §131E-23, (b).
Applicability of provisions, §131E-23, (d).
Certain provisions not applicable to authority, §131E-23, (d).
Corporate agents, §131E-23, (b).
Eminent domain, §131E-10.
Enumeration, §131E-23, (a) to (d).
Exercise of powers through agents, §131E-23, (b).
Generally, §131E-23, (a) to (d).
Implied powers, §131E-23, (c).
Property exempt from taxes, §131E-28, (b).
Purchase money security interests.
Contract in amount less than $750,000.
Power without local government commission approval, §131E-32, (b).

HOSPITAL AUTHORITIES —Cont'd
Purchase money security interests —Cont'd
Contract in amount more than $750,000.
Local government commission approval, §131E-32, (b) to (d).
Power to purchase real or personal property under, §131E-32, (a).
Purpose, §131E-15, (b).
Removal of commissioners, §131E-22, (a) to (d).
Reports.
Audit report to be filed, §131E-29.
Sale of hospital facilities to certain nonprofit corporations, §131E-14.
Sanitation.
Subject to sanitary laws, ordinances and regulations, §131E-25.
Short title, §131E-5, (a).
United States.
Contracts with federal government, §131E-27.
Willful violation of laws or contract.
Removal of commissioner acquiescing in, §131E-22, (b).
Zoning.
Subject to zoning laws, ordinances and regulations, §131E-25.

HOSPITAL DISTRICTS, §§131E-40 to 131E-47.
Additional and alternative methods, §131E-40, (c).
Board of county commissioners.
Alternative procedures for creation of district, §131E-41, (b).
Creation of district.
Alternative procedures, §131E-41, (b).
Governing body of district, §131E-47.
Citation of part.
Hospital district act, §131E-40.
Construction and interpretation.
Liberal construction, §131E-40, (d).
Creation of district.
Adoption of resolution, §131E-42, (c).
Alternative procedures, §131E-41, (b).
Designation, §131E-42, (d).
Limitation of actions, §131E-43.
Methods of creation, §131E-41, (a), (b).
Notice of creation, §131E-42, (e).
Resolutions.
Adoption, §131E-42, (c).
Creation by resolution, §131E-41, (b).
Elections.
Referendum on repeal of tax levy, §131E-46, (a) to (d).
Equipment.
Tax levy for equipment, §131E-45.
Referendum on repeal of tax levy, §131E-46, (a) to (d).
Fiscal impact of bills, resolution or rules.
Local government fiscal information, §§120-30.41 to 120-30.49.
General powers, §131E-44, (a), (b).
Health care facilities finance act.
Additional powers of public agencies, §131A-6.
Hearings.
Petition for formation of hospital district, §131E-42, (a), (b).
Result of hearing, §131E-42, (c).
Liberal construction of part, §131E-40, (d).
Limitation of actions.
Creation of district, §131E-43.
Maintenance of district.
Tax levy for maintenance, §131E-45.
Referendum on repeal of tax levy, §131E-46, (a) to (d).

HOSPITAL DISTRICTS —Cont'd
Municipal corporations.
Body corporate and politic, §131E-44, (a).
Municipal hospital facilities act.
Applicability of provisions, §131E-47.
Name of district, §131E-42, (d).
Notice.
Creation of district, §131E-42, (e).
Operation of district.
Tax levy for operation, §131E-45.
Referendum on repeal of tax levy, §131E-46, (a) to (d).
Petitions.
Formation of hospital district, §131E-41, (a).
Hearing on petition, §131E-42, (a), (b).
Powers, §131E-44, (a), (b).
Purpose of part, §131E-40, (b).
Referendum on repeal of tax levy, §131E-46, (a) to (d).
Tax levy for operation, equipment and maintenance, §131E-45.
Referendum on repeal of tax levy, §131E-46, (a) to (d).
Title.
Hospital district act, §131E-40, (a).

HOSPITAL EXPENSES.
Offer to pay, admissibility, §8C-1, Rule 409.

HOSPITAL, MEDICAL AND DENTAL SERVICE CORPORATIONS, §§58-65-1 to 58-66-40.
Acknowledgment of claims, §58-3-100, (c).
Failure to acknowledge after receiving notice.
Civil penalty, §58-3-100, (c).
Action for negligent decisions.
Health care liability, §§90-21.50 to 90-21.56.
See HEALTH CARE LIABILITY.
Additional coverage mandates prohibited, §58-50-63, (a).
Employer not prohibited from expanding coverage, §58-50-63, (b).
Insurer and health benefit plan defined, §58-50-63, (c).
Advance practice registered nurse.
Payment or reimbursement, §58-50-30, (d).
Right to choose services, §58-50-30, (a1) to (a3), (g), (h).
Agents licensing, §58-65-115.
Associations to transact business through licensed agents only, §58-65-120.
Required, §58-65-120.
Amendments to charter, §58-65-130.
Conversion of corporation, §58-65-131, (d).
Applicability of other laws, §58-65-2.
Applicability of provisions.
Preexisting hospital service corporations, §58-65-145.
Single employer plans, §58-65-150.
Boards of directors.
Amendments to charter, §58-65-130.
Composition, §58-65-20, (b).
Defined, §58-65-20, (a).
Breast cancer.
Mammograms.
Coverage, §58-65-92.
Cancer treatment.
Breast cancer.
Mammograms.
Coverage, §58-65-92.
Cervical cancer screening.
Coverage, §58-65-92.

HOSPITAL, MEDICAL AND DENTAL SERVICE CORPORATIONS —Cont'd
Cancer treatment —Cont'd
Colorectal cancer examinations, laboratory tests and screening.
Coverage required of all health benefit plans, §58-3-179, (a).
Limitations applicable to services, §58-3-179, (b).
Coverage of certain prescribed drugs for.
Exceptions, §58-65-94, (b), (c).
Generally, §58-65-94, (a).
Mammograms.
Coverage, §58-65-92.
Certificate of authority or license.
Applications, §58-65-50.
Fee, §58-65-55, (b).
Issuance, §58-65-55, (a).
Monetary penalty for violations, §58-2-70, (c), (d), (g).
Restitution for violations, §58-2-70, (e) to (g).
Revocation.
Notice and hearing, §58-2-70, (b).
Surrender, §58-2-65.
Suspension.
Applicable provisions, §58-2-70, (h).
Criminal convictions, §58-2-60, (b).
Notice and hearing, §58-2-70, (b).
Cervical cancer.
Screening for early detection.
Coverage requirements, §58-65-92, (a), (e).
Defined, §58-65-92, (a1).
Chemical dependency.
Contracts to cover treatment, §58-65-75, (a) to (e).
Chiropractors.
Right to choose services, §58-50-30, (a1) to (a3), (g), (h).
Choice of providers, §58-65-1, (a).
Choice of service providers, §58-50-30, (a1) to (a3).
Pediatrician for minors, §58-3-240.
Provider directories, §58-3-245.
Specialist selected as primary care provider, §58-3-235.
Uniform provider credentialing, §58-3-230.
Claim denial, notice, §58-3-172, (a).
Health benefit plans defined, §58-3-172, (b).
Claim forms.
Uniform claim forms, §58-3-171, (a).
Health benefit plans defined, §58-3-171, (c).
Workers' compensation included in health benefit plan, §58-3-171, (b).
Claims.
Acknowledgment of claims, §58-3-100, (c).
Failure to acknowledge after receiving notice.
Civil penalty, §58-3-100, (c).
Clinical social workers.
Defined, §58-50-30, (c).
Right to choose services, §58-50-30, (a1) to (a3), (g), (h).
Clinical trials, coverage, §58-3-255, (b).
Costs not required to be covered, §58-3-255, (d).
Covered clinical trials defined, §58-3-255, (a).
Definitions, §58-3-255, (a).
Medical necessary costs covered, §58-3-255, (c).
Closed formularies or restricted access to prescription drugs, §58-3-221.
Colorectal cancer examinations, laboratory tests and screening.
Coverage required of every health benefit plan, §58-3-179, (a).

HOSPITAL, MEDICAL AND DENTAL SERVICE CORPORATIONS —Cont'd
Colorectal cancer examinations, laboratory tests and screening —Cont'd
Limitations applicable to services, §58-3-179, (b).
Commissioner of insurance.
Examinations by, §58-65-105.
Exemptions from provisions.
Determination, §58-65-165.
Expenses in connection with solicitation of subscribers.
Subject to inspection by commissioner, §58-65-110.
Merger or consolidation.
Approval, §58-65-155.
Readable insurance certificates act.
Filing of certificates with commissioner, §58-66-30, (a).
Applicability of provisions, §58-66-35, (a).
Approval by commissioner, §58-66-30, (a).
Disapproval by commissioner, §58-66-30, (a).
Grounds, §58-66-30, (b).
Reports filed with, §58-65-100.
Visitations, §58-65-105.
Consolidation, §58-65-155.
Continuing care retirement community residents, §58-3-200, (f).
Contraceptive drugs or devices and outpatient contraceptive services.
Coverage by insurer providing health benefit plan, §58-3-178, (a), (b).
Definitions, §58-3-178, (c).
Prohibited acts, §58-3-178, (d).
Religious employer requesting exclusion of coverage, §58-3-178, (e).
Contracts.
Chemical dependency treatment.
Contracts to cover, §58-65-75, (a) to (e).
Dentists' services, §58-65-30.
Generally, §58-65-25, (a).
Hemoglobin seed trait.
Contracts to cover persons possessing, §58-65-70.
Merged or consolidated corporations, §58-65-155.
Required provisions, §58-65-25, (b).
Sickle cell trait.
Contracts to cover persons possessing, §58-65-70.
Subscribers' contracts.
Dependents, §58-65-60, (b).
Forms, §58-65-40.
Group contracts, §58-65-60, (c).
Master group contracts, §58-65-60, (e) to (e2).
Rate schedule.
Filing as prerequisite, §58-65-40.
Revision hearing, §58-65-45.
Renewal, §58-65-60, (a), (f).
Term, §58-65-60, (a).
Written contracts, §58-65-60, (c), (d).
Tax-supported institutions.
Coverage for active medical treatment in, §58-65-65, (a) to (c).
Conversion.
Attorney general.
Enforcement authority, §58-65-132, (d).
Foundation to receive fair market value of corporation.
Approval of determination of fair market value, §58-65-133, (h).
Certificate of authority.
Issuance, §58-65-132, (a).
Effect, §58-65-132, (b).

HOSPITAL, MEDICAL AND DENTAL SERVICE CORPORATIONS —Cont'd
Conversion —Cont'd
Charter amendment for conversion, §58-65-131, (d).
Compliance with provisions required, §58-65-131, (c).
Definitions, §58-65-131, (b).
Foundation to receive fair market value of corporation.
Advisory committee, §58-65-133, (d).
Attorney general.
Approval of determination relating to fair market value, §58-65-133, (h).
Board of directors, §58-65-133, (c).
Costs, §58-65-133, (g).
Creation, §58-65-133, (a).
Independent of corporation, §58-65-133, (e).
Purpose, §58-65-133, (b).
Voting and stock registration agreement, §58-65-133, (f).
Legislative declaration, §58-65-131, (a).
Plan.
Approval, §58-65-132, (a).
Filing, §58-65-131, (e).
Legal action on validity of plan, §58-65-132, (d).
Public comment on, §58-65-131, (g).
Public record, §58-65-131, (h).
Requirements, §58-65-131, (f).
Review.
Approval, §58-65-132, (a).
Costs, §58-65-131, (e).
Final decision and order by commissioner, §58-65-132, (c).
Public records.
Applications, reports, plans, and other documents, §58-65-131, (h).
Cost plus plans, §58-65-135.
Coverage, §58-65-93, (a), (c).
Credentialing providers.
Health benefit plan and insurer defined, §58-3-230, (c).
Process requirements, §58-3-230, (a).
Time limit on processing applications, §58-3-230, (a).
Uniform provider credentialing application form.
Commissioner to adopt by rule, §58-3-230, (b).
Definitions, §58-65-1, (a).
Accident, accidental injury, and accidental means, §58-65-80, (a), (b).
Indemnification of directors, officers, employees, etc, §58-65-166, (b).
Mentally ill and chemically dependent, §58-65-90, (a).
Readable insurance certificates act, §58-66-15.
Dental procedures performed in hospital or ambulatory surgical facility.
Children under age nine, persons with serious mental and physical condition and persons with significant behavior problems.
Definitions, §58-3-122, (b).
Health benefit plans to provide coverage for payment of anesthesia and facility charges, §58-3-122, (a).
Dentists.
Right to choose services, §58-50-30, (a1) to (a3), (g), (h).
Determinations as to coverage, §58-3-200, (c).
Diabetes.
Coverage for certain treatment, §58-65-91, (a).
Definition of "physician," §58-65-91, (b).
Directories of providers, §58-3-245.

HOSPITAL, MEDICAL AND DENTAL SERVICE CORPORATIONS —Cont'd
Direct payment to government agency, §58-3-175, (b).
Health benefit plan defined, §58-3-175, (a).
Inapplicability of provisions, §58-3-175, (c).
When direct payment not required, §58-3-175, (d).
Disclosure requirements for health benefit plans, §58-3-191, (b).
Discrimination.
Mentally ill and chemically dependent.
Applicability of section, §58-65-90, (d).
Coverage, §58-65-90, (b1), (c).
Definitions, §58-65-90, (a).
Prohibited acts, §58-65-90, (b).
Exceptions, §58-65-90, (c).
Prohibited practices, §58-65-85.
Drive-thru deliveries, §58-3-169.
Electronic or on-line system for up-to-date network information.
Plan to provide, §58-3-245, (a).
Emergency care.
Coverage required, §58-3-190.
Entitlement to payment or reimbursement, list of providers, §58-65-1, (a).
Evidence of coverage.
Notice, expenses may exceed covered amount, §58-3-250, (b).
Payment obligations, explanation by insurer, §58-3-250, (a).
Exemptions from provisions.
Determination by commissioner of insurance, §58-65-165.
Single employer plans, §58-65-150.
Expenses.
Solicitation of subscribers.
Subject to inspection by commissioner of insurance, §58-65-110.
External review of health benefit plan, §§58-50-75 to 58-50-95.
See ACCIDENT AND HEALTH INSURANCE.
Fee based pastoral counselor.
Defined, §58-50-30, (c1).
Right to choose services, §58-50-30, (a1) to (a3), (g), (h).
Fees.
Certificate of authority or license, §58-65-55, (b).
Financial incentives to delay, deny or reduce coverage.
Plan prohibited from offering provider, §58-3-265.
Foreign or alien corporation not authorized to do business, §58-65-1, (d).
Genetic information in health insurance, §58-3-215.
Grandfather clause.
Preexisting hospital service corporations, §58-65-145.
Grievance procedures for insurers, §58-50-62.
External review of decision, §§58-50-75 to 58-50-95.
Health benefit plans generally, §§58-3-167 to 58-3-178, 58-3-190 to 58-3-265.
See ACCIDENT AND HEALTH INSURANCE.
Health maintenance organizations.
Contracts with health maintenance organizations, §58-67-95, (b).
Power to organization and operate health maintenance organization, §58-67-95, (a).
Provisions not applicable to health maintenance organizations, §58-67-170, (a).

HOSPITAL, MEDICAL AND DENTAL SERVICE CORPORATIONS —Cont'd
Hearings.
Rate schedule.
Revision of existing schedule or establishment of new schedule, §58-65-45.
High-risk populations.
Nondiscrimination against, §58-3-200, (e).
Incentives to delay, deny or reduce coverage.
Plan prohibited from offering provider, §58-3-265.
Indemnification of directors, officers, employees, etc.
Additional indemnification, §58-65-173, (a), (b).
Advance for expenses, §58-65-169.
Applicability of part, §58-65-174, (a) to (c).
Articles of incorporation.
Mandatory indemnification not limited by, §58-65-168.
Unless articles provide otherwise, §58-65-172.
Authority, §58-65-167, (a) to (f).
Court-ordered indemnification, §58-65-170.
Determination and authorization of indemnification, §58-65-171, (a) to (c).
Unless articles of incorporation provide otherwise, §58-65-172.
Court-ordered indemnification, §58-65-170.
Definitions, §58-65-166, (b).
Determination of indemnification, §58-65-171, (a) to (c).
Expenses.
Advance for, §58-65-169.
Insurance, §58-65-173, (c).
Mandatory indemnification, §58-65-168.
Policy statement, §58-65-166, (a).
Prohibited matters, §58-65-167, (c).
Scope of part, §58-65-174, (a) to (c).
Insurance companies generally.
See INSURANCE COMPANIES.
Investments in securities, §58-65-95, (a).
Laws governing, §58-65-1, (a).
License.
Revocation and suspension.
Grounds, §58-65-125, (a).
Natural persons, made applicable to, §58-65-125, (b).
Long-term care insurance, §§58-55-1 to 58-55-50.
See LONG-TERM CARE INSURANCE.
Mammograms.
Coverage requirements, §58-65-92, (a), (c).
Low dose screening mammography defined, §58-65-92, (b).
Reimbursement, §58-65-92, (d).
Marriage and family therapists.
Defined, §58-50-30, (c4).
Right to choose services, §58-50-30, (a1) to (a3).
Mastectomy.
Coverage for reconstructive breast surgery following, §58-65-96, (a).
Definitions, §58-65-96, (b).
Notice of available coverage, §58-65-96, (d).
Prohibited acts, §58-65-96, (c).
Maternity coverage requirements, §58-3-170, (a).
Health benefit plans defined, §58-3-170, (b).
Minimum hospital stay following birth, §58-3-169.
Medical necessity.
Requirements when health benefit plans that limit coverage to medically necessary services and supplies, §58-3-200, (b).
Merger, §58-65-155.

HOSPITAL, MEDICAL AND DENTAL SERVICE CORPORATIONS —Cont'd
Negligent decisions of plan providers.
Health care liability, §§90-21.50 to 90-21.56.
See HEALTH CARE LIABILITY.
Newborn hearing screening.
Coverage required, §58-3-260, (b).
Health benefit plan and insurer defined, §58-3-260, (a).
Notice.
Amendments to charter, §58-65-130.
Claim denial, §58-3-172.
Conversion.
Public comment on plan of conversion, §58-65-131, (g).
Merger or consolidation, §58-65-155.
Rate schedule.
Hearing on revision of existing schedule or establishment of new schedule, §58-65-45.
Nurses.
Rendition of services by registered nurse, §58-65-35.
Offset or reversal of payment, §58-50-57, (a).
Contract with provider not to contain provision authorizing, §58-50-57, (b).
Optometrists.
Right to choose services, §58-50-30, (a1) to (a3), (g), (h).
Osteoporosis or low bone mass.
Bone mass measurement for diagnosis and evaluation.
Health benefit plan to provide coverage, §58-3-174, (a).
Definitions, §58-3-174, (d).
Frequency of coverage, §58-3-174, (b).
Screening for nonqualified individuals not covered, §58-3-174, (c).
Payment obligations for covered services.
Explanation by insurer, §58-3-250, (a).
Notice that actual expenses may exceed covered amount, §58-3-250, (b).
Payment to government agency.
Direct payment, §58-3-175.
Pediatrician.
Direct access for minors, §58-3-240.
Pharmacist.
Payment or reimbursement, §58-50-30, (e).
Right to choose services, §58-50-30, (a1) to (a3), (g), (h).
Physician assistant.
Payment or reimbursement, §58-50-30, (f).
Providing services for agency, institution or physician entitle to payment, §58-65-36.
Right to choose services, §58-50-30, (a1) to (a3), (g), (h).
Plans.
Cost plus plans, §58-65-135.
Plan summaries.
Notice, expenses may exceed covered amount, §58-3-250, (b).
Payment obligations, explanation by insurer, §58-3-250, (a).
Podiatrists.
Right to choose services, §58-50-30, (a1) to (a3), (g), (h).
Policies and contracts.
Insurance policies and contracts generally.
See INSURANCE POLICIES OR CONTRACTS.
Prescription drug identification cards.
Plan issuing prescription drug cards to issue uniform identification cards, §58-3-177, (a).
Definitions, §58-3-177, (e).
Electronic verification of claim, §58-3-177, (d).

HOSPITAL, MEDICAL AND DENTAL SERVICE CORPORATIONS —Cont'd
Prescription drug identification cards —Cont'd
Plan issuing prescription drug cards to issue uniform identification cards —Cont'd
Exceptions, §58-3-177, (f).
Information contained in card, §58-3-177, (a), (b).
Issued annually if change in coverage, §58-3-177, (c).
Prescription drugs.
Closed formularies or restricted access to perspiration drugs or devices.
Definitions, §58-3-221, (c).
Medically necessary nonformulary or restricted access drug or device prescribed.
Voiding or refusing to renew contract prohibited, §58-3-221, (b).
Payment for drugs or devices specifically excluded from coverage not required, §58-3-221, (d).
Requirements of insurers maintaining, §58-3-221, (a).
Contraceptive drugs or devices.
Coverage by insurer providing health benefit plan, §58-3-178.
Primary care provider, specialist selected.
Insured diagnosed with serious or chronic degenerative, disabling or life threatening disease, §58-3-235, (a).
Care authorized by specialist, §58-3-235, (b).
Denial of access by insurer, §58-3-235, (a).
Treatment plan approved by insurer, selection under, §58-3-235, (b).
Professional counselor.
Defined, §58-50-30, (c3).
Right to choose services, §58-50-30, (a1) to (a3), (g), (h).
Prostate-specific antigen (PSA) tests.
Defined, §58-65-93, (b).
Provider credentialing.
Health benefit plan and insurer defined, §58-3-230, (c).
Process requirements, §58-3-230, (a).
Time limit on processing applications, §58-3-230, (a).
Uniform provider credentialing application form.
Commissioner to adopt by rule, §58-3-230, (b).
Provider directories.
Allied health professionals, listing, §58-3-245, (c).
Information included in directory listing, §58-3-245, (b).
Plan required to provide, §58-3-245, (a).
Provider networks.
Services outside networks, §58-3-200, (d).
Psychologists.
Defined, §58-50-30, (b).
Right to choose services, §58-50-30, (a1) to (a3), (g), (h).
Readable insurance certificates act, §§58-66-1 to 58-66-40.
Alteration of legal effect of provisions of certificates or contracts.
Provisions not to require or allow, §58-66-40, (b).
Applicability of provisions, §58-66-10, (a).
Exceptions, §58-66-10, (b).
Non-English language certificate, §58-66-10, (d).
Citation of act.
Short title, §58-66-1.
Construction and interpretation, §58-66-40.

HOSPITAL, MEDICAL AND DENTAL SERVICE CORPORATIONS —Cont'd
Readable insurance certificates act —Cont'd
Cover, first or insert page of certificate.
Statement required, §58-66-20, (a).
Definitions, §58-66-15.
Exclusive nature of provisions, §58-66-10, (c).
Filing of certificates, §58-66-30, (a).
Applicability of provisions, §58-66-35, (a).
Approval by commissioner, §58-66-30, (a).
Disapproval by commissioner, §58-66-30, (a), (b).
Flesch scale analysis readable score.
Definitions of "text," §58-66-25, (e).
Procedure generally, §58-66-25, (c), (d).
Required, §58-66-25, (a).
Samples which must be analyzed, §58-66-25, (b).
Format requirements, §58-66-20, (a).
Factors used in determining compliance, §58-66-20, (b).
Index of major provisions of certificate.
Required, §58-66-20, (a).
Language on which actions may be based, §58-66-40, (c).
Non-English language certificate, §58-66-10, (d).
Other laws.
Insurers not relieved from provisions, §58-66-40, (a).
Purpose of act, §58-66-5.
Title of act.
Short title, §58-66-1.
Reconstructive breast surgery.
Coverage following mastectomy, §58-65-96.
Definitions, §58-65-96, (b).
Notice of availability, §58-65-96, (d).
Prohibitions, §58-65-96, (c).
Scope of required coverage, §58-65-96, (a).
Records.
Conversion.
Public access to records, §58-65-131, (h).
Reports.
Annual report to commissioner of insurance, §58-65-100.
Health benefit plan reporting requirements, §58-3-191, (a).
Access to reports, §58-3-191, (b1).
Reserve requirements, §58-65-95, (b) to (d).
Risk based capital requirements.
Insurance companies, §§58-12-2 to 58-12-70.
See INSURANCE COMPANIES.
Sickle cell anemia.
Contracts to cover persons possessing sickle cell trait, §58-65-70.
Single employer plan.
Exemptions as to, §58-65-150.
Specialist care referral.
In-plan specialists.
Definitions, §58-3-223, (b).
Duties of insurer providing health benefit plan, §58-3-223, (a).
Specialist selected as primary care provider.
Insured diagnosed with serious or chronic degenerative, disabling or life threatening disease, §58-3-235, (a).
Care authorized by specialist, §58-3-235, (b).
Denial of access by insurer, §58-3-235, (a).
Treatment plan approved by insurer, selection under, §58-3-235, (b).
Substance abuse professional.
Defined, §58-50-30, (c2).

HOSPITAL, MEDICAL AND DENTAL SERVICE CORPORATIONS —Cont'd
Substance abuse professional —Cont'd
Right to choose services, §58-50-30, (a1) to (a3), (g), (h).
Telephone system for up-to-date network information.
Plan to provide, §58-3-245, (a).
Treatment discussions.
Limiting prohibited, §58-3-176.
Unfair trade practices, laws applicable, §58-65-125, (c).
Uniform claim forms, §58-3-171.
Uniform prescription drug identification cards, §58-3-177.
Uniform provider credentialing, §58-3-230.
Utilization review.
External review, §§58-50-75 to 58-50-95.
Generally, §58-50-61, (a) to (o).

HOSPITALS.
Abortion.
Lawful abortions.
Requiring hospital to perform abortion, §14-45.1, (f).
Abused juveniles brought for medial diagnosis or treatment.
Obtaining judicial authority to retain physical custody of juvenile when abuse suspected, §7B-308.
Abuse of patients, §14-32.2.
Administrative procedure.
Contested case hearings.
Petition time limit, §131E-2.
Licenses.
Adverse action on licenses, §131E-78, (a) to (c).
Denial or revocation of license, §131E-78, (a).
Alcohol detoxification programs.
Specialty hospitals, §131E-65.
Alcoholic beverage control.
Exemption from provisions, §18B-103.
Ambulatory surgical facilities.
Licenses, §§131E-145 to 131E-152.
See AMBULATORY SURGICAL FACILITIES.
Anatomical gifts.
Federally designated organ procurement organizations and tissue banks.
Access to patient's medical records, §130A-412.1, (b).
Hold harmless provision.
Hospital made party to action arising out of failure of federally designated organ procurement organization, §130A-412.2, (f).
Medical records.
Access by federally designated organ procurement organization and tissue bank.
Deceased patient's medical records, §130A-412.1, (d).
Protocols for organ procurement, §130A-412.1, (a).
Immunity of hospitals and hospital personnel in good faith compliance, §130A-412.1, (g).
Requirements not to exceed protocol provisions of Title XI of social security act, §130A-412.1, (f).
Signed statement with federally designated organ procurement organization, §130A-412.1, (a).
Authorities.
General provisions, §§131E-15 to 131E-34.
See HOSPITAL AUTHORITIES.
Automated external defibrillator (AED), §90-21.15.

HOSPITALS —Cont'd
Bed capacity, temporary increase, §131E-83.
Bills.
Itemized charges.
Discharged patient's bill, §131E-91.
Bomb scares, §§14-69.1, 14-69.2.
Bond issues.
Authority to finance by bond issue, Const. N. C., art. V, §8.
Branch facilities.
County hospitals, §131E-14.1.
Cancer.
Cancer clinics, §130A-207.
Capacity, temporary increase, §131E-83.
Cardiac rehabilitation certification program, §§131E-165 to 131E-170.
Certificate of public advantage, §§131E-192.1 to 131E-192.13.
See HEALTH CARE FACILITIES.
Certificates of need.
General provisions, §§131E-175 to 131E-190.
See HEALTH CARE FACILITIES.
Charitable hospital purposes.
Property tax exemption, §105-278.8.
Claims against the state.
Assignment of claims against state.
Section inapplicable to assignments in favor of hospitals, §143-3.3, (c).
Commission for health services.
Regulation of sanitation by commission, §130A-235.
Committees.
Medical review committee, §131E-95, (b), (c).
Communicable diseases.
Emergency departments, surveillance by state health director, reporting requirements, §130A-480, (a), (b).
Medical facilities may report, §130A-137.
Confidentiality.
Emergency response plans, §132-1.6.
Employee personnel files, §131E-257.2.
Health care contracts, §131E-99.
Construction and enlargement of local hospitals, §131E-70.
Federal aid, §131E-70, (c), (e).
Unallocated federal sums or balances, §131E-70, (g).
Grants-in-aid to acquire real estate and construct facilities, §131E-70, (f).
Rules and regulations, §131E-70, (d).
State agency for setting up and administering statewide plan, §131E-70, (b).
Surveys conducted by department of health and human services, §131E-70, (a).
Cooperative agreements.
Between physician, hospital or other person, §§90-21.24 to 90-21.26.
Certificate of public advantage, §§131E-192.1 to 131E-192.13.
See HEALTH CARE FACILITIES.
County health services, §153A-249.
County hospitals.
Branch facilities, §131E-14.1.
Criminal record checks of personnel, §114-19.3.
Definitions, §131E-1.
Certificate of need law, §131E-176.
County-city hospital facilities for the poor
Garnishment for debts owed public hospitals, §131E-48.
Licenses, §131E-76.
Municipal hospitals, §131E-6.

HOSPITALS —Cont'd
Department of health and human services.
Inspections, §131E-80, (a) to (e).
Licenses.
Enforcement of article and rules, §131E-79, (b).
Program of hospital care, §131E-70.
Specialty hospitals.
Control of certain hospitals transferred to department of health and human services, §131E-67.
Designated development agency, §131E-177.
Discharge from hospital.
Authority of administrator or superintendent, §131E-90.
Itemized charges, §131E-91.
Refusal to leave after discharge, §131E-90.
Districts.
See HOSPITAL DISTRICTS.
Donation of medical equipment no longer needed.
Public or state hospitals, §131E-250, (a), (b).
Eastern North Carolina hospital.
Control of certain hospitals transferred to department of health and human services, §131E-67.
Emergency medical services.
Generally, §§143-507 to 143-519.
See EMERGENCY MEDICAL SERVICES.
Regulation of emergency medical services, §§131E-155 to 131E-161.
See EMERGENCY MEDICAL SERVICES.
Eminent domain.
Municipal hospitals, §131E-10.
Powers of local public condemnors, §40A-3, (b).
Employees.
Criminal record checks, §114-19.3.
Garnishment for debts owed public hospitals.
Discharge or disciplinary action because employee subject to garnishment, §131E-50.
Public hospital personnel, §§131E-257 to 131E-257.2.
Benefit plans for employees.
Payment of cost of, §131E-257.1, (b).
Confidentiality of information in employee's personnel file, §131E-257.2, (c).
Employee's personnel file defined, §131E-257.2, (a).
Inapplicability of certain provisions, §131E-257, (c).
Incentive compensation plans.
Public hospital may establish, §131E-257.1, (a).
Information that need not be disclosed to employee or to other persons, §131E-257.2, (d).
Information with respect to employee matter of public record, §131E-257.2, (b).
Investment of escrowed or trusteed retirement and deferred compensation fund, §131E-257.1, (c).
Pay expense allowances and other compensation.
Public hospital to determine, §131E-257.1, (a).
Personnel policies and procedures.
Hospital may adopt, §131E-257.1, (b).
Physician classification and pay plans.
Public hospital may establish, §131E-257.1, (a).
Provisions controlling over other inconsistent laws, §131E-257, (d).
Public hospital defined, §131E-257, (e).

HOSPITALS —Cont'd
Employees —Cont'd
Public hospital personnel —Cont'd
Public hospital personnel act.
Provisions known and cited as, §131E-257, (a).
Purposes of provisions, §131E-257, (b).
Removal of inaccurate or misleading information from employee's personnel file, §131E-257.2, (f).
Severance payments and other severance benefits.
Hospital may pay and provide, §131E-257.1, (b).
Training, research or academic institutions.
Access to selected files permitted, §131E-257.2, (e).
Unlawful access or use of employee's personnel file, §131E-257.2, (h).
Unlawful disclosure of information in employee's personnel file, §131E-257.2, (g).
Work hours, work days and holidays.
Hospital may determine, §131E-257.1, (b).
Establishment of hospital.
License required, §131E-77, (a).
Federal aid.
Construction and enlargement of local hospitals, §131E-70, (c), (e).
Unallocated federal sums or balances, §131E-70, (g).
Municipal hospitals, §131E-11.
Financing health care facilities generally, §§131A-1 to 131A-25.
See HEALTH CARE FACILITY FINANCING.
Fraud.
Information obtained from patients.
Acquisition and use of information for fraudulent purposes, §14-118.3.
Garnishment for debts owed public hospitals.
Definitions, §131E-48.
Discharge or disciplinary action because employee subject to garnishment, §131E-50.
Exclusive nature of provisions, §131E-51.
Notice.
Motion for garnishment, §131E-49, (b).
Order of court.
Duty of garnishee upon receipt, §131E-49, (g).
Entry of order, §131E-49, (b).
Restrictions, §131E-49, (c), (d).
Prerequisites for motion, §131E-49, (a).
Review, §131E-49, (f).
Processing fee, §131E-49, (e).
Satisfaction of judgment, §131E-51.
Grants.
Construction and enlargement of local hospitals, §131E-70, (f).
Health care personnel registry, §131E-256.
Health education facilities.
AHEC program.
Conveyance of hospital facilities to, §131E-8.1, (c).
Sale or lease.
Applicability of section, §131E-8.1, (a).
Continued access to identical or equivalent facilities, §131E-8.1, (c).
Effect of provisions on operating contracts, §131E-8.1, (d).
Notice of intent, §131E-8.1, (b).
Hiring nurses.
Verification of licensure status, §90-171.43A, (a), (b).

HOSPITALS —Cont'd
Home care agencies.
Licenses, §§131E-135 to 131E-142.
See HEALTH CARE FACILITIES.
Hospital districts.
See HOSPITAL DISTRICTS.
Immunities.
Directors, trustees or officers of public hospitals.
Limited liability, §131E-47.1, (a), (b).
Medical review committee, §131E-95, (a).
Infirmaries.
Licenses.
Definition of infirmary, §131E-76.
Not required to obtain license, §131E-77.
Inspections by department, §131E-80, (a).
At all times subject to, §131E-80, (a).
Confidential or privileged information.
Disclosure, restriction, §131E-80, (d).
Delegation of authority, §131E-80, (b).
Disclosure of information, §131E-80, (d), (e).
Examination of records, §131E-80, (d).
Immunity for disclosing information.
Persons interviewed, §131E-80, (d).
Names of persons furnishing information.
Disclosure, prohibition, §131E-80, (d).
Review of writing or other record, §131E-80, (d).
Right of proper entry, §131E-80, (c).
Licenses.
Administrative procedure.
Adverse action on licenses, §131E-78, (a) to (c).
Denial or revocation of license, §131E-78, (a).
Adverse action on licenses, §131E-78, (a) to (c).
Appeals.
Adverse action on licenses, §131E-78, (c).
Application for license, §131E-77, (c).
Disclosure of information, §131E-80, (e).
Definitions, §131E-76.
Denial of license, §131E-78, (a).
Judicial review, §131E-78, (c).
Department of health and human services.
Enforcement of article and rules, §131E-79, (b).
Disclosure of information, §131E-80, (e).
Enforcement of article and rules, §131E-79, (b).
Hearings, §131E-78, (a), (b), (c).
Hospital.
Defined, §131E-76.
Immunity from liability.
Reports of disciplinary action, §131E-87.
Infirmaries.
Definition of infirmary, §131E-76.
Not required to obtain license, §131E-77.
Information to be disclosed, §131E-80, (e).
Injunctive relief, §131E-82, (a) to (c).
Inspections and consultations, §131E-80, (a) to (e).
Issuance of license, §131E-77, (d), (e).
Legislative purpose, §131E-75, (b).
Nursing homes, §§131E-100 to 131E-110.
See NURSING HOMES.
Penalties for violations of licensing act, §131E-81, (a), (b).
Posting of license, §131E-77, (f).
Purpose of article, §131E-75, (b).
Renewal of license, §131E-77, (d).
Reports.
Disciplinary actions, §131E-87.
Required, §131E-77, (a).
Revocation of license, §131E-78, (a).
Judicial review, §131E-78, (c).
Risk management.
Requirement for issuance or renewal of license, §131E-96, (b).

HOSPITALS —Cont'd
Licenses —Cont'd
Rules and regulations, §131E-79, (a), (b).
Submission of plans and specifications, §131E-77, (b).
Title of article.
Hospital licensure act, §131E-75, (a).
Violations of licensing act.
Penalties, §131E-81, (a), (b).
Lien for services rendered injured persons, §44-49.
Accounting for disbursements, §44-50.1, (a) to (c).
Attorneys' fees, §44-50.
Charges, §44-50.
Evidence, §44-50.
Funds for purposes stated.
Duty of receiving person, §44-50.
Limit on recovery, §44-50.
Settlement.
Disputed claims to be settled before payment, §44-51.
Local government finance.
Application of article to public hospitals, §159-39, (b).
Assets.
Authority of local government commission, §159-39, (e).
Audit.
Public hospitals, §159-39, (f).
Bond issues.
Public hospitals, §159-39, (k).
Budgets.
Public hospitals to operate under balanced budget, §159-39, (c).
Deposits, §159-39, (h), (i).
Electronic payments, §159-39, (i), (i1).
Finance officers of public hospitals.
Powers and duties, §159-39, (d).
Investments.
Public hospitals, §159-39, (g).
Public hospitals defined, §159-39, (a).
Regulations.
Special regulations pertaining to public hospitals, §159-39, (e).
Reports.
Public hospitals, §159-39, (j).
Revenue bonds.
Anticipation notes.
Nonprofit corporation or association operating or leasing public hospital, §159-170, (d).
Maintenance of hospital.
License required, §131E-77, (a).
Malpractice actions generally, §§90-21.11 to 90-21.14.
See MEDICAL MALPRACTICE.
Medical care commission.
Appointments, §143B-166.
Officers, §143B-168.
Bond issues, §131A-18.
Chairman, §143B-168.
Compensation, §143B-166.
Creation, §143B-165.
Definition, §§131A-3, 131E-76.
Duties, §143B-165.
Licenses.
Promulgation of rules, §131E-79, (a).
Meetings, §143B-167.
Members, §143B-166.
Officers.
Appointment, §143B-168.
Powers, §§131A-4, 143B-165.

HOSPITALS —Cont'd
Medical care commission —Cont'd
Quorum, §143B-166.
Refunding bonds, §131A-18.
Selection of members, §143B-166.
Special meetings, §143B-67.
Vice-chairman, §143B-168.
Medical records.
See MEDICAL RECORDS.
Medical review committee.
Definitions, §131E-76.
Immunity of members, §131E-95, (a).
Introduction of records into evidence, §131E-95, (b), (c).
Limited liability of members, §131E-90.
Testimony of members of committees, §131E-95, (b), (c).
Mental health, developmental disabilities and substance abuse.
General provisions.
See MENTAL HEALTH, DEVELOPMENTAL DISABILITY, SUBSTANCE ABUSE.
Motor vehicle accidents.
Notification to medical examiner of death within hospital from accident, §20-166.1, (f).
Municipal hospitals, §§131E-5 to 131E-14.2.
See MUNICIPAL HOSPITALS.
Nurses.
General provisions.
See NURSES.
Nurses, hiring.
Verification of licensure status, §90-171.43A, (a), (b).
Nursing homes.
Licenses, §§131E-100 to 131E-110.
See NURSING HOMES.
Obstruction of health care facility, §14-277.4.
Occupational diseases.
Reports, §130A-457.
Patients.
Abuse, §14-32.2.
Discharge from hospital, §§131E-90, 131E-91.
Fraudulently obtained information.
Acquisition and use of information for fraudulent purposes, §14-118.3.
Statements obtained from persons in shock or under influence of drugs.
Presumption of fraud, §8-45.5.
Personnel files of employees.
Privacy, §131E-257.2.
Physical abuse of patients, §14-32.2.
Planning and development agency, §131E-177.
Prescriptions.
Patient counseling, §131E-79.1, (a).
Prisons and prisoners.
Inmate's medical records, §131E-98.
Surgical operations on inmates of state institutions.
Juveniles in juvenile facilities, §143B-526.
Procedure when surgical operations necessary, §148-22.2.
Private hospitals.
Regulation of sanitation by commission for health services, §130A-235.
Privileges to practice in hospitals.
Compliance with bylaws, rules and regulations, §131E-85, (d).
Granting or denial of privileges, §131E-85, (a).
Immunity from liability.
Reports of disciplinary action, §131E-87.
Limited privileges, §131E-86, (a), (b).

HOSPITALS —Cont'd
Privileges to practice in hospitals —Cont'd
Procedures for considering applicants for hospital privileges, §131E-85, (b), (e).
Reports of disciplinary action, §131E-87.
Immunity from liability, §131E-87.
Suspension, revocation or modification of privileges, §131E-85, (c).
Professional counselors.
Person performing counseling as employee of a hospital.
Exemption from licensure, §90-332.1.
Program of hospital care.
Department of health and human services, §131E-70.
Property tax exemption.
Property used for charitable hospital purposes, §105-278.8.
Provider sponsored organizations.
General provisions, §§131E-275 to 131E-314.
See PROVIDER SPONSORED ORGANIZATIONS.
Records.
Documentary evidence.
Copies of medical records, §8-44.1.
Medical review committee.
Introduction of records into evidence, §131E-95, (b), (c).
Personal data concerning persons admitted or confined.
Persons required to keep records, §130A-117, (a), (d).
Retention of records, §130A-117, (d).
Subpoena commanding custodian to appear for purpose of producing, §1A-1, Rule 45, (c).
Remains of terminated pregnancies.
Manner of disposal, §130A-131.10.
Reports.
Certain wounds, injuries and illnesses, §90-21.20.
Emergency departments, reports to state health director.
Public health threats, detection of, §130A-480, (a), (b).
Licensing.
Reports of disciplinary actions, §131E-87.
Public hospitals.
Deposits and investments, §159-39, (j).
Right of proper entry.
Authority of department, §131E-80, (c).
Risk management.
Program required, §131E-96, (a), (b).
Sales and use tax.
Refunds.
Nonprofit hospitals, §105-164.14, (b).
Sanitation.
Regulation of sanitation by commission, §130A-235.
Adoption of rules, §130A-235, (a).
License or approval revocation for violation of rules, §130A-235, (c).
Water supply wells.
Setback requirements applicable to certain wells, §130A-235, (b).
Smoking in public places.
No smoking in hospital, §143-599.
Specialty hospitals.
Alcohol detoxification programs, §131E-65.
Control of certain hospitals transferred to department of health and human services, §131E-67.
Other programs controlled by department, §131E-67.

HOSPITALS —Cont'd
State aid.
Municipal hospitals, §131E-11.
State of North Carolina.
Assignments of claims against state.
Assignment in favor of hospitals.
Section not applicable to, §143-3.3, (c).
Surplus medical equipment.
Donation by public or state hospital, §131E-250, (a), (b).
Swine houses, lagoons and land areas.
Siting requirements near, §106-803, (a), (b).
Telephone service.
Shared use and or resale of service, §62-110, (d).
Terrorist incident using nuclear, biological or chemical agents.
Emergency departments, surveillance by state health director, reporting requirements, §130A-480, (a), (b).
Trespass.
Obstruction of health care facility, §14-277.4, (a).
Patient discharged from hospital, §131E-90.
University of North Carolina hospital at Chapel Hill.
Bond issues, §116-187.
Employment of attorney for hospital, §114-4.2B.
Liability insurance or self-insurance generally, §§116-219 to 116-223.
See UNIVERSITY OF NORTH CAROLINA.
Sales and use tax refunds, §105-164.14, (c).
Setoff debt collection.
Generally, §§105A-1 to 105A-16.
See SETOFF DEBT COLLECTION.
Workers' compensation.
Reimbursement allowed, §97-26, (b).

HOSTAGES.
Electronic surveillance orders for taking of hostage, §15A-290, (b).
Foreign countries.
Missing persons.
Applicability of provisions, §28C-20.
Seizing building or facility.
Disorderly conduct, §14-288.4.
Taking of hostage by prisoner, §14-258.3.

HOSTILE WITNESSES.
Examination, §1A-1, Rule 43, (b).
Leading questions, §8C-1, Rule 611, (c).

HOTCHPOT.
Advancements generally, §§29-23 to 29-29.
See INTESTATE SUCCESSION.

HOTELS, INNS AND OTHER TRANSIENT LODGING PLACES.
Alcoholic beverage permits, §§18B-1000, 18B-1001.
Alcoholic beverages possessed by resident in hotel room, §18B-300, (a).
Alcoholic beverages possessed for special occasions, §18B-301, (c).
Animals.
Admitting to rooms, §72-7.1.
Assumed names.
Registration of guests to be in true name, §72-30.
Baggage.
Liability for loss of baggage, §72-2.
Bed and breakfast inn.
Defined, §130A-247.
Brown-bagging permit.
Kind of permit that may be issued, §18B-1001.

HOTELS, INNS AND OTHER TRANSIENT LODGING PLACES —Cont'd
Child care facilities.
Drop-in or short-term child care not included in term child care, §110-86.
Contracts.
Written statement of time period guest may occupy room, §72-1, (b).
Copies of provisions.
Posting, §72-6.
Culinary ABC permit.
Kind of permit that may be issued, §18B-1001.
Definitions.
Sanitation of food and lodging establishments, §130A-247.
Defrauding innkeeper, §14-110.
Duties of innkeepers.
Safekeeping of valuables, §72-3.
Suitable lodging accommodations, §72-1, (a).
Fees, §130A-248, (d).
Fire prevention, §§58-81-5 to 58-81-15.
Building inspectors.
Powers and duties not limited, §58-81-15.
Careless or negligent setting of fires, §58-81-5.
Fire chiefs.
Powers and duties not limited, §58-81-15.
Loss by fire.
Liability, §72-4.
Negligent or careless setting of fires, §58-81-5.
Noncompliance with provisions, §58-81-10.
Game fish, unlawful possession for resale.
Prima facie evidence, §113-302, (a).
Guest room cabinet ABC permit.
Kind of permit that may be issued, §18B-1001.
Guests' negligence, §72-5.
Handicapped persons.
Right to use of public accommodations, §168-3.
Husband and wife.
Falsely registering as husband and wife, §14-186.
Immoral purposes.
Opposite sexes occupying same bedroom for immoral purposes, §14-186.
Inspections.
Sanitation of food and lodging establishments, §130A-249.
Jewelry and other valuables.
Safekeeping, maximum amount, §72-3.
Liability of innkeepers.
Loss by fire, §72-4.
Loss of baggage, §72-2.
Negligence of guest may be shown, §72-5.
Safekeeping of valuables.
No liability for loss or damage to money or jewels not deposited, §72-3.
Liens.
Possessory liens on personal property.
Persons entitled to lien, §44A-2, (b).
Mixed beverage ABC permit.
Kind of permit that may be issued, §18B-1001.
National historic landmark district, §18B-1006, (n).
Mixed beverages catering ABC permit.
Kind of permit that may be issued, §18B-1001.
Motor vehicles owned or operated by.
Exemption from provisions, §62-260, (a).
Negligence of guests, §72-5.
Off-premises malt beverage ABC permit.
Kind of permit that may be issued, §18B-1001.
On-premises fortified wine ABC permit.
Kind of permit that may be issued, §18B-1001.

HOTELS, INNS AND OTHER TRANSIENT LODGING PLACES —Cont'd
On-premises malt beverage ABC permit.
Kind of permit that may be issued to, §18B-1001.
On-premises unfortified wine ABC permit.
Kind of permit that may be issued, §18B-1001.
Parks in which department of environment and natural resources has jurisdiction.
Department not to construct, maintain, operate or lease, §66-58, (b).
Permits or transitional permits, §130A-248, (b) to (c).
Pets.
Permitting in room, §72-7.1.
Posting of copies of provisions, §72-6.
Railroad corporations.
Establishment of hotel, §136-190.
Registration of guests.
Falsely registering as husband and wife, §14-186.
Tourist camps and homes.
See TOURIST CAMPS AND HOMES.
Removal of property by innkeeper after expiration of time period on written statement, §72-1, (b).
Restraining lodger from entering room after expiration of time period on written statement, §72-1, (b).
Room occupancy tax.
Uniform provision for counties authorized to levy, §153A-155.
Uniform provision for municipalities authorized to levy, §160A-215.
Safekeeping of valuables generally, §72-3.
Sales and use tax.
Rate, §105-164.4, (a).
Sanitation of food and lodging establishments, §§130A-247 to 130A-250.
Bed and breakfast establishments.
Exemption, §130A-250.
Definitions, §130A-247.
Establishments providing food or lodging to regular boarders or permanent house guest only.
Exemption, §130A-250.
Exemptions from provisions, §130A-250.
Grade cards, §130A-249.
Inspections, §130A-249.
Occasional fundraising events.
Exemption, §130A-250.
Permanent house guests.
Defined, §130A-247.
Private clubs.
Defined, §130A-247.
Exempted from provisions, §130A-250.
Regular boarder.
Defined, §130A-247.
Rules, adoption, §130A-248, (a1), (a3).
Sexual offenses.
Husband and wife.
Falsely registering as husband and wife, §14-186.
Opposite sexes occupying same bedroom for immoral purposes, §14-186.
Special occasion ABC permit.
Kind of permit that may be issued, §18B-1001.
Tourist camps and homes.
General provisions.
See TOURIST CAMPS AND HOMES.

HOTELS, INNS AND OTHER TRANSIENT LODGING PLACES —Cont'd
University of North Carolina and constituent institutions.
Information supplied legislative commission on governmental operations.
Prior to issuing debt or executing contract on transient lodging facility, §66-58, (h).

HOT PURSUIT.
Arrest.
Campus police officers.
Immediate and continuous flight, §15A-402, (f).
Company police.
Power to make arrest, §74E-6.
County and city officers.
Immediate and continuous flight, §15A-402, (d).
Officers from other states, §15A-403.
Police chases, speed limits not applicable, §20-145.

HOT WATER HEATERS.
Baffles, heat traps, etc., testing requirements, §66-27.2.
Boilers generally.
See BOILERS.
Safety.
Baffles, heat traps, etc., testing requirements, §66-27.2.
Local regulation, §66-27.4.
Relief valves.
Approved relief valves required, §66-27.1, (a).
Installation or sale of unapproved relief valves.
Prohibited, §66-27.1, (b).
Thermostat settings.
Presetting, §66-27.1A, (a).
Resetting by occupant, §66-27.1A, (b).
Warning tags or stickers, §66-27.1A, (c).
Violations, §66-27.3.

HOURS OF LABOR.
Wage and hour act.
General provisions.
See WAGE AND HOUR ACT.

HOUSE ARREST, §15A-1343, (b1).
Delinquent juveniles, ordering to submit to, §7B-2506.
Electronic monitoring devices, §15A-1343, (b1).
Costs, §148-10.3.
House arrest with electronic monitoring, defined, §15A-1340.11.
Impaired driving.
Level one punishment.
Special probation, §20-179, (g).
Level two punishment.
Special probation, §20-179, (h).

HOUSEBREAKING.
Burglary, §§14-51 to 14-57.
See BURGLARY.

HOUSE CARS.
Defined, §20-4.01.
Safety inspections, subject to, §20-183.2, (b).

HOUSEHOLD CLEANERS, §§66-85 to 66-88.
Containing phosphorus.
Manufacture, storage or sale.
Prohibition, exceptions, penalties, §143-214.4, (a) to (g).
Labeling cleaners containing volatile substances capable of producing toxic effects.
Applicability of provisions after enactment of federal legislation, §66-88.

HOUSEHOLD CLEANERS —Cont'd
Labeling cleaners containing volatile substances capable of producing toxic effects —Cont'd
Definition, §66-85.
Injunctions.
Sales in violation of provisions, §66-87.
Required, §66-85.
Sales in violation of provisions.
Injunction, §66-87.
Misdemeanor, §66-86.

HOUSEHOLD FURNISHINGS.
Decedents' estates.
Sale or lease, §28A-16-3.
Exempt property from enforcement of claims of creditors, §1C-1601, (a).
Intestate succession.
Payment of debts from estate of deceased, §29-30, (g).
Possessory liens on personal property.
Persons entitled to lien, §44A-2, (e).
Usurious loans on furniture, §14-391.

HOUSEHOLD GOODS.
Exempt property from enforcement of claims of creditors, §1C-1601, (a).

HOUSEMOVERS, §§20-356 to 20-372.
Injunctions, §20-371, (b).
Motor vehicles.
Compliance with municipal regulations, §20-368.
Equipment, §20-360.
Escort vehicles, §20-360.
Injunctions, §20-371, (b).
Insurance requirements, §20-359.1.
Invalid sections, §20-372.
Liability, §20-362.
Licenses.
Certificates of insurance providing for continuous coverage, §20-359.1, (b).
Duration, §20-359.
Insurance requirements, §20-359.1, (a).
Obtaining by fraud, §20-367.
Out-of-state housemovers, §20-369.
Qualifications, §20-358.
Required, §20-357.
Obstructions, §20-363.
Permits, §20-360.
Applications, §20-361.
Obtaining by fraud, §20-367.
Out-of-state housemovers, §20-369.
Qualifications, §20-358.
Right-of-way, §20-365.
Routes, §§20-361, 20-364.
Severability of provisions, §20-372.
Speed limits, §20-370.
Violations constitute misdemeanor, §20-371, (a).
Weather.
Effect of weather, §20-366.
Rules and regulations.
Municipal regulations.
Compliance with, §20-368.

HOUSE OF REPRESENTATIVES.
State house of representatives.
See GENERAL ASSEMBLY.
United States house of representatives.
See CONGRESS.

HOUSES OF MIRRORS.
Amusement device safety generally, §§95-111.1 to 95-111.18.
See AMUSEMENT DEVICE SAFETY.

HOUSE TRAILERS.
Brake requirement, §20-124, (f).
Lighting equipment, §20-129.2.
Two door requirement, §66-27.5.
Window tinting exceptions, §20-127, (c).

HOUSING.
Cooperative associations.
Authorized purposes, §§54-111, 54-124.
Disclosures.
Death, serious illness or certain criminal convictions of previous occupant.
Deemed not a material fact in real property transactions, §42-14.2.
Discrimination.
Fair housing, §§41A-1 to 41A-10.
See FAIR HOUSING.
Handicapped persons.
Right to housing, §168-9.
Domestic violence.
Orders for relief, §50B-3, (a).
Fair housing act.
Administration by human relations commission, §143B-391.
General provisions, §§41A-1 to 41A-10.
See FAIR HOUSING.
Geographically based field programs.
Safe and sanitary housing, eligible cases, §7A-474.3, (b).
Handicapped persons.
Right to housing, §168-9.
Heating and air.
Weatherization assistance program, §108A-70.30.
Housing assistance information.
Economic and community development department.
Toll-free telephone number to provide information, §143B-431.1.
Local governments, §§160A-441 to 160A-450.
See LOCAL GOVERNMENTS.
Low-income housing tax credits, §§105-129.40 to 105-129.45.
Migrant farm workers.
Standards for housing, §§95-222 to 95-229.
See MIGRANT FARM WORKERS.
Minimum housing standards proceedings.
Filing of lis pendens by cities or counties, §1-120.2.
Municipal corporations.
Lease of land for housing, §160A-278.
Public assistance.
Weatherization assistance program, §108A-70.30.
Relocation assistance, §§133-5 to 133-18.
See RELOCATION ASSISTANCE.
Rents.
Control of rents, §42-14.1.
Death, serious illness or certain criminal convictions of previous occupant.
Deemed not a material fact in real property transactions, §42-14.2.
Trespass.
Injuring houses, §14-144.
Taking possession of house without consent, §14-159.
Veterans.
Property tax exemption.
Housing of disabled veterans, §105-275.
Weatherization assistance program, §108A-70.30.

HOUSING AUTHORITIES AND PROJECTS, §§157-1 to 157-70.
Abolition of authority, §157-4.1, (b).

HOUSING AUTHORITIES AND PROJECTS —Cont'd
Accounts and accounting.
System as part of city or county accounting system, §157-4.2.
Actions.
Remedies of obligee, §§157-18 to 157-22.
Alternative organization for authorities, §157-4.1, (a).
Appeals.
Eminent domain.
Issuance of certificate of public convenience and necessity, §157-28.
Area of operation.
Authority to operate in municipality.
Findings required, §157-39.6.
City authorities, §157-39.1, (a), (b).
County authorities, §157-39.1, (a).
Indian housing authority, §157-69.
Regional housing authority.
Decreasing area of operation, §157-39.3.
Hearings.
Increasing or decreasing area of operation, §157-39.4.
Increasing area of operation, §157-39.2.
Rural housing authorities, §157-39.1, (a).
Barbed wire, fences and gates.
Prohibition, §157-9, (d).
Bond issues.
Covenants.
Authority to covenant, §157-16.
Cumulative nature of obligee's remedies, §157-20.
Definitions, §157-3.
Form of bonds, §157-15.
Legal investments, §157-25.
Liability of commissioners, §157-14.
National defense housing projects.
Obligations made legal investments, §157-57.
Validation of previous issues, §157-58.
Negotiability, §§157-15, 157-25.
Power to purchase own bonds, §157-15.
Provisions, §157-16.
Refunding bonds.
Authority to issue, §157-14.
Remedies of obligee, §§157-18 to 157-22.
Sales, §157-15.
Types of bonds to be issued, §157-14.
Validation.
Proceedings for issuance, §§157-32, 157-32.3.
Boundaries.
Area of operation, §157-39.1, (a) to (c).
Budgets.
Local government finance.
Special provisions pertaining to public housing authorities, §159-42, (c).
System as part of city or county budget system, §157-4.2.
Building regulations.
Applicability of building regulations, §157-13.
Cancellation of certificate of incorporation, §157-4.
Citation of article, §157-1.
Commissioners.
Appointment, §157-5, (a).
City authority operating beyond 10 mile limit, §157-39.1, (c).
Compensation, §157-5, (d).
Conflicts of interest, §157-7.
County authorities, §157-34.
Defined, §157-3.
Indian housing authority, §157-68.

HOUSING AUTHORITIES AND PROJECTS —Cont'd
Commissioners —Cont'd
Meetings.
Location, §157-39.7.
Qualifications, §157-5, (a), (b).
Regional housing authority, §157-36, (a) to (k).
Removal.
Grounds, §157-8.
Residence requirements, §157-39.7.
Tenure, §157-5, (d).
Vacancies in office, §157-5, (d).
Violation of law.
Removal, §157-8.
Community facilities.
Defined, §157-3.
Compliance with provisions.
Duty of authority, §157-6.
Composition of authority, §157-5, (a), (c).
Conflicts of interest.
Commissioners or employees, §157-7.
Consolidated housing authorities.
Establishment, §157-39.5.
Contracts.
Federal aid, §157-39.8.
Power to contract with federal government, §157-23.
Validation, §§157-31, 157-32.2, 157-32.4.
Cooperation of authorities, §157-10.
Council.
Abolition of authority, §157-4.1, (b).
Exercise of powers of authority, §157-4.1, (a).
Counties.
Area of operation, §157-39.1, (a) to (c).
Commissioners, §157-34.
Creation of authority, §157-33.
Low- and moderate-income housing programs.
Authority to establish and develop, §153A-378.
Powers of authority, §157-34.
Counties of 250 square miles or less and population of more than 100,000, §157-9.2, (e).
Bonds or debt, issuing or incurring, §157-9.2, (d).
Definitions, §157-9.2, (b).
Findings and purpose, §157-9.2, (a).
Powers generally, §157-9.2, (c).
Proposed financing, notice of, §157-9.2, (f).
Creation of authority.
Procedure, §157-4.
Validation, §157-30.
Declaration of necessity, §157-2, (a), (b).
Definitions, §157-3.
Eminent domain.
Housing project, §157-49.
Fraudulent misrepresentation in obtaining housing assistance.
Person, §157-29.1, (c).
Municipal cooperation and aid, §157-41.
National defense housing projects, §157-53.
Deposits.
National defense housing projects.
Security for public deposits, §157-57.
Security for funds deposited, §157-24.
Development zone project tax credit, §105-129.13, (b).
Donations.
Advances and donations by city and municipality, §157-43.
Duties of authority, §157-6.
Electrified fences and gates.
Prohibition, §157-9, (d).

HOUSING AUTHORITIES AND PROJECTS —Cont'd
Eminent domain, §§157-48 to 157-50.
Certificate of convenience and necessity.
Required, §157-28.
Declaration of necessity, §157-48.
Exercise of right, §157-50.
Finding and declaration of necessity, §157-48.
Housing project.
Defined, §157-49.
Municipal cooperation and aid.
Restrictions on exercise of right, §157-45.
Power of eminent domain, §§40A-3, (c), 157-11, 157-50.
Restrictions on right, §157-28.
Employees.
Conflicts of interest, §157-7.
Establishment of authority.
Procedure, §157-4.
Validation, §157-30.
Eviction of tenants, §157-29, (c).
Exemptions.
Executions.
Property of authority, §157-21.
Real estate licensure requirements, §157-26.1.
Taxation, §157-26.
Farmers of low income.
Defined, §157-3.
Housing applications by farmers, §157-39.
Rural housing projects, §157-38.
Federal aid.
Authority to secure federal aid, §157-23.
Contracts, §157-39.8.
Fences.
Electrified fences, spikes or barbed wire prohibited, §157-9, (d).
Fiduciaries.
Bond issues.
Legal investments, §157-25.
Finding of necessity, §157-2, (a), (b).
Foreclosure sale.
Title subject to agreement with government, §157-22.
Fraudulent misrepresentation in obtaining housing assistance.
Felony, §157-29.1, (b).
Misdemeanor, §157-29.1, (a).
Person defined, §157-29.1, (c).
Gates.
Electrified gates, spikes or barbed wire prohibited, §157-9, (d).
Housing finance agency, §§122A-5.8, 122A-5.9.
Indian housing authority, §§157-66 to 157-70.
Applicability of chapter, §157-67.
Appointment, §157-68.
Area of operation, §157-69.
Commission of Indian affairs.
Authority, §157-67.
Composition, §157-68.
Creation, §157-66.
Governor.
Powers, §157-67.
Powers, §157-67.
Rentals.
Applicability of section 157-29, §157-70.
Tenants.
Selection.
Application of section 157-29, §157-70.
Vacancy, §157-68.
Local government finance.
Special provisions pertaining to public housing authorities, §159-42.

HOUSING AUTHORITIES AND PROJECTS —Cont'd
Local government risk pools, §§58-23-1 to 58-23-40.
See LOCAL GOVERNMENT RISK POOLS.
Low and moderate income, §157-9.1, (a).
Applicability of provisions, §157-9.1, (b) to (d).
County authority to establish and develop projects, §153A-378.
Mixed income projects.
Operating expenses of project.
Payment, §157-9.3.
Mortgages and deeds of trust.
Approval of mortgages.
Local government commission, §157-17.1, (a).
Consideration of commission, §157-17.1, (b).
Rules and regulations, §157-17.1, (c).
Defined, §157-3.
Foreclosure sale.
Limitation on remedies of obligee, §157-21.
Title subject to agreement with government, §157-22.
Power to mortgage.
Project financed with governmental aid, §157-17.
Remedies conferrable by mortgage, §157-19.
Multi-family rental housing projects.
Persons of low income.
Setting aside of units, §157-9.4, (a), (b).
Municipal cooperation and aid, §§157-40 to 157-47.
Actions to be by resolution, §157-44.
Advances.
Advances and donations by city and municipality, §157-43.
Agreement in aid of housing project, §157-42.
Conveyances in aid of housing projects, §157-42.
Declaration of necessity, §157-40.
Definitions, §157-41.
Donations.
Advances and donations by city and municipality, §157-43.
Eminent domain.
Restrictions on exercise of right, §157-45.
Findings, §157-40.
Intent of article, §157-46.
Investigation of projects, §157-45.
Leases.
Aid of housing project, §157-42.
Purpose of article, §157-46.
Resolutions.
Actions to be by resolution, §157-44.
Supplemental nature of article, §157-47.
Utilities commission.
Duties, §157-45.
National defense housing projects, §§157-52 to 157-60.
Administration.
Defined, §157-53, (a).
Bond issues.
Validation of previous issues, §157-58.
Cooperation with federal government, §157-55.
Definitions, §157-53.
Deposits.
Security for public deposits, §157-57.
Development.
Defined, §157-53, (b).
Federal government.
Cooperation with federal government, §157-55.
Defined, §157-53, (c).
Sale of projects to federal government, §157-55.

HOUSING AUTHORITIES AND PROJECTS —Cont'd
National defense housing projects —Cont'd
Housing authority.
Cooperation with federal government, §157-55.
Defined, §157-53, (d).
Further declaration of powers, §157-59.
Powers conferred supplemental, §157-60.
Rights and powers relative to projects, §157-54.
Initiated.
Defined, §157-53, (e).
Investments.
Obligations made legal investments, §157-57.
Persons engaged in national defense activities.
Defined, §157-53, (f).
Persons of low income.
Defined, §157-53, (g).
Powers conferred supplemental, §157-60.
Purpose of article, §157-52.
Sale of projects to federal government, §157-55.
Security for public deposits, §157-57.
State public body.
Cooperation in developing projects, §157-56.
Defined, §157-53, (h).
Obligee of the authority, remedies.
Additional remedies conferrable by mortgage or trust indenture, §157-19.
Cumulative remedies, §157-20.
Defined, §157-3.
Foreclosure sale.
Title subject to agreement with government, §157-22.
General provisions, §157-18.
Limitation on remedies, §157-21.
Officers of authority, §157-5, (e).
Operation of authority in municipality.
Findings required, §157-39.6.
Ownership and operation.
Expenses of operating.
Mixed income projects, §157-9.3.
Housing finance agency, §122A-5.9.
Persons of low income.
Defined, §157-3.
Persons of moderate income.
Defined, §157-3.
Planning.
Applicability of planning regulations, §157-13.
Powers of authority.
Counties of 250 square miles or less and population of more than 100,000, §157-9.2, (a) to (f).
Eminent domain, §157-11.
General provisions, §157-9, (a), (b).
Guest and visitors to properties.
Rules governing lawful entry, §157-9, (c).
Property.
Acquisition for government, §157-12.
Redevelopment commissions.
Designation as housing authority, §157-4.1, (a), (c), (d).
Regional housing authority.
Area of operation, §157-39.1, (a) to (c).
Decreasing area of operation.
Hearings, §157-39.4.
Procedure, §157-39.3.
Increasing area of operation.
Hearings, §157-39.4.
Procedure, §157-39.2.
Commissioners.
Appointment, §157-36, (a) to (g).
Certificate of appointment, §157-36, (e).

HOUSING AUTHORITIES AND PROJECTS —Cont'd
Regional housing authority —Cont'd
Commissioners —Cont'd
Removal, §157-36, (i).
Terms of office, §157-36, (h).
Composition, §157-36, (j).
Consolidated housing authority, §157-39.5.
Creation.
Hearings, §157-39.4.
Procedure, §157-35.
When authorized, §157-35.
Officers, §157-36, (k).
Powers, §157-37.
Rentals.
Distressed rental housing projects.
Housing finance authority, §122A-5.8.
Establishment, §157-29, (a), (b).
Indian housing authority.
Applicability of section 157-29, §157-70.
Termination of rental agreement, §157-29, (c).
Waiver of default or failure.
Acceptance or receipt not to constitute, §157-29, (d).
Reports.
Annual report of authority, §157-27.
Rural housing projects.
Farmers of low income, §157-38.
Housing applications, §157-39.
Security for funds deposited, §157-24.
Spikes, fences and gates.
Prohibition, §157-9, (d).
Taxation.
Exemptions from taxation, §157-26.
Tenants.
Eviction, §157-29, (c).
Selection.
Indian housing authority.
Applicability of section 157-29, §157-70.
Procedure, §157-29, (a), (b).
Summary ejectments, §157-29, (e).
Title of article, §157-1.
Utilities commission.
Municipal cooperation and aid.
Duties of commission, §157-45.
Powers of commission, §157-28.
Validation.
Bond issues.
Proceedings for issuance, §§157-32, 157-32.3.
Contracts, agreements, etc., §§157-31, 157-32.2, 157-32.4.
Creation and establishment validated, §§157-30, 157-32.1.
National defense housing projects.
Previous bonds, notes, etc., §157-58.
Violation of law.
Removal of commissioners, §157-8.
Zoning.
Applicability of zoning regulations, §157-13.

HOUSING COORDINATION AND POLICY COUNCIL, §§122A-5.10 to 122A-5.12.
Abrogation of responsibilities, §122A-5.10, (b).
Appointment, §122A-5.11, (b), (c).
Creation, §122A-5.10, (a).
Duties, §122A-5.10, (a).
Expenses, §122A-5.11, (d).
Meetings, §122A-5.12, (a).
Membership, §122A-5.11, (a).
Quorum, §122A-5.11, (e).
Reports, §122A-5.12, (b).

HOUSING COORDINATION AND POLICY COUNCIL —Cont'd
Support services, §122A-5.11, (f).

HOUSING DEVELOPMENTS.
Environmental impact statements.
Ordinances requiring for major development projects, §113A-8, (a) to (c).

HOUSING FINANCE AGENCY, §§122A-1 to 122A-23.
Actions.
General power of agency to sue and be sued, plead and be impleaded, §122A-5.
Adult care home, group home, and nursing home fire protection fund.
Authorized, §122A-5.13, (a).
Rules for management and use, §122A-5.13, (b).
Applicability of provisions.
Inconsistent laws inapplicable, §122A-23.
Appropriations.
Authorization to accept appropriated moneys, §122A-18.
Receipt, administration and compliance with conditions and requirements of appropriation.
General power of agency, §122A-5.
Board of directors.
Appointment, §122A-4, (c), (d).
Composition, §122A-4, (b).
Executive committee, §122A-4, (f).
Oath of office, §122A-4, (e).
Officers, §122A-4, (f).
Quorum, §122A-4, (f).
Reappointments, §122A-4, (e).
Removal from office, §122A-4, (d).
Secretary, §122A-4.
Terms, §122A-4, (d).
Vacancies in office, §122A-4, (d).
Bond issues.
Authentication, §122A-8.
Collection and payment of reasonable fees and charges in making, purchasing and servicing bonds.
General power of agency, §122A-5.
Defined, §122A-3.
Denominations, §122A-8.
Execution, §122A-8.
Exemption from taxation, §122A-19.
Form, §122A-8.
Interest, §122A-8.
Interim receipts or temporary bonds, §122A-8.
Investments.
Obligations eligible for investment, §122A-14.
Issuance, §122A-8.
Liability of officers of agency, §122A-17.
Maturity, §122A-8.
Maximum amount, §122A-8.
Negotiable instruments, §122A-13.
Payment, §122A-8.
Proceeds.
Investment, §122A-11.
Trust funds, §122A-11.
Use of proceeds, §122A-8.
Redemption, §122A-8.
Refunding obligations, §122A-15.
Remedies of bondholders and trustees, §122A-12.
Replacement of lost or mutilated bonds, §122A-8.
Sale, §122A-8.
Security.
Trust agreement or resolution, §122A-9.
State treasurer.
Powers of state treasurer, §122A-8.1.
Tax exemption, §122A-19.

HOUSING FINANCE AGENCY —Cont'd
Bond issues —Cont'd
Temporary bonds, §122A-8.
Trust agreement or resolution.
Security for agency obligations, §122A-9.
Trust funds, §122A-11.
Validity of any pledge, §122A-10.
Borrowing money.
General power of agency, §122A-5.
Bylaws.
Adoption of bylaws.
General power of agency, §122A-5.
Citation of act, §122A-1.
Compensation, §122A-4.
Conflicts of interest, §122A-20.
Construction and interpretation.
Liberal construction of chapter, §122A-22.
Coordination and policy council, §§122A-5.10 to 122A-5.12.
See HOUSING COORDINATION AND POLICY COUNCIL.
Counseling services.
General power of agency to provide counseling service, §122A-5.
Creation, §122A-4, (a).
Credit of state.
Not pledged, §122A-6.
Satisfying liabilities under energy conservation loan guarantees, §122A-6.1.
Definitions, §122A-3.
Distressed rental housing projects.
Adjustment of income requirements, §122A-5.8, (c) to (e).
Powers of board of directors, §122A-5.8, (c), (d).
Defined, §122A-5.8, (b).
Legislative declaration, §122A-5.8, (a).
Energy conservation loan authority.
Authorized expenditures, §122A-5.3, (b).
Credit of state.
Not pledged to satisfy liabilities under energy conservation loan guarantees, §122A-6.1.
Expenditures authorized, §122A-5.3, (b).
Guaranteeing payment or collection of energy conservation loans, §122A-5.3, (a).
Liabilities under energy conservation loan guarantees.
Credit of state not pledged to satisfy, §122A-6.1.
Outstanding loan guarantees.
Limitations on amounts remaining unspent, §122A-5.3, (b).
Rules and regulations.
Adoption, modification or repeal, §122A-5.3, (c).
Executive director, §122A-4, (f).
Federal aid.
Participation in federally assisted lease program for housing for persons of lower income, §122A-5.
Federally insured securities.
Purchase, §122A-5.
Purchase, approval, commitments by lender, §122A-5.1, (c).
Fees.
Mortgage insurance authority.
Application fee prescribed, §122A-5.2, (c).
Fire protection fund proceeds.
Use to provide staff support for loan processing, §122A-5.13, (c).
Funds.
Adult care home, group home, and nursing home fire protection fund, §122A-5.13.

HOUSING FINANCE AGENCY —Cont'd
Funds —Cont'd
Authorization to accept appropriated moneys, §122A-18.
Bonds and notes.
Trust funds, §122A-11.
Home ownership assistance fund, §122A-5.7.
Housing trust fund.
General provisions, §§122E-1 to 122E-9.
See HOUSING TRUST FUND.
Mortgage insurance authority.
Payments into housing mortgage insurance fund, §122A-5.2, (h).
General assembly.
Finance committees of general assembly.
Oversight by committees, §122A-16.
Legislative findings and purposes, §122A-2.
Moderate income persons and families.
Legislative findings and determinations, §122A-5.4, (a).
Gifts.
Receipt, administration and compliance with conditions and requirements of gift, §122A-5.
Grants.
Receipt, administration and compliance with conditions and requirements of grant, §122A-5.
Home ownership assistance fund, §122A-5.7.
Housing projects.
Distressed rental housing projects, §122A-5.8.
Ownership and operation.
Authorized, §122A-5.9, (a).
Certain statutory provisions not applicable, §122A-5.9, (c).
Subsidiary corporations to own and operate.
Authorized, §122A-5.9, (b).
Housing trust fund.
General provisions, §§122E-1 to 122E-9.
See HOUSING TRUST FUND.
Inconsistent laws inapplicable, §122A-23.
Insurance.
Mortgage insurance authority, §122A-5.2.
Procuring insurance against losses, §122A-5.
Interest.
Bonds and notes, §122A-8.
Loans.
To and by mortgage lenders, §122A-5.6, (b).
Modification of terms of interest.
General power of agency, §122A-5.
Rules and regulations governing agency activity, §122A-5.1, (b).
Investments, §122A-11.
Bonds and notes, §122A-14.
Legislative findings, §122A-2.
Loans.
Collection and payment of reasonable fees and charges in connection with making, purchasing and servicing loans, §122A-5.
Energy conservation loan authority, §122A-5.3.
Rehabilitation loan authority, §122A-5.5.
To and by mortgage lenders, §122A-5, (4a).
Terms and conditions of loans, §122A-5.6, (a) to (e).
Collateral security, §122A-5.6, (d).
General obligations, §122A-5.6, (d).
Interest, §122A-5.6, (b).
Objectives of chapter, §122A-5.6, (a).
Origination of new mortgage loans, §122A-5.6, (c).
Representations and warranties, §122A-5.6, (e).

HOUSING FINANCE AGENCY —Cont'd
Loans —Cont'd
To and by mortgage lenders —Cont'd
Terms and conditions of loans —Cont'd
Rules and regulations, §122A-5.6, (a).
Moderate income persons and families.
Definitions, §122A-5.4, (b), (c).
Legislative findings, §122A-5.4, (a).
Mortgage insurance authority.
Applications for mortgage insurance, §122A-5.2, (a), (c).
Fee, §122A-5.2, (c).
Claims for benefit of insurance, §122A-5.2, (g).
Defaults by mortgagor, §122A-5.2, (e).
Eligibility of mortgage payments for insurance, §122A-5.2, (b).
Fund.
Payments into housing mortgage insurance fund, §122A-5.2, (h).
Premiums for insurance of mortgage payments, §122A-5.2, (d).
Release of mortgagor from liability, §122A-5.2, (f).
Mortgages and deeds of trust.
Insurance.
Mortgage insurance authority, §122A-5.2.
Loans to and by mortgage lenders, §122A-5.6.
Making of mortgage loans to sponsors of residential housing.
General power of agency, §122A-5.
Mortgage insurance authority, §122A-5.2.
Public or private sale.
General power of agency, §122A-5.
Purchase, approval, commitments by lender, §122A-5.1, (c).
Rehabilitation loan authority, §122A-5.5, (a), (b).
Notes.
Anticipation notes authorized, §122A-8.
Authentication, §122A-8.
Collection and payment of reasonable fees and charges in connection with making, purchasing and servicing notes.
General power of agency, §122A-5.
Defined, §122A-3.
Denominations, §122A-8.
Execution, §122A-8.
Exemption from taxation, §122A-19.
Form, §122A-8.
Interest, §122A-8.
Investments.
Obligations eligible for investment, §122A-14.
Issuance, §122A-8.
Liability of officers of agency, §122A-17.
Maturity, §122A-8.
Maximum amount, §122A-8.
Negotiable instruments, §122A-13.
Payment, §122A-8.
Proceeds.
Trust funds, §122A-11.
Use of proceeds, §122A-8.
Redemption, §122A-8.
Refunding obligations, §122A-15.
Remedies of bondholders and trustees, §122A-12.
Sale, §122A-8.
Security.
Trust agreement or resolution, §122A-9.
State treasurer.
Powers of state treasurer, §122A-8.1.
Tax exemption, §122A-19.
Trust agreement or resolution.
Security for agency obligation, §122A-9.
Trust funds, §122A-11.

HOUSING FINANCE AGENCY —Cont'd
Notes —Cont'd
Validity of any pledge, §122A-10.
Oaths.
Board of directors, §122A-4, (e).
Officers.
Bonds and notes.
Liability of officers, §122A-17.
Conflicts of interest, §122A-20.
Offices.
Establishment and maintenance of office, §122A-5.
Maintenance of office.
General power of agency, §122A-5.
Personnel.
Conflicts of interest, §122A-20.
Employment of fiscal consultants, engineers, etc.
General power of agency, §122A-5.
Subject to state personnel act, §122A-4, (f).
Persons and families of moderate income.
Definitions, §122A-5.4, (b), (c).
Legislative findings, §122A-5.4, (a).
Pledges.
Bonds and notes.
Validity of any pledge, §122A-10.
Powers, §122A-5.
Supplemental and additional powers, §122A-21.
Purposes of chapter, §122A-2.
Real property.
Acquisition on temporary basis.
General power of agency, §122A-5.
Refunding obligations, §122A-15.
Rehabilitation.
Defined, §122A-3.
Purchase of mortgage loans for rehabilitation of existing residential housing, §122A-5.5, (a).
Rules and regulations, §122A-5.5, (b).
Releases.
Mortgage insurance authority.
Release of mortgagor from authority, §122A-5.2, (f).
Reports.
Annual report of activities, §122A-16.
Budget expenditures, §122A-16.
Rules and regulations.
Adoption, modification or repeal of rules and regulations, §122A-5.1, (a).
Conditional purchases, §122A-5.1, (b).
Effectuation of general purposes of chapter, §122A-5.1, (a).
Energy conservation loan authority.
Adoption, modification or repeal of rules and regulations, §122A-5.3, (c).
Governing agency activity, §122A-5.1.
Homeownership assistance fund.
Adoption of rules, §122A-5.7.
Interest rates, §122A-5.1, (b).
Making and publishing of rules and regulations.
General power of agency, §122A-5.
Rehabilitation loan authority, §122A-5.5, (b).
Specific objectives effectuated, §122A-5.1, (a).
Seals and sealed instruments.
Adoption of official seal.
General power of agency, §122A-5.
Duties of secretary of agency, §122A-4, (f).
Short title, §122A-1.
State treasurer.
Powers of state treasurer, §122A-8.1.

HOUSING INSPECTORS.
County inspection departments.
Generally, §§153A-350 to 153A-375.
See COUNTY INSPECTION DEPARTMENTS.

HOUSING TRUST FUND.
Accounts and accounting.
Separate accounts, §122E-5, (c).
Allocation of funds, §122E-8, (a).
Applications for funds.
Eligible applicants, §122E-7.
Priorities, §122E-8, (c), (d).
Rules and regulations, §122E-8, (b).
Beneficiaries, §122E-6, (a).
Citation of act.
Short title, §122E-1.
Composition, §122E-3, (b).
Conflicts of interest.
North Carolina housing partnership, §122E-4, (i).
Definitions, §122E-2.
Displacement, §122E-9.
Established, §122E-3, (a).
Housing finance agency.
Administration of provisions, §122E-5, (a).
Definition of "agency," §122E-2.
Reports, §122E-5, (d).
Responsibilities, §122E-5, (b).
Investments, §122E-3, (c).
North Carolina housing partnership.
Chairman, §122E-4, (b).
Compensation of members, §122E-4, (e).
Composition, §122E-4, (b).
Conflicts of interest, §122E-4, (i).
Creation, §122E-4, (a).
Duties, §122E-4, (f).
Executive director, §122E-4, (g).
Meetings, §122E-4, (h).
Powers, §122E-4, (f).
Purposes, §122E-4, (a).
Quorum, §122E-4, (b).
Terms of members, §122E-4, (c).
Vacancies, §122E-4, (d).
Voting on issues, §122E-4, (b).
Projects.
Eligible projects, §122E-6, (b).
Reports.
Housing finance agency, §122E-5, (d).
Rules and regulations.
Applications for funds, §122E-8, (b).
Displacement, §122E-9.
Equitable distribution of funds, §122E-7.
State treasurer.
Trustee of fund, §122E-3, (c).
Title of act.
Short title, §122E-1.
Use of funds, §122E-6.
Eligible uses, §122E-6, (c), (d).

HOV LANES, §20-146.2.

HULL INSURANCE, PROTECTION AND INDEMNITY CLUBS, §§58-20-1 to 58-20-40.
Audit, §58-20-20.
Board of trustees.
Duties, §58-20-15, (a).
Immunity, §58-20-40.
Operation of clubs, §58-20-15.
Prohibited actions, §58-20-15, (b).
Citation of article, §58-20-1.
Definitions, §58-20-5.
Evaluation of clubs, §58-20-30.
Financial monitoring of clubs, §58-20-30.
Immunity.
Administrators and boards of trustees, §58-20-40.
Indemnification.
Mutual agreement, §58-20-20.
Optional provisions, §58-20-20, (b).
Required provisions, §58-20-20, (a).

HULL INSURANCE, PROTECTION AND INDEMNITY CLUBS —Cont'd
Insolvency or impairment of club, §58-20-35.
Assessment of members, §58-20-35, (b).
Procedure once revealed, §58-20-35, (a).
Loss and loss adjustment expenses, actuarial evaluation, §58-20-20.
Membership termination, §58-20-25.
Mutual agreement for indemnification.
Optional provisions, §58-20-20, (b).
Required provisions, §58-20-20, (a).
Organization.
Authorized, §58-20-10.
Notice of intent to organize, §58-20-10.
Purposes, §58-20-10.
Short title of article, §58-20-1.
Termination of membership, §58-20-25.

HUMAN BURIAL AND HUMAN SKELETAL REMAINS.
Unmarked human burial and human skeletal remains protection, §§70-26 to 70-40.
See UNMARKED HUMAN BURIAL AND SKELETAL REMAINS PROTECTION.

HUMANE ORGANIZATIONS.
Solicitation of contributions, §§131F-1 to 131F-24.
See CHARITABLE SOLICITATION.

HUMAN PEDIGREE.
Hearsay exception.
Records of religious organizations, §8C-1, Rule 803.
Statement of personal or family history, §8C-1, Rule 804, (b).

HUMAN RELATIONS COMMISSION.
Civil rights, interference with.
Action on behalf of person subject to violation, §99D-1, (b1).
Clerical and support services, §143B-392, (d).
Creation, §143B-391.
Within department of administration, §143B-391.
Duties, §143B-391.
Equal employment practices.
Citation of article, §143-422.1.
Conciliations, §143-422.3.
Investigations, §143-422.3.
Legislative declaration, §143-422.2.
Purpose of article, §143-422.2.
Receipt of charges, §143-422.3.
Short title, §143-422.1.
Expense reimbursement, §143B-392, (b).
Fair housing act.
Administration by commission, §143B-391.
Members, §143B-392, (a).
Powers and duties, §143B-391.
Quorum, §143B-392, (c).
Terms, §143B-392, (a).
Vacancies, §143B-392, (a).

HUMAN SERVICE AND VOLUNTEER TRANSPORTATION, §§62-289.1 to 62-289.7.
Carriers.
Inapplicability of laws and regulations, §62-289.5.
Classification of transportation, §62-289.4.
Commercial transportation.
Inapplicability of laws and regulations, §62-289.5.
Common carriers.
Inapplicability of laws and regulations, §62-289.5.
Counties.
Local licenses and taxes prohibited, §62-289.7.
Definitions, §62-289.3.

HUMAN SERVICE AND VOLUNTEER TRANSPORTATION —Cont'd
Human service agency.
Defined, §62-289.3.
Human service transportation.
Classification, §62-289.4.
Defined, §62-289.3.
Inapplicability of certain laws and regulations, §62-289.5.
Insurance.
Classification of transportation, §62-289.4.
Volunteer transportation, §62-289.6.
Intention of general assembly, §62-289.2.
Licenses.
Municipal licenses and taxes.
Prohibited, §62-289.7.
Motor carriers.
Inapplicability of laws and regulations, §62-289.5.
Municipal corporations.
Local licenses and taxes prohibited, §62-289.7.
Nonprofit.
Defined, §62-289.3.
Person.
Defined, §62-289.3.
Purpose of act, §62-289.2.
Short title of act, §62-289.1.
Taxation.
Municipal licenses and taxes.
Prohibited, §62-289.7.
Volunteer transportation.
Classification, §62-289.4.
Defined, §62-289.3.
Insurance, §62-289.6.

HUMAN SKELETAL REMAINS AND UNMARKED HUMAN BURIAL PROTECTION ACT, §§70-26 to 70-40.
See UNMARKED HUMAN BURIAL AND SKELETAL REMAINS PROTECTION.

HUMAN TISSUE.
Anatomical gifts, §§130A-402 to 130A-412.1.
See ANATOMICAL GIFTS.
Donation cards.
Availability at division of motors offices, §20-7.3.
Donation program, §130A-413.
Medical examiners.
Discovery of anatomical matter.
Report to medical examiner, §130A-383, (b).
Red lights used on organ procurement organization vehicles, §20-130.1, (b).

HUMAN TISSUE DONATION PROGRAM.
Cooperation between state departments and agencies, §130A-413, (c).
Coordinated program, §130A-413, (b).
Cooperation between state departments and agencies and law-enforcement agencies, §130A-413, (c).
Establishment, §130A-413, (a).
Law-enforcement agencies.
Cooperation in coordinated program, §130A-413, (c).
Legislative findings and purpose, §130A-413, (a).
Purposes of program, §130A-413, (a).
State departments and agencies.
Cooperation in coordinated program, §130A-413, (c).
Coordinated program established, §130A-413, (b).

HUNG JURY, §15A-1235.
Grounds for mistrial, §15A-1063.

HUNTER SAFETY COURSE, §113-270.1A.

HUNTERSVILLE.
Traffic control photographic systems, §160A-300.1, (d).

HUNTING AND WILDLIFE.
Accounts and accounting.
Wildlife conservation account, §143-247.2.
Acquiring or disposing of wildlife.
Dead wildlife, §113-291.3, (b) to (d).
Live wildlife, §113-291.3, (a).
Adverse possession of property subject to public trust rights.
No adverse possession, §1-45.1.
Agents to sell licenses, §113-270.1.
Animal fights and baiting.
Exception as lawful taking or training of animals, §14-362.1, (e).
Applicability of provisions, §143-252.
Arrest.
Fees, §113-303.
Protectors.
Arrest without warrant, §113-136, (d).
Search on arrest, §113-137, (a).
Service of arrest warrants, §113-136, (e).
Article subject to chapter 113, §143-252.
Attorney general.
Attorney for agency, §113-131, (d).
Bag limits, §113-291.2, (a) to (e).
Foxes.
Open seasons for taking foxes with firearms, §113-291.4A.
Bald eagles.
Unlawfully taking, possessing, etc., §113-294, (l).
Beagles.
Field trials for beagles.
Hunting license exemption, §113-276, (k).
Bear, §113-291.7.
Sale of parts prohibited, §113-291.3, (b).
Unlawfully taking, possessing or transporting, selling, etc., §113-294, (c1).
Beaver, §113-291.9.
Damage control program, §113-291.10.
Trapping.
Use of trap number 330 of connibear type, §113-291.6, (d).
Unlawfully selling, possessing for sale or buying, §113-294, (f).
Beaver damage control advisory board, §113-291.10.
Big game animals.
Handguns and handgun ammunition, §113-291.1, (g1).
Kill reports, §113-270.3, (c).
Bird sanctuaries.
Municipalities, §160A-188.
Black-tailed deer.
Unlawfully transporting or possessing, §113-294, (p).
Boats.
Taking wild animals or birds from vessels equipped with motors, §113-294, (g).
Bobcats.
Sale of parts, §113-291.3, (b).
Bow and arrow.
Method of taking wildlife, §113-291.1, (a).
Nongame fish.
Taking in inland and joint fishing waters, §113-275, (k).
Captivity license, §113-272.5.
Captivity permits, §113-274, (c).

HUNTING AND WILDLIFE —Cont'd
Child support enforcement.
Forfeiture of licensing privilege, §50-13.12.
Suspension or revocation of hunting licenses, §§110-142, 110-142.2.
Closing forests and woodlands to hunting, fishing and trapping, §113-60.1.
Publication of proclamation and annulment, §113-60.2.
Violation of proclamation a misdemeanor, §113-60.3.
Clothing.
Hunter orange material, §113-291.8, (a) to (c).
Coastal reserves, §113A-129.2, (a).
Confiscation.
Fruits and instrumentalities of offenses in question, §113-137, (i).
Controlled hunting preserve operator licenses, §113-273, (g).
Cooperative agreements, §113-305.
Cougars.
Unlawfully taking, possessing, transporting, etc., §113-294, (c2).
Coyotes.
Hunting preserves, §113-273, (g).
Unlawfully transporting or breeding, §113-294, (o).
Criminal law enforcement authority of wildlife protectors, §113-136, (d1).
Criminal negligence.
Enforcement of article, §113-290.1, (e).
Impaired at time of violation.
Aggravating factor, §113-290.1, (b).
Penalties, §113-290.1, (a).
Resulting in death of another person.
Involuntary manslaughter, §113-290.1, (f).
Suspension of hunting privileges, §113-290.1, (c).
Hunting while license suspended, §113-290.1, (d).
Unlawful use of firearms, §113-290.
Currituck county game commission.
Authority not repealed or abridged by limitation upon local regulation, §113-133.1, (d).
Dangerous animals.
Possessing or harboring in city, §160A-187.
Possessing or harboring in county, §153A-131.
Dare county game and wildlife commission.
Authority not repealed or abridged by limitation upon local regulations, §113-133.1, (d).
Dealer licenses, §113-273.
Deer.
Deer swimming or in water above knees.
Unlawful to take, §113-291.1, (j).
Dogs hunting deer.
Muzzle loading firearms season.
Dogs not used for hunting, §113-291.2, (a).
Regulation of use, limitations, §113-291.5, (a) to (f).
Muzzle loading firearms season.
Dogs not used for hunting, §113-291.2, (a).
Taking one antlerless deer, §113-291.2, (a).
Night hunting with artificial lights, §113-294, (e).
Overpopulation of landowners land.
Survey to determine, special antlerless tags issued to owner, §113-291.2, (e).
Special antlerless deer tags, §113-291.2, (e).
Spotlighting.
Prima facie evidence, §113-302, (b).
Survey of deer population to determine overpopulation, §113-291.2, (e).

HUNTING AND WILDLIFE —Cont'd
Deer —Cont'd
Sweeping area with lights at night, §113-291.1, (e1), (e2).
Unlawfully selling, possessing for sale or buying, §113-294, (b).
Unlawfully taking, possessing or transporting, §113-294, (d).
Definitions.
Dealer, §113-273, (a).
Dealing in furs, §113-273, (f).
Endangered and threatened wildlife and species of special concern, §113-331.
Hunting and fishing on registered property of another, §113-281.
Public trust resources, §113-131, (e).
Department of environment and natural resources.
Powers, §113-131, (b).
Scientific investigations, §113-261, (a).
Taking wildlife in generally prohibited manner.
Authority, §113-261, (c).
Depredation permits, §113-274, (c).
Disabled persons.
Crossbow or other specially equipped bow.
Permission to use, §113-297, (b).
Method exemptions for, §113-297, (a).
Unlawful use of facilities provided for disabled sportsman, §113-298.
Disabled sportsman program.
Application, §113-296, (c).
Eligibility for participation, §113-296, (b).
Established, administration, §113-296, (a).
Fee, §113-296, (c).
Number of special activities per year, §113-296, (f).
Publicizing activities, §113-296, (e).
Requirements in establishing, §113-296, (d).
Dogs.
Dangerous dogs.
Dogs used in lawful hunt.
Inapplicability of provisions of article to, §67-4.1, (b).
Field trials with dogs, §113-291.1, (d).
Foxes, §113-291.4, (b).
Muzzle loading firearm deer season.
Using dogs to hunt deer prohibited, §113-291.2, (a).
Raccoon and opossum hunting at night, §113-291.1, (e).
Regulation of dogs used in hunting, §113-291.5, (a), (b).
Closed deer season.
Chasing deer, prohibition, §113-291.5, (e).
Game land, wildlife refuges and public hunting grounds, §113-291.5, (c).
Leashing or confining of pet dogs.
Section not intended to require, §113-291.5, (f).
Number of dogs or breed of dogs.
Regulations on prohibited, §113-291.5, (d).
Training during closed season, §113-291.1, (d1).
Use in taking wildlife, §113-291.1, (a).
Drainage districts.
Conservation and replacement, §156-69.
Drugs.
Taking by using drugs.
Permits issued by department and commission authorizing, §113-261, (b).
Prohibited, §113-262, (a), (b).

HUNTING AND WILDLIFE —Cont'd
Eagles.
Unlawfully taking, possessing, etc., §113-294, (l).
Eddie Bridges fund, §143-250.1, (a) to (h).
Electricity.
Taking by using electricity.
Permits issued by department and commission authorizing, §113-261, (b).
Prohibited, §113-262, (a), (b).
Endangered and threatened wildlife and species of special concern, §§113-331 to 113-337.
Declaration of policy, §113-332.
Definitions, §113-331.
Nongame wildlife advisory committee, §113-335.
Powers and duties, §113-336.
Placement of animals on protected animal list, §113-334.
Policy of state, §113-332.
Unlawful acts, §113-337, (a).
Misdemeanors, §113-337, (b).
Wildlife resources commission.
Conservation plan, §113-333, (b), (c).
Powers and duties, §113-333, (a).
Enjoyment of wildlife resources belongs to people of state, §113-133.1, (a).
Evidence.
Possession of illegally killed fish as evidence, §113-262, (b).
Spotlighting deer.
Prima facie evidence, §113-302, (b).
Warning tickets not to constitute evidence of commission of offense, §113-140, (g).
Exotic species.
Releasing for hunting or trapping, §113-292, (e).
Explosives.
Taking by using explosives.
Permits issued by department and commission authorizing, §113-261, (b).
Prohibited, §113-262, (a), (b).
Exportation or importation permits, §113-274, (c).
Falconry.
Method of taking wildlife, §113-291.1, (a).
Federal laws and regulations.
Adoption by wildlife resources commission, §113-307.
Legislative assent to specific federal acts, §113-307.1.
Fees.
Arrest, §113-303.
Licenses, §113-270.2.
Captivity license, §113-272.5, (b).
Collection licenses, §113-272.4, (c).
Combination fishing and hunting licenses, §113-270.1C, (b).
Controlled hunting preserve hunting license, §113-270.2, (c).
Controlled hunting preserve operators, §113-273, (g).
Disposition of license funds, §113-306, (b).
Furbearer propagation, §113-273, (i).
Fur-dealers, §113-273, (f).
Fur-dealer stations, §113-273, (f).
Game bird propagation, §113-273, (h).
Government-owned property.
Collecting fees for hunting on government-owned property, §113-39.
Guides, §113-270.4, (b).
Lifetime resident comprehensive hunting license, §113-270.2, (a), (c).

HUNTING AND WILDLIFE —Cont'd
Fees —Cont'd
Licenses —Cont'd
New license to replace lost or destroyed license, §113-275, (c1).
Nonresident license fee increase, §113-275, (a1).
Nonresident state hunting license, §113-270.2, (a), (c), (d).
Resident annual comprehensive hunting license, §113-270.2, (a), (c).
Resident county hunting license, §113-270.2, (a), (c).
Resident state hunting license, §113-270.2, (a), (c).
Special activity licenses, §113-270.3, (b).
Sportsmen licenses.
Annual license, §113-270.1D, (a).
Disabled resident sportsman license, §113-270.1D, (b).
Lifetime license, §113-270.1D, (b).
Taxidermy, §113-273, (k).
Trapping licenses, §113-270.5, (b).
Service of process, §113-303.
State forests.
Collection of reasonable fees for privileges, §113-35, (b).
Witnesses, §113-303.
Felony convictions.
Forfeiture of license privilege after conviction, §15A-1331A.
Field trials with dogs, §113-291.1, (d).
Beagles, hunting license exemption, §113-276, (k).
Fines.
Limitation upon penalty for offense created by rules of wildlife resources commission, §113-135.1, (a), (b).
Refusal to stop in obedience to directions of protector, §113-136, (j).
Firearms.
Beaver.
Open season with firearm, §113-291.9, (a).
Big game animals.
Handguns and handgun ammunition, §113-291.1, (g1).
Foxes, §113-291.4, (c).
Method of taking wildlife, §113-291.1, (a).
Misdemeanor for using certain firearms, §113-291.1, (c).
Pistols of twenty-two caliber.
Use in taking rabbits, squirrels, etc., §113-291.1, (g).
Unlawful use of firearms.
Criminal negligence, §113-290.
Fires.
Use in taking wild animals or birds, §113-291.1, (b).
Food servers.
Preparation of edible wildlife, §113-276, (i).
Forfeiture of licensing privilege for failure to pay child support, §50-13.12.
Foxes.
Hunting preserves, §113-273, (g).
Open seasons for taking foxes with firearms, §113-291.4A, (a), (b).
Regulation of foxes, §113-291.4.
Sale of parts prohibited, §113-291.3, (b).
Study of fox and fur-bearer populations, §113-291.4.
Trapping unlawfully, §113-294, (j).
Furbearer propagation.
Licenses, §113-273, (i).
Fur-dealer licenses, §113-273, (f).

HUNTING AND WILDLIFE —Cont'd
Fur-dealer station licenses, §113-273, (f).
Game bird propagation.
Licenses, §113-273, (h).
Golden eagles.
Unlawfully taking, possessing, etc., §113-294, (l).
Governor.
Closing forests and woodlands to hunting and trapping.
Authority, §113-60.1.
Publication of proclamation, §113-60.2.
Violation of proclamation as misdemeanor, §113-60.3.
Guides.
Licenses, §113-270.4.
Handguns.
Big game animals, §113-291.1, (g1).
Rabbits, squirrels, etc.
Use of pistol of twenty-two caliber, §113-291.1, (g).
Handicapped persons.
Special vehicular access identification card and permit.
Violation of rules restricting access to holders, §113-294, (n).
Harassment.
Persons taking wildlife resources, §113-295.
Heads, antlers, horns, hides, skins, plumes, feet and claws.
Sale, §113-291.3, (b).
Hiring hunter or trapper to take game.
Person hiring deemed buyer, hunter or trapper deemed seller, §113-291.3, (d).
Hours for hunting, §113-291.1, (a).
Hunter orange material.
Display required, §113-291.8, (a) to (c).
Hunter safety course.
Required to procure license or hunt in state, §113-270.1A, (a), (a1).
Wildlife resources commission.
Duties, §113-270.1A, (b).
Lifetime licenses.
Sale not prohibited, §113-270.1A, (d).
Prohibited acts, §113-270.1A, (c).
Hunting and fishing on registered property of another.
Affirmative duty of sportsman to determine if property is registered and posted, §113-284.
Definitions, §113-281.
Entry permits.
Forms to be furnished, §113-283, (a).
Issuance and dating, §113-283, (b).
Not substitute for hunting or fishing licenses, §113-287, (d).
Request that individual produce valid entry permit, §113-287, (b).
Required, §113-285, (a), (b).
Violations of provisions as misdemeanors, §113-285, (c).
Evidence.
Registration of property, §113-287, (a).
Law enforcement officers.
Duties, §113-287, (c).
Loss of rights by registrant, §113-282, (e), (f).
Removal, destruction or mutilation of posted notices, §113-286.
Posting of property, §113-282, (d).
Affirmative duty of sportsman to determine if property is registered and posted, §113-284.
Consent from owner or agent required, §14-159.8.

HUNTING AND WILDLIFE —Cont'd
Hunting and fishing on registered property of another —Cont'd
Posting of property —Cont'd
Enforcement by peace officers, §14-159.10.
Entrance on navigable waters not prohibited for purpose of fishing, hunting or trapping, §14-159.9.
Failure to keep registered property posted.
Notification of registrant, §113-282, (g).
Misdemeanor offense when written consent not obtained, §14-159.6, (a).
Mutilation, etc., of posted signs, §14-159.8.
Posting signs without consent, §14-159.8.
Regulations as to posting, §14-159.7.
Removal, destruction or mutilation of posted notices, §113-286.
Removal of signs after receipt of notice that tract has been deleted from registration.
Failure to remove, §113-282, (h).
Wildlife protectors authorized to execute process, §14-159.10.
Registration of property.
Application, §113-282, (a), (b).
Action on, §113-282, (c).
Fee, §113-282, (b).
Evidence, §113-287, (a).
Hunting guide licenses.
Fees, §113-270.4, (b).
Nonresidents, §113-270.4, (a).
Qualifications and duties, §113-270.4, (c).
Required, §113-270.4, (a).
Hunting preserves.
Controlled preserve operator licenses, §113-273, (g).
Hunting stands.
Use in taking wild animals or wild birds, §113-291.1, (b).
Income tax credit.
Donations of real property for fish and wildlife conservation, §105-151.12.
Injunctions.
Authority of commission to institute action for, §113-306, (e).
Encroachment upon usurpation or otherwise violating public trust rights of people, §113-131, (c).
Interference with taking of wildlife resources, §113-295, (b).
Inspection of licensed or commercial premises, §113-302.1.
Interference with taking of wildlife resources, §113-295.
Jurisdiction.
Wildlife protectors, §113-136, (c).
License agents.
Informational materials prepared by commission.
Distribution to agents, §113-301.1, (a).
Licenses.
Administrative control of licensees.
Applicability of section, §113-276.2, (a).
Investigations, §113-276.2, (i).
Notice of refusal to issue or reissue, §113-276.2, (d).
Orders limiting licensees, §113-276.2, (j).
Prohibited acts as misdemeanors, §113-276.2, (g), (i).
Reapplication after refusal of issuance or reissuance, §113-276.2, (h).
Refusal to issuance, §113-276.2, (b).
Reissuance review, §113-276.2, (c).

HUNTING AND WILDLIFE —Cont'd
Licenses —Cont'd
Administrative control of licensees —Cont'd
Return upon revocation, §113-276.2, (g).
Revocation, §113-276.2, (e).
Agents to sell.
Appointment, §113-270.1, (a).
Fee deducted from amount collected for license, §113-270.1, (b).
Hearing on suspension, revocation or nonrenewal of appointment, §113-270.1, (f).
Misdemeanors, §113-270.1, (d).
Notice of revocation or nonrenewal, §113-270.1, (g).
Penalty for late remission of license, §113-270.1, (c).
Reapplication for appointment after termination or denial, §113-270.1, (i).
Record of evidence considered in findings made at hearings, §113-270.1, (j).
Return of record books, reports, etc., upon termination, §113-270.1, (h).
Suspension, revocation or refusal to renew appointment, §113-270.1, (e).
Termination of appointment, §113-270.1, (h).
Term of appointment, §113-270.1, (c).
Beagles.
Field trials for, hunting license exemption, §113-276, (k).
Big game hunting licenses, §113-270.3, (b).
Bow and arrow.
Nongame fish.
Taking in inland and joint fishing waters, §113-275, (k).
Captivity license, §113-272.5, (a).
Black bears, applicability to, §113-272.5, (f).
Caging and care, standards, §113-272.5, (c).
Cougar, issuing for, §113-272.5, (e).
Deviation from requirements, possession unlawful, §113-272.5, (d).
Duration, §113-272.5, (b).
Fee, §113-272.5, (b).
Certificate of competency.
Required to procure license, §113-270.1A, (a), (a1).
Child support enforcement.
Forfeiture of licensing privilege, §50-13.12.
Suspension or revocation of license, §§110-142, 110-142.2.
Collection licenses.
Issuance by wildlife resources commission, §113-272.4, (a).
Assistants in taking, utilization by licensees, authorization, §113-272.4, (e).
Authority delegated to executive director, §113-272.4, (b).
Duration period, §113-272.4, (c).
Fee, §113-272.4, (c).
Restrictions imposed, §113-272.4, (d).
Combination hunting and fishing licenses, §113-270.1C, (a), (b).
Controlled hunting preserve operators, §113-273, (g).
Conviction of suspension offense.
Mandatory suspension, §113-276.3.
Dealers, §113-273.
Controlled hunting preserve operators, §113-273, (g).
Dealer defined, §113-273, (a).
Furbearer propagation license, §113-273, (i).
Fur-dealers, §113-273, (f).

HUNTING AND WILDLIFE —Cont'd
Licenses —Cont'd
Dealers —Cont'd
Game bird propagation, §113-273, (h).
Required, §113-273, (b).
Rules governing, §113-273, (b).
Taxidermy, §113-273, (k).
Disclosure of information by license applicant, §113-275, (d).
Duration of validity, §113-270.1B, (b).
Effective dates of license issued, §113-275, (b).
Enumeration of licenses issued by wildlife resources commission, §113-270.2, (c).
Exemptions and exceptions, §113-276, (c) to (m).
Exhibit or display.
Refusal, §113-275, (h).
Failure to comply with provisions of article or rules and regulation, §113-275, (i).
Falconry, §113-270.3, (b).
False or misleading statements to secure, §113-294, (h).
Fees, §113-270.2.
Captivity license, §113-272.5, (b).
Collection licenses, §113-272.4, (c).
Combination fishing and hunting licenses, §113-270.1C, (b).
Controlled hunting preserve hunting license, §113-270.2, (c).
Controlled hunting preserve operators, §113-273, (g).
Disposition of license funds, §113-306, (b).
Furbearer propagation, §113-273, (i).
Fur-dealers, §113-273, (f).
Fur-dealer stations, §113-273, (f).
Game bird propagation, §113-273, (h).
Government-owned property.
Collecting fees for hunting on government-owned property, §113-39.
Guides, §113-270.4, (b).
Lifetime resident comprehensive hunting license, §113-270.2, (a), (c).
New license to replace lost or destroyed license, §113-275, (c1).
Nonresident license fee increase, §113-275, (a1).
Nonresident state hunting license, §113-270.2, (a), (c), (d).
Resident annual comprehensive hunting license, §113-270.2, (a), (c).
Resident county hunting license, §113-270.2, (a), (c).
Resident state hunting license, §113-270.2, (a), (c).
Special activity licenses, §113-270.3, (b).
Sportsmen licenses.
Annual license, §113-270.1D, (a).
Disabled resident sportsman license, §113-270.1D, (b).
Lifetime license, §113-270.1D, (b).
Taxidermy, §113-273, (k).
Trapping licenses, §113-270.5, (b).
Felony convictions.
Forfeiture of privilege after conviction, §15A-1331A.
Field trials for beagles.
Hunting license exemption, §113-276, (k).
Furbearer propagation, §113-273, (i).
Fur-dealers, §113-273, (f).
Fur-dealer stations, §113-273, (f).
Game bird propagation, §113-273, (h).
General provisions respecting licenses issued by wildlife resources commission, §113-275.

HUNTING AND WILDLIFE —Cont'd
Licenses —Cont'd
Guides, §113-270.4.
Hunter safety course, §113-270.1A.
Individual license required, §113-275, (f).
Kept about person, §113-275, (f).
Landholders, exemption from license requirement, §113-276, (c).
Lost or destroyed licenses, §113-275, (c1).
Mail, issuance by.
Information on laws and rules applicable to type of license.
Furnishing licensee, §113-301.1, (b).
Mandatory suspension.
Conviction of suspension offense, §113-276.3.
Migratory waterfowl, §113-270.3, (b).
Minors.
Persons under 16 years of age, license exemption, §113-276, (d).
Misdemeanors, §113-275, (j).
New license to replace lost or destroyed license, §113-275, (c1).
Nonresident license fee increase, §113-275, (a).
Probation.
Purchase of certain licenses required, §15A-1343, (b1).
Reciprocal agreements, §§113-275, (a), 113-304.
Regulatory authority of commission, §113-276.1.
Removal of residence of licensee to another state.
Continued validity, §113-275, (b1).
Required, §113-270.1B, (a).
Revocation or suspension.
Discretionary revocation or suspension by court, §113-277.
Mandatory suspension.
Conviction of suspension offense, §113-276.3.
Separation of revenues.
Precondition for receiving funds under cooperative program, §113-307.1, (d).
Sold for full amount prescribed, §113-275, (c), (e).
Special activity licenses, §113-270.3, (a), (b).
Sportsmen combination licenses, §113-270.3, (d).
Sportsmen licenses, §§113-270.1D, 113-270.3, (d), (e).
Taxidermy, §113-273, (k).
Transfers, §113-275, (f).
Trapping, §113-270.5, (a).
Duration of validity of license, §113-270.1B, (b).
Fees, §113-270.5, (b).
Requirement of license, §113-270.1B, (a).
Unlawful acts, §113-275, (g) to (j).
Voluntary contributions to hunters safety education program.
Authorized, §113-270.2A, (a).
Collection, §113-270.2A, (b).
Lights used to take wild animals or birds, §113-291.1, (b).
Live wildlife.
Taking, possessing, buying, selling, §113-291.3, (a).
Local regulation of wildlife resources.
Limitation upon local regulations, §113-133.1, (d).
Repeal generally of special, local and private acts, §113-133.1, (b).
Repeal specifically of local acts, §113-133.1, (g).
Retention of specific local acts or portions of local acts, §113-133.1, (e).
Review of local acts by wildlife resources commission, §113-133.1, (f).
Magistrates' powers in cases involving hunting offenses, §7A-273.

HUNTING AND WILDLIFE —Cont'd
Manner of taking wild animals and wild birds, §113-291.1.
Methods for taking wildlife, §113-291.1, (a).
Migratory game birds.
Managed hunts, §113-291.2, (a).
Methods of taking.
Expansion to conform with federal law, §113-291.1, (f).
Shooting hours, bag limits and seasons.
Federal law observed, §113-291.2, (a).
Unlawfully taking, possessing or transporting, §113-294, (m).
Misdemeanors.
Endangered and threatened wildlife and species of special concern.
Unlawful acts, §113-337, (b).
Seized property left with defendant.
Failure or inexcusable neglect of defendant to keep property, §113-137, (f).
Specific violations, §113-294.
Violations of rules adopted by wildlife resources commission, §113-135, (a) to (c).
Limitation upon penalty for offense created by rules, §113-135.1, (a), (b).
Motor vehicles.
Taking wild animals or birds from or with use of vehicle, §113-291.1, (b).
Temporary stops by protectors, §113-136, (f), (g), (j).
Mule deer.
Unlawfully transporting or possessing, §113-294, (p).
Negligence.
Criminally negligent hunting, §113-290.1.
Nesting or breeding areas.
Intentional destruction of impairment, §113-291.1, (i).
Nests and nest eggs.
Taking, possessing, buying, selling, §113-291.3, (a).
Nets, traps, snares used in taking wild animals or birds, §113-291.1, (b).
Night hunting deer with artificial light, §113-294, (e).
Prohibiting intentional sweeping of area with lights, §113-291.1, (e1), (e2).
Night hunting for raccoons and opossums, §113-291.1, (e).
Nuisance species.
Authority of commission to introduce, §113-292, (d).
Open season.
Bears, §113-291.7.
Foxes.
Taking foxes with firearms, §113-291.4A, (a), (b).
Opossums.
Night hunting with dogs, §113-291.1, (e).
Sale of parts, §113-291.3, (b).
Orange hat, cap or other garmet.
Display of hunter orange required, §113-291.8, (a) to (c).
Otter.
Trapping.
Use of trap number 330 of connibear type, §113-291.6, (d).
Packages, crates or containers used for shipping wildlife.
Marking, adoption of regulations, §113-291.3, (c).

HUNTING AND WILDLIFE —Cont'd
Parks.
Collection of reasonable fees for privileges in state forests and parks, §113-35, (b).
Penalties.
Taking fish by illegal means, §113-262, (a), (b).
Permits.
Administrative control of permittees, §113-276.2.
Captivity permit, §113-274, (c).
Defined, §113-274, (a).
Depredation permit, §113-274, (c).
Drugs, electricity, explosives or poisons.
Authorizing wildlife to be taken by use of, §113-261, (b).
Exemptions and exceptions, §113-276, (c) to (m).
Exportation or importation permit, §113-274, (c).
General provisions respecting licenses and permits issued by wildlife resources commission, §113-275.
Possession permit, §113-274, (c).
Required, §113-274, (b).
Revocation or suspension.
Discretionary revocation or suspension by court, §113-277.
Mandatory suspension.
Conviction of suspension offense, §113-276.3.
Transportation permit, §113-274, (c).
Trophy wildlife sale permit, §113-274, (c).
Pesticides.
Unlawful use in taking animals or birds.
Criminal penalties, §113-300.3, (b), (c).
Separate offense, §113-300.3, (a).
Wild animal or bird declared pest.
Use in taking, §113-300.2.
Pests, wild animal or bird declared.
Action by commission after notification, §113-300.2, (c).
Agencies that may declare animal or bird pests, §113-300.2, (a).
Concurrence of commission required, §113-300.2, (b), (e), (f).
Criminal penalty.
Neglect to observe restrictions, §113-300.3, (c).
Notice to commission of action taken, §113-300.2, (b).
Poisons or pesticides, animal or bird taken with, §113-300.2, (d).
Poisons.
Permits issued by department and commission authorizing.
Taking wildlife by poison, §113-261, (b).
Prohibited taking, §113-262, (a), (b).
Unlawful use in taking animals or birds.
Criminal penalties, §113-300.3, (b), (c).
Separate offense, §113-300.3, (a).
Use, §113-300.1.
Wild animal or bird declared pest, §113-300.2.
Possession and transportation of taken animals, §113-291.2, (c).
Carcasses known or suspected to carry infectious or contagious diseases, §113-291.2, (c1).
Closed seasons, §113-291.2, (d).
Possession permits, §113-274, (c).
Posted property.
Affirmative duty of sportsman to determine if registered and posted, §113-284.
Consent from owner or agent required, §14-159.8.
Definitions, §113-281.
Entrance on navigable waters for purposes of fishing, hunting or trapping, §14-159.9.
Entry permits, §§113-283, 113-285, 113-287.

HUNTING AND WILDLIFE —Cont'd
Posted property —Cont'd
Failure to keep registered property posted.
Notification of registrant, §113-282, (g).
Misdemeanor offense when written consent not obtained, §14-159.6, (a).
Mutilation, etc., of posted signs, §14-159.8.
Peace officers to enforce, §14-159.10.
Posting of property generally, §113-282, (b).
Posting signs without consent, §14-159.8.
Registration of property, §113-282.
Regulations as to posting, §14-159.7.
Removal, destruction or mutilation of posted notices, §113-286.
Removal of signs after receipt of notice that track deleted from registration.
Failure to remove, §113-282, (h).
Wildlife protectors authorized to execute process, §14-159.10.
Property of another.
Hunting and fishing on registered property of another, §§113-281 to 113-287.
Posted property, §§14-159.6 to 14-159.10.
Protectors.
Arrest powers, §113-136.
Arrest warrants, search warrants, etc.
Service by protectors, §113-136, (e).
Criminal laws, enforcement, §113-136, (d1).
Exhibiting upon request items required to be carried by law or rule, §113-136, (k).
Jurisdiction, §113-136, (c).
Peace officer powers, §113-136, (a).
Search on arrest, §113-137, (a).
Seizure of lawfully discovered property.
Evidence of crime, §113-137, (b), (c).
Leaving property with defendant, §113-137, (f).
Return to owner, §113-137, (h).
Safeguarding pending trial, §113-137, (e).
Sale of perishable wildlife pending trial, §113-137, (g).
Summary disposition of live or perishable wildlife, §113-137, (d).
Stopping temporarily persons or motor vehicles, §113-136, (f), (g), (j).
Warning tickets, §113-140.
Public lands.
Hunting licenses.
Collecting fees for hunting on government-owned property, §113-39.
Public hunting grounds.
Coordination with private landowners in establishing, §113-264, (c).
Regulatory power over property belonging to commission, §113-264, (a).
Public trust resources.
Defined, §113-131, (e).
Public trust rights, no adverse possession, §1-45.1.
Rabbits.
Sale of edible parts, §113-291.3, (b).
Rabies emergency for particular county.
Plan to reduce exposure by foxes, raccoons, skunks and bobcats, §113-291.2, (a1).
Raccoons.
Night hunting with dogs, §113-291.1, (e).
Sale of parts, §113-291.3, (b).
Reciprocity.
Licenses, §113-304.
Recorded animal or bird calls.
Use in taking wild animals or birds, §113-291.1, (b).

HUNTING AND WILDLIFE —Cont'd
Refuges and sanctuaries.
Municipal corporations, §160A-188.
Reports.
Big game kill reports, §113-270.3, (c).
Restrictions generally, §113-291.
Restrictions, new rules, adopting.
Notification to public, §113-301.1, (c), (d).
Revisions of subchapter.
General statement of purpose and effect, §113-316.
Revocation or suspension of license or permit.
Discretionary revocation or suspension by court, §113-277, (a), (a1).
Concurrent or consecutive, §113-277, (a2).
Conviction defined, §113-277, (a3).
Criminal offenses during period of suspension, §113-277, (b).
Surrender, §113-277, (a4).
Mandatory suspension of license or permit.
Conviction of suspension offense, §113-276.3, (a).
Beginning of period of suspension, §113-276.3, (a).
Discretionary court suspension supersedes section's provisions, §113-276.3, (e).
Offenses requiring suspension, §113-276.3, (d).
Period of suspension, §113-276.3, (d).
Reporting convictions and suspensions, §113-276.3, (c).
Surrender of licenses and permits, §113-276.3, (b).
Rifles.
Method of taking wildlife, §113-291.1, (a).
Rules and regulations.
Federal laws and regulations.
Adoption, §113-307.
Legislative assent to specific federal acts, §113-307.1.
Notification to members of general public.
New laws and rules affecting public, §113-301.1.
Wildlife resources commission, §113-134.
Violations as misdemeanors, §113-135, (a) to (c).
Limitation upon penalty for offense created by rules, §113-135.1, (a), (b).
Sales.
Seized or confiscated property, §113-137, (i).
Trophy wildlife sale permit, §113-274, (c).
Unlawfully selling, possessing for sale or buying wildlife, §113-294, (a).
Bear, §113-294, (c1).
Beaver, §113-294, (f).
Cougars, §113-294, (c2).
Deer or wild turkey, §113-294, (b).
Sales and use taxes.
Wildlife resources fund.
Transfer of taxes on hunting and fishing supplies and equipment, §105-164.44B.
Searches and seizures.
Exhibiting upon request of protector items required to be carried by law or rule, §113-136, (k).
Game birds.
Disposition of seized, confiscated or unclaimed property.
Provisions not to apply to game birds, §15-17.
Issuance of search warrants by wildlife protectors, §113-136, (e).
Search on arrest by protector, §113-137, (a).

HUNTING AND WILDLIFE —Cont'd
Searches and seizures —Cont'd
Seizure of lawfully discovered evidence by protectors, §113-137, (b), (c).
Leaving property in possession of defendant, §113-137, (f).
Return to owner, §113-137, (h).
Safeguarding pending trial, §113-137, (a).
Sale of seized property, §113-137, (i), (j), (k).
Summary disposition of live or perishable wildlife, §113-137, (d).
Temporary stops by protectors, §113-136, (f), (g), (j).
Unreasonable searches and seizures prohibited, §113-136, (l).
Seasons.
Bears, §113-291.7.
Foxes.
Continuance of open seasons, §113-291.4, (f1).
Training dogs during closed season, §113-291.1, (d1).
Seasons and bag limits.
Authority of commission to fix, §113-291.2, (a).
Closed seasons.
Authority to fix included, §113-291.2, (a).
Deer.
Special antlerless deer tags, §113-291.2, (e).
Different seasons and bag limits.
Setting in different areas, §113-291.2, (a).
Dog use in hunting deer prohibited, §113-291.2, (a).
Foxes.
Open seasons for taking foxes with firearms, §113-291.4A, (a), (b).
Migratory game birds.
Federal seasons and bag limits observed, §113-291.2, (a).
Muzzle-loading firearms season for deer.
One antlerless deer taken, §113-291.2, (a).
Possession and transportation of taken animals, §113-291.2, (c).
Carcasses known or suspected to carry infectious or contagious diseases, §113-291.2, (c1).
Closed seasons, §113-291.2, (d).
Setting of season and possession limits.
Authority to fix bag limits includes, §113-291.2, (a).
Special antlerless deer tags, §113-291.2, (e).
Special or extended seasons, §113-291.2, (a).
Survey of deer population to determine overpopulation, §113-291.2, (e).
Transportation of taken animals, §113-291.2, (c).
Carcasses known or suspected to carry infectious or contagious diseases, §113-291.2, (c1).
Closed seasons, §113-291.2, (d).
Wounded or disabled animals.
Reasonable effort to capture and kill, §113-291.2, (b).
Selling, buying, possessing, importing, exporting.
Dead wildlife, §113-291.3, (b) to (d).
Live wildlife, §113-291.3, (a).
Service of process.
Fees, §113-303.
Service by protectors.
Arrest warrants, search warrants, orders for arrest, etc., §113-136, (e).
Shooting preserves.
Manner of taking wild animals or birds.
Relaxing requirements on controlled shooting preserves, §113-291.1, (h).

HUNTING AND WILDLIFE —Cont'd
Shotguns.
Method of taking wildlife, §113-291.1, (a).
Special activity licenses, §113-270.3, (a), (b).
Special conservation officers.
Conference of law enforcement powers, §113-138, (a).
Jurisdiction and powers generally, §113-138, (d).
Limitation on exercise of authority to confer powers, §113-138, (d).
Specification of particular officers or classes of officers, §113-138, (c).
Sportsmen licenses, §§113-270.1D, 113-270.3, (d), (e).
Spotlighting deer.
Prima facie evidence, §113-302, (b).
Squirrels.
Sale of edible parts, §113-291.3, (b).
State forests.
Collection of reasonable fees for privileges, §113-35, (b).
Statutes.
Repeal of certain public, public-local, special and private acts, §113-377.8.
Subpoenas.
Service by protectors, §113-136, (e).
Sunday hunting, §103-2.
Taxidermist.
Possessing wildlife authorized to handle, §113-291.3, (b).
Taxidermy licenses, §113-273, (k).
Transitional provisions.
Purpose and effect of revisions of subchapter, §113-316.
Transportation.
Permits, §113-274, (c).
Transportation of taken animals, §113-291.2, (c).
Carcasses known or suspected to carry infectious or contagious diseases, §113-291.2, (c1).
Closed seasons, §113-291.2, (d).
Transporting lawfully taken wildlife, §§113-291.2, (c), (d), 113-291.3, (b) to (d).
Transporting live wildlife, nests and nest eggs, §113-291.3, (a).
Trapping.
Beaver.
Snares used, §113-291.9, (d).
Trapping pursuant to beaver damage control program, §113-291.10, (d).
Foxes, §113-291.4, (f), (f1).
Hiring hunter or trapper to take game.
Person hiring deemed buyer, hunter or trapper deemed seller, §113-291.3, (d).
Licenses, §113-270.5, (a).
Duration of validity of license, §113-270.1B, (b).
Fees, §113-270.5, (b).
Required, §113-270.1B, (a).
Methods of taking wildlife, §113-291.1, (a).
Regulation, §113-291.6.
Restrictions, new rules, adopting.
Notification to public, §113-301.1, (c), (d).
Violations generally, §113-294, (i), (j).
Trespass.
Hunting, fishing or trapping on "posted" property, §§14-159.6 to 14-159.10.
Registered property, §§113-281 to 113-287.
Land under option by federal government, §14-131.
Trophy wildlife sale permits, §113-274, (c).
United States agencies.
Scientific investigations, §113-261, (a).

HUNTING AND WILDLIFE —Cont'd
United States agencies —Cont'd
Taking wildlife in generally prohibited manner.
Authority, §113-261, (c).
Unlawfully selling, possessing for sale or buying, §113-294.
Unlawfully taking, possessing, transporting, §113-294.
Venue.
Interference with taking of wildlife resources.
Injunctive relief, §113-295, (b).
License agents.
Appointment.
Suspended, revoked or not renewed.
Hearings, §113-270.1, (f).
Vessels.
Taking wild animals or birds from vessels equipped with motors, §113-294, (g).
Violations generally.
Specific violations, §113-294.
Voluntary migratory waterfowl conservation print.
Exclusive production rights, §113-270.2B, (a).
Ownership rights, §113-270.2B, (a).
Proceeds, §113-270.2B, (b).
Warning tickets.
Accounting for and recording of issuance, §113-140, (e).
Conditions for issuance, §113-140, (c).
Evidence of commission of offense.
Issuance not to constitute, §113-140, (g).
Inappropriate issuance, §113-140, (d).
Issuance generally, §113-140, (a).
Powers of protectors or law enforcement officers not restricted, §113-140, (f).
Standards for issuance, §113-140, (b).
Watersheds of navigable streams, protection of.
Legislative assent to specific federal acts, §113-307.1, (a).
Weapons.
Beaver.
Open season with firearm, §113-291.9, (a).
Big game animals.
Handguns and handgun ammunition, §113-291.1, (g1).
Foxes, taking with firearms, §113-291.4, (c).
Method of taking wildlife, §113-291.1, (a).
Misdemeanor for using certain weapons, §113-291.1, (c).
Pistols of twenty-two caliber.
Use in taking rabbits, squirrels, etc., §113-291.1, (g).
Unlawful use of firearms, §113-290.
Wildlife endowment fund.
Appropriations and agency receipts.
Fund not to take the place of, §143-250.1, (g).
Assets, §143-250.1, (c).
Board of trustees.
Accumulation of investment income, §143-250.1, (e).
Created, §143-250.1, (b).
Officers, §143-250.1, (b).
Powers and duties, §143-250.1, (b).
Created, §143-250.1, (a).
Declared special trust, §143-250.1, (d).
Dissolution of wildlife resources commission.
Assumption of trusteeship of fund, §143-250.1, (h).
Eddie Bridges fund.
Fund to be known as, §143-250.1.
Expenditures of income, §143-250.1, (f).

HUNTING AND WILDLIFE —Cont'd
Wildlife endowment fund —Cont'd
Supplemental to other income and appropriations, §143-250.1, (g).
Use of income and principal, §143-250.1, (a).
Wildlife management areas.
Dogs.
Killing or injuring deer or bear.
Dog may be killed without liability, §67-14.1, (a).
Running at large.
Unmuzzled dogs running at large.
Impoundment, §67-14.1, (b) to (e).
Wildlife management plan.
Development, §113-306, (d).
Wildlife resources belong to people of state, §113-131, (a).
Wildlife resources commission.
Notification to public affected by laws and rules, §113-301.1.
Scientific investigations, §113-261, (a).
Taking wildlife in generally prohibited manner.
Authority, §113-261, (c).
Wildlife restoration projects.
Legislative assent to specific federal acts, §113-307.1, (b).
Wild turkey.
Sale of parts prohibited, §113-291.3, (b).
Unlawfully selling, possessing for sale or buying, §113-294, (b).
Unlawfully taking, possessing or transporting, §113-294, (c).
Witnesses.
Fees, §113-303.
Wounded or disabled animals.
Reasonable effort to capture and kill, §113-291.2, (b).

HUNTING GUIDES.
Licenses, §113-270.4.

HUNTING PRESERVES.
Controlled preserve operator's license, §113-273, (g).

HURRICANE FLOYD RESERVE FUND PAYMENTS.
Deductions to taxable income, §§105-130.5, (b), 105-134.6, (b).

HURRICANES.
Flood and hurricane protection works.
Appropriations, §153A-438.
Flood protection and beach erosion control project revolving fund, §143-215.62.
Removal of property deposited by hurricane, §104B-1.
Special assessments by counties generally, §§153A-185 to 153A-206.
See SPECIAL ASSESSMENTS BY COUNTIES.

HUSBAND AND WIFE.
Abandonment.
Acts barring rights of spouse, §31A-1, (a).
Guardian's sale of abandoned incompetent spouse's estate, §35A-1306.
Willful abandonment, §14-322.
Absentees in military service.
Appointment as receiver, §28B-4, (b).
Transfer of property valued at less than $5,000.
Application to superior court, §28B-9, (a).
Abuse or neglect of children.
Waiver of husband-wife privilege in child abuse cases, §8-57.1.

HUSBAND AND WIFE —Cont'd
Acknowledgments.
Absence of wife does not affect deed as to husband, §39-9.
Before different officers, §39-8.
Certain conveyances not affected by fraud, §39-11.
Different times and places, §39-8.
Husband's and wife's acknowledgment before same officer, §47-40.
Order immaterial, §39-8.
Powers of attorney.
Acknowledgment of spouse of grantor unnecessary, §39-12.
Actions.
Quieting title, §41-10.
Torts.
Acts arising outside state, §52-5.1.
Torts between husband and wife, §52-5.
Acts barring property rights of spouse, §31A-1, (a).
Acts specified barring rights, §31A-1, (a).
Pleading in bar, §31A-1, (c).
Rights lost, §31A-1, (b).
Sale or conveyance of property without joining spouse at fault, §31A-1, (d).
Adoption.
Death of joint petitioner pending final decree, §48-2-204.
Prohibition on adoption, §48-1-103.
Spouse of petitioner must join in petition, §48-2-301, (b).
Alimony.
See ALIMONY.
Anatomical gifts.
Persons who may execute anatomical gift, §130A-404, (b).
Annulment of marriage.
General provisions.
See ANNULMENT OF MARRIAGE.
Antenuptial contracts.
Generally, §§52B-1 to 52B-11.
See ANTENUPTIAL AGREEMENTS AND CONTRACTS.
Liability of married persons for debts, contracts or damages incurred before marriage, §52-11.
Bail and recognizance.
Crimes of domestic violence, §15A-534.1, (a).
Retention of defendant in custody without action, time limitation, §15A-534.1, (b).
Capacity of married persons to contract, §52-2.
Child custody.
General provisions.
See CHILD CUSTODY.
Child support.
General provisions.
See CHILD SUPPORT.
Community property, divorce.
Equitable distribution of marital property generally, §§50-11, 50-20 to 50-22.
Cross-actions, jurisdiction, §7A-244.
Mediated settlement conferences, district courts, §7A-38.4A.
Community property rights, disposition at death, §§31C-1 to 31C-12.
See COMMUNITY PROPERTY RIGHTS, DISPOSITION AT DEATH.
Constitution of North Carolina.
Women.
Property of married women secured to them, Const. N. C., art. X, §4.

HUSBAND AND WIFE —Cont'd
Contracts.
Antenuptial contracts.
Generally, §§52B-1 to 52B-11.
See ANTENUPTIAL AGREEMENTS AND CONTRACTS.
Liability of married persons for debts, contracts or damages incurred before marriage, §52-11.
Between husband and wife.
Judgment of superior or other court.
Inapplicability to, §52-10, (c).
Not inconsistent with public policy, §52-10, (a).
Required to be in writing and acknowledged, §52-10, (a).
Certifying officer, §52-10, (b).
Statute of fraud.
Required to be in writing and acknowledged, §52-10, (a).
Capacity to contract, §52-2.
Distribution of marital property agreements, §50-20, (d).
Examinations.
Validation of contracts where wife is not privately examined, §52-8.
Joint execution by husband and wife.
Married persons under 18 made competent as to certain transactions, §39-13.2, (a), (b).
Notaries public.
Validation of certificates as to contracts between husband and wife, §52-7.
Recovery by person suing alone, §52-4.
Separation agreements, §52-10.1.
Validation.
Contracts failing to comply with provisions of former section 52-6, §52-8.
Validation of contract executed by married women without private examination.
Contracts executed prior to Feb. 7, 1945, §39-13.1, (b).
Contracts executed since Nov. 7, 1944, §39-13.1, (a).
Conveyances.
Acknowledgments.
Absence of wife's acknowledgment does not affect deed as to husband, §39-9.
Different times and places, §39-8.
Acts barring property rights.
Conveyance of property by spouse not at fault, §31A-1, (d).
Conveyance by spouse to both spouses.
Tenants by the entirety, interest vested as, §39-13.3, (b).
Conveyance by spouse to other spouse.
Interest vested in grantee spouse, §39-13.3, (a).
Tenants by the entirety, dissolution of interest held as, §39-13.3, (c).
Deed of separation.
Conveyance by husband or wife under deed, §39-13.4.
G.S. 52-10 or 52-10.1.
Applicability of provisions to conveyances by spouses to spouses, §39-13.3, (e).
Instruments affecting married woman's title.
Validation of instruments not executed by husband, §39-7.1.
Joinder of spouse, §39-7, (b).
Grantor's spouse, §39-13.3, (d).
Married persons under 18 made competent as to certain transactions, §39-13.2, (a), (b).

HUSBAND AND WIFE —Cont'd
Conveyances —Cont'd
Notaries.
Validation of certificates as to conveyances between husband and wife, §52-7.
Party to convey without joinder, §39-7, (b).
Purchase-money mortgages.
Spouse need not join, §39-13.
Validation of conveyance executed by married women without private examination.
Conveyances executed prior to Feb. 7, 1945, §39-13.1, (b).
Conveyances executed since Nov. 7, 1944, §39-13.1, (a).
Validation of instruments not executed by husband, §39-7.1.
Waiver of elective life estate.
Execution of conveyance, §39-7, (a), (c).
Corporate stock and investment securities, joint ownership, §41-2.2, (a).
Death of joint tenant, §41-2.2, (c).
Inheritance laws unaffected, §41-2.2, (d).
When joint tenancy and shares if corporate stock or investment securities exist, §41-2.2, (b).
Costs.
Judgments against married persons for costs.
Levy and collection out of separate estate, §1-223.
Credit.
Equal availability of credit for women, §25B-1, (a).
Criminal law and procedure.
Postnuptial crimes, §52-12.
Curtesy.
Abolished, §§29-4, 41-4.
Renunciation by married person under 21 years, §39-13.2, (c).
Damages.
Judgments against married persons for damages.
Levy and collection out of separate estate, §1-223.
Recovery by person suing alone, §52-4.
Tort actions arising out of acts occurring outside state, §52-5.1.
Torts between husband and wife, §52-5.
Deeds.
Acknowledgments.
Absence of wife's acknowledgment not to affect deed as to husband, §39-9.
Different times and places, §39-8.
Certain conveyances not affected by fraud if acknowledgment or privy examination regular, §39-11.
Conveyances under deed of separation, §39-13.4.
Married persons under 18 made competent as to certain transactions, §39-13.2, (a), (b).
Power to convey property without joinder, §39-7, (b).
Probates.
Different officers of deeds, §47-87.
Validation of deed executed by married women without private examination.
Deeds executed prior to Feb. 7, 1945, §39-13.1, (b).
Deeds executed since Nov. 7, 1944, §39-13.1, (a).
Validation of instruments not executed by husband, §39-7.1.
Definitions.
Abandonment and failure to support spouse and children, §14-322, (a).
Dependent spouse.
Duty of supporting spouse, §14-322.

HUSBAND AND WIFE —Cont'd
Divorce.
See DIVORCE.
Domestic violence, §§50B-1 to 50B-9.
See DOMESTIC VIOLENCE.
Dower.
Abolished, §29-4.
Renunciation by married person under age of 21 years, §39-13.2, (c).
Duress.
Certain conveyances not affected by fraud or duress, §39-11.
Earnings and damages.
Recovery by person suing alone, §52-4.
Elective life estate, §29-30.
Waiver, §39-7, (a), (c).
Executions.
Married women.
Levy and collection from separate property, §1-304.
Exemptions.
Property of married women secured to them, Const. N. C., art. X, §4.
Property passing by bequest, devise, intestate succession or gift to dependent spouse.
Continuation of exemption, §1C-1604, (b).
Falsely registering as husband and wife, §14-186.
Fire insurance.
Policy issued to husband or wife on joint property, §58-44-45.
Forms.
Acknowledgments.
Husband's and wife's acknowledgment before same officer, §47-40.
Fraudulent conveyances.
Certain conveyances not affected by fraud, §39-11.
Free trader agreements, §52-10.
Guardian ad litem for minor in domestic relations actions.
When not required, §1A-1, Rule 17, (b).
Guardians.
Abandoned incompetent spouse's estate.
Sale of spouse's separate property by guardian, §35A-1306.
Sale of ward's estate.
Spouse entitled to special proceeding for sale of real property, §35A-1307.
Homesteads.
Acts barring rights of spouse, §31A-1, (b).
Hotels.
Falsely registering as husband and wife, §14-186.
Immunities.
Inter-spousal immunity.
Abolished, §52-5.1.
Actions arising out of acts occurring outside state, §52-5.1.
Income tax.
Individual income tax.
Joint returns, §105-152, (e).
Payment of tax, §105-157, (a).
Insurance.
Fire insurance.
Policy issued to husband or wife on joint property, §58-44-45.
Life insurance.
Rights of beneficiaries, §58-58-95.
Married person may insure spouse's life, §52-3.
Inter-spousal immunity.
Abolished, §52-5.1.
Actions arising out of acts occurring outside state, §52-5.1.

HUSBAND AND WIFE —Cont'd
Intestate succession.
Acts barring rights of spouse, §31A-1, (b).
Joint bank accounts.
Right of survivorship, §41-2.1.
Joint ownership of corporate stock and investments securities, §41-2.2, (a).
Death of joint tenant, §41-2.2, (c).
Inheritance tax laws unaffected, §41-2.2, (d).
When joint tenancy exists, §41-2.2, (b).
Judgments against married persons.
Levy and collection out of separate estate or property, §1-223.
Judgments construed to be contract or release between spouses.
Inapplicability of provisions concerning contracts and releases, §52-10, (c).
Jurisdiction.
Personal jurisdiction.
Marital relationship, §1-75.4.
Leases.
Power to lease without joinder of spouse, §39-7, (b).
Validation of leasehold executed by married women without private examination.
Leasehold executed prior to Feb. 7, 1945, §39-13.1, (b).
Leaseholds executed since Nov. 7, 1944, §39-13.1, (a).
Life estates.
Elective life estate, §29-30.
Waiver, §39-7, (a), (c).
Waiver of elective life estate.
Execution of instruments affecting estate, §39-7, (a), (c).
Life insurance.
Rights of beneficiaries, §58-58-95.
Magistrates.
Contracts.
Power of magistrate to take acknowledgment of written contract, §7A-292.
Separation agreements.
Power of magistrate to take acknowledgment of agreement, §7A-292.
Marriage.
See MARRIAGE PROCEEDINGS.
Minors.
Conveyances.
Married persons under 18 competent as to certain transactions, §39-13.2, (a), (b).
Missing persons.
Property owned as tenants by the entirety.
Power of receiver to partition, §28C-8.
Mobile homes.
Tenancy by the entirety in mobile home, §41-2.5, (a), (b), (d).
Definition of "mobile home," §41-2.5, (c).
Mortgage or sale of estates held by the entireties, §§35A-1310 to 35A-1314.
Approval by judge, §35A-1311.
Authorized, §35A-1310.
Clerk of court.
Powers, §35A-1310.
Funds.
Clerk may direct application, §35A-1313.
General law applicable, §35A-1311.
Petition.
Authority to file, §35A-1310.
Contents, §35A-1310.
Prior sales and mortgages validated, §35A-1314.
Purchasers and mortgagees protected, §35A-1313.

HUSBAND AND WIFE —Cont'd
Mortgage or sale of estates held by the entireties —Cont'd
Title.
Acquisition of title unaffected by provisions, §35A-1313.
Proceeding valid in passing title, §35A-1312.
Validation of prior sales and mortgages, §35A-1314.
Mortgages and deeds of trust.
Joint execution.
Married persons under 18 made competent as to certain transactions, §39-13.2, (a), (b).
Power to mortgage without joinder of spouse, §39-7, (b).
Purchase-money mortgages.
Spouse need not join in, §39-13.
Spouse of mortgagor has right to redeem, §45-45.
Nonsupport.
Duty of supporting spouse, §14-322.
Notaries public.
Contracts or conveyances between husband and wife.
Validation of certificates of notaries, §52-7.
Opposite sexes occupying same bedroom for immoral purposes, §14-186.
Partition.
Creation of tenancy by entirety in partition of real property, §39-13.5.
Paternity proceedings, §8-57.2.
Personal property.
Acts barring property rights.
Acts specified, rights lost, §31A-1.
Property of married persons secured, §52-1.
Pleading.
Acts barring rights of spouse, §31A-1, (c).
Postnuptial crimes and torts, §52-12.
Powers of attorney.
Authorized to execute, §39-12.
Validation of instruments not executed by husband, §39-7.1.
Premarital agreements generally, §§52B-1 to 52B-11.
See ANTENUPTIAL AGREEMENTS AND CONTRACTS.
Privilege.
Abused, neglected or dependent juvenile actions.
Inapplicable when guardian ad litem demands information, §7B-601.
Abuse or neglect of children.
Husband-wife privilege not grounds for excluding evidence of abuse or neglect, §8-57.1.
Child support actions instituted by designated representatives of county commissioners, §110-130.
Civil actions, §8-56.
Criminal actions, §8-57, (a) to (c).
Paternity proceedings, §8-57.2.
Probate and registration.
Before different officers, §47-68.
Free trader.
No examination of husband's assent where wife free trader, §47-69.
Probate by different officers of deeds by husband and wife, §47-87.
Wrong order, §47-67.
Property, §52-1; Const. N. C., art. X, §4.
Acts barring rights of spouse, §31A-1, (b).
Property rights barred.
Acts specified, rights lost, §31A-1.

HUSBAND AND WIFE —Cont'd
Purchase-money mortgages.
Spouse need not join in, §39-13.
Real property.
Acts barring property rights.
Acts specified, rights lost, §31A-1.
Registration.
Absence of wife's acknowledgment.
Registration of instrument, §39-9.
Release and quick claim of rights.
Judgment of superior or other court.
Inapplicability to, §52-10, (c).
Not inconsistent with public policy, §52-10, (a).
Required to be in writing and acknowledged, §52-10, (a).
Certifying officer, §52-10, (b).
Statute of fraud.
Required to be in writing and acknowledged, §52-10, (a).
Residential property disclosure act.
Transfers resulting from divorce.
Applicability of act, §47E-2.
Resumption of marital relations, §52-10.2.
Sale of personal or real property.
Acts barring property rights.
Sale without joining spouse at fault, §31A-1, (d).
Securities.
Joint ownership of investment securities, §41-2.2, (a).
Death of joint tenant, §41-2.2, (c).
Inheritance tax laws unaffected, §41-2.2, (d).
When joint tenancy in investment securities exist, §41-2.2, (b).
Separation agreements.
Authorization and requisites, §52-10.1.
Distribution of marital property agreements, §50-20, (d).
Sexual offenses.
Bail and recognizance, §15A-534.4.
Victim is spouse of person committing act.
Defense that victim is spouse, §14-27.8.
Stock, joint ownership, §41-2.2.
Death of joint tenant, §41-2.2, (c).
Inheritance tax laws unaffected, §41-2.2, (d).
When joint tenancy and shares of corporate stock exist, §41-2.2, (b).
Support and maintenance.
Child support.
General provisions.
See CHILD SUPPORT.
Failure to support dependent spouse, §14-322.
Generally.
See SUPPORT AND MAINTENANCE.
Interstate family support, §§52C-1-100 to 52C-9-902.
See INTERSTATE FAMILY SUPPORT.
Surviving spouses.
See SURVIVING SPOUSES.
Taxation.
Combined returns, §105-152, (e).
Excess funds, §28A-15-9.
Federal income tax refunds.
Death of spouses, §28A-15-6.
Federal marital deduction on distribution of estates, §28A-22-6.
Joint returns.
Federal income tax refunds, §28A-15-6.
When not authorized, §105-152, (e).
Separate returns.
Federal income tax refunds, §28A-15-7.

HUSBAND AND WIFE —Cont'd
Taxation —Cont'd
State income tax returns.
Death of spouse, §28A-15-8.
Tenancy by the entireties.
Absentees in military service.
Partition of property, §28B-6.
Control of real property held in tenancy by the entirety.
Applicability of section, §39-13.6, (c).
Equal rights to control, §39-13.6, (a).
Vesting of title, §39-13.6, (b).
Conveyance by spouse to other spouse.
Dissolution of interest held as, §39-13.3, (c).
Conveyance spouse to both spouses.
Interest created, §39-13.3, (b).
Creation in partition of real property, §39-13.5.
Killing decedents.
Disposition of property, §31A-5.
Mobile homes, §41-2.5, (a), (b), (d).
Definition of "mobile home," §41-2.5, (c).
Mortgage or sale of estates held by the entireties, §§35A-1310 to 35A-1314.
Renunciation by surviving tenant, §31B-1.
Title.
Mortgage or sale of estates held by the entireties.
Incompetent spouses.
Proceeding valid in passing title, §35A-1312.
Quieting title, §41-10.
Torts.
Actions arising out of acts occurring outside state, §52-5.1.
Antenuptial torts, §52-11.
Between husband and wife, §52-5.
Earnings and damages.
Recovery by person suing alone, §52-4.
Postnuptial torts, §52-12.
Uniform interstate family support act, §§52C-1-100 to 52C-9-902.
See INTERSTATE FAMILY SUPPORT.
Waiver, release or renunciation of interest.
Married persons under 18 made competent as to certain transactions, §39-13.2, (a).
Wills.
Acknowledgments.
Different officers, §39-8.
Different times and places, §39-8.
Not revoked by marriage, §31-5.3.
Witnesses.
Child abuse cases.
Waiver of husband-wife privilege, §8-57.1.
Child support actions instituted by designated representative of county commissioners.
Inapplicability of husband-wife privilege, §110-130.
Civil actions, §8-56.
Criminal actions, §8-57, (a) to (c).
Wrongful death.
Acts occurring outside state, §52-5.1.

HUSBAND-WIFE PRIVILEGE.
Abused, neglected or dependent juvenile actions.
Inapplicable when guardian ad litem demands information, §7B-601.
Child abuse or neglect.
Waiver, §8-57.1.
Child custody jurisdiction and enforcement, §50A-310, (d).
Child support actions instituted by designated representative of county commissioners.
Inapplicability, §110-130.
Civil actions, §8-56.

HUSBAND-WIFE PRIVILEGE —Cont'd
Criminal actions, §8-57, (a) to (c).
Interstate family support, §52C-3-315, (h), (i).
Paternity proceedings, §8-57.2.
Termination of parental rights proceedings.
Inapplicability, §7B-1109, (f).

HYBRID SEEDS, §106-277.17.

HYDE COUNTY.
Ambulances.
Obtaining ambulance services without intending to pay, §14-111.2.
Board of county commissioners.
Filling vacancies on board, §153A-27.1.
Cropper or tenant refusing to perform terms of contract.
Forfeiture of right of possession to premises, §42-27.
Dog collars.
Unlawful removal of electronic dog collars, §14-401.17.
Forestland sales, distribution of funds, §113-38.
Foxes, open seasons for taking.
Wildlife resources commission authorized to continue from year to year, §113-291.4, (f1).
Game laws, local acts not repealed, §113-133.1, (e).
Grants in navigable waters, registration, §113-205, (a).
Housing authority commissioners.
Tenant as commissioner, exemption from provision of law allowing, §157-5.
Maps in special proceedings, recording of photographic copies, §47-32.
Violation as misdemeanor, inapplicability of provisions, §47-32.2.
Northeastern North Carolina regional economic development commission, §158-8.2.
Open fires, high hazard counties.
Applicability of provisions, §113-60.23, (a).
Ground clearing activities, special permit, §113-60.23, (c).
Woodland fires, permit required, §113-60.23, (b).
Registration of deeds.
Tax certification that no delinquent taxes due, §161-31, (b).
School property.
Acquisition and improvement, §153A-158.1.
Sheriff.
Vacancy, performance of duties until vacancy filled, §162-5.1.
Special school tax, election to abolish.
Petition required, §115C-505.
Swimming, surfing and littering in Atlantic Ocean.
City ordinances effective, §160A-176.1.
Tax sales, notices by publication validated.
Inapplicability of provisions, §47-108.24.

HYDRAULIC BRAKE FLUIDS.
Types and brands approved by commissioner of motor vehicles, §20-124, (h).

HYDRAULIC POWER CORPORATIONS.
Eminent domain.
Use or occupancy of public highway, §62-181.

HYDROELECTRIC GENERATORS.
Business and energy tax credits, §§105-129.15 to 105-129.19.

HYDROPHOBIA.
Generally, §§130A-184 to 130A-201.
See RABIES.

HYPODERMICS AND SOPORIFICS.
Controlled substances generally, §§90-86 to 90-113.8.
See CONTROLLED SUBSTANCES.

HYPOTHETICAL CLAIMS OR DEFENSES, §1A-1, Rule 8, (e).

I

ICE.
Insurance.
Farm owners' and other property policies.
Damage from ice, snow or sleet, §58-44-55.
Tire chains, permissible use, §20-122, (b).

ICEBOXES.
Discarding or abandoning iceboxes, §14-318.1.

ICE CREAM PLANTS, CREAMERIES AND CHEESE FACTORIES, §§106-246 to 106-255.
Animals.
Prohibited, §106-246.
Board of agriculture.
Test by board, §106-250.
Butterfat, §106-250.
Certificate to district attorney.
Closure of plants for violation of article, §106-252.
Cleanliness.
Receivers of products to clean utensils before return, §106-249.
Required, §106-246.
Vessels and utensils, §106-247.
Closure of plants.
Certificate to district attorney, §106-252.
Violations of article, §106-252.
Compliance with standards, §106-248.
Desserts.
Frozen or semifrozen desserts.
Regulating trade or brand names, §106-253.
District attorney.
Closure of plants for violation of article.
Certificate to district attorney, §106-252.
Enforcement of provisions.
Department of agriculture and consumer services, §106-251.
Fees.
Inspection fees, §§106-254, 106-267.1.
Frozen or semifrozen desserts.
Regulating trade or brand names, §106-253.
Inspections.
Board of agriculture, §106-251.
Fees, §§106-254, 106-267.1.
Living and sleeping rooms, §106-246.
Misdemeanors.
Violations of article, §106-255.
Purity of products, §106-248.
Standards of purity and sanitation, §106-253.
Receivers of products.
Cleaning utensils before return, §106-249.
Right of entry to make inspections, §106-251.
Sanitation.
Required, §106-246.
Standards of purity and sanitation, §106-253.
Semifrozen desserts.
Regulating trade or brand names, §106-253.
Sleeping rooms, §106-246.
Sterilization.
Vessels and utensils, §106-247.
Test of butterfat, §106-250.
Toilets, §106-246.

ICE CREAM PLANTS, CREAMERIES AND CHEESE FACTORIES —Cont'd
Trade or brand names.
Frozen or semifrozen desserts, §106-253.
Utensils.
Cleaning and sterilization of utensils, §106-247.
Receivers of products to clean utensils before return, §106-249.
Vessels.
Cleaning and sterilization of vessels, §106-247.
Violations of article.
Closure of plants, §106-252.
Misdemeanor offenses, §106-255.
Washrooms and toilets, §106-246.

ICE SKATING RINKS.
Amusement device safety.
Amusement device defined as not including, §95-111.3, (a).

IDENTIFICATION.
Alcoholic beverage sales to or purchases by underage persons.
Fake identification, §18B-302, (d) to (f).
Cigarettes and tobacco products.
Proof of age.
Fake identification offered by minor for purchase of tobacco product, §14-313, (c).
Concealed handgun permits.
Identification required to be carried, §14-415.11, (a).
Dead bodies before burial or cremation, §90-210.29A.
Delinquent or undisciplined juvenile actions.
Fingerprinting and photographing juveniles, §7B-2102.
Nontestimonial identification order procedures generally, §§7B-2103 to 7B-2109.
DNA analysis, §§15A-266 to 15A-270.
See DNA DATABASE AND DATABANKS.
False or fraudulent, §14-100.1.
Foreign birth.
Certificate of identification, §130A-108.
Health care practitioners, §90-640.
Applicability, §90-640, (a).
Contents, §90-640, (b).
Disciplinary action, §90-640, (e).
Display required, §90-640, (b).
Exception, §90-640, (c).
Practitioner's office, exception, §90-640, (c).
Rules for exemptions, §90-640, (d).
Violation, §90-640, (e).
Identification cards for nonoperators of motor vehicles, §§20-37.7 to 20-37.9.
Leases, UCC.
Identification of goods, §25-2A-217.
Casualty to identified goods, §25-2A-221.
Insurable interest in existing goods.
Vesting in lessee, §25-2A-218.
Lessor's right to identify goods upon lessee's default, §25-2A-524.
Livestock.
Brucellosis.
Sale of diseased animals.
Removal of identification marks, §106-390.
Public livestock markets.
Cattle removed from market for slaughter and nonslaughter purposes, §106-409.
Removal of identification.
Disease control purposes, §106-414.
Swine removed from market for slaughter and nonslaughter purposes, §106-410.

IDENTIFICATION —Cont'd
Machines and apparatus, identification marks.
Removing, defacing, etc., §14-401.4.
Motor vehicle engine numbers.
Altering or changing.
Prohibited acts, §20-109, (a).
Intent to conceal or misrepresent true identity of vehicle, §20-109, (b).
New engine.
Division to be notified on installation, §20-70, (a).
Surrender of certificate of title and registration card on installation, §20-70, (b).
Vehicles without manufacturer's numbers.
Prohibitions as to, §20-108.
Nontestimonial identification, §§15A-271 to 15A-282.
Attorneys at law.
Copy of results.
Providing to person involved or his attorney, §15A-282.
Right to counsel, §15A-279, (d).
Bodily fluids.
Extraction.
Who may extract, §15A-279, (a).
Contempt.
Failure to obey order to appear, §15A-276.
Resistance to compliance with procedures, §15A-279, (e).
Copy of results.
Providing to person involved, §15A-282.
Defined, §15A-271.
Delinquent or undisciplined juvenile actions, §§7B-2103 to 7B-2109.
Destruction of products.
Motion by suspect, §15A-280.
Detention.
Length of detention, §15A-279, (c).
Failure to appear, §15A-276.
Force.
Unreasonable or unnecessary force not to be used, §15A-279, (b).
Investigations.
Additional investigative procedures not precluded, §15A-272.
Modification of order, §15A-275.
Order must state that person may request, §15A-278.
Order.
Application for.
Time for, §15A-272.
Contents, §15A-278.
Failure to obey, §15A-276.
Grounds for issuance, §15A-273.
Implementation, §15A-279.
Issuance, §15A-274.
Authority to issue, §15A-271.
Grounds, §15A-273.
Modification, §15A-275.
Order must state that person may request, §15A-278.
Previous orders.
Effect, §15A-279, (f).
Request of defendant, §15A-281.
Return, §15A-280.
Service, §15A-277.
Time for, §15A-274.
Request by defendant for order, §15A-281.
Resistance.
Contempt, §15A-279, (e).
Evidentiary effect, §15A-279, (g).

IDENTIFICATION —Cont'd
Nontestimonial identification —Cont'd
Return, §15A-280.
Service of order, §15A-277.
Time for, §15A-274.
Time limit on procedure, §15A-279.
Pawnbrokers.
Requirements, §91A-7, (b).
Personal property.
Trespasses to personal property.
Alteration, destruction or removal of permanent identification marks, §14-160.1.
Proof of age of minors.
Alcoholic beverage sales to or purchases by underage persons, §18B-302, (d) to (f).
Cigarettes and tobacco products, sales or distribution to, §14-313, (b).
Sale of goods, UCC.
Identification of goods, §25-2-501, (1).
Casualty to identified goods, §25-2-613.
Manner of identification, §25-2-501, (1).
Seller's right to identify notwithstanding breach, §25-2-704.
Searches and seizures.
Item subject to seizure under search warrant, §15A-242.
State departments and agencies.
Cards for field agents or deputies, §128-14.
Termination of parental rights.
Unknown parent, preliminary hearing to ascertain identity, §7B-1105.
Vital statistics.
Birth certificate where parentage cannot be established.
Certificate of identification in lieu of birth certificate, §130A-107.
Foreign birth.
Certificate of identification for person of foreign birth, §130A-108.

IDENTIFICATION CARDS.
Alcoholic beverage sales to or purchases by underage persons.
Allowing use of identification, §18B-302, (f).
Fraudulent use of identification, §18B-302, (e).
Production of identification card showing age to be at least required age for purchase, defense, §18B-302, (d).
Bail bondsmen and runners, §58-71-40, (d).
Cigarette and tobacco product purchases by minors, §14-313, (c).
False or fictitious names.
Possession or manufacture of cards, §14-100.1.
Presenting identification card with fake name in commission of felony, §20-37.8, (b).
Locksmith licensing.
Photo identification card, §74F-11.
Medicaid cards.
Medicaid recipient fraud.
Misuse of card, §108A-64, (b1).
Prescription drug identification cards.
Uniform identification cards issued by health benefit plan, §58-3-177.
Special identification cards for nonoperators of motor vehicles, §§20-37.7 to 20-37.9.
Applications, §§20-7, (b), 20-37.7, (b).
Change of address.
Notice, §20-37.9, (a).
Change of name, §20-37.9, (b).
Color photocopies or color reproductions.
Prohibition, §20-30.

IDENTIFICATION CARDS —Cont'd
Special identification cards for nonoperators of motor vehicles —Cont'd
Confidentiality of photographic image or signature, §20-43, (a).
Electronic system to verify information, §20-37.02.
Eligibility, §20-37.7, (a).
Expiration, §20-37.7, (d).
Fees, §§20-37.7, (d), 20-37.9, (c).
Form, §20-37.7, (c).
Fraud or misrepresentation in application.
Misdemeanor, §20-37.7, (e).
Fraudulent use.
Misdemeanor, §20-37.8, (a).
Prohibited, §20-37.8, (a).
Informing residents of provisions, §20-37.7, (h).
Nonliability of state, §20-37.7, (g).
Notification of change of address, §20-37.9, (a).
Organ, eye and tissue donor cards.
Availability at division offices issuing cards, §20-7.3.
Record of all recipients of special identification card, §20-37.7, (f).
Residency of state.
Proof required for issuance, documents evidencing, §20-7, (b2), (b3), (b4).
Social security number or tax payer identification number.
Providing required for issuance of license, §20-7, (b1).
Wrongful issuance, §20-34.1.
Structural pest control.
Certified applicators.
Issuance, fee, renewal, reissuance, new card, §106-65.31, (a).
Employees.
Issuance, renewal, fees, §106-65.31, (b1).
Issuance licensees and certified applicators, §106-65.25, (h).
Rules, committee may provide for, §106-65.31, (c).
Voter registration cards, §163-82.8.

IDENTIFICATION CERTIFICATE FOR INDIVIDUAL OF FOREIGN BIRTH, §130A-108, (a).
Readoption in state, §130A-108, (b).

IDENTIFICATION NUMBERS.
Commercial fishing boats.
False information, §75A-5.1, (d).
Renewal of number, §75A-5.1, (a), (c).
Motor vehicle engine numbers.
Altering or changing.
Prohibited acts, §20-109, (a).
Intent to conceal or misrepresent true identity of vehicle, §20-109, (b).
New engine.
Division to be notified on installation, §20-70, (a).
Surrender of certificate of title and registration card on installation, §20-70, (b).
Vehicles without manufacturer's numbers.
Prohibitions as to, §20-108.

IDENTIFICATION OF TOXIC OR HAZARDOUS SUBSTANCES, §§95-173 to 95-218.
See TOXIC SUBSTANCES.

IDENTITY FRAUD.
Applicability of provisions, §14-100.1, (c).
Damages, §1-539.2C, (a).
Additional nature of rights and remedies, §1-539.2C, (d).

IDENTITY FRAUD —Cont'd
Damages —Cont'd
Deceased person.
Recovery by estate, §1-539.2C, (b).
Venue of action for, §1-539.2C, (c).
Expungement of criminal records.
Dismissal or finding of not guilty.
Crime committed by another using defendant's identifying information, §15A-147.
Financial identity fraud, §§14-113.20 to 14-113.25.
Identification, defined, §14-100.1, (d).
Obtaining identification using false or fictitious information, §14-100.1, (b).
Penalties, §14-100.1, (e).
Possession or manufacture of false or fraudulent identification, §14-100.1, (a).

IGNITION INTERLOCK SYSTEM.
Impaired driving conviction.
Restoration of license conditioned on use of interlock.
Duration of condition, §20-17.8, (c).
Limited driving privilege, effect, §20-17.8, (d).
Notice of requirement, §20-17.8, (e).
Scope, §20-17.8, (a).
Violation as driving while license revoked, §20-17.8, (f), (g).
Commencement of revocation, §20-17.8, (h).
Hearings, §20-17.8, (j).
Notification of revocation, §20-17.8, (i).
Restoration after revocation for, §20-17.8, (k).
When required, §20-17.8, (b).
Vehicles subject to requirement, §20-17.8, (c1).
Limited driving privileges.
When required as condition, §20-179.3, (g5).

ILLEGITIMACY, §§49-1 to 49-17.
Aid to dependent children.
Reports to district attorney of illegitimate births, §§15-155.1 to 15-155.3.
Artificial insemination.
Status of child born as a result of, §49A-1.
Bigamy.
Children born of voidable marriage legitimate, §50-11.1.
Birth certificates.
Affidavit acknowledging paternity.
Listing declaring father on birth certificate and presumption as natural father, §130A-101, (f).
Legitimation.
New certificate upon legitimation, §49-13.
Legitimation when mother married, §49-12.1, (e).
Names entered upon birth certificates, §130A-101, (f).
Clerks of court.
Paternity of illegitimate children judicially determined.
Furnishing state registrar with facts as to paternity, §130A-119.
Confidentiality of information.
District attorneys.
Reports to district attorneys of aid to dependent children and illegitimate births, §15-155.3.
Constitution of North Carolina.
Local, private and special legislation prohibited, Const. N. C., art. II, §24.
Construction and interpretation.
Jurisdiction over nonresident persons.
Construction of section, §49-17, (b).

ILLEGITIMACY —Cont'd
Costs.
Allowance of costs to either party or apportioned in discretion of court, §6-21.
Custody.
Establishment of paternity, §49-15.
District attorneys.
Reports to district attorneys of aid to dependent children and illegitimate births, §§15-155.1 to 15-155.3.
Divorce.
Effects of absolute divorce.
No judgment to render children illegitimate, §50-11, (b).
Voidable marriages.
Children born legitimate, §50-11.1.
General assembly.
Local, private and special legislation prohibited, Const. N. C., art. II, §24.
Intestate succession.
Descent and distribution upon intestacy, §29-20.
Legitimated children.
Succession by, through and from, §29-18.
Person's illegitimate child entitled to take by, through and from, §29-19, (b).
Shares of others than surviving spouse, §29-22.
Succession by, through and from, §29-19, (a).
Surviving spouses.
Share of surviving spouse of illegitimate intestate, §29-21.
Shares of others than surviving spouse, §29-22.
Jurisdiction.
Construction of section, §49-17, (b).
Nonresidents, §49-17, (a).
Legitimation.
Birth certificates.
New certificate upon legitimation, §49-13.
Legitimation when mother married, §49-12.1, (e).
Civil action to establish paternity.
Establishment not to have effect of legitimation, §49-14, (a).
Effects, §49-11.
Legitimation when mother married, §49-12.1, (b).
Marriage.
By subsequent marriage, §49-12.
Legitimation when mother married, §49-12.1.
Order of court, §49-10.
Parties, §49-10.
Petition, §49-10.
Special proceedings, §49-10.
Legitimation when mother married.
Putative father may file, §49-12.1, (a).
Subsequent marriage, §49-12.
When mother married, §49-12.1.
Marriage.
Legitimacy.
By subsequent marriage, §49-12.
Legitimation when mother married, §49-12.1.
Misdemeanors.
Nonsupport of illegitimate child by parents, §49-2.
Nonresidents.
Construction of jurisdictional basis, §49-17, (b).
Jurisdiction over nonresident or nonresident persons, §49-17, (a).
Nonsupport, §49-2.
Parties.
Proceedings may be brought by certain parties, §49-16.

ILLEGITIMACY —Cont'd
Paternity.
Blood tests and samples.
Competency of blood test, §8-50.1.
Civil action to establish.
Action brought more than three years after birth of child.
Evidentiary requirements, §49-14, (d).
Authorized, §49-14, (a).
Establishment not to have effect of legitimation, §49-14, (a).
Invoices for services rendered.
Admissibility, §49-14, (e).
Limitations on commencement, §49-14, (c).
Proof to be beyond reasonable doubt, §49-14, (b).
Temporary order of child support, §49-14, (d).
Trial at first session after docketing, §49-14, (e).
Custody and support of illegitimate children.
When paternity established, §49-15.
Legitimation when mother married.
Special proceeding brought by putative father, §49-12.1, (a).
Witnesses.
Presumed father or mother as witnesses where paternity at issue, §8-57.2.
Support of illegitimate children.
Amount.
Determination by court, §49-7.
Bonds, surety.
Future appearance of defendant, §49-9.
Child defined, §49-2.
Continuances, surety of person accused of being father, §49-5.
Death of mother not bar to proceedings, §49-5.
District attorneys.
Reports to district attorneys of aid to dependent children and illegitimate births, §§15-155.1 to 15-155.3.
Immunity of mother testifying, §49-6.
Issues.
Determination by court, §49-7.
Misdemeanors.
Willful nonsupport of illegitimate child, §49-2.
Orders, §49-7.
Power of court to modify, §49-8.
Paternity.
Custody and support when paternity established, §49-15.
Temporary order of support.
Entry when determination of paternity pending, §49-14, (f).
Paternity, preliminary determination, §49-5.
Place of birth of child.
Not consideration, §49-3.
Self-incrimination.
Mother not excused on grounds of self-incrimination, §49-6.
Sentencing.
Power of court to suspend sentence, §49-8.
Time for commencing prosecution, §49-4.
Title of article, §49-1.
Venue, §49-5.
When prosecution may be commenced, §49-4.
Willful nonsupport.
Misdemeanor, §49-2.
Vital statistics.
Birth certificates.
Affidavit acknowledging paternity.
Listing declaring father on certificate and presumption as natural father, §130A-101, (f).

ILLEGITIMACY —Cont'd
Vital statistics —Cont'd
Birth certificates —Cont'd
Children born out of wedlock, §130A-101, (f).
Illegitimate children judicially determined.
Furnishing facts as to paternity, §130A-119.
Legitimation.
New certificate upon legitimation, §49-13.
Legitimation when mother married, §49-12.1, (e).
Names entered upon birth certificates, §130A-101, (f).
When mother married.
Burden of proof.
Presumption of legitimacy.
Overcoming by clear and convincing evidence, §49-12.1, (b).
Consent order, §49-12.1, (c).
Effect of legitimation under section, §49-12.1, (d).
Guardian ad litem.
Appointment, §49-12.1, (a).
Presumption of legitimacy.
Overcoming by clear and convincing evidence, §49-12.1, (b).
Special proceeding.
Putative father may file, §49-12.1, (a).
Vital statistics.
New birth certificate.
Certified copy of order of legitimation sent to state registrar, §49-12.1, (e).
Wills.
Revocation by subsequent entitlement of after-born children, §31-5.5.
Witnesses.
Paternity.
Presumed father or mother as witnesses where paternity at issue, §8-57.2.

ILLITERACY.
Executors and administrators.
Persons disqualified to serve, §28A-4-2.

IMITATION FOODS.
Food, drug and cosmetic act.
Foods deemed misbranded, §106-130.

IMMEDIATE CIVIL LICENSE REVOCATION, §20-16.5.
Implied consent violations.
Civil actions, §20-16.5, (o).
Costs, §20-16.5, (j).
Definitions, §20-16.5, (a).
Effect of revocation, §20-16.5, (i).
Exceptions, §20-16.5, (n).
Hearing, contesting validity, §20-16.5, (g).
Limited driving privilege, §20-16.5, (p).
Modification of order, §20-16.5, (m).
Persons charged with violations, §20-16.5, (b).
Precharge test results basis for revocation, §20-16.5, (b1).
Refusal to submit to chemical analysis, §20-16.5, (b).
Report to division, §20-16.5, (k).
Report to judicial officials.
Duty of charging officers, §20-16.5, (c).
Judicial officer with whom report filed, §20-16.5, (d).
Person not present, procedure for filing, §20-16.5, (f).
Person present, procedure for filing, §20-16.5, (e).

IMMEDIATE CIVIL LICENSE REVOCATION —Cont'd
Implied consent violations —Cont'd
Restoration fee, person with no license, §20-16.5, (l).
Return of license, §20-16.5, (h).

IMMIGRATION.
Constitution of the United States, Const. U. S., art. I, §9.
Fair housing, §§41A-1 to 41A-10.
See FAIR HOUSING.

IMMIGRATION AND NATURALIZATION SERVICE.
Officers authorized to enforce criminal laws, §15A-406.

IMMUNITY.
Abandonment of child.
Temporary custody of infant without court order.
Immunity from civil and criminal liability, §7B-500, (e).
Abused, neglected or dependent juvenile actions.
Volunteers participating in local guardian ad litem program, §7B-1204.
Abused, neglected or dependent juvenile reports or investigations.
Persons making report and cooperating in investigation, §7B-309.
Address confidentiality program, §15C-11.
Adult care homes.
Criminal history record checks of employees, §131D-40, (g).
Quality assurance, medical, or peer review committees, §131D-21.2, (a).
Advance health care directive registry, §130A-471.
Aged persons.
Long-term care ombudsman program.
Good faith performance of official duties, §143B-181.24.
Agricultural finance authority, §122D-23.
Arbitration.
Arbitrators, immunity of, §1-569.14, (a).
State court-ordered nonbinding arbitration in certain civil actions.
Arbitrators.
Immunity as judges from civil liability for official conduct, §7A-37.1, (e).
Architects.
Volunteers during an emergency or disaster.
Qualified immunity, §83A-13.1.
Athletic trainers.
Good faith reports of misconduct or incapacity, §90-539.
Attorneys at law.
Disciplinary proceedings.
Persons immune from suit, §84-28.2.
Automated external defibrillator (AED).
First-aid or emergency medical personnel, §90-21.15, (c), (d).
Baby drop off.
Temporary custody of infant without court order.
Immunity from civil and criminal liability, §7B-500, (e).
Cancer.
Reports.
Persons who report cancer, §130A-211.
Charities.
Defense of charitable immunity abolished, §1-539.9.

IMMUNITY —Cont'd
Charities —Cont'd
Volunteers for charitable organizations, §1-539.10, (a) to (c).
Definitions, §1-539.11.
Child care provider criminal history record check, §110-90.2, (f).
Child support actions instituted by designated representative of county commissioners.
Parent required to answer, §110-130.
Communicable diseases.
Investigations.
Persons permitting access to medical records, §130A-144, (c).
Reports.
Immunity of persons who report, §130A-142.
Compromise and settlement.
Mediated settlement conferences in superior court civil actions.
Judicial immunity of mediators, etc., §7A-38.1, (j).
Consent to health care for minors.
Reliance and authorization, §32A-33, (b).
Constitution of the United States, Const. U. S., art. IV, §2.
Corneal tissue removal, §130A-391, (b).
Corporations.
Nonprofit corporations.
Acceptance or rejection of member's vote.
Corporate action in good faith, §55A-7-27, (d).
Directors and officers, §55A-8-60.
Director's compliance with standards of conduct, §55A-8-30, (d).
Officers, discharging duties, §55A-8-42, (d), (e).
Crematory licensee.
Authorization form.
No liability of licensee for cremation pursuant to, §§90-210.45, (c), 90-210.51, (b).
Dentists.
Peer review committees.
Members, §90-48.8.
Witnesses, §90-48.9.
DNA database and databanks.
DNA analysis.
Persons authorized to draw blood, §15A-266.6, (b).
Donated food, §99B-10.
Dry-cleaning solvent cleanup.
State, agencies, officers, employees and agents, §143-215.104T, (b).
Education.
Local boards of education, §115C-42.
Electrologists.
Reports of violations of chapter, §88A-23.
Emergency management, §§166A-14, 166A-15.
Emergency war powers of governor, §147-33.4.
Employee assistance professionals.
Good faith report of violations, §90-510.
Employer disclosing information about employee's job history or performance, §1-539.12, (a) to (d).
Engineers.
Volunteer engineers during emergency or disaster, §89C-19.1.
Enhanced 911 wireless system for wireless communications.
Limitation of civil liability, §62A-31.
Equine activity liability, §99E-2, (a).
Expedited evictions.
Civil liability, §42-76.

IMMUNITY —Cont'd
Extradition.
No immunity from other criminal prosecution while in this state, §15A-748.
Financial records privacy.
Disclosure of financial records by financial institution, §53B-9, (c).
Fish and fisheries resources.
Hull insurance and protection and indemnity clubs.
Administrators and boards of trustees, §58-20-40.
Forest and forestry.
Prescribed burning of forestlands, §113-60.42, (b), (c).
Fraternal benefit societies.
Officers.
Civil liability for monetary damages, §58-24-35, (d).
Gambling contracts.
Confessions of witnesses, §16-2.
Governmental immunity.
Community colleges.
Negligence of agents and employees of institutions.
Waiver of governmental immunity by act obtaining liability insurance, §115D-24.
Counties.
Liability insurance.
Purchase as waiver of governmental immunity, §153A-435, (b).
Emergency management, §166A-14, (a).
Emergency war powers of governor, §147-33.4.
Mental health, developmental disabilities and substance abuse.
Area authorities.
Waiver of immunity as to torts of agents, employees and board members, §122C-152, (a) to (f).
Municipal corporations.
Tort liability.
Waiver of immunity through insurance purchase, §160A-485.
University of North Carolina.
Insurance.
Provisions not deemed to waive sovereign immunity of state, §116-221.
Guardian ad litem program providing services to abused, neglected or dependent juveniles.
Volunteers participating in local program, §7B-1204.
Guardians.
Guardian of the person.
Acting within limits imposed by powers and duties or order of appointment, §35A-1241, (c).
Hazardous materials emergency response.
Regional response team personnel, §166A-24.
Health care institutions reporting disciplinary actions against physicians, §90-14.13.
Health care powers of attorney.
Reliance on health care power of attorney, §32A-24, (c).
Hospitals.
Directors, trustees or officers of public hospitals.
Limited liability, §131E-47.1, (a).
Exception, §131E-47.1, (b).
Medical review committee, §131E-95, (a).

IMMUNITY —Cont'd
Husband and wife.
Inter-spousal immunity.
Abolished, §52-5.1.
Actions arising out of acts occurring outside state, §52-5.1.
Insurance.
Fraud.
Immunity from liability for reporting fraud, §58-2-160, (a), (b).
Market assistance program.
Good faith immunity for operation of, §58-40-135.
Insurance commissioner.
Examinations, §58-2-133, (d).
Insurance consumer and customer information privacy.
Disclosure in accordance with article, §58-39-110.
International commercial arbitration and conciliation.
Conciliators and parties, §1-567.87.
Inter-spousal immunity.
Abolished, §52-5.
Actions arising out of acts occurring outside state, §52-5.1.
Juvenile code.
Abuse or neglect of children.
Reporting abuse or neglect of child.
Immunity of persons reporting, §7B-309.
Law enforcement officers.
Assistance to individuals intoxicated in public.
Use of reasonable measures, §122C-301, (b).
Mediated settlement conferences in superior court civil actions.
Judicial immunity of mediators, etc., §7A-38.1, (j).
Mediated settlement conferences or other settlement procedures in district court.
Actions involving equitable distribution, alimony or support.
Mediators and neutrals acting pursuant to provisions, §7A-38.4A, (h).
Medical assistance provider false claims.
Persons furnishing information to officials, §108A-70.15, (a).
Medical board members and staff, §90-14, (e).
Medical examiners.
Corneal tissue removal.
Immunity from liability, §130A-391, (b).
Mental health, developmental disability, substance abuse.
Advance instruction for mental health treatment.
Providing treatment in reliance on instruction, §122C-75, (b).
Area authorities.
Waiver of immunity as to torts of agents, employees and board members, §122C-152, (a) to (f).
Consumer advocacy program, §122C-19.
Disclosure of confidential or privileged information during inspection, §122C-192, (b).
Facilities, staff, physicians, etc., §122C-210.1.
Methamphetamine watch program.
Immunity from civil and criminal liability.
Good faith actions, §114-43.
Minors.
Motor vehicles.
Parent-child immunity.
Abolition in motor vehicle cases, §1-539.21.
Monopolies and restraint of trade.
Examinations by attorney general.
Person examined exempt from prosecution, §75-11.

IMMUNITY —Cont'd
Motor vehicles.
Parent-child immunity.
Abolished in motor vehicle cases, §1-539.21.
Rendering first aid or emergency assistance at accident scene, §20-166, (b).
Municipal corporations.
Exercise in conformity with charter and general laws, §160A-11.
Exercise of corporate powers, §160A-12.
Tort liability.
Waiver of immunity through insurance purchase, §160A-485.
National guard or state defense militia members, §127A-150, (a) to (c).
Nonprofit corporations.
Acceptance or rejection of member's vote.
Corporate action in good faith, §55A-7-27, (d).
Directors and officers, §55A-8-60.
Director's compliance with standards of conduct, §55A-8-30, (d).
Officers, discharging duties, §55A-8-42, (d), (e).
Nurses.
Nurse licensure compact.
Officers, employees or agents of state licensing boards, §90-171.90.
Reports of violations.
Immunity from suit, §90-171.47.
Nursing homes.
Medically necessary actions.
Action taken pursuant to physician's order, §131E-124, (d).
Occupational diseases.
Reportable diseases, illnesses and injuries.
Immunity of persons who report, §130A-459.
Oil pollution and hazardous substances control.
Removal of oil discharges.
Limitation on liability of persons engaged in, §143-215.93A, (a).
Exceptions, §143-215.93A, (b).
Parent and child.
Motor vehicles.
Abolition of parent-child immunity in motor vehicle cases, §1-539.21.
Parking in fire lane.
Law enforcement officers carrying out or enforcing provisions, §20-162, (b).
Pathologists.
Corneal tissue removal.
Immunity from liability, §130A-391, (b).
Pharmacists and pharmacies.
Impaired pharmacist peer review organizations, §90-85.41, (f).
Physicians and surgeons.
Advance instruction for mental health treatment.
Providing treatment in reliance on instruction, §122C-75, (b).
Aircraft pilot's disability or infirmity.
Report or testimony as to mental or physical disability or infirmity, §90-21.20A.
Health care institution reporting disciplinary actions, §90-14.13.
Peer review agreements.
Peer review activities conducted in good faith, §90-21.22, (f).
Reporting or investigating alleged misconduct.
Good faith immunity, §90-14, (f).
Principal and income act.
Conversion to uniturst.
Good faith immunity, §37A-1-104.8.

IMMUNITY —Cont'd
Public health authorities.
Medical review committee, §130A-45.7, (a).
Railroad passenger injured while in prohibited place.
Nonliability of railroad, §136-196.
Recreational trespass.
Limitation of liability, §38A-4.
Renunciation of property or interest.
Distributing or disposing of property in reliance upon terms, §31B-4, (b).
Rescue squads.
Volunteer rescue squad members.
Civil liability, §§58-82-5, (c), 90-21.14, (a), (b).
Residential school personnel.
Low-performing schools.
Negligence in carrying out provisions relating to personnel, §143B-146.8, (e).
Retirement system for counties and cities.
Management of funds, §128-29, (f).
Safe haven for infants.
Temporary custody of infant without court order.
Immunity from civil and criminal liability, §7B-500, (e).
School buses.
Waiver of immunity as to certain acts of bus drivers, §115C-255.
School employee personnel evaluations.
Persons carrying out provisions, §115C-333, (e).
Schools.
Criminal record checks of school personnel, §115C-332, (g).
Secured transactions.
Limitation on liability of secured party, §25-9-628.
Skateboarding, inline skating and freestyle bicycling.
Activities on governmental entity's property.
Limitation of liability, §99E-25.
Assumption of inherent risks, limitation on liability, §§99E-21 to 99E-25.
Social services.
Adult protection.
Certain persons immune from civil or criminal liability, §108A-102, (c).
Emergency services.
Petitioners, §108A-106, (g).
Sport shooting range protection.
Persons owning, operating or using sport shooting ranges, §14-409.46, (a), (b).
Support of illegitimate children proceeding.
Mother testifying, §49-6.
Telecommunications companies.
Discontinuation of telecommunications services used for unlawful purposes, §15A-299, (e).
Terrorist incident using nuclear, biological or chemical agents.
Reports.
Immunity of persons making, §§130A-476, (d), 130A-480, (c).
Volunteer fire department members.
Civil liability, §58-82-5, (c).
Volunteer health care providers, §90-21.16.
Volunteers.
Civil liability, §§58-82-5, (c), 90-21.14, (a), (b).
Immunity from civil liability, §1-539.10, (a) to (c).
Definitions, §1-539.11.
Witnesses.
Alcoholic beverages.
Illicit sale.
Testimony enforced in certain criminal investigations, §8-55.

IMMUNITY —Cont'd
Witnesses —Cont'd
Argument to jury as to impact of immunity, §15A-1055, (b).
Arrest in civil cases, §8-64.
Child support actions instituted by designated representatives of county commissioners, §110-130.
Contempt.
Criminal contempt.
Refusal to testify or produce information, §5A-11, (a).
Evidence of grant of immunity may be fully developed, §15A-1055, (a).
Gaming.
Testimony enforced in certain criminal investigations, §8-55.
Jury.
Argument to jury as to impact of immunity, §15A-1055, (b).
Monopolies and restraints of trade.
Persons compelled to testify, §75-11.
Mother in support of illegitimate child proceeding, §49-6.
Order to testify of produce other information, §15A-1051, (a).
Application for.
Court proceedings, §15A-1052, (a), (b).
Grand jury proceedings, §15A-1053, (a), (b).
Court proceedings, §15A-1052, (a).
Definition of "other information," §15A-1051, (c).
Grand jury proceedings, §15A-1053, (a).
Application, §15A-1053, (a), (b).
Jury trial.
Judge to inform jury of grant of immunity, §15A-1052, (c).
When effective, §15A-1051, (b).
Self-incrimination, §15A-1051, (a).
Sentence concessions, §15A-1054, (a).
Evidence of testimonial arrangement may be fully developed, §15A-1055, (a).
Jury.
Argument to jury as to impact of agreement, §15A-1055, (b).
Notice of agreement, §15A-1054, (c).
Recommendations, §15A-1054, (b).
Supplemental proceedings.
Incriminating answers not used in criminal proceedings, §1-357.

IMMUNITY OF WITNESSES.
Alcoholic beverage illicit sales.
Testimony enforced in certain criminal investigations, §8-55.
Argument to jury as to impact of immunity, §15A-1055, (b).
Arrest in civil cases, §8-64.
Child support actions instituted by designated representatives of county commissioners, §110-130.
Criminal contempt.
Refusal to testify or produce information, §5A-11, (a).
Evidence of grant of immunity may be fully developed, §15A-1055, (a).
Gaming investigations.
Testimony enforced, §8-55.
Monopolies and restraint of trade.
Persons compelled to testify, §75-11.
Mother in support of illegitimate child proceeding, §49-6.

IMMUNITY OF WITNESSES —Cont'd
Order to testify or produce other information.
Application for.
Court proceedings, §15A-1052, (a), (b).
Grand jury proceedings, §15A-1053, (a), (b).
Court proceedings, §15A-1052, (a).
Definition of "other information," §15A-1051, (c).
Grand jury proceedings, §15A-1053, (a).
Application, §15A-1053, (a), (b).
Jury trial.
Judge to inform jury of grant of immunity, §15A-1052, (c).
When effective, §15A-1051, (b).
Self-incrimination, §15A-1051, (a).
Sentence concessions, §15A-1054, (a).
Evidence of testimonial arrangement may be fully developed, §15A-1055, (a).
Jury.
Argument to jury as to impact of agreement, §15A-1055, (b).
Notice of agreement, §15A-1054, (c).
Recommendations, §15A-1054, (b).
Supplemental proceedings.
Incriminating answers not used in criminal proceedings, §1-357.

IMMUNIZATION, §§130A-152 to 130A-158.
Adult care homes.
Residents and employees, §131D-9.
Certificate of immunization, §130A-154.
Adults attending school, §130A-155, (d).
Child-care facilities.
Maintenance of record, §130A-155, (b).
Report to be filed, §130A-155, (c).
Submission of certificate to facility, §130A-155, (a).
Information to be contained, §130A-154, (a).
Maintenance of record, §130A-155, (b).
School authorities.
Report to be filed, §130A-155, (c).
Submission of certificate to authorities, §130A-155, (a).
State other than North Carolina, §130A-154, (b).
Submission of certificate to child-care facility, preschool and school authorities, §130A-155, (a).
Universities and colleges.
Records to be maintained, §130A-155.1, (b).
Reports.
Filing of immunization report with department, §130A-155.1, (c).
Submission of certificate to, §130A-155.1, (a).
Charge for obtaining immunization, §130A-153, (a).
Child-care facilities.
Certificate of immunization.
Maintenance of record, §130A-155, (b).
Report to be filed, §130A-155, (c).
Submission of certificate to facility, §130A-155, (a).
Childhood vaccine-related injury compensation, §§130A-422 to 130A-434.
See CHILDHOOD VACCINE-RELATED INJURY COMPENSATION.
Commission for health services.
Promulgation of rules concerning implementation of program, §130A-152, (c).
Contracts for purchase of covered vaccines.
Authority of secretary of health and human services, §130A-433, (a).

IMMUNIZATION —Cont'd
Department of health and human services.
Enforcement of rules concerning implementation of program, §130A-152, (c).
Distribution of covered vaccines.
Local health departments' responsibility, §130A-433, (a).
Exemption.
Medical exemption, §130A-156.
Religious exemption, §130A-157.
Fees.
Administering covered vaccines, §130A-433, (b).
Adoption of rules establishing, §130A-152, (c1).
First responders, smallpox vaccination.
Sick leave and salary policy, time off due to adverse reaction, §160A-164.1.
Flu vaccination information.
Charter school students parents or guardians.
Information provided, §115C-238.29F, (a).
Church schools and schools of religious charter.
Information provided parents and guardians of students, §115C-548.
Home schools.
Information provided, §115C-565.
Local boards of education.
Information provided parents and guardians, §115C-47.
Implementation of program.
Promulgation and enforcement of rules concerning implementation, §130A-152, (c).
Medical exemption, §130A-156.
Medical plan for teachers and state employees, §135-40.5, (f).
Meningococcal disease vaccination information.
Charter school students parents or guardians.
Information provided, §115C-238.29F, (a).
Church schools and schools of religious charter.
Information provided parents and guardians of students, §115C-548.
Home schools.
Information provided, §115C-565.
Local boards of education.
Information provided parents and guardians, §115C-47.
Universities and colleges.
Providing students information, §116-260.
Minors, §130A-153, (d).
Negligence.
Restitution.
Vaccine spoiled due to provider negligence, §130A-158.
Nursing homes.
Residents and employees, §131E-113.
Obtaining immunization, §130A-153, (a).
Charge, §130A-153, (a).
Poultry.
Quarantine of inoculated poultry, §106-307.4.
Records.
Access to records, §130A-153, (c).
Certificate of immunization.
Maintenance of record.
By child-care facility and school authorities, §130A-155, (b).
By college or university, §130A-155.1, (b).
Religious exemption, §130A-157.
Reports, §130A-153, (b).
Certificate of immunization.
Filing of report.
By child-care facility and school authorities, §130A-155, (c).

IMMUNIZATION —Cont'd
Reports —Cont'd
Certificate of immunization —Cont'd
Filing of report —Cont'd
By college or university, §130A-155.1, (c).
Required, §130A-152, (a).
Additional immunization, §130A-152, (e).
Requirements that can be placed on child or parent.
Adoption of rules, §130A-152, (c1).
Restitution.
Vaccine spoiled due to provider negligence, §130A-158.
Rules and regulations, §130A-152, (c).
School authorities.
Certificate of immunization.
Maintenance of record, §130A-155, (b).
Report to be filed, §130A-155, (c).
Submission of certificate to authorities, §130A-155, (a).
Smallpox.
Claims arising from vaccinations of state employees.
Employment vaccination pursuant to homeland security act, §143-300.1A.
County employees.
Vaccination incident to homeland security act.
Adverse reaction, sick leave policy, counties to enact, §153A-94.1.
First responders, smallpox vaccination.
Sick leave and salary policy, time off due to adverse reaction, §160A-164.1.
Public officers and employees.
Sick leave for adverse reaction to vaccination, §126-8.4, (a) to (c).
Workers' compensation.
Occupation diseases.
Infection or adverse medical reaction.
Employment vaccination incident to homeland security act, §97-53.
Spoiled vaccine.
Restitution.
Vaccine spoiled due to provider negligence, §130A-158.
Standards of vaccine preparations used, §130A-152, (d).
Universities and colleges.
Certificate of immunization.
Records.
Maintaining immunization records, §130A-155.1, (b).
Reports.
Filing of immunization report with department, §130A-155.1, (c).
Submission of certificate, §130A-155.1, (a).
Vaccine preparations, §130A-152, (d).

IMPAIRED DRIVING.
Aider and abetter punishment, §20-179, (f1).
Alcohol and drug education traffic (ADET) school.
Limited driving privilege, §20-179.3, (g2).
Restoration of license after conviction.
Obtaining certificate of completion, §20-17.6, (c).
Arrest, §15A-534.2.
Bicycles.
Definition of vehicle does not include, §20-138.1, (e).
Boating under the influence, §75A-10, (b), (b1).
Check of drivers, §20-16.3A.

IMPAIRED DRIVING —Cont'd
Chemical analysis of impairing substances in blood.
Additional analysis.
Right of person tested, §20-139.1, (d).
Administration of analysis.
Additional analysis.
Right of person tested, §20-139.1, (d).
Arresting or charging officer may not perform, §20-139.1, (b1).
Requisites, §20-139.1, (b).
Who may withdraw blood, §20-139.1, (c).
Affidavits.
Use in district courts, §20-139.1, (e1).
Alcohol.
Department of health and human services.
Rules and regulations concerning ingestion of controlled amounts, §20-139.1, (g).
Alcohol concentration.
Defined, §20-4.01.
Alcohol screening tests.
Approval of devices and manner of use, §20-16.3, (b).
To be made with approved devices and in approved manner, §20-16.3, (c).
Use of results, §20-16.3, (d).
When test may be required, §20-16.3, (a).
Arrest.
Test as condition of release, §15A-534.2.
Availability of records, §20-27, (b).
Basis for officer to require analysis, §20-16.2, (a).
Breath analysis.
Introducing routine records kept as part of breath testing program, §20-139.1, (b4).
Results inadmissible if preventive maintenance not performed, §20-139.1, (b2).
Sequential breath tests required, §20-139.1, (b3).
Commercial drivers' licenses.
Refusal to submit to chemical test.
Disqualification, §20-17.4, (a).
Effect, §20-17.5, (c).
Commercial vehicles.
Impaired driving in commercial motor vehicle.
Applicability to offense, §20-138.2, (g).
Controlled-drinking programs, §20-139.1, (g).
Definitions, §20-16.2, (a1).
Department of health and human services.
Alcohol.
Rules and regulations concerning ingestion of controlled amounts, §20-139.1, (g).
Duty of law enforcement officer, §20-16.5, (c).
Evidence.
Admissibility of results, §20-139.1, (a).
Qualification of person withdrawing blood, §20-139.1, (c).
Refusal to submit to analysis.
Admissibility of evidence of refusal, §20-139.1, (f).
Immediate revocation of driving privileges.
Alcohol concentration, §20-16.2, (a).
Refusal of test, §20-16.2, (a).
Implied consent, §20-16.2, (a).
Commercial vehicles.
Impaired driving in commercial vehicles.
Implied consent offense, §20-138.2, (d).
Habitual impaired driving as implied consent of offense, §20-138.5, (c).
Unconscious or otherwise incapable of refusal, §20-16.2, (b).

IMPAIRED DRIVING —Cont'd
Chemical analysis of impairing substances in blood —Cont'd
Liability.
Nonliability of person administering analysis, §20-139.1, (c).
Mandatory revocation of license in event of refusal to submit to analysis, §20-16.2, (d).
Designation of proceedings, §20-16.5, (o).
Effect of revocation, §20-16.5, (i).
Exception for license already revoked, §20-16.5, (n).
Hearing, §20-16.2, (d), (e).
Immediate civil revocation, §20-16.5.
Limited driving privilege.
Person's license indefinitely revoked, §20-16.5, (p).
Limited driving privilege after six months, §20-16.2, (e1).
Modification of revocation order, §20-16.5, (m).
Notice, §20-16.2, (d), (f).
Report to division, §20-16.5, (k).
Restoration fee for unlicensed persons, §20-16.5, (l).
Return of license, §20-16.5, (h).
Review de novo, §20-16.2, (e).
Revocation report, §20-16.5, (c) to (f).
Negligence.
Person administering analysis liable for negligent act, §20-139.1, (c).
Notification of rights, §20-16.2, (a).
Nurses.
Administration of analysis, §20-139.1, (c).
Additional analysis, §20-139.1, (d).
Physicians and surgeons.
Administration of analysis, §20-139.1, (c).
Additional analysis, §20-139.1, (d).
Procedures.
Conforming procedures to those approved by commission for health services, §20-139.1, (b).
Performed by licensed individuals, §20-139.1, (b).
Qualification of person withdrawing blood.
Evidence, §20-139.1, (c).
Records, §20-139.1, (e).
Availability, §20-27, (b).
Refusal to submit to analysis, §20-16.2, (c).
Admissibility of evidence of refusal, §20-139.1, (f).
Consequences, §20-16.2, (d).
Case involving death or critical injury, §20-16.2, (d1).
Evidence inadmissible, §20-139.1, (f).
Hearings before division, §20-16.2, (d).
Reporting refusals, §20-16.2, (c1).
Request to submit to analysis, §20-16.2, (c).
Right of drivers to request, §20-16.2, (i).
Results.
Reporting, §20-16.2, (c1).
Right to chemical analysis before arrest or charge, §20-16.2, (i).
Unconscious person may be tested, §20-16.2, (b).
Who may administer analysis, §20-139.1, (c).
Commercial drivers' licenses.
Disqualification.
Grounds, §20-17.4, (a).
Commercial vehicles.
Chemical analysis of impairing substances in blood.
Applicability, §20-138.2, (g).

IMPAIRED DRIVING —Cont'd
Commercial vehicles —Cont'd
Defenses.
Legally entitled to use alcohol or drug.
Defense precluded, §20-138.2, (b).
Effect when impaired driving offense also charged, §20-138.2, (e).
Implied consent offense, §20-138.2, (d).
Misdemeanor, §20-138.2, (e).
Offense defined, §20-138.2, (a).
Pleading.
Sufficiency, §20-138.2, (c).
Restoration of license after conviction, §20-17.6.
Special information inquired in judgment for conviction, §20-24, (e).
Community service.
Alternative punishment program conducted by department of correction, §20-179.4, (a).
Coordinator assigned to district court districts, §20-179.4, (b).
Coordinators to report violations of terms, §20-179.4, (e).
Fee paid for serving community service sentence, §20-179.4, (c).
Deposit in general fund, §20-179.4, (d).
Hearings on violations, §20-179.4, (e).
Time limit for performing, §20-179, (n).
Concealed handgun permit.
Conviction is grounds for denial of permit, §14-415.12, (b).
Consolidating two or more charges for judgment prohibited, §20-179, (f2).
Credit for first 24 hours of time spent in incarceration pending trial.
Judge not to give, §20-179, (p).
Credit for good behavior, §15A-1355, (c).
Credit on term of imprisonment for inpatient treatment, §20-179, (k1).
Defenses.
Commercial vehicles.
Legal entitlement to use alcohol or drug.
Defense precluded, §20-138.2, (b).
Preclusion of certain defense, §20-138.1, (b).
Definitions.
Offenses involving impaired driving, §20-4.01, (24a).
Dismissal of charge.
Prosecutor to explain, §20-138.4.
Drivers' licenses.
Immediate revocation of driving privilege.
Chemical analysis of impairing substance in blood.
Alcohol concentration, §20-16.2, (a).
Refusal of test, §20-16.2, (a).
Issuance to habitual drunkard.
Prohibited, §20-9, (c).
Mandatory revocation.
Period of suspension or revocation, §20-19, (c1) to (e).
Permanent revocation.
Habitual impaired driving, §20-138.5, (d).
Provisional licensees.
Revocation or suspension, §20-13.2, (b), (c).
Restoration after conviction, §20-17.6.
Ignition interlock as condition.
Duration of condition, §20-17.8, (c).
Limited driving privilege, effect, §20-17.8, (d).
Notice of requirement, §20-17.8, (e).
Scope, §20-17.8, (a).
Violation as driving while license revoked, §20-17.8, (f), (g).
Commencement of revocation, §20-17.8, (h).
Hearings, §20-17.8, (j).

IMPAIRED DRIVING —Cont'd
Drivers' licenses —Cont'd
Restoration after conviction —Cont'd
Ignition interlock as condition —Cont'd
Violation as driving while license revoked —Cont'd
Notification of revocation, §20-17.8, (i).
Restoration after revocation for, §20-17.8, (k).
When required, §20-17.8, (b).
Driving by person less than 21 years old after consuming alcohol or drugs.
Impaired driving offense also charged, §20-138.3, (c).
Driving on license revoked for prior impaired driving offense.
Seizure, impoundment and forfeiture of vehicle, §§20-28.2 to 20-28.9.
Evidence.
Chemical analysis of impairing substances in blood.
Admissibility, §§20-16.3, (d), 20-139.1, (a).
Alcohol screening tests.
Admissibility of results, §20-16.3, (d).
Qualification of person withdrawing blood, §20-139.1, (c).
Refusal to submit to analysis.
Admissibility of evidence of refusal, §20-139.1, (f).
Records of division of motor vehicles.
Admissibility of records as prima facie evidence of convictions, §8-35.1.
Felonies.
Habitual impaired driving, §20-138.5, (b).
Forfeiture of motor vehicle.
Accidents.
Motor vehicles involved in, §20-28.2, (c1).
Affidavit of impoundment.
Presented to magistrate by seizing officer, §20-28.3, (c).
Appearance by county board of education, §20-28.3, (k).
Bond, pretrial release of vehicle, §20-28.3, (e).
Civil judgment for cots docketed against defendant, §20-28.3, (l).
Continuance of trial involving forfeiture, §20-28.3, (m).
Costs of towing, storage and sale, §20-28.3, (l).
Payment of towing and storage costs on release of vehicle, §20-28.3, (n).
County board of education, constructive possession, §20-28.3, (d).
Custody of vehicle, §20-28.3, (d).
Definitions, §20-28.2, (a), (a1).
Department of public instruction.
Contracts to tow, store, process, maintain, and sell seized vehicles.
Authorized, §20-28.9, (a).
Fees, §20-28.9, (b), (c).
Department of public instruction, constructive possession, §20-28.3, (d).
Division of motor vehicles.
Reports to division, §20-28.8.
Responsibility, §20-28.7.
Driver not convicted.
Release of vehicle to driver, §20-28.4, (a).
Duty of charging officer to seize and impound vehicle, §20-28.3, (b).
Effecting order of seizure, §20-28.3, (c1).
Facsimile notification of impoundment to lienholder, §20-28.3, (b2).

IMPAIRED DRIVING —Cont'd
Forfeiture of motor vehicle —Cont'd
Force used to seize vehicle, §20-28.3, (c1).
Hearing, §20-28.2, (d).
Hearing on pretrial release of vehicle.
Defendant owner, §20-28.3, (e2).
Impounded vehicles.
Appeal of order, §20-28.5, (e).
Proceeds of sale, §20-28.5, (b).
Retention of vehicle, §20-28.5, (c).
Sale, §20-28.5, (a).
Innocent parties.
Duty of prosecutor to notify, §20-28.2, (c).
Insurance proceeds accruing to defendant.
Payment into court, §20-28.3, (h).
Magistrate review of seizure and impoundment, §20-28.3, (c2).
Mechanic's lien on seized vehicle, §20-28.4, (b).
Notice of hearing on pretrial release of vehicle, §20-28.3, (e2).
Notice to county board of education of proceeding, §20-28.3, (k).
Notification of impoundment, §20-28.3, (b1), (b2).
Order of seizure, §20-28.3, (c), (c1).
Participation by county board of education, §20-28.3, (k).
Personal property not affixed to vehicle, retrieval by owners, §20-28.3, (j).
Petition for pretrial release of vehicle.
Defendant owner, §20-28.3, (e2).
Lienholder, §20-28.3, (e3).
Nondefendant owner, §20-28.3, (e1).
Pretrial release of vehicle.
Defendant owner, §20-28.3, (e2).
Lienholder, §20-28.3, (e3).
Nondefendant owner, §20-28.3, (e), (e1).
Payment of towing and storage costs, §20-28.3, (n).
Priority of trial of offenses involving forfeiture, §20-28.3, (m).
Probable cause to seize and impound, §20-28.3, (b).
Release of vehicle pending trial.
Defendant owner, §20-28.3, (e2).
Lienholder, §20-28.3, (e3).
Nondefendant owner, §20-28.3, (e), (e1).
Payment of towing and storage costs, §20-28.3, (n).
Release of vehicle to innocent owner, §20-28.2, (e).
Release of vehicle to insurance company.
Vehicle declared total loss, §20-28.3, (h).
Release of vehicle to lienholder, §20-28.2, (f).
Release of vehicle upon conclusion of trial, §20-28.4, (a).
Rental vehicles.
Charging officer not seize or impound, §20-28.3, (b).
Reports to division of motor vehicles, §20-28.8.
Responsibility of division of motor vehicles, §20-28.7.
Restitution.
Costs of towing, storage and sale, §20-28.3, (l).
Sale of vehicle by county board of education.
Expedited sale to avoid towing and storage costs, §20-28.3, (i).
Search warrant for purposes of seizing concealed vehicle, §20-28.3, (c1).
Stolen vehicles.
Charging officer not to seize or impound, §20-28.3, (b).

IMPAIRED DRIVING —Cont'd
Forfeiture of motor vehicle —Cont'd
Towing and storage charges, payment.
Order authorizing release vehicle to require, §20-28.2, (h).
Towing of seized vehicle, §20-28.3, (d).
Vehicle subject to seizure, §20-28.3, (a).
When vehicle becomes property subject to forfeiture, §20-28.2, (b).
Habitual impaired driving.
Forfeiture of vehicle, §20-138.5, (e).
Implied consent offense, §20-138.5, (c).
Revocation of license.
Permanent revocation, §20-138.5, (d).
Sentence and punishment, §20-138.5, (b).
What constitutes, §20-138.5, (a).
Homicide.
Special information if conviction of homicide involves, §20-24, (e).
Horses.
Definition of vehicle does not include, §20-138.1, (e).
Ignition interlock system.
Impaired driving conviction.
Restoration of license conditioned on use of interlock.
Duration of condition, §20-17.8, (c).
Limited driving privilege, effect, §20-17.8, (d).
Notice of requirement, §20-17.8, (e).
Scope, §20-17.8, (a).
Violation as driving while license revoked, §20-17.8, (f), (g).
Commencement of revocation, §20-17.8, (h).
Hearings, §20-17.8, (j).
Notification of revocation, §20-17.8, (i).
Restoration after revocation for, §20-17.8, (k).
When required, §20-17.8, (b).
Limited driving privilege.
Ignition interlock allowed, §20-179.3, (g3).
Vehicles subject to requirement, §20-17.8, (c1).
Immediate civil license revocation.
Civil actions, §20-16.5, (o).
Costs, §20-16.5, (j).
Definitions, §20-16.5, (a).
Effect of revocation, §20-16.5, (i).
Exceptions, §20-16.5, (n).
Hearing, contesting validity, §20-16.5, (g).
Limited driving privilege, §20-16.5, (p).
Modification of order, §20-16.5, (m).
Persons charged with violations, §20-16.5, (b).
Precharge test results basis for revocation, §20-16.5, (b1).
Refusal to submit to chemical analysis, §20-16.5, (b).
Report to division, §20-16.5, (k).
Report to judicial officials.
Duty of charging officers, §20-16.5, (c).
Judicial officer with whom report filed, §20-16.5, (d).
Person not present, procedure for filing, §20-16.5, (f).
Person present, procedure for filing, §20-16.5, (e).
Restoration fee, person with no license, §20-16.5, (l).
Return of license, §20-16.5, (h).
Impairing substances.
Defined, §20-4.01, (14a).

IMPAIRED DRIVING —Cont'd
Implied consent, §20-16.2.
Driving by person less than 21 years old after consuming alcohol or drugs.
Offense subject to implied consent law, §20-138.3, (b).
Open container law offense subject to implied consent law, §20-138.7, (b).
Impoundment of vehicles.
Forfeiture of vehicles, §§20-28.2 to 20-28.9.
Inpatient treatment.
Credit on term of imprisonment, §20-179, (k1).
Lawnmowers.
Definition of vehicle does not include, §20-138.1, (e).
Limited driving privilege.
After six months, §20-16.2, (e1).
Eligibility of persons convicted of offense of impaired driving, §20-179.3, (b).
Indefinite revocation for refusal to submit to chemical analysis, §20-16.5, (p).
Restoration of license after conviction.
Persons subject to section not eligible for limited driving privilege, §20-17.6, (a).
Mandatory minimum period of imprisonment to be served, §20-179, (p).
Mandatory revocation of driver's license by division, §20-17, (a).
Motor vehicle registration.
Revocation of registration.
Impaired driving while license revoked as result of prior impaired driving license revocation, §20-54.1.
Offenses involving.
Commercial vehicles.
Offense defined, §20-138.2, (a).
Defined, §20-4.01, (24a).
Open container law violations.
Impaired driving offense also charged, §20-138.7, (e).
Parole, §20-179, (p).
Applicability of article 85, §15A-1370.1.
Community service parole, §15A-1371, (h) to (j).
Eligibility, §15A-1371, (a).
Habitual impaired driving, §20-138.5, (b).
Release on parole, §15A-1371, (g).
Pleading, §20-138.1, (c).
Commercial vehicles.
Sufficiency, §20-138.2, (c).
Presentence investigation of person convicted, §20-179.1.
Probation.
Unsupervised probation unless judge determines supervised probation necessary, §20-179, (r).
Prosecutor.
Reduction or dismissal of charge.
Prosecutor to explain, §20-138.4.
Provisional licensee.
Restoration of license after conviction, §20-17.6.
Punishment.
Aider and abetter punishment, §20-179, (f1).
Amelioration.
Limit on, §20-179, (p).
Community service alternative punishment, §20-179.4.
Community service time limit, §20-179, (n).
Credit for inpatient treatment, §20-179, (k1).
Good or gain time credit not used to reduce mandatory minimum period, §20-179, (p).
Level one punishment, §20-179, (g).
Level two punishment, §20-179, (h).

IMPAIRED DRIVING —Cont'd
Punishment —Cont'd
Level three punishment, §20-179, (i).
Level four punishment, §20-179, (j).
Level five punishment, §20-179, (k).
Mandatory minimum period of imprisonment to be served, §20-179, (p).
Method of serving sentence, §20-179, (s).
Probation.
Unsupervised probation unless judge determines supervised probation necessary, §20-179, (r).
Punitive damages.
Exemption from cap, §1D-26.
Railroads.
Operating trains or streetcars while intoxicated, §14-281.
Reduction of charge.
Prosecutor to explain, §20-138.4.
Restoration of driver's license after conviction, §20-17.6.
Certificate of completion.
Required for restoring license, §20-17.6, (b).
Requirements for obtaining certificate, §20-17.6, (c).
Limited driving privileges.
Persons subject to section not eligible, §20-17.6, (e).
Notice of requirement of section, §20-17.6, (d).
Requirements for restoring license, §20-17.6, (b).
Scope of section, §20-17.6, (a).
Road block checks, §20-16.3A.
Seizure of vehicles.
Forfeiture of vehicles, §§20-28.2 to 20-28.9.
Sentencing.
Amelioration of punishment, limit on, §20-179, (p).
Community service alternative punishment, §20-179.4.
Community service time limit, §20-179, (n).
Consolidating two or more charges for judgment prohibited, §20-179, (f2).
Credit for first 24 hours of time spent in incarceration pending trial.
Judge not to give, §20-179, (p).
Credit for good behavior, §15A-1355, (c).
Credit for inpatient treatment, §20-179, (k1).
Good or gain time credit not used to reduce mandatory minimum period, §20-179, (p).
Habitual impaired driving, §20-138.5, (b).
Level one punishment, §20-179, (g).
Level two punishment, §20-179, (h).
Level three punishment, §20-179, (i).
Level four punishment, §20-179, (j).
Level five punishment, §20-179, (k).
Mandatory minimum period of imprisonment must be served, §20-179, (p).
Method of serving sentence, §20-179, (s).
Parole of defendant, §20-179, (p).
Probation.
Unsupervised probation unless judge determines supervised probation necessary, §20-179, (r).
Sentencing hearing.
Aggravating factors to be weighed, §20-179, (d).
Chemical analysis made of defendant.
Prosecutor to present evidence of resulting alcohol concentration, §20-179, (a).
Evidentiary standards, §20-179, (o).
Grossly aggravating factors, determining existence, §20-179, (c).

IMPAIRED DRIVING —Cont'd
Sentencing hearing —Cont'd
Mitigating factors to be weighed, §20-179, (e).
Prior convictions, proof of, §20-179, (o).
Record of traffic convictions furnished defendant, §20-179, (a).
Required, §20-179, (a).
Weighing aggravating and mitigating factors, §20-179, (f).
Streetcars.
Operating trains or streetcars while intoxicated, §14-281.
Substance abuse services.
Assessments, §122C-142.1, (b).
Certificate of completion, §122C-142.1, (e).
Compliance with rules, §122C-142.1, (d).
Curriculum compliance, §122C-142.1, (d).
Fees, §122C-142.1, (f).
Multiple offenses for which certificate of completion required, §122C-142.1, (f1).
Multiple offenses for which certificate of completion required, §122C-142.1, (f1).
Out-of-state services, §122C-142.1, (g).
Private providers.
Authorization to provide services, §122C-142.1, (a1).
Providing services, §122C-142.1, (a).
Reports, §122C-142.1, (i).
Restoration of license after conviction.
Obtaining certificate of completion, §20-17.6, (c).
Rulemaking authority, §122C-142.1, (h).
Compliance with rules, §122C-142.1, (d).
School or treatment, §122C-142.1, (c).
Standards, §122C-142.1, (d).
Supervising or instructing of minor, §20-12.1, (b).
Treatment of persons convicted, §20-179.1.
When driving impaired, §20-138.1, (a).

IMPAIRED DRIVING CHECKS, §20-16.3A.

IMPAIRED PHARMACIST PEER REVIEW ORGANIZATIONS, §90-85.41.

IMPEACHMENT, §§123-1 to 123-13.
Articles of impeachment preferred.
Procedure in impeachment, §123-6.
Attorneys at law.
Accused entitled to counsel, §123-9.
Causes for impeachment, §123-5.
Chief justice.
Governor.
Presiding officer in impeachment of governor, §123-2.
Constitution of the United States, Const. U. S., art. I, §§2, 3; art. II, §4; art. III, §2.
Court of impeachment.
Chief justice presides in impeachment of governor, §123-2.
Quorum, §123-1.
Senate is court of impeachment, §123-1; Const. N. C., art. IV, §4.
Power of presiding officer, §123-4.
Power of senate as a court, §123-3.
Quorum, §123-1.
Vesting of judicial power, Const. N. C., art. IV, §1.
Effect of impeachment, §123-13.
Suspension of accused during trial, §123-12.
Felonies.
Causes for impeachment, §123-5.
General assembly.
House of representatives.
Power to impeach, Const. N. C., art. IV, §4.

IMPEACHMENT —Cont'd
General assembly —Cont'd
Senate.
Trial of impeachments, Const. N. C., art. IV, §4.
Governor, Const. N. C., art. III, §3.
Chief justice.
Presiding officer in impeachment of governor, §123-2.
Hearing time fixed, §123-10.
House of representatives.
Power to impeach, Const. N. C., art. IV, §4.
Indictments.
Effect of impeachment, §123-13.
Judges.
Habeas corpus.
Refusal to grant precepts to bring up party detained, §17-20.
Refusal to make attachment for failure to obey writ, §17-17.
Judgments.
Effect of impeachment, §123-13.
Misdemeanors.
Causes for impeachment, §123-5.
Modes of prosecution, Const. N. C., art. I, §22.
Notice.
Procedure in impeachment.
Accused to be given notice, §123-8.
Oaths.
Procedure in impeachment.
Administering oath to members, §123-11.
President of senate.
Power, §123-4.
When president of senate impeached, §123-7.
President of the United States, Const. U. S., art. II, §4.
Procedure in impeachment.
Articles of impeachment preferred, §123-6.
Counsel.
Accused entitled to counsel, §123-9.
Notice given to the accused, §123-8.
Oath administered to members, §123-11.
Time of hearing fixed, §123-10.
Quorum.
Court of impeachment, §123-1.
Senate.
Court of impeachment, §123-1; Const. N. C., art. IV, §4.
Power of presiding officer, §123-4.
Power of the senate as a court, §123-3.
Quorum, §123-1.
President of senate.
Power, §123-4.
When president of senate impeached, §123-7.
Suspension of accused during trial.
Effect of impeachment, §123-12.
Time of hearing fixed, §123-10.
Vice-president, Const. U. S., art. II, §4.
Witnesses.
See IMPEACHMENT OF WITNESSES.

IMPEACHMENT OF WITNESSES.
Character and conduct of witness, §8C-1, Rule 608.
Conviction of crime, §8C-1, Rule 609.
Hearsay declarant, §8C-1, Rule 806.
Hostile witnesses, §1A-1, Rule 43, (b).
Religious beliefs or opinions, §8C-1, Rule 610.
Use of depositions, §1A-1, Rule 32, (a).
Utilities commission proceedings, §62-65, (a).
Who may impeach, §8C-1, Rule 607.

IMPERSONATION.
Bail bondsmen and runners.
Personation of law-enforcement officer, §58-71-95.
Emergency medical services personnel, §14-276.1.
Felonies.
Law enforcement or other public officer, §14-277, (d1).
Firemen, §14-276.1.
Misdemeanors.
Law enforcement or other public officer, §14-277, (d1), (e).
Peace officers.
Elements of offense, §14-277, (a), (b).
Exceptions to provisions, §14-277, (c).
Punishment, §14-277, (d1), (e).
Public officers and employees, §14-277, (e).
Law enforcement officers, §14-277, (a) to (d1).
Soil scientists.
Misdemeanor, §89F-22.
Weights and measures.
Public weighmasters.
Prohibited, §81A-55, (b).

IMPLIED CONSENT.
Chemical analysis of impairing substances in blood, §20-16.2.
Commercial vehicles.
Impaired driving in commercial vehicles.
Implied consent offense, §20-138.2, (d).
Operating a commercial vehicle after consuming alcohol, §20-138.2A, (b).
Driving by person less than 21 years old after consuming alcohol or drugs.
Offense subject to implied consent law, §20-138.3, (b).
Habitual impaired driving.
Offense under implied consent, §20-138.5, (c).
Money transmitters.
Delegates.
Consent to inspection, §53-208.20, (d).
Open container law.
Offense subject to implied consent law, §20-138.7, (b).
School buses.
Operating a school bus, school activity bus, or child care vehicle after consuming alcohol.
Implied-consent offense, §20-138.2B, (b).

IMPLIED WARRANTIES.
Condominiums.
Implied warranty of quality.
Exclusion or modification.
Agreement or expression, §47C-4-115, (a).
Purchaser of unit used for residential purposes, restrictions, §47C-4-115, (b).
Leases, UCC.
Exclusion or modification, §25-2A-214, (2), (3).
Express warranties displace inconsistent implied warranties, §25-2A-215, (c).
Fitness for particular purpose, §25-2A-213.
Merchantability, §25-2A-212.
Third-party beneficiaries, §25-2A-216.
Products liability.
Action directly against manufacturer for breach of implied warranty, §99B-2, (b).
Privity requirements, §99B-2, (b).
Sale of goods, UCC.
Course of dealing, §25-2-314, (3).
Exclusion or modification by course of dealing, §25-2-316, (3).
Cumulation and conflict, §25-2-317.

IMPLIED WARRANTIES —Cont'd
Sale of goods, UCC —Cont'd
Fitness for a particular purpose, §25-2-315.
Merchantability, §25-2-314.
Third party beneficiaries, §25-2-318.
Usage of trade, §25-2-314, (3).
Exclusion or modification, §25-2-316, (3).

IMPORTS AND EXPORTS.
Alcoholic beverages.
Denatured alcohol.
Exemption from provisions, §18B-103.
Liquor importer/bottler permit, §18B-1105.1.
Malt beverages.
Importer.
Authorization of permit, §18B-1108.
Unauthorized imports and exports prohibited, §18B-102, (a).
Violation a misdemeanor, §18B-102, (b).
Wine importer.
Authorization of permit, §18B-1106, (a).
Distribution agreements, §18B-1106, (b).
Ammunition.
Teflon-coated bullets, §14-34.3.
Constitution of the United States, Const. U. S., art. I, §§9, 10.
Fertilizers.
Commercial fertilizers.
Sales or exchanges between imports, §106-676.
Livestock.
Tubercular animals.
Importation of cattle, §106-345.
Pesticides.
Foreign exports.
Exceptions, §143-445, (b).
Sales and use tax.
Exemptions, §105-164.13.
Wildlife exportation or importation permits, §113-274, (c).

IMPOSSIBILITY OF PERFORMANCE.
Sale of goods, UCC.
Excuse by failure of presupposed condition, §25-2-615.
Procedure on notice claiming excuse, §25-2-616.
Substituted performance, §25-2-614.

IMPOTENCE.
Food, drug and cosmetic act.
Drug or device, false advertising, §106-138, (b).
Void marriages, §51-3.

IMPOUNDED WATER.
Navigable waters.
Impoundment not included in definition of navigable waters, §76-40, (d).
Right of withdrawal.
Applicability of provisions, §143-215.50.
Assignment of right of withdrawal, §143-215.45.
Community water supplies.
Right of withdrawal for use, §143-215.49.
Definitions, §143-215.44, (b) to (d).
Determining streamflows.
Authority to make determinations, §143-215.48, (b).
Minimum average flow, §143-215.48, (a).
Discharges of water.
Effect of right of withdrawal, §143-215.47.
Exercise of right of withdrawal, §143-215.46.
Generally, §143-215.44, (a).
Interpretation with other statutes, §143-215.50.
Transfer of right of withdrawal, §143-215.45.
Use in community water supplies, §143-215.49.

IMPOUNDMENT.
Dogs.
Wildlife management areas.
Unmuzzled dogs running at large, §67-14.1, (b) to (e).
Livestock.
Any person may impound livestock at large, §68-17.
Costs and damages.
Demand upon owner, §68-18.
Determination by selected landowners or by referee, §68-19.
Right of impounder to recover, §68-17.
Feeding and watering impounded livestock.
Any person may feed and water, §68-23.
Owner liable, §68-23.
Failure to feed and water.
Misdemeanor, §68-21.
Illegally releasing or receiving impounded livestock.
Misdemeanor, §68-21.
Notice.
Actual notice when owner known, §68-19.
Sale where owner fails to redeem or is unknown, §68-20.
When owner not known, §68-18.1.
Outer Banks.
Stock running at large.
Applicability of general provisions, §68-45.
Sale where owner fails to redeem or is unknown, §68-20.
Violations of provisions, §68-24.
Motor vehicles.
Impaired driving offenses, §§20-28.2 to 20-28.9.
Property impounded for evidence, §15-11.1.

IMPRISONMENT.
Jails.
See JAILS.
Prisons and prisoners.
See PRISONS AND PRISONERS.

IMPROPER BACKING.
Movement not safe or interfering with traffic, §20-154.

IMPROPER GOVERNMENT ACTIVITIES.
Communications with members of the general assembly, §126-90.
Limitation of actions, §1-54.
Reporting.
Attorneys' fees, §126-87.
Civil actions for injunctive relief or other remedies, §126-86.
Costs, §126-87.
Injunctive relief, §126-86.
Notice of employee protections and obligations.
Posting by employer, §126-88.
Policy of state, §126-84.
Protection from retaliation, §126-85.
Posting notice of employer protection, §126-88.
Remedies, §§126-86, 126-87.
Retaliation.
Employees retaliating against other employees.
Illegal activities, §126-85, (a1).
Refusal to carry out directive, §126-85, (b), (b1).
Head of department or agency.
Illegal activities, §126-85, (a).
Refusal to carry out directive, §126-85, (b).
Notice of employee protection, posted by employer, §126-88.

IMPROPER GOVERNMENT ACTIVITIES —Cont'd
Reporting —Cont'd
Retaliation —Cont'd
Scope, §126-85, (c).
Statement of policy, §126-84.

IMPROPER VENUE.
Defense by pretrial motion, §1A-1, Rule 12, (b).

IMPROVEMENT OF COUNTY LAND RECORDS PROGRAM, §102-15.

IMPROVEMENTS.
Betterments, §§1-340 to 1-351.
See BETTERMENTS.
Bond issues.
State debt, §§142-1 to 142-29.7.
See STATE DEBT.
Budget.
Building and permanent improvement funds.
Spending in accordance with budget, §143-31.
Studies and reviews, §143-31.1.
Capital improvements.
Construction of improvements not specifically authorized or provided for, §143-18.1, (c).
Increase or decrease of projects, §143-18.1, (a), (b).
Contracts to improve real property.
Provisions making contract subject to laws of another state.
Void and against public policy, §22B-2.
Counties.
Ordinances.
Submission of statement concerning improvements, §153A-325.
Special assessments.
Street light assessments, §153A-206.
Subdivision and residential streets, §153A-205.
Drainage districts.
Assessments.
Renovation, enlargement and extension of canals, structures and boundaries, §156-93.5.
Bonds.
Increase to extinguish debt, §156-122.
Proceedings as for original bond issue, §156-123.
Redress to dissatisfied landowners, §156-121.
Renovation, enlargement and extension of canals, structures and boundaries, §156-93.5.
Canals, structures and boundaries.
Renovation, enlargement and extension.
Procedures generally, §§156-93.2, 156-93.3.
Construction.
Commissioners.
Control and repairs by commissioners, §156-92.
Contracts, §§156-84 to 156-86.
Improvement, renovation, enlargement and extension of canals, structures and boundaries, §§156-93.2 to 156-93.7.
Lateral drains, §156-93.
Payments, §156-85.
Public or private ways.
Maintenance of drainage across, §156-88.
Railroads, §§156-89 to 156-91.
Right of entry, §156-87.
Superintendent of construction, §156-83.
Estimates.
Monthly estimates for work and payments thereon, §156-85.

IMPROVEMENTS —Cont'd
Drainage districts —Cont'd
Construction —Cont'd
Superintendent of construction —Cont'd
Removal, §156-136.
Trees and timber.
Removal of timber, §156-87.
Easements.
Renovation, enlargement and extension of canals, structures and boundaries, §156-93.6.
Fairs.
State fair.
Board authorized to construct and finance facilities and improvements, §106-503.1.
False statements as to improvements.
Misdemeanor for furnishing, §44A-24.
Highways.
Connection of highways with improved streets, §136-27.
Municipal participation in improvements to state highway system.
County participation.
Specified counties, §136-66.3, (k).
Development related improvements, §136-66.3, (d).
Limitations on agreements, §136-66.3, (c3).
Population of municipalities.
Maximum participation, §136-66.3, (f).
Project additions, §136-66.3, (e).
Proposals, §136-66.3, (b).
Reimbursement of department of transportation for costs, §136-66.3, (e1).
Reimbursement procedure, §136-66.3, (e1).
Report on agreements, §136-66.3, (f).
Rights of way.
Acquisition, §136-66.3, (g) to (j).
State funds, distribution, §136-66.3, (c2).
TIP projects, effect, §136-66.3, (c1), (c3).
Types of the participation, §136-66.3, (c).
Urban area streets.
Reduction in traffic congestion, §136-66.5.
Limitation of actions.
Injuries arising from defective or unsafe condition, §1-50, (a).
Local improvement districts.
Bankruptcy and insolvency.
Authority to avail of provisions of bankruptcy law, §23-48.
Municipal corporations.
Urban area streets.
Reduction in traffic congestion, §136-66.5.
Public schools.
School building improvement reports.
Administrative units, §115C-47.
State board of education.
Development of system of reports, §115C-12.
Real property.
Contracts to improve real property.
Subject to laws of another state, §22B-2.
Defective or unsafe condition.
Limitation of actions, §1-50, (a).
Subcontractors, payments to, §§22C-1 to 22C-6.
State debt, §§142-1 to 142-29.7.
See STATE DEBT.

IMPUTED NEGLIGENCE.
Dogs.
Dangerous dogs causing injury or property damage, §67-4.4.
Injuring livestock or fowl, §67-1.

IMPUTED NEGLIGENCE —Cont'd
Dogs —Cont'd
Running at large at night, §67-12.
Motorboat and vessel operation.
Family purpose doctrine applicable, §75A-10.1.
Motor vehicle owned or operated by parent or child.
Abolition of parent-child immunity in motor vehicle cases, §1-539.21.

INAUGURAL CEREMONIES COMMITTEE.
Allowances of members, §143-539.
Appointments, §143-533.
Time of appointments, §143-534.
Appropriations.
Payments from appropriations, §143-539.
Chairman.
Election, §143-536.
Created, §143-533.
Definitions, §143-532.
Duties.
Generally, §143-538.
Expenses, §143-539.
Filling vacancies, §143-535.
Inaugural period.
Defined, §143-532.
Inaugural planning period.
Defined, §143-532.
Meetings, §143-537.
Members, §143-533.
Mileage.
Per diem and allowances of members, §143-539.
Offices, §143-539.
Powers.
Generally, §143-538.
Qualifications of members, §143-533.
Quorum, §143-536.
Rules and regulations.
Procedural rules, §143-536.
Terms of office, §143-534.
Time of appointments, §143-534.
Vacancies.
Filling, §143-535.

IN-CAMERA HEARINGS.
Rape shield law.
Relevance of victim's past behavior, §8C-1, Rule 412.
Trade secrets, actions for misappropriations, §66-156.

INCAPACITY OF BENEFICIARY.
Custodial trusts.
Determination, §33B-10.
Generally, §§33B-1 to 33B-22.
See CUSTODIAL TRUSTS.

INCAPACITY OF DEFENDANT TO PROCEED.
Capacity regained by defendant, §15A-1006.
Commitment.
Civil commitment, §15A-1003, (a), (b).
Evidence admissible at proceedings, §15A-1003, (c).
Institution of proceedings, §15A-1002, (b).
Observation and treatment, §15A-1002, (b).
Confidentiality of information.
Reports to court, §15A-1002, (d).
Determination of incapacity, §15A-1002, (b).
Dismissal of charges, §15A-1008.
Supplemental hearing, §15A-1007, (c).
Dismissal with leave, §15A-1009.
Hearings.
Supplemental hearings, §15A-1007, (a).
Court's own determination, §15A-1007, (b).
Dismissal of charges, §15A-1007, (c).

INCAPACITY OF DEFENDANT TO PROCEED —Cont'd
Motion, §15A-1002, (a).
No proceedings when defendant mentally incapacitated, §15A-1001, (a).
Exception as to motions which can be handled by counsel without assistance of defendant, §15A-1001, (b).
Orders for safeguarding defendant, §15A-1004, (a) to (c).
Amendment or supplementation, §15A-1004, (f).
Reports to court, §15A-1004, (d).
Return of defendant to stand trial, §15A-1004, (e).
Reports to court, §15A-1002, (b), (b1), (d), 15A-1005.
Hospital or institution with custody of defendant, §15A-1002, (d).
Return of defendant for trial upon gaining capacity, §15A-1004, (e), 15A-1006.
Temporary confinement of defendant, §15A-1002, (c).

INCAPACITY OF PRINCIPAL.
Durable power of attorney.
Generally, §§32A-8 to 32A-14.
See DURABLE POWER OF ATTORNEY.

INCENDIARIES.
Drivers' licenses.
Revocation or suspension of license.
Minors, §20-13.2, (c2).
Explosives generally.
See EXPLOSIVES.

INCEST, §14-178.
Bail and recognizance, §15A-534.4.
Child abuse, §14-318.4.
Defenses.
Child under age of sixteen, when other person at least four years older, §14-178, (c).
Elements of offense, §14-178, (a).
Intercourse and sexual offenses with certain victims, §14-27.7, (a).
Marriage, prohibited degrees of kinship, §51-4.
Punishment, §14-178, (b).
Rehabilitative treatment.
Defendant may pay cost as condition of probation, §15A-1343, (b1).
Venue, §15A-136.

IN CHAMBERS.
District court proceedings, hearings and acts conducted by judge, §7A-191.
Interlocutory orders, §7A-192.
Injunctions.
Judges having jurisdiction, §1-493.
Jurisdiction of emergency superior court judges, §7A-48.

INCINERATION.
Disposal of certain wastes by, §130A-309.10, (f1), (f2), (i), (j).

INCITEMENT TO RIOT, §14-288.2.
Riots and civil disorders.
Generally.
See RIOTS AND CIVIL DISORDERS.

INCLEMENT WEATHER.
General court of justice.
Cancellation of court sessions, §7A-39, (a).
Chambers or ex parte jurisdiction, §7A-39, (c).

INCLINED OR VERTICAL WHEELCHAIR LIFT.
Elevator safety act generally, §§95-110.1 to 95-110.15.
See ELEVATORS.

INCLINED STAIRWAY CHAIRLIFT.
Elevator safety act generally, §§95-110.1 to 95-110.15.
See ELEVATORS.

INCOME.
Loss of income.
Mortality tables as evidence, §8-47.
Principal and income act.
General provisions, §§37A-1-101 to 37A-6-602.
See PRINCIPAL AND INCOME ACT.

INCOME TAX.
Bank holding companies.
Dividends.
Adjustment to expenses related to, §105-130.6A, (c), (e), (f), (h).
Banks.
Refund anticipation loans, §§53-245 to 53-254.
Bond issues.
Exemption from federal income taxation.
Registered public obligations act.
Generally, §§159E-1 to 159E-15.
See REGISTERED PUBLIC OBLIGATIONS.
Purpose of act, §159E-3, (a), (b).
Federal tax reform allocation committee.
Duties, §143-433.8.
Formulas for allocation, §143-433.9.
Generally, §143-433.7.
Legislative findings, §143-433.6.
Port authority bonds.
Gain from transfer not exempt from taxation, §143B-456, (g).
Refunding obligations issued by state.
Gain from transfer not exempt from taxation, §142-29.6, (f).
State bonds, act authorizing not addressing exemption from taxation.
Not exempt from income taxes on gain from transfer, §142-12.
Business and energy tax credits, §§105-129.15 to 105-129.19.
Business investments.
Tax credit for qualified business investments, §§105-163.010 to 105-163.015.
Checkoffs.
Refund contributions.
Candidates financing fund, §105-269.6.
Wildlife conservation account, §105-269.5.
Child tax credit, §105-151.24, (a).
Nonresident or part-time resident claiming, limitation, §105-151.34, (b).
Cigarettes manufactured for exportation, credit, §105-130.45.
Amount of credit allowed, §105-130.45, (b).
Cap, §105-130.45, (c).
Definitions, §105-130.45, (a).
Increasing employment and utilizing state ports.
Allocation, §105-130.46, (f).
Allowance of credit, amount, §105-130.46, (d).
Carryforward, §105-130.46, (h).
Ceiling, §105-130.46, (g).
Definitions, §105-130.46, (b).
Documentation, §105-130.46, (i).
Employment level, eligibility for full credit, §105-130.46, (c).
No double credit, §105-130.46, (j).
Partial credit, §105-130.46, (e).
Purpose, §105-130.46, (a).
Reports, §105-130.46, (k).

INCOME TAX —Cont'd
Cigarettes manufactured for exportation, credit —Cont'd
Information required by corporation attaining credit, §105-130.45, (d).
No double credit, §105-130.45, (e).
Clergymen.
Withholding of income taxes from wages.
Ordained or licensed clergymen may elect to be self-employed, §105-163.1A.
Cogenerating power plants.
Credit for constructing in state.
Corporation or partnership not public utility, §105-130.25, (a).
Application for credit, §105-130.25, (d).
Ceiling on credit, §105-130.25, (e).
Cogenerating power plant defined, §105-130.25, (b).
Cost paid during earlier year, alternative method, §105-130.25, (c).
Collection of taxes.
Assignments, §105-269.13, (c).
Debts not collectible, §105-269.13, (a).
Retailer debts, §105-269.13, (b).
Conservation tillage equipment.
Corporations, §105-130.36.
Individual income tax.
Credit for installation, §105-151.13.
Constitution of North Carolina.
Limitations and restrictions, Const. N. C., art. V, §2.
Constitution of the United States, Const. U. S., amd. XVI.
Corporations.
Accelerated depreciation.
Determining state net income, §105-130.5, (a), (b).
Additional nature of tax, §105-130.1.
Additions to federal taxable income in determining state net income, §105-130.5, (a).
Adjustments to federal taxable income in determining state net income, §105-130.5, (a) to (e).
Affiliated corporations, §105-130.6.
Air and water transportation corporations.
Allocation and apportionment of income.
Revenue ton mile, §105-130.4, (s).
Air-cleaning devices.
Amortization, §105-130.10.
Allocation and apportionment of income, §105-130.4, (b).
Air and water transportation corporations, §105-130.4, (s).
Apportionable income, §105-130.4, (i).
Defined, §105-130.4, (a).
Excluded corporations, §105-130.4, (r).
Motor carrier of passengers, §105-130.4, (p).
Motor carriers of property, §105-130.4, (o).
Payroll factor, §105-130.4, (k).
Property factor, §105-130.4, (j).
Railroad companies, §105-130.4, (m).
Sales factor, §105-130.4, (l).
Telegraph companies, §105-130.4, (q).
Telephone companies, §105-130.4, (n).
Definitions, §105-130.4, (a).
Hearings, §105-130.4, (t).
Interest and net dividends, §105-130.4, (f).
Nonapportionable income, §105-130.4, (c) to (h).
Defined, §105-130.4, (a).
Intangible property.
Royalties or similar income received from use of, §105-130.4, (g).

INCOME TAX —Cont'd
Corporations —Cont'd
Allocation and apportionment of income —Cont'd
Nonapportionable income —Cont'd
Sale or other disposition of real property, §105-130.4, (e).
Rents and royalties, §105-130.4, (c), (d).
Sale or other disposition of real property, §105-130.4, (e).
Amortization.
Air-cleaning devices, §105-130.10.
Equipment mandated by OSHA.
Defined, §105-130.10A, (b).
Generally, §105-130.10A, (a).
Recycling facilities, §105-130.10.
Waste treatment facilities, §105-130.10.
Bank holding companies.
Dividends.
Adjustment to expenses related to, §105-130.6A, (c), (e), (f), (h).
Building and loan associations.
Exemption, §105-130.11, (a).
Chambers of commerce.
Exemption, §105-130.11, (a), (b).
Charities.
Contributions.
Deductions, §105-130.9.
Exemption of charitable corporations, §105-130.11, (a), (b).
Cigarettes manufactured for exportation, credit, §105-130.45.
Amount of credit allowed, §105-130.45, (b).
Cap, §105-130.45, (c).
Definitions, §105-130.45, (a).
Increasing employment and utilizing state ports, §105-130.46.
Information required by corporation attaining credit, §105-130.45, (d).
No double credit, §105-130.45, (e).
Citation of act.
Short title, §105-130.
Civic leagues.
Exemption, §105-130.11, (a), (b).
Cogenerating power plants.
Credit for construction, §105-130.25.
Condominium associations.
Exemption, §105-130.11, (a).
Contributions.
Deductions, §105-130.9.
Cooperative associations.
Exemption, §105-130.11, (a), (b).
Credits.
Cigarettes manufactured for exportation, §105-130.45.
Amount of credit allowed, §105-130.45, (b).
Cap, §105-130.45, (c).
Definitions, §105-130.45, (a).
Increasing employment and utilizing state ports, §105-130.46.
Information required by corporation attaining credit, §105-130.45, (d).
No double credit, §105-130.45, (e).
Cogenerating power plants, §105-130.25.
Conservation tillage equipment.
Definition of "conservation tillage equipment," §105-130.36, (b).
Generally, §105-130.36, (a).
Gleaned crop.
Definitions, §105-130.37, (b).
Generally, §105-130.37, (a).

INCOME TAX —Cont'd
Corporations —Cont'd
Credits —Cont'd
Handicapped persons.
Construction of dwelling units for, §105-130.22.
Methane gas facility construction
Ports authority wharfage, handling and throughput charges, §105-130.41.
Real property donations, §105-130.34.
Renewable energy equipment facility construction.
Cap on credit, §105-130.28, (c).
Definitions, §105-130.28, (b).
Double credit not allowed, §105-130.28, (d).
Generally, §105-130.28, (a).
S corporation shareholders, §105-131.8.
Telephones.
Providing service to low-income residential consumers at reduced rates, §105-130.39.
Deductions.
Amortization of equipment, §§105-130.10, 105-130.10A.
Contributions, §105-130.9.
Net economic loss, §105-130.8.
Allowance as deduction, §105-130.8, (a).
Limitations, §105-130.8, (a).
Records to determine and verify amount, maintaining, inspection, §105-130.8, (b).
Redetermination of item closed by statute of limitations, §105-130.8, (b).
Definitions, §§105-130.2, 105-130.4, (a).
Biomass equipment, §105-130.28, (b).
Estimated tax, §105-163.38.
Renewable energy equipment, §105-130.28, (b).
Solar electric or thermal equipment, §105-130.28, (b).
Wind energy equipment, §105-130.28, (b).
Depreciation.
Recapture of depreciation required under internal revenue code.
Inclusion in state net income, §105-130.5, (e).
Dividends.
Adjustment for expenses related to.
Bank holding companies, §105-130.6A, (c).
Cap, §105-130.6A, (e).
Credits, §105-130.6A, (f), (h).
Definitions, §105-130.6A, (a).
Electric power holding companies, §105-130.6A, (d).
Credits, §105-130.6A, (g), (h).
General rule.
Corporations other than bank holding companies and electric power holding companies, §105-130.6A, (b).
Allocation and apportionment of income.
Interest and net dividends, §105-130.4, (f).
Information filed with secretary of revenue.
Persons receiving dividends, §105-130.21, (b).
Information to be filed with secretary of revenue, §105-130.21, (b).
S corporations.
Distributions to shareholders, §105-131.6.
Donation of harvested crops to nonprofit organization.
Credit for gleaned crops, §105-130.37.
Donation of interest in real property, credit, §105-130.34, (a).
Amount, §105-130.34, (b).
Carry forward of unused portion, §105-130.34, (c).

INCOME TAX —Cont'd
Corporations —Cont'd
Donation of interest in real property, credit —Cont'd
Not eligible for deduction as charitable contribution, §105-130.34, (d).
Electric power holding companies.
Dividends.
Adjustment for expenses related to, §105-130.6A, (d), (g), (h).
Estimated tax.
Declaration.
Amendment, §105-163.39, (c).
Time for filing, §105-163.40, (b).
Contents, §105-163.39, (b).
Filing.
Amendments to declaration, §105-163.40, (b).
Short taxable year, §105-163.40, (c).
Time for, §105-163.40, (a).
Required, §105-163.39, (a).
Definitions, §105-163.38.
Electronic funds transfer, payment by, §105-163.40, (d).
Overpayment.
Refund, §105-163.43.
Payment.
Electronic funds transfer, §105-241, (b).
Payment of tax.
Electronic funds transfer, §105-163.40, (d).
Overpayment.
Refund, §105-163.43.
Underpayment, §105-163.41.
Penalties.
Underpayment, §105-163.41.
Refund of overpayment, §105-163.43.
Underpayment.
Penalty, §105-163.41, (a).
When not imposed, §105-163.41, (d).
Period of underpayment, §105-163.41, (c).
What constitutes, §105-163.41, (b).
Exemptions.
Organizations exempt, §105-130.11, (a).
Conditional exemptions, §105-130.11, (b).
Federal taxable income.
Adjustments in determining state net income, §105-130.5, (a) to (c).
Change, §105-130.20.
Deductions in determining state net income, §105-130.5, (b).
Fiscal year.
Defined, §105-130.2.
Foreign corporations.
Defined, §105-130.2.
Installment method of reporting income.
Prerequisites for use, §105-130.15, (c).
Fraternal beneficiary societies.
Exemption, §105-130.11, (a), (b).
Fuel ethanol distilleries.
Credit for construction, §105-130.27.
Gleaned crops, credit, §105-130.37, (a).
Definitions, §105-130.37, (b).
Handicapped persons.
Dwelling units for.
Credit for construction of, §105-130.22.
Hearings.
Allocation and apportionment of income, §105-130.4, (t).
Homeowner association income, §105-130.11, (c).
Hurricane Floyd reserve fund payments.
Deductions to taxable income, §§105-130.5, (b).

INCOME TAX —Cont'd
Corporations —Cont'd
Income year.
Change of income year, §105-130.15, (b).
Defined, §105-130.2.
Information filed with secretary, §105-130.21, (a).
Dividend payments, §105-130.21, (b).
Insurance companies.
Exemption, §105-130.11, (a).
Intangible property.
Royalties or similar income received from use of.
Allocation and apportionment of income, §105-130.4, (g).
Interest.
Allocation and apportionment of income.
Interest and net dividends, §105-130.4, (f).
International banking facilities.
Deductions in determining state net income, §105-130.5, (b).
Levy, §105-130.3.
Merger or consolidation.
Corporation using installment method of reporting income, §105-130.15, (d).
Motor carriers.
Allocation and apportionment of income.
Business income of motor carriers, §105-130.4, (o), (p).
Net economic loss, §105-130.8.
Net income.
Computation, §105-130.15, (a).
Federal taxable income.
Adjustments in determining state net income, §105-130.5, (a) to (c).
Recapture of depreciation required under internal revenue code.
Inclusion in state net income, §105-130.5, (e).
Subsidiary and affiliated corporations, §105-130.6.
Payment of tax.
Estimated tax.
Overpayment, §105-163.43.
Underpayment, §105-163.41.
Generally, §105-130.19, (a).
Ports authority.
Credit for ports authority wharfage, handling and throughput charges, §105-130.41.
Poultry composting facility.
Credit limitations, §105-130.44.
Purpose of provisions, §105-130.1.
Railroads.
Application and apportionment of income.
Business income of railroad companies, §105-130.4, (m).
Rate of tax, §105-130.3.
Real estate investment trust, §105-130.12.
Real estate mortgage investment conduits.
Exemption, §105-130.11, (d).
Real property donations, credit, §105-130.34, (a).
Amount, §105-130.34, (b).
Carry forward of unused portion, §105-130.34, (c).
Not eligible for deduction as charitable contribution, §105-130.34, (d).
Recapture of depreciation.
Inclusion in state net income, §105-130.5, (e).
Recycling facilities.
Amortization, §105-130.10.
Regulated investment companies, §105-130.12.
Renewable energy equipment facility.
Credit for construction, §105-130.28.

INCOME TAX —Cont'd
Corporations —Cont'd
Rents and royalties.
Allocation and apportionment of income, §105-130.4, (c), (d).
Returns.
Affirmation verifying return, person signing, §105-130.16, (a).
Consolidated returns for federal income tax purposes, §105-130.14.
Correction of net income by secretary, §105-130.16, (b), (c).
Dissolution or withdrawal from state, time for filing, §105-130.17, (e).
Distortion of net income, correction by secretary, §105-130.16, (b).
Exempt organizations, filing, §105-130.17, (d1).
Extension of time to file, §105-130.17, (d).
Failure to file.
Supplementary returns, §105-130.18.
Filing, §105-130.17, (a).
Time for filing, §105-130.17, (b) to (e).
Marketing associations, §105-130.17, (c).
Mutual associations to conduct agricultural business, §105-130.17, (c).
Required, §105-130.16, (a).
S corporations, §105-131.7.
Signing, §105-130.16, (a).
Supplementary returns, §105-130.18.
Time for, §105-130.17, (b) to (e).
Royalty payments for use of trademarks.
Optional methods for reporting income, §105-130.7A, (a).
Definitions, §105-130.7A, (b).
Election, §105-130.7A, (c).
Indirect transactions, same effect, §105-130.7A, (d).
Savings and loan associations.
Exemption, §105-130.11, (a).
Supervisory fees.
Credit limitations, §105-130.43.
S corporations.
Adjustment of basis, §105-131.3.
Adjustment of income, §105-131.2, (a).
Individual income tax, §105-134.6, (a).
Citation of division, §105-131, (a).
Corporation exempt from corporate income tax, §105-131.1, (a).
Credits, §105-131.8.
Definitions, §105-131, (b).
Distribution, §105-131.6.
Individual income tax, §105-134.5, (d).
Interpretation of division, §105-131, (c).
Net income.
Characterization of income, §105-131.2, (c).
Shareholders.
Pro rata share of net income, §105-131.1, (b).
Returns, §105-131.7.
Shareholders.
Basis, §105-131.3.
Credits, §105-131.8.
Part-year resident shareholder, §105-131.5.
Pro rata share of net income, §105-131.1, (b).
Short title, §105-131, (a).
Subsidiary corporations, §105-130.6.
Taxable year.
Defined, §105-130.2.
Telegraph companies.
Allocation and apportionment of income.
Business income of telegraph companies, §105-130.4, (q).

INCOME TAX —Cont'd
Corporations —Cont'd
Telephone companies.
Allocation and apportionment of income.
Business income of telephone companies, §105-130.4, (n).
Credits for providing service to low-income residential consumers at reduced rates, §105-130.39.
Title of act.
Short title, §105-130.
Waste treatment facilities.
Amortization, §105-130.10.
Withdrawal from state.
Corporation using installment method of reporting income, §105-130.15, (d).
Counties.
Levy prohibited, §105-247.
Credits.
Business and energy tax credits, §§105-129.15 to 105-129.19.
See BUSINESS AND ENERGY TAX CREDITS.
Corporations. See within this heading, "Corporations."
Renewable energy equipment facility construction, §105-130.28, (a) to (d).
S corporation shareholders, §105-131.8.
Estates and trusts, §105-160.3.
Income taxes paid to other states, §105-160.4.
Historic structure rehabilitation tax credit, §§105-129.35 to 105-129.37.
Individual income tax. See within this heading, "Individual income tax."
Long-term care insurance, §105-151.28.
Low-income housing tax credits, §§105-129.40 to 105-129.45.
Partnerships, §105-269.15.
Ports authority.
Wharfage, handling and throughput charges, §105-130.41.
Poultry composting facility.
Construction, §105-151.25, (a).
Property owned by the entirety, §105-151.25, (b).
Qualified business investments, §§105-163.010 to 105-163.015.
Recycling facilities.
Tax credit for large or major recycling facility investment, §§105-129.25 to 105-129.28.
Renewable energy investment tax credit, §105-129.16A.
Research and development tax credit, §§105-129.50 to 105-129.55.
S corporation shareholders, §105-131.8.
Tax incentives for new and expanding businesses generally, §§105-129.2 to 105-129.13.
See TAX INCENTIVES FOR NEW AND EXPANDING BUSINESSES.
Telephone service to low-income residents at reduced rates.
Credit to corporation providing, §105-130.39, (a), (b).
Crops.
Gleaned crops.
Individual income tax.
Credits, §105-151.14, (a), (b).
Decedents' estates.
Excess funds, §28A-15-9.
State income tax returns, §28A-15-8.
Deductions.
Corporations.
Amortization of equipment, §§105-130.10, 105-130.10A.

INCOME TAX —Cont'd
Deductions —Cont'd
Corporations —Cont'd
Contributions, §105-130.9.
Net economic loss, §105-130.8.
Deficiency.
Penalty for large income tax deficiency, §105-236.
Definitions.
Corporations, §§105-130.2, 105-130.4, (a).
Conservation tillage equipment, §105-130.36, (b).
Estimated tax, §105-163.38.
Gleaned crop, §105-130.37, (b).
Renewable biomass resources, §105-129.15, (b).
S corporations, §105-131, (b).
Estates and trusts, §105-160.1.
Individual income tax, §105-134.1.
Conservation tillage equipment, §105-151.13, (b).
Gleaned crops, §105-151.14, (b).
Taxable income, §105-134.5.
Refund anticipation loans, §53-246.
Tax credit for qualified business investments, §105-163.010.
Withholding of income taxes from wages, §105-163.1.
Dividends.
Corporations.
Adjustment to expenses related to, §105-130.6A.
Information filed with secretary of revenue.
Persons receiving dividends, §105-130.21, (b).
S corporations.
Distributions to shareholders, §105-131.6.
Elections.
Individual income tax refund.
Contribution to candidates' financing fund, §105-269.6.
Electric power holding companies.
Dividends.
Adjustment for expenses related to, §105-130.6A, (d), (g), (h).
Estates and trusts, §§105-160 to 105-160.8.
Amount of tax, §105-160.2.
Changes, §105-160.8.
Corrections, §105-160.8.
Credits, §105-160.3, (a).
Credits not allowed, §105-160.3, (b).
Income taxes paid to other states, §105-160.4.
Definitions, §105-160.1.
Imposition of tax, §105-160.2.
Payment.
Place of payment, §105-160.7, (a).
Returns, §105-160.5.
Place of filing, §105-160.6.
Time of filing, §105-160.6.
Short title, §105-160.
Taxable income, §105-160.2.
Title of provisions, §105-160.
Estimated tax.
Corporations.
Declaration, §105-163.39.
Filing, §105-163.40.
Definitions, §105-163.38.
Refund of overpayment, §105-163.43.
Underpayment, §105-163.41.
Individuals.
Definition of "tax," §105-163.15, (g).
Liberal construction of provisions, §105-163.24.
Overpayment.
Refund, §105-163.16.

INCOME TAX —Cont'd
Estimated tax —Cont'd
Individuals —Cont'd
Required installments, §105-163.15, (c).
Amount, §105-163.15, (d), (e).
Underpayment, §105-163.15, (a), (f), (h).
Amount of underpayment, §105-163.15, (b).
Exemptions.
Organizations exempt, §105-130.11.
Port authority bond issues.
Gain from transfer not exempt, §143B-456, (g).
Refunding obligations issued by state.
Gain from transfer not exempt from taxation, §142-29.6, (f).
State bonds, act authorizing issue not addressing exemption.
Not exempt from income taxes on gain from transfer, §142-12.
Withholding of income taxes from wages.
Allowable exemptions, §105-163.5, (a).
Certificates, §105-163.5, (b), (c), (e).
New withholding exemption certificate, §105-163.5, (d).
Farm machinery.
Credit for property taxes paid, §105-151.21.
Federal government workers.
Credit or partial refund for tax paid on certain federal retirement benefits, §105-151.20.
Fiduciaries.
Individual income tax.
Filing returns, §105-152, (b).
Guardian of estate, specific duties, §35A-1253.
Handicapped persons.
Individual income tax.
Credits.
Construction of dwelling units for, §105-151.1.
Credit for the disabled, §105-151.18.
Definitions, §105-151.18, (c).
Disabled dependent, §105-151.18, (b).
Disabled taxpayer, §105-151.18, (a).
Limitations, §105-151.18, (d).
Historic structure rehabilitation tax credit, §§105-129.35 to 105-129.37.
Hurricane Floyd reserve fund payments.
Deductions to taxable income, §§105-130.5, (b), 105-134.6, (b).
Husband and wife.
Excess funds, §28A-15-9.
Individual income tax.
Joint returns, §105-152, (e).
Payment of tax, §105-157, (a).
State income tax returns.
Death of spouse, §28A-15-8.
Income tax credit for property taxes.
Farm machinery, §105-151.21, (a).
Adjustments, §105-151.21, (c).
Definitions, §105-151.21, (b).
Income tax credit for qualified business investments.
Definitions, §105-163.010.
Individual income tax.
Additions to taxable income, §105-134.6, (c).
Adjustments to taxable income.
Charitable contribution credit by nonitemizers, §105-151.26.
Other adjustments, §105-134.6, (d).
S corporations, §105-134.6, (a).
Transitional adjustments.
Transition to tax changes, §§105-131 to 105-134.7, (a), (b).
Applicability of provisions, §105-163.15, (j), (k).

INCOME TAX —Cont'd
Individual income tax —Cont'd
Charitable contribution tax by nonitemizers, §105-151.26.
Child care.
Credit for certain employment-related expenses, §105-151.11, (a).
Applicable percentage, §105-151.11, (a1).
Limitations, §105-151.11, (b), (c).
Children.
Credits, §105-151.24.
Citation of act.
Short title, §105-133.
Conservation tillage equipment.
Credit for installation.
Definition of "conservation tillage equipment," §105-151.13, (b).
Generally, §105-151.13, (a).
Tenants by the entireties, §105-151.13, (c).
Credits.
Charitable contributions by nonitemizers, §105-151.26.
Child care.
Employment-related expenses, §105-151.11.
Children, §105-151.24.
Conservation tillage equipment, §105-151.13.
Disabled persons, §105-151.18.
Definitions, §105-151.18, (c).
Dependents, §105-151.18, (b).
Limitations, §105-151.18, (d).
Taxpayers, §105-151.18, (a).
Donation of certain real property, §105-151.12.
Fuel ethanol distillery.
Construction, §105-151.6.
Gleaned crops.
Generally, §105-151.14.
Government retirement benefits, §105-151.20.
Handicapped persons.
Construction of dwelling units for, §105-151.1.
Income taxes paid other states, §105-151, (a).
Refund, §105-151, (b).
Long-term care insurance.
Premiums paid, §105-151.28.
Ports authority wharfage, handling and throughput charges, §105-151.22, (a).
Definitions, §105-151.22, (c).
Limitations, §105-151.22, (b).
Poultry composting facility, §105-151.25.
Qualified business investments, §§105-163.010 to 105-163.015.
Real property donations, §105-151.12.
Withheld amounts, §105-163.10.
Deductions to taxable income, §105-134.6, (b).
Definitions, §105-134.1.
Conservation tillage equipment, §105-151.13, (b).
Gleaned crops, §105-151.14, (b).
Taxable income, §105-134.5.
Donations of interest in real property, credit, §105-151.12, (a).
Amounts, §105-151.12, (b).
Carry over of unused portion, §105-151.12, (b).
Married couples, §105-151.12, (d).
Marshland, §105-151.12, (e).
Partners of partnership qualifying for credit.
Maximum dollar limit, §105-151.12.
Requirements for claiming, §105-151.12, (c).
Estimated tax.
Construction and interpretation.
Liberal construction of provisions, §105-163.24.

INCOME TAX —Cont'd
Individual income tax —Cont'd
Estimated tax —Cont'd
Definition of "tax," §105-163.15, (g).
Overpayment.
Refund, §105-163.16.
Required installments, §105-163.15, (c).
Amount, §105-163.15, (d), (e).
Underpayment, §105-163.15, (a), (f), (h).
Amount of underpayment, §105-163.15, (b).
Federal government workers.
Credit or partial refund for tax paid on certain federal government benefits.
Credit, §105-151.20, (b).
Deceased taxpayers, §105-151.20, (d).
Definitions, §105-151.20, (a).
Establishment of claims, §105-151.20, (d).
Federal retiree accounts, §105-151.20, (e).
Purposes, §105-151.20, (a).
Refund alternatives, §105-151.20, (c).
Fiduciaries.
Returns.
Filing by, §105-152, (b).
Fuel ethanol distilleries.
Credit for construction.
Application for credit, §105-151.6, (c).
Ceiling, §105-151.6, (d).
Expiration, §105-151.6, (g).
Carrying over credit, §105-151.6, (e).
Definitions, §105-151.6, (b).
Generally, §105-151.6, (a).
Gleaned crops.
Credits.
Definitions, §105-151.14, (b).
Generally, §105-151.14, (a).
Government retirement benefits.
Credits, §105-151.20.
Handicapped persons.
Credits, §105-151.18.
Construction of dwelling units for, §105-151.1.
Definitions, §105-151.18, (c).
Disabled dependent, §105-151.18, (b).
Disabled taxpayer, §105-151.18, (a).
Limitations, §105-151.18, (d).
Heads of households.
Rate of tax, §105-134.2, (a).
Hurricane Floyd reserve fund payments.
Deductions to taxable income, §105-134.6, (b).
Husband and wife.
Payment of tax, §105-157, (a).
Returns.
Joint returns, §105-152, (e).
Imposition of tax, §105-134.2, (a).
Alternative tax, §105-134.2, (b).
Indian tribe or Indian reservation activities.
Deductions from income, §105-134.6, (b).
Inheritance tax.
Adjustments to taxable income, §105-134.6, (d).
Inventories, §105-134.8.
Investments.
Tax credits for qualified business investments, §§105-163.010 to 105-163.015.
Long-term care insurance.
Credit for premiums paid, §105-151.28.
Married individuals filing joint returns.
Rate of tax, §105-134.2, (a).
Married individuals not filing jointly.
Rate, §105-134.2, (a).
Military affairs.
Abatement of income taxes of certain members of armed forces upon death, §105-158.

INCOME TAX —Cont'd
Individual income tax —Cont'd
Nonresidents, §105-134.5, (b).
Partnerships, §105-134.5, (d).
Payment of tax.
Additional tax, §105-159.
Estimated tax.
Overpayment, §105-163.16.
Underpayment, §105-163.15.
Time for payment, §105-157, (a).
Year for which paid, §105-134.3.
Persons affected, §105-134.
Political contributions.
Designation of tax by individual to political party, §105-159.1, (a).
Paid preparer of tax returns, §105-159.1, (e).
Remission of funds by secretary, §105-159.1, (b).
Return to indicate contribution neither increases or decreases tax liability, §105-159.1, (d).
Ports authority.
Credit for wharfage, handling and throughput charges, §105-151.22, (a).
Definitions, §105-151.22, (c).
Limitations, §105-151.22, (b).
Poultry composting facility.
Credit, §105-151.25.
Public campaign financing fund.
Allocation to fund by individual, §105-159.2, (a).
Instructions for individual to designate allocation, §105-159.2, (c).
Returns to give individual opportunity to designate allocation, §105-159.2, (b).
Purpose of provisions, §105-134.
Qualified business investments.
Tax credits, §§105-163.010 to 105-163.015.
Rate of tax, §105-134.2, (a).
Alternative tax, §105-134.2, (b).
Real property donations, credit, §105-151.12, (a).
Amount, §105-151.12, (b).
Married couples, §105-151.12, (d).
Marshlands, §105-151.12, (e).
Partners of partnership qualifying for credit.
Maximum dollar limit, §105-151.12.
Requirements for claiming, §105-151.12, (c).
Refunds.
Contribution to candidates' financing fund, §105-269.6.
Contribution to wildlife conservation account, §105-269.5.
Retired federal government workers.
Partial refund or alternative, §105-151.20, (c).
Required installments.
Farmer or fisherman, §105-163.15, (i).
Residents, §105-134.5, (a).
Retired federal government workers.
Credit or partial refund for tax paid on certain federal retirement benefits, §105-151.20.
Returns.
Agent filing, §105-152, (b).
Corrections and changes, §105-159.
Deceased persons, §105-152, (b).
Executors and administrators.
Filing for deceased persons, §105-152, (b).
Failure to file.
Supplementary returns, §105-156.
Forms, §105-155, (d).
Guardians.
Filing by, §105-152, (b).

INCOME TAX —Cont'd
Individual income tax —Cont'd
Returns —Cont'd
Husband and wife.
Joint returns, §105-152, (e).
Information at the source returns.
Nonresident owner or partner.
Payment of tax on behalf of, §105-154, (d).
Partnerships, §105-154, (c).
Payment of tax on behalf of nonresident partner, §105-154, (d).
Payers, §105-154, (b).
Time for filing, §105-155, (a).
Information required with return, §105-152, (c).
Secretary may require additional information, §105-152, (d).
Joint returns.
Husband and wife, §105-152, (e).
Place of filing, §105-155, (a).
Supplementary returns, §105-156.
Time for filing, §105-155, (a).
Extension, §105-155, (a).
Who required to file, §105-152, (a).
S corporations, §105-134.5, (d).
Taxable income.
Adjustments to taxable income, §105-134.6, (d).
Additions, §105-134.6, (c).
Deductions, §105-134.6, (b).
S corporations, §105-134.6, (a).
Transitional adjustments, §105-134.7.
Computation, §105-134.4.
Defined, §105-134.5.
Inventories, §105-134.8.
Part-year residents, §105-134.5, (c).
Transitional adjustments, §105-134.7.
Taxable year, §105-134.4.
Title of act.
Short title, §105-133.
Transition to tax changes.
Transitional adjustments, §§105-131 to 105-134.7, (a), (b).
Trusts and estates.
Provisions not to apply to, §105-163.15, (k).
Unmarried individuals.
Rate of tax, §105-134.2, (a).
Withholding of income taxes from wages, §§105-163.1 to 105-163.24. See within this heading, "Withholding of income taxes from wages."
Year of assessment, §105-134.3.
Inheritance tax.
Individual income tax.
Adjustments to taxable income, §105-134.6, (d).
International banking facility.
Deductions in determining state net income, §105-130.5, (b).
Limited liability companies, §57C-10-06.
Loans.
Refund anticipation loans, §§53-245 to 53-254.
Long-term care insurance.
Credit for premiums paid, §105-151.28, (a).
Double benefit prohibited, §105-151.28, (b).
Qualified long-term care insurance defined, §105-151.28, (c).
Low-income housing tax credits, §§105-129.40 to 105-129.45.
Marital deduction.
Fiduciaries.
Incorporation by reference of certain powers, §32-26.

INCOME TAX —Cont'd
Military affairs.
Individual income tax.
Abatement of income taxes of certain members of armed forces upon death, §105-158.
Municipal corporations.
Levy prohibited, §105-247.
Natural and scenic rivers system.
Contribution or donation of scenic easement.
Deemed contribution to state of North Carolina, §113A-39.
New and expanding businesses.
Tax incentives generally, §§105-129.2 to 105-129.13.
See TAX INCENTIVES FOR NEW AND EXPANDING BUSINESSES.
Partnerships.
Credits.
Allowance, §105-269.15, (b).
Distributive share, determination, §105-269.15, (c).
Qualification, §105-269.15, (a).
Real property donations.
Maximum dollar limit, §105-151.12, (d).
Subject to taxation according to classification, §59-84.1, (b).
Penalty for large income tax deficiency, §105-236.
Pension payments, withholding, §105-163.2A.
Political parties.
Designation of tax by individual to political party financing fund, §105-159.1.
Ports authority.
Bond issues.
Gain from transfer not exempt from taxation, §143B-456, (g).
Credits.
Wharfage, handling and throughput charges, §§105-130.41, (a), 105-151.22, (a).
Definitions, §§105-130.41, (c), 105-151.22, (c).
Limitation, §§105-130.41, (b), 105-151.22, (b).
Sunset, §§105-130.41, (d), 105-151.22, (d).
Poultry composting facility.
Credit for construction, §105-151.25, (a).
Property owned by the entirety, §105-151.25, (b).
Principal and income act.
Allocation of disbursements during administration of trust, §37A-5-505, (a) to (d).
Public campaign financing fund.
Allocation to fund by individual, §105-159.2, (a).
Instructions for individual to designate allocation, §105-159.2, (c).
Returns to give individual opportunity to designate allocation, §105-159.2, (b).
Public works.
Relocation assistance.
Payments not to be considered as income, §133-15.
Qualified business investment tax credit, §§105-163.010 to 105-163.015.
Amount of credit allowed, limitation, §105-163.012, (a), (b).
Application for credit, §105-163.011, (c).
Brokered investments, no credit, §105-163.011, (a).
Carry-over, §105-163.012, (a).
Definitions, §105-163.010.
False application, §105-163.014, (b).
Forfeiture.
Effect, §105-163.014, (e).
False application, §105-163.014, (b).

INCOME TAX —Cont'd
Qualified business investment tax credit —Cont'd
Forfeiture —Cont'd
Location out-of-state, §105-163.014, (c).
Participation in business, §105-163.014, (a).
Transfer or redemption of investment, §105-163.014, (d).
Individuals, §105-163.011, (b).
Pass-through entities, §105-163.011, (b1).
Penalties, §105-163.011, (d).
Qualified business defined, §105-163.010.
Qualified business ventures, §105-163.012, (b).
Defined, §105-163.010.
Registration, §105-163.013, (b).
Qualified grantee businesses.
Defined, §105-163.010.
Registration, §105-163.013, (c).
Qualified licensee business.
Defined, §105-163.010.
Registration, §105-163.013, (b1).
Redemption of investment, §105-163.014, (d).
Reduction of credit, §105-163.012, (c), (d).
Registration.
Application, §105-163.013, (d).
Fees, §105-163.013, (d).
Qualified business ventures, §105-163.013, (b).
Qualified grantee businesses, §105-163.013, (c).
Qualified licensee business, §105-163.013, (b1).
Report, §105-163.013, (g).
Revocation, §105-163.013, (e).
Transfer, §105-163.013, (f).
Repeal, §105-163.015.
Transfer of investment, §105-163.014, (d).
Rate of tax.
Limitation, Const. N. C., art. V, §2.
Reciprocity.
Withholding of income taxes from wages, §105-163.22.
Recycling facilities.
Tax credit for large or major recycling facility investment, §§105-129.25 to 105-129.28.
Refunds.
Anticipation loans.
Appeals.
Decision of commissioner, §53-252.
Cease and desist orders, §53-251, (a).
Commissioner.
Appeal of decisions, §53-252.
Definitions, §53-246.
Disclosures, §53-249, (d).
Enforcement of article, §53-253.
Exemptions from article, §53-254.
Facilitator of loans.
Prohibited activities, §53-250.
Fees.
Filing of fee schedule, §53-249, (a).
Notice of unconscionable fee, §53-249, (b).
Posting of schedule, §53-249, (c).
Informal hearings, §53-248, (d).
Penalties.
Civil penalty, §53-251, (c).
Failure to register, §53-247, (b).
Prohibited activities, §53-250.
Registration.
Display of certificate, §53-248, (c).
Exemptions, §53-247, (c).
Failure to register.
Penalties, §53-247, (b).
Initial registration, §53-248, (a).
Renewal, §53-248, (b).

INCOME TAX —Cont'd
Refunds —Cont'd
Anticipation loans —Cont'd
Registration —Cont'd
Required, §53-247, (a).
Revocation, §53-251, (b).
Rules and regulations.
Promulgation, §53-253.
Scope of article, §53-245, (b).
Title of article, §53-245, (a).
Individual income tax.
Contribution to candidates' financing fund, §105-269.6.
Contribution to wildlife conservation account, §105-269.5.
Restoration of item of income.
Included in taxpayer's gross income for earlier taxable year, §105-266.2.
Renewable energy investment tax credit, §105-129.16A.
Research and development tax credit, §§105-129.50 to 105-129.55.
Restrictions and limitations, Const. N. C., art. V, §2.
Retired federal government workers.
Individual income tax.
Credit or partial refund for tax paid on certain federal retirement benefits, §105-151.20.
Returns.
Corporations.
Affirmation verifying return, person signing, §105-130.16, (a).
Consolidated returns for federal income tax purposes, §105-130.14.
Correction of net income by secretary, §105-130.16, (b), (c).
Dissolution or withdrawal from state, time for filing, §105-130.17, (e).
Distortion of net income, correction by secretary, §105-130.16, (b).
Exempt organizations, filing, §105-130.17, (d1).
Extension of time to file, §105-130.17, (d).
Failure to file.
Supplementary returns, §105-130.18.
Filing, §105-130.17, (a).
Time for filing, §105-130.17, (b) to (e).
Marketing associations, §105-130.17, (c).
Mutual associations to conduct agricultural business, §105-130.17, (c).
Required, §105-130.16, (a).
S corporations, §105-131.7.
Signing, §105-130.16, (a).
Supplementary returns, §105-130.18.
Time for filing, §105-130.17, (b) to (e).
Individuals.
Agent filing, §105-152, (b).
Corrections and changes, §105-159.
Deceased persons, §105-152, (b).
Executors and administrators.
Filing for deceased persons, §105-152, (b).
Failure to file.
Supplementary returns, §105-156.
Forms, §105-155, (d).
Guardians.
Filing by, §105-152, (b).
Husband and wife.
Joint returns, §105-152, (e).
Information at the source returns, §105-154.
Information required with return, §105-152, (c).
Secretary may require additional information, §105-152, (d).

INCOME TAX —Cont'd
Returns —Cont'd
Individuals —Cont'd
Joint returns.
Husband and wife, §105-152, (e).
Place of filing, §105-155, (a).
Supplementary returns, §105-156.
Time for, §105-155, (a).
Who required to file, §105-152, (a).
Royalty payments for use of trademarks.
Corporations.
Optional methods for reporting income, §105-130.7A.
S corporations.
Adjustment of basis, §105-131.3.
Adjustment of income, §105-131.2, (a).
Individual income tax, §105-134.6, (a).
Carrybacks.
Restrictions, §105-131.4, (a).
Carryforwards.
Restrictions, §105-131.4, (a).
Citation of division, §105-131, (a).
Corporation exempt from corporate income tax, §105-131.1, (a).
Credits, §105-131.8.
Definitions, §105-131, (b).
Distribution, §105-131.6.
Dividends.
Distributions to shareholders, §105-131.6.
Individual income tax, §105-134.5, (d).
Interpretation of division, §105-131, (c).
Losses and reduction.
Restrictions amount, §105-131.4, (b) to (d).
Net income.
Characterization of income, §105-131.2, (c).
Shareholders.
Pro rate share of net income, §105-131.1, (b).
Payments.
Agreements by nonresident shareholders to file return and pay tax, §105-131.7, (c) to (e).
Composite payments, §105-131.7, (b).
Returns, §105-131.7, (a).
Agreements by nonresident shareholders to file return and pay tax, §105-131.7, (c) to (e).
Composite returns, §105-131.7, (b).
Shareholders.
Agreements by nonresidents to file return and pay tax, §105-131.7, (c) to (e).
Basis, §105-131.3, (a).
Acquisition received by gift, time, §105-131.3, (g).
Adjustment, §105-131.3, (b).
Nonresident, §105-131.3, (d).
Nonresident, §105-131.3, (c).
Adjustment, §105-131.3, (d).
Reduction, §105-131.3, (e), (f).
Credits, §105-131.8, (b).
Taxes paid to other states, §105-131.8, (a).
Distributions to shareholders.
Accumulated adjustments account, §105-131.6, (c).
Adjusted basis of stock defined, §105-131.6, (c).
Taxable distributions, §105-131.6, (a), (b).
Dividends.
Distributions to shareholders, §105-131.6.
Part-year resident shareholder, §105-131.5.
Pro rate share of net income, §105-131.1, (b).
Short title, §105-131, (a).
State bonds, act authorizing issuance not addressing exemption from taxation.
Not exempt on gain from transfer of instrument, §142-12.

INCOME TAX —Cont'd
State refunding obligations.
Gain from transfer not exempt from taxation, §142-29.6, (f).
Tax incentives for new and expanding businesses generally, §§105-129.2 to 105-129.13.
See TAX INCENTIVES FOR NEW AND EXPANDING BUSINESSES.
Telephone service to low-income residents at reduced rates.
Credits.
Credit to corporation providing, §105-130.39, (a), (b).
Tenants by the entireties.
Husband and wife.
Control of real property held in tenancy by the entirety, §39-13.6, (c).
Trusts and trustees.
Estates and trusts generally, §§105-160 to 105-160.8. See within this heading, "Estates and trusts."
Individual income tax.
Estimated tax.
Provisions not to apply to estates or trusts, §105-163.15, (k).
Unemployment compensation.
Withholding of income tax from unemployment compensation, §96-12, (g).
United States.
Withholding from federal employees, §105-163.23.
Wildlife.
Individual income tax refund.
Contribution to wildlife conservation account, §105-269.5.
Withholding of income taxes from wages, §§105-163.1 to 105-163.24.
Amount withheld, §105-163.2, (a).
Calculating employee's anticipated income tax liability, §105-163.2, (a).
Clergymen.
Ordained or licensed clergymen may elect to be an employee, §105-163.1A.
Construction and interpretation.
Liberal construction of provisions, §105-163.24.
Crediting of amounts withheld to individual for calendar year, §105-163.10.
Definitions, §105-163.1.
Employer required to deduct and to withhold, §105-163.2, (a).
Estimated withholding, §105-163.2, (d).
Exemptions.
Allowable exemptions, §105-163.5, (a).
Certificates, §105-163.5, (b), (c), (e).
New withholding exemption certificate, §105-163.5, (d).
Federal corrections, §105-163.6A.
Federal employees, §105-163.23.
Information to secretary.
Required, §105-163.7, (b).
Liability of withholding agents and others.
Others, §105-163.8.
Withholding agents, §105-163.8.
Miscellaneous payroll period, §105-163.2, (c).
Nonresident withholding agent's act in compliance with provisions.
Not evidence that nonresident doing business in state, §105-163.4.
Other persons withholding.
Liability, §105-163.8.

INCOME TAX —Cont'd
Withholding of income taxes from wages —Cont'd
Overpayment.
Refund, §§105-163.9, 105-163.16.
Payment of amounts withheld, §105-163.6, (a).
Categories, §105-163.6, (e).
Monthly, §105-163.6, (c).
Quarterly payments, §105-163.6, (b).
Refund of overpayment, §§105-163.9, 105-163.16.
Payors paying contractors' certain amount required to withhold, §105-163.3, (a).
Annual statement, report to secretary, §105-163.3, (d).
Exemptions, §105-163.3, (b).
Records, §105-163.3, (e).
Repaying amounts withheld improperly, §105-163.3, (f).
Returns, due date, §105-163.3, (c).
Penalty for improper withholding, §105-163.5, (f).
Pension payers must withhold taxes, §105-163.2A, (b).
Amount withheld, §105-163.2A, (c).
Definitions, §105-163.2A, (a).
Election by recipient not to have taxes withheld, §105-163.2A, (d).
Exempted pension payments, §105-163.2A, (e).
Liability for withholding and payment of taxes, §105-163.2A, (b).
More than one arrangement for making payments.
Separate treatment for each arrangement, §105-163.2A, (b).
Nonperiodic distribution, amount withheld, §105-163.2A, (c).
Notice to recipient of right to elect not to withhold, §105-163.2A, (d).
Periodic payment, amount withheld, §105-163.2A, (c).
Residents of state, applicability of provisions, §105-163.2A, (b).
Reciprocity, §105-163.22.
Refund to employer, §105-163.9.
Returns.
Federal corrections, §105-163.6A.
When employer must file return, §105-163.6, (a).
Categories, §105-163.6, (e).
Monthly, §105-163.6, (c).
Quarterly, §105-163.6, (b).
Semiweekly, §105-163.6, (d).
Statement to employees.
Required, §105-163.7, (a), (b).
Tables and rules adopted by secretary, §105-163.2, (b).
Alternatives to tables, §105-163.2, (b).
Alternative tables, §105-163.2, (e).
Withholding agents.
Liability, §105-163.8.
Withholding of income tax from unemployment compensation, §96-12, (g).

INCOME TAX CHECKOFFS.
Refund contributions.
Candidates financing fund, §105-269.6.
Wildlife conservation account, §105-269.5.

INCOME TAX RETURN PREPARERS.
Defined, §105-228.90.
Designation of tax by individual to political party.
Preparer not to designate, §105-159.1, (e).

INCOME TAX RETURN PREPARERS —Cont'd
Fraudulently evading tax on return.
Aiding or assisting, penalty, §105-236.
Unauthorized disclosure of tax information, §75-28.

INCOME WITHHOLDING.
Alimony.
Limitation on amount withheld, §110-136.6, (b1).
Child support.
Assignment of wages, §110-136.1.
Employer reporting to directory of new hires.
Notice to employer to withhold, §110-129.2, (f).
Garnishment.
Continuing wage garnishment proceedings, §110-136, (b), (b1).
Wage garnishment order, §110-136.
Generally, §§110-136.3 to 110-136.14.
See CHILD SUPPORT.
Interstate family support act, §§52C-5-501 to 52C-5-507.
See INTERSTATE FAMILY SUPPORT.
National medical support notice, §§110-136.11 to 110-136.14.
Unemployment compensation benefits, §110-136.2, (f).
Education.
Local board of education employees.
Charitable organization approved by local board.
Deduction of contribution from salary or wage, §143-3.3, (i).
Garnishment.
Child support.
Continuing wage garnishment proceedings, §110-136, (b), (b1).
Wage garnishment order, §110-136.
Withholding of income generally, §§110-136.3 to 110-136.14.
See CHILD SUPPORT.
Wages.
Limitation on wage garnishment, §1-362.
Income tax.
Withholding of income taxes from wages, §§105-163.1 to 105-163.24.
See INCOME TAX.
Withholding of income tax from unemployment compensation, §96-12, (g).
Interstate family support act, §§52C-5-501 to 52C-5-507.
See INTERSTATE FAMILY SUPPORT.
Postseparation support.
Limitation on amount withheld, §110-136.6, (b1).
Public officers and employees.
Annuity contracts.
Salary deductions, §147-9.3.
Charitable organization.
Approved by local board of education or community college board.
Deduction of contribution from salary or wages, §143-3.3, (i).
Approved by University of North Carolina constituent institutions.
Deduction of contribution from salary or wages, §143-3.3, (j).
Credit union.
Member of state employee credit union.
Deductions from salary or wages authorized, §143-3.3, (f).
Employee organizations.
Deductions from salary or wages authorized, §143-3.3, (g).

INCOME WITHHOLDING —Cont'd
Public officers and employees —Cont'd
Insurance.
Payroll deduction.
Competitive selection of products, §58-31-60, (c).
Payroll savings plans, §§143-301 to 143-305.
Repayment of money owed to state, §§143-552 to 143-562.
See PUBLIC OFFICERS AND EMPLOYEES.
State employees combined campaign.
Deduction of employee's pledge from salary or wages, §143-3.3, (h).
Public schools.
Charitable organization approved by local board of education.
Contributions.
Deduction from local board employee's salary or wage, §143-3.3, (i).
Employees.
Repayment of money owed state, §§143-552 to 143-554.
Retirement system for teachers and state employees.
Consolidated judicial retirement act.
Contributions by members, §135-68, (a), (b).
Social security.
Coverage under Title II of social security act.
Contributions by state employees, §135-22.
Supplemental retirement income act.
Contributions, §135-93.
University of North Carolina.
Charitable organization approved by constituent institution.
Contributions.
Deduction from employee's salary or wage, §143-3.3, (j).

INCOMPETENCE.
Administration of estates, costs.
Additional costs assessed before clerk, §7A-307, (d).
Assessment of costs, §7A-307, (a).
Completeness and exclusivity of costs, §7A-307, (c).
Courtroom and related judicial facilities.
Amount of facilities fee, §7A-307, (b).
Use of facilities, §7A-307, (a).
General court of justice.
Support of court, §7A-307, (a).
Liability of parties for costs, §7A-307, (e).
Custodial trusts.
Determination on incapacity of beneficiary, §33B-10.
Generally, §§33B-1 to 33B-22.
See CUSTODIAL TRUSTS.
Determination of incompetence, §§35A-1101 to 35A-1116.
Adjudication orders, §35A-1112, (d).
Affidavit.
Proving mailing of notice and petition, §35A-1109.
Appeal from order adjudicating incompetence, §35A-1115.
Appointment of guardian, §35A-1120.
Appointment of guardian following adjudication, §35A-1112, (e).
Appointment of interim guardian, §35A-1114.
Attorney general to represent petitioner on appeal by respondent.
Court of appeals may request, §35A-1115.

INCOMPETENCE —Cont'd
Determination of incompetence —Cont'd
Attorneys' fees, §35A-1116, (a).
Court-appointed counsel, §35A-1116, (c).
Autism defined, §35A-1101.
Cerebral palsy defined, §35A-1101.
Certificate of acceptance.
Proving mailing of notice and petition, §35A-1109.
Certified copy of adjudication sent to clerk in county of ward's legal residence, §35A-1112, (f).
Change of venue, §35A-1104.
Clerk of superior court.
Original jurisdiction over proceedings, §35A-1103, (a).
Clerk having interest in proceedings, jurisdiction vested in superior court judge, §35A-1103, (d).
Transfer of proceedings, exceptions, §1-301.2, (g).
Continuance of hearing.
Multidisciplinary evaluation ordered, §35A-1108, (b).
Costs.
Applicability to all parties to any proceeding under chapter, §35A-1116, (d).
Assessment in taxing, §35A-1116, (a).
Multidisciplinary evaluation, §35A-1116, (b).
Witness fees and fees of court-appointed counsel or guardian ad litem, §35A-1116, (c).
Definitions, §35A-1101.
Dismissal of proceedings.
Finder of fact not finding respondent incompetent, §35A-1112, (c).
Voluntary dismissal, §35A-1112, (g).
Appointment of interim guardian, §35A-1114, (f).
Epilepsy defined, §35A-1101.
Exclusive procedure for adjudicating person to be incompetent adult or incompetent child, §35A-1102.
Guardian ad litem.
Attorney as guardian ad litem, §35A-1107, (a), (b).
Fees of court-appointed guardian ad litem, §35A-1116, (c).
Hearing.
Appointment of interim guardian, §35A-1114, (c), (d).
Dismissal if finder of fact does not find respondent incompetent, §35A-1112, (c).
Incompetence determined in another state, §35A-1113.
Open to public unless respondent requests otherwise, §35A-1112, (a).
Place of hearing, §35A-1112, (a).
Rights of petitioner and respondent, §35A-1112, (b).
Time for holding, §35A-1108, (a).
Extension if multidisciplinary evaluation ordered, §35A-1108, (b).
Incompetence determined in another state.
Hearing, §35A-1113.
Incompetent adult defined, §35A-1101.
Incompetent child defined, §35A-1101.
Indigent defined, §35A-1101.
Inebriety defined, §35A-1101.
Interim guardian, appointment.
Bond, posting, §35A-1114, (e).
Hearing, §35A-1114, (c), (d).

INCOMPETENCE —Cont'd
Determination of incompetence —Cont'd
Interim guardian, appointment —Cont'd
Notice of hearing, §35A-1114, (c).
Order appointing, §35A-1114, (d), (e).
Termination of guardianship, §35A-1114, (e).
Verified motion, filing, §35A-1114, (a).
Contents, §35A-1114, (b).
Voluntary dismissal of petition of adjudication of incompetence, §35A-1114, (f).
Jurisdiction over proceedings under subchapter.
Clerk of superior court has original jurisdiction, §35A-1103, (a).
Jury trial, right to, §35A-1110.
Mailing notice and petition to respondent, §35A-1109.
Mental illness defined, §35A-1101.
Mental retardation defined, §35A-1101.
Multidisciplinary evaluation.
Clerk may order respondent to attend, §35A-1111, (d).
Consideration at hearing for adjudication of incompetence, §35A-1111, (e).
Costs, §35A-1116, (b).
Defined, §35A-1101.
Designated agency to prepare or assemble, §35A-1111, (b).
Evaluation not containing medical, psychological or social work evaluations, filing, §35A-1111, (c).
Evaluation not to be public record, §35A-1111, (b).
Extension of time for hearing upon ordering, §35A-1108, (b).
Requesting and ordering evaluations, §35A-1111, (a).
Time for filing with clerk, §35A-1111, (b).
Notice of hearing.
Appointment of interim guardian, §35A-1114, (c).
Service, §35A-1109.
Time clerk to file, §35A-1108, (a).
Notices, service of subsequent notices, §35A-1108, (c).
Order adjudicating respondent incompetent, §35A-1112, (d).
Petition, verification, §35A-1105.
Contents, §35A-1106.
Service, §35A-1109.
Restoration to competency, §35A-1130.
Right to counsel, §35A-1107, (a).
Right to jury, §35A-1110.
Service of application for appointment of guardian when joined with petition for adjudication of incompetence, §35A-1211, (b).
Service of notice of hearing in petition, §35A-1109.
Service of subsequent notices to parties, §35A-1108.
Sheriff to serve notice and petition without demanding fees in advance, §35A-1109.
Stay of appointment of guardian.
Appeal of order adjudicating incompetence, §35A-1115.
Superior court judges jurisdiction.
Clerk having interest in proceedings, §35A-1103, (d).
Transfer of proceeding for appointment of guardian, §35A-1112, (e).
Venue for proceedings, §35A-1103, (b).
Change of venue, §35A-1104.

INCOMPETENCE —Cont'd
Determination of incompetence —Cont'd
Venue for proceedings —Cont'd
Proceedings involving same respondent brought in more than one county, §35A-1103, (c).
Voluntary dismissal, §35A-1112, (g).
Interim appointment of guardian, §35A-1114, (f).
Witness fees, §35A-1116, (c).
Durable power of attorney.
Incapacity or incompetence of principal.
Generally, §§32A-8 to 32A-14.
See DURABLE POWER OF ATTORNEY.
Guardians.
Generally.
See GUARDIANS.
Insurance proceeds or money belonging to incapacitated adult.
Payment to and receipt by clerks of superior courts or public guardians, §7A-111, (b), (d).
Judicial sales.
Confirmation of public sale of real property, §1-339.28, (b).
Mental health, developmental disability, substance abuse.
See MENTAL HEALTH, DEVELOPMENTAL DISABILITY, SUBSTANCE ABUSE.
Restoration to competency.
Accounts from guardian, filing an approval, §35A-1130, (e).
Appeal from clerks order denying petition, §35A-1130, (f).
Discharge of guardian, §35A-1130, (e).
Guardian ad litem.
Appointment, §35A-1130, (c).
Hearing, §35A-1130, (c).
Setting for hearing, §35A-1130, (b).
Jury trial, §35A-1130, (c).
Motion, §35A-1130, (a).
Multidisciplinary evaluation, §35A-1130, (c).
Order adjudicating restoration to competency, §35A-1130, (d).
Order denying petition, §35A-1130, (f).
Right to representation by counsel or guardian ad litem, §35A-1130, (c).
Service of notice and motion on guardian and ward, §35A-1130, (b).

INCOMPETENCY ADJUDICATION, §§35A-1101 to 35A-1116.
See INCOMPETENCE.

INCONVENIENT FORUM.
Change of venue, §1-83.
Stay of proceeding to permit trial in foreign jurisdiction, §1-75.12.

INCORPORATION.
Business corporations.
Formation generally.
See CORPORATIONS.
Commercial banks, §§53-2 to 53-17.1.
See BANKS.
Municipal corporations.
General assembly to provide for local government, Const. N. C., art. VII, §1.
Joint legislative commission on municipal incorporation, §§120-158 to 120-174.
See MUNICIPAL CORPORATIONS.
Nonprofit corporations.
Formation generally.
See NONPROFIT CORPORATIONS.

INCORPOREAL HEREDITAMENTS.
Limitation of actions.
Injury to, §1-50, (a).

INCRIMINATION.
Self-incrimination generally.
See SELF-INCRIMINATION.

INDECENCY.
Obscenity.
General provisions, §§14-190.1 to 14-190.20.
See OBSCENITY.

INDECENT EXPOSURE, §14-190.9.
Breastfeeding excluded from definition, §14-190.9, (b).
Elements of offense, §14-190.9, (a).
Local government regulation, §14-190.9, (c).
Sexual offenses generally.
See SEXUAL OFFENSES.

INDECENT LIBERTIES BETWEEN CHILDREN.
Elements of offense, §14-202.2, (a).
Misdemeanor offense, §14-202.2, (b).

INDECENT LIBERTIES WITH A MINOR.
Bail and recognizance, §15A-534.4.
Electronic surveillance orders, §15A-290, (c1).
Elements of offense, §14-202.1, (a).
Felony offense, §14-202.1, (b).

INDEMNIFICATION.
Business corporations.
Additional indemnification, §55-8-57, (a), (b).
Agents, §55-8-56.
Articles of incorporation.
Restrictions on indemnification, §55-8-58, (a).
Conflicts of interest.
Court-ordered indemnification, §55-8-54.
Expenses.
Certain powers of corporation not limited, §55-8-58, (b).
Evaluation as to reasonableness, §55-8-55, (c).
Expenses in defending proceedings.
Advance for expenses, §55-8-53.
Indemnification not void or voidable on grounds of, §55-8-51, (f).
Mandatory indemnification, §55-8-52.
Restrictions on indemnification, §55-8-51, (d), (e).
Court-ordered indemnification.
Directors, §55-8-54.
Directors.
Advance for expenses, §55-8-53.
Authority to indemnify, §55-8-51, (a) to (c).
Determinations required, §55-8-55, (a), (b).
Manner of authorization, §55-8-55, (c).
Effective date of article.
Restriction on applicability of provisions, §55-8-58, (c).
Employees, §55-8-56.
Insurance.
Purchase and maintenance, §55-8-57, (c).
Mandatory indemnification.
Directors, §55-8-52.
Officers, employees and agents, §55-8-56.
Officers, §55-8-56.
Report to shareholders, §55-16-21, (a).
Construction indemnity agreements, §22B-1.
Contribution.
Joint tort-feasors.
Right of indemnity not impaired, §1B-1, (f).

INDEMNIFICATION —Cont'd
Electric membership corporations.
Directors, officers, employees and agents, §117-46.
Executors and administrators.
Rights of surety in danger of loss, §28A-8-5.
Farm machinery franchises.
Supplier to indemnify dealer against judgment for damages or settlement, §66-187, (b).
Fraternal benefit societies.
Officers, directors, employees or agents, §58-24-35, (b).
Improvement to real property defective or unsafe.
Limitation of action for indemnification, §1-50, (a).
Insurance agents.
Credit information or credit scores of insurer used.
Action, error or omission from use, §58-36-90, (e).
Limited liability company managers, directors, executives and members, §57C-3-31.
Permissive indemnification, §57C-3-32, (a).
Livestock.
Diseased animals.
Compensation for killing.
Owner's claim for indemnity supported by reports, §106-334.
Hog cholera.
Destruction of swine affected with or exposed to hog cholera, §106-322.2.
When indemnity payments not to be made, §106-322.3.
Local boards of education members or employees.
Paying judgment against member or employee, §115C-43, (b), (c).
Nonprofit corporations.
Additional indemnification and insurance, §55A-8-57.
Advance for expenses, §55A-8-53.
Agents, §55A-8-56.
Applicability of part, §55A-8-58.
Authority to indemnify, §55A-8-51.
Authorization of indemnification and evaluation to reasonableness of expenses, §55A-8-55.
Court-ordered indemnification, §55A-8-54.
Definitions, §55A-8-50, (b).
Determination, §55A-8-55.
Directors.
Notice to members, §55A-16-21.
Employees, §55A-8-56.
Expenses.
Advance for expenses, §55A-8-53.
Insurance, §55A-8-57.
Mandatory indemnification, §55A-8-52.
Officers, §55A-8-56.
Policy statement, §55A-8-50, (a).
Powers generally, §55A-8-51.
Partnerships.
When partnership must indemnify partner, §59-48.
Public policy.
Construction indemnity agreements invalid, §22B-1.
Savings and loan associations.
Blanket indemnity bond, §54B-109, (a).
Fines and penalties.
Indemnification of persons fined or penalized.
Prohibited, §54B-72.
Rules and regulations, §54B-109, (f).

INDEMNIFICATION —Cont'd
Savings and loan associations —Cont'd
Unauthorized investments.
Indemnity bond, §54B-109, (c), (d).
Withdrawable accounts.
New account books.
Loss that might result from issuance, §54B-134.
Savings banks.
Fines or penalties.
Reimbursement or indemnification prohibited, §54C-85.
Structural pest control.
Financial responsibility, §106-65.37, (a).
Telephone membership corporations.
Directors, officers, employees and agents, §117-46.
Trust companies.
Directors.
Surety and indemnity bond, §53-358, (a), (b).

INDEPENDENCE DAY.
Public holiday, §103-4, (a).

INDEXES.
Clerks of superior courts.
Immediate indexing.
Documents received for docketing, §7A-109, (c).
Minimum criteria, §7A-109, (b).
Record-keeping requirements generally, §7A-109, (a) to (e).
General assembly.
Journals indexed by clerks, §120-28.
Local legislation.
Published by division of publications, §147-54.1.
Session laws, §120-34, (b).
Judgments, §1-233.
Motor vehicles.
Registration records, §20-56, (a).
Stolen vehicles.
Index of seized, stolen or recovered vehicles.
Examination of receipt of application for registration, §20-55.
Public lands.
Grants.
Index system for grants, §146-44.
Record of surveys, §§146-40 to 146-42.
Registers of deeds.
Indexing procedures, §161-14.2.
Board of county commissioners may require transcribing and indexing of books, §161-18.
General index, §161-21.
Index and cross-index of immediate prior owners of land, §161-22.1.
Index of registered instrument, §161-22.
Land records management.
Minimum standards for, §161-22.3.
Parcel identifier number indexes, §161-22.2.
Public lands.
Entries.
Record of surveys, §§146-40 to 146-42.
Registered instruments, §161-22.
Standards.
Land records management, §161-22.3.
Secretary of state.
Public lands.
Index system for grants, §146-44.
Torrens system registration.
Cross-indexing of lands by register of deeds, §43-14.
Trusts and trustees.
Wills.
Rules and regulations concerning registration and indexing of testamentary trusts, §36A-108.

INDEXING JUDGMENTS, §1-233.

INDIAN BEACH.
Eminent domain.
Exercise of power, purposes, modified provisions, §40A-3, (b1).
Vesting of title and right to possession, §40A-42, (a).

INDIAN DAY.
Designation, §147-18.

INDIAN HOUSING AUTHORITY, §§157-66 to 157-70.
Applicability of chapter, §157-67.
Appointment, §157-68.
Area of operation, §157-69.
Commission of Indian affairs.
Authority, §157-67.
Composition, §157-68.
Creation, §157-66.
Governor.
Powers, §157-67.
Powers.
General provisions, §157-67.
Rentals.
Applicability of section, §§157-29, 157-70.
Tenants.
Selection, §§157-29, 157-70.
Vacancy, §157-68.

INDIANS.
Adoption.
Adoptee subject to Indian child welfare act, §48-1-108.
Antiquities, §§70-1 to 70-4.
Department of cultural resources.
Possessors of relics urged to commit them to custody of state agencies, §70-2.
Destruction or sale of relic from public lands, §70-4.
Private landowners urged to refrain from destruction, §70-1.
Public lands.
Destruction or sale of relic from public lands, §70-4.
Preservation of relics on public lands, §70-3.
State museum.
Possessors of relics urged to commit them to custody of state museums, §70-2.
Archaeological resources protection.
Permits for archaeological investigations.
Procedure when permit may harm cultural or religious site, §70-13, (d).
Burial grounds.
Relics generally, §§70-1 to 70-4.
Unmarked human burial and human skeletal remains protection generally, §§70-26 to 70-40.
See UNMARKED HUMAN BURIAL AND SKELETAL REMAINS PROTECTION.
Cherokee Indians of Robeson county.
Provisions not applicable to certain bands of Cherokees, §71A-2.
Rights and privileges, §71A-1.
Child custody jurisdiction and enforcement, §50A-104.
Child welfare.
Collaboration between division of social services and commission of Indian affairs, §143B-139.5A.

INDIANS —Cont'd.
Citizenship, §§71A-3 to 71A-7.2.
Coharie Tribe of North Carolina.
Rights, privileges, immunities, obligations and duties, §71A-6.
Commission of Indian affairs.
Chairman, §143B-407, (b).
Clerical staff, §143B-410.
Compensation, §143B-407, (c).
Creation, §143B-404.
Purposes, §143B-405.
Duties, §143B-406, (a).
Employees, §143B-411.
Executive director, §143B-411.
Fiscal records, §143B-410.
Meetings, §143B-408, (a).
Membership, §143B-407, (a).
Name, §143B-404.
Proxy vote, §143B-408, (c).
Purposes for creation, §143B-405.
Quorum, §143B-408, (b).
Records.
Fiscal records, §143B-410.
Reports.
Preparation and submission of annual report by commission, §143B-409.
Rulemaking, §143B-406, (b).
Terms, §143B-407, (b).
County inspection departments.
Tribal lands, §153A-350.1.
Day.
Designation of Indian day by governor, §147-18.
Eastern band of the Cherokee.
Advisory council.
Appointment, §143B-411.1.
Chairman, §143B-411.3.
Clerical and administrative support, §143B-411.4.
Compensation, §143B-411.3.
Composition, §143B-411.1.
Creation, §143B-411.1.
Duties, §143B-411.2.
Meetings, §143B-411.3.
Powers, §143B-411.2.
Purpose, §143B-411.2.
Quorum, §143B-411.3.
Terms of office, §143B-411.1.
Full faith and credit.
Considered a foreign judgment, §1E-1, (b).
Subject to certain provisions, §1E-1, (b).
Tribal Court.
Subject to full faith and credit of Tribal Court, §1E-1, (a).
Motor fuels and special fuel taxes refunds.
Definitions applicable, §105-449.114, (b).
Memorandum of understanding or agreement to make refunds, §105-449.114, (c).
Recognition as possessing sovereign legal rights, §105-449.114, (a).
Education.
State advisory council.
Chairperson.
Election, §115C-210.3, (a).
Compensation, §115C-210.3, (c).
Composition, §115C-210.1.
Created, §115C-210.
Duties, §115C-210.4.

INDIANS —Cont'd
Education —Cont'd
State advisory council —Cont'd
Established, §115C-210.
Expenses paid, §115C-210.3, (c).
Meetings.
Generally, §115C-210.3, (b).
Members, §115C-210.1.
Powers, §115C-210.4.
Terms of office, §115C-210.2.
Subsequent terms, §115C-210.2.
Gaming.
Authorization for federally recognized tribes, §71A-8.
Governor.
Designation of Indian day, §147-18.
Haliwa Saponi Tribe of North Carolina.
Rights, privileges, immunities, obligations and duties, §71A-5.
Housing authority.
Applicability of chapter, §157-67.
Appointment, §157-68.
Area of operation, §157-69.
Commission of Indian affairs.
Authority, §157-67.
Composition, §157-68.
Creation, §157-66.
Governor.
Powers, §157-67.
Powers.
General provisions, §157-67.
Rentals.
Applicability of section 157-29, §157-70.
Tenants.
Selection.
Application of section 157-29, §157-70.
Vacancy, §157-68.
Income tax.
Individual income tax.
Deductions from income, §105-134.6, (b).
Lumbee Tribe of North Carolina.
Rights, privileges, immunities, obligations and duties, §71A-3.
Marriage proceedings.
Solemnization by federally recognized tribe or nation, §51-3.2, (a).
Applicability of chapter, §51-3.2, (b).
Meherrin tribe of North Carolina.
Rights, privileges, immunities, obligations and duties, §7A-7.1.
Misdemeanors.
Relics.
Destruction or sale of relic from public lands, §70-4.
Motor vehicle license plates.
Special native American plates, §20-79.4, (b).
Occaneechi band of Saponi nation in North Carolina.
Rights, privileges, immunities, obligations and duties, §71A-7.2.
Person county.
Sappony.
Designated as, rights, privileges, immunities, obligations and duties, §71A-7.
Records.
Fiscal records.
Commissioner, §143B-410.
Relics.
Department of cultural resources.
Possessors of relics urged to commit them to custody of state agencies, §70-2.

INDIANS —Cont'd
Relics —Cont'd
Misdemeanors.
Destruction or sale of relic from public lands, §70-4.
Private landowners urged to refrain from destruction, §70-1.
Public lands.
Destruction or sale of relic from public lands.
Misdemeanors, §70-4.
Preservation of relics on public lands, §70-3.
State museum.
Possessors of relics urged to commit them to custody of state museums, §70-2.
Reports.
Preparation by commissioner, §143B-409.
Sappony.
Tribe residing in Person county.
Rights, privileges, immunities, obligations and duties, §71A-7.
Solidarity week, §103-8.
Taxation.
Constitutional provisions, Const. U. S., art. I, §2; amd. XIV.
Waccamaw Siouan Tribe of North Carolina.
Rights, privileges, immunities, obligations and duties, §71A-4.

INDIAN SOLIDARITY WEEK.
Designation, §103-8.

INDICTMENTS.
Accomplices and accessories.
Before the fact accessories.
Accessory before fact punishable as principal felon, §14-5.2.
Attorneys at law.
Unauthorized practice of law.
Duty of district attorney to indict persons upon receipt of information of violation, §84-7.
Bribery of officials.
Public officers and employees, §14-217, (b).
Bullet-proof vests.
Defendant wearing or having in possession during commission of felony.
Allegations, §15A-1340.16C, (c).
Capital punishment.
Waiver.
Indictment may not be waived in capital case, §15A-642, (b).
Child support.
District attorneys.
Reports to district attorneys of aid to dependent children and illegitimate births.
Criminal offenses, §15-155.2, (b).
Consolidation of charges, §15A-643.
Constitution of North Carolina.
Modes of prosecution, Const. N. C., art. I, §22.
Right of accused to be informed of accusation, Const. N. C., art. I, §23.
Constitution of the United States, Const. U. S., amd. V.
Contents, §15A-644, (a).
Corporations.
Securing attendance of organizations as defendants, §15A-773.
Defective indictments.
Limitation on subsequent prosecution for same offense, §15-1.
Definitions.
Defects which do not vitiate, §15-155.
Generally, §15A-641, (a).

INDICTMENTS —Cont'd
Dismissal.
Motion to dismiss.
Grounds, §15A-955.
Domestic violence.
Violation of valid protective order as felony, §50B-4.1, (e).
Embezzlement.
Description in bill for embezzlement of money, §15-150.
Enhanced sentence.
Bullet-proof vests.
Defendant wearing or having in possession during commission of felony.
Allegations, §15A-1340.16C, (c).
Firearms.
Use or display during commission of felony.
Allegations, §15A-1340.16A, (d).
Methamphetamine manufacture.
Serious injury inflicted on law enforcement or emergency personnel.
Allegations, §15A-1340.16D, (b).
False pretenses and cheats.
Sufficiency, §14-100, (a).
Firearms.
Felony firearms act.
Possession of firearms, etc., by felon prohibited, §14-415.1, (c).
Use or display during commission of felony.
Enhanced sentence.
Allegations, §15A-1340.16A, (d).
Forgery.
Intent to defraud.
Sufficiency of allegation, §15-151.
Forms.
Defects which do not vitiate, §15-155.
Informality.
Bill or warrant not quashed for informality, §15-153.
Perjury.
Bill for perjury, §15-145.
Fraud.
Intent to defraud.
Sufficiency of allegation, §15-151.
Grand jury.
Confidentiality of information.
Bill of indictment, §15A-623, (f).
Foreman.
Signature, §15A-644, (a).
Notice.
True bill of indictment.
Notice to defendant, §15A-630.
Number of members required to concur, §15A-623, (a).
Return of bill of indictment, §15A-628, (a), (c).
Not true bill, §15A-628, (a).
Institution of new charge, §15A-629, (b).
Procedure upon finding of not true bill, §15A-629, (a).
True bill, §15A-628, (a).
Notice to defendant, §15A-630.
Submission of bill of indictment by prosecutor, §15A-627, (a).
Offenses within original jurisdiction of superior court, §15A-627, (b).
True bill.
Return as not true bill, §15A-628, (a).
Institution of new charge, §15A-629, (b).
Procedure upon, §15A-629, (a).
Return as true bill, §15A-628, (a).
Notice to defendant, §15A-630.

INDICTMENTS —Cont'd
Grand jury —Cont'd
Validity inquiry.
Testimony of jurors, §8C-1, Rule 606.
Venue to present or indict, §15A-631.
Habitual felons, §§14-7.2, 14-7.3.
Violent habitual felons, §14-7.9.
Hazing.
Self-incriminating testimony.
No indictment to be founded on self-incriminating testimony, §14-38.
Homicide.
Essentials of bill for homicide, §15-144.
Impeachment.
Effect of impeachment, §123-13.
Informality.
Bill or warrant not quashed for informality, §15-153.
Joinder.
Offenses and defendants, §15A-643.
Joint tenants and tenants in common.
Manner of alleging joint ownership of property, §15-148.
Jury.
Reading of indictment to prospective jurors or to jury.
Prohibited, §15A-1221, (b).
Larceny.
Description in bill for larceny of money, §15-149.
Separate offenses.
Charging in same indictment, §15-151.
Life imprisonment without parole.
Second or subsequent conviction of class B1 felony, §15A-1340.16B, (d).
Manslaughter.
Essentials of bill, §15-144.
Methamphetamine manufacture.
Serious injury inflicted on law enforcement or emergency personnel.
Enhanced sentence.
Allegations, §15A-1340.16D, (b).
Money.
Description of money.
Bill for embezzlement, §15-150.
Bill for larceny, §15-149.
Murder.
Essentials of bill, §15-144.
Necessity, Const. U. S., amd. V.
Organizations or groups, §15A-773.
Partnerships.
Securing attendance of organizations as defendants, §15A-773.
Perjury.
Form of bill for perjury, §15-145.
Subornation of perjury.
Sufficiency of bill, §15-146.
Pleadings in felony cases and misdemeanor cases initiated in supreme court division.
Amendment.
No amendment of indictment, §15A-923, (e).
Form of indictment, §15A-923, (b).
Prosecution on indictment, §15A-923, (a).
Waiver of indictment, §15A-923, (c).
Plea of guilty or no contest in district court, §15A-644.1.
Previous convictions.
Allegations, §15A-645.
Property.
Joint ownership of property.
Manner of alleging, §15-148.

INDICTMENTS —Cont'd
Quashing.
Defects which do not vitiate, §15-155.
Informality.
Bill or warrant not quashed for informality, §15-153.
Rape.
Essentials of bill, §15-144.1, (a).
Age.
Victim female child under age of 13, §15-144.1, (b).
Mentally ill.
Victim mentally defective or incapacitated, §15-144.1, (c).
Minors.
Victim female child under 13, §15-144.1, (b).
Physically helpless victim, §15-144.1, (c).
Sexual offenses.
Essentials of bill, §15-144.2, (a).
Age.
Victim 13 years of age or less, §15-144.2, (b).
Mentally ill.
Victim mentally defective or incapacitated, §15-144.2, (c).
Minors.
Victim age 13 or less, §15-144.2, (b).
Physically helpless victim, §15-144.2, (c).
Signatures.
Required signatures, §15A-644, (a).
Stolen goods.
Receiving stolen goods.
Charging with separate offenses in same indictment, §15-151.
Subornation of perjury.
Sufficiency of bill, §15-146.
Superior court.
Prosecutions originating in superior court to be upon indictment or information, §15A-642, (a).
Superseding indictments, §15A-646.
Time.
Defects which do not vitiate, §15-155.
Venue.
Grand jury.
Venue to present or indict, §15A-631.
Violent habitual felons, §14-7.9.
Waiver, §15A-642, (b), (c).

INDICTMENTS, ESSENTIALS OF BILL, §15-144.2, (a).
Age.
Victim 13 years of age or less, §15-144.2, (b).
Mentally incapacitated.
Victim mentally defective or incapacitated, §§15-144.1, (c), 15-144.2, (c).
Minors.
Victim age 13 or less, §15-144.2, (b).
Physically helpless victim, §15-144.2, (c).

INDIGENT DEFENSE SERVICES.
Abused, neglected or dependent juvenile proceedings.
Payment of appointed counsel.
Office responsible for providing counsel, §7A-603, (b).
Administrative support to office.
Director of administrative office of the courts to provide, §7A-498.2, (c).
Appellate counsel.
Appointment, compensation eligibility.
Capital cases, IDS Rules 2B.1 to 2B.4.
Standards for, IDS Appx. 2B.1 to 2B.3.

INDIGENT DEFENSE SERVICES —Cont'd
Appellate counsel —Cont'd
Appointment, compensation eligibility —Cont'd
Non-capital criminal and non-criminal cases, IDS Rules 3.1 to 3.7.
Appellate defender, §7A-498.8.
Appointment by commission, §7A-498.8, (a).
Appointment fee in criminal cases.
Assessment, §7A-455.1, (e).
Crediting of fees collected, §7A-455.1, (f).
Generally, §7A-455.1, (a) to (c).
Nonpayment, §7A-455.1, (b), (d).
Rulemaking, §7A-455.1, (g).
Appropriated funds.
Allocation and disbursement by office, §7A-498.3, (d).
Use, commission approval, §7A-498.2, (e).
Budget of office, §7A-498.2, (d).
Reduction or modification.
Approval of commission required, §7A-498.2, (e).
Capital cases.
Appellate defender.
Additional conditions of appointment, setting, IDS Rule 2B.4.
Appeal to IDS commission.
Determination that lawyer not qualified, IDS Appx. 2B.2.
Appointment and representation, IDS Rule 2B.2.
Conflict of interest, IDS Rule 2B.2.
Application for appointment, IDS Appx. 2B.2.
Appointment of appellate counsel, IDS Rule 2B.2.
Capital appeals roster.
Creation, IDS Appx. 2B.2.
Removal from, IDS Appx. 2B.3.
Certiorari.
When appointed counsel required to file writ, IDS Rule 2B.4.
Compensation, IDS Rule 2B.3.
Conditions of appointment, IDS Rule 2B.4.
Conflict of interest in appellate defender, IDS Rule 2B.2.
Contract services.
Recoupment of services, IDS Rule 2B.3.
Coverage of part, IDS Rule 2B.1.
Experts, appointment and compensation, other expenses.
Appointment of experts.
Application to court, IDS Rule 2D.4.
Confidentiality of applications, IDS Rule 2D.2.
Notice of disapproval of application, IDS Rule 2D.3.
Disapproval of application, IDS Rule 2D.3.
Notice of disapproval, IDS Rule 2D.3.
Other programs, plans or contracts.
Authority to implement, IDS Rule 2D.5.
Payment.
Application to IDS, IDS Rule 2D.1.
Retention of expert.
Application to IDS, IDS Rule 2D.1.
Knowledge and experience.
Standards and qualifications, IDS Appx. 2B.1.
On-going training.
Required to retain eligibility for appointment, IDS Appx. 2B.3.
Other appellate counsel.
Assignment to defendant, IDS Rule 2B.2.
Other programs, plans and contracts.
Authority to implement, IDS Rule 2B.1.
Post conviction counsel.
Application for appointment, IDS Appx. 2C.2.
Appointment of counsel, IDS Rule 2C.2.

INDIGENT DEFENSE SERVICES —Cont'd
Capital cases —Cont'd
Post conviction counsel —Cont'd
Compensation, IDS Rule 2C.3.
Conditions of appointment, requirements, IDS Rule 2C.4.
Contract services.
Recoupment, IDS Rule 2C.3.
Coverage of part, IDS Rule 2C.1.
Experience and knowledge.
Standards for, IDS Appx. 2C.1.
List of eligible lawyers, IDS Rule 2C.2.
On-going training.
Required to remain eligible, IDS Appx. 2C.3.
Other programs, plans and contracts.
Authority to implement, IDS Rule 2C.1.
Post-conviction roster.
Creation, IDS Appx. 2C.2.
Removal from, IDS Appx. 2C.3.
Recoupment of fees, IDS Rule 2C.3.
Replacement of counsel.
Appointment of substitute, IDS Rule 2C.5.
Standards for, IDS Appx. 2C.
Submissions with application for appointment, IDS Appx. 2C.2.
Substitution of counsel.
Replacement of counsel, IDS Rule 2C.5.
Training session.
Required to remain eligible, IDS Appx. 2C.3.
Two lawyers appointed, IDS Rule 2C.2.
Waiver of experience and knowledge standards, IDS Appx. 2C.1.
Recoupment of fees, IDS Rule 2B.3.
Replacement of counsel, substitute appointed, IDS Rule 2B.4.
Standards and qualifications, IDS Appx. 2B.
Submissions with application for appointment, IDS Appx. 2B.2.
Substitution of counsel.
Replacement of counsel, IDS Rule 2B.4.
Training session.
Required to retain eligibility for appointment, IDS Appx. 2B.3.
Trial counsel.
Appeal to IDS commission.
Review of determination that attorney not qualified, IDS Appx. 2A.2.
Appointment of trial counsel, IDS Rule 2A.2.
Application for appointment as lead or associate counsel, IDS Appx. 2A.2.
Capital defendant defined, IDS Rule 2A.1.
Capital offense defined, IDS Rule 2A.1.
Capital trial roster.
Creation, IDS Appx. 2A.2.
Removal for, IDS Appx. 2A.3.
Compensation, IDS Rule 2A.4.
Conditions of appointment, requirements, IDS Rule 2A.5.
Contract services.
Recoupment, IDS Rule 2A.4.
Coverage of subpart, IDS Rule 2A.1.
First lawyer appointed, IDS Rule 2A.2.
Lead and associate counsel, appointment, IDS Rule 2A.2.
Standards for, IDS Appx. 2A.
List of lawyers eligible for appointment, IDS Rule 2A.2.
Local counsel, provisional appointment, IDS Rule 2A.2.
Non-capital charges joined with capital charges, applicability to, IDS Rule 2A.1.

INDIGENT DEFENSE SERVICES —Cont'd
Capital cases —Cont'd
Trial counsel —Cont'd
Notification by court of need to appoint counsel, IDS Rule 2A.2.
On-going training to remain eligible for appointment, IDS Appx. 2A.3.
Other programs, plans and contracts.
Implementation authorized, IDS Rule 2A.1.
Provisional appointment, local counsel, IDS Rule 2A.2.
Qualifications and experience.
Standards for lead and associate counsel, IDS Appx. 2A.1.
Recoupment of compensation, IDS Rule 2A.4.
Replacement of counsel with new counsel, IDS Rule 2A.5.
Second trial counsel appointed, IDS Rule 2A.2.
Standby counsel.
Waiver of counsel by defendant, IDS Rule 2A.3.
Submissions with application for appointment, IDS Appx. 2A.2.
Substitution of counsel.
Replacement of counsel with new counsel, IDS Rule 2A.5.
Training session.
Required to remain eligible for appointment, IDS Appx. 2A.3.
Waiver of counsel, IDS Rule 2A.3.
Waiver of qualifications and experience standards.
Standards for lead and associate counsel, IDS Appx. 2A.1.
Waiver of knowledge and experience requirements.
Standards and qualifications, IDS Appx. 2B.1.
Commission on indigent defense services.
Approval of office budget, §7A-498.5, (g).
Chair, §7A-498.4, (h).
Compensation, §7A-498.4, (j).
Compositions, §7A-498.4, (b).
Conflicts of interest, §7A-498.4, (d).
Delivery of service methods, §7A-498.5, (d).
Consultation with district bar, §7A-498.5, (e).
Development of standards, §7A-498.5, (c).
Direction to attend meetings, §7A-498.4, (i).
Director of office.
Appointment, §§7A-498.5, (b), 7A-498.6, (a).
Establishment, §7A-498.4, (a).
Inaugural meeting, §7A-498.4, (k).
Powers and duties, §7A-498.5.
Procedures for distribution of appropriated funds, §7A-498.5, (f).
Purpose, §7A-498.5, (a).
Quorum, §7A-498.4, (g).
Rulemaking authority, §7A-498.5, (h).
Term of office, §7A-498.4, (c).
Vacancies, §7A-498.4, (f).
Voting, §7A-498.4, (e).
Counties not served by office of indigent defense services.
Superior court clerk informed if person without counsel for 48 hours, §7A-453, (b).
Defendant states indigency and desire for counsel.
Custodial authority's duty to inform superior court clerks or office of indigent defense services, §7A-453, (c).
Defender districts, §7A-498.7, (a).

INDIGENT DEFENSE SERVICES —Cont'd
Determination of indigency.
Policies and procedures, office to develop and implement, §7A-498.3, (b).
Preliminary determination by office of indigent defense services, §7A-453, (a).
Director of office.
Acceptance of gifts or bequests, §7A-498.6, (b).
Administration of office, §7A-498.6, (b).
Appointment, §§7A-498.5, (b), 7A-498.6, (a).
Assistance to commission, §7A-498.6, (b).
Budget submission, §7A-498.6, (b).
Conduct of training programs, §7A-498.6, (b).
Duties as assigned, §7A-498.6, (b).
Financial recordkeeping, §7A-498.6, (b).
Hiring professional staff, §7A-498.6, (b).
Intergovernmental cooperation, §7A-498.6, (b).
Powers and duties, §7A-498.6, (b).
District or regional public defender offices.
Establishing, §7A-498.7, (a).
Establishment of office within judicial department, §7A-498.2, (a).
Experts.
Capital cases.
Appointment and compensation, other expenses, IDS Rules 2D.1 to 2D.5.
Fees paid by state, §7A-454.
Fees.
Appointment fee in criminal cases, §7A-455.1.
Independent of administrative office of the courts, §7A-498.2, (b).
Indigent services act of 2000.
Article cited as, §7A-498.
Interstate compact on juvenile.
Return of escapees or absconders.
Appointment of counsel in accordance with rules of, §7B-2805, (c).
Liens.
Counsel services for indigents.
Petitions for value of legal services, §7A-455, (b1).
Money value of services rendered by counsel.
Counsel services for indigents.
Judgment lien on amount.
Petitions for value of legal services, §7A-455, (b1).
Non-capital criminal and non-criminal cases.
Appellate counsel.
Appellate roster.
Creation, IDS Rule 3.4.
Removal from, IDS Rule 3.6.
Appointment of appellate defender, IDS Rule 3.2.
Assignment to private counsel or public defender, IDS Rule 3.2.
Compensation, IDS Rule 3.3.
Conditions of appointment, requirements, IDS Rule 3.4.
Conflicts of interest.
Appellate defender, IDS Rule 3.2.
Contract services.
Recoupment, IDS Rule 3.3.
Coverage of part, IDS Rule 3.1.
Experience and knowledge requirement, IDS Rule 3.4.
Fee application.
Private assigned counsel, IDS Rule 3.3.
Judgment or decree and appellate entries and rulings.
Forwarding to appointed counsel, IDS Rule 3.2.

INDIGENT DEFENSE SERVICES —Cont'd
Non-capital criminal and non-criminal cases —Cont'd
Appellate counsel —Cont'd
Notice of assignment, IDS Rule 3.2.
Other programs, plans and contracts.
Authority to implement, IDS Rule 3.7.
Recoupment of fees, IDS Rule 3.3.
Replacement of counsel.
Substitute, IDS Rule 3.5.
Review of appellate defender decision.
Attorney not eligible for appointment, IDS Rule 3.4.
Roster of attorneys, IDS Rule 3.4.
Setting fee.
Private assigned counsel, IDS Rule 3.3.
Standards, IDS Rule 3.4.
Submissions with application for appointment, IDS Rule 3.4.
Substitution of counsel, IDS Rule 3.5.
Training session to remain eligible, IDS Rule 3.4.
Trial level.
Affidavit of Indigency.
Required, IDS Rule 1.4.
Appellate case, defined, inapplicability of part, IDS Rule 1.1.
Appointment procedure, IDS Rule 1.5.
Capital case, defined, inapplicability of part, IDS Rule 1.1.
Clerk of superior court.
Responsibilities as to in-custody defendants, IDS Rule 1.3.
Compensation of appointed counsel, IDS Rule 1.9.
Continued representation, obligation of appointed counsel, IDS Rule 1.7.
Contract with IDS, IDS Rule 1.8.
Compensation of contract counsel, IDS Rule 1.9.
Recoupment for services of contract counsel, IDS Rule 1.11.
Withdrawal of contract counsel, IDS Rule 1.7.
Coverage of rule, IDS Rule 1.1.
Determining Indigency.
Procedure, IDS Rule 1.4.
District bar.
Plan for appointment, district without public defender, IDS Rule 1.5.
Experts, fees for, IDS Rule 1.10.
Fee schedules, IDS Rule 1.9.
Fees for support services, IDS Rule 1.10.
In-custody defendants.
Responsibilities of public defenders and clerks, IDS Rule 1.3.
Indigency defined, IDS Rule 1.4.
Indigency, determining, IDS Rule 1.4.
Investigators, fees for, IDS Rule 1.10.
Non-criminal cases defined, IDS Rule 1.1.
Obligation of appointed counsel, IDS Rule 1.7.
Outside compensation prohibited, IDS Rule 1.9.
Payment of appointed counsel, IDS Rule 1.9.
Plan for appointment, IDS Rule 1.5.
Procedure for determining indigency, IDS Rule 1.4.
Public defenders.
Appointment procedure in districts with, IDS Rule 1.5.
Responsibilities as to in-custody defendants, IDS Rule 1.3.

INDIGENT DEFENSE SERVICES —Cont'd
Non-capital criminal and non-criminal cases —Cont'd
Trial level —Cont'd
Record keeping.
Plans for assignment of counsel, IDS Rule 1.5.
Recoupment of fees, IDS Rule 1.11.
Special counsel office.
Procedure for appointment, districts with, IDS Rule 1.5.
Standard of indigency, IDS Rule 1.4.
Standby counsel in criminal case.
Waiver of counsel by defendant, IDS Rule 1.6.
Support services. fees for, IDS Rule 1.10.
Trail level defined, IDS Rule 1.1.
Waiver of counsel, IDS Rule 1.6.
Withdrawal of appointed counsel, IDS Rule 1.7.
Office of indigent defense services.
Legislative reporting.
Local government services contracts, §7A-346.2, (a).
Offices of public defenders.
Counties in which established, §7A-498.7, (a).
Partial indigency.
Liens.
Amount of money value of counsel services.
Petitions for value of legal services, §7A-455, (b1).
Petitions.
Money value of services rendered by counsel.
Judgment lien on amount.
Petitions for value of legal services, §7A-455, (b1).
Post-conviction counsel.
Appointment, compensation, eligibility.
Capital cases, IDS Rules 2C.1 to 2C.4.
Standards for, IDS Appx. 2C.1 to 2C.3.
Powers, §7A-498.2, (b).
Public defenders.
Appointment, duties, §7A-498.7, (b) to (k).
Purpose of article, §7A-498.1.
Reports.
Office of indigent defense services.
Legislative reporting on local government services contracts, §7A-346.2, (a).
Rules and procedures adopted by office, §7A-498.3, (c).
Supporting services.
Fees and expenses paid by state, §7A-454.
System for providing legal representation.
Responsibility of office to establish, §7A-498.3, (a).
Trial counsel.
Appointment, eligibility, compensation.
Capital cases, IDS Rules 2A.1 to 2A.5.
Standards for, IDS Appx. 2A.1 to 2A.3.
Non-capital criminal and non-criminal cases, IDS Rules 1.1 to 11.

INDIGENT PERSONS.
Abused, neglected or dependent juvenile actions.
Appointment of counsel for parent, §7B-602.
Payment of court-appointed counsel, §7B-603, (a) to (c).
Access to civil justice act, §§7A-474.1 to 7A-474.5.
See GEOGRAPHICALLY BASED FIELD PROGRAMS.
Affidavit as to inability to advance court costs.
Required to sue as indigent, §1-110, (a).
Appeals in forma pauperis, §1-288.

INDIGENT PERSONS —Cont'd
Appearances.
First appearance before district court judge.
Determination whether defendant has been assigned counsel.
Duty of judge, §15A-603, (a).
Proceedings when defendant asserts indigence and desires counsel, §15A-603, (c).
Right to be furnished counsel.
Defendant to be informed by judge, §15A-603, (b).
Arbitration and award.
Hearings.
Proceedings in forma pauperis, Arbitration Rule 3.
Arrest in civil cases.
Order for arrest.
Information to be included in order, §1-413.
Attorneys at law.
Geographically based field programs.
Access to civil justice act, §§7A-474.1 to 7A-474.5.
See GEOGRAPHICALLY BASED FIELD PROGRAMS.
Indigent defense services act, §§7A-498 to 7A-498.8.
See INDIGENT DEFENSE SERVICES.
Legal services provided by law students.
Rules governing, Bar Rules & Regs., C, §§.0201 to .0207.
Authority to sue as indigent.
Court authorized to allow, §1-110, (a).
Blind persons.
Aid to the blind, §§111-13 to 111-35.
See BLIND PERSONS.
Cancer.
Financial aid for diagnosis and treatment, §130A-206.
Capital punishment.
Representation of indigent persons.
Appointment of counsel in capital cases, §7A-451, (c) to (e); Indigent Rep., Model Plan, Arts. VII, VIII, §8.2.
Indigent defense services act, §§7A-498 to 7A-498.8.
See INDIGENT DEFENSE SERVICES.
Commitment.
Involuntary outpatient commitment, §7A-451.1.
Costs.
Payment of costs, §6-24.
Criteria for suing as indigent, §1-110, (a).
Delinquent and undisciplined juvenile actions.
Appointment of counsel for juvenile, §7B-2000, (a).
Payment, §7B-2002.
Presumption of indigence, §7B-2000, (b).
Secure or nonsecure custody hearings.
Appointment of counsel for juvenile, §7B-1906, (c).
Summons to notify parent of right to counsel and appointment of counsel, §7B-1805, (b).
Department of health and human services.
Costs of care paid by persons admitted to institutions of department.
Power to admit indigent persons, §143-123.
District courts.
Small claims actions.
Appeals, §7A-228, (b).
Executions.
Execution against the person.
Appointment of counsel, §1-311.
Contents of execution, §1-313.

INDIGENT PERSONS —Cont'd
Fees.
Representation of indigents, §7A-452, (b).
Frivolous complaint.
Prisoners filing pro se motions to proceed as indigent.
Determination by court, dismissal, §1-110, (b).
Geographically based field programs.
Access to civil justice act, §§7A-474.1 to 7A-474.5.
See GEOGRAPHICALLY BASED FIELD PROGRAMS.
Guilty pleas.
Waiver of right to counsel, §7A-457, (b).
Incompetence, restoration.
Guardian ad litem appointed, §35A-1130, (c).
In forma pauperis.
See IN FORMA PAUPERIS.
Involuntary outpatient commitment, §7A-451.1.
Judicial department.
Appointment of assistant counsel for representation, §7A-450, (b1).
Landlord and tenant.
Summary ejectment.
Stay of judgment.
Indigent defendant appellant, §42-34, (c1).
Law students providing legal services.
Rules governing, Bar Rules & Regs., C, §§.0201 to .0207.
Marriage proceedings.
Guardian ad litem for underage parties, §7A-451, (f).
Mental health, developmental disability, substance abuse.
Attorneys at law.
Appointment, §122C-270.
Involuntary commitment.
Appointment of counsel.
Substance abuser's commitment hearing, §122C-286, (d).
Duty of assigned counsel.
Substance abusers, §122C-289.
Outpatient commitment.
Representation.
Counsel fees, §7A-451.1.
Motion for appropriate relief, §15A-1421.
Appointment of counsel for indigent defendant, §15A-1421.
Parolees.
Entitlement to counsel, §148-62.1.
Prisoners.
Frivolous complaint.
Determination by court, dismissal, §1-110, (b).
Pre se motions to proceed as indigent, §1-110, (b).
Public schools.
Compulsory attendance law.
Investigation of indigency, §115C-382.
Representation of indigent persons, §§7A-450 to 7A-458.
Abused, neglected or dependent juvenile actions.
Appointment of counsel for parent, §7B-602.
Payment of court-appointed counsel, §7B-603, (a) to (c).
Notice in summons of right to counsel and appointment information, §7B-406, (b).
Access to civil justice act, §§7A-474.1 to 7A-474.5.
See GEOGRAPHICALLY BASED FIELD PROGRAMS.
Acquittals.
Applicability of partial payments and liens provisions when indigent not finally convicted, §7A-455, (c).

INDIGENT PERSONS —Cont'd
Representation of indigent persons —Cont'd
Appointment of counsel, §7A-452, (c).
Appellate appointments, Indigent Rep., Model Plan, art. VIII, §8.1.
Capital cases, Indigent Rep., Model Plan, art. VIII, §8.2.
Capital cases, Indigent Rep., Model Plan, art. VII, §7.2.
Appellate appointments, §7A-451, (c) to (e); Indigent Rep., Model Plan, art. VIII, §8.2.
Applicability of provisions, Indigent Rep., Model Plan, art. VII, §7.1.
Qualifications of appointed attorneys, Indigent Rep., Model Plan, art. VII, §7.3.
Clerks of court.
Appointment by, Indigent Rep., Model Plan, art. VI, §6.7.
Record of attorney subject to appointment.
Maintenance, Indigent Rep., Model Plan, art. VI, §6.2.
Committee on indigent appointments.
Authority, Indigent Rep., Model Plan, art. IV, §4.6.
Chairman, Indigent Rep., Model Plan, art. IV, §4.4.
Deletion of attorneys from lists, Indigent Rep., Model Plan, art. V, §§5.6 to 5.8.
Established, Indigent Rep., Model Plan, art. IV, §4.1.
Lists of attorneys.
Development, Indigent Rep., Model Plan, art. III, §3.5.
Review, Indigent Rep., Model Plan, art. III, §3.7.
Meetings, Indigent Rep., Model Plan, art. IV, §§4.5, 4.7, 4.8.
Members, Indigent Rep., Model Plan, art. IV, §§4.2, 4.3.
Quorum, Indigent Rep., Model Plan, art. IV, §4.7.
Requests for placement on lists.
Review, Indigent Rep., Model Plan, art. V, §§5.2, 5.4, 5.5.
Discretion of court, Indigent Rep., Model Plan, art. VI, §6.3.
Inherent discretionary power, Indigent Rep., Model Plan, art. X, §10.2.
Generally, Bar Rules & Regs., D, §.0404.
General provisions, §§7A-450 to 7A-458.
See INDIGENT DEFENSE SERVICES.
Lists of attorneys, Indigent Rep., Model Plan, arts. III, V.
Appointment in accordance with, Indigent Rep., Model Plan, art. VI, §6.1.
Defendant's attorneys on list may be appointed to represent, Indigent Rep., Model Plan, art. III, §§3.2 to 3.4.
Deletion from, Indigent Rep., Model Plan, art. V, §§5.6 to 5.7.
Development by committee on indigent appointments, Indigent Rep., Model Plan, art. III, §3.5.
Placement on, Indigent Rep., Model Plan, art. III, §3.1.
Requests for, Indigent Rep., Model Plan, art. V, §§5.1 to 5.5.
Public defender.
Consultation of lists, Indigent Rep., Model Plan, art. VI, §6.6.

INDIGENT PERSONS —Cont'd
Representation of indigent persons —Cont'd
Appointment of counsel —Cont'd
Lists of attorneys —Cont'd
Requirements for inclusion, Indigent Rep., Model Plan, art. III, §3.6.
Review by committee on indigent appointments, Indigent Rep., Model Plan, art. III, §3.7.
Supplying to clerks, Indigent Rep., Model Plan, art. VI, §6.1.
Model plan, Indigent Rep., Model Plan, arts. I to X.
Administrator, Indigent Rep., Model Plan, art. IX, §§9.1 to 9.3.
Applicability, Indigent Rep., Model Plan, art. II.
Authority for issuance, Indigent Rep., Model Plan, art. X, §10.1.
Clerks of superior court.
Duties, Indigent Rep., Model Plan, art. IX, §§9.4, 9.5.
Construction of regulations.
Liberal construction, Indigent Rep., Model Plan, art. X, §10.3.
Effective date of regulations, Indigent Rep., Model Plan, art. X, §10.4.
Generally, Indigent Rep., Model Plan, arts. I to X.
Inherent discretionary power of court, Indigent Rep., Model Plan, art. X, §10.2.
Purpose, Indigent Rep., Model Plan, art. I.
Multiple defendants.
Appointment to represent in single case, Indigent Rep., Model Plan, art. VI, §6.5.
Notice of appointment, Indigent Rep., Model Plan, art. VI, §6.4.
Record of attorney subject to appointment.
Clerks to maintain, Indigent Rep., Model Plan, art. VI, §6.2.
Assignment of counsel, §7A-452, (a).
Authority for rules and regulations of state bar relating to, Bar Rules & Regs., D, §.0401.
Authority to issue rules and regulations, Indigent Rep., §1.1.
Capital cases.
Appellate level, §7A-451, (c) to (e); Indigent Rep., §4.10.
Assistant counsel, Indigent Rep., §4.8.
Postconviction counsel, §7A-451, (c) to (e).
Qualifications, Indigent Rep., §4.9.
Change of status, §7A-450, (d).
Commitment.
Counsel fees, §7A-451.1.
Committee on indigent appointments. See within this subheading, "Appointment of counsel."
Compensation of counsel, §7A-452, (d).
Appellate level, Indigent Rep., §6.2.
Copies of orders, Indigent Rep., §6.4.
Entry of orders, Indigent Rep., §6.3.
Judgment against defendant, Indigent Rep., §6.1.
Judgment for payment, Indigent Rep., §6.5.
Orders, Indigent Rep., §6.1.
Outside compensation, Indigent Rep., §6.6.
Procedure for payment, Bar Rules & Regs., D, §.0406.
Continuation of entitlement to services of counsel, §7A-451, (b).
Counsel fees for outpatient involuntary commitment proceedings, §7A-451.1.

INDIGENT PERSONS —Cont'd
Representation of indigent persons —Cont'd
Custodian of possibly indigent person, duties.
In addition to duties imposed upon arresting officers, §7A-453, (d).
In counties designated by office of indigent defense services, §7A-453, (a).
In counties not designated by office of indigent defense services, §7A-453, (b).
Statement that defendant desires counsel, §7A-453, (c).
Definition of indigent person, §7A-450, (a).
Delinquent and undisciplined juvenile actions.
Appointment of counsel and payment of fees, §§7B-2000, 7B-2002.
Secure or nonsecure custody hearings, §7B-1906, (c).
Summons to notify parent of right to counsel and appointment of counsel, §7B-1805, (b).
Determination of fiduciaries at indigency determination, §7A-450.2.
Determination of indigency, Bar Rules & Regs., D, §.0402; Indigent Rep., §2.4.
Affidavit, Indigent Rep., §§2.1, 2.3.
Authority to make determinations, §7A-452, (c).
Bases for determination, Indigent Rep., §2.4.
Examination of defendants, Indigent Rep., §2.2.
Preliminary determination by office of indigent defense services, §7A-453, (a).
Duty of custodian of possibly indigent person, §7A-453, (a) to (d).
Eligible counsels.
Maintenance of records, Indigent Rep., §4.6.
Entitlement to counsel, §§7A-450, (b), 7A-452, (c).
Actions and proceedings where indigent entitled to services of counsel, §7A-451, (a).
Beginning of entitlement to services of counsel, §7A-451, (b).
Capital cases.
Postconviction counsel, §7A-451, (c) to (e).
Continuation of entitlement through critical stages of action or proceeding, §7A-451, (b).
Counsel fees for outpatient involuntary commitment proceedings, §7A-451.1.
Responsibility for payment by certain fiduciaries, §7A-450.1.
Determination of fiduciaries, §7A-450.2.
Determination of responsibility at hearing, §7A-450.3.
Exemptions, §7A-450.4.
Scope of entitlement, §7A-451, (a).
When entitlement begins, §7A-451, (b).
False material statements as to Indigency.
Felony, §7A-456, (a).
Notice to person of penalty, §7A-456, (b).
Fees of counsel, §7A-452, (d).
Fixing of counsel fees, §7A-458.
Liability for payment of fees, §7A-452, (b).
Generally, Indigent Rep., §4.1.
Geographically based field programs.
Access to civil justice act, §§7A-474.1 to 7A-474.5.
See GEOGRAPHICALLY BASED FIELD PROGRAMS.
Guilty pleas.
Waiver of right to counsel, §7A-457, (b).
Hearing impaired.
Interpreters, §7A-450, (a).
Indigent defense services.
See INDIGENT DEFENSE SERVICES.

INDIGENT PERSONS —Cont'd
Representation of indigent persons —Cont'd
Interstate compact on juvenile.
Return of escapees or absconders, §7B-2805, (c).
Law students, legal services provided by, Bar Rules & Regs., C, §§.0201 to .0207.
Liens.
Counsel services for indigent.
Judgment lien on amount, §7A-455, (b).
Lists of attorneys. See within this subheading, "Appointment of counsel."
Marriage proceedings.
Guardian ad litem for underage parties, §7A-451, (f).
Mental health, developmental disability, substance abuse.
Involuntary commitment.
Substance abuser's commitment hearing, §122C-286, (d).
Model plan, Indigent Rep., Appx.
Adoption, Indigent Rep., §4.1.
Certification, Indigent Rep., §4.2.
Compliance, Indigent Rep., §4.2.
Filing, Indigent Rep., §4.5.
Model plan of the state bar, Bar Rules & Regs., D, §§.0501 to .0510.
Administrator of regulations, Bar Rules & Regs., D, §.0509.
Appellate appointments, Bar Rules & Regs., D, §.0508.
Applicability of regulations, Bar Rules & Regs., D, §.0502.
Appointment in capital cases, Bar Rules & Regs., D, §.0507.
Appointment in noncapital cases, Bar Rules & Regs., D, §.0506.
Appointment of members to committee on indigent, Bar Rules & Regs., D, §.0504.
Construction of regulations, Bar Rules & Regs., D, §.0510.
Discretion of court to decline appointment, Bar Rules & Regs., D, §.0510.
Effective date of regulations, Bar Rules & Regs., D, §.0510.
List of attorneys, Bar Rules & Regs., D, §§.0503, .0505.
Purposes of regulations, Bar Rules & Regs., D, §.0501.
Money value of services rendered by counsel.
Judgment lien on amount, §7A-455, (b).
Murder.
Appointment of assistant counsel, §7A-450, (b1).
Orders for appointment of council, Indigent Rep., §4.7.
Out-of-court proceedings.
Waiver of right to counsel, §7A-457, (c).
Partial indigency, §7A-455, (a).
Applicability of provisions when indigent not finally convicted, §7A-455, (c).
Liens.
Amount of money value of counsel services, §7A-455, (b).
Pleas of guilty.
Waiver of counsel, §7A-457, (b).
Professional relationship of counsel to indigent person, §7A-450, (b).
Public defender appointments, Indigent Rep., §§4.11, 4.12.
Redetermination of indigency, §7A-450, (c).
Residency requirement, Indigent Rep., §4.3.

INDIGENT PERSONS —Cont'd
Representation of indigent persons —Cont'd
Responsibility for payment by certain fiduciaries, §7A-450.1.
Determination of fiduciaries, §7A-450.2.
Determination of responsibility at hearing, §7A-450.3.
Exemptions, §7A-450.4.
Selection by defendant prohibited, Indigent Rep., §4.4.
Social security.
Obtaining number when judgment to be entered, §7A-455, (d).
Source of counsel, §7A-452, (a).
Specialized programs, Indigent Rep., §4.13.
State bar council.
Implementing regulations by council, §7A-459.
Capital cases.
Appointment and compensation of postconviction counsel to comply with rules and regulations, §7A-451, (d).
Termination of parental rights proceedings.
Adjudicatory hearing, appointment for parents, §7B-1109, (b).
Appointment of counsel, payment of fees, §7B-1101.
Waiver of right to counsel, §7A-457, (a); Bar Rules & Regs., D, §.0403.
Acceptance, Indigent Rep., §3.3.
Form, Indigent Rep., §3.1.
Matters to be considered in determining acceptance of waiver, §7A-457, (a).
Out-of-court proceedings, §7A-457, (c).
Personal inquiry by judge, Indigent Rep., §3.2.
Pleas of guilty, §7A-457, (b).
Refusal to execute, Indigent Rep., §3.1.
Withdrawal by counsel, Bar Rules & Regs., D, §.0405; Indigent Rep., §5.1.
Appellate level, Indigent Rep., §5.2.
Good cause, Indigent Rep., §5.3.
Permission to withdraw, Indigent Rep., §5.1.
Small claims actions.
Appeals, §7A-228, (b1).
Social services.
See SOCIAL SERVICES.
Suits by indigent.
Payment of costs, §6-24.
Termination of parental rights.
Indigent defense services act, §§7A-498 to 7A-498.8.
See INDIGENT DEFENSE SERVICES.
Termination of parental rights proceedings.
Adjudicatory hearing, appointment of counsel for indigent parents, §7B-1109, (b).
Appointment of counsel, payment of fees, §7B-1101.
Welfare policy of state, Const. N. C., art. XI, §4.
Wills.
Contests.
Provisions for bringing suit in forma pauperis.
Provisions applicable to section, §31-34.

INDIRECT CRIMINAL CONTEMPT, §5A-13, (b).

INDIVIDUAL RETIREMENT ACCOUNTS OR ANNUITIES.
Exempt property from enforcement of claims of creditors, §1C-1601, (a).
Renunciation of succession, §31B-1.

INDORSEMENTS.
Check-cashing business.
Instrument presented by licensee for payment, §53-280, (d).

INDORSEMENTS —Cont'd
Commercial code generally.
Unauthorized indorsement defined, §25-1-201, (43).
Commercial paper.
See NEGOTIABLE INSTRUMENTS.
Documents of title, §25-7-501, (1).
Compelling indorsement.
Right to compel, §25-7-506.
Delivery to compel indorsement, §25-7-506.
Indorser not guarantor for other parties, §25-7-505.
Power to compel indorsement, §25-7-506.
Requirements of due negotiation, §25-7-501.
Investment securities, §25-8-107.
Assurance that indorsements are effective, §25-8-402.
Warranties in direct holding, §25-8-108.
Negotiable instruments generally.
See NEGOTIABLE INSTRUMENTS.
Uttering instrument containing forged endorsement, §14-120.

INDUCEMENTS.
Wine distribution agreements.
Prohibited, §18B-1202.

INDUSTRIAL AND POLLUTION CONTROL FACILITIES FINANCING, §§159C-1 to 159C-27.
Applicability of article.
Additional methods, §159C-24.
Inconsistent laws inapplicable, §159C-26.
Liberal construction, §159C-25.
Authorities.
Annual reports, §159C-22.
Commissioners.
Appointment, §159C-4, (a).
Compensation, §159C-4, (e).
Officers, §159C-4, (c).
Qualifications, §159C-4, (b).
Quorum, §159C-4, (d).
Removal from office, §159C-4, (b).
Term of office, §159C-4, (a).
Conflict of interest of officials, §159C-16.
Consultants and employees.
Powers as to, §159C-5.
Creation.
Authorized, §159C-4, (a).
Ratification, §159C-27.
Dissolution of authorities, §159C-21.
Notification of department of commerce of formation, §159C-4, (f).
Powers, §159C-5.
Ratification of creation, §159C-27.
Bond issues.
Approval bonds by local government commission.
Application for approval, filing, §159C-8, (a).
Factors considered on determining whether to approve, §159C-8, (b).
Obligor's ability to perform, evaluation, §159C-8, (d).
Refunding bonds, §159C-19, (a1).
Required for issuance, §159C-8, (a).
Special purpose project, public hearing, required for approval, §159C-8, (c).
Capital facilities finance agency, §§159D-1 to 159D-27.
Credit of state not pledged, §159C-17.
Eligibility for investment, §159C-18.
Financing agreements, §159C-11.

INDUSTRIAL AND POLLUTION CONTROL FACILITIES FINANCING —Cont'd
Bond issues —Cont'd
Immunity of commissioners.
No personal liability for executing or issuing, §159C-23.
Interest.
Exemption from taxation, §159C-14.
Issuance.
Approval, §159C-4, (d).
Authority.
Refunding bonds, §159C-19, (a).
Purposes.
Refunding bonds, §159C-19.
Refunding bonds, §159C-19, (a).
Proceeds.
Exemption from taxation, §159C-14.
Trust funds, §159C-13.
Public or private sale of bonds, §159C-9.
Refunding bonds.
Approval of local government commission, §159C-19, (a1).
Issuance, resolution, purposes, §159C-19, (a).
Sale or exchange, §159C-19, (c).
Sale of bonds, §159C-9.
Refunding bonds, §159C-19, (b).
Security documents, §159C-12.
Taxation.
Exemption from taxation, §159C-14.
Trust agreements.
Security by agreements, §159C-12.
Bonds.
Approval of project before issued, §159C-7.
Authorization to issue, §159C-6, (a).
Consent of state, political subdivision, etc., not required, §159C-6, (g).
Interim receipts or temporary bonds, issuance, §159C-6, (f).
Loans to obligor, §159C-6, (e).
Preliminary expenditures, reimbursement from proceeds, §159C-6, (d).
Proceeds, use, §159C-6, (b).
Refinancing costs, proceeds not used for, §159C-6, (c).
Terms and conditions, §159C-6, (a).
Capital facilities finance agency, §§159D-1 to 159D-27.
Bonds.
Approval by local government commission prior to issuance.
Application for approval, filing, §159D-8, (a).
Factors considered, §159D-8, (b).
Financial date and information, submittal, §159D-8, (c).
Required, §159D-8, (a).
Approval of project by secretary of commerce prior to issuance.
Certificate approval, §159D-7, (h), (i).
Certification of department of environment and natural resources, §159D-7, (e).
Findings required, §159D-7, (b).
Forms and rules, data and information about project, §159D-7, (g).
Initial operator, identified in application, §159D-7, (c).
Public hearing required by county, §159D-7, (d).
Required, §159D-7, (a).
Wage requirement, waiver, §159D-7, (f).
Authority to issues, §159D-6, (a).

INDUSTRIAL AND POLLUTION CONTROL FACILITIES FINANCING —Cont'd
Capital facilities finance agency —Cont'd
Bonds —Cont'd
Banks and trust companies acting as depository of proceeds, §159D-12, (b).
Board of directors not personally liable, §159D-24.
Consent of state or political subdivision.
Issuing without obtaining, §159D-6, (e).
Consent to location by board of commissioners required, §159D-10.
Credit of state not pledged, §159D-17.
Financing agreements, §159D-11.
Legal to invest in bonds, §159D-18.
Payment from revenues and other funds, statement, §159D-17.
Preliminary expenditures, reimbursement from proceeds, §159D-6, (d).
Proceeds, use, §159D-6, (b).
Refinancing cost of project, use of proceeds, §159D-6, (c).
Refunding bonds.
Approvals required, §159D-19, (a1).
Authorization to issue, §159D-19, (a).
Purposes, §159D-19, (a).
Sale or exchange, §159D-19, (b).
Terms and conditions, provisions governing, §159D-19, (a1).
Sale, §159D-9.
Security documents securing, §159D-12, (a).
Sinking fund, §159D-12, (a).
Tax exemption, interest on bonds, §159D-14.
Terms and conditions, §159D-6, (a).
Trust funds, proceeds, §159D-13.
Conflict of interest, disclosure, §159D-16.
Consent to location by board of commissioners.
Required prior to issuance of bonds, §159D-10.
Construction contracts.
Agreement that contract solicited, negotiated, awarded and executed by operator, §159D-15.
Definitions, §159D-3.
Eminent domain, no power of, §159D-20.
Exemption from taxes, §159D-14.
Financing agreements.
Additional provision if necessary, §159D-11, (g).
Assignment of agency rights, §159D-11, (f).
Interest of agency in project under agreement, §159D-11, (e).
Nature of agreement, §159D-11, (b).
Provision required, §159D-11, (a).
Purchase of project by obligor, requirement, lease agreement, §159D-11, (c).
Rights and remedies of agency in event of default, §159D-11, (d).
General powers, §159D-5.
Inconsistent laws inapplicable, §159D-27.
Interest directly or indirectly in contract, disclosure, §159D-16.
Investing in bonds, §159D-18.
Jurisdiction, §159D-4.1.
Legislative findings and purpose, §159D-2, (a), (b).
Liberal construction of article, §159D-26.
Location of projects, §159D-10.
North Carolina industrial and pollution control facilities financing act.
Short title, §159D-1.
Project approval by secretary of commerce.
Required prior to issuance of bonds, §159D-7.

INDUSTRIAL AND POLLUTION CONTROL FACILITIES FINANCING —Cont'd
Capital facilities finance agency —Cont'd
Public hearing on project by county.
Required for approval by secretary of commerce, §159D-7, (d).
Refunding bonds, §159D-19.
Secured transactions article of UCC, applicability, §159D-23.
Security documents securing bonds, §159D-12, (a).
Supplemental and additional method, §159D-25.
Tax exemption, §159D-14.
Transfer of duties, powers, jurisdiction and responsibilities to agency, §159D-4.1.
Trust funds, money received, §159D-13.
UCC secured transactions article, applicability, §159D-23.
Citation.
Short title, §159C-1.
Conflict of laws.
Inconsistent laws applicable, §159C-26.
Conflicts of interest.
Public officers, §159C-16.
Construction contracts, §159C-15.
Construction of article.
Inconsistent laws applicable, §159C-26.
Liberal construction, §159C-25.
Contracts.
Construction contracts, §159C-15.
Credit of state not pledged, §159C-17.
Definitions, §159C-3.
Dissolution of authorities, §159C-21.
Eminent domain.
No power of eminent domain, §159C-20.
Exemptions from taxation, §159C-14.
Financing agreements.
Assignment of authority's interest, §159C-11, (c).
Authority's interest in project under agreement, §159C-11, (c).
In the nature of lease, purchase by obligor on expiration or termination, §159C-11, (b).
Provisions required, §159C-11, (a).
Interstate environmental compact.
Citation of article, §113A-21.
Compact provisions, §113A-23.
Legislative findings, §113A-22.
Provisions generally, §113A-23.
Purpose, §113A-22.
Short title, §113A-21.
Investments.
Bonds eligible for investment, §159C-18.
Legislative findings and purposes, §159C-2, (a) to (c).
Location of projects, §159C-10.
Municipal corporations.
Emission of pollutants.
Prohibited, §160A-185.
Nonpoint source pollution control program.
Committee.
Composition, §143-215.74B.
Duties, §143-215.74B.
Creation of program, §143-215.74, (a).
Participation in program, §143-215.74A.
Requirements of program, §143-215.74, (b).
Review of program, §143-215.74, (c).
Committee, §143-215.74B.
State funds for program to remain available until expended for the program, §143-215.74, (d).
Voluntary participation, §143-215.74A.
Plastic yokes or ring type holding devices.
Containers, §14-399.2.
Policy of state, Const. N. C., art. XIV, §5.

INDUSTRIAL AND POLLUTION CONTROL FACILITIES FINANCING —Cont'd
Pollution prevention pays programs.
Department of environment and natural resources, §113-8.01.
Projects.
Approval by secretary of commerce.
Certificate of approval, §159C-7, (g).
Department of environment and natural resources.
Certificate of, §159C-7, (d).
Findings, §159C-7, (b).
Initial operator, findings as to, §159C-7, (b1).
Public hearings, §159C-7, (c).
Required, §159C-7, (a).
Rules, §159C-7, (f).
Wage requirement, §159C-7, (b).
Waiver, §159C-7, (e).
Location, §159C-10.
Public hearings.
Special purpose project.
Required for approval of bond issuance, §159C-8, (c).
Public officers.
Conflicts of interest, §159C-16.
Refunding bonds, §159C-19.
Reports.
Annual reports of authorities, §159C-22.
Revenues.
Trust funds, §159C-13.
Special purpose project.
Public hearing.
Required for approval of bond issuance, §159C-8, (c).
State.
Credit of state not pledged, §159C-17.
Taxation.
Exemptions from taxation, §159C-14.
Title.
Short title, §159C-1.
Trust agreements.
Security for bonds, §159C-12.
Trust funds.
Revenues and proceeds of bonds constitutes trust funds, §159C-13.
Water and air resources, §§143-211 to 143-215.9B.
See WATER AND AIR RESOURCES.

INDUSTRIAL BANKS, §§53-136 to 53-145.
Applicability of general provisions, §53-143.
Powers generally, §53-141.
Branch banks.
Power to establish, §53-141.
Commissioner of banks.
Supervision by, §53-144.
Consumer finance act.
Exemption, §53-191.
Defined, §53-136.
Depositories.
Designation, §53-142.
Incorporation, §53-137.
Minors.
Deposit account.
Operating in name of minor, §53-43.5, (a).
Safe deposit boxes.
Leasing or renting to minors, §53-43.5, (b), (c).
Names.
Certificate of incorporation to set forth, §53-137.
Corporate title, §53-138.
Powers, §53-141.

INDUSTRIAL BANKS —Cont'd
Rules and regulations.
State banking commission, §53-144.
Stock and stockholders.
Amount of authorized capital stock, §53-139.
Certificate of incorporation to set forth, §53-137.
Sale of capital stock, §53-140.
Supervision.
Applicability of general law, §53-145.
Commissioner of banks, §53-134.

INDUSTRIAL CLEANERS.
Containing phosphorus.
Manufacture, storage or sale.
Prohibition, exceptions, penalties, §143-214.4, (a) to (g).

INDUSTRIAL COMMISSION.
Administrative procedure act.
Full exemption, §150B-1, (c).
Administrator, §97-78, (b).
Salary, §97-78, (b1).
Appeals.
Administrative decisions appealed, I.C. Rule 703.
Appeal to court of appeals, I.C. Rule 702.
Awards of commission, §97-86.
Payment of award pending appeal in certain cases, §97-86.1.
Commission appeals, I.C. Rule 701.
Court of appeals.
Review of final orders, §7A-250, (b).
Insurers.
Expenses of appeals brought by insurers, §97-88.
Right of appeal from industrial commission to court of appeals, §7A-29, (a).
Appointment of members, §97-77, (a).
Awards, §§97-85 to 97-87.
Blank forms and literature.
Providing, §97-81, (a).
Business transacted by commission, I.C. Rule 102.
Chairman, §97-77, (a).
Child vaccine-related injury compensation, §§130A-422 to 130A-434.
See CHILDHOOD VACCINE-RELATED INJURY COMPENSATION.
Clerical assistance, §97-78, (b).
Commissioner.
Contested cases.
Disqualification, I.C. Rule 615.
Composition, §97-77, (a).
Compromise and settlement.
Approval of settlements, §97-17.
Contempt, §97-80, (g), (h).
Court of appeals.
Remedial writs.
Power of court to issue, §7A-32, (c).
Review of final orders, §7A-250, (b).
Right of appeal from industrial commission to court of appeals, §7A-29, (a).
Creation, §97-77, (a).
Death benefits act.
Rules, I.C. Death Benefits Rules I to V.
See DEATH BENEFITS.
Definition of "commission," §97-2.
Depositions, §97-80, (d).
Deputies.
Appointment, §97-79, (b).
Determination of disputes by, §97-84.
Disqualification in contested cases, I.C. Rule 615.
Powers, §97-79, (b).

INDUSTRIAL COMMISSION —Cont'd
Discovery.
Power to limit, §97-80, (f).
Disputes.
Appeals, §97-86.
Payment of award pending appeal in certain cases, §97-86.1.
Award.
Authority of clerk to enter judgments, §1-209.
Conclusive as to facts, §97-86.
Hearings.
Interest on awards after hearing, §97-86.2.
Payment of award pending appeal in certain cases.
Generally, §97-86.1, (a), (b).
Not admission of liability or estoppel to deny liability, §97-86.1, (c).
Repayment, §97-86.1, (d).
Review, §97-85.
Certified questions of law, §97-86.
Commission to determine all questions, §97-91.
Hearings, §§97-83, 97-84.
Facilities, §97-83.1.
Security, §97-83.1.
Review of award, §97-85.
Employers report of injury, I.C. Rule 104.
Executive secretary, §97-78, (b).
Salary, §97-78, (b1).
Expenses of members, §97-78, (c), (d).
Forms.
Official forms, I.C. Rule 103.
Habeas corpus.
Issuance of writs, §97-101.1.
Hearings.
Attorneys' fees, §97-88.1.
Agreements for fees.
Approval, §97-90, (c).
Approval by commission, §97-90, (a), (b).
Conduct of hearings, §97-79, (d).
Disputes, §§97-83, 97-84.
Facilities, §97-83.1.
Security, §97-83.1.
Hours of business, I.C. Rule 101.
Tort claims rules, Tort Claim Rule T101.
Information to commissioner of labor upon request, §97-81, (e).
Insurance.
Proof of insurance coverage, I.C. Rule 301.
Interrogatories.
Power to limit, §97-80, (f).
Liability.
Referral of suspected fraud case, §97-88.2, (d).
Managed care organizations.
Application of provisions.
Waiver, I.C. Managed Care Orgs. R. X.
Construction of provisions.
Purpose of rules, I.C. Managed Care Orgs. R. I.
Contract provisions, I.C. Managed Care Orgs. R. VI.
Definitions, I.C. Managed Care Orgs. R. II.
Department of insurance.
Qualification, I.C. Managed Care Orgs. R. III.
Employee information, I.C. Managed Care Orgs. R. VII.
Employer.
Defined, I.C. Managed Care Orgs. R. II.
Employer network.
Defined, I.C. Managed Care Orgs. R. II.
Health care provider.
Defined, I.C. Managed Care Orgs. R. II.

INDUSTRIAL COMMISSION —Cont'd
Managed care organizations —Cont'd
Inclusive provider panels, I.C. Managed Care Orgs. R. VIII.
Information for employee/patient, I.C. Managed Care Orgs. R. VII.
Lists of physicians, I.C. Managed Care Orgs. R. VIII.
Managed care organization (MCO).
Defined, I.C. Managed Care Orgs. R. II.
Notice to commission, I.C. Managed Care Orgs. R. V.
Patient information, I.C. Managed Care Orgs. R. VII.
Purpose, I.C. Managed Care Orgs. R. I.
Qualification.
Department of insurance, I.C. Managed Care Orgs. R. III.
Generally, I.C. Managed Care Orgs. R. IV.
Qualified physicians, I.C. Managed Care Orgs. R. VIII.
Quality assurance, I.C. Managed Care Orgs. R. IX.
Required contract provisions, I.C. Managed Care Orgs. R. VI.
Revocation, I.C. Managed Care Orgs. R. IV.
Utilization review, I.C. Managed Care Orgs. R. IX.
Waiver, I.C. Managed Care Orgs. R. X.
Mediated settlement and neutral evaluation conferences.
Agreement of parties.
Compensation of mediator, I.C. Mediated Settlmt. Conf. R. 7(a).
Order for, I.C. Mediated Settlmt. Conf. R. 1(a).
Selection of mediator, I.C. Mediated Settlmt. Conf. R. 2(a).
Appeals.
Motions, I.C. Mediated Settlmt. Conf. R. 10.
Application of provisions.
Waiver of rules, I.C. Mediated Settlmt. Conf. R. 9.
Appointment from lists, I.C. Mediated Settlmt. Conf. R. 8(c).
Appointment of mediator, I.C. Mediated Settlmt. Conf. R. 8(b).
Attendance, I.C. Mediated Settlmt. Conf. R. 4(a).
Waiver of attendance requirement, I.C. Mediated Settlmt. Conf. R. 4(b).
Attorneys' fees.
Sanctions for failure to attend, I.C. Mediated Settlmt. Conf. R. 5.
Authority of mediators, I.C. Mediated Settlmt. Conf. R. 6(a).
Commission, appointment of mediator, I.C. Mediated Settlmt. Conf. R. 2(b).
Commission, order of, I.C. Mediated Settlmt. Conf. R. 1(c).
Compensation of mediator, I.C. Mediated Settlmt. Conf. R. 7(b).
Commission, waiver of rules, I.C. Mediated Settlmt. Conf. R. 9.
Completion.
Request to extend date, I.C. Mediated Settlmt. Conf. R. 3(c).
Content of order, I.C. Mediated Settlmt. Conf. R. 1(f).
Costs.
Sanctions for failure to attend, I.C. Mediated Settlmt. Conf. R. 5.
Delay of other proceedings, I.C. Mediated Settlmt. Conf. R. 3(e).

INDUSTRIAL COMMISSION —Cont'd
Mediated settlement and neutral evaluation conferences —Cont'd
Duties of mediators, I.C. Mediated Settlmt. Conf. R. 6(b).
Duties of parties, representatives and attorneys, I.C. Mediated Settlmt. Conf. R. 4.
Exemptions, I.C. Mediated Settlmt. Conf. R. 1(r).
Fees.
Payment of mediator's, I.C. Mediated Settlmt. Conf. R. 4(e).
Sanctions for failure to attend, I.C. Mediated Settlmt. Conf. R. 5.
Finalizing agreement, I.C. Mediated Settlmt. Conf. R. 4(d).
Neutral evaluation procedures, I.C. Mediated Settlmt. Conf. R. 9(I).
Generally, I.C. Mediated Settlmt. Conf. R. 3.
Lists of mediators, I.C. Mediated Settlmt. Conf. R. 8(c).
Mediation coordinator.
Motions, I.C. Mediated Settlmt. Conf. R. 10.
Mediators.
Appointments from lists, I.C. Mediated Settlmt. Conf. R. 8(b).
Authority, I.C. Mediated Settlmt. Conf. R. 6(a).
Certification and decertification, I.C. Mediated Settlmt. Conf. R. 8.
Compensation, I.C. Mediated Settlmt. Conf. R. 7.
Duties, I.C. Mediated Settlmt. Conf. R. 6(b).
Failure to appear at conference, I.C. Mediated Settlmt. Conf. R. 8(d).
Fees.
Payment, I.C. Mediated Settlmt. Conf. R. 4(c), (e).
Sanctions for failure to attend, I.C. Mediated Settlmt. Conf. R. 5.
Payment of fees, I.C. Mediated Settlmt. Conf. R. 4(c), (e).
Selection by mutual consent, I.C. Mediated Settlmt. Conf. R. 2, 8(a).
Motions, I.C. Mediated Settlmt. Conf. R. 11.
Authorization of use of neutral evaluation procedures, I.C. Mediated Settlmt. Conf. R. 1(i).
Dispense with or defer conference, I.C. Mediated Settlmt. Conf. R. 1(g).
Neutral evaluation.
Applicability of mediation rules and duties, I.C. Mediated Settlmt. Conf. R. 9(j).
Authority of evaluator to assist negotiations, I.C. Mediated Settlmt. Conf. R. 9(h).
Duties of evaluator, I.C. Mediated Settlmt. Conf. R. 9(g).
Ex parte communications.
Prohibited, I.C. Mediated Settlmt. Conf. R. 9(k).
Finalizing agreement, I.C. Mediated Settlmt. Conf. R. 9(i).
Motion to authorize use of procedures, I.C. Mediated Settlmt. Conf. R. 1(i).
Nature of neutral evaluation, I.C. Mediated Settlmt. Conf. R. 9(a).
Pre-conference submissions, I.C. Mediated Settlmt. Conf. R. 9(c).
Replies to, I.C. Mediated Settlmt. Conf. R. 9(d).
Procedure for conference, I.C. Mediated Settlmt. Conf. R. 9(e).
Modification, I.C. Mediated Settlmt. Conf. R. 9(d).

INDUSTRIAL COMMISSION —Cont'd
Mediated settlement and neutral evaluation conferences —Cont'd
Neutral evaluation —Cont'd
Standards of conduct for neutrals.
Adherence to, I.C. Mediated Settlmt. Conf. R. 9(l).
When conference held, I.C. Mediated Settlmt. Conf. R. 9(b).
Notice of mediation order, I.C. Mediated Settlmt. Conf. R. 4(c).
Order for, I.C. Mediated Settlmt. Conf. R. 1.
Payment of mediator by parties, I.C. Mediated Settlmt. Conf. R. 7(c).
Pro se representation.
Cases involving plaintiffs not represented by counsel, I.C. Mediated Settlmt. Conf. R. 1(j).
Recesses, I.C. Mediated Settlmt. Conf. R. 3(d).
Referral upon receipt of form 33 request for hearing, I.C. Mediated Settlmt. Conf. R. 1(b).
Reports.
Duties of mediators, I.C. Mediated Settlmt. Conf. R. 6(b).
Request of a party.
Order for, I.C. Mediated Settlmt. Conf. R. 1(d).
Sanctions, I.C. Mediated Settlmt. Conf. R. 5.
Saturdays, Sundays and legal holidays.
References to number of days to include, I.C. Mediated Settlmt. Conf. R. 12.
Scheduling of conference.
Duties of mediators, I.C. Mediated Settlmt. Conf. R. 6(b).
Time conference held, I.C. Mediated Settlmt. Conf. R. 3(b).
Timing of order, I.C. Mediated Settlmt. Conf. R. 1(e).
Waiver of rules, I.C. Mediated Settlmt. Conf. R. 10.
When conference held, I.C. Mediated Settlmt. Conf. R. 3(b).
Where held, I.C. Mediated Settlmt. Conf. R. 3(a).
Mediation to order, §97-80, (c).
Medical examinations.
Qualified physician to make examinations.
Appointment, §97-89.
Fees, §97-89.
Approval by commission, §97-90, (a), (b).
Recovery from third-party tort-feasor is not prevented, §97-90, (d).
Modification of award, §97-47.
Notice.
Employment covered by act, I.C. Rule 201.
Number of members, §97-77, (a).
Offices, §97-79, (a).
Location, I.C. Rule 101.
Tort claims rules, Tort Claim Rule T101.
Ombudsman program, §97-79, (f).
Parties to proceedings.
Power to make additional parties plaintiff or defendant, §97-79, (e).
Penalties.
Collection of fines and penalties.
Actions, §97-101.
Powers, §97-80, (b).
Public school employee injured during episode of violence.
Entitlement to salary and other benefits.
Appeal of board of education decision, §115C-338, (c).

INDUSTRIAL COMMISSION —Cont'd
Questions arising under provisions.
Determination by commission, §97-91.
Records.
Not open to public, §97-92, (b).
Rehabilitation professionals, I.C. Util. Rehab. Profs. I to X.
Application of rules, I.C. Util. Rehab. Profs. III.
Cases rules applicable to, I.C. Util. Rehab. Profs. III.
Communication, I.C. Util. Rehab. Profs. VII.
Definitions, I.C. Util. Rehab. Profs. I.
Enumeration of qualifications, I.C. Util. Rehab. Profs. V.
Goals of rehabilitation, I.C. Util. Rehab. Profs. IV.
Interaction with physicians, I.C. Util. Rehab. Profs. VIII.
Interpretation of rules, I.C. Util. Rehab. Profs. II.
Medical rehabilitation, I.C. Util. Rehab. Profs. I.
Medical rehabilitation goals, I.C. Util. Rehab. Profs. IV.
Motions.
Change of rehabilitation professional, I.C. Util. Rehab. Profs. X.
Notice, I.C. Util. Rehab. Profs. VII.
Parties.
Defined, I.C. Util. Rehab. Profs. I.
Physician.
Defined, I.C. Util. Rehab. Profs. I.
Professional responsibility, I.C. Util. Rehab. Profs. VI.
Purpose of rules, I.C. Util. Rehab. Profs. II.
Qualifications, I.C. Util. Rehab. Profs. V.
Records, I.C. Util. Rehab. Profs. VIII.
Reports, I.C. Util. Rehab. Profs. VII.
Return to work, I.C. Util. Rehab. Profs. IX.
Responsibility of professionals, I.C. Util. Rehab. Profs. VI.
Return to employment.
Goals of rehabilitation, I.C. Util. Rehab. Profs. IV.
Return to work, I.C. Util. Rehab. Profs. IX.
Defined, I.C. Util. Rehab. Profs. IX.
Second opinions, I.C. Util. Rehab. Profs. VIII.
Suitable employment.
Defined, I.C. Util. Rehab. Profs. I.
Vocational rehabilitation.
Defined, I.C. Util. Rehab. Profs. I.
Work restrictions.
Return to work, I.C. Util. Rehab. Profs. IX.
Reports.
Annual report of administration of article, §97-78, (e).
Tabulation of accident reports, §97-81, (b).
Rules and regulations, §97-80, (a).
Procedure for rulemaking, I.C. Rule 803.
Waiver, I.C. Rule 801.
Rules of civil procedure.
Court actions before commission.
When rules to govern, §1A-1, Rule 1.
Salaries, §97-78, (a), (d).
Administrator, §97-78, (b1).
Executive secretary, §97-78, (b1).
School employee injured during episode of violence.
Entitlement to salary and other benefits.
Appeal of board of education decision, §115C-338, (c).
Sessions.
Place for, §97-79, (c).
Studies and investigations, §97-81, (c), (d).

INDUSTRIAL COMMISSION —Cont'd
Subpoenas, §97-80, (e).
Superior courts.
Authority of clerk to enter judgments, §1-209.
Terms of members, §97-77, (a).
Tort claims against state departments and agencies.
Tort claim rules, Tort Claim Rules T101 to T502.
See TORT CLAIMS AGAINST STATE DEPARTMENTS AND AGENCIES.
Transaction of business, I.C. Rule 102.
Utilization of rehabilitation professionals, I.C. Util. Rehab. Profs. I to X. See within this heading, "Rehabilitation professionals."
Vice-chairman, §97-77, (b).
Witnesses.
Powers as to, §97-80.

INDUSTRIAL DEVELOPMENT, §§158-16 to 158-24.
Applicability of article.
Counties to which article applies, §158-24.
Commission, §158-21.
Board of county commissioners.
May function and carry out duties of commission, §158-23.
Bureau.
Annual audit, §158-22.
Counties to which article applies, §158-24.
Environmental impact statements.
Ordinances requiring for major development projects, §113A-8, (a) to (c).
Taxation.
Authorized activities, §158-7.1, (b).
Elections.
Announcing results, §158-19.
Calling for tax election, §158-16.
Canvassing of results, §158-19.
Counting of ballots, §158-19.
Designation of ballot box, §158-18.
Form of ballot, §158-18.
Registration of voters, §158-17.
Supervision of county board of elections, §158-17.
When ballot supplied, §158-18.
Levy, §158-20.
Rate, §§158-16, 158-20.

INDUSTRIAL DEVELOPMENT FINANCING.
Authority.
Bond issues.
Capital projects for industry.
County may create authorities to issue bonds, Const. N. C., art. V, §9.
Capital projects for industry.
Authorities may issue bonds, Const. N. C., art. V, §9.
Local government finance.
General provisions, §§159-1 to 159-188.
See LOCAL GOVERNMENT FINANCE.
Bond issues.
Authority.
Capital projects for industry.
Authorities may issue bonds, Const. N. C., art. V, §9.
Constitution of North Carolina.
Capital projects for industry.
Bond issues to finance.
County may create authorities to issue bonds, Const. N. C., art. V, §9.

INDUSTRIAL DEVELOPMENT FINANCING —Cont'd
Industrial and pollution control facilities financing.
Industrial and pollution control facilities financing act, §§159C-1 to 159C-27.
See INDUSTRIAL AND POLLUTION CONTROL FACILITIES FINANCING.
North Carolina capital facilities financing act.
North Carolina industrial and pollution control facilities financing act, §§159D-1 to 159D-27.
See INDUSTRIAL AND POLLUTION CONTROL FACILITIES FINANCING.

INDUSTRIAL DEVELOPMENT FUND, §143B-437.01.
Job development investment grant program.
Transfer of funds upon disbursement of grant, §143B-437.61.

INDUSTRIAL ESPIONAGE.
Larceny of secret technical processes, §14-75.1.

INDUSTRIAL HYGIENE.
Safety professionals, §§90-671 to 90-674.

INDUSTRIAL HYGIENISTS.
Definitions, §90-515.
Engineers.
Engaging in practice of, §90-516, (f).
Injunctions.
Illegal practices, §90-516, (d).
Issues of title, §90-516, (a) to (c).
Venue.
Actions brought under article, §90-516, (e).

INDUSTRIAL PARKS.
Seafood industrial park authorities, §§113-315.25 to 113-315.39.
See SEAFOOD INDUSTRIAL PARK AUTHORITY.

INDUSTRIAL SICK BENEFIT INSURANCE.
Accident and health insurance generally.
See ACCIDENT AND HEALTH INSURANCE.
Defined, §58-51-65.
Policy provisions, §58-51-70.

INEFFECTIVE ASSISTANCE OF COUNSEL.
Motion for appropriate relief.
Waiver of attorney-client privilege, §15A-1415, (e).

INFANTILE PARALYSIS.
Food, drug and cosmetic act.
Drug or device, false advertising, §106-138, (b).

INFANTS.
Abandonment of child, §§14-318.2, 14-318.4, 14-322.3, (c).
Abused, neglected or dependent juveniles.
Generally, §§7B-100 to 7B-1414.
See CHILD ABUSE, NEGLECT OR DEPENDENCY.
Adoption.
General provisions.
See ADOPTION.
Baby drop off, §§14-318.2, 14-318.4, 14-322.3, (c).
Bastardy.
General provisions.
See ILLEGITIMACY.
Child care facilities.
See CHILD CARE FACILITIES.
Child placement.
See CHILD PLACEMENT.

INFANTS —Cont'd
Children and minors generally.
See CHILDREN AND MINORS.
Consent to health care for minors, §§32A-28 to 32A-34.
Custody.
See CHILD CUSTODY.
Family preservation act, §§143B-150.5, 143B-150.6.
General provisions.
See CHILDREN AND MINORS.
Health care for minors, consent to, §§32A-28 to 32A-34.
Illegitimacy.
General provisions, §§49-1 to 49-17.
See ILLEGITIMACY.
Juvenile code.
Abused, neglected or dependent juveniles.
Generally, §§7B-100 to 7B-1414.
See CHILD ABUSE, NEGLECT OR DEPENDENCY.
Generally.
See JUVENILE CODE.
Juvenile services.
See YOUTH SERVICES.
Minors generally.
See CHILDREN AND MINORS.
Parent and child.
See PARENT AND CHILD.
Safe haven for infants, §§14-318.2, 14-318.4, 14-322.3, (c).
Youth services.
See YOUTH SERVICES.

INFECTIOUS DISEASES.
Communicable diseases generally.
See COMMUNICABLE DISEASES.
Nuclear, biological or chemical agents.
Terrorist incident using, §§130A-475 to 130A-479.
See TERRORIST INCIDENT USING NUCLEAR, BIOLOGICAL OR CHEMICAL AGENTS.

INFERENCES.
Sexual exploitation of minor.
Depiction of minor, §§14-190.16, (b), 14-190.17, (b), 14-190.17A, (b).

INFLUENCING EMPLOYEES IN VIOLATING DUTIES OWED EMPLOYERS, §§14-353, 14-354.

INFORMANTS.
Criminal investigation and intelligence records.
Law enforcement not required to disclose, §132-1.4, (h).
Criminal procedure.
Identity to be disclosed, §15A-978, (b).

IN FORMA PAUPERIS.
Appeals, §1-288.
Bonds, App. Proc. Rule 17, (d).
Cost.
Security for cost, App. Proc. Rule 6, (b).
Extraordinary writs, App. Proc. Rule 24.
Record on appeal, App. Proc. Rule 6, (c).
Costs.
Appeals.
Security for cost, App. Proc. Rule 6, (b).
Dismissal of actions.
Rules of civil procedure, §1A-1, Rule 41, (d).
Supreme court.
Appeal bonds, App. Proc. Rule 17, (d).

INFORMATIONS.
Consolidation of charges, §15A-643.
Contents, §15A-644, (b).
Defined, §15A-641, (b).
Informality.
Bill or warrant not quashed for informality, §15-153.
Joinder.
Offenses and defendants, §15A-643.
Pleadings in felony cases and misdemeanor cases initiated in supreme court division.
Amendment, §15A-923, (d).
Form, §15A-923, (b).
Prosecution on information, §15A-923, (a).
Plea of guilty or no contest in district court, §15A-644.1.
Previous convictions.
Allegations, §15A-645.
Superior court.
Prosecutions originating in superior court to be upon indictment or information, §15A-642, (a).
Superseding informations, §15A-646.

INFORMATION TECHNOLOGY SERVICES.
Biennial state information technology plan, §147-33.72B.
Business and disaster plan with respect to information technology.
State agencies to develop and review, §147-33.89, (a).
Cost-sharing basis.
Office providing services on, §147-33.83, (c).
Disaster recovery plan.
State agencies to establish, §147-33.89, (a).
State agencies to submit to office annually, §147-33.89, (b).
Disaster recovery planning team.
State agencies to establish, §147-33.89, (a).
Dispute resolution panel, §147-33.93.
Disputes between CIO and agencies.
Resolution, procedure, §147-33.72D.
Information resource management commission.
Administrative procedure.
Special provisions, §§150B-38 to 150B-42.
School computer purchases.
Guidelines for useful life of computers purchased, §115C-529.
Information technology advisory board.
Conflicts of interest, §147-33.72G, (b).
Created, §147-33.72G, (a).
Meetings, §147-33.72G, (d).
Membership, §147-33.72G, (a).
Powers and duties, §147-33.72G, (c).
Information technology fund, §147-33.72H.
Joint legislative oversight committee on information technology, §§120-230 to 120-235.
Legacy information technology systems assessment.
Analysis for needs, costs and time frame, §147-33.90, (a) to (c).
Local governmental entities.
Procurement of information technology, §147-33.96, (b).
Telecommunications services for, §147-33.92, (a), (b).
Use of services, programs and contracts, §147-33.82, (b).

INFORMATION TECHNOLOGY SERVICES —Cont'd
Office of information technology services, §§147-33.75 to 147-33.103.
Applicability of provisions.
Exempt agencies, §147-33.80.
Budgets, §147-33.88, (a).
Confidentiality, §147-33.83, (b).
Cost-sharing basis.
Office providing services on, §147-33.83, (c).
Definitions, §147-33.81.
Local governmental entities, §147-33.82, (b).
Duties, §§147-33.82, (a), 147-33.83, (a).
Procurement of information technology, §147-33.95, (b).
Electronic procurement.
Application service provider, §143-48.3, (c).
Authority to use, §147-33.95, (e).
Exempt agencies, §147-33.80.
Governor.
Authority over office, §147-33.75, (b).
Transferred to office of Governor, §147-33.75, (a).
Information technology advisory board, §147-33.72G.
Liaison to coordinate with chief information officer, §147-33.82, (f1).
Powers, §147-33.83, (a).
Procurement of information technology, §147-33.95, (b).
Reports, §§147-33.87, 147-33.88, (b).
Procurement of information technology, §147-33.97, (b), (c).
Webportal system.
Development and implementation, §66-58.20, (b).
Procurement of information technology, §§147-33.95 to 147-33.102.
Aggregation of purchases.
Cost savings, §147-33.72F.
Attorney general.
Assistance by, §147-33.103, (a).
Board of awards.
Review, §147-33.101, (a).
Bribery, §147-33.99.
Certification that information technology bids submitted without collusion, §147-33.100.
Cost savings, §147-33.72F.
Director of the budget.
Review and approval, §147-33.101, (b).
Electronic bidding, §147-33.95, (d).
Electronic procurement system, authority to use, §147-33.95, (e).
Financial interest of officers in sources of supply, §147-33.99.
Generally, §147-33.95, (a).
Liability for violations, §147-33.102.
Local governments, §147-33.96, (b).
Policy of state, §147-33.97, (a).
Powers and duties, §147-33.95, (b).
Reporting, §147-33.97, (b), (c).
Reverse auctions, §147-33.95, (c).
Rules.
Authority to adopt, §147-33.95, (f).
State agency contractual authority restricted, §147-33.96, (a).
Unauthorized use of public purchase or contract procedures for private benefit, §147-33.98, (a).
Criminal penalty, §147-33.98, (c).
Exceptions to prohibition, §147-33.98, (b).
Public contracts, §143-129.8.

INFORMATION TECHNOLOGY SERVICES —Cont'd
Revenue department.
Deviations authorized for department.
Generally, §147-33.84, (a).
Plans, policies and rules to be adopted by, §147-33.84, (b), (c).
Review, §147-33.84, (d).
Security for information technology services.
Approval of technology purchased or use by state agency, §147-33.111, (a).
Assessment of agency compliance with standards, §147-33.112.
Contracts for assessment of network vulnerability.
Approval by CIO, §147-33.111, (c).
Cooperation by heads of state agencies, §147-33.113, (a), (b).
State entities establishing own security standards, §147-33.111, (b).
Statewide standards.
CIO to establish, §147-33.110.
State chief information officer.
Agency information technology projects.
Review and approval, §147-33.72C, (a).
Suspension of approval, §147-33.72C, (c).
Appointment, §147-33.76, (a).
Approval of technology purchased or use by state agency, §147-33.82, (d), 147-33.111, (a).
Assessment of agency compliance.
Security standards, §147-33.112.
Biennial state information technology plan.
Development, §147-33.72B, (a).
Budget requests, §147-33.77, (e).
Contracts for assessment of network vulnerability.
Approval, §147-33.111, (c).
Custody of books and records of office, §147-33.77, (d).
Disputes between officer and agencies.
Resolution, procedure, §147-33.72D.
Head of office, §147-33.76, (a).
Liaison to coordinate with, §147-33.82, (f1).
Long-range plan.
Responsible for developing and administering, §147-33.76, (b1).
Powers, §147-33.77, (a) to (c), (f).
Project management assistant.
Designation, duties, §147-33.72E, (b).
Salary, §147-33.76, (c).
Statewide security standards.
CIO to establish, §147-33.110.
State information technology management.
Agency information technology projects.
Contracts between agency and private party.
Vendor performance review and accountability, §147-33.72C, (e).
Implementation, §147-33.72C, (b).
Performance contracting.
Vendor performance review and accountability, §147-33.72C, (e).
Quality assurance.
Projects not subject to review and approval, §147-33.72C, (d).
Review and approval, §147-33.72C, (a).
Suspension of approval, §147-33.72C, (c).
Agency responsibilities, §147-33.72E, (a).
Biennial state information technology plan.
Agency plan developed by executive agencies, §147-33.72B, (c).
Development by chief information officer, §147-33.72B, (a).
Elements, §147-33.72B, (b).

INFORMATION TECHNOLOGY SERVICES —Cont'd
State information technology management —Cont'd
Cost savings, procurement procedures, §147-33.72F.
Disputes between CIO and agencies.
Agency request for review, §147-33.72D, (a).
Review process, §147-33.72D, (b).
Purposes, §147-33.72A.
State chief information officer responsibilities, §147-33.72E, (b).
Telecommunications services.
Local governmental units and other entities, §147-33.92, (a), (b).
State agencies, §147-33.91.

INFRACTIONS.
Appeals.
Review of disposition by superior court, §15A-1115.
Appeal of district court decision, §15A-1115, (a).
Review of infractions originally disposed of in superior court, §15A-1115, (b).
Appearances.
Appearance bonds, §15A-1113, (c).
Failure to appear to answer charge.
No order for arrest, §15A-1116, (b).
Arrest.
Detention of person charged, §15A-1113, (b).
Territorial jurisdiction, §15A-1113, (d).
Failure to appear to answer charge.
No order for arrest, §15A-1116, (b).
Bonds, surety.
Appearance bonds, §15A-1113, (c).
Burden of proof, §15A-1114, (f).
Child bicycle safety act, §20-171.9, (d).
Cigarettes and tobacco products.
Fake identification offered by minor for purchase of tobacco product, §14-313, (c).
Purchased by minors, §14-313, (c).
Cleaning agents containing phosphorus.
Water and air resources.
Using agents, §143-214.4, (g).
Concealed handgun permit, §14-415.21, (a).
Contempt.
Enforcement of sanctions.
Use of contempt procedures, §15A-1116, (a).
Costs, §15A-1118.
Defined, §14-3.1, (a).
District attorneys.
Hearing procedure.
Duties, §15A-1114, (e).
Preparation of trial dockets, §7A-61.
District courts.
Costs in criminal actions.
Applicability of section to infractions disposed of in district courts, §7A-304, (e).
Hearings conducted in open court, §7A-191.
Jurisdiction for adjudication and disposition, §7A-253.
No right to trial by jury in adjudicatory hearings, §7A-196, (c).
Reporting not provided in hearings to adjudicate, §7A-198, (e).
Education.
Motor vehicles.
Powers of local boards of education to regulate parking.
Violations of regulations of local boards of education, §115C-46, (a).

INFRACTIONS —Cont'd
Enforcement of sanctions.
Order of arrest.
Not to be used, §15A-1116.
Financial identity fraud.
Cash registers and other receipt printing machines.
Sale of, §14-113.25, (b).
Credit, charge, or debit card numbers on receipts, §14-113.24, (c).
Fines.
Enforcement of sanctions.
Use of fine collection procedures, §15A-1116, (a).
Handicapped persons.
Motor vehicles.
Parking violations, §20-37.6, (f).
Hunting and wildlife.
Hunter orange material.
Violations of requirements, §113-291.8, (b).
Jurisdiction.
Adjudication and disposition, §15A-1114, (a).
Detention of person charged.
Territorial jurisdiction, §15A-1113, (d).
District courts, §7A-253.
Jury.
District court adjudicatory hearings for infractions.
No right to trial by jury, §7A-196, (c).
No trial by jury, §15A-1114, (b).
Landlord and tenant.
Smoke detectors, §42-44, (a1), (a2).
Lasers.
Criminal use of laser device, §14-34.8, (c).
Magistrates.
Powers in infraction actions, §7A-273.
Mopeds, §20-140.4, (c).
Motor carrier safety regulation unit.
Safety inspection of vehicles.
Failure to conduct inspection, §20-384.
Motorcycles, §20-140.4, (c).
Motor vehicle license plates.
Covering or making illegible plate or renewal sticker, §20-63, (g).
Motor vehicles.
Commercial drivers' licenses, §20-37.21, (b), (c).
Driving without license, §20-37.21, (a).
Violations of driver notice requirements, §20-37.21, (b).
Fire department vehicles.
Motorist approach violation, §20-157, (a).
Handicapped persons.
Parking violations, §20-37.6, (f).
Inspections, §20-183.8, (a).
Lights.
Requirement violations, §20-129, (a).
Passing vehicles.
Driver of overtaken vehicle not giving way to right in favor of overtaking vehicle, §20-149, (b).
Penalty not specified, §20-176.
Public schools.
Powers of local boards of education to regulate parking.
Violations of regulations of local board of education, §115C-46, (a).
Railroad grade crossings.
Crossing gate violation, §20-142.1, (d).
Heavy equipment.
Moving at railroad grade crossing.
Violations of requirements, §20-142.4, (f).
Stop sign violation, §20-142.2.

INFRACTIONS —Cont'd
Motor vehicles —Cont'd
Railroad grade crossings —Cont'd
Vehicles required to stop, §20-142.3, (c).
Seat belt.
Violations of mandatory use provision, §20-135.2A, (e).
Speedometer.
Requirement violations, §20-123.2, (b).
Stopping.
Traffic obstructed, §20-142.5.
Tandem trailers and subtrailer.
Load limitation violations, §20-115.1, (h).
Transporting children under 12 years of age in open bed or open cargo area of vehicle, §20-135.2B, (c).
Municipal corporations.
Violation of ordinance is misdemeanor or infraction, §160A-175, (b).
Parking on community college campuses, §115D-21, (b).
Parking on public school grounds, §115C-46, (a).
Penalties, §14-3.1, (a).
Authorized penalties, §15A-1361.
Pleas, §15A-1114, (d).
Procedure for hearing and disposition.
Appeals.
Review of disposition by superior court, §15A-1115.
Appeal of district court decision, §15A-1115, (a).
Review of infractions originally disposed of in superior court, §15A-1115, (b).
Appearance bonds, §15A-1113, (c).
Arrest.
Failure to appear to answer charge.
No order for arrest, §15A-1116, (b).
Burden of proof, §15A-1114, (f).
Contempt.
Enforcement of sanctions.
Use, §15A-1116, (a).
Costs, §15A-1118.
Detention of person charged, §15A-1113, (b).
Territorial jurisdiction, §15A-1113, (d).
Disposition, §14-3.1, (b).
General procedure, §15A-1111.
Review by superior court, §15A-1115.
District attorneys.
Duties, §15A-1114, (e).
Enforcement of sanctions, §15A-1116.
Fines.
Enforcement of sanctions.
Use of fine collection procedures, §15A-1116, (a).
General procedure for disposition, §15A-1111.
Hearing procedure, §15A-1114.
Burden of proof, §15A-1114, (f).
Civil or criminal sessions, §15A-1114, (c).
District attorneys.
Duties, §15A-1114, (e).
Jurisdiction, §15A-1114, (a).
Jury trial.
No trial by jury, §15A-1114, (b).
Pleas, §15A-1114, (d).
Recording not necessary, §15A-1114, (g).
Jurisdiction, §15A-1114, (a).
Jury trial.
No trial by jury, §15A-1114, (b).
Pleas, §15A-1114, (d).
Prehearing procedure, §15A-1113.
Appearance bonds, §15A-1113, (c).

INFRACTIONS —Cont'd
Procedure for hearing and disposition —Cont'd
Prehearing procedure —Cont'd
Detention of person charged, §15A-1113, (b).
Territorial jurisdiction, §15A-1113, (d).
Process, §15A-1113, (a).
Use of same process for two offenses, §15A-1113, (e).
Recordings.
Not necessary, §15A-1114, (g).
Sanctions.
Enforcement, §15A-1116.
Summons and process, §15A-1113, (a).
Use of same process for two offenses, §15A-1113, (e).
Superior courts.
Review of disposition, §15A-1115.
Appeal of district court decision, §15A-1115, (a).
Review of infractions originally disposed of in superior court, §15A-1115, (b).
Venue, §15A-1112.
Public schools.
Motor vehicles.
Powers of local board of education to regulate parking.
Violations of regulations of local board of education, §115C-46, (a).
Records.
Hearing procedure.
Recording not necessary, §15A-1114, (g).
Smoke detectors.
Landlord and tenant, §42-44, (a1), (a2).
Solid waste management.
Landfill fees.
Failure to collect or report revenue, §130A-309.27, (c).
Streets and highways.
Obstructing highway drains, §136-92.
Summons and process, §15A-1113, (a).
Use of same process for two offenses, §15A-1113, (e).
Superior court jurisdictions, §7A-271, (d).
Superior courts.
Costs in criminal actions.
Applicability of section to infractions appealed to superior court, §7A-304, (e).
Review of disposition, §15A-1115.
Appeal of district court decision, §15A-1115, (a).
Review of infractions originally disposed of in superior court, §15A-1115, (b).
Venue.
Hearing and disposition of infractions, §15A-1112.
Water and air resources.
Cleaning agents containing phosphorus.
Using agents, §143-214.4, (g).

INFRINGEMENT.
Leases, UCC.
Warranty against, §25-2A-211.
Exclusion or modification, §25-2A-214, (4).
Sale of goods, UCC.
Buyer's obligation against infringement, §25-2-312, (3).
Notice of claim or litigation to person answerable over, §25-2-607.
Warranty against infringement, §25-2-312, (3).
Trademarks.
Counterfeit trademarks, §§80-11, 80-11.1.
Criminal use of counterfeit trademark, §80-11.1.
Deceptive or unfair trade practices, §80-12.

INHERENT RISKS.
Equine activity liability, §§99E-1 to 99E-3.
Roller skating rink safety and liability, §§99E-10 to 99E-14.

INHERITANCE.
Decedents' estates.
General provisions.
See DECEDENTS' ESTATES.
Executors and administrators.
General provisions.
See EXECUTORS AND ADMINISTRATORS.
Inheritance tax.
See INHERITANCE TAX.
Intestate succession.
General provisions.
See INTESTATE SUCCESSION.
Simultaneous death act, §§28A-24-1 to 28A-24-7.
See SIMULTANEOUS DEATH.
Small estates, §§28A-25-1 to 28A-25-6.
See SMALL ESTATES.
Surviving spouses.
General provisions.
See SURVIVING SPOUSES.
Wills.
General provisions.
See WILLS.

INHERITANCE TAX.
Bond issues.
Port authority bonds.
Gain from transfer not exempt, §143B-456, (g).
Refunding obligations issued by state.
Gain from transfer not exempt from taxation, §142-29.6, (f).
State bonds, act authorizing not addressing exemption from taxation.
Not exempt from tax on gain from transfer, §142-12.
Corporations.
Joint ownership of corporate stock and investment securities.
Inheritance tax laws unaffected, §41-2.2, (d).
Estate tax.
Apportionment of federal estate tax, §§28A-27-1 to 28A-27-9.
See FEDERAL ESTATE TAX APPORTIONMENT.
Exemptions.
Port authority bond issues.
Gain from transfer not exempt, §143B-456, (g).
Refunding obligations issued by state.
Gain from transfer not exempt from taxation, §142-29.6, (f).
State bonds, act authorizing not addressing exemption from taxation.
Not exempt on gain from transfer, §142-12.
Intestate succession.
Descent and distribution subject to payment, §29-13.
Investments.
Joint ownership of corporate stock and investment securities.
Inheritance tax laws unaffected, §41-2.2, (d).
Joint tenants and tenants in common.
Joint ownership of corporate stock and investment securities.
Inheritance tax laws unaffected, §41-2.2, (d).
Port authority bond issues.
Gain from transfer not exempt from taxation, §143B-456, (g).

INHERITANCE TAX —Cont'd
Probate and registration.
Inheritance and estate tax waiver.
Registration, §47-18.2.
Registration.
Inheritance and estate tax waiver, §47-18.2.
Renunciation of property and fiduciary powers, §31B-1, (b).
Savings banks.
Joint accounts.
Provisions not to repeal or modify estate tax law, §54C-165, (b).
Trust accounts.
Provisions not to repeal or modify estate tax law, §54C-166, (d).
Securities.
Joint ownership of investment securities.
Inheritance tax laws unaffected, §41-2.2, (d).
State bonds, act authorizing not addressing exemption from taxation.
Not exempt from tax on gain from transfer, §142-12.
State refunding obligations.
Gain from transfer not exempt from taxation, §142-29.6, (f).
Waiver.
Registration, §47-18.2.

INITIATIVE.
Referenda.
See REFERENDUM.

INJUNCTIONS.
Abortion.
Obstruction of abortion clinic, §14-277.4, (d).
Adoption.
Prohibited placement activities, §48-10-101, (d).
Unlawful payments related to adoption, §48-10-102, (c).
Affidavits.
Preliminary injunction.
Issuance, §1-485.
Air pollution control.
Enforcement procedures, §143-215.114C.
Airports.
Zoning.
Violations of provisions, §63-35.
Alarm systems licensing.
Violations of provisions, §74D-11, (a).
Alcoholic beverages.
Beer franchises.
Wrongful termination of agreement, §18B-1306, (a).
Alimony.
Remedy available, §50-16.7, (f).
Ambulatory surgical facilities.
Licensing of facilities, §131E-152, (a) to (c).
Antifreeze.
Violations of article.
Applying for and granting preliminary or permanent injunction, §106-579.12, (d).
Appeals.
Pending appeal, §1A-1, Rule 62, (c).
Restraining orders and injunctions in effect pending appeals, §1-500.
Aquatic weed control.
Violation of article, §113A-226, (b).
Arbitration.
Motion to compel arbitration, §1-569.7, (a).
Architects.
Violations of provisions, §83A-17.

INJUNCTIONS —Cont'd
Athletic trainers.
Illegal practices, §90-537.
Atomic energy.
Radiation protection.
Violations of provisions, §104E-23, (b).
Attachment.
Stock and stockholders.
Transfer of certificate of stock, §1-440.19, (c).
Warehouse receipts.
Transfer of negotiable warehouse receipts, §1-440.20, (b).
Attorneys at law.
State bar.
Discipline.
Practice of law by attorney, §84-28, (f).
Unauthorized practice, §84-37, (b).
District attorneys to bring injunction proceedings upon application, §84-7.
Auctions and auctioneers.
Violations of provisions, §85B-9, (b).
Automobile dealers associations, §20-308.1, (d).
Bankruptcy and insolvency.
Trespass on land.
Insolvency of defendant.
When allegation of insolvency unnecessary, §1-486.
Banks.
Dissolution and liquidation.
Taking possession by commissioner, §53-20, (f).
Barbers.
Illegal practice, §86A-20.1.
Bills of lading.
Enjoining negotiation of document, §25-7-602.
Biologics.
Violations of provisions, §106-714, (b).
Blue Ridge parkway.
Control of outdoor advertising.
Violations, §113A-170.
Boilers.
Commissioner of labor.
Uniform boiler and pressure vessel act.
Power to enjoin violations, §95-69.11.
Bonds, surety, §1A-1, Rule 65, (c).
Appeals.
Restraining orders and injunctions in effect pending appeals, §1-500.
Boxing, §143-658, (c).
Building code.
Code officials qualification board.
Certificates for code enforcement officials.
Violations, §143-151.18.
Business combinations, §75E-4.
Business corporations.
Judicial dissolution.
Powers of court, §55-14-31, (c).
Business opportunity sales.
Violations of provisions, §66-100, (c).
Cable television systems.
Theft of services, §14-118.5.
Cemeteries.
Commission.
Power to bring action for, §65-53.
Certified public accountants.
Power of board of examiners to apply to courts for injunctive relief, §93-12.
Charitable solicitation.
Power of attorney general to seek, §131F-24, (a).
Power of department to seek, §131F-23, (c).
Child care facilities, §110-104.

INJUNCTIONS —Cont'd
Child custody.
Enforcement of custody orders.
Power of court having jurisdiction, §50-13.3, (b).
Simultaneous proceedings, §50A-206, (c).
Child placing agencies.
Interference department carrying out duties, §131D-10.8, (b).
Operating without license, §131D-10.8, (a).
Child support.
Enforcement of support, §50-13.4, (f).
Chiropractors.
Unlicensed practice, §90-147.
Civil no-contact orders.
Workplace violence prevention, §§95-265 to 95-276.
See WORKPLACE VIOLENCE PREVENTION.
Civil rights, interference with, §99D-1, (b), (b1).
Claim and delivery.
Notice containing order enjoining defendant from disposing of property, §1-474.1, (a).
Closing-out sales.
Violations of provisions, §66-83.
Coastal area management.
Permits.
Violations, §113A-126, (a).
Collection agencies.
Violations of provisions.
Restraining orders, §58-70-40, (a).
Commercial code.
Enjoining negotiation of document, §25-7-602.
Commercial feed.
Relief from violations of article, §106-284.44, (d).
Commodities.
Enforcement of act, §78D-22, (b).
Power of court to grant injunctive relief, §78D-23.
Consumer finance act.
Powers of commissioner of banks, §53-187.
Contents, §1A-1, Rule 65, (d).
Contractors.
Electrical contractors.
Violations of provisions, §87-48, (b).
General contractors.
Violations of provisions, §87-13.1.
Plumbing, heating and fire sprinkler contractors.
Violations of provisions, §87-25.1.
Refrigeration contractors.
Violations of provisions, §87-61.1.
Control share acquisitions, §75E-4.
Cooperative associations.
Unauthorized use of term "mutual" in name.
Violators may be enjoined from doing business, §54-112.
Corporations.
Nonprofit corporations.
Corporate power to act.
Ultra vires, §55A-3-04.
Cosmetic art, §88B-28.
Cotton gins.
Operation without registration, §106-451.44.
Cotton merchants.
Operation without registration, §106-451.44.
Cotton warehouses.
Operation without registration, §106-451.44.
Counties.
Inspection departments.
Equitable enforcement of article, §153A-372.
Ordinances.
Enforcement, §153A-123, (d).
Subdivisions.
Transferring lots in unapproved subdivisions, §153A-334.

INJUNCTIONS —Cont'd
Credit.
Women.
Right of action to enforce article, §25B-3, (b).
Credit device fraud.
Telecommunication services, §14-113.6, (c).
Credit repair services.
Violation of provisions, §66-225.
Cruelty to animals.
Civil remedies generally, §§19A-1 to 19A-4.
Permanent injunction, §19A-4.
Preliminary injunction, §19A-3.
Dams.
Dam safety law.
Violations, §143-215.36, (c).
Debt adjusting, §14-425.
Dentists.
Unauthorized practice, §90-40.1.
Dietitians and nutritionists.
Violation of provisions, §90-367.
Disabled persons.
Protection act.
Relief available, §168A-11, (b).
Discrimination.
Discrimination in business.
Enforcement of provisions, §75B-4.
Dissolution.
Damages on, §1A-1, Rule 65, (e).
District courts.
Enforcement or invalidation of statutes.
Injunctive and declaratory relief to enforce or invalidate.
Grounds for transfer, §7A-245, (b).
Extension, modification or vacation.
Applications.
Before whom heard, §1-498.
Jurisdiction of judge, §1-493.
Return, §1-494.
Divorce.
Distribution by court of marital and divisible property.
Equitable distribution, §50-20, (i).
Order for custody of minor child.
Enforcement, §50-13.3, (b).
Documents of title.
Enjoining negotiations of document, §25-7-602.
Dry-cleaning solvent cleanup, §143-215.104R.
Eggs.
Granting temporary or permanent injunction for violations, §106-245.24, (b).
Elections.
Contributions and expenditures in political campaigns.
Violations of provisions, §163-278.28, (a).
Electrologists.
Violations of chapter, §88A-22, (a).
Electronic commerce in government.
Jurisdiction over transactions, §66-58.6, (b).
Eminent domain.
Private condemnors.
Provisions not to preclude injunctive relief, §40A-28, (g).
Public condemnors.
Remedy not precluded by provisions, §40A-42, (f).
Employee assistance professionals.
Enforcement of article, §90-506, (a).
Employment security.
Contributions.
Injunction to restrain collection.
Not to be issued, §96-10, (f).

INJUNCTIONS —Cont'd
Employment security —Cont'd
Operation by employer in violation of provisions, §96-10, (g).
Energy.
Crisis administration.
Enforcement of act by injunction, §113B-24, (c).
Enforcement or invalidation of statute, ordinance or regulation.
Superior court jurisdiction, §7A-245, (a).
Engineers and land surveyors.
Violations of provisions, §89C-10, (c).
Execution sales.
Dissolution of order restraining or enjoining sale.
Procedure upon, §1-339.59, (a), (b).
Expedited evictions.
Preliminary injunction against illegal activity pending completion of discovery, §42-70, (e).
Preliminary injunction in emergency situation, §42-74.
Fair housing.
Appropriateness of relief, §41A-7, (j).
Family law arbitration, §50-44, (c).
Findings of fact and conclusions of law on preliminary injunction, §1A-1, Rule 52, (a).
Fish and fisheries resources.
Buoys, nets, markers, stakes, etc.
Robbing or injuring, §113-268, (e).
Encroachment upon, usurpation or otherwise violating public trust rights of people, §113-131, (c).
Interference with taking of wildlife resources, §113-295, (b).
Floodplain regulations.
Restraining violations of ordinances, §143-215.58, (c).
Flour, corn meal and grain.
Grain dealers.
Violations of article, §106-615.
Food, drugs and cosmetics.
Inspections of donated food.
Restraining violations of article, §106-141.1, (b).
Restraining violations of provisions, §106-123.
Forest protection and development corporations.
Secretary of environment and natural resources.
Power to apply for injunctions, §113-65.
Fraternal benefit societies.
Application or petition for.
Attorney general upon request of commissioner, §58-24-155.
Fraud.
Removal or disposition of property with intent to defraud plaintiff.
Issuance of preliminary injunction when threatened, §1-485.
Funds transfers, UCC, §25-4A-503.
Funeral service.
Violations of provisions.
Power of board to seek injunction, §90-210.25, (f).
Geologists.
Violation of chapter, §89E-23.
Harmful materials, protection of minors.
Disobedience.
Contempt, §19-20, (a).
Permanent injunction, §19-18, (b).
Preliminary injunction, §19-19, (c), (d).
Notice of issuance, §19-19, (d).
Temporary restraining order, §19-19, (a), (b).

INJUNCTIONS —Cont'd
Hazardous waste management.
Inactive hazardous sites.
Failure to submit data or comply with orders, §130A-310.1, (d).
Imminent hazard.
Violation of orders, §130A-310.5, (b).
Health.
Secretary of environment and natural resources or local health directors, §130A-18, (b).
Secretary of health and human services or local health directors, §130A-18, (a).
Health care facilities.
Certificates of need.
Noncompliance with representations in application for certificate, §131E-190, (i).
Home care agencies, §131E-142, (a) to (c).
Hospices.
Violation of article, §131E-206, (a) to (c).
Health maintenance organizations.
Violations of provisions, §58-67-165, (e).
Hearing aid dealers and fitters.
Board.
Actions for, §93D-4.
Hearings.
Extension, modification or vacation.
Applications.
Before whom heard, §1-498.
Judges.
Before what judge returnable, §1-494.
Stipulation as to judge to hear, §1-495.
Return, §1-494.
Stipulation as to judge to hear, §1-495.
Historic districts and landmarks.
Violations of part, §160A-400.11.
Home care agencies, §131E-142, (a) to (c).
Home inspectors.
Violations of provisions, §143-151.60.
Hospices.
Violation of article, §131E-206, (a) to (c).
Hospitals.
Certificate of need law.
Enforcement and sanctions of article, §131E-190, (h).
Licensing act, §131E-82, (a), (b), (c).
Household cleaners.
Labeling cleaners containing volatile substances capable of producing toxic effects.
Sales in violation of provisions, §66-87.
Housemovers, §20-371, (b).
Hunting and wildlife.
Authority of commission to institute action for, §113-306, (e).
Encroachment upon usurpation or otherwise violating public trust rights of people, §113-131, (c).
Interference with taking of wildlife resources, §113-295, (b).
Industrial hygienists.
Illegal practices, §90-516, (d).
Insurance.
Accident and health insurance.
Pharmacy of choice.
Violations of provisions, §58-51-37, (h).
Holding companies.
Mandatory injunction directing commissioner to act, §58-19-70, (b).
Violations of provisions, §58-19-45, (a).
Supervision, rehabilitation and liquidation of insurers, §58-30-20.
Supervision proceedings.
Enforcement of supervision order, §58-30-60, (i).

INJUNCTIONS —Cont'd
Insurance —Cont'd
Unauthorized insurers.
Powers of commissioner, §58-28-20.
Unfair trade practices.
Undefined practices, §§58-63-40, (b) to (d), 58-63-45.
Violations of provisions.
Restraining orders, §58-2-60, (a).
Interpreters and transliterators.
Violations of license provisions, §90D-13.
Investment advisers.
Violation of chapter, §78C-28, (a).
Issuance.
Judges.
Preliminary injunction.
When issued, §1-485.
What judges have jurisdiction, §1-493.
Judges.
Extension, modification or vacation.
Applications.
Before whom heard, §1-498.
Hearings.
Before what judge returnable, §1-494.
Stipulation as to judge to hear, §1-495.
Issuance.
Preliminary injunction.
When issued, §1-485.
What judges have jurisdiction, §1-493.
Return.
Before what judge returnable, §1-494.
Jurisdiction.
What judges have jurisdiction, §1-493.
Labor.
Retaliatory employment discrimination.
Relief granted in civil actions, §95-243, (c).
Landscape architects, §89A-8, (b).
Landscape contractors.
Violations of provisions, §89D-10.
Letters of credit.
Fraud or forgery.
Injunction on honoring, §25-5-109, (b).
Limitation of actions.
Time of stay by injunction.
Not considered part of time limited for commencement of action, §1-23.
Limited liability companies.
Foreign limited liability companies.
Actions by attorney general, §57C-7-13.
Liquefied petroleum gases.
Violations of provisions, §119-59, (b).
Littering.
Violations of section, §14-399, (f).
Loan brokers.
Violations of provisions, §66-111, (b).
Local government finance.
Offending officers, §159-182.
Local governments.
Housing.
Petition for injunction restraining public officer from carrying out order or decision, §160A-446, (f).
Locksmith licensing, §74F-17.
Manufactured homes.
Enforcement of provisions, §143-151.1.
Marketing associations.
Breach of marketing contract, §54-152, (c).
Marriage and family therapists.
Violations of provisions, §90-270.62.
Massage and bodywork therapy.
Violations of provisions, §90-634, (c).

INJUNCTIONS —Cont'd
Medical assistance provider false claims, §108A-70.14, (j).
Membership camping contracts violations, §66-247, (c).
Mental health, mental retardation and substance abuse.
Facilities.
Licenses.
Enjoining violations of provisions, §122C-29, (a), (b).
Mines and minerals.
Safety and health.
Powers of commissioner of labor, §74-24.12.
Uranium.
Exploration for uranium.
Violations of provisions, §74-87, (b).
Money transmitters, §53-208.25, (a).
Monopolies and restraint of trade.
Action to obtain mandatory order, §75-14.
Lender requiring borrower to deal with particular insurer, §75-19.
Mortgages and deeds of trust.
Enjoining or restraining sale.
Equitable grounds, §45-21.34.
Sales under power of sale.
Procedure upon dissolution of order restraining or enjoining, §45-21.22.
Motion pictures.
Fair competition.
Enforcement of provisions, §75C-5.
Motor carriers.
Unlawful operation, §62-279.
Motor fuel marketing violations, §75-86.
Motor vehicle repairs.
Remedies for violation of article, §20-354.9.
Motor vehicles.
New motor vehicles warranties act, §20-351.8.
Odometers.
Violations of provisions, §20-349.
Municipal corporations.
Enforcement of ordinances.
Real property violations, §160A-175, (e).
Zoning.
Remedies for violations, §160A-389.
Nonprofit corporations.
Attorney general.
Exercise of corporate franchises not granted, §55A-3-05.
Corporate power to act.
Ultra vires, §55A-3-04.
Judicial dissolution, §55A-14-31, (c).
Notaries public.
Violations of chapter, §10A-12, (f).
Notice.
Preliminary injunction, §1A-1, Rule 65, (a).
Temporary restraining order, §1A-1, Rule 65, (b).
Nuisances.
Abatement of offenses against public morals, §§19-1 to 19-8.3.
See NUISANCES.
Nurses.
Nursing pools, §131E-154.7.
Violations of provisions, §90-171.46.
Nursing pools, §131E-154.7.
Nursing homes.
Patients' bill of rights.
Civil action for injunctive relief to enforce provision of article, §131E-123.
Restraining or preventing establishment, conduct, management or operation of nursing home without license, §131E-110, (a) to (c).

INJUNCTIONS —Cont'd
Obstructing justice.
Violating orders of court, §14-226.1.
Obstruction of health care facilities, §14-277.4, (d).
Occupational safety and health.
Imminent danger, §95-140, (b).
Occupational therapists.
Violation of article, §90-270.80.
Oil and gas conservation.
Violations of laws and regulations, §113-408.
Oil pollution and hazardous substances control.
Offshore oil and gas activities.
Violations of part, §143-215.94FF, (a).
Opticians.
Violations of provisions, §90-254.
Optometrists.
Illegal practices, §90-121.1.
Ordinances.
Real property.
Enforcement of violation of real property, §160A-175, (e).
Pastoral counselors.
Certification of fee-based practicing pastoral counselors.
Injunctive relief against violations, §90-393.
Pharmacists and pharmacies.
Board of pharmacy.
Authority, §90-85.39.
Physical therapists.
Violations of provisions.
Actions for injunctive relief, §90-270.37, (a).
Venue, §90-270.37, (b).
Physicians and surgeons.
Violations of provisions, §90-14.12.
Pipelines.
Safety standards for gas pipeline facilities.
Violations of provisions, §62-50, (f).
Plant protection and conservation.
Violations of article, §106-202.19, (c).
Podiatrists, §90-202.13.
Pollution control.
Sedimentation pollution control act of 1973.
Violations of programs, §113A-65.
Power of sale, sales under.
Dissolution of order restraining or enjoining sale.
Judge ordering sale, §45-21.22, (a), (b).
Preliminary injunctions.
Extension.
Application.
Before whom heard, §1-498.
Findings of fact and conclusions of law necessary, §1A-1, Rule 52, (a).
Issuance.
Grounds, §1-485.
Modification.
Application.
Before whom heard, §1-498.
Notice required, §1A-1, Rule 65, (a).
Vacation.
Application.
Before whom heard, §1-498.
When issued, §1-485.
Preneed funeral contracts and funds.
Violations of article, §90-210.70, (e).
Private personnel services.
Violations of provisions, §95-47.10.
Private protective services.
Violations of provisions.
Powers of board, §74C-17, (a).

INJUNCTIONS —Cont'd
Professional counselors.
Board not required to post bond, §90-342.
Professional employer organizations, §58-89A-165, (a), (e).
Psychologists.
Violations of provisions, §90-270.19.
Public officers and employees.
Improper government activities.
Reporting.
Civil actions for injunctive relief, §126-86.
Public utilities.
Violations of provisions applicable to water or sewer utilities service, §62-310, (b).
Quo warranto.
Possession of office not enjoined pending trial, §1-524.
Racketeer influenced and corrupt organizations.
Prohibited activities, §75D-8.
Real estate brokers and salespersons.
Violations of provisions, §93A-6, (c).
Records.
Public records.
Regaining custody of public records, §132-5.1.
Rerefined or reprocessed oil.
Injunctions following multiple offenses, §119-13.3.
Respiratory care practitioners.
Regulatory violations, §90-663.
Retaliatory employment discrimination.
Relief granted in civil actions, §95-243, (c).
Return.
Judges.
Before what judge returnable, §1-494.
Safety professionals.
Unlawful representation, §90-672, (a).
Sanitarians.
Violations, §90A-66.
Savings and loan associations.
Interstate branches, §54B-274, (c).
Violations of provisions, §54B-8, (d).
Commissioner may request attorney general to institute action for, §54B-65, (c).
Savings banks.
Dissolution.
Involuntary liquidation.
Continued operation of savings bank, §54C-83, (l).
Interstate branch banks, §54C-208.
Unlawful operation as savings bank, §54C-8, (c).
Scope, §1A-1, Rule 65, (d).
Secured transactions.
Remedies for noncompliance with article, §25-9-625, (a).
Limitation of liability, §25-9-628.
Securities regulation.
Violations of provisions, §78A-47, (a).
Security, §1A-1, Rule 65, (c).
Sewers.
Violations of public utilities provisions applicable to sewers, §62-310, (b).
Sheriffs' education and training standard commission.
Violation of chapter by justice officer, §17E-9, (c).
Social workers, certification and licensure.
Violations of provisions, §90B-13.
Soil additives act, §106-50.38.
Soil scientists.
Power of board to seek injunction, §89F-23.
Speech and language pathologists and audiologists.
Violations of provisions.
Power of board to bring action, §90-304, (a).

INJUNCTIONS —Cont'd
State of emergency.
Public or private educational institutions, §14-288.18, (a), (b).
Stays.
Exceptions to automatic stay, §1A-1, Rule 62, (a).
Substance abuse professionals.
Illegal practices, §90-113.45.
Superior courts.
Enforcement or invalidation of statutes.
Injunctive and declaratory relief to enforce or invalidate, §7A-245.
Extension, modification or vacation.
Applications.
Before whom heard, §1-498.
Jurisdiction of judge, §1-493.
Return, §1-494.
Swine farms.
Relief generally, §106-804, (a).
Taxation.
Property taxes.
Restrictions on use of injunction, §105-379, (a).
Telephone solicitations.
Action by subscriber seeking, §75-105, (b).
Temporary restraining orders.
Duration, §1A-1, Rule 65, (b).
Extension.
Application.
Before whom heard, §1-498.
Hearing, §1A-1, Rule 65, (b).
Modification.
Application.
Before whom heard, §1-498.
Notice, §1A-1, Rule 65, (b).
Vacation.
Application.
Before whom heard, §1-498.
Therapeutic recreation personnel.
Certification.
Violations of provisions, §90C-19.
Time shares.
Violations of provisions, §93A-54, (c).
Trade secrets.
Misappropriation, §66-154, (a).
Tramways.
Passenger tramways.
Restraining operation of tramways or compelling compliance with commissioner's orders, §95-123.
Trees and timber.
Title to timberlands.
Trial of title, §1-487.
When timber may be cut, §1-488.
Trespass.
Trial of title to timberlands, §1-487.
When timber may be cut, §1-488.
When solvent defendant restrained, §1-486.
Trespass.
Insolvency of defendant.
When allegation of insolvency unnecessary, §1-486.
Trees and timber.
Solvent defendant.
When restrained, §1-486.
Trial of title to timberlands, §1-487.
When timber may be cut, §1-488.
Trust companies.
Seizure by commissioner.
Objection and response to seizure, §53-382, (a).
Unauthorized disclosure of information, §48-10-105, (c).

INJUNCTIONS —Cont'd
Unit ownership.
Relief for noncompliance with regulations and covenants, §47A-10.
Uranium.
Exploration for uranium.
Violations of provisions, §74-87, (b).
Veterinarians.
Violations of provisions, §90-187.13.
Viatical settlements, §58-58-290, (a).
Violating orders of court, §14-226.1.
Wage and hour act.
Violations of provisions, §95-25.24.
Warehouse receipts.
Enjoining negotiation of document, §25-7-602.
Water and air resources.
Enforcement procedures, §143-215.6C.
Water and air quality reporting, §143-215.69, (c).
Waters and watercourses.
Natural and scenic rivers system.
Violations of provisions, §113A-42, (a).
Use of water resources.
Capacity use areas.
Enforcement procedures, §143-215.17, (c).
Water supply and waterworks.
Violations of public utilities provisions applicable to water service, §62-310, (b).
Weights and measures.
Violations of provisions, §81A-30.
Well contractors, §87-98.13.
Wells.
Construction.
Violations of provisions, §87-95.
Wildlife resources commission.
Prevention of irreparable injury to wildlife, §113-306, (e).
Wine distribution agreements, §18B-1207.
Women.
Credit rights.
Actions to enforce article, §25B-3, (b).
Workplace violence prevention.
Civil no-contact orders, §§95-265 to 95-276.
See WORKPLACE VIOLENCE PREVENTION.

INJURING MOTOR VEHICLE, §20-107.

IN KIND DISTRIBUTIONS.
Powers of fiduciaries incorporated by reference, §32-27.

INKJETS.
Agreement prohibiting reusing, remanufacturing or refilling.
Void and unenforceable, §75-36.

INLAND FISHING LICENSES.
Generally.
See FISHING LICENSES.

INLAND WATERWAYS.
Acquisition of land for, §§104-12, 104-19, 104-25.
Bridges over waterways, §§104-17, 104-23.
Condemnation of land, §§104-13, 104-20.
Expenses and awards.
Method of payment, §§104-15, 104-22.
Public purpose.
Use declared paramount public purpose, §§104-14, 104-21.
Jurisdiction.
Concurrent jurisdiction over waterways, §§104-18, 104-24.
Public purpose.
Use declared paramount public purpose, §§104-14, 104-21.

INLAND WATERWAYS —Cont'd
Right of entry.
Private lands.
Utilities commission to secure, §§104-13, 104-20.
State and United States may enter upon lands, §104-16.
Steam vessels not having United States licensed pilots subject to pilot laws, §76-44.
Surveys and surveyors.
State and United States may enter upon lands for survey, §104-16.
Vessels exempt from pilot laws, §76-44.

INLINE SKATING.
Assumption of inherent risk, §99E-24, (a).
Governmental entities.
Limitation of liability, §99E-25, (b).
Duty of care not created, §99E-25, (d).
Exceptions, §99E-25, (c).
Independent concessionaires or other persons or organizations.
Liability not limited by section, §99E-25, (e).
Insurance carried by entity.
Not waiver of liability limits, §99E-25, (f).
Sovereign immunity not waived, §99E-25, (d).
Specifically designated areas for activities.
Requirement to participate on property owner or controlled by entity, §99E-25, (a).
Responsibilities of participants, §99E-24, (b).

INMATE GRIEVANCE PROCEDURE, §§148-118.1 to 148-118.9.
See PRISONER'S GRIEVANCE PROCEDURE.

INMATE LABOR, §§148-26 to 148-49.
See PRISONER LABOR.

INMATES OF STATE INSTITUTIONS.
Mental health, developmental disabilities and substance abuse generally.
See MENTAL HEALTH, DEVELOPMENTAL DISABILITY, SUBSTANCE ABUSE.
Prisons and prisoners.
See PRISONS AND PRISONERS.

INNS.
Hotels.
See HOTELS, INNS AND OTHER TRANSIENT LODGING PLACES.

INOCULATIONS.
Immunization generally, §§130A-152 to 130A-158.
See IMMUNIZATION.
Rabies.
Vaccinations.
See RABIES.

INORGANIC SALTS.
Antifreeze solutions compounded with, manufacture or sale prohibited, §66-66.

INQUESTS.
Compensation of jurors at inquest, §152-9.
Duties of coroners, §152-7.
Medical examiners to be notified of certain deaths.
Holding of inquests by coroner, §130A-394.

IN REM JURISDICTION.
Grounds, §1-75.8.
Interlocutory orders for protection of rem, §1-75.9.
Manner of exercising, §1-75.9.

IN REM JURISDICTION —Cont'd
Proof of jurisdiction.
Judgment against nonappearing defendant, §1-75.11.
Quasi in rem jurisdiction.
Grounds, §1-75.8.
Interlocutory orders for protection of rem, §1-75.9.
Manner of exercising, §1-75.9.
Proof of jurisdiction.
Judgment against nonappearing defendant, §1-75.11.
Requirements, §1-75.3, (c).
Requirements, §1-75.3, (c).
Service of process.
Manner of service to exercise, §1A-1, Rule 4, (k).

IN REM PROCEEDINGS.
Torrens system registration, §§43-1 to 43-64.
See TORRENS SYSTEM REGISTRATION.

INS.
Officers authorized to enforce criminal laws, §15A-406.

INSANITY.
Generally.
See MENTAL HEALTH, DEVELOPMENTAL DISABILITY, SUBSTANCE ABUSE.

INSANITY DEFENSE.
Civil commitment of defendant found not guilty by reason of insanity, §15A-1321.
DNA sample required for certain crimes, §15A-266.4.
Temporary restraint, §15A-1322.
Verdicts to so state, §15A-1237, (c).
Incapacity of defendant to proceed, §§15A-1001 to 15A-1009.
Notice of intent to raise, §15A-959.
Pretrial determination of insanity, §15A-959.

INSECTICIDES.
Pesticide applicators, §§143-452 to 143-459.
See PESTICIDE APPLICATORS.
Pesticide board generally.
See PESTICIDE BOARD.
Pesticide consultants, §§143-455, 143-456.
Pesticide dealers and manufacturers licenses, §§143-448 to 143-451.
Pesticide registration.
See PESTICIDE REGISTRATION.
Pesticides generally.
See PESTICIDES.

INSECTS.
Boll weevil eradication, §§106-65.67 to 106-65.78.
Mosquito and vector control program, §§130A-346 to 130A-349.
Mosquito control districts, §§130A-352 to 130A-358.
Pest control.
See PEST CONTROL.
State insect.
Honeybee, §145-7.
Structural pest control.
See STRUCTURAL PEST CONTROL.

INSECT STINGS.
Life-saving treatment to persons suffering severe adverse reaction.
Department of health and human services to promote means of training individuals to administer, §143-509.

INSIDER INFORMATION.
Public officers and employees.
Misuse of confidential information, §14-234.1.

INSIGNIAS.
Insurance companies, §58-3-50.
Motor vehicles.
Operation of vehicles resembling law enforcement vehicles prohibited, §20-137.2, (a).
Misdemeanor, §20-137.2, (b).

INSOLVENCY.
Bankruptcy and insolvency.
See BANKRUPTCY AND INSOLVENCY.
Banks.
See BANKS.
Prisoners.
Generally.
See DISCHARGE OF INSOLVENT PRISONERS.

INSPECTION OF MOTOR VEHICLES.
Generally, §§20-183.2 to 20-183.8G.
See MOTOR VEHICLE INSPECTIONS.

INSPECTIONS.
Administrative search and inspection warrants.
Authorized, §15-27.2, (a).
Construction and interpretation.
Not to be regarded as search warrants for certain purposes, §15-27.2, (g).
Evidence.
Use of facts obtained, §15-27.2, (f).
General search warrant provisions not to apply, §15A-259.
Health purposes, §130A-17.
Issuance.
Conditions, §15-27.2, (c).
Requirements, §15-27.2, (d).
Who may issue, §15-27.2, (b).
Period of validity, §15-27.2, (e).
Adult care homes, §131E-105.
Bill of rights.
Refusal to allow inspection, §131D-34, (d).
Agriculture.
Marketing and branding farm products.
Authorized inspections, §106-194.
Authorized inspectors, §106-190.
Farm product inspection account, §106-194.1.
Alcoholic beverages.
Authority to inspect licensed premises, §18B-502, (a).
Disposition of seized beverages, §18B-503.
Interference with inspections, §18B-502, (b).
State warehouse.
Private warehouses, §18B-204, (b).
Ambulatory surgical facilities.
Licensing of facilities, §131E-150, (a), (b).
Animal waste management, §143-215.10F.
Arson.
Failure of property owner to comply with public authorities, §14-68.
Barbers, §86A-15, (b).
Bees and honey.
Conduct of inspections and other activities, §106-643.
Moveable frame hives.
Inspection for disease or disorder, §106-641.
Penalties for preventing inspection, §106-644, (a), (b).
Boilers.
Certificates.
Defined, §95-69.9, (e).
Refusal to issue or renew, §95-69.17, (b), (c).
Required, §95-69.18.

INSPECTIONS —Cont'd
Boilers —Cont'd
Inspectors, §95-69.15.
Misrepresentation as inspector, §95-69.18.
Qualifications, §95-69.15, (c).
Powers and duties of commissioner, §95-69.11.
Required, §95-69.16.
Boll weevil eradication.
Entry of premises, §106-65.71.
Budgets.
Advisory budget commission.
Biennial inspection of physical facilities, §143-4.1.
Surveys, studies and examinations of departments and institutions, §143-22.
Building codes.
Local inspection departments.
Code officials qualification board.
Defined, §143-151.8, (a).
Building inspections.
County inspection departments, §§153A-350 to 153A-375.
See COUNTY INSPECTION DEPARTMENTS.
Buildings.
Municipal building inspection, §§160A-411 to 160A-438.
See MUNICIPAL BUILDING INSPECTION.
Cardiac rehabilitation certification program, §131E-170, (a), (b).
Clean water revolving loans and grants.
Inspection of project, §159G-14.
Commercial feed.
Description of samples obtained, §106-284.42.
Presentation of appropriate credentials, §106-284.42, (b).
Purpose of enforcement of article, §106-284.42, (a).
Refusing admission of commissioner or agent, §106-284.42, (d).
Reports and inspection fees, §106-284.40.
Cosmetic art, §88B-27.
Shops and schools, §88B-4, (b).
Operation of shop while board inspects for compliance, §88B-14, (c).
County inspection departments, §§153A-350 to 153A-375.
See COUNTY INSPECTION DEPARTMENTS.
County inspectors of articles of commerce, §§66-1 to 66-6.
Dams.
Dam safety law, §143-215.32.
Plans and specifications of dams, §113-263.
Right of entry, §143-215.37.
Donated food.
By department of agriculture and consumer services, §106-141.1.
Drugs.
Controlled substances, §90-107.
Economic and community development department.
Main street financial incentive fund, §143B-472.35, (j).
Emergency medical services.
Equipment sanitation, supply and design.
Inspection of ambulance for compliance, §131E-157, (b).
Fertilizers.
Commercial fertilizers.
Duty of commissioner to inspect, §106-662, (a).
Fees for inspection, §106-671, (a), (b).
Fire investigations and inspections of premises, §§58-79-1 to 58-79-45.

INSPECTIONS —Cont'd
Fires and fire protection, §58-79-20.
Fish and fishing.
Inspectors, §113-136.
Conflicts of interest, §113-225.
Seizure of lawfully discovered evidence, §113-137.
Warning tickets, §113-140.
Jurisdiction of fisheries agencies generally.
Seafood industrial park authority, §113-315.34.
Food, drug and cosmetic act.
Additives deemed unsafe, §106-132.
Donated food to be inspected, §106-141.1.
Manufacture of foods subject to contamination with microorganisms.
Permits governing manufacture, §106-131, (c).
Food, drugs and cosmetics.
Power of commissioner, §106-140, (a) to (c).
Gasoline and oil inspection, §§119-14 to 119-47.
See GASOLINE AND OIL INSPECTION.
Health care facilities.
Cardiac rehabilitation certification program, §131E-170, (a), (b).
Home care agencies, §131E-141.
Hospices, §131E-204.
Confidentiality of information, §131E-207, (a) to (c).
Hogs.
Feeding garbage to swine, §106-405.7, (a).
Home inspectors.
General provisions, §§143-151.43 to 143-151.63.
See HOME INSPECTORS.
Hospitals.
Licenses, §131E-80, (a) to (e).
Hotels, inns and other transient lodging places.
Sanitation of food and lodging establishments, §130A-249.
Ice cream plants, creameries and cheese factories generally, §§106-246 to 106-255.
Jails.
Local confinement facilities, §§153A-221.1, 153A-222.
Labor.
Commissioner of labor.
Powers generally, §95-4.
Department of labor.
Inspection service fees, §§95-107, 95-108.
Law enforcement agents.
Inspection of licensed premises, §18B-502.
Limestone, marl and landplaster.
Sale of agricultural liming materials and landplaster, §106-92.10.
Livestock.
Cattle tick.
Local state inspectors, §106-354.
Control of livestock diseases, §106-401.1.
Diseases.
Examination before slaughter, §106-549.17.
Hog cholera, §106-318.
Threat of disease imminent.
Warrantless inspection of vehicles, §106-399.5.
Local ABC officers.
Inspection of licensed premises, §18B-502.
Lubricating oils.
Commissioner of agriculture.
Duties of inspection devolve upon commissioner, §119-6.
Maternity homes.
Licensing of homes, §131D-1, (a).
Facilities subject to provisions, §131D-1, (b).

INSPECTIONS —Cont'd
Mattresses and bedding.
Examination of records of bedding, §130A-271, (d).
Opening seams of bedding to examine filling, §130A-271, (d).
Meat generally, §§106-549.15 to 106-549.39.
See MEAT INSPECTIONS.
Mental health, developmental disabilities and substance abuse.
Facilities.
Licenses, §122C-25.
Migrant farm workers.
Preoccupancy inspection.
Housing standards.
Application for inspection, §95-226.
Heating equipment.
When not required, §95-225, (e).
Milk and milk products.
Definitions, §106-268.
Enforcement, §106-268.
Promulgation of rules and regulations for inspection, §106-267.
Records and reports of milk distributors and processors.
Commissioner of agriculture authorized to inspect, §106-264.
Mines.
Reclamation, §74-56, (a).
Safety and health, §74-24.7, (a).
Authorized representative of miners to be allowed to accompany commissioner, §74-24.7, (g).
Request for inspection.
Notice to commissioner or director, §74-24.7, (f).
Right of entry, §74-24.7, (b).
Mobile homes.
Uniform standards code.
Inspection of service records, §143-143.22.
Mosquito control districts.
Corporate powers of board of commissioners, §130A-355.
Motor carrier safety regulation unit.
Penalty for failure to conduct safety inspection, §20-384.
Motor vehicles generally, §§20-183.2 to 20-183.8G.
See MOTOR VEHICLE INSPECTIONS.
Nurses.
Nursing pools, §131E-154.5.
Nursing homes, §131E-105, (a) to (c).
In accordance with rules adopted by commission, §131E-105, (a).
Patients' bill of rights.
Refusal to allow inspection.
Civil penalty, §131E-129, (d).
Review of records, §131E-105, (b).
Right of entry, §131E-105, (c).
Occupational safety and health.
Commissioner of labor.
Right of entry, §95-136, (a).
Subpoenas, §95-136, (b).
Director.
Powers as to, §95-133, (b).
Right of entry, §95-136, (a).
Employer and employee representatives.
Right to accompany and consult with commissioner or director, §95-136, (c).
Information obtained.
Powers of commissioner as to, §95-136, (e).

INSPECTIONS —Cont'd
Occupational safety and health —Cont'd
Notice, §95-136, (f).
Unauthorized advance notice.
Penalty, §95-139.
Reinspection.
Willful serious violation found, §95-136, (a).
Request for inspection, §95-136, (d).
Rules and regulations as to, §95-136, (g).
Special emphasis inspection program, §95-136.1.
Oil pollution and hazardous substances control, §143-215.79.
Confidential information, §143-215.80.
Pawnbrokers.
Law enforcement officers.
Pawn transactions, §91A-7, (d).
Personnel system.
Records.
Privacy of state employee personnel records.
Certain records to be kept by state agencies open to inspection, §126-23.
Files not subject to inspection, §126-22.
Pesticides.
Board may provide inspections, §143-466, (c), (d).
Plant pests.
Agents of board, §106-422.
Narcissus inspection, §106-423.
Nursery inspection, §106-423.
Pollution control.
Sedimentation pollution control act of 1973.
Land-disturbing activities.
Periodic inspections, §113A-61.1, (a), (b).
Poultry products, §§106-549.49 to 106-549.69.
See POULTRY PRODUCTS INSPECTIONS.
Private schools.
Sanitation, §130A-237.
Proprietary schools, §115D-89.
Public building contracts.
Safety officers, §143-135.7.
Public schools.
Fire hazards.
Inspection of schools for fire hazards, §115C-525, (b).
Sanitation, §130A-237.
Rabbits.
Poultry products inspection.
Applicability of article to domesticated products, §106-549.51A.
Records.
Public records, §132-6.
Right of entry generally.
See RIGHT OF ENTRY.
Riots.
Motor vehicles in or approaching riots area, §14-288.11.
Sale of goods, UCC.
Buyer's right to inspect goods, §25-2-513.
Disputed goods.
Preserving evidence of goods in dispute, §25-2-515.
Sales.
Disposition of seized alcoholic beverages.
Procedure, §18B-503, (e).
Proceeds of sale, §18B-503, (f).
Schools.
Sanitation standards.
Principal to make inspection, §130A-237.
Seeds.
Agricultural and vegetable seeds to be inspected, §106-277.21.

INSPECTIONS —Cont'd
Seeds —Cont'd
Right of entry for purpose of inspection, §106-277.20.
Social services.
Local confinement facilities, §131D-11.
Soil additives act.
Sampling and inspection of additives, §106-50.36.
Solid waste management.
Projects for which loans made, §159I-27, (a), (b).
Structural pest control.
Violations of article, §106-65.30, (a), (c).
Toxic substances.
Identification.
Fire chief, §95-194, (c).
Tramways.
Passenger tramways.
Commissioner of labor, §95-121.
Transportation department.
Highway inspection reports.
Falsifying reports, §136-13.2.
Vegetables, §106-284.19.
Veterinarians.
Power of board, §90-186.
Wage and hour act.
Commissioner of labor, §95-25.15, (a).
Warrants.
Administrative search and inspection warrants, §15-27.2.
Wastewater systems.
Required before systems covered or placed into use, §130A-337, (a).
Waters and watercourses.
Use of water resources.
Capacity use areas, §143-215.19, (a) to (e).
Weights and measures.
Duties of commissioner, §81A-15.
Wildlife protectors.
Entry and inspection of licensed or commercial premises, §113-302.1.

INSPECTION SERVICE FEES BY DEPARTMENT OF LABOR.
Assessment and collections, §95-107.
Certificates of safe operation, §95-107.
Disposition of fees, §95-108.

INSTALLATION CHARGES.
Sales and use tax.
Exemption, §105-164.13.

INSTALLMENT CONTRACTS.
Leases, UCC.
Default.
Defined, §25-2A-103, (1).
Lessee's rights and remedies, §25-2A-508.
Rejection and default, §25-2A-510.
Sale of goods, UCC, §25-2-612.

INSTALLMENT LAND SALES DISCLOSURES, §§47E-1 to 47E-10.
See RESIDENTIAL PROPERTY DISCLOSURE ACT.

INSTALLMENT LOANS.
Corporations, §53-176, (f).
Due date of first payment, §53-176, (e).
Election to make loan under, §53-176, (d).
Loan processing fee, §53-176, (b).

INSTALLMENT PURCHASE CONTRACTS.
Department of administration.
Purchasing buildings , utilities and structures, §143-341.

INSTALLMENT PURCHASE CONTRACTS —Cont'd
Public school equipment, §115C-528.

INSTALLMENT SALES.
See RETAIL INSTALLMENT SALES.

INSTITUTE OF MEDICINE, §90-470.

INSTITUTIONAL FUNDS.
Management of institutional funds, §§36B-1 to 36B-10.
See MANAGEMENT OF INSTITUTIONAL FUNDS.

INSTRUCTIONS TO JURY.
Comment on verdict prohibited, §1A-1, Rule 51, (c).
Criminal procedure, §§15A-1231, 15A-1232.
Additional instructions, §15A-1234.
Capital punishment.
Consequences of guilty verdict, §15-176.4.
Conference on instructions, §15A-1231, (b).
Deliberations.
Instructions as to, §15A-1235, (a), (b).
Error in instructions to prejudice of defendant.
Grounds for correction of errors by appellate division, §15A-1442.
Failure to object not waiver of right to appeal, §15A-1231, (d).
Impaneling jury.
Instruction by clerk, §15A-1216.
Opinion.
Prohibited, §15A-1232.
Removal of disruptive defendant.
Instruction that removal not to be considered in deliberations, §15A-1032, (b).
Tender of instructions by parties, §15A-1231, (a).
Judge to explain law but give no opinion on facts, §1A-1, Rule 51, (a).
Judicial notice of adjudicative facts, §8C-1, Rule 201, (g).
Limiting instruction on admissibility, §8C-1, Rule 105.
Opinion of facts.
Judge to explain law but give no opinion on facts, §1A-1, Rule 51, (a).
Punitive damages, §1D-40.
Special instructions.
Requests for, §§1-181, (a) to (c), 1A-1, Rule 51, (b).
Violent habitual felons, §14-7.11.

INSUFFICIENCY OF PROCESS OR SERVICE.
Defense by pretrial motion, §1A-1, Rule 12, (b).

INSUFFICIENCY OF THE EVIDENCE.
New trial.
Grounds for motion, §1A-1, Rule 59, (a).

INSULIN.
Food, drug and cosmetic act.
Drugs deemed misbranded, §106-134.
Sales and use tax exemption, §105-164.13.

INSURABLE INTEREST.
Artworks on consignment, §25C-5.
Life insurance, §§58-58-70 to 58-58-86.
See LIFE INSURANCE.

INSURANCE.
Accident and health insurance.
Generally.
See ACCIDENT AND HEALTH INSURANCE.
Health insurance portability and accountability, §§58-68-25 to 58-68-75.
See HEALTH INSURANCE PORTABILITY AND ACCOUNTABILITY.

INSURANCE —Cont'd
Accident and health insurance —Cont'd
Hospital, medical and dental service corporations, §§58-65-1 to 58-66-40.
See HOSPITAL, MEDICAL AND DENTAL SERVICE CORPORATIONS.
Jurisdiction over providers of health care benefits.
Determination generally, §§58-49-1 to 58-49-25.
See HEALTH CARE BENEFITS PROVIDERS.
Life and health insurance guaranty association, §§58-62-2 to 58-62-95.
See LIFE AND HEALTH INSURANCE GUARANTY ASSOCIATION.
Long-term care insurance, §§58-55-1 to 58-55-50.
See LONG-TERM CARE INSURANCE.
Medicare supplement insurance, §§58-54-1 to 58-54-50.
See MEDICARE.
Multiple employer welfare arrangements.
Regulation generally, §§58-49-30 to 58-49-65.
See HEALTH CARE BENEFITS PROVIDERS.
Small employer group health coverage, §§58-50-105 to 58-50-150.
See SMALL EMPLOYER GROUP HEALTH COVERAGE.
Third party administrators, §§58-56-2 to 58-56-66.
See THIRD PARTY ADMINISTRATORS.
Actions.
Health care liability.
Negligent decision of health benefit plan providers, §§90-21.50 to 90-21.56.
Actuaries.
See ACTUARIES.
Adjusters.
See INSURANCE ADJUSTERS.
Administrative procedure.
Hearings.
Department of insurance and commissioner of insurance.
Special provisions, §§150B-38 to 150B-42.
Aged persons.
Accident and health insurance.
Joint action to insure elderly, §§58-52-1 to 58-52-25.
See ACCIDENT AND HEALTH INSURANCE.
Agencies.
Examination.
Commissioner of other authorized employee, §58-2-195, (e).
Records.
Commissioner may require, §58-2-195, (a).
Employee responsible for keeping.
Required, §58-2-195, (b).
Enforcement of provisions, §58-2-195, (d).
Violations of provisions, §58-2-195, (c).
Reports.
Commissioner may require, §58-2-195, (a).
Employee responsible for making.
Required, §58-2-195, (b).
Violations of provisions, §58-2-195, (c), (d).
Agents.
See INSURANCE AGENTS.
Agricultural finance authority.
Agricultural loans, §122D-9.
Alarm systems licensing.
Liability insurance.
Cancellation of policy, §74D-9, (e).

INSURANCE —Cont'd
Alarm systems licensing —Cont'd
Liability insurance —Cont'd
Certificate of insurance to be maintained on file, §74D-9, (f).
Requirements, §74D-9, (d).
Alcoholic beverages.
County alcoholic beverage control board.
Defense of employees and officers.
Insurer provides defense, §160A-167.
Alien insurance companies.
Generally.
See FOREIGN OR ALIEN INSURANCE COMPANIES.
Amusement device safety.
Liability insurance, §95-111.12.
Annuities.
See ANNUITIES.
Artwork on consignment.
Provisions as to insurable interest.
Not affected, §25C-5.
Assessment companies.
See ASSESSMENT COMPANIES.
Attorneys' fees.
Allowance of counsel fees as part of costs, §6-21.1.
Authorized kinds of insurance, §58-7-15.
Banks.
Deposit insurance.
Requirements, §53-9.1.
Beach area essential property insurance.
Generally, §§58-45-1 to 58-45-90.
See BEACH AREA ESSENTIAL PROPERTY INSURANCE.
Underwriting associations, §§58-45-10 to 58-45-80.
See BEACH AREA ESSENTIAL PROPERTY INSURANCE.
Brokers.
See INSURANCE BROKERS.
Building code council.
Department of insurance.
Transfer to department, §143A-78.
Burial insurance.
Mutual burial associations, §§90-210.80 to 90-210.107.
See MUTUAL BURIAL ASSOCIATIONS.
Cancellation of insurance.
See INSURANCE POLICIES OR CONTRACTS.
Ceding insurer.
Generally.
See REINSURANCE.
Childbirth.
Maternity coverage, §§58-3-169, 58-3-170.
Child support.
Medical insurance, §50-13.11.
Citation of law.
Short title, §58-1-1.
Claims.
Secured transactions.
Inapplicability of article 9.
Transfers of policy interest or assignment of claim, §25-9-109, (d).
Transfer of interest or claims in policy excluded, §25-9-104, (g).
Supervision, rehabilitation and liquidation of insurers, §§58-30-185 to 58-30-235.
See INSURER SUPERVISION, REHABILITATION AND LIQUIDATION.
Claims against the state.
Assignments of claims against state.
Medical, hospital, disability or life insurance.
Assignment in favor of company for, §143-3.3, (c).

INSURANCE —Cont'd
Collision insurance.
Authorized, §58-7-15.
Commercial code generally.
Policy or certificate as prima facie evidence, §25-1-202.
Commissioner, §§58-2-1 to 58-2-230.
See INSURANCE COMMISSIONER.
Community colleges.
Annuity contracts, §115D-25.
Fire and casualty insurance on institutional buildings and contents.
Funding, §115D-58.11, (b).
Purchase authorized, §115D-58.11, (c).
Purchase required, §115D-58.11, (a).
Health insurance for employees, §115C-340, (a), (b).
Liability insurance, §115D-58.12, (a) to (e).
State funds to pay premiums, §115D-31.1.
Companies.
Generally.
See INSURANCE COMPANIES.
Company police, §74E-3.
Compromise and settlement.
Advance or partial payments.
Effect, §1-540.3, (a).
Motor vehicles.
Property damage claims arising from motor vehicle collisions or accidents.
Settlement not to constitute admission of liability nor bar party seeking damages for bodily injury or death, §1-540.2.
Condominiums.
Property and liability insurance, §47C-3-113.
Assessment to pay costs, §47C-3-115, (c).
Confidentiality.
Consumer and customer information.
Generally, §§58-39-1 to 58-39-165.
See INSURANCE CONSUMER AND CUSTOMER INFORMATION PRIVACY.
Continuing care retirement communities.
General provisions, §§58-64-1 to 58-64-85.
See CONTINUING CARE RETIREMENT COMMUNITIES.
Continuing education program for licensees, §§58-33-130, 58-33-135.
Contribution.
Joint tort-feasors.
Rights of liability insurer, §1B-1, (e).
Cotton.
Warehouses, §106-451.11, (b).
Counties.
Defense of employees and officers.
Civil and criminal actions.
Insurer provides defense, §160A-167.
Liability insurance, §153A-435, (a), (b).
Public officers and employees, §153A-92.
Rail transportation liability.
Contracts allocating financial responsibility.
Insurance required, §153-279, (c).
Credit cards.
Credit card guaranty or collateral.
Prohibited, §58-3-147.
Solicitation, negotiation or payment of premiums through credit card facilities, §58-3-145.
Credit insurance, §§58-57-1 to 58-57-115.
See CREDIT INSURANCE.
Credit scoring.
Motor vehicle or property insurance, §58-36-90.

INSURANCE —Cont'd
Credit unions.
Members.
Cooperative marketing arrangements to facilitate members' purchase of, §54-109.75, (b).
Purchase of insurance for, §54-109.75, (a).
Officers.
Liability insurance for, §54-109.76.
Share and deposit insurance, §54-109.78, (a).
Prerequisite to granting of charter, §54-109.78, (b).
Customer information safeguards act.
Generally, §§58-39-130 to 58-39-165.
See INSURANCE CONSUMER AND CUSTOMER INFORMATION PRIVACY.
Decedents' estates.
Killing decedents.
Proceeds payable to slayer, §31A-11, (a).
Deceptive trade practices.
Generally, §§58-63-1 to 58-63-70.
See INSURANCE UNFAIR TRADE PRACTICES.
Definitions, §58-1-5.
Accident, accidental injury and accidental means, §58-3-30, (b).
Applicability of definitions, §58-3-30, (a).
Accident and health insurance.
Blanket accident and health insurance, §58-51-75, (a).
Credit accident and health insurance, §58-51-100.
Franchise accident and health insurance, §58-51-90.
Group accident and health insurance, §58-51-80, (a).
Hospitalization insurance, §58-51-105.
Industrial sick benefit insurance, §58-51-65.
Joint action to insure elderly, §58-52-1.
Pharmacy of choice, §58-51-37, (b).
Beach area property essential property insurance, §§58-45-5, 58-45-6.
Credit insurance, §58-57-5.
Credit property insurance.
Dual credit property, §58-57-90, (a).
Personal household property, §58-57-90, (a).
Single interest credit property, §58-57-90, (a).
"Equity security," §58-7-145, (f).
Health insurance portability and accountability, §58-68-25, (a), (b).
Guaranteed availability of individual coverage to certain individuals with prior group coverage, §58-68-60, (b), (h).
Preexisting condition exclusion, §58-68-30, (b).
Holding companies, §58-19-5.
Insurance premium financing, §58-35-1.
Life and health insurance guaranty association, §58-62-16.
Life insurance.
Credit life insurance, §58-58-10.
Domestic insurance companies, §58-7-15.
Employee life insurance, §58-58-150.
Industrial life insurance, §58-58-5.
Policies.
Interest rates on life insurance policy loans, §58-61-5.
Prearrangement insurance policy provisions, §58-60-35, (a).
Requisites of contract, §58-58-1.
Solicitation, §58-60-10.

INSURANCE —Cont'd
Definitions —Cont'd
Long-term care insurance, §58-55-20.
Facilities, services and conditions, §58-55-35.
Medicare supplement insurance, §58-54-1.
Motor vehicle reinsurance facility, §58-37-1.
Post-assessment insurance guaranty association, §58-48-20.
Preferred providers, §58-50-56, (a).
Rates, §§58-40-5, 58-40-10.
Readable policies, §58-38-15.
"Text," §58-38-25, (e).
Reciprocal insurance, §58-15-5.
Reinsurance intermediary, §58-9-2, (a).
Risk retention groups, §58-22-10.
Small employer group health coverage, §58-50-110.
Supervision, rehabilitation and liquidation of insurers, §58-30-10.
Surplus lines, §58-21-10.
Third party administrators, §58-56-2.
Unauthorized insurers false advertising process act, §58-29-5.
Unfair trade practices, §58-63-5.
Utilization review, §58-50-61, (a).
Department.
See INSURANCE DEPARTMENT.
Deposits.
Banks.
Requirements as to deposit insurance, §53-9.1.
Disability income insurance.
Standards for policies, §58-51-130.
Disability insurance.
Accident and health insurance generally.
See ACCIDENT AND HEALTH INSURANCE.
Discovery.
Scope of discovery.
Insurance agreements, §1A-1, Rule 26, (b).
Discrimination by insurance companies.
Prohibited acts, §58-3-120.
Domestic reciprocals, §§58-15-100 to 58-15-150.
See RECIPROCAL INSURANCE.
Drive-thru deliveries, §58-3-169.
Duress.
Statements, releases, etc., obtained from persons in shock or under the influence of drugs.
Presumption of fraud, §8-45.5.
Education.
Continuing education program for licensees, §§58-33-130, 58-33-135.
Local boards of education.
Liability insurance, §115C-42.
Electrical materials, devices, appliances and equipment sales.
Acceptable listings as to safety of goods, §66-25.
Legal responsibility for proper insulation unaffected, §66-26.
Liability.
Effect of provisions, §66-26.
Elevator insurance.
Authorized, §58-7-15.
Embezzlement.
Agents, brokers or administrators embezzling money or substitutes for money, §58-2-162.
Reports, §58-2-163.
Emblems.
Companies, §58-3-50.
Emergency care.
Coverage required, §58-3-190.

INSURANCE —Cont'd
Employer discrimination against lawful use of lawful products during nonworking hours.
Health, disability or life insurance policies distinguishing between employees, §95-28.2, (b).
Employment security.
General provisions, §§96-1 to 96-29.
See UNEMPLOYMENT COMPENSATION.
Evidence.
Documents executed by commissioner.
Certificate as evidence of authority to do business, §58-2-115.
Originals and certified copies, §58-2-110.
Liability insurance.
Existence inadmissible, §8C-1, Rule 411.
Mental health area authorities, §122C-152, (f).
Tort action against community college trustees, §115D-58.12, (d).
Policy or certificate as prima facie evidence, §25-1-202.
Examinations by commissioner.
Generally.
See INSURANCE COMMISSIONER.
Exemptions from general insurance laws, §58-24-110.
Fair access to insurance requirements, §§58-46-1 to 58-46-60.
See PROPERTY INSURANCE.
False statement to procure or deny benefit, §58-2-161.
Family leave credit insurance, §58-57-115.
Fidelity and surety insurance, §58-7-15.
Foreign or alien insurance companies.
Deposits.
Required, §58-5-10.
Fiduciaries, §32-27.
Financial responsibility.
Motor vehicles generally, §§20-279.1 to 20-284.
See MOTOR VEHICLE FINANCIAL RESPONSIBILITY.
Fire department.
Volunteer fire department.
Defense of employees and officers.
Insurer provides defense, §160A-167.
Fire insurance.
See FIRE INSURANCE.
Fish and fisheries resources.
Hull insurance, protection and indemnity clubs, §§58-20-1 to 58-20-40.
See HULL INSURANCE, PROTECTION AND INDEMNITY CLUBS.
Foreign or alien insurance companies.
See FOREIGN OR ALIEN INSURANCE COMPANIES.
Fraternal benefit societies.
Directors, officers, employees or agents.
Powers of society to purchase and maintain insurance, §58-24-25, (c).
Fraternal orders.
General provisions, §§58-25-1 to 58-25-70.
See FRATERNAL ORDERS.
Fraud.
Arson, §14-65.
Burning of personal property, §14-66.
Statements, releases, etc., obtained from persons in shock or under the influence of drugs.
Presumption of fraud, §8-45.5.
General contractor's board.
Liability insurance, authority to purchase, §87-9.1, (b).

INSURANCE —Cont'd
Group insurance.
Accident and health insurance.
Generally.
See ACCIDENT AND HEALTH INSURANCE.
Annuities.
Group annuity contracts, §58-58-145.
Assignment of interest in, §58-58-155.
Commissioner.
Approval of master plan and certificates, §58-3-20.
Life insurance generally.
See LIFE INSURANCE.
Restrictions on group plans, §58-3-20.
Small employer group health coverage, §§58-50-100 to 58-50-150.
See SMALL EMPLOYER GROUP HEALTH COVERAGE.
Guardian's powers in administering incompetent's estate, §35A-1251.
Handicapped persons.
Discrimination.
Prohibited, §168-10.
Health benefit plan external review, §§58-50-75 to 58-50-95.
See ACCIDENT AND HEALTH INSURANCE.
Health benefit plans.
Generally, §§58-3-167 to 58-3-178, 58-3-190 to 58-3-265.
See ACCIDENT AND HEALTH INSURANCE.
Health care benefits providers.
Determination of jurisdiction over, §§58-49-1 to 58-49-25.
See HEALTH CARE BENEFITS PROVIDERS.
Regulation of multiple employer welfare arrangements, §§58-49-30 to 58-49-65.
See HEALTH CARE BENEFITS PROVIDERS.
Health care liability.
Negligent decision of health benefit plan providers, §§90-21.50 to 90-21.56.
Health care providers insurance payment claims not timely processed due to year 2000 date change.
Definitions, §58-2-235, (c).
Interim payments by insurer to providers, §58-2-235.
Payment in full, when considered, §58-2-235, (c).
Recovery of excess payment, §58-2-235, (c).
Report by insurer, §58-2-235, (a).
Health departments.
District health departments.
District boards of health.
Authority to provide liability insurance, §130A-37, (k).
Health insurance.
Accident and health insurance generally.
See ACCIDENT AND HEALTH INSURANCE.
Credit insurance generally, §§58-57-1 to 58-57-115.
See CREDIT INSURANCE.
Group insurance.
Student coverage, §58-51-81, (a).
Health insurance portability and accountability, §§58-68-25 to 58-68-75.
See HEALTH INSURANCE PORTABILITY AND ACCOUNTABILITY.
Health maintenance organizations, §§58-67-1 to 58-67-185.
See HEALTH MAINTENANCE ORGANIZATIONS.

INSURANCE —Cont'd
Holding companies, §§58-19-1 to 58-19-70.
See INSURANCE HOLDING COMPANIES.
Home appliance service agreement companies, §§58-1-25 to 58-1-36.
See HOME APPLIANCE SERVICE AGREEMENT COMPANIES.
Homicide.
Killing decedents.
Additional liability for insurance company, §31A-11, (c).
Decedent beneficiary, §31A-11, (b).
Proceeds payable to slayer, §31A-11, (a).
Hospital, medical and dental service corporations, §§58-65-1 to 58-66-40.
See HOSPITAL, MEDICAL AND DENTAL SERVICE CORPORATIONS.
Housing finance agency.
Mortgage insurance authority, §122A-5.2.
Procuring insurance against losses.
General power of agency, §122A-5.
Hull insurance, protection and indemnity clubs, §§58-20-1 to 58-20-40.
See HULL INSURANCE, PROTECTION AND INDEMNITY CLUBS.
Human service and volunteer transportation.
Classification of transportation, §62-289.4.
Volunteer transportation, §62-289.6.
Incapacitated persons.
Proceeds belonging to incapacitated adult as beneficiary on death of insured.
Payment to and receipt by clerk of superior court or public guardian, §7A-111, (b), (d).
Information privacy protection.
Consumer and customer information.
Generally, §§58-39-1 to 58-39-165.
See INSURANCE CONSUMER AND CUSTOMER INFORMATION PRIVACY.
Information to be furnished to commissioner, §58-6-20.
Insurance information and privacy act.
Generally, §§58-39-1 to 58-39-76.
See INSURANCE CONSUMER AND CUSTOMER INFORMATION PRIVACY.
Insurance regulatory information system.
Test data.
Not public records, §58-2-220.
Insurance scores.
Motor vehicle or property insurance, §58-36-90.
Jurisdiction.
Personal jurisdiction.
Grounds, §1-75.4.
Kinds of insurance authorized, §58-7-15.
Labor.
Discrimination against lawful use of lawful products during nonworking hours prohibited.
Health, disability or life insurance policies distinguishing between employees, §95-28.2, (b).
Landlord and tenant.
Lien on crops, §42-15.1.
Law-enforcement officers.
Separate insurance benefits plan for law-enforcement officers, §143-166.60, (a) to (h).
Leases, UCC.
Leased goods, §25-2A-218.
Lending institutions.
Not to require insurance as condition of loan, §58-3-135.

INSURANCE —Cont'd
Liability insurance.
Counties.
Purchase, waiver of governmental immunity, §153A-435, (a), (b).
District health departments.
District boards of health.
Authority to provide insurance, §130A-37, (k).
General contractor's board.
Authority to purchase, §87-9.1, (b).
Mental health, developmental disabilities and substance abuse.
Area authorities.
Agents, employees and board members to secure insurance, §122C-152, (a) to (f).
Motor vehicle insurance generally.
See MOTOR VEHICLE INSURANCE.
Occupational licensing boards, §93B-16, (a), (b), (c).
Personal watercraft rental businesses, §75A-13.3, (c1).
Failure to carry, misdemeanor, fine, §75A-18, (c1).
Risk retention groups generally, §§58-22-1 to 58-22-70.
See RISK RETENTION GROUPS.
Structural pest control.
Financial responsibility of licensee or certified applicator or other applicants, §106-65.37, (a).
Volunteer immunity.
Volunteers performing services for charitable organizations.
Waiver of immunity if covered by liability insurance, §1-539.10, (b).
Liability insurance commission, §§58-32-1 to 58-32-30.
See LIABILITY INSURANCE COMMISSION.
Life and health insurance guaranty association, §§58-62-2 to 58-62-95.
See LIFE AND HEALTH INSURANCE GUARANTY ASSOCIATION.
Life insurance.
Credit life insurance generally, §§58-57-1 to 58-57-115.
See CREDIT INSURANCE.
Generally, §§58-58-1 to 58-61-15.
See LIFE INSURANCE.
Life and health insurance guaranty association, §§58-62-2 to 58-62-95.
See LIFE AND HEALTH INSURANCE GUARANTY ASSOCIATION.
Third party administrators, §§58-56-2 to 58-56-66.
See THIRD PARTY ADMINISTRATORS.
Viatical settlements, §§58-58-200 to 58-58-310.
See VIATICAL LIFE INSURANCE SETTLEMENTS.
Limited liability companies.
Purchase on behalf of managers, directors, executives, employees or agents of company, §57C-3-32, (c).
Limited representatives.
See INSURANCE LIMITED REPRESENTATIVES.
Liquefied petroleum gas.
Dealers.
Liability insurance or substitute required, §119-56.
"Lloyds" insurance association, §58-17-1.
Loans.
Interest rates on life insurance policy loans, §§58-61-1 to 58-61-15.

INSURANCE —Cont'd
Loans —Cont'd
Lender requiring borrower to deal with particular insurer, §§75-17 to 75-19.
Local government risk pools, §§58-23-1 to 58-23-40.
See LOCAL GOVERNMENT RISK POOLS.
Long-term care insurance, §§58-55-1 to 58-55-50.
See LONG-TERM CARE INSURANCE.
Managing general agents, §§58-34-2 to 58-34-15.
See MANAGING GENERAL INSURANCE AGENTS.
Mandatory or voluntary risk sharing plans, §§58-42-1 to 58-42-50.
See MANDATORY OR VOLUNTARY RISK SHARING PLANS.
Marine insurance.
Foreign or alien insurance companies.
Deposits.
Required, §58-5-5.
Limitation of risk.
Exception as to, §58-3-105.
Mutual insurance companies.
Surplus.
Requirements, §58-7-75.
Market assistance program.
Good faith immunity from operation of programs, §58-40-135.
Marriage.
Married may insure spouse's life, §52-3.
Mass gatherings.
Provisional permit.
Liability insurance, §130A-255, (c).
Maternity coverage, §§58-3-169, 58-3-170.
Mediation.
Prelitigation mediation of insurance claims, §7A-38.3A.
Medicaid.
ERISA plans may not require Medicaid to pay first, §58-51-116.
Medical service corporations.
Hospital, medical and dental service corporations, §§58-65-1 to 58-66-40.
See HOSPITAL, MEDICAL AND DENTAL SERVICE CORPORATIONS.
Medicare supplement insurance, §§58-54-1 to 58-54-50.
See MEDICARE.
Mental health, developmental disabilities and substance abuse.
Area authorities.
Agents, employees and board members to secure liability insurance, §122C-152, (a) to (f).
Minors.
Administration of insurance proceeds to which minor entitled, §35A-1227, (a).
Proceeds belonging to minor as beneficiary on death of insured.
Payment to and receipt by clerk of superior court or public guardian, §7A-111, (a), (c).
Missing persons.
Absentee insurance fund, §28C-19, (a), (b).
Determination that absentee not dead, §28C-18, (d).
Failure of insurer to pay, §28C-18, (b).
Payment of insurance policies, §28C-18, (a).
Required survivor of beneficiary.
Failure to establish, §28C-18, (c).

INSURANCE —Cont'd
Monopolies and restraint of trade.
Lender requiring borrower to deal with particular insurer.
Contempt.
Disregard of injunction or other court order, §75-19.
Injunction, §75-19.
Nondiscriminatory approval of insurer.
Lender may require, §75-18.
Penalty, §75-19.
Prohibited, §75-17.
Mortality tables, §§8-46, 8-47.
Mortgage guaranty insurance, §§58-10-120 to 58-10-135.
Mortgage insurance authority, §122A-5.2.
Mortgage insurance consolidations.
Commissioner authorized to adopt rules, §58-2-210.
Mortgages and deeds of trust.
Advances and future obligations.
Priority of payments, §45-70, (c).
Motor carriers.
Liability insurance, §62-268.
Motor clubs and associations, §§58-69-2 to 58-69-55.
See MOTOR CLUBS AND ASSOCIATIONS.
Motor vehicle insurance.
Financial responsibility generally, §§20-279.1 to 20-284.
See MOTOR VEHICLE FINANCIAL RESPONSIBILITY.
Generally.
See MOTOR VEHICLE INSURANCE.
Reinsurance facility generally, §§58-37-1 to 58-37-65.
See MOTOR VEHICLE INSURANCE.
Motor vehicle service agreement companies, §§58-1-25 to 58-1-36.
See MOTOR VEHICLE SERVICE AGREEMENT COMPANIES.
Multiple employer welfare arrangements.
Regulation generally, §§58-49-30 to 58-49-65.
See HEALTH CARE BENEFITS PROVIDERS.
Municipal corporations.
Defense of employees and officers.
Civil and criminal actions.
Insurer provides defense, §160A-167.
Employees.
Council may purchase life, health and other forms of insurance, §160A-162, (b).
Health insurance for employees, §160A-163, (e).
Railroads.
Contracts allocating financial responsibility.
Insurance required, §160A-326, (c).
Tort liability.
Waiver of immunity through insurance purchase, §160A-485.
Mutual burial associations, §§90-210.80 to 90-210.107.
See MUTUAL BURIAL ASSOCIATIONS.
Mutual insurance companies, §§58-8-1 to 58-8-60.
See MUTUAL INSURANCE COMPANIES.
Mutual life insurance companies.
Conversion of society into company, §58-24-70.
NAIC filing requirements.
Applicability of article, §58-4-1.
Filing requirements, §58-4-5, (a), (b).
Immunity of members of NAIC, §58-4-10.

INSURANCE —Cont'd
NAIC filing requirements —Cont'd
Revocation or suspension of certificate of authority, §58-4-15.
Scope of article, §58-4-1.
Test ratios, data or information generated.
Dissemination, §58-4-25.
Negligent decision of health benefit plan providers.
Health care liability, §§90-21.50 to 90-21.56.
Nonprofit corporations.
Purchase on behalf of directors, officers or employees, §55A-8-57, (b).
North Carolina rate bureau, §§58-36-1 to 58-36-110.
See RATE BUREAU.
Occupational licensing boards.
Commercial liability insurance, §93B-16, (a), (b), (c).
Pest control.
Insurance fund.
Articles of compact, §106-65.55.
Cooperation of state agencies with fund, §106-65.56.
Request for assistance.
Pest control compact, §106-65.59.
Physicians and surgeons.
Professional liability insurance.
Reports.
Award of damages or cancellation or nonrenewal of policy, §90-14.13.
Planned community act.
Common elements, §47F-3-113.
Policies.
See INSURANCE POLICIES OR CONTRACTS.
Post assessment insurance guaranty association, §§58-48-1 to 58-48-130.
See POST ASSESSMENT INSURANCE GUARANTY ASSOCIATION.
Powers of attorney.
Powers conferred by statutory short form, §32A-2.
Premium financing, §§58-35-1 to 58-35-100.
See INSURANCE PREMIUM FINANCING.
Premiums.
See INSURANCE PREMIUMS.
Premium tax, §§105-225.5 to 105-228.10.
Preneed funeral contracts and funds.
Sales of insurance policies not regulated by article, §90-210.71.
Privacy protection.
Consumer and customer information.
Generally, §§58-39-1 to 58-39-165.
See INSURANCE CONSUMER AND CUSTOMER INFORMATION PRIVACY.
Private protective services.
Adjusters.
Exemption from act, §74C-3, (b).
Certificate of liability insurance.
Cancellation by insurance carriers, §74C-10, (f).
Employees not required to obtain, §74C-10, (g).
Required, §74C-10, (e), (h).
Trainee permit.
Holder not required to obtain, §74C-10, (g).
Products liability.
Risk retention groups.
Generally, §§58-22-1 to 58-22-70.
See RISK RETENTION GROUPS.
Professional liability insurance.
Statements.
Annual statements by professional liability insurers, §58-2-170.

INSURANCE —Cont'd
Professional liability insurance —Cont'd
State officials and employees, §58-31-25.
Property insurance.
Beach area property essential property insurance, §§58-45-1 to 58-45-90.
See BEACH AREA ESSENTIAL PROPERTY INSURANCE.
Credit property insurance, §58-57-90.
Fair access to insurance requirements, §§58-46-1 to 58-46-60.
See PROPERTY INSURANCE.
Fire insurance.
Generally.
See FIRE INSURANCE.
Residential real property insurance.
Claim closed without payment.
Termination or refusal to issue or renew.
Prohibition, §58-36-115.
Inquiry as to policy provisions not resulting in claim.
Termination or refusal to issue or renew.
Prohibition, §58-36-115.
Protected cell companies, §§58-10-75 to 58-10-110.
See INSURANCE COMPANIES.
Public officers and employees.
Defense of state employees.
Coverage afforded excess coverage over any commercial liability insurance, §143-300.6, (c).
Employee insurance committee, §58-31-60, (b).
Selection of insurance product proposals.
Procedure, §58-31-60, (c1).
Payroll deductions, §58-31-60, (c).
Public school property.
State insurance, §§115C-533 to 115C-543.
See SCHOOL BUILDINGS AND PROPERTY.
Public schools.
Health insurance.
School employees, §115C-340, (a), (b).
Liability insurance.
Powers of local boards to secure, §115C-47.
Proceeds of claims, §115C-449.
School buses.
Liability insurance, §§115C-255, 115C-262.
Public works.
Design and construction insurance.
Purchase, §58-31-65, (a).
Owner controlled or wrap-up insurance program, §58-31-65, (a).
Definitions, §58-31-65, (b).
Self-insurance.
Providing, §58-31-65, (a).
Rate bureau, §§58-36-1 to 58-36-110.
See RATE BUREAU.
Rates, §§58-40-1 to 58-40-140.
See INSURANCE RATES.
Readable policies generally, §§58-38-1 to 58-38-40.
See INSURANCE POLICIES OR CONTRACTS.
Real property.
Warranties.
Real property warranty as contract of insurance, §58-1-20, (a).
Rebates.
Prohibited.
Premiums on credit insurance, §58-57-95.
Unfair trade practices.
Prohibited acts, §58-63-15.

INSURANCE —Cont'd
Reciprocal insurance, §§58-15-1 to 58-15-150.
Actions
Regional public transportation authority.
Contracts allocating financial responsibility.
Insurance required, §160A-626, (c).
Registers of deeds, §161-4.2.
Reinsurance.
See REINSURANCE.
Reinsurance intermediaries, §§58-9-2 to 58-9-26.
See REINSURANCE INTERMEDIARIES.
Rental car companies.
Limited license to sell insurance, §58-33-17.
Rescue squads.
Defense of employees and officers.
Civil and criminal actions.
Insurer provides defense, §160A-167.
Retail installment sales.
Certificates of insurance, §25A-36, (a).
Consumer credit installment sales contracts.
Additional charges for insurance, §25A-17, (c).
Premium included in contract.
Crediting to unpaid balance of the contract, §25A-36, (b).
Revolving charge account contracts.
Additional charges for insurance, §25A-17, (a).
Risk based capital requirements.
Insurance companies, §§58-12-2 to 58-12-70.
See INSURANCE COMPANIES.
Risk retention groups, §§58-22-1 to 58-22-70.
See RISK RETENTION GROUPS.
Sale of goods, UCC.
C.I.F. and C. & F. terms, §25-2-320.
Form of bill of lading required in overseas shipment, §25-2-323.
Net landed weight, §25-2-321.
Payment on arrival, §25-2-321.
Warranty of condition on arrival, §25-2-321.
Insurable interest in goods, §25-2-501.
Salvage vehicles.
Surrender of title to vehicle deemed salvage vehicle, §20-109.1.
Savings and loan associations.
Accounts.
Requirements, §54B-17.
Loans.
Insured or guaranteed loans, §54B-158.
Savings banks.
Accounts.
Required insurance, §54C-17.
School buildings and property.
State insurance of public school property, §§115C-533 to 115C-543.
See SCHOOL BUILDINGS AND PROPERTY.
School buses.
Liability insurance, §§115C-255, 115C-262.
Secured transactions.
Inapplicability of article 9.
Transfers of policy interest or assignment of claim, §25-9-109, (d).
Self-service storage companies.
Rental insurance.
Limited license, §58-33-18.
Service agreement companies.
Home appliances and motor vehicles generally, §§58-1-25 to 58-1-36.
Insurance requirements, §58-1-36.
Simultaneous death act.
Contracts of insurance.
Provision for distribution of property different from provisions of article, §28A-24-5.

INSURANCE —Cont'd
Simultaneous death act —Cont'd
Disposition of proceeds, §28A-24-4.
Small employer group health coverage, §§58-50-105 to 58-50-150.
See SMALL EMPLOYER GROUP HEALTH COVERAGE.
State fire and rescue commission, §§58-78-1 to 58-78-20.
See FIRE AND RESCUE COMMISSION.
State of North Carolina.
Assignment of claims against state.
Medical, hospital, disability or life insurance.
Section inapplicable to assignment in favor of insurance company for, §143-3.3, (c).
State property fire insurance fund, §§58-31-1 to 58-31-50.
See FIRE INSURANCE.
Structural pest control.
Liability insurance.
Financial responsibility of licensee or certified applicator or other applicants, §106-65.37, (a).
Supervision, rehabilitation and liquidation of insurers.
Generally, §§58-30-1 to 58-30-310.
See INSURER SUPERVISION, REHABILITATION AND LIQUIDATION.
Surplus lines, §§58-21-1 to 58-21-105.
See SURPLUS LINES INSURANCE.
Third party administrators.
Generally, §§58-56-2 to 58-56-66.
See THIRD PARTY ADMINISTRATORS.
Title insurance.
Generally, §§58-26-1 to 58-27-15.
See TITLE INSURANCE.
Title of law.
Short title, §58-1-1.
Town or county mutual insurance companies, §58-7-75.
Transfers to minors.
Investments and premiums on life insurance or endowment policy, §33A-12.
Transportation department.
Vessels operated by department.
Authority to insure vessels, §136-82.1.
Trusts and trustees.
Powers of trustees under express trust generally, §36A-136.
Trusts of death benefits.
Interest of trustee as beneficiary of life insurance policy.
Interest sufficient to support inter vivos or testamentary trust, §36A-100, (a).
Twisting with respect to insurance policies.
Insurance producers, prohibition, §58-33-75.
Unauthorized insurers.
Generally, §§58-28-1 to 58-28-45.
See UNAUTHORIZED INSURERS.
Unauthorized insurers false advertising process act.
Generally, §§58-29-1 to 58-29-25.
See UNAUTHORIZED INSURERS.
Unclaimed property generally, §§116B-51 to 116B-80.
See UNCLAIMED PROPERTY.
Underground storage tanks.
Leaking petroleum cleanup.
Pools authorized, §143-215.94I.
Underinsured motorists, §20-279.21, (b).

INSURANCE —Cont'd
Underwriting association.
Beach area essential property, §§58-45-10 to 58-45-80.
See BEACH AREA ESSENTIAL PROPERTY INSURANCE.
Undue influence.
Statements, releases, etc., obtained from persons in shock or under the influence of drugs.
Presumption of fraud, §8-45.5.
Unemployment insurance, §§96-1 to 96-29.
See UNEMPLOYMENT COMPENSATION.
Unfair trade practices.
Generally, §§58-63-1 to 58-63-70.
See INSURANCE UNFAIR TRADE PRACTICES.
Uninsured motorists, §20-279.21, (b).
Unit ownership, §47A-24.
University of North Carolina.
Board of governors.
Further action authorized, §116-223.
Power to secure insurance or provide self-insurance, §116-219.
Confidentiality of records, §116-222.
Defense of actions against covered persons, §116-220, (d).
Liability insurance trust fund council, §116-220, (c).
Nuclear reactors.
Purchase of insurance in connection with construction and operation, §116-40.2.
Self-insurance, §§116-220 to 116-220.2.
Sovereign immunity.
Provisions not deemed to waive sovereign immunity of state, §116-221.
Vessels.
Department of transportation.
Authority to insure vessels operated by department, §136-82.1.
Viatical settlements, §§58-58-200 to 58-58-310.
See VIATICAL LIFE INSURANCE SETTLEMENTS.
Violations of provisions.
Civil penalties or restitution, §58-2-70.
Volunteer fire department.
Department of insurance.
Transfer to department, §143A-79.
Warehouses.
Public warehousemen.
When insurance required, §66-38.
Western residence of the governor, §143-345.7.
Wills.
Renunciation.
Beneficiaries of life insurance policies.
Right to renounce succession, §31B-1, (a).
Mailing copy to insurance company, §31B-2, (c).
Workers' compensation insurance.
Generally.
See WORKERS' COMPENSATION INSURANCE.
Self-insurance, §§58-47-60 to 58-47-205.
See WORKERS' COMPENSATION.
Self-insurance guaranty association, §§97-130 to 97-143.
See SELF-INSURANCE GUARANTY ASSOCIATION.
Year 2000 date change.
Health care providers insurance payment claims not timely processed due to year 2000 date change.
Definitions, §58-2-235, (c).

INSURANCE —Cont'd
Year 2000 date change —Cont'd
Health care providers insurance payment claims not timely processed due to year 2000 date change —Cont'd
Interim payments by insurer to providers, §58-2-235.
Payment in full, when considered, §58-2-235, (c).
Recovery of excess payment, §58-2-235, (c).
Report by insurer, §58-2-235, (a).

INSURANCE ADJUSTERS.
Agent or limited representative.
Acting as adjuster, §58-33-70, (b).
Assumed name, operating under, §58-33-83.
Authorized companies.
Acting for, §58-33-115.
Bankruptcy, insolvency or receivership.
Commissioner to be notified, §58-33-46, (c).
Continuing education program for licensees, §58-33-130, (a).
Advisory committees, §58-33-135.
Compliance with provisions.
What constitutes, §58-33-130, (h).
Courses of study.
Approval by commissioner, §58-33-130, (i).
Fees established by commissioner, §58-33-130, (j).
Hour requirements, §58-33-130, (d), (e), (g).
Powers and duties of commissioner generally, §§58-33-130, 58-33-135.
Renewal of license.
Requirements for, §58-33-130, (c).
Discrimination.
Prohibited, §58-33-80.
Emergency insurance adjustments.
Permitted without license, §58-33-70, (e).
Learner's permit, §58-33-70, (c).
Licenses.
Acting without license, §§58-30-130, 58-33-120.
Applicability of article, §58-33-1.
Application, §58-33-31, (a).
Documents necessary to verify information, requiring, §58-33-31, (c).
Required, §58-33-30, (a).
Continuing education program for licensees, §§58-33-130, 58-33-135.
Definitions, §58-33-10.
Denial, §58-33-30, (g).
Duplicate licenses.
Lost, stolen or destroyed license, §58-33-50, (d).
Education and training, §58-33-30, (d).
Examination, §58-33-30, (e).
Exemptions, §58-33-35.
Exceptions to requirement, §58-33-26, (n).
Insurers, §58-33-26, (o).
Fees, §58-33-125, (a) to (g).
General requirements, §58-33-26, (a).
Interstate reciprocity.
Administrative action against licensee, reporting, §58-33-32, (k).
Application requirements, waiver, §58-33-32, (i).
Conditions for receiving nonresident license, §58-33-32, (c).
Continuing education requirements, satisfaction, §58-33-32, (j).
Criminal prosecutions, reporting, §58-33-32, (l).
Examination, when not required, §58-33-32, (g).
Greater fee not to be assessed, §58-33-32, (h).
Purposes of section, §58-33-32, (a).

INSURANCE ADJUSTERS —Cont'd
Licenses —Cont'd
Nonresident, §58-33-30, (h).
Interstate reciprocity, §58-33-32.
Reciprocity, §58-33-30, (j).
Retaliatory provisions, §58-33-30, (i).
Notice.
Suspension, revocation or nonrenewal, §58-33-50, (a), (b).
Reciprocity.
Interstate reciprocity, §58-33-32.
Required, §§58-33-5, 58-33-26, (b).
Surrender.
Termination of residency, §58-33-50, (c).
Suspension, revocation, refusal to renew, placing licensee on probation.
Authority of commissioner, §58-33-46, (a).
Grounds, §58-33-46, (a).
Issuance of another license, requirements, §58-33-46, (d).
Notice, §58-33-50, (a), (b).
Other provisions, applicability, §58-33-46, (b).
Temporary licensing.
Authority of commissioner to issue, §58-33-66, (a).
Grounds for issuing, §58-33-66, (a).
Limiting authority of temporary licensee, §58-33-66, (b).
Revoking, §58-33-66, (b).
Sponsor, requiring temporary licensee to have, §58-33-66, (b).
Termination on transfer of business, §58-33-66, (b).
Violations of insurance laws.
License not to be issued, §58-33-46, (e).
Violations of licensing laws.
Impositions of penalties or remedies, §58-33-46, (f).
Misdemeanors, §58-3-130.
Penalties.
Violations of insurance law generally, §58-3-130.
Practice of law.
Engaging in prohibited, §58-33-70, (a).
Referral of business to repair source.
Gratuity accepted for referral, prohibition, §58-33-76, (b).
Prohibition, §58-33-76, (a).
Violations, §58-33-76, (c).
Violation of insurance laws, §58-33-120.

INSURANCE AGENTS.
Actions.
Soliciting agent represents the company, §58-58-30.
Adverse underwriting decisions.
Reasons for making, obligation to give, §§58-39-55 to 58-39-65.
Agreements restricting agent's commission.
Prohibited, §58-43-30.
Applications for insurance.
False statement, §58-33-105.
Appointment as agent for insurer.
Accepting insurance application from person not appointed.
Prohibition, §58-33-40, (h).
Appointment fee, insurer to remit, §58-33-40, (d).
Authority upon being appointed, §58-33-40, (b).
Duration of appointment, §58-33-40, (e).
Agents with license in effect prior to statute's enactment, §58-33-40, (g).

INSURANCE AGENTS —Cont'd
Appointment as agent for insurer —Cont'd
Filing information on newly appointed agents.
Duty of insurer, §58-33-40, (c).
Malice in reporting, failure to report as required, §58-33-56, (l).
Notification of termination.
Additional information discovered, §58-33-56, (c).
Authority of commissioner as to materials received, §58-33-56, (i).
Comments concerning substance of notification, filing, §58-33-56, (e).
Confidentiality of materials obtained by commissioner, §58-33-56, (h).
No waiver of privilege or claim of confidentiality, §58-33-56, (j).
Copy of notification mailed to producer, §58-33-56, (d).
Grounds for suspension or revocation of license reason for termination, §58-33-56, (a).
Immunity for statements or information provided, §58-33-56, (f), (g).
Other grounds as reason for termination, §58-33-56, (b).
Releasing information on final adjudicated actions, §58-33-56, (k).
Renewal appointment fee, insurer to remit, §58-33-40, (f).
Required to act as agent for insurer, §58-33-40, (a).
Required to place insurance, §58-33-26, (i).
Revocation.
Suspension, revocation or refusal to renew license, §58-33-46, (d).
Temporary license because of death or disability of agent.
Representation of insurers that had appointed agent, §58-33-66, (e).
Termination.
Notification to commissioner, §58-33-56.
Who may be appointed, §58-33-40, (b).
Assumed name, operating under, §58-33-83.
Bankruptcy, insolvency or receivership.
Commissioner to be notified, §58-33-46, (c).
Charges in excess of premium prohibited, §58-33-85, (b).
Commissions.
Agreements restricting, §58-43-30.
Commissions, brokerage, service fee or other valuable consideration.
Assigning or directing payment, §58-33-82, (e).
License required to accept, §58-33-82, (d).
Renewal or other deferred commissions, §58-33-82, (c).
Unlicensed person, paying to or accepting, §58-33-82, (a), (b).
Companies not licensed to do business in state.
Soliciting for prohibited, §58-33-26, (h).
Confidentiality.
Consumer and customer information.
Generally, §§58-39-1 to 58-39-165.
See INSURANCE CONSUMER AND CUSTOMER INFORMATION PRIVACY.
Consumer reports.
Investigative consumer reports, §58-39-40.
Continuing education program for licensees, §58-33-130, (b).
Advisory committees.
Appointment, §58-33-135, (a).
Composition, §58-33-135, (b), (c).

INSURANCE AGENTS —Cont'd
Continuing education program for licensees —Cont'd
Commissioner.
Powers and duties of commissioner generally, §§58-33-130, 58-33-135.
Compliance with provisions.
What constitutes, §58-33-130, (h).
Courses of study.
Approval by commissioner, §58-33-130, (i).
Fees.
Establishment by commissioner, §58-33-130, (j).
Hour requirements, §58-33-130, (d), (e).
Carrying over to subsequent calendar year, §58-33-130, (g).
Renewal of license.
Requirement for, §58-33-130, (c).
Countersignatures, §58-33-60.
Credit information or credit scores of insurer used.
Indemnification.
Action, error or omission from use, §58-36-90, (e).
Customer information safeguards act, §§58-39-130 to 58-39-165.
See INSURANCE CONSUMER AND CUSTOMER INFORMATION PRIVACY.
Discrimination.
Prohibited, §58-33-80.
Embezzlement by insurance agents, §58-2-162.
Report to commissioner, §58-2-163.
Examination.
Commissioner or other authorized facility, §58-2-195, (e).
Indemnification.
Credit information or credit scores of insurer used.
Action, error or omission from use, §58-36-90, (e).
Information practices.
Notice, §§58-39-25 to 58-39-28.
Information privacy protection.
Consumer and customer information.
Generally, §§58-39-1 to 58-39-165.
See INSURANCE CONSUMER AND CUSTOMER INFORMATION PRIVACY.
Information security program, §§58-39-130 to 58-39-165.
Licenses.
Acting without license, §§58-3-130, 58-33-120.
Agent for United States military personnel in foreign countries, §58-33-15.
Applicability of article, §58-33-1.
Application, §58-33-31, (a).
Business entities, §58-33-31, (b).
Documents necessary to verify information, requiring, §58-33-31, (c).
Required, §58-33-30, (a).
Business entities, §58-33-26, (j).
Definitions, §58-33-10.
Denial, §58-33-30, (g).
Duplicate licenses.
Lost, stolen or destroyed license, §58-33-50, (d).
Education and training, §58-33-30, (d).
Examination, §58-33-30, (e).
Exemptions, §58-33-35.
Exceptions to requirement, §58-33-26, (n).
Insurers, §58-33-26, (o).
Fees, §58-33-120.
General requirements, §58-33-26, (a).

INSURANCE AGENTS —Cont'd
Licenses —Cont'd
Interstate reciprocity.
Administrative action against licensee, reporting, §58-33-32, (k).
Application requirements, waiver, §58-33-32, (i).
Conditions for receiving nonresident license, §58-33-32, (c).
Continuing education requirements, satisfaction, §58-33-32, (j).
Criminal prosecutions, reporting, §58-33-32, (l).
Examination, when not required, §58-33-32, (g).
Greater fee not to be assessed, §58-33-32, (h).
Purposes of section, §58-33-32, (a).
Surplus lines license, §58-33-32, (d).
Viatical settlement broker or provider, §58-33-32, (e).
Kinds of insurance agent may be licensed for, §58-33-26, (c).
Life and health insurance license.
Medicare supplements and long-term care insurance, authorized to sell, §58-33-26, (f).
Required to sell accident and health insurance, §58-33-26, (d).
Variable contracts, authorized to sell, §58-33-26, (e).
Name, social security number or other identifying number, §58-33-26, (k).
Nonresident, §58-33-30, (h).
Interstate reciprocity, §58-33-32.
Reciprocity, §58-33-30, (j).
Retaliatory provisions, §58-33-30, (i).
Notice.
Suspension, revocation or nonrenewal, §58-33-50, (a), (b).
Property and liability licensee.
Selling accident and health insurance prohibited, §58-33-26, (d).
Reciprocal insurance, §58-15-55.
Reciprocity.
Interstate reciprocity, §58-33-32.
Renewal, §58-33-26, (m).
Rental car companies.
Limited license to sell insurance, §58-33-17.
Required, §§58-33-5, 58-33-26, (b).
Restricted license for overseas military agents, §58-33-15.
Self service storage renter's insurance.
Limited license.
Issuance to self service storage company, §58-33-18.
Surplus lines insurance, §58-21-65.
Surrender.
Termination of residency, §58-33-50, (c).
Suspension, revocation, refusal to renew, placing licensee on probation.
Authority of commissioner, §58-33-46, (a).
Grounds, §58-33-46, (a).
Issuance of another license, requirements, §58-33-46, (d).
Notice, §58-33-50, (a), (b).
Other provisions, applicability, §58-33-46, (b).
Return to commissioner, §58-33-26, (l).
Revocation of appointment, §58-33-46, (d).
Temporary licensing, §58-33-65.
Authority of commissioner to issue, §58-33-66, (a).
Death or disability of agent.
Representation of insurers that had appointed agent at time of death or disability, §58-33-66, (c).

INSURANCE AGENTS —Cont'd
Licenses —Cont'd
Temporary licensing —Cont'd
Grounds for issuing, §58-33-66, (a).
Limiting authority of temporary licensee, §58-33-66, (b).
Revoking, §58-33-66, (b).
Sponsor, requiring temporary licensee to have, §58-33-66, (b).
Termination on transfer of business, §58-33-66, (b).
Title insurance company agents.
Annual license, §58-26-10.
Violations of insurance laws.
License not to be issued, §58-33-46, (e).
Violations of licensing laws.
Impositions of penalties or remedies, §58-33-46, (f).
Life insurance solicitation.
Information to be given prospective purchasers, §58-60-20, (b).
Misleading titles prohibited, §58-60-20, (c).
Regulation of solicitation generally, §§58-60-1 to 58-60-35.
See LIFE INSURANCE.
Limited representatives generally.
See INSURANCE LIMITED REPRESENTATIVES.
Liquidation of insurers.
Duties of agents.
Failure to provide information to liquidator, §58-30-127, (c).
Generally, §58-30-127, (a).
Policy issued through an agent, determination of, §58-30-127, (b).
Provisons of section are additional to other duties, §58-30-127, (d).
Managing general agents, §§58-34-2 to 58-34-15.
Misdemeanors.
Acting without license, §58-3-130.
Premiums.
Obtaining by fraud, §58-33-100, (b).
Notice.
Information practices, §§58-39-25 to 58-39-28.
Penalties, §58-3-130.
Policies.
Signing certain blank policies, §58-33-110.
Premiums.
Obtaining by fraud, §58-33-100, (b).
Payment to agent valid, §58-33-100, (a).
Privacy protection.
Consumer and customer information.
Generally, §§58-39-1 to 58-39-165.
See INSURANCE CONSUMER AND CUSTOMER INFORMATION PRIVACY.
Rebates.
Credit life and credit accident and health insurance, §58-33-90.
Rebates or discounts prohibited, §58-33-85, (a).
Reciprocal insurance.
Licenses, §58-15-55.
Records.
Commissioner may require, §58-2-195, (a).
Enforcement of provisions, §58-2-195, (d).
Violations of provisions, §58-2-195, (c).
Referral of business to repair source.
Gratuity accepted for referral, prohibition, §58-33-76, (b).
Prohibition, §58-33-76, (a).
Violations, §58-33-76, (c).

INSURANCE AGENTS —Cont'd
Rental car companies.
Limited license to sell insurance, §58-33-17.
Repair source, referral of business to, §58-33-76.
Reports.
Commissioner may require, §58-2-195, (a).
Enforcement of provisions, §58-2-195, (d).
Violations of provisions, §58-2-195, (c).
Representations.
Controversies between insured and insurer, §58-33-20.
Retention of funds by agent.
Credit life and credit accident and health insurance, §58-33-90.
Security program.
Information security program, §§58-39-130 to 58-39-165.
Self service storage renter's insurance.
Limited license.
Issuance to self service storage company, §58-33-18.
Supervision, rehabilitation and liquidation of insurers.
Duties of agents.
Failure to provide information to liquidator, §58-30-127, (c).
Generally, §58-30-127, (a).
Policy issued through an agent, determination of, §58-30-127, (b).
Provisons of section are additional to other duties, §58-30-127, (d).
Surplus lines insurance.
Licenses, §58-21-65.
Title insurance company agents.
Annual license, §58-26-10.
Twisting.
Prohibited, §§58-3-115, 58-33-75.
Unauthorized insurers.
Soliciting, negotiating or selling insurance for.
Civil action or license revocation proceeding, §58-33-95, (b).
Criminal penalty, §58-33-95, (a).
Strict liability for losses or unpaid claims, §58-33-95, (a).
Terms defined, §58-33-95, (c).
Violation of insurance laws, §58-33-120.

INSURANCE BROKERS.
Assumed name, operating under, §58-33-83.
Bankruptcy, insolvency or receivership.
Commissioner to be notified, §58-33-46, (c).
Charges in excess of premium prohibited, §58-33-85, (b).
Commissions, brokerage, service fee or other valuable consideration.
Assigning or directing payment, §58-33-82, (e).
License required to accept, §58-33-82, (d).
Renewal or other deferred commissions, §58-33-82, (c).
Unlicensed person, paying to or accepting, §58-33-82, (a), (b).
Companies not licensed to do business in state.
Soliciting for prohibited, §58-33-26, (h).
Continuing education program for licensees, §58-33-130, (b).
Advisory committees.
Appointments, §58-33-135, (a).
Composition, §58-33-135, (b), (c).
Compliance with provisions.
What constitutes, §58-33-130, (h).

INSURANCE BROKERS —Cont'd
Continuing education program for licensees —Cont'd
Courses of study.
Approval by commissioner, §58-33-130, (i).
Fees.
Establishment by commissioner, §58-33-130, (j).
Hour requirements, §58-33-130, (d), (e).
Carrying over to subsequent calendar year, §58-33-130, (g).
Powers and duties of commissioner generally, §§58-33-130, 58-33-135.
Renewal of license.
Requirement for, §58-33-130, (c).
Countersignatures, §58-33-60.
Discrimination.
Prohibited, §58-33-80.
Embezzlement by insurance brokers, §58-2-162.
Report to commissioner, §58-2-163.
Insurer-controlled brokers.
Definitions, §58-3-155, (a).
Determination of control, §58-3-155, (b).
Disclosures by broker, §58-3-155, (c).
Policyholders, claimants, etc.
Section not to affect rights of, §58-3-155, (d).
Licenses.
Acting without license, §§58-3-130, 58-33-120.
Applicability of article, §58-33-1.
Application, §58-33-31, (a).
Business entities, §58-33-31, (b).
Documents necessary to verify information, requiring, §58-33-31, (c).
Required, §58-33-30, (a).
Bond and other requirements, §58-33-30, (f).
Business entities, §58-33-26, (j).
Continuing education program for licensees, §§58-33-130, 58-33-135.
Definitions, §58-33-10.
Denial, §58-33-30, (g).
Duplicate licenses.
Lost, stolen or destroyed license, §58-33-50, (d).
Education and training, §58-33-30, (d).
Examination, §58-33-30, (e).
Exemptions, §58-33-35.
Exceptions to requirement, §58-33-26, (n).
Insurers, §58-33-26, (o).
Fees, §58-33-125, (a) to (g).
General requirements, §58-33-26, (a).
Interstate reciprocity.
Administrative action against licensee, reporting, §58-33-32, (k).
Application requirements, waiver, §58-33-32, (i).
Conditions for receiving nonresident license, §58-33-32, (c).
Continuing education requirements, satisfaction, §58-33-32, (j).
Criminal prosecutions, reporting, §58-33-32, (l).
Examination, when not required, §58-33-32, (g).
Greater fee not to be assessed, §58-33-32, (h).
Purposes of section, §58-33-32, (a).
Surplus lines license, §58-33-32, (d).
Kinds of insurance, §58-33-26, (c).
Name, social security number or other identifying number, §58-33-26, (k).
Nonresident, §58-33-30, (h).
Interstate reciprocity, §58-33-32.
Reciprocity, §58-33-30, (j).
Retaliatory provisions, §58-33-30, (i).
Notice.
Suspension, revocation or nonrenewal, §58-33-50, (a), (b).

INSURANCE BROKERS —Cont'd
Licenses —Cont'd
Reciprocity.
Interstate reciprocity, §58-33-32.
Renewal, §58-33-26, (m).
Required, §§58-33-5, 58-33-26, (b).
Surplus lines insurance, §58-21-65.
Surrender.
Termination of residency, §58-33-50, (c).
Suspension, revocation, refusal to renew, placing licensee on probation.
Authority of commissioner, §58-33-46, (a).
Grounds, §58-33-46, (a).
Issuance of another license, requirements, §58-33-46, (d).
Notice, §58-33-50, (a), (b).
Other provisions, applicability, §58-33-46, (b).
Temporary licensing, §58-33-65.
Authority of commissioner to issue, §58-33-66, (a).
Grounds for issuing, §58-33-66, (a).
Limiting authority of temporary licensee, §58-33-66, (b).
Revoking, §58-33-66, (b).
Sponsor, requiring temporary licensee to have, §58-33-66, (b).
Termination on transfer of business, §58-33-66, (b).
Violations of insurance laws.
License not to be issued, §58-33-46, (e).
Violations of licensing laws.
Impositions of penalties or remedies, §58-33-46, (f).
Limited representatives generally.
See INSURANCE LIMITED REPRESENTATIVES.
Misdemeanors, §58-3-130.
Premiums.
Obtaining by fraud, §58-33-100, (b).
Penalties, §58-3-130.
Premiums.
Obtaining by fraud, §58-33-100, (b).
Payment to broker valid, §58-33-100, (a).
Rebates or discounts prohibited, §58-33-85, (a).
Representation.
Controversies between insured and insurer, §58-33-20.
Surplus lines insurance.
Licenses, §58-21-65.
Twisting.
Prohibited, §58-33-75.
Unauthorized insurers.
Soliciting, negotiating or selling insurance for.
Civil action or license revocation proceeding, §58-33-95, (b).
Criminal penalty, §58-33-95, (a).
Strict liability for losses or unpaid claims, §58-33-95, (a).
Terms defined, §58-33-95, (c).
Violation of insurance laws, §58-33-120.

INSURANCE COMMISSIONER, §§58-2-1 to 58-2-230.
Accident and health insurance.
Credit insurance generally, §§58-57-1 to 58-57-115.
See CREDIT INSURANCE.
Forms.
Approval, §§58-51-85, 58-51-95, (a).
Group accident and health insurance.
Conversion privileges.
Premium rates and adjustments to be filed with commissioner, §58-53-60, (c).

INSURANCE COMMISSIONER —Cont'd
Accident and health insurance —Cont'd
Hearings.
Withdrawal of approval of forms, §58-51-95, (e).
Premiums.
Approval of rates, §58-51-95, (f).
Increased rates, §58-51-95, (f).
Actuaries, §58-2-25, (a).
Chief actuary, §58-2-20.
Qualifications of, §58-2-171.
Adjusters.
Generally.
See INSURANCE ADJUSTERS.
Aged persons.
Accident and health insurance.
Joint action to insure elderly, §§58-52-1 to 58-52-25.
See ACCIDENT AND HEALTH INSURANCE.
Agents.
Generally.
See INSURANCE AGENTS.
Annuities.
Generally.
See ANNUITIES.
Assessment companies, §§58-11-1 to 58-11-35.
See ASSESSMENT COMPANIES.
Beach area essential property insurance, §§58-45-1 to 58-45-90.
See BEACH AREA ESSENTIAL PROPERTY INSURANCE.
Cease and desist orders.
Unauthorized insurers, §§58-28-20 to 58-28-35.
Chief actuary, §58-2-20.
Chief deputy commissioner, §58-2-15.
Chief officer of department, §58-2-5.
Committees.
Appointment, §58-2-30.
Companies.
Authority over all insurance companies, §58-2-125.
Generally.
See INSURANCE COMPANIES.
Consultants.
Contracts for consultants, §58-2-25, (a).
Continuing care retirement communities.
Registration, disclosure, contract, etc., requirements, §§58-64-1 to 58-64-85.
See CONTINUING CARE RETIREMENT COMMUNITIES.
Continuing education program for licensees.
Instructor qualifications, §58-33-132.
Powers and duties of commissioner generally, §§58-33-130, 58-33-135.
Contracts.
Consulting contracts, §58-2-25, (a).
Councils.
Appointment, §58-2-30.
Credit insurance.
Generally, §§58-57-1 to 58-57-115.
See CREDIT INSURANCE.
Defined, §58-1-5.
Deposits.
Selection of bank or trust company, §58-5-1.
Deputies, §58-2-25, (a).
Chief deputy commissioner, §58-2-15.
Dissolution of insurers, §58-7-73.
Documents executed by commissioner.
Evidence.
Certificate as evidence of authority to do business, §58-2-115.

INSURANCE COMMISSIONER —Cont'd
Documents executed by commissioner —Cont'd
Evidence —Cont'd
Original and certified copies, §58-2-110.
Duties.
Investigation of charges, §58-2-155.
Election, §58-2-5.
Examinations, §58-2-50.
Conduct, §58-2-131, (c) to (e).
Conflicts of interest, §58-2-133, (a).
Contempt of court, §58-2-131, (j).
Definitions, §58-2-131, (b).
Dispensing with further examination, §58-2-131, (g).
Fees, §58-6-5.
Foreign or alien insurers.
Report by domiciliary insurance regulator accepted in lieu of, §58-2-131, (f).
Frequency, §58-2-131, (d).
Holding companies, §58-19-35, (a), (b), (d).
Confidentiality of information, §58-19-40.
Immunity, §58-2-133, (d).
Life and health insurance guaranty association, §58-62-66.
Impaired insurers, §58-62-56, (e).
Notice, §58-2-131, (h).
Post assessment insurance guaranty association, §58-48-65.
Insolvent insurers, §58-48-60, (b).
Report, §58-48-60, (c).
Powers in connection with, §58-2-131, (i) to (m).
Public reports.
Hearings before information made public, §58-2-131, (l).
Purposes, §58-2-131, (a).
Rates.
Commissioner to examine organizations, §58-40-90.
Refusal to submit to examination, §58-2-133, (c).
Reimbursement by insurer, §58-2-134, (a).
Limited on amount paid by insurer, §58-2-134, (b).
Reinsurance intermediaries, §58-9-21, (f).
Report, §58-2-132.
Confidential information, §58-2-132, (e), (f), (h), (i).
Contents, §58-2-132, (a).
Definitions, §58-2-132, (j).
Filing, §58-2-132, (b).
Review, §58-2-132, (c), (d), (g).
Retention of professionals and specialists, §§58-2-131, (k), 58-2-133, (b).
Scheduling.
Criteria for determining, §58-2-131, (d).
Scope.
Criteria for determining, §58-2-131, (d).
Subpoena power, §58-2-131, (j).
Termination or suspension, §58-2-131, (m).
Unfair trade practices.
Power of commissioner, §58-63-20.
Workers' compensation self-insurance.
Employer groups, §58-47-100.
Third-party administrators and service companies, §58-47-195.
Fair access to insurance requirements.
Appeals, §58-46-30.
Immunity of commissioner from liability, §58-46-35.
Plan.
Action on, §58-46-20, (b).

INSURANCE COMMISSIONER —Cont'd
Fees and charges.
Schedule, §58-6-5.
Financial analyst and examiners.
Education requirements, §58-2-25, (b).
Employment, §58-2-25, (a).
Fire insurance.
Generally.
See FIRE INSURANCE.
Firemen's relief fund.
Certificate of eligibility, §58-84-46.
Treasurer of state firemen's association.
Payment of fund to treasurer by commissioner, §58-84-25.
Foreign or alien insurance companies.
Generally, §§58-16-1 to 58-16-55.
See FOREIGN OR ALIEN INSURANCE COMPANIES.
Forms.
Approval, §58-3-150, (a).
Fraternal benefit societies.
Directors, officers, employees or agents.
Powers of society to purchase and maintain insurance, §58-24-35, (c).
Exemptions from general insurance laws, §58-24-110.
Mutual life insurance companies.
Conversion of society into company, §58-24-70.
Reinsurance, §58-24-60, (a).
Consolidation or merger, §58-24-60, (b).
Fraud.
Immunity from liability for reporting, §58-2-160, (a), (b).
Request for and release of information, §58-2-160, (c).
Group insurance.
Approval of master plan and certificates, §58-3-20.
Health benefit plan external review, §§58-50-75 to 58-50-95.
See ACCIDENT AND HEALTH INSURANCE.
Health care benefits providers.
Determination of jurisdiction over, §§58-49-1 to 58-49-25.
See HEALTH CARE BENEFITS PROVIDERS.
Multiple employer welfare arrangements.
Regulation generally, §§58-49-30 to 58-49-65.
See HEALTH CARE BENEFITS PROVIDERS.
Health insurance.
Credit insurance generally, §§58-57-1 to 58-57-115.
See CREDIT INSURANCE.
Generally.
See ACCIDENT AND HEALTH INSURANCE.
Health maintenance organizations, §§58-67-1 to 58-67-185.
See HEALTH MAINTENANCE ORGANIZATIONS.
Hearing officers.
Designating, §58-2-55.
Hearings, §58-2-50.
Accident and health insurance.
Withdrawal of approval of forms, §58-51-95, (e).
Appeals.
Rules for hearing of, §58-2-52, (a), (c).
Applicable procedural provisions, §58-2-52, (b).
Filing of approvals and disapprovals.
Agency decision for certain purposes, §58-2-53.
Rates, §58-40-105, (a).
Imposition of penalties or suspension of licenses, §58-40-110, (c).

INSURANCE COMMISSIONER —Cont'd
Hearings —Cont'd
Unfair trade practices, §58-63-25.
Holding companies generally, §§58-19-1 to 58-19-70.
See INSURANCE HOLDING COMPANIES.
Hospital, medical and dental service corporations, §§58-65-1 to 58-66-40.
See HOSPITAL, MEDICAL AND DENTAL SERVICE CORPORATIONS.
Hull insurance, protection and indemnity clubs, §§58-20-1 to 58-20-40.
See HULL INSURANCE, PROTECTION AND INDEMNITY CLUBS.
Immunity.
Examinations, §58-2-133, (d).
Fraud.
Immunity from liability for reporting, §58-2-160, (a), (b).
Information furnished to commissioner, §58-6-20.
Insurance policies or contracts.
Generally.
See INSURANCE POLICIES OR CONTRACTS.
Interagency consultation.
Authority of commissioner, §58-2-128, (b).
Definitions, §58-2-128, (d).
Privileged information, §58-2-128, (c).
Purpose of provisions, §58-2-128, (a).
Investigations, §58-2-50.
Complaints of violations, §58-2-155.
Life and health insurance guaranty association.
Generally, §§58-62-2 to 58-62-95.
See LIFE AND HEALTH INSURANCE GUARANTY ASSOCIATION.
Life insurance.
Generally, §§58-58-1 to 58-61-15.
See LIFE INSURANCE.
Limited representatives generally.
See INSURANCE LIMITED REPRESENTATIVES.
Local investigators of fire and fire prevention inspectors.
Supervision, §58-2-95.
Longevity pay, §58-2-10.
Long-term care insurance.
Generally, §§58-55-1 to 58-55-50.
See LONG-TERM CARE INSURANCE.
Managing general agents.
Generally.
See MANAGING GENERAL INSURANCE AGENTS.
Master trusts.
Use, §58-5-1.
Mortgage guaranty insurance, §§58-10-120 to 58-10-135.
Mortgage insurance consolidations.
Commissioner authorized to adopt rules, §58-2-210.
Motor vehicle insurance.
Generally.
See MOTOR VEHICLE INSURANCE.
Motor vehicle safety program, §58-31-52, (a) to (e).
Multiple employer welfare arrangements.
Regulation generally, §§58-49-30 to 58-49-65.
See HEALTH CARE BENEFITS PROVIDERS.
Mutual insurance companies.
Generally, §§58-8-1 to 58-8-60.
See MUTUAL INSURANCE COMPANIES.

INSURANCE COMMISSIONER —Cont'd
Office of commissioner to be a public office, §58-2-100.
Orders.
Judicial review, §58-2-75.
Appeals from supreme court, §58-2-75, (d).
Credit insurance, §58-57-75.
Jurisdiction of trial judge, §58-2-75, (c).
Motor vehicle reinsurance facility, §58-37-65, (f).
Orders as to plan of operation, §58-37-40, (d).
Petition, §58-2-75, (a).
Place of hearing.
Change, §58-2-75, (b).
Post-assessment insurance guaranty association, §58-48-45, (c).
Premiums.
Rate, §§58-2-80 to 58-2-90.
Presumption of correctness and propriety, §58-2-75, (b).
Rates, §58-40-105, (b).
Stay.
Commencement of proceedings not to operate as stay of commissioner order, §58-2-75, (e).
Transcript of hearing.
Commissioner to provide, §58-2-75, (b).
Unauthorized insurers.
Domestic companies, §58-14-15.
Signing, §58-2-45.
Writing.
Required, §58-2-45.
Post assessment insurance guaranty association.
Generally, §§58-48-1 to 58-48-130.
See POST ASSESSMENT INSURANCE GUARANTY ASSOCIATION.
Powers, §§58-2-40, 58-2-95, 143A-74.
Transfer to department of insurance, §143A-75.
Protected cell companies, §§58-10-75 to 58-10-110.
See INSURANCE COMPANIES.
Rate bureau.
Generally, §§58-36-1 to 58-36-110.
See RATE BUREAU.
Rates.
Regulation generally, §§58-40-1 to 58-40-140.
See INSURANCE RATES.
Readable insurance policies generally, §§58-38-1 to 58-38-40.
See INSURANCE POLICIES OR CONTRACTS.
Reciprocal insurance.
Generally, §§58-15-1 to 58-15-150.
See RECIPROCAL INSURANCE.
Records.
Inspection.
Subject to, §58-2-100.
Reinsurance.
Fraud.
Reporting and investigation, §58-2-160, (a), (b).
Request for and release of information, §58-2-160, (c).
Generally.
See REINSURANCE.
Reinsurance intermediaries.
Generally, §§58-9-2 to 58-9-26.
See REINSURANCE INTERMEDIARIES.
Reports.
Fees and taxes received, §58-6-1.
Reports to governor and general assembly, §58-2-120.

INSURANCE COMMISSIONER —Cont'd
Risk retention groups.
Generally, §§58-22-1 to 58-22-70.
See RISK RETENTION GROUPS.
Rules and regulations, §58-2-40.
Salary, §58-2-10.
Schedule of fees and charges, §58-6-5.
Seal, §58-2-35.
Service of process.
Fire insurance.
Unauthorized insurers, §58-28-45, (e).
Reciprocal insurance, §58-15-85.
Unauthorized insurers false advertising process act.
Acts appointing commissioner as attorney for service, §58-29-20, (a).
Manner of service on commissioner, §58-29-20, (b), (c).
Small employer group health coverage.
Generally, §§58-50-105 to 58-50-150.
See SMALL EMPLOYER GROUP HEALTH COVERAGE.
Statements.
Duties as to, §58-2-40.
False statements, §58-2-180.
Professional liability insurers.
Filing with commissioner, §58-2-170, (a), (b).
Supervision, rehabilitation and liquidation of insurers.
Generally, §§58-30-1 to 58-30-310.
See INSURER SUPERVISION, REHABILITATION AND LIQUIDATION.
Surplus lines insurance.
Generally, §§58-21-1 to 58-21-105.
See SURPLUS LINES INSURANCE.
Taxes relating to insurance.
Collection of certain taxes and administration, §105-228.9.
Term of office, §§58-2-5, 163-1, (a).
Third party administrators.
Generally, §§58-56-2 to 58-56-66.
See THIRD PARTY ADMINISTRATORS.
Title insurance.
Generally, §§58-26-1 to 58-27-15.
See TITLE INSURANCE.
Transfer of powers to department of insurance, §143A-75.
Unauthorized insurers.
Domestic companies.
Cease and desist orders, §58-14-15.
Generally, §§58-28-1 to 58-28-45.
See UNAUTHORIZED INSURERS.
Unauthorized insurers false advertising process act.
Action by commissioner under unfair trade practices act, §58-29-15.
Attorney for service of process.
Act constituting appointment as, §58-29-20, (a).
Manner of service on, §58-29-20, (b).
Generally, §§58-29-1 to 58-29-25.
See UNAUTHORIZED INSURERS.
Notice of unlawful advertising, §58-29-10.
Underground petroleum storage tank leak cleanup.
Insurance pools by owners and operators of underground storage tanks, §143-215.94I.
Unfair trade practices.
Generally, §§58-63-1 to 58-63-70.
See INSURANCE UNFAIR TRADE PRACTICES.

INSURANCE COMPANIES.
Accident and health insurance.
Credit insurance generally, §§58-57-1 to 58-57-115.
See CREDIT INSURANCE.
Generally.
See ACCIDENT AND HEALTH INSURANCE.
Small employer group health coverage, §§58-50-105 to 58-50-150.
See SMALL EMPLOYER GROUP HEALTH COVERAGE.
Actions for negligent decision.
Health care liability, §§90-21.50 to 90-21.56.
Adjusters.
Generally.
See INSURANCE ADJUSTERS.
Adverse underwriting decisions.
Defined, §58-39-15.
Reasons for making, obligation to give, §§58-39-55 to 58-39-65.
Affidavit of company president or other chief officer.
Compliance with insurance law.
Required to do business, §58-2-150.
Aged persons.
Accident and health insurance.
Joint action to insure elderly, §§58-52-1 to 58-52-25.
See ACCIDENT AND HEALTH INSURANCE.
Agents generally.
See INSURANCE AGENTS.
Alien insurance companies.
Generally.
See FOREIGN OR ALIEN INSURANCE COMPANIES.
Annual report, §55-16-22, (a1).
Annuities.
See ANNUITIES.
Applicability of provisions, §58-7-1.
Approval of formation or initial license.
Refusal to approve, §58-7-37, (c), (d).
Assessment companies, §§58-11-1 to 58-11-35.
See ASSESSMENT COMPANIES.
Assets.
Acceptance of assets subject to lien in favor of claimants, §58-13-25, (c).
Acquisition.
Securities or investments.
Purchasing above market value, §58-7-167, (b).
Violation of law.
Disallowing of amounts of assets, §58-7-160.
Admitted assets, §58-7-162.
Alien insurers, §58-7-198.
Allowable assets, §58-7-162.
Cash, §58-7-172.
Deposit, §58-7-172.
Disposal.
Ineligible property.
Effect of failure to dispose, §58-7-188, (a).
Time limit, §58-7-188, (a).
Unqualified investments, §58-7-167, (c).
Foreign or alien insurers, §58-7-198.
Free and unencumbered assets, percentage required, §58-13-25, (a).
Investments.
Disposal of ineligible property.
Effect of failure to dispose, §58-7-188, (b).
Time limit, §58-7-188, (a).

INSURANCE COMPANIES —Cont'd
Assets —Cont'd
Investments —Cont'd
Disposal of unqualified investments, §58-7-167, (c).
Permitted investments, §58-7-173.
Real estate, §58-7-187, (a) to (d).
Special consent investments, §58-7-183, (a) to (c).
Valuation.
Real property, §58-7-193, (c), (d).
Maintenance of assets in state, §58-7-50, (b).
Exceptions to provisions, §58-7-50, (d), (e).
Not allowed, §58-7-163.
Prior and preferential claim of claimants, §58-13-25, (d).
Protected cell companies, §§58-10-75 to 58-10-110.
Protection.
Applicability of article, §58-13-10.
Citation of article, §58-13-1.
Definitions, §58-13-15.
Examination by commissioner, §58-13-20, (b).
Exceptions, §58-13-20, (a).
Hypothecation, prohibition, §58-13-25.
Pledge of assets restricted, §58-13-25.
Purposes of article, §58-13-5.
Reasons, §58-13-5.
Scope of article, §58-13-10.
Short title of article, §58-13-1.
Publication, §58-3-60.
Removal from state, §58-7-50, (c).
Replacing of certain assets, §58-7-197, (a) to (e).
Statement filed by insurer, §58-13-25, (b).
Authorization upon submission of fees, §58-6-15.
Authorized kinds of insurance, §58-7-15.
Background check of applicants for new license, §58-7-37.
Banks.
Disclosure of regulatory rating prepared by bank commissioner, §53-99, (d).
Beach area essential property insurance, §§58-45-1 to 58-45-90.
See BEACH AREA ESSENTIAL PROPERTY INSURANCE.
Boards of directors.
Classes of directors, §58-7-45, (a).
Election, §58-7-45, (a).
First meeting, §58-7-40.
Investments in or loans to, §58-7-200, (c) to (e).
Vacancies.
Filling, §58-7-45, (a).
Bylaws.
Adoption, §§58-7-40, 58-7-45, (a).
Amendments.
Filing, §58-7-45, (b).
Cancellation of insurance.
Generally.
See INSURANCE POLICIES OR CONTRACTS.
Capital.
Amount required, §58-7-75.
Casualty, fidelity and surety companies.
Loss and expense reserves, §58-3-81.
Premium deficiency reserves, §58-3-72.
Cease and desist orders.
Producer-controlled property or casualty insurers.
Lack of material compliance with section, §58-3-165, (l).
Ceding insurer.
Generally.
See REINSURANCE.

INSURANCE COMPANIES —Cont'd
Certificates of authority.
Required before issuing policies, §58-7-10.
Cessation of business.
Statements or communications made in good faith.
No liability for, §58-41-40, (a).
Charters.
Extension of existing charters, §58-7-5.
Chattel mortgages.
Investments, §58-7-180, (a) to (d).
Child support.
Lien on insurance settlements, §§58-3-135, 58-3-185, (a), (b).
Settlement payments, receiving person's duty to retain funds, §44-50.
Claims.
Acknowledgment of claim, §58-3-100, (c).
Civil penalty for failure to acknowledge, §58-3-100, (c).
Failure to acknowledge after receiving notice.
Civil penalty, §58-3-100, (c).
Commissioner.
Authority over all insurance companies, §58-2-125.
Taxes relating to insurance.
Collection and administration, §105-228.9.
Compliance with law required, §58-2-150.
Confidentiality.
Consumer and customer information.
Generally, §§58-39-1 to 58-39-165.
See INSURANCE CONSUMER AND CUSTOMER INFORMATION PRIVACY.
Risk based capital requirements.
Hearings on commissioner's determinations, §58-12-30.
Information filed with commissioner, §58-12-35, (a).
Consolidation, §58-7-150.
Authorized, §58-7-150, (a).
Conditions, §58-7-150, (a).
Fees, §58-7-150, (c).
Reinsurance by other insurer deemed consolidation, §58-7-150, (b).
Consumer reports.
Investigative consumer reports, §58-39-40.
Controlling shareholders.
Investments in or loans to, §58-7-200, (c) to (e).
Conversion of domestic mutual to stock insurer, §58-10-10, (a).
Approval of plan, §58-10-10, (b).
Insurer with guaranty capital, §58-10-10, (c).
Distribution of assets, surplus or capital.
Director, officers or employees not to receive, §58-10-10, (g).
Experts for reviewing plan, retention by commissioner at insurer's expense, §58-10-10, (e).
Fee, commission, compensation, etc.
Director, officers or employees not to receive, §58-10-10, (g).
Plan of conversion.
Acquisition of beneficial interest, §58-10-12, (e).
Application for approval of plan and charter amendment, §58-10-12, (c).
Definitions, §58-10-12, (a).
Distributing consideration to members.
Delaying or restricting, time period, §58-10-12, (d).
Requirements, §58-10-12, (b).

INSURANCE COMPANIES —Cont'd
Conversion of domestic mutual to stock insurer —Cont'd
Plan of conversion —Cont'd
Sale or transfer of stock.
Delaying or restricting, time period, §58-10-12, (d).
Public hearing, scheduling, §58-10-10, (d).
Rules, adoption by commissioner, §58-10-10, (h).
Transfer of assets, rights, franchises, etc., to stock company, §58-10-10, (f).
Conversion of stock corporations into mutual corporations, §§58-10-1, 58-10-5.
Corporation law.
Applicability of general corporation law, §58-7-1.
Credit insurance.
Generally, §§58-57-1 to 58-57-115.
See CREDIT INSURANCE.
Criminal history record search of applicants for new license, §58-7-37.
Customer information safeguards act, §§58-39-130 to 58-39-165.
See INSURANCE CONSUMER AND CUSTOMER INFORMATION PRIVACY.
Death benefits paid in services or merchandise.
Issuing contracts prohibited, §58-3-55.
Deceptive trade practices.
Generally, §§58-63-1 to 58-63-70.
See INSURANCE UNFAIR TRADE PRACTICES.
Definitions.
Generally, §§58-1-5, 58-12-2.
Department of insurance generally.
See INSURANCE DEPARTMENT.
Depository institutions.
Affiliations with.
Gramm-Leach-Bliley act.
Compliance with provision required, §58-19-2, (b).
Depository institution defined, §58-19-2, (a).
Deposits.
Foreign or alien insurance companies, §§58-5-5 to 58-5-40.
See FOREIGN OR ALIEN INSURANCE COMPANIES.
Derivative transactions.
Investments, §58-7-205.
Discrimination.
Between individuals of same class, prohibition, §58-3-120, (b).
In favor of any person, prohibition, §58-3-120, (a).
Dissolution of insurers, §58-7-73.
Dividends or other distributions.
Conversion of stock corporations into mutual corporations.
Repayment of dividends to corporation for beneficiaries, §58-10-5.
Impairment of capital.
Dividends not payable when capital impaired, §58-7-125.
Liability of stockholders for unlawful stockholders, §58-7-125.
Liability of stockholders not restricted, §58-7-130, (d).
Other requirements and limitations, §58-7-130, (e).
Rate bureau.
Payment of dividends not prohibited or regulated by rate bureau division, §58-36-60.

INSURANCE COMPANIES —Cont'd
Dividends or other distributions —Cont'd
Restricted by commissioner, grounds, §58-7-130, (a).
Transfer out of paid-in and contributed surplus, §58-7-130, (c).
Unassigned surplus, declared from, §58-7-130, (b).
Domestic reciprocals, §§58-15-100 to 58-15-150.
See RECIPROCAL INSURANCE.
Electioneering communications.
Prohibited disbursement for, §163-278.82, (a), (b).
Mass mailings and telephone banks, §163-278.92, (a), (b).
Penalties, §163-278.93.
Penalties for violations, §163-278.83.
Emblems, §58-3-50.
Examinations.
Generally.
See INSURANCE COMMISSIONER.
Reimbursement of costs by insurers, §58-2-134, (a).
Limit on amount paid, §58-2-134, (b).
Fair access to insurance requirements, §§58-46-1 to 58-46-60.
See PROPERTY INSURANCE.
Fees.
Consolidation, §58-7-150.
License fees.
Annual continuation fee, §58-6-7, (a), (b).
Defined, §58-6-15.
When submitted, §58-6-15.
Financial disclosure, §§58-3-65, 58-40-130, (a) to (e).
Designation of rating or advisory organizations, §58-40-130, (b).
Publication of financial information, §58-3-65.
Rate regulation, §58-40-130, (a), (d).
Financial statements, §58-2-165, (a).
Format, to, §58-2-165, (b).
Preparation, §58-2-165, (c).
Town or county mutual, §58-2-165, (a1).
Fire insurance.
Generally.
See FIRE INSURANCE.
Foreign or alien insurance companies.
Generally.
See FOREIGN OR ALIEN INSURANCE COMPANIES.
Franchise tax.
Exemption, §105-125, (a).
Group insurance.
Accident and health insurance generally.
See ACCIDENT AND HEALTH INSURANCE.
Life insurance generally.
See LIFE INSURANCE.
Health care liability, §§90-21.50 to 90-21.56.
Health care providers insurance payment claims not timely processed due to year 2000 date change.
Definitions, §58-2-235, (c).
Interim payments by insurer to providers, §58-2-235.
Payment in full, when considered, §58-2-235, (c).
Recovery of excess payment, §58-2-235, (c).
Report by insurer, §58-2-235, (a).
Health insurance.
Credit insurance generally, §§58-57-1 to 58-57-115.
See CREDIT INSURANCE.

INSURANCE COMPANIES —Cont'd
Health insurance —Cont'd
Generally.
See ACCIDENT AND HEALTH INSURANCE.
Health maintenance organizations, §§58-67-1 to 58-67-185.
See HEALTH MAINTENANCE ORGANIZATIONS.
Hearings.
Refusal to approve formation or initial license, §58-7-37, (d).
Risk based capital requirements.
Confidential hearing on commissioner's determination, §58-12-30.
Hedging transaction.
Authority to enter into, §58-7-205, (d).
Holding companies.
Generally, §§58-19-1 to 58-19-70.
See INSURANCE HOLDING COMPANIES.
Hospital, medical and dental service corporations, §§58-65-1 to 58-66-40.
See HOSPITAL, MEDICAL AND DENTAL SERVICE CORPORATIONS.
Hull insurance, protection and indemnity clubs, §§58-20-1 to 58-20-40.
See HULL INSURANCE, PROTECTION AND INDEMNITY CLUBS.
Impairment.
Contributing to impairment.
Acts resulting in, §58-30-12, (c).
Penalties, §58-30-12, (c).
Duty to report, §58-30-12, (b).
Definitions, §58-30-12, (a).
Income generation transaction, §58-7-205, (e).
Incorporation.
Background check of applicants for new license, §58-7-37.
Capital and/or surplus.
Amount required, §58-7-75.
Certificate of incorporation, §58-7-35.
First meeting, §58-7-40.
Procedure, §58-7-35.
Refusal to approve formation.
Grounds, §58-7-37, (c).
Notice, hearing, §58-7-37, (d).
Information practices.
Notice, §§58-39-25 to 58-39-28.
Information privacy protection.
Consumer and customer information.
Generally, §§58-39-1 to 58-39-165.
See INSURANCE CONSUMER AND CUSTOMER INFORMATION PRIVACY.
Information security program, §§58-39-130 to 58-39-165.
Insignias, §58-3-50.
Insurance regulatory fund.
Created, use of proceeds, §58-6-25, (d).
Investments.
Acquisition.
General qualifications, §58-7-167, (a) to (c).
Purchasing above market value, §58-7-167, (b).
Authorization, §58-7-168.
Derivative transactions.
Conditions, §58-7-205, (b).
Counterparty exposure amount, §58-7-205, (f).
Definitions, §58-7-205, (a).
Documentation and records required, §58-7-205, (i).
Guidelines and internal procedures, §58-7-205, (h).
Hedging transaction, §58-7-205, (d).

INSURANCE COMPANIES —Cont'd
Investments —Cont'd
Derivative transactions —Cont'd
Income generation transaction, §58-7-205, (e).
Other transactions, approval, §58-7-205, (g).
Requirements for derivative instruments, §58-7-205, (j).
Rules, adoption by commissioner, §58-7-205, (c).
Directors, officers, controlling stockholders or other persons.
Investments in limited, §58-7-200, (c) to (e).
Disposal of ineligible property.
Effect of failure to dispose, §58-7-188, (b).
Time limit, §58-7-188, (a).
Diversification.
Amount of investments required to be maintained, §58-7-170, (a).
Deposits with financial institutions, limiting, §58-7-170, (j).
Limitations on eligible investments, §58-7-170, (b).
Medium or low quality obligations, limitation, §58-7-170, (d).
Documentation that limit not exceeded, §58-7-170, (f).
Effective date of limitation, §58-7-170, (g).
Failure to obtain approval for investment in excess of limitation, §58-7-170, (i).
Investments prior to effective date, §58-7-170, (g).
Medium or low quality obligations defined, §58-7-170, (e).
Separate schedule, noncompliance with limitation, filing, §58-7-170, (h).
Mortgages, limitation on percentage of investments in, §58-7-170, (c).
Provision supersede inconsistent provisions, §58-7-170, (k).
Eligible investments, §58-7-165.
Foreign or territorial investment.
Canadian securities inapplicability of provision, §58-7-178, (c).
Insurers authorized to transact business in foreign country or territory, §58-7-178, (a).
Insurers not authorized to transact business in foreign country or territory, §58-7-178, (b).
Hedging transaction, §58-7-205, (d).
Income generation transaction, §58-7-205, (e).
Medium or low quality obligations, §58-7-170, (d) to (h).
Mortgages, §58-7-179, (a) to (e).
Chattel mortgages, §58-7-180, (a) to (d).
Limitation, §58-7-170, (c).
Permitted insurer investments, §58-7-173.
Prohibited investments, §58-7-185, (a).
Securities or property of other persons, §58-7-185, (b).
Real estate, §58-7-187, (a) to (d).
Valuation, §58-7-193, (c), (d).
Replacing of certain assets, §58-7-197. (a) to (e).
Securities approved by secretary of housing and urban development, federal housing administration and veterans administration, §53-45.
Special consent investments, §58-7-183, (a) to (c).
Title insurers, §58-7-182.
Transactions allowed or prohibited, §58-7-200, (a).
Derivative transactions allowed, §§58-7-200, (b), 58-7-205, (b).
Directors, officers, controlling stockholders or other persons.
Investments in prohibited, §58-7-200, (c) to (e).

INSURANCE COMPANIES —Cont'd
Investments —Cont'd
Unlawful acquisition.
Disallowance of amounts of assets, §58-7-160.
Valuation, §58-7-192, (d).
Kinds of insurance authorized, §58-7-15.
Liabilities.
Publication, §58-3-60.
Reporting certain liabilities, §58-7-197, (b).
Licenses.
Background of incorporators and key personnel.
Criminal history search of applicants for new license, §58-7-37, (a).
Fingerprints and photograph of applicants for new license.
Submission to commissioner required, §58-7-37, (a).
Key person defined, §58-7-37, (b).
Power of commissioner, §58-7-37, (e).
Rules for obtaining background information, adoption, §58-7-37, (f).
Fees.
Annual continuation fee, §58-6-7, (a), (b).
Rating bureau exempt from, §58-6-7, (d).
When submitted, §58-6-15.
Foreign companies.
Conditions of licensure, §58-16-8.
Restricting license.
Prohibiting or limiting kinds or amount of insurance, §58-3-100, (e).
Revocation, suspension or refusal to renew.
Notice to agents in state, writing new business prohibited, §58-3-100.
Issuance.
New company, §58-7-40.
Misdemeanors.
Failure to secure license, §58-3-85.
Notification by license applicants to insurance commissioner.
Criminal convictions, §58-2-69, (c).
Definitions, §58-2-69, (a).
Residential address, §58-2-69, (b).
Service of notice, §58-2-69, (d), (e).
Perpetual license, §58-6-7, (a).
Refusal to approve initial license.
Grounds, §58-7-37, (c).
Notice, hearing, §58-7-37, (d).
Renewal, §58-6-15.
Required to do business, §§58-3-85, 58-6-7, (a).
Restricting license.
Prohibiting or limiting kinds or amount of insurance, §58-3-100, (e).
Revocation, suspension or refusal to renew.
Authority of commissioner, §58-3-100, (a).
Foreign insurance companies.
Notice to agents in state, writing insurance prohibited, §58-3-100, (d).
Grounds, §58-3-100, (a).
Holding companies.
Violations of provisions, §58-19-65.
Individuals, making applicable to, §58-3-100, (b).
"Twisting," §58-3-115.
Sale or major reorganization of company.
License to be restricted, §58-3-160.
Self-service storage companies.
Rental insurance.
Limited license, §58-33-18.
Term, §58-6-15.
Lien for services rendered injured persons.
Accounting for disbursements, §44-50.1, (a) to (c).

INSURANCE COMPANIES —Cont'd
Liens.
Child support obligors.
Lien on insurance settlements, §§58-3-135, 58-3-185, (a), (b).
Life and health insurance guaranty association, §§58-62-2 to 58-62-95.
See LIFE AND HEALTH INSURANCE GUARANTY ASSOCIATION.
Life insurance.
Generally, §§58-58-1 to 58-61-15.
See LIFE INSURANCE.
Reinsurance, §58-58-65.
Reserve fund.
Calculation of reserve fund of domestic companies, §58-58-45.
Limitation of risk.
Exceptions, §§58-3-105, 58-3-110.
Fidelity or surety business.
Limitations on exposure, §58-3-110, (a).
Limitations on guarantees of any single institution, §58-3-110, (c).
Transportation or warehousing bonds, §58-3-110, (b).
Generally, §§58-3-105, 58-3-110.
Liquidation generally, §§58-30-1 to 58-30-310.
See INSURER SUPERVISION, REHABILITATION AND LIQUIDATION.
Loans.
Authorization, §58-7-168.
Eligible investments, §58-7-165.
Mortgage loans, §58-7-179, (a) to (e).
Policy loans, §58-7-175.
Securities approved by secretary of housing and urban development, federal housing administration and veterans administration, §53-45.
To directors, officers, controlling shareholders or others, §58-7-200, (c) to (e).
Long-term care insurance.
Generally, §§58-55-1 to 58-55-50.
See LONG-TERM CARE INSURANCE.
Loss and expense reserves.
Casualty insurance or surety company, §58-3-81.
Managing general agents, §§58-34-2 to 58-34-15.
See MANAGING GENERAL INSURANCE AGENTS.
Mortgage guaranty insurance, §§58-10-120 to 58-10-135.
Contingency reserve.
Annual contribution, factors to determine, §58-10-135, (a).
Calculations to develop, sequence, §58-10-135, (g).
Larger reserve maintained under laws or regulations of another jurisdiction, §58-10-135, (h).
Liability, reported as, §58-10-135, (c).
Rate formula factor.
Commissioner may establish, §58-10-135, (b).
Withdrawals, §58-10-135, (d) to (f).
Definition, §58-10-120.
Minimum policyholder position, §58-10-125, (a).
Cessation of new business.
Company not having minimum position, §58-10-125, (b).
Group of loans subject to aggregate loss limit, §58-10-125, (d).
Insuring loans with percentage claim settlement option, §58-10-125, (c).

INSURANCE COMPANIES —Cont'd
Mortgage guaranty insurance —Cont'd
Minimum policyholder position —Cont'd
Layers of coverage, deductibles or excess reinsurance provided, §58-10-125, (e).
Leases, coverage on provided, §58-10-125, (g).
Loans secured by junior liens, §58-10-125, (f).
Percentage loss settlement option provided, §58-10-125, (h).
Unearned premium reserve.
Computation, §58-10-130, (a).
Loss reserve, case basis method used to determine, §58-10-130, (c).
Special contingency reservation, reported as liability, percentage, §58-10-130, (b).
Mortgage loans.
Investments, §§58-7-170, (c), 58-7-179, (a) to (e).
Motor vehicle declared total loss.
Total loss claim.
Marking registration card and title certificate, §20-71.3, (a1).
Motor vehicle insurance.
Generally.
See MOTOR VEHICLE INSURANCE.
Mutual insurance companies, §§58-8-1 to 58-8-60.
See MUTUAL INSURANCE COMPANIES.
Names, §58-7-35.
Companies must do business in own names, §58-3-50.
Words which must be included, §58-7-35.
Negligent decisions.
Health care liability, §§90-21.50 to 90-21.56.
Nonrenewal of business.
Entire book of business, §58-41-45, (a).
Loss of reinsurance, §58-41-30.
Notice, §58-41-20, (a) to (c).
Timing of notice to insured, §58-41-40, (b).
Penalties, §58-41-55.
Statements or communications made in good faith.
No liability for, §58-41-40, (a).
North Carolina rate bureau, §§58-36-1 to 58-36-110.
See RATE BUREAU.
Notice.
First meeting, §58-7-40.
Information practices, §§58-39-25 to 58-39-28.
Refusal to approve formation or initial license, §58-7-37, (d).
Oath as to compliance with insurance law.
Required to do business, §58-2-150.
Officers, §58-7-140.
Investments in or loans to, §58-7-200, (c) to (e).
Penalties.
Failure to acknowledge claim after receiving notice.
Civil penalty, §58-3-100, (c).
Publication of assets and liabilities.
Violations of provisions, §58-3-60.
Violations of article.
Misdemeanors, §58-21-105, (a).
Policies or contracts generally.
See INSURANCE POLICIES OR CONTRACTS.
Pool of assets and liabilities.
Protected cell companies, §§58-10-75 to 58-10-110.
Post assessment insurance guaranty association, §§58-48-1 to 58-48-130.
See POST ASSESSMENT INSURANCE GUARANTY ASSOCIATION.

INSURANCE COMPANIES —Cont'd
Premium deficiency reserves.
Acquisition costs and premium taxes previously incurred not considered, §58-3-72, (c).
Anticipates investment income, reduction not taken, §58-3-72, (d).
Calculation for recorded unearned premium reserves, §58-3-72, (b).
Date of determination, §58-3-72, (a).
Financial statement or report to include in liabilities, §58-3-72, (a).
Grouping policies for determining if deficiency exists, §58-3-72, (e).
Other basis use to produce adequate or reasonable reserves, §58-3-72, (f).
Premiums.
Generally.
See INSURANCE PREMIUMS.
Premium tax, §§105-225.5 to 105-228.10.
Privacy protection.
Consumer and customer information.
Generally, §§58-39-1 to 58-39-165.
See INSURANCE CONSUMER AND CUSTOMER INFORMATION PRIVACY.
Producer-controlled property or casualty insurers.
Business transacted with, §58-3-165, (a) to (n).
Cease and desist orders.
Lack of material compliance with section, §58-3-165, (l).
Definitions, §58-3-165.
Professional liability insurance.
Reports to commissioner, §58-2-170, (c).
Property insurance.
Beach area essential property insurance, §§58-45-1 to 58-45-90.
See BEACH AREA ESSENTIAL PROPERTY INSURANCE.
Fair access to insurance requirements, §§58-46-1 to 58-46-60.
See PROPERTY INSURANCE.
Fire insurance generally.
See FIRE INSURANCE.
Protected cell companies.
Administrative and accounting procedures, §58-10-85, (e).
Assessment by guaranty fund or association, prohibited, §58-10-95, (d).
Assets owned by company, §58-10-85, (c).
Attribution of assets and liabilities, §58-10-85, (b).
Availability of assets to creditors, §58-10-95, (a).
Charging assets with liabilities of other business, §58-10-90, (a).
Closing out protected cell account.
Cessation of business, §58-10-90, (g).
Conservation, rehabilitation or liquidation, §58-10-100, (a).
Amount recoverable, §58-10-100, (b).
Contributions to guaranty fund or association, prohibited, §58-10-95, (d).
Definitions, §58-10-80.
Duties of directors, §58-10-85, (e).
Establishment, §58-10-85, (a).
Fraudulent purpose or fraudulent conveyance.
Establishment of cell does not constitute, §58-10-95, (e).
Income, gains and losses, §58-10-90, (b).
Insurance securitization, §58-10-90, (d).
Contracts or other documentation, requirements, §58-10-90, (e).

INSURANCE COMPANIES —Cont'd
Protected cell companies —Cont'd
Issuing insurance or reinsurance.
Directly to policyholders or reinsureds, prohibition, §58-10-90, (f).
Legal person separate from company.
Creation of protected cell does not create, §58-10-85, (c).
Name, §58-10-85, (a).
Obligations, creditor's recourse, §58-10-95, (b), (c).
Plan of operation, §58-10-85, (a).
Protected cell accounts.
Holding assets in accounts, requirement, §58-10-85, (a).
Transfer of assets to, §58-10-85, (a).
Protection from creditors, §58-10-95, (a).
Purpose and legislative intent, §58-10-75.
Rules, adoption by commissioner, §58-10-110.
Satisfaction of protected cell liabilities.
Only protected cell assets available, §58-10-90, (a).
Security interest attaching to protected cell assets, §58-10-85, (c).
Third party managing protected cell assets or protected cell, §58-10-85, (d).
Transaction of insurance business.
Not deemed, §58-10-105.
Trustee of protected cell assets, §58-10-85, (c).
Value of protected cell assets, §58-10-85, (f).
Fair market value, §58-10-90, (c).
Protection.
Hypothecation.
Restrictions, §58-13-25.
Rate bureau, §§58-36-1 to 58-36-110.
See RATE BUREAU.
Rate regulation generally, §§58-40-1 to 58-40-140.
See INSURANCE RATES.
Readable insurance policies generally, §§58-38-1 to 58-38-40.
See INSURANCE POLICIES OR CONTRACTS.
Real property.
Investments, §58-7-187, (a) to (d).
Authorized by section, §58-7-187, (a).
Conditions, §58-7-187, (c).
Limitation on amount of property, §58-7-187, (d).
Types of property, §58-7-187, (b).
Valuation, §58-7-193, (c), (d).
Rebates.
Prohibited.
Premiums on credit insurance, §58-57-95.
Reciprocal insurance.
Generally, §§58-15-1 to 58-15-150.
See RECIPROCAL INSURANCE.
Records.
Agencies, agents, brokers and producers of record, §58-2-195.
Exhibiting books and papers to commissioner.
Required, §58-2-200.
Inspection by commissioner, §58-2-185.
Maintenance in state.
Exceptions, §58-7-55.
Maintenance of records, §58-7-50, (a).
Exceptions to provisions, §58-7-50, (d), (e).
Removal from state, §58-7-50, (c).
Exceptions, §58-7-55.
Requirements, §58-2-185.
Refusal to approve formation, §58-7-37, (c), (d).
Regulatory charge.
Computation, §58-6-25, (a).
Definitions, §58-6-25, (e).

INSURANCE COMPANIES —Cont'd
Regulatory charge —Cont'd
Insurance regulatory fund.
Created, use of proceeds, §58-6-25, (d).
Levy, §58-6-25, (a).
Payment, §58-6-25, (c).
Rate, §58-6-25, (b).
Returns, §58-6-25, (c).
Rehabilitation generally, §§58-30-1 to 58-30-310.
See INSURER SUPERVISION, REHABILITATION AND LIQUIDATION.
Reinsurance.
See REINSURANCE.
Reinsurance intermediaries, §§58-9-2 to 58-9-26.
See REINSURANCE INTERMEDIARIES.
Reorganization.
License.
Restricted, §58-3-160.
Reports.
Agencies, agents, brokers and producers of record, §58-2-195.
Annual report, §55-16-22, (a1).
Financial data, §58-40-130, (a), (d), (e).
Financial statements, §58-2-165.
Health care providers claims not timely processed due to year 2000 date change, §58-2-235.
Liabilities.
Reporting certain liabilities, §58-7-197, (b).
Special reports.
Commissioner may require, §58-2-190.
Reserves.
Contingency reserve.
Mortgage guaranty insurers, §58-10-135.
Fire and marine insurance companies.
Loss reserves, §58-3-75.
Loss and expense reserves.
Casualty insurance or surety company.
Date of determination, §58-3-81, (a).
Diminished by allowance or credit for reinsurance covenable, §58-3-81, (a).
Financial statement or report to include in liabilities, §58-3-81, (a).
Other basis for adequate or reasonable reserves, §58-3-81, (e).
Outstanding losses and loss expenses, §58-3-81, (b).
Record of losses and claims notices to be kept, §58-3-81, (f).
Workers' compensation insurance, minimum loss and loss expense, §58-3-81, (c).
Fire and marine insurance companies, §58-3-75.
Mortgage guaranty insurers.
Contingency reserve, §58-10-135.
Unearned premium reserve, §58-10-130.
Premium deficiency reserves.
Acquisition costs and premium taxes previously incurred not considered, §58-3-72, (c).
Anticipates investment income, reduction not taken, §58-3-72, (d).
Calculation for recorded unearned premium reserves, §58-3-72, (b).
Date of determination, §58-3-72, (a).
Financial statement or report to include in liabilities, §58-3-72, (a).
Grouping policies for determining if deficiency exists, §58-3-72, (e).
Other basis use to produce adequate or reasonable reserves, §58-3-72, (f).
Reciprocal insurance, §58-15-75.
Unearned premium reserves.
Computation, §58-3-71, (b) to (f).
Rules, §58-3-71, (g).
Mortgage guaranty insurance, §58-10-130.

INSURANCE COMPANIES —Cont'd
Reserves —Cont'd
Unearned premium reserves —Cont'd
Required, §58-3-71, (a).
Requirements.
Reciprocal insurance, §58-15-75.
Risk based capital requirements, §§58-12-2 to 58-12-70.
Additional capital endorsed by General Assembly, §58-12-4.
Announcements as to risk based capital levels prohibited, §58-12-35, (b).
Authorized control level event.
Actions taken by commission, §58-12-21, (b).
Defined, §58-12-21, (a).
Company action level event.
Defined, §58-12-11, (a).
Financial plan in event of, §58-12-11, (b).
Copies submitted to other state, §58-12-11, (f).
Time for submitting, §58-12-11, (c).
Unsatisfactory, commissioner determining, §58-12-11, (d), (e).
Confidential hearing on commissioner's determination, §58-12-30.
Confidentiality of information filed with commissioner, §58-12-35, (a).
Definitions, §58-12-2.
Exemptions from provisions, §58-12-40, (c).
Foreign insurers.
Mandatory control level event, §58-12-45, (c).
Risk based capital plan.
When commissioner may require, §58-12-45, (b).
Submission of report.
Request of commissioner, §58-12-45, (a).
Health organization's risk based capital.
Determining, §58-12-6, (d).
HMO net worth requirement, §58-12-70.
Legislative findings, §58-12-4.
Life or health insurer's risk based capital.
Determination, §58-12-6, (b).
Mandatory control level event.
Defined, §58-12-25, (a).
Foreign insurers, §58-12-45, (c).
Life and health insurers, §58-12-25, (b).
Property and casualty insurers, §58-12-25, (c).
Notices resulting in regulatory action.
Effective date, §58-12-50.
Phase in provision, §58-12-55.
Health organization, §58-12-65.
Property or casualty, §58-12-60.
Property or casualty insurer's risk based capital.
Determining, §58-12-6, (d).
Rate making.
Information not used by commissioner for, §58-12-40, (b).
Regulatory action level event.
Actuaries and investment experts, retaining, §58-12-16, (d).
Corrective actions, determining, §58-12-16, (c).
Defined, §58-12-16, (a).
Risk based capital plan.
Submission, §58-12-16, (b).
Report of risk based capital levels.
Adjustment by commission, report inaccurate, §58-12-6, (c).
Filing, filing date, §58-12-6, (a).
Risk based capital plan.
Company action level event, §58-12-11, (b) to (f).
Regulatory action level event, §58-12-16, (b).
Supplemental nature of provisions, §58-12-40, (a).

INSURANCE COMPANIES —Cont'd
Risk retention groups.
Generally, §§58-22-1 to 58-22-70.
See RISK RETENTION GROUPS.
Sale of company.
License.
Restrictions, §58-3-160.
Salvage vehicles.
Surrender of title to vehicles deemed salvage vehicle, §20-109.1.
Secretary of state.
Incorporation.
Certificate of secretary of state, §58-7-35.
Securities or property of other persons.
Underwriting or participating in offering, prohibition, §58-7-185, (b).
Security program.
Information security program, §§58-39-130 to 58-39-165.
Segregated and insulated pool of assets and liabilities.
Protected cell companies, §§58-10-75 to 58-10-110.
Self-service storage companies.
Rental insurance.
Limited license, §58-33-18.
Service of process.
Unauthorized insurers false advertising process act, §§58-29-1 to 58-29-25.
See UNAUTHORIZED INSURERS.
Small employer group health coverage.
Generally, §§58-50-105 to 58-50-150.
See SMALL EMPLOYER GROUP HEALTH COVERAGE.
Special act.
Domestic companies incorporated by special acts.
Extension of charters, §58-7-5.
Statements.
Filing with commissioner
Professional liability insurers, §58-2-170.
Publication of financial information, §58-3-65.
Stock and stockholders.
Amount of capital required, §58-7-75.
Assessment of stock, §58-7-110.
Controlling shareholders.
Investments in or loans to, §58-7-200, (c) to (e).
Conversion of stock corporations into mutual corporations, §§58-10-1, 58-10-5.
Dividends or other distributions.
Liability not restricted, §58-7-130, (d).
Other requirements and limitations, §58-7-130, (e).
Restricted by commissioner, grounds, §58-7-130, (a).
Transfer out of paid-in and contributed surplus, §58-7-130, (c).
Equity securities.
Defined, §58-7-145, (f).
Exemptions from provisions, §58-7-145, (g).
Rules and regulations, §58-7-145, (h).
Sale.
Arbitrage transactions, §58-7-145, (e).
Dealers, §58-7-145, (d).
Delivery of security sold, §58-7-145, (c).
Equity securities held less than six months, §58-7-145, (b).
Severability of provisions, §58-7-145, (i).
Statement of ownership, §58-7-145, (a).
Impairment of capital, §58-7-75.
Assessment of shares, §58-7-110.
Dividends not payable when capital impaired.
Liability of stockholders for unlawful dividends, §58-7-125.

INSURANCE COMPANIES —Cont'd
Stock and stockholders —Cont'd
Impairment of capital —Cont'd
Reduction of capital stock, §§58-7-105, 58-7-120, 130A-45 to 130A-45.12.
Increase of capital stock, §§58-7-105, 58-7-115.
Certificate of authority to transact new business, §§58-7-105, 58-7-115.
Payment in cash for capital stock, §58-7-80.
Reduction of capital stock, §§58-7-105, 58-7-120.
Certificate of authority to conduct new business, §§58-7-105, 58-7-120.
Supervision generally, §§58-30-1 to 58-30-310.
See INSURER SUPERVISION, REHABILITATION AND LIQUIDATION.
Surplus.
Amount required, §58-7-75.
Impairment of surplus, §58-7-75.
Surplus lines insurance.
Generally, §§58-21-1 to 58-21-105.
See SURPLUS LINES INSURANCE.
Taxation.
Commissioner of insurance.
Election of certain taxes relating to insurance, §105-228.9.
Counties.
No additional local taxes, §105-228.10.
Credits.
Gross premiums tax.
Assessments paid to insurance guaranty associations, §105-228.5A.
Definitions, §105-228.3.
Gross premiums tax, §§105-228.5, 105-228.6.
Information to be furnished to commissioner, §58-6-20.
Local taxes.
No additional local taxes, §105-228.10.
Municipal corporations.
No additional local taxes, §105-228.10.
Persons procuring insurance directly with unlicensed insurer.
Collection of tax by commissioner of insurance, §105-228.9.
Premiums tax.
Additional local fire and lightning rate, §105-228.5, (d).
Measurement of additional tax imposed, §105-228.5, (b).
Additional statewide fire and lightning rate, §105-228.5, (d).
Article 65 corporations.
Measurement of tax imposed, §105-228.5, (b).
Rate of tax, §105-228.5, (d).
Calculation of tax base, §105-228.5, (b1).
Credits.
Assessments paid to insurance guaranty associations, §105-228.5A.
Exclusions, §105-228.5, (c).
Exemptions, §105-228.5, (g).
Installment payments, §105-228.5, (f).
Levy, §105-228.5, (a).
Payment, §105-228.5, (e).
Rate of taxes, §105-228.5, (d).
Reports, §105-228.5, (e).
Retaliatory taxes, §105-228.8.
Self-insurers.
Measurement of tax imposed, §105-228.5, (b).
Tax base, §105-228.5, (b).
Calculation, §105-228.5, (b1).
Withdrawal from state.
Taxes in case of, §105-228.6.

INSURANCE COMPANIES —Cont'd
Taxation —Cont'd
Premiums tax —Cont'd
Workers' compensation.
Rate of tax, §105-228.5, (d).
Retaliatory premium taxes, §105-228.8.
Risk retention groups.
Collection of tax by commissioner of insurance, §105-228.9.
Surplus lines.
Collection by commissioner of insurance, §105-228.9.
Third party administrators.
Generally, §§58-56-2 to 58-56-66.
See THIRD PARTY ADMINISTRATORS.
Title insurance.
Generally, §§58-26-1 to 58-27-15.
See TITLE INSURANCE.
Total loss claim.
Motor vehicle declared total loss.
Marking registration card and title certificate, §20-71.3, (a1).
Types of business entitled to do.
Upon payment of license fees and taxes, §58-6-7, (c).
Unauthorized insurers.
Generally, §§58-28-1 to 58-28-45.
See UNAUTHORIZED INSURERS.
Unauthorized insurers false advertising process act.
Generally, §§58-29-1 to 58-29-25.
See UNAUTHORIZED INSURERS.
Unclaimed property generally, §§116B-51 to 116B-80.
See UNCLAIMED PROPERTY.
Unfair claims settlement practices, §58-63-15.
Applicability to risk retention groups, §58-22-20.
Unfair trade practices.
Generally, §§58-63-1 to 58-63-70.
See INSURANCE UNFAIR TRADE PRACTICES.
Valuation of securities and investments, §58-7-192, (d).
Year 2000 date change.
Health care providers insurance payment claims not timely processed due to year 2000 date change.
Definitions, §58-2-235, (c).
Interim payments by insurer to providers, §58-2-235.
Payment in full, when considered, §58-2-235, (c).
Recovery of excess payment, §58-2-235, (c).
Report by insurer, §58-2-235, (a).

INSURANCE CONSUMER AND CUSTOMER INFORMATION PRIVACY, §§58-39-1 to 58-39-165.
Access to individual's personal recorded information.
Request by individual, §58-39-45.
Account numbers.
General prohibition on disclosure, §58-38-76, (a).
Definitions, §58-38-76, (b).
Exceptions, §58-38-76, (c).
Action by individual for violations.
Costs and attorney's fees, §58-39-105, (c).
Damages, §58-39-105, (b).
Equitable relief, §58-39-105, (a).
Exclusive remedy, §58-39-105, (e).
Statute of limitations, §58-39-105, (d).

INSURANCE CONSUMER AND CUSTOMER INFORMATION PRIVACY —Cont'd
Adverse underwriting decisions.
Defined, §58-39-15.
Notice of reasons, §58-39-55, (a).
Orally giving reasons and summary of rights, §58-39-55, (d).
Other agent or institution satisfying obligations, §58-39-55, (c).
Previous decisions.
Basing decision on, §58-39-65.
Seeking information concerning, prohibition, §58-39-60.
Rights of applicant or policyholder or individual upon request, §58-39-55, (b).
Summary of rights, providing, §58-39-55, (a).
Appeal of right.
Final order of commissioner, §58-39-100.
Authorization for disclosure, §58-38-75.
Cease and desist orders, §58-39-90.
Penalty for violating, §58-39-95, (b).
Civil penalties, §58-39-95, (a).
Civil penalty and forfeiture fund.
Proceeds of civil penalty remitted to, §58-39-95, (c).
Conditions for disclosure, §58-38-75.
Consumer reports.
Defined, §58-39-15.
Investigative consumer reports, §58-39-40.
Correction, amendment or deletion of individual's recorded information.
Request by individual, §58-39-50.
Credit insurance, applicability to, §58-39-10, (e).
Criminal activity, fraud or misrepresentation suspected.
Pretext interview, use to obtain information, §58-39-20.
Customer information safeguards act, §§58-39-130 to 58-39-165.
Definitions, §58-39-140.
Purpose, §58-39-130.
Scope, §58-39-135.
Short title, §58-39-1.
Definitions.
Account numbers, disclosure, §58-39-76.
Customer information safeguards act, §58-39-140.
Insurance information and privacy act, §58-39-15.
Disclosure authorization forms.
Personal or privileged information disclosure, requirements, §58-39-35.
Disclosure limitations and conditions, §58-38-75.
Effective date of rights granted, §58-39-120.
Examinations and investigations by commissioner.
Affairs of insurance institution or agent, §58-39-125, (a).
Affairs of insurance-support organization, §58-39-125, (b).
False pretenses.
Obtaining information under, criminal penalty, §58-39-115.
Governmental authority records, information gathered from.
Inapplicability of act, §58-39-10, (d).
Hearing on violations, §58-39-80, (b).
Immunity.
Disclosure in accordance with article, §58-39-110.
Individual remedies, §58-39-105.
Information security program, §58-39-145.
Effective date, §58-39-165.
Objects, §58-39-150.

INSURANCE CONSUMER AND CUSTOMER INFORMATION PRIVACY —Cont'd
Information security program —Cont'd
Rules, §58-39-155.
Violations, §58-39-160.
Institution, agents or insurance-support organizations.
Applicability of act to, §58-39-10, (a).
Insurance information and privacy protection act, §§58-39-1 to 58-39-76.
Definitions, §58-39-15.
Purpose of article, §58-39-5.
Short title, §58-39-1.
Standards for collection, use and disclosure of information.
Purpose of article, §58-39-5.
Investigative consumer reports.
Defined, §58-39-15.
Personal interview, §58-39-40, (b), (c).
Requirements before making, §58-39-40, (a).
Limitations on disclosure, §58-38-75.
Market and research survey information.
Specification of questions designed to obtain, §58-39-30.
Medical-record information.
Access to individual's personal recorded information, §58-39-45, (c).
Mortgage guaranty insurance company.
Notice of insurance information practices, §58-39-28, (b).
Notice of hearings on violations, §58-39-80, (a).
Notice of insurance information practices.
Abbreviated notice in lieu of notice, §58-39-25, (c).
Blanket or group insurance plan, §58-39-27, (g).
Combined or separate notices, §58-39-27, (c).
Exceptions to required notice, §58-39-27, (d) to (f).
Federal privacy disclosure, §58-39-26, (a).
Information included, §58-39-26, (b).
When provided, §58-39-26, (c).
Joint notice provided by institution or agent, §58-39-27, (a).
Mortgage guaranty insurance company, §58-39-28, (b).
Other institution or agent satisfying obligation, §58-39-25, (d).
Provided applicants and policyholders, §58-39-25, (a).
Requirements, §58-39-25, (b).
Single notice to two or more policyholders or applicants, §58-39-27, (b).
Title insurance company, §58-39-28, (a).
When provided, §58-39-25, (a).
Written notice required, contents, §58-39-25, (b).
Penalties, §58-39-95.
Personal information.
Access to individual's recorded information.
Request by individual, §58-39-45.
Correction, amendment or deletion of individual's recorded information.
Request by individual, §58-39-50.
Disclosure authorization forms, requirements, §58-39-35.
Disclosure limitations and conditions, §58-38-75.
Persons rights extended to, §58-39-10, (b).
Powers of commissioner, §58-39-125.
Pretext interview.
Defined, §58-39-15.
Use to obtain information, §58-39-20.
Reasons permitting disclosure, §58-38-75.

INSURANCE CONSUMER AND CUSTOMER INFORMATION PRIVACY —Cont'd
Request by individual.
Access to individual's personal recorded information.
Consumer reporting agency.
Not included in term insurance-support organization, §58-39-45, (g).
Duties owed individual requesting, §58-39-45, (a).
Fee to cover costs, charging, §58-39-45, (d).
Identification of source of information, §58-39-45, (b).
Medical-record information, §58-39-45, (c).
Natural persons, extension of rights to, §58-39-45, (f).
Other institution or agent satisfying obligation, §58-39-45, (e).
Rights of individual requesting, §58-39-45, (a).
Correction, amendment or deletion of recorded information.
Consumer reporting agency.
Not included in term insurance-support organization, §58-39-50, (f).
Duties and rights owed individual, §58-39-50, (a).
Natural persons, extension of rights to, §58-39-50, (e).
Notice to individual, furnishing information, §58-39-50, (b).
Refusal, disagreement with, §58-39-50, (c), (d).
Resident of state, when considered, §58-39-10, (c).
Security program, §58-39-145.
Effective date, §58-39-165.
Objects, §58-39-150.
Rules, §58-39-155.
Violations, §58-39-160.
Service of process on support organization.
Organization outside state, §58-39-85.
Statement of charges.
Violations, service, §58-39-80, (a).
Title insurance company.
Notice of insurance information practices, §58-39-28, (a).
Violations.
Cease and desist orders, §58-39-90.
Hearing and procedures, §58-39-80.
Individual remedies, §58-39-105.
Information security program, §58-39-160.
Penalties, §58-39-95.

INSURANCE CONSUMER PROTECTION FUND, §58-2-215.

INSURANCE DEPARTMENT.
Accident and health insurance.
Credit insurance generally, §§58-57-1 to 58-57-115.
See CREDIT INSURANCE.
Generally.
See ACCIDENT AND HEALTH INSURANCE.
Adjusters.
Generally.
See INSURANCE ADJUSTERS.
Aged persons.
Accident and health insurance.
Joint action to insure elderly, §§58-52-1 to 58-52-25.
See ACCIDENT AND HEALTH INSURANCE.

INSURANCE DEPARTMENT —Cont'd
Agents.
Generally.
See INSURANCE AGENTS.
Annuities.
Generally.
See ANNUITIES.
Assessment companies, §§58-11-1 to 58-11-35.
See ASSESSMENT COMPANIES.
Beach area essential property insurance, §§58-45-1 to 58-45-90.
See BEACH AREA ESSENTIAL PROPERTY INSURANCE.
Brokers.
Generally.
See INSURANCE BROKERS.
Building code council.
Transfer to department, §143A-78.
Commissioner generally, §§58-2-1 to 58-2-230.
See INSURANCE COMMISSIONER.
Companies generally.
See INSURANCE COMPANIES.
Consumer protection fund.
Appropriations, §58-2-215, (c).
Creation, §58-2-215, (a).
Uses, §58-2-215, (b).
Continuing care retirement communities.
Generally, §§58-64-1 to 58-64-85.
See CONTINUING CARE RETIREMENT COMMUNITIES.
Creation, §§58-2-1, 143A-73.
Credit insurance.
Generally, §§58-57-1 to 58-57-115.
See CREDIT INSURANCE.
Defined, §58-1-5.
Duties, §58-2-1.
Established, §58-2-1.
Fair access to insurance requirements, §§58-46-1 to 58-46-60.
See PROPERTY INSURANCE.
Fire insurance.
Generally.
See FIRE INSURANCE.
Foreign or alien insurance companies.
Generally.
See FOREIGN OR ALIEN INSURANCE COMPANIES.
Fraternal benefit societies.
Directors, officers, employees or agents.
Powers of society to purchase and maintain insurance, §58-24-35, (c).
Exemptions from general insurance laws, §58-24-110.
Generally.
See FRATERNAL BENEFIT SOCIETIES.
Mutual life insurance companies.
Conversion of society into company, §58-24-70.
Reinsurance, §58-24-60, (a).
Consolidation or merger, §58-24-60, (b).
Health care benefits providers.
Determination of jurisdiction over generally, §§58-49-1 to 58-49-25.
See HEALTH CARE BENEFITS PROVIDERS.
Regulation of multiple employer welfare arrangements generally, §§58-49-30 to 58-49-65.
See HEALTH CARE BENEFITS PROVIDERS.
Health insurance.
Credit insurance generally, §§58-57-1 to 58-57-115.
See CREDIT INSURANCE.

INSURANCE DEPARTMENT —Cont'd
Health insurance —Cont'd
Generally.
See ACCIDENT AND HEALTH INSURANCE.
Health maintenance organizations, §§58-67-1 to 58-67-185.
See HEALTH MAINTENANCE ORGANIZATIONS.
Holding companies generally, §§58-19-1 to 58-19-70.
See INSURANCE HOLDING COMPANIES.
Hospital, medical and dental service corporations, §§58-65-1 to 58-66-40.
See HOSPITAL, MEDICAL AND DENTAL SERVICE CORPORATIONS.
Hull insurance, protection and indemnity clubs, §§58-20-1 to 58-20-40.
See HULL INSURANCE, PROTECTION AND INDEMNITY CLUBS.
Insurance policies or contracts.
Generally.
See INSURANCE POLICIES OR CONTRACTS.
Liability insurance commission.
Generally, §§58-32-1 to 58-32-30.
See LIABILITY INSURANCE COMMISSION.
Transfer to department, §143A-79.1.
Life and health insurance guaranty association, §§58-62-2 to 58-62-95.
See LIFE AND HEALTH INSURANCE GUARANTY ASSOCIATION.
Life insurance.
Generally, §§58-58-1 to 58-61-15.
See LIFE INSURANCE.
Limited representatives generally.
See INSURANCE LIMITED REPRESENTATIVES.
Long-term care insurance.
Generally, §§58-55-1 to 58-55-50.
See LONG-TERM CARE INSURANCE.
Managing general agents.
Generally.
See MANAGING GENERAL INSURANCE AGENTS.
Motor vehicle insurance.
Generally.
See MOTOR VEHICLE INSURANCE.
Mutual insurance companies.
Generally, §§58-8-1 to 58-8-60.
See MUTUAL INSURANCE COMPANIES.
Personnel.
Powers of commissioner, §58-2-25, (a).
Placing of insurance for state agencies by, §58-31-55.
Post assessment insurance guaranty association, §§58-48-1 to 58-48-130.
See POST ASSESSMENT INSURANCE GUARANTY ASSOCIATION.
Powers of insurance commissioner.
Transfer to department, §143A-75.
Rate bureau.
Generally, §§58-36-1 to 58-36-110.
See RATE BUREAU.
Rate regulation generally, §§58-40-1 to 58-40-140.
See INSURANCE RATES.
Readable insurance policies generally, §§58-38-1 to 58-38-40.
See INSURANCE POLICIES OR CONTRACTS.
Reciprocal insurance.
Generally, §§58-15-1 to 58-15-150.
See RECIPROCAL INSURANCE.

INSURANCE DEPARTMENT —Cont'd

Reinsurance.
Generally.
See REINSURANCE.

Reinsurance intermediaries, §§58-9-2 to 58-9-26.
See REINSURANCE INTERMEDIARIES.

Risk retention groups.
Generally, §§58-22-1 to 58-22-70.
See RISK RETENTION GROUPS.

Seal, §58-2-35.

Small employer group health coverage.
Generally, §§58-50-105 to 58-50-150.
See SMALL EMPLOYER GROUP HEALTH COVERAGE.

State agencies.
Placing of insurance for state agencies by, §58-31-55.

State fire and rescue commission.
Transfer to department, §143A-79.2.

Supervision, rehabilitation and liquidation of insurers.
Generally, §§58-30-1 to 58-30-310.
See INSURER SUPERVISION, REHABILITATION AND LIQUIDATION.

Surplus lines insurance.
Generally, §§58-21-1 to 58-21-105.
See SURPLUS LINES INSURANCE.

Third party administrators.
Generally, §§58-56-2 to 58-56-66.
See THIRD PARTY ADMINISTRATORS.

Title insurance.
Generally, §§58-26-1 to 58-27-15.
See TITLE INSURANCE.

Transfer of powers of insurance commissioner to department, §143A-75.

Unauthorized insurers.
Generally, §§58-28-1 to 58-28-45.
See UNAUTHORIZED INSURERS.

Unauthorized insurers false advertising process act.
Generally, §§58-29-1 to 58-29-25.
See UNAUTHORIZED INSURERS.

Unfair trade practices.
Generally, §§58-63-1 to 58-63-70.
See INSURANCE UNFAIR TRADE PRACTICES.

Volunteer fire department.
Transfer to department, §143A-79.

INSURANCE DISCRIMINATION.

Accident and health insurance.
Coverage of bones and joints, §58-3-121, (a) to (c).
Group accident and health insurance.
Mentally ill and chemically dependent.
Applicability, §58-51-55, (d).
Coverage, §58-51-55, (b1), (c).
Definitions, §58-51-55, (a).
Prohibited acts, §58-51-55, (b), (c).

Bones, coverage of, §58-3-121, (a) to (c).

Employer discrimination against lawful use of lawful products during nonworking hours.
Health, disability or life insurance policies distinguishing between employees, §95-28.2, (b).

Handicapped persons.
Prohibited, §168-10.

Joints, coverage of, §58-3-121, (a) to (c).

Life insurance.
Prohibited acts, §58-58-35.

Motor vehicles.
Prohibited practices, §58-3-25.

INSURANCE DISCRIMINATION —Cont'd

Race, color or national or ethnic origin.
Prohibited acts, §58-3-25, (c).

Rates not to be unfairly discriminatory, §58-40-20, (a), (e).
Method of rate making, §58-36-10.

Unfair trade practices.
Prohibited acts, §58-63-15.

INSURANCE FRAUD.

Burning dwelling, §14-65.

Burning personal property, §14-66.

False statement to procure or deny benefit of policy or certificate, §58-2-161, (b).
Action, §58-2-161, (b).
Criminal penalties, §58-2-161, (b).
Insurer defined, §58-2-161, (a).
Statement defined, §58-2-161, (a).

Immunity from liability for reporting, §58-2-160, (a), (b).

Life insurance.
Creditors deprived of benefits of policies except in cases of fraud, §58-15-115.
Misrepresentation of policies prohibited, §58-58-40.

Reinsurance.
Reporting and investigation, §58-2-160, (a), (b).
Request for and release of information, §58-2-160, (c).

Twisting, §58-3-115.

INSURANCE HOLDING COMPANIES, §§58-19-1 to 58-19-70.

Acquisition of control of or merger with domestic insurer.
Approval by commissioner, §58-19-15, (d), (f).
Exceptions to provisions, §58-19-15, (h).
Foreign or alien insurer.
Report of change of control, §58-19-17, (b).
Definitions, §58-19-17, (a).
Hearing, §58-19-15, (e).
Jurisdiction of courts, §58-19-15, (j).
Mailing of notices and other materials.
Expenses, §58-19-15, (g).
Prohibited acts, §58-19-15, (i).
Restrictions, §58-19-15, (a).
Statement to be filed, §58-19-15, (a) to (c).
Contents of statement, §58-19-15, (b).
Oath or affirmation, §58-19-15, (b).
Violations of provisions, §58-19-15, (i).

Appeals.
Orders of commissioner, §58-19-70, (a).

Cease and desist orders.
Violations of provisions, §58-19-50, (c).

Commissioner.
Acquisition of control of or merger with domestic insurer.
Approval by commissioner, §58-19-15, (d), (f).
Appeals from order of commissioner, §58-19-70, (a).
Examinations, §§58-19-35, 58-19-40.
Mandatory injunction or writ of mandamus directing commissioner to act, §58-19-70, (b).

Confidentiality of information.
Information obtained by commissioner, §58-19-40.

Definitions, §58-19-5.

Dividends.
Extraordinary dividends, §58-19-30, (c).
Reporting of dividends by registered insurers, §58-19-25, (d).

Examinations, §58-19-35, (a), (b), (d).
Confidentiality of information, §58-19-40.

INSURANCE HOLDING COMPANIES —Cont'd
Felonies.
False statements or reports, §58-19-50, (e).
Findings of legislature, §58-19-1, (a).
Gramm-Leach-Bliley act.
Affiliations with depository institutions, §58-19-2.
Injunctions.
Mandatory injunction directing commissioner to act, §58-19-70, (b).
Violations of provisions, §58-19-45, (a).
Investments, §58-19-10, (b), (d).
Disposal of investments if insurer ceases to control subsidiary, §58-19-10, (e).
Exemption from certain provisions, §58-19-10, (c).
Liquidation or rehabilitation of domestic insurer.
Recovery.
Generally, §58-19-60, (a).
Liability, §58-19-60, (c), (e).
Maximum amount recoverable, §58-19-60, (d).
Restrictions, §58-19-60, (b).
Mandamus.
Writ of mandamus directing commissioner to act, §58-19-70, (b).
Penalties.
Criminal penalties for violations, §58-19-50, (d).
Registration statement.
Failure to file, §58-19-50, (a).
Transactions or investments in violation of provisions.
Director of officer, §58-19-50, (b).
Policy of state, §58-19-1, (b).
Purposes of provisions, §58-19-1, (b).
Registration of insurers.
Affiliated insurers.
Disclaimer of affiliation with authorized insurer, §58-19-25, (j).
Registration on behalf of, §58-19-25, (i).
Disclaimer of affiliation with authorized insurer, §58-19-25, (j).
Dividends and distributions.
Reporting to commissioner by registered insurers, §58-19-25, (d).
Exemption from provisions of section, §58-19-25, (i).
Information necessary to comply with provisions.
Persons required to provide to insurers, §58-19-25, (e).
Required, §58-19-25, (a).
Statements, §58-19-25, (a) to (c).
Consolidated registration statement, §58-19-25, (g).
Contents, §58-19-25, (b).
Failure to file, §58-19-25, (k).
Penalty, §58-19-50, (a).
Termination of registration, §58-19-25, (f).
Subsidiaries, §58-19-10.
Cessation of control of subsidiary.
Disposal of investments therein, §58-19-10, (e).
Defined, §58-19-5.
Organization or acquisition, §58-19-10, (a).
Surplus.
Determination of reasonableness, §58-19-30, (d).
Transactions.
Standards, §58-19-30, (a), (b).
Violations of provisions.
Cease and desist orders, §58-19-50, (c).
Injunctions, §58-19-45, (a).
Receivership, §58-19-55.
Revocation or suspension, §58-19-65.

INSURANCE HOLDING COMPANIES —Cont'd
Voting securities.
Prohibitions against voting, §58-19-45, (b).
Sequestration, §58-19-45, (c).

INSURANCE INFORMATION AND PRIVACY PROTECTION ACT, §§58-39-1 to 58-39-76.
See INSURANCE CONSUMER AND CUSTOMER INFORMATION PRIVACY.

INSURANCE INSTRUCTOR LICENSES, §58-33-132, (a).
Summary suspension, §58-33-132, (b).

INSURANCE LIMITED REPRESENTATIVES.
Assumed name, operating under, §58-33-83.
Bankruptcy, insolvency or receivership.
Commissioner to be notified, §58-33-46, (c).
Charges in excess of premium prohibited, §58-33-85, (b).
Commissions, brokerage, service fee or other valuable consideration.
Assigning or directing payment, §58-33-82, (e).
License required to accept, §58-33-82, (d).
Renewal or other deferred commissions, §58-33-82, (c).
Unlicensed person, paying to or accepting, §58-33-82, (a), (b).
Companies not licensed to do business in state.
Soliciting for prohibited, §58-33-26, (h).
Discrimination.
Prohibited, §58-33-80.
Licenses.
Acting without license, §58-33-120.
Applicability of article, §58-33-1.
Application, §58-33-31, (a).
Business entities, §58-33-31, (b).
Documents necessary to verify information, requiring, §58-33-31, (c).
Required, §58-33-30, (a).
Business entities, §58-33-26, (j).
Definitions, §58-33-10.
Denial, §58-33-30, (g).
Duplicate licenses.
Lost, stolen or destroyed license, §58-33-50, (d).
Education and training, §58-33-30, (d).
Examination, §58-33-30, (e).
Exemptions, §58-33-35.
Exceptions to requirement, §58-33-26, (n).
Insurers, §58-33-26, (o).
Fees, §58-33-125, (a) to (g).
General requirements, §58-33-26, (a).
Interstate reciprocity.
Administrative action against licensee, reporting, §58-33-32, (k).
Application requirements, waiver, §58-33-32, (i).
Conditions for receiving nonresident license, §58-33-32, (c).
Continuing education requirements, satisfaction, §58-33-32, (j).
Criminal prosecutions, reporting, §58-33-32, (l).
Examination, when not required, §58-33-32, (g).
Greater fee not to be assessed, §58-33-32, (h).
Limited lines license, §58-33-32, (f).
Purposes of section, §58-33-32, (a).
Kinds of licenses representative may qualify for, §58-33-26, (g).
Name, social security number or other identifying number, §58-33-26, (k).
Nonresident, §58-33-30, (h).
Interstate reciprocity, §58-33-32.
Reciprocity, §58-33-30, (j).

INSURANCE LIMITED REPRESENTATIVES —Cont'd
Licenses —Cont'd
Nonresident —Cont'd
Retaliatory provisions, §58-33-30, (i).
Notice.
Suspension, revocation or nonrenewal, §58-33-50, (a), (b).
Reciprocity.
Interstate reciprocity, §58-33-32.
Renewal, §58-33-26, (m).
Required, §§58-33-5, 58-33-26, (b).
Surrender.
Termination of residency, §58-33-50, (c).
Suspension, revocation, refusal to renew, placing licensee on probation.
Authority of commissioner, §58-33-46, (a).
Grounds, §58-33-46, (a).
Issuance of another license, requirements, §58-33-46, (d).
Notice, §58-33-50, (a), (b).
Other provisions, applicability, §58-33-46, (b).
Temporary licensing, §58-33-65.
Authority of commissioner to issue, §58-33-66, (a).
Grounds for issuing, §58-33-66, (a).
Limiting authority of temporary licensee, §58-33-66, (b).
Revoking, §58-33-66, (b).
Sponsor, requiring temporary licensee to have, §58-33-66, (b).
Termination on transfer of business, §58-33-66, (b).
Violations of insurance laws.
License not to be issued, §58-33-46, (e).
Violations of licensing laws.
Impositions of penalties or remedies, §58-33-46, (f).
Misdemeanors.
Premiums.
Obtaining by fraud, §58-33-100, (b).
Policies.
Signing certain blank policies, §58-33-110.
Premiums.
Obtaining by fraud, §58-33-100, (b).
Payments to limited representatives valid, §58-33-100, (a).
Rebates or discounts prohibited, §58-33-85, (a).
Representation.
Controversies between insured and insurer, §58-33-20.
Twisting.
Prohibited, §58-33-75.
Unauthorized insurers.
Soliciting, negotiating or selling insurance for.
Civil action or license revocation proceeding, §58-33-95, (b).
Criminal penalty, §58-33-95, (a).
Strict liability for losses or unpaid claims, §58-33-95, (a).
Terms defined, §58-33-95, (c).
Violation of insurance laws, §58-33-120.

INSURANCE POINTS.
Motor vehicle insurance.
At-fault accidents and certain moving violations, §58-36-75, (a) to (g).
Classifications and safe driver incentive plan, §58-36-65, (a) to (m).

INSURANCE POLICIES OR CONTRACTS.
Accident and health insurance.
Adopted children.
Policies to cover, §§58-51-30, (a) to (f), 58-51-125, (a) to (c).
Age limits, §58-50-20.
Applications for, §58-50-5, (a).
Alteration, §58-50-5, (b).
False statements.
Effect, §58-50-5, (c).
Blanket accident and health insurance, §58-51-75, (a).
Approval of forms, §58-51-85.
Disability income insurance.
Standards for policies, §58-51-130.
Exemption of certain policies from provisions, §58-50-65.
Filing.
Rules and regulations as to, §58-51-15, (g).
Forfeiture.
Notice of nonpayment of premium required before forfeiture, §58-50-35.
Forms, §58-51-5, (a).
Approval by commissioner, §58-51-1.
Other states, §58-51-5, (b).
Group accident and health insurance, §58-51-80, (a), (b).
Approval of forms, §58-51-85.
Renewal, §58-51-110, (a).
Replacement, §58-51-110, (b).
Industrial sick benefit insurance.
Provisions, §58-51-70.
Intoxicants and narcotics, §58-51-16, (a) to (c).
Mentally retarded or physically handicapped children.
Policy coverage to continue as to, §58-51-25.
Narcotics and intoxicants, §58-51-16, (a) to (c).
Newborn infants.
Policies to cover, §58-51-30, (a) to (f).
Nonconforming policies, §58-50-15, (b).
Preexisting condition exclusion.
Clarification, §58-51-15, (h).
"Preexisting conditions."
Meaning of term, §58-51-60.
Provisions.
Generally, §58-51-15, (a), (b).
Inapplicable or inconsistent provisions, §58-51-15, (c).
Industrial benefit insurance, §58-51-70.
Order of certain policy provisions, §58-51-15, (d).
Other policy provisions.
Effect, §58-50-15, (a).
Requirements of other jurisdictions, §58-51-15, (f).
Renewability.
Applicability of provisions, §58-51-20, (d).
Notice, §58-51-20, (a).
Policies issued during grace period construed to be continuation of first policy, §58-51-15, (c).
Unilateral acts by insurers prohibited, §58-51-15, (b).
Requirements, §58-51-5, (a).
Other states, §58-51-5, (b).
Return of policy.
Notice of right to return policy, §58-51-10.
Third-party ownership not precluded, §58-51-15, (e).
Actions or suit on policies or contracts.
Conditions or stipulations.
Court or jurisdiction for bringing action or suit.
Prohibited, §58-3-35, (a).

INSURANCE POLICIES OR CONTRACTS —Cont'd
Actions or suit on policies or contracts —Cont'd
Conditions or stipulations —Cont'd
Prohibited conditions or stipulations void, §58-3-35, (c).
Time for bringing action or suit.
Less than period prescribed by law, prohibited, §58-3-35, (b).
Additional insurance clauses.
Prohibited, §58-3-15.
Annuities.
Standard nonforfeiture law for individual deferred annuities, §58-58-61.
Standard provisions, §58-58-23.
Assessment companies.
"Assessment plan" to be printed on, §58-11-10.
Revocation for noncompliance, §58-11-15.
Conformance with charter and bylaws required, §58-11-5.
Binders.
Lenders engaged in mortgage or deed of trust loans.
Acceptance or denial of temporary insurance contracts, §58-3-140.
Cancellation.
Applicability of article, §58-41-10, (a).
Citation of article, §58-41-1.
Commercial general liability insurance.
Extended reporting periods, §58-40-140.
Grounds, §58-41-15, (a).
Intent of legislature, §58-41-5, (a), (b).
In-term cancellation of entire book of business, §58-41-45, (b).
Legislative findings, §58-41-5, (a), (b).
Loss of reinsurance, §58-41-30.
Nonpayment of premium, §58-41-15, (d).
Notice.
Copies sent to agent or broker, §58-41-15, (e).
Required, §58-41-15, (b).
Timing of notice to insured, §58-41-40, (b).
Penalties, §58-41-55.
Policy in effect for less than sixty days, §58-41-15, (c).
Provisions not exclusive, §58-41-10, (b).
Short title, §58-41-1.
Statements or communications made in good faith.
No liability for, §58-41-40, (a).
Workers' compensation insurance.
Before expiration of policy, §58-36-105.
Certificates of authority.
Prerequisite to issuance of policies, §58-7-10.
Charitable gift annuities, §58-3-6.
Choice of law provisions.
Court or jurisdiction in which action or suit may be brought.
Condition or stipulation in policy prohibited, §58-3-35, (a).
Coinsurance clauses, §58-3-15.
Commercial general liability insurance.
Extended reporting periods, §58-40-140, (a).
Health care provider professional liability insurance, §58-40-140, (b), (c).
Conditions.
Court or jurisdiction action may be brought.
Prohibited, §58-3-35, (a).
Forbidden conditions or stipulations void, §58-3-35, (c).

INSURANCE POLICIES OR CONTRACTS —Cont'd
Conditions —Cont'd
Time within which suit or action may be commenced.
Less than period prescribed by law, prohibited, §58-3-35, (b).
Construction, §58-1-10.
Credit insurance.
Amounts authorized, §58-57-15.
Contents, §58-57-25, (b).
Credit unemployment insurance.
Provisions, §58-57-110, (a) to (c).
Insurance to be evidenced by individual policy, §58-57-25, (a).
Issuance, §58-57-55.
Kinds of policies authorized, §58-57-10.
Notification when policy not delivered to debtor, §58-57-25, (e).
Prohibited provisions, §58-57-25, (d).
Required provisions, §58-57-25, (c).
Death benefits.
Interest of trustee as beneficiary.
Sufficient to support inter vivos or testamentary trust, §36A-100.
Death benefits paid in services or merchandise.
Issuance of contract providing prohibited, §58-3-55.
Deductibles.
Requirements for additional insurance or coinsurance clauses, §58-3-15.
Deemer provisions.
Law has deemed filing or contract to be approved, §58-3-151.
Disability income insurance.
Standards for policies, §58-51-130.
Discrimination by insurance companies.
Prohibited acts, §58-3-120.
Documents submitted to department.
Paper size, stapling or binding, §58-3-150, (c).
Excess liability policies.
Uninsured and underinsured motorist coverages, §58-3-152.
Exclusive nature of provisions, §58-3-5.
False statement to procure or deny benefit, §58-2-161.
Family leave credit insurance, §58-57-115.
Farmowners' and other policies.
Ice, snow or sleet damage, §58-44-55.
Fire insurance.
Amount.
Limitation, §58-43-5.
Conditions of insurance to be stated, §58-44-1.
Devices.
Performance of contracts as to devices not prohibited, §58-43-1.
Encumbrances.
Notice to encumbrance.
Effect of failure to give, §58-44-40.
Functional replacement, §58-43-5.
Husband and wife.
Policy issued to husband or wife on point property, §58-44-45.
Indemnity contracts for difference in actual value and cost of replacement, §58-43-5.
Items to be stated in policies, §58-44-5.
Mortgagees.
Policies for benefit of, §58-43-15.
Standard fire insurance policy, §58-44-15, (a), (b).
Form, §58-44-15, (c).

INSURANCE POLICIES OR CONTRACTS
—Cont'd
Fire insurance —Cont'd
Standard fire insurance policy —Cont'd
Increase of hazard, unoccupancy and other insurance.
Notice by insured or agent as, §58-44-30.
Nuclear reaction, nuclear radiation or radioactive contamination.
Optional provisions as to loss or damage from, §58-44-25.
Permissible variations, §58-44-20.
Umpire.
Judge to select, §58-44-35.
Term.
Limitation, §58-43-5.
Forms.
Approval, §58-41-50, (a).
Commissioner of insurance, §58-3-150, (a).
Existing policy forms, §58-40-115.
Group and blanket accident and health insurance and group life insurance policies, §58-3-150, (b).
Lost forms.
Proof furnished, §58-3-40.
Information as to.
Furnishing to commissioner, §58-6-20.
Interest rates on life insurance policies loans.
Purpose of provisions, §58-61-1.
Law has deemed filing or contract to be approved.
Deemer provisions, §58-3-151.
Life and health insurance guaranty association.
Powers and duties of association generally, §58-62-36, (a) to (t).
Life insurance.
Forfeiture.
Notice of nonpayment of premium required, §58-58-120.
Group insurance.
Authorized policies, §58-58-135.
Standard provisions, §58-58-140.
Interest rates on life insurance policy loans, §§58-61-1 to 58-61-15.
Renunciation, §58-58-100.
Standard nonforfeiture law, §58-58-55, (a) to (i).
Standard provisions, §58-58-22.
Annuity and pure endowment contracts, §58-58-23.
Standard valuation law, §58-58-50, (a) to (l).
Statements required, §58-58-1.
Survivorship fund in life insurance contract.
Prohibited, §58-58-15.
Viatical life insurance settlements, §§58-58-200 to 58-58-310.
See VIATICAL LIFE INSURANCE SETTLEMENTS.
Limitation of action.
Condition or stipulation in policy or contract.
Prohibition, less time than that prescribed by law, §58-3-35, (b).
Long-term care insurance.
Generally, §§58-55-1 to 58-55-50.
See LONG-TERM CARE INSURANCE.
Medicare supplement insurance.
Generally, §§58-54-1 to 58-54-50.
See MEDICARE.
Misdemeanors.
Willful violations of provisions, §58-50-70.

INSURANCE POLICIES OR CONTRACTS
—Cont'd
Missing persons.
Payment on policies, §28C-18.
Mortgage or deed of trust loans.
Temporary contracts.
Acceptance or denial binders by lenders, §58-3-140.
Motor vehicle insurance.
Information to be contained in policies, §20-279.21, (d).
Liability policies, §20-279.21.
Cancellation or nonrenewal.
Notice, §20-279.22.
Surrender of license, §20-279.30.
Other policies not affected, §20-279.23.
Termination.
Notice, §20-279.22.
Surrender of license, §20-279.30.
Multiple policies, §20-279.21, (j).
Operator policies, §20-279.21, (c).
Other than auto liability, §20-279.23.
Owner's policies, §20-279.21, (b).
Taxicab operators, §20-279.21, (c).
Mutual insurance companies.
Assignment, §58-8-45.
Contingent liability printed on policy, §58-8-35.
Nonassessable policies.
Foreign or alien companies, §58-8-40.
Prerequisites to issuance, §58-8-1.
Nature of insurance contracts, §58-1-10.
Paper size, stapling or binding.
Documents submitted to department, §58-3-150, (c).
Principal and income act.
Allocation of receipts not normally apportioned during administration of trust, §37A-4-407, (a) to (c).
Proof of lost forms.
Furnishing, §58-3-40.
Punishment for violations, §58-50-70.
Rate regulation generally, §§58-40-1 to 58-40-140.
See INSURANCE RATES.
Readable policies, §§58-38-1 to 58-38-40.
Actions arising from policies approved pursuant to provisions.
Language on which actions may be based, §58-38-40, (c).
Applicability of provisions, §58-38-10, (a).
Exceptions, §58-38-10, (b).
Filing requirements, §58-38-35, (a).
Citation of act.
Short title, §58-38-1.
Construction and interpretation, §58-38-40, (a), (b).
Definitions, §58-38-15.
"Text," §58-38-25, (e).
Disapproval of policy by commissioner.
Grounds, §58-38-30, (b).
Exclusive nature of provisions, §58-38-10, (c).
Exemptions from provisions, §58-38-10, (b).
Filing policies with commissioner, §58-38-30, (a).
Applicability of requirements, §58-38-35, (a).
Flesch scale analysis readability score.
Defined, §58-38-15.
Procedures, §58-38-25, (a) to (d).
Format requirements, §58-38-20, (a).
Determination of whether policy in compliance.
Factors to be considered, §58-38-20, (b).

INSURANCE POLICIES OR CONTRACTS —Cont'd
Readable policies —Cont'd
Hospital, medical and dental service corporations.
Readable insurance certificates act, §§58-66-1 to 58-66-40.
See HOSPITAL, MEDICAL AND DENTAL SERVICE CORPORATIONS.
Legislative declaration.
Purpose of act, §58-38-5.
Non-English language policies.
When deemed in compliance, §58-38-10, (d).
Purpose of act, §58-38-5.
Scope of application, §58-38-10.
Title of act.
Short title, §58-38-1.
Real property warranties, §58-1-20, (a).
Reciprocal insurance, §58-15-50.
Additional nature of authority to enter into reciprocal insurance contracts, §58-15-20, (b).
Assessable policies.
Subscribers contingent assessment liability, §58-15-60.
Eligible contracting persons, §58-15-20, (a).
Nonassessable policies.
Certificate authorizing, §58-15-65, (a), (b).
Revocation upon impairment of surplus, §58-15-65, (c).
Surplus requirement, §58-15-65, (d).
Reinsurance.
Assumption reinsurance.
Notice, §58-10-30, (a) to (h).
Policyholder rights, §58-10-35, (a) to (d).
Renewal.
Notice, §58-41-25.
Policies with premium or coverage changes, §58-41-25, (a) to (e).
Timing of notice to insured, §58-41-40, (b).
Secured transactions.
Inapplicability of article 9.
Transfers of policy interest or assignment of claim, §25-9-109, (d).
Service of process.
Violations as to.
Penalty, §58-43-35.
Simultaneous death of insured and beneficiary.
Contract provision for distribution of proceeds, §28A-24-5.
State law governs, §58-3-1.
Exclusive nature of law, §58-3-5.
Statute of limitations.
Condition or stipulation as to time for bringing action.
Prohibited, period less than prescribed by law, §58-3-35, (b).
Stipulations.
Court or jurisdiction action may be brought.
Prohibited, §58-3-35, (a).
Forbidden conditions or stipulations void, §58-3-35, (c).
Time within which suit or action may be commenced.
Less than period prescribed by law, prohibited, §58-3-35, (b).
Supervision, rehabilitation and liquidation of insurers.
Liquidation.
Continuance of coverage, §58-30-110.
Surplus lines.
Valid and enforceable, §58-21-55.

INSURANCE POLICIES OR CONTRACTS —Cont'd
Temporary contracts.
Lenders engaged in mortgage or deed of trust loans.
Acceptance or denial binders, §58-3-140.
Twisting.
Insurance producers, prohibition, §58-33-75.
Venue for bringing action or suit.
Condition or stipulation prohibited, §58-3-35, (a).
Viatical life insurance settlements, §§58-58-200 to 58-58-310.
See VIATICAL LIFE INSURANCE SETTLEMENTS.
Warranties.
Manufacturers, distributors or sellers of goods or services, §58-1-15.
Statements in policies not warranties, §58-3-10.

INSURANCE PREMIUM FINANCING, §§58-35-1 to 58-35-100.
Agents.
Exemptions from license requirement, §58-35-10, (c).
Banks.
Exemption from license requirement, §58-35-10, (a).
Bonds, surety.
Licensees, §58-35-15, (a).
Brokers.
Exemptions from license requirements, §58-35-10, (c).
Cancellation of insurance contract upon default.
Procedure, §58-35-85.
Cash surrender value.
Cancellation of insurance contract upon default.
Collection of cash surrender value, §58-35-85.
Commissioner of insurance, §58-35-25.
Confession of judgment.
Provisions in agreements giving power of attorney to confess judgment in state.
Prohibited, §58-35-60.
Copies of agreements, §58-35-65.
Credit unions.
Exception to license requirement, §58-35-10, (a).
Definitions, §58-35-1.
Fees.
Disposition, §58-35-95.
Excessive finance charges, §58-35-35.
Licenses, §58-35-5, (d), (e).
Nonrefundable, §58-35-100.
Forms.
Filing with and approval by commissioner, §58-35-45, (a).
Insurance premium finance agreements, §58-35-50, (a).
Blanks.
Filling out before signing, §58-35-50, (d).
Hearings.
Power of commissioner of insurance, §58-35-25.
Insurance companies.
Exemption from license requirement, §58-35-10, (b).
Insurance premium financing agreements.
Assignment, §58-35-40, (b), (c).
Filing on notice not necessary to validity, §58-35-40, (b).
Payments by insured without notice of assignment, §58-35-70.
Contents, §58-35-50, (b), (c).

INSURANCE PREMIUM FINANCING —Cont'd
Insurance premium financing agreements —Cont'd
Copies.
Delivery of copy to insurer, §58-35-65.
Defined, §58-35-1.
Delinquency and collection charge on installments in default.
Agreements may provide for, §58-35-55, (f).
False information.
Penalty, §58-35-90.
Forms, §58-35-50, (a).
Blanks.
Filling out before signing, §58-35-50, (d).
Prohibited provisions, §58-35-60.
Investigations.
Power of commissioner of insurance, §58-35-25.
Licenses.
Applications, §58-35-5, (b), (c).
Bond, surety, §58-35-15, (a).
Branch office licenses, §58-35-5, (e).
Change of office location.
Notice to commissioner by licensee, §58-35-15, (f).
Display, §58-35-15, (e).
Engaging in business without license.
Penalty, §58-35-90.
Fees, §58-35-5, (d), (e).
Issuance, §58-35-15, (a).
One office per license, §58-35-15, (d).
Refusal, §58-35-15, (a).
Grounds, §58-35-20, (a).
Notice to applicant, §58-35-15, (b).
Renewal, §58-35-15, (c).
Refusal to renew.
Grounds, §58-35-20, (a).
Required, §58-35-5, (a).
Exceptions, §58-35-10.
Surrender of license, §58-35-20, (b).
Suspension or revocation, §58-35-20.
Grounds, §58-35-20, (a).
Term, §58-35-15, (c).
Transfer or assignment prohibited, §58-35-15, (e).
Types, §58-35-5, (e).
Misdemeanors.
Records.
Prohibited acts as to, §58-35-30, (b).
Violations of provisions, §58-35-90.
Notice.
Cancellation of insurance contract upon default, §58-35-85.
Payments by insured.
Assignment of agreement.
Payments without notice of assignment, §58-35-70.
Credit upon anticipation of payment.
Amount, §58-35-80, (b).
Authorized, §58-35-80, (a).
Default.
Cancellation of insurance contract upon default.
Procedure, §58-35-85.
Release on payment in full, §58-35-75, (b).
Statement of account, §58-35-75, (a).
Penalties.
Excessive finance charges, §58-35-35.
Violations of provisions, §58-35-90.
Rebates.
Prohibited, §58-35-40, (a), (c).
Records.
False statements.
Misdemeanor, §58-35-30, (b).
Licensees, §58-35-30, (a).

INSURANCE PREMIUM FINANCING —Cont'd
Records —Cont'd
Refusal to exhibit to commissioner.
Misdemeanor, §58-35-30, (b).
Reports.
Licensees, §58-35-30, (a).
Savings and loan associations.
Exemption from license requirement, §58-35-10, (a).
Service charges.
Authorized, §58-35-55, (b), (d).
Computation, §58-35-55, (c), (d).
Limitations on, §58-35-55, (a).
Multiple agreements for obtaining excessive charges prohibited, §58-35-55, (e).
Rate plan.
Filing with commissioner, §58-35-45, (b).

INSURANCE PREMIUMS.
Absentees in military service.
Receivers' power to pay, §28B-6.
Accident and health insurance.
Approval of rates by commissioner, §§58-51-1, 58-51-95, (f).
Increased rates, §58-51-95, (f).
Filing of rates.
Group or blanket accident and health insurance, §58-51-85.
Group accident and health insurance.
Adjustment of rate, §58-51-80, (g).
Continuation privileges.
Payment of premiums, §58-53-30.
Conversion privileges, §58-53-60.
Joint action to insure elderly.
Approval of rates by commissioner, §58-52-15.
Nonpayment.
Notice required before forfeiture, §58-50-35.
Refund.
Notice of right to return policy and have premium refunded, §58-51-10.
Credit cards.
Solicitation, negotiation or payment of premiums through credit cards facilities.
Prohibited, §58-3-145.
Credit insurance.
Credit property insurance, §58-57-90, (b).
Credits, §58-57-50, (e).
Rate standards, §§58-57-35 to 58-57-45.
Refunds.
Generally, §58-57-50, (a) to (e).
Minimum amount, §58-57-50, (d).
Reducing term insurance, §58-57-50, (b).
Financing, §§58-35-1 to 58-35-100.
See INSURANCE PREMIUM FINANCING.
Fire insurance.
Excess over actual cash value of property.
Reimbursement, §58-43-10.
Information as to.
Furnishing to commissioner, §58-6-20.
Life insurance.
Assessment life insurance companies.
Minimum premium rates, §58-58-125.
Default.
Notice of nonpayment.
Required before forfeiture, §58-58-120.
Employee life insurance.
Payment, §58-58-150.
Missing persons.
Receivers.
Authorization to pay, §28C-8.

INSURANCE PREMIUMS —Cont'd
North Carolina rate bureau, §§58-36-1 to 58-36-110.
See RATE BUREAU.
Rate regulation generally, §§58-40-1 to 58-40-140.
See INSURANCE RATES.
Supervision, rehabilitation and liquidation of insurers.
Recovery of premiums owed, §58-30-175, (a).
Obligation of insurer to pay unpaid premiums, §58-30-175, (b).
Surplus lines.
Effect of payment of licensee, §58-21-60.

INSURANCE PRODUCERS.
Insurance adjusters.
See INSURANCE ADJUSTERS.
Insurance agents.
See INSURANCE AGENTS.
Insurance brokers.
See INSURANCE BROKERS.
Insurance limited representatives.
See INSURANCE LIMITED REPRESENTATIVES.
Motor vehicle damage appraisers.
See MOTOR VEHICLE DAMAGE APPRAISERS.

INSURANCE RATES, §§58-40-1 to 58-40-140.
Accident and health insurance.
Exceptions to applicability of rating provisions, §58-40-15.
Group accident and health insurance.
Conversion privileges.
Premium rates and adjustments, §58-53-60.
Acting in concert.
Insurers authorized to act in concert, §§58-40-65, 58-40-70.
Advisory organizations.
Defined, §58-40-5.
Examination by commissioner, §58-40-90.
Filings required, §58-40-55, (a).
Changes or amendments to documents, §58-40-55, (b).
Licenses.
Required, §58-40-55, (a).
Unfair or unreasonable practices.
Prohibited, §58-40-55, (c).
Agreements among insurers.
Adherence agreements.
Prohibited, §58-40-75.
Apportionment agreement, §58-40-95.
Annuities.
Exemption from applicability of rating provisions, §58-40-15.
Appeals.
Orders and decisions of commissioner, §58-40-105, (b).
Applicability of provisions, §58-40-15.
Apportionment agreements among insurers, §58-40-95.
Beach area essential property insurance.
Applicability of rates, rating plans, rate rules and forms to insurance written by association, §58-45-45, (a).
Change in coverage or rates.
Notice, §58-41-20, (d) to (f).
Timing of notice to insured, §58-41-40, (b).
Commissioner.
Disapproval of rates, §58-40-45, (a).
Examination of organizations, §58-40-90.

INSURANCE RATES —Cont'd
Commissioner —Cont'd
Hearings, §58-40-105, (a).
Imposition of penalties or suspension of licenses, §58-40-110, (c).
Notice, §58-40-105, (a).
Joint underwriting and joint reinsurance organizations.
Unfair or unreasonable practices.
Cease and desist orders, §58-40-60, (c).
Judicial review of orders and decisions, §58-40-105, (b).
Willfully withholding or furnishing false or misleading information, §58-40-45, (c).
Construction and interpretation, §§58-40-120, 58-40-125.
Credit insurance.
Premium rates, §§58-57-35 to 58-57-45, 58-57-90, (b).
Credit property insurance, §58-57-90.
Criteria for determining compliance with standards, §58-40-25.
Definitions, §§58-40-5, 58-40-10.
Discrimination.
Rates not to be unfairly discriminatory, §58-40-20, (a), (e).
Dividends.
Payment of dividends not affected, §58-40-120.
Examinations.
Commissioner to examine organizations, §58-40-90.
Excessive rates, §58-40-20, (a).
Method of rate making, §58-36-10.
Existing rates, §58-40-115.
Filing, §§58-40-30, (a) to (d), 58-41-50, (a) to (g).
Charging unfiled rates, §58-41-50, (f).
Construction of provisions, §58-40-30, (d).
Exceeding filing, §58-40-30, (c).
Inspection, §58-40-35.
Prior to effective date, §58-40-30, (a).
Rates prepared by rating organization, §58-40-40, (b).
Statistical and rating information required, §58-41-50, (c) to (e).
Supporting data, §58-40-30, (b).
Inspection, §58-40-35.
Hearings.
Commissioner, §58-40-105, (a).
Rate bureau.
Disapproval of rates, §58-36-20, (a).
Violations of provisions.
Imposition of penalty or suspension of license, §58-40-110, (c).
Inadequate rates, §58-40-20, (a), (d).
Method of rate making, §58-36-10.
Insurers authorized to act in concert, §§58-40-65, 58-40-70.
Joint underwriting and joint reinsurance organizations.
Examination by commissioner, §58-40-90.
Filings required, §58-40-60, (a).
Changes or amendments to documents, §58-40-60, (b).
Unfair or unreasonable activities.
Cease and desist orders, §58-40-60, (c).
Judicial review of commissioner's decisions and orders.
Compelling action withheld or delayed by commissioner, §58-2-40.
Extent of review, §58-2-90, (a), (b).
Generally, §58-2-80.

INSURANCE RATES —Cont'd
Judicial review of commissioner's decisions and orders —Cont'd
Ground for relief limited to those set forth in, §58-2-90, (c).
Notice of appeal.
Time for, §58-2-85.
Presumption of correctness and propriety, §58-2-80.
Prima facie correct, §§58-2-40, 58-2-90, (e).
Procedure, §58-2-85.
Stay of commissioner's order or decision.
Appeal to operate as, §58-2-85.
Title of cause on appeal, §58-2-85.
Withheld or delayed actions, §58-2-90, (d).
Legislative declaration.
Purposes of provisions, §58-40-1.
Life insurance.
Exceptions to applicability of rating provisions, §58-40-15.
Lists.
Commissioner to compel and make available to public, §58-2-40.
Loss and expense experience, §58-40-85.
Method of rate making, §58-36-10.
Modification.
Financial disclosure of companies, §58-40-130, (a) to (e).
Review and modification by commissioner, §58-40-130, (c).
Upon financial disclosure of companies, §58-40-130.
North Carolina rate bureau, §§58-36-1 to 58-36-110.
See RATE BUREAU.
Notice.
Coverage or rate change, §§58-36-45, 58-41-20, (d) to (f).
Timing of notice to insured, §58-41-40, (b).
Hearings.
Commissioner, §58-40-105, (a).
Imposition of penalties or suspension of licenses, §58-40-110, (c).
Penalties.
Violations of provisions.
Notice and hearing required for imposition of penalty, §58-40-110, (c).
Policy forms.
Existing policy forms, §58-40-115.
Purposes of provisions, §58-40-80.
Rating organizations.
Consultation with other rating organizations and insurers, §58-40-80.
Defined, §58-40-5.
Examination by commissioner, §58-40-90.
Exchange of information or experience data, §58-40-80.
Filing requirements.
Rates prepared by organizations, §58-40-40, (b).
Licenses.
Applications.
Action on, §58-40-50, (d).
Amendments, §58-40-50, (e).
Supporting information, §58-40-50, (c).
Required, §58-40-50, (a).
Suspension, §58-40-110, (b), (c).
Refusal to supply services.
Prohibited, §58-40-50, (b).
Saving clause, §58-40-50, (f).
Use of rates prepared by.
Authorized, §58-40-40, (a).

INSURANCE RATES —Cont'd
Reinsurance.
Exception to applicability of rating provisions, §58-40-15.
Reports.
Loss and expense experience, §58-40-85.
Request for review of rate, rating plan, rating system or underwriting rule, §58-40-100, (a).
Rejection of request.
Complaint to commissioner, §58-40-100, (a).
Standards.
Applicable standards in making and using rates, §58-36-10.
Determination of compliance.
Criteria, §58-40-25.
Generally, §58-40-20.
Noncomplying rates.
Interim use, §58-40-45, (b).
Orders of commissioner as to, §58-40-45, (a).
Uniqueness of risk.
Use of individual form or rate, §58-41-50, (g).
Violations of provisions.
Hearings.
Required, §58-40-110, (c).
Suspension of licenses, §58-40-110, (b).

INSURANCE REGULATORY CHARGE, §58-6-25.

INSURANCE REGULATORY INFORMATION SYSTEM.
Test data not public records, §58-2-220.

INSURANCE SCORES.
Motor vehicle or property insurance, §58-36-90.

INSURANCE-SUPPORT ORGANIZATIONS.
Defined, §58-39-15.
Information privacy protection.
Consumer and customer information generally, §§58-39-1 to 58-39-165.
See INSURANCE CONSUMER AND CUSTOMER INFORMATION PRIVACY.

INSURANCE UNDERWRITING ASSOCIATION.
Beach area essential property, §§58-45-10 to 58-45-80.
See BEACH AREA ESSENTIAL PROPERTY INSURANCE.

INSURANCE UNFAIR TRADE PRACTICES, §§58-63-1 to 58-63-70.
Acts prohibited, §58-63-10.
Additional nature of provisions, §58-63-55.
Advertisements.
False advertising.
Prohibited acts, §58-63-15.
Appeals.
Cease and desist orders.
Judicial review, §58-63-35.
Undefined practices.
Judicial review by intervenor, §58-63-45.
Boycotts.
Prohibited acts, §58-63-15.
Cease and desist orders.
Effect.
No person absolved from liability under other law, §58-63-35, (d).
Finality.
When order becomes final, §58-63-35, (c).
Issuance, §58-63-32, (a).
Judicial review, §58-63-35.
Additional evidence, §58-63-35, (b).
Order of court, §58-63-35, (b).
Effect, §58-63-35, (d).
Petition, §58-63-35, (a).

INSURANCE UNFAIR TRADE PRACTICES —Cont'd
Cease and desist orders —Cont'd
Modification or setting aside, §58-63-32, (b), (c).
Violations.
Penalty, §58-63-50.
Coercion.
Prohibited acts, §58-63-15.
Commissioner.
Additional nature of powers, §58-63-55.
Powers.
Examination and investigation, §58-63-20.
Rule-making authority, §58-63-65.
Confidentiality of information.
Misuse of borrowers' confidential information, §58-63-15.
Defamation.
Prohibited acts, §58-63-15.
Definitions, §58-63-5.
Discrimination.
Prohibited acts, §58-63-15.
Enumerated, §58-63-15.
Examinations.
Power of commissioner, §58-63-20.
Fraud.
Prohibited acts, §58-63-15.
Health care service discount practices by insurers and service corporations, §58-63-70, (a).
Substantial assistance in accomplishing, §58-63-70, (b).
Hearings, §58-63-25, (b), (c).
Immunity from prosecution, §58-63-60.
Notice, §58-63-25, (a).
Service, §58-63-25, (e).
Powers and duties of commissioner as to, §58-63-25, (d).
Undefined practices, §58-63-40, (a).
Witnesses.
Immunity from prosecution, §58-63-60.
Powers of commissioner as to, §58-63-25, (d).
Injunctions.
Undefined practices, §§58-63-40, (b) to (d), 58-63-45.
Intimidation, §58-63-15.
Investigations.
Power of commissioner, §58-63-20.
Legislative declaration.
Purpose of provisions, §58-63-1.
Life insurance.
Solicitation.
Failure to comply with requirements, §58-60-30.
Prohibited, §58-63-10.
Purpose of provisions, §58-63-1.
Rebates.
Prohibited acts, §58-63-15.
Rules and regulations, §58-63-65.
Settlements.
Unfair claim settlement practices, §58-63-15.
Statements.
False financial statements.
Prohibited acts, §58-63-15.
Unauthorized insurers false advertising process act.
Action by commissioner under unfair trade practices act, §58-29-15.
Undefined practices.
Hearing, §58-63-40, (a).
Notice, §58-63-40, (a).
Injunctions.
Judicial review by intervenor, §58-63-45.

INSURANCE UNFAIR TRADE PRACTICES —Cont'd
Undefined practices —Cont'd
Injunctions —Cont'd
Petition by commissioner for, §58-63-40, (b).
Action by court on, §58-63-40, (c), (d).
Judicial review by intervenor, §58-63-45.
Report by commissioner, §58-63-40, (a).
Viatical life insurance settlement, §58-58-295.
Witnesses.
Immunity from prosecution, §58-63-60.
Workers' compensation self-insurance.
Third-party administrators and service companies.
Applicability of provisions to, §58-47-200.

INSURER SUPERVISION, REHABILITATION AND LIQUIDATION, §§58-30-1 to 58-30-310.
Actions.
Liquidation.
Actions by and against liquidator, §58-30-130.
Rehabilitation.
Actions by and against rehabilitator, §58-30-90.
Administrative supervision.
Administrative supervisor, §58-30-62, (g).
Applicability of section, §58-30-62, (b).
Compliance with requirements of commissioner.
Time limitation, §58-30-62, (e).
Confidentiality, §58-30-62, (f).
Contesting action of commissioner, §58-30-62, (h).
Exceeding powers, §58-30-62, (a).
Liability of commissioner, §58-30-62, (k).
Meetings between commissioner and supervisor, §58-30-62, (j).
Notice to insurer, §58-30-62, (d).
Section not to limit powers granted to commissioner, §58-30-62, (i).
When subject to administrative supervision, §58-30-62, (c).
Agents.
Liquidation.
Failure to provide information to liquidator, §58-30-127, (c).
Generally, §58-30-127, (a).
Policy issued through an agent, determination of, §58-30-127, (b).
Provisons of section are additional to other duties, §58-30-127, (d).
Applicability of provisions.
Persons covered, §58-30-5.
Attachment.
Prohibited during pendency of liquidation proceeding, §58-30-295.
Audits.
Books or records.
Person defined, §58-30-22, (a).
Powers of commissioner and receiver, §58-30-22, (b).
External audit of receiver's books, §58-30-255.
Bonds, surety.
Claims of surety, §58-30-210.
Commissioner and deputies.
Responsibility on official bonds, §58-30-30.
Claims, §§58-30-185 to 58-30-235.
Contingent claims, §58-30-195, (a), (b).
Denial of claim.
Notice, §58-30-205, (a).
Objections, §58-30-205, (a).
Hearing, §58-30-205, (b).
Employment contracts, §58-30-195, (e).
Filing, §58-30-185, (a).

INSURER SUPERVISION, REHABILITATION AND LIQUIDATION —Cont'd
Claims —Cont'd
Foreign or alien insurers.
Domiciliary liquidators in other states.
Filing of claims with, §58-30-270, (c).
Interstate priorities generally, §58-30-300.
Resident's claims against insurers domiciled in reciprocal states, §58-30-290.
Subordination of claims for noncooperation, §58-30-305.
Guaranty associations.
Claims of, §58-30-190, (e).
Late filings, §58-30-185, (c).
Interest on claims, §58-30-230, (b).
Interstate priorities.
Generally, §58-30-300, (a).
Secured claims, §58-30-300, (c).
Special deposit claims, §58-30-300, (b).
Late filings, §58-30-185, (b) to (d).
Guaranty associations, §58-30-185, (c).
Other claimants not previously considered, §58-30-185, (d).
Sharing in distributions, §58-30-185, (b).
Nonresident's claims against insurers domiciled in this state.
Filing, §58-30-285, (a).
Proof of claims, §58-30-285, (b).
Periodic payment of judgments, §58-30-195, (d).
Priority of distribution, §58-30-220.
Proof of claim.
Contents of statement, §58-30-190, (a).
Form, §58-30-190, (b).
Incomplete claims, §58-30-190, (b).
Judgment or order against insured, §58-30-190, (d).
Other information and documents, §58-30-190, (b).
Requests for information or evidence, §58-30-190, (c).
Recommendations of liquidator to court.
Action by court on, §58-30-225, (b).
Generally, §58-30-225, (a).
Third party claims, §58-30-200, (c).
Resident's claims against insurers domiciled in reciprocal states.
Allowance of claim.
Effect of final allowance by court, §58-30-290, (c).
Filing, §58-30-290, (a).
Proof of claims, §58-30-290, (b).
Secured claimants, §58-30-195, (c).
Secured creditors.
Determination of claim by court, §58-30-215, (a).
Surrender of security.
Effect, §58-30-215, (b).
Structured settlements, §58-30-195, (d).
Sureties, §58-30-210.
Third party claims, §58-30-200, (a), (b).
Guaranty associations.
Exception of claims covered by, §58-30-200, (d).
Recommendations to court by liquidator, §58-30-200, (c).
Unclaimed funds, §58-30-235, (a).
Commissioner.
Bond, surety.
Responsibility on official bond, §58-30-30.
Cooperation of officers, owners and employees, §58-30-25, (a), (c).
Failure to cooperate, §58-30-25, (d).

INSURER SUPERVISION, REHABILITATION AND LIQUIDATION —Cont'd
Commissioner —Cont'd
Fees.
Exemptions, §58-30-310.
Obstruction or interference with commissioner, §58-30-25, (b).
Powers of commissioner not limited by provisions, §58-30-1, (a).
Confidentiality of information.
Hearings, §58-30-70.
Construction and interpretation, §58-30-1, (a), (b).
Continuances.
Delinquency proceedings, §58-30-50.
Contracts.
Executory contracts and unexpired leases.
Acceptance or rejection by receiver.
Authority of receiver, subject to court approval, §58-30-35, (a).
Breach of contract or lease, §58-30-35, (g).
Defaults in contracts or leases, requirements to assume, §58-30-35, (b).
Lessee's rights and options, §58-30-35, (h).
Prohibitions on assignment or assumption, §58-30-35, (c).
Termination or modification, §58-30-35, (e).
Time period, §58-30-35, (d).
Assignment, §58-30-35, (f), (k).
Breach of contract.
When rejection constitutes, §58-30-35, (g).
Defaults in contracts or leases.
Requirements for receiver to assume, §58-30-35, (b).
Lessee's rights and options after rejection by receiver, §58-30-35, (h).
Prohibitions on assignment or assumption by receiver, §58-30-35, (c).
Termination or modification, §58-30-35, (i), (j).
Restrictions, §58-30-35, (e).
Custodian.
Turnover of property by.
Definition of "custodian," §58-30-40, (a).
Generally, §58-30-40, (b), (c).
Powers and duties of court, §58-30-40, (d), (e).
Definitions, §58-30-10.
Delinquency proceedings.
Condition on release from delinquency proceedings, §58-30-55.
Continuation, §58-30-50.
Release from delinquency proceedings.
Condition on, §58-30-55.
Dissolution of insurer, §58-30-115.
Duty to report impairment, §58-30-12.
Execution.
Levy of execution.
Prohibited during pendency of liquidation proceeding, §58-30-295.
Fees.
Commissioner.
Exemption from filing fees, §58-30-310.
Foreign or alien insurers.
Ancillary formal proceedings, §58-30-275.
Order appointing ancillary receiver, §58-30-275, (b).
Petition for appointment of ancillary receiver, §58-30-275, (a).
Powers of ancillary receiver, §58-30-275, (c), (d).
Ancillary summary proceedings, §58-30-280.
Claims.
Domiciliary liquidators in other states.
Filing of claims with, §58-30-270, (c).
Interstate priorities generally, §58-30-300.

INSURER SUPERVISION, REHABILITATION AND LIQUIDATION —Cont'd
Foreign or alien insurers —Cont'd
Claims —Cont'd
Resident's claims against insurers domiciled in reciprocal states, §58-30-290.
Subordination of claims for noncooperation, §58-30-305.
Conservation of property found in state.
Liquidation of assets.
Petition for order, §58-30-260, (d).
Order, §58-30-260, (a) to (c).
Termination of conservation.
Petition for order, §58-30-260, (e).
Interstate priorities generally, §58-30-300.
Liquidation of property found in state.
Claims of residents of state.
Payment, §58-30-265, (f).
Federal courts.
Appointment as receivers, §58-30-265, (e).
Liquidator as ancillary receiver, §58-30-265, (d).
Orders of court, §58-30-265, (a) to (c).
Liquidation of property in other states.
Domiciliary liquidators in other states, §58-30-270, (a), (b).
Claims to be filed with, §58-30-270, (c).
Summary proceedings.
Ancillary summary proceedings, §58-30-280.
Garnishment.
Prohibited during pendency of liquidation proceeding, §58-30-295.
Grounds for liquidation, §58-30-100.
Grounds for rehabilitation, §58-30-75.
Hearings.
Claims.
Denial.
Objections, §58-30-205, (b).
Confidentiality of hearings, §58-30-70.
Seizure order by court.
Hearing and review, §58-30-65, (e), (f).
Immunity and indemnification of receiver and employees.
Administrative expenses of insurer.
Indemnification, §58-30-71, (e).
Applicability of provisions, §58-30-71, (k), (m).
Attorneys' fees.
Payment, §58-30-71, (d).
Generally, §58-30-71, (b), (c), (l).
Other rights not affected, §58-30-71, (j).
Persons entitled to protection, §58-30-71, (a).
Segregation of funds for, §58-30-71, (f), (g).
Settlements.
Payment of settlement amount, §58-30-71, (h), (i).
Injunctions, §58-30-20, (a).
Out-of-state courts, §58-30-20, (b).
Supervision proceedings.
Enforcement of supervision order, §58-30-60, (i).
Jurisdiction, §58-30-15, (a) to (c), (e).
Voidable preferences and liens, §58-30-150, (g).
Liens.
Voidable preferences and liens, §§58-30-150, 58-30-155.
Limitation of actions.
Rehabilitation.
Actions by and against rehabilitator, §58-30-90, (b).
Liquidation.
Accounting by liquidator.
Declaration of insolvency, §58-30-105, (d).
Orders to require, §58-30-105, (e).

INSURER SUPERVISION, REHABILITATION AND LIQUIDATION —Cont'd
Liquidation —Cont'd
Actions by and against liquidator.
Generally, §58-30-130, (a), (b).
Guaranty associations.
Standing to appear, §58-30-130, (c).
Agents.
Failure to provide information to liquidator, §58-30-127, (c).
Generally, §58-30-127, (a).
Policy issued through an agent, determination of, §58-30-127, (b).
Provisons of section are additional to other duties, §58-30-127, (d).
Assessments.
Court order adjudging liability, §58-30-165, (e).
Failure to pay assessment.
Court order adjudging liability, §58-30-165, (e).
Proceedings upon, §58-30-165, (c) to (f).
Levy of assessment, §58-30-165, (b).
Report by liquidator to court, §58-30-165, (a).
Show cause orders.
Court order adjudging liability, §58-30-165, (e).
Failure to pay assessment, §58-30-165, (c) to (f).
Notice, §58-30-165, (d).
Assets.
Distribution, §58-30-230, (a).
Claims generally, §§58-30-185 to 58-30-235. See within this heading, "Claims."
Priority, §58-30-220.
Proposal by domiciliary liquidator to distribute assets, §58-30-180.
Reciprocal insurance, §58-15-145.
Unclaimed funds, §58-30-235, (a).
Withheld funds, §58-30-235, (b).
List of assets, §58-30-135, (a), (c).
Reduction to liquidity, §58-30-135, (b).
Claims.
Generally, §§58-30-185 to 58-30-235. See within this heading, "Claims."
Continuation of coverage, §58-30-110, (a), (b).
Life or health insurance or annuities, §58-30-110, (c), (d).
Dissolution of insurer, §58-30-115.
Distribution.
Guaranty associations.
Proposal by domiciliary liquidator to distribute assets, §58-30-180, (d).
Proposal by domiciliary liquidator to distribute assets.
Amount relative to claim payments, §58-30-180, (c).
Contents, §58-30-180, (b).
Guaranty associations, §58-30-180, (d).
Notice, §58-30-180, (e).
Time for, §58-30-180, (a).
Fraudulent transfers after petition.
Generally, §58-30-145, (a), (b).
Negotiability of instruments not affected, §58-30-145, (c).
Fraudulent transfers prior to petition.
Generally, §58-30-140, (a), (b).
Liability of persons receiving, §58-30-140, (d).
Reinsurer.
Transactions with, §58-30-140, (c).
Grounds, §58-30-100.

INSURER SUPERVISION, REHABILITATION AND LIQUIDATION —Cont'd
Liquidation —Cont'd
Guaranty associations.
Proposal by domiciliary liquidator to distribute assets, §58-30-180, (d).
Notice, §58-30-125, (a).
Effect, §58-30-125, (c).
Potential claimants, §58-30-125, (b).
Orders, §58-30-105, (a).
Effect, §58-30-105, (b), (c), (e).
Petition for liquidation.
Rehabilitator, §58-30-95, (a).
Powers of liquidator, §58-30-120, (a).
Enumeration not exclusive, §58-30-120, (b).
Premiums.
Recovery of premiums owed, §58-30-175.
Proposal by domiciliary liquidator to distribute assets.
Amount relative to claim payments, §58-30-180, (c).
Contents, §58-30-180, (b) to (d).
Guaranty associations, §58-30-180, (d).
Notice, §58-30-180, (e).
Time for, §58-30-180, (a).
Reciprocal insurance.
Domestic reciprocals, §§58-15-145, 58-15-150.
Records.
Disposition during and after termination of liquidation, §58-30-250.
Reinsurers.
Liability, §58-30-170.
Reopening liquidation, §58-30-245.
Termination of proceedings.
Application, §58-30-240, (b).
Liquidator, §58-30-240, (a).
Records.
Disposition during and after termination of liquidation, §58-30-250.
Reopening liquidation, §58-30-245.
Voidable preferences and liens.
Generally, §§58-30-150, 58-30-155.
Notice.
Assessments.
Show cause order, §58-30-165, (d).
Liquidation, §58-30-125.
Proposal by domiciliary liquidator to distribute assets, §58-30-180, (e).
Orders, §58-30-20, (a).
Dissolution of insurer, §58-30-115.
Liquidation orders, §58-30-105.
Out-of-state courts, §58-30-20, (b).
Rehabilitation orders, §58-30-80.
Seizure order by court.
Generally, §58-30-65, (b) to (d).
Hearing and review, §58-30-65, (e), (f).
Petition for, §58-30-65, (a).
Supervision proceedings.
Summary orders generally, §58-30-60.
Policies.
Liquidation.
Continuance of coverage, §58-30-110.
Premiums.
Recovery of premiums owed, §58-30-175, (a).
Obligation of insurer to pay unpaid premiums, §58-30-175, (b).
Purpose of provisions, §58-30-1, (c).
Reciprocal insurance.
Liquidation of domestic reciprocals, §§58-15-145, 58-15-150.

INSURER SUPERVISION, REHABILITATION AND LIQUIDATION —Cont'd
Records.
Audits.
Person defined, §58-30-22, (a).
Powers of commissioner and receiver, §58-30-22, (b).
Rehabilitation.
Accounting by rehabilitator, §58-30-80, (b).
Actions by and against rehabilitator.
Generally, §58-30-90, (a).
Guaranty associations.
Standing to appear, §58-30-90, (c).
Limitation of actions, §58-30-90, (b).
Fraudulent transfers.
Power of rehabilitator to avoid, §58-30-85, (f).
Grounds, §58-30-75.
Orders, §58-30-80, (a), (b).
Anticipatory breach of contract.
Order not to constitute, §58-30-80, (c).
Powers and duties of rehabilitator.
Enumerated, §58-30-85, (a).
List not limiting, §58-30-85, (b).
Fraudulent transfer, avoidance of, §58-30-85, (f).
Legal remedies, authority to pursue, §58-30-85, (d).
Life insurers, powers relative to, §58-30-85, (e).
Necessary and appropriate actions, §58-30-85, (c).
Termination of rehabilitation.
Petition, §58-30-95, (b).
Reinsurers.
Liquidation.
Liability of reinsurer, §58-30-170.
Scope of provisions.
Persons covered, §58-30-5.
Setoffs.
Accounting statements, §58-30-160, (d).
Exceptions, §58-30-160, (b).
Generally, §58-30-160, (a).
Local agents.
Setoffs permitted to, §58-30-160, (c).
Reinsurance, §58-30-160, (e).
Supervision proceedings, §58-30-60, (b), (c).
Compliance with requirements of commissioner.
Time for, §58-30-60, (d).
Hearings, §58-30-60, (e).
Notice of hearing, §58-30-60, (e).
Request for administrative hearing, §58-30-60, (f).
Injunctions.
Enforcement of supervision order, §58-30-60, (i).
Review of action of supervisor.
Request for commissioner to review, §58-30-60, (g).
Summary orders, §58-30-60, (a).
Violation of orders, §58-30-60, (h), (j).
Penalty, §58-30-60, (h).
Utility service.
Alteration, refusal or discontinuance, §58-30-45, (b).
Restriction, §58-30-45, (a).
Venue, §58-30-15, (d), (e).
Voidable preferences and liens.
Attorneys at law.
Payments or transfers to for services rendered, §58-30-150, (j).
Bonds, surety.
Discharge of liability of surety under releasing bond, §58-30-150, (h).

INSURER SUPERVISION, REHABILITATION AND LIQUIDATION —Cont'd
Voidable preferences and liens —Cont'd
Bonds, surety —Cont'd
Lien dissolved by furnishing of bond, §58-30-150, (e).
Claims of holders of void or voidable rights, §58-30-155, (a).
Late filing, §58-30-155, (b).
Further credit extended to insure in good faith, §58-30-150, (i).
Generally, §58-30-150, (a) to (f).
Jurisdiction.
Summary jurisdiction of court, §58-30-150, (g).
Liability, §58-30-150, (h), (k).
Lien defined, §58-30-150, (c).
Preference defined, §58-30-150, (a).
Transfer defined, §58-30-150, (b).
New and contemporaneous consideration, §58-30-150, (d).

INSURRECTION OR REBELLION.
Constitution of the United States, Const. U. S., art. I, §8.
Militia.
Unorganized militia.
Ordered out for service, §127A-87.
Rebellion against state, §14-8.
Riots and civil disorders, §§14-288.1 to 14-288.20.
See RIOTS AND CIVIL DISORDERS.
Secret political and military organizations, §14-10.
Subversive activities, §§14-11 to 14-12.1.

INTAKE SERVICES.
Delinquent and undisciplined juveniles, §7B-1700.

INTANGIBLE PERSONAL PROPERTY.
Applicability of provisions, §105-276.
Collection of taxes.
Subject to attachment or garnishment, §105-242, (b).
Exempt property, §105-242, (e).
Defined, §105-273.
Listing of property.
Place for listing, §105-305.
Applicability of provisions, §105-305, (a).

INTELLECTUAL PROPERTY.
Constitutional protection, Const. U. S., art. I, §8.
Corporate income tax.
Allocation and apportionment of income, §105-130.4.
International commercial arbitrations.
Arbitration deemed commercial, §1-567.31, (e).
Invention developed by employees.
Employee's rights, §66-57.1.
Employer's rights, §66-57.2.
Invention development services contracts, §§66-209 to 66-216.
Bond or other financial requirements, §66-214.
Contracting requirements, §66-212.
Cover sheet, notice, §66-211.
Definitions, §66-209.
Disclosure prior to contract, §66-210.
Enforcement, §66-216.
Mandatory terms, §66-213.
Remedies, §66-215.
Recorded musical performances.
Common law right restrict or collect royalties on commercial use abrogated, §66-28.

INTELLECTUAL PROPERTY —Cont'd
Trademark registration, §§80-1 to 80-14.
See TRADEMARKS.

INTENT.
Special matters, pleading, §1A-1, Rule 9, (b).

INTERCEPTION OF COMMUNICATIONS.
Electronic surveillance generally, §§15A-286 to 15A-298.
See ELECTRONIC SURVEILLANCE.

INTERCHANGE OF GOVERNMENT EMPLOYEES, §§126-51 to 126-58.
See PERSONNEL SYSTEM.

INTEREST.
Accident and health insurance.
Prompt claim payments under health benefit plans, §58-3-225, (e).
Accounts and accounting.
Default judgments.
Clerk to ascertain interest upon default judgment on account, §24-6.
Accrual.
Time from which interest runs, §24-3.
Agriculture.
Assessment of fees and taxes.
Procedure for assessment, §106-9.3, (h).
Bills of exchange.
Default judgments.
Clerk to ascertain interest upon default judgment on bill of exchange, §24-6.
Bond issues.
Corporate bonds may be sold below par, §24-2.
Refunding bonds.
State debt, §§142-29.6, (a), 142-29.7.
Bonds, surety.
Default judgments.
Clerk to ascertain interest, §24-6.
Penal bonds.
Exceptions to contract rate, §24-5, (a).
Legal rate from date of entry of judgment, §24-5, (a1).
Brownfields property reuse.
Unpaid fees, §130A-310.39, (c).
Charge cards.
Disclosure requirements.
Generally, §24-11.2.
Community colleges.
Deposits.
Investment of idle cash, §115D-58.6.
Compound interest.
Guardians.
Obligations due guardians to bear compound interest, §24-4.
Condominium common expenses.
Past due assessment, §47C-3-115, (b).
Construction loans.
Definition, §24-10, (c).
Maximum fees on loans secured by real property, §24-10, (a).
Less than three hundred thousand dollars, §24-10, (d).
Prepayment, §24-10, (b).
Consumer finance act.
Computation of charges, §53-173, (b).
Insurance.
Credit life and credit accident and health insurance.
Premiums not deemed interest or charges, §53-189, (b).

INTEREST —Cont'd
Consumer finance act —Cont'd
Judgments.
Limitation on interest after judgment, §53-173, (c).
Maturity of loans.
Limitation of interest after, §53-173, (d).
Optional maturities, §53-176.
Maximum rate, §53-173, (a).
Further charges prohibited, §53-178.
Optional rates, §53-176, (a).
Schedule of charges, §53-181, (b).
Contractors.
Subcontractors.
Payments to subcontractors.
Late payments, §22C-5.
Contract rates and fees, §24-1.1.
Contracts.
Bearing of interest, §24-5, (a).
Penal bonds.
Exception as to, §24-5, (a).
Maximum fees on loans secured by real property, §24-10, (a).
Rates, §24-1.
Real property.
Maximum fees on loans secured by real property.
Construction loans construed, §24-10, (c).
Prepayment, §24-10, (b).
Corporations.
Sale below par permitted, §24-2.
Costs.
Attorneys' fees in notes, conditional sale contracts, etc., in addition to interest, §6-21.2.
Interest from verdict to judgment added as costs, §24-7.
Covenants.
Default judgments.
Clerk to ascertain interest upon default judgment on covenant to pay money, §24-6.
Credit cards.
Disclosure requirements.
Generally, §24-11.1.
Loans exempt from interest rate and fee limitations, §24-9, (d).
Credit unions.
Defined, §54-109.65.
Rate, §54-109.65.
Default judgments.
Clerk to ascertain upon default judgment on bond, bill, note or signed account, §24-6.
Definitions.
Construction loans, §24-10, (c).
Drainage districts.
Assessment anticipation notes, §156-97.1.
Bond issues, §§156-95, 156-97.
Payment.
Duty of treasurer, §156-112.
Economic development loans.
Certain fees or other funds paid by borrowers.
Not subject to claim or defense of usury, §24-9.3.
Eminent domain.
Public condemnors.
Compensation.
Interest as part of just compensation, §40A-53.
Employment security.
Contributions.
Past-due contributions, §96-10, (a).

INTEREST —Cont'd
Energy conservation finance act.
Certificates of participation, §142-67, (b).
Financing contract.
Calculation of interest component of installment payments under, §142-65, (f).
Equity lines of credit.
Loans exempt from interest rate and fee limitations, §24-9, (c).
Rates of interest, §24-1.2A.
Exemption of loans from rate and fee limitations.
Credit card plans, §24-9, (c).
Definitions, §24-9, (a).
Equity lines of credit, §24-9, (c).
Usury prohibited as defense, §24-9, (b).
Family law arbitration, §50-51, (c).
Fiduciaries.
Reduction of interest rates.
Powers which may be incorporated by reference in trust instrument, §32-27.
Finance.
Cash management plan, maximization, §147-86.11, (g).
Foreign-money claims.
Increase or decrease, §1C-1828, (b).
Rate of interest, §1C-1828, (a), (c).
Funds transfers, UCC.
Rate of interest, §25-4A-506.
Global TransPark authority.
Bond issues, §63A-9, (a).
Guardians.
Compound interest.
Obligations due guardians to bear compound interest, §24-4.
Health care facilities.
Finance act.
Bonds and notes, §131A-11.
Housing finance agency.
Bonds and notes, §122A-8.
Loans.
To and by mortgage lenders, §122A-5.6, (b).
Modification of terms of interest.
General power of agency, §122A-5.
Rules and regulations governing agency activity, §122A-5.1, (b).
Insurance.
Foreign or alien insurance company deposits, §58-5-63, (a).
Life insurance policy loans, §§58-61-1 to 58-61-15.
See LIFE INSURANCE.
International commercial arbitration and conciliation.
Authority to award, §1-567.61, (f).
Judgments, §24-5, (a).
Clerk to ascertain interest upon default judgment on bond, covenant, bill, note or signed account, §24-6.
Interest from verdict to judgment added as costs, §24-7.
Legal rate, §24-1.
Limitation on interest after judgment, §53-173, (c).
Prejudgment interest, §24-5, (b).
Late payment charges.
Authorized, §24-10.1, (a).
Home loans, §24-10.1, (c).
Restrictions, §24-10.1, (b).
Legal rate, §24-1.
Lenders.
Mortgage bankers and brokers as lenders, §24-2.5.

INTEREST —Cont'd
Letters of credit.
Damages for wrongful dishonor or breach, §25-5-111, (d).
Life insurance.
Interest on death benefits, §58-58-110.
Interest rates on life insurance loans, §§58-61-1 to 58-61-15.
See LIFE INSURANCE.
Loan-related goods, products and services.
Collection of payment for, §24-8, (d).
Insurance proceeds to lender, §24-8, (e).
Items included, §24-8, (d).
Loans exempt from rate and fee limitations.
Credit card plans, §24-9, (c).
Definitions, §24-9, (a).
Equity lines of credit, §24-9, (c).
Usury prohibited as defense, §24-9, (b).
Loans generally.
See LOANS.
Maximum rates.
Contract rates, §24-1.1.
Conveyance of property other than collateral in consideration for loan, §24-8, (c).
Forfeitures for usury, §24-2.
Guardians.
Obligations due guardians to bear compound interest, §24-4.
Insurance proceeds to lender, §24-8, (e).
Late fees, §24-10.1.
Legal rate, §24-1.
Loan amount $300,000 or less, §24-8, (a).
Loan-related goods, products and services.
Collection of payment for, §24-8, (d).
Mortgages and deeds of trust.
First mortgages and deeds of trust, §24-1.1A.
Secondary or junior mortgages, §24-14.
Second or junior lien on real property, §24-10, (g).
Penalty for usury, §24-2.
Real property.
Maximum fees on loans secured by real property, §24-10, (a).
Revolving credit charges, §24-11.
Small business investment companies.
Applicability of provisions, §24-8, (f).
Mortgage bankers and brokers.
Lenders.
When bankers and brokers considered lenders, §24-2.5.
Mortgages and deeds of trust.
First mortgages and deeds of trust, §24-1.1A, (a).
Additional charges allowed.
Certain lenders, §24-1.1A, (c2).
Small loans, certain lenders, §24-1.1A, (c1).
Compensation to mortgage banker, broker, etc., for services rendered, §24-1.1A, (i).
Deferred payments of interest, §24-1.1A, (g).
Exemption of certain investments, §24-1.1A, (d).
Fee chargeable, §§24-1.1A, (c), 24-10.
Graduation of periodic payments, §24-1.1A, (h).
"Home loan" construed, §24-1.1A, (e).
Maximum fees on loans secured by real property, §24-10.
Prepayment fees, §24-1.1A, (b).
Saving clauses, §24-1.1A, (f).
High cost home loans, §24-1.1E.
Increased interest rate.
Limitations on loans, §24-1.1E, (b).
Reverse mortgages.
Shared appreciation.
Defined, §53-257.

INTEREST —Cont'd
Mortgages and deeds of trust —Cont'd
Reverse mortgages —Cont'd
Total annual percentage rate.
Defined, §53-257.
Secondary or junior mortgages, §24-10, (g).
Limitations, §24-14.
Motor vehicles.
Retail installment sales.
Credit installment sale contracts.
Finance charge.
Used cars, §25A-15, (c).
Municipal corporations.
Assessments.
Delinquent assessments, §160A-233, (a).
Joint municipal electric power and energy act.
Bond issues.
Rate, §159B-15, (a).
Variable rates, §159B-15, (a).
Negotiable instruments, §25-3-112.
Notes.
Default judgments.
Clerk to ascertain interest upon default judgment on note, §24-6.
Occupational licensing boards.
State treasurer's investment program.
Use of interest earned by occupational licensing boards under program, §93B-11.
Partition.
Owelty, §46-11.
Pawnbrokers.
Municipal or county authority to regulate, §91A-12.
Rates of interest, §91A-8.
Payment.
Time from which interest runs, §24-3.
Penal bonds, §24-5, (a), (a1).
Penalties.
Usury, §24-2.
Prejudgment interest, §24-5, (b).
Prepayment of loan.
No prepayment terms or prepayment terms not in accordance with law, §24-2.4.
Public utilities.
Certain repayments to consumers not subject to claim or defense of usury, §24-9.1.
Refunds to customers for over collections or advancements, §62-130.
Railroads.
Internal improvements, §124-5.1, (b).
Rates of interest.
Contract rates, §24-1.1.
Conveyance of property other than collateral in consideration for loan, §24-8, (c).
Equity lines of credit, §24-1.2A.
Extension of credit by banks and savings and loan associations, §24-2.2.
Forfeitures for usury, §24-2.
Funds transfers, UCC, §25-4A-506.
Guardians.
Obligations due guardians to bear compound interest, §24-4.
Insurance proceeds to lender, §24-8, (e).
Late fees, §24-10.1.
Legal rate, §24-1.
Loan amount $300,000 or less, §24-8, (a).
Loan-related goods, products and services.
Collection of payment for, §24-8, (d).
Mortgages and deeds of trust.
First mortgages and deeds of trust, §24-1.1A.
Secondary or junior mortgages, §24-14.

INTEREST —Cont'd
Rates of interest —Cont'd
Mortgages and deeds of trust —Cont'd
Second or junior lien on real property, §24-10, (g).
Penalty for usury, §24-2.
Real property.
Maximum fees on loans secured by real property, §24-10, (a).
Revolving credit charges, §24-11.
Savings and loan associations, §24-1.4, (b).
Associations domiciled in North Carolina, §24-1.4, (a).
Extensions of credit, §24-2.2.
Small business investment companies.
Applicability of provisions, §24-8, (f).
Real property.
Maximum fees on loans secured by real property, §24-10, (a).
Construction loan construed, §24-10, (c).
Less than three hundred thousand dollars, §24-10, (d).
Prepayment, §24-10, (b).
Second or junior lien on real property, §24-10, (g).
Retail installment sales finance charges.
Consolidation and refinancing, §25A-31, (c).
Consumer credit installment sale contracts.
Division of simple transaction into two or more sales to avoid limitations prohibited, §25A-15, (e).
Rates, §25A-15, (a).
Determination, §25A-15, (b).
Residential manufactured homes.
Sale secured by first lien, §25A-15, (f).
Security interest.
Rates chargeable, §25A-15, (d).
Used cars.
Rate chargeable, §25A-15, (c).
Defined, §25A-8, (a).
Exclusions from definition, §25A-8, (b).
Refinancing, §25A-31, (c).
Remedies and penalties, §25A-44.
Revolving charge account contracts.
Default or deferral charges, §25A-14, (c).
Insurance.
Additional charges for insurance, §25A-17, (b).
Rates, §25A-14, (a).
Security interest.
Rates, §25A-14, (b).
Security interest.
Transactions in which seller acquires security interest, §25A-8, (c).
Unearned finance charge credits.
Prepayment of real property and mobile home loans, §25A-32.1.
Retirement system for counties and cities.
Management of funds.
Annual allowance of regular interest, §128-29, (b).
Retirement system for teachers and state employees.
Consolidated judicial retirement act.
Assets of retirement system.
Regular interest allowance, §135-67, (e).
Definition of regular interest, §135-1.
Consolidated judicial retirement act, §135-53.
Management of funds.
Regular interest allowance, §135-7, (b).
Revolving credit charges, §24-11.

INTEREST —Cont'd
Savings and loan associations.
Effect of loan provisions, §54B-167.
Rates, §24-1.4, (b).
Associations domiciled in North Carolina, §24-1.4, (a).
Extensions of credit, §24-2.2.
Savings banks.
Forced retirement of deposit accounts, §54C-179, (b), (c).
Loans.
Maximum rates.
Applicable law, §54C-125, (c).
Securities regulation.
Exemptions, §78A-63, (i).
Security interests.
Revolving credit charges, §24-11.
Small business investment companies.
Applicability of provisions, §24-8, (f).
State debt.
Attachment of interest coupons, §142-1.
Bond issues.
Reimbursement of treasurer for interest, §142-15.
Coupons.
Attachment, §142-1.
Registration as to principal and interest, §142-6.
Refunding bonds, §142-29.7.
Registration.
Conversion and reconversion, §142-6, (b).
Reimbursement of treasurer for interest, §142-15.
State treasurer.
Reimbursement of treasurer for interest, §142-15.
Taxation.
Exemption from taxation, §142-12.
Continuation of state tax exemption, §142-12.1, (c), (d).
Federal taxation of interest income on state or local bonds, effect, §142-12.1, (a), (b).
State employees.
Retirement system for teachers and state employees.
Definition of regular interest, §135-1.
State funds.
Investments of general fund and highway funds, §147-69.1, (d).
State literary fund.
Terms of loans, §115C-459.
State treasurer.
Depositories.
Contracts as to payment interest, §147-81.
Statewide accounts receivable program, §147-86.23.
Streets and highways.
Condemnation proceedings.
Part of just compensation, §136-113.
Subcontractors, payments to.
Late payments, §22C-5.
Taxation.
Assessment of tax, exclusive of penalties assessed on tax, §105-241.1, (i).
Delinquent taxes, §105-241.1.
Exemption from taxation.
Interest on state or local bonds, §142-12.
Property taxes.
Nonpayment of taxes, §105-360, (a).
Refund of overpayment, §105-266, (e).

INTEREST —Cont'd
Teachers.
Retirement system for teachers and state employees. See within this heading, "Retirement system for teachers and state employees."
Time from which interest runs, §24-3.
Time shares.
Independent escrow agent.
Escrow account.
Interest-bearing account, §93A-42, (d).
Trust companies.
Seizure by commissioner.
Dividends to shareholders and creditors.
Unclaimed dividends, §53-392.
Unclaimed property act.
Failure to report, pay or deliver property, §116B-77.
Unclaimed property generally, §§116B-51 to 116B-80.
See UNCLAIMED PROPERTY.
Underground storage tanks.
Leaking petroleum cleanup.
Groundwater protection loan fund, §143-215.94P, (a).
Usury.
Affirmative defense, pleading, §1A-1, Rule 8, (c).
Bond issues.
Corporate bonds sold below par, §24-2.
Consumer credit installment sale contract.
Finance charge rates, §25A-15.
Contract rates, §24-1.1.
Corporations.
Bonds may be sold below par, §24-2.
Cost to be recovered by parties seeking recovery on usurious contracts, §6-25.
Economic development loans.
Certain fees or other funds paid by borrowers.
Not subject to claim or defense of usury, §24-9.3.
Forfeitures of usurious interest, §24-2.
Household and kitchen furniture loans.
Usurious late loans on furniture, §14-391.
Judgments.
Legal rate of interest, §24-1.
Late fees, §24-10.1.
Legal rate, §§24-1, 24-1.1.
Loans exempt from rate and fee limitations.
Credit card plans, §24-9, (c).
Definitions, §24-9, (a).
Equity lines of credit, §24-9, (c).
Usury prohibited as defense, §24-9, (b).
Maximum rates.
Transactions governed by chapter, §24-2.1.
Mortgages and deeds of trust.
First mortgages and deeds of trust, §24-1.1A.
Late payment charges, §24-10.1, (c).
Maximum fees on loans secured by real property, §24-10.
Secondary or junior mortgages, §24-14.
Penalty, §24-2.
Policy of state, §24-2.1.
Public utilities.
Certain repayments to consumers not subject to claim or defense of usury, §24-9.1.
Real property.
Maximum fees on loans secured by real property, §24-10.
Retail installment sales finance charge.
Consumer credit installment sale contract rate, §25A-15.

INTEREST —Cont'd
Usury —Cont'd
Revolving credit charges, §24-11.
State opt-out from federal preemption, §24-2.3, (a), (b).
Transactions governed by chapter, §24-2.1.
Wage assignments.
Usurious loans on assignment of wages, §14-391.
Workers' compensation.
Rates of compensation.
Commuted values.
Discount table to be used, I.C. Rule 406.

INTERESTED PARTIES.
Habeas corpus.
Notice, §17-29.
Letters testamentary and of administration.
Grounds for revocation, §28A-9-1.
Missing persons.
Notice of action for receiver, §28C-4.
Probate of wills.
Clerk of superior court.
Conflicts of interest, §28A-2-3.
Public officers or employees benefiting from public contracts, §14-234.

INTERESTED WITNESSES.
Competency of witnesses, §§8-49, 8-57.2.
Disqualification, §8C-1, Rule 601, (c).
Not excluded by interest or crime, §8-49.
Paternity cases.
Presumed father or mother as witness, §8-57.2.

INTEREST ON LAWYER'S TRUST ACCOUNTS.
Rules governing administration of plan, Bar Rules & Regs., D, §§.1301 to .1316.
See ATTORNEYS AT LAW.

INTEREST RATE SWAP AGREEMENTS FOR GOVERNMENTAL UNITS, §§159-193 to 159-200.
See SWAP AGREEMENTS.

INTERFERENCE WITH ABUSE, NEGLECT OR DEPENDENCY OF JUVENILE INVESTIGATION, §7B-303.

INTERFERENCE WITH CIVIL RIGHTS, §99D-1.
Civil action.
Compensatory and punitive damages, §99D-1, (b), (b1).
Costs and attorney's fees, §99D-1, (b), (b1).
Government unit or government official.
Restriction on bringing against, §99D-1, (c).
Human relations commission bringing, §99D-1, (b1).
Personal action, §99D-1, (b).
Conduct constituting, §99D-1, (a).
Future acts.
Restraining and enjoining, §99D-1, (b), (b1).

INTERFERING WITH EMERGENCY COMMUNICATIONS, §14-286.2.

INTERLOCAL COOPERATION.
Appropriations.
Joint agencies, §160A-462, (b).
Authorized, §160A-461.
Contracts or agreements.
Authorized, §160A-461.
Provisions, §160A-464.
Regional councils of governments.
Power to contract, §160A-475.

INTERLOCAL COOPERATION —Cont'd
Contracts or agreements —Cont'd
Revenue and expenses for joint undertakings, §160A-466.
Definitions, §160A-460.
Economic development, interlocal agreements, §158-7.4.
Expenses for joint undertakings, §160A-466.
Industrial or commercial parks or sites.
Interlocal agreements concerning economic development, §158-7.4, (a).
Binding effect, action to specifically enforce, §158-7.4, (c).
Length of undertaking, §158-7.4, (b).
Joint agencies, §160A-462, (a).
Appropriations for, §160A-462, (b).
Personnel, §160A-463, (a).
Personnel.
Joint agencies, §160A-463, (a).
One officer exercising function for all participating units, §160A-463.
Regional councils of governments.
Power to employ personnel, §160A-475.
Project development financing debt instruments.
Interlocal agreement for purposes of issuing.
Private development project benefited, §159-103, (c).
Regional councils of governments.
Charter, §160A-470.
Contents, §160A-472.
Contracts or agreements.
Power to contract, §160A-475.
Creation, §160A-470, (a).
Fiscal affairs, §160A-476.
Meetings, §160A-473.
Membership, §160A-471.
Officers.
Election, §160A-473.
Personnel.
Power to employ personnel, §160A-475.
Powers, §160A-475.
Supplementary nature of powers, §160A-478.
Reports, §160A-477.
Sales and use tax refunds, §105-164.14, (c).
Units of local government.
Appropriations to council, §160A-476.
Creation of councils, §160A-470, (a).
Defined, §160A-470, (b).
Membership in council, §160A-471.
Withdrawal from council, §160A-474.
Withdrawal from council, §160A-474.
Reports.
Regional councils of governments, §160A-477.
Revenue for joint undertakings, §160A-466.

INTERLOCUTORY DECREES.
Appeals.
Court of appeals.
Appeals of right from the courts of the trial divisions, §7A-27, (d).
District courts.
Appeals of right from district courts to court of appeals, §7A-27, (d).
Review on appeal from judgment, §1-278.
Superior courts.
Appeals of right from superior courts to court of appeals, §7A-27, (d).
Supreme court review.
Discretionary review on certification, App. Proc. Rule 15, (h).

INTERLOCUTORY DECREES —Cont'd
District courts.
Appeals of right from district courts to courts of appeals, §7A-27, (d).
Exercise of power to issue interlocutory orders, §7A-192.
Letters testamentary and of administration.
Revocation of letters, §28A-9-5.

INTERLOCUTORY ORDERS.
Jurisdiction in rem or quasi in rem.
Protection of res while action pending, §1-75.9.

INTERLOCUTORY SUMMARY JUDGMENTS, §1A-1, Rule 56, (c).

INTERMEDIATE CARE FACILITIES.
Certificates of need, §§131E-175 to 131E-190.
See HEALTH CARE FACILITIES.
Financing health care facilities generally, §§131A-1 to 131A-25.
See HEALTH CARE FACILITY FINANCING.
Long-term care ombudsman program, §§143B-181.15 to 143B-181.24.
See LONG-TERM CARE OMBUDSMAN.

INTERMENT.
Cemeteries.
General provisions, §§65-1 to 65-73.
See CEMETERIES.
Cremation.
General provisions, §§90-210.40 to 90-210.54.
See CREMATION.

INTERNAL IMPROVEMENTS.
Appropriations.
State deemed shareholder in corporation accepting appropriation, §124-2.
Council of state.
Control of internal improvements, §124-1.
Investigation of corporations.
Power of investigation, §124-7.
Encumbrances.
Approval of encumbrance on state's interest in corporations, §124-5, (a).
Governor.
Control of internal improvements, §124-1.
Investigation of corporations.
Power of investigation, §124-7.
Proxies.
Appointment of proxies, etc., §124-6, (a).
Investigations.
Power of investigation of corporations, §124-7.
Proxies.
Appointment of proxies, etc., §124-6, (a).
Railroad companies.
Appointment of directors, §124-6, (b).
Report by railroad, canal or other public work.
Additional information provided by state owned railroad.
Request of governor or general assembly, §124-3, (b), (c).
Attorney-client privilege not waived.
State owned railroad providing information, §124-3, (b).
Confidential information.
State owned railroad providing information, §124-3, (c).
Contents, §124-3, (a).
President or chief officer to make, §124-3, (a).
Stock and stockholders.
Proxies.
Appointment of proxies, etc., §124-6, (a).

INTERNAL IMPROVEMENTS —Cont'd
Stock and stockholders —Cont'd
State deemed shareholder and corporation accepting appropriation, §124-2.
INTERNAL MEDICINE.
Primary care physicians, medical education, §143-613.
INTERNAL REVENUE SERVICE.
Agents authorized to enforce criminal laws, §15A-406.
INTERNATIONAL ASSOCIATION OF FIRE FIGHTERS.
Motor vehicle license plates.
Special license plates, §20-79.4, (b).
INTERNATIONAL BANKING, §§53-232.1 to 53-232.17.
Agencies.
Authority to establish and operate, §53-232.3, (c), (d).
Restrictions, §53-232.8, (d), (e).
Defined, §53-232.2, (a).
Termination of operation, §53-232.13, (b).
Appeals.
Commissioner's decisions, §53-232.17.
Applicability of North Carolina business corporation act, §53-232.5.
Applicability of provisions, §53-232.4, (a).
Exceptions, §53-232.4, (b).
Branches.
Authority to establish and operate, §53-232.3, (c), (d).
Restrictions, §53-232.8, (d), (e).
Defined, §53-232.2, (a).
Termination of operation, §53-232.13, (b).
Business corporation act.
Applicability, §53-232.5.
Cease and desist orders, §53-232.16.
Citation of act.
Short title, §53-232.1, (a).
Commissioner of banks.
Appeal of commissioner's decisions, §53-232.17.
Cease and desist orders, §53-232.16.
Definition of "commissioner," §53-232.2, (a).
International representative offices.
Review of operations, §53-232.14, (c).
Corporate income tax.
Deductions in determining state income, §105-130.5, (b).
Corporations, §§53-232.10, (d), 53-232.12.
Actions against.
International banking corporation or nonresident of state, §53-232.7, (b), (c).
Resident of state, §53-232.7, (a).
Defined, §53-232.2, (a).
Dissolution, §53-232.13, (a), (c).
Financial certification, §53-232.11, (a).
Home state, §53-232.3, (e).
Investments.
Restrictions, §53-232.11, (b).
Licenses.
Applications.
Approval or disapproval by commissioner, §53-232.8, (c).
Contents, §53-232.8, (a).
Documents to accompany, §53-232.8, (b).
Effect of issuance, §53-232.9, (a), (e), (f).
Issuance by commissioner, §53-232.6, (b).
Renewal, §53-232.9, (b).
Surrender of license on refusal to renew, §53-232.9, (d).

INTERNATIONAL BANKING —Cont'd
Corporations —Cont'd
Licenses —Cont'd
Requirement for carrying on banking business, §53-232.6, (a).
Revocation, §53-232.9, (c).
Surrender of license, §53-232.9, (d).
Loans.
Restrictions, §53-232.11, (b).
Powers, §53-232.3, (a) to (d).
Reports, §53-232.12, (a).
Exemption from certain requirements, §53-232.12, (b).
Securities held in state, §53-232.10, (d).
Securities to be held in state.
Generally, §53-232.10, (a).
Powers of commissioner, §53-232.10, (c).
Reports, §53-232.10, (d).
Valuation of securities, §53-232.10, (b).
Transacting business in state.
Requirements, §53-232.6, (a).
Definitions, §53-232.2, (a).
Federal international bank institutions.
Authority to establish and operate, §53-232.3, (a), (b).
Defined, §53-232.2, (a).
International bank agencies.
Authority to establish and operate, §53-232.3, (c), (d).
Restrictions, §53-232.8, (d), (e).
Defined, §53-232.2, (a).
Termination of operation, §53-232.13, (b).
International bank branches.
Authority to establish and operate, §53-232.3, (c), (d).
Restrictions, §53-232.8, (d), (e).
Defined, §53-232.2, (a).
Termination of operation, §53-232.13, (b).
International banking corporations, §§53-232.10, (d), 53-232.12.
Actions against.
International banking corporation or nonresident of state, §53-232.7, (b), (c).
Resident of state, §53-232.7, (a).
Defined, §53-232.2, (a).
Dissolution, §53-232.13, (a), (c).
Financial certification, §53-232.11, (a).
Home state, §53-232.3, (e).
Investments.
Restrictions, §53-232.11, (b).
Licenses.
Applications.
Approval or disapproval by commissioner, §53-232.8, (c).
Contents, §53-232.8, (a).
Documents to accompany, §53-232.8, (b).
Effect of issuance, §53-232.9, (a), (e), (f).
Issuance by commissioner, §53-232.6, (b).
Renewal, §53-232.9, (b).
Surrender of license on refusal to renew, §53-232.9, (d).
Requirement for carrying on banking business, §53-232.6, (a).
Revocation, §53-232.9, (c).
Surrender of license, §53-232.9, (d).
Loans.
Restrictions, §53-232.11, (b).
Powers, §53-232.3, (a) to (d).
Reports, §53-232.12, (a).
Exemption from certain requirements, §53-232.12, (b).

INTERNATIONAL BANKING —Cont'd
International banking corporations —Cont'd
Reports —Cont'd
Securities held in state, §53-232.10, (d).
Securities to be held in state.
Generally, §53-232.10, (a).
Powers of commissioner, §53-232.10, (c).
Reports, §53-232.10, (d).
Valuation of securities, §53-232.10, (b).
Transacting business in state.
Requirements, §53-232.6, (a).
International representative offices.
Authority to establish and operate, §53-232.3, (c), (d).
Conversion to international branch bank or international bank agency, §53-232.14, (d).
Defined, §53-232.2, (a).
Generally, §53-232.14, (a).
Powers, §53-232.14, (e).
Registration, §53-232.14, (b).
Review of operations by commissioner, §53-232.14, (c).
Termination of operation, §53-232.13, (b).
Investments.
Restrictions on international banking corporations, §53-232.11, (b).
Legal and financial terms used in article.
Reference to equivalent terms used in foreign country, §53-232.2, (b).
Legislative declaration.
Intent of provisions, §53-232.1, (b).
Licenses.
International banking corporations, §§53-232.8, 53-232.9.
Reports.
International banking corporations, §§53-232.10, (d), 53-232.12.
Representative offices.
Authority to establish and operate, §53-232.3, (c), (d).
Conversion to international branch bank or international bank agency, §53-232.14, (d).
Defined, §53-232.2, (a).
Generally, §53-232.14, (a).
Powers, §53-232.14, (e).
Registration, §53-232.14, (b).
Review of operation by commissioner, §53-232.14, (c).
Termination of operation, §53-232.13, (b).
Rules and regulations.
Banking commission, §53-232.15.
State banking commission.
Rules and regulations, §53-232.15.
Title of act.
Short title, §53-232.1, (a).

INTERNATIONAL COMMERCIAL ARBITRATION AND CONCILIATION, §§1-567.30 to 1-567.87.
Agreements expressly excluding applicability of article, §1-567.31, (g).
Amiable compositeur (amicable compounder).
Tribunal deciding on, §1-567.58, (c).
Appeals, §1-567.67, (a), (b).
Applicability of article, §1-567.31, (a).
Arbitral tribunal.
Conducting arbitration in manner deemed appropriate.
No agreement on procedure, §1-567.49, (b).
Decisions made by majority, §1-567.59.

INTERNATIONAL COMMERCIAL ARBITRATION AND CONCILIATION —Cont'd
Arbitral tribunal —Cont'd
Interim measures.
Power to order, §1-567.47.
Jurisdiction.
Competence to rule on, §§1-567.46, (a), 1-567.47.
Place of meetings for consultation, §1-567.50, (b).
Arbitration agreement.
Defined, §1-567.37, (a).
Valid, enforceable and irrevocable, §1-567.37, (c).
Written agreement, §1-567.37, (b).
Arbitration institution.
Appointing to conduct arbitration, §1-567.41, (g).
Arbitrators.
Agreement on appointment, §1-567.41, (b), (c).
Appointment, §1-567.41, (b) to (g).
Substitute or replacement arbitrator.
Termination of mandate, §1-567.45, (a) to (c).
Arbitration institution, appointing, §1-567.41, (g).
Challenges to, §1-567.42, (d), (e).
Agreement on procedure, §1-567.43, (a).
Arbitral tribunal to decide issue, §1-567.43, (b).
Rejection of challenge, request to superior court to decide, §1-567.43, (c).
Written statement of reasons for challenge, §1-567.43, (b).
Compensation, §1-567.41, (h).
Disclosure required.
Information causing impartiality to be questioned, §1-567.42, (a).
Continuing duty, §1-567.42, (c).
Mandatory and not waived, §1-567.42, (b).
Failure to act.
Termination of mandate, §1-567.44, (a) to (c).
Nationality, §1-567.41, (a).
Number, §1-567.40.
Procedure for appointment, §1-567.41, (b) to (g).
Substitute or replacement arbitrator.
Termination of mandate, §1-567.45, (a).
Previously held hearing, repeal, §1-567.45, (b).
Validity of ruling of tribunal not effected, §1-567.45, (c).
Superior court appointing.
Failure to agree, §1-567.41, (d) to (f).
Termination of mandate.
Substitute or replacement arbitrator, §1-567.45, (a) to (c).
Termination of proceedings, §1-567.62, (c).
Unable to perform or failure to act, §1-567.44, (a).
Arbitrator withdraws or agrees to termination, effect, §1-567.44, (c).
Decision by superior court, request for, §1-567.44, (b).
Unable to perform.
Termination of mandate, §1-567.44, (a) to (c).
Attorneys at law.
Representation by attorney, §1-567.48, (b).
Conciliation proceedings, §1-567.79.
Attorneys' fees.
Awarding, order of costs, §1-567.61, (h).
Award.
Additional award.
Extension of period for making, §1-567.63, (d).
Forma and content requirements, §1-567.63, (e).
Request, time, §1-567.63, (c).
Confirmation, §1-567.65.
Copies delivered to parties, §1-567.61, (d).

INTERNATIONAL COMMERCIAL ARBITRATION AND CONCILIATION —Cont'd

Award —Cont'd
Correction or interpretation.
Extension of time, §1-567.63, (d).
Forma and content requirements, §1-567.63, (e).
Request, time for, §1-567.63, (a).
Tribunal correcting on own initiative, time, §1-567.63, (b).
Costs, awarding, §1-567.61, (h).
Date and place of arbitration, stating required, §1-567.61, (c).
Enforcement, §1-567.65.
Foreign currency, denominated in, §1-567.61, (e).
Interest, authority to award, §1-567.61, (f).
Modification, §1-567.64.
Reasons upon which based not stated, §1-567.61, (b).
Settlement.
Agreed terms, status and effect, §1-567.60, (c).
Signature of arbitrators required, §1-567.61, (a).
Specific performance, awarding, §1-567.61, (g).
Vacating of award, §1-567.64.
Writing required, §1-567.61, (a).

Burden of proof.
Tribunal conducting proceeding, §1-567.49, (b).

Challenge to arbitrators appointed or designated, §§1-567.42, 1-567.43.

Claims.
Stating, requirements, §1-567.53, (a).
Amending or supplementing, §1-567.53, (b).
More than two parties to arbitration, §1-567.53, (c).

Commencement of proceedings, §1-567.51.

Commercial arbitration or conciliation considered, §1-567.31, (e).

Compelling arbitration, stay of judicial proceedings.
Application to superior court for order, §1-567.38, (a).
Beginning or continuing arbitration while application pending, §1-567.38, (b).

Conciliators.
Conduct of proceedings, §1-567.78, (c).
Draft conciliation agreement.
Preparation, §1-567.80, (a).
Duties, §1-567.78, (b).
Immunities, §1-567.87, (b).
Selection, §1-567.78, (a).
Service of process.
Not subject to service or matters related to conciliation, §1-567.87, (a).
Settlements.
Acceptance by parties, §1-567.80, (b).

Conflict of laws.
Application of law as determined by conflict rules.
Failure of parties to designate applicable law, §1-567.58, (b).
Dispute decided on rules of law as chosen by parties, §1-567.58, (a).
Substantive law, designation construed to refer to, §1-567.58, (a).

Consolidation of arbitration agreements, §1-567.57, (b).

Construction and interpretation.
Severability of provisions, §1-567.33A.

Contracts.
Severability of arbitration laws, §1-567.46, (a).

Cost of arbitration.
Awarding, §1-567.61, (h).

INTERNATIONAL COMMERCIAL ARBITRATION AND CONCILIATION —Cont'd

Cost of conciliation.
Borne equally by parties, §1-567.85, (b).
Expenses of party borne by party, §1-567.85, (b).
Giving notice of costs, §1-567.85, (a).
Included in costs, §1-567.85, (a).
Setting costs on termination, §1-567.85, (a).

Counterclaims.
Stating, requirements, §1-567.53, (a).
Amending or supplementing, §1-567.53, (b).
More than two parties to arbitration, §1-567.53, (c).

Courts.
Applications to superior court, §1-567.66.
Extent of intervention, §1-567.35.

Default of party, §1-567.55.

Defenses.
Stating, requirements, §1-567.53, (a).
Amending or supplementing, §1-567.53, (b).
More than two parties to arbitration, §1-567.53, (c).

Definitions, §1-567.32, (a).
Arbitration agreement, §1-567.37, (a).

Designation of law or legal system, §1-567.58, (a), (b).

Discovery.
Assistance of superior court in obtaining, request, §1-567.57, (a).
Tribunal conducting proceeding, §1-567.49, (b).

Draft conciliation agreement.
Acceptance of settlement, §1-567.80, (b).
Preparation, §1-567.80, (a).

Enforceability of decree, §1-567.84.

Equal treatment of parties, §1-567.48, (a).

Evidence.
Admission made in course of conciliation.
Admissibility, §1-567.81, (a).
Documentary evidence, translation, tribunal ordering, §1-567.52, (b).
Documents prepared, §1-567.81, (c).
Offering in violation of provisions, §1-567.81, (b).
Tribunal conducting proceeding.
Not limited to rules of evidence, §1-567.49, (b).

Ex aequo et bono (on the basis of fundamental fairness).
Tribunal deciding on, §1-567.58, (c).

Expenses of party to conciliation.
Borne by party, §1-567.85, (b).

Experts.
Appointment by tribunal, §1-567.56, (a).
Hearings.
Participation in, §1-567.56, (b).
Relevant information or property.
Parties providing access to, §1-567.56, (a).

Hearings.
Closing at conclusion of evidence, §1-567, (f).
Confidentiality of matters, §1-567, (d).
Experts.
Participation in, §1-567.56, (b).
Held at appropriate stage of proceedings, §1-567, (a).
In camera, held in, §1-567, (d).
Notice for purposes of inspection property or documents, §1-567, (b).
Record or transcript, agreement on, §1-567, (e).
Service of statements, documents or other information, §1-567, (c).
Tribunal to decide whether to hold, §1-567, (a).

INTERNATIONAL COMMERCIAL ARBITRATION AND CONCILIATION —Cont'd
Immunities.
Conciliators and parties, §1-567.87.
Interim relief.
Arbitral tribunal.
Power to order, §1-567.47.
Interim relief directly from superior court.
Arbitrator not available or not appointed, §1-567.39, (a).
Relief granted, §1-567.39, (c).
Finding of fact of arbitral tribunal.
Preclusive effect given, §1-567.39, (d), (e).
Limiting availability by written agreement, §1-567.39, (f).
Other cases, §1-567.39, (b).
International agreements.
Article subject, §1-567.31, (a).
International arbitration or conciliation considered, §1-567.31, (c), (d).
Jurisdiction, §1-567.36, (a), (b).
Arbitral tribunal.
Competence to rule on its jurisdiction, §§1-567.46, (a), 1-567.47.
Ruling on jurisdiction as preliminary question.
Appeal of ruling to superior court, §1-567.46, (c).
Ruling on jurisdiction in award on the merits, §1-567.46, (c).
Time for raising plea of lack of jurisdiction, §1-567.46, (b).
Effect of consenting to conciliation, §1-567.86.
Language or languages to be used.
Agreement by parties, §1-567.52, (a).
Documentary evidence, translation, tribunal may order, §1-567.52, (b).
Translators, employing, §1-567.52, (c).
Tribunal determining.
No agreement by parties, §1-567.52, (a).
Limitation of actions.
Tolling on beginning of conciliation proceedings, §1-567.82, (b).
Mediation, conciliation or other procedures.
Settlement of dispute, §1-567.60, (a).
Number of arbitrators, §1-567.40.
Objection to noncompliance.
Waiver of right to object, §1-567.34.
Other dispute resolution laws.
Not affected, §1-567.31, (f).
Parties.
Default, §1-567.55.
Equal treatment, §1-567.48, (a).
Place of arbitration, §1-567.50, (a).
Place of arbitration in state.
Required for provisions to apply, §1-567.31, (b).
Policy of state, §1-567.30.
Purpose of article, §1-567.30.
Rules of interpretation, §1-567.32, (b) to (d).
Rules of procedure.
Agreement of parties on, §1-567.49, (a).
Decisions on, §1-567.59.
Tribunal conducting arbitration in manner deemed appropriate.
No agreement on procedure, §1-567.49, (b).
Setoffs.
Stating, requirements, §1-567.53, (a).
Amending or supplementing, §1-567.53, (b).
More than two parties to arbitration, §1-567.53, (c).

INTERNATIONAL COMMERCIAL ARBITRATION AND CONCILIATION —Cont'd
Settlement.
Award.
Agreed terms, status and effect, §1-567.60, (c).
Mediation, conciliation, use to settle, §1-567.60, (a).
Termination of proceedings, §1-567.60, (b).
Tribunal may encourage, §1-567.60, (a).
Severability of provisions, §1-567.33A.
Short title of article, §1-567.30.
Site of arbitration, §1-567.50, (a).
Specific performance, awarding, §1-567.61, (g).
Statute of limitations.
Tolling at beginning of conciliation proceedings, §1-567.82, (b).
Stay of arbitration.
Submitting dispute to conciliation, §1-567.82, (a).
Stay of judicial proceeding and compel arbitration.
Application to superior court for order, §1-567.38, (a).
Beginning or continuing arbitration while application pending, §1-567.38, (b).
Termination of arbitrators mandate.
Substitute or replacement arbitrator, §1-567.45, (a) to (c).
Termination of proceedings, §1-567.62, (c).
Unable to perform or failure to act, §1-567.44, (a) to (c).
Termination of conciliation.
All parties, §1-567.83, (a).
Particular party or parties, §1-567.83, (b).
Termination of proceedings, §1-567.62, (a).
Mandate of tribunal terminates, §1-567.62, (c).
Order of termination, §1-567.62, (b).
Settlement, §1-567.60, (b).
Terms of contract.
Deciding in accordance with, §1-567.58, (d).
Translators, employing, §1-567.52, (c).
Tribunal exceeding scope of authority.
Time for raising of plea, §1-567.46, (b).
Usage of trade, taking into consideration, §1-567.58, (d).
Venue, §1-567.36, (a), (b).
Waiver.
Right to object, §1-567.34.
When proceeding starts, §1-567.51.
Written agreement.
Effect, §1-567.84.
Written communications or submissions.
Court, administrative or special proceedings, §1-567.33, (c).
Receipt, §1-567.33, (a).
Last known place of business, domicile or mailing address, §1-567.33, (b).

INTERNATIONAL FESTIVAL OF STATE.
Folkmoot USA, §145-19.

INTERNATIONAL LAW.
Congress.
Power to punish offenses against, Const. U. S., art. I, §8.

INTERNATIONAL RELATIONS.
Secretary of state, powers and duties, §147-54.6.

INTERNET.
Advance health care directive registry.
Access to registry, §130A-469.
Cyberstalking, §14-196.3.

INTERNET —Cont'd
Electronic auction service.
State surplus property.
Sale or disposal using, §143-64.03, (d).
E-NC authority, §§143B-437.44 to 143B-437.47.
Health benefit plans.
Electronic or on-line system for up-to-date information, §58-3-245, (a).
Money transmitters licenses.
Engaged in the business of money transmission.
Website available to in-state citizens, §53-208.3, (c).
Organ donation records.
Access by organ procurement organizations, §20-43.2.
Property tax information contained on web site.
Amount of taxes due.
Person relying on information, §105-361, (e).
Understatement of taxes and special assessment.
Liability of tax collector, §105-361, (e).
Records of superior courts in clerks offices.
Electronic access to records.
Contracts to provide access to public, §7A-109, (d), (e).
Sales and use tax on telecommunications services.
Excluded from gross receipts, §105-164.4C, (c).
Sexual offenses.
Solicitation of child by computer, §14-202.3, (a).
Turnpike authority.
Internet report of funds expended, §136-89.195.

INTERNSHIP COUNCIL.
Applications.
Committees for screening applications, §143B-419.
Members, §143B-418.
Powers and duties, §143B-417.

INTERPLEADER AND INTERVENTION.
Administrative procedure.
Appeals.
Motion to intervene, §150B-46.
Right to judicial intervention when agency unreasonably delays decision, §150B-44.
Hearings.
Motion to intervene, §§150B-23, (d), 150B-38, (f).
Attachment.
Third persons claiming attached property, §1-440.43.
Bills of lading.
Determination of conflicting claims, §25-7-603.
Child support.
Action for support of minor child, §50-13.5, (e).
Complaint for interpleader and declaratory relief.
Form, §1A-1, Rule 84.
Delivery of property to intervener, §1-483.
Documents of title, §25-7-603.
Determination of conflicting claims, §25-7-603.
Funds subject to competing claims.
Deposit of funds in interest bearing accounts, §1A-1, Rule 22, (b).
Interpleader generally, §1A-1, Rule 22.
Intervention of right, §1A-1, Rule 24, (a).
Permissive intervention, §1A-1, Rule 24, (b).
Plaintiff exposed to double or multiple liability.
Persons having claims against plaintiff joined as defendants and required to interplead, §1A-1, Rule 22, (a).

INTERPLEADER AND INTERVENTION —Cont'd
Procedure for intervention, §1A-1, Rule 24, (c).
Property claimed by third person, §1-482.
Public utilities.
Attorney general.
Intervention in commission proceedings, §62-20.
Right to intervene, §1A-1, Rule 24, (a).
Sale of goods, UCC.
Documents of title.
Determination of conflicting claims, §25-7-603.
Notice of claim or litigation to person answerable over, §25-2-607, (5).
Utilities commission proceedings, §62-73.
Warehouse receipts.
Determination of conflicting claims, §25-7-603.

INTERPRETERS.
Educational agency employed interpreters and transliterators.
Annual job related training, number of hours, §115C-110, (n).
Fraud.
Licenses.
Revocation, suspension or denials of licenses, §90D-12.
Grand jury.
Permitted in grand jury room during proceedings, §15A-623, (d).
Hearing impaired, interpreters for.
Administrative proceedings.
Appointment if deaf person party or witness before, §8B-2, (c).
Appointment.
Compensation, §8B-8.
Waiver of appointed interpreter, §8B-3, (a), (b).
Arrest of deaf person.
Arresting officer to procure, §8B-2, (d).
Civil, criminal or juvenile proceedings.
Appointment if deaf person party or witness, §8B-2, (a).
Compensation, fees and expenses.
Administrative agencies.
Payment for services before, §8B-8, (e).
City or county administrative proceedings.
Payment for services, §8B-8, (f).
Civil cases and special proceedings.
Payment for services, §8B-8, (c).
Criminal and juvenile proceedings.
Payment for services, §8B-8, (b).
Fixed by appointing authority, §8B-8, (a).
Legislative bodies.
Payment for services before, §8B-8, (d).
Reasonable fee for services, entitlement, included in, §8B-8, (a).
Travel and subsistence expenses, §8B-8, (a).
Competence.
Determination, §8B-1.
Confidentiality.
Privileged communications, §8B-5.
Coordination of interpreter services, §8B-6.
Definitions, §8B-1.
Licensure act, §90D-3.
Determination of competence, §8B-1.
Educational agency employing interpreters and transliterators.
Annual job related training, number of hours, §115C-110, (n).
Fees.
Licenses, §90D-10, (b).

INTERPRETERS —Cont'd
Hearing impaired, interpreters for —Cont'd
Fees —Cont'd
Training and licensing preparation program fee, §8B-10.
Funds.
Responsibility for payment to implement chapter, §8B-9.
Legislative committees.
Appointment if deaf person witness before, §8B-2, (b).
Licensure of interpreters and transliterators generally, §§90D-1 to 90D-13.
Lists of interpreters, §8B-6.
Notice.
Need for interpreter, §8B-4.
Oath, §8B-7.
Parent of juvenile brought before court deaf.
Appointment for parent, §8B-2, (e).
Preliminary determination for appointment, §8B-2, (f).
Privileged communications, §8B-5.
Proof of deafness, §8B-4.
Removal, §8B-2, (g).
Responsibility for payment of funds to implement chapter, §8B-9.
Right to interpreter, §8B-1.
Training and licensing preparation program fee, §8B-10.
Waiver of appointed interpreter, §8B-3, (a), (b).
Injunctions.
Violations of license provisions, §90D-13.
Licenses, §§90D-1 to 90D-13.
Applicability of provisions, §90D-4, (b).
Board, §90D-5.
Compensation, §90D-5, (f).
Creation, §90D-5, (a).
Duties, §90D-6.
Fees and expenses, §90D-10, (a), (b).
Meetings, §90D-5, (h).
Members, §90D-5, (b), (c), (d), (e).
Officers, §90D-5, (g).
Powers, §90D-6.
Continuing education.
Provisional licenses, §90D-8, (a).
Renewals, §90D-11.
Criminal records checks for license applicants, §90D-7, (c).
Definitions, §90D-3.
Disciplinary actions, §90D-12.
Exemptions, §90D-4, (b).
Fees, §90D-10, (b).
Injunctions, §90D-13.
Legislative intent, §90D-2.
Nonresidents.
Reciprocity, §90D-9, (a), (b).
Provisional licenses, §90D-8, (a), (b), (c).
Purpose of act, §90D-2.
Qualifications, §90D-7, (a), (b).
Provisional licenses, §90D-8, (a), (c).
Reciprocity, §90D-9, (a), (b).
Renewals, §90D-11.
Provisional licenses, §90D-8, (b).
Required, §90D-4, (a).
Revocation, suspension or denials of licenses, §90D-12.
Short title, §90D-1.
Titles, use of, §90D-4, (a).
Violations of provisions, §90D-12.
Injunctions, §90D-13.

INTERPRETERS —Cont'd
Reciprocity.
Licenses, §90D-9, (a), (b).
Witnesses.
Subject to provisions relating to qualifications as expert, §8C-1, Rule 604.

INTERRACIAL MARRIAGES.
Validated, §51-3.1.

INTERROGATION OF DELINQUENT OR UNDISCIPLINED JUVENILE.
Procedures generally, §7B-2101.

INTERROGATION OF WITNESSES.
Interrogation by court, §8C-1, Rule 614.
Leading questions, §8C-1, Rule 611, (c).
Procedure, §8C-1, Rule 611, (a).
Scope of cross-examination, §8C-1, Rule 611.

INTERROGATORIES.
Answers, §1A-1, Rule 33, (a).
Availability, §1A-1, Rule 33, (a).
Limited liability companies.
Interrogatories by secretary of state, §§57C-1-31 to 57C-1-33.
Assets of judgment debtor, discovery, §1-352.1.
Business records.
Option to produce, §1A-1, Rule 33, (c).
Civil investigative demand.
Medical assistance provider false claim, §108A-70.14.
Corporations.
Business corporations.
Secretary of state, §§55-1-31 to 55-1-33.
Depositions.
See DEPOSITIONS.
Discovery.
See DISCOVERY.
Discovery methods, §1A-1, Rule 26, (a).
Discovery of assets of judgment debtor, §1-352.1.
Executions.
Discovery of assets of judgment debtor, §1-352.1.
Expedited evictions.
Time for response, §42-70, (d).
Failure to serve answers to interrogatories, §1A-1, Rule 37, (d).
Filing, §1A-1, Rule 5, (d).
Larceny.
Mutilation, larceny or destruction of public records and papers, §14-76.
Limited liability companies.
Interrogatories by secretary of state, §§57C-1-31 to 57C-1-33.
Medical assistance provider false claim.
Civil investigative demand, §108A-70.14.
Nonprofit corporations.
Failure to answer, §55A-1-32.
Information disclosed by.
Confidentiality, §55A-1-33.
Secretary of state, §55A-1-31.
Procedure, §1A-1, Rule 33, (a).
Scope, §1A-1, Rule 33, (b).
Secretary of state.
Interrogatories to limited liability companies, §§57C-1-31 to 57C-1-33.
Nonprofit corporations, §55A-1-31.
Summary judgment.
Affidavit supplemented or opposed by answers to, §1A-1, Rule 56, (e).
Supplemental proceedings.
Discovery of assets of judgment debtor, §1-352.1.
Use at trial, §1A-1, Rule 33, (b).

INTERROGATORIES —Cont'd
Workers' compensation.
Industrial commission.
Power to limit, §97-80, (f).

INTERSECTIONS.
Authority of local officials to regulate turning, §20-153, (c).
Blind pedestrians, §20-175.1.
Defined, §§20-4.01, (16), 20-150, (c).
Lanes.
Keeping to right in crossing intersections or railroads, §20-147.
Left turns, §§20-153, (b), 20-155.
Modification of method of turning, §20-153, (c).
Overtaking and passing.
Limitations on privilege, §20-150, (c).
Parking near, §20-162, (a).
Railroad intersections.
Automatic signals at railroad intersections.
Commission may require, §136-20.1, (b).
Grade crossings generally.
See RAILROAD GRADE CROSSINGS.
Highways.
Intersection with, §136-191.
Powers of railroad corporations, §136-190.
Powers of railroad corporations, §136-190.
Red lights, §20-158, (b).
Right of way, §20-155, (a).
Stop signs and traffic lights, §20-158, (b).
Yield signs, §20-158.1.
Right side of highway.
Vehicle crossing intersection to keep to, §20-147.
Right turns, §20-153, (a).
Modification of method of turning, §20-153, (c).
Right turn on red, §20-158, (b).
Stop lights, §20-158.
Stopping.
Certain highways, §20-158.
Traffic obstructed, §20-142.5.
Stop signs, §20-158, (a), (b).
Traffic lights, §20-158, (a), (b).
Walk or don't walk traffic-control signals or devices, §20-172, (a), (b).

INTER-SPOUSAL IMMUNITY.
Abolished, §52-5.1.
Tort action arising out of acts occurring outside state, §52-5.1.

INTERSTATE AGREEMENT ON DETAINERS, §§15A-761 to 15A-767.
Appropriate court.
Defined, §15A-762.
Cooperation in enforcement, §15A-763.
Designation of enforcement officers, §15A-766.
Distribution of copies of provisions, §15A-767.
Escape from temporary custody, §15A-764.
Text of agreement, §15A-761.
Warden's, etc., duties, §15A-765.

INTERSTATE AGREEMENT ON QUALIFICATIONS OF EDUCATIONAL PERSONNEL, §§115C-349 to 115C-358.
See SCHOOL EMPLOYEES.

INTERSTATE BRANCH BANKING.
Generally, §§53-224.9 to 53-224.31.
See BRANCH BANKS.
Savings and loan associations.
Out-of-state branch offices, §§54B-265 to 54B-278.
See SAVINGS AND LOAN ASSOCIATIONS.
Savings banks.
Out-of-state branch banks, §§54C-199 to 54C-212.
See SAVINGS BANKS.

INTERSTATE COMMERCE.
Congress, Const. U. S., art. I, §§8, 9.
Constitution of the United States, Const. U. S., art. I, §§8, 9.
Earnings of employees in interstate commerce.
Collections out of state to avoid exemptions.
Abetting.
Resident not to abet collection out of state, §95-74.
Actions.
Institution of foreign suit as evidence of intent to violate, §95-76.
Construction and interpretation, §95-77.
Evidence of intent to violate provisions, §95-76.
Penalties for violations, §95-75.
Prohibited, §95-73.
Remedies for violations, §95-75.
Resident not to abet collection out of state, §95-74.
Limited liability companies.
Applicability of provisions to, §57C-10-02.
Occupational safety and health.
Standards not to unduly burden interstate commerce, §95-131, (e).
Public utilities.
Separation or allocation of revenue and costs of.
Commission may require, §62-35, (b).
Sales and use tax.
Refunds, §105-164.14, (a).

INTERSTATE COMPACT FOR THE SUPERVISION OF ADULT OFFENDERS, §§148-65.4 to 148-65.9.
Citation, §148-65.4.
Form, §148-65.5.
Governor.
Execution of compact, §148-65.5.
Executive orders for implementation, §148-65.6, (f).
Hearings on interstate parole and probation, §148-65.8, (a), (b).
Alleged parole or probation violations, §148-65.8, (d).
Rights of offender, §148-65.8, (c).
Sentences.
North Carolina sentence to be served in other jurisdiction, §148-65.9.
Short title, §148-65.4.
State council for interstate adult offender supervision.
Established, §148-65.6, (a).
Meetings, §148-65.6, (b).
Members, §148-65.6, (a), (d).
Powers and duties, §148-65.6, (c), (e).
Supervision fee, §148-65.7.
Text, §148-65.5.

INTERSTATE COMPACT ON JUVENILES, §§7B-2800 to 7B-2827.
Absconders.
Out-of-state confinement amendment, §7B-2827.
Return, §7B-2805.
Voluntary return procedure, §7B-2806.
Administrators.
Authority to enter into supplementary agreement, §7B-2817.
Designation by governor, §§7B-2812, 7B-2816.
Discharging financial obligations imposed, §7B-2818.
Hearings before, §7B-2823.

INTERSTATE COMPACT ON JUVENILES —Cont'd
Amendment to compact concerning interstate rendition of juveniles alleged to be delinquent.
Additional remedies and binding between party states, §7B-2826, (a).
Construction of provisions, §7B-2826, (b).
Petition, §7B-2826, (b).
Requisition, §7B-2826, (b).
Binding upon executing state until renounced, §7B-2814.
Confinement of probationers or parolees, escapees or absconders.
Out-of-state confinement amendment, §7B-2827.
Cooperative care, treatment and rehabilitation of delinquents.
Supplementary agreement, §7B-2810.
Cost, payment of, §7B-2808, (a).
Asserting right against person, agency or other entity, §7B-2808, (b).
Court defined, §7B-2803.
Definitions, §7B-2803.
Juvenile.
Return of runaways, §7B-2804, (c).
Sending state.
Out-of-state confinement amendment, §7B-2827.
Delinquent juvenile defined, §7B-2803.
Detention practices, §7B-2809.
Donations, gifts and grants, acceptance by party state, §7B-2811.
Due process at parole or probation violation hearing, §7B-2824.
Effectuation of purposes and intent, enforcement generally, §7B-2819.
Enforcement of compact, §7B-2819.
Escapees.
Out-of-state confinement amendment, §7B-2827.
Return, §7B-2805.
Execution of compact on behalf of state.
Governor authorized and directed to execute, §7B-2800.
Federal and other aid, acceptance, §7B-2811.
Financial obligations imposed, discharging, §7B-2818.
Findings, §7B-2801.
Full force and effect of law within state, §7B-2813.
Governor authorized and directed to execute compact, §7B-2800.
Governors of party states to designate administrators, §§7B-2812, 7B-2816.
Hearing officers, §7B-2823.
Hearing on return of runaways, §7B-2821.
Hearing procedures for parolees or probationers, §7B-2822.
Interstate rendition of juveniles alleged to be delinquent.
Amendment of compact binding on party states, §7B-2826, (a).
Construction of provisions and procedures, petition, requisition, §7B-2826, (b).
Jails, juvenile not to be placed or detained in, §7B-2809.
Lockups, juvenile not to be placed or detained in, §7B-2809.
Notice of renunciation, §7B-2814.
Operative immediately upon execution, §7B-2813.

INTERSTATE COMPACT ON JUVENILES —Cont'd
Out-of-state confinement amendment, §7B-2827, (a), (b).
Confinement or ordering confinement of delinquent juvenile in compact institution, §7B-2827.
Parental rights and responsibilities, compact not in derogation of, §7B-2802.
Parole and probation hearing procedures, §7B-2822.
Parole or probation violation hearings.
Due process rights, §7B-2824.
Effect of hearing outside state, §7B-2825.
Payment of cost, responsibility, §7B-2808, (a).
Asserting right against person, agency or other entity, §7B-2808, (b).
Petition appropriate court in demanding state for issuance of requisition.
Return of runaways, §7B-2804, (a).
Policy of states party to compact, §7B-2801.
Prisons.
Juvenile not to be placed or detained in, §7B-2809.
Probationer or parolee residing in receiving state, §7B-2807, (a), (b).
Officers of sending state entering receiving state and apprehending and retaking juvenile, §7B-2807, (c).
Transporting juvenile to sending state, payment of cost, §7B-2807, (d).
Visitation and supervision duties.
Exercise by receiving state, §7B-2807, (a), (b).
Probationers or parolees, confinement.
Out-of-state confinement amendment, §7B-2827.
Probation or parole defined, §7B-2803.
Provisions severable, §7B-2815.
Purposes, §7B-2801.
Reasonable and liberal construction of compact, §7B-2801.
Remedies and procedures in addition to and not in substitution for other rights, remedies and procedures, §7B-2802.
Renunciation of compact, §7B-2814.
Requisition.
Return of runaways, §7B-2804, (a).
Residence defined, §7B-2803.
Return of escapees or absconders.
Counsel or guardian ad litem, appointment, §7B-2805, (c).
Detention order, §7B-2805, (a).
Requisition for return, §7B-2805, (a).
Taking juvenile into custody without requisition, §7B-2804, (a).
Transportation cost, responsibility for payment, §7B-2805, (b).
Voluntary return procedure, §7B-2806.
Return of runaways.
Additional procedures not precluded, §7B-2820.
Detention order, §7B-2804, (a).
Hearing on petition, §7B-2804, (a).
Hearing to determine whether petitioner entitled to legal custody, §7B-2821.
Juvenile defined, §7B-2804, (c).
Period of time for holding juvenile in custody, §7B-2821.
Petitioning appropriate court in demanding state for requisition, §7B-2804, (a).
Procedures for return, §7B-2821.
Requisition, §7B-2804, (a).

INTERSTATE COMPACT ON JUVENILES —Cont'd
Return of runaways —Cont'd
Taking juvenile into custody without requisition, §7B-2804, (a).
Testing legality of proceedings, §7B-2821.
Transportation cost, responsibility for payment, §7B-2804, (b).
Runaways.
Return, §7B-2804.
Additional procedures not precluded, §7B-2820.
Proceedings for return, §7B-2821.
Severability of provisions, §7B-2815.
State defined, §7B-2803.
Supplementary agreement, §7B-2810.
Authority of compact administrator, §7B-2817.
Time for sending notice of renunciation, §7B-2814.
Voluntary return procedure, §7B-2806.

INTERSTATE COMPACT ON THE PLACEMENT OF CHILDREN, §§7B-3800 to 7B-3806.
See CHILD PLACEMENT.

INTERSTATE COMPACTS.
Adoption.
Interstate compact on adoption and medical assistance, §§7B-3900 to 7B-3906.
See ADOPTION.
Atlantic States Marine Fisheries Compact and Commission, §§113-251 to 113-257.
Child placement.
Interstate compact on the placement of children, §§7B-3800 to 7B-3806.
Corrections, §§148-119 to 148-121.
Detainers.
Interstate agreement on detainers, §§15A-761 to 15A-767.
See INTERSTATE AGREEMENT ON DETAINERS.
Driver's license compact, §§20-4.21 to 20-4.30.
See DRIVER'S LICENSE COMPACT.
Education, §115C-104.
Educational personnel.
Interstate agreement on qualifications, §§115C-349 to 115C-358.
See SCHOOL EMPLOYEES.
Emergency management assistance compact, §§166A-40 to 166A-53.
Environmental compact, §§113A-21 to 113A-23.
Forest fire protection.
Southeastern interstate forest fire protection compact, §§113-60.11 to 113-60.15.
High-speed rail transportation.
Virginia-North Carolina interstate high-speed rail compact, §§136-220 to 136-222.
Juveniles.
Interstate compact on juveniles, §§7B-2800 to 7B-2827.
See INTERSTATE COMPACT ON JUVENILES.
Libraries, §§125-12 to 125-16.
See LIBRARIES AND LIBRARIANS.
Marine fisheries compact, §§113-251 to 113-257.
Mental health, developmental disabilities and substance abuse.
Interstate compact on mental health, §§122C-361 to 122C-366.
See MENTAL HEALTH, DEVELOPMENTAL DISABILITY, SUBSTANCE ABUSE.
Mines and minerals.
Interstate mining compact, §74-37.

INTERSTATE COMPACTS —Cont'd
Motor vehicles.
Driver's license compact, §§20-4.21 to 20-4.30.
See DRIVER'S LICENSE COMPACT.
Vehicle equipment safety compact, §§20-183.13 to 20-183.21.
See MOTOR VEHICLE EQUIPMENT.
National guard.
Mutual assistance compact, §§127A-175 to 127A-184.
See NATIONAL GUARD.
Parole.
Interstate compact for the supervision of adult offenders, §§148-65.4 to 148-65.9.
See INTERSTATE COMPACT FOR THE SUPERVISION OF ADULT OFFENDERS.
Pest control compacts, §§106-65.55 to 106-65.61.
Placement of children, §§7B-3800 to 7B-3806.
See CHILD PLACEMENT.
Probation.
Interstate compact for the supervision of adult offenders, §§148-65.4 to 148-65.9.
See INTERSTATE COMPACT FOR THE SUPERVISION OF ADULT OFFENDERS.
Southeastern interstate forest fire protection compact, §§113-60.11 to 113-60.15.
Southern dairy compact, §§106-810, 106-811.
Southern growth policies agreement, §§143-490 to 143-506.
See SOUTHERN GROWTH POLICIES AGREEMENT.
Southern states energy compact, §§104D-1 to 104D-5.
Vehicle equipment safety compact, §§20-183.13 to 20-183.21.
See MOTOR VEHICLE EQUIPMENT.

INTERSTATE FAMILY SUPPORT, §§52C-1-100 to 52C-9-902.
Actions.
Minor parent, §52C-3-302.
Act or similar law not enacted by responding state.
State tribunal may make findings required by law of responding state, §52C-3-304, (b).
Additional nature of remedies, §52C-1-103.
Application of provisions, §§52C-3-301, (a), 52C-9-901.
Law of this state, §52C-3-303.
Severability, §52C-9-902.
Attorney-client relationship.
Support enforcement agency, §52C-3-307, (c).
Attorneys' fees, §52C-3-312, (b).
Bases for jurisdiction over nonresident, §52C-2-201.
Child.
Defined, §52C-1-101.
Child support orders generally. See within this heading, "Support orders."
Child support payments.
Certified copies.
Admissibility as evidence, §52C-3-315, (c).
Choice of law, §52C-6-604.
Commencement of proceedings, §52C-3-301, (c).
Communications between tribunals, §52C-3-316.
Confidentiality, §52C-3-311.
Confirmed orders, §52C-6-608.
Conflict of laws.
Act or similar law not enacted by responding state.
State tribunal may make findings required by law of responding state, §52C-3-304, (b).

INTERSTATE FAMILY SUPPORT —Cont'd
Contesting validity of orders, §52C-6-606.
Continuing, exclusive jurisdiction, §52C-2-205, (f).
Enforcement powers, §52C-2-205, (c).
Exercise of jurisdiction, §52C-2-205, (a).
Initiating tribunal, §52C-2-206, (a).
Modification of child support order of another state, §§52C-2-205, (f), 52C-6-611, (d).
No continuing, exclusive jurisdiction, §52C-2-206, (c).
No exercise of jurisdiction, §52C-2-205, (b).
Recognizing jurisdiction of another state, §52C-2-205, (d).
Responding tribunal, §52C-2-206, (b).
Spousal support orders, §52C-2-205.
Temporary support orders, §52C-2-205, (e).
Controlling order.
Two or more orders issued, §52C-2-207.
Costs, §52C-3-312.
Prevailing party, §52C-3-312, (b).
Credit for payments, §52C-2-209.
Cumulative nature of remedies, §52C-1-103.
Defenses.
Nonparentage, §52C-3-314.
Definitions, §52C-1-101.
Delay tactics.
Costs and fees imposed, §52C-3-312, (c).
Disbursement of payments, §52C-3-318.
Discovery.
Tribunal requesting assistance with, §52C-3-317.
District attorney.
Representation of obligee, §52C-3-308.
District court jurisdiction, §52C-1-102.
Due process.
Issuance of support orders, §52C-4-401.
Duty of support.
Defined, §52C-1-101.
Enumeration of proceedings, §52C-3-301, (b).
Evidence.
Special rules of evidence and procedure, §52C-3-315.
Exclusive jurisdiction, §52C-2-205.
Exemptions.
Limited immunity of petitioner, §52C-3-313, (c).
Extradition.
Conditions of rendition, §52C-8-802.
Grounds for rendition, §52C-8-801.
Fax.
Admissibility as evidence, §52C-3-315, (e).
Fees, §52C-3-312.
Filing fee, §52C-3-312, (a).
Governor.
Defined, §52C-8-801, (a).
Health care bills.
Admissibility as evidence, §52C-3-315, (d).
Home state.
Defined, §52C-1-101.
Husband-wife privilege, §52C-3-315, (h), (i).
Immunity, §52C-3-315, (i).
Inappropriate tribunal, §52C-3-306.
Income.
Defined, §52C-1-101.
Income-withholding orders of another state.
Administrative enforcement.
Sending documents to be registered to state support enforcement agency, §52C-5-507, (a).
Enforcement of order by agency, §52C-5-507, (b).

INTERSTATE FAMILY SUPPORT —Cont'd
Income-withholding orders of another state —Cont'd
Compliance with law of obligor's principal place of employment.
Duty of employer, §52C-5-502, (d).
Compliance with terms of order.
Employer to withhold and distribute funds, §52C-5-502, (c).
Contest of validity or enforcement by obligor, §52C-5-506, (a).
Notice of contest, obligor to give, §52C-5-506, (b).
Copy of order supplied obligor.
Duty of employer on receiving order, §52C-5-502, (a).
Defined, §52C-1-101.
Effect of registration for enforcement, §52C-6-603.
Employment security commission.
Sending order to, obligor receiving unemployment compensation, §52C-5-501, (a).
Immunity of employer complying with order, §52C-5-504.
Multiple orders, compliance with, §52C-5-503.
Notice of registration of order, §52C-6-605.
Penalties for noncompliance, §52C-5-505.
Procedure to register for enforcement, §52C-6-602.
Registration for enforcement, §52C-6-601.
Sending to obligor's employer.
Filing petition, pleading or registering not required, §52C-5-501, (a).
Treating order as if issued by court of this state.
Duty of employer receiving order, §52C-5-502, (b).
Inference affect.
Refusal to answer on grounds of self-incrimination, §52C-3-315, (g).
Initiating state.
Defined, §52C-1-101.
Initiating tribunal.
Act or similar law not enacted by responding state.
Issuance of certificate and findings required by law of responding state, §52C-3-304, (b).
Authority to act as, §52C-2-203.
Defined, §52C-1-101.
Enforcement and modification of support order, §52C-2-206, (a).
Forwarding copies of petition and other documents.
Duty, §52C-3-304, (a).
Proceeding to determine parentage, §52C-7-701, (a).
Responding tribunal.
Proceeding to determine parentage, §52C-7-701, (a), (b).
Interstate rendition, §§52C-8-801, 52C-8-802.
Issuing state.
Defined, §52C-1-101.
Governing law, §52C-6-604, (a).
Issuing tribunal.
Defined, §52C-1-101.
Jurisdiction.
Extended personal jurisdiction, §52C-2-201.
Generally, §52C-1-102.
Limited immunity of petitioner, §52C-3-313, (a).
Simultaneous proceedings in another state, §52C-2-204, (a).
No jurisdiction exercised, §52C-2-204, (b).

INTERSTATE FAMILY SUPPORT —Cont'd
Law.
Defined, §52C-1-101.
Limitation of actions.
Proceeding for arrears, §52C-6-604, (b).
Mail.
Duties and powers of responding tribunal, §52C-3-305, (a), (e).
Inappropriate tribunal, §52C-3-306.
Registered orders.
Contesting validity or enforcement, §52C-6-606, (c).
Minor parents.
Actions by, §52C-3-302.
Modification of orders, §52C-6-609.
Effect of registration for modification, §52C-6-610.
Orders of another state.
Continuing, exclusive jurisdiction, §§52C-2-205, (f), 52C-6-611, (d).
Filing of certified copy, §52C-6-611, (e).
Non-modifiable orders, §52C-6-611, (c).
Notice to issuing tribunal, §52C-6-614.
Recognition of order modified in another state, §52C-6-612.
Requirements, procedures and defenses, §52C-6-611, (b).
Responding tribunal, §52C-6-611, (a).
Modification of support orders.
Orders of another state.
Jurisdiction of state tribunal, parties residing in state, §52C-6-613, (a).
Provision of act, procedure and substantive law of state, applicability, §52C-6-613, (b).
Multiple child support orders.
Two or more obligees, §52C-2-208.
Nondisclosure of information, §52C-3-311.
Nonparentage.
Defenses, §52C-3-314.
Nonresidents.
Bases for jurisdiction over, §52C-2-201.
Procedure when exercising jurisdiction over, §52C-2-202.
Notice.
Income-withholding order from another state.
Contest by obligor, §52C-5-506, (b).
Issuance of support orders, §52C-4-401, (c).
Modification of orders of another state.
Notice to issuing tribunal, §52C-6-614.
Order issued in another state, §52C-6-605, (a).
Contents of notice, §52C-6-605, (b).
Registration of order, §52C-6-605, (c).
Obligee.
Defined, §52C-1-101.
Obligor.
Defined, §52C-1-101.
Parentage bills.
Admissibility as evidence, §52C-3-315, (d).
Parentage proceedings, §52C-7-701.
Parent and child defense of immunity, §52C-3-315, (i).
Paternity.
Choice of law, §52C-7-701, (b).
Initiating or responding tribunal, §52C-7-701, (a).
Nonparentage as defense, §52C-3-314.
Proceeding to determine parentage, §52C-7-701.
Payments.
Credit for payments, §52C-2-209.
Receipt and disbursement, §52C-3-318.
Petitions.
Copies forwarded by state tribunal, §52C-3-304, (a).

INTERSTATE FAMILY SUPPORT —Cont'd
Petitions —Cont'd
Establishing support order, §52C-4-401.
Registration, §52C-6-602, (c).
Requirements, §52C-3-310, (b).
Verification, §52C-3-310, (a).
Admissibility as evidence, §52C-3-315, (b).
Photocopies.
Admissibility as evidence, §52C-3-315, (e).
Physical presence of petitioner.
Special rules of evidence and procedure, §52C-3-315, (a).
Pleadings and accompanying documents, §52C-3-310.
Privileged communications.
Husband and wife, §52C-3-315, (h).
Procedure.
Special rules of evidence and procedure, §52C-3-315.
Procedure to register.
Orders of another state.
Modification of orders, §52C-6-609.
Procedure when exercising jurisdiction over nonresident, §52C-2-202.
Proceedings under this chapter.
Commencement of proceedings, §52C-3-301, (c).
Enumeration, §52C-3-301, (b).
Receipt and disbursements of payments, §52C-3-318.
Recognition of order modified in another state, §52C-6-612.
Recognition of support orders.
Continuing, exclusive jurisdiction, tribunal with, §52C-2-207, (d).
Only one tribunal issuing order, §52C-2-207, (a).
Two or more orders issued.
Determining which order to recognize.
Basis for determination stated in order, §52C-2-207, (e).
Certified copy of order, filing by party obtaining, §52C-2-207, (f).
Rules, §52C-2-207, (b).
Request by resident obligee for state tribunal to determine, §52C-2-207, (c).
Register.
Defined, §52C-1-101.
Registering tribunal.
Defined, §52C-1-101.
Registration of orders, §52C-6-601.
Confirmed order, §52C-6-608.
Contesting validity or enforcement, §52C-6-606.
Burden of proof, §52C-6-607, (a).
Confirmation of order, §52C-6-607, (c).
Defenses, §52C-6-607, (b).
Failure to contest in timely manner, §52C-6-606, (b).
Hearing, §52C-6-606, (a), (c).
Effect of registration for enforcement, §52C-6-603.
Effect of registration for modification, §52C-6-610.
Generally, §52C-6-601.
Issued in another state, §52C-6-603, (a).
Enforceability of order, §52C-6-603, (b).
Modification, §52C-6-603, (c).
Notice of registration order, §52C-6-605.
Petition to establish, §52C-4-401.
Procedure to register for enforcement, §52C-6-602.
Recognition of order modified in another state, §52C-6-612.
Registration of order of another state for modification, §52C-6-609.

INTERSTATE FAMILY SUPPORT —Cont'd
Rendition.
Child support proceedings, §52C-8-802, (a), (b).
Decline to honor demand, §52C-8-802, (c).
Delay of proceedings, §52C-8-802, (b).
Demand by governor, §52C-8-801, (b).
Applicability of demand, §52C-8-801, (c).
Demand of governor.
Decline to honor demand, §52C-8-802, (c).
Governor.
Defined, §52C-8-801, (a).
Representation of obligee, §52C-3-308.
Responding state.
Defined, §52C-1-101.
Responding tribunal.
Application of law of this state, §52C-3-303.
Authority to act as, §52C-2-203.
Calculations on which support order is based, §52C-3-305, (c).
Conditioning payment of support order, §52C-3-305, (d).
Defined, §52C-1-101.
Enforcement and modification of support order, §52C-2-206, (b).
Filing of papers, §52C-3-305, (a).
Forwarding of papers from inappropriate tribunal, §52C-3-306.
Issuance of support order, §52C-4-401, (a).
Mailing of copies of order, §52C-3-305, (e).
Modification of child support order of another state, §52C-6-611, (a).
Powers and duties, §52C-3-305, (b).
Self-incrimination.
Refusal to answer on grounds of, §52C-3-315, (g).
Service of process.
Limited immunity of petitioner, §52C-3-313, (b).
Severability, §52C-9-902.
Short title, §52C-1-100.
Simultaneous proceedings in another state, §52C-2-204.
Spousal-support order.
Defined, §52C-1-101.
State.
Defined, §52C-1-101.
State information agency.
Department of health and human services.
Division of social services, §52C-3-309, (a).
Powers and duties, §52C-3-309, (b).
Statute of limitations.
Proceeding for arrears, §52C-6-604, (b).
Support enforcement agency.
Defined, §52C-1-101.
Fiduciary relationships, §52C-3-307, (c).
Provision of services, §52C-3-307, (a).
Enumeration of services, §52C-3-307, (b).
Support orders.
Defined, §52C-1-101.
Registration.
Filing of documents, §52C-6-602, (b).
Pleadings and petitions, §52C-6-602, (c).
Procedure to register, §52C-6-602, (a).
Telephone conversation.
Testimony or deposition by telephone, §52C-3-315, (f).
Transmission of documentary evidence, §52C-3-315, (e).
Temporary child support order, §52C-4-401, (b).
Title of provisions, §52C-1-100.
Transmitted documents from another state.
Admissibility as evidence, §52C-3-315, (e).

INTERSTATE FAMILY SUPPORT —Cont'd
Tribunal.
Communications between, §52C-3-316.
Defined, §52C-1-101.
Two or more obligees.
Multiple child support orders, §52C-2-208.
Two or more orders issued.
Controlling order, identifying, §52C-2-207.
Uniformity of application and construction, §52C-9-901.
Verification of petition, §§52C-3-310, (a), 52C-3-315, (b).
Videotape.
Testimony or deposition of witness, §52C-3-315, (f).

INTERSTATE HIGHWAYS.
Litter enforcement signs.
Placement, §136-32.3.
Maximum speed vehicle to be operated, §20-141, (d).
Minimum speed vehicle to be operated, §20-141, (c).
Tandem trailers and semitrailers.
Operated on, §20-115.1.
Unlawful use of national system of interstate and defense highways, §20-140.3.

INTERSTATE LAW FIRMS.
Interstate and international law firm registration, Bar Rules & Regs., E, §§.0201 to .0206.
Registration, Bar Rules & Regs., E, §§.0201 to .0205.

INTERSTATE RECIPROCITY IN INSURANCE PRODUCER LICENSING, §58-33-32.

INTERSTATE SAVINGS AND LOAN BRANCH ASSOCIATIONS.
Out-of-state branch offices, §§54B-265 to 54B-278.
See SAVINGS AND LOAN ASSOCIATIONS.

INTERSTATE SAVINGS BRANCH BANKS.
Out-of-state branch offices, §§54C-199 to 54C-212.
See SAVINGS BANKS.

INTERVAL OWNERSHIP.
Time shares, §§93A-39 to 93A-57.
See TIME SHARES.

INTERVENTION.
As of right, §1A-1, Rule 24, (a).
Attachment.
Third persons claiming attached property, §1-440.43.
Delivery of property to intervener, §1-483.
Of right, §1A-1, Rule 24, (a).
Property claimed by third person, §1-482.
Termination of parental rights proceedings.
Who may intervene, §7B-1103, (b).
Utilities commission proceedings.
Persons authorized to file complaint, §62-73.

INTER VIVOS GIFTS.
Intestate succession.
Presumed.
Absolute gift and not advancement, §29-24.

INTER VIVOS TRUSTS.
Community property rights at death.
Defection of title of surviving spouse, §31C-4.
Renunciation of succession by beneficiary, §31B-1.

INTESTATE SUCCESSION.
Adopted children.
Adoptive parents and heirs of adoptive parents.
Succession from adopted children, §29-17, (c).
Natural parents and heirs of natural parents, §29-17, (b).
Succession from adopted children, §29-17, (d).
Succession by, through and from adopted children, §29-17, (a).
When adopted child considered child of natural parents for purposes of intestate succession, §29-17, (e).
Adoption.
Inheritance rights of child subject to adoption.
Consequences of consent by parent to adoption, §48-3-607, (c).
Advancements.
Death of advancee before intestate donor, §29-27.
Defined, §29-2.
Effect, §29-25.
Generally, §29-23.
Gift inter vivos.
Presumption of gift, §29-24.
Inventory.
Failure to give inventory, §29-28.
Release by advancee, §29-29.
Taking into account and computation of estate, §29-23.
Valuation.
Determination, §29-26.
Aliens, §29-11.
Ancestral property.
Distinctions between ancestral and nonancestral property.
Abolished, §29-3.
Brothers and sisters.
Distribution among classes, §29-16, (b).
Certain distinctions as to intestate succession abolished, §29-3.
Claims against the estate.
Descent and distribution subject to payment, §29-13.
Collateral succession.
Limitation, §29-7.
Computation of next of kin, §§29-5, 104A-1.
Costs of administration.
Descent and distribution subject to payment, §29-13.
Curtesy.
Abolished, §29-4.
Definitions, §29-2.
Descent and distribution, §29-13.
Distinctions between real and personal property abolished, §29-3.
Distribution among classes.
Brothers and sisters and their lineal descendants, §29-16, (b).
Lineal descendants, §29-16, (a).
Uncles and aunts and their lineal descendants, §29-16, (c).
Dower abolished, §29-4.
Elective share of surviving spouse, §§30-3.1 to 30-3.6, 31-5.3.
Elective shares, §§29-14, 29-15.
Escheats, §29-12.
Estate.
Defined, §29-2.
Estate taxes.
Descent and distribution subject to payment, §29-13.

INTESTATE SUCCESSION —Cont'd
Excise stamp tax on conveyances.
Exempted transfers, §105-228.29.
Exemptions.
Continuation of exemption of property, §1C-1604, (b).
Gifts.
Advancements.
Gift inter vivos presumed absolute gift, §29-24.
Heirs.
Defined, §29-2.
Homicide.
Killing decedents.
Slayer barred from intestate succession, §31A-4.
Household furnishings.
Payment of debts from estate of deceased, §29-30, (g).
Husband and wife.
Acts barring rights of spouse, §31A-1, (b).
Illegitimate children.
Descent and distribution upon intestacy, §29-20.
Legitimated children.
Succession by, through and from, §29-18.
Person's illegitimate child entitled to take by, through and from, §29-19, (b).
Shares of others than surviving spouse, §29-22.
Succession by, through and from, §29-19, (a).
Surviving spouses.
Share of surviving spouse of illegitimate intestate, §29-21.
Shares of others than surviving spouse, §29-22.
Inheritance taxes.
Descent and distribution subject to payment, §29-13.
Inventories.
Advancements.
Failure of donor to give inventory on oath, §29-28.
Jury.
Election of surviving spouse to take life interest.
Appointment of jury, §29-30, (d).
Final report of jury, §29-30, (e).
Kinship.
Degrees of kinship.
Computation, §§29-5, 104A-1.
Legitimated children.
Succession by, through and from, §29-18.
Legitimation, effect, §49-11.
Mother married, legitimation when, §49-12.1.
Subsequent marriage, legitimation by, §49-12.
Lineal descendants.
Defined, §29-2.
Determination of share, §29-16, (a).
Unlimited, §29-6.
Motor vehicles.
Transfer of title or interest, §20-77, (b).
Net estate.
Defined, §29-2.
Next of kin, §41-6.1.
Defined, §41-6.1.
Notice.
Election of surviving, §29-30, (c).
Parent and child.
Acts barring rights of parents, §31A-2.
Partial intestacy, §29-8.
Personal property.
Distinctions between real and personal property abolished, §29-3.
Presumptions.
Gift inter vivos presumed gift and not advancement, §29-24.

INTESTATE SUCCESSION —Cont'd
Pretermitted children, §29-9.
Real property.
Distinctions between real and personal property abolished, §29-3.
Relations of the whole blood.
Distinctions between relations of the whole blood and those of the half blood.
Abolished, §29-3.
Renunciation, §29-10.
Acceptance of property, interest or benefit.
Effect on right of renunciation, §31B-4, (e).
Applicability of chapter, §31B-1, (b).
Application of chapter, §31B-6.
Bar, §31B-4, (a).
Disposition of property in reliance on invalid renunciation.
Immunity from liability, §31B-4, (d).
Effect of renunciation, §31B-3, (a).
Exclusiveness of remedy, §31B-5.
Future interests.
When instrument filed, §31B-2, (b).
Instruments.
Contents, §31B-1, (c).
Copies, §31B-2, (c).
Indexing, §31B-2, (c).
When filed, §31B-2, (a).
Where filed, §31B-2, (c).
Record of renunciation.
Contents, §31B-2, (c).
Right to renounce succession, §31B-1, (a).
Short title, §31B-7.
Tax consequences, §31B-1, (b).
Waiver, §31B-4, (a).
Binding on certain persons, §31B-4, (b).
Disposition of property in reliance on invalid renunciation.
Immunity from liability, §31B-4, (d).
Shares.
Defined, §29-2.
Shares of others than surviving spouse, §29-15.
Short title of act, §29-1.
Simultaneous death act, §§28A-24-1 to 28A-24-7.
See SIMULTANEOUS DEATH.
Small estates, §§28A-25-1 to 28A-25-6.
See SMALL ESTATES.
Surviving spouses.
Illegitimate children.
Share of surviving spouse, §29-21.
Shares of others than surviving spouse, §29-22.
Life estates.
Appointment of jury, §29-30, (d).
Contents, §29-30, (b).
Final report of jury, §29-30, (e).
Waiver, §29-30, (h).
Life interest.
Election to take life interest in lieu of intestate share, §29-30, (a).
Share of surviving spouse.
Equitable distributions of property, §29-14, (c).
Personal property, §29-14, (b).
Real property, §29-14, (a).
Shares of others than surviving spouse, §29-15.
Time.
Election of surviving spouse to take life interest.
Filing of notice, §29-30, (c).
Title of act, §29-1.
Unborn infants, §29-9.
Uncles and aunts.
Distribution among classes, §29-16, (c).

INTESTATE SUCCESSION —Cont'd
Uniform simultaneous death act, §§28A-24-1 to 28A-24-7.
See SIMULTANEOUS DEATH.
Unlimited lineal succession, §29-6.
Waiver.
Renunciation, §31B-4.
Surviving spouses.
Election to life interest in lieu of intestate share, §29-30, (h).
Waste.
Heirs.
Action by heirs, §1-537.

INTIMIDATION.
Elections.
Officers of election.
Felony, §163-275.
Voters.
Intimidation by officers, §163-271.
Misdemeanor, §163-274.
Ethnic intimidation, §14-401.14, (a), (b).
Insurance.
Unfair trade practices.
Prohibited acts, §58-63-15.
Involuntary servitude, §14-43.2.
Obstructing health care facilities, §14-277.4.
Secret societies.
Placing exhibit with intention of intimidating, §14-12.13.
Wearing of disguise, §14-12.14.
Witnesses, §14-226, (a).
Electronic surveillance orders, §15A-290, (c3).

INTOXICATING LIQUORS.
See ALCOHOLIC BEVERAGES.

INTOXICATION, §§14-443 to 14-447.
Acquittal of defendant because of alcoholism.
Disposition of defendant, §14-446.
Aircraft operation while impaired, §§63-27, 63-28.
Alcohol detoxification programs.
Specialty hospitals, §131E-65.
Alcoholic beverage sales to intoxicated persons prohibited, §18B-305, (a).
Alcoholism.
Defined, §14-443.
Barbers.
Disqualifications for certificates or permits, §86A-18.
Boating safety.
Operation of boat or manipulation of water skis while intoxicated, §75A-10, (b), (b1).
Penalty, §75A-18, (b).
Carriers.
Ejection of intoxicated person, §62-151.
Ticket may be refused intoxicated person, §62-150.
Carrier ticket agent.
Refusing ticket to intoxicated person, §62-150.
Chemical analysis of impairing substances in blood generally.
See IMPAIRED DRIVING.
Chiropractors.
Addiction or severe dependency upon alcohol.
Grounds for disciplinary action, §90-154, (b).
Grounds for disciplinary action, §90-154, (b).
Criminal procedure.
Notice to state of defenses, §15A-905, (c), (d).
Defense of alcoholism, §14-445, (a).
Disposition of defendant acquitted because of alcoholism, §14-446.

INTOXICATION —Cont'd
Defense of alcoholism —Cont'd
Request for additional information, §14-445, (b).
Dental hygienists.
Grounds for disciplinary measures, §90-229, (a).
Drivers' licenses.
Issuance to habitual drunkard.
Prohibited, §20-9, (c).
Revocation of license of habitual users of alcohol and narcotics, §20-17.1.
Impaired driving generally.
See IMPAIRED DRIVING.
Incompetence, determination of, §§35A-1101 to 35A-1116.
See INCOMPETENCE.
Law enforcement officers.
Assistance to individual intoxicated in public.
Actions permitted to be taken, §122C-301, (a).
Immunity for reasonable measures taken, §122C-301, (b).
Reasonable force to restrain individual, §122C-301, (b).
Removal of unfit officers, §128-16.
Nursing home administrators.
Grounds for denial, revocation or suspension of license, §90-285.1.
Osteopaths.
Habitual drunkenness as grounds for refusal, revocation or suspension of license, §90-136.
Physical therapists.
Grounds for disciplinary action, §90-270.36.
Physicians and surgeons.
Ground for denial, revocation or suspension of license, §90-14, (a).
Public conveyances.
Driver of public conveyance preventing intoxicated person from entering, §62-150.
Driver of public conveyance putting intoxicated person off of conveyance, §62-151.
Public intoxication.
Assistance to individual intoxicated in public.
Detention by facility to which officer takes individual.
Time limits on detention, §122C-301, (c).
Employment of officers to assist.
Cities and counties, §122C-302.
Involuntary commitment.
Person assisted to facility substance abuser, §122C-301, (d).
Jails, use for care of, §122C-303.
Law enforcement officers.
Actions permitted to be taken, §122C-301, (a).
Immunity for reasonable measures taken, §122C-301, (b).
Reasonable force to restrain individual, §122C-301, (b).
Cities.
Employment of officers to assist individual intoxicated in public, §122C-302.
Counties.
Employment of officers to assist individual intoxicated in public, §122C-302.
Definitions.
Alcoholism, §14-443.
Intoxication, §14-443.
Public intoxication, §14-443.
Public place, §14-443.
Entering plea to charge, §14-445, (c).
Home of individual intoxicated in public.
Transportation by officer to, §122C-301, (a).

INTOXICATION —Cont'd
Public intoxication —Cont'd
Hospital of physician's office.
Transportation by officer to, §122C-301, (a).
Detention of individual, time limits, §122C-301, (c).
Involuntary commitment.
Assistance to individual intoxicated in public.
Officer detaining individual, §122C-301, (a).
Person assisted to facility substance abuser, §122C-301, (d).
Jails.
Use for care of intoxicated individuals, §122C-303.
No prosecution for public intoxication, §14-447, (a).
Officers to assist individuals intoxicated in public.
Cities and counties, §122C-302.
Penalties.
Ways of being intoxicated and disruptive in public, §14-444, (b).
Prehearing review of drinking history, §14-445, (d).
Public place.
Defined, §14-443.
Residence of another willing to accept intoxicated person.
Transportation by officer to, §122C-301, (a).
Shelter facility.
Transportation by officer to, §122C-301, (a).
Detention of individual, time limits, §122C-301, (c).
Shelter or health-care facility.
Transport and release of person to appropriate facility, §14-447, (b).
Ways of being intoxicated and disruptive in public, §14-444, (a).
Penalty for violation of provisions, §14-444, (b).
Railroads.
Ejection of passenger who becomes intoxicated, §136-198.
Ticket may be refused intoxicated person, §136-197.
Specialty hospitals.
Alcohol detoxification programs, §131E-65.
Workers' compensation.
Injury or death caused by intoxication of employee.
No compensation payable, §97-12.
Use of intoxicant or controlled substance, §97-12.

INTRAGOVERNMENTAL SERVICE FUNDS.
Financial plans.
Generally, §§159-11, (d), 159-13.1.

INTRASTATE SYSTEM AND TRANSPORTATION IMPROVEMENT PROGRAM.
Distribution formula for funds expended, §136-17.2A.

INVALID AGREEMENTS.
Construction indemnity agreements, §22B-1.
Contract provisions waiving jury trial, §22B-10.
Contracts to improve real property.
Provisions making contract subject to laws of another state, §22B-2.
Contracts with forum selection provisions, §22B-3.

INVASION OF PRIVACY.
Confidentiality.
See CONFIDENTIALITY.
Freedom of information, §§132-1 to 132-10.

INVASION OF PRIVACY —Cont'd
Insurance consumer and customer information privacy.
Immunity from suit.
Disclosure in accordance with article, §58-39-110.
Privacy of state employer personnel records, §§126-22 to 126-29.
Searches and seizures generally.
See SEARCHES AND SEIZURES.

INVASIONS.
Constitution of the United States, Const. U. S., art. I, §§8 to 10; art. IV, §4.
Unorganized militia.
Ordered out for service, §127A-87.

INVENTION DEVELOPMENT.
Definitions.
Invention development services, §66-209.
Employers and employees.
Inventions developed by employees, §§66-57.1, 66-57.2.
Employment agreements.
Certain agreements void, §66-57.1.
Reporting inventions to employer.
Employer may require, §66-57.2.
Right of employees to certain inventions, §66-57.1.
Rights of employers, §66-57.2.
Larceny of secret technical processes, §14-75.1.
Patents.
Constitutional provisions, Const. U. S., art. I, §8.
Services.
Contracts.
Contents, §66-213.
Cover notice, §66-211.
Disclosures made prior to contract, §66-210.
Financial requirements, §66-214.
Requirements for contracting, §66-212.
Standard provisions for cover notice, §66-211.
Voidable contracts, §66-215.
Damages.
Violations of provisions, §66-215.
Definitions, §66-209.
Disclosures made prior to contract, §66-210.
Enforcement of article, §66-216.
Financial requirements, §66-214.
Violations of provisions.
Civil penalties, §66-216.
Damages, §66-215.

INVENTIONS.
Larceny of secret technical processes, §14-75.1.

INVENTORIES.
Absentees in military service.
Final inventory upon termination of receivership, §28B-8, (c).
Receiver to file, §28B-5, (b).
Accounts and accounting.
Trusts and trustees.
Wills.
Filing inventories and accounts, §36A-107, (a).
Assignments for benefit of creditors.
Trustee of deed of trust to file with clerk of superior court, §23-2.
Cigarettes and tobacco products.
Cigarette tax.
Tax with respect to inventory on effective date of tax increase, §105-113.7.

INVENTORIES —Cont'd
Cigarettes and tobacco products —Cont'd
Tobacco products tax.
Recordkeeping requirements, §105-113.40.
Closing-out sales.
Required of applicants for licenses, §66-77, (a).
Coal and petroleum suppliers.
Reporting petroleum fuel capacity, §§143-345.13, 143-345.14.
Conservation easements, §113A-235, (c).
Decedents' estates.
Appraisers, §28A-20-4.
Compelling inventory, §28A-20-2, (a).
Failure to file.
Liability for costs, §28A-20-2, (b).
Removal of representative, §28A-20-2, (a).
Required within three months, §28A-20-1.
Supplemental inventory.
Enforcement, §28A-20-3, (b).
Erroneous or misleading inventory, §28A-20-3, (a).
Durable power of attorney.
Incapacity or incompetency of principal.
Filing inventory of principal's property with clerk, §32A-11, (b).
Guardians.
Accounts and accounting.
Inventory or account required within three months, §§35A-1261 to 35A-1262, (b).
Procedure to compel inventory, §35A-1262.
Supplemental inventory, §35A-1263.1.
Intestate succession.
Advancements, §29-28.
Missing persons.
Filing by temporary receiver, §28C-3.
Permanent receivers, §28C-7.
Power of attorney.
Durable power of attorney.
Incapacity or incompetency of principal.
Filing inventory of principal's property with clerk, §32A-11, (b).
Receivers.
Corporate receivers, §1-507.3.
Searches and seizures.
List of items seized pursuant to search warrant, §15A-254.
Trust companies.
Seizure by commissioner.
Inventory of assets and liabilities, §53-385.
Trustees of deeds of trust.
Assignment for benefit of creditors, §23-2.
Trusts and trustees.
Class in esse.
Sale of property held by, §41-11.1, (l).
Wills.
Filing inventories and accounts, §36A-107, (a).

INVENTORY SHORTAGES.
Deductions from employees' wages, §95-25.9.
Combined amounts of deductions and recoupments, §95-25.10.
Employers' remedies preserved, §95-25.11.

INVERSE CONDEMNATION, §40A-51.

INVESTIGATIONS.
Abandonment.
Welfare recipients, §15-155.2.
Abused, neglected or dependent juveniles.
Criminal investigation upon director finding evidence of abuse, §7B-307.

INVESTIGATIONS —Cont'd
Abused, neglected or dependent juveniles —Cont'd
Immunity of persons reporting and cooperating in investigation, §7B-309.
Physician or medical facility receiving judicial authority to retain custody of abused juvenile.
Notice to director of social services, treatment as report of suspected abuse, §7B-308, (b).
Receipt of report by director.
Interference with investigation, §7B-303.
Adult care homes.
Death of resident within seven days of use of physical restraint, §131D-34.1, (c).
Residents' bill of rights, §131D-26, (a1), (b).
Agriculture.
Marketing and branding farm products.
Board of agriculture to investigate marketing of farm products, §106-187.
Air pollution control.
Permits, §143-215.108, (d).
Alarm systems licensing.
Background investigation of license applicant, §74D-2, (d).
Powers of board, §74D-5, (a).
Alcoholic beverages.
Expenses.
Restitution, §18B-505.
Law enforcement agents, §18B-500.
Local ABC officers, §18B-501.
Permits.
Prior to issuance, §18B-902, (b).
Restitution.
Expenses, §18B-505.
Arson.
Public officers and employees.
Failure of officers to investigate incendiary fires, §14-69.
Auctions and auctioneers.
Commission, §85B-8, (e).
Banks.
Commissioner of banks.
Confidentiality of official records, §53-99.
Insolvent banks.
General or special investigations, §53-100.
Official communications relating to, §53-109.
Insolvent banks.
General or special investigations, §53-100.
Blind persons.
Aid to the blind.
Determining eligibility of applicant, §111-14.
Cemeteries.
Commission.
Powers and duties, §65-53.
Check-cashing businesses.
Licensing, §53-278, (b).
Child placing agencies.
Death of resident of facility within seven days of use of physical restraint, §131D-10.6B, (c).
Children.
Abandoned or neglected.
Welfare recipients, §15-155.2.
Child support.
District attorneys.
Reports to district attorneys of aid to dependent children and illegitimate births.
Action on, §15-155.2, (a).
Commodities, §78D-21.
Continuing care retirement communities, §58-64-50, (a).
Powers of commissioner, §58-64-50, (b), (c).

INVESTIGATIONS —Cont'd
Disability income plan.
Medical board, §135-102, (d).
Elections.
County boards of elections, §163-33.
State board of elections, §163-22, (d).
Electrologists.
Board of electrologist examiners.
Powers, §88A-6.
Elevators.
Accidents, §95-110.9, (b).
Employee assistance professionals.
Violations of provisions, §90-510.
Engineers and land surveyors.
Duties of board, §89C-10, (f).
Extradition.
Fugitives from other states.
Governor may cause investigation to be made, §15A-724.
Fair housing complaints, §§41A-7, (e), 41A-8.
Financial identity fraud.
Attorney General, §14-113.23.
Fire investigations and inspection of premises, §§58-79-1 to 58-79-45.
See FIRES AND FIRE PROTECTION.
Flour, corn meal and grain.
Grain dealers.
Authority to investigate, §106-612.
Food, drugs and cosmetics.
Conduct of investigations, §106-141, (b).
Geologists, §89E-17, (b).
Confidentiality of proceedings, §89E-17, (c).
Grand jury.
Powers, §15A-628, (a).
Health.
Communicable diseases, §130A-144, (a) to (c).
Hogs.
Feeding garbage to swine, §106-405.7, (a).
Housing authorities and projects.
Municipal cooperation and aid.
Investigation of projects, §157-45.
Illegitimacy.
Child support.
Reports to district attorneys of aid to dependent children and illegitimate births.
Action on, §15-155.2, (a).
Insurance commissioners, §58-2-50.
Complaints of violations, §58-2-155.
Insurance premium financing.
Power of commissioner of insurance, §58-35-25.
Insurance unfair trade practices.
Power of commissioner, §58-63-20.
Internal improvements.
Power of investigation of corporations, §124-7.
Judicial standards commission.
Preliminary investigations, Jud. Stds. Comm. Rule 7.
Labor.
Retaliatory employment discrimination, §95-242, (a).
Lead poisoning hazard, §130A-131.9A.
Meat and meat products.
Biological residues in animals.
Discovering violations of article, §106-549.86.
Mental health, developmental disability, substance abuse.
Death of client, §122C-31.
Reports of abuse or exploitation.
Investigation required, §122C-66, (f).

INVESTIGATIONS —Cont'd
Milk and milk products.
Records and reports of milk distributors and processors.
Commissioner of agriculture authorized to investigate, §106-264.
Mine safety and health, §74-24.7.
Modification of safety and health standards, §74-24.5.
Monopolies and restraint of trade.
Attorney general, §75-9.
Power to compel examination, §75-10.
False swearing by persons examined.
Perjury, §75-12.
Immunity of person examined from prosecution, §75-11.
Refusal to furnish information, §75-12.
False swearing by persons examined.
Perjury, §75-12.
Mortgage bankers and brokers.
Disciplinary action, §53-243.12, (g).
Motor clubs and associations.
Powers of commissioner of insurance, §58-69-20.
Motor vehicle accidents.
Appropriate law enforcement officers, §20-166.1, (e).
Motor vehicles.
Impaired driving.
Presentence investigation of persons convicted, §20-179.1.
Police authority of division, §20-49.
Nurses.
Nurse licensure compact.
Change of residence.
Pending investigations, completion, §90-171.85, (b).
Current significance investigative information, §90-171.86.
Practices violating provisions, §90-171.37.
Nursing homes.
Patients' bill of rights, §131E-124, (a1), (b).
Occupational safety and health.
Director.
Powers, §95-133, (b).
Parole.
Investigators and investigations of cases of prisoners, §148-53.
Personnel system.
Political hirings.
Violations, §126-14.4.
Physical therapists.
Board of examiners, §90-270.26.
Post-assessment insurance guaranty association.
Duty to investigate claims, §58-48-35, (a).
Preneed funeral contracts and funds.
Violations, §90-210.70.
Presentence investigations.
Criminal law and procedure, §15A-1332.
Prisons and prisoners.
Administrative remedy procedure.
Grievance resolution board.
Powers of board, §148-118.9.
Private personnel services.
Overstated earnings expectations from employers, §95-47.3A, (b).
Private protective services.
Powers of attorney general, §74C-7.
Powers of board, §74C-5.
Proprietary schools, §115D-89, (c).

INVESTIGATIONS —Cont'd
Real estate brokers and salespersons.
Private real estate schools.
Commission, §93A-33.
Report of abuse, neglect or dependency of juvenile.
Interference with director's investigation, §7B-302.
Retirement system for counties and cities.
Board of trustees.
Duties of actuary, §128-28, (n), (o).
Retirement system for teachers and state employees.
Actuary to make investigations, §135-6, (m), (n).
Savings and loan associations.
Examination and investigation.
See SAVINGS AND LOAN ASSOCIATIONS.
Interstate branches.
Regulatory and supervisory oversight, §54B-273.
Savings banks.
Interstate branch banks.
Regulatory and supervisory oversight, §54C-207, (c).
Securities regulation.
Obstruction of investigation, §78A-58.
Seeds.
Complaints by buyers, §106-277.30, (a).
Damages recoverable, §106-277.34, (b).
Evidence introduced in action, §106-277.34, (a).
Referral of investigation to seed board, §106-277.30, (c).
Requesting investigation, §106-277.30, (b).
Social services.
County directors of social services, §108A-14, (a).
State departments and agencies.
Conduct, §143-160.
Governor given authority to direct, §143-159.
Special investigations, §143-158.
Conduct, §143-160.
Stenographic record of proceedings, §143-161.
Subjects, §143-159.
Structural pest control.
Licensees or identification card holders.
Denial, revocation or suspension of license or identification card, §106-65.28, (e).
Superintendents of schools.
Failure to perform duties, §115C-274, (b).
Therapeutic recreation personnel.
Certification.
Violations of provisions, §90C-17.
Trust companies.
Merger or consolidation.
Articles of merger, §53-360, (a).
Investigation of proposed transaction, §53-361, (b).
Seizure by commissioner.
Claims against company, §53-387.
Urban redevelopment.
Powers of redevelopment commissions, §160A-512.
Utilities commission.
Accidents involving public utilities, §62-41.
Duty to investigate books and papers of utilities, §62-34, (a).
Initiation of investigations, §62-13, (d).
Powers, §62-37, (a).
Report of findings, §62-37, (b).
Veterinarians.
Powers of board, §90-185.
Viatical settlements.
Fraudulent acts, §58-58-240.
License applicants, §58-58-210, (f).

INVESTIGATIONS —Cont'd
Weights and measures.
Duties of commissioner, §81A-15.

INVESTIGATIVE DEMAND.
Medicaid.
False claims by providers.
Civil investigative demand, §108A-70.14.

INVESTIGATORIAL ASSISTANTS.
District attorneys' offices, §7A-69.

INVESTING IN BUSINESS PROPERTY TAX CREDIT.
Business and energy tax credits, §§105-129.15 to 105-129.19.

INVESTING IN MACHINERY AND EQUIPMENT TAX CREDIT.
Tax incentives for new and expanding businesses, §105-129.9.

INVESTMENT ADVISERS.
Actions.
Civil liabilities for violations, §78C-38.
Administration of chapter, §78C-26, (a).
Advisory activities.
Prohibited activities, §78C-8, (a).
Exemptions, §78C-8, (f).
Appeals.
Judicial review of orders, §78C-29.
Bonds, surety, §78C-17, (e).
Burden of proof.
Civil or administrative proceedings, §78C-40.
Child support enforcement.
Forfeiture of licensing privilege, §50-13.12.
Citation of chapter, §78C-1.
Civil liabilities.
Contract violations.
Suit not based on contract, §78C-38, (e).
Controlling persons, §78C-38, (b).
Generally, §78C-38, (a).
Limitation of action, §78C-38, (d).
Survival of action, §78C-38, (c).
Confidentiality of information, §78C-26, (b).
Construction and interpretation.
Severability of provisions, §78C-48.
Statutory policy, §78C-47.
Contempt.
Violation of order of court, §78C-27, (c).
Contracts.
Contents, §78C-8, (c).
Exemptions, §78C-8, (d).
Crimes at common law or by statute.
Punishment for, §78C-39, (c).
Criminal penalties, §78C-39, (a) to (a4).
Criminal prosecution.
Referral of evidence to prosecutors, §78C-39, (b).
Custody of security or funds.
Violation of rule or order of administrator, §78C-8, (e).
Definitions, §78C-2.
False or misleading filings, §78C-9.
Fees.
Disposition, §78C-26, (c).
Felony convictions.
Forfeiture of license, §15A-1331A.
Filing of documents, §78C-31, (a), (c1) to (c3).
Hearings.
Public hearing, §78C-30.
Information furnished to clients, §78C-18, (b).
Injunctions.
Violation of chapter, §78C-28, (a).

INVESTMENT ADVISERS —Cont'd
Interpretive opinions by administrator, §78C-31, (e).
Investigations, §78C-27, (a), (b).
Files and records relating to criminal investigations, §78C-31, (c1).
Investment advisor representatives.
Registration.
Required, §78C-16, (a1), (b).
Misleading filings, §78C-9.
Misrepresentations, §78C-8, (b).
Penalties for violations.
Civil penalties, §78C-28, (c).
Policy of state, §78C-47.
Prudent person rule.
Investment and deposit of funds, §36A-2, (a).
Records, §78C-18, (a).
Amendment, §78C-18, (d).
Examination, §78C-18, (e).
Financial records.
Amendment, §78C-18, (d).
Public records.
Administrator may make available, §78C-31, (d).
Registration.
Application, §78C-17, (a).
Consent appointing administrator as attorney to receive service of process, §78C-46, (b).
Filing, §78C-20, (a).
Information may be made available to public, §78C-31, (c).
Register of applications, §78C-31, (b).
Bar or censure of registrant, §78C-19, (a), (b).
Notice, §78C-19, (f).
Bonds, surety, §78C-17, (e).
Cancellation, §78C-19, (d).
Notice, §78C-19, (f).
Denial, §78C-19, (a), (b).
Notice, §78C-19, (f).
Exercise of authority of administrator not prevented, §78C-20, (c).
Expiration, §78C-16, (c).
Federal law.
Compliance with state requirements, §78C-16, (d).
Fees, §78C-17, (b).
Fraudulent representations, §78C-10.
Investment advisor representatives.
Required, §78C-16, (a1), (b).
Minimum net capital requirement, §78C-17, (d).
Required, §78C-16, (a).
Revocation, §78C-19, (a), (b).
Notice, §78C-19, (f).
Successor, §78C-17, (c).
Felony convictions, §15A-1331A.
Suspension, §78C-19, (a), (b).
Notice, §78C-19, (f).
Summary postponement or suspension of registration, §78C-19, (c).
Unlawful representations, §78C-10.
Withdrawal from registration, §78C-19, (e).
Reports.
Financial reports, §78C-18, (c).
Rights and remedies in addition to other rights and remedies, §78C-38, (g).
Rules and regulations.
Adoption, amendment, etc., §78C-30.
Scope of provisions, §78C-46, (a).
Service of process.
Administrator as attorney to receive service of process, §§78C-46, (b) to (d).

INVESTMENT ADVISERS —Cont'd
Severability of provisions, §78C-48.
Short title of chapter, §78C-1.
Subpoenas.
Enforcement, §78C-27, (d).
Violation of chapter.
Cease and desist orders, §78C-28, (b).
Civil penalties, §78C-28, (c).
Criminal penalties, §78C-39, (a) to (a4).
Injunction, §78C-28, (a).
Referral of evidence to prosecutors, §78C-39, (b).
Waiver of compliance with provisions.
Void, §78C-38, (f).

INVESTMENTS.
Absentees in military service.
Receivers.
Power to invest property or income, §28B-6.
Agricultural finance authority.
Bond issues.
Legal investments, §122D-17.
Moneys of authority.
Authorized investments, §122D-16, (b).
Banks.
See BANKS.
Capital facilities finance act.
Special indebtedness, §142-93.
Cemeteries.
Corporate trustees, §65-60.1, (e).
Trust funds for care of cemeteries, §65-10.
Community college investment of idle cash, §§115D-58.6 to 115D-58.10.
Credit unions.
Authorized investments, §54-109.82.
Crime victims compensation.
Crime victims compensation fund.
Investments by state treasurer, §15B-23.
Decedents' estates.
Powers of personal representative or fiduciary, §28A-13-3, (a).
Disability income plan.
Trust fund.
Assets of fund, §135-110, (d).
Drainage districts.
Surplus funds, §156-135.1.
Education.
State board of education.
Authority to invest school funds, §115C-411.
Education assistance authority.
Bond issues.
Eligibility for investment, §116-209.10.
Energy conservation finance act.
Financing contracts and certificates of participation.
Investment eligibility, §142-70.
Facility authorities.
Bonds eligible for investment, §160A-480.13.
Fiduciaries.
Investment and deposit of trust funds, §§36A-1 to 36A-7.
Securities approved by secretary of housing and urban development, federal housing administration and veterans administration, §53-45.
Fraternal benefit societies.
Funds, §58-24-100.
Health care facilities.
Finance act.
Bonds or notes eligible for investment, §131A-17.
Refunding bonds or notes, §131A-18.

INVESTMENTS —Cont'd
Health maintenance organizations, §58-67-60.
Hospital, medical and dental service corporations.
Investments and reserves, §58-65-95, (a) to (d).
Housing authorities and projects.
Local government finance.
Special provisions pertaining to public housing authorities, §159-42, (i).
National defense housing projects.
Obligations made legal investments, §157-57.
Housing finance agency, §122A-11.
Bonds and notes.
Obligations eligible for investment, §122A-14.
Housing trust fund, §122E-3, (c).
Husband and wife.
Joint ownership of corporate stock and investment securities, §41-2.2, (a).
Death of joint tenant, §41-2.2, (c).
Inheritance tax laws unaffected, §41-2.2, (d).
When joint tenancy exist, §41-2.2, (b).
Income tax.
Tax credits for qualified business investments, §§105-163.010 to 105-163.015.
Inheritance taxes.
Joint ownership of corporate stock and investment securities.
Inheritance tax laws unaffected, §41-2.2, (d).
Insurance companies.
See INSURANCE COMPANIES.
Local government finance.
Bond issues.
Bonds or notes eligible for investment, §159-140.
Capital reserve funds, §159-21.
Fiscal control.
Idle funds, §159-30.
Public hospitals, §159-39, (g).
Reports.
Semiannual report on status, §159-33.
Management of institutional funds.
Governing board.
Authority, §36B-4.
Delegation of investment management, §36B-5.
Standard of conduct, §36B-6.
Release of restrictions on investment, §36B-7.
Missing persons.
Receivers.
Power to invest or reinvest property or income, §28C-8.
Municipal corporations.
Joint municipal electric power and energy act.
Bonds eligible for investment, §159B-21.
Mutual burial associations.
Funds of association, §90-210.86.
911 system.
Emergency telephone system fund, §62A-7.
North Carolina enterprise corporations.
Primary investments, §53A-43.
Prohibited investments, §53A-44.
Parking authorities.
Bonds legal investments for public officers and fiduciaries, §160A-560.
Pollution control.
Industrial and pollution control facilities financing act.
Bonds eligible for investment, §159C-18.
Post-war reserve fund, §143-192.
Principal and income act.
General provisions, §§37A-1-101 to 37A-6-602.
See PRINCIPAL AND INCOME ACT.

INVESTMENTS —Cont'd
Private protective services recovery fund, §74C-30, (d).
Prudent investor act, §§36A-161 to 36A-173.
See TRUSTS AND TRUSTEES.
Prudent person rule, §36A-2, (a).
Public schools.
Critical school facility needs fund, §115C-489.1.
Endowment funds, §115C-491.
Idle cash, §115C-443.
Public school building capital fund, §115C-546.1, (b).
Reports on status, §115C-446.
State board of education.
Authority to invest school funds, §115C-411.
Qualified business investments tax credits, §§105-163.010 to 105-163.015.
Real estate brokers and salespersons.
Real estate recovery fund, §93A-16, (c).
Retirement system for counties and cities.
Common and preferred stocks.
Authority to invest in certain stocks, §128-29.1.
Retirement system for teachers and state employees.
Consolidated judicial retirement act.
State treasurer to invest assets of system, §135-66.
Savings and loan associations, §§54B-180 to 54B-197.
See SAVINGS AND LOAN ASSOCIATIONS.
Savings banks, §§54C-129 to 54C-142.
See SAVINGS BANKS.
Holding companies, §54C-195, (d).
State funds.
Administration of state treasurer's programs, §147-69.3.
General fund, §147-69.1.
State psychiatric hospital financing act.
Special indebtedness, §142-112.
State treasurer.
Administration of state treasurer's investment programs, §147-69.3.
General fund.
Authorized investments, §147-69.1.
Highway fund.
Authorized investment, §147-69.1.
Highway trust fund.
Authorized investments, §147-69.1.
Special funds held by state treasurer, §147-69.2.
Superior courts.
Clerks of court.
Funds in clerk's hands which may be invested, §7A-112.
Fees, §7A-308.1.
Tax credits for qualified business investments, §§105-163.010 to 105-163.015.
Title insurance.
Companies, §§58-7-182, 58-26-15.
Torrens system registration.
Assurance fund, §43-49.
Transfers to minors, §33A-12.
Trust companies.
Bonds.
Purchase for own account, §53-342, (e).
Securities, §53-342.
State trust company facilities, §53-340, (a).
Types not specified, §53-342, (f).
Uniform trusts act.
Investments in securities by banks or trust companies, §36A-66.1.

INVESTMENTS —Cont'd
Trusts and trustees.
Charitable trusts.
Annuity trusts and unit trusts, §36A-59.4, (e).
Costs of investing trust assets, §36A-167.
Diversification of investments, §36A-163.
Investment and deposit of trust funds, §§36A-1 to 36A-7.
Powers of trustees under express trust generally, §36A-136.
Prudent investor act, §§36A-161 to 36A-173.
See TRUSTS AND TRUSTEES.
Uniform trusts act.
Funds held by corporation exercising fiduciary powers awaiting investment or distribution, §36A-63, (a), (c).
Fee for temporary investment, §36A-63, (d).
Investments in securities by banks or trust companies, §36A-66.1.
University of North Carolina.
Distinguished professors endowment trust fund, §116-41.14.
School of science and mathematics.
Endowment fund, §116-238, (e), (f).
Urban redevelopment.
Powers of redevelopment commissions, §160A-512.
Workers' compensation.
Self-insurance.
Employer groups, §58-47-80.

INVESTMENT SECURITIES, §§25-8-101 to 25-8-511.
Acquisition of security, asset or interest therein, §25-8-104.
Generally, §25-8-104, (a).
Satisfying requirement of transfer or delivery, §25-8-104, (d).
Security entitlement, §25-8-104, (b), (c).
Applicability of provisions, §25-8-110.
Assurance that indorsement or instruction is effective.
Additional assurance, §25-8-402, (b).
Allowed required assurance, §25-8-402, (a).
Appropriate evidence of appointment or incumbency, defined, §25-8-402, (c).
Guarantee of the signature, defined, §25-8-402, (c).
Authenticating trustee, transfer agent and registrar, §25-8-407.
Bona fide purchasers.
Enforcement of completed or altered instrument, §25-8-206.
Choice of law, §25-8-110.
Citation of chapter, §25-8-101.
Clearing corporation rules, §25-8-111.
Completion of instrument.
Contains all necessary signatures, §25-8-206, (a).
Enforceable only to its original terms, §25-8-206, (b).
Control, §25-8-106.
Bearer form certificated securities, §25-8-106, (a).
Registered form certificated securities, §25-8-106, (b).
Required, §25-8-106, (g).
Security entitlements, §25-8-106, (d), (e).
Substitutions or changes, §25-8-106, (f).
Uncertificated securities, §25-8-106, (c).
Creditor's legal process, §25-8-112.
Certificated securities, §25-8-112, (a).
Creditor whose debtor is owner of, §25-8-112, (e).

INVESTMENT SECURITIES —Cont'd
Creditor's legal process —Cont'd
Certificated securities —Cont'd
In possession of another, §25-8-112, (d).
Security entitlements, §25-8-112, (c).
Uncertificated securities, §25-8-112, (b).
Defenses.
Issue and issuer, §§25-8-202, 25-8-203.
Additional issuer's defenses, §25-8-202, (d).
Entitlement holders, §25-8-202, (f).
Issuer asserts security is not valid, §25-8-202, (b).
Lack of genuineness of certificated security, §25-8-202, (c).
Material change, §25-8-202, (e).
Purchaser for value without notice, §25-8-202, (a).
Definitions, §25-8-102.
Index of definitions, §25-8-102.
Investment company security, §25-8-103.
Issuer's jurisdiction, §25-8-110.
Demand that issuer not register transfer.
Liability, §25-8-403, (d), (e).
Notice, §25-8-403, (a).
Withholding registration of transfer, §25-8-403, (b).
Time period for withholding, §25-8-403, (c).
Determination of security or financial asset, §25-8-103.
Application of provisions, §25-8-103, (d).
Clearinghouse corporations, §25-8-103, (e).
Commodity contract, §25-8-103, (f).
Investment company security, defined, §25-8-103, (b).
Issued by corporation or similar entity, §25-8-103, (a).
Partnership or limited liability company, §25-8-103, (c).
Duty of issuer to register transfer.
Generally, §25-8-401, (a).
Liability, §25-8-401, (b).
Evidentiary rules concerning certificated securities, §25-8-114.
Husband and wife.
Joint ownership, §41-2.2.
Indorsement, §25-8-304.
Effectiveness of endorsement, instruction or entitlement.
Appropriate person, defined, §25-8-107, (a).
Change of capacity, §25-8-107, (d).
Change of circumstances, §25-8-107, (e).
Conditions for effectiveness, §25-8-107, (b).
Additional conditions, §25-8-107, (c).
Intermediary as purchaser for value, §25-8-116.
Issuer, §25-8-201.
Assurance that indorsement or instruction is effective, §25-8-402.
Demand that issuer not register transfer, §25-8-403.
Duty of issuer to register transfer, §25-8-401.
Effect of unauthorized signature, §25-8-205.
Generally, §25-8-201, (a).
Guarantors, §25-8-201, (b).
Jurisdiction, §25-8-110, (a).
Defined, §25-8-110, (d).
Lien, §25-8-209.
Liability to adverse claimant, §25-8-115.
Registered owners.
Rights of issuer with respect to registered owners, §25-8-207, (a).
Interpretation of provisions, §25-8-207, (b).

INVESTMENT SECURITIES —Cont'd
Issuer —Cont'd
Signature.
Effect of signature authenticating trustee, registrar or transfer agent, §25-8-208.
Transfer, §25-8-201, (c).
Effect of issuer's restrictions on transfer, §25-8-204.
Effect of signature authenticating trustee, registrar or transfer agent, §25-8-208.
Warranties.
Effect of signature authenticating trustee, registrar or transfer agent, §25-8-208.
Joint ownership, §41-2.2.
Lost, destroyed or wrongfully taken security certificates, §25-8-405.
Issuance of new certificate, §25-8-405, (a).
Obligation to notify issuer, §25-8-406.
Registration, §25-8-405, (b).
Notice of adverse claim, §25-8-105.
Events which do constitute notice, §25-8-105, (d).
Events which do not constitute notice, §25-8-105, (c).
Filing of a financial statement, §25-8-105, (e).
Generally, §25-8-105, (a).
Transfer of financial asset or interest therein, §25-8-105, (b).
Overissue, §25-8-210.
Application of provisions, §25-8-210, (b).
Compelling purchase, §25-8-210, (c).
Generally, §25-8-210, (a).
Recovery of price, §25-8-210, (d).
Registration.
Demand that issuer not register transfer, §25-8-403.
Duty of issuer to register transfer, §25-8-401.
Effect of signature authenticating trustee, registrar or transfer agent, §25-8-208.
Indorsement or instruction effective, §25-8-402.
Wrongful registration, §25-8-404.
Secured transactions.
Priority of security interests, §25-9-331.
Provisions concerning investment property.
See SECURED TRANSACTIONS.
Securities intermediary's jurisdiction, §25-8-110, (b), (e), (f).
Security entitlements.
Assertion of adverse claim against entitlement holder, §25-8-502.
Priority among security interests and entitlement holders.
Asset held by securities intermediary, §25-8-511, (b).
Clearing corporations, §25-8-511, (c).
Generally, §25-8-511, (a).
Rights of purchaser from entitlement holder, §25-8-510.
Assertion of adverse claims, §25-8-510, (b).
Cases not covered by priority rules, §25-8-510, (c).
Notice of adverse claims, §25-8-510, (a).
Priority of securities intermediary as purchaser over conflicting purchaser, §25-8-510, (d).
Securities account, defined, §25-8-501.
Securities intermediary.
Acquisition of security entitlement from.
Generally, §25-8-501, (b).
Holding of financial asset, §25-8-501, (c), (d).
Issuance of security, §25-8-501, (e).
Securities account, defined, §25-8-501, (a).

INVESTMENT SECURITIES —Cont'd
Security entitlements —Cont'd
Securities intermediary —Cont'd
Duty to change holder's position to other form of holding, §25-8-508.
Duty to comply with entitlement order.
Generally, §25-8-507, (a).
Transfer pursuant to ineffective order, §25-8-507, (b).
Duty to exercise rights as directed by entitlement holder, §25-8-506.
Duty to maintain financial asset.
Clearing corporations, §25-8-504, (d).
Generally, §25-8-504, (a).
Granting of security interests in, §25-8-504, (b).
Satisfying duty, §25-8-504, (c).
Duty with respect to payments and distributions.
Generally, §25-8-505, (a).
Obligation to entitlement holder, §25-8-505, (b).
Property interest of entitlement holder in financial asset held by.
Actions, §25-8-503, (e).
Creditors' claims, §25-8-503, (a).
Enforcement, §25-8-503, (c), (d).
Pro rata interest, §25-8-503, (b).
Specification of duties by other statute or regulation, §25-8-509.
Short title of chapter, §25-8-101.
Signatures.
Effect of signature authenticating trustee, registrar or transfer agent, §25-8-208.
Effect of unauthorized signature, §25-8-205.
Statute of frauds, §25-8-113.
Transfer.
Delivery, §25-8-301.
Certificated security, §25-8-301, (a).
Uncertificated security, §25-8-301, (b).
Effect of guaranteeing signature, indorsement or instruction, §25-8-306.
Effect of signature authenticating trustee, registrar or transfer agent, §25-8-208.
Indorsement, §25-8-304.
Assumption of obligations, §25-8-304, (f).
Bearer form, §25-8-304, (e).
Blank or special, §25-8-304, (a).
Effect of guaranteeing, §25-8-306.
Interpretation of provisions, §25-8-304, (c).
Missing necessary indorsement, §25-8-304, (d).
Separately transferable units, §25-8-304, (b).
Instruction, §25-8-305.
Effect of guaranteeing, §25-8-306.
Generally, §25-8-305, (a).
Obligations assumed, §25-8-305, (b).
Protected purchaser, §25-8-303.
Defined, §25-8-303, (a).
Free of adverse claims, §25-8-303, (b).
Rights of purchaser, §25-8-302.
Extent of rights acquired, §25-8-302, (b).
Generally, §25-8-302, (a).
Registration of transfer, §25-8-307.
Taking from protected purchaser, §25-8-302, (c).
Signature.
Effect of guaranteeing, §25-8-306.
Warranties.
Additional assumptions of liability, §25-8-208, (b).
Direct holding, §25-8-108.
Agents, §25-8-108, (g).
Brokers, §25-8-108, (i).

INVESTMENT SECURITIES —Cont'd
Warranties —Cont'd
Direct holding —Cont'd
Certificated securities, §25-8-108, (f).
Generally, §25-8-108, (a).
Indorsements.
Security certificates, §25-8-108, (d).
Person who originates registration of transfer, §25-8-108, (b).
Redelivery, §25-8-108, (h).
Uncertificated securities, §25-8-108, (c), (e).
Effect of signature authenticating trustee, registrar or transfer agent, §25-8-208.
Indirect holding, §25-8-109.
Delivering security certificate, §25-8-109, (b).
Entitlement holders, §25-8-109, (c).
Generally, §25-8-109, (a).
Uncertificated security credited to securities account, §25-8-109, (b).
Person signing security as authenticator, §25-8-208, (a).
Where security certificate located, §25-8-110, (c).
Wrongful registration.
Liability, §25-8-404, (a).
Effective indorsement or instruction, §25-8-404, (c).
Restitution, §25-8-404, (b).

INVESTOR PROTECTION AND EDUCATION TRUST FUND, §147-54.5, (a) to (f).

INVISIBLE FENCES.
Electronic dog collars.
Unlawful removal, §14-401.17.

INVOICES.
Alcoholic beverages transported by motor carriers, §18B-1115, (d).
Eggs, §106-245.19.
Enhanced 911 wireless system for wireless communications.
Reimbursement from fund, §62A-25, (c), (d).
Motor vehicle repairs.
Contents, §20-354.6.
Providing upon completed repair, §20-354.6.
Paternity, civil action to establish.
Admissibility of invoices for services rendered, §49-14, (g).
Simulation.
Prohibited, §75-35.

INVOLUNTARY COMMITMENT.
Mental health, developmental disabilities and substance abuse.
See MENTAL HEALTH, DEVELOPMENTAL DISABILITY, SUBSTANCE ABUSE.

INVOLUNTARY DISMISSAL OF ACTION, §1A-1, Rule 41, (b).

INVOLUNTARY MANSLAUGHTER.
Death by vehicle.
Double jeopardy.
Subsequent prosecution prohibited, §20-141.4, (c).
Mandatory revocation of driver's license.
Permanent revocation, §20-19, (i).
Indictments.
Essentials of bill, §15-144.
Motor vehicles.
Death by vehicle, §20-141.4.
Revocation or suspension of license, §20-17, (a).
Permanent revocation, §20-19, (i).
Punishment, §14-18.

INVOLUNTARY SERVITUDE.
Constitution of North Carolina.
Prohibited, Const. N. C., art. I, §17.
Constitution of the United States, Const. U. S., amds. XIII, XV.
Elements of offense, §14-43.2, (a).
Kidnapping and abduction, §14-39.
Marriage.
Validation of marriage between slaves, §51-5.
Prohibited, §14-43.2, (b).
Relationship between unemancipated minor and parent or guardian.
Effect, §14-43.2, (c).
Reports, §14-43.2, (d).

IOLTA, Prof Cond. Rule 1.15-4.
Rules governing administration of plan, Bar Rules & Regs., D, §§.1301 to .1316.

IONIZING RADIATION.
Radiation protection act generally, §§104E-1 to 104E-29.
See RADIATION PROTECTION.

IRA'S.
Exempt property from enforcement of claims of creditors, §1C-1601, (a).
Renunciation.
Right to renounce by beneficiary, §31B-1, (a).

IREDELL COUNTY.
Acquisition of property, power, §153A-158.1, (a).
Ambulances.
Attachment or garnishment and lien for, §§44-51.4 to 44-51.8.
Obtaining ambulance services without intending to pay, §14-111.2.
Blank or master forms of mortgages, deeds of trusts, etc.
Indexing and recording, inapplicability of provisions, §47-21.
Condemnation or acquisition of land by local government unit outside county.
Consent of board of commissioners necessary, §153A-15.
Counties generally.
See COUNTIES.

IREDELL COUNTY —Cont'd
Game laws, local acts not repealed, §113-133.1, (e).
Oil, gas and mineral interests separated from surface fee, extinguished, title in surface fee holder.
Interest not listed for tax purposes for 10 years prior to January 1, 1971.
Protection of surface interest from surface estate holder, §1-42.2, (d).
Probates and registration orders before clerks of inferior courts validated, §47-59.
Registration of deeds.
Tax certification, no delinquent taxes due, §161-31, (b).
School property.
Acquisition and improvement, §153A-158.1.
Special school tax, election to abolish.
Petition required, §115C-505.
Tax sales, notices by publication validated.
Inapplicability of provisions, §47-108.24.

IRRIGATION.
Cooperative associations.
Authorized purposes, §§54-111, 54-124.
Drainage, §§156-1 to 156-141.
See DRAINAGE.

IRS.
Agents authorized to enforce criminal laws, §15A-406.

ISLANDS.
Public lands.
Title to lands formed by acts of nature, §146-6, (d).

ISRAEL.
University of North Carolina.
North Carolina-Israel visiting scholar program, §116-230.

ITINERANT MERCHANTS.
Generally, §§66-250 to 66-258.
See PEDDLERS, ITINERANT MERCHANTS AND SPECIALTY MARKETS.
Regulation of itinerant merchants, §153A-125.
Municipalities, §160A-178.

Clark–
It was the best of
times . . .

George

Four Fathers

Volume Four

Inside a Pair of Dice

Illustrations by Lesley Etters

Dear Reader-

This is fiction. No character in this book is based upon anyone, real or imaginary. The incidents portrayed are entirely figments of the author's overworked imagination. No shoe is fit to be worn.

"For My Dad"

Table of Contents

XXIII. Begin the Beguine 13

Shamble 14

A. A Natural Firmness Not Unlocked By Trifles 14

B. Deserves The Love And Thanks of Man And Woman 16

C. Dearness Only Gives Every Thing Its Value. 18

D. The Harder the Conflict, The More Glorious the Triumph 20

E. What We Obtain Too Cheap, We Esteem Too Lightly 21

F. Heaven Knows How to Put a Proper Price Upon Its Goods 22

G. It Would Be Strange Indeed If So Celestial An Article As Freedom Should Not Be Highly Rated 24

H. Declared Too Soon, Or Delayed Too Long 26

I. Tried Men Sole 27

J. Shrink From the Service 29

K. He That Stands By It Now 30

L. The Spirit of the Jerseys 31

M. None To Blame But Ourselves But No Great Deal Is Lost Yet 32

N. The Expression is Impious 33

O. The Independence Of The Incontinent 35

P. Tyranny Like Hell Is Not Easily Conquered 36

Q. As Little Superstition In Me as Any Man Living 39

R. Every Decent Method Which Wisdom Could Invent.. 40
S. We Did Not Make a Proper Use of Last Winter.. 42
T. If Being Bound In That Manner, Is Not Slavery, Then is There Not Such a Thing as Slavery Upon Earth. 44
U. A Right to Bind Us in All Cases Whatsoever... 45
V. We Have This Consolation With Us.. 47
W. An Army to Enforce Her Tyranny 49
X. While We Were In A Dependent State... 51
Y. Rather A Ravage Than A Conquest.. 53
Z. My Own Simple Opinion... 55
AA. Quickly Repulsed... 58
BB. Time And A Little Resolution Will Soon Recover.. 59
CC. So Earnestly And So Repeatedly Sought To Avoid 60
DD. Given Us Up To The Care Of Devils... 63
EE. My Secret Opinion Has Ever Been 64
FF. Now Enter Into.. 65
GG. Touchstones Of Sincerity And Hypocrisy... 67
HH. Our Situation There Was Exceedingly Cramped.. 69
II. We Shut Ourselves Up And Stood On Our Defence 71
JJ. The Best Part Of Our Stores Had Been Removed 72
KK. God Almighty Will Not Give Up A People.. 73
LL. The Fault, If It Were One, Was All Our Own 75
MM. Only For Temporary Purposes 79
NN. Endeavor To Penetrate.. 83
OO. On The Apprehension 87
PP. It Must Occur To Every Thinking Man 88
QQ. Our Numbers Were Greatly Inferior 91
RR. Bore It With A Manly And Martial Spirit 94
SS. Their Folly Or Their Baseness... 96
TT. The Line Of Irrecoverable Separation Be Drawn 99
UU. Greeks Baring Gifts... 100
VV. The Calamities of War... 103

WW. So Much Of The Infidel In Me 105
XX. Look Up To Heaven For Help 108
YY. Leave Them Unsupportedly To Perish 110
ZZ. Suppose That He Has Relinquished 112
AAA. Cannot See On What Grounds 114
BBB. Would Have Been Much Better 117
CCC. The Simple Object 120
DDD. Our First Object Was To Secure 121
EEE. As Much Baggage As The Wagons Could Contain 122
FFF. March Them On Till They Could Be Strengthened 124
GGG. Enabled To Make A Stand 127
HHH. The Rest Was Lost 129
III. Marched Out Twice To Meet The Enemy 132
JJJ. Trusted Our Cause To The Temporary 134
KKK. In The World For A Sudden Exertion 136
LLL. Will Not Do For A Long Campaign 140
MMM. Give Him Encouragement To Come 143
NNN. Appropriate Their Possessions 149
OOO. A Common Murderer, A Highwayman, Or A House-breaker, Has As Good A Pretence ... 151
PPP. Confiscation Of The Property Of Disaffected Persons 154
QQQ. The Far And The Near, The Home Counties And The Back, The Rich And The Poor 157
RRR. The Hangman's Beautiful Daughter 159
SSS. Throw Not The Burden Of The Day Upon Providence 161
TTT. A Little Might Have Saved The Whole 163
UUU. Reason To The Root Of Things 165
VVV. Grow Brave By Reflection 166
WWW. Fall An Easy Prey 168
XXX. Defection At Pleasure 170
YYY. Once More We Are Again Collected And Collecting 172
ZZZ. To Open The Next Campaign 174
AAAA. To Ravage The Defenceless Jerseys 177
BBBB. 'Tis The Business Of Little Minds To Shrink 179

CCCC. A Peace Which Passeth All Understanding 182
DDDD. Say Not That Thousands Are Gone, Turn Out Your Tens Of Thousands 184
EEEE. The Heart That Feels Not Now Is Dead 185
FFFF. The Relief Of Those Who Have Suffered In Well-Doing 186
GGGG. Call It Rather The Soft Resentment Of A Suffering People 188
HHHH. No Object In View But The Good Of All 190
IIII. Eloquence May Strike The Ear 191
JJJJ. Flock To His Standard Folly To Argue Against Determined Hardness 192
KKKK. Used Numberless Arguments To Show Them 193
LLLL. One Or Both Must Fall 196
MMMM. Under Some Providential Control 200
NNNN. The Particulars Of Our Retreat 202
OOOO. Those Who Live At A Distance Know But Little Or Nothing 205
PPPP. No Army At Hand To Have Relieved The Garrison 206
QQQQ. All Nations And Ages Have Been Subject To Them 208
RRRR. If We Believe The Power Of Hell To Be Limited 211
SSSS. The Inevitable Consequences Of A Long Retreat 213
TTTT. There Are Cases Which Cannot Be Overdone By Language 215
UUUU. See Not The Full Extent Of The Evil Which Threatens 221
VVVV. Where Conquest Is The Object 223
WWWW. Dwell Not Upon The Vapors Of Imagination 226
XXXX. Hold Up Truth To Your Eyes 229
YYYY. Let Them Call Me Rebel And Welcome 234
ZZZZ. 'Tis Surprising To See How Rapidly A Panic Will Sometimes Run Through A Country 236
5A. Never Appeared To Full Advantage But In Difficulties And In Action 240
5B. Intercepted Our March 241
5C. Suffice It For The Present 242
5D. Wisdom Is Not The Purchase Of A Day 246
5E. An Excess Of Tenderness 247
5F. The Flame Of Liberty May Sometimes Cease To Shine, The Coal Can Never Expire 250
5G. A Man Can Distinguish Himself Between Temper And Principle 253
5H. She Has Nothing To Do But To Trade 255

5I. Never Be Happy Till She Gets Clear 257
5J. She Whose Heart Is Firm And Whose Conscience Approves Her Conduct 258
5K. The Warm Ardor Of A Friend To Those Who Have Nobly Stood 261
5L. Sustained An Orderly Retreat 266
5M. A Few Broken Forces Collected And Headed By A Woman 268
XXIV. Get Out of Town 270
A. Punctuated Absence 270
Bramble 273
B. The Pan Within 273
C. Bring ‘Em All In 275
D. Peace of Iona 277
E. Fisherman's Blues 279
F. Medicine Bow 280
G. Long Way To The Light 285
H. The Whole of the Moon 293
I. Open 297
J. My Dark Side 306
K. A Song for the Life 311
L. Love You To 313
M. Tomorrow Never Knows 315
N. Taxman 320
O. She Said She Said 327
P. Come Live with Me 329
Q. The Return Of Jimi Hendrix 332
R. I Want To Tell You 334
S. Here There And Everywhere 336
T. Yellow Submarine 339
U. I’m Only Sleeping 342
V. Doctor Robert 346
W. For No One 349
X. And Your Bird Can Sing 353
Y. Good Day Sunshine 358

Z. Got To Get You Into My Life 363
AA. 99 and 44/100 years Of Gratitude 366
BB. It's As Easy As ABC 371
CC. In The Shadow Of Young Girls In Flower 378
DD. Swann's Way 381
EE. Sodom And Gomorrah 383
FF. The Guermantes Way 385
GG. The Fugitive 388
HH. The Prisoner 393
II. Time Regained 396
JJ. Simple Joy 399
KK. Shared Joy 401
LL. Solemn Joy 407
MM. Spirited Joy 412
NN. Only God Can Make A Tree 417
OO. Lodi 420
PP. The Night Time Is The Right Time 423
QQ. Tombstone Shadow 426
RR. Bad Moon Rising 427
SS. Sinister Purpose 434
TT. Start Stark Spark 435
UU. Start Stare Share 438
VV. Green River 439
WW. Fore Sore Bore 443
XX. In A Cloud Of Dust I Met Two Jinn 446
YY. Commotion 448
ZZ. Cross-Tie Walker 451
AAA. The Big One Looked A Lot Like You The Other One Looked Just Like You Too 457
BBB. A Score Of Lies They Swore Were True 463
CCC. My Strange Heroes Lead Me On 469
DDD. Karma To Burn 473
XXV. Too Darn Hot 475

A. Claim on Me 475
B. Coyote 477
Scramble 479
C. Hejira 479
D. The Silky Veils of Ardor 482
E. Song for Sharon 484
F. One Day I Walk 487
G. Ladies Love Outlaws 489
H. The Tenth World 490
I. Paprika Plain 493
J. Jericho 494
K. Jenny Lynn 497
L. Hobo's Mandolin 499
M. Furry Sings the Blues 501
N. A Strange Boy 504
O. Black Magic Gun 506
P. Talk to Me 509
Q. No Regrets 513
R. Desperados Waiting for a Train 514
S. Black Crow 518
XXVI. "Ridin' High" 523
A. All Down The Line 523
B. Let It Loose 525
C. Rip This Joint 527
Wamble 529
D. Sweet Virginia 529
E. Casino Boogie 533
F. Turd on the Run 535
G. Sweet Black Angel 538
H. I Just Want to See His Face 541
I. Soul Survivor 543
J. Don Juan's Reckless Daughter 545

K. Refuge of the Roads 548
L. Loving Cup 550
M. Blue Motel Room 552
N. Overture - Cotton Avenue 555
O. Shine A Light 557
P. Happy 559
Q. Off Night Backstreet 562
R. Torn And Frayed 564
S. Tumbling Dice 567
T. Stop Breaking Down 573
U. Rocks Off 575
V. Dreamland 578
W. Indian Woman from Wichita 580
X. Shake Your Hips 582
Y. Ventilator Blues 584
Z. Coming Out 587
XXVII. "Easy To Love" 589
A. Lullaby 589
B. Time to Run 592
C. Brother 594
Sonamble 596
D. The Host on the Shore 596
E. In the Wind 597
F. I Will Be Back One Day 599
G. I'll Always Know 602
H. In the Good Old Days (When Times Were Bad) 604
I. Run 'Em Off 606
J. Green, Green Grass of Home 607
K. Teach Me to Forget 609
L. Little Ole Wine Drinker Me 612
M. The Sunny Side of My Life 614
N. Folsom Prison Blues 616

O. I Could Have Gone Right 617

P. You'll Never Love Me Now 619

Q. She Lit a Fire 620

R. Ends of the Earth 622

XXVIII. "Don't Fence Me In" 623

A. Willie the Wandering Gypsy And Me 623

B. Too Many Bridges to Cross Over 627

C. Lonesome Dreams 629

Gamble 631

D. Black Rose 631

E. Mama Tried 633

F. We Had it All 636

G. You Asked Me To 639

H. Honky Tonk Heroes 642

I. Old Five And Dimers Like Me 646

J. Literate Iterate Irate Rate Rat 649

K. Low Down Freedom 651

L. Omaha 654

M. Tequila Mockingbird 657

N. Ride Me Down Easy 662

O. My Silver Spoon's This Beggar's Cup And When It's Empty I Fill Up All I Have To Do Is Just Show Up 666

P. Dreams Are Lies, It's The Dreaming That's Real 668

Q. Ain't No God In Mexico 670

R. In A World That We Can't See, To Sing Drunk With The Angels, Play Again For Free 674

S. The Man Who Lives Forever 676

XXIII. Begin the Beguine

The Sun Is Out

The Sky Is Blue

It’s beautiful

And So Are You

Lennon/McCartney

Shamble

A. A Natural Firmness Not Unlocked By Trifles

Things never really change. Through all American epochs, from pre-revolutionary times to the present, the same tableau presents itself on Nassau Street in the slumbering burg of Princeton, New Jersey. This main thoroughfare endures, even if it once existed in a nominally different place, upstate in North Jersey. Nassau Street is the line of demarcation between town and gown. In the beginning, a row of dandy commerce separated the town of Princeton from the College of New Jersey, a seat of learning where hell, fire, and brimstone marked its inception. Only on very few occasions, in the many years that have followed, did easy virtue slither between cracks formed by the tectonic forces created when duty to hearth and to patria clash with heaven's own righteousness. First established in 1746 by the right Reverend Jonathan Edwards, the place is now known as Princeton University.

For many years students and townies were kept separate and apart, but not equal, a space between maintained by well more than six degrees. The tall iron FitzRandolph Gate guarded the main entrance to Nassau Hall keeping cloistered academe from the town. FitzRandolph opened only for reunions and for commencement or to greet visiting dignitaries such as President Grover Cleveland. In 1970 the imposing gate was unlocked and wrought welcome on behalf of the college, not to be closed again. An inscription is now welded into its strong steel, "Together for Community." Intertwined numerals comprising the year, 1970, are part of the inscription. Into the center of the zero is a "peace sign."

The high hopes for world harmony have long gone up in smoke. The puffs of peace are now as dispersed as the small pipes of the sixties, once proliferating, from whence impudent aspiration idealistically sprouted. Even if those gathering relevant data ignored the press of the parade of world history which preceded it, any realistic chance ever given for tranquility on earth and for good will towards men was obliterated by failing case after failing case in the bellicose years that would follow 1970. The open FitzRandolph Gate, an iron-scuffed suggestion of the naïve desire to end all armed conflict is a quaint sentiment long gone from the dark labyrinth that is now the American psyche. Even those with the equanimity of Gandhi fairly sigh in disgust. "And Jesus wept" has taken on an entirely new meaning.

B. Deserves The Love And Thanks of Man And Woman

The ever recurring scene is a simple one. A young man and a young woman walk before the stores that line Nassau Street. Ignoring theology, world order, and dashed faint hopes, the time-tested promenade continues, true to its own fashion. From the days horses harnessed to carriages plied rutted paths in the unpaved mud of the streets of its original location, Elizabeth, New Jersey to the current day when a Smartphone appended to a once free hand navigates invisible wave troughs connecting to portals wherein data packets from anywhere and everywhere may be harnessed, there is an unhurried do-si-do. Again and again, it involves the same core, a well-worn touching scene. A Princeton Gentleman, as they were oft known, walks arm in arm with his weekend date. This tender is the night foray involves crossing the street to leave the security and the sheltering shade of the ever-burgeoning historic Campus, once the cradle of our Republic. It is always the same as it ever was.

Two saunter serenely, matched for the moment, perhaps not in the moment. The pair stride in front of merchandise galore. Well designed store fronts are full of items needed for the elite to finish college or, at least, to find their way to the heart of Saturday night. The interloping fairer gender, once from one of the Seven Sisters, Briarcliff, Pine Manor, Swarthmore, Bennett, or the aptly-named Marymount keeps stride. She moves closer to her man diverting attention from her stolen glances through the windows to inspect the items for sale. Thoughts of silent congratulation abound. Her fate will soon be well-placed good fortune. The Princeton man, in escort of his three day prey never even peeks inside the windows. His eyes steel unwaveringly upon his own image in the glass. Self-love is its own reward. Who knows where through the looking glass might lead?

From then until now, the iteration is replayed, stuck in a groove like an old phonograph needle. Similar sounds bounce, again and again, with only slight variations. A cornucopia of sense data is captured when consciousness contains what apparent reality presents, each in the eye of its beholder. Two reflections in a golden eye flow from the same stroll. One, ordinate, slinks through the surface to wallow in mundane superficiality. The other, inordinate, is canny in finding only itself lurking everywhere.

C. Dearness Only Gives Every Thing Its Value.

More often than not, what first appears a glaring counterexample, after close scrutiny, is discerned to be just another variation on a theme. On a day in late May, 1974, there was nothing but blue skies that never saw the sun shining so bright, never saw things going so right. Joseph Pantritus Cebellum stands astride a small patch on the Princeton campus. The massive, cathedral-sized University Chapel with four story stained glass windows looms large behind him. To his left, Murray-Dodge Hall is a place with a small stage for Theater Intime and with smaller solemn rooms used by religious groups and the Gay Alliance. Murray-Dodge squats consonant with tiny significance. To Joe's right, standing taller is East Pyne Hall. This building holds offices and precept rooms. It is connected to Chancellor Green, a building that houses the Student Center and the Pub. The Pub was once the library. Bricks and mortar from the Nineteenth Century abound.

Joe surveys two rows of Princeton alumni, each eight or more deep. They have all returned to line a campus pathway, both sides now, all in place in a place well trod with fond habituation during each of their four years past. The long lines are motionless but for their sway of ready surge and the animation of flowing conversation. Joe stands apart, but will soon be a part of the large group. The throng extends past the matching Whig and Clio Halls, white pristine cubes fronted by grand stairs that lead up to large Greek columns which divide the space to enter. Whig and Clio belong to a time preceding even those days in the Eighteenth Century when ground was broken for their construction. For those who value freedom, these are sacred places. If you listen closely, the echoes of earth-shattering vigorous and free debate can still be heard.

Joe lingers in the surrounding magnificence. Slowed synapses cause his eyes to savor the languor. The two rows of alumni strand into the bosom of the Campus, past two more two hundred year old buildings West College, the admissions office, and Witherspoon Hall, a Freshman dormitory. That new morning the grounds and those peopling it are all part of the depth and beauty of history itself.

D. The Harder the Conflict, The More Glorious the Triumph.

The epicenter of reunions, the P-Rade, is about to reach its full blossom. Far from the gladdened crowd, President Richard M. Nixon frets in the oval office. The full weight of the Watergate Investigation bears down upon his administration where the bloom is surely off the rose. In brazen contrast to the splendid fabric from which freedom has been woven and now from which education reigns supreme, Nixon's superficial view of history as that which expedience requires has caused a festering sore which will not even fool some of the people some of the time. Even the bright rays of the New Jersey sun which shine chiefly upon a heritage of celebration cannot focus all attention away from the Imperial calumny. The silent majority will soon be silenced.

E. What We Obtain Too Cheap, We Esteem Too Lightly

Behind Joe, the Firestone Library gives the entire campus quiet comfort. Harvey Firestone sold tires tirelessly. One result of this enterprise was the largest open stack library in the world, one of the largest libraries of any kind. This stronghold of the written word speaks volumes for the open exchange of ideas. In solemn testament to that which faith alone will not provide, the imposing light brick cenotaph towers gracefully at one side of the Princeton Chapel. On the other side of the Chapel, there is a two story fortress of free thinking, a sprawl of lecture halls and classrooms in the buildings known as McCosh Hall and Dickinson Hall, places where Firestone books are carried. In the courtyard separating the secular and the sacred, in the midst of many crossing paved paths, the Mather Sundial keeps time in the sunshine, as it has for about seventy-five years. One ideal for higher learning is "the human nature of a university," the phrase Princeton's President Robert Goheen used to title a book of his thoughts on the subject. Erudition should start with a cornerstone of daft and deft ambition. Into every nine pound abyss, scholars try to pour ten pounds of understanding. What starts as empty is nevertheless full of infinity. Learning is the effort of pouring content into seamless obscurity, giving borders to the unbounded, adding shape, frame, and lattice, as needed.

F. Heaven Knows How to Put a Proper Price Upon Its Goods

Afloat in the restrained furor of energy that will soon erupt, it is not surprising that Joe does not notice a man sitting on a bench to the left of the front of Firestone. A man outwardly bland as milk toast is quaintly oblivious to the impending harmless tumult. The man is John Nash. If President Nixon lurks on one end of a continuum where thoughts divagate to the narrow, twisted paths of power and persuasion to mold public opinion with the use of the propaganda of crass half-truths and of craven obfuscation, then John Nash is aspree, unleashed at the other end. Nixon's demons exist in a practical reality. Nash is schizophrenic. His mind freely flows with thoughts renegade and with ruminations galore. In those same cerebral nooks and crannies, Nash holds involuntarily to imaginary friends, hallucinations who lack the grace to have acceded from his consciousness while he was still a whining schoolboy. Nash sits by the library with his left shoe in his left hand. He is using that which belongs on his foot as a phone to talk to his right brain. The active mind of John Nash wended its way recklessly through intricate labyrinths wild and wonderful to merge concepts purely mathematical with the applications of economics to garner the respect of serious scholars in both disciplines and to win a Nobel Prize. Princeton lives so that John

Nash and many others less peculiar may thrive and go forth, with a full bounty of ideas. That veracity and vivacity is reason sufficient for the assembled multitude to engage in a three day celebration. The sixties made sure that the staid did not stay for long. Weird geniuses with schizophrenic hallucinations like Nash would soon walk Princeton pathways with colleagues, peers, and students who voluntarily caused their brains to have chemically induced eye-opening massive clusterfucks.

G. It Would Be Strange Indeed If So Celestial An Article As Freedom Should Not Be Highly Rated

Back at the bustle which will soon be the unique spectacle of the P-Rade in full flow, Joe is surrounded by a trifle of like-minded confreres and consouers. All in his small group of twenty odd wear the same yellow t-shirt and "Groucho Marx" glasses. The cotton undershirts are emblazoned with a simple pen and ink drawing- a bestubbled Richard Nixon has been bonked in the head with a lit-fuse bomb whose vintage is Napoleon, or more precisely Voltaire. The legend below the assaulted Presidential noggin reads, "The Terrace Conspiracy."

Terrace Club is one of the many Eating Clubs. All but Terrace line the opportunely named Prospect Street. Princeton students refer to Prospect as "The Street." Eating Clubs started as fraternal social organizations serving meals where the members did not sleep. Terrace Club is on Washington Road just behind Tower Club which sits near the corner of Prospect and Washington. Thus, Terrace is "the only Club on the Street, not on the Street." As the yellow t-shirts show, this impertinence in location is only the beginning.

Joe muddied the yellow sentiment of dissent by wearing a Phoenician purple hat, possibly fashioned from some royal court in the Dumas era. The brimmed, banded, and indented head garment is adorned with a large peacock feather. It is more likely that the chapeau did not actually hearken from the court of Louis XIV but rather was purloined from the property room for the set of an Errol Flynn swashbuckler.

H. Declared Too Soon, Or Delayed Too Long

The Terrace Conspiracy stands engulfed by a larger group, one which approaches one thousand in number. Their peers are wearing authorized and approved class outfits, a different set of matching shirts that make no reference to any U.S. President. Everyone is wearing the same matching lenseless black rimmed glasses with attached large plastic nose with a black mustache which flows from the nostrils. It is not clear why some disguise is in order for any but those wearing yellow t-shirts. All in all, this is a proud group whose metal has been forged and whose mettle has been tested by the fierce and fine heat of academic fire. It is the Princeton graduating class of 1974. In three days, the Commencement Ceremony will put the final icing on the cake, the reward for meeting all requirements to receive a degree.

The assembled class of 1974 forms the end of a long line of all returning alums. The P-Rade is about to start. The Class of 1973 stands next. The Class of ’73 sports Hunter Thompson-style aviator goggles and white shirts with black and orange epaulettes. The drug induced renegade diversion from the path to diploma suggested by the mirrored lenses and by the ornamental codpieces is all hat and no cattle. Few from the class years close to 1973 had imbibed real fear and loathing as part of the Princeton experience. To mark the flow of years toward the past, each newer class wears its own time-honored costume.

I. Tried Men Sole

1973 and 1974 are the first two classes to have Princeton "co-eds" in the P-Rade. These women are proud in all the silliness that wearing a class outfit entails. These are the first two class years with women who are entitled to full diplomas after four years of study.

A gale which may have steadied its nascent sea legs in earning the right to vote forged further fount in the crucible of another conflict. A *force mujere* had been conceived then bottled up in the factories of war. Spiraling circles were then released never to be recorked. When the boys marched home from war, Rosie the Riveter and her brood toiled for what was presumed to be their last. World War II was over. Explicably but ineffectually, someone said, "You're in the wrong place my friend, you'd better leave."

It was only a matter of time. After helping to liberate Europe and the Pacific, the mortar and pestle of women's liberation would go forth from piecework on the assembly line inexorably to give birth to acts of legislative assembly. Moreover, right thinking sentiment was set in concerted action without force of law. The swirling whirlwinds swept over many places. Some tornados will themselves touch ground. Some tornados will themselves to touch down. Critical mass forms when those who are touched, reach out and touch, in turn. The turn, turn, turn becomes the right place and the right time. One locus which gave the storm comfort was the Princeton campus in the fall of 1969. The eye of this hurricane would breed a furor of its own. Nevertheless, the condition was fulfilled. For the first time, four year female students were no longer part of an assembly line of dreams not yet forged and welded. Fruition found its full reward, once and for all.

J. Shrink From the Service

Today was Saturday, the first full day of Princeton Reunions. The pomp and circumstance of the graduation ceremony was seventy-four hours away. Much frivol would ensue before that "Day of the Locusts," which was how Bob Dylan reported his Princeton Commencement experience in a song of the same name. In 1970, he received his honorary degree as a "Doctor of Music." David Crosby and Dylan took a private limousine from Greenwich Village to the bowels of New Jersey. The dope they smoked in the back seat of the chauffeur-driven long black Cadillac only heightened Dylan's already keen acuity.

Dylan was honored as he stood in front of Nassau Hall facing Nassau Street looking through FitzRandolph Gate. The black robed academics scurried everywhere with their own special purpose. The image of infestation of periodic insects was apt. The line in the song that Dylan was afraid he was too close to someone whose head was about to explode also hit the mark. Bob Dylan received his honorary degree about a month after Nixon's decision to expand the war. The commander-in-chief who had yet to stand naked had said he was in the midst of winding down "The War." The invasion of Cambodia was a plague on the Princeton campus as it was on almost every campus in the United States. But that was Zen and this is Tao.

K. He That Stands By It Now

The unfolding spectacle was as big as any scene seen in a Hollywood epic, even as large as Marc Antony standing before his revenging legions at Philippi in the Burton and Taylor, *Cleopatra*. Princeton Reunions are more decadent, however. The time is gathered and grabbed furiously. Men, whose purposeful little feet regularly race rattedly through the corridors of power, take the short-lived moments of a long weekend to reflect upon their own significance and to congratulate themselves upon their good station. Much back-slapping and many fond reminiscences build their own crescendo. The roar of a tide formed by squeals of approbation and by laughs of self-congratulation swallows innate campus serenity.

Princeton Reunions are governed by the rule of major classes. Each five year leap from graduation is deemed its own monument. In 1974, the major classes were 1969, 1964, 1959, and all the way back to 1894 where one Princeton man survived another year, if only to find his way back to Old Nassau, that "best damn place of all."

A different dormitory is assigned the task of holding every five years of alums. Each dormitory surrounds its own open spaces. As reunions find full swing, courtyard after quaint courtyard fall into the lapse of time. There is true glee in the communion of brethren once again assembled. Classmates and contemporaries all hoist and quaff, one after another, as in days gone by, cans of Budweiser beer, all brewed from the once pristine waters which flow from the industrialized North Jersey aquifer into the Anheuser-Busch facility in Newark, New Jersey.

L. The Spirit of the Jerseys

Alumni reunions are big events throughout the Ivy League. Nowhere does the fever pitch reach full trill as on the campus which houses Nassau Hall, the virtual seat of fledgling Colonial independence. 1974 was no different than any other year. Much of the P-Rade marches past Cannon Green. Whig Hall and Clio Hall are on one side. On the other, Nassau Hall spreads maternally. This was the green where Victory bonfires consumed celebratory smoke and fire. Orange and black flames reflected beer soaked revelry. The alums were back to recreate.

What would soon enfold was nothing short of a *bona fide* historical monument. Next to the graduating class, stood the members of the Class of 1973, then the members of the Class of 1972. Each and every class year with even one returning alumni took its place. The returning alums formed a chronological order, in this instance all the way back in time to the 1800s. The last twenty odd years of classes are known, with true affection, as the "Old Guard." A few of the Old Guard will walk with canes. Most are driven in golf carts. The purpose of this line-up of classes was to form the "P-Rade," a silly name for an, oh so, serious ritual. The oldest of the Old Guard steps into the path as he marches in front of all his younger fellows. Each newer class than follows in turn. The metaphor of the march of time is soon in full motion. By the time the P-Rade reaches the graduating class, in this case the Class of 1974, the entire body of returning alumni passes before those soon to be baptized to then partake in this singular rite of passage. Those new to the fold will experience a true sense of brotherhood. More than camaraderie, the graduating class breathes a deep breath of history, a history in which it is now a part.

M. None To Blame But Ourselves But No Great Deal Is Lost Yet

The Terrace "Conspirators" watched the awe without the shock. Each class year has its own Black and Orange banner. Princeton is firmly in the firmament of the House of Orange, the orange greater than the black as the Princeton Tiger burns bright. For the weekend, each class ignores the motto, "Princeton in the Nation's Service," as it focuses inward. Each group that graduated together wears a different topical "outfit." Every five years, the powers that govern each class determine what costume will be worn during reunions for the next five years, and especially as part of the spectacle of the P-Rade. At the twenty-fifth reunion, school boy regalia are given over to black and orange sport jackets. Each class wears a Blazer with a different pattern, usually some form of plaid. As much dignity as is possible is regained by wearing intersecting lines rather than helicopter beanies. Princeton students are forever denominated by their class year. "So and So" becomes "So and So '73" if the fall of 1969 is the first semester. Wives and off-spring march with the alums, unless they walk with their own alumni class.

N. The Expression is Impious

The Terrace Conspiracy did not know it was bad form to defile the office of the leader of the free world. They did know it was not good form to fire up a joint while the P-Rade was gathering together while everyone readied for the festivities to begin. They might have to share a puff or two with people they did not know very well. It therefore became necessary, if not sufficient, to take a few tokes back at the Club before heading onto campus. Before donning the 1974 class glasses, noses, and moustaches, the group of yellow shirts peaceably assembled in the large sunken sitting room down a few short steps to the right of the Terrace Club entrance. With just the right amount of transcendent reverence, the smoke from seven or eight "big bomber" joints was inhaled and held even more deeply, into expanded lungs. Those who were about to become stoned saluted a large stuffed moose-head facing the smokers from the front wall. A red and green Christmas Tree ornament has been hung from its left antler without care. Joe Cebellum remembered to notice that a roach, that very tasty end of a marijuana cigarette, dangled from the mouth of the moose as it had for almost two school years. It is never a good idea to look a gift moose in the mouth. Nevertheless the stuffed presence which presided over the room was relieved of that small sacrilege. Three Conspirators took short last puffs from the stub of resin-stained rolling paper. Throughout the ceremony, some to receive this strange communion here for the last time, a liturgy of songs spilled forth from the speakers in the walls of the Terrace Club sound system. The music shifted from Bruce Springsteen, "Blinded by the Light," to Neil Young, "After the Gold Rush," to Elton John, "Good-bye Yellow Brick Road, then to the Grateful Dead, "Truckin.'"

O. The Independence Of The Incontinent

The Groucho Marx masks were part of the official 1974 Class costume. The yellow Nixonbomber shirts were not. The Conspirators did not need to be stoned to do what they were about to do; but it helped. As the classes from the first five years of the '30s walked in front of the graduating class, the 1920s just before them, and the 1940s soon to follow, the Conspirators and a few others started booing. Did the privileged upper crust society set who had lived in the grace and comfort of the Princeton cocoon during the Great Depression really deserved to be booed? It is said that when you are stoned you lose your sense of time. Here the Conspirators surely had done so. They had neglected to consider that even the class of 1939 started its tenure in the fall of 1935, and those classes too, in the interest of fairness, should have been given their own share of Bronx cheers, derision which was, so much, not a part of the Princeton experience.

P. Tyranny Like Hell Is Not Easily Conquered

The Great Depression crippled even the very wealthy, but not all. In the fall of 1935, John F. Kennedy came to Princeton, New Jersey as a member of the Class of 1939. He took with him his roommates from The Choate School, Kirk LeMoyne Billings and Rip Horton Jr. Billings later "roomed" with JFK in an apartment kept for him at the Camelot White House. Kennedy entered the University despite his father's desire that he go to Harvard. Joe, Sr. had not yet heard the story which accurately described the functional distinction between educations gleaned from the two institutions of higher learning. A Princeton man and a Harvard man are in the Waldorf-Astoria bathroom while attending a society dance. The Harvard man notices the Princeton man has not washed his hands before leaving.

"At Hahvahd, we leahrned to wahshh our hahnhds ahfter we uhrhinate."

"At Princeton, we don't piss on our hands."

All truisms aside, the "Southern hospitality" that marked Princeton did not suit the gastrointestinal health or the spirit of the young Irish Catholic. No records exist showing how those chaps from families who had attended Princeton for generations treated a Papist-come-lately. Sunday Chapel was no longer compulsory but was still rigorously attended. Services were held in

English which did not worship the Virgin Mary. It may well be that a liturgy omitting the Holy Mother caused Kennedy's cavalier attitude towards women in his later life. Perhaps, he never understood the Latin sanctimony in the first instance. Surely not a White Anglo Saxon Protestant patrician, Kennedy smoothed over his lack of heritage and true lineage by adopting the nickname, "Ken."

Guesswork being what it is, it may have been the secular, not the sacred, which started Kennedy feeling out of sorts. It is easy to imagine a Hotchkiss fellow telling JFK the story of an Irish Rover asking the consummate Ladies' Man how he attracts so many women,

"Why Ken, I am sure you have heard this one, maybe at Friday night mass in Roxbury, an Irishman is told the secret of how to worm his way into the affection of the lassies, one which I am sure you will surmise given the cuisine from your country of origin,

'You start with a potato. You then put it in your pants.'

The Erin Go Bragh fish worshipper later sees the guy who clued him into this technique. He tells him,

'I tried the potato trick but the women-folk seemed more repelled than usual.'

'Show me how you used the potato.'

He hands him a large White Russet. The 'Mc' suppresses his urge to eat the potato then puts it in his pants.

'Why no, my good fellow. You should put the potato in the front of your pants.'"

Rather than gleeful schoolboy renditions intended to offend all sensibilities, what could well have caused the milk to curdle in Kennedy's stomach might have been the vintage gold brocade of Princeton's quilted *tout ensemble*, one which reeked of the sweet smell of success wafting fatuously from the sullen trough of birthright. That JFK had, himself, been fed with a silver spoon was no real solace since his family fineware was of recent purchase.

Q. As Little Superstition In Me as Any Man Living.

Keeping a stiff upper lip is not just for the British. Bearing up does not make discomfiture disappear. After what was no doubt a fall of acclimatization if not assimilation, Kennedy persuaded his two friends from Choate to collaborate on a glossy 1935 Christmas card. They are photographed wearing top hats and tails in homage to Fred Astaire's film "Top Hat," which opened earlier that year. It would have only been a little more expensive, with a trifle logistical difficulty, to add Fred and Ginger to the sitting for the photo. The non-denominational Christmas card showed Kennedy, fit, fare, and formal, donning gay apparel at a time when, for many, the problem was scrounging their next meal. The money the Choate boys spent on the card would have fed the entire dust bowl for the Holiday Season. Spreading the good word about the birth of Jesus is no doubt better than actually following the words, “Feed the Hungry.” Thankfully, Joseph Kennedy, Sr. picked up the Yuletide slack with his continuing contributions to the Teamsters who, some say, in the days of Prohibition, helped him truck Bronfman family Seagram product to the Genovese family in New York City. It is heart-warming to know that the precept of Peace on Earth and Good Will Towards men was furthered when Canadian Jewish kith and kin got together with Sicilian *famiglia* all with the help of an Irish clan.

R. Every Decent Method Which Wisdom Could Invent

Notwithstanding the full born sentiment of Christmas spirit, the many weeks of running into the impervious wall of cold staid WASP diffidence and retrenchment was more than the young Kennedy could stomach. He was, none too soon, hospitalized. The campus infirmary staff sought diagnosis more hospitable. It might have been the wassail. It might have been a case of too much food while most of the rest of America was finding too little. There is also the possibility that JFK may have ingested moth ball vapors as those holiday tuxedo tails were "brushed off." At least one future President learned not to inhale. It was not unusual for a young Princeton Gentleman just starting his academic career to find himself too close to his own gentleman's gentleman. Princeton dormitory rooms were tight by the standards of those brought up in a way to which we would all like to be accustomed. Each room was designed as a single with a floor plan holding a large sitting room complete with working fireplace, a large bedroom of emolument, and a smaller one of indenture. Honorary degree in hand, Bob Dylan worried he was dangerously proximate to a brain brimming with too much wrong-headedness. Learning to live in such nearness to his live-in help served Kennedy well when he shook hands, cradled babies, and kissed mothers on the campaign trail. When all is said and done, the cause of the persistent Princeton-induced Kennedy nausea may have been the effect of injecting Irish Lace into the long-established wasps' nest.

There is a persistent rumor that walks the Princeton campus. In those days, it was civilized practice for the transcripts of students who failed their early exams to show those so privileged stricken with infirmity. It will never be known what swirled to send JFK from the only Ivy League school well suited for Southern Gentlemen. It is, however, known that the man voted by the Choate Class of 1935 as "Most Likely to Succeed" then entered his father's first choice to graduate in 1940. The rest is history.

S. We Did Not Make a Proper Use of Last Winter

As Joe Cebellum started Freshman Orientation Week in 1969, the buildings on the Princeton campus were essentially the same. For almost three hundred years, the grounds were scrupulously manicured from an endowment specifically limited to gardening and lawn maintenance. The army of Italian greenskeepers was fortunate to be paid from a fund larger than the general endowments of most U.S. universities. Nevertheless, Joe would find Princeton a place quite different from that experienced by those who entered in 1935.

Joseph and Della drove Joe to Princeton from Barrington. The Cebellum's Dodge Coronet 440 was filled with all Joe's earthly possessions- almost entirely clothes. On the road headed East, mother and father alike beamed proudly. Joseph, the Cubs' fan in the family, was happy for another reason. On August 19th, the day before the Cebellum trio started the drive to New Jersey, Kenny Holtzman threw a Wrigley Field no-hitter. It was a *rara avis* with an even rarer *avis* inside, no hits but not one strike out. Only once before had this anomaly of anomalies occurred. More unusual yet, the Cubs were in first place late in the season, a solid 8.5 games ahead of the second place St Louis Cardinals and 9.5 games ahead of the New York Mets.

First there was the hubbub of Freshman Week orientation then the pother of a campus teeming with a full complement of students. Joe lost track of the baseball season. In a crucial two game series at Shea Stadium on September 8th, Cubs' starter Bill Hands threw at Mets' lead-off hitter, Tommy Agee. Mets' lefty, Jerry Koosman then pitched with purpose to hit the next batter he faced, breaking the hand of the Cubs' beloved third baseman, Ron Santo. Agee hit a two-run homer the next time at bat as the Mets won the game 3-2. On the next day, the ninth day of the ninth month in the year of our Lord, 1969, the Mets beat the Cubs 7-1. In the course of that game, a black cat jumped out of the stands to cross the path of Ron Santo as he left the on deck circle.

September 10th sealed the Cubs' fate. The Mets swept a doubleheader as the Cubs' lost one. Thereafter, first place remained the sole property of those amazing Mets as the Cubs suffered one of the greatest collapses in the history of competitive endeavors. The Mets were charmed. In a late season game, the Phillies' Steve Carlton strikes out 19 but loses.

T. If Being Bound In That Manner, Is Not Slavery, Then is There Not Such a Thing as Slavery Upon Earth.

In getting ready for college, Joe lost track of other current events. Max Yasqur's farm was overrun with rain, peace, love, and many forms of happiness. It was originally billed as an "Agrarian Exposition in White Lake, New York." For three days, thirty-two acts performed musical magic before the Woodstock Nation, 400,000 strong. To use the Buddy Holly vernacular, the Cubs were fading away but love and popular music would not. At Woodstock, Sha Na Na underscored the point "Rock and Roll is Here to Stay."

In all prior times, for those who walked the Princeton Campus, class station reigned supreme. In the sixties, young men left Andover, Lawrenceville, Groton, St, Paul's, and other Strunk & White driven places of that ilk. The campus was peopled with preppies wearing pink cashmere cable knit sweaters, lime green wide-wale corduroy pants and Topsiders. In the fall of 1969, however, all good men came to the aid of the party by dressing down. It didn't matter what you wore as long as it was bell-bottom Levi blue jeans, a denim work shirt or plaid flannel shirt with Wellington boots. It was not just the casual observer who could not tell the public school kids from the preppies. For only a brief window in time, it was almost *gauche* to be rich. If you asked a fellow student about his family background, the answer was invariably the diminutive, "upper middle class."

U. A Right to Bind Us in All Cases Whatsoever

With fanfare befitting a proclamation before the royal court, the Admissions office made clear its guidelines. Students were admitted on the basis of merit without regard to need. By defining terms carefully, no lies are ever told. In this case, there is a large difference between admission decisions from the "student" applicant pool and the pool of legacy applicants. The dice are not really loaded from the start. Some say sixty percent of each new class is "legacies" or those who rub elbows with that special class. The actual number is likely lower. In theory and practice, to ensure that those who have bestowed large largesse by way of Alumni Giving will see their off-spring attend Princeton is more than just a case of Princeton feathering its own nest. It could be argued that the Princeton endowment is larger than reasonably needed to weather even the worst imaginable storm. Princeton would not enjoy the highest regard and most elite status it holds among Universities everywhere if it was not able to provide lavishly in all veins needed to remain superlative. Whether the sixty percent number is true or not, even forty percent culled from the oligarchy furthers laudable goals. Six-tenths of a loaf is better than none, even if the remaining four out of ten hail from the "let 'em eat cake" school. Whether or not the statement that all admissions are on the basis of merit was fudged, there is no doubt financial aid on the basis of "need" was forthcoming. No one admitted could say the school was too expensive. The financial aid package was clearly defined. Once need was established by way of clear mathematical formula, the amount "needed" was covered with one-third grant, one-third low interest, subsidized student loan not due until all schooling, graduate or professional included, was completed, and one-third campus employment. In practice, the work portion of the "aid package" could be earned with a decent summer job. Further, it was not a long walk to the Financial Aid office to plead your case before a sympathetic University official in order to receive a favorable modification or additional low cost student loan. The Princeton general endowment has been so large for so long that the loan portion of the package has now been eliminated to now provide two-thirds grant.

V. We Have This Consolation With Us

In those days, very few Princeton students did not receive some portion of financial aid. Sophomore year, Joe had a roommate, Joshua Matthew Relioport from Allentown, Pa. His daddy was a postman who saved and saved for college from the day his son was born. “Thew,” as he was known, received no scholarship at the cost of an entire lifetime of family vacations, scrimped bare-boned meals, and many other corners cut.

One Princeton Freshman in the year in which women were first admitted, was Charles Scribner. Scribners had been going to Princeton for generations. It seemed every other one was Charles Scribner III, there being neither strict Roberts’ Rule of Order nor Dewey Decimal System for the Roman Numeral system of denominating same-named aristocrats. There may have been a time when the “Scrivener” family came through Ellis Island and some border security official accidentally changed the family name to “Scribner,” but if so, it was likely before the French gave us the Statue of Liberty. If ever, it had been eons since any Scribner was part of any tired, poor, or huddled mass. One common truth marks all American “royal” families. What is now sweet harmony was once crude hominy.

Given the publishing business in which the Scribner family engaged, it was mellifluous fortuity that they now bore their name, a quasi-homonym worn like a proud coat of arms. One day in the fall of 1969, the wind was briefly taken out the sails of the smooth-sailing pleasured-harbor vessel that the most recent Scribner had set ashore on the Princeton Campus. No amount of prior paternal admonitions given to Charles III (or was it IV or V?) to maintain composure and embouchure above all else, prevented the portrait of the artist as a young man from sliding onto a coarse canvas hang-jawed, stunned, and aghast. It could not be denied that there was scribblin' on Scribner's Door. The dandy wood had been defaced. The Vietnam Moratorium and the free spirit that flowed therefrom had reared its ugly radical head to ruffle fine feathers.

W. An Army to Enforce Her Tyranny

Since before the time some prior Scribner scion founded the Eating Club, “Ivy Club,” Princeton's answer to the Yalie Senior Year Secret Society, Skull and Bones, the Scribner family had been more accustomed to the polite knocking of good folks like Hemingway, Fitzgerald, and Wolfe upon their Maxwell Perkins' guided door of literary opportunity. Bright-eyed and bushy-tailed Charles Scribner returned from class only to discover someone had scrawled primitively upon his door. Before him was an indelicate, indeed indecorous, and above all pejorative exclamation concerning his wealth and his station. When does a door become a wall? Furthermore, when you see the writing on the wall, is it better to count the flowers or to seek the shade of Plato's Cave to reflect whether the forms of all that is proper and good themselves are achangin.’ Like a prohibitionist who was shocked to find one dandelion among his otherwise pure bent grass front lawn, Scribner may have over-reacted. The inscription was not “Fuck you, you rich fuck,” but rather, from the writings of F. Scott Fitzgerald, “Let me tell you about the very rich. They are different from you and me.” The gentility that is Princeton remained essentially unsullied. Scribner’s reaction was consistent with the new ethos of near shame. The scarlet dollar sign was not to be worn. After all, he was really not that rich, at least not by Fitzgerald’s “standards.”

The young Scribner was actually an interesting case study. Joe Cebellum was developing the working hypothesis that we are all wounded birds. No matter how normal, well-positioned, or well put-together someone first appears, it was only a short matter of time before Joe would discern, again and again, that we are all cut from the same crazy quilt. Years later Charlie Scribner converted to Roman Catholicism. A well-intentioned "pleasant chap," did what his faith deemed best to spread his wings to exceed the limitations of his parochial, stilted upbringing. In the fall of 1969, however, he was shocked at the criticism, tepid in form and substance, that anyone would think that he fell among the wealthy.

X. While We Were In A Dependent State

Freshman Week was a mélange of method over mandate. There were more mixed messages than installed institutional inculcation. Joe looked forward to finding himself in the midst of the world of ideas, a confluence of the rich and the strange. There was one odd little requirement. Before school started all incoming students are thrown off the end of the pier, to complete a graduation requirement. Not really off the pier but rather into the Olympic size swimming pool beneath Dillon Gymnasium.

Dillon sits in the middle of campus. For many years, the tradition that was Princeton's pride, basketball, was centered there. For the first time that coming winter, basketball would be played in a large structure that looks like a landed zeppelin, more modern than the one pictured on the cover of the seminal soon to be iconic first Led Zeppelin album, the blimp that blew up over Lindenhurst, New Jersey to the north. The "Jadwin Cage," as it is known, is perhaps better described as a large spaceship donated to Princeton by Steven Spielberg after he used it in the closing scene of "Close Encounters of the Third Kind." With two other giants, Jadwin lords over Washington Road near Palmer Stadium where Ivy football games are played which, in turn, is near New Fine Tower where the much heralded Princeton Mathematics department keeps quarters.

The need to swim for all Princeton Gentlemen may have been a throwback to that time ocean liners and zeppelins ferried the wealthy between North

America and Europe. In time of unthinkable disaster, staying afloat until someone from the crew brings you a lifejacket is a worthwhile skill. More likely, when Princeton men reach the summer of their first, and soon to be many, Tanqueray and tonics, there is a very real need to learn to swim given the danger of falling overboard while wobbling weak-kneed on the deck of the family yacht.

Joe was sure it was an oversight, the result of benign inadvertence. Princeton was now accepting Afro-Americans. Some of those black kids were from the Deep South. They had never seen the deep end, much less any part, of a swimming pool. Classmate Walter Baker was a case in point. Walter lived in Alabama. The thought of this rite of baptism terrified him. Another classmate, Barry Richardson, had been recruited to play at Palmer Stadium, a defensive back from Maine. Technically Princeton did not recruit. Some of the coaches did have some hand in the admissions selection process, however. Barry was now a friend to Walter and to Joe.

Joe was barely able to follow the exchange, a thick Maine accent issuing words of reassurance, then a Southern drawl reciting serious doubt. Barry's smile and warmth and Walter's tight shoulders and shaking head were enough to convey the meaning. Joe stepped in.

"Walter, we will hold you up. Barry and I are both strong swimmers. You will see."

Walter Baker had no other choice. Over 100 young men tread water for twenty minutes. The coaches overseeing the exercise were kind in overlooking the fact Walter was buoyed by his new buddies. For the first thirty seconds Walter was one tense muscle, his entire body an involuntarily nervous knot. The Southern "boy" soon relaxed. The rest of the time was a walk in the park.

Y. Rather A Ravage Than A Conquest

In those days, the few blacks on campus formed a group known by the acronym, "ABC." The Association of Black Collegians became a tightly knit group. Malcolm X propagated the idea that the white people were devils. The ABC officers did go quite that far. Distrust was the watchword. Walter Baker and the other black students were given counsel to maintain more than a Chinese wall to safely separate themselves from the whites. Intermingling should be avoided. If it was necessary to interact, the white students and teachers should be viewed with a disdain, bordering upon contempt. Skeptical aloofness was not enough. The swimming requirement was just another friendly reminder that blacks must tread carefully, even, or perhaps especially, in this pastoral and idyllic white world.

Barry Richardson is one of life's great people. None were a more affable chair for the Class of 1973 reunions than he. He has known Walter through the day they both graduated, and beyond. In the closeness of guarded conversation, Barry will express his view that he feels great pain that he did not get to know Walter better, even though he is sure he understands the reasons ABC members took the stance they did. There is no doubt that it is also Walter Baker's loss not to know Barry better. Joe came to realize that the essence of the Princeton experience was the deep camaraderie developed with friends in those years. It was more than school boy kinship. Bonds of love are forged as Princeton students even, almost inexplicably, between classmates who would not meet until years later.

The swimming requirement for a Princeton diploma satisfied, Joe walked out of Dillon Gym. He was headed back to his dorm room, 22 Little Hall. Little is a long two-story building which has its start near the lower base of Witherspoon separated by an opening guarded by two large stone Tigers. Little's stately elongation turns two corners before its walls meet the walls of Dillon. Where the two buildings connect, an archway covers stairs which lead down to the concrete path to Pyne Hall where Princeton's women students first lived.

Z. My Own Simple Opinion

A short classmate with red-tinted yellow hair, and a smile which evinced studied wry boredom walked with purpose to step into Joe's path. Here in front of Joe stood a young man whose diminutive stature bundled more energy than the average Princeton Crew. The motion from two short legs in full pace was now channeled to speech,

"Why, y'all, I daresay you and that fellow from Maine have the best intentions. But y'all may wish to consider something you can't be expected to know..."

Phil "Red" Light spoke freely without fear of contradiction or recrimination. Four years at the exclusive and highly regarded, Washington, D.C. Prep School, "St. Augustine's" fortified rather than removed his Southern drawl and his slurped "Y'alls." Few could afford to attend St. Augustine's. Fewer still were accepted. There was no coincidence that the leading prep school for fine Southern gentleman was located at the location where the boarding house of Mary Surratt once sat, the place where John Wilkes Booth kept a room before heading off to the Ford Theater.

Red hailed from a fine Southern family, really two fine South Carolina families, one finer than the next. His father's side manufactured lamps making a fortune that Croesus would admire. The maternal fortune, larger and bordering on the enormous, was derived from selling chandeliers. The recent upswing in sales of Lava lamps had no effect on the bottom line of either business. Red left St. Augustine's cocksure and infallible. Nothing could take the briskness from his step or the wind from his pure white, billowing sails. The world around him was only occasionally a small bother. Fools were ignored entirely and never, ever suffered since those beneath both his station and his superior learning did not sully his brow and never, ever sent even a small shot across the deck of his dominion. Anything anyone said which did not fall within that tight, unerring set of his beliefs was simply ignored. Actually, that which countervailed Red's steady self-assurance was not even really disregarded since that would imply some initial recognition in his consciousness. Red saw not as far as his arms stretched, not even as far as beyond his upturned nose. Red's entire being smacked with the supercilious notion that either you were like-minded or you did not matter, with the important caveat that there are few perspicacious enough to be of the same feather,

"...These porch monkeys have been shown a great disservice by well-intentioned folks who have put them here, in a place they do not belong..."

"Excu-use me, who are you?"

"My name is Phil Light, but everyone calls me, 'Red.' And you?"

"I'm Joe Cebellum."

"As I was saying folks like y'all, I am sure y'all mean well but the truth of the matter is that these boys were all much better off when they were slaves. Their masters sought only their better interests. Interests the surface of which they themselves cannot even begin to scratch..."

"Red, are you fucking kidding me?"

“These boys were much better off with order and stability on the plantation. Now they are lost and no amount of words on a blackboard or high minded speeches will ever reach them. Although, even where they are now, mired in their God-given lethargy, they are much better off than when we brought them from Africa. Genetic limitations can neither be ignored nor transcended.”

“Red, I’ve got to go. I just remembered I have an appointment to have the shit scraped off my shoes.”

“Funny, but you and your lobster trapping friend might have helped keep that little Sambo afloat for twenty minutes, but he, and all those like him, will surely sink of their own weight, all in the fullness of the Good Lord’s time. The world is a treacherous place for the unworthy and the incapable.”

“Red, it is so nice to hear your concerns.”

AA. Quickly Repulsed

Joe turned tail. He walked away taking full strides. He did not look back. This would not be the last time a fellow Princeton student would be comfortable around him, just because they had the same skin color, to heap insipid platitudes his direction. It was not always Southerners. Boston had its own strange niche. Women and colored folk could not keep pace, hampered by the limitations given by their Creator. One group was better off in the kitchen or the boudoir. The other was better off in another form of slavery now abolished by law. Both groups had masters, blessed by divinity, who treated them with kindness and with care.

As Joe walked up the stairs of the second entry of Little Hall that afternoon, his hair was still wet from the Dillon swimming pool. As he opened the door, he shook his head trying to make his meeting with Red disappear as if it had never happened. A few drops floated to the landing barely leaving a watermark. The picture in Joe's head did not as easily evanesce. Blacks and women stood obsequiously in line. Each waited to be polished and buffed like so many antique grandfather clocks given due care in some proud antebellum collection.

BB. Time And A Little Resolution Will Soon Recover

As everyone on the Princeton campus was soon to know, women have their own unique position. Joe sat on the lower bunk bed in his dorm room, taking off his shoes and his socks. He considered the issue whether blacks should use their best efforts to breach the gap created by prejudice in an effort to stand on equal or greater footing with their "betters," thereby improving everyone. This predicament was really beyond his ken. So Joe leaned back into his bed, rolled in, and took a short nap.

Perhaps only Gandhi or Mandela would answer with a "yes." For the Association of Black Collegians in those days, it was not enough that the force of law, affirmative action, required they be given that first step into the stream from manifold oppression. Taking courses and passing tests presented difficulty enough. The black students preferred not to test the waters. At Princeton, the whole quandary was redoubled. It was a legitimate fear that they could not ever weave themselves into the depth of a pale white fabric long ago milled and, as yet, not interspersed with any of the colors of the rainbow. Changes in the mosaic that is the heritage and the history of Princeton occur slightly more quickly than mountains rising. Patience of geological proportion is difficult when you know, in your head and in your heart of hearts, that your time has come.

CC. So Earnestly And So Repeatedly Sought To Avoid

One of the first leaders of the ABC was Jerome Davis. After Princeton, Jerome attended the Harvard Business School. In the next three years, his younger brother, Legrome, became a Princeton student, as did a third brother, Alan. Alan was more comfortable mingling with the white folk even in those few short years of difference. Joe and his buddies smoked marijuana with Alan, as they listened to what they called rock and roll. Alan politely suggested that white people's music was horrible. Joe put his arm around him as Alvin Lee played a long blues based solo.

"Astrodome, tell me this is not what music is all about."

Ignoring the preposterous but playful nickname visited upon him from the natural progression of the names of his older brothers, Alan shook his head clenching a closed mouth smile not showing too many teeth,

"Joe, Joe, it is a white guy's idea of what the blues is all about, try listening to Buddy Guy or better yet, early B.B.King. Second thought, maybe you should start one small step at a time, some James Brown or Curtis Mayfield."

Even small progress leads to great inroads. Before starting his political life, Woodrow Wilson was President of Princeton where he discovered that politics was tame compared to the tooth and claw tension that existed when he ran Princeton. Starting in 1902, Woodrow Wilson nurtured the imperative that demanded better facilities, better and larger faculty, and better curriculum. Progressive improvement in the field of higher education followed, among them the “precept,” small groups of six or less where students met with professors in addition to course lectures. In their last two years, students picked a discipline in which to concentrate. Raising money from the Trustees for these improvements was not a problem.

Wilson and the Trustees started butting heads when Wilson tried to raise admission standards and to abolish the prevalent, perfunctory, and lackadaisical “Gentleman’s C” and replace it with the rigors of serious study. Wilson informed legacy alumni that he wished to "to transform thoughtless boys performing tasks into thinking men."

Wilson and the Trustees locked horns in 1906 when Wilson tried to curtail the influence of the social elites by abolishing the upper-class Eating Clubs. He wished to move the students into college quadrangles. The “Quad Plan” met fierce opposition from Princeton alumni, notably Moses Taylor Pyne, Princeton's most powerful Trustee. Not politic, Wilson tried to hold his ground, saying that giving in "would be to temporize with evil."

In October 1907, due to the intensity of alumni opposition, the Board of Trustees withdrew support for the Quad Plan. Wilson was instructed to table the plan. Wilson’s final effort in the struggle of Alpha males involved a confrontation with Andrew Fleming West, Dean of the graduate school, and West's ally former President Grover Cleveland who was a trustee. Wilson wanted to integrate the Graduate and undergraduate campuses. West wanted them to remain separate. The national press portrayed the dispute as a battle between elitist separatism and democratic intermingling. West prevailed. Favorable publicity in what was only a moral victory may have led to Wilson’s decision to turn tail, scarred by the fight with the existing order for territorial imperative, and leave the cloistered acrimony for the relative calm of public life. Only a few years into politics, Wilson would make the first of many comments that politics was less brutal than university administration. When all was said and done, Wilson set Princeton on the path to becoming one of America's great universities.

DD. Given Us Up To The Care Of Devils

Woodrow Wilson was not Branch Rickey. As U. S. President, Woodrow Wilson segregated Federal offices stating that white women would not wish to work with Negroes. On February 8, 1903, at a Trustees' meeting on campus, Wilson criticized federal appointments of blacks by President Theodore Roosevelt. According to Edmund Morris, Wilson joked with alumni that the groundhog had returned to its burrow fearful that Teddy Roosevelt would put a "coon" in it.

Nevertheless, it was none other than Woodrow Wilson who set the wheels of change in motion. In the sixties, meritocrats met plutocrats on an essentially level playing field with almost equal footing. A separate peace produced huge gains. The Eating Clubs still thrived but "Bicker" did not have the power to make or break a student as it once did. Bicker is to the Eating Clubs as "Rush" is to fraternities. Prospective members are judged worthy on the basis of important factors such as family background. The unacceptable are left by the wayside to cry in their beer. At Princeton, however, the beer mugs are fine pewter not plastic cups. Stories still ring true that more than one Princeton Gentleman killed himself when he was not accepted to the Club he, and his ancestors, fancied. By school year 1970-1971, many Eating Clubs became "non-selective." Some admitted women. In the late '70s, a Princeton student, Sally Frank, commenced what would become a torturous procedural path in an effort to force Ivy Club to accept women.

EE. My Secret Opinion Has Ever Been

It was Wednesday afternoon. Joe woke up from his afternoon cat nap. Some deep thinking about the predicament of black people in the United States turned to selfish consideration of something he now sorely missed. That summer had been pure joy. Sarah Foreswallow and Joe had long been delectably running together, smoothly using all Sarah's cylinders. In the heat of Midwestern dog days, they secured their own special swelter. Sarah and Joe discovered that fucking was sometimes foreplay and that post-coital sixty-nine would soon turn pre-coitus. Joe kept the position they both liked best in a firm place in his mind, through his whole psyche to the very tip of the toes of his being. It was the activity that always brought down, if not burned down, the house. Sarah faced Joe straddling him as he lay on his back. Sarah would glide her soft, wet pussy up and down the full length of his shaft which stood at full attention. She kept to a slow rhythm which made tactile eternity not nearly long enough. At some point Sarah would decide the time was right. She would lean forward, her pussy still in place. Joe would lift his head. Slow and elaborate wet kisses hinted at the way each would soon be greeting the other's genitals. Soon, the kisses turned frantic. Joe would grab Sarah's hips to hold her still her legs spread wide, as he pumped up into her gaping under carriage with full thrusts formed by his own synchronized hip and knee bends. Their kisses became pure slobber. This scene had been part of a nightly summer's entanglement. It had now been almost a week with no end to the drought in sight. Joe's hand was on his hard cock, squeezing it just below its bulb to give him just the right tingle. With three roommates, taking things into his own hand presented a problem in seizing the moment. The next time he was sure to be alone, for even fifteen minutes, his rod in his hand would comfort him.

FF. Now Enter Into

22 Little was a suite. The foyer held two desks, one on either side of the ash-worn fireplace which still functioned. The windows on the outer wall had beneath them a window seat with wooden panels which lifted up to spaces which held firewood. The wall to the opposite of the fireplace had room for a full sofa, in this case a chocolate brown corduroy hide-a-bed with three plush deep cushions. Two maple wood lamp tables had been placed at either end of the sofa. Two identical couch pillows sat on the hide-a-bed. Each showcased the head of a vigilant wide-eyed tiger. The maple set also included a chair with two foam cushions covered with a fabric of muted medium and light browns. The reading chair sat between another matching piece, a rectangular coffee table, and the fireplace. On the wall away from the windows two speakers sat on the floor, either side of a stereo in a cabinet which also held record albums.

There were two bedrooms. Each held a bunk bed, two bureaus, and a desk which sat below a window which looked out the back of Little Hall. Joe shared a bunk with Joel Frites, from Lakeland, Ohio.

The smaller room in this quad which was once a single, the one for the valet, still held ample space for two students. Ronald George "Ronny" Hoyle, from Cherry Hill, New Jersey and Mel Rothstein from Shawnee Mission, Kansas shared that room. Ron Hoyle swam freestyle on the Princeton swim team. He was already practicing twice a day, the morning in a large outdoor for longer workouts and the late afternoon in the Dillon pool. Joel and Joe were both about 6’3” tall. Frites was more muscular. Joel lifted weights every day. Joe had brought his weight set from home with the best intentions. Even back in Tower Lakes, near the Sleepy Little Village of Barrington, Illinois, Joe never worked out with the weights which had been given to him as a Christmas present two years ago. There was room in the Cebellum car so the barbell set made the trip East. Joel was happy to use them at the room when he did not have time to go to the weight room in Dillon.

Mel was the only one of the three was not an athlete. He was also the only one of the three who did not fall into the category of handsome. Short, fat, and plain was a description about which there could be no disagreement. Nevertheless, Mel’s intelligence prevailed through his happy smile and his sharp eyes. Above all, Mel was a likeable guy who seemed interested in more than his own puffy visage and his plump stance.

GG. Touchstones Of Sincerity And Hypocrisy

It was Frites who Joe saw first when he walked out of the bedroom after his nap.

“Joe, let’s go to the Pyne Hall courtyard tonight. One of the guys I met over in the Dodd Hall courtyard told me that for the last two nights a large group has formed at Pyne to drink beer and to check out the new Princeton women. Maybe we will get lucky.”

“An exercise in utter futility given the very long odds, 100 to 3000 or so, but the opportunity to drink beer should not be passed over without good reason.”

Mel, still sitting on the living room couch, jumped in even though, strictly speaking, he had not been invited,

“For my people, ‘Passover’ is a term not used lightly. Plus I do not drink. You guys have fun. I’ll stay here and watch t.v.”

Mel had brought a small portable television which had an alarm clock feature. He kept it to himself on the top of his bedroom bureau. Ron Hoyle had already left for practice. Even in two days, it was clear to the other three that twice a day work outs took their toll. All waking hours were spent sleeping, as were the night time sleeping hours. Frites and Joe followed the opposite schedule. They stayed awake long into the night, even if it was just the two of them talking well into the wee hours comparing the differences between growing up in their home states. Their discussions had, at the kernel, the thread of one-upmanship until the last word was popped.

For that evening, at least in its beginning, this most recent incarnation of the ongoing war of words between two bunkmates had been circumscribed.

Frites summed up,

“So two ‘Ayes’ have it.”

“To be sure but I fear in this case the ‘Ayes’ will be windows to the sole.”

Joel swallowed a chortle which burped up silently as a small tart smile. He was not willing to acknowledge Joe’s levity. He squinted his eyes,

“Joe, I get it- two guys alone, left to their own devices. I hear that Pyne Hall now is a dorm with four and twenty windows with a woman’s face in ev’ry one.”

“Frites, I am not sure the odds are improving. The good news is that we are assured two nights of good sleep before we go to the gym on Friday to try out for Cane Spree basketball.”

“Our class has some good players. I have seen them in the gym, lots of pick-up games.”

“Whether I make the Cane Spree squad or not, I think I will start playing in the gym.”

HH. Our Situation There Was Exceedingly Cramped

Princeton has a long, devout tradition of hazing Freshmen, both informal and institutional. In an 1895 collection called, "Princeton Stories," Jesse Lynch Williams, one of the sons of Old Nassau wrote this unnervingly arcane description-

"...In the glorious old days of untrammeled class activity when everyone recognized that there were certain duties owed the freshman by the sophomore class...you had only casually to drop word to a freshman on the way to recitation to wait for you when night came, back of Witherspoon — as you would bid a classmate come to a spread in your room — and he would turn up promptly and smilingly, take his little dose meekly and cheerfully, and go to bed a better boy for it and brag about it every time he dined out on Christmas holidays..."

In 1865, thirty years before the strange activity described by Williams, some upperclassmen deemed the freshmen unfit to carry the canes of gentlemen. In an act of awesome violence, they attacked members of the freshman class, seizing their canes. Thus, Cane Spree was born. Perhaps to protect the incoming students, for too many years to count, the University now sanctions and oversees the "competition."

Harvard students are neither impartial observers nor do they have clean skirts. A now unknown Harvard Crimson reporter had the cheek to make this toothy description,

"The 'Cane Spree' at Princeton.
October 31, 1885 [N.B. The date is not April 1st]

The 'cane spree' is an institution peculiar to Princeton, and a description of it may interest our readers. It is in no sense a cane rush, and must not be confused with the disgraceful struggles which occur at some colleges between the sophomore and freshman classes en masse. It is merely a species of wrestling by representatives of the two classes for the possession of three canes. A heavy weight, middle weight, and light weight champion is selected from each class. At the appointed time, a great crowd collects in a ring on the campus, and then the heavy, middle, and light weight couples contest separately for the canes. Last Tuesday the annual cane spree occurred at Princeton. The first spree, the light weight, was won by a freshman, who, as the *Daily Princetonian* says, 'after four rounds had been vigorously fought, secured the cane by a twist, and was carried off on the shoulders of his enjoyed classmates.' The middle weight spree was won by a sophomore. In the heavy weight spree, we see evidence of the spirit in which Princeton is conducting foot-ball mattes this year. The candidates selected were foot-ball men, but, as the managers of the spree were unwilling that foot-ball men should incur the danger of a heavy fall, the candidates were barred out, and without protest acquiesced to the decision of the managers. The freshmen had no man to put up against the other candidate of the sophomores, and so lost the heavy weight."

II. We Shut Ourselves Up And Stood On Our Defence

The Cane Spree grew from seeds sown by a small group. James Madison had twelve classmates. It is fair to say that in the beginning, Princeton meant high handed, top hatted, and circumspectly devout. It was not just Jonathan Edwards. Aaron Burr's father was a minister who next followed Edwards at the helm of a God-fearing proper, upright education. No theologian or critic has ever suggested that Jesus was self-satisfied. That cannot be said for the young minds that gave breath to the revolution from England. The only similarity between James Madison and his Princeton fellows and Jesus and his disciples was their number, thirteen.

As Gandhi put it, "I like your Christ. I do not like your Christians. Your Christians are so unlike your Christ."

Aaron Burr settled a score by killing Alexander Hamilton in a duel in the north New Jersey highlands. Both gentlemen with a full entourage of seconds engaged in a ritual where insult requires honor. The idea that one has a place to preserve and to protect became an integral part of hazing and of the Cane Spree itself. Some would say it is all in the name of good clean fun. Others might disagree. Even the strong and mighty suffer their own bitter form of insecurity.

JJ. The Best Part Of Our Stores Had Been Removed

Joe had not spent much time thinking about the idea of "hazing," extenuating the idea of a rite of passage to add the elements of unnecessary pain and ridicule. He hoped the times they were achangin' with the dull-witted soon to be the last to notice that the waters were rising. Joe had not expected to see the lock stepped mentality of boot camp traipsing about the Princeton Campus.

As Frites and Joe bid goodbye to Mel, before rushing out the door, each with a self-confident bounce in stride both carefree and deliberate, the stereo speakers held a distinctive nasal intonation,

"...In the dime stores and bus stations,
People talk of situations,
Read books, repeat quotations,
Draw conclusions on the wall.
Some speak of the future..."

Some say Bob Dylan is obscure. By 1969 this sort of forthright clarity sashayed its way to a larger in-crowd, a group too hip for any regimentation. Not one coffee shop visionary from Greenwich Village had even a small measure of success in predicting the course of history, a path where the squares will have it and where circle never takes the square. Hazing reinforces the concept that it is acceptable to show the unworthy where they belong. It wrings all guilt from the consciences of the privileged as all lessers are kept in their place in later life.

KK. God Almighty Will Not Give Up A People

As a Freshman Horned Toad at Texas Christian University, Tommy Wanderby encountered Lone Star variations on the teachings of Our Savior aplenty. Joe's lessons came face-to-face or in small informal groups. For Tommy, as befit the nature of a large University, a mass instruction was afoot. The Fort Worth campus was abuzz. A special mandatory meeting had been called for all students. As far back as anyone could remember this was unprecedented. Meetings for the entire student body had, of course, been needed many times over the long and the illustrious history of Texas Christian University. The learned and the anointed knew that to use the Amon G. Carter Stadium for anything but Football, sacrilege was approached. A dispute akin to a bona-fide range war ensued. The coaching staff did not feel it was proper to use their facility for education or for religious upbringing. Only cattle rustling was less forgivable. The coaches were finally persuaded that insidious influences, driven by the devil himself, were threatening to undermine every value all Christians hold dear. Football would just be the next item on the diabolic agenda of subversion. It was necessary for the school administrators to enlist the hierarchy of the Disciples of Christ. More than the slogan from the days of the Stone-Campbell movement, *"In essentials, Unity; In non-essentials, Liberty; and in all things, Charity"* was needed to persuade the Football regime and the alumni booster club. But in the end, everyone was reminded that the roots of TCU ran deep. Horned Toads harkened back even before their gunslinging days as just another baptizing college in Waco. Finally, the imperative of the moment prevailed. The coaches agreed to re-arrange to twice-a-day practice schedule to accommodate an aggregation which would be as near to Pentecostal as anyone could imagine, never before seen in Texas or anywhere near the Panhandle.

LL. The Fault, If It Were One, Was All Our Own

The atmosphere that night smacked of an old fashioned tent revival. As a new pledge, Tommy was told he was proud to sit with his Sigmund Albert Estragon fraternity brothers at the fifty yard line, the best seats in the house. There he sat with the entire student body. To fill the stadium, high school students and church congregations had also been invited. The word of the Lord would follow but right now, right here a festival of exuberance overflowed out of the stands, onto the field. Even the Horned Toad cheerleading squad, enlisted to frame the event, was dwarfed. All present were overawed by the energy of expectation.

Suddenly in one dark flash, all the stadium lights were doused. Only hushed whispers remained. Three seconds seemed a holy eternity. A huge spotlight circled the Reverend Timothy Galatian. The circumference of clean white light surrounded the minister effusively. The bright coned beam was solemn as the man on a mission swaggered toward the stage. Even those who had ventured small sounds to be heard only for the next ear were now significantly silent. The spotlight informed the twelve stairs Galatian climbed to reach the speaker's platform which had been set carefully at midfield on the fifty. His last six sufficiently humble, head-bowed lopes were proud processional. The clean light shone only within its edifying limits making a bold contrast to the surrounding sea of heathen darkness, just as Galatian's white clerical collar was all that smiled out from his black suit.

Galatian picked up the microphone. He tapped it on the front of the podium. The three little metal bumps were magnified to force a shiver through the assembled multitude. The Reverend looked down. He raised his right hand, forefinger pointing to heaven. The group festival rivaling a Saturday half-time show had been shushed without the first word,

"Let us pray. Dear Lord let us learn to know that what we know are words which seem to have one meaning but with the Holy Spirit become words that only God in all His glory can really know. Humble man, with all his imperfections cannot assume to know that which only God and His Perfect Son, His great gift to mankind to be sacrificed as the lamb of peace do know..."

The stadium had stood as one. Now the Reverend raised his left hand then lowered both arms to signify the time to sit.

"...This University is a gift from God started by a group called 'The Disciples of Christ.' Some may say that there are only twelve Disciples of Christ. Words have the meaning God wishes them to have. Our holy ancestors, seeing the true path, left the Presbyterians to become again, the 'Disciples of Christ.' For God, at that moment, those who saw the light were given the power to Judge no matter what has been said by the name of God before. Today, we are again, asked to look more closely at scripture to find the true light in the word of God..."

At that moment all the stadium lights were again turned on, blinding everyone.

"It is said Jesus said, 'Love thy enemy.' There is no doubt that what God means by this is that after, and only after, our enemy is conquered, vanquished, or even obliterated, you should love him as the brother he might have been had he not been the enemy in the first place…"

The stadium lights again went dark. The spotlight surrounded Galatian.

"…We may come to understand true meaning by understanding other New Testament words that are often misunderstood, 'Turn the other cheek.' Obviously God does not want His chosen children, those who walk in His grace and His Light…"

The stadium lights again flood the gathering.

"…to be hurt. 'Turn the other cheek' means give your enemy one last chance to see the light before conquering, vanquishing, or obliterating him to maintain God's order of righteousness and good…"

The lone spotlight again became preeminent as the stadium lights were turned off.

"…The best way to see this point is truly, to understand, some other words of Jesus. 'Blessed are the peacemakers' is a good example although what I am saying, or I should say what the Holy Spirit is saying through me, works equally well for 'the poor' or any other group Jesus ever mentioned. Everyone knows that final 'Blessing'' is something that happens only by God. It is therefore irrefutable, and all else is unholy sacrilege to suggest that we give any help to peacemakers, poor, or anyone who has not been anointed with the God's goodness and God's light since that is beyond our capabilities as imperfect men, no matter how some of us may have greater insight into the Word of the Lord…"

All the stadium lights were again turned on, this time to stay.

"...The final clear and compelling evidence God has given us is that which Jesus told us, the passage about the birds in the air and the lilies of the field. God will take care of everyone in good time. We need not be concerned with our enemies, the peacemakers, the poor, or any other group except those who truly belong as the Disciples of Christ. Knowing this gives great comfort to all of us. Now that the Holy Spirit has filled us with God's will and understanding, I must discuss the reason we are all here tonight. We must not allow those who do not belong among us to be among us. God will take care of everyone as His will be done. That is not our role. When a 'peacemonger' seeks to invade out Holy Fellowship, we are duty bound, as Christians, to just say, 'No.' Therefore the speech that Jane Fonda was to give here on campus later this year has now been canceled. Without further notice, you must all strive to seek the unjust and remove them from your presence. It is God's will. The Holy Spirit and Jesus tell us so. Let the Lord be with you, now and forever, especially when the temptation to help an enemy, a peacemonger, or a poor person threatens the essence of your God-given Christianity. Let us pray the prayer Jesus taught us to pray, 'Our Father, who art in Heaven, hallowed be Thy Name..."

With the word, 'Amen,' the lights went out on the field and the speaker's platform, leaving only the stands shining with God's light. The entire multitude left Amon G. Carter Stadium knowing that what they had witnessed was authentic and inalterable.

MM. Only For Temporary Purposes

That same night, Sam Thorn fully expected the unexpected. He had so far stranded himself only in the comfort of his own habits. Norman, Oklahoma was surely to his liking. The University of Oklahoma, "OU" as it is known, was so large Sam could hide himself amidst a throng. For Sam, commonality was a concept honored only in its breach. His pride hoisted itself from the rooftops of singularity far above the troughs tread by the Middle America in which he was awash. Sam was unique even as he followed the well-trod paths of others. For the young Thorn, comfort in chaos would soon supplant static repose.

Sam's dad, Phil, was glad. Sam was going to college far from home. At long last he would have the Pickwick Place Townhouse to himself. He lavished upon his son the full affection that only material objects will bring. Sam sat as the lord of the manor, in this case a large one bedroom apartment, awash in the lap of luxury. Watson, Holmes, and Moriarty would be forced to agree, Sam's sitting room was a far better place than the digs at 221B Baker Street. Manliness had come home to roost. The two windows which faced the street one flight below were superfluous, not even second thoughts. The grey grimed glass was almost fully covered with pasty once flesh-colored window shades. They had been rolled down to stay. The bottom weighted creases of the shades both rested uncomfortably upon the grubby brass handles at the bottom of the window frames, just above sills that held a shiny layer of beige lacquer which covered strata of lead based paint from before the Dust bowl days. Prior layers had only been partially scraped before another coat was applied. The uneven surface with its small craters did not diminish the gestalt. Only some picky aesthete, probably feminine to the core, would quibble with the essence of what surrounded Sam.

The windows served the purpose of balanced framing the showpiece of Sam's Oklahoma nest. The top shelf of the mahogany cabinet held a 27" RCA color television. On the waist high shelf below the t.v., Sam had carefully placed and leveled a Fisher 550T 90 watt stereo receiver upon which sat a Bang and Olufsen Beogram 1800 turntable. Below that sturdy shelf there were two doors with shiny brass handles which enclosed three more shelves. Those three lower shelves were proud in their bounty. Playboy Magazines going back to the one with Marilyn Monroe scantily clad on the cover and wearing less on the inside had been religiously placed in piles. To the side of the entertainment center, beneath each window sat Bose 901 reflecting speakers. Sam was more than a few steps ahead of "state of the art." Those speakers barely contained Sam's current choice, Cream's last album, *Goodbye*. Sam had just played the side with "Badge" and "What a Bringdown." He flipped the vinyl over to the Skip James' classic blues number, "I'm So Glad." Deft and brazen notes blared from the defunct power trio.

The wall space on the outer sides of both windows was covered with matching Mahogany Bookcases. The one to the left, held five shelves of books, mostly murder mysteries Phil had given Sam. The book case to the right had its shelves adjusted down to four to provide the needed space to hold Sam's ever burgeoning album collection. The current number of 1620, a momentarily good place to land, would continue to increase at the rate of five to ten records a week. Sam kept his collection in an order driven by his sense of quality. The best, like the band, Cream, rose to the top shelf. Those groups no longer favored slumped on the path of least resistance to the bottom shelf. The records on the two shelves in between could go up or down with the vagaries of Sam's muse. Thus, The Beatles, The Rolling Stones, Cream, Blind Faith, Steely Dan, and the Moody Blues started the collection on the far left of the top shelf. All the way to right of the bottom shelf was a virtual dust bin of unlamented disfavor, Sopwith Camel, Bubble Puppy, The Brooklyn Bridge, Gary Puckett and the Union Gap, The New Vaudeville Band, and Tommy James and the Shondells. Trial and error is necessary for any superlative rock and roll collection.

A "Hide-a-Bed" pull-out couch faced the middle cabinet. Its fabric was navy blue thin corduroy. The three cushions and stuffed backing provided ample comfort. Even the pullout bed was top drawer. Many a sound night's sleep had been had and would be had in the deep support of its Sealy Posturepedic mattress. Sam's caramel leather reclining reading chair was placed at an angle of 45 degrees to the left of the couch. To its left was a small table which held an ashtray, three rumpled empty packs of cigarettes, and a few books and magazines. A brass floor lamp comprised of rings of embossed Egyptian hieroglyphic patterns which alternated with pure gleaming golden metal rings rose to the height of five feet at which point the column of circles met bulb and socket. A large canvas tent shade forced a tent of white light. There was more than plenty illumination for the many hours Sam spent reading. At the other side of the couch, perpendicular to it, Sam placed a burgundy red and masculine dark pink paisley wing back chair. In front of the couch, there was an incongruously dark-stained oak coffee table with four short legs. Four curved edges were hinged to the rectangular center each with an oval void presumably crafted to allow the placing of a hand for movement up and down. Books, magazines, two more empty packs of Tareytons, and the Beatles' album, *Rubber Soul,* were strewn around a large ceramic diamond shaped ashtray which sat in the center.

The front door faced a hallway. The hallway led behind the living room to the door to a large bedroom with master bath and tub. The bedroom held a king-sized bed with brass-frame, a tall dressing bureau and another shorter chest of drawers with an attached mirror. The only framed item in the entire apartment hung above the arched seven-rung headboard, the poster which showed John, Paul, George, and Ringo and proclaimed, "The Beatles' Command Performance at the Royal Albert Hall with Sam Thorn." This was a treasure given to him by his dad that Sam was sure would follow him wherever he went, for the rest of his life. The hallway continued past the door to the bedroom to a formal dining room. It was furnished with a large white painted hutch, eight maple dining room chairs, and a matching maple round table which could hold one or two leaves to seat eight. Between the bedroom and the dining room was a full guest bath with shower. The last room was a large kitchen with a back door to stairs that led down to the place where Sam parked his 1964 White Comet.

NN. Endeavor To Penetrate

Sam sat in the leather chair as the needle scored the last groove in *Goodbye*. Sam smoked his last Tareyton down to the point where the tobacco ended and the filter started. He rubbed the stub into the ashtray on his left. The way Sam always heard it, “the exception proved to rule.” Previously, Sam had no actual experience which poured any content into this ungainly anomaly. Tonight would be his completely, however. Sam locked the door to his apartment. He pulled the handle to be sure it was latched. Sam turned a crisp military about-face but then relapsed to his true character, just enough insouciance to saunter down the worn, polished wooden stairs to the street. Sam’s attention, if that was fair denomination for his special brand of consciousness divided into one, was above noticing the dust cowering in the corners of each of the seven stairs which met his tread. There was always more to meet Sam’s eye which prevented him from seeing. The matter at hand was to buy more cigarettes. It looked like every four days; Sam would be buying another carton.

Sam took his dilly-dally left to head for the cigarette counter of his local Rexall Drug Store. Suddenly, there was a bounce to his step as his right heel landed off the little stoop on the street where he lived. Sam was almost entirely self-absorbed but not mired in neglect. Anyone, and especially Sam, could not fail to notice the form of pure beauty that approached, one block in the distance, half-way between him and the pharmacy. All that was female floated over the sidewalk on the side he stepped, his right, her left. Sam hoped all her attitudes about convention would be similarly carefree.

No matter how much Sam's universe of prior attendant failures suggested the contrary, he always harbored the hope pure bliss would surely follow. In just a few seconds, each one seeming to last longer than the next, the two would cross paths. Sam was sure the mental picture of his own graceful accession and bow as he gave way to the slow simmering sensuality which girdled his field of vision would be realized. She, whoever she was, had a presence stronger than the meander of Sam's thoughts of future possibilities, the only realm where he had ever thrived. Each guileful step, each artful turn of her hip, and each planed shoulder was steeped in the rhythm of her motion. Her every breath raised her breasts even a little more than gravity would allow. Her carriage gave succor to some greater primeval force. She now filled Sam's full attention and his other important body part. He shifted his blue jeans. She was a shimmer of flawless harmony. Stepping towards him, directly in his path, she was not nervous. From a sly glance below his belt to his face, her eyes met his. Once she was sure he was engaged, she smiled with a serenity that escaped from the bounds of sweetness to the declivity of suggestion.

The two continued to walk toward one another. Sam really wanted to pinch himself. It was bad enough he was sporting a bulge in his pants. The young woman bore the color of chocolate, a skin tone in the middle between dark chocolate and light. Her face, arms, and legs visible from the knees down glowed with a fine brown, better than the tan Sam had seen on any girl, ever. She was not tan, however. Her dark black hair was pulled behind her head. Sam could see her pony tail bounce with her sultry natural rhythm. Her skirt was a royal blue with gold lines flowing from the waist. The skirt clung to her hips. It showed only a touch of her thighs, slightly above her knees. She was wearing a blouse, really a jacket that was almost ceremonial. It had square shoulders and flowed in a straight line down both sides of her body. The apple red fabric was silk, a coarse silk. It was alive with many golden threaded triangles forming larger and larger triangle patterns. Sam did not get lost in this optical confection because the way the cloth clung to her breasts, or rather the way her breasts pushed against the straining silk. All that was right and good suggested to Sam that her bosom wanted to find a way out, sooner rather than later. Given her 5'4" height, her 34 D cup breasts captured Sam's gaze for a split-second too long, perhaps longer. He was pleased she kept smiling as he raised his glance. Something in the way she moved attracted him as never before. The beauty of any of her particular body parts was consumed by her effortless grace. All that is, except her face. Sam was overtaken by perfection. Her deep brown almond shaped eyes were alive with an electricity he could feel. Her cheek bones and forehead formed a stunning border for her eyes. There was a small, dark circle in the middle of her forehead, just above her symmetrical and full black eyebrows. There was time to reflect later that in the midst of the state where many Native Americans had been herded, Sam was about to cross paths with a *bona fide* Indian Princess from Punjab or Bombay. Now her thin perfect nose led Sam's eyes to a mouth in full delectation. Sam could feel his lips touch hers. He could see a small space in her mouth open as her tongue made her lips slightly wet, but fully salacious.

The moment to meet arrived. Sam stumbled on a crack in the sidewalk as he moved to his left to grant free stroll to the girl of his newest dream.

"I guess you do your own choreography," was all she said.

The only item she held now lost its place under her arm. It was a book. Did it fall or had she let it slip? Sam recovered his balance in time to catch the book before it hit the ground.

“Thanks, you know you just made me realize I could use someone to help me with my new book.”

Sam looked at the cover. There were two words in some sort of ancient printed text at the top. Beneath the words was an Asian painting of two bodies deliciously interknit. The two words were, “Kama Sutra.”

OO. On The Apprehension

Back in the Sleepy Little Village, Joe, Tommy, and Sam had left Fred to his own devices. Even Tim Camphor had headed up to college in Fargo, North Dakota. Felina Woodworrell was now a Freshman at New York University. Sally Sensabell and five Barrington classmates had matriculated to the University of Southern California, actively recruited to try to fill the void left by the senseless killing of Brock Argil the year before. Of course, Fred had Martha Buchanan, now in her Senior year. The bad news was that her father, Howard, was still steadfast in his rule that she could go out only one night a weekend and be home by 11 p.m. The death of Martha's mother, Marcie, covered the three sisters with more than the pall of mourning.

Joe's mother, Della, always said Fred was like a cat. He would always land on his feet. Fred, himself, knew there were many ways to skin a cat, curious or otherwise. Other high school girls displayed interest in his 1967 Chevy Camaro SS blue convertible. Fred discovered they fancied him, not the purr of his four barreled carburetor as he screamed down the local roads approaching 100 miles an hour. There was a new universe for Fred. Young women were bountiful in and around Harper Junior College, the local community college in Palatine where he was now enrolled. Fred worked, earning wages around his first semester course load. He had the way and the means to wine and to dine the girls he met with from the Sleepy Little Village to the many communities that surrounded Harper. Now Fred needed to find one who had just the right similar inclination.

PP. It Must Occur To Every Thinking Man

It was an autumn morning with a slight nip. Half the leaves had changed color. All of them were stiff and ready to crackle. The dog day heat of August had wrenched all summer's green moisture from maple, oak, and hickory alike. Fred stood near the outer sidewalk of the Harper administration building facing Roselle Road.

"You're Fred Etheridge, right?"

The tentative voice came from a conservatively attired fellow. He had horn-rimmed glasses, spit-shined cordovan Oxfords, pressed tan Khaki pants, and a full-starched white dress shirt with a button-down collar. The guy's height was about 5 feet 10 inches. He had a wry smile which seemed inconsistent with the rest of his manner which cried only, "President of the Future Accountants Club."

"Yep, and you?"

"I'm Bob Garvin. We are taking Basic Bookkeeping together."

"I misread the course description. I had an entirely different idea about where 'spread sheets' would lead…"

Garvin giggled.

"…two girls in a class of thirty five and both would surely turn the least picky to study animal husbandry."

Now Garvin was in full laugh, to the point he needed to suppress a sneeze. Neither Bob nor Fred noticed that a sleek 1962 Ford Galaxie convertible, red with a wide white stripe from the back half way into the hood, slid top down up to the curb.

"Excuse me."

This voice was more than an annoyed peep. The hurried strain of feminine frustration emerged from lips wearing too much dark red lipstick. Somehow, beyond the pout, her mouth gave promise of a tender interlude. The girl teased her bangs and her brown hair curled as it hit her shoulders. Her eyeliner was dark and thick. Her eye lashes were caked with mascara. She curled them up to a point where that they could support a surfboard. Her eyes were nevertheless deep and engrossing. They were filled with liveliness more than the small hurry of the moment. All her dark features stood to underscore her lily white skin. She was wearing a lime green light wool sweater, the kind that buttoned up the back. Her 34 C-cup white bra was too much for the loose knit. The undergarment peeked out everywhere yet nothing showed through the old fashioned, some sort of opaque, thick material. All signs of life underneath were successfully obscured. Two impatient but nicely curved hips hung from a woolen skirt of red, blue, and yellow plaid woolen skirt with too much brazen yellow. Her posture of bother was accentuated by the hand palm down on her right hip as she lowered her left side. The black pumps with three inch heels did not belong on this, or any, campus but they did underscore pure attitude. She pulled her shoulders back. Her breasts heaved forward, still entombed. She made a dismissive motion with her left hand in an effort to banish both Bob and Fred from her path.

She smacked her chewing gum,

"Excuse me Bob and whoever you are."

In two short steps, she bustled her way in between, brushed both breasts *seriatim* against Fred's shoulder. The driver stretched to open the passenger door to the Galaxie. She slid into the front seat. Fred twice felt soft fullness even the Iron Maiden bra could not occlude. She granted Fred an unnecessary view of her legs as she swiveled to face forward, almost up to where her right thigh met her hip. It was apparent the thought of not being the center of attention was too much for her.

"Who the fuck was that? Like she could easily have walked around us."

The driver of the Galaxie had skulked through some crack in the time-space continuum. He sported a crooked, satisfied smirk and placid, dark eyes. His thick black hair was greased straight back. Rudolph Valentino prettiness eclipsed the crude beauty of the girl now bouncing slightly in the seat to his right. He was wearing black dungarees and a white t-shirt. From the left short sleeve, he unfolded a pack of Marlboros. He lit one with the car's cigarette lighter then handed it over to try to slow the nervous energy to his side. Next he lit another one for himself. He took a deep drag then slowly let the smoke out both nostrils before he screeched away from the curb. In one last motion in this skit of imagined imperiousness, he turned his head to smile at all those about to be in his wake.

QQ. Our Numbers Were Greatly Inferior

"Her name is Delilah Pellioni. I went to Hoffman Estates High School with her. She is an honest-to-God Mafia Princess. Her dad is Giacomo Pellioni. He and his brother Carlo now report directly to Sam Giancana, the guy they call 'Momo.' Governor Fricke Wanderby chased all those guys, unsuccessfully, when he was a special prosecutor, back in the days when he tried and convicted Tony 'The Big Tuna' Accardo."

"One of my best buddies is Wanderby's nephew, a really cool guy from Texas who moved up here just last summer, Tommy Wanderby. I miss him already. He is going to Texas Christian near Dallas."

"Delilah's Uncle Carlo is not cut of the same cloth as our Governor but he may be equally powerful. He lives in Tiperrary..."

"That's the wannabe subdivision south of Barrington, really small lots with lots of lawn sculptures and with bird baths with yellow globes on them."

"I would love to live there. You people from Barrington are spoiled."

"Not me. My dad is a bricklayer. I live in a house he built himself. Sorry I interrupted you telling me about Uncle Carlo."

"Listen to this. Carlo has a daughter, Delilah's cousin, Minerva. She wanted to take riding lessons. The snot-nosed brats in Barrington would not let her join any of their riding clubs so Carlo elected to use a stable down Highway 59 near Lake Street. Anyway, Minerva was thrown by her horse during her second lesson. Carlo went to the stable that night. His hands are as big as ham hocks. Carlo is reputed to have been a very active street Lieutenant after Tony 'Big Tuna' Accardo went from underboss to boss of the 'Outfit,' the name the Chicago mob now uses. Carlo and Giacomo were there when the Outfit added their luster to Las Vegas as New York's Five Families had done…"

Fred's eyes got big.

"You guys from Hoffman Estates know lots of stuff."

"It gets better. Delilah's dad was in charge of bootlegging…"

"Come on Bob. Prohibition ended in the '20s."

"Not in Oklahoma and Kansas. Those guys made *mucho dinero* in those two states. Anyway, Carlo goes back to the stable after the horse threw Minerva. With his right ham hock he clocks the poor horse right between the eyes. The poor animal fell over dead on the spot."

"Whoa. What?"

"Yep. Then the real fun starts. The Mayor of Tiperrary pays Carlo an 'informal visit' to set things right. The next thing you know they find the guy who owns the stable hanging upside down, tied at both ankles from the top of his main barn, gagged. His wife did not find him until the next morning, none the worse for wear really. The Mayor received his own surprise. Somebody, I guess more than one somebody, snuck into his garage to adorn his brand new pink Cadillac. The dead horse was cut into three pieces, one for the front seat- hoofs on the dashboard, head looking over the steering wheel, the torso placed front to back in the back seat, and the horse's ass stuck right out of the trunk, back feet tucked in. It was one bloody mess. That Caddy was never the same. Now, just for fun, for the next two or three months, somebody, or somebodies, kept letting the air out of the tires of the cars owned by all the Tiperrary Village Board, sometimes by pulling the pin from the middle of that gizmo where you fill the tires. More often the tires were just punctured by a stiletto. Sometimes this happened when the cars sat together at a board meeting in front of God and everybody, everybody other than the malefactors that is. The police thought they had some leads to follow but the Village Board and Mayor were united. They all said they preferred not to prefer charges. The F.B.I. is looking into the reason the whole matter settled down. Apparently, Minerva now owns, not one, but two, really nice Lipizzaner Stallions, docile as church mice, given to her by the Tiperrary Board of Realtors."

"Bob, I gotta run. See you soon. I guess I am going to cross Delilah off my list of girls I want to meet."

"She has a friend, Madeleine Palmisano. The word on the street is that you might want to meet her, flat-chested but hips that do not quit, or her younger sister, Cassandra whose tits are bigger but the same commodious carriage. Hoffman Estates has lots of beautiful Italian girls, and some real Irish beauties, too."

"So much talent, so little time. I only wish."

Bob nodded his head in agreement, on both counts.

"See you later, Fred."

RR. Bore It With A Manly And Martial Spirit

It was a spritely dusk on the Princeton campus. Joe and Frites walked the lightly shadowed pathways to Pyne Hall. The tall trees that surrounded them were impervious to small matters such as the first group of Princeton coeds. More than a few Princeton men were not. Joe walked up the steps into Pyne courtyard. The space was spoked with seven or eight walkways leading to entry doors. The quadrangle lay spooked with Princeton past. Only two of the entries held dorm rooms for Freshmen men. The courtyard space was also manned with people talking without listening, spoken words discerned as banter, some soon to be slurred by beer.

Some guy ran up to Joe,

"You're not gonna believe this guy, Sammy Rice, what a pissah, and from Detroit who would have thought?"

"Excuse me, what in the name of the Good Lord is a 'pissah?'"

"Hi, I'm Sean McManana. I live in a quad up three flights of stairs in the entry on the right, the one in the middle just to the right of the arch."

The Boston accent was thick.

"Me, I'm Joe Cebellum. This is one of my roommates over at Little Hall, Joel Frites. So, what the fuck is a 'pissah?'"

Frites tried to help,

“I think he is saying ‘pisser.’”

Sean nodded assent.

“And a ‘pisser’ is what exactly?”

“Joel, Joe right? Follow me. You’ll see.”

The three headed closer to the entry to Sean’s room. A small group surrounded the center of attention. The man in the middle was short, squat, and round. Most of the other guys were looking at him with raised eyes. A couple of the onlookers went beyond askance to glare pure skepticism. The Pillsbury doughboy version of Henny Youngman had escaped from the Catskills. Recycled jokes, most of them starting with, “Take my wife…please” were followed with some vintage Rodney Dangerfield, “my wife used to be afraid of the dark until one night she saw me naked…”

Sean McManana bellied up to Sammy and pointed,

“This guy is a pissah, a real pissah.”

Sean laughed and laughed. Sammy formed a full minstrel smile which somehow reached beyond ear to ear. Praise of any sort was just what the doctor ordered. He really did not need any encouragement,

“…so this is coyote ugly, the guy wakes up next this really ugly girl still drunk from the night before. She is sleeping on his arm. He decides it is better to chew off his arm at the armpit rather than face the wretched creature when she wakens.”

Sean was laughing. He hopped up and down like he hadn’t peed in two days. Joe looked around for help.

SS. Their Folly Or Their Baseness

Two guys walked out from the arch. Help had arrived. He recognized one of the guys, Ron Streeter, the older brother of his high school biology lab partner, Bruce. Joe had planned to look him up when classes started. Here he was, a Senior on campus a few days early in the middle of Freshman Week.

"Hey Ron"

Ron smiled as he saw Joe,

"Come on over here. I want you to meet somebody."

Joe was more than happy to oblige, the Sammy-Sean sideshow had run its feeble course.

"Joe, this is Steve Puissant. Steve meet Joe Cebellum, a friend of my little brother, Bruce."

"Yea Ron, I've met your little brother. He is twice your size. Hey Joe, nice to make your acquaintance."

"Ron, why are you here so early?"

"Steve is the President of Cannon Club. I am the Treasurer. We came back to campus early to get the Club going full bore, ready for the wave of beer drinking that will soon commence and not subside until Christmas break. We are here, at Pyne Hall, to inspect Miss Bikini's bicycle. Everybody has heard that this girl from Southern California, Hermosa Beach, Manhattan Beach, or somewhere around there. She not only won a swim suit contest but was accepted here. Beauty and brains. Anyway, somebody said her parents gave her a tiger striped bike with black and orange streamers out the holes in the rubber handle grips, and a bicycle seat where she sits on a roaring tiger's face- a nice picture no?"

Steve Puissant jumped in,

"The weird thing is the bike has a little white woven basket hanging from the handlebars with plastic pink and yellow flowers stuck into it. Like Toto is missing from the whole picture."

Joe smiled,

"I guess she has to put all her school books somewhere."

"Joe, Steve and I just spotted it under the arch. Go take a look. You can see how even a few women are gonna fuck up what was once a perfectly nice campus, where men were men..."

Puissant could not resist,

"And the cows jumped at any sudden movement."

Joe now noticed two things. First these two guys each held a beer in their right hands. Second, in his left hand, Steve Puissant held a set of six plastic rings with four beers still hanging in place. Ron noticed Joe looking at the cans of Rolling Rock.

"Joe, the liquor store on the corner of Nassau Street and Witherspoon, the one next to the Porn Shop, was out of Iron City, so any port in a storm. You want one?"

Steve had already removed a beer can from its plastic collar and flipped it Joe's direction. Joe popped the beer can open, took an appropriately large, manly swallow, and headed to see Miss Bikini's bicycle. Sure enough, under the arch, leaning on its right side, the kick stand up, was a bicycle that met the description. Ron and Steve followed Joe back to the scene of the perceived sacrilege.

"Saturday night, Cannon Club is gonna throw a big unauthorized beer blast here in the middle of Pyne, welcoming the coeds with four or five kegs of beer..."

Ron lifted his head back to chug half a beer so Steve finished,

"We have a guy at the Club, 'No Neck' we call him. Nobody really remembers his last name. We are all pretty sure he was once a student here but who really knows. No Neck is old school. He will be the master of ceremonies Saturday. I can tell you this. He will not like that bicycle..."

Ron wiped some foam from his upper lip,

"Listen, why don't we share these remaining three beers on the way back across campus to Cannon? We're not supposed to have any kegs open yet, but, you know, boys will be boys."

"Ron, Steve, that sounds great. Is it o.k. to bring my roommate Joel along?"

Joe punctuated the question with a long gulp from the green can of beer.

Ron nodded, "Sure, the more the merrier."

Steve furrowed his brow but came to a quick solution,

"O.K. for sure but you two have to share one beer on the walk back."

TT. The Line Of Irrecoverable Separation Be Drawn

The next morning Joe woke up bilious swallowing one burp after another. The first sound he heard was from Frites in the top bunk. Joe had won the toss for the bottom bunk. From above came one long profuse beer fart. Joe was wobbly. He was more than a little bleary-eyed as he headed down two flights of stairs to the bathroom in the basement halfway between the first and second entries.

The bathroom had four sinks with mirrors, a large shower with six shower heads, and four toilet stalls with no doors. The hangover dizziness had subsided in the course of the long walk. A large guy, 6'3" tall and a muscular 260 lbs, stood shaving. He turned, the left half of his face still covered with shaving cream. His first words to Joe were simple and plenary,

"Do you smoke dope?"

This is how Joe met John Paul "Lemming" Cello. In a large sense all that would follow sprung forth from this one point in time.

UU. Greeks Baring Gifts

Stuck inside of Fraternity Row at TCU, Tommy did his best to remain positive. He could not help feel out of sorts. While Joe drank beer in the dank, mildew infested unfinished basement which Cannon Club members called, “the party room,” Tommy sat, more than a little uncomfortably, in the dining room at the Sigmund Albert Estragon fraternity house. He and all the other pledges were waiting. Five upperclassmen, all his new brothers, had headed somewhere into Fort Worth. Their mission was to bring back a “skank” or a “pig.” Whatever the right word, the girl cajoled, enticed, or kidnapped would soon be the center of the final rite of SAE initiation, the new pledge gangbang. At first Tommy thought this could not really be happening. He and his Freshmen fraternity brothers would not have to go through with it. Campus folklore must be exaggerated. Why a fat, ugly poor black or poor Mexican? Cruelty must have some limits. The whole idea was disgusting- guys cheering while you fucked a strange girl, her pussy dripping and sopping wet from the guys who preceded you. Then the part where all was said and done, the new pledges, still naked post-tumescent penises aflop, formed a circle. Each guy now used his right hand to wipe his prick clean. Hands were held to penises not quite long enough for a mass jerk off. The unwritten rules provided your cock had to return to attention. Each pledge had an SAE sponsor who then sniffed his pledge’s hand for “authenticity.” The final trifle of humiliation, each pledge put his hand up to the pledge to his right who sucked each finger and licked the palm clean. For the next two months, the guys whose cocks reacted as fingers were sucked would be reminded about their true inclinations.

The moment had arrived. The fat black chick was actually smiling. She was 5'2" tall, really a round bowling bowl. Through her one piece plantation style dress, right off the set of Porgy and Bess, seven rolls of fat were living easy. Her triple chin was her most attractive feature. Her thighs were three feet in circumference and her calves were not too much smaller. The girl made the Oprah Winfrey character from "The Color Purple" look sleek.

The new pledges walked up to the Fraternity President who was holding a fishbowl.

"Pick a number," he said to one pledge after another until the fishbowl no longer held even one folded piece of paper.

Tommy picked number thirteen.

"O.K. boys, show Louella what you've got. Remind me to tell the incoming President about an idea I have for next year's last rite, the new pledges should line up by the size of their pricks, should make it more fun for the girl if she gets it tiny tot to tree trunk size."

It seemed inexplicable. The girl was still smiling as she dropped her dress to the floor. She lowered panties the size of a six man tent to her ankles, turned around, bent over, and held the edge of the head table in the dining room. It turned out that part of the initiation dues had been given to her. Apparently, five hundred bucks was more than enough happy inducement to let a bunch of rich white college boys stick their pricks into her. She was sure she had been treated worse in her own neighborhood.

Being the guy that made a baker's dozen was bad, but not as bad as the guy who was number twenty-nine. Tommy walked up behind Louella. The rolls of fat in her thighs were scored with cellulite. Sweat rolled down her legs. Her pussy dripped whitish-yellow from sperm and vaginal discharge.

"Grab those ass cheeks, Tommy. Give Louella all you've got."

Tommy's prick went limp as he placed his hands on buttocks the size of basket balls.

VV. The Calamities of War

“Sorry, Tommy, you know the rules. You have to go to the end of the line. Try stroking that pathetic penis of yours. See if you can get to the size and hardness so that Louella will feel more than you are ringing her doorbell.”

Laughter cascaded all around Tommy as he turned to take his place behind the sixteen guys who had not yet conjoined in this perversion of camaraderie. Everyone was surprised he kept his head up as he walked to the end of the line.

“Well folks, we have had an unexpected break in the action. I hope we can pick up where we left off without any further lapses.”

Everyone, upperclassmen and pledges alike, again joined chorus in laughter. Tommy looked at the entire array around him. He did not feel an iota of shame for his lost erection, but rather guilt and sorrow for his willingness to be a part of this sordid group.

Just as the twenty-ninth brother, as that term is used in its lily white sense, did his worst. The President held up his hand,

“Tommy the officers have held an impromptu meeting. We will hold a special rite of passage just for you in one month. Until then you will be on probationary status, walking on very thin ice, not quite as thin as that droopy little thing suffering between your legs. I suspect that if you were not a National Champion A.A.U. swimmer, SAE would have no place for you. The officers will assign you special chores that only a plebe such as yourself will throw yourself into fully, with proper 'thank yous.' Come here, I have a toothbrush, start by scrubbing the floor under where Louella has been standing. I'll be back to make sure everything is ship shape."

Laughter again reigned supreme. The President did not know that this sort of rigorous cleaning was just another day's work for him back home as directed by his fastidious German mother, Wanda.

"Thank you Mr. President" was all Tommy said as he got on his hands and knees to clean the slimy mess his brothers had created.

WW. So Much Of The Infidel In Me

To the East, in New Jersey, “Lemming” Cello and Joe agreed to meet in half an hour to smoke a joint. Joe was sure that the American Medical Association would soon approve marijuana as the best cure for too much booze and for many other ailments.

Joe walked up to the second floor of the first entry of Little. He knocked on the door marked, ‘12.’ Cello’s roommate, a guy named, Daniel Ferraro opened the door. Since Princeton did not “recruit” both Ferraro and Cello had been admitted with only a sly wink from the head football coach, Jake McCandless. Dan and John shared a one-room double, really just a bunk bed and two desks. There was barely enough room for Cello’s stereo under the one window that looked out at the back of Laughlin Hall.

“Lemming” Cello was bent over the turntable,

“Hey Joe, come on in. Dan this is a guy I just met in the basement latrine. We are gonna get stoned.”

“John, I told you that I do not take marijuana and that it is against training.”

“Hey Dan, no worries, I decided I am not gonna go out for football. There will be more tokes for the two of us if you don’t want to partake.”

“Aren’t you worried the Football coaches will say that you are no longer an athlete here?”

“Right, after all that bullshit about no recruiting, do you think they can afford someone telling it like it is. One thing I learned from my dad who is CEO of Lovable Bra Company, if you are unconscious from an accident and your underwear ain’t dainty, you better watch out. Hey Joe, how does Led Zeppelin’s first album sound to you?”

“Don’t know it but right now, you are the songmeister.”

“Lemming” Cello dropped the tone arm on side one. He then grabbed a joint he already rolled from his shirt pocket and twisted both ends to be sure it was ready to be fired up. He handed it to Joe as he grabbed a butane disposable plastic lighter from the right front pocket of his Levis.

The words of “Your Time is Gonna Come” sprang from the speakers like an animal released from a cage,

“Lying cheating, that’s all you ever do…”

Page, Plant, Bonham, and Jones were in top form,

Joe inhaled, held the smoke in his lungs for about a minute into the song, then exhaled through his nose,

“Cello, this is great.”

“The dope or the music?”

“I meant the music but the dope ain’t bad either.”

Dan Ferraro opened the door, walked out, and slammed the door behind him.

Cello handed the joint back to Joe as he exhaled and raised his eyes into his head. Joe took the joint between his right thumb and forefinger, and as he raised it to his lips,

"Each to his own, and let the music play."

For more than three hours "Lemming" Cello and Joe got really stoned. Three joints were history as both sides of *Led Zeppelin I*, the self-titled Crosby, Stills, and Nash, Jeff Beck's *Truth* with vocals *extraordinaire* by Rod Stewart, Neil Young's *Everyone Knows This is Nowhere*, and the *piece de resistance,* Procol Harum's *A Salty Dog* spun freely. The dope favored crescendo would soon be circadian, reached whenever a deft hand dropped the tone arm in place. For Cello, Joe, and their many new friends, the song would remain the same. From yesterday to today, only the music would change as, over and over, they would find just the right note, spinning vinyl and more vinyl at high volume. Joe had come to Princeton without a single album. That would change.

XX. Look Up To Heaven For Help

Cello looked at Joe,

"Let's go see what the campus looks like. We can come back for more later, after the buzz wears off."

"A more perfect plan has never been devised. Wanna head over to Pyne Hall?"

"I am not sure those girls will meet our standards. Think about the girls in your high school that got the best grades."

As they headed out the door, Joe looked at John. He had not paid attention to his face before. Cello had jet black, thick hair, brown eyes that were bright and permanently mischievous, and a round even face with a winning smile. The dimple on his chin completed the picture. Here was the Italian Laurence Olivier standing next to him.

Joe was sure that if the campus ratio of women to men was not in the realm of the ridiculous, "Lemming" Cello would surely have his pick of the litter.

"Lemming" Cello continued as they headed down the stairs,

"Since we don't have any real chance since all the upperclassmen will soon be around, it doesn't matter that Princeton has admitted One Hundred girls, none of whom we would ask out if we were back home, legends in our own minds."

“Cello, think of it this way, there is good reason to complain- the food is bad and the portions are too small.”

As they walked out the first entry door, their surroundings captured them as time almost stopped. The mid-day light left no shadows, just bright and solid images. The large trees, the black lampposts guiding the geometry of the campus walkways, the movement of bustling, purposeful students on their way, and the looming presence of large dormitories all formed a mixture of impressions though definitely here and now, were part of some past time, in any decade spanning the last One Hundred years or so. The transcendent beauty would again and again strike a chord that crossed from all those thens to one abiding present.

“Hey let’s go towards Witherspoon rather than through the Dillon Arch.”

“We can take a look at Blair Tower with that huge clock, the arch where those Nassoons do all that *A capella* singing, and all those marble steps.”

“Is it marble?”

“O.K. some kind of fancy rock forming thirty odd wide steps up. Every other one belongs adorned with two or three sitting women, their knees up, their legs barely covered by their skirts, just waiting…”

“You wish.”

YY. Leave Them Unsupportedly To Perish

Cello and Joe made a left to pass the two stone Tigers who seemed to be smiling approval. Perched atop their two posts holding shields Joe imagined inscriptions, "All Ye Who Enter Are Lost" for one and "The Grass Is Always Greener" for the other. Joe wasn't sure which direction was in and which was out.

They entered the courtyard below Blair Hall. Cello pointed to the Princeton University Store, the "U-Store."

"Joe, let's go get some chocolate bars. They have Droste and Cadbury in there, lots of dark chocolate with good flavors, orange, hazelnut...Shit, my mouth is watering at my own suggestion."

The munchies had kicked in. The left turn towards Pyne was postponed in order to satisfy their taste buds.

The U-store was a book store that had everything. The candy was on the first floor near the books needed for the Religion and Philosophy courses. Food for the consciousness and for the taste buds. Upstairs was where the albums were sold. Alphabetically ordered bins held every kind of LP from classical to bubble gum. Rock and roll was the flavor of the month which would last well past the time they were expected to graduate. "Lemming" Cello and Cebellum did not make it to the second floor this trip. In a matter of days spurred by lacunas in the collections of "Lemming" Cello and his 22 Little roommates, Joe's first acquisitions in what would become a definitive 3500 title rock and roll collection were Moody Blues, *To Our Children's Children's Children*, B.B. King, *Alive and Well*, Ten Years After, *Sshhh*, Jethro Tull, *Stand Up*, and Buffalo Springfield, *Retrospective*.

Now, however, the reality was simply two kids in a candy store. Lingering over all that chocolate was its own pleasure. The classical approach-approach conflict led to gleeful indecision. The cannabis prolonged the experience, heightening all five senses. Finally, slowed synapses landed upon then claimed Cadbury Hazelnut light chocolate bars. Joe took one, Cello two. From the checkout counter to the outer doors, twenty feet at the most, only half of "Lemming" Cello's second candy bar was not yet part of confectionary history. If candy was this dandy, it was easy to conclude that other experiences would reach a monumental proportion, a landslide that would start with music and end with free love.

ZZ. Suppose That He Has Relinquished

Life was pure youth abloom. Cello and Joe walked out of the U-Store. Lockhart Hall, Foulke Hall, and Henry Hall flowed to their right. Henry was a sight to behold with its magnificent five story Tower and a fortress size turret on top. Laughlin Hall and 1901 Hall rambled on to their left. The wind whisked slightly through the leaves. The lead glass windows which dotted left and right captured the early afternoon light without really reflecting it. The colors were alive.

As they passed Henry Tower, a left turn led them to the Pyne Hall Arch, near were Joe, Ron, and Steve met the night before. At mid-day all the bicycles were somewhere else. Pyne Courtyard was empty. As they headed in their plan was to go left and down the stairs to complete a circle back to Little by going up the stairs through Dillon Arch. As they entered the courtyard, a guy popped out of the first entry door to their right. He was 6 feet tall, blonde, and wiry. When he noticed Joe and Cello to his left, he did a double take and then repeated his last stride while standing in place. His face was seriously pockmarked with acne but somehow not marred in the slightest. The guy was all grin and no gripe.

With that last move, feet forward and back while not going anywhere, Joe and "Lemming" Cello looked at each other and smiled settling on the same wavelength,

“Hi, I’m Joe Cebellum. This is my new stoned soul buddy, John Cello.”

Joe extended his hand.

“I’m Timothy Parsley Fief. Call me Tim or Fief, either one will do. Good to know you guys. Let’s make it a full-blown picnic. I’ve got some pretty good hash. Let’s go back to my room, first door on the left in the entry I just left. It’s a one room double. What am I blathering about? I am ripped. Just follow me. My, roommate Josh Relioport won’t be there not that it matters. I had a gram. He and I smoked half of it already. The other half will soon be ours.”

“Lemming” Cello smiled in way which would soon be a well-known trademark, like a Buddha crossing from serenity to contentment. He licked his lower lip to be sure no Cadbury chocolate was lurking,

“I’m there.”

Fief turned with military precision to his right. He then bobbed his head and arched his upper back and shoulders as he loped toward the door he had just left. The picture of a capricious camel was complete. Joe shook his head and laughed with him.

AAA. Cannot See On What Grounds

In the room Cello settled into one of the desk chairs, Joe perched on the bottom bunk, and Fief sat upright in front of his desk which held two KLH speakers, an AR turntable, and a small Heathkit amplifier. It was little but it had enough power to drive the speakers. Albert King's *Born Under a Bad Sign* was on the turntable.

While the stereo cranked pure blues, Fief reached into the top right desk drawer. He pulled out a hash pipe made of a copper tube with some plastic to protect the draw and a little silver colored metal cup at the other end to hold the hash. He next grabbed a Kodak film canister, opened it, and flopped a piece of hash onto his hand. It was that light green almost powdery kind, not really resinous. He clipped the piece in half with his thumbnail then put one half in the little silver bowl. Fief placed the other half back in the yellow canister before screwing the top back on. Cello had his lighter out of his pocket. He added blue-yellow flame to the hash. Fief took the first hit. He held his breath as he put his thumb to cover the tiny bowl.

Still holding his breath, he mouthed,

"I think it's still going."

Joe nodded, grabbed the middle of the stem of the little pipe and inhaled. As Joe held the strong fumes in his lungs, he covered the bowl. Joe handed the pipe to "Lemming" Cello. Just in time. Joe started coughing. The stuff was powdery but powerful.

Cello was undeterred. He lit the little lump then sucked from the end of the pipe. He smiled as he held the fumes in his lungs.

There was enough hash to complete one more hit for each of the three before it was played out.

“So where you guys from?”

Cello started since Joe was looking at the album cover for the Incredible String Band, *Wee Tam and the Big Huge* which had been left on the bed.

“I’m from Bergen County, Demarest, a little north of the Bridge, the George Washington Bridge for you Midwestern Boys,”

“Lemming” Cello looked at Joe,

“Right, I am from Barrington a town northwest of Chicago, about fifty miles, sort of the last commute, almost exurban more than suburban. And you Tim?”

“Scarsdale, Westchester County near the Tappan Zee Bridge”

Joe got up. He leafed through Fief’s record collection which was sitting in a six foot long, legal paper sized, stiff cardboard storage box, Rahsaan Roland Kirk, *Volunteered Slavery*, Sun Ra and His Solar Arkestra, *The Magic City*, Miles’ Davis *Nefertiti*, Buddy Guy *A Man and the Blues,* Albert Collins *Love Can Be Found Anywhere (Even in a Guitar)*, Otis Spann *The Biggest Thing Since Colossus*, all three Volumes of Vanguard’s, *Chicago/The Blues/Today!*, and James Brown *Say It Loud, I’m Black and I’m Proud Pt. 1.*

“You guys play basketball?”

Joe stopped flipping through the albums. He looked up,

“Sure.”

Cello shook his head no.

“Joe, How ‘bout you and I meet tomorrow morning to see if we can get into Dillon and shoot a few hoops?”

“I hear Dillon is closed.”

“I think I know a way to get in. I’ve got a basketball. I’ll meet you there at ten.”

“Cool.”

The three new friends listened to some more of Fief’s albums. Nary a pop selection cluttered the collection. One of the few rock and roll records in the corrugated baker’s box was the Grateful Dead, *Workingman’s Dead*. There was also some Dylan. After three and one-half hours of conversation, here and there, North Jersey this, Westchester county that, and Northern Illinois so far away, they headed up to Commons, the underclassmen dining hall.

BBB. Would Have Been Much Better

It was overcast and a little muggy, when ten o'clock rolled around the next morning. As planned, Joe met Fief outside Dillon Gym. They were about to head to the entrance near Patton Hall when a happy-go-lucky guy accosted them,

"You guys gonna shoot some hoops?"

They introduced each other. The third for basketball that morning was David Donald Tunney. Soon everyone was calling him, "DDT." He came to Princeton to play baseball. He threw a knuckleball and a slider. His own patience nearly always prevailed over eager hitters. DDT had the most amazing eye to hand coordination Joe had ever seen. Above his dexterity was his willingness to get together to do stuff, to have fun no matter what the time or place.

Fief, DDT, and Joe entered Dillon after Fief played a little trick with one of the outer doors. He pushed it in, pulled it up while pushing down on the door handle. "Eh, voila," the three were inside the gym.

The three trespassers were surprised. Three other guys had beat them onto the hardwoods that morning. Not just any three other guys. The new arrivals stopped dead in their tracks. Warming up with a full court three man weave were Bill Bradley, Dave DeBusschere, and Brian Taylor. Bradley was the most famous athlete ever to play sports at Princeton. He had written a book, *A Sense of Where You Are*. "Dollar Bill" took time in merry old England before playing in the NBA with the New York Knicks. Bradley was a Rhodes scholar. DeBusschere also had interests other than playing for the Knicks. He had been a major league baseball player, pitching for the Detroit Tigers. DDT hailed from St. Clair Shores, Michigan, part of the Detroit Metropolitan area, an exclusive suburb abutting the even more exclusive Grosse Pointe. DeBusschere was DDT's pitching idol. At first, they did not know the third guy. Then a light went on in Fief's head,

"That's our classmate, from Orange, New Jersey, first team All-state, Brian Taylor. The pro scouts are already looking at him. It is no surprise he is working out with Bradley and DeBusschere."

Joe marveled as the warm-up drill continued. He had never seen more precise passing than Bill Bradley's chest passes or more perfect footwork as Bradley cut behind the man to whom he had just given up the ball. It was also clear that Brian Taylor had pure natural talent. Joe saw Taylor carry a smile as he picked up Bradley's passion for minute detail. For the ten years that followed the Presidential election of Ronald Reagan, Joe would be persistent in predicting that the 2000 Presidential election will be Clint Eastwood v. Bill Bradley. Who would know that things would return to the Ivy elitism that made Nixon cringe? First a Harvard man Al Gore (who did have a Hollywood college roommate in Tommy Lee Jones) ran to lose against New Haven's George W. Bush. Then the same Bush beat the Yalie JFK, John Kerry, when Skull and Bones pitted two of its pride against one another in a race to see who would govern from sea to shining sea.

Bill Bradley noticed Fief, DDT, and Joe standing just off the court below the basket,

"Will you guys join in? Let's see you do some passing and cutting. We are going to take a short break."

Fief dribbled once, looked up from under the basket and then flipped a reverse lay-up off the glass and through the net. Joe grabbed the ball as it dropped. He took four dribbles from the basket to the free throw line extended, then hit a turn-around jump shot, nothing but net. Fief captured the ball to hit DDT at the opposite corner. DDT hit the center of the cylinder with a standing set shot.

DeBusschere and Taylor smiled. Bradley ran under the basket with the ball. He motioned to DDT to cut to the middle. Bradley then snapped a succinct pass right to DDT's navel, and cut behind him. Joe completed the trio for the drill. For six lengths, Bill Bradley maintained devotion to a drill most basketball players see only as mere tedium. Joe made a mental note that *joie de vivre* is everywhere, in any undertaking. Then Bradley, Taylor, and DeBusschere headed for the locker room but not before Brian Taylor reminded his Freshmen classmates that the Cane Spree basketball tryouts are that afternoon.

CCC. The Simple Object

Joe, DDT, and Fief stay on the floor. They shoot for awhile then play a few games of horse. Horse is a game where you take a shot. If you make it, the next guy must make the exact same shot or he gets a letter. Five letters, H-O-R-S-E then you are out of the game. You get two tries to stay in on the last letter. DDT displayed an amazing repertoire of trick shots. It was just a matter of time. First Fief, then Joe are out. DDT wins all five games. Basketball involves shooting skill but also requires the ability to get open, both to receive a pass and to free yourself to take a decent shot. In addition to being the slowest guy on his high school Varsity team, Joe was the worst pure shooter. Nevertheless he worked hard with the ball and away from the ball to lead the conference in scoring. Joe was thinking that Joel, Tim, DDT, Barry, and he would be an excellent core to a very good Freshmen intramural team.

DDD. Our First Object Was To Secure

On the way out of Dillon Gym, DDT moved the discussion to another important part in the rich fabric that is tradition at Princeton, "The Clapper,"

"For the Freshman class to take the first step to success at Princeton, it is necessary to silence 'The Clapper.' If the bell atop Nassau Hall does not ring next Monday, classes cannot start. This nice trod on the road of wishful thinking has led to an hoary mandate. Steal the clapper…"

In an uncharacteristic homage to the current musical landscape, Fief popped in,

"Wishful, Sinful."

"How 'bout we get together right after dark tonight to try to figure our way into the bell tower to purloin that dangling augury?"

Fief smiled, twisting both corners of an imaginary villain's moustache,

"I am always game for petty larceny."

Joe pipes in,

"Yea, I heard about this bit of tomfoolery. My friends at Cannon Club say the bell is now electric. I'll try to get this guy I met the other day, Barry Richardson, to join us. After all, it's the thought that counts. See you guys on the Cannon Green side of Nassau Hall at the filching hour."

EEE. As Much Baggage As The Wagons Could Contain

Lunch at Commons was the usual meal of high starch, limp vegetables, and meat of unknown origin. The mess hall for underclassmen resembled the Great Hall where Errol Flynn's Robin Hood confronts Claude Rain's Prince John near the beginning of *The Adventures of Robin Hood*. The dignity of the surroundings did nothing to improve the cafeteria quality of the food. Bad food was no reason not to eat three platefuls.

Joe headed back to his room to kill the time before Cane Spree tryouts started. Mel Rothstein was there. Cebellum, Frites, and Hoyle would later find it strange that Rothstein never went to Commons for a meal, not even once. Stranger still, as the first semester progressed, Mel was gaining weight. Strangest of all, Mel was never in the shower but he was always clean. The only record album Rothstein brought from Kansas was the four sided, *Diana Ross and the Supremes Greatest Hits*. As Joe entered 22 Little, "You Can't Hurry Love" was issuing sweet, rhythmic admonition. Mel was in front of the turntable. He caught himself in time to stop dancing as Joe broke the threshold.

"Hey, Joe Good luck with the Cane Spree tryouts."

"Thanks, Mel. The Supremes can really weave some soulful happy songs."

"My girlfriend, Shelley, and I wiled away the hours listening to this record. I can't wait until she comes to visit this November."

"I'll be glad to meet her."

Mel had a photo of Shelley, on the top of his bureau right next to his portable t.v. The girl in the photo was beautiful by any standards complete with bedroom eyes that would stir any man to the depth of his pith or any other applicable body part. Joe, Joel, and Ronny agreed that Mel must have some secret, not apparent to anyone, to be able to call Shelley his girlfriend. It turned out that the secret was the boudoir photographer. If there was a Pulitzer Prize for transforming reality to fantasy, the guy who took Shelley's picture would win it.

FFF. March Them On Till They Could Be Strengthened

As Joe headed over to Dillon for the tryouts, he thought to himself, “Mel has to be the only guy I know who owns a *Supremes* record.”

Princeton’s Freshmen basketball coach, Art Hyland, presided over the tryouts. Hyland had played with Bill Bradley. He parlayed his position on that storied team to be hired by Pete Carril, the man who succeeded legendary coach Butch van Breda Kolff. Van Breda Kolff coached the Bill Bradley team to the final four. They lost to the eventual National champions, Michigan with Cazzie Russell, one of the best players in the history of Chicago inner city basketball. Van Breda Kolff is one of four men to coach a final four team and an NBA final team, the Lakers in 1968 and 1969. Carril would become a legend of his own by playing a methodical slowdown style of basketball that ran contrary to the beauty, flow, and meter of the game played everywhere else in the country. The “disciplined” style was so unique that the better teams Princeton played outside the Ivies did not spend much time trying to unravel its intricacies or break it down in order to win the one game a year they would play against Princeton. That is until the NCAA playoffs, when more time for scouting and focused practices was available and necessary. The Ivy League schools knew the Princeton style but Princeton’s players were better. The Bradley legacy left its mark. Many bright basketball players who could attend other Ivy League schools were earmarked and picked, although not recruited, to come play in Dillon Gym. As a result, Princeton usually contended for the Ivy crown and the anachronistic NCAA playoff berth which goes with it.

One example of a player guided to Princeton was a Senior when Joe was a Freshman, Geoff Petrie. Petrie and his teammate, John Hummer were both All-Ivy. Petrie had the best pure jump shot Joe had ever seen. He could shoot falling off to either direction, even it seemed as he was heading upside down straight to the floor. Bill Bradley's style fell in the category of standing set shot when compared to Petrie. Even an artist like Lynn Shackelford who fired from the corner on the John Wooden coached Alcindor/Jabbar UCLA teams had to admire Petrie's studied and practiced artistry. Petrie played in the NBA with Portland where he was rookie of the year. After he retired, he was a natural for the front office. Until June, 2013, he was President of Basketball Operations for the Sacramento Kings.

Hyland was cut of different cloth, a journeyman with no real talent, just lucky to be in the right place at the right time with no better player to take his place on the floor. Cane Spree tryouts started with Joe guarding Brian Taylor. Joe noticed that Taylor liked a spin move to his left, the defender's right. He also noticed that the dribble prior to the spin move made a nearly forty-five degree angle with the floor rather than one almost perpendicular. The third time down the floor, Joe recognized the change in dribble angle. Like an arrow, Joe stretched his right hand to meet the ball just prior to the point it hit the floor. His flicked the ball back towards his own basket with the only contact his hand and the ball. Joe had a breakaway since Taylor had started his spin move towards his own basket. Hyland blew his whistle, calling a foul on Joe. Joe kept dribbling. He sank an unmolested lay-up. Hyland's whistle reached staccato pitch. Joe cradled the ball as it fell through the net. He placed it carefully on the hardwood underneath the basket. Hyland was now at half court, his face red from blowing the whistle. It was not clear whether he was out of breath or embarrassed by Joe's crass insubordination. Joe took three steps to the free throw line,

"If I were Brian Taylor, I would be insulted knowing a so-so like you feels the need to protect your star player in such an egregious fashion."

Joe then turned away from Cane Spree group, and walked out the front of Dillon. Hyland was again blowing his whistle. Later, Brian Taylor told Joe it was a clean steal. One of the nice things about playing basketball without referees is that the game is much cleaner. The players know if there is a foul. There is a true sense of honor in the game of street ball. Ethics of a much higher order prevail when players play one another. Princeton has long prided itself on its "Gentleman's Honor Code." Suffice to say, that while exams are not proctored and signing a blue book or a paper is an affirmation of integrity, there have been occasions where a Princeton Gentleman treated the Princeton Honor Code as operating in a milieu with referees rather than one where the participants, fully aware of all conditions, call their own fouls.

GGG. Enabled To Make A Stand

It was just after dark Friday night, Joe and Joel waited at the center of Cannon Green near the cannon heavy with years of painted coats of black shellac. This relic was half-submerged, muzzle first. Fief arrived a few minutes after they did.

As Timothy Parsley Fief's approach was near, Joe spoke,

"Hey, Fief. I want you two guys to meet. This is my roommate Joel Frites. Joel this is a Tim Fief. Joel and I stopped by Cannon Club the other night. We drank of few beers with a guy I know from back home and some of his Cannon buddies. As you walk up to the Club, halfway down the sidewalk...

Joe pointed to the cannon,

"...they have one of these same black lacquered Revolutionary War cannons, only that one is on its proper station, or whatever you would call it. Anyway, the long held lore of Cannon Club is that their cannon will go off if a virgin ever walks out of the Club."

"Right, and if you eat the right wafer and drink the right wine, you will spend eternity in paradise. Let me tell you some stuff that is true. My Junior year at Scarsdale High, my dad and mom drove me down here to see the campus. My dad is an alum, a lot of family on both sides actually, so I had been here to Palmer Stadium for lots of tailgate parties and football games. But I had never taken the Key Club guided tour which goes into the history. Nassau Hall was held by the Colonials during the Revolutionary War, at the Battle of Princeton. The British fired on it. So did George Washington. Both sides struck the walls with their cannonballs. Tomorrow in the daylight, I'll show you. You can still see some of the marks from almost two hundred years ago. The Redcoats then took over the building as their headquarters. You know the place where Washington crossed the Delaware is not too far from here, just up the river from Trenton. Nassau Hall is most famous as the site of the Second Constitutional Convention. In 1783, Princeton graduated fourteen of the landed gentry's best and brightest. George Washington attended along with a remarkable number of those who signed the Declaration of Independence and who would sign the Constitution, just 'cause they were in the neighborhood. Reminds me of some recent rock lyrics I'd like to mix together, 'Their walls are built of *cannonballs*, their motto is 'don't tread on me.'' 'But the answer my friend is blowin' in the wind,' the answer is that 'the waters are rising and you'll sink like a stone…'"

The three now waited for Barry Richardson and DDT who were both coming from Witherspoon Hall, 'Spoon as it was called, a Freshmen dorm they could see from where they stood. There were two other Freshmen dorms, Dodd, eclipsed by Whig and Clio, and Brown, set back further behind the Art Museum. This clear, warm August night was a long way off from the foggy, damp nights of the New Jersey winter. For too many years to count, the first semester wore on to propagate revelry and chicanery known with affection as the "Brown-Dodd Riots."

HHH. The Rest Was Lost

Barry Richardson's thick Maine accent was the next thing heard,

"Let's get the clapper theft going. I've got to get back to my room. I promised to call my girlfriend, Celeste. Do any of you nit wits have a plan?"

"We should wait for DDT. Barry, first things first, go make your call, wack off, and we'll be happy to wait. Just wash your hands. We don't want the clapper desecrated with the stick of your jism."

"Ah, a man who has been there and done that. Joe, what's your girlfriend's name?"

"Sarah"

Fief and Frites laughed. Barry continued,

"I appreciate your genuine, heartfelt concern but I have time now. I am not calling until ten."

Barry looked at Fief,

"By the way I know Joe and Joel. I'm Barry and you?"

Joel jumped in,

"I just met Tim, too. A good guy from Scarsdale. Timothy Parsley Fief meet Barry Richardson, the pride of Maine as in so goes the country, or in this case, there goes the neighborhood. Richardson meet Fief."

Joe responded to the question of nit wits with a plan.

“It looks like DDT has been lost on his way to the purloinery. If it were not Princeton, I would say he was ‘waylaid’ but…”

Fief was Johnny on the spot,

“A certain statistical sufficiency of necessary counterparts is lacking for the latter.”

Everybody laughed. They did not yet realize the situation was not the proper subject for levity.

“…I noticed there is a door that Fief is fully capable of jimmying on the side of the building near the student center. Let’s go in the easy way up the stairs all the way to the bell tower.”

Barry looked serious,

“And we are standing here now with our thumbs up our asses, why?”

The four incipient culprits turned to their right. Fief played the same trick he did with the Dillon door earlier in the day. It was dark. None of the nit wits brought a flashlight. Small ancient steps up cramped dark passages led only to a couple stubbed toes, three banged knees, and four bumped heads. Joel hit his head squarely in his right eye on a low corner he did not expect. The four climbed to the entrance to the bell tower. There they were stymied. The trapdoor to the bell tower had a deadbolt. To make matters worse, Nassau Hall had a silent alarm system. Two uniformed proctors, who did have flash lights came quickly up the stairs. One was a middle aged white guy. The other, a young, round genial black guy spoke first,

"O.K. gentlemen. I think the best route from here is back down the stairs and out the front door, the place where you will get your diplomas, assuming you get smarter in the next four years."

Now the white guy shined his flashlight in each of their faces,

"Nice shiner" was all he said as he noticed the swelling around Frite's eye.

III. Marched Out Twice To Meet The Enemy

Nassau Hall stood large. Fief looked at Joel. Joel, with a squint in one eye, looked at Barry. Barry looked at Joe.

"Do we have Plan B?"

"Barry of little faith. I noticed the army of Italian gardeners that tends the grounds keeps an equipment shed at the far South end of campus near the student parking lot. I also noticed those guys have a long extension ladder."

Barry looked up,

"Joe, it looks to me like the overhang to the roof of Nassau Hall is about three stories up..."

Fief added, "Copping a ladder from the Princeton Fire Department might be better."

Joel said his piece,

"Or one of their fire trucks."

Joe regained the floor,

"Nope I have seen the ladders, aluminum with two inner extensions. Fief, come with me. We can get in to the maintenance area to borrow a ladder. Barry, go make your call. Joel, you guys meet us back here in one-half hour in case those two proctors make a quick loop back. And tell Celeste, I love her."

“Wait ‘til you meet her to tell her yourself.”

Joel volunteered, “I better go with you guys. Getting the ladder over the fence might require a third guy.”

Joe was right. There was a large ladder lying on the ground outside the shed. Joel was right, too. Three guys were needed to liberate the ladder. Fief, Frites, and Cebellum used serpentine stealth on their clandestine mission back to Nassau Hall. Shadows and bushes covered their tracks. Barry was right on time.

“I called but Celeste wasn’t in her room. Let’s get this show on the road.”

The very top of the third extension barely made it to the rain gutter at the edge of the overhang.

Joe pushed the ladder against the edge. It wobbled.

Joel looked up through his good eye. His right one had swollen shut. He was quick to volunteer for the work on the ground,

“I’ll hold the base of the ladder.”

Barry said, “I’ll go up.”

Joe hugged Barry, “What’s Celeste’s number so I can call her to tell her where to send the flowers.”

Fief said, “Don’t worry Barry, Joel, and I will hold the ladder, lest Joe’s vested interest in the girl from Maine he has never met gets in the way.”

JJJ. Trusted Our Cause To The Temporary

Somehow Barry made it up to the top of the roof. He carefully crept on all fours up the roof's incline. He shimmied up the base of the bell tower. Barry then disappeared into the tower. After grabbing an edge with one hand, he lifted one leg to catch the flat border top. Barry then pulled himself all the way up, over, and in.

Joel, Fief, and Joe stood gleefully on the ground. Their ear to ear smiles came to a quick halt. The two proctors were back.

The white proctor was serious, "Which one of you three geniuses was going to plummet to certain injury going up this ladder? It is barely long enough and surely not sturdy enough."

The ladder made unsteady arcs as the proctors rolled both extensions back down. Before carrying the ladder back to the proctor's station on campus, the black proctor grinned,

"Fun for the night is over. I suggest you guys go back and see if it's not too late to sign up for remedial Physics. You missed that day in high school when they went over Newton and that falling apple."

Joel, Tim, and Joe bowed their heads. They turned tail towards Little Hall taking the path between Clio and 'Spoon. DDT rushed towards them,

"Sorry guys. I called my girlfriend, actually my fiancé, Peggy Sue. The phone call lasted a long time."

"Don I want you to meet Joel. Joel Frites please meet David Donald Tunney. But we have an immediate problem. Richardson is stuck on the roof of Nassau Hall. The proctors have taken our ladder."

"Where the fuck did you guys get a ladder?"

Fief put both palms up. He lifted his head a little while raising his eyebrows,

"There will be time to give you the straight skivvy later. The proctors do not know you are one of us. Will you go down the steps into the proctor's office to create a diversion, like tell them somebody stole one of your goldfish for tomorrow's swallowing contest..."

"Funny."

"...and ask to fill out a report, while we take back our ladder to get Barry."

DDT created just the right diversion or the proctors didn't care. At the top of the stairs that led to the proctor's command center, there was an old iron fence with the same black lacquer as the cannons on the green and in front of Cannon Club. The proctors had handcuffed the ladder to the fence.

The good news was that Barry got the clapper. The bad news was that he had to wait until morning to escape. The bell tower trapdoor could be opened from above. When Barry heard people enter Nassau Hall, he knew the alarm was off. He left the bell tower. Then Barry snuck to the first floor undiscovered. Once there, he just rolled up a window, leaped down, and returned to his room at 'Spoon. Notwithstanding Barry's protestations of true love and fidelity, Celeste was not happy. Barry's mettle aside, she might have been given greater comfort had she been known that there were really no females on campus. At least the clapper belonged to the Class of 1973.

KKK. In The World For A Sudden Exertion

No matter how much faith Sam had in the unexpected, he would soon be surprised more than anybody. His Saturday night was about to receive five stars from any reviewer. There was no doubt that OU was a party school. Party school or not, Sam's luck was about to change. The name of the girl with her own copy of the Kama Sutra was Abha Vasudha. Abha asked Sam to meet her at her apartment Saturday evening. Sam knew something would happen to interfere. Sam's best laid plans always suffered some fly in the ointment, some sand in the Vaseline, or worse. Abha answered the door. She was wearing a purple flowing skirt with a gold pattern, this time some kind of large birds, probably geese. Her blouse was pure white with wide cuffs, two petite rounded scoops for a collar, and little pearl buttons. Abha was one smile,

"Sam, I am so pleased that you are here."

Sam put both hands on her shoulders. He looked directly in her eyes. For him, this way of connection was a parlor trick he had picked up reading the Playboy Advisor.

"Abha, you are beautiful, even more so as I gaze through your eyes gleaning just a glimpse of the depth of your *elan vital*."

"Sam, you are sweet, something trite out of Thomas Hardy, but sweet. I think our night will unfold so that we both find many things about one another and ourselves."

Sam scanned Abha's small studio apartment. The little kitchenette held a sink, a small stove, and a tiny refrigerator in the far left corner. A rice cooker sat on the counter to the left of the. On the right wall, Abha had hung a large Indian cotton print. It was cobalt blue with squares of yellow. Within each square, diamonds turned smaller and smaller, each more and more faint yellow as the points of each diamond bisected the lines of each outer square. On the wall across from the cloth with the nightfall of diamonds was a Brocade piece from Burma. The hanging dangled with sequins, plastic pearls of all sizes, opaque white plastic gems, all intricately stitched. It had twelve squares one for each of the signs of the Zodiac. The little kitchen table to the right approached the kitchenette. There was incense smoke pluming gently from a small blue and white ceramic bowl on the table. To Sam's immediate right was a 1950's style phonograph. Sam expected to see a forty-five with one of those orange or yellow adapters to meet the 33 spindle in its center. Instead, the album playing was Ravi Shankar. To the left of the stereo, underneath the descending diamonds were two deep covered cushions, red almost burgundy. Sam could see a fold where the two cushions connected down their center.

Abha noticed Sam eyeing the horizontal, "That's my futon. It is dual purpose, perhaps even multi- purpose."

Abha caught Sam's eyes. He averted her gaze. He was a little embarrassed at the boldness of her suggestion.

"I have never seen one before."

"It folds up to the perpendicular, if you wish to sit."

Sam gathered his courage to return Abha's gaze, "I like the way you have it now."

Abha took Sam's right hand in her left hand. She led him to the futon bed.

As they reached the side of the double-wide cushion, Abha unbuckled Sam's belt, undid his pants button, and lowered his zipper. She was then gentle, but with purpose. Abha lowered Sam's pants. He stepped out of his shoes. He was not wearing socks. Abha then stood close to Sam. She started kissing him, stretching up on her tip toes. Abha made sure her body made full contact with Sam's crotch as she first unbuttoned then removed his shirt. She unbuttoned and removed her blouse. Abha then unzipped her skirt before stepping out it. She was not wearing a bra. The two kissed, standing up. Abha was reduced to her panties, Sam only his white cotton Jockey shorts. Sam could not believe how aroused he was, almost as if he were alive for the first time. Sam was not sure whether it was Abha's broad, moist lips meeting his, whether it was her tongue on his lips then into his mouth, whether it was her breasts and nipples on his abdomen, or whether it was her leg and hip as she moved turning into his crotch using his penis for a fulcrum in some ancient carnal dance of the spirits.

Abha pointed to the little bookcase between the futon and the kitchenette. The Kama Sutra was on top.

"Why don't you open it to a random page?"

Sam got the book, opened it. By the time he turned around, Abha had removed her pink satin bikini panties. She gathered herself on the futon. Her legs were spread slightly in no small invitation. The first two fingers of her right hand were centered between her labia. Thick, black pubic hair covered the area above her hand.

"I wanted to see how wet I really am. But, tell me what you think. Get rid of your underwear and join me."

Sam needed no further prompt. His underwear hit the floor in less than a second. His unbundled prick sprang instantaneously to a full ninety degree position. Sam rested on his side next to Abha. With the first two fingers on his right hand he touched her pussy lips. Sam then pushed both fingers inside her. Abha made a tiny gasp as his first then second knuckles entered her but then she smiled. She was sopping.

Abha took the book from Sam's left hand.

"Let's see how many of these we can do."

Abha arched her back. She opened her legs wide. Sam's fingers were soon third knuckle flush inside her.

All that followed from Abha's tender touch, warm kisses, and open embraces was a night which Sam should remember, cherish, and hold within his spirit as more than a fond memory, even to his old age. Sam, however, had a tendency, a dull proclivity, to be mired in his perverse capacity to focus on what he did not have and what he thought he should have had. He thereby created his own scratchy surfaces from even the most silky and gossamer. He met rough sailing in even the most sublime, smooth waters. At first, Sam's unsteady inability to attain equilibrium affected even the moment. Abha, however, was too pure in her own full gratitude and in the gracious gift of herself. She made those vibrant hours electric. That night she was able to transform the dull clay of Sam's being to make him one with her joy. At the very least, Sam was learning to communicate, to actually touch another, perhaps not deep down to the marrow. Sam was also learning to express himself, not just from reading Playboy magazine, but from the drawings in the Kama Sutra. This alone might hold him in great stead.

LLL. Will Not Do For A Long Campaign

For Fred, it was the night before. Friday night in the Sleepy Little Village was the one night in the week that the bank was open late. Fred stood in line to cash his pay check. He was not sure what he would do that evening. Saturday, for her one night out, Fred was taking Martha to the movies. The iconic *Easy Rider* was at the Drive-In with the soon to be forgotten, *Thank You All Very Much* with Sandy Dennis. Fred was "underage." A bar in Fox River Grove, Helen and Wally's, was gracious in allowing Fred to drink. More and more, Fred spent his work nights and free weekend time sitting with those friendly folk, where everyone knew your name. That particular Friday night, however, Fred thought he might go bowling at The Ten Pin. He could stop in the bar, just to say hello to his dad, Red, who ruled the roost there.

Fred did not notice the young woman who walked into the bank behind him. She was short, about 5'4" tall. Her eyes were green, her hair tawny brown, and her skin porcelain. She formed true Irish beauty. Her rounded, but pronounced hips flowed from her tiny waist and swayed subtly from side to side. She was careful to keep her shoulders pulled back, her head up. This was the best way to emphasize her average to small sized breasts. Her slightly suggestive motion behind Fred did not capture his attention.

The line moved up. Fred would be the next one to the teller. Tiffany Wallett decided she better not rely upon the small signals of sexual energy she was sending. She tapped Fred's right shoulder from behind. As Fred turned around Tiffany took a small step toward him with her right foot at the same time increasing the space between her legs. She was still wearing her school clothes, a pink lambswool cardigan sweater and a knee-length blue corduroy skirt that hung straight down from hips that were clearly her best feature.

Tiffany was careful to innocently brush the edge of her right hand along Fred's arm as she lowered it from his shoulder,

"Fred, Hi."

"Hey, It's Tiffany right, Sear's little sister."

"I am not so little anymore. I have started Freshmen year in high school."

"Not little at all, and I would have guessed a junior or senior by looking at you if I did not know your age."

Tiffany licked her lower lip lightly with the tip of her tongue. She rolled her right hip towards Fred,

"You know I always wanted to get to know you better. Sears and my parents are away for the weekend. They are going to look at Bradley University. Sears is thinking he will apply there. Would you like to come back to my house with me? There's lots of cold beer there."

"You cross 59 right after it turns away from Barrington Road at Dundee Avenue then keep going. It's a big house on the left, right?"

"Would you drive me? I walked to the bank. I hung around Cancer Corner after school then went with some friends to listen to the new Blind Faith album. I came to the bank to get money. I want to buy it. Maybe we can go pop out of the bank to the right. The record store could not be closer..."

Tiffany moved closer. Fred could almost feel her breathing.

"...I wasn't looking forward to the long walk home. I hope you will be my knight in shining armor. When we get to my house, we can listen to this very cool LP, especially the long and lingering song, 'Do What You Like' with the Ginger Baker drum solo. I won't mind if you add a little mimic of your own."

Tiffany now put her left hand on Fred's left hip.

One of the most beautiful women in town was the head teller, Melody Dunsinane. Fred and Tiffany were in her line. Friday was always a long day. She was now waiting. Since her lover was one of Fred's many cousins, she feigned patience. But Melody, too, had places to go.

"Next please."

MMM. Give Him Encouragement To Come

Tommy Wanderby was surprised he no longer felt at home in Texas. It was not just that he had new friends, really good friends, in Fred, Sam, Joe, and Tim Camphor. He felt stifled, almost choked back in his old home state. It wasn't just the hazing from his fraternity brothers. It wasn't just that he was a student on a campus for the self righteous that had been born when the Disciples of Christ decided their Savior was the right savior. It wasn't just that every day he walked by the library he was reminded of the story of Mary Couts Burnett, and her three million dollar bequest. She was the widow of Texas rancher, Samuel Burk Burnett. Burnett made one fortune on the hoof in Texas, then another with his partner, Quanah Parker, when Burnett's buddy, Teddy Roosevelt "facilitated" the lease of Comanche and Kiowa land in Oklahoma for even more cattle grazing. It was not just TCU and the library, but the entire state of Texas was tainted, tainted in too many ways to list. Mary Couts Burnett threatened to divorce her husband when she tired of Samuel Burnett's relationship with his granddaughter, Ann Burnett Tandy, whose fourth husband was the entrepreneur, Charles David Tandy, the man who turned Radio Shack into a successful chain. For first response to threat of divorce, Samuel Burk Burnett threatened to kill Mary Couts. She started telling all her friends of the threats. Burnett took the next logical Lone Star step. He had his lawfully wedded wife legally committed to a private insane asylum. On the day he died, she broke out and soon had the insanity finding reversed. It took a little longer to successfully contest Burnett's will which provided that Ann Burnett Tandy was the sole beneficiary. The courts granted Mary Couts Burnett her spousal share, one-half. In 1922, Texas Christian University received all but $12,000 of her estate. From those funds, the library was built and named after her. For Tommy, the straw that broke the camel's back, the thing about Texas that became the most tiresome was that everyone who was anyone was called by three names.

To take a deep, free breath was all he wanted. He needed to walk steps of his own, away from all that stultifying institutional madness. It was more than an itch that needed to be scratched. For Tommy, to be free was not a matter of selfishness, but more a matter of doing the right thing no matter the consequences, no matter what the consensus opinion would dictate. There was a young woman who sat next to Tommy in the orientation meeting for the English Class, *Introduction to Prose and Poetry*. With four thousand other kids, the two sat in a large lecture hall. Her name was Abby. Abby dropped her pencil, and again. Twice Tommy leaned into Abby to retrieve her pencil from the floor and return it to her. For the third nuzzle, the pencil was unnecessary. As they walked out of class, Abby turned to Tommy,

"This weekend, at the Dallas International Motor Speedway, they are having the first follow up to Woodstock. I am sure there will be many more, well into the next millennium."

"Tell me more, Abby."

"It is called the Texas International Pop Festival, three days of really good music."

Abby pulled the promotional brochure out of her tan leather shoulder bag,

"Listen to this-

Saturday, August 30

1. Canned Heat
2. Chicago Transit Authority
3. James Cotton Blues Band
4. Janis Joplin
5. B.B. King
6. Herbie Mann
7. Rotary Connection
8. Sam & Dave

Sunday, August 31

1. Chicago Transit Authority
2. James Cotton Blues Band
3. Delaney & Bonnie & Friends
4. Incredible String Band
5. B.B. King
6. Led Zeppelin
7. Herbie Mann
8. Sam & Dave
9. Santana

Monday, September 1

1. Johnny Winter
2. Delaney & Bonnie & Friends
3. B.B. King
4. Nazz
5. Sly and the Family Stone
6. Spirit
7. Sweetwater
8. Ten Years After
9. Tony Joe White

The bands are better than Woodstock."

"If you don't count The Who, Jefferson Airplane, The Grateful Dead, Jimi Hendrix, and a few others."

"Well can we say, as good? Some of the ones that will be here that were not there, especially, the blues bands are better than Sha Na Na and John Sebastian. Don't mess with Texas."

"I'm sold. Let's go."

Abby and Tommy camped in a tent on the grounds near Lewisville Lake. They both joined in the free spirited skinny dipping. Not on the schedule, Grand Funk opened at 4 p.m. each of the three days. B.B. King also played all three days, with the exact same stories, jokes, and other patter. That the same 150,000 people were there for all his shows did not seem to affect his choice of stage banter. Led Zeppelin was introduced as "The Led Zeppelin," prescient and fitting. Led Zeppelin played with fire and force. They transcended both blues and rock and roll. Their legacy was now riding high in the saddle. Heavy Metal was here to stay.

Tommy was amused by the Merry Pranksters' Bus, "Further," and the weird people that ambled in and out. He admired the help they gave kids freaking out on acid at the "trip tent." This was the first time Kesey's number two man, Hugh Romney was dubbed, "Wavy Gravy." Tommy and Abby did not take any L.S.D. Most of the people who did spouted consciousness raising pap which Tommy did not really understand. As far as he was concerned, where he stood was the best place he could be. His own brain and his own two feet would take him where he wanted to go. Abby was more than happy to go with him.

Abby Diane Host was her full name. She was a blonde beauty with the body of Greek Goddess. It was not the cold water that gave Tommy goose bumps when Abby pulled her light blue cotton dress over head. She followed him into the water, stepping out of lace pink bikini panties. She had blue eyes. The water was fine but Tommy wanted to swim in Abby's azure pools of kindness. Porcelain cheek bones, a slender nose that came to a point above her sweet lips, and her soft symmetrical chin completed a picture of allure. Abby's body would not quit. Strong shoulders gave way to round firm, very white breasts with pink areola the size of half dollars. Abby's nipples stood out the instant her toes touched the water. She was in the water before Tommy really got to see below her belly button.

Saturday night after the music, with Santana's "Soul Sacrifice" still ringing in their ears, Tommy got to know Abby's slender hips and her long legs. With knees bent she beckoned him from her back. Her blonde pussy captured his attention. Pink labia matched the center of her breasts. Apparently rock and roll was the work of the devil, or some special angel, take your pick. Abby was wet. Tommy slid inside her like he belonged there.

"Tommy, I knew you would feel really good."

Tommy lifted himself up using only his knees. His thumb and index fingers lightly squeezed Abby's nipples. Their two mouths tried to devour one another as Tommy slowly lifted his penis out of Abby's pussy. He then slowly used its tip and first inch to barely enter and to leave her. In about two minutes, Abby grabbed Tommy with both hands behind his neck.

"I want all of you, all the way inside of me."

Abby lifted her mouth to Tommy's right ear. She whispered,

"Take another piece of my heart now baby,"

Janis Joplin had sounded great earlier that night but Abby's performance was forthright and historically informed. Just like B.B. King, Tommy and Abby reprised their own *verbatim* tryst every night after the last band played, well into the early morning as the sun rose over the lake. Nobody was up early. With more than words of love, soft and tender, Tommy was able to get Abby where she wanted to go.

Tommy and Abby both felt liberated as they bonded. Tommy did not know it yet but what ailed him was not just Texas. History, even rock and roll history, has now long forgotten those three days in Dallas. Far away in New York, the first ATM hit the street on Tuesday, September 2, 1969. That day in history is also long forgotten but it has a much more significant aftermath. It is a telling comment about all that America holds dear, all that is now held in the special death grip of a society gone wrong, that technology triumphed, in spades, over the essence of youth. 1969 was also the year the academic community got together to form a network of large mainframe computers to enable easy sharing of data, monographs, and other intellectual output. Those internet pioneers would undoubtedly be distressed to see how the information highway has been strewn with debris with commercial billboards placed to monitor traffic and to collect their toll. It seems reasonable to argue that all hope for a culture that thrives on love, peace, and happiness has been dashed. The realistic and the cynical are not surprised. Freedom's just another word for nothing left to lose, more chimera than even Jimi Hendrix and his castles made of sand.

NNN. Appropriate Their Possessions

Good jokes travel quickly, bad ones faster yet. The word on the Princeton campus was that those first coeds had all been christened, "Sue Pyne." To be sure, it was a clever quip. From the women's dorm, Pyne Hall, to 'supine,' the horizontal position many men fantasize all women should find when not barefoot in the kitchen, chained to the stove. At the same time Tommy and Abby were spellbound by James Cotton as he closed his set with the classic, "Rocket 88," Joe decided to get "Lemming" Cello so he could meet Ron Streeter, Steve Puissant, and the other Cannon Club guys assembled around their keg of beer in Pyne Hall Courtyard. When Cello and Joe arrived, they saw twelve guys wearing white canvas jackets standing around three kegs.

"Joe, I have heard about Princeton beer jackets. Now we see them."

In 1912, some Princeton Gentlemen hosted a few mugs of beer in a restaurant on Nassau Street. Even the most well-bred cannot avoid the occasional slobber or spill. Inadvertent jostles can also have an ill effect on items procured at the best Madison Avenue haberdashers. Then, there is that occasional overly exuberant pat on the back that will cause beer to go back up out the mouth, or worse, up and out the nose. For the privileged, every problem has a solution. That night an innocent bartender made the suggestion that if the boys could not keep the beer in either the mugs or down the hatch, they might consider bibs. If a napkin around the neck was good, a full dress ensemble would be better. Initially, white denim jackets with matching trousers became what suited serious Princeton beer drinkers, which was all Princeton men. Drinking beer was a long-standing accepted form of behavior. Until 1969, it was really the only game in town. Beer was still much embraced even when other ways of altering consciousness became popular. The white trousers soon fell out of fashion. Then more practical white canvas replaced denim. Canvas makes a good canvas. Stencils of Tigers, monikers, and other whimsy were tattooed to the cloth making each identical beer jacket unique.

OOO. A Common Murderer, A Highwayman, Or A House-breaker, Has As Good A Pretence

That night, Cannon Club's famous "No Neck" was in top form. How was Miss Bikini to know? The arch near the entry to her dorm room seemed like the perfect place. Some say all college pranksters belong in the loony bin. In fact, insane asylums are most often filled with patients like Job. No Neck invented a new Cannon Club diversion, especially devised for that time and place. Sometimes evolution is its own reward. Heretofore the common attitude from Princeton men about women was akin to pathological. Margaret Mead would have understood. Young girls are best served like a virgin, sacrificed to the volcano god. No matter the motivating male eruptions are of a much, much smaller scale. Any anthropologist who considered the circumstance would agree. Cultural developments start slowly with their first steps often backwards. First No Neck amused himself, both hands on the handlebars of Miss Bikini's bicycle, his nose to the grindstone, so to speak.

Steve Puissant added a pinch of Cannon levity,

"No Neck, my good man, I prefer the air around Tom Paine, and he has been smolderin' in the grave, rotting for almost 200 years."

If sniffing is good, pissing is better, particularly if a dollop of beer jacket hubris befitting an all male institution is added. No Neck took the next step forward in the progress of early man confronting women for the first time as full time students. Chug a beer, piss on a coed's bike. What was first a whim became a ritual. Twelve Cannon Club members took their turn. Miss Bikini's bicycle was the first to be so baptized. There were many coed bicycles in the arch. It was difficult to get twelve guys to share communion around one bicycle. Steve Puissant was the first to follow No Neck to Miss Bikini's bicycle. The next ten chugged then took their turns.

Sammy Rice stood in one of the triangles formed by the pathways which led to Pyne entries. He was again performing his stale comedy routine. Sammy could not see beyond himself. There was a new guy there that Saturday night, a skinny tall freshman, George Demondrone, the younger brother of Jason, Tommy's AAU swimming buddy and the inaugurating member of the Grassy Knoll Club. Each Demondrone had his own way of being a fool on the hill. George noticed what the guys in the beer jackets were doing. He was about to find slippery footing on dry, flat land. The younger Demondrone ran to the arch,

"What the heck do you guys think you're doing?"

No Neck had a ready answer. He grabbed George Demondrone from behind and pinned his elbows behind him. One of the other apostles of unseemly urinary foment gave George a right hook, blackening his left eye. There were many ways a Princeton Freshman could bump into trouble.

The final step in the evolution of man is communication and folklore. In some cases, a collected unconscience ensues. Princeton male word of mouth followed suit. Just as the nickname "Sue Pyne" soon swelled in craven hands, ugly rumor on campus reared its ugly head. The first object of mean spirited gossip was Ruth George. The word on the street was that for Ruth, like Einstein, love not duty guided her best efforts. If it was not love, it was surely fascination. The frequency of the falsehood gained amplitude. It was said Ruth so loved to have a penis in her mouth that she sucked cock on campus wherever her knees might land. The Ruth George prevarication made knee pads the stuff of lore long before Monica Lewinsky, at her mother's suggestion, brought some with her to be a true beltway insider. The problem with tall tales is that sometimes later events fit. It is now said that Ruth followed her real interest, a firm fascination with penises, even so far as ending in the locker room of the New York Knicks, Willis read dropping his towel, for her benefit, to look but not to touch, as a sports reporter for the New York Times. Ruth said she was only trying to gather all that will fit.

What is hazing among men is abuse if visited upon the fairer gender. Equality does not include belittling sophomoric high jinks if aimed at feminism's most emancipated. The Princeton Cane Spree is a case in point. Women would never wrestle in the mud, or jello for that matter. Ruth George is the flip side of the coin of harmless campus traditions. Even if it is o.k. for a man to be on the receiving side, a woman should not have to address the issue of wanton giving.

The epilogue but not the end to that No-Neck driven spectacle ended in a shroud of secrecy. Beaming hope and pure expectation were stopped in their tracks. Fresh innocence was dashed. No one knew who raised the point of contention to the next level in this archetypal primitive conflict, turning medium to message. Soon everyone saw Miss Bikini's bicycle dangling in the wind aptly tied with ribbons atop the Blair Arch flagpole, one of the most prominent and visible places on campus. It was a shot across the bow. The men from Cannon Club must have known, however, that they were shadowboxing the apocalypse, trying to end run the ineffable. It is impossible to win the endgame against inevitability, especially if it is an idea, a right, an entitlement whose time has come.

PPP. Confiscation Of The Property Of Disaffected Persons

When "Lemming" Cello and Joe got closer to the Cannon Club contingent, they wanted no part of the beer bladder tango they saw choreographed before their very eyes. "Lemming" Cello looked at Joe, turning his gaze to Tim Fief's entry. Joe got the message. Ron Streeter and the other Cannon guys were too busy marking their turf to notice Cebellum and Cello slink by them.

Fief responded to the knock on his door in seconds. With the door open, there was Dylan's singing voice, if it could be called such,

"...The Vandals stole the handle."

"Hey John. Hey Joe. Please enter our humble home. I want you to meet somebody..."

Joe interrupted,

"Your roommate, Josh Relioport?"

"Nope I am sure you will meet Josh Matthew Relioport in good time. Here is a guy who lives in this same entry, upstairs, Fenton Appleseed, a good old boy from Chestnut Hill Academy. a place more mainline than the Philadelphia mainline itself..."

The picture of all that is blue blood and social register extended his right hand to no one in particular,

"Hi, I'm Fenton Appleseed."

Joe blurted,

"Jesus Christ, you are the spitting image of Teddy Kennedy."

"Lemming" Cello smiled. He pulled a joint out of his front Levi pocket. The white Ron Jon Surf shop t-shirt he was wearing had no pockets.

"You know I have tried dope but I never have been able get stoned. I am having my fourth gin and tonic of the evening, however."

"Lemming" Cello was now a man on a mission,

"Fenton, do you mind if we call you 'Teddy,' I have the cure for what ails you, some really good homegrown. Let's toke up."

Fief had switched the record. He put the tone arm in the middle of side two of *John Mayall and The Bluesbreakers with Eric Clapton*. Before they joined Peter Green and became the rhythm section of Fleetwood Mac, John McVie, and Mick Fleetwood added to the quintessential slow blues, "Have You Heard."

Appleseed was not the sharpest knife in any drawer. At "PU" or "PrU" as those who are the really effete like to denominate Princeton, Fenton was in way over his head, except for his lineage. Generation after generation of Appleseeds had joined generations of Scribners to study at Old Nassau with the onspring of other fine families. Quite a few Parsleys went way back, too. Fief's father and the males in his mother's family were all Old Princeton. In fact Fief's first cousin, Kent Parsley also entered Princeton in the Fall of 1969.

It was not the gin. Whether it was aloof disinterest or an utter lack of perspicacity, Fenton was genuinely unable to follow the thread of the simplest conversation,

“Hey, Fief. I just noticed the bunk bed. You have a roommate?”

“Yea ‘Teddy,’ I was just talking about him, Josh Relioport.”

Joe interrupted,

“I am sure we will all meet ‘Thew’ in due course.”

“I didn’t realize there are one room doubles, I have a single all to myself.”

It might have been coincidence. Scribner and Appleseed were lucky Freshmen. Neither shared even one roommate.

QQQ. The Far And The Near, The Home Counties And The Back, The Rich And The Poor

Good breeding alone did not pave the road for admission to Princeton. Attending certain schools also helped. The secondary school did not have to be a prep school. In Illinois, New Trier in the north shore suburbs of Chicago and Oak Park-River Forest in the west side suburbs both acted as proud Ivy League feeders. Timothy Parsley Fief attended Scarsdale High, another public school that had all the right stuff. One of Fief's high school classmates was one of the first full time women. Her name was Lisa Birdor. Her older brother Carl was a Princeton sophomore. Sibling connections may have also helped gain admission. A couple years later, Cheryl Fullglass followed her brother, Filbert. It also helped that their grandfather was a U.S. Senator from Illinois. Their father, a Princeton grad, was CEO of Python Zinc, a large South American mining conglomerate. Perhaps the most famous brother and sister at Princeton are come-latelies. Craig and Michelle Robinson came from the Southside Chicago Ghetto. Craig was a basketball star at Princeton. He now coaches basketball at Oregon State University. Michelle wrote her senior thesis on the subject of the rocky road to civil rights for blacks. She married a guy who was Editor of the Harvard Law Review before he was elected President of the United States.

Fief got up to play another record. “Lemming” Cello caught Joe’s eye then looked at the door. Appleseed was of the same mind. He finished his gin and tonic and stood up,

“John, I don’t think that marijuana got me stoned.”

“App, I promise we will apply ourselves until the dime drops.”

Cebellum and Cello both got up.

“Guys, there is a high school friend here that I’d like you to meet, Lisa Birdor. She is stunning and sharp.”

Fief did his best Grouch Marx eye rolls complete with waggle of an imaginary cigar.

Cello managed a fake chortle,

“I hope her sense of humor is better than yours.”

Joe opened the door,

“Let’s do this again.”

“Teddy” said,

“You name the time and the place.”

Fief put his right hand in front then his left hand behind him before giving a full bow. “Teddy,” “Lemming” Cello, and Joe sauntered out.

RRR. The Hangman's Beautiful Daughter

"Teddy" headed up the stairs. John and Joe took the Dillon Arch route back to Little. They were both definitely stoned as they headed up the stairs into the arch. "Lemming" Cello nudged Joe. It was not necessary. Lisa Halaby took her first step down those same stone stairs. Lisa's gait personified the term, "carriage." She glided, almost off the ground in complete conformity with her background as a Park Avenue debutante. She was tall, blonde, with pale blue eyes. Her yellow hair was pulled straight back from the top of her forehead. It formed an upward crest, short of full tiara, before luxuriating to a mantle of nobility on, around, and down her shoulders. Lisa Halaby wore a light grey cashmere sweater, the kind with only one button at the top of a large teardrop opening on the back. No girl ever looked better in a pair of straight leg khaki pants, even if they were starched and military pressed.

"Lemming Cello" actually missed the fourth step up. Lisa Halaby had too much dignity to notice. Her head-turning visage remained taciturn. Young girls from New York, walking in public, learn early not to smile, and never to make eye contact. It was not snobbishness, just self-protection.

Neither Joe nor John could find words. Lisa Halaby walked oblivious to their awkward silence. She was now out of earshot. They passed the first few Little entries to the left of the corner that met Dillon.

"Joe, I was wrong. I am man enough to admit it. That woman hovers over this mortal ground perhaps only shining upon us a few moments of her grandeur, an angel brought to torture us all. The admissions office definitely made a mistake when they admitted her."

"Whoa, Cello. The better she is, and she is, the more likely some smug prick driving a Ferrari his daddy gave him for his 20th birthday is going to find his way into her affections."

"I am not gonna give up the ship. Damn the torpedoes, full speed ahead. It is better to have crashed and burned than to never have taken wing at all."

"O.K. O.K. Slow down big fellow."

It turned out neither Joe nor John was right. It was true Lisa Halaby was out of their league. She was also beyond the reach of even the biggest man on the PU campus. Her father was CEO of Pan American Airlines. Najeeb Halaby was a Texan of Jordanian descent whose money, power, and affiliation with the Rockefellers granted him access to East Coast High Society and a high berth on Nixon's enemies' list. Lisa was the cookie cutter image of her mother. Najeeb "Robert" Halaby's best friend was Jordan's King Hussein. Following Middle East protocol rather than Upper Eastside custom, Lisa's daddy introduced her to His Royal Highness. Queen Noor is the name she took. Years later, Joe was watching C-Span, the Ninety-fifth Street Book Club. Queen Noor deigned to discuss her autobiography. The moderator asked her about the solution for peace in the troubled region where she reigned. Queen Noor said, the solution was simple, "Until there is justice, there will be no peace." Upon further query, Queen Noor explained that justice meant merely that a promise be kept. In exchange for the agreement to spill blood fighting the Turks in World War One, France and England long ago assured the Arab world that Palestine would be an Arab state.

SSS. Throw Not The Burden Of The Day Upon Providence

In theory there may have been a few women, very few whose pedigree transcended their gender. Even so, the fall of 1969 was literal for many Alumni. The "First 100" entered Princeton's hallowed halls. It was not propitious that an early cold spell caused the ivy that clung to historic old walls to shrivel in shock. The full-time women undergraduates started a ripple of Alumni unrest which culminated with a large wave of hate finding its way ashore in one of the places where the Constitution and the Bill of Rights first held dominion. Asa Bushnell and Shelby Cullom Davis bankrolled the Concerned Alumni of Princeton "CAP." *Prospect*, a new glossy magazine, was delivered free to the doorsteps of all students and was also mailed free to the full extent of the considerable reach of the ensconced WASP power base. Proud to pick up the retrogauntlet were T. Harding Jones and the Brutusally honorable Andy Napolitano. Once a group starts rooting out evil, it is hard to stop. CAP's platform evolved with its own simple stench, "No women, no Jews, no blacks." Later U.S. Supreme Court Justice, Samuel Alito Princeton Class of 1972, listed membership in CAP simply to enhance his ability to find work. Even later, Alito really did not remember that he was a member. After all was said and done, it was likely that he only read the magazine for the pictures.

Everybody always wants to bring back the good old days, even, to quote Merle Haggard, "when times were bad." In 1969, depending upon your point of view, women either invaded the Princeton Campus or received what was long overdue. Either way, the women are still there. For some, the Id is a labyrinth that only having a roommate in prep school can truly dulcify. At the time of that first incursus, some old school alumni suggested the only step in the right direction was to take "Cane Spree" to its most logical extension and bring back those ancient days of fully naked Greco-Roman style wrestling. Some alum wanted it entirely Greek.

All this coeducation was not just a problem at Princeton. Trouble was brewing as far below as the "Elicave," the secret headquarters of Yale's famed Skull and Bones, hidden craftily somewhere under the teeming metropolis of New Haven. The secret society had an important function, well more than the induction promise all make, even George W. Bush to John F. Kerry, to protect each others' family fortunes above all else, all else. Skull and Bones was charged with maintaining the integrity of a gallery of headshots broken down by visiting girls' schools. This was well more than Mitt Romney's bevy of ring binders with "women in them." A crack in the stele had materialized. Should these catalogs of possible blind dates include Yalie women, or God forbid, Princeton women? The dispute over the content of these "Facebooks" as they were called was not a faint little ferment.

Clamor and furor did not really describe the brewing brouhaha. At Princeton, "parietals" had just been abolished. This meant that women could now stay through the night. Proctors could no longer prowl dorms to determine whether the "three feet on the floor" rule was strictly followed by a student intertwined on a bed with his weekend date. Concerned Alumni put one and one together. One wag issued a way out of the dilemma. Yale also had coeds for the first time. Send the Yalie women to Princeton and vice-versa, so to speak. Tradition dictated that there would be no hand wringing if a Princeton man fucked a Yalie. Two years later, Joyce Maynard was in her first few months as a Yale Freshwoman. No doubt concerned that this plan might yet be implemented, she fled Connecticut to the arms of the essentially barren and less than sporadically capable J.D. Salinger. The possibility that a 53 year old starter wouldn't start did not enter the star cross of her ambition.

TTT. A Little Might Have Saved The Whole

Abha and Sam were going strong. At first Sam thought he'd better pinch himself. Then he decided that if it was all a dream why take even the remote chance a pinch would wake him up. The ball was in Abha's court. Few men realize that is where you will always find the ball. Abha, just like a woman, wanted to improve the relationship. She looked Sam in his middle eye, touched his hand, and nestled in just the right spot finding the center of his energy zone. Abha suggested lovingly that the Kama Sutra was not enough. Now Sam felt the urge to pinch himself.

Their first prong of the road to taking a grand song and trying to make it better was a visit to the nearest, neighborhood Native American sweat lodge. Sopping wet, Sam came to the fair conclusion that sitting in an enclosed hut, with perspiring peers was just too darned hot.

Abha was not one to give up on an idea whose time had come,

"Let's cut to the chase. Why sweat to reach nirvana. Peyote gets us where we want to go with only a little vomiting."

"Abha, I think you are onto something here. I have read the back cover of that Carlos Castaneda book at your place. A plethora of splashing colors and vibrant patterns with stanzas of bliss is just what the doctor ordered."

Abha and Sam tripped together once. Sam is one who starts the day with introspection then goes deeper inside from there. With peyote, he moved wholly into his own dark recesses. Abha could not, or would not, pull Sam from his own drug soaked reticence. It was too bad for Sam, since Abha was in free flow, playing a major part in her own full Technicolor VistaVision sensory experience. She was a hair trigger touch away from taking sexual union beyond the Kama Sutra on any of its many best days. Sadly for Sam, he was unable to send even one soft caress Abha's direction. Someone else, not Sam, would soon be buried in a full avalanche of her sexual energy. Abha was on the precipice of finding frisson from extroverted embrace. The ensuing tingle of slight shivers would send her around the corner to warm waves then a standing pattern formed by echoes of convulsions. Sam sat physically proximate to Abha's constant craving, but yet so far away.

By early the next morning, the peyote had worn off. During the night Abha had raised the window in Sam's bedroom to let in the cool night air. Now the morning breeze was a co-conspirator with the window shades. The dawn tentatively blew open the curtains allowing the sun to pierce the room with sporadic colors. Sam had come down alone, fully clothed on top of the bed sheets. Abha was gone. She did not need to leave a note. Sam resigned himself to the conclusion that he and Abha were now worlds apart. Sam looked only on the dark of it all. He did not, and could not, realize that a short interlude of intense heat is better than none. Moreover, from positive little steps, soon spring great strides. Advances Sam could never seem to enjoy.

UUU. Reason To The Root Of Things

In the Sleepy Little Village, Fred was not having problems with the palpable. It was easy for Tiffany Wallett to convince Fred to drive her to school every morning. Fred was an open book to Tiffany. She had the perfect sense of Fred's internal rhythms and the ability to bring Fred to full conclusion. Fred was not sure whether she had natural talent or whether her technique was honed after much practice. What Fred did know was that when his 1967 Blue Camaro crossed the E, J & E railroad tracks three blocks from the High School, the bump of those tracks gave Tiffany the signal to shift to high gear. When Fred turned the corner onto the high school grounds, like clockwork Tiffany lifted her head from his lap, another morning's magic had come to a head. Tiffany swallowed but she always kept a few drops on her tongue. She always gave Fred a very sloppy French kiss before thanking him for the ride. The effect was always the same. Fred sat in glorious discomfort. It did not help to shift his position in his seat while he drove away. With everyone milling about to get to school on time, Fred kept his crotch covered with his left hand. He was barely able to shift and steer with his right. Once he made the turn back on to County Line Road, he was able to force his slumped penis back into his pants and to zip up. Fred was never late for work.

VVV. Grow Brave By Reflection

Joe would have been equally happy with a leisurely drive to school before the work day started. The bright lines from lucid lectures and that which could be drawn from the intersecting exchanges in the small group precepts was not what Joe chose to take from Princeton's rich bounty. Joe's mother, Della, would have gone to as many classes as the day permitted while reading anything and everything in the evening hours, well into the night. For Joe, reading, without more, was sufficient. Moreover, Joe did not subscribe to the view that a student only "read philosophy" while it was necessary to sink your teeth into the rigors of science. To Joe, science, engineering, and mathematics were plain and simple. Literature, philosophy, and religion presented the greatest difficulties in understanding, analysis, and articulation. The big lie about the body of scientific knowledge was one masked by nomenclature then propagated by men of science, predominantly medical doctors. The large remuneration doctors received was justified by the asserted difficulty of learning what they needed to learn. Socrates grappled with more than either Archimedes or Hippocrates. The greatest hypocrites of all were doctors foisting themselves up on their own pedestals while besmirching and belittling the liberal arts, ignoring the cerebration and ratiocination necessary to be steeped and to be versed in those necessarily imprecise and veiled disciplines. Scientists should know first that everything is connected, including the areas of learning least hospitable to quantification, fine tuning, and resolution. You cannot press into one area without necessarily encountering conundrums that thrive in another area far off. Of course, there are many big lies. It is hard to measure and judge which one is the biggest. The best you can do really is pick your favorite one of the moment. Joe had many favorites. The idea that philosophy was a waste of time, only for pursuit by school boys before they attained maturity, something to be discarded as men, was right at the top. Socrates had been put to death because he could not put juvenile pursuits to rest.

WWW. Fall An Easy Prey

Joe walked back into the second entry of Little Hall. Professor Sonnenfeld had just smiled knowingly and sneered imperiously through another superficial exegesis. This time it was Mann's *Death in Venice.* Joe would have preferred fanciful rhetoric about Evelyn Waugh's *The Loved One* and Thanatopsis. Today's mail had been delivered. There was a light purple envelope, for him as it turned out. The return address was Merryl Lithekenner, 41 Haskell Hall, Jackson University, Somerville, Mass. The letter was sweet and short. Merryl inquired how Joe was doing. She disclosed that she was finding Boston and Jackson, the girls' school for Tufts, both full of possibilities, that she was fond of a new song which made her think of Joe. The song was "Sunlight" by the Youngbloods off the *Elephant Mountain* album. Merryl hoped that Joe might come to Boston for a visit some weekend. Merryl closed by giving Joe her phone number.

Joe knew "Lemming" Cello had that record. He stopped in to give it a listen. First things first, on the way to hearing "Sunlight," John played "Ride the Wind." They listened to that song four times. Four was a good start. When John finally put the tone arm needle on the "Sunlight" groove, Joe heard all he needed to hear-

Have you seen the sunlight pourin' through her hair
Felt her warm mouth on you in the summers' air
Runnin' in a field of brown
Laughin', rollin' on the ground now
Smilin' as she pulls you down

That's the way she feels about you
That's the way she feels about you

If your dreams can wake you screaming in the night
She can touch your face and take away your fright
Like a tree in the meadow wind
She will bend to take you in now
Makes no difference where you been

That's the way she feels about you
That's the way she feels about you

In the mornin' wake up laughing with the day
She will smile and ask you with her eyes to stay
Like the sunshine warms the sand
She will touch you with her hands now
Touchin' makes you understand...

XXX. Defection At Pleasure.

“Lemming” Cello and Joe bumped into Barry Richardson on the way to Commons for lunch that day.

“Hey, Barry. Did Celeste forgive you yet?”

“Joe, this Friday I am flying up to see her for the weekend. Why don’t you come with me to ask her yourself?”

“Lemming” Cello nodded his head up and down, in full assent with Barry’s wry sentiment. He was becoming more and more fond of Barry’s glib, positive spin on everything.

“Eastern Airlines has two-thirds student reserve- twelve bucks each way. We can catch the last flight out.”

“Barry, I like that idea. I will go with you.”

“Lemming” Cello shook his head from side to side. If there was a place which had a beat all its own, Joe was forging his way to it.

Barry was kind and thoughtful,

“Joe, sit by the window. It’s a short flight but you should see the Eastern Seaboard at night.”

Joe was surprised. It was more than the quantum mess that had become Manhattan. It was more than the Hudson, more than the East River, and more than the Connecticut Coast and Long Island Sound,

“Barry, I have never seen so many lights.”

The dense, urban sprawl was unrelenting from Newark to Logan. There was no open space along the coast from North Jersey to Boston. Joe kept his nose to the window for the entire thirty minute flight. Logan landings seem precarious. The jet touched down at the exact point Massachusetts Bay gave way to the runway

“Barry, after you introduce me to Celeste at Simmons tonight, I am going to indulge the presumption that she and you have some, shall I say, catching up to do. I will beg your leave.”

“Well put my good man, well put.”

“I’ll meet up with you at the airport Sunday night in time to catch our plane back.”

YYY. Once More We Are Again Collected And Collecting

September in Boston has its own idyllic glow. Somehow the spectacle of changing colors in Vermont, New Hampshire, and Maine weaves a spell which reaches all the way to Lexington, Concord, Boston Harbor, and the Back Bay. Fall foliage coupled with the energy of all those college kids back in school turns Boston into a bustle serene. The message that winter is not far behind is not lost. If spring turns a young man's fancy to romance, in autumn the urge becomes the imperative of finding a companion for the winter. The cold season must be spent with someone, anyone who knows the importance of cuddling. Two bodies touching all the night long will permaseal their warmth. Otherwise, any mix of comforters, quilts, and blankets will seem insufficient. Gathering nuts and seeds cannot provide full sustenance. Survival, during even a short winter, requires the heat of two bodies under the covers. Passion between the sheets is good as far as it goes. To secure golden slumbers, two bodies press close together for the long nights, with close breaths more apurr than aheave.

The sharp autumn sunlight forces discrete, sharp images in late afternoon. Those underscored, pronounced points and counterpoints then give way to the gentle shadows and the dusk of days still long causing even the best gatherers and storers to lose their way. Plus, Princeton was unlikely to provide even the least acceptable winter consort. In any event, seizing the moment always seems right. Joe could not wait to see Merryl again. His own impetuousness had ended their relationship almost a year ago. Joe regretted that Merryl's friend Trudy Harrison had discovered him with Vicky Allash when Merryl and her parents had gone to Boston to visit the Jackson campus. He was not sure he regretted that he spent time with Vicky. Some regret is better than none. If the song, "Sunlight" was any indication, fences would soon be mended.

It was fun to meet Celeste. For all Joe could understand, her Maine patois might as well have been Norwegian. Joe did not need to know what she was saying. Celeste was tall, halfway between bird-boned and big boned. Her hair was a mane, dark but bright auburn. She had brown eyes, an oval face with proportional features, and a lively smile that sent dark clouds on their way. Celeste turned her head when she talked which flipped her hair just off one shoulder then the other. Knowing Celeste was in his corner went well on the way to give Barry his optimism, more than just a winning attitude.

Barry walked Joe out of the Simmons dorm. Celeste had figured out a way to sneak Barry into her room for the weekend. Joe's best guess was that they would not leave the room.

"Surely, you are a man most fortunate. It is too bad Celeste does not have a twin sister."

Barry grinned from ear to ear,

"Joe, but she does. And don't call me Shirley."

Before Joe could say anything, Barry closed the door then headed to the elevator.

ZZZ. To Open The Next Campaign

At the first sight of Merryl, Celeste and her twin sister, real or imagined, were gone and forgotten. Merryl picked the place they would meet- Harvard Square in front of the Coop, even though it was closed. As Joe walked up the Redline subway stairs, Merryl waved. She kept her elbow tight to her side, her palm up to the side of her face, just a small rotation of the wrist. She was restrained but not tentative. A guy and a girl stood to her right. They were both smiling. Merryl introduced Joe to her roommate, Judy Bass, and to Judy's boyfriend, Lenny Siegman.

Lenny held up his car keys.

"I have been conscripted to give you a ride back to Tufts, I mean Jackson. My friends against the war better not find out how easy I was to enlist."

"Thanks, Lenny. Your secret is safe with me."

Merryl's restraint lapsed to reserve. She brightened the evening light. Keeping her elbow to her side, she grasped Joe around his upper arm. She took firm hold then squeezed his biceps from front to back. Joe smiled. Merryl stood on her toes. She kissed him lightly on his cheek.

"Judy, it looks like it is a good idea you will be spending the night with me. These two might abrogate all of Queen Victoria's rules of deportment between a lady and a gentleman."

"Lenny, I think I will show you how I think a man and a woman should behave tonight."

"So all the stuff before has just been a dry run."

"I guess if dry means wet."

Joe smiled at Merryl,

"These two have met before?"

"Joe, Boston is the cradle of freedom."

Judy, Merryl, Lenny, and Joe took feverish banter to a new level through the car ride back and for another two hours. Lenny looked at his watched to pretend he was tired and the hour was late. No one argued. Joe and Merryl rejoined their special bond. Merryl's body again spoke to Joe in a language only for him, an idiom Joe was just beginning to learn when the two had parted ways. As brimming and bountiful as was Merryl's mind, her body was as sleek and as slender. She stood slightly rounded, but not drooping, shoulders, 5'8" tall. Her face beamed only noble gentility. When she walked, she swayed slightly, just enough to know there was purpose and poise in her poised sensual being. Joe caught up to the incipient swelter of her hips. He put his arm around her at the shoulder. They moved side to side, their hips touching just enough to feel each other's expectation.

Merryl and Joe woke up the next morning feeling the after effects of reaching a lather that only the concentrated and repeated sexual intimacy of youth can raise. The toothy, emancipated grins the two exchanged when they awoke and looked at one another in the early light of morning would have caused any uninformed onlooker to conclude that they portrayed only childish, innocent delight. That onlooker would have formed the correct conclusion. They wiped the sleep from their eyes. Merryl made circles on the tip of Joe's penis with her thumb and her forefinger. If nerve end study volunteers were ever needed, Joe would be first in line.

"Do we have time before we meet Judy and Lenny for that walk around campus?"

Joe assented involuntarily, the best way he knew how.

AAAA. To Ravage The Defenceless Jerseys

In those days new friends rambled everywhere. Deep bonds formed easily. Hands clasped together were the natural product of bright trust and the prospect of a world of new hope. The four new friends wandered the campus. Bright chatter reigned everywhere they went. That morning the Tufts Jumbos, the football team, played the Rensselaer Polytechnic Sliderules, or whatever they were called. With no particular place to go, Judy, Merryl, Lenny, and Joe now sat in the small bleachers. Their number increased the spectators to twelve. Their lively jibber jabber raised the good feelings between the four to a level of exuberance that a wave of fans in a standing room only NFL stadium could not match.

At eleven, each couple went back to their two rooms after agreeing to meet after lunch. They would meet in front of the television on the first floor of Haskell Hall. Both thought they would be keeping the other two waiting. Some free spirit had synchronized their watches. "Fashionably late" had a new incarnation in the revel of free love. As they walked into the room, the television was turned to football. It was halftime. The American college pageant held special meaning that Saturday, September 27, 1969. The setting was New Brunswick, New Jersey for the 100th meeting of Princeton and Rutgers in the longest football rivalry. In 1869 they played the first ever college football game. ABC was showing the centennial as its game of the week. While Rutgers would win 29-0, the PU Band scored its own brand of victory. They formed the letters, "ABC," on the field. As the live cameras zoomed in, the letters became, "NBC."

Lenny laughed, pointing to the television screen,

“I’m glad we all got here in time for that.”

“So Lenny, how much money did Eddie Haskell give of his *Leave it to Beaver* earnings to get a dorm named after him?”

Judy bass laughed. They were the only four in the room. The swift, energetic flow of ramble lasted until the game was over, not that anyone was watching. Judy Bass really thought Joe was funny. The more Judy laughed. The more Joe said things he knew would make her laugh. Joe felt all was well with the world when a woman laughed at his patter. He now realized why he did not enjoy going to class, either lectures or precept. There was no doubt that the lecturers at Princeton were among the best. Precepts were also unique opportunities that were unavailable at any other college. Either they did not to exist at all or they were not conjoined with the same verve. Leading Professors, not just earnest, dedicated grad students, led lively precept discussions. There was one small impediment for Joe. In the midst of Princeton all maleness (minus 100), he did not have the opportunity to make girls giggle. Going to class for the love of learning was not part of what moved Joe.

BBBB. 'Tis The Business Of Little Minds To Shrink

Had Merryl, Judy, Lenny, and Joe not been awash in quick witted laughter and relevant repartee, what they would have seen was Rutgers destroy the last remnants of Princeton's quaint single wing offense. Princeton was still considered Division I. In reality the Black and Orange did not perform much better than the Jumbos. To add to alumni grumbling about the decline of once great prominence, there would soon be racial turbulence in the small pond at Palmer Stadium.

It is hard to raze iconic folklore from any tabula. Ivy memories die hard. Princeton had been preeminent on the gridiron when slow white preppies were all who donned cleats. Cheered autumn accomplishments were now held dear in recollections seemingly more indelible as time passed. In the days of Amos Alonzo Stagg, in places of storied ilk like the University of Chicago football Stadium, Saturday stalwarts tried to split the space between guard and tackle. Now Princeton's Old Guard reveled in memories of a past unstained by time. Reminiscences became real to remain of seemingly much more consequence than that which Fermi would later spawn under those same bleachers as he led experiments aimed at splitting the space between neutrons and electrons.

Until that Miltonian fall of 1969, football was important, with a capital, "I," to all male, testosterone infused places of collegiality like Princeton. Much of the social life, alas laden but not laid, took place around football weekends when women were scarcely bussed after being bused in from the Seven Sisters and places like Sweet Briar, Centenary, and various other schools. When Joe, Barry, Frites, Relioport, Rothstein, and Cello arrived with those first One Hundred women, football weekends became less important. Women, soon to be more and more, were in residence all the week long.

Coincidence or calumny, Princeton elevated an assistant coach, Jake McCandless, to the position of head coach. He immediately set out to change the nature of Princeton Football. As the last bastion of single wing football, Princeton was unique. Jake abandoned the single wing and, in doing so, he relegated the Team Captain, a Canadian by the last name of Bracken, to the bench. Bracken had been a star in prior years but the "new" system had no place for him. Bracken took the demotion as a Princeton Gentleman would take any "C" grade, in stride with class.

McCandless elevated the second string single wing tailback to the new leading position of quarterback. It was previously a blocking position. The single wing was delicately dropped in the scrap bin of history. The legacies of those like Cosmo Iacavazzi and Dick Kazmaier were all that remained. Rod Plummer was now the quarterback. In a time of racial unrest, social turmoil, SDS, and a host of protests, it was beyond ironic that Jake McCandless would lose his job amid allegations of racism even though Plummer was black. Allegations of white blindness centered around Bill Early. Barry Richardson, a safety on that football team, termed Early the greatest running back he ever saw in person. Bill Early had the misfortune of being on the same team as Hank Bjorkland who had tenure and who was good enough to be drafted by the New York Jets.

The bottom line was simple. If you are a football coach under attack, losing is the only issue. The reasons there for simply do not matter. Criticism will mount and ride from all perspectives. Stated cause will match the peculiar predilection of the particular Sunday morning quarterback. When all was said and done, the single wing, but not the memory of its glory days, was gone. While the coarse male Cannon Club antics would soon lead to the Club's well-deserved demise, Tiger Inn ("TI") would thrive. Some silly male bonding behavior remained alive and well. Every Saturday night that TI hosted a party, as the moon struck the like-minded lunatics, the members would divide themselves by their sizes, tall, small and average- trees, trolls, and 'tweens. At the ring of a bell or the blow of a whistle, some sort of organized melee would then ensue where trolls jumped, trees withstood, and 'tweens bore the brunt of institutionalized, orchestrated clashes. The piles of drunken future leaders would unravel, bloodied with few serious injuries, to live to fight another day. Such was the Princeton that Joe, his new buddies, and the first One Hundred women would soon find themselves as presumptive interlopers.

CCCC. A Peace Which Passeth All Understanding

All this remained on a campus branded by tradition. Back in Massachusetts, at Haskell Hall on the Jackson Campus, an undeniable fact remained. Black and white or color, watching Princeton single wing football was about as much fun as watching the three legged race at the 4th of July picnic. To again breath in the good air, that night Joe and Merryl headed for Cambridge, to the soon to be legendary, Joe's Club. Normally, some Chicago Blues Master commanded the stage. Some local boys, "The J. Geils Blues Band," were just what the doctor ordered.

Sunday followed with a full day and night of "rapping," the hip word for lively conversation. The four new friends explored and dissected many interesting topics. Even topics which lacked real substance became springboards for giddy comment and for wry provocation. Merryl and Joe were also able to find time for brief respite, shortly after lunch and after dinner. Time after midnight was spent well into the night as again they sequestered themselves in Merryl's bed. Lenny and Judy were not offended when left to their own devices since they would go to Lenny's room. Their two points of separate but presumably equal white lightning, red heat would then cool sufficiently to gather for another quadrangle of angular billiard ball bouncing banter. Throughout Sunday, Judy continued to be Joe's tuning fork of laughter, capturing not just the tenor but the encompassing vibrations of his incisive wit and shrewd silliness. As the clock struck twelve, Judy had an idea,

"Merryl, don't you think Joe should stay one more day? Arlo Guthrie is going to perform 'Alice's Restaurant' from beginning to end, on campus tomorrow."

Joe planned to take the early flight out Monday morning,

"And one more night."

It was not clear who smiled at the other first, Joe or Merryl.

"Joe, my bed is your bed."

"Say no more."

Joe called Celeste's room,

"Celeste please tell Barry. I am going to stay another day. It was great to meet you. I look forward to meeting your twin sister."

"Will do and what?"

"We'll talk about that later. Bye for now."

DDDD. Say Not That Thousands Are Gone, Turn Out Your Tens Of Thousands

The concert voiced the naive hope of that time. Arlo Guthrie captured the full the rapt attention of a buzzing throng there to listen and to be part of the scene. He was more than just a guy who sang the first day at Woodstock while an airplane flew overhead behind him whisping a large white peace sign on the pale blue firmament. As corny as the whole idea was, The Beatles had set The Magical Mystery Tour in full motion. The attitude of young people everywhere was each person was one singer and the song was clear, "You can get anything you want." It would not be long before the Rolling Stones hit the true nail on the head. Not less optimistic, but more sanguine, a chorus sang, "You can't always get what you want but if you try some time you just might find you get what you need..." The tide had turned. Just as in 1965, Bob Dylan had turned abrasively to amplified electric music at the Newport Jazz festival, music would soon turn it up a notch, away from one guy with an acoustic guitar singing, "I gave my love a cherry..." From the Rolling Stones' album cover of *Let it Bleed*, this admonition seared into the fray, "**Play It Loud**."

Merryl, Judy, Lenny, and Joe floated on tranquil waters as the concert ended with the double encore, "The City of New Orleans" and "Coming in to Los Angeles." The crowd roared when Guthrie rhymed a "couple of keys" with "Los Angeles."

EEEE. The Heart That Feels Not Now Is Dead

Merryl was on Joe's left. Judy walked to his right with Lenny to her right. Joe's attention was entirely to his immediate right,

"You know, a long train ride from Chicago to New Orleans would be idyllic. Even without the contraband."

Judy looked up at Joe,

"I know what you mean."

Merryl had reached the limit of her patience,

"Joe, you can sleep on the floor tonight. Enough is enough."

Joe squinted. He pulled his head into his neck. Judy moved to the other side of Lenny. Merryl was mad. More than mad she was hurt. Just as Joe would soon learn the difference between getting everything you want and getting what you need, he received another first lesson- forgiving was easy and forgetting was the hardest part. No matter how cozily well matched they were, and they were, Merryl could not put out of her mind the fact that Joe had strayed. What she had buried in the back of her mind, hoping it would be lost forever, came rushing out. Thus it ended. The way Merryl felt about Joe succumbed to rushes of irrepressible memory. Lenny, Judy, and Joe were all sure that Joe and Judy were just having harmless, albeit ubiquitous, fun.

FFFF. The Relief Of Those Who Have Suffered In Well-Doing

The next day, Joe walked in the door at 22 Little. He greeted Mel as he looked up from his desk,

"Mr. Rothstein, may I thank you again for turning in my Philosophy 101 paper that was due yesterday."

"Joe I was happy to do it. I actually did you one better. I typed it up for you. I know handwritten is o.k. but is it really?"

"Thanks, Mel I hope those guys don't get the idea all my papers are going to be typed. What about my signature as required by the Honor Code?"

"Joe, since you gave me your proxy to hand the paper in, I am sure the ambit of that which you delegated includes authority to sign your name."

"Mel, are you sure you want to go into advertising or the creative arts? It sound to me like you should be a lawyer for God's sakes."

"By the way, I read the paper. The subject of ethical relativism versus moral absolutism is interesting. Like is it o.k. to eat a guy who is dead to survive, when, if ever is it o.k. to kill a guy who would die anyone to keep five or six other people alive. I think the army does that sort of mercy killing all the time- It is o.k. to kill people in Vietnam to be sure they don't become communists. But, Joe are you sure it is a good idea to write a paper that ends with fifteen questions piled on top of one another?"

"You could see they were rhetorical, no?"

"Well, I hope your professor sees it that way."

Princeton may have been missing the fairer gender piece of the puzzle but it was running on all cylinders in almost every other area. There were two movies theatres in town. New York and Philadelphia were both cultural Meccas quite close. Even Boston and Washington, D.C. were not that far away. Activities on the Princeton campus were bountiful. There was really no reason to leave the sheltering umbrella of academe. Different student groups showed movies of current interest. Cream's Farewell Concert was shown at the lecture hall, McCosh 10. Joe could leave Little to head to McCarter Theatre or to go the other direction to Alexander Hall. At McCarter, he and his buddies saw the international film, *Battle of Algiers*. and then the virtuoso pianist, Vladimir Ashkenazy.

Alexander Hall was the perfect venue for a concert. The stage sat in front of a large round stained glass window which loomed high above it. There was seating on the floor with more seats in a balcony that made a crescent up to the corners of the stage. In the month of October, Joe and his friends attended two Alexander concerts. They "saw" "Chicago Transit Authority" before they became merely "Chicago" and the folk artist, Tim Buckley. In November, Alexander would showcase "The New York Rock & Roll Ensemble" and later, on the Saturday before Thanksgiving, the "James Cotton Blues Band." December would bring the 81st Annual Princeton Triangle Club Show to McCarter. This year, "Call a Spade a Shovel" included the usual irreverence and kept the "Kickline" where Princeton men gave up their beer jackets to dress in drag and prance onstage like gangly rejects from *The Folies Bergere*.

GGGG. Call It Rather The Soft Resentment Of A Suffering People

From October 10 to October 12, as part of a comprehensive and a thorough TCU campaign, Tommy and his fellow students were all handed a piece of paper. The same paper was handed to every student each time they entered a classroom, lecture hall, or laboratory. As Tommy sat down in his Trigonometry class, he opened an open letter to all students-

"TCU hereby declares a Moratorium on the upcoming 'Vietnam Moratorium' currently slated by subversive elements for October 15 in the year of our Lord, 1969. Texas and Christians, after all are one and the same. We must all stand tall, rise up in the saddle with our spurs shining as exemplars. October 15th shall be a day where there shall be all business as usual with no funny business. Anyone engaged in the mildest sort of shut down shall be subject to severe academic discipline and shall be severed from the University. Furthermore, anyone seen suffering the antics of the misguided anti-war protest groups, shall be similarly subject to castigation and censure, including but not limited to, suspension and expulsion. Upstarts must know they cannot speak freely when they are not wanted. Texans do not stand silent when their most sacred principles have been attacked. The legacy of Texas Christian University is seen in its fight with the sin and carnage in the neighboring district known as Hell's Half Acre. More than the move to Waco to find purity, more than the new principles of our founders and our guiding light, 'The Disciples of Christ,' Good always triumphs. TCU is back where it belongs. 'Hell's Half Acre' is now just an unfortunate memory, dirt washed off the hands by those who have been purified by the blood of the Lamb. TCU did not succumb to evil then. It will not fall prey to the devil now."

Later that day Tommy sat at lunch in the SAE dining room. He was no longer surprised. One of his brothers held forth,

"It is bad enough we have to observe Columbus Day. Like anyone from a Mediterranean Country had any real influence on the development of this great country of ours."

Tommy mused to himself, "If the idea of transitivity could be extended to oxymorons, 'Texas Christian University' would surely belong on the short list of leading candidates."

The day after the Nationwide Moratorium to stop the war, *The San Antonio Evening Light* published a photograph of Paul Newman in London. He was holding up a placard which read, "Moratorium." Apparently, the Moratorium had international sway. Nobody knew who he was at the time, but standing next to Paul Newman on the United States Embassy steps was a Rhodes Scholar. He held a petition to stop the war to deliver to the U.S. Ambassador. It was signed by many interested citizens of the United States and Great Britain, citizens of the world. This young activist had worked in the office of Senator William Fulbright, who as head of the Senate Committee on Foreign Affairs was an outspoken critic of Johnson and his conduct of the Vietnam War. His name was William Jefferson Clinton.

HHHH. No Object In View But The Good Of All

Princeton's spin on the Moratorium differed from TCU. First they added a day. Both days had many "workshops" with Princeton Professors guiding the way. Throughout the nation, the academic community joined hands in public protest against the war. Additionally, professors throughout the land led small learning groups, "teach-ins." MIT's Noam Chomsky traveled down to Princeton to give a "teach-in." High in Chomsky's thoughts in those days was the issue of the responsibility of the intellectual. Kennedy's Harvard cadre, Galbraith and others, then McNamara, and finally Kissinger, all incanted a variation on the old chestnut, "Trust us, we're from the government, and we're smart." with its implicit, "You're not so smart."

Chomsky was marked with Jeffersonian brilliance. He felt people who could think, had a duty to think, especially when the banner of patriotism was unfurled and waved.

Joe, "Lemming" Cello, and Appleseed spent the day in their own little seminar, trying to teach "Teddy" to get stoned. Some synapses take longer than others to get with the program. Only Thomas Parsley Fief found salve for that which grieved within his lily white bosom. Fief always bought the Black Panther newspaper on Nassau Street. His commitment to the cause took off from there. Later, he joined his friends. Procol Harum was playing the song, "The Devil Came From Kansas." Fief was bubbling with radical energy, ready to step forward against the war and the military industrial complex. After three or four hits of dope, he settled down and listened to the music. By the time everyone but Fenton Appleseed was good and ripped, Grace Slick was bellowing, with Jefferson Airplane wailing behind her, "Somebody to Love."

IIII. Eloquence May Strike The Ear

Oklahoma was a state of a different color. The Vietnam War was not a significant part of the Norman campus. Back in high school, Sam Thorn was as content as someone who was missing the main axle of his gyroscope could be. A dizzy amble was the best he could muster. Away from the Sleepy Little Village of Barrington, Sam discovered two things. First, there were many girls at OU, who thought he was good-looking and interesting. With that positive feedback, he came to the second revelation that he had a way with words. Sam soon realized that if the audience liked you, they were predisposed to like what you had to say. Sam had a wry way of turning a phrase. He met one girl after another who gleaned only positive humor, even in Sam's most surly observations. Slowly the sardonic skew turned tranquil. From there, what began a sullen song, suddenly turned happy tune. Sam was no longer mired in the blasé. Best of all, he now knew the modern twist to all the world's a stage. Sam was in a play where first act, second act, third act, and encore all involved free love, often with different partners. It was an easy step for Sam to take. From his newfound ability to worm his way into the affection of the many, he stumbled upon his one true calling. His conclusion was a simple one. He would become a huckster in the world of advertising. Tricks of the trade still guided, and limited, Sam's vision.

JJJJ. Flock To His Standard Folly To Argue Against Determined Hardness

For Fred the world was not complicated. It was an open book. Each day was a different page, each connection a different chapter. Everyone Fred met was grist for his happy mill. He sent his own bright light onto and into even the most casual acquaintance. Those he met could not help reflect that which they had just been given. Fred's beacon was unbridled positive energy. Fred was an everyman stoking the good that lies within us all. Many of the young women Fred met were ensnared by the hurly burly of Fred's dynamic surge. Some of them thanked him with intimate physical contact. It was all just another piece in the jigsaw puzzle that formed the satisfaction of innocent release. Fred always came back to Martha. What she did not know could not hurt her.

KKKK. Used Numberless Arguments To Show Them

Princeton lacked the same oceans of possibility that engulfed, Tommy, Sam, and Fred. Joe was not one to be caught forever in the horse latitudes of lonely seas. Doldrums would always give way. So far, however, fresh warm breezes were subdued and without vigor. Joe always made the best of everything, taking what he could. He played basketball at Dillon. More and more, he smoked dope and listened to music, usually with "Lemming" Cello. Music soothed whatever ailed you. Marijuana gave it all a nice edge. Joe also attended concerts, movies, and plays with his buddies. Princeton, like many same sex schools for many years, held dances joined by members of the opposite sex from other schools, the "mixer." Mixers were soon to be quaint relics of the past.

For Joe, mixers would be, at best, a mixed-bag. Later that year in December, "Come and Get It," Badfinger's only big hit from the movie, *The Magic Christian*, may have said it best. "It" in this case was a bag of shit, but not "good shit," the term used for potent marijuana.

Joe's first mixer was at Dillon Gym. The factitious nature of the undertaking should have been its own warning. With the possibility of meeting a girl, however, Joe did not give up easily. The clothes he bought on State Street in downtown Chicago before heading East were another story. To go to the mixer, Joe put on dark green iridescent bell bottoms and a glossy sheen chocolate brown shirt with a wide sharp-pointed open collar and cuffs with four buttons. The outfit was designed by someone lost somewhere between Carnaby Street and the Chicago Ghetto. It was easy to see why, in only a matter of short time; Joe would be wearing the ubiquitous bell-bottom blue jeans and unobtrusive shirts.

There was no doubt Joe's awkward Mod/Superfly attire made him a target. A mousy little preppy girl walked up to Joe. Her self-satisfied smirk matched her thin cranberry cable knit sweater and her khaki trousers. Her outfit covered the possibility of even remote sensuality. She was only a few prosperous pounds overweight. Her ebbing eyebrows and evanescent eyelashes blended into her pale, almost colorless blue eyes. She had a thin smile, almost no lips. Her cute little button nose, round cherub's cheeks, and symmetrically round chin completed the picture of preppiness. She was, however, a woman, and this was a "mixer."

The preppy girl spoke first,

"I can tell by your fashion statement that you are not from the East Coast, at least not my neck of the woods."

"Near Chicago, a little town called Barrington."

"Are there more dressed you like back there?"

Joe held out his hand,

"Hi, I'm Joe Cebellum. And you are?"

Her tone was studied nasal,

"Samantha Trover, but my friends call me 'Muffy.'"

“Samantha, what else do you do other than walk up to guys you don’t know and criticize their choice of outer garments?”

Muffy laughed,

“You are not really trying to blame me for noticing the gold iridescence in your green polyester, creaseless trousers and the shiny shirt with the sixteen odd large buttons up and down the front and on the cuffs?”

“So, does this mean you want to dance?”

With that Muffy raised her right hand, stepped on her tippy toes, wiggled her formless hips, and shook like a bowl full of Dundee’s orange marmalade. Some guy Joe did not know slithered toward them. He was another preppy to be sure, wearing the same Khakis as Muffy and a heavy-starched light blue dress shirt with button down collar, His cordovan loafers were tasseled, just like Muffy’s. He had about twenty extra pounds of privilege on his amorphous frame.

“Joe Cebellum, I’d like you to meet Pen Swill. Pen meet Joe. Pen, Joe just asked me to dance.”

Muffy held out her hand. Pen handed her a dollar. The two preppies left Joe in the wake of their cackle.

LLLL. One Or Both Must Fall

The next mixer started better. The whole night looked much better but the laws of physics intervened. Dillon was again the scene of another stilted boy meets girl artifice. This time Joe learned not to stand by himself. Fief and he were together. Joe marched his way down Witherspoon Street to the Army-Navy store. He was now wearing time and coast appropriate clothes. He did not stand out like a Hollywood extra who had been strewn aside on the cutting floor from the movie, *Barbarella.* Fief was wearing light brown wide wale corduroy pants and a barely ironed button collar blue dress shirt. Three girls from Bennett latched onto them. As the mixer ended, Joe seized the moment,

"Why let the fun stop when we are just really getting to know one another. Tippy, Missy, and Sloopy, how 'bout joining Tim and me back at my room? We could all smoke some dope."

Three yesses confirmed the enthusiasm of the hour.

Joe's roommate Joel Frites was spending the weekend in New York with his stepmother and father. They were celebrating. Joel's dad had divorced his mother long ago. Mr. Frites remarried a woman from Argentina. Not surprisingly the new Mrs. Frites was a devout Roman Catholic. Joel and his dad were more or less average North American papists. Mr. Frites now feigned the posture of one fully devout. Nothing would make the new bride happier than if Mr. Frites could take communion. Catholic orthodoxy is rigid and unbending unless the correct procedure is followed, one which usually involves a joyful giving of *mucho dinero*. The correct protocol of crossing a bishop's palms sufficiently was followed. The canon's wheels moved slowly to correct what was now deemed a clerical error in the roles of what only God may set asunder. The marriage of Mr. Frites to Joel's mother was annulled. By fiat, Joel was now numbered among those born out of wedlock. The good news was that Mr. Frites could now partake of the sacrament of the blood and body of the Lamb.

Moreover, Joe and Fief could go back to Joe's bedroom with Tippy, Missy, and Sloopy. Fief, Tippy, and Sloopy climbed into the top bunk. Joe and Missy rolled onto the bottom. The lower two settled in, under the covers. All five flicked their clothing to the floor. Fief and his two new friends enjoyed the exhilarating height with a tad too much exuberance. The top bunk came off its posts. The roof caved in upon Missy and Joe. By instinct, Joe tried to protect Missy from the falling bunk bed. He held up his left hand. You can't close the door when the walls cave in. Or perhaps, it was better to say that the horses were out of the barn. The issue of proper metaphor was moot. The metal edge of the bottom of the top bunk mashed the top of the third finger on his left hand into the wall.

One-half inch of the tip of Joe's finger, almost down to the bottom of his nail hung precariously from the rest of the finger. The tip was listless. The throbbing finger below was bloody. It was a warm, starry night for the walk to the Infirmary. Joe wore only his blue and red boxer shorts with a blanket draped over his shoulders. Fief expressed his concern and regrets,

"Joe, shit. I am sorry. I had no idea that top bunk would spring loose, a bucking bronco of its own accord."

"Don't worry Tim. I am sure I will be o.k. I guess the lesson is that a man should only try to break in one saddle at a time. It is good that Tippy, Sloopy, and you all landed on your feet, unharmed."

"All three girls got out of Dodge even before the last stage."

"Do we even know their last names?"

"Barely, and I do mean barely, their first names."

The campus was quiet at three in the morning. Fief and Joe walked into the Infirmary. A sign directed them up the stairs to the second floor where the night nurse's station was located."

"I think we need some medical attention"

The nurse, in full white dress, little white triangular hat included, put her finger to her lips,

"Shh, shhh."

Joe showed her his finger.

"You will have to sign in."

"Listen Nurse Ratched, I am left-handed, Please call an ambulance since it appears you are the only one here."

This would be Joe's only visit to the Princeton Infirmary. It was a quick trip up Washington, over on Nassau Street, then down Witherspoon past the Army-Navy store to the emergency room of the Princeton Hospital. Once there, it was a three hour wait. Gauze around the tip of Joe's finger stopped the bleeding. The emergency room surgeon was involved in a serious case. A man had been shot in the head. The victim hailed from the Princeton neighborhood which held the blacks who worked as cooks and waiters for the Eating Clubs and as janitors on campus. The Friday night argument started in a bar. It was about a woman. The operation was long and delicate. The surgeon removed the bullet successfully. The E.R. doctor was bleary-eyed by the time he attended to Joe. He saved the tips of Joe's finger with six stitches. Joe's finger was set back in place only a little cock-eyed. The nail was in the proper place but the tip beneath was slightly skewed. The next night Joe went to see the movie, *Bullit*. The Darvon that the doctor prescribed for Joe's pain enhanced the dizzying effects of the famous San Francisco car chase scene. Joe's finger was still healing when basketball tryouts for the Freshmen team started. Bad digit on his shooting hand or not, Joe was sure he would have been fingered by Coach Hyland as a bad apple not to spoil the barrel picked to ply the Princeton hardwoods. Once healed, the finger was fine. Joe's jump shot and all his other activities suffered no long term affect.

MMMM. Under Some Providential Control

The third mixer was the charm. Fief, Appleseed, and Cebellum headed to Manhattan. Finch College, the upper Eastside girl's finishing school, had issued a blanket invitation to Princeton which Fief glibly noted would likely end between the sheets. Finch was a school for girls from privileged families who had neither the aptitude nor the achievement to attend the Seven Sisters or other places of higher learning. Tricia Nixon and Grace Slick were both alumnae. When Tricia invited her Finch schoolmates to the White House for a "tea party" on April 24th, 1970, the lead singer for the Jefferson Airplane was invited. Belying her stage name, Slick lacked the Grace to send regrets. She also decided to bring Abbie Hoffman along for the ride. The idea was to turn the cozy event into something the Mad Hatter would hanker. Grace Slick was on Nixon's "Enemies List." LSD in hand, she was recognized at the door then denied admission. The Secrets Service stalwarts did not recognize Federal criminal conspiracy defendant, Abbie Hoffman.

Back in late 1969, the hopeful trio of Teddy, Tim, and Joe headed up to the Big Apple with Tim at the wheel in the Fief family Chrysler. Joe was armed with a pint of Southern Comfort in his back pocket. When Teddy suggested Joe's choice of booze was not fitting for the occasion, Joe replied,

"What's good enough for Janis Joplin is good enough for New York's most pliable debutantes."

The mixing part of the evening went better than expected. Joe, Tim, and Teddy met three girls willing to squeeze every last drop out the night. The girl that latched on to Teddy had her own Park Avenue apartment, actually a co-op, and all to herself. Her daddy wanted her to have all the comforts of home. The three couples were all the better for drink as they poured themselves into Fief's car to head up Park Avenue. It was not clear whether it was simple sloppy drunkenness or the complication of unbuttoning dress buttons while driving. Tim did not notice the light had turned red. The Fief Chrysler plowed into the back of a car stopped at the intersection. The impact caused the trunk of the stopped car to lose its latch. None of the latchees or the latchors in the Chrysler were hurt. It was Timothy Parsley Fief's lucky night. The light turned green. The car in front of the Chrysler sped away. No one will ever know what was in that trunk. The open trunk bounced up and down but neither drugs nor dead body spilled out.

What was left of that night and the rest of the weekend was spent in Park Avenue opulence. The Penthouse apartment was fully furnished, no doubt by one of New York's leading interior decorators. No detail or expense was spared. More importantly, the place had four bedrooms, one more than necessary. The comfort of the surroundings was surpassed by the comely hospitality that can only be enjoyed during a weekend in the sack with a daughter of free market success who has fully and completely given herself over to the idea and the practice of free love.

NNNN. The Particulars Of Our Retreat

In between the interludes provided by mixers, Joe procured other diversions, on and off campus. Joe's best friend in the fifth and sixth grades, and on again off again buddy thereafter, Felina Woodworrell entered New York University in Greenwich Village. Joe visited Manhattan for the first time to see Felina, weeks before the Finch Mixer. Joe took the bus to New York's Port Authority Bus Station. He got off the bus then took the subway to NYU. Joe walked up from the subway then directly into Felina's dorm which fronted Washington Square with its smaller Arch de Triomphe. Joe was intent upon seeing Felina. He did not notice the hip Dylan/Baez influenced semi-bustle that marked Greenwich Village. Nor did he feel the sunny, light-aired grace of a perfect autumn day. Joe's hurried failure to observe his surroundings made the time with Felina all the more spectacular. Up the dorm elevator, in the cramped shaded single room, Joe and Felina smoked a couple of joints.

The two melded as one from their first warm embrace and polite kiss. They were together again. It was not necessary to hold hands to be close. Side by side, Joe and Felina left her room. They took the elevator down to the dorm lobby then stepped from the steps out to the sidewalk. Joe and Felina whirled through the subway turnstiles to go uptown. The two were stoned, immersed in one another. It was not just their syncopated waves of reflexive conversation which made them both oblivious to all else.

The subway ride muted the effects of the dope. The clank, clank, clang of the train wheels on the tracks and the artificial yellow underground light were a strange and dull prelude to the full exuberance of what would soon glimmer before them. They exited the subway at 86th Street on the west border of

Central Park. They walked, shoulder touching shoulder up into a gentle melee.

There is a reason “Autumn in New York” is a jazz standard. The golden light of late afternoon framed Felina and Joe. It also demarked everything all around them. Tall trees had not yet lost their green. Large sprawling meadows were trimmed with light green spaces of grass interspersed with brown patches occasioned by the rub of baseball, soccer, and football. People were everywhere to inhale vigorously one more last gasp of warmth before the chill of November and the damp cold of December and of the winter.

Everywhere you looked the temper of the times added its own brush stroke. Colors flashed tempo. Clothing was worn to make a statement. Cacophony and clash prevailed over fashion sense and style. Vintage boutiques, second-hand stores, and Salvation Army resale shops had all been plundered. It did not matter what you wore as long as it could not be worn by the nine to five militia. The cadre of conformity was the unknowing enemy of the self-proclaimed free spirited. Splashes of fabric, pattern, sheen, and tint created a canvas with no regard for the bounds of taste.

The flurry of the moment did not require clothing. Atop the Winged Angel of the Waters on Bethesda Fountain, a young man danced in a light blue Speedo. He moved to the rhythm of the earth and to the syncopation of the crowd below. People in rowboats on a little lake stood up. Instability sent ripples and waves to meet gentle propagations from boats nearby. So many landlubbers without sea legs, pivoted perilously towards the tipping point without capsizing. Remarkably, no ballast, human or otherwise, became flotsam or jetsam, unless, balance was neglected in the throes of battle when oars crossed precariously. Near the shore, two Rubenesque women and a Van Gogh guy stood bare-chested, waist deep in the water. The only element missing was an Impressionist with his easel.

Calculated promenade had given way to steps turning circles, ovals, and inadvertent figure eights. Geometry in turn disappeared. Sway, swirl, and sashay cut to the core of music driven motion. Near one frenetic group was a steel drum trio. Another band of merry makers was led by two guitars and a bongo drum. Three young girls were dressed in Indian pattern one piece cotton cloths, one purple, one chartreuse, and one deep blue, all three knotted above their breasts. It was something drawn from Jules Feiffer. They matched the movement created by a lonely saxophone player. In most places, the sound of the rustle of the wind in the leaves sufficed to give the throng its impetus. Somehow the omnipresent city street noises had been eclipsed.

Felina and Joe clasped five fingers. They walked around the park until they saw a tree trunk they could call their own. The two old friends sat under the shelter of tender branches. They did not say a word. As the sun set, the time of day which is neither daylight nor dark refreshed their spirits. The day quenched the need to roam. Joe and Felina fetched simple harmony, within themselves, with each other, and with their surroundings.

OOOO. Those Who Live At A Distance Know But Little Or Nothing

Joe took the bus back to Princeton. Neither the chemical smells along the Turnpike from the Lincoln tunnel to the Oranges nor the grey squalor of the swampy landscape darkened Joe's mood even an iota. When Joe got off the bus in Princeton, Joe was happily confronted with the fact that Nassau Street and the campus were a different world, a singularly better place than either Manhattan or its North Jersey curtilages. Princeton consumes everything within its open arms. The University is neither twister nor hurricane. Students reach beyond the comfort of their outstretched arms and legs buoyed by the amniotic emulsion of unreined discourse. A vivacious mix of thoughts, pure and applied, is sustained by a viscous stasis. Intellectual and scientific pursuits are folded carefully, yet prominently within the envelope of history to spread to the four corners of its unbounded shelter. It was not surprising that within this swarm of fetal nurture, Joe lost track of the baseball season. *The New York Times*' sports page reports Ivy league squash results but not yesterday's baseball scores. The writers for *The Daily Princetonian* aspire to follow in those footsteps. While the Fall Classic was in full swing, *The Prince* reported mainly on the Vietnam War Moratorium. October 14th and 15th marked the days "teach-ins" spotted the academic landscape to upset the Nixon administration. At Shea Stadium, a larger upset was a foot. The Amazing Mets won Games Three and Four. On October 16th, in Game Five the Mets clinched the series. It was one of the greatest upsets in the history of baseball against the Baltimore Orioles, a team many, even today, consider to be one of the best teams in the history of the game. It was the second time in the span of one year that a team from New York had wrested the National Championship from a team from Baltimore. In January, Joe Namath and the New York Jets took The Baltimore Colts to task in the Super Bowl.

PPPP. No Army At Hand To Have Relieved The Garrison

Fred and Sam kept their full attention on the baseball season. Fred followed the Cubs in pain, Sam with glee. The Cubs blew a seemingly insurmountable first place lead with little time left in the season.

From Norman, Oklahoma, Sam called Fred at home.

Betty called Fred from upstairs,

"Fred, the phone for you, It's Sam."

"Hullo"

"You know ineptness is something at which the Cubs excel better than any other team."

Fred was terse,

"Sam, your snide comments are something up with which I will not put. It is only fitting that one of your chosen few will soon be banned forever from our National Pastime. I see that the Cardinal's Center Fielder has taken the notion of the abolition of slavery to extreme limits. On October 7th, Curt Flood was traded and now refuses to go where he has been sent. When those cotton pickers get rotten, you can't pick very much cotton. Curt Flood has confused roaming the outfield with callus forming hard work."

“Fred, Baseball will always survive.”

“I guess you are right, we survived the Cardinal’s owner, Bill Veeck with that midget, Eddie Gaedel, going to bat to make a mockery of the game. Jackie Robinson even survived the Cardinals’ Enos ‘Country’ Slaughter when he spiked Robinson, half way up his leg, out of mean, sheer spite.”

“Veeck was the St. Louis Browns not the Cardinals”

“St. Louis is St. Louis”

“But, you are right, it is a short step from integration to having the inmates running the asylum. Next thing you know the players will be making a million dollars a year, white, black, and even Latin guys like Roberto Clemente. Plus what they can make on underwear ads.”

“Sam, all I know is that the Cubs keep the true spirit of the game, fielding a team of guys who can barely play, keeping the doormat dusted and with no lights so you have to watch the game the way God intended.”

QQQQ. All Nations And Ages Have Been Subject To Them

Upperclassmen and pledges alike were all perched on the edge of their seats in the dining room of the Sigmund Albert Estragon house. The lights were all on Tommy.

Even though the object of the exercise was clear, the President of the fraternity said his piece,

"Tommy Wanderby, fallen pledge, we will give you one last chance to resurrect your own standing in our Fraternity, in our state, and in our race. There are limits to human compassion for the inferior races. If you do not treat a dog with discipline, when you least expect it, that dog will bite you. Show your brothers, and come clean for all mankind that you were mistaken when you befriended that Spic girl, Clavita however you pronounce that weird Mexican last name; and that you doubly erred when you stood up in Court to testify against one of your own kind when your Clavita was righteously killed the day you brought her to a place she did not belong where she did not have proper respect or behavior for and towards her betters."

The President's mean spirited remarks oozed unwholesome slime over the sordid setting. His venom was devoid of even one drop of the milk of human kindness or the life blood of Christ's compassion. While the words of spite dripped capaciously out of all sides of a mouth which voiced volumes of engrained hate and bigotry, a young Mexican girl stood naked and shivering.

She was not over the age of sixteen, most likely only fourteen. Her hands were bound behind her. She did not look up.

“O.K. Tommy, give her all you’ve got.”

It was a miracle Tommy Wanderby remained composed. He walked quietly towards the young girl who flinched as he drew near. He removed his shirt.

His assembled brothers cheered. Tommy then reached behind the young girl. He untied her hands then placed his shirt over his shoulders. Tommy took the sobbing and shuddering girl from the dining hall, neither to return.

The catcalls and slurs were loud and unanimous,

“Spic lover.” “Pussy boy” “You won’t pledge here or anywhere on this campus.” “You are a lame excuse for a Texan” “Only a Commie Fag would do what you just did.” “Take your chicken acts and that little piece of chicken shit wearing your shirt the hell out of here now.” “And don’t come back unless you want to have the wrath of the Good Lord come down upon you like Jacob’s hammer.”

Tommy thought, “Ladder, hammer what’s the difference.”
The point had been made. The next day Tommy informed the Dean of the University of his formal intention to withdraw from TCU.

His mother, Wanda was beside herself,

“F. Scott, I warned you about our son. The minute, I mean the second, he started that friendship with Alberto, I knew his days were numbered as an upright Christian in Texas or any God-fearing community. What can we do? What will we tell our friends?”

“Wanda, you should be proud of our son. He took a stand for what he believes. Not only that, what he believes is right.”

“F. Scott, there are subversive elements everywhere. Look at the way the kids dress. Look at the hair on the boys. The girls’ hair is even worse, never curled, never permed, and no make-up or brassieres. God made us all to wear clothes, especially underwear. The world as we know it will soon be over. Next thing you know someone will say that money is the root of all evil,”

“Wanda, I do not think we have to worry. Money will always have its day in the sun. There is never a real setback for the buck. The Almighty dollar will always reign supreme. Even the Communists will soon be clamoring for currency. I fear the day when that happens. Bottom line, we do not need to worry about the dollar. Greed has the time-proven historical propensity to take care of itself. Let us do our best to let Tommy know we are here to help him.”

“F. Scott, really?”

RRRR. If We Believe The Power Of Hell To Be Limited

In the next two weeks, Wanda's pouting was never too far away. Finally, F. Scott called his brother, Fricke, who was still Governor of Illinois. Fricke was never too busy to help his brother. He called President Nixon who gave him the name of the right guy to call at the Pentagon. Fricke made the call. The matter was set. Tommy joined the Army. He would go to basic training with the unspoken assurance that he would not be sent to Vietnam. Tommy knew none of this. He would have been happy to serve. It was more than the war. It was strange times everywhere. Yet, for four close friends, it really was the same story, just different variations on two major themes in learning and in growing. Each traveled his own way, with his own limits and horizons. Joe both knew and felt that everything was connected but he also knew and felt he did not fit in. Fred had no sense anything was connected. He did not care. Fred, however, fit in wherever he went. Sam could not find even the first connection. He did not believe there was or could be any positive intricacy or pattern to the world around him. Beyond his skepticism, Sam knew he could not really fit in, anywhere. For Sam, any possibility of insight or sight was fettered by sorrow and by self-pity. Tommy knew and felt a strong connection with all humanity. That Tommy ultimately made the decision that he would not fit in with his SAE Fraternity brothers was a testament to the fact that he would fit in everywhere, an everyman with true warm feelings for all those he would meet and those he might help. For both Tommy and Joe, security was an illusion but was not something that was needed. They both had confidence that brimmed of its own accord. Joe did not trust in anything specific but he knew whatever happened would come out all right.

Tommy held a calm faith with a world view of giving back all that you wish to take thereby receiving more in the end. Fred needed something beyond the ease with which he made friends. He did not want to spend a lot of time thinking about it, but he did need someone to tell him that everything would turn out right. Sam just didn't give a fuck. He wanted everyone to like him. He yearned to be admired as somebody. Sam was never comfortable in his own skin.

SSSS. The Inevitable Consequences Of A Long Retreat

It was early November when Tommy was inducted. He would report for duty at the beginning of the New Year, 1970. Tommy decided to spend the last two months of 1969 with Alberto Faltenada in counties along the Texas-Mexican border, helping the cause of migrant farm workers. While Fred was helping Tiffany get to school on time, while Sam was vainly fluttering from flower to floor adroitly refining his skills as a word merchant, and while Tommy was across the borderline to help the poor marking time before basic training started, Joe was settling into the *tout ensemble* that was and would be Princeton.

It was sweater weather. The afternoon was sunny and decidedly cool. After two months, Joe's days were blending into routine. He would sleep late. The night before was always well spent into the wee hours listening to music with John "Lemming" Cello and anyone else who would help fill the air with music, bonhomie, and exhaled marijuana smoke. The march to Commons for lunch was always the same. Joel Frites and Joe would argue about whatever topic piqued their interest, eat four or five plates of mystery meat, starch, and canned vegetables, then head back to share a few tokes before heading to Dillon to play basketball pick-up games, usually half court where the winners held the floor. After basketball, Joe would read. Sometimes he took a cat nap before dinner at Commons. Dinner was unremarkable except in its nutritional similarity to lunch. Sometimes, Joe and "Lemming" Cello would break up the afternoon with Yogurt at the Student center. They both felt virtuous for not eating French fries. It had to be Dannon yogurt, the kind with the fruit on the bottom. The truth was that a diet of Yogurt might be healthy if it were not a snack in addition to a three meal regimen. The third meal was a late night meal, more than a snack. At times it was brought to the entry door by the Hoagie Man or the Pizza Man, both whom roamed the campus in the afterhours. Other times a trip off the campus was required, a hoagie from A&S on Nassau Street near Witherspoon Street, a pizza at The Annex on Nassau towards Washington Street, or a Sandwich at the Diner on Witherspoon Street just across the street but down a little from the Army-Navy store. When you skipped breakfast, a late night meal was necessary. Dope induced munchies added, hand in hand, to the pleasure of the taste and to the relief of hunger. By Christmas break Joe and "Lemming Cello" had gained twenty to twenty-five pounds. This was the heaviest Joe would be until he stopped smoking cigarettes when he turned thirty.

As far as routines go, this was a good one. This first semester Joe attended all his classes and all his precepts. The only other part of the day which occurred regularly, with some frequency, involved making phone calls. After dinner, and before music and drugs, sadly without the sex, Joe would call home. He spent so much time on the phone that the amount of his share of long distance charges on the 22 Little phone bills might have covered a lot of airplane travel. He spent most of his time talking to Sarah Foreswallow. He called her almost every day. Joe also frequently called his mom and dad. He also occasionally called Fred and other high school buddies still back in the Sleepy Little Village. It was too hard to try to hook up with Tommy and Sam as they tramped through their own college experiences.

TTTT. There Are Cases Which Cannot Be Overdone By Language

Basketball that afternoon was fun. His finger was completely healed. Joe noticed his stamina and his shooting were both markedly better than when he played in high school, no doubt predominantly a function of maturity and growing into his adult frame. Rather than go back to his bunk to read after showering, Joe decided to go to Pyne Hall, one entry towards the middle arch from Fief and Thew's room. It was a coed entry. He wanted to see if Lisa Birdor was around. Fief had introduced the two very early in the semester. Lisa was outgoing and pleasant. Joe was not sure whether the better description of the group of upperclassmen interested in Lisa was "throng" or "swarm." Lisa was friendly to everyone. Joe knocked on her door.

"Who is it, please?"

"Lisa, Hi. It's Joe Cebellum. You know the guy who says hello to you whenever our paths cross on campus, the guy Tim Fief knows."

Lisa opened the door.

"Sure, come on in. Grab a chair..."

Lisa pointed to the empty desk chair. She reclined amidst five or six pastel shaded pillows on her bed. Sitting or standing, Lisa was a picture of subtle confidence. She was wearing hip hugger bell bottom blue jeans. Her hips gave the pants just the right oomph. Lisa's slender legs led her body with grace. The space between her thighs issued suggestion if not invitation. Lisa's light pink man-tailored blouse flowed elegantly from her shoulders to her slender waist until it was lost in her jeans. Her soft bra, likely one of those that unsnapped in the front, pushed softly against the double packets of the blouse. As she leaned against the head of her bed, she pulled her knees up to her chin. There is nothing warmer than a pair of intelligent eyes engaging you in just the right way, even if you are only imagining that it is in just the right way. Lisa's elegance started with her thin nose. Her chin found a small but perfect round arc. Her cheeks were understated, leaving her eyes their true place of prominence. Lisa pursed her lips. Her smile shone breezy with a gentleness that fell short of coquetry. Joe's imagination took the next step, a look from someone else, Lisa's head tilting up, her eyes focused down, her mouth opened to show just a peal of white glimmering top teeth. It was Gene Tierney's overbite, the essence of sensual.

"...I don't think Layla will mind you sitting on her chair while she's out. My chair is full of laundry that needs to be folded."

Lisa wrapped her arms around her upbent knees. She leaned her head forward maintaining eye contact, a plumb not quite a pierce.

Joe sat down. He leaned toward Lisa. He was thinking he would follow her anywhere, but he said,

"I didn't know Layla Lungadont is your roommate."

"Yea, since she is not here studying. I think I will play a record. Would you mind closing the door so I can crank the volume?"

"A pleasure."

Lisa got up then removed Joe Cocker's *With a Little Help from My Friends* from its jacket, then the dust cover. In seconds, side one, "Feeling Alright" was blaring. Lisa again took to the comfort of her array of pillows,

"So to what do I owe the pleasure of this visit?"

"I am transparent in carrying the burden of ulterior motive. Before I seek to impose upon you, please tell me what is like to be the most popular girl on an Ivy men's campus."

"Lisa blushed and turned her eyes down. You know there's June and another Lisa, Halaby, just to name two."

"No one is, or is it has, the entire package. That in which I am luxuriating right now."

Lisa deflected the overly profuse compliment with a tight smile and a slight rear of her head,

"This may sound peevish and ungrateful, but the attention is wearing. I feel like any second I might be trampled by a pack of horny dogs. God knows what will happen if I were actually to go into heat..."

Joe laughed.

"...I am not being snotty or arrogant, just overwhelmed by testosterone. I feel like everyone is just trying to cut to the chase. Life demands that you taste first. Then add a little flavor of your own. My sense is that I am worshipped, or at least, revered like some cold marble Greek statute in some fucking museum."

The song switched to "Bye Bye Blackbird."

“A problem I do not think I will ever have. But there are worse traps in which to be caught, I suppose”

“Do you have time to smoke a joint? I have some dope at the right of my middle desk drawer, near the back, in an envelope, if you want to roll a joint. The rolling papers are there too.”

Joe opened the desk drawer then reached to the back.

“Smells good”

“Yep, a friend of mine gave me a lid. This is all that is left. She says some guy laid it on her at Woodstock. So we can imagine Joe Cocker is singing for us right there, right then.”

“Right On.”

They took three tokes each, not even half a joint.

Lisa rubbed the joint out in a little ashtray on her desk. Satisfied it was played out, she dipped the resinous remaining half into the horizontal right front pocket of her hip huggers.

“Wow, thanks. I am definitely ripped.”

“Me, too. So tell me Joe. What is the favor you came to ask?”

“I almost forgot. You see, I have this girlfriend back home.”

“This is a pick-up line I have not heard on campus yet.”

Joe laughed,

“Right you will have to excuse me for not finding my way into the pack, or is it now a herd. You may rest assured I have a sense of my own limits and an astute fear of rejection, more than the fact I have the old steady back home, the girl that's just like the girl that married dear old dad, or not as the case may be."

"You Midwestern boys have your bumbly charm."

"Anyway, Sarah, her name is Sarah, will come to visit soon. How do you feel about lying for a good cause, if not for the greater good of one lonely boy from Illinois?"

"You tug at my heart strings. Telling the truth is important"

"How 'bout we call it a statement of future intention- in circumstances where it is hard to predict what will transpire. Lying, if I may be permitted to use that word here, somewhere between a fact and an opinion."

"Law school is in your future."

"May the Good Lord strike me down where I sit. Anyway, I noticed in your desk drawer that your stationary is ever so lavender, just the right color for an expedient prevarication."

"I will be writing a letter?"

"I'll provide the postage."

"And the address"

"Mr. and Mrs. Vincent Foreswallow Fox Point, 44 Old Mill Road, Barrington, Illinois 60010. Please tell them that their lovely and innocent daughter, Sarah, may stay in your room during her visit here, thereby propriety will be served. After all, it's the thought that counts."

"For Sarah and you, consider pen will soon be to paper."

“Thanks, Lisa I’ll stop by promptly upon my return from my trip up to Boston this weekend for the Harvard game.”

“No need, I’ll mail it. Foreswallow, 44 Old Mill, Barrington, 60010.”

“Charm and full attention. So this is how the consummate lure men to their doom.”

Joe left the room. Joe Cocker sang Dylan, “…she makes love just like a woman…”

UUUU. See Not The Full Extent Of The Evil Which Threatens

Joe would never admit this to Sam or to Tommy but the first time he walked into Palmer Stadium to see a Princeton football game, he thought he had mistakenly wandered in to see Princeton High School play. The Barrington team his Senior year would certainly have given Princeton all they would ask. Football played at OU and at TCU was from a different universe. Princeton alumni never lost homage or reverence to the glory days when ineffectual slow social register players became first mired in their own fantasies. What Princeton lacked in athleticism it soon picked up in the realm of espionage and matters of state. The spy game was not just for Skull and Bones Yalies. William Colby '40 became head of the CIA. The Dulles Brothers, Allan '14 and John Foster '08 were a double threat propped by the Rockefellers, but not on the gridiron. The word on campus was that George Schultz '42 had a tattoo of a Princeton tiger on his ass. Before Princeton, Adlai Stevenson '22 was a Northern Illinois farm boy who hailed from a large farm on Route 22 due east of the Sleepy Little Village on the way back to the North Shore town of Lake Forest. The Stevenson Estate was located in the town of Half Day, so-called because it was a half day away from Chicago, by horseback, back in the day. Adlai had left his less than humble roots to attend Choate where, like Kennedy, surrounded by the cream of the elite, he learned that the poor were people too. Adlai was prey to the same influence as JFK. The Choate headmaster, George St. John, told the young men in his charge, "Ask not what Choate can do for you, ask what you can do for Choate." For Adlai Stevenson '22, too, Choate was alive with the same sentiment. He failed in his run for President against a *bona fide war hero.* When Kennedy succeeded where Stevenson had not, JFK '39 broadened the scope of that charge for his fellow prep school students to citizens of the nation as a whole.

All exclusive clubs, thrive with the same unwavering imperative, "Take Care of Our Own." Kennedy's original Princeton class, 1939, exemplified this limited stricture. In a fashion probably best explained by the notion, "there but for the grace of God goes I," they all rallied around one besotted fellow from their year, Freddy Fox. In the fall of 1969, it was common to see Fox, a hapless but privileged drunk, pedal his bicycle, in and around campus. The state of New Jersey had, for some time, revoked his driver's license. While Kennedy and Stevenson asked what they could do for everyone, the good folks named Colby, Dulles, Schultz asked what they could do for their own, to protect U.S. business interests here and abroad. The dominos that were feared to fall if Communism spread were U.S. owned businesses operated overseas in both hemispheres. Nationalization was the dirtiest of dirty words.

VVVV. Where Conquest Is The Object

It mattered to Joe, not a whit, that the Princeton-Harvard game was not really football. The time honored motto, "Princeton in the Nation's Service" in the sense of protecting old money legacies mattered even less. Joe was going up to see Peter Valpeter, his buddy from Senior Year of high school. Peter was starting his first year at Harvard. Joe also thought he would stop by Wellesley College to see Kay Paulson, a girl he once fancied. Kay, a devout Christian Scientist had thrown him over Junior year of high school when Fred and he snuck a bottle of Vodka into the Paulson's kitchen.

As you walked into the lower level of the U-Store, there was a "ride board." It was a bulletin board where students would offer to give other students rides, usually back home for Christmas, Thanksgiving, School End, or Spring Break. Pinned notes offering rides to Florida and to away football games were also common. Joe had seen one for the Harvard football weekend. The offer was by George Demondrone. Joe called him. George, another guy named Fred Alexander from Indiana, and Joe headed North through New Jersey, into New York over the George Washington Bridge, on to the Cross Bronx Expressway. Then Demondrone exited south on the Major Deegan expressway. In minutes, a modern shrine to success loomed before them.

"George, Fred. You know, I play basketball in Dillon Gym five or six days a week. It is nice to pound the hardwoods in the house that Bill Bradley built. But to see Yankee Stadium, the house that Ruth built, this is one of life's true pleasures. I can now almost hear Lou Gehrig, dying in front of a standing room only crowd clamoring appreciation, 'Today, I am the luckiest man on the face of the earth.' I can see Mickey Mantle standing at the plate admiring one of his long home runs, just like George Herman Ruth and many others before and after him. You know Mickey Mantle and I have the same birthday, October 20th, although he is ten years older…"

"Why I'll be a blue nosed gopher, my mama gave me my first breath on that same day in a little bitty hospital in Houston."

Fred could not resist,

"Why I'll be a spring peeper, I was born in Indianapolis on a cold Kentucky morning, in the ghetto. And by the way, you went south on 87 when you were supposed to head north on 95."

George interrupted the chortles of Fred and Joe. He tried to sweep his small *faux pas* under the floorboards.

"Gentlemen, in Texas for fun, we go fishing or catch some cattle rustlers, then celebrate with an old fashioned barbecue. The Houston Colt '45s, I mean Astros, have proved that the only sport men in Texas really play is football. And my ole' buddy Fred here, back home in Indiana, for fun they watch the corn grow."

"Demondrone, and I do mean drone, at least in Indiana only the women are scared, not like in Texas where you have to include sheep and heifers."

Demondrone merged to the next exit to head back north.

For Joe there were no wrong turns,

“Well, I, for one, am glad we saw Yankee Stadium. Next spring I will go to see a game.”

Soon they were in Connecticut. Joe noticed it was starting to snow, just a sprinkle.

“George, have you ever driven in snow before?”

“Nope but don’t worry your little Northern head about it. I think I told you, Fred anyway, my daddy owns the biggest Buick dealer in Houston. This here Buick, if I may leave our studied shores and lapse back into the vernacular of my homeland, has General Motors, state of the art, road handling technology. They call it, ‘positraction.’”

Fred added,

“I haven’t had as much experience with snow in Southern Indiana as Joe, but I do know steering and suspension will not correct hydroplaning.”

The snow began to fall in earnest. Interstate 95 was now wet and slushy. The Demondrone Buick swerved then spun to a safe stop on the shoulder.

Fred kept pointing to the road sign while, between words, laughing his best Indiana farmer nasal guffaw,

“Ride ‘em cowboy. A stop even a rodeo clown would admire. New Haven sixteen miles, I guess, George old boy, you heaved into a new haven right here.”

Demondrone got out of the front seat of the car. He flipped his car keys to Joe. Joe drove the rest of the way to Boston without incident.

WWWW. Dwell Not Upon The Vapors Of Imagination

It was great to see Peter Valpeter. He lived in a Freshmen dorm in Harvard Yard. Joe arrived in time for a Friday night party. There was beer and loud music plus girls from all over the Boston area. The nearest school to PU that had girls was Rider College to the South, the nearest girls' school was Centenary. Harvard was luxuriating in women freely given to good times and to friendly persuasion. Princeton had no counterpart to Radcliff. Peter handed Joe a beer,

"Good to see you. You made it safe and sound. Why not take the mingling by the horns, so to speak?"

"Thanks, Peter. I can see you left three doting girls in the lurch."

"I will wander the land in search of the next honest gam."

"Go forth and stultify."

Joe walked up to a young woman with brown hair that curled at her shoulders, bangs that broke a straight line just above her hazel eyes, and an uncertain smile. Her skin was pale white. She was sitting comfortably. Her blue chinos were loose. Her navy sweater held her ample round breasts without a bra.

Joe smiled and raised what was formed as a question,

“Are you now, or have you ever been, a negro?”

“No, I’m a Sagittarius”

The ball was rolling. Somewhere in the genetic mapping of his male driven anima, Joe knew that if you approached a woman with a comment that was not really funny, and she then responded in a friendly way, all was not yet lost. Joe mimicked a variation of Richard Benjamin’s first phone call to Ali MacGraw in the movie, *Goodbye Columbus*. In that movie, the two had not met face-to-face. Joe hoped that sprinkling a little HUAC humor would help screen out the Republicans and the overly serious alike. The “Sagittarius” response was directly from the same movie. Joe and Janet were on the same page.

Their discussion roared from that small joined point of departure to cover movies, music, and current events. Finally, it was time to get personal. Janet was a sophomore at Radcliff. She grew up in Waltham, Massachusetts. She had a roommate who that night had their room exclusively to entertain. After three hours, Peter’s dorm room was afloat with sloppy drunks. Even if Janet were willing, there was no place for them to go. It was too cold to sit outside. They left the party in full swing to go sit on the stairs on the first floor inside the entry to Valpeter’s second floor room. It was warm enough. They greeted passersby. The outside door only opened long enough to give them both a nice touch of fresh air, cold but not for too long. Janet and Joe talked for another three hours. Finally, the party upstairs winded down. It was now late enough, or early enough. Janet headed back to her own dorm room. She kissed Joe goodbye on his forehead. The message was clear but she explained anyway,

“I have a steady boyfriend. He rows for Harvard. The crew team is away this weekend. Anyway, I hope I did not lead you down the garden path. I really enjoyed the time we spent. The conversation was gripping and engrossing. There are only a few guys who can keep up with me. I had trouble staying with your pace."

"As much as I enjoy words minced and other literal grounds, conversation is not my preferred way of communicating."

"I believe you. Sometimes two ships pass in the night but that is all there is to it. Anyway, I am beat. I can now head back home for some sleep. The coast is clear. My roommate and I agree, eight is enough, hours in this case. So, Shelley's visitor for the night, whoever he might be, has now been given his walking papers."

"Sounds like I met the wrong roommate. Just kidding. I had a great time. Another time, another place, as the saying goes."

Janet kissed Joe, again on the forehead. Twice now, faint hope politely dashed. Joe sought slumber on Valpeter's lumpy couch. He slept a deep sleep. The trip up and the late hour discussion mixed to make him quickly dead to the world.

XXXX. Hold Up Truth To Your Eyes

Saturday noon came early. The entire Harvard Yard slept soundly in a community of beer induced aporia. As Joe changed position within furrows now creased into slightly threadbare couch cushions, he heard the slight tap of four knuckles on a wooden door. Joe got up. He lumbered his way to turn the door knob. Through his grogginess, Joe's face turned ear to ear smile. It was not thaumaturgy from heavens beseeched, but it was nevertheless some sort of intercessory delectation of the highest order. Janet had returned to land on the landing outside Valpeter's room. By comparison, there was no doubt that finding Plymouth Rock in 1620 was overwhelmingly propitious. Nevertheless, Joe was delighted to indulge his senses given Janet's one small step in furtherance of the legacy of the Bay Colony pilgrims' progress. As she looked at the semi-somnambulating Joe, Janet slipped from proper reticence to return her own full-face sincere grin. Janet glanced down at Joe's boxers. Her tongue seemed to stumble over an upper front tooth as she licked her lip,

"Put your clothes on. I know a place where we can discuss the great books and can drink our fill of espresso."

Janet and Joe spent the afternoon on the other side of the Harvard "Coop," the side away from the Redline Station in the middle of the Square. It has been said that the roads in Cambridge, and perhaps Boston as a whole, were established when an early road surveyor followed a drunken cow as it meandered about on a particularly dark New England night. Brattle Street was no exception. Janet knew the way to the Casablanca Restaurant. Since the Fifties, this was a place to eat, drink, and be hip. The room matched Rick's Place from the set of the Bogart-Bergman classic. As they sat drinking dark coffee, it seemed only a matter of minutes before Claude Rains would rush in, blow his whistle to close the place down because he was "shocked, shocked" to discover there was gambling in a backroom on the premises while at the same time he is handed his winnings from that evening. They sat astride in a script of their own making, inserted into the midst of a big screen panorama. It was not apparent to Joe that Janet and he were on their way to commit their own closed room small screen peccadillo.

Janet directed the conversation to a point of purely conjectural or hypothetical interest, or so it seemed,

"Joe, our generation now thrives in the full flush of free love. I believe it is time for the death of the double standard. Men can do what they want but women must toe the line. Women's liberation demands this, at a minimum. More importantly, women must, and should, find their bodies to be the same source of raw physical pleasure as men."

"Interpersonal ethics and cultural mores are interesting from a variety of points of view, to be sure. I like the idea that two people have an obligation to enhance, to enjoy each other in as many permissible ways as possible, and to use your term, to thrive together within the acceptable limits of connection and interaction. Plus men and women owe each other all they can do to be sure that full expression and replete response follow from, at one end, the most intricate and complicated, to at the other, even the simplest form of communication."

"Joe, I like this way of looking at things. There is something I have never understood in the realm of fidelity, not bright, clear and pure sensory experiences, but rather the faithfulness that is, let us say, 'owed' when two people are together..."

"Like you to your away this weekend rower..."

"Right, but on one hand all sorts of intimate intellectual connections and closeness are allowed both on an interpersonal level and as sanctioned by cultural mores or community standards, while simple physical joint gratification and pleasure giving is a long standing taboo. To the extent this no-no is part of the idea that a woman is part of the universe of property owned by a man..."

"There may be a more simple reason for the prohibition. The simple touching of two souls, a goal which, for me, has no worthy rival, for which there is no higher purpose, is, in theory, benign and wonderful when tethered to a purely intellectual plane. The catch with physical intimacy, which surely, while having its own sense of wonder, cannot blossom in the myriad marvelous ways expression with words and exchanges of ideas will enrapture and enthrall, is that while it is ostensibly harmless, but is, in all actuality, primordially fraught with danger..."

Smiles again met and eyes settled in a short but deep gaze.

Joe continued, with only a small blush,

"... Words alone do not lead to pregnancy. Therein, I think is the basis and foundation for the moral stricture against free love as opposed to free conversation."

"And since I am on the pill..."

The ‘p’ in the word ‘pill’ while a mere puff released between Janet’s sultry lips was a fully salacious suggestion. At that split-second, the waiter arrived to suggest a second two double espressos. The moment coursed within Joe even though their conversation then wended to and fro then hither and yon. Rapt immersion in the here, there, and all around was something Janet and Joe had captured in full relish. Anticipation of fruition added fire to the present heat. After a fourth espresso over the line and much in the way of hyper-animated engaging verbal back and forth, with slight, no longer innocent, touching added for good measure, Janet leaned across their little round table. With one hand she squeezed Joe’s right elbow with the force of true intent. She lightly brushed her lips across Joe’s right cheek. She next brought her mouth to Joe’s ear. Janet’s words were barely louder than her soft breath.

“Let’s go kill a couple hours at the Blue Parrot, just around the corner. By then Shelley will have vacated the premises. Tonight, it is my eight hours.”

Logistical impediments had fallen by the wayside. It was now just a matter of sweet time. The Blue Parrot followed the lead of the Casablanca Restaurant. Only Sidney Greenstreet’s character, Signor Ferrari, the man who controlled all organized crime in Casablanca, was missing from this small but cozy faithful living replica. The two hours alinger over dinner seemed to last forever. At long last Janet looked at her wristwatch,

“I think it is now time to connect and embrace the way, last night, you suggested was your métier.”

“I hope my bravado has not caused you to have expectations beyond that which I am capable of meeting.”

“I am sure that, we together, can meet all comers.”

“I am certain that you, on your own, can increase the flow of great rivers and part the seas.”

“I think proper focus is the flow of our own energy and juices as our bodies seize the moment.”

The next eight hours together passed as quickly as the two hours before had slowly creeped. Janet and Joe touched each other. It was spectacular to behold, a spectacle partaken just for the two of them. Joe would never have imagined that a few lines from *Good Bye Columbus*, would lead to an afternoon sparked in joy framed by the classic, *Casablanca*. What then ensued was something beyond the realm of prediction. Tactile pleasures abounded about which not even the best cinema, literature, or words could hint. Mind and body are really always one. That point is made sublimely, to the point of transcendental tremble, when two, each as one, together change a genuine duality to simple, serene unity. It is more than holding each other, more than shared breaths, more than touching which has been transposed to pure sensation. There is a province beyond the point of knowing where waves of true ecstasy cannot be recognized or claimed as having been given or received. At this point no small miracle has been delivered. All feelings simply are.

The time came. Shelley knocked on the door to intrude upon still bliss. Joe and Janet kissed sweetly. Janet squeezed Joe’s hand with the same force she had earlier forced her fingertips into his elbow. The question of what wrong had been done was left for their betters.

YYYY. Let Them Call Me Rebel And Welcome

Joe returned to the Harvard Yard to sleep at Peter Valpeter's dorm room. The rest of that Saturday night Joe was wide awake in the wake of vibrant glow. He was so sated he did not need to find sleep. Joe arose early. He left Peter a note. After words of thanks which did not begin to express his full feelings for that which Peter would never know had been conferred upon Joe, Joe wrote he was going to visit Kay at Wellesley. From there he would head back to New Jersey.

In comparison, the visit with Kay was no more than a social call. Kay was the same, gracious and kind but stiff. Joe was tentative, not sure why he felt the need to give her his regards. The ties formed from four years walking the same halls in the high school at the Sleepy Little Village were profound. Nevertheless, it was common background and no more. Whatever Kay and Joe had approached together before Kay served Joe his walking papers was gone. It evanesced as two planets, or more aptly, molecular particles, spun their own paths, never to meet again. Kay and Joe had touched, but only briefly and never with vigor, not even rigor. Kay extended her hand to stop Joe as he leaned in to kiss her good-bye. Joe had decided to hitchhike back to the Best Damn Place of All. A Volkswagen microbus stopped to pick him up as he walked on the entrance ramp of the Mass Turnpike. "Get-in" was all that was said. Here was a world of difference from Kay's aloof, dismissive clasp. The back of a van was packed with the children of the day. Even before Joe was all the way in, somebody he did not even know was warm with greeting. A soft hand firmly part of the counter-culture extended to Joe half a joint, still fired up. The blue haze of smoke in the van was interspersed with raw conviviality. The skinny blonde girl next to Joe smiled. She pressed her shoulder into his as he sat down. They both exhaled the same dope at the same time adding to the hue. With the wafts, music played. Crosby, Stills, and Nash, “Marrakesh Express,” gave way to Judy Collins with the Sandy Denny song, “Where Does the Time Go?,” next Dylan’s, “Visions of Johanna,” then “The Circle Game,” by Tom Rush. Somewhere in the middle of the song by the Incredible String Band, “Painting Box.” the music became the canvas upon which the small band of fellow travelers was now aflourish. Nine new friends would be whisking to and fro all the way to New Jersey.

ZZZZ. 'Tis Surprising To See How Rapidly A Panic Will Sometimes Run Through A Country

Joe returned with all his better instincts rejuvenated. Time again surged wave and trough as the measure met the circumstance. As the distance from the idyllic interlude *non pareil* with Janet widened, the time for Sarah to arrive seemed to barely shorten. She would visit the week before Thanksgiving Week. In the days between, the pace slowed with the full realization that women were among the missing. The expectation attendant with Sarah's visit coupled with the recent memory of Janet added resin to the sands of time. Minutes, hours, and days bottlenecked. The span might well have clogged, frozen like maple sap resolutely stuck to the stiff, cold bark of a tree on a winter day in Maine. Joe never let any interval stand still for long. Music and camaraderie helped to increase the tempo of all passing hours.

The week before Sarah was going to fly back to New Jersey, once her home, the "Armistice Day Blizzard" cut a 1000 mile swath through the Midwest from Kansas to Michigan. Just as the snow started to sprinkle lightly down Sarah drove to the Barrington Post Office to post a letter thanking Lisa Birdor for her kind offer of hospitality. No snow would slow her down. Sarah would soon be on her way.

Sarah Foreswallow knew New Jersey weather. Winter may encumber the Midwest but in New Jersey, in comparison to Chicagoland, snow only sprinkled, if at all. A few days later, on November 14th, a sonic flurry hit the campus. The Byrds filled Princeton's Dillon with white man's magic. Dorm rooms filled with smoke as everyone toked up while they cued *Untitled* the Byrds live double record or the *Easy Rider* soundtrack. The die was cast. For Joe, his buddies, and many others, "Eight Miles High" became a floor not a ceiling.

The next day was the second Vietnam Moratorium that Fall. For Joe, Teddy, and "Lemming" Cello, it was another day to listen to music and to smoke grass.

"Hey Teddy where'd you get this *Life* magazine?"

"It came in the mail from a kid I went to Chestnut Hill Academy with, Dustin Sharpley."

An irresistible impulse surged through Fief, "Teddy, how did you find it buried under all those dividend check envelopes you get every day?"

It was true Fenton Appleseed received at least ten checks every week.

"Tim, it is not my fault the benefits of the long labors of my family have borne fruit in the way of many envelopes."

"Lemming" Cello grabbed the magazine away from Joe, "To change the subject to somebody really rolling in dough, what the fuck is Paul McCartney doing on the cover? I thought he was dead."

Teddy shook his head, "And with Linda, Jeez."

"Joe, you know I did exhaustive research into all the Beatle albums and their lyrics. There is no doubt Paul is dead. I even listened to that F. Lee Bailey radio program where he cross-examined witnesses then let the listeners draw their own conclusion."

Teddy rolled his eyes, "And with Linda, Jeez."

“I can tell you this. Paul is dead. Lennon played live in Toronto with Clapton and the Plastic Ono Band this September last.

Teddy looked glum, “Yoko Ono, Jeez.”

“I guess it is a metaphor. Paul is the dog that didn’t bark in the night.

Teddy scrunched his face, “Yoko Ono. Linda Eastman, Jeez.

“Listen to this. Paul should stick to writing silly love songs,

‘Perhaps the rumour started because I haven't been much in the press lately. I have done enough press for a lifetime, and I don't have anything to say these days. I am happy to be with my family and I will work when I work. I was switched on for ten years and I never switched off. Now I am switching off whenever I can. I would rather be a little less famous these days.’”

“Yeah and *Life* should stick to publishing photos not notable quotes.”

Teddy’s neck knotted to the left, “Yoko Ono, Linda, Jeez…There is no number of women that can fail to fuck up a perfectly good rock and roll band.”

Fief added his two cents, “There is a primal bond. The universe is one large omnipresence with vital and subtle connections that defy categorization. You need only inhale to get that clear sense. Nevertheless, I continue to be amazed by the capacity of the human mind to dedicate itself to finding connections with humanity that are simply not there, and worse yet, to draw firm and abiding conclusions from flimsy, non-existence evidence. Paul is dead, my ass.”

“Lemming” Cello looked hurt, “Teddy, light one up. Fief is right. It is time to inhale again.”

Teddy finally smiled, “Hear, hear ‘Lemming’ Cello.”

The Beatles officially disbanded in November.

The news reached Oklahoma. Sam was frantic with sorrow. This was worse than reading Sir Arthur Conan Doyle and the death of Sherlock Holmes for the first time. He raised Joe on the telephone,

“There is a heavy burden in my heart. The days of our youth, the days of wine and roses are gone with the wind. Some rosebuds may no longer be gathered...”

“Sam, that homegrown in Oklahoma must be damned good.”

“Seriously Joe, how much would you pay to go to a Beatles’ Concert- third row center? The best songwriting team, since Ira met George, since Cole met Porter, is now *kaput*. Women should be kept out of the recording studio. Their place is in the hotel room, part of room service. Not since the Garden of Eden has the fairer gender had such a profound deleterious effect.”

“Bring some of that weed back home for Christmas.”

“Joe, I didn’t tell you or Fred. I am gonna stay in Oklahoma. The weather forecast is better. It is going to be raining young girls.”

“What happened to all that misogyny of moments ago?”

“Theory and criticism is one thing, practice and immersion quite another.”

5A. Never Appeared To Full Advantage But In Difficulties And In Action

Finally, it was the time for Sarah to come. Joe took all necessary steps for Sarah's arrival. He hung a blanket from the open entrance to the 22 Little living room. Satisfied some privacy was secured, Joe then opened the hide-a-bed, added two pillows, two sheets, and a blanket. The stage was set. Joe borrowed "Lemming" Cello's car to pick Sarah up from the airport. Joe and Sarah walked through the campus from the student parking lot. Sarah punctuated the beauty and the history with "ooh" and "ah." This was the only sightseeing they would do. For the next seventy two hours, the two sequestered themselves between the sheets. Joe had forgotten the tingle, the electricity, and then the full charge. Sarah maintained succinct response, Her "oohs" and "ahhs" were rounded by a sound that was neither purr nor coo, something guttural in full supplication to the joy of her winsome body fully spent, then arising to arousal only to be spent again, and again. Joe peaked beyond his capacity to become peeked surpassing blithe enervation. Words cannot be substituted for either arousal or climax. Then there is the persistent afterglow. Sarah smiled from limb to limb.

"Joe, how will we find a place to do this again next week when you return home for Thanksgiving?"

"If anyone can do it, we are the two who will."

5B. Intercepted Our March

Joe stayed on the East Coast for Thanksgiving. This was the first rift in the structure of Sarah Foreswallow's grand plan for future happiness ever after. "Lemming" Cello had tickets to see the Rolling Stones at Madison Square Garden, both shows on November 28th, the day after Thanksgiving. Joe told Sarah she should understand first things first. Over the phone Joe did not see her pained cringe. Sarah would never understand. With the Beatles gone, Joe was not going to miss his chance to see the Stones. Jagger pranced onstage like a peacock guarding the henhouse. Keith Richards played rock and roll guitar the way Chuck Berry intended. Mick Taylor added the full luster of the slow blues imperative. This was the first time Joe attended a concert that would be released as a "live" record, *Get Your Ya-Yas Out*. It would not be the last.

5C. Suffice It For The Present

Joe was happy to be home for Christmas break. He arrived late on a Wednesday night. The next morning he was happy to wipe the sleep from his eyes then join the whole family, Della, Joseph, Susan, and Victoria. It was too early in the morning for much talk. They were all together at the breakfast table for the first time since the summer. The fellowship of the bond of family preserved a calm warm peace in the face of windows thick with frost. The bitter cold of the Chicago winter was barely restrained. Mom and Dad left the table first. They would take the Northwestern commuter train downtown. Joe's friends reported that his parents held hands as they sat together on the train. Joseph had been promoted to corporate headquarters in the big city. Van Yost Brady had moved The Heart in Hand Bookstore. Della continued as manager. No longer did she hear unhurried light steps along the tree lined asphalt streets of Long Grove. Now Della was surrounded by the snappy bustle of feet pounding the concrete pavement on Michigan Avenue's Magnificent Mile. In another thirty minutes, Joe's two sisters headed out the door to go up the hill to the bus stop.

Joe retreated to his bed. Two sets of wool blankets and a large down comforter would keep him warm. The window shades were down. Joe languished in the haze of light sleep for a good one-half hour. He did not hear the click when the front door opened. He may have heard the hinges of his bedroom door. What he did hear was the delicate rustle of clothes hitting the ground. Sarah's naked body nestled against his.

It was a faint whisper,

"Time to take those plaid boxers off."

Sarah Foreswallow was firm but gentle as she pulled Joe's underwear down his legs and off his feet.

"Now, where we when I last left you at college?"

"Remind me."

Sarah surged to her favorite spot. She straddled Joe. Her wet, tight little pussy surrounded Joe's cock. Sarah placed a palm on each of Joe's shoulders as he tried to sit up.

"Stay where you are. Let me take it from here."

Sarah settled into a smooth glide. Joe's penis was her only guide. She arched her back then leaned forward. Sarah kissed Joe's mouth. It was difficult to tell whether her pussy or her mouth was wetter, a point of only academic interest to be sure. Sarah played with the tiny round tips of her nipples as she continued the slow surge and ebb over Joe's cock. Tongues darted in and out with a faster tempo of their own. They both knew, by heart, the music they were making. Joe liked to keep his eyes closed. He would then concentrate on his body, the feelings pouring from its highest and best use. Sarah was like-minded. She knew just the right way to keep them both at a peak of pleasure without it turning the corner, at least not yet. The path they were taking was more than a road that went on forever. An hour of a slow, slippery slide was an acceptable minimum. Joe moved with Sarah as she reached top then struck bottom, to be sure he would make the moment last. In this case, the moment was going on forty-five minutes. The phone rang, once, twice, then a third time.

Joe reached for the receiver. Sarah continued to keep perfect time.

"Hello"

"Yes, this is Joe Cebellum"

"Yes, I got home last night."

"Sarah Foreswallow, no, I haven't seen her yet."

It was true. Joe had never opened his eyes.

"There is always the possibility that she had car trouble on the way to school."

"Yes, if I see her I will be sure to tell her to get to school."

Joe placed the receiver back on its cradle. In one motion he rolled Sarah on her back. She spread her legs as wide as she could. Joe pumped her pussy for only thirty seconds. He pulled out. His spurt soon oozed from her.

"So you can come quickly if you need to."

"Can you believe it? That was the Attendance Office. If you get to the High School right away they will look the other way. The lady on the phone was serious but all smirk."

Sarah talked as she put her clothes back on,

"I love life in a small town. Everybody knows your next move even before you do. Remind me that when we grow up we should live in the big city."

Sarah gave Joe a very wet sloppy kiss.

"Joe, I'll see you after school. We have many bridges to cross, at least 69."

"That is a good starting number."

"Our favorite."

Sarah wrapped her mouth around the tip of Joe's penis. Then she smacked her lips to let Joe loose from this short lived clutch.

"I love that little devil, especially deep inside me."

The two walked to the door.

"See you later this afternoon, after school. I'll think of a place where we can go."

5D. Wisdom Is Not The Purchase Of A Day

It was not going to be easy to tell Sarah that they were through. Added to that, Christmas break was not going to be all play. There would be enough work to dull the sheen of even the most intrepid fun lover. Della knew the folks at the Lake Zurich Post Office. Lake Zurich delivered a ton of mail, maybe two tons, to The Heart in Hand Book Store for the many years it maintained premises in Long Grove. She also knew that the Seasonal mail crunch required each normal route be cut in two. It was an easy matter to see that Joe was hired to drive one-half a route. For a college kid, the Federal pay scale made this an opportunity that could not be refused. Joe was lucky his mother had an "in." Otherwise there was no way he would be hired. Joe would make enough money in two weeks to provide for the whole next semester. The only drawback to all earning all those sawbucks was the schedule. The hours were imposing- at work at six and then not back home until after dark, six at the earliest. Joe was going to repeat the prior summer. There would be no sleep between work all day and then all night, Sarah, or some other tomfoolery. He could catch up on his sleep back at school.

5E. An Excess Of Tenderness

Chance or circumstance, call it what you will. The point was to pick. Joe preferred to think that opportunity was more than pure potential. Unlimited potential was simply another way of saying never comes the day. Action was simply a matter of assiduously tumbling with the march of time wherever the roll may lead. As long as you liked the bounce, the spin, and the turns, the ultimate place of rest may not matter. Better yet, there may be no stopping point. Giving the world the benefit of the doubt, going forward with an open positive mind only added to the mix. Driving home from his first day of work from the Lake Zurich Post Office, Joe met one more case in point. It had been dark for ninety minutes. The darkness added to the glisten of white snow banks struck by headlights. Only about one foot of snow had fallen that December. Joe drove toward home on Lake Shore Drive. He was about to turn to the right as the road met the lake shore. Joe spotted Carol Eton. She was framed by gleaming white as she stood in the middle of her family's well lit driveway. The path from the front door of her house to the mailbox was shoveled and was broom tidy. The snow was piled up around her two feet above the twelve or so inches that had fallen. Joe slid to a stop with only a slight swerve not a full fishtail. The evening drop in temperature had given the road a slippery crust. Joe leaned to his right to lower the passenger side window,

"Whoa, Nelly Bell"

"After being back east Joe, did you forget how to drive?"

"Sometime I will tell you the story about a Texan driving through a slight snowfall in Connecticut with only positraction as his guide."

"Is 'Positraction,' the contraction for positive attraction?"

"Carol, how do you like Shimer so far?"

"Joe let's finish this chat somewhere warm like my living room."

"Is later tonight too soon? I have to head home for dinner."

"O.K. it's a date. See you in an hour or so."

"Sounds great."

"I second that emotion."

Carol and Joe were all smiles. Only their ears and their noses felt cold from the cold night air.

It was a little less than ninety minutes when Joe walked back the three blocks from his house to the Etons. He knocked on the front door.

Once again, ears and nose bore the brunt of winter.

Carol opened the wooden door. Joe opened the metal storm door.

"Please come on in."

"I hope I am not too late."

"How do you like the idea of heading to the living room, playing some music to try to make up for lost time?"

"Am I that late?"

“Not at all, I was just thinking we spent the last three years of high school walking the same halls but never really even said, ‘hello.’ I’d like to remedy that.”

“You’re the doctor. Will you be spending time with Buzz this winter break?”

Carol and Jim “Buzz” Scutner had been joined at the hip, and likely other body parts, a couple going seriously steady from Sophomore year on.

“Jim is staying at USC.”

“Not a bad decision weatherwise but leaving the playing fields of Eton to her own devices...”

“Joe you are funny. I always heard...”

“I was goofy.”

“Wanna follow me to my parents’ living room? Bring your light hearted whimsy with you.”

5F. The Flame Of Liberty May Sometimes Cease To Shine, The Coal Can Never Expire

In a world blessed with much beauty and many beautiful women, Carol Eton struck a vein of magnificence few could rival. Her hair was dark, dark brown, almost black, straight and thick. It ran down her back and over her shoulders, its tips touching the full contour of her breasts. Carol's skin was white but not pale. A light from within her made her complexion sunny. It also made her deep brown eyes as bright as the new day. Her face was a perfect oval. On some it might be solemn but for Carol evoked only pure tranquility. She had round cheeks separate and pronounced but not stranded from either her forehead or her nose. Carol's nose formed a gentle thin vertical line pointing down to its point of three rounded ridges which no plastic surgeon could possibly improve. Her mouth was her *piece de resistance.* Carol had firm but soft lips, not too fat, not too thin. Her lips enchanted with each word she spoke. Each breath Carol took directed attention to her mouth, a precipice of two tawny blooms waiting, almost wanting to be kissed.

Carol had slight shoulders but with no suggestion of cower. Her hips matched her shoulders. Carol's figure did not form an hourglass but its shape delicately framed her slender abdomen to showcase her 36 D-cup breasts. Her hips and calves pushed against blue denim hip huggers, tight but not too tight. She needed no belt. Carol's short legs were bowed. The right hint of pleasure was suggested between them. Beyond her size and her shape, she carried herself with a pride that did not repel. Her manner suggested communion with the universe, with mankind, with the person she just met or the one she would next meet. After only one semester at that very liberal, perhaps radical, Shimer College, Carol was free to shimmer and to shine.

“Joe, you look tired.”

Carol stacked three records onto the spindle of the BSR turntable in the console stereo, sides one and three of the Chicago Transit Authority, and side one of *Child is the Father to Man* by Blood, Sweat, and Tears The small casket of tawny stained wood made first a metal to metal click as the spindle dropped the lowest LP, then a plop as that vinyl platter hit the spinning platform, and then a dull stereophonic scrape, as the tone arm dropped to the outer most groove. Sweet music was resurrected to fill the room.

Carol pulled her cranberry wool sweater over her head then off. She sat at the end of the plush beige Victorian couch,

“Would you like to rest that goofy head of yours on my lap?”

Carol beamed as she pointed to where she sat.

In a matter of seconds, Joe was stretched out, taking the full length of the couch, his feet and his ankles hung over the armrest. Joe’s head nudged against this perfect place of rest at the end of a long day. He looked up at Carol’s breasts. They were covered by a blue blouse, its thin fabric stretched before his eyes. He then closed his eyes. He turned his face toward her. Carol lightly stroked Joe’s head. Next she ran her fingers through his hair with one hand while rubbing his neck with her other hand.

The sensual blur of music slipped into occasional focus. “Does Anyone Really Know What Time It Is?” “I’m a Man,” and “I Can’t Quit Her” sprung to center stage. Joe got up to flip the three discs adding Simon and Garfunkel's *Bridge Over Troubled Water* to the queue. The music played on. The next selection of the evening was all four sides from The Who, their "Rock Opera," *Tommy*. The last side standing was Rare Earth, their long version of the Temptation's "Get Ready," weaving one more strand of magic into the well-suited fabric that embraced them. Carol and Joe kissed once lightly, the electricity of their effortless connection sprinkled all around. Four eyes atwinkle, the two said good night.

It is rare when one can attain both aspiration and world view. In later life Carol attained her métier, her real place. She led an organization, AGNT. It marched forward for world peace. Carol joined hands with the Dalai Lama, to help set up meetings in the United States and beyond. There was no doubt even as the year 1969 swelled to a close, Carol brimmed with contentment. Joe shared in some small part of her positive nature that night and in the few nights that followed.

5G. A Man Can Distinguish Himself Between Temper And Principle

Early the next morning, Joe whistled his way to work. One of the songs from *Tommy* still echoed in his head, “But somehow, when you smiled I could brave bad weather…” The guys at the post office had developed a nice holiday routine. Ceremony is its own reward. Most good religions have an offering, if not a sacrifice for the greater good. The ranking member from the front counter was appointed. The men on the dock gathered two items of parcel post, one more hated by postal workers than the next. The first was a large cardboard box of grapefruits, fresh from Florida. Those citrus fruit shipments to celebrate the birth of peace on Earth may not have been the heaviest for their size but there were too many of them. The second was the “fragile” package. Telling a postman that you do not trust him is never a good idea. Even the most indolent government employee takes great pride in the rudiments of the work day. Certainly, all postal workers know that packages are not to be dented, dropped, or crushed. More than one “Fragile” label is too many. The package with the most “Handle with Care,” “Fragile,” and “Precious Cargo” stickers and legends was taken to a special place. The superstition that you should not walk under a ladder is a good one. The winner of the award for the most fragile package of the day was placed directly under a twelve step ladder. The front counter man was then anointed with a box of grapefruits, the box cradled on his shoulder with one arm. The sacred procession to the top of the ladder was cheered by the entire congregation of support persons who now encircled the altar of doom. There was no need for anyone to announce their name and acknowledge any sort of addiction. The fruit box was dropped, not thrown. Gravity did the heavy lifting. The over-labeled package was flattened and decimated, not to be rehabilitated.

The next part of the morning ritual was even more serious. The rank and file was always careful to be sure that management arrived after the twelve step the program. This time, the card carrying community and management alike formed a full circle. Everyone grabbed a coin. The postal workers played “odd man out.” The coins were flipped and counted. If there were more heads, the heads left. If the next toss had more tails, the tails left the circle. If one person was left, the loneliest number was the loser. Two can be as sad as one but only for a short time. If the group was whittled down to two, then, the coins were tossed. Someone called even or odd. The loser, however finally determined, was now obliged to buy cokes for the entire group. In the two weeks Joe was there, he was never the last man standing.

5H. She Has Nothing To Do But To Trade

After the morning was spent sorting the mail for the day, Joe drove the route, delivering the mail. One day Joe was half-way home when he noticed Sarah Foreswallow was following him in her daddy's Lincoln Continental.

"Sarah, you are aware it is a federal offense to waylay a postal employee in the course of his duties."

Sarah was in no mood to be amused.

"Joe, I have not heard from you since the morning the attendance office called. Your mother, Victoria, and Susan have all taken a dozen messages that I called."

"A dozen each."

"What? You know I have called?"

"You know I know you have called."

"If this is about buying me a Christmas present, you are all I need."

"Sarah, Jim Morrison of the Doors, the master of turning a quaint phrase, put it this way, 'When the music's over, turn off the lights.'"

"What? How? Why? You and I are meant for each other, I know we will live happily ever after."

"I am sure we will, just not together."

"What did I do? What happened?"

"Sarah, I like sex as much as the next guy, and your body speaks volumes. But other than those great, wonderful, and exciting conversations, we have nothing to say to one another. Your values and mine have taken different paths."

"I can change."

"Nope you are who you are, a wonderful person who will make someone totally happy. Sooner or later we will make each other miserable."

Sarah sobbed. Tears streamed down her face freezing on her skin before they reached her chin. She got back into the Lincoln, slammed the door, and drove away without looking back. Joe was sure Sarah would not give up easily. Telling her was unpleasant but it was a necessary first step in a process that he hoped would not last too long. The coming exposition of her pain was not going to be pretty. Joe was sure that Sarah would take all steps she felt necessary to underscore the drama in the next scenes of the passion play. Only the audience would be feeling any real pain. Sarah was not a girl who wasted her feelings on emotion. What Joe said was true, he liked ideas. He liked talking the way he talked with Sally and Felina. While women and men reached incomparable utility when their bodies were sweating together, the whole package required more than just arousal and the scintillating path to orgasm. The connection must be multifaceted.

5l. Never Be Happy Till She Gets Clear

Christmas was on a Thursday. For five full days before, Sarah Foreswallow kept calling. Joe kept not calling her back. Three times she drove to the Cebellum house, once to deliver Christmas cookies, the really good peanut butter ones with the Hershey kiss in the middle. Next Sarah delivered fruit cake. The last trip was to bring Joe a framed picture. It showed the two of them each holding one of the four Cebellum cats in front of the Christmas tree. Sarah and Joe were wearing winter coats and stocking caps. Their cheeks were rosy red from the cold. Two smiles consumed the winter holiday scene. The frame was not a Christmas frame. It was something for Valentine's Day. It was wide gold metal embossed with the red outlines of hearts. The photo came with a note,

"Joe I know you love me as I love you. I know that someday we will again be together. I will always be true to you in my fashion. Please always know that you are the one who fills my heart with joy, night and day, day and night. Our love will never die even though every time we say goodbye, I cry a little, die a little. Your little bundle of joy, Sarah"

Joe decided that before he returned to school he would give the empty frame to Fred. Fred could give it to Martha on the next Valentine's Day. He returned the photo to one of the many Cebellum family photo albums. Joe wondered when Sarah got her hands on it.

5J. She Whose Heart Is Firm And Whose Conscience Approves Her Conduct

Friday night after Christmas, Felina threw a party. Everyone who was back home from the first semester from college was going to be there. Janet Feralposey was back from William Smith, the girl's school for Hobart, the liberal arts school in Ithaca not too far from Cornell. Kiefer Mandolin was back from Michigan. Glenn Reaper was back from the University of Iowa. Virgil Chausseur had returned from Washington University near St. Louis. Karen Orbble came back from U.S.C. Like Buzz Scutner, Sally Sensabell did not make it back from the West Coast. Prince Bastion was back from Boulder, Colorado. Joe was happy the Post Office was closed for four days straight then closed again the following week for the four days around New Year's Day. He would have some time to see everybody before he headed back to Princeton.

It started with Felina's party then continued with a wave of parties that followed for the next ten days. Those who returned to the Sleepy Little Village that Christmas break grabbed each moment. Every drop of camaraderie, affection, love, and warmth was squeezed to be savored then cherished. Everywhere there was an unstated sense, a profound gnawing sadness hovered in the wings. Everyone knew that they would never all be together again. Their frenzied cocoon would be lost forever. Rather than succumb to the inevitable, Joe and his high school classmates clung to the illusion of the impassable now.

Felina's townhouse at Pickwick Place reached exuberance running amok. Then the fervency spiked. Frank Lee Gonzo was back from Western Illinois University, a school in the little town of Macomb on the Mississippi River. Frank Lee was a guy everyone liked. He was bright, a very good golfer, an exceptional singer, and a piano player. His talents gave way to pleasant simple, humility. His father was a middle school math teacher. Frank Lee's mother was complected entirely of sweetness and light. Frank Lee knew that his family lacked nothing even though they were among those in Barrington who were not blessed by the glow of the almighty dollar. No matter how balanced and well-centered he was, nothing in Frank Lee's family background, knowledge, or experience prepared him for Sarah Foreswallow.

That Friday night about ten o'clock, Sarah walked into Felina's front door. She made sure she did not look for Joe. Her innate sense of where he was gave her the strange ability to shower him with neglect. Frank Lee Gonzo was standing in the kitchen drinking a beer. His innocence was soon subject to stampede. Sarah looked at Frank Lee,

"Would you help me with my coat?"

Frank Lee helped remove Sarah's lambswool half length coat. It had a thick fleece collar. Sarah rubbed the collar against her face. She purred,

"Fr-r-r-ank, this feels so good."

She brought the fleece to his face then placed her thigh in his crotch. She put her hand behind him so he could not step back. Sarah was wearing tight straight leg blue jeans and a violet cashmere sweater.

"Do you like that?"

Frankly, he did not know what to say. Sarah took the sleeve of her sweater to his face rubbing her chest up against Frank Lee's arm and front while taking her palm and pushing into the inside of his thigh. Sarah moved her hip out of the way so she could slide the edge of her hand against his penis.

"How does my cashmere feel to you?"

Sarah's prey was trapped.

"Mr. Gonzo, would you drive me to get some cigarettes?"

No one noticed the time when the two left the townhouse.

5K. The Warm Ardor Of A Friend To Those Who Have Nobly Stood

At one in the morning, Kiefer and Virgil were sitting on the living room couch smoking a joint with Karen Orbble and Janet Feralposey. Ten people were upstairs in Felina's room listening to Richie Havens, Felina, Fred, and Joe included. The upstairs was filled with the blue grey of tobacco and marijuana smoke. Everyone was drunk. There was no knock.

Two Barrington cops burst in, Officers Theodore "Krupke' Fozcube and "Fast Eddy" Halfcone. It was hard to say who sprang up from the couch more quickly or who spoke first. Virgil and Kiefer played a duet from the sheet music of today's revolution, a loud crescendo reaching a screech in a few short seconds,

"Pigs, get the fuck out"

"Fucking pigs, get your fascist asses out of here"

"Goddamned pigs"

Joe sobered himself by way of some instinct of preservation. He bounded down the stairs. His agility belied his dope and alcohol altered mental state,

"Officers, please pay no attention to Kiefer or Virgil. They have seen one too many CBS six o'clock news shows."

Somehow not one word was slurred, not one ‘s’ Joe uttered was sibilant.

“Do you guys have a warrant?”

Krupke smiled sheepishly,

“No”

Felina and Fred now stood behind Joe. Joe was the picture of seriousness,

“Kiefer, Virgil, shut the fuck up.

The two radicals sat down. Joe looked directly at Virgil Chausseur’s five inch long, slightly curved finger nails. Virgil was half-Japanese. He wanted to make a statement about the ancient culture of his Asian heritage. Joe flipped his head to the right. Virgil put his hands behind him but not before the only occasionally observant Officer Krupke noticed the long nails.

“I have a question for the sort of yellow Chinaman over there on the settee. Do those long nails serve to overcompensate for a Mousey Dong, if I may take the name of your fearless leader in vain?”

“Fast-Eddy” was the only one to laugh. Virgil’s actual heritage did not matter. All the slanty-eyed yellow people were the same to Krupke. Kiefer Mandolin raised his hand and pointed a finger. Before he could say a word to support his friend, Virgil came to his own rescue,

“Tell you what copper, I’ll show you mine, if you show me yours.”

The Officer stood silent.

Joe again jumped in to defuse a volatile situation,

“Officers, what may we do for you?”

"O.K. no one will leave. If you do we will arrest you for driving under the influence. Agreed?"

Felina spoke,

"Officers, I'll make sure everyone stays until breakfast. My mother is a sound sleeper but she makes a great pot of coffee. I'll cook the bacon and eggs."

"Great, now I need everyone's name."

Kiefer started to stand up.

Joe took one step towards him,

"Mandolin sit the fuck down and keep your mouth shut."

Krupke remembered Felina and Joe from the time Marcie Buchanan was discovered dead in the two car garage under the Palace of Thorns, the townhouse inhabited by Sam and his dad, Phil. Officer Krupke turned to them,

"So really, why does your weird friend sit there with those long nails?"

Felina smiled,

"He turned Chinese Gothic too late to have his feet bound."

Joe added,

"And he's the wrong gender."

The cops wrote down all the names. They left by way of reminding everyone they should stay there until they were sober.

Fred turned to Joe,

"How did those inept cops find out about this party?"

Sarah Foreswallow walked into the front door,

“You guys have to help. The cops have arrested Frank Lee Gonzo.”

Fred now stood between Sarah and Joe,

“Arrested for what?”

“Well frankly my dears, I did not know I could have such an effect on a young man. We pulled out of Pickwick Place onto Easter toward County Line. There was a car approaching. I told Frank Lee it would be fun to flash his headlights on and off while swerving back in forth of the oncoming car.”

Joe said,

“Gonzo does not know how to hold his liquor.”

“Anyway, it turned out it was a Barrington cop car, Officer Krupke at the wheel of the oncoming car.”

Fred shook his head,

“Nice”

Felina did not like Sarah to start with,

“So why did the cops come here?”

“Krupke told Gonzo he would not arrest him if he told him where the party was where he got drunk.”

Joe and Fred looked at each other. Fred looked at Sarah,

“So where is our friend, Gonzo, now?”

“The police station I expect. Halfcone drove me home. I snuck out to tell you guys.”

Joe and Fred drove to the Barrington police station. They walked in. Frank Lee Gonzo was sitting by the front counter. He saw Joe and Fred,

He got up then walked towards them. Tears swelled from his eyes,

"I love you guys."

Krupke was less emotional,

"You guys, get out of here. I mean it."

Fred held out his arms in front of him, palms up,

"We just want to help out a friend."

"If I we're you..."

Joe interrupted,

"I'd be leaving."

Krupke made the point again,

"Right."

Fred and Joe did an about-face then turned tail.

5L. Sustained An Orderly Retreat

Three days later, R.O. Johnson called Joe's dad.

"Yes Chief, this is Joseph Cebellum."

Joseph pointed to a dining room chair. Joe sat down

"Let me be sure I understand, Chief. There is a meeting you have called for tomorrow night for the parents of kids who attended a party Friday night."

Joe scrunched his eyes together and grimaced. Then he turned his head down.

"Let me be sure I also understand, no one, my son Joe, included, is, or will be, under arrest."

Joe brought his arms to his side, pulled his shoulder into his body, and sat upright in the wooden chair.

"O.K. I appreciate your concern and your stated notion about respect for the community but since there are no, and will not be, any charges, I will not attend."

Joseph put the receiver back on its latch on the kitchen wall.

"Joe, try to avoid doing things that might cause the police to call me."

"Will do, Dad."

Nothing more was said or done. Fred's dad, "Red" went to the meeting. It turned out that the cops expressed their concerns about teenage drinking and drug use. The parents expressed their concerns, too. As soon as the meeting was over Red drove straight to the Ten Pin Bowling Alley Bar to hoist a few with his old friend, E.Z. Sinon.

5M. A Few Broken Forces Collected And Headed By A Woman

The New Year's Eve Party lasted three days. It seemed that the more champagne they drank, the more champagne somebody else brought. On the first night Fred was relieving himself of some very cold Mumm's Cordon Rouge. He forgot to lock the door. There was no need for Kelly Shaunton to come in through the bathroom window. Chris Shaunton's little sister was an auburn haired beauty, fit and fair. Kelly was an equestrienne. She had won more trophies than any other girl in the Sleepy Little Village. Apparently she liked to take free rein, on more than one kind of little wild ride. Kelly locked the door behind her. Fred finished peeing. He shook the last two drops of urine from the tip of his penis. Kelly put both hands on his hips and turned him towards her. She got on her knees in front of Fred before he could zip up. Fred was not that drunk. Nine glorious minutes was all Kelly needed. They were done before anyone else needed that bathroom.

Kelly Shaunton licked her lips,

"You know Fred, my friend, Tiffany Wallet is right. Sucking your prick is a lot of fun."

The third night Joe again broke the cardinal rule. He would never do it again. He drank an entire bottle of champagne after two glasses of stiff scotch on the rocks. That was not the problem. Then he smoked a joint. He was basically immobilized from dizziness. He poured himself into a plush wingback chair. The party was in full swing all around him. Laurie Foil had her eye on Joe since he was in Little League, when they were ten years old. Joe was never interested in Laurie, not for a second. Here was her chance. Laurie was a redhead, carrot topped with pale pasty skin. She was not the sort of redhead men desired. She sat down on Joe's lap. She started stroking the hair on the back of his neck with her clumsy fat fingers. Joe was too drunk for those hairs to stand on end. Laurie's lips were now perilously close to his mouth. All he could do was squirm, a mixed signal to be sure. Joe summoned all his inner strength to control his dizziness. He had a serious case of the whirlies. He did not want to throw up. Joe had heard Dean Martin joke on television about being so drunk he would see double. Joe had it worse. He was now seeing three Laurie Foils. To make matters worse, Joe was unable to get up as she sat on his lap, lavishing her full attention to all parts of his body. This was no way to start the New Year.

XXIV. Get Out of Town

"Look upon the ruins of the Castle of delusion..."

A. Punctuated Absence

"Reading period" was the beginning of what would surely mete the end. Means and outcomes aside, Joe gave the full heave of a long breath of relief as he returned to the Princeton campus in early January of 1970. The activities that consumed his time prior to Christmas Day led to sweet enervation. Joe was weakened further by the week of round the clock revelry that marked the last real New Year celebration the High School Class of 1969 would visit upon the Sleepy Little Village. The young Cebellum was now fully prepared for a long winter's nap. Princeton maintained a longstanding academic schedule which afforded its students nearly a month for studying for final exams and for writing term papers. Exam period followed. After that, there was a semester break. By the time second semester classes commenced spring was a lively reality, more than just around the corner.

Students who planned well could indulge in a veritable hibernation from *academe* while remaining in the sheltering cocoon of the campus. Joe was a quick study. Of his first semester courses, only one had a final exam. So the New Year, 1970, started on easy street. Joe resolved to make all future reading periods footloose and fancy free. A course with a final exam would never again darken his door.

Who knew the promise of the lilt of spring would lead to rough sledding, even if the track was one of Joe's own choice. The means to what seemed a certain end for Joe were threefold- music, drugs, and card games. Princeton had recently eliminated the requirement of mandatory attendance at the Chapel on Sunday. Even if Joe had the benefit of stern warnings from the pulpit about deadly sins, those admonitions would have fallen well short of deaf ears. Echoes of sermons from Jonathan Edwards, Aaron Burr, Sr. and those theologians who stood at Princeton's helm as late as 1937 had long since dissipated to stoned silence. Cautionary messages well supported by scripture were supplanted by all the devil holds dear, music with a beat, intemperance fueled by booze and drugs, and that sad substitute for time spent wantonly with the opposite sex, a deck of cards. Whether poker or bridge, card playing was a poor substitute for the third and the best prong of the unholy trinity- carnal knowledge. Joe was never one to complain about the hand he had been dealt. As with many who are inclined, for whatever reason, to slide intransigently down the slippery slope of the road to perdition, Joe's first steps in the realm of campus card games were bathed in innocence.

The double room right around the corner from the double shared by Fief and Relioport held Malcolm Richard "Dick" Spinepounds from Willard, Ohio and T. William Solder from Nashville, who was soon known as "Nash." The bridge games started there. Dick Spinepounds and "Nash" Solder were later both able to wash their hands of a winter and spring spent shuffling, dealing, and drawing trumps. Dick and "Nash" cleanly extricated themselves from the fray to then devote full measure to their studies in the years that followed. This seriousness, with their innate acumen, served them both well. In later life, Solder helicoptered from his home Greenwich, Conn to Manhattan to fulfill his duties as head of Deutsche Bank. Spinepounds attained prominence in Atlanta as the managing partner for the South's most powerful law firm, King & Spaulding. Bridge and gambling remained a consuming dimension for Joe.

Bramble

B. The Pan Within

During reading period and exams, it was always easy to find four players, even if they were not always the same four. Writing a paper, cramming for an exam or taking a final did consume large chunks of time from the otherwise bridge-minded. Joe, Spinepounds, and Solder were joined, variously by Tim Fief, "Thew" Relioport, "Teddy" Appleseed, and Sean McManus. Barry Richardson played football not any sort of silly kids' game. "Lemming" Cello never touched a card. He held only disdain for the limitations of a deck of fifty-two. Cello felt that the real array of probabilities was much larger. Whether meeting the future or the past, possibility was something to be taken religiously, especially in ever increasing doses. Edgar Cayce, with astral projection, and Paul Twitchell with his Eckankar version of soul traveling, struck John's fancy and captured his equilibrium. When there was no bridge game afoot, Joe's feet would not fail to guide him to visit "Lemming" Cello for one more interlude that only high decibel rock could fashion. Seeing Joe enter the room, Cello would come back from whatever plane that day he was trying to attain. They would then smoke some dope and wind up the stereo. Once Joe opened the door to Cello's room, it was only a matter of seconds. Loud music surrounded them like the four winds, always blowing them safely home. All confusion was rendered moot in the moment as sounds spun free. Dan Ferraro studied at the library. Upon his return to bunk with John Cello, Dan always slept a deep sleep, even with speakers in full blare and thump. The London Blitz would not have awakened him.

C. Bring 'Em All In

For a short time, there was another bridge game in Pyne, down the hall in the quad where Sammy Rice lived. Only the Spinepounds/Solder game survived to continue into the semester. Dick and "Nash" were serious about studying and class attendance so the game broke up around eleven or twelve. Once McManus and Appleseed got the bridge bug, there was more than sufficient critical mass to sound a battle cry. "The game must go on" figuratively shook Pyne Hall's centuries old, ivied walls. Logistics reared its ugly head. There was no place to play. Everyone involved had roommates who propriety or the threat of force dictated should not be disturbed. Even though roommates Fief and Relioport were committed regulars, "Thew" always hit the sack no later than midnight. Unlike Ferraro, Josh was a very light sleeper.

"The game must go on" is more than just a pleasant old saying. It was a simple matter to head upstairs to the showers and bathroom that served that entire Pyne corner entry. It was easy to turn a large waste basket upside down. Somebody's desk blotter became a sturdy playing surface once placed on top of the solid rim of the waste basket. Like the Van Gogh painting, players bent forward from desk chairs as they surrounded the make shift knee high card table. The game lasted through the night. Morning greetings were exchanged as students less succumbed to fritter entered to shower and to shave. The guys on their way to the first classes of the day at first gave casual, quizzical greetings to the hearty bunch of all night card players, usually Joe, Fenton, Sean, and Tim. As the game around the waste basket became a fixture, the morning hellos sometimes led to the delay of ablutions. Young men in towels would “kibitz.” They would stand around the players then follow the hand being played. The scene vaguely resembled that famous painting of Socrates’ last day. In fact, Fenton Appleseed’s fall from grace started as a kibitzer. He had now found the depths as a regular player.

D. Peace of Iona

Joe's first semester courses were Literature 141, "An Introduction to European Literature," Philosophy 101, "An Introduction to Philosophy," French 103 (after five years of high school French, Joe had placed out of only one semester of the four semesters needed for the Princeton Foreign language requirement), and Mathematics 441, "The Philosophy of Mathematics." Only Math 441 had a final exam. Its professor was the renowned Albert W. Tucker, head of the vaunted Princeton Math Department since 1954. Mr. Tucker had joined the faculty in 1933. All professors at Princeton were "Mr." This two-letter appellation would not sit well with the PH.D. types who fancy themselves "Doctor" or, at the very least, "Professor." At Princeton "Mr." rang just the right bell of stature. Tucker was a giant by any name. He retired in 1974. Anecdotes from his twenty years as head of the department became the stuff of true "oral history." Even before, legendary tales abounded. Stories about Tucker, his colleagues, and his Ph. D. students start with the vivacious Princeton mathematics community in the 1930's and end forty-one years later. Those stories memorialized legendary steps in modern mathematical theory. Mr. Tucker made important contributions in the areas of topology, game theory, and non-linear programming. At a class in the fall of 1969, during Tucker's exposition of the fourth dimension and beyond, Joe interjected,

"Now I get the course title, 441 and one for four."

Tucker did not mind the interruption. The cornerstone of his muse was mussing to delve into intricate, connected concepts by way of some simple seemingly facile starting point, a point of departure which sounded with its own internal interwoven structure. Mathematics 441 wended its way from the problem of crossing the Seven Bridges of Konigsberg, once and only once, to the "Prisoner's Dilemma," the game theory paradox involving benefits and betrayal that he had named. Tucker embodied genial joy and calm. The kind-eyed Canadian was of slight physical stature and gentle features well worn and worn well all befitting the professorial. His understanding smile dominated his presence. He was a gaunt Buddha meditating in the world of dancing numbers and the choreographed and improvised steps of their propinquities, near and far. Tucker was always soft spoken but firm. He gave students the glow of "show me that I am everywhere but bring me home for tea." It was not clear whether he had always known, or had come to find, secure involvement in the undertaking and life path which he loved and embraced. His understated enthusiasm was infectious both for the content of his subject and the overall impression that doing what you liked was to achieve the only real goal. Tucker projected the ambience of a television show moderator, comfortably deposited in a fat- cushioned leather armchair, teeming book cases behind him, smoking a pipe from which wafted smoke in the form of a genie to grant the wishes of all those who wanted things to know. It did not matter that Tucker actually sat in front of a class of six, in the same straight back chair as his students, perched and reclining upon stiff pastel polyethylene quadrangles fastened bottom and back to an unpersuasive frame of hollow metal tubes. A green chalkboard full of scattered hieroglyphics and strange arrows leading here and there was prepossessed behind him, as he was armed only with a stub of chalk. Fundamentally Tucker had come to understand and embrace the pure love of learning. Any love for matters that engaged the mind had merit.

E. Fisherman's Blues

January in New Jersey brings a couple of cold days. Cloistered once again in the Pyne Hall second floor bathroom, Fief, "Teddy," McManus, and Joe were warm as they huddled around the wastebasket. As the morning sun peeked in, Dick Spinepounds, wrapped in a towel with his dopp kit in hand, walked to one of the old leaded glass windows and turned the handle to open it.

"Fuck guys, it's hot in here."

Cold air blew in. Teddy shivered. He could now see his breath, "So now you feel at home, Dick?"

The cold air seemed to bring Joe to attention, "I have the last four tricks making six no-trump as bid, a vulnerable 1440. I'll add that to the totals for Teddy and me. It looks like I am plus 15,550. At the usual tenth of a cent, 15 dollars and 55 cents. Appleseed is plus 25 cents-not bad for a winter's night work. So Fief, you owe ten bucks and seventy five cents and Sean you owe an even fin. Sorry to break up the game so early but I have to go take a final. No doubt Tucker will be posing some knotty questions."

McManus looked a Joe and shook his head, "A 400 level course on the philosophy of math and you play bridge all night then waltz right over to New Fine Hall. What is the matter with you?"

In Joe's time at Princeton, Tucker's course was the only course in which Joe got an "A."

F. Medicine Bow

Boot camp is the opposite of Princeton's Reading Period. The Fort Bragg Army base in Fayetteville, North Carolina was no exception. For Tommy Wanderby, Texas Christian University and the Sigmund Albert Estragon fraternity were gone but not necessarily forgotten. Now saddled with the reality of enlistment, an instinct more than self- preservation suggested to Tommy that joining the Army as a Green Beret was not a step in the right direction, even though his uncle had pulled strings to see he would train as part of the Military Police to assure he would not fight in Vietnam. It was more than the debasing, dehumanizing Pavlovian qua Jim Crow regimen that darkened Tommy's psyche. The forced physical exertion pushed beyond the limits of even the highly-trained capabilities of a multiple National championship level swimmer. Then there was the incessantly abusive, strident Special Forces browbeating. Fort Bragg was taking its toll upon Tommy.

Tommy dialed the pay phone in the Mess Hall. It was the evening of the 17th day of February. Even though it was the middle of the month, Tommy was at the end of his tether.

"Hi, Uncle Fricke."

"Hey, Tommy. It's always good to hear your voice."

"I am always glad that you can talk to me. I know how busy you are as Governor."

“I always have time for my favorite nephew. How is that problem about your missing trigger finger being resolved? I’ll never understand how they missed that at your enlistment physical.”

“Well, it is only the tip. I lack only the top knuckle down to the second knuckle. Someday science will march forward to permit weapons to be fired with the thumb and any other finger, from the safety of hearth and home, at targets on the other side of the world. Hold on a second I have to put some more coins in the pay phone.”

“Tommy, what is the number on the pay phone. I’ll call you back so we can chew the fat for a good while.”

The pay phone rang. Tommy picked up the receiver, “Uncle Fricke. Thanks for making this your dime.”

“My pleasure, Tommy. Let’s chat ‘til the cows come home.”

“Or until they blow Taps”

“Right. Where were we? Oh yea. Only men who have never fought will glamorize combat. I still shiver cold when my dreams take me back to the Ardennes as my battalion is blown up around me. Some day the asserted sanctity of the mother’s price for patriotism in the loss of a son will not prevent a cogent, balanced discussion of the horror of war.”

“I wish it was just war. I still wake up in a cold sweat with the murder of Clavita pulsing vividly through my veins. I wish I could say it was cold blooded but the white supremacist woman who poured gasoline on Clavita, threw a match on her, then shot her as the flames surged felt nothing more than someone swatting a mosquito. Uncle Fricke, Clavita’s trial is the reason I am calling you. As an experienced prosecutor, I need your help to straighten me out. I have the deep feeling there is no real justice, at least not in the courts. Last night, today I should say, in the early morning hours, there were brutal murders here in Fort Bragg-a pregnant wife and their two daughters, one five, the other two. As an M.P. trainee, I observed the scene as it was investigated. The husband, a Green Beret doctor named Jeffrey MacDonald was injured but not as brutally as his wife and his little kids. It looks like he will survive. His only major wound is a concise stab wound between two of his ribs, causing a partial collapse of one lung. At first blush, this stab wound seems too precise when compared with the other stab wounds which were scattered and furious, or even if you consider the type of wound one would likely receive in a fight with three other men. The rest of his family was battered and was stabbed, heads crushed by a wooden, multiple, vicious stab wounds. The weapons were recovered just outside the family's apartment. On the headboard of the marital bed, someone had written the word, 'Pigs...'"

Governor Fricke Wanderby could only muster, "Jesus."

"...Written in blood with a surgical glove it appears. It looks like the daughters were killed somewhere else then returned to their own beds, in the positions in which they normally slept, positions likely no longer possible given their massive injuries. The investigators, and I agree with them, think the scene has been staged. Jeffrey MacDonald claims three men and one woman entered his home, killed his family in the bedroom area, and then tried to kill him. He had been sleeping on the couch, awakened as he heard screaming and cries for help. The killers came to him to kill him but he was able to save himself. He claims he fought the other three men successfully to save himself, even though it turned out his family had been all killed. While the four men fought MacDonald says the woman stood in front of him, her face appeared to have a light upon her as she chanted, 'Acid is groovy' among other things. Nobody says 'groovy' anymore. There is at least one nagging loose end. The early morning hours were rainy. There appears to be insufficient evidence that four strangers, in from the rain, entered the house. Nevertheless, the stage has been set to inflame the passions of the trier of fact- a doped up cult like the Manson family, real or not, will be the culprit. I am afraid common fears and prejudice will rule the day, perhaps, in a slightly different way than the racism of the jurors who declared Clavita's killer innocent, in the face of my sworn testimony as a first-person witness."

"Tommy, first let me say I respect you for testifying against the White Supremacist who killed your friend as if she was merely an insect on the windshield, a kind blot on a depraved world view. Having said that, there are times when you must realize that you are pissing into the wind. Regarding these brutal murders you are helping to investigate..."

"I am not really helping. As a trainee, I mostly stand around with my thumb up my ass."

Tommy, I am sure that is not true. Your whole life you have been a perspicacious sponge soaking up everything that is important. I do hope you are wrong about these brutal murders. Let me make sure I understand what you are saying. This Doctor MacDonald fellow, stabbed himself, wrote in blood, and made up the four acid crazed hippies..."

"Yea, I forgot to tell you. There was a magazine with the Manson murder story in it in the living room."

"I have no doubt a surgical doctor would know how to safely slit himself, causing a real injury but nothing life threatening. Let me see. Let's say, the husband and wife had not been getting along. Suppose, one of the young daughters came in to stop a quarrel. The husband violently over-reacted and accidentally killed the little girl. Scared with only his own self-preservation, he acted instinctually again, to kill his pregnant wife. At some point, lucidity, such as it is, in this case, took over. The idea was hatched. Cover up the crime with the idea of four hippie intruders. The other daughter was also killed since she may have heard…"

"Uncle Fricke, I think you are on the right track. One of the daughters wet her parents' bed, sleeping with her mother, before Doctor MacDonald came to bed. This may have caused him to erupt, initially not to kill, of course. Jeffery MacDonald is a very smart guy, quite handsome, and apparently quite well put together. He finished his Princeton education in three years. Then he went to medical school near where you and Dad grew up, Northwestern University. After a stint as an intern, which has to be hard on any family, he enlisted as a Green Beret in the medical corps. I heard the army is currently using his expertise as a surgeon to make sure the latrines are kept disinfected. One of the M.P.s who is training me said MacDonald is known on the base as a guy who has had a lot of extramarital affairs…"

"Tommy, is it likely a rag tag band of hippies can wander the base?"

"Well, Fort Bragg is an open base. The town of Fayetteville has a lot of these new counter-culture types, plus drugs from Vietnam, are often smuggled onto the base, sometimes even in body bags. I am not sure L.S.D. 'tripping' as they call it, is conducive to concerted group activities or even violence. I heard that the Manson killers were not actually under the influence of acid at the time of their rampage. But back to the base at Fort Bragg, while it is open, M.P.s and army guys and their families all are quite aware of who is visiting. So far there are no reports of three men and a woman traipsing about."

G. Long Way To The Light

"Tommy, you know I went to Yale. In New Haven, there is a clear idea that Princeton is its own special haven for the pretty and the prissy. Narcissism is the *sine qua non* for that college of good ole boys since the days of the studied self-absorption of Aaron Burr, Jr. If your conclusions are remotely true, MacDonald would be the Narcissist's narcissist..."

"A bit of an oxymoron Eh, Uncle Fricke."

"Indeed."

Many miles of telephone lines separated the Governor's mansion in the state capitol of Springfield, Illinois and the mess hall at Ft. Bragg. The distance of opaque cables did not prevent Tommy from having a clear picture of his uncle's well-known wry smile.

Governor Fricke Wanderby continued,

"The flipside of the coin, however, would be the Army's interest in maintaining the veneer of safety at the base and the desire to minimize fears that drug people are running all around the place, starting with the cold and crass retrieval of drugs from the bodies of those soldiers who gave their all in a foreign land. Having said that please allow me to address the issue you fear, wherever it bears. Justice is a lofty goal. I would like to think that the good is well served. Even when you get a conviction, however, sometimes the defendant never serves jail time. Look at my most famous case. Accardo never spent any time in stir for his sentence. Federal Judge Julius Hoffman presided. In reversing the verdict, the Seventh Circuit decried trial publicity more than judicial error. More than that small bump in the road, justice, particularly in celebrated cases with the attention of the newspapers and now television, other agendas are often served, not just those of press. Money and power sometimes serve to subvert the judicial process. I am not sure whether those with power are not worse than those with money, but quite often the two are inextricably complicit.

Let me tell you the story of a freshman Congressman from California. First I need to tell you about another man, one who toiled for the State Department, a lawyer named, Alger Hiss. He clerked for United States Supreme Court Justice Oliver Wendell Holmes. He was in law school at Harvard when Sacco and Vanzetti were convicted of murder. This was another celebrated case where many think prejudice, this time against 'foreign born anarchists' reared its ugly head to pervert justice. Alger Hiss and his lifelong mentor, Felix Frankfurter, who later served on the U.S. Supreme Court, were among those who felt Sacco and Vanzetti were wrongly convicted. Another problem with murder cases is that the police and prosecutors are motivated by the idea that public wounds must be salved, and soon. Furthermore, the public outcry to find the evildoers requires speedy resolution. Anyway, Alger Hiss was accused, not only of being a communist but also of using his State Department position to commit treason. A man named Whittaker Chambers accused Hiss. At the time of the accusation, Chambers was an editor at Henry Luce's *Time* magazine. But let me lay out the simple facts that seem indisputable-

1. Chambers was a communist, a Soviet spy, a man who acted predominantly as a courier of sensitive documents in a chain of spies which led back to Russia.

2. Alger Hiss and his wife Priscilla were 'well-bred' from good families but in the throes of the economic suffering that affected millions in the 1930s, both leaned to the left with their sympathies for the poor. A number of Harvard Law School friends and acquaintances, particularly from the time Hiss was a member of the prestigious Harvard Law Review, developed or maintained socialist/communist tendencies, which at the time were a matter of politics- not an issue of 'national security.'

3. As the 'New Deal' unfolded many conservative people equated the New Deal with communism. In some quarters, even extreme ones peopled both those with a long reach, that attitude has not diminished today.

4. Hiss worked at prestigious corporate law firms, first in Boston then in Manhattan, by day. At night he and his wife joined a very left leaning group, espousing liberal, let us say socialist ideas to help the poor. Many of their friends were communists, communist 'sympathizers' or what became to be known as fellow travelers. Left leaning was perhaps incongruous in a prominent family with maids with a breadwinner whose real life work was keeping large corporations large and prosperous, no matter where the chips may fall in regard to the rest of the people in the states.

5. In 1939, the ever-so humble Whitaker Chambers asked to speak to President Roosevelt, claiming he was now a defector from the communist party and a former Russian spy. He wanted to tell about his knowledge of the network which included communists and spies in the State department upon condition that he not be prosecuted. As you would expect, FDR would not see him, but the fellow who made inquiries on his behalf, a guy named

Levine, was able to set up a meeting with the assistant in charge of internal security at the State Department, a man named Berle if memory serves. Berle indicated he was acting on behalf of FDR and that, of course, Chambers would not be prosecuted. Chambers insisted the meeting be held somewhere other than the State department. Here is an interesting point. He said he would not go there. He had no doubt that he would be recognized by the network of former communist confederates who still worked there. The meeting occurred the day before World War II started in Europe. Chambers named names. He described what he said was the full breadth of Russian espionage activities. Berle took copious notes. Two of the names named were Alger Hiss and his brother, Don, also a Harvard Law grad who was a partner at the powerful D.C. firm of Covington and Burling.

6. As a result of this meeting J. Edgar Hoover ordered an almost two year long wire tap of the telephone of Priscilla and Alger Hiss, recorded to whom articles were mailed and from whom mail was sent, and upon sufficient impetus, opened Hiss mail. The F.B.I. intercepted Hiss telegrams and engaged in occasional round the clock surveillance with spot surveillance added for good measure. Intercepted mail was copied. Later, one letter was sent to the Hiss perjury prosecutor with express instruction that he not show it to any of his higher ups in the Justice Department. The F.B.I. commenced this investigation based upon the information disclosed by Chambers. Later, Chambers was adamant that he had never received 'immunity' for his testimony. The facts about the Berle meeting with the promise not to prosecute are not in dispute as is the simple fact that Chambers, an admitted spy was never prosecuted.

7. Another fact is that Hiss with his wife and Chambers with his wife became friends.

8. In Maryland, there was a catholic priest named Cronin, who infiltrated the communist party. He also told Hoover and later told the House Un-American Activities Committee that Alger Hiss was a communist spy. The F.B.I. interviewed Alger Hiss. Nixon spent many hours with Cronin. Later Nixon and Chambers met many times, including meetings where the only record which was kept was Nixon's notation that the content of the meeting was 'off the record.'

10. Hiss became a member of the state Department. He traveled to the Yalta conference. He negotiated the United Nations Charter, in fact bringing the original document back to Washington for Truman's signature. John Foster Dulles was the head of a peace organization who hired Hiss as its president. The future looked bright and rosy for Alger Hiss, possibly even a cabinet position as Secretary of State was on his horizon.

11. Almost ten years later, after investigation by the F.B.I., HUAC, as the House Committee became to be known, called Whitaker Chambers as a witness. At this point in time, the prevailing view was that it was not acceptable to be, or to have been, a 'communist' and to be part of the U.S. Government. Chambers was placed under oath. Chambers testified that he had was once a communist, part of a group he termed the Ware group, some of whose members acted as spies. Chambers did not, at this time, include Hiss in this group. Alger Hiss was called to testify. Hiss was shown a picture of Chambers which he claimed he could not identify. Hiss asked to see the man in the photo.

12. Now here is where things get interesting. The sordid issue aside of government 'stool pigeons' and their motivation in testifying, but moreover the issue of that which might actually motivate those who use them for the 'greater good,' Hiss had not informed John Foster Dulles that he had been

the subject of F.B.I. inquiry. As a man who was on the brink of realizing his career ambition, Hiss was acutely aware that being tied to Chambers would be the death knell. And therein you find the Achilles' heel of Alger Hiss. While at the time in the 1930s, Hiss was doing nothing wrong in espousing very liberal, socialist views. But, and a big practical 'But' it is, he and his wife were close friends with Chambers and his wife and this reflected directly upon his judgment, not necessarily because Chambers was a communist but necessarily because Chambers was a spy. At the very least, Hiss was subject to the claim he lacked sufficient discretion. He did not know to avoid stepping on dog shit as he walked down the street. And as we all know, you cannot wiggle crap off your shoes.

13. Finding himself painted into this rather unfortunate corner, Hiss then turned pragmatic, dropping whatever moral compunction he carried with him by the wayside. Hiss decided to deny he knew Chambers, with the first step being he would fail to recognize the photo. Perhaps he thought Chambers would never appear. Perhaps he knew the F.B.I. investigation had led nowhere. Hiss did not know about Nixon and the priest, Cronin, nor did he know Nixon and Chambers had become their own version of fellow travelers. Nor did Hiss know about the Berle meeting with Berle's extensive notes still preserved. Nixon requested the role as head of a HUAC sub-committee to determine which of the two, Chambers or Hiss, had committed perjury- knowing full well that Hiss was lying about the friendship with Chambers. The ultimate stumbling block, among many, was that Nixon had, or would have Berle's notes and much other evidence to prove the Chambers-Hiss connection. There is no doubt Hiss committed perjury. But I also have no doubt that Hiss was not a spy. His lied to protect his judgment under the false apprehension that his station and position of power with

powerful friends at his beck and call would trump Chambers' ostensible lack of position and power."

"It looks like Hiss never considered either the desire for power of HUAC in general, and Nixon in particular, nor did he consider Chamber's testimony could be given the legs of truth informed by details from the F.B.I. investigation and the other many resources of HUAC and Hoover."

"An excellent point, Tommy. I believe that may well be what actually happened with the additional help of some other forces which sought to conspire against liberal Democrats and which happened to catch Hiss along the way. Hiss had great acumen and self- reliance. He did not however, look deeply into the position in which he was trapped and where it was leading. Swirling forces would swallow up his denial. It would soon be shown to fall out of the realm of the plausible. Not only Princeton, which by the way is where John Foster Dulles and his brother Allen, whom I will mention in a moment, were schooled, but Harvard Law School seems to have its own breeding ground for those who like their own reflections above all else, a place for the further nurturing of arrogance and pride all to the end of its own special form of narcissism."

"Jesus, Uncle Fricke. How do you know all this stuff?"

"Most of it was in the press at the time. T.V. was on its infant legs. HUAC in the Hiss and Chambers probe was the first televised congressional committee. Some of it I know from Hoover or Nixon directly, other things from those close to both of them. As I will explain in a minute, there is also an intelligence community involvement, so some of the information comes from people I know personally in the C.I.A., especially as part of the Johnson and Nixon sanctioned joint venture between the F.B.I and C.I.A., Operation CHAOS as it is called. Let me go back to the Hiss case itself and how it evolved for Nixon to bring down Hiss. He was convicted for perjury since the statute of limitations had run on espionage…"

"Uncle Fricke, it may be the case was too thin to prove espionage, statute of limitations or not, if, as you say, Hiss was not a spy."

"In a better world you would be right Tommy, but as you will see I am not so sure. In any event Hiss served jail time for perjury. The end result of all of these Machiavellian machinations, some of which I have yet to tell you, catapulted Nixon from first year California congressman to U.S. Senator in 1950, then Vice President in 1952 and ultimately, our President."

"It looks like you are right. Justice and truth are only minor issues, especially as the press shines a light making everything under its microscope bigger than life with political futures hanging in the balance."

H. The Whole of the Moon

"Tommy, there is no doubt about that. I am Governor today, in part, because I successfully prosecuted Al Capone's number one man, Tony Accardo."

"You should be proud."

"I am but sometimes political expediency is the sole focus of a prosecutor, or someone like Nixon, as head of an investigating committee. Committees, even those with independent, special prosecutors, have too much power. Acts which are not the legitimate basis for culpability, like the Hiss' friendship with Chambers, may nevertheless work to seal the fate of the person caught in the cross hairs of the aim of a single-minded committee. It is too easy to prove that someone is hiding something whether it is a politically motivated crime or even a socially unacceptable trifle of misfeasance, like sexual misconduct. In the Hiss' case an act that was entirely without blame, at the time it occurred led to a cascade of prevarication from which Hiss could not stop his own fall."

"So Uncle Fricke, Washington with his little hatchet chopping down the cherry tree and Lincoln with his 'all of the people all of the time' were both right. Honesty is the best policy."

"Right you are in the ideal world. Political motivation should never be that which motivates an honest politician. I hope we never reach the day where executive decisions are made with an eye to how the voting public will receive them. Sometimes those in the know must do what they know to be right. The people must be served. I am sure I will not be re-elected because of something I will implement, something which Illinois must have, a state Income Tax. I am proud to serve the people, and not my own career. Others do not so guide themselves."

"I am really proud of you Uncle Fricke. But please tell me more. Why do you think the Hiss case did not serve the ends of justice? I do not want to become cynical but, at the time, I thought the Clavita murder trial was an unusual perversion of justice, and now with this Jeffrey MacDonald case likely to become a matter of sensational reporting, I am wary. I hope the t.v. people do not feast like vultures on the bones of those caught in the criminal justice system. There is also the issue you mention. The very real threat of prosecution taints the promise of immunity especially when it is given to testifying witnesses who are no better, and could be worse, than those targeted by the zealots on Crusade. All this becomes essentially worse than trial by combat since the accusers bring weapons to bear that are much more powerful than those used by knights jousting."

"Or two gentlemen with pistols pointed standing at twenty paces..."

"There is no doubt government 'stool pigeons' sully the whole system."

"Well put, Tommy, in the Hiss case, Chambers was able to claim he testified against 'his friend, Alger Hiss' because Hiss turned against him and his wife by suing him for slander. Nixon established that either Hiss or Chambers had committed perjury, knowing full well that Hiss had (and would) lie to protect his reputation and career. Hiss fell into the trap. He sued Chambers for slander to further protect his 'good name.' The wheels of doom were set in motion. Chambers then produced documents and microfilm incriminating Hiss not just as a communist but as a spy. And here is where the whole matter becomes really, really interesting in a number of different realms for the power hungry or mere human dynamics, not the least of which was Hiss' willingness to believe that his own position, acumen, and power would win the day against an admitted spy, communist, and as events have shown a homosexual. Hiss was willing to produce evidence at his trial that Chambers was gay, but he never did even though our own Intelligence community stepped in to make sure Chambers appeared credible. It is not clear to me whether Nixon, or even Hoover, knew this would happen, but let me go back a few steps first. The lawyers that represented Hiss were essentially inept. Harvard's stalwarts, in this case the emphasis is on 'warts,' should stick to that which they know, keeping the fat of big companies out of the various fires in which they routinely find themselves. I am not saying these powerful, highly compensated lawyers do not know about callous lawbreakers. Those who run with the big dogs are all aswim in the same kettle of lawlessness, the lawyers included. 'Cost-benefit' or 'Risk versus gain' analysis lives beyond Harvard Business School and the way Robert McNamara ran Ford Motor Company. The concept of what best runs to the bottom line feasts in the board rooms where sometimes it is not at all clear ultimately whose flesh is being eaten or upon what shores all the ripples will finally come to rest.

"If you lose your soul..."

"Exactly, Tommy, in heaven as it is on earth. Look at the whole unholy process. First, powerful lawyers sometimes control the laws and regulations themselves. Sometimes the lawyers simply have influence over policies that govern detection and prosecution. Sometimes knowledge of the principles that guide the regulating agencies is enough to suggest a course of conduct or ultimate defense. Even if the board with legal counsel present determines they are running afoul of the law, and that they may get caught, the likelihood of actual cases filed, then the quantification of actual dollars lost is considered. The decision to engage, or continue, in a patently illegal course of conduct is then made. Moral principles do not affect that determination or analysis. The sole concern of a corporation is that which flows to its bottom line. Extrinsic factors beyond profit cannot be considered. There is no big picture, only trying to squeeze it all through the eye of a camel. So, Tommy, you can see that large corporations, have complex, intricate decision trees, or more aptly decision forests, in which to find their own single purposed way. Their lawyers are highly skilled, highly trained, highly intelligent, and highly experienced, but not in the simple sort of hand-to-hand combat necessary to conduct even a simple jury trial seeking conviction for two counts of perjury."

"So the betters are led down the garden path by their inferiors. I guess if you know the way, no amount of superiority joined against you will cause you to change your path."

I. Open

“Interesting, Tommy. Let us look at the ‘whole picture,’ the one the Hiss’ trial team somehow missed. They were not alone. The television commentators and newspaper scribes at the time and the writers who have since written books all failed to see a simple fact- the issue of our own intelligence community’s later manipulation aside...”

“Boy, Uncle Fricke, this is interesting, and all of this I am sure will bear upon the Dr. Jeffrey MacDonald case, since the facts of the murders are so gruesome and the networks are such willing handmaidens in the effort to titillate the public with gory details and vivid horror.”

“Once again, Tommy, I am sure you are right. It is loathsome that he who manipulates best is the one man surviving when the conflagration is over. Counting the bodies on a bloody field is all that remains to be done. Sometimes the battle itself rages on; other times it is never ending comment and review that continues to breathe life into a controversy. But let me go back to the one winning point that Hiss and his team of shining Harvard stars all missed, more than the eventual outmaneuvering I promised to tell you about. Everyone presumes Chambers made an ‘honest defection.’ Chambers was no different than the many intellectuals who embraced socialist principles in the 1930s and then fell into the arms of Russian communism and an apparatus carefully designed for espionage. Just as our intelligence people are highly capable. The Russian spies who implemented and who executed espionage activities here were no fools. Not getting caught is a major consideration. Ongoing activities are protected from their inception. A plan to keep an agent, once planted, in place, is part of any successful intelligence scheme. It is an easy assumption to make. Chambers did not defect. He simply received an assurance that he would not be prosecuted, technically not a grant of 'immunity' which is a formal, written act. Splitting hairs is not just the act of a lawyer. Nixon was accused of spending the weekend with Chambers to help Chambers prepare testimony showing his knowledge of the personal habits of Alger and Priscilla Hiss. Nixon was comfortable in his categorical denial. He felt that since he went home between all day Saturday and all day Sunday sessions, he had not 'spent the weekend.' So, Tommy, we are now just beginning to see how truth, with justice its companion, falls quickly to further the means of some perceived laudable goal- ferreting out all communists in the case of Nixon and our Republicans. In the case of Russian spies, the laudable goal, the end that justifies the means, is freeing the oppressed working peoples from the yokes of their masters holding all dat *Das Capital*. It is easy to imagine that Chambers was instructed to curry friendship with Hiss. In the 1930s, Hiss and Priscilla leaned to the left with real concern for the many poor, some whom they saw everyday in Manhattan, on the streets, or in the tent cities of Hooverville that grew up on the shores then teeming, not with hope but only the tired, the poor, and other huddled masses. Chambers might not have been told this is so many terms but he may well have been charged by his handler or handlers with an activity more important than that of a document courier. His role was to protect the real agent or agents working in the State Department. To defend himself, Hiss needed only to say that Chambers was inherently not trustworthy. The communist spy apparatus was alive and real. Great care was taken to prevent and avoid detection. We now know the high level Soviet operatives examined by HUAC all took the fifth and gave no real information. Chambers said he kept the documents he said he got from Hiss to protect himself. Even the documents in Hiss' own handwriting could have been purloined by the actual Soviet operatives still working in the State Department, the person, but more likely, persons Chambers was enlisted, perhaps unwittingly, as a pawn to protect. It is also interesting that the documents Chambers produced, microfilm included were all relatively benign. Another interesting question, not raised by Hiss' lawyers, was how did Chambers make the copies he kept? Chambers' friendship with the Hisses was nurtured to create a scapegoat, a deflection from the real Soviet embedded State Department spies. It was a huge error that the best the defense could muster was that Chambers was a 'sociopathic' liar. Even though it turns out Nixon and Hoover had Chambers' own admissions about his extensive homosexual encounters, Hiss did not have enough 'evidence' of his homosexuality, even though it was well-known. Hiss had retained so-called experts to testify that homosexuality causes a strange personality disorder. Just to have this wrongheaded defense at the ready shows how the team had dropped the ball. Why get into the realm of conjecture…"

"Uncle Fricke, it is a fine world in which we live, when one prejudice is used to win the day over another pile of bigotry."

"'Tis true Tommy, but there are those who believe that in desperate times, any sort of desperate measures may be used. The Hiss defense missed the evidence right under their swanky noses. It is a believable, and not a particularly elaborate, scheme to protect the existing Russian spy apparatus. Well known principles of espionage or rather self- preservation, principles even well-known in the 1930s, in an environment of schemes acknowledged by Chambers to be one where great care was taken to preserve secrecy. It is a simple next step to assume that those in charge had the chutzpah to deceive in order to lead the bloodhounds sniffing down the wrong trail particularly given the amount of energy and resources, Hoover, the CIA, and military counter-intelligence were and would bring to bear to uncover the covert. Beyond all that, think of another simple point. It was wildly unlikely the leaders or handlers of Chambers and Hiss, assuming they were both Russian spies, would throw the two of them together as close family friends. There was risk enough in the weekly, or every ten day, meetings about which Chambers testified when Hiss would bring home sensitive documents to return them the next day."

"So, Uncle Fricke, Hiss was more a deflection than a red herring."

"Tommy, it is funny you would use that term. Truman called the HUAC hearings a 'red herring.' The Hiss lawyers should have figured this out. It is more than plausible. But now listen to this. Let me tell you about the typewriter, a tale where the better and his team of betters were all one-upped. So Tommy here we go. What I am about to tell you is all about what you never want to know. Shakespeare and his cauldrons boiling and bubbling never had a plot as good as this one. There is this powerful New York lawyer Donovan. His firm is called Donovan-Leisure. They are so big the two names do not even need a conjunction."

"Funny."

"Hiss was a powerful force at Yalta, and even more powerful with the U.N. Charter. He successfully negotiated with Stalin to reduce the number of U.N. votes. Stalin wanted one vote for each Socialist Republic. Hiss knocked it down to four, including the U.S.S.R. Hiss was not only the man who brought the original U.N. Charter, once in final form, back to Washington for Truman's signature. But let me take a step back. Tommy, remember if you start with the 'right' premise or premises, you can then use ironclad logic to prove anything. In the 1930s, the conservative folks felt that Roosevelt's New Deal was exactly the same as communism. The second premise, of course, is that 'socialism' is the same as 'communism,' particularly after the war when Russian Communism became particularly unpalatable, or now as Mao's Red China is totally abhorrent. Who would have guessed Stalin would kill more than Hitler and that Mao would kill more than Stalin? It is easy to see why 'communism' is a blot on the world of human rights. It is not as easy to see why the New Deal is as bad, unless, of course you have money, and do not want to pay taxes. The issue of what motivates people with money aside, and who knows whether Marx was not right in his views on capital being the key to history, the conservative right wanted the New Deal, and those who supported it and implemented it, dead. The only good red is a dead one is still the banner philosophy of newspapers like the Chicago Tribune. Hiss fell into the category of a New Deal propagator. He wrote for a publication that espoused forming a union for tenant farmers and share croppers. He worked at the American Agricultural Association, the 'AAA.' The AAA was a Federal agency so far to the left that it did not last long, even in King Roosevelt's four term tenure. Naturally the war produced a significant military intelligence community. When the war ended, many of those guys were now 'all dressed up, with nowhere to go.' Donovan was part of that group. Just as Patton wanted to keep going right past Berlin and take the Third Army all the way to Moscow, a lot of the members of the intelligence community wanted to stamp out all vestiges of communism, especially within our home shores. Allen Dulles was another guy like that. In 1945, Hiss had a bright future. The word was he would be the first Secretary General of the United Nations. Since 'New Deal' equals 'Communism,' this was not acceptable to some, Donovan among them. Through an aide he warned the State Department not to support Hiss. It is ironic that John Foster Dulles appointed Hiss as the head of his peace organization. I guess brothers do not talk about everything although other circumstances in the Hiss case seem to indicate the Dulles boys later had their oars in the water pulling in the same direction."

"Jeez Uncle Fricke, I thought Jack and Bobby were powerful brothers, but the Secretary of State and the head of the C.I.A., cornering the market on foreign affairs. Who knows how long it will be before one family will have such control?"

"Tommy right again, and that's just the tip of the iceberg if the little bump in the road for Alger Hiss is any indication. Before the CIA, there was the OSS, Donovan ran the show and Allen Dulles was a big part. There was this guy Howard Schmahl who worked with Donovan at the OCI, the 'Office of Counter-Intelligence' if I am remembering the acronym correctly. There was another guy who worked in this milieu named Adam Kunze. Anyway, and this is hard to believe but true, the Hiss defense team hired Schmahl as part of its investigation team. When the typed documents produced by Chambers, from inside a pumpkin no less, the Hiss lawyers thought if they produced Hiss' old typewriter, the documents would not match, and that would be that. Well that was that, but not the way they thought. The military intelligence community was well-versed in forging typed documents for travel into countries with assumed names. This Kunze guy was an expert in the field of changing the type set on typewriters to match. So one day Schmahl shows up with Hiss' old typewriter. That was the good news. The bad news was that the type set matched the Pumpkin Papers. That was the end for Alger Hiss. To the day he died, Hiss said he would get to the bottom of the issue of 'forgery by typewriter.' Once again the prissy boys that Hiss hired to keep his skirts clean may have known how to sign a debutante's dance card at a coming out ball, but they never formed the simple conclusion that the intelligence community long had the means to copy so-called 'unique' type set."

"You know Uncle Fricke. Every kid that has ever read Arthur Conan Doyle knows that Sherlock Homes always says, when you eliminate the impossible, you have the solution. So dance cards and debutantes asides, it is hard to see how so many people had a blind spot."

"No one knew the depth and the reach of the intelligence communities. So Hiss had two extremely capable and adroit spy groups working against him. There is no doubt, however, the two intelligence communities, ours and theirs, dovetailed in the areas of illicit intent and smoke screens for cloak and dagger covert activities and in so many ways, plots and sub-plots, parries and counter-parries, that those activities were masked and carefully, ingeniously hidden."

"So is this how Nixon became known as 'Tricky Dickie?'"

"At first, I do not think Nixon had the full sense of the scope and breadth of all the merging intelligence communities which became the CIA. I do know Nixon kept issuing subpoenas for U.S. Intelligence agents to testify before HUAC. The C.I.A kept screaming like a stuck pig- why give the public and the Russians too much info about our spies. Nixon agreed to stop. It is not a far stretch to imagine that the then not yet fully 'Tricky Dick,' sought and received the agreement from Dulles and his people, guys like Donovan to feed HUAC with information. Nixon was single minded. He may not be a quick study but he is facile enough, an opportunist who was probably not privy to intelligence community information at the beginning. At a point in time, no doubt Nixon saw which side of the bread that the butter was on. There are some coincidences which are simply too complex to be solely the matter of chance. After the Hiss trial, where John Foster Dulles testified against Hiss, where Allen Dulles brought his resources to bear, Nixon became Vice President, one Dulles the Secretary of State, and the other to head the C.I.A. It is funny how during all this Hiss stuff, Hoover and the F.B.I. kept away from Nixon, at least not as close as Nixon would have liked. I did not mention some other things about Schmahl who was a German National and Donovan. Donovan served as Schmahl's character reference on his Personal History Statement for OSS. After Schmahl's penetration and Hiss's subsequent conviction, Donovan recommended Schmahl for Special Operations at the CIA. Nowadays, years later, I have heard from others, some close to Nixon, that Nixon is fond of reminiscing about the salient point of the case that catapulted him to prominence, about the Kunze-Schmahl typewriter, 'We built one in the Hiss case.'"

"It is always a good idea to take credit whether credit is due or not, whether you were a pawn on the outside or part of the deep scheme from the outset."

"That is funny but true, Tommy. Many people like to think they have earned what they have the hard way after they have been given it. After I finish with Hiss, let's talk about your missing finger. Then, if we have time, I'll tell you about some of those who take greed to its lowest level- two sons of a guy name Koch, one of the founders, with Robert Welch, of that group of patriots for their own accounts, the John Birch Society. While I am sure the Birchers slither I am not sure whether they act only to line, no to **keep** lined, their own significant corporate pocket books. Nixon is a snake in the grass but he is our snake. The one thing Nixon learned as a man new to Washington was that the corridors of power do exist and where they are, thus, maintained. Nixon speaks often and freely about his distrust and disdain for the East Coast/Ivy league closed group with its old money. From his first days on the hill, Nixon saw the elite first hand, those surrounding the Dulles boys and Hiss alike. I wonder whether he should now fear the middle class meritocrats, those who now, like the way he was in 1948, have fire in their bellies. Or does real power still firmly repose with those who roam the long standing corridors, rooted through history and *noblesse oblige* as if it is all theirs and all theirs alone? It may well be that it will be easy to divert the wannabes, with their rage to succeed, to Wall Street where significant sums of money will turn the compulsive overachievers from the public schools away from seeking life for the public good. The ubiquitous ambitious will turn instead to line up to take their turn to put on the feed bag for large executive bonuses. I hope the day never comes where the politicians serve only their golfing buddies."

"A shuddering thought Uncle Fricke. A country run to protect and serve the haves and the 'have mores.''

"Yes and without *mores*. The land of the crass and the home of the craven. One final point before I mention the Hiss aftermath- McCarthyism and the John Birch Society- the absurdities reached from logical extensions on a path wrought from overstated premises, then add to the mix a self-serving agenda of pure avarice. But first what's going on with your missing trigger finger?"

J. My Dark Side

"Uncle Fricke, I think you know the army has its own version of red tape. Initially they were red-faced that my enlistment physical failed to disclose the obvious missing tip on my index finger. Now it looks like once I complete basic training, I will work at a desk for the M.P.s. and never leave the base at Fort Bragg."

"Let me call some folks. I think the army, red scare aside, has a mechanism for honorable discharge. It may take to the end of the year. Worst case, you can continue to have Carolina on your mind. You definitely need not worry about Southeast Asia and falling dominos. Before I talk about the ripples of fear that keep the voting public lined up to vote against the democrats who are soft on the red menace, I want to conclude my thoughts on the Hiss case. Closing argument must fit the facts presented a trial. This is the one point I did not reach in regard to the utter failings of the Hiss defense team. Eloquence alone will never win the day. A stammering fool who can point to the important evidence adduced at trial will always beat the most eloquent warbler whose song is a thing of beauty but does not match or ring true with the evidence in the case. The Hiss team may have had its hands tied because Hiss was unwilling to tell the truth about how well he and his wife knew Chambers and his wife, and about their left leaning inclinations in the 30s. Nevertheless, in any trial you have to tell a story, a story that makes sense and that is believable. The prosecution case lived and breathed with the communist spy threat- so the defense needed only to wrap it up in one neat package. Hoist 'em with their own petard I always say. A scenario involving an intricately interwoven Russian spy network was there- a credible threat, a delicious icing... "

"A cakewalk for the Hiss defense."

"You are right in stride, Tommy. The Russians used Chambers to set up Hiss to protect their real spies long planted in the State Department. The defense did not need to suggest that our spies forged the Hiss typed documents. It would have been an easy reach to suggest only that those very scary and highly motivated Russians, a cabal of evil, had the means and the need to immerse themselves in all they could do to further their nefarious agenda. The prosecution would then have been hamstrung, really unable to argue that communism is bad, but not that bad. The story told at trial, through the evidence need only be believable, a place where a juror can hang his hat. A lawyer must believe his client even if he knows his client is lying because he must show to the jury that his client's cause can be followed in a clear path to its ultimate conclusion. To see how wanting and how far from obtaining a not guilty verdict Hiss was, look at his character witnesses. Never has there been anything like it. Two sitting United States Supreme Court Justices, Frankfurter and Reed, and John W. Davis, the Democrats' candidate who lost twice to Hoover, and Adlai Stevenson, then Governor, placed in the same Governor's mansion where I now sit, yet to run and lose twice against Ike, all four testified as to the sterling and pristine reputation of Alger Hiss for veracity- truth telling and honesty. These were formidable witnesses with impeccable integrity, but perhaps, this was more than a case of gilding the lily, more than a case of the lady protesting too much. Without a storyline upon which to hang the evidence for a case-winning theory no number of witnesses will win the day. John Foster Dulles was all the prosecution needed to say Hiss was not trustworthy and disingenuous because Hiss failed to mention to him that the F.B.I. had investigated him at the time Duller was appointed heads of Dulles' peace commission. Even that should have played into the hands of the defense hands. The drum they had to beat was that the F.B.I investigated and unearthed nothing. "

"Uncle Fricke. I think you would have won the Hiss case. Plus I think Hiss suffered from a serious case of thinking his shit did not smell. How hard would it have been to tell Dulles he had been the subject of an F.B.I. interview with no further steps taken?"

"Hiss read too much Roman history, I fear. Feet of clay and all that. His own character flaws aside, for his lawyers, jury trial experience is essential. I can see the day when a large company loses a big criminal anti-trust case by using its large corporate firm to cross swords with the Department of Justice wits its best jury trial lawyers. These big firms have what they call, 'litigation departments.' Those officious little pricks are too smug and too sophisticated to call themselves 'trial lawyers,' much less to wrestle in the mud of the realm of juries. These 'white shoes' lawyers may look down their upturned noses. But mark my words, if a big firm department head and the lawyers actually handling the case have never picked a jury, then Katie bar the door. There is another factor. I think I would have won the Hiss case, too- had I tried either side. All good trial lawyers know that jury trials are seduction- pure and simple- after much hard preparation, of course. You cannot be overprepared. All good trial lawyers think that if you can seduce a woman, you can seduce a jury. The same skill set."

"It's not just lawyers Uncle Fricke. I have been spending time with a nurse at the base hospital. Doctors and nurses are like lawyers and juries. My nurse friend tells me that the word at the nursing stations is that Jeffrey MacDonald is no exception. In any pressure cooker, the participants find nature's best way to relieve the stress."

"Yes, Tommy, and seduction is sometimes a question of 'did I jump or was I pushed?' Realizing the need for an oasis of calm, whether it is two in a bed in the nearest empty hospital room or in a room full with the heated deliberations of twelve angry men, the man who can give just the right suggestion of having a sturdy rudder in turbulent waters will invariably right the ship in just the right way. Your mother better never hear us talking like this. I do think the concepts are analogous, however. Both women and juries have an innate, primordial desire to be pushed in the direction of natural inclination whether it is that which furthers the preservation of the species or that which serves the ends of justice. Both objects of persuasion fall prey to the same sort of flattery. They must be shown not pointed, however. The must reach the path seemingly of their own choice and initiative."

"I am sure even his wife, Pat, would agree that Nixon could not seduce his way out of a paper bag, even if his face was covered with one. Nevertheless in the Hiss trial, first term Congressman Richard Nixon engaged in our modern version of trial jousting knights at odds to uphold honor. Televised legislative hearings are surely not more interesting than justice or honor upheld at the end of a pistol with dainty, well-dressed seconds surrounding men like Burr and Hamilton…"

"Tommy, keep in mind Nixon set the wheels in motion. He did not bring Hiss to the mat. Only a good trial lawyer could have saved him once he was bruised, bloodied, dazed, and down for the count. There is a funny anecdote that was spawned in the throes of all this anti-Communist hysteria. The head of Time magazine, Henry Luce was shocked that Chambers, as one of his editors, had not disclosed to him that he was a former spy, now on the side of the right and the good. Chambers was supercilious in saying, 'Luce you are a grown man, you must know all communist party members engage in espionage.' Chambers started believing the new party line. And thus the crucible became the cauldron. Hiss and all 'communists' were tarred and feathered, then pilloried. McCarthyism became bigger than life after the Hiss debacle had run its course. By its own fiat, the John Birch Society maintained that all who were soft on communism were communists. Even Ike was put on their enemies list. The New Deal/Communist equation was yanked to its utmost extension. To mollify the hardliners, Nixon and Dulles, among others were added to surround Eisenhower so the claim he did not march the troops from Berlin to Moscow would not stick to hurt him. One Birch Society founding father, Fred C. Koch, was a Wichita oil and gas magnate who initially lost, through his own long and bitter experience in the judicial system, when the big oil companies sued him for impinging upon their exclusive rights..."

K. A Song for the Life

"So, Fred Koch was initially communist minded, at least in the "to each" prong, ignoring the property rights of others."

"Until the courts slapped his hand. Koch then did what he was trying to do here, fracking mostly whatever that is, in foreign lands. Russia was where he made the most money back then. On the steppes was where his true antipathy to socialism was born. For Koch, the John Birch Society..."

"A skeptic might suggest that Koch is motivated to see that Russia is a free market simply to feather his own nest even more."

"Yes, Tommy there is always a pot of gold at the end of any spectrum of zealotry and self-aggrandizement. There is a rumor about Koch's sons, not sure which of the four, a rumor which will not die. Sometime after their dad died, they got together socially with some other well-to-do types. The Kochs raised their glasses for a toast to making their fortunes the way God intended, the hard way, by inheriting it."

"Wealth, or at least, money in hand, is not just for the astute and opportunistic business man or the beneficiaries of the trust funds they accumulate. Chambers had the unmitigated gall to fan the flames of anti-communist sentiment while at the same time extolling his new born virtue..."

"Nothing worse than a reformed hooker, eh Uncle Fricke?"

“Or an anti-communist with a profit motive, perhaps. Plus the human need to fly the flag of self-righteousness is strong. Chambers wrote a book, *Witness*. I am, more and more, amazed how writers swim circles safely around a bait ball where the accused and the titillated public are trapped alike. Once the media are done picking over the bones, some other fascinating subject becomes the news, writers make a name by writing about these high profile trials. This is another subversive incentive for those actually involved- dollars down the road. Chambers’ book has been picked up by the right. The Governor of California, Ronald Reagan, once the head of the Screen Actor’s Union who calls himself a former New Deal democrat, says that after he read Chambers’ book with its clear exposition of where communism will lead and had gone, he has now been transformed a true freedom fighter, a conservative Republican ready to bring down the Iron Curtain.”

“Hey Uncle Fricke. The bugler is blowing lights out.”

“Wow, where did the time go. We talked forever about a range of interesting topics, but it seemed like only a few minutes.”

“For me, too. Thanks for making a lonely recruit feel like he was back home.”

“Keep me in the loop or better yet, let me know if there is anything I can do. Good night, Tommy.”

“Good night, Uncle Fricke.”

L. Love You To

The two Wanderbys hung up their phones at the same time. For one night in Fort Bragg, Tommy slept the sleep of a baby rocked in a cradle, not the enforced sleep of a man pushed to the limits of physical exertion, a mental calm beyond the rest his tired body craved every night. Tommy awoke refreshed. All 6'3" inches of his lean and muscular swimmer's frame was ready for action. His sharp blue eyes were shiny and bright, the perfect accompaniment to the winning smile that always completed his handsome visage.

Shortly after again reporting for duty to the M.P. station that morning, Tommy persuaded the C.I.D. investigator in charge of the MacDonald murders that he should check with the nurses to confirm the scuttlebutt about MacDonald. Tommy's inquiries were stopped dead in their tracks by the first nurse he encountered. Uncle Fricke had just made droll reference to two in a hospital bed. Tommy started and ended in a place he had come to know and to like. In this instance it, or she to be more apt, was Nurse Cheryl Stubblefill, a sassy lass who hailed from Savannah. She was a red head, lanky and lean but with hips that moved with just the right subtle suggestion. Her freckles formed a galaxy of invitation below her ever-welcoming green eyes. To put her in the class of the pride of Georgia did not overstate the case. Cheryl had an earthy, down home attitude about everything physical. The ethos of free love that ruled the day added to her geniality. The nurses had a long standing agreement concerning an off duty fringe benefit. Whoever covered the nursing station, when given a wink and an empty room number, would hand the off duty nurse one of those "highly contagious" placards then make sure that room was kept safe and sound from outside interruption. Fever would then rule the roost. That day Tommy and Cheryl spent six hours with Tommy on his back in the full comfort of a hospital bed, the back raised to just the right point where so Cheryl could ride Tommy and lean forward grasping the top of his shoulders with both hands. Tommy did not need to lift his head to find Cheryl's nipples with his mouth. Cheryl kept Tommy's prick inside her as she slid slow from side to side using the same rhythm with her hips that made her gentle amble so alluring. Four times, Cheryl rocked Tommy to sweet peace. The fourth time Cheryl finished in full flush together with Tommy,

"Tommy, do you mind if I tell the other girls that you are the hardest working man in slow business?"

Tommy was dazed in delight,

"Cheryl, you ride in little circles which compress the beauty as motion transcends time into one long lingering taut rope which then flails and explodes- one multi-colored sunset after another. So the other nurses may be disappointed."

"Not about the way you can keep it up and then rise again. Are you sure your family is not from Dixie?"

M. Tomorrow Never Knows

Usually, at the end of the day, Tommy left the Mess Hall with his legs like jelly from U.S. Government approved Army maneuvers. Cheryl improved the way to his wobble immeasurably. After the long talk with Uncle Fricke the night before, Tommy thought he would see what Joe Cebellum had to say, and see if Joe was faring better than he had at college. He was out of coins so he called Joe collect, person to person.

“Sure operator, I accept the charges. Hey Tommy this is great. Are you wearing your olive drab in the North Carolina dusk?”

“Standing at the pay phone, the best sort of military attention I can muster. You cannot believe how I spent the day, fit as a fiddle, in a hospital bed with a nurse who takes her Clara Barton vows very seriously, extending them to help a young soldier in need.”

“I knew you would find a way to fit in as one of America’s elite fighting forces.”

“One small spurt for mankind, one after another.”

“Stop you forget I am in the midst of the last bastion of male celibacy, enforced by an almost utter lack of gender dear, willing or otherwise.”

“Sounds bleak.”

“Bleak appears to be only the tip of the iceberg of solitude.”

“And no way a superman such as yourself can find a way to fly out? Oh wait, that is the fortress of solitude.”

“Right church wrong pew. But Princeton makes kryptonite seem like a placebo. Tommy, let me call you back right now. My phone bill is a study in deficit spending. My long distance charges have now increased to equal two trips home a month but I do get to talk to lots of people all over, like you, which I could not do if I flew home. Tommy what is the number there? It is cheaper if I call direct. That way we can talk well into the wee hours.”

“Or at least until the Fort Bragg Montgomery Clift bugling wannabe blows taps?”

“Unlike you, we students can stay up all night, from here to eternity, but with no place to put the point of our desire.”

“You can always hope that every dog will have his place in the sun.”

With that Tommy returned the receiver to its cradle. In a few short seconds the pay phone rang. Tommy noticed the sun was still twenty degrees off the horizon. He heard Joe’s voice in full stride.

“So, Tommy, as one dog to another, to what do I owe the pleasure of this call? More than just scant reference to mussing infirmary sheets…”

“Joe, did you read about this Dr. Jeffrey MacDonald family mass murder, or see it on t.v.?”

“Nope, I have been spending all my outward attention playing cards or turning up the stereo. Music soothes the savage beast…”

“Especially with no savage breasts in hand. This MacDonald guy is a Green Beret doctor. He graduated from Princeton a few years before you got there…”

Tommy then gave Joe the gory details of the gruesome mass murder.

"Tommy, this turns my stomach. If there is no forensic evidence of any outside interlopers after the crime scene investigation you just described, the conclusion is inescapable. The press will have a field day, anything to sell commercial time during the news hour. Either way the viewing public will not want to change the channel, Green Beret Doctor goes berserk or Drug Crazed Hippies again on the loose, a national epidemic playing right into the hand of Nixon and his silent majority. Our President is going to teach those doped up war protesters a sharp lesson."

"Ironic, Vietnam is fueling the influx of grass and heroin but that war is o.k. with the White House. Some soldiers are making a killing selling contraband."

"No matter what you hear, Art Linkletter's daughter trying to fly out of an upstairs window to her death in the middle of an acid trip, hallucinogens-LSD, mescaline, psilocybin, tripping really incapacitates you from any sort of gainful activity, just a happy mush of sense perceptions- violence, especially orchestrated mayhem is simply not possible once the doors of perception have been opened wide with the psychedelic experience."

"What about somebody like Manson using acid for purposes of mind control, then conditioning his subjects to kill?"

"I guess history will show whether LSD is a viable agent for mind control. Ken Kesey and the Merry Prankster, including some of the guys in the Grateful Dead were all paid by the Army to take acid in a hospital bed, probably not having as much fun as you had today, but all the while those paid subjects are zonked to the gills, the V.A. Hospital doctors in Palo Alto, right by Stanford, recorded the effects and ran some experiments to boot."

"I hear that it's not only the army who wants to duplicate the steely eyed possessed killer from the Manchurian Candidate. The CIA wants to avail itself of the full benefits of drug induced hypnosis, from truth serum to turning an enemy spy to do our bidding. The experimental program, of which the Palo Alto hospital is one small part, is called MK-Ultra. It has been going on in earnest since after the Korean War, in response to the Russian and Chinese intelligence communities' use of mind control."

"Joe, my Uncle told me about Alger Hiss. How hysteria was whipped up about Soviet spying, I guess just another way to justify spending taxpayer funds."

"Tommy, let's talk more about Alger Hiss next. It is a subject which is, now more than ever, fascinating. My mom always says Nixon railroaded Hiss but I do not know too much more than that. Current events and the recent past do not interest me as much trying to uncover whether the women in the photo shoots in Playboy magazine bear relationship to the everyday articles."

"With the emphasis on 'bare.'"

"Bare-naked is the best kind of naked. I want to say one more thing about MacDonald before we bat the ball around about the Hiss case. If he did it, it is hard to imagine how even the most self-centered egotist could live with himself- pregnant wife and two young daughters lay battered and bloodied before him- all dead at his own hand. We are coming to a place in our culture where right and wrong have become totally blurred. It is well more than the notion of mistaking paradise for the house down the road. Self-importance cannot justify the exclusion of everything but our own trample to the material excesses of the American dream. I hate to think that Princeton had a hand in this sort of wayward Narcissism either by creating a magnet for those special elite born to be above the law or whether with the Ivy version of an aberrant Pygmalion's touch, the students once here learn to have their sense of free reign cultivated to the point it runs unfettered, after being told, again and again, in so many ways, that what is good for themselves is the ultimate good. Achievement is measured only in terms of the almighty dollar. Then money becomes the only Holy Grail sought."

"Joe, I hate to think the elite, born or groomed, will become the super-rich taking it all and leaving none for the middle class or that MacDonald, if he did the murders, is some sort of Through the Looking Glass example of a huge ego beyond good and evil let loose to prowl without inhibition or restraint. It is bad enough that the woman who killed Clavita got away scot-free because of the sense of the community that whites are superior, but to think all dimensions of the way we live will be dominated by actors who justify their sense that the rules do not apply to them if the object sought is deemed to be so valuable, whether it is ego or dollars, which I guess amount to the same thing, as to justify any means to the end. The first step to a total breakdown of any real morality is the demise of institutional justice. The first step has been taken for the most part. The rich and powerful, the elite answer to no one. That is why my Uncle Fricke was telling me about the Hiss case- the course of history and the coarse hands now guiding it are subverting what should be the path to fairness. I am going to give serious consideration to finding a path that does not include money as the way to happiness and more so to find a mate who does not fit the pattern of virtue extolled by those who toil only to find all that they have is nothing and that the more they have, the less they know."

"I hope events and time, the full plod of history in the coming years will prove our fears unfounded. Tell me what the Governor of the Great State of Illinois, one of today's leading Republicans, said about Alger Hiss."

Tommy told Joe the whole tale- straight from the mouth of Fricke Wanderby.

"HUAC- I recently made reference to their favorite question in an effort to ingratiate myself with a girl from Radcliff."

"'Ingratiate?' It is all too precious for my taste. Why can't you just get 'em drunk and let the advanced wiggling begin from there like everybody else?"

"All the world is not like Texas or Fort Bragg."

"I am pleased to report that it is unless, of course, you have the dubious distinction of going to Princeton. When I get out I will have to come visit to see how bad it really is."

"The semesters of my discontent aside, the 1929 stock market crash had more ripples than just the catastrophe of the Great Depression."

"History books cannot contain all the episodes staged by those hell bent upon unseemly overcompensation. The backlash of repercussion is profound as the pendulum once set in motion swings back to its opposite extreme. What caused the initial cataclysm is never blamed, particularly if it is the inexorable result of conservative dogma running free on the open range."

"Shit Tommy, a day in the sack and you wax poetic. The big picture aside, Whittaker Chambers is an interesting character study, with or without the aid of the two largest clandestine intelligence hunters and gatherers on the planet, ours and theirs."

"How so?"

"I just took a course from this famous math guy, Tucker. He knows lots of advanced theory about math and philosophy. Chambers found himself, or placed himself in an interesting variation in what Tucker calls the 'Prisoner's Dilemma.' He was able to assure very favorable treatment from those who had him by the short hairs by ratting out confederates but he also was able to increase his stature immeasurably, at the time, and by later writing his book, by implicating a person against whom his captors had a real interest in neutralizing. This adds an additional dimension to the benefits achieved by a prisoner who can dummy up or sing like a bird. It seems the bird is always better in all variations. Whittaker Chambers took all necessary steps to maximize what could be gained from his predicament. Once Chambers was in the briar patch, whether initially he acted alone, or as part of a greater Communist plot, with the forces of anti-Communist next taking aim, Hiss could only wiggle and squirm, and not in the way you were talking about earlier, like a girl with a few beers in her. The Hiss trial was more than a zero sum game where when one loses, another must have an equivalent win. HUAC, Nixon, Chambers, and the Russian spies preserved in the State Department and elsewhere in these great United States were all clear front line winners. Hiss was the only loser, really collateral damage in a game where he was more minuscule than a fleck of dust on a chess board."

"Jesus, Joe, you better find a woman fast. Next thing I'll hear you are running for student government, or joining the debate society."

"Tommy, perish the thought. Finding my way into the arms and affection of the fairer gender is my only goal. Getting back to the dilemma of a Prisoner, even if in name only, Chambers gained more than the initial immunity he was assured. He was guaranteed ongoing favorable treatment, by the conservative right, by saying just what they wanted to hear. Hiss could not guess what was going on in the black box. He did not understand the nature of the game Nixon and Chambers were playing. Thus, he could not win. He was stuck in his own maze, trying to protect his good name and career. No defense, no matter how good, can ever win against an even better offense."

"So Newton was wrong for every action there is not an equal and opposite reaction."

"Well said Private Wanderby. Where you stand inevitably affects what there is, not just what there is to see. Hiss and his lawyers only saw the typewriter as an innocent machine. Rather, the typewriter is another interesting variation of an old puzzle this math genius Tucker guy talked about briefly in the class I just took, 'The Liar's Paradox.' There are lots of variations but basically you come to a fork in a road in a land where all the people are either people who always lie or always tell the truth. Two guys who know the way are there to help you find the way- one a liar, the other stuck in the mire of veracity. You have to form a question that will get you were you wish to go. So you have to ask something like, 'If I ask you whether the left fork is the way I wish to go, will you say yes?' The truth-teller will say yes if it is the right way. The liar also says 'yes,' a lie since he would actually say 'no.' If it is not the right way, the truthsayer says 'no.' and the liar again concurs with his counterpart since he would actually say 'yes.'"

"Fuck, Joe you better find yourself in the arms of a good woman fast. So the typewriter the enemy was so kind to provide to the Hiss defense team is a shrewd version of the 'Liar's paradox.' Whether it typed the documents or not, it is gonna say, yes I did the typing.' And thereby, Hiss had his goose cooked."

"Because he did not know the correct question to ask or where to ask it. In this case, it was simple enough, 'could you be altered to type the documents?' He did not know enough to assume that the typewriter could or would lie. Hiss and his lawyers did not understand where they were, or the game they were playing."

"Joe it is also interesting that nobody ever said to Chambers that he was required to sing like a canary about the other spies he named in that meeting with Berle and Levine. I see what you are saying. The game was only to capture Hiss."

"Later, the game changed. Once HUAC obtained an air of legitimacy in capturing Hiss, McCarthy implemented his own version of 'scorched earth.' From there the scare of worldwide domination took on a life of its own ending with Chicken Little rhetoric from those like the John Birch Society. Did I ever tell you that I caddied at Barrington Hills Country Club for a couple of regular members in a foursome that included, a Bircher guy who I think was named Koch, a guest that day, and a Texan who I think was a country club member even though he lived in Texas. For eighteen holes, the talk of the four fine feathered friends was pure vitriol and entirely mean-spirited- Blacks, Mexicans, Jews, Homosexuals and Women- each had their turn as institutionalized derision was brewed to a not particularly clever foment. It was pick a minority and tether them to the precept that they were mired in their own God-given inferiority. Eventually the golfers tired of showing their utter disdain for their lessers. The discussion turned to the free market and Ayn Rand. As far as I can tell, once you have it, there should be no governmental interference to take it away from you- no matter how the government may have helped you get it and keep it. This free market idea is entirely a figment of the imagination of economists who wish to rationalize that the wealthy should remain the wealthy. The four golfers had a real laugh about how the taxes upon the lower classes were used to fund the police to maintain order and keep the minions in their place at home, and were used to fund the armed forces lest the foreign poor rise up. The smug gratuitous back-slapping was sickening. The rich and powerful really see Karl Marx as a straw man, an easy caricature, one that can be vilified to rouse the rabble into a quake of fear. Koch got a real kick out of repeating that the workers of the world would arise to pay the cost of their own yokes. They all thought it was funny, really funny that, and I quote, 'that the yokes on them.'"

Tommy focused on the vile bigotry,

"Fucking racists. Their willingness to run ramshackle and rough over those beneath them is acceptable mainly because those culturally denominated and institutionally accepted as inferiors are dehumanized, and from there deserve only the business end of a boot. A collective foot on the throats of the inferiors keeps them, those who deserve nothing more, subjugated, but not with so much pressure to stop their breathing, since you still need the bottom of the barrel to do the heavy lifting, and the other wet work- *el trabajo sucio*."

"Shit, Tommy. You sound like you are ready to join the SDS."

"Nope, but those rich fucks are going to get us all in trouble one way or the other. You can change the rules but you can never change the game-the unwavering philosophy of those with capital willing to protect what they think they have at all costs. Unfairness rankles me."

"You hit the nail on the head, Tommy. But remember, as bad as it is, and it is, the world is a wild and wonderful place. I say, cut the cards and deal and see the hand you are dealt. Times 'awasting. There is always a way to have a good time, even if you find yourself *in extremis* and the fairer gender is unfairly omitted. I leave the world bettering to those whose ideals can do no better. You should, too. We all have our own crosses to bear. By the way how did you manage to spend the day in a hospital bed with a nurse when you are supposed to be climbing over artificial hedgerows and other obstacles, jumping into puddles and what not, with some Sergeant with a small man's complex yelling obscenities in your ears?"

"The medical examiners missed that I am missing the important digit needed for the war effort. I am now in the army equivalent of limbo, an M.P. trainee with a desk job pending ultimate disposition, mustering, duty rostering, and final orders..."

"But not necessarily in that order."

"Yesterday I investigated MacDonald's reputation in the medical community but was diverted by the first witness I interviewed."

"So you see, just another briar patch. No amount of adversity cannot be turned to your own advantage. The case of the missing top of the trigger finger has come to the rescue. When will you know the decision of those charged with army protocol such as it is?"

"Uncle Fricke just said he was going to make a call to bird dog that very issue. In the meantime, I have nowhere to point my stub but towards myself as I study the role of the M.P. The investigation continues and the party never ends."

Two nights in a row Tommy heard Taps standing at the same pay phone.

"Hey Joe, Sorry to interrupt but duty calls. The trumpet blows for me."

"You better run. You have to rest up for another bout with a nurse in heat, cutting hospital corners, in a ward that is its own reward."
"The first day's ward is the next day's re-ward. I only wish I could keep doing it until I get it exactly right"

"Trying to find just the right note, quite an aspiration. Listen, learn..."

"And keep her hips to the mill."

"Where do I go to enlist?"

"Before you hang up, all our worries about a total breakdown of ethical conduct aside, think about where we are today, we have the laws against drugs, abortions, and we have the draft for a war of dubious intentions. It all seems unjust. "

"Nevertheless, Tommy, I want you to know that I do like rules as long as I am not the one who has to follow them. They arc comfort and stability."

"No doubt. All sons of the Lone Star know that you, yourself should obey only what you know is right. Remember you are a rugged individualist, just like everyone else with boots, spurs, and a six gun."

Tommy's receiver made a metal clank. Joe's sounded a plastic clunk. Even an hour after the phone call ended, Joe could feel the gleam of Tommy's smile, that well-known Wanderby toothy grin even though he had not seen it.

O. She Said She Said

Tommy's conversation with Joe brightened Tommy's outlook, almost as much as the time he spent with Nurse Stubblefill. Joe's positive nihilism was contagious. For Tommy, it would be only an efficacious stop gap. Tommy was sure he would find a purely positive world view where peace and love were real not just a few hours well spent. After those two long phone calls, Tommy also became sure that what society saw as justice was not fair. His choice of lifetime companion would not be restricted to a girl like the one who married dear old dad, one with a proper upbringing, or even one where traditional values composed her.

The situation at Princeton that Joe described to Tommy was not as bad as he had said. It was worse. There is a scene early in the movie, *Casablanca*, where Rick Blaine, the Humphrey Bogart character, sends a girlfriend, Yvonne, out of his bar after this tried and true man-woman exchange-

"Where were you last night?"

"I can't remember that far into the past."

"Where will you be later tonight?"

"I never make plans that far into the future."

Yvonne makes clear she is not pleased. Rick has her whisked away.

Claude Raines, the Inspector Renault character, sees Yvonne has been dismissed. His admonition to Rick is curt,

"Some day they may be scarce."

Rick gives Renault a look of serious doubt.

The compelling weight of demographic data aside, it appeared that Joe had stumbled into a black hole the existence of which was not contemplated in any physicist's worst nightmare. It was not the weather that made winter in New Jersey bitter, bleak, and oppressive. Occasional aberrations serve only to underscore the point. Each and every new class at Princeton has many more Captains of their high school Football, Basketball, and Baseball teams than any other college. Business recruiters like the idea that true leadership is developed when young men compete against one another in front of cheering crowds. It is no accident that the last four letters of 'Princeton' are 'Eton.' Nearby Hightstown High School employed a particularly limber and flexible physical education teacher. This not too particular thirty year old woman decided she would fill her sexual history resume with as many former high school sports captains as time allowed. Word of this exuberant woman's new exercise regimen spread quickly. To pass the time as the long winter turned to late February, Sean McManus and Sammy Rice joined the passing parade. Sean was Football captain, Massachusetts State Champion, and All-State Quarterback. Sammy had not even a varsity letter to his name. When a line forms, not everyone in the queue gets fully vetted. Sean and Sammy both belonged in the second long line that formed, this one at the student infirmary. It is sad but true. "Penis all in" sometimes spells "penicillin." Syphilis was nothing to write home about. As luck would have it, neither Sean nor Sammy needed to pen even a penny postcard. Apparently, the clap has a mind of its own.

P. Come Live with Me

Sammy Rice was also involved in another less poignant counterexample proving the depths of a true void. On the Beatles' great album, *Sgt. Pepper's Lonely Hearts Club Band*, there is a song, "She's Leaving Home." With the fanfare from the Summer of Love in full blossom, young girls did not need to listen to the song to feel the urge to leave strict parents.

Whether Sammy Rice took the first step to meet the Scandinavian girl he nicknamed, "Norwegian Would," or whether she took the first step in taking full advantage of a collective desperation did not change the outcome. "Norwegian Would" was soon known on campus as "NW." For NW, Princeton became a providential stop gap but sadly just another whistle stop before she would become another forlorn nameless statistic lost to unforgiving urban streets. For about six weeks, love, peace, and happiness pervaded as Princeton's gentlemen garnered as much comfort as the circumstances allowed. Sammy Rice used his job at James Madison Hall, the full and formal name for Commons, to see that NW got three squares a day. NW, a beacon of promiscuity, made sure she had at least three square young men a day. Early in her forays, NW discovered that no one really hip could be found.

Marcel Proust rationalized the view of those who lacked the luxury of selection best, "Let us leave pretty women to men with no imagination." NW required imagination's full measure. She fell somewhere on the spectrum between a frumpy, forlorn peasant lost from a Brueghel farming landscape to one of Picasso's undecipherable cubist swoops of lines and tangents. Normally, Scandinavian beauty is something to behold. NW hailed from some dark, neglected corner where Laps and reindeer ran amuck. Only at Princeton would she be held. NW had an unfortunate slope to her forehead. Her nose was too prominent forming an inelegant slant from the line of her thin eyebrows. The skin and pores on her upper cheeks were coarse, uneven, and bore the suggestion of teenage acne. NW's eyelids were bulbous and overpowered her eyes. Her whole face flowed to a chin that sought a permanent place to duck for cover. Even her pouting, sultry lips could not cure the overall mish mash of misdirected facial features which ultimately spelled fish face. To top it all off, NW was plump to the point of truly dumpy. None of this mattered as February wore on. Standards fly out the window when instinct demands even the most docile zippers be untoothed. Even on a good day, Joe was more akin to a force of nature than tepid quietude.

NW had now bounced around more than a few top and bottom bunks for about four weeks. It was a Wednesday. The straw breaking the camel's back of prudence and restraint was the afternoon mail. It was a plain brown wrapper with no return address. There was no note inside, just the '45- the single, "Ain't No Mountain High Enough." Joe did not need to be a forensic specialist. The package had Sarah Foreswallow's fingerprints all over it. Thinking about Sarah was not good for a guy whom she had taken to the top of the mountain when he was now mired without hope or prospect. Joel Frites said he was going to a movie that night. Joe brought NW back to his bottom bunk. His release lacked both humanity and joy. It brought only a large wet spot. 22 Little was now just one more dorm NW had sullied with unbridled freedom. When all was said and done, Joe was lucky. From

Norwegian Would, nobody on campus suffered a case of what was then called a “social disease.”

Joel Frites had returned to the room. He stuck his head in for only a brief second as the sordid episode was in full throttle. Frites told “Lemming“ Cello who voiced his disapproval. He was concise. Even masturbation had to be better. Cello, however, had the luxury of retreat, at least every two weeks, to his hometown of Demarest. Returning from his last visit home, Cello was wide-eyed in reporting that the drug culture in North Jersey had taken an interesting turn. Girls he knew from high school were getting stoned, snorting cocaine, getting naked and then rubbing the expensive white powder between their pussy lips in prelude to fucking their brains out. If this sort of thing was happening at Princeton, it was only in the psych labs where white mice could get an experimental overdose of endorphins by hitting a little metal bar as often as their little feet could move to send the desired effect their way, until they could pump the little metal bar no longer.

Q. The Return Of Jimi Hendrix

Eye opening will sometimes lead those who could not see to reach a strange set of conclusions. When your eyes are closed, with your perceptions restricted, you have the luxury of knowing everything you need to know. Joe and “Lemming” Cello were about to run smack dab into the middle of this simple truth.

It was early in March, not yet warm and definitely not cold. As Joe walked from the University Store that morning, a mild, cool breeze wisped was almost unnoticeable. Joe shuddered as he thought about the March winds ravaging the Midwest, going in like a lion and out like a lion. He had just bought some new records. Rather than take them back to 22 Little, Joe headed straight to “Lemming” Cello’s where John and he could toke a few, listen to some tunes, and talk over the top of the loud speakers.

“Hey, Joe. I have been reading this Edgar Cayce Book. Did you ever notice when it is really quiet, the in-bred cockroaches that have inhabited these hallowed halls for centuries are so big you can actually hear them walking.”

“Another good reason to play loud music. On that note, I just bought some new stuff to hear.”

“For a guy who arrived here naked, with nary a record, you have caught up to the curve and assembled a pretty good collection, in, what is it, ‘sheeks’ we have been stuck here for half a year.”

"Most of 'em I bought at the U-Store, although I did pilfer my sisters' Beatles albums when I came back from Christmas break. I think I have been buying records at a clip of about five a week. I guess I should count them all."

"Play 'em, don't count 'em."

Cello got up. What have we here? He stopped with the first record, ripped the shrink wrap, opened the cover, and freed the music from the dust jacket. The turntable was again a carousel in full swing. The album spinning merrily was *Déjà Vu* by Crosby, Stills, Nash, and Young.

"Good point, so what's going on? Reading Edgar Cayce. Have you turned traitor to Paul Twitchell and his happy band on the Eckankar soul parade?"

"Edgar focuses on reincarnation not Twitchell's exalted idea of leaving this plane upon which we are otherwise mired for other, higher strata. I hope someday to master Eckankar, leave my body and spend the day reading dialogues with Plato."

"You will have better luck kneading little dogs out of Playdough. And by the way, what's wrong with where we find ourselves, one obvious deficiency aside. I love the here and now. The present is amazing, really a path more than a place, even with all its blotches and omissions."

"So you keep saying. For me, there is a fine line between going with the locus and going loco. Present reality is fine, as far as it goes. Joe, I am trying to find the way to immerse myself in the real P.U., not Princeton University, but the moment's foremost and matchless Parallel Universe."

R. I Want To Tell You

The music took over. The song, “Teach Your Children” moved front and center. There are times closing your eyes and drifting with the harmonies is all you need. The record ended. Joe opened his eyes, looked at Cello, and smiled,

“So the dope you just brought back from Demarest is better than usual?”

“I got the stuff we are about to smoke from my high school buddy, Dino DeMirror. He is just down the road on the way to Trenton, a freshman at Rider College. He has great connections. I have an idea. Let’s buy stuff in quantity from him, sell the larger portion in smaller sizes to our buddies, and smoke what’s left for free. That reminds me, the 5th Dimension will be playing at Rider. Not a great band, but the girls like them. Wanna go with me? We can see where going to a concert in a normal co-educated environment might lead.”

“Do you think you will be back in time from dallying with Socrates?”

Cello got up to unwrap then play *Delaney & Bonnie On Tour with Eric Clapton*. He started with side two. All this talk was between puffs with lungs expanded to hold the smoke from deep inhales. Joe and “Lemming” Cello were now officially ripped, a state they had attained everyday that they were both on campus from Freshman Week going forward.

“Joe, how many dimensions do you think there are?”

“I am going to guess that ‘three’ is not the right answer.”

“Well shit, most people allow four- length, width, depth, and time.”

“This Tucker guy in the Philosophy of Math course I just took, says the fourth dimension is similar to taking a movie from above a green on a golf course. The green has many contours. There is a guy lining up a long put. He hits the ball in exactly the right way taking into account the distance and the effects of all the undulations. When you watch the movie all you see is the ball making a straight line to the hole as the guy sinks the put.”

“What the fuck is that supposed to mean?”

“I guess you better go ask Plato yourself.”

“O.K. let’s say there are the four I mentioned. I think we can add perspective, place, and motion.”

A few notes from Clapton’s guitar on the song “Where There’s a Will There’s a Way” pounced upon their ears.

“Fuck, John. I know we just heard the tip of the fretted iceberg but I have no doubt that there is an eighth dimension. It is the only one that really matters- Eric Clapton in full flail, changing all of the first seven all at once with his trademark- a loud, improvisational, electric guitar solo. Time stops with all those other dimensions falling to the wayside.”

“Lemming” Cello shook his head from side to side in a frantic effort to eradicate the image of Clapton stealing the moment,

“I guess I always knew there was a reason I listen to music and play my guitar.”

“I like the word, ‘absorbed’ in this context.”

S. Here There And Everywhere

Joe then returned to query Cello's about his three new dimensions,

"So why are perspective and place not the same dimension?"

"Perspective implies the limitations of the observer, all that the observer brings with him to distort that which he is seeing. Place is the point in the universe where the observer stands indelibly affecting what is seen, actually what is there."

"And motion?"

"That's easy- the same thing at rest is not the same thing as it goes from place to place. What if the observer is in motion, too?"

"So the variables of dimension are not just one set of variables but rather more. To keep the discussion simple to illustrate the point, one die has six possibilities, two dice, each with six sides, have thirty-six possibilities. Some possibilities are more likely than another if the number is seven- are 4-3 and 5-2 are the same?"

Cello got up to free The Doors' *Morrison Hotel* from its plastic wrapper before unleashing its undeterred frolic.

"I get it. Snake-eyes and box cars are more difficult to roll than some of the other numbers since there is only one way to get those 'hard numbers.'"

"Speaking of numbers, let's light up another one."

Cello pulled a fat joint from the pocket of his blue denim work shirt. The smoke wended its way to waiting lungs. Happily slowed synapses soon dripped with the effect of the dope.

"This Tucker guy was telling us about this other famous Princeton mathematician, Hugh Everett III, or maybe he was a physicist."

"At some point all that unknowable stuff essentially merges together into one ball of smooth and shiny wax."

"Coalescence is its own reward, the best damn melt down of all. It avoids going around in circles with the sense of déjà vu chasing its own tail. Anyway, Everett was around in the fifties in the days Hugh Hefner was duly propagating his many women theory."

"The dearth of which we are now both so painfully aware, given our own perspective, place of observation, and unavailing motions which have now given way to the unwanted acquiescence of full rest."

The Doors now required the studied listening that only silence will bring. The song, "Land Ho," captured the attention of the two fellow travelers. Side one ended. Cello snapped to attention to attend to the deafening silence. He arose to unwrap the fourth new record, *Moondance* by Van Morrison. The turntable lifted the music to a new level or was it the other way around. "Lemming" Cello fired up another joint.

"Back to what I was saying, at the same time that nearly naked women like Marilyn Monroe are adorning glossy centerfolds, high atop an ivory tower at Princeton..."

"Then as now, with the reality of no women in sight."

"...no doubt by way of contrite proof, Hugh Everett III opened a door that Aldous Huxley only imagined, 'The Many Universe' theory. Whatever is lacking is not really lacking. Sameness would never be the same."

"And you were belittling Edgar Cayce and Eckankar."

"Theory ain't practice. But let me tell you what I do think..."

"...One good misconception is better than a thousand dull realities..."

T. Yellow Submarine

Again silence captured the moment. Rapt attention became the watchword halfway into "And It Stoned Me." That first song swept into the soul sweet lilt of "Moondance." "Crazy Love" sashayed into "Caravan." Then Van Morrison's "Into the Mystic" overwhelmed Cello and Cebellum. The sensory flow of the music formed palpable, savory morsels. It was not only Clapton who could stop time. *Moondance* Side One raised the bar for those devoted to listening pleasure. It was not until two years later that anybody who Joe knew would think to play Side Two. Much music had been missed as the needle stuck, again and again, on the first side of the marvelous record, *Moondance*.

The quintessence of a full blown marijuana ramble now ensued,

"Now that is what 'mystic' is all about. Cello, the way you are going about it, 'mystic' sounds more like mistake to me. It is all right here in front of our small faces. Quantum forces liken themselves to their own conclusion. There are many examples of the same thing. The interesting thing is they all get pressed together. There is One/Many/Both. Then On/Off/Both. And Beginning/End/Both. I really like Positive/Negative or Both and also Quantum ethics- Absolute/Relative or Both. But my favorite is Quantum Ontology- What/Is/What Is."

"Is it 'is' or 'are'? Sounds like it all boils down to the same Zen kettle of fish"

“The confection of confusion belies the unity of time, place and action or the sudden sameness of times, places and actions.”

“Joe I like structure, an ordered universe where description forces dialogue which breeds tension to reach the birth of the ideas. And this I will go forth and find.”

“Cello, my good man, I prefer the path itself, footsteps swirling about with forces alive, dead, and both.

They both noticed nothing was coming forth from the stereo. “Lemming Cello” got up, and quickly dismantled the wrapping. The song “Roll Away the Stone” from the self-titled *Leon Russell* now enlivened the room.

“Joe, what now passes as pure science is really the study of the past and is the final conversation stopper-the ultimate gelid. My goal is to transcend the limits of what we know as alive or dead.”

“You want to unleash swirling forces in a chorus belaboring the oblivious?”

“Say what you may but they laughed at Columbus.”

“Cello, even at Princeton I can keep my feet on the ground, my consciousness in my body. Everett set forth the proposition that there are ‘many universes’ but the paradox is irrefutable, however many there are, they all amount to one and, the one that is, Leibniz’ optimism aside, is the best damn place of all.”

“So how did Hugh Everett prove the ‘many universes’ that I know exist from some inner place of faith or intuition.”

“One…two…many…His proof disproved all else leaving only a negative conclusion to show what remains….”

"The same, or not, as the case may be."

"I think the conclusion is that a positive force moves everything to be connected. The negative is only a non-existent shadow, and is never what is left. Probability governs the path but our fate is what we make of the moments we are given."

"Joe, all this leads me to confirm my initial inclinations. We are embedded in a mystery of words which cognizance must unlock. The flip side of any parallel universe is all part of the same form, each propagated in many varied iterations. The trick is to find the way to get there."

"The trick is to understand that you are already there and then put it all on the back burner so that the steps you take are not consumed by cerebration or questions of faith. The mind is driven to solve problems even when there is no answer..."

"But Joe, remember that whether there is no answer is always the subject of dispute and the soluble tomorrow is the imponderable today and the inconceivable yesterday."

"Cello, have no doubt that therein is the rub."

Cello got up to unwrap the last record from the orange and white striped U-Store paper bag. It was *Climbing!* by Mountain. Soon "Theme from an Imaginary Western" loomed large. All alternate realities aside, that spring semester, while the music played, more and more of Joe's time was spent playing cards. The shuffle, the deal, and the play became the ever varying constant.

U. I'm Only Sleeping

Fred Etheridge was still groggy. It had been a long night at the Highway 53 Drive-In with Martha Buchanan. The heat from their own bodies added to the profusion of direct hot air from the space heater. Fred's Camaro became more furnace than greenhouse. During the incongruous double bill of *Patton* then *Mash,* an uncomfortable too-many-beer inspired sweatiness dripped over both Fred and Martha making intimacy perfunctory and sticky. Fred thought it was never really good when Martha was wetter on the outside. But as the saying goes, the nice thing about sex, even when it is bad, it's good.

Now Fred was sure, in the space between sleeping and waking, it was his mother's voice from the top of the stairs.

With an mild insistence that existed somewhere between exasperation and boredom, Betty again called down,

"Fred, did you drink too much last night? I have been calling you for five minutes. There is a girl on the phone for you. It is not Martha, and she is sobbing-three heaves for every word-either the world has ended or we have quite a good little method actress."

"Sorry, mom. I'll be right up. Thanks."

Fred stood up wearing only his white jockey shorts. His blue jeans were right where he left them on the floor at the foot of the bed. There was time only to grab his navy blue sweater. He had carelessly draped it to hang over the lower ledge of the basement fireplace. As Fred took two stairs at a time up to the kitchen telephone, hangover was the operative word as he noticed his chest tingled from the coarse tight-knit wool.

Fred followed the chord from the phone hanging on the wall to the receiver where Betty had left it on the counter top to the right of the refrigerator. As Fred picked up the hand piece, he smiled. He saw his mother was making pancakes.

"Hello"

Fred followed the words between sobs and deep ineffectual breaths.

"Fred, my life is over. I will die an old maid."

"What? Is this Sarah?"

"I had my birthday yesterday. I turned 18 on Friday the 13th and spent the day in my room, all by myself. My parents and even my little sister forgot it was my birthday."

Sarah Foreswallow did not know that her family had planned a big surprise party for her the next night. Her dad could not return from a business trip out west until Saturday afternoon.

"Sarah. Take a deep breath. Relax. You are the last person I know who will be an old maid."

The sobs continued. Heavy heaving became hiccups.

“Fred, you are so nice to say that. Would you meet me at the Bread Basket? I need to see a friendly face. I am sure the world will soon end. I do not want to die unhappy.”

“Sarah, please. It will all straighten out for the best for you. I will leave in fifteen minutes to meet you. In the mean time, dry your eyes. Fill your lungs with the good air, breathe out the bad air.”

Little sobs and tiny pauses replaced the grand vocal gestures.

“I will try but what is there left for me?”

“Joe was talking to Sam once, and I am not sure I understood what he said until now as I hear you falling into pieces. Here is how I remember it, ‘While every step falls on one path to the same end, each step is aspree in its own identity. All steps should fancy their own reward, an unmeasured pace wandering free of its own accord.’”

The feminine overplaying returned with choking and stuttering added to the mix.

“Joe…J-J-Joe…please never mention that name in my presence again. Fred, will you h-h-help me learn to walk again?”

“Sarah, time heals all wounds.”

Six uninterrupted words flowed succinctly,

“And I hope wounds all heels.”

“Joe is not that bad. You guys just could not get along. Perhaps you will in some other time, some better place. I’ll see you in a booth where we can really talk in twenty minutes, as long as you like. In the meantime try to compose yourself. When I sit down, I hope I will see, across the table from me, the beauty of the coming spring not watery eyes, a red nose, and a sad face."

Sarah was back in stride,

"Do you think we can sit side by side?"

Fred reassured himself that Martha's one night out a week was last night. Sarah's surprise party started at eight. He would pick Stephanie Wallet up at seven. Fred would take the long way from South Barrington to Fox Point, their ten minute morning ride would expand to an experience for Fred that Stephanie had turned into an art form- one slurpy oral hour.

V. Doctor Robert

Joe's Saturday morning lacked both the histrionics and possibilities in which Fred was now awash. Joe would go to the Chambers Brothers Concert at Dillon that night, with his new buddies- no woman in sight or on the horizon. A week later, he would be on a plane back home to the Sleepy Little Village for Spring Break. Joe was looking forward to seeing his old buddies.

Joe was on his way to the showers in the basement wearing only a towel with bar soap, shaving cream, and razor in hand.

Mel Rothstein wore his friendly, soft smile as he looked up from Samuelson's *Economics*,

"Joe, I know you do all the reading. But why did you stop going to classes?"

"You mean other than French 105?"

"Right if you miss more than the allotted absences, they flunk you."

"Even Napoleon skipped Corsica, at least once. Mel, I see you are reading the ultimate bed time story for all those who aspire to fly business class. I am afraid it may be turning your agile brain to mush. Why worry about my class attendance? It does not affect the supply and demand curves of the real world. The so-called discipline of Economics, all that data assembled to justify large bank deposits."

Mel gulped,

“Sorry I asked. I admire your independence and self-assurance, skipping classes is something I could never do.”

“Mel, my sense of humor got the worse of me. Sorry, but I do not think studying what is the best way to accumulate as much money as possible is part of any valid intellectual pursuit nor does it belong in the curriculum of a liberal arts or classical education, but it is not as bad as being pre-med I suppose.”

“Hippocratic hypocrisy- a dog without a leash trying to heel thyself, grinding the unfortunate with the rear of the boot, the finely honed art of heeling, with the fulsome expectation that those within the group so treated will assemble and exclaim, ‘All healed, Seizers.’ The budding doctors feel the need to take Economics as an elective. It helps enliven an innate pre-disposition which appears to me to course in the veins of the privileged, and those who so aspire, among those anointed in these parts- that the less deserving are those who have nothing and should be accustomed to it.”

“Mel- you’ve got the real sense of humor and a critical, incisive point of view. But I am getting cold standing in this towel. So it is down to the lavatory dungeon for me. Talk to you later, man.”

Mel beamed a pleasant good-bye.

Mel’s question started Joe thinking about how he was mired where he was. Lingering winter could easily hatch the heat of a maze of intrepid introspection. One did not need to be Raskolnikov confined to a small rented garret. That morning the point of departure rightly belonged to the thoughts of someone else. Joe’s brain was spinning its wheels. He expected The Chamber Brothers concert would breathe some vitality. Some spirit of joy was needed to thaw the cold ground just ahead of the time little sprigs break the surface to make their slight green vernal appearance. Ever so serious students, perhaps not Mel, had a point of view as to the rigors of proper conduct. The walkways of Princeton brimmed with the earnest steps of those always on the lookout for the future. Little buds at their feet usually went unnoticed. Stopping to smell is not an issue if you do not see even the flower beds in the first place. Until the first note was played that night, Joe's mind rambled with discordance amplified to polyphonia.

W. For No One

Even the day before the Ides of March will cause those ever concerned about how the future will shine upon them to be wary. Foreboding signs are helpful to highlight the bumps in the road for those whose manner always includes a plod designed to order all the steps to come. Joe and his new band of cohorts did not number among the careful. That semester Joe did not attend classes other than the "First Meeting." If you failed to attend the first class, you were fined.

It was unusual for Joe to reflect upon the error of his ways. His own judgment, his own self-reliance left little room to consider that others may judge him more harshly. Princeton teemed with people of exceptional intelligence. It was a good idea to pause to consider the comments of friends and of those who knew him more than superficially. To yourself you must be true. That did not mean you should never change. Keeping an open mind meant not just seeing without constriction but also meant considering what weight to give the opinions of those whose intelligence was undeniable. This sort of self-examination was not part of the Narcissist's playbook.

Even staid places with unchanging values could suffer superficial change. No longer did clothes make the man on campus. Nevertheless, some simple primordial instincts form the core of untremoring bedrock stability. Some urges go to the essence of the beast. At the top of the list is what Mick Jagger pouts in the song, "(I Can't Get No) Satisfaction," the words, "…I am trying to make some girl." The essence does not change whether you frame the quandary as "you don't know what you've got 'til it's gone" or the more quaint aphorism, "you don't miss the water until the well's gone dry." There is no doubt that the women are the thing. In the instant predicament, One Hundred of the terrific and the nonpareil were not nearly enough. Joe was not alone in feeling stranded in the large group of all-male loneliness. This was not the scourge suffered in the first years of high school. There were not nearly enough women on the Princeton campus to feel the snub of neglect. Just once, Joe wished he could accost a Princeton woman who could, in good faith, say, "I don't have the time to ignore you." The simple fact of the matter was that, all craven images aside, those first coeds were spread too thin, not really even there at all.

Joe had not felt the full brunt of isolation from the fairer gender in the fall semester but by the middle of the third month of 1970, the bleakness of the harsh landscape was undeniable. It was not until winter waned that Joe was certain that a black vicious boom of unintended celibacy had been unavoidably lowered. It was immaterial whether the cruel penance had been imposed by Jonathan Edward's God of Hell, Fire, and Brimstone or by the Devil himself.

For months, Joe had lapsed into a weekday routine. He was happy to fill his days by sleeping late then reading for a few hours. He would then play pick-up basketball at Dillon for a couple hours after lunch. Next on the agenda was smoking dope and listening to music before and/or after another starch filled dinner at Commons. At some point in the evening, Joe would then head to Pyne Hall to play bridge, first to the one room single of Solder and Spinepounds, four players crudely huddled around the lower bunk, then, as the moon struck twelve, to the second floor bathroom to huddle once again around the overturned wastebasket, sometimes until the morning sun rose to signal the end of the game. It was more than the fact that going to classes simply did not fit into Joe's schedule. Joe loved to read. His mind was nimbled and humbled by the written thoughts of others. Joe sharpened his outlook and his critical abilities as his mind ran efficiently through the pages of book after book. Two or three hours of reading would equal eight or ten hours of listening whether it be in the large lecture halls or the smaller rooms for cozy formal preceptorials.

For Joe, it did not matter how eminent or how capable. A professor, preceptor, or teacher could only do two things- tell you something you did not know or guide you back to a path you did know. Joe had always used and he would always use his own guile and compass for those two purposes, all aided by the next book. The course syllabus, required and recommended reading, was sufficient road map for Joe's learning experience. What rankled Joe most was the stench of self-importance which accompanied banging the gong about the serious value of the body of work to which the professor had devoted his life. Books are not sacred objects which require genuflection and due deference. Books are the best things ever invented to make fun of people.

Apart from the proven efficacy of his own abilities, Joe did not like ass-kissing. He preferred wise-cracking. The professors at Princeton seemed to thrive on brown-nosing. It did not matter to Joe that the lickspittles he observed were facile, well-versed, and profoundly adept. Joe had never been interested in impressing the person who was giving him the grade. For whom the cleverness tolled made all the difference. The real problem for Joe was more of the same. There were never enough women in the class to justify arriving and acting up. Standing out in class remained an exercise Joe developed in order to worm his way into a present or possible object of female affection. Princeton, at least in the first two years of coeducation, was a bane worse than a monastery. Only the wool shirts and self-flagellation were missing. Plus all the banter with Joe's "stoned out" buddies was more than sufficient intellectual involvement. Bridge and poker kept Joe's mind sharp, too.

On the weekends, concerts and movies filled the evenings. That night, The Chambers Brothers made the joint go 'round and 'round. It was not only the extended cadence pounding version of their big hit, "Time Has Come Today" that enthralled an audience ready to find the blossom of rhythm and blues in full rockin' incarnation. The band delivered more than the beat. Dillon Gym was magically transformed into a hothouse of meter and of sultry swagger. This was the real thing, not the never-break-a-sweat saunter of the imperious elite. The crowd was transfixed by its own motion, generating one sweltering wave after another. It would have been better with a woman but the music sufficed to thaw what ailed a restless campus. The message, whether anti-war or anti-bigotry, added to the ferment.

X. And Your Bird Can Sing

Seven days later, on the 21st of March, Joe was back home in the Sleepy Little Village. Spring Break would last one week. Fred was there. Sam stayed in Norman, Oklahoma. Tommy was still in the grasp of the U.S. Army at Fort Bragg. Felina flew back from NYU. Kiefer Mandolin drove from Ann Arbor. Prince Bastion made the short trip back from Shimer College. Joe and Fred saw each other the first day Joe was back. After that, Fred had to work. He now had a job driving a truck for a customs broker at O'Hare Airport, a German named, Rolfe. He got the job through Bob Garvin, his new buddy from Harper Junior College. The rest of Fred's free time, he had his hands, and other body parts, full with Martha and Stephanie. Since Fred was unavailable, Joe and Felina headed to Belmont Harbor. Chris Shaunton still had his apartment on Melrose Place. Now Chris was studying filmmaking at Columbia College just north of the Chicago River on Ohio Street. Kiefer and Prince also like getting together at Shaunton's apartment.

Kiefer brought his girlfriend, Laura Splendifera. They met at a meeting to mobilize against The War. They were two among four hundred or more on the campus of the University of Michigan. One thing led to another, as it happened in those free spirited days among those in the "revolution." Usually birth control was involved- girls' choice, the pill or a diaphragm. Kiefer, adopting the role of ardent bull in a china shop, assumed the ball was in Laura's court. Laura was all dressed up and ready to go, except for the birth control. Their trip to Chicago from Michigan was not part of Spring Break. School was on that week. Laura wanted an abortion. Kiefer said he knew someone in Chicago. It turned out the practitioner who performed the illegal abortion was not having one of his better days. Two hours after the backroom procedure, Laura was back at Shaunton's, bleeding profusely. Joe and Felina arrived an hour later. Laura had absolutely no color. Even the wan had deserted her. Joe insisted. Kiefer and he drove to the emergency room at Henrotin Hospital on LaSalle. Laura would live to tell the tale.

That night after visiting hours were over, Kiefer, Prince, Felina, Chris, and Joe sat in the small living room on Melrose. Shaunton had a stereo but his entire record collection was show tunes. No one was in the mood for "Oh What a Beautiful Morning" or "There is Nothing Like a Dame." It was unusual to get stoned and talk without music forming an ocean of waves upon which to float and to drift. The conversation ranged from catching up, to the horrors of The War, how drugs make everything better, and finally a topic more pointed- what was a good way to stay out of the mainstream in order to avoid corporate America and the military-industrial complex. Prince, Kiefer, and Joe formed a conclusion after traverse and wander through their notions of the landscape of opportunity. If you know how to short order cook, you can get a job anywhere, and you will never go hungry. Kiefer and Joe really liked the idea. Prince was willing to concur in the merit of the suggestion but he voiced a higher goal,

"Listen guys, it is great that you can take care of yourselves, and there are many who cannot. I want to help the really poor, the really helpless- the people in foreign lands who starve, without clothes, without even basic medicine. I am going to devote my life to helping others."

Felina stood up from the couch. She had been leaning innocently upon Joe's shoulder. Felina took Prince's hands in hers, pulled him up from his cross-legged position on the floor, gave him a strong hug, then a light, sweet little kiss,

“Prince, God bless you. May the road always rise up to meet you. Your burden will lighten the load for many others…”

Prince smiled a sheepish smile and looked down closing his eyes, “…I wish I had the guts to do what I know you will do.”

Kiefer stepped up to Felina and Prince and hugged them both, “Felina I know you are the best of souls in a world that has not always been kind to you. Your presence reflects a new light, your step now finds the inner music of the universe, and joviality will soon be yours.”

Joe piped in, “Mandolin has been toking up some of his own stash, stuff clearly trippier than the dope we just smoked.”

Joe then walked over to join the group hug.

Chris Shaunton was one of those people who became totally lost in his own shell when he got stoned. When he was ripped, everything happening around him was too much. He wasn’t born to follow- in this case even a slow moving conversation. Chris sat in the far corner of the couch, lost in the morning Chicago Tribune, the 24th of March. He looked up and wondered why his four friends were huddled together in the center of the room, their arms a crazy mish-mash.

“Hey, Joe, Felina- did you see this? The Air Traffic Controllers are going to have a ‘Sick Out.’ Apparently it is illegal for Federal Employees to strike. Starting tomorrow, there will be massive absences, especially at O’Hare. Everyone will call in sick, kind of like when the cops have the ‘blue flu.’”

Kiefer liked this, “Power to the People.”

Felina looked at Joe with nervous eyes that voiced a more practical concern,

“Joe we are both flying back on Sunday…”

Chris added, “It says here the ‘sick out’ will last at least through the weekend. The Air Traffic Controllers are doing it now since Easter is the busiest time of the year.”

Kiefer was on a roll, “From ‘love-ins’ to ‘sick-outs,’ to ‘be-ins’ to ‘bed-ins,’ it all leads to ‘over, under, sideways, down.’ Turn everything on its head. We’ve got the whole world in our hands. Power to the people.”

“While Kiefer waxes poetic, please know Felina, I will look into taking the bus. I hear the stop in Cleveland is the highlight of the trip.”

“Right, first prize one week in Cleveland, Second prize two weeks in Cleveland. Maybe we can see the river that runs through it burst into flame.”

“Spontaneous combustion is its own reward.”

“Joe, you have a way of making everything fun. I can’t wait to ride back to school on a Greyhound bus- never been on one before. We can be just like Clark Gable and Claudette Colbert in Frank Capra’s *It Happened One Night*.”

At the thought of a classic movie, Shaunton was now bedazzled, in full twinkle, “That is the only movie to win all five major Oscars, “Best Picture, Best Director, Best Actor, Best Actress….”

Kiefer was not so stoned that he could not count to five, “Maybe there are only four major categories. The point of that movie and all the point of everything that we all now know today, and should never forget that we know now and heretofore, is that the rich do not have as much fun as the poor and those who know how to light one up to raise everyone’s consciousness are the ones with life’s real riches- just like Clark Gable saved

Claudette Colbert from the drab existence that only money can bring. I think I am gonna go forth and wander like a wild beast in the west."

Joe shook his head in amazement, "When you get there, try to derail the ramble at the first hitching post you see."

Prince dropped his almost permanent mantle of seriousness, "Now that Laura is recovering, and I am so happy she is, please allow me to say this, I hope that your Wild West experience will not include the Biblical. You need not go forth and multiply, at least not until you can add, in this case add something to the mix. Your repertoire needs more than a raised fist of exhortation for the proletariat."

Chris looked up again from the Tribune, "I think now is a good time for me to something on the stereo. How 'bout 'Wouldn't It Be Loverly?'"

Y. Good Day Sunshine

It was early Sunday morning. Della and Joseph drove Felina and Joe to the bus station. The Greyhounds left from downtown Chicago, near the corner of Randolph and State. The day was pure Chicago. The calendar could read spring or fall but the weather would be the same. It was gray, a gray gray, a thick envelope of fog, really a cloud adhered to the ground, not just to visit but to stay. The sun was not part of the picture. Adding to the dreariness was moisture, spitting and sputtering, not really rain, but damp, wet enough to punctuate a final point of dank unpleasantness.

Joe hugged his mother. Della hugged Felina, a strong hug of real warmth,

“Felina, I so enjoyed spending time with you on the car ride this morning. You say so many interesting and perceptive things.”

Felina felt bright and shiny. Joe and Joseph shook hands. To Felina, Joseph tipped his hat goodbye. The bus would leave in one-half an hour. The trip would take morning into night. Felina and Joe bought their tickets. The bench at the very back of the bus was unoccupied.

“Joe, why don’t you go in first? Then I will snuggle next to you.”

Two old friends could find peace with just tender touching, no words were needed. As the bus headed on the Dan Ryan Expressway south before it turned east into Indiana, Felina pursed her lips on Joe’s neck as she rested her head on his shoulder. Joe put his right arm around her drawing her closer. Joe’s jacket was open. Felina unbuttoned the top of Joe’s shirt. She slowly drew her right hand across his chest. Her touch was light but firm. Felina turned sideways to Joe but kept her head and lips in place. She pulled his shirt tail out of his pants. She then rubbed her thumb up and down Joe's lower spine from below his pants to one-third up his back. Joe tried to reach his free hand into Felina's blouse. Since Felina was on his right, her blouse buttons were oriented just the right way for easy unbuttoning. Felina sighed, then twice bit Joe's neck with approval as his left thumb and forefinger rubbed her left nipple, then her right.

Felina whispered, "Joe, let's wait until it gets dark. I think we can finish what we've started then. Your jacket is pretty big."

The rhythm of the wheels made the ride relaxing. Waiting for the time until it was dark gave the relaxation a nice edge. The bus seemed to stop everywhere. Since time was the order of the day, the distance traveled did not concern them. Felina and Joe maintained silence. They now touched each other only above their clothing with an innocence that belied where they were headed no matter how far the bus progressed. Neither made the suggestion, but they both became lost in each other's breathing. The bus informed subtle movements of their bodies.

The trip was a far cry from the trip in *It Happened One Night*. There was no group sing-a-long. No friendly stranger came to add his two cents about the human condition. Best of all, there was no need to get off the bus to escape reward hunters willing to turn over a runaway heiress to her father.

Felina drew her head to find Joe's ear, "I am going to change out of my jeans. I'll put on a skirt. There is enough room for me, when the time is right, to straddle you where you sit."

Felina changed into a light blue skirt with little yellow smiling suns. Before she moved back close to Joe, she caught his eye. Felina opened her shoulder bag. With just the right ceremony, she placed her panties inside. Joe moved his hand then started to slide Felina's skirt up her left thigh.

Felina again whispered, really a purr, "Wait Joe, it is going to be a long night ride home. Let's go slow to make it last. Let me be the laboring oar for a while. Take off your jacket."

Joe and Felina snuggled their way under Joe's jacket. Joe was covered from waist to knees. Felina unzipped Joe's zipper. She undid his belt then unbuttoned the top button of his jeans. There was now plenty of space to bring his cock to full attention, his and hers. Felina licked the palm of her right hand. The moisture was just enough to make the pleasure linger without taking Joe to the point of no return. It seemed like an hour but it was more likely thirty minutes.

"Joe, this is fun."

First making sure Felina was covered as was necessary, Joe concurred in one smooth motion. With his left hand, he first freed Felina from her blue and yellow covering by bunching it half way up her thighs. Next, Joe's forefinger creased the space between Felina's outer lips. She was wet. Felina continued to slowly stroke his cock. She slid forward so she could spread her legs to make herself more available to Joe's hand. Joe inserted two fingers then moved them in and out. He matched the slow tempo now a permanent part of their ride. They were now in Pennsylvania. It did not take more than twenty minutes. Joe rubbed his thumb, not too lightly, into Felina's clit. She shook a polite shudder. The she opened her legs. Joe dipped his two fingers three knuckles deep. He lifted Felina slightly off the bench seat. In a good, very good five minutes, Felina resumed normal breathing.

Joe whispered, “Let me try to see if I can replicate that last little interlude.”

“Be my guest.”

Twice more Felina squeezed Joe’s left hand hard, clamped tight until again recapturing calm composure. The first half of the Keystone State was a blur of quivers.

In the flurry of all this attention, Felina had stopped stroking Joe’s cock. Everyone on the bus was asleep, or at least had the civility to pretend. Joe lowered his jeans below his knees. They dropped to the floor. Felina dropped the jacket to the floor covering indiscreet denim. Joe grabbed Felina by both hips. She helped him lift her over his lap with her legs spread around him. She dropped her skirt. It fell to form an updated version of the protection of circling the wagons. Felina bent her knees, jutting forward and arching her back to fit into the limited space. She used her hands to hold Joe’s shoulders. With Joe’s guiding hands still on her hips, she dropped her pussy onto the plumb. Joe was swallowed inside her in two delicious wet seconds.

Face to face, Felina broke the silence with soft words spoken only to Joe’s ear, “Let’s do this without kissing. My roommate stays nights with her boyfriend. I hope you will stay a few days with me at Washington Square. We can kiss then.”

Felina then dragged her dry tongue on an imaginary straight line up the center of Joe’s ear. Then she moistened her tongue slightly before slowly basting the entirety of Joe’s ear with the sweetened broad base of the middle of her tongue. Felina then used the tip of her tongue to swirl smaller and smaller little circles until she finished by whetting the exact middle of his ear. Joe almost came. If Felina had moved her pussy up and down his cock, even one centimeter, he was sure the matter would be *fait accompli*. As it was, the two captured a slow motion which lasted hours. Neither of them had yet heard of Tantric Yoga, but they had achieved that which many in a California hot tub have sought. As the bus entered the Lincoln Tunnel, Joe's slow arcs became thrusts of full insistence. Felina smiled as she felt his spurt. Her slightly sore and dry pussy felt a gush of relief. Felina was surprised. Joe's enthusiasm made her come for the fourth time. She had never had an orgasm before. Now she had four under her belt. The expression, "you're either on the bus or off the bus" had new meaning for her.

On the subway down to Greenwich Village, Felina looked at Joe and smiled. He returned the smile and gave her an across the top of her shoulders hug.

"Joe, I have never told anyone this..."

Joe hoped this was not going to be a new born Felina professing true love. There was no doubt they loved each other.

"... I am so against this immoral war I am going to Canada."

"Felina, guys go to Canada to avoid the draft. I am now quite sure you are not a guy."

"I know but women must make a statement, too. And this shall be mine."

"Let's talk about this later. I feel too good, from head to toe, to talk politics."

For the next two nights, with many cups of coffee and lots of talk, Felina and Joe rode a wave they started on the bus. They achieved a totality of feeling that they, two together, were in the best place they could be, the best there ever is, and the world be damned. Three nights later, Joe was back at 22 Little. He had missed one more French 105 class. It was the last absence the course permitted.

Z. Got To Get You Into My Life

Joe returned to campus having traveled with Felina much more than a long days' journey into night. Princeton would now envelope him in his first real experience with Springtime. When he awoke Thursday morning, there was more than the song of the birds announcing the freshness of a new day, more than the gentle touch of a light airy breeze finally free of the last clasp of cold, and more than the bounty of yellow green new leaves sprouted from the sparkling promise of tiny buds. A multitude of flower beds line the outer squares of the campus walkways which border Princeton's many courtyards. Dormant for months, those many rectangles and squares now teemed with the maternity of *terra firma*. Colors burst forth from the simplicity of rows of standing slender reeds and from the complexity of myriad shades and variations of ground cover, tidy blankets of nicely mannered geometric patterns and uneven lattices strewn in eclectic aggregations. The diagonal walkways which criss-cross the courtyards are framed by triangles of monochromatic lawns. There is nothing monotonous about these green spaces, vibrant with new grass. Some mornings, trees, lawns, and flower beds alike are all charmed to wear jewels of morning dew. The sun of the early hours stokes color. Then the light meets the prisms of water condensed on leaves and on reeds of grass. The ensuing kaleidoscope strikes even the most studied unobservant.

Princeton does not permit cars on campus. Without motor vehicles, the architecture which looms left and right during any walk gives no clue which century is being traversed. You do not need to be stoned to be lost in time; but dope does give the marvelous *tout ensemble* a nice sheen. The effect is enhanced in the evening when the cast iron lamp posts which light the ways, now electric, effectively resemble the gas-fired glass globes and translucent cylinders which lined the streets in Victorian England and here in times going back before the American Revolution. Being lost momentarily by not knowing the time of day is nice, but not knowing the era is an even better way to take free steps aloof from the pedestrian stops which pace the hours. Added to the quaint charm are stone tigers sitting atop square pillars with burning bright smiles of feline omniscience for all who pass below. There is no doubt that the stately buildings and the other structures that dot the campus pale in comparison to nature abounding. Spring achieves the pinnacle of a landscape of surrounding beauty.

Even before Joe got out of bed that morning, he knew there was a new bounce to his step. He was not sure what made his glad heart gladder. Was it the music now within him, now part of his everyday, never more than one pulse away? Was it the ethereal serenity of two spirits touching, even in cramped quarters in the back of a Greyhound bus? Or was it simply the warm air which entered the open window? Everything was connected- music, natural beauty, and that which seized the flesh.

The sunlight cascaded all around Joe as he walked towards Pyne Hall that afternoon. As he approached the open gate at the end of Henry Hall, Joe stopped alive in his tracks. To his right, the magnolia trees lining University Place spoke full splendor. He had never seen a Magnolia tree in full blossom. The twenty foot high trees wore a preponderance of flowers. Their thick garland almost formed a globe. The sight was breathtaking. It demanded sole attention obliterating everything else which might otherwise draw a glance. Magnolia blossoms are pulpy thick flowers the size of an open palm with fingers extended upward. Five or six petals ring from a common point below to surround a smaller cup, all of delicate white or serene pink silk. Joe's appreciation was as palpable as the elegant flesh of these transcendent subtle blooms. It was not a far step to picture Scarlet O'Hara sitting beneath one of those magnificent trees, waiting for suitors to join her for "picnic" or some such antebellum ritual. The very thought almost made Joe wish he was a Southern Gentleman rather than a commoner from the Midwest, the realm of the coarse hog butcher. The moment shutter-stopped then inhaled in this place full of wonder was there to stay. Full of whimsy inspired by joy, Joe reflected, "Until now, I have never seen the face of Spring. Someday I will find a place where flowers are so profuse, it is impossible to name them all."

AA. 99 and 44/100 years Of Gratitude

If Prospect Street is your cup of tea, then magnolias are nice but prospective buds welcoming you with open arms at the end of Bicker cause real delight. Bicker begins the week following "intercession." The theological underpinnings of Princeton pop up everywhere. Other schools have Spring break. For the same week-long time off from studies, Princeton uses a term that belongs in the milieu of the original etymology of 'holiday,' a time for devotion and for prayer rather than for beer blasts and for wet t-shirt contests. During Bicker week, some Clubs conduct structured interviews, with those aspiring, hat-in-hand, answering all the hard questions. Other Clubs favor friendly competitions like blow-pong, a drinking game where nearly grown men huddle on their knees around a ping pong table blowing their best whenever a ping pong ball comes near. When the selection process open only to Sophomores has been completed, Club members meet in closed session to assess the supplicants. The fortunate are informed. The next weekend is used to host parties welcoming the lucky new members. Each Eating Club has a different initiation ritual, some more secret than others. By 1970, many students and many more outsiders were critical of a selection process deemed demeaning and dehumanizing. More to the point, some of the Clubs could not maintain sufficient members given the sixties ethos of free-spirited independence which managed to marginally intrude into the fabric of the Princeton social structure. As a result of dwindling memberships some Eating Clubs would permit "sign-ins." Anyone could step right up and join. It would not be long that some of the Eating Clubs would go the way of all flesh. For Cannon Club, the writing was on the wall. There was no doubt that an environment of slobbering drunks staggering around slurring their words had its own special allure in an earlier time. This sloppy sort of male bonding was further enhanced by herd behavior, in the bathroom, or not, members summoned by the impetus of bladders overfull with beer, all indexterously trying to avoid urinating on their own feet (or the feet of the guy standing nearby). Added to the sordid stank of stale beer and dry urine that claimed Cannon Club was the long indulged fiction that Cannon members could, and would, treat women as pieces of meat. Their tombstone had been sculpted from some ancient rudiment once thought to be bed rock. The epitaph chiseled in stone which would proclaim Cannon's demise was just one more beer belch away. The mood at Cannon that second weekend started somber. Only four new members would be initiated Saturday night. One thing all good Cannon members knew was that the reality of implosion is no reason to cry in your beer. By eight o'clock Saturday night, the mood was lightened as a second keg of Rolling Rock was emptied. Intersecting paths are neither the product of fate nor the result of coincidence. Sometimes an event occurs just because it can.

Earlier that evening, at 22 Little, Mel Rothstein's clock television read 6:30 p.m. Joel Frites, John "Lemming" Cello, and Joe Cebellum sat on the couch listening to a song turned up loud. It was *Sgt. Pepper's Lonely Hearts Club Band*. As the song ended with words, "now the singer's gonna sing a song" and Ringo again introduced the notion "I get by with a little help from my friends," Frites had a surprise.

Joel held his palm open. He carefully cupped three gelatin capsules.

"Three hits of really good mescaline. Shall we take it for a spin around the block?"

Cello and Cebellum were game. Three gulps later, "Lucy in the Sky with Diamonds," started to tell the tale, "...with tangerine trees and marmalade skies....cellophane flowers of yellow and green towering over your head....look for the girl with the sun in her eyes and she's gone..." The proceedings were furthered edified by the rest of side one. Then side two of that epochal Beatles' record crystallized into an inexplicable but clear sense all that was left. With Frites still steady hand, the first album of Crosby, Stills, and Nash then joined the fray.

By the time the song, "Long Time Gone" spun its own sweet Everly Brothers harmonies, Joe was propitious to suggest,

"Let's head over to Prospect Street. Most of the Clubs are open to Freshmen this weekend...

Cello was not persuaded,

"So we can all see what joy Club membership will bring."

Frites, however, grasped the essence of the situation,

"Free beer."

The mescaline kicked in. It is a new vision when the mind's eye makes an earmark. The experience is more than a current of flowing and ebbing guideposts, more than the clear sense of remembering things you don't know. The walk across campus was a light and shadow created delight. Patterns appeared everywhere to dance without moving. Joe smiled the big smile of a guest who had been issued a special invitation to immerse himself into the depths of the patina of the profound. Joel could only cackle and point. John was all business. He started by taking one gentle step after another. He then held spread his arms away from his tentative sides, to keep his balance. Thus anchored, his gait increased as he swayed to the music of the motion of the buildings on both sides of the walkways. By the time the trip reached the arch of 1879 Hall, the Philosophy Department to the right and the Religion Department on the left, the three all stopped dead in their tracks, as if on cue. Across Washington Road, the fountain at the Woodrow Wilson School spit succinct luminous beads of water, up and down, into that good night. The water held in the rectangular basin that framed the fountain formed a surface with the subtle slight roll of waves which reflected bars and spots of pea green light.

Joel mustered a verbal consensus,

"Whoa."

Minutes last a long time when slow synapses are at the helm. An eternity of marvel gave way to further trek. Men milled both sides of Prospect Street. That night, the footsteps of F. Scott Fitzgerald were nowhere to be heard. Frites, Cello, and Cebellum meandered to their right. Tower Club was an uninviting blur. The boys strolled past still measuring full wonder of all that was about. Cannon Club next loomed forward. The black lacquer cannon in the walkway on the front lawn silently absorbed light from the nearest street lamp.

"Hey, Frites, let's introduce Cello to those guys from Cannon."

No one knew what happened next or whether anything happened in any sensible order. The conclusion was clear. As Freshmen, Joe, John, and Joel had been initiated illegally. They were not only knighted new members but they were given the permanent honor of becoming Cannon Club members emeritus, in perpetuity with all rights and privileges appurtenant thereto. Stuck in Joe's mind was the group of Cannon members below him as he was passed up the stairs in the final rite of initiation. As he looked behind down the stairs, the larger, heavier and more cumbersome, "Lemming" Cello crested more slowly. The stair stuck membership was unable to lift Cello above the large stuffed Elk who presided at the turn in the stairway. The sight of Cello momentarily unsprung amidst sixteen point antlers was memorable, all mescaline aside. In those days, Saks Fifth Avenue was proud to have a store on Nassau Street. The following Monday, Joe walked, a little sheepishly, into the men's section to buy his Cannon Club tie- dark green silk with little colonial era cannons in abundance. His new membership had been memorialized. In order to buy any Club's tie, your name had to appear on the authorized list. The list was checked. The salesman accepted Joe's money then proudly handed him the tie from the soon to be long besmirched.

BB. It's As Easy As ABC

In Norman, Oklahoma, Spring was equally balmy and commensurately full of the energy of blooms that had waited long enough. It lacked only the arcane ritual of Princeton's Eating Club selection process. Sam Thorn was not sure exactly when it happened. But one morning, he awoke aware of a strange metamorphosis. Sam had been transformed to swim in rich waters, languid ripples of luxuriousness to which he was unaccustomed. Sam not only had his pick of the litter, he was having a lick at the fitter. Strangely it all started with fitness, a place Sam did not really belong. One morning, Sam came upon another in a long list of reasons to cut class. This time he followed a girl who walked out of an apartment building soon after he left his own front stoop. The glimpse he caught of long brown hair was enough suggestion to lead him to follow the hypnotic motion of her hips. Three steps behind for four blocks, Sam tried to think of just the right thing to say to her, the perfect opening gambit in a game only he was playing. Sam drew a blank. He never guessed she was going to the gym. Sam followed her. As Sam lifted ten pound barbells, the girl rode the stationary bicycle. Sam still did not see her from the front. Nor could she see the odd picture of a guy in blue jeans, sandals, and a starched light blue dress shirt trying his best to affect the look of someone who did arm curls with some regularity. Focus and concentration were never Sam's strong suits. Pumping iron was not what Borges recommended for transfixed meditation to lead to higher planes. Nevertheless, Sam was overcome with a day dream of lost thoughts and of forgotten locutions.

Things he had never seen or considered before seemed to pop up again from some dusty corner of a consciousness he had yet come to know. Normally, Sam would spend his mental energies trying to guess the size of the breasts of the girl he had not yet seen turnaround. Today his spirit was incandescent and reborn from mirth. Before the apocalypse of full epiphany, Sam was struck with a happy memory. In the sweaty must of the workout room, he was touched with a breath of warm fresh air. Abha's bright charm and zest for life was still winnowing through his consciousness. At first Sam thought Abha and he had traveled back to her home in India. The sun made shimmers of many sided diamonds on the moving points of blue water flowing across a large oval lake. An opal fishing boat surged with the motion of the waves. Twelve men stood in the boat, facing a man with his arms out-stretched. Now the scene challenged that which had been long well-known. Sam shook his head, but what he heard was repeated,

"Retep, I will teach you manners of fish."

Sam would tell this story many more times. It became the cornerstone of a new religion, one for which Sam became the first prophet. This was a way of life, more than a religion. Sam unfurled its name, "Alphabetology."

That first reverie led Sam to discover the existence of the Zuider Zee Zchrolls. He had never been to even one of the low countries in Europe. The Three Zs, as they were now heralded throughout the land of Will Rogers and Woody Guthrie, had been raised up to the heights of mercy me from below zee-level. They formed the cornerstone of a miracle which was not built by human hands nor ever actually touched by anyone, Sam included. In the Three Zs, the unalterable words of the omnipotent were a part, a large part, of the all that comprises everything- thus shown to Sam for the benefit of all mankind.

The Church of Alphabetology, with Sam manning the pulpit, spread like wildfire on the campus, and into the town. Many beliefs which only made sense to those truly enlightened were propagated by this new man of the cloth. The belief that was the cement, or, if you preferred, the straw that stirred the holy emulsion was the notion that there is a trinity, heel, instep, and toe taking thirty-one steps up, or turning the numerals around, thirteen on the way down in order to follow the equally appropriate, but not numerically equivalent, transitive path. The Zuider Zee Zchrolls contained, in their three insoluble corners, many erstwhile mysteries, some yet to be discovered. In the table of contents at the very forefront of the infallible unwritten word was the mapped excursus of some important missing years. This *Itinerati* 'twas brillig, full of content for the soon to be contented. But the real breakthrough which led to the "trancelation" of the profound and the unerring was unleashed in the duality of the alphabetic letters of the Rosetta Store. From land once overcome by the calm and shallow waters of the Zuider Zee, three more tablets were revealed from green growth. These three hits or three doses were soon a part of the vernacular of Alphabetology. The recollection of things no longer moss led fortuitously to a rolling rock, which once gathered, came to land upon the discovery of the fertile field from which all good things flowed. The good earth which heaved what it had henceforth was a plot of rock hard land situate behind a crooked windmill which nevertheless always captured just enough of life's true breeze. This sacred igneous ground was and would be forever known as "The Rich Yard Stone." In the Rich Yard Stone, there lay what could only be seen by the righteous as remnants of a burnt row of corn stalks. At its head, from remains surely charred by the fire of the Almighty, peered up what was obvious, the two, and only two letters, 'C' and 'A.' With the help of the three doses and the Rosetta Store, Sam was blessed with first and last true insight.

It could not be gainsaid, and not just because it defied human understanding. It was a manifold conclusion to form. According to the orthodoxy of Alphabetology, all you need was channeled through three great thinkers whose last names started with the most important tertiary and primary letters the alphabet has ever known, 'CA.' From this point of sturdy embarkation, it was an easy step for Sam to give literal transcription to the heaving shelves of the Rosetta Store. Thus the twenty-one abiding tenets of Alphabetology were now inscribed, here and there, for all eternity. Sam laid the First Missive of Three Zs down in the Ark of the Covered Net, a fine inlaid wooden box which sat at the feet of his favorite pulpit. The Holy Words read, "This is more than in the beginning."

The liturgy required, with wafting smoke and dinging bells, a formal salute in the direction of the solid form of the sacred twenty-one to acknowledge the gifts from the generous hand of the Creator which had been granted undespoiled to even sinners undeserving. Holding the printed words high above his head, Sam then read aloud and slowly,

"Camus-

1. You will never be happy if you continue to search for what happiness consists of. You will never live if you are looking for the meaning of life.

2. The only way to deal with an unfree world is to become so absolutely free that your very existence is an act of rebellion.

3. Autumn is a second spring where every leaf is a flower.

4. Don't wait for the last judgment it takes place every day.

5. The struggle itself for the heights is enough to fill every man's heart. One must imagine Sisyphus happy.

6. You cannot create experience. You must undergo it.

Carroll-

7. Sometimes I have believed as many as six impossible things before breakfast.

8. Contrariwise, if it was so, it might be and if it were so, it could be; but as it isn't, it ain't. That's logic.

9. 'But I don't want to go among mad people,' said Alice. "Oh you can't help that,' said the cat. 'We're all mad here.

10. Begin at the beginning till you come to the end; then stop.

11. The rule is jam tomorrow and jam yesterday- but never jam today.

12 That's the reason they are called lessons because they lesson from day to day.

13. Take care of the sense and the sounds will take care of themselves.

14. If you don't know where you are going any road will get you there.

Castaneda-

15. A man of knowledge lives by acting, not by thinking about acting.

16. To seek freedom is the only driving force I know. Freedom to fly off into that infinity out there. Freedom to dissolve; to lift off; to be like the flame of a candle, which, in spite of being up against the light of a billion stars,

remains intact, because it never pretended to be more than what it is: a mere candle.

17. You say you need help. Help for what? You have everything needed for the extravagant journey that is your life.

18. Forget the self and you will fear nothing, in whatever level or awareness you find yourself to be.

19. The secret is to be hooked only to infinity.

20. Life in itself is sufficient, self-explanatory and complete.

21. Beware of those who weep with realization, for they have realized nothing."

Alphabetology did not require that all faithful followers memorize the ritual and the printed words all together forming that which first begun, and now continued preserved forever, as the twenty-one salute to all that is sacred and holy. The fundament of unassailable scriptural reading became more than pure rote reincantation, even if babbling was involved. Those whose ministrations were loved the best did often remember many of the words with a devotion to their clear intent, striving to spend eternity in peace.

Sam was able to breathe full impressions and further meaning into the twenty-one salute with wholly homily,

"It is surmised and thus conceived that the path untraveled led from India, Tibet, Persia, Assyria, Greece and Egypt. Then on to England to correct the future site of Hadrian's wall before wading on the wetlands in what would become the Netherlands where it is said to be said, 'Go forth with dykes, two lips, and stealth waters will be parted until Levis are everywhere,' or some similar set of homonyms."

This pithy parable became known throughout Norman, Oklahoma as "The Churlish One Foundation." Brevity being the soul of wit, this early motto of distillation stuck, and helped bring members of all ages into the fold, many of whom followed only those four simple words. Most of the newly congregated were young girls. Innocent souls who wished to have their yearnings quenched. From all that had been revealed the morning Sam's arms curled revealing sublime openness to salve the souls of the seekers, Sam had insight to impart and inject for the benefit of all who wished to come. Sam was more busy than worn. He did not realize that religion could take so much of a man's time. Getting to know as many as possible of the newly devout in special intimacy was part of Sam's new road of best intentions. This new purpose put a veritable bounce in his step. Sam was now infused with positive meaning. This optimism was new and wonderful for him. Sam now embraced life as never before.

CC. In The Shadow Of Young Girls In Flower

The myriad hints of middle March in New Jersey gave way to nature's full revel. The campus was consumed with more than brilliant sunlight with warm, crisp, and refreshing breezes. As the saying goes, it was Spring, and at Princeton, a young man's fancy turns to wiffleball. Most of the time, Joe walked from 22 Little to Pyne Hall to play bridge. Now that weather permitted, Joe and his card-playing cronies would join up in the afternoon to smoke a joint and then play "home run derby" or "strike-out." The game was a version of stickball, played on city streets everywhere in the states. The name varied with the region. This version replaced a broom handle and tennis ball with a yellow plastic bat and a white waffle-holed wiffleball. The rules varied only slightly. The pitcher plied his trade right in front of the center arch. The batter stood ready on the walkway platform directly in front, just in front of a small magnolia. The steps behind the walkway led either to the rear of the 1901 and the Laughlin dorms on the long route which crossed McCosh Walk before leading up through Blair Arch and then on to Commons or led to the walkway veering right to Dillon and Little. The catcher's task was to keep the ball from bouncing down the steps in either direction. If the batter hit the long wall of Pyne anywhere above the tip of the center arch, it was a home run. If the hitter was able to send the wiffleball into an open window, it was a grand slam. Anything else was an out. Soon other guys from Pyne joined the game. Smoking dope was not required but was encouraged. Even a senior, Peter Orton, an active member of the SDS, and not an athlete by any means, joined the fray with the inducement of cannabis. Orton was Princeton's version of one of the Fabulous Furry Freak Brothers from Zap Comix. He was that other brother who had the lights on with somebody home. Orton had shoulders slumped forward in a permanently stoned posture in a full state of readiness for truckin', traveling low to the ground to be sure that the next deal went down. With shoulder length black hair, full beard, and a complete scraggly appearance, Orton made a perfect match with the R. Crumb characters. That drugs would get you through times of no money better than money will get you through times of no drugs was an ethos shared by the head shop comic book characters and one of Princeton's true revolutionaries. In later years, many would say that the SDS guys at Princeton soon sold out for six figure jobs. Those many so saying, however, in the fullness of time, had glided their way to seven figure incomes with eight figure bonuses.

Evolution being what it is, it was only a matter of time before sound was added to the wiffleball game. Speakers were propped from the two windows of the dorm room of "Thew" and Parsley Fief. *Led Zeppelin II* dominated the games. Whether it was "Whole Lotta Love" or "Live in-Love in Maid," the sex driven music and lyrics of Led Zeppelin's monster of a best-selling album could not have gilded a more unlikely environment. On a day still talked about in hushed, reverent tones, Joe brought Son Seals first record to the game. It was the second blues record issued by the Chicago label, Alligator Records. The record had a track, "Hot Sauce." It was really a searing, soaring guitar solo by a man who would soon become a blues legend. What soon transpired on the playing fields of Pyne became the stuff of legend. The annals of wiffleball report the game started in the morning that day. A short, round freshman, Mike Marx, from Philadelphia, was diverted on his way to Organic Chemistry. In the vortex of Spring, it was not difficult to persuade Mike to lay down his pre-med Bible. The first time up, the Son Seals instrumental was spinning frantically on the Fief turntable. Marx hit a home run to claim, ever after, the nickname "Hot Sauce." Josh "Thew" Relioport did not play that morning. He sat at his desk near the Fief stereo. His Calculus book was open but unattended. Each of the five times Mike Marks next batted, "Thew" placed the stylus needle back in the "Hot Sauce" groove. The record of achievement that morning stands unblemished- six at bats with five home runs and a grand slam which flashed through a window in the coed entry to the left of the arch.

Other favorites which filled the air to enliven the games were *Let it Bleed* by the Rolling Stones, the Allman Brothers' first album, *Willy & the Poorboys* by Creedence Clearwater Revival, and *Yer Album* by the James Gang. Baseball, even as modified for urban streets and Ivy League courtyards, belonged to Apollo. Bright, unwavering lines ruled its conduct. Static joy existed within clear regimentation. The music threw rigidity a curve. Dionysius took over as pounding speakers pumped peaks and troughs of pure frenzy. Even without the marijuana, the music would have made it difficult for the players to stay between the lines. Baseball and rock were Yin and Yang, 1970 American all-male campus style. The internal and external beauty of sport augmented by notes aplenty lacked only that which left the whole scene mired in a parched void. At Princeton the notion of handling curves was loaded with the suggestion of the unattainable. A bunch of guys throwing an array of pitches and swinging flexed bats was no substitute for a slow walk in the midst of nature reborn, arm-in-arm with a girl, a pace short of prance enlivened by the breath of a new season that made all women young and all young women beautiful. Spring spawned a collective dream. Suggestion, anticipation, and possibility led to infinite rooms woven with pulsing feminine sensuality. At Princeton, in those days, as before, the dreamer always awoke back in that one room of reality, only Spartan, drab, and male-nourished. Joe learned that sometimes things are not gray and white, sometimes they are black. Joy taken as, when, and where it could be found, and it always could be found, was better than self-pity wallowing in the mire of dilemma, waiting for heaven or a better day. Nevertheless, Joe and his cohorts had to tread carefully. The insidious trap that even nascent nostalgia offers must be avoided. It may have seemed a pleasant interlude to remember the "good old days" of only the year before. Thinking back to a world peopled with the fairer gender did not further well-being.

DD. Swann's Way

By the Spring of 1970, in a world slow turning, Joe now placed his faith only in music. The catechism required a diurnal trip to the U-Store. For Joe and Cello, for Joe and Fief, or for Joe alone, the ritual was the same. The spirit moved Joe to a trip up to the second floor and to the record department. Bins with albums were divided into broad categories. The categories were Classical, Jazz, Show tunes, "Foreign Lands," and "Current." Current music included rock, pop, blues and folk. Joe was religious in his inspection of all the "Current" bins. Everyday Joe purchased the new arrivals of the music which interested him. His record collection now numbered over six hundred records. Music was the perfect complement to smoking marijuana every day, two or three times a day. Rock and roll reached a fitting and proper place, a high decibel intensity that no cloud of smoke could obscure. Grass made all sensations all the more worthwhile. By ten or eleven, every weekend night and the occasional evening when there was no bridge game at Pyne, brimming with pot, Joe and "Lemming" Cello would make their way to Nassau Street and "A&S," The Porn Shop. They were sometimes accompanied by Parsley Fief, Joel Frites, and/or "Teddy" Appleseed. Inappropriate sexual content was not the object of the exercise. The Porn Shop was a long thin store front next to the liquor store on the corner of Nassau and Witherspoon Streets. As you entered, a little man with a haphazard shave and the stub of an oversoaked cigar stuck on his lower lip sat at the cash register on the left. There were "girlie magazines" behind him. To the right were shelves and shelves of prurient paperbacks, all written without redeeming content. Joe and his confederates were on a different mission. The real treasure trove was the back of the store. Two guys took and cooked orders for hoagies. Porn Shop hoagies were the perfect way to end a womanless evening. Cheesesteak, Tuna, or Eggplant Parmesan were all good, really good. Cheesesteak hoagies were always number one in the hearts of Princeton men, stoned or straight. You could almost taste the dense wafts of simmering onions, peppers, and shaved marinated sirloin. The smells alone made the trip off campus worthwhile. It was one of life's great culinary experiences to ravenously devour the crusty Italian bread that surrounded the grilled steak slices and accompaniments topped with melted mozzarella cheese then covered with shredded lettuce, chopped tomatoes, red wine vinegar, and olive oil. No matter how many times the same hoagie was swallowed in what seemed a large stoned gulp, the trip back to the Porn Shop for the next time was more than a new day yesterday or an old day now. Whether oil and warm grease, or mayo and tomato seeds dripped down your chin, the moment was savored. Tomorrow never comes when any sensual experience is truly relished. No amount of anticipation or planning will ever take the place of even two small minutes in the moment.

EE. Sodom And Gomorrah

It was an unlikely coincidence that the trip back from A&S intersected with the closing of Firestone Library. Only occasionally did "Lemming" Cello and the others walk and watch as unattainable co-eds removed themselves from the library after a night of studying. In reference to real deprivation, Joe was fond of saying that if it was not next to you touching you; it did not matter whether that which you sought was beyond you, beside you, or beneath you. The law of supply and demand had some strange effects that even Milton Friedman could not predict. Young women who had never once been accosted during four years of high school were now Cinderella, before midnight. Even a journeyman economist could predict the evolution of one predictable change in Princeton culture. In the beginning, before coeducation, nobody went to the library except to use the carrels assigned to upperclassmen. The carrels existed on the lower floors of the open stacks. They were used to assemble and ferret primary and secondary sources for footnotes to then put pen to paper for two independent graduation requirements, the Junior Paper ("JP") and the Senior Thesis, a massive scholarly undertaking which bore no diminutive appellation. Now those few first women used the library for more than just a place to study at night. The reading rooms were a place of quiet refuge, away from the storm of would-be suitors and other gawkers. Somebody once said that where the righteous go, the mighty follow. More accurate for Princeton's first full-time women, "as the first One Hundred go, many sorely interested men would follow."

It was a clear and starry night. The campus beamed its own gentle charm. Buildings loomed an almost archaeological presence. The stories those walls might tell if not constrained to further the polite strictures of uppercrust silence. That night, amidst premature summer warmth, the walkways were filled with young women scurrying back to Pyne Hall. Female footsteps which followed the march of history now made their own place. Joe and three buddies came close to one of the One Hundred.

The long winter brought out “Lemming” Cello’s least noble side. He had coined the description, “Radioactive Ugly,” which soon became “RAU” (pronounced Ray-Ooh). As “Lemming” Cello approached the worse than plain but serious student, he mimicked a Geiger counter. As the distance between shortened, intermittent soft clicks reached a crescendo of loud constant clucks, Joe, Fief, and Appleseed gave up trying to get “Lemming” Cello to stop. They had learned to give no notice to John’s uncharitable but apt commentary. The young woman knew something odd was occurring, but not that she bore the brunt of unkind mischief.

Joe interrupted Cello’s Geiger counter in full eruption, “John, that idea you have about buying hash is worth exploring.”

Fief added his two cents, “Cebellum since when are you buying any dope? You and Teddy both seem quite content to smoke everyone else’s stash.”

“Parsley, old boy, our spiritual leader and profferor of all that is green or gooey is hell-bent on turning on the world. Just like the Beatles chant in *I am the Walrus*, ‘smoke pot smoke pot everybody smoke pot.’ With ‘Lemming’ Cello at the helm it will all soon come to pass. Anyway, when you guys light up, I am here to help the joint pass from hand to hand. I have always assumed it would be rude to turn down any gracious offer.”

FF. The Guermantes Way

Except when Joe was back home in the Sleepy Little Village, he never bought even a nickel bag. His friends resigned themselves to the fact Joe's contribution would be an ever growing record collection. Tunes added to the mix. The dope went up in smoke. Joe's records lived to fight another day. The real impetus for sharing grass with everyone in the room was a dynamic of psychology- the need for the addict to be normal. That need was furthered if everyone within reach was a like-minded pot-head. Fenton Appleseed, in his own way, also preyed upon a variation. Appleseed pretended the smoke he was inhaling did not get him stoned. More and more was Cello's response. It was clear to everyone but "Lemming" Cello that "Teddy" Appleseed was glassy-eyed and ripped. As long as "Teddy" feigned he could not get off the dime, John would make sure he got three or four times the number of tokes everyone else received, all without Teddy spending even one nickel.

Cello stopped his loud clucking,

"So Joe, that means you will ante up one-half for my suggested money-saving idea?"

"John, Normally, I prefer to sit back and watch the river flow..."

"Right, I contact Dino, buy an ounce of hash..."

Teddy was right there,

"An ounce, Jesus, that's a mountain of a rock of hashish."

Fief rendered a variation,

"Unless it is a large dung heap of medicated goo."

"In point of fact, my old high school buddy, Dino, down the road to Trenton at Rider College, has scored a prodigious amount of Nepalese finger hash. I hear naked women run through awaiting fields of gold. After the resin adheres lusciously to their wanting pores, highly trained workers have the pleasure of scraping pure potency from their skin."

"Now where do I sign up for that job? It sounds finger lickin' good."

"Joe, yeah, right- fingers, that's what you'd be wanting to lick."

Cello brought the group back to the matter at hand,

"So Dino will sell us this primo stuff at a very good price. We can shave off a big piece for our own consumption, then sell the rest in littler gram pieces. All to break even or to make a little profit with the real inducement being all the hash we smoke for free. Plus the stuff is so THC laden, it is almost like you are tripping. I've tried it. Who's in?"

Joe stepped out of character,

"I'll contribute my share of the capital needed."

Fief and Teddy remained silent.

"O.K. Joe, it's you and me, in for one-half each. Happy days are here again."

"It seems to me the music never stopped."

"Good point, I should have said, 'the more, the merrier.' I'll call Dino and get the hash rolling."

Fief followed his own tangent,

“You know I like satisfying the munchies as much as the next guy. That tuna fish hoagie was dynamite but it seems like the more you eat, the less you’re stoned.”

“Lemming” Cello never needed a prompt. He pulled a fat joint out of the front shirt pocket of his blue denim work shirt. Surrounded by the rectangles of dorm room lights from Witherspoon, Edwards, and Little, the four stood in Little courtyard. Cello fired one more up before Fief and Teddy took their leave to return to Pyne,

Teddy was always polite,

“Joe and John, we bid you goodnight.”

Fief touched his imaginary top hat, twirled a half turn on his toe tops. The two then disappeared between the two tigers that guarded McCosh Walkway within the inner sanctum of the campus.

GG. The Fugitive

The next morning Joe did not hear the phone ring. Joel Frites gave Joe a slight shake,

“Cebellum, the phone’s for you.”

Joe wiped the sleep out of his eyes as he suppressed a yawn. Frites handed him the black rotary dial phone. The cradle had an extended cable which allowed the phone to stretch to the bunks in either bedroom.

“Thanks, Joel.”

Joe did not recognize the voice,

“Slow down, what?”

“It’s Prince. I’m with Chris Shaunton.”

“Prince why are you causing Ma Bell to ring into the pastoral peace of a bright New Jersey morning, with Shaunton at your side, to boot?”

“Joe, a matter of some gravity has arisen.”

“I thought only hot air rose.”

“Seriously, there is trouble here in the land of Hough and…”

“Puff.”

“Well worse than anything that ever happened to Little Jackie Paper, once again, seriously,”

“O.K. Prince play it, if you can take it, I can take it.”

Shaunton grabbed the phone. He had been overspilling with the precarious,

“Joe, Chris here. Disaster is at our door. Only you can prevent it.”

“That reminds me, what is Smokey the Bear’s middle name?”

“Joe would you drop the funny patter, remember a long distance call is the equivalent of a telegram in the old days.”

“Shit, did somebody die?”

“No, worse than that.”

“’The,’ Smokey’s middle name is ‘the.’”

“If today was not so dire, I would laugh. Your best friend and buddy to us all has been imprisoned and is being led around by one of his less gallant body parts.”

Prince recaptured the phone,

“Joe, let me try to put the whole disaster in two words, ‘Sarah Foreswallow.’ She has her claws into Fred, deeply and indelibly it appears.”

“What?”

“Seriously. Fred and Sarah are engaged to be married. The matter has attained an absurd proportion. They have opened a joint checking account to save money for their first refrigerator.”

"And I thought 'joint' was just a way to get high, not to get handcuffed. What about Martha? What about Fred's brain?"

"Sarah's feminine wiles are a force beyond Mother Nature's wildest imagination particularly when applied to anyone unsteady and unsturdied by blood flow between the legs. Remember the power she had over Frank Lee Gonzo last Christmas."

Shaunton wrested the phone from Bastion,

"We have all tried driving sense into Fred's thick skull, but to no avail. You have to catch the next plane back here. Fred is talking about driving to Arkansas, to the Ozarks. Apparently he has an uncle who likes to perform marriages."

"At least there is some chance the ceremony would not be legal then. Are you guys sure? This whole scenario seems ridiculous to the point of the absurd."

"Sarah has Fred following one pace behind her, bobbing his head like some kind of Asian monk. He has seen the light. I am pretty sure it is not a spiritual awakening."

Bastion now had the receiver as Joe said,

"I guess one good head bob leads to another. How 'bout I just call Fred?"

"Joe, it is not Fred you have to see to save him. No amount of persuasion will cause him to deviate from this path to certain doom."

"What?"

"You have to go see Sarah, to take one for the team."

“Well I suppose this sort of sacrifice could be just what the doctor ordered for all hands on deck, especially knowing what I know about what she knows. I had not considered that this was a gambit, one even Scarlet O’Hara would not have conceived on her darkest day-simply Sarah trying to get me back…”

“Get back to where you once belong.”

“…O.K. I’ve got the picture. I am happy to return to save my friend’s life. Why not spend a few days in the sack with a talented amateur. The only problem is that there is a class here I cannot miss. I have used up all the absences allowed for third semester French. Let me talk to the grad student who teaches the class. Demonstrated proficiency in a foreign language is required for graduation.”

Later that morning Joe walked past Whig and Clio on his right, Cannon Green, and Nassau Hall to his left, then into East Pyne Hall and up the stairs to the second floor where the French Department had some offices. Joe knocked on the door.

“Come in.”

Joe entered the small room with a faint odor of grass lingering around the small man behind the desk, bearded like Van Gogh, but with shoulder length black hair and an ear-to-ear illegal smile, both ears.

“You caught me just finishing my coffee break.”

“Too bad I did not arrive a little earlier. I would have enjoyed sharing a cup.”

Joe’s French professor, Lucien Petard, was not yet fully married to the rigors of academia. It wasn’t just the laissez faire attitude of the sixties stoked by getting stoned. Since the days of Thomas Jefferson and the seven elements of classical education, the historical basis for the modern liberal arts, consisted of the trivium (grammar, logic, and rhetoric) and the quadrivium (arithmetic, geometry, astronomy, and music). For Jefferson and Benjamin Franklin, French was needed for the Royal Court. Whether the impetus was need or tradition, in the modern world, particularly for business, English was the spoken language. Many educators thought Princeton's foreign language requirement was only slightly less quaint than throwing a Freshman in the pool before school started. Nevertheless Petard feigned an interest in holding the line.

He scrunched his forehead, causing no small squint of doubt,

"Joe, no let me make sure I understand. You have to fly back to the Chicago area to sleep with an old girlfriend and, in so doing; you will save your best friend from a fate worse than death..."

"I know it sounds like a preposterous excuse to get laid, even for someone mired here. But this girl makes Mata Hari seem like Shirley Temple. My best friend Fred is in over his head. No matter how delicious a regimen of being led around by your dick might now seem to him, I can assure you I must step into the breach, no matter how nice a little breach it is. I can stand the repercussions. Fred might not. I cannot take the chance."

"I believe you. Not only that, I admire your loyalty. I will look the other way about class absences until you return."

HH. The Prisoner

The next night Fred picked Joe up at O'Hare. The two slept together in Joe's large bed at the Cebellum's in Tower Lakes.

After discussing the upcoming baseball season and what music they now liked the best, Joe tested the waters. After Fred confirmed the main points of the Bastion-Shaunton phone call, he filled Joe in about a few other things.

"Let me see if I understand the situation. You and Martha are still going steady?"

"Yep."

"You see Martha one night a week since her dad, Howard, still enforces that silly rule. And, at the same time, you and Sarah are engaged to be married?"

"Yep."

"All the while Martha has no suspicion about this minor intrusion upon her ultimate happiness?"

"'Tis true."

"And Sarah does not know that you still see Martha?"

"Yep."

"And you drive Tiffie Wallet to school every day while she wets your whistle so you can spend the rest of your work day in the midst of a happy tune?"

"Yep."

Joe was now convinced Fred would not be horribly upset if Sarah jilted him. The next morning Fred left early to pick up Stephanie Wallet. Joe then called the Foreswallow's to catch Sarah before she left for school.

"Why Joe whatever are you doing back in Barrington?"

"Sarah, it is important that we get together to talk."

"Whatever will we talk about, Joe?"

"Let's say it is a matter in which we both have a genuine interest. Can you do it?"

"It turns out my mother will be leaving in about one-half hour for the day. I'll tell her I am under the weather, just a few sniffles, an easy performance. Daddy is away on a business. Once my little sister leaves for school, the coast will be clear here."

"I'll be there in forty-five minutes."

Joe dropped his parents at the train station for their downtown commute. He drove into Fox Point, pulled into the Foreswallow driveway, and then lifted the brass knocker from the front door. Sarah opened the door before metal hit metal. She was all smiles. Her pink baby doll night gown had little string ties at her shoulders. As she turned when Joe followed her in, she wiggled her tiny WASP behind as she stretched the lower elastic on the matching pink panties with both thumbs,

"I hate when these things encumber my easy movement."

Joe shook his head.

"Sarah, are you really going to go forward with this idea to marry Fred?"

"Joe, you know we have even opened a bank account. We are saving for our first kitchen appliances."

"A sensible plan, but is it really for the best for Fred, and for you?"

"Why Joe whatever could be the problem? You and I are over. I know that. Are you jealous?"

Joe looked at her. She then rubbed the middle of the small of her back with her right hand.

"Joe, all this talk about the complications of our lives has given me a pain in my shoulders and back. Would you be wonderful and rub my back?"

For Sarah, the world was her stage whether it was the sniffles or a crick in her neck. She led Joe into the living room. There was no piece of furniture and no place on the floor in that formal sitting room those two had failed to brand with their fervent sexuality. Sarah was now face down on the thick carpet in front of the large couch. Joe started to straddle her thighs. Instead she spread her legs,

"Joe, why I do believe, you will be able to apply just the right pressure to my back if you kneel between my legs. Plus do you mind untying the bows on the top of my nightgown. I fancy it will be much more therapeutic if I can feel the touch of your hands on my neck and back."

Sarah and Joe finished curing what ailed her up in the four poster bed in her pink bedroom. Well before that, there was no doubt the engagement was off. That night Sarah stopped to see Fred to give him the sad news.

II. Time Regained

The next day Sarah could not skip school. There were tests to take. It was felicitous coincidence. Mr. and Mrs. Shaunton were again in the Virgin Islands for a month. This time, in order to avoid the devastation of last year's now legendary banister parties, they thought prudence dictated that they hire a college age girl to housesit and to take care of Kelly. Their plan had only one minor hiccup. Last year the wreckage started with a grand banister and ended everywhere. The girl they hired was Katherine Ziffle. She was from a fine Brinker Road family. Kate was one of the leading equestrians at the Barrington Hills Riding Club. The flaw in the plan was that Kate liked to ride boys almost as much as she enjoyed riding English side saddle.

A polite line of Seniors from Barrington High school formed outside the Shaunton master bedroom. Each waited his turn to see how long he could last while Kate did her finest impression of a bucking Bronco. It was the best damned rodeo any kid could ever imagine. Needless to say, this left the rest of the Shaunton house in the same peril that wrecked it the year before. Kelly took charge of the upstairs bathroom. It turned out her bedroom was often otherwise engaged. Fred again fell into Kelly's trap. Before he could lock the door behind him to take a piss in peace, Kelly had slid in behind him. She then locked the door. Kelly dropped her dress to the floor. She was not wearing underwear. She whispered in Fred's ear,

"This time how 'bout you lick my pussy?"

Kelly sat on the sink and spread her legs leaving her crotch open at the front edge. Fred licked until Kelly reached the end of all that there is. Kelly's little white clit glistened in full prominence. Fred turned Kelly to the corner of the sink. He grabbed Kelly's ankles. He then settled her hips back from the edges. Fred stood tiptoed as he pounded her pussy to again reach the point of no return. Kelly clung to the two sides of the sink to keep herself from bouncing off. The Senior boys in line at the end of the hall were now hearing unbridled "oohs" and "ahhs" in stereo.

At the same time, Joe was in Kelly's bedroom. Candy Fraines was a girl from Joe's high school class who worked evenings at the Lamplighter, "from lamps to chandeliers, the store with everything to light up your life and to decorate your inner most passions." Candy and he were both naked in between Kelly's horse and saddle motif high count cotton sheets. Joe's mouth was giving Candy's left nipple his full attention. Her nipple responded in kind. Candy managed a gasp,

"My breasts are just too tiny."

Joe knew what to say,

"Anything more than mouthful is a waste."

Women were equally kind, "It's how you use it."

Both genders quickly learn the benefit of kind words when there are bigger fish to fry. Candy cooed. She arched her back and spread her legs. The smell of her pussy was strong. Joe followed his nose. Soon his hand was two fingers deep into her wetness.

"Joe, I am about to have my period. I think it is safe to fuck."

When Sarah came home from school that afternoon, she freshened up, and then knocked on her next-door neighbor's door. The second annual banister party was in full swing. Seventy-five kids were sprawled and wandering everywhere. Joe was in the living room smoking a joint with Prince Bastion and Chris Shaunton. They had both congratulated him for a job well done,

"Mission Accomplished."

JJ. Simple Joy

Sarah and Joe walked upstairs, the banister still intact. Sarah smiled when she saw the line in front of the door to the master bedroom. Joe took Sarah's hand to lead her into Chris' old bedroom. Sarah pretended not to notice that Joe was covered in Candy's scent.

At the end of Joe's short return to the Sleepy Little Village, Joe and Sarah had reached the limits of sweet enervation. Fred dropped his bleary-eyed friend off at O'Hare on his way to work. Joe would fly back to school. Fred would drive a truck ferrying packages from the airport customs warehouse and back.

"Joe, it's great Sarah and you are back together. There is one thing I did not tell you. Sarah and I developed this habit. We park in front of your parents' house. Something about being close to your bedroom in the front of the house seems to put Sarah in the woman on a mission mode. Anyway, it's a habit I am not yet ready to break."

"Fred, you and I have always said that no woman will ever break up a perfectly good little friendship."

"A sound principle to guide us all our lives, no doubt. So after you return to Princeton, is it o.k. if I continue to take Sarah to the small parking place of marvel where the road is level before the lawn slopes to your front door?"

"Try to maintain your balance, you drunken sailor, as the two of you slink into the back seat. Not at all, Fred. I know Sarah has her own, unique special charms."

What constitutes prevarication is a labyrinth of its own meander. Joe was sure he had not really lied to Sarah, at least not in any pernicious sense. It could not be contradicted. They were "back together." As Sarah just proved, promises about the future are tenuous at best. Joe had looked into her eyes with full sincerity. He told Sarah he looked forward to renewing the passion they had more than rekindled. There is no doubt sincerity finds its purest form in an erection. Deception is often necessary to further that which is most earnest. In this case Joe was also prodded by a genuine interest in disentangling Fred from an artifice that would lead to the depths of destruction for any man, no matter how the wrong path might be pure joy. Joe's last words to Sarah were that he hoped he could be back for Sarah's Senior Prom, but he did allow that the demands of the Princeton campus were onerous. The trip back to the Sleepy Little Village did set the future in one particular. Joe had heard Jim Hill, the head lifeguard at the Barrington Hills Country Club pool, had still not replaced Brock Argil. Joe called. Then the two met. Joe got the job. Joe tried not to think of the young bright-eyed college freshman, Brock, and his brutal murder by unknown black assailants on the street where U.S.C. fraternities border the Watts ghetto in the fall of 1968. Once back at school, far from any urban influences of any sort, Joe would complete the American Red Cross Water Safety Instructor course given in the pool beneath Dillon Gym.

The summer of 1970 was full of bright promise with only the small matter of again extricating himself from the devious clutches of Sarah Foreswallow. At least now, Fred Etheridge was safe, and Martha Buchanan would never know about Fred's tiny misstep.

KK. Shared Joy

The afternoon of the day before Fred drove Joe to O'Hare Airport, Joe went to see a dress rehearsal at Harper Junior College. Sarah was at high school. Longtime friend and old poker buddy, Tim Camphor, was the director. Tim spent one semester in the theater department up at North Dakota State. He then discovered he would receive the full amount of Veterans benefits to spend as he wished whether he was enrolled out of state or in the much cheaper local junior college. The fold and crackle of spending money in Tim's pocket led him back to live with 'Ma' Camphor two doors down from the Etheridges. Now Tim was a big fish in a little pond. His first effort as a director was ambitious, George Bernard Shaw's *Man and Superman*.

Backstage after rehearsal ended, Joe and Tim mused about the famous scene with Don Juan and the Devil. The discussion then turned to a few words about the part that evil plays in any good theology, In the midst of Tim reiterating a line from the *Epistle Dedicatory,* "This is the true joy in life, the being used for a purpose recognized by yourself as a mighty one; the being thoroughly worn out before you are thrown on the scrap heap; the being a force of Nature instead of a feverish selfish little clod of ailments and grievances complaining that the world will not devote itself to making you happy," Joe noticed an attractive young woman talking to one of the cast members. She appeared to have him cornered, really talking at him rather than to him. Conversational skills aside, she was a dark-eyed, Italian beauty.

To Joe, it appeared the guy did not seem to mind he was not getting even one word in sideways.

"Tim, who's the Gina Lollobrigida wannabe?"

"Delilah Pellioni. She is Harper's *prima donna*. I plan to cast her in the lead for the next couple of plays I direct. I think she will be great as Joan of Arc in *The Lark*. Her daddy is some higher-up in the Chicago mob. Her mom divorced him and somehow lived to tell the tale. Delilah lives with her mom and step-father in Hoffman Estates."

Delilah Pellioni was the case-study *de tutti* case-studies. She had only marginally above-average looks coupled with an above-average body all bundled together with minimal mental acuity. Her assessment of herself, however, was decidedly different. Severe limitations gave way to an expansive view of her own unlimited potential. The source of her self-confidence could not be more crude or more base. From the cradle to her teenage years, Delilah enjoyed abundant family praise, lavish superlatives for small talent with heaps of genuine demonstrative affection. The effect of praise every day, as it would have had on any child, was to give Delilah a strong sense of inner worth. Delilah knew she was the best. Over and over again, Joe had seen this phenomenon in kids in Barrington whose often absent parents imparted in them a swagger of importance simply from the material well-being which encompassed them. When a child's course of development lacks nothing in the way of food and shelter, and the press of parental affection from both parents at home is added, a spoiled skew in the perception of a child's place on this planet is the fortuitous and irretrievable result. Delilah was a shining example. All that she lacked was nothing in comparison to that which she thought she had been blessed. Her family had instilled in her a pronounced sense that all she spun was pure gold. Objective reality was immaterial.

While nobody in Delilah's family ever told her that her family was "connected," an environment of scorn for law and authority was part of her upbringing. By way of comparison, Sarah Foreswallow was a rustic innocent. Delilah developed what now seemed innate, a peculiar variant of free market thinking, take what you can. With the idea that 'what is mine is mine and what is yours is mine,' Delilah developed an almost sociopathic disregard for all conventions, rules, and societal norms except the ones which applied to everyone else.

"Tim, let's go over there to see if either one of us can get a word in edgewise."

As Joe and Tim headed in the direction of Delilah and the young man trapped in her conceit, Joe realized he was wrong in thinking the guy was happy to be caught in the clutches of this siren. A look of genuine relief swelled over the face of the current object of Delilah's ongoing explanation of her own wonderfulness.

"Hi Delilah, I'd like you to meet one of my best friends, Joe Cebellum."

Delilah kept talking to the man entangled in her obvious charms. She failed to notice that he slipped away with Tim's first words.

"You know I think that one day I will be on stage not just Broadway, but in Italy singing Opera, the true path for any thespian."

Delilah let the last word linger on her tongue. It was always important for the listener to know that you knew you were using a big word. Plus Delilah thought the word sounded naughty if not pronounced correctly. Joe held out his hand,

"Delilah, I am glad to meet you. Tim tells me he has great plans for you in his upcoming productions."

Delilah cooed,

"Tim understands the theater and talent like few people I have ever met."

"The roar of the greasepaint and the smell of the crowd."

"Tim, are all your friends from Barrington clever and handsome like this one? It's Joe, right?"

Joe nodded. Delilah stepped into the area directly in front of Joe. She then leaned into him. She stopped just before her modest but pert breasts almost touched him. She then inhaled. An immodest brush of their two bodies was the intended result. Joe could feel Delilah's breath on his neck as she continued to speak,

"Tim, what else will you bring forth from your hometown or have we reached the limits?"

On the outside Tim was full of smiles. Inwardly, Tim was not amused since the only attention Delilah ever gave him was directed to what lead she would next be given with not a hint of *quid pro quo*. Tim was fully aware that he would never play a male lead, even if he lost the extra one hundred and fifty pounds he carried on his small frame. He also had taken the hint. In his nineteen short years, the notion approached a certainty. Tim knew he would spend his life relegated to the part of confidant and close friend, with romance never part of the picture.

Joe decided to let Delilah know she was treading onto dangerous ground. Remembering rubbing Sarah's back, Joe put both hands on Delilah, the rounded places of her shoulders where they started to turn down to her upper arms. Joe then glided his hands down slowly. He touched the back of her shoulders as he pushed his thumbs precisely below the identical spaces halfway below her collar bones. Delilah was not sure what Joe was doing but the way he made her feel made her nervous.

As she stepped uncomfortably away from Joe, Joe made full eye contact. As he dropped his hands from her upper body, Delilah was disarmed,

"Delilah, Barrington is full of surprises. Sadly, I leave to go back to school tomorrow. Next time I am back I hope I will see you perform."

Delilah's face turned roseate. It may have been a real blush. Who knew?

Tim and Joe headed to the student parking lot to drive back home to play poker with Ma, Fred, and Fred's brother, Fanta. First, Joe would spend a few final hours doing what Sarah and he did best before he joined his cronies in the Camphor kitchen. They hopped into Tim's car. Tim started the car. The oldies station was still on. The song now playing was "Mona Lisa." Tim's eyes twinkled. He was all one cherubic smile, a proverbial bowl full of jelly but with Christmas nowhere near.

"Joe what was that all about, the hands-on-the-shoulders move with Delilah? Something you learned back East?"

"I wish. You forget that I am one-quarter Italian which makes me at least one-half Italian. I can tell you this. Delilah is trouble."

Tim confirmed the obvious,

"Delilah only thinks of Delilah. Accolades have been heaped upon her by her doting parents and her family. She now knows she is the belle of the ball even though she has never been to one. For her, the clock will never strike twelve. She has been trying to get me to direct *A Streetcar Named Desire*. I don't think she understands point one about the play but she does know that Vivien Leigh played the lead, Blanche DuBois, in the movie and that Marlon Brando played the earthy, strong noble savage, Stanley Kowalski. Delilah told me she wants to find her very own Stanley. She really has no idea about the Blanche character, and she has Blanche and Stella confused but, hey, that is only a small detail. It does not change the full scope of what I am trying to tell you. Delilah says she is sure she can soon make her Stanley shipshape, to toe the line just the way she wants him, the improved image of everything any girl would ever want."

"I would hate to be that lucky guy. I like the idea of going from barbarism to decadence without stopping at civilization. Blanche or Delilah and their many see only the middle ground. But, I think a new day is coming. In any event, you can be sure of one thing. Delilah will never need to rely upon the kindness of strangers."

LL. Solemn Joy

As Joe's plane is made its "final descent" into Newark, Tommy was again using the pay phone outside the Fort Bragg mess hall. He talked with his Uncle Fricke. Coincidence or not, the talk would soon turn to the Pellionis.

"Tommy, it's great to hear your voice."

"You, too Uncle Fricke, I mean, Governor Wanderby."

"Let us dispense with the formalities, but speaking of formal process, how is the progress of the Army in granting your early release?"

"The Army is never wrong, only slow. At first, my missing trigger finger was a minor curiosity. The brass did not know whether to give me a medal for valor in the face of adversity or a discharge me for patent deficiency..."

"Things never change."

"...There was also some talk of starting a special program for teaching recruits with unique deficits to learn to fight but I think the Army could not find more recruits with special problems akin to my missing fickle finger of fate..."

"Funny."

"...Unless, more 'hurry up and wait' finds its way to my file, it looks like I will return to civilian life in the fall. I will live with my parents in Tower Lakes and attend the local community college..."

"Harper, in Palatine?"

"Right, I am not sure I am made out for book learning but I will give it one more try."

"Tommy, you are one smart Wanderby. I am sure you will fare well no matter where your steps will take you."

"Thanks, Uncle Fricke, so what's going on with governing the Great State of Illinois?"

"I will tell you about two interesting items- one that affects the nation as a whole and the other an interesting anecdote peculiar to Chicago and its Mafia culture. Right before you called, I was reading a document prepared by a multi- state organization of local police forces. It is being disseminated jointly by J. Edgar Hoover and President Nixon. The document contains verified statistics of politicized acts of violence. In the last two years there were the occasional white racist violent acts against civil rights activists and other blacks, the less occasional Nazi acts against Jews and retaliation by the Jewish Defense League..."

"Two years do not a prison make."

"...To be sure. The really serious activity, however, falls in two separate categories. First, black militants nationwide persist in shooting at the local police. Chicago seems to have one of the more exacerbated situations. A couple of police officers were killed. Naturally, the Chicago cops retaliated, this time a raid last December against the Black Panther hideout. One leader, Fred Hampton was killed with some other active members. The black community has been further aroused by the raid. The claim is that police attacked the Black Panthers while they slept. There were eighty shots fired by the police and only one shot fired by the Black Panthers. There is another interesting angle to all this, one that touches Barrington. Do you know of the Botch family there?"

"Everybody in town knows Elvira Botch, the real estate broker. She lives with her husband in Biltmore. He is some kind of Army General. They have a son, Lonnie, and a daughter, Maggie. Maggie is pretty wild. She hangs around with my sister, Glenda. The stories about Lonnie are legendary. He got his dad really mad one day. The General was about to start a round of golf at Biltmore when Lonnie, who was on leave or was between tours of duty, landed an Army helicopter he had commandeered from Fort Sheridan, in the middle of the putting green…"

"So that story is more than folklore. I was about to tell you about Lonnie. He spent two tours in Vietnam. Then he decided to 'debrief' as a Chicago cop on the Southside. Apparently he does not like the idea of Chicago's boys in blue being target practice for the Southside's boys, I mean guys, in black. Lonnie Botch has been involved in a number of alleged and confirmed shootings-incidents where he has shot blacks on the street. The ACLU came in to town to investigate these incidents and others. Anyway, the head of the investigation is a pretty accomplished civil rights lawyer. The newest allegation is that Lonnie and a couple of like minded Chicago cops arrested this ACLU lawyer, on some pretext or another but the gist of the *geste* is that as the ACLU would get a Federal writ of habeas corpus to release the guy, Lonnie and his cohorts would move their prisoner to another precinct jail. The ACLU would have to get another writ, directed to a different precinct desk sergeant. They say Lonnie just kept moving the ACLU lawyer around for weeks until they were finally able to serve the writ."

"Funny. How many walls does it take to keep a guy in jail?"

“Yeah but no one is amused. The second part of all this political violence is new. Many people who know Nixon think he is paranoid about the students being at war with the U.S. Government. Hoover, of course, says it is the Commies and persists in looking under everyone’s beds, but he does avoid looking in his own closet for other activities many consider subversive, or at least repugnant. I am not sure how well the students are organized, or whether the activities are orchestrated, but the evidence is undeniable, student violence is increasing and is nothing with which to trifle. More and more campuses have been struck with violence, mostly explosions at National Armories and ROTC buildings, but also draft boards off campus have been hit. Two years ago, the incidents were a couple times a month if that. Now there are ten or more serious incidents of violence a month, with the trend increasing. Strangely, the students at my alma mater, Yale, have made their mark in a way which indicates the boys in New Haven don’t quite get the object of the exercise. There have been two violent acts at Yale- one destroying property in the Art Museum and the other in the Law Library.”

“If those weird Yalies are the example, it appears there is no real nationwide monolithic student network of radicals bent upon violence…”

“Good point. In any event Nixon and Hoover, with his idea that Communists are hiding everywhere but in his closet, are justifiably concerned. The documented evidence about escalating violence in the ghetto and on the campus is undeniable. I also saw a memo today which some might say is pretty funny. As Governor, of course, I am appalled at the conduct.”

“Do tell.”

“There are these two brothers, pretty well-known in the Chicago mob, Giacomo and Carlo Pellioni. About a month ago, these two guys decided to go sport fishing in St. Augustine, Florida. In the old days Al Capone, ran a casino and whorehouse right in the middle of town. Nowadays, guys like the Pellionis go down there just for the fishing. Apparently, the fishing wasn't good or they just got bored. So they rented an office, got some stationary and a telephone number then formed their own bank. To add to the merriment, they got some title officer at Chicago Title to wire around 26 million dollars to this new bank."

"Pretty funny."

"Chicago Title is embarrassed. The title officer has been arrested and the bank has disappeared into thin air, all the money too. The rumor is the Pellionis did this but so far there appears to be no hard evidence and the guy they arrested from Chicago Title is not talking."

"Fun is fun, and they say crime does not pay."

Fricke Wanderby suppressed a laugh. He was ever mindful that his phone was bugged, "for his own protection," by Hoover, acting for the FBI or for Operation CHAOS, the joint venture with the CIA,

"Now, Tommy you know there is nothing fun, or funny about 26 million dollars. These criminals must be brought to justice, along with anyone bent upon violence whether it is shooting police, or blowing up buildings..."

"Or fine art and law books. Uncle Fricke, it has been great hearing all this stuff. I am now hearing taps as we speak."

"Call me soon, Tommy. Let's get together when you get out of olive drabs. I'll buy you a drink at the Chicago Bar Association or the Union League Club."

"Sounds great. Good Night, Uncle Fricke."

"'Night, Tommy."

MM. Spirited Joy

As Tommy walked back to his barracks, Joe rode the Penn Central back to Princeton Junction. This was as close as the main commuter line from New York to Philadelphia got to the town of Princeton. He then took the "Dinky" from Princeton Junction to campus. The "PJ & B" or the Dinky, take your pick, was the shortest regularly scheduled train line, really shorter than a spur. Just as everything else on the Princeton campus, the Dinky was filled with legend and folklore. Since the tracks were first laid, the train would be filled with women on the weekends that the Clubs had parties. The biggest weekend of the year, rivaled only by the grand culmination of Bicker, was simply denominated, "Houseparties." This bacchanalia lasted over a long weekend to proclaim the end of classes. Only reading period and exam period followed with Reunions and commencement the last official activities of the school year. The many women who joined to make the festivities festive arrived by way of the Dinky. To celebrate the eagerness which only the fairer gender will engender, on more than one occasion, Princeton's privileged few rented horses. Then donning the full regalia of cowpokes from the Wild West, or at least, wearing what was worn on some dude ranch in Reno, the Princeton buckaroos would ambush the Dinky and ride off into the sunset of Prospect Street with the objects of their affection for that weekend. The Clubs had "dorms" at their top with rows and rows of beds to be filled with comely lasses. The Club Manager acted as chaperone to keep the wolves at bay in the days of parietals.

That weekend Joe had a blind date, for the whole weekend. Once parietals were abolished, dorms and chaperones became unnecessary. The reality of sleeping in the same room for two nights with someone you just met presented its own set of difficulties. The rampant notion of Free Love added to the complexity. Kris Kristofferson wrote the words, but Janis Joplin sang 'em best, "Freedom's just another word for nothing left to lose and nothin' ain't worth nothin' but it's free." Parsley Fief had a date for the weekend from back home in Scarsdale. Her name was Lil MaGill but everyone knew her as "Nancy." She went to Centenary, a North Jersey private girls' school, a rung or two up the ladder from a full-fledged finishing school but certainly not a college in the realm of the Seven Sisters. Fief's friend had a friend. The fix-up was on. So far, Joe only knew her name, Loretta Sweet. Meeting the Dinky on horseback was not in Joe's bag of tricks. It was just before dusk on Friday afternoon the 17th of April. Fief and Joe waited for the train's metal wheels to slow to a slight squealed stop. This trip was the railroad version of *Operation Petticoat*. One girl after another loped off the train. Pressed blue jeans and pastel front-buttoned blouses were the travel outfit of choice. Almost all wrestled with a suitcase big enough for a summer trip to Europe. Most girls also sported a large, commodious shoulder bag in addition to a purse.

As the off-loading continued, Fief made eye contact with a brown-eyed girl with dark brown hair. She was medium height, an athletic body that moved free and easy in a wholesome suggestion of good clean fun. The swift, short buff on the cheek Nancy granted Fief in greeting confirmed the Platonic nature of the friendship.

Loretta walked two steps behind Nancy. She was blonde, big boned, and 5' 10" tall. She walked carefully but without suggestion of trepidation. She did not seem she would stumble but her gait was not one that had been practiced with a thin book balanced on the top of her head. Loretta's bangs were cut straight, about one inch above thin eyebrows. Her eyes were pale blue. Her broad cheeks were lightly freckled. She had a pleasant nose, neither thin nor bulbous. Her lips smacked an outgoing smile. Loretta's chin was round and made a small jut forward to meet the imaginary line that started straight downward at the point of her nose. In short, she was a slightly more simian version of Doris Day, and equally wholesome as any girl-next door. Loretta carried a purse in her left hand which nested into the crook of her elbow as it rested on her forearm. Only a small pale blue round Samsonite overnight bag swayed carefree in a light dangle from her left hand.

Joe stepped past Nancy and Fief,

"Hi, I'm Joe. You must be Loretta. I have been looking forward to meeting you."

Loretta exhaled. She then dropped her shoulders. Her whole body relaxed a she inhaled,

"This whole Ivy League weekend blind date thing scared me. It is nice to see you are a normal All-American boy, not some stuffed-shirt tight-assed taken-with-himself preppy."

"I like how you speak your mind and how you string together your thoughts. I am not sure how you made such a fast assessment, except for the stuffed-shirt preppy part. Tim, Nancy, I am going to take Loretta back to my room so she can freshen up. We can get to know each other before dinner. Let's meet for dinner later at the Annex about seven?"

Nancy nodded. Fief shook his head and said,

"Sure. Italian sounds good to me. You, too Nancy?"

"Red sauce it is."

Nancy and Fief walked away towards Pyne Hall. Joe turned to Loretta,

"Let me take your bag."

Within the bounds of propriety, Loretta then held Joe's right elbow with the tips of her thumb and first two fingers of her left hand as they walked up the walkway past Henry Hall. Joe thought they could talk on the slightly longer way back to Little. Loretta could also see the enormous Blair Arch clock and its impressive stone steps. The clean late afternoon light made sharp the shapes of everything on campus.

"Joe, may I ask you something?"

"Shoot."

"I have some synthetic mescaline, powder not cut with anything. The buzz is pure and good. Wanna do some? It'll last about twelve hours."

Joe smiled gently. He turned his head at a forty-five degree angle away from Loretta. His look was pleasant surprise.

"It is a perfect night to enjoy the splendor that surrounds us. I'll call Tim to beg off. Eating will only mar the effect."

"Good idea, Nancy is looking forward to catching up with Tim. They have not seen each other since last summer."

For the next hour Loretta and Joe talked with the same vibrant energy of the bright light that would soon give way to the end of the afternoon. The conversation ranged from sketches of family history, high school experiences, favorite television shows, pet peeves, stuff they liked to do now, and stuff they wanted to do. Joe and Loretta dropped their guards. Both of them felt safe.

“Joe I have only one other outfit and another blouse, in addition to pajamas even a nun would approve. I’d like to change into a light spring dress. I can wear my blue jeans tomorrow and Sunday. It doesn’t matter what I wear when I leave.”

“Blue jeans will be *de rigueur* for the Country Joe and the Fish concert at Alexander Hall tomorrow night. Will you be wedded to the pajama idea?”

Joe had not yet learned that if you have to ask, the answer will not be the one you want.

“As the Mother Superior in her marriage to Jesus. But, I am sure you and I will have a great time. Let’s drop the mescaline.”

They each ingested a tiny amount of the grey power Loretta provided from some folded aluminum paper.

“Joe, I am going to change. I want feel the freedom of wearing a dress as we wander wherever our trip takes us tonight.”

NN. Only God Can Make A Tree

In five minutes, Loretta walked out of Joe's room. She was wearing a muted yellow dress. It buttoned down the front. Perhaps it was caused by Loretta's stated reticence but Joe now focused on her almost clumsy big-boned manly manner. More likely, it was the simple fact Loretta looked awkward in the dress. In less than an hour, the drug had taken charge. The two were peaking. As the sun set, a bird on the horizon sitting on a fence sang a song for them at his own expense. The dusk fell. Joe was not sure where they walked or how long they had walked. The lively static sensations bounced all around from everywhere and nowhere. Joe was sure neither spoke a word. The look on their faces gave each other comfort. They each had visages which held the gleam of new amazement, the discovery of what was neglected around them every day. Joe was also sure he was now lying on his back looking straight up. The direction of the focus of his vision was the only straight part of the whole picture. Loretta was next to him. She was also on her back looking up. The grassy ground provided sufficient soft repose. They had come to rest in defiance of Newton's law that objects in motion tend to stay in motion. The place of supple inertia was a square patch of lawn across from Patton Hall in the space between Dillon Gym and the tennis courts below. They captured a little overlook above the courts. High ground never felt better. The tennis courts and the buildings around them were now lost to the ages. For the next eight hours, until sunrise provided a diverting spectacle, a large soft wood tree spread its many arms over the two trippers. It was the intricate network of branches and the varying lattices of leaves that captured and kept their full attention. Silence was the watchword. No words were necessary to speak the truth of the moment, no matter how long the moment lasted. It was unnecessary to change the channel. Under the influence of fascinating patterns infinite in form and in changes, one umbrella of verity presented itself, "The deeper you go the higher you fly. The higher you fly the deeper you go." Looking would never be the same. No matter what tomorrow would bring, eyes had been opened to stay.

All day Saturday, Loretta and Joe wore tired smiles. They had joined in some monumental significance. They had not slept but had rested in a larger sense. Saturday night broke the spell but spun its own web to enmesh all within earshot. Loud electronically amplified rock and roll, especially screaming lead guitar can only be experienced and can never be adequately described. To say it is visceral, felt in the gut more than heard only begins to tell the tale. The band was the one-dimensional Country Joe and the Fish. It didn't matter as long as you were there. Radical politics did not interest Joe. Nevertheless, the lyric, "send your son home in a box" stuck in Joe's head. Princeton's sheltering cocoon stood in stark contrast to the notion of U.S. soldiers returning dead from Vietnam, whether it was body bag or wooden coffin. After the concert, Loretta and Joe got back to the serenity of the cosmos from the night before. They walked from Alexander Hall to Firestone Library past the Chapel, McCosh, and then to Prospect House. Prospect House was a large building in which the faculty could find respite. A grand garden well conceived and better maintained graced the view of the faculty dining hall. Loretta and Joe continued their nocturnal promenade after sitting on a stone bench in the garden. Joe twice suppressed the urge to say something to Loretta about the "nearness of you." They strolled in peace behind Brown Hall, and to the side of Dodd Hall since the traditional and long-standing freshman rioters from those dorms had long petered themselves out mid-winter. In what seemed a profuse encounter in short time, Loretta and Joe returned to second entry Little. This time of its own accord, unaided by any hallucinogen, the night again branded profound impressions. For the rest of night the two looked across from one another at rest on Joe's lower bunk bed. Joel was up visiting his dad and step-mom in Manhattan where his dad had traveled for business from Argentina. Now sitting cross-legged rather than legs astride cross-walks, the grandeur of pure quiet sensations gave way to criss-crossed conversation. Two nights in a row, Loretta and Joe were awake to observe the sun appear to dissolve the darkness and to announce the beginning of one more beautiful spring day. In the morning light, Joe realized he had learned something among the many other things he had just discovered. Had Princeton's winter buried a once strong sexual urge? No, Joe was sure that if celibacy did not work on monks, it did not work to diminish that which was foremost in guiding his motivations. Joe realized that physically intimacy was not the only way to get close, to become connected in a meaningful way. The extended ramble with Loretta was a spectacular retreat. Joe realized he missed the chats with Sally and Felina, like the days with Felina after their time "on the bus." Sex was basic. It is possible to find satisfying currency in hand and roll it around in your palm in other ways, however. Two could connect with the exchange of ideas or experiences, or even in the simplicity of fingers interlaced while immersed in the world all around, whether the moment was formed by nature, music, or the many other man-made points of interest. Joe had no doubt. While he would probably never see Loretta gain, the moments they achieved were not time sold short. Even the smallest point of connection could expand to shine a bright light. Joe was still sure that sex was the best way a man and a woman could indulge themselves. It was not only his weekend blind date with Loretta and the unsatisfying quick fuck with NW which led Joe to the conclusion that merit required some real point where two together intersected.

OO. Lodi

A few weeks before returning home to save Fred's life, Joe was playing wiffleball in Pyne Courtyard. "Foxy Lady" by Jimi Hendrix regaled and taunted the players with that to which they all should aspire. "Hot Sauce" peaked out as he opened the door from his entry.

Parsley Fief was the first to acknowledge his presence,

"Hey Mike, wanna give a try at duplicating that which the Great Bambino never accomplished? Five swings five round-trippers."

"Hot Sauce" was not as strictly polite as the old Princeton would demand. Two girls followed him out of the entry.

"Sorry guys, not today. My sister, Brenda, is visiting me for a few days before the weekend. She brought her best friend, Viola Lee with her. They are both high school seniors."

The wiffleball game took a back seat to proper introductions. Viola Lee and Joe looked at each other. Their eyes met to celebrate a coterminous sparkle. Viola Lee was a young girl untouched by staid solemnity. Freedom coursed through her veins like a carnival. From under her feet to the top of her head, she reveled in the manifestations of the droll design she discovered wherever she went. Whether or not anyone else would think Joe was amusing or entertaining, Viola Lee saw the humor in his comments and observations. Forget about the alimentary route, the way to a man's heart is through his own sense of his sense of humor. From the point of Joe's first few words, Viola Lee laughed and giggled. Joe was sure she joined him tripping the light fantastic. Brenda, Viola Lee, "Hot Sauce," and Joe spent the better part of the rest of the day, and then the next, as a foursome. This was the way it should be, not around a bridge table, nor on any back nine. In the course of wise-cracking and clowning around the campus with Mike and Brenda Marks, Joe regained his stride. With each new Viola Lee giggle and nod of agreement, Joe felt he was back on a bicycle he had never forgotten to pedal. No man likes it better than when he thinks he is ringing clear as a bell. Whether contrived or genuinely conjoined, Viola Lee's embellishments caused Joe to feel he again had good reason to puff up his chest. Once down this path of felicity, there is really no way to unring the bell. Joe told the story about one of the Cebellum family cats.

"My mom, Della, loves all living things. We take spiders and other bugs out of the house to let them go free. We have four cats who do not share this perspective. The largest is a male we call him, 'Brown.' He is an honest-to-God twenty four pound Persian. With his fur he looks even bigger..."

Hot Sauce interjected,

"Next year he will be drafted by the Green Bay Packers."

Brenda, Viola Lee, and Joe all laughed.

"...my mom was concerned at the number of animals Brown would drop on the front stoop of our house, to proudly show us his accomplishment, some dead, some kept alive to play with and to torment a little more..."

Hot Sauce continued the motif,

"A fifteen yard penalty for unnecessary roughness."

Everybody laughed and Viola added her two cents,

"The late hits, out-of bounds are the real killers."

Brenda kept a slight audible, 'ha-ha' within her mouth. Hot Sauce hit more of a smiling, closed lipped 'tee-hee,' while Joe opened his mouth to let go a laugh that started in his belly.

"...It's not funny if you are one of the little animals, released then captured over and over, thinking, 'Oh Lord stuck in Brown's clutches again.' My mom got the idea she should make Brown wear a collar with a bell..."

Borrowing from one of the more well-known television commercials for laundry detergent of the day, Brenda popped in,

"To keep a ring around his collar."

Hot Sauce added,

"In the hope the cat could not unbell a ring."

The others shook their heads but could not suppress their laughter.

"So the next day of the new regime, Brown shows up at the front door step. This time he has a mouse. My mom was appalled when she opened the front door to see what Brown had in his mouth. When Brown saw my mom, he dropped the dead mouse and then, but not before apparently, shook his head to make the bell ring. Even my mom thought this was funny."

PP. The Night Time Is The Right Time

Viola Lee laughed. She took a step toward Joe to brush her hip slightly against his thigh. In addition to the vivacious way she grasped the humor in things big and small and the joyful way she rushed toward the intrinsic beauty of life, Viola Lee held her own true beauty. Her hair was auburn, that rare tumultuous blend of deep brown with interwoven fiery red. Her brown eyes almost matched her hair but held a gleam more than a flame. Viola's skin captured pale white but did not diminish her round cheeks. Her nose sloped to meet her cheeks on middle ground. She had an arc to her chin that seemed to capture a tender innocence. Viola's full lips freed the full red that had been subsumed into her wild mane. She was an average height with only a suggestion of slight corpulence. She was not really plump but in no way was she skinny. Her legs carried her torso in a motion which accentuated the sly motion of her lower body as her hips almost seemed to rotate contradicting the lack of experience in her face. At the same time, she seemed to hover to give her carriage a graceful steadiness. She walked with her shoulders pulled only slightly back; proud she could emphasize her 36" C- cup breasts. As Viola started to speak, Joe hoped she did not catch him admiring her ass, one more part in a body which was grounded in pleasing circles.

"Joe, I have two tickets to see Phil Ochs at the Electric Factory in Philly tomorrow night..."

Brenda started to say,

"I thought you and I…"

"Right, Brenda, I **was** looking forward to going with you. It's too bad you had that other prior engagement come up."

"Oh, right. I forgot."

Brenda was not all smiles.

"I am sure my parents would be happy to let you sleep in the pull-out couch in the downstairs family room. I hope I am not being too forward…"

Brenda regained her equilibrium,

"I hope Joe you can help out here since I had to cancel at a time later than even I thought."

Viola Lee laughed.

"This sounds great to me. Phil Ochs is just the cherry on top of…"

"I hope we both get to enjoy the full menu with dessert only the beginning of more to come."

Joe did not understand how parents thought it was o.k. to allow some guy from Princeton they did not know to molest their daughter, in their own house. But there he was. The Electric Factory was fine but the basement was better. Phil Ochs spit out "I Ain't Marching Anymore" to lead the parade. Another highlight was "Outside of a Small Circle of Friends." 311 Phil Ochs fans could not be wrong. After a great concert, Joe and Viola kissed. They fondled for a couple hours in the family room. Viola Lee helped Joe pull out the hide-a-bed before saying good night. Six minutes later, Joe was on his back. Viola Lee returned. She lifted her night gown over her head to expose a body that spoke youthful beauty, a continual breaking dawn. Viola Lee then pulled Joe's red and blue boxer shorts down and off his legs before climbing on top of his hips for a ride that led them both to quiet bliss. Her movements captured something folk music could not even begin to attempt. Viola Lee exerted just the right pressure just the right force, just the right tension, and just the right push. Joe replied in kind. Jazz is the musician's attempt to capture in sound that which strikes both the ear and the visceral. The beauty of the movement and the feeling Viola Lee and Joe attained in the family room was its own tactile improvisation. Joe was surprised to get a call from Viola Lee two days later. She had a steady boyfriend who attended Dartmouth. He had returned to surprise her that very day. He asked for her hand in marriage. Viola Lee had accepted his proposal. Joe was happy. He reflected that once was better than never. Viola Lee's fiancé was one very lucky guy. The issue of connection aside, when all is said and done, sex in just the right way, with a person of similar sympathies, is what it is all about.

QQ. Tombstone Shadow

Given the short nature of the tryst, it was not a fair characterization to say Viola Lee broke up with Joe. For different reasons, it may not have been fair to say Paul McCartney broke up with the Beatles.

On April 11th, Sam called Joe. He was out of breath.

"This is earth shattering ridiculousness."

"Sam, what catastrophe has befallen us now?"

"Yesterday, Paul McCartney issued a press release. He has left the Beatles. They are no more. McCartney thinks this is some sort of laughing matter. The press release is in the form of an interview that never happened. Well, I hope Linda and he are proud of themselves, breaking up the greatest band that ever was or ever will be."

"Sam, no rock and roll band performing in 1970 will be around in ten years, much less the turn of the century. All that drug use cannot breed longevity. Keith Richards may not last through the next week."

"Well it was airplanes that killed Buddy Holly and Patsy Cline. Drugs are the brave new world, the opening of glorious horizons, the enlightenment of walking through the doors of perception. Mescaline and marijuana will lead our generation to new heights and to new accomplishments, even without the Beatles. May they rest in peace."

RR. Bad Moon Rising

Mescaline and marijuana are wonderful drugs. Most days that Spring, however, Joe and "Lemming" Cello smoked the surfeit turned subsistence of Nepalese hash until the music which they heard and the surroundings which they saw all lingered with the force of a slow seriously non-transcendental drip. Put into the strain of strenuous circumstances, a short-lived burst of mean spirit can bubble up from even those with the most admirable equanimity. Even though John did head back to the normal male-female balanced environment of his hometown in Demarest every couple of weekends, the dreary and dull all male cauldron spelled his doom. At first the void was the subject of slow incredulity, but now the bane from the absence was deep-rooted. There would likely be permanent effects on anyone who had spent four years of some prominence in a public school peopled with boys and girls.

Beeping crescendos of RAU were not enough. In the serious context of the sullen traipse most acutely felt on the Princeton campus, "Lemming" Cello utilized the idea of desperation for the name for any group of young men gripped in the unnatural throes of any non-sexual environment perceived as hostile whether fleeting or enduring. Thus the club, "The Horny Toad Desperadoes," was born. The Princeton Chapter was not the seminal group. "Lemming" Cello's high school buddies back home in Bergen County held that honor. Princeton, however, nurtured the essence of pointed vacuity which marked the ambit of all for which the "Horny Toad Desperados" stood. Soon there would be an active chapter in the Sleepy Little Village.

In underlined counterpoint to this diversion of silliness was "tripping." "Lemming" Cello now spent all his waking and sleeping hours trying to find a higher plane. Hallucinogens seemed as good a way to go as any. Cello's path was driven by more than the gravity's rainbow of a furrowed brow bridled by the concerns of what were and what might have been. He strove to discover and to know more than what is, more than even what lies beneath and more than where or what is the virtual lynchpin of meaning and knowledge. In short, the chaos that surrounded "Lemming" Cello perplexed him to the point that his every breath, his full being, cried out for order, a structure that only even more flux could provide.

It was Wednesday night following the Country Joe and the Fish concert. Cello was alone. There was a knock on the door. It was James Southdrown, a guy from Upstate New York. He was one of the few to whom Joe and Cello sold some of their stash of finger hash in their early days of their best intentions to get ripped for free. The rap of Southdrown's knuckles his door interrupted Cello in the third hour of an acid trip. Music was the key for the evening. The heightened experience started with a familiar listen to the Beatles' album, *Yesterday and Today*. From that vantage, Cello was pointed in the direction of the music and words as agglomerated by Procol Harum. From their first album, "A Whiter Shade of Pale" and "Repent Walpurgis" sprang forth elliptically. After only short ellipsis, there came forth the title track from their third album, "A Salty Dog." That night the song was born anew. It painted a roving picture in stride with some unspoken everlasting fancy which captured Cello's full attention. John stood up in the first step to disentangle himself from the lavish panorama of sound that surrounded him. He opened the door, his wits now about him,

"Hey Sergeant Southdrown, what brings you here?"

Southdrown was wearing his crisply pressed and brightly clean Navy R.O.T.C uniform. His officer's military hat with the insignia centered above the brim glistened to catch Cello's gaze. "Lemming" Cello made a mental note to spin the Procol Harum second album, *Shine On Brightly* when "Salty Dog" returned home from the sea.

"Cello, you see I am a Navy man. We do not have Sergeants."

"Well Captain, what can a like-minded seafarer do for you? I was just listening to the lyrics, "all hands on deck, I heard the Captain call…."

"It all sounds like loud weird music to me but then that is why I am here. I need to get in the right frame of mind. I smoked all that hash Joe and you sold me."

Cello looked sad and serious,

"My Captain, the ship has sailed. The fearful trip is almost done. Cebellum and I have decided to keep the small remainder of what was once a glorious ounce safe at shore for ourselves."

"That is bad news. I was hoping to continue to join you in the pleasures of the harbor. Is there anyway, I can get someone from the guy who sold it to you?"

"It's funny you just used that phrase from the great Phil Ochs' song, Joe just went to Philadelphia, the weekend before last. He saw Phil Ochs' live, said it was great show of a guy who stands toe-to-toe with Dylan in the halcyon days of the folk protest movement."

“I had no idea I was quoting a folk singer. And what is there really to protest? Plus I never heard of Phil Ochs. I will have to look into the stuff we’re listening to now….”

“Procol Harum.”

“…and Phil Ochs. It seems like I never get enough of Bob Dylan. I love that song, ‘Mr. Tambourine.’ I hope Dylan has some other big hits soon. Play another song for me. I’m not sleepy and there is no place I’m going to. Although if you are gonna write one great song, that one has to be it. I am not sure exactly why but some of my ROTC buddies think Bob Dylan is subversive. But I believe in free thinking. Those other folks’ ideas should not be repressed, especially if the main point is singing for people. Music is not just for the church choir. Speaking of repressive tolerance Herbert Marcuse was here on campus speaking on that subject. I thought Marcuse was dead, just like Nietzsche said God was. I never quite got how the Germans are able to mix so much structure with so much philosophy. It is like they are able to go beyond the two really good musical art forms they dominate- military marches and waltzes. ”

“What?”

“Cello, do you think you can tell me how to get in touch with the guy who sold you that humongous amount of hash?”

“I wish Princeton would bring some more mystical deep thinkers to the campus. It seems they think that one local yoga guy is enough. Like who trusts a yoga instructor with a name like a Wall Street banker?”

“Hey, John, there is a song written by somebody with the recurring line, ‘When will it ever end.’ Maybe that songwriter fellow, whoever he is, is talking about things like west and east being separate when the west will soon spread its wings over all the civilized parts of the world? Plus I think Princeton is really helping about all that. Just think about the stuff that has been on campus this spring. Charles Evers, the brother of the civil rights leader who was shot in Mississippi was here, talking about how everything is improving for his people all over the South."

Cello shook his head when he realized Southdrown did not know Dylan wrote "Blowin' In The Wind." Cello's eyes got big as Southdrown described the campus visit of the brother of Medgar Evers.

"Are you sure that was what he was saying?"

"Well, I wasn't there. You do remember that George Wallace was helping to hold open the door when Lyndon Johnson's Attorney General, Nicholas Katzenbach, one of our great recent Princeton alumni, brought federal government troops to assist those two Negro students find their way into the campus."

At this point "Lemming" Cello hoped he was hallucinating, but knew he was not. Could anyone really think Governor Wallace, the staunch small-minded segregationist, did anything other than reluctantly budge from his personal barricade of the door to permit entry only when he realized Katzenbach and the troops behind him meant business.

"Plus that well meaning but misguided Ralph Nader, another alum Class of '55, was here. No doubt he was preaching that consumers need to be protected from big business. The free market operates just fine, thank you very much. If Nader keeps saying American made cars are unsafe at any speed, who knows what might happen. People could actually start buying more and more foreign cars. Next thing you know, they will be making cars in Korea, well only South Korea, of course."

“Lemming” Cello was beginning to think he was going to need divine intervention to escape from the inane web in which he was now caught. This sort of thing might explain why Art Linkletter’s daughter jumped out of window in the middle of an acid trip.

“Southdrown, I can tell you this. Our buddy, Joe took a one-time job at the Faculty Lounge, Prospect House...”

“Oh yeah, the place that used to be the President’s house on campus back in the day of Woodrow Wilson.”

“...Yea, Joe was a waiter for a special dinner for Benny Carter when he was here in February giving a few seminars on Jazz, finishing it all up with that really tasty concert by his trio.”

“You know I think jazz is for misguided pop culture followers. The days of hep cats shooting heroin will not last forever. I prefer the more intellectual offerings given here in the full smorgasbord of interesting campus activities. I missed it but I am sure the recent talk on ‘The Allocation of Time over Time’ had to be fascinating as was, although I missed this one too, the symposium, ‘Can the Natural Scientists Solve the Social Problems Better Than the Social Scientists?’ And then there was just another one from the Institute for Advanced Studies, really too deep for me, or probably anyone really, ‘Degeneracy of the Mass Spectrum for Local Infinite Component Fields.’ It is great all these presentations are open to the public, not just to quench the thirst for knowledge of the students...”

“When will it ever end” was now echoing in Cello’s head.

“...One talk I did really want to attend was by Shelby Cullom Davis under the auspices of the Princeton Historical Society. I do admire the way he adheres to his principles in fighting to keep Princeton the way it was in the days of the deep traditions which are now firmly part of the fabric which makes it a great university…"

"Lemming" Cello was sure that if there was an end to Southdrown's love of the sound of his own voice, he was nowhere near finding it. There was no light at the end of the tunnel. Cello's active mind now latched itself upon simple wordplay, "historical" in this case was "hysterical" both funny and that which finds its derivation in hysteria, mass or massive, all leading to a mission of promulgating missives hastened by hate and hauteur.

"…So John, it looks like I better get back to do some studying. May I call the guy who sold you that really good stuff?"

SS. Sinister Purpose

"Lemming" Cello gave Dino's phone number to Southdrown. Southdrown called Dino then bought some stuff. Two days later Dino was arrested. It turned out Cebellum and Cello dodged a bullet. James Southdrown, Navy R.O.T.C. officer and solid citizen, was also a "narc," an undercover operative to interdict the illegal flow of drugs that was now overwhelming our otherwise great country. Southdrown was a volunteer. Since only Dino was busted, Joe and John always presumed the protected cocoon that is Princeton saved their asses. It was likely the administration suffered a student narc only upon the express assurance that off-campus dealers would be the only focus of the undercover operation. Under fire from a significant number of alumni like Shelby Cullom Davis for allowing women, blacks, and more and more Jews to be Princeton students, the last thing needed was the bad publicity that would result if there was a campus drug bust. The prevailing principle that Princeton Gentlemen were never the subject of unseemly intrusion by local law enforcement allowed parents to rest easily. It was no coincidence that the immunity ensured on a campus where the police were kept at bay flowed to the direct benefit of powerful forces in the Nation's service, who did or would make significant contributions to support Old Nassau. No matter how well-bred, well brought up, or well-schooled, even for the best of sons favored, favorite, or prodigal, the dictum obtained, "Boys will be boys."

TT. Start Stark Spark

The last weekend in April was also the last weekend before "Houseparties." Saturday night would lead to the Eating Clubs where practice runs were always reason enough to have a party. Saturday would wait. Friday night, Joe and his buddies got stoned then went to the movies. Nassau Street had two movie theatres, "The Playhouse" near one end of the campus in Nassau Square and "The Garden" which sat at the other end on the corner of Washington Road where the Nassau Street shopping area ended. Movies were also shown by student organizations intent on furthering some agenda, or were screened simply as art for art's sake. Joe's favorite movies from those shown on campus during the second semester of his Freshman year were *Witness for the Prosecution*, *A Hard Day's Night*, *La Dolce Vida*, *Dinner at Eight*, and *On the Waterfront*.

In 22 Little Joe toked up before the movie with Appleseed, Fief, and Relioport.

As he exhaled, "Thew" intoned, "You know what I like about going to the movies? You can put aside that old saying, 'A book in the hand is worth two on the shelf.'"

Fief did his best to move the conversation forward, "Thew, it has also been said that professors either adore or abhor. In your case I am going with the word with fewer vowels."

No matter what was going on around him, "Teddy" Appleseed maintained his well-known shit-faced grin. He rarely said a word. This silence was not a case of "still waters run deep" but rather "little things come in small packages."

“Teddy” learned quickly. In the battles of wits which were fought incessantly around him, he was essentially unarmed. He was happy as a stoned clam in his role was neutral observer. Stepping into the fray would lead to more than putting his foot into it. Invariably, he would have to slink away, tail between his legs.

“Fief, and to think I thought sweet nothings were the best you could whisper. The empty concussion of your words which show you are able to count very small numbers will not affect your sense of balance or harmony. You are a man not accountable to himself but rather a cannibal to himself.”

Fief and Joe laughed. Teddy remained in character, his own special version of Cigar Store Indian. Fief came to his own aid,

“Well put my little friend Thew. Keep in mind, however, if someone is only talking and not paying attention, it doesn’t matter what anyone else might say…”

Thew was right there, on the spot, “Unless, of course your own inner ear and personal pride become an issue.”

Joe changed tack, “Now I know you boys are having fun but I would like to propose that we give those Juniors on the first floor in the room below a little retribution. Last night, they were not even cordial in their refusal to let Frites and me go into their living room and blast Jethro Tull. They have set up a sound system integrated with these two cool light boards with triangles of Christmas tree light bulbs, one side green, one side blue, and one side red, one board set for the left channel, the other for the right. Each different color lights up with the different frequencies of sound on the stereo. It is perfect for two guys who are stoned. They only use it to gawk at, background lights veiled by the cloud of inebriation gained from drinking one beer after another…”

Fief was impatient, "And you were about to get to the point."

"I have this M-80 and a nickel. I am going to pin their door closed by shoving the nickel between the door latch and the doorjamb. I will light the M-80 then deposit it into the mail slot in their door. As Sartre would say, 'No Exit…'"

"As Sartre would say?"

"Thew" oozed compassion, "I know those guys, just three science geeks who pedal their bikes back and forth almost every day off campus to the Engineering Quad, that big building near where the Prospect Street Clubs end that no one studying liberal arts has ever seen. The finely honed applied knowledge they gain fuels a waiting nation. Two electric engineers and a mechanical engineer…"

"Finely honed? Those E-Quad wonks get their just desserts as they become slaves to their own greed tethered to U.S. business interests…"

"Nevertheless whatever else may await them, immediate mean retribution and vengeance, even for imagined wrongs, is its own impetus. Follow me boys, we will have bang and whimper both."

"Thew" shook his head from side to side, "Thank God you did not say anything about the Chattanooga Choo Choo."

"Teddy" was not really paying attention, "God Bless You."

UU. Start Stare Share

The operation was a success but the smoke alarm brought the proctors. Joe acknowledged his part in creating a dangerous amount of smoke, particularly since the three drunken predecessors to "The Big Bang Theory" had been trapped in its midst. Joe's *mea culpas* were necessary but not sufficient. The two responding proctors told him that he would hear from the Dean. Joe received only a letter, a written reprimand. He was warned that future malfeasance or miscreance might lead to more drastic consequences or some such Ivy League mumbo jumbo not likely to strike fear into the heart of anyone. Calm indifference was the administration's watchword. During the first semester, Joe and Barry Richardson smoked a joint setting off the smoke detector in Barry's Witherspoon room. Both tobacco and dope did the trick. The proctors could not tell which room was the culprit, so they just showed up to be sure no fire had been started, and to turn off the din.

Back at Little Hall, the proctors had used all necessary force to pry open the door. Smoke rushed out to reveal three triangles of fiercely flashing colored lights. Two open windows did not vent enough. The Wollensak reel-to-reel tape recorder was last heard playing a "Group Called Smith," *Baby, It's You*. After the hubbub down below, the four boys missed the movies. Adventure and punctuality do not often cross swords. Those two strangers rarely meet. Being at the right place at the right time implies a lack of planning. Rarely does true chaos start at an appointed hour. Accidents will happen, however. The mescaline adventure on Prospect Street landed Joe, Joel, and John at Cannon's front door just as the initiation ritual started, welcoming them with open antlers. So some sprees can benefit from prompt attendance.

VV. Green River

The next night was one more Saturday. Frites, Cello, and Cebellum reprised their mescaline trip to Prospect Street. This time they were moved by the same acid Cello had the interrupted pleasure of doing when Southdrown darkened his door. Timeliness was not on the agenda that evening. The brave new world that night was one which skipped over Cannon to pass directly to Dial Lodge. There were two jock Clubs on the street. Dial Lodge and Tiger Inn. Dial Lodge members could be easily mistaken as belonging to Cannon. Interior linemen foot the bill best. Tiger Inn was filled with athletes with fine motor skills. That night Dial Lodge had an "open party." Frites, Cello, and Cebellum were thus able to slip in and out of Dial with beer after beer from a never empty keg which greeted incoming guests near the front door. Once their three plastic cups were again filled, the three space cadets did a slow scurry back to sit on Dial's front lawn near the sidewalk that lined that side of Prospect Street. The kept their eyes open wide that see the chance and take it. Time and again they would return to the front door once their cups were again empty so they could be full again. The three reveled in this repeating process. Even after sixteen such trips, the L.S.D., though dulled, still overpowered the alcohol. If they were getting drunk, they would be the last to know. This was a worthwhile experiment elucidating a truth of advanced physics- Relativity of Mind Alteration. As they kept returning to the same point of observation on the front lawn, having again discovered the fountain of suds, they attained that which quantum theory had only heretofore hypothesized- a state of tripping, drunk, and both. In a conjoined condition transcending the existential, from their *terra firma* vantage point, all that passed them by filled them with wonder of the depth of inconsequence.

Three young women stopped to express their curiosity about the lawn loungers. What ensued could not be accurately described as conversation. Frites, Cello, and Cebellum later agreed. The three faces were somehow disembodied. They disagreed about the visages, however. Cello went with gaunt, sad echoes of Modigliani inspiration. Frites insisted upon Botticelli's fine-featured alabaster. Joe remembered only Renoir, sensual and bright-eyed.

They did agree that Cello spoke first,

"Positive energy and love equals joy."

One of the girls was up to the task,

"Is that the beer talking?"

The second gave away her inner urge,

"Love in the active sense?"

The third was all business,

"Is what you just said better framed as concoction rather than equation?"

"Lemming" Cello took it all in and redrafted accepting all suggested amendments,

“Consciousness forces the conclusion that positive energy and the love that connects us all make joy.”

“You guys wanna go with us to Quadrangle? I hear they have a good band there. The lead singer sings just like Sam Cooke.”

Cello answered,

“Wouldn’t you rather join us here on Planet Earth?”

“Sorry, dancing, not grass stains are what we are into tonight.”

The three girls turned to cross the street then disappeared into the night.

Frites shook his head,

“It is darkest just before reality fades into the shadows.”

Cello was not persuaded,

“I think we just experienced was not a rebuke but rather a circumstance akin to the one when a lady stood up to look out the window to see her home country. Reality is what you make of it, not merely what happens to you.”

Frites’ mind was the first to leave the immediate surroundings,

“Now Live Evil Won. Able Was I Ere I Saw Elba.”

Joel stood up fixing an imaginary hole between two non-existent buttons, into which he placed his right hand. With his left hand, he adjusted the cock of the tri-colored, three-sided hat that wasn’t there. He then pointed his left hand forward to the magnetic, or in this case, the electric North. Two military steps rallying imaginary troops and cheering countrymen then followed.

Frites cackled liked the devil himself. He then continued,

"So there you have it. I have enunciated the essential difference between palindrome and palimpsest. One is merely letters back and forth, the other a slate of double blind tales where its newest reincarnation covers what was once some prior deviation of its own accord. The past gives way to the present never learning what happened before since it is all covered up. As in Napoleon's return from exile, past events are prolegomena to future failure. Repetition accedes to the oneness of then, now, and both.

Joe followed the bouncing sine-trough,

"Quantum History dovetails with acid dreams."

There was no doubt that a critical juncture had been reached. From what was now left, the straggled remnants of the Sixties, "The Lost Generation" had been recomposed with the deft touch of Don Quixote.

WW. Fore Sore Bore

On the afternoon of Tuesday April 28th Joe was on his way off-campus to visit the anthropologist, Ashley Montagu. Joe's mom, Della, was friends with Montagu. Their first contact was correspondence. Della was initially engaged to find rare books. Their exchange of letters blossomed to friendship. At the time the Brits, Ashley Montagu and his wife, invited Joe to tea, he was better known as a humorist guest on the Johnny Carson show than as the man who questioned the idea of race as a biological concept and the author of the UNESCO Statement on Race and *Man's Most Dangerous Myth- The Fallacy of Race.* Among his sixty or so other books, Montagu authored, *The Natural Superiority of Women*. Montagu now lived in Princeton. He had taught and lectured at Harvard, Princeton, Rutgers, New York University, and the University of California. His academic career ended in 1955. His connection with the UNESCO Statement on Race made him a target for the anti-communist elite who saw equality among men as the ultimate subversion. Untenured, he was dismissed from Rutgers. All other academic avenues were blocked. It was then he moved to the town of Princeton.

Joe was not really sure why he was going to tea. Della told Joe he would enjoy both Ashley Montagu and his wife, Marjorie. Joe was nervous about leaving campus to have tea and crumpets with a popular television personality. On the way to Nassau Street, Joe stopped by 'Spoon to see Barry Richardson. Barry was not in his room. Some of the first floor dorms had windows which opened onto the front stoop of Witherspoon. The windows were open to the room of three Freshmen, Daniel Lichty, Colin Femgris, and Richard Eugene Boehm. Lichty was prominent in the campus chapter of the SDS. He was vocal in opposition to the war and to the military-industrial complex. Lichty also espoused socialism. He did not yet know he was a fish out of water. Colin Femgris would major in Biology and was, even now, spending many hours in the laboratory. By sophomore year, Colin was happy to test the hallucinogens Joe and his cohorts would ingest. This was a good way to avoid ingesting strychnine cut with speed that had been proffered as pure synthetic mescaline or acid from Owsley and Timothy Leary's "Brotherhood." Rick Boehm would become Joe's best friend at Princeton and his favorite bridge partner.

Joe's nervousness led him to stick in his head to say hello. Joe was greeted in kind so he joined the three roommates. He came in through the front room window.

"Hi guys, you will never guess where I am going?"

Ever the scientist, Colin replied,

"I am sure you are right."

Lichty was as friendly as any marginalized student radical would ever be,

"Do tell us if you are so inclined."

"I am going to have tea with Ashley Montagu and his wife."

The three had no idea who Montagu was. Joe really did not either.

Boehm was not amused,

"Do tell."

One quaint now not often used name for marijuana was "tea." Lichty had been smoking dope,

"I hope that means you are getting stoned, not sipping warm water with stuff legally grown in Ceylon dipped into it."

"My thought exactly, sad to say, it will be high tea but not in the sense of altitude that we like."

Lichty persisted in his friendly fellowship for all comrades,

"Fare thee well. Go forth and don't choke on any scones."

Richard Eugene Boehm thought Joe was as pretentious a prick as he had ever met. Some guy not one of the guys in his room knew, had slithered in to tell them he was going to meet some famous guy. Joe spent his life overcoming unfavorable first impressions. By sophomore year, Cebellum and Boehm were fast friends. R.B., as he was soon known by everyone on campus, loved telling everybody what an obnoxious asshole Joe was when they first met that April afternoon. Those who knew Joe were quick to agree. Joe accepted the judgment of his peers. The beauty of Princeton was that Joe had many close friends.

Rick Boehm was an interesting case study. He came to Princeton by way of airplane, taxi, and train. It was the first time he traveled by any of those means. Boehm's father was a postman, like "Thew's." He delivered the mail through snow, sleet, and hail in Tallmadge, Ohio, a suburb of Akron, which was in turn a suburb of Cleveland. R.B. attended an all boy Catholic school. Without knowing the real reasons, his mother went to church everyday to pray for her son. It was not chutzpah, but very limited means. Princeton was the only college to which Boehm applied. R.B. exuded only innocence, kindness, and warmth. It was not until after college graduation that R.B. had his first date. Princeton's all-male regime did not faze him in the least.

XX. In A Cloud Of Dust I Met Two Jinn

Having said his goodbyes to new 'Spoon acquaintances, Joe walked the eight or ten blocks beyond Nassau Street into one of the many nice residential areas in the town of Princeton. Joe was warmly greeted by Marjorie. Ashley was equally hospitable. In a matter of minutes, it was apparent that Della and Montagu shared the same passion for books. Montagu's immense library held everything intellectual. Like in Joe's home, worthwhile but non-popular books of every type and description teemed from the shelves. No confections could be observed. Tripe was nowhere to be seen. Some of the books Joe saw were authored by those with whom Montagu studied, in anatomy by Arthur Keith in psychology by Karl Pearson and Charles Spearman, in anthropology by Grafton Eliot Smith, Earnest Hooton, "Papa" Franz Boas, Ruth Benedict, and Charles Gabriel Seligman. One book was from a broad and glorious horizon all its own. Ashley Montagu was one of the first students of Bronislaw Malinowski at the London School of Economics. When Montagu left England for the States, he falsely claimed to Harvard anthropologist Earnest Hooton that he had attended Cambridge, Oxford, London, Florence, and Columbia where he earned M.A. and PhD degrees. Montagu did not graduate from Cambridge or Oxford. He did not receive a PhD degree until later. At Columbia University, Montagu's PhD dissertation, sounded in cultural anthropology, *Coming into being among the Australian Aborigines: A study of the procreative beliefs of the native tribes of Australia*, led to Montagu's first doctorate. Joe was amidst a mountain of hard backs. Their titles cascaded from all quarters, whichever direction he turned. Whether a matter of cultural anthropology or mere fidget blossomed to predilection, people will tend to climb into a shell or create a cocoon with hobby, collection, game, or any obsession. No matter how formed, with structure or with chaos, there is then a place where no storm will enter. In the eye of this particular calm, Montagu took extreme pride in his collection of first editions. Many of them were signed. From that special section of the library, after first lifting the full protection of a hinged glass cover, Montagu handed to Joe a small book. The cover read, On Liberty. Joe opened the cover to find the signature, "John Stuart Mill." Once the cordial afternoon was over, Joe walked briskly back to campus. His path was crisply illuminated by the late afternoon sun. Objects all around him were set off in clear contrast by the scintillating backlighting which is only provided late in the day. Joe reckoned that soon he would be back on campus, with "Lemming" Cello and loud music, once again getting stoned.

YY. Commotion

Two nights later, trouble was afoot. The United Nations treads water in a pond that exists only in the realm of ideals. The first tenet of International Law protects the sovereign borders of all nations. On April 30, 1970, the United States went on the record that it was above that law. President Richard M. Nixon announced the invasion of Cambodia.

In response, student protest reached violent proportions, crossing the boundaries of restraint and non-violent civil disobedience. Two of Joe's lifelong buddies were among those who lead the charge on their respective campuses. Kiefer Mandolin was involved in blowing up a building on the Michigan Wolverine campus. There was collateral damage. One innocent bystander, a janitor was killed. At the University of Iowa, Glenn Reaper led a student demonstration that quickly turned ugly. Students incensed with the callous indifference of the Nixon administration took their own version of the end justifies the means to the streets. Property was destroyed as protesters trampled everything in their path. The thundering mob followed Reaper off the campus onto city streets. Glenn Reaper became disgusted with Nixon and the War. He concluded America was not a better place. Reaper moved to Squaw Valley where, since 1970, he has his own special brand of spreading rainbows over the blues. In the winter, Glenn Reaper jumps off rock promontories with only his skis to break his fall. In summer he races down steep mountain roads riding state of the art bicycles with the wind in his face.

Until the events following Nixon's invasion of Cambodia, Sam was blissfully untouched by politics and protest. The Church of Alphabetology proclaimed that its adherents must render to "see-ers" that which the eye could see. Sam called this point of demarcation and cornerstone of tolerance "The Church's First Sound Principle."

It was an easy matter then, with that small phrase of self-serving dogma so denominated, for Sam to lead members of the flock, usually one or two young girls at a time, to places where music was played. Musicians who hailed from Oklahoma became crowd pleasers for those who had successfully rendered to see-ers. Sam and his flock were particularly fond of hearing J. J. Cale, Merle Haggard, Leon Russell, and Jesse "Ed" Davis, the Native American who played a mean slide guitar harkening back to the roots of Taj Mahal. Jesse "Ed" taught Duane Allman to play in the bottleneck style.

Since Sam felt he was not a good dancer he guided another dictum into "all that churned in the large mixing bowl of our thick kneading." So said Sam, "The inert lets love swirl all around." By holding a young girl close to him on the dance floor, feet in place, with only their two bodies touching in a motion that pleased each other, Sam would ensure Alphabetologists avoided floundering on the reefs of melodic mix-up. By so doing, they could stand in place and thereby dance until the dawn. Initially, religions seek means to bring new members into the fold. Sam's Alphabetology was full of the type of fresh ideas upon which young people of the day wished to grasp, latch, and feast. By the time Nixon spoke of the Cambodian invasion, organized religion stood in a different role. As religion matures it becomes defensive. It does so as the empire will have it. The impetus of God and King or the Unites States version, Manifest Destiny, gives way to notions like the Monroe Doctrine. Conservative thinking to preserve the status quo replaces the liberal notion of change for the better originally needed to bring new members to join the congregation. Christ once stood for the Crusades and before that he stood for his own death. Now it would be uncomfortable for those settled into Christianity to become unsettled by notions of witnessing for the good of all mankind. There is no need to expand for everyone that which has already been acquired and vouchsafed for those in the fold. The days of Alphabetology were numbered.

At OU, the prophylactic apparatus to interdict all steps of misguided youth was in place. In Oklahoma prior to 1970, antiwar demonstrations were a *rara avis*. Nevertheless, the Sooner State became part of the expansive focus by the federal government to minimize the influence of radical student groups and dissident activities. Responding with due care to the emergence of the Students for a Democratic Society and other unseemly college radical groups, FBI Director J. Edgar Hoover, in an abundance of caution, authorized countermeasures to infiltrate, disrupt, and discredit the dissident activity Hoover viewed as driven by Communism. As one example of Hoover style "dirty-tricks," in 1968 the FBI fabricated and distributed a letter to local newspapers. The purported author was a concerned parent of an Oklahoma State University (OSU) student. The letter voiced complaint about the "immoral character" and criminal activities of members of the SDS at OSU and OU. Even thought dissident sentiment was slow to develop in Oklahoma during the 1960s, Vietnam War protests followed the televised announcement of escalation into neighboring Cambodia. As elsewhere throughout troubled academia, the shooting deaths of four students by National Guard troops at Kent State University in Ohio led to a sharp increase in protests.

ZZ. Cross-Tie Walker

On May 4 the OU R.O.T.C. building on the Norman campus suffered minor damage. The Selective Service office in Norman was firebombed with little damage. There was no loss of the draft records that the military-industrial complex needed to fuel the fight that had now reached Cambodia. On May 6, 1970, concerned OU students called for a general strike to support the antiwar movement. Several hundred assembled. One unfurled a Vietcong flag. The protester and the flag were both arrested under Oklahoma state law forbidding the display of a procommunist flag. An angry clash followed. Students and "two busloads" of police joined by thirty-five Oklahoma Highway Patrol officers followed a script that would be repeated from sea to shining sea. Several protesters were injured in the demonstration. Three more were arrested. Nearly two thousand gathered to march in a peaceful protest against the arrest of the flag-bearing student clothed in the protection of the First Amendment. Five hundred demonstrators occupied campus buildings demanding university administrators acknowledge students' rights. Red-faced verbal exchanges led to inconsequential shoving matches. Will Rogers was not smiling. The OU student body voted 3,831 to 3,628 not to boycott classes. By the following week the wave of protest was a small trickle. Only a few students carried picket signs outside campus buildings. Young men, fewer still, burned their draft cards. Disciplinary proceedings were started against seven students for activities during the demonstrations. The wheels had been set in motion. It was a logical and easy next step for the newly implemented dragnet of exorcism to bring Sam in to answer for Alphabetology. Although bringing Alphabetology to task was a foreseeable event, the circumstances were not. One OU administrator, while unable to avoid mixing metaphors, was prophetic, “Once the netting is rigged, why not use it to sweep the streets clean.”

Sam was invited to attend the hearing, so it would not be said he did not have the opportunity to defend himself. Nominal due process was due even the most wayward and subversive. Sam sat for five days while the evidence against the seven Vietnam War protesters was adduced. Sam hated being an afterthought. Finally, Alphabetology took center stage. Those from the days of the inquisition would be proud at the way the “fact finding” was conducted.

An English professor, Marshall Vouchsafe Haynought, limited by his knowledge of Milton and pre-Elizabethan Drama made what served as an opening statement,

“I have read the liturgy and all that passes for the teachings of this blot on all religions, this…”

The word caught in his throat. Eventually he voiced just the right sputter,

“… ‘Alphabetology.’ Sam Thorn is a sad case, surely not one who studies English. He is a young lad who deserves our pity. His writing can appear to be composed exclusively of digressions from an absent center. There are rarely introductory overviews or concluding summaries, and transitions appear interchangeable with non-sequiturs. Puns, jokes, lists, slippery metaphors, and webs of allusions supplant arguments. Sam wrenches nouns into verbs writes, a follower ‘landscapes action.’ Mr. Thorn may have slept through four years of high school English, although the evidence strongly suggests the graduation requirements of his Northern Illinois High School did not require the study of grammar, writing, or the great body of American language literature. This self-proclaimed vanguard of Alphabetology has discovered the Zuider Zee Zchrolls, writings obviously concocted by a nitwit who cannot even spell 'scroll.' Mr. Thorn...

Marshall Vouchsafe Haynought marshaled another pregnant pause before pursing another set of sputters,

"...sustains strings of divergent, perhaps irreconcilable adjectives such that praise can seem inseparable from censure, arriving at a kind of backdoor poetry: not lyrical, or routinely poetic, but original only startling all conventions adopted by the just and the good. Ultimately satire reaches the point of sacrilege. An unwashed heathen strikes cajolery at the heart of that which many have held precious and dear, not just Presbyterians, Methodists, and Baptists, but even, I dare say, Roman Catholics. The sum of the absurd suggests that there is now a rent in the fabric of all that for which we now stand proudly in our joint (and I do not mean that in any sort of drug sense) rule of a silent majority who does not even need to vote to express proper views."

Next came the OU Chancellor. Obviously all this acrimony had upset his normal quiet demeanor. Usually he greeted visitors, smiled, and showed them a tour of the campus. To participate in the trial of seven criminals and of a heretic was not that for which he had on to signed,

"I daresay we are more than troubled, more than shocked. For five days we have heard about students who think that war is a bad thing, not the stuff of which great nations have been formed and now so forged, going forth fashioned, fabricated, and framed ultimately unperturbed by the notions of foment, which have been aroused, incited, and agitated by delusion, deviation and misapprehension of what is agreeable, admirable, and commendable for the gratification of the business of America which is business itself no matter what the actual toll, outlay, or tariff. On this the sixth day, and as the Bible demands on the seventh we must rest, in this case uneasily, uncomfortably and excruciatingly, it is now necessary to retrieve that which has been absconded from hallowed ground. So before this day is over, we will meet and vote for the fate of all eight. Mr. Sam Thorn really needs no more consideration. To do what he has done, to take the Ten Commandments turning them asunder in the lowlands of Northern Europe a place where God intended only tulips and wooden shoes not sacred words, too flippantly, too fast and too loose, to fracture the teachings of Our Savior, to take, to choke, to crush between closed fingers and a clenched fist, the Lord's name, appellation, and by all that he is known, as subterfuge, deception, and underhanded pretext, will cause the great winds that devastated our Great State in the days of the Dust Bowl to again swirl, wail, and cycle to take all that is good from this place where we learn what we need to go forward, hence, and hereafter, to become part of the cogs, spokes, and inner tubes of the wheels of commerce which we all enjoy from the depths of belief, faith, and submission to the one Holy Word, infallible, unceasing, and inalterable. Need I say another word, make another joyful noise, or sing another Psalm? Enough is enough and in this case, too much."

Proving once around the Thesaurus was enough, the Chancellor rested. Now it was Sam's turn. Sam stayed up late the night before. For five days he attended a hearing Judge Roy Bean would admire. "Let's give 'em a fair trial then hang 'em," was the clear design. Sam knew the die had been cast and the bell rang for him. He could roll them bones. After bouncing off the back rail and coming to rest on the house's green felt, this time Sam would only see "snake-eyes" and hear church bells ring behind him as he was blindfolded to walk the plank. Sam decided the best way to defend was to offend. It would be easy to annoy those stuffed shirts that had taken the dais. Sam knew he had been included as a matter of convenience. Why not throw him out, just more scum when the other *enfants terrible* were thrown out with the bath water so sullied? It may not have been a good plan but it was his plan. Sam devised an incorrigible and unyielding scenario, one which would astonish and unnerve those assembled to serve Sam his just desserts. More than humble pie would be set before them. His answer in advance would bring disgust to the haughty. Sam decided the way to ready himself for the mischief he planned was to awaken that morning and one hour before the hour again continued in order to do a hit of mescaline. "Better living through Chemistry" was the now popular quip.

The time had come. Neither the chickens nor the roost were yet anywhere to be seen. Sam stood up. The faculty conference hall was latticed in a combination of artificial light and natural beams from the windows. The two slightly different colors sent pale yellow and light white. Shadows fluttered even though the objects blocking the light were not really moving.

Somehow Sam's words came easily, if not coherently,

"Assembled witch doctors, village idiots, and book urned, sometimes a blimp is a blip is a lip. From that which is large, intractable, and obsolete, tiny notions of challenge ensue. Some voice must then be given to them. Math more than biology leads to the conclusion that mankind is the sum or product of one or more episiotomies. This is some quiet epiphany. As we travel and explore, unless we sit self-satisfied and smug in our own material surroundings, no matter what the cost, we must then ignore these disquieting truths-

1. Perception is not possible without immersion which in turn is not meaningful without depth.
2. Mapping a flat surface is not possible without three dimensional depth
3. The contours of the topology of our everyday existence cannot be rightly navigated without plumbing their depth

I for one, do not need to seek knowledge from the teachers, here and wherever, who seek to impart knowledge from texts devoid of meaning, from models intended only to preserve the status quo. There have many words bandied about today, flung far and wide. I leave you with this one word, 'susurrant.' Susurrant is the condition where a subservient state may only act within itself to govern itself without the ability to take international action independent of the dominant state. That which is susurrant is no longer possible, if it ever really was. You may think you are protecting the American Dream. But the American Dream entails a cost which cannot be calculated or contained. An idea whose time has come, once set in motion, cannot subside, by operation of law or by imposition of the strictures of institutionalized faith, within any borders. That which you do here to the eight of us, that which America does overseas or does at home to those who beg to differ, that which established religions see as their God-given right to smear and to smudge, then eradicate, only exposes a total lack of necessary depth. The present artifices exist only in the thinness of their own sordid veneer. No pomp and circumstance will serve to give depth where none exists."

AAA. The Big One Looked A Lot Like You The Other One Looked Just Like You Too

Needless to say, before sundown on the sixth day, Sam was expelled from OU. For the first time of many times to follow, Sam was a bit player on the broader canvas of someone else's hallucination. The written findings were succinct, "Mr. Samuel Thorn formed a religion and took aggrieved steps in furtherance of that formation (but not in the permitted football sense)..." Like most pioneers for institutions that fall in the category of religious, Sam paid not even a whit of attention to the gravamen of the complaint against him. His own slim consciousness was not sullied with even an iota of substance. The precepts he had declared or unfurled walked on skinny legs. In its report, the Faculty Disciplinary Committee did get to the heart of the matter. It also cited that Sam's congregation consisted almost entirely of underage girls.

Alphabetology was effectively destroyed. Sam was defrocked by fiat of the OU administration. He was not content with the remaining young girls who still believed. What had been the bounty of a seven course meal were now table scraps, few and far between. Once you have seen the bright lights of Paris, you cannot go back to the farm. As before, Sam wandered the land of the lost. Everything had been there for Sam. Yet Sam again missed the point. Sam was mired in the malaise of his own vanity. The desire to be seen as more than you are, driven by how others see you is a waste of time.

Examining your own self-image is even more unprofitable. True ego satisfaction comes only when you are able to shed your ego and throw what is left into the heat and light. Sam had not experienced the "moment." He gleaned no benefit from where he had been. He had never really been there. Even though Sam's religion coursed powerfully from Euripides to Yogi Berra, Sam saw only the shadows on the wall. Once you learn to learn, the rigor is over, doors open to paths which lead to unbundled joy. Sam could not even find the door. Like Fredo in the Godfather movies, Sam was the proverbial second son. He had the expectation of entitlement. Sam wallowed "I'm smart, too." It is the essence of irony. The deficient do not know what they lack. Knowing what they do know, they never yearn to learn. You are never limited by your own capacity. You cannot see beyond by comparing yourself to others with the inherent limitations of your own light. Thus bounded, you will only know what you know, and no more. You ain't gonna learn what you don't want to know.

Constricted by his fall from grace, Sam fell back into an old path. He called Fred to tell him he would be returning to the Sleepy Little Village. The comfort of the carpet of Alphabetology had been pulled from under him. Sam was not repentant. He was discouraged but Fred did not need to know. Sam feigned pride and accomplishment,

"You know Fred, there's nothing which when viewed in the proper context cannot lead the onlooker to the wrong conclusion. Thus I shall make my way through this world in the field of advertising. A wordsmith I shall be. As I decided once before, my career has now been ratified. I am again on the road to find out."

Fred was never one to be deflected from the right path,

“Sam, hurry back. We can get stoned and listen to music. There are plenty of girls here, too.”

“That sounds good as far as it goes, but I now know that there are bigger fish to fry. I am gonna right a book, ’For Whom the Phone Rings.’ Do you think anyone will ever be able to tell who is calling without picking the receiver from its cradle?”

“I think someday we will all be off the hook without lifting a finger, simply by trusting in something bigger than all of us.”

“Fred you know it is easy to play with words and, even more so, ideas. Faith is not all it is cracked up to be. What has happened is all that matters. We are doomed by the past. I am now sure the devil has won in his rebellion with God. He is now sitting on the throne without revealing his true identity to the unwary.”

“’Ratified,’ the word sounds like someone who has rodent to town…”

“Not funny.”

“Sam, by no means am I a wordsmith whatever that is. Quite the opposite, I walk out the door in the morning and I walk back in at the end of the day. What is sandwiched between those two simple steps is the bounty of what is for me. Why waste time thinking about it?”

“Thoughts are the ultimate Trojan Horse. Watch out for Greeks bearing gifts.”

“Not to mention gift horses’ mouths.”

“You will always get lost in reflection. Ramblin’ becomes ramble on.”

“Which brings us to rock and roll. Sam. Led Zeppelin’s ‘Ramble On’ is all you ever need to know, and who knows what that is. Plus I prefer the beauty of a naked girl no matter what nationality. Any bare gift is fine with me.”

“Funny, but that just brings us back to meaningless word play. You can rhyme until the cows come home and never say a thing. Gamble, Bramble, Wamble, Shamble, Scramble…”

“Right, you cannot unscramble an omelet.”

“…Somnable, Postamble, Revelamble, Rebelamble…”

“I get the point. But do you? Plus some of those words aren’t even words, are they?”

“My point exactly. We must keep asking the perennially unanswered questions that plague us, forthwith or with force of all that cannot be said.”

Fred shook his head. Why did Sam not see the steps? He saw only their descriptions. Sam thought he was on a roll but he never fully realized why he was out of kilter. A palpable sense nagged at him unceasingly. “If you look around the table and cannot figure out who is the mark, you are.” Sam was not content in the knowledge that in life you always look up to people but there are always those who look up to you. Perhaps he did not even know it. More likely he wanted everyone to look up to him. This unrealistic aspiration had the inevitable effect of making Sam uncomfortable in his own skin.

Fred knew that some have more, some have less, some things change but you are always only where you are. You cannot be anywhere above or below your own self-assurance limited by imperfection. Satisfaction and happiness depend upon the realization that your place will always be in between the above and below. Even more so, Fred knew that security is an illusion but there is certain strength in the knowledge of your own frailty. Those who seek freedom from all harm in this world create an expectation that will never be achieved. Surrounded by the trappings of a safe port the deluded are saddled with an environment difficult to change or to surmount. For too many, bad music you know is better than good music you do not know. There is a scene in the movie, *Gone With the Wind.* Scarlett O'Hara sits at her vanity. Rhett Butler comes into her room smiling. For the first time, they are both satiated from their togetherness the night before. Their two spirits have finally touched. All is well until Rhett sees the picture of Ashley Wilkes that Scarlett once kept closest to her heart; but she no longer cares about Ashley. The extrinsic new reality fades to black. Rhett cannot lift himself past the "comfort" of his knowledge that, come hell or high water, Scarlett will always love Ashley, even though he is wrong.

Within minutes of his phone call with Fred, Sam's phone rang. The guy on the other end of the line said he was an Assembly of God Minister from Crossett, Arkansas, Jimmy Canker. He had heard about Sam and the demise of Alphabetology. He said he thought Sam had just the right charisma for the 20th century's Charismatic Branch of Christianity, teaching the Pentecostal, evangelical mysteries, and Jesus' spiritual path. Sam said he was not sure that he was the right man. Jimmy asked Sam to think about how he could further the good word-

1. Jesus taught his followers that they would get whatever they prayed for if they had faith.

2. Jesus did faith healing by putting his hands on his believers.

3. Jesus spent all night in prayer.

4. Jesus was full of the Spirit and led by the Spirit, and

5. Jesus could heal people with his clothes.

Sam asked Jimmy whether it was possible to do the second and third things at the same time. Jimmy told Sam he was a very quick learner. Jimmy closed by saying he thought Sam would be particularly good at speaking in tongues. Sam was hooked. So Sam did not return to the Sleepy Little Village that summer. Instead he became a summer intern for Reverend Jimmy Canker in the quest to show the world that preaching the word of Jesus was best suited for television. Strange chickens had come home to roost. Sam was, once again relegated to his status as an expert practitioner of the law of diminishing returns.

BBB. A Score Of Lies They Swore Were True

Nixon's televised address was met in Princeton with an immediate, but measured, response. The word spread like wildfire throughout the campus. Concerned faculty and students were going to meet at the Chapel. Within one-half hour of Nixon's address to the nation, the front half of the Chapel was full with the idealism of the Ivory Tower and youth alike. Approximately 1000 students hovered beneath 10,000 square feet of stained glass. The Princeton Chapel was built to resemble an English Cathedral with a style which reflects both English and French influences. Inside it has a height is 78.5 feet, a width of 93.5 feet, and a length of 249 feet. The Princeton Chapel remains a grand place for a mass meeting.

The speaker everyone would soon be talking about was Mr. Malcolm Diamond, a full tenured professor from the Religion Department. In his latter day inquisition, Sam Thorn had been derogated when the disciplinary committee called him, "Mr." As with Mr. Tucker, the "Mr." added to Malcolm Diamond's name confirmed the elevation of his status. Diamond talked in terms of men of conscience and moral imperative. The throng left the Chapel in a sea of focused energy. "Shine On You Crazy Diamond" was not yet part of the popular lexicon but the description was apt for the impetus given to the concerned. A near consensus was reached in regard to Houseparties. The gravity of the situation demanded that a weekend of parties was out of the question. The sole remaining issue became what was the better way to more properly indicate the moral objection against the immoral war. Should the students and faculty strike against the University or against the Vietnam War? Ivy League semantic hairsplitting is a thing of its own special beauty.

Action gave way to debate sparked by long-learned effete prep school notions of the best way to draw distinctions without a difference. Presumably it was the SDS. The next day, May 1st, the Princeton R.O.T.C. building was firebombed. On May 2d, the Princeton Armory was firebombed. For years, the SDS had been vociferous in its criticism of the administration for allowing the Institute for Defense Analyses ("IDA") to be part of the Campus, even if was really on its curtilage near Prospect Street. The SDS objection was the Institute likely operated euphemistically. Its critics feared IDA was a government think tank cerebrating the best ways to use the instrument of war as a good offense to achieve the best defense for a grateful nation. Whether good or evil, or beyond, IDA had borne the brunt of SDS contempt. The demands for its removal were a cliché. The University raised its own analysis of the issue in its own defense. Princeton merely rented the property to IDA, thereby washing its hands of the whole matter. Had the SDS known then what is generally accepted to be known now, the tenor of criticism leveled at Princeton would have been made those radical hoarse with a different color. There is an acknowledged Princeton facility, The Forrestal Campus. Its location is far from the Princeton Campus proper across Route One, closer to RCA's David Sarnoff Research Center, the Princeton Diner, and the nearest Mecca for Chinese food, "The A Kitchen" and, as such, did not touch and concern the daily activities of undergraduates and most other students. Forrestal was insulated from criticism by the hardcore left simply because the University proudly held it out as a cutting edge facility for advanced research with particle accelerators and other capital intensive scientific research paraphernalia. The CIA's connection to Princeton and its professors was also part of the dialogue of criticism led by the SDS. That which was asserted to be a pure research facility was named after James Forrestal, a man who attended Princeton without graduating. He distinguished himself in the Navy and as a Presidential Cabinet Member. Forrestal was the man who pointed the Navy in the tactical direction of using

air craft carrier task forces. In later life Forrestal was "troubled." In the last days of
his life, he was institutionalized in a Navy hospital. He fell from his hospital room to his death leaving this passage from Sophocles' tragedy Ajax:

> ...Fair Salamis, the billows' roar,
> Wander around thee yet,
> And sailors gaze upon thy shore
> Firm in the Ocean set.
> Thy son is in a foreign clime
> Where Ida feeds her countless flocks,
> Far from thy dear, remembered rocks,
> Worn by the waste of time–
> Comfortless, nameless, hopeless save
> In the dark prospect of the yawning grave....
> Woe to the mother in her close of day,
> Woe to her desolate heart and temples gray,
> When she shall hear
> Her loved one's story whispered in her ear!
> "Woe, woe!' will be the cry–
> No quiet murmur like the tremulous wail
> Of the lone bird, the querulous nightingale...

Over many years, the amount of money Princeton University received from the Federal Government for various projects maintained at the Forrestal project has been a significant boon. There is no doubt the posture of the Princeton Administration and its trustees would be that those dollars were not needed for the protection of an age old campus thereby preserving a conscience of enlightenment. It is quaint and charming to believe that by keeping facilities separate and far apart, the pristine purity of academia is untainted. It is theoretically possible that the salient, perhaps even important, aims of the military-industrial complex could be served. The stated position of the Princeton administration is that no weapons research has ever occurred at Princeton, either on the Forrestal campus or on the main campus. Professor John Wheeler, a man who worked in the physics department for more than 60 years, had a different account. Wheeler was clear. He and other physics researchers used the Palmer Physics Lab on campus for nuclear weapons research in the 1930s and '40s. Wheeler also said that he developed components for the hydrogen bomb on campus at the Forrestal Research Center. Princeton's position would make the CIA proud. Princeton's Vice President and Secretary, Thomas Wright '62, reiterated, to make perfectly clear. He did not know whether any weapons research had been conducted at the University during the 1930s and '40s, but a policy change in 1970 forbade any government-related classified research. This left open the question of nuclear waste. The Palmer Physics building was once directly across Washington Road from the Terrace Club. Nuclear waste in that vicinity could explain the mutated behavior of the members of Terrace.

It is perhaps fair admonishment that IDA and the Forrestal campus were not within the province of any Princeton student, especially if perspective and judgment were germinated and cultivated in a hot bed of the leftist idealism. In 1970, Princeton's ties to the CIA, had they not been "classified," might make the University less circumspect. Initial disclosures about Princeton and the CIA were limited to close ties in three areas: (1) ongoing recruitment (including extensive CIA collaboration with former Dean of Students, William D'O. Lippincott '41 and former Director of Career Services Newell Brown '39); (2) research carried out on the Princeton campus (including the secret MK-ULTRA mind control program); and (3) indubitable institutional ties (several Princeton alumni have served as CIA Director, Deputy Director, or Director of Personnel). Two persons affiliated with the University conducted secret research for the Central Intelligence Agency's MK-Ultra project as early as the 1950s. The controversial project experimented with L.S.D. as a chemical agent to "brainwash." Some involved in the project used volunteers but also used the unsuspecting. The full breadth of the project will never be known because all records were ordered destroyed. Some MK-Ultra records were misfiled to become the subject of Congressional investigation. It is known that many of the West Coast "merry pranksters," Ken Kesey and Robert Hunter, the lyricist for the Grateful Dead, included, were paid to volunteer to ingest L.S.D. at the Palo Alto, California, Veterans Administration Hospital. It is no small irony that students on campuses throughout the United States, Joe Cebellum and his buddies included, were now taking L.S.D. as a tool for learning. Inspired by Huxley and others, acid was a tool for independent enlightenment, not part of a CIA program to test the limits of mind control or brainwashing. MK-Ultra was started by Princeton alumni, Allen W. Dulles on April 13, 1953. The CIA also ran a "covert-op" in Vietnam. William Colby '40, later head of the CIA, was stationed in Vietnam during the War to head the "Phoenix Program." Colby took charge of those covert activities that included infiltration, terrorism, capture, torture, and assassination.

There were also CIA activities involving Princeton Professors who acted as paid "consultants." One professor was glib in denying he was ever "employed" by the CIA, since he was a consultant not an employee. Throughout the 1960s, and possibly longer, at least five Princeton professors worked secretly as high-level consultants for the CIA, according to documents contained in the personal papers of former CIA director Allen W. Dulles. These papers were not disclosed until many years after 1970. The Professors developed data for the "National Board of Estimates." The Board assembled demographic information to determine the number of people in a foreign country who had political beliefs which were not in the interest of the United States and American businesses which operated in that country. The Board also developed estimates to help determine "enemy intention." The Board prepared "Blue books" for each country. Many colleges, including Princeton and other Ivy League schools, use the term "blue book" for the little blue covered booklets with lined pages used for answering final exam questions. The Blue Books of the National Board of Estimates, prepared by Princeton Professors (and professors elsewhere) were considered the highest form of national intelligence. Estimates also covered foreign military capabilities. Princeton consultants were members of committees whose conclusions were sent directly to the White House. One such committee was an interdepartmental panel responsible for overseeing the CIA's high-risk covert-action operations. The Princeton Consultants' work could have served as an intelligence base for the series of brutal and often illegal covert operations of against the democratically elected or constitutional governments of Mohammed Mossadegh in Iran (1953); Patrice Lumumba in the Congo (1961); Joao Goulart in Brazil (1964); Juan Balaguer in the Dominican Republic (1965); Cheddi Jagan in Guyana (1962-66); and Salvador Allende in Chile (1973). Princeton professors were again smug when later queried about their activities. They had no reason to believe the information they assembled was used for any covert purpose. One Professor answered that any such conclusion would be "sheer speculation." A rhetorical question gave the blue book data estimators comfort, "Are these people [the consultants] responsible for the uses to which their estimates are put?"

It also became known that Princeton Consultants operated during a sizable segment (and possibly all) of the Vietnam War. The question arises whether their "estimates" of "enemy intentions" were an input into the CIA's Phoenix Program of torture and assassination, which led to the death, between 1968 and 1972, of some 20,000 Vietnamese citizens.

There was no doubt that, before and after the Invasion of Cambodia, the dissenting college students, such as those in the SDS, felt they were engaged in an open debate in the exercise of the right to Free Speech. Critics of the student movement in those days often made the point that the students did not know what they were talking about. Vigorous debate stands tall and proud much different than the students' one-sided harangue. Those critics were correct. Had the students known what is now known, the discussion would have been very different. It is surely coincidence that those radical knee-jerk responses have been ratified by information unavailable at the time.

CCC. My Strange Heroes Lead Me On

It was not a matter of chance that Joe and "Lemming" Cello missed the Chapel meeting. It was more that the music was too loud than that they were too stoned to notice students scurrying about the campus on the way to the Chapel. James Southdrown did attend, taking down names and making other notes. Cello and Joe were again engaged in that which they did best, letting the music fly. That night they started with some of The Who. The song "Sensation" was a stand out. Center stage was soon captured by The Rolling stones' album, *Beggar's Banquet*. The song, "No Expectations" struck just the right chord. The night ended with the now almost ceremonial blaring of The Beatles, this time *The White Album*, The curtain call, before the two friends went their own way to find a night's sleep, was its own exemplar, a brusque watermark in fine stationary, "Everyone's Got Something to Hide Except for Me and My Monkey."

The next day Joe and John again met to smoke some finger hash. The possibility of a strike to end classes and cancel exams did not seem propitious. Neither "Lemming" Cello nor Joe had sufficient passing grades at mid-terms. That night the issue of which particular large axe loomed over their heads did not interest either as much as a discussion of the inherent deception of the description of events whether as history in the fullness in the passage of time, or as the attempt to put current events in sufficient false light to fool a sufficiency of some of the people some of the time.

"John, the facts are unimportant. It is how what is said, or what is done, that is the only thing that matters."

"So truth is a fairytale for only the littlest babes in the woods."

"Right, the madding throng, or the electorate call them what you will, are little lost sheep with no little Bo Peep in sight. Let me give you a couple of examples, in 1969, Creedence Clearwater Revival sold more records than the Beatles. Their lead singer and lead guitar, John Fogarty was interviewed and said Creedence was 'bigger' than the Beatles. John, Paul, George, and Ringo were not offended. But their following horde took up figurative arms at this gross impertinence. Back some time ago, Spring 1966 maybe, Time Magazine had a cover exclaiming that 'God is Dead.' Did God send even one lightning bolt at Henry Luce or any Time editor? Not as far as we know. But we do know that God's merry men were wounded to their very souls. The outcry from the pulpit was strenuous and unyielding."

"For me God cannot be dead since God was never alive in the first place."

"Yes but public perception, no matter that the public is never in accord, is what matters, not yours. Who knows, even though I sincerely doubt it, there may be a band someday that will be more popular than the Beatles. They will not need to say so. Their tribe of followers will call the tune. It has been many moons that God has been offended by man. Blasphemy rankles the faithful."

"Let us get ready for the Concert tomorrow night. I am not crazy about seeing John Sebastian but I think Seals and Crofts will be interesting. I think I'll play some now. Should we do mescaline for the concert?"

"Nah, let's just get good and ripped. Cello you know what I like?"

"I have a feeling you are going to tell me."

"I like that Rock and Roll Music has intruded onto the Princeton Campus and has overtaken the WASP tradition of Opera and Stuffed Shirt seamless Classical elevator music."

"Be careful of the hordes of Wagner's warriors who will impale you and then deprive you of your private parts."

Cello exhaled then handed to Joe the hash pipe. Joe filled his lungs, held the smoke for one-half the song, "Summer Breeze," and then slowly exhaled. The song ended on a high note. The discussion continued its meander.

"I don't like authority. Not just about music. You do not need to grasp the intricacies of some old dead guys' conceit to enjoy music. Authorities of ideas and words are even worse. If chiseled on some sacred tablet, words must be taken to task. If not so relegated to a presumed body of knowledge, words are tools to be used as playthings, particularly to shine light on the failings of the structures deemed important. Those superficially making rules, and abiding by their own mandate, will necessarily be left out of the whimsy."

"Speaking of being left out, I decided that if you and I roomed together we would be on a hell bound train, or some sort of train wreck we should try to avoid. Anyway, right or wrong, Barry Richardson and Rick Boehm asked me to room with them next year. I said, yes."

"I can stand a single but I prefer the idea of roommates. I will ask Fief and those guys at Pyne what they are doing."

The stereo now blasted Neil Young and Crazy Horse, *Everybody Knows This Is Nowhere*. The song, "Cowgirl in the Sand" prodded much elation. Music was more than balm. It pounded pure ecstasy. Concerts were the icing on the cake. Loud music in the dorm rooms and louder music out dorm windows was everywhere. From Fall of 1969 to Spring, 1970, a real musical awakening fell into the spring of full stride. The first step in the process was rhythm. Did the music you enjoy evoke your mother's heartbeat? Does arrhythmia lead to a love of syncopation? Are there different genetic heart tones? No matter what the genesis, Joe was now praying at the altar of music. The crucible of rhythm forged steadfastly forward, giving a place upon which lead guitar could settle and soar. Music gave Joe an irrepressible positive urge. Many of the uninitiated, not just Southern Baptist ministers felt into the misguided fallacy that black music was the devil's work. For Joe, the problem with classical music and opera was that it had no beat. The appeal of classical music is for the prepubescent and those who wish to remain in some safe harbor that precedes or avoids the discovery of sexual energy. After all is said and done the Southern Christian ministers who wanted to burn all the Beatles albums and ban or ignore black music were right. Whether it is the simple heavy beat of Duke Ellington influenced swing or the repetitive pounding of techno or rap, the bass line is the force that moves the body to ignore the limits of propriety. Rock and Roll practitioners like Neil Young had captured the understanding of this fundamental truth.

The next day Joe discovered that Fief, "Thew," and Fenton were going to room with "Dick" Spinepounds. At the last minute before roommate decisions were to be sent to Dormitory and Food Services, Spinepounds decided that one year of the "Princeton experience" was enough. He asked his hometown girlfriend, Betsy, to marry. Betsy said, "Yes." She would drop out of Ohio State and join Dick at the married housing near campus that Princeton provided. Joe was asked to join to replace Spinepounds.

DDD. Karma To Burn

The silence of the campus was deafening. Everywhere, almost everyone seemed to be holding a collective breath in anticipation of the determination of the steps to be taken to respond to the escalation of the war Nixon had previously promised he was ending. Houseparties had been cancelled. The members of four Clubs who decided to ignore the times that were achangin' kept the celebration close to their chest. The steady girlfriends of those Club members from schools up and down the East coast sighed in collective relief. Their hope of arriving on campus to have that long desired engagement ring appropriately bestowed a few days before graduation was not dashed. Only a tiny fraction of the usual drunken revelry splashed about anywhere. A few drunken preppies sullied all due solemnity with a desecrating wet-clothed knee-deep dance in the Woodrow Wilson School Fountain. The four Clubs that remained open for Houseparties followed their own rules. No blood oaths of allegiance were needed. What needs to be expressly agreed in New Haven is implicitly understood at Princeton. Ivy Club makes Skull and Bones seem like the Y.M.C.A. Those from the Social Register, have no friends, only interests. When all is said and done, there are those with background and breeding which makes them better than their lessers, even those who are well enough off but nevertheless under them. Whether the place is Princeton or is the Sleepy Little Village of Barrington, the special and the blessed stand above mores, strictures, and inconvenience.

The weekend came to its own small conclusion. On May 4, four students were killed by the National Guard at Kent State. On May 6, putting all dangling prepositions aside, the Princeton Student body, as then so constituted, voted to "strike the war." Princeton was now parsing on to victory. An important codicil to the strike was added and accepted by the Princeton administration. No matter what the student's mid-term grades, the political importance of the strike was paramount. All striking students, all men of conscience, were to receive a "Pass." The Dissident's "P" was added to the Gentlemen's C. There was joy in Mudville. There was no doubt. By invading Cambodia, Richard Milhouse Nixon saved Joe's chances for a Princeton diploma. Chance more than merit was the prevailing wind. Joe called to tell his parents he was on his way back home. Joseph wondered out loud whether Joe would be better served taking his exams. Joe assured his dad that taking exams was not a good idea. Joe then headed to Pyne to play some wiffleball. The game was interrupted when Pete Orton appeared with a suitcase in each hand and a large duffle bag slung from his shoulder. He was headed for the Dinky, a man of serious purpose. Joe wished Pete well and suggested the war would be soon over. Pete was sanguine. This was the fourth year he left campus with that thought. Someday, the War would not cast a long, black veil over the nation. The wiffleball game resumed. The song playing, full decibels out the window of the Fief and "Thew" double was The Doors' "When the Music's Over (Turn Out the Lights)." It came to pass that fewer Princeton students took their exams than those who stood on their clubbable principles rather than strike Houseparties. The Princeton campus was a ghost town by the time Townes Van Zandt and Mandrake Memorial played Alexander Hall on May the 8th.

XXV. Too Darn Hot

"If wealth was the inevitable result of hard work and enterprise, every woman in Africa would be a millionaire."

A. Claim on Me

Within ten minutes, Joe knew he was going to enjoy his summer job. The life of a lifeguard at the Barrington Hills Country Club pool was the life for him. Princeton University and the Barrington Hills Country Club were the same despite their many differences. At Princeton, the buildings and the surrounding landscape were much older. At Barrington Hills, the average intelligence was lower. One place was created to be set apart from everyday mundane realities, where the focus was quiet discourse and knowing acquiescence which would allow nurture and development of important efforts to further greater goals. The other was a place where childish games were played for four years in the hope grown men would find maturity to then venture forth to find a place in the slipstream of commerce. Princeton prided itself upon the fact it was a place for the elite, thereby excluding the unworthy. Barrington Hills Country Club stayed the course by assiduously keeping its membership limited to white Anglo-Saxon protestants, excluding all other races, nationalities, and creeds. The traditional *sine qua non* was more than unbridled racism and bigotry. The majority in both institutions fancied themselves lifted by a strong sense of gallantry even though no real adventure was afoot. Both places permitted women but not at the core. Princeton's first One Hundred had yet to climb the walls of tradition to step into sacrosanct chambers. At Barrington Hills, there were two epicenters, the men's locker room and the golf course, men only except Ladies' Day on Tuesday and Sunday afternoon when husband and wife would golf together. Women and children were allowed on the tennis courts and in the pool. Upstairs, women could eat in the restaurant. There was an area where they could also play bridge. An essential and fundamental attribute was shared. Its singular thrust was best framed by Bertrand Russell.

"Advocates of capitalism are very apt to appeal to the sacred principles of liberty, which are embodied in one maxim: The fortunate must not be restrained in the exercise of tyranny over the unfortunate,"

To Joe, none of this mattered a whit as he sat watching the members' little kids splash in the water while their mothers played tennis at the other end of the Clubhouse or while they sat poolside sunning themselves or reading something off somebody's summer list of "must-reads." What Joe had on his mind was Sarah Foreswallow. The plan to extricate himself by gently dropping Sarah was taking longer than he expected. It had been easier to get his Red Cross Water Safety Instructor certification in the pool beneath Dillon gym than to loose himself from Sarah.

B. Coyote

It was an azure, bright summer day. The fresh, light air gave no hint of the sweltering humidity and the oppressive heat sure to come. Joe sat in his red swimming trunks with white stripes on both sides into which the large blue letters, "LIFEGUARD" had been stenciled. He remembered the day of the final test. It was simple and straight forward. First, the easy part, dive to the bottom of the deep end of the pool, under the diving boards and the ten meter platform, over 16 feet of water. While his ears felt the pressure, Joe had to retrieve a thirty pound weigh then bring it to the surface. The hard part was second. An upperclassman volunteered to pretend he was in peril. The final test scenario allowed the rescuer to subdue the victim in a "cross-chest carry." Once the rescuer restrained the drowning man by reaching an arm over his front taking firm hold of the victim by his armpit, the volunteer now had *carte blanche* to use any means to escape. In real life, those who could not swim, thrashing in deep waters, would panic and irrationally attack their would-be rescuers. To get certified, Joe had to save a 6'8" Senior who weighed about 280 pounds. He was not a football player. Joe had never seen him before, except perhaps in some forgotten bad dream. Once in Joe's grasp, the gambit raised both his feet straight up, plummeting both of them about eight feet to the bottom of the pool. Joe realized he would not win any physical struggle. So he merely kept pawn and preserver both at the bottom. Joe could hold his breath longer than the large hireling he held. The kids at Tower Lakes had taught Joe a useful skill. They had dunked him and held him under water for two minutes, then more. It was a rite of passage when he moved from Chicago's Southside at the age of ten, when the water and he were virtual strangers. Whenever the culprit he was about to save feigned panic, Joe raised his own two feet straight up, returning set-up and saver both to the bottom of the pool. Finally, short of breath, choking and sputtering, the over-strong cretin capitulated to rescue. After Joe received confirmation he had passed, he asked the 6'8" nearly three hundred pounds in front of him why he had been so driven to try to drown both of them. Only a Princeton man would find such an answer, particularly when he was still trying to regain normal breathing,

"Responsibility I believe accrues through privilege. People like you and me have an unbelievable amount of privilege and therefore we have a huge amount of responsibility. We live in free societies where we are not afraid of the police; we have extraordinary wealth available to us by global standards. If you have those things, then you have the kind of responsibility that a person does not have if he or she is slaving seventy hours a week to put food on the table; a responsibility at the very least to inform yourself about power. Beyond that, it is a question of whether you believe in moral certainties or not."

Joe shook his head sending water from his hair all around. Joe was pretty sure the big wet baboon was quoting something but he was not sure what.

Scramble

C. Hejira

In the refreshing early summer sun in Barrington, Joe had no doubt Sarah had greater stamina. It was more than the ability he had gained to hold his breath. He was also certain that Sarah would not panic. Joe and Sarah continued to enjoy the way they had learned to stretch their many moments of pure physical bliss together. When Joe called from Princeton to give Sarah the sad news that to say, because of circumstances beyond his control, he was going to miss her Senior Prom, she indulged the fiction. Sarah showed soothing grace, a picture of equipoise. Joe was not sure how Sarah's disappointment would show its face. So far, in the early days of summer, there had not been a trace of resentment or a hint of retribution. If Sarah were not only a serious practitioner of all things Sybaritic, it might have been a different story. It was odd for Joe to admit it, but Sarah's finely honed skills in the sack, or wherever the spirit moved them, were not enough to keep him in the fold, as nice a place of frolic and repose as it was. For some reason Sarah and Joe had yet to find a way to have their connection spill over into the areas of conversation or common interests.

The Barrington Hills Country Club Pool did not open until Memorial Day Weekend. Three weeks before, Joe arrived home from Princeton late in the evening. The next morning, after dropping his mom and dad off at the train, Joe was back in bed. Entitled or not, he was enjoying the deep sleep only the fully innocent deserve. Joe was still groggy when he realized his left ear was favored with light licking. He turned his head. Their lips met briefly.

"I let myself in."

"The front door is never locked."

The past echoed into the present. Sarah and Joe were well onto their way to their own little bit of rapture when the telephone rang. It was the high school attendance office again looking after Sarah. There were no secrets in the Sleepy Little Village. Sarah decided that this time the high school could wait. Two hours later, together in the shower, Joe and Sarah splashed and soaped the sweat off their sated bodies. Sarah toweled off then pulled her wet hair into a pony tail. She kissed Joe goodbye before jumping into her dad's ivory Lincoln Continental to drive to school in time for lunch hour.

Since the revolution was not televised, Joe wanted to see, first hand, the course of local campus protest. Joe drove west to Evanston. He had not been back to Northwestern for two summers, when he was a cherub in the Engineering program. Even then the study of science was ebbing as a possibility. One of the first things Joe did at Princeton was drop Physical Chemistry, leaving the serious sciences in his wake. The class met at 7:40 which alone was good reason to remove it from the schedule he had picked from home when his admissions package had arrived in the mail. 7:40 on paper is one thing, the reality of an early morning class quite another. Moreover, the objective rigors of science with exams and lab requirements did not fit with the *laissez faire* Joe embraced within his first two days on the campus, even before classes started. Back in Evanston, Joe fondly recalled the places Fred and he had wandered with relish. The only difference now was that Sheridan Road, which bordered Northwestern by the West, was a mess. It was a major commuter route. The tall iron fence that lined the campus had been uprooted to form barricades barring traffic in either direction. The French could not have done it better. In addition, the student body voted. Northwestern students were not concerned with striking this or striking that. Half measures were inadequate. Northwestern seceded from the Union. The U.S. Post Office responded in kind. It refused to deliver the mail to the upstart vanguards of protest.

D. The Silky Veils of Ardor

Most of the time before Joe's full time summer job started was spent with Sarah. Joe agreed to open the pool on Mondays for caddy day. It was a good way to earn a few extra bucks. It was also a good way for Sarah to dip her toe into the water.

"Joe, my dad says I should not be wearing my bikini in public. I had to sneak it out of the house under these blue jeans and this yellow blouse."

Joe noticed Sarah's jeans were ironed with a crisp crease, something he had not seen on jeans worn on campus, even by the most fastidious of the first One Hundred. The little rounded collar, front button panel, and cuffs of Sarah's blouse was starched. Style and fashion was another area where Joe and Sarah did not intersect.

"Let me see if I agree with your dad."

Sarah was out of her pants and her top in seconds. She stood before Joe, right foot forward, knee bent slightly. Sarah placed her hands on her hips. She turned a few degrees to the left. For her last move, she pulled her shoulders back. Vince was right. The public at large was not ready for Sarah's bikini. The top had little ruffles which amply covered her chest. There was no doubt that the source of paternal objection was the bikini bottoms. The back did not cover the bottom of Sarah's ass cheeks. The ruffled front did little to hide the triangle between her legs. The fabric did manage to obscure the outline of her pussy lips.

Joe grabbed Sarah's hand. They jumped into the deep end of the pool together. Fifteen caddies were on and off the low dive. Two or three were brave enough to try the high dive. All told, twenty odd caddies filled the pool. Sarah and Joe swam to the shallow end, joining four caddies in the midst of a splash fight. Sarah and Joe stood face to face and moved closer to one another,

“Your dad was right.”

Sarah again gave Joe’s ear her best hush, “I guess you’d better take them off me then.”

Sarah then pulled Joes’ red trunks to his knees. Joe was quick to follow the game plan. He dipped below the surface of the water. Joe grabbed the bottom ruffles with both hands. He pulled them to the pool bottom. Sarah stepped out of her bikini bottoms. Joe held them in his right hand as he again stood to face Sarah. Sarah then gave herself a little lift in the water, wrapped her arms around Joe’s shoulders, clasping her hands behind his head. At the same time she wrapped her legs around Joe’s waist and dropped herself onto Joe’s prick. Somehow not one caddy noticed. They were all too busy enjoying their one day in the rich peoples’ pool.

Joe closed the pool before following Sarah home. Mrs. Foreswallow invited Joe to have dinner with the family. Sarah and Joe then headed out for an ice cream at Baskin-Robbins and a movie. Sarah slid into the front seat. Joe had the underground FM station from Woodstock on the radio. Sarah switched to WLS 89 on the AM dial. Joe winced. Music and drugs were two more areas were Sarah had not yet caught up with Joe. The movie they were about to see at the Catlow Theater in the Sleepy Little Village was “A Man Called Horse” with Richard Harris. As Barrington’s leading (and only) Indian Princess, Sarah agreed with Joe that the movie might be interesting. This movie was an exception to their divergent interests. Joe’s thoughts kept coming back to the same point. It was going to take more than Sarah’s Native American heritage to get them both on the same page in their choice of movies.

E. Song for Sharon

The Franticones were a younger couple who lived on West County Line Road, just east of the Country Club. Both in their thirties, they were among the Club members who threw the wildest and the most wonderful parties. On their small estate, they had a barn. The barn was kept spic and span, spit-shined really. It was used for extravagant, loud carrying on. Music in the barn bounced between a live band and a fully stocked juke box with all the popular hits, current number ones to tried-and-true oldies. Mick Franticone was a handsome ne'er-do-well. He had bootstrapped himself to this rarefied echelon by marrying Ellen Ball, a Muncie, Indiana socialite. The Ball family, made rich by selling canning jars, was really the only family from Muncie in the thin social register for the state of Indiana. Mick knew Joe from the days he shined shoes in the Mens' Locker Room. Mick and Ellen both followed Joe's career as a hometown hero on the basketball hardwoods and the baseball diamond. The Franticones were about to open the summer party season. They asked Joe if he wanted to bartend. This was a really good way to earn a few extra bucks. Plus they needed another bartender. Joe was happy to get Fred to join the fray.

The Franticones had two little kids. Plus they were happy to provide a place in the main house for the children of everyone they invited. They needed two girls to tend the children. Sarah Foreswallow and Terry Touche, a Senior girl everyone knew well, were both glad to help out.

Joe and Fred stood behind the bar. The music was blasting. Forty people were alive with drink. Heavy drinking was the order of the night even though there was a big Golf Calcutta the next day at the Club. The Franticone's party had started that Friday night after the Calcutta auction in the Mens' Locker Room. Twenty people were dancing.

A tall blonde with long, straight shoulder length hair walked with purpose straight to Joe. Her name was Cecelia Odewon. Joe had coveted her since the first day he caddied at the Club, all the way back to the sixth grade. In those days, while he waited for an assignment or for his foursome to go out, Joe would sit high up the staircase that nobody used, steps that led to the kitchen in the Clubhouse. Looking over the top of the pop machine, Joe could watch Cecelia play tennis. And watch he did. Cecelia had long slender legs, small hips that flowed to a tiny waist. Her square, athletic shoulders framed her high breasts. She played tennis without a bra. Her taut, C-cup breasts somehow maintained appropriate contact with her chest. It was Cecelia's face that most drew Joe's attention. She had light green eyes. Their color was the stuff of song and poem. Her long thin nose came to a ski-jump point. Her cheek bones and chin shone patrician simplicity. Her mouth was formed by subtle, thin lips. She was ready with just the right hint of smirk needed to emphasize a quiet understatement that somehow nevertheless said, "Let's go." If Grace Kelly ever wanted to switch faces, this was the face she would pick. Joe had no doubt the story was true when the assistant golf pro told him Cecelia Odewon was a Northwestern sorority queen.

As Cecilia was three steps from Joe, she made eye contact. Her hips were in free sashay as her lips slipped past their usual restraint. Joe was unnerved. He had to look down and away. He was beginning to think Cecelia could read his mind. She reached the front of the bar. Her light pink cashmere sweater was perfect for the cool May evening. Her blue chinos strained only at her hips.

"What ma'am may I get for you..."

Joe was sure her smile now turned salacious.

"...to drink?"

"Do the Franticones let the bartenders dance?"

Joe looked at Fred with wide eyes, "I don't see why not. Right now we are not too busy."

Fred nodded with a smirk. "Don't worry Joe, I can hold down the fort."

F. One Day I Walk

Cecelia held out her hand to lead Joe to the well-waxed shiny squares of latticed wood. As they reached the edge of the dancing area, Joe looked to down to watch his step. The alternating tan and mahogany rectangles within each square were not what captured his attention. The band was on break. The next record from the jukebox was a slow song, actually one of the worst songs ever pressed to vinyl, The Brooklyn Bridge, “The Worst that Could Happen.”

Almost before they started dancing, Cecelia moved close to Joe. She stood on her toes to whisper in his ear as she rubbed her breast into his chest. She pushed her left hip into his crotch. Joe decided if this was the worst that could happen he could not wait for the next thing.

“Is your back o.k.?”

Joe turned to whisper back. It was now really a lost battle to keep a proper distance.

“My back?”

“Yes I was wondering if your back is healing.”
“I don’t think it’s been hurt.”

“Last night, you know, where I dug my fingernails deep into your back as I climaxed.”

"I think you have mistaken me for someone else."

Cecelia left the space near Joe's ear. She kept her breasts and hip in contact. Her green eyes almost made him melt. She smiled with pursed lips which did not open as she spoke,

"I don't think so."

Cecelia took Joe's hand then led him out of the barn. There was a field next to the main house on the other side of the area where everyone parked their cars. When they walked into the middle of the field, Cecelia continued her direct approach,

"Lay me down in the tall grass and let me do my stuff."

Later that night Cameron Odewon, Cecelia's husband asked Joe to fix him a stiff vodka tonic. Joe was not a seasoned mixologist. He should not have been concerned about the interlude with Cameron's wife. Odewon, as always, had spent the evening with his golfing buddies while they regaled one and another with stories they had all heard before. Nevertheless Joe was embarrassed. He feared Cameron suspected. Distracted, he mixed a new drink- half vodka and half gin, a little more potency than Carl actually wanted. Odewon and C.O. Race were the favorites to win the Calcutta. They had gone at auction for high six figures. It was late in the evening so Cameron Odewon finished the drink in a flash. The next day he barely made it through the front nine. His round ended abruptly as he vomited capaciously in a sand trap at the ninth green.

G. Ladies Love Outlaws

While Cameron was unaware and uncaring, Sarah sensed the non-existent scratch marks on Joe's back. She had not seen Joe and Cecelia in the field. Sarah was not prescient. There are other tell tale indications. Joe drove Sarah home after they parked at Bateman Circle. On the way there before they fucked, Sarah sucked Joe's cock. He kept his eyes on the road and his hands upon the wheel. On the way back, Sarah massaged Joe's crotch through his pants,

"Joe, you know, this is the second time now. The first was when you came back to town and we had sex at the Shaunton's at the second annual banister party. I like the taste of another woman's pussy when I slurp your penis dry. Put your prick wherever you want, I promise you, I will lick it clean."

To extricate or not to extricate, there seemed to be no end in sight. Sarah agreed to water the plants and feed the pets at the Bastions for the week before Memorial Day while they were away. Each afternoon, into the evening, Sarah and Joe took full advantage of the empty house. They would start in Prince's bed, sixty-nine, sweat and shower. As cool water cascaded around them, they would fuck standing up. Sarah clenched passionately but did not use her nails. Joe's back was unblemished as he started work at the pool. The regimen had its own independent force, sixty-nine until frothing a full lather of sweat, then sex in the shower. Repeat as was necessary, until Joe's weak knees and rubber legs could not support Sarah. The position that evolved from standing in the pool's buoyant water required more strength than, at the end of the day, Joe could summon, even with Sarah's legs wrapped around him, her hands clasped behind his head.

H. The Tenth World

Joe stood at the edge of the Barrington Hills Country Club pool. He was awakened from his review of the events before his first day of work. A good lifeguard could scan the pool and still indulge in reverie or fantasy. Joe was beginning to wonder whether he was living a life where those two worlds met. Now to his right appeared Cecelia Odewon. She was wearing a two-piece with pink and white hound's-tooth checks. It was more modest than a bikini.

"Now this is a surprise."

Joe returned his eyes to the pool,

"Why, whatever do you mean, Mrs. Odewon?"

"Please call me Ce Ce. I never did catch your name."

"Joe Cebellum. I will be your lifeguard this summer. I look forward to giving swimming lesson to your daughter and two younger sons. Your oldest should be ready for swim team. And your boys, one for intermediate class and one for beginners."

Ce Ce held a book up to her chest. It was *The Sensuous Woman* by "J."

"I did not realize that my life was an open book. I think I'll go find one of those chaise lounges by the kiddy pool. If you get a break, come over. You might be able to help me get through some of the parts of this book I don't quite get."

Joe wondered whether Ce Ce was the "J" who wrote the book.

"I am sure you will have no trouble deciphering, since you are a happily married woman."

"I could read some of it to you to see what happens."

In the weeks that followed, Ce Ce read to Joe whenever he was on a break. The first day no other adult was at the pool, so Ce Ce reveled in reading *The Sensuous Woman* aloud to Joe. She continued the book on other days when she was the only woman at the pool. Joe could stand near her and watch the kids. He also had to watch his bathing trunks. Sometimes he could not adjust them to hide how his interest was piqued.

When some other women were poolside, Ce Ce would pull another book out of her beach bag. If someone else was listening, she always started the same way,

"Joe you are a student radical from one of those liberal Ivy League schools. In the unlikely event you are able to watch the pool and listen at the same time, what do you think of this?"

Some of the passages Ce Ce read were thought provoking, especially from the mouth of a sorority queen who lived in the lap of luxury,

"Yes, there's sense in that. But the suddenly rich are on a level with any of us nowadays. Money buys position at once. I don't say that it isn't all right. The world generally knows what it's about, and knows how to drive a bargain. I dare say that it makes the new rich pay too much. But there's no doubt but money is to the fore now. It is the romance, the poetry of our age. It's the thing that chiefly strikes the imagination. The Englishmen who come here are more curious about the great new millionaires than about anyone else, and they respect them more. It's all very well. I don't complain of it," William Dean Howells, The Rise of Silas Lapham

"I've never understood it,' continued Wilfred Carr, yawning. 'It's not in my line at all; I never had enough money for my own wants, let alone for two. Perhaps if I were as rich as you or Croesus I might regard it differently.'

There was just sufficient meaning in the latter part of the remark for his cousin to forbear to reply to it. He continued to gaze out of the window and to smoke slowly.

'Not being as rich as Croesus - or you,' resumed Carr, regarding him from beneath lowered lids, 'I paddle my own canoe down the stream of Time, and, tying it to my friends' doorposts, go in to eat their dinners.' W.W. Jacobs, The Monkey's Paw and Other Tales of Mystery and Macabre

"Why are you not smarter? It's only the rich who can't afford to be smart. They're compromised. They got locked years ago into privilege. They have to protect their belongings. No one is meaner than the rich. Trust me. But they have to follow the rules of their shitty civilised world. They declare war, they have honour, and they can't leave. But you two. We three. We're free." Michael Ondaatje, The English Patient

I. Paprika Plain

Working at the country club was not entirely a bed of roses. The little rich brats at Barrington Hills were worse than he imagined that some of his privileged pampered preppy Princeton classmates were at the same age. Discipline and order were not the rule of the day. Blowing the whistle did little. Timing the kid out until the end of the next rest period usually helped, if only because the malefactor had to stay out of the pool. Joe narrowly avoided trouble one day. One of the kids was proud to take a shit right in the middle of boys' locker room floor. Joe determined which little fuck it was. He grabbed the annoying twerp, a scrawny ten year old named, Ben Veldon. Joe turned him upside down, grabbed him by his legs and stuffed him head first into a large wire mesh wastebasket by the snack bar. Ben turned red with embarrassment, from the ketchup in his hair, and from blood where the metal diamonds dug into his back. Ben's mother was playing tennis. Alerted by his older brother, the eleven year old Will, Marcia Veldon came charging over to the pool, waving her finger.

"This will be your last day working here, young man."

Marcia's finger was now directly in Joe's face.

"Mrs. Veldon, would you be so kind as to follow me to the Boys' Locker Room."

Joe pointed to the pile of crap between two benches, "This belonged to your son."

Joe was given a warning not to again use force on the members' children.

J. Jericho

Finally providence struck. Her name was Jen Quenaciendo. She and Patricia Von Pattersfeet had just finished their Freshman year at Barrington High making her a full five years younger. Joe played basketball with her brother, Brant. When Joe first saw her, she was still in Junior High School, an awkward ugly duckling to be sure. Jen had turned the corner. She now glided with the indubitable beauty of a swan. The Beatles song, "I Saw Her Standing There" starts with the lyric, "She was just seventeen if you know what I mean." Jen and Patricia had two years to go to reach that age when they would still be jail-bait.

Sarah Foreswallow seethed dark sensuality. Jen Quenaciendo oozed white heat. The two girls were even better than Alfred Hitchcock's best display of counterpoised black and white objects of desire. An enticing approach-approach conflict, Sarah and Jen would send even the most virtuous man, beyond full bristle, into a doozy tailspin. Joe would soon be waving the white flag. With Sarah alone, he was in over his head, in spades.

Jen was an alabaster queen with whom Joe would soon be happy to be in foolsmate. She had blonde hair. Thin, straight strands of gold flowed below her shoulders, down her back. The round whites of her eyes encircled sky blue centers. Her eyes beckoned with a glint, an entreaty of pure innocence. Jen had full red lips. Her smile matched her eyes' sly invitation. Pale peach skin covered her fine porcelain features. Jen was tall, 5'10" with proportionate long legs. Her round behind flowed to curved hips. Jen's hips met a slender waist which then pleasantly burgeoned to her torso. Her large oval breasts formed a full cantilever from her upper chest. With broad shoulders, Jen maintained a sense of perpendicular independence. She moved showing only self-assuredness. Jen was a primer in royal bearing.

Fred, everyman's knight errant, joined Joe's footsteps with Jen's best friend, Patricia Von Pattersfeet. In time, Fred would go on to blaze a trail all his own. Spending time with Fred made double dating even more appealing. The two sets of best friends were happy whatever they were doing. Most often they collected themselves in the downstairs library at the Von Pattersfeets. Two bookends met two bookends. The stereo was always playing loud. The summer of 1970 cast a musical spell. *Let it Be*, The Beatles' denouement, was released on May 8th. Joe and Fred did not hear it until that summer. At first they were not on board. As Patricia played the record again and again, the simple songs soon carved a niche, making their own bittersweet indelible impression. Two days after Flag Day, June 14th, Patricia unwrapped *Workingman's Dead*. Once again Joe and Fred were not impressed. Soon, however, the songs stuck. The summer also spawned "live" recordings to remember, The Who *Live at Leeds*, *Live Cream*, The Doors *Absolutely Live*, Joe Cocker's *Mad Dogs and Englishmen*, and Hot Tuna's first release. They all glistened from the loudspeakers in opposite corners of the Von Pattersfeet's wall-to-wall built-in oak bookcase. Fred and Joe would argue which music was the best. Patricia or Jen would turn up the volume. Then the two would ride the music. No dope was needed.

The parade of records continued through the summer, exploring the depths and stretching the borders of rock and roll. Creedence released *Cosmo's Factory*. Traffic let loose with their swansong, *John Barleycorn Must Die*. Then there were The Moody Blues' *A Question of Balance*, The Band, *Stage Fright*, Neil Young's *After the Gold Rush*, and Eric Clapton's self-titled first solo record. England added to the patchwork quilt of folk rock with Fotheringay. With the release of the self-titled *Poco* and The Flying Burrito Brothers' *Burrito Deluxe*, a new branch, country rock, but definitely rock, settled into the midst of the studied chaos. Rock and roll was here to stay. Outside the Von Pattersfeet basement, The Who presented its "rock-opera" Tommy at the New York City Metropolitan House. For the first time that holy place of arias opened its arms to electronically amplified inanity. Woodstock was reprised in England at the Isle of Wight. Jimi Hendrix, The Moody Blues, The Who, The Doors, Jethro Tull, Joni Mitchell, and Ten Years After all appeared in full blossom.

K. Jenny Lynn

Joe enjoyed Jen's bright and shiny company. Jen kept Joe within her virgin boundaries. Joe and Fred each kept other irons in the fire. Fred spent many a late evening well into the wee hours with Sarah in the back seat of her father's Continental parked in front of the Cebellum's. In the beginning of the summer, the insatiable Sarah would often first wind herself up with Joe. As summer lingered, Joe was able to finally cut the cord. It was an exercise more difficult than trying to solve the Gordian knot. Joe did not realize that the same simple surgical exigency solved both quandaries. By the time he headed back to school towards the end of the summer, Joe was unencumbered. Sarah was gone by way of the force of his own extrication, Jen from his simple lack of serious commitment.

In the meantime, for Patricia, Fred, Jen, and Joe summer was getting hotter and hotter. Heat and humidity could be mollified in many ways. As the heat of the summer of 1970 dragged on, cool water invited skinny dipping. Relaxed standards led to even more relaxed standards. After a soothing dip in a dark lake, the four would take a ride in Fred's convertible Camaro. At 120 mph with the top down, there was a free, cool breeze that no amount of heat could overwhelm. To divert attention from any long, hot summer, music would serve to run the gamut from giving a small pool of relief to a full sea of joy. The summer of 1970 was no exception. Again and again, whether from tiny reservoirs or great oceans, Joe dipped his toe into waters that lapped gracefully onto the shores of his consciousness. After reluctantly pulling the plug on Sarah and her reign of free love, Joe spent most of his time that summer working at the pool and running around with Jen, Patricia, and Fred, Time is interesting. It is a commodity that cannot be traded. It is fungible yet unique. Sometimes you have too much, sometimes not enough. Joe always adopted the idea that it was best to keep busy. Quality was a wasted goal, if idle moments resulted. What you did carried more weight than with whom you did it. It was how not what or who.

L. Hobo's Mandolin

Joe always enjoyed seeing Sally Sensabell. Her dad had a grey-white Karmann Ghia convertible. This Volkswagen was just a small sliver slicing into the American market. Joe and Sally enjoyed a peek into what would soon be an avalanche of foreign cars. In the evenings, it was fun to drive and talk. With the top down, the rushing air formed the contour of a cocoon of privacy. The radio was broken so the two longtime friends sat ear to ear. The words flowed. One night they drove to the movie theater in Elgin to see one of the worst movies in the history of cinema, *Myra Breckinridge*. It was disturbing that the best acting, to use that term loosely, was by the lightweight movie critic, Rex Reed. Both Raquel Welch and Mae West stayed true to form, one dimensional caricatures of sex objects, now and haggard.

"Joe, from what you are telling me, and what I know about you, Princeton is one of the worst places you could ever be. Listen to this. There are so many beautiful girls at Southern Cal. When the television show, *The Dating Game* needs girls to sit in those tall chairs to be picked by some eligible guy, the director calls any sorority. He asks for volunteers. A casting call with no screening needed."

"Sally, plus the beach is nearby so I am sure there are bikinis galore. I am sure your male-female ratio is much healthier. If I had to do it all over again, I would skip over U.S.C. and go right to heaven on earth. At the University of Florida in Gainesville, the girls wear their bathing suits to classes. Let me switch the subject. I'd like to tell you something interesting. I know I can trust your discretion. My dad will soon be traveling to Russia on business. The polyethylene wrap his company manufactures is part of a small exemption to the cold war mutual trade embargo. Oil is as important there as it is here. He was serious, almost solemn. He sat the whole family down to tell us about it. He was emphatic. He almost seemed scared. My dad said that no one was to speak a word about where he was or what he was doing. He is afraid that the conservatives will paint ugly messages on the white siding of our house, or worse."

"I will not say a word. I promise. On the good side, this could be a first step that will lead to the end of the cold war then lead to world peace in our time. No more wars of any kind, ever again."

"I am not going to hold my breath."

M. Furry Sings the Blues

Joe did not see Felina until the month of August. Felina was having a difficult time with her mother, Ethel. Her drinking had become an epidemic problem. Ethel would wake up only to pass out. Her waking time was spent mumbling incoherently. She was a Lady Macbeth whose best lines were gibberish. Felina knew her mother was deeply troubled but she never knew what her mother was trying to say. Now Felina cooked, cleaned, and did the laundry. The ghost of her father did not haunt her. Felina had long ago put behind her any guilt for his strange death. While her mother walked an uneasy sleep with ineradicable blood on her hands, Felina stayed the course. She had returned from college to find her mother living in disarray. Her younger brother, Scottie, had moved out. He was now living in Toronto with their older sister. All the rooms in the house were a dirty, dusty mess. The kitchen was worse. It was filled with dirty dishes each its own little biology experiment. The garbage was fecund. Her mother wore the same clothes for days on end. Felina toiled like Cinderella. Felina's mother managed to maintain a strange hold over her. Felina was doing everything to help her mother. The one who was ineffectual held the reins. When her mother would briefly arise from her alcohol induced stupor, she invariably took brush in hand to swipe Felina's bangs from her forehead, or Ethel would tell Felina that her blouse was coming out of the back of her skirt. The mother-daughter dance of the ages reared its ugly head. Ethel was still able to touch a chord to mar Felina's inner child. Felina knew the motivation was maternal love. Felina could not help but feel that the message was she did not meet her mother's approval. None of this made any sense, given Ethel's clear debility. Nevertheless, old patterns of behavior die hard.

“Joe, I am so relieved you have called. I am sorry I have been only able to spend time on the phone with you.”

“Felina, I love our long phone calls, but enough is enough. I have two tickets for Janis Joplin at Ravinia. You are going with me, no ifs, ands, or buts.”

Felina did not recognize the feeling, but she was being asked to the ball. Relief turned to the excitement of anticipation. No matter the clock would strike twelve.

“Joe. Let’s do it.”

On the evening of August 4th, Joe and Felina drove to Ravinia, an outdoor venue. Ravinia is the summer home of the Chicago Symphony. The orchestra performs under a roofed Pavilion on a stage. Full covered seating gives way to a huge lawn with only the sky above. The Ravinia Festival always adds other musical events. In the summer of 1970, rock and roll was the major ingredient in the Festival menu.
The folks with general admission tickets always turn the lawn area into a large, elegant picnic. Large blankets are surrounded by baskets of food and coolers of white wine or beer. Many other music-goers add to the elegance with French red wine. Some turn it up a notch from there by centering candelabras on their picnic blankets. Only an impressionist could have enhanced the picture. Well-amplified music creates an aura which makes attending Ravinia a mid-summer’s night dream.

That night, it did not matter that the heat and humidity stifled even the most enterprising mosquito. The setting and the music created the illusion of an ebullience which somehow expelled the blister and the muggy smarm of a dog day’s night. Joe and Felina added their own sense of proportion. They lit up a joint. Janis Joplin belted the blues through the saturated stagnant air. The grainy dust in her voice moved the crowd down the road. One song after another lifted the mood. “Down on Me,” “Cry, Baby,” “Piece of My Heart,”

“Try (Just a Little Bit Harder),” “Ball and Chain,” “Get It While You Can,” “Bye, Bye Baby,” “Move Over,” and “Me and Bobby McGee.” Nobody knew this would be the alpha and omega of her greatest hits. Janis Joplin would not live out the year. One of her last encores was perfect, the song, “Summertime.” Her voice gave gravelly and gravely contradiction to the smooth Gershwin lyric. The still night swelter was left in her wake. Hot as it was, Joe and Felina secured their comfort wrapped in a blanket. The darkness of the night obscured the movement of their bodies and hid the clothes they had discarded to the side. One of the anomalies of human sexuality is that Felina and Joe did not wilt under the covers.

N. A Strange Boy

In June and July, Joe and Fred met at North Park, home of Barrington's Little League. Together they were coaching a minor league team, the eight and nine year old kids still learning the game. One practice and two games a week compassed their *bona fide* labor of love. The team Fred and Joe coached finished with the worst record last season. When this season ended, they had captured the minor league championship. On the field of battle, their team running on all nine cylinders, the sun gathered in a bright spotlight. Fred was sure that in those moments, with only a backstop added to the playing field, there was no better showcase. Big League Baseball sets grand stages with state-of-the-art, stunning artificial illumination which beams down from the prolific and massive artificial lights arrayed high upon large stanchions. In the eye of the mind of Fred Etheridge, Major League Parks, like the two most recently opened, Riverfront Stadium for the Cincinnati Reds and Three Rivers Stadium for the Pittsburg Pirates, were bigger but not better. It was not only that their minor leaguers finished in first place. Fred and Joe experienced the truth that passion and duty together make grace. Joe decided that they would run the team in the opposite way little league teams were traditionally coached. The rule was that every kid on the team had to play two innings or more. The worst kids sat on the bench until late in the game. Thus, they were marked as "benchwarmers," a term worse than incompetents. Fred and Joe flipped standard practice on its head. They started their worst players then replaced them after two or three innings. This vote of confidence produced remarkable effects. In the beginning, the parents of the better kids would yell from the stands complaining that Joe and Fred had no idea what they were doing, leaving the best players on the bench. The Little League mothers were soon silenced.

Mitch, the shortstop was a case in point. During practices, Mitch would try to field 100 or more groundballs. Not one time would he both cleanly field and accurately throw. In the games, however, on the field of battle he was buoyed by the confidence of being a "starter." In sixteen chances, he did not make one error. Fred would always smile and shake his head. The impossible was happening over and over again.

July 2nd was the hottest day of the year. It had been 108 degrees in the shade. The night did not offer relief. Fred and Joe again fielded their new group of winners. This time they soundly beat a team that featured one of the sons of Mr. Key, Joe's 8th grade principal.

"Congratulations, Joe. Fred and you have done a wonderful job with your kids. Quite an accomplishment. I saw most of those kids play last year. Miracles can happen."

"Thanks, Mr. Key."

"Joe, it has been over five years. I think it is now safe to admit that you are the one who tied the flagpole line to Mr. Cubley's bumper."

"Principal Key, that is something I will never admit."

They both smiled.

O. Black Magic Gun

After the championship game, Joe and Fred bathed in the lavish praise given by their kids' parents and many of the parents of the opposing team. Accolades are nice but poker is better. Fred and Joe headed to Camphors to play with, Tim, "Ma," and Fred's brother, Fanta.

"Fred, I just bought an ounce of Kansas homegrown from Warren Harbinger. He says it was grown along some river from hemp originally planted on the banks of a navigable waterway by the Army Corps of Engineers. Warren says who knows who figured out a way to re-pollinate the plants by adding a few female plants. Five bucks seems like a lot to spend on a bag of dope, but Warren says it will knock our socks off..."

"So stop talking, light it up, and pass me the pipe."

Fred and Joe were ripped. Fred pulled to a smooth stop in front of the Camphors. Joe's front door opened to the sidewalk to the step up to the front porch door.

"Whose Harley is that, Fred?"

"A friend of Laura Camphor. Her name is Kathy Harden."

When the game ended, Kathy was still there. One nice thing about working as a life guard is that, when there are no lessons, the pool opens at 1 p.m. Joe walked to the Etheridge driveway on Lageschulte Drive. He got into his car, turned right on Lake and followed Kathy home. She was twenty-two years old. Joe was not sure whether her sex drive was something she always had or whether the large motorcycle engine vibrating between her legs was the thing that really got her going. Kathy worked the second shift at the phone company. Joe went straight to the pool the next day, without sleep. It was a Friday. Joe had every other Saturday and Sunday off. This was one of those weekends. That Friday night Joe headed straight home to catch up on his sleep. Saturday afternoon came early. Fred was shaking him in his bed.

"Get up you lazy fuck."

Joe looked at the clock,

"4:15. I guess so."

"I have an idea. Chris Shaunton says he has some really good synthetic mescaline. He says he got it from his older brother, you know the guy who promotes rock and roll concerts in South America, mostly Brazil. Prince Bastion is with Shaunton."

"Let's do it."

Two hours later, Prince Bastion was weaving in his seat. Chris, Joe, and Fred, swayed with his motion. The room was still but they might have been on the ocean with gentle rolling waves.

"I liked the radical atmosphere at Shimer College, but I have decided the liberal arts curriculum is not for me. I have enrolled at the Boulder, the University of Colorado. I am going to study agribusiness. I want to help underdeveloped countries all over the world."

Chris Shaunton got up to turn up the stereo. The speakers crackled Eric Clapton's guitar, pounded Jack Bruce's bass, and rang Ginger Baker's cymbals. The song was the long version of the Willie Dixon blues classic,

"Spoonful," performed live at the Fillmore West. In the middle of the Shaunton living room coffee table was a large yellow wax candle which had been made in the form of indiscriminately shaped undulations.

"Wait 'til you see this."

Chris Shaunton let the candle's very thick wick. In five minutes all four boys were transfixed by the standing waves of light from the strobe candle. Nobody said a word for the next twenty minutes. They had been served an eternity of sight and sound. Cream played "Spoonful." The rhythm matched, note for note, beat for beat, the waves of light that formed rigorous patterns. It all filled the living room in a way no interior decorator ever imagined. The music finally stopped.

Fred was the first to speak,

"I know this song. It ain't never gonna end."

P. Talk to Me

For Sam the summer shaped up quite differently. His love of music took a temporary back seat. Crossett, Arkansas was more than a horse of a different color- more than a small town where everyone knew your name. The pride of Crossett and the nearby town of Hamburg was Barry Switzer. He was an Assistant Football coach at the University of Oklahoma. He brought the "Wishbone" offense to college football. It was ironic that Barry's life fell more into the category if wishes were horses, beggars would ride. It was more than that his dad committed suicide. His mother eked out a living from her trailer. The poverty, black and white in Southern Arkansas, caused a theological bent quite different from that which was preached from the pulpits in communities overflowing with God's grace like the Sleepy Little Village. Crossett was blessed with a village idiot, a town drunk, and the local whore. It was a small town peopled with Opie, Aunt Bea, Andy, Barney, Gomer, and Goober. Ladies night at the bowling alley ended at the Holiday Inn. It was a "dry" county. So the bowlers were "members" of a club that bore a strange resemblance to a neighborhood bar. Membership has its privileges, in this case, the right to consume alcohol. The bartender, Zeke, knew the sexual proclivities of every bowler, married or not. Business men staying at the Holiday Inn could also buy a "membership." Traveling salesmen were happy to hear Zeke's recommendations and warnings. The hypocrisy of faith-based Christians has its own special affectations. Restaurants had skinny cardboard partitions- on one side sat the teetotalers, on the other side, the loud drunks, having paid one thin dollar for admission to a club where they could buy an empty glass into which they could pour booze they owned which was kept in a cupboard or behind the bar.

The here and now for the faithful poor is quite different from that experienced by the "haves." Doctrine dictates the "world" is a place where Jesus says the members of the church, his bride, must separate themselves- since the devil is all that is there. The reward of heaven is all the Numismatic, Charismatic, spirit-filled, baptized have. There is no bounty here. The "world" must be kept at arm's length. The unfortunate "withouts" have never felt the light of God's grace. The actualization of the Holy Spirit has not covered them with material wealth. The present is a nightmare only the Pentecost will reverse when Jesus returns to take his flock to sit as his side near the throne. The race is on for poor Christians. For what seems to be an eternity, they are coming up the backstretch evermore behind.

For Sam, the end came sooner than prophesy could foresee. The full summer had been spent reading scripture and learning to comfort the devout, reassuring them that Jesus was coming soon. Sam knew all the best words to describe all that is holy. It was now the end of August, still hotter than a pistol. The temperature of 93 almost matched the 95% humidity. The pine trees stood still in the heat. The only real movement in the air was when one of Georgia Pacific's lumber trucks whisked its way down the road. All timber rights, for miles and miles around, had long been owned by that large company.

"Sam, I know it sounds like it should be the other way around, isn't that often the way it often is now that the good Lord has left the world in the Devil's hands. But we can cool off in a steam bath."

Sam and his new mentor, Jimmy Canker, sat on the slats of a wooden bench. They were naked but for the towels that covered their laps.

"Sam, I think you are ready to guide the flock. Let us see where we should take you, where the Holy Spirit will move you. Our God-given vigilance is part of a man's better instincts. The male of the species is always on the look-out. We act as sensors, for any slight movement, for any slight sound, for any deviation from our immediate surroundings. We tingle with the readiness the good Lord has given us. Deep down in our souls, to the very essence of our nature, all the way into our bones, so to speak…"

Sam did not notice. Jimmy had one hand under his towel which now formed a tiny tent.

"…waiting to sense the approach of danger or the nearnesss of a woman, which are really the same thing. The Bible warns us over and over that women will lead even a good man down the path where all is lost. There is a reason we preach that women should not wear make-up, fancy clothes, or jewelry. Women should never reveal their bodies. In the days of the book of Genesis, the book from the Apocrypha, 'Enoch,' tells us how the angels came down to fornicate with women. Women must wear head covering to hide from the angels. No part of a women's body should ever make a suggestion. Think if an angel can be enticed to fly down from the celestial, how mere mortal men are affected?"

Sam was leaning back, his eyes closed, listening. Jimmy's tent was now rising and falling as he spoke with stroke of the power all women held over all men, angels and mortals alike.

"Know this Sam, we are in the midst of the devil's music. We must close our ears. It does not matter whether it is the country blues, the simple sounds from the cotton fields or jazz, that urban music which delights in the sounds of evil from the city streets. Since unsuspecting white boys and girls fall prey, rock and roll is worse. It is the blues emanating from some Godless garage. Even rhythm and blues is an unwanted bastard- thrown out of the churches for improper conduct in the choir loft, caught when the errant think that nobody is looking. But praise there be. The Good Lord is ever present. Time should not be used to meter music. The passage of time only distracts the faithful from the true articles of faith. Is time a useful commodity? I can only say this. Sometimes it is, sometimes it isn't."

Jimmy had dropped the artifice of his towel to the floor. He was on his knees at Sam's feet. Sam was suddenly vigilant, perched to alight, all alarm bells ringing.

"Sam, let me show you the miracle of the laying on of hands."

Sam shot out of the steam bath like somebody had stepped on his tail. The next morning he made the decision to leave Arkansas. He needed a few days to recharge his batteries and to recover from all that had been wrought. Sam was skittish, a cat trapped in a tar paper shanty. He longed for fresh air. He might as well head back to Norman, Oklahoma. There he was well-neigh a cult figure. Sam was sure young girls would offer to buy him drinks in every bar in town. He liked nothing better than the idea he would wake up in the morning then raise his head from his pillow to see a couple of small size cowboy boots assembled at the foot of the bed.

Q. No Regrets

The summer ended on an unexpected note for Fred and Patricia Von Pattersfeet. Patricia took a jet to Switzerland to terminate an unwanted pregnancy. Fred had not stayed within the bounds of Patricia's virginity. As Patricia's plane touched down in Geneva, Fred bid fond farewells to Martha Buchanan. She would soon start school in Columbia, Missouri, Stephens College.

"Martha, I will miss you so much. The only thing that will keep me from absolute sadness is my knowledge that someday we will be married and live happily ever after. You are the love that lights up my life, Martha, my dear."

It was sheer randomness. Probability did not enter into the equation. Sarah Foreswallow was headed to Missouri. She would attend William Woods, the girls' school for Westminster College. Located in Fulton, Missouri, Sarah and Martha were again near neighbors. Winston Churchill gave the famous speech when he coined the phrase, "Iron Curtain," at the chapel at Westminster College. There was no one to say good-bye to Sarah except her family as she headed to start her freshman year. Sarah remained secure in her solid belief. No Iron Curtain, no Berlin Wall would ever persist to stand between Joe and her. Time would heave all. Even if now Joe had gone his way and she was about to go hers, most likely, no it was a statistical certainty, the walls would come tumbling down leaving only their true love amidst the rubble of chance.

R. Desperados Waiting for a Train

Earlier that summer Tommy had been discharged from the army. It was the end of August when he called Uncle Fricke. Fricke Wanderby had spoken with William Colby about Tommy. From that conversation, Tommy volunteered for covert training.

"Uncle Fricke, I am disturbed by forces that are aligned in seeming lock-step, all marching in a direction to protect only material well-being, only things gathered. The phrase, '…If you lose your soul…' continues to reverberate through my head throughout my very being."

"You are supposed to be at spy school not poetry class, for Chrissakes. But I think I know what you mean. The way things are going has even affected my thick skinned WWII hardened, Republican sensibility, if that is the right word."

"Funny."

"Tommy I like to sneak out at night away from the agents of the Illinois Bureau of Investigation who are assigned to protect me…"

"The I.B.I. is lax afoot."

"Praise the Presbyterian God in Heaven. When I drive the car all by myself, I get a renewed sense of freedom, like I am sixteen years old again driving on a brand new license. I heard some words from a song on the radio. I was stopped at a red light with my windows down. The young man in the car next to me had the volume up way too high. Here is what I think I heard-

'Up on Housing Project Hill
It's either fortune or fame
You must pick up one or the other
Though neither of them are to be what they claim
If you're looking' to get saved
You better go back to from where you came'"

"That's Bob Dylan. If you listen to him we are on a path which has passed the eve of destruction, hell bent on the road to nowhere. I know those words. They are from a song, 'Just Like Tom Thumb's Blues,' from the *Highway 61 Revisited* album. In the four years since it was released it is now an iconic record. That song is just like real life six verses and no chorus. Dylan started in Greenwich Village writing songs with the conviction that social change is inevitable, now he seems to have taken a step back, he writes wry commentary perhaps with faint hope that he will be heard. Dylan himself has issued his own rationale from his step back from the protest podium, perhaps an apology,

'Equality, I spoke the word, as if a wedding vow
But I was so much older then, I'm younger than that now.'"

"Tommy, I hope the current energy of the youth movement reaching to grasp change does not fade into the mist of insight without action, eschewing hope and faith. So what do you see is the problem with becoming a spook in Vietnam?"

"As you know I signed up for the 'Phoenix Program.' The idea is to quote, supervise, close quote the South Vietnamese in ferreting out and removing the civilian Vietcong from South Vietnam. Based on what I know now, from those who have trained me, those with firsthand knowledge as to the particulars of this undertaking, the C.I.A. has fallen into a plod that furthers what cannot be considered anything more than the protection of U.S. business interests, all we hold holy. I need your help to see that I am released from the special C.I.A. training program I joined. I know I volunteered as a way to get out of the army."

"Tommy, I will help you no matter what. You will get out. I am interested in hearing what you know."

"Uncle Fricke, the whole idea is called, 'counter terror,' a type of terrorism that they argue is a legitimate tool to use in unconventional warfare, and that counter-terrorism should be applied strategically to 'enemy civilians' in order to reduce civilian support for the Viet Cong. Originally, the CIA covert units were known as 'Counter Terror' teams, but they were renamed to 'Provincial Reconnaissance Units,' ('PRUs') after CIA officials worried about adverse publicity which the word, 'terror.'"

"Counter-terror- one man's terror is another man's fight for liberty- Tommy, I worry as you do. I saw too much killing in the Europe in World War II. The rules of civilized war are a mockery. Now it is worse. It cannot be the case that violence from either quarter is justified simply because of the righteousness of the cause. It is a simple truth, both sides cannot be right, but both sides can be wrong. I once heard there are languages with double negatives, twice can make it a positive or just reinforce the negative. One thing I do know is that no language uses two positives to make a negative..."

"Yeah, right. Uncle Fricke what troubles me, right or wrong, central to the Phoenix Program is the fact that it targets civilians, not soldiers. 'Neutralization' takes place under special laws that allow the arrest and prosecution of suspected communists all with the stilted end to prevent nationalization of our businesses. The model for the operation is the unsuccessful program the French undertook in Algiers..."

"Tommy, I question the wisdom of adopting a program, no matter how well-thought out, how thorough, and how comprehensive if it failed for the French in Algeria."

"Uncle Fricke, the methods of torture taught by the CIA to the South Vietnamese who actually do the wet work at PRU Interrogation Centers make me shudder, including rape, gang rape, rape using eels, snakes, or hard objects, and rape followed by murder; electric shock (they think they are funny in calling it the 'the Bell Telephone Hour') rendered by attaching wires to the genitals or other sensitive body parts like the tongue; the 'water treatment'; the 'airplane' in which the prisoner's arms were tied behind the back, and the rope looped over a hook on the ceiling, suspending the prisoner in midair, after which he or she is beaten; beatings with rubber hoses and whips; the use of police dogs to maul prisoners."

"It's not just colonial places like Algeria where European business interests were derogated to freedom through successful revolution. Capture, torture, and killing heretics did not work for the Vatican and the Catholic churches who derived their imperative at the time of the Inquisition either. In a better world, the CIA and the Catholic Church would make strange bedfellows, if at all. To me it seems the CIA acts against communism with full disdain since its precepts threaten the free market and the bottom lines of U.S. businesses. The Vatican has spurned communism since the result of the Russian Revolution was the prohibition of all religion with Christianity especially caught in the cross hairs."

"If you extrapolate the 'results' since 1968, by 1972 the Phoenix Program will have 'neutralized' 81,740 suspected as civilian enemies, of whom 26,369 will have been killed. William Colby is now stationed in Saigon to head the project. He claims that the program does not sanction the 'premeditated killing of a civilian in a non-combat situation…'"

S. Black Crow

"President Nixon told me the other day that I am the only Ivy League brat he trusts. While you might be careful because of my New Haven bias, since William Colby graduated from Princeton, what I have to say will open your eyes..."

"You know my friend, Joe Cebellum, goes there."

"I hope he does not become one of thus smug little pricks, if he is not already."

"Nope he likes sex, drugs, and rock and roll too much to be bothered by politics and by trying to improve the world."

"Sometimes it is the frying pan or the fire. What I am about to tell you came up very recently. My gubernatorial duties led me to consult with a New York lawyer, a black man named, Bruce Wright. I think his statistical information and history are reliable for reasons you will soon hear. At Princeton, in 1932, the students were 85% from private schools. 18% had fathers who were alums. Fifteen prep schools provided nearly one-half the freshman class. While a handful of blacks attended Princeton in 18th and 19th centuries, in the 20th century before World War II, not one black successfully enrolled. 'Hebrews,' as they were called at Princeton, were also 'unwelcome' but not prohibited. It was said they would not be admitted to the Eating Clubs, that they were 'unclubbable...'"

"I am sure the Princeton Admissions Office took a long time to learn the hard earned lesson that without money, even the fitted sheets don't fit."

"No doubt. All this stuff I am telling you is from the time between World Wars. 90% of Princeton students were in Eating Clubs, private social places with a well-established hierarchy. The top four, in an order no one disputed in those days, were Ivy, Cottage, Cap & Gown, and Colonial. The class of 1932 was 30% Presbyterian and 33% Episcopal. 87% of the student body was white and protestant. Remember the class of 1932 entered before the great crash of 1929. 2/3 had a parent who went to college. By 1932 Princeton's financial situation was precarious. It took in the largest freshman class in history. The student's ability to pay without help was taken into account. Harvard, Yale and Princeton all used the same unfortunate phrase, the 'Jewish problem.' At Princeton, so-called Hebrews never exceeded 2.3% of the total student body. One PU Admissions Dean said one class had 10 Hebrews, 7 of whom admit it since Hebrews 'unable to be loyal to anything frequently deny their origins.' Starting with the class of 1937, the Princeton administration and admissions office developed something they called, 'Plan C.' From my point of view, the idea was to preserve the so-called, Gentlemen's C."

"What the fuck is that?"

"The idea of the Gentlemen's C embodies all that keeps Princeton the great club it is. Once your family gets you in, neither hell nor high water will get you out. Even the biggest dullards receive a 'C' grade. Back to Plan C, in 1937 Princeton said the plan was adopted to 'find exactly the type of boys Princeton wants and needs.' They said they were looking for sports and leadership from schools away from the East Coast to develop a geographical diversity. 5 out of the first 29 Plan C students came from our Chicago area public high school, New Trier. By taking more white Anglo-Saxon Protestants from coast to coast, Plan C did not upset the character of an overwhelming white upper and upper middle class protestant institution keeping it attractive to the off-spring of the eastern upper class. Before Plan C, high college boards were all you needed. If I did the math of his class years right,

William Colby snuck in under the radar the year before Plan C. He had high board scores so that he was a Roman Catholic from Minnesota did not matter.

“Colby got away from the shores of Lake Superior before the reigning Lutherans ran him out of town on a rail. Although up there, tar and feathers have a nice warming effect. But Uncle Fricke, how do you know all this stuff?”

“The reason I know all these stats is that Bruce Wright just told me about all this, Wait ‘til you hear this. Princeton engaged in the systematic exclusion of Negroes ostensibly to protect southern lads from discomfiture. In fact only 10% of the student body hailed from below the Mason Dixon line, with most of them from Maryland and the District of Columbia. Even the best laid plans sometimes run afoul. In 1939 Bruce Wright was accidentally admitted, with full scholarship. The happy young man stood ready to enter Princeton, on campus for registration. An upperclassman confronted him to say he must see the dean immediately. Bruce Wright was pulled from the line of remaining deserving white boys. He was escorted to the dean’s office. Bruce says the Dean of Admissions looked at him as if he were a disgusting specimen under a microscope. The admissions dean told him, ‘The race problem is beyond solution in America…If you’re trying to come here, you’ll be in some place where you’re not wanted.’ The dean concluded by telling him he should go to a college for ‘his own kind.’”

“Uncle Fricke, it appears that just like in Texas, while some like Negros as far they go, nobody wants a Negro next dorm.”

“Tommy needless to say, Wright left ‘shattered.’ He was persistent. He wanted to attend. He kept pushing. He finally received this letter from the Dean of Admissions. I’ll read it to you. Bruce Wright gave me a copy,

‘Dear Mr. Wright-

Princeton does not discriminate against any race, color, or creed. This is clearly set forth in the original charter of the college and the tradition has been maintained throughout the life of the university…

Let me give you a purely personal reaction and I speak as one who has always been particularly interested in the colored race and I have always had pleasant relations with your race both in civilian life and in the army. I cannot conscientiously advise a colored student to apply to Princeton simply because I do not think he would be happy in this environment. There are no colored students in the university and a member of your race might feel very alone.

There are, moreover, a number of Southern students in the college. This has been a tradition of long standing at Princeton, and as you know, there is still a feeling in the south quite different from that existing in New England. My personal experience would enforce my advice to any colored student that he would be happier in an environment with others of his race.

Yours Sincerely, Radcliffe Heermance'"

"Fucking A"

"Tommy, Wright won a bronze star and purple heart in WWII. He has a distinguished career as a lawyer after attending Lincoln College with his 'kind.' I am reminded of a G. K. Chesterton quote which I fear hits its mark, 'Among the rich you will never find a really generous man even by accident. They may give their money away, but they will never give themselves away; they are egotistic, secretive, dry as old bones. To be smart enough to get all that money you must be dull enough to want it.'"

"Uncle Fricke, I am now quite certain everyone creates realities based on their own personal beliefs. These beliefs are so powerful that they can create expanding realities which entrap them, over and over."

"I hate to think that William Colby who is called the warrior priest is motivated as a Roman Catholic against communism- to deter it at all costs. I am further troubled by a conceptual framework that suggests the existence of ‘enemy civilians’ within borders outside our own. U.S. soldiers are injected into a weird hegemony. What is the tipping point? One man’s terror is another man’s righteous revolution, with God on our side. Like with another Princeton guy, Allen W. Dulles, it looks like Colby will be sternly at the helm. I hope Princeton’s special brand of narcissism does not run amok, where the inquisition takes another incarnation.”

“Uncle Fricke, here is another quote I like. I forget who said it, ‘A man is like a fraction whose numerator is what he is and whose denominator is what he thinks of himself. The larger the denominator, the smaller the fraction.’”

Fricke Wanderby made the necessary calls. Tommy was cut loose to return to live with his parents in Tower Lakes, not too far from the Cebellums, seven short miles from the Sleepy Little Village. He, too, would attend Harper Junior College, full time in the fall.

The summer waned. A principal principle was firmly established to add to the propinquity of time and place for Joe, Fred, Sam, and Tommy. Loyalty to one’s own independence and a healthy disregard for institutional authority were the moving forces. Strong bonds had formed and were forming stronger.

XXVI. "Ridin' High"

A. All Down The Line

Joe returned to campus the week before first semester classes started. He noticed it immediately. It was not thrust upon him as much as it enveloped him. There was a common, all too common, thread above the bustle of returning students. Call it what you will, one name is as good as another. "Aural wallpaper" makes it sound a lot better than ambient noise. Whether the Princeton campus ever had it before, it surely had it now. From dorm windows everywhere, it was surely a sonic plague. What should have been a crazy quilt of contrasting rhythms, melodies, and lyrics was, instead, a collaborative chorus. Take your pick; it could be the nasal din of James Taylor's album, *Sweet Baby James* or the light lilt of Joni Mitchell's, *Ladies of the Canyon*. Even the best of the best could be run aground. Anything played over and over again, was too much, especially when the world, from every corner, from every nook and cranny, was brimming with creative bounty. Music, sweet music, music was everywhere. But instead the needle was stuck in the groove. The campus air was impregnated with the soon stale repetition of a groovy kind of love. The song "Big Yellow Taxi" was "doo bop bop bopping" from every window sill. Either that or it was the lyric "...There is a young cowboy, he lives on the range. His horse and his cattle are his only companions..." By the next Spring, these redundant strains were pasted over by Carole King's *Tapestry*, "...I feel the earth move..." That Fall Joe was sure and by the next Spring, he was double-sure, it was not as good for him as it was for them.

The wallow of repetition glissaded to the place it was due in the back of Joe's mind. Sophomore year would soon begin. Now the moment struck him, "You never know when it will be the last." Almost in rebuttal, strolling towards Joe was a large man with a gentle lope. The round upbeat visage of his friend, John "Lemming" Cello was dominated by an illegal smile. In those days the opposite of a furtive grin was a shit-faced smirk. Both crossed Cello's countenance simultaneously.

"Let's Go," was all he said.

B. Let It Loose

Two steps at a time, the like-minded day trippers headed up the four flights of stairs to Joe's new room, a quad over the north arch in Holder Hall. It said, “8A” on the door. Two of Joe's three roommates were there, Timothy Parsley Fief and Joshua Matthew Relioport. Cello could roll a joint with one hand, even when he was driving. So the honors were his. It was not long before Cello, his own lungs full of smoke, passed the carefully crumpled and glued rolling papers to his right.

Fief took a long toke, stood up, shook himself off. He then did a Charlie Chaplin, Little Tramp shuffle as he headed to switch records. Eric Clapton's new solo record, the side with "Let it Rain" had just finished. Stephen Stills' fused wah-wah runs and Clapton's crisp clean notes still lingered delectably. Now came Jimi Hendrix, side three of *Electric Ladyland*, the one that starts with "Rainy Day, Dream Away." It didn't matter that the skies were not cloudy all day.

“Lemming” Cello leaped up, stood near the stereo, grabbed the headphones, and found his ears.

"I cannot believe how the tide of the music laps from one side of your head to the other,"

Joe looked at Fief and mouthed the word,

"Laps?"

That same day, on the German Isle of Fehmarn, Hendrix played his last concert. It had been a short but brilliant orbit circumscribed atop the rock and roll world. In twelve more days, Jimi Hendrix was dead from drowning in the rushing tide of his own alcohol enlivened vomit.

“Thew” looked up from the book he had in front of his nose, as the song, "1983 (A Merman I Should Turn To Be),” spewed lavishly from the turntable.

"Two peas do not make a pod but listen to this- 'I must be a mermaid, Rango. I have no fear of depths and a great fear of shallow living.'"

“Thew” issued the devilish smile of unique understanding. With a full body, "A-Ha," he slapped the weathered volume on the burnt orange coffee table which had been spray painted antique-style, just for times like this. The book was Anais Nin, *The Four Chambered Heart*. Fief started to lurch towards the junk shop table. He stopped when he realized that the open baggie of dope was not in jeopardy from “Thew's” careless release.

Fief then looked to Joe and mouthed,

"Peas? Pod?"

“Lemming” Cello noticed the joint was spent. He lifted his headphones off,

"Let's fire up another one."

By the time the boys were back puffing halfway through their second joint together, the record spinning was the new Moody Blues album, *A Question of Balance*, The song, "How Is It (We Are Here) pivoted fluently to "And The Tide Rushes In..."

C. Rip This Joint

There was knock on the door. It was the fourth roommate, Fenton "Teddy" Appleseed. He had forgotten his key.

Fief sampled just the right swatch of absurdity,

"Sign-in, please."

"Tim, It's Teddy."

"Lemming" Cello, stuck to his favorite chorus,

"Teddy, you are just in time to smoke a joint."

"Hey guys, I just bumped into Joel Frites. Apparently Colonial Club has gone non-selective. Not only that, they are really hurting for members, they think they will soon not be able to cover their overhead..."

"Covering overhead. It sounds a trifle difficult at that."

"Whatever, Frites suggests we all sign-in right now- they are having 'early-sign-in.' Sophomores don't become members 'til next spring, since that is the earliest time the University allows but they have sophomore Club intramural teams, including bridge."

"Will we fit in? Those guys are kind of high brow, no?"

"There are enough of us that we will make merry no matter what the rest are doing, or not doing, to be more to the point."

"Thew" took a pass. He was angling for Quadrangle Club where he knew some of the guys from the Triangle Show where he had been very active in the previous year. Everybody else was on-board. Fief, Cello, Appleseed, Frites, and Joe all signed in together. Over time Colonial members had evolved into short, intellectuals who were hell bent on hearing classical music and opera. One of the senior class members was an effete little fellow aptly named, Norman Flitt. After dinner, the membership would congregate in the living room to the left of the main entrance. While the other members sipped sherry or turned their noses in just the right way, Norman Flitt would play the grand piano, going for baroque for the most part. The tinkle of dainty keys being ruffled in just the right way could be heard between the massive three story white-ribbed ante-bellum pillars that dominated the front of the place. Whether it was Twelve Oaks or Tara, the architecture of Colonial Club evoked better days. While the roof was not quite ready to fall in, there was no doubt the Club had fallen on hard times. Joe and his buddies did not meet the profile. If nothing else, their average height was seven inches taller than the average of the upper class membership.

Wamble

D. Sweet Virginia

On the Saturday before classes started, Joe and Teddy introduced themselves to the three guys in the triple of the first floor their entry, Peter Laughline, Dan Parka, and Al Woodart. That fall proper introductions involved passing a joint around. Woodart exhaled to clear his lungs of blue smoke before he got up to switch the record from the Mothers of Invention, *We're Only in it For the Money*, to Free's self-titled second album, the one with the amazing blue cover a woman astride the cosmos with a sparkling star consuming the place from which all life has come.

Joe was always trying to find birds of a feather,

"Any of you guys like to play bridge?

You never knew when you would need a fourth.
Woodart and Parka both said, "Yes."

"Well, let's deal the cards."

Teddy was rarely the wet blanket,

“I have to do some laundry at the Laundromat on Witherspoon. Wanna go with me? We can eat some Chinese next door.”

“Another time, Fenton my good man. I think I know where we can find a fourth. You guys wanna go with me to the Street, to Colonial? I think George Demondrone will be there. We can play up stairs in the library.”

“Let’s do it.”

Colonial was even more pasty, quiet, and ghoulish than usual. It was empty. That afternoon, the gentlemen ghosts of its glorious past did not wander its once charmed corridors.

“Shit sorry, to drag you guys across campus.”

“Shh, Shh, Shhhh.”

“What the fuck is that? Mice?”

At first it seemed an apparition from some Victorian penny novel. A strange woman took form at the top of the stairs. Her name was Deborah Teagarden. She was a Senior, one of the few women who was admitted as a full-time transfer when the first One Hundred were admitted as Freshmen.

“Hi, I’m Deborah Teagarden. Please call me Deb-o-rah.”

She was 5’4” tall with long unexceptionally brown hair which she managed to wrap around her head in some sort of scrawny semi-turban. She wore a blouse with a pink-cream-pale yellow muted pattern. It was not tucked into her burgundy flowing floor length skirt. Her clothes obscured her shape, if she had one. Her face sufficiently possessed the geometry, color, and hastily scrawled features of Edvard Munch's "The Scream" that it merited no further attention.

"Deborah, I hope I am pronouncing that correctly. I am Joe Cebellum. I am one of the five guys who signed in early a couple of days ago. These are my friends, Al Woodart and Dan Parka. They are thinking of joining Cannon. Al plays the tuba and Dan plays the fife. You don't play the snare drum by any chance?"

Parka and Woodart smirked, squinted, and swallowed incipient chortles. "What?"

"Just kidding Deborah, we were looking for George Demondrone, one of the other early Sophomore sign-ins. We need a fourth for bridge."

"I play"

"Wunnerful."

"What?"

"Would you care to play upstairs or down?"

"Let's play downstairs. I have books all over the table in the library up here. I am trying to get a head start for my class on Early Middle Age Iconic Non-Devotional Art."

"Well by all means, let's not muss that up."

The game was uneventful. Too much talk from the Teagarden side of the table impeded actually playing the game. As anyone would have predicted, there soon came the straw that broke the camel's back.

Deborah Teagarden thought she was among her usual array of like-minded fancy fellows,

"I just finished reading Jerzy Kosinsky's *Steps*. It is a voluptuous book, filled with great insight and finely sculptured prose..."

Woodard had had enough. No card game was worth this sort of pretentious nonsense,

"I just saw the movie, *The Dirty Dozen*. I can't wait for the book to come out."

Deborah Teagarden had suffered enough of the never washed. She took her leave without even a small effort at bidding polite farewells. Huff, puff, and slight stomp were all she could muster as she almost fell off her chair on her way back to prepare for her understanding of the then next big art history movement.

E. Casino Boogie

It was not just the abolition of mandatory chapel and of parietals that led to chaos. For many years Princeton had a first meeting requirement. If a student did not attend the first meeting of a class, there was a fine imposed. In those days it was fifty dollars. In the freedom of the fall of 1970, the Nassau Hall administration lifted the fines for missing the first meeting. If there was ever a stodgy cause for celebration, this was it. For one entire week an intrepid group of Colonial's early Sophomore sign-ins camped in the library, playing bridge around the clock. Cebellum, Fief, Appleseed, and Demondrone were all gleeful participants. Daniel Deadknee, Fred Alexander, and Samuel Shankleweight also joined the ensemble. Tim Parsley Fief and Fenton Appleseed decided not to play on the Colonial bridge team. Sophomores were eligible for the Club Championship. Joe and the other four guys did play. Colonial won its first University bridge championship since Andrew Johnson was President and the game was called, "Whist."

More surprisingly, Colonial fielded an intramural basketball team. The Colonial basketball players were Joe and his buddies. It was not improbable but well-nigh impossible. All the jock Clubs fell to defeat. After each game, first the members of Dial, then Tower, and finally Tiger Inn, the places where true athletes would join, all returned to their Clubs, heads hanging low. At first the other members thought their mates were making a bad joke.

"Colonial?"

"You have to be fucking kidding me?"

Yet, it was true. The Colonial basketball team had won Colonial's second Club championship. This was the first athletic team Colonial Club ever fielded, all the way back to the days Naismith hung a couple peach baskets up in a gym in Massachusetts.

And so it came to pass, Colonial was not all aria and adagio. Even the year before, there had been a leak in the dike. Barry Miles '69 came back to Colonial to play his unique form of jazz, not really even jazz, some hybrid without pedigree, an incorporation of rock and roll with the tasteless title, "fusion." There were still many able to uphold the true Colonial banner. The new vanguard of cretinism, cards and sports had its limits. Not only were the upperclassmen all cut of the same cloth. One early-sophomore sign-in was a fellow named, Marshall "Mug" Quartzite. Mug's father was one of the great living English philosophers, perhaps the only one. The Quartzite school developed around the linguistic conundrum that no matter how much shale was shaved from the mica; there was always a bedrock which could refract the prism of great ideas into the bosom of discourse and redaction- or some similar construct. No one really knew.

F. Turd on the Run

Functionally as short-lived as the Teagarden bridge game, the days Joe and his buddies would spend as Colonial members were numbered. As much fun as they were having, they did not really hanker to tawny port and tone poems. Joe and "Lemming" Cello made extra money working meals, as waiters, or as dishwashers, a couple of days a week. This was the only reason they hung on as long as they did. Even though there were plenty of all night bridge games in the Colonial library, when push came to shove, 8A Holder became the place to be.

Princeton maintained a requirement that all graduates pass a laboratory course. The indolent, which means all those who were not pre-med, had two choices- Geology 101 or Psychology 101, "Rocks for Jocks" or "Rat Psych." Joe chose Rat Psych. The course required an experiment. Joe decided upon simplicity itself. In the classical style of psychology, he would prove, something about which there was no real doubt-- people who smoked pot were better than people who did not. As undertakings go, psychology falls somewhere in the dark and murky area between science and faith. Many have tried the dress up psychology as a science, to make it part of the scientific method. That same many have failed. Joe understood this. He would take two groups, those who smoked dope and the control group, those who did not. It would be easy to apply the existing methodology of "tests" to determine whether or not his presumption was correct. For his experiment, Joe chose two of the well respected personality tests. Both were long embraced by the community of those who sought to be seen as true scientists, "The Minnesota Multiphasic Personality Inventory" and "Cattell's

Sixteen Personality Factors." As far as Joe was concerned, hocus pocus had never sounded so good.

As with any faith based undertaking there was a Rorschach blotch that stood in the way. That which the believer wanted to believe could not be substantiated. Usually it was the higher being that had to be taken on faith. Here Joe could not find the lower. He searched, far and wide, through the entire campus. Joe could not find sufficient numbers for the control group. There were simply no people on campus who did not smoke marijuana.

Actually, there was one. Upstairs from 8A Holder was another quad, a large room which sat over the arch. Joe and his buddies knew one of the guys already, David Donald Tunney, "DDT." Joe and DDT had taken more than a few trips to the U-Store. Their quarry was LPs and Droste or Cadbury chocolate bars, proof, if more was needed, that DDT fell in the stoned-out category. DDT's three other roommates were Dave Major, Bill Fitts, and Dan Wigodsky. Wigodsky was a Texan. That was not the reason he did not toke up. He was an Olympic fencer. It was not the fear of drug testing but rather the need for precision. Dan feared he would lose his eye-to-hand coordination if any sort of fuzziness befell his brain from Tetrahydrocannabinol ("THC"). Wigodsky was the only guy Joe could find who would admit he had never smoked pot. Not smoking marijuana seemed to work well for him. Dan Wigodsky could point his foil at the ceiling, flick his wrist, and then kill some unsuspecting fly with its tip. He never missed. Of course, you had to be stoned to really appreciate the full nature and extent of this feat. Years later, anyone who remembered the way it was in the eastern seaboard colleges in the late sixties and early seventies knew the statement by Bill Clinton that he never inhaled was absurd on its face.

Joe was now confronted with a dilemma, a problem shared by theologians and psychologists alike. He lacked sufficient empirical evidence for that which he wished to prove. Joe now stepped forward to do what either of those two groups would do. Data being what it is, Joe contrived the control group. This not only saved time but made proving the truth of his working hypothesis all that much more easy. As Joe filled out test questionnaire after questionnaire for the imaginary participants in his control group, he was struck with the thought that "culture" is all the same and always the same. It is no different whether it is in a Petrie dish, throughout an entire campus, or throughout this great nation. Once his Rat Psych experiment was completed, Joe now understood the efficacy of shooting loaded dice. Getting the result you wanted was easier than Cain shooting Abel back in the day before the Ten Commandments or before any other scientific stricture or ethical prohibition. Science is looking at all the empirical evidence in order to try to discover the truth. Conclusions based on faith simply skip a step or two of that needless rigor. Those justifying their Faith need not even look at partial examples just ratifying flashes. As a lawyer in later life, Joe learned that trying cases involves assembling only the evidence that supports a position and ignoring, rebuking, or minimizing what seems to be contrary. It is easy to get the multitudes to follow that sort of lead. The dance is one you can all join in. The imagined sins of those who doubt serve better than supporting facts. Newton was wrong. There is always a reaction greater and more expansive than any initial action. Or, of course, there are cases where there is no reaction at all. The internet now serves to give many examples. Here is just one, if not a just one. Conservatives led a boycott of "Hanoi Jane" Fonda's products on the QVC/Home Shopping Network at a time in her later life she could no longer play *Barbarella*. She had reached the point in her career that she was minimized as a woman, cast in the role of Nancy Reagan. There are never measured limits in the response to perceived heresy. Viral proportion is an easy hurdle to attain when conscientious sheep are reminded that someone did something horrible, once upon a time, long, long ago. Reasoned balancing and weighing all available evidence are left in the wake as the crowd rushes to the right conclusion.

G. Sweet Black Angel

Satisfied his experiment was a success, Joe turned to other fish to fry. He had his eye on one of the new Freshmen co-eds. Her name was Sarah Reposehomme. Since Pyne Hall could not hold all the newly registered women, the newest were shuffled off to Witherspoon. Sarah was from the Philadelphia mainline. The same divination that allowed Fenton Appleseed and Charlie Scribner, a single when "all" Freshman had one or more roommates, gave Sarah her choice of roommates, in this case, Martha Sharpley, a girl with a proper upbringing, whose brother, Dustin, once attended Chestnut Hill Academy with Teddy. Joe tagged along with Teddy the day he stopped to say hello to Martha and to welcome her on campus. Joe was immediately struck and stricken. Here in the same room were Princeton's transmogrification of Barrington's Martha Buchanan and Sarah Foreswallow. It was at that moment Joe decided that if he ever wrote a book, he would call it *4,000 Pounds*. The two tons with which he was familiar Barring*ton* and Prince*ton* weighed in to give what Joe was sure would be a splendid story. The Martha and Sarah from the Sleepy Little Village had none of the breeding or bearing of either Martha '74 or Sarah '74. Martha '74 had all the self-assuredness that Martha lacked. Sarah '74 had all the refinement that Martha was missing. Of course when you have one thing you are missing something else. Martha had the God-given sense that she was always right no matter how many counter-examples obstructed her path. Sarah, on the other hand, seethed a sensuality that only being free of reins will engender. Joe was stricken, or to be more apt, smitten. In a few short minutes Sarah Reposehomme had captured his fancy. She had beady, little eyes and a snub of a nose. Her chin did not quite reach the plane derived from her forehead to her nose. Her lips were wan and thin. She was short with an amorphous shape. It may have been uncharitable but it was certainly not unfair to say that Sarah '74 was among the best of a bad lot. Martha '74 was prettier but she oozed hauteur with aloof chill that was definitely not cool. The squinty eyes of Sarah '74 did sparkle with *savoir faire* of some kind. Joe fell prey to the notion she was interesting and canny. The die was cast. The possibility of having a regular girlfriend was all the impetus Joe needed. He visited Sarah '74, four or five times. If Joe was paying attention, he might have noticed Sarah '74 was not interested, even in the slightest. Persistence is its own reward, however. Finally, with the long winter approaching, Joe threw caution, and good judgment, to the wind. He bought two tickets, third row center for the Miles Davis concert November 14th at Alexander Hall. He asked Sarah '74 if she wanted to go with him. Sarah '74 said,

"Why not."

The big night finally arrived. There they were, sitting in the best seats in the house. It could have been a great concert, the first step in a long and lasting relationship. The only thing missing was Miles Davis. The thought of performing on the Princeton campus, for all those honkies, made his blood run cold, more than any Bitches Brew. Miles' body was there but he was miles away. The performance that night did not even rise to the level of perfunctory. The best part of the evening was the venue. Alexander Hall was, as usual, an unusual building. Folklore or the fancy of some wag, the story on campus was that the architect who designed Alexander Hall donated it to the school as no small retribution. The architecture department had forced him to redo his senior thesis project. No matter what the origin, Alexander Hall formed an imposing figure. The side that faced the campus was piled high with large grey stone rectangles which came to a point. The other sides were dark brown brick. People who claimed to know architecture called it "Federal" style. The stage fronted a main floor. There was a balcony that ringed the stage, sort of a semi-circle in the round. Behind the stage, below the point of the wall on the campus side, there loomed that full circle of stained glass. No light really ever peered in or out of its circumference. In any event, it was a significant presence which gave any performance a serious, mystical quality, almost any performance. The music that night was devoid of content. The second and only other interesting part of the evening was that Miles Davis wore a long cape, deep dark purple. He turned his back on the audience for the entire show. It would have been easy for Joe to blame the performer.

The reality was that Sarah ’74 and Joe ’73 were not to be. When they shared a joint before the concert, Joe began to take notice. Sarah inhaled and exhaled but never came out her shell. They had talked together before. Not once had they really connected. Sarah spoke to show those around her that she was perceptive and articulate. That night Miles Davis and Sarah shared the same warmth. In the right place, at the right time, the milk of human kindness would flow, but not for Joe. Joe had seen Van Morrison with “Lemming” Cello at McCarter Theater. He had skipped the James Taylor performance in Dillon Gym on October 17th. The weekend following Miles Davis, Joe would again return to seeing shows with his buddies. On November 21st, Delaney and Bonnie and Friends blew the crowd away.

H. I Just Want to See His Face

Princeton's most famous contribution to the stage derives from the Triangle Club. Founded in 1891, the Triangle review has oft maintained a level of professionalism. The Kickline is Triangle's most visible and enduring feature. After all, there is an almost universal appeal whenever a bunch of spoiled preppies go on stage arm-in-arm, dressed like women. The 1969-1970 Triangle Show, *Call a Spade a Shovel*, maintained the Kickline tradition, but little else. The year before, one woman performed. She was part of the "critical languages" program, where women were first suffered on the all male campus as a quaint anomaly. *Call a Spade a Shovel* featured six co-eds in a seventeen member cast. The social and political commentary, started with the titled reference to slang for a black man, and from there, sprang to pervasive criticism of the Vietnam War. The show caused an enormous backlash of alumni protest. Princetonians have long adhered to the precept that what is sauce for the goose is sauce for the gander. There was a mass walk-out at the Grosse Pointe, Michigan stop on the Triangle tour. One of the skits in the show attempted to do one better than the Kicklines of yore. Some guys dressed in Gorilla suits danced around in a scene meant to evoke primeval creation, or whatever it was Kubrick tried to suggest in the scene that ended *2001, A Space Odyssey*. One of the costumed proponents of the evolution of a mono solution was none-other than Josh "Thew" Relioport. Early in the Fall, realizing the show was threatening, of its own accord, to wane into a black hole, an effort to promote the tour of *Call a Spade* was devised. One of the Gorillas your dream climbed high atop Blair Arch to wave at imaginary bi-planes and to save a Fay Wray wannabe. The Triangle guys and dolls were confused. They had skipping effusively from the *2001* theme Strauss, "Thus Sprekinzee Zarathustra," to the silent movie, *King Kong*.

Joe soon learned that a boy and his gorilla outfit are difficult to part. It might have been the dope or it might have been the occasional hallucinogen. More likely, it was just the thrill of reaching into the depths of unnatural selection after listening to a Firesign Theater record one too many times. Whatever the cause, "Thew" was wedded to his Gorilla outfit. He would walk around campus wearing it, sometimes even attending classes so attired. Wherever he went, everyone knew him. The choruses of "Hey, Josh, How you doin' today?" were met with animated armpit scratching, sloop shouldered, bent knee jumping, and Relioport's best effort at gorilla grunts. Joe decided Thew needed help with his routine. It started with Joe following behind the Gorilla. He would yell, "Duck Walk," then "Duck Quack," then "Duck Tail," and finally, the *piece de resistance*, simply the one word, "Duck." Thew would imitate Chuck Berry. He would then make sounds that sounded more like gobbles than quacks. This was actually much better than the way he aped gorilla sounds. Next he would wag his tail like a duck trying to shake off water from a recent swim. At last, he would hit the deck avoiding some imaginary but imminent collision. Looking at Joe and Thew together, it was never clear who was the organ grinder and who was the primate. Suffice to say, perhaps only two people were amused.

I. Soul Survivor

Later that fall, back in Barrington, Fred, Sam, and Tommy, all fully re-assembled, did their own version of monkeys in a barrel. Tommy returned home from covert training. He was looking for that one honest man, or woman. Sam's return to Norman after Good Lord training in Arkansas was short-lived. He was back living with his dad at the Palace of Thorns in Pickwick Place. Fred's state of mind was still to stay in the state he knew the best, even if it was the only one he knew Confluences being what they are, Tim Camphor became the inadvertent ringmaster for a circus that somehow threatened to go on forever even though it never actually started.

One simple innocent suggestion led to all the fuss. Tim was directing the play by Jean Anouilh, *The Lark*. Tommy was a full-time Harper student. Fred and Sam would enroll for the Winter term. Tim thought anyone had the right to answer a casting call, God-given or natural, it mattered not. He invited Fred, Tommy, and Sam to tryout. He was wrong. The content of the *The Lark* aside, the error fell in the realm of execution rather than eligibility. In this case, the forecast was dim. In addition to the three-fold difficulty of trying to put multi-faceted pegs into round holes, there was the play itself. The French playwright Jean Anouilh was an existentialist in the finest tradition of that fine tradition. It might have been a simple story. A young peasant girl dons armor. She then leads her rag tag troops to save France. The French King whom she just led to coronation leaves her in the lurch An English bishop crosses the channel to transgress the line between fairness and injustice. Joan is given all the courtesy of a hearing before judgment is rendered against her. Anouilh adds a wrinkle. As the stakes are increased, the prosecutor who also just passed sentence pulls the reality of the blazing inferno from underneath her. Joan is left holding only a cross in her right hand to save her soul. Anouilh's curtain falls with the certainty of history left up in the air. A better ending is left to the imagination of the audience and, perhaps, of those who would later gave Joan of Arc reprieve and canonization. Anouilh peppered the script with humor and dangerous foreboding which enlivened the foreshadowing of life's horrible outcome. Even the best existentialist would prefer not to act if the dilemma ended only to be burnt at the stake. Then, of course, there was the complication of the voices. If Joan of Arc heard voices, was she blessed or delusional? Grace can be a difficult state to find yourself, especially when one King's God says, "No" and another King's God rains diffidence.

J. Don Juan's Reckless Daughter

All this theological, historical, and philosophical confusion was then exacerbated by Lillian Hellman's English language adaptation, a text bearing her two-edged three day old fish to fry. Of course, Feminism had to have its day in court. More, so Lillian Hellman had her own stinking agenda. She had been summoned to her own modern version of a fair hearing. Hellman had her day in court before the House Un-American Activities Committee. She was then blacklisted. In this case, from Hellman's point of view, the rule of the day was that the heresy of Godless Communism was better the object of scorched earth even if all innocent bystanders standing in an expansive landscape were presumed guilty until further notice. This revisionist complexity with unerring fine points then plagued a pre-existing script which simmered with a surfeit of its own hysteria, doom, and predestination. These were dangerous waters for even the best honed thespian. Delilah Pellioni was oblivious to the niceties of nuance or the ravages of fate. She saw only her name in lights. The die was cast. Delilah was given the part she was born to play. It was not enough she had been crowned "Miss Hoffman Estates." For her one reign, she would drive a brand new lime green Plymouth Satellite convertible. Her status as *bona fide* beauty queen was borne emblazoned in blaring block letters in two identical white squares also naming the car dealer donor glued to both of the car's two doors. Adding Joan of Arc to her resume was another feather for Delilah's strange bonnet. Born and raised a sociopath, Delilah knew she was perfect for the role. The other players had their entrances and their exits, small players in the shadows around a spotlight that always fell only on Delilah.

Tim gave Fred the part of the skulking Dauphin, a French King whose light would remain in a bushel until after this particular drama ran its course. Fred felt the idea of lurking in the background to be inconsistent with his every breath. Tim kept insisting that the no show must go on. Fred's sulking lent itself delightedly to the character of Charles the 7th.. Sam presented a real problem. Nothingness was what best tried Sam's being. Since Delilah had been given the part of The Lark herself, Tim could find no place for Sam's special brand of wooden conformity to a position transfixed by conviction, especially since Sam's spin on fate was a sense that disaster lurked around the corner where it was waiting to meet him. Tim was not sure. It might have been one of his own thoughts or a preternatural voice that spoke only to him. No matter the source, the solution was one of rare beauty and practicability. Tim told Sam he wanted him to achieve that which had heretofore never been attempted. Sam would take up the gauntlet of an "all-purpose" understudy ready to jump in at a moment's notice to save the day no matter which character could not find a way to the stage. Again, Sam was back in his old stomping grounds, paralyzed by infinite possibility. Tim made sure the day would never come when any understudy was actually needed.

Tim cast Tommy perfectly as the simple English foot soldier who, throughout the entire play, stood immobile at attention with his eyes straight ahead. Tommy may have lost his animate vitality but he did gain the leading lady. From Delilah's first gander, Tommy's goose was cooked. Tommy had been centered in the cross-hairs of unmaidenly desire. Now in Delilah's grasp, Tommy was a goner. He took it on faith that he was just another guy caught in the intricate web of feminine wiles. *The Lark* was an unmitigated success from all quarters. Unlike the disgruntled Princeton Alumni from Grosse Pointe who walked out on the faithless reveries of disgruntled ingrates, the many points and missteps of *The Lark* were lost on the faithful Harper Community College theatre goers who heaped praise upon Tim's efforts and the willingness of the cast to throw themselves full force into an undertaking of any magnitude. When all was said and done, the play was a mélange of vision and ideas, all wrapped in butcher paper. Back for Thanksgiving break,

Joe saw the last performance. He really expected the cast party would lead to his own feet being held to the fire by one of Harper's erstwhile maidens. He hoped angelic words would soon have his ear. At the *bonne fete* following the performance, Joe rushed to give to Tim hearty congratulations,

"In the existentialist play 'No Exit,' Jean Paul Sartre suggested that we all have our own version of hell. Tim, you prodded your players to the point that the audience has been delightfully browbeaten with the versimilitude that the subjectively faithful will either rue or rule the day."

"Joe, you know I never thought of it quite like that. But, I do believe I have so said. Faith is what should be blacklisted and burned at the stake."

The cast party did not lead Joe to find fruitful acquaintance to raise his faith. A voyage best taken by two did not ensue. Joe did not even find an opening to pay his respects to Delilah. She was surrounded by an admiring throng, reveling in the limelight. What she had long known from hearing the adoring clucks of her family, Delilah knew again. She had her own special roost. Tommy wanted only to find that which he was looking for. So he sat with benign obeisance to Delilah- off stage right, waiting patiently to kiss her ring, or to otherwise engage in some sort of intimacy. Even Sam derived some benefit from his brief parry into the world of theatrical production. Sam decided that if he was going to be out of place wherever he was, it really did not matter where was. So, forsooth he reasoned to himself, his only real listener, why not continue to relax in the comfort of the Palace of Thorns. Sam was sure much merriment would follow. A coterie of Harper woman would soon breathe life into his one and only brand of bob. Sam was convinced he would soon be part of the madding crowd.

K. Refuge of the Roads

Earlier that fall, Joe's movements away from Princeton were more predictable. Prior to going back to the Sleepy Little Village for Thanksgiving, just in time to see *The Lark*, Joe left campus twice. The first time was to stand up at a wedding. Joe's sister, Susan, was now a Freshman at the University of Illinois, the main campus downstate at Champaign-Urbana. Mid-summer Susan left the Cebellum nest early to take some orientation classes for the Russian language curriculum. Shortly after arriving on campus, Susan met a very nice young man who was studying to be a doctor. Jim Black and Susan surrendered to the whirlwind of romance. The day for their wedding was set at the end of the fourth week of regular classes. The ceremony would be in the sanctuary of one the many the local First Methodist churches, this one in the town of Champaign, cake and punch reception to follow in the church basement. Most of the Cebellum clan and many long-time family friends gathered to celebrate the nuptials, and then to do whatever one did with what was left of the nuptials. Fred joined to meet Joe if only to cajole a buddy who was forced to wear an Edwardian tuxedo, grey with black trim. There was no doubt Fred was one of the family. His sense of proportion, a voice he rarely heard, insisted he travel south to the wedding. Another voice pushed Fred west from there. This one reminded him that Stephens College and Martha Buchanan were a mere hop, skip, and jump away. As the receiving line was forming, Fred summoned Joe aside,

"I am going to Missouri to see what Martha can show me."

"Right now?"

“As soon as the reception gets to a point where I will not be missed.”

“You really do not expect me to leave that statement alone, do you?”

“O.K. how ‘bout when the time is right to make an unassuming exit? You know Sarah Foreswallow is right down the road from Martha. Who knows? We could improve upon Lewis and Clark’s journey if you joined me to haplessly half-step our ways across the Mississippi. Plus from there, we can visit Sam in Oklahoma.”

“Really?”

“And listen to this, I have cut the umbilical cord. I have enrolled in college at North Texas State, in the town of Denton, not too far from Dallas. They have accepted me a couple weeks late. I have mailed all my belongings directly to my new dorm. The guys at the Barrington Post Office helped me. The postage for seven big boxes was one thin regular stamp.”

“We’re from the government and we’re here to help you. O.K. I’m in. Let’s go.”

L. Loving Cup

Even before Susan and Jim cut the cake, Fred and Joe had hitched their first ride, all the way to St. Louis. Three hours later, they were in Columbia, Missouri. Fred headed directly to see Martha. Joe stopped in to see Aunt Bess and Uncle Reggie. The Tetherfasts had seven kids. The oldest, Melinda, was Joe's favorite paternal cousin. When they were little, on a rare Tetherfast visit north to Chicago, Melinda grabbed Joe and kissed him. They ended innocently panting in the pantry of Grandma Cebellum's house. It was a strange bond but a real one. Melinda had a mischievous smile and a twinkle in her eyes. The Tetherfasts were surprised to see Joe. Small town America formed the limit of their universe. The visits to Chicago were few and far between. Even forty years later, few Tetherfasts had ever been on an airplane. The trip to Susan's wedding was beyond the edge of the flat earth they inhabited. After a pleasant evening, a good night's sleep, and a hearty breakfast, Joe said exuberant good-byes before setting out to Fulton.

Sarah at first appeared nonplussed, "Why, Joe. You are the last person I would have expected to see here at William Woods. It is too bad, you didn't call first."

"I didn't know your number. Besides, what would you have said?"

Sarah was a fast worker. Not quite as quick as Susan whose romance was a sweet whirlwind. Sarah was her own version of a tempest on cat feet, stealth with a knockout punch to relish,

"I would have saved you a trip. I am engaged to be married. I would have told you not to come."

"Who is the lucky guy?"

"This is not the time for sarcasm. But I am touched by the hint of jealousy."

"No, I'd like to meet him. Tell me about him."

"Stanley Mirk is his name. He is a senior at Westminster. He is from a prosperous hop growing family from Milwaukee. Stosh, as he likes to be called, I prefer 'Stanley,' was engaged to one of the girls here, a sophomore named, Cynthia Clare. They got real drunk one night just before school started and he totaled his Cadillac."

"I was able to nursemaid him back to full recovery. 'Cyn' smashed her face into the windshield. Her face is permanently messed up. My Stanley no longer felt he could marry her. Sad, but true. Anyway, I know he felt guilty about the accident. I have managed to make him forget it happened."

"You should be a candidate for this year's Florence Nightingale award for kindness above and beyond the call of duty."

"I only did what any girl would have done."

"Any girl like you."

Sarah introduced Joe to Stanley. As the three walked around the campus to see where Winston Churchill spoke, they bumped into Cyn. Joe liked her immediately. Cyn had something to prove. Once she knew Joe was once the object of Sarah's affection, she lavished Joe with attention. They spent two nights together sweating until their bodies both waved the white flag of surrender. Sarah was not the only one who knew how to lead the troops into battle. Cyn had proved her point. Joe was happy to be a pawn in the game.

M. Blue Motel Room

Fred and Joe agreed to meet back at Stephens before heading to see Sam at Norman. The two sat in the waiting room of Martha's dorm. The television was on. It was NBC's Major League game of the week. The Pittsburg Pirates were playing. Joe and Fred watched Roberto Clemente make a great play in right field to end the inning. The game faded to commercials.

"Fred, you know and I know that three is not a crowd. Three always thrive..."

"Especially if two of the three are you and me."

"Poetic and apt. Getting back to what I was saying, this season in baseball there have been some special sets of threes. Get this Fred, in less than a month, the Yankees' Horace Clarke breaks up three no-hitters in the ninth, Joe Niekro, Jim Rooker, and Sonny Siebert."

"The Yankees' hitting is that bad, eh?"

"Sad but true."

"Here's another set of trios. Johnny Bench hits three straight homers off Steve Carlton..."

"No mean feat."

"...A wily, powerful lefty, headed to the Hall of Fame. And on the same day Orlando Cepeda hits three consecutive homers against the Cubs."

"Shiver me timbers, laddies. Let's get off the three thing if my Cubbies are on the wrong end of it."

"And when pray tell are your Chicago Cubs not looking up from the depths of the bottom of the barrel?"

"To change the subject, remember the All-Star Game at Riverfront, Pete Rose breaks catcher Ray Fosse's collar bone scoring the winning run. Fosse is in the way, but he does not have the ball. Rose is one prickly pear."

"Yep the National league wins the All Star game after you guessed it, scoring three runs in the ninth off Catfish Hunter, down 3-0."

"So why didn't they have a reliever in for the ninth?"
"Good point. And the National League had only three hits through the first eight innings."

Later that fall the Reds eliminate the Pirates in the playoffs. In the fall classic, threes would come home to roost against Pete Rose. Three times the Reds are up 3-0 only to lose as the Baltimore Orioles win a three game advantage 4-1. At third base, the human vacuum cleaner Brooks Robinson puts on a defensive display in the five game series to garner Series MVP, putting on such a show that the Red's right fielder, Pete Rose, is left in the dust. The next year the Pirates would win the World Series. Clemente is one of the greatest who has ever played the game. In his last season, 1972, he reaches the rarefied atmosphere of the 3,000 hit plateau. Roberto Clemente will die New Year's Eve 1972 in a plane crash going to do some charity work after a devastating earthquake in Nicaragua. For many winters, Clemente left his homeland in Puerto Rico to help the poor and the disadvantaged throughout Latin America. Roberto Clemente was one of the first in a wave a Latin players whose talent would eclipse the endeavors of all the others who ever played, white or black.

"Joe, I decided to stay one more day here with Martha. We are going to check into a hotel tonight. It is a big football weekend her for Mizzou. The University of Missouri Tigers are taking the field. So I was lucky to get a room."
"Well, do your best to make good use of that which the Good Lord has given you,"

"That I shall. Plus I visited a travel agent. I booked a flight out tomorrow."

"Let me see your ticket."

Fred handed Joe the ticket jacket.

"Sam and I will pick you up when your plane lands at Will Rogers International Airport. I assume I will have hitchhiked my way all the way there by then if I leave now. An International Airport in Oklahoma, what will they think of next?"

"I think they fly to Juarez."

N. Overture - Cotton Avenue

Joe hitched a ride on the interstate all the way to Joplin, Missouri. The fifty year old guy who picked Joe talked about how his wife did not understand him. Joe feigned sympathy until the driver put his right hand on Joe's left thigh. Joe looked the guy in the eye,

"That is not going to happen. Do you want to let me out of the car right now?"

"No, I'll keep my hands to myself and take you all the way to Joplin. You can't blame a fella for trying."

For the next two hours nobody said a word. Joe got out of the car. For the next six hours, nobody stopped to pick up Joe. Four other hitchhikers were now standing in the same place, looking for a ride. Joe noticed that the lightpole next to him had some graffiti. "You are gonna die in Joplin" was the scrawl.

Finally a guy driving a panel truck, a laundry truck stopped. Everyone piled in. A one hour ride from that hell hole to Tulsa was better than anyone hoped. Joe got out. Three of the other guys had reached their destination. The fourth guy was a native American named, Quentin Thundercloud. He claimed he was the ceremonial chief of the Wisconsin Winnebago Tribe. He was on his way to a council of tribal chiefs which would be meeting Monday near a town called Shawnee, near Oklahoma City and Norman. The two took their position on the shoulder of the Will Rogers Turnpike. Joe wondered whether Oklahoma named everything in the state after the toothsome lariat spinning homespun philosopher who never met a man he did not like. It was now late Saturday night, two in the morning Sunday to be exact. Finally, a drunk pulled over. In desperate times, desperate measures are required. After standing for a near eternity at Joplin, Joe was sure even a bad ride was better than no ride. The driver claimed he was once a rodeo star. Watching the guy weave from the left shoulder to the right without falling out of the front seat, Joe was sure he was telling the truth. Joe sat in the front passenger seat. Quentin sat in the back. The situation was precarious. When they got in, the drunk told them how far he was going, the name of the exit in Oklahoma City. Joe and Quentin made eye contact as the drunk rambled about how you had to be careful not to land just the wrong way on a rodeo bull or you'd end up with your balls in your mouth. His shoulder to shoulder one car weave continued. Quentin confirmed the guy's intended exit. Joe had no other choice. He smacked the guy full force on the side of his head. It was a solid right hook. It did not take a lot for the guy to see alcohol induced stars. Joe grabbed the steering wheel first, before bringing the car to a stop with a full extension of his leg to put his left foot on the brake. At rest on the right shoulder, Joe and Quentin lifted the guy out of the driver's seat before depositing him into the back seat. His snoring confirmed he was out for the count. Joe drove. When they got to the guy's exit, Joe pulled over. He hung the keys from the driver's side visor. He was sure the guy would see them dangling in front of him if the keys did not put his eye out when he got into the front seat.

O. Shine A Light

The two guys walked to the nearest phone booth. Joe called Sam who was not happy about the time, 5:00 in the morning. But what is a friend for if not to disturb a sound slumber? Sam did not believe their story but Joe persuaded him it was not a good idea to drive by the car in case the guy regained consciousness at just the wrong moment.

Joe looked at Sam. Sam looked at Joe. They were stuck with Quentin. Apparently, he thought he was now one of the gang. The three headed back to Sam's apartment. There were no small sized cowboy boots on the floor at the foot of the bed. In fact, the free drinks had been few and far between, and were now even fewer and farther. Womenwise, Sam had struck out, down on his luck. Drugwise, he had scored some synthetic mescaline.

"I know it's not quite six in the morning but let's say we have a hit of mescaline to start the day."

"Sunday morning going up."

Quentin never really talked. He did hold out his hand when Sam offered Joe the hallucinogen. Fred's flight was scheduled to arrive at noon. Fred's flight was on time. Sam and Joe met Fred at the gate. They walked back to Sam's white 1964 Comet. As Sam threw Fred's small bag into the trunk, Fred noticed Quentin in the back seat. He scrunched his face into a question,

"Fred Etheridge, allow me to introduce to you Quentin Thundercloud, Chief of the Winnebago Indians."

Quentin did not even say "Ugh."

Joe got into the back seat.

Sam gave Fred a status report,

"I am sorry to inform you that you are one hit of mescaline behind us."

He handed him a gelatin capsule.

"Well I smoked three joints with Martha as we spent the morning in bed until I had to race to the airport with a happily limp dick. I still have a one in my hard pack of Winston's."

Joe could not resist,

"I hope you are talking about a joint and not your penis."
Sam stayed on point,

"O.K. so light one up and pass it around. You are one joint ahead of us."

The cigarette lighter popped out. Fred pulled it from its place in the Comet's ashtray.

"I think in order to find the great equalizer. We should stop and buy a case of Coors. Is there a liquor store open on Sunday?"

"Nope, we are just going to have to suffer with the mind-altering substances that we now enjoy."

P. Happy

The mescaline made a strong suggestion. There was a lake nearby. They could walk around the water admiring nature and the Sunday picnickers to take full advantage of the bright sunny day. By nine that night, they were back at Sam's. The sunset had been a spectacular display of oranges, reds, and yellows splurging across a turquoise background. The four guys watched. The colors across the sky moved. There was no doubt they were watching Claude Monet or God paint, which was really the same thing. Finally the background framed darker and darker blues to reach a final dank gray. As the pastels dissolved into darkness, the first stars twinkled.

Back at Sam's, the consensus was three "yays" with one affirmative silence. His own idea, with the added peer group acclamation, sent Sam back into his baggy full of mescaline capsules. The sun was down and the time was right for loud music. Sam cranked the stereo. All four sides of The Beatles' *White Album* never sounded better. Fred decided he did not have to report for classes until Wednesday. Once the liquor stores opened on Monday, the boys retrieved a case of Coors. Back at Sam's there was more music, The Rolling Stones' Live record, *Get Your Ya Yas Out*,

Joe started to say,

"I was at Madison Square..."

"Yeah, yeah, we know."

"You heard the Stones play this music live, in full ear shattering splendor."

"Dare, I say earth shattering…"

"You have and I am sure we will hear it again…"

"And again."

Next Sam played The Allman Brothers' second record, *Idlewild South*. The icing on any cake was to then spin Santana's *Abraxas*. The music was interspersed with the chatter of exuberance. Many of the world's problems were discovered and solved. For the sake of issues long forsaken, the tide of discussions turned and stemmed. Not needing a grinding halt, Sam got up to play Cream, *Goodbye*. Both sides screamed rancorous beauty. The next record which blared in full big screen Panavision was from Jefferson Airplane, *Surrealistic Pillow* front and back. The music stood still while the room moved in pleasing waves to pick up the slack. Some unknown moderator turned the discussion to all things female. Once again a consensus was reached. Nobody ever thought Sarah would just say, "No." Beyond that, Fred was smitten with the course of his own fate. He could not wait for the happy day. He and Martha would tie the knot, find wedded bliss, and live happily ever after.

Sam was first,

"Fred do you think wedded bliss will be any different than the time you now spend with Martha in the sack?"

Joe jumped in,

"A bed blessed with the sanctimony of the holy rite of matrimony must be a wonder to behold."

Sam then queried,

“Do you think married people ever fuck standing up? Or in the back seat of a car?”

Joe added,

“What about the cold tiles on the kitchen floor?”
“Would you guys cut it out? Martha and I are meant for each other. Once the children…”

“Ah yes, the mewling and puking little darlings …”

Quentin broke his silence,

“Anybody got any dope?”

They passed another joint around. Monday night they bought another case of Coors. The plan was a simple one. Nothing could go wrong. It had the minimum required moving parts. They would head out Tuesday morning to drop Quentin at the closest sweat lodge and then head south to North Texas State. Tuesday morning came. Just as the doctor ordered, the regimen of hits of mescaline kept on coming.

Q. Off Night Backstreet

As they loaded up the car to hit the road, something struck Sam,

“It’s been 49 hours. Do you think we will ever sleep again?”

Fred was paying attention, “49?”

Joe waxed with a pure sense of Tao what you like, “I read somewhere that you can catch up on your sleep after you die.”

“Well, one more day tripping never hurt anybody.”

The car was stocked with all the necessaries, the new case of Coors, a bag of clean homegrown buds, and the remaining seven hits of mescaline. Once they started on the road, it was time to crack open an ice cold Coors, before the beer got too warm. Everything was as good as it could be. That was, until Sam decided to take a short cut. Later, he said everybody did it. Rather than pull up to a stop sign and stop to turn right, Sam simply glided through the open pavement of the gas station to his right, an impermissible end run. The cop Sam did not notice behind him was not amused. It looked like there was going to be more than a five yard penalty. Somehow Sam established his wits. He removed himself from the front seat, stood up straight, and walked with almost military, if not regal, bearing, directly to the cop car behind them, the one with the pretty red light on the top still flashing. If there had been a rational mind present, the conclusion would have been clear, Sam would not pass go.

“Officer, what may I do for you this fine morning?”

Back at the Comet, Quentin remained wooden stoic. Joe started extemporating pure paranoia.

"I never thought I would spend the rest of my life in prison in Oklahoma. Fred, let's make a dash for it. I am sure we can out run that cop."

Without looking to the back seat Fred intervened, "Joe, settle down. I am looking into the side view mirror. So far, Sam is talking to the cop at his car. His gun is still holstered."

"That is not funny. I am going to make a break for it."

Fred was all calm and common sense, "Wait, wait, wait. Do nothing 'til you hear for me, and I hope you never will. Sam, I know it is hard to believe, appears to have things well in hand."

In what seemed a month of Tuesdays, Sam walked back to the car. He was carrying only a warning ticket. Fred's reasoned restraint had prevailed. Joe did sit still. The urge to run for his life had somehow been suppressed.

They soon dropped Quentin near the reservation where all the tribal chiefs had been meeting,

"I am only a little late. It has been for a good cause. Stoned spiritual enlightenment is always better than a bunch of prima donnas invoking Robert's Rules of Orders. Like, we're gonna get reparations for Wounded Knee. They might as well ask for all the oil in Oklahoma, throw in Texas to boot, and while the gettin' is good, admit Little Big Horn was all Custer's fault."

Quentin ambled on his way.

R. Torn And Frayed

Sam finally had his opening.

"Joe, where did you find that guy?"

Fred added,

"And how did we not get rid of him?"

Joe told the story of their Joplin's last stand and the drunken goat roper they had to knock unconscious.

"Sam, how did you pull of what you pulled off with that cop?"

"I guess he never figured we would have a case of beer, a bag of dope and some hallucinogens all with some crazed Indian in the back seat that early on a Tuesday morning."

"And thanks, Fred, for keeping me in the back seat."

Sam was unnerved,

"Fuck, Joe. You were gonna bolt. We'd all be in jail, as in lock the door and throw away the key."

"All's well that ends well."

Fred had a question,

"Joe, with all the poker and bridge you play, you'd think you'd know by now how to sit in your chair and not give anything away even when the chips are down, the writings in the wall, the chickens..."

"I get it."

They were out of harm's way. The pressure was off Sam drove amidst cackles and giggles. There was never anything good on the A.M. radio. The billboards for Jesus, Your Savior which were everywhere soon lost their allure. At one point, they knew they were lost, perhaps even in a time warp. They drove down an old dirt farm road. Dust squeezed from four wheels. Red rectangles advertising Burma-Shave flew past them to the right. Finally they stopped the car. They had traversed the way to admire another sunset. They were down to their last hit of mescaline. They each had one. With the one they shared with Quentin right before he got out of the car, this left three, just enough for now. It might not be a Guinness World Record, but it was official- a three day mescaline binge.
For the most part, the happy travelers had the mescaline under control. Only a few times did Sam slam on the breaks to avoid hitting a really large shadow that crossed the road. Intersections were a problem, each one a new experience. Sam would stop. Fred and Sam would discuss the signs. Then they would go through without turning. Joe was head to foot across the backseat. He was watching a really bad version of the Honeymooners with Jackie Gleason and Art Carney on vacation away from the Big Apple. Sam and Fred laughed with Joe, even if he was laughing at them.

It was soon time to stop the car even though there was no crossroad to consider. It was always good idea to stretch your legs and walk around, even it was night. A million stars were bright pin pricks dotting the night sky. The firmament was all anyone ever needed to see. Sam led. Joe and Fred followed. They were soon into the woods. The Comet and the road were somewhere behind, but this was no time to look back. At the same broad and lasting mescaline measured second, all three stopped dead in their tracks. As they came out of the woods, before them was a freshly plowed field, eerie with moist furrows of new soil. Smack dab in the middle was a large white cross. Six eyes scanned for tell-tale signs of robes and hoods. If it were possible to sneak up on an inanimate object, that was what they were doing. Fred, Sam, and Joe traipsed separate paths to the middle, each with his own impression of serpentine stealth. Once again, at the same elongated breath of time, the three pointed. This time their eyes were wide but smiling. Their prey was neither animal nor vegetable. Up this close, their twenty questions were answered. The terrifying cross in the Texas field was part of a pipeline. The twenty-four-inch circumference tube arched up from the ground in two places. The middle where the pipeline reached its highest point was a large valve. The large wheel, needed in an emergency to turn the flow of oil on and off, made a parallel with the ground below. It rested on a perpendicular stem. From a distance its round depth lacked dimension. Seeing they were safe from threats heaven above, white-hooded here, or the other world below, the three star troopers crossed the field to walk a dry creek bed. The stars shone upon marvel after marvel until they came full circle.

They got back in the car to head for the place where the road and the sky collide. The next stop was a roadside picnic area overlooking Denton. Here there was nothing better than what life had to offer. First stand on a picnic bench. Next lift yourself up to a big branch of an accommodating large Oak. Then pull yourself up to the next available large branch. Finally, straddle like you are on a horse and rest your palms in front of you. From their separate but equal perches, the city lights did battle to blur the canopy of stars above.

S. Tumbling Dice

The second time he left campus, Joe stayed closer to 8A Holder. It was "political break." When Nixon first heard of it, the President was not happy. College students let loose before mid-term elections. If the practice continued, re-election was in two years, the menace might be palpable. There was no doubt for anyone in the administration. The college students would be aligned against Nixon, full force. Years later, in the Sleepy Little Village, the old men having their morning coffee at the Towne Shoppe all agreed. It must have been Hank Paulson. He was working as a White House intern. Princeton was the first to announce that the school would give two weeks off from classes to aid the political campaign of choice. Nixon was sure other schools would follow. Someone suggested that the idea of a political break was sufficient for a university to lose its tax exempt status. It was only the tax code but Nixon liked it. An Assistant U.S. Attorney by the name of William H. Rehnquist was assigned the task of doing the research necessary to nip the whole peril in the bud. Nixon would put the fear of God into Princeton and anyone else who might wish to follow along. Free speech has its limits. Taxes were the best way to hit the point home hard. Hank Paulson was the guy who knew all that Treasury stuff. It might have been conjecture but who, other than Old Hank, would run such an idea up the flagpole. Eventually, no one saluted it. For whatever the reason, the 1971, "Political Break" lived to tell the tale. Everybody got two weeks off. Joe was not inclined to volunteer to help fight the futile battle against the re-election of "his" Congressman, Donald Rumsfeld. He would pick his spots if he wanted to go piss into the wind. Joe called Fred who was happy to join Parsley Fief, Appleseed, and Joe for the freefall Greenwich Village and the rest of Manhattan would offer. Felina had a weak moment. She agreed that all four of the guys could crash at her apartment. She told her roommate, who had just dumped her boyfriend, that they were all attractive guys, even though she had yet to meet Tim or Teddy, and she knew Fred and Joe were neither worth writing home to mother.

The late afternoon autumn sun sent waning beams through recently windexed window panes. Felina welcomed Teddy, Tim, and Joe with open arms. She fully anticipated that a good time would be had by all. The close quarters of her small two bedroom virtually assured her roommate would share a bed with one or both of Joe's Princeton friends. Felina and Joe would sleep together. Their whole lives they had been more siblings than lovers so who knew where the two would land this time. Once Fred arrived, he would be on his own. The principle of first come, first served left him late and never. The next morning Joe got up to take the subway to Grand Central Station where Fred and he agreed to meet. Felina was right. Fenton Appleseed discovered the comfort of her roommate's bed. Tim Parsley Fief slept on the couch.

Joe's ride uptown was uneventful. He stood at the appointed intersection, as he watched the Grand Central Clock click thirty minutes past the time Fred said he would be there. Ten minutes later, Joe did not see Fred. Fred was on time. He leaned against a lamp post directly across the street. Standing in a sea of commuters, a bustling throng worming its way through the Big Apple, neither Fred nor Joe could keep heads above water long enough to see one another. This is not the sort of thing that would ever happen in the Sleepy Little Village or up a tree in North Texas. It was a bump in the road that lasted less than an hour. Fred could not believe New York. Even the subway ride back downtown held his interest. Everything he saw was exotic. Fred did not need to tell Joe had not stayed long at North Texas State. Two weeks later, Fred returned home. It was not just the billboards that read "Turn in a Pusher Today." Being away from the Sleepy Little Village was really not part of the genetic predisposition of any Etheridge, unless it was only a trip to visit his best friend back East.

Two at a time, Fred and Joe took the steps to Felina's apartment. Teddy had picked some music to play. The stereo was in fine tune. The old floor boards heaved with the bass notes from the speakers. First it was Pink Floyd's *Atom Heart Mother* then Emerson, Lake, and Palmer's self-titled first album. The "Lucky Man" synthesizer solo was in full regalia when Felina made a suggestion,

"The two records you just played, even though brand new, were accidentally left here by my roommate's old boyfriend. They parted ways the day before you guys got here. Would you guys mind if we play the other stuff in the bin, the kind of music girls tend to like? I have a record I just bought, brand new, too."

Felina handed to Teddy Elton John's *Tumbleweed Connection.* "Come Down in Time" soon had the six a crowd mesmerized. That night, Teddy opted to stay with Felina's roommate. Felina had to go to work. She was a waitress at a Greenwich Village coffee shop. Fred, Joe, and Tim decided to go to Washington Square. The new freedom milled everywhere. They smoked a joint before they left. Soon they were standing under a tree. The New York City Park District had installed a large tree house in the lower branches. Their intention was that little kids would play there. That night it was all for big little kids. Two girls invited the three boys up to see if they would like some of the blotter acid they had just taken. In a short time, the tree seemed to grow and spread its wings, five people who did not know each other were now like one old married couple, cozy but with nothing to say. The parade below and all around offered its own intricate pulse. Joe quickly learned not to turn his head too fast. The best way to observe was slowly, a little at a time.

Felina was not happy when Joe returned to her bed at four in the morning, "I thought you came here to see me."

"The best laid plans…"

“Do not involve that activity right now, or anytime soon.”

Felina’s feelings were hurt. Even through the lens of the acid, Joe was sure of that. The flow of the drug through his body also made sure he felt too good to get upset about the whole thing.

The next day was Saturday, October 24th. Felina was still in a tiff. Joe was back on an even keel.

“Felina, this is not really like you. Please tell me what is bothering you.”

“You are right Joe. It is not really you. I hoped we could recreate the magic bus and our real intimacy in those couple of days that followed. I see it was a time we will always treasure. Time and space will keep us apart, more than even now. I really do not like it here, not just New York, the whole fester that is the United States. I have decided to move to Toronto. My sister works for the CBC there, doing serious public television news. I can get a job with her.”

“Sounds cool.”

“I hope so. Anyway, I am working a double shift at the coffee shop. I was going to spend the evening with you but a friend asked me to cover for her, and I will need the money to move across the border.”

Joe kissed Felina on her forehead. The fraternal irony struck both of them.

It was the night to set the clocks back. In the Village in those days, hallucinogens or not, time was never a factor. Teddy decided to join his buddies to go to the Fillmore East. Now there were two disgruntled girls at Felina’s. The Fillmore that night had the usual three acts- a band nobody had ever heard of, Ballin’ Jack, Humble Pie with Steve Marriot and Peter Frampton, two confections followed by a real concoction, Clapton’s Derek and The Dominos. Fief, Appleseed, Etheridge, and Cebellum left the roost three hours before show time. It never hurt to wander the never-ending gala of the Village streets. Three girls and a cat sat on the front steps of a walkup. Fred tottered but did not tip when he sensed he had been relegated to the cat, a calico with an unerring aura of calm. The other six chattered before and during the mescaline the girls had to offer. The four boys were peaking when they walked up the Fillmore's balcony steps, the best seats that could get. The balcony was plenty close enough. The music drew them in. The light show gave them images upon which they could ride. Afterwards, they each had a different song to exclaim. Fred won the award for best choice of the night. It was the Blind Faith song, *Presence of the Lord.* Clapton's solo reached notes of a new depth. The light show usually splatted a bunch of amorphous blobs behind the band. Fred decided he had willed his own order upon the blobs, transforming them into photos. One European Cathedral after another loomed large as it flashed across Fred's psyche. Fred was convinced that he had a religious experience all his own with everyone else mired in amorphous blobs. While Teddy was on a magic carpet ride of his own somewhere else, Joe and Tim described the same churches. Fred allowed that a group hallucination had transcribed their attention.

"Joe and Fief, I am convinced God spreads His hand out to grasp His love, and that only the special chosen, the elected few will see to answer the call."

"So Fred, what did you think of the way Clapton segued 'Blues Power' to the Freddy King classic, 'Have You Ever Loved a Woman?'"

"That was so cool. I could not help thinking about Martha. Someday she and I will raise a large family of happy kids."

"You are hopeless. At least, you have a short attention span that always relapses into the mode of fun, full speed ahead."

"Right you are."

Joe, Fred, Tim, and Teddy spent the rest of the night, taking full advantage of the extra hour from the time change. Their footsteps were afrolic. It did not matter whether you danced to music heard externally, heard just in your head, or both at the same time.

T. Stop Breaking Down

By December, music gained tenure to reign supreme at 8A Holder. Night and Day, the stereo blasted without rest. There was a little bridge, poker, and the game of "hearts" thrown in to fill the time until the next joint was passed around. The hardest part for Joe was making sure the discs were put back without harm. His roommates and the other guys who wandered in to play some tunes left the discs anywhere and everywhere. Joe was the guy who slipped the records back into their paper dust jackets, and then back into their album covers. Occasionally, Joe would wait a little. Someone needed to use one of the album covers which opened up at the middle to clean some dope of seeds and stems before rolling a joint. With new releases in November and December, the music fashioned its own history, Derek and the Dominos, *Layla*, Van Morrison, *His band and Street Choir*, Stephen Stills self-titled solo album, Cat Stevens, *Tea for the Tillerman*, George Harrison's monumental, *All Things Must Pass*, the Grateful Dead, *American Beauty*, Jefferson Starship, *Blows Against the Empire*, Spirit, *Twelve Dreams of Dr. Sardonicus*, Ry Cooder, *Into the Purple Valley*, Ten Years After, *Watt*, Peter Green, *The End of the Game*, and Savoy Brown *Looking In*.

"Thew" insisted upon adding the soundtrack from *Jesus Christ Superstar* to the mix. Once Yvonne Elliman started singing, "I don't' know how to love him..." he would walk behind the bar, open the little refrigerator, grab the brown bottle of amyl nitrate, and inhale. He was the only one who did "poppers." He claimed the rush overtook him. Hearing Yvonne Elliman over and over again, Joe came very close to crucifying "Thew" or, worse yet, throwing the Jesus Christ Superstar disc out the third floor window.

Music guided every step. It started slowly, whether you knew it or not. The Grateful Dead's "Ripple" soon sent ever burgeoning circles everywhere.

"If my words did glow with the gold of sunshine
And my tunes were played on the harp unstrung,
Would you hear my voice come thru the music,
Would you hold it near as it were your own?

It's a hand-me-down, the thoughts are broken,
Perhaps they're better left unsung.
I don't know, don't really care
Let there be songs to fill the air.

Ripple in still water,
When there is no pebble tossed,
Nor wind to blow.

Reach out your hand if your cup be empty,
If your cup is full may it be again,
Let it be known there is a fountain,
That was not made by the hands of men.

There is a road, no simple highway,
Between the dawn and the dark of night,
And if you go no one may follow,
That path is for your steps alone...
...You who choose to lead must follow
But if you fall you fall alone,
If you should stand then who's to guide you?
If I knew the way I would take you home."

With the abundant help of albums strewn all about, L.S.D. came to stand on its own two legs.

U. Rocks Off

The locus with the focus was not invariably 8A Holder. One night, Joe decided to go see “Lemming” Cello. Cello shared a room with Barry Richardson and Rick Boehm in the corner entry of Joline Hall. It was early November and unseasonably warm. Rick Boehm was in the living room nodding at the stereo. The Band was playing “Across the Great Divide.” R.B. did not look up when Joe entered the room and said, “Hey Boehm.” Joe walked into the single bedroom Barry needed when Celeste visited. He was on his hands and knees, looking under the bed.

“Hey Barry, what’s going on?”

“Joe maybe you can help me. I have dropped my left eyeball. I think it rolled under the bed.”

“O.K. now I get it. When do you and Boehm do the hallucinogens?”

“Not just the two of us, ‘Lemming’ Cello too. The physics major we bought it from said it was really good and laughed diabolically. I had no idea how right he was. Anyway I think I am going to need my other eyeball very soon.”

Joe showed Barry he had both eyes in their sockets,

“I guess I found it under the bed and forgot I put it back in...”

Cello came running into room. He slammed the door behind him then looked all around,

"Run for your lives and hide while you still have the chance."

Cello then ran into the bedroom he shared with Boehm. All of John's 6 feet and 3 inches and 260 lbs then scrunched itself under the lower bunk.

Joe was calm. He peered under the bed.

"So tell me my good friend. Something is happening and it isn't exactly clear..."

"The acid we took hit me very hard while I was waiting tables at Colonial. At first it was all too beautiful then it was entirely too much. I took off my serving apron and left the Club. I walked across campus. At first the lights from the Martian space ships were sporadic. So I started to run. Then the lights were everywhere, all pointing at me. Thank God I am now safe. You guys better find a place to hide before it is too late."

Joe reflected upon all the flashing lights,

"Cello, listen to me. What you saw was only the normal lights on campus- bright and electric- brazen from the acid you are doing, as you ran the lights surrounded you, seeming to come from everywhere. I'll go outside but I am pretty sure there are no flying saucers out there."

"Thanks man, please check it out."

As Joe passed Barry,

"Thanks, Joe for helping me find my eyeball."

Boehm looked up as Joe left the room. Somehow the stereo was now playing from a collection called something like *Twang To Remember*. It was the Ventures, “Walk Don’t Run.”

It turned out that the only aliens on campus were space cadets like Joe and his buddies. The admissions office could not be pleased by the rising tide of their numbers. “Lemming” Cello was relieved it was only a paper sun. He somehow unwedged himself from under the bed.

V. Dreamland

Another time Frites, Fief, Cello, and Cebellum decided to drive to Route One after they were peaking on some windowpane. Cello drove there but Joe drove back. The diner was all plastic and primary colors, illuminated by really crisp electric lights. Somehow the four guys ordered. Three of them sat quietly observing obscenely large pieces of heavily frosted cake waiting for their next move. If the pieces of cake started talking, or, at the very least inhaling and exhaling, no one would have been at all surprised. Joe ate his four layers of Black Forest cake, frosting and all. He then did his best to eat the others' three pieces. His stomach ran out of room half way through the last piece, the Diner's signature New York Cheesecake with Strawberries and a red, really sweet glaze. The glaze matched the color and vibrations of the neon lights that formed the top border outside.

On the liner notes for *Surrealistic Pillow* by Jefferson Airplane, the lead guitar player for the Grateful Dead, Jerry Garcia was listed as "Capt. Trips." Whenever Joe went back home to the Sleepy Little Village, not one person ever believed he was the stabilizing influence among his band of merry pranksters. "Lemming" Cello delighted in calling Joe, "Straight Arrow Cebellum."

Cello coined the name the first time Joe happened upon John trying to hypnotize Rick Boehm while R.B. was sleeping.

"R.B. you are getting sleepy, sleepy. Watch my forefinger. Your eyes are getting tired. R.B. you are getting sleepy. Sleepy, slee..."

It was unexpected but predictable, R.B. started to snore.

“Lemming” Cello was now certain. He could not be persuaded his hypnosis had not worked.

The more Joe tried, the more John knew his friend was a straight arrow, unable to understand the universe of soul traveling, astral projection and other marvels into the mystic. It turned out R.B. could sleep anywhere under the influence of any drug. He visited 8A Holder one day. Fief, Appleseed, Cebellum and he did a hit of acid, one little yellow dot on a sugar cube each. This was the third time they got L.S.D. from some physics major. The regimen of very high volume started with the side of *All Things Must Pass* that had Dylan’s “If Not For You,” then both sides of Dave Mason’s *Alone Together*, the side of Traffic’s *John Barleycorn Must Die* with the song “Glad,” and finally the side of Eric Clapton’s solo album with the song, “Blues Power.” Even without the L.S.D., they had all the ingredients for a plentitude of understated reverence.

Rick Boehm got up at the same time Joe did to change the record,

“Hey guys. I’ve got to go to work at 6 a.m. at Commons, the breakfast shift. I’ll see you later.”

The way out of 8A Holder posed some confusion. It did not matter that R.B. had gone out the correct door one hundred times before or that it was then one hundred years from now. There was a door to the left which led out. There was also a door to the right, just in front of the bar. It opened into a closet. As the stereo played the George Harrison song, “Behind That Locked Door,” Boehm picked door number two. No one was surprised when R.B. emerged from the closet five hours later, just in time to make it to work. The music was still playing as the sun sparkled on the morning dew in Holder Courtyard. The evidence was anecdotal but it seemed to confirm that one door is as good as another when you are doing L.S.D.

W. Indian Woman from Wichita

More and more that fall, Fief returned to Nassau Street near Palmer Square. Two or three Black Panthers were often there handing out pamphlets and their magazine. Parsley Fief had one of the more severe cases of white upper-middle class guilt complex that the world has ever known. At first, the black guys were not amused when Fief would try to give them high fives and say stuff like "Tell it brother, tell it like it is." Eventually they figured there was no harm in letting Fief hand out printed materials when they were not there. One day Fief was proselytizing for the proletariat. A girl from Princeton High School took an interest. Her name was Doris Concave. She was in her Junior year. One thing led to another. She and Fief soon became fast friends. Joe was never bothered when Doris and Fief would close the door to the bedroom he shared. Joe was always outside around the burnt orange coffee table listening to music, playing cards or not. Other times, when the Concave house was empty, Fief and Doris would camp out there. Doris was an only child whose parents liked to spend the weekend up in Manhattan taking in a Broadway show or two. One afternoon in mid- November Doris brought a friend for Teddy Appleseed. Her name was Cathy Forsch. She was also a Junior. Doris was skinny with dirty blonde hair. She had a bad complexion, roseated blotches more than the pimples that Fief sported. Cathy fell on the side of the well-fed. Her tawny brown hair was naturally curly, tight curls that the young Shirley Temple would have coveted. Teddy and Cathy would be together three years later when he was forthright in his devotion,

"Cathy, I love you, all of you, even your double chin."

Seeing the progress to the bedroom, doors closed behind them, for both Fief and Appleseed, Joe finally decided it might be a good idea if Doris and Cathy found someone for him. It was an appealing idea, to go into the bedroom he shared with Fief then close the door while the music played on.

Joe and his buddies had an established rule. Whenever anyone proposed a bet, the person to whom the bet was proposed could take either side. The idea was to ensure fundamental fairness in the terms of the wager, or at least what the proponent thought was fair.

“Joe, Doris says she is going to bring a friend for you to meet this weekend. She says you will like her.”

“I’ll bet five bucks I like her.”

“I’ll bet you five bucks you do, too.”

Teddy wanted some of the action,

“I’ll bet you that you like her, too.”

Fenton Appleseed, with his at least one dividend check a day to keep a lot of things away, was imposing,

“Teddy, I cannot afford your stakes. How ‘bout we say another fin?”

“It’s a bet.”

X. Shake Your Hips

It was cold that December Friday. Doris and Cathy walked into 8A Holder bringing the cold in with them. As they both took off their navy pea jackets, Joe noticed the girl who was tentative in following them in.

"Hi Joe, This is Mary Davis. She is one of our classmates and a good friend."

Mary was medium height, a little shorter. She was wearing hip hugger blue denim bellbottoms. Her synthetic light blue blouse clung to her body. Joe could tell she was wearing one of those new smooth cupped bras that unsnapped in the front. It took him years to master the one handed unsnap from the back. Now they were doing this to him. Mary's breasts formed only a slight contour away for her chest. Her small bottom gave her blue jeans shape. She was not overweight but she still had a slight hint of baby fat, especially in her round pleasing pink cheeks. Mary's eyes were very pale blue, almost no color at all. She looked at the world with comfort that might have been mistaken for complacency. Mary mirrored contradiction. It started with soft aquiline lines and ended with a small mouth with thin pink lips that beckoned for attention. Her contradictions did not conflict. Joe immediately fell in with her harmony, a fragile balance that drew great strength from a bright inner light, a beacon beaming only for him. Mary held out her hand as she stepped toward Joe. The hesitation she showed when she entered the room was gone. Her motion spoke of some selfless knowledge, inside and out. Mary Davis lacked the pride of beauty which kept track of men's glances in her direction as so many notches on her belt. She jitterbugged to feel the flow not to show off what she had. At Benny Goodman's 1939 Carnegie Hall concert, the society folk got up to fill the aisles with the motion they could not contain as the band played *One O'Clock Jump*. The main floor ticketholders were released to full freedom. For Mary Davis, no restrictions were part of her natural gait. Her inner tempo so moved her. Tranquility and solace formed the base for her meter. She was not reticent but rather an inviting calm looking for a spark. Circumstances would soon show Joe's spinning fervor was just what the doctor ordered.

The next night there was an open party at 8A Holder. DDT and his roommates, Dave Major and Bill Fitts attended. Dan Wigodsky spent the night studying at the Architecture Building, across McCosh Walk from McCosh Hall, only a stone's throw across Washington road to the Woodrow Wilson School of Public Affairs. Mary and Joe snuck up the stairs to the empty room. A long and happy concupiscence was quietly, but fervently consummated in an unused bed. From the outset their intimacy was not only juicy but sweet. It would blossom to a proportion Joe could not then imagine.

Y. Ventilator Blues

It was a Thursday night in December, right before Christmas Break. It had happened before. It was now threatening to become habit. One weekday night during the school week, usually Thursday, Joe and his buddies all did acid or mescaline. The weekends were also used for intermittent tripping. What would soon to be habitual was not that they would all hallucinate every Thursday night, but rather, an attendant ritual. When Joe could feel the early effects of the drug which would soon more steadily influence his buddies and him, he would pop up to put side one of The Beatles' *Abbey Road* on the turntable, full volume. As that side's last song, "I Want You (She So Heavy)" tried to find a way to end itself and the needle ricocheted in the last groove, Joe would flip the record to ring in the aural splendor of side two. It may seem trite but "Here Comes the Sun" and the seamless songs that followed were the perfect place to peak. The twenty-three seconds of "Her Majesty" had just ended. Teddy got up. He accidentally looked out the window,

"What the fuck?"

Fief joined him,

"Will you look at that? It's like they have never seen snow before, and not very much at that, either. It was the first snow for many Southerners. From the Princeton University Internet archives, here is how some historians have recorded how it happened one night, something which the Daily Princetonian at first dubbed the "Christmas Carouse."

“...by 1970 many of the restrictive rules of campus life from prior eras, including mandatory chapel attendance and parietals, gave way to a more liberal set of behaviors...

...Broadway theater included nudity in plays such as "Hair" and "Oh, Calcutta," and the first Woodstock Concert (1969) was often characterized as a Three Day Love-In of 500,000 young people.

...According to well documented reports, one resident of the third entry of Holder from a group called the Bachelors Six was especially known for his antics, that sometimes included Reading Period tension reduction tactics with bottle rockets, unauthorized bonfires, and occasional sprints around the courtyard in the buff. Most times he soloed, but on rare occasion that year, he managed to coerce another to participate, jokingly dubbing the activity "Nude Relays."

In December of 1970, their junior year, a surprise snowstorm settled across campus on a Thursday evening, only days before Holiday Recess was to commence. One of them, John Leidy '72, telephoned Public Safety to complain that several naked students were cavorting in Holder Courtyard. At the time of his call, nothing had in fact happened. Immediately thereafter, he also telephoned the offices of the Daily Princetonian with a similar report and asking if they would be covering the "Nude Olympics." When the Prince confessed ignorance of said event, Leidy then suggested they get verification by calling the Proctor's Office. When the inquiring Prince reporter phoned the Proctor's, his inquiry was met with the response, "We just received a call about that, and are sending an officer to look into it."

Not long thereafter, a handful of individuals were indeed cavorting in the snowy courtyard in various states of undress, at times racing one another across the courtyard. Whenever a Proctor appeared on the scene, these "athletes" would disappear into one of Holder's many entryways, and then run through the underground corridors, to resurface on the other side of the courtyard, much to the delight of the growing crowd of onlookers who cheered their many escapes.

Whether or not there was full fledged nudity on this occasion is subject to some debate, but this event became known as the "snow riot" or "nude Olympics" and these antics were spoken of laughingly across campus by the following morning.

"...using the stimulant of choice in those days. That coupled with loud music and an unexpected snowfall caused Tom to open up the ground floor window and announce in his booming, melifluous voice, "IT'S SNOWING" (Tom always did have a keen sense of the obvious)...Lee K. was among the first to respond to Tom's riotous mating call and within minutes at least a dozen of us were swirling around in the snow in Holder courtyard. At this point people like S. and K. were certainly involved...

My recollection was that there was a big parade in Holder on the first snowfall. However, I'm not sure how much clothing was worn because it was all-male in Holder at the time.

I also recall that Santa Claus made an appearance!

...On April 11, 1999, the Board of Trustees voted to ban the annual tradition... The following August, prior to the beginning of the academic year, each undergraduate received a personal letter calling his/her attention to this ban. In addition, their Parents and Guardians also received a similar letter, that included the sentence, "I want to encourage you to be sure that your student also is fully informed."

Z. Coming Out

To Joe the ruckus was absurd. Snow was nothing new. The attitude that there's no business like snow business had lost its luster by the time he entered kindergarten. Beyond that, Joe was a major proponent of the point of view that nudity should not be wasted on a bunch of guys running around. Everyone's scope and vision is limited by their upbringing and environment. Even Joe showed his hand. The embarrassing stripes of the prison from which had hailed were hidden only slightly below the surface. Over a year ago, still brand new to the campus during Freshmen Week, Joe stood on the front porch of Witherspoon. He and Bill Goldberg, a guy from New York, had introduced themselves to one another. They discussed the practice whereby the guys who lived in the room the previous year would sell the refrigerator to those new to that room. An improvident word left Joe's lips. It would never happen again. Joe said to Bill,

"Everyone seems to enjoy Jewing about the price of the beat up old refrigerators."

It was a gerund of common usage in the Sleepy Little Village. The sad and surprised look on Bill Goldberg's face made Joe realize he was not in Kansas anymore. One of the professors in Princeton's philosophy department which was the best in the English speaking world, was a guy named Richard Rorty. Rorty always stuck to the guns he was predisposed to stick, "The way you constitute the world determines the way you constitute the world." Most reasonable historians agree that Charlie Scribner did not participate in that first Nude Olympics. It was beneath his dignity to spend a Thursday evening running around in his birthday suit. More likely, two nights later the fourth young Charlie would be in his proper place standing forth in that which is the opposite of nudity. It did not matter whether it was a white tail debutante ball or some other type of Christmas coming out. The quintessence of formalwear is what the invitation demands. It is indeed a pretty picture to imagine Charlie Scribner amidst his peers, a few other fledgling traditional backbones of the social register, all properly attired. A tidy group assembled in someone's private suite at the Waldorf Astoria, white bows firmly tied around their necks, the circulation in their stiff upper lips unaffected. Since there are few so privileged, most must guess the content of the polite, but simply marvelous chit chat and the restrained glee that follows when St. Paul's school chums reunite after semesters at Cambridge, New Haven, and Princeton. One can only suppose the words used while they wait, in the lap of luxury, to escort fair haired maidens presently engaged in powdering their noses.

Some are building monuments, others jotting down notes...

XXVII. "Easy To Love"

A. Lullaby

Joe and Sally Sensabell were still stoned. The dope they smoked on the way to see the move, *Love Story* had not worn off. The movie was ridiculous. Fortunately, marijuana allows a different perspective, always creating many new points of interest. That night sitting before the silver screen watching a movie that even ogling Ali McGraw would not save, Joe soon skipped over the lame plot and the sophomoric acting. His attention quickly turned to the transitions, fades, and dissolves which all approached the interminably funny.

"Sally do you remember that part where the door opened to the next scene?"

"Yep, I giggled the same time you did. Somebody in the editing room was overworked. I don't think we should have snickered over all that sadness at the end."

"Hooray for Hollywood. They say a camel was devised by committee..."

"This movie was deranged by those who should be committed."

"Exactly where I was going. And Erich Segal. He should stick to teaching Latin and Greek."

"Money means never having to say you're sorry."

"Joe, have you met Martha Sharpley?"

"Yep, I had one ill-fated date to a Miles Davis concert with her roommate."

"I got no kick against modern jazz. But I am pretty serious about her brother, Dustin. He and I are taking some classes together at S.C."

"Sally, you deserve the best. Thanks for going to the movies with me. I look forward to seeing you this summer."

Joe walked Sally to her front door.

"You wanna come in. It looks like my parents are still out we can blast some music 'til they get back."

It was the same couch they had commandeered many times before. Sally lay down her head on Joe's lap. He stroked her hair with fond caresses. That night they were soon on an interstellar flight deck. The Jefferson Starship commanded its own special version of space travel. The song, "Have You Seen the Stars Tonight," from *Blows Against the Empire* rang loud and true. If sound gliding from a stereo could do it, it had. The two old friends touched one another again. The evening spoke softly for the next two hours. Neither said a word as Sally rested in Joe's arms. The Sensabells came home. It was time for Joe to go. Sally walked him to the front door. He kissed her lightly. She pressed back after making her winter dry lips moist with her tongue.

"Happy New Year, Sally."

"You are two days early."

"I know but tomorrow I am playing poker with 'Ma' Camphor and the gang. New Year's Eve, Fred and Tommy have fixed me up with someone from Harper. There is a party in Arlington Heights in somebody's fixed-up basement Rec Room."

Sally kissed Joe. It was a kiss she hoped would last until the summer.

B. Time to Run

It had now been confirmed. In fact, it was old news. Tommy had fallen prey to the Wanderby genetic yearning for beauty queens. Delilah Pellioni was now sitting in the director's chair. She had taken to wearing rings on every finger. Delilah followed a time-honored principle. The number of rings on your fingers governs how much you move your hands when you talk. She could thus add emphasis to her imperatives with every wave of her hand.

She insisted that Fred take Madeleine Palmisano. Martha had not come home from Stephens. She said she did not want to be home at Christmas. Since her mother was dead, their house in Tower lakes was more mausoleum than family home. Fred was always true to Martha in his fashion. Madeleine was the kind of girl you would not want to take home to meet mom. She was perfect for all sorts of all night revelry. Delilah also corralled a friend for Joe, Sheila O'Brian. She was a true Irish beauty who would win any Katherine Ross look-a-like contest. Joe looked forward to replaying the scene from *Butch Cassidy and The Sundance Kid* where Redford watches while Katherine Ross untimorously drops her undergarments to the floor in front of him. Redford's Sundance added some steam to the scene by pointing a pistol he did not need. Joe did not own a gun. He hoped Sheila would be cooperative without the prop. When he picked her up for the blind date that New Year's Eve, he knew he was overmatched by her wholesome allure. One of the things Joe noticed as he grew up in Barrington was that, as a general rule, there was no doubt that people who have money are prettier than those who do not. Some beauty does transcend its humble circumstances. Sheila was heads above the pack. New Year's Eve ended the way it usually did when Fred was around. After everyone dropped their dates back home, Tommy and Joe drove around trying to find the snow bank where Fred had come to rest. No one wanted Fred to spend his remaining New Years frozen to death.

C. Brother

It had been long decided to play poker at Camphors, on the first day of 1971 starting right around noon as soon as everyone got up. They could play in the kitchen. The t.v. would be on in the living room so they would not miss the bowl games or the Rose Parade.

Sam and Joe waited for Tommy and Fred to arrive. Tim was up showering. "Ma" was washing the dishes from a late breakfast.

"Sam do you really think it was a good idea to tell Delilah she had no sense of history, especially the history that surrounded Joan of Arc."

"I don't even hold reverence in reverence. I tell it like it is, brother. "

"Was it really worth running the risk of the Pellioni Harper College girlwide blacklist that has now been visited upon you?"

"We will see. I have a new working hypothesis. A bad idea incubated by the passage of time is better than any new idea."

"You do know that there is no hypothetical construct which will fail to find support in some array of facts. Sam it may be that it is infinitely more interesting and rewarding to find ways in which someone is right than to simply enumerate the faults of another. Your entire perspective is turned topsy-turvy."

Sam had not learned that he should not be afraid to amplify, underscore, or backlight prior footsteps,

“For me, life is all about latching upon a different niche.”

“Sam, when there is no gentle breeze, the adroit have learned to sway. The trick is to avoid letting your own motion make you too light-headed. What did you do last night?”

“I listed to the Stones’ new release, *Let it Bleed.* The liner notes say, ‘PLAY IT LOUD’ and they mean it. I played it over and over again. I can assure you the louder it is, the higher you go.”

“Cool, I am sure we will give it good play back in New Jersey.”

“Yea, wait ‘til you hear, ‘Midnight Rambler.’”

Sonamble

D. The Host on the Shore

The was the first day the television did not feature talking packs of cigarettes or catchy jingles espousing the virtue of lighting one up to catch a lady's eye. Even the Virginia Slims catchphrase, "You've Come a Long Way, Baby" would not be heard as an ad on t.v. ever again. Cigarette advertising had been banned. Sam Thorn predicted the result would be cataclysmic, the downfall of the United States of America. With certain deleterious and permanent repercussions, the Marlboro man would be supplanted with ads for feminine hygiene deodorant spray. The national psyche would be scarred forever. It was abundantly clear. Sam hoped to live in a world where he did not disgrace the party, to be a big part of something he could never attain. On the other hand, Fred knew he was alive and lively. Wherever he walked, the party followed him. To prove the point, Fred walked into the Camphor living room carrying a case of beer.

E. In the Wind

Two days later, Joe was happy to be back at Princeton. It was not just he would soon see Mary Davis. It was more than the fact she carried an unlimited number of discrete packets of sexual energy ready to be unbundled at the drop of a hat. Something had happened. Now there was something about the place itself. After three semesters, Joe was more than pleased, more than comfortable. It had only been a matter of time. Whether immersed in the rigors and discipline of study or not, all who go to Princeton become part of Nature-knitted hedges trimmed with the notion of pleasing angles and imposing hightowers taking geometric cues, adorned with non-offending ornaments. Joe also loved hanging around with his buddies. Music and cards all interspersed then doused with talk. The word in those days was "rapping." To rap trivialized the conversation that any two guys at Princeton, friends or strangers, could, and would have. When good friends with the bond of camaraderie sat down to smoke a joint, the words that flowed were full of life and substance, even if nobody really knew either the course of the conversation or the meaning of the meander. Being right was not the issue. The process ruled the day.

Rick Boehm came back from Christmas Break. He had been home in Tallmadge, Ohio. He brought with him a new poker game. One of his Catholic high school buddies had introduced it to his group. It was not really poker. It resembled "Three Card Gut." During the fall, Three Card Gut became the game of choice at 8A Holder. You anteed and were dealt three cards. Then, everybody put a closed fist over the table. All hands opened at the same time. If you had a chip you were in. If not you were out and waited for your next three cards. The game lasted as long as there was money in the pot. If you were in and held the high hand, you took the pot. If you were in and you lost, you matched the pot. More than one loser would increase the size of the pot. The many alums who were free market proponents would be proud. At the burnt orange coffee table, in a sonic envelope, there was no "maximum burn." The game was unregulated. The players did their best to avoid the finger that pointed. Nobody wanted to be the last man standing. Figuratively or not, "it points for thee" were words no one wanted to hear.

F. I Will Be Back One Day

In the beginning the 8A Holder poker games were straight five card draw and straight seven card stud. Then a lot of wild-card perversions were added. It was more than drug induced hysteria. The next illogical step was the game of Gut. It was fast and full of cheap thrills. The biggest kick was winning. Next came losing. Gambling addicts could not ask for more. What came to be called, "The Boehm Game" was similar to Three Card Gut. Both involved matching the pot with the strong possibility that the pot would increase in size to unwieldy proportions with no government bailout on the horizon. You were soon playing a game where the pot made its prior exponents seem small numbers. Avarice marked a treacherous landscape. The Boehm Game took greed up a notch by injecting another element of skill. It was a trick taking game. Three cards were dealt. Then a card was turned up. That card was trump. Like three card gut, you could be in or out, hand empty or full, all opened at once. Now came the crazy part, you could take up to three new cards. If you threw your hand away, you were taking a "Boehm." You did not need to have anything to stick. Pure potential added a dimension for any true thrillseeker. The next step was for the guy next to the dealer to lead. So in addition to the slight skill involved in the play of a three card trick taking game, there was a decided advantage to be dealer, the last to play to the first trick. It also could help to be the one who made the opening lead. If you were in and did not take a trick, you matched the pot. For each trick you did take, you received one-third of the pot.

Reading period and exam period were over. It was the first day of classes. Nobody had classes that day. Or if they did, The Boehm Game seemed a better use of time. Bill Fitts made a small mistake. He stuck his head in the door. Fitts was Mississippi cordial. On a different day, he might have headed to class. Fitts sat down to play. The game started with a few straight seven card stud games. Then "Thew" fell from grace,

"Let's play The Boehm Game."

Fitts was apprised. Things seemed to be going well for him. He had one hundred dollars plus the fifty with which he started. The moving finger could not sit still. The pot tripled to four hundred and fifty dollars. It then doubled to nine hundred. Fitts looked at his cards. There was no doubt Christmas was here again, and so close to the last one. The four of diamonds had been turned to name trumps. Fitts was looking at the Jack, ten, and nine of diamonds. Only the Ace, King, and Queen were higher. Sixteen cards had been dealt, including the one that had been flipped. Nobody threw their hand in take three new cards. That meant thirty-six cards which were not in the game could include the higher face cards or one of them. Two other players, Boehm and Joe, stayed in the game. Victory seemed assured. One of them could not hold all three of the relevant high diamonds. If Fitts was on lead, he would almost certainly get one trick to avoid matching the pot. Joe was on lead, however. Joe had the King and Queen of diamonds and the Ace of spades. He led the spade. Fitts played next. The nine of diamonds, the curse of Scotland hit the table. Rick Boehm had the Ace and King of hearts and the Ace of Diamonds. Boehm over-ruffed, playing the diamond Ace. Joe showed his hand. Since the Ace was just played, the King and Queen were now high. The Jack, ten and nine of diamonds held by Bill Fitts had improbably bit the dust. Fitts did not hear "Thew" say,

"Read 'em and weep."

If he had heard "Thew" continue who knows what might have happened. Fitts was in a non-sentient daze.

"If the shoe Fitts, wear it."

Bill Fitts was a stunned zombie. He lost eight hundred dollars in less than an hour, a lot less. He moped upstairs carrying his befuddled blur with him. The phone rang. It was the Dean's office. In another fifteen minutes, he sat in a chair in front of a solemn Dean Rudenstine. The news was not good. Bill Fitts had flunked out. All Six Feet Four Inches and Two Hundred and Twenty Pounds of Bill Fitts were not too big to fail. For many years, both Princeton Charlie and the Gentlemen's "C" were inviolate fixtures. You had to try hard, really hard, to flunk out. The primary motivating force for such drastic steps was simple unhappiness. The bevy of Prep school kids that had historically peopled Princeton had learned to become inured to their predicament. It would be odd to go from a public school environment where the males and females met in balance to Princeton with no female off-set in sight and then not be miserable. In a twice-told tale, Bill Fitts learned the hard way. Like when the Pope blessed of Philip II's Invincible Armada or when Heinz Ketchup Company Offered Joe DiMaggio a bonus if he hit in that 57th variety of games, extrinsic factors may subvert an otherwise flawless design.

G. I'll Always Know

On the Sunday morning that followed the first week of classes, Joe awoke smiling. Mary Davis was snuggled next to him in the lower bunk. Parsley Fief and Fenton spent the night at the Concave's with Doris and Cathy. The nearest bathroom was in the basement. Joe did not consider navigating five flights of stairs with sleep still in his eyes. The "Old" all-male Princeton had many fine traditions. One of them was pissing out the window. The bedroom window overlooked a slate roof with a gutter. Beyond that was a large tree which stood between Alexander Hall and the Nassau Presbyterian Church. The gutter served to keep the urine from dripping onto the sidewalk below. When the large oak had leaves, privacy was secured. January meant only bare branches. There was no doubt that worshippers leaving the sanctuary were entitled to the serenity from the morning sermon unbroken by the picture of Joe standing with only his dick in his hand. History had visited worse. The Nassau Presbyterian Church building was occupied by both British and American soldiers during the Revolution. The pews and galleries were stripped for firewood to be burned in a makeshift fireplace inside the sanctuary. After the war, the devastated building was restored and services resumed in 1784. The original building burned to the ground in 1813 when a sexton accidentally stored live coals in a closet. It was rebuilt in eight months, but that building was destroyed by fire in 1835 when a skyrocket fired in celebration of Independence Day landed on the roof. The current building, in some form, was constructed in 1836. No point of contention concerning students' penises ever arose. Fortunately, the churchgoers' peace was largely undisturbed. Their thoughts were in heaven but their gazes were upon the cold ground, or at the highest, eyes straight ahead. More likely, those from the congregation had long ago learned not to look up at any of the windows in Holder Hall. In the middle of the campus, in dorms like Little, it was not uncommon for a student pissing out a window to greet passersby with a free hand. Minimum rules of polite behavior dictated no less, unless the student below was showing his parents around campus, or some such thing. Then the student on the ground was obliged to divert the attention from those in his midst. Once urine started flowing, even though modesty might have required it, logistics made getting zipped up in time an exercise in futility, even if stream or drop could be prevented from landing inward.

Joe zipped up. He walked into the living room to grab a Marlboro from the burnt orange coffee table. Joe pulled two new records from his collection, now almost 1,000 records strong. The first Joy of Cooking album gave way to Lowell George and the first Little Feat release. A groggy "Threw" entered the living room in time to share the first joint of the day. The music played on. Joe and Mary spent the day taking the few steps back and forth between living room and lower bunk. "Thew" seized opportunities to play *Jesus Christ Superstar*, Lee Michaels, Mark-Almond, Mott the Hoople's *All the Young Dudes*, David Bowie's *Space Oddity*, and The Velvet Underground album *Loaded* with the song, "Sweet Jane." On their intermittent returns to the living room, Joe and Mary were able to prevail upon the turntable to play Santana's first album, the one with "Soul Sacrifice," Crosby, Stills, Nash first album, Neil Young's *After the Gold Rush*, and the Mountain album with "Mississippi Queen."

H. In the Good Old Days (When Times Were Bad)

It would not be long before Spring. The music continued to play constantly. Current events would intrude briefly, if at all. One day Teddy Appleseed was reading the Philadelphia Enquirer,

"Whoa, Stella Stevens was just elected the first President of Sierra Leone?"

Parsley Fief grabbed the newspaper,

"Teddy, give me that. **Siaka** Stevens not Stella. Whoever gave you that speed reading course at Chestnut Hill Academy should have his last three Christmas Bonuses rescinded."

In the course of the next few months, attention to the news was equally partly clouded, if noticed at all.

One April morning "Thew" looked up from the New York Times,

"The Middle east is one big fucking mess. I wonder how long chaos and contention will rule the day. It says here Libya, Syria, and Egypt have formed a confederation."

Fief looked jump from the Zap Comix he was reading,

"Wake me when Georgia, Mississippi, and Alabama get together again."

"Shit, Tim. Earlier this year, Palestinian troops fought their way into Jordan all the way to Amman, now they have been pushed back."

"And the Light Brigade has headed north from Sebastopol."

"The south may well rise again, with the Northern big cities joining ranks. Mark my words, that *Swann* case the U.S. Supreme Court decided saying busing was constitutional is going to create a fine kettle of fish, way worse than forcing the South to integrate their schools and their lunch counters. The urban centers of the North are fine with de-segregation as long as their own ethnic and racial neighborhoods are left alone."

"Shit, 'Thew,' even Princeton came around, not just nowadays. But even during World War II. In those days, 85% of Princeton students were Republicans, quite a few relatives of mine... and Teddy's. Ninety-percent on campus made their voices known by saying how can we be fighting a war against racism and anti-Semitism when we attend a college with the same policies."

"It is nice to live in a country where the two major political parties will come together on important issues without divisive rancor."

"And even if they disagree, compromise is always just around the corner."

Joe walked into the room, "I prefer when rock musicians get together, throwing contractual agreements to the wind, to play on one another's records- so the best play with the best without artistic compromise."

In February, David Crosby issued a record, *If I Could only Remember My Name.* Anybody who was anybody on the west coast played on that record. It was not an artistic or commercial success. Just as the "super group" had gone the way of all flesh, Crosby's feeble effort may have signaled the end of super artists conjoining for tea and sympathy. That February the 8A Holder turntable was well more fond of *The Yes Album* and *Cry of Love* by Jimi Hendrix.

I. Run 'Em Off

In March, Jethro Tull released *Aqualung*. That month no record was played more often or louder. On March 13th, Joe and Mary Davis were going to take the bus to Port Authority. They waited outside the bus station. Neither one of them paid much attention to the systematic parade of underage boys and the occasional Princeton Professor in and out of the men's bath room, even though not one appeared to be taking the bus. The concert than night at the Fillmore East was monumental. Elvin Bishop opened. What came next was the stuff of legend. The Allman Brothers Band was in top form running on all eight cylinders, or in this case, two of the finest guitar players that ever picked up an electrically amplified rock and roll guitar. That would have been enough but then John Winter And blew the crowd away. As they walked out of the Fillmore East, Mary Davis and Joe Cebellum were buzzing with energy, stuck on the Allman Brothers.

"I hate to admit it. Teddy was right. He has been touting The Allman Brothers as one of the best bands ever for some time."

"One song after another, the next better than the last. 'Whipping Post' really was totally cool."

"I liked the instrumental Dickie Betts wrote, 'In Memory of Elizabeth reed."

"Yea, and the really, really long version of Donovan's 'first there is a mountain then there is no mountain, then there is' all without a word ever being sung."

"We could go on and on."

J. Green, Green Grass of Home

Two days later Joe had a surprise, a big surprise. Tommy Wanderby, Fred Etheridge and Tim Camphor knocked on the door of 8A Holder. What was first intended to be a visit for one week, telescoped to a full, glorious month. The three back home had begged Sam Thorn to come along. Sam was resolute if not dissolute. He said why leave the comfort of the Palace of Thorns with its state of the art stereo, his never-ending bag of dope, and visits from the occasional Harper girl who were now daring to run the Delilah Pellioni blockade. Tommy put it best. Sam wanted to stay home with his thumb comfortably up his ass. In fact, Sam was more than happy at home. He listened to the same music that dominated the aural spectrum at 8A Holder. Both places played synchronously, including the next month's new releases, Crosby, Still, Nash, and Young's Live album *Four Way Street*, The Doors last studio album, *L.A. Woman*, and the Rolling Stones with the over-the-top, *Sticky Fingers*.

Almost every morning, as the three interlopers from the Sleepy Little Village camped in the 8A Holder living room, Fred Etheridge was the first to arise. He always started the day the same way. He would walk to the turntable to play The Doors, *Morrison Hotel*, the side with "Roadhouse Blues." As Jim Morrison sang, "I woke up this morning and had myself a beer," Fred would mosey behind the bar to the little refrigerator and grab a cold Rolling Rock or a Schaefer. Fred stayed away from the Budweiser brewed in Newark or the

Schlitz brewed in Brooklyn. It seemed the act of traitor when he could go back home and have a St. Louis "Bud" or a Milwaukee brewed Schlitz.

It was not long into their stay. Fred was on his second can of beer. Everyone was up. The poker game would soon start.

"It is a sad day. Let us all enjoy a moment of silence. The Ed Sullivan show will be no more."

Teddy was surprised,

"I wonder who will pick up the rights to Topo Gigio."

Joe mourned utter loss,

"I guess we will never hear the Rolling Stones sing 'Let's Spend Some Time Together' rather than 'Let's Spend the Night Together."

Fred turned the page of the newspaper,

"That lunatic Manson is going to be sentenced. And Lieutenant Calley has been convicted of multiple murders, too."

"Opposite ends of the same continuum of craziness."

During the month of poker and music, the only time Joe went to class was every other week to take the weekly quiz in Philosophy 201, "Logic." His plan was one Mr. Spock, the Leonard Nimoy character on Star Trek would approve. The tests Joe took, he passed perfectly. The tests he skipped he failed with flying colors. An "A" and an "F" always averages to a "C."

K. Teach Me to Forget

It was one more Spring morning. After the obligatory side one of *Morrison* Hotel, the boys were blasting "Sway" from *Sticky Fingers,*

Fief was chortling. Beer slobbered out of his nose,

"God must hate those Southerners. Wait 'til I tell my Black Panther brothers on Nassau Street. Fifty tornados have ravaged Mississippi. Seventy-four are dead."

"Fief, while I am sure the Lord works in strange ways, I would venture to guess that at least one of the seventy four is an unfortunate poor black person."

"Don't rain on my parade. It's the thought that counts. And look at this, justice is being done in South America, too. The Bolivian government has nationalized a U.S. owned mining operation."

"Thank God for American business interests the C.I.A. is around."

"I fear the traditional values of our youth will disappear, never to rise again. The white picket fences seen in television shows like 'Leave it to Beaver' will soon be long forgotten in the brave new world."

"Back in our home town of Barrington, there are many families who still live this idyllic existence, especially if three or four martinis back home from the commuter train are part of the picture."

"Especially the Bebidons."

"Or most of the Biltmore Country Club members."

"Why stop there? The Sleepy Little Village is a place all its own."

It was time to deal the cards.

Tommy cut the deck. "Thew" picked up the cards to shuffle. Tommy took his right index finger. He pointed it in "Thew's" direction. As Tommy pushed his finger into "Thew's" sternum, he said,

"Boop"

"Thew" laughed with glee. He had been disarmed. His inner child was all that was left.

Soon everyone, and the moment was always propitious, was "booping" everyone.

It was early one morning, the sun was shining. Joe knocked on "Thew's" door. Teddy was with Fief, spending the weekend at the Concaves.

"Josh, I need some money to go to New York. Can you part with some of what you owe me from playing poker for a good cause?"

"Is Mary Davis going with you?"

"Nope, my Barrington buddies and I are going to hit the Fillmore then spend Easter Sunday tipping a few in some bar in Manhattan. Mary is having a big family gathering. I was invited but she understands about my buddies being here."

"I don't understand how someone with a penis your size..."

“Don’t you know when you stand next to a guy at a urinal you are not supposed to look?”

“Convention be damned. I was just reading that George Bernard Shaw felt that one of life’s great pleasures was the actual act of taking a shit.”

“Are you sure that was not Oscar Wilde? Anyway I feel a man, especially a white man, should be judged on the basis of the principle of erect penis utilization, rather than statistical measurement. Anyway fork over some dough.”

“Thew” handed Joe fifty bucks and said,

“I have always thought the America dream was to have rather than to use.”

L. Little Ole Wine Drinker Me

The show that night at the Fillmore East was another good one. The pills of some moment, in this case LSD, enhanced the *tout ensemble.* The first act, Wishbone Ash, was better than usual, almost as good as Elvin Bishop had been almost a month before. The headliner was Elton John. Joe, Fred, Tim, and Tommy all agreed. The second act, Seatrain, stole the show, just as The Allman Brothers had done before Johnny Winter And played.

The next day the venue was Jack Dempsey's Bar near Penn Station and Madison Square Garden. The Barrington boys put on a memorable performance of their own. Tommy, Fred, and Tim had twenty-six ten ounce glasses of draft beer. Joe had twenty-four. He fell behind when he excused himself to call home to wish his mother, "Happy Easter." Everybody was drunk, a trip back to the urinal every ten minutes drunk. Somehow, they were able to keep their bladders under control on the bus ride home. Tim had a problem of a different sort. He threw up all over himself. He was now passed out and snoring peacefully. The bus back to Princeton stopped in New Brunswick. Two black guys sauntered to the back of the bus. In those days all the black guys, who were not actually in the Black Panthers, wanted to look like "Superfly." These two guys were no exception. Indescribable colors that clashed jacket, shirt, and pants all of extravagant cut and odd material. The look was all topped off by hats that heretofore belonged only on jesters in some medieval royal court. Joe and his buddies knew the hats were no laughing matter. One of the black guys moved to sit next to Tim, not noticing the puke or the pungent smell of regurgitated beer.

Tommy sat across from Tim. He held up a hand,

"You can't sit there."

"What you say?"

"O.K. Be my guest."

The black guy came to the party,

"Oh, she-eet. No kidding. Thanks my man."

On April 14th, Tim, Fred, and Tommy flew back to O'Hare.

"I gotta get back to pay my taxes" was all Fred said.

Tommy gave "Thew" one last "Boop."

M. The Sunny Side of My Life

On a bright note of history, more remembered and more chronicled than the "Nude Olympics," The Grateful Dead played Dillon Gymnasium on a Saturday night. The date was April 17th to be exact. Though still in full voice, Pigpen is less than a year away from his last breath. When Garcia sings, "Sugaree," the exuberant Texan, Gary Martin, further fueled by some pure synthetic mescaline, jumps on stage and kisses Jerry. This is not the reason Garcia vows never to return to the Princeton campus. The Proctors are steadfast in refusing to let him smoke a tobacco cigarette behind the stage.

Princeton Charlie and Cosmic Charlie are worlds apart but once in a while you get shown the light in the strangest of places if you look at it right. Before the concert, Alexander Randall V '73, better known as "Louie Motherball," Michaelangeloed his way to the ceiling of Dillon Gym to hang one solitary microphone above the stage. He recorded the Grateful Dead playing two sets. The "bootleg" vinyl LP was soon everywhere on Campus.

What was the next move to top the Dead show? Two Princeton Charlies cut of some new cloth, Charlie Hitchcock '73 and Charlie Black '73 sat stoned with the light all shining on them until they could barely see. Naturally, an idea was hatched. They wrote to the Hydrox Cookie Company telling it they had formed "The Hydrox Club" at Princeton. Would the Sunshine Cookie Company send them some free promotional samples? The "goof" was on.

One more Saturday night was soon to be magically adjusted to suit even the Merriest of Pranksters. It was the first ever Hydrox Party complete with *creme* filled cookies. The date was set. Invitations were issued with a sly wink of the middle eye. The place was the now defunct Cannon Club, where, if legend was true, Jane Fonda, down for the weekend from Vassar, once swung naked from the large chandelier in the main foyer. Clinically-tested LSD was added to the punchbowl.

Needless to say, sooner rather than later, the joint was going 'round and 'round, reelin' and arockin' what a crazy sound. Fathers of two high school senior girls from Trenton were not amused when their daughters came home tripping the light fantastic. Both Charlies had some "splainin' to do" to Dean Rudenstine. It turned out that new lore is better than old lore. Everyone who attended said to the Charlies, "I want to thank you for a real good time."

N. Folsom Prison Blues

Almost entirely, the rest of the spring was one huge afterthought. The calm of another budding spring ruled the zeal. It has been said that some get strong; some get strange.

Sometime in May, Boehm and Cebellum marched up the stairs one entry away from 8A Holder. They knocked on the dorm room door to meet some physics major they had never met. The word was he had some acid to sell. Once again the caveat was issued, "It's really good." An hour later, DDT, R.B., and Joe sat in the living room of Boehm's room in Joline Hall. R.B. reposed in the infinite fascination that only a light bulb will bring. He had removed the lampshade from a table lamp. There he sat, his jaw agape with new marvel. DDT sat at a nearby desk. For the next three hours he would peruse the same two pages of the telephone book open before him. Joe sat on the window seat looking out the window, watching the bright lights and the passing humanity. Joe even managed discourse. A couple of football players, "Barto" and Barisich stopped to wonder why Joe's gaze seemed so determined. Keeping his eye on the ball, Joe regaled them with tales of the great rum runners. Unsatisfied, they politely took their leave. It was time to study "orgo," organic chemistry. The *piece de resistance* was Dan Wigodsky. Dan happened by not knowing it was better to walk on by. Joe was not so wasted as to fail to see the ironic, if not bizarre, possibilities. Joe invited Dan up to see his buddy, DDT. Wigodsky did his best to pursue a course of polite conversation. In minutes he realized something was amiss. Not long after that he backed out of the room. It was some type of careful retreat he learned in the art of fencing.

O. I Could Have Gone Right

Occasionally Joe needed more money than poker would provide. He would take one time gigs. Twice more, he worked as a bartender at the faculty lounge. The Prospect House mansion was interesting but the garden was even more fascinating. Rows of special hybrids, black tulips and orange tulips framing exceedingly well- trimmed short hedgerows, which, in turn, surround blooming bushes, all framed with a background of small trees. Interspersed everywhere in between were more flowers, myriad types of joyful blooms. Those bartending jobs did not come up often enough. Boehm was a Commons Captain, one of the rising stars in the on-campus underclassmen food delivery apparatus. The structure for operations and promotion from within was one that even those involved in mapping the most intricate and enticing business plans for an M.B.A. at Harvard would admire. R.B was on his way to the top rungs of the corporate ladder. Sean McManus and Sammy Rice were not far behind. Joe was the only blot on his record. Twice Joe asked for a job as a dishwasher. He worked one week both times, then quit. This sort of sporadic lack of loyalty was not part of the standard operating procedure. Now for the third time, Joe was begging R.B. for a job as a dishwasher.

"Joe, do you promise not to quit after one week?"

"Honest, R.B. my word is my bond."

Boehm gave Joe the job. True to his word, this time Joe quit after four days. R.B. finally learned his lesson. Joe would not be seen working at the Commons dining halls again.

P. You'll Never Love Me Now

That second spring on campus was more beautiful than the first, with better weather. One day after another mounted refreshing breezes and summer temperatures. 8A Holder continued to play the best music in the land. New releases were prominent, and something to behold. Rod Stewart came into his own with *Every Picture Tells a Story.* Magnificent songs with his raspy voice filled the air. This record was even better than the one Stewart released with the Faces, *Long Player* which had a cover of the McCartney tune, "Maybe I'm Amazed." Rod Stewart's version answered the question for all time. There was now no doubt why Paul wrote "silly love songs." McCartney released *Ram* but as far as Joe was concerned, the song "Admiral Halsey" should be played one time, and one time only. "Thew" would spin the disc only when Joe was way out of earshot. Marvin Gaye took soul music into the serious arena of protest with *What's Going On?* Linda Ronstadt also came into her own. She once performed at McCarter Theater. The highlight was "Love Has No Pride." Close behind was her version of Jackson Browne's "Rock Me on the Water." The best part of the show was the intrusion of the "Old" Princeton. Linda pulled on the elastic at the top of her white pleasant blouse, just above some Mexican stitched colors. Some in the predominantly male audience hooted. Linda looked down at her breasts, and said,

"There is nothing here for you guys to get excited about."

The she scanned the crowd and became very serious,

"On second thought…."

From the hooting and hollering that followed, it might have been mistaken for a U.S.O. show.

Q. She Lit a Fire

Sammy Rice and Parsley Fief decided to drive down to Washington to protest the war by "disrupting" the government. History does not record nor long remember whether they were among the 12,000 arrested in the course that May's D.C. protest. Most were later released with no blotch on their "permanent record."

On the way there, Sammy was succinct,

"It looks like the strike last year really worked. This year South Vietnamese troops, backed by U.S. air support, invaded Laos."

Everyone has his own idea of disruption. It was two weeks later on May 15th. In a matter of days, everyone would leave campus for the summer. Joe, Mary Davis and "Thew" walked out of McCarter. They enjoyed a good buzz from The Incredible String Band concert, a repeat performance after their well received show at Alexander Hall on January 5th 1969.

Mary Davis walked four steps ahead of "Thew" and Joe. "Thew" whispered to Joe,

"When she first walked in, the night of your blind date, I thought she was o.k. But now I honestly declare. Mary Davis is one of the most beautiful, graceful, and charming women I have ever seen."

“Thew” had purchased all three tickets to the concert. Fitts was not the only one burned into oblivion by The Boehm Game. “Thew” owed over $1000.00 to Joe. For the next two years, Joe would formally call in a chit or two. More often, he would just walk into “Thew’s” room to take whatever he wanted. Joshua Matthew Relioport did not like to be reminded of the error of his ways. He opted out as a next year roommate, even though he had never been asked. Fief, Cello, Appleseed, Boehm, Cebellum, and a guy named Don Markedup had agreed to take two three man suites. They were “lucky” in room draw. R.B. helped a little in their lottery pick since he had now achieved high ranking status with Dormitory & Food Services. Junior year, they would live the across the hall from one another on the second floor of third entry Patton just across from the entrance to Dillon nobody ever used, right above the tennis courts which preponderated to the left, near a tree Joe once came to know.

R. Ends of the Earth

That Spring, there did remain one point of special demarcation. On April 27th, Joe and Mary Davis had tickets to again see The Grateful Dead, this time with The Beach Boys at the Fillmore East. They took the bus to Manhattan. As they rushed to get on the bus, Joe did not notice John Nash or the Princeton Philosophy Professor, Ron Angle, a man whose academic reach was likely limited to the position of untenured Department Head. Had Joe seen them he would not have failed to observe a tell-tale slink as both men exited the bus stop bath room. Two heads were on the lookout, bobbing in many directions to see if they were noticed.

Once at the Fillmore after the subway ride downtown to the Village from Port Authority, Joe had no reason to notice a girl who was now in her junior year at Nightingale-Bamford School, an exclusive private school for girls. She would enter Princeton the next fall. Her name was Leslie Friedan. Joe had three or four chances to see her as she passed him that night. Leslie's seat was ten rows in front of Joe, third row center. Her date was a guy who took some great photographs of Jerry Garcia during the show. During the encore, when The Dead and the Beach Boys did a spirited version of the Merle Haggard song, "Okie from Muskogee," Joe again missed the chance to pick Leslie out of the crowd. She was one of the first off her feet, laughing, as everybody in the place sang, "...like the hippies out in San Francisco do..."

It would be a little more than two years before serendipity would intervene to see Joe and Leslie share a snug pillow of wanderlust.

XXVIII. “Don't Fence Me In”

A. Willie the Wandering Gypsy And Me

“Joe, I’d like for you to tell me what you think.”

“And whenever have I had any trouble in that vein?”

“’Tis true. But I’d like to hear my thoughts out loud. You are the nearest sounding board.”

“Flattery will get you everywhere.”

Tommy and Joe were standing on the bottom of the Barrington Hills Country Club Pool. They were painting the sides. The troublesome task of painting the bottom without painting themselves into a corner was not yet before them. It was one week before the pool would open. Joe was now the head lifeguard.

“I brought Delilah home to meet my parents.”

"You mean your mother, Wanda. You are a brave man. To think I believed you left the army then the C.I.A. from fits of rampant cowardice."

"Joe, we do not say, 'C.I.A.' out loud, remember."

"Sorry, I forget those spooks have plenary power, here and abroad."

"Anyway, things went well when Delilah met my mom for about twelve seconds..."

"The over-under was ten seconds and the smart money was on less than."

"Delilah was the one who struck first. She told my mom she looked great for a woman her age and asked what beauty contests were like thirty years ago."

"The first cut is the deepest. What did Wanda, I mean your mom, do, pray tell."

"It was scary. She was the perfect hostess. Delilah never had a clue she was about to enter the realm of beauty contestant *non grata.*"

"And girlfriend thrown under the bus."

"No kidding. The second I returned home, I received a curt, 'Tommy, may I please see you for just a moment? I think there is something we must discuss.' My mom continued to maintain composure. Icy cold she was."

"Oh, Christ. And the ultimatum was?"

"If I wanted to live under her roof, I must never see Delilah Pellioni again."

"Wait 'til your mom finds out who her dad is."

"That's just it. You know I really like that her family has no compunction about breaking the law. As Dylan says, 'If you live outside the law you must be honest.'"

"I don't think he had the Mafia in mind. Those guys operate on brawn, 'muscle' as they put it. If you don't do it their way, they just remove you from the picture."

"Well, and you are right, I prefer honest dishonesty to my mom's superficial pretentiousness. It is only a thin veil for bigotry. All those others are merely there for my mom to walk over with a sullen distaste for their presence. So I will not kowtow to her worldview nor will I be duplicitous."

"I have always preferred mendacity to womendacity. So your honest streak means you are not gonna sneak around with Delilah behind your mom's back?"

"Right."

"Do you think Wanda, I mean your mom will let you live in the garage if you vacuum it Saturday and Wednesday night? What about your dad?"

"My dad walks into the house. As the Jefferson Airplane put it, 'your friends treat you like a guest.'"

"You hit the nail on the head with that one."

"Yep, he tries to stay under the radar so he will avoid agreeing with that which does not sit well with him."

"Marriage is the place where cognitive dissonance comes home to roost."

"I wonder if having sex is worth it."

"Well you know the answer to that but I wonder if they are even having sex."

"This is a lot to suffer if you are not getting laid. Although one never really pictures one's parents..."

"Now, Tommy. I am not sure Delilah Pellioni is not simply a newer model so to speak. But everyman has the right to pick the way he will ultimately go down in flames, or is it up in flames? Getting back to the subject at hand, I'll ask my parents. I am sure they will let you move in with me."

"That'll be great. Joe, I am so glad I met you guys when I moved up from Texas. Plus I do know Delilah has really got a hold on me."

"The power a woman has over a man. And most of the little darlings know it. I suppose the trick is to find one that doesn't or knows but doesn't use it. The girl I am seeing back at Princeton, you met her, Mary Davis allows me the illusion that I am in charge."

"I liked her a lot. I am glad you are still together."

B. Too Many Bridges to Cross Over

A voice from the top of the pool reached the point somewhere between amusement and derision,

"Why you boys are smarter than I thought."

Joe looked up at the face now leaning over the pool,

"Janet Feralposey, how long have you been eavesdropping?"

Another face popped into the picture. Joe's face went from beam to beamier,

"Anne Argil, you are here, too. Unlike your friend, I am sure you are not too indelicate to listen without making your presence known. Tommy, I am pleased to introduce two girls from Barrington High School, and they are both the class of the Class of 1969."

Tommy was ever the gentleman,

"Janet Feralposey, Anne Argil, it is my pleasure. Please forgive me for not coming up to shake your hand. I am sure you can see both of us have painted all over ourselves, hands included."

Janet smiled from ear to ear,

"We are wearing our bathing suits. May we sun ourselves by the pool?"

"Tommy, I think it is time for a break. Anne and Janet, we will be right up to get you both chaise lounges."

Janet stood waiting with her hands on her hips. Her bikini left her body with the sight of all any man could ever want. She knew it. She also knew standing there, her best hip forward, summoned thanks enough. Anne actually looked better. Anne, however, was raised in a home where civility was an important hallmark,

"Joe, that'll be great. Thanks. Tommy, it is very nice to meet you."

Tommy and Joe feasted their eyes. Joe opened the girls' locker room to retrieve to lounges. Tommy did his best to maintain eye contact as he talked.

"And to think the womenfolk in Texas think they are the best in the land..."

Janet grabbed her bottle of baby oil to which she had added a little iodine,

"Why, Tommy you are a true gentleman. I once swam at a swim meet in Dallas..."

Tommy grinned with sudden recognition, "I was there, too. You do breaststroke right?"

Janet nodded. Her face took a serious turn.

"I think you, what is the right word, 'met,' a guy I was lucky to beat for the butterfly championship, Jason Demondrone. I think he told me he was going to show you around the 'Grassy Knoll.' I think the Grassy Knoll Club will go down in history as more elite, with its members more in demand, than even the Mile High Club."

Janet blushed. Anne and Joe both looked surprised. The sudden lack of composure was not part of Janet's repertoire. Tommy knew. Jason told him about Janet. They had sex on the Grassy Knoll, up and down the slope, or so he said. Tommy had not believed him. Janet's blush confirmed what Tommy thought had been pure bravado.

C. Lonesome Dreams

Joe looked at Anne,

"Will you walk with me to the practice green? It appears Janet has a thing for Texans."

Janet had been tweaked,

"Joe Cebellum, you think you are funny, but you are not."

"Seriously, Anne, Let's talk a short walk."

"Sure, Joe."

Once Tommy and Janet were out of earshot,

"Anne, you know I still feel bad about breaking down crying which caused you to lose your composure in the receiving line after Brock's memorial service. I could not help it. Senselessly killed, so you young and so alive. I mean, what the fuck."

Anne's eyes got soft with extra fluid, but no tears,

"I know. I know. That day it was a short step to full tears. We all miss Brock. I wanted to come here with Janet since he worked here as a lifeguard before you. Who would think walking out of fraternity at night would lead to getting stabbed and killed? Some black guys, just because he was white..."

"And the fair blue eyed, All American boy. What a sad, sad fucking waste."

"My family, all the guys, like you, who played sports with him, the whole town of Barrington really, we'll all miss him. Your thoughts, everyone's thoughts have given us great comfort. But I will always miss him. Thanks for walking with me so we could talk. Joe, you are an amazingly nice person. You know I am not going steady anymore."

Joe was surprised with the direct turn of the conversation. Joe was able to keep a poker face at the card table but not here,

"R-r-really. I thought you and J-j-jerry Saxon were joined at the hip."

If Joe had an A-game, he was not bringing it.

"Me, too but it is, we are now over."

A double stammer was better than a triple,

"W-would you go to the Catlow with me Friday night?"

Anne touched Joe, just below his elbow,

"That will be nice, thanks."

Gamble

D. Black Rose

Friday evening was a disaster. It was not he was thinking about Mary Davis. He should have been but he did not. It wasn't the movie. *The Summer of '42* was bad. It did make Joe think about his time with Diane Isis, but not to the point of preoccupation, as it once would. It was not that he drove the car like he had never been behind the wheel. He was distracted but not by Anne. For four years of high school, Joe had pined for Anne Argil. She sat next to him on the ride back to her house. She was beautiful, body and inner being. Anne was also attractive with the way she carried her vulnerability, not just from the cruel, senseless death her brother suffered on the border of Watts in L.A. in the fall of 1968, not just she was now without a boyfriend after going steady for over four years. Anne begat the sense she was an innocent frail flower in a world that would soon turn to winter, a flower that craved the right kind of nurture and love. What kept Joe from falling, hook, line, and sinker? It was more than the high pedestal Joe always felt he could not reach. Anne was ground floor, right before him. The immediate reality was actually better than what Joe saw from afar. Something stood in the way, however. It was like a stone in his shoe, an itch, only worse. There was a spark in the back of his mind. As odd as it seemed, Joe decided that the tiny speck of deflecting light was Janet Feralposey.

Saturday morning, Joe and Tommy woke up together. Della and Joseph welcomed Tommy with open arms. Tommy was always upbeat and positive,

"Let's go get some of those waffles your dad likes to make, the ones he makes with crisp bacon in the batter."

"Shit, Tommy I hate to share."

"I talked to your dad. He is going to make three times the normal amount, starting with a full pound of bacon."

"Bring on the maple syrup."

"Then I am going to take Delilah on a picnic. There's a place overlooking the Fox River, near the bar Fred's uncle owns, 'The Broken Oar.' If things keep going the way they are, I can hear wedding bells."

"My advice is get your ears cleaned. Tinnitus will take strange forms. Then listen to the song, 'When the Hunter Gets Captured By the Game,' the title not the words."

"This is a trap I will willingly become ensnared."

"And so you have, but I suppose it is better than going to fight in Vietnam."

Thirty-six waffles were consumed that morning at the Cebellum breakfast table overlooking a blossoming pear tree with Tower Lake in its own spring shimmer, sunlight dancing on green undulations.

E. Mama Tried

Tommy headed out the front door with waffles dancing in his head. Joe picked up the telephone then dialed,

"Hello Mrs. Feralposey. May I please speak to Janet?"

"This is Joe Cebellum."

"Yes, I just finished my second year at Princeton."

"I will study Philosophy."

"I think I will teach."

"You may be right. Law school is something I have never considered. I may also venture into the world of advertising, now that you mention other possibilities."

Janet and Joe spent Saturday night driving to downtown Chicago. For many years, The Prudential Building was the tallest building in Chicago. Janet had never been to the observation deck, right above the Prudential Insurance Company logo, The Rock of Gibraltar. This emblem was not the worst bit of puffing an insurance company ever visited upon an unwary public. The summer night was spectacular and clear- Grant Park and the Band Shell, the Art Institute, the Shedd Aquarium, Adler Planetarium, The Field Museum, Soldier's Field, and the tiny airport, Meigs Field. Michigan Avenue sprawled to the South in front of a hundred storefronts, The Palmer House, and the Conrad Hilton.

"Joe, look at the lake. Will you take me sailing sometime?"

"We could retrace the route of the Kon-Tiki, the two of us lost at sea, our very own little shipwreck to Tahiti."

"You have romantic vigor."

Joe dropped Janet back home on Donlea Road in Barrington Hills.

"Why don't you come in? It was a little strange. My mom made a point of saying that if we closed the door to the family room, she would make sure we would have our privacy."

"What about your dad?"

"My dad long ago surrendered the rule of the roost."

"And your sister..."

"To think I thought I was once an attractive proposition."

Janet took Joe by the hand. The family room had a nice built-in sitting area on one wall. The cushions were comfortable. Soon, Joe and Janet succeeded in short breath and rapid heartbeat. Janet did not allow Joe's hand inside her pants. From their outside, Joe pursued a spot Janet liked. Janet fixed her teeth lightly into Joe's lower lip. She grabbed Joe's hand pressing it full force into the space between her legs. Janet finished by crossing her legs and lifting her hips off the cushion. Joe left the Feralposey's that night with a small hitch in his step. More than that was a crimp in his style. On the way out of the family room, Joe whispered the suggestion that next time they could go to spend some unsupervised time at Sam's, The Palace of Thorns.

"Joe, I think we have to go slow. You do know I have a steady boyfriend back at school. William Smith is the girl's school for Hobart. My guy will be a senior there next fall."

As soon as Janet closed the door, her mother, ever the eavesdropper, rushed at her.

"What is the matter with you? I will never allow you to marry a sociology major, or even a psychology major, for that matter. Get it into that pretty little head of yours. Why do I have to repeat myself over, and over again? It is equally easy to marry a rich boy as a poor boy?"

Even though they Janet knew Mrs. Feralposey was dead serious, "Mother, I cannot believe you. Plus Joe is studying, if he is studying at all, philosophy."

"Janet, my darling dimwit. You will never make your way on your own in this world. You know as well as I do that Joe is exceptional, one of those who does not have to work hard to succeed. Plus I am sure his Princeton pedigree will be all else that he needs to become a success in life."

"Different people have different ideas of the meaning of 'success.'"

"Janet, you little dunce, if you have started smoking grass, you'd better stop. There is only one meaning to success. Money is the way you are graded in real life. Joe is the first to know that."

"He may know it but I am sure he will not abide by it."

"My sweet dumkopf, everyone knows that our way of life, our quality of living, requires money and that is all there is."

"Well, I'll be surprised if Joe calls me again. I saw his face when I told him about my boyfriend."

"Then you call him."

"Mother, really."

F. We Had it All

The next night Patricia and Jen invited Fred and Joe to listen to music in the Von Pattersfeet library. Jen was happy to see Joe. You can forget quite a bit in a school year. Joe was happy to be back in the fold. Patricia cued up Joni Mitchell's brand new, *Blue*. Fred and Joe listened patiently. The record was good, too good, but not what they called rock and roll. Patricia acceded to next play two less recent records the The Lovin' Spoonful's Greatest Hits and the self-titled Doors record, the one with "Light My Fire."

Joe I have always said,

"First things first..."

Joe could never avoid a quip,

"Then the second and third can be better than none."

Both boys eyed the Joni Mitchell jacket taking its rightful place beneath the John Sebastian and Jim Morrison album covers. While most Aristotelian scholars do not know the meaning, all mathematicians do. Some ideas are simpler left to their bare bones. Fred was about to learn the lesson he had taught Joe after Sam ran the stop sign in Oklahoma. Don't run if there is no place to hide or as Morrison was singing what Willie Dixon once wrote, "The men don't know what the little girls understand."

As the music ended, Joe spun the group down the wayward path,

"Fred, Jen, Patricia, I have an idea. Tommy and I just filled the pool at the Club. The time is right to test drive the water."

Jen issued a qualm,

"I don't have a bathing suit."

Patricia was her dear friend,

"None of mine will fit you. In the interest of fairness, I won't wear one either."

"Joe and I will follow your cue."

"Good 'cause if we swim in cut-offs. The filter might get clogged with loose threads."

It was a short drive from the Von Pattersfeet mansion to the Club. For years, Patricia had walked down West County Line Road to take golf or tennis lessons. Her three companions that night were not proper guests, a mere employee and two non-members.

The four were barely making a splash. Fred and Patricia stood kissing in the shallow end in the near corner. Jen clung to Joe's shoulders while Joe held on to the side of the pool at the near corner of the deep end. It was not a lightning bolt. Bright light filled the darkness in one fell swoop. The flood lights at the top of that side of the Clubhouse were all in full blare. Joe craned his neck to look up over the snack bar. One of the French doors on the second floor was open. There stood the Club Manager, Steve Carson. Joe could see Carson could not see any of the four of them since they were eclipsed by the awning which covered the area between the snack bar and the pool. Fred fell from the grace that inspired him that morning in Oklahoma. He did not know Carson could not see them. Buck naked, Fred jumped out of the pool. He ran across the old practice tee and across the eighteenth green. It goes unsaid, but bears repeating, lifeguards, golf pros, and tennis instructors can, and perhaps should, mess around with the members' wives but never, ever go near their daughters. Joe was given his walking papers. All that remained from Joe's many jobs at Barrington Hills Country Club- caddy, shoeshine boy in the Mens' Locker Room, grounds crew, and lifeguard- was some junk in the back of his mind.

G. You Asked Me To

When it rains it pours. Two nights later Joe and Fred hosted a dinner party at the Cebellums. Sam declined to attend. Tommy brought Delilah and another blind date for Joe. Delilah was going to see that Joe would be as happy as Tommy, whether he liked it or not. Joe's date that night was Delilah's latest best friend, Jocelyn Round. Patricia presented an impediment. Fred brought little Miss Von Pattersfeet. She did not mind that Joe had another date. Jen Quenaciendo was another story, however. Joe and Jen were finished. Joe and Jocelyn never got started. To her credit, Jocelyn could not keep up with the group. Delilah really couldn't either. But that's the way the guys in Texas like their women folk. It was more apt that Tommy saw only the good, although Joe, Fred, and Sam all agreed it took an electron microscope.

The next unfortunate occurrence, another weird scene in the gold mine, was the dinner itself. Joe and Fred were a good cooking team. Eventually, whiskey sours will do ill to even the best chefs. The beef stroganoff with broad Polish egg noodles, green beans almandine, and Caprese salad were all fine and good. The Baked Alaska was another story. The dessert itself made a grand entrance from the oven. All was well. The cognac flame was a different story. No one told Joe or Fred that it was necessary to heat the brandy before ignition. Match after match hit the booze that doused the ice cream *en croute*. No pretty blue flambé ever resulted. The Baked Alaska was all wet.

The worst news of the evening was that Fred did get a match to burn. Later back in the Von Pattersfeet basement library, one of Fred's swimmers did find its way all the way home. Although they would not know it for another six weeks, Patricia was again pregnant. Joe would remain successful, or was it just dumb luck, at the alleged birth control method known as "pulling out." In fact with Fred for comparison, Joe was beginning to think he was shooting blanks.

Patricia's story was a sad one, a true horror. Actually, the misery is unimaginable, a circumstance that no parent ever contemplates. Patricia would marry happily. A wonderful man named Peter and she would bring two children into the world, an older son, Mark, and a daughter, Miriam. Mark would die at the age of seventeen, dehydrated to the point of no return. He was an accomplished long distance runner for which the cause of death was beyond oddity, a totally freak circumstance, but fatal. The thought was always near the surface of Patricia's dank depression. The sins of two abortions had been visited upon the mother. Moral issues be damned. To call it Karma without no ethical component did not a whit of good. There were really no words to describe the unbearable weight. Patricia was wrapped in a ball of confusion. Her feelings kept turning, bouncing from top to bottom, side to side, trapped in a revolving drum that never stopped cycling. She kept looking and hoping to find some solution, some answer, some way to exist in peace. The thoughts in the back of her mind surfaced incessantly. Back or front it did not matter. Patricia was plagued. What parent would not so suffer. It was not her fault but she never could be persuaded otherwise. Her only son, Mark, was always standing at the top of the stairs, calling for Patricia. She knew all the time that she wanted to die as black thoughts sullied her psyche and a cold wind blew constantly through the hole in her heart. Those that knew Patricia hoped or prayed that the tiny glow that resides within us all, which must always be there, would make a fire for the very first time from some branches of trust and a kindling of faith. Fred, to his credit, not counting tiny fetuses, had saved the life of Sarah, Martha's sister who had gone under the rusty knife of a back alley abortion. Being happy-go-lucky was Fred's mainstay. Whatever was served up to slow his steps was confounded. For Fred, the end of the tunnel never came up. Patricia was still living and breathing, but barely more than a phantasm. She had come to the end of the line. It remains to be seen whether this was the best of all worlds. Patricia might ultimately discover the precipice upon which her toes were precariously tucked was like the horizon. For the ancients, it was an apparent point of no return. We now know our world is round and without those sorts of infernal cliffs. Fred, like Tommy and Joe, would always see the light they'd been hoping to see.

In two more days, good fortune smiled upon Joe. Tower Lakes was looking for a life guard to work the 5 to 8 dusk shift. Even though it was not full time pay, Joe gladly took the job. Then even better fortune smiled upon him. The head lifeguard was a girl a year older, about to enter her Senior year. Allison Truame was her name. Her boyfriend apparently had sent a missile in the right direction. The obstetrician said her pregnancy would be complicated. Allison took permanent maternity leave. The head lifeguard job landed in Joe's lap.

H. Honky Tonk Heroes

It was the day after the fourth of July. Sam, Fred, and Joe were driving to see Creedence Clearwater Revival at the International Amphitheater near the old Chicago Stockyards. They wanted Tommy to go with them but Delilah had her own ideas. Her dad's side of the family celebrated the 195th birth of our great nation for two straight days. The Chicago Mafia was pleased to show its gratitude for good fortune. Organized crime had landed in the welcoming embrace of the land of opportunity.

Sam was behind the steering wheel. Joe won the toss for the front seat. Fred sat in the middle of the back seat so he could look out the front window between Sam and Joe. As they drove north on Barrington Road, the F.M. radio played The Doors, "Riders on the Storm." As the song ended, the D.J. spoke in a solemn hush, "On July 3rd, Jim Morrison was found dead in a bathtub in Paris, an apparent drug overdose. May he rest in peace. We must all play on no matter how many of the mighty fall among us. And now to the National News. On June 30th The United States Supreme Court denied the request of the U.S. Government to censor the publication of the Pentagon Papers. The Washington Post has joined the fray with the New York Times. From these Department of Defense documents generated at the behest of Robert McNamara, documents classified Top Secret and Sensitive, we now know that the Johnson Administration 'systematically lied, not only to the public but also to Congress.'

More specifically, the Pentagon Papers reveal that the U.S. concocted the reasons for entering the war. It is clear that Hanoi was provoked, and provoked again until it retaliated so the U.S. could then claim it had to itself respond to North Vietnamese aggression. To make matters worse, the U.S. secretly enlarged the scale of the Vietnam War with the bombings of Cambodia and Laos, coastal raids on North Vietnam, and Marine Corps attacks. None of the bombings, raids, or attacks, these real acts of aggression, had been reported in the mainstream media, until now."

The Beatles song, "A Day in the Life" haunted the airwaves,

"I read the news today, oh boy…"

Sam shook his head,

"Our government, right or wrong. What the fuck?"

Fred leaned into the space between his two friends,

"No matter how fucked up things get, we will always have each other."

Joe put his hand on Fred's shoulder,

"You don't mind if we bring some women along for the ride, too?"

Sam did his best demonic guffaw,

"Don't forget the drugs and loud music."

They entered the Northwest Tollway. The route was next to the Tri-State South, then the Eisenhower before heading South to the Amphitheater. As they drove past the Gunboard Crane headquarters and storage yard just before O'Hare, Fred opened his palm.

"I think this is a good time to take some mescaline."

“It is always a good time to take mescaline.”

“Excellent point, Sam you just keep right on thinking. That’s why we pay you the big bucks.”

“Joe, I have been wounded to the quick.”

Fred would have been right but for a three car accident which gridlocked the Eisenhower. Sam’s word choice of “quick” was wrong.

As the mescaline peaked inside the Comet which was now moving only bumper to bumper, Fred grew impatient. It was not only the long Chicago winter that could lead to cabin fever.

“Are we ever going to get there? I feel like we are three tuna fish in a can.”

Sam looked at his watch,

“We have plenty of time to get there before the concert starts. Don’t you mean sardines? It would have to be a pretty big can for three tuna.”

Joe pondered as was his wont, mescaline or no,

“Let us not lose our stride from the bump in the road as we sit in stalled traffic. I have been prompted by the apparent malapropism of our dear friend. Did you ever consider the knotty question, ‘Do sardines consider themselves fungible?’ But first let me add this possibility. The brain is a computer which will stop working when its components fail. There is no heaven or afterlife for broken down computers. Heaven is a place where nothing ever happens. People, like little children who are afraid of the dark, need a father figure to read them a bedtime story, a fairy tale. Let us take a moment of silent meditation to consider this, that, and the other thing.”

The radio D.J. interrupted the short silence,

“For those of you stuck on the Eisenhower on your way to the Creedence Concert, allow me to play three in a row to prime the pump.” The song, “Have You Ever Seen the Rain” was followed by “Fortunate Son,” then “Traveling Band.”

The International Amphitheater shook with live rock and roll. John Fogarty and the band were never better. Creedence played their asses off. Their music was a place to ride. “Shelter from the storm” was a Creedence lyric before Dylan adopted the phrase as a song title. The encore said it all, “Who’ll Stop the Rain?”

I. Old Five And Dimers Like Me

Sam never took the shelter, only the storm. He made a point of always being his own special failing case. He needed no reason to be bleak. His very being was being lost in the back of his mind. The buoy of Alphabetology had been a round float that he once grasped only to have it float away. Sam did not allow the possibility that another lifesaver might drift his way. Even if one did, he would go out of his way not to recognize it. There is a joke where a devout man stands on the roof of his house. The flood waters rise perilously around him. First, a rowboat comes to his rescue. "No thanks, I have the Good Lord to save me. Next, a motor boat arrives. "The Lord shall save me." Third as the waters threaten the very point of the rooftop of his home, a rescue helicopter arrives to save the day. He waves the helicopter away, "The Lord is my salvation." Up in heaven the man kneels before God, "I was a faithful and good man, Lord. Why was I not saved?" "I sent a rowboat, a motor boat, and a helicopter."

For Sam there was always music. Sometimes Sam preferred the offbeat to show everyone his ability to discern that which no other could without his fine artistic sensibility. At first it was Todd Rundgren and Nazz. Next, it was Robert Fripp and King Crimson. In later years, it would be Steely Dan. Even Sam knew this music did not cast a real lifeline. All the beatitude of celibacy aside, the way to grace is in a woman's arms. There was a reason Sam declined to attend the night Joe's parents gave Fred and Joe the run of the kitchen during which the now legendary soggy Baked Alaska was showcased. Fred's younger sister Lee was showing Sam some interest. It started out innocently sharing a joint and the Moody Blues record, *A Question of Balance.* Next they shared a couple of beers and a joint. Sam bought Lee a pair of cowboy boots, light blue with yellow rhinestones. He soon found out that Lee was a cowgirl. She could ride Sam's best bucking bronco. Her real talent was she could suck the chrome off a trailer hitch. For Sam, all good things ended, often abruptly and for no apparent reason. One night Tommy stopped at the Palace of Thorns on his way home to the Cebellums after work. Delilah had seen that Tommy got a job with her step-father, Farley Gunboard. He owned Gunboard Crane rentals. Tommy started as an entry level, union crane operator. Farley told Delilah that Tommy would meet all expectations.

"Tommy, Good to see you away from 'Ma' Camphor's kitchen and the poker table. Shall we have a beer?"

"I thought you would never ask."

On the living room couch, Sam and Tommy shot the breeze. One beer led to two, then three. They had just opened their fourth beer when Sam came clean,

"Tommy, I have been fucking Fred's sister, Lee. I would never have guessed that she has very talented Velcro tonsils."

"You are a lucky man."

Tommy had not yet persuaded Delilah that they should not wait for their wedding night.

“Yes, but the problem with Lee is that the elevator does not go up to the top floor, the lights are on…

Sam had left the front door open. Lee had just stepped onto the front stoop, well within earshot, as Sam gave Tommy his grim assessment. Lee was to the point,

“As fucking idiots go Sam, you are the biggest one I have ever met.”

Lee cried only the little tears. Lee was not dumb. Sam did not deserve her.

Lee ceremoniously slammed the front door to the Palace of Thorns behind her.

J. Literate Iterate Irate Rate Rat

"Tommy I guess we should all learn a lesson today. Never forget to turn on the stereo. Cranking *Let it Be* over our light conversation would have saved me from another cranky female. Even though my dad was only out for a short walk with Skitch, we should have blasted some tunes- even though we would have had to turn them down when those two got back,"

"Yea, Skitch, let's blame that yippy schnauzer of yours."

Phil and Skitch walked in the door.

"Sam, I just got the mail. There are those who would say that if you sit around the house all day, doing nothing..."

"Nothing."

"Yes, nothing, the least you could do is go get the morning mail. In this case your own indolence has come to bite you in the ass. I opened a letter from town hall, Norman, Oklahoma. They claim you have 'collected,' if I may use that word for this sort of lawless ridiculousness, one hundred and thirty-six parking tickets which you neglected to pay. So with fines, interest and court costs you owe over $11,000.00"

"Dad, why are you opening my mail?"

Tommy's eyes were as bright as they could be. He grinned from ear to ear at the corner into which Sam had painted himself.

"Your car, which I am about to sell to pay the parking tickets, is registered in my name, for insurance purposes."

"Dad, I need the car."

"To drive between the living room, the kitchen, and your bedroom, while my stereo plays loud rock and roll?"

"Seriously, there must be another way out."

"You could get a job."

Sam cringed. Tommy held his hands at the side of his head to keep himself from laughing.

"Don't you know somebody from American Can? Or your days in the F.B.I.?"

"While there is no doubt American Can can, I think this time I will call somebody who knows somebody down in that neck of the woods."

"Dad, that would be great. Just when it looked like the storm would brew to sweep me away, you come to the rescue. That reminds me, I think you might like this record I picked up, just released in May. The band is called *Weather Report.* I would say they play on the forefront, a place where jazz deigns to meet rock on some imaginary middle ground."

"Sam, I read about this band in one of the recent articles on jazz in *Playboy* magazines."

Now, Tommy was really smirking. He finally met somebody who read the *Playboy* articles.

K. Low Down Freedom

It turned out that Phil Thorn knew just the right people. All but one ticket were mysteriously expunged from the annals of Norman parking misfeasance. Sam did have to return to Norman on the court date. It turned out the trip was everything Sam might ever dream. After he paid the $88.13 fine, interest and court costs included, he decided to call Sarah Foreswallow. Her parents had moved from Fox Point back to Oklahoma City, their original hometown, even before they lived in New Jersey. That night Sarah and Sam met in a cowboy bar near her parents' neighborhood.

"I am glad I could shoehorn you in. My flight leaves in the morning."

"I would think you would be more interested in me shoehorning you in."

Sarah liked to dress to fit the part. She was wearing crimson, white and indigo. Her top was a crimson and white trail shirt, the kind with a shoulder hood, in this case crimson over a white chemise. Below the blouse she wore a short, very short, indigo mini-skirt. Sam was trying to figure out how she was able to walk with the skirt tightly wrapped around her cute little behind squeezing her legs too close together. Sarah bottomed the whole outfit with a pair of cowboy boots, white with crimson rhinestones.

Sam saw her cowboy boots. He was struck, almost frozen in the thought. More than a couple of his wildest dreams were about to be realized. Sam shook his head.

“Sam, let’s go back to your hotel room. I heard about your stint as the head of the Church of Alphabetology. I have always wanted to make a minister come, come again, and praise all that is young and beautiful.”

“Sarah, I have always wanted to fuck a girl wearing only cowboy boots.”

“O.K. Sam we can both have our way. One more thing, I sometimes masturbate with this fantasy- I grab on to a window sill, the drapes pulled open, and the shade up. I am bent over looking out at the night sky. I am fucked from behind until I am sure I am standing on the moon.”

“With only cowboy boots on?”

“Why not?”

The window shade and drapes were still open wide. Sarah was now on her back on the bed, her legs spread wide. She insisted Sam lick her pussy while she wiggled to a safe landing, retro rockets firing, back to earth.

“Sam, I’d like to see you masturbate. Will you jack yourself off and talk to me?”

To say Sam was wound up tight, did not give full expression to all that was, in a few short minutes, again coiled up within him.

“Stand in front of the window, sideways so I can see you, too. Now start talking. The topic presented to the third of our finalists is ‘World Peace.’”

“Third?”

“Yep, first Joe, then Fred, now you. I have your new friend, Tommy on my short list. Did you forget the topic?”

Sam noticed Sarah’s legs were still spread wide. Her right index finger was gently massaging her clit.

"If people just stopped fighting, there'd be no reason to fight."

"Is that your best answer? No tell me a little about yourself."

"My world extends to the reach of my penis."

"So when you stir the rubber ducky in the bathtub, do you think you are Magellan? Is it true that God gave you that little bulb at the tip of your dick so your fist wouldn't skip off at the height of self-gratification?"

Sam spurted.

L. Omaha

A thunderstorm caused Sam's plane to touch down in Nebraska. Once the flight back landed after resuming its intended course, Sam raced to the O'Hare parking lot. He could not wait to return to the Sleepy Little Village to tell all who would listen about this recent turn. It didn't matter that no one would believe him. This time the story of his exploits was true.

The second place Sam visited after unpacking at the Palace of Thorns was Tower Lakes Beach.

"Sam, nothing Sarah does surprises me. She has a delightful way of trampling all the better rainbows. Her own sweet steps do add to the myriad, bright colors..."

"You mean you believe, I mean, I'll say."

"Did you know Fred and Sarah used to drive up to the front of my parents' house, park on the little parking space at the top of the front yard, and then just fuck and fuck, sometimes in the back seat, sometimes Fred would bend Sarah over the front hood of his Camaro?"

Sam was disappointed that he had not been the first to desperately seek Sarah in that position.

"Hey, that sounds like fun."

Joe and Sam looked to the left. They had not noticed the approach of Beatrice "Beat" Wetter. The Wetter family lived in North Lake a few houses up the street from the Wanderbys. Her siblings included an older brother, Fred, who dated Carol Grove and was cornerstone of the High School Gymnastics team. Beat had a wild mane of deep red hair and green eyes that spoke volumes. Her lips pierced into all that was sexual. Guys were an open book in front of this free and easy minx.

Sam said, "I'm game."

Joe was uncharacteristically late,

"Me, too."

"First come, first served, first come. Let's go big boy."

Joe realized he could not leave his life guarding duties in any case. Sam was on a roll. Joe was sure he would hear about it later, whether it happened or not. Joe had agreed to cover the short late shift. So he would leave the beach then go directly to the poker game at "Ma's." It was dusk. The sun was low in the sky. On the right side of the beach there were three dredging pipes. A barge was tied to Rest Island, across from where Joe sat on Play Island. Tower Lakes had a mud bottom. It was dredged around the beach regularly, to add depth before more sand was dumped in the first twenty feet of water that served the front of the sandy beach area. With their first steps off the bridge to Play Island, it was obvious. Dirk Alford, Warren Harbinger, and Victor Slimdeuce were stoned. The giveaway was not just the group giggle. Assembled loosely, they wandered to their right. It was a three man weave that could only have been choreographed by cannabis. Dirk noticed the dredging pipes. They were ten feet long, eighteen inches in diameter, and sturdy steel. The pipes were heavier than they looked, too heavy for these three. What unfolded was for the cartoon ages. Dirk picked up the front end of the pipe. Victor picked up the middle. Warren lifted the opposite end. The three then lifted the pipe over the heads. As they took three steps forward they resembled some hieroglyphic from the wall of a tomb in the Valley of the Kinks. Three steps was one more than the limit. First Warren succumbed. Then the weight of the pipe forced Victor to release. The end of the pipe hit the ground sending a wave within it. Dirk still held up his end over his head. The pipe was over his head as it made one full length internal ripple. What Joe saw next appeared to be slow motion. First, Dirk lost his grip. Then the pipe fell to hit Dirk squarely on his head. The pipe bounced off Dirk's skull, landing on the ground to his right in three ever smaller bounces. Dirk took two steps. He was apparently o.k. Dirk then did a loopy about-face before falling to the ground in an unconscious heap.

Joe yelled at Victor to run across the bridge and get to the nearest house where someone was home to call Gunnar Jackson, Tower Lakes' only cop. Jackson's 1960 Rambler pulled into the parking area between the two islands. The fat old cop moved as fast as he could across the bridge.

"I know these guys. Nothing but a bunch of trouble makers since they were ten. Too bad it isn't Warren on the ground, I mean I'll call the Wauconda Fire Department. They'll send an ambulance right away."

Dirk lived to tell the tale. He might have suffered closed head trauma, or it might have been some other aberration, genetic or dope induced. Most likely, the dreaded dredge pipe incident was the reason Dirk volunteered to become one of the Jonestown followers.

M. Tequila Mockingbird

That same night, after work, Fred walked into the Yankee Doodle to have one beer before going next door to Village Liquor to buy a case of beer for the poker game at the Camphors. Apparently the stars that night were aligned for sex. It may have been set in motion the night before with Sarah at the window starstruck, dressed only in her cowgirl boots. Sitting at the end of the bar was Lynnette Slouch, a girl from high school, the class of 1969. The Slouch family lived in Biltmore, on Castleview Drive, just below the Club. Lynnette stepped off the commuter train then headed straight to the Doodle. Two gin and tonics in the bar car were not enough.

"Hi, Lynn."

"Hey, Fred. I have not seen you in a hundred years."

"At least three or four blue moons."

Lynnette Slouch was the picture of wanton ready-to-go. Her thin straight black hair sat pertly on her shoulders. Her bangs formed a horizontal line that broke just above her eyelashes. Her dark brown eyes twinkled best in the firmament of sin.

Fred's mind was alive with possibility. He pictured the morning light streaming over Lynn's porcelain skin and facial features spelling pure sexuality. He was sure in that new morning they would then do it again to brush in the missing colors for each other's paint by number dreams. It struck

Fred hard. He was overtaken with the notion of wanting to be a one night veteran with Lynn, dreaming of a fight that only their two bodies could bring to frothy fruition. Lynn sat perched atop the barstool wearing a conservative pearl color front-buttoned blouse on top of a bra with a thick cover which diminished that part of her sensuality. She added a workday appropriate navy cotton skirt that broke just below her knees. There is no limit to where Fred's thoughts would have raced had he known that Lynn was wearing only a garter belt, no panties, and no stockings. Lynn's boss was married. He liked to fuck her in the afternoon before he drove home to the wife and kids. During her three o'clock cigarette break, Lynn would stand in the alley near the front entrance of the office building where she worked in downtown Chicago. She liked to be ready for her boss since it meant she had to do less work. When the moment was right, Lynn would stub the end of her cigarette on the side of a metal dumpster and then, as smoothly and surreptitiously as possible, she would deposit her underwear and nylon hosiery into the dumpster.

The Doodle Juke box was playing the Doors, "Love Me Two Times." Fred knew he only wanted to go full speed ahead, up periscope, torpedo armed and ready for firing. The circumstances dictated a little light conversation which Fred hoped would serve as foreplay. Unlike Sam, Fred now knew that however much foreplay he thought was enough, he had to triple it.

"Lynn, what do you think about ole Tricky Dick and his war on drugs? As of June 28, 1971, drugs have now been named, 'Public Enemy Number One.'"

Ignoring her actual circumstance Lynn replied,

"The injustice of Nixon's stupidity is what gets my panties in a bunch."

Fred did not really care about politics but he knew it was best to take up the gauntlet of a position the girl favored to get on her good side. Ingratiation was Fred's strong suit.

"Joe Cebellum said something interesting the other day at our regular poker game. We play five or six nights a week."

"How is Joe? He once dated my friend Debby Harlow, back when we were Sophomires."

The ingratiation continued,

"Funny,"

"Joe would step past me like I wasn't even there, just to give Debby his full attention."

"I would have stopped right there in front of you."

"I think you have forgotten what Debby looks like, and how she is brimming with get up and go, to all the places boys like. So what did the intrepid Mr. Cebellum say?"

"Joe is always positive, hard to believe anyone can be so. Anyway, it was something like, 'To be good you do not have to be perfect, you do not have to be right all but one time, you just have to be right often, but most of all you must always be fair, magnanimous, and maintain as much equanimity as possible."

"I prefer an occasional fit of savagery, wildness followed by sweet rest."

It seemed Fred was not paying attention to where things had proceeded. In fact, he was prolonging the foreplay.

"I think the idea that the Chinese will be a savage force..."

"Not quite the type of savage I had in mind."

Fred smiled. He felt he was on the right path. He did not know he had to pick up the pace. The last thing he wanted was to be on anyone's list of ingrates,

"I am sure we will get to explore your feelings in the vein you suggest. Anyway I do not understand why Nixon ended the trade embargo with China. On one hand we fight in Vietnam to stem the surge of Chinese Communism. On the other, our own businesses demand they step up to the trough and further fatten themselves. In any event, Communism is on the way of the dinosaurs. My friend, Tommy Wanderby told me this one. Sam played his straight man."

"I like the looks of Tommy Wanderby. I saw him at Tower Lakes Beach talking to Joe when Joe was lifeguarding. My friend, Nancy Gage and I were there to sunbath. Joe was kind to slowly rub iodine tinctured baby oil up and down my back. But, please tell me the joke."

"Tommy played the communist proponent. Sam played the peasant. Tommy says, 'You are gonna love communism. Here is how it works. If a man has two houses, he has to give one to a poor person.' Sam says, 'That sounds good.' Tommy says, 'If a man has two cars, he has to give one for the poor people.' Sam says, 'That sounds fair.' Tommy then says, 'If a man has two chickens...' Sam jumps in, 'Wait, I have two chickens.'"

"Fred, I see you're done with your beer. I just finished my third gin and tonic, one here, two on the Northwestern. Do you have any more bright ideas or current event topics you wish to discuss?"

For emphasis, Lynn touched Fred on the elbow, since her obvious words had so far not been clear enough. She wanted Fred to finish what her boss had only started earlier that afternoon. Lynn wished she was wearing a shorter skirt so she could flash Fred her clear intention.

The light finally went on,

"I know a place where we can go, Sam Thorn's townhouse at Pickwick Place. His dad is out of town. I have a key. If Sam's there, he doesn't mind if we pop over and ignore him."

Two hours later which lasted more like twenty minutes,

"Lynn, I love eating pussy, especially yours."

"I guess you do."

"It's like the salt and the lime before a shot of tequila. Only you don't need the tequila."

"Never heard anybody talk about it that way. Maybe I should try it myself sometime. On second thought, you always need the tequila."

They both laughed the laughs of close friends.

N. Ride Me Down Easy

Fred dropped Lynnette Slouch back at her car at the train station. He bought that case of beer and headed to the poker game, just in time. He also vacated the Palace of Thorns in the nick of time. Sam was still in the throes of discovering how bendy Beat Weeter really was. He had parked his car in a field way behind the Tower Lakes dam. His imagination had been fueled to the stout first by her hands on the passenger windowsill then the front hood. Sam was surprised that Beat never wanted to stop. He'd get soft but Beat would bring him back from the dead. Sam decided he would add a little Hindu reincarnation to the New Revised Version of Alphabetology, if there ever was going to be one.

That night, Phil Thorn flew home a day early from a company wide sales meeting in Manhattan. As Vice President/Controller, he was the number cruncher who presented the relevant historical data and the future projections with the newest bonus schedule. Phil decided to skip the "Circle the Wagons" sales pow- wow and the other "inspirational" meetings only dyed in the wool salesmen would find worthwhile. Mindless pep talks, no matter how much they were money driven, were not Phil's cup of tea. That night, as coincidence demanded, Sudsie McDolick sat next to Phil in American Airlines First Class. Sudsie was a Barrington Hills socialite. She really belonged at a cocktail party on the North Shore or at some Art Institute Board meeting. Although, as Phil would soon discover, she was sufficiently randy to be part of the Barrington Hills wife swapping ethos. The sexual incandescence that had long been added to the beauty of the rolling hills and mature trees that arched the ambling roads would soon be adopted and ratified as part of popular culture. In Barrington Hills there was never a need to throw a party the whole purpose of which was to throw car keys in a hat to see who goes home with whom. That which had been going on for many years among those who made their own rules now seeped into the lower echelons supplanting more strict mores.

Neither Sudsie nor Phil had a spouse with which to barter. Phil had been long divorced. Sudsie was more recently set on the loose. Once landed and curbside, Sudsie cancelled the airport limo she had reserved to take her home. Phil offered that he give her a ride. As Phil's card exited the Northwest Tollway at Barrington Road,

"Sudsie, how would you like a snifter of fine Napoleon Brandy? I have been keeping some back at my place for just the right occasion. We can stop there before I drop you off at Bateman Circle."

Sudsie was not bashful. The two soon slipped in between Phil's satin sheets. Phil's brain was willing but his flesh was weak. Part of him kept glancing over to the Diane Von Furstenberg, cream and shamrock green patterned dress that Sudsie had flung to the floor at the side of the bed. Phil was in the right place, but was not resolute. Sloppy sex with a slightly flaccid penis is good as far as it goes but Sudsie had a better idea. With her thumb in Phil's asshole, Phil's prick came to attention.

"Ten hut, quartermaster, why Phil you are now a fullmaster. Since you like where my thumb is, I have a better idea. Let me reach into my bag of tricks to see what I can find."

Sudsie got out of bed. She walked to the bureau and opened her large, designer travelling bag. Better than a garter belt with no panties, Sudsie pulled out a strap-on harness and a good-sized dildo. Phil's eyes got big. His prick was now harder than it had ever been in the presence of a woman.

Sudsie wore the harness like she had done this before. Her dildo was now predominant.

"Phil, you little pussy. Suck my dick."

Phil did not need to be asked a second time.

"Now that my cock is nice and slurpy wet. Another part of you is going to get up close and personal with it. I am going to stick this nice little prick of mine right up your ass without any lube, just to see you squirm."

Phil was on all fours in three seconds. Sudsie was on two feet behind him with one idea in mind.

"Phil, you've got some tales to tell about your tail. It looks like your asshole has been the place to meet and greet for some time now."

Phil was about to turn the tables.

"Just fuck me you little bitch, then I will fuck you hard, in every place you have."

It was more than the flat end of the dildo which the harness pressed tight into Sudsie's clit. Her pussy gushed in favor of the suggestion. Phil and Sudsie finished the night in the missionary position. Phil was on top, in charge for the first time ever. He pumped hard into Sudsie. He could feel her pussy clamp down and cramp around his prick engulfing it in waves. Phil came, a man finally resplendent.

“Phil, next time I want you to finish in my ass. But rest assured, your ass will always get full abuse first. I can tell you like it so much.”

“Yes, I like it like that. But, Sudsie, I can tell that you are the real cock whore.”

“Indeed, I am.”

O. My Silver Spoon's This Beggar's Cup And When It's Empty I Fill Up All I Have To Do Is Just Show Up

The Palace of Thorns was not just a place for felicitous meetings for Phil and Fred. Rarely was it for Sam. More and more, it was summer commonplace for Joe and Sally Sensabell. They started listening to Rod Stewart's *Every Picture Tells a Story*. The two sides played while they were alone in Sam's bedroom. It became an artistic study, delving into the depths of Sally's bronze and beautiful shape. From the curves of her hip to her square shoulders and her round white breasts with chocolate centers and light brown attentive nipples, Joe was overtaken. Joe and Sally both knew they had waited a longtime for Joe to enter her, slide in and out, pulsing together. It was better than either ever thought it would be. June turned to July, then August. Joe and Sally could only smile. They used to love to talk. Now they just wanted to feel. Once inside, it did not even matter that there was no movement. They both felt they belonged coupled. It was a deep feeling that gave "wasted words" true meaning. They played the Rod Stewart classic over and over again. Their bodies sang electric to the tender point of final relapse. Next it was Herbie Mann's *Push Push*, music with a sexually charged jazz flute and a bossa nova tinge, featuring Duane Allman one of the last times he would play on any album. Then they listened, deliciously woven together, to The Beach Boys' *Surf's Up.* Brian Wilson touched all the bases in a feast of arousing revelry.

The summer ended on three high notes dangling deliciously around their higher love. First Sally and Joe became further enmeshed, two bodies drawing from the same well, in a way only the blues will map the libidinous. The record was called the *London Howlin' Wolf Sessions*. Behind Chester Burnett aka Howlin' Wolf was the greatest white blues band ever assembled. To the Rolling Stones' rhythm section, Charlie Watts on drums and Bill Wyman on bass were added Steve Winwood on keyboards with the icing on the cake, Eric Clapton on lead guitar. From there they thought there was no place to go but down. But the crescendo waxed. Two bodies blossomed, opening buds as they met one another on more and more familiar ground. What for others would have been merely luscious sonic wallpaper, the music sprang to capture their entireties with all walls crashing down. Sally and Joe melted into one another to become one fleshy accumulation, greater than the sum of its parts, all spent of its own accord. The penultimate summer album was the self-titled first release by *The New Riders of the Purple Sage*, the quintessence of sybaritic country rock with Jerry Garcia added to play pedal steel guitar. The sound that surrounded their nakedness as they became one for the last time was *A Space in Time* by Ten Years After. The music seized upon heavy hedonism which somehow transcended the cliché of cosmic conception. Sally and Joe, their two bodies together sang sweet songs. The music gave their yin a yang, or vice-versa. It did not matter which was which or what was what. Sally and Joe flowed to synchronous virtue. Sally headed back to Los Angeles. Joe would head back to Princeton. They both had waiting sweethearts. Their time together was a treasure only they would ever really know. From that point forward for many years, they would, from time to time, think of the other with body brimming broad inner smiles. Sally and Joe had gone from satisfaction to satisfied to sated.

P. Dreams Are Lies, It's The Dreaming That's Real

Only once did Tommy visit the Palace of Thorns to avail himself of Phil's amenities. Phil's Napoleon brandy got Delilah to just the right point of dizzy delirium. Tommy hoped it would be better. Even bad sex is good. Tommy noticed only that Delilah's pussy was not very wet. Delilah noticed the mirror that hung from the wall above Phil's four foot high chest of drawers.

"Tommy, help me prop my head up with a couple of pillows."

The thought of seeing herself in the mirror made Delilah wet.

Tommy was making love with Delilah. Delilah now saw her face in the mirror. She found making love with herself the best of all. Soon Delilah was dripping. Tommy would have added to the mix but he was wearing a condom.

Tommy panted as he put on his pants,

"Delilah, the pillow idea was a good one."

Delilah had heard that the suites at Caesar's Palace in Las Vegas had mirrors on the ceiling.

"Tommy, when we get married, I think I know where I would like to honeymoon."

Tommy had more than his share of the Napoleon brandy. He left the spent rubber in Phil's bed. Sam's dad was none too pleased with the latex bedfellow. Sam took the logical course of action. He blamed Joe. Two years before, Joe had admitted guilt after throwing champagne bottles on the neighbor's lawn when Candy Cunegonde and Lacey Doniteros invited Sam and Joe to the Dames Dance. Since that time, Joe was always the culprit. Joe could not argue with sound policy. Sam was right. It was better to have his dad mad at only one of his friends, not all of them. Until the day he died, Phil Thorn always looked at Joe with unequivocal disgust.

Q. Ain't No God In Mexico

Martha Buchanan returned to the Sleepy Little Village in late August. She seemed more confused and disgruntled than Joe remembered her. Her second night back, Fred, Martha, and Joe decided to go see a White Sox game, a night game at Comiskey Park. Major League Baseball should cure what ailed anyone.

Fred drove the Blue Camaro. The top was down. Now Joe stuck his head between Martha and Fred to join the conversation. Martha had the floor,

"I am finished with finishing school. I think I will return to college at Champaign-Urbana but not this Fall."

Fred's eyes lit up.

"Martha, my dear. I am so glad we can be together. Why not skip college? We can be married and live happily ever after."

There were no secrets among Fred, Martha, and Joe.

"Fred, I love you but I have serious doubts about many things, you included. I now know never to grab something that cannot support my weight."

"Let me show you the bearable lightness of marriage, my darling."

"When you visited me in Missouri in early July, all you wanted to do was talk about the Creedence concert..."

“That was true if you mean, between the times we spent together as consenting adults.”

“That gives me an idea. How ‘bout we start by going to the Palace of Thorns after the ballgame?”

“Fred you know, or you should know, it is just too eerie and fucking depressing for me to go back to the place where my mother died in the garage. I don’t even like to think of Pickwick Place at all.

“So sorry, Martha.”

“I’d like to talk about the recent source of what has become my summer of discontent. I didn’t tell you ‘cause it was my decision, my body. I got pregnant during all that consenting adult time with you in July. Anyway, a week ago, my dad flew with me to Panama. We went to a military hospital there, at a place called Fort Gulick. The abortion was a simple procedure, no complications. I guess my dad and the army doctor thought I was going to be unconscious for some time. Their discussion was eye-opening even though I had to keep my eyes closed to hear all that they had to say. I don’t know why I pretended to be asleep. The conversation I heard started to be innocuous enough. They were talking about how, on August 15, Nixon ended the gold standard and put a 90 day freeze on wages, prices, and rents. They both chuckled when they said the effect on the financial circumstances of some foreign regimes might be vast. Then they started talking about something they called, Operation Chaos. As far as I can tell, the F.B.I and the C.I.A. have a nationwide domestic operation which monitors threats to national security-a blanket fear of communism but stretched beyond all reasonable limits. From what I heard, it is not just the Black Panthers, the student movement, but it is also the B’Nai B’rith, what exactly is that? The thing that really sticks in my craw, Operation Chaos has now targeted the Women’s Liberation

Movement as part of Communism's attempt to take away our way of life. What they started talking about next really made my blood boil, but I maintained the pretense I was still under the anesthetic. Why do they call it that? It is hardly the opposite of 'esthetic…'"

Both Fred and Joe suppressed the urge to comment on Martha's use of the word, "pretense" in the context of her lying comatose.

"So you are not gonna believe this. In March of this year my dad was involved in smuggling swine flu into Cuba to infect the pigs and mess up the Cuban economy."

"To think our very own Howard Buchanan…"

"Seriously, the doctor asked my dad about his trip with the vial of swine flu virus. He recounted the journey which started at Fort Gulick. From there my dad was on a ship which made a rendezvous to change ships off the coast of Panama near a place called Boca del Toro…"

"Good thing it wasn't cattle flu virus…"

"You think you are funny, Joe. But this is very serious. From there my dad stopped at a U.S. island I never heard of, Navassa Island 100 miles south of Cuba. The last stop was the south Cuban coast, not too far from our base at Guantanamo where my dad gave some covert operatives the virile vial…"

"I think you mean virulent."

"You say potato and I say tomato, any way I considered getting up but then they started talking about covert operations, military involvement in Bolivia to stop the government there form nationalizing U.S. interests in mining. Apparently from August 19-22 there was a re-coup of the U.S. backed coup which was turned back. Then it got worse. The C.I.A. is going to overthrow some guy named Allende in Chile. There are over 300 U.S. businesses there which the C.I.A. fears will be lost to the Communists- they really mean socialists but hey. I am so upset about all of this I cannot even sleep at night."

Fred, Martha, and Joe bought last minute seats in the right field bleachers. Unlike Wrigley Field which had a bunch of Andy Frain ushers dressed in movie theater uniforms, the White Sox ushers wore yellow vinyl jackets, necessary for cover when beer is thrown at them. More importantly, Andy Frain ushers were normal sized men, sometimes even women. The Comiskey Park security yellowjackets were all the size of refrigerators or bigger, all with the bearing of interior linemen. It was time to play the National Anthem. Everyone stood. Everyone except Martha that is. Fred and Joe both told her to stand up.

"It's not just the Vietnam War. Did you guys listen when I told you what the C.I.A., my own father for Godssakes, is up to?"

"Martha, stand the fuck up."

It was not just the guys who surrounded them in the right field bleachers who were threatening serious violence and certain bodily harm, not to Martha, but to Fred and to Sam, since they could not control "their woman." Now the yellowjacket security refrigerators had joined the menace. Fred and Joe each grabbed one armpit and lifted. Martha was pulled to her feet, kicking and screaming the whole way. Two weeks later in the comfort of her home in Northlake, Tower Lakes, Martha had a nervous breakdown. She was soon heavily sedated.

R. In A World That We Can't See, To Sing Drunk With The Angels, Play Again For Free

As Fred, Martha, and Joe were driving back from the baseball game, Phil Thorn drove Sudsie McDolick home after another close encounter at the Palace of Thorns. They had the place to themselves. Sam spent the evening with Beat Wetter. It was a position Beat quickly grew to love, her skinny legs spread-eagled both hands on the hood of Sam's Comet. Sam was the farthest thing from Phil's thoughts. He was in love, for the first time. Inebriated with flying endorphins, Phil's mind was singing a happy tune. The speedometer of his Thunderbird as he traveled west on County Line between Donlea and Bateman was also not part of his consciousness. A Barrington Hills cop pulled him over. The cop was Lonnie Botch.

"Officer, I am so sor...Lonnie Botch as I live and breathe. What the fuck brings you to don the uniform of one of Barrington Hills' finest?"

"Phil Thorn, how the fuck are you? Oh sorry Mrs. McDolick. I did not see you there."

Sudsie had been hunched over Phil's lap when Lonnie pulled the Thunderbird to the right shoulder.

"No mind Officer Botch."

Lonnie formed the distinct impression that Sudsie could not take her eyes off his handcuffs."

"So there I am a Chicago cop, in the middle of what they now call racial unrest. Apparently some of the Southside locals, let me call them that, do not appreciate the special Botch brand of law and order. Alex MacArthur, one of Barrington Hills' leading citizens, helped to get me this job. If you think you can get post-traumatic stress disorder after two tours of duty in Vietnam, try being a cop patrolling Cottage Grove and 85th. There is a lot less civil unrest here in Barrington Hills, unless you count tax evasion which is not within my jurisdiction.

S. The Man Who Lives Forever

The next night, Sam, Fred, and Joe were sitting comfortably in the Cebellum living room. The rest of the Cebellums had taken a family vacation. Joe had a few more days as the Tower Lakes lifeguard before heading back to Princeton. The stereo was loud. The album was a new release, *Who's Next*. The three old friends were on a path like a runaway train, a steam locomotive going down the track, flyin' blind with a monkey as the engineer. The trio had been shot from the dark, catapulted from the back of the same single-mindedness. They had each taken a full clinical dose of L.S.D. Loud, really loud rock and roll had never sounded so good- "Baba O'Riley," "Bargain," "Love Ain't for Keeping," "My Wife," "The Song Is Over, "Getting in Tune," "Going Mobile," "Behind Blue Eyes," "Won't Get Fooled Again." Each song spun in turn, creating grooves of its own vitality. It was more than the synthesizer The Who added, more than the "dead-on" lyrics.

The record ended. There was calm after the storm. Joe looked out the window. The unilluminated lake was wine-dark. On the shore to the right, the large willow tree rustled waves of premonition. Joe held the *Who's Next* cover in his hands. It was a sacred artifact.

"The Who teach what is taut, well beyond that suggested by this photo where they have just pissed on Stanley Kubrick's trite and trooped 2001 movie monolith."

Sam shook his head,

"Trooped?"

Joe changed the subject,

"Look outside. We are about to see something that will make both sides of *Who's Next* at full volume seem like a tempest in a teacup."

Lifeguards on the flatlands learn the signals that precede major storms. Joe was a quick study. His meteorological conclusion was accurate. Imbued with the sense abilities of L.S.D. coursing through their veins, Fred, Sam, and Joe were about to experience nature's remarkable energy. For now there were only calm dark waters and solemn dark pea-green skies partially eclipsed by clouds darker yet. The looming large puffs overburdened with their own vapor made faint reflections on still waters. The three who would soon find dire saluted each other. They then sauntered toward the small wooden rowboat the Cebellums kept tied to the shore to the left of the willow. The tendrils of the large tree now hushed stillness. Before the torment, there is always an interlude which gives those in its midst the sense they have been bestowed with a lasting case of revelation. That is until it is time to ride the storm. The clouds started to grow. The scene was set as the rowboat coursed to the middle of the small lake. Sam rowed. Fred stood in the front of the boat. He adopted the pose of Washington crossing the Delaware. Joe stood at the back. There was an imaginary kettle drum in front of him. Both his hands held supposed timpani sticks which he pounded up and down, matching the tempo of Sam's oars as they broke the water. With the first break of pure white light and its jagged bolt downward, all three riders on the storm were now consumed by the Doors' lyric, "...into this house we're born." The lightning was voracious but it started slow and easy. The strikes soon formed a full circle of sky top to lake surface flashes. "There once was a note pure and easy" now echoed in their heads between flashes and thunderclaps. Soon there was no time between strikes. The smash and mash of electrical ions traveling down from all directions encompassed all else to mesmerize them. No more spectacular light show had ever been seen anywhere. The bang of thunder filled their stomachs, resonating to stay. White jagged light pounded the skies with a visual cacophony. More thunder rocked their very souls. The tale has been told that the Light Brigade rode into the Valley with the intense boom and flash of cannon fire from above. The little lighter rowboat was immersed in a sound and fury immeasurably larger, cascading from higher heights. Joe, Fred, and Sam were smack dab in the middle of the ultimate in titillation. Each intermittent burst took a still photograph, stopping time with its own slow shutter. Even though it was all black and white, the colors were there, seen through an imaginary prism of refracted darkness. Consciousness contended with external presence. The fantastic scored and scoured. The beauty of L.S.D., even in time of great danger, is that if you stand still, don't shake your head, and above all, don't duck for cover, slow motion rules the landscape of sense-data from your feet to the horizon. Joe and Fred should have been scared, scared out of their wits, but they were not.

Sam always wanted to be everyone's saving grace, he issued a gratuitous and unnecessary reassurance,

"Don't worry. If I see one coming at us, I will row safely out of harm's way."

The willow which bends to the tempest, often escapes better than the oak which resists it; and so in great calamities, it sometimes happens that light and frivolous spirits recover their elasticity and presence of mind sooner than those of a loftier character.
Albert Schweitzer

41296240R10381

Made in the USA
Charleston, SC
24 April 2015